The evangelical expositor: or, a commentary on the Holy Bible. Wherein the sacred text of the Old and New Testament is inserted at large; ... By the Reverend Thomas Haweis, ... Vol. II. Volume 2 of 2

ECCO
PRINT EDITIONS

The evangelical expositor: or, a commentary on the Holy Bible. Wherein the sacred text of the Old and New Testament is inserted at large; ... By the Reverend Thomas Haweis, ... Vol. II.
Volume 2 of 2
Multiple Contributors, See Notes
ESTCID: T091134
Reproduction from British Library
With the text in the Authorised version. The titlepage to volume 2 is dated 1766. With a divisional title to the N.T. No Apocrypha.
London : printed for Edward and Charles Dilly, 1765-66.
2v. ; 2°

Gale ECCO Print Editions

Relive history with *Eighteenth Century Collections Online*, now available in print for the independent historian and collector. This series includes the most significant English-language and foreign-language works printed in Great Britain during the eighteenth century, and is organized in seven different subject areas including literature and language; medicine, science, and technology; and religion and philosophy. The collection also includes thousands of important works from the Americas.

The eighteenth century has been called "The Age of Enlightenment." It was a period of rapid advance in print culture and publishing, in world exploration, and in the rapid growth of science and technology – all of which had a profound impact on the political and cultural landscape. At the end of the century the American Revolution, French Revolution and Industrial Revolution, perhaps three of the most significant events in modern history, set in motion developments that eventually dominated world political, economic, and social life.

In a groundbreaking effort, Gale initiated a revolution of its own: digitization of epic proportions to preserve these invaluable works in the largest online archive of its kind. Contributions from major world libraries constitute over 175,000 original printed works. Scanned images of the actual pages, rather than transcriptions, recreate the works ***as they first appeared.***

Now for the first time, these high-quality digital scans of original works are available via print-on-demand, making them readily accessible to libraries, students, independent scholars, and readers of all ages.

For our initial release we have created seven robust collections to form one the world's most comprehensive catalogs of 18th century works.

Initial Gale ECCO Print Editions collections include:

> ***History and Geography***
> Rich in titles on English life and social history, this collection spans the world as it was known to eighteenth-century historians and explorers. Titles include a wealth of travel accounts and diaries, histories of nations from throughout the world, and maps and charts of a world that was still being discovered. Students of the War of American Independence will find fascinating accounts from the British side of conflict.

Social Science
Delve into what it was like to live during the eighteenth century by reading the first-hand accounts of everyday people, including city dwellers and farmers, businessmen and bankers, artisans and merchants, artists and their patrons, politicians and their constituents. Original texts make the American, French, and Industrial revolutions vividly contemporary.

Medicine, Science and Technology
Medical theory and practice of the 1700s developed rapidly, as is evidenced by the extensive collection, which includes descriptions of diseases, their conditions, and treatments. Books on science and technology, agriculture, military technology, natural philosophy, even cookbooks, are all contained here.

Literature and Language
Western literary study flows out of eighteenth-century works by Alexander Pope, Daniel Defoe, Henry Fielding, Frances Burney, Denis Diderot, Johann Gottfried Herder, Johann Wolfgang von Goethe, and others. Experience the birth of the modern novel, or compare the development of language using dictionaries and grammar discourses.

Religion and Philosophy
The Age of Enlightenment profoundly enriched religious and philosophical understanding and continues to influence present-day thinking. Works collected here include masterpieces by David Hume, Immanuel Kant, and Jean-Jacques Rousseau, as well as religious sermons and moral debates on the issues of the day, such as the slave trade. The Age of Reason saw conflict between Protestantism and Catholicism transformed into one between faith and logic -- a debate that continues in the twenty-first century.

Law and Reference
This collection reveals the history of English common law and Empire law in a vastly changing world of British expansion. Dominating the legal field is the *Commentaries of the Law of England* by Sir William Blackstone, which first appeared in 1765. Reference works such as almanacs and catalogues continue to educate us by revealing the day-to-day workings of society.

Fine Arts
The eighteenth-century fascination with Greek and Roman antiquity followed the systematic excavation of the ruins at Pompeii and Herculaneum in southern Italy; and after 1750 a neoclassical style dominated all artistic fields. The titles here trace developments in mostly English-language works on painting, sculpture, architecture, music, theater, and other disciplines. Instructional works on musical instruments, catalogs of art objects, comic operas, and more are also included.

THE

Evangelical Expositor:

OR, A

COMMENTARY

ON THE

HOLY BIBLE.

WHEREIN

The Sacred TEXT of the OLD and NEW TESTAMENT is inserted at Large, the Sense Explained; and the more difficult Passages Elucidated:

WITH

PRACTICAL OBSERVATIONS.

ALSO

References to Parallel Scriptures: the Marginal Readings; and a Chronology.

For the Use of Families and Private Christians of every Denomination.

By the Reverend THOMAS HAWEIS,

Rector of Aldwinckle, Northamptonshire, and Chaplain to the Right Honourable the Earl of PETERBOROW.

VOL. II.

LONDON.

Printed for EDWARD and CHARLES DILLY, in the Poultry, near the Mansion House.

MDCCLXVI

PREFACE.

THE prophetical books of the Old Testament, properly so called, are generally divided into the greater and lesser prophets, not that there subsists any difference in their inspiration, but with reference to the length of their several prophecies, the first four being far more voluminous than the sixteen latter.

The word Prophet *is, by the learned, usually derived from an Arabic word, signifying to be lifted up, because, like men on an eminence, the prophets were enabled to descry distant objects beyond the reach of others sight, or as raised to a state of high dignity, by this distinguishing mark of divine favour, or as standing above their audience, that they might be better heard. The word signifies also to publish, or deliver a message, it being the chief employment of these divinely inspired ministers, not merely to predict future events, but also to deliver God's admonitions to the people, to remonstrate against their sins, to invite them to repentance, and return to God; and to denounce the wrath of God on the obstinately impenitent.*

Prophesying, taken in the more enlarged sense, includes all the exercise of God's gifts in speaking, preaching, prayer, or singing psalms, see Exod. vii. 1. 1 Cor. xiv. 1—32. Gen. xx. 7. 1 Cor. xi. 4. 1 Chron. xxv. 1—3. 1 Sam. xix. 20. *but more strictly, is usually confined to the foretelling things to come, or declaring the past, present, or future events, which were so concealed and secret, as to be incapable of being known but by divine revelation, and in this sense chiefly the prophecies before us are to be regarded, where the chief matter is the prediction of future events, interspersed with divine admonitions, doctrines, consolations, and instructions.*

The learned Witsius defines Prophecy to be "A knowledge and manifestation of secret things which a man "attains, not from his own sagacity, or the relations of others, but by an extraordinary revelation from "heaven." A knowledge, *because it was not merely their organs of speech which were employed, but such a clear copy of the truth revealed was imprinted on their minds, and their intellects preserved so entire, that what they delivered they understood, as a man describes in words the thoughts of his own mind.* A manifestation, *because what was revealed to them, they were appointed to declare to others.* The things were secret, *such as no human reason could have known and foreseen, nor any learning have taught, and therefore, though there seem to have been schools of the Prophets very early established, seminaries where young men were trained up in sacred knowledge, and employed in religious exercises, and out of these God might sometimes select particulars for the extraordinary work of revealing his will, yet it was not always the case, God's choice in this matter being sovereign, and he sending by whom he would send. Amos was not a prophet by education, nor the son of a prophet by birth, or from the schools, but a herdsman, when God sent him to prophecy,* Amos vii. 14, 15. For prophecy came not in old time by the will of man, but holy men spake as they were moved by the Holy Ghost, 2 *Pet.* i. 21. *who conveyed the revelation of God's will to their mind, by secret impulse directed and constrained them what and how to speak, and when his divine afflatus was withdrawn, they were no more acquainted with the secrets of God than other holy men.*

The ways in which this divine inspiration was conveyed to their minds were by vision, or dream, Numb. xii. 6. *whether sleeping or waking, by day or night, by external appearances to their bodily sight, or representations made to their imagination, by angelic ministers, by secret impulse or an audible voice, by symbols and and figures, of the meaning and design of which they were informed, and instructed how to explain them to others, and herein they were under the immediate and supernatural guidance of God. An instance or two there is wherein God made use of evidently wicked men to prophecy, as Balaam,* Numb. xxiv. 17. *and Caiaphas,* John xi. 49—52. *but in all other cases, the persons selected were men as eminent for their piety, as distinguished by their prophetical character.*

Prophecy began almost with the creation, in the antediluvian world Adam, Enoch, Noah possessed that high gift, Abraham, Job, Moses succeeded, after a considerable interval it revived in Samuel, and was continued in a succession of holy men, raised up by God, till the canon of the Old Testament closed with Ma-

lachi, more than three hundred years before our Lord's appearing, when in John the Baptist, his forerunner, the prophetic spirit was restored, and in the Revelation of John the Apostle, the vision and prophecy were finally sealed up

The great subjects of the prophetic writings are,

1 Christ, his person, offices, and character, his incarnation, humiliation, sufferings, with the glory which should follow, and these described with such minuteness respecting the time, place, with all the circumstances of his afflicted life, miserable death, glorious resurrection, ascension, and future judgment, that when we compare them with his history in the New Testament, we see them so exactly fulfilled in Jesus the son of Joseph, that nothing but judicial blindness, and wilful rejection of the truth, can leave a suspicion in the mind, but that this is he that should come, neither look we for another

2 His church, the perpetuity of it, amidst all the variety of attacks made on it by men and devils, and the final triumphs of the truth over all the powers of darkness and error

3 The people of the Jews, their various captivities, sufferings, restoration, present dispersion, and their expected conversion in the last days

4. The kingdoms of the earth, the rise and fall of the four great monarchies, the Babylonian, Persian, Grecian, and Roman, together with the particular fate of the nations bordering on Judea, the Egyptians, Philistines, Edomites, Ammonites, Tyrians, &c whereunto may be added, the fall of the Ottoman Empire, the ruin of all the antichristian powers, and the seat of the papacy, events which remain yet to be accomplished

5 The great doctrines of salvation and redemption through the offering of Jesus, and the various duties of all God's people, strongly inculcated, and enforced by admonitions, cautions, exhortations, consolations, and this with such sublimity, purity, simplicity, and uniformity, as carries the strong and striking evidence of the divine authority from whence they proceed

That there should be many passages in the prophets difficult to be understood, cannot be wondered at, when many of the events predicted wait for the comment of time to explain them but by prayer, meditation, and diligent comparing scripture with scripture, we may, through the assistance of that blessed Spirit who dictated the prophecies, come to the understanding of them

The learned Vitringa, in his Typus Doctrinæ Propheticæ, has laid down several rules or canons, very useful and helpful in investigating the true sense of the prophets, which I shall not think it too much labour to transcribe, and are as follow

1 In all interpretation of prophecies, care and pains must be taken, and means used, in the first place, that the subject of the prophecy may be truly known, whether the prophet speaks of himself, or of others; and whether of things in his own time, or of things to come, and of these, whether he speaks of them properly and literally, or improperly and figuratively, See Acts viii 34

2 That we may come to an accurate and distinct knowledge of the subject, we should diligently attend to all the attributes and characters which are applied to that subject in the prophecy for, if the subject is not mentioned by name, it may be found out by the characteristics of it, such are many of the predictions concerning Christ, and if it is expressly named, it should be enquired, whether it is to be taken properly or mystically, or partly properly, and partly mystically, as when any one by name is spoken of, as a type of the Messiah

3 From the literal sense of the subject, when called by its own proper name, we must never depart, if all the attributes, or the more remarkable, noted, and principal ones, agree with the subject of the prophecy, this rule is of considerable use in the prophecies concerning Israel, Judah, Babylon, Egypt, Tyre, and others

4 If the attributes by no means agree with the subject expressed in the prophecy by its own name, we must think of another subject answerable to it, which is mystically called by this name, because of the agreement between the type and the antitype, examples of this are in Edom, Isa lxiii 1 in David, Jer xxx 20 Ezek xxxiv 23, 24 in Elijah, Mal iv 5

5 If, in prophecies, the subject is treated of under its express name, so that it will bear both the proper and mystical interpretation, and the attributes of the prophetic discourse are such, that some of them more rightly agree with the subject mystically taken, and others are more rightly predicated of it, in a literal and grammatical sense, we must take the subject of the prophecy not to be simple, but complex, and that the prophet, being acted and illuminated by the Spirit, so speaks, as that he would be understood of both, and the reader is to be advised of the mystical or allegorical sense, as wrapped up in the literal sense thus, in many of the prophecies concerning Egypt, Babylon, Tyre, and Edom, there are such august and magnificent things, which, if properly taken, will admit but of a very poor and barren exposition, and therefore it must be presumed, that the Holy Ghost designed something more, and to lead our minds to spiritual Egypt, &c and so

sometimes, such grand things are said of the people of the Jews returning from the Babylonish captivity, and of such blessings bestowed upon them, as necessarily oblige us to look out for a further accomplishment in redemption by Christ, and the spiritual blessings of grace bestowed upon the people of God under the gospel dispensation, specimens of which may be seen in Isa lii 1, 2, 3. Jer iii. 14, 15, 16

6 *In continued prophecies, which are not distinguished one from another by titles or inscriptions, we should carefully attend both to the beginning and end of the prophetic sermons, both to the epocha of the time in which the scene of the prophetic vision is fixed, and its termination the former of these especially has its use in the sermons of* Isaiah, *which follow the fortieth chapter of that book*

7 *It is probable, that those prophecies, whose* terminus a quo *demonstrates the beginning of the time of Christ's kingdom, and the* terminus ad quem, *the end of that time, give a narration of the chief things that shall befal the church in a continued series, unless any thing hinders, which obliges us to go back to former times The interpretation of the prophecy of* Isaiah, *from chap* liv 1 *to chap* lx 22 *depends on this foundation The beginning of this prophecy, without all doubt, is to be applied to the beginning of the kingdom of Christ, the term or end falls upon the most flourishing state of that kingdom, which is to follow the conversion of the Jewish nation, and the vindication of the afflicted church, of which* Isa lix 19, 20, 21 *which flourishing state of the kingdom of Christ is described throughout the whole sixtieth chapter It is very likely therefore, that what is intermediate, treats of the affairs or fates of both terms I affirm not this however as absolutely certain, but rather refer it to more accurate enquiry, for I do not deny that there are specious objections*

8 *Yet it is to be observed, that some prophecies, whose context is continued, admit of resumptions, repetitions of sayings, and retrograde leaps, or scattered or detached pieces, belonging to superior times, which are inserted into the context, for the sake of illustrating this or that part of the prophecy, examples of which are in* Zech xiii 7 *and in* Isa xl xli xlii

9 *To these also may be rightly referred the excursions and digressions, in which the prophets, whilst they really have before their eyes some object of more remote time, suddenly leave it, and by way of excursion turn themselves to men of their own time, or the next, that from the subject of their prophecy, they may admonish, exhort, and convince them, which when they have done, they resume the thread of their prophecy, an instance of which is in* Joel iii *from* ver 1 *to* ver 9

10. *That interpretation of the word of God, and especially of the prophecies, is to be accounted the best, which attends to, pursues, and demonstrates the greatest emphasis of the oration or speech, and the wisdom of the Holy Ghost, a good and sure rule, and yet to be applied prudently to the subject-context of the prophecy*

11. *A sure key for the interpretation of prophecy is, a true understanding of Christ Jesus, and of righteousness to be procured by him for the church, and of the spiritual kingdom to be founded by him in the world, according to that of the apostle,* Rom xii 6 let us prophesy according to the proportion *or* analogy of faith, *for the prophets prophesied chiefly of the Messiah and his kingdom, and of the times and prerogatives of it*

12. *Wherefore, when there is a twofold method of interpreting prophesies, the one barren, the other liberal, of which, those that follow that, with difficulty, and more rarely, find Christ Jesus and his kingdom, and those who adopt this, more frequently find Christ, and things that belong to him it seems not to be doubted of, but the latter is to be preferred to the former This is a rule of great use and profit certainly the Spirit, which was in the prophets, either is not Christ's, or he directly speaks of Christ, if he speaks directly and clearly of Christ, it is the business of a good interpreter, first indeed to seek diligently after Christ in the prophetic word, then, if occasion favours, to demonstrate it, but never to shun any opportunity, when it offers itself, but willingly take it*

13 *Since it is not only probable, but certain, that there are in the prophetic part of the word, distinct delineations of the whole counsel of God, interpreters act rightly, who in prophecies, which, it is plain, treat of the kingdom of Christ, and the affairs of it, industriously attend to the events of the church of Christ, known from history, and produce them from the same, so that it is done without offering any violence to the scripture, since God does nothing but he reveals his secret to his servants the prophets,* Amos iii 7

14 *The interpretation of the word of prophecy made by Christ, and by the apostles, and by the Holy Ghost, in the* Revelation, *is a rule and key of rightly explaining the prophecies which they have touched upon, who can doubt of this? since every one is the best interpreter of his own words, so it should be thought that the Holy Ghost, in more recent prophecies, alludes to ancient ones, yea, often uses the same words, phrases and images, and the like, which he did formerly, designing thereby, to lead us by the hand to the true understanding of those oracles*

15 *Whatsoever excellently, gloriously, emphatically, characteristically, is predicted of some certain person, not called by his own name, in the prophecies, or in the psalms, so that the singular predicates can be demonstrated in no singular subject of that or any other time, it must be taken as said and predicted of the Messiah This rule will deceive no man*

16. *In prophecies which treat of Christ and his kingdom, that sense is the best, which is the most spiritual This canon hath a certain and easy demonstration; for the kingdom of Christ is no other foretold in prophecies, than it is manifest in time, but that is not of this world, it is spiritual,* John xviii. 36 Rom xiv 17. *therefore no interpretation is of avail, none is right and good, which understands those things corporally, which are predicated of a thing spiritual; for the attributes and predicates of a spiritual thing are spiritual*

17 *In prophecies, in some places prudently to be distinguished, there obtains an* ὕστερον πρότερον, *so that on which we must dwell, should be put in the last place, that it may be carried on without interruption to the end*

18 *The writers of the New Testament, in confirmation of their doctrines from the prophetic writings, oftentimes borrow words from one prophet, and take the thing from another.*

19 *In things future, we must not indulge our conjectures, but as it becomes the faith and modesty of Christians; what are indefinitely said, and not determined by parallel prophecies, we must reckon that God wills those things should be put in his own power, as to mode, persons, times, places, and species*

THE

EVANGELICAL EXPOSITOR;

OR, A

PRACTICAL COMMENT

Upon the Book of the PROPHET

ISAIAH.

ISAIAH *is the first of the prophets, not that his prophecy was first written, but because it is the largest, and fullest of the notices of the Messiah, concerning whose person, offices, and kingdom, he hath spoken so clearly, that he hath justly obtained the name of the Evangelical Prophet. Hence in the New Testament we find more quotations taken from this book, than from any other part of Scripture, the Psalms excepted.*

Who Isaiah was, is uncertain: the Jewish tradition is that he was of the seed-royal, and nearly allied to Amaziah; but there appears no proof of this assertion. Certain it is, he was much at court, and his stile and manner refined, and peculiarly elegant and lofty. It being a very reasonable observation made concerning those whom God employed, that though they were under the immediate influence of his Spirit, he acted upon them as men, not merely as machines; and therefore, though the matter and substance was from him, they were to make use of their several natural faculties in expressing and conveying the notices given them of the Divine Will.

That he lived to a good old age, the length of the time he prophesied shews; but when he died is uncertain, some extending his life to the time of Manasseh, when they say he suffered martyrdom, and was sawn asunder, to which Heb. xi. 37. *is supposed to allude; but it is more generally supposed, that he died before Hezekiah, the name of Manasseh not being mentioned among the kings under whose reigns he lived and prophesied,* Chap. i. 1.

The contents of this book are partly historical, partly prophetical, relative to the state of the Jews and other nations, and more especially to the kingdom and church of Christ; and this sometimes expressed clearly and distinctly, sometimes more obscurely, under the type of the Jewish captivity and deliverance.

The beginning of the prophecy abounds most with reproofs for sins, and threatenings of judgment; the conclusion, with bright displays of the Redeemer's kingdom, and the grace to be brought to light in the gospel. They will give the glad tidings of a Saviour's grace the most hearty welcome, who are most deeply sensible of their sin, guilt, and danger.

Before Christ 760

CHAP. I.

The prophecy opens with, 1. A high charge against the Jewish church and nation, (1.) For their ingratitude, ver. 2, 3. (2.) For their incorrigibleness, ver. 5. (3.) For the universal degeneracy of the people, ver. 4, 6, 21, 22. (4.) For their rulers perverting of justice, ver. 23. 2. A sad complaint of the judgments of God, which their sins had brought upon them, ver. 7—9. 3. A just rejection of their formal worship amidst this general defection and apostasy, ver. 10—15. 4. An earnest call to repentance and reformation, setting before them life and death, life if they complied with the call, and death if they did not, ver. 16—20. 5. A threatening of ruin to those that would not be reformed, ver. 24, 28—31. 6. A promise of a happy reformation at last, and a return to their primitive purity and prosperity, ver. 25—27.

1 [a]THE vision of Isaiah the son of Amoz, which he saw concerning Judah and Jerusalem, in the days of Uzziah, Jotham, Ahaz, *and* Hezekiah, kings of Judah. Before Christ 760

a Num. xii. 6.

Ver. 1. The first verse is a kind of title to the whole book. The author is Isaiah, which signifies *the salvation of the Lord*; his father was Amoz, not Amos the prophet, but a different person, and of a different name. It is called his vision, as being delivered to him in this way; and, as he had himself a clear understanding of what he spoke, he delivered it very perspicuously to others. The great subject of the prophecy is said to be Judah and Jerusalem, little mention being made of the rest of the revolted Israelites; and when notice is taken of other nations, it is because of their connection with the Jews, and their captivity by them, or deliverance from them. Under four

kings,

kings his ministry continued, but in what year of Uzziah he began, or in which of Hezekiah he finished, is uncertain. Certain however it is, that he lived to see the best and worst of times, and under both proved himself alike faithful. They who live long may expect to see strange alterations; happy if with the prophet they can in all states and conditions approve their unshaken fidelity to Jesus.

2 Hear, O heavens, and give ear, O earth: for the
LORD hath spoken, I have nourished and brought up
children, and they have rebelled against me. 3 The
ox knoweth his owner, and the ass his master's crib:
but Israel doth not know, my people doth not consider.
4 Ah sinful nation, a people laden with iniquity, a
seed of evil doers, children that are corrupters: they
have forsaken the LORD, they have provoked the
holy One of Israel unto anger, they are † gone away
backward. 5 ¶ Why should ye be stricken any more?
ye will revolt more and more: the whole head is sick,
and the whole heart faint. 6 From the sole of the
foot even unto the head, *there is* no soundness in it;
but wounds, and bruises, and putrifying sores: they
have not been closed, neither bound up, neither mollified
with ‡ ointment. 7 Your country *is* desolate, your
cities *are* burnt with fire: your land, strangers devour
it in your presence, and *it is* desolate as overthrown by
strangers. 8 And the daughter of Zion is left as a
cottage in a vineyard, as a lodge in a garden of cucumbers,
as a besieged city. 9 Except the LORD of
hosts had left unto us a very small remnant, we should
have been as Sodom, *and* we should have been like
unto Gomorrah.

Ver. 2—9. Dark and dismal is the prospect with which the prophet opens his discourse.

1. He begins with an address to the heavens and the earth, ver. 2. as if turning from an incorrigible people, deaf to reproof, to the inanimate creation, or appealing to the hosts above, and men in general, to record God's mercies and his people's impenitence.

2. He charges them with black ingratitude. *I have nourished and brought up children*, or, *I have magnified and exalted them*, not only preserved them from their state of infancy, but distinguished them with such peculiar marks of honour, *and they rebelled against me*, made him such base requital for his mercy, rejecting his government, and apostates from his worship. *Note*, (1.) Ingratitude is justly reckoned among the greatest crimes. (2.) As no kindness can equal that which God hath shown to the sons of men in creation, and especially in redemption, so can no ingratitude be so great and criminal as that of the impenitent sinner.

3. He upbraids them with the more than brutish stupidity of their conduct. The dull ox appears sensible of the hand that feeds him, and knoweth his owner's voice; and the very ass the crib that feeds him, *but* more stupid *Israel doth not know*, or acknowledge the gracious care of God, nor make the least suitable returns of love, *and my people doth not consider*, they pay no regard to the ordinances of God's service, and, wilfully obstinate, neither know nor desire to know him. *Note*, (1.) When men chuse dissipation, and fly from every means which would lead them to consider their ways, they cannot but be led captive by the devil at his will. (2.) Many are in profession God's people, whose practice is utterly opposite thereto, and their sin highly aggravated. (3.) Negligence about God and our soul must necessarily end in ruin.

4. He dwells upon their wretched state, either as threatening them with the consequences of their sins, or lamenting the evils he foresaw. *Ah, sinful nation!* what will be thine end? How grievous the prospect! universal apostasy reigned, *a people laden with iniquity*, sinking under the heavy load and curse of it, *a seed of evil doers*, degenerated utterly from their pious ancestors; *children that are corrupters*, not content with being abandoned themselves, but doing the devil's work, in turning tempters to others. *They have forsaken the Lord*, his ways and worship; *they have provoked the holy One of Israel unto anger*, justly incensed at such rebellious conduct: *they are gone away backward*, vile apostates from their holy profession. *Note*, When God comes to visit for sins, he will be minute; and every aggravation of them will be remembered, to fill up the measure of wrath.

5. They were incorrigible under every visitation, and their case desperate. *Why should ye be stricken any more?* when all the past visitation produced no gracious effects. *Ye will revolt more and more*; made desperate, and hardened by the correction which should have led them to repentance. *The whole head is sick, and the whole heart is faint*, which may respect their sufferings; or, that, though reaching from the highest to the lowest, produced no reformation of their sins, which had so thoroughly infected priests and people, that, like a leper, from head to foot

not a sound part was left, and, impenitently obstinate, none thought of repentance, or laboured to avert the heavy judgments under which they groaned, ver. 6. *Note*, (1.) We have here a lively picture of the corruption of the human heart, universally defiled by sin, loathsome before God, and incurably desperate for ought that man can do to help himself. (2.) Afflictions, though a bitter potion, are the means God often employs to awaken the sinner's conscience, and restore health to his soul. (3.) When sinners refuse to answer the gracious visitations of God, instead of being humbled by them, they grow more hardened. (4.) The case of that soul is desperate indeed, concerning which God saith, Let him alone.

6. He laments the desolations of Zion that are begun, or rather foretels what will be shortly her sad case. *Your country is*, or shall be, *desolate*, ravaged by their enemies, the cities burnt, their land devoured by strangers, whilst they looked on, unable to prevent their ruin; their country a desert, the holy city and temple depopulated, deserted, despicable, ruinous, as the wretched hut which the keeper of the vineyard forsakes when the vintage is gathered, and the lodge, where the gardener watched till his fruit was safe, and then is overturned with winter's blasts. Or like a besieged city, from which escape is so difficult and dangerous, and which none care to approach. This was the case, 2 *Chron.* xxviii. 17—19. under Ahaz, during whose wicked reign it is supposed this was written; or it refers to the desolations which at first the Babylonians, and afterwards, more dreadfully, the Romans brought upon them. *Note*, They who will not be warned, must smart for it: whether it be a nation or individual, impenitence and perdition are inseparable.

7. A few, and but a few, still remained, thro' divine grace, firm to God amidst the general apostacy; and, but for these, utter extirpation must have ensued, dreadful as that which fell upon the devoted cities of Sodom and Gomorrah. The Apostle quotes this as applicable to his own times, and descriptive of them, *Rom.* ix. 29. when, except the few who received the gospel, the rest of the Jewish nation persisted in unbelief and hardness of heart. *Note*, (1.) It is a mercy, that God reserves a few faithful in the worst of times. (2.) The fewer they are, and the more wicked the days, the greater diligence should we give to be of that few. (3.) If ever we are saved out of this world, which lieth in wickedness, we shall be convinced it is by sovereign and almighty grace alone. (4.) To go with the multitude is the sure way to hell. (5.) The more we reflect upon the wonders of grace, in plucking us as brands from the burning, the more should our hearts abound in love and praise.

10 ¶ Hear the word of the LORD, ye rulers
of Sodom; give ear unto the law of our God, ye
people of Gomorrah. 11 To what purpose *is* the multitude
of your sacrifices to me? saith the LORD:
I am full of the burnt-offerings of rams, and the fat of
fed beasts; and I delight not in the blood of bullocks,
or of lambs, or of he-goats. 12 When ye come to
appear before me, who hath required this at your
hand to tread my courts? 13 Bring no more vain
oblations; incense is an abomination to me; the
new moons and sabbaths, the calling of assemblies, I
cannot away with; *it is* ‖ iniquity, even the solemn meeting.
14 Your new moons, and your appointed feasts
my soul hateth: they are a trouble unto me; I am
weary to bear *them*. 15 And when ye spread forth
your hands, I will hide mine eyes from you: yea, when
ye make many prayers, I will not hear: your hands
are full of blood.

Ver. 10—15. We have here,

1. An awful address to the rulers and people, to hear God's word. He calls them rulers of Sodom, and people of Gomorrah, because, like them, they were *sinners before the Lord exceedingly*, Gen. xiii. 13. and magistrates, priests, and people, sunk in the deluge of iniquity. Perhaps he has reference here to the gospel, which the Jewish people were called to receive, and for rejecting which, it will be more tolerable in the day of judgment for Sodom, than for them, *Mat.* xi. 24.

2. He rejects all their hypocritical services and sacrifices. Their most solemn assemblies, their feasts, sabbaths, incense, prayers, were an abomination. What purpose could they answer, when their hands were defiled with blood, and remaining pride, impenitence, and unbelief, made these outward ceremonies, however expensive, but solemn mockery of God. This is especially applicable to the time of Christ, when with the greatest zeal the Scribes and Pharisees maintained the temple worship, whilst they rejected him who was prefigured in their institutions, and exclusive of whom God never delighted in the most expensive sacrifices; and after having imbrued their hands in the Saviour's blood, though by his death an end was put to all the ritual service, yet they persisted in them, till God

dissolved

Before Christ 760.

destroyed their city and temple together *Note*, (1) The greatest enemies to the power of godliness are often those who are most rigid observers of the form (2) Whilst inward iniquity is harboured, and the heart continues estranged from God, the most liberal charities, or the largest gifts to God's altar, will be rejected with abhorrence (3) Many in a fright will be driven to their knees and their prayers, who are not driven from their sins, and therefore pray in vain (4) So far are all the outward services of religious worship from pleasing God, where the soul is unconverted and self-righteous, that he abhors the sabbaths and the solemn meeting, so that the very duties on which the formalists depend, will prove their damnation

b Jer iv 14 c Ps xxxiv 14 & xxxvii 27 Amos v 15 Rom xii 9 1 Pet iii 11 † Or, right d Chap xliii 26 e Ps li 7 Rev vii 14 f Tit i 2

16 ¶ [b] Wash ye, make you clean, put away the evil
of your doings from before mine eyes, [c] cease to do evil,
17 Learn to do well, seek judgment, † relieve the op-
pressed, judge the fatherless, plead for the widow 18
Come now and [d] let us reason together, saith the LORD
though your sins be as scarlet, [e] they shall be as white as
snow though they be red like crimson, they shall be
as wool 19 If ye be willing and obedient, ye shall eat
the good of the land. 20 But if ye refuse and rebel,
ye shall be devoured with the sword for [f] the mouth
of the LORD hath spoken *it*.

v 16—20 Since the ceremonial worship was declared ineffectual, the prophet directs them to the only sufficient means of acceptance with God

1 By washing and making themselves clean, which all their ritual ablutions never could effect, and therefore they must come by faith, under the sense of their guilt and pollution, to the fountain which should be opened in a Saviour's blood *Note*, We might as soon think to wash the Ethiopian white, as to remove one spot of sin from our souls by any other method, than through the atoning blood of Jesus

2 As washed from their sins they must amend their lives, putting away all known evil, making restitution for every act of injustice, and ceasing from allowed sin They must not merely rest in negative holiness, but exercise themselves unto godliness in the practice of every good word and work, under the influence of divine grace, and with a single eye to the divine glory And he instances wherein this course of well-doing consists, under the two great points of mercy and justice, which would please the Lord better than the most costly sacrifices *Note*, (1) Where the blood of Jesus cleanses from the guilt of sin, the Spirit of Jesus will deliver from the power of it, and in vain do they hope for the one, who continue strangers to the other (2) Though perfectly to cease from sin is the blessedness reserved for us above, yet here we shall obtain the testimony of a good conscience, that in simplicity and godly sincerity we have our conversation in the world (3) A Christian has no time to be idle, much hath he to learn, much to do, and all his attention and care will be little enough for the great work that is before him

3 He silences an objection which might be raised in the minds of those, whose deep views of past guilt might discourage them from returning to God, as if their sins were beyond pardon and hope *Though your sins be as scarlet, they shall be as white as snow though they be red like crimson, they shall be as wool* how very great and aggravated their iniquities, they need not be discouraged nay, are invited to *come*, yea, to *come now* without delay, *and let us reason together, saith the Lord*, though on the footing of their own deeds or duties they could not appear in any wise at God's bar, yet, when God put that prevailing argument in their mouths of the promises of full and free pardon through the blood and righteousness of a Redeemer, then they might come boldly to the throne, and fear no condemnation, the plea would be accepted, the sinner justified from all things *Note*, That blood of Jesus which alone can cleanse from the least sin, can fully and effectually cleanse from the greatest let no returning sinner despair

4 He sets before them the blessing and the curse *If ye be willing* to submit to this advice, to wash and be clean, *and obedient* to the word and ways of God, *ye shall eat the good of the land*, the land of Canaan, in which their abode would be sure, as long as their fidelity was maintained, and a better country than this also is the portion of the faithful servants of God *But if ye refuse* to hearken to these admonitions, *and rebel* against the government and ministers of God, and against his incarnate word the Messiah, then their ruin was determined, *the mouth of the Lord hath spoken it*, the sentence is fixed and irrevocable, *ye shall be devoured with the sword* of the Babylonian and Romans, executing upon them God's temporal judgments, and by the sword of eternal vengeance after death pursuing them to the lowest hell *Note*, (1) If sinners perish, it will not be for lack of warning, their blood is upon their own heads (2) They who will not submit to God's sceptre, must suffer under his sword (3) When sinners perish in their rebellion, they reject their own mercies, and God's justice in their condemnation will be manifest to all

Before Christ 760.

g Jer ii 21 h Jer vi 28 30 Ezek xxii 18 19 i Hos iv 18 k Hos ix 15 l Ezek xxii 12 Hos iv 18 Mic iii 11 m Jer v 28 Zech vii 10 n Deut xxviii 63 Ezek v 13 o Jer v 9 p Jer vi 29 & ix 7 Mal iii 3 q Jer xxxiii 7 r Chap ix 18 Zech viii 3 † Or, they that return of her s Job xxxi 3 Ps i 6 & xcii 9 & civ 35 t Chap lvii 5 u Chap lxv 3 & lxvi 17 x Jer xvi 6 y Ezek xxxii ‡ Or, his work z Chap xxxiv 10 Rev xiv 11

21 ¶ [g] How is the faithful city become an harlot! it
was full of judgment, righteousness lodged in it, but
now murderers 22 Thy silver is become dross, [i] thy
wine mixt with water 23 [k] Thy princes *are* rebel-
lious, and companions of thieves [l] every one loveth
gifts, and followeth after rewards, [m] they judge not the
fatherless, neither doth the cause of the widow come
unto them. 24 Therefore saith the LORD, the LORD
of hosts, the mighty One of Israel, Ah, [n] I will ease me
of mine adversaries, [o] and avenge me of mine enemies
25 ¶ And I will turn my hand upon thee, and [p] purely
purge away thy dross, and take away all thy tin 26
And I will restore thy judges [q] as at the first, and thy
counsellors as at the beginning afterward [r] thou shalt
be called, the city of righteousness, the faithful city
27 Zion shall be redeemed with judgment, and † her
converts with righteousness 28 ¶ And [s] the destruction
of the transgressors and of the sinners *shall be* together,
and they that forsake the LORD shall be consumed.
29 For they shall be ashamed of [t] the oaks which ye
have desired, [u] and ye shall be confounded for the gardens
that ye have chosen 30 For ye shall be [x] as an oak
whose leaf fadeth, and as a garden that hath no water
31. And [y] the strong shall be as tow, and ‡ the maker of
it as a spark, and they shall both burn together, and
[z] none shall quench *them*

v 21—31 As Jesus wept over the devoted city, the prophet, moved with a portion of his compassionate spirit, laments the wickedness he beheld

1 An aweful change had passed on Jerusalem the once faithful city is become an harlot, turning from the worship and service of God, and prostituting herself to all the abominations of iniquity It was in past days famed for justice, *full of judgment*, her magistrates distinguished for integrity, *righteousness lodged in it*, as it chosen for her favoured abode But how awful the contrast! *now murderers*, who first massacred the prophets who witnessed of the just One, and then at last murdered the Son of God, *Mat* xxiii 37 *Acts* vii 52 Pure once, and bright as silver, dross now only remained, their practice corrupt, and their principles depraved *Thy wine is mixed with water*, the lively oracles of God adulterated and debased by false glosses, and human traditions, so that it was become of no effect *Thy princes are rebellious*, ringleaders in sin, *and companions of thieves*, conniving at their crimes, and, for the protection they afforded, sharing of the fruits of their robberies Gifts and bribes were then known delight, and ever carried the cause at their bar, whilst the poor, the fatherless, and widow, who had nothing to give, were suffered to be oppressed without redress; and such was exactly the character of the Jews in our Saviour's days, *See Rom* ii *Note*, (1) Prostitution of justice for gain is more infamous than the prostitution of the harlot for hire (2) Injustice and bribery on the seat of judgment are heavier curses on any people, than the ravages of the worst banditti against the one we may guard, from the other there is no redress. (3) We must not only abstain from injuring the poor, we are criminal if we neglect to vindicate them from oppressors, and to espouse the cause of the afflicted (4) The former good examples of preceding magistrates, or illustrious progenitors, reflect double darkness on their degenerate successors

2 God with indignation awakes to execute vengeance on his enemies *Ah, I will ease me* of them, as a load under which the earth groaned or, *I will take comfort of* them, pleased with the execution of righteous judgment upon them And this he confirms by a recital of his glorious titles, *The Lord of hosts, the mighty One of Israel*, able to fulfil all his threatenings, and before whom every foe must fall Terrible was the execution of this threatening in their first destruction by the Babylonians, but most fearful, when, having rejected and murdered the Lord of life, he employed the Roman sword, and commanded these his enemies, who would not that he should reign over them, to be slain before him

3 A part shall be recovered, converted, and saved *I will turn my hand upon thee*, revive the decayed state of religion, purging their dross away in the furnace of affliction, and taking away the tin, the adulteration they had mixed in their worship, and the corruptions of their practice, restoring their judges as at the first, and counsellors as at the beginning, and then they would recover their former credit and honour, as *the city of righteousness*, *the faithful city*, redeemed by judgment executed on their foes, and being now converted unto God, his righteousness became engaged for their recovery And this was the case in some measure under Hezekiah's reformation, and may look to their restoration from Babylon but especially regards the day of Christ, when, by the powerful grace of God in the gospel, such multitudes of Jews were converted, their sin, as dross, purged away, their self-righteousness, like tin, renounced, as false and base alloy The apostles, as judges, were

raised

Before Christ 760

raised up to recover them from the worst enemies, sin and Satan, and to counsel and direct them in the way of truth and holiness Being incorporated in Christ's church, they would become a praise in the earth, a people clothed with righteousness imputed and impressed, and faithful to Christ, his gospel, and ordinances His Zion is thus redeemed by the judgment executed on the divine Redeemer in her stead, and *her converts with righteousness*, in a way perfectly consistent with the holiness of God, whose righteousness eminently appears displayed in the salvation of the gospel *Note*, (1) Every man by nature and practice is the slave of sin, that worst of slavery, till redeemed by grace (2) The work of conversion belongs to God alone, he must turn us, or we never shall be turned (3) The Redeemer's righteousness is the great meritorious cause of our conversion, whereby God can be just, when he is the justifier of him that believeth on Jesus (4) When we recover the favour of God we had forfeited, we shall be restored to the honour we had lost

4 The destruction of the enemies of Christ and his people is as sure as their salvation Together they will perish, *v* 28 Their false confidence shall fail and confound them, *v* 29 Stripped as the oak in winter, they shall be left naked and bare, and withered as the garden that hath no water, *v* 30 The strong shall be as unable to resist, as the tow before the devouring fire, and *the maker of it*, the idol, or *his work*, all the devices of the transgressors, shall be *as a spark* of fire, *and they shall burn together, and none shall quench them*, which will eminently be fulfilled in the day of final recompense, when God shall execute judgment upon the ungodly, and the man of sin and all his followers, who have forsaken the ways of truth for lying vanities, human traditions, false doctrines and worship, and abominable idolatries, will have their portion together in the lake which burneth with fire and brimstone, which is the second death, *See Rev* xx 10

CHAP II

With this chapter begins a new sermon, which is continued in the two following ones The subject of it is Judah and Jerusalem, ver 1 The prophet foretels, 1 The glory of the gospel-church in the latter days, ver 2, 3 and the great peace it should introduce into the world, ver 4 whence he infers the duty of the house of Jacob, ver 5 2 The rejection of the Jews for their sins, ver 6—9. 3 That God by his judgments would humble them, ver 10—17. 4 That they should themselves be ashamed of their confidence in their idols, and in an arm of flesh, ver 18—22

1 THE word that Isaiah the son of Amoz saw, concerning Judah and Jerusalem 2 And [a] it shall
come to pass in the last days, *that* [b] the mountain of the
LORD's house shall be established in the top of the
mountains, and shall be exalted [c] above the hills, and
[d] all nations shall flow unto it 3 And many people
shall go and say, [e] Come ye, and let us go up to the
mountain of the LORD, to the house of the God of
Jacob, and [f] he will teach us of his ways, and we will
walk in his paths, for [g] out of Zion shall go forth the
law, and the word of the LORD from Jerusalem, 4
And he shall judge among the nations, and shall [h] rebuke many people and [i] they shall beat their swords
into plow-shares, and their spears into pruning-hooks
nation shall not lift up sword against nation, neither
shall they learn war any more 5 O house of Jacob,
come ye, and [k] let us walk in the light of the LORD

a Mic iv 1 &c
b Zech viii 3
c Mat v 14
d Chap xi 10 Jer iii 17 & xxxi 12
e Jer xxxi 6 & l 5 Zech viii 20—23
f Ps lxxxvi 11
g Luke xxiv 47
h John xvi 8
i Ps xlvi 9 Hos ii 18 Zech ix 10
k Ps lxxxix 15 John xii 35 Eph v 8

v 1—5 We have here a glorious prophecy of the establishment of the kingdom and church of Christ in the last days, the days of the Messiah The gospel is the last dispensation, nothing now remains but the great consummation of all things at the second appearing of the great God and Saviour

1 *The mountain of the Lord's house*, his church, firm and immoveable, *shall be established on the top of the mountains*, in Christ, who is the head of all principalities and powers, *and*, with a supremacy over all the kingdoms of the earth, *shall be exalted above the hills*, the antichristian powers, whether papal, pagan, or Mahometan, being subdued before it *Note*, Whatever oppressions the church for a time may groan under, in the end she will see all her enemies at her feet

2 *All nations shall flow unto it*, many out of all lands shall be incorporated into it, and, having tasted the blessedness of Christ's service, shall be zealously solicitous to propagate his holy religion, and engage others to go with them *Many people shall go and say, Come ye*, along with us, *and let us go up to the mountain of the Lord*, his church, *and to the house of the God of Jacob*, the place he hath chosen for his blessed abode And, as an argument to enforce their exhortation, they urge, *and he will teach us of his ways*, his holy happy ways of grace, mercy, and peace, *and we will walk in his paths* instructed by his word, and strengthened by his Spirit *Note*, (1) The gospel shall have a more glorious and universal spread than ever yet it hath had (2) They who are Christ's people, are not only made willing to follow him themselves, but are zealous to engage others to come and partake of the same blessing (3) None can teach us effectually, but God himself Though the best means may be employed, unless he gives the increase, Paul plants and Apollos waters in vain (4) They who would go to the mount of God, must go *up*, in opposition to corrupt nature, and expect many difficulties in the ascent from the world and Satan, but every pain will be amply repaid, when we shall reach the summit (5) They who are taught of God are made obedient to his holy will, their knowledge hath a sanctifying influence, engaging them to walk and please God

3 The means God will employ for this purpose *Out of Zion shall go forth the law*, or *doctrine*, the gospel, the law of the Spirit of life *and the word of the Lord from Jerusalem*, where the incarnate word appeared, and from whence he sent forth his apostles to preach the gospel unto every creature, which hath been done in a measure, continues still to be spread, and will more eminently be propagated than ever, before the second coming of Christ

4 The blessing of Christ's government is declared *He shall judge among the nations*, holding the reigns of universal dominion, and ruling with the most consummate equity, *and shall rebuke many people*, convince and convert them from the error of their ways by his word and Spirit Peace then will bless the earth, such as hath never yet been known *They shall beat their swords into plough-shares, and their spears into pruning-hooks nation shall not lift up sword against nation, neither shall they learn war any more* In part we see this fulfilled, so far as the gospel obtains power and influence on the heart, it leads us to follow peace with all men, but the state of perfect harmony here described remains yet to come, when Christ shall reign over his saints gloriously

5 The Gentile church addresses the Jewish people, sollicitous for their conversion *O house of Jacob, come ye*, and join us in the worship and ordinances of the gospel, *and let us walk in the light of the Lord*, in the light of the Sun of Righteousness, the divine Redeemer, whose word is our bright guide through time unto eternity, and whilst by faith and love we cleave to him, and look up in prayer for continued support, he will lead us by his counsel, till he shall bring us to his glory

6 ¶ Therefore [l] thou hast forsaken thy people, the
house of Jacob, because they be replenished ‖ from the
east, and [m] *are* soothsayers like the Philistines, and [n] they
please themselves in the children of strangers 7 [o] Their
land also is full of silver and gold, neither *is there any*
end of their treasures their land is also full of horses,
neither *is there any* end of their chariots 8 [p] Their land
also is full of idols they worship the work of their own
hands, that which their own fingers have made 9 And
the mean man boweth down, and the great man humbleth himself [q] therefore forgive them not

l Rom xi 20
‖ Or more than the east
m Deut xviii 14
n Jer x 2
o Deut xvii 16 17
p Jer ii 28
q Chap xxvii 11

v 6—9 These words contain a reason for the divine conduct in the rejection of the Jews, and vocation of the Gentiles

1 Their sins were great they introduced the magic and sorceries of the east, imitated, in their arts of divination, the Philistines, and preferred the children of strangers to native Israelites, *v* 6 Though God had forbidden them to multiply riches, and chariots, and horses, to appear formidable to their neighbours, yet they anxiously laboured to procure these as their confidence, instead of God's promise and care, *v* 7 Though he had so awfully warned them against idols, they had filled their land with them, *v* 8 and high and low joined in the idolatrous service, *v* 9 This description suits the times in which the prophet spoke, better than their state after their return from Babylon, and every preceding generation, as well as that which immediately rejected Christ, contributed to fill up the measure of their nation's guilt Some refer this to Antichrist and his followers, who call themselves the people of God, but shew the marks of an apostate church The [illegible], trick, and frauds of Romish priests are well known, their convents filled with children of strangers, or they please themselves in unnatural lust with such, whence Rome is called spiritually Sodom, *Rev* xi 8 They enrich themselves by masses, indulgences, &c and, attended with great pomp of chariots and horses, their ecclesiastics appear in all the magnificence of worldly splendor Full of idols, worshipping images of pretended saints, and of many who never existed, and all sunk in the same idolatrous folly like priest, like people

2 Their doom was heavy God had forsaken them, given them up to a reprobate mind, they would never be forgiven, either in this world or that which is to come, but all such practices be punished with eternal vengeance This was verified in the [illegible] desolations the Romans brought upon the Jewish people, when the body of the nation was so terribly destroyed,

Before Christ 760

ſtroyed, and ſhall be more fully accompliſhed in the eternal ruin of all the impenitently wicked in the day of God

10 ʳ ¶ Enter into the rock, and hide thee in the duſt,
for fear of the LORD, and for the glory of his majeſty
11 ˢ The lofty looks of man ſhall be humbled, and the
haughtineſs of men ſhall be bowed down, and ᵗ the
LORD alone ſhall be exalted in that day 12 For the
day of the LORD of hoſts *ſhall be* upon every *one that is*
proud and lofty, and upon every *one that is* lifted up,
and he ſhall be brought low, 13 And upon all ᵘ the
cedars of Lebanon, *that are* high and lifted up, and up-
on all the oaks of Baſhan, 14 And upon all ˣ the
high mountains, and upon all the hills *that are* lifted up,
15 And upon every high tower, and upon every fenced
wall, 16 And ʸ upon all the ſhips of Tarſhiſh, and upon
all † pleaſant pictures 17 And ᶻ the loftineſs of man
ſhall be bowed down, and the haughtineſs of men ſhall
be made low . and the LORD alone ſhall be exalted in
that day 18 And the idols he ſhall utterly aboliſh
19 And ᵃ they ſhall go into the holes of the rocks, and
into the caves of the earth, for fear of the LORD, and
ᵇ for the glory of his majeſty, when he ariſeth to ſhake
terribly the earth 20 In that day ᶜ a man ſhall caſt
his idols of ſilver, and his idols of gold, which they
made, *each one* for himſelf to worſhip, to the moles, and
to the bats 21 ᵈ To go into the clefts of the rocks,
and into the tops of the ragged rocks, for fear of the
LORD, and for the glory of his majeſty, when he
ariſeth to ſhake terribly the earth 22 Ceaſe ye from
man, ᶠ whoſe breath *is* in his noſtrils for wherein is he
to be accounted of ?

r Ver xix 21 Rev vi 15
s Ver 17 Chap v 15 & xxiv 21 t 1 Cor i 31
u Ezek xxxi 3—11 Amos ii 9 Zech xi 1, 2
x 2 Cor x 5
y Pſ xlviii 7
† Heb Pictures of deſire
z Ver 11 Chap xiii 11
a Ver 10 Hoſ x 8 Luke xxiii 30 Rev vi 16 & ix 6
b 2 Theſ i 9
c Chap xxx 22 & xxxi 7
d Ver 19
e Pſ cxlvi 3 Jer xvii 5
f Job xxvii 3

v 10—22 When God does not forgive, he will deſtroy We have here the deſolations denounced, either upon the Jewiſh people, or upon the antichriſtian foes, to both which the words are applicable

1 He bids them *enter into the rock*, as deriding their vain confidence, and ſhewing them how unable they will be to eſcape, when *for fear of the Lord, and the glory of his majeſty*, they ſhould ſeek to hide their guilty heads *Note*, (1) At God s bar, the ſtouteſt hearted ſinner will tremble (2) Vain will be every refuge in the day of judgment, no rock, no mountain can cover the guilty, when God ariſeth to ſhake terribly the earth

2 The pride of ſinners ſhall then be laid low, the lofty looks ſhall ſink into dejection and deſpair, and the haughtineſs of the inſolent lick the duſt, *and the Lord alone ſhall be exalted in that day*, in his judgments executed upon his enemies, and in his kingdom, which then ſhall be eſtabliſhed for ever, and never more be diſturbed by any antichriſtian foe *Note*, Pride muſt come down, if we now fall not on our knee in humiliation, we muſt fall deep into hell under our ſins

3 The particulars of God s judgments upon the proud and lofty are mentioned Though firm as mountains, and tall as cedars, they will be overturned, though guarded by the ſtrongeſt fortreſſes, they cannot ſtand, all their confidence will fail them, and their glory vaniſh, their ſhips be deſtroyed, their pleaſant pictures defaced, their idols aboliſhed The kings of the earth, and great men, and chief captains, who ſupported the beaſt, and the falſe prophet, and committed fornication with the great whore, will be ruined with her, their armies fitted out to war againſt the ſaints of God, will be diſperſed and deſtroyed, their curious paintings of madonnas, ſaints, crucifixes, and the like idolatrous ornaments of their churches, will periſh together, and their images, to which they paid their blind devotions, be for ever aboliſhed

4 The worſhippers, convinced of the vanity of their idols, will renounce them, or deſpairing of relief, in anger caſt them to the moles and the bats, frighted with God s judgments, and flying to the clefts of the rocks for ſhelter *Note*, (1) Sooner or later the vanity of idols will appear, whether the groſſer idolatry of images, or the more refined, yet equally abominable idolatry of inordinate affection, placed on gold and ſilver, or any other creature, none of which will profit in the day of wrath (2) Many are driven from their ſins who never repent of them, either are so terrified, that conſcience deters them, or the inconveniences and ſufferings they ſuſtain, withhold them; or opportunity is wanting to commit them, but ſtill the unmortified love of them remains in their hearts

5 The prophet concludes with an exhortation *to ceaſe from man*, either directed to the Jews, who truſted on Egypt for help againſt the Babylonians, or to the followers of antichriſt, who put ſuch truſt in the blaſphemous pardons and indulgences iſſued from the papal chair, or in general to all, not to truſt in man, even the greateſt, for ſalvation, becauſe he is a worm, *for wherein is he to be accounted of?* the Egyptians would help in vain, the great vaunts of the man that calls himſelf Chriſt's vicar, and God upon earth, are empty boaſts of arrogance, and all human excellence nothing, and leſs than nothing, and vanity *Note*, We cannot put too little truſt in man, nor too great confidence in God They who ceaſe from the one, to live wholly upon the other, will find a rock inſtead of a reed

Before Christ 700

CHAP III

The prophet in this chapter goes on to foretel the deſolations that were coming upon Judah and Jeruſalem for their ſins God threatens, 1 To deprive them of all the ſupports, both of their life and government, ver 1—3 2 To leave them to fall into confuſion and diſorder, ver 4, 5, 12 3 To deny them the bleſſing of magiſtracy, ver 6—8 4 To ſtrip the daughters of Sion of their ornaments, ver 17—24 5 To lay all waſte by the ſword, ver 25, 26 The ſins that provoked God to deal thus with them, were, (1) Their defiance of God, ver 8 (2) Their impudence, ver 9 (3) The abuſe of their power, ver 12—15 (4) The pride of their daughters, ver 16 And in the midſt of the chapter the prophet, [1] Aſſures the righteous that it ſhould be well with them, notwithſtanding thoſe general calamities, ver 10 [2] That it ſhould go ill with the wicked at laſt, however God might now in judgment remember mercy, ver 11 O that the nations of the earth at this day, would hearken to the rebukes and warnings which this chapter gives!

1 FOR behold, the LORD, the LORD of hoſts
ᵃ doth take away from Jeruſalem, and from Ju-
dah, ᵇ the ſtay and the ſtaff, the whole ſtay of bread, and
the whole ſtay of water, 2 ᶜ The mighty man and the
man of war, the judge, and the prophet, and the pru-
dent, and the ancient, 3 The captain of fifty, and †
the honourable man, and the counſeller, and the cun-
ning artificer, and the eloquent orator 4 And I will
give ᵈ children *to be* their princes, and ‡ babes ſhall rule
over them 5 And the people ſhall be oppreſſed, ᵉ
every one by another, and every one by his neighbour
the child ſhall behave himſelf proudly againſt the an-
cient, and the baſe againſt the honourable 6 When a
man ſhall take hold of his brother of the houſe of his
father, *ſaying*, Thou haſt clothing, be thou our ruler,
and *let* this ruin *be* under thy hand 7 In that day ſhall
he ‖ ſwear, ſaying, I will not be an § healer, for in my
houſe *is* neither bread nor cloathing, make me not a
ruler of the people 8 For Jeruſalem is ruined, and
Judah is fallen becauſe ᶠ their tongue and their doings
are againſt the LORD, to provoke the eyes of his
glory

a Jer xxxviii. 9
b Lev xxvi. 26
c 2 Kings xxiv 14
† Heb. A man eminent in countenance
d Eccleſ. x. 16
‡ Heb Men of illuſions
e Chap ix. 19, 21.
‖ Heb Lift up the hand Gen xiv 22. Rev x 5.
§ Heb Binder up.
f Chap v 19

v 1—8 God had commanded them to ceaſe from man and creature-confidences theſe he here threatens to deſtroy, and mentions his glorious titles, *the Lord, the Lord of hoſts*, able to the uttermoſt to execute the ſentence he pronounces

1 Famine ſhould come upon them, *v* 1 and terribly it raged in Jeruſalem, both when beſieged by Nebuchadnezzar, and afterwards by Titus, which laſt deſtruction ſeems to be chiefly the ſubject of this prophecy

2 Deſolation ſhould be ſpread on every ſide, their mighty warriors fallen, and none remain to lead their armies, no judge left to adminiſter juſtice, no prophet to inſtruct or comfort them The power had been taken from them to decide in matters of life and death, forty years before their deſtruction, *John* xviii 31 but after they had revolted, and were beſieged by the Romans, a ſtate of utter confuſion began within the walls, the prudent and the ancient were removed by famine, or the ſword, *v* 2 Not ſo much as an inferior officer left, or one honourable man or counſellor to be found, or when all order was diſſolved, neither office, honour, or wiſdom maintained any longer reverence or attention The cunning artificer ceaſed, when all buſineſs was at a ſtand, and the eloquent orator ſilenced, when his voice could be no longer heard for the tumult, *v* 3

3 The government devolved on thoſe who were weak as infants, and unable to reſtrain the general diſorder, *v* 4 or *men of illuſion*, as in the margin, every arrogant factious ſpirit, who headed the populace, and from whence a ſcene of violence and ſtrange diſorder muſt enſue, as was the caſe when, during the ſiege of Jeruſalem, factions rent them in pieces, and every ſtreet afforded ſcenes of murder, rapine, and violence, all reſpect for age and ſtation was loſt, and lawleſs anarchy reigned, *v* 5

4 So deſperate would be their ſtate, ſo ruined and deſolate, that every one who had ought to loſe, would decline the adminiſtration, though preſſed to be their ruler, as having cloathing when the reſt were naked, as well as furniſhed, and that *this ruin might be under their hand*, in order to alleviate, or extricate them from it, *v* 6 but not a man could be found, who would accept the office ſeeing their ſtate deſperate and incurable,

each

Before Christ 760.

each would ſwear himſelf incapable of healing the deadly breaches, and that he had neither food nor cloathing to maintain ſuch dignity, or relieve their wants, v 7

5 The cauſe of all this miſery was their ſins *becauſe their tongue and their doings are againſt the Lord*, and eſpecially againſt his Chriſt, in their malignity and cruelty, reviling him as an impoſtor, and crucifying him as the greateſt of malefactors *to provoke the eyes of his glory*, who, juſtly offended with ſuch inſult and rejection of himſelf and his goſpel, cauſed this wrath to come upon them to the uttermoſt

From the whole, we may learn, (1) That ſin unrepented of, will be ſooner or later the ruin of every nation, and each individual ſinner (2) It is among the ſad ſymptoms of God's abandoning a people, when he ſends them a famine of his word, and removes the miniſtry of his goſpel from them (3) The kingdom is in the way to ſpeedy ruin, when folly and weakneſs are at the helm, and popular tumults dare interrupt the adminiſtration of juſtice (4) There is no healing thoſe whom God hath wounded, vain are all the means of grace to a reprobate mind

9 ¶ The ſhew of their countenance doth witneſs
againſt them, and they declare their ſin g as Sodom, they
hide *it* not h Wo unto their ſoul, for they have rewarded
evil unto themſelves 10 Say ye to the righteous, i that
it ſhall be well *with him* for k they ſhall eat the fruit of
their doings 11 Wo unto the wicked, l *it ſhall be* ill
with him for m the reward of his hands ſhall be given
him 12 ¶ *As for* my people, n children *are* their op-
preſſors, and women rule over them O my people, o
they which † lead thee, cauſe *thee* to err, and deſtroy
the way of thy paths 13 The LORD ſtandeth up to
plead, and ſtandeth to judge the people 14 The
LORD will enter into judgment with the ancients of
his people, and the princes thereof for ye have eaten
up p the vineyard, the ſpoil of the poor *is* in your houſes
15 What mean ye q *that* ye beat my people to pieces,
and grind the faces of the poor? ſaith the LORD God
of hoſts

g Gen xiii 13 & xviii 20 & xix 5
h Lam v 16
i Eccleſ viii 12
k Pſ cxxviii 2
l Eccleſ viii 13
m Prov i 31 Rom ii 8, 9 Gal vi 8
n Ver 4
o Chap ix 16 Jer i 6
† Or call thee bleſſed
p Jer vi 13 Ezek xxii 22
q Mat xxi 33
r Mic iii 2, 3.

v 9—15 We have here,

1 An awful woe denounced upon a wicked people *Wo unto their ſouls!* the judgments were great, through the weakneſs and wickedneſs of their rulers, who, though effeminate as women, and unable as children to protect them from their enemies, harraſſed and oppreſſed them, v 12 this was the leaſt part of their miſery, their ſouls, their immortal ſouls, were more terribly expoſed to the eternal wrath and curſe of God *they have rewarded evil to themſelves*, their ruin is their own choice, and their ſufferings the juſt reward of their ſins *Note*, (1) If we loſe our ſouls, we loſe our all (2) In the day of God, the ſinner will have none to blame for his miſery, but himſelf Several grievous provocations are here mentioned,

[1] They ſin with an high hand, take no pains to conceal it, nor bluſh, with hardned impudence, openly avowing their abominations as Sodom, ſhameleſs before men, and fearleſs of God, v 9 *Note*, (1) Habitual ſin hardens the conſcience (2) They who are paſt ſhame, are on the brink of ruin (3) Sodom's ſin will have Sodom's vengeance

[2] Their prieſts were their corrupters, they who ſhould have led, deceived them by falſe doctrines, they who ſhould have rebuked, cried peace to them, they whoſe examples ſhould have reformed, hardened them, v 12 ſuch were the Phariſees in our Lord's day But were they the only falſe teachers, the exalters of human merit, the falſe prophets of peace, and examples of iniquity? How many a prieſt will this ſuit in every age?

[3] Their magiſtrates were oppreſſive, devouring the poor whom they ſhould have protected, and greedy of gain, ſought only to fill their coffers, inſtead of exerciſing mercy and doing juſtice, v 14

2 For theſe things *the Lord ſtandeth up to plead*, expoſtulating with them on the wickedneſs of their ways, *What mean ye*, &c *and ſtandeth to judge the people*, either to vindicate his people from their oppreſſors, or rather to execute judgment upon the wicked, and this without reſpect of perſons, the ancient, and princes, as deepeſt in guilt, will be the firſt in puniſhment *Note*, (1) When God ſtandeth up to plead, what ſinner but muſt tremble? why will they not conſider their ways, and prevent their ruin? (2) The greateſt muſt ſtand at his tribunal, none can appeal from his ſentence, height of ſtation only brings aggravation of ſin and ſuffering

3 A diſtinction will be made amidſt theſe judgments The righteous few ſhall not ſuffer with the wicked *Say ye to the righteous*, who in Chriſt Jeſus is accounted ſuch, and by his grace renewed in the ſpirit of his mind, *it ſhall be well with him*, peace of conſcience, the ſenſe of God's love, and the hope of his glory ſhall be his ſupport in whatever national viſitation he may be involved, *for they ſhall eat the fruit of their doings*, a

they have not provoked the judgments, they ſhall be delivered from them, or ſupported under them *Wo unto the wicked, it ſhall be ill with him* in time and in eternity, all his ſufferings embittered, his proſpects dark, his life miſerable, his death terrible, and after death accurſed, he is doomed to devouring fire, and everlaſting burnings Wo indeed to the wicked, when *the reward of his hands ſhall thus be given him!*

16 ¶ Moreover, the LORD ſaith, Becauſe the
daughters of Zion are haughty, and walk with ſtretched
forth necks, and r wanton eyes, walking, and † mincing
as they go, and making a tinkling with their feet 17
Therefore s the LORD will ſmite with a ſcab the crown
of the head of the daughters of Zion, and the LORD
t will diſcover their ſecret parts 18 In that day the
LORD will take away the bravery of *their* tinkling or-
naments *about their feet*, and *their* ‡ cauls, and *their* round
tires like the moon, 19 The ‖ chains, and the brace-
lets, and the § mufflers, 20 The bonnets, and the or-
naments of the legs, and the head bands, and the tablets,
and the ear-rings, 21 The rings, and noſe-jewels,
22 The changeable ſuits of apparel, and the mantles,
and the wimples, and the criſping pins, 23 The glaſſes,
and the fine linen, and the hoods, and the veils 24
And it ſhall come to paſs, *that* inſtead of ſweet ſmell,
there ſhall be ſtink, and inſtead of a girdle, a rent,
and inſtead of well ſet hair, u baldneſs, and inſtead of a
ſtomacher, a girding of ſackcloth, *and* burning inſtead
of beauty 25 Thy men ſhall fall by the ſword, and thy
mighty in the war 26 And x her gates ſhall lament
and mourn and y ſhe *being* † deſolate, ſhall ſit upon the
ground.

r 2 Pet ii 14
† Or tripping.
s Deut xxviii 27.
t Chap. xlvii 3 Nah iii 5.
‡ Or net work
‖ Or ſweet balls
§ Or ſpangled ornaments
u Mic i 16
x Lam i 4.
y Lam ii 10 Luke xix 44
† Heb Cleanſed, emptied of all ſubſtance.

v 16—26 The daughters of Zion had contributed to ſwell the national guilt, and muſt therefore ſhare in their plagues

1 Their ſins are vanity and lewdneſs Proud of their perſons and ornaments, with elevated heads, and ſtretched forth necks, they treated with an air of diſdain their inferiors, whilſt wantonly they caſt their amorous glances around, and all their motions beſpoke deſire of admiration *Note*, (1) Vanity is woman's beſetting ſin (2) They who lay ſnares for others, are juſtly chargeable with every evil conſequence that follows (3) A wanton eye betrays an impure heart

2 Their puniſhments would correſpond with their ſins Loathſome diſeaſe ſhould deform and humble the proud beauty, v 17 inſtead of their full wardrobes of various dreſſes, they ſhould be ſtripped naked to their ſhame, their ornaments (the exact meaning of the ſeveral particulars of which is ſcarcely to be aſcertained, and is of little moment) which ſiſh on dictated, and their vain hearts affected, pleaſed with the finery, and never thinking they had enough, muſt all be plundered, themſelves enſlaved, and led into captivity, a girding of ſackcloth would be their miſerable covering inſtead of perfumes and fragrance, they would be nauſeous through poverty and ulcers, their ſhining girdles would give place to rags, tattered and rent, their braided locks, dreſſed with ſuch curious art, now torn for anguiſh, or falling off through ſickneſs, would leave them bald, and the ſcorching ſun, or burning carbuncles, disfigure that fair face, which in the glaſs had led ſo often to ſelf-idolatry, whilſt their huſbands ſhould be ſlain by the ſword, and no man left to marry them Thus ſunk under univerſal deſolations, the gates of the very city would mourn, and Jeruſalem, as a diſconſolate widow, in the duſt bewail her irreparable ruin *Note*, (1) The ſins of lewdneſs often make thoſe loathſome, who were once moſt lovely (2) Extravagant finery eaſily lead to pinching poverty (3) Beauty is a dangerous gift, and often proves the bane of its poſſeſſor (4) Dreſs according to our ſtation is becoming, but to be curious and expenſive is to turn the covering of our ſhame into an incentive of our ſin

CHAP IV

In this chapter is foretold, 1 The ſcarceneſs of men that ſhould be left in Jeruſalem, ver 1 2 The reſtoration to peace and purity in the days of the Meſſiah, ver 2—6

1 AND a in that day ſeven women ſhall take hold of
one man, ſaying, We will eat our own bread,
and wear our own apparel only let us be called by thy
name, b to take away our reproach

a Chap iii 25
b Luke i 25.

v 1 This verſe properly belongs to the foregoing chapter, where the ravages of the ſword are mentioned, and ſhould be ſo great, that by reaſon of the few men left, contrary to the eſtabliſhed rule of their ſex, and the ordinance of God, *ſeven women ſhould take hold of one man*, preſſing him to their bed, and content to ſhare him as their huſband, and inſtead of expecting a main-

tenance

Before Christ 760.

tenance from him, offering to provide for themselves, is an argument to gain his consent to their proposals, at any rate desiring to have a husband, and not to be compelled to a single life, which among the Jews was reckoned very reproachful. Perhaps it intimates also the immodesty of their hearts, as if the reproach of virginity to them was more irksome, than the reproach of vice. *Note*, As modesty is the great ornament of the female sex, the want of it makes them most detested and loathsome.

c Jer. xxiii. 5. Zech. iii. 8. & vi. 12.

2 In that day shall [c] the branch of the LORD be
beautiful and glorious, and the fruit of the earth *shall be*
excellent and comely for them that are escaped of Israel.
3 And it shall come to pass, *that he that is* left in Zion,
and *he that* remaineth in Jerusalem, [d] shall be called holy,
even every one [e] *that is* written † among the living in Jerusalem.
4 When [f] the LORD shall have washed away the filth of the daughters of Zion, and shall have
purged the blood of Jerusalem from the midst thereof,
by the spirit of judgment, and by the spirit of burning.
5 And the LORD will create upon every dwelling-place of mount Zion, and upon her assemblies [g] a cloud,
and smoke by day, and the shining of a flaming fire by
night: for upon all the glory [h] *shall be* ‡ a defence.
6 And there shall be a tabernacle for a shadow in the day
time from the heat, and for [i] a place of refuge, and for a
covert from storm and from rain.

d Chap. iv. 21. e Ps. lxix. 28. Rev. iii. 5. xvii. 8. † Or to life. Acts xiii. 48. f Mal. iii. 2, 3. g Exod. xiii. 21. h Zech. ii. 5. ‡ Heb. A covering. Chap. vii. 14. i Chap. xxv. 4. Heb. vi. 18.

V. 2—6 In the midst of these terrible threatnings, a bright beam of hope dawns from the great and precious promises of the Messiah, whose kingdom and glory should then be exalted, when those who had rejected him, received their righteous doom.

1. *In that day* of Jerusalem's desolations, *shall the branch of the Lord*, the Messiah, that should shoot from the stem of Jesse, Zech. iii. 8. Jer. xxiii. 5. Isa. xi. 1. *be beautiful and glorious*, laden with the precious fruits of pardon, grace, and glory, and though springing in his humiliation as a root out of a dry ground, yet in his exaltation shining brighter than the sun, glorified of his saints, and admired of all that believe: *and the fruit of the earth*, Christ Jesus incarnate on the earth, *shall be excellent and comely*, though once a worm, and no man, his visage marred more than any, now become the chief of ten thousand, and altogether lovely; *for them that are escaped of Israel*, the chosen few, whom he hath reserved for himself, whose eyes are opened to know his excellencies, and who are ordained to eternal life, that they may behold his glory. *Note*, (1.) Though in the eyes of a carnal world there is no beauty in Jesus, wherefore they should desire him, faith can descry excellencies, that make him above all things precious, so that we can say, Whom have I in heaven but thee? and there is nothing I desire upon earth in comparison of thee. (2.) In the Saviour all fulness dwells; do we want pardon, peace, grace, comfort, we may come to him, and freely take, enough to supply the most enlarged desires of our souls.

2. When the Messiah comes, to him will the gathering of the people be. *It shall come to pass, that he that is left in Zion*, the remnant, according to the election of grace, *and he that remaineth in Jerusalem*, the gospel church, *shall be called holy*, accounted such, in virtue of their complenteness in Jesus Christ, and really made such, in a measure, by the powerful operation of the spirit of holiness on their hearts and lives, *even every one that is written among the living*, or *unto life in Jerusalem*, that is, they, and only they, who, by God's sovereign choice, are ordained unto eternal life, and whose names are written in the book of life of the Lamb slain from the foundation of the world: and this separation of his people for himself will then appear, *when the Lord shall have washed away the filth of the daughters of Zion, and shall have purged the blood of Jerusalem in the midst thereof, by the spirit of judgment, and by the spirit of burning*, which may signify the judgments God would bring upon the wicked, till they were utterly consumed, or rather the purging thoroughly the church of his redeemed, and the daughters of Zion, particular believers, in the furnace of affliction, in order to cleanse them from their remaining corruptions and defilement; and this the Lord would also further effectually accomplish, by raising up ministers and magistrates, endued with a spirit of wisdom, and animated with holy zeal for the perfecting of the saints, for the edifying of the body of Christ. *Note*, (1.) They whom Jesus writes among the living, shall never taste of death, not one of them can be lost. (2.) Every elect vessel is before prepared unto glory, through sanctification of the Spirit: vain are their hopes of an interest in heaven, whose hearts continue earthly, sensual, devilish. (3.) When the Lord is pleased to work, he can easily find instruments, furnish them abundantly for their labour, and bless them with success. (4.) What very gracious changes are produced on a people, or an individual, we may be assured that it is the Lord's doing, whose power alone can convert the sinner's soul.

3. The church of the redeemed, and every believer, will in the Lord enjoy protection, guidance, comfort, and security. As Israel's camp of old was preserved by God's pillar of the cloud and of fire, safely led through the howling wilderness, and hid from the scorching sunbeams, and as the tabernacle was defended by several coverings from the storm and tempest, so shall God's people still enjoy as real, if not as sensible, tokens of his care in their passage through this wilderness; neither the storms of persecution, nor the blasts of temptation; nor the scorchings of affliction, nor the burning wrath of a broken law, shall be able to hurt them. He will defend *their glory*, their souls, glorious in holiness, lead them safe through every trial, comfort them with a sense of his love, hide them in the day of wrath, as under the shadow of a great rock in a weary land, and after beholding the destruction of the ungodly, bring them safe to that blest tabernacle he hath pitched in heaven for their everlasting abode.

CHAP. V.

The prophet in this chapter declares the sins of his people, and the judgments which would ensue. 1. By a parable of an unfruitful vineyard, representing the great favours God had bestowed upon them, their disappointing of his expectations, and the ruin they had thereby deserved, ver. 1—7. 2. *By an enumeration of the sins that did abound among them, with a threatening of punishments corresponding to their sins. (1.) Covetousness, which will be punished with famine*, ver. 8—10. (2.) *Rioting and drunkenness*, ver. 11, 12, 22. *to be punished with captivity*, ver. 13—17. (3.) *Presumption in sin, and defying God's justice*, ver. 18, 19. (4.) *Confounding the distinctions between vice and virtue, and so undermining the principles of religion*, ver. 20. (5.) *Self-conceit*, ver. 21. (6.) *Perverting justice, for which a great and general desolation is threatened*, ver. 24, 25. *by a foreign invasion*, ver. 26—30.

1 NOW will I sing to my well-beloved a song of
my beloved touching [a] his vineyard. My well-
beloved hath a vineyard in † [b] a very fruitful hill. 2
And he fenced it, and gathered out the stones thereof,
and planted it with the choicest vine, and built a tower
in the midst of it, and also made a wine-press therein:
and he looked that it should bring forth grapes, and it
brought forth wild grapes. 3 And now, O inhabitants
of Jerusalem, and men of Judah, [c] judge, I pray you,
betwixt me and my vineyard. 4 What could have been
done more to my vineyard, [d] that I have not done in it?
wherefore when I looked that it should bring forth grapes,
brought it forth wild grapes? 5 And now go to; I
will tell you what I will do to my vineyard: [e] I will take
away the hedge thereof, and it shall be eaten up; *and*
break down the wall thereof, and it shall be trodden
down. 6 And [f] I will lay it waste: it shall not be
pruned, nor digged, but there shall come up briers and
thorns: I will also command the clouds that they rain no
rain upon it. 7 For the vineyard of the LORD of
hosts *is* the house of Israel, and the men of Judah ‡ his
pleasant plant, and he looked for judgment, but [g] behold || oppression; for righteousness, but behold [h] a cry.

a Ps. lxxx. 8. Cant. viii. 11. Chap. xxvii. 2. Jer. ii. 21. Mat. xxi. 33. Luke xx. 9. † Heb. The horn of the son of oil. b Deut. viii. 7—9. c Rom. iii. 4. d 2 Chron. xxxvi. 15. Mat. xxiii. 37. e Ps. lxxx. 12. f Deut. xxviii. 51. ‡ Heb. The plant of his pleasures. g Eccles. iii. 16. || Heb. A scab. h Exod. xxii. 23, 27.

V. 1—7 To bring these sinners to a sense of their guilt and danger, they have line upon line, and precept upon precept, every winning means is tried, whether by affecting parables, or plain address. The prophet here in poetic measure and parabolic figure warns them. He calls it a song, of the well-beloved, and addressed to him, to Christ, the beloved Son of the Father, and the object of chief regard and affection to every faithful soul. Under the parable of a vineyard, he shews,

1. The peculiar care God had taken of them. He had placed his vineyard *in a very fruitful hill*, where corn, wine, oil, and every earthly blessing abounded, *fenced it in* from the rest of the world, by a covenant of peculiar separation, and protected them night and day by his Almighty power, *gathered out the stones thereof*, the Canaanites, hard and obdurate as stones, *planted it with the choicest vine*, the seed of Abraham his chosen, and gave them the knowledge of his true religion and pure worship, *and he built a tower in the midst of it*, the temple where his presence rested in the midst of them, their glory and defence, *and also made a wine-press therein*, his altar, on which their oblations might be poured out, and their sacrifices offered. *Note*, In all our privileges and blessings, whether temporal or spiritual, God's hand should be acknowledged by us.

2. The reasonable expectations he entertained, and the disappointment he met with. *He looked that it should bring forth grapes, and it brought forth wild grapes*: instead of the fruit of righteousness, poisonous principles, hypocritical professions, or openly impious practice. *Note*, (1.) If God hath given us

D outward

Before Christ 760.

outward privileges, he justly expects suitable returns. It is not merely the leaves of profession, nor the green grape of future purposes, but the sound fruit of purity and holiness he demands. (2) When God is said to be disappointed, it means not that he did not foresee, or know what would be the event, but this is spoken after the manner of men, according to what we, in a like case, should have expected. (3) They who produce the wild grapes, will set an edge on their own teeth, when God's righteous vengeance awakes to punish the transgressors.

3. He appeals to the men of Judah and Jerusalem. In a case so very evident, he might rest it on their own consciences what more could have been done? what greater advantages, civil and religious, could they desire to have enjoyed? wherefore then have they acted so vile a part, and made such unsuitable returns? or it may be rendered, *Why have I expected that it should bring forth grapes, seeing it brought forth wild grapes?* why have I born with them so long, or why should they be longer spared? *Note*, (1) The sinner acts most unreasonably, as well as most ungratefully, and will in the day of God, appear without excuse. (2) When we consider our mercies, who need not tremble for his own unprofitableness? (3) Though God's patience last long, it will not endure for ever: when the wicked are incorrigible, their ruin is near.

4. God pronounces judgment upon them. *I will take away the hedge thereof*, remove their defence, and give them for a prey to their enemies, *and it shall be eaten up* by wild beasts, such as were the Roman soldiers, massacring without pity; *and break down the walls thereof, and it shall be trodden down*, when the besiegers entered at the wide breaches, utterly destroying all before them, laying both city and people in the dust. *And I will lay it waste*, without inhabitant; *it shall not be pruned nor digged*, neither magistrates, prophets, nor ministers should any longer attempt to cultivate it; *but there shall come up briers and thorns*, errors and immoralities, fatal as universal. *I will also command the clouds that they rain no rain upon it*, no dew of heaven, no influence shall descend upon them, but they shall be left to their hard and impenitent hearts, as is the case with the Jews to this very day. *Note*, That nation and people are in a miserable way, from which God in displeasure withdraws his ordinances, his ministers, and his grace, and gives them up to their own hearts.

5. The prophet applies the parable to the Jewish people; the commonwealth of Israel was the vineyard, and the members of it the once pleasant plants, but now become the degenerate plants of a strange vine. The fruits God expected were righteousness and judgment, honesty and impartial administration of justice; but instead thereof, the cry of oppression went up to God, and called down vengeance on the guilty land. *Note*, Men's sins pass not unnoticed: God sees, and will assuredly visit for these things.

8 ¶ Wo unto them that [i] join house to house, *that*
lay field to field, till *there be* no place, that † they may
be placed alone in the midst of the earth. 9 [k] In mine
ears *said* the LORD of hosts, Of a truth many houses
shall be desolate, *even* great and fair without inhabitant.
10 Yea, ten acres of vineyard shall yield one [l] bath, and
the seed of an homer shall yield an ephah. 11 ¶ [m] Wo
unto them that rise up early in the morning, *that* they
may follow strong drink, that continue until night, *till*
wine inflame them. 12 And [n] the harp and the viol,
the tabret and pipe, and wine are in their feasts: but [o]
they regard not the work of the LORD, neither consider
the operation of his hands. 13 ¶ [p] Therefore my peo-
ple are gone into captivity, because *they have* no know-
ledge: and their honourable men *are* famished, and their
multitude dried up with thirst. 14 Therefore hell hath
enlarged herself, and opened her mouth without measure:
and their glory, and their multitude, and their pomp,
and he that † rejoiceth shall descend into it. 15 And
[q] the mean man shall be brought down, and the mighty
man shall be humbled, and the eyes of the lofty shall
be humbled: 16 But [r] the LORD of hosts shall be
exalted in judgment, and God *that is* holy, shall be
sanctified in righteousness. 17 Then shall [s] the lambs
feed ‖ after their manner, and the waste places of the fat
ones shall strangers eat.

[i] Mic. ii. 2. † Heb. Ye. [k] Chap. xxii. 14. [l] Ezek. xlv. 11. [m] Prov. xxiii. 29, 30. Eccles. x. 16. Ver. 22. [n] Amos vi. 5, 6. [o] Job xxxiv. 27. Ps. xxviii. 5. [p] Hos. iv. 6. † Or, revelleth. [q] Chap. ii. 9, 11, 17. [r] Ps. ix. 16. [s] John xxi. 15. ‖ Or, guide them. Mic. ii. 12.

v. 8—17. We have two heavy woes denounced against two crying sins, worldly-mindedness and sensuality, the common iniquities, not of the Jews only, but of our own days, and which will as assuredly now bring down the wrath of God as then.

1. They were insatiable, and ever coveting to enlarge their possessions, to engross every spot around; and whilst they might gratify their own covetousness, careless what inconveniencies others suffered thereby, or what injuries they sustained, so themselves might but be accommodated, v. 8, 9. therefore God threatens them by a revelation made to his prophet, *Many*, or *great houses shall be desolate*, when their avaricious owners and chief men went into captivity, or were slain by the sword; and none left to dwell in those gorgeous palaces they with so much solicitude had raised; and instead of the plenty they expected from joining field to field, such a curse should be upon the land, that ten acres of a vineyard should not produce half so many gallons of wine, nor their ground yield scarce a tenth of the seed they had sown. *Note*, (1) They who set their hearts on worldly things, are sure to be disappointed. (2) Though it be no sin to purchase what our neighbour is willing to part with, yet to be ever casting about how to increase our stores, to have a greedy eye on every adjoining field, to make our own estate more complete, *O si angulus ille, proximus accedat qui nunc denormat agellum*, this is to provoke God to smite our possessions with a curse.

2. They were sunk in sensuality and pleasure. Eager to quench, or rather inflame their raging thirst, they rose early, and began the day with strong drink, protracted their carousals till night, flushed with wine, no evil stuck with them, rage, revelling, lust, reigned uncontrouled, v. 11. Music prostituted, served to heighten their passions; drunken, lewd, light the song, with pleasing sound, stole deeper into the heart, and no place left for serious recollection—God, his judgments, works and ways, his Christ and gospel, were disregarded, v. 12. *Note*, (1) Drunkenness is not only a vice most brutal and odious in itself, but the pregnant author of every abomination. (2) The most innocent things are liable to grievous abuse; even music may lull the soul into eternal ruin. (3) When the mind is enslaved by lust and pleasure, God is forgotten, and every thought of him and his judgments that would enter, thrust out as irksome intruders. Wo therefore unto them! the judgment near and terrible approaches. *Therefore my people are gone, or are going into captivity*, by the Babylonians first, and afterwards by the Romans, *because they have no knowledge*, by their sins are become brutish, insensible of their danger, and wilfully blind to their impending ruin: *their honourable men are famished, and their multitude dried up with thirst*, a just judgment on those who wasted so much in rioting and drunkenness: and dreadful but to read of were their sufferings, during the sieges they sustained, even so far as to eat their own children. *Therefore hell hath enlarged herself*, a pit, deep like Tophet, is dug to receive the corpses, perishing so numerous by famine, pestilence, and the sword; or the place of torment yawns to ingulph their polluted souls, *and hath opened her mouth without measure*, insatiate to devour the wicked, *and their glory*, the nobles, *and their multitude*, the populace, or the rulers, though never so many as well as mighty, *and their pomp*, their rich ones who lived in splendor, *and he that rejoiceth* in careless gaiety and carousing, *shall descend into it*, into the grave, or afterward into hell together; where, instead of mirth and riot, their everlasting portion will be weeping and wailing, and gnashing of teeth. Thus shall the mean and mighty perish together, and leave a warning to others, of the danger of their ways. Let the drunkard solemnly peruse this judgment, let the careless pleasure-loving world behold the appointed end, that before it be too late they may consider their ways, and prevent so fearful a destruction.

3. By the execution of such just judgments would God be glorified, his holiness, and hatred of sin appear, his righteousness in executing vengeance be manifested, v. 16. *Then also shall the lambs feed after their manner*, or according as they are led, the lambs of Christ's flock, fed by his word, and walking in all his holy ways, *and the waste places of the fat ones shall strangers eat*, the Gentiles shall possess both the country of Israel, and partake of those gospel blessings, which the proud and self-righteous Jews despised and rejected. *Note*, (1) God will not want a people; if some are obstinate, others will hear and obey him. (2) If sinners will not glorify God's mercy by their humble acceptance of his grace and redemption, they must glorify his justice in the place of torment.

18 Wo unto them that draw iniquity with cords of
vanity, and sin as it were [t] with a cart-rope: 19 [u] That
say, Let him make speed, *and* hasten his work, that
we may see *it*: and let the counsel of the holy One of
Israel draw nigh and come, that we may know *it*. 20
¶ Wo unto them that call evil good, and good evil,
that put darkness for light, and light for darkness; that
put bitter for sweet, and sweet for bitter. 21 Wo
unto *them* [x] *that are* wise in their own eyes, and prudent
in their own sight. 22 [y] Wo unto *them that are* mighty
to drink wine, and men of strength to mingle strong
drink: 23 Which [z] justify the wicked for reward, and
[a] take away the righteousness of the righteous from him.
24 Therefore [b] as ‖ the fire devoureth the stubble, and
the flame consumeth the chaff, *so* [c] their root shall be as
rottenness, and their blossom shall go up as dust: be-
cause they have cast away the law of the LORD of
hosts, and despised the word of the holy One of Israel.
25 Therefore [d] is the anger of the LORD kindled

[t] Job iv. 8. [u] Chap. lxvi. 5. Jer. v. 12; xvii. 15. Amos v. 18. 2 Pet. iii. 3, 4. [x] Prov. iii. 7. Rom. xii. 16. [y] Ver. 11. [z] Prov. xvii. 15; & xxiv. 24. [a] 1 Kings xxi. 13. [b] Exod. xv. 7. ‖ Heb. The tongue of fire. [c] Job xviii. 16. Amos ii. 9. [d] 2 Kings xxii. 13.

Before Chriſt 760.

againſt his people, and he hath ſtretched forth his hand
againſt them, and hath ſmitten them, and [e] the hills did
tremble, and their carcaſes *were* torn in the midſt of the
ſtreets [f] For all this his anger is not turned away, but
his hand *is* ſtretched out ſtill 26 ¶ And he will lift up
[g] an enſign to the nations from far, and will [h] hiſs unto
them [i] from the end of the earth, and behold they ſhall
come with ſpeed ſwiftly 27 [k] None ſhall be weary nor
ſtumble amongſt them none ſhall ſlumber nor ſleep
[l] neither ſhall the girdle of their loins be looſed, nor the
latchet of their ſhoes be broken. 28 Whoſe arrows *are*
ſharp, and all their bows bent, their horſes hoofs ſhall
be counted like flint, and their wheels like a whirlwind
29 Their roaring *ſhall be* like a lion, they ſhall roar like
young lions yea, they ſhall roar and lay hold of the
prey, and ſhall carry *it* away ſafe, and none ſhall deliver
it 30 And in that day they ſhall roar againſt them,
like the roaring of the ſea and if *one* [m] look unto the
land, behold darkneſs *and* ſorrow, ‡ and the light is dark-
ned in the heavens thereof

e Jer iv 24
f Chap ix 12, 17 21 & x. 4
g Chap xi 12
h Ibid vii 18
i Deut xxviii 49 Jer v 15
k Joel ii 7, 8
l Dan v 6
m Chap viii 22 Jer iv 23, Lam iii 2 Ezek xxxii 7 8
‡ Or when it is light, it ſhall be dark in the deſtructions thereof

v 18—30 Two woes are denounced, but there are others yet to come equally grievous, and all dating their origin from ſin, which then, now, and ever is the cauſe of all our miſery Happy, did we but take warning by others woes, and flee their iniquities

1 Their ſins are many

(1) *They draw iniquity with cords of vanity, and ſin as it were with a cart rope*, ſtrain every nerve, uſe every argument to accompliſh their wicked purpoſes, ruſhing into temptation, and bent on gratifying their luſts at all events

(2) They defied God, deſpiſed the warnings of his prophets, and when his Son appeared, treated his pretenſions with contempt *They ſay, let him make ſpeed, and haſten his work*, the men of that generation ſaid, where are the threatned judgments? deriding their prophets who brought the meſſage the Jews ſaid, if he be the Son of God, let him come down from the croſs, and the infidel ſinner continues thus to treat God's warnings in every age

(3) They ſought to confound good and evil, wilfully miſrepreſented truth as falſhood, branding the ways of godlineſs as miſerable, and boaſting the paths of ſin to be the only ſubſtantial bliſs, *v* 20 *Note*, The devil and wicked men ſtudy ever to dreſs up religion and its profeſſors in the moſt forbidding colours, whilſt every glaring vice is palliated with ſome ſoft name, or pleaded for as commendable Seriouſneſs and ſingularity are termed pride and moroſeneſs, whilſt a life of diſſipation is called a little innocent pleaſure, a debauch, good company, ſordid parſimony, frugality, and daring infidelity, free-thinking but names alter not things, nor change their nature, the ſweetneſs of God's good ways abides the ſame, and all the gloſſes of ſinners will not prevent their feeling the bitterneſs of the flames of hell

(4) They were proud and ſelf-ſufficient, *wiſe in their own eyes*, though ſo infatuated, *and prudent in their own ſight*, valuing themſelves on their underſtanding and management Thus the Phariſees ſaid, we ſee, when moſt deeply their ſin remained *Note*, Conceit of our own wiſdom and righteouſneſs, is among the moſt fatal errors

(5) They were *mighty to drink wine*, ſtrong heads, and gloried in the quantity of liquor they could carry off, *and men of ſtrength to mingle ſtrong drink*, delighting in being able to drink others down *Note*, (1) They who were mighty to drink wine, muſt ſhortly drink of the wine of the wrath of God (2) The ſtrength of a man's conſtitution will not exculpate him from the guilt of drunkenneſs To ſit long at the cups, and delight in them, is as evil as to fill the table with vomit, or ſtagger in their walk (3) They who glory now in their ſhame, of having out-drunk their companions, in hell will find ſmall joy in theſe exploits

(6) They baſely perverted juſtice for gain Their magiſtrates *juſtified the wicked for reward*, money covered all crimes, whilſt *they take away the righteouſneſs of the righteous from him*, the poor that cannot bribe, or the upright that dare not, however juſt their cauſe, are ſure to be caſt for iniquities like theſe, God will viſit, and his ſoul be avenged of ſuch a people as this Therefore,

2 He denounces their doom *Becauſe they have caſt away the law of the Lord*, the doctrine ſent them by his prophets, and the goſpel preached by his Son, *and deſpiſed the word of the holy One of Iſrael*, treated it with contempt and diſregard, *therefore as the fire devoureth the ſtubble, and the flame conſumeth the chaff*, ſo ſudden, terrible, reſiſtleſs, and irreparable ſhould their deſtruction be, ſo that *their root ſhall be as rottenneſs*, and therefore the whole political tree muſt periſh, *and their bloſſom go up as the duſt*, all their pomp, riches, and glory be diſperſed, as withered bloſſoms before the wind *Therefore is the anger of the Lord kindled againſt his people*, once his choſen, now apoſtate from him, and expoſed to his wrath Preſent judgments were upon them, their princes ſlain in their ſtreets, and none to bury them, yet these but the beginning of ſorrows God's anger was far from being turned away, and greater woes to come, his hand being ſtretched out ſtill, *v* 25 *He will ſet up an enſign*, as the ſignal for marching, *to the nations from far*, the Romans, compoſed of various people, and bringing their troops from diſtant provinces *He will hiſs unto him*, or *them*, the army, or the general, as a ſhepherd whiſtles his dog to come Inſtantly they will obey, marching ſpeedily, no wearineſs ſhall retard, or difficulty ſtumble them ſo eager would they be to haſten to the ſiege, that they would march day and night, and not even undreſs themſelves, or looſe their ſhoes, to lie down to ſleep by the way expreſſions denoting their indefatigable diligence, *v* 27 Their archers ready to ſhoot, their cavalry ſtrong, their chariots as whirlwind rattling and thundering along, *v* 28 Fierce as lions, their roar would intimidate, ſtrong as lions, their defenceleſs prey would fall, and none be able to deliver the devoted people of Judea from the ravening Roman ſoldiers *v* 29 In that day of the ſiege of Jeruſalem, they ſhould roar with their ſhouts and battering engines, as the tempeſtuous ſea, and the land of Judah be ravaged and ſunk under its diſtreſs, as if the luminaries of heaven were extinguiſhed, *Matth* xxiv 29 their whole polity, civil and eccleſiaſtical, be utterly diſſolved, and prieſts, princes, and people, ſink in one promiſcuous ruin *Note*, (1) When ſinners reject the counſel of God againſt their own ſoul, they bring upon themſelves ſwift deſtruction (2) God never wants inſtruments to execute his vengeance upon a guilty nation (3) When the Lord gives the word the damnation of the wicked no longer ſlumbers (4) They who have fled from the light of truth to the darkneſs of ſin, are juſtly conſigned to the eternal darkneſs

CHAP VI

In this chapter we have, 1 The viſion which Iſaiah ſaw of the glory of God, ver 1—4 The fright it put him into, ver 5 and the relief given him, by an aſſurance of the pardon of his ſins, ver 6, 7 2 The commiſſion which he received, ver 8 3 The obſtinacy of the Jews notwithſtanding their deſolation foretold, ver 9 4 The remnant he ſhould be ſaved, amidſt the general deſtruction, ver 13

758

1 IN the year that [a] king Uzziah died, I [b] ſaw alſo the
LORD [c] ſitting upon a throne, high and lifted up,
and his † train filled the temple 2 Above it ſtood [d] the
ſeraphims each one had ſix wings, with twain he co-
vered his face, and [e] with twain he covered his feet, and
with twain he did [f] fly 3 And one cried unto another,
and ſaid, [g] Holy, holy, holy *is* the LORD of hoſts, [h] the
whole earth *is* full of his glory 4 And [i] the poſts of
the door moved at the voice of him that cried, and [k] the
houſe was filled with ſmoke

a 2 Kings xv 7
b John xii 41
c 1 Kings xxii 19
† Or ſkirts
d Pſ civ 4
e Ezek i 11
f 1 Cor x 20 Dan ix 21
g Rev iv 8
h Pſ lxxii 19
i Chap v 25
k Exod xl 34 1 Kings viii 10 Rev xv 8.

v 1—4 Iſaiah had before, at God's command, begun his prophetic employment, a ſolemn confirmation of it is made in this auguſt viſion, as a means to ſtrengthen his faith, and quicken his diligence in the diſcharge of his important office The date of the viſion is the year Uzziah died, after a long and pious reign of fifty-two years, though during the latter part of it, the leproſy, under which he laboured, excluded him from the adminiſtration, which was lodged in the hands of his ſon

1 What the prophet ſaw; *I ſaw alſo the Lord ſitting upon a throne*, the Lord Jeſus Chriſt enthroned in the glory which he had with the Father before the worlds were, for to him is this expreſly applied, *John* xii 41 and contains one of the moſt incconteſtible proofs of the eſſential Godhead of our incarnate Redeemer, *high and lifted up*, exalted above all bleſſing and praiſe, infinitely tranſcending all created excellence, the King eternal, to whom every knee muſt bow, and every tongue confeſs *and his train filled the temple*, either the bright angelic ſpirits, who graced his preſence, or the irradiation that beamed around him, or perhaps it may refer to his church on earth, filled with the gifts and grace which, on the day of Pentecoſt, were ſo eminently beſtowed upon the apoſtles, by whoſe preaching, a vaſt acceſſion of converts was quickly made *Above it*, or *near him*, *ſtood the ſeraphims*, the burners, the heavenly hoſts, or thoſe emblematic repreſentatives of the miniſters of the goſpel, *Rev* i 13 *each one had ſix wings*, *with twain he covered his face*, as unable to bear the tranſcendent brightneſs of the Redeemer's glory, *with twain he covered his feet*, as in his beſt ſervices unworthy of God, *and with twain he did fly*, delighted, ready and ſwift to obey God's high commands Thus do Chriſt's miniſters with ſhame acknowledge their ſinfulneſs and unworthineſs to look up to God, and own the imperfection of their holieſt walk; whilſt burning with zeal, they are ready to fly at his word to preach his goſpel, and fulfil his pleaſure *Note*, (1) We cannot entertain apprehenſions of the glory of our Immanuel, according to his excellent greatneſs, it ſurpaſſeth knowledge (2) Before God, the higheſt creature ſtands aſhamed,

Before Christ 758

ſhamed, and how much more cauſe hath man, a ſinful worm, to bluſh and be confounded, when he appears before the throne of Jeſus (3) Burning zeal for God, is the character of his faithful miniſters (4) Delight and chearful readineſs for God's work and will, is the way to riſe to fellowſhip with angels

2 What he heard *One cried unto another*, with fervency and unanimity, *Holy, holy, holy, is the Lord of hoſts*, the triune God, glorious in all his attributes, and eſpecially in his holineſs, *the whole earth is full of his glory*, manifeſted in all the works of creation and providence, but eſpecially of redemption and grace Thus do God's miniſters of flame on earth unite in preaching the one glorious goſpel, and giving to Father, Son, and Holy Ghoſt, the praiſe of that holineſs diſplayed in the juſtification of the ſinner's perſon, and the ſanctification of his ſoul, by the atoning blood of Jeſus, and his efficacious grace

3 The effect of this cry *The poſts of the door moved at the voice of him that cried*, denoting the removal of the temple worſhip and ſervice, or the powerful effect of the goſpel on men's conſciences, ſhaking their vain confidence, and awakening their ſouls to a ſenſe of ſin *and the houſe was filled with ſmoke*, in alluſion to the cloud of incenſe, which covered the mercy ſeat on the day of atonement, and intimating God's acceptance of his miniſters ſervices, or ſignifying the judgments that would come upon the Jewiſh people, when their city and temple ſhould be deſtroyed, or finally, the ſmoke of the ſinner's torment that aſcendeth up for ever and ever

l Jer iv 31 22 & xix 2 Job xl 6 m Jam iii 2 n Pſ cix 20 o Heb xiii 10 p Jer i 9 Dan x 16 † Heb Cauſed it to touch q John xii 41 Acts xxviii 25 r Gen i 26 & iii 22 & xi 7 ‡ Heb Behold me

5 ¶ Then ſaid I, ˡ Wo *is* me, for I am undone, be-
cauſe I *am* a man ᵐ of unclean lips, and I dwell in the
midſt of a people of unclean lips for mine eyes have
ſeen the King, the LORD of hoſts 6 Then ⁿ flew
one of the ſeraphims unto me, having a live coal in his
hand, *which* he had taken with the tongs from off ᵒ the
altar 7 And ᵖ he † laid *it* upon my mouth, and ſaid,
Lo, this hath touched thy lips, and thine iniquity is
taken away, and thy ſin purged 8 Alſo I heard the
voice of ᑫ the LORD, ſaying, Whom ſhall I ſend, and
who will go for ʳ us? Then ſaid I, ‡ Here *am* I, ſend
me.

v 5—8 Struck with the aſtoniſhing viſion, the prophet is confounded, conſcious of his own ſinfulneſs, and inability to ſtand before this holy Lord God

1 He laments over himſelf *Wo is me*, a ſinful worm, *for I am undone*, if this holy God be ſtrict to mark what is amiſs, *becauſe I am a man of unclean lips*, defiled in nature, and probably conſcious of fear, and want of boldneſs in the delivery of the awful meſſages with which he was charged, *and I dwell in the midſt of a people of unclean lips*, whoſe iniquities were, to his bitter ſorrow, ready to draw down the heavy judgments of God upon them *for mine eyes have ſeen the King, the Lord of hoſts*, the Lord Chriſt, whoſe perfection of holineſs, like the bright beams of day, diſcovered thoſe ſpots and impurities that in the dark before he did not perceive *Note*, (1) The more we know of God's purity and perfections, the more we ſhall diſcover of our own vileneſs and pollution (2) The higheſt ſaints of God, who know him beſt, are moſt lowly in their own eyes (3) A good man not only laments over his own corruption, but when he looks around, his heart is grieved with the filthy converſation of the wicked, and he trembles for their approaching ruin

2 A gracious meſſage is ſent him for his encouragement *Then flew one of the ſeraphims unto me*, on his humbling confeſſion, *having a live coal in his hand*, ſignifying the powerful and lively word of the goſpel, *which he had taken with the tongs from off the altar* of burnt-offering, which was the type of the Lord Chriſt, whoſe atoning ſacrifice alone can procure the ſinner's pardon, *and he laid it upon my mouth*, not to conſume his unclean lips, but to purify them from their pollution, *and ſaid, Lo, this hath touched thy lips*, intimating the application of the pardoning word of God to the ſinner's ſoul, by which he is enabled to take the comfort of the promiſe, *and thine iniquity is taken away, and thy ſin purged*, or *expiated*, utterly blotted out before God, wiped away from his conſcience, and perfectly expiated by the ſacrifice of Jeſus *Note*, (1) God delights to comfort the mourners in Zion, penitent prayers will find an anſwer of peace and joy (2) Nothing can heal the heart-broken under ſin, but the precious balm of atoning blood applied by faith in the word of promiſe It muſt be this coal from the altar, not ſtrange fire, that can quicken the periſhing ſoul (3) They who would ſpeak to God, or for God, with confidence, muſt firſt hear him ſpeak to them pardon and peace (4) None are ſo fit or able ſo feelingly to preach to ſinners the grace of a Redeemer, as they who have, by experience, taſted the riches of his love to their own ſinful ſouls (5) The miniſters of God, like burning ſeraphs, ſhould fly to the relief of the poor and broken-hearted ſinner, with the invigorating word of kind conſolation

3 Having offers himſelf for God's ſervice. God is intro-

duced deliberating on the choice of a meſſenger, and the prophet is ready to go *Alſo I heard the voice of the Lord*, the Father, ſpeaking with his coequal Son and Spirit, *whom ſhall I ſend* on this dangerous errand, to reprove a hardened nation, *and who will go for us?* John xii 41 Acts xxviii 25 an evidence of the trinity of the perſons in the unity of the Godhead *Then ſaid I, Here am I, ſend me* Since God had purged his pollution, he is now ready to undertake any ſervice for his glory, however difficult or dangerous *Note*, (1) None can rightly ſpeak for God, who have not a divine miſſion from him, and have heard his voice teaching their own hearts the truths they muſt deliver to others (2) The ordination of a miniſter is a matter of ſolemn weight, ſeeing it is ſo rare to find that zeal for God, that love for men's ſouls, that acquaintance with the myſteries of godlineſs, which are ſuch eſſential qualifications for a preacher of the goſpel (3) If a deſire to glorify God, and a delight to ſerve him in the goſpel of his dear Son, does not engage us as volunteers in the ſervice, excluſive of all worldly proſpects, and regardleſs of all ſufferings, it were a horrid profanation to offer ourſelves for the miniſtry, merely becauſe deſtined by our parents, or to procure a maintenance

9 ¶ And he ſaid, Go and tell this people, ˢ Hear ye
† indeed, but underſtand not, and ſee ye ‡ indeed, but
perceive not 10 Make ᵗ the heart of this people fat,
and make their ears heavy, and ſhut their eyes ᵘ leſt
they ſee with their eyes, and hear with their ears, and
underſtand with their heart, and convert and be healed
11 Then ſaid I, LORD, how long? And he anſwer-
ed, Until ˣ the cities be waſted without inhabitant, and
the houſes without man, and the land be ‖ utterly deſo-
late, 12 And the LORD have removed men far away,
and *there be* a great forſaking in the midſt of the land
13 ¶ But yet in it *ſhall be* a tenth, § and *it* ſhall return,
and ſhall be eaten as a teil tree, and as an oak, whoſe
ſubſtance *is* in them, when they caſt *their leaves* ſo ʸ the
holy ſeed *ſhall be* the ſubſtance thereof

s Chap xliii 8 Mat xiii 14 Mark iv 12 Luke viii 10 John xii 40 Acts xx viii 26 Rom xi 8 † Heb In hearing ‡ Heb In ſeeing t Pſ cxix 70 Chap lxiii 17 u Deut xxix 4 Chap xliv 20 Jer v 21 x 2 Kings xxv 9 &c ‖ Heb Deſolate with deſolation Mic iii 12 § Or when it is returned and hath been browſed. † Or as the ſupport at Shallecheth is in the elms and the oaks, ſo the holy ſeed is the ſubſtance thereof y Job xiv 7—9 z Pſ lxxv 3, Chap i 9

v 9—13 Iſaiah having offered himſelf, his ſervice is accepted, and his commiſſion given him, *Go*, but he is informed, though to the moſt it would be utterly ineffectual, to a few it would be bleſſed with ſucceſs

1 He is commanded to *tell this people*, now abandoned to their own hearts luſts, *Hear ye indeed* the words of the prophets, but eſpecially of Chriſt and his apoſtles, in reference to whoſe preaching this ſcripture is ſeveral times quoted in the New Teſtament, *but underſtand not*, either the glories of his perſon, or his doctrine, *and ſee ye indeed* his miracles ſo great and ſtrange, *but perceive not* the proof of his divine miſſion therein contained *Make the heart of this people fat, and make their ears heavy, and ſhut their eyes* God gives them up to judicial hardneſs and blindneſs, because they deſire not the knowledge of the truth, in judgment they ſhall be deprived of it, and and the goſpel which was ordained unto life, to them a ſavour of death unto death *leſt they ſee with their eyes, and hear with their ears, and underſtand with their heart, and convert and be healed*, to which the preaching of the word was adapted, or at leaſt might ſee ſo far as to make ſome national reformation, which might avert the judgments God had reſolved to bring upon them for the rejection of his Son, and therefore he left them to a reprobate mind *Note*, (1) Many are called by the goſpel word, few ſaved by goſpel-grace (2) The cleareſt truths of God's word are darkneſs to the fallen mind, the natural man receiveth not the things of the Spirit of God, they are fooliſhneſs to him, neither can he know them, becauſe they are ſpiritually diſcerned (3) Wherever God's word is preached, it ſerves to harden thoſe who receive it not in the light and love of it (4) They who are converted, will find the wounds healed which ſin had made in their ſouls, whilſt the impenitent periſh in their iniquities

2 He is informed of the deſolations to be accompliſhed upon them, in anſwer to his queſtion, *How long* ſhould this impenitence and divine judgment upon them continue? even till the whole nation was deſtroyed and diſperſed, the country depopulated, and utter ruin brought upon them by the Roman ſword, *v* 11, 12 and to this day, both their hardneſs of heart, and their terrible judgments are continued *Note*, (1) The ruin of men's ſouls is the neceſſary conſequence of rejection of the goſpel (2) Temporal judgments are often the puniſhment of national ſins

3 Though to the moſt the prophetic word would be fruitleſs, a remnant would be ſaved *But yet in it ſhall be a tenth*, alluding to the Lord's portion of the tythes, a few reſerved amidſt the general apoſtacy, *and it ſhall return, and ſhall be eaten*, or *be burnt*, after their return from Babylon, the city and people ſhould be conſumed with fire by the Romans *as a teil tree, and as an oak, whoſe ſubſtance is in them*, though in winter they are ſtripped of all their verdure the principle of life ſtill remains, *ſo the holy ſeed is the ſubſtance thereof* they ſhall ſubſiſt, though in their wretched condition, a ſeparate people to the

Before Chriſt 758. elect's ſake that ſhall at laſt be gathered in, or for Chriſt's ſake, who ſhall at laſt turn away ungodlineſs from Jacob. *Note*, (1.) Though the labours of God's miniſters may not be ſo extenſively uſeful as they wiſh, they ſhall not be in vain, a few ſhall appear ſeals of their fidelity. (2.) For the ſake of the faithful that remain, the world is preſerved; when they are gathered out, then cometh the end. (3.) Though our ſouls may ſometimes, through temptation and deſertion, appear as the trees in winter, if there be ſpiritual life within, we ſhall again bud and bloſſom as the roſe.

CHAP. VII.

In this chapter we have, 1. The fright of Ahaz, occaſioned by an attack which the confederate forces of Syria and Iſrael made upon Jeruſalem, ver. 1, 2. 2. The aſſurance which God gave him that the attempt ſhould be defeated, ver. 3—9. 3. The confirmation of this by a ſign, ver. 10—16. 4. A threatening of the great deſolation that God would bring upon Ahaz and his kingdom by the Aſſyrians, notwithſtanding their eſcape of this preſent ſtorm, becauſe they went on ſtill in their wickedneſs, ver. 17—25.

742. 1 AND it came to paſs in the days of Ahaz the ſon
of Jotham, the ſon of Uzziah king of Judah,
[a] *that* Rezin the king of Syria, and Pekah the ſon of Re-
maliah king of Iſrael, went up towards Jeruſalem to war
againſt it, [b] but could not prevail againſt it. 2 And it
was told the houſe of David, ſaying, Syria † is confede-
rate with Ephraim. And [c] his heart was moved, and
the heart of his people, as the trees of the wood are
moved with the wind. 3 Then ſaid the LORD unto
Iſaiah, Go forth now to meet Ahaz, thou and ‡ Shear-
jaſhub thy ſon, at the end of [d] the conduit of the upper
pool in the highway of the fuller's field; 4 And ſay
unto him, Take heed, and [e] be quiet; fear not, ‖ nei-
ther be faint hearted, for the two tails of theſe ſmoking
firebrands, for the fierce anger of Rezin with Syria, and
of the ſon of Remaliah. 5 [f] Becauſe Syria, Ephraim,
and the ſon of Remaliah, have taken evil counſel againſt
thee, ſaying, 6 Let us go up againſt Judah, and § vex
it, and let us make a breach therein for us, and ſet a
king in the midſt of it, *even* the ſon of Tabeal: 7 Thus
ſaith the Lord GOD, [g] It ſhall not ſtand, neither ſhall it
come to paſs. 8 For the head of Syria *is* Damaſcus,
and the head of Damaſcus *is* Rezin; and within three-
ſcore and five years [h] ſhall Ephraim be broken, that it be
not a people. 9 And the head of Ephraim *is* Samaria,
and the head of Samaria *is* Remaliah's ſon. [i] † If ye will
not believe, ſurely ye ſhall not be eſtabliſhed.

[a] 2 Kings xvi. 5. [b] Pſ. cxxix. 2. † Heb. reſteth on. Chap. x. [c] Mat. ii. 3. ‡ i. e. A remnant ſhall return. Chap. vi. 13. & x. 21. [d] 2 Kings xviii. 17. Chap. xxxvi. 2. [e] Chap. xxx. 15. ‖ Heb. Let not thy heart be tender. Deut. xx. 3. [f] Pſ. ii. 2. & lxxxiii. 3. § Or weaken. [g] Pſ. xxxiii. 10. Prov. xxi. 30. Chap. viii. 10. [h] 2 Kings xvii. 10, 11. 2 Chron. xx. 20. † Or do ye not believe? it is becauſe ye are not ſtable.

v. 1—9. A new prophecy begins in this chapter, that bears date in the reign of Ahaz, when the confederate forces of Syria and Iſrael, which had before committed great ravages and miſeries in the country, 2 *Kings* xv. 37. 2 Chron. xxviii. 5—7. united to beſiege Jeruſalem the capital, and utterly to deſtroy the kingdom of Judah; though, by divine interpoſition, their deſign was baffled, *v.* 1.

1. This formidable invaſion put the king and his ſubjects into great confuſion. *It was told the houſe of David*, of which though Ahaz was a degenerate branch, yet for his father's ſake, not forſaken, *ſaying, Syria is confederate with Ephraim*; and before two ſuch potent monarchs, whoſe power ſeparately he had been unable to cope with, nothing but ruin ſeemed approaching, *and his heart was moved, and the hearts of the people, as the trees of the wood are moved with the wind*, weak, bending, diſordered, and ready to fall before theſe mighty foes. *Note*, (1.) Bad news flies faſt. (2.) They who have accuſing guilt on their conſciences, are in terrors at the approach of danger.

2. God ſends to comfort and encourage them. Though perplexed, they need not be in deſpair; Iſaiah, the meſſenger of warning to them, is now the meſſenger of mercy, little as they deſerved it, to prove them whether the goodneſs of God might lead them to repentance. He is commanded to go with his ſon, whoſe ſignificant name, Shear-jaſhub, *a remnant ſhall return*, carried in it a token for good, and meet Ahaz *at the conduit of the upper pool, in the highway of the fuller's field*, where probably he was making ſome preparations for the approaching ſiege, by fortifying his capital, introducing plenty of water into the city, or cutting it off from ſupplying the beſiegers. *Note*, (1.) God is thinking of ſinners, and preventing them with the bleſſings of his grace, when he is not in all their thoughts. (2.) Seaſonable relief in time of helpleſs diſtreſs, is doubly welcome. The meſſage with which the prophet is ſent, is moſt encouraging.

(1.) He bids them not fear foes ſo deſpicable. Though to human view ſo potent, in God's regard they were but as the tails of firebrands when they are burnt out, and then worth no more to be regarded than the ſmoke of an extinguiſhed taper. *Take heed and be quiet*, beware only of unbelieving diſtruſt, and wait in confidence of the ſalvation of God, *neither be faint-hearted*, or *be not ſoft* as wax, melted before the ſun. *Note*, (1.) Nothing lays the ſoul ſo open to the inroads of ſin, as unbelieving fear. (2.) The greateſt dangers will not diſturb their peace, whoſe minds are ſtayed upon God. (3.) The enemies of God's people are raging as firebrands, but all their wicked purpoſes will end in ſmoke.

(2.) He foretells the diſappointment of the preſent attempt: though their ſchemes were deep laid, and full of malice, deſigning nothing leſs than the ravaging the whole country, dethroning the king, and ſetting up a tributary of their own, and ſo ſecure were they of ſucceſs, that they had pitched on the perſon already, had taken the city in imagination, and divided the ſpoil; yet one word of God defeats the plan. *It ſhall not ſtand, neither ſhall it come to paſs.* He who ſets bounds to the ſea, can as eaſily ſtill the ragings of the mighty. *Note*, (1.) The ſinner's confidence ſerves but to increaſe the confuſion of his diſappointment. (2.) They who are purpoſing to vex others, will often ſee the miſchief return on their own heads. (3.) God delights to humble the proud. They ſhall ſee whoſe word ſhall ſtand.

(3.) From the preſent defeat, he paſſes on to their future deſtruction. Far from being able to extend their territories, their kingdoms ſhould never be enlarged; and Ephraim, perhaps the moſt inveterate of the two, within ſixty-five years, ceaſe to be a people, which ſome compute from the prophecy of Amos, two years before Uzziah was ſmitten with leproſy, to the ninth year of Hoſea, when Samaria was taken, 2 *Kings* xviii. 10. but others more properly reckon from the preſent date, the fourth year of Ahaz, and ſee the completion of the prophecy, not in the demolition of the kingdom of Iſrael, but in that entire tranſlation of the whole inhabitants, which Eſarhaddon made in the Twenty-ſecond year of Manaſſeh, when colonies from Babylon, Cuthah, Hamath, &c. were brought, and dwelt ever after in the cities of Samaria.

4. They are enjoined to credit his meſſage; for *if ye will not believe, ſurely ye ſhall not be eſtabliſhed*, faith in the divine promiſe was that which could alone abidingly ſecure their ſafety, whatever temporary deliverances might be vouchſafed them. *Note*, The word of promiſe only brings comfort, when it is mixed with faith in them that hear it.

10 ¶ Moreover the LORD ſpake again unto Ahaz,
ſaying, 11 Aſk thee a ſign of the LORD thy God,
aſk it either in the depth, or in the height above. 12
But Ahaz ſaid, I will not aſk, [k] neither will I tempt the
LORD. 13 And he ſaid, Hear ye now, O houſe of
David, *Is it* a ſmall thing for you to weary men, but
will ye [l] weary my God alſo? 14 Therefore [m] the
LORD himſelf ſhall give you a ſign, [n] Behold, a virgin
ſhall conceive and bear [o] a ſon, and † ſhall call his name
‡ Immanuel. 15 Butter and honey ſhall he eat, [p] that he
may know to refuſe the evil, and chooſe the good. 16
For [q] before the child ſhall know to refuſe the evil, and
chooſe the good, the land that thou abhorreſt ſhall be
forſaken of [r] both her kings.

[k] Deut. vi. 16. [l] Amos ii. 13. [m] Ezek. xxxvi. 32. [n] Mat. i. 23. Luke i. 31. [o] Chap. ix. 6. † Or thou, O virgin, ſhalt call. ‡ i. e. God with us. Chap. viii. 8. John i. 14. [p] Luke ii. 52. [q] Chap. viii. 4. [r] 2 Kings xv. 30. & xvi. 9.

v. 10—16. To confirm by miracle the veracity of the prophetic word, Iſaiah,

1. Bids Ahaz aſk a ſign of the Lord his God; for though he was a wicked king, God had not yet caſt off his national relation to him and his people, and was ready to grant him every evidence to engage his truſt and dependance.

2. Ahaz wickedly rejects the offer, pretending piety, *v.* 12. but there could be no fear of tempting God in aſking a ſign, when himſelf had made the offer; the true reaſon ſeems to be, he was unwilling to be quiet, and truſt the caſe with God, expecting more from the help of the Aſſyrians and his own fortifications, than from the word of promiſe.

3. The prophet rebukes the high affront herein ſhown, not to himſelf merely as a prophet, but more eſpecially to that God who ſent him, *v.* 13. And ſince he diſdains to aſk a ſign, God will give him one ſtrange and marvellous; a ſign that relates in a double reſpect to the preſent and eternal good of his people. *Behold* a ſtrange unheard of wonder, *a virgin ſhall conceive* without the knowledge of man, *and bear a ſon, and ſhall call his name Immanuel*, God with us in our nature, conceived of a virgin, by the power of the Holy Ghoſt, that he might have the human nature pure from our original defilement, and add infinite dignity thereunto, by uniting it to the divine nature in that myſterious perſon God and man in one Chriſt. *Butter and honey ſhall he eat*, partaking of a real human nature, ſupported by food and water, and growing to maturity of underſtanding, by progreſſive ſteps, *that he may know*, or *until he ſhall know to refuſe the evil, and chooſe the good*. Now this was a ſign of preſent deliverance for Judah, as well as future ſafety, ſince, till the time of the coming of this wonderful perſonage, the ſceptre ſhould not depart finally from them: and for this more imme-

Before Christ 742

of the comfort it is added, *Before this child*, probably pointing to Shear-jashub his little son, or *before the child*, any child that is born, *shall know to refuse the evil, and chuse the good*, shall come to the exercise of reason, *the land thou abhorrest*, or Syria and Israel, now confederate, *shall be forsaken of both her kings* Pekah and Rezin, which was quickly fulfilled in the death of Rezin, slain by the king of Assyria, 2 *Kings* xvi 9 and Pekah by Hoshea, 2 *Kings* xv 30 *Note*, (1) Insults cast on God's prophets, is in silence against himself, and will be highly resented by him (2) The great comfort in every distress, is not so much the hope of present deliverance, as the prospect of eternal blessedness in our Immanuel (3) The more we examine the word of prophecy, the more confirmed shall we be in the faith of Jesus, in whom it is so perfectly fulfilled

17 ¶ The LORD shall bring upon thee, and upon
thy people, and upon thy father's house, days that have
not come, from the day [a] that Ephraim departed from
Judah, *even* the king of Assyria 18 And it shall come
to pass in that day, *that* [t] the LORD shall hiss for the fly
that *is* in the uttermost part of the rivers of Egypt, and
for the bee that *is* in the land of Assyria 19 And they
shall come, and shall rest all of them in the desolate val-
leys, and in the holes of the rocks, and upon all thorns,
and upon all † bushes 20 In the same day shall the
LORD shave with a razor *that is* hired, *namely* by them
beyond the river, by the king of Assyria, the head and
the hair of the feet and it shall also consume the beard.
21 And it shall come to pass in that day, *that* a man
shall nourish [x] a young cow and two sheep 22 And
it shall come to pass for the abundance of milk *that* they
shall give, he shall eat butter for butter and honey
shall every one eat *that is* left in the land 23 And it
shall come to pass in that day, *that* every place shall be
where there were a thousand vines at a thousand silver-
lings, [y] it shall *even* be for briers and thorns 24 With
arrows and with bows shall *men* come thither, because [z]
all the land shall become briers and thorns 25 And *on*
all hills that shall be digged with the mattock, ‡ there
shall not come thither the fear of briers and thorns but
it shall be for the sending forth of oxen, and for the
treading of lesser cattle

a 1 Kings xii. 16
t Chap. v 26
† Or, commendable trees
u 2 Kings xvi 7, 8
x Jer. xxxix 10
y Chap. v 6
z Ibid. xxxii 13
‡ Or, none shall come thither for fear

v 17—25 Though God will now appear for Zion's sake, let not Ahaz think his unbelief shall go unpunished

1 A sore judgment is threatned, such as before the land of Judah never knew, since the grand revolt of the ten tribes, *v* 17 *Note*, Though God may have long patience, the impenitent must not promise themselves impunity

2 The instrument to be employed, was chiefly the king of Assyria Nebuchadnezzar, and Pharoah-Nechoh, the king of Egypt, helped forward their destruction, 2 *Kings* xxiii 29—35 As readily as the shepherd's dog obeyed the whistle, would their armies come up at God's call, thick as swarms of bees and flies, *v* 18 resting in the desolate valleys like flights of locusts not a green leaf should be left, so thoroughly would they devour the land, and climb every fortress, though seated on the craggy rocks, *v* 19 As a sharp razor, passing from head to foot, shaves off the hair, so should the king of Assyria make an entire conquest of Judea, receiving the spoil as his hire or alluding to the present Ahaz sent him, to engage his assistance, 2 *Kings* xvi 7—9 which in the end turned to his own damage, and brought upon him the continual inroads of the Assyrians, till the fatal captivity arrived *Note*, (1) When God will chastise a guilty nation, he will not want a scourge (2) It is just in God to make that creature the instrument of our vexation, we have made the object of our confidence, and to let men see thereby the misery as well as folly of changing a rock for a reed

3 Terrible would be the consequence of these invasions instead of lowing herds and grazing flocks, a man would think himself happy if he had one young cow, and two poor sheep remaining, *v* 21 So desolate would every family be, and such plenty of pasture in the depopulated country, that this small flock of cattle would yield a full sufficient butter and honey would be their only diet, for meat could not be afforded in the scarcity of beasts that remained, *v* 22 and vineyards and tillage would be utterly neglected the spot that paid a yearly rent of a thousand shekels (*about the value of half a crown*) for a thousand vines, so fruitful were they, now overgrown with briers and thorns, yielded no revenue, *v* 23 Instead of pruning their vineyards, men must now go armed to protect them from the wild beasts, or robbers that lodged in their thickets, where fruitful vineyards grew, *v* 24 and the hills and fields untilled, where once the rich harvest stood, now, no longer fenced with hedges of thorns, are left quite open as a wild waste, where the cattle roamed without controul, *v* 25 How terrible are the desolations which sin, and war, the effects of it, makes in the earth? What sinful nation need not tremble on beholding Judea's wretched fate, and read an alarming call to repentance in her overthrow?

Before Christ 742

CHAP VIII

Amidst dark threatnings to the ungodly, bright beams of hope break forth on the faithful In this chapter we have, 1 A prophecy of the destruction of the confederate kingdoms of Syria and Israel by the king of Assyria, ver 1—4 2 Of the desolations that should be made by that proud victorious prince, in the land of Israel and Judah, ver 5—8 3 Great encouragement given to the people of God in the midst of these distractions they are assured, (1) That their enemies shall not gain their point against them, ver 9, 10 (2) That if they kept up the fear of God, and kept down the fear of man, they would find God their refuge, ver 11—14 And while others stumbled, and fell into despair, they should be enabled to wait on God, and see themselves reserved for better times, ver 15—18

1 MOREOVER, the LORD said unto me,
Take thee a great roll, and [a] write in it with a
man's pen, concerning † Maher-shalal-hash-baz 2
And I took unto me faithful [b] witnesses to record, [c]
Uriah the priest, and Zechariah the son of Jeberechiah
3 And I ‡ went unto the prophetess, and she conceived
and bare a son, then said the LORD to me, Call his
name Maher-shalal-hash-baz 4 For [d] before the child
shall have knowledge to cry, My father and my mo-
ther, § the riches of Damascus, and the spoil of Sa-
maria shall be taken away before the king of Assyria
5 ¶ The LORD spake also to me again, saying, 6
Forasmuch as this people refuseth the waters of Shiloah
that go softly, and rejoice in Rezin and Remaliah's son
7 Now therefore behold, the Lord bringeth up upon them
the waters of the river, strong and many, *even* the king
of Assyria, and all his glory and he shall come up over
all his channels, and go over all his banks 8 And he
shall pass through Judah, he shall overflow and go over,
[g] he shall reach *even* to the neck, and the stretching out
of his wings shall fill the breadth of thy land, O [h] Im-
manuel

a Hab. ii 2
† i.e. Make speed to the spoil, hasten to the prey
b 2 Cor. xiii 1
c 2 Kings xvi 11
‡ Heb. Approached unto, Lev. xviii 6
d Chap. vii 16
About 741
§ Or, he that is before the king of Assyria, shall take away the riches, &c.
e 2 Kings xv 29 & xvi 9
f Chap. xvii.
Chap. xxviii 2
g Ibid. xxx 28
h Ibid. vii 14

v 1—8 The destruction of Damascus and Samaria are here threatned, and the rod of warning shaken over Judah

1 The prophet is commanded to write this, with the four following chapters, on a large roll, and as a title to inscribe on it Maher-shalal-hash-baz, *hasten to the spoil, hasten to the prey*, an invitation to the king of Assyria, and repeated to shew the certainty of the event *Note*, It is an unspeakable mercy the holy scriptures are committed to writing, and not handed down to us by uncertain tradition

2 The prophet having obeyed the Divine injunction, gets it attested by two credible witnesses, Uriah the priest, and Zechariah, probably a Levite, 2 *Chron* xxix 13 that when the event corresponded with the prediction, his Divine mission might incontestibly appear

3 On the conception of the prophetess his wife, so called from her relation to him, and the birth of a second son, to engage greater attention to the prophecy, he by Divine command gives the child the same name as was inscribed on the roll. The design of which,

4 He explains, *v* 4 That before the infant could speak plainly, Damascus and Samaria should be spoiled by the Assyrian king, which was fulfilled, 2 *Kings* xvi 9, xvii 3 and more fully xviii 10 *Note*, (1) War is God's scourge over guilty lands (2) They who have been troublers of others repose, are justly doomed to suffer in return

5 Judah also shall not go unpunished, because many of the faithless Jews despised the waters of Shiloah that go softly, the gentle government of David's race, or the weakness of their kingdom, eclipsed by the greater dominion of Rezin and Pekah, whom, though avowed enemies, these traitors of their country applauded and honoured, *v* 6 therefore to punish them the Assyrian king, like a flood, with his armies should cover the land, rapid and irresistible, reaching to the neck, even to Jerusalem the metropolis, 2 *Kings* xviii 13—17 and spreading his wings *should fill the breadth of Immanuel's land*, so called, because there he should in the fulness of time be born, live, and die *Note*, (1) To affect the fashions, admire the manners and government of our inveterate enemies, and to despise our own, betrays a heart destitute of the love of our country (2) Though the waters of trouble reach to the neck, yet even then in God trust, Here shall thy proud waves be stayed, and save us out of the floods, when we seem in our own eye most desperate (3) If the Lord Jesus have possession of our hearts, though

Before Christ 741

though corruption often ſpreads its wings, he will never give us up for a prey to our ſpiritual enemies

[i] Chap. xvii. 12, 13. Mic. iv. 11—13

[k] Job v. 12. Pſ. xxxiii. 10. Prov. xxi. 30. Chap. vii. 7.
[l] Chap. vii. 14. Jer. xx. 11. Rom. viii. 31.
[m] Jer. xv. 19.
[n] 1 Pet. iii. 14, 15.
[o] Ezek. xi. 16.
[p] Chap. xxviii. 16. Luke ii. 34. Rom. ix. 33. 1 Pet. ii. 8.
[q] Mat. xxi. 44. Luke xx. 18.

9 ¶ [i] Aſſociate yourſelves, O ye people, and ye ſhall
be broken in pieces, and give ear all ye of far countries
gird yourſelves, and ye ſhall be broken in pieces 10
Take counſel together, [k] and it ſhall come to nought,
ſpeak the word, and it ſhall not ſtand, for [l] God *is* with
us 11 ¶ For the LORD ſpake thus to me with a ſtrong
hand, and [m] inſtructed me that I ſhould not walk in the
way of this people, ſaying, 12 Say ye not, A confe-
deracy, to all *them* to whom this people ſhall ſay, A con
federacy, [n] neither fear ye their fear, nor be afraid
13 Sanctify the LORD of hoſts himſelf, and *let* him
be your fear, and *let* him *be* your dread 14 And he
ſhall be for a ſanctuary, but [p] for a ſtone of ſtumbling,
and for a rock of offence to both the houſes of Iſrael,
for a gin, and for a ſnare to the inhabitants of Jeruſalem
15 And many among them [q] ſhall ſtumble and fall,
and be broken, and be ſnared, and be taken

v. 9—15 In Judah's diſtreſſed caſe, the prophet encourages and inſtructs them,

1 With a promiſe of their enemies diſappointment and defeat though ſtrongly confederate, the expedition deeply planned, and the troops well armed and ready for the battle, they ſhall be broken to pieces This is repeated to ſhew the certainty of the event and the vanity of their hopes of ſucceſs, when God will infatuate their councils, and Immanuel defend his own land, v. 9, 10 *Note*, (1) Though power and policy unite to cruſh the church of Chriſt, their efforts will prove the confuſion of her enemies (2) God's promiſe is ſure, and they who truſt it will never be diſappointed (3) If God be with us and for us, we need neither fear nor care who are againſt us

2 He directs them how to ſpeak and act in their preſent ſituation *The Lord ſpake unto me with a ſtrong hand*, in the ſpirit of prophecy, *not to walk in the way of this people*, dejected with their fears, or flying with them to Aſſyria, for help againſt their invaders, Pekah and Rezin, *ſaying*, *Say ye not, A confederacy, to all them to whom this people ſhall ſay, A confederacy*, join not in the general cry for a foreign aid, or in any factious party at home, *neither fear ye their fear, nor be afraid* on account of the confederate armies of Syria and Iſrael *Sanctify the Lord God of hoſts*, by your profeſſed dependance upon, and ſubjection to him, *and let him be your fear, and let him be your dread*, who is the only worthy object *And he ſhall be for a ſanctuary*, a ſure protection to thoſe who truſt him in every time of trial and diſtreſs *Note*, (1) In time of danger good men need encouragement againſt their fears (2) They who would follow Chriſt, muſt renounce the ways of a wicked world, a holy ſingularity is the inſeparable badge of a holy converſation (3) When God teaches us with a ſtrong hand, then ſhall we be enabled to walk aright ourſelves, and to direct others in the way (4) In whatever difficulties we are involved, let us never uſe undue means for relief (5) The fear of God upon the heart, will preſerve us from being terrified with the threatenings of men (6) God is ſanctified, when by patient reſignation we are content to wait for his ſalvation (7) If we have taken the Lord Jeſus for our ſanctuary, all the powers of earth and hell can never pluck us thence, nor endanger our ſafety

3 He threatens thoſe who continued rebellious with ruin, if they would not truſt God as their ſanctuary, they ſhould find him *a ſtone of ſtumbling, and rock of offence to both the houſes of Iſrael, and for a gin and a ſnare to the inhabitants of Jeruſalem*, which was ſoon verified in the deſtruction the king of Aſſyria, at God's command, brought upon them, and hath a further reference to the day of Chriſt, *ſee* 1 *Cor* i 30 when, offended at the Lord Jeſus, his character, birth, diſciples, &c the Jews, unable to reconcile it to their proud expectations of a conquering Meſſiah, rejected him, *many among them ſtumbled and fell, and were broken, and ſnared, and taken*, as was here predicted, and thereby periſhed under their unbelief and hardneſs of heart *Note*, The ſame Jeſus that is a ſanctuary to the poor and helpleſs ſinner, to the proud and ſelf-righteous is ſtill a ſtone of ſtumbling, they will not renounce themſelves to truſt in him, and therefore periſh in their iniquities.

[r] Dan. xii. 4.
[s] Chap. xxv. 9. Mic. vii. 7.
[t] Chap. liv. 8. lvii. 17.
[u] Heb. ii. 13.
[x] Pſ. lxxi. 7. Zech. iii. 8.
[y] Chap. xxix. 4.
[z] 1 Sam. xxviii. 8.

16 Bind up the teſtimony, [r] ſeal the law among my
diſciples 17 And [s] I will wait upon the LORD [t] that
hideth his face from the houſe of Jacob, and I will look
for him 18 [u] Behold, I and the children whom the
LORD hath given me, [x] *are* for ſigns, and for wonders
in Iſrael, from the LORD of hoſts. which dwelleth in
mount Zion 19 ¶ And when they ſhall ſay unto you,
Seek unto them that have familiar ſpirits, and unto wi
zards [y] that peep, and that mutter ſhould not a people
ſeek unto their God? for the living, to the dead?
20 [a] To the law and to the teſtimony if they ſpeak not
according to this word, *it is* becauſe [†] *there is* no light
in them 21 And they ſhall paſs through it, hardly be-
ſtead and hungry and it ſhall come to paſs, that when
they ſhall be hungry, [c] they ſhall fret themſelves, and
curſe their king, and their God, and look upward 22
And [d] they ſhall look unto the earth and behold, trouble
and darkneſs, dimneſs of anguiſh, and *they ſhall be* driven
to darkneſs

Before Christ 741

[a] Luke xvi. 29.
[b] Mat. xv. 14.
[†] Heb. Morning light
[c] Rev. xvi. 10, 11.
[d] Chap. v. 30.

v. 16—22 We have here,

1 The command given to the prophet *Bind up the teſtimony*, the prophetic word concerning the Meſſiah, more precious than bags of gold, to be preſerved for futurity, *ſeal the law among my diſciples*, the diſciples of Jeſus, to whom the law of the ſpirit of life was intruſted, and though a ſealed book to others, revealed to them, and tranſmitted faithfully to their ſucceſſors *Note*, (1) We can never enough be thankful for the ineſtimable treaſure of God's word (2) Till God opens our underſtanding to underſtand the ſcriptures, they are a book ſealed, and a goſpel hid

2 The prophet profeſſes his earneſt expectation and hope *I will wait upon the Lord*, the Redeemer of his people *that hideth his face from the houſe of Jacob*, either in frowns of diſpleaſure, or as being yet hid from them until his glorious manifeſtation in the fleſh, *and I will look for him*, in confidence of his coming, and in joyful hope of the bleſſed iſſue of his appearing *Note*, (1) Patient waiting upon God will never be diſappointed (2) When God hides his face, we muſt not think he hath forſaken us, but be ſtirred up to pray, Lift up again upon us the light of thy countenance

3 Chriſt, in anſwer to the prophet's expectation, appears to cheer and comfort him, of whom the words ſeem rather ſpoken than of the prophet himſelf and his two ſons, though they were probably types of Chriſt and his people, for to him the words are expreſsly aſcribed, *Heb* xi 13 *Behold, I and the children whom the Lord hath given me*, in virtue of the everlaſting covenant, in which it was promiſed, that he ſhould ſee his ſpiritual ſeed, *Iſa* liii 10 but the world knoweth them not, becauſe they knew him not, they *are for ſigns, and for wonders in Iſrael*, ſigns and wonders were wrought by them, yet Iſrael would not believe, yea, derided and reviled them, and ſtill they continue in the world a people every where ſpoken againſt, and bearing the reproach of the croſs, *from the Lord of hoſts, which dwelleth in mount Zion*, who freely gave his Son for us, and in his ſovereign grace beſtowed on him that peculiar people, the travail of his ſoul *Note*, (1) The relation between a miniſter, and thoſe who are begotten by him in the goſpel, is near and dear as between the parent and his natural offspring (2) We muſt not be aſhamed of the reproach of Chriſt, nor, however ſtrange the world may think us, join with them in their ways

4 Chriſt cautions his diſciples to beware of deceivers, and to keep cloſe to the word of revelation primarily it may refer to the Jews, who in their diſtreſſes were readier to recur to any help than to God, 2 *Kings* i 2 but it contains a warning againſt the falſe doctrines of the Scribes and Phariſees, who were much given to ſorcery and enchantments, and in their principles and practices were as contrary to God as wizards, them therefore it were folly to conſult *ſhould not a people ſeek unto their God?* who beſides the Redeemer can give a ſatisfactory anſwer to the queſtions of the guilty, and the cries of the diſtreſſed ſoul? it were highly abſurd *for the living* to apply *to the dead*, to magians, or necromancers, or the Scribes and Phariſees, and all like them, who, tho pretending to teach others, are themſelves dead in treſpaſſes and ſins *To the law and to the teſtimony*, the ſcriptures, which are the only teſts of truth *if they ſpeak not according to this word, it is becauſe there is no light in them*, they are blind leaders of the blind *Note*, (1) The ſuperſtitious folly of many profeſſed chriſtians, who truſt in charms, and fortune-tellers, and the like, is ſcandalous as unlawful (2) If God be our God, we may always ſeek, and always find help in him in every trial (3) The more we examine the Bible for ourſelves, the leſs liable ſhall we be to be deceived (4) No doctrine is to be received as genuine, which hath not ſcripture proof to ſupport it (5) A miniſter whoſe own ſoul hath never felt the enlivening influences of God's word and ſpirit, can ſcarce be expected to guide others aright in the way to glory, the living might as ſoon expect inſtruction from the dead, as the ſoul edification from ſuch

5 The doom of the wicked is read, who forſake God for familiar ſpirits, the truth for falſhood *And they ſhall paſs through it* (the land) *hardly beſtead and hungry* when in their captivity, they ſhould ſcarce have bread to ſupport their miſerable lives, are with madneſs and vexation under their calamities blaſpheme God, and their king Meſſiah, and look upwards in vain for help from him till Chriſt, having rejected the true Redeemer whenever they turned their eyes, darkneſs, diſtreſs, and wretchedneſs ſhould appear, till a miſerable life ſhould cloſe in a

Before Christ 740

more miserable death, which was fully verified in the judgments brought on the Jews by the Roman sword *Note*, (1) The unhumbled fret and kick against the pricks, but they only thereby aggravate their own sufferings (2) God's judgments upon sinners, instead of bringing them to repentance, provoke their blasphemies (3) They who forsake the God of their mercies, in death find all their prospects terminated with darkness and despair

CHAP. IX.

The prophet in this chapter begins, 1 With comforts to God's people (1) In the doctrine of the Messiah, ver 1—3 (2) His victories, ver 4, 5 (3) His government and dominion, as Immanuel, ver 6, 7 2 With dreadful threatnings against the people of Israel, that had revolted from, and were enemies to the house of David, that they should be brought to utter ruin, ver 18—21 And this is typical of the final destruction of all the enemies of the Son of David and his kingdom.

About 740

1 NEVERTHELESS, ᵃ the dimness *shall* not
be such as *was* in her vexation, when at the first
ᵇ he lightly afflicted the land of Zebulun, and the land
of Naphtali, ᶜ and afterward did more grievously afflict
her by the way of the sea, beyond Jordan in Galilee †
of the nations 2 ᵈ The people that walked in darkness,
have seen a great light they that dwell in the land
of the shadow of death, upon them hath the light shined
3 Thou hast multiplied the nation, *and* ‡ not increased
the joy ᵉ they joy before thee, according to the joy in
harvest, ᶠ *and as men* rejoice when they divide the spoil
4 For thou hast ᵍ broken the yoke of his burden, and
the staff of his shoulder, the rod of his oppressor, ʰ as in
the day of Midian 5 For every battle of the warrior
is with confused noise, and garments rolled in blood, but
ⁱ *this* shall be with burning *and* fuel of fire 6 For unto
us a child is born, unto us ᵏ a son is given, and the government
shall be upon his shoulder and his name shall
be called, ˡ Wonderful, Counsellor, ᵐ The mighty God,
§ The everlasting Father, ⁿ The Prince of peace. 7 Of
the increase of *his* government and peace ᵒ *there shall be*
no end, upon the throne of David, and upon his kingdom,
ᵖ to order it, and to establish it with judgment and
with justice, from henceforth even for ever ᑫ the zeal of
the LORD of hosts will perform this.

ᵃ Chap. viii 22
ᵇ 2 Kings xv 29
ᶜ Ibid xvii 5, 6
† Or, populous
ᵈ Mat iv 16. Eph v 14
‡ Or, to him
ᵉ Ps iv 7
ᶠ Ibid cxix 162
ᵍ Chap x 27 & xiv 5 Jer xxx 8
ʰ Judges vii 22 Chap x 26.
ⁱ Mal iii 3
ᵏ Chap vii 14 Luke ii 11
ˡ John iii 16
ᵐ Tit ii 13
§ Heb. The father of eternity, John x 28 Heb v 9
ⁿ Eph ii 14 Col i 20
ᵒ Luke i 32, 33
ᵖ Zech vi 13
ᑫ 2 Kings xix 31 Chap xxxvii 32

v 1—7 The former chapter concluded with a dismal scene of desolations, but here to the righteous there ariseth up light in the darkness, through that glorious Saviour, whose coming, like the sun, should dispel the clouds, and whose power should subdue every foe before him

1 He is spoken of as the light of his people There had been grievous vexations and ravages committed by Pul and Tilgath-pilnezer, kings of Assyria, and more deplorable ones when Salmanezer carried away the Jews captive into Assyria, but though the last under the Romans should be most terrible, there should be one alleviation of them, which the former had not *The people that walked in darkness, have seen a great light*, Christ the sun of righteousness arisen, who favoured Galilee with so much of his presence, preaching, and miracles *they that dwell in the land of the shadow of death*, in a state of affliction under the Roman yoke, but more especially under the blindness and ignorance of their fallen minds, and exposed to eternal death, by reason of sin, *on them hath the light shined*, the light of the glorious gospel, dispensed by Jesus and his apostles *Note*, (1) In the midst of the deepest distresses, a sense of Christ's presence and love alleviates every burden (2) Every man by nature is a child of darkness, and his ways lead down to death and hell, till Christ the light of life arises upon his soul, pardoning, quickening, and leading him into the paths of peace (3) We might much better want the light of the sun, than the light of the gospel, with the gospel the blind may find the way to heaven, without it the sun can only light us into eternal darkness

2 As the Saviour of his people, causing them to rejoice in him *Thou hast multiplied the nation*, increased the number of faithful converts, either among the Jews in Galilee, or from the nations who dwelt among them, from whose sojourning there it was called, *Galilee of the nations*, v 1 *and hast increased the joy of it*, (we read *not increased*, but the marginal reading seems much preferable); the gospel being glad tidings of great joy to all who receive it *they joy before thee, as the joy of harvest*, more delighted with the blessed fruits of gospel grace, than with plenty of corn and wine; *and as men rejoice when they divide the spoil* of conquered enemies, such is now sin, Satan, death, and hell, are become, through the victory of our Redeemer *For thou hast broken the yoke of his burden, and the staff of his shoulder, the rod of his oppressor, as in the day of Midian*; Christ, like the mighty Gideon, by the trumpet of his gospel, and the light of truth committed to earthen vessels, his ministers, hath delivered his people from the yoke of Satan, sin, and the law, more burdensome to the soul than the oppression of Midian to Israel *For every battle of the warrior is with confused noise, and garments rolled in blood, but this* of a different nature, *shall be with burning and fuel of fire*, by the power of the spirit of God, operating like fire upon the sinner's heart, and burning up his vile affections, as fire doth the fuel Though some read the words, *which shall be for burning the fuel of fire*, it being usual for conquerors to burn the armour and spoil of their enemies *Note*, (1) When Christ entered the lists in the behalf of his people, his foes fell as lightning from heaven before him, and with the shout of victory he expired, crying, It is finished (2) Whoever hath felt the bitterness and bondage of sin, and groaned under it, being burdened, will hear the glad tidings of salvation, through the Redeemer, with transport (3) They who are delivered from the power of sin and Satan, will ascribe the whole of their salvation to the Redeemer's Almighty grace, for it is his right hand hath gotten for us the victory

3 The glorious person of our Redeemer and Saviour, is set forth under a variety of views, expressive of his excellent greatness, and admirably adapted to encourage the faith and hope of his people *For unto us a child is born*, one in the human nature, born for our sake, to be a Saviour to the uttermost, *unto us a son is given*, the Son of God, already in the eternal counsels appointed, and as certainly to be incarnate as if he had then been on the earth, and least the views of his humanity might lessen him in our eyes, the infinitely transcendent dignity of his person is insisted upon; *and the government shall be upon his shoulders*, though an infant, yet a king, invested with all power in heaven and earth, and especially establishing his throne in the hearts of his people *and his name shall be called, Wonderful*, his incarnation, life, death, resurrection, ascension, are full of wonders, his love, grace, redemption, amazingly great and glorious, and all he is and doth, justly challenges the admiration of angels as well as men, *Counsellor*, which may be joined with wonderful he is of the sacred Three, by whose infinite wisdom all things were created, and by whose designs of providence and grace the whole world above and beneath is administered, and to his teaching are his people indebted for their salvation, who, in every difficult, guided by his counsel, are safely brought at last to glory, *The mighty God*, or *God the mighty One*, very God as well as very man, sharing in all the incommunicable attributes of Deity, self-existence, eternity, omnipotence, &c and mighty therefore to save all that come to him as their Redeemer, *The everlasting Father*, though in person distinct from the God the Father, yet one with him in essence and the unity of the godhead, and particularly the everlasting Father of his people, the children given him according to the tenor of the eternal covenant of grace, and to whom he is the author of everlasting salvation, *The Prince of peace*, the procurer of peace between God and man, the giver of it to the troubled conscience, his subjects are all peaceable, and ruling in their hearts, he keeps them in perfect peace whilst stayed upon him, and will bring them shortly to everlasting peace and rest in glory *Of the increase of his government and peace there shall be no end*, from small beginnings it shall increase more and more, till the ends of the earth remember themselves, and turn unto the Lord, and the peace he gives shall be eternal as his throne, *Ephraim shall not envy Judah, nor Judah vex Ephraim*, all animosities between his people will subside, and, Oh that the time were come for this happy union of all true believers in one heart and one mind! *upon the throne of David, and upon his kingdom*, the Redeemer, the Son of David after the flesh, will be exalted, *to order it*, the kingdom of his Israel, and *to establish it with justice and judgment*, confirming his people in righteousness and true holiness, and executing judgment on their enemies, *henceforth even for ever* for his dominion is that which shall not be destroyed, he ever lives and ever reigns, not only in time, but to eternity *the zeal of the Lord of hosts will perform this*, his faithfulness is engaged to fulfil his promise, his power almighty to accomplish his purpose, and therefore not a jot or tittle shall fail Happy therefore, eternally happy, are those souls who are brought under the government of Jesus, and, by experience of his power establishing that kingdom within them, which is righteousness and peace, and joy in the Holy Ghost, can say with humble confidence, *My King* and *my God*

8 ¶ The LORD sent a word unto Jacob, and it hath About 738
lighted upon Israel 9 And ʳ all the people shall know, ʳ Heb known
even Ephraim, and the inhabitants of Samaria, that say in
the pride and stoutness of heart, 10 ˢ The bricks are ˢ Mal i 4
fallen down, but we will build with hewn stones the
sycamores are cut down, but we will change *them into*
cedars 11 Therefore the LORD shall set up the adversaries
of Rezin against him, and † join his enemies † Heb mingle

Before Christ 738

together 12 The Syrians before, and the Philiſtines
behind, and they ſhall devour Iſrael with open mouth
ᵗ for all this his anger is not turned away, but his hand
is ſtretched out ſtill 13 For ᵘ the people turneth not
unto him that ſmiteth them, ᵛ neither do they ſeek the
LORD of hoſts 14 Therefore the LORD will cut
off from Iſrael head and tail, branch and ruſh in one
day 15 The ancient and honourable, he *is* the head
and ʸ the prophet that teacheth lies, he *is* the tail 16
For ‡ the leaders of this people cauſe *them* to err, and
they that are § led of them *are* ‖ deſtroyed 17 There-
fore the LORD ſhall have no joy in their young men,
neither ſhall have mercy on their fatherleſs and widows
for ᶻ every one *is* an hypocrite, and an evil doer, and
every mouth ſpeaketh † folly ᵃ for all this his anger is
not turned away, but his hand *is* ſtretched out ſtill 18
¶ For ᵇ wickedneſs burneth as the fire, it ſhall devour the
briers and thorns, and ſhall kindle in the thickets of the
foreſt, and they ſhall mount up *like* the lifting up of
ſmoke 19 Through the wrath of the LORD of hoſts
is ᶜ the land darkned, and the people ſhall be as the fuel
of the fire ᵈ no man ſhall ſpare his brother 20 And
he ſhall ſnatch on the right hand, and be hungry, and
he ſhall eat on the left hand, and ᵉ they ſhall not be ſa-
tisfied ᶠ they ſhall eat every man the fleſh of his own
arm 21 Manaſſeh, Ephraim, and Ephraim, Ma-
naſſeh, *and* they together *ſhall be* againſt Judah ᵍ for
all this his anger is not turned away, but his hand *is*
ſtretched out ſtill

ᵗ Chap v 25 & x 4 Jer iv 8 ᵘ Jer v 3 Hoſ vii 7 ᵛ Mal ii 8, 9 ‡ Heb They that call them bleſſed Chap iii § Heb called bleſſed &c ‖ Heb. Swallowed up ᶻ Chap x 6 † Or, villany. ᵃ Ver 12, 21 Chap v 25 & x 4 ᵇ Mal iv 1 Pſal lxxxiii 14 ᶜ Chap viii 22 ᵈ Mic vii 2 ᵉ Lev xxvi 26 ᶠ Chap xlix 26 Jer xix 9 ᵍ Ver 12, 17

v 8—21 The ſame prophetic word which brings tidings of mercy to ſome, denounces the judgments of God on others They who diſregard his anger, ſhall feel the lighting down of his indignation, and know by dire experience how fearful a thing it is to fall into the hands of the living God The kingdom of Iſrael hath no ſhortly approaching doom denounced, a moment's reſpite is in mercy given, before God ſtrikes he warns, not willing that any ſhould periſh, but that all ſhould come unto repentance

1 A high charge is brought againſt them for ſundry crimes and miſdemeanours againſt the Majeſty of heaven

(1) They braved God's threatnings with daring inſolence Though the Aſſyrians had demoliſhed their houſes in the ſiege, they vaunted how ſoon they would reſtore them in greater magnificence, changing the bricks for hewn ſtone, and when the ſycamores were cut down for the beſieger's uſe, to burn or facilitate their approaches, they boaſted they would ſupply their place with cedars *Note*, Impenitence under warning providences, is a ſad ſymptom of approaching ruin

(2) They were incorrigible, *v* 13 nor in their deepeſt diſtreſſes deigned to humble their ſouls and ſeek to God *Note*, If corrections bring us not to our knees now, God's fierce wrath will be poured out, and prayer come too late to be heard

(3) Their magiſtrates and miniſters concurred in haſtening the judgment by their ill examples and lying promiſes *The leaders of this people*, or *they who bleſs this people*, deceive them, encouraging their falſe hopes, and ſeeing viſions of peace for them when there is no peace *Note*, When miniſters, inſtead of zeal againſt men's ſins, ſuffer them to continue undiſturbed, and ſpeak ſmooth things to flatter them to their ruin, the caſe is deſperate The ſick patient muſt needs die, if the phyſician adminiſters poiſon inſtead of medicine

(4) Hypocriſy, falſhood, and wickedneſs, were reigning ſins, *v* 17 They who kept up the form of religion, were as abominable as the profane and abandoned ſinner, the one renounced openly all reſpect to God, the other approached him with their lips, whilſt their hearts were far from him, or, truſting on the meritoriouſneſs of their outward duties and devotions, more fatally deceived themſelves to their ruin

2 A heavy puniſhment is threatned, temporal and eternal

[1] The ruin of their country, *v* 11, 12 The adverſaries of Rezin, whom Ahaz had hired, 2 *Kings* xvi 7—9 had ſcarce ſooner ſucceeded in the reduction of Damaſcus, than incorporating the Syrian forces with their own, they ſhould fall upon Iſrael on one ſide, and the Philiſtines on the other, ſo that they ſhould be grievouſly ſpoiled *Note*, God ſends leſſer judgments firſt, and if these prove ineffectual, he hath heavier in ſtore, for,

[2] Becauſe, by their continued impenitence, his wrath was not turned away, but his hand ſtretched out ſtill, he will make a more terrible havock among them, *v* 14, 15 neither young nor old, high or low, prieſt or people, ſhould eſcape nor would God extend the leaſt compaſſion to the moſt miſerable objects, *v* 17 *Note*, (1) When God viſits for ſin, the higheſt in ſtation ſhall be among the firſt to ſuffer, crowns plead no privilege at his bar (2) The miniſter that ſpeaketh lies, to curry favour with the great, connives at their ſins, or indolently negligent, is a blind leader of the blind will ſhortly appear a character the moſt deteſtable and baſe, and receive a puniſhment proportioned to his guilt and perfidy (3) The wickedneſs of the poor is as much remembered as the ſins of the rich, and their want and wretchedneſs here will be no exculpation, rather an aggravation of their ſins that when they had leſs of this world to enſnare them, they did not more carefully ſeek a better

[3] Inteſtine broils ſhall deſtroy them as well as the ſword of the enemy, *v* 20, 21 they ſhould bite and devour one another, and even the neareſt relations not ſpare their own fleſh and blood, various inſtances of which appeared when their deſolations drew near, and the ravages the tribes made on each other, opened an eaſier conqueſt for their enemies *Note*, Nothing ſo weakens God's church as cauſeleſs diviſions, and perverſe diſputes, for in the heat of religious controverſy, the power of godlineſs is uſually loſt, and Satan reaps the ſpoil

[4] The wrath of God, terrible and eternal, would yet purſue them their wickedneſs would kindle a fire of vengeance, which nothing could quench, and the ſmoke of their torment would aſcend up for ever and ever the darkneſs and diſtreſs of their outward ſituation, was but a faint image of their future proſpects, when, as fuel for the flames, they ſhould lie down in torment without meaſure and without end, *v* 18, 19 for as in all their temporal judgments, their obſtinacy provoked a repetition of the ſtrokes, ſo in the eternal puniſhment of the wicked, God's wrath will never be turned away, but his hand be ſtretched out ſtill, for his wrath is for ever wrath to come

CHAP X.

The prophet in this chapter threatens, 1 *The proud oppreſſors of his people at home,* ver 1—4 2 *Sennacherib then avowed enemy, concerning whom obſerve,* (1) *The commiſſion given him to invade Judah,* ver 5, 6 (2) *His pride and inſolence in the execution of that commiſſion,* ver 7—11, 13, 14 (3) *A rebuke given to his haughtineſs, and a threatning of his ruin,* ver 12, 15—19 (4) *A promiſe of grace to the people of God, to enable them to bear up under the affliction,* ver 20—23 (5) *Great encouragement given to them not to fear this threatning ſtorm, for there is yet hope,* ver 24—34

About 713

1 WO unto them ᵃ that decree unrighteous de-
crees, and † that write grievouſneſs *which* they
have preſcribed 2 To turn aſide the needy from judg-
ment, and to take away the right from the poor of my
people, that widows may be their prey, and *that* they may
rob the fatherleſs 3 And ᵇ what will ye do in the day
of viſitation, and in the deſolation *which* ſhall come from
far? ᶜ to whom will ye flee for help? and where will ye
leave your glory? 4 Without me they ſhall bow down
‡ under the priſoners, and they ſhall fall under the ſlain
ᵈ for all this his anger is not turned away, but his hand
is ſtretched out ſtill

ᵃ Pſal lviii & xciv 20 † Heb To the writers that write. ᵇ Job xxxi 14 ᶜ Job vi ‡ Or, among ᵈ Chap v. 25 & ix 12, 17, 21

v 1—4 God proceeds in his controverſy with Iſrael in their four verſes, which might more properly have concluded the foregoing chapter

1 He accuſes their governors of oppreſſion and injuſtice, by framing ſuch laws as immediately tended to diſtreſs the poor, or by making the proceedings ſo tedious and expenſive, that the needy never could afford to maintain his right, or in their adminiſtration they were ſo corrupt, that they enriched themſelves with the ſpoil of the fatherleſs and widows, and feared not to rob and plunder thoſe who were too weak to reſiſt, *v* 1, 2 *Note*, There is a lawgiver, to whom the oppreſſed may appeal, and wo to thoſe whoſe unrighteous decrees ſhall come before his bar

2 He warns them of the folly, ſin, and danger of their ways They braved it out now, *but what will ye do in the day of viſitation*, when God riſes up to judge? *and in the deſolation which ſhall come from far*? from the king of Babylon *to whom will ye flee for help*, in that day of calamity? *and where will ye leave your glory*? the riches, which they accounted their great ſupport, but in that day would periſh irrecoverably. *Without me*, when forſaken of my help, *they ſhall bow down under the priſoners*, or *among the priſoners, and ſhall fall under*, or *among the ſlain*, either in chains led captive, or left dead by the enemies ſword, and after all, greater judgments are ſtill in ſtore, *v* 4 *Note*, (1) As there is an awful day of enquiry approaching, it becomes every ſoul ſeriouſly to conſider what he ſhall then do, and how he ſhall be able to ſtand before the eternal judge (2) Whatever greatneſs and glory a ſinner may acquire, he muſt leave it all behind, and go a naked criminal to a righteous bar, where no covering or excuſe can hide his iniquities, and from whence there lies no appeal (3) They who live without God, will die without hope, the priſoners of

Before Christ 713

of the grave, and lying down among the slain in the second
death (4) It will be the consummation of misery to the dam-
ned that no gleam of hope will ever chear their darkness, nor
the least prospect appear of God's anger being ever turned a-
way

5 ¶ † O Assyrian, ᵉ the rod of mine anger, and the
staff in their hand is mine indignation 6 I will send
him against ᶠ an hypocritical nation, and against the peo-
ple of my wrath ᵍ will I give him a charge to take the spoil,
and to take the prey, and to tread them down like the
mire of the streets 7 ʰ Howbeit, he meaneth not so,
neither doth his heart think so, but *it is* in his heart to
destroy, and cut off nations not a few 8 For ⁱ he saith,
Are not my princes altogether kings? 9 *Is* not ᵏ Cal-
no, ˡ as Carchemish? *is* not Hamath, as Arpad? *is* not
Samaria, ᵐ as Damascus? 10 As my hand hath found ⁿ
the kingdoms of the idols, and whose graven images did
excel them of Jerusalem, and of Samaria, 11 ⁿ Shall
I not, as I have done unto Samaria and her idols, so do
to Jerusalem and her idols? 12 Wherefore it shall
come to pass, *that* when the Lord hath performed his
whole work ᵒ upon mount Zion and on Jerusalem, ᵖ I
will punish the fruit of the stout heart of the king of
Assyria, and the glory of his high looks 13 For he
saith, ᵍ By the strength of my hand I have done *it*, and
by my wisdom, for I am prudent and I have re-
moved the bounds of the people, and have robbed their
treasures, and have put down the inhabitants † like a
valiant *man* 14 And my hand hath found as a nest
the riches of the people and as one gathereth eggs *that*
are left, have I gathered all the earth, and there was none
that moved the wing, or opened the mouth, or peeped
15 Shall ʳ the ax boast itself against him that heweth
therewith? *or* shall the saw magnify itself against him
that shaketh it? as if the rod should shake *itself* against
them that lift it up, *or* as if the staff should lift up *itself* ˢ
as if it were no wood 16 Therefore shall the Lord, the
Lord of hosts, send among his fat ones leanness, and un-
der his glory he shall kindle a burning like the burning
of a fire 17 And the light of Israel ᵘ shall be for a fire,
and his holy One for a flame and ˣ it shall burn and de-
vour his thorns and his briers in one day 18 And shall
consume the glory of his forest, and of his fruitful field,
both soul and body and they shall be as when a standard
bearer fainteth 19 And the rest of the trees of his
forest shall be few, that a child may write them

† Or, woe to Assur
ᵉ Jer li 20
ᶠ Chap ix 17
ᵍ Jer xxxiv 22
ʰ Gen l 20
ⁱ 2 Kings xviii 24 & xix 10, &c
ᵏ Am vi 2
ˡ 2 Chron xxxv 20
ᵐ 2 Kings xvi 9
ⁿ Chap xxxvi 18—20 & xxxvii 10—13
ᵒ 2 Kings xix 31
ᵖ Jer l 18
ᵍ Deut viii 17 Dan iv 30 Am vi 13
ʳ Hab i 16
† Or, like many peo-ple
ˢ Jer li 20
ᵗ Ps lxxxiii 7 Ezek xxviii 9
ᵘ Is xlvi...
ˣ Chap xxvii 4

v 5—19 Desolations upon Israel being accomplished, let not Judah think to go unpunished Sennacherib is commissioned to shake the rod over them, yet God prescribes bounds to his path, and saith, Hither to shalt thou come, and no further

1 The Jews are described as *an hypocritical nation*, for though they complied with the reformation of Hezekiah, their hearts remained unchanged, and their religious services were but vain formality, and therefore they are called, *The people of my wrath*, nothing being in God's sight more detestable than hypocrisy, yet no sin so common among professors

2 God hath a rod prepared to scourge them, the Assyrian monarch is commissioned from him to ravage and spoil their country and as mire in the streets to tread them under foot, *v* 6 *Note*, (1) The tyrants of the world are but the tools of providence (2) They who most impiously employ their power against God, receive it from him, and he can make their wickedness subservient to his glory (3) When God chastises his own children, he intends their profiting, not their perdition

3 The proud instrument employed, thinks not who employs him, nor means to answer God's purposes but his own, *v* 7 to establish universal monarchy, and to gratify his ambition boasting therefore his power and conquests, he promises himself success against Jerusalem, as well as the other cities he had taken, his princes, equal to kings, were able to supply him ... for the accomplishment of the extensive conquests he meditated, *v* 8 A variety of cities, the capitals of vanquished countries, he enumerates, over which his arms had proved successful, *v* 9 and whose inhabitants he had transplanted into other countries, *v* 13 after having plundered their houses of their treasure, as eggs taken from the nest whilst the dam is absent, so that no resistance was made, and none had to withstand him of all the nations he or his predecessor had invaded, *v* 14 and thus he vainly imputes to his own strength and wisdom, which his policy none could defeat, and his power none could withstand *v* 13 From whence he concludes that as the preservation of the heathen he had subdued was

5

more and more precious than the gods of Jerusalem and Samaria, *v* 10 and the latter already fallen a prey, the former would afford him as easy a victory, blasphemously comparing Judah's God to the idols of the nations, and supposing him equally unable to protect his votaries, *v* 11 *Note*, (1) Nothing is farther from the hearts of sinners than to serve God's designs, but whilst they mean only their own ends, they are made to answer his (2) What is a worm of earth, though princes bow before him, compared with him, whom angels, principalities, and all the powers above obey? (3) To leave out God in the account of our gains, and to ascribe them to our own prudence, is direct atheism (4) Vanity and self-sufficiency generally issue in shame and disappointment

4 God by his prophet rebukes the insolent boaster, and foretells his approaching ruin Not more absurd would be the boast of the ax or saw in the craftsman's hand, as if the work done was theirs, not his who used them, than for this proud king, the rod of God's anger, to vaunt his conquests, or for this staff of God's indignation to arrogate the glory of his victories to himself, as if not an instrument, but the self-sufficient agent in those atchievments but God will make him know his folly in his fall, when he hath done his work of chastising and correcting God's people, for which he is employed, *v* 12 then shall his pride and haughtiness be humbled, his mighty army, the glory of his strength, like a body emaciated with consumption, shall pine away, and as fuel for the fire shall be burnt to ashes, *v* 16 God, the light and holy One of Israel, the Messiah, shall, by his angel, in one day consume the whole army, as easily as briers and thorns fall before the devouring fire, *v* 17 Though thick as a forest his tents, or the jewelry of his soldiers, and tall as cedars his mighty captains, they shall be consumed together, body and soul, *as when a standard-bearer fainteth*, and the rout is universal or it may be rendered, *as the dust of the worm that eats wood*, so easily and utterly would they be destroyed, *v* 18 and so few escape the general ruin, that instead of a muster-master, a little child might number them, *v* 19 *Note*, (1) The most proud and insolent, God can abase (2) In all the visitations on his people, God hath some gracious design to answer, when that is done, the rod will be burnt (3) In the midst of our trials, if God be our light, we shall see a door of escape, or be comforted with his presence, which can make the heaviest afflictions light (4) None ever hardened his heart against him and prospered (5) When God arises to judge the wicked, he will destroy both body and soul together in hell

20 ¶ And it shall come to pass in that day, *that* the
remnant of Israel, and such as are escaped of the house
of Jacob, ʸ shall no more again stay upon him that smote
them, but shall stay upon the LORD the holy One of
Israel in truth 21 ᶻ The remnant shall return, *even*
the remnant of Jacob, unto ᵃ the mighty God 22 For
ᵇ though thy people Israel be as the sand of the sea, ᶜ *yet*
a remnant of them shall return ᵈ the consumption de-
creed shall overflow with righteousness 23 For the Lord
GOD of hosts shall make a consumption, even deter-
mined in the midst of all the land

ʸ 2 Kings xvi 7 Hos v 13
ᶻ Chap vii 3
ᵃ Ibid ix 6
ᵇ Rom ix 27
ᶜ Chap vi 13
ᵈ Ibid xxviii 22 Dan ix 27 Rom ix

v 20—23 When judgment is executed on the enemies of God's church, mercy is reserved in store for his own people Amidst the general desolations, a remnant should be preserved, and return to their old habitations after Sennacherib raised the siege of Jerusalem, or from the Babylonish captivity but this prophecy looks farther also, and especially regards the time of the Messiah, *Rom* ix 27

1 A remnant of Israel should then be saved, escaping from the general blindness and unbelief which were upon the rest of their countrymen, renouncing their vain confidence as now they were taught by sad experience the vanity of trusting on Assyria for help, and therefore, in faith and truth placing all their hopes of salvation on the power and grace of their Redeemer alone, *v* 21 *Note*, (1) Among the numbers of religious professors, the chosen and faithful are but few (2) When we return to God, renouncing our self dependance and our sins, God will return to us in pardon and peace

2 When the mighty God the Saviour hath secured his own people, the remnant of Jacob, *v* 21 then vengeance will, according to God's decree, be executed on the more numerous part of Israel that have rejected his salvation the consumption is decreed, the exact time and number are fixed of those appointed unto destruction, and herein God will abundantly manifest his righteousness, when in all the land a consumption shall be made of the obstinately unbelieving, *v* 22, 23 Some understand these words in a different sense, and interpret *the consumption decreed*, &c as God's decree for the salvation of his people, wherein his righteousness shall be gloriously manifested, and apply it as speaking comfort to the chosen few, in the view of the certainty of their salvation but the former sense seems preferable

24 ¶ There-

Before Christ 713

24 ¶ Therefore thus saith the Lord GOD of hosts,
O my people that dwellest in Zion, [e] be not afraid of the
Assyrian: he shall smite thee with a rod, and shall lift up
his staff against thee, [f] after the manner of Egypt. 25
[g] For yet a very little while, and [h] the indignation shall
cease, and mine anger in their destruction. 26 And the
LORD of hosts shall stir up [i] a scourge for him, accord-
ing to the slaughter of [k] Midian at the rock of Oreb:
and *as* his rod *was* upon the sea, so shall he lift it up
after the manner of Egypt. 27 And it shall come to
pass in that day, *that* [m] his burden † shall be taken a-
way from off thy shoulder, and his yoke from off thy
neck, and the yoke shall be destroyed [n] because of the
anointing. 28 He is come to Aiath, he is passed to Mi-
gron; at Michmash he hath laid up his carriages: 29
They are gone over [o] the passage: they have taken up
their lodging at Geba; Ramah is afraid; [p] Gibeah of Saul
is fled. 30 ‡ Lift up thy voice, O daughter of [q] Gallim:
cause it to be heard unto [r] Laish, [s] O poor Anathoth.
31 [t] Madmenah is removed; the inhabitants of Gebim
gather themselves to flee. 32 As yet shall he remain [u]
at Nob that day: he shall shake his hand *against* the
mount of the daughter of Zion, the hill of Jerusalem.
33 Behold, the LORD, the LORD of hosts shall lop
the bough with terror: and [x] the high ones of stature
shall be hewn down, and [y] the haughty shall be humbled.
34 And [z] he shall cut down the thickets of the forest
with iron, and Lebanon shall [a] fall by a mighty one.

v. 24—34. Since God was determined to save a remnant for himself, he here,

1. Encourages them to trust, and not be afraid: terrible as Sennacherib's invasion appeared, God had set bounds to his ambition, though for a while they should suffer, as when their fathers were in Egypt, under the scourge, or be distressed as at the red sea, when the Egyptians pursued them, *v.* 24. yet in a moment the cause of their fears would cease, and God's anger, which seemed to threaten them in this invasion, be removed by the destruction of the Assyrians, *v.* 25. A destroying angel, his scourge, should pass through their host with sudden and terrible destruction by night, as the sword of Gideon smote the Midianites, and the sea swallowed up the Egyptians, when Moses stretched out his rod, *v.* 26. Their enemies defeated, the burden of tribute imposed on them, *2 Kings* xviii. 14. would be taken off, and their yoke of bondage to Assyria be destroyed, *because of the anointing*, for the sake of the redeemed, who have an unction from the holy One, or for the sake of the Messiah, who is the author of every mercy and blessing which descends on his people. *Note*, (1.) God's people need never fear with any amazement, there is hope for them in the darkest day. (2.) The unfaithfulness of God's own people provokes his displeasure, but it is short, and in wrath he remembers mercy. (3.) Though believers now groan, being burdened under their sins and corruptions, the redemption of their souls is secured, and shall quickly be perfected, when every yoke shall be broken for ever from their necks, by the grace of the anointed Jesus, and by the power of the anointing Spirit.

2. He describes the rapid progress of the Assyrian king advancing to the siege, and the ravages and dismay which he shall spread around him: without the least resistance he marches from Aiath to Migron, and thence to Michmash, where he establishes his magazines, *v.* 29. and hastening through the noted pass, 1 *Sam.* xiv. 4. encamps for a night at Geba in Benjamin. Frighted at his approach, the inhabitants sought only to save themselves by flight: whilst detachments from his army ravaged the country, and the cries of the poor people, plundered by the soldiers, were heard from one end of Judea to the other, *v.* 30, 31. Nob was his last station, where he halted within sight of Jerusalem, and, shaking his hand in threatening, promised himself a speedy conquest of their high battlements. *Note*, Success is apt to intoxicate, and the confidence of the proud turns to their destruction.

3. His overthrow is determined. The Lord, the Lord of hosts, before whom the mightiest are but as dust before the whirlwind, will stretch out his hand, confound his aspiring hopes, and all his army and chief captains, as the cedars of Lebanon fall under the stroke of the ax, shall perish by the sword of the destroying angel. *Note*, (1.) The terrors of God in the day of wrath, will overwhelm the proudest, and sink the mightiest in despair. (2.) None ever persecuted God's church and people with impunity.

CHAP. XI.

From the temporal deliverance of the Jews, the prophet makes a pleasing transition to the greater and eternal salvation of the Messiah, of which this was the type and figure. He describes, 1. His rise out of the house of David, ver. 1. 2. His qualifications for his great undertaking, ver. 2, 3. 3. The equity of his government, ver. 3—5. 4. The peace blessings of his kingdom, ver. 6—9. 5. The accession of the Gentiles to it, ver. 10. and with them the remnant of the Jews, that shall be united with them in the Messiah's kingdom, ver. 11—16.

Before Christ 713

1 AND [a] there shall come forth a rod out of the
stem of Jesse, and [b] a branch shall grow out of
his roots: 2 And [c] the Spirit of the LORD shall rest
upon him, the Spirit of wisdom and understanding, the
Spirit of counsel and might, the Spirit of knowledge,
and of the fear of the LORD; 3 And shall make him
of † quick understanding in the fear of the LORD: and
he shall not judge after the sight of his eyes, neither re-
prove after the hearing of his ears: 4 But [d] with
righteousness shall he judge the poor, and reprove with
equity, for the meek of the earth: and he shall smite
the earth with the rod of his mouth, and with the breath
of his lips shall he slay the wicked. 5 And righteous-
ness shall be the girdle of his loins, and faithfulness the
girdle of his reins. 6 [f] The wolf also shall dwell with
the lamb, and the leopard shall lie down with the kid;
and the calf and the young lion, and the fatling toge-
ther; and a little child shall lead them. 7 And the
cow and the bear shall feed; their young ones shall lie
down together: and the lion shall eat straw like the ox.
8 And the sucking child shall play on the hole of the
asp, and the weaned child shall put his hand on the
cockatrice-den. 9 [g] They shall not hurt nor destroy
in all my holy mountain: for [h] the earth shall be full
of the knowledge of the LORD, as the waters cover the
sea.

v. 1—9. As the coming of the glorious Messiah was the great hope of God's people of old, in every time of trouble, the prophet directs them to look above their temporal deliverance from the power of Sennacherib, to the eternal salvation their great Redeemer would accomplish for them.

1. His descent is spoken of. *As a rod out of the stem of Jesse*, it being promised to David, that from him Christ should spring, *and a branch shall grow out of his roots*, signifying the meanness of his appearance in the flesh, as a tender branch compared with the tall cedars of this world's princes; and intimating the low estate to which the family of Jesse would be reduced, when all the former royalty it possessed would be gone, as the tree cut down, whose stump only remains in the earth. And such was the case with the family of Joseph and Mary, when Jesus was born.

2. His qualifications for the work appointed him are mentioned. *The Spirit of the Lord shall rest upon him*, even the fulness of the Godhead bodily; and with this text he opened his ministry, *Luke* iv. 18. *the Spirit of wisdom and understanding*, the hid treasures of which are all resident in Jesus; *the Spirit of counsel and knowledge*, how to execute the plan of redemption, to preach the gospel, instruct his people, and order the affairs of his spiritual kingdom, to God's glory, and the salvation of his chosen; *the Spirit of might*, to conquer all his foes, and accompany his word of truth with effectual demonstration and power unto the consciences of men, *and of the fear of the Lord*, being the perfect pattern of all godliness, and setting us an example that we should follow his steps: *and shall make him of quick understanding in the fear of the Lord*, or of acute smell, intimating the thorough discernment he shall possess of the hearts of men. See *John* ii. 17. *Note*, (1.) When we have such a Redeemer, of wisdom and might to counsel and support us, how firm and unshaken ought our confidence in him to be. (2.) A quick understanding in the fear of God, is the gift of God; the brightest genius without his grace, is in spiritual things dark and ignorant.

3. His throne shall be established in righteousness. As he knows men's hearts, he can judge of their characters, not by their outward appearance, but their inward tempers and principles, detecting the hypocrite under all the disguise of outward formality and religious profession, *Matt.* xxiii. 28. The poor and humbled sinner that flies to him for pardon and grace, he will justify by his righteousness, and rescue the meek from their oppressors, whether Satan or wicked men, whom he will rebuke in equity; and smite the earth with the rod of his mouth, in warnings against those who place their affection upon it, and with the breath of his lips slay the wicked, by present judgment, or more terrible and eternal vengeance, *v.* 4. 2 *Thess.* xi. 8. In all which dispensations of mercy and judgment, the righteousness of his government shall appear as a glorious ornament, and his faithfulness in accomplishing the promise made to his people, and completing the ruin denounced on his enemies, shall be manifested to his everlasting praise, *v.* 5.

4. His

Before Christ 713

4 His kingdom ſhall enjoy the moſt happy union and concord ſuch a change will paſs upon the ſpirits of men, by the grace of Jeſus, that the moſt perſecuting, fierce, and untractable, ſhall become meek, lowly, and gentle as the lamb, all animoſities ſubſide, and no more venom remain in the human boſom The knowledge of the Lord, which ſhall be diffuſed through the earth, ſhall produce this marvellous renovation of our fallen nature, and all united in love and peace, under the divine Redeemer, become one fold under one ſhepherd The fulfilment of which appears now wherever the power of the goſpel is known and felt, as in Saul, and innumerable others, whoſe hearts the grace of a Redeemer hath aſtoniſhingly changed and we hope to ſee a day when not partially, but univerſally, this wonder-working Jeſus ſhall make his power to appear, and all ſhall know him, love him, and ſerve him, from the leaſt unto the greateſt

l Rom xv 12 Rev v 5
k Rom xv 10
† Heb Glory
l Zech x. 10
m Chap. xlix 2
n John vii 35 James i 1
‡ Heb Wings
o Jer iii 18 Ezek xxxvii 16, 22 Hoſ i 11
§ Heb Their obedience
p Zech x. 11
q Chap. xix 16 Zech. x 9
r Chap xix 23
s Ex xiv 29 Chap li 10

10 ¶ And in that day l there ſhall be a root of Jeſſe,
which ſhall ſtand for an enſign of the people k to it ſhall
the Gentiles ſeek, and his reſt ſhall be † glorious 11.
And it ſhall come to paſs in that day, *that* the LORD
ſhall ſet his hand again the ſecond time, l to recover the
remnant of his people which ſhall be left, from Aſſyria,
and from Egypt, and from Pathros, and from Cuſh, and
from Elam, and from Shinar, and from Hamath, and
from the iſlands of the ſea 12 And m he ſhall ſet up an
enſign for the nations, and ſhall aſſemble the out-caſts
of Iſrael, and gather together n the diſperſed of Judah,
from the four ‡ corners of the earth 13 o The envy al-
ſo of Ephraim ſhall depart, and the adverſaries of Judah
ſhall be cut off Ephraim ſhall not envy Judah, and Ju-
dah ſhall not vex Ephraim 14 But they ſhall fly upon
the ſhoulders of the Philiſtines towards the weſt, they
ſhall ſpoil them of the eaſt together they ſhall lay their
hand upon Edom and Moab, and the children of Am-
mon § ſhall obey them 15 And p the LORD ſhall ut-
terly deſtroy the tongue of the Egyptian ſea, and with his
mighty wind q ſhall he ſhake his hand over the river, and
ſhall ſmite it in the ſeven ſtreams, and make *men* go over
dry-ſhod. 16 And r there ſhall be an highway for the
remnant of his people, which ſhall be left from Aſſyria,
s like as it was to Iſrael in the day that he came up out
of the land of Egypt

v 10—16 We have here a farther prophecy of the glory and enlargement of the Meſſiah's kingdom, which, whatever regard it may have to the times of Hezekiah, or their recovery from Babylon, which was but a partial deliverance, certainly looks forward to the days of the goſpel, when Jews and Gentiles were incorporated in one church, and will have, we truſt, its final accompliſhment when the fulneſs of the Gentiles ſhall be come in, and all Iſrael ſhall be ſaved

1 The great author of the ſalvation is *the root of Jeſſe*, the Lord Jeſus, before called the rod and branch, for he is both *the root and offspring of David*, Rev v 5 He *ſhall ſtand for an enſign of the people*, lifted up in the preaching of the goſpel among all nations, who ſhall be invited to liſt under his banners, and *to it ſhall the Gentiles ſeek* for pardon and peace through his blood and righteouſneſs, deſiring to become willing ſubjects of his government, and live in ſafety under his care and protection, *and his reſt ſhall be glorious*, either Chriſt's, when, having in his ſufferings and death, finiſhed the work of his people's ſalvation, he entered into his reſt above in glory everlaſting or it refers to his redeemed, who in him find a preſent happy reſt to their ſouls from guilt and fear, and expect an eternal reſt with him hereafter in his kingdom

2 The completion of the ſalvation is deſcribed, *v* 11 Notwithſtanding every oppoſition, God is ſaid to do it *the ſecond time*, alluding to the firſt deliverance of the people from Egypt, when not a hoof was left behind The redeemed are called *a remnant*, or thoſe that remain, ſome in all former ages having been called already into the church, but now, more univerſally than ever, the goſpel ſhall go forth into all lands, to gather from the four corners of the earth, and moſt diſtant iſles of the ſea, the diſperſed Jews, as well as the Gentiles, among whom they dwell, *v* 11, 12 All enmity between Jew and Gentile, as ſubſiſted of old between Judah and Ephraim, ſhall be at an end, *v* 13 uniting in the ſervice of their Redeemer, the inveterate enemies of Chriſt and his people, whether Papal or Pagan, &c as the Philiſtines, Moabites, Ammonites were to the Jews, ſhall be vanquiſhed by the powerful word of the goſpel, and be brought to the obedience of the faith, *v* 14 And Antichriſt and his followers, compared to Egypt, for their enmity againſt the church, *Rev* xi 8 who will riſe up to make war with the ſaints, ſhall be utterly deſtroyed, *Rev* xvi 16—19 as when God, by the rod of Moſes, opened a way for his redeemed to paſs over, but overwhelmed their enemies in the Red ſea, and the Ottoman empire, ſignified by the river Euphrates, *Rev* xvi 12 *ſhall be ſmitten in the ſeven ſtreams*, perfectly deſtroyed, *ſeven* being a number denoting perfection and thus every enemy being removed, *the way of the kings of the eaſt*, Rev xvi 12 *ſhall be prepared*, and converts from every ſide be added to the church daily, of ſuch as ſhall be ſaved *Note*, Whenever God's appointed time is come, whether to convert a ſoul, or exalt the univerſal dominion of his ſon, all difficulties will be removed, the mountain becomes a plain, the river dry

CHAP XII

As the glorious ſalvation of the former chapter ſecured the church's ſafety, it here engages her praiſes 1 For the bleſſed change of her ſtate, ver 1 2 For the ſtrength engaged to ſupport her, ver 2 3 For the plentiful joy in the goſpel, ver 3 4 A mutual exhortation is given to join in exalting the great Redeemer, ver. 4—6

a Chap xi 11, 16.
b Pſ lxxxv 3 Chap x 25
c Chap xl 1 & li 3, 12
d Ex xv 2 Pſ cxviii 14
e John iv 10, 14 & vii 37, 38

1 AND a in that day thou ſhalt ſay, O LORD, I
will praiſe thee though thou waſt angry with
me, b thine anger *is* turned away, and c thou comforteſt
me 2 Behold God *is* my ſalvation. I will truſt, and
not be afraid, for the LORD JEHOVAH *is* d my
ſtrength and *my* ſong, he alſo is become my ſalvation 3
Therefore with joy ſhall ye draw e water out of the wells
of ſalvation

v 1—3 As Iſrael eſcaped from the Red ſea, when they beheld the floating corpſes of the Egyptians, ſang praiſe for their deliverance, with greater joy ſhall the redeemed of the Lord in the day of their ſalvation, adore the power and grace of their exalted Lord

1 For the bleſſed change which is paſſed *Though thou waſt angry with me, thine anger is turned away, and thou comforteſt me*, not that we muſt impute to God our infirmities, as either that he is capable of change of purpoſe, or that anger, ſuch as dwells in our boſom, knows a place in his we ſpeak after the manner of men, God's anger is his righteous purpoſe to puniſh ſin, and if he changes his diſpenſations, it is according to the eternal counſels of his will We have by our ſins deſerved puniſhment, but when God turns us to himſelf, we feel a bleſſed alteration, and, no longer terrified as before, rejoice in the comfort of his ſalvation *Note*, (1) Every faithful ſoul will own how often and how juſtly he hath by his ſins provoked God's wrath and indignation againſt him (2) The deeper views we have of our own guilt, the more enlarged will our hearts be with love, and our lips with praiſe, when we experience a ſenſe of his returning favour (3) The pardon and reconciliation of the ſinner's ſoul to God, is only through the blood and righteouſneſs of the Redeemer Jeſus

2 They will triumph in the ſtrength engaged for them, and in the ſecurity of their hopes *Behold*, with wonder and love I record it, *God is my ſalvation*, Jeſus hath given himſelf for me, able to ſave to the uttermoſt, and on him alone I depend, renouncing every other hope *I will truſt* with quietneſs and confidence, *and not be afraid*, though ſin, Satan, and conſcience accuſe, or corruption, temptation, affliction, war againſt me, *for the Lord Jehovah is my ſtrength*, how then ſhould I fail, when his everlaſting arms are under me? *and my ſong*, which, whilſt I pay as the grateful tribute for his mercies, increaſes my own conſolations, *he alſo is become my ſalvation*, I am complete in him, and can wiſh for nothing more, he is all my ſalvation, and all my deſire *Note*, (1) They who have God for their ſtrength, need not dread who are their foes (2) Confidence in Chriſt's power and love, will keep the mind eaſy amidſt every ſtorm (3) If God be our ſalvation, he deſerves to be our ſong, yea every redeemed ſoul will think eternity too ſhort to ſpeak his praiſe

3 From what God hath done, we are encouraged to expect what he will continue to do, *therefore with joy ſhall ye draw water from the wells of ſalvation*, or *the Saviour* in Chriſt are the living waters, all fulneſs dwells in him for his people's uſe, they have free acceſs to him at all times, and it is both their duty and delight, by faith to draw continual ſupplies of grace from him, in the exerciſe of prayer, meditation, the word, and ſacraments Surely bleſſed are the people who are in ſuch a caſe!

f 1 Chron xvi 8 Pſ cv 1
‖ Or proclaim
g Pſ cxlv 4—6
h Phil ii 9.
i Zeph iii 14
‡ Heb Inhabitreſs
k Pſ xlvi 5

4 And in that day ſhall ye ſay, f Praiſe the LORD, ‖
call upon his name, g declare his doings among the people,
make mention that h his name is exalted 5 Sing
unto the LORD, for he hath done excellent things this
is known in all the earth 6 i Cry out and ſhout, thou ‡
inhabitant of Zion for k great *is* the holy One of Iſrael
in the midſt of thee.

Before Christ 712

v 4—6 They who have learnt God's praise, and know the blessedness of the employment, will be sollicitous to stir up others to join in the grateful service. *In that day* of the soul's conversion, and specially in the great day when the Redeemer's glory shall appear in his universal dominion, *shall ye say, Praise the Lord, call upon his name*, in every act of religious worship due to the exalted Jesus, *declare his doings among the people*, seek to diffuse the knowledge of his grace, the fulness of his atonement, the perfection of his righteousness, the power of his Spirit, the glory of the purchased possession, *make mention that his name is exalted* above all principalities and powers, and every name that is named, not only in this world, but in that which is to come, and let him be thus exalted in every heart, by every tongue. *Sing unto the Lord* loud songs of praise, making melody in the heart to him, *for he hath done excellent things*, wrought out for us an everlasting righteousness, offered himself a perfect sacrifice in our stead, vanquished sin, death, and hell for us, led our captivity captive, opened heaven's gates, prepared our thrones in glory everlasting. *This is known in all the earth*, by the gospel, before preached among all nations. *Cry out and shout*, with the voice of triumphant exultation, *thou inhabitant of Zion*, the church of the redeemed, *for great is the holy One of Israel in the midst of thee*, there he delights to take up his abode, and there must reign till every foe is subdued, every faithful soul brought home. The expected end shall come, and in his eternal kingdom he will make the fullest displays of his excellent greatness to his people, and be the object of their everlasting praise. Amen, and Amen!

CHAP. XIII.

God is king in all the earth, and by him the fate of empires is determined. The nations here spoken of were all conversant with the Jews, and are treated according to their behaviour towards his people, who are his peculiar care, and therefore he will espouse. Babylon comes first into the account, and affords a type of the ruin of Babylon mystical in the book of Revelations. *In this chapter we have, 1. A general rendezvous of the forces that were to be employed against Babylon*, ver. 1—5. *2. The dreadful work that those forces should make in it*, ver. 6—18. *3. The utter ruin of Babylon which this should end in*, ver. 19—22.

712 a Chap. xxi. 1. & xlvii. 1. Jer. l. & li.
1 [a]THE burden of Babylon, which Isaiah the son
of Amoz did see. 2 [b]Lift ye up a banner
b Chap. xviii. 3. Jer. l. 2.
upon the high mountain, exalt the voice unto them,
shake the hand, that they may go into the gates of the
nobles. 3 I have commanded my sanctified ones, I
have also called my mighty ones for mine anger, *even*
c Ps. cxlix. 2. † Heb. In praise
them [c]that rejoice † in my highness. 4 The noise of
a multitude in the mountains, like as of a great people;
d Jo. iii. 27, 28.
a tumultuous noise of the kingdoms of nations gathered
together: the LORD of hosts mustereth the host of the
e Jer. l. 26.
battle. 5 [e]They come from a far country, from the
end of heaven, *even* the LORD, and the weapons of his
indignation, to destroy the whole land.

v 1—5 A new vision here is given the prophet concerning the fate of the neighbouring kingdoms; and as the captivity of the Jews in Babylon approached, before the time comes they have this prophecy to comfort them, that the rod of their oppressor should be broken. It is called *the burden of Babylon*, a prophecy concerning it, denouncing her heavy doom, crushed in pieces under the combined forces of Medes and Persians, and this Isaiah saw in prophecy clearly revealed to him.

1. God gave the command, his standard is unfurled, the forces haste to join their colours, and he mustereth them armed for the battle. The kings of Media and Persia, with their officers, were employed to summon the soldiers, beckon them to enlist, and lead them to the gates of the nobles, the proud walls of Babel; but it was God's secret impulse which stirred up their spirit, strengthened them for the battle, and crowned their arms with success. *Note*, Whatever is done among the inhabitants of the earth, it is the Lord's doing, and his hand is to be acknowledged.

2. The persons employed are his *sanctified ones*, the Medes and Persians; not that they were really gracious souls, but raised up to serve his purpose, and qualified by him for their work. *His mighty ones*, Cyrus and Darius, who were instruments in his hand, and cloathed with strength to execute his decree; *even them that rejoice in my highness*, or *that rejoice my highness*, they rejoiced in their success, whereby God was glorified, and a vast army followed them from different nations, (*See Jer.* li. 27, 28.) from the end of the earth, the furthest part of their dominion, and very distant from Babylon; but, when sent on God's errand, no distance or danger could deter them.

3. The design of them is, as *weapons of the Lord's indignation*, to destroy the whole land of Chaldea, and Babylon the metropolis. *Note*, When God gives the word, against a sinful nation

Vol. II.

(i)

tion, to pluck up and to destroy, his armies are quickly ready, and resistance is vain.

6 ¶ Howl ye; for [f]the day of the LORD *is* at f Jer. l. 27.
hand; [g]it shall come as a destruction from the Almighty. g Job xxxi. 23. Joel i. 15.
7 Therefore [h]shall all hands † be faint, and every man's h Jer. l. 43. † Heb. fall down.
heart shall melt: 8 And they shall be afraid: [i]pangs and i Is. xlviii. 6.
sorrows shall take hold of them; they shall be in pain as a
woman that travaileth: they shall be amazed one at another;
their faces *shall be* ‡ *as* flames. 9 Behold, the day ‡ Heb. faces of the flames. Lam. iv. 8.
of the LORD cometh, cruel both with wrath and
fierce anger, to lay the land desolate: and he shall destroy
the sinners thereof out of it. 10 For the stars of
heaven, and the constellations thereof shall not give their
light: [k]the sun shall be darkned in his going forth, and k Chap. xxiv. 21. Ezek. xxxii. 7. Joel ii. 31. & iii. 15. Mat. xxiv. 29. Mar. xiii. 24. Luke xxi. 25.
the moon shall not cause her light to shine. 11 And I
will punish the world for *their* evil, and the wicked for
their iniquity; and I will cause the arrogancy of the
proud to cease, and will lay low the haughtiness of the
terrible. 12 I will make a man more precious than fine
gold; even a man than the golden wedge of Ophir. 13
[m]Therefore I will shake the heavens, and the earth shall l [illegible]
remove out of her place, in the wrath of the LORD m Hag. ii. 6.
of hosts, and in the day of his fierce anger. 14 And
it shall be as the chased roe, and as a sheep that no
man taketh up: [n]they shall every man turn to his own n Jer. l. 16. & li. 9.
people, and flee every one into his own land. 15 Every
one *that is* found shall be thrust through; and [o]every o Rev. xviii. 3.
one *that is* joined *unto them*, shall fall by the sword. 16
Their children also shall be [p]dashed to pieces before their p Ps. cxxxvii. 9. Nah. iii. 10.
eyes; their houses shall be spoiled, and their wives ravished.
17 Behold, [q]I will stir up the Medes against q Chap. xxi. 2. Jer. li. 11, 28. Dan. v. 28.
them, which shall not regard silver; and *as for* gold,
they shall not delight in it. 18 *Their* bows also shall
dash the young men to pieces; and they shall have no
pity on the fruit of the womb; their eye shall not spare
children.

v 6—18 The destruction of Babylon being commanded, we have here an awful account of its accomplishment.

1. It is the day of the Lord's wrath, and therefore must be terrible; and destruction from the Almighty, and therefore irresistible, *v.* 1. Though God for just correction suffered them to bring his people into bondage, he will avenge their ill usage at the hands of their enemies.

2. Dismay and terror would overtake the hosts of Babylon. Howling for distress, and trembling, their courage should fail them, *v.* 7. pangs like those of a travailing woman should seize them, and each increase the panic by communicating their fears; their faces dark, as if burnt to a coal, or red as flame, *v.* 8. the terrible wrath and fierce anger of the Lord upon them, and certain ruin, the wages of sin, approaching, *v.* 9. the very heavens black and lowring, and the bright luminaries hid; or this is figuratively expressed to describe the ruin of their kings and princes, and the dreadful gloom of horror which surrounded them, whilst no openings appeared for their escape, *v.* 11. and all irreparable by continual revolt, of which this is the just punishment. God will lay low the arrogance of Nebuchadnezzar and Belshazzar, and bring their pride in to the dust, *v.* 11. their country and capital so ruined, that a man should scarce be left, or so merciless their conquerors, that no ransom would engage them to spare their captives, *v.* 12. The thunder above, and the quaking earth beneath, should help forward their destruction; or by these may be intimated the utter dissolution of the government, *v.* 13. Like a chased roe their warriors should flee, and like a sheep straying from the flock defenceless become a prey to the wolf, so should they be devoured. Their auxiliary forces shall desert their sinking cause, and, glad with life to escape to their own country, leave the devoted city to ruin, *v.* 14. *Note*, (1.) That is complete misery upon earth, where the terrors of a guilty conscience are added to the heavy judgments of affliction. (2.) Sin, sin is the cause of all human wretchedness. (3.) They who have [illegible] here, shall in the day of God be covered with shame, and the boldest countenance turn pale at God's frown. (4.) When God devotes a nation to ruin, all her allies will desert her, and fly as from a falling house.

3. The executioners of God's vengeance approach, the Medes, more thirsty for blood than for spoil, *v.* 17. shall even like lions unmercifully shed the blood of all that were found in arms, whether Babylonian or auxiliaries, *v.* 15. The laws of humanity find no place in a city taken by storm; and God, in just retribution for the cruelties offered to his people, (*Psalm* cxxxvii. 8, 9. *Lam.* v. 11.) will suffer their children to be dashed in pieces, and their wives ravished before their eyes, *v.* 16. Not content with plunder, they would pierce their young men with arrows, and pluck the infant [illegible]

Before Christ 712.

the womb ript up, *v* 18 *Note*, (1) When the native cruelty of the heart is unrestrained, no beast of the forest is more savage than man (2) If we shudder at the infinite miseries, let us remember how bitter and evil a thing sin is, and read in their sufferings a pregnant evidence of original guilt (3) They who are companions with the wicked will share in their plagues

r Chap xiv 4. s Gen xix 24. Jer l 40. t Jer l 39. & li 43. u Chap xxxiv 11—15 Rev xviii 2. † Heb Daughters of the owl. ‡ Or, palaces

19 ¶ And ʳ Babylon the glory of kingdoms, the beauty of the Chaldees excellency, shall be ˢ as when God overthrew Sodom and Gomorrah 20 ᵗ It shall never be inhabited, neither shall it be dwelt in from generation to generation neither shall the Arabian pitch tent there, neither shall the shepherds make their fold there 21 ᵘ But wild beasts of the desert shall lie there, and their houses shall be full of doleful creatures, and † owls shall dwell there, and satyrs shall dance there 22 And the wild beasts of the islands shall cry in their ‡ desolate houses, and dragons in *their* pleasant palaces and her time *is* near to come, and her days shall not be prolonged

v 19—22 The inimitably lively and striking images of the utter desolation of Babylon here displayed, cannot be read without admiration

1 Her former towering height of glory serves to strengthen the contrast of misery into which Babylon, the beauty of Chaldea, must fall Utter destruction, like that of Sodom and Gomorrah, approached, instead of crouded streets, not an inhabitant should remain among the dreary ruins for ever instead of a fertile soil, such barrenness should succeed, that not even an Arabs tent, nor a shepherd's fold, should be seen, *v* 20. Those late proud palaces, where riot, mirth, and pleasure reigned, abandoned, ruinous, are become the dens of ravening beasts, and owls, dragons, satyrs, and every doleful creature, occupy the desolate mansions, *v* 21, 22 And this prophecy the relations of travellers verify, who report, that the venomous creatures which lodge there, made it highly dangerous even to approach the ruins

2 The nearness of this heavy judgment is intimated, *v* 22 for the comfort of God's Israel when in their captivity It was more than two hundred years from the time of the prophecy, but that with God is but a moment, it would be quickly at hand, *for her days shall not be prolonged*, but a final period put to her prosperity and power, yea, to her very being And thus shall mystical Babylon also perish, when the day of her recompence, appointed in the eternal counsels, shall arrive, *Rev* xviii 2, 4, 21

CHAP XIV

For Zion's comfort, and her enemies confusion, we have here, 1 Israel's deliverance from captivity, ver 1—3 2 Babylon and her king fallen and insulted over, ver 4—20 3 The whole people destroyed, ver 21—23 4 It is fixed by divine decree, ver 24—27 5 Philistia's fate and Judah's triumphs are recorded, ver 28—32

a Ps cii 13. b Zech i 17 & ii 12. c Chap xiv 1 & lxvi. d Chap lx 5 Zech ii 11. e Chap lx 14 & lxi 5. f Chap lx 14.

1 FOR ᵃ the LORD will have mercy on Jacob, ᵇ and will yet choose Israel, and set them in their own land and ᶜ the strangers shall be joined with them, and they shall cleave to the house of Jacob 2 And the people shall take them, ᵈ and bring them to their place and the house of Israel shall possess them in the land of the LORD, ᵉ for servants and handmaids and they shall take them captives, whose captives they were, and ᶠ they shall rule over their oppressors 3 And it shall come to pass in the day that the LORD shall give thee rest from thy sorrow, and from thy fear, and from the hard bondage wherein thou wast made to serve,

v 1—3, It was for Zion's sake that God visited her oppressors, both to avenge her quarrel, and by their ruin to procure the liberty of his people, which Cyrus, on his conquest of Babylon, sent back to their own land

1 God encourages his people with promises of mercy in general, that they might not think, because of their sufferings they were utterly rejected No, it was his eternal purpose to chuse Israel, and he will now make it manifest in their restoration *Note*, (1) All our salvation must be ascribed to the rich and sovereign mercy of God (2) It is God's election of grace, not any free will and power in man, which can bring the soul to the inheritance among the saints (3) Whatever discouragements they may meet with, or however dark their path may be, God will not cast away his people

2 He engages in particular, to bring them once more into their own land, to increase their number by faithful proselytes, *v* 1 to open the hearts of Cyrus and his subjects to help them on their journey, *See Ezra* i 4 to give them servants and handmaids out of the land of their captivity, and to make them their captives, whose captives they were, and these were either the proselytes from Babylon, who chose rather to serve in the meanest offices of the Lord's land, where his worship was established, than stay behind or such as the Medes might have sold for slaves to the Israelites, when Babylon was taken, *v* 2 Thus God having restored them with honour, and replenished them, they would no longer be under servitude, distressed and sorrowful, but enjoy a happy rest in Canaan's fertile land, *v* 3 And this seems to look forward to the times of the gospel, when, through the preaching of Jesus and his apostles, multitudes of Jews and Gentiles should be converted and brought home to the church, *the land of the Lord*, and lead their captivity captive, no more the servants of corruption, nor distressed with terrifying and guilty fears, but entering into pardon, peace, and rest, through Jesus, here below, as an earnest of that eternal rest which remaineth for them above

g Chap xiii 19 Hab ii 6. † Heb Taunting speech. ‡ Or the exactress of gold. h Ps cxxv 3. i Chap ix 4. k Jer l 34. l Ezek xxxi 16. m Ezek xxxii 21. § Or, the grave. || Heb. Leaders. n Ps lxxxix 6 7. o Rev xviii 22. p Job xxi 26. † Or day-star. q 2 Thes ii 4. r Dan viii 10, 11 & xi 36. s Ps xlviii 2. t Chap xlvii 8. u Rev xiv 20. x Jer l 23. y Jer l 33.

4 ¶ That thou ᵍ shalt take up this † proverb against the king of Babylon, and say, How hath the oppressor ceased! the ‡ golden city ceased! 5 ʰ The LORD hath broken the staff of the wicked, *and* the sceptre of the rulers 6 He who smote the people in wrath with a continual stroke, he that ruled the nations in anger, is persecuted, *and* none hindreth 7 The whole earth ⁱ is at rest *and* is quiet ᵏ they break forth into singing 8 ˡ Yea, the fir-trees rejoice at thee, *and* the cedars of Lebanon, *saying*, Since thou art laid down, no feller is come up against us 9 ᵐ § Hell from beneath is moved for thee, to meet *thee* at thy coming it stirreth up the dead for thee, *even* all || the chief ones of the earth, it hath raised up from their thrones all the kings of the nations 10 All they shall speak and say unto thee, Art thou also become weak as we? ⁿ art thou become like unto us? 11. Thy pomp is brought down to the grave, ᵒ *and* the noise of thy viols the worm is spread under thee, ᵖ and the worms cover thee 12 How art thou fallen from heaven, O † Lucifer, son of the morning! *how* art thou cut down to the ground, which didst weaken the nations! 13 For thou hast said in thine heart, ᵠ I will ascend into heaven, ʳ I will exalt my throne above the stars of God I will sit also upon the mount of the congregation, ˢ in the sides of the north 14 I will ascend above the heights of the clouds, ᵗ I will be like the most High 15 Yet ᵘ thou shalt be brought down to hell, to the sides of the pit 16 They that see thee, shall narrowly look upon thee, *and* consider thee, *saying*, ˣ *Is* this the man that made the earth to tremble, that did shake kingdoms? 17 *That* made the world as a wilderness, and destroyed the cities thereof, ʸ *that* opened not the house of his prisoners? 18 All the kings of the nations, *even* all of them lie in glory, every one in his own house 19 But thou art cast out of thy grave, like an abominable branch *and as* the raiment of *those that are* slain, thrust through with a sword, that go down to the stones of the pit, as a carcase trodden under feet 20 Thou shalt not be joined with them in burial, because thou hast destroyed thy land, *and* slain thy people ᶻ the seed of evil doers shall ‖ never be renowned 21. Prepare slaughter for his children ᵃ for the iniquity of their fathers, that they do not rise, nor possess the land, nor fill the face of the world with cities 22 For I will rise up against them, saith the LORD of hosts, and cut off from Babylon ᵇ the name, and remnant, ᶜ and son, and nephew, saith the LORD 23 ᵈ I will also make it a possession for the bittern, and pools of water and I will sweep it with the besom of destruction, saith the LORD of hosts

z Job xviii 19 Ps xxi 10 & xxxvii 28 & cix 13. a Exod xx 5 Mat xxiii 35. b Deut xxv 19. c Job xviii 19. d Chap xxxiv 11 Zeph ii 14.

v 4—23 The triumphs of God's people, and the vast baseness to which their proud conqueror shall be reduced, are here most elegantly displayed The description is called a proverb, a taunting speech, full of freedom and zeal

1 With admiration and exultation the people of God behold the fall of Babylon, the golden city, full of splendor, and her oppressive king, *v* 4 For his wickedness, cruelty, and tyranny, God hath broken his sceptre, and hurled him from his throne, overtaken by just judgments, and none either able or willing to deliver him, *v* 5, 6 *Note*, (1) Riches profit not in the day of wrath (2) When [illegible] turn tyrant, the [illegible]

of

Before Christ 71-

of kings justly breaks the staff of their government, and by their fall makes them know he is greater. (3.) When God in wrath seizes the sinner, none can stay his vengeance, or deliver out of his hand.

2. The fall of this oppressive power would be the peace and joy of the nations of the earth. Their troubles removed, quietness would be restored, and with gladness the people would exult at their deliverance, v. 7. The very firs and cedars are represented as rejoicing, since now no feller would hew them down, to build gorgeous palaces for these proud monarchs. Or rather, the kings and princes of the earth, hereby represented, are happy to be delivered from the bondage and fears under which they groaned during the tyrannic sway of Babylon's monarchs. *Note*, (1.) The fall of tyrants is the joy of the oppressed people. (2.) Peace and quietness in a nation is matter of great thankfulness.

3. Whilst earth rejoices in being rid of such a burden, those who are in hell, or the state of the dead, are represented as welcoming the king of Babylon with sarcastic taunts to their dark abode. They are all in motion, hasting to congratulate him on his arrival. *It stirreth up the dead*, Rephaim, the giants, the chief ones of the earth: these, informed of his approach, are represented as going to meet him; and the kings of the nations, as rising from their thrones, in derision to pay him that homage that in his life time they had been obliged to render, v. 9. These all with affected wonder shall say, *Art thou become also weak as we?* a boasted god, but found, like us, a dying worm, v. 10. How short-lived is thy glory! how despicable thy end! Thy pomp is faded in the dust, thy music lost in groans, and that gorgeous body, which glittered on a throne, clothed in purple and fine linen, and faring sumptuously every day, is now loathsome in corruption, and meat for worms, v. 11. How wondrous the change! *How art thou fallen from heaven, O Lucifer, son of the morning!* proud as the prince of darkness, like him once shining as the morning star, and in glory exalted high as heaven, but now cut down even to the ground, low as the nations thou hast wasted, v. 12. How vain thy former pride and boast! nothing once seemed too high for thy aspiring ambition: thou hast said, I will establish a monarchy as wide as the heavens, bring suppliant kings to the footstool of my throne, and sit as conqueror on Zion's holy mount, v. 13. Yea, not content with earthly dignity, affecting divine honours, as if thou couldst ascend above the clouds, and rival the Most High, v. 14. But how different thy catastrophe! brought down to hell, and numbered among the dead. *Note*, (1.) Pride is the bosom-sin of fallen man: since first our parents, affecting God-like wisdom, were undone, we have inherited their guilty ambition. (2.) It seems intimated here, that there is an intercourse and knowledge among departed spirits in the unseen world. (3.) They who go down to the pit in their iniquities, will be thrust down into hell as their eternal punishment.

4. The living can scarce believe their own eyes, when they behold him fallen from his high estate, and weltering in his blood. So different his ghastly countenance, deformed with wounds, and pale in death, from what he once appeared, and therefore insulting over him they shall say, *Is this the man*, the mighty conqueror that shook the thrones, and humbled the monarchs of the earth, v. 16. that by his ravages depopulated the nations, destroyed their cities, and made the world a wilderness, and whose captives groaned under a heavy yoke, without hope of being ever loosed? v. 17. Yes, this is he, once higher than the highest, now more despicable than ever he was dignified. Whilst other kings in pomp are carried to the tomb, the clods of the valley made sweet unto them, and stately monuments erected over them to perpetuate their memory, destitute even of a grave, thy corpse is cast out as an abominable branch, and, like the raiment of those who are slain with the sword, clotted with blood, which none cared to touch as ceremonially unclean, trodden under foot as mire by men and horses in the battle, and afterwards cast into the pit, and covered with a heap of stones, v. 19. Such shall be thy vile end, denied a place among the tombs of thy ancestors, because of thy wanton cruelty, murders, and arbitrary oppression; for this is God's righteous decree, *that the seed of evil doers shall never be renowned*, or *not for ever*, their momentary blaze of glory being quickly extinguished, and their honour laid in the dust. *Note*, (1.) In the blaze of conquest we admire the hero, and are apt to overlook the murderer, the robber, and the scourge of mankind. (2.) The pomp of a gorgeous sepulchre is a poor distinction; yet, for the punishment of iniquity to be denied a grave, is a brand of real infamy. (3.) Strange changes are soon brought about when God will work; and it is a wretched greatness to be proud of, which stands in so slippery a place, and may so quickly be dashed in pieces.

5. The utter ruin of the royal family, and Babylon the seat of their majesty, is declared. The Mede and Persian are commanded to prepare slaughter for them, to visit on them the sins of their fathers, and not spare the most distant branch, but utterly extirpate the name of the Babylonish monarch, that they might no more succeed to the throne of their ancestors, or fill the world with cities, to perpetuate their fame, or extend their grandeur; and their metropolis, utterly ruined, should become a marsh, and the abode of bitterns, swept with the besom of destruction, and scarce a stone left upon another; all which was literally accomplished.

Before Christ 71-

The whole of this awful and terrible destruction also looks forward to the ruin of Babylon mystical, whose pride, impiety, tyranny, and cruelty, will meet with as condign punishment, and be matter of the like joy to the saints of God, as fully appears from the book of *Revelations*. Compare v. 7, 8. with *Rev.* xv. 2, 3. xix. 2, 3, 20. v. 9, 10. with 2 *Thess.* ii. 4, 8. *Rev.* xiii. 4. xx. 10. v. 11. with *Rev.* xviii. 22. v. 12. with *Rev.* xi. 7. xiii. 7, 15. xvii. 21. v. 13, 14. with *Rev.* xviii. 7, 8. 2 *Thess.* ii. 4. v. 19. with *Rev.* xix. 20. v. 20. with *Rev.* xiii. 10, 13. xix. 2. v. 21. with *Rev.* ii. 23. v. 23. with *Rev.* xviii. 21.

24 ¶ The LORD of hosts hath sworn, saying,
Surely as I have thought, so shall it come to pass; and
as I have purposed, *so* shall it stand: 25 That I will
break the Assyrian in my land, and upon my mountains
tread him under foot: then shall his yoke depart from
off them, and his burden depart from off their shoulders.
26 This *is* the purpose *that is* purposed upon the
whole earth: and this *is* the hand that *is* stretched out
upon all the nations. 27 For the LORD of hosts hath
purposed, and who shall disannul *it?* and his hand *is*
stretched out, and who shall turn it back? 28 In the
year that king Ahaz died, was this burden. 29 ¶
Rejoice not thou whole Palestina, because the rod of
him that smote thee is broken: for out of the serpent's
root shall come forth a cockatrice, and his fruit *shall be*
a fiery flying serpent. 30 And the first-born of the
poor shall feed, and the needy shall lie down in safety:
and I will kill thy root with famine, and he shall slay
thy remnant. 31 Howl, O gate; cry, O city; thou
whole Palestina *art* dissolved: for there shall come from
the north a smoke, and † none *shall be* alone in his appointed
times. 32 What shall *one* then answer the
messengers of the nation? That the LORD hath
founded Zion, and the poor of his people shall ‡ trust
in it.

Chap. xxxvii. 36. Chap. ix. 4. & x. 27. 2 Chron. xx. 6. Job ix. 12. & xxiii. 13. Psal. xxxiii. 11. Prov. xix. 21. & xxi. 30. Chap. xlvi. 13. Dan. iv. 35. 2 Kings xvi. 20. 2 Chron. xxvi. 6. 2 Kings xviii. 8. † Or, He shall not be alone in his assemblies. Chap. xxxix. 1. Psal. lxxxvii. 1, 5. & cii. 16. Zeph. iii. 12. Zech. xi. 11. ‡ Or, betake themselves unto it.

v. 24—32. Whilst the more distant events of the utter destruction of Babylon, and the deliverance of God's people, are expected, an earnest of their fulfilment is given in two signal instances of a nearer date, the destruction of Sennacherib's army, and the subdual of the Philistines.

1. The Assyrians shall be broken, when invading God's land, and be trodden under foot on the mountains of Israel, who now should be delivered from the yoke of bondage, and, with the ruin of their oppressors, regain their freedom, v. 25. The work God undertakes himself to accomplish, according to his eternal purpose, ratified by his solemn oath, v. 24. His hand is stretched out upon the mighty army of Assyria, composed of all nations brought under his tyrannic sway. Or this is his purpose throughout the earth, to punish universally the persecutors of his people, v. 26. And who can defeat the counsels of infinite wisdom, or oppose the arm of omnipotence? v. 27. *Note*, (1.) They who are the enemies of God's people will smart for it. (2.) God's purposes are from eternity; he never changes; and therefore since his gifts and calling are without repentance, his people may trust him for their stability; from his hand none can pluck them. (3.) To be delivered from the burden and yoke of sin is a greater mercy, than to be redeemed from the heaviest chains, and most abject bodily servitude.

2. The victory over the Philistines is foretold, and the happy state of Israel under Hezekiah. This is a new prophecy revealed in the year the wicked Ahaz died, and his pious son succeeded him; and therefore here the fifteenth chapter would most properly begin.

[1.] The ruin of Palestine is foretold. *Rejoice not*, as they did at Uzziah's death, who had smitten them, 2 *Chron.* xxvi. 6, 7. and during the reign of Ahaz, when they ravaged Judea, 2 *Chron.* xxviii. 18. and trusted they should be greater gainers under the new king; but found to their cost, that Hezekiah, sprung from Uzziah, the serpent who had stung them, more fierce and fatal, a cockatrice, and fiery flying serpent, would rush upon them, and ravage their coasts, v. 29. Soon would their shouts of triumph give place to the howl of bitter lamentation, and the cry of the vanquished, their whole country wasted, their cities destroyed. From the north the lowering storm arises, the smoke thereof; *none shall be alone in his appointed place*, but each man ready in his post, and then them [illegible] his companion to rush upon them as their prey, v. 31. and whilst within the beleaguered city a part perished miserably by famine, the remainder fell by the sword of their conqueror Hezekiah,

Before Christ 714.

zekiah, (*see* 2 Kings xviii 8) and were utterly conſumed ſhortly after by the Aſſyrians, *Jer* xlvii 2 *Note*, (1) The joy of the ſinner is deceitful, he ſings on the brink of perdition (2) If God removes one faithful inſtrument from his people, he will raiſe them up another to carry on his work

[2] The happy ſtate of Iſrael is deſcribed At reſt from their enemies under Hezekiah's government, the pooreſt Iſraelite ſhould have plenty, and the weakeſt enjoy protection, *v* 30 Triumphant over their foes, when neighbouring nations ſhould ſend to congratulate their victory, they would aſcribe their greatneſs to the Lord, the founder and defender of his Zion, and truſting on his conſtant care over it, reſt in comfort and ſafety *Note*, (1) The character of a great king is not merely to be formidable to his foes, but a father to his people (2) They who have God for their founder, and are fixed on Jeſus the rock of ages, may well truſt, and not be afraid (3) When others, led by what they have ſeen, enquire of us how the happy change of our circumſtances was wrought, we ſhall delight with Judah to aſcribe the whole to the rich grace of our God, and own, *that to him we are indebted for every mercy*

CHAP XV

This chapter, and that which followeth it, are the burden of Moab a prophecy of the deſolation that was coming upon that country, which bordered upon the land of Iſrael, and had often been injurious and vexatious to it We have, 1 Great lamentation made by the Moabites, and by the prophet himſelf for them, ver 1—5 2 *The calamities which ſhould occaſion that lamentation,* ver 6—9

a Jer xlviii 1 Ezek xxv 8 Amos ii 1 · b 1 Theſ v 3 · c Num xxi 28 · † Or, cut off · d Chap. xvi 12 · e Lev xxi 5 Jer xlviii 37 · f Jer xlviii 38 · ‡ Or, coming down weeping · g Gen xxvii 46 Job iii 20 · h Chap xvi 11 Jer xlviii 31, 36 · i Jer xlviii 31

1 [a] THE burden of Moab, becauſe [b] in the night
[c] Ar of Moab is laid waſte, *and* † brought to
ſilence, becauſe in the night Kir of Moab is laid waſte,
and brought to ſilence 2 [d] He is gone up to Bajith,
and to Dibon, the high places, to weep Moab ſhall
howl over Nebo, and over Medeba, [e] on all their heads
ſhall be baldneſs, *and* every beard cut off 3 In their
ſtreets they ſhall gird themſelves with ſackcloth [f] on
the tops of their houſes, and in their ſtreets every one
ſhall howl, ‡ weeping abundantly 4 And Heſhbon
ſhall cry, and Elealeh their voice ſhall be heard *even*
unto Jahaz therefore the armed ſoldiers of Moab ſhall
cry out, [g] his life ſhall be grievous unto him 5 [h] My
heart ſhall cry out for Moab, his fugitives *ſhall flee* unto
Zoar, [i] an heifer of three years old for by the mount-
ing up of Luhith with weeping ſhall they go it up
for in the way of Horonaim they ſhall raiſe up a cry
of deſtruction

v 1—5 This prophecy is either the ſame with *chap* xvi 14 and was to be quickly accompliſhed, within three years, when Salmaneſer ravaged the country, or, as ſome think, diſtinct from that, and relative to the final deſtruction of Moab by Nebuchadnezzar, *Jer* xlviii

We have here a picture of the moſt affecting diſtreſs

1 Sudden and terrible would be the ſtroke Some of their cities ſurprized in the night, ſacked, and demoliſhed, *v* 1 others, in terror at the expectation of the ſame fate, with tokens of bittereſt anguiſh upon them, diſfigured with baldneſs, and girt with ſackcloth, and every place full of weeping and tears, *v* 3 loud as the heifer bellows, and reaching to the diſtant cities, whither they fly for ſhelter from the approaching ruin, *v* 3—5 *Note*, (1) Death often ſeizes the ſinner in the night with terrible ſurprize (2) When we lie down on our beds, by ſome unexpected ſtroke our bed may be quickly made our grave let us therefore be always ready (3) It will be too late for thoſe to cry, when God's wrath overtakes them, who before never cried to avert it

2 All help ſhould fail them their mighty warriors ſhould faint under their fears, and their life be a burden to them Or it may be rendered, *His ſoul ſhall cry out for himſelf*, each bemoaning his wretched caſe nor ſhall their idols afford them more help, *v* 2 Though they go up to their high places to weep, no anſwer ſhall be given them, and weeping they ſhall deſcend, *v* 5 as in the margin *Note*, Creature-confidences, like idol gods, will utterly fail us in time of trouble

3 The prophet himſelf in pity drops a tear over their deſolation, though enemies Such tender and compaſſionate hearts ſhould miniſters poſſeſs, and, like their divine Lord, weep over thoſe ſinners that will not be warned

k Jer xlviii 34 · † Heb De-ſolations · † Or, valley of the Arabians

6 For the waters of [k] Nimrim ſhall be † deſolate for
the hay is withered away, the graſs faileth, there is no
green thing 7 Therefore the abundance they have
gotten, and that which they have laid up, ſhall they
carry away to the † brook of the willows 8 For the
cry is gone round about the borders of Moab the
howling thereof unto Eglaim, and the howling thereof
unto Beer-elim 9 For the waters of Dimon ſhall be
full of blood for I will bring § more upon Dimon,
[l] lions upon him that eſcapeth of Moab, and upon the
remnant of the land

Before Christ 713. · § Heb Additions · l Lev xxvi 22 2 Kings xvii 25

v 6—9 From one corner to the other of the land, the cry of Moab ſhould be heard, *v* 8 and no marvel, when her deſolations were ſo great

1 The country ſhould be devoured and waſted, either by drought, or eat up as forage by theſe invaders, ſo that not a blade of graſs ſhould remain, and their abundance, with ſo much care collected and laid up, *be carried away to the brook of the willows*, either by themſelves to hide it, or rather by their enemies to Babylon, ſo called from its marſhy ſituation *Note*, This world's riches are often a ſhort-lived poſſeſſion, ſo ſoon do they make themſelves wings and fly away

2 The waters of Dimon ſhall be full of blood, the numbers of the ſlain ſo great, that her ſtreams ſhould be dyed thereby and *more*, or *additions*, of trouble be brought upon them, the lions ſhall glean thoſe which are eſcaped from the ſword, *v* 9 *Note*, When God in wrath begins with ſinners, he will make an end, and whilſt they continue hardened, he will not be weary in ſmiting them

CHAP XVI.

This chapter concludes the burden of Moab In it, 1 The prophet counſels the Moabites to reform what was amiſs among them, and particularly to be kind to God's people, as the likelieſt way to prevent the judgments before threatened, ver 1—5 2 *Fearing they would not take this counſel, they were ſo proud, he goes on to foretel the lamentable devaſtation of their country, and the confuſion they ſhould ſoon be brought to,* ver 6—14

a 2 Kings iii 4 · † Or Ezra vii 17 · b 2 Kings xiv 7 · † Or, Petra · ‡ Or, elſe · c Num xxi 14 · d Dan iv 27 · e Mat xxv 35 Heb xiii 2 · § Heb Wringer · f Prov xx 28 & xxix 14 · g 2 Sam xxiii 3

1 [a] SEND ye the lamb † to the ruler of the land
from [b] Sela to the wilderneſs, unto the mount of
the daughter of Zion 2 ‡ For it ſhall be *that* as a
wandring bird caſt out of the neſt *ſo* the daughters of
Moab ſhall be at [c] the fords of Arnon 3 [d] Take coun-
ſel, execute judgment, make thy ſhadow as the night in
the midſt of the noon-day, hide the out-caſts, bewray
not him that wandereth 4 [e] Let mine out-caſts dwell
with thee, Moab, be thou a covert to them from the
face of the ſpoiler for the § extortioner is at an end,
the ſpoiler ceaſeth, the oppreſſors are conſumed out of
the land 5 And [f] in mercy ſhall the throne be eſta
bliſhed, and he ſhall ſit upon it in truth, in the taber-
nacle of David, [g] judging and ſeeking judgment, and
haſting righteouſneſs

v 1—5 To prevent the threatened ruin, the prophet warns them what ſteps to take, to do juſtice, and ſhew mercy, and leaves them inexcuſable if they reject the admonition

1 He adviſes them to ſend their tribute, laid on them by David, 2 *Sam* viii 2 which was paid in lambs and rams, 2 *Kings* iii 4, 5 *from Sela*, their capital, *to the wilderneſs*, the neareſt road which led to Zion, *to the ruler of the land*, to Hezekiah, David's rightful ſucceſſor, or, *O ruler of the land*, the king of Moab, whoſe duty it was to pay it, and that on the peril of being ejected from his country, *for it ſhall be*, or, *otherwiſe it ſhall be*, if the juſtice be not done, then, as a wandering bird ſhould they be driven from their houſes to the borders of their country, and in conſternation uncertain whither to flee

2 He counſels them to ſhew mercy to the outcaſts of Iſrael, who, on the invaſion of the Aſſyrians, ſhould fly to hide themſelves from their fury They ſhould protect and cheriſh them, as a thick ſhadow, from the ſcorching heat of perſecution, conceal them from their enemies, and never betray them if purſued, *v* 3 but let them dwell in ſafety in their land till the tyranny was overpaſt, which ſhould not laſt long, whether that of Salmanezer, who, after ravaging the country, returned, or that of Sennacherib, whoſe army was ſo quickly deſtroyed *Note*, (1) God's people are often perſecuted and driven from their homes, but God is with them, and will ſeek them a covert from the ſtorm (2) They who are kind to God's outcaſts, ſhall find him abundantly recompenſing the favour

3 It would be their intereſt as well as duty thus to act As God would eſtabliſh the throne of Hezekiah and long continue him in the tabernacle of David, executing righteous judgment, and readily adminiſtring juſtice to the needy, he would be enabled to return the kindneſs to Moab, when her diſtreſs ſhould arrive *Note*, We ſhould ſtudy to oblige every man, as we know not what need we may have of their aſſiſtance before we die

Before Christ 747

6 ¶ We have heard of [h] the pride of Moab, (he *is* very
proud) *even* of his haughtiness, and his pride, and his
wrath, *but* [i] his † lies *shall* not *be* so 7 Therefore shall
Moab [k] howl for Moab, every one shall howl for the
foundations of Kir-hareseth shall ye ‡ mourn, surely *they*
are stricken 8 For [l] the fields of Heshbon languish,
and [m] the vine of Sibmah, the lords of the heathen have
broken down the principal plants thereof, they are come
even unto Jazer, they wandered *through* the wilderness,
her branches are stretched out, they are gone over the sea
9 ¶ Therefore I will bewail with the weeping of Jazer,
[n] the vine of Sibmah I will water thee with my tears,
[o] O Heshbon, and Elealeh for § the shouting for thy
summer fruits, and for thy harvest, is fallen 10 And
[p] gladness is taken away, and joy out of the plentiful field,
and in the vineyards there shall be no singing, neither shall
there be shouting the treaders shall tread out no wine in
their presses, I have made *their vintage*-shouting to cease
11 Wherefore [q] my bowels shall sound like an harp for
Moab, and mine inward parts for Kir-haresh 12 ¶ And
it shall come to pass, when it is seen that Moab is weary
on [r] the high place, that he shall come to his sanctuary
to pray, [s] but he shall not prevail 13 This *is* the
word that the LORD hath spoken concerning Moab
since that time 14 But now the LORD hath spoken,
saying, Within three years, [u] as the years of an hireling,
and the glory of Moab shall be contemned, with all
that great multitude, and the remnant *shall be* very small
and || feeble

h Jer xlviii 29 Zeph ii 10
i Chap xxviii 15
† Or, vain counsels
k Chap xlv 24
l Jer xlviii 20
‡ Or, mutter
m Chap xlv 24 — Ver 9
n Jer xlviii 32
o Chap xv 4
§ Or, the alarm is fallen upon
p Jer xlviii 33
q Jer xlviii 36
r Chap xv 2
s Jer xlviii 35
t Chap xv
u Chap xiv 23
|| Or, not many

v 6—14 Because Moab haughtily rejected the prophetic counsel, his doom is near

1 His sins were great and notorious, with haughtiness and pride he treated the poor refugees of Israel, and in wrath persecuted rather than protected them *But his lies*, or *his strength*, *shall not be so* He hath mischievous designs against Israel, but God will disappoint his wiles, or break his power, so that his wicked purposes shall not be brought to pass *Note*, (1) Pride in God's sight is most abominable (2) It is a mercy for God's people, that the power of their enemies is not proportioned to their malice

2 The sorrows of Moab would be increased, their strongest fortresses levelled with the ground, and their fertile land wasted The vine of Sibmah, that spread her tendrils even unto Jazer, a city in Gilead, and to the Dead Sea, the borders of their country, now languishes, broken down by the lords of the heathen, the Assyrian army, and Heshbon's fruitful fields, no longer cheared with the songs of reapers, or the shouts of those who trod the wine-press, in mournful solitude and silence lie desolate and barren The prophet, whilst he denounces the judgment, weeps for their ruin, and, like the trembling strings of the harp, his bowels yearn in compassion over them, *v* 7—11 *Note*, (1) Sorrow and sin are twin sisters (2) The miseries even of the wicked move a gracious heart to pity them

3 All applications to their idol gods would be in vain tho' they went from one high place to another, as Balak of old, till they wearied themselves with sacrifices, their miseries would not abate, and as fruitless would be their prayers before the shrine of Chemosh Though some suppose the sanctuary refers to the temple of God, whither in their distresses they would be driven, but God would reject their prayers, *v* 12 The decree was gone forth, *since that time*, the date of the prophecy in the first year of Hezekiah, and was now irreversible *Note*, (1) When prayer is the extorted cry of suffering, and not the voice of repentant sorrow, no marvel it is rejected (2) There is a time when prayer comes too late to profit it will be in vain to knock when the door is shut

4 The day of execution is fixed for Moab's destruction, when their glory should be despicable, their multitude of soldiers cut off, and the remnant weak and disabled to make head against their invader In three years, as the years of an hireling, who waits with earnestness the expiration of his contract, the people of God might expect the fulfilment of the prophecy, *v* 14 Some regard this as a distinct vision, referring the former part to the total destruction of the whole people by Nebuchadnezzar *But now the Lord hath spoken* concerning a nearer event, which was fulfilled in the fourth of Hezekiah, when Shalmaneser conquered Samaria, and ravaged Moab in his way, 2 *Kings* xviii 9 which was a warning to them, and a prelude to their final ruin

CHAP XVII

Syria and Ephraim were confederate against Judah, chap vii 1, 2 *Here they are joined in ruin, for companions in sin will ever be companions in suffering* 1 *The destruction of the strong cities both of Syria and Israel is here foretold*, ver 1—5 *and again*, ver 9—11 2 *A gracious promise is made, that a remnant should be preserved from these calamities, and should get good by them*, ver 6—8 3 *The overthrow of the Assyrian army before Jerusalem is pointed at*, ver 12—14 *In order of time this chapter should be placed next after chap ix for the destruction of Damascus here foretold happened in the reign of Ahaz*, 2 Kings xvi 9

Before Christ 741

1 [a] THE burden of Damascus Behold, [b] Damas-
cus is taken away from *being* a city, and it shall
be a ruinous heap 2 The cities of Aroer *are* forsaken,
they shall be for flocks which shall lie down, and none
shall make *them* afraid 3 [c] The fortress also shall cease
from Ephraim, and the kingdom from Damascus, and
the remnant of Syria they shall be as the glory of the
children of Israel, saith the LORD of hosts 4 And
in that day it shall come to pass, *that* the glory of Ja-
cob shall be made thin, and the fatness of his flesh shall
wax lean 5 And it shall be [d] as when the harvest-
man gathereth the corn, and reapeth the ears with his
arm, and it shall be as he that gathereth ears in the val-
ley of Rephaim

747
a Jer xlix 23, Amos i 3 Zech ix 1
b Fulfilled in 740 2 Kings xvi 9
c Chap viii 4 & chap vii 16 & ix
d Rev xiv 15 16

v 1—5 The cup of trembling goes round, Syria and Israel must drink of it They were closely allied, but the strongest confederacies in sin will fail The burden begins with Syria, Damascus, the capital, is doomed to fall, and lie for a while in ruins, her fertile villages desolate, the deserted houses become shepherds huts, and in the streets, once thronged with crowds of citizens, the sheep shall graze unmolested The few who remain poor and despicable, shall be as the glory of Israel, an ironical expression, since Israel's glory too was alike departed, and her fate as desperate The fortress of Ephraim, Samaria, shall be demolished, the government dissolved, so that it should no more recover and all the fatness of Israel, her riches, and multitudes, once her glory, like a man wasted with a consumption, shall pine away, destroyed by famine or the sword, ripe for ruin as the corn in harvest, and cut down by the armies of the Assyrians, as the reaper gathers the sheaf, and with as much care as the husbandman in the vale of Rephaim, where the corn was peculiarly excellent, collected every ear *Note*, (1) If pining consumption seize the body natural or politic, we may quickly trace the origin of the disease to sin, the cause of every human misery (2) The strongest fortress hath no defence, when God stretches out his arm to destroy (3) When the sinner is ripe for destruction, death, as the harvest-man, will put in the sickle, and none can deliver out of his hands

6 (¶ [e] Yet gleaning grapes shall be left in it, as the
shaking of an olive-tree, two *or* three berries in the top
of the uppermost bough, four *or* five in the outmost
fruitful branches thereof, saith the LORD God of Israel
7 At that day [f] shall a man look to his Maker, and his
eyes shall have respect to the holy One of Israel 8 And
[g] he shall not look to the altars, the work of his hands,
neither shall respect *that* which his fingers have made,
either the groves, or the † images)

e Chap xxiv 13
f Chap x 20 21 & xix 22 Hos xiv 8
† Or, sun images

v 6—8 One gleam of mercy beams through the darkness, to comfort the hearts of God's faithful amidst these desolating judgments They shall be preserved from the destruction, and hid in the day of the Lord's fierce anger, by escaping to Judah, or being overlooked by the Assyrians

1 They are but few, very few, like the gleaning grape when the vintage is over, or two or three olives left on the topmost bough, which were not shaken down *Note*, (1) They who are led captive by the devil at his will are many, whilst those who escape his bondage are, comparatively, few (2) Such as are careful in the evil day to keep close to God, he will keep them from the hour of temptation

2 They are drawn nearer to God by their danger *At that day of Israel's calamity shall a man look to his Maker, and his eyes shall have respect to the holy One of Israel* In prayer the faithful will spread their case before God their Saviour, and cast their care on him, renouncing every vain confidence, such as the idol altars and images of their apostate countrymen, which themselves might have formerly worshipped, but now abhorred and rejected, they cleave to the Lord alone, as able to save them in the day of evil *Note*, (1) They are blessed afflictions that bring us nearer to God (2) As naturally as a child runs to its parent for protection, so doth the child of God in the day of distress in prayer betake himself to the arms of Jesus his Saviour (3) Nothing serves more to detach the soul from earth and creature-comforts and confidences, than those strokes of Providence that convince us of their vanity

Before Christ 741

9 ¶ In that day shall his strong cities be as a forsaken
bough, and an uppermost branch which they left, be-
cause of the children of Israel and there shall be deso-
lation 10 Because thou hast [h] forgotten the God of
thy salvation, and hast not been mindful of [i] the rock
of thy strength therefore shalt thou plant pleasant
plants, and shalt set it with strange slips 11 In the
day shalt thou make thy plant to grow, and in the
morning shalt thou make thy seed to flourish but [k] the
harvest *shall be* † a heap in the day of grief, and of de-
sperate sorrow

h Ps cvi 21 Hos viii 14 i Ps xxxi 2 k Lev xxvi 16 Deut xxviii 38 † Or, removed in the day of inheritance and there shall be deadly sorrow

v 9—11 The prophet having said to the righteous, it shall be well with them, returns to cry woe to the wicked, for it shall be ill with them

1 The cause of all their misery is their departure from God, *v* 10 They had forgotten his wonders of mercy and grace, neglected his worship, disregarded his commands, and forsaking the rock of their strength, were justly forsaken by him *Note*, (1) Negligence about the things of God, and their souls, is the [illegible] sin and ruin of mankind (2) They who forsake the God of their strength, renounce their own mercies

2 The consequence of their apostacy is their destruction As desolate as the cities of Canaan were made when first Israel seized them, so desolate should their own cities become through the sword of the Assyrians, as a withered branch stripped of its leaves, and the topmost bough blasted and dead Their country, cultivated with such assiduity, full of pleasant fruits, its native produce, and improved by foreign trees and plants, promised a great increase but, ere the day of harvest comes, all is blasted, *a heap in the day of grief*, or *inheritance*, when they expected to reap, the enemy should collect their fruits into a heap, destroying what he did not use, and leaving them nothing but *desperate sorrow* not only their land wasted, but themselves carried captive, without any hope of ever returning to it again *Note*, (1) If the wicked Canaanites were cast out of their cities, let not wicked Israelites think to escape (2) When worldly hopes and cares engross our hearts, God justly blasts our prospects, and punishes our creature-idolatry

† Or noise l Jer vi 23

12 ¶ Wo to the † multitude of many people, *which*
make a noise [l] like the noise of the seas, and to the
rushing of nations, *that* make a rushing like the rushing
of mighty waters 13 The nations shall rush like the
rushing of many waters [m] but *God* shall rebuke them,
and they shall flee far off, [n] and shall be chased as the
chaff of the mountains before the wind, and like ‡ a
rolling thing before the whirlwind 14 And behold,
at evening tide trouble, *and* [p] before the morning he *is*
not this *is* the portion of them that spoil us, and the
lot of them that rob us

m Ps xciii 4 n Ps lxxxiii 13 Hos xiii 3 ‡ Or, thistle-down o Chap xxxvii 36 p 2 Kings xix 35

v 12—14 This prophecy concerns the destruction of Sennacherib and his army

1 Their multitude and impetuosity is described, like raging seas rolling their furious billows to the shore, and foaming out, in Rabshakeh's blasphemy, their own shame, *v* 12

2 Their woe is denounced God will take the cause into his own hand, and rebuke the wrath of these fierce enemies They shall rush upon their ruin, his angel, like chaff, shall beat them small, and, as the down of thistle before the whirlwind, so easily shall they be dispersed, and the few that remain from the sword of the destroyer, flee far away, *v* 13 *Note*, The mightiest foes of the church and people of God, before the Almighty, are less than nothing and vanity

3 A quick period is put to the distress of God's people Though troubled at the evening, when they beheld the approaching host of Assyria, one night removed their fears, and the next morning shewed them their dead corpses *Note*, Tho' the faithful may be now and then dismayed, their heaviness endureth but for a night, and joy cometh in the morning

4 Such shall be the case of all the enemies of God's church, and his servants must remember it for their comfort, for *this is the portion of them that spoil us, and the lot of them that rob us* *Note*, The past experience of God's people should be treasured up as a ground of present confidence in the like temptations

CHAP XVIII

A woe is pro-nounced against the land shadowing with wings, *for God watcheth upon his people's account against it* 1 *They threaten God's people*, ver 1, 2 2 *All the neighbours are hereupon called to take notice what would be the issue*, ver 3 3 *Though God seem unconcerned in the distress of his people for a time, he would arise to appear against their enemies, and will cut them off*, ver 4—6 4 *Jews shall yet make* [illegible] ver 7

Before Christ 741

1 WO to the land [a] shadowing with wings, which
is beyond the rivers of † Ethiopia 2 That
sendeth ambassadors by the sea, even in vessels of bul-
rushes upon the waters, *saying*, Go ye swift messengers
to [b] a nation scattered and peeled, to a people [c] terrible
from their beginning hitherto, a nation ‡ meted out and
trodden down, whose land the rivers § have spoiled 3
All ye inhabitants of the world, and dwellers on the
earth, see ye, [d] when he lifteth up an ensign on the
mountains, and when he bloweth a trumpet, hear ye
4 For so the LORD said unto me, I will take my rest,
and I will || consider in my dwelling-place, like a clear
heat ‡ upon herbs, *and* [e] like a cloud of dew in the
heat of harvest 5 For afore the harvest when the bud
is perfect, and the sour grape is ripening in the flower,
he shall both cut off the sprigs with pruning-hooks, and
take away *and* cut down the branches 6 They shall
be left together unto the fowls of the mountains, and
to the beasts of the earth and the fowls shall summer
upon them, and all the beasts of the earth shall winter
upon them 7 ¶ In that time [f] shall the present be
brought unto the LORD of hosts, of [g] a people ‡ scat-
tered and peeled, and from a people terrible from their
beginning hitherto a nation meted out and trodden
under foot, whose land the rivers have spoiled, to the
place of the name of the LORD of hosts, the mount
Zion

a Chap viii 8 † Heb Cush b Ver 7 c Deut xxviii 50 ‡ Or, that meteth out and treadeth down § Or despise d Chap xiii 2, 4 || Or regard my dwelling place 1 Kings viii 39 † Or, after rain e 2 Sam xxiii 4 Ps lxxii 6 f Ps lxviii 31 & lxxii 10 Chap xvi 1 Zeph iii 10 g Ver 2 ‡ Or outspread and polished

v 1—7 Various have been the conjectures of the learned concerning the people meant by *the land shadowing with wings* Some have thought it to be Judea, who sought to find shelter under the shadow of Egypt and Ethiopia against the Assyrians Others interpret it of one of these nations, leagued with Judah to oppose Sennacherib's invasion I rather incline to suppose it the Assyrians themselves, (*See chap* viii 8) and to be a sequel to the former chapter, since by Cush, or Ethiopia, is rather meant Arabia, than that country so called in Africa, and Assyria lying beyond the Euphrates and Tigris, the borders of Arabia, more aptly suits the description here given

1 A woe is pronounced on the land, whatever it be, which sendeth embassadors to form alliances, and to engage auxiliary forces, in order to strengthen their army, *v* 1, 2

2 God prepares to disappoint their designs, and gives his orders *Go, ye swift messengers* of his vengeance, *to a nation scattered and peeled*, which, with the following words, some suppose addressed to Judea, harrassed by the Assyrians, but seem rather spoken of these invaders, who, though terrible hitherto, were destined to ruin, and therefore, though laden with spoils, are spoken of as a people *scattered and peeled, a nation meted out and trodden down*, such being their appointed portion, *whose land the rivers have spoiled*, smitten by the sword of the destroyer, as rivers swelled with rain overflow their banks, and deluge the country

3 All the people of the earth are called to be spectators of the controversy, *v* 3 when on the mountains of Judea the proud Assyrian monarch should lift up his banners, and sound the dread alarm However intimidating his appearance, God bids them see and hear, and mark the end *Note*, God's hand of providential interposition is carefully to be remarked, and, when dangers are most alarming, he is nearest to defend and save us As it is written, *in the mount of the Lord it shall be seen*

4 For a while God seems to give up his people for a prey *So the Lord said unto me, I will take my rest*, as on sleep, and disregarding the distress of his people, *and I will consider in my dwelling-place* what I resolve to do, or, *I will look upon my dwelling-place*, Jerusalem, so called from the Shechinah of glory abiding in the temple, *like a clear heat on herbs, and like a cloud of dew in the heat of harvest*, either reviving them, as the sun quickens the grass after a shower, and a cloud allays the scorching heat of harvest, or, suffering them for a while to be afflicted, as the sun burns up the grass, and as rain is hurtful in the time of harvest And this may refer to his dealings with his people, whom he would comfort and protect, or the invading Assyrians, whose devices he would thus consider and disappoint *Note*, (1) God's repose can never be disturbed by all the impotent rage of his foes (2) He seems, respecting his people, sometimes to have forgotten and forsaken them, when he is just ready to display his determination of grace for their deliverance

5 His enemies, when ready in their own conceits to reap the fruits of their conquests, are destroyed *afore the harvest, even the bud is perfect*, their designs formed for execution *and the sour grape*, the mischievous purpose, *is ripening in the flower*, ready to be accomplished, *he shall both cut off the sprigs with pruning-hooks, and take away and cut down the branches*, destroy both the soldiers of the army and the chief captains by the sword of the angel, and such a slaughter shall be made, that enough

to d

Before Christ 741

food will be provided from the carcases of the slain, during summer and winter, for the fowls and the wild beasts, v. 6. *Note,* The deepest laid schemes against God's people, in which their adversaries already triumph in the certainty of success, God can easily counteract to their confusion.

6 God's people, delivered by his wondrous interposition, would bring to his altar a grateful present from the spoil of their enemies, who are described as v. 3. Or this may refer to future times, when these, as well as other antient enemies of God's church, should present themselves to him; and, wretched and vile as before their character was esteemed, being converted by grace, their offering would be accepted, and they admitted into the church of Christ, *the place of the Lord of hosts, the spiritual mount Zion.* *Note,* (1.) If God enriches us by his providence, we are bound to bring the grateful present to him, and the poor are his receivers. (2.) They who design the ruin of others, are themselves justly given up for a prey.

CHAP. XIX.

This is the burden of Egypt. 1. It should be greatly weakened, and become as contemptible among the nations as it was once considerable, through a complication of judgments which God would bring upon them, ver. 1—17. *2. At length God's holy religion should be established in it,* ver. 18—25.

714
a Jer. xlvi. 13. Ezek. xxix. & xxx.
b Psal. xviii. 10. & civ. 3.
c Exod. xii. 12. Jer. xliii. 12. & xlvi. 25.
d Ver. 1.
e Job v. 13.
† Or, shut up.
f Ezek. xxx. 12.
g 2 Kings xix. 24.
‡ Heb. shall not be.
h 1 Kings x. 28. Prov. vii. 16.
i Num. xiii. 22.
k Rom. i. 22. 1 Cor. i. 20.
l Jer. ii. 16.
§ Heb. the corners, or governors.
m 1 Kings xxii. 22.
n Chap. xxviii. 8.
o Chap. ix. 14.
p Jer. li. 30. Nah. iii. 13.
q Chap. xi. 15.
r Chap. xiv. 1.

1 aTHE burden of Egypt. Behold, b the LORD
rideth upon a swift cloud, and shall come into
Egypt, and c the idols of Egypt shall be moved at his
presence, and the heart of Egypt shall melt in the midst
of it. 2 And I will set the Egyptians against the
Egyptians: and they shall fight every one against his
brother, and every one against his neighbour; city
against city, *and* kingdom against kingdom. 3 And
d the spirit of Egypt shall fail in the midst thereof;
and e I will destroy the counsel thereof: and they shall
seek to the idols, and to the charmers, and to them
that have familiar spirits, and to the wizards. 4 And
the Egyptians will I † give over into the hand of a
cruel lord; and a fierce king shall rule over them,
saith the LORD, the LORD of hosts. 5 And f the
waters shall fail from the sea, and the rivers shall be
wasted and dried up. 6 And they shall turn the rivers
far away; *and* g the brooks of defence shall be emptied
and dried up: the reeds and flags shall wither. 7 The
paper-reeds by the brooks, by the mouth of the brooks,
and every thing sown by the brooks shall wither, be
driven away, and ‡ be no *more.* 8 The fishers also shall
mourn, and all they that cast angle into the brooks shall
lament, and they that spread nets upon the waters shall
languish. 9 Moreover, they that work in h fine flax,
and they that weave net-works shall be confounded. 10
And they shall be broken in the purposes thereof, all that
make sluices *and* ponds for fish. 11 ¶ Surely the princes
of i Zoan k *are* fools, the counsel of the wise counsellors of
Pharaoh is become brutish: how say ye unto Pharoah, I
am the son of the wise, the son of ancient kings? 12
Where *are* they? where *are* thy wise *men*? and let them
tell thee now, and let them know what the LORD of
hosts hath purposed upon Egypt. 13 The princes of
Zoan are become fools, l the princes of Noph are deceived,
they have also seduced Egypt, *even* § they that are the stay
of the tribes thereof. 14 The LORD hath mingled m a
perverse spirit in the midst thereof; and they have caused
Egypt to err in every work thereof, n as a drunken *man*
staggereth in his vomit. 15 Neither shall there be *any*
work for Egypt, which o the head or tail, branch or rush
may do. 16 In that day shall Egypt p be like unto
women: and it shall be afraid and fear, because of q the
shaking of the hand of the LORD of hosts, which
he shaketh over it. 17 And r the land of Judah shall
be a terror unto Egypt, every one that maketh mention
thereof, shall be afraid in himself, because of the coun-
sel of the LORD of hosts which he hath determined
against it.

v. 1—17. Egypt had often been a broken reed to the house of Judah, who, notwithstanding the misery their fathers had there endured, were ever flying thither for help, and making this their confidence, though ever to their hurt. God therefore will in the destruction of Egypt cut off this false resource. We have here,

Before Christ 714

1 The terror of Egypt, and the helplessness of their idol-gods, when the Lord cometh on the swift cloud, in terrible majesty, hastening as a judge to condemn the malefactors, or as a general at the head of his troops, with impetuous speed, and irresistible power, to lay the country waste before him. At his presence the idols, like Dagon's image before the ark, shall be confounded, and their courageous soldiers be utterly dispirited, v. 1. *Note,* Before an avenging God who can stand?

2 Intestine feuds shall embroil them, and lay them more open to the invader, v. 2. which may refer to the civil war, when Psammiticus seized the kingdom, or to that between Apries and Amasis, in the time of Nebuchadnezzar. *Note,* They are the greatest enemies of their country, who foment a spirit of faction, and seek to embroil brother against brother.

3 A spirit of infatuation and folly shall seize the Egyptians, v. 3. Their princes and wisest counsellors, notwithstanding their boasts of science, and descent from a long train of illustrious ancestors, are become brutish and fools, unable to discover the divine purposes; neither can their idols or magicians inform them, v. 11, 12. Deceived themselves, their princes have deceived their country; and they who should have been the stay thereof, hasten its destruction, v. 13. Like men intoxicated with wine, they have drunk of the cup of error, and every step they take is wrong. Their counsels weak, unsteady, perverse, and by them the state is led to the precipice of ruin, v. 14. *Note,* It is a needful and weighty petition of our Litany, *That it may please thee to endue the Lords of the council and all the nobility with grace, wisdom, and understanding.*

4 They shall be sold into the hand of a cruel lord, or *lords,* either the twelve tyrants who succeeded Sethon, or Psammiticus, who united the monarchy under himself; or rather the Persian emperors, Cambyses and Ochus, to whom the character highly agrees. *Note,* (1.) A tyrant king is the scourge of his land. (2.) What reason have we to bless God for the mild government we enjoy!

5 The sources of their riches and commerce should be cut off, and want and wretchedness ensue. The Nile, the great cause of Egypt's fertility, shall fail them, occasioned by such a drought as would prevent its usual overflowing, v. 5. or by the imprudent attempts of their kings, one of whom, Pharaoh Necho, by endeavouring to join the Nile with the Red Sea, is said to have greatly weakened its force; the consequence of which would be, [1.] That their defence would be gone, the ditches which the water of the Nile filled round their fortified places being drained, v. 6. [2.] That famine would be in their land, because, as they have no rain in Egypt, the Nile not rising as usual, nothing would grow; and if the reeds on its banks, from whence paper and a variety of other things were made, withered for want of moisture, much more would all the fruits of the ground, v. 7. [3.] Even their fish, of which such vast plenty abounded, would be no more: the river dried up, the fishermen destitute of employment would mourn, and the people who generally fed thereon be reduced to deep distress. Nor shall the rich be able to supply their tables, when their sluices and ponds should alike be exhausted, v. 8—10. [4.] Their manufactures for want of flax should be at a stand: they who wove in the loom, or spun, or made their nets, now unemployed, in want would pine away, v. 11. and an entire stop be put to their trade and commerce, there being no work *which head or tail, branch or rush may do,* ver. 15. *Note,* Our common blessings are grievously overlooked; but one year of drought, that should destroy our harvest, would sensibly teach us the value of the mercies we disregard. May our ingratitude and unmindfulness of God never provoke him thus to plague us!

6 The ruin of Judea by the Assyrian hosts would spread panic among them; pangs shall come upon them as on a travailing woman, beholding the hand of the Lord thus lifted up, justly apprehensive of the vicinity of the victorious army, and fearing, that if God's own people are not spared, Egypt may not hope to escape, against which the decree is gone forth, v. 16, 17. *Note,* (1.) When one sinner is cut down, it becomes the survivors to look and tremble. (2.) When the wicked persist in their perverse way, the counsel of the Lord is determined for their destruction.

s Zeph. iii. 9.
t Deut. x. 20. Or, Neh. x. 29.
‡ Or, Jer. xii. 16.
† Or, the sun.
u Gen. xxviii. 18.
x Josh. xxii. 27.
y Jer. iii. 15.
z Zeph. iii. 10.
a Mal. i. 11.

18 ¶ In that day shall five cities in the land of
Egypt s speak the language of Canaan, and t swear to
the LORD of hosts: one shall be called the city of
‡ destruction. 19 In that day u shall there be an altar
to the LORD in the midst of the land of Egypt, and a
pillar at the border thereof to the LORD. 20 And
x it shall be for a sign, and for a witness unto the
LORD of hosts in the land of Egypt: for they shall
cry unto the LORD, because of the oppressors, and
he shall send them y a saviour and z a great one, and he
shall deliver them. 21 And the LORD shall be
known to Egypt, and the Egyptians shall know the
LORD in that day, and a shall do sacrifice and oblation,
yea, they shall vow a vow unto the LORD,

all

Before Christ 714

and perform *it* 22 And the LORD ſhall ſmite Egypt,
c he ſhall ſmite and heal *it*, and they ſhall return, *even*
to the LORD, and he ſhall be intreated of them, and
ſhall heal them 23 ¶ In that day d ſhall there be a
high-way out of Egypt to Aſſyria, and the Aſſyrian
ſhall come into Egypt, and the Egyptian into Aſſyria,
and the Egyptians ſhall ſerve with the Aſſyrians 24
In that day ſhall Iſrael be the third with Egypt, and with
Aſſyria, *even* a bleſſing in the midſt of the land 25
Whom the LORD of hoſts ſhall bleſs, ſaying, Bleſſed
be Egypt e my people, and Aſſyria f the work of my
hands, and g Iſrael mine inheritance

c Hoſ vi 1 Heb xii 11
d Chap xi 16
e Hoſ ii 23
f Pſ c 3 Chap xxix 23 Eph ii 10
g Jer x 16

v 18—25 In the midſt of wrath a beam of mercy gladdens the dreary ſcene There is yet hope in their end, and ſpiritual bleſſings in ſtore, which would infinitely outweigh the heavieſt temporal calamities The accompliſhment of this prophecy ſome refer to the converſion of many of them by the Jews, who fled into Egypt from the Aſſyrians, but it ſeems rather to refer to the times of the goſpel, when Egypt, by the preaching of St Mark and others, was early converted to the Chriſtian faith

1 Their cities ſhall ſpeak the language of Canaan, becoming acquainted with the word of God, and converſing with the people of God *One ſhall be called the city of deſtruction*, or, *of the ſun*, where idolatry was moſt rooted, the grace of God ſhall be moſt prevalent, or, the city that refuſed the goſpel, would be devoted to ruin *Note*, (1) When the ſoul is converted to God, we learn a new language, the love of God in Chriſt, and his rich ſalvation known and believed, is the pleaſing ſubject of our converſation, a language that to the world appears ſtrange and unknown (2) That ſoul is doomed to deſtruction, who continues a ſtranger to the divine teachings, and experimentally unacquainted with the truths of goſpel-grace

2 The worſhip of God ſhould be publicly eſtabliſhed The name of idols ſhould come no more into their lips, but their appeals be made to the heart-ſearching Jehovah, and to the Lord Jeſus would they pledge their fidelity, *v* 18 To him ſhall they go, as the only altar where atonement had been made for their ſins, and where acceptance of their ſervices can be alone obtained And in the utmoſt borders a pillar ſhall be erected, intimating the general profeſſion of the faith of Chriſt throughout the land *Note*, (1) An oath is a ſolemn act of religion, and therefore to God alone muſt we appeal (2) Chriſt is our altar, in and by whom alone our perſons and ſervices can be accepted of God (3) If there be but one true altar, what a pity is it, yea, what a ſin, for the profeſſors of the religion of Jeſus by cauſeleſs diviſions to ſet up altar againſt altar

3 God's truth being thus embraced, and his ordinances of worſhip eſtabliſhed, they would be a ſign between him and his people In time of diſtreſs, when they cry unto him, he will hear and anſwer them, and by a Saviour, a great one, yea, an almighty Saviour, Jeſus, deliver them from every oppreſſor, from ſin, Satan, death, hell, and every foe, *v* 20 Some interpret this of Ptolemy Soter, or the Saviour, one of their kings, but the former ſenſe ſeems much preferable *Note*, (1) God's ears are ever open to the prayer of his people, and Jeſus ever near to help his afflicted ones Whilſt we pray, he will never leave nor forſake us (2) They who feel they have great ſins, and tremble under their great corruptions, ſhould remember they have a great Redeemer, able to ſave to the uttermoſt

4 They ſhall be brought to the knowledge of God, and, as the bleſſed effect of it, ſhall have their hearts engaged to him, paying the grateful tribute of praiſe and thankſgiving for his mercies, *v* 21 By the tranſlation of the Hebrew ſcriptures into Greek at Alexandria, the knowledge of divine truth was, in a meaſure, laid open, but more eſpecially were they enlightened, when the miniſters of Chriſt carried the goſpel thither, and preached unto them the grace which is in Jeſus Chriſt

5 By his word and providences he will ſmite their hearts, effectually awakening their conſciences, and as he wounds, healing them, forgiving their ſins, and converting their ſouls, *v* 22 *Note*, When God wounds, it is to heal, not to deſtroy

6 They ſhall be admitted into the communion of God's ſaints All quarrels now terminated, Egypt and Aſſyria ſhould become friends, and maintain intimate intercourſe, and both unite in the ſervice of the ſame God, *v* 23 and Iſrael, which lay between them, through the Saviour, who was of their ſtock, ſhould become a bleſſing to them, and, cordially uniting with them, the diſtinction of Jew and Gentile ſhall ceaſe, when they become one fold under one ſhepherd, *v* 24 For their God, as their common Father, will regard them Egypt is equally his people with Iſrael his inheritance, and bleſſed in the ſame covenant of peace, and Aſſyria, alike the work of his hand, choſen, called and created anew in Chriſt Jeſus, and all united in him, and members one of another, *v* 25 *Note*, They who are the ſervants of the ſame God, bought with the ſame blood and begotten by the ſame ſpirit, ſhould unite in love, lay aſide all animoſities, and with one mind and one mouth join in his worſhip and praiſe

Before Christ 714

C H A P XX

This chapter is a prediction of the captivity of the Egyptians and the Ethiopians by the king of Aſſyria Here is, 1 The ſign by which this was foretold, ver 1, 2 2 The explication of the ſign, ver 3—5 3 The uſe which the people of God ſhould make of it, ver 6

1 IN the year that a Tartan b came unto Aſhdod
(when Sargon the king of Aſſyria ſent him) and
fought againſt Aſhdod, and took it 2 At the ſame
time ſpake the LORD by Iſaiah the ſon of Amoz, ſaying,
Go, and looſe c the ſackcloth from off thy loins,
and put off thy ſhoe from thy foot and he did ſo,
d walking naked and barefoot 3 And the LORD ſaid,
Like as my ſervant Iſaiah hath walked naked and barefoot
e three years f *for* a ſign and wonder upon Egypt
and upon Ethiopia, 4 So ſhall the king of Aſſyria
lead away the Egyptians priſoners, and the Ethiopians
captives, young and old, naked and barefoot, g even
with *their* buttocks uncovered, to the † ſhame of Egypt
5 And h they ſhall be afraid and aſhamed of Ethiopia
their expectation, and of Egypt their glory 6 And
the inhabitant of this ‡ iſle ſhall ſay in that day, Behold,
ſuch *is* our expectation whither we flee for help
to be delivered from the king of Aſſyria and how
ſhall we eſcape ?

a 2 Kings xviii 17
b Ibid 8
c Zech xiii 4 Mat iii 4
d Mic i 8.
e Ezek iv 4—6
f Chap viii 18
g Jer xiii 22
† Heb. Nakedneſs.
h Chap xxx. 3, 7, 31 & xxxvi. 6
‡ Or, country Job xxii 30 Jer xlvii 4.

v 1—6 We have here,

1 The date of the prophecy, in the year of the ſiege of Aſhdod, or Azotus, *Acts* viii 40 by Tartan, one of the chief captains of the hoſts of Aſſyria, *whom Sargon, the king of Aſſyria, ſent*, which ſome ſuppoſe to be Salmanezer, and then this event will fall in the fourth year of Hezekiah, when Samaria was taken, 2 *Kings* xviii 9 Others think him to be Eſarhaddon, called Sarchedon, *Tob* i 21 and then it muſt fall about the twenty-ſecond year of Manaſſeh, but he is generally thought to be Sennacherib, among whoſe captains Tartan is reckoned, 2 *Kings* xviii 17 and the time about the fourteenth of Hezekiah

2 The ſign given of the deſtruction to be brought on Egypt and Ethiopia Iſaiah is commanded to take off his habit of ſackcloth, (which, as a prophet, he wore to ſignify his deadneſs to the ornaments of dreſs, or as mourning over the deſolations of Judah and Iſrael) to put off his ſhoes, and to walk naked, probably not abſolutely ſo, but ſtripped of his upper garment, and barefoot How long he continued to go thus is not certain, whether once, or three days, a day for a year, or three years, as our tranſlation ſeems to imply, though the three years rather refer to the prophecy, which ſhould be accompliſhed after that time, or ſo long the Aſſyrian king would employ in ſubduing them The prophet without heſitation, as a faithful ſervant, obeys the divine command, dangerous as it might be to his health, and however much it expoſed his perſon to contempt And God explains the ſign, as prefiguring the miſerable and ſhameful captivity of the Egyptians and Ethiopians, who ſhould thus be led away priſoners by the Aſſyrians, *v* 4 *Note*, (1) When duty calls we muſt truſt health, character, and all in God's hands If he ſays, Well done, good and faithful ſervant, it will infinitely overbalance every inconvenience or inſult we may have received (2) Miſerable is the plight of theſe poor captives, but how much more miſerable thoſe ſlaves of ſin, who are led captive by the devil at his will ? What confuſion will cover them, when in the preſence of God, his ſaints, and angels, the ſhame of their nakedneſs ſhall appear, and no eye pity them ?

3 The warning given the Jews of the folly of depending on theſe nations Ethiopia was their truſt, and Egypt the ally in which they gloried but now, afraid at the ruin of theſe potent neighbours, and confounded at ſeeing their ſupport thus removed, *the inhabitants of this iſle*, Judea ſo called, *ſhall ſay, Behold, ſuch is our expectation*, ſo vain, ſo fooliſh, *whither we flee* for help to thoſe who cannot help themſelves, and *how then ſhall we eſcape*, when mightier foes are unable to withſtand the victorious arms of the Aſſyrian army ? *Note*, Creature confidences will aſſuredly fail us, and they who have neglected to make God their refuge, in the day of calamity, will be abandoned to deſpair, and too late bewail their folly

C H A P

Before Christ 714

CHAP XXI.

In this chapter we have a prophecy of ſad times coming, 1 Upon Babylon, that it ſhould be deſtroyed by the Medes and Perſians, and that God's people ſhould receive benefit from it, ver 1—10 2 Upon Dumah, ver 11, 12 3 Upon Arabia, or Kedar, the deſolation of which country was very near, ver 13—17

1 THE burden of the deſert of the ſea [a] As whirl-
winds in the ſouth paſs through, *ſo* it cometh
from the deſert, from a terrible land 2 A grievous vi-
ſion is declared unto me, the treacherous dealer † dealeth
treacherouſly, and the ſpoiler ſpoileth [b] go up, O Elam
beſiege, O Media all the ſighing thereof have I made
to ceaſe 3 Therefore are my loins filled with pain,
[c] pangs have taken hold upon me, as the pangs of a wo-
man that travaileth I was bowed down at the hearing
of it, I was diſmayed at the ſeeing *of it* 4 My heart
panted, fearfulneſs affrighted me [d] the night of my
pleaſure hath he turned into fear unto me 5 [e] Prepare
the table, [f] watch in the watch-tower, eat, drink arise,
ye princes, *and* anoint the ſhield 6 For thus hath the
LORD ſaid unto me, Go, ſet a watchman, let him de-
clare what he ſeeth 7 And [g] he ſaw a chariot *with* a
couple of horſemen, a chariot of aſſes, *and* a chariot of
camels, and he hearkned diligently with much heed
8 And ‡ he cried, [h] A lion my lord, [i] I ſtand conti-
nually upon the watch-tower in the day-time, and I am
ſet in my ward whole nights 9 And behold, here
cometh a chariot of men, *with* a couple of horſemen
and he anſwered and ſaid, [k] Babylon is fallen, is fallen,
and [l] all the graven images of her gods he hath broken
unto the ground 10 [m] O my threſhing, and the § corn
of my floor that which I have heard of the LORD of
hoſts the God of Iſrael, have I declared unto you

a Zech ix 14
† Or, hath found a treacherous dealer and the ſpoiler or, that ſpoileth
Chap xxxiii 1 Mat vii 2
b Chap xiii 17 Jer li 11
c Chap xiii 8 Jer l 43
d Dan v 1, 30
e Dan v 2, &c
f Jer li 12
g Ver 9
‡ Or, he cried as a lion
h Jer l 14
i Hab ii 1
k Jer li 8 Rev xiv 8 & xviii 2
l Chap xlvi 1 Jer l 2 & li 44
m Jer li 33
§ Heb ſon

v 1—10 As Babylon was appointed for a houſe of bondage to God's people, to comfort them in their low eſtate, her deſtruction is repeatedly foretold, and when captives there, they may confidently expect to ſee her ruin, and their deliverance This prophecy is intitled, *The burden of the deſert*, or plain, *of the ſea*, as lying in a flat country, ſurrounded with rivers and lakes, and *a burden*, becauſe of the heavy doom denounced

1 The invaſion of the Medes is deſcribed, ſwift and reſiſtleſs as the whirlwind from the ſouth, ſweeping all before it *From the deſert it*, or *he*, *cometh*, Cyrus marching his troops through a deſert in his way to Babylon, *from a terrible land*, ſuch as Media was, producing fierce warriors, terrible to their enemies *A grievous viſion is declared to me*, full of wrath againſt the Chaldeans *The treacherous dealer dealeth treacherouſly, and the ſpoiler ſpoileth*, Belſhazzar, whoſe wickedneſs and oppreſſion of God's people brought deſtruction upon him Or, as ſome render the words, *the treacherous dealer* hath found *a treacherous dealer, and the ſpoiler one that ſpoileth*, the Babylonians being repaid in kind by the Perſians for their former ravages in Judea *Go up, O Elam, beſiege, O Media, all their ſighing hath he made to ceaſe*, either that of the Medes and Perſians, fatigued with the length of their march, and the labour of draining the river, in order to open a way into the city, or the ſighing of the captive Jews and others in Babylon, who, when the city was taken, regained their liberty

2 The diſtreſs of the king of Babylon is ſet forth under the image of a travailing woman, *v* 3, 4 Amidſt the revels of that fatal night, when rioting with his princes, the ſacred veſſels of the ſanctuary were prophaned, the hand-writing on the wall ſtruck with ſudden pangs the impious king, and ſpoke his approaching doom, which is ſcarce ſooner pronounced than executed, the city that very night being taken, and Belſhazzar ſlain *Note*, Though the midnight revels of pleaſure, and the board of drunkenneſs, may not be interrupted with ſuch a miraculous hand-writing on the wall, and ſinners, joyous and thoughtleſs, to dance and ſong devote the day, did they but ſee what is written in God's book, how quickly would their mirth, like Belſhazzar's, be turned into mourning, and their joy into heavineſs?

3 The entertainment is made ready at command, *v* 5 and whilſt they ſit around the feſtal board, the watch is ſet to prevent ſurprize, and in ſecurity they carouſe *Note*, The ſecurity of ſinners haſtens their ruin

4 In that critical moment the beſiegers are preparing for the aſſault The princes ariſe, the ſhields are ready, and ſudden deſtruction approaches, *v* 5

5 The prophet is appointed of God, as a watchman poſted on the walls, to declare what he ſees, *v* 6 On looking he beheld a chariot with two horſemen, perhaps alluding to Cyrus and Darius, and *a chariot of aſſes*, and *another of camels*, repreſenting the two nations of Medes and Perſians, and, on *hearkening diligently*, he perceived the ſound of the army ruſhing on the city, and *he cried*, *A lion*, Cyrus, for ſtrength and courage compared to that king of beaſts, haſting to ſeize the prey of Babylon Thus with unwearied vigilance, day and night, the prophet diſcharged his truſt, *v* 8 and now perceiving the chariot and horſemen above deſcribed, the Perſian and Median army under their generals entering the city, he cries, *Babylon is fallen, is fallen, and all the graven images of her gods he hath broken unto the ground*

In the ſtate and ruin of this proud city we have a figure of Babylon myſtical, which ſhall thus be ſurprized and deſtroyed, and many of the expreſſions in the *Revelations* are borrowed from this deſcription, *Rev* xvii 1—15 xviii 2, 7, 8 xiv 8

6 The prophet addreſſes the people of God, aſſuring them of the certainty of the events he foretold He calls them, *My threſhing*, either as being ſmitten with God's word, or afflicted by his providences, *and the corn of my floor*, as dear and valuable to him, and carefully preſerved, as the choiceſt wheat, when the chaff is winnowed away *Note*, (1) God's deareſt children have the ſharpeſt trials, but it is only to purify and cleanſe them (2) The church is God's floor, where the faithful, his corn, are collected, whilſt all falſe profeſſors and careleſs ſinners are the chaff, which will be burnt with unquenchable fire (3) What miniſters receive from God they muſt carefully and diligently deliver, keeping back from the people nothing of the whole counſel of God

11 ¶ [n] The burden of Dumah He called to me out
of Seir, Watchman, what of the night? watchman,
what of the night? 12 The watchman ſaid, The morn-
ing cometh, and alſo the night if ye will enquire, en-
quire ye return, [o] come

n Jer xlix 7 Ezek xxxv 2 Obad 1
o Luke xiii 3
p Chap lv 6

v 11, 12 We have here,

1 The burden of Dumah, which ſome ſuppoſe a part of Arabia, *See Gen* xxv 14 but more generally it is interpreted Idumea What temporal judgment it referred to is uncertain, probably they ſuffered with their neighbours from the Aſſyrian army

2 A queſtion put by one of mount Seir, *Watchman, what of the night? watchman, what of the night?* what hour, how much remains, or *what from the night?* what tidings? what danger? The queſtion is repeated, as from a perſon eager to be reſolved; or from ſeveral coming quickly after each other, ſo great is their anxiety, that a ſecond calls before the watchman can anſwer the firſt *Note*, (1) Every miniſter is a watchman; he is to ſpread the alarm, and the people are to enquire at his mouth (2) It is a mercy when a ſenſe of danger drives us to a ſollicitous enquiry how to eſcape (3) Every ſoul is by nature in darkneſs, till Chriſt, the Sun of righteouſneſs, ariſes with healing in his wings (4) The people of God experience dark nights of temptation, affliction, deſertion, and wait for a returning ſenſe of God's light and love, more eagerly than they who look for the morning

3 *The watchman ſaid, The morning cometh*, ſome reſpite from the calamity Or, if we ſuppoſe the queſtion put by a proſelyte Idumean, waiting for the conſolation of Iſrael under the darkneſs of the Moſaic diſpenſation, the anſwer is, that the morning cometh, when Chriſt, the day-ſtar, ſhould ariſe, and light and joy be diffuſed by his goſpel But he adds, *and the night alſo*, their ruin by the army of the Aſſyrians Or, taken more generally, it may imply a ſtate of perſecution ſucceeding the firſt propagation of the goſpel, or a ſtate of darkneſs in the church, when the prevalence of mahomediſm and popery ſhould almoſt utterly extinguiſh the light of truth *If ye will enquire, enquire ye* diligently and earneſtly, by prayer, meditation, reading God's word, and conſulting his miniſters, in order to *return* and *come* to him, either to God, by repentance under the affliction, or to the watchman, for conſtant information and advice *Note*, (1) In the day of proſperity we muſt not forget to prepare for the night of adverſity (2) If the morning of our life be loſt in vanity, the night of age and death will ſurprize us unprepared for eternity (3) The ſoul that is enquiring after Chriſt, is already come to the dawning of the day (4) The goſpel preaches free grace, whoſoever will, let him come, and welcome, to Jeſus Chriſt (5) Since our time is ſo ſhort, it ſhould quicken our diligence to improve it we have no moment to ſpare

13 ¶ [q] The burden upon Arabia In the foreſt in
Arabia ſhall ye lodge, O ye travelling companies of
Dedanim 14 The inhabitants of the land of Tema
‖ brought water to him that was thirſty, ‖ they pre-
vented with their bread him that fled 15 For they fled
from the ſwords, from the drawn ſword, and from the
bent bow, and from the grievouſneſs of war 16 For
thus hath the LORD ſaid unto me, Within a year, [r] ac-
cording to the years of an hireling, and all the glory of

q Jer xlix 28
‖ Or, bring ye
‖ Or, prevent with your bread, &c
r Chap xvi 14

Before Christ 712

Kedar shall fail 17 And the residue of the number of
|| archers, the mighty men of the children of * Kedar
shall be diminished for the LORD God of Israel hath
spoken it

|| Heb bows
* Ps cxx 5 Chap l 7

v 13—17 As they lying in the way of the Assyrian army, it is probable their detachments ravaged the country, or subdued it, as they advanced towards Judea

1 The miserable case of the travelling companies of Dedanim is set forth, (they were descendants of Abraham, by Keturah, as Tema and Kedar were of Ishmael, *Gen* xxv 3—15) terrified by the sword of the Assyrians, they fled to the forest to save themselves from the grievousness of war, *v* 15 They are called *travelling companies*, because their traffic was carried on by large caravans, or alluding to their wandering life in tents and herds, without any settled abode, *v* 13 In their distress their friendly neighbours supplied them, fainting and famished, with bread and water, or as the margin reads it, they are commanded to do so, *v* 14 such kind compassion being ever due to the afflicted

2 Kedar shares the same fate, *v* 16, 17 All their glory, their riches, their flocks and herds plundered, and their mighty warriors, that stood to defend their country, diminished by the sword of the Assyrians, and few men left So poor and uncertain a thing is this world's glory, so easily tarnished, and our abundance often proving our ruin, and exposing us to dangers we otherwise might have escaped

3 The time is fixed for their ruin *within one year, according to the years of an hireling*, who precisely marks the day when his contract expires And since Israel's God affirms it as sure, his people are warned not to trust on Arabia as friends, or to fear them as foes

CHAP XXII

We have here, 1 The distress of Jerusalem, probably on Sennacherib's invasion, ver 1—7 2 Their weakness exposed, and vain confidence, ver 8—11 3 Their unhumbled state, ver 12—14 4 The change in Hezekiah's court, by the displacing of Shebna, and the advancement of Eliakim, ver 15—25

712

a Ps cxxv 2

1 THE burden of a the valley of vision What
aileth thee now, that thou art wholly gone up
to the house tops? 2 Thou that art full of stirs, a
tumultuous city, b a joyous city thy slain *men are* not
slain with the sword, nor dead in battle 3 All thy
rulers are fled together, they are bound || by the archers
all *that are* found in thee are bound together, *which*
have fled from far 4 Therefore said I, c Look away
from me, I will weep bitterly, labour not to comfort
me, because of the spoiling of the daughter of my
people 5 For d *it is* a day of trouble, and of treading
down, and of perplexity by the Lord GOD of hosts
in the valley of vision, e breaking down the walls, and
of crying to the mountains 6 And f Elam bare the
quiver with chariots of men *and* horsemen, and Kir
uncovered the shield 7 And it shall come to pass
that thy choicest valleys shall be full of chariots, and
the horsemen shall set themselves in array || at the gate

b Chap xxxii 13
|| Heb Of or from the bow
c Jer ix 19 & iv Luke xix 41
d Chap xxxvii 3
e 2 Kings xxv 4
f Jer xlix 35
|| Or to wards

v 1—7 The object of this prophecy is the burden of the valley of vision, alluding to the name of Jerusalem, which signifies the vision of peace, or because that was the place where God made known his will in visions to the prophet It is called a valley, the hills surrounding it on every side, and the vision is a burden, a heavy calamity, though not utterly consuming, yet greatly terrifying them

1 Their consternation at the approach of the Assyrian army is great, running to the tops of their houses, to see if any help was at hand, or to observe the approach of the enemy, *full of stirs* or *cries*, preparing to oppose their invaders, or *thou that art full of stirs*, the streets crowded with people, *a tumultuous city*, populous and noisy with the din of trade, *a joyous city*, rich and revelling But now the voice of mirth is ceased, the horrid sound of war is heard alone, and fear and consternation are spread abroad Though the sword had not reached them, the famine was felt, or the fright they were put into, sunk them spiritless, as if thrust through with a sword, *v* 2 Nor was this panic among the people only, their rulers increased it, flying from all the neighbouring cities to Jerusalem, without attempting to defend them, *chap* xxxvi 1 or many of Jerusalem, instead of encouraging the people, thought only to secure themselves by flight instead of preparing for a vigorous defence, they surrendered themselves to be bound, or were so disheartened, that they had not courage to draw an arrow as it may be rendered, *bound by the bow*, *v* 3 *Note*, The alarm of war is terrible;

may we never, by our abuse of the blessings of peace, provoke God to bring the scourge upon us, for, if under his wrath, our dispirited fleets and armies could yield us small protection

Before Christ 712

2 Great is the prophet's grief at the scene of desolation before him He desires his friends not to attempt to comfort him, but to leave him bitterly to weep over the spoiling of the daughter of his people, *v* 4 and abundant cause there is for his tears, when trouble is on every side, the people as mire in the streets trodden down by the Assyrians, the walls of the fortified cities battered into dust, all the land full of distress and perplexity, and the Lord's correcting hand seen in the judgment adds bitterness to the affliction, *v* 5 *Note*, (1) Every good man is a patriot, and when he can do no more to save his country, will weep over its ruins (2) Whatever we feel of afflictions from man, we must look farther to the hand of God who sends them

3 The vast hosts, composed of different nations, Persians, and Medes, which were in Sennacherib's army, fill the country with chariots and horsemen, and prepare for the siege of Jerusalem, make ready their shields, and place their advanced guard, to intercept any going in, or coming out of the gates of the city, *v* 6, 7 How melancholy a change to see those valleys, once so thick with corn, now yield an iron harvest of erected spears

8 ¶ And he discovered the covering of Judah, and
thou didst look in that day to the armour of g the house
of the forest 9 h Ye have seen also the breaches of the
city of David, that they are many and ye gathered together
the waters of the lower pool 10 And ye have
numbred the houses of Jerusalem, and the houses have ye
broken down to fortify the wall 11 Ye made also a
ditch between the two walls, for the water of the old
pool but ye have not looked unto i the maker thereof,
neither had respect unto him that fashioned it long
ago 12 And in that day did the Lord GOD of hosts
call to weeping and to mourning, and k to baldness, and
to girding with sackcloth 13 And behold, joy and
gladness, slaying oxen, and killing sheep, eating flesh,
and drinking wine, l let us eat and drink, for to morrow
we shall die 14 And m it was revealed in mine
ears by the LORD of hosts, n Surely this iniquity shall
not be purged from you, till ye die, saith the Lord
GOD of hosts

g 1 Kings vii 2 & x 17
h 2 Chron xxxii 4, 5
i Chap xxxvii 26.
k Ibid xv 2 Mic i 16
l Chap lvi 12 Wisd ii 6 1 Cor. xv 32
m Chap v 9
n 1 Sam iii 14 Ezek. xxiv 13

v 8—14 When recovered a little from their terrors they began to think what was to be done *He discovered the covering of Judah*, either Hezekiah opened his magazines, or God detected their hypocrisy in this time of danger, by the temper they discovered, or rather Sennacherib having taken the surrounding fortresses that covered the city, came in full view of it, ready to begin the siege Hereupon we are told,

1 The steps they took to put Jerusalem in a posture of defence Their first concern was to arm the people, for which purpose, the armoury of the house of the forest of Lebanon, built by Solomon, 1 *Kings* vii 2 is opened, they next surveyed the fortifications, and set themselves to repair the breaches of the fortress, called the city of David, 2 *Sam* v 7 which in times of peace had been greatly neglected To secure plenty of water, they collected together those of the lower pool, and having raised another wall, drew the water out of the old pool into the ditch between the walls, to strengthen the place, as well as to distress the enemy for want of it The houses are numbered, that each may furnish its quota of men, money, or provisions, for the use of the soldiery, and those in the suburbs, which might facilitate the approaches of the besiegers, or too near the wall within, so as to prevent an easy communication from one part to another, are demolished, and the materials applied to strengthen the walls *Note*, (1) In times of danger we must exert our utmost efforts, and trust God with the issue (2) Times of peace are often times of waste, because war seems distant, a provision against it is neglected, and that is a temptation to the enemy to attack us unprepared

2 Amidst their warlike preparations they neglected the God of war they fortified the city, but forgot the maker of it, without whom, the watchman waketh in vain Their king indeed looked up to him, 2 *Kings* xviii 5 2 *Chron* xxxii 8 but his irreligious council, with Shebna at their head, seemed to have no thought of divine assistance, and trusted only to the arm of flesh *Note*, Though a king may make religion fashionable, by espousing the profession of it, it is not in their power to convert the heart A greater King than they must come, or their courtiers, though complaisantly submissive, will be mere outward conformists, not internal converts

3 Their unhumbled temper under the visitation is remarked to their shame God called to weeping and mourning, *&c* the expressive signs of true penitential sorrow, to produce which, was the great end of their affliction, and his prophets recom-

Before Christ 712

seconded the providence with their preaching, but vain was the call Having, as they thought, secured the city, they set danger at defiance, and mirth, jollity, and riot reigned, they treated the prophetic warnings with contempt, and since the prophet urged their danger, and death at their door, as an argument to humble their souls in sorrow, for their sins before God, they, with infidel disregard, made it a plea for their impiety, *let us eat and drink, for to morrow we die*, it is but a short life, let it be a merry one, and disbelieving the doctrine of a future state, appeared fearless of the consequences of their sins, 1 Cor xv 32 *Note*, (1) A life of pleasure naturally leads to a state of infidelity (2) They who risk eternity on the miserable hope that at death their being is at an end, will find too late their dreadful delusion

4 God, in displeasure against such impiety, denounces his wrath on these proud mockers, v 14 They contemned the prophet's warning, but they shall feel the wrath they despised, *and neither in this world, or that which is to come, should* their iniquity ever be forgiven Mark the end of impiety and infidelity

15 ¶ Thus saith the Lord GOD of hosts, Go, get
thee unto this treasurer, *even* unto Shebna, which *is*
over the house, *and say*, 16 What hast thou here? and
whom hast thou here, that thou hast hewed thee out a
a 2 Sam xviii 18 sepulchre here *as he* a that heweth him out a sepulchre
on high, *and* that graveth an habitation for himself in
a rock? 17 Behold, the LORD will carry thee a-
b Esth vii 8 way with a mighty captivity, and will surely b cover
thee 18 He will surely violently turn and toss thee,
† Heb a country large of spaces *like* a ball into † a large country there shalt thou die,
and there the chariots of thy glory *shall be* the shame of
thy lord's house 19 And I will drive thee from thy
c Psal lx 5 station, and c from thy state shall he pull thee down
20 ¶ And it shall come to pass in that day, that I
d 2 Kings xviii 18 will call my servant d Eliakim the son of Hilkiah 21
e Ps xlv 4 And I will e clothe him with thy robe, and strengthen
f Chap xi 5 him with f thy girdle, and I will commit thy g govern-
g Isa ix 6 ment into his hand, and he shall be a father to the in-
habitants of Jerusalem, and to the house of Judah 22
h Rev iii 7 And h the key of the house of David will I lay upon
his shoulder so he shall open, and none shall shut, and
he shall shut, and none shall open 23 And I will
i Ezra ix 8 fasten him i *as* a nail in a sure place, and he shall be
k Rev iii 21 for a k glorious throne to his father's house 24 And
they shall hang upon him all the glory of his father's
house, the offspring and the issue, all vessels of small
‡ Or instruments of viols quantity from the vessels of cups, even to all the ‡
vessels of flagons 25 In that day, saith the LORD
of hosts, shall the nail *that is* fastened in the sure place
l Verse 3 be removed, and be cut down and fall, and l the burden
that *was* upon it shall be cut off for the LORD hath
spoken *it*

v 15—25 We have here a prophecy of a domestic occurrence in the household of Hezekiah, which foretells the disgrace of Shebna, and the advancement of Eliakim What was Shebna's particular crime which occasioned his being degraded, does not appear the Jews say he was a traitor, and had agreed to give up the city to the Assyrians, but being disappointed in the *attempt, was carried away captive by them, and severely used* for deceiving them

1 His fall is declared to him by Isaiah, v 15 Though a great man, and high in office, both treasurer and steward of the household, he is not too great to be faithfully admonished *What hast thou here?* what estate, or what business? being, it is supposed, a foreigner promoted by Ahaz, and continued in office by Hezekiah, to whose reformation he conformed, and *whom hast thou here?* or what friend to prevent thy ruin, or what family, *that thou hast hewed thee out a sepulchre?* an habitation in a rock, with a stately monument erected over it, where his remains, with pomp, must be deposited vain preparation! when doomed to captivity, sudden and terrible, and covered as a criminal led to execution, v 17 Tossed to and fro, as a ball in that strange land, he should lead a wretched life, and die there, destitute of all his former splendor, a shame to his master's house, to Ahaz, who promoted him, v 18 Suspected, probably before, and now degraded by Hezekiah, he shall fall from his high station, in which he seemed fixed as a nail in a sure place, and all his dependents and followers, as is the case when favourites are disgraced, sink with him, v 19, 25 *Note*, (1) High places are slippery, they who seem most firmly fixed, are often nearest the precipice of ruin (2) Pride looks even to the tomb, and the lying monument is taught to flatter, when the corpse is turning to putrefaction (3) A faithful minister of God must not fear to deliver his message boldly to the greatest, however offensive it may appear

2 Eliakim's advancement is foretold, a faithful servant of God, promoted at his instigation, who inclined Hezekiah to put so worthy a man in Shebna's stead, v 20 and it would be a deep mortification to the disgraced minister, to see the ensigns of office he wore, now transferred to another, the robe, the girdle, and the key, v 21 A worthy magistrate would he prove, a father to the people, strengthened of God to discharge the trust reposed in him, v 21 having the entire management of affairs committed to him, v 22 fixed in his office through God's blessing, an honour to his family, v 23 and kindly regarding them, from the least unto the greatest, and according to their several abilities and capacities, employing and rewarding them, v 24 *Note*, (1) When preferment comes, not hunted down by sollicitation in the way of pride and covetousness, but unsought for from the hand of providence, and conferred as the wages of desert, then it is truly honourable (2) When God calls us into office, we may expect from *him strength to discharge it* (3) They who would rule well, must regard their subjects as children display parental affection with authority, and shew that the great end of all they do, is the public good and then *Pater patriae*, the father of their country, will be their most honourable title (4) The higher the office, the heavier the burden, and the greater diligence, fidelity, and zeal is required to discharge it (5) Eliakim was herein the type of the Lord Jesus, the servant of God, emphatically so called, *chap* xlii 1 appointed by his Father to the office of ruler in his church, and upheld by him in the discharge of his arduous undertaking, invested with the ensign of royalty, and possessed of all power, having the keys of wisdom and grace to unlock the treasures of his word, the keys of heaven, to open the kingdom to all believers, and of death and hell, which he shuts, and none can open, he opens, and none can shut. His government is fixed and established for ever, he is the brightness of his Father's glory, his people's happiness and honour are derived from him, and careful of the interests of his spiritual offspring, from the least to the greatest they receive out of his fulness, according to their wants and capacities are supported by him, so that they cannot fall and perish, and have a mansion eternal in the heavens provided for them among the houshold of God

CHAP XXIII

Tyre, the great mart of nations, had been closely allied with Israel, but must fall with it In this chapter is foretold, 1 The lamentable desolation of Tyre, by Nebuchadnezzar, about the same time that he destroyed Jerusalem, ver 1—14 2 Its restoration after seventy years, and return to trade again, ver 15—18

715
1 THE burden of a Tyre b Howl, ye ships of Tar- a Jer xxv 22 & xlvii 4 Ezek xxvi 27 28
shish, for it is laid waste, so that there is no
house, no entring in from c the land of Chittim it is re-
vealed to them 2 Be still, ye inhabitants of the isle, Amos i 9 Zech ix 2
thou whom the merchants of Zidon that pass over the
sea, have replenished 3 And by great waters the seed b Ver 14 c Ver 12
of Sihor, the harvest of the river *is* her revenue, and d Ezek
d she is a mart of nations 4 ¶ Be thou ashamed, O xxvii 3
Zidon, for the sea hath spoken, *even* the strength of the
sea, saying, I travail not, nor bring forth children, nei-
ther do I nourish up young men, *nor* bring up virgins
5 e ‡ As at the report concerning Egypt, *so* shall they e Chap xix 16
be sorely pained at the report of Tyre 6 Pass ye over ‡ Or when
to Tarshish, howl ye inhabitants of the isle 7 *Is* this the report cometh to
your joyous *city*, whose antiquity *is* of ancient days? Egypt they shall &c
f her own feet shall carry her far off to sojourn 8 f Eccles x 7
Who hath taken this counsel against Tyre, the crowning
city, whose merchants *are* princes, whose traffickers *are*
the honourable of the earth? 9 The LORD of hosts
hath purposed it, || to stain the pride of all glory, *and* to || Heb to pollute
bring into contempt all the honourable of the earth
10 Pass through thy land as a river, O daughter of
Tarshish *there is* no more || strength 11 He stretch- || Heb girdle
ed out his hand over the sea, he shook the kingdoms Psal xxix
the LORD hath given a commandment § against § the
merchant *city*, to destroy the strong holds thereof 12 § Heb Canaan
And he said, Thou shalt no more rejoice, O thou op- g Rev xviii 22
pressed virgin, daughter of Zidon arise, pass over to
h Chittim, there also shalt thou have no rest 13 Be- h Ver 1
hold the land of the Chaldeans, this people was not *till*
the Assyrian founded it for them that dwell in the wil-
derness they set up the towers thereof, they raised up ‡ Or shall hurt
the palaces thereof, *and* he ‡ brought it to ruin 14
i Howl, ye ships of Tarshish for your strength is laid i Ver 1
waste

Before Christ 715

v 1—14 Tyre was a city in Phœnicia, of great antiquity, and the grand mart of trade for all the commodities of the East and West It stood on an island, about half a mile from the sea, strongly fortified by art and nature, and deemed impregnable but when God hath a controversy with any people, their strength is weakness We have here,

1 Her prosperity She was a mart of nations, enriched by the traffick of all people, whose merchants resorted thither, at first by a colony from Zidon, a few leagues distant from Tyre, and therefore called her daughter, *v* 12 though soon eclipsing her mother city Thither the products of Egypt were carried, and her revenue increased with the harvest, which the river Sihor, or Nile, by overflowing, produced, *v* 3 A city full of wealth, and, as the sad effect of it, grown proud and haughty, *v* 9 A joyous city, where pleasure as well as business abounded, and sitting as a queen on the seas, her seat of empire seemed established for ever her citizens great as princes, and her merchants among the honourable of the earth, *v* 8 *Note, The ships which plow the main produce a larger harvest to a land, than the plough which breaks the soil*

2 Her fall by Nebuchadnezzar, after a siege of thirteen years, and then when it could hold out no longer, the inhabitants stripped the place of every thing valuable, and sailed away, leaving little but empty houses, and a naked rock The ships of Tarshish, which some suppose Tartessus, in Spain, and others Tarsus, in Cilicia, or more generally the ships of the sea of all nations, are called upon to howl over her desolations no house being left standing by the conqueror, nor is there any more entering into the port, her traffic being utterly ruined, *v* 1 *From the land of Chittim it is revealed to them*, the Tyrians are informed of the preparations made against them by the Babylonians, or there is *no entering in from the land of Chittim*, the merchants of Greece and Italy can no longer carry on their trade thither *it is revealed to them* that Tyre is destroyed In mournful silence the inhabitants would sit astonished at their overthrow, *v* 2 and Zidon her neighbour, and nearly connected with her, be ashamed, having placed such confidence in Tyre, that it could not be taken, but the waves of the sea carry the tidings, and this proud city, late *the strength of the sea*, so fortified and strengthned by it, bemoans her desolations, no longer full of inhabitants, and sending out her colonies to distant parts, but now a widow, bereaved of her children, *v* 4 Not Egypt's fall, though so potent a kingdom, would spread a greater terror, *v* 5 or, as the words may be rendered, *when the report cometh to the Egyptians, they will be in pain at the report of Tyre*, trembling for themselves, when this bulwark between them and the Chaldeans is fallen Hasting now to forsake the place, the inhabitants are enjoined to embark for Tarshish, and *her own feet shall carry her away*, those that should be seized by the conqueror, would be led into captivity, or this may signify her ships, whose oars and mariners would serve her instead of feet to escape, *v* 7 Swift as a river the merchants of Tarshish, who were at Tyre, or the people so called, are urged to hasten away, because the place is no longer defensible, and is ready to fall, *v* 10 Thus for a season her joy should be silenced *The oppressed virgin, the daughter of Zidon*, that had never been conquered before, must pass over to the isles of Chittim, Greece or Italy, or the islands of Corsica, Sardinia, and Sicily, where colonies of the Tyrians were planted, and yet even there *thou shalt have no rest*, these countries being doomed to fall under the yoke of their enemies *Note*, (1) When God pursues, there is no flying from our misery (2) They who think themselves most secure, feel the heavier anguish in their falls

3 If it be asked, who hath taken this counsel against Tyre, *v* 8 the answer is, one that is fully able to execute his designs, the Lord of Hosts, who would abase their pride, and stain all human glory, that others, warned by their fall, might be admonished of the vanity of every temporal possession, and the folly of being proud, and trusting on that which can profit so little in the day of wrath As he did of old, when Egypt was smitten under his mighty hand, *v* 11 so hath he now given commandment to the destroyer, and is pleased to use the Chaldean sword Though *this people was not* of note and figure *till the Assyrian founded it for them that dwelt in the wilderness*, who drove out the original inhabitants of Mesopotamia, and transplanted thither the Chaldeans, who before dwelt scattered in the wilderness, *they set up the towers thereof, they raised up the palaces* of Babylon, greatly augmenting and fortifying it, *he brought it*, or *he shall bring it, to ruin*, these Chaldeans shall be instruments to execute the divine judgments

15 And it shall come to pass in that day, that Tyre
shall be forgotten [k] seventy years, according to the days
of one king after the end of seventy years || shall
Tyre sing as an harlot 16 Take an harp, go about
the city, thou harlot that hast been forgotten, make
sweet melody, sing many songs, that thou mayst be remembered
17. ¶ And it shall come to pass after the
end of seventy years, that the LORD will visit Tyre,
and she shall turn to her hire, and shall commit fornication
with all the kingdoms of the world upon the face
of the earth 18 And [l] her merchandise, and her hire,
[m] shall be holiness to the LORD it shall not be treasured
nor laid up for her merchandise shall be for them
that dwell before the LORD, to eat sufficiently, and
for durable clothing

[k] Jer xxix 10
|| Heb It shall be unto Tyre, as the song of an harlot
[l] Chap ix 6
[m] Zech xiv 20, 21

Before Christ 715

v 15—18 The desolations of Tyre are not designed to be perpetual

1 Seventy years are appointed for the term of her captivity, as of the Jews, during the days of *one king*, or kingdom, for so long Nebuchadnezzar and his family reigned before Babylon was taken and on the conquest Cyrus made, these, among other captive nations, were permitted to resettle in their own country

2 On their return, Tyre is represented under the character of a harlot, returning from confinement, or recovering from sickness, when all her paramours had forsaken her, and resuming all her former arts to recover her trade, and to engage the return of her merchants, as a harlot with the harp, by her voice and music seeks to draw in her lovers, and enrich herself by the wages of her fornication and so far she would succeed, as to become again a general mart, and to increase her wealth, as in her former days of prosperity *Note*, (1) This world's wealth carries a harlot's smiles, and too often seduces the heart into spiritual whoredom (2) Though our case be reduced never so low, we need not despair when God will turn our captivity, he can bring back our lost prosperity

3 A better state than that of her worldly prosperity closes the prophecy In the days of the Messiah her gains should be employed in the service of his kingdom, to support the preachers of his gospel, and be consecrated to his glory, *v* 18 which was fulfilled, *Acts* xxi 3 when we find Christianity planted there, and according to the custom of the primitive church, 1 *Cor* xv 1 no doubt their being rich, contributed liberally to the necessities of the saints Some suppose from their acquaintance with the Jews in Babylon, and their prophets, they contracted a veneration for their God, and his worship; and on their return sent liberal presents to the temple, but the former sense seems preferable *Note*, (1) If God gives abundance, it becomes then a blessing, when he gives us withal a desire to employ it to his glory (2) The ministers of the sanctuary have a just claim to a liberal maintenance, and they who honour the master they serve, will be happy to support his ministers for his sake (3) They who devote themselves to God's work, must desire no great things in this world, if they have sufficient bread, and durable cloathing, they want not niceties and elegance

CHAP XXIV

In this chapter we have, 1 A threatning of desolating judgments for sin, ver 1—12 To which is added an assurance, that in the midst of them, good people should be comforted, ver 13—16 2 A further threatning of the like desolations, ver 16—22 to which is added an assurance, that in the midst of all God should be glorified, ver 23

1 BEhold the LORD maketh the earth empty, and 712.
maketh it waste, and | turneth it upside down,
and scattereth abroad the inhabitants thereof 2 And
[a] it shall be, as with the people, so with the ‡ priest,
as with the servant, so with his master, as with the maid,
so with her mistress, as with the buyer, so with the seller,
as with the lender, so with the borrower, as with
the taker of usury, so with the giver of usury to him
3 The land shall be utterly emptied, and utterly spoiled.
for the LORD hath spoken this word 4 The earth
mourneth *and* fadeth away, the world languisheth *and*
fadeth away, [b] || the haughty people of the earth do languish
5 [c] The earth also is defiled under the inhabitants
thereof because they have transgressed the laws,
changed the ordinance, broken the everlasting covenant
6 Therefore hath the curse devoured the earth,
and they that dwell therein are desolate therefore the inhabitants
of the earth are burned, and few men left 7
[d] The new wine mourneth, the vine languisheth, all the
merry hearted do sigh 8 [e] The mirth of tabrets ceaseth,
the noise of them that rejoice endeth, the joy of the
harp ceaseth 9 They shall not drink wine with a
song, strong drink shall be bitter to them that drink
it 10. [f] The city of confusion is broken down, every
house is shut up, that no man may come in 11 *There
is a* crying for wine in the streets, all joy is darkned,
the

| Heb Perverteth the face thereof
[a] Chap v 15 Hos 9
‡ Or prince
[b] Chap ii 12
|| Heb The height of the people
[c] Gen iii 17
[d] Chap xvi 8, 9 Joel i 10, 12
[e] Jer vii 34 & xvi 9 & xxv 10 Ezek xxvi 13 Hos ii 11 Rev xviii 22
[f] Chap xxvii 10.

Before Christ 712

the mirth of the land is gone 12 In the city [h] is left
deſolation, and the gate is ſmitten with deſtruction

g Amos viii 10
h Ps cxii 3?

v 1—12 The ſubject of this prophecy ſeems to be the earth in general laid under the deſolating judgments of God Some refer it to the ravages of Salmaneſer, and of Sennacherib, in Judea, others to the more extenſive conqueſts of Nebuchadnezzar The celebrated Vitringa ſuppoſes, it refers to the times of the Maccabees, perhaps it hath its fulfilment in the conſtant deſolations which, by wars, are made in the earth; and may foretel the ruin of Antichriſt

1 The earth, either the land of Judea in particular, or the world in general, is repreſented in ſuch confuſion and deſolation, as in its chaotic ſtate, emptied of inhabitants, as a veſſel turned upſide down, v 1 without diſtinction of age, ſex, ſtation, or office, v 2 utterly ſpoiled and waſted, v 3 mourning under the judgments inflicted, fading like a flower, languiſhing, as one under a ſevere diſeaſe, v 4 burnt up as with fire, and ſo deſolate, that few men remain, v 6 The proud and haughty are laid low before the heavy ſcourge, v 4 The fruit of the vine is deſtroyed by the inclement ſeaſons, or the trees cut down by the ravagers, and thoſe who ſpent in jollity the day, now ſigh out their inconſolable ſorrows, v 7 All joyful ſounds are baniſhed, and muſic is forgotten amidſt the dreary ſcene, v 8 The ſongs of the voice of feaſting are at an end, and ſtrong drink no longer pleaſant, when mingled with their tears, or become taſteleſs through their ſickneſs and diſeaſes, v 9 The city of confuſion is broken down, the houſes empty, the inhabitants ſlain by famine or the ſword, and none remaining, v 10 Reduced to the deepeſt diſtreſs, their ſtores fail them in the ſiege, their joys are fled, their hopes deſperate, v 11 Deſolation reigns through the city, and the defences are ruined, v 12 If this be applied to Judea, it paints the terrible deſtruction made by Nebuchadnezzar, or Antiochus, if to the fall of Antichriſt, we may ſee the like judgments predicted, *Rev* xi 13 xviii 2—22 It ſhould teach us, (1) The vanity of the creature, and the neceſſity of ſeeking a better portion, than that which is ſo tranſitory and uncertain (2) Death is making continually its ravages, we need be always ready (3) We ſhould rejoice as if we rejoiced not, when we ſtand thus daily in jeopardy, of having our joy turned into mourning (4) If the prieſt join the people in their iniquities, he will be the firſt and deepeſt in the puniſhment, which God threatens to inflict

2 The cauſe of this judgment is ſin, provoking moſt juſtly the divine wrath and indignation, v 5 They have tranſgreſſed God's laws, changed his ordinances and worſhip, in oppoſition to his preſcribed appointment, and broken the everlaſting covenant, and therefore the curſe of God terribly deſcends This was fully verified in the Jews, whoſe diſobedience to God's laws, and inſtituted ordinances of worſhip, brought on their ruin, and forfeited all the mercies promiſed in the everlaſting covenant of grace Nor leſs applicable is it to the Romiſh church, where diſpenſations for ſin give a licenſe for iniquity, and all the ordinances of Chriſt are corrupted, or mutilated, the ſcriptures themſelves perverted, and ſo far as human power can do it, an attempt made to break the everlaſting covenant of grace, and to prevent its becoming effectual to the ſalvation of the redeemed

13 ¶ When thus it ſhall be in the midſt of the land
among the people, [i] *there ſhall be* as the ſhaking of an
olive tree, *and* as the gleaning grapes when the vint-
age is done 14 They ſhall lift up their voice, they
ſhall ſing for the majeſty of the LORD, they ſhall cry
aloud from the ſea 15 Wherefore [k] glorify ye the
LORD, in the ‖ fires, *even* the name of the LORD God
of Iſrael in the iſles of the ſea

i Chap xvii 5 6
k 1 Pet ii 12 ?
‖ Or valleys

v 13—15 In the midſt of the deſolations threatned, a few eſcape the general ruin

1 They are like the berries left on the olive-tree, after it hath been ſpliſhed or ſhaken, and like the gleaning grapes, one here and there, that eſcaped obſervation, when the reſt were gathered for the vintage *Note*, (1) God hath a people, when iniquity is moſt prevalent (2) They are but few in any age, yet known by him, and dear to him (3) Whatever judgments he inflicts, they ſhall be hid in the day of his fierce anger

2 A ſenſe of the mercy manifeſted in their deliverance will awaken their gratitude and praiſe, v 14 Into whatever diſtant land they may have been diſperſed, *they ſhall ſing for the majeſty of the Lord*, magnified now in the deſtruction of their enemies *Note*, The people of God will never want matter for their praiſe In the days of deepeſt viſitation, to the godly there ariſeth up light in the darkneſs

3 They call upon to improve theſe judgments, exhorting each other *to glorify God in the fires*, or *the valleys*, in the ſharp ſtings of ſorrow, and the loweſt ſtate of abatement, acknowledging their ſuffering to be the juſt deſert of their ſins, and humbling themſelves for them before God, in the moſt diſtant iſles of the ſea, whither they fled *Note*, (1) They who are God's people, cannot but be zealous for his glory (2) When we are in the furnace of affliction, we have a peculiar call to confeſs our ways, and turn unto the Lord (3) We glorify God eſpecially, when in our deepeſt diſtreſſes we truſt his promiſes

This may be applied to the Jewiſh people, among whom, in the worſt times, God had a choſen few, and when he turned their captivity under Cyrus, they rejoiced over their oppreſſors fallen and in the places whither they had been diſperſed, glorified God for his mercy remembered in the midſt of judgment But it may alſo regard the faithful, under the oppreſſion of Antichriſt, preſerved for God, *Rev* xviii 4 rejoicing at the fall of Rome *Rev* xi 3 xix 1, 2 whereof the iſles of the ſea, and our own particularly, will be glad, and glorify God for his righteous judgments

16 ¶ From the uttermoſt part of the earth have we
heard [l] ſongs, *even* glory to the righteous but I ſaid,
† My leanneſs, my leanneſs, wo unto me the trea-
cherous dealers have dealt treacherouſly, yea, the trea-
cherous dealers have dealt very treacherouſly 17
[m] Fear, and the pit, and the ſnare *are* upon thee, O in-
habitant of the earth 18 And it ſhall come to paſs,
that he who fleeth from the noiſe of the fear, ſhall fall
into the pit; and he that cometh up out of the midſt of
the pit, ſhall be taken in the ſnare for [n] the windows
from on high are open, and [o] the foundations of the earth
do ſhake. 19 [p] The earth is utterly broken down, the
earth is clean diſſolved, the earth is moved exceedingly
20 The earth ſhall reel to and fro like a drunkard, and
[q] ſhall be removed like a cottage, and the tranſgreſſion
thereof ſhall be heavy upon it, and it ſhall fall, and
not riſe again 21 And it ſhall come to paſs in that
day, *that* [r] the LORD ſhall ‡ puniſh the hoſt of the high
ones *that are* on high, and the kings of the earth upon
the earth 22 And they ſhall be gathered together ‖ *as*
priſoners are gathered in the pit, and ſhall be ſhut up in
the priſon, and after many days ſhall they be § viſited
23 Then [s] the moon ſhall be confounded, and the
ſun aſhamed, when the LORD of hoſts ſhall reign in
mount Zion and in Jeruſalem, and before his ancients
† glorioully.

l Rev xv 3 & xix 1, &c.
† Heb. Leanneſs to me, or my ſecret to me
m 1 Kings xix 17 Jer xl viii 43, 44 Amos v 19
n Gen vii. 11
o Pſ xviii 7.
p Jer iv 23.
q Rev xx. 11
r Pſ lxxvi 12
‡ Heb Viſit upon
‖ Heb With the gathering of priſoners
§ Or found wanting
s Chap. xiii 10 Ezek xxxii 7 Joel ii 31 & iii 15
† Or in glory

v 16—23 To what particular event, theſe words relate, is dubious They may be well applied to the ruin of Babylon, and the joy of the Jews, on their return from thence, or to the conqueſts of the Maccabees over the armies of Antiochus, or, which ſeems a more noble view of the prophecy, to the triumphs of the ſaints, when Chriſt ſhall have ſubdued every foe, and ſhall reign over his ancients glorioully in the new Jeruſalem

1 The joy of the redeemed in all lands is heard, giving glory *to the righteous*, to the Lord Jeſus Chriſt, for the propagation of his goſpel, and the ſubdual of the enemies of the Chriſtian name, *Rev* xix 1—7 or *ſaying glory to the righteous* ones, who, oppreſſed and perſecuted as they had been, now will ſhine as ſtars in the firmament for ever and ever

2 The prophet mourns in the proſpect of the evil days, which ſhould precede the coming of Chriſt, v 16 when ſuch perfidy would reign among men, and ſo general a departure from God prevail, that he ſhould ſcarce *find faith in the earth* *Note*, The true prophets cannot behold a wicked world, without feeling diſtreſs for their impending miſeries

3 The perplexity and diſtreſs of men's minds, *Luke* xxi 25—35 at the approach of the day of Chriſt, are deſcribed by an elegant paronomaſia *Pachad, Pachath, Pach*, fear, the pit, the ſnare are upon thee, O inhabitant of the earth, no place affords ſhelter or refuge for the ſinner's ſoul *Note*, When the day of the Lord cometh, it will be too late to flee, and impoſſible to eſcape The way to prevent our terrors, is now to fly to the arms of Jeſus for pardon and grace, that then we may confidently appear before our judge

4 The deſtruction of the world is repreſented by expreſſions drawn from its diſſolution at the deluge It is utterly ſhaken in pieces, and reduced to its chaotic ſtate of confuſion, removed as a cottage, and doomed to eternal deſolations, for the heavy iniquity that lies thereon, v 18, 19 *Rev* xx 11 *Note*, Sin is the burden under which the world groans, unto this origin may every evil we ſuffer be traced, and for this is the curſe upon the earth, till the day it ſhall be utterly conſumed

5 As an introduction to that great day, God *will puniſh the hoſts of the high ones that are on high*, or *the army of that high one*, of the king of Babylon; or it may be the man of ſin, that exalteth himſelf above all that is called God, ſurrounded by an army of jeſuits, monks, and friars, his champions, *and the kings of the earth*, who have ſubjected themſelves under his dominion, and make war againſt the ſaints, to ſupport the uſurpations of the idolatrous church of Rome, *Rev* xvii 2—14 being vanquiſhed and ſubdued, they ſhall be ſhut up as priſoners in

Before Christ 712

in the pit, reſerved in chains of darkneſs to the judgment of the great day, when they ſhall finally receive their doom, *v* 22 See *Rev* xix. 21 xx 5—10

6 The glorious triumphs of the Redeemer will appear, when all the powers of earth are fallen before him, repreſented by the ſun and moon, or when theſe luminaries of heaven are blotted out, becauſe in the new Jeruſalem there will be no need of the light of the ſun or the moon, the Lamb being the light thereof, *Rev* xxi 23 then will he reign before *his ancients*, the ſaints of old, and all whoſe names are written in the book of life of the Lamb, from the foundation of the world, *gloriouſly*, or *his antients in glory*, reigning with him, and made to ſit down together on his eternal throne *Bleſſed and holy is he that hath part in the firſt reſurrection, on ſuch, the ſecond death hath no power*, Rev xx 6

C H A P. XXV.

After the threatnings of wrath in the foregoing chapter, we have, 1 *Thankful praiſes for what God had done*, ver 1—5 2 *Precious promiſes of what God would yet further do for his church*, ver 6, 7, 8 3 *The church's triumph in God over her enemies thereupon*, ver 9—12,

a Rev xix 1, 2
1 O LORD, thou art my God, I will exalt thee, [a] I
will praiſe thy name, for thou haſt done won-
derful things, *thy* counſels of old *are* faithfulneſs *and*
b Chap. xxi 9. Jer li 37 Rev xviii 2
truth 2 For thou haſt made [b] of a city, an heap, *of*
a defenced city, a ruin a palace of ſtrangers, to be no
city, it ſhall never be built 3 Therefore ſhall the
c Pſ lxxii 9, 10
ſtrong people glorify thee, the city of [c] the terrible na-
tions ſhall fear thee. 4 For thou haſt been a ſtrength to
d Chap iv 6 & xxxii 2
the poor, a ſtrength to the needy in his diſtreſs, [d] a refuge
from the ſtorm, a ſhadow from the heat, when the blaſt
of the terrible ones *is* as a ſtorm *againſt* the wall. 5
Thou ſhalt bring down the noiſe of ſtrangers, as the
heat in a dry place, *even* the heat with the ſhadow of
e Chap xiii 11
a cloud the branch of [e] the terrible ones ſhall be
brought low

v 1—5 We have here the triumphant ſong of God's people for their deliverance, whether of the Jews, for the ruin of Babylon, or of the redeemed at the laſt day, for the fall of ſpiritual Babylon, or of both, the former being typical of the latter

1 The prophet in the perſon of the redeemed reſolves to praiſe and exalt the name of God, for all his wondrous works of mercy to his people, and judgment on their enemies, according to his eternal counſels, and according to his faithfulneſs in the never-failing promiſes of his word And nothing would engage him to this honourable work ſo heartily, as the conſciouſneſs of an intereſt in the favour of this faithful and exalted Jehovah, *thou art my God, and I will praiſe thee* *Note*, (1) They who can ſay, *My God*, are bound to praiſe him evermore (2) The wonders of providence and creation are marvellous, but thoſe of redemption greater ſtill, and will be the everlaſting ſubject of the ſongs in glory

2 He particularly mentions two inſtances of God's faithfulneſs and truth, for which he would exalt him (1) For the deſtruction of the oppreſſor, *thou haſt made of a city, an heap*, &c *v* 2 As Babylon now is, Rome will be, the former was a *palace of ſtrangers*, chap xxiii 13 ſo is the latter, ſucceeding to the former Pagan inhabitants, and though profeſſing Chriſtianity, ſtrangers to the covenants of promiſe the one now lieth in ruins, and ſuch will the fate of the other be, to periſh for ever, and *never built* again (2) For the protection of the poor, *v* 4 whoſe ſtrength God is in every time of trial, covering them as with a cloud, from the ſcorching heat of temptation, and preſerving them from the ſtorm of the terrible ones, interpoſing as a wall, to ward off the tempeſt Thus God preſerved his people in Babylon, and brought them out ſafely, and ſo will do under all the perſecutions of Antichriſt, and in general, under every diſtreſs, his people who fly to him will find him *a very preſent help in trouble*

3 The effect of God's interpoſition would be either the humiliation and conviction, or the utter ruin of his foes They are *called ſtrong people, terrible nations, terrible ones*, but however dreadful they may appear to others, they muſt ſtoop before God, and bow in fear before his rod of correction, repenting and glorifying his mercy, or breaking under the rod of his judgments, and glorifying his juſtice *their branch*, or *their ſong*, brought low, either in the duſt of abaſement, or in the place of torment, where, as a branch caſt out, they would be burned, and their mirth be changed into eternal mourning *Note*, (1) The formidable appearance of our foes is often ready to intimidate us, but if the Almighty God be for us, the terrible ſhall be brought low, and even death, the king of terrors, be ſubdued (2) When the judgments of God, however heavy, lead men to fear before him, and do no more wickedly, they become the choiceſt bleſſings, and judgment, as well as mercy, ſhall then furniſh matter for a ſong

Before Christ 712

f Prov ix 2 Matt xxii 4
6 ¶ And in this mountain [f] ſhall the LORD of
† Or drawn from the lees
hoſts make unto all people a feaſt of fat things, a feaſt of
wines † on the lees, of fat things full of marrow, of wines
‡ Or face covering
on the lees well refined 7 And he will deſtroy in this
g 2 Cor iii 15 Eph iv 18
mountain the face of the ‡ covering caſt over all people,
and [g] the vail *that is* ſpread over all nations 8 He will
h Hoſ xiii 14 1 Cor xv 54 Rev xx 14 & xxi 4
[h] ſwallow up death in victory, and the LORD God will
i Rev vii 17 & xxi 4
[i] wipe away tears from off all faces, and the rebuke of
his people ſhall he take away from off all the earth. for
the LORD hath ſpoken *it* 9 ¶ And it ſhall be ſaid in
k John xx 28
that day, Lo, [k] this *is* our God, [l] we have waited for
l Gen xlix 18 Chap xxvi 8
him, and he will ſave us this *is* the LORD, we have
m Pſ xx 5 & xxi 1
waited for him, [m] we will be glad, and rejoice in his ſal-
vation 10 For in this mountain ſhall the hand of the
n Mal iv 3
LORD reſt, [n] and Moab ſhall ‖ be troden down under
‖ Or threſhed
him, even as ſtraw is troden down for the dunghill 11
And he ſhall ſpread forth his hands in the midſt of them,
as he that ſwimmeth ſpreadeth forth *his hands* to ſwim
o Chap xvi 6 Jer xlviii 29
and he ſhall bring down [o] their pride together with the
ſpoils of their hands 12 And [p] the fortreſs of the high
p Chap xxvi 5
fort of thy walls ſhall he bring down, lay low, *and*
bring to the ground, *even* to the duſt.

v 6—12 We have a key to open this ſcripture, 1 *Cor* xv 54 and ſee therein ſome of the great and precious promiſes of life and immortality brought to light by the goſpel

1 Under the image of a royal feaſt, *Matt* xxii 1 a view is preſented to us of the goſpel-diſpenſation *The Lord of hoſts*, the Lord Jeſus, the great maſter of the feaſt *in this mountain*, the church of his redeemed, *makes unto all people a feaſt*, ſome of all nations will partake of it, Gentiles as well as Jews, and the invitation thereto is general, *whoſoever will, let him come*, there is here enough and to ſpare, *for it is a feaſt of fat things, full of marrow, and of wine on the lees well refined*, plenty, and of the beſt ſort, is provided, there is nothing wanting that a ſoul hungring and thirſting after righteouſneſs can need, pardon, peace, grace, ſtrength, conſolation, glory, all are ready, and a more refreſhing proviſion to the ſoul, than the beſt ſpread table to the famiſhed, or than the ſtrongeſt wines to the faint Bleſſed and happy are they, who are called to this feaſt!

2 The Lord Jeſus *will alſo deſtroy in this mountain the face of the covering caſt over all people* as malefactors led to execution with their faces covered, ſo had the ſons of men by ſin forfeited their lives to divine juſtice, or as the dead wrapped in grave cloaths, ſo were we dead in treſpaſſes and ſins, till Chriſt came to redeem us from going down to the pit, by paying the ranſom for us, and to reſcue us from the death of ſin by his quickning ſpirit *and the vail which is ſpread over all nations* of groſs darkneſs and ſpiritual ignorance, now diſpelled before him the light of life, like the ſhadows of the night before the riſing ſun

3 Even death itſelf ſhall be a vanquiſhed foe *He will ſwallow up death in victory*, not only by his own reſurrection leading captivity captive, and quickning his people dead in treſpaſſes and ſins, but by the final deſtruction of death, when all the bodies that ſleep in duſt ſhall riſe at the great day of Jeſus' appearing and glory, and eſpecially thoſe of his ſaints be raiſed to glory and honour, and mortality be thus ſwallowed up of life *Note*, (1) What joy and conſolation doth the faith of Jeſus impart, that thus enables us to triumph over the king of terrors, and cry, *O death, where is thy ſting?* (2) Whatever burdens this corruptible body feels now, we may well ſay they are light afflictions, but for a moment, and may patiently and cheerfully endure them, becauſe then hope in the end of a glorious reſurrection

4 All grief and ſhame will then be done away As a tender parent, our divine Lord ſhall dry up his children's tears, no ſins will then awaken their ſorrows, or afflictions diſturb their repoſe, no reproach blacken their character, or oppreſſor vex and grieve them, but everlaſting joy be upon their heads, their beauty of holineſs without ſpot, and clothed with glory, their enemies will behold them, and wonder and periſh How light then ſhould every ſorrow ſit, how eaſy ought we to be under the malignant aſperſions, or perverſe unkindneſs of men, when we ſhall in a moment come to endleſs bliſs, and ſhine as ſtars in the firmament for ever and ever?

5 Great will be the joy of the redeemed in that day By faith and hope, they often triumphed here below, but the conſummation of their bliſs in glory they waited and devoutly wiſhed for And lo! glad tidings of great joy He is come! he is come! *this is our God*, our Jeſus, our ſalvation, our joy, eternity ſhall hear his praiſe, *v* 9 *Note*, (1) They who by faith wait in hope, ſhall not be diſappointed (2) In glory all the praiſe will be aſcribed to Jeſus, and every crown be laid at his bleſſed feet

6 The perpetuity of this bleſſedneſs is enſured by the Lord's dwelling in the midſt of his people In this mountain his hand ſhall reſt, his preſence be ever manifeſted, his power employed to

Before Christ 712

preſerve them, and all his goodneſs to make them eternally happy

7 The enemy ſhall be utterly deſtroyed Moab, the repreſentative of all the foes of God's church and people, ſpiritual and temporal, ſhall be trodden down, as mire in the ſtreet, *v* 10 As the ſwimmer ſpreads his hands, ſo will the Lord ſtretch forth his arm of vengeance, executing his judgment on the proud, and ſpoiling the ſpoiler, *v* 11 All the fortreſſes of Moab ſhall fall, and their utter deſtruction be certain, ſudden, and irrecoverable, *v.* 12 And thus ſhall all the Antichriſtian powers periſh at laſt, and Satan, Death, and Hell, be caſt together into the burning lake, *Rev* xix 20 xx 14, 15

CHAP XXVI

This chapter is a ſong of holy joy and praiſe, it is prepared to be ſung when the foregoing prophecy ſhould be accompliſhed The people of God are taught, 1 To rejoice in their ſafety under the divine protection, ver 1—4 2 To triumph over all oppoſition, ver 5, 6 3 To walk with God, and wait for him in the worſt of times, ver 7, 8, 9 4 To lament the ſtupidity of thoſe who regard not the providence of God, either merciful or afflictive, ver 10, 11 5 To aſcribe to God all the good that is in them, and the victories that are obtained for them, ver 12, 14 and to engage themſelves to continue in his ſervice, ver 13 6 To recollect God's dealings with them, and their own zeal and earneſtneſs in afflictions, ver 15—18 7 To rejoice in hope of a glorious reſurrection, ver 19 and of preſent ſecurity, whilſt God puniſhes the wicked, ver 20, 21

a Chap. xxv 6 b Ma. xvi 18 Rev xxi 2 c Chap lx 18 Zech ii 5 d Pſ cxviii 19 20 † Heb Peace, peace e Rom iv 20, 21 f Pſ xxxvii 40 g Chap xlv 17 ‡ Heb Jah Pſ lxviii 4 || Heb The rock of ages Deut xxxii 4

1 IN [a] that day ſhall this ſong be ſung in the land of
Judah, We have [b] a ſtrong city, [c] ſalvation will
God appoint *for* walls and bulwarks. 2 [d] Open ye the
gates, that the righteous nation which keepeth the truth
may enter in 3 Thou wilt keep *him* in † perfect
peace, [e] *whoſe* mind *is* ſtayed *on thee* [f] becauſe he truſt-
eth in thee 4 Truſt ye in the LORD for ever for
[g] in the LORD ‡ JEHOVAH *is* || everlaſting
ſtrength

v 1—4 The work of heaven is everlaſting praiſe, and the redeemed delight to begin the ſervice upon earth We have here the ſong which, in the latter day, ſhall be ſung in the land of Judah, the church of the firſt-born, whoſe names are written in heaven

1 God hath prepared for his people a city, his church, or the new Jeruſalem, *Rev* xxi 2—11 *a ſtrong city*, againſt which the gates of hell cannot prevail It needs no human defences, when God himſelf is in the midſt of her, and *his ſalvation her walls and bulwarks*, *v* 1 *Note*, They are ſafe lodged who have fled to Jeſus, the city of refuge, and have God's everlaſting promiſes for their protection

2 He commands the gates to be opened for the admiſſion of the righteous nation, that keepeth the word of his truth All that in Jeſus Chriſt the way, the truth, and the life, draw near to God, are now accepted as righteous, welcome to partake of the ordinances of his church below, and ſhall have hereafter an entrance miniſtered to them abundantly, into the everlaſting kingdom of our God and Saviour above

3 The prophet exults in the ſecurity of thoſe who thus receive and truſt God's promiſes *Thou wilt keep him in perfect peace, whoſe mind is ſtayed on thee*, peace with God, peace of conſcience, peace under every provocation, peace in every trial, peace that paſſeth all underſtanding ſhall the ſoul enjoy, that is content to truſt his all in the hands of Jeſus Lord increaſe our faith! increaſe our peace!

4 He exhorts at all times to exerciſe faith in the Saviour, and under all difficulties to truſt on his blood, and his righteouſneſs for pardon and acceptance, on his grace for ſtrength, on his promiſes for perſeverance, and he will never diſappoint our hopes, for in the Lord Jah Jehovah is *everlaſting ſtrength*, or *the rock of ages*, he is able to ſave to the uttermoſt; from his everlaſting arms none can pluck us, fixed on him, we ſhall be immoveable, ſince the rock of ages is our foundation *Note*, Had we a heart to truſt God more firmly, we ſhould certainly find cauſe to praiſe him more frequently and joyfully

h Chap xxv 12 i Jer l 45 ‖ Or the way of the Lord is the juſt is even neſſes k Pſ xi 4 l Chap lxiv 5 m Cant. iii 1

5 ¶ For he bringeth down them that dwell on high,
[h] the lofty city he layeth it low, he layeth it low, *even*
to the ground, he bringeth it *even* to the duſt 6 The
foot ſhall tread it down, [i] *even* the feet of the poor, *and*
the ſteps of the needy 7 ‖ The way of the juſt *is* up-
rightneſs [k] thou moſt upright doſt weigh the path of
the juſt 8 Yea, [l] in the way of thy judgments, O
LORD, have we waited for thee; the deſire of *our* ſoul
is to thy name, and to the remembrance of thee 9
[m] With my ſoul have I deſired thee in the night, yea,
with my ſpirit within me will I ſeek thee early for
when thy judgments *are* in the earth, the inhabitants
of the world will learn righteouſneſs 10 [n] Let favour
be ſhewed to the wicked, *yet* will he not learn righte-
ouſneſs in the land of uprightneſs will he deal unjuſt-
ly, and will not behold the majeſty of the LORD 11
LORD, *when* thy hand is lifted up, [o] they will not ſee
but they ſhall ſee, and be aſhamed for ‡ *their* envy at
the people, yea the fire ‖ of thine enemies ſhall devour
them

n Eccleſ viii 10 Rom ii 4 o Job xxxiv 27 Pſ xxviii 5 Chap v 12. ‡ Or thy zeal towards thy people Chap ix 7 ‖ Or ſhall devour theſe thine enemies

v 5—11 We have here,

1 The humiliation of the proud, and the deſtruction of the lofty city, Babylon, now trod upon by thoſe, who before were oppreſſed by her, or of ſpiritual Babylon, on which the poor perſecuted ſaints of the moſt high ſhall trample, when utterly laid waſte before the Lord in the latter day, *v* 5, 6

2 The regard God ſhews his people *The way of the juſt is uprightneſs*, or *evenneſſes*, a ſtrait path of uniform and ſteady obedience, or *the way* of the Lord *to the juſt is evenneſſes*, agreeable to his own perfections of wiſdom, goodneſs, truth, and equity, ſo that they have ever cauſe to addreſs him as *thou moſt upright*, whoſe ways of providence and grace are perfectly pure, and tranſcendently excellent, *thou doſt weigh*, or *make even the path of the juſt*, conſider and approve it as good, or removing every obſtacle, enable him to walk in the paths of holineſs.

3 The people of God profeſs their attendance on him, and deſires after him *In the way of thy judgments*, thy word, and ordinances, or thy chaſtiſements which we have endured, *we have waited for thee*, patiently expecting to ſee thy ſalvation *the deſire of our ſoul is to thy name, and to the remembrance of thee*; in the midſt of our heavieſt afflictions, to thee our affections go forth, we think upon thee, and derive ſupport from the remembrance of thy grace, power, love, and faithfulneſs. *With my ſoul ardently have I deſired thee in the night*, literally waking when others ſlept, or under the darkeſt diſpenſations of providence, *yea, with my ſpirit within me will I ſeek thee early*, not forgetting him in proſperity, but when the day returned, with the dawn meeting him with prayer and praiſe *for when thy judgments are in the earth*, thoſe that ſhall be laid upon the ſinners, and followers of Antichriſt, *the inhabitants of the world*, ſome of them, the faithful, who are called and choſen, *will learn righteouſneſs*, the juſtice of God in his judgments on others, and his afflictions on themſelves, and profiting under them, bring forth the peaceable fruits of righteouſneſs, in penitence, patience, and perſeverance *Note*, (1) They who wait for God in his ways, ſhall aſſuredly meet him to their comfort (2) If our affections are not warm towards God, we need be jealous leaſt there is a rival in our hearts (3) The earlier in life we begin to ſeek God, the pleaſanter ſhall we find his ways (4) Under our own corrections we muſt humble our ſouls, and from his viſitations on others take warning, then however heavy the ſtroke, the iſſue will be to us righteouſneſs and peace

4 The impenitence of the wicked is obſerved as the prelude to their ruin *Let favour be ſhewed to the wicked, yet will he not learn righteouſneſs*, providential mercies are no more effectual to lead him to repentance, than judgments to drive him *in the land of uprightneſs*, where the moſt plentiful knowledge of goſpel-truth is diffuſed, and the power of goſpel grace moſt eminently diſplayed, *he will deal unjuſtly*, perſiſt in his iniquities, in oppoſition to every warning of God's word and miniſters, *and will not behold the majeſty of the Lord*, acknowledge his power, providence, and goodneſs, nor worſhip, ſerve, and obey him, as in duty bound *Lord, when thy hand is lifted up*, or *thy high hand, they will not ſee* God's hand in their mercies, or in the judgments viſible in the earth, and hanging over their own heads, obſtinately hardened, and wilfully ſhutting their eyes againſt conviction *Note*, (1) To dwell in a land of uprightneſs is an ineſtimable mercy, and there to dwell in ſin and darkneſs, where light and grace plentifully abound, will be aggravated guilt (2) Forgetfulneſs of God, and inattention to his word and works, are the ruin of men's ſouls (3) They who will not ſee, are juſtly given up to judicial blindneſs

5 Then deſtruction is near and ſure The judgments they would not fear, they muſt feel *They ſhall ſee* the proſperity of God's people, *and be aſhamed for their envy*, or *the zeal towards the people*, the Lord's regard for them, and his care to vindicate their wrongs *yea, the fire of thine enemies ſhall devour them*, or *the fire ſhall devour theſe thine enemies*, the fire of preſent judgments, or the unquenchable fire that ſhall torment their bodies and ſouls in hell Let the enemies of God's people hear and tremble!

12 ¶ LORD, [p] thou wilt ordain peace for us; for
thou alſo haſt wrought all our works ‖ in us. 13 O
LORD our God, [q] *other* lords beſides thee have had do-
minion over us *but* by thee only will we make men-
tion of thy name 14 *They are* dead, they ſhall not
live, [r] *they are* deceaſed, they ſhall not riſe ‡ therefore
haſt thou viſited and deſtroyed them, and made [s] all their

p Chap lx 17, 18 John xvi 33 ‖ Or for us q 2 Chron xii 8 Jer l 17 r Pſ xxxvi 12 ‡ Or becauſe s Prov

[illegible]

Before Chriſt 712

memory to periſh 15 Thou haſt increaſed the nation,
O LORD, thou haſt increaſed the nation, thou art glori-
fied, thou hadſt removed *it* far *unto* all the ends of the
earth 16 LORD, in trouble have they viſited thee,
they poured out ‖ a prayer *when* thy chaſtening *was* upon
them 17 Like as ᵘ a woman with child *that* draweth
near the time of her delivery, is in pain, *and* crieth out
in her pangs, ſo have we been in thy ſight, O LORD
18 We have been with child, we have been in pain, we
have as it were brought forth wind, we have not wrought
any deliverance § in the earth, neither have the inhabi-
tants of the world fallen 19 ˣ Thy dead *men* ſhall live,
ʸ † *together with* my dead body ſhall they ariſe ᶻ awake
and ſing, ye that dwell in duſt for thy dew *is as* the
dew of herbs, and the earth ſhall caſt out the dead.

t 2 Chron xxxiii 12 Hoſ v 15. ‖ Heb, A ſecret ſpeech, or prayer u John xvi 21 § Or for our land x Ezek xxxvii 11—14 Dan xii 2 y Mat. xxvii 52, 53 † Or as my dead body z Eph v 14 or Dan xii 2 John v 28

v 12—19 We have here,

1 The church's dependance on God, aſcribing to his grace alone all the good that was found in her, v 12 *Lord, thou wilt ordain peace for us,* whatever enemy without or within ſeeks to trouble our repoſe, and wilt at laſt bring us to the eternal reſt which remaineth for the people of God *for thou alſo haſt wrought all our works in us,* or *for us,* whatever good is in our ſouls, thou, Lord, art alone the author of it, whatever good we are the inſtruments of communicating to others, thy grace is alone to be acknowledged, whatever bleſſings or comforts we receive, from thy hand alone they come

2 The humbling confeſſion and gracious purpoſe of God's people, v 13 *O Lord our God,* whoſe we are, and whom we ought and deſire to ſerve, yet with ſhame acknowledge *other lords beſides thee have had dominion over us,* either this is the confeſſion of the Jews, bewailing their captivity and idolatries, or of the church, oppreſſed by the perſecuting powers of Antichriſt, or more generally of every faithful ſoul, who laments the bondage of corruption, every vile affection being a tyrant, and Satan, in a ſtate of nature, having led us captive at his will But now recovered by grace, we ſhall be enabled to ſay, *by thee only,* by thy grace ſupported, and by thy power delivered, *will we make mention of thy name,* cleave alone to thee as our God and guide, and aſcribe to thee the praiſe of all our ſalvation

3 They triumph over their oppreſſors, v 14 *They are dead, they ſhall not live, they are deceaſed, they ſhall not riſe,* either the Babyloniſh monarchs, whoſe kingdom never roſe from its ruins, or the enemies of the church in general, whether Pagan, Papal, or Mahomedan, who will be finally deſtroyed, and no more oppreſs the redeemed, *therefore,* or *becauſe thou haſt viſited and deſtroyed them, and made all their memory to periſh,* conſigned them to eternal ſhame in the place of torment

4 The great increaſe of the church is declared *Thou haſt increaſed the nation, O Lord, thou haſt increaſed the nation,* either the Jewiſh nation by proſelytes, or rather the Chriſtian church, called the righteous nation, v 2 by numerous converts of Jews and Gentiles and this is ſpoken as already done, becauſe ſuch is God's purpoſe in the latter day, who calleth the things that are not, as though they were *thou art glorified* in the ſalvation of thy people, and the ruin of their enemies *thou hadſt removed it far unto all the ends of the earth,* in a ſtate of diſperſion, from whence they are now delivered, or he had ſpread into every land the knowledge of his grace, and gathered a people for himſelf out of all nations

5. Before their reſtoration, a ſtate of great trouble is foreſeen and lamented, either of the Jews groaning under their captivity, or the church, under the perilous times that precede the deſtruction of Antichriſt, v 16—18 *Lord, in trouble have they viſited thee,* this being the great uſe and benefit of afflictions, to bring us nearer to God, from whom proſperity is too apt to alienate our hearts *they poured out a prayer when thy chaſtening was upon them;* for this is the conſtant method of all God's people, in prayer and ſupplications to make their requeſts known unto him nor ſhall we ever be ſo earneſt and importunate, as when we feel his chaſtiſements bringing to remembrance our ſins *Like as a woman with child that draweth near the time of her delivery, is in pain, and crieth out in her pangs,* which are the moſt acute and bitter, *ſo have we been in thy ſight, O Lord,* in deep diſtreſs, and crying for deliverance *we have been with child,* big with hopes; *we have been in pain,* travailing in prayers and tears, yet diſappointed, and our hopes abortive, ſo long is our ſalvation delayed *we have brought forth wind,* our prayers ineffectual and unanſwered, *we have not wrought any deliverance in the earth,* ſo as to regain our liberty, or *ſalvations have not been wrought in the earth,* to deliver us from our enemies; *neither have the inhabitants of the world fallen,* but continue to oppreſs the cauſe of godlineſs and truth *Note,* (1) God may for wiſe ends long ſuffer his own cauſe and people to be oppreſſed by wicked men (2) However long or ſore our trial, we muſt continue to pray, and not faint (3) If we do ſo, we ſhall aſſuredly not be diſappointed at the laſt For,

6 Chriſt anſwers his people's prayers *Thy dead men ſhall live,* ſpiritually, by the power of Jeſus, the dead in ſin ſhall be quickned, and in the latter day vaſt additions of living ſouls be made to the church, or it refers to the reſurrection, when the dead in Chriſt ſhall riſe firſt, and reign with him, *together with my dead body ſhall they ariſe,* as the bodies of many ſaints did, when Jeſus himſelf aroſe, *Matt* xxvii 51, 53 or *as my dead body ſhall they ariſe,* certainly, and as glorioufly: *awake and ſing, ye that dwell in the duſt,* awake at the goſpel call, ye dead in ſin, or awake from the duſt of death, ye ſleeping ſaints, ariſe to meet your Lord in the air, and join in ſongs of praiſe that never will have an end *for thy dew is as the dew of herbs,* thy ſpirit as effectual to quicken the ſouls and bodies of the ſpiritually and naturally dead, as the dew cauſes the herb to ſhoot that ſeemed dead in the ground, during the ſleep of winter, *and the earth ſhall caſt out the dead,* when, at the word of Jeſus, they that are in their graves, ſhall hear and live *Note,* Whatever our afflictions here may be, if we have but a part in the reſurrection of the juſt, we need not aſk or wiſh for more

20 Come, my people, enter thou into thy cham-
bers, and ſhut thy doors about thee hide thyſelf as it
were ᵃ for a little moment, until the indignation be over
paſt 21 For behold, the LORD ᵇ cometh out of his
place to puniſh the inhabitants of the earth for their ini-
quity ᶜ the earth alſo ſhall diſcloſe her † blood, and
ſhall no more cover her ſlain

a Pſ xxx 5 Chap liv 7, 8 2 Cor iv 17, b Mic i 3 Jude 14 c Rev xviii 24 † Heb Blood

v 20, 21 Theſe verſes are either the concluſion of the former ſong, or the introduction of the next chapter, to which they are uſually referred

1. Chriſt calls his people to a place of ſafety, when he is about to execute his wrath on the wicked *Come, my people,* the endearing title of property and relation, and the aſſurance of ſafety, for if we are his, none ſhall pluck us out of his hand, *enter thou into thy chambers,* where they may be ſafe, as Rahab, when Jericho was taken, or the Iſraelites, when the deſtroying angel paſſed through the land, *and ſhut thy doors about thee,* to be ſecure and private, to pour out the voice of prayer when danger threatens *hide thyſelf* from the impending ſtorm, under the ſhadow of Almighty grace, *as it were for a little moment, until the indignation be overpaſt,* the time will be momentary, for a ſhort work will God make on the earth, his wrath, when it begins to conſume the wicked, will quickly make an end of them, *Rev* ii. 10 xi 7—11

2 He goes forth, to execute his judgments *For behold,* to the aſtoniſhment of the ſurprized world, *the Lord cometh out of his place,* with clouds deſcending, in terrible majeſty *to puniſh the inhabitants of the earth for their iniquity,* be they never ſo great, never ſo numerous, their iniquity will receive a juſt recompence of reward *the earth alſo ſhall diſcloſe her blood, and ſhall no more cover her ſlain,* the blood of ſaints and martyrs, from Abel to the laſt perſecuted believer, ſhall then be brought to light, and however ſecretly murders may have been committed, blood will cry for vengeance, or it may ſignify the immenſe carnage to be made in the battle of Armageddon, ſo that the earth ſhall not be able to drink up the blood, nor ſuffice for graves to the ſlain, *Rev* xi 13 xiv 20 xix 17, 18 *Note,* The day is near when God will bring every ſecret thing into judgment Let the guilty tremble

CHAP XXVII

In this chapter the prophet goes on to ſhew, (1) *What great things God would do for his church and people,* 1 *That proud oppreſſors ſhould be reckoned with,* ver 1 2 *That care ſhould be taken of God's vineyard,* ver 2, 3 3 *That God would let fall his controverſy with his people upon their return to him,* ver 4, 5 4 *That he would greatly increaſe them,* ver 6 5 *That as to their afflictions, they were comparatively ſmall,* ver 7, 8 *and ſanctified,* ver 9 6 *That though their city might be laid waſte for a time,* ver 10, 11 *yet it ſhould be reſtored, and the ſcattered members gathered together again,* ver 12, 13

1. IN that day the LORD with his ſore and great
and ſtrong ᵃ ſword ſhall puniſh leviathan the ‡
piercing ſerpent, even leviathan that crooked ſerpent,
and he ſhall ſlay the dragon that *is* in the ſea 2 In
that day ᶜ ſing ye unto her, A vineyard of red wine 3
I the LORD do keep it, I will water it every moment,
leſt *any* hurt it, I will keep it night and day 4 Fury
is not in me who would ſet the briers *and* ᵉ thorns a-
gainſt me in battle? I would ‡ go through them, I
would burn them together 5 Or ‖ let him ᶠ take hold
of my ſtrength, *that* he may make peace with me, *and*
he ſhall make peace with me 6 ᵍ He ſhall cauſe them
that come of Jacob to take root Iſrael ſhall bloſſom
and bud, and fill the face of the world with fruit

a Rev xix 15 b Ibid. xii 9 & xx 2 ‡ Or, ſlid ing or croſſing like a bar c Chap v 1 d Pſ cxxi 4 e 2 Sam. xxiii 6 ‡ Or march againſt ‖ Or if he will &c or O that he would, &c f Job xxii 21 Luke xiv 32 g Chap xxxvii 31.

3 v 1—6 We

Before Christ 712

v 1—6 We have here,

1 The execution of judgment on the great enemy of God's people, called leviathan, the serpent, the dragon, either Nebuchadnezzar, or Antiochus, or Antichrist, *Rev* xii 3 or Satan himself Though strong, furious, crafty, and poisonous, God's sword can reach him, and as he hath destroyed the persecuting powers of old, he will as surely destroy those that still rage, by the two-edged sword of his gospel, expelling their poisonous errors, or by the sword of his judgments, punishing them with everlasting destruction, *Rev* xx 1—10

2 In the day of vengeance on his enemies, his grace and mercy to his church will eminently appear, and she shall sing for joy over her persecutors fallen, and her peace and comfort everlastingly restored, *Rev* xv 1—3 xix 1—7

(1) The church is represented as a *vineyard of red wine*, a people separated by sovereign grace, secured by the wall of everlasting love, ingrafted on Christ the living vine, and thence enabled to bring forth the choicest fruits of faith and holiness *I the Lord do keep it*, though his church lies in the midst of an howling wilderness, where wicked men, more savage than beasts of prey, roam continually, and threaten to break through and spoil, yet it is safe under his protection, and flourishing under his care *I will water it* with the dew of heavenly influences *every moment*, for every moment we need his gracious help, *lest any hurt it*, or *lest he may* ... *it*, the enemy of souls intent to deceive and destroy, *I will keep it night and day*, in prosperity and adversity, at all times, amidst every danger, he that slumbereth not, nor yet sleepeth, will preserve his chosen *Note*, The more we know of the riches and fulness of the divine promises, the more will our hearts be filled with thankfulness, and our lips with praise

(2) The people of God are assured of his favour *Fury is not in me*, however terrible to his enemies, to his chosen God is all love, and their iniquities cancelled in redeeming blood, no wrath remains against them, even their chastisements are the rod of mercy *who would set the briars and thorns against me in battle? I would go through them, I would burn them together*, or *I would step into it, and burn them out of it*, meaning either that should he contend with them for their sins, his own people would be but as briars and thorns before the consuming fire, or rather that when hypocrites and false teachers, like briers and thorns, sprung up to trouble his people, he would step into his vineyard as a man of war, and quickly destroy and burn them up Some render the words, *who will set me as a brier or thorn in battle, that I should go against it, and burn it up together?* What provocation should ever lead him to destroy his own people? None, for fury is not in him though he visit their offences with the rod, his loving-kindness will he never take from them

(3) God directs them how abidingly to preserve the sense of his regard to them *Or let him*, which some render *if he will*, and *O that he would take hold of my strength*, in times when his corrections are on his people, they need not be terrified, but apply to that Almighty Saviour the strength of God, who is their ever-living and all-prevailing advocate, *that he may make peace with me*, by pleading the blood which he once shed for the redemption of his people, and *he shall make peace with me*, God, for his sake, will be perfectly pacified toward the believing soul, and comfort him with the confidence of his mercy

(4) The church shall have a great increase *He shall cause them that come of Jacob*, the spiritual Israel of God, *to take root*, to be firmly fixed, and spread their branches on every side some read, *in times to come he shall cause*, &c in the latter day of gospel truth, when *Israel shall bud and blossom, and fill the face of the world with fruit*, as in the days of the apostles, *Col* i 6 and shall, we trust, be more abundantly fulfilled hereafter

7 ¶ Hath he smitten him, as he smote those that
smote him? *or* is he slain according to the slaughter of
them that are slain by him? 8 [h] In measure, [i] when it
shooteth forth, thou wilt debate with it, [i] he stayeth his
rough wind in the day of the east wind 9 [k] By this
therefore shall the iniquity of Jacob be purged, and this
is all the fruit to take away his sin, when he maketh all
the stones of the altar as chalk-stones *that are* beaten in
sunder, the groves and [‡] images shall not stand up 10
[l] Yet the defenced city *shall be* desolate, *and* the habitation
forsaken, and left like a wilderness there shall the
calf feed, and there shall he lie down, and consume the
branches thereof 11 When the boughs thereof are
withered, they shall be broken off, the women come *and*
set them on fire for [m] it *is* a people of no understanding
therefore he that made them will not have mercy
on them, and he that formed them will shew them no
favour 12 ¶ And it shall come to pass in that day,
that the LORD shall beat off from the channel of the
river unto the stream of Egypt, and ye shall be gathered
one by one, O ye children of Israel 13 And it shall
come to pass in that day, *that* [n] the great trumpet shall
be blown, and they shall come which were ready to perish
in the land of Assyria, and the outcasts in the land of
Egypt, and [o] shall worship the LORD in the holy
mount at Jerusalem

Marginal notes: [h] Job xxiii 6 Jer x 24 & xxx 11 & xlvi 28 1 Cor x 13 † Or, when thou sendest it forth ‖ Or, he removeth [k] Chap xlvi 11 [i] Ps lxxviii 38 ‡ Or, sun images [l] Chap xxxii 14 [m] Deut xxxii 28 Jer viii 7 [n] Lev xxv 9 Rev xi 15 [o] Chap lxvi 20

v 7—13 Though God had intimated that sometimes afflictions would fall upon his people, yet very different would his dealings with them be, from his judgments on their enemies

1 Respecting the measure of them Though he should smite them, yet not as he smote those that smote him, *v* 7 his strokes on his people would be mitigated, and however rough the wind blew for a season he would say, Peace, be still, *v* 8 But their enemies would be utterly consumed, their fortresses destroyed, their country a wilderness, where cattle would feed, *v* 10 Like a withered tree they would be condemned to the flames, and this in just judgment, because they are a people of no understanding, and being ungrateful and disobedient to their Maker, receive the reward of their deeds in utter destruction, *v* 11 This may primarily refer to the Jewish nation and their foes, but it hath a more enlarged view to all the people of God and their enemies *Note*, (1) If we are God's children, we shall, because we deserve it, feel his gracious rod (2) Though involved in the same outward calamities, there is at all times a wide difference between those who are corrected in mercy, and those who suffer in wrath (3) They who obstinately reject God's warnings may expect in a judgment-day no mercy

2 The end God proposed in correcting his people, was their repentance and salvation *By this therefore shall the iniquity of Jacob be purged, and this is all the fruit to take away his sin*, and a gracious end this, for which every faithful soul hath reason to bless God, who can say, before I was afflicted I went astray The particular sin here to be removed is idolatry *when he maketh all the stones of the altar*, erected for idol-worship, 2 *Kings* xvi 10—12 *as chalk-stones that are beaten in sunder, the groves and the images shall not stand up* And after the captivity, the Jews were so thoroughly cured of that idolatry, to which before they were so prone, that the least traces of it no longer appeared among them *Note*, It is a blessed symptom for good, when our sin, our bosom sin, that did most easily beset us, is thus radically mortified

3 When God hath for their good corrected his people, he will gather them together wherever dispersed, and however distressed *It shall come to pass in that day, that the Lord will beat off*, and collect his chosen, as fruits to be laid up in store, or corn separated from the chaff, *from the channel of the river (Euphrates) unto the river of Egypt, and ye shall be gathered one by one*, with such care, and so completely, that not one shall be lost, *O ye children of Israel And it shall come to pass in that day, that the great trumpet shall be blown*, which, if referred literally to the Jewish people, signifies the proclamation of Cyrus, by which they were restored to their own land from all places of their dispersion, but rather it refers to the collection of the Israel of God, by the trumpet of the everlasting gospel, recovering those who *were ready to perish*, and *the outcasts*, like the wretched infant in Ezekiel, lying in their blood, outcasts from God's church, and perishing in their sins, till called, quickened, and restored by the power of divine grace through the word of the gospel, and brought to join the holy worship of the saints in God's church on earth, and to prepare for the everlasting service of God in glory *Note*, (1) Amidst all the troubles and trials of God's Israel, not one will be lost (2) Whenever the gospel-trumpet is blown, they who know the joyful sound will assemble thither (3) When God opens the heart to hear his word, he brings the conscience to a deep and humbling sense of its misery and lost estate by reason of sin, and then by to Christ, whose gospel is to the lost the trump of jubilee, glad tidings of great joy (4) It is a mercy when we have liberty to worship God, and a greater to delight in the service, and to say of God's courts, Here would I dwell for ever

CHAP XXVIII

In this chapter, 1 Ephraim is threatened for their pride and drunkenness, their security, and sensuality, ver 1—5 But in the midst of this, a gracious promise is given to the remnant of his people, ver 5, 6 2 They are likewise threatened for their stupidity and unteachableness, ver 9—13 3 The rulers of Jerusalem are threatened for their insolent contempt of God's judgments, 14, 15, 17 22 4 A gracious promise intervenes, ver 16 for the comfort of the faithful 5 The certainty of God's judgments is illustrated by the ploughman's sowing and threshing, under divine instruction, ver 23 29

1 WO to [a] the crown of pride, to the drunkards of
Ephraim, [b] whose glorious beauty *is* a fading
flower, which *are* on the head of the fat valleys of *them*

Marginal notes: [a] Ver 3 [b] Ver 4

Before Christ 725

that are overcome with wine 2 Behold, the LORD
hath a mighty and strong one, which c as a tempest of
hail, and a destroying storm, as a flood of mighty wa-
ters overflowing, shall cast down to the earth with the
hand 3 The crown of pride, the drunkards of E-
phraim shall be troden under feet 4 And the glorious
beauty which is on the head of the fat valley, shall be a
fading flower, and as the hasty fruit before the summer
which when he that looketh upon it seeth it, while it is
yet in his hand, he † eateth it up 5 ¶ In that day
shall the LORD of hosts be for a crown of glory, and
for a diadem of beauty unto the residue of his people
6 And for a spirit of judgment to him that sitteth in
judgment, and d for strength to them that turn the battle
to the gate 7 ¶ But e they also f have erred through
wine, and through strong drink are out of the way
g the priest and the prophet have erred through strong
drink, they are swallowed up of wine, they are out of
the way through strong drink, h they err in vision, they
stumble in judgment 8 For all tables are full of vomit
and filthiness, so that there is no place ‡ clean

c Chap xxx 30
† Heb Swalloweth
d 2 Kings xviii 8
e Jer iii 10
f Prov xx 1 Hos iv 11
g Chap lvi 10 2
h Jer xiv 14 Lam ii 14
‡ Heb Or free

v 1—8 Though judgments are denounced on all their foes, yet they will first begin at the house of God, and the sinners in Zion must feel the heaviest scourge Such is the woe pronounced here on Ephraim, and Samaria the capital of the ten revolted tribes

1 The sins charged upon them are pride and drunkenness Their country being rich and fertile, abundance swelled their vain hearts, and sensual appetite abused their distinguished mercies Carousing at the festal board, their heads with garlands crowned, they proudly defied sorrow, fearless of the wrath they provoked *Note*, (1) Pride on God's gifts is the sure way to provoke him to deprive us of them (2) A drunkard is a monster in nature, and he that thus basely chuses to degrade himself into a brute, justly deserves to be made a companion of devils

2 Heavy is the curse the prophet is commissioned to pronounce on these proud drunkards As they gave up their senses to the base servitude of lust, and drowned their reason in excess, in just judgment they should be delivered to their foes The king of Assyria, Salmanezer, like a resistless hail storm, or winter's flood, should bear down all before him, *v* 2 *The crown of pride*, their king and his mighty men, or Samaria the metropolis, or the crowns of garlands on the drunkard's head, surprized in this defenceless and intoxicated state, he would cast down, and tread the drunkards under his feet, reducing them to state of most abject wretchedness, *v* 3 *Their glorious beauty*, their numerous inhabitants, or their country decked with vineyards, and vallies thick with corn, shall fade as quickly as the flowers bloom departs, and be devoured by the hosts of Assyria, as greedily as the first ripe fruit, *v* 4 so that nothing but desolation should be seen *Note*, (1) They who give the reins to their appetites, and to drunkenness especially, are voluntary slaves, and court a servitude most wretched even now, issuing at present in the ruin of their health, fortune, and families, and bringing them hastily to that place of torment, where a drop of water will be sought in vain to cool a flaming tongue (2) God's ministers must denounce his woes against men's sins freely and plainly (3) Whatever the sinner here is proud of, it is but a fading flower, and at death at furthest, if not before, will vanish

3 In the midst of the desolations of Ephraim, Judah and Benjamin, the residue of God's people, have a gracious promise made to them *The Lord shall be a crown of glory, and a diadem of beauty to them*, eminently distinguishing, and protecting them from the power of the Assyrians, under Hezekiah, a type of that Son of David, in whom the offices of King and Priest should be united *And for a spirit of judgment to him that sitteth in judgment*, which God would bestow on the king and his magistrates, to execute righteous judgment, which is the great happiness of every state, *and for strength to them that turn the battle to the gate*, enduing their generals and soldiers with courage to vanquish their enemies, and pursue them to the gates of their city *Note*, (1) Christ is his people's glory, and in his wisdom, righteousness, and strength, they are made more than conquerors over all their enemies (2) Whatever the Lord is to us, or doth for us, we are bound to ascribe the praise of all to him

4 A heavy complaint is lodged against Judah for their sins In her were found the sins of Israel, and the same drunkenness led them astray from God Yea, so generally had this scandalous sin spread, that priest, prophet, and people were alike infected with it The consequence of which was, that the pretended prophet uttered the fancies of his inflamed brains for visions, deceiving, and being deceived, the priests, instead of the conscientious discharge of their office, mistook God's law, misinterpreted his oracles, and led their hearers into fatal error or on the bench, decided wrong, to the great injury of truth and justice, *v* 7 Yea, so common and infamous was their drunkenness, that every table was full of vomit, and no place clean, a scene as loathsome in the eyes of sober men, as detestable in the sight of God *Note*, Drunkenness is vile and brutish in every man, but in a priest, a minister of the sanctuary, what words can express the infamy, impiety, and scandalousness of the crime!

9 ¶ i Whom shall he teach knowledge? and whom
shall he make to understand doctrine? k *them that are*
weaned from the milk, *and* drawn from the breasts 10
For l precept † *must be* upon precept, precept upon pre-
cept, line upon line, line upon line, here a little *and*
there a little 11 For m with stammering lips, and a-
nother tongue, will he speak to this people 12 To
whom he said, This *is* n the rest *wherewith* ye may cause o
the weary to rest, and this *is* the refreshing yet they
would not hear 13 But the word of the LORD was
unto them, precept upon precept, precept upon precept,
line upon line, line upon line, here a little *and* there a
little, p that they might go and fall backward, and be
broken, and snared, and taken

i Jer vi 10.
k Ibid. iv 22
l 2 Chron xxxvi 15 Chap v 4
† Or hath been
m Jer v 15. or 1 Cor xiv 21
n Jer vi 16
o Mat xi 28
p 2 Cor ii 16

v 9—13 Drunkenness necessarily brought stupidity upon their minds, and steeled them against all the warnings of God

1 In vain were all the teachings of the prophets, sollicitous as they were to make them understand, waiting upon them with patient perseverance, and daily inculcating their lessons, *v* 10 and so plainly and affectionately withal, shewing them how nearly they were interested in the matter, as being the only way for them to obtain deliverance from the threatned evils, or refreshing to their guilty consciences, *v* 12 Yet sooner might a child at the breast be taught, *v* 9, so stupified were they with their drunkenness, and so obstinate, *they would not hear*, tho' the word was ever sounding in their ears, it never reached their hearts, and they seem to have turned it into ridicule, repeating it after the prophet in mockery, *Tsau latsau, kau lakau*, or at their drunken feasts jesting with the sacred words of scripture, *v* 13 *Note*, (1) God condescends to teach us as babes, his word is the sincere milk, and as a nurse cherisheth her children, his ministers are sent to wait upon us with unwearied patience (2) Children's minds must not be over burthened, a little, as they are able to receive it, will be the most profitable instruction (3) There is rest for the weary in Jesus, and refreshing for the miserable it argues our folly as great as our wickedness to reject our own mercies, and refuse his calls to come to him, that we may find rest to our souls (4) Many hear the word of God, whose hearts continue impenetrable, yea, they will not understand, and none so blind as these (5) The last step of hardened wickedness is making a jest of things sacred

2 In just judgment God gives them up to the ruin they have chosen *With stammering lips and another tongue shall he speak to this people*, when foreign armies shall waste their country, or it refers to the gift of tongues, which the apostles possessed, 1 *Cor* xiv 21 against which, miraculous as it was, they continued hardened, so that their destruction was determined, *that they might go and fall backward, and be broken, and snared, and taken*, as the punishment of their apostacy from God, first given up to the Babylonians, and at last their country utterly destroyed by the Romans *Note*, They who will not attend to God's calls to repentance, will hear his terrible voice of judgment, when their ruin is past recovery

14 ¶ Wherefore hear the word of the LORD, q ye
scornful men that rule this people which *is* in Jerusalem
15 Because ye have said, We have made a covenant
with death, and with † hell are we at agreement, when
the overflowing scourge shall pass through, it shall not
come unto us, for we have made lies our refuge, and
under falshood have we hid ourselves 16 ¶ Therefore
thus saith the Lord God, Behold, I lay in Zion for r a
foundation, s a stone, ‖ a tried stone, a t precious u cor-
ner *stone*, a sure foundation he that believeth w shall not
make haste 17 Judgment also will I lay to the line,
and righteousness to the plummet, and the hail shall
sweep away x the refuge of lies, and the waters shall over-
flow the hiding-place 18 ¶ And your covenant with
death shall be disannulled, and your agreement with hell
shall not stand, when the overflowing scourge shall pass
through, then ye shall be troden down by it 19 From
the time that it goeth forth, it shall take you for morn-
ing by morning shall it pass over, by day and by night,
and it shall be a vexation, only ‖ *to* understand the re-
port 20 For y the bed is shorter, than that *a man* can
stretch himself on *it* and the covering narrower, than
that

q Chap v 19
† Or the grave Chap xiv 15
r 1 Cor iii 11 Psal cxviii 22 Mat xxi 42 Acts iv 11 Rom ix 33 x 11 1 Pet ii 6, &c
‖ Heb A stone of proof, or trial
t 1 Pet ii 7
u Eph ii 20
w Psal cxvi...
x Ver 15
‖ Or when he shall make you to understand doctrine Ver 9
y Chap lix 5, 6

Before Christ 725

that he can wrap himself in it 21 For the LORD
shall rise up ^a as *in* mount Perazim, he shall be wroth ^a
as *in* the valley of Gibeon, that he may do his work,
^b his strange work, and bring to pass his act, his strange
act 22 Now therefore be ye not ^c mockers, lest your
bands be made strong for I have heard from the Lord
GOD of hosts ^d a consumption, even determined upon
the whole † earth

a 2 Sam v 20 a Josh x 12 or 1 Chron xiv 16. b Jer xxx 14 Lam iii 33 c Chap v 19 d Ibid x 22, 23 Dan ix 27 † Or land

v 14—22 This prophecy some apply to the men of Judah, and their destruction by the Assyrians, but it seems to belong especially to the Jews in Christ's day, and the desolations which the Romans shortly after brought upon them

1 The scornful men who rejected the prophetic admonition, too great to take rebuke, and infatuated to their ruin, boasted themselves secure The death and hell the prophet threatned, they feared not they thought themselves as safe, as if they had made a compact with the grave, and were confident whatever overflowing scourge passed through the land, it should not come to them, making lies their refuge, and hiding themselves under falshood, the lying prophets, who encouraged them, or their own strength, wealth, and policy, to overcome or over-reach their adversaries By the overflowing scourge, the Roman army seems intended, against which they thought themselves safe, but found, too late, their sad delusion *Note*, (1) When we are in covenant with God through a Redeemer, and at peace with him through the blood of sprinkling, then, and only then, have we made a covenant with death, and cannot be hurt thereby (2) Vain confidence buoys up sinners to the last, but there will then be found a lie in their right hand

2 The prophet admonishes them, where alone they can safely place their confidence *Behold, I lay in Zion a foundation*, the Lord Jesus Christ, other foundation than whom no man can lay, *a stone*, a rock, firm and immoveable, *a tried stone*, who hath been proved the sure support of his saints in every age, *or a stone of trial*, by whom men's states are discovered, and their characters determined, *a precious corner-stone*, supporting the whole spiritual building, and inestimably prized by every believer, who knows the value of such a Redeemer, *a sure foundation*, that will stand for eternity, and on which we may safely trust body and soul *he that believeth, shall not make haste*, but under every trial patiently wait the Lord's leisure, and thus will never be confounded, or *ashamed*, as it is rendered, 1 *Pet* ii 6 for he hath never failed those who trust him, and never can or will disappoint their hopes

3 He warns them of the folly, sin, and danger of their conduct, in trusting on lying vanities For when the Lord shall lay judgment to the line, and righteousness to the plummet, as builders, to prove their work strait, their ways will be found perverse, and their judgment ensue, then their vain hopes shall fail, and the hail-storm sweep away their refuge of lies The army of the enemy is easily and utterly overwhelming them, their lying prophets, their riches and temple together, or whatever else they trust in, as the waters of the deluge did the sinners of old, *v* 17 Then their covenant with death would be proved a delusion, and the sword of the Chaldeans, or rather the Romans, as an overflowing scourge, pass through, and as mire in the streets they should be trodden down, *v* 18 *From the time it goeth forth*, neither policy nor power will be able to oppose it, *it shall take you* as prisoners for captivity, or seize you as criminals for the sword, and thus continually and thoroughly, till God's judgments are executed *Morning by morning it shall pass over, by day and by night* without interruption the siege would be carried on, and the devastations increase, *and it shall be a vexation only to understand the report*, so terrible would the tidings be which those who fled into Jerusalem should carry of the ravages of the Chaldean or Roman army *For the bed is shorter, than that a man can stretch himself on it and the covering narrower, than that he can wrap himself in it*, which either describes the insufficiency of their projects, and the uncomfortableness of their state, when their beds would give them no repose, or the case of Jerusalem, crouded with those who fled thither, whose useless number increased the miseries of the besieged *For the Lord shall rise up as in mount Perazim*, and against his arm resistance is vain, *he shall be wroth as in the valley of Gibeon*, two eminent instances wherein he displayed his terrible majesty against his enemies, 2 *Sam* v 20 *Josh* x 10—13 *that he may do his work, his strange work, and bring to pass his act, his strange act*, he used to fight for them, but now is turned to be their enemy, and their fall is sure *Note*, (1) If God lay judgment to the line, and righteousness to the plummet, who can stand, or bear the scrutiny? (2) It is the folly of the self-righteous and the hypocrite that they cry peace, when there is no peace (3) If sinners cannot bear the report of God's terror without vexation, nor hear of hell, and torments, and eternal despair without commotion, how will they endure them? (4) They who think their moral duties will yield them a covering in the day of God, and seek repose in their own righteousnesses, will find the bed too short, the covering too narrow,

and perish in their own deceivings (5) Vengeance is God's strange work, he delighteth not in the death of a sinner

4 The whole is pressed upon their consciences for their conviction and reformation *Now therefore*, to-day, whilst it is called to-day, and yet there is mercy, *be ye not mockers*, despising these divine notices, *lest your bands be made strong*, and aggravated guilt provoke a heavier judgment *for I have heard from the Lord of hosts*, who cannot lie, and is able to make good his word, *a consumption, even determined upon the whole earth*, or *land* of Judea, it shall be swept as with the besom of destruction, *See Dan* ix 27 *Note*, (1) It is merciful in God to give sinners warning, he leaves them then without excuse (2) Mockers will be strangely disappointed, when the terrors they despised seize them, and the warnings they ridiculed are proved dreadful realities

Before Christ 712

23 ¶ Give ye ear, and hear my voice, hearken and
hear my speech. 24 Doth the plowman plow all day to
sow? doth he open and break the clods of his ground?
25 When he hath made plain the face thereof, doth he
not cast abroad the fitches, and scatter the cummin, and
cast in ‖ the principal wheat, and the appointed barley,
and the rie in their place? 26 ‡ For his God doth instruct
him to discretion, *and* doth teach him 27 For
^e the fitches are not threshed with a threshing-instrument,
neither is a cart-wheel turned about upon the cummin
but the fitches are beaten out with a staff, and the cummin
with a rod 28 Bread *corn* is bruised, because ^f
he will not ever be threshing it, nor break *it* with the
wheel of his cart, nor bruise it with his horsemen
29 This also cometh forth from the LORD of hosts,
^g *which* is wonderful in counsel, *and* excellent in working

‖ Or the wheat in the principal place and the barley in the appointed place ‡ Or, and he bindeth it in such sort as his God doth instruct him e Chap xxvii 7 f Psal ciii 9 g Ibid xcii 5 Jer xxxii 19

v 23—29 The prophet, in God's name, calls on them for attention, *v* 23 and gives them a parable of warning

1 He bids them regard the husbandman, what various methods he uses, how prudently he plows and sows, casting the seed into the proper soil, and in the appointed season; and when he hath gathered his fruits, how wisely he manages them, using more force with the seeds that are more firm and difficult to be beat out of the ear, and less with such as would be liable to be bruised, *v* 27 And when the bread corn is beat out with the threshing instrument, (which was a kind of low cart, drawn by horses or oxen, with iron spikes at the bottom) he does not suffer it to be trampled on too much, or broken with the wheel on the floor, but carries it to the mill to be ground So,

2 God would not always be warning, and making preparations for the execution of his judgments, but inflict them according to the several deserts of sinners *Note*, (1) All wisdom cometh from above If the husbandman is taught to plow and sow aright, he owes it to God wonderful in counsel (2) The heart of man is as the fallow ground, obdurate and unfruitful, till God in his word breaks up the stubborn soil, and awakens the sinner's conscience (3) Christ is the living seed, the heart that receives him will yield fruit unto God (4) God knows the several dispositions of his people, and dispenses his word and providences in such a way towards them, as may most effectually answer the purposes of his grace (5) In proportion to their guilt and provocations will be the execution of the divine vengeance on the wicked (6) In all his ways and works God will manifest his own glory, and appear *wonderful in counsel, and excellent in working*

CHAP XXIX

This prophecy is against the city of Jerusalem 1 *The event itself is foretold, that Jerusalem should be greatly distressed*, ver 1—6 *but that their enemies should be disappointed*, ver 7, 8 2 *A reproof is given to three sorts of sinners* (1) *Those that were stupid and regardless of the prophet's warnings* ver 9—12 (2) *Those that were formal and hypocritical in their religious performances*, ver 13 (3) *Those politicians that atheistically and profanely despised God's providence, and set up their own projects in competition with it*, ver 14—16 3 *Precious promises of grace are made to a remnant whom God would sanctify, and in whom he would be sanctified, when their enemies and persecutors should be cut off*, ver 17—24

1 WO to ^a † Ariel, to Ariel, the city *where* David
‡ dwelt ^b ‖ add ye year to year; let them kill
sacrifices 2 Yet I will distress Ariel, and there shall
be heaviness and sorrow and ^c it shall be unto me as
Ariel 3 And I will camp against thee round about,
and will lay siege against thee with a mount, and I will
raise

712 a Ezek xliii 15 † i e The lion of God. ‡ Or, encamped b Ezek xxxi 11 ‖ Or, cut off the heads c 2 Kings xix 7

Before Christ 712

raise forts against thee 4 And thou shalt be brought
down, *and* shalt speak out of the ground, and thy speech
shall be low out of the dust, and thy voice shall be as of
d Chap viii 19 one that hath d a familiar spirit out of the ground, and
† Heb chirp thy speech shall † whisper out of the dust 5 Moreover,
the multitude of thy strangers shall be like small dust,
e Job xxi 18 Chap xvii 13 and the multitude of the terrible ones *shall be* e as chaff
that passeth away yea, it shall be f at an instant sud-
f Chap xxx 13 denly 6 Thou shalt be visited of the LORD of hosts
with thunder, and with earthquake, and great noise,
with storm and tempest, and the flame of devouring
fire 7 ¶ And the multitude of all the nations that
fight against Ariel, even all that fight against her, and
her munition, and that distress her, shall be as a dream
g Ps lxxiii 20 of a night-vision 8 g It shall even be as when a hun-
gry *man* dreameth, and behold he eateth, but he a-
waketh and his soul is empty or as when a thirsty *man*
dreameth, and behold he drinketh, but he awaketh, and
behold *he is* faint, and his soul hath appetite so shall
the multitude of all the nations be, that fight against
mount Zion

v 1—8 The subject of this prophecy, is Jerusalem, the place where David *dwelt*, or *encamped*, it is called Ariel, *the lion of God*, some think in reference to the altar, that consumed the sacrifices as a lion his prey, or more probably as the metropolis of Judah, called the lion's whelp, *Gen* xlix 9 and whose standard was a lion

1 The ruin of it is foretold, which all their sacrifices, because hypocritical, cannot prevent Vain were the oblations from year to year, whilst their iniquities were unrepented of, v 1 God threatens to distress them, to fill every heart with heaviness and sorrow, and make the city like the altar of God, surrounded with the blood and carcasses of the slain, and fire kindled in the midst of it, v 2 The besiegers under a Divine support should surround it with mounts and forts without, v 3 beat down the walls, and reduce them to the most abject subjection, or bring them so low by famine, that their voices should through weakness scarce be heard, like those who pretending to familiar spirits, whispered and muttered out of the dust, v 4 With marks of Divine displeasure, God would assist their foes with thunder, earthquake, and tempest, and give them up at last into their hands, who should consume their city and temple with fire, v 6 *Note*, (1) Formal services, whilst the heart continues unchanged and unhumbled, are but an abomination in the sight of God (2) Wo unto those against whom God contends, against him there is no defence (3) The proudest sinner will sooner or later be laid in the dust, either in willing penitence, or terrible perdition

2 God would disappoint their foes, they in their turn should suddenly be destroyed, v 5 their vain hopes of success be as a vision in the night, v 7 and their disappointment like the man who dreams of meat and drink, yet awakes hungry and thirsty, v 8 Which some refer to the ruin of Sennacherib's army, though that will not agree with v 3 as they never raised any mount there others apply the words to the Roman army, and suppose, v 5 to mean their sudden irruption, and numerous forces rushing to the siege, and, v 7, 8 their disappointment, when the spoil they promised themselves would be so little answerable to their expectations some think the whole appertain to the Jews, expressing the *destruction of the succours they expected*, v 5 and the vanity of the hopes with which they flattered themselves, that their city would not be taken till dreadful experience at last awaked them from their fatal reverie

† Heb Take your pleasure and riot 9 ¶ Stay yourselves and wonder, † cry ye out, and
cry h they are drunken, but not with wine, they stag-
h Chap xxviii 7 8 ger, but not with strong drink 10 For i the LORD
i Rom xi 8 hath poured out upon you the spirit of deep sleep, and k
k Chap xliv 18 hath closed your eyes the prophets and your rulers, the
seers hath he covered 11 And the vision of all is be-
l Chap viii 16 come unto you, as the words of a book l *that is* sealed,
Dan xii 4 Rev v 1 which *men* deliver to one that is m learned, saying, Read
this, I pray thee, and he saith, I cannot, for it *is* sealed
m Mat xi 25 & xiii 11 12 And the book is delivered to him that is not learned,
saying, Read this, I pray thee, and he saith, I am not
learned 13 ¶ Wherefore the LORD said, Forasmuch
n Ez xxxiii 31 Mat xv 8 Mar vii 6 as n this people draw near *me* with their mouth, and
with their lips do honour me, but have removed their
heart far from me, and their fear towards me is taught o
o Col ii 22 by the precept of men 14 p Therefore behold, I will
p Hab i 5 proceed to do a marvellous work amongst this people,
q Jer xlix 7 Obad 8 1 Cor i 19 *even* a marvellous work and a wonder for q the wisdom
of their wise *men* shall perish, and the understanding of

their prudent *men* shall be hid 15 r Wo unto them
Before Christ 712
r Chap xxx 1 that seek deep to hide their counsel from the LORD,
and their works are in the dark, and s they say, Who
s Ps xciv 7 Ecclus xxiii 18 seeth us? and who knoweth us? 16 Surely your
turning of things upside down shall be esteemed as the
t Chap xlv 9 potters clay for t shall the work say of him that
made it, He made me not? or shall the thing fram-
ed say of him that framed it, He had no under-
standing?

v 9—16 Whatever fulfilment these words had in the men of that generation, it is plain, from *Rom* xi 7, 8 they refer to the times of Christ

1 The prophet calls aloud with the voice of warning *Stay yourselves*, consider your ways, and run no more madly in the way of sin and ruin, *and wonder* at the long patience of God, *and cry ye out, and cry* at the impending judgments of God, if yet there may be hope or it may be read, *delight yourselves*, either mocking at their peril in the ways of iniquity, or by returning to God for his pardoning mercy

2 The prophet describes their stupidity and judicial blindness They were drunken, not merely with wine, but with corrupt principles, staggering, unsteady in their conduct, and ever turning aside from the right way, v 9 And to this God had in righteous judgment given them up, because they refused the knowledge of the truth, priests, prophets, and rulers, were all under this spirit of darkness and infatuation, v 10 The prophecies were as a sealed book, the wise no more understanding them than the ignorant, v 11, 12 Which was eminently verified, when, in opposition to the brightest evidence, and fullest completion of the prophecies concerning the Messiah, the Jews obstinately rejected the Lord Jesus, and the rulers and priests were the chief in the transgression, blind leaders of the blind, hardened themselves, and hardening others against conviction *Note*, (1) They who will not take warning, will be given up to their own hearts lusts (2) It is a woful case, when they who should teach others, are blind and ignorant themselves (3) Multitudes, in the midst of the plainest light of gospel truth, are still so overcharged with surfeiting and drunkenness, and the cares of this life, that their eyes are closed in darkness, and they are led captive by the devil at his will

3 He charges them with vile hypocrisy *They draw near me with their mouth, and with their lips do honour me*, giving him the formal services of the lip and knee, *but have removed their heart far from me*, their affections being supremely placed on the world, and the things of it, and their souls utter strangers to any inward heart-approach to God, *and their fear towards me is taught by the precept of men*, their religion was mere educational, not derived from God's word, and their worship destitute of spirituality, and suited to lull their souls asleep in stupid formality Such was the case with the Jews, *see Matt* xv 3—9 and such is still the case with multitudes, who call themselves, and are counted by the world, good christians, whose prayers are as regular as the hour returns, whilst their hearts are utter strangers to converting grace and communion with God, and take away their books of devotion, they know no more how to draw near to God, than the cushion on which they kneel *Note*, (1) That is no prayer which is not the soul's work (2) The prayers of the worldling and formalist, are no better than a solemn mockery of God

4 God threatens them with condign punishment a marvellous work he would work, at which they should be astonished

[1] The understanding of their wise men should perish, v 14 Though their schemes were laid so deep against the Lord, and against his anointed, and so concealed, that they atheistically promised themselves not even God could see or disappoint them, v 15 Yet wo unto them! their politics were as absurd as wicked their attempts to hide their counsel from him, and counteract his designs, were vain, since as easily as the potter mould the clay, so could he turn their schemes, or fashion them after his own will, *for shall the work say of him that made it, He made me not? or as it less created, or shall the thing framed say of him that framed it He had no understanding?* which they in fact did, by such conduct, though the folly of it was so evident *Note*, (1) They who set up for wise men and free-thinkers, and discard their Bibles, will prove at last the most egregious fools (2) A disbelief of God's all seeing eye and universal agency, is at the bottom of every work of darkness

[2] The Gentiles should shortly be called into the church, and the Jews rejected, v 17 Though the one was now like a forest, it should, by the preaching of the gospel, become as a fruitful field, and the other, though long favoured in a peculiar manner of God, hereupon, should be utterly laid waste for their impenitence, and especially for their rejection of Christ and his gospel and this in the eyes of the Jews, and even of the apostles themselves, too partial at first to their own nation, appeared a marvellous work

Before Christ 712

17 *Is* it not yet a very little while, and [u] Lebanon
shall be turned into a fruitful field, and the fruitful field
shall be esteemed as a forest? 18 ¶ And in that day [x]
shall the deaf hear the words of the book, and [y] the eyes
of the blind shall see out of obscurity, and out of darkness
19 The meek also shall [z] increase *their* joy in the LORD,
and the poor among men shall rejoice in the holy One of
Israel 20 For the terrible one is brought to nought,
and the scorner is consumed, and all [a] that watch for ini-
quity are cut off 21 [b] That make a man an offender
for a word, and [c] lay a snare for him that reproveth in the
gate, and turn aside the just for a thing of nought 22
Therefore thus saith the LORD, who redeemed Abra-
ham, concerning the house of Jacob, Jacob shall not now
be ashamed, neither shall his face now wax pale 23
But when he seeth his children, [d] the work of mine hands
in the midst of him, they shall sanctify my name, and
sanctify the holy One of Jacob, and shall fear the God
of Israel 24 They also that erred in spirit shall come
to understanding, and [e] they that murmured, shall learn
doctrine

u Chap xxxii 15. x Chap xxxv 5. y Luke vii 22. Acts xxvi 18. z John xv 11. a Mark ii 2. b Mat xxii 15. c Amos v 10. d Chap xix 25. Eph ii 10. e Luke xv 2.

v 18—24 It having been foretold in the former verse, that the Gentiles should be called, and the Jews rejected we have here the blessings the church should in that day of gospel grace enjoy

1 They who before were deaf to God's calls, and blind to any spiritual knowledge of the truth, should by the preaching of the gospel, in demonstration of the spirit and power, have the eyes of their mind enlightened, and be enabled to hear and receive the word of truth, *v* 18 *Note,* (1) Every soul is by nature spiritually blind (2) The preaching of the gospel is the means God uses to bring the soul out of darkness into his marvellous light (3) He must open the understanding to understand the scriptures, or else the light shineth in darkness, and the darkness comprehendeth it not

2 Joy and gladness shall revive the meek and the poor in spirit Such as are brought to a view of their own sinfulness, and humbly submissive to every dispensation of providence, silent under provocation, and in their own eyes poor and perishing, these shall increase their joy in the Lord, under the experience of his love and care of them, and rejoice in the holy One of Israel as their rich portion and exceeding great reward *Note,* (1) God hath in general chosen the poor among men for heirs of his kingdom (2) It is not external poverty, but internal lowliness of heart, to which the promise is made (3) Whatever injuries we receive, or wants we endure, if in the midst of all, our hearts are quietly stayed upon God, we have cause of abundant joy

3 The erroneous shall be convinced, and they who murmured at God's word as hard sayings, be silenced, and humbly submit to his truth, *v* 24

4 Their enemies and persecutors shall be destroyed, *v* 20 *By the terrible one* may be meant the rulers of the Jews, or the persecuting power of the pagan Roman emperors, or it may have respect to antichrist, whose kingdom shall be brought to nought, as the former enemies of Christ and his gospel have been broken *The scorner* signifies the philosophers of the Gentiles, or the Jews, that scoffed at the doctrine of the cross, whose inveterate enmity against Christ and his apostles, kept them always on the watch, *v* 20 and any word which could be misapprehended, served for a ground of accusation they laid snares for their faithful reprovers, that they might entangle them in their talk, and without proof or evidence condemned the just, *v* 21 And this was abundantly fulfilled in the conduct of the Scribes and Pharisees, *Matt* xxii xxiii but they received their just doom, and were cut off according to the prophetic word in their iniquities *Note,* (1) They who are Christ's servants, must expect the threatenings of the terrible, and the ridicule of the scorner (2) The enemies of religion are ever on the watch to catch at every slip or failing of the professors of it as matter of railing accusation against them Let it make us the more watchful to cut off occasion from those who desire occasion (3) We may not think it strange, to have a word dropped unadvisedly, construed into a heavy charge, or an innocent expression perverted to a most criminal meaning, when seekers come to hear God's ministers, not for edification, but to lay snares for their reprovers So persecuted they the prophets that were before us (4) If in the faithful discharge of our office, we find a wicked world opposing, and with every base and malignant insinuation seeking to blacken us, it is a consolation that we are the more like our Lord (5) Whatever success at present may seem to attend those who oppose the cause of God and truth, they shall be cut off at the last

5 The church should be gloriously enlarged, by the accession at last of the seed of Jacob *Therefore thus saith the Lord, who redeemed Abraham* from Ur of the Chaldees, and out of all his troubles, till he obtained eternal salvation, *concerning the house of Jacob* his posterity, *Jacob shall not now be ashamed, neither shall his face wax pale,* as when his degenerate seed rejected and crucified the Lord Jesus *But when he seeth his children* recovered from their apostacy, *the work of my hands,* by converting grace fashioned anew, *in the midst of him* assembled together, *they shall sanctify my name,* by believing in the Redeemer, and receiving his gospel, *and sanctify the holy One of Jacob, and shall fear the God of Israel,* returning to his worship and service By Jacob here also the church of Christ may be meant, rejoicing in the conversion of all the spiritual seed, whether Jews or Gentiles, in the latter day, who shall then together unite in the praises of their Lord

CHAP. XXX

This chapter contains the sins and destruction of the Jews Herein, 1 A just reproof to those who in their distress trusted to the Egyptians for help, ver 1—7 2 *A terrible threatening against those that slighted the advice which God by his prophets gave them,* ver 8—17 3 *Gracious promises to those who trusted in God,* ver 18—26 4 *A prophecy of the total rout and ruin of the Assyrian army, which should be an occasion of great joy to God's people,* ver 27—33

About 712

1 WO to the rebellious children, saith the LORD,
[a] that take counsel, but not of me, and that
cover with a covering, but not of my Spirit, that
they may add sin to sin 2 [c] That walk to go down
into Egypt, (and [d] have not asked at my mouth) to
strengthen themselves in the strength of Pharaoh, and
to trust in the shadow of Egypt 3 [e] Therefore shall
the strength of Pharaoh be your shame, and the trust in
the shadow of Egypt *your* confusion 4 For [f] his princes
were at Zoan, and his ambassadors came to Hanes 5
[g] They were all ashamed of a people [h] *that* could not pro-
fit them, nor be an help nor profit, but a shame and
also a reproach 6 The burden of [i] the beasts of the
south into [k] the land of trouble and anguish, from
whence *come* the young and old lion, the viper, and
fiery flying serpent, they will carry their riches upon the
shoulders of young asses, and their treasures upon the
bunches of camels, to a people *that* shall not profit
them 7 For the Egyptians shall help in vain, and to
no purpose therefore have I cried ‖ concerning this, [l]
Their strength *is* to sit still

a Chap xxix 15. b Deut xxix 19. c Chap xxxi 1. d Numb xxvii 21. Josh ix 14. 1 Kings xxii 7. e Chap xx 5. f Ibid xix 11. g Jer ii 36. h Chap xxxvi 6. i Ibid lvii 9. k Exod i 13, 14. ‖ Or, to her. l Chap vii 4. Ver 15.

v 1—7 It was the sin and folly of the Jews to leave the rock of ages to trust on the broken reed of human supports, and they severely smarted for it

1 A woe is pronounced on the rebellious children of Judah, and the cause of it declared In the day of danger, instead of applying to God, and seeking his guidance and protection, they placed their confidence in the wisdom of their own measures, and the alliance they sought with Egypt, expecting from them a shelter against the impending storm of the Assyrians and thus by sin not only provoked God to chastise them, but also by their disregard of him under their corrections, filled up the measure of their iniquities, his children in profession, but rebels in their practice *Note,* (1) Distrust of God's providence, is virtually to deny his government of the world, and to turn rebels, nay, atheists (2) Rebellion in those who in profession were once his children, is peculiarly provoking (3) If afflictions bring us not nearer to God, they will exceedingly harden and drive us further from him

2 Their confidence would fail them, whatever cost they were at, whatever difficulties they were put to, in order to obtain the alliance of Egypt, or however fair the promises of Pharaoh to support them God was near to be consulted and to help them, and required nothing from them but a humble supplication, yet they rather chose to encounter the dangers of the road that led to Egypt, through deserts abounding with lions and serpents, to burden the weary beasts with their choicest riches, as presents to purchase Pharaoh's aid to go so far as Hanes and Zoan for help, and though so long and cruelly their house of bondage, to seek relief from them [illegible] therefore doth God warn them, *The strength of Pharaoh shall be your shame, and the trust of the shadow of Egypt your confusion,* failing and deceiving them, and making them vexed at their own folly, so hard to purchase an ally, who instead of help or profit, should be their reproach, *chap* xxxvi 6 *Note,* (1) The self-righteous, like these Jews, grudge no expence or trouble in labouring to establish their own righteousness, which must prove their ruin, instead of accepting Christ and his righteousness, freely offered, and which would never fail them (2) When we leave God in our trials to trust on men, we deserve well to rue our folly and be ashamed of [illegible]

Before Christ 713.

3 The prophet warns them of their only method of ſafety *Then ſtrength is to ſit ſtill*, inſtead of ſending their embaſſadors, or ſeeking foreign aſſiſtance, to keep at home, and patiently expect the ſalvation of God *Note*, If we deſire to extricate ourſelves from diſtreſs, it muſt not be by the uſe of undue means, or impatient ſtruggles, but by patient dependance and waiting upon God

m Hab ii 2
† Heb The latter day
n Deut xxxii 20 Chap i 4 Acts vii 51
o Jer xi 21 Amos ii 12 & vii 13 Mic ii 6
p Mic ii 11
q Acts xiii 8
‡ Or fraud
r Pſal lxii 3
s Chap xxix 5
t Jer xix 11
u Chap xlvii 14
x Ver 7 Chap vii 4
y Lev xxvi 8 Deut xxviii 25 & xxxii 30
§ Or, a tree bereft of branches.

8 ¶ Now go, m write it before them in a table, and
note it in a book, that it may be for † the time to come
for ever and ever 9 That n this is a rebellious peo-
ple, lying children, children *that* will not hear the law of
the LORD 10 o Which ſay to the ſeers, See not ;
and to the prophets, Propheſy not unto us right things, p
ſpeak unto us ſmooth things, propheſy deceits 11 Get
you out of the way, q turn aſide out of the path, cauſe
the holy One of Iſrael to ceaſe from before us 12
Wherefore thus ſaith the holy One of Iſrael, Becauſe ye
deſpiſe this word, and truſt in ‡ oppreſſion and perverſe-
neſs, and ſtay thereon 13 Therefore this iniquity ſhall
be to you r as a breach ready to fall, ſwelling out in a
high wall, whoſe breaking s cometh ſuddenly at an in-
ſtant 14 And t he ſhall break it as the breaking of
the potter's veſſel, that is broken in pieces, he ſhall not
ſpare, ſo that there ſhall not be found in the burſting
of it, u a ſherd to take fire from the hearth, or to take
water *withal* out of the pit 15 For thus ſaith the Lord
God, the holy One of Iſrael, x In returning and reſt ſhall
ye be ſaved, in quietneſs and in confidence ſhall be your
ſtrength, and ye would not 16 But ye ſaid, No, for
we will flee upon horſes, therefore ſhall ye flee and we
will ride upon the ſwift, therefore ſhall they that purſue
you be ſwift 17 y One thouſand *ſhall flee* at the rebuke
of one at the rebuke of five ſhall ye flee, till ye be left
as § a beacon upon the top of a mountain, and as an en-
ſign on an hill

v 8—17 For a teſtimony againſt them, for a warning to others, and to vindicate God's juſtice in their puniſhment, the prophet is commanded to write their ſins, and threatned deſtruction on a table, that it might be hung up in ſome conſpicuous place, and note it in a book for future times, *v* 9 *That this is*, or *becauſe this is a rebellious people* this was either the ſubſtance of the writing, or the cauſe why God would have it recorded, they were rebels againſt God, *lying children*, a ſpurious brood, who bore a relation to God in profeſſion, but in practice they denied him, *children that will not hear the law of the Lord*, pay no regard to it, but caſt the word behind their back Two heavy charges are particularly laid againſt them, and each hath a terrible threatning annexed thereto

1 They ſaid *unto the ſeers, See not*, as if they wanted them to connive at their ſins, endeavouring to diſcountenance the freedom of their reproofs, or to ſilence them utterly, *and to the prophets, Propheſy not right things*, the truths of God's word, the evil and guilt of their conduct, and the threatned judgment, *ſpeak unto us ſmooth things, propheſy deceits*, not the harſh words of wrath and damnation, but viſion of peace and proſperity *get you out of the way, turn aſide out of the path*, not obſtruct them in their ſinful courſes, by remonſtrating againſt their iniquities, nor turn aſide with them, and join in their wickedneſs, *cauſe the holy One of Iſrael to ceaſe from before us*, by no more urging their awful miſſion from him, or prefacing their threatnings with the view of the character of God, as the jealous and ſin avenging God *Note*, (1) They are in a dangerous way that are diſguſted at the fidelity, plainneſs, and ſeriouſneſs with which God's miniſters reprove their ſins (2) Though Men's ears are offended at the harſh terms, damnation, hell, eternity of torments, and unquenchable fire, the faithful preacher may not pleaſe them by ſoftening thoſe terrors with which he is commanded to perſuade men (3) A zealous miniſter is a burdenſome ſtone in the ſinner's way, and robs him of the peace he ſeeks in his deluſions (4) They who propheſy ſmooth things, to lull the ſinner aſleep, and flatter the confidence of the formal, will be indeed highly acceptable to the world, but muſt expect from God the doom of perfidy and falſhood (5) If a prophet can be ſeduced to turn aſide, ſinners then ſecurely tranſgreſs, countenanced by ſuch an example

God pronounces their doom, *that holy One of Iſrael*, whoſe name was burdenſome to them, will execute it, and that word they have deſpiſed, ſhall riſe in judgment againſt them, becauſe they rejected his warnings, and truſted *in oppreſſion and perverſeneſs*, in the wealth got by ſuch wicked methods, or their allies which led them aſtray Their deſtruction ſhould come ſudden and terrible, *as a breach ready to fall, ſwelling out in a high wall*, which before the ſtorm ruſhes ſuddenly down, and cruſhes thoſe who fled thither for ſhelter under its ruins, and irreparable as the potter's veſſel, daſhed in pieces by an iron rod, that never

can be reunited *Note*, (1) Whether men will hear, or whether they forbear, we muſt not ceaſe to warn them ſolemnly from God (2) The confidence of the ſinner, and the ſelf-righteous, is like the tottering wall, in the day of wrath it will overwhelm them, and their damnation be not only unexpected and terrible, but irrecoverable and eternal

2 They oppoſed the plaineſt and moſt ſalutary advice *For thus ſaith the Lord God, the holy One of Iſrael*, whoſe burdenſome name they could not bear, though his holineſs was the great ſecurity of his promiſes, *In returning and reſt ſhall ye be ſaved* this is the path of ſafety, to return from their evil ways, and inſtead of truſting on Egypt, to wait patiently on God, *in quietneſs* expecting help from above, *and confidence* in the ſalvation of God *ſhall be your ſtrength*, for thus no enemy could prevail againſt them, *and ye would not*, they obſtinately refuſed to leave the matter in God's hand *But ye ſaid, No*, bent on their own devices, *but we will flee upon horſes*, to ſecure their perſons or treaſures, or to ſeek foreign aſſiſtance, *therefore ſhall ye flee*, be left to your own folly, and be chaſed by their foes *and we will ride upon the ſwift*, in hopes to eſcape, but in vain, *therefore ſhall they that purſue you be ſwift*, and arreſt you in your flight Utterly diſpirited, *one thouſand ſhall flee at the rebuke of one*, See Lev xxvi 7, 8 *at the rebuke of five*, before the moſt inconſiderable number of enemies *ſhall ye flee, till ye be left as a beacon upon the top of a mountain, and as an enſign on an hill*, ſcattered and ſolitary, and almoſt utterly conſumed *Note*, (1) When we truly return to God, we may aſſuredly expect his ſalvation (2) In every trial it ſhould be much more our concern to have our heart brought to quietneſs and reſt in God, than to be anxious about the means of our deliverance (3) They who are enabled wholly to place their confidence in Chriſt, can then do all things, he ſtrengthening them (4) They who will not make uſe of the medicine which never fails to cure, deſerve to die of their diſeaſe (5) When the ſinner ſeeks to fly from God's vengeance, he will quickly feel how vain is the attempt

† Or yet notwithſtanding
z 2 Pet iii 9
a Pſ ii 12 & xxxiv 8 Prov xvi 20 Jer xvii 7
b Ezek xx 40
c 1 Kings xxii 27
‡ Or oppreſſion
d Pſ lxxiv 9 Amos viii 11 12
e 1 John ii 20
f Chap xxxv 8
g Joſh xiv 6
h Chap ii 20 & xxxi 7
i Hoſ xiv 8
k Mat vi 33 1 Tim iv 8
l 1 Cor ix 9
m Chap xxxvii 36

18 ¶ ‖ And therefore will z the LORD wait that he
may be gracious unto you, and therefore will he be exalt-
ed, that he may have mercy upon you for the LORD
is a God of judgment, a bleſſed *are* all they that wait for
him 19 For b the people ſhall dwell in Zion at Jeruſa-
lem thou ſhalt weep no more he will be very graci-
ous unto thee at the voice of thy cry, when he ſhall
hear it, he will anſwer thee 20 And *though* the Lord
give you c the bread of adverſity, and the water of ‡ af-
fliction, yet d ſhall not thy teachers be removed into a
corner any more, but thine eyes ſhall ſee thy teachers
21 And e thine ears ſhall hear a word behind thee, ſay-
ing, f This *is* the way, walk ye in it, g when ye turn to
the right hand, and when ye turn to the left 22 h Ye
ſhall defile alſo the covering of thy graven images of ſil-
ver, and the ornament of thy molten images of gold
thou ſhalt caſt them away as a menſtruous cloth, i thou
ſhalt ſay unto it, Get thee hence 23 k Then ſhall he
give the rain of thy ſeed that thou ſhalt ſow the ground
withal, and bread of the increaſe of the earth, and it
ſhall be fat and plenteous in that day ſhall thy cattle
feed in large paſtures 24 l The oxen likewiſe, and
the young aſſes that ear the ground, ſhall eat clean pro-
vender which hath been winnowed with the ſhovel and
with the fan 25 And there ſhall be upon every high
mountain, and upon every high hill, rivers *and* ſtreams
of waters, in the day of m the great ſlaughter, when the
towers fall 26 Moreover, the light of the moon ſhall
be as the light of the ſun, and the light of the ſun ſhall
be ſeven-fold, as the light of ſeven days, in the day that
the LORD bindeth up the breach of his people, and
healeth the ſtroke of their wound

v 18—26 After the former threatnings, ſome conſolation is promiſed to the faithful

1 In the midſt of judgment God would remember mercy *and therefore*, or *nevertheleſs*, *will the Lord wait that he may be gracious unto you* the choſen remnant, whom, as the word ſignifies, he *pants* to deliver out of their troubles, *and therefore will he be exalted*, or will exalt his Son as a prince and Saviour in the midſt of them, *that he may have mercy upon you for the Lord is a God of judgment*, faithful to his promiſes, as juſt in his correction, and therefore *bleſſed are all they that wait for him*, they will in the iſſue be made happy, in a ſalvation, and their patient hope be crowned with deliverance *For the people ſhall dwell in Zion at Jeruſalem*, ſafe amidſt all the threatnings of Sennacherib *thou ſhalt weep no more*, as they did in the day of their diſtreſs *he will be very gracious unto thee*, exceeding thy moſt ſanguine hope, *at the voice of thy cry, when he ſhall hear it, he will anſwer thee*, as he did Hezekiah's prayer, when he ſpread

Before Christ 713.

spread their afflicted case before the Lord *Note*, (1) God waits to be gracious no sooner does the sinner return, than he is ready to receive him (2) Persevering prayer ever brings an answer of peace (3) We shall find every trial a rich blessing to us in the issue, whenever it hath served to excite our faith, and quicken our application to God

2 The Lord will provide them with the rich means of grace, to preserve them in the path of duty, afflicted they might be, as is the frequent lot of his people, but never deserted In the times of persecution, probably under Ahaz, their faithful teachers were driven into obscurity but God promises now to restore them, that they might publickly and quietly enjoy the benefit of their ministrations, and to preserve a constant succession of them, v 20 And they should hear a voice behind them, the Spirit of truth, who should be sent to guide them into all truth, *saying*, *This is the way, walk ye in it*, directing them to the written word as their rule, and enlightening their minds to see and follow it, when they turned to the right hand or the left, from the strait way of God's commandment And this is particularly applicable to the times of Christ, when he raised up his faithful servants, and sent his Spirit to direct his people in the way of life and glory, and to bring them to himself, who is the way, the truth, and the life *Note*, (1) Among the greatest afflictions God's people lament, and what is worse than a famine of bread and water, is the famine of the word (2) Though the church may be under persecution, and faithful ministers especially driven into a corner, yet God will rebuke the storm, and bring them from their concealment again, to the joy of his people (3) It becomes us to be attentive to the voice of conscience, and the secret warnings of God, when tempted and in doubt how to act (4) Disposed we are continually to turn aside, if the preventing and restraining grace of God did not preserve us

3 They should then renounce their idolatry, their besetting and most provoking sin Their idols now, though made of richest metal, nicely engraved, and curiously adorned, with abhorrence should be cast away, as polluted and nauseous, v 22 And this was fulfilled on their deliverance from Sennacherib, *see 2 Kings* xviii 4 2 *Chron* xxix 16 and after the Babylonish captivity, this evil was radically cured *Note*, (1) Nothing engages the heart so much to God as a sense of his goodness (2) True penitents abhor their sins, and put from them as far as possible whatever they have found a means of temptation to them in the time past

4 Plenty shall be restored to them Their ground, watered with the dew of heaven, should yield abundant increase, v 23 *See chap* xxxvii 30 Their cattle fatten in rich pastures, and eat provender winnowed, such plenty being in the land, v 24 The rain descending as rivers from the hills, should make their vallies fruitful, that they may stand thick with corn, and add to the joy of their deliverance from the Assyrian army, slaughtered by the sword of the destroying angel, v 25 And this may well be applied to the abundance of gospel grace, that will be dispensed in the latter day, when the high towers of Babylon mystical shall fall, and the earth be filled with the knowledge of the Lord, as the waters cover the sea *Note*, The minister, like the husbandman, may sow the seed, but it is God alone that giveth the increase, yet this must not supersede, but quicken our labours

5 Uncommon light and joy would then be diffused *The light of the moon shall be as the light of the sun, and the light of the sun shall be seven-fold, as the light of seven days*, expressive of their exultation on the destruction of the Assyrians, when their breaches made by that army should be repaired, and the wounds of their state healed and may be referred to the day of Christ at present, when every awakened sinner, brought out of darkness into God's marvellous light, rejoices with joy unspeakable, and full of glory, at seeing the breach, which sin had made, bound up by the sacrifice of a Redeemer, and experiences the healing of this blessed Saviour's grace in his soul and perhaps it looks forward to the expected glorious spread of the gospel, when all afflictions of God's people are at an end, the nation of the redeemed shall for ever walk in the light of the Lord

27 ¶ Behold, the name of the LORD cometh from far, burning with his anger, and the burden *thereof is* heavy his lips are full of indignation, and his tongue as a devouring fire 28 And his breath, as an overflowing stream, ⁿ shall reach to the midst of the neck, to sift the nations with the sieve of vanity and *there shall be* ᵒ a bridle in the jaws of the people, causing *them* to err 29 Ye shall have a song as in the night, ᵖ *when* a holy solemnity is kept, and gladness of heart, as when one goeth with a pipe to come into the mountain of the LORD, to the ‖ mighty One of Israel 30 And the LORD shall cause ‡ his glorious voice to be heard, and shall shew the lighting down of his arm, with the indignation of *his* anger, and ᵠ with the flame of a devouring fire, *with* scattering, ʳ and tempest, ˢ and hail-stones 31 For ᵗ through the voice of the LORD shall the Assyrian be beaten down ᵘ *which* smote with a rod 32 And in every place where the grounded staff shall pass, which the LORD shall § lay upon him, ˣ it shall be with tabrets and harps and in battles of shaking will he fight ‖ with it 33 For ʸ Tophet *is* ordained of old yea, ᶻ for the king it is prepared, he hath made *it* deep *and* large the pile thereof *is* fire and much wood, the breath of the LORD, like a stream of brimstone, doth kindle it

ⁿ Chap viii 8 ᵒ Chap xxxvii 29 ᵖ Ps xlii 4 ‖ Heb Rock Deut xxxii 4 18 xviii 31 ‡ Heb The glory of his voice ᵠ Chap xxix 6 & xxxvii 36

Before Christ 713 ʳ Chap xxviii 2 & xxx ᵗ Josh x 11 ᵘ Chap xxxvii 36 ˢ Chap x 24 § Heb cause to rest upon him ˣ Ib Lam 10 & lxviii 25 Rev xx 1, 2 ‖ Or, against them ʸ Josh xv 8 & viii 10 Mat v 22 ᶻ Chap xxxvii 38

v 27—33 The happiness of God's people being intimately connected with the destruction of their foes, the prophet foretells their utter ruin

1 The great agent in this, is God himself, from heaven sending forth his terrible wrath against the army of Sennacherib, v 27 swallowing up the hosts of Assyria, as a deluge, and sifting them in the sieve of vanity, the whole being chaff, dispersed with the breath of his displeasure his bridle in their jaws should cause them to err, turned backwards from their designs of destroying Jerusalem, as a horse is governed by its rider, v 28 At his voice his minister of wrath shall go forth armed with lightning, tempest, and hail-stones, and stretching forth his more than mortal arm, spread universal destruction around, v 30 The rod which smote God's people, shall now be broken, v 31 before the *grounded staff*, the judgment grounded on God's eternal decrees, and lying so heavy on the Assyrians, that none should be able to withstand it, in that night of terror, v 32 Tophet, in the valley of the son of Hinnom, where they encamped, is ordained for their slaughter-house, deep and large, so often defiled with the abominable idolatries of those who passed their children through the fire to Moloch, rendered abominable, as covered with the blood and corpses of the slain, which the lightning of God scorched, or where the Jews burnt the bodies when they found them dead in the morning *Note*, (1) It is a fearful thing to fall into the hands of the living God (2) The burnings of Tophet represent the eternal punishment of impenitent sinners Our Saviour calls the place of the damned, Gehenna, in allusion to this valley of Hinnom, there the greatest kings, as well as the meanest slaves, whose guilt provokes the wrath of God, lie down in flames that never can be quenched, and there the multitude of sinners, with the devil and his angels, are tormented day and night in those everlasting burnings, which *the breath of the Lord, like a stream of brimstone, doth kindle*

2 As when the smoke of the sinners torment ascendeth for ever and ever, the saints of God say Hallelujah, *Rev* xix 3 so here the Jews are represented as rejoicing over their proud oppressors fallen, in solemn thanksgivings with tabret and harp, transported at the miraculous interposition, and ascribing to the mighty One of Israel the praise of all his wondrous works *Note*, However now the wicked triumph, the time is short, their fall determined, their ruin terrible, and God's just judgments upon them, will minister matter for his saints everlasting praises

CHAP XXXI

This chapter is an abridgment of the foregoing, the heads of it are much the same Here is, 1 A woe to those that when the Assyrian army invaded them, trusted to the Egyptians and not to God for succour, ver 1—3 2 Assurance given that God would defend Jerusalem in that time of danger, ver 4, 5 3 A call to repentance and reformation, ver 6, 7 4 A prediction of the fall of the Assyrian army, and the fright which the Assyrian king should thereby be put into, ver 8, 9

1 WO to them ᵃ that go down to Egypt for help, and ᵇ stay on horses, and trust in chariots, because *they are* many, and in horsemen, because they are very strong but they look not unto the holy One of Israel, neither seek the LORD 2 Yet ᶜ he also *is* wise, and will bring evil, and will not call back his words but will arise against the house of the evil doers, and against the help of them that work iniquity 3 Now the Egyptians ᵈ *are* men and not God, and their horses flesh and not spirit, when the LORD shall stretch out his hand, both he that helpeth shall fall, and he that is holpen shall fall down, and they all shall fail together 4 For thus hath the LORD spoken unto me, Like as the lion and the young lion roaring on his prey, when a multitude of shepherds is called forth against him, he will not be afraid of their voice, nor abase himself for the ‖ noise of them ᵉ so shall the LORD of hosts come down to fight for mount Zion, and for the hill thereof 5 ᶠ As birds flying,

ᵃ Deut xvii 16 Chap xxx 2 Jer xlvii ᵇ Ps xx 7 ᶜ 1 Cor i 25 ᵈ Ps cxlvi 3 4 ᵉ Hos xi 10 Amos iii 8 ‖ Or, multitude ᶜ Chap xlii 13 ᶠ Deut xxxii 11 Ps xci 4

Before Christ 713

flying, so will the LORD of hosts defend Jerusalem, [h]
defending also he will deliver *it*, *and* [i] passing over he will
preserve *it*

[h] Ps xxxvii 40
[i] Ex xii 13

v 1—5 Repeated woes are denounced to awaken the sinners in Zion, if still they persist in their wicked way, surely their blood will be on their own heads

1 The charge laid against them, is their recourse to Egypt, and neglect of God, v 1 The numerous hosts of Pharaoh, his chariots and horsemen, seemed to afford greater security to the eye of sense, than the word of promise, and therefore they are more sollicitous to engage his friendship, than spread their case before the holy One of Israel *Note*, They who consult with sense, take a bad guide

2 The folly and danger of their conduct is exposed If they wanted wisdom, lo! God is all wise, and they should consult him if they wanted might, God was almighty, and could protect them, but when he was slighted and neglected, his wisdom and power, that might have been engaged for them now are armed against them and what then can the wisdom or power of Egypt do to save them? he will counteract all the schemes of their allies, and execute the threatning he hath pronounced against the workers of iniquity, v 2 and by sad experience they shall be taught the vanity of that strength of Pharoah, which they idolized The Egyptians shall be found men frail, false, foolish, and not God, as they by their confidence in them seemed to make them, and their horses flesh and not spirit, and therefore when the Lord should stretch forth his hand, they and their unprofitable helpers must fall together, v 3 *Note*, (1) They who affect to be wiser than their Bibles, will only in the end expose their own folly (2) The more we know of men, the more we shall see cause to cease from human dependance, the more we know of God, the more shall we be engaged to trust him (3) There are many truths evident and allowed by all, and yet in practice we are apt glaringly to contradict them (4) The sinner in the day of wrath shall find little comfort or help in his companion, when they shall fall together, and receive the reward of their iniquities

3 Those in Zion, who, without having recourse to Egypt, trusted God for their safety, should find him a sure refuge in the day of calamity, as a lion seizing his prey, that cannot be intimidated by the shouting of the shepherds, who, daring not to approach him, seek to scare him with their noise, so impotent will be the army of the Assyrians, when the lion of the tribe of Judah shall come to fight for his Zion, v 4 swift as the eagle will he fly to their succour, and safe preserve them, when the destroying angel shall pass over to smite their enemies, and by their destruction deliver Jerusalem *Note*, In the midst of danger they are safe whom God with tenderness unutterable covers under his wings, as a hen gathereth her chickens, and defends with an arm of almighty and irresistible power Oh, that we did but trust him!

[k] Hos ix 9
[l] Chap ii 20 & xxvii 9 & xxx 22
[m] Chap. xxxvii 36
[||] Heb for melting, or tribute
[n] Chap xxxvii 37
[‡] Heb his rock shall pass away for fear
[o] Lev vi 13 or 1 C xxi 9 Zech ii 5

6 ¶ Turn ye unto *him from* whom [k] the children of
Israel have deeply revolted 7 For in that day every
man [l] shall cast away his idols of silver, and his idols of
gold, which your own hands have made unto you *for* a
sin 8 ¶ Then [m] shall the Assyrian fall with the
sword, not of a mighty man, and the sword, not of a
mean man shall devour him but he shall flee from the
sword, and his young men shall be [||] discomfited 9 [n]
And [‡] he shall pass over to his strong-hold for fear,
and his princes shall be afraid of the ensign, saith the
LORD, [o] whose fire *is* in Zion, and his furnace in Jerusalem

v 6—9 We have here,

1 A gracious call to repentance God had not cast them off, though they had basely forsaken him, and deeply revolted from him he calls them children of Israel as a reproach for their ingratitude, to beget conviction of their baseness, and encourage their hope, seeing, though they deserved to be disowned, he still regarded them as his sons and daughters, and invited them to turn to him, with assurances of kind acceptance *Note*, (1) If the goodness of God will not lead us sinners to repentance nothing will (2) It is never too late to return to God, the deepest revolters will find their king, on humble submission, very inexorable

2 A blessed reformation wrought *In that day*, when their deliverance should appear so evidently the work of God's hand, vanquished by almighty grace, they should cast away their idols of gold and silver the work which their own hands had made to sin so bent were they upon idolatry, that no cost or pains were spared, but now their sin is their burden, and their idols detested and abhorred *Note*, (1) In a day of repentance our tempters to sin will be loathed more than ever they have been loved (2) Every man hath his peculiar idol lust, the indulgence of which will be his bitterest burden when God awakens his conscience, and against which he must place an especial guard

3 A glorious victory obtained The Assyrian shall fall, not by an arm of flesh, but by the immediate stroke of God and whilst the army is discomfitted, their king in terrors shall flee, and his princes, the few who escape with him, shall pass over to his strong-hold, or, *his rock shall pass over for fear*, his mighty warriors who were left, trembling at the terrible ensign in the air, the destroying angel with his drawn sword, or least they should be pursued by the Jews in their flight, and dreading that fiery furnace of wrath that burns so hot against the enemies of Zion Some interpret the last words, of God's altar at Jerusalem, on which the fire burned continually, and of his constant residence there as in his own house *Note*, (1) When God contends, he will overcome (2) In present judgments are so terrible, what must be the fire of hell, and the furnace of eternal wrath! (3) The same God which is a consuming fire to his enemies, is a wall of fire around his people to protect them, and a fire of love within their hearts to comfort them

CHAP XXXII

Hezekiah is here the type of Christ, to whom this chapter most properly belongs We have here, 1 The blessing of his people under his government, procured by his grace, and taught by his word, ver 1—4 2 The hypocrisy and outrageousness of the foes, ver 5—8 3 The destruction threatened, which they are called to lament, ver 9—14 4 The happy times that should succeed, ver 15—20

Before Christ 713

[a] Jer xxiii 5 Dan ix 24 Zech ix 9
[†] Or the
[b] Ps xxxi
[c] Chap iv 6
[d] John xii 37 38
[e] Chap xxix 4
[f] Chap. xxxv 5 6
[‡] Heb Hasty
[§] Or elegantly
[||] Heb Nabal, the fool 1 Sam xxv 25
[g] Mal ii 18
[h] Luke xi 52
[†] Or he speaketh against the poor in judgement
[i] 2 Cor ix 9
[‡] Or be established, Prov xii 7

1 BEHOLD, [a] a king shall reign in righteousness,
and princes shall rule in judgment 2 And a
man shall be [b] as an hiding place from the wind, and [c]
a covert from the tempest as [†] rivers of water in a dry
place, as [c] the shadow of a great rock in a weary land
3 And [d] the eyes of them that see, shall not be dim,
and the ears of them that hear shall hearken 4 The
heart also of the [‡] rash shall understand knowledge, and
the tongue of the stammerers shall be ready to speak [§]
plainly 5 [||] The vile person [g] shall be no more called
liberal, nor the churl said *to be* bountiful 6 For the
vile person will speak villany, and his heart will work
iniquity, to practise hypocrisy, and to utter error against
the LORD, to make empty the soul of the hungry, and
[h] he will cause the drink of the thirsty to fail 7 The
instruments also of the churl *are* evil he deviseth
wicked devices to destroy the poor with lying words,
even when [†] the needy speaketh right 8 But [i] the
liberal deviseth liberal things, and by liberal things shall
he [‡] stand

v 1—8 Under Hezekiah's government the people enjoyed great blessings himself a righteous governor, his princes copying his example, by them the oppressed were protected, the ignorant instructed, the law of God both taught and understood, and as the consequence thereof, a right estimation made of the characters of men, as viewed in this light of truth And to this the prophecy primarily may refer, but we may say of it truly, a greater than Hezekiah is here

1 The righteous government of Christ is foretold *Behold*, with transport and joy, *a king*, the Lord upon his throne, *shall reign in righteousness*, protecting his people, and punishing his enemies, his laws most equitable, and his administration altogether righteous *and princes shall rule in judgment*, the bishops and pastors ordained by him to have rule in the church, who preach his gospel, administer his ordinances, and execute their office according to his appointment

2 His people shall be saved from wrath by him *A man*, or *that man*, *shall be as an hiding-place from the wind and a covert from the tempest*, by him the sinner's soul is sheltered from the storm of Divine vengeance, which by the interposition of his own body on the tree, he hath endured for them, and from the fiery darts of Satan, and the fierce temptations of sin, that else would overwhelm them *as rivers of water in a dry place*, refreshing, quickening, and comforting the souls of his people, when parched up as the dry ground for want of rain, or fainting with thirst under the assaults of corruption, *as the shadow of a great rock in a weary land*, such as we infer the christian pilgrim finds this world, and scorched with the sultry beams of persecution, affliction, and temptation must utterly fail but for this hospitable shadow, which Christ his rock spreads over him, there he feels support ministered, there he is hid in the hour of trial, and under this shadow sitting with great delight, renews his strength, and is enabled for the remainder of life's journey, till in the grave he shall find his home and rest

3 Great light and knowledge shall be diffused *The eyes of them that see, shall not be dim*, but discern the truth as he hath discovered the light of the glory of God in the gospel of his dear

I Son

Before Christ 713

Son, and shall know him from the least to the greatest, *and the ears of them that hear shall hearken*, earnest to search the scriptures, and to obtain deeper discoveries of Divine truth *The heart also of the rash shall understand knowledge*, to which they before paid no regard, or hastily mistook the meaning of the sacred oracles, *and the tongue of the stammerers shall be ready to speak plainly*, or *elegantly*, as when illiterate Galileans were endued with wisdom from above, or, as is still the case, when by Divine grace the soul is led into the knowledge of the gospel, and taught of the spirit, and then even a child can speak more distinctly of the things of God, than the wisest unenlightened man

4 Eminent discernment, to distinguish the characters of men, and fidelity to reprove, shall then be in the ministers of Christ, weighing persons in the balance of the sanctuary, they shall not give flattering titles, but charge men's sins home upon their consciences, *v* 5 or the meaning is, that then *the vile person Naval*, a fool, *shall be no more called Nadib* a prince, nor put in trust with the gospel, which his folly must disgrace, nor *the churl*, the covetous person, *be called bountiful* or honourable, since ignorance in understanding, and covetousness in temper, would be a scandal to the ministry *For the vile person*, or *the fool, will speak villany*, or *folly*, advancing doctrines opposite to the oracles of wisdom, such as the rectitude of human nature, the freedom of man's will, the merit of works, &c *and his heart will work iniquity*, which is the natural fruit of false principles, *to practise hypocrisy*, pretending regard for the interests of piety and religion, when most effectually sapping the foundations of true holiness, *and to utter error against the Lord*, denying the Godhead, or debasing the glory of the Redeemer, *to make empty the soul of the hungry*, by withholding from them the bread of life, *and he will cause the drink of the thirsty to fail*, by turning them away from the doctrines of the free, all-sufficient, and sovereign grace of God, the fountain of living waters, to the empty and broken cisterns of good resolutions formed in man's self-sufficient strength *The instruments also of the churl are evil*, his methods to gratify his covetousness, being more sollicitous about his own gain, than the good of the souls committed to him *he deviseth wicked devices to destroy the poor*, or *afflicted*, *with lying words, even when the needy speaketh right things*, if any under soul-concern come to enquire, he gives them bad advice how to get rid of their convictions, and heals the hurt slightly, contriving to prejudice them against those who were able to extricate them from their troubles, in the way of grace and truth Such is the character of a false and faithless minister *but the liberal deviseth liberal things*, being possessed of a princely spirit, meet for a ruler in God's church fraught with Divine grace, or perhaps enjoying the blessings of providence, he contrives how to be useful, dispensing the doctrines of the gospel zealously, not for filthy lucre's sake, but of a willing mind, and is an example to believers in charity and liberality, *and by liberal things he shall stand*, or *be established*, his own spirit strengthened, and a blessing bestowed on his labours

9 ¶ Rise up, ye women that are [h] at ease, hear my
voice, ye careless daughters, give ear unto my speech
10 † Many days and years shall ye be troubled, ye care-
less women for the vintage shall fail, the gathering
shall not come 11 Tremble, ye women [k] that are at
ease; be troubled, ye careless ones [l] strip ye and make
ye bare, and gird *sackcloth* upon your loins 12 They
shall lament for the teats, for the pleasant ‡ fields, for
the fruitful vine 13 [m] Upon the land of my people
shall come up thorns *and* briers, § yea, upon all the
houses of joy in the ‖ joyous city 14 Because [n] the
palaces shall be forsaken, the multitude of the city shall
be left, the forts and ‡ towers shall be for dens for ever,
a joy of wild asses, a pasture of flocks 15 Until the
Spirit be poured upon us from on high, and [p] the wil-
derness be a fruitful field, and the fruitful field be counted
for a forest 16 Then judgment shall dwell in the wil-
derness, and righteousness remain in the fruitful field
17 And [q] the work of righteousness shall be peace, and
the effect of righteousness, quietness, and assurance for
ever 18 And my people shall dwell in a peaceable
habitation, and in sure dwellings, and in quiet resting-
places 19 [r] When it shall hail, coming down on the
forest, and the city shall be low in a low place 20
Blessed *are* ye [s] that sow beside all waters, that send forth
thither the feet of the ox and the ass

† Heb Days above a year
k Amos vi 1
l Chap iii 24
‡ Heb Fields of desire
m Chap xxxiv 13 Hos ix 6
n Chap vii 23
§ Or, burning upon
‖ Or, revelling
n Chap xxvii
o 2 Kings xxv 9
‡ Or clifts and towers
p Chap xliv 3 Joel ii 28
q Chap xxix 17 & xxxv 2
r James iii 18
r Chap xxx 30 Rev xvi 21
s Eccles xi 1 Matt viii 4 1 Cor ix 10

v 9—20 We have here,

1 A warning of approaching judgments, directed to the daughters of Zion, whose wantonness, pride, and vanity, had contributed to fill up the measure of the nation's iniquity They are represented as *careless*, or *confident*, and *at ease*, without any concern, either about their sin or danger, but they are called to hear the word of God and tremble, and by immediate humiliation, *v* 11 prevent, if possible, the impending wrath of the Almighty, or prepare to meet it Heavy is the threatened judgment, the vintage failing through drought or consumed by the enemy, *v* 10 the pastures ravaged, or withered away, so that the kine should not give their milk, *v* 12 the land desolate, and producing only briars and thorns, their joyous houses, where mirth and pleasure reigned, ruined, *v* 13 the palaces forsaken, the city deserted, the fortifications mouldering away, and Zion become the den of beasts and wild asses, whilst flocks graze in the streets, once crowded with inhabitants, and this desolation abiding *for ever*, which directs us to apply this catastrophe not to the destruction of Jerusalem by the Chaldeans, but to the final ruin it afterward underwent, and in which it lies to this day *Note*, (1) When men live careless, and at ease, in their sins, death will come upon them with a terrible surprize (2) They who have abused their plenty to pride and excess, justly are made to feel the miseries of want (3) The only way to prevent our eternal sorrows, is by a timely regard to God's warnings, and by present humiliation for our sins (4) They who continue impenitent, will quickly experience an awful change, when their houses of joy and pleasure must be quitted for an abode in everlasting burnings, where there is weeping, and wailing, and gnashing of teeth

2 A promise of future blessings which looks forward to the latter days of the gospel dispensation for so long will Jerusalem be trodden down of the Gentiles, *Luke* xxi 24

(1) *The Spirit shall be poured out from on high*, from heaven, as in the days of pentecost, and this shall be again abundantly the case in the last days, when Jews and Gentiles shall be converted, and made one fold under one shepherd *Note*, The desolations of every fallen soul must for ever continue, unless the Spirit from on high be poured out to convert and renew the heart of the sinner

(2) A mighty change shall be produced by his Divine power *The wilderness shall be a fruitful field, and the fruitful field be counted for a forest*, the world that was as a wilderness, full of impiety and iniquity, now, by grace renewed, shall bring forth the fruits of righteousness and true holiness, and numerous converts, thick as the trees of the forest, be added to the church daily *Then judgment shall dwell in the wilderness*, the word of God, and the doctrines according to godliness, be received and embraced by those who before were utterly ignorant of them, or at enmity against them, *and righteousness remain in the fruitful field*, those who are effectually wrought upon, shall abide faithful, and increasing in every Divine temper and disposition *And the work of righteousness shall be peace*, either the work of Divine grace, which the Spirit works in the heart, shall produce peace, as it is the evidence of our reconciliation with God, or rather the perfect work of righteousness, wrought out by the Redeemer, shall give us the most solid grounds of peace with God, and in our own consciences, *and the effect of righteousness, quietness and assurance for ever*, so if interested in the Redeemer's perfect work, no troubles need disturb, no accusations of sin or Satan distract us, we may rest satisfied in him, and with unfailing confidence expect the constant supplies of his grace, strength, and consolations on earth, and the certain possession of the inheritance purchased for us in glory everlasting *And my people shall dwell in a peaceable habitation, and in sure dwellings, and in quiet resting-places*, the enmity between Jew and Gentile being utterly abolished, their foes of earth and hell restrained from disturbing their repose, their comfort and prosperity secured for ever, and none to make them afraid *when it shall hail, coming down on the forest*, the storm of wrath being poured on the ungodly, *see Rev* xvi 21 and the seat of antichristian oppression and tyranny laid in the dust, *Rev* xvi 19—21 *Note*, (1) Wherever the spirit of God is poured out on a soul, immediately the fruit will be holiness to the Lord (2) A clear discovery, and a full persuasion of the all-sufficiency of the finished righteousness of a Redeemer, is the solid ground of peace within, and whilst our souls fix on this alone, we may rest assured, there neither is nor can be any condemnation (3) Whenever the soul, complete in Jesus, makes mention of his righteousness only, then will the heart experience most abundantly the transforming power of Divine grace, and grow like him, from whom cometh our salvation (4) Whatever troubles disturb our present repose; if we are found in Christ, we know there is a mansion of eternal rest provided for his redeemed (5) When storms of vengeance descend on the ungodly, they who have fled for refuge to the hope set before them, are sure to be hid in the day of the Lord's fierce anger

(3) An especial blessing is promised to the ministers of God, and their labours as diligent husbandmen cast their seed on well watered lands, and see it springing up to fill, that their cattle are let in to crop it, or at harvest bring home the corn, so shall the word of God be in their mouths, attended by the Spirit, producing an abundant harvest of souls, in whom they see the fruit of their labours, and who will be their crown,

and

Before Christ 713

and rejoicing in the day of the Lord Jesus *Note*, They who *ſow beſide all waters*, take every opportunity of doing good, ſhall find God not unrighteous to forget their works of faith and labours of love

CHAP. XXXIII

This chapter relates to the ſame events with the foregoing, wherein the invaſion of Sennacherib, and the deliverance of Jeruſalem, are a figure of the ſufferings and deliverance of the church from the power of Antichriſt 1 *Here is a wo denounced*, ver 1 2 *The prayer of God's people*, ver 2 3 *An anſwer given them*, ver 2—6 4 *The diſtreſs which would precede their deliverance*, ver 7—12 5 *Notice given of it, for the confuſion of hypocrites, and the comfort of the faithful*, ver 13—19 6 *The church of Chriſt finally triumphant*, ver 20—24

1 WO to thee [a] that ſpoileſt, and thou *waſt* not
ſpoiled, and dealeſt treacherouſly, and they
dealt not treacherouſly with thee [b] when thou ſhalt
ceaſe to ſpoil, thou ſhalt be ſpoiled, *and* when thou ſhalt
make an end to deal treacherouſly, [c] they ſhall deal
treacherouſly with thee 2 O LORD, be gracious un-
to us, [d] we have waited for thee be thou their arm every
morning, [e] our ſalvation alſo in the time of trouble 3
At the noiſe of the tumult [f] the people fled at the lift-
ing up of thyſelf the nations were ſcattered 4 And
your ſpoil ſhall be gathered *like* the gathering of the cater-
piller as the running to and fro of locuſts ſhall he run
upon them 5 The LORD is exalted for [g] he dwell-
eth on high, he hath filled Zion with judgment and
righteouſneſs 6 And [h] wiſdom and knowledge ſhall be
the ſtability of thy times, *and* ſtrength of ſalvation the
fear of the LORD is his treaſure. 7 Behold, their †
valiant ones ſhall cry without [i] the ambaſſadors of peace
ſhall weep bitterly 8 [k] The high-ways lie waſte, the
way-faring man ceaſeth, [l] he hath broken the covenant,
[m] he hath deſpiſed the cities, he regardeth no man 9
The earth mourneth *and* languiſheth [n] Lebanon is a-
ſhamed *and* hewn down Sharon is like a wilderneſs, and
Baſhan and Carmel ſhake off *their fruits* 10 [o] Now will
I riſe, ſaith the LORD now will I be exalted, now will
I lift up myſelf 11 Ye ſhall [p] conceive chaff, ye ſhall
bring forth ſtubble your breath *as* fire ſhall devour
you 12 And the people ſhall be *as* the burnings of
lime · *as* thorns cut up ſhall they be burnt in the fire

[a] Chap xxi 2. Hab ii 8
[b] Rev xiii 10
[c] Mat vii 2
[d] Chap xxv 9 & xxvi 8
[e] Pſ xxi 4, 5
[f] Chap xxxvi 37
[g] Pſ xciii 4
[h] Eccleſ vii 12
† Or, meſſengers
[i] Chap xxxvi 22
[k] Judges v 6
[l] 2 Kings xviii 14, &c
[m] 2 Chron xxxii 1
[n] Chap xxiv 8 & xxxvii 24
[o] Pſ xii 5 & cii 13
[p] Pſ vii 14

v 1—12 The ſubject of this prophecy is variouſly interpreted, ſome refer it to the ſtate of the Jews under Hezekiah, when Sennacherib diſtreſſed them and was deſtroyed, others to the deſolations made by Antiochus, and to the victorious arms of the Maccabees over him, others to the church of Chriſt, oppreſſed by the antichriſtian foe, and his final ruin, and all theſe may be comprehended herein, and the former deliverances of God's church prefigure thoſe of the latter day Herein,

1 The wo denounced on the ſpoiler and treacherous dealer for a while his politics would ſucceed, and his power prevail, however cruelly or unjuſtly exerciſed, but God will return his evil upon his own head, and at the appointed time viſit upon him his wickedneſs and this was the caſe with Sennacherib and Antiochus, as it will be of the Romiſh antichriſt, whoſe politics, craft, and deceivableneſs of unrighteouſneſs, are well-known, and by theſe, long hath he made a prey of men's goods, bodies, and ſouls, but at laſt God will viſit him according to his deſerts See *Rev* xiii 11 xvii 12—16 *Note*, (1) To compaſs their ends, the wicked heſitate not at falſhood, fraud, or violence, but God knows how to repay them in their own coin (2) There are appointed bounds ſet to men's wickedneſs, and when they have filled up the meaſure of their iniquities, God will awake to judgment

2 The people of God in prayer fly to him in the day of their calamity *O Lord, be gracious unto us*, interpoſe to ſave us from every enemy, *we have waited for thee*, not fainting in the time of adverſity, but expecting thy ſalvation *be thou their arm every morning*, which either is a requeſt for Hezekiah and the princes, that they might be ſtrengthened for their work; or rather it is the interceſſion of the members of the church one for another, every morning offered, for grace to enable them for the work of every day *be thou our ſalvation alſo in time of trouble*, from all the perſecutions and diſtreſs under which in body or ſoul we groan, being burdened *Note*, (1) When we have a gracious God to go to, there is comfort under every affliction (2) They who wait on him, will never be forſaken by him (3) Every morning our prayer muſt be renewed, for every day we may expect freſh trials, and need renewed ſupports, for we have no power of ourſelves to help our ſelves (4) We muſt be advocates for each other, and eſpecially remember thoſe who are afflicted in our prayers (5) The higher the ſtorm of temptation blows, the faſter ſhould we cling to the rock of our ſalvation

Before Christ 713

3 An anſwer of peace is given Their enemies, the Aſſyrians, ſhall be terrified before the deſtroying angel, and whilſt ſome flee, and more are ſlain, they have nothing to do but ruſh on the ſpoil without reſiſtance, as when a flight of locuſts devours the field, *v* 4. And thus ſhall it be in the laſt days, when the ruin of the antichriſtian armies is completed, the conquerors ſhall devour the ſpoil *See Rev* xvii 16 *Note*, (1) God not only anſwers our prayer, but often exceeds all our expectations (2) To ſpoil the ſpoiler is a juſt repriſal

4 The people of God celebrate the praiſe of their deliverer, they adore him for the manifeſtation of his glory, made in the deſtruction of the Aſſyrians, and for the bleſſed effects his mercy produced among themſelves, filling Zion with judgment and righteouſneſs From what they had experienced, they encourage Hezekiah to proceed in his pious work of reformation, ſince *wiſdom and knowledge* of God's will and worſhip, by his care diffuſed, would be *the ſtability* of his *times*, and the beſt means of ſecuring their preſent happy ſtate, *and the ſtrength of ſalvation* their ſecurity againſt every invader and *the fear of the Lord*, either in his own heart, or in the hearts of his ſubjects, *is his treaſure*, a better portion, and a ſurer protection againſt his enemies than all other riches ſuch will alſo be the praiſes aſcribed to their Redeemer, when the antichriſtian foe is fallen, *Rev* xv 1, 2 and the kingdom of Chriſt eminently eſtabliſhed, then wiſdom and knowledge will be abundantly diffuſed, and thoſe times be bleſſed with durable peace and joy, the ſalvation of God's people be ſure and eternal, and their hearts enriched with the beſt treaſure, even that fear of the Lord which will keep them that they ſhall never depart from him *Note*, (1) Since the work of our ſalvation is from Chriſt alone, we are moſt bounden to aſcribe to him alone the praiſe (2) Wherever the kingdom of Jeſus is eſtabliſhed in any heart, there juſtice towards men, and righteouſneſs towards God, will immediately take place (3) A true knowledge of the grace of God, is the great ſtability of the ſoul (4) The fear of God is the chriſtian's beſt treaſure

5 The diſtreſſed ſtate they would be in, ſhall ſerve to heighten the joy of their deliverance *Their valiant ones* are repreſented as crying in deſpair, their embaſſadors weeping over their diſappointment from Egypt, *v* 7 all trade ſtagnated, and no traveller daring to go to the ſolemn feaſts, or on any buſineſs, whilſt the Aſſyrians waſte the country, the covenant is violated by Sennacherib, *ſee 2 Kings* xviii 14—17 their fortified cities taken, and *no man regarded*, or compaſſion ſhown to any, *v* 8 the country utterly waſted, and the moſt fruitful ſpots turned into a wilderneſs, *v* 9 And ſuch will be the deſolate condition of God's church, when the Lord in the latter day ſhall ariſe to deliver his redeemed the miniſters, who were valiant for truth, ſhall cry out under perſecution, and be ſlain publickly, *ſee Rev* xi 3—8 the ambaſſadors of peace be ſilenced, and weep in ſecret over the miſeries of the church, *v* 7 none daring to frequent the ordinances of God's worſhip, *becauſe of the pains* and penalties inflicted by the perſecuting power of Antichriſt, whom no covenants can bind, it being a maxim with him, that no faith is to be kept with heretics his power will then prevail over the reformed countries, and their cities be taken and inſulted, *v* 8 The world will groan under his yoke, and where pure chriſtianity moſt flouriſhed, it will be deſtroyed the miniſters, like cedars of Lebanon, againſt whom the greateſt enmity is ſhown, will be hewn down, and the people compelled to receive the mark of the beaſt, or be deſtroyed, *v* 9

6 At laſt theſe deſolations ſhall come to an end, when the Aſſyrians are in the heighth of their triumph *Now will I ariſe, ſaith the Lord*, at the critical time *now will I be exalted*, in the reſcue of his people, and the ruin of his enemies, *now will I lift up myſelf* to judgment the conſequence of which will be, the abortion of the ſanguine hopes of the Aſſyrians, and their blaſphemies, like fire among the ſtubble, will provoke God to burn them up, *v* 11 miſerably and utterly conſumed, as ſtones burnt to lime, or thorns ſuddenly vaniſhing into flame and ſmoak, *v* 12 And thus will the Lord alſo ariſe, when ſunk to the loweſt ebb his church is trampled down, and antichriſt triumphant his vengeance ſhall be poured on his foes, their politics confounded, and their ſchemes fruſtrated, their power broken, and all their rage and perſecution of his people, and blaſphemies againſt himſelf, ſhall kindle that fire which never can be quenched, where they muſt lie down together, as ſtones collected in the lime-kiln, and as thorns bound in bundles for the burning *See Rev* xvii 16 xix 20 *Note*, (1) When we are moſt diſtreſſed and deſperate, then is God's time to appear for our ſalvation (2) They that are hardened, as the ſtones againſt God's warnings, and hurtful and noxious as the thorns in the field, are nigh unto curſing, whoſe end is to be burned

Before Chriſt 713

13 ¶ Hear ye *that are* far off, what I have done,
and ye *that are* near, acknowledge my might 14 ª
The ſinners in Zion are afraid, fearfulneſs hath ſurpriſed
the hypocrites who among us ſhall dwell with the de-
vouring fire? who amongſt us ſhall dwell with everlaſt-
ing burnings? 15 He that ʳ walketh † righteouſly, and
ſpeaketh uprightly, he that deſpiſeth the gain of oppreſ-
ſions, that ſhaketh his hands from holding of bribes,
that ſtoppeth his ears from hearing of blood, and ˢ
ſhutteth his eyes from ſeeing evil 16 He ſhall dwell
on ‡ high his place of defence *ſhall be* the munitions
of rocks, bread ſhall be given him, his waters *ſhall be*
ſure 17 Thine eyes ſhall ſee ᵗ the king in his beauty
they ſhall behold the land that is very far off 18 Thine
heart ſhall meditate terror ᵘ Where *is* the ſcribe? where
is the § receiver? where *is* he that counted the towers?
19 ˣ Thou ſhalt not ſee a fierce people, ʸ a people of a
deeper ſpeech than thou canſt perceive, of a ‖ ſtammer-
ing tongue, *that thou canſt* not underſtand 20 Look
upon Zion the city of our ſolemnities thine eyes ſhall
ſee Jeruſalem a quiet habitation, ᶻ a tabernacle *that* ſhall
not be taken down, not one of the ſtakes thereof ſhall
ever be removed, neither ſhall any of the cords thereof
be broken 21 But there the glorious LORD *will be*
unto us a place of † broad rivers *and* ſtreams, wherein
ſhall go no galley with oars, neither ſhall gallant ſhip
paſs thereby 22 For the LORD *is* our judge, ª the
LORD *is* our law-giver, the LORD *is* our king, ᵇ he
will ſave us 23 Thy tacklings are looſed, they could
not well ſtrengthen their maſt, they could not ſpread the
ſail then is the prey of a great ſpoil divided, ᶜ the lame
take the prey. 24 And the inhabitant ſhall not ſay, I
am ſick ᵈ the people that dwell therein *ſhall be* forgiven
their iniquity

q Job xv 24. r Pſ xv 2 & xxiv 3, 4. † Heb in righteouſneſſes. s Pſ cxix 37. ‡ Heb heights, or high places. t Pſ xlviii 2. 1 John iii 2. u 1 Cor i 20. § Heb Weigher. x 2 Kings xix 32. y Deut xxviii 49. Jer v 15. ‖ Or, ridiculous. z Pſ xlvi 5 & cxxv 1. 2. Neh xvi 18. † Heb Broad of ſpaces or hands. a James iv 12. b Pſ lxix 35. Chap xxxvii 35. c Pſ lxviii 12. d Jer l 20.

v 13—24 When the eternal Jehovah ſpeaks, let every mortal hear, and all the world acknowledge his power and glory, *v* 13 which appear eſpecially,

1 In the terror and deſtruction of the wicked and the hypocrite As the ſinners and hypocrites in *Zion* have peculiar guilt, they may well tremble at their full meaſure of judgment, *v* 14 when they ſee Jeruſalem ready to be beſieged, and expect to have their houſes fired, they are in diſtraction, have no hope in God, and Egypt hath failed them, or when they ſaw the Aſſyrians ſo terribly conſumed, they trembled leaſt the devouring fire ſhould reach them alſo *Note*, (1) Of all men they are moſt guilty, who amidſt the light of goſpel truth perſiſt in the ways of ſin and formality (2) The day will come when the moſt ſecure ſinner will be ſtartled (3) If men would ſeriouſly put the queſtion to their ſouls, how they can dwell with devouring fire, and endure the everlaſting burnings, it might awaken their conſciences, and prevent their ruin (4) This terrible portion muſt they ſhortly and ſurely receive, who neglect to fly from the wrath to come, to that Redeemer who alone can hide them in the day of judgment

2 In the ſalvation of the righteous, whoſe character is here diſplayed *He that walketh righteouſly*, making God's word his rule, conſcientious in all his dealings, and perſevering in the worſhip of the Lord, *and ſpeaketh uprightly*, his word is ſacred, his converſation gracious, and ſuited to miniſter edification to others *he that deſpiſeth the gain of oppreſſion*, who thinks it infamous to fatten upon the ſpoil of the injured, and means as wicked to commit injuſtice, *that ſhaketh his hands from holding of bribes*, rejects them, when offered, with indignation, *that ſtoppeth his ears from hearing of blood*, cannot be brought to liſten to any cruel or oppreſſive propoſal, *and ſhutteth his eyes from ſeeing evil*, cannot bear to ſee others ſin, and ſtops up that dangerous avenue at which temptation might enter *he ſhall dwell on high*, ſecure in the everlaſting love of God from all thoſe evils that terrify the wicked *his place of defence ſhall be in the munition of rocks*, even Chriſt the rock of ages, his impregnable fortreſs, againſt which the gates of hell, and the floods of temptation, rage in vain, *bread ſhall be given unto him, and his water ſhall be ſure*, when famine rages, he ſhall not want in the ſiege, or rather he ſhall eat the living bread, of which the world knoweth not, and be refreſhed with the ſtreams of Divine grace, and eternal conſolations, when the ſinner and hypocrite in flames cannot obtain one drop of water to quench their raging thirſt

3 Many great and diſtinguiſhing mercies are here promiſed, applicable not only to the Jews, but more generally to all the faithful, who ſhall be delivered at the laſt day from the power of the wicked one

(1) They ſhall ſee the king in his beauty, Hezekiah in his royal robes, and the land afar off, whither for fear of the Aſſyrians before they dared not go, *v* 17 And how much greater joy will it afford to the faithful ſoul, in that diſtant realm of eternal day, to ſee Jeſus their king, brighter than the ſun, ſitting on his throne of glory, and themſelves as ſtars ſhining around him?

(2) Their fears ſhall be at an end, and ſerve them but for matter of grateful meditation, the terrors that compaſſed them are fled, they hear no more the voice of commanders within, collecting the ſupplies, or numbering the people for the battle, or the captains and engineers of Aſſyria without, threatning their ruin, *v* 18 They ſee no longer a fierce nation, whoſe ſpeech they could not underſtand, and whoſe voice ſpread diſmay, all are now dead corpſes, or fled Thus when our ſouls ſhall reach the heavenly Zion, our paſt trials, however grievous, ſhall be remembered with delight, and all our foes, which bred in us ſo many fears, be for ever ſunk in darkneſs, and incapable ever more of troubling our repoſe

(3) They ſhall look with tranſport on Zion, the city of their ſolemnities during the ſiege theſe had been interrupted, and they might fear never would be reſtored, but lo, once more in peace, their habitation is quiet, and God promiſes long to preſerve his tabernacle among them, and to diſappoint the malice of thoſe who ſought to deſtroy it, *v* 20 The earthly Zion is long ſince indeed demoliſhed, but we look for a city which hath foundations, whoſe maker and builder is God, even the new Jeruſalem, to which this prophecy hath eſpecial regard, where God's ſaints night and day ſhall ſerve him, and go out no more for ever, having found their glorious reſt, and dwelling ſafe from fear of evil *See Rev* iii 12

(4) They ſhall have the Lord, glorious in power and holineſs, for their protector, law-giver, judge, and Saviour Though Jeruſalem had no navigable river to further commerce, or ſerve for a ſecurity againſt their enemies, God would be all that to her in his bleſſing, no galley, or gallant ſhip, could bring an invading army againſt her, and inacceſſible would he preſerve her from every foe their judge to avenge his people's wrongs, their law-giver to direct their conduct, their king to govern with gentleneſs, and protect them from danger, in ſhort, their Saviour to the uttermoſt *Note*, (1) If God be ours, all thing are ours, every bleſſing is then ſecured in time and eternity (2) The Lord Chriſt is this judge, law-giver, king, and Saviour, to his redeemed, and if, as his ſubjects, our ſouls are yielded up to his government, who can pluck us out of his hands?

(5) Their enemies, like a ſhip in a ſtorm, diſmaſted, and the rigging torn in pieces, a perfect wreck, and ready to be daſhed in pieces againſt the rocks, ſhould ſee all their hopes blaſted, and themſelves a prey, ſo helpleſs to defend themſelves, that even the lame ſhould divide their ſpoil, *v* 23

(6) Sickneſs ſhall be removed, and ſin pardoned The diſeaſes of Jeruſalem, ariſing from their confinement, would be at an end, and the people, returning to God under a ſenſe of Divine mercy, obtain pardon and acceptance with him and this will be emphatically fulfilled in the days of the church's proſperity, when, with the pardon and grace, then abundantly diſpenſed, Chriſt will heal all the ſickneſs of the ſouls of his people, and at laſt, when mortality ſhall be ſwallowed up of life, ſin, ſorrow, ſickneſs, pain, and death, ſhall be for ever baniſhed from the eternal ſtate of bliſs and glory

CHAP XXXIV.

In this chapter we have the fatal doom of all the nations that are enemies to God's church and people Edom is only mentioned, but we have reaſon to ſuppoſe it is intended as a denunciation of the wrath of God againſt all thoſe who fight againſt the intereſts of his kingdom among men, and will have its full accompliſhment in the fall of Antichriſt, and finally in the diſſolution of all things at the day of judgment, and perdition of ungodly men Here is, 1 *A demand of univerſal attention,* ver 1 2 *A direful ſcene of blood and confuſion preſented,* ver 2—7 3 *The reaſon given for theſe judgments,* ver 8 4 *The continuance of this deſolation, the country being made like the lake of Sodom,* ver 9, 10 *and the cities abandoned to wild beaſts and birds,* ver 11—15 5 *The ſolemn ratification of all this,* ver 16, 17 *Let us hear and tremble*

1 COME near, ye nations, to hear, and hearken, ye
people ª let the earth hear, and † all that is
therein, the world, and all things that come forth of it
2. For ᵇ the indignation of the LORD *is* upon all na-
tions, and *his* fury upon all their armies he hath utter-
ly deſtroyed them, he hath delivered them to the ſlaugh-
ter. 3. Their ſlain alſo ſhall be caſt out, and ᶜ their
ſtink ſhall come up out of their carcaſes, and the moun-
tains ſhall be melted with their blood 4 And ᵈ all the hoſt
of heaven ſhall be diſſolved, and the heavens ſhall be ᵉ rol-
led together as a ſcroll ᶠ and all their hoſt ſhall fall
down as the leaf falleth off from the vine, and ᵍ as a
falling *fig* from the fig tree 5 For ʰ my ſword ſhall be
bathed

a Deut iv 26 Chap i 2. † Heb The fulneſs thereof. b Jer xxv 15. c Chap lxvi 24 Joel ii 20. d Pſ cii 26 Ezek xxxii 7 Joel ii 31 & iii 15 Mat xxiv 29 2 Pet iii 10. e Rev vi 14. f Chap xiv 12. g Rev vi 13. h Jer xlvi 10.

Before Chriſt 713.

l Jer xlix 7. k Mal i 4. l Chap lxiii 1. Zeph i 7. † Or, rhinoceros. m Chap xxxv 4 & lxi 18.

bathed in heaven behold, [l] it ſhall come down upon
Idumea, and upon [k] the people of my curſe to judgment
6 The ſword of the LORD is filled with blood, it is
made fat with fatneſs, *and* with the blood of lambs and
goats, with the fat of the kidneys of rams for [l] the
LORD hath a ſacrifice in Bozrah, and a great ſlaughter
in the land of Idumea 7 And the ‡ unicorns ſhall come
down with them, and the bullocks with the bulls, and
their land ſhall be ſoked with blood, and their duſt made
fat with fatneſs 8 For *it is* the day of [m] the LORD's
vengeance, *and* the year of recompences for the contro-
verſy of Zion.

v 1—8 We have here,

1 The awful ſummons ſent forth to the nations of the world, and the earth, and things therein called upon to hearken, as if the irrational, or inanimate creatures, were more attentive than hardened ſinners, *v* 1

2 The univerſality of the approaching judgments of God is declared, *v* 2 againſt all the nations and their armies, who have committed fornication with the great whore, *ſee Rev* xvii 3 and therefore are doomed to utter deſtruction, *Rev* xix 21

3 The execution of this terrible doom is diſplayed in the moſt awful colours The carcaſſes of the ſlain will be unburied, and ſend forth peſtilential vapours, the very mountains are melted with blood, like rivers running down, *v* 3 The hoſts of heaven, ſun, moon, and ſtars, dropping as untimely figs, and the firmament wrapped up as a ſcroll, repreſenting the utter ruin of the ſtates and kingdoms of the followers of the man of ſin, with their princes and mighty men, *v* 4 (*compare Rev* xix 17, 18 *Rev* xiv 20 *Rev* vi 13, 14) and this is effected by the ſword of the Lord, *bathed in heaven*, well-tempered, drawn according to his eternal decree, and deſcending with fury irreſiſtible on Idumea, probably the Romiſh ſtate, the implacable enemies of the church of Chriſt, as the Edomites were of the Jews, and therefore called *the people of my curſe*, lying under it, and doomed to this due judgment, *v* 5 Before this ſword the armies of Antichriſt, the common ſoldiers, as lambs and goats, like hecatombs at the altar, fall ſacrifices to divine juſtice at Bozrah, a city of Idumea, repreſenting Rome, the capital of the antichriſtian powers, *v* 6 And their chief captains, fierce as bulls and ſtrong as unicorns, ſhall periſh together, and the land be ſoked with their blood and fattened, or *made drunk*, as with ſhowers of rain, ſuch vaſt quantities ſhould be ſhed *See Rev* xvi 6 xvii 6 xiv 20 *Note*, (1) Miſerable, eternally miſerable are they, who by their ſins provoking God's curſe, awaken his ſword of judgment (2) If it be terrible but to hear the report, ſinner, how wilt thou endure when this great day of his wrath is come? (3) The ſinners in hell are eternal ſacrifices to God's juſtice, and therefore, when the ſmoke of their torment aſcends, his ſaints adore him (4) However long triumphant, and cruelly oppreſſive, the enemies of God's people may have been, their doom is determined, and God will give them blood to drink

4 The equity of the procedure is remarked, this day of vengeance is the year of recompenſes for the controverſy of Zion, and the time is fixed in the eternal counſels to do her juſtice, when the church of God, and every perſecuted member of it will find a righteous judge eſpouſing their quarrel, and recompenſing to the full the injuries they have endured *See Rev* xiii 10 xi 18 *Note*, When we are ſuffering for the teſtimony of the truth, and a good conſcience, we ſhould be comforted in patient hope, that the year of recompenſe is at hand, for Zion's friends and Zion's enemies

n Deut xxix 23. o Rev xiv 11 & xviii 18 & xix 3. p Mal i 4. q Chap xiv 23 Zeph ii 14 Rev xviii 2. r 2 Kings xxi 13 Lam ii 8. s Hoſ ix 6. t Chap xiii 21. ‡ Or, oſtriches. † Or, night monſter.

9 And [n] the ſtreams thereof ſhall be turned into pitch,
and the duſt thereof into brimſtone, and the land thereof
ſhall become burning pitch 10 It ſhall not be quench-
ed night nor day, [o] the ſmoke thereof ſhall go up for
ever [p] from generation to generation it ſhall lie waſte,
none ſhall paſs through it for ever and ever 11 ¶ [q] But
the cormorant and the bittern ſhall poſſeſs it, the owl al-
ſo and the raven ſhall dwell in it, and [r] he ſhall ſtretch
out upon it the line of confuſion, and the ſtones of
emptineſs 12 They ſhall call the nobles thereof to the
kingdom, but none *ſhall be* there, and all her princes ſhall
be nothing 13 And [s] thorns ſhall come up in her pa-
laces, nettles and brambles in the fortreſſes thereof, and [t]
and it ſhall be an habitation of dragons, *and* a court for
‡ owls 14 The wild beaſts of the deſert ſhall alſo meet
with the wild beaſts of the iſland, and the ſatyr ſhall cry to
his fellow, the † ſcreech-owl alſo ſhall reſt there, and find
for herſelf a place of reſt 15 There ſhall the great owl
make her neſt, and lay and hatch, and gather under her
ſhadow there ſhall the vultures alſo be gathered every
one with her mate 16 ¶ Seek ye out of the book of
the LORD, and read no one of theſe ſhall fail, none
ſhall want her mate for my mouth it hath commanded,
and his ſpirit it hath gathered them 17 And he hath
caſt the lot for them, and his hand hath divided it unto
them by line they ſhall poſſeſs it for ever, from gene-
ration to generation ſhall they dwell therein

v 9—17 Awful and moſt awakening are the images here uſed to diſplay the utter ruin and deſolations of the enemies of Chriſt and his people, and which ſeem to look forward to the fall of Antichriſt, and may alſo be applied to that great and terrible day of the Lord, when the ſinner's torment in body and ſoul will be completed

1 Their land is deſcribed as the land of Sodom Since ſin hath rendered it as fuel for the flames, the wrath of God ſhall kindle the inextinguiſhable burnings, *v* 9, 10 and their cities deſerted, deſolate, ruinous, ſhall become the abode of every unclean bird and ravenous beaſt, *v* 11—15 the elegance and dignity of which deſcription cannot be equalled, and which every comment muſt debaſe Only we may obſerve, (1) The dreadful evil of ſin, the cauſe of all theſe deſolations (2) The folly and madneſs of attempting to fix our abode on earth, doomed ſo ſhortly, with all the works on it, to be burnt up (3) The terrible end of the ungodly, when wrath to the uttermoſt is poured out upon them, and they are caſt into the lake of brimſtone and fire which burneth for ever and ever

2 An aſſurance is given of the moſt minute fulfilment of the prophecy, *v* 16, 17 And when the deſtruction cometh, they are commanded to compare the event with the prediction, and not a tittle will be found to fail Since God's word hath commanded, his ſpirit will accompliſh it, collecting in exact order, as at the deluge, theſe monſters with their mates to their appointed abode, and by an eternal decree, according to the dictates of juſtice, dooming the place to everlaſting ruin Theſe, with the correſpondent prophecies in the book of Revelations, are yet in the womb of time, but ſhall as ſurely be accompliſhed in their ſeaſon, as thoſe we have ſeen already fulfilled And when we read in the book of the Lord, the ſure expectation thereof ſhould comfort and ſupport the ſuffering ſaints of God

CHAP XXXV

The flouriſhing ſtate of the goſpel church is here ſet forth, as a contraſt to the dreadful devaſtations of the preceding chapter 1 The Gentiles ſhall be brought into it, ver 1, 2, 7 2 The weak and timorous ſhall be encouraged, ver 3, 4 3 Miracles ſhall be wrought both on the ſouls and bodies of men, ver 5, 6 4 It ſhall be conducted in the way of holineſs, ver. 8, 9 5 It ſhall be brought at laſt to endleſs joys, ver 10

a Chap lv. 12. b Ibid xxxii 15. c Job iv 4 Heb. xii 12. † Or haſty. d Chap xxxiv 8. ‡ Or the God of recompence. e Mat i.21.

1 [a] THE wilderneſs and the ſolitary place ſhall be
glad for them and the deſert ſhall rejoice, and
bloſſom as the roſe 2 [b] It ſhall bloſſom abundantly,
and rejoice even with joy and ſinging, the glory of Le-
banon ſhall be given unto it, the excellency of Carmel
and Sharon they ſhall ſee the glory of the LORD, *and*
the excellency of our God 3 ¶ [c] Strengthen ye the
weak hands, and confirm the feeble knees 4 Say to
them *that are* of a † fearful heart, Be ſtrong, fear not
behold, [d] your God will come *with* vengeance, *even* ‡
God *with* a recompence, he will come and [e] ſave you.

v 1—4 When the Aſſyrian army was deſtroyed, the country of Judea, which had been waſted as a wilderneſs before them, quickly reſumed its verdure and fruitfulneſs To this the prophecy may in part refer, but it chiefly regards,

1 The flouriſhing ſtate of the church, when the Gentile world, before a barren wilderneſs, by the preaching of the goſpel puts on a new face, bloſſoming with the joys of divine conſolations, bringing forth the moſt excellent fruits of grace, and with ſuch abundance, is to be compared to Lebanon, where the choiceſt cedars grew, and to Carmel and Sharon, the richeſt ſpots of Judea for Corn and paſturage ſuch ſtrength, beauty, and fruitfulneſs ſhould eminently unite in the goſpel church, and *they ſhall ſee the glory of the Lord*, and *the excellency of our God*, the Lord Jeſus Chriſt, his perſon, offices, and complete redemption, wherein God is ſo tranſcendently magnified, and appears ſo amiable and glorious in the eyes of the redeemed *Note*, A believing view of the Redeemer's grace and glory brings joy to the heart, and is the effectual means of quickening it to bring forth much fruit

2 By the miniſtry of the word, they are encouraged and ſupported to bear up under the temptations and ſufferings to which, for the ſake of Chriſt, they would be expoſed *Strengthen ye the weak hands, and confirm the feeble knees*, thoſe who from an awakened ſenſe of guilt and wrath were ready to ſink down in deſpair, unable to lift up the hands of prayer, muſt be encou-

raged,

Before Christ 713

hand, and those, whose knees trembled under the load of their trials, from corruption or persecution, the ministers of God must confirm, by pointing them to the great and precious promises *Say to them that are of a fearful heart, be strong, fear not*, though you are weak, your enemies mighty, and in your own strength you feel yourselves utterly unable to cope with them, yet help is laid for you on one mighty to save, therefore, be strong in the Lord, look to him, and then your fears will vanish, for who can pluck you out of his hand? *behold*, see your deliverance near and sure, *your God*, your reconciled God and Saviour, *will come with vengeance*, to cover your enemies with confusion, *even God with a recompence*, or *the God of recompence*, to give a reward to his saints, and tribulation to them that trouble them, *he will come and save us*, as sure as ever he once appeared in the flesh, victorious over the powers of darkness, so surely will he in every time of our distress appear for our succour, and when the appointed hour arrives, be revealed the second time from heaven to compleat in us the salvation he hath begun

5 ¶ Then [f] the eyes of the blind shall be opened, and
[g] the ears of the deaf shall be unstopped 6 Then shall
[h] the lame *man* leap as an hart, and [i] the tongue of the
dumb sing for in the wilderness [k] shall waters break out,
and streams in the desert 7 And the parched ground
shall become a pool, and the thirsty land springs of
water in [l] the habitation of dragons, where each lay,
shall be grass with reeds and rushes 8 And an high-
way shall be there, and a way, and it shall be called the
way of holiness, [m] the unclean shall not pass over it, but
† it *shall be* for those [n] the way-faring men, though
fools, shall not err *therein* 9 [o] No lion shall be there,
nor *any* ravenous beast shall go up thereon, it shall not
be found there but the redeemed shall walk *there* 10
And [p] the ransomed of the LORD shall return and come
to Zion with songs, and [q] everlasting joy upon their
heads they shall obtain joy and gladness, [r] and sorrow
and sighing shall flee away

[f] Chap xxix 18 & xxxii 3 & xlii 7 Mat ix 27—29, 30 & xx 30 & xx 30, &c John ix 6 7 Acts xxvi 18 2 Cor iv 6
[g] Mat vii 32 &c
[h] Mat xv 30 John v 8 9 Acts iii 6 7
[i] Mat ix 33 Col i 11
[k] Chap xli 18 & xliii 19 John vii 38 39
[l] Chap xxxv 1
[m] Chap lii 1 Joel iii 17 Rev xxi 27
† Or, for he shall be with those
[n] Psal xxv 8, 9 & cxix 130
[o] Chap xi 9 1 Pet v 8
[p] Chap li 11
[q] John xvi 22
[r] Chap xxv 8 Rev vii 17 & xxi 4

v 5—10 We have here,

1 The wonders that shall be wrought at Christ's coming, on the bodies and souls of men The blind shall see, the deaf hear, the lame walk, the dumb speak, which we see literally fulfilled, *Mat* ix 27 *Mark* vii 34 *Acts* iii 8 *Mat* ix 32 but greater works than these shall he do, enlightening the blindness of the fallen mind, causing the spiritually deaf to hear and receive the gospel, strengthening those who were helpless, to walk in the ways of truth and righteousness, and teaching those to sing his praise whose lips before had been sealed up in silence Lord, continue still to make thy glorious power to appear!

2 The remarkable out-pouring of the spirit in the days of Christ, and the blessed effects thereby produced *In the wilderness shall waters break out, and streams in the desert*, such a copious effusion of divine gifts, graces, and consolations shall then be made on the Gentile world, that *the parched ground and thirsty land*, the sinner's soul, barren or scorched up with the sense of divine wrath, *shall become a pool and springs of water* refreshed and fertilized *in the habitation of dragons, where each lay*, the places where Satan, the great dragon, hath fixed his abode, and men resembling him in fierceness and cruelty, such as the Pagan emperors, or Papal powers, *shall be grass with reeds and rushes*, a number of converts to the gospel, thick as grass, and flourishing as the reeds in the brook and this was fulfilled when the Pagan temples were changed into places for Christian worship, and shall be farther accomplished when Babylon mystical is fallen, and the church of God triumphant over her

3 The way that then will be opened for all nations, Jew and Gentile, to draw nigh unto God, and that way is Christ, emphatically so called, because no man cometh to the Father but by him, nor can there be any access to an offended God, but through his blood and righteousness He is *a high way* ordained by the King of heaven, free and open to all, and where every obstruction from sin and Satan are utterly removed, *a way of holiness*, or *holy way*, where the grace of sanctification, as well as the gift of justification, is bestowed, and strength communicated to the soul, enabling those who are in Christ to walk and please God, where all holy means and ordinances are found, where all the travellers are in temper and conduct in a measure holy, and which will infallibly conduct them to the perfection of holiness Love *the unclean shall not pass over it*, those being justly excluded who persist in the love and service of their sin, *but it shall be for those* justified and renewed souls above described, or as it may be rendered, *he shall be with them*, Christ, their companion, guide, and support *the way-faring men, though fools, shall not err therein*, counted such of the world, after their conversion to God, and spiritually indeed such before they were taught of him, these travellers to Zion shall not err, the way is plain before them, the bible is their sure directory, and the spirit of truth their guide, not that every christian is infallible, but he shall not greatly, or fatally err *No lion shall be there, nor any ravenous beast shall go up thereon, it shall not be found there*, none of such fierce and turbulent dispositions, none to disturb the peace of the happy traveller, and especially the old lion, that goeth about seeking whom he may devour, shall not be able to approach to destroy any soul that is found in this holy way *but the redeemed shall walk there*, those whom Divine Grace hath chosen, and Jesus hath purchased by his blood, they shall in safety travel without being weary, and reach at last their blessed journey's end, which will be,

4 Their everlasting joy For *the ransomed of the Lord shall return* from the state of sin and darkness, in which like others they lay, to the shepherd and bishop of their souls, Christ Jesus, *and*, under his guidance, *come to Zion*, that mount of God in glory, appointed for their eternal residence, and, whilst *with* grateful *songs* they celebrate redeeming love, and ascribe to sovereign grace their whole salvation, *everlasting joy* shall be *upon their heads*, joy that shall never again be interrupted by sin, temptation, or suffering, but be permanent as God's everlasting love, the source of it *They shall obtain joy and gladness*, unspeakable and full of glory, as much exceeding all they tasted here below, as the boundless ocean exceeds the drop of the bucket, *and sorrow and sighing shall flee away*, when every cause that could produce them are for ever removed, and perfect holiness and perfect happiness flow from the uninterrupted beatific vision of the triune God O may my soul possess this everlasting joy!

CHAP XXXVI

The prophet Isaiah is here an historian, and the events of the following chapters serve to explain and confirm the foregoing prophecies The story here recorded is nearly the same as 2 Kings xviii xix *and* 2 Chron xxxii *to which you may look back for a larger exposition We have here,* 1 *Sennacherib's descent and success against Judah,* ver 1 2 *The conference he desired to have with Hezekiah, and the managers on both sides,* ver 2, 3 3 *Rabshakeh's railing blasphemous speech,* ver 4—10 4 *His attempt to persuade the people to desert Hezekiah, and so force him to surrender,* ver 11—20 5 *The report of this made to Hezekiah by his agents,* ver 21, 22

1 [a] NOW it came to pass in the fourteenth year of
king Hezekiah, *that* Sennacherib king of Assy-
ria came up against all the defenced cities of Judah, and
took them 2 And the king of Assyria sent Rabshakeh,
from Lachish to Jerusalem, unto king Hezekiah, with a
great army and he stood by the conduit of the upper
pool in the high-way of the fullers field 3 Then came
forth unto him Eliakim, Hilkiah's son, which *was* over
the house, and Shebna the scribe, and Joah Asaph's son
the recorder 4 ¶ And Rabshakeh said unto them, Say
ye now to Hezekiah, Thus saith [b] the great king, the king
of Assyria, [c] What confidence *is* this wherein thou trustest?
5 I say, *sayest thou*, (but *they are but* vain words) [d] *I have*
counsel and strength for war now on whom dost thou
trust, that thou rebellest against me? 6 Lo, thou trustest
[e] in the staff of this broken reed, on Egypt, whereon if
a man lean, it will go into his hand and pierce it [f] so *is*
Pharaoh king of Egypt to all that trust in him 7 But
if thou say to me, We trust in the LORD our God
is it not he [g] whose high places, and whose altars Hezekiah
hath taken away, and said to Judah and to Jerusalem, Ye
shall worship before this altar? 8 Now therefore give
† pledges, I pray thee, to my master the king of Assyria,
and [h] I will give thee two thousand horses, if thou be
able on thy part to set riders upon them 9 How then
wilt thou turn away the face of one captain of the least
of my master's servants, and put thy trust on Egypt for
chariots and for horsemen? 10 And am I now come
up without the LORD against this land to destroy it?
[i] the LORD said unto me, Go up against this land, and
destroy it

14
[a] 2 Kings xviii 13, &c 2 Chron xxxii 1, &c
710.
[b] 2 Kings xviii 19
[c] Psal xlix 6, 7, 13 & lxxviii 22
[d] Ezek xxix 6, 7
[e] 2 Kings xvii 21
[f] Ezek xxix 6
[g] 2 Kings xviii 4 2 Chron xxxi 1 & xxxii 12
† Or, hostages
[h] 2 Sam xvi 14 Neh iv 2
[i] 2 Kings xix 1 Chap x 5, 6

v 1—10 As this transaction hath been treated of at large, 2 *Kings* xviii xix 2 *Chron* xxxii A few remarks will here suffice, and we may observe, (1) How apt success is to intoxicate, and prosperity to puff men up with pride Because the other defenced cities were taken, Rabshakeh already reckoned Jerusalem as a prey (2) When, like Hezekiah, we are found in the zealous discharge of our duty, and may be hoping for signal blessings from God, we may meet with the severest conflicts and discouragements for the exercise of our faith, the brightening our graces, and the increase of our joy (3) The people of God must expect sometimes the threats, sometimes the mockery of men, to intimidate and [illegible] them from following the good way of the Lord, but [illegible] tell,

Before Chriſt 710

ſiſt, and truſt ſtill on him (1) Many, like Rabſhakeh, pre-
tend the Lord's commiſſion, who will be found to have a lie in
their right hand, v 10

k 2 Kings xviii 26, &c

11 ¶ k Then ſaid Eliakim, and Shebna, and Joah unto
Rabſhakeh, Speak, I pray thee, unto thy ſervants in the
Syrian language, for we underſtand it and ſpeak not to
us in the Jews language, in the ears of the people that *are*
on the wall 12 ¶ But Rabſhakeh ſaid, Hath my maſ-
ter ſent me to thy maſter and to thee, to ſpeak theſe
words ? *hath he* not *ſent me* to the men that ſit upon the
wall, l that they may eat their own dung, and drink † their
own piſs with you ? 13 Then Rabſhakeh ſtood and cri-
ed with a loud voice in the Jews language, and ſaid, Hear
ye the words of the great king, the king of Aſſyria
14 Thus ſaith the king, Let not Hezekiah deceive you,
for m he ſhall not be able to deliver you 15 Neither let
Hezekiah make you truſt in the LORD, ſaying, The
LORD will ſurely deliver us, this city ſhall not be deli-
vered into the hand of the king of Aſſyria 16 Hearken
not to Hezekiah for thus ſaith the king of Aſſyria,
Make an agreement with me by a preſent, and come out
to me and eat ye every one of his vine, and every one
of his fig-tree, and drink ye every one the waters of his
own ciſtern 17 Until I come and take you away to a
land n like your own land, a land of corn and wine, a
land of bread and vineyards 18 *Beware* leſt Hezekiah
perſuade you, ſaying, o The LORD will deliver us
p Hath any of the gods of the nations delivered his land
out of the hand of the king of Aſſyria ? 19 Where *are*
q the gods of Hamath and Arphad ? where *are* the gods
of Sepharvaim ? and have they delivered Samaria out of
my hand ? 20 Who *are they* amongſt all the gods of
theſe lands, that have delivered their land out of my
hand, r that the LORD ſhould deliver Jeruſalem out
of my hand ? 21 But s they held their peace, and u an-
ſwered him not a word for the king's commandment
was, ſaying, Anſwer him not 22 ¶ Then came Eli-
akim the ſon of Hilkiah, that *was* over the houſhold,
and Shebna the ſcribe, and Joah the ſon of Aſaph the
recorder, to Hezekiah x with *their* clothes rent, and told
him the words of Rabſhakeh

l Exod xv 9 1 Kings xx 10 Pſ lxxiii 8 † Heb The water of their feet
m Dan iii 15 & vii 25, Rev xiii 6
n Exod iii 8 Deut xxxii 13, 14
o 2 Pet ii 9
p Hab i 15, 16
q Iſ x 9—8
r John xix 11
s Rev xiii 6
t Pſ xxxviii 13 14
u Prov ix 7 & xxvi 4 Mat vii 6
x Jer xxxvi 24 Mat xxvi 65

v 11—22 With civil entreaty the perſons appointed by Hezekiah for the conference with Rabſhakeh, beg the favour of him to ſpeak to them in the Syriac tongue, as his diſcourſe had in the Hebrew [illegible] bad tendency to diſcourage thoſe who were within hearing to which he makes a reply as indecent as inſolent, v 12 and addreſſing his ſpeech, in the Jews language, to the people on the wall, with blaſphemous reflections on Iſrael's God, endeavours to ſpread a ſpirit of mutiny amongſt them v 13—20 But they are forbidden to reply, v 21 and, ſhocked at the blaſphemy, or grieved at their diſtreſs, the meſſengers return unto the king, and report the words of this impious Aſſyrian, v 22 *Note*, (1) Inſolent language betrays a baſe ſpirit (2) The devil, like Rabſhakeh, would inſinuate, that it is our advantage to ſerve him, but his fair promiſes are foul lies (3) Silence is often the propereſt anſwer to railing accuſations (4) It were folly to attempt replying to thoſe who are as unreaſonable as they are wicked (5) It is a grief to the gracious ſoul, to hear the name of God diſhonoured

C H A P XXXVII

Hezekiah, 1 Hezekiah's reſentment of Rabſhakeh's impious diſcourſe, ver 1 2 The meſſage he ſent to Iſaiah to deſire his prayers, ver 2—5 3 The encouraging anſwer which Iſaiah ſent him from God, ver 6, 7 4 An abuſive letter which the king of Aſſyria ſent to Hezekiah, ver 8—13 5 Hezekiah's humble prayer to God upon the receipt of it, ver 14—20 6. The further anſwer which God ſent him by Iſaiah, promiſing him ſpeedy and full deliverance, ver 21—35 7 The immediate accompliſhment of this prophecy in the ruin of his army, ver 36 and the murder of Sennacherib, ver 37, 38 All which was largely opened, 2 King xix

a 2 Kings xix 1 &c
b 2 Chron vii 15
c 2 Kings xix 2 Luke iii 2

1 a AND it came to paſs when king Hezekiah
heard *it*, that he rent his clothes, and covered
himſelf with ſackcloth, and b went into the houſe of the
LORD 2 And he ſent Eliakim, who *was* over the
houſhold, and Shebna the ſcribe, and the elders of the
prieſts covered with ſackcloth, unto Iſaiah c the prophet,
the ſon of Amoz 3 And they ſaid unto him, Thus

ſaith Hezekiah, This day *is* d a day of trouble, and of
† rebuke, and of e blaſphemy for the children are come
to the birth, and f *there is* not ſtrength to bring forth
4 g It may be the LORD thy God will hear the
words of Rabſhakeh, whom the king of Aſſyria his
maſter hath ſent to reproach the living God, and h will
reprove the words which the LORD thy God hath
heard wherefore i lift up *thy* prayer for the remnant
that is left 5 So the ſervants of king Hezekiah came
to Iſaiah 6 ¶ And Iſaiah ſaid unto them, Thus ſhall
ye ſay unto your maſter, Thus ſaith the LORD, k Be
not afraid of the words that thou haſt heard, wherewith
the ſervants of the king of Aſſyria have blaſphemed me
7 Behold, I will ſend a ‡ blaſt upon him, and he ſhall
hear a rumour, and return to his own land, and I will
cauſe him l to fall by the ſword in his own land

Before Chriſt 710
d Pſ l 15
† Or, reviling Pſal cxxiii 3
e Chap xxxvi 20
f Hoſ xiii 13
g Exod ii 24 & vi 12
h Pſ l 21
i 1 Sam xii 19 Joel ii 17 1 Tim ii 1 2
k Exod xiv 13
‡ Heb. Spirit Ver 36
l Ver 38

v 1—7 Shocked at the tidings he received, Hezekiah in ſackcloth falls down before God in his ſanctuary, v 1 and ſending his chief officers to Iſaiah, repreſents his deplorable ſituation, as a woman in travail exhauſted with her pains, and ſinking under her weakneſs, ſo ready he ſeemed to periſh, unleſs the Lord interpoſed to vindicate his own honour, for which he begs the prophet's prayers, v 2—5 Nor was his requeſt in vain Iſaiah ſoon diſpatches the meſſengers with an anſwer of peace to the king, and bids him, fearleſs of danger, be confident of ſeeing the ſpeedy deſtruction of his enemies, v 4— *Note*, (1) A day of trouble ſhould be a day of humiliation and prayer, and whatever drives us thus nearer to God, muſt in the iſſue prove a bleſſing (2) The prayers of good men are to be earneſtly ſought, and it is a great encouragement to have them interceding with God in our behalf (3) When we are ready to deſpair, God will often moſt eminently magnify his power and grace in our deliverance (4) They who ſeek to terrify God's people from their holy profeſſion, will ſoon be made a terror to themſelves

8 ¶ m So Rabſhakeh returned, and found the king
of Aſſyria warring againſt Libnah for he had heard
that he was departed from Lachiſh 9 And n he heard
ſay concerning Tirhakah king of Ethiopia, He is come
forth to make war with thee and when he heard *it*,
he ſent meſſengers to Hezekiah, ſaying, 10 Thus
ſhall ye ſpeak to Hezekiah king of Judah, ſaying, o Let
not thy God p in whom thou truſteſt deceive thee, ſay-
ing, Jeruſalem ſhall not be given into the hand of the
king of Aſſyria 11 Behold, thou haſt heard what the
kings of Aſſyria have done to all lands, by deſtroying
them utterly, and ſhalt thou be delivered ? 12 q Have
the gods of the nations delivered them which my fathers
have deſtroyed, *as* Gozan, and Haran, and Rezeph, and
the children of Eden which *were* in Telaſſar ? 13
Where *is* the king of Hamath, and the king of Arphad,
and the king of the city of Sepharvaim, Hena and Ivah ?
14 ¶ And Hezekiah received the letter from the hand
of the meſſengers, and read it and Hezekiah r went
up unto the houſe of the LORD, and s ſpread it before
the LORD, 15 And Hezekiah prayed unto the LORD,
ſaying, 16 O LORD of hoſts, God of Iſrael, t that
dwelleſt *between* the cherubims, thou art the God, *even*
thou alone, of all the kingdoms of the earth, u thou haſt
made heaven and earth. 17 x Incline thine ear, O
LORD, and hear y Open thine eyes, O LORD, and
ſee and hear all the words of Sennacherib, which hath
ſent to reproach the living God 18 Of a truth,
LORD, the kings of Aſſyria have laid waſte all the
nations, and their countries 19 And have caſt their
gods into the fire, for they *were* no gods, but the
work of men's hands, wood and ſtone therefore they
have deſtroyed them 20 Now therefore, O LORD
our God, ſave us from his hand, that all the kingdoms
of the earth a may know, that thou *art* the LORD, *even*
thou only

m 2 Kings xix 8, &c
n Gen xxii. 14. 1 Sam xxiv 2— Rev xii. 16
o Chap xxxvi. 20
p Ibid 15
q Ibid 18
r Ver 1
s 1 Tim ii 8
t 1 Sam iv 4 Pſ lxxx 1
u Jer x 12
x Pſ v 1 2 Sam xxvi Dan ix 18
y 2 Chron vi 40
z Chap xl 19 Jer x 3
a Joſh iv 24 1 Kings viii 43 Pſ lxxxiii 18

v 8—20. Unable to prevail by threatnings and inſult, Rabſhakeh reports to his maſter the iſſue of the conference, v 8 and the king of Aſſyria, in hopes yet to force Hezekiah to ſubmit, before the news ſhould reach him of Tirhakah's armament in his favour, v 9 writes a boaſting and blaſphemous letter to the king of Judah, in order to terrify him into a ſurrender, v 10—13 which Hezekiah ſolemnly ſpreads before the Lord in prayer, and reſts the cauſe with him to give an anſwer to the impious blaſphemer, v 14—20 *Note*, (1) Though craft and power unite againſt the faithful, impotent will be the at-

tempts

Before Chriſt 710

tempts of the r enemies (2) Blaſphemous diſcourſe is terrible, but to propagate by writing ſentiments of irreligion and infidelity, is perpetuating the dire contagion to the lateſt times, and will more exceedingly aggravate men's guilt (3) When we have God for our friend, and have acceſs with confidence to pour all our complaints into his compaſſionate boſom, we may reſt in peace, and expect him to appear for us

21 ¶ [b] Then Iſaiah the ſon of Amoz [c] ſent unto Heze-
kiah, ſaying, Thus ſaith the LORD God of Iſrael,
Whereas thou haſt prayed to me againſt Sennacherib
king of Aſſyria 22 This *is* the word which the
LORD hath ſpoken concerning him, The virgin, the
daughter of Zion, hath deſpiſed thee, *and* laughed thee
to ſcorn, the daughter of Jeruſalem hath ſhaken her
head at thee 23 Whom haſt thou reproached and
blaſphemed? and againſt whom haſt thou exalted *thy*
voice, and lifted up thine eyes on high? [d] *even* againſt
the holy One of Iſrael 24 † By thy ſervants haſt thou
reproached the LORD, and [e] haſt ſaid, [f] By the multi-
tude of my chariots am I come up to the height of the
mountains, to the ſides of Lebanon and I will cut
down the tall cedars thereof, *and* the choice fir-trees
thereof and I will enter into the height of his border,
and the foreſt ‡ of his Carmel 25 I have digged, and
drunk water, and with the ſole of my feet have I dried
up all the rivers of the beſieged places 26 Haſt thou
not heard long ago *how* I have done it, *and* of ancient
times that I have formed it? now have I brought it to
paſs, [h] that thou ſhouldſt be to lay waſte defenced cities
into ruinous heaps 27 Therefore their inhabitants *were*
§ of ſmall power, they were diſmayed and confounded
[i] they were *as* the graſs of the field, and *as* the green
herb, [i] *as* the graſs on the houſe tops, and *as corn* blaſted
before it be grown up 28 But [k] I know thy abode,
and thy going-out, and thy coming in, and [l] thy rage
againſt me 29 Becauſe thy rage againſt me and thy
tumult is come up into mine ears, therefore [m] will I put
my hook in thy noſe, and [n] my bridle in thy lips, and I
will turn thee back by the way by which thou cameſt
30 And [o] this *ſhall be* a ſign unto thee, [p] Ye ſhall eat
this year ſuch as groweth of itſelf, and [q] the ſecond
year [r] that which ſpringeth of the ſame and in the
third year ſow ye, and reap, and plant vineyards, and
eat the fruit thereof 31 And the remnant that is
eſcaped of the houſe of Judah [s] ſhall again take root
downward, and bear fruit upward 32 For [t] out of
Jeruſalem ſhall go forth a remnant, and they that eſcape
out of mount Zion [u] the zeal of the LORD of hoſts
ſhall do this 33 Therefore thus ſaith the LORD
concerning the king of Aſſyria, He ſhall not come into
this city, nor ſhoot an arrow there, nor come before it
with ſhields, nor caſt a bank againſt it. 34 [x] By the
way that he came, by the ſame ſhall he return, and ſhall
not come into this city, ſaith the LORD 35 For I
will defend this city to ſave it for mine own ſake, and
[y] for my ſervant David's ſake 36 ¶ [z] Then the angel
of the LORD went forth, and [a] ſmote in the camp of
the Aſſyrians an hundred and fourſcore and five thou-
ſand and when they aroſe early in the morning, [b] be-
hold, they *were* all dead corpſes 37 ¶ So Sennache-
rib king of Aſſyria departed, and went and return-
ed, and dwelt at Nineveh 38 And it came to paſs
as he was worſhipping in the houſe of Niſroch his
god, that Adrammelech and Sharezer [c] his ſons ſmote
him with the ſword, and they eſcaped into the land
of ‖ Armenia and Eſar-haddon his ſon reigned in his
ſtead

‖ Heb Ararat

v 21—38 In anſwer to Hezekiah's prayer, Iſaiah tranſmits him a meſſage from God, *v* 21 eſpouſing his people's quarrel as his own, *v* 22, 23 He looks with contempt on the impotent threats of Sennacherib Elated on his paſt ſucceſſes, he thought he could carry the whole world before him, and, utterly inſenſible that it was from God alone that he had prevailed hitherto, he aſcribes it impiouſly to his own arm, *v* 24—27 But God, who ſees his proud deſign, will blaſt them ſuddenly to his confuſion, and ſtop his mad career, as eaſily as the rider governs his ſteed, *v* 28, 29 As a ſign of the continuance of the divine favour, plenty ſhould be reſtored as well as peace, notwithſtanding the harveſt was ruined by the Aſſyrians, and the ſucceeding year, as ſabbatical, admitted no tillage, *v* 30 The people thus eſcaped, though but a remnant, ſhould yet take root, and greatly increaſe, *v* 31, 32 and ſo far ſhould the enemy be from deſtroying Jeruſalem, that he ſhould not ſo much as ſhoot an arrow againſt it, *v* 33—35 for before the ſiege was formed, God would ariſe to defend them, and his judgment was accordingly executed by an angel, to the entire deſtruction of the army, *v* 36 and though the king eſcaped to Nineveh, he there met a more grievous death from his own unnatural ſons, *v* 37, 38 *Note*, (1) The inſults caſt on his people God reſents, as affronts againſt himſelf, and will remember them (2) Whatever wiſdom or prudence we may poſſeſs, it is atheiſm to aſcribe to ourſelves the glory of our enterprizes (3) The wicked can go no farther than the Lord permits, and he can quickly hurl them headlong into ruin in the midſt of their career of proſperity (4) When one diſtreſs is removed, another may be in proſpect, as here famine threatened though the ſiege was raiſed, but he who ſaves us from all our ſpiritual foes, can alſo relieve all our temporal wants, and they who are enabled to truſt him in the way of duty, ſhall not be deſtitute (5) If one angel in a night could ſpread ſuch fearful havock, how ſafe are they who have the God of angels for their protector, and theſe his hoſts their miniſtring ſpirits

CHAP XXXVIII

This chapter proceeds with the hiſtory of Hezekiah Here is, 1 His ſickneſs, and the ſentence of death he received, ver 1 2 His prayer in his ſickneſs, ver 2, 3 3 The anſwer of peace which God gave to that prayer, and the ſign given to confirm his faith, ver 4—8 And this we read and explained before, 2 Kings xx. 1 &c *But, 4 Here is Hezekiah's thankſgiving for his recovery, on uſing the means preſcribed,* ver 9—22 *which was not mentioned before, and contains much precious matter for the encouragement of our faith and hope at all times, and in ſickneſs particularly*

710

1 [a] IN thoſe days was Hezekiah ſick unto death and
Iſaiah the prophet the ſon of Amoz came unto
him, and ſaid unto him, Thus ſaith the LORD, † Set
thine houſe in order for thou ſhalt die, and not live
2 Then Hezekiah [b] turned his face unto the wall, and
[c] prayed unto the LORD, 3 And ſaid, [d] Remember
now, O LORD, I beſeech thee, how I have walked be-
fore thee in truth, and [e] with a perfect heart, and have
done *that which is* good in thy ſight and Hezekiah
[f] wept ‡ ſore 4 ¶ Then came the word of the LORD
to Iſaiah, ſaying, 5 Go, and ſay to Hezekiah, Thus
ſaith the LORD, the God of David thy father, I have
heard thy prayer, [i] I have ſeen thy tears behold, [i] I
will add unto thy days fifteen years 6 And [k] I will
deliver thee and this city out of the hand of the king of
Aſſyria and [l] I will defend this city 7 And [m] this
ſhall be a ſign unto thee from the LORD, that the
LORD will do this thing that he hath ſpoken 8 Be-
hold, I will bring again the ſhadow of the degrees which
is gone down in the ſun dial of Ahaz ten degrees back-
ward So the ſun returned ten degrees, by which de-
grees it was gone down

† Heb Give charge concerning, &c

‡ Heb With great weeping

v 1—8 To what hath been obſerved before on theſe words, we may add,

1 That ſince death is the common lot, it is our duty, before it approaches, to provide for it, both by a ſettlement of all our worldly concerns, that they may not at that time occupy our thoughts, and more eſpecially by ſuch a daily dying to the world and ſin, as may make the day of our removal neither unexpected nor unacceptable

2 In every ſituation, ſick, afflicted, or tempted, prayer is the great relief It is the heart's eaſe to unboſom ourſelves to God

3 It will be a comfort in every calamity, and a joy in the hour of death, to have our conſcience bear us witneſs in the Holy Ghoſt, that in ſimplicity and godly ſincerity we have had our converſation in the world

4 God regards every tear which falls from the eye of his mourners, and will give them quickly the garment of praiſe for the ſpirit of heavineſs

5 The proſperity promiſed to Zion, *v* 6 was better to Hezekiah than the reſtoration of his health, as the welfare of the church, and the intereſt of the Redeemer's kingdom, are ever dearer to the faithful, than any other concern merely relative to themſelves

6 One miracle ſerved to confirm Hezekiah's faith, we have ſeen the glorious Redeemer work innumerable, and ſhall we diſtruſt him?

Before Christ 714

9 ¶ The writing of Hezekiah king of Judah, when
he had been sick, and was recovered of his sickness
10 I said in [n] the cutting off of my days, I shall go to the
gates of the grave I am deprived of the residue of my
years 11 I said, [o] I shall not see the LORD, *even*
the LORD in the land of the living I shall behold
man no more with the inhabitants of the world 12
Mine age is departed, and is removed from me as a
shepherd's tent [p] I have cut off like a weaver my life
he will cut me off † with pining sickness from day
even to night wilt thou make an end of me 13 I reck-
oned till morning, *that* as a lion, so [q] will he break all
my bones from day *even* to night wilt thou make an
end of me 14 Like a crane *or* a swallow, so did I
chatter [r] I did mourn as a dove mine eyes fail *with*
looking upward, [s] O LORD, I am oppressed, ‡ under-
take for me 15 What shall I say? he hath both
spoken unto me, and himself hath done *it* I shall go
softly all my years in the bitterness of my soul 16
O LORD, [u] by these *things men* live, and in all these
things is the life of my spirit so wilt thou recover me,
and make me to live 17 Behold, for peace I had
great bitterness, but thou hast § in love to my soul *de-*
livered it from the pit of corruption for [x] thou hast cast
all my sins behind thy back 18 For [y] the grave can-
not praise thee, death can*not* celebrate thee they that
go down into the pit cannot hope for thy truth 19
[z] The living, the living, he shall praise thee, as I *do* this
day [a] the father to the children shall make known thy
truth 20 The LORD *was ready* to save me there-
fore we will sing my songs to the stringed instruments
all the days of our life in the house of the LORD 21
[c] For Isaiah had said, [d] Let them take a lump of figs,
and lay *it* for a plaister upon the boil, and he shall reco-
ver 22 Hezekiah also had said, What *is* the sign,
that [e] I shall go up to the house of the LORD?

n Ver 1
o Ps xxvii 4 & xlii 2 & xvi 9
p Job vii 6
† Or, from the thrum
q 1 Cor xi 32
r Chap lix 11
s Ps cxix 122
‡ Or, ease me
t Job vii 11 & x 1
u Deut viii 3 Chap lxiv 5
§ Heb loved my soul from the pit
x Ps xxxii 1
y 2 Chap xliii 25 Mic vii 19
z Ps vi 5 & xxx 9 & lxxxviii 11 & cxv 17
a Eccles ix 10
b Ps lxxviii 3 4
c Ps xxvii 4
d 2 Kings xx 7
e John ix 6
f Ps xlii 2 & lxxxiv 2 & cxxii 1

v 9—22 In grateful acknowledgment of the divine mercy shown him in his recovery, Hezekiah composed this sacred thanksgiving, and such memorials are not only profitable to keep alive our own gratitude, but stand as monuments of God's mercy, and an encouragement to trust him for future generations We have here,

1 The desperateness of his case *I said in the cutting off of my days, I shall go to the gates of the grave*, though in the prime of life, he saw the gates of the grave open to receive him *I am deprived of the residue of my years*, which, in the course of nature, he might have expected to have lived, but his grief was more that he was removed in the midst of his usefulness, than in the midst of his days *I said, I shall not see the Lord, even the Lord in the land of the living*, no more frequent the courts of his house, and join in the ordinances of his worship, encouraging by his example the piety of his people *I shall behold man no more with the inhabitants of the world*, or time, and be no longer able to serve the interests of God among his subjects, or be the instrument of [illegible] their reformation and happiness, and also no more enjoy the company of those near and dear to him, with whom, in the house of God, he used to hold sweet communion *Mine age is departed, and is removed from me as a shepherd's tent*, or my habitation, the tabernacle of the body, ready to return to dust, as the shepherd's tent, is quickly and easily removed *I have cut off like a weaver my life* who, when his piece is finished, cuts it out of the loom, and his sins might be regarded by him as the cause of his days being shortened *He will cut me off with pining sickness*, or, *from the thrum*, alluding to the metaphor of the weaver, and acknowledging the hand of God in the affliction, in whose hand are life and death *I reckoned till morning*, or, *set my time till morning*, concluding it impossible longer to survive, *that as a lion, so will he*, or it, *break all my bones*, the Lord's afflicting hand, or his disease, the pains of which were as acute as if he had been torn and gnawed by a lion *From day even to night wilt thou make an end of me*, though beyond expectation he saw the light of another day, he had no hope of seeing a third Note, (1) When we are in distress, we are too apt to sink into despondence (2) A solicitude for God's glory, and his interest among men, is the only truly laudable motive that can make a good man prefer abiding in the body to a departure to his Lord (3) The gates of the grave stand open day and night, it becomes us frequently to think of passing through them (4) Our most settled abode here is but as a poor shepherd's tent, and our passage through time swift as the weaver's shuttle it should therefore awaken our solicitude to secure a more durable mansion, that when the days of time are cut off, we may be enabled with joy to step forward into eternity

[illegible] his [illegible] prayer in his distress *Like a crane or a swallow, so did I chatter*, sometimes aloud, in extremity of pain, sometimes low, worn out with anguish, or so interrupted and broken were his prayers, through the torment he endured *I did mourn as a dove*, bemoaning himself over his transgressions *mine eyes fail with looking upward*, ready to close in death, despairing of relief *O Lord, I am oppressed*, or, *it oppresseth me*, my disease *undertake for me*, to pluck me from the bars of the pit, or it may be rendered, *I have no righteousness, be surety for me*, as containing his humble confession, and his dependance for pardoning grace on that Redeemer, who, in the fulness of time, should be his people's surety *Note*, (1) Nothing can make a dying bed easy, but confidence in the sufficiency of our divine surety to undertake for us in the great day (2) Till our eyes are closed, our lips ought not to be silent, yea, when our tongue can no longer perform its office, to this dear Redeemer should our soul aspire, till we breathe it forth into his bosom

3 His grateful acknowledgments *What shall I say?* where words are wanting to express the gratitude I feel *He hath both spoken unto me, and himself hath done it* sure is every word of his promise, and now by experience he can bear testimony thereto *I will go softly all my years in the bitterness of my soul*, meditating upon the mercies received, and ashamed of his own sinful distrust Or rather, *I will go chearfully all my years, after the bitterness of my soul*, the storm blown over, peace and prosperity shall crown all the years God doth prolong *O Lord, by these things men live*, by the word of divine promise, and the gracious providence of God *and in all these things is the life of my spirit*, the power, providence, and grace of God appearing thus wonderfully for him, gave renewed life to his soul as well as his body, filling him with faith, and love, and joy He instances several particulars that call for especial praise

(1) His recovery *So wilt thou recover me, and make me to live*, or, *so hast thou recovered me, and made me to live*, and every new life bestowed justly calls on us to adore the gracious giver

(2) The pleasing contrast of ease for pain, health for sickness *Behold, for peace I had great bitterness* or, as it may be rendered, *behold, into peace hath he changed my great bitterness*

(3) The love of God seen in his case made the mercy unspeakably sweeter, and more endeared to him *Thou hast in love to my soul delivered it from the pit of corruption*, the grave or, *with tender love thou hast embraced my soul from the pit of corruption*, snatching me from it, as a tender parent, when I was rushing into the horrible pit *Note*, Health restored is doubly pleasing, when we can see it is in love to our souls

(4) His sins pardoned, fully, freely, for ever *for thou hast cast all my sins behind thy back* And herein every redeemed soul is called upon to join the thanksgiving of this pious king, for, (1) Our souls and bodies, by reason of sin original and actual, in heart and life, are forfeited, and ready to fall into the bottomless pit of eternal perdition (2) The transcendently rich and gracious love of God in Christ Jesus hath interposed to pluck us from ruin, and to this alone we are indebted (3) Whom God loves in Christ, he pardons, and not only forgives, but forgets their provocations, be they never so great, numerous, or aggravated (4) All the bitterness which a sense of guilt and danger awakens in the conscience, God's love removes, and fills the soul, O blessed change! with joy and peace in believing (5) The souls thus rescued shall never taste of death, the pit of corruption is for ever shut, and the golden gates of life and immortality unfolded

4 His resolution to continue himself, and excite others to join him, in this constant and delightful work of praise *For the grave cannot praise thee, death cannot celebrate thee* silence there reigns, no grateful songs ascend from the dust, and no more service can be rendered to God's interests here below, by those who are departed *They that go down into the pit cannot hope for thy truth*, there God can be no longer glorified by faith or hope in his promise, but *the living, the living, he shall praise thee, as I do this day* those whose bodily lives are through mercy renewed, and their souls spiritually alive also, these would join him in God's praise *The father to the children shall make known thy truth*, transmitting to posterity the memorial of God's faithfulness, to encourage their trust, and awaken their gratitude *The Lord was ready to save me*, instant as I called, what happened *therefore we will sing my songs to the stringed instruments all the days of our life*, I, and all the faithful rejoicing in my mercies, will render the ceaseless tribute of our songs *in the house of the Lord* *Note*, (1) Since in the grave we can no more glorify God, what now our hand findeth to do for him, let us do it with our might (2) Who shall praise him, if they do not, who have been recovered from going down to the pit? (3) Whilst life and breath endure, so long should our praise last and then we shall go where they will never end (4) Godly parents will not fail to transmit to their children the memorial of their fathers mercies, and to encourage them to trust the same promises which themselves have proved so faithful

5 At the close of this history it is remarked, as in 2 *Kings* xx 7, 8 that the sign, v 8 was given at Hezekiah's request, and

Before Chriſt 714.

and a lump of figs, at Iſaiah's command, laid on the boil, either as a means to procure his recovery, or as a ſign to aſſure him of it *Note*, (1) Though in ſickneſs our dependance muſt not be on the medicines, yet we are to truſt God in the uſe of means (2) The great comfort of health is ability to attend on God's worſhip, and be employed actively in his ſervice, and this is the great end for which a good man wiſhes to live

CHAP XXXIX

The ſtory of this chapter likewiſe we had before, 2 Kings xx 12, &c We have here, 1 Hezekiah's pride in ſhewing his treaſures to the king of Babylon's ambaſſadors that were ſent to congratulate his recovery, ver 1, 2 2 Iſaiah's enquiry, and Hezekiah's acknowledgment what he had done, ver 3, 4 3 The ſentence paſſed upon him for it, ver 5—7 4 Hezekiah's penitent and patient ſubmiſſion to it, ver 8

a 2 Kings xx 12, &c b 2 Chr xxxii 31

1 [a] AT that time Merodach-baladan, the ſon of Ba-
ladan king of Babylon, [b] ſent letters and a pre-
ſent to Hezekiah for he had heard that he had been
ſick, and was recovered 2 And Hezekiah was glad
of them, and [c] ſhewed them the houſe of his † precious
things, the ſilver, and the gold, and the ſpices, and
the precious ointment, and all the houſe of his ‡ armour,
and all that was found in his treaſures [d] there was no-
thing in his houſe, nor in all his dominion, that Heze-
kiah ſhewed them not 3 ¶ Then came Iſaiah the
prophet unto king Hezekiah, and ſaid unto him, What
ſaid theſe men? and from whence came they unto thee?
And Hezekiah ſaid, They are come from a far country
unto me, *even* from Babylon 4 Then ſaid he, What
have they ſeen in thine houſe? And Hezekiah an-
ſwered, [e] All that *is* in mine houſe have they ſeen
there is nothing among my treaſures that I have not
ſhewed them

c 2 Chron xxxii 25, 31 † Or, ſpicery ‡ Heb Veſſels, or inſtruments d Eccl ſ vii 20 1 John i 8 e Job vii 16 Job xxxi 33

v 1—4 Though nothing could appear more promiſing than Hezekiah's late profeſſions, and in general he did approve himſelf faithful, yet in ſome things he failed, as in the ſtory here recorded, where his pride and vanity ſeduced him, ſo that, as it is obſerved by the ſacred hiſtorian, 2 *Chron* xxxii 25 *He rendered not again according to the benefit done to him*

This hiſtory we have had before, 2 *Kings* xx 12 and may juſt add to what was there obſerved, (1) How hard it is to be kept humble under diſtinguiſhed mercies and this world's wealth (2) They will be courted in proſperity, who in adverſity would be deſpiſed (3) When it becomes their intereſt, the enemies of religion will careſs God's people, but their kiſſes are commonly deceitful (4) An affectation of diſplaying our improvements, wealth, buildings, &c to ſtrangers, and taking a ſecret pleaſure in doing ſo, evidences the vanity of the heart, and that often moſt, when we affect to call them trifles (5) God will not ſee his children puffed up without ſending them the needful rebuke it is well if, as Hezekiah, we take ſhame to ourſelves, and confeſs our folly

f 2 Kings xx. 16, &c g Jer lii 17 Dan i 2 h Dan i 3, 7 i 1 Sam iii 18 Job i 21 Pſal xxxix 9

5 [f] Then ſaid Iſaiah to Hezekiah, Hear the word of
the LORD of hoſts 6 Behold, the days come, that
all that *is* in thine houſe, and *that* which thy fathers have
laid up in ſtore until this day, [g] ſhall be carried to Baby-
lon nothing ſhall be left, ſaith the LORD 7 And
of thy ſons that ſhall iſſue from thee, which thou ſhalt
beget, ſhall they take away, and [h] they ſhall be eunuchs
in the palace of the king of Babylon 8 Then ſaid He-
zekiah to Iſaiah, [i] Good *is* the word of the LORD which
thou haſt ſpoken he ſaid moreover, For there ſhall be
peace and truth in my days

v 5—8 It was a mortifying meſſage the prophet brought him, but a bleſſed ſymptom of Hezekiah's gracious ſpirit, that ſo humbly he acquieſced in the divine decree It may teach us, (1) That it is juſt in God to take from us the gifts we abuſe (2) Not to be deſirous of, or value ourſelves upon, the reſpect paid us by the children of this world our intimacy and connection with them uſually in their iſſue prove our plague (3) True prophets of God muſt not ſpare the faithful reproof, and true penitents will, ſo far from being offended, receive it with thankfulneſs (4) When God is pleaſed to reſume his gifts we have abuſed, or to puniſh us by afflictions in this world for our ſins, it becomes us to bear the rod with quietneſs, and juſtify him in his judgments Whilſt we are out of hell, all our ſufferings are infinitely leſs than we deſerve (5) Though we cannot but be concerned about the evils which we foreſee, yet every moment's reſpite is a mercy to be acknowledged

Before Chriſt 714

CHAP XL

At this chapter begins the latter part of the prophecy of this book the concluſion of the former chapter ſpread a dark cloud over Judah and its princes, but before God ſent his people into captivity, he furniſhed them with precious promiſes for their ſupport and comfort in their trouble, and we may well imagine of what great uſe to them this gracious prophecy was in that cloudy and dark day, and how much it helped to dry up their tears by the rivers of Babylon Much of Chriſt and goſpel grace we meet with in the foregoing part of this book, but in this latter part we ſhall find much more, and as if it were deſigned for a prophetical ſummary of the New Teſtament, it begins with that which begins the goſpels, the voice of one crying in the wilderneſs, *chap* xl 3 *and concludes with that which concludes the book of the Revelation,* the new heavens and the new earth, *chap* lxvi 22

In this chapter we have, 1 Orders given to publiſh abroad the glad tidings of redemption, ver 1, 2 2 Theſe glad tidings introduced by a voice in the wilderneſs, which gives aſſurance that all obſtructions ſhall be removed, ver 3—5 and that though all creatures fail and fade, the word of God ſhall be eſtabliſhed and accompliſhed, ver 6—8 3 A joyful proſpect given to the people of God of the happineſs which this redemption ſhould bring along with it, ver 9—11 4 The ſovereignty and power of that God magnified, who undertakes to work out this redemption, ver 12—17 5 Idols therefore triumphed over, and idolaters upbraided with their folly, ver 18—26 6 A reproof given to the people of God for their fears and deſpondencies, and enough ſaid in a few words to ſilence thoſe fears, ver 27—31 And we through patience and comfort of this ſcripture may have hope

1 COmfort ye, comfort ye my people, ſaith your 712
God 2 Speak ye † comfortably to Jeruſalem,
and cry unto her, that her ‡ warfare [a] is accompliſhed,
that her iniquity is pardoned for ſhe hath received of
the LORD's hand [b] double for all her ſins

† Heb To the heart of ‡ Or, appointed time a Pſ cii 13 b Chap lxi 7

v 1, 2 The concluſion of the prophet's meſſage in the former chapter ſpoke terror and conviction, the opening of this, joy and conſolation for though it be a needful ſeverity to wound, it is the more pleaſing part of our office to bind up the broken-hearted, and to preach the goſpel of peace

It would afford the pious Jews a beam of chearing hope amidſt the evils that were expected, and ſupport the fainting ſpirits of the poor captives, to have theſe great and precious promiſes ſet before them, and be aſſured, whatever they ſuffered, there was hope in the end We have here,

1 The commiſſion given *Comfort ye, comfort ye, my people, ſaith your God Speak ye comfortably to Jeruſalem,* or, *to the heart of Jeruſalem, and cry unto her* (1) The perſons addreſſed are *my people*, this is their character, they are choſen, and faithful, and called (2) The perſon ſpeaking, *your God*, your reconciled God in Jeſus Chriſt, in whoſe love preſent and eternal his people are intereſted, and therefore may expect all that almighty power, boundleſs mercy, infinite wiſdom, and unchangeable faithfulneſs can beſtow (3) The employment of God's miniſters is to comfort his people, who are often greatly dejected through affliction, temptation, corruption, and deſertion (4) The order is repeated, and they are commanded not only to ſpeak, but cry aloud, for though it be the privilege of God's people to rejoice, and his will concerning them that they ſhould be happy in him, yet they are apt to write bitter things againſt themſelves, and ſcarce can be perſuaded to receive the bleſſings God hath in ſtore for them

2 The mercies promiſed, and theſe are, (1) The pardon of ſin *Her iniquity is pardoned*, however deep the die, and aggravated the guilt, it is pardoned freely, fully, for ever The blood and righteouſneſs of Jeſus have obtained eternal redemption for us, and there is no more condemnation (2) Victory over all our enemies *Her warfare is accompliſhed* Chriſt, the captain of our ſalvation, hath vanquiſhed for us ſin, Satan, death, and hell, hath entered into the land of glory as conqueror, to take poſſeſſion for us, and we are already triumphant in our exalted head, and what he hath done for us, he will do in us Though we have a warfare to maintain whilſt we are in the body, againſt fleſh and blood, corruption within, and the world without, and Satan tempts, and death threatens, yet by his grace we ſhall be more than conquerors, and ſee quickly all our enemies put under our feet (3) *She hath received of the Lord's hand double for all her ſins* God ſpeaks as a tender parent, whoſe love makes him think the corrections he had given his dear children beyond meaſure or rather the words intimate the full ſatisfaction God hath taken of Chriſt our ſurety, exacting from him to the uttermoſt the deſert of our iniquities,

c Mat iii 3, Mark i 3 Luke iii 4 John i 23 d Mal iii 1 e Pſ lxviii 4

3 ¶ [c] The voice of him that crieth in the wilderneſs,
[d] Prepare ye the way of the LORD, make ſtraight in the
deſert a high way for [e] our God 4 Every valley ſhall
be

Before Christ 714.

be exalted, and [f] every mountain and hill shall be made
low and [g] the crooked shall be made straight, and the
rough places plain 5 And [h] the glory of the LORD
shall be revealed, and all flesh shall see *it* together for
the mouth of the LORD hath spoken *it* 6 The
voice said, Cry And he said, What shall I cry? [i] All
flesh *is* grass, and all the goodliness thereof *is* as the
flower of the field 7 The grass withereth, the flower
fadeth, [k] because the Spirit of the LORD bloweth up
on it surely the people *is* grass 8 The grass with-
ereth, the flower fadeth but [l] the word of our God shall
stand for ever

f Zech iv 7
g Chap. xlv 2
h John i 14
i Job xiv 2 Ps xc v & cii 11 & ciii 15 Jam i 10 1 Pet i 24
k Ps ciii 16
l Rom iii 3 1 Pet i 25

v 3—8 The scriptures of the New Testament have not left us uncertain whose voice this is which crieth in the wilderness John, like the morning-star, the harbinger of day, appears to usher in the Sun of righteousness, and to awaken, by his preaching, the souls of sinners to turn their eyes towards the Lamb of God which taketh away the sins of the world,

1 The cry is, *Prepare ye the way of the Lord, make straight in the desert a high-way for our God* Jehovah, our God, here spoken of, is the glorious Redeemer, whose eternal godhead is asserted Our hearts are a desart, till his presence and love change the dreary scene Where his footsteps tread, waters break forth in the wilderness, and streams of grace and consolation in the desart The preparation for him must be from him, and he that commands must give the hearing ear, the contrite heart, and dispose us to welcome him into our souls

2 Where Jesus comes, *every valley shall be exalted, and every mountain and hill shall be made low, and the crooked shall be made strait, and the rough places plain* Such will be the effects of his grace upon the souls of his people those who were sunk into the lowest deep under the sense of guilt, shall be raised up by divine mercy and exalted the proud, who in their own eyes before were high in conceit of their own worth and excellence, shall be brought low, and acknowledge their sin and vileness the crooked and rough ways of men of perverse minds shall be made strait, their errors removed, their corrupt practices reformed, and their hearts renewed in holiness

3 *The glory of the Lord shall be revealed*, the Redeemer Jesus, the brightness of his father's glory, and the express image of his person, *and all flesh shall see it together*, he being the universal Saviour, not of the Jews only, but also of the Gentiles *for the mouth of the Lord hath spoken it*, and therefore no jot or tittle of his promises shall fail

4 A farther commission is given the preacher, and at his request he is instructed what to cry, *v* 6—8 which may refer to the weakness and impotence of the Babylonians, to detain the Jews in their captivity, when the Lord should arise to save them, or more generally may be applied to all men, where the word of the gospel is preached, as an alarming motive to attend to the great and precious promises of a better world, seeing this is so frail and fading *All flesh is grass*, weak and withering, *and all the goodliness thereof as the flower of the field*, which, though it looks more gay and beautiful, is as frail and feeble Such are all human gifts and greatness, and such the best works of man's righteousness, which however specious, quickly fade *The grass withereth, the flower fadeth, because the spirit of the Lord bloweth upon it*, then drooping, dying, all our beauty and glory languishes health loses its bloom, our possessions fade away, and death closes the scene or when this Spirit breathes upon us in conversion, our best doings and duties appear poor and wretched, and those things on which we prided ourselves we count dung and loss, that we may win Christ *Surely the people is grass*, all people of every age, rank, and degree, *the grass withereth, the flower fadeth*, such perishing things are all human excellence, *but the word of our God shall stand for ever*; and therefore when all besides perishes, and every earthly comfort or possession in death are for ever lost, they who make the great and precious promises of the gospel their stay, will find, to their everlasting comfort, a portion which cannot fail them in the better world of glory

9 ¶ † O Zion that bringest good tidings, get thee
up into the high mountain, ‡ O Jerusalem, that bring-
est good tidings, lift up thy voice with strength lift it
up, be not afraid, say unto the cities of Judah, Be-
hold your God 10 Behold, the LORD God will
come § with strong *hand*, and his arm shall rule for
him behold, [m] his reward *is* with him, and his ‖ work
before him 11 He shall [n] feed his flock like a shep-
herd he shall gather the lambs with his arm, and car-
ry *them* in his bosom, *and* [o] shall gently lead those that
¶ are with young.

† Or, O thou that bringest good tidings to Zion Chap lii 7
‡ Or, O thou that bringest good tidings to Jerusalem
§ Or, against the strong
m Chap lxii 11 Rev xxii 12
‖ Or, recompense for his work
n Ezek xxxiv 23 John x 11
o Chap xlii 3 Mat xi 28 Rom xiv 1
¶ Or that give suck,

v 9—11 Great was the joy when, by the edict of Cyrus, once more the Jews were permitted to return to their own land, and loudly was it proclaimed by those who had at heart the prosperity of Zion To this the prophecy may refer, but it evidently was designed for the days of Christ, and respects his incarnation.

1 His manifestation in the flesh is proclaimed to sinners, as their greatest happiness *O Zion, that bringest good tidings*, when his ministry chiefly was exercised, or better, it may be rendered, *O thou that bringest good tidings to Zion*, as addressed to John the Baptist, and all the ministers of the gospel, whose office it is to proclaim the divine glories and transcendent excellence of the Redeemer, in all his offices and undertakings, for the salvation of sinners, *get thee up to the high mountain*, to the most public places, such as the mount of the Lord's house *O Jerusalem, &c* or, *O thou that bringest good tidings to Jerusalem, lift up thy voice with strength lift it up, be not afraid* of the opposition and revilings of men, who would persecute the preachers of the gospel *Say unto the cities of Judah*, where Christ appeared, *Behold your God* incarnate, the promised Emmanuel, a man, and yet the eternal Jehovah, come with the most joyful tidings that can greet a sinner's ears, to proclaim pardon, grace, and salvation, freely and to the uttermost

2 His power and all-sufficiency are declared *Behold, your God shall come*; that desire of all nations, and especially the glory of his Israel, he shall come *with a strong hand*, mighty to save his people, and punish his enemies or, *against a strong one*, to destroy the works of the devil, and break his hateful power in the hearts of men *and his arm shall rule for him*, self-sufficient, and designing his own glory or *against him*, the great enemy of souls, who must yield to this conqueror *Behold!* with joy, ye people of God, *his reward is with him*, to bestow eternal life on as many as believe in him *and his work before him*, the glorious work of redemption he came fully acquainted with the steps necessary thereto, and perfectly able and willing for the undertaking

3 His grace and love are tenderly displayed under the character of a watchful shepherd *He shall feed his flock like a shepherd* his people are his sheep, bought at the price of his blood, and therefore with tenderest regard he feeds them in the green pastures of his ordinances, bestows on them the waters of consolation, watches over them night and day, defending them from every danger, seeking them when strayed, and suffering none of them to be lost *He shall gather the lambs with his arm, and carry them in his bosom*, as when the cold is ready to kill the new-cast lamb, or it is so weak that it cannot follow the dam, the shepherd in his bosom bears and cherishes it, so doth Christ the lambs of his flock, pitying their weakness, helping their infirmities, and in the bosom of his love cherishing and strengthening their souls *and shall gently lead those that are with young*, whose circumstances are embarrassed, and trials difficult, he leads them gently as they are able, and safely, so that they do not miscarry, nor finally come short of the glory of God. Let the under-shepherds learn of their chief shepherd to partake of his Spirit, and tread in his steps, consulting the weakness and ministring to the wants of those sheep and lambs of his flock entrusted to their care

12 ¶ [p] Who hath measured the waters in the hollow
of his hand? and meted out heaven with a span, and
comprehended the dust of the earth in a † measure, and
weighed the mountains in scales, and the hills in a ba-
lance? 13 [q] Who hath directed the Spirit of the LORD,
or *being* ‡ his counseller hath taught him? 14 With
whom took he counsel, and *who* instructed him, and
taught him in the path of judgment, and taught him
knowledge, and shewed to him the way of understand-
ing? 15 Behold, the nations *are* as a drop of a bucket,
and are counted as the small dust of the balance be-
hold, he taketh up the isles as a very little thing 16
And Lebanon *is* not sufficient to burn, nor the beasts
thereof sufficient for a burnt-offering 17 [r] All nations
before him *are* as nothing, and they are counted to him
[s] less than nothing and vanity.

p Prov xxx 4
† Or, a tierce
q Job xxi 22 & xxxvi 22, 23 Wisd ix 13 Rom xi 34 1 Cor ii 16
‡ Heb The man of his counsel
r Dan iv 35
s Ps lxii 9

v 12—17 These words speak consolation to God's people, they declare the infinite power and wisdom of their God His captives in Babylon need not fear his ability to compleat their deliverance, and his chosen now and ever may be assured, that he, who in his condescensions is their shepherd, suffers no diminution of his uncreated glory thereby The description here given of our Redeemer is unutterably grand Such his immensity, the vast depths of waters to him are but as a few drops in the hollow of his hand, the expanded heaven to him is but a span, the ponderous globe but is a few particles of dust, and the mountains and hills, so prodigious in height and breadth, weighed in his scales, appear as grains of sand, and all nicely proportioned for the purposes they were designed to serve, *v* 12 In his amazing work of creation he needed no adviser, himself the fountain of wisdom, all receiving from him, none capable of adding to him, *v* 13 Before him the mightiest nations are but as the drop of the bucket, or the small dust of the balance, so light, as not to turn the poised scale The isles he *taketh up*,

or

Before Christ 712.

or *caſteth away*, as chaff, or the down of thiſtles, *v* 15 Were Lebanon with all its foreſts hewn down for fuel, and the innumerable herds which feed thereon ſlain for a ſacrifice, utterly inſufficient would they have been to expiate the ſins of men no leſs than the incarnate Jehovah could offer the propitiation, *v* 16 before whom all nations are as nothing, and, as if words were wanting to expreſs their inſignificance, they are *counted leſs than nothing and vanity* Note, (1) The more we ſee of the Redeemer's greatneſs and glory, the more ſhould our hearts be eſtabliſhed in the fulneſs of his ſalvation (2) The leſs we are in our own eyes, and the more we ſee our own vanity, as well as ſin, the more ſhall we admire the infinite love and condeſcenſion of our Immanuel

18 ¶ [t] To whom then will ye liken God? or what
likeneſs will ye compare unto him? 19 [u] The work-
man melteth a graven image, and the goldſmith ſpreadeth
it over with gold, and caſteth ſilver chains 20 He that
is ſo impoveriſhed, that he hath no oblation, chooſeth a
tree *that* will not rot, he ſeeketh unto him a cunning
workman [x] to prepare a graven image *that* ſhall not be
moved 21 Have ye not known? have ye not heard?
[y] hath it not been told you from the beginning? have
ye not underſtood from the foundations of the earth?
22 *It is* he that ſitteth upon the circle of the earth, and
the inhabitants thereof *are* as graſhoppers, [z] that ſtretch-
eth out the heavens as a curtain, and ſpreadeth them out
as a tent to dwell in 23 That bringeth [a] the princes
to nothing, he maketh the judges of the earth as va-
nity 24 ¶ Yea they ſhall not be planted, yea they
ſhall not be ſown, yea their ſtock ſhall not take root in
the earth and he ſhall alſo blow upon them, and they
ſhall wither, and the whirlwind ſhall take them away as
ſtubble 25 [b] To whom then will ye liken me, or ſhall
I be equal? ſaith the holy One 26 Lift up your eyes
on high, and behold who hath created theſe *things*, that
bringeth out their hoſt by number [c] he calleth them all
by names, by the greatneſs of his might, for that *he is*
ſtrong in power, not one faileth.

[t] Ver 25 Chap xlvi 5 Act xvii 29
[u] Chap xli 6 & xliv 12 Jer x 3
[x] Chap xli 7
[y] Pſ xix 1 Rom i 20
[z] Job ix 8 Pſ civ 2 Chap xliv 24 Jer x 12
[a] Job xii 21 Pſ cvii 40
† Or, ſo that they are as if they had not been planted nor ſown &c
[b] Ver 18
[c] Pſ cxlvii 4

v 18—26 The ſin and folly of idolaters is here upbraided

1 The abſurdity of idolatry is here deſcribed, *v* 19, 20 Mad in the purſuit of idol vanities, the founder caſts the figure, and, laviſh of their riches, they deck the ſenſeleſs image, it is overlaid with plates of gold, or adorned with chains of ſilver Yea, he that cannot afford an offering will have a god, tho' carved from a tree, and chuſing the wood that is moſt incorruptible, has it faſhioned into ſhape, and fixed in its place Amazing ſtupidity! to pay adoration to a ſenſeleſs log, or expect ſupport from that which cannot ſtand without being faſtened *Note*, (1) The idolatry that hath prevailed ſo univerſally is a ſtriking proof of the fall of man, and of the dreadful darkneſs of the human underſtanding (2) The continuance of this abominable practice in the church of Rome is among the ſtrong proofs of her utter apoſtacy (3) Beware of ſpiritual idolatry to place a confidence in gold, or ſet up the creature above God in our affections, is equally criminal as to bow the knee to a ſtock or a ſtone

2 The prophet expoſtulates with them, *Have ye not known? have ye not heard? hath it not been told you from the beginning? have ye not underſtood from the foundations of the earth?* From the viſible creation the great Author's eternal power and godhead might be clearly ſeen, and traditionary notices of his Being were handed down from the beginning, yet they degraded him into an image made like to corruptible man, and worſhipped him not as God, ſo that they were without excuſe, *See Rom* i 20 A glorious deſcription then follows of the great Jehovah On the circle of the heavens he ſitteth, by his power and providence upholding all things on this terreſtrial ball he looks, an atom in the vaſt expanſe, and puny mortals appear but as graſhoppers or locuſts before him As a curtain he ſtretches out the firmament, and in the heavens, hid from mortal eye, ſpreads his radiant tabernacle, *v* 22 In his view earth's mightieſt princes ſhrink into *nothing*; *their perſons, counſels, power, are all vanity*, *v* 23 Fixed as their thrones appear, and great as they ſeem to worms like themſelves, one breath of his diſpleaſure blaſts them as graſs, and hurls them from the earth as ſtubble before the whirlwind, *v* 24

3 He directs them whither to turn their eyes, nor more attempt to liken God, the eternal Spirit, to any corporeal form *Lift up your eyes on high, and behold who hath created theſe things*, read in the expanded volume above, the legible characters of the Creator's glory, *that bringeth out their hoſt by number*, marſhalled in exact order *he calleth them all by names* ſuited to their poſition and influence *by the greatneſs of his might, for that he is ſtrong in power, not one faileth*, bound by omnipotent power, each in his ſeveral orbit performs his revolution, and uſes his influence according to his Creator's will Since then God is ſo infinitely above the higheſt creatures and all theſe the works of his hands, every repreſentation of him by them muſt be a debaſement of his glory

27 Why ſayeſt thou, O Jacob, and ſpeakeſt, O Iſ-
rael, [d] My way is hid from the LORD, and [e] my judg-
ment is paſſed over from my God? 28 ¶ Haſt thou
not known? [f] haſt thou not heard, *that* the everlaſting
God, the LORD, the Creator of the ends of the earth,
fainteth not, neither is weary? [g] *there is* no ſearching of
his underſtanding 29 [h] He giveth power to the faint,
and to *them that have* no might, he increaſeth ſtrength
30 Even [i] the youths ſhall faint, and be weary, and the
young men ſhall utterly fall 31 But they that wait
upon the LORD [k] ſhall † renew *their* ſtrength they
ſhall mount up with wings as eagles, they ſhall run and
not be weary, *and* they ſhall walk and not faint.

[d] Job iii 23
[e] Mal ii 17
[f] Pſ xliv 1
[g] Pſ cxlvii 5 Rom xi 33
[h] 2 Cor xii 9
[i] Pſ xxxiii 16
[k] Pſ ciii 5
† Heb. Change, or double

v 27—31 Their long captivity was ready to diſcourage the hearts of the Jews, and ſome of them, under the power of unbelief, were ready to conclude themſelves forgotten and forſaken of God, for which the prophet here reproves them, and their rebuke is deſigned for our admonition, who are ready to ſay it when we are corrected of him

1 He expoſes their impatience and unbelief *Why ſayeſt thou, O Jacob, and ſpeakeſt, O Iſrael, My way is hid from the Lord*, he diſregards my afflictions, *and my judgment is paſſed over from my God?* he hears not my appeals, nor gives me the expected redreſs *Note*, (1) Unbelieving ſuggeſtions ariſe often in the hearts of true Iſraelites (2) Such queſtions as our impatience utters, muſt be ſilenced *Why and* wherefore do we complain? God is not ſlack in his promiſes, but we are haſty in ſpirit *The viſion is for an appointed time* (3) It argues our folly, as well as ſin, to ſuppoſe God doth not ſee our diſtreſs, or is not able to relieve us

2 Two things he reminds them of, which they ought to have known and conſidered the infinite power, and unſearchable wiſdom of God *Haſt thou not known?* after all the wonders diſplayed in behalf of his people, *haſt thou not heard*, from the experience of paſt ages, as well as the oracles of truth, *that the everlaſting God, the Lord, the Creator of the ends of the earth, fainteth not, neither is weary?* His power is never exhauſted, nor his government enfeebled he is from eternity unchangeably the ſame, and, as the Creator of all, muſt needs be able to govern the work of his own hands, and therefore, however low his church may be reduced, it is not owing to weakneſs or wearineſs that he doth not appear for their relief When his time is come, he will ſave them to the uttermoſt, nor can be at a loſs for the means, when infinite wiſdom is joined with almighty power, for *there is no ſearching of his underſtanding*, therefore we are bound at all times to truſt him, and patiently expect the ſalvation of God

3 When we do ſo, we are ſure of being holpen *He giveth power to the faint, and to them that have no might, he increaſeth ſtrength* ſuch as, ſeeing their own ſpiritual weakneſs and helpleſſneſs, apply to him, find him a very preſent help *When I am weak, then am I ſtrong* *Even the youths ſhall faint, and be weary, and the young men ſhall utterly fall* ſuch as truſt on an arm of fleſh, and, ſelf confident, think they are able to extricate themſelves from their difficulties, or, by the ſtrength of their own endeavour, to overcome the power of their corruptions; theſe ſhall prove their inſufficiency, and utterly fail *but they that wait on the Lord*, both for righteouſneſs and ſtrength, and in every trial caſt their care upon him, ſenſible of their own ſinfulneſs, ignorance, and weakneſs, theſe *ſhall renew their ſtrength*, be enabled to ſtand in the evil day, and ſupported under the ſore burden of their temptations, affliction, and corruption yea, more than ſupported, *they ſhall mount up with wings as eagles*, ſo ſwift and ſtrong, and their trials ſerve to ſtrengthen their graces, and lift their ſouls farther from earth, and nearer heaven *they ſhall run, and not be weary*, in the way of God's commandments, pleaſed in his happy ſervice, and accounting it perfect freedom *and they ſhall walk, and not faint*, though long their journey, and difficult the way, the everlaſting arms of Jeſus's love ſhall bear them up, and bring them ſafe at laſt to their eternal home Hold out then, faith and patience!

CHAP. XLI

This chapter contains a challenge to the enemies of Chriſt, to try their cauſe before God, and is full of comfort to God's people, and confuſion to idolaters, 1 God ſhews the folly of thoſe that worſhipped idols, ver 1—9 2 He encourages his faithful ones with an aſſurance that he would make them victorious over their enemies, and bring about a happy change of their affairs, ver 10—20 3 He challenges the idols to vie with him either for knowledge or power, ver 21—24, 26 4 He mentions a glorious perſonage who ſhall ariſe to deſtroy his idolatrous foes, ver. 25, 27—29

1 KEEP

Before Christ 712

1 [a] KEEP ſilence before me, O iſlands, and let the
people renew *their* ſtrength let them come
near, then let them ſpeak let us come near together to
judgment 2 Who raiſed up † the righteous man [b]
from the eaſt, called him to his foot, [c] gave the nations
before him, and made *him* rule over kings? he gave
them as the duſt to his ſword, *and* as driven ſtubble to
his bow 3 He purſued them, *and* paſſed ‡ ſafely,
even by the way *that* he had not gone with his feet 4
Who hath wrought and done *it*, calling the generations
from the beginning? I the LORD [d] the firſt, and with
the laſt, I *am* he 5 The iſles ſaw *it* and feared, the
ends of the earth were afraid, drew near, and came
6 [e] They helped every one his neighbour, and *every one*
ſaid to his brother, ‖ Be of good courage 7 [f] So the
carpenter encouraged the § goldſmith, *and* he that ſmooth-
eth *with* the hammer him that ſmote the anvil, ¦ ſaying,
It *is* ready for the ſodering and he faſtned it with nails,
[g] *that* it ſhould not be moved 8 But thou Iſrael *art*
my ſervant, Jacob [h] whom I have choſen, the ſeed of
Abraham [i] my friend 9 *Thou* whom I have taken from
the ends of the earth, and called thee from the chief
men thereof, and ſaid unto thee, Thou *art* my ſervant,
I have choſen thee, [k] and not caſt thee away

a Zech ii 13 † Heb Righteouſneſs b Gen xii 31, or Chap xlvi 11 c Gen xiv 15 or Chap xlv 1 ‡ Heb In peace d Chap xliii 10 & xliv 6 & xlviii 12 Rev i 17 & xxii 13 e Chap xl 19 & xliv 12 ‖ Heb Be ſtrong f Chap xl 19 § Or founder ¦ Or ſaying of the ſoder, it is good g Chap xl 20 h Deut vii 6 & x 15 Pſ cxxxv 4 i 2 Chron xx 7 Jam ii 23 k 1 Sam xii 22 Pſ xciv 14

v 1—9 We have here,

1 A challenge given to idolaters, to try their cauſe before God, or as ſome ſuggeſt the matter of the controverſy here intended is the divine power and godhead of the Redeemer, ſpoken of in the former chapter, which Heretics, antient and modern, denied, who are cited to produce their evidence, though the firſt ſenſe ſeems moſt natural The court is ſet, the citation ſent forth, ſilence proclaimed, the defendants of idolatry called to plead, and aſſured of a fair hearing, if they dared bring the matter to an iſſue *Note*, (1) We may ſafely challenge the enemies of the religion of Jeſus to do their worſt, ſince their oppoſition will iſſue in their greater confuſion (2) The truths of the goſpel will bear the ſtricteſt ſcrutiny, they who moſt attentively read their bibles, and weigh the arguments there advanced, will be unmoved with the wretched cavils of infidelity

2 He mentions an inſtance of his glorious power, to which the idols cannot pretend, v 2—4 The righteous man here ſpoken of, many interpret of Abraham, called of God from Ur of the Chaldees, obedient inſtantly to the divine admonition, though he knew not whither he went, eminently rewarded of God for his faith and obedience by preſent bleſſings, and the victory he obtained over the kings, *Gen* xiv having a grant of the land of Canaan for himſelf and poſterity, and appointed a father of many nations Some ſuppoſe the righteous man here deſcribed is Cyrus, and that what ſhould be done hereafter is in the prophetic language ſpoken of as already accompliſhed, others, that the prophecy relates to the apoſtle Paul, though the firſt ſenſe appears moſt natural and preferable, and was a glorious manifeſtation of the Almighty power with which the eternal and unchangeable Jehovah had once delivered their great progenitor from the midſt of idolaters, and therefore the captives of Babylon might ſee both the vanity of idols, and the reaſon they had to hope for the ſame interpoſition of God's arm to reſcue them, and bring them back again to their own land *Note*, (1) The wonders of old time wrought for our anceſtors ſhould be an encouragement to us in time of trial (2) When God calls us to his foot, we may ſafely commit ourſelves to his guidance, though the way in which he is pleaſed to lead us be dark, and the iſſue unknown (3) All our enemies muſt bow before us, when the Lord is our ſtrength, and our Redeemer

3 He repreſents the vain oppoſition of the idolaters, v 5 When they ſaw what God had done for Abraham and his ſeed, they were alarmed, as if the cauſe of idolatry was in danger, and therefore, with eagerneſs united to prevent it, by increaſing the number of their idols, v 6, 7 This is by ſome applied to the diſturbance St Paul's preaching gave the idolaters at Epheſus, *Acts* xix 20 and other places, and the oppoſition made againſt him It ſhews, (1) The jealouſy of the world and the devil, againſt the encroachments of religion (2) That the ſinner's heart is often exaſperated by the means which were deſigned for his converſion (3) How ready the wicked are to unite for purpoſes of evil, and ſhould the ſervants of the bleſſed God be leſs active in his ſervice?

4 He encourages his Iſrael to truſt him *Thou, Iſrael, art my ſervant*, and being owned by him will be aſſuredly protected, *Jacob, whom I have choſen* as a veſſel of mercy ſeparated for God's ſervice from the world of idolaters, *the ſeed of Abraham my friend*, that high and honoured character, and therefore beloved for their father's ſake, *whom I have taken from the ends of the earth, and called thee from the chief men thereof* whither they were diſperſed, *and ſaid unto thee, thou art my ſervant, I have choſen thee, and not caſt thee away*, notwithſtanding all their provocations. And this is true alſo of the ſpiritual ſeed, choſen of God's grace, called by his word, appointed to be his faithful ſervants, owned and acknowledged by him as ſuch, and ſecured in a covenant of everlaſting love, from being finally caſt away

Before Christ 712

10 ¶ [l] Fear thou not, [m] for I *am* with thee be not
diſmayed, for I *am* thy God I will ſtrengthen thee, yea,
I will help thee, yea, [n] I will uphold thee with the right
hand of my righteouſneſs 11 Behold, all *they that*
were incenſed againſt thee, [o] ſhall be aſhamed and con-
founded they ſhall be as nothing, and † they that ſtrive
with thee ſhall periſh 12 Thou ſhalt ſeek them, and
ſhalt not find them, *even* them that contended with thee
they that war againſt thee ſhall be as nothing, and as a
thing of nought 13 For [p] I the LORD thy God will
hold thy right hand, ſaying unto thee, Fear not, I will help
thee 14 [q] Fear not, thou worm Jacob, *and* ye men of
Iſrael I will help thee, ſaith the LORD, and thy Re-
deemer, the holy One of Iſrael 15 Behold, [r] I will
make thee a new ſharp threſhing inſtrument having teeth
thou ſhalt threſh the mountains, and beat *them* ſmall, and
ſhalt make the hills as chaff 16 Thou ſhalt fan them,
and the wind ſhall carry them away, and the whirl-
wind ſhall ſcatter them and thou ſhalt rejoice in the
LORD, *and* ſhalt glory in the holy One of Iſrael
17 *When* the poor and needy ſeek water, and *there is*
none, *and* their tongue faileth for thirſt, I the LORD
will hear them, *I* the God of Iſrael will not forſake
them 18 I will open [s] rivers in high places, and foun-
tains in the midſt of the valleys I will make [t] the wil-
derneſs a pool of water, and the dry land ſprings of
water 19 I will plant in the wilderneſs the cedar, the
ſhittah-tree, and the myrtle, and the oil-tree I will ſet
in the deſert the fir-tree, *and* the pine, and the box-tree
together 20 [u] That they may ſee, and know, and
conſider, and underſtand together, that the hand of the
LORD hath done this, and the holy One of Iſrael hath
created it

l Ver 14 m Rom viii 31 n Deut. xxxiii 27 o Exod xxiii 22 Chap xlv 24 & lx 12 Zech. xii 3 † Heb The men of thy ſtrife p Pſ lxxiii 23 Chap xlv 1 q Ver 10 r Mic iv 13 2 Cor. x 4, 5. s Chap. xxxv 6, 7 & xliii 19 & xliv 3 t Pſ cvii. 35 u Job xii 9

v 10—20 To ſilence the fears, and encourage the faith and hope of God's people in their diſtreſſes, they are called upon to look to the rock which is higher than they

1 God, their covenant God, is with them to ſtrengthen, help, and uphold them with the right hand of his righteouſneſs, v 10 and then of whom need they be afraid? If he ſtrengthen, what foe can prevail? If he help, what greater ſupport can they need? If he uphold with his right hand, who ſhall pluck them from it? *Note*, (1) If God, by his preſence and effectual grace, be with us, then in every trial, under every temptation, in the hour of death, and the day of judgment, we muſt be ſafe (2) Faith in the promiſe is the ſovereign antidote againſt all fear, and we can be in no ſituation wherein this very promiſe may not be produced to encourage us

2 They ſhall be victorious over all their foes, to their great joy Incenſed as they were againſt the faithful, ſeeking with implacable enmity their ruin, confuſion ſhall cover them, v 11. and mighty as they were in power and policy, their ſtrength ſhall fail, their devices be diſappointed, v 12 Whilſt Iſrael victorious, like a ſharp threſhing inſtrument, ſhall beat them ſmall as the duſt, humble the loftieſt, and abaſe the proud, v 15 and ſcattering them as chaff before the wind, they ſhall rejoice in the great ſalvation of God herein ſo glorioully diſplayed, v 16 which may refer literally to the victories of the Maccabees, but ſpiritually regards the conqueſts of God's people over the great enemies of their ſouls For however weak they may be, as worms of Jacob, their Redeemer is mighty, and though earth and hell without, and corruption within, daily fight and trouble them, yet their mightieſt inbred luſts, as well as their ſtrongeſt perſecutors, God can ſubdue before them; and a day of joy indeed will it be to ſee them fall *Note*, (1) Every chriſtian hath a hard warfare to maintain, and there are many adverſaries (2) Fear is often apt to beſet us, when we ſee ourſelves compaſſed about on every ſide, and feel how impotent we are to withſtand them (3) If God were not in ſuch ſeaſons to ſpeak a word of comfort to our ſouls, we muſt utterly faint (4) Tho' the conteſt be hard, the victory is ſure, they cannot faint whom God never fails to uphold (5) The greater our enemies, the more ſhall the power of God be magnified in our deliverance (6) Whatever victories we, through grace, are enabled to obtain, our glorying muſt be in the Lord, not in ourſelves; the work is his, and to him muſt be aſcribed the praiſe

3 In their deepeſt diſtreſſes the people of God ſhall find him a very preſent help in trouble When oppreſſed with thirſt they cry, inſtant ſhall their prayer be heard and anſwered, v 17 From the high places the guſhing ſtream ſhall burſt, in the vallies the fountains ſhall flow, the very deſert ſhall abound with pools and ſprings, v 18 and every beautiful and ſpreading tree

Before Christ 712

tree spring up to shelter them, *v* 19 A work so wonderful, that they would with wonder and surprize own, This hath God done, *v* 20 And this was eminently the case when, by the preaching of the gospel, the Gentile world heard and turned to the Lord, and such a wondrous change was wrought on the hearts of men, as if the desart had been cloathed with trees and pasture and such also every truly converted soul experiences to be his very condition, when the Spirit of God renews his heart (1) He is described as poor and needy, sensible of his deep spiritual wants and wretchedness (2) He cries, and is heard, for prayer is the breath of an awakened soul (3) He thirsts for the pardon of his sins, a sense of the divine favour, and the supports of divine grace and lo! the Lord quenches his thirst with views of the redeeming blood, sheds abroad in his heart a sense of his love, and implants in the soul a living principle of grace, like a well of water springing up into everlasting life (4) When this is the case, the whole heart is changed, the miserable sinful soul becomes pure, peaceable, heavenly-minded, holy, happy (5) This miracle of grace marks the finger of God evident and to him the praise of this glorious work alone must be ascribed

† Or cause to come near
x Chap xlv & xliv 21
y John xiii 19
z Jer x 5
a Chap xliv 9 1 Cor viii 4
‡ Or worse than nothing
‖ Or worse than a viper
b Chap xli 25
c Ibid xliii. 9
d Chap. xl. 9
e Ibid lxiii. 5
§ Heb. Return
f Jer x 3

21 † Produce your cause, saith the LORD, bring
forth your strong *reasons*, saith the king of Jacob 22
x Let them bring *them* forth, and shew us what shall
happen let them shew the former things what they *be*,
that we may consider them, and know the latter end of
them or declare us things for to come 23 y Shew
the things that are to come hereafter, that we may know
that ye *are* gods yea, z do good, or do evil, that we
may be dismayed, and behold *it* together 24 Behold,
a ye *are* ‡ of nothing, and your work ‖ of nought an
abomination *is he that* chooseth you 25 I have raised
up *one* from the north, and he shall come b from the
rising of the sun shall he call upon my name, and he
shall come upon princes as *upon* mortar, and as the potter
treadeth clay 26 Who hath declared from the begin-
ning, that we may know? c and before time, that we
may say, *He is* righteous? yea, *there is* none that shew-
eth, yea, *there is* none that declareth, yea, *there is* none
that heareth your words 27 The first *shall say* to Zion,
Behold, behold them, and I will give to Jerusalem d one
that bringeth good tidings 28 For e I beheld, and
there was no man, even amongst them, and *there was* no
counseller, that when I asked of them, could § answer a
word 29 Behold, they *are* all f vanity, their works *are*
nothing their molten images *are* wind and confusion

v 21—29 The Lord having comforted his people, resumes his controversy with the idolaters his enemies

1 He challenges them to produce their arguments, *v* 21 let their Gods be brought forth and speak for themselves, if they have knowledge, or prescience, let them shew it; if power, let them exert it, can they either describe the past, or foretell the future? do good or hurt to their foolish votaries? *v* 22, 23 not the least they are nothing, a work of vanity, and justly are they counted an abomination, who forsake the living God for such senseless deities

2 God declares his own work and design *I have raised up one from the north, and he shall come, from the rising of the sun shall he call upon my name* this is usually interpreted of Cyrus, by his father, a Mede, by his mother, a Persian, which countries lay, the one to the north, the other to the east of Babylon, whose princes he trod down as mortar, and proclaimed deliverance, in God's name, to the captives Some apply this to Constantine, a native of Britain, who, after triumphing over his Pagan competitors, established the profession of Christianity throughout the whole Roman empire

3 God, in foretelling this, convinces them of the vanity of the idols, who could never inform them of any such future transactions, *v* 26 *The first shall say to Zion, or I, the first, do say to Zion, Behold, behold them, and I will give to Jerusalem one that bringeth good tidings* Cyrus, who issued the edict for their restoration, or the Lord Christ, with his fore-runner John Baptist, preaching the gospel of the kingdom events, whichever of them be referred to, concerning which the worshippers of idols foresaw nothing, nor had a word to plead in vindication of their abominable practices, *v* 28 Their idols evidently proved mere vanities, and their curiously molten images utterly useless and unprofitable, *v* 29

CHAP XLII

This chapter contains an eminent prophecy of the Messiah We have here 1 His coming to do the work of a Redeemer, ver 1—4 2 His commission opened, ver. 5—9 3 The joy with which the glad tidings of this should be received, ver 10, 11, 12 4 The success of the gospel, and the overthrow of the devil's kingdom, ver 13—17 5 The rejection and ruin of the Jews for their unbelief, ver 18—25

Before Christ 712

a Chap xlix. 6 & lii 13 Mat xii 18, &c
Phil ii 7
b Mat iii 17
& xvii 5
Eph i 6
c Chap xi 2 & lxi 1
John iii 34
d Ps lxxii 2
e Mat xii 28
‖ Or burn dimly
f Gen xlix 10

1 BEHOLD a my servant whom I uphold, mine
elect b *in whom* my soul delighteth c I have put
my spirit upon him, d he shall bring forth judgment to
the Gentiles, e He shall not cry, nor lift up, nor cause
his voice to be heard in the street 3 e A bruised reed
shall he not break and the ‖ smoaking flax shall he not
quench he shall bring forth judgment unto truth 4
He shall not fail, nor be discouraged, till he have set
judgment in the earth and f the isles shall wait for his
law

v 1—4 That these words belong to Christ we are assured, *Mat* xii 17—21 We have,

1 His designation to his office, and qualification for it *Behold!* with wonder and love, *my servant*, though equal with the Father as touching his godhead, yet humbling himself to the form of a servant, for us men and our salvation, *whom I uphold*, for as man, Christ received power and strength from the Father, to enable him to accomplish the arduous work of redemption, or *on whom I lean*, expressive of the confidence God reposed in him, to fulfil the work appointed him, as much to his glory as his people's good, *mine elect*, chosen and designed for the work from the foundation of the world, *in whom my soul delighteth*, his righteousness, sufferings, sacrifice, and all that he did, being always highly pleasing to his Father, *I have put my spirit upon him*, fully qualifying and enabling him for the execution of all he hath undertaken *Note*, (1) The highest honour is to be an elect servant of God (2) There never was but one under the sun in whom, for his own sake, God could say my soul delighteth (3) If God bid us minister, he will supply the ability

2 His exercise of his office *He shall bring forth judgment to the Gentiles*, the gospel, which is to be the rule and guide of all his converted people *He shall not cry, nor lift up, nor cause his voice to be heard in the streets*, as coming with human pomp and grandeur, for his kingdom was not of this world *A bruised reed shall he not break*, so tender are his compassions toward the weak and tempted, who are cast down under their trials, but supported and strengthened by him, that they may not utterly faint, *and the smoaking flax shall he not quench*, where the smallest gracious appearances are seen, he will not despise, but cherish them, and fan the smoaking flax into a flame *he shall bring forth judgment unto truth*, accompanying the word of his truth with such effectual power, as to accomplish the thing whereunto he sends it *He shall not fail, nor be discouraged* amidst the arduous work in which he shall be engaged, *till he have set judgment in the earth*, established his glorious gospel, which is so productive of judgment and righteousness among men, *and the isles shall wait for his law*, the distant nations of Gentiles offering themselves willing scholars at the feet of his ministers The Septuagint, from whence the passage is quoted, *Mat* xii 20 *Acts* xxviii 25 renders it, *And in his name shall the Gentiles trust*

g Chap xliv 24
h Zech xii 1
i Ps cxxxvi 6
l Chap xlix 8
m Luke ii 32
Acts xiii 47
& xxvi 18
n Chap lxi 1
Luke iv 18
2 Cor iv 6
Col i 13
o Chap xlviii 11
p Ps xcviii 1
q Chap xxiv 16

5 ¶ Thus saith God the LORD, g he that created the
heavens, and stretched them out, h he that spread forth
the earth and that which cometh out of it, he that giveth
breath unto the people upon it, and spirit to them that
walk therein 6 I the LORD have called thee in
righteousness, and will hold thine hand, and will keep
thee, l and give thee for a covenant of the people, for a
light of the Gentiles, 7 m To open the blind eyes, n to
bring out the prisoners from the prison, *and* them that
sit in darkness out of the prison house 8 I *am* the
LORD, that *is* my name, and o my glory will I not give
to another, neither my praise to graven images 9 Be-
hold, the former things are come to pass, and new things
do I declare before they spring forth I tell you of
them 10 p Sing unto the LORD a new song, *and* his
praise from the end of the earth ye that go down to
the sea, and all that is therein, the isles and the inhabi-
tants thereof 11 Let the wilderness, and the cities
thereof lift up *their voice*, the villages *that* Kedar doth
inhabit let the inhabitants of the rock sing, let them
shout from the top of the mountains 12 Let them
give glory unto the LORD, and declare his praise in the
islands

v 5—12 God having ushered in the glorious personage appointed by him for the work of his people's salvation, here encourages and authorizes him to proceed in his undertaking

1 He gives him his orders, as the Almighty Creator of all, able abundantly to support him in the exercise of his office, *v* 5 He calls him *in righteousness*, in a way wherein the divine per-

Before Christ 712

perfections were eminently to be magnified, or *with righteouſneſs*, being himſelf a righteous perſon, and in his nature and practice knew no ſin, he promiſes to uphold and keep him, that no difficulties may diſcourage, nor enemies prevail againſt him, to give him for a covenant of the people, to be their great covenant head, by him all the terms of the covenant being fulfilled, and through him all the bleſſings of it are to be freely received two of the moſt eminent of which are mentioned, (1) He is given *for a light to the Gentiles, to open the blind eyes*, both to be the light of the world which lay in darkneſs and the ſhadow of death, and alſo to beſtow power on the fallen mind of man to ſee this light of life, without which it ſhineth in darkneſs *Note*, The mind of man, yea, of the wiſeſt, continues in utter darkneſs reſpecting ſpiritual things, without divine illumination (2) He is ſent *to bring the priſoners from the priſon, and them that ſit in darkneſs out of the priſon-houſe*, we are by nature the ſlaves of ſin and Satan, and though we may have light enough to ſee and deplore our miſery, we have no power to help ourſelves, till the Lord Jeſus interpoſes to break our bands, and bring us forth into the glorious liberty of the ſons of God

2 He confirms his commiſſion by his great name, Jehovah, *v* 8 who, in this inveſtiture of the Redeemer, intends to exalt his own glory, and will not ſuffer idols to be his rivals, but will condignly puniſh thoſe who aſcribe to them the praiſe due to him alone And as he has fulfilled his former promiſes, ſo will he alſo accompliſh the new things he now declares, relative to the deliverance of the Jews under Cyrus, the incarnation of the Meſſiah, and the ſucceſs of his goſpel, which, *before they ſpring forth* into act from the divine decree, he foretells, and ſhall be as ſurely fulfilled in their ſeaſon, as any paſt prophecies had been *Note*, God hath ſtill new mercies in ſtore, if we have faith to truſt him, he will not, cannot fail us

3 The whole church is called upon to exalt God's praiſe for the redemption of Jeſus From the ends of the earth, to which the goſpel ſhould be ſpread, the grateful ſong muſt ariſe, thoſe who go down to the ſea, the Tyrians and Phœnicians, and other maritime places, the Arabians, and the moſt ſavage inhabitants of the deſert and the rock, civilized by the preaching of the goſpel, muſt join in the work of praiſe, till the ſound ſhould be univerſal, and the knowledge of the glory of God be wafted to the moſt diſtant iſles of the ſea This was in a meaſure the caſe under the miniſtry of the apoſtles, and we expect a ſtill more glorious day, when praiſes for redeeming love ſhall be ſung from pole to pole

13 The LORD ſhall go forth as a mighty man, he
ſhall ſtir up jealouſy like a man of war he ſhall cry,
[r] yea, roar, he ſhall prevail againſt his enemies 14 [s] I
have long time holden my peace, I have been ſtill, *and*
refrained myſelf *now* will I cry like a travailing woman,
I will deſtroy and || devour at once 15 I will make
waſte mountains and hills, and dry up all their herbs,
and I will make the rivers iſlands, and I will dry up the
pools 16 And I will bring the blind [t] by a way *that*
they knew not, I will lead them in paths *that* they have
not known I will make darkneſs light before them, and
crooked things ſtraight Theſe things will I do unto
them, and not forſake them 17 ¶ They ſhall be turned back, [u] they ſhall be greatly aſhamed that truſt in
graven images, that ſay to the molten images, Ye *are*
our gods

r Chap xxxi 4
s Pſ l 21 Luke xviii 7
|| Heb ſwallow up
t Luke i 79 Heb x 20
u Pſ xcvii 7 Chap i 29 & xliv 11 & xlv 16

v 13—17 We have here,

1 The victory the Lord will obtain over his enemies As a man of war he will ruſh upon them with a cry, and prevail, his goſpel being made effectual to the caſting down all the ſtrong holds of darkneſs, *v* 13 For a long while he ſeemed to pay no regard to the heathen world, winking at the times of their ignorance, but now when he ſends his elect miniſter Jeſus, he will deſtroy and devour at once, they who ſubmit not to the calls of his mercy, muſt periſh under the rod of his judgments, *v* 14 The greateſt, high as mountains, are not too mighty to eſcape, nor the leaſt, though mean as the graſs, too ſmall to be overlooked and every impediment ſhall be removed, as at the paſſage of Iſrael through the Red ſea, that his word may have free courſe, and run, and be glorified, *v* 15 *Note*, When God will work, none can let it

2 He will bring home his people to himſelf *I will bring the blind*, thoſe that were ſpiritually ignorant of the ways of God, *by a way that they knew not*, even Chriſt the living way, hid from ages and generations, but now revealed to the Gentiles, *I will lead them in paths that they have not known*, the path of holineſs and life eternal; *I will make darkneſs light before them*, ſhining on their path, and making it plain before their faces, *and crooked things ſtraight*, removing all obſtructions, and forming their once crooked and perverſe ways by his divine grace, conformably to his holy mind and word *Theſe things will I do unto them, and not forſake them*, but to eternity perfect in them the ſalvation here begun And bleſſed truly are they to whom the Lord is pleaſed to ſhew ſuch continuing and effectual grace

3 The idolaters being converted, ſhall now be made aſhamed of their idols, or thoſe who perſiſted in their worſhip be confounded to find how little they can profit them in a day of wrath, *v* 17

18 Hear, [x] ye deaf, and look, ye blind, that ye may
ſee 19 [y] Who *is* blind, but my ſervant? or deaf, as my
meſſenger *that* I ſent? who *is* blind as *he that is* perfect,
and blind as the LORD's ſervant? 20 Seeing many
things, [z] but thou obſerveſt not opening the ears, but
he heareth not 21 The LORD is well pleaſed for his
righteouſneſs ſake, he will magnify the law, and make † *it*
it honourable 22 But this *is* a people robbed and
ſpoiled, ‡ *they are* all of them ſnared in holes, and they
are hid in priſon houſes they are for a prey, and none
delivereth, for a ſpoil, and none ſaith, Reſtore 23
Who among you will give ear to this? [a] *who* will hearken, and hear for the time to come? 24 Who gave
Jacob for a ſpoil, and Iſrael to the robbers? did not the
LORD, he againſt whom [b] we have ſinned? for they
would not walk in his ways, neither were they obedient
unto his law 25 Therefore he hath poured upon him
the fury of his anger, and the ſtrength of battle and
it hath ſet him on fire round about, [c] yet he knew not,
and it burned him, yet he laid *it* not to heart

x Ezek xii 2
y Chap lv 10 M… xv 14
z Rom ii 22
† Or him
‡ Or inſnaring all the young men of them
a Jer x…
b Lam v 8
c Jer v 3 Hoſ vii 9

v 18—25 We have here,

1 A general exhortation addreſſed to the ſpiritually deaf and blind, whether Jews or Gentiles, to hear and ſee For though more was needful in order to divine knowledge, than the mere exerciſe of their natural faculties, yet as they had ears to hear, and eyes to ſee the word of truth, they were bound to make uſe of the appointed means *Note*, They who wilfully turn away their eyes from the truth, and will not uſe them to examine the ſcriptures, juſtly are given up to judicial blindneſs

2 A ſharp reproof is given to the Jewiſh people *Who is blind as my ſervant*, or *deaf as my meſſenger that I ſent*? or as ſome render it, *thoſe to whom I ſend my meſſenger*? They who had every opportunity of ſpiritual knowledge, were more criminally ignorant than their Gentile neighbours, and their teachers blind leaders of the blind *Who is blind as he that is perfect, and blind as the Lord's ſervant*? the Scribes and Phariſees, who moſt boaſted their high attainments, were moſt obſtinate in rejecting Chriſt and his goſpel *Seeing many things*, or pretending to ſee at leaſt, *but thou obſerveſt not* the evidences of Chriſt's divine miſſion in his miracles, *opening the ears* to the preaching of Chriſt and his apoſtles, *but he heareth not* to any ſaving purpoſe, but cavilled, and rejected the counſel of God againſt their own ſouls *Note*, (1) Spiritual blindneſs is grievouſly common, even among the profeſſors of religion (2) They who have the higheſt conceit of their own perfection and excellence, are moſt grievouſly ignorant both of God, his law, and their own vile hearts (3) It is a deplorable caſe when they, who ſhould be teachers of others, are blind and erroneous themſelves (4) None uſually are ſo obſtinate in prejudice and ignorance as thoſe who, having aſſumed the character of God's meſſengers, count it a diſhonour to have it but ſuggeſted that they themſelves are out of the way (5) They who, through ignorance in their miniſtry, miſlead and ruin other's ſouls as well as their own, may expect to receive greater damnation

3 God will be glorified, notwithſtanding their obſtinacy *The Lord is well pleaſed for his righteouſneſs ſake, he will magnify the law, and make it honourable*, either by the execution of juſt judgment on the rejecters of his truth, or rather this refers to Chriſt, for whoſe righteouſneſs ſake God is well pleaſed, and with all who are found in him, ſince by his obedience unto death, he hath in the higheſt meaſure magnified the divine law in their behalf, and reſtored the honour it had loſt by their violations of it

4 The deſtruction of the whole people is foretold, becauſe of their rejection of the goſpel They are given up to the Romans to be robbed, ſpoiled, and ſnared, dragged from their lurking-places, and impriſoned, without proſpect of deliverance or reſtoration, *v* 22 They would not be admoniſhed of the judgment coming upon them, till it was impoſſible to avert it, 23 God's hand in their ruin was evident, and acknowledged even by Titus, their deſtroyer, becauſe of their obſtinate diſobedience, *v* 24 Therefore wrath to the uttermoſt overtook them, and to this day the heavy ſtroke is ſtill upon them, yet they will not acknowledge the rejection of Jeſus as the cauſe, nor lay it to heart, the veil being yet unremoved, and their meaſure of chaſtiſement not yet full *Note*, (1) Of the many who hear God's word, few pay it the attention it deſerves (2) Diſregard of God's warnings is ſure to bring down his wrath

(3) All

Before Christ 712

(3) All ſuffering comes ultimately from God's hand, whatever inſtruments are employed (4) Sin that now provokes God's anger againſt the ſinner in temporal afflictions, will, if unrepented of, ſhortly kindle that fire of eternal wrath which never can be quenched

CHAP XLIII

The contents of this chapter are much the ſame with that of the foregoing, deſcribing the releaſe of the Jews out of their captivity, but looking through and beyond that, to the great work of man's redemption by Chriſt, and the grace of the goſpel, which, through him, believers partake of Here are, 1 *Precious promiſes made to God's people in their affliction,* ver 1—7 2 *A challenge to idols to vie with the omniſcience and omnipotence of God,* ver 8—13 3 *Encouragement given to the people of God to hope that they ſhould aſſuredly be delivered out of Babylon, as their fathers were out of Egypt,* ver 14—21. 4 *The people are reminded of their ſins, by which they had provoked God to ſend them into captivity, in order that they might repent, and ſeek for pardoning mercy,* ver 22—28

1 BUT now, thus ſaith the LORD [a] that created
thee, O Jacob, and [b] he that formed thee, O Iſ-
rael, [c] Fear not for I have redeemed thee, [d] I have cal-
led *thee* by thy name, thou *art* mine 2 [e] When thou
paſſeſt through the waters, I *will be* with thee, and
through the rivers, they ſhall not overflow thee when
thou walkeſt through the fire, thou ſhalt not be burnt,
neither ſhall the flame kindle upon thee. 3 For I *am*
the LORD thy God, the holy One of Iſrael, thy Savi-
our [f] I gave Egypt *for* thy ranſom, Ethiopia and Seba
for thee 4 Since thou waſt precious in my ſight, thou
haſt been honourable, and I have loved thee therefore
will I give men for thee, and people for thy life 5 [g]
Fear not, for I *am* with thee [h] I will bring thy ſeed from
the eaſt, and gather thee from the weſt 6 I will ſay
to the north, Give up, and to the ſouth, Keep not back,
bring my ſons from far, and my daughters from the
ends of the earth, 7 *Even* every one *that is* called by
my name for [i] I have created him for my glory, I have
formed him, yea, I have made him

a Ver 7
b Chap xliv 2, 21
c Chap xli 10
d Ex xxxiii 17
e Pſ lxvi 12 & xci 3, &c 1 Cor x 13
f Prov xi 8 & xxi 18
g Chap xli 10. Jer xxx 10 & xlvi 27
h Ezra i 3, 4 or Chap lxvi 19 Zech viii 7
i Pſ c 3 Chap xxix 23 John iii 3, 5 2 Cor v 17 Eph ii 10

v 1—7 This gracious prophecy in its primary ſenſe probably reſpects the recovery of the Jews from their captivity in Babylon, but moſt eminently refers to the goſpel days, when the church ſhould, amidſt all perſecutions, riſe great and glorious, and be increaſed with converts on every ſide

1 God encourages them, from the moſt endearing views of his regard for them, and relation to them *But now, thus ſaith the Lord that created thee, O Jacob,* created thee anew in Chriſt Jeſus, *and he that formed thee, O Iſrael,* the peculiar work of his hands, *fear not* under any trials or diſcouragements, *for I have redeemed thee* by the blood and righteouſneſs of Jeſus, *I have called thee by thy name,* every faithful ſoul being written in the book of life of the Lamb, *thou art mine,* in a covenant of everlaſting love which cannot be broken, mine for ever

2 He aſſures them of his conſtant ſupport under every trial, *v* 2 However threatning, violent, or ſevere their ſufferings, his preſence and power ſhould both ſtrengthen, comfort, and deliver them, ſo that they ſhould receive not the leaſt hurt or damage *Note,* If God be for us, and with us, then in the midſt of danger we are ſafe, and even in the jaws of death can triumph

3 He mentions the former inſtances of his care as the earneſt of his preſent ſalvation of them He calls himſelf, *v* 3 their God, in a covenant that is everlaſting, their Saviour from every foe As of old he had deſtroyed Egypt for their ſake, and overthrown the Ethiopians, 2 *Chron* xiv 9, 13 or turned the arms of Sennacherib upon them inſtead of Jeruſalem, ſuch ſhould be ſtill his regard towards them, their enemies ſhall be all deſtroyed, becauſe they were precious in his ſight, through that Saviour in whom they were accepted, and honoured with the higheſt titles, the ſons and daughters of the Lord Almighty, and as ſuch beloved by him with affection unchangeable and everlaſting, *v* 4

4 He promiſes a great increaſe of converts under the preaching of the goſpel They need not fear, however diminiſhed or brought low, for God is with them, and at his word, from the four quarters of the earth converts ſhall flock into his church, as doves to their windows, *v* 5, 6 even as many as, being choſen in the divine purpoſe, are called by his grace, renewed by his Spirit, and prepared to ſhew forth his praiſe in all holy converſation and godlineſs, *v* 7 This may be applied particularly to the collecting the Jews from their captivity, but ſeems more plentifully fulfilled in the converſion of the Gentiles, by the preaching of the goſpel *Note,* (1) Every one called by Chriſt's name, is bound to ſet forth his glory (2) The work of regeneration is God's own, we are the clay, he is the potter, if we are veſſels of honour, it is becauſe his ſovereign and ſaving grace hath made us ſuch (3) They who by divine grace are gathered in to Jeſus now as their Saviour, ſhall be ſhortly raiſed from the duſt of death, caught up to meet him in the air, and ſo ſhall be ever with the Lord

8 ¶ [k] Bring forth the blind people that have eyes, and
the deaf that have ears. 9. Let all the nations be ga-
thered together, and let the people be aſſembled [l] who
among them can declare this, and ſhew us former
things? let them bring forth their witneſſes, that they
may be juſtified or let them hear and ſay, *It is* truth
10 [m] Ye *are* my witneſſes, ſaith the LORD, and [n] my
ſervant whom I have choſen that ye may know and be-
lieve me, and underſtand that I *am* he before me there
was no God formed, neither ſhall there be after me 11
I, *even* [o] I *am* the LORD, and beſide me *there is* no ſa-
viour. 12 I have declared, and have ſaved, and I have
ſhewed, when [p] *there was* no ſtrange *god* among you
therefore ye *are* my witneſſes, ſaith the LORD, that I
am God 13 [q] Yea, before the day *was,* I *am* he, and
there is none that can deliver out of my hand I will
work, and [r] who ſhall † let it?

k Chap xlii 19 20 Ezek xii 2
l Chap xli 22, 26
m Chap xliv 8
n Ibid xlii 1
o Ibid xlv 21 Hoſ xiii 4
p Deut xxxii 12
q John viii 58
r Job ix 12, Chap xiv 27
† Heb Turn it back, or reverſe

v 8—13 The worſhippers of idols are called to appear and confront God's witneſſes, if they dared maintain their wretched cauſe God calls them the *blind who have eyes,* and the *deaf who have ears,* becauſe though they have the faſhion of men, by ſuch abominable idolatries they ſeem to have loſt their reaſon and faculties They cannot prove the divinity of their idols to juſtify their worſhip, they are the work of men's hand, and blinder and more impotent than their fooliſh votaries, *v* 8—10 But let God's witneſſes appear, his Iſrael, and his ſervant, either the prophet Iſaiah, or rather the Meſſiah, emphatically ſo called, *chap* xlii 1 to prove his unrivalled godhead and glory, he alone was from eternity, the ſole exiſtent, ſelf-exiſtent God and Saviour, and beſides him, there neither is nor can be any other In proof of which, two arguments are urged, drawn from his preſcience and his power (1) He hath declared things to come, his people's deliverance of old from Egypt, when as yet no ſtrange God was among them, and now from Babylon, with numberleſs other things concerning the coming of the Meſſiah and his church, and ſurely none of the idols can pretend to ſuch fore-knowledge (2) He hath ſaved his people, from his hand, none can deliver, and when he works, none can let, whilſt all the idols of the heathen are unprofitable and vain, unable in the leaſt to aſſiſt or protect their worſhippers This they ſhould obſerve to their conviction, and ſay, *it is truth,* acknowledging the folly of truſting to other gods, and giving the Lord alone the glory due unto his name

14 ¶ Thus ſaith the LORD your Redeemer, the
holy One of Iſrael, [s] For your ſake I have ſent to Baby-
lon, and have brought down all their nobles, and the
Chaldeans, [t] whoſe cry *is* in the ſhips 15 I *am* the
LORD, your holy One, the creator of Iſrael, your
king 16 Thus ſaith the LORD, [u] which maketh a
way in the ſea, [x] and a path in the mighty waters 17.
[y] Which bringeth forth the chariot and horſe, the army,
and the power, they ſhall lie down together, they ſhall
not riſe they are extinct, they are quenched as tow
18 ¶ [z] Remember ye not the former things, neither
conſider the things of old. 19. Behold, [a] I will do a
new thing now it ſhall ſpring forth, ſhall ye not know
it? I will even make [b] a way in the wilderneſs, [c] *and*
rivers in the deſert 20. The beaſt of the field ſhall
honour me, the dragons and the ‖ owls becauſe [d] I
give waters in the wilderneſs, *and* rivers in the deſert,
to give drink to my people, my choſen 21 [e] This
people have I formed for myſelf, they ſhall ſhew forth
my praiſe

s Luke xviii 7
t Rev xviii 11
u Exod xiv 16 21 Chap li 10.
x Joſh iii 13, 16
y Exod xiv 4—9, 23
z Jer xvi 14 & xxiii 7
a 2 Cor v 17 Rev xxi 5
b Chap xl 3
c Ibid xxxv 6 & xli 18.
‖ Or oſtriches
d Chap xlviii 21.
e Pſ cii 18 Luke i 74, 75

v 14—21 Great was the deliverance from Egypt, great the recovery from Babylon, but greater ſtill the recovery of loſt ſouls by Jeſus Chriſt, whoſe redemption is here ſpoken of

1 For the encouragement of his people, God calls himſelf their Redeemer, the holy One of Iſrael, their Creator, their King For though they ſeemed now caſt off, their ſtate diſſolved, and their kingdom deſtroyed, yet God calleth the things that are not, as though they were, becauſe he only ſpeaks, and it is done

2 He tells them what he intended to do for their ſake, which he ſpeaks of as already accompliſhed, even to deſtroy the Babylonians, who fly in vain to their ſhips to eſcape, or, bound captives by the Medes and Perſians with [illegible] were [illegible]-

ported

Before Christ 712.

ported far away, *v* 14 Some translate it, *brought down all the nobles, brought forth all the fugitives*, as spoken of the Jews, who would be brought forth from the house of their prison, when their proud oppressors were broken

3 He reminds them of what he had done for them, when, at the Red sea, the chariots and horses of Pharoah were utterly overthrown, and such would be the case of their present enemies, and as then he opened a path in the Red sea for their passage, so would he, amidst all difficulties, bring them safe once more to their own land, *v* 17 *Note*, In our deepest afflict on we should remember God's wonders of old time, and wait in faith for his salvation

4 Yet greater things than these would he do for them such miracles of grace as would, as it were, obliterate the remembrance of all that was past *Behold, I will do a new thing*, which would astonish and surprize them, even the incarnation of Jesus Christ, *now it shall spring forth* as a branch in a short time, *shall ye not know it*, and thankfully receive this great Redeemer? In consequence of whose appearing, a wondrous change will be wrought in the world, the Gentile nations, before like a wilderness, impassable, uncultivated and barren, shall be laid open for the gospel, and become fruitful like a well-watered land, *v* 19 Men, whose tempers before were savage as the beasts, fierce as dragons, and stupid as the owls, shall be renewed and turned to the worship and service of the true God, and in this once desolate world of heathenism, there shall be a plentiful effusion of gospel-grace, like the waters of a river, *v* 20 and God will own the Gentile converts as his chosen, formed by his Spirit for his glory, and designed to shew forth his praise to all eternity *Note*, (1) Man does not naturally differ more from the beasts, than man does from man, when divine grace hath changed his heart (2) Wherever the gospel comes, powerful and blessed are its effects the wilderness then becomes a fruitful field (3) All that is good in the hearts of men, is God's own work, and designed for his own glory (4) It must be our labour, study, and prayer to correspond with the divine intentions, and to shew forth his praise who hath called us out of darkness into his marvellous light

22 ¶ But thou hast not called upon me, O Jacob,
but [f] thou hast been weary of me, O Israel 23 [g] Thou
hast not brought me the † small cattle of thy burnt-of-
ferings, neither hast thou honoured me with thy sacri-
fices I have not caused thee to serve with an offering,
nor wearied thee with incense 24 Thou hast bought
me no sweet cane with money, neither hast thou filled
me with the fat of thy sacrifices but thou hast made
me to serve with thy sins, [h] thou hast wearied me with
thine iniquities 25 I, *even* I *am* he [i] that blotteth out
thy transgressions for mine own sake, [k] and will not re-
member thy sins 26 Put me in remembrance [l] let us
plead together declare thou, that thou mayst be justi-
fied 27 Thy first father hath sinned, and thy teachers
have transgressed against me. 28 Therefore [m] I have
profaned the ‡ princes of the sanctuary, and have given
Jacob to the curse, and Israel to reproaches

[f] Mal i 13 [g] Amos v 25 † Heb Lambs, or kids. [h] Chap i 14 Amos ii 13 Mal ii 17 [i] Chap xliv 22 & xlviii 9 Jer l 20 Ezek xxxvi 22 &c [k] Chap i 18 Jer xxxi 34 [l] Mic vi 3 [m] Chap xlvii 6 Lam ii 2 ‡ Or holy princes.

v 22—28 The unworthiness of the sinner the more exalts and magnifies the glory and grace of the Saviour We have here,

1 A heavy charge brought against Israel They had neglected prayer and the worship of God, yea, had counted his service wearisome, and wanted to be rid of it, *v* 22 Though dwelling in a land of plenty, they grudged the expence of God's temple, with-held their burnt-offerings and sacrifices, and prepared no sweet cane for the holy anointing oil and the sweet incense Yet God *had not caused them to serve with an offering, nor wearied them with incense*, did not exact from them difficult or burdensome services the idolaters paid much greater honours, and offered more expensive sacrifices to their false gods, than they were required to offer to the living Jehovah whereas they not only neglected his worship, but openly violated his laws; till weary with their iniquities, nothing seemed to await them but just and condign punishment, *v* 24

2 A wondrous promise comes in When we might have expected to hear, I, even I am he that blotteth out their name from under heaven, God, in mercy transcendently glorious, declares, *I, even I am he that blotteth out thy transgressions for mine own sake, and will not remember thy sins* *Note*, (1) Forgiveness of sin is the great glory of the gospel, of all sin, and the vilest need not despair (2) When God forgives, he forgets, and though we are ever bound to remember and abhor ourselves, God will never remember our sins, to upbraid or confound us. (3) It is an act of sovereign grace in God to forgive sin; the least sin is in its nature deadly, and nothing we can do could ever save us from eternal ruin, unless his rich mercy interposed to pardon it:

3 God commands his people to put him in remembrance, and plead his promises with him, that they may be justified, *v* 26

Though some understand this as a reproof to the self-righteous, challenging them to produce the good works on which they depend for justification, the vanity of which would be manifested, and they reduced to seek the free pardon offered, or perish in their pride

4 He reminds them that all their sufferings proceeded from their sins, to repent of which, his gracious promises were the greatest encouragement *Thy first father hath sinned*, Adam, or rather their more immediate ancestors, *and thy teachers have transgressed against me*, they who should have directed others, erred themselves, and led their brethren astray In consequence of which, God had afflicted them, or would, for it seems spoken of their captivity in Babylon, or their last visitation by the Romans *Therefore I have profaned the princes of the sanctuary*, the Priests and Levites, *and have given Jacob to the curse, and Israel to reproaches*, under which they still lie, monuments of God's righteous judgments, till the spirit shall be poured on them from on high, and at last they shall return to him, from whom they have so greatly departed, and find that pardon and grace in Jesus which they have despised

CHAP XLIV

God by the prophet goes on in this chapter as before, 1 To assure his people that he had great blessings in store for them at their return out of captivity, and those typical of much greater, which the gospel-church should partake of in the days of the Messiah and hereby he proves himself to be God alone against all pretenders, ver 1—8 2 To expose the amazing folly of idol-makers and idol-worshippers, ver 9—20 3 To ratify the assurances he had given his people of those great blessings, and to raise their joyful and believing expectations of them, ver 21—28

1 YET now hear, O Jacob [a] my servant, and Israel
whom I have chosen 2 Thus saith the LORD
that made thee, [b] and formed thee from the womb, *which*
will help thee, Fear not, O Jacob my servant, and thou
[c] Jesurun, whom I have chosen 3 For [d] I will pour
water upon him that is thirsty, and floods upon the dry
ground I will pour my Spirit upon thy seed, and my
blessing upon thine offspring 4 And [e] they shall spring
up *as* among the grass, as willows by the water-courses
5 One shall say, I *am* the LORD's and another shall
call *himself* by the name of Jacob and another shall
subscribe *with* his hand unto the LORD, and surname
himself by the name of Israel

[a] Chap xli 8 & xliii 1 Jer xxx 10 & xlvi 27 [b] Chap xliii 1, 7 [c] Deut xxxii 15 [d] Chap xxxv 7 Joel ii 28 John vii 38 Acts ii 18 [e] 2 Pet iii. 8

v 1—5 Amidst the threatned judgments which closed the former chapter, a chosen generation is reserved for God, to whom he addresses himself in these words, for their comfort and encouragement

1 Their character and relation to him are mentioned, *v* 1, 2 They bear the honourable title of *his servants*, whom he will protect, they *are his chosen*, that with peculiar regard he hath distinguished, they are called *Jesurun, upright*, such being their temper, or *prime ones*, to whom the glory of God in the gospel of his Son hath been manifested, they are God's *creation*, his spiritual seed, whom he will help, and therefore whatever trouble fall on others, they need not fear Happy are the people that are in such a case, so near and dear to the blessed God

2 God promises to do great things for them *I will pour water on him that is thirsty, and floods on the dry ground*, the soul that under a sense of sin, is the parched ground, thirsts for pardon, grace, and consolation, shall be replenished abundantly out of God's fulness *I will pour my Spirit*, that best of gifts, *on thy seed*, the spiritual seed of Christ, *and my blessing upon thy offspring*, the blessed effect of which will be, *they shall spring up as among the grass, as willows by the water courses*, numerous, flourishing, and increasing in all the gifts of grace, and fruits of holiness. *Note*, The soul is then truly happy, when, watered by the divine Spirit, it daily grows in grace, and in the knowledge and love of the Lord Jesus Christ

3 They shall make open and public profession of their adherence to the Lord Christ, and not only the Jews, but the Gentiles, called to the knowledge of the gospel, shall rank themselves among the Israel of God, join in communion and worship with them, and become one fold under one shepherd, *v* 5 *Note*, (1) It is the duty and delight of every faithful soul to surrender up himself into the arms of Jesus, and he is then happy when he can say, I am the Lord's, my beloved is mine, and I am his (2) An Israelite indeed is a greater name, and more to be envied, than that of the highest monarchs of the earth

6 Thus saith the LORD the King of Israel, and [f] his
Redeemer the LORD of hosts, [g] I *am* the first, and I *am*
the last, and besides me *there is* no God 7 And [h] who,

[f] Chap xli 14 [g] Ibid xli 4 & xlviii 12 Rev i 8, 17 & xxii 13 [h] Chap xli 26

Before Christ 712 as I, shall call, and shall declare it, and set it in order
for me, since I appointed the ancient people? and the
things that are coming, and shall come, let them shew
unto them 8 Fear ye not, neither be afraid have not
I told thee from that time, and have declared it? i ye
i Chap xliii 10 12 are even my witnesses Is there a God besides me? yea,
k Deut iv 35 39 & xxxii 39 k there is no + God, I know not any 9 ¶ l They that
1 Sam ii 2 make a graven image are all of them vanity, and their
Chap xlv 5 delectable things shall not profit, and they are their own
+ Heb. Rock. witnesses, m they see not, nor know, that they may be
Deut xxxii 4 ashamed 10 Who hath formed a god, or molten a
l Chap xli 24 29 graven image n that is profitable for nothing? 11 Be-
m Ps cxv 4, &c hold, all his fellows o shall be ashamed and the work-
n Hab ii 18 men, they are of men let them all be gathered toge-
o Ps xcvii 7 Chap i 29 & xlii 17 & xlv 16 ther, let them stand up, yet they shall fear, and they
shall be ashamed together 12 p The smith with the
p Chap xl 19 & xli 6. Jer x 3 Wisd xiii 11 tongs both worketh in the coals, and fashioneth it with
hammers, and worketh it with the strength of his arms
yea, he is hungry, and his strength faileth he drinketh
no water, and is faint 13 The carpenter stretcheth out
his rule he marketh it out with a line he fitteth it with
planes, and he marketh it out with the compass, and
maketh it after the figure of a man, according to the
q Judg xvii 5 beauty of a man, that it may remain q in the house 14
He heweth him down cedars, and taketh the cypress and
the oak, which he strengthneth for himself among the trees
of the forest he planteth an ash, and the rain doth nou-
rish it 15 Then shall it be for a man to burn for he
will take thereof and warm himself, yea, he kindleth it,
and baketh bread, yea, he maketh a god, and worship-
peth it he maketh it a graven image, and falleth down
thereto. 16 He burneth part thereof in the fire with
part thereof he eateth flesh he rosteth rost, and is satis-
fied yea, he warmeth *himself*, and saith, Aha, I am
warm, I have seen the fire 17 And the residue thereof
he maketh a god, *even* his graven image he falleth down
unto it, and worshippeth it, and prayeth unto it, and
r Chap. xlv 20. Jer x 8 saith, Deliver me, for thou *art* my god 18 r They have
s 2 Thess ii 11 not known, nor understood for s he hath shut their eyes,
that they cannot see, *and* their hearts, that they cannot
understand 19 And none considereth in his heart, nei-
ther *is there* knowledge nor understanding to say, I have
burnt part of it in the fire, yea, also I have baked bread
upon the coals thereof I have rosted flesh and eaten it,
and shall I make the residue thereof an abomination?
shall I fall down to the stock of a tree? 20 He feedeth
t Hos iv 12 of ashes t a deceived heart hath turned him aside, that
he cannot deliver his soul, nor say, *Is there* not a lie in
my right hand?

v 6—20 Never was controversy so unequal as this between the living Jehovah and dead idols

1 God displays his own greatness and glory, eternal and omniscient, let his Israel hear and believe He is their King, their Redeemer, and in that peculiar relation to them demands their love and fidelity He is also the Lord of Hosts, the universal Sovereign, the first and the last, from eternity to eternity, and beside him, there is no God No other can foresee and declare as he hath done the events of futurity, or give an exact account of his works from the days of old, since he appointed the ancient people the first inhabitants of the earth even of the minutest occurrence which should happen, the idol gods could not inform them, *v* 7 therefore they need neither fear them, nor ought to serve them, but be witnesses for God and his truth, besides whom, there is no other that can at all pretend to claim their notice, or deserve their worship

2 He exposes the folly and stupidity of idolaters, as a warning to his people not to follow their abominable ways, and especially to guard them in Babylon, the city of idols, from joining in that worship so hateful to him, and so absurd in itself The makers of the idol are all vanity, prove themselves empty and foolish; they call their idols *delectable things*, but they are unprofitable and vain, can neither know nor see the wants of their votaries, who seem equally blind in paying worship to the senseless stock, and witness to their own folly, *v* 9 for how wretched must be the god, of which man himself is the maker, *v* 10 and well may they be ashamed of the work, *v* 11 The description of it alone is sufficient to expose both the maker and the idol to ridicule The smith labours at the forge to prepare the iron work, and the carpenter with his tools fashions and planes the tree into shape and form, and when made, fastens it in his place He plants a log of durable wood, or an ash of his own planting, and whilst one part of the loppings are employed to the use of his kitchen, to dress his victuals, or warm him, the residue is made a god, and with senseless stupidity he falls down to worship it, never reflecting on the ignoble use to which the remainder of the tree was applied, and that his own folly only made the difference between the log he worshipped, and the coals on his hearth, and all proceeds from the darkness of a deceived heart, the Devil, the god of this world, having blinded the eyes of idolaters, that they cannot see the lie that is in their right hand *Note*, (1) When once the human heart is abandoned to itself, there is nothing so brutish and absurd it may not be brought to do (2) The pains idolaters take to honour and worship their idols, is a just reproof of those who are negligent in the worship of the living and true God (3) They who place their affections on worldly things, are in fact idolaters, and will find, to their everlasting disappointment, a lie in their right hand (4) The serious consideration of the evil of our ways, is the first step towards our recovery

Before Christ 712 21 ¶ Remember these, O Jacob and Israel, for thou
art my servant, I have formed thee, thou *art* my ser-
vant O Israel, thou shalt not be forgotten of me 22 u u Chap xliii 25
I have blotted out as a thick cloud thy transgressions, and
as a cloud thy sins return unto me, for I have redeemed
thee 23 x Sing, O ye heavens, for the LORD hath x Ps lxix 34 & xcvi 11 12
done *it* shout ye lower parts of the earth break forth Chap xlix 13
into singing ye mountains, O forest, and every tree there Jer li 48 Rev xviii 20
in for the LORD hath redeemed Jacob, and glorified
himself in Israel 24 Thus saith the LORD thy re-
deemer, and y he that formed thee from the womb, I *am* y Chap xliii 1
the LORD that maketh all *things*, z that stretcheth forth z Job ix 8
the heavens alone, that spreadeth abroad the earth by
myself 25 That a frustrateth the tokens of b the liars, Chap xl 22 & xlii 5
and maketh diviners mad, that turneth wise *men* back- a Chap xlvii 13
ward, and maketh their knowledge foolish 26 That b Jer l 36
confirmeth the word of his servant, and performeth the
counsel of his messengers, that saith to Jerusalem, Thou
shalt be inhabited; and to the cities of Judah, Ye shall
be built, and I will raise up the decayed places thereof
27 c That saith to the deep, Be dry, and I will dry up thy c Jer l 38 & li 36
rivers 28 That saith of Cyrus, *He is* my shepherd, Rev xvi 12
and shall perform all my pleasure, even saying to Jeru- 2 Chron. xxxvi 22 23
salem, d Thou shalt be built, and to the temple, Thy d Ezra i 1 &c Chap xlv 13
foundation shall be laid

v 21—28 God having exposed the folly of idolatry, here addresses himself to his own people

1 He bids them remember these things, and in the land whither they were about to be carried captive, beware of these abominations to which they would be tempted, and to which also to their shame in time past they had been so prone *Note*, It becomes us to remember our own evil ways, that we may loath and abhor ourselves for them

2 He gives them the most endearing promises, claiming them as his own, and assuring them of his kind and constant remembrances, and as that was among the most eminent of all mercies, he particularly promises them the pardon of all their great and numerous transgressions, *v* 22 to blot them out as a cloud, and as a thick cloud to disperse them *Note*, (1) Our sins, like the dark cloud, intercept the beams of God's favour, and expose us to the storm of divine wrath (2) When God speaks the pardoning word, the clouds pass away, and the sun of righteousness arises with healing in his wings (3) It is matter of transporting joy to the soul when this blessed change is effected, and when in Jesus we, who were in darkness and the shadow of death, behold the light of life

3 He exhorts them in the view of these great and precious promises to return unto him without delay They had greatly departed from him, and deserved his wrath and indignation, but he is become their Redeemer, and therefore invites them to the arms of his mercy *Note*, (1) The promise of pardoning grace is the great argument and inducement for the miserable sinner to return to God (2) Whenever he doth, he will find a complete redemption wrought out for him, both from the guilt and power of sin, and from death and hell its consequences

4 A triumphant song is put in the mouth of the redeemed, not merely of the Jews delivered from Babylon, but of all the Israel of God, who, through Jesus Christ, have obtained victory over the powers of sin and Satan The joy is great, the heavens are called upon to join the song, and angels on their golden harps to speak the wonders of redeeming love, whilst earth, with all its inhabitants, from every forest and mountain echoes back the grateful sound of thanksgiving, to the God of their mercies, *v* 23 *Note*, (1) Praise is the bounden tribute due from every redeemed soul (2) There is joy in heaven over every soul recovered by divine grace from the bondage of corruption

Before Christ 712

5 The Lord the Redeemer of Israel encourages them to trust in his promises, which, as the Almighty Creator, and governor of all, he was fully able to accomplish, v 24 particularly he engages to confound the wise men and diviners of Babylon, who saw for it lying visions of peace, and would be mad with vexation when the event corresponded so little with their prophecies, v 25 whilst his own word should receive the fullest accomplishment in their deliverance The cities of Zion would shortly be desolate indeed, without inhabitants, but their desolations should not continue, God will restore her decayed palaces, and rear again the temple from its ruins Cyrus by name is appointed as his shepherd, the great instrument which the Lord meant to employ, first to destroy Babylon, the oppressor of his people, which he did by turning the course of the river, which ran through the place, and thereby entered the city, v 27 and then to proclaim deliverance to the captive Jews, and restore their civil and ecclesiastical polity, giving them leave to rebuild their city and temple, and fixing them again in their own land *Note*, (1) When God hath designs to fulfil, he cannot want the means, difficulties before him are nothing, the mountain becomes a plain, the river dry (2) The character of a good king, is to be God's shepherd to protect and provide for his people, and be a nursing father to his church (3) Whatever the greatest conquerors propose to themselves, they are raised up purely to fulfil God's pleasure, and perform his purposes

CHAP XLV

We have here, 1 The great things which God would do for Cyrus, to enable him to release God's people, ver 1—4 2 The proof God would hereby give of his eternal power and godhead, ver 5—7 3 A prayer for the hastening of this deliverance, ver 8 4 A check to the unbelieving Jews, who quarrelled with God for the lengthening out of their captivity, ver 9, 10 5 An assurance given to the believing Jews, that God would in due time accomplish this work by the hand of Cyrus, ver 11—15 6 Confusion threatened to the worshippers of idols, and salvation promised to the worshippers of the true God, with an eye to the Mediator, who is made of God to us both righteousness and sanctification, ver 16—25 And here, as in other parts of this prophecy, there is much of Christ and gospel-grace

1 THUS saith the LORD to his anointed, to Cy-
rus, whose right hand I have † holden to subdue
nations before him and I will loose the loins of kings, to
open before him the two-leaved gates, and the gates shall
not be shut 2 I will go before thee, and [a] make the
crooked places straight I will break in pieces the gates
of brass, and cut in sunder the bars of iron 3 And I
will give thee [b] the treasures of darkness, and hidden
riches of secret places, [c] that thou mayst know, that I
the LORD which call *thee* by thy name, *am* the God
of Israel 4 For Jacob my servant's sake, and Israel [d]
mine elect, I have even called thee by thy name I
have surnamed thee, though thou hast not known
me.

† Or strengthened

a Chap xl 4

b Jer l 37

c Exo [illegible]

d Eph [illegible]

v 1—4 Cyrus was the type of the great Redeemer, and in his deliverance of the captive Jews, prefigured the greater redemption which Jesus should obtain for his people of all nations more than two hundred years before the event came to pass, we have him particularly named and pointed out, and his great conquests described, which, through the mighty hand of God upon him, he was enabled to obtain over kingdoms which seemed much more powerful than his own, and which opened a way at last to him, in conjunction with the Persians, for the conquest of Babylon We have here,

1 The conquests he should obtain Nations are subdued before him, and kings submit to his yoke, the strongest cities cannot resist his arms, nor the most difficult passes stop his march, God goes before him, and therefore resistance is vain, v 1, 2 The treasures of his enemies become his spoil, v 3 and among them, those of Croesus, king of Lydia, the richest monarch of that age and by these he was enabled to pursue his victories, to the final overthrow of the Babylonish monarchy

2 God's design in this was purely to serve his Israel Cyrus himself was a stranger to the true God and meant no doubt his own grandeur and glory alone, but it was for Jacob's sake God had raised him up, and ordained him to be such a conqueror, in order that he might be their deliverer, v 4 *Note*, (1) In all God's providences, in the revolutions of states and kingdoms, there is wheel within wheel, and God hath purposes to answer for the good of his people, which the great agents employed in these things little think of (2) Christ is exalted to the throne for the sake of his Israel, hath all power given him, and all the unsearchable riches of grace to bestow,

therefore they may expect at his hands every mercy and blessing they can need

Before Christ 712

5 ¶ I *am* the LORD, and [e] *there is* none else, *there*
is no God besides me [f] I girded thee, though thou hast
not known me 6 [h] That they may know from the
rising of the sun, and from the west, that *there is* none
besides me, I *am* the LORD, and *there is* none else 7
I form the light, and create darkness I make peace,
[i] and create evil I the LORD do all these *things* 8
[k] Drop down, ye heavens from above, and let the skies
pour down righteousness let the earth open, and let
them bring forth salvation, and let righteousness spring
up together I the LORD have created it 9 Wo unto
him that striveth with his maker *let* the potsherd *strive*
with the potsherds of the earth [l] Shall the clay say to
him that fashioneth it, What makest thou? or thy work,
He hath no hands? 10 Wo unto him that saith unto
his father, What begettest thou? or to the woman, What
hast thou brought forth

e Deut iv 35 39 & xxxii 39 Chap xliv 8

f Ver 14 18 21

g Psal xviii 32

h Mal i 11

i Job ii 10. Amos iii 6

k Psal lxxxv 11.

l Chap xxix 16 Jer xviii 6 Rom ix 20

v 5—10 The design of God in raising up Cyrus, was to make his own power and glory to appear therefore,

1 He asserts his own Godhead, and besides him there is no other his works declare his universal dominion, light and darkness, good and evil, not the evil of sin, but of suffering, are all from him and if Cyrus was so wonderfully strengthened for his conquests, the world must take notice to whom he stands indebted, though he knew not the hand who supported him, in this prophetic word, it evidently appears the work was of God, v 5, 6 *Note*, Since prosperity and adversity both come from God, in both he is to be acknowledged, and our duty is to correspond with his designs

2 A glorious prophecy is revealed, of the abundance of blessings, that by the incarnation of the Redeemer, should descend on the Israel of God *Drop down, ye heavens, from above and let the skies pour down righteousness*, or *the righteous One*, the Lord Jesus, who descending from above, as the rain waters the earth, would cause the souls of men to bring forth the blessed fruits of grace and holiness *let the earth open*, the human hearts of men, that are like dead earth, till enlivened by the precious influences of the spirit of Jesus, *and let them bring forth salvation, or the Saviour, and let righteousness spring up together*, that righteousness which is the work of the incarnate Redeemer, and that salvation which is the issue of his work of grace upon the soul *I the Lord have created it*; the work is wholly Divine in the contrivance and execution of it, and our righteousness and salvation derived from him alone

3 A wo is pronounced on the rebellious, either the enemies of God, who opposed his people's deliverance, or the faithless Jews who despaired of it Poor worms of dust, as potsherds of the earth, may strive with each other, but to contend with God, or find fault with him, is as absurd as for the clay to pretend greater wisdom than the potter, and unnatural as for the child to quarrel with his parents for having begotten and brought him forth God's sovereignty, wisdom, justice, and goodness, in all his works and ways, are incontestible, and it is as wicked as foolish to find fault with or oppose them *Note*, (1) They who quarrel with God and his providences, only aggravate their own sufferings (2) Nothing can be a greater argument for entire resignation to the Divine will, than the consideration, what God is, and what we are, and we then act as becomes creatures, when, as clay in the hand of the potter, we are content to be just what our maker pleases

11 Thus saith the LORD, the holy One of Israel,
and his maker, Ask me of things to come concerning
my sons, and concerning the work of my hands com-
mand ye me. 12 [m] I have made the earth, and created
man upon it I, *even* my hands have stretched out the
heavens, and all their hosts have I commanded 13 I
have raised him up in righteousness, and I will direct
all his ways [o] he shall build my city, and he shall let
go my captives, [p] not for price nor reward, saith the
LORD of hosts 14 Thus saith the LORD, [q] The la-
bour of Egypt, and merchandise of Ethiopia, and of
the Sabeans, men of stature, shall come over unto thee,
and they shall be thine, they shall come after thee, in
chains they shall come over and [r] they shall fall down
unto thee, they shall make supplication unto thee, *say-
ing*, Surely [s] God *is* in thee, and [t] *there is* none else,
there is no god 15 Verily thou *art* a God [u] that hidest
thyself, O God of Israel the saviour 16 They shall
be ashamed, and also confounded all of them, [x] they
shall go to confusion together *that are* makers of idols
17 [y] *But* Israel shall be saved in the LORD with an

m Psal [illegible]

n Chap xlv 13

n Gen i 2

o Ver [illegible] Chap xliv 28

p Chap lii 3

q Psal lxviii 31 & lxxii 10, 11

Dan vii 14

r Chap lx 14 Rev iii 9

s Zech viii 23 1 Cor xiv 25

t Ver 5

u Chap viii 17 & [illegible] 17

x Chap xliv 11

y Chap xxvi 4

Before Christ 712

everlasting salvation: ye shall not be ashamed nor con-
founded world without end.
18 For thus saith the
LORD [z] that created the heavens, God himself that
formed the earth and made it, he hath established it,
he created it not in vain, he formed it to be inhabited,
[a] I *am* the LORD, and *there is* none else.
19 [b] I have
not spoken in secret, in a dark place of the earth: I said
not unto the seed of Jacob, Seek ye me in vain: I
the LORD speak righteousness, I declare things that are
right.

z Chap. xlii. 5.
a Ver. 5.
b Deut. xxx. 11. Chap. xlviii. 16. John xviii. 20.

v. 11—19. We have here,

1. The encouragement God gives to his people to wait upon him in prayer, and to enquire concerning the great events he had foretold, either the restoration of his people from their captivity, or the glorious increase of the sons of God, which should be raised up by the preaching of the gospel, v. 11. The words also may be read interrogatively, in correspondence with the former verse, as implying a reproof to those who questioned the fitness of his dispensations.

2. God displays his own glorious power, in the creation of all things, as a ground to engage his people's confidence, v. 12. and particularly mentions their deliverance by Cyrus; it is spoken of as already done, because determined in the Divine mind. God had raised him up in righteousness, and directed all his ways, and he should without price disengage them, and with his favour assist them to rebuild Jerusalem, v. 13. This also may refer to the greater than Cyrus, that Messiah whom God would raise up in righteousness, not for one nation only, but for all people, whose way he directed to the full accomplishment of their salvation; and who, having by his own arm wrought out redemption for them, discharges them from all the arrests of sin, and from the bondage of corruption, without money and without price.

3. He promises a great increase should be made to them, v. 14. Many of the neighbouring nations, probably on their return, became converts to their religion: or rather this refers to gospel times, when, by the word of truth, the Gentiles, Egyptians, Ethiopians, and Sabeans, gladly received Christ's gentle yoke, and yielded themselves up to God, in the gospel of his dear Son.

4. Though sometimes in their afflictions he appeared to hide himself, yet he was still *the God of Israel the saviour*, ready in due time to appear for their help and consolation, v. 15. *Note*, (1.) There are dark days when God's face is hid from his people, and they go mourning without the sun. (2.) God is not the less tender of us, or farther from our help, when he seems to forget us: if he hides himself, it is to engage us more earnestly to seek him.

5. The idolaters should be confounded and ashamed, v. 16. as the Babylonians were, when their gods, as well as themselves, went into captivity; and as was more abundantly seen when the gospel triumphed over the powers of darkness, and idolatry was generally abolished.

6. God promises his Israel an everlasting salvation. *Israel shall be saved* IN, or BY, *the Lord*; the work is his, and shall be surely accomplished; not merely from Babylon, and the yoke of their captivity, but *with an everlasting salvation* through the Lord Jesus: *ye shall not be ashamed nor confounded world without end*, or *unto the ages of eternity*; so permanent is that salvation which Christ by his blood and righteousness hath purchased, and will bestow on his chosen.

7. God gives his Israel the strongest assurances of the eternal salvation he promised them, v. 18, 19. He who made the heavens with such admirable wisdom, and fashioned the earth so beautifully and wonderfully, the only true God and Creator, v. 18. he speaks the never-failing promise, not with a muttering low voice in secret, as the oracles of the heathens were delivered, but openly and publickly: and none of the seed of Jacob ever did, or shall seek his face in vain; he will ever hear and answer them; and his word of righteousness is a full ground for their trust and confidence, v. 19. *Note*, (1.) The word of promise is the great argument for the prayer of faith. (2.) If none seek God's face in vain, how inexcusable are they who reject their own mercies, and restrain prayer before God. (3.) Whatever God saith or doth is altogether righteous and true, and the faithful soul ever acquiesce therein.

20 ¶ Assemble yourselves and come; draw near to-
gether, ye *that are* escaped of the nations: [c] they have no
knowledge that set up the wood of their graven image,
and pray unto a god *that* cannot save.
21 Tell ye,
and bring *them* near; yea, let them take counsel toge-
ther: [d] who hath declared this from ancient time? *who*
hath told it from that time? *have* not I the LORD?
and [e] *there is* no God else beside me; a just God and a
Saviour; *there is* none beside me.
22 [f] Look unto
me, and be ye saved, all the ends of the earth: for I
am God, and *there is* none else.
23 I have sworn by
myself, the word is gone out of my mouth *in* righteous-
ness, and shall not return, that [g] unto me every knee shall
bow, [h] every tongue shall swear.
24 Surely, shall *one*
say, [i] In the LORD [1] have I righteousness and strength:
even to him shall *men* come; and [k] all that are incensed
against him shall be ashamed.
25 [l] In the LORD shall
all the seed of Israel be justified, [m] and shall glory.

c Chap. xliv. 9.
d Chap. xli. 22. xliii. 9. xliv. 7.
e Ver. 5.
f Chap. xlv. 9.
i Psalm xxii. 27.

Before Christ 712

g Rom. xiv. 11. Phil. ii. 10.
1 Or, Surely he shall say of me, In the Lord is all righteousness and strength.
k Chap. xli. 11.
l Acts xiii. 39. Rom. iii.
m 1 Cor. i. 31.

v. 20—25. The folly of idolaters had before been declared. Here,

1. God calls his people, the converts from heathenism, to see the vanity of those who persisted in the abominable worship of idols, v. 20. and to remonstrate with them against it: they *pray unto a god that cannot save them*; though all the votaries of idols consulted together, they cannot bring a proof of any one instance wherein their false gods shewed the least prescience of future events, for they are no gods; the living Jehovah alone claims this as his prerogative, and *besides him there is no other*, *a just God*, whose works and words are all righteousness and truth, and *a Saviour*, able to the uttermost to bless and protect his worshippers. *Note*, They who by Divine grace have themselves been converted to God, are especially called upon to shew zeal for his glory, in order to the conviction and conversion of others.

2. All nations are called upon to look to Jesus and be saved by him: the everlasting salvation promised is obtained, and through him alone to be received, for *there is none else*. Becoming incarnate, and by an obedience unto death, even the death of the cross, lifted up as the serpent in the wilderness, every perishing sinner may look to him and live: *he is God*, and therefore he saves to the uttermost; the guilty, the weary, the tempted, the disconsolate, have all their fears silenced, and their countenance lightened by the bright beams of grace and mercy that flow from the crucified Jesus.

3. According to his solemn oath, the nations of the redeemed must become subject unto him, and his enemies bow before him. *I have sworn by myself, the word is gone out of my mouth in righteousness*, and shall, both respecting the promise and the prophecy, be assuredly fulfilled, *and shall not return void*, *that unto me every knee shall bow, every tongue shall swear*, pay their allegiance, and join the worship of him their Redeemer, as will be seen in the day when the kingdoms of the world shall become the kingdoms of the Lord and his Christ; and especially in the judgment day, to which the apostle refers this passage, Rom. xiv. 10, 11. *Surely, shall one say*, triumphing in their interest in the glorious Redeemer, *In the Lord*, or *only in the Lord, have I righteousness and strength*, renouncing every thing in themselves, and by faith laying hold of the perfect righteousness and all-sufficient grace of Jesus their Lord, to justify, sanctify, and save them: *even to him shall men come*, all that are his chosen, *and all that are incensed against him*, who are either careless transgressors of his law, or proudly reject his righteousness and strength to trust on their own, they *shall be ashamed* at the vanity of their confidence, and the misery which their iniquities will bring upon them, whilst the humble believer will rejoice, for *in the Lord shall all the seed of Israel*, the living members of Christ's church, *be justified* from every accusation of sin, the law, and their own consciences, *and shall glory*, not in themselves, but in the Lord their righteousness, at whose feet their crown is laid, and to whose rich and sovereign grace the whole of their salvation is ascribed.

CHAP. XLVI.

The destruction of Babylon and her idols is here displayed. 1. To warn God's people not to fear them, but trust in God, their Saviour of old, ver. 1—4. 2. They are cautioned not to make, or worship such false gods, ver. 5—8. 3. They are reminded of the prophecies of God, especially concerning Cyrus, which should be accomplished, ver. 9—11. 4. The stout hearted are admonished to observe God's work and its fulfilment, ver. 12, 13.

1. [a] BEL boweth down, Nebo stoopeth, their idols
were upon the beasts, and upon the cattle:
your carriages *were* heavy laden; *they are* a burden to
the weary *beast*.
2. They stoop, they bow down toge-
ther, they could not deliver the burden, but [1] them-
selves are gone into captivity.
3 ¶ Hearken unto me,
O house of Jacob, and all the remnant of the house
of Israel, [b] *which are* born *by me*, from the belly, *which*
are carried from the womb:
4 And *even* to *your* old
age I *am* he; and *even* to hoar hairs [c] will I carry *you*:
I have made, and I will bear; even I will carry and will
deliver *you*.

a Chap. xxi. 9. Jer. l. 2. & li. 44.
1 Heb. Their soul.
b Deut. i. 31. & xxxii. 11. Psalm lxxi. 6. Chap. xlvi. 9.
c Psal. xlviii. 14.

v. 1—4. Two things are here foretold,

1. The miserable state to which Babylon and her idols would be reduced. Bel and Nebo, the deities they worshipped, so far from being able to protect their votaries, would not be able

Before Christ 712.

able to ſave themſelves, but, among other ſpoil, be plucked from their pedeſtals, and laid as heavy burdens on the weary beaſts who carried them. Iſrael therefore muſt not fear, or worſhip ſuch wretched and impotent idols.

2. When Babylon's gods would fail her, the Lord will eminently appear the protector of his people; great had been the care he had ſhown them from their infant days, when firſt they began to grow into a nation, and never would he leave or forſake them in their old age, but bear them above their difficulties, carry them back to their own land, and deliver them from all their oppreſſors; and ſuch is ſtill his tender regard towards his people. From the womb he took us, and preſerved our natural life amidſt the perils of helpleſs infancy; but more, he took us from the womb of nature, that we might become children of grace, bore with our weakneſs and infirmities, and watched over us with more than maternal tenderneſs: nor will he ever fail us, when the infirmities of old age creep upon us, and infantile weakneſs returns; his hoary-headed ſaints are precious in his ſight, and he will bear them through all the ſtorms of life, and land them ſafe on the bliſsful ſhores of immortality, where their youth will be renewed as the eagle.

5 ¶ [d] To whom will ye liken me, and make *me*
equal, and compare me, that we may be like? 6 [e]
They laviſh gold out of the bag, and weigh ſilver in
the balance, *and* hire a goldſmith, and he maketh it a
god: they fall down, yea, they worſhip. 7 [f] They
bear him upon the ſhoulder, they carry him, and ſet
him in his place, and he ſtandeth; from his place ſhall
he not remove: yea, [g] *one* ſhall cry unto him, yet
can he not anſwer, nor ſave him out of his trouble.
8 Remember this, and † ſhew yourſelves men: bring
it again to mind, O ye tranſgreſſors. 9 Remember the
former things of old; for [h] I *am* God, and [i] *there is*
none elſe; I *am* God, and *there is* none like me, 10 [k]
Declaring the end from the beginning, and from ancient times *the things* that are not *yet* done, ſaying, [l]
My counſel ſhall ſtand, and I will do all my pleaſure:
11 Calling a ‡ ravenous bird [m] from the eaſt, the man
§ that executeth [n] my counſel from a far country: yea,
I have ſpoken *it*, I will alſo bring it to paſs; I have
purpoſed *it*, I will alſo do it. 12 ¶ Hearken unto
me, ye ſtout hearted, that *are* far from righteouſneſs:
13 I bring near [o] my righteouſneſs; it ſhall not be
far off, and my ſalvation ſhall not tarry: and I will
place ſalvation in Zion for Iſrael my glory.

d Chap. xl. 18. 25. e Chap. xl. 19. & xli. 6. & xliv. 12. 19. Jer. x. 3. f Jer. x. 5. g Chap. xlv. 20. † Or, be ye ſtrong. h Ps. xlv. 11. i Chap. xlv. 5. & xliv. 8. k Chap. xlv. 21. l Pſ. xxxiii. 11. Prov. xix. 21. & xxi. 30. Acts v. 39. ‡ Or, ſwift winged. m Chap. xli. 2. § Heb. Of my counſel. n Jer. l. 45. o Chap. li. 5. Rom. iii. 21.

v. 5—13. Iſrael's beſetting ſin was idolatry, and many of them, it is to be feared, in Babylon would eaſily be brought to worſhip the gods of their conquerors: to them theſe words ſeem eſpecially addreſſed.

1. God ſhows them the folly of the moſt expenſive idols. Though they laviſhed gold and ſilver out of the bag, it were vain to attempt repreſenting the eternal Spirit, or equalling him who is above all, v. 5, 6. Their richeſt gods were motionleſs and ſenſeleſs, muſt be carried to their places, and neither could hear or grant the prayer of their petitioners, v. 7. *Note*, To ſerve their idol luſts men grudge no expence; to ſerve the glorious God ſhall we count any thing too much to beſtow on his ſervice? Theſe idolaters ſhall riſe up in judgment againſt niggardly profeſſors.

2. He calls upon them to remember and repent of theſe ſinful works. *Shew yourſelves men*, for ſuch ſervice is brutiſh; or, *be ye ſtrong* to oppoſe the torrent of idolatry; or, *be fired with zeal* againſt the diſhonour hereby ſhown to God. *Bring it again to mind, O ye tranſgreſſors*; remember your evil ways, and, as ſinners, with ſhame return to God, who is the only true God; the evidence of which he hath given in all the prophecies, that from the beginning have been exactly accompliſhed according to his word, and which continue daily fulfilling, and ſhall all come to paſs in their appointed time; for his counſel muſt ſtand, and he will do all his pleaſure, v. 10. particularly his deſign of delivering his people ſhall be accompliſhed by Cyrus, called a *ravenous*, or *ſwift-winged bird*, with impetuoſity advancing againſt the Babylonians, to execute God's counſel in their deſtruction, which, as he hath purpoſed and foretold, he will perform, and prove therein his Divine power and preſcience. *Note*, (1.) It is good for us often to remember and reflect upon our ways, and we ſhall find much in them to bewail, repent of, and amend. (2.) As God in all his providences fulfils his own pleaſure, it becomes us ever to reſt ſatisfied in his diſpenſations, and to acknowledge he doth all things well. (3.) God's people may comfort themſelves in the confidence of the accompliſhment of thoſe prophecies which are yet unfulfilled, as ſurely as they have ſeen the former ones verified. Rome, with her idols, as Babylon, muſt fall, and God's kingdom be more eminently than ever yet exalted in the earth.

3. God addreſſes the ſtout-hearted Jews, that were far from righteouſneſs, who continued unhumbled under all their viſitations, diſtruſted God's faithfulneſs, or though they kept up an exterior of religion, and truſted that they were righteous, yet being ignorant of God's righteouſneſs, and proud of their own, were ſo much the farther removed from the way of ſalvation, v. 12. God ſaith, *I bring near my righteouſneſs*, either his faithfulneſs in the fulfilment of his promiſes, or that glorious diſplay of his righteouſneſs, manifeſted in the Redeemer, his work and ſufferings: *it ſhall not be far off*, but in the word of the goſpel brought near to every awakened ſinner, to believe in and truſt upon; *and my ſalvation ſhall not tarry*, it ſhall quickly be accompliſhed, the deliverance of the Jews from their captivity, and the greater deliverance which Jeſus ſhould work for all his redeemed ones; *and I will place ſalvation in Zion for Iſrael my glory*, when they were reſtored to their own land; or more eminently when the Lord Jeſus came to Zion, publiſhing the goſpel of the kingdom, and his Iſrael received him, glorifying God for the gift of his Son, and eminently ſhewing forth his praiſe, both in their lips and in their lives. *Note*, (1.) Nothing is ſo fatal to the ſoul as pride and conceit of our own righteouſneſs. (2.) A free and full ſalvation is now offered to the periſhing ſinner. (3.) The ſtout-hearted, who reject Jeſus as a Saviour, will find their ſtout hearts fail them, when they ſhall meet him as their judge. (4.) His Iſrael is the Redeemer's glory; for this he hath formed us; let it be our conſtant care to approve ourſelves to him, that he may be glorified in us and by us.

CHAP. XLVII.

In this chapter we have the fall of Babylon foretold. 1. The greatneſs of the ruin threatened, ſunk from the height of proſperity into the depth of adverſity, ver. 1—5. 2. The ſins that provoked God to bring this ruin upon them. (1.) Their cruelty to the people of God, ver. 6. *(2.) Their pride and carnal ſecurity,* ver. 7—9. *(3.) Their confidence in themſelves, and contempt of God,* ver. 10. *(4.) Their dependence upon enchantments and ſorceries, which ſo far from defending them, would haſten their ruin,* ver. 11—15.

1 [a] COME down and ſit in the duſt, O virgin
daughter of Babylon, ſit on the ground: *there is*
no throne, O daughter of the Chaldeans: for thou ſhalt
no more be called tender and delicate. 2 Take the
millſtones and [b] grind meal: uncover thy locks, [c] make
bare the leg, uncover the thigh, paſs over the rivers.
3 Thy nakedneſs ſhall be uncovered, yea, thy ſhame
ſhall be ſeen: [d] I will take vengeance, and [e] I will not
meet *thee as* a man. 4 *As for* [f] our redeemer, the
LORD of hoſts *is* his name, the holy One of Iſrael. 5
Sit thou ſilent, and get thee into darkneſs, O daughter
of the Chaldeans: for thou ſhalt no more be called [g] the
lady of kingdoms.

a Jer. xlviii. 18. b Lam. v. 13. c Chap. xx. 4. Jer. xiii. 22. d Rom. xii. 19. e Chap. xxxi. 4. Rev. xviii. 8. f Chap. xliv. 11. g Chap. xiii. 19. ver. 7. Dan. ii. 37.

v. 1—5. Babylon had long ſat as a queen, and ſeen her captives proſtrate at her feet, a virgin kingdom, whom no conqueror had yet ſubdued; but now her doom is read: into the duſt ſhe muſt fall low; no more her monarchs grace the throne, ſeized by the Perſian king; no more rioting in luxury and delicacies, v. 1. her miſerable inhabitants are reduced to the loweſt drudgery, to grind at the mill, or driven in herds as captives before their lordly maſters, v. 2. ſtripped naked, without compaſſion or humanity; for the vengeance is from God, v. 3. and he, as Iſrael's Redeemer, now returns the cruelty they had ſhown his people, v. 4. The noiſe which once reſounded in the ſtreets of Babylon, is ſilenced; and in darkneſs, whither they retired, or in their priſon-houſes, in vain they lamented the loſs of their kingdom, which ſhould be no more reſtored, v. 5. *Note*, (1.) They who abuſe their power, and walk in pride, God delights to abaſe. (2.) It is well to be inured to hardſhip; thoſe who are moſt delicately brought up, will feel every reverſe of ſtation with deeper anguiſh. (3.) When God viſits in vengeance, the ſinner may expect judgment without mercy.

6 ¶ [h] I was wroth with my people, [i] I have polluted
mine inheritance, and given them into thine hand: thou
didſt ſhew them no mercy; [k] upon the ancient haſt thou
very heavily laid thy yoke. 7 ¶ And thou ſaidſt, I
ſhall be [l] a lady for ever: *ſo* that thou didſt not lay theſe
things to thy heart, [m] neither didſt remember the latter
end of it. 8 Therefore hear now this, thou *that art*
given to pleaſures, that dwelleſt careleſly, that ſayeſt in
thine heart, [n] I *am*, and none elſe beſide me; I ſhall not
ſit *as* a widow, neither ſhall I know the loſs of children:
9 But [o] theſe two *things* ſhall come to thee in a moment
in one day, the loſs of children and widowhood: they
ſhall

h Zech. i. 15. i Chap. xliii. 28. k Deut. xxviii. 50. l Ver. 5. Rev. xviii. 7. m Deut. xxxii. 29. n Ver. 10. Zeph. ii. 15. 2 Thess. ii. 4. o Chap. li. 19.

Before Christ 712

shall come upon thee in their perfection, for the multi-
tude of p thy sorceries, *and* for the great abundance of
thine inchantments
10 ¶ For q thou hast trusted in
thy wickedness thou hast said, None seeth me r thy
wisdom and thy knowledge, it hath perverted thee and
s thou hast said in thine heart, I *am*, and none else be-
sides me
11 Therefore shall evil come upon thee,
thou shalt not know † from whence it riseth: and t mis-
chief shall fall upon thee, thou shalt not be able to ‡
put it off and desolation shall come upon thee suddenly,
which thou shalt not know
12 Stand now with thine
inchantments, and with the multitude of thy sorceries,
wherein thou hast laboured from thy youth, if so be
thou shalt be able to profit, if so be thou mayest prevail
13 Thou art wearied in the multitude of thy counsels
u let now the astrologers, the star-gazers, § the monthly
prognosticators stand up, and save thee from *these*
things that shall come upon thee
14 Behold, x they
shall be as stubble the fire shall burn them they shall
not deliver themselves from the power of the flame
y *there shall* not *be* a coal to warm at, *nor* fire to sit be-
fore it
15 Thus shall they be unto thee z with whom
thou hast laboured, a *even* thy merchants from thy youth,
they shall wander every one to his quarter, none shall
save thee

p Nah iii 4 Rev ix 21 & xviii 23
q Ps lii 7
r Ver 8
s Ver 8
† Heb The morning of it
t 1 Thes v 3
‡ Heb Expiate
u Chap xlv 25
§ Heb That give knowledge concerning the months
x Nah i 10 Chap xxx 14
z Ver 12
a Rev xviii 11

v 6—15 All God's dealings are according to the strictest equity, if Babylon suffers, her sins have given abundant provocation We have here,

1 The black catalogue of her crimes

(1) Cruelty to God's people God was wroth with his people, and meant to visit their iniquities with the scourge, and therefore gave them into the hands of the Chaldeans, but they unmercifully chastised them with scorpions, paying no regard to age or station, but *on the ancients*, whose hoary locks, or honours, should have pleaded for compassion, *making their yoke heavy*. *Note*, They who cruelly oppress God's people, however they may triumph for a moment, will find a day of awful reckoning at hand

(2) Pride and security, *v* 7 Because her monarchy seemed established, she promised herself that her throne should be coeval with the days of time, and neither regarding her sins, nor warned by the threatnings denounced against her, sat secure in her own sufficiency, and despised her enemies *Note*, They who are most self-confident and secure, are nearest the precipice of ruin

(3) Love of ease and pleasure, *v* 8 Given up to the indulgence of sensual appetite, and confident that every day should return fraught with mirth and jollity, and no sorrow interrupt the jocund hours

(4) Detestable sorceries, and magical arts, in which from their youth they were trained up, and placed therein their chief dependence and all these are sins, which are remarked as found in Babylon mystical, and the causes of her destruction, *Rev* xviii 4—7, 23

2 The doom of Babylon is read She trusted in her wisdom, policy, wealth, and wickedness, but deceived herself, as sinners usually do her boasts end in shame only in her confusion, *v* 10 Vain is her confidence, in one day the evils from which she thought herself so secured, shall overtake her, her king and nobles be slain, her people captives, *v* 9 So sudden and terrible the destruction, she could neither foresee nor avert it, *v* 11 Fruitless would be every attempt of her astrologers and diviners; vexed with disappointment, despair should seize her, when all the counsels of her magicians failed, and ruin approached, *v* 12, 13 Her wise men, so far from delivering their country, should be unable to save themselves, utterly consumed by the Divine judgment, as fuel reduced by the flames to dust, *v* 14 Her merchants, either those astrologers who had enriched themselves by their pretensions to science, or rather those who traded to Babylon, shall flee to secure themselves, *every one to his quarter*, or *passage*, glad to desert the devoted city, and eager to save themselves from the impending danger in their own lands *See Rev* xviii 15 *Note*, (1) Sinners are strangely apt to promise themselves secrecy and impunity, and this hardens their heart against the Divine admonitions (2) The dangers, of which the proud and secure were least apprehensive, often suddenly surprize them, and too late, to their astonishment, they discover the ruin they cannot escape (3) The greatest monarch sits on a tottering throne, when wickedness loosens the pillars of it (4) Wisdom or wealth are no defence against the judgments of God (5) They who are the instruments of man's vengeance, shall themselves feel the heaviest strokes of vengeance

CHAP XLVIII

God having resolved to destroy Babylon, and release his Israel, seeks here to bring them to repentance for their sins, before they should be delivered from their sufferings 1 *He charges them with hypocrisy in his service, and obstinacy in evil, especially in their idolatry*, ver 1—8 2 *He assures them that their deliverance would be wrought purely for his own sake*, ver 9—11 3 *He encourages them to depend wholly upon his power and promise for their deliverance* ver 12—15 4 *He shews them that as it was for their own sins that they were brought into captivity, so it would be only by the grace of God that they would obtain the necessary preparatives for their enlargement* ver 16—19 5 *He proclaims their release, yet with a promise, that the wicked shall have no benefit by it*, ver 20—22

1 HEAR ye this, O house of Jacob, *which are*
called by the name of Israel, and a are come
forth out of the waters of Judah, b which swear by the
name of the LORD, and make mention of the God of
Israel, c *but* not in truth, nor in righteousness
2 For
they call themselves of d the holy city, and e stay them-
selves upon the God of Israel, the LORD of hosts *is* his
name.
3 f I have declared the former things from the
beginning and they went forth out of my mouth, and
I shewed them, I did *them* suddenly, and g they came
to pass
4 Because I knew that thou *art* † obstinate,
and thy neck *is* an iron sinew, and h thy brow brass
5 I have even from the beginning declared *it* to thee,
before it came to pass I shewed *it* thee lest thou
shouldst say, Mine idol hath done them, and my graven
image, and my molten image hath commanded them
6. Thou hast heard, see all this; i and will not ye
declare *it*? I have shewed thee new things from this
time, even hidden things, and thou didst not know them
7 They are created now, and not from the beginning,
even before the day when thou heardst them not, lest
thou shouldst say, Behold, I knew them
8 k Yea, thou
heardest not, yea, thou knewest not; yea, from that time
that thine ear was not opened for I knew that thou
wouldst deal very treacherously, and wast called l a trans-
gressor from the womb.

a Deu xxxiii 28 Ps lxviii 26
b Chap lxv 16
c Jer v 2 Zeph i 5
d Chap lii 1
e Mic iii 11 Rom ii 17
f Chap xlii 9 & xliv 7, 8 & xlv 21 & xlvi 10
g Josh xxi 45
† Heb Hard
h Jer iii 3
i Ps xl 10
k Deut xxx 4
l Ps lviii 3

v 1—8 The prophet here addresses the house of Jacob, in order to bring them to a conviction of their hypocrisy and idolatry, and to engage their humble return to God, from whom they had so greatly departed

1 He charges them with the false and hypocritical professions they made They valued themselves highly, as being called by the name *of Israel*, and boasted their lineage *from Jacob*, they were of the royal race *of Judah*, the tribe that adhered to the temple, and the successors of David, when the rest revolted, they swore *by the name of the Lord*, owning him as their God and king, and engaging their fidelity to him, and made *mention of the God of Israel*, addressing him in their prayers and exercises of religious worship they called themselves of the holy city, as counting it an honour to have a name in the church of God, and stayed themselves upon the God of Israel, at least pretended to do so, as if the Lord of hosts was the name on which alone their dependance was fixed, but all was false and faithless, *not in truth nor in righteousness* *Note*, (1) Many claim the name of christian, who continue strangers to the power of christianity (2) It is mere hypocrisy when persons only draw near to God with their lips, whilst their heart are far from him (3) We have to do with a heart-searching God, and if our souls are insincere before him, vain is all the pageantry of external profession

2 He urges what he had done to convince and convert their souls to him as the only true God, and preserve and reclaim them from the damning idolatry, to which they were so addicted from the beginning he had foretold what should happen to them, their sojourning in Egypt, deliverance, conquest of Canaan, and all came to pass suddenly and certainly, God's power in the fulfilment of his prophetic word appearing evident, as his prescience in the prediction, *v* 3 This they might easily discern, and ought to declare to the glory of God a new revelation also God now gave them, which they never could have known, nor could their idols have informed them, concerning their captivity in Babylon, and their deliverance by Cyrus, with all the other prophecies, more immediately relative to the gospel dispensation and in all these things God intended to engage them to cleave to, and depend upon him, as the only true God, besides whom there was none other

3 God gives the reasons of his dispensations towards them

Before Christ 712

(1) Becauſe he knew they were obſtinate, their neck an iron ſinew, and their brow braſs, ſtubborn and hard-hearted, rigid againſt conviction, and impudently diſpoſed to deny God's work, if by his prophecies foregoing he had not indiſputably proved that he was the author of all their mercies (2) He would cut off all pretence of aſcribing theſe events to their idols, as they would elſe be vainly diſpoſed to do, v 5 it being evident by his foretelling thoſe things, which their idol prieſts never could, that the work was from God alone (3) He would ſtop their boaſting, who might pretend when the event came to paſs, that they had foreſeen it, but now it was clear they had not the apprehenſion of what was coming, till God's prophets revealed the hidden counſels of God, decreed from the beginning, but now created and brought to light in the prophetic word (4) He would leave them inexcuſable Notwithſtanding all he had ſpoken their ear was not opened, and their hearts inattentive to the predictions God had given he knew them to be treacherous dealers, who had often backſlidden from him, and from their firſt formation into a people had been tranſgreſſors, but he now left them without excuſe, if they ſtill refuſed to pay regard to his word, ſo plain, evident, and clear *Note*, (1) It is the true and humbling character of every man, that he is a tranſgreſſor from the womb (2) Original ſin, in which we are born, is the pregnant ſource of all the actual evil that afterwards appears in our hearts and lives (3) God knows and remarks the inmoſt diſpoſition of our ſouls, and an apoſtate nature is in his eyes the ſin exceeding ſinful (4) The word of God is deſigned to ſtain all human glory, and to ſhow us how ignorant, as well as wicked, we muſt have been without Divine revelation (5) They who proudly and obſtinately reject God's word, deſervedly are left to periſh in their native guilt and blindneſs

9 ¶ [m] For my name's ſake [n] will I defer mine anger,
and for my praiſe will I refrain for thee, that I cut thee
not off 10 Behold, I have refined thee, but † not
with ſilver, I have choſen thee in the furnace of affliction
11 [o] For mine own ſake, *even* for mine own ſake
will I do *it*, [p] for how ſhould *my name* be polluted? and
[q] I will not give my glory unto another 12 Hearken
unto me, O Jacob, and Iſrael my called, I *am* he, [r] I
am the firſt, I alſo *am* the laſt 13 [s] Mine hand alſo
hath laid the foundation of the earth, and ‡ my right
hand hath ſpanned the heavens *when* [t] I call unto them
they ſtand up together 14 All ye aſſemble yourſelves
and hear [u] which among them hath declared theſe
things? [x] the LORD hath loved him he will do his
pleaſure on Babylon, and his arm *ſhall be on* the Chal
deans 15 I, *even* I have ſpoken, yea, I have called him
I have brought him, and he ſhall make his way proſperous

m Chap xliii 24 n Pſ lxxviii 38 † Or, not as ſilver, Pſal cxvi 9 Chap lvii 16 o Pſ lxxix 9 [illegible] 9 p Deut xxxii 27 Chap lii 5 Ezek xx 14, 22 q Chap xlii 8 r Ibid xli 4 & xliv 6 Rev i 17 & xxii 13 s Chap xlii 5 John i 3 ‡ Or, the palm of my right hand hath ſpread out t Pſ cxlvii 4 Chap xl 26 u Chap xli 22 & xliii 9 & xliv 7 & xlv 21 x Chap xlv 1, &c

v 9—15 Their guilt was a circumſtance very diſcouraging, how could they hope for God's interpoſition? and their oppreſſors were ſo powerful that no proſpect of human relief appeared To ſupport them therefore againſt their juſt fears,

1 God, not out of reſpect to them, but for his own glory, declares he will deliver them though they deſerved to be utterly cut off, he will defer his anger, and leſt the heathen nations might reproach him, as if he was unable to ſave his people, or count their gods above him he will refrain his arm from deſtroying them, and ſave them from their enemies, *v* 9, 11 Behold, and admire the grace, *I have refined thee*, by theſe ſufferings to which they had been expoſed, *but not with ſilver*, or *among ſilver*, have not kept them in the furnace till all their droſs was purged away, for then the ſpirit muſt fail before him, if he dealt with them in ſtrict juſtice, *but I have choſen thee in the furnace of affliction*, he made the afflictions they endured the means of calling them home to himſelf, and by their trials exerciſed and brightened their graces, and purified their ſouls from ſin *Note*, (1) If God dealt with us according to our iniquities, there could no fleſh living be ſaved (2) It is not for our deſerts but to manifeſt the glory of his grace, that God is pleaſed to ſpare and pardon (3) Affliction is often the bleſſed means of bringing thoſe home to God who had before wandered far from the right way (4) It is a gracious ſign of God's paternal affection towards us, when he is pleaſed in mercy to correct us, and not to leave us wholly unpuniſhed

2 Though they could not help themſelves, God will raiſe up a deliverer for them, who ſhall overthrow the kingdom of Babylon Let Jacob hear the Divine determination, and Iſrael, called of God and choſen, believe what he ſpeaks, who is the ſelf-exiſtent, eternal, and immutable Jehovah, *v* 12 He whoſe hand laid the foundation of the earth, and ſtretched out the heaven with ſuch eaſe as if they had been but a ſpan's breadth, at whoſe word the aſſembled hoſts of both ſtand up, ready to execute his high behests, he is able to accompliſh their ſalvation, *v* 13 Let Iſrael therefore attend to the prophetic word, of which none among the gods of the heathen, or the wiſe men, could ever inform them Cyrus, the beloved of the Lord, is appointed for their deliverer, to execute God's pleaſure on Babylon, and to lift his arm of vengeance on the Chaldeans, *v* 14 God hath ſpoken, and his word is irreverſible, he will enable him for the work, bring him to the ſiege from a far country, and make his way proſperous, giving him victory in the battle, and ſucceſs in all his enterprizes, *v* 15 *Note*, (1) Cyrus is the type of God's beloved Son, ſent down from heaven, and riding on proſperouſly, the conqueror of death, hell, and ſin, and the Redeemer of his Iſrael (2) We may ſafely depend on the fulfilment of God's promiſes, however to human view the difficulties in the way of their accompliſhment ſeem inſurmountable Is any thing too hard for God? (3) They who have a Divine call, and are under Divine guidance, may be ſure their way ſhall be proſperous

16 ¶ Come ye near unto me, hear ye this, [y] I have
not ſpoken in ſecret from the beginning, from the time
that it was, there *am* I and now [z] the LORD God and
his Spirit hath ſent me 17 Thus ſaith [a] the LORD
thy redeemer, the holy One of Iſrael, I *am* the LORD
thy God which teacheth thee to profit, which leadeth
thee by the way that thou ſhouldſt go 18 [b] O that
thou hadſt hearkned to my commandments! [c] then had
thy peace been as a river, and thy righteouſneſs as the
waves of the ſea, 19 Thy ſeed alſo had been as the
ſand, and the offſpring of thy bowels, like the gravel
thereof, his name ſhould not have been cut off, nor deſtroyed
from before me 20 ¶ [d] Go ye forth of Babylon,
flee ye from the Chaldeans, [e] with a voice of ſinging declare
ye, tell this, utter it *even* to the end of the earth
ſay ye, [f] The LORD hath redeemed his ſervant Jacob
21 And [g] they thirſted not *when* he led them through
the deſerts he cauſed the waters to flow out of the rock
for them [h] he clave the rock alſo, and the waters guſhed
out 22 [i] *There* is no peace, ſaith the LORD, unto
the wicked

y Chap xlv 19 z Chap xi 2 Zech ii 9, 11 [illegible] a Chap xliii 14 b Deut v 29 & xxxii 29 Pſal lxxxi 13 c Pſ cxix 165 d Chap lii 11 Jer l 8 & li 6, 45 Zech ii 6 Rev xviii 4 e Pſ cxxvi 1, 2 Chap xxvi 1 Rev xix 1 f Pſ cvii 2 Luke i 68 g Chap xli 17, 18 h Ex xvii 6 Num xx 11 i Chap lvii 21

v 16—22 We have here,

1 The call of God to attend the miniſtry of the prophet, or rather the call of Chriſt, who ſeems to be ſpoken of, to the Jews to hear and receive his goſpel, and acknowledge his Divine miſſion *I have not ſpoken in ſecret from the beginning*, but preached publickly in the ſynagogues, *from the time that it was*, from the beginning of his miniſtry, *there am I*, openly teaching the goſpel of the kingdom, or, *before the time that it was*, ere he was become incarnate, *there was I*, exiſting from eternity in the boſom of the Father *and now the Lord and his Spirit hath ſent me*, or *the Lord hath ſent me*, having the fulleſt commiſſion for the execution of the work of redemption, and his Spirit to make that work effectual, by bringing it near to the ſouls of men *Note*, (1) We have here the Trinity of perſons in the Godhead clearly aſſerted (2) When God ſends he will qualify us for his ſervice (3) It becomes us to hear with ſolemn reverence and attention the words of him whom God hath ſent

2 The Lord Jeſus informs them of his character and deſign *I am the Lord thy God*, without which, he could not have been the Redeemer of his Iſrael, nor could they have been able comfortably and confidently to truſt their ſouls in his hands, *which teacheth thee to profit*, or *profitable things*, the doctrines of truth and holineſs, ſuch as their fallen ſtate, their guilt and danger, the grace revealed for ſinners in the goſpel, the perfection of atonement and righteouſneſs wrought out by him, and the fulneſs of the Spirit which reſided in him, to be communicated to his people, *which leadeth thee by the way which thou ſhouldſt go*, Chriſt himſelf is the living way, his word is our guide, his grace our ſupport, and all the diſpenſations of his providence concur to lead his redeemed towards their glorious reſt

3 He laments over thoſe poor ſouls that ſinned againſt their own mercies, *Mat* xxiii 37 *O that thou hadſt hearkened to my commandments!* which though ſome did, yet we ſee the generality of the Jewiſh people rejected Chriſt and his goſpel, and thereby forfeited all the mercies which had been promiſed to the obedient, and brought heavy deſolation upon them Had they heard and believed them *their peace had been as a river, and their righteouſneſs as the waves of the ſea*, abundant and permanent, *v* 18 Their nation would have been increaſed exceedingly, and their ſtability ſecured to ever, but now, for their unbelief and impenitence, the very reverſe is their caſe *Note*, (1) Sin robs us of all our joys (2) The remembrance of the mercies they have forfeited, as well as the torment they endure, will aggravate the miſery of the ungodly (3) It is a grief to the Saviour, to ſee poor ſouls rejecting their own mercies, and ruſhing on their ruin (4) They who periſh eternally will have no blame to caſt on God's mercy, but muſt confeſs that their own obſtinacy and hardneſs of heart procured their deſtruction

4 By the proclamation given to the Jews to depart from Babylon is prefigured the great deliverance of ſinners' ſouls from the bondage of corruption, which, through the preaching of the

the gospel, should be effected They are called to go forth from Babylon and flee, not as by stealth, but with the voice of singing, openly exulting in their escape With gladness they are commanded to publish their glorious redemption, wrought out for them by the power of God, v 20 and as God in their first great deliverance from Egypt, led them through the wilderness safely, and brought water from the rock to slake their thirst, such would be still his care over them in their return from Babylon to Judea, v 21 And this is most applicable to the state of all God's people who go forth with joy from the house of their prison, and from the bonds of sin and Satan, publish to God's glory the redemption wrought out by Jesus for them, are safely led through all the dangers of this world, to them an howling wilderness, refreshed and comforted with the streams of divine grace, and brought at last to their native land, better than Canaan, even the inheritance provided for them among the saints in light

5 The obstinately impenitent are excluded from all the promised mercies *There is no peace, saith the Lord, to the wicked*, which may refer to those who chose their abode in Babylon, preferably to a return to Judea, or more particularly to the Jewish nation, who, after their rejection of Christ and his gospel, became a miserable, harrassed, and troubled people, and continue so to this day Or more generally it includes all impenitent sinners, who have no peace with God, no solid rest in their own consciences, no comfort in death, no hope in eternity, but the wrath of God present and eternal abideth on them

CHAP XLIX

The deliverance of the Jews from the Babylonish yoke, and the prophecies going before concerning it, were designed to direct their eyes to the greater salvation which the Messiah was ordained to accomplish for his people In this chapter we have, 1 *The designation of Christ to his office as Mediator*, ver 1—3 2 *The assurance given him of the success of his undertaking among the Gentiles*, ver 3—8 3 *The redemption that should be wrought by him, and the progress of that redemption*, ver 9—12 4 *The encouragement given from hence to the afflicted church*, ver 13—17 5 *The addition of many to it, and the setting up of a church among the Gentiles*, ver 18—23 6 *A ratification of the prophecy of the Jews release out of Babylon, which was to be the figure and type of all these blessings*, ver 24—26

1 LISTEN, O isles, unto me, and hearken ye
people from far, [a] The LORD hath called me
from the womb, from the bowels of my mother [b] hath
he made mention of my name 2 And he hath made
[c] my mouth like a sharp sword, in the shadow of his
hand hath he hid me, and made me [d] a polished shaft,
in his quiver hath he hid me, 3 And said unto me,
[e] Thou *art* my servant, O Israel, [f] in whom I will be
glorified 4 Then I said, [g] I have laboured in vain, I
have spent my strength for nought, and in vain, [h] *yet*
surely my judgment is with the LORD, and my work
with my God 5 ¶ And now saith the LORD,
that formed me from the womb *to be* his servant, to
bring Jacob again to him, [i] Though Israel be not gathered,
yet shall I be glorious in the eyes of the LORD,
and my God shall be my strength 6 And he said, It
is a light thing that thou shouldst be my servant to
raise up the tribes of Jacob, and to restore the ‖ preserved
of Israel I will also give thee [k] for a light to
the Gentiles, that thou mayest be my salvation unto the
end of the earth

[a] Jer i 5 [b] Mat i 21 Luke i 31 [c] Chap xi 4 & li 16. Heb iv 12 Rev i 16 [d] Pf xlv 5 [e] Chap xlii 1 Zech iii 8 [f] John xvii 4 [g] Chap liii 3 & lxv 2 Mat xvii 17 John i 11 [h] v 10 1 Cor iii 8 [i] Mat xxiii 37 ‖ Or, desolations [k] Chap xlii 6 & ix 3 Luke ii 32 Acts xiii 17 & xxvi 18

v 1—6 The former chapter related chiefly to the salvation of the Jews, this looks much farther, even to the salvation of Gentiles as well as Jews, through the preaching of the gospel

1 The isles are summoned to attend the word of their God and Saviour, which should go forth into all lands, and distant realms are called to hear the glad tidings of salvation through a Redeemer, v 1

2 His mission and authority are set forth *The Lord hath called me from the womb*, from eternity, to be a prophet, priest, and king to his people *from, or before, the bowels of my mother hath he made mention of my name*, his name Jesus being given him by the angel, before his conception *And he hath made my mouth as a sharp sword*, so piercing and powerful his word, that the powers of darkness fall down before it, and deep conviction seized the sinner's heart, *in the shadow of his hand hath he hid me*, during the days of infancy, when Herod sought to destroy him, *and made me a polished shaft, or choice arrow*, bright and sharp *In his quiver hath he hid me*, till the fulness of time came that he should be manifested in the flesh, *and said unto me, Thou art my servant*, (for in this form he consented to appear) *O Israel*, the representative and covenant head of his people, *in whom I will be glorified*, God's perfections being never so eminently displayed, as in the salvation wrought out by his incarnate Son

3 He complains of the little effect his preaching produced on the Jewish people he laboured in vain, and spent his strength for nought They paid no attention to his miracles, nor were convinced by his word, yet God knew the fidelity with which he discharged his trust, and his work was approved, and would be rewarded by him, v 4 *Note*, (1) It is no uncommon complaint ministers make, that to the most of their congregations they labour in vain (2) We must not be discouraged if we see not all the success we hoped for the work is God's, when we are conscious of our own simplicity, we may quietly leave the matter in his hand (3) It is not always lost labour, where the effects are not immediately seen the seed Christ sowed in his life grew most plentifully after his death (4) Our success enters not into our reward, but our fidelity

4 With two encouraging promises God answers his complaints He had formed him to be his servant, and appointed him to seek and save the lost sheep of the house of Israel But though the people in general rejected his gospel, yet, [1] He should be glorious in the eyes of the Lord, and God would be his strength, to carry him through all the difficulties of his arduous work Thus we see him attended by angels at his birth, ministred to by them in his agony, transfigured on the mount, ascending from the dead, and exalted to the right hand of the majesty on high [2] He should not merely be a Saviour to the preserved of Israel, and raise up God's elect among the Jews, but on the Gentiles his light should arise, and his salvation be spread to the ends of the earth, from whence converts would be gathered into the church, unspeakably more numerous than those of his own nation who should reject him and this we see in part fulfilled, and fulfilling daily, till the fulness of the Gentiles shall come in *Note*, (1) The soul is in utter darkness till Christ in his gospel enlightens the eyes of our minds, and guides us into paths of peace (2) God's Israel are preserved for him, kept by eternal love, and none can separate them from him (3) Christ is the only salvation for lost man, out of him there is no hope

7 Thus saith the LORD the Redeemer of Israel,
and his holy One, to him [l] whom man despiseth, to him
[m] whom the nation abhorreth, to a servant of rulers,
[n] Kings shall see and arise, princes also shall worship, because
of the LORD that is faithful, *and* the holy One
of Israel, and he shall choose thee 8 Thus saith the
LORD, [o] In an acceptable time have I heard thee, and
in a day of salvation have I helped thee and I will preserve
thee, and give thee [p] for a covenant of the people,
to † establish the earth, to cause to inherit the desolate
heritages, 9 That thou mayest say [q] to the prisoners,
Go forth, to them that *are* in darkness, Shew yourselves
they shall feed in the ways, and their pastures *shall be* in
all high places 10 [r] They shall not hunger nor thirst,
[s] neither shall the heat nor sun smite them for he that
hath mercy on them shall lead them, even by the springs
of water shall he guide them 11 And I will make all
my mountains a way, and my high-ways shall be exalted.
12 Behold, [t] these shall come from far and lo,
these from the north and from the west, and these from
the land of Sinim

[l] Chap liii 3 [m] Acts iii 14 [n] Pf lxxii 10, 11 Ver 23 [o] Pf lxix 13 2 Cor vi 2 [p] Chap xlii 6 † Or, raise up [q] Chap xlii 7 Zech ix 12 [r] Rev vii 16 [s] Pf cxxi 6 [t] Chap xliii 5 6 Mat viii 11

v 7—12 We have here,

1 The humiliation and exaltation of the Lord Jesus God the Father, the Redeemer of Israel, encourages his dear Son under his abasement in the days of his flesh he would be *despised* of men, *abhorred* of his own nation, and crucified; *a servant of rulers*, insulted by the Jewish and Roman chiefs yet great was the glory to which he should be advanced the kings of the earth should do him homage, and princes bow down to him; as was the case, when the Roman empire under Constantine embraced the profession of Christianity, and will be more abundantly fulfilled, when all nations shall come and worship before him

2 God promises him all support in the day of his trouble He will answer his prayer, and help him in the trying hour, when on the cross, he hung, accomplishing the salvation of his people, v 8 *Note*, (1) Whenever [illegible] inclined to look up in prayer to God, he will find it an acceptable time (2) God never forsakes his chosen in their distress, but will succour and save them at their cry

3 He is assured he shall see of the travail of his soul in the salvation of his people *I will give thee for a covenant of the people*, as their great covenant-head and representative, in whom they would be accepted, and entitled to the blessings of grace and glory, which by his blood and righteousness he obtained for them *to establish or raise up the earth, and cause to inherit the desolate heritages*, by the preaching of his gospel, replenishing his church from the Gentile world,

which

Before Chriſt 712.

which before was deſolate, and the members of it comparatively few *v* 8 *that thou mayeſt ſay to the priſoners, Go forth*, *to them that are in darkneſs, Shew yourſelves*, the ſinner's ſoul being under the bonds of iniquity, ſhut up in the darkneſs of ignorance and error, and obnoxious to the juſtice of God, till Chriſt by his pardoning word cancels our guilt, by his renewing grace enlightens our minds, and brings us forth into the glorious liberty of the ſons of God, to ſhew forth the change he hath wrought, and therein to make his glory to appear And whom he thus redeems, he preſerves *they ſhall feed in the ways*, in the word and ordinances of God, *and their paſtures ſhall be in all high places*, where there is plenty of nouriſhment, and they are ſafe from all attacks *They ſhall not hunger nor thirſt*, ſhall want no temporal or ſpiritual good, *neither ſhall the heat nor ſun ſmite them*, God will preſerve them from the power of temptation, and cover them from the ſeverity of perſecution *For he that hath mercy on them ſhall lead them*, with all the tenderneſs of a ſhepherd *even by the ſprings of water ſhall he guide them*, filling their ſouls with conſolations, and, as they are under divine conduct, making them happy in divine comfort Every obſtacle in their way to glory ſhall be removed, *I will make all my mountains a way*, *and my high-ways ſhall be exalted*, that the redeemed may ſee the ſtrait path before them, and walk ſafely and ſecurely therein and, as at Cyrus's proclamation the Jews aſſembled from all parts of the land of Chaldea to return to Zion, ſo, in greater numbers, ſhall converts flock into the church of Chriſt *Behold!* the glorious ſight, *theſe ſhall come from far and lo, theſe from the north and from the weſt, and theſe from the land of Sinim*, from all quarters of the globe, whither his goſpel ſhould go forth, multitudes ſhould join themſelves to the Lord, which, in the apoſtles days, was eminently verified, and ſhall be yet more abundantly ſeen in the latter days *Note*, (1) Chriſt is our covenant, all the conditions of the covenant of grace were fulfilled by him, and by faith all the bleſſings of it are derived from him (2) Miſerable is the ſinner's ſtate, till Chriſt comes to ſet him free, yet how many ſleep careleſs in their chains, and never conſider that the darkneſs of ſin muſt ſhortly iſſue in the outer darkneſs of hell! (3) The redeemed are the Saviour's peculiar care, and he will ſee they ſhall want no manner of thing that is good (4) The way to glory hath difficulties, but none ſo great but that almighty Grace can make us more than conquerors (5) Were we left to ourſelves a moment, how quickly ſhould we like ſilly ſheep go aſtray? Bleſſed be God, we are not left to our own keeping, but are under the care of that watchful ſhepherd, who can ſay of his flock, I have loſt none

13 ¶ [u] Sing, O heavens, and be joyful, O earth, and
break forth into ſinging, O mountains for [x] the LORD
hath comforted his people, and will have mercy upon
his afflicted 14 But Zion ſaid, [y] The LORD hath
forſaken me, and my LORD hath forgotten me 15
[z] Can a woman forget her ſucking child, [a] that ſhe
ſhould not have compaſſion on the ſon of her womb?
[b] yea they may forget, [c] yet will I not forget thee 16
Behold, [d] I have graven thee upon the palms of *my*
hands; thy walls are continually before me 17. Thy
‖ children ſhall make haſte, thy deſtroyers, and they
that made thee waſte, ſhall go forth of thee

[u] Chap. xliv 23 & lv 12 [x] Chap. xl 1 & li 3 [y] Chap. xl 27 [z] Mat vii 11 [a] 1 Kings iii. 26 [b] Lam iv 3 [c] Chap. xliv 21 Jer xxxi 20 [d] Cant viii 6 ‖ Or build ers 1 Cor iii 10

v 13—17 The deliverance of Iſrael from Babylon was juſt matter of abundant joy, but how much greater is due for the redemption of Jeſus, the deſire of all nations?

1 The whole creation is repreſented as burſting forth into ſongs of joy on this glorious event The afflicted are comforted, the miſerable find mercy, and heaven and earth unite to celebrate the Saviour's praiſe, *v* 13 *Note*, We can never enough be thankful to redeeming love, nor will eternity ſuffice to ſpeak the praiſes of our Lord

2 The ſtate of deſpondence into which Zion had fallen, ſerved to heighten the joy of their deliverance *Zion ſaid*, or *hath ſaid, The Lord hath forſaken me, and my Lord hath forgotten me* in their long captivity they were ready to faint, and deſpair of relief, and many a time the church of God hath been reduced ſo low, driven by perſecution into the deſert, that it ſeemed forſaken of God And thus it is alſo with the ſouls of believers in a ſtate of temptation, when under darkneſs they are ready to deſpair, and give up all for loſt But this is our infirmity, for he is,

3 God's anſwer to Zion's complaint nothing can be conceived more expreſſive of his love, tenderneſs, care, and the unchangeableneſs of his regard towards his people *Can a woman forget her ſucking child, that ſhe ſhould not have compaſſion on the ſon of her womb?* Strange as it may appear, ſuch an unnatural monſter might perhaps be found, but with tenderneſs infinitely ſurpaſſing, God never forgets, never ceaſes to love and protect the children of his grace On his hands they were engraved, ever before him in his remembrance, and as a ſignet precious to him Perhaps ſome alluſion may be had to the prints of the nails in the hands of Jeſus, the love-marks he bears for his peo-ple's ſake, *v* 16 and being remembred of him, they ſhall be ſaved by him *Thy children ſhall make haſte*, or *thy builders*, either goſpel-miniſters, who ſhould aſſiduouſly labour to build up the church, or converts that ſhould flock into it, whilſt *thy deſtroyers, and they that made thee waſte, ſhall go forth of thee*, the Babylonians, or rather all the perſecutors and corruptors of God's church, ſuch as Antichriſt and his followers, who ſhall be deſtroyed at the coming of Jeſus, and caſt into outer darkneſs *Note*, (1) The love of Chriſt towards his people is ſo ſurpaſſing great, that wherever it is truly believed and known, it cannot but powerfully conſtrain the heart (2) When Chriſt calls, we muſt make no delay (3) The damnation of the wicked is as ſure as the ſalvation of the redeemed

18 ¶ [e] Lift up thine eyes round about, and behold
all theſe gather themſelves together, *and* come to thee
as I live, ſaith the LORD, thou ſhalt ſurely clothe thee
with them all, as with an ornament, and bind them *on*
thee as a bride *doth* 19 For thy waſte and thy deſolate
places, and the land of thy deſtruction, [f] ſhall even now
be too narrow by reaſon of the inhabitants, and they
that ſwallowed thee up ſhall be far away 20 [g] The
children which thou ſhalt have, after [h] thou haſt loſt the
other, ſhall ſay again in thine ears, The place is too
ſtrait for me give place to me that I may dwell 21
Then ſhalt thou ſay in thine heart, Who hath begotten
me theſe, ſeeing I have loſt my children, and am deſo-
late, a captive, and removing to and fro? and who hath
brought up theſe? Behold, I was left alone, theſe, where
had they *been*? 22 Thus ſaith the LORD God, Be-
hold, [i] I will lift up mine hand to the Gentiles, and ſet
up my ſtandard to the people and they ſhall bring thy
ſons in *their* † arms, and thy daughters ſhall be carried
upon *their* ſhoulders 23 [k] And kings ſhall be thy
nurſing-fathers, and their ‡ queens thy nurſing-mothers
they ſhall bow down to thee with *their* face toward the
earth, and [l] lick up the duſt of thy feet, and thou ſhalt
know that I *am* the LORD. for [m] they ſhall not be
aſhamed that wait for me

[e] Chap lx 4 [f] Chap liv 1 Zech ii 4 & x 10 [g] Chap lx 4 [h] Rom xi 15, 20 [i] Chap lx 4 lxvi 20 [i] 1 1 † Heb boſom [k] Pſ lxxii 11 Ver Chap lii 15 & lx 16 ‡ Heb. Princeſſes Sarah, Gen xvii 15 [l] Pſ lxxii 9 [m] Pſ xxv 22 Rom ix. 33 & x 11.

v 18—23 Great and precious promiſes of the increaſe and glory of the church are here revealed A glympſe of this appeared when the Jews returned from their captivity, a brighter diſplay of it was made when the goſpel was firſt preached, but the full blaze ſeems yet reſerved for the times to come, when all nations ſhall be called to the obedience of the faith

1 A vaſt increaſe ſhall be made to the church *Lift up thine eyes*, behold the numerous converts aſſembling from every quarter, ornaments to their profeſſion by the holineſs of their lives, as the jewels which adorn a bride, *v* 18 *The waſte and deſolate places*, the countries before deſtitute of true religion, ſhall be filled with faithful ſouls, and all their enemies confounded ſhall periſh, *v* 19 *The children thou ſhalt have, after thou haſt loſt the other*, cut off by the perſecuting powers of the earth, ſhall ſpring up, as a plenteous harveſt, from the blood of the ſlain martyrs, or, *the children of thy widowhood*, when the church ſeemed bereft of all her ſons and daughters by the prevalence of the man of ſin, *ſhall ſay again*, or, *ſhall yet ſay in thine ears, The place is too ſtrait for me*, ſuch a ſudden and ſtrange increaſe of converts ſhall be made, *v* 20 With pleaſing ſurprize the glad mother ſhall behold the children God hath given her, and, wondering, enquire who hath begotten them, and whence they come, ſo unexpected a comfort to her widowed ſtate, *v* 21 and the anſwer is, They come from Gentile lands, called by the word of goſpel-grace, and liſted under the banner of a crucified Jeſus, and ſo eager are they to have a place in the ſpiritual Zion, that the weak and feeble are borne upon the ſhoulders of the ſtrong or, they will bring their children with them, and enroll them in the viſible church or perhaps it may refer to the aſſiſtance the Gentiles ſhall give the Jews, when their day of grace arrives, *v* 22 *Note*, (1) However low the church may be reduced, her latter end ſhall have great increaſe (2) They who have a concern for their own ſouls, cannot but be ſollicitous that others, eſpecially their own children, may be brought to the knowledge of Chriſt and his goſpel

2 The church ſhall not only be increaſed in number, but be highly honoured Kings ſhall be nurſing-fathers, and queens nurſing-mothers to it ſuch as Cyrus, Ahaſuerus, and Eſther, were to the Jews, or rather ſuch as Conſtantine and Helena, and other Chriſtian monarchs have been, and which will be ſtill farther ſeen, when all the kingdoms of the world ſhall become the kingdoms of the Lord and his Chriſt *They ſhall bow down to thee with their face towards the earth*, with profoundeſt ſubmiſſion, *and lick up the duſt of thy feet*, ready to ſerve the church in the loweſt offices, and to ſhew affection and regard to the meaneſt of Chriſt's members *And thou ſhalt know that I am the Lord*, by ſuch wondrous exertion of his power to make all

Before Christ 712.

all nations obedient to the faith, *for they shall not be ashamed that wait for me*, the performance of all his promises shall be seen in their season, and the hopes of his waiting people shall never be disappointed, therefore, my soul, trust thou still in the Lord!

24. ¶ [n] Shall the prey be taken from the mighty, or
† the lawful captive delivered? 25 But thus saith the
LORD, Even the captives of the mighty shall be taken
away, and the prey of the terrible shall be delivered
for I will contend with *him* that contendeth with thee,
and I will save thy children 26 And [o] I will feed
them that oppress thee, with their own flesh, and they
shall be drunken [p] with their own blood, as with sweet
wine, and [q] all flesh shall know that I the LORD
am thy saviour, and thy redeemer, the mighty One of
Jacob

n Luke xi. 21, 22. † Heb. The captivity of the just. o Chap. ix. 20. p Rev. xiv. 20. & xvi. 6. q Ps. ix. 16.

v 24—26 Deliverance is promised, but great difficulties are in the way

1 We have an objection raised, either by their proud oppressors, as despising the prophetic word, or by the unbelieving Jews, as distrusting it *Shall the prey be taken from the mighty?* such as were the Babylonian monarchs, *and the lawful captive*, or *the captivity of the righteous, be delivered?* of which so little probability appeared And this is applicable to our souls taken captive by the devil, and by our willing servitude surrendered into his hands, who is strong to keep his prisoners; and it is a miracle of mercy if any sinner is rescued from his bands

2 God, by express promise, assures his people it shall be done Mighty as their oppressors are, and terrible, they are not too great for God to cope with He will espouse their quarrel, overcome their foes, and save their children, plucking them from the power of their enemies, *v* 25 Nay, he will do more, he will utterly consume them, will visit them with the sorest judgments, and make the world acknowledge his power to abase his foes, and his love towards the children of his grace, *v* 26 And this is spiritually fulfilled daily in the souls of sinners, by divine grace delivered from the bonds of sin and Satan, that strong man armed, and saved with an everlasting salvation from all their enemies, and will also literally be fulfilled in the destruction of Antichrist, and the persecuting powers of popery, paganism, and Mahometism, when Christ shall make his glory to appear, and all the world be forced to own both his power to save and to destroy to the uttermost

CHAP L

In this chapter we have, 1 The rejection of the Jews signified by a divorce, because of their contempt of the Messiah, who was so able to save them, ver 1—3 2 *Christ produces his commission, and professes his readiness to suffer*, ver 4—6 3 *He expresses his confidence in God's support*, ver 7—9 4 *He comforts his desponding saints, and threatens the self righteous and presuming sinners*, ver 10, 11

1 THUS saith the LORD, Where *is* [a] the bill of
your mother's divorcement whom I have put
away? or which of my creditors *is it* to whom I have
sold you? Behold, [b] for your iniquities have you sold
yourselves, and for your transgressions is your mother
put away 2 Wherefore [c] when I came, *was there* no
man? when I called, *was there* none to answer? [d] Is
my hand shortned at all, that it cannot redeem? or
have I no power to deliver? behold, [e] at my rebuke
[f] I dry up the sea [g] I make the rivers a wilderness
[h] their fish stinketh, because *there is* no water, and dieth
for thirst 3 [i] I clothe the heavens with blackness,
[k] and I make sackcloth their covering

a Deut. xxiv. 1. Hos. ii. 2. b Chap. lii. 3. c John i. 11. d Num. xi. 23. Chap. lix. 1. e Nah. i. 4. f Exod. xiv. 21. g Josh. iii. 16. h Exod. vii. 18. i Exod. x. 21. k Rev. vi. 12.

v 1—3 God will vindicate his ways to men, and prove his justice in the rejection of the Jewish people

1 He desires the cause of their rejection may be examined *Where is the bill of your mother's divorcement?* intimating, either that God had not cast them off, but they, like an adulteress, had treacherously departed from him, or, that if he had divorced them, if the bill was produced, the cause would be found abundantly to vindicate his proceeding *or which of my creditors is it to whom I have sold you?* fathers having such a right over their children among the Jews, but God owed nothing either to the Babylonian or Romans, and therefore if they were captives, it was not of him, but themselves *Behold, for your iniquities have you sold yourselves, and for your transgressions is your mother put away*, to gratify their vile lusts, they provoked God, by their idolatries especially, and at last, by crucifying the Redeemer, they brought upon themselves destruction. *Note*, (1) Though all who are saved owe it to God's sovereign grace, none are damned but must own it the just reward of their own obstinate impenitence (2) If sinners sell themselves to work wickedness, they can only hope to earn the wages of sin

2 He upbraids them with their inattention to his calls by all his prophets, and especially by his Son, who came himself to warn them, yet none regarded They paid no credit to his word, nor would be persuaded, that he who appeared in circumstances so mean was the almighty Redeemer promised, tho' he had given such instances of his glorious power in their former deliverances At his rebuke the sea was divided, by him Jordan became dry ground, he slew the fish of Egypt, when the rivers were turned into blood, *v* 2 and covered the Egyptians with that thick darkness which might be felt, *v* 3 Or it may refer to his power in raising the thick clouds, and, when he pleases, eclipsing the luminaries of heaven, in all which works his omnipotence is manifested

4 [l] The Lord GOD hath given me the tongue of
the learned, that I should know how to speak a word
[m] in season to *him* [n] *that is* weary he wakeneth morning
by morning he wakeneth mine ear to hear as the
learned 5 ¶ [o] The Lord GOD hath opened mine ear,
and I was not [p] rebellious, neither turned away back
6 [q] I gave my back to the smiters, [r] and my cheeks to
them that plucked off the hair I hid not my face from
shame and spitting 7 ¶ For the Lord GOD will help
me, therefore shall I not be confounded therefore have
[s] I set my face like a flint, and I know that I shall not
be ashamed. 8 [t] *He is* near that justifieth me, who will
contend with me? [u] let us stand together who *is* † mine
adversary? let him come near to me 9 Behold, the
Lord GOD will help me, who *is* he *that* shall condemn
me? [x] lo, they all shall wax old as a garment [y] the
moth shall eat them up

l Exod. iv. 11. m Prov. xxv. 11. n Mat. xi. 28. o Ps. xl. 6. p John xiv. 31. Phil. ii. 8. Heb. x. 5, &c. q Mat. xxvi. 67. & xxvii. 26. r Lam. iii. [illegible] s Ezek. iii. 8, 9. t Rom. viii. 32, &c. u Exod. xxii. 9. Deut. xix. 17. † Heb. The master of my cause. x Chap. li. 6. y Chap. li. 8.

v 4—9 We have here our Lord proceeding in his work of redemption, for which he is every way so fully qualified

1 As endued with the highest wisdom, that he might know how to preach the gospel which brings rest to the weary soul, and constantly receiving from his Father, is the great prophet of his church, those lessons of instruction, which, with fidelity and zeal, rising up early he inculcated on his disciples, *v* 4 *Note*, (1) The greatest qualification of a minister of God is to know how to address the troubled conscience, and to speak the seasonable word to calm the tumult of the soul (2) It is God that gives the ability, and he alone can add the blessing (3) They who would serve God in the gospel of his Son, must attentively hear him speaking in his revealed word, for there are all the hid treasures of wisdom (4) Morning by morning must we be found upon our knees, asking the wisdom which cometh from above, for the most laborious researches of the human understanding in the scriptures, without the teaching of God's Spirit, will never make us wise unto salvation

2 Patiently suffering He voluntarily yielded himself up to his Father's will, as the servant who had his ear bored, *Exod* xxi 5, 6 became his master's property for ever, and when he was called to the severest trials, in the course of his obedience unto death for our redemption, he cheerfully met his sufferings, *v* 5 submitting to all that shame, insult, pain, and agony, which he endured from his wicked persecutors, *v* 6 *See Mat* xxvi 67 xxvii 26 *Mark* xiv 65 *John* xviii 22 *Note*, The more we consider what Jesus so readily submitted to on our behalf, the more should our hearts be comforted in the persuasion of his willingness to save all who come to him

3 Powerfully supported, and boldly accomplishing his work in the face of all opposition *For the Lord God will help me*, as man, he needed support from his Father, and found it in the day of his calamity, *therefore shall I not be confounded*, so as to faint under his sufferings *Therefore have I set my face as a flint*, to resist all the ignominious treatment to which he was exposed; *and I know that I shall not be ashamed*, his cause was good, and he was assured in the issue he should not be disappointed, but see the redemption of his people compleated *He is near that justifieth me, who will contend with me? Let us stand together who is mine adversary? let him come near to me* The charges that were laid against him, from Satan, from the law, from his malicious persecutors, were all answered, and God, by his resurrection from the dead, declared him fully acquitted of every accusation, and that he had made compleat satisfaction for the sins of his people. Thus holpen of God, no condemnation remained against him, whilst all his enemies, doomed to ruin, like a moth eaten garment, should utterly and irrecoverably perish, *v* 9 *Note*, (1) They who are called to stand up for Christ, have need of courage, and to set their faces as a flint against the revilings of men (2) Christ's service will bear us out, and, however shameful in the eyes of men the preaching of the cross may appear, it is our greatest glory (3) Whilst our hearts are led up to

Before Christ 712

God for strength, he will not fail us (4) A believer in Jesus may now challenge every accuser, the resurrection of his Lord gives him a plea that silences all condemnation (5) The enemies of Christ and his people, however they may prevail for a time, are doomed at last to perish for ever, and the worm which dieth not shall feed upon them

a Mal iii 16 · a Ps xxiii 4. Chap viii 22 · b Ps xxvii 13 Hab ii 4 · c Chap x 20 1 Pet v 7 · d Ps xvi 4. John ix 39

10 ¶ Who *is* among you [a] that feareth the LORD,
that obeyeth the voice of his servant, [a] that walketh *in*
darkness, and hath no light ? [b] let him trust in the name
of the LORD, [c] and stay upon his God 11 Behold,
all ye that kindle a fire, that compass *yourselves* about
with sparks walk in the light of your fire, and in the
sparks *that* ye have kindled [d] This shall ye have of mine
hand, ye shall lie down in sorrow

v 10, 11 The sufficiency of the Lord Jesus for his undertaking being shewn, he here addresses saints and sinners, comforting the one, and warning the other

1 He speaks a word of kind encouragement to his people Their character is drawn as *fearing the Lord*, with child-like reverence and regard, and *obeying the voice of his servant*, receiving by faith his promises of gospel grace, and yielding a willing submission to his commands and ordinances *Yet they walk in darkness, and see no light*, exposed to severe afflictions, or suffering under desertions, destitute of their wonted comfort, and reduced to fears and doubts about their interest in the Redeemer In such a state of distress he bids them *trust in the name of the Lord*, against hope believing in hope, *and stay themselves on their God*, who, though they are in darkness, never quits his relation to them, and they must plead still his unchangeable covenant of grace, and never cast away this hope of their confidence *Note*, (1) God's children are sometimes left to great darkness, and reduced very low, in order more eminently to exercise their faith, and to manifest more abundantly God's love towards them (2) In the darkest dispensations of providence and grace there is still ground to say, *My God*, and as long as our faith doth not fail, we shall not be cast away

2 He speaks a word of conviction to the presumptuous *Behold, all ye that kindle a fire, that compass yourselves about with sparks*, like Nadab and Abihu offering strange fire, setting up the light of nature instead of revelation, seeking by works of righteousness that they can do, to recommend themselves to God's favour, instead of renouncing themselves, to trust alone in the righteousness of a Redeemer *Walk in the light of your fire, and in the sparks that ye have kindled*, ironically spoken, as intimating the vanity and insufficiency of the methods they pursued *this shall ye have of my hand, ye shall lie down in sorrow* The issue of your ways will be fatal the light of nature can only lead you to outer darkness, and dependence on your own deserts and duties, prove at last your eternal ruin *Note*, Creature-comforts may administer a short-lived enjoyment, and self-dependence flatter us with a momentary hope, but soon will these sparks be extinguished, and death undeceive those, who would not be undeceived before

CHAP LI

This chapter is designed for the comfort of the church of God in her distress 1 God, who raised his church at first out of nothing, will take care it shall not perish, ver 1—3 2 The righteousness and salvation he designs for his church are sure and near, ver 4—6 3 Her persecutors are weak and dying creatures, ver 7, 8 4 The same power which did wonders for the church formerly, is now engaged for her protection and deliverance, ver 9—11 5 God himself, the maker of the world, had undertaken to deliver his people out of their distress, and to comfort them under it, ver 12—16 6 As deplorable as the condition of the church now was, ver 17—20 to the same woful circumstances her persecutors should shortly be reduced, ver 20—23.

a Mat v 6 & vi 33 Rom ix 30 & 1 Thes iii 9 · b Rom iv 1 · c Gen xii 1 · d Gen xiii 10

1 HEARKEN to me, [a] ye that follow after
righteousness, ye that seek the LORD look
unto the rock *whence* ye are hewn, and to the hole of
the pit *whence* ye are digged 2 [b] Look unto Abraham
your father, and unto Sarah *that* bare you ; for [c] I called
him alone, and blessed him, and increased him 3 For
the LORD shall comfort Zion he will comfort all her
waste places, and he will make her wilderness like Eden,
and her desart [d] like the garden of the LORD, joy and
gladness shall be found therein, thanksgiving, and the
voice of melody

v 1—3 This was probably designed primarily for the comfort of Israel in Babylon, but is equally applicable to the whole church

1 The character of God's people is here described *Ye that follow after righteousness, ye that seek the Lord*, who earnestly embrace the righteousness of faith, seek the Lord in all his appointed ordinances, and desire to walk before him in all holy conversation and godliness

2 Their duty is set before them in general, to hearken to all God's words, and particularly to look back with humility on their low original, and with faith to trust God in the time of their deepest distress, who is as able to save them, and increase his church, as to deliver Abraham from his idolatrous country, and make him the father of many nations, *v* 2 *Note*, (1) It is good for a child of God to be often remembering the hole of the pit, the state of nature and sin, from whence he hath been digged, to keep him ever humble before God (2) What God hath done of old for those who trusted, as Abraham, implicitly on his promise, should encourage us to follow their faith, and hope for their blessing

3 In the way of duty God will meet them with his consolations *The Lord will comfort Zion*, his church, and every member of it, with the discoveries of his love *He will comfort all her waste places*, where, through the ravages of persecution, or decays of vital godliness, few faithful remained, *and he will make her wilderness like Eden, and her desart as the garden of the Lord*, so flourishing and fruitful, and this will yield matter of abundant consolation to the saints, as well as glory to God *joy and gladness shall be found therein, thanksgiving, and the voice of melody* *Note*, (1) It is matter of greatest joy to the soul, when God is pleased to change its desart state of nature, and by his grace renewed, to make it flourish as the garden of Eden (2) The tribute of praise is the least we can render for the mercies we continually receive from God

e Chap ii 3 · f Luke ii 32 · g 1 Thes v 24, 2 Thes i 6 · h Ps cii 26 Mat xxiv 35 2 Pet iii 10 · i Chap l 9 · k John iii 16 · l Ps xxxvii 31 · m Mat x 28 · n Chap l 9 · o Ver 6

4 ¶ Hearken unto me, my people, and give ear
unto me, O my nation for [e] a law shall proceed from
me, and I will make my judgment to rest [f] for a light
of the people 5 [g] My righteousness *is* near my sal-
vation is gone forth, and mine arms shall judge the peo-
ple the isles shall wait upon me, and on mine arms
shall they trust 6 Lift up your eyes to the heavens,
and look upon the earth beneath for [h] the heavens shall
vanish away like smoke, and the earth shall wax old like
a garment, and [i] they that dwell therein shall die in
like manner but [k] my salvation shall be for ever, and
my righteousness shall not be abolished 7 ¶ Hearken
unto me, ye that know righteousness, the people [l] in
whose heart *is* my law, [m] fear ye not the reproach of
men, neither be ye afraid of their revilings 8 For
[n] the moth shall eat them up like a garment, and the
worm shall eat them up like wool [o] but my righteous-
ness shall be for ever, and my salvation from generation
to generation

v 4—8 God promises to comfort his church, and we have here abundant ground of consolation set before us, from the views of the transcendently glorious and everlasting righteousness of God our Saviour

1 We are told who they are that have an interest in it *My people*, the elect of God, *my nation*, the chosen generation of Jews and Gentiles incorporated, that make one body, of which Christ is the living head, *ye that know righteousness*, are thoroughly acquainted with, and believe in the righteousness of Jesus, as wrought out for the sinner's justification, *in whose heart is my law*, faith working by love, and engaging a willing obedience to all God's commandments Reader, is this thy case ?

2 A repeated and solemn call is given to these, to hear him who speaketh from heaven, and brings to men the knowledge of salvation *Note*, They who would know God's mind and will, must be attentive to his word

3 The glad tidings Christ brings are delivered

(1) *A law shall proceed from me*, the law of the Spirit of Life, the gospel, *and I will make my judgment to rest for a light of the people*, his word shall gain a firm establishment, and be not merely the light of Israel, but of the ends of the earth

(2) In this gospel the grand object is the righteousness of the Redeemer, wrought out in behalf of his people, and the meritorious cause of the salvation, which is, in consequence thereof, bestowed upon them, *v* 5

(3) This righteousness is *near*, and this salvation *gone forth* openly preached in the word of the gospel, and is near to every sinner, from whom no previous qualifications are required whenever he receives God's record as true, that moment he becomes entitled to the salvation promised

(4) *Mine arm shall judge the people* ; either the arm of the Lord shall be revealed to them in mercy, and they shall trust upon it, as will be the case of those who embrace the proffered salvation ; or he will visit those who neglect so great a mercy, and punish them for their unbelief, *v* 5

(5) The righteousness and salvation of the Redeemer shall be eternal it is not only free for all nations, but enduring through all ages The heavens will decay, and the earth be destroyed

Before Christ 712

destroyed, but this will abide unchangeably the same When all created nature sinks in ruins, the saints of God therein arrayed, shall appear compleat before the throne of judgment, and plead this righteousness, as their only title to eternal glory, v 6

(6) They need not fear the reproaches and revilings of men, who have an interest in this righteousness and salvation they are to expect their cross, but it is their glory, not their shame

(7) Christ will silence and destroy shortly all their enemies, and when, through the ages of eternity, those who have made his righteousness their trust, shall be rejoicing in glory, they who have rejected it must lie down in torment, where their worm dieth not, and their fire is not quenched, v 8

9 ¶ [p] Awake, awake, [q] put on strength, O arm of
the LORD, awake as in the ancient days, in the gene-
rations of old [r] Art thou not it that hath cut Rahab,
[s] and wounded the dragon? 10 Art thou not it [t] which
hath dried the sea, the waters of the great deep, that
hath made the depths of the sea a way for the ransomed
to pass over? 11 Therefore [u] the redeemed of the
LORD shall return, and come [x] with singing unto Zion,
and everlasting joy shall be upon their head they shall
obtain gladness and joy, and sorrow and mourning shall
flee away 12 [y] I, even I am he that comforteth you
who art thou, [z] that thou shouldst be afraid of a man
that shall die, and of the son of man [a] which shall be
made as grass? 13 And forgettest the LORD thy
maker, [b] that hath stretched forth the heavens, and laid
the foundations of the earth? and hast feared con-
tinually every day, because of the fury of the oppressor,
as if he were ready to destroy? and [c] where is the fury
of the oppressor? 14 The captive exile hastneth, that
he may be loosed, [d] and that he should not die in the
pit, nor that his bread should fail 15 But I am the
LORD thy God, [e] that divided the sea, whose waves
roared the LORD of hosts is his name 16 And [f] I
have put my words in thy mouth, and have covered
thee in the shadow of mine hand, [g] that I may plant the
heavens, and lay the foundations of the earth, and say
unto Zion, Thou art my people

p Ps xliv 23. q Rev xi 17. r Ps lxxxix 10. s Ps lxxiv 13, 14 Chap xxvii 1 Ezek xxix 3. t Exod xiv 21 Chap lxiii 16. u Chap xxxv 10. x Chap xlvii 20. y 2 Cor i 3. z Ps cxviii 6. a Chap xl 6. 1 Pet i 24. b Job ix 8 Ps civ 2 Chap xl 22 & xlii 5 & xliv 24. c Chap xiv 4. d Zech ix 11. e Job xxvi 12 Jer xxxi 35. f Deut xviii 18 John iii 34. g Chap lxv 17 & lxvi 22 Rev xxi 1. Or, Eph i 10. Col i 20.

v 9—16 God had promised to bring near his salvation, the church immediately in prayer cries to him to hasten it in his time

1 His people pray that he would awake, and put forth his mighty power for their salvation not that he ever sleeps or slumbers, but, when the faithful are diminished and brought low, he seems to forget their distresses Confident of his power, they plead their former experience of it, when in the plagues of Egypt he made bare his arm, and, in the deliverance of Israel from that house of their prison, wrought such miracles on their behalf Confident of his love, they promise themselves a speedy answer, that he will bring them to Zion with songs, banish their sorrows, and crown them with everlasting joy, v 9—11 This may refer to the restoration of the Jews from Babylon, or to the church of Christ, when Babylon mystical is fallen And it is applicable to every believer, who here, beset with enemies, is driven to God in continual prayer for help and succour, through grace is enabled to triumph over all difficulties, and in death goes to the heavenly Zion, where all his tears will be for ever wiped away, his sorrows be eternally banished, and joy unspeakable and full of glory glow in his bosom, whilst amidst the enraptur'd hosts of saints and angels he joins in the everlasting song of a Redeemer's praise

2 God, whose ears are ever open to the prayers of his people, answers them to their utmost satisfaction I, even I am he that comforteth you, and when he, who is the fountain of mercy, and the God of all consolations, gives such an assurance, what can we need more?

(1) He comforts them under their fears Who art thou, that thou shouldst be afraid of a man that shall die, &c However the oppressors threatned, the greatest before God were but dying worms, and frail as the withering grass, and therefore their continual fears were groundless and unreasonable, v 12 Nay, they were dishonourable to God, and shewed a forgetfulness and distrust of his almighty power and grace, who hath established his church more firmly than the pillars of heaven, or the foundations of the earth, and in an instant could slay the oppressors, as in the case of Pharaoh and Sennacherib, v 13 Note, (1) A sense of the vanity of man will greatly tend to deliver us from the fear of offending in the way of our duty, for what is the wrath of a dying worm, compared with the frown of the living God? (2) We often create ourselves needless disquiet, and tremble at consequences and events which never come to pass (3) The cause of all tormenting fear is our unbelief, One thought of God, with fixed dependance upon him, would bear us above all frowns and threatnings

(2) He will loose them from their bonds The captive exile hastneth that he may be loosed it is a natural desire, and he is sollicitous for the time to come, and that he should not die in the pit, the house of his prison, nor that his bread should fail, and he be famished And such might be the fear of some of the Jews in Babylon, and is the case of the faithful at times, when under temptation they are ready to despair of themselves, but God will not suffer them to perish I am the Lord thy God, and therefore will never leave nor forsake thee, that divided the sea, whose waves roared, as when he once opened a way for his ransomed to escape out of Egypt, so will he from Babylon, and thus shall all his captive exiles be set free, whatever spiritual bondage for a time they may endure the Lord of hosts is his name, and therefore able to accomplish all his promises

(3) He will fulfil his word to the uttermost in the establishment of his church I have put my words in thy mouth, Christ, the great prophet, being authorized and sent of the Father to publish the gospel and have covered thee in the shadow of my hand, protected him, and his ministers commissioned by him to preach his word, with whom God is to the end of the world, maintaining them against all opposition, that I may plant the heavens, and lay the foundations of the earth, the gospel church, bright as the heavens in purity of doctrine and worship, and fixed and strong as the foundations of the earth, against which the gates of hell can never prevail and say unto Zion, Thou art my people, the spiritual Zion, where Jews and Gentiles, incorporated together, become one fold under one shepherd

17 ¶ [a] Awake, awake, stand up, O Jerusalem, which
[b] hast drunk at the hand of the LORD the cup of his
fury, [c] thou hast drunken the dregs of the cup of trem-
bling, and wrung them out 18 [d] There is none to guide
her among all the sons whom she hath brought forth
neither is there any that taketh her by the hand, of all
the sons that she hath brought up 19 [e] These two
things are come unto thee who shall be sorry for thee?
desolation, and destruction, and the famine, and the
sword [f] by whom shall I comfort thee? 20 [g] Thy sons
have fainted, they lie at the head of all the streets as
a wild bull in a net they are full of the fury of the
LORD, the rebuke of thy God 21 ¶ Therefore
hear now this, thou afflicted, and drunken, [h] but not with
wine 22 Thus saith thy Lord, the LORD, and
thy God [i] that pleadeth the cause of his people, Behold,
I have taken out of thine hand the cup of trembling,
even the dregs of the cup of my fury, thou shalt no
more drink it again 23. But [k] I will put it into the
hand of them that afflict thee [l] which have said to thy
soul, Bow down, that we may go over and thou hast
laid thy body as the ground, and as the street to them
that went over

a Chap lii 1. b Jer xxv 15 16. c Deut xxviii 28 Ps lx 3 Zech xii 2. d Mat ix 36. e Chap xlvii 9. f Amos vii 2. g Lam ii 11, 12. h Lam iii 15 Rev xiv 10. i Jer l 34. k Prov xi 8 Jer xxv 26, 29. l Ps lxvi 11, 12.

v 17—23 Jerusalem here appears sunk under her calamities into the stupor of despair, or, like Ezekiel's dry bones, in a state of death

1 God calls aloud, Awake, awake! and his voice can raise the dead, and rouse the soul from the depths of despair Deplorable indeed was her case, for grievous provocations she had been made to drink the cup of fury and trembling to the dregs Most awful judgments had been poured upon her, and, like one intoxicated with wine, weak and feeble, she became an easy prey to the invader, v 17 None of all her sons was able to help or support her, king, priest, and prophet had failed, v 18 Two things had come upon her, a state of abject misery, and not a friend to comfort her Famine, desolation, destruction, and the sword, had cut off all ranks, v 19 and the few who were left, though despairing, were furious, though fainting with hunger, impatient under God's rebukes, and quarrelling with his providences, instead of meekly humbling themselves for their sins, v 20 Note, (1) If judgment thus begin at the house of God, where will the ungodly and the sinner appear? (2) When we have been unfaithful to God, let it not be thought strange, if our nearest relatives prove unfaithful to us (3) None can comfort the soul, against whom God rises up in displeasure (4) Too many under God's visitations, instead of being abased by them, madly quarrel with his providences (5) They but entangle themselves the more, and add to their plagues, who struggle in his net

2 God's compassions towards them fail not though they deserve wrath to the uttermost, in the midst of judgment he remembers mercy Therefore hear now this thou afflicted, and drunken, but not with wine, stupified with the weight of calamities, and an object of God's pity Thus saith thy Lord, the Lord thy God, who, notwithstanding all provocations, hath not utterly cast off his people, nor will renounce his relation to them, that pleadeth the cause of his people, to the confusion of their enemies, Behold, I have taken out of thine hand the cup of trembling,

Before Chriſt 712

trembling, even the dregs of the cup of my fury, the puniſhment inflicted is enough *thou ſhalt no more drink it again*, the ſin forgiven, there ſhall be no more curſe *and I will put it into the hand of them that afflict thee*, of the Babylonians, and, in future time, of Babylon myſtical, *which have ſaid to thy ſoul, Bow down, that we may go over*, not only enſlaving their bodies, but tyrannizing over the ſouls of men, the diſtinguiſhing mark of the antichriſtian church, who ſet up an infallible head, and require implicit obedience *and thou haſt laid thy body as the ground, and as the ſtreet to them that went over*, reduced to the moſt abject ſtate of diſtreſs, *See Rev* xi 2 but now the time is come to vindicate their quarrel, and execute judgment on their oppreſſors *Note*, (1) It is often the caſe of God's people to be in tribulation, and greater afflictions ſeem yet to await the church, than any ſhe hath yet experienced (2) It is the ſupport of the faithful in all times of ſuffering, that they cannot be ſeparated from the love of God (3) However the cauſe of godlineſs may be oppreſſed, it will appear triumphant at the laſt (4) They who have been perſecutors of God's people, will find him the avenger of their wrongs.

CHAP LII.

This chapter contains a prophecy of the glorious ſtate of the church of Chriſt, typified by the deliverance of the Jews 1 God promiſes them a free and full ſalvation, ver 1—6 *2 There ſhall be great rejoicing upon that occaſion*, ver 7—10 *3 Thoſe that remained in captivity are called to depart, and directed how to proceed*, ver 11, 12 *4 A ſhort idea is given us of the Meſſiah, which is enlarged upon in the next chapter*, ver. 13—15

a Chap li. 17
1 [a] AWAKE, awake, put on thy ſtrength, O Zion,
put on thy beautiful garments, O Jeruſalem,
b Chap xxxv 8 & lx 21 Rev xxi 27
the holy city for [b] henceforth there ſhall no more
come into thee the uncircumciſed, and the unclean 2
Shake thyſelf from the duſt ariſe, *and* ſit down, O
c Zech. ii 7
Jeruſalem [c] looſe thyſelf from the bands of thy neck,
O captive daughter of Zion 3 For thus ſaith the
d Pſ xliv. 12 Chap xlv 13 Jer xv 13
LORD, [d] Ye have ſold yourſelves for nought and ye
e 1 Pet i 18.
ſhall be redeemed [e] without money. 4 For thus ſaith
f Gen xlvi 6
the Lord GOD, My people went down aforetime [f] into
Egypt to ſojourn there, and the Aſſyrian oppreſſed them
without cauſe. 5 Now therefore, what have I here,
ſaith the LORD, that my people is taken away for
nought? they that rule over them, make them to howl,
g Ezek xxxvi 20, 23 Rom ii 24
ſaith the LORD, and [g] my name continually every day
is blaſphemed 6 Therefore my people [h] ſhall know
h Pſ ix, 16
my name therefore *they ſhall know* in that day, that I
am he that doth ſpeak, behold, *it is* I.

v 1—6 *By an elegant figure Jeruſalem is here deſcribed as a mourner in the moſt abject diſtreſs, ſitting in the duſt, ſtripped of every ornament, waſted with ſorrow, and ready to ſleep the ſleep of death. And herein ſhe is the figure of the church, under the prevalence of Antichriſt, when the power of true religion will be reduced to the loweſt ebb In this afflicted ſtate,

1 God awakens her with his calls, bids her ariſe, and ſhake herſelf from the duſt, put on her beautiful garments, recover her decayed ſtrength, and looſe the captive bands from her neck, and what he commands, he will enable her to perform *Note*, When the calls of goſpel grace reach the ſinner, he is the deplorable captive of ſin, ſtripped of all righteouſneſs and ſtrength, and doomed to the duſt of death and hell, but, awakened by the voice of God, the beautiful garments of a Redeemer's righteouſneſs are provided for him, ſtrength miniſtered to break the band of ſin, and riſing from the duſt of ſpiritual death, he ſits down among the living ſaints of God

2 He promiſes to preſerve her from the future power of her enemies *For henceforth there ſhall no more come into thee the uncircumciſed, and the unclean*, which can only agree with Jeruſalem myſtical, the church of God in the latter day, *See Rev* xxi 27 ſince Jeruſalem, after the return from the captivity, was profaned by Antiochus and the Romans, and is poſſeſſed by the Turks at this day

3 God will redeem his Iſrael freely *Ye have ſold yourſelves for nought*; for whatever pleaſure and enjoyment ſin promiſes, miſery and vanity are found the only fruits of it *and ye ſhall be redeemed without money*, corruptible things, ſuch as ſilver and gold, were of no avail to redeem the ſoul, but the precious blood of Chriſt alone, and though the purchaſe was dearly made by him, yet the ſalvation obtained by his bloodſhedding comes to us entirely free, without money and without price

4 The Lord will magnify his own glory in the deliverance of his people from the antichriſtian bondage, as he did of old *from the priſon of Egypt*, when the Jews, who went to ſojourn there, were oppreſſed, and as he reſcued them from the yoke of the Aſſyrians, who unreaſonably and cruelly afflicted them, *v* 4. God's glory ſuffered whilſt they were enſlaved tyrannically treated, they howled for anguiſh, and their proud maſters, far from acknowledging God in their conqueſts, blaſphemed his name, as if unable to deliver them, *v* 5 *Therefore* he will make his glory appear, and his people ſhall know his ſalvation, and acknowledge, in the day of their deliverance, the faithfulneſs of God in his promiſes, *v* 6 Thus when Babylon myſtical is fallen, then Jeſus will be eſpecially adored by his redeemed, as the faithful and true witneſs

7 ¶ [i] How beautiful upon the mountains are the feet i Nah i 15. Rom x 15.
of him that bringeth good tidings, that publiſheth peace,
that bringeth [k] good tidings of good, that publiſheth k Luke ii 10
ſalvation, that ſaith unto Zion, [l] Thy God reigneth! l Pſ xciii 1
8 Thy [m] watchmen ſhall lift up the voice, with the voice xcvi 10. & xcvii 1
together ſhall they ſing for they ſhall ſee eye to eye, Mic iv 7
when the LORD ſhall bring again Zion. 9 ¶ Break Rev xi 15
forth into joy, ſing together, ye waſte places of Jeruſa- m Ezek iii. 17
lem for the LORD hath comforted his people, he
hath redeemed Jeruſalem 10 The LORD hath made
bare his holy arm in the eyes of all the nations, and
[n] all the ends of the earth ſhall ſee the ſalvation of our n Pſ xcviii 3 Luke iii. 6
God 11 ¶ [o] Depart ye, depart ye, go ye out from
thence, touch no unclean *thing*, go ye out of the midſt o Chap xlviii 20.
of her, be ye clean that bear the veſſels of the LORD Jer l 8 & li 6, 45
12 For [p] ye ſhall not go out with haſte, nor go by 2 Cor vi. 17 Rev. xviii 4.
flight for [q] the LORD will go before you and the p Exod xii 33, 39
God of Iſrael *will be* your rere-ward q Exod xiv. 21 Mic. ii 13 r Num x 25 Chap. lviii 8

v 7—12 Great was the joy which Cyrus's proclamation occaſioned, and happy were the Jews to ſpread the report, but the Apoſtle, *Rom* x 15 plainly intimates, that a greater cauſe of joy is here ſignified, even the coming of Chriſt, and the preaching of his goſpel, to which theſe words are to be referred

1 A bleſſed meſſenger is ſent publiſhing the happieſt tidings which ever greeted mortal ear Some refer this to John the Baptiſt, but it may well be applied to the Redeemer himſelf and his apoſtles The tidings they bring are *tidings of peace, tidings of good things, tidings of ſalvation*, pardon of ſin obtained, God's favour reſtored, victory over our ſpiritual foes, deliverance from the bondage of corruption, and, above all, *our God reigneth*, Jeſus is riſen, is aſcended up on high, hath led captivity captive, ſits on the throne of glory to bleſs, preſerve, protect his people, and bring them to be with him, where he is, that they may behold his glory Theſe are the tidings publiſhed *in the mountains* publickly, and beautiful are the feet of thoſe who bring them, worthy to be had in honour for their works ſake

2 With greateſt joy the meſſage is received *Thy watchmen*, the miniſters of the goſpel, *ſhall lift up the voice*, and publiſh aloud the glad news that is arrived of pardon, peace, and ſalvation through Jeſus *With the voice together ſhall they ſing*, with delight and joy ſhall they execute their miniſtry *for they ſhall ſee eye to eye*, clearly and diſtinctly, the great truths they are authorized to proclaim, ſo as to have the fulleſt conviction of them in their own ſouls, *when the Lord ſhall bring again Zion*, revive his work, enlarge his church, and by an abundant outpouring of his Spirit in the latter day, call in Jews as well as Gentiles to the communion of his ſaints

3 The waſte places of Jeruſalem are called upon to rejoice and ſing for this great and general redemption Long had deſolations been ſpread around, but now God will build up her breaches *For the Lord hath comforted his people*, with the diſcoveries of his rich grace in the goſpel of his Son *he hath redeemed Jeruſalem*, his church, by the offering of the body of Jeſus once for all And this ſalvation now no longer, as of old, is confined to one peculiar people, but *the Lord hath made bare his holy arm in the eyes of all the nations*, diſplayed his power and holineſs in the work of the Redeemer, *and all the ends of the earth ſhall ſee the ſalvation of our God* manifeſt in the fleſh, whoſe redemption is univerſal, not confined to one nation or people, but free for all, whoſoever will, may come and partake of it *Note*, The ſubject of redeeming love will afford matter for praiſe that never will be exhauſted

4 An inſtant and urgent command is given to *depart*, and the Lord himſelf promiſes to be *their rere-ward*, that their march may be ſafe and uninterrupted This may primarily refer to the return from Babylon, but is applied by the apoſtle, 2 *Cor* vi 17 to the ſeparation from ſin and idolatry, which, by the preaching of the goſpel, would be effected in the Gentile world *Depart ye, depart ye*, make no delay *go ye out from thence*, from the kingdom of darkneſs *touch no unclean thing*, keep back no allowed ſin, nor have fellowſhip with the workers of iniquity *go ye out of the midſt of her*, of Babylon, or rather the houſe of Satan's bondage *be clean, ye that bear the veſſels of the Lord*, not merely be ceremonially clean, ye Jewiſh prieſts, who bear the veſſels of the ſanctuary Cyrus reſtored

le

Before Christ 712.

It belongs rather to gospel ministers, whose purity of life must adorn the doctrines they preach, or to every Christian who is consecrated a priest unto God, and keeps himself pure in his ordinances and worship *For ye shall not go out with haste, nor go by flight*, but openly, and boldly casting off the yoke of sin, and asserting their glorious liberty wherewith Christ hath made them free, *for the Lord will go before you*, as in the pillar of fire of old, to guide and lead you safe from every danger, *and the God of Israel will be their rere-ward*, so that, though Satan pursues with all his power and wiles, he shall never be able to bring back to the house of his prison one soul which Jesus hath redeemed He will keep them in all their journey, and bring them safe with himself to the inheritance provided for them in glory May we trust in him, and chearfully and steadily hold on, and hold out!

13 ¶ Behold ' my servant shall † deal prudently,
' he shall be exalted and extolled, and be very high
14 As many were astonished at thee, (his ' visage was
so marred more than any man, and his form more than
the sons of men) 15 * So shall he sprinkle many na-
tions, ' the kings shall ' shut their mouths at him for
* that which had not been told them, shall they see, and
that which they had not heard, shall they consider

* Chap xlii 1 † Or prosper Chap lii 10 Jer xxiii 5 ‖ Phil ii 9 ‖ Chap liii 2 * Ezek xxxvi 25 Acts ii 33 Heb x 22 1 Pet i 2 ‖ Chap xlix 7 Job xxix 9 10 & xl ‖ Rom xv 21

v 13—15 These three verses, with the following chapter, set forth the person, offices, humiliation, and exaltation of the Lord Christ, and may justly be reckoned among the clearest prophecies of the sufferings of the son of God, and of the glory which should follow

1 God points him out to our notice and regard *Behold! my servant*, appointed and commissioned for the work of redemption, and fully qualified for it, he *shall deal prudently*, with unerring wisdom ordering all his ways or, he *shall prosper* in all his undertakings, and accomplish thoroughly the salvation of his people

2 His humiliation and exaltation are described [1] *His humiliation* *As many were astonished at thee*, to see him who was so high, abased so low to the form of a servant, to the death of a malefactor *His visage was so marred more than any man, and his form more than the sons of men*, though fairer than the children of men, yet worn down with sorrows, like unto which were no sorrows, his temples pierced with thorns, his face buffeted and spit upon, the form of his countenance was changed, and he appeared a spectacle of woe [2] *His exaltation* *He shall be exalted*, by his resurrection from the dead, ascension into heaven, and session on the throne of glory, *and extolled*, men and angels shall adore him *and be very high*, all things in heaven and earth being made subject unto him *So shall he sprinkle many nations*, by the word of his gospel, *See Deut* xxxii 2 and the effusion of his Spirit, which he sent down from on high, by the application of his blood to men's consciences, and by the ordinance of baptism, which he instituted as the sign and seal of admission into his kingdom *The kings shall shut their mouths at him*, with reverence silent before him, and submissive to his will *for that which had not been told them, shall they see, and that which they had not heard, shall they consider*, the glorious truths hid from ages and generations, which the light of nature could not teach, nor any of their wise men and philosophers discover, concerning the trinity in unity, the incarnation of Jesus, the justification of the sinner through his atonement and righteousness, the resurrection of the body, and the like; these by the preaching of the gospel were brought to light, and they now became acquainted with *the unknown God*, and saw his glorious salvation in the Redeemer

C H A P LIII

That Christ ought to suffer, and then enter into his glory, Luke xxiv 26, 27 *according to the word of prophecy, we see clearly in this chapter, where we may observe, 1 The reproach of Christ's sufferings, the meanness of his appearance, the greatness of his grief, and the prejudices which many conceived from thence against his doctrine*, ver 1—3 2 *The rolling away of this reproach, and the conferring of an immortal honour upon his sufferings, notwithstanding the infamy and ignominy of them, by four considerations* (1) *That therein he did his Father's will*, ver 4, 6, 10 (2) *That thereby he made atonement for the sin of man*, ver 4, 5, 6, 8 11, 12 *For it was not for any sin of his own that he suffered*, ver 9 (3) *That he bore his sufferings with an invincible and exemplary patience* ver 7 (4) *That he should prosper in his undertaking, and his sufferings should end in his immortal honour*, ver 10—12

‖ John xii 38 Rom x 16 ‖ Or doctrine ‖ Chap lii 10 ‖ Chap xi 1

1 * WHO hath believed our ‖ report? and to
whom is ' the arm of the LORD revealed?
2 For ' he shall grow up before him as a tender plant,
and as a root out of a dry ground ' he hath no form
nor comeliness and when we shall see him, *there is* no
beauty that we should desire him 3 ' He is despised
and rejected of men, a man of sorrows, ' and acquainted
with grief and ‡ we hid as it were *our* faces from him,
he was despised, and ' we esteemed him not

Before Christ 712. ' Chap lii 14 ' Ps xxii 6 Chap xlix 7 & liii 14 ' Heb iv 15 ‡ Or he hid as it were his face from us ' John i 10, 11

v 1—3 Whilst Gentile nations and kings with wonder heard and believed the gospel word, the Jews, obstinate in unbelief, rejected the counsel of God against their own souls

1 The chapter opens with a complaint against them for rejecting the gospel *Who hath believed our report? and to whom is the arm of the Lord revealed?* Wondrous as the miracles were which Jesus wrought, and powerful as the doctrine was he taught, yet very few embraced it, and in general they shut their eyes against all evidence, and would not hear nor understand *Note*, (1) Of multitudes that still hear the gospel word, few receive it in the light and love of it (2) Till the Spirit of God give an inward revelation of Jesus to the soul, the most powerful preaching will be ineffectual

2 The reason of their disregard to Christ was the meanness of his appearance *For he shall grow up before him as a tender plant*, or *sucker*, which every foot might crush, *and as a root out of a dry ground*, or a branch of *a root*, that for want of moisture is withered, and stinted in its growth, his family being reduced to the meanest circumstances, and nothing great was hoped for out of Nazareth *He hath no form nor comeliness*, either respecting his person, which was not distinguished by beauty, or any extraordinary majesty, as might be expected in the countenance of God incarnate, or rather his appearance was unpromising, brought up in a mean cottage, his dress agreeable to his station, his followers poor fishermen, and in every respect unlike the personage which the carnal Jews expected *And when we shall see him, there is no beauty that we should desire him*, no pomp, no splendor attending him, but poor and abject in their eyes, they could not desire him as the Messiah, who seemed so unable to rescue them from the Roman yoke *He is despised*, as a person mean and contemptible, *and rejected of men*, his pretensions treated with disdain, and his company shunned as ignominious or, *destitute of men*, no persons of distinction, no rulers or pharisees, believing on him, or following him as his disciples *a man of sorrows, and acquainted with grief*, his whole life, especially from the time he entered on his ministry, being a scene of troubles, from the temptations of Satan, and the malice of his persecutors, whilst his own heart, affected with human miseries, groaned over the desolations of his enemies, which he foresaw, and caused the tears of tenderest compassion to flow above all, the wrath of God, which our sins had deserved, was laid upon him, and filled his soul with bitterest anguish *And we hid as it were our faces from him*, as a loathsome object *he was despised, and we esteemed him not*, all consented to treat him with disregard, and to reject his claim as the Messiah But let not the humiliations of Jesus make him appear little in our eyes, never were his grace and glory more manifested; never did he appear more lovely, than when for our sakes he stooped so low, to make satisfaction for the dishonour we had brought on God by our sins, and by humbling himself to obtain our exaltation

4 ¶ Surely ' he hath born our griefs, and carried our
sorrows yet we did esteem him stricken, smitten of
God, and afflicted 5 But ' he *was* ‖ wounded for our
transgressions, he was bruised for our iniquities ' the
chastisement of our peace *was* upon him, and ' with his
‖ stripes we are healed 6 ' All we like sheep have gone
astray we have turned every one to his own way, and
the LORD hath § laid on him the iniquity of us all
7 He was oppressed, and he was afflicted, yet ' he
opened not his mouth ' he is brought as a lamb to the
slaughter, and as a sheep before her shearers is dumb,
so he openeth not his mouth 8 He was taken ‖ from
prison and from judgment and ' who shall declare his
‖ generation? for ' he was cut off out of the land of the
living for the transgression of my people was he stricken
9 And ' he made his grave with the wicked, and with
the rich in his death, because he had done no violence,
' neither *was any* deceit in his mouth

' Mat viii 17 ' Pet ii 24 ' Rom iv 25 1 Cor xv 3 ‖ Or, tormented ' Rom iii 25 2 Cor v 19 1 Pet ii 24 ‖ Or bruise ' Ps cxix 176 1 Pet ii 25 § Heb Made to meet ' Mat xxvi 63 & xxvii 12, 14 ' Acts viii 32 ‖ Or by distress and judgment ‖ Rev vii 9 ‖ Or, ' Dan ix 26 ' Mat xxvii 57 58 ' 1 Pet ii 22 1 John iii 5

v 4—9 We have a further account of the Redeemer's sufferings

1 The cause of them, our sins and transgressions, *v* 5 by which God had been dishonoured, his wrath provoked, and our souls lost and undone, and this universally the case, for *all we like sheep have gone astray*, from the womb, foolish, disobedient, deceived, in nature corrupt, and in all our ways perverse before God *We have turned every one to his own way*, fulfilling the desires of the flesh and of the mind, and each, as inclination led, pursuing with wilful perseverance the iniquity which most

Before Christ 712.

moſt eaſily beſet him *Note*, We can never know Chriſt aright, nor the wonders of his grace, till we become acquainted with our fallen ſtate, and ſee the depths of ſin in which we were by nature and practice ſunk irrecoverably, but for his interpoſition

2 The nature of them Griefs and ſorrows, like unto which were no ſorrows, reckoned by his enemies as the abhorred of God, and all his ſufferings reputed as juſt judgments for his crimes, *v* 4 *Wounded* with the thorns, the nails the ſpear, bruiſed with ſtrokes and buffetings, his back ploughed up with *ſtripes* and ſcourgings, *v* 5 *Oppreſſed*, though innocent, condemned as guilty, *afflicted* with every ſpecies of miſery and woe, *v* 7 and ending his days on the croſs, a death the moſt painful, ignominious, and accurſed, *v* 8

3 His behaviour under his ſufferings, and his innocence *He opened not his mouth*, except in prayers for his murderers no complaint was heard of their injuſtice or cruelty *He is brought as a lamb to the ſlaughter, and as a ſheep before her ſhearers is dumb, ſo he openeth not his mouth*, and of him we muſt learn the like patient ſilence before our bittereſt perſecutors *And he made his grave with the wicked, and with the rich in his death* it was intended he ſhould be buried, as well as die, with malefactors, but God ordered it otherwiſe, though his death was with the wicked, his grave was with the rich, Joſeph of Arimathea laying his body in his *own new tomb*, and this honour was done him, *becauſe he had done no violence, neither was guile found in his mouth* though he was accuſed as an enemy to the ſtate, a mover of ſedition, and deceiver of the people, the charge was infamous and falſe He was holy, harmleſs, undefiled, and ſeparate from ſinners, and, from the cradle to the grave, in ſpotleſs innocence always did the things which pleaſed his Father, and was thereby qualified to bear the ſins of others, having of his own none to anſwer for

4 The end and deſign of his ſufferings was to make atonement for the ſins of his people, and by paying the penalty due to them, thereby to obtain their diſcharge *He hath borne our griefs, and carried our ſorrows* he not only healed the diſeaſes of men's bodies, touched with tender ſympathy for their ſuffering, See *Mat* viii 17 but the griefs and ſorrows due to our ſins he took upon himſelf *The Lord laid upon him the iniquity of us all*, appointed him as the ſinner's ſubſtitute, and conſented to accept his ſufferings in their ſtead, and having made him to be ſin for us, *He was ſtricken and ſmitten of God*, with the ſword of divine juſtice, *for the tranſgreſſion of my people was he ſtricken*, ſtanding in their name and character, the wrath of God they had provoked lighted upon his devoted head Hence *he was wounded for our tranſgreſſions, he was bruiſed for our iniquities, the chaſtiſement of our peace was upon him, and by his ſtripes we are healed* Great, numberleſs, aggravated, were the ſins of his people, wide, and irreparable by any human means, the breach made between God and us But lo! Jeſus hath found a ranſom a bleſſed commutation is made of our guilt, miſery, and ſin to our Redeemer, of his infinite merits to us, bringing pardon, peace, and healing to our periſhing ſouls, in virtue of his ſufferings and death on our behalf This is a pleaſing theme, upon it we can never ſufficiently dwell, for on this all our everlaſting hopes depend We may obſerve here, (1) The encouragement given to the chief of ſinners, *that come to God by him*, *Heb* vii 25 If Jeſus, as the ſcape goat in the day of expiation, hath borne *all* our iniquities, then we are aſſured of redemption through his blood, even the forgiveneſs of ſins (2) This is God's own conſtitution, accepting the juſt for the unjuſt, and therefore we may with perfect ſatiſfaction reſt therein (3) The vicarious ſubſtitution of the Saviour's obedience unto death in the ſinner's ſtead, is the grand peculiarity, and the diſtinguiſhing glory of the goſpel diſpenſation

5 God teſtified his approbation and ſatiſfaction of the Redeemer's undertaking by raiſing him from the dead *He was taken from priſon, and from judgment, and who ſhall declare his generation?* which ſome interpret of the wrong done him in the unjuſt ſentence paſſed upon him, when, as a malefactor, he was condemned at Pilate's tribunal, and crucified by the men of that generation, whoſe cruelty and inhumanity are paſt deſcription But it may better refer to his glorious reſurrection he had been conſigned to the grave, under the juſt ſentence of death due to our iniquities, and on his reſurrection from thence reſted the grand proof of the ſufficiency of the ſatiſfaction he had made for ſin, God therefore on the third day ſent his angel as the officer to diſcharge him from the priſon of the grave, the judgment paſſed and executed upon him having fully reſtored the honour of God's government, violated by the ſin of man, and therefore it was impoſſible he ſhould be holden longer of death He is raiſed therefore for our eternal juſtification; *and who can declare his generation?* ſince death hath now no more dominion over him, and he hath obtained for himſelf and his redeemed, whom no man can number, an eternity of glory

10 ¶ Yet it pleaſed the LORD to bruiſe him, he
hath put *him* to grief when † thou ſhalt make his ſoul
an offering for ſin, he ſhall ſee *his* ſeed, he ſhall pro
long *his* days, and the pleaſure of the LORD ſhall
proſper in his hand 11 He ſhall ſee of the travel of
his ſoul, *and* ſhall be ſatisfied [u] by his knowledge ſhall
[x] my righteous ſervant juſtify many for [y] he ſhall bear
their iniquities 12 [z] Therefore will I divide him *a*
portion with the great, and [a] he ſhall divide the ſpoil with
the ſtrong becauſe he hath poured out his ſoul unto
death and [b] he was numbered with the tranſgreſſors,
and he bare the ſin of many, [c] and made interceſſion for
the tranſgreſſors

† Or, When thou ſhalt make [illegible]

Before Chriſt 712.

u John xvii 3
x Chap xlii 1
y Ver 5.
z Pſ ii 8 Or, Phil ii 9
a Col ii 15
b Mark xv 28 Luke xxii 37
c Luke xxiii 34 Rom. viii 34 Heb vii 25 & ix 24 1 John ii 1

v 10—12 Theſe words are by ſome connected with the foregoing verſe, thus, *Though he had done no violence*, &c *yet it pleaſed the Lord to bruiſe him*, and they contain the ſame ſubject as was before treated of, the ſufferings of Chriſt, and the glory which ſhould follow

1 His ſufferings *It pleaſed the Lord to bruiſe him*, exacting from him the puniſhment due to our iniquities *He hath put him to grief*, Jeſus, in his human nature, enduring the ſevereſt anguiſh in his body, and agony in his ſoul, when he ſubſtituted himſelf in our ſtead, and made *his ſoul an offering for ſin*, yielding up himſelf to ſuffer, not of conſtraint, but freely and willingly and ſince ſuch was the demand of juſtice, that nothing but the Saviour's life could ſatisfy for the ſinner, *he poured out his ſoul unto death*, as a libation, ſhedding his blood for the remiſſion of ſin *And he was numbered with the tranſgreſſors*, not only as he was reviled as ſuch, and joined with them at his crucifixion, but as *he bore the ſins of many*, died under the imputation of their guilt, *and made interceſſion for the tranſgreſſors*, when on the croſs he cried, "Father, forgive them," and this in virtue of thoſe very ſufferings he there endured, which were then, are now, and ever, the only effectual plea on which forgiveneſs of ſin can be obtained

2 His glory, in virtue of theſe ſufferings, which was engaged for in the covenant of redemption, and for the ſake of which he endured the croſs, deſpiſing the ſhame We have here ſeveral particulars of this glory

[1] *He ſhall ſee his ſeed*, he ſhall not die in vain, or be uncertain about the effects of his oblation a ſpiritual ſeed is given him, a people who ſhall call him father, and *he ſhall prolong his days*, himſelf ſhall live for evermore, and ſee the children of his grace all brought home to him in time, and gathered to him in eternity, to reign with him in glory everlaſting

[2] *The pleaſure of the Lord ſhall proſper in his hand*, the work of man's redemption, in which God delights, ſhall be effectually accompliſhed by him, to his Father's glory, his own everlaſting praiſe, and our eternal comfort

[3] *He ſhall ſee of the travail of his ſoul, and be ſatisfied*, his pangs ſhall not prove abortive, but with fulleſt ſatisfaction to his ſoul he ſhall behold all thoſe the Father hath given him, with him in glory, and not one loſt of the innumerable multitude *Note*, (1) The ardent longing of the Redeemer after his people, and the travail he bore for them well may we ſay, Behold, how he loved them! (2) The certainty of the ſalvation of all for whom Chriſt died, ſince he is ſatisfied in the fruit of his labour

[4] *By his knowledge ſhall my righteous ſervant juſtify many for he ſhall bear their iniquities* He is *righteous* himſelf, and the author of everlaſting righteouſneſs to his redeemed They are *juſtified*, acquitted at God's bar from every accuſation, for their ſins have been borne in Chriſt's body on the tree, and *many* declared perfectly righteous, and therefore entitled to all the bleſſings of obedience, as found in Chriſt, and compleat in him They are *many*, not all mankind, but as many as the Lord our God hath choſen, and beſtowed on his dear Son The way in which they become poſſeſſed of the bleſſing of juſtification to life, is by the *knowledge of him*, becoming acquainted with his character and tranſactions, and receiving the record which God has given of his Son, no qualification or previous good diſpoſitions in us being at all required, for we are to be ſaved by grace alone It is enough that we ſee the fulneſs of Jeſus to ſupply our wants, and are content to reſt our ſouls on his finiſhed ſalvation this is to give him the glory due to his name

[5] His kingdom ſhall be great, his ſubjects numerous, *therefore will I divide him a portion with the great, and he ſhall divide the ſpoil with the ſtrong*, as ſome mighty conqueror, that by his arms ſubdues the nations under him, and takes their ſpoils Or, *I will allot him a multitude of nations*, and *for a prey many ſhall fall to his ſhare*, even very many of all nations, kindred, tongues, and people, brought by the preaching of the goſpel to the obedience of the faith *Note*, (1) Every redeemed ſoul is Chriſt's ſpoil, reſcued out of the hands of Satan, ſin, and death (2) Though there may be but few faithful in any age or place, yet when they ſhall be collected together at the laſt day they will appear an hoſt that no man can number

Before Christ 712

CHAP LIV

The death of Christ is the life of the church, and of all that truly belong to it, and therefore very fitly, after the prophet had foretold the sufferings of Christ, he foretels the flourishing of the church, which is a part of his glory Whatever reference this hath to the Jewish church, it is evident, Gal iv 26, 27 *that it looks farther to the church of Christ among the Gentiles* 1 *God promises, that though she had hitherto been in a state of widowhood, he would, as an husband, give her a numerous offspring,* ver 1—5 2 *That though sometimes he might seem to withdraw from her, and suspend the tokens of his favour, yet he would return in mercy, and not contend with her any more,* ver 6—10 3 *That though for a while she was in sorrow, and under oppression, yet she should at length be advanced to greater honour and splendor than ever,* ver 11, 12 4 *That knowledge, righteousness, and peace, should flourish and prevail,* ver 13, 14 5 *That all attempts against the church should be baffled, and she secured from the malice of her enemies,* ver 14—17

a Zeph iii 14 Gal iv 27 b 1 Sam ii 5 c Chap. xlix 20. d Chap. lv 5 & lxi 9 e Jer iii 14 Eph v 25 f Chap. xlviii 4

1 [a] SING, O barren, thou *that* didst not bear, break
forth into singing, and cry aloud, thou *that* didst
not travail with child for [b] more *are* the children of the
desolate, than the children of the married wife, saith the
LORD 2 [c] Enlarge the place of thy tent, and let
them stretch forth the curtains of thine habitations spare
not, lengthen thy cords, and strengthen thy stakes 3
For thou shalt break forth on the right hand, and on
the left, and [d] thy seed shall inherit the Gentiles, and
make the desolate cities to be inhabited 4 Fear not,
for thou shalt not be ashamed neither be thou confounded,
for thou shalt not be put to shame for thou
shalt forget the shame of thy youth, and shalt not remember
the reproach of thy widowhood any more 5
For [e] thy maker *is* thine husband, (the LORD of hosts
is his name) and [f] thy redeemer the holy One of Israel,
the God of the whole earth shall he be called

v 1—5 Jerusalem, during her captivity, like a widow bereaved of her children, lamented her sad desolations, but when God restored her palaces they were quickly repeopled, and they soon, under the divine blessing, increased exceedingly But this prophecy seems more particularly to relate to the gospel church, and the quotation the apostle makes, *Gal* iv 26 is the sure key for the interpretation of it We have here,

1 The low estate of the church, signified by a barren woman, or one desolate, bereft of husband and children, which may fitly represent her state when Christ came into the world, and till the day of Pentecost, when the Gentiles universally were in blindness, and among the Jews very few received the gospel he preached unto them

2 The joy arising from the glorious increase which should be made to the church, by the preaching of the apostles, and in future times *More are the children of the desolate,* the Gentiles, *than the children of the married wife,* in which relation the Jewish church had stood, and few of them, comparatively, believed *Enlarge the place of thy tent, and let them stretch forth the curtains of thine habitations,* the church of old being reduced within so small a compass, but now, by the accession of the Gentile converts, it spreads on every side, therefore, *spare not, lengthen thy cords, and strengthen thy stakes,* where the same image of a tent, to which the church is compared before, is continued, and the ministers are especially called upon to spare no labour or pains, but to spread abroad the gospel, and confirm the disciples, that they may grow stronger in faith, as they grew more numerous, and God promises abundantly to bless their labours, *v* 3 *Note,* (1) It is a matter of great joy to every true member of Christ, to see his kingdom flourish, and his gospel preached (2) They who enjoy fewer means and ordinances are yet often seen to exceed others in their growth in grace, who possess much greater privileges (3) It will be the labour of every faithful soul, to lengthen the cords, and strengthen the stakes, to spread the knowledge of Christ, and build up each other on their most holy faith

3 The Lord encourages his church against all fear and shame Unlikely as such a work appeared, she may trust God's promise, and wait confidently the accomplishment *For thou shalt forget the shame of thy youth,* &c when her members were few, and none of the wise and noble embraced the gospel, but quickly the scene was changed, when the Roman empire became Christian, and men of all ranks embraced the religion of Jesus

4 The blessed author of this happy change is Christ, the Maker, Husband, and Redeemer of his church, for in these glorious and endeared relations he stands, able to the uttermost to protect and preserve her, as the Lord of hosts, faithful to his promises, as the holy One of Israel, and having universal dominion, as the God of the whole earth, to enlarge her borders according to the counsel of his own will *Note,* (1) There is a union between Christ and believing souls nearer than that between husband and wife they indeed are one body, but he that is joined to the Lord is one spirit (2) If our Maker be our husband, then we are deeply bound in love and duty to approve our fidelity to him (3) Our Redeemer is mighty, and the more firmly we trust him, the more surely we shall stand

g Chap lxii 4 h Jer iii 1 Ezek xvi 8 i Pf xxx 5 Chap xxvi 20 2 Cor iv 17 k Deut xxxii 20 Chap viii 17 & lvii 17 l Jer xxxi 3 m Gen ix 11 n Chap lv 11 Jer xxxi 36 o Pf xlvi 2 Mat v 18 p Chap li 6 q Eph ii 4 Tit iii 5

6 For the LORD [g] hath called thee as a woman
forsaken and grieved in spirit, [h] and a wife of youth,
when thou wast refused, saith thy God 7 [i] For a
small moment have I forsaken thee, but with great
mercies will I gather thee 8 In a little wrath [k] I hid
my face from thee, for a moment, [l] but with everlasting
kindness will I have mercy on thee, saith the LORD
thy Redeemer 9 For this *is as* the waters of Noah
unto me for *as* [m] I have sworn that the waters of
Noah should no more go over the earth, [n] so have I
sworn that I would not be wroth with thee, nor rebuke
thee 10 For [o] the mountains shall depart, and the
hills be removed, [p] but my kindness shall not depart
from thee, neither shall the covenant of my peace be removed,
saith the LORD [q] that hath mercy on thee.

v 6—10 We have here, comfort promised to the disconsolate church of God

1 She is represented by a woman forsaken of her husband, either dead, or divorced by him, and grieved at parting, and as a wife of youth refused, which made the separation more painful And this seems to regard the state of the church, when, at the beginning, Christ was taken away by death, and the disciples were so disconsolate or it describes the distress which ensued on the first publishing of the gospel, when so many of the preachers and professors were cut off by the sword of persecution, which is signified by the little wrath, *boiling wrath,* as the word means, *v* 8 when God's face was hid, and for *a small moment* he seemed to *forsake* his people, *v* 7 *Note,* (1) A child of God may be at times in great bitterness of soul, under the sense of his displeasure (2) Whatever we feel of chastisement, we must own it little, in comparison of what we have deserved (3) We must not be discouraged under present afflictions, however sharp, they are but for a moment, a little faith and patience will bring us through them

2 God promises a gracious return of mercy *With great mercies will I gather thee,* from the dispersion during the persecutions, as was fulfilled in the days of Constantine, when the profession of Christianity was established peaceably throughout the Roman empire Yea, *With everlasting kindness will I have mercy on thee, saith the Lord thy Redeemer,* for all his dispensations, however dark for a season they may appear, are perfectly consistent with his everlasting love towards his people and because of the relation he stands in towards them as their Redeemer, he will not suffer any of his chosen to perish *Note,* (1) It is purely of the Lord's mercies we are not consumed, and not for any desert in us (2) Nothing can be a more reviving consideration to the dejected heart, than that God's kindness is everlasting, and though he may cast us down with affliction, he will not cast us off in displeasure (3) Our present sufferings, however severe, are, comparatively with what we deserve, light and momentary, but they will be succeeded with a far more exceeding and eternal weight of glory

3 To confirm the faith of his people in the immutability of his counsel of peace with them, and the perpetuity of his regard, he confirms it by an oath As he engaged to Noah, that the waters should never again deluge the earth, so hath he sworn to his people, that he will never in wrath rebuke them, so as to cast them off utterly, or renounce his relation to them, *v* 9 and sooner shall the mountains that lift their summits to the skies be removed, or all the mightiest monarchies of the earth, prefigured by these, be dissolved, than his kindness depart, or his covenant of peace fail yea, when these mountains are departed, the hills fled, and all created nature sunk in ruins, still the everlasting covenant of peace shall stand, *saith the Lord that hath mercy on thee* As it springs from the mercy of God, not the merits of man, the fulfilment of it is sure for ever, for he changeth not

r Rev xxi 6 s 1 Chron xxix 2 Rev xxi 18, &c t Chap. xi 9 Jer xxxi 34 John vi 45 1 John ii 27 u Pf cxix 165 Chap xlviii 18

11 ¶ O thou [r] afflicted, tossed with tempest, *and* not
comforted, behold, I will lay thy stones [s] with fair colours,
and lay thy foundations with sapphires 12 And
I will make thy windows of agates, and thy gates of
carbuncles, and all thy borders of pleasant stones 13
And all thy children *shall be* [t] taught of the LORD,
and [u] great *shall be* the peace of thy children. 14 In
righteousness shalt thou be established thou shalt be far
from oppression, for thou shalt not fear, and from terror,
for it shall not come near thee 15. Behold, they
shall

Before Christ 712

shall surely gather together, *but* not by me [x] whosoever
shall gather together against thee, shall fall for thy sake
16 Behold, I have created the smith that bloweth the
coals in the fire, and that bringeth forth an instrument
for his work, and I have created the waster to destroy.
17 ¶ No weapon that is formed against thee shall prosper, and [y] every tongue *that* shall rise against thee in
judgment, thou shalt condemn This *is* the heritage of
the servants of the LORD, and [z] their righteousness *is*
of me, saith the LORD

x Ps xxxvii 1—15
y Chap l 8 Acts vi 10 Rom viii 33
z 1 Cor v [illegible]

v 11—17 Glorious things are spoken of thee, O thou city of God! We have,

1 The church in distress *O thou afflicted*, with persecutions without, and heretical teachers within or, *O thou indigent* (for of the poor the church ever chiefly consisted), *and tossed with tempests*, as a feeble bark, ready to be swallowed up in the stormy billows, *and not comforted*, no kind friend to support, no magistrate to protect her from oppression, as was the case under the pagan emperors, and is still under the papal tyranny; but God will be his people's everlasting friend, and never leave nor forsake them Therefore,

2 He engages to raise up his church, a glorious church, and set it above the enmity of every foe

[1] He will raise it up a glorious church The foundations, pavement, windows, gates, shall be of the most precious jewels, emblematical of Christ, and the gifts and graces of his Spirit, which should be abundantly dispensed, compared with which, all the splendor of this world's brightest gems vanishes, as the stars before the rising sun Particularly, 1 Divine wisdom shall be plentifully dispensed *All thy children shall be taught of the Lord*, not only by the word and the ministry, but by the illumination of the Spirit of truth, who shall lead them into all truth, opening their understandings, and giving them that experimental knowledge of Jesus and his salvation, which no other teacher can communicate to the soul 2 Abundance of peace shall be diffused *Great shall be the peace of thy children*, internal peace of conscience from a sense of God's love, external peace and harmony among the faithful, when, loving each other out of a pure heart fervently, all contentions and disputes shall be for ever banished 3 *In righteousness shalt thou be established*, in the doctrine of justification by the righteousness of Jesus and in the practice of holiness, the blessed fruit and effect of it, which is the great ornament and support of the church, and without which it must quickly decay

[2] No foe shall be able to prevail against her, God will defend her, 1 From all *fear and terror* *Thou shalt be far from oppression, for thou shalt not fear, and from terror, for it shall not come near thee* However great the fury and threatening of the oppressors, God will not only restrain their violence, but keep the mind of his people in perfect peace, whilst stayed upon him, and a great mercy it is to be delivered from the power of tormenting fear 2 Every attempt made against them should end in the destruction of their enemies *Behold, they shall surely gather together* the enmity of Satan and the world is implacable against the saints, and they will seek to trouble them [illegible] *but not by me*, [illegible] they have God against them, their designs must prove abortive *Whosoever shall gather together against thee, shall fall for thy sake*, be they never so mighty, or numerous, they rush only on their own ruin, God in love to his people will cast them down 3 As all the power which wicked men possess comes from God, he can, whenever he pleases, restrain the exercise of it If the smith forges the military weapons, or the waster employs them to destroy, they are both the creatures of God, raised up by his providence, and subject to his over-ruling power, and therefore whatever desolations they are permitted to work in the earth, they shall be restrained from hurting God's people *No weapon that is formed against thee shall prosper*, all the secret contrivances, as well as the avowed opposition against God's church, shall be disappointed. 4 Every accusation shall be refuted, to the confusion of the accuser *Every tongue that shall rise against thee in judgment*, either seeking to calumniate and blacken their character, to misrepresent them to the civil magistrate, to claim authority over men's consciences, or to lay to their charge their sins at God's bar, for which according to the law, they must be cast and punished, *thou shalt condemn*, having a full answer to every accusation In Christ the law is satisfied, by well-doing, the malicious insinuations of foolish men will be put to silence, and God, at last in the great day, will make our righteousness appear as the light, condemn the enemy and avenger, and give a verdict for his people against every accuser

Lastly, All these invaluable privileges are *the heritage of the servants of the Lord* It is secured to them as the estate that descended to the heir, and not only here do they enjoy a part in present grace and protection, but look for an inheritance incorruptible and undefiled, that fadeth not away, reserved for them in heaven, *and their title to it is clear and acknowledged*, *for their righteousness is of me, saith the Lord*, a divine righteousness, that can justify them from every charge, and standing in this before the throne of judgment, God will vindicate their cause and character, and give them the reward of the purchased possession, which their divine and glorious Saviour hath obtained for them

Before Christ 712

CHAP. LV.

As we had much of Christ in the fifty-third, and much of the church of Christ in the fifty fourth chapter, so in this we have much of the covenant of grace made with us in Christ The sure mercies of David which are promised here, ver 3 are understood by the apostle of the benefits which flow to us from the resurrection of Christ, Acts xiii 34 which may serve as a key to this chapter, Here is, 1 A gracious invitation to all, to come and take the benefit of gospel grace, ver 1 2 Pressing arguments to enforce this invitation ver 2—4 3 A promise of the success of this invitation among the Gentiles, ver 5 4 An exhortation to repentance and reformation, with great encouragement given to hope for pardon and forgiveness thereupon, ver 6—9 5 The ratification of all this, with the certain efficacy of the word of God, ver 10, 11 6 The [illegible] this will produce, and the glory that will accrue to God thereby, ver 12, 13

1 HO, [a] every one that thirsteth, come ye to the
waters, and he that hath no money, come ye,
[b] buy and eat, yea, come, buy wine and milk [c] without
money, and without price 2 Wherefore do ye spend
money for [d] *that which is* not bread? and your labour for
that which satisfieth not? hearken diligently unto me,
and eat ye *that which is* good, and let your soul delight itself in fatness 3 Incline your ear, and [e] come
into me hear, and your soul shall live, and [f] I will
make an everlasting covenant with you, [g] *even* the sure
mercies of David 4 Behold, I have given him *for*
a witness to the people, [h] a leader and commander to
the people 5 [i] Behold, thou shalt call a nation *that*
thou knowest not, and nations *that* knew not thee shall
run unto thee, because of the LORD thy God, and for
the holy One of Israel, for he hath glorified thee.

a 1 John iv 14 & vii 37 Rev xxi 6 & xxii 17
b Matt xiii 44, 46 Rev iii 18
c Acts viii 20 Or Rom iii 24 Eph ii 8
d Phil iii 4—7
e Matt x 28
f Chap lix [illegible]
g 2 Sam vii 8 Ps lxxxix 28, 29 [illegible] 3 3, Acts xiii 34
h Matt ii 6
i Chap lii 15 Eph ii 11 12

v 1—5 We have here,

1 A gracious invitation to sinners in general, to come and partake of the benefits and ordinances of the gospel *Ho, every one that thirsteth*, no exception is made, the invitation is general and universal to sinners of all ranks and degrees if they thirst for pardon, righteousness, and salvation, as those who see themselves perishing without it, then they are welcome and welcome to Jesus Christ *come unto the waters*, Christ is the fountain of living waters, his Spirit is usually represented by this emblem, and his ordinances are the pools, in these the soul maintains communion with the Saviour, and he dispenses out of his fulness to the thirsty *and he that hath no money*, free and gracious is the salvation of the gospel, requiring no meritorious qualifications, nothing of our own to recommend us to the divine favour, for indeed we have nothing worth his acceptance, we are utterly corrupt and sinful, our best is bad, and our spiritual poverty most abject and miserable, yet that is no discouragement no, it is such, and such alone, whom Christ invites, and who will be persuaded to come to him to *buy and eat* As food eaten and digested nourishes the body, so doth the promises of the gospel, when mixed with faith, profit our souls Christ in his ordinances is to be fed upon, his word is the bread of life, and in the sacraments we eat his flesh and drink his blood, the sweetest and most nourishing food for our souls, called therefore wine and milk *come, buy wine and milk*, the invitation is repeated, because of our stupid backwardness, and Christ urges our acceptance of his mercy, as if it were a favour done to him, instead of an unutterable obligation conferred on us And least we should hesitate, because mention is made of a purchase, and we have nothing to pay, the whole is offered *without money, and without price*, Christ indeed hath paid for all the blessings he bestows to the full, but to us they come free as the light which shines on us, or the air we breathe

2 Christ expostulates with those who seek righteousness and comfort out of him *Wherefore do ye spend your money for that which is not bread, and your labour for that which satisfieth not?* All the toil and pains of the worldly minded can never procure them solid satisfaction, corroding cares leaven their gains, corrupt their enjoyment, the pleasures they seek in present vanities, are found husks instead of bread, and disappointments perpetual bid them seek a better and more enduring portion And they who, by their [illegible] and duties, would [illegible] establish a righteousness before God [illegible] but in the [illegible] their bread [illegible] portion, their toil [illegible], the more they seek thus to enter into life, the further they advance in the path of death, for [illegible] Christ there is no justifying righteousness, [illegible] all worldly enjoyment without his love and favour, are but flattering dreams, and death, too late, will awaken the soul to perceive the [illegible] delusion Happy they who are led to seek their happi-

Before Christ 712

ness from Christ alone, and from him to expect righteousness and salvation.

3. He exhorts them to hearken to his word, and embrace the true good, which he proffers to bestow upon them. *Hearken diligently unto me*, with such serious attention as the importance of the salvation of an immortal soul demands, *and eat ye that which is good*, the glad tidings of good things, which the word of truth in the gospel proclaims, such good things as pass man's understanding, *and let your soul delight itself in fatness*, in the pardon and peace, righteousness and joy in the holy ghost, which are provided as the richest feast for the believing soul. *Incline your ear, and come unto me*, Jesus would kindly, would earnestly court the sinner to taste the riches of his grace. Strange! that we should need entreaty to come to him and be happy! *hear, and your soul shall live*, or that *your soul may live*, life spiritual and eternal being derived from the word of Jesus, and they who hear and believe in him can never die. *and I will make an everlasting covenant with you, even the sure mercies of David*, to strengthen our faith, God condescends to bind himself under a covenant with his people, a covenant of his own contriving from everlasting, and which will endure to everlasting. The blessings of the covenant are called *mercies*, because man's desert is utterly excluded, and mercies of every kind, whether respecting grace or glory, *sure mercies*, confirmed by the faithfulness of the unchangeable God, and as being the *mercies of David*, that is, of Christ his Son, by whom they were obtained, through whom they are dispensed, and in whom all the promises of God are yea and amen. Blessed, for ever blessed be God, for Jesus Christ.

Christ is promised for *a witness to the people*, him hath God the Father sent, to bear witness to the truth, and he is faithful and true. He came in the flesh, to publish to all nations the great salvation of God, and by his works and miracles sufficiently proved his divine mission: him we are commanded to hear and obey, for he is *a leader and commander to the people*, a *leader*, as he instructs and guides his people to walk in the ways of truth and righteousness, and having led them by his counsel, will bring them at last to his glory; *a commander*, the captain of our salvation, who will subdue all our enemies before us, and make us more than conquerors, who bids us follow him, and leads the way to victory and everlasting triumphs. *Note*, They who receive Christ's word as true, will follow his example as their pattern, and manfully fighting under his banners, win through his grace, and wear the crown of righteousness.

5. Vast and numerous shall be the converts, that at the invitation of Jesus shall come to him. *Behold, thou shalt call a nation that thou knowest not*, the nations of the Gentile world, that before were not acknowledged as God's people, *and nations that knew not thee shall run unto thee*, denoting the eagerness with which the Gentiles would receive and embrace the gospel, *because of the Lord thy God*, because of the demonstration of the spirit and power accompanying the word, and the grace and love of God in the gospel, which are most mightily constraining, and because they now perceive there is no approaching a holy God but through a Saviour, *and for the holy one of Israel*, trusting on his faithfulness, or *to the holy One of Israel*, to Christ, the holy Saviour, on whose atonement, righteousness, and grace, they alone depend, *for he hath glorified thee*, God the Father hath exalted his Son Jesus, given him to be head over all, committed all power into his hands, and he is glorified when sinners come to him, out of his fulness to receive an abundant supply of all their wants, and this is an encouragement to draw near to him, since our salvation is his glory.

k Pf. xxxii 6. Mat. v. 25. Heb. iii. 7.
l Obs. i. 16.
n Jer. iv. 14.
o Pf. cxxx.
† Heb. Multiply to pardon.
p 2 Sam. vii. 19.
q Pf. ciii. 11.
r Deut. xxxii. 2.
s Ez. l. xii. 25.
t Chap. xlv. 23.
u Chap. xliv. 10. & lxii. 11.
x Pf. xcvi. 11, 12. & xcviii. 8.
Chap. xliv. 8.
z Chap. xli. 19.
b Jer. xxxiii. 9.
c Chap. liv. 10. or Jer. 1. 5.

6 ¶ [k] Seek ye the LORD while he may be found,
call ye upon him while he is near. 7 Let the wicked
forsake his way, and the unrighteous man his [m] thoughts:
and let him return unto the LORD, and he will
have mercy upon him, and to our God, for [o] he will
† abundantly pardon. 8 ¶ For [p] my thoughts *are* not
your thoughts, neither *are* your ways my ways, saith the
LORD. 9 [q] For *as* the heavens are higher than the
earth, so are my ways higher than your ways, and my
thoughts than your thoughts. 10 For [r] as the rain cometh
down, and the snow from heaven, and returneth
not thither, but watereth the earth, and maketh it bring
forth and bud, that it may give seed to the sower, and
bread to the eater: 11 [s] So shall my word be that goeth
forth out of my mouth: [t] it shall not return unto me
void, but it shall accomplish that which I please, and
it shall prosper *in the thing* whereto I sent it. 12 For
[u] ye shall go out with joy, and be led forth with peace:
[x] the mountains and the hills shall break forth before
you into singing, and [y] all the trees of the field shall
clap *their* hands. 13 [z] Instead of [a] the thorn shall
come up the fir tree, and instead of the brier shall come
up the myrtle-tree: and [b] it shall be to the LORD for
a name, [c] for an everlasting sign *that* shall not be cut
off.

v. 6—13. We have here the same subject of the return of sinners to God farther prosecuted.

1. They are urged to seek God from the consideration of his rich grace and readiness to receive the miserable that fly to him for mercy. (1.) The persons addressed are *the wicked* and *unrighteous*, for such we all are, and such Christ Jesus came to seek and save; they who know not this to be their character, have no part nor lot in his salvation. (2.) The way in which they are directed to proceed. In faith, prayer, and penitence. *Seek ye the Lord while he may be found, call upon him while he is near*, God will be found of them that seek him; this is his promise: therefore on our knees we must cry for the pardon and mercy we need, and he proffers to bestow, and this without delay, before his abused patience cast us off, and say, my spirit shall no longer strive; or death carry us to the tomb, when it will be too late to knock, because the door is shut. Oh how should this awful consideration awaken our importunity, whilst the day of life and mercy lasts! *Let the wicked forsake his ways*, let him turn from the paths of sin with loathing and abhorrence, nor suffer one darling lust, *and the unrighteous man his thoughts*, let not one allowed desire of evil remain; the views of promised grace must constrain the sinner to part with all readily, cheerfully, entirely, and to cleanse the temper as well as reform the practice, *and let him return unto the Lord*, from whom he had so greatly departed, to stand before him as a criminal seeking pardon, as a helpless worm to find grace, and as a redeemed soul now engaged in his service, and desiring to follow him in all his holy ways; whoever thus seeks, will find. For, (3.) God promises *he will have mercy upon him*, yea, *will abundantly pardon*, no guilt so great, no iniquity so aggravated, but that there is with him grace abounding for the chief of sinners. And this is mentioned, not as the condition and reward of our repentance and prayers, but as the argument to engage us thereto, seeing we can neither repent nor pray till we see this pardoning mercy and grace extended towards us in the Redeemer. (4.) He answers an objection their fears might raise, guilt being ever ready to drive us to despair. They indeed who have never known the burden of sin, think it easy to believe in God's mercy, whilst they who have once felt it, are soon convinced of the unbelief of their hearts. *My thoughts*, says God, *are not your thoughts*, in general with regard to sin, Christ, happiness, &c. and particularly which seems here intended respecting the manner of the sinner's acceptance: for when we scarce dare believe he can receive such vile wretches as we are, he knows how to glorify himself in being the justifier of him who believeth in Jesus; *neither are your ways my ways*, ours are perverse, his pure; ours lead to death and hell, his to life and glory: we never could forgive one who had offended us as we have God, yet he can and doth freely and fully both forgive and forget it. *Thus as the heavens are higher than the earth*, so incomparably transcendent are his thoughts and ways of mercy and grace beyond all that we can ask or think.

2. The Lord engages to make his own word effectual. For as in the kingdom of nature, the rain and snow directed by Divine Providence water the earth, and cause its fertility, accomplishing God's purposes of mercy in providing food for men's bodies: *So, says he, shall my word be that goeth forth out of my mouth*, the word of the gospel, of which Christ is the sum and substance, *it shall not return unto me void, but*, accompanied with divine energy, *it shall accomplish that which I please*, be made effectual to the conversion of as many as the Lord our God shall call, *and it shall prosper in the thing whereto I sent it*, producing a plenteous harvest of converted souls, and leaving those inexcusable who reject it. *Note*, All God's purposes and promises must infallibly take effect, and it is a great encouragement to all his faithful ministers to be assured that they shall not labour in vain in the Lord: to some they will be a savour of life unto life, to others a savour of death unto death, and in both God will be glorified.

3. The word being made effectual to the conversion of men's souls, will produce great joy in the hearts of the redeemed, as was the case with the Jews when released from Babylon, to whom this may primarily be applied, and who herein represented the people of God going forth from the slavery of sin, their bands loosed, and they rejoicing in the glorious liberty of the sons of God, whilst the mountains and hills break forth into singing, as if congratulating their deliverance, and all the trees of the field clap their hands for joy: which may express the delight of the apostles and ministers of the word, when they saw their labours so abundantly owned, and so many converted by their preaching, who rejoiced with them in so blessed an event. And the consequence of this is a wondrous change in men's tempers and dispositions. *Instead of the thorn shall come up the fir tree, and instead of the brier shall come up the myrtle-tree*, and being thus renewed in the spirit of their minds, *it shall be to the Lord for a name, for an everlasting sign that shall not*

Before Christ 712.

not be cut off, God having taken them for his own, will preserve them by his grace below, and bring them to be everlasting monuments of his mercy, love and power in his kingdom of glory above

CHAP LVI

After the exceeding great and precious promises of gospel grace, typified by temporal deliverances which we had in the foregoing chapter, we have here, 1 A solemn charge given us to make conscience of our duty, as we hope to have the benefit of those promises, ver 1, 2 2 *Great encouragement given to strangers that were willing to come under the bonds of the covenant,* ver 3—8 3 *A high charge drawn up against the watchmen of Israel that were careless and unfaithful in the discharge of their duty,* ver 9—12

† Or equity a Mic vi 8 b Chap xlvi 13 & li 5 Mat iv 17 Rom xiii 11 c Ps xv 5 d Chap lviii 13 Jer xvii 21, 22

1 THUS saith the LORD, Keep ye † judgment,
and [a] do justice for [b] my salvation *is* near to
come, and my righteousness to be revealed 2 Blessed
is the man *that* doth this, and the son of man *that*
layeth hold on it [d] that keepeth the sabbath from polluting it, and keepeth his hand from doing any evil

v 1, 2 From the privileges of the gospel, the Lord enforces obedience to the precepts of it

1 The privileges are inestimable *My salvation is near to come, and my righteousness to be revealed* He calls it *my salvation*, because the contrivance and execution of it was wholly his own, *and my righteousness*, because in this salvation the most eminent display was to be made of the divine justice in the sufferings and obedience of Jesus, and in the acceptance of sinners through him, in a way whereon God might at the same time glorify his righteousness, and yet be the justifier of him that believeth in Jesus And the time was now near when the Saviour should be revealed, comparatively speaking in the view of the time elapsed since the first promise was made, *Gen* iii 15

2 The duty of those who partook in this salvation is enforced For they who truly understand the doctrine of God's free grace in the salvation of sinners, will ever feel the obligation it lays upon them to walk in all holy conversation and godliness (1) *Keep judgment, and do justice*, let God's word be the rule of your conduct, and in all your ways approve yourselves to him in uprightness, fidelity, simplicity, and godly sincerity (2) *Keep the sabbath from polluting it*, that being God's day, should be wholly devoted to his service, and employed in his worship, not only must we rest from servile employments, but seek to improve the sacred hours in every exercise of piety and devotion, that may contribute to raise up our affections to heavenly things, and promote in others the same gracious dispositions (3) *Keep thy hand from doing any evil*, preserve a conscience void of offence towards God and towards man, abstain from every known sin, and though absolute perfection is not in man, let it be your labour, study, and prayer to cleanse yourselves from all filthiness of flesh and spirit, perfecting holiness in the fear of God

3 God pronounces his blessing on all such *Blessed is the man that doth this, and the son of man that layeth hold on it*, who embraces the salvation and righteousness of Jesus, and adorns the doctrine of God the Saviour in all things

e Deut xxiii 1 Acts x 34 Rom ii 10 11 f Deut xxiii 1 g Acts viii 27, 38 h Mat xx 28 1 Tim iii 15 i John i 12 1 John iii 1 k Acts ii 41 † Or keepeth still So Ver 4, 1 Chap ii 2 l Mat xxi 13 Mark xi 17 Luke xix 46 n Rom x 12 John x 16 Eph ii 11

3 ¶ Neither let [e] the son of the stranger, that hath
joined himself to the LORD, speak, saying, The
LORD hath utterly separated me from his people
[f] neither let the eunuch say, Behold, I *am* a dry tree
4 For thus saith the LORD unto the eunuchs that
keep my sabbaths, and choose the things that please me,
and take hold of my covenant 5 [h] Even unto them
will I give in [g] mine house, and within my walls, a place
and a [i] name better than of sons and of daughters I
will give them an everlasting name, that shall not be
cut off 6 Also the sons of the stranger [k] that join
themselves to the LORD, to serve him, and to love
the name of the LORD, to be his servants, every
one that keepeth the sabbath from polluting it, and †
taketh hold of my covenant 7 Even them [l] will I
bring to my holy mountain, and make them joyful in
my house of prayer their burnt-offerings and their
sacrifices *shall be* accepted upon mine altar, for [m] mine
house shall be called an house of prayer [n] for all people
8 The Lord GOD which gathereth the outcasts of
Israel saith, Yet will I gather *others* to him, besides
those that are gathered unto him.

[illegible]—8 We have here the encouragement given to those who, though willing to join themselves to the Lord, were [illegible]

Before Christ 712.

1 The eunuch might lament his unhappy case, saying, *I am a dry tree*, under the reproach of being written childless, and expressly excluded from the congregation of the Lord, *Deut* xxiii 1 yet God speaks comfort unto such *Thus saith the Lord unto the eunuchs which keep my sabbaths*, religiously observant of God's worship on that holy day, and all the instituted ordinances of the gospel, *and choose the things that please me*, attentive to God's revealed will in his word, and delighting in that which he commands, serving not of constraint but willingly, *and take hold of my covenant*, embrace it as their only hope, trust on it with unshaken confidence, and walk under the influence of the blessed promises contained therein, *even to them will I give in my house, and within my walls, a place and a name better than that of sons and daughters* children are a precious gift, they are like arrows in the hand of the giant, and father's an honourable title, but every honour, every possession, every enjoyment here is trivial, compared with an interest in God's regard, and a name in his book of life, this is for eternity, *I will give them an everlasting name which shall never be cut off* *Note*, (1) When we set temporal blessings against spiritual, time against eternity, the infinite disproportion between them should instantly and constantly determine our choice to the better part (2) All real good we ever can enjoy here or hereafter, comes from God's free gift, and must be acknowledged to his glory

2 The Gentile alien might fear, *v* 3 that God had utterly separated him from his people, *See Deut* xxiii but his fears are groundless, the wall of separation between Jew and Gentile being cast down, and therefore, if he *joined himself to the Lord*, renouncing all other gods, and cleaving to him alone, *to serve him* with fidelity and constancy, *to love the name of the Lord*, deeply sensible of his amazing grace, and powerfully constrained by the views of it, *to be his servant*, in all willing and cheerful obedience, counting his service perfect freedom, *every one that keepeth the sabbath from polluting it*, diligent and conscientious in the observance of this sacred day of rest, *and taketh hold of my covenant*, the everlasting covenant of love and peace in a Redeemer, as the foundation of all his hopes, such need apprehend no exclusion from the divine favour, or the assembly of the faithful *Even them will I bring to my holy mountain*, the church of the redeemed, and give them a right to partake of all the blessings and privileges bestowed upon it, *and make them joyful in my house of prayer*, or, *the house of my prayer*, where prayer and supplications are offered to God, and he meets his people with joy and gladness, giving an answer to the prayer of the afflicted, and comforting his mourners *Their burnt-offerings and their sacrifices shall be accepted upon mine altar*, their prayers, praises, works of faith, and labours of love, shall thro' Christ, the altar which sanctifieth the gift, become a sacrifice of a sweet smell, well-pleasing to God *for mine house shall be called an house of prayer for all people*, no distinction any longer subsisting between Jew and Gentile, but incorporated in one holy church, of which Christ is the living head

3 God having provided a house of prayer for all people, will furnish it with worshippers *The Lord God which gathereth the outcasts of Israel*, the spiritual Israel, that in a state of nature lay exposed, as the infant in Ezekiel, in their blood, *saith, Yet will I gather others to him, besides those that are gathered unto him*, to Christ, or his church, to which, in every age and generation, multitudes shall be gathered And it may particularly be applied to those, who, being persecuted by the pagan emperors, were, under Constantine, peaceably settled in their assemblies, and to the conversion of numerous nations which followed, till then strangers to the Christian faith, and this may look for its final accomplishment in the latter day, when *the fulness of* the Gentiles shall be come in, and all Israel, till then dispersed, shall be converted and saved

p Rev xix 17 18 q Mat xv 14 r Hos iv 6 ‖ Or talking in their sleep s Mic iii 11 ‡ Heb know not to be satisfied t Mic iii 11 u Chap xxviii 7 x Chap xxii 13

9 ¶ [p] All ye beasts of the field, come to devour, *yea*,
all the beasts in the forest 10 [q] His watchmen *are*
blind [r] they *are* all ignorant, they *are* all dumb dogs,
they cannot bark, ‖ sleeping, lying down, loving to
slumber 11 Yea, *they are* greedy dogs, [s] *which* ‡ can
never have enough, and they *are* shepherds *that* cannot
understand they all look to their own way, every one
for his gain, from his quarter 12 Come ye, *say they*,
[u] I will fetch wine, and we will fill ourselves with strong
drink, [x] and to morrow shall be as this day, *and* much
more abundant

v 9—12 After all the comfort and promises [illegible] before, here a scene of desolation [illegible] continued in the following chapter [illegible] to the sin and punishment of the Jewish people by the Babylonians and Romans, or [illegible] the ravages of the Goths and Vandals, and other barbarous people, which were sent to punish the [illegible] corruption which had crept into the Christian Roman empire

1 The beasts of prey are summoned to execute God's judgment [illegible] Who would not [illegible] the [illegible] from blood [illegible]

[illegible]

Before Christ 7 2 ments ever at his beck, to execute his wrath Woe to the sinners, to the nation, that by their iniquities and impenitence provoke it!

2 The principal cause of these judgments is, a lazy, ignorant, worldly-minded, covetous, drunken, careless ministry Such was probably the case in Isaiah's day, happy were it, if future times had afforded no parallel! A dreadful character is here drawn *His watchmen are blind*, they who are appointed to descry the approaching enemy, and give warning, are themselves blind and insensible unawakened in their own souls, they never saw their guilt and danger of sin, therefore cannot blow the alarm, and persuade others by the terrors of the Lord *They are all ignorant* of the scriptures, and that knowledge which maketh wise unto salvation, and cannot preach a gospel they have not themselves understood *They are all dumb dogs, they cannot bark*, never reprove men's sins, and hate the work of the ministry in which they are engaged, ordained to lift up their voice like a trumpet, but *sleeping, lying down, loving to slumber*, slothful, indolent, glad to devolve on others the irksome task of preaching and prayer, and seeking ease, instead of enduring hardness, as good soldiers of Jesus Christ *Yea, they are greedy dogs, that can never have enough*, of the duty of the ministry, the least part is sufficient, of the gain of it, nothing can satisfy them, infinitely more solicitous in prosecuting preferment, than seeking lost souls, and never enquiring the weight of the charge, but the value of the benefice The words may be rendered, *of insatiable appetite, that never can be filled*, whose belly is their god, and eating and drinking their supreme happiness *And they are shepherds*, or, *though they are shepherds*, pretend to be so, *they cannot understand*, not acquainted with divine things themselves, and therefore utterly incapable of teaching others *They look to their own way*, follow their own pleasures and worldly advantage, careless of the cause of God and truth, *every one for his gain from his quarter*, this is their grand object, and on this their chief pains are bestowed *Come ye, say they, I will fetch wine, and we will fill ourselves with strong drink*, their bottle is more beloved than their books pleased to see the wine sparkle in the glass, they put it round, sit long at the cups, till bloated, inflamed, or drunken, their time and their faculties are destroyed, and, far from being ashamed of such scandalous immoralities, their great concern is to renew the entertainment, and make a fresh appointment for the next day *for to-morrow shall be as this day, and much more abundant* Supine and secure, they forget eternity, promise themselves days and years to come, consider neither the guilt of their course, nor the uncertainty of their enjoyments, but encourage each other to mutual neglect of God and their souls, till he, in an unexpected hour, with terrible surprize calls them to give account of their ministry, and arraigns them at his tremendous bar

CHAP LVII

The prophet in this chapter makes his observations, 1 Upon the deaths of good men, their comfortable end, and reproves those that did not make a due improvement of such providences, ver 1, 2 2 Upon the gross idolatries and spiritual whoredoms of the people, and the destroying judgments they were thereby bringing upon themselves, ver 3--12 3 Upon the gracious returns of God to his people, ver 13--19. 4 Upon the character and misery of the wicked, ver 20, 21

1 [a] THE righteous perisheth, and no man layeth
it to heart, and † merciful men *are* taken
away, none considering that [b] the righteous is taken
away from the evil *to come* 2 He shall ‡ enter into
peace [c] they shall rest in their beds, *each one* walking *in*
his uprightness

a Ps. [illegible] Mic vii 2 † Heb Men of kindness, or godliness b 2 Kings xxii 20 [illegible] Wisd iv 10 &c ‡ Or Go in peace [illegible] c Eccles xii 7

v 1, 2 If the watchmen were blind and careless, no wonder the people were stupid and negligent, and disregarded the notices of Divine Providence

1 *The righteous perisheth, and the merciful man is taken away* Death delivered them from their burdens, and God in mercy took them away from a wicked world *Note*, Piety is no protection from death, nay, in time of persecution the righteous are most exposed The sufferers in this dead, died in mercy

2 It was a mark of great hardness of heart, and inattention to the calls of God, that *no man laid it to heart, nor considered it* The removal of the righteous is a grievous loss to the church, and to the nation, a mark of God's displeasure, and a warning of approaching judgment, and they who hear not the rod, and repent, will quickly feel its smart, and perish under the stroke

3 The blessedness of the righteous in their removal is great, to them to die is gain *They are taken away from the evil to come*, as Noah into the ark before the deluge came they see not the evil that is coming on a wicked world, but take their happy flight to the mansions prepared for them in glory *He shall enter into peace*, or, *go in peace*, no fears dismay his dying hour, having seen the salvation of God, he departs with joy to the full possession of it, to enter that blest abode where sin, sorrow, or sufferings, shall never more disturb his repose *They shall rest in their beds* no bed so welcome to the weary, as that bed of dust, where the saints sweetly sleep in Jesus, and wait a joyful resurrection, *each one walking in his uprightness*, either such was their conduct upon earth, or such is now the state of their departed souls, delivered from the burden of the flesh, and joined to the spirits of just men made perfect, or, *before him*, admitted to the beatific vision and fruition of the blessed God

Before Christ 699

3 ¶ But draw near hither, ye sons of the sorceress,
the seed of the adulterer, and the whore 4 [d] Against
whom do ye sport yourselves ? against whom make ye a
wide mouth, *and* draw out the tongue ? *are* ye not chil-
dren of transgression, a seed of falshood ? 5 Inflaming
yourselves with idols [e] under every green tree, [f] slaying
the children in the valleys under the clifts of the rocks ?
6 Among the smooth stones of the stream *is* thy por-
tion, they, they *are* thy lot even to them hast thou
poured a drink offering, thou hast offered a meat offer-
ing [g] Should I receive comfort in these ? 7 [h] Upon
a lofty and high mountain hast thou set thy bed even
thither wentest thou up to offer sacrifice 8 Behind
the doors also and the posts hast thou set up thy re-
membrance for thou hast discovered *thyself to another*
than me, and art gone up thou hast enlarged thy bed,
and † made thee *a covenant* with them, [i] thou lovedst
their bed where thou sawest *it* 9 And [k] thou ‡ wentest
to the king with ointment, and didst increase thy per-
fumes, and didst send thy messengers far off, and didst
debase *thyself even* unto hell 10 [l] Thou art wearied in
the greatness of thy way, *yet* saidst thou not, There is
no hope thou hast found the life of thine hand, there-
fore thou wast not grieved 11 And of whom hast
thou been afraid or feared, that [m] thou hast lied, and
hast not remembred me, nor laid *it* to thy heart ? [n] have
not I held my peace even of old, and thou fearest me
not ? 12 [o] I will declare thy righteousness, and thy
works, for they shall not profit thee.

d Exod xvi 8 Luke x 16 1 Thess iv 8 e 2 Kings xvi 4 & xvii 10 f Lev xviii 21 & xx 2 2 Kings xvi 3 & xvii 17 Ezek xvi 20 & xx 26 g Chap lxvi 3 Jer vii 9 10 h Ezek xvi [illegible] † Or hewed it for thyself larger than theirs i Ezek xvi 6 25 k Chap xxx 6 Ezek xvi 33 ‡ Or prefented l Jer ii 25 m Chap lix 13 n Ps l 21 o Jer ii 35

v 3--12 We have here a strong character drawn of the wicked abovementioned, who were well-pleased to be rid of the righteous who troubled them and this may belong either to the Jews under their latter monarchs, especially Ahaz, in whose reign Isaiah lived, or to the apostate church of Rome, where all the idolatries of the heathen are revived, and, with the name of Christian, paganism is in a measure re-established,

1 They are summoned to God's bar *Draw near hither*, to hear your fearful doom, and the title given them marks their character, *ye sons of the sorceress, ye seed of the adulterer and the whore*, or *who commit whoredom*, *children of transgression, a seed of falsehood*, the whore of Babylon, the sons of that idolatrous church, committing whoredom with her, given up to iniquity, embracing false doctrines, and propagating them *Note*, The practice of sin is spiritually sorcery and adultery, it is a virtual contract with the devil, and an open breach of our baptismal engagements

2 The crimes alledged against them are produced, and they are many and aggravated

[1] Contempt of God and his warnings, in the person of his ministers They ridiculed the preachers, treated them with derision and scorn, and shewed them such insult and ill manners, as themselves would have counted a flagrant injury, if done to the meanest of their servants whom they had sent with a message *Note*, (1) They who deliver faithfully God's message to a wicked world, may often expect to meet insult and reproach (2) When religion is in the case, they who on other occasions pique themselves on their behaviour as gentlemen, here count all manners laudable, and esteem the minister of God as excluded from the common right of civility (3) They who thus insolently treat God's servant, need well consider against whom they sport themselves their master is not thus to be mocked with impunity

[2] Idolatry They were mad upon their idols, and, as is the nature of vile affections, the more they are indulged, the more they are inflamed, and hurry men on to greater excesses Under every green tree they had their images and so besotted were they, that even their own children were not too dear to offer to them, for when a man is given up to his heart's lust, he becomes unnatural even to his own flesh and blood, and, to gratify his raging appetites, cares not what sufferings his children and family undergo, *v* 5 Innumerable were their idols all they found in the streams of the valleys a smooth stone, they set it up for worship, and valued it as their portion and inheritance, pouring out their drink offering and meat offering before it as the papists do the images of their saints, and set up the [illegible] of their [illegible],

Before Christ 699

consisting of bread and wine, in honour of their idols *Shall I receive comfort in these?* says God, No, they are his utter abhorrence, v 6 On the hills they have set up their bed, their idolatrous altars, and thither went up to offer sacrifice to their idols alluding, it may be, to the city of Rome, the seat of idolatry, situate on seven hills, or to their high altars, where they celebrate their masses, v 7 yea, every house has its tutelar saint, as the heathen Lares and Penates *Behind the doors also and the posts hast thou set up thy remembrances*, their images, crucifixes, and superstitious pictures, *for thou hast discovered thyself to another than to me*, or *from me*, apostate from God's true worship, and prostituted to idolatry *and art gone up*, openly and publicly without blushing, to these unhallowed altars *Thou hast enlarged thy bed*, their idol temples, *and made a covenant with them*, joined in league with others like themselves, *See* Rev xiii 15—17 *Thou lovedst their bed where thou sawest it*, took delight in the places and altars for idolatrous worship, as Ahaz, 2 Kings xvi 10 or, *where thou sawest a statue*, didst fall down and worship it

[3] Their zeal to make proselytes to their idolatry *Thou wentest up to the king with ointment*, &c Some refer this to the trust the Jews reposed in the foreign assistance they courted, but it may be applied to Rome the mother of harlots, who, decking herself with all the pomp and splendor of outward devotion and gaudy worship, invites the kings of the earth to commit fornication with her, *and didst increase thy perfumes*, to make herself appear amiable, pretending to antiquity, infallibility, the power of miracles, and authority to bestow plenary indulgences for sin *and didst send thy messengers afar off*, nuncios and legates to the courts of her kings, to establish her authority, and missionaries and emissaries to promote her interests, and spread her false religion *and didst debase thyself even to hell*, making pretences to the deepest humility, in order to ensnare the unwary, or, *didst bring low even to hell*, making her converts sevenfold more the children of hell than before, and destroying the souls of those she pretended to save

[4] Their obstinate perseverance in those ways of wickedness *Thou art wearied in the greatness of thy way*, or, *the multiplicity of thy ways*, the many stratagems and the vast pains taken to compass the subjection of kingdoms, and all churches to the church of Rome, which were enough to have wearied out invention and patience, before they could be brought to take effect *Yet saidst thou not, There is no hope*, no disappointments deterred the Roman see from persevering in her ambitious designs, till at last they prevailed *Thou hast found the life of thy hand*, the dominion over men's consciences, and over all other churches which they sought, with all the wealth that accrued from thence *therefore thou wast not grieved*, or *sick*, not sorry for the pains bestowed, or sick of the undertaking, from whence they hoped at last all their pains would be recompensed And this may be applied to sinners in general, (1) The happiness they seek in creature-comforts wearies them in the pursuit, and ever disappoints their expectations (2) Though experience should teach him, by repeated disappointment, the vanity of the creature, so infatuated is the sinner, that he still entertains hopes, that by and by he shall find the joy he pursues (3) Sometimes he flatters himself he hath attained his point, and saith to his soul, Take thine ease, but most fatally is he then deluded, when most securely he cries, Peace, peace

[5] Long impunity had bred confidence of its continuance, notwithstanding the repeated provocations given *Of whom hast thou been afraid or feared?* intimating either, that she had cast off all fear of God, or that it was through fear of losing her influence over her votaries, *that thou hast lied*, stuck at no fraud and falsehood to carry her point *and hast not remembered me*, paid no regard to God, nor shewed any apprehension of his judgments *Have I not held my peace even of old, and thou fearest me not?* or, *therefore thou fearest not*, emboldened to sin by the patience God had shown in bearing her provocations *Note*, (1) Fear of men often leads to the sin of lying (2) They can have no fear of God, who dare tell a deliberate lie (3) Because vengeance is not speedily executed on an evil worker, presumptuous sinners harden themselves in their iniquities

3 God threatens to bring them to an awful reckoning, to detect their hypocrisy, and visit them for their sins *I will declare thy righteousness*, for this the Jews boasted of, and went about to establish, as the church of Rome also vaunts her purity, teaching the meritoriousness of men's duties, and even pretends to works of supererogation but these pretences shall quickly be confuted and confounded, either by the preaching of the pure gospel, as at the reformation, and hereafter, when the Romish harlot shall be destroyed, or at God's bar of judgment, *for* then it will appear how vain is their plea, *they shall not profit thee*, cannot justify them before God, nor in any measure secure them from his wrath, which shall be revealed from heaven against all such [illegible] pretenders to merit and human righteousness *Note*, (1) No delusion is more fatal than the conceit of our own righteousness (2) The doctrine of the merit of works is the grand pillar of popery would God the leaven were not still deeply spread in many a professing Protestant's heart

13 ¶ p When thou criest, let thy companies deliver
thee but the wind shall carry them all away, vanity
shall take *them* q but he that putteth his trust in me,
shall possess the land, and shall inherit my holy moun-
tain 14 And shall say, r Cast ye up, cast ye up, pre-
pare the way, take up the stumbling-block out of the
way of my people 15 For thus saith the high and
lofty One s that inhabiteth eternity, whose name *is* Holy,
t I dwell in the high and holy *place*, u with him also *that*
is of a contrite and humble spirit, x to revive the spirit of
the humble, and to revive the heart of the contrite ones
16 For y I will not contend for ever, neither will I be
always wroth for the spirit should fail before me, and
the souls z *which* I have made

p Pf xviii 41 q Pf xxxvii 3 Jer xvii 7 8 r Chap xl 3 s Job vi 10 s 1 Tim vi 16 t Pf lxviii [illegible] Zech ii 13 u Pf xxxiv 18 & cxxxviii 6 Chap lxvi 2 x Pf cxlvii 3 Chap lxi 1 y Pf lxxxv 5 & ciii 9 Mic vii 18 z Num xvi 22

v 13—16 We have here,

1 The vanity of idols in the day of calamity *When thou criest, let thy companies deliver thee*, but utterly unable will they be found to help The sinner's confidences will then fail him, *the wind*, or lightest breath of air, *shall carry them away*, the works of the self-righteous will all prove at the bar of God altogether lighter than vanity itself

2 The insufficiency of idols and creature-confidences serves to magnify the all-sufficiency of God, which will never disappoint those who make him their rock alone *He that putteth his trust in me shall possess the land, and shall inherit my holy mountain*, which refers either to the restoration of the Jews to their own land from Babylon, or, spiritually, contains a promise of blessing to all the faithful, who shall inherit the heavenly Canaan, and come to the eternal mount of God in glory *Note*, Abiding faith in God is the surest way to secure a blessed portion in time and eternity

3 Proclamation is made to prepare the way for the return of the captive Jews, v 14 Or this may be considered as the call of God by his ministers to his people, to come out of Babylon mystical, or, more generally, to depart from all the ways of sin *He shall say, Cast ye up, cast ye up, prepare the way*, that it may be plain and strait, for such is God's way, *a highway, a way of holiness, the wayfaring men, though fools, shall not err therein*, and to this way it is the business of the spiritual guide to conduct men's souls *Take up the stumbling-block out of the way of my people* he who calls them forth, will bring them safely home Whatever difficulties stand in their way, from fightings without, or corruptions within, they shall be removed and overcome

4 The humble and contrite shall find the power and love of God engaged for them *For thus saith the high and lofty One that inhabiteth eternity*, in the contemplation of whose transcendent perfections, greatness, and glory, our thoughts are lost in wonder and adoration, *whose name is Holy*, essentially so in himself, the source of holiness to all his creatures, and whose works and ways are so ordered, as most eminently to display this adorable perfection, *I dwell in the high and holy place*, heaven is his throne, where he is pleased to make the brightest manifestations of his presence, and whither we are taught to look up to him yet, not confined to the skies, he fills heaven and earth, and condescends to take up his avowed abode *with him also that is of a contrite and humble spirit*, cheering and comforting the soul of the sinner abased with the views of guilt, and healing with his precious grace the heart broken under a sense of sin, supporting his afflicted ones oppressed and persecuted of men, and as their tribulations abound, making their consolations abound also *to revive the spirit of the humble, and to revive the heart of the contrite ones*, that they may not sink under their burdens, or faint in despair, but by faith and patience bear up under their trials, and cheerfully and steadily hold on their heavenly way The celebrated Vitringa particularly applies this to the sufferings of the Waldenses and Bohemians, so cruelly persecuted by the pope and his adherents, and others, to the latter days, when the antichristian powers shall prevail *Note*, (1) A humble and contrite spirit is among the best gifts of God (2) There is an endeared communion to be enjoyed with God, which only they can tell, in whose hearts he is pleased to manifest himself, as he doth not unto the world (3) Where God dwells no evil can approach, no real good be absent

5 Though God in merciful correction visits his people, he will quickly remove the rod, when in humiliation the soul bows down before it *For I will not contend for ever, neither will I be always wroth*, the Father's heart is ready to relent, but his anger is only for a moment, like a tender father, whose bowels yearn even when he chastises his child, so doth the Lord haste to end his controversy with his people, ready to pardon them instantly at their cry, and to support them under, or save them out of, all their troubles *for the spirit should fail before me, or be overwhelmed, and the souls which I have made*, which God gives as a reason for his compassions he knows our weakness, and will not lay upon us more than we can bear *Note*, (1) Our souls are God's, not merely by creation, but much more by redemption and regeneration (2) He

has

Before Christ 699

heavy trials our hearts are ready to deſpair, but God is faithful, and will never leave nor forſake us

17 *For the iniquity of his covetouſneſs was I wroth,
and ſmote him* [a] *I hid me, and was wroth, and* [b] *he
went on frowardly in the way of his heart* 18 *I have
ſeen his ways,* [c] *and will heal him I will lead him alſo,
and reſtore comforts unto him,* [d] *and to his mourners*
19 *I create the fruit of the lips, peace, peace* [e] *to him
that is far off, and to him that is near, ſaith the LORD,
and I will heal him* 20 *But* [f] *the wicked are like the
troubled ſea,* [g] *when it cannot reſt, whoſe waters caſt up
mire and dirt* 21 [h] *There is no peace, ſaith my God,
to the wicked*

a Chap xlv 15 b Chap liii 6 c Jer iii 22 d Chap lxi 3 Ezek ix 4 Mat v 4 e Acts ii 39 Eph ii 17 f Job xv 20, 21 & xx 25 g Prov iv 16 h Chap xlviii 22

v 17—21 We have here, reproofs, promiſes, and warnings, according to the ſeveral ſtates of the people to whom the prophecy is addreſſed, and they are levelled either againſt the Jews of that day, or thoſe ſad declenſions among Chriſtians, for which God for a while in anger ſuffers the man of ſin to prevail againſt them

1 Their covetouſneſs was among their crying ſins, Spiritual as well as corporal idolatry defiled them they prized gold more than God, and gain than godlineſs, and therefore God was wroth, ſold them into the hands of the Chaldeans, and ſeemed for a while utterly to turn away from them And this is remarkable, the predominant ſin of the miniſters in proteſtant churches, who, while they are only ſeeking their own advantage and preferment, are loſing the ſouls of their people, ſeduced by the emiſſaries of popery, and for this God hath a controverſy againſt them *Note,* (1) Covetouſneſs, though covered with many a ſpecious guiſe, is the ſin God abhors, and in miniſters of the goſpel is moſt peculiarly guilty (2) God's wrath, however little feared, will be proved terrible where it falls

2 Their hearts were obſtinate, and, inſtead of being reformed by their afflictions, *they went on frowardly*, fretting againſt the Lord, inſtead of falling low at his foot-ſtool, and perſiſting in the way of their covetouſneſs, inſtead of returning from it *Note,* The wicked heart of man is often made more furious by reſtraint, and the ſevereſt afflictions are ineffectual to convert him, unleſs the grace of God accompanies them

3 God's mercy triumphs over their perverſeneſs We might well have expected to have heard him ſay, *I have ſeen thy ways, and will deſtroy thee* but lo! the very reverſe, *I have ſeen his ways, and will heal him* We cannot heal or help ourſelves, our nature is utterly corrupt, unleſs ſovereign grace interpoſe, we are undone for ever This God ſees and knows, therefore he pardons freely, and, by the powerful influences of his Spirit, converts our ſouls, heals their inveterate diſeaſes, and draws us powerfully that we may follow him *I will lead him alſo* in the paths of righteouſneſs for my name's ſake, and hold up his goings in the way, *and reſtore comforts to him and to his mourners* brought to a deep and humbling ſenſe of their guilt, and, tho once hardened, now by divine grace melted down with ſorrow and ſhame God will therefore bind up their bleeding wounds, ſpeak comfortably to his people, and wipe every tear from their eyes *Note,* (1) It is a bleſſed ſymptom for good, when the ſoul begins to mourn over ſin (2) It is of God alone that our ſtubborn ſouls are ever brought to ſee and lament the evil of our ways (3) They who ſow in tears, are ſure to reap in joy

4 The comfort God will reſtore ariſes eſpecially from a ſenſe of the peace and reconciliation made between him and the ſinner *I create the fruit of the lips*, God gives both the cauſe for thankſgiving, and opens the heart and lips to ſpeak his praiſe *Peace, peace to him that is far off, and to him that is near, ſaith the Lord*, peace with God, peace of conſcience, peace from all enemies, peace preſent and eternal and to this the apoſtle ſeems to refer, *Eph* ii 17 and applies it to the preaching of the apoſtles, when not only the Jews, but the diſtant Gentile lands, heard the goſpel of peace, found pardon through the blood of the croſs, and were joined in one body, holding the unity of the Spirit in the bond of peace *and I will heal him*, recovering them from all their ſins and backſlidings, reſtoring them to a ſtate of purity, and healing all their diviſions *Note,* (1) None can ſpeak peace to the troubled ſoul, till God create that fruit of the lips, and make the word of goſpel grace in the mouth of his ſervants effectual (2) All who are reſtored to peace with God, from that moment begin to experience the ſanctifying influence of his grace

5 The impenitently wicked will finally periſh They *are like the troubled ſea, when it cannot reſt*, agitated by the winds of raging paſſion, toſſed to and fro with the ſtruggles of vile affection and innate corruption, and reſtleſs under the terrifying apprehenſions of the wrath which is revealed from heaven againſt all ungodlineſs and unrighteouſneſs of men *whoſe waters caſt up mire and dirt*, foaming out their own ſhame, polluting and defiling in their converſation, and all their comforts rendered bitter and loathſome by the curſe of God which mingles with them *There is no peace, ſaith my God, to the wicked*, no peace with God, no true peace of conſcience, no peace in death, no peace in eternity, but the wrath of God abideth on them

CHAP LVIII

This chapter is a reproof to all hypocritical profeſſors, and deſigned for thoſe who, under Hezekiah, conformed to his reformation, but continued unrenewed, it is highly applicable alſo to the Scribes and Phariſees in our Saviour's time, and ſtands as a perpetual rebuke to all who follow their ſteps in every age, and which the faithful miniſters muſt boldly urge on mens conſciences, ver 1 Obſerve, 1 The plauſible profeſſion of religion which they made, ver 2 2 The boaſts they made of that profeſſion, and the blame they laid upon God for taking no more notice of it ver 3 3 The ſins they are charged with, which ſpoiled their faſts, ver 4, 5 4 Inſtructions given them how to faſt aright, ver 6, 7 5 Precious promiſes made to thoſe who faſt aright, ver 8—12 6 The like precious promiſes made to thoſe that ſanctify ſabbaths aright, ver 13, 14

1 CRY † aloud, ſpare not, lift up thy voice like a
trumpet, and [a] ſhew my people their tranſgreſ-
ſion, and the houſe of Jacob their ſins. 2 Yet [b] they
ſeek me daily, and delight to know my ways, as a na-
tion that did righteouſneſs, and forſook not the ordinance
of their God they aſk of me the ordinances of juſtice
they take delight in approaching to God

† Heb With the throat a Ezek iii 17 b Chap xxix 13 Ezek xxxiii 31

v 1, 2 A commiſſion is given to the prophet to remonſtrate againſt the iniquity and hypocriſy of the people

1 He is commanded to be earneſt and bold in the diſcharge of his office *Cry aloud, ſpare not, lift up thy voice like a trumpet* Sinners are dull of hearing, they need ſons of thunder to ſpread the dire alarm of their danger, and miniſters who would be faithful to their truſt, muſt be free, bold, and earneſt in their reproofs, and accept no man's perſon *and ſhew my people their tranſgreſſion, and the houſe of Jacob their ſins*, in which, notwithſtanding their pious profeſſions, they lived, and which, diſtinctly and particularly, God's miniſters muſt charge home upon their conſciences, particularly their formality, ſelf-dependence, and hypocriſy

2 Their pretences to religion muſt not impoſe upon him, they were but an aggravation of their guilt, and called for a ſharper rebuke *Yet they ſeek me daily*, affect to appear ſollicitous in the ordinances of worſhip, make it their conſtant practice to attend their devotions public and private, *and delight to know my ways*, in appearance, take pleaſure in attending the moſt powerful and evangelical preachers, and deſire to furniſh their heads with right ſentiments of religion, *as a nation that did righteouſneſs*, they would fain appear righteous unto men, *and forſook not the ordinance of their God*, to whoſe favour they made a ſtrong claim, and joined in the exerciſe of worſhip, praying, reading, ſinging, communicating *They aſk of me the ordinances of juſtice*, enquiring of God's miniſters, and in their prayers teſtifying an earneſt concern to know the right way, and walk in it *They take delight in approaching to God*; pleaſed with their own ſervices, and either counting them meritorious in the eye of God, or expecting from them men's eſteem and admiration *Note,* (1) The moſt deteſtable character before God is the hypocrite (2) How far, how very far may men go, to appearance, in the way to heaven? even to be admired and envied for their gifts and piety, and yet in fact be only hastening to their own damnation, and ſo much nearer the belly of hell

3 ¶ [c] Wherefore have we faſted, *ſay they*, and thou
ſeeſt not? *wherefore* have we ‖ afflicted our ſoul, and
thou takeſt no knowledge? Behold, in the day of your
faſt you find pleaſure, and exact all your ‖ labours 4
Behold, ye faſt for ſtrife and debate, [h] and to ſmite
with the fiſt of wickedneſs ye ſhall not faſt as *ye do*
this day, to make your voice to be heard on high 5
Is it [i] ſuch a faſt that I have choſen? [k] ‖ a day for a
man to afflict his ſoul? *Is it* to bow down his head as
a bulruſh, and [l] to ſpread ſackcloth and aſhes under
him? wilt thou call this a faſt, and an acceptable day
to the LORD? 6 *Is* not this the faſt that I have
choſen? [k] to looſe the bands of wickedneſs, to undo the
heavy burdens, and [l] to let the § oppreſſed go free, and
that ye break every yoke? 7 *Is it* not [m] to deal thy
bread to the hungry, and that thou bring the poor
[n] ‖ that are caſt out, to thy houſe? [o] when thou ſeeſt the
naked, that thou cover him, and that thou hide not
thyſelf from [p] thine own fleſh?

c Mal iii 14 Luke xviii 9 &c d Lev xvi 29 31 & xxiii 27 ‖ Heb griefs e 1 Kings xxi 9 12 Luke xx 17 f Zech vii 5 g Lev xvi 29 ‖ Or, to afflict his ſoul for a day h Mic vi 16 i Neh ix 1 Joel ii 12 Dan ix 3 k Mic vi 10 l Jer xxxiv 9 § Or, broken m Ezek xviii 7 16 Mat xxv 35 n Heb xi 37 ‖ Or, afflicted o Job xxxi 19 20 Mat xxv 36 p Neh v 5 Luke x 31

Before Christ 699

v 3—7 Because these hypocrites had so many good things to say of themselves, they are here

1 Reprehended as expostulating with God for paying no more regard to them Having an high opinion of themselves, their doings and duties, they would fain have God express the like approbation of them *Wherefore have we fasted, and thou seest not? wherefore have we afflicted our soul, and thou takest no knowledge?* Note, (1) There are those who fast and afflict their souls from a principle of pride and self-righteousness, as well as from a spirit of real humiliation (2) Many flatter themselves God will reward the services he in fact abhors (3) Nothing more highly exasperates those who value themselves on their own goodness, than to have the vanity of their self-dependence shewn them, and the folly of their hopes detected

2 The hypocrisy of their duties is rebuked If God disregarded them, he had abundant cause to do so They *took pleasure*, and prided themselves in their fasts, as if they were more righteous than others, they *exacted all their labours*, rigorous and severe with their servants, and unrelenting towards their poor debtors *They fasted for strife and debate*, appointing these solemn seasons to perpetuate divisions among them, by pretending to cast the cause of their national afflictions on others sins, instead of their own, or making their fast days occasion of strife and debate, when and how they should be observed, *and to smite with the fist of wickedness*, oppressing and ill-using the poor insolvent debtors, whilst they pretended to be humbling their souls for their own offences before God *Ye shall not fast as ye do this day, to make your voice to be heard on high*, either clamorous against their debtors, or threatening their servants, or disputing with each other, or with their pompous and loud devotions affecting extraordinary piety *Is it such a fast that I have chosen? a day for a man to afflict his soul?* the mere wretched work of abstaining from meat for a few hours, whilst the heart continues utterly unhumbled and unrenewed? *Is it to bow the head like a bulrush, and to spread sackcloth and ashes under him?* Is this enough, to make a parade of the external tokens of pretended humiliation? *wilt thou call this a fast, and an acceptable day to the Lord?* can it be possible, that he should be pleased or approve such a farce of religious ceremony? No, God searcheth the heart, he seeth falsehood and hypocrisy, and will not accept the services of feigned lips Note, (1) To pretend a zeal for religion, and live in the indulgence of iniquity, is to be hypocritical, and the sure way to destroy our own souls (2) A demure look, and affectation of sanctity, may pass upon men for eminent piety, but God requireth truth in the inward parts

3 God prescribes the true nature of a religious fast He wills the soul should be afflicted for sin, whilst the body is humbled in the dust, and, as the surest proof of it, that there be a change wrought in our lives *Is not this the fast that I have chosen, to loose the bands of wickedness?* in general, to break off from every known sin, from every wicked combination, *to undo the heavy burdens* from the poor servant, who groaned under unreasonable commands, or from the poor debtor loaded with chains, who had really nothing to pay, *and to let the oppressed go free*, obtain his discharge from vexatious suits, or hard servitude, *and that ye break every yoke*, no more enslaving or harrassing their brethren *Is it not to deal thy bread to the hungry?* whom want compels to crave relief, and needs the bread, which in our fasts we are called to deny ourselves, *and that thou bring the poor that are cast out to thy house*, those who shiver in the cold, and have no covering, or the poor refugees *that suffer persecution*, as the word may be rendered, for conscience sake, and are driven from their own homes *When thou seest the naked, that thou cover him*, not say, be warm, be filled, and give him not the things he needs, but clothe him, *and that thou hide not thyself from thine own flesh*, not only those near relatives, who have the first claim to our bounty, but esteeming every man a brother, as of the same blood, and especially those of the houshold of faith Note, (1) If any man seeth his brother in need, and shutteth up his bowels of compassion from him how dwelleth the love of God in him? (2) They who have the deep sense of the divine charity of Jesus to them, will ever be most ready to open their hearts and their hands to relieve the distresses of others

8 ¶ Then shall thy light break forth as the morn-
ing, and thine health shall spring forth speedily and
thy righteousness shall go before thee, the glory of
the LORD shall be thy rereward 9 Then shalt
thou call, and the LORD shall answer, thou shalt
cry, and he shall say, Here I *am* If thou take away
from the midst of thee the yoke, the putting forth of
the finger, and speaking vanity 10 And *if* thou
draw out thy soul to the hungry, and satisfy the af-
flicted soul then shall thy light rise in obscurity, and
thy darkness *be* as the noon day 11 And the LORD
shall guide thee continually, and satisfy thy soul in
drought, and make fat thy bones and thou shalt be
like a watered garden, and like a spring of water, whose
waters ‡ fail not 12 And *they that shall be* of thee,
shall build the old waste places thou shalt raise up the
foundations of many generations, and thou shalt be cal-
led, The repairer of the breach, the restorer of paths
to dwell in

‡ Or, lie, *or* deceive
a Chap. lxi. 4. & lxi.
b Mat. xvii. 11

v 8—12 They who walk in the ways of grace, will ever find them paths of blessedness We have here,

1 The gracious conduct enjoined *If thou take away from the midst of thee the yoke*, abstaining from every oppression and severity towards their brethren, and labouring, as far as their influence and authority prevail, to restrain it in others, *the putting forth of the finger*, either as a mark of threatening or correction, or as a token of contempt and derision, *and speaking vanity*, hypocritical addresses to God, flattering speeches to men, or falsehood and lying in their dealings one with another *And if thou draw out thy soul to the hungry*, not only relieving their wants, but expressing for them the tenderest compassion, which doubly enhances the favour, *and satisfy the afflicted soul*, whatever are the causes of his distress, kindly affording him every assistance for his body, or soul, then God will reckon these works of faith and labours of love Note, The world is full of compassionate objects, we shall not want opportunity, if we do not want a heart to do good

2 Many and rich blessings are promised to those who thus walk in love, and live to be useful

(1) God will remember them in the day of affliction, and cause their light to shine *Then shall thy light rise in obscurity, and thy darkness be as the noon day*, out of every trouble God would deliver them Swiftly, as the morning breaks, and plentifully, as the rising sun dispels the shadows of the night, so should *thy light break forth*, their comfort, credit, and prosperity, shining more and more unto the perfect day, *and thine health shall spring forth speedily*, if they had been afflicted in body or soul, the affliction shall be removed Note, They will be no losers who lend unto the Lord, by relieving his people in distress, he will repay, nay, over-pay them for their kindness

(2) The Lord will be their protector and guide *thy righteousness shall go before thee*, as the evidence of their fidelity, or rather, the Lord their righteousness would go before them, make their title good to the heavenly glory, and answer every charge which might be brought against them, *and the glory of the Lord shall be thy rereward*, or *shall gather thee* as a strong body of troops, that protects the rear, and gathers up the stragglers that none be lost, so the Lord will preserve them safe in all their ways, and magnify his own glory in their salvation *The Lord shall guide thee continually*, by his word, spirit, and providences, and this continually, night and day, lest any hurt them Note, They are happily secured, who see the righteousness of the Redeemer before them as their sure acceptance, and the glory of God engaged for their support and perseverance

(3) All their prayers shall be heard and answered *Thou shalt call, and the Lord shall answer, thou shalt cry, and he shall say, Here am I*, a very present help in trouble, whilst they are speaking, he will hear, he will be near them when frighted they cry to him, and he is ready to do more and better for them than they are able to ask or think Note, If we have so great, so kind a friend ever at hand, so willing, so able to help us, let us never neglect to apply to him, and then, who can harm us?

(4) God will supply all their wants, spiritual and temporal *He will satisfy thy soul in drought*, when the lions lack and suffer hunger, they shall be fed, or when thirsting in this barren land for Christ, the water of life, for his righteousness and grace, for his presence and spirit, he will refresh them, *and make fat thy bones*, giving them plenty, or rather comforting and strengthening the souls of his people, and causing them to increase with the increase of God *And thou shalt be like a watered garden*, adorned with divine graces as a garden blooming with beauty, breathing fragrance, and laden with the choicest fruits, *and like a spring of water, whose waters fail not*, the heavenly principle of grace implanted never failing, but springing up into everlasting life

(5) They shall be honoured as the instruments of building up the church of God *And they that shall be of thee shall build the old waste places*, which may refer to those of the Jews, who, on their return from Babylon, restored the cities, and especially Jerusalem, that had lain in Ruins, or to those God will employ in the gospel to build up *the waste places of the world*, as it may be rendered, the whole earth having been covered with the desolation of ignorance and sin, till by the preaching of the word the Gentiles were converted, and christianity established, *and thou shalt raise up the foundations of many generations*, as when the temple was raised from its rubbish, so shall the church of Christ rise beautiful and glorious, and endure to all generations *and thou shalt be called the repairer of the breach, and the restorer of paths to dwell in*, they shall be honoured by those who have been called through their ministry, the breach which abounding iniquity had made shall be repaired, all divisions healed, and by their means the paths of truth and holiness become happily frequented

13 ¶

Before Christ 698.

13 ¶ [c] If thou turn away thy foot from the sabbath,
from doing thy pleasure on my holy day, and call the
sabbath [d] a delight, the holy of the LORD, honour-
able, and shalt honour him, not doing thine own ways,
nor finding thine own pleasure, nor speaking *thine own*
words: 14 Then [e] shalt thou delight thyself in the
LORD, and I will cause thee [f] to ride upon the high
places of the earth, and feed thee with [g] the heritage of
Jacob thy father: for the mouth of the LORD hath
spoken *it*.

c Chap. lvi. 2. d Pf. xl. 4. e Job xxii. 26. f Deut. xxxii. 13. Chap. xxx. 1. g Pf. cxxxv. 12.

v. 13, 14. A serious and conscientious observance of the sabbath day, is one of the best evidences, and surest means of having the heart devoted to God.

1. The sanctification of this day is described, *v.* 13. *If thou turn away thy foot from the sabbath*, from trampling upon it, by profane neglect, making it a day of travelling, idleness, or visiting; *from doing thy pleasure on my holy day*, not making it a day of vain amusements, or spending it in those recreations, that at another season may be lawful; *and call the sabbath a delight*, welcoming its return with gladness, counting these sacred hours the happiest portion of our time, and spending them with joy in his blessed service of prayer, praise, meditation, godly conversation; *call the holy of the Lord*, respecting its divine institution, *and honourable*, employing ourselves in it as may most conduce to advance the honour and glory of God; *and shalt honour him*, who appointed this day of rest, *not doing thine own ways* in any secular business, or the work of common life; *nor finding thine own pleasure*, turning it into a day of hunting, diversion, or vanity; *nor speaking thine own words*, the thoughts of this world, and the cares of it should be banished from our minds, and all our conversation be employed about the things of God, and how we may secure to ourselves a part in his eternal rest.

2. The benefit of such an improvement of the Lord's day, will be great; for *then shalt thou delight thyself in the Lord*, abundant consolation will be the blessed fruit, and clearer discoveries of the riches of the grace and love of Christ be made to the soul, so that by experience we shall say, one day in thy courts is better than a thousand; *and I will cause thee to ride upon the high places of the earth*, in safety from every enemy, exalted to honour; or, spiritually, to live above the earth, and have our conversation in heaven, enjoying the comfort and dignity of being sons of God; *and feed thee with the heritage of Jacob thy father*, with all the blessings of the covenant of promise, and the foretastes of eternal bliss, more precious than the richest provision of Canaan, the heritage of Israel: *for the mouth of the Lord hath spoken it*, and therefore we may confidently trust him, for he will never disappoint our hopes. Heaven and earth shall pass away, but his word shall never pass away, until the whole be fulfilled.

CHAP. LIX.

In this chapter we have, first, a strong and affecting description of a sinful and generation, and of what [illegible] the sinner's sin, ver. 7, 8. is applied to the general corruption of mankind, Rom. iii. 15. [illegible] what is here said [illegible] a Redeemer, ver. 20. is applied to Christ, Rom. xi. 26. 1. The particular sins are explained which kept good things from God's people, ver. 1—8. 2. They are told both what the judgments were which they had brought upon their own heads, ver. 9—11. and that the sins which provoked God to send these judgments, ver. 12—15. 3. It is here promised, that notwithstanding this, God would work deliverance for them, purely for his own name's sake, ver. 16—19. and would reserve mercy in store for, and extend it upon them, ver. 20, 21.

a Numb. xi. 23. b Chap. lviii. 17. [illegible]

1 BEHOLD, the LORD's hand is [a] not shortned,
that it cannot save: neither his ear heavy,
that it cannot hear: 2 But your iniquities have sepa-
rated between you and your God, and your sins have
[b] hid his face from you, that he will not hear. 3 For
[c] your hands are defiled with blood, and your fingers
with iniquity; [d] your lips have spoken lies, your tongue
hath muttered perverseness. 4 None calleth for justice,
[e] nor *any* pleadeth for truth: they trust in vanity, and
speak lies; they [f] conceive mischief, and bring forth in-
iquity. 5 They hatch cockatrice eggs, and weave the
spider's web: he that eateth of their eggs dieth, and
that which is crushed breaketh out into a viper.
6 [h] Their webs shall not become garments, neither
shall they cover themselves with their works: their works
are works of iniquity, and the act of violence *is* in
their hands. 7 [i] Their feet run to evil, and they make
haste to shed innocent blood: their thoughts *are* thoughts
of iniquity; wasting and destruction *are* in their paths.
8 The way of peace they know not; and *there is* no
judgment in their goings: [k] they have made them
crooked paths: whosoever goeth therein shall not know
peace.

Before Christ 698.

v. 1—8. They had complained before of God's inattention to their fasting and prayers. God here in these convinces them that the fault was in themselves.

1. It was their sins, not want of power or grace in him, that occasioned the continuance of their afflictions. *Behold, the Lord's hand is not shortened, that it cannot save*, he is the same, yesterday, to-day, and for ever; length of time, or strength of foes, make no difference with him; *neither his ear heavy, that it cannot hear*, his regard for, and attention to his people, is unchangeable, and they who cry to him in simplicity will find him ever near to answer and relieve them: if our prayers return not with a blessing, it is because we ask amiss, or grow weary and faint in our minds. *But your iniquities have separated between you and your God, and your sins have hid his face from you, that he will not hear*. Here is the grand obstacle, and this remaining, how can we hope to succeed with him? See Pf. lxvi. 18. *Note*, (1.) Though God may be really our God, yet by our perverseness we may provoke him to withdraw, and in their sins he justly leaves his own people in darkness to lament his absence. (2.) Sin is the accursed thing that breeds all our sorrows: oh that we saw it in its true colours, and hated it as it deserves! (3.) It is in vain for us to hope for any return of peace to our prayers, while we allow iniquity to cut off the intercourse between God and our soul.

2. God had charged them with sin in general; here a variety of particulars is alledged, fully vindicating the divine procedure against them.

[1.] Their hearts were desperately wicked; *their thoughts are thoughts of iniquity*, this is ever uppermost in their minds; *they conceive mischief*, as the embryo is formed in the womb, so in their hearts the purpose of sin ripens into act, *and they bring forth iniquity*. *They hatch cockatrice eggs, and weave the spider's web*, their schemes are curiously formed, with much art and labour, and though they appear fair without, they are big with poison, and the most pernicious consequences. *He that eateth of their eggs dieth*, whoever credulously embraces the false doctrines they broach, or is seduced to follow the evil practices they patronize, brings upon himself swift destruction; *and that which is crushed breaketh out into a viper*, either the foot that incautiously treads in the way of such, is in danger of being stung, or the very attempt to crush them is dangerous, as exposing those who do it to [illegible] and persecution. *Their webs shall not become garments, neither shall they cover themselves with their works*. They who build on them [illegible] will be finally disappointed, and be left naked before the wrath of God; [illegible] will especially be the case of all who set up their own works and duties as the ground of their acceptance with God, which can no more serve for a robe of righteousness, than a spider's web for a garment.

[2.] Out of the abundance of their heart, their mouth speaketh; *your lips have spoken lies, and your tongue hath muttered perverseness*, false and fraudulent in their dealings, backbiters, and whisperers, or it may refer to the heretical tenets they broached and openly supported, to the great ruin of men's souls.

[3.] Their actions corresponded with their evil heart; *your hands are defiled with blood, and your fingers with iniquity*, either shed in passion, or under pretext of justice, or rather with the blood of martyrs, who, opposing their wicked ways, suffered for their fidelity. This left upon their conscience deep defilement, and cried for vengeance. *Their feet run to evil*, eager in the pursuit, and impatient to gratify their malice and revenge; *they make haste to shed innocent blood: wasting and destruction are in their paths*, they spread desolation around them, ruining both body and soul, and their ways will conduct them at last to everlasting perdition.

[4.] All truth and justice is banished; *none calleth for justice*, the injured dare not complain, because power is with their oppressors, and none will interest themselves in their behalf, or see them righted: *nor any pleadeth for truth*, supporting the cause of oppressed innocence, or vindicating the truths of God [illegible] the errors and heresies with which these wicked men have obscured and perverted them. *They trust in vanity*, deceive themselves as well as others with false confidence; or they trust in lies, hoping, by bold and confident assertions, to carry the cause against truth and justice. *The way of peace they know not*, how should they, when all their thoughts, words, and deeds, are opposite to God and holiness? *and there is no judgment in their goings*, no justice in their dealings with men, no discernment of the right way before God, no apprehension of their own danger. *They have made them crooked paths*, all their ways are perverse before God: *whosoever goeth therein shall not know peace*, no true peace of conscience, or solid satisfaction, but misery, like their shadow, must attend them, and the wrath of God, present and eternal, abide upon them. *Note*, Many cry peace to their souls, whose ways inevitably tend to everlasting perdition.

k Chap. lvii. 20, 21. [illegible]

Before Christ 699

‖ Jer viii 15
m Deut xxviii 29 Job v 14 Lam iv 14
n Ps xxii 1 & xxxviii 8
o Chap xxxviii 14 Ezek vii 16
‖ Chap i 4 & ii 4
r Mat xii 34
‖ Or is accounted mad see 2 Sam ix 1 1 Pet iv, 4

9 ¶ Therefore is judgment far from us, neither doth justice overtake us ‖ we wait for light, but behold obscurity, for brightness, *but* we walk in darkness 10 m We grope for the wall like the blind, and we grope as if *we had* no eyes we stumble at noonday as in the night, *we are* in desolate places as dead *men* 11 We n roar all like bears, and o mourn sore like doves we look for judgment, but *there is* none, for salvation, *but* it is far off from us 12 For our p transgressions are multiplied q before thee, and our sins testify against us for our transgressions *are* with us, and *as for* our iniquities, we know them 13 In transgressing and lying against the LORD, and departing away from our God, speaking oppression and revolt, conceiving and r uttering from the heart words of falshood 14 And judgment is turned away backward, and justice standeth afar off for truth is fallen in the street, and equity cannot enter 15 Yea, truth faileth, and he *that* departeth from evil ‖ maketh himself a prey and the LORD saw *it*, and it displeased him that *there was* no judgment

v 9—15 Tho in general there appears to have been a grievous departure from God, yet in every age a few faithful are found, and they are here represented confessing and bewailing the prevailing sins and misery of their people

1 Their misery was great under the power of their oppressors No justice could be obtained from man, and God in righteous judgment refused to vindicate their quarrel and execute vengeance on their foes Their expectations were grievously disappointed, they waited *for light, but beheld obscurity*, for *brightness*, or *brightnesses*, some eminent interposition of God to rescue them from their afflictions, *but we walk in darkness*, in thickest darkness, their troubles increasing rather than diminishing, and their hopes sinking fast into black despair, v 9 Totally at a loss what way to direct their course, like blind men they groped for the wall, and, though they had God's word, as a light shining in a dark place, they neglected or misunderstood it, so that in *the noon-day they stumbled as in the night*, they were ready to give up all for lost, *in desolate places*, dejected, and retiring to mournful solitudes to pour out their griefs, or *in fatnesses*, where they had abundant means of grace, yet not quickened by them others render the word, *in sepulchres, as dead men*, their state desperate and irrecoverable as that of the dead, v 10 under which calamities, bitter were their groanings, roaring as bears, or mourning as doves, they saw no prospect of deliverance, and God seemed to have utterly withdrawn from them his salvation, v 11 *Note*, (1) When power is in the hands of oppressors, little justice can be expected (2) They who hope for the light of God's countenance, yet walk in the way of iniquity, must needs be disappointed (3) None so blind as those, who in the midst of gospel day, hate the light of truth justly doth God leave them to the darkness they have chosen (4) Sinners are ever swinging to extremes, in prosperity secure, in adversity despairing (5) When the mourning of the sufferer is more for his sins than his calamities, there is then hope of relief

2 The faithful, who in the name of the people lament their sufferings, confess their sins as the just cause of them all the charges God had brought against them are acknowledged to be altogether righteous and true Their transgressions were many, great, and aggravated, especially as a professing people, for which their conscience condemned them and which it were folly to attempt concealing from God, v 12 particularly *in transgressing and lying against the Lord*, being false to their vows, and faithless in breaking their allegiance to him, or misrepresenting his truth, as now is done, by robbing the Redeemer of the glories of his godhead, and denying his vicarious righteousness and atonement *and departing away from our God*, from his commands, worship, and ordinances, *speaking oppression and revolt*, not merely rebels themselves, but daring to utter their treasonable designs against God's honour and glory, in order to seduce others to join in their defection, and where they have power, oppressing those that are zealous to oppose their false doctrines and pernicious ways, *conceiving and uttering from the heart words of falshood*, contriving how to propagate their errors, and earnest in maintaining them, v 13 Justice had ceased to exert herself, and truth was no longer regarded by which all the bonds of civil society were dissolved, or it may respect the state of the decayed churches of protestantism, where the true doctrines of the gospel are generally exploded and trampled upon Those who should be the first to see them maintained, are the chief apostates from them, whilst the few that remain [illegible] to the principles of free grace in Jesus Christ, are oppressed without redress, and find no advocate, and the door of admission into the ministry shut against them, v 14 So that truth faileth, *yea, and he that departeth from evil maketh himself a prey*, when falshood and iniquity are become fashionable, it is dangerous to be singularly faithful, it ruins a man's interest in the world, and exposes him to the persecution of his brethren, who cannot bear the reproof of his words and ways so opposite to their own, or it may be rendered, *is reckoned a madman*, treated as an enthusiast, as melancholic, or disturbed in his senses, for such his conduct makes him appear to those, who, destitute of all zeal for God's glory themselves, and only anxious about worldly advantage, regard others, who act on principles so utterly different, as fools or mad *And the Lord saw it, and it displeased him that there was no judgment*, he observed it, and was justly displeased at the abounding iniquity, peculiarly criminal in a people professing godliness

s Ezek xxii 30
t Ps xcviii 1 Chap lxiii 5
u Eph vi 14, 17 1 Thess v 8
x Chap lxiii 6
† Heb recompences
y Ps cxiii Mal i 11
z Rev xii 15
a Zech iv 6
‡ Or put him to flight
b Rom xi 26
c Chap i 27
d Deut xxx 3 Acts ii 36
e Heb viii 10 & x 16
f Rom ix 8 Gal iii 29

16 ¶ And s he saw that *there was* no man, and wondered that *there was* no intercessor therefore t his arm brought salvation unto him, and his righteousness, it sustained him 17 For u he put on righteousness as a breast plate, and an helmet of salvation upon his head, and he put on the garments of vengeance *for* cloathing, and was clad with zeal as a cloak 18 x According to *their* † deeds, accordingly he will repay, fury to his adversaries, recompence to his enemies, to the islands he will repay recompence 19 So y shall they fear the name of the LORD from the west, and his glory from the rising of the sun when the enemy shall come in z like a flood, a the Spirit of the LORD shall ‡ lift up a standard against him 20 ¶ And b the Redeemer shall come to c Zion, and d unto them that turn from transgression in Jacob, saith the LORD 21 As for me, e this *is* my covenant with them, saith the LORD, My Spirit that *is* upon thee, and my words, which I have put in thy mouth, shall not depart out of thy mouth, nor out of the mouth of thy f seed, nor out of the mouth of thy seed's seed, saith the LORD, from henceforth and for ever

v 16—21 We have heard before how sin abounded, we see here how grace much more abounded.

1 God beheld their deplorable case with an eye of pity *He saw that there was no man*, none, comparatively speaking, for some few, as appears, lamented their unhappy case, but in general, there was no man who cared to espouse the sinking cause of justice and truth, or laid to heart the evil of their ways, *and wondered that there was no intercessor* to stand in the gap, and plead, like Abraham for Sodom, if it were possible to avert the impending judgments At this God is said *to wonder*, for, speaking after the manner of men, considering what means and mercies he had vouchsafed them, such a general apostacy was strange *Note*, It is very bad with a nation, when her praying advocates cease, or are few, it is to be feared then destruction is near

2 To save them from utter ruin, God is pleased graciously to interpose *Therefore his arm brought salvation to him*, when they had no power nor resolution to help themselves, he magnified his strength in their weakness, and by himself, and for his own glory, arose to save them, which may be applied to the deliverance of the Jews from Babylon, but according to the following verses, more eminently refers to the great salvation of Jesus, who by his own arm vanquished the spiritual enemies of his people, and wrought out a complete salvation for them; *and his righteousness it sustained him*, his own divine righteousness was his support, and enabled him effectually to accomplish the redemption of his people, or his faithfulness to his promise, notwithstanding their provocations, engaged him to deliver them, *for he put on righteousness as a breast-plate*, being in his own person perfectly pure and holy, all the fiery darts of the enemy were repelled, and when the prince of the world came to tempt him, he found him invulnerable, or by his righteous procedure, in delivering his people, and destroying their enemies, he eminently secured his own honour and faithfulness, *and an helmet of salvation upon his head*, clad in that divine panoply, which renders him terrible to his foes, and most adorable and amiable in the eyes of his friends *and he put on the garments of vengeance for cloathing, and was clad with zeal as a cloak*, zeal for his own glory, and his people's cause, [illegible] against his enemies and theirs, which now to the uttermost he resolves to execute *According to their deeds, accordingly he will repay, fury to his adversaries, recompence to his enemies, to the islands he will repay recompence*, a just retaliation for the wrongs they have committed against his people, and which will extend to all, even the most distant nations, that have any way oppressed or persecuted them *Note*, (1) Let not wicked men think with impunity to trample on the faithful, their day is coming, big with wrath and fury, the day of vengeance of our God (2) Let not the persecuted saints of God faint under their trials, their Lord is at hand, and he will shortly save them to the uttermost

3 The glory of God in the salvation shall be spread far and wide *So shall they fear the name of the Lord from the west, and his glory from the rising of the sun* from east to west the knowledge

Before Christ 699

knowledge of the Redeemer's work ſhall be ſpread, and God be magnified for his grace, who hath viſited and redeemed his people, and he will alſo continue to protect and preſerve them for ever *When the enemy ſhall come in like a flood, the Spirit of the Lord ſhall lift up a ſtandard againſt him*, which ſome interpret of a flood of hereſy and perſecution, which under the reign of antichriſt ſhall break in upon the nations others of the irruption of the Turks and Tartars in the eaſt, and the Goths and Vandals in the weſt, and it may more generally be applied to the floods of ungodlineſs that the great enemy of mankind in every place is ſeeking to raiſe, in order to overwhelm the cauſe of God and truth but in vain, for the Lord will, in his appointed time, break the Mahomedan and Popiſh yoke, and by his Spirit, wherever the goſpel is preached, doth continually glorify his grace in the ſalvation of ſinners from the power of ſatan, and the dominion of ſin

4 This ſalvation will moſt eminently be manifeſted in that day of the Redeemer's appearing, when he ſhall take to him his great power and reign and hereunto the apoſtle applies the words, *Rom* xi 25 26 *And the Redeemer ſhall come to Zion, and unto them that turn from tranſgreſſion in Jacob, ſaith the Lord*, when having gathered in the fulneſs of the Gentiles, his ancient people the Jews ſhall at laſt be converted to him, and turning from their long courſe of tranſgreſſion, and their inveterate rejection of the Meſſiah, they ſhall receive him, and enter into the common fold of the church, where all diſtinction between Jew and Gentile will ceaſe *As for me, this is my covenant with them*, for God hath not caſt away his people, whom he foreknew, but there are covenant bleſſings ſtill in ſtore for them, *my Spirit, which is upon thee, and my words, which I have put in thy mouth*, the Redeemer having received his meſſage from his Father, and the Spirit without meaſure for the diſcharge of his office as Mediator, and in order to furniſh his miniſters and people out of his fulneſs unto the end of time, *ſhall not depart out of thy mouth, nor out of the mouth of thy ſeed, nor out of the mouth of thy ſeed's ſeed, ſaith the Lord, from henceforth and for ever* God will have alway a church, and maintain the miniſtry of his goſpel in the world, and by his Spirit will conſtantly make it effectual to the converſion of mens ſouls, and eſpecially in the laſt days a more abundant out-pouring of this word and Spirit will be ſeen, and the knowledge of the Lord cover the earth, as the waters cover the ſea *Note*, (1) The church of Chriſt is founded on a rock, againſt which the floods ſhall not prevail (2) It is by the miniſtry of the word that the church is maintained and preſerved (3) The word is made effectual by the Spirit, which accompanies it to the heart, and Chriſt hath promiſed, in the power of his grace, to be with his miniſters always, even to the end of the world (4) When the Spirit of God is pleaſed to convert the ſoul, his work is for ever, he will keep thoſe whom he calls, and they ſhall never periſh

CHAP LX

The vaſt extent of the goſpel church is the ſubject of this chapter, in which it is promiſed, 1 That the church ſhall be enlightened, ver 1, 2 2 That it ſhould be greatly enlarged, ver 3—8 3 That the new converts ſhould be very ſerviceable to it, ver 9—13 4 That it ſhould be in great honour and repute among men, ver 14—16 5 That it ſhould enjoy a profound peace and tranquillity, ver 17, 18 6 That the members of it being all righteous, the glory and joy of it ſhall be everlaſting, ver 19—22

1 ARISE, ſhine, for [b] thy light is come, and [c] the
glory of the LORD is riſen upon thee
2 For behold, [d] the darkneſs ſhall cover the earth, and
groſs darkneſs the people but the LORD ſhall ariſe
upon thee, and his glory ſhall be ſeen upon thee
3 And [e] the Gentiles ſhall come to thy light, and kings
to the brightneſs of thy riſing 4 [f] Lift up thine eyes
round about, and ſee, all they gather themſelves toge-
ther, [g] they come to thee, thy ſons ſhall come from far,
and thy daughters ſhall be nurſed at *thy* ſide 5 Then
thou ſhalt ſee and flow together, and thine heart ſhall
fear, and be enlarged, becauſe [h] the ‖ abundance of the
ſea ſhall be converted unto thee, the † forces of the
Gentiles ſhall come unto thee 6 The multitude of
camels ſhall cover thee the dromedaries of Midian and
Ephah all [i] they from Sheba ſhall come they ſhall
bring [k] gold and incenſe, and they ſhall ſhew forth the
praiſes of the LORD 7 [l] All the flocks of Kedar
ſhall be gathered together unto thee, the rams of Ne-
baioth ſhall miniſter unto thee they ſhall come up
with acceptance on mine altar, and I will glorify the
houſe of my glory 8 Who *are* theſe *that* fly as a cloud,
and as the doves to their windows?

v 1—8 The glory and increaſe of the church of Chriſt are here beautifully repreſented

1 Great light and glory are beſtowed on her *Ariſe, ſhine, for thy light is come*, the light of the goſpel illuminating a benighted world, wakening up ſinners from the ſleep of ſpiritual death, and turning their miſery into joy and gladneſs, *for the glory of the Lord is riſen upon thee*, Chriſt, the ſun of righteouſneſs, with healing in his wings, manifeſting, in the moſt tranſcendent manner, the glory of God, in the pardon and ſalvation of his people *For behold, the darkneſs ſhall cover the earth, and groſs darkneſs the people* either when this light ſhould break forth it would be the more welcome and ſurprizing, becauſe of the darkneſs, ignorance, idolatry, and ſuperſtition, which every where prevailed, or it ſpeaks the diſtinguiſhing privilege of thoſe to whom the goſpel was preached, who, like Iſrael in Goſhen, had light in their dwellings, whilſt the reſt of the world, to whom it hath not come, or who have rejected it, are like the land of Egypt, covered with darkneſs that may be felt *but the Lord ſhall ariſe upon thee, and his glory ſhall be ſeen upon thee*, as it reſted on the tabernacle in the pillar of a cloud and fire, not only protecting his church ſafely, but making her appear beautiful and glorious, the joy of the whole earth *Note*, (1) Without the light of the goſpel, the higheſt attainments of human wiſdom are but folly and darkneſs (2) They who have ſeen Chriſt ariſing upon their ſouls in his glory, are bound to ſhine to his praiſe, and let their light appear before men, that they may take knowledge of them that they have been with Jeſus

2 A great increaſe of the church is promiſed Allured by the goſpel word, and ſtruck with the bright examples of believers, the Gentiles ſhall become converts, and bow down before Chriſt the Sun of Righteouſneſs, *v* 3 On every ſide behold, they flock together, as children to their parents, to be nouriſhed with the ſincere milk of the word *See Acts* xi 5 With pleaſing ſurprize the church will behold this ſtrange acceſſion, and in a tranſport of joy receive the multitude of minners, and armies of Gentile ſoldiers, that among others ſhall be converted unto the truth, *v* 5 From Midian and Ephah they ſhall come in vaſt companies, riding on camels and dromedaries From Sheba they ſhall bring gold and incenſe, *See Matt* ii 11 and ſhew forth the praiſes of the Lord, for his mercy in calling them to himſelf *v* 6 The inhabitants of Kedar and Nebaioth, in Arabia, whoſe riches chiefly conſiſted in their flocks, ſhall offer themſelves and their ſubſtance up to God, and through Chriſt their ſpiritual ſacrifices ſhall be accepted, and God glorified in their converſion, *v* 7 As a cloud before the wind, and as the doves flying to their windows, ſo thick, unanimous, openly, and eagerly, ſhall the Gentiles haſten into the church of God, whilſt with wonder and delight, the faithful welcome them to their reſt *Note*, (1) When our ſouls, like the dove, are weary with wandering, or purſued by our ſpiritual enemies, as birds of prey, we muſt fly to Chriſt for ſhelter, and under the ſhadow of his wings ſhall be ſafe, and find a pleaſing reſting-place (2) It is among the chief delights of a ſoul that loves the Lord Jeſus Chriſt in ſincerity, to behold his kingdom eſtabliſhed, and many converted unto him

9 [a] Surely the iſles ſhall wait for me, and the ſhips
of Tarſhiſh firſt, [o] to bring thy ſons from far, [p] their
ſilver and their gold with them, [q] unto the name of the
LORD thy God and to the Holy One of Iſrael,
becauſe he hath glorified thee 10 And [r] the ſons of
ſtrangers ſhall build up thy walls, and [s] their kings ſhall
miniſter unto thee for in my wrath I ſmote thee, but
in my favour have I had mercy on thee 11 There-
fore [t] thy gates ſhall be open continually, they ſhall not
be ſhut day nor night, that *men* may bring unto thee
the ‖ forces of the Gentiles, and *that* their Kings *may*
be brought 12 For [u] the nation and kingdom that will
not ſerve thee, ſhall periſh yea, *thoſe* nations ſhall be
utterly waſted. 13 [x] The glory of Lebanon ſhall come
unto thee, the fir-tree, the pine-tree, and the box to-
gether, to beautify the place of my ſanctuary, and I
will make [y] the place of my feet glorious 14 The
ſons alſo of them that afflicted thee, ſhall come bend-
ing unto thee, and all they that deſpiſed thee, [z] ſhall
bow themſelves down at the ſoles of thy feet, and they
ſhall call thee, The city of the LORD, the Zion of
the Holy One of Iſrael

v 9—14 The ſame ſubject is here purſued as in the foregoing verſes

1 *The church ſhall gain vaſt acceſſions of ſtrength and wealth* The diſtant iſles ſhall wait for, and welcome the Saviour, the ſhips of Tarſhiſh readily convey the ſons of God to Zion, the ſpiritual church, with all their riches, willingly offering themſelves, and all they have, to be employed in his bleſſed ſervice, as the grateful return for the grace and glory he hath

Before Chriſt 698

hath beſtowed upon them, v 9 The ſons of ſtrangers, ſuch as were the Gentile nations, ſhall now greatly contribute to build up the church, and kings miniſter in the bleſſed work, as when Conſtantine, and other Chriſtian emperors and kings, eſpouſed the cauſe of truth, and as will be more eminently the caſe in the days to come *For in my wrath I ſmote thee*, which may refer to the days of pagan perſecution, or to the prevailing power of Antichriſt, permitted for the coldneſs, formality, corruptions, and diviſions, among God's profeſſing people *but in my favour have I had mercy on thee*, as when under the Chriſtian emperors the church enjoyed reſt, and as will be the caſe when Chriſt, having ſubdued the oppreſſors of his people, will ſet up his kingdom univerſally in the world, v 10 and great will be the glory of it, v 13 As the cedars of Lebanon, and every beautiful tree, contributed to the ſplendor of the temple, ſo ſhall thoſe who by the goſpel are called into the church, by the purity and holineſs of their lives adorn their profeſſion, and bring glory to God *Note*, (1) When the heart is truly given up to God, we ſhall liberally employ our wealth and influence in ſupport of his cauſe (2) The higheſt honour of kings is to be miniſters for good to Chriſt's people

2 Many of the enemies of the church ſhall become converts Thoſe who deſpiſed and afflicted the people of God ſhall be brought in deep humiliation to acknowledge their ſin, and highly reſpect thoſe they before inſulted and abuſed, v 14 Thus the ſufferings of the martyrs often confounded their perſecutors, and many who have with bitter enmity oppoſed the goſpel, have been at laſt convinced by the word, and joined the people they had before reviled And this will be more eſpecially the caſe in the expected day of power and grace, when many papiſts, pagans, and Mahometans, will be turned from darkneſs unto light, and make open profeſſion of the goſpel

3 The gates of the church are open night and day continually, all are welcome to enter, and multitudes are daily coming in of all ranks and degrees and this denotes the ſecurity in which they dwell, for none can diſturb their repoſe, v 11 *Note*, The gate of mercy in Chriſt is ever open, and ſinners of every rank and degree are ſure of admiſſion into the city of God, whenever in faith and prayer they return to him

4 Thoſe who obſtinately refuſe the proffers of grace, and periſh in their impenitence, muſt rue for it They will periſh, and be utterly waſted, be they never ſo many, never ſo mighty, v 12 *Note*, They who bow not before the calls of grace, muſt be broken under the iron rod of vengeance, 2 *Theſ* 1 8

15 Whereas thou haſt been forſaken and hated, ſo
that no man went through *thee*, I will make thee an
eternal excellency, a joy of many generations 16 Thou
ſhalt alſo ſuck the milk of the Gentiles, and [a] ſhalt ſuck
the breaſt of kings, and thou ſhalt know that [b] I the
LORD *am* thy ſaviour and thy redeemer, the mighty
One of Jacob 17 [c] For braſs I will bring gold, and
for iron I will bring ſilver, and for wood braſs, and for
ſtones iron I will alſo make thy officers peace, and
thine exactors righteouſneſs 18. [d] Violence ſhall no
more be heard in thy land, waſting nor deſtruction
within thy borders, but thou ſhalt call [e] thy walls ſal-
vation, and thy gates praiſe 19 [f] The ſun ſhall be
no more thy light by day, neither for brightneſs ſhall
the moon give light unto thee but the LORD ſhall
be unto thee an everlaſting light, and [g] thy God thy
glory 20 [h] Thy ſun ſhall no more go down, neither
ſhall thy moon withdraw itſelf for the LORD ſhall
be thine everlaſting light, and the days of thy mourning
ſhall be ended 21 [i] Thy people alſo *ſhall be* all righte-
ous [k] they ſhall inherit the land for ever, [l] the branch
of my planting, [m] the work of my hands, [n] that I may
be glorified 22 [o] A little one ſhall become a thouſand,
and a ſmall one a ſtrong nation. I the LORD [p] will
haſten it in his time

[a] Chap. lx. 16. [b] Chap. xlix. 26. [c] 1 Kings x. 21. [d] Chap. xxvi. 1. [e] Rev. xxi. 23. [g] Zech. ii. 5. [h] Amos viii. 9. [i] Chap. lii. 1. [k] Pſ. xxxvii. 11, 22. Matt. v. 5. [l] Chap. lx. 21. Matt. xv. 13. [m] Eph. ii. 10. [p] Hab. ii. 3.

v. 15—22 What honour and reſpect ſhould be paid the church by thoſe who were once enemies and perſecutors, hath been intimated, v 14 and here we ſee what juſt reaſon there would appear for it

1 Her excellence and ſtability are for ever ſecured by the power and grace of the Saviour *Whereas thou haſt been forſaken and hated*, to appearance deſerted of God, and the object of the world's enmity, *ſo that no man went through thee*, a place unfrequented, like the ruin of Jeruſalem, whither none went up to worſhip *I will make thee an eternal excellency*, to be had in the higheſt eſteem, adorned with the righteouſneſs of Jeſus, and all the graces of the Spirit, brighter than robes of wrought gold, ſhining with goſpel light, beautiful in diſcipline, and in the dignity, decency, ſimplicity, and order of her worſhip *a joy of many generations*; as long as time ſhall laſt, ſo long muſt the church be the joy of all its members on earth, and to eternity its glory will extend, when in heaven the col-

lected body ſhall for ever ſhine with their exalted head, and this ſhall be done, that all Chriſt's people may acknowledge the power, grace, faithfulneſs, and love of the Lord their Saviour and Redeemer, the mighty One of Jacob, v 16 *Note*, Deſpicable as the church of Chriſt and her poor members now may appear, they will ſhortly be ſeen in a different point of view, when all thoſe who deſpiſed and hated them will wonder and periſh

Before Chriſt 698

2 Her riches will be great *Thou ſhalt ſuck the milk of the Gentiles, and the breaſt of kings*, their richeſt treaſures ſhall be offered to ſerve the intereſts of the church of Chriſt The moſt precious metals ſhall be ſo plentiful, that gold and ſilver will be as common as braſs and iron, and iron and braſs become as wood and ſtones, which ſome refer to the excellence of the goſpel diſpenſation above the Moſaical, and others, to the glory of the latter day, when in ſpiritual gifts and graces, and in purity of doctrine and diſcipline, the church will as much exceed its preſent ſtate, as gold and ſilver do the baſer metals

3 The governors, whether civil or eccleſiaſtical, ſhall be men of juſtice and uprightneſs No oppreſſion will be committed, no injuſtice patronized, but *the officers ſhall be* men of *peace*, that ſeek to heal all differences, and accommodate every diſpute, and *the exactors*, the tax-gatherers, who uſed to fleece the people, ſhall be *righteouſneſs*, approve themſelves with the greateſt honeſty and integrity, v 17

4 All wars and rumours of wars ſhall ceaſe, and perſecution be at an end, and the moſt uninterrupted peace and proſperity will be eſtabliſhed Salvation, ſtronger than walls and bulwarks, ſhall keep the people of God ſafe from every enemy. All their gates, the places of concourſe, ſhall be called praiſe, their aſſemblies continually reſounding with ſongs of triumph for redeeming love, a ſtate of bliſs and happineſs to which the church hath never yet arrived, v 18

5 God will be the everlaſting light and glory of his redeemed, v 19, 20 And here the prophet ſeems to riſe from the happy days of the church on earth, to the conſummation of her bliſs in heaven, where they ſhall need neither ſun nor moon, but ſhall enjoy the brighter preſence of God, *their everlaſting light and glory* No clouds ſhall ever interrupt the bliſsful viſion, no darkneſs of affliction, deſertion, or temptation, for a moment intervene, but bleſſedneſs, abiding and eternal as the ſource from whence it flows, be the portion of the redeemed *Thy ſun ſhall no more go down*, but ſhine with unclouded ſplendor through the ages of eternity, *nor thy moon withdraw itſelf*, never will there be the leaſt diminution of their bliſs, *for the Lord ſhall be thine everlaſting light*, when this bright ſun plucked from his ſphere ſhall be extinguiſhed, and this pale moon in darkneſs hide her head, with infinitely tranſcending brightneſs ſhall the eternal God ſhine on his choſen, and everlaſting as his being ſhall be their joy and glory *And the days of thy mourning ſhall be ended*, a period put to all their ſorrows, every tear wiped from their eye, and the cauſe of all, ſin and ſuffering, be for ever baniſhed from the place O Lord! thy kingdom come!

6 They ſhall be perfected in holineſs *Thy people alſo ſhall be all righteous*, not only as they are accepted in Chriſt, but as they are by the Holy Ghoſt ſanctified wholly in body, ſoul, and ſpirit, and made meet for the inheritance among the ſaints in light *They ſhall inherit the land for ever*, the heavenly Canaan, *the branch of my planting*, ingrafted into Chriſt, and, after flouriſhing on earth, tranſplanted with him to the paradiſe of God, *the work of my hands* the whole of ſalvation, from beginning to end, will in heaven be evidently ſeen and acknowledged to be God's own work, to the glory of his rich and ſovereign grace, *that I may be glorified*, as he will then be, in and by all his ſaints

7 They ſhall be an innumerable multitude *A little one ſhall become a thouſand, and a ſmall one a ſtrong nation* few and feeble as the ſaints of God were in every age and place, when collected they will appear numerous and formidable, a hoſt like the hoſt of God *I the Lord will haſten it in his time*, however difficult it may appear, or long as the final ſalvation of the faithful may ſeem to be delayed, the event is ſure, and in God's appointed ſeaſon it ſhall be accompliſhed May we with faith and patience wait for it

CHAP. LXI.

In this chapter we have, 1 Chriſt publiſhing to a loſt world the everlaſting goſpel, ver 1—3 2 The proſperity and [illegible] of his church, ver 4—9 3 The [illegible], and a promiſe made her of manifeſting her righteouſneſs and glory to all nations, ver 10, 11

1 [a] THE Spirit of the Lord GOD *is* upon me,
because [b] the LORD hath anointed me to
preach good tidings unto the meek, he hath ſent me
[c] to bind up the broken hearted, [d] to proclaim liberty to
the captives, and the opening of the priſon to *them*
that

[a] Chap. xi. 2. Luke iv. 18. John i. 32. [c] Chap. lvii. 15. Pſ. cxlvii. 3. [d] Chap. xlii. 7.

Before Christ 698

f Lev. xxv 9 · g Chap. lxiii 4 · h Chap. lvii 18 Matt. v 4 · Or for · i Ps. xxx 11 · k Chap. lx 21

that are bound 2 To proclaim f the acceptable year
of the LORD, and g the day of vengeance of our God,
h to comfort all that mourn 3 To appoint unto them
that mourn † in Zion, i to give unto them beauty for
ashes, the oil of joy for mourning, the garment of praise
for the spirit of heaviness, that they might be called
trees of righteousness, k the planting of the LORD,
that he might be glorified

v 1—3 Our Lord, in the opening of his ministry at Nazareth, *Luke* iv 17—21 hath left us no doubt to whom this prophecy belongs We have here,

1 His qualifications for, and ordination to, the office of Mediator *The Spirit of the Lord God is upon me*, without measure the Father had given it unto him, that he might be enabled for the arduous work he had undertaken *because the Lord hath anointed me*, he invested him with full power and authority for the discharge of his offices, as the prophet, priest, and king of his people

2 In consequence of this appointment he opens his commission, which was, *to preach good tidings unto the meek*, those who are lowly in their own eyes, to whom free pardon and grace will be welcome news or *the poor*, as *Luke* xi 18 both in spirit and purse, for unto these the gospel is preached *He hath sent me to bind up the broken-hearted*, those, whose bleeding hearts, pierced with a sense of guilt and sin, no other physician can cure, he is sent to bind up, to comfort, and heal them *to proclaim liberty to the captives, and the opening of the prison to them that are bound* Captives are we all to sin and Satan, not even born free, and by willing subjection also under heavier bondage, from which, by reason of our native corruption, we are utterly unable to deliver ourselves He is come *to purchase* our liberty respecting God, by paying a ransom for us in satisfaction to the divine justice, which had delivered us up to the executioner of wrath to *rescue* us by his power from the hands of our enemy, *destroying death, and him that had the power of it*, and providing a sufficiency of grace and strength to loose our captive bands, and enable us to come forth at his call, delivered alike from the power and punishment of our sins *To proclaim the acceptable year of the Lord*, as the jubilee trumpet proclaimed the release of servants, the restoration of lost inheritances, and rest from all labour, so doth the gospel proclaim, with more acceptable sound, a glorious liberty among the sons of God, a restoration to our forfeited inheritance, through the blood and righteousness of a Redeemer, and an eternal rest in glory, secured not for a year, but for the ages of eternity *and the day of vengeance of our God*, the day of vengeance taken on Christ for our sins, or rather on the powers of darkness, when he triumphed over them on his cross, and which the sinner, who obstinately rejects his salvation, may expect, when he cometh on the clouds of heaven with power and great glory *To comfort all that mourn* under a sense of guilt, or corruption, or affliction, or who compassionately melt at others woes or danger, and this he doth by his great and precious promises, which afford balm for every grief *To appoint unto them that mourn in Zion*, or the mourners of Zion, whose hearts are tenderly affected with her corruptions, divisions, declensions, and sufferings *to give unto them beauty for ashes* In the original there is an elegant paronomasia, Pheer for Epher, they who lay in ashes, and were disfigured with dust, shall be raised up in beauty *the oil of joy for mourning*, for in seasons of affliction they neglected to anoint themselves, as at other times *the garment of praise for the spirit of heaviness*, their sackcloth changed for brighter robes expressions which are designed to describe the blessed change which is wrought upon the sinner's heart by the gospel of Jesus, when from the dust of death and hell, from the depths of despair and misery, he is rescued, refreshed with the oil of Divine Grace, adorned with robes of a Redeemer's righteousness, and his natural deformity removed, through that new creation in Christ Jesus, whereby he puts on the image of God in righteousness and true holiness, and rejoices in God his Saviour with that holy cheerfulness which adorns his profession *That they might be called trees of righteousness*, whose blessed fruit proves the soundness of their root, *the planting of the Lord*, to whose rich grace they are indebted for all, *that he may be glorified*, this being his great design, and to shew forth his glory in our lips and our lives, must be our chief labour

l Chap. lviii 12 · m Ch. lx 10 · n Chap. lx 10 · o Exod. xix 6 · p Rev. i 6 · q Chap. lx 5, 16 · r Chap. xl 2 · s Zech. ix 12

4 ¶ And they shall l build the old wastes, they shall
raise up the former desolations, and they shall repair the
waste cities, the desolations of many generations 5
And strangers shall stand and m feed your flocks, and
the sons of the alien *shall be* your plowmen, and your
vine dressers 6 But n ye shall be named the priests of
the LORD *men* shall call you the ministers of our
God o ye shall eat the riches of the Gentiles, and in
their glory shall you boast yourselves 7 ¶ p For your
shame *you shall have* double ; and *for* confusion they shall
rejoice in their portion therefore in their land they shall
possess the double everlasting joy shall be unto them
8 For q I the LORD love judgment, I hate robbery
for burnt-offering, and I will direct their work in truth,
and s I will make an everlasting covenant with them 9
And their seed shall be known among the Gentiles, and
their offspring among the people all that see them shall
acknowledge them, that t they *are* the seed *which* the
LORD hath blessed

Before Christ 698

q Ps. xi 7 · r Chap. i 11 13 · s Chap. lv 3 Jer. xxxii 40 · t Chap. lxv 23

v 4—9 The promises here made might be designed for the encouragement of the Jews on their return from Babylon, but they extend to the church of Christ, and every sinner delivered from the bonds of corruption

1 They shall be enabled to rebuild their waste places, and repair their former desolations, v 4 and when deeper desolations were spread over the world by sin, ignorance, and idolatry, God was pleased to send his Son, and by his ministry, and those whom he hath ordained, to raise up a glorious church in the midst of a desart world and in every soul recovered by divine grace, the ruins of corruption are also repaired, and the heart renewed as a holy temple, an habitation for God through the Spirit

2 They should no longer be in subjection to others, but have plenty of servants at their command, v 5 Or this may better refer to those of the Gentile converts, who being put in trust with the gospel, became pastors to the flock of Christ, and husbandmen in his field, labouring assiduously in the work of the ministry, to sow the seed of eternal life in men's hearts

3 They shall be exalted and enriched, honoured as priests of God, and enriched by the treasures of the Gentiles, the kings of Persia liberally assisting them at their return, v 6 But this belongs more particularly to the church of Christ, where every member is consecrated a priest unto God, into which the riches of the Gentiles are brought, who at first contributed abundantly to the relief of the poor saints at Jerusalem, and whose wealth is still devoted to the service of Christ and his people *and in their glory shall you boast yourselves*, in Christ, the glory of all the faithful Or it means, that the Jewish believers would rejoice to see the honour put upon the Gentiles, in making them fellow heirs, and of the same body *Note*, (1) Despicably as the men of the world account of God's ministers, their honour in his sight is great (2) They employ riches aright, who use them to promote the interests of Christ, and to serve his church and people

4 They shall have abundant cause of joy and rejoicing, v 7 *For your shame you shall have double*, or, *for your double shame*, for that load of ignominy which the profession of the gospel at first exposed them to, God would doubly repay them in inward consolations, *and for confusion they shall rejoice in their portion*, God can make them take pleasure in reproaches, and his love will be a portion that will abundantly satisfy them in spite of all tribulations they may be called to endure *Therefore in their land they shall possess the double*, whatever loss they sustain for Christ he can give them in this world more in kind, or, what is better, double their inward comfort and joy, which is the best possession *everlasting joy shall be unto them*, they shall not only here be satisfied with the fulness of his house, but inherit an eternity of glory as their exceeding great reward

5 God will be their guide, v 8 to teach them his will, and how to please him *I the Lord love judgment*, and therefore will right the wrongs of his people or he urges it as an argument for them to walk in uprightness before him, and in the paths of justice respecting each other *I hate robbery for burnt-offering*, as when by their own deeds and duties men pretend to offer an acceptable sacrifice to God, which is regarded as the highest robbery of the Redeemer's glory, in whose righteousness alone we can be accepted or it is a rebuke to those who, like the Pharisees, were strict in the observance of their ceremonial offerings, yet in temper were covetous, and offered in sacrifice the fruits of their oppression From a heart enslaved by iniquity no pleasing service can be rendered to God *And I will direct their work in truth*, his people shall be taught of him the true worship and way to please him *and I will make an everlasting covenant with them*, in which he engages to make them his people, and be their God for ever and ever, and happy are the people who are in such a case!

6 Their posterity shall be blessed *Their seed shall be known among the Gentiles, and their offspring among the people*, distinguished for their sound faith and unfeigned piety *all that see them shall acknowledge them, that they are the seed which the Lord hath blessed*, the spiritual seed of Abraham, and blessed with all spiritual blessings in Christ Jesu And this, with all the foregoing verses, some apply to the calling of the Jews in the latter day, when they shall possess an honourable place in the church of God *Note*, Though to affect or desire esteem even from good men for our conduct would be evil, yet when, without it, known godliness engages their regard, it is an honourable distinction

Before Christ 698

10 [u] I will greatly rejoice in the LORD my soul
shall be joyful in my God, for [x] he hath clothed me
with the garments of salvation, he hath covered me
with the robe of righteousness, as a bridegroom † deck-
eth *himself* with ornaments, and [y] as a bride adorneth
herself with her jewels 11 For as the earth bringeth
forth her bud, and [z] as the garden causeth the things
that are sown in it to spring forth so the Lord GOD
will cause righteousness and praise to spring forth before
all the nations

u Chap lxvi 10 Luke i 46, 47 x Ps cxxxii 9, 16 Phil iii 9 † Heb. Decketh as a priest Exod xxviii 2 y Rev xxi 2 z Num xxiv 6 Chap xviii 11

v 10, 11 These seem to be the words of the church triumphing in God her Saviour

1 For what he *hath* done for her *I will greatly rejoice in the Lord, my soul shall be joyful in my God*, an interest in his love known and believed, cannot but fill the soul with joy unspeakable, and full of glory When we can say he is *my God*, we may well rejoice in him *greatly* here we need fear no excess, whilst he is the glorious object of our delight *For he hath clothed me with the garments of salvation, he hath covered me with the robe of righteousness*, without, most splendidly adorned with the complete robe of a Redeemer's righteousness, spotless and pure, within, all glorious with the garments of salvation, the divine tempers and graces, with which the Spirit of God arrays the souls of the redeemed *as a bridegroom decketh himself with ornaments*, coming from his chamber compleatly dressed, or in sacerdotal robes, glorious as those the high-priest wore, *and as a bride adorneth herself with jewels*, glittering and splendid for the day of her espousals and thus are believers presented to Christ, perfect in the comeliness he hath put upon them, and decked with the beauty of holiness May my soul be thus arrayed!

2 For what he *will* do for her These robes of righteousness and garments of salvation shall endure for ever, nor can time ever change their glorious hue *For as the earth bringeth forth her bud, and as the garden causeth the things that are sown in it to spring forth*, so that from year to year, in regular succession, the earth brings forth her increase, *so the Lord God will cause righteousness and praise to spring forth before all the nations* To the end of time this divine righteousness shall be the ornament of every believer, and the subject of our ceaseless praise, and as it is wholly the Lord's prerogative both to work it out for us, and to apply it to us, to him alone must all the glory be ascribed

CHAP. LXII

The business of prophets was both to preach and pray In this chapter, 1 The prophet determines to apply himself closely and constantly to this business, ver 1. 2 God appoints him and others of his prophets to continue to do so, for the encouragement of his people during the delays of their deliverance, ver 6, 7 3 The promises are here repeated and ratified of the great things God would do for his church, (1) It shall be made honourable in the eyes of the world, ver 2 (2) It shall appear to be very dear to God, precious and honourable in his sight, ver 3—5 (3) It shall enjoy great plenty, ver 8, 9 (4) It shall be released out of captivity, and grow up again into a considerable nation, particularly owned and favoured by heaven, ver 10—12

1 FOR Zion's sake will I not hold my peace, and
for Jerusalem's sake I will not rest, [a] until the
righteousness thereof go forth as brightness, and the sal-
vation thereof as a lamp *that* burneth 2 And the
Gentiles shall see thy righteousness, and all kings thy
glory and [b] thou shalt be called by a new name, which
the mouth of the LORD shall name 3 Thou shalt
also be a crown of glory in the hand of the LORD,
and a royal diadem in the hand of thy God 4 [d] Thou
shalt no more be termed, [e] Forsaken, neither shall thy
land any more be termed desolate but thou shalt be
called † Hephzi-bah, and thy land, ‡ Beulah for the
LORD delighteth in thee, and thy land shall be married
5 For *as* a young man marrieth a virgin, *so* shall thy
sons marry thee and *as* the bridegroom rejoiceth over
the bride, [f] *so* shall thy God rejoice over thee

a Ps xxxvii 6 b Ver iv 2. Chap lxv 15 c Zech ix 16 d Hos i 10 e Chap liv 6 † i e My delight is in her ‡ i e Married f Chap lxv 19 Zeph iii 17

v 1—5 With much zeal the prophet professes

1 His determined purpose to labour constantly in the execution of his office *For Zion's sake will I not hold my peace, and for Jerusalem's sake I will not rest* the concerns of God's church and people lay deep imprinted on his heart, and therefore his sermons are frequent and urgent, and his prayers to God fervent in their behalf *until the righteousness thereof go forth as brightness, and the salvation thereof as a lamp that burneth*, either till her cause should be clearly vindicated, and her enemies destroyed, or rather, till Christ, whose righteousness and salvation are wrought out for her, shall cloath her therewith, and perfect her in holiness and so long will this prophecy endure, for Isaiah, though dead, yet speaketh *Note*, (1) The interests of Christ's kingdom are the great concern which lies upon a faithful minister's heart (2) In the service of immortal souls he is ready to spend and be spent (3) They who labour in faith, will assuredly see the fruit of their labours

2 The prophet expresses his confidence that God would hear and answer him *And the Gentiles shall see thy righteousness*, the perfection of righteousness the church possesses in Christ, or the justice of her cause *and all kings thy glory*, shall behold and admire, and desire to partake of it, as when Constantine the Roman emperor, and others after his example, declared themselves Christians, and will be more universally the case in the day of the church's triumphs *And thou shalt be called by a new name, which the mouth of the Lord shall name*, as a mark of that distinguished honour and dignity to which she shall be advanced by him who is the fountain of honour, who speaks and it is done, *See Rev.* ii 17 iii 12 *Thou shalt also be a crown of glory in the hand of the Lord*, glorious in his righteousness and grace, valued by him as the richest crown that shall for ever adorn his brows, and held in his hand, that none may pluck his people from him, nor rob him of the glory of their salvation *and a royal diadem in the hand of thy God* Thus distinguished, *thou shalt no more be termed forsaken, neither shall thy land any more be termed desolate*, as the Gentile world seemed to be, before the preaching of the gospel *but thou shalt be called Hephzi-bah*, a new and honourable title, signifying, *My delight is in her*, *and thy land, Beulah, or married*, *for the Lord delighteth in thee*, and in his love and favour all bliss and blessedness is comprehended *and thy land shall be married*, from eternity the contract subsisted, but the Lamb's wife hath not yet made herself ready, till the fulness of the Gentiles is come in, then the heavenly bridegroom shall bring her home to himself, to his eternal mansions in glory *For as a young man marrieth a virgin*, fond of his bride, delighting in her company, and from the union a numerous offspring is expected, *so shall thy sons marry thee*, united to the church in warm affection, joining in her ordinances, delighting in the communion of the saints, and seeking to increase their number *and as a bridegroom rejoiceth over the bride, so shall thy God rejoice over thee* the church of the redeemed are the joy of the Redeemer's soul, in whose present conversion he is happy, and in them to all eternity will be his delight

6 [g] I have set watchmen upon thy walls, O Jerusa-
lem, *which* shall never hold their peace day nor night,
ye † that make mention of the LORD, keep not si-
lence, 7 And give him no ‡ rest, till he establish,
and till he make Jerusalem a praise in the earth 8
The LORD hath sworn by his right hand, and by
the arm of his strength, § Surely, [h] I will no more
give thy corn *to be* meat for thine enemies, and the sons
of the stranger shall not drink thy wine, for the which
thou hast laboured 9 But they that have gathered
it, shall eat it, and praise the LORD, and they that
have brought it together, shall drink it [i] in the courts
of my holiness

g Ezek iii 17 xxxiii 7 † Or that are the Lord's remembrancers ‡ Heb Silence § Heb If I give &c h Deut xxviii 31 &c Jer v 17 i Deut xii 12 & xiv 26 & xvi 11

v 6—9 The gracious provision God hath made for his people is here declared

1 For their spiritual wants, giving them faithful ministers, and pouring out a spirit of prayer and supplication on them

[1] *I have set watchmen on thy walls, O Jerusalem, which shall never hold their peace day nor night* The church militant is a city, defended by the walls of God's everlasting love, yet besieged by the powers of sin, Satan, and the world incessantly, who fight, but cannot prevail The ministers of the gospel are the watchmen appointed to give warning of approaching danger, and their station demands, (1) Fidelity and zeal for the cause of Christ and his people (2) Constancy and watchfulness, that in season, out of season, they preach, rebuke, exhort (3) Willingness to endure hardship, and not shrink from any danger or reproach, to which they may be exposed (4) Incessant prayer, that they may be enabled to discharge their ministry, and be supported by that almighty grace, without which mortal spirits must faint and fail

[2] The prayers of the people must second the preaching of the word *Ye that make mention of the Lord*, his professing people, *keep not silence*, but be still at the throne of grace, *and give him no rest*, for importunity will not offend him, *till he establish, and till he make Jerusalem a praise in the earth*, by the purity of her doctrine and discipline, by eminent holiness in the members, by their fervent love and charity one towards another, by vast accessions of converts, and, among these, the honourable of the earth *Note*, (1) God's people delight to mention his name, and to speak to his praise of the things he hath done for their souls (2) Prayer is the natural and constant language of the heart touched by redeeming grace (3)

Before Christ 698

Nothing lies nearer the hearts of the faithful, than the interests of the Redeemer's kingdom (4) Persevering importunity in prayer is sure to find an answer of peace

2 For their temporal wants When their enemies prevailed, their country was ravaged, and their harvest and vintage served for a spoil, but now God, having for ever broken their arm, will feed his people with abundance of good things they shall eat their bread and drink their wine with a merry heart in the courts of his holiness, as the priests and Levites there partook of the consecrated things, with holy sobriety, and enlarged thankfulness This may refer in part to the people of the Jews, but though for a while they enjoyed their land, they soon were, and continue to be, dispossessed of it therefore this must chiefly refer to the happy days of the church's prosperity, when God will give his people the abundance of outward blessings or, as corn and wine may also figuratively signify the rich provisions of the gospel, which for ever undisturbed the redeemed shall possess, and by an oath God confirms their faith in the immutability of his counsel and the eternity of their inheritance *Note*, (1) Whatever labours we employ, even for the things of this life, it is God only who giveth the increase (2) Temporal gifts are then truly blessings, when we receive them as coming from God's hand, and employ them for his glory (3) God, who gives us of this world's good, wills that we should richly enjoy it, and praise him for his bounty (4) God's wine is to be drunk in the courts of his holiness with temperance and sobriety, else our blessings, abused, will prove our greatest curse

k Chap xl 3 & lvii 4

10 ¶ Go through, go through the gates, [k] prepare
you the way of the people, cast up, cast up the high-
way, gather out the stones, lift up a standard for the
people 11 Behold, the LORD hath proclaimed [l] un-
to the end of the world, [m] Say ye to the daughter of
Zion, Behold, thy salvation cometh, behold, [n] his re-
ward *is* with him, and his † work before him 12
And they shall call them, [o] The holy people, the redeem-
ed of the LORD and thou shalt be called, Sought
out, a city [p] not forsaken

l Rom x 18 m Zech ix 9 Mat xxi 5 John xii 15 n Chap xl 10 Rev xxii 12 † Or recompense o Chap lx 21 p Ver 4

v 10—12 Though there may be here an allusion to the return of the Jews from Babylon at Cyrus's proclamation, this seems, with the preceding part of the chapter, to belong to the gospel church

1 Preparation is made for the return of captive souls *Go through, go through the gates*, the prison-doors are thrown open for their escape *prepare you the way of the people, cast up, cast up the high-way, gather out the stones* the ministers of God, as John the Baptist, must prepare the way, remove all obstacles, and make plain the road before their face, and especially *lift up a standard for the people*, display the banner of Christ in the gospel, around which they must assemble, that in a body, under his guidance and protection, they may march in the high-way of holiness, towards the heavenly mount of Zion

2 The glorious appearance of Christ in his church proclaimed, who comes as the Captain of their salvation to lead the way *Behold, the Lord hath proclaimed unto the end of the world*, to all nations under heaven, among whom the gospel shall be preached, *Say ye to the daughter of Zion*, the members of the church, not only among the Jews, but the gentiles also, *Behold, thy salvation*, or *thy Saviour, cometh*, with power and great glory, as when he first appeared in the flesh, or rather as he will appear hereafter, when his kingdom shall be established in all the world *Behold, his reward is with him*, either the glory himself should receive as the reward of his sufferings, or that which he hath to bestow on his faithful people *and his work before him*, which he undertakes to accomplish for them, and in them, even their compleat salvation from Satan, sin, death, and hell

3 His people will then become dignified with the most honourable titles *They shall call them the holy people*, for this is their distinguishing character and their honour, that they are consecrated to God, and pure in heart *the redeemed of the Lord*, this being their singular mercy, and the source of all their holiness and happiness, for both of which they are indebted to the redemption of Jesus *and thou shalt be called, Sought out, a city not forsaken* Desolate as before the church appeared, now the greatest resort shall be made thither, and she shall be no more forsaken of her members, who will take up in her their continual abode, nor of her God, who will preserve all who resort thither, that they may never perish, but have everlasting life

CHAP LXIII

In this chapter we have, 1 God coming towards his people in ways of mercy and deliverance, ver. 1—6 2. God's people meeting him with their devotions, and addressing him with suitable affections, where we have, (1.) A thankful acknowledgment of the great favours God had bestowed upon them, ver 7 (2) The magnifying of these favours, from the consideration of God's relation to them, ver 8 His compassionate concern for them, ver 9 Their unworthiness, ver 10 And the occasion which it gave both him and them to call to mind former mercies, ver 11—14 (3) A very humble and earnest prayer to God to appear for them in their present distress, pleading God's mercy, ver 15 their relation to him, ver 16 their desire towards him, ver 17 and the insolence of their enemies, ver 18, 19

Before Christ 698.

1 WHO *is* this [a] that cometh from Edom, with
dyed garments from Bozrah? this *that is*
† glorious in his apparel, travelling in the greatness of
his strength? I that speak in righteousness, [b] mighty to
save 2 Wherefore *art thou* [c] red in thine apparel, and
thy garments like him that treadeth in the wine fat?
3 [d] I have trodden the wine-press alone, and [e] of the
people *there was* none with me for I will tread them
in mine anger, and trample them in my fury, and their
blood shall be sprinkled upon my garments, and I will
stain all my raiment 4 For [f] the day of vengeance *is*
in mine heart, and the year of my redeemed is come
5 And [g] I looked, and [h] *there was* none to help, and
I wondered that *there was* none to uphold therefore
[i] mine own arm brought salvation unto me, and my
fury, it upheld me 6 And I will tread down the peo-
ple in mine anger, and [k] make them drunk in my fury,
and I will bring down their strength to the earth

a Chap xxxiv 6 † Heb Decked b Heb viii 25 c Rev xix 13 d Rev xiv 19 20 & xix 15 e Chap lix 16 Ver 5 f Chap xxxiv 8 & lxi 2 g Chap xli 28 & lix 16 h John xvi 32 i Ps xcviii 1 Chap lix 16 k Rev xvi 6

v 1—6 The former chapter closed with the promise of the Saviour's appearing, this opens with the fulfilment of that promise, and the glorious victory obtained by the Redeemer over the powers of darkness, through his incarnation, or it points to the overthrow of all the enemies of his church in the last days

1 The prophet, as suddenly surprized with the appearance of this glorious personage, with abrupt enquiry asks, *Who is this?* Is the form human or divine, that I behold? *He cometh from Edom*, the country of the professed enemies of the church, *with dyed garments from Bozrah*, like some victorious conqueror, who, having sacked the capital of his foes, returns in triumph, his sword yet reeking from the slaughter, and his garments dyed with the blood of the slain *this that is glorious in his apparel*, bearing in his person, aspect, and dress, the marks of transcendent dignity *travelling in the greatness of his strength*, not faint through fatigue, nor weary with his march, but with power irresistible, and zeal unquenchable, advancing with majestic stateliness to new conquests, till every foe becomes his footstool

2 The great God-man approaches this devout enquirer, and, terrible as his aspect seemed, his lips are full of grace, and his answer unspeakably kind and gracious *I that speak in righteousness*, whose word is truth itself, and his promises unchangeably faithful, or *of righteousness*, that divine righteousness, to accomplish which, is the great design of my appearance, and to reveal it, the office of my Spirit; in virtue whereof I am *mighty to save*, to save to the uttermost from sin, corruption, death, and hell, and none so guilty, none so desperate, as to be beyond the power of my grace

3 Encouraged by the condescensions he had experienced, the prophet humbly presumes to renew his enquiry If thou art come not to destroy men's lives, but to save, *Wherefore art thou red in thine apparel, and thy garments like him that treadeth in the wine-fat?* These bloody ensigns seem to bespeak destruction, not salvation; and mark the arm of inexorable justice, rather than forbearing mercy *Note*, Though doubts disturb, and fears dismay, the further we enquire into the divine word, the more will they be removed and silenced

4 The Saviour with fullest satisfaction resolves his question *I have trodden the wine-press*, and underneath my feet sin, death, and hell, as vanquished foes, are fallen, and with the blood of these adversaries of my people is my raiment discoloured This victory have I gained *alone*, too great to need an associate, and infinitely too jealous of my own honour to accept assistance *Of the people there was none with me*, none of the inhabitants of heaven or earth to afford the least succour, or take the least share in the glorious work The salvation of sinners, their eternal redemption from wrath to glory, is my act alone yours be the benefit, mine the honour *For I will tread them in mine anger, and trample them in my fury*, my former victories ensure my future what foes soever yet remain, in wrath unquenchable, and fury irresistible, will I tread into the dust, *and their blood shall be sprinkled upon my garments, and I will stain all my raiment* the powers of antichristian tyranny shall be broken, and my garments dipt in blood, *Rev* xix 13 *for the day of vengeance is in my heart*, fixed and immutable is the decree, the day determined, when the blood of my martyrs and suffering saints shall be recompensed; *and the year of my redeemed is come*, when all my chosen shall be collected, and their triumphs be-

Before Chriſt 698

gin *And I looked, and there was none to help*; as at the firſt, when, ſunk in helpleſs miſery, the race of men lay weltering in their blood, ſo under the power of Antichriſt, proſtrate in the duſt, the Redeemer beholds his church in the latter day *and I wondered there was none to uphold* the ſinking cauſe, and the afflicted people None, none were found able or willing to eſpouſe their quarrel, or attempt their deliverance, *therefore mine own arm brought ſalvation unto me*, that arm of omnipotence, which alone could accompliſh it *and my fury, it upheld me*, zeal for his people's ſafety and honour, indignation againſt their enemies, burned in his boſom, and urged him to take vengeance to the uttermoſt *And I will tread down the people in mine anger, and make them drunk in my fury*, putting into their hands the cup of the wine of the wrath of God, and making them drink the dregs thereof *and I will bring down their ſtrength to the earth*, giving them an utter overthrow, and covering them with everlaſting deſolations *Note*, (1) When all other help fails, Chriſt never fails thoſe that truſt him (2) Though our deliverance may ſeem long delayed, and our enemies triumphant, the decree is gone forth againſt them, and he that cometh, will come, and will not tarry (3.) They who perſiſt to drink of the intoxicating cup of ſin, will ſhortly be made to drink the cup of trembling

7 ¶ [l] I will mention the loving-kindneſſes of the
LORD, *and* the praiſes of the LORD, according to all
that the LORD hath beſtowed on us, and the great
goodneſs towards the houſe of Iſrael, which he hath be-
ſtowed on them, according to his mercies, and according
to the multitude of his loving kindneſſes 8 For he
ſaid, Surely they *are* my people, children *that* will not
lie ſo he was their Saviour 9 ¶ [m] In all their af-
flictions † he was afflicted, and [n] the angel of his pre-
ſence ſaved them [o] in his love and in his pity he re-
deemed them, and [p] he bare them, and carried them all
the days of old 10 ¶ But [q] they rebelled, and [r] vexed
his holy Spirit [s] therefore he was turned to be their
enemy, *and* he fought againſt them 11 Then he re-
membred the days of old, Moſes *and* his people, *ſaying*,
Where *is* he [t] that brought them up out of the ſea, with
the ‡ ſhepherd of his flock? where *is* he [u] that put his
holy Spirit within him? 12. That led *them* by the
right hand of Moſes, with his glorious arm, [x] dividing
the water before them, to make himſelf an everlaſting
name? 13 That led them through the deep as an
horſe in the wilderneſs, *that* they ſhould not ſtumble?
14 As a beaſt goeth down into the valley, the Spirit
of the LORD cauſed him to reſt ſo didſt thou lead thy
people, to make thyſelf § a glorious name

l Pſ lxxvii 5, 10.
m Judg x 16 Zech ii 8 Acts x 4
† Or, He afflicted them not
n Ex xxiii 20, 21 & xxxiii 14 Mal iii 1 1 Cor x 9
o Deut vii 7 8
p Ex xix 4 Deut i 31 & xxxii 11 Chap xlvi 3, 4
q Ex xv. 24 Num xiv 11 Pſal lxxviii 56. & xcv 9
r Pſ lxxviii 40 Acts vii 51 Eph iv 30
s Ex xxiii 21
t Ex xiv 30 Jer ii. 6
‡ Or ſhepherds, as Pſ lxxvii 20
u Neh ix 20 Dan iv. 8 Hag ii 5
x Ex xiv 21 Joſh iii 16
§ Heb A name of glory

v. 7—14. As an encouragement to hope for future mercies, the prophet takes a review of the paſt, ſo wonderfully and graciouſly vouchſafed unto them

1. He makes a grateful acknowledgment in general of all the mercies and loving-kindneſſes of God to his people, ſo numberleſs, ſo great, that they were more than he is able to expreſs, and all the effects of his boundleſs grace and undeſerved favour, *v* 7 *Note*, (1) When we review God's mercies towards us with an enlightened mind, we ſhall be loſt in wonder, love, and praiſe (2) Every bleſſing we enjoy of providence, grace, or glory, in time or eternity, flows not from the leaſt merit in us, for we have none, but from God's infinitely rich and ſovereign mercy

2 He mentions ſome eſpecial inſtances of his kindneſs *For he ſaid, Surely they are my people*, he had taken them for his own in a covenant of everlaſting love, and he juſtly expected they would approve themſelves to him in all fidelity and truth *children that will not lie*, neither be falſe to their vows, nor hypocritical in his ſervice *ſo he was their Saviour*, from their houſe of bondage in Egypt particularly, and as he ever was and is, of all his people from every enemy, from every danger *In all their afflictions he was afflicted*; he felt with tender ſympathy every burden under which they groaned, and came with kindeſt compaſſion and welcome relief to deliver them Or it may be read, *In all their afflictions there was no affliction*; the ſenſe of his love alleviated their ſorrows, and made every burden light; *and the angel of his preſence ſaved them*; the Lord Jeſus Chriſt, the uncreated angel, who was with Iſrael in the wilderneſs, and whoſe voice they were enjoined to obey, *Exod* xxiii. 20, 21 *In his love and in his pity he redeemed them* from their ſtate of hard ſervitude; *and he bare them* in his arms, as a ſhepherd the weak lambs of his flock; *and carried them all the days of old*; amidſt their manifold provocations his paternal heart bore with them, and, as on eagles wings, he brought them ſafe to their promiſed reſt in Canaan And thus doth the Redeemer regard all his people, carries them ſafe amidſt their trials and temptations, patiently in pity bears with their folly and perverſeneſs, and never leaves them till they are ſafe lodged in their eternal reſt *Note*, (1) The children of God will not lie; for they who do ſo, prove their parentage to be of their father the devil. (2) It is a comfort to God's afflicted people, that they have a compaſſionate high-prieſt, who can be touched with the feeling of their infirmities (3) They who look for their portion in a better world, ſit eaſy under this world's troubles they know, that they are both light and momentary (4.) If the angel of God's preſence had not born us up, many a time muſt we have utterly fainted in our journey to glory

Before Chriſt 698

3 Their repeated and long-continued ingratitude, at laſt brought his rod upon them, *v* 10 *They rebelled, and vexed his holy Spirit*, rejected God from being their king, caſt off their allegiance, and, by their unbelief, murmuring, and idolatry, forſook his covenant, deaf to the warnings of Moſes and the prophets, as the Scribes and Phariſees in our Lord's day, the true children of their fathers, always reſiſted the Holy Ghoſt; in conſequence of which, *God*, that offended God, whoſe favour they had ſo abuſed, *turned to be their enemy, and fought againſt them*, with repeated ſtrokes of his indignation, both in the wilderneſs, and after their ſettlement in Canaan, till their captivity in Babylon, and as he did afterwards, till the Romans came and deſtroyed them *Note*, (1) Sin is the cauſe of all our miſery if God from our friend becomes our foe, ſurely this makes the quarrel (2) It is baſe as wicked, when God's children grieve that holy Spirit, whereby they are ſealed unto the day of redemption, and they will ſmart for it

4 They reflect upon the particular favours of God when firſt he formed them into a people, *v* 11—14 Some underſtand theſe as the words of God, calling to mind his own mercies of old, as an argument ſtill to do them good, and not caſt them away Others ſuppoſe theſe to be the reflections of the few faithful among them, ſtill encouraging themſelves from paſt experience to hope for his mercy *Then he remembered the days of old, Moſes and his people, ſaying, Where is he that brought them up out of the ſea, with the ſhepherd*, or *ſhepherds, of his flock?* Moſes, Aaron, and the elders of Iſrael, *where is he that put his holy Spirit within him?* in Moſes, or the people of Iſrael, who were taught and inſtructed of God and this they mention as mourning over the ſad change, and complaining of the abſence of God's Spirit, or as in humble expoſtulation and prayer for the return of his bleſſed influences *That led them by the right hand of Moſes*, ſtrengthening and proſpering him as their captain, *with his glorious arm*, enabling their leader to perform miracles for their preſervation, *dividing the water before them*, at the Red Sea, *to make himſelf an everlaſting name?* by their miraculous deliverance, and the deſtruction there brought upon their enemies *That led them through the deep as an horſe in the wilderneſs*, or *in the plain, that they ſhould not ſtumble?* as eaſy their paſſage between the divided waters, as dry and ſafe, as when a horſe travels on a level road *As a beaſt goeth down into the valley*, ſoftly and gently, *ſo the Spirit of the Lord cauſed them to reſt*, either when they deſcended from the ſhore into the depths of the ſea, they did it gently, and without precipitation, ſecure in the divine protection, or it refers to their ſeveral ſtations in the wilderneſs, where, under God's direction, they reſted, till they were brought to their journey's end *So didſt thou lead thy people, to make thyſelf a glorious name*, his honour being concerned in their ſalvation, and this being the ultimate deſign of all his works and ways to manifeſt his own glory, and engage the everlaſting praiſe of his redeemed people *Note*, (1) If God calls us to paſs through the depths of the ſea, the ſoreſt trials, or the moſt imminent dangers, he can make the path plain, and enable us in confidence and peace to go ſafely through (2) If we ever find true reſt to our ſouls, it muſt come from the Eternal Spirit, for this world ſaith, It is not in me (3) When God's glory is the great end we aim at in all our works and ways, then we truly correſpond with the divine will.

15 ¶ [y] Look down from heaven, and behold from
the habitation of thy holineſs and of thy glory, where
is thy zeal and thy ſtrength, † the ſounding of [z] thy
bowels, and of thy mercies towards me? are they re-
ſtrained? 16 [a] Doubtleſs thou *art* our father, though
Abraham [b] be ignorant of us, and Iſrael acknowledge us
not thou, O LORD, *art* our father, our redeemer,
thy name *is* from everlaſting 17 ¶ O LORD, why
haſt thou made us to err from thy ways? *and* hardned
our heart from thy fear? [c] Return for thy ſervants ſake,
the tribes of thine inheritance 18 The people of thy
holineſs have poſſeſſed *it* but a little while [d] our adver-
ſaries have troden down thy ſanctuary 19 We are
thine, thou never bareſt rule over them, ‡ they were not
called by thy name

y Deut xxvi 15 Pſ lxxx 14
† Or, the multitude
z Jer. xxxi 20 Hoſ xi 8
a Chap lxiv 8
b Job xiv. 21 Eccleſ ix 5
c Num x 36 Pſ xc 13
d Pſ lxxiv 7
‡ Or, thy name was not called upon them

v 15—19 We have here the importunate prayer of God's people, which is continued through the following chapter It was penned for their uſe in captivity, either in Babylon, or in their preſent diſperſion, and is applicable to the church of God, during its afflicted ſtate, as well as to particular believers.

1 They

Before Christ 698.

1. They desire a gracious hearing *Look down from heaven*, not that his eyes ever cease to go to and fro in the earth, but they beg a look of tender pity and regard, and that God would bend his ear to the voice of their humble petitions, *and behold from the habitation of thy holiness and of thy glory*, the place where he is pleased to fix his radiant throne, within the highest heavens, where the most Holy dwells, and holy angels celebrate his praise *Note*, When we consider what a holy God we approach, and what sinful dust and ashes we are, it becomes us ever to appear before him with deepest humility, reverence, and godly fear

2 They lament their miserable case *O Lord, why hast thou made us to err from thy ways? and hardened our heart from thy fear?* They had erred from God's ways and worship, and hardened themselves against his fear and his warnings, and God had now given them up to their own hard hearts in just judgment; and this was matter of deep complaint to those whose eyes were opened to see their people's state They did not charge God with their sins, as the author of them, but lamented the sore visitations they had provoked by them, and no sufferings are more deplorable than these spiritual judgments *Our adversaries also have troden down thy sanctuary* the ruin of their land, the losses of their own family, were to the faithful, no doubt, heavy afflictions, but God's temple fallen, his service interrupted, this swallowed up every other grief

3 They make their plea for mercy to the God of all mercy

[1] They urge his former dealings with them *Where is thy zeal*, thy jealousy for thy own glory, whilst the enemies of Zion blaspheme, *thy fervent love* towards thy people, that of old appeared, *and thy strength?* Is thine arm shortned that it cannot save? *the sounding of thy bowels*, that used to melt over every distress of Israel, *are they restrained?* Hath the Lord forgotten to be gracious? will he be no more intreated? No, it cannot be thou wilt surely turn and refresh us, and bring us from the depths of the earth again For,

[2] *Doubtless thou art our Father*, provoking as our transgressions have been, we cannot quit the dear relation in which once we stood and shall not the meltings of thy paternal heart still admit the claim, and receive the returning prodigals? *Though Abraham be ignorant of us, and Israel acknowledge us not*, either they are gone, neither know our case, nor can assist us with their advice and prayers, or rather, though, were they again on earth, they might be led to disown such degenerate children, yet, greater are thy compassions, *O Lord, thou art our Father*, faith cannot quit the plea, unworthy as we are to be called thy sons; *our Redeemer, thy name is from everlasting*, the same in mercy and grace for ever, or, *Our Redeemer from everlasting, is thy name*, having chosen us from eternity in Jesus, thou never wilt, thou never canst, (pardon the boldness thy faithfulness encourages!) thou never canst utterly cast us away

[3] They plead the covenant established with their fathers and them *Return for thy servant's sake*, return in mercy, or *turn* from thy wrathful indignation, for the sake of Abraham, Isaac, and Jacob, with whom the covenant was made, or for the sake of the few faithful which remained, *the tribes of thine inheritance*, by right thine, and in duty and gratitude bound to be thy servants, save us, that we may be such, nor suffer us longer to serve strangers, or strange gods in a strange land

[4] They urge the short enjoyment they had of the promised land and the sanctuary of God *The people of thy holiness have possessed it but a little while* separated as they were from all others, and consecrated to God, they hoped to have possessed the land for ever; but short was comparatively their abode in Canaan, about 1400 years in all, and seldom in peace and quietness, whilst their temple had a much shorter duration, and stood little more than 400

[5] They plead, *We are thine* they were so in profession, they continued such in the covenant, and promised to be such in practice, when the Lord should turn their captivity *Thou never barest rule over them*, their conquerors and oppressors, to whom God had not stood in that relation of King and Saviour, as he had done to the Jews *they were not called by thy name*, not regarded as his children, nor professed his blessed service and surely God will not suffer these to trample down that people, who, though they have been unfaithful, yet bore his name, and desired to be re-admitted to his favour, and to yield themselves up to his service *Note*, When we return unto God, we may be fully sure he will return unto us

CHAP. LXIV.

The prayer of the church is continued in this chapter 1 *She prays for some visible display of God's power, as in time past*, ver 1, 2. 2 *She confesses her sins, and implores the divine mercy*, ver 5—9. 3 *She represents her distressed case, as an argument to obtain it*, ver 10—12

1 OH that thou wouldst ᵃ rend the heavens, that thou wouldst come down, that ᵇ the mountains
might flow down at thy presence 2. As *when* the
† melting fire burneth, the fire causeth the waters to
boil, ᶜ to make thy name known to thine adversaries,
that the nations may tremble at thy presence. 3 When
ᵈ thou didst terrible things *which* we looked not for,
thou camest down, the mountains flowed down at thy
presence 4 For since the beginning of the world, ᵉ *men*
have not heard, nor perceived by the ear, neither hath
the eye ‡ seen, O God, besides thee, *what* he hath prepared
for him that waiteth for him 5 Thou meetest
him that rejoiceth, and worketh righteousness, ᶠ *those that*
remember thee in thy ways behold thou art wroth,
for we have sinned ᵍ in those is continuance, and we
shall be saved

a Ps. cxliv. 5.
b Mic. i. 4.

Before Christ 698.
† Heb. The fire of meltings.
c Ps. ix. 16.
d Ex. xxxiv. 10. Judg. v. 4, 5. Ps. lxvi. 3. Hab. iii. 6.
e Ps. xxxi. 19. 1 Cor. ii. 9.
‡ Or, seen a God besides thee, which doth so for him, &c.
f Chap. xxvi. 8.
g Rom. xi. 4.

v 1—5 We have here,

1 The church's request, v 1, 2 desiring some glorious manifestation, as in the days of old that God would appear for the salvation of his people, and, with vengeance burning as the most vehement fire, terrify and consume their enemies And this may respect either Christ's first coming in the flesh, to destroy the spiritual enemies of his people; or that manifestation of his glory which shall be made, when fire shall come down from heaven, devour the seat of Antichrist, and destroy his tyranny, or that appearance of Jesus on the clouds of heaven, when he shall come to judge the world, and all created nature be dissolved in one universal conflagration Note, God will make himself known to all, to his people in mercy, to his enemies in terrible judgment!

2 God had wrought strange wonders of old, therefore his praying people hope for the same interposition *When thou didst terrible things which we looked not for*, when dejected in Egypt they saw no hopes of deliverance, then did God shew his wonders great and terrible, *thou camest down*, as on mount Sinai, in all the pomp of awful majesty, *the mountains flowed down at thy presence*, and if he is pleased still to appear, all mountains of difficulty shall quickly vanish, and all oppressors, though lofty as the summit of these mighty hills, be laid in the dust

3 The promises of the great things in store for God's people, more than eye hath seen, or ear heard, strengthened their faith, and quickened their desires of his appearing gloriously and speedily to help them *For since the beginning of the world, men have not heard, nor perceived by the ear, neither hath the eye seen, O God, besides thee, what he hath prepared for him that waiteth for him* great as the wonders of God's mercy in the deliverance of his people have appeared, yet other wonders of mercy and grace, known only to God in his secret counsels, are yet in store for them The apostle, 1 Cor. ii. 9. particularly applies these words to the knowledge of the gospel truths, which neither the light of nature, nor the deepest researches of human wisdom, could discover, without a revelation from God, nor even then, till he give the seeing eye, and opened the understanding to understand the scriptures and when the eyes are in a measure enlightened, and we comprehend many truths, we still know but in part, many revealed truths are still mysterious and incomprehensible, and we wait for a more perfect state, when we shall know even as we are known *Thou meetest him that rejoiceth, and worketh righteousness*, rejoiceth in God his Saviour, in the grace bestowed, and the glory promised, and, in consequence, walks under the influence of the Spirit of holiness, desiring to please God in all things *those that remember thee in thy ways*, in all instituted ordinances, means of grace, and providences, improving them, in order to maintain nearer communion with God Now, where a soul is thus found waiting on God, he will *meet* such with his mercies, denoting his readiness to hear, pardon, and save them out of all their troubles *Note*, (1) Faith in God will produce patient waiting upon him, and that shall never be disappointed (2) Much is yet unknown by us of the riches of grace to which in this life we may attain, and more with respect to the glory prepared for us in eternity (3) They who would meet God, must be found in the way of righteousness; out of that we may not expect his presence or blessing (4) Cheerfulness in the ways of God is the ornament of our walk, as well as highly our duty Gloomy and melancholy Christians are a discouragement to his service (5) As all God's ways are right, in all let us remember him, in prosperity thankful and humble, in adversity resigned and patient, praising him in all and for all, and assured that all shall work together for our good

4 They trust in the unchangeableness of his promises, not withstanding their sins *Behold, thou art wroth, for*, or *because, we have sinned*, and justly provoked God's displeasure; but he will not finally destroy his people, though he long and severely correct them *In those is continuance* in the ways of righteousness God's favour would be secured to them, or in the ways of God's grace and mercy there is continuity and perpetuity; his covenant is everlasting, and his gifts and callings without repentance *and we shall* therefore *be saved*, finally and eternally Some translate the words, *In these*, our sins, *we have been ever*, being thus conceived, and from the womb transgressors, *yet we shall*

Before Chriſt 698

ſhall be ſaved, through the riches of a Redeemer's grace extending to the caſe of the moſt deſperate ſinner *Note*, (1) If the covenant of grace were not everlaſting, and the bleſſings of it ſecured by a better obedience than our own, we muſt ſink into deſpair (2) Whilſt we ſee and lament our ſins, acknowledge God's juſtice in our puniſhment, and caſt our ſouls at his feet, we cannot periſh there

6 But we are all as an unclean *thing*, and all our
righteouſneſſes *are* as † filthy rags, and ʰ we all do fade
as a leaf, and ⁱ our iniquities like the wind, have taken
us away 7 And ᵏ *there is* none that calleth upon thy
name, that ſtirreth up himſelf to take hold of thee for
thou haſt hid thy face from us, and haſt ‡ conſumed us,
ˡ becauſe of our iniquities 8 ᵐ But now, O LORD,
thou *art* our father we *are* the clay, ⁿ and thou our
potter, and ᵒ we all *are* the work of thy hand 9 ¶ ᵖ Be
not wroth very ſore, O LORD, neither remember iniquity for ever behold, ſee, we beſeech thee, we *are*
all thy people 10 ᑫ Thy holy cities are a wilderneſs,
Zion is a wilderneſs, Jeruſalem a deſolation 11 Our
holy and our beautiful houſe, where our fathers praiſed
thee, ʳ is burnt up with fire and all our pleaſant things
are laid waſte 12 ˢ Wilt thou refrain thyſelf for theſe
things, O LORD? ᵗ wilt thou hold thy peace, and afflict us very ſore?

† Heb A garment of rags, or of ſeparation, Ezek xxxvi 17
h Pſ xc 5, 6
i Chap. lvii 13
k Hoſ vii 7
‡ Heb Melted us by thy hand
l Job viii 4
m Chap lxiii 16
n Chap xlv 9
Jer xviii 6
Rom ix 20 21
o John x 8—
p Pſ cxix 73
q Pſ lxxix 8
r Chap i 7
s 2 Chr on xxxvi 19
t Chap xlii 14
u Pſ xxxiii 1, 2

v 6—12 They had confeſſed, *We have ſinned*, here they enlarge on their tranſgreſſions, confeſſing and bewailing them, juſtifying God in their afflictions, acknowledging their own unworthineſs of the grace they craved, and, pleading their miſery, caſt themſelves on his mercy

1 They confeſs their guilty ſtate *But we are all as an unclean thing*, or *perſon*, which is the ſtate of every man by nature, and they, whoſe eyes are moſt enlightened to know their real condition, will moſt lament their deep and deſperate corruption within This alſo particularly reſpected the deplorable eſtate of the Jewiſh people, who were ſunk almoſt univerſally into the dregs of iniquity *And all our righteouſneſſes are as filthy rags*, or *a menſtruous cloth*, impure and nauſeous, which is true, not only of the ceremonial righteouſneſs of forms, and rites, and outward devotions, but of all moral righteouſneſs, which, however plauſible, and wrought with greateſt exactneſs, if truſted upon to commend us to God, or to embolden us to appear in his preſence, can ſtand us in no more ſtead, than rags to cover our nakedneſs, can no more adorn us, than filthy rags can fit us to appear in the preſence of a king for to all we can do ſo much pollution and impurity cleaves, that our righteouſneſs muſt be our ruin, and our very duties damn us, if on them we were to truſt for acceptance

2 They acknowledge the general careleſſneſs and neglect of God's worſhip *And there is none that calleth upon thy name*, none, comparatively ſpeaking, that had any deſire to ſeek to God for pardon or grace *There is none that ſtirreth up himſelf to take hold of thee*, they who performed their devotions, did it either to ſupport a good opinion of themſelves, or merely to ſatisfy conſcience, or through the force of habit, and were ſo lifeleſs, lukewarm, and negligent in them, that they knew nothing of the importunity of prayer, or the wreſtlings of faith, and ſuch ſervices added but to the number of their ſins *Note*, (1) There is not a ſurer proof of a careleſs and loſt ſoul, than the neglect of private prayer (2) The life of prayer is faith, that layeth hold of God's promiſes, and will not quit him without a bleſſing (3) Our cold hearts need much to be ſtirred up to the work of prayer, for ſpiritual ſloth is grievouſly apt to creep even upon the faithful

3 They own their afflictions to be the fruit of their ſins *We do all fade as a leaf*; our profeſſions wither, our root is ſapleſs, our boughs blaſted, *and our iniquities, like the wind, have taken us away* As the autumnal blaſts ſhake down the withered leaf, and hurl it away, ſo did the wrath of God, becauſe of their iniquities, diſperſe them firſt in Chaldea and the countries of the Babyloniſh monarchy, and now the diſperſion is become univerſal *For thou haſt hid thy face from us* in diſpleaſure, *and haſt conſumed us, becauſe of our iniquities* *Note*, (1) Falſe profeſſors, however blooming they may for a time appear, will quickly be blaſted uſually in this world their decays are manifeſt; at leaſt, at death their leaf falls and the wind of vengeance hurls them into hell (2) As God is of purer eyes than to behold iniquity, they who have no better covering than the filthy rags of their own miſerable performances, may never hope to ſee his face with comfort

4 They plead their relation to God, notwithſtanding the prevailing iniquity Some were ſtill found faithful, and, as a people, God had not caſt them away *But now, O Lord, thou art our father*, though we have done ſo much againſt thee, we cannot quit this endeared relation correct us as a father, but do not utterly diſinherit us *We are the clay, and thou our potter*; mould us to thy will; we are content to be and ſuffer according to thy pleaſure, only remember, *we are all the work of thy hands*, created by thy power, by peculiar mercy collected into a people, therefore deſtroy not thine own work

Before Chriſt 698.

5 They intreat, if not the removal of their ſufferings, yet a mitigation of them, and ſome proſpect of their end *Be not wroth very ſore, O Lord*, correct us, but in meaſure, not in fierce anger, leſt we be utterly conſumed *neither remember iniquity for ever*, but forgive at laſt, and remove from us thy heavy hand *Behold, ſee, we beſeech thee, we are all thy people*, in covenant, and therefore, according to the tenor of that, though thou viſit our iniquities with the rod, and our ſin with ſcourges, thou haſt promiſed that thy loving-kindneſs thou wilt not utterly take from us, nor ſuffer thy truth to fail

6 They ſpread their miſerable ſtate before God Their cities deſolate and in ruins, their country a wilderneſs, and Zion's palaces lying in the duſt, and, what was ſtill a bitterer cauſe of anguiſh, their *holy and beautiful houſe*, that temple, ſo magnificent and glorious, where the Shechinah once abode, and holy worſhip was offered to God, where their fathers of old praiſed the Lord, is now *burnt with fire*, which was the conſummation of their miſeries *and all our pleaſant things are laid waſte*, not merely their palaces and poſſeſſions ruined, but, above all, their ſacrifices ceaſed, their feaſts of gladneſs at an end, the worſhip of God interrupted, and no more ſongs of praiſe reſound in the courts of the Lord's houſe *Note*, (1) Human miſery is an object of the divine compaſſions (2) They who have truly at heart the intereſts of God's kingdom, are more concerned for the deſolations of the temple, than for any loſſes of their own

7 They humbly and earneſtly expoſtulate with the Lord on their unhappy caſe *Wilt thou refrain thyſelf for theſe things?* ſhall not jealouſy for thy own glory awake? thy bowels of mercy yearn over our miſeries? *Wilt thou hold thy peace*, as an unconcerned ſpectator of theſe things, *and afflict us very ſore?* ſhall there be no end nor abatement of our ſufferings? ſurely thou wilt not contend for ever ariſe, O Lord, plead thy own and thy people's cauſe! *Note*, Though God long and heavily afflict his people, let them not utterly deſpair, there is yet hope in their end

C H A P. LXV.

This propheſy looks forward to goſpel times, and, as ſome think, to the latter days of it, when Jews, as well as Gentiles, ſhould come in, and the new heaven and earth appear, wherein righteouſneſs ſhould dwell We have, 1 The preventing of the Gentiles with the goſpel call, ver 1 2 The rejection of the Jews for their obſtinacy and unbelief, ver 2—7 3 The ſaving of a remnant of them, ver 8—10 4 The judgments of God that ſhould purſue the rejected Jews ver 11—16 5 The bleſſings reſerved for the Chriſtian church, which ſhould be its joy and glory, ver 17—25

1 ᵃ I AM ſought of *them that* aſked not *for me* I am
found of *them that* ſought me not I ſaid, Behold
me, behold me, unto a nation *that* was not called by my
name 2 I have ſpread out my hands all the day unto
a rebellious people, which walketh in a way *that was* not
good, ᵇ after their own thoughts 3 A people ᶜ that
provoked me to anger continually to my face, ᵈ that ſacrificeth in gardens, and burneth incenſe † upon altars
of brick 4 ᵉ Which remain among the graves, and
lodge in the monuments, ᶠ which eat ſwines fleſh, and
‡ broth of abominable *things is in* their veſſels 5
ᵍ Which ſay, Stand by thyſelf, come not near to me,
for I am holier than thou theſe *are* a ſmoke in my
§ noſe, a fire that burneth all the day 6 Behold, ʰ *it
is* written before me, I will not keep ſilence, but ⁱ will
recompenſe, even recompenſe into their boſom, 7
Your iniquities, ᵏ and the iniquities of your fathers together (ſaith the LORD) which have burnt incenſe
upon the mountains, ˡ and blaſphemed me upon the
hills therefore will I meaſure their former work into
their ‖ boſom

a Rom ix 24 &c & x 20 &c & ii 12, 13
b Pſ lxxxi 12
c Chap iii 8 Acts vi 51
d Chap i 29 & lxvi 17
† Heb Upon bricks
e Chap lxvi 17
f Deut iv 8
‡ Or pieces
g Jude 19
§ Or anger
h Deut xxxii 34 Mal iii 16
i Pſ lxxix 12
k Ex xx 5
l Ezek xx 27 28
‖ Or lap, as Ver 6

v 1—7 The application of theſe words to the converſion of the Gentiles, and the rejection of the Jews, is fixed by an infallible expoſitor, *Rom* x 20, 21

1 The Gentiles, by divine grace and mercy, are brought into the church, and this not only when they had no deſert, but no deſire after God He ſought them firſt, calling to them to *behold* him, his Son, his goſpel, when they had no thoughts about his ſalvation, nor ſtood, as the Jews, in any near relation to him as a people; but they were not diſobedient to the heavenly viſion, when he called, they anſwered, when he drew them, they ſought him early, *Acts* xiii 42—48 *Note*, (1) If God did not firſt ſeek us, we ſhould never have enquired after him (2) When he is graciouſly manifeſting himſelf in

mercy

Before Chriſt 698

mercy to us, it becomes us to ſeek him earneſtly in all his appointed ways

2 The Jews for their impenitence and rebellion are rejected by him With long patience God bore with them, by a variety of means and methods he had ſought to reclaim them, after ſending all his prophets, he laſt of all ſent his Son, yet vain was every attempt of Chriſt and his apoſtles, inviting them by every endearing plea to turn from the evil of their ways, they obſtinately perſiſted in their own inventions, ſeeking to eſtabliſh a legal righteouſneſs, and riveted in their pride and prejudices to the ceremonial inſtitutions, rejected the counſel of God againſt themſelves, *v* 2 Their fathers ſin had been groſs and impious idolatry, forſaking God for ſtocks and ſtones, and leaving his temple and altar for groves and altars of their own erecting, where they burnt incenſe, and offered ſacrifices to their idols, and this openly without a bluſh, as if wilfully deſigning to provoke God to his face, by their daring impiety, and contempt of his ſervice, *v* 3 Addicted to necromancy, and among the graves and monuments conſulting the dead, or the evil ſpirits that were ſuppoſed to haunt thoſe melancholy abodes, paying no regard to the diſtinctions of clean and unclean ordained by the law, but eating ſwine's fleſh, and broth of abominable things, *v* 4 Now theſe iniquities of their fathers, whoſe meaſure they filled up, God would viſit upon them, for though the Jews of our Saviour's day were cured of their idolatries, yet their pride and hypocriſy were yet more deteſtable, *which ſay, Stand by thyſelf, come not near to me, for I am holier than thou*, ſo high in their own conceits, and ſo holy, that they looked down with contempt on others, and thought defilement was contracted even by their touch *Theſe are a ſmoke in my noſe*, offenſive and loathſome, *a fire that burneth all the day*, a continual provocation, againſt which his indignation and wrath burned like fire For theſe abominations God will plead with them, and with juſt judgment recompenſe them for their iniquities, and all the former ſins ſhould come into the dreadful account, and be required of the men of that generation, *Luke* xi 51 *Note*, (1) Sooner or later God will viſit for ſin, and woe to the ſoul on whom the vengeance due to it ſhall be laid! (2) Nothing is in God's ſight more odious, than a ſinner vaunting his own holineſs, and proudly looking down with contempt on others (3) Though vengeance may be long delayed, it will ſurely come at laſt, when the meaſure of the ſinner's iniquity is full

n Rom xi 5
8 ¶ Thus ſaith the LORD, n As the new wine is
found in the cluſter, and *one* ſaith, Deſtroy it not,
n Joel ii 14 for n a bleſſing *is* in it ſo will I do for my ſervants
ſakes, that I may not deſtroy them all 9 And I will
o Rom xi 29. bring forth o a ſeed out of Jacob, and out of Judah an
inheritor of my mountains and mine elect ſhall inherit
it, and my ſervants ſhall dwell there 10 And Sharon
p Hoſ ii 15 ſhall be a fold of flocks, and p the valley of Achor a place
for the herds to lie down in, for my people that have
ſought me.

v 8—10 Though the generality of the Jewiſh people were rejected for their unbelief and rebellion, there was yet a remnant ſaved, according to the election of grace

1 This is repreſented by a cluſter of grapes, hanging on a blighted vine, which the dreſſer of the vineyard, ſeeing it in general withered, is ready to cut down, but the maſter ſtays his hand for the ſake of that one cluſter, and becauſe it ſhews alſo there is ſtill life, and the tree may again revive *Deſtroy it not, for a bleſſing is in it* *Note*, (1) The faithful are few, as one cluſter of grapes upon a vine, yet for their ſakes God ſpares the land (2) Wherever the truth of grace is found, though but in the weakeſt meaſure, the ſoul ſhall not periſh

2 God promiſes, not only for his ſervants ſake, not to deſtroy them all, but to bring *a ſeed out of Jacob and Judah*, to inherit his holy mountain, the church, and *his elect ſervants ſhall dwell there*, ver 9 enjoying all the ordinances, and enriched with all ſpiritual gifts and graces, as the flocks and herds that fed in the green paſtures of Sharon and Achor, which was fulfilled in the multitude of thoſe Jewiſh converts called by the preaching of the apoſtles, who were alſo themſelves all of the ſtock of Judah, and by whoſe labours the ſpiritual ſeed of Jacob throughout the world was ſo exceedingly increaſed *Note*, (1) The elect of God are known by their earneſtneſs in ſeeking God, and their fidelity in ſerving him (2) None ever ſought God in truth, but found him their exceeding great reward

11 ¶ But ye *are* they that forſake the LORD, that
forget my holy mountain, that prepare a table for that
† Or Gad † troop, and that furniſh the drink-offering unto that
‡ Or Meni ‡ number 12 Therefore will I number you to the
q Iſai i 24 &c Chap lxvi 4 Jer vii 13 ſword, and ye ſhall bow down to the ſlaughter q be-
cauſe when I called, ye did not anſwer, when I ſpake,
ye did not hear, but did evil before mine eyes, and did
choose *that* wherein I delighted not 13 Therefore
thus ſaith the Lord GOD, Behold, r my ſervants ſhall r Pſ xxxv 19, 20
eat, but ye ſhall be hungry behold, my ſervants ſhall
drink, but ye ſhall be thirſty behold, s my ſervants ſhall s Prov xxiv 6.
rejoice, but ye ſhall be aſhamed 14 Behold, my ſer-
vants ſhall ſing for joy of heart, but ye ſhall cry for
ſorrow of heart, and ſhall howl for § vexation of ſpirit § Or breaking
15, And ye ſhall leave your name for a curſe unto my
choſen for the Lord GOD ſhall ſlay thee, and t call t Chap lxii 2 John i 12 or Acts xi 26
his ſervants by another name 16 u That he who
bleſſeth himſelf in the earth, ſhall bleſs himſelf in the u Pſ lxxii 17 Jer iv 2
God of truth, and x he that ſweareth in the earth, ſhall
ſwear by the God || of truth, becauſe the former trou- x Deut vi 13 Pſ lxiii 11 Chap xlv 18 & xlv 23 Zeph i 5
bles are forgotten, and becauſe they are hid from || Heb. Amen Rev, iii 14
mine eyes

v 11—16 The body of the Jewiſh people perſiſted in their impiety and infidelity to them theſe words are addreſſed

1 They are upbraided with their ſins

[1] Apoſtacy from God and his ſervice *Ye are they that forſake the Lord, that forget my holy mountain*, they rejected his government, and neglected his worſhip *Note*, They who forſake the Lord, forſake their own mercies

[2] Idolatry *That prepare a table for that troop, and that furniſh the drink-offering unto that number*, their idols ſo multiplied, and yet ſo liberally ſupplied with offerings, whilſt God's altar was utterly neglected Some ſuppoſe the words *Gad* and *Meni*, rendered by *troop* and *number*, to be the names of their idols, and to ſignify the ſun and moon *Note*, Men to gratify their luſts grudge no expence, and ſhall we then be niggards in the ſervice of the Lord?

[3] Obſtinate impenitence The former more properly were their fathers ſins, though to be viſited upon them, this the eſpecial guilt of the Jews in our Saviour's day *When I called, ye did not anſwer, when I ſpake, ye did not hear* nay, though he became incarnate in his own glorious perſon, to preach and teach the way of life, they rejected his words and warnings, contradicting and blaſpheming, *but did evil before mine eyes*, following determinedly the imaginations of their own evil hearts, and adding to all the reſt that daring conſummation of their evil, the crucifying the Lord of life and glory, *and did chooſe that wherein I delighted not*, the traditions of the elders, and thoſe falſe gloſſes which deſtroyed the ſpirit of God's word, and ſhewed that pride, hypocriſy, and enmity againſt the goſpel, which were ſo peculiarly provoking to him

2 Their puniſhment is denounced *I will number you to the ſword, and ye ſhall bow down to the ſlaughter*, and dreadful was the maſſacre which the Roman ſoldiers made of them *Note*, (1) When the ſword devours, the number is fixed for the ſlaughter, and every bullet has its billet (2) When God fights againſt the ſinner, reſiſtance is vain, for he will overcome

3 The bleſſedneſs of God's people, as contraſted with their miſery, will aggravate their doom *Note*, It will be an additional torment to the miſeries of the damned, to ſee the righteous in the kingdom of God, and themſelves caſt out This is inſiſted on in three particulars

[1] The one ſhall be conſumed with famine and want, the other enjoy plenty and affluence, *v* 13 which was literally the caſe, when the Chriſtians, before the ſiege of *Jeruſalem*, removed to Pella; whilſt the Jews, who were beſieged, terribly periſhed by famine And alſo ſpiritually, thoſe who reject Chriſt and his goſpel, and ſeek to fill themſelves with the comforts of earth, will ever be unſatisfied here, and in hell want a drop of water to aſſuage their raging thirſt, whilſt his people, who feed upon him in his promiſes, find the hidden manna, ſweet and nouriſhing to their ſoul, and drink of thoſe conſolations which are better than wine, and theſe but foretaſtes of the proviſion God hath made for them in the eternal world, where they ſhall hunger no more, nor thirſt any more, the moſt boundleſs deſires of their ſouls being ſatisfied in the fruition of God

[2] God's ſervants ſhall rejoice and ſing, when his enemies are aſhamed, and with anguiſh cry out in their pangs. The paths of heavenly wiſdom are full of preſent peace and joy; the paths of ſin all lead to ſhame and miſery And how much greater ſtill will the difference appear, when theſe ſhall be rejoicing in glory, and joining the ſongs of angels, whilſt the ſinner is covered with everlaſting confuſion, and gnawing his tongue for pain, in thoſe eternal torments, where the worm dieth not, and the fire is not quenched

[3] The one ſhall be deteſted and infamous, the other honourable and diſtinguiſhed, *v* 15 Hence the very name of *Jew* is become execrable, they are ſtigmatized for knavery and covetouſneſs, but God's people have a new and honourable name, *Chriſtians*, or *Hephzibah and Beulah*, intimating the Lord's love and delight in them *That he who bleſſeth himſelf in the earth*, who looks for God's bleſſing, or thankfully acknowledges the mer-

Before Christ 698

cies received from him, *shall bless himself in the God of truth*, as the faithful servants of God ever do, esteeming God as their great portion, and expecting from him all their mercies or, *shall bless themselves in God, Amen*, in Jesus Christ, who is the *Amen*, the faithful and true witness, *Rev* iii 14 *And he that sweareth in the earth*, which is an act of religious worship, *shall swear by the God of truth*, to whom alone the solemn appeal ought to be made, *because the former troubles are forgotten, they are hid from my eyes*, either the idolatry and superstition of the Gentile world, which were a grief to God's people, but now are destroyed, or the carnal ordinances, which were a heavy yoke, and were by Christ's sacrifice abolished, and this sense seems best to suit the following words

17 ¶ For behold, I create [y] new heavens, and a new
earth and the former shall not be remembered, nor
come into mind 18 But be you glad and rejoice for
ever *in that* which I create for behold, I create Jeru-
salem a rejoicing, and her people a joy, 19 And [z] I
will rejoice in Jerusalem, and joy in my people, and
[a] the voice of weeping shall be no more heard in her,
nor the voice of crying 20 There shall be no more
thence an infant of days, nor an old man [b] that hath not
filled his days for the child shall die an hundred years
old, but [c] the sinner *being* an hundred years old shall be
accursed 21 And [d] they shall build houses and inhabit
them, and they shall plant vineyards, and eat the fruit
of them 22 They shall not build, and another inha-
bit, they shall not plant, and another eat for [e] as the
days of a tree, *are* the days of my people, and mine elect
shall long enjoy the work of their hands 23 They
shall not labour in vain, [f] nor bring forth for trouble
for they *are* the seed of the blessed of the LORD, and
their offspring with them 24 And it shall come to
pass, that [g] before they call, I will answer, and while
they are yet speaking, I will hear 25 [h] The wolf and
the lamb shall feed together, and the lion shall eat straw
like the bullock and [i] dust *shall be* the serpent's meat
They shall not hurt nor destroy in all my holy moun-
tain, saith the LORD.

[y] Chap li 16 & lxvi 22 2 Pet iii 13 Rev xxi 1
[z] Chap lxii 5
[a] Chap xxxv 10 & li 11 Rev vii 17 & xxi 4
[b] Job v 26
[c] Eccles viii 12
[d] Lev xxvi 16 Deut xxviii 30 Am ix 14
[e] Ps xcii 12
[f] Deut xxviii 41 Hos ix 12 [illegible] 1 Cor xv
[g] Ps xxxii 5 [illegible]
[h] Chap xi 6 7 9
[i] Gen iii 14

v 17—25 We see here,

1 A new creation rise at God's command, new heavens expanded, a new earth framed, and these so glorious, that they obliterate the remembrance of the former, which some refer to the gospel day, when such a wondrous change should be wrought in the hearts of men, that it should be said, *Old things are past away, behold, all things are become new*, 2 Cor v 17 Others suppose this will be literally fulfilled after the dissolution of all things, and that Christ will come and reign with his saints upon earth a thousand years, and to this they conceive the apostles to refer, *Rev* xxi 1—[illegible], 2 *Pet* iii 13, whilst others look farther, and interpret this of the state and blessedness of the saints of God in glory everlasting

2 This will give occasion to God's saints of everlasting joy *But be you glad and rejoice for ever in that which I create*, as partaker of the blessed change, the gospel works, and inheritors of the eternal glory God bestows *For behold, I create Jerusalem a rejoicing, and her people a joy*, with such consolation shall the church and every member of it be filled, and all her friends rejoice with and over her, because of her prosperity *The voice of weeping shall no more be heard in her*, there shall be no allay or interruption of her joys, but they shall be endless as the source from whence they flow

3 God himself will rejoice in his own work *And I will rejoice in Jerusalem, and joy in my people*, when, through the righteousness of Jesus, and the effectual work of the Divine Spirit, they shall be wholly renewed in body, soul, and spirit, and become the object of God's eternal complacence

4 In this blessed state there shall be no untimely deaths, as now, when we see the infant carried almost from the womb to the grave, and few, even of those who are aged, reach the full limits appointed to the life of man the contrary to which some suppose will literally be the case in the latter day, when, among other instances of temporal blessings, long life shall be enjoyed I rather incline to interpret this spiritually, as intimating that the youngest convert who departs, shall be raised in the fulness of the measure of the stature of Christ, as if he had lived an hundred years, and those whose lives have been longer spent in Christ's service, shall have their full reward in glory, whilst the sinner, to whatever extent God lengthens out his days, will be accursed at the last *Note*, (1) We need not grieve for early converts snatched away by death; they are happily entered into their rest, and the space taken from the labours of time, shall be added to the rewards of eternity (2) An aged saint is a venerable object, an aged sinner the most pitiable and deplorable (3) However long God's patience bears with the sinner, his curse will overtake him at last

5 Their possessions shall not be precarious, nor their enjoyments interrupted The houses they build, the vineyards they plant, no enemy shall possess, nor spoiler destroy, but the elect of God shall long peaceably and comfortably enjoy the blessings he bestows upon them *for as the days of a tree, are the days of my people*, as the days of an oak, which lives for ages, or the tree of life in the paradise of God, to which there seems to be an allusion and this will be eminently true, when the redeemed enter their mansions in glory, and drink the new wine in the kingdom of God

6 Their children after them shall inherit their blessings *They shall not labour in vain*, but see the blessing of God upon all the work of their hands *nor bring forth trouble*, their children shall be their comfort, not their sorrow *for they are the seed of the blessed of the Lord, and their offspring with them* their mercies descend to their posterity, together interested in a covenant of grace, and prevented and followed with the blessings of divine goodness

7 A wondrous change shall pass upon the tempers of men *The wolf and the lamb shall feed together*, Gentiles and Jews shall now become one fold, and men of the most savage dispositions be brought to the meekness of the lamb *and the lion shall eat straw like the ox*, ravening persecutors not only brought to be men of peace, but laborious ministers, as in the case of Paul and others *and dust shall be the serpent's meat*, the sentence pronounced on the devil, *Gen* iii 14 and, in him, on all the enemies of God's church and people, shall be fulfilled, they shall be trodden under the feet of God's victorious saints *They shall not hurt or destroy in all my holy mountain*, but their power be utterly broken, and themselves ruined, *saith the Lord*, whose word is faithful, and the accomplishment of it sure

CHAP LXVI

The first verse of this chapter is applied by Stephen to the dismantling of the temple and the planting of the Christian church, Acts vii 49 50 *which may serve as a key to the whole We have here*, 1 *The contempt God puts upon ceremonial services, in comparison with moral duties, and an intimation therein of his purpose shortly to put an end to them*, ver 1—4 2 *The salvation God will in due time work for his people, out of the hands of their oppressors*, ver 5 *speaking terror to the persecutors*, ver 6 *and comfort to the persecuted a speedy and compleat deliverance*, ver 7—9 *a joyful settlement*, ver 10, 11 *the accession of the Gentiles to them, and abundance of satisfaction therein*, ver 12—14 3 *The terrible vengeance which God will bring upon the enemies of his church and people*, ver 15—18 4 *The happy establishment of the church upon large and sure foundations, its constant attendance on God, and triumph over its enemies*, ver 19—24 *And we may well expect that this evangelical prophet, here in the close of his prophecy, should (as he doth) look as far forward as to the latter days, to the last day, to the days of eternity*

1 THUS saith the LORD, [a] The heaven *is* my
throne, and the earth *is* my footstool where
is the house that ye build unto me? and where *is* the
place of my rest? 2 For all those *things* hath mine
hand made, and all those *things* have been, saith the
LORD but [b] to this *man* will I look, *even* to *him that*
is poor and of a contrite spirit, [c] and trembleth at my
word 3 [d] He that killeth an ox, *is as if* he slew
a man he that sacrificeth a † lamb, *as if* he [e] cut off a
dog's neck he that offereth an oblation, *as if he offered*
swine's blood he that ‡ burneth incense, *as if* he bles-
sed an idol yea, they have chosen their own ways, and
their soul delighteth in their abominations 4 I also
will choose their § delusions, and will bring their fears
upon them; [f] because when I called, none did an-
swer, when I spake, they did not hear but they did
evil before mine eyes, and chose *that* in which I de-
lighted not

[a] 1 Kings viii 27 2 Chron vi 18 Matt v 34 35 Acts vii 49 & xvii 24
[b] Chap lvii 15 & lxi 1
[c] [illegible]
[d] [illegible]
[e] [illegible]
† Or kid
[illegible] Deut xxiii 18
‡ Heb maketh a memorial of Lev ii 2
§ Or devices
[f] [illegible] Chap lxv 12 Jer vii 13

v 1—4 The grand delusion of the Jewish people was the confidence they placed in their outward privileges and ritual services, their temple and sacrifices To undeceive them herein, the prophets and evangelists warn them of the vanity of these things, and that the temple they so highly prized, would soon be razed from its foundations, as it was by the Chaldeans, and more entirely afterwards by the Romans

1 The prophet rebukes their mean and unworthy notions of God, as if confined to the temple they had built, whom heaven, and the heaven of heavens cannot contain *Thus saith the Lord, Heaven is my throne*, where most transcendently he displays the infinite brightness of his glory, *and the earth is my footstool*, subject to his government, and at his disposal *Where is the house that ye build unto me?* that can contain his immensity, or be worthy of his dignity, who is exalted above all

Before Christ 698

bleſſing and praiſe, *and where is the place of my reſt?* who needs no repoſe, and can take no ſatisfaction in the wretched fabrics of puny mortals *for all theſe things hath mine hands made*, heaven and earth, and the inhabitants of both *and all thoſe things have been*, or *are*, *ſaith the Lord*, were created by his power, and ſubſiſt by his providence how impoſſible therefore for this eternal Creator of all to need a temple made with hands, or this omnipreſent Deity to be circumſcribed within theſe narrow bounds?

2 The temple he delights in is not that which conſiſts of hewn ſtones, and cedars overlaid with gold, a far nobler manſion he hath formed for himſelf *To this man will I look, even to him that is poor and of a contrite ſpirit, and trembleth at my word*, which ſome interpret of Chriſt, in whom dwelt all the fulneſs of the godhead bodily, but more generally may be applied to every believer, who is an habitation of God through the Spirit, and whoſe character is here delineated, *poor* in his own eyes, ſenſible of his abject ſpiritual wants and wretchedneſs, *of a contrite heart*, broken with conviction of his guilt and danger, *and trembleth at my word*, with that reverence and godly fear which faith inſpires, ſuch a heart is the living temple of the Deity

3 Their ſacrifices are rejected, aboliſhed, abhorred they were ever deteſtable, when offered by thoſe whoſe ways were wickedneſs, but now to perſiſt in them, and depend upon them for acceptance with God, when the one great ſacrifice once offered put a period to the ritual ſervice, was utterly abominable Murder, idolatry, and the moſt unclean and forbidden ſacrifices, as the offering of a dog, or the blood of ſwine, were not more highly criminal, and abhorred of God, nor would be attended with deeper and more condign puniſhment, than the continuance of their incenſe and oblations, which was now in effect to trample under foot the blood of the Son of God, to reject his goſpel, and do deſpite to the ſpirit of grace *Note*, Many think they take great pains to ſave their ſouls by their duties and ſervices, and will not be perſuaded, that their truſt in theſe only brings upon them more ſure deſtruction

4 God gives them up to their own inventions, and woe to that ſoul whom he abandons! *Yea, they have choſen their own ways*, cleaving to the law for righteouſneſs, they wilfully and obſtinately rejected Chriſt and his ſalvation, *and their ſoul delighteth in their abominations*, they are pleaſed with their own ſervices, and flatter themſelves God approves them, when in fact he abhors them Therefore, ſays he, *I alſo will chooſe their deluſions*, giving them up to their own deceived hearts, *and will bring their fears upon them*, the calamities they dreaded, eſpecially the horrible devaſtations of the Romans, who they feared would take away their place and nation, *John* xi 48 which, whilſt they crucified the Redeemer to prevent, they thereby moſt effectually drew upon their heads the judgments which they ſought to avoid *becauſe when I called, none did anſwer, when I ſpake they did not hear*, deaf to the preaching of Chriſt and his apoſtles, they hardened their hearts in unbelief and impenitence *But they did evil before mine eyes*, reviling, blaſpheming, perſecuting, and at laſt murdering the Lord Jeſus, and utterly rejecting his goſpel, *and choſe that in which I delighted not*, not only the ways of wickedneſs and ſin, but the falſe confidences of legal righteouſneſs, and the vain interpretations of oral tradition *Note*, (1) They who are deaf to God's warnings, will be made to feel his wrath (2) Wilful rejection of the light is juſtly puniſhed by God's leaving a ſinner to the deluſions he hath choſen, and giving him up to a reprobate mind (3) Nothing more is needful to kindle up a hell within ſinners hearts, even on this ſide the grave, than to *bring their own fears upon them*

5 ¶ Hear the word of the LORD, ye that tremble
at his word, your brethren that hated you, that caſt
you out for my name's ſake, ſaid, Let the LORD be
glorified but he ſhall appear to your joy, and they
ſhall be aſhamed 6 A voice of noiſe from the city, a
voice from the temple, a voice of the LORD that
rendeth recompenſe to his enemies 7 Before ſhe
travailed, ſhe brought forth before her pain came, ſhe
was delivered of a man child 8 Who hath heard ſuch
a thing? who hath ſeen ſuch things? ſhall the earth be
made to bring forth in one day, *or* ſhall a nation be
born at once? for as ſoon as Zion travailed, ſhe brought
forth her children 9 Shall I bring to the birth, and
not cauſe to bring forth? ſaith the LORD ſhall I
cauſe to bring forth, and ſhut *the womb*? ſaith thy
God 10 Rejoice ye with Jeruſalem, and be glad with
her, all ye that love her rejoice for joy with her, all ye
that mourn for her 11 That ye may ſuck, and be
ſatisfied with the breaſts of her conſolations that ye
may milk out, and be delighted with the abundance of
her glory 12 For thus ſaith the LORD, Behold, I
will extend peace to her like a river, and the glory of
the Gentiles like a flowing ſtream Then ſhall ye
ſuck, ye ſhall be born upon *her* ſides, and be dandled
upon her knees 13 As one whom his mother com-
forteth, ſo will I comfort you and ye ſhall be com-
forted in Jeruſalem 14 And when ye ſee *this*, your
heart ſhall rejoice, and your bones ſhall flouriſh like
an herb and the hand of the LORD ſhall be known
towards his ſervants, and *his* indignation towards his
enemies

Before Christ 698

Chap xlix 22 & lx 4 — Chap li 3 — John xvi 22 — Ezek xxxvii 1, &c

v 5—14 The prophet turns from the diſobedient, againſt whom God's judgments were denounced, to thoſe who trembled at his word, and encourages the humble and contrite with the aſſurances of God's regard, and his bleſſing upon them

1 God will appear to vindicate them againſt their perſecutors *Your brethren that hated you, that caſt you out for my name's ſake*, as the Jews did the apoſtles and diſciples of Chriſt, tho' their brethren, excommunicated them from their ſynagogues, and were their bittereſt and moſt implacable enemies, ſtirring up the Gentiles againſt them in every place, *ſaying*, *Let the Lord be glorified*, pretending zeal for his honour, and many really thinking, that he who killed them did God ſervice *but he ſhall appear to your joy*, ſupporting and ſtrengthening them againſt all oppoſition, giving ſucceſs to their labours, and comforting them in all their tribulation *and they ſhall be aſhamed*, all their devices baffled, the goſpel ſpreading in ſpite of their oppoſition, and ſpeedy deſtruction haſtening upon their own heads *Note*, (1) A Chriſtian's bittereſt foes are often thoſe of his own houſe (2) Church rulers have been in general the chief perſecutors, and cover with the fair pretext of zeal for religion, the enmity of their hearts againſt thoſe more faithful miniſters, whoſe boldneſs, diligence, and exemplary lives reproach their ſloth, negligence, and carnality (3) They who ſuffer for their fidelity, ſhall find the comforts of God an abundant ſupport and recompenſe

2 Heavy will be the vengeance of God on their enemies, *v* 6 *A voice of noiſe from the city*, the ſhrieks of the wounded, the groans of the dying, and the ſhouts of the conquerors *a voice from the temple* of lamentation, when ſet on fire by the Romans, or that which Joſephus reports was heard in the temple ſhortly before its deſtruction, when the doors flew open of their own accord, and a voice iſſued from the holy place, crying, *Let us depart hence* *A voice of the Lord that rendeth recompenſe to his enemies*, by whoſe direction and order all theſe judgments came upon them

3 To the wonder and joy of his people, and the confuſion and aſtoniſhment of his enemies, God will enlarge and eſtabliſh his church in the earth, *v* 7—9 *Before ſhe travailed, ſhe brought forth before her pain came, ſhe was delivered of a man-child* The church of Chriſt is repreſented as a pregnant woman, that immediately, with little or no pain, brings forth her ſon, ſo ſpeedily and eaſily, by the preaching of a ſingle ſermon, *Acts* ii 41 were multitudes regenerate and converted to Chriſt *Who hath heard ſuch a thing? who hath ſeen ſuch things?* ſo ſtrange and uncommon *Shall the earth be made to bring forth in one day?* ſince the creation the ſeaſons go on in gradual ſucceſſion, and the fruits require time to ripen them or *ſhall a nation be born at once?* which is uſually the work of ages *for as ſoon as Zion travailed, ſhe brought forth her children*, no ſooner began the goſpel to be preached, than multitudes both of men and women, as the drops of dew from the womb of the morning, were added to the church daily, *Pſ* cx 3 *Acts* iv 4 *Shall I bring to the birth*, in conviction, *and not bring forth*, in converſion and regeneration? *Shall I cauſe to bring forth*, in one place and age, *and ſhut the womb, ſaith thy God?* that there ſhould not be a conſtant ſucceſſion of ſpiritual births? No God's work is perfect when he begins he will make an end, and, till time ſhall be no more, he will add unto the church daily ſuch as ſhall be ſaved *Note*, (1.) Whatever labour, pains, and prayer miniſters uſe, ſo as to be ſaid to travail in birth, till Chriſt be formed in their hearers, it is God's work alone to regenerate the ſoul, and every real convert is born of him (2) God will maintain his church in the world to the end of time, and we may expect the fulfilment of this prophecy more eminently hereafter, both reſpecting Jews and Gentiles, *Hoſ* i 10, 11 *Rom* xi 25, 26

4 All the friends of Jeruſalem are called to rejoice with her, as we congratulate each other on the birth of a ſon *Rejoice ye with Jeruſalem, and be glad with her, all ye that love her rejoice for joy with her, all ye that mourn for her* They who love God, love his church and people, have their intereſts at heart, pray for their peace and proſperity, take delight in her communion, and mourn over her ſorrows, afflictions, declenſions, and perſecutions, and therefore they cannot but partake in her joys as their own *That ye may ſuck, and be ſatisfied with the breaſts of her conſolations* as full breaſts afford the ſweeteſt nouriſhment to the infant, and abundantly ſupply its wants, ſo plenteous, ſo precious, ſhall the conſolations of God's Spirit be to the ſoul that by faith feeds on the ſincere milk of the word, and on thoſe great and precious promiſes contained in the covenant of God's everlaſting love *that ye may milk out, and be delighted*

Before Christ 698

with the abundance of her glory, a glorious Saviour, a glorious Spirit, a glorious proviſion of promiſes, a glorious hope, a glorious inheritance these are the delight of the believing ſoul, and there is abundance for all who ſeek it, they may come and milk out from theſe breaſts of glory, to the ſatisfying the moſt boundleſs deſires of their ſouls

5 God will give them moſt abundant cauſe for joy in the gathering the Gentiles, and the ruin of every enemy *For thus ſaith the Lord, I will extend peace to her as a river*, ſo plentiful, ſo perpetual, peace with God, peace of conſcience, peace among themſelves, and, like a river full to its margin, it ſhall flow uninterrupted into the boundleſs ocean of eternal joy *and the glory of the Gentiles like a flowing ſtream*, multitudes of converts ſhall be made, and theſe of the mighty and noble, numerous as the drops of water in the river, or as Egypt by the overflowing of the Nile, the church ſhall be enriched with their abundance of good things *Then ſhall ye ſuck the milk*, the riches, *of the Gentiles*, or the breaſts of the church's conſolations *ye ſhall be borne upon her ſides*, or *at her ſide*, as the nurſe carries her infant charge, tenderly and ſafely, *and be dandled on her knees*, as the mother with fond delight dandles her darling boy And this repreſents the tenderneſs with which young converts muſt be treated, and the delight of the church, her members, and eſpecially her miniſters, in thoſe that are born unto her *As one whom his mother comforteth, ſo will I comfort you*, with that unutterable affection that mothers only know, yea, with tenderneſs infinitely greater than theirs, will God comfort his people If he chides, their ſorrows melt his heart, and he returns with the kiſſes of his love to dry up the falling tear if they fall, he raiſes them up, ſooths their anguiſh, and heals their hurt if they are afflicted, he feels with more than human ſympathy, with his kind arm ſupports their reclining head, refreſhes them with his conſolations, and recovers them from the bed of languiſhing. *And ye ſhall be comforted in Jeruſalem*, in the church and her ordinances, where God eſpecially manifeſts his favour towards his people *and when ye ſee this*, experiencing the wondrous grace of this compaſſionate God and Saviour, *your heart ſhall rejoice*, with joy unſpeakable and full of glory, *and your bones ſhall flouriſh like an herb*, you ſhall both be ſtrengthened and comforted with divine conſolations, ſpringing up within the heart, as an herb in a well-watered garden, and which will be as marrow to the bones, *Prov* xvii 22 *And the hand of the Lord ſhall be known towards his ſervants*, his care and protection of them, and kindneſs towards them, ſhall be manifeſted to their comfort and honour, and his great glory, *and his indignation towards his enemies*, upon whom his vengeance will fall ſo remarkably and terribly, that they who behold it will own, that it is the finger of God

y Ezek xxxviii 22 · z 2 Theſ i 8 · * Pſ l 3 — 15 For behold, [y] the LORD will come with fire,
and with his chariots like a whirlwind, [z] to render his
anger with fury, and his rebuke with flames of fire
16 For by fire, and by his ſword, will the LORD
a Rev xix 18 — plead with all fleſh and [a] the ſlain of the LORD ſhall
b Chap lxv 3 4 — be many. 17 [b] They that ſanctify themſelves, and pu-
rify themſelves in the gardens, † behind one *tree* in the
† Or one after another — midſt, eating ſwines fleſh, and the abomination, and the
mouſe, ſhall be conſumed together, ſaith the LORD
c Rev ii 2 — 18 For [c] I *know* their works and their thoughts it
ſhall come, that I will gather all nations and tongues,
d Luke ii 34 — and they ſhall come and ſee my glory 19. And [d] I
will ſet a ſign among them, and I will ſend thoſe that
e Mat xxviii 19 — eſcape of them [e] unto the nations, *to* Tarſhiſh, Pul, and
Lud, that draw the bow, *to* Tubal and Javan, *to* the iſles
afar off, that have not heard my fame, neither have
f Mal i 11 — ſeen my glory, and [f] they ſhall declare my glory among
the Gentiles 20 And they ſhall bring all your bre-
g Rom xv 16 — thren [g] *for* an offering unto the LORD, out of all na-
‡ Or coaches — tions, upon horſes, and in chariots, and in ‡ litters, and
upon mules, and upon ſwift beaſts, to my holy moun-
tain Jeruſalem, ſaith the LORD, as the children of Iſ-
rael bring an offering in a clean veſſel into the houſe of
h Exod xix 6 Chap lxi 6 1 Pet ii 9 Rev i 6 — the LORD 21 And I will alſo take of them [h] for
i Chap lxv 17 2 Pet iii 13 Rev xxi 1 — prieſts, *and* for Levites, ſaith the LORD 22 For as
[i] the new heavens, and the new earth which I will make,
ſhall remain before me, ſaith the LORD, ſo ſhall your
k Zech xiv 16 — ſeed and your name remain 23 And [k] it ſhall come
l Pſ lxv 2 — to paſs, *that* from one new-moon to another, and from
one ſabbath to another, [l] ſhall all fleſh come to worſhip
before me, ſaith the LORD 24. And they ſhall go
m Mark ix 44, 46 48 — forth, and look upon the carcaſes of the men that have
tranſgreſſed againſt me for [m] their worm ſhall not die,
neither ſhall their fire be quenched, and they ſhall be
an abhorring unto all fleſh

v 15—24 We have here an awful diſplay of the wrath of God revealed from heaven againſt the ungodlineſs of men, and a bright proſpect of the glory and triumphs of the redeemed, that, like the pillar of the cloud, gives light to God's Iſrael, but hangs louring with vengeance over his enemies

Before Christ 698

1 Chriſt will appear, to the terror of the wicked, in flaming fire, and with fury like a whirlwind, his judgments irreſiſtible as terrible, *v* 15 Arraigned at his bar, and their guilt too glaring to be denied, the ſword of inexorable juſtice is unſheathed, and the multitude of criminals executed, *v* 17 Their crimes are idolatry, ſuperſtition, and every abomination committed in defiance of God's law *They purify themſelves in gardens*, according to their idolatrous rites, *behind one tree in the midſt* Some ſuppoſe *Achad*, which we render *one*, to be the name of their idol, and others read the words, *one after another*, eagerly crouding to this hated worſhip, *eating ſwines fleſh, and the abomination, and the mouſe*, unclean and forbidden animals, and therefore *they are conſumed together* God being privy to their works and thoughts, and ſeeing their utter apoſtacy from his worſhip and ſervice, executes vengeance upon them This relates either to the Jews, as ſome interpret it, who might have brought back with them, and practiſed in ſecret, thoſe idolatries they had learnt in Babylon or, as others, to the Antichriſtian church, in which idolatry ſhall revive, and Chriſt's ordinances be diſregarded or it may more generally refer to all the wicked who rebel againſt God We have ſeen fire and ſword terribly devour Jeruſalem, with the ſame temporal judgments ſhall the ſeat of Antichriſt be deſtroyed, *Rev* xviii 8 and we expect Jeſus, the Judge of all, to be at laſt revealed from heaven in flaming fire, taking vengeance on all who know not God, and obey not his goſpel

2 He will ſet up his kingdom in the world, to the great joy of his people, as he did at the firſt preaching of the goſpel, or as he will do more univerſally at laſt, when his name will be ſpread from pole to pole

[1] All nations ſhall hear the goſpel word, and be gathered in to Chriſt *It ſhall come, that I will gather all nations and tongues, and they ſhall come and ſee my glory*, the glory of Chriſt in his perſon and offices, or of his goſpel, in the great and precious promiſes of it, or of the church, into which they will be gathered, and where the members ſhall in purity of manners, beauty of order, and unity of affection, eminently adorn their profeſſion, and glorify their Lord *And I will ſet a ſign among them*, an enſign, ſuch as Chriſt is, lifted up in the goſpel word, to whom the gathering of the people will be, or ſome miraculous ſign, as when on the day of Pentecoſt the Holy Ghoſt was poured out upon the apoſtles, and, to the aſtoniſhment of the different nations aſſembled at Jeruſalem, they heard them ſpeak all their ſeveral languages and it is not improbable, that before the great day of the Lord's power, theſe miraculous gifts may be again reſtored Others ſuppoſe this ſign will be the converſion of the Jews, or ſome diſtinguiſhing mark put upon the foreheads of God's people, but the former ſenſes are much preferable

[2] Preachers ſhall for this purpoſe be ſent forth *I will ſend thoſe that eſcape of them unto the nations*, either the apoſtles and converts of the Jews, who eſcaped the general impenitence of their countrymen, and went forth into every place preaching the goſpel, or thoſe who eſcape when the Antichriſtian powers ſhall be broken, and are as brands plucked out of the burning, will be enabled feelingly to preach the grace of a Redeemer, and the dreadful danger of ſin *to Tarſhiſh, Pul and Lud, that draw the bow, to Tubal and Javan, and the iſles afar off* Concerning the countries here meant interpreters are divided and uncertain, but the ſenſe is clear, that they ſhould go into all lands far and near, even to the moſt diſtant iſles of the ſea, preaching the goſpel to thoſe *that have not heard my fame, nor ſeen my glory*, ſtrangers to Chriſt and his word, and to whom his fame had never reached *and they ſhall declare my glory among the Gentiles*, the glory of the pardoning, ſanctifying, comforting, and ſaving grace of the Redeemer

[3] The effect of their miniſtry in the converſion of the Gentiles would be great *They ſhall bring your brethren*, the Gentiles, and all converts who have one father, *for an offering to the Lord out of all nations*, either the miniſters ſhall preſent them before the Lord, as the fruit of their labours, or they ſhould offer up themſelves, their bodies, ſouls, and ſpirits, as *living ſacrifices*, Rom xii 1 *Upon horſes, and in chariots, and in litters, and upon mules, and upon ſwift beaſts*, according to the condition and circumſtances of the ſeveral converts, ſome rich, ſome poor, ſome weak, ſome ſtrong, but all eager to come into the church of Chriſt, or rather theſe carriages repreſent the goſpel miniſters, by which the ſouls of men are brought home to Chriſt, *to my holy mountain Jeruſalem, ſaith the Lord*, the place of general reſort, *as the children of Iſrael bring an offering in a clean veſſel into the houſe of the Lord*, ſo ſhall the Gentiles be preſented to God in the beauty of holineſs, their hearts purified by faith, and ſanctified by the Holy Ghoſt, as veſſels of honour, and accepted as a well-pleaſing oblation, *Rom* xv 16 *Note*, (1) They who are brethren in Chriſt, muſt love as brethren (2) The moſt acceptable offering is the ſinner's heart, for this ſhall *pleaſe the Lord better than a bullock that hath horns and hoofs*

[4] God

Before Christ 698 4 God will appoint the miniſters of his ſanctuary out of these Gentile converts *I will alſo take of them for prieſts, and for Levites, ſaith the Lord* Though the Aaronical prieſthood is deſtroyed, God reſerves this prerogative to himſelf, to appoint his own ambaſſadors, and no man who is not called of God, as was Aaron, has any right to miniſter, no ordination of man being able to make thoſe miniſters of God, who are not firſt inwardly moved by the Holy Ghoſt to take this office upon them Let thoſe who dare make that profeſſion, in order to intrude into the ſacred office, whilſt conſcious of their utter unacquaintedneſs with any inward call, tremble at the complicated guilt they incur, by lying not only againſt their own conſciences, but againſt the Holy Ghoſt

5 There ſhall be a ſucceſſion of ſuch goſpel miniſters to the end of time *For as the new heavens, and the new earth which I will make, ſhall remain before me, ſaith the Lord*, the goſpel diſpenſation, which ſucceeded the Moſaical, wherein all things are become new, a new covenant eſtabliſhed, new inſtitutions made, new commandments given, and theſe to abide for ever, *ſo ſhall your ſeed and your name remain*, a ſpiritual ſeed, both of miniſters and people, who ſhall have a name in the earth, and in whom the church will be maintained and preſerved againſt all the powers of darkneſs

6 The ſolemn, frequent, and conſtant returns of worſhip in the goſpel church, are deſcribed in terms borrowed from the Jewiſh diſpenſation Their new moons indeed and ſabbaths are aboliſhed, but in their ſtead the Lord's-day is appointed for the religious aſſemblies of Chriſtians for prayer, the preaching of the word, and joining in the Lord's Supper, and all true believers are careful to maintain and keep up theſe ſtated opportunities of worſhip, *not forſaking the aſſembling of themſelves together, as the manner of ſome is*

Laſtly, They ſhall with joy behold the Redeemer's triumphs in the final and eternal deſtruction of his enemies and theirs *They ſhall go forth, and look upon the carcaſes of the men that have tranſgreſſed againſt me*, either of the Jews who ſhould be maſſacred by the Roman ſword, whom the Chriſtians would ſee lying unburied on the earth, or of the Antichriſtian powers overthrown and deſtroyed, *Rev* xix 19—21 by *the word of God* or rather at the reſurrection-day, the ſaints of God going forth from their graves, ſhall ſee the wicked, loathſome and abhorred as putrid carcaſes, caſt into the everlaſting burnings of hell *for their worm ſhall not die*, eternal horrors gnawing inceſſantly their guilty conſciences *neither ſhall their fire be quenched*, conſuming, yet unconſumed, curſed with immortality, amidſt the unutterable tortures of thoſe raging flames no death, though courted, ſhall come to their releaſe, but, tormented day and night for ever, they ſhall have no reſt *and they ſhall be an abhorring to all fleſh*, the ſaints of God beholding them with abhorrence, applauding the juſtice of God in their damnation, and admiring the diſtinguiſhing grace of their Redeemer, which plucked them as brands from the burning *Note*, (1) Let ſinners hear and fear, ſin will certainly receive its wages at the laſt, and it is a fearful thing to fall into the hands of that God who is a conſuming fire (2) In eternity God will be magnified for his judgments executed on the wicked, as well as for his grace manifeſted to his people, and they who join the ſongs of angels in celebrating redeeming mercy, will find matter for their praiſes alſo even in the miſeries of the damned, for when *the ſmoke of their torment aſcendeth up for ever and ever, the ſaints of God* will cry *Allelujah!* Rev xix 2, 3 Before Christ 698

THE

EVANGELICAL EXPOSITOR;

OR, A

PRACTICAL COMMENT

Upon the BOOK of the PROPHET

JEREMIAH.

THE prophecy of Jeremiah succeeds that of Isaiah, not as being next in order, but in bulk. His name is by some interpreted, The Lord shall exalt, *he being raised up of God to this high dignity. Others derive it from a word signifying* to cast down, *this being the great subject of his prophecy, that God would destroy the Jewish people and nation. He began to prophesy young, in the 13th year of Josiah, which Archbishop Usher places in the 629th before Christ, and of the Julian period from the creation, 4085, and continued upwards of forty years in Judea. How long he prophesied after he was carried into Egypt, is uncertain, where antient tradition reports he was stoned for his fidelity and zeal.*

This book contains many discourses of the prophet, delivered to his rebellious countrymen, testifying against their sins, inviting them to repentance, and warning them of their ruin, if they persisted in their iniquities; particularly foretelling the destruction of their city and temple, and the captivity in Babylon; amidst which threatned judgments some gracious promises of the Messiah's kingdom are interspersed, to comfort the few faithful, and support their hopes amidst their desolations. There are also several predictions in this book relative to other nations.

Some chapters are purely historical, and give a particular account of the taking of Jerusalem, the miseries the Jews endured, the captivity that followed, the sad dispersion of the remnant that was left; and to his bitter sorrow he lived to see his prophecies accomplished, and in the book of Lamentations, *generally ascribed to him, with deepest anguish bewailed their desolations.*

Before Christ 628.

CHAP. I.

In this chapter we have, 1. The title of the book, with the time of the continuance of Jeremiah's public ministry, ver. 1—3. 2. His call to the prophetical office, ver. 4—10. 3. The visions of an almond rod and a seething pot, signifying the approaching ruin of Judah and Jerusalem by the Chaldeans, ver. 11—16. 4. Encouragement given to the prophet to go on undauntedly in his work, in consideration of God's presence with him, ver. 17—19.

1 THE words of Jeremiah the son of Hil-
kiah, of the priests that *were* in Ana-
thoth in the land of Benjamin: 2 To
whom the word of the LORD came in
the days of Josiah the son of Amon king of Judah, in
the thirteenth year of his reign. 3 It came also in the
days of Jehoiakim the son of Josiah king of Judah, un-
to the end of the eleventh year of Zedekiah the son of
Josiah king of Judah, unto the carrying away of Je-
rusalem captive in the fifth month.

Ver. 1—3. We have here an account of the prophet's parentage, and the time of his prophecy.

1. He was of the sacerdotal race, the son of Hilkiah, not the high priest, nor of that family, but probably a descendant from Ithamar, of whose line Abiathar was the last high-priest, whose possessions were at Anathoth, *see* 1 *Kings* ii. 26. a city about three miles from Jerusalem, in the tribe of Benjamin.

Before Christ 628.

2. He began to prophesy in the thirteenth year of Josiah, and, no doubt, was a great encourager of that pious king in his work of reformation, and countenanced by him in his labours to bring Israel to repentance: but the attempts of both were fruitless, the people continued hypocritical, even when they pretended to reform, and thus filled up the measure of their iniquities, and brought down those judgments Jeremiah was commissioned to denounce against them. He continued to prophesy during the wicked reigns of Josiah's successors, when the destruction of the people was hastening apace, till he saw Jerusalem, under Zedekiah, miserably destroyed, and the people enslaved. *Note*, (1.) All attempts to save a people devoted to ruin come too late. (2.) They who will not be reformed, must be destroyed.

4 Then the word of the LORD came unto me,
saying, 5 Before I formed thee in the belly, I
knew thee; and before thou camest forth out of the
womb, I sanctified thee, *and* I ordained thee a prophet
unto the nations. 6 Then said I, Ah, Lord GOD,
behold, I cannot speak: for I *am* a child. 7 ¶ But the
LORD said unto me, Say not, I *am* a child: for thou
shalt

Before Christ 628

shalt go to all that I shall send thee, and [k] whatsoever I
command thee thou shalt speak. 8 [l] Be not afraid of
their faces: for I [m] *am* with thee to deliver thee, saith
the LORD. 9 Then the LORD put forth his hand,
and [n] touched my mouth, and the LORD said unto
me, Behold, I have [o] put my words in thy mouth.
10 [p] See, I have this day set thee over the nations,
and over the kingdoms, [q] to root out, and to pull
down, and to destroy, and to throw down, to build,
and to plant.

v. 4—10. The designation of the prophet to his office, and God's encouragement of him to proceed in it, are here set forth.

1. His designation. God, before he formed him in the womb, had foreknown and predestinated him in his eternal counsels to be his servant, and sanctified or separated him for this peculiar service, in which he was to be employed, *as a prophet to the nations*, not only to the Jews, but to other nations also, against whom his word should go forth. *Note*, (1.) God from eternity knoweth those that are his. (2.) What he predestinates us to, must infallibly take place. (3.) The eternal designs of God's mercy towards us are known by his word coming unto us, and calling us to the work and office he hath appointed us. (4.) None can minister acceptably before God whom he hath not first sanctified and ordained.

2. His distress, under the apprehension of his own insufficiency. *Ah, Lord God! I cannot*, or *I know not how to speak*, as such an office requires, *for I am a child*, in wisdom, [illegible] probably also in years, it being certain he began to prophesy very early. *Note*, (1.) The work of the ministry is an arduous task; they may well tremble for themselves who are called to undertake it. (2.) It becomes young men especially to entertain a diffidence of their own abilities. No fool so great as a youth who is self-conceited.

3. God encourages him for his work. *Say not, I am a child*: though never so insufficient of ourselves, we may not draw back when we have God's mission and promise of support: his strength shall be perfected in our weakness. Three arguments he urges. (1.) *I send thee*, and under a divine call we may be assured of divine help. (2.) I will instruct thee; *what I command thee thou shalt speak*, and therefore he should never be at a loss for matter or words. (3.) *I am with thee*, to uphold thee with my arm, to comfort thee with my presence, *to deliver thee* from all danger; *be not afraid of their faces*. He might expect opposition, to be brow-beat, threatned, and insulted on account of his ministry; but he need not fear when God's omnipotence is engaged for him. *Note*, (1.) If God pleases, out of the mouth of babes and sucklings he can shew forth his praise. (2.) A faithful reprover must expect to meet a frowning world; but we must not fear the faces of men, nor need we, if God's power protect, and his love comfort us; what can man do against us?

4. God gives him a sign to confirm his word to him. *The Lord put forth his hand*, the Lord Jesus, the God of his holy prophets, who appeared now in a human form, *and touched my mouth*, intimating that it was sanctified, and fitted for his service; *and the Lord said unto me, Behold, I have put my words in thy mouth*, that he might with freedom and boldness deliver the message he had received from his Master, and in what [illegible] it was. *See, I have set thee over the nations, and over the kingdoms*, as a prophet, whose word concerning them should infallibly come to pass, *to root out, and to pull down, and to destroy, and to throw down*, to pronounce their doom, and foretel the judgment that should overturn them, as a house or a tree rooted up and thrown down by the whirlwind; *and to build, and to plant*, to prophesy the restoration of the Jews after their captivity, or to call them to repentance, that when others perished, they might be preserved. *Note*, (1.) The sword of God's word in the mouth of his ministers is more to be feared than the glittering spear. (2.) The same prophetic word which is to some a savour of death unto death, because they harden their hearts against the warning, becomes, through Divine Grace, to the penitent a savour of life unto life.

11 ¶ Moreover, the word of the LORD came unto
me, saying, Jeremiah, what seest thou? and I said, I
see [r] a rod of an almond-tree. 12 Then said the LORD
unto me, Thou hast well seen: for I will hasten my
word to perform it. 13 And the word of the LORD
came unto me the second time, saying, What seest thou?
and I said, I see [s] a seething pot, and the face thereof
is [†] toward the north. 14 Then the LORD said
unto me, [u] Out of the north an evil shall break forth
upon all the inhabitants of the land. 15 For lo, [x] I
will call all the families of the kingdoms of the north,
saith the LORD, and they shall come, and [y] they shall
set every one his throne at the entering of the gates of
Jerusalem, and against all the walls thereof round about,
and against all the cities of Judah. 16 And [z] I will
utter my judgments against them touching all their
wickedness, who have forsaken me, and have burnt incense
unto other gods, and worshipped the works of
their own hands. 17 ¶ Thou therefore [a] gird up thy
loins and arise, and speak unto them all that I command
thee: [b] be not dismayed at their faces, lest I
[†] confound thee before them. 18 For behold, I have
made thee this day [c] a defenced city, and an iron pillar,
and brasen walls against the whole land, against the
kings of Judah, against the princes thereof, against the
priests thereof, and against the people of the land. 19
And they shall fight against thee, [d] but they shall not
prevail against thee: for I *am* with thee, saith the
LORD, to deliver thee.

v. 11—19. Jeremiah having received his mission, hath here a general view of the [illegible] subject of his prophecy, the destruction of the Jews [illegible].

1. Their ruin is foretold by two signs, shewing how speedily and certainly it approached. The first is *an almond rod*, which is presented to his view, and which God explains, as signifying that the destruction of the Jews should be very soon, as the almond tree hastens before any other tree to put forth her blossoms. The other is *a seething pot, with its face towards the north*. This pot is Jerusalem, and the fire under it the Chaldeans, as God explains it, tumbling out of the north, under the conduct of Nebuchadnezzar, called of God [illegible] 15 to execute his judgment, coming under the divine direction, and therefore sure to prevail. They shall set up not only their tents as besieging foes, but their thrones as triumphant conquerors, in the gates of Jerusalem, having subdued it, with all the defenced cities of Judah. *Note*, (1.) God will never want enemies to execute his vengeance against a devoted people; at his summons instantly they stand. (2.) Ministers clearly in the Bible foretel the ruin of sinners, and forewarn them, but they will not believe, till too late they feel their doom inevitable.

2. The cause of their ruin is their sins, especially their idolatry. *I will utter my judgments against them*, pass sentence upon them, and execute it, *touching all their wickedness*, which was great and aggravated, *who have forsaken me*, apostatized from God's worship and service, *and have burnt incense to other gods*, they have *worshipped the works of their own hands*, gods of their own fancy, and the images of their own making, which argued their stupidity and ignorance, strong as their impiety and ingratitude.

3. God directs him how to proceed, and encourages him to be faithful. *Gird up thy loins*, alluding to the long garments they wore in the east, which, when they went in haste, they girt about their waist. He must be expeditious and diligent. *Arise, and speak unto them all that I command thee*, not intimidated by any fears or dangers, *all that I command thee*, without adding thereto, or diminishing therefrom, however offensive and provoking the message might appear, and however great the persons to whom it must be delivered, to their kings, princes, priests, and people. The dignity of the [illegible] doth not [illegible] reproof, nor the sacredness of the priestly office [illegible] exempt those who dishonour it from rebuke; rather, as their influence and example is so pernicious, [illegible] they are chief in the transgression, they deserve the severest rebuke. [illegible] to discharge his mission, God warns and promises. He warns him of his danger, if he proved fearful or faithless, *be not dismayed at their faces, lest I confound thee before them*, and put such a mark of his displeasure upon him, as would be his greatest confusion. He promises, in [illegible] to maintain him in the discharge of his duty, to protect and preserve him [illegible] *a defenced city*, strong *as an iron pillar*, and unshaken *as walls of brass*. Though all rose up against him, as he might expect they would, kings, priests, and people, *yet shall they not prevail to destroy thee, for I am with thee, saith the Lord, to deliver thee* in every day of danger and difficulty. *Note*, (1.) The ministers of God must shew no respect to persons when they are delivering his word, nor dare to dilute the awful truths of God, by softening the expressions, or seeking to make them less offensive. (2.) It requires much grace to stand against the torrent of [illegible] and [illegible] to [illegible] the judgment of God. (3.) Nobles and faithless priests were ever the bitterest enemies of God's prophets. (4.) We have need of every argument to work on our fears, as well as hope, and all little enough to keep us unshaken against the revilings and opposition we must expect to meet in the zealous discharge of our ministry. (5.) If God be with us, though princes threaten, and priests thunder their anathemas, and the people join the cry, we shall be enabled, unmoved and steadfast, to witness to their face their iniquities, and declare the wrath of God revealed against them.

CHAP.

Before Christ 628 / Before Christ 628

CHAP II

Jeremiah here opens his ministry with a most pathetic discourse on the evil and danger of their sins, and particularly of their shameful idolatries They are told, 1 That this was ungrateful to God, who had been so kind to them, ver 1—8 2 That it was without precedent, that a nation should change their god, ver 9—13 3 That hereby they had disparaged and ruined themselves, ver 14—19 4 That they had broken their covenants, and degenerated from their good beginnings, ver 20, 21 5 That their wickedness was too plain to be concealed, and too bad to be excused, ver 22, 23, 25 6 That they were irreclaimable and indefatigable in their idolatries, ver 24, 25, 33, 36 7 That they shamed themselves by their idolatry, and should shortly be made ashamed of it, ver 26—29, 37 8 That they had not been reformed by the rebukes of providence, ver 30 9 That they had put a great contempt upon God, ver 31, 32 10 That with their idolatries they had mixed the most unnatural murders, ver 34 And O that by meditating on this chapter we might be brought to repent of our spiritual idolatries, giving that place in our souls to the world and the flesh, which should have been reserved for God only

1 MOREOVER the word of the LORD came to
me, saying, 2 Go, and cry in the ears of
Jerusalem, saying, Thus saith the LORD, I remember
thee, the kindness of [a] thy youth, the love of thine es-
pousals, when thou wentest after me in the wilderness,
in a land *that was* not sown 3 [b] Israel *was* holiness
unto the LORD, *and* [c] the first-fruits of his increase [d]
all that devour him, shall offend, evil shall come upon
them, saith the LORD 4 Hear ye the word of the
LORD, O house of Jacob, and all the families of the
house of Israel 5 ¶ Thus saith the LORD, [e] What
iniquity have your fathers found in me, that they are
gone far from me, and [f] have walked after vanity, and
are become vain? 6 Neither said they, Where *is* the
LORD, [g] that brought us up out of the land of Egypt,
[h] that led us through the wilderness, through a land of
deserts, and of pits, through a land of drought, and of
the shadow of death, through a land that no man pas-
sed through, and where no man dwelt? 7 And I
brought you into a plentiful country to eat the fruit
thereof, and the goodness thereof, but when ye enter-
ed, ye [i] defiled my land, and made mine heritage an
abomination 8 The priests said not, Where *is* the
LORD? and [k] they that handle the law, knew me not
the pastors also transgressed against me, and [l] the pro-
phets prophesied by Baal, and walked after *things that*
do not profit

a Ezek xvi 8 22 b Exod xix 5 6 c James i 18 Rev xiv 4 d Chap xii 14 Chap l 7 e Isa v 4 Mic vi 3 f Jonah ii 8 g Isa lxiii 11 13 Hos xiii 4 h Deut viii 15 & xxxii 10. i Ps lxxviii 58 & cvi 38 k Mal ii 7 Rom ii 20 l Chap xxiii 13

v. 1—8 Being ordained a prophet to the Lord, Jeremiah hath his message delivered to him, and is commanded to go to Jerusalem from Anathoth, the place of his residence, and there publickly declare the word of God, that all may hear, and either repent of their iniquities, or be left inexcusable in their unbelief and hardness of heart

1 He reminds them of their own former professions, and God's dealing with them, when by every instance of kindness he had engaged their affections, and they had given such fair expectations of their making a suitable return *I remember thee, the kindness of thy youth*, either God's kindness to them in their early days, or rather their affection to regard to him, *the love of thine espousals*, when their warm hearts, filled with affection, as a new married bride, sought only how to please their Lord, *when thou wentest after me in the wilderness*, trusting on his guidance, and depending on his providence, *in a land that was not sown*, and where none of the necessaries of life were to be obtained, but they were fed by daily miracles *Israel was holiness to the Lord*, separated for him, consecrated to him, and in the bonds of his covenant solemnly engaged to be his, and his alone, *and the first fruits of his increase*, presenting themselves, bodies, souls, and spirits, as the first fruits at the temple, a holy offering unto him Thus they did run well, and God's blessing was in the midst of them *all that devour him shall offend, evil ... guilty*, God protected them, they were as the apple of his eye dear to him, none dared touch them with impunity, *evil shall come upon them, saith the Lord*, God will be the avenger of their wrongs, and their enemies shall perish From Egyptian bondage he brought them, led them *through the wilderness* by his pillar of a cloud and fire, *through a land of deserts, and of pits*, where venomous creatures lodged, scorpions, and fiery flying serpents, *through a land of drought*, where no water could be found, *and of the shadow of death*, dismal and lonely *through a land that no man passed through, and where no man dwelt*, pathless, without inhabitant, and yet amidst difficul-

ties so insurmountable by human power, God safely conducted them, covered them with the shadow of his cloud from the scorching sun, fed them with plenty of the richest food, opened streams from the rock, protected them from every danger, and brought them safe at last to his promised rest, to *a plentiful country, to eat the fruit thereof, and the goodness thereof*, to a land flowing with milk and honey, the glory of all lands, for which unspeakable favours he justly might expect from them the deepest returns of duty, love, and service *Note*, (1) Our first love should be often remembered, to humble us for our departure from God, and to hasten our return to him, *Rev* ii 4, 5 (2) God takes pleasure in beholding the affections of his people placed upon him (3) When we love God in sincerity, we shall follow him implicitly, and fear no dangers even in the wilderness (4) God's Israel are a holy people, they who answer not this character, have no lot nor portion among them (5) They who persecute God's chosen, will find him the avenger of their quarrel (6) The way to heaven lies through difficulties impassable for mortal strength, and if ever our souls are safely led to the heavenly Canaan we must acknowledge ourselves intirely indebted to his everlasting arms of power and love (7) The greater our trials, the more is the grace of God magnified in our deliverance (8) For all the wonders of his grace, God hath the deepest and most just demands of love and service from us (9) The promising beginnings we have shewn, and the fair professions we have made, will greatly aggravate our guilt, should we begin in the spirit and end in the flesh

2 He upbraids them with their black ingratitude *Thus saith the Lord, What iniquity have your fathers found in me?* Had he done them injustice, been a hard master, or unfaithful to any of his promises? No, there is no unrighteousness in him they who forsake him, forsake their own mercies, and out of their own mouths will be condemned—*that they are gone far from me*, apostates from his service and worship, for those who depart from a religious profession, become usually viler than those who never pretended to it, *and have walked after vanity*, after idols, which are the greatest vanities, *and are become vain?* corrupt in their practice, as dark in their imaginations, defiling the good land, into which the Lord had brought them, with their abominations, and which they held only on condition of their fidelity God was utterly forgotten, *none said, Where is the Lord?* notwithstanding all his miracles of mercy shewn them any, the priests, who should have been the first to restrain others, were chief in the transgression, *the priests said not, Where is the Lord?* and if they, who were their guides, took no pains to acquaint themselves with him, no marvel the people forgot God *and they that handle the law knew me not*, pretending to instruct others, but totally ignorant themselves, and strangers to all experimental knowledge of God and his truth *The pastors also transgressed against me*, civil, as well as ecclesiastical, casting off all fear of God, *and the prophets prophesied by Baal*, pretending inspiration from their idol to contradict the prophets of the Lord, and supported by the princes and priests in their impiety, *and walked after things that do not profit*, their false gods, from whom no blessing could be derived *Note*, When blind priests lead a blind people, no marvel they perish together

9 ¶ Wherefore I will yet plead with you, saith the
LORD, and [m] with your children's children will I
plead 10 For [‖] pass over the isles of Chittim, and
see, and send unto Kedar, and consider diligently,
and see if there be such a thing 11 [n] Hath a nation
changed *their* gods, [o] which *are* yet no gods? [p] but
my people have changed their glory for *that which* doth
not profit 12 [q] Be astonished, O ye heavens, at this,
and be horribly afraid, be ye very desolate, saith the
LORD 13 For my people have committed two
evils they have forsaken me [r] the fountain of living
waters, *and* hewed them out cisterns, broken cisterns
that can hold no water

m Exod xx 5 Lev xx 5 ‖ Or pass over to n Mic iv 5 o Chap xvi 20 p Ps cvi 20 Rom i 23 q Isa i 2 Chap vi 19 r Ps xxxvi 9 Chap xvii 13 & xviii 14 John iv 14

v 9—13 Having rebuked their ingratitude, God pleads against them the unprecedented folly of their conduct He desires to convince sinners, and therefore he uses every argument, and at least will leave them inexcusable in their impenitence

1 They were in this respect more false and fickle, even than the idolatrous nation they affected to resemble They retained a veneration for their fathers gods base as the idols were which they worshipped, nothing could prevail with them to forsake the religion of their ancestors Go to the isle of Chittim, Greece, or Italy, or to Kedar in Arabia, and not an instance would be found of a nation that had changed their gods, *but my people have changed their glory*, have forsaken the living, true, and only God, whose service they should have accounted their highest honour, and their distinguished a portion for him their most exalted glory, *for that which doth not profit*, for idols, for Baal, in whose worship neither honour nor advantage could be found, but the very contrary

2 The heavens are called upon with wonder and horror to behold

Before Christ 628

behold this ſcene of aggravated guilt and folly *Be aſtoniſhed, O ye heavens, at this*, the inhabitants of them, or the very inanimate creation might well be amazed, *and be ye horribly afraid*, trembling for ſins ſo great, and that muſt bring down judgments ſo heavy *be ye very deſolate, ſaith the Lord*, as if the ſun ſhould refuſe his light to ſuch miſcreants, the clouds thicken with thunder and lightning over them, and ſweep them from the earth with the beſom of deſtruction *For my people*, ſeparated for God, once profeſſors of his truth, and thereby every departure from him being rendered more infamous and exceeding ſinful, my people *have committed two evils*, their tranſgreſſions are numberleſs, but theſe are capital ſins, and the ſources of all the reſt *they have forſaken me the fountain of living water*, rejecting his government, neglecting his ordinances, and leaving him far above, out of their ſight, and in ſo doing, have cut themſelves off from the fountain of living waters, from that God of all grace and conſolation, in whom they might have for ever found a rich ſupply for all their wants, *and hewed them out ciſterns, broken ciſterns that can hold no water*, ſuch were their idols, that after all the pains and expence beſtowed on them, did not afford the leaſt conſolation, not even the miſerable relief of a drop of putrid ſtagnating water, to quench the thirſt of their votaries *Note*, (1) They who forſake God, forſake their own mercies (2) As long as our ſouls come to Jeſus the living fountain, ſo long ſhall we find the waters of his grace within us a well of water, ſpringing up to everlaſting life (3) Whatever creature enjoyments in ſ promiſe, they will deceive our expectations if we ſeek our happineſs from wealth, honour, or indulgence, toil as we can to ſecure the bliſs, we ſhall find the ciſterns empty, but one portion can adequately ſatiſfy an immortal ſoul, and that is, the love of the eternal God

14 ¶ *Is* Iſrael a ſervant? *Is* he a home-born *ſlave*?
Why is he † ſpoiled? 15 ˢ The young lions rored upon him, *and* ‡ yelled, and they made his land waſte
His cities are burnt without inhabitant 16. Alſo the
children of Noph and ᵗ Tahapanes ‖ have broken the
crown of thy head 17 ᵘ Haſt thou not procured this
unto thyſelf, in that thou haſt forſaken the LORD thy
God, when he led thee by the way? 18 And now what
haſt thou to do ˣ in the way of Egypt, to drink the waters of Sihor? or what haſt thou to do in the way of
Aſſyria, to drink the waters of the river? 19 ʸ Thine
own wickedneſs ſhall correct thee, and thy backſlidings
ſhall reprove thee know therefore and ſee, that *it is* an
evil *thing* and bitter, that thou haſt forſaken the LORD
thy God, and that my fear *is* not in thee, ſaith the
LORD God of hoſts

† Heb. Become a ſpoil
ˢ Chap iv 7
‡ Heb Gave out their voice
ᵗ Chap xliv 1, 9
‖ Or feed on thy crown
ᵘ Deut xxxii 12 Iſa liii 8
ˣ Chap iv 18
ˣ Iſa xxx 2
ʸ Iſa iii 9 Hoſ v 5

v 14—19 The miſeries coming upon them for their ſins are ſpoken of as already preſent, becauſe they were ſo near and certain

1 By their iniquities they had brought themſelves into ſlavery, were defeated by their enemies, and their country ravaged *Is Iſrael a ſervant? Is he a home-born ſlave?* whence comes this grievous change, how is their glorious liberty loſt? *Why is he ſpoiled?* ſurely ſome awful provocation hath brought on him this calamity, ſo terrible are his deſolations *The young lions roared upon him, and yelled, and they made his land waſte*, his invading foe, the King of Aſſyria with his army, fierce and cruel as thoſe ravening beaſts, roaring and yelling with all the horrid din of war, hath plundered the country, *and his cities are burnt without inhabitant*, all led captives, or ſlain by the ſword, and none left to reſtore them from their ruins *Alſo the children of Noph and Tahapanes have broken the crown of thy head*, the Egyptians, whoſe chief cities theſe were, as well as the Aſſyrians, contributed to their ruin, Joſiah being ſlain by Pharaoh Nechoh, his ſon dethroned, Jeruſalem plundered, and a tribute ſet upon them, 2 Kings xxiii 29—35 *Haſt thou not procured this unto thyſelf?* yea, verily, none but themſelves had they to blame for their ſufferings, *in that thou haſt forſaken the Lord thy God*, him, who was ſo able to protect them, who ſtood in a relation to them ſo glorious, and from whom it was ſo fooliſh as well as wicked, to depart him they forſook for idols, and human confidences, changing a rock for a reed, *when he led thee by the way*, the right way, the path of duty, in which had they abode, they would have certainly found it the way of ſafety, but they deſpiſed his guidance, and ruſhed on their own ruin *Note*, Whatever miſeries a ſinner is involved in, whether in time or eternity this bitter reflection will ſharpen their edge, *Haſt thou not procured this unto thyſelf?*

2 The ſinful methods they took to extricate themſelves from their troubles, ſerved but to haſten their deſtruction Inſtead of looking unto God for help againſt their enemies, they ſought other ſupports When threatened by Aſſyria, they ran to Egypt for ſuccour, when invaded by Egypt, they courted the Aſſyrian help *What haſt thou to do with theſe*, who in their turn will deceive, oppreſs, and plunder thee? *Thine own wickedneſs* in general, or this in particular, of truſting, in the ſe vain helpers,

ſhall correct thee, bring ſevere chaſtiſement upon them, *and thy backſlidings*, their treacherous departure from God, *ſhall reprove thee Know therefore, and ſee, that it is an evil and bitter thing, that thou haſt forſaken the Lord thy God, and that my fear is not in thee, ſaith the Lord God of hoſts* The event would prove to their terrible conviction, the evil and miſery of the ways which they had choſen, and ſinners will find this truth univerſally verified Obſerve, (1) The root of all ſin *My fear is not in thee*, there is deep unbelief in the natural heart, God's warnings make no impreſſion, and the practice can riſe no higher than the principle Hence, (2) The effect produced *Thou haſt forſaken the Lord*, when the heart is not reſtrained by his fear, corrupt nature, prone to ſin, eaſily hurries on the ſoul to all the forbidden indulgencies of fleſh and ſpirit (3) The iſſue of ſin is evil and bitter It is not only evil in its own nature, as oppoſite to God's purity and perfections, but the conſequences are ever evil and bitter to the ſoul, the curſe follows the ſinner cloſer than his ſhadow, his miſeries and diſappointments are many, his enjoyments embittered, and death, eternal death, ſtares him in the face, the terrible wages of ſin (4) It is happy for thoſe who are brought to ſee and know this, before it is too late, and all God's viſitations have this deſign to lead us to repentance for our ſins, that we may not periſh in them

20 ¶ For of old time I have broken thy yoke, *and*
burſt thy bands, and ᶻ thou ſaidſt, I will not † tranſgreſs
when ᵃ upon every high hill, and under every green tree,
thou wandereſt, playing the harlot 21 Yet I had ᵇ
planted thee a noble vine wholly a right ſeed how then
art thou turned into ᶜ the degenerate plant of a ſtrange
vine unto me? 22 For though thou ᵈ waſh thee with
nitre, and take thee much ſope, *yet* ᵉ thine iniquity is
marked before me, ſaith the Lord GOD 23 ᶠ How
canſt thou ſay, I am not polluted, I have not gone after
Baalim? ᵍ ſee thy way in the valley, know what thou
haſt done *thou art* a ſwift dromedary traverſing her
ways 24 ʰ A wild aſs ‡ uſed to the wilderneſs, *that*
ſnuffeth up the wind at her pleaſure, in her occaſion who
can ‖ turn her away? all they that ſeek her, will not
weary themſelves, in her month they ſhall find her
25 Withhold thy foot from being unſhod, and thy
throat from thirſt but ⁱ thou ſaidſt, § There is no hope
No, for I have loved ſtrangers, and after them will I go
26 As the thief is aſhamed when he is found ſo is the
houſe of Iſrael aſhamed, they, their kings, their
princes, and their prieſts, and their prophets, 27 Saying to a ſtock, Thou *art* my father, and to a ſtone,
Thou haſt † brought me forth for they have turned
their back unto me, and not *their* face but ᵏ in the
time of their trouble they will ſay, Ariſe, and ſave us
28 But ˡ where *are* thy gods that thou haſt made thee?
let them ariſe, ᵐ if they can ſave thee in the time of
thy ‡ trouble for ⁿ *according* to the number of thy
cities are thy gods, O Judah

ᶻ Exod xix 8
† Or ſerve
ᵃ Iſa lvii 5, 7 Chap iii 6
ᵇ Exod xv 17 Pſ xliv 2 & lxxx 8 Iſa v 1, &
ᶜ Iſa i xxi 3
ᶜ Deut xxxii 32 Iſa i 21
ᵈ Job ix 30.
ᵉ Deut xxxii 34 Job xiv 17 Hoſ xiii 12
ᶠ Prov xxx 12
ᵍ Chap iii 2
ʰ Job xxxix 5 &c Chap xiv 6
‡ Heb Taught
‖ Or reverſe it
ⁱ Chap xviii 12
§ Or is the caſe deſperate?
† Or begotten me
ᵏ Iſa xxvi 16
ˡ Deut xxxii 37 Judg x 14
ᵐ Iſa xlv 20
‡ Heb Evil
ⁿ Chap. xi 13

v 20—28 The prophet proſecutes his charge againſt this rebellious people

1 Their crying ſin was idolatry, and when they had left the one true God, their wanderings were endleſs, and their idols innumerable, every city had its god and tutelar deity, *v* 28 On every hill their idols ſtood thick, and not a ſpreading tree or grove was there, where their incenſe had not ſmoaked, and where they had not *played the harlot*, committing ſpiritual adultery, *v* 20 Nor was this the crime of the refuſe of the people only, their kings, princes, prieſts and prophets, horrible to tell! theſe were the patrons of idolatry, and the moſt bigotted votaries, *ſaying to the ſtock, thou art my father, and to the ſtone, thou haſt brought me forth*, and whilſt infatuated, and more ſenſeleſs than the images they worſhipped, to theſe they aſcribed divine honours, they *turned their backs on God*, with inſolent contempt of his worſhip and ſervice *Note*, When a ſinner is given up to his own heart, there are no lengths of folly, iniquity, and impiety to which he may not run

2 Their attempts to deny it were vain, and the methods they uſed to expiate their ſins uſeleſs Like the adultreſs, *Prov* xxx 20 they diſowned the charge of idolatry, when the evidence was ſo notorious. In the valley, probably of Hinnom, where they burnt their children to Moloch, the monuments of their ſin teſtified againſt them, *v* 23 And their excuſes were frivolous when God had, in his omniſcience, marked their iniquities with a brand they never could waſh out, or rather, as *v* 22 may ſignify, their ceremonial ablutions and ſacrifices to which they had recourſe, could never cancel the guilt of their ſins, or remove the ſtain of them from their conſcience *Note*, (1) To deny, or ſeek to palliate the evil of our ſins, is the ſure ſign of an impenitent heart (2) Nothing can waſh

out

Before Christ 628

out the stain of sin's black guilt, but the blood of Jesus, every other method will but fix the dye deeper and stronger

3 Their sins were abundantly aggravated by the mercies they had received, and the fair promises they had made Of old God had delivered them from the Egyptian yoke, v 20 planted them in the promised land as *a noble vine wholly a right seed*, v 21 both with respect to their worthy ancestors, and their own gracious conduct on their first possessing their inheritance, *Josh* xxiv 31 nor could there be more solemn engagements, than they had repeatedly made of their perpetual fidelity, v 20 *Exod* xix 8 xxiv 7 yet like a broken bow they had started aside, degenerated from their primitive piety, and became as wild gourds, not only useless but noxious *Note*, (1) The greatness of God's mercies aggravates our guilt and ingratitude (2) We need often reflect with shame on the promises we have made, and on our repeated unfaithfulness

4 They are represented as pursuing their idolatries with determined waywardness in spite of all warnings, as the dromedary and wild ass, when in *their occasion* they are seeking the males, are so eager in running from place to place to find them, that every attempt to restrain them is vain, and will only weary those that pursue them, till their month comes, when big with young, they might more easily be found and caught So were this people raging in their idolatrous lusts, and no hope remained of reclaiming them, till the judgments of God were heavy upon them, and stopped their career *Note*, (1) Nothing so lawless as brutal lust, vain are all the restraints of reason, conscience, honour, when appetite seizes the reins (2) However headstrong in the vigour of health men are in the pursuit of their forbidden gratifications, the hours will come of deep remorse, when their career will be stopped, and when *the joys of sin* no more inebriate, *the sting of sin*, like a scorpion, will torment the guilty conscience

5 Fair warning is given them of the issue of their ways, and they are admonished by repentance to prevent their captivity *Refrain thy foot from being unshod, and thy throat from thirst*, for unless they repented of their evil ways, and turned from them, this would be the consequence, that barefoot, and ready to be choaked with thirst in the journey, they should be led captives into a distant land Some understand it as an admonition, not to wear out the shoes of their messengers, and be at the pains of sending to Egypt or Assyria for help, since these succours would be of no use to them, but the former sense seems best

6 Their obstinacy, or their despair, is rebuked *But thou saidst, there is no hope*, bidding the prophets cease their attempts, for they would never attend to them, either to quit their idolatries, or to desist from seeking the help of their heathen neighbours, they liked, and would pursue their own inventions Or this is the language of despair, as if their case was past hope either for God to pardon, or their corruptions so strong, that to attempt to resist them was vain, therefore they desperately abandon themselves to their iniquities *Note*, Nothing so effectually enslaves the soul to sin, as despair, and therefore whilst Satan is ever a preacher of presumption to the careless, he fails not to be a preacher of despair to the awakened, as if their iniquities were too great to be forgiven, or their corruptions too strong to be subdued, and therefore that it were best to banish their convictions, and abandon themselves to their lusts, but he was a liar from the beginning No sin can be too great for sovereign grace to pardon, no corruption so strong, that Almighty grace cannot subdue Let us take to us words, and return unto the Lord, and then there is surely yet hope in our end

7 If they persisted in their ways, confusion would cover them in the day of their calamity, as a thief detected in the fact, when their false gods cannot relieve them, and the true God, whom they have forsaken, will refuse to hear their prayer, v 27, 28 *Note*, (1) In the day of calamity, many who never thought of him before, are driven to God to cry, save us, but when the fear of hell merely, not the sense of the evil of sin, dictates the prayer, no marvel it is rejected (2) Whatever the impenitent sinner places his comfort or confidence in, the day will come when it will prove a refuge of lies

29 Wherefore will ye plead with me? ye all have
transgressed against me, saith the LORD 30 In
vain have l I smitten your children, they received no
correction m your own sword hath devoured your pro-
phets, like a destroying lion 31 ¶ O generation, see
ye the word of the LORD n Have I been a wilderness
unto Israel? a land of darkness? wherefore say my
people, We ‡ are lords, we will come no more unto
thee? 32 Can a maid forget her ornaments, *or* a bride
her attire? yet my people o have forgotten me days
without number 33 Why trimmest thou thy way to
seek love? therefore hast thou also taught the wicked
ones thy ways 34 Also in thy skirts is found the blood
of the souls of the poor innocents I have not found it
by ‡ secret search, but upon all these 35 Yet thou
sayest, Because I am innocent, surely his anger shall turn
from me behold, s I will plead with thee, because t
thou sayest, I have not sinned 36 u Why gaddest
thou about so much to change thy way? x thou also
shalt be ashamed of Egypt, y as thou wast ashamed of
Assyria 37 Yea, thou shalt go forth from him, and
z thine hands upon thine head for the LORD hath
rejected thy confidences, and thou shalt not prosper in
them

l Isa i 5 ix 13 Chap v 3

m Mat xxiii 29, &c

n Ver 5

‡ Heb Have dominion

o Hos iv 6

Before Christ 628

‡ Heb Digging

s Ezek xvi 20

t Prov xxx 20 Ver 23

u Chap xxxi 22

x Isa xxx 3

y 2 Chron xxviii 16, 20

z 2 Sam xiii 19

v 29—37 It is the folly and wickedness of sinners that they complain against God, as if his punishments were severe, and his ways unequal, when they alone are the authors of their own misery, and their punishment less than their iniquities deserve

1 God vindicates his justice *Wherefore will ye plead with me?* when their case was so indefensible, *ye all have transgressed against me*, and therefore could neither exculpate themselves from guilt, nor justly complain of their sufferings *Note*, We are all sinners at God's bar, every mouth must be stopped, we have nothing to do but to confess our guilt, justify his judgments, and cast ourselves wholly on his mercy

2 He charges upon them their incorrigibleness In vain had been all the afflictions he had brought upon them, hardened under the rod, *they received no correction*, were not brought to any repentance Nay, as if exasperated by what they suffered, when he seconded the rebukes of his providences by the word of his prophets, like furious lions they rushed on these ministers of God, and cruelly shed their blood for their fidelity, v 30 *Note*, (1) They who will be zealous in rebuking men's sins, must put their life in their hands (2) It is the sign of a desperate state when afflictions harden, instead of softening the heart

3 He expostulates with them on their ingratitude Had he shewn them unkindness, or brought them into darkness and distress, they might have had some plea for their revolt, but his conduct to them in the wilderness, the rich provision he made for them, the light with which he led them, and the land in which he placed them, all evidenced his unutterable kindness, and the least attention to his dealings with them might convince them of it how ungrateful then was their rebellion, thus to cast off his government, and reject his worship and service? v 31 *Note*, (1) They who cleave to God, find all his ways pleasantness and peace if sinners are entangled in a wilderness, or inveloped with darkness, it is because of their departures from him (2) They who affect to emancipate themselves from God's government, only exchange his service, which is perfect freedom, for the base and tyrannical servitude of their lusts

4 He accuses them of sundry crimes against him (1) Forgetfulness of him It would be counted strange if a maid forgot her ornaments, and a bride her attire, *yet*, stranger still, *my people have forgotten me days without number* They were his professing people, and therefore the more criminal their neglect of him, and especially when so long persisted in (2) They were corrupters of others Like a lewd harlot that decks and paints, to inveigle men into her snare, so had they sought to engage their heathen neighbours to become their confederates, and join in their idolatries *therefore hast thou also taught the wicked ones thy ways*, instructing them in their superstitions, and vile as they were before, making them worse by the connection *Note*, (1) They who entice others into sin, will have most aggravated guilt on their heads (2) Fellowship with the workers of iniquity is dangerously infectious, and diligently to be avoided (3) They were polluted with innocent blood, v 34 of the children whom they sacrificed to Moloch, or of innocent persons, especially the prophets and faithful men, who were murdered for reproving their impieties, 2 *Kings* xxi 16 and this openly and notoriously, it needed no search, nor deep enquiry, their skirts were dyed with blood, and the corpses cried for vengeance against them And therefore, (4) Their plea of innocence, v 35 was presumptuous, and their expectation of God's wrath being removed, vain *Behold, I will plead with thee, because thou sayest, I have not sinned*, which was an aggravation of their sin, and provoked God the more to enter in judgment against them *Note*, (1) If we say we have not sinned, we make God a liar (2) Until a sinner is brought to acknowledge the justice of God's wrath, it will never depart from him

5 Their confidences should at last fail them and they be led into a miserable captivity Like an adulteress that gads about to gratify her lewdness, so had they gone to Assyria and Egypt, making league with them in turn for their assistance, as they were pressed by either, but they would disappoint them Assyria had distressed them formerly, as allies, 2 *Chron* xxviii 20 and the Egyptians would alike be their confusion, as they afterward proved, when against Nebuchadnezzar, they promised help in vain, so that *thou shalt go forth with thine hands upon thine head*, as a mourner, led into a shameful captivity; *for the Lord hath rejected thy confidences*, their allies, in whom

Before Christ 628

whom they trusted, *and thou shalt not prosper in them*, but he gives them up for a prey to their enemies. *Note*, (1) The soul that leaves God wanders endlessly, seeking rest, and finding none. (2) Human confidences and comforts in the day of evil will prove a broken reed, unable to support the soul.

CHAP. III.

The foregoing chapter was wholly taken up with reproofs and threatnings against the people of God for their apostasies from him; but in this chapter gracious invitations and encouragements are given them to repent and turn, notwithstanding the multitude and greatness of their provocations. Here, 1. It is farther shewn how bad they had been, and how well they deserved to be abandoned, and yet how ready God was to receive them into his favour, ver. 1—5. 2. The impenitency of Judah is aggravated from the judgments of God upon Israel, ver. 6—11. 3. Great encouragements are given to these backsliders to repent, and promises made of great mercy which God had in store for them, ver. 12—19. 4. The charge renewed against them for their apostasy from God, and the invitation repeated to repent, to which are added the words which they should make use of in their return to God, ver. 20—25.

1 THEY say, If a man put away his wife, and
she go from him, and become another man's,
[a] shall he return unto her again? shall not that land be
greatly polluted? but [b] thou hast played the harlot with
many lovers; [c] yet return again to me, saith the LORD.
2 Lift up thine eyes unto the high places, and see
where thou hast not been lien with. [d] In the ways hast
thou sat for them, as the Arabian in the wilderness; and
thou hast polluted the land with thy whoredoms, and
with thy wickedness. 3 Therefore [e] the showers have
been withholden, and there hath been no latter rain;
and thou hadst a whore's forehead, thou refusedst to be
ashamed. 4 Wilt thou not from this time cry unto
me, My Father, thou *art* [g] the guide of my youth?
5 [h] Will he reserve *his anger* for ever? will he keep *it*
to the end? Behold, thou hast spoken and done evil
things as thou couldst.

[a] Deut. xxiv. 4. [b] Chap. ii. 20. [c] Chap. iv. 1. [d] Gen. xxxviii. 14. Ezek. xvi. 25. [e] Deut. xxviii. 24. Chap. ix. 12. [f] Chap. v. 25. & viii. 3. Ezek. iii. 7. Zeph. iii. 5. [g] Prov. ii. 17. [h] Psal. ciii. 9. Isa. lvii. 16. Ver. 12.

v. 1—5. When for our sins we deserve to be abandoned, our God is merciful, and not willing that any should perish; as here most eminently appears.

1. Their iniquities were great, numberless, and aggravated. Like the most infamous prostitute, *thou hast played the harlot with many lovers*, multiplying their idols as their cities, *chap.* xi. 28. and not an high place was in the land where their spiritual adulteries had not been committed, *v.* 2. Nay, they had courted others to join them, as a prostitute sits by the way, soliciting the traveller; or as the Arabian robber, lying in wait for his prey. Brazen against reproof, with a whore's forehead they blushed at none of their abominations; but as if trying how wicked they could be, *thou hast spoken and done evil things as thou couldst*; they gloried in their wickedness, and studied to provoke God to the uttermost. *Note*, (1.) Lewdness indulged by degrees banishes shame; and this last relic of virtue lost, there is no hope of recovery. (2.) The thief that lies in wait for our purse is innocent, compared with the tempter, that by leading us into sin, would rob us of our souls. (3.) They are advanced to the summit of wickedness, who give an unbounded loose to all their appetites, and know no restraint from sin, but the want of ability.

2. God would be perfectly justified in giving them up to destruction. The law was express in case of an adulteress divorced, that she could no more be restored to her husband's bed, for the land would have been polluted thereby. God might therefore well treat them in the same manner, by an utter rejection, especially after he had in vain chastised them, by withholding their rain in its season; and instead of repenting, they continued hardned under his judgments, *v.* 3. *Note*, (1.) If sinners had to do with man instead of God, all reconciliation must be despaired of. (2.) When the heart is stubborn under the rod of correction, it is much to be feared the stroke of final judgment is near.

3. Notwithstanding all that was past, God invites them to return, and directs them in the way. *Return again unto me, saith the Lord*, which contains a gracious intimation that he was yet ready to receive them. And the chief of sinners may be assured, whenever they in penitence cry to him, he will yet speak to them pardon; and therefore *wilt thou not from this time cry to me?* After so long and treacherous departures, it is high time at last, though late, to begin; and now is the accepted time, when the invitations of mercy are pleading, and without delay to be embraced. And lest, confounded at their guilt, they should not know what to say, God puts words in their mouth, *My Father, thou art the guide of my youth*, as returning prodigals, unworthy to be called children, yet hoping to find in God a merciful father; and as those, that since they have left him, have ever erred and wandered to and from misery, and therefore desire to be taken under his care, and henceforward, as in the days of youth, to be guided by his will and word. *Will he reserve his anger for ever? will he keep it to the end?* No, he is God, and not man, and as his majesty is, such is his mercy. *Note*, (1.) If a sense of God's grace does not engage the sinner's heart to return, nothing can. (2.) They who begin to be sensible of their departures from God, will be importunate on their knees, to be restored to his forfeited favours. (3.) Whatever fears unbelief may suggest, God is a father, whose tender compassions fail not, and we may confidently trust in his mercy.

Before Christ 628

6 ¶ The LORD said also unto me in the days of
Josiah the king, [i] Hast thou seen *that* which backsliding
Israel hath done? [k] she is gone up upon every high mountain,
and under every green tree, and there hath played
the harlot. 7 And I said, after she had done all these
things, [l] Turn thou unto me. [m] But she returned not.
And her treacherous sister [n] Judah saw *it*. 8 And I saw,
when for all the causes whereby backsliding Israel committed
adultery, I had put her away, and given her a
bill of divorce; yet her treacherous sister Judah feared
not, but went and played the harlot also. 9 And it
came to pass through the † lightness of her whoredom,
that she defiled the land, and committed adultery with
stones and with stocks. 10 And yet for all this, her
treacherous sister Judah hath not turned unto me [p] with
her whole heart, but ‡ feignedly, saith the LORD.
11 And the LORD said unto me, [q] The backsliding
Israel hath justified herself more than treacherous Judah.

[i] Ver. 11. [k] Chap. ii. 20. [l] 2 Kings xvii. 13. [m] Hos. v. 1. [n] 2 Kings xvii. 14. Hos. vi. 6. Ezek. xvi. 46. & xxiii. 2, 4. Ezek. xxiii. 9. † Or, fame. [p] 2 Chron. xxxiv. 33. Hos. vii. 14. ‡ Heb. in falsehood. [q] Ezek. xvi. 51. & xxiii. 11.

v. 6—11. Josiah heartily laboured after the reformation of the people, and the prophet, with his sermons, seconded his pious design; but we find the labours of both were ineffectual. The kingdom of Judah was become apostate as the kingdom of Israel, and must shortly share her fate.

1. The sin and ruin of backsliding Israel are observed. The prophet, in the history of that kingdom, and seen their miserable end about ninety years before. They first revolted from David's successors, and then left God's worship for idolatry, not only in Dan and Bethel, but on every mountain and under every green tree their spiritual adulteries were committed, *v.* 6. In vain the prophets warned, in vain the patience of God waited, in vain were all his gracious invitations to return; they persisted in their impenitence, *v.* 7. and that produced their ruin. God gave them a divorce, thrust out of his protection, and then they were quickly enslaved, and became a prey to their enemies, *v.* 8. *Note*, Backslider shall sooner or later be filled with their own ways, and rue their choice.

2. Judah took no warning by the judgment. She is called *her treacherous sister*, sprung from the same stock of Jacob, and though affecting to cleave to God's temple and worship, false and faithless in her professions, *v.* 7. Instead of being awed, or reformed by her sister's ruin, she plunged into the same sins, and *played the harlot also*, *v.* 8. As abominable as ever Israel had been, she defiled the land, and with such base gods as stocks and stones committed adultery, *v.* 9. Yea, notwithstanding the efforts made by the gracious monarch Josiah, and those who assisted him in the work, though for a time the people outwardly appeared reformed, their hearts were as unrenewed as ever, and their professions utterly hypocritical, *v.* 10. *Note*, (1.) Appearances may impose upon men, but God trieth the heart. (2.) Hypocrisy is among the greatest sins, and the false-hearted professor may expect to meet an avenging God, as much as the abandoned profligate. (3.) They who will not take warning by others falls, are hastening to their own ruin.

3. God justifies backsliding Israel more than treacherous Judah. They had greater means, greater warnings, and made greater professions, therefore their guilt was more aggravated. This doth not excuse Israel, but it adds to Judah's iniquity. *Note*, The more we have received from God of mercies and means, the heavier will be our judgment, if we have neglected and abused them.

12 ¶ Go, and proclaim these words toward the north,
and say, Return, thou backsliding Israel, saith the
LORD; *and* I will not cause mine anger to fall upon
you: for [r] I *am* merciful, saith the LORD, *and* I will
not keep *anger* for ever. 13 Only acknowledge thine
iniquity, that thou hast transgressed against the LORD
thy God, and hast scattered thy ways to the strangers
under every green tree, and ye have not obeyed my
voice, saith the LORD. 14 Turn, O backsliding
children, saith the LORD; for [s] I am married unto you:

[r] Psal. lxxxvi. 15. Chap. xxxiii. 8. Ver. 5. [s] Chap. xxxi. 32.

and

Before Chriſt 612.

and I will take you one of a city, and two of a family,
and I will bring you to Zion 15 And I will give you
ᵗ paſtors according to mine heart, ᵘ which ſhall feed you
with knowledge and underſtanding 16 And it ſhall
come to paſs when ye be multiplied and increaſed in the
land, in thoſe days, ſaith the LORD, ˣ they ſhall ſay
no more, The ark of the covenant of the LORD nei-
ther ſhall it come to mind, neither ſhall they remember
it, neither ſhall they viſit *it*, neither ſhall † *that* be done
any more. 17 At that time they ſhall call Jeruſalem
the throne of the LORD, and all the nations ſhall be
gathered unto it, ʸ to the name of the LORD, to Jeru-
ſalem neither ſhall they ᶻ walk any more after the ‡
imagination of their evil heart 18 In thoſe days ᵃ the
houſe of Judah ſhall walk with the houſe of Iſrael, and
they ſhall come together out of the land of the north,
to the land that I have ‖ given for an inheritance unto
your fathers 19 But I ſaid, How ſhall I put thee a-
mong the children, and give thee ᵇ a § pleaſant land, †
a goodly heritage of the hoſts of nations? and I ſaid,
ᶜ Thou ſhalt call me, My father, and ſhalt not turn a-
way from me

ᵗ Chap xxiii 4 Ezek xxxiv 23 Eph iv 11 ᵘ Chap xx 25 ˣ Heb x 8, 9 † Or it be magnified ʸ Iſa lx 9 ᶻ Chap xi 8 ‡ Or ſtubbornneſs ᵃ Iſa xi 13 Ezek xxxvii 16, 22 Hoſ i 11 ‖ Or cauſed your fathers to poſſeſs ᵇ Pſ cvi 24 Ezek xx 6 Dan viii 9 & xi 16, 41, 45 § Heb Land of deſire † Heb A heritage of glory, or beauty ᶜ Rom viii 15

v 12—19 Seldom do the prophets proclaim any ſingular mercies to the Jewiſh people, but they interſperſe ſome glorious promiſes of that mercy of all mercies, the coming of the Redeemer, to ſet up his church univerſally in the world, to be the light of the Gentiles, and the glory of his people Iſrael We have here,

1 An invitation to Iſrael to return This muſt be proclaimed towards the north, where now they were captives *Return, thou backſliding Iſrael*, ver 12 and again, *turn, O backſliding children*, ver 14 *Children*, yet *backſliders*! aſtoniſhing ingratitude *Backſliders*, yet *children*! amazing mercy! God, even when his children backſlide, will not renounce his relation to them, when ſeduced by temptation, overcome by corruption, plunged into guilt, diſcouraged from prayer, their conſcience ſtupified, they ſeem without power or inclination to return, even then he will not caſt them off, his voice can reach them, his grace conſtrain them, his word direct them how to come to him, and what to ſay, for *he is merciful*, and therefore there is hope *Only acknowledge thine iniquity*, and what leſs can be enjoined? yea, how can we do otherwiſe, when we reflect confounded on the paſt? *that thou haſt tranſgreſſed againſt the Lord thy God*, which relation to him aggravates their guilt, and every penitent ſinner deſires never to extenuate his ſins, but to behold them in all their malignity, *and haſt ſcattered thy ways to ſtrangers under every green tree*, committing idolatry, as a proſtitute, who follows every ſtranger ſhe meets Thus our particular ſin muſt be confeſſed, the time, place, circumſtances reflected upon with ſhame and horror *and ye have not obeyed my voice, ſaith the Lord*, and ſuch rebellion againſt the divine law, and rejection of God's warnings, call for deepeſt humiliation

2 The great and precious promiſes made them to engage their return, which have a particular relation to their deliverance from captivity, when many of the ten tribes joined thoſe of Judah and Benjamin, and embraced the proclamation of Cyrus, but they look farther, and are to be extended to all the Iſrael of God in goſpel times, that ſhould be collected into his church

(1) God's anger ſhall remove, in conſequence of their ſins being forgiven, on their penitent return, *v* 12 *Note*, The moſt powerful means to engage the ſoul to repent, is the promiſe of pardon

(2) They ſhould be taken into the ſame endeared relation to God as ever, for *I am married unto you*, and he would receive them into his arms, and give them the ſame place in his heart, as if they had never treacherouſly departed from him *Note*, God not only forgives, but forgets the ſins of his people, they are as if they had never been committed, and when they return to him, they are reſtored to the ſame favour, as if no variance had ever ſubſiſted

(3) God will bring them to Zion, into the goſpel-church *I will take you one of a city, and two of a family*, ſeparating them by diſtinguiſhing grace for himſelf, and though they were few comparatively who returned, none of them ſhould be loſt *Note*, (1) Backſliders recovered, are few, very few (2) If any ſuch be called, and reſtored, it is of God's rich and ſovereign mercy (3) When God engages *to take and bring* his people to the heavenly Zion, no difficulties are inſurmountable to him

(4) God will give them paſtors after his own heart, *to feed them with knowledge and underſtanding*, and under ſuch gracious miniſtration their ſouls will grow in grace and in meetneſs for glory, *v* 15 *Note*, (1) They are no paſtors who intrude into the miniſtry without a divine call, but wolves in ſheep's clothing (2) Chriſt's true miniſters reſemble their maſter in zeal, charity, and labour, the ſame mind is in them, and by their fruits ye ſhall know them (3) God's word is the food with which Chriſt's flock muſt be fed, and every paſtor muſt be a wiſe houſeholder, thoroughly acquainted with theſe ſacred ſtores, and ſkilful to produce what is moſt ſuited to the variety of the wants of thoſe to whom he miniſters

(5) The typical and ceremonial inſtitutions ſhall be all aboliſhed Chriſt, who is the ſum and ſubſtance of them, being come, the ark, that was of old their glory, ſhould be no more eſteemed or remembered, when the church was increaſed, and the Meſſiah's kingdom ſhould be ſet up, *v* 16

(6) The church of God, adorned with his preſence and the acceſſion of the Gentiles, would be more glorious and more reſorted to, than the temple with its Shechinah, and Jeruſalem in the moſt frequented ſolemnities *They ſhall call Jeruſalem the throne of the Lord*, where his glory eminently appears, and his government is with delight obeyed, *and all nations ſhall be gathered into it* from the Gentile lands, *neither ſhall they walk any more after the imagination of their evil heart*, being effectually turned from idols to ſerve the living and true God *Note*, Our hearts are evil, very evil, yea, the imaginations of them only evil, till by divine grace renewed, God gives a new heart, and puts a right ſpirit within us

(7) All enmity between Iſrael and Judah ſhall ceaſe They ſhall be united in affection, and become one people, *v* 18 and this was the caſe after their return from Babylon, and prefigured the union of Jews and Gentiles, and that perfect harmony which ſhall ſubſiſt between them when joined in the ſame body, of which Chriſt is the living head

3 Though on their part they were utterly unworthy of theſe mercies, yet God directs their plea, and will accept it *How ſhall I put thee among the children?* ſo undeſerving as they were of the relation, and of all the great bleſſings provided, of *a pleaſant land*, and *goodly heritage of the hoſts of the nations* who poſſeſſed it, till God caſt them out, to make room for his people Of ſuch favours they might well deſpair, but he contrives a way for overcoming the objections drawn from their unworthineſs, conſiſtent with his own glory *Thou ſhalt call me, My father*, returning in faith to him, through the Son of his love, *and ſhalt not turn away from me*, but approve henceforward their fidelity unſhaken, *Note*, (1) When we conſider what we are by nature, and what we have been in practice, we may well wonder how it is poſſible God ſhould ever put us among his children (2) When by faith we truly turn to God, the vileſt ſinners, and the fouleſt backſliders, ſhall be advanced to the tranſcendent dignity of being counted the ſons of God (3) God will keep his children that they ſhall not depart from him, and will engage them to ſtand faſt in his covenant (4) They who are called to be the ſons of God on earth, will be the heirs of glory, and poſſeſs that heavenly Canaan, that goodly heritage among the ſaints, prepared for them before the foundation of the world

20 ¶ Surely, *as* a wife treacherouſly departeth from
her † huſband ſo ᵈ have you dealt treacherouſly with
me, O houſe of Iſrael, ſaith the LORD 21 A voice
was heard upon the high places, weeping *and* ſupplica-
tions of the children of Iſrael for they have perverted
their way, *and* they have forgotten the LORD their
God 22 ᵉ Return, ye backſliding children, *and* ᶠ I will
heal your backſlidings behold, we come unto thee,
for thou *art* the LORD our God 23 Truly in vain
is ſalvation hoped for from the hills, *and from* the mul-
titude of mountains ᵍ truly in the LORD our God
is the ſalvation of Iſrael 24 For ‡ ſhame hath devour-
ed the labour of our fathers from our youth, their
flocks and their herds, their ſons and their daughters
25 ʰ We lie down in our ſhame, and our confuſion
covereth us for we have ſinned againſt the LORD
our God, we and our fathers, ⁱ from our youth even
unto this day, and have not obeyed the voice of the
LORD our God

† Heb friend ᵈ Chap v 11 ᵉ Hoſ xiv 1 ᶠ Ibid v 1 & xiv 4 ᵍ Pſ cxxi 1, 2 ‡ Or that ſhameful thing Chap xi 13 Hoſ ix 10 ʰ Ezra ix ⁱ Chap xxii 21

v 20—25 According to God's gracious invitation, we have Iſrael's penitent return Like an adulterous wife, *v* 20 that had eloped from her huſband, ſo had they departed from God, but now they begin to be convinced of their guilt and danger, and lament them

1 They openly and aloud bewail their iniquities, on thoſe high places before the ſcene of their abomination, and with tears in prayer acknowledge that they have perverted their way, and forgotten the Lord their God, *v* 21 *Note*, (1) When do we ſo much need *that our head ſhould be waters*, and our eyes a fountain of tears, as when we remember our paſt rebellions againſt, and ingratitude toward the bleſſed God? (2) Forgetfulneſs of God is at the root of all our ſin (3) When the ſinner is driven to a throne of grace, to unboſom his bitter anguiſh, he will ever find a God that heareth prayer

2 God graciouſly invites them to come to him, backſliding

children

Before Christ 612.

children as they had been, and promises to heal their backslidings and restore them again to his grace and favour. *Note*, (1.) God is more willing to hear than we to pray, and not a tear falls from the eye of his penitents but it is noted in his book. (2.) The sinner's backslidings are then healed, when God pardons the past, and by his grace renews the heart, and prevents it from relapsing again into sin.

3. God's children earnestly and instantly accept his call, and echo back, *Behold we come unto thee*, without delay, without reserve, *for thou art the Lord our God*, once our offended but now our reconciled God, in whose favour we have a sure interest, to whose service we devote ourselves, and on whom alone our dependance is placed. *Truly in vain is salvation hoped for from the hills, and from the multitude of mountains*: their idol gods and human confidences they now renounce, convinced of their vanity and insufficiency. *Truly in the Lord our God is the salvation of Israel*: out of him there is no salvation, in him there is all sufficiency to save to the uttermost, and he is *our God*: we may be assured of his power and grace to interpose on our behalf. Whilst thus they express their confidence in him, they own their sin and shame, especially their idolatry, which they and their fathers had committed, and the dreadful consequences of which they felt to their confusion, in the curse of God upon all the labour of their hands, on their families and possessions, and own that the visitation was altogether righteous, because they obeyed not the voice of the Lord their God, v. 24, 25. *Note*, (1.) Penitent sinners ever take shame and confusion of face to themselves, and justify God in his judgments. (2.) The sense of our own great unworthiness must not discourage us from exercising faith on the divine promises. (3) There is a salvation wrought out for Israel, by which the most desperate may still find mercy through a Redeemer, and a reconciled God. (4.) When we return to Christ, we must renounce all other confidences, and make mention of his strength and righteousness only.

CHAP IV.

The two first verses, as the foregoing chapter, are directed to Israel; the rest of the chapter concern Judah and Jerusalem. 1. *They are called to repent and reform*, ver. 3, 4. 2. *They are warned of the advance of Nebuchadnezzar against them, and told that it is for their sins, from which they are again exhorted to wash their hearts*, ver. 5—18. 3. *To affect them the more with the greatness of the desolation that was coming, the prophet himself bitterly laments it, as a reduction of the world to its first chaos*, ver. 19—31.

1 IF thou wilt return, O Israel, saith the LORD,
ᵃ return unto me: and if thou wilt put away
thine abominations out of my sight, then shalt thou not
remove. 2 And ᵇ thou shalt swear, The LORD liveth,
ᶜ in truth, in judgment, and in righteousness; and the
nations shall bless themselves in him, and in him shall
they ᵈ glory.

ᵃ Chap. iii. 1, 22. Joel ii. 12. [illegible] ᵇ [illegible] Zech. viii. 8. ᶜ Isa. xlv. [illegible] ᵈ 1 Cor. i. [illegible]

v. 1, 2. Israel had made penitent professions of returning, God accepts them, and directs them in the way.

If thou wilt return, O Israel, saith the Lord, return unto me; or, *If thou wilt return unto me, thou shalt return*, either let them immediately execute their purpose, or it is promised that, on their doing so, God will bring them back from their dispersion, *and if thou wilt put away thine abominations out of my sight*, all their idolatrous practices and images, *then shalt thou not remove* into captivity again, or, *if thou shalt not move to and fro*, be fickle and wavering, but stedfast in their adherence to God, then his blessing would be upon them. *And thou shalt swear, The Lord liveth*, making no more mention of their idle gods, *in truth, in judgment and in righteousness*, solemnly, and with strictest regard to truth. *And the nations shall bless themselves in him*, being called into communion with God's Israel, and counting themselves happy in the pardon, grace, and glory, revealed in the Redeemer: *and in him shall they glory*, renouncing all other confidence, and glorying in the fulness of the Lord Jesus Christ. *Note*, (1.) They who truly turn to God must put away *all* their abominations, and no allowed sin be spared. (2.) An oath is an act of religious worship, and therefore to swear by any creature is blasphemy against God. (3.) Every oath should be taken *in truth*, with scrupulous adherence to it, asserting nothing of which we have not the fullest assurance, nor promising aught we *do not really intend to perform*: *in judgment*, when called upon before a magistrate, or solemnly, not rashly, or in common conversation, but where the importance of the subject makes such an appeal to God lawful: *and in righteousness*, that justice may be done, and God glorified.

3 ¶ For thus saith the LORD to the men of Judah
and Jerusalem, ᵉ Break up your fallow ground, and
ᶠ sow not among thorns. 4 ᵍ Circumcise yourselves to
the LORD, and take away the foreskins of your heart,
ye men of Judah and inhabitants of Jerusalem: lest my
fury come forth like fire, and burn that none can quench
it, because of the evil of your doings.

ᵉ Hos. x. 12. ᶠ [illegible] ᵍ [illegible]

v. 3, 4. The prophet, having discharged his message to the men of Israel, and set forth their repentance, here addresses himself to the men of Judah and Jerusalem, whom he would provoke to jealousy by their example, and excite to the like repentance. We have,

1. Their Duty. This is represented to them by two familiar images. (1.) *Break up your fallow ground, and sow not among thorns*. Not that of their own ability they could do this. What God calls them to, he would enable them by his grace to perform. This is a striking image of man's natural heart, bringing forth no fruit to God, barren of all grace, hard and impenitent, unfenced, where every lawless appetite ranges uncontrouled, overgrown with the briars and thorns of vile and corrupt affections, and therefore *nigh unto burning*, Heb. vi. 7, 8. This fallow ground must be broken up before it can produce fruit, and this is done by the word of God, *convincing the sinner's conscience*, and opening his heart to receive the seed of the gospel, as the plough divides the soil, *Heb.* iv. 12. and the briars and thorns being rooted up, the seed is not choaked, but brings forth fruit unto perfection. (2.) *Circumcise yourselves to the Lord, and take away the foreskins of your heart*. They placed great dependance on circumcision: but without the circumcision of the heart, and cutting off their corrupt affections, that which was outward in the flesh signified nothing. *Note*, All institutions and forms, however strictly observed, can profit us nothing, if the spirit and power of Godliness be wanting within us; they serve but to delude and deceive the soul that trusts in them.

2. Their danger great and imminent. *Lest my fury come forth like fire, and burn that none can quench it, because of the evil of your doings*. Delays are dangerous. To-day, whilst it is called to day, they are warned not to harden their hearts. *Note*, (1.) It is sin that provokes God's wrath, and kindles the unquenchable flames of hell. (2.) Nothing is so terrible as falling impenitent into the hands of that God who is a consuming fire. (3.) The moment of delay God affords us should be eagerly seized, before the flames kindle round us, for then it would be too late to call or return.

5 Declare ye in Judah, and publish in Jerusalem,
and say, Blow ye the trumpet in the land: cry, gather
together, and say, ʰ Assemble yourselves, and let us go
into the defenced cities. 6 Set up the standard towards
Zion: † retire, stay not: for I will bring evil ⁱ from the
north, and a great ‡ destruction. 7 ᵏ The lion is come
up from his thicket, and the destroyer of the Gentiles is
on his way; he is gone forth from his place ˡ to make
thy land desolate; *and* thy cities shall be laid waste, with-
out an inhabitant. 8 For this ᵐ gird you with sackcloth,
lament and howl: for the fierce anger of the LORD is
not turned back from us. 9 And it shall come to pass
at that day, saith the LORD, *that* the heart of the king
shall perish, and the heart of the princes; and the priests
shall be astonished, and the prophets shall wonder. 10
Then said I, Ah LORD God, ⁿ surely thou hast greatly
deceived this people, and Jerusalem, ᵒ saying, Ye shall
have peace; whereas the sword reacheth unto the soul.
11 At that time shall it be said to this people, and to
Jerusalem, ᵖ A dry wind of the high places in the wilder-
ness toward the daughter of my people, not to fan, nor
to cleanse, 12 *Even* § a full wind from those *places* shall
come unto me: now also will I ‖ give sentence against
them. 13 Behold, he shall come up as clouds, and ᵠ his
chariots *shall be* as a whirlwind: ʳ his horses are swifter
than eagles. Wo unto us, for we are spoiled. 14 O
Jerusalem, ˢ wash thine heart from wickedness, that thou
mayest be saved. How long shall thy vain thoughts lodge
within thee? 15 For ᵗ a voice declareth from Dan, and
publisheth affliction from mount Ephraim. 16 Make
ye mention to the nations; behold, publish against Jeru-
salem, *that* watchers come from a far country, and give
out their voice against the cities of Judah. 17 As keep-
ers of a field are they against her round about; because
she hath been rebellious against me, saith the LORD.
18 ᵘ Thy way and thy doings have procured these *things*
unto thee, this *is* thy wickedness, because it is bitter,
because it reacheth unto thine heart.

ʰ Chap. viii. 14. † Or strengthen. ⁱ Chap. i. 14, 15. & vi. 22. ‡ Heb. Breaking. ᵏ Dan. vii. 4. ˡ Chap. ii. 15. ᵐ Chap. vi. 26. ⁿ Ezek. xiv. 9. ᵒ Chap. v. 12. & xiv. 13. ᵖ Hos. xiii. 15. § Or a fuller wind than those. ‖ Heb. Utter judgements. ᵠ Isa. v. 28. ʳ Hab. i. [illegible] ˢ Isa. i. 16. ᵗ Chap. viii. 16. ᵘ Ps. cvii. 17. Isa. l. [illegible] Chap. ii. 17, 19.

v. 5—18. The judgments coming upon Judah and Jerusalem are foretold, as an awakening motive to their speedy repentance.

1. The alarm is spread through the land of the invading foe coming from the north, and they who are dispersed in the country are called to flee for safety to the defenced cities; but it being thought that only a [illegible] [illegible]

The

Before Christ 612.

2 The approach of the Chaldeans, with Nebuchadrezzar at their head, is described by a variety of images, expressive of *the great destruction* and ravages which would ensue. *As a lion*, v. 7. pinched with hunger, sallies furiously from his thicket on the defenceless flocks, so fierce, so cruel, would the king of Babylon come at the head of his armies, *the destroyer of the Gentiles*, and now of the Jews, to spread desolations on every side; *as a dry wind*, sharp and piercing, violent and raging, that, instead of fanning or cleansing the grain, would sweep with resistless fury all before it, v. 11, 12. Thick as *clouds* they advance, and swift as the *whirlwind*; their *horses are swifter than eagles*, and therefore flight as impracticable as opposition was vain. *From Dan*, the most northern border, the first alarm is spread, v. 15. that the nations may hear who were to drink of the same cup, and especially *Jerusalem*, against whom this armament is intended. *Behold watchers come from a far country*, or besiegers, threatening ruin to all the cities of *Judah*, and shouting, as confident of victory, v. 16. *As keepers of a field*, who guard the corn, and prevent all entrance into it, so should these cut off from Jerusalem all supplies, and suffer none to escape. See 2 Kings xxv. 4.

3 The cause of these judgments is their sin. *Thou hast been rebellious against me, saith the Lord*, v. 17. *Thy way and thy doings have procured these things unto thee*; they had none to blame but themselves for what they suffered, it was the just recompence of their iniquities: *this is thy wickedness*, the fruit of it, *because it is bitter*, both the sin and the punishment, *because it reacheth to the heart*, a mortal blow, an utter destruction. *Note*, (1.) Whatever we suffer, we have only ourselves to blame; our sins are our tormentors. (2.) If we feel not the bitterness of sin to repent of it, we shall feel the bitterness of the punishment when repentance will come too late.

4 The terrible consequences of these judgments are described. Their hearts fail them. The king and princes, that should have roused the people to a brave defence, have lost all spirit, and cannot conceal their coward fears; the priests, whose office it was to animate them to the battle, are themselves astonished, and unable to sound a blast from the silver trumpets; and the false prophets, who had deceived them with visions of peace, are dumb with horror and amazement. Every warrior is sunk in despair, every face gathers blackness, and one universal groan is heard, *woe unto us, for we are spoiled*, v. 13. In vain then will they *gird themselves with sackcloth, lament and howl*, their desolations are determined, and *the fierce anger of the Lord is not turned back*; the decree of their ruin is gone forth, *I will give sentence against them*, and their destruction is inevitable, because the measure of their iniquities is full. *Note*, (1.) A sense of guilt makes men cowards. (2.) Wicked priests and false prophets, who deceived the people with visions of peace, in a judgment-day will find God's terrors around them.

5 The prophet laments the deceptions of the people through their false prophets, v. 10. to believe whose lies God in just judgment gave them up, which was among the sorest of their visitations. They had promised them peace, *but now the sword reached unto the soul*, drenched in the blood of the slain. *Note*, (1.) Among the heaviest curses of God this may be justly reckoned, when he gives up the heart to delusion, and suffers the blind to lead the blind. (2.) The faithful ministers of God behold with deep concern those who pretend to be teachers of God's word vending their false doctrines, and lulling the souls of sinners into a fatal security, endeavouring to prejudice them against the truth, and prevent every awakening impression, which the zealous and true preachers seek to make upon their hearts.

6 He seeks to snatch them as a brand from the burning. *O Jerusalem, wash thine heart from thy wickedness, that thou mayst be saved*. He deals faithfully, not as the false prophets, glossing over their iniquities, but charging them home upon their conscience. Their heart was wicked, there the deep root of bitterness lay, and from that they must be cleansed, if they would be saved. And he expostulates on the folly and danger of delaying their repentance, *How long shall vain thoughts lodge within thee?* too long had they done so, 'twas high time to awake out of sleep, the judgments of God were hastening on, in a moment it would be too late to prevent them. *Note*, (1.) Whilst wickedness continues indulged in the heart, there can be no salvation hoped for. (2.) There is but one fountain that is capable of washing the sinner's heart from his iniquities, and that was opened in the Redeemer's side, of blood and water: *blood*, to pardon the deepest guilt of sin; *water*, to purify from every stain of corruption. The pardoning and sanctifying grace of Jesus are inseparable. (3.) Vain thoughts are sinful, and if our hearts are not purged from their imaginations, our ways will be quickly perverse. (4.) When we consider how short our life is, how much is past, how uncertain the moment yet to come, it should be an awakening admonition to seize the present *now*, and seek to God to day, whilst it is called to day.

19 ¶ y My bowels, my bowels, I am pained at ‡ my
very heart; my heart maketh a noise in me; I cannot
hold my peace, because thou hast heard, O my soul, the
sound of the trumpet, the alarm of war. 20 z Destruction
upon destruction is cried; for the whole land is
spoiled: suddenly are my tents spoiled, *and* my curtains
in a moment. 21 How long shall I see the standard,
and hear the sound of the trumpet? 22 For my people
is foolish, they have not known me; they *are* sottish
children, and they have none understanding: a they *are*
wise to do evil, but to do good they have no knowledge.
23 b I beheld the earth, and lo, *it was* without form,
and void; and the heavens, c and they *had* no light.
24 I beheld the mountains, and lo, d they trembled,
and all the hills moved lightly. 25 I beheld, and lo,
there was no man, and e all the birds of the heavens were
fled. 26 I beheld, and lo, the fruitful place *was* a
wilderness, and all the cities thereof were broken down
f at the presence of the LORD, *and* by his fierce anger.
27 For thus hath the LORD said, The whole land
shall be desolate; g yet will I not make a full end. 28
For this shall the earth mourn, and h the heavens above
be black: because I have spoken *it*, I have purposed *it*,
and will not repent, neither will I turn back from it.
29 The whole city shall flee for the noise of the horsemen,
and bowmen; i they shall go into thickets, and
climb up upon the rocks: every city *shall be* forsaken,
and not a man dwell therein. 30 And *when* thou *art*
spoiled, what wilt thou do? Though thou clothest thyself
with crimson, though thou deckest thee with ornaments
of gold, k though thou rentest thy ‡ face with
painting, in vain shalt thou make thyself fair; *thy* lovers
will despise thee, they will seek thy life. 31 For I have
heard a voice l as of a woman in travail, *and* the anguish
as of her that bringeth forth her first child, the voice of
the daughter of Zion, *that* bewaileth herself, m *that*
spreadeth her hands, *saying*, Woe *is* me now, for my soul
is wearied, because of n murderers.

y Isa. xv. 5. & xvi. 11. & xxi. 3. & xxii. 4. Chap. ix. 1, 10. ‡ Heb. The walls of my heart. z Psal. xlii. 7. Ezek. vii. 26.

a Rom. xvi. 19. b Gen. i. 2. Isa. xxiv. 19. c Isa. v. 30. d Isa. v. 25. Ezek. xxxviii. 20. e Zeph. i. 3. f Nah. i. 5. g Isa. vi. 13. Chap. v. 18. & xxx. 11. & xlvi. 28. h Isa. v. 30. & l. 3. i 2 Chron. xxxiii. 11. k Ezek. xxiii. 40. ‡ Heb. Eyes. l Chap. vi. 24. m Lam. i. 17. n 2 Chron. xxxvi. 17.

v. 19—31. With deep concern and anguish the prophet beheld the miseries coming upon his people: his bowels yearned over the distress of his country, and his heart throbbed with bitter anguish.

1. For their sins. *My people is foolish*. This is the character God gives them, for sin is the greatest folly. Yet not abandoned, he acknowledges them for his people still, though *they have not known me*. In name and in profession they had owned him, but had no experimental knowledge of him as their God. *They are sottish children*, stupid and untractable; *and they have no understanding*, respecting their true happiness, or the means of attaining it. *They are wise to do evil*, cunning to contrive and accomplish their sinful schemes, a wisdom which is their curse; *but to do good they have no knowledge*, nor desire to know, their inclination is averse to it. Such is the character of every natural man, till God takes away the blindness, and cures the perverseness of his heart, by bestowing on him the wisdom and grace which come from above.

2. For their sufferings, and these are enlarged upon and strongly described. The trumpet spreads the alarm of war, v. 19. swift and sudden the destruction spreads, and, successive as Job's messengers of evil, the dreadful tidings fly, of one city taken after another, till the whole land is spoiled, and all the country where the shepherds pitched their tents ravaged, v. 20. no end of the calamity appears. The banners of the invading foe are displayed, and their warlike instruments are heard on every side, v. 21. The country, utterly wasted, appears like the first chaos, when the earth was without form and void, and darkness upon the face of the deep; or it may be applied to the utter confusion of their affairs, political and ecclesiastical, and the heavens, as if unwilling to look upon their abominations, veil their bright luminaries with darkness; or so darkened and bewildered were their kings and princes, not knowing what course to take, v. 23. The mountains trembled and the hills fled before the face of the offended God, such terrors seized the most stout-hearted warriors, v. 24. Universal desolation seems to reign through that once populous and fruitful land; the cities, without an inhabitant, lye in ruins, the country is wasted and barren as a rock, the very birds are fled, no food remaining for them; and all this arising from God's fierce anger, which is itself the heaviest part of the judgment, v. 25, 26. And this is not the case with one city or part of the country, the whole is utterly ruined, v. 27, 28. Affrighted at the horsemen and bowmen, they flee to rocks and thickets to hide themselves; the cities are deserted and destroyed, and not a living soul remains in them, v. 29. and, but for one word of mercy, v. 27. they might expect a total extirpation, and their very name to be blotted out from under heaven; but *God will not make a full end*, a remnant shall escape. *Note*, (1.) These awful images of Judea's destruction give some faint description of that great and terrible day of the Lord, when his wrath shall finally be poured out on the ungodly, the heavens be dissolved, the earth burnt up, and all created nature return to its original chaos. (2.) What-

ever

Before Christ 612

ever visitations come upon us from the hands of men, we must look farther for the cause of them, if we would profit under them (3) In all God's judgments below some mercy is mingled with vengeance, but hereafter there will be judgment without mercy

3 Their sufferings are remediless God will not help them, they cannot deliver themselves, and their human confidences will fail, and leave them in despair If the earth mourn, and the heavens are black with storms of wrath, 'tis because God hath spoken their doom His purpose is fixed, his sentence irrevocable since they refused to repent of their sins, he will not repent of his judgments for them, v 28 He being against them, what can they do, whither can they go Their own force is insufficient to resist the invading foe, and as vain their hope in their confederates Though like a prostitute, that by painting and dress seeks to conceal her wrinkles, and hide her decays, Judah courted her allies, *in vain shalt thou make thyself fair*, every wile she can use will no longer secure her gallants sensible of her ruined state, they will forsake her in the day of her calamity, and help forward her destruction, v 30 In agonies, as a woman in the pangs of the most difficult travail, the daughter of Zion shall cry out, *Wo is me now*, her sufferings so intolerable, her case so desperate, *my soul is wearied because of murderers*, either those that dwelt in Jerusalem, at whose hands the blood they had shed was now required, or through those horrid massacres made by the Chaldean sword *Note*, (1) They who fall into adversity will generally feel, to their cost, the vanity of creature confidences The friendships of the world are faithless God is the only friend who never fails (2) The paint of duties and devotions can stand us in little stead, if the deformity of sin continues underneath (3) They are remediless indeed whom God abandons

CHAP V

Reproofs for sin and threatnings of judgment are intermixed in this chapter (1) The sins they are charged with are, Injustice, ver 1. Hypocrisy in religion, ver 2 Incorrigibleness, ver 3 Both poor and rich are corrupt, ver 4, 5 Idolatry and adultery, ver 7, 8 Treacherous departures from God, ver 11 An impudent defiance of him, ver 12, 13 And that which is at the bottom of all this, want of the fear of God, ver 20—24 Violence and oppression, ver 26—28 And a combination of those to debauch the nation that should have been active to reform it, ver 30, 31 (2) The judgments they are threatned with are very terrible In general, they shall be reckoned with, ver 9, 29 A foreign enemy shall be brought in upon them, ver 15—17 Shall set guards upon them, ver 6 Shall destroy their fortifications, ver 10 Shall carry them away into captivity, ver 19 And keep all good things from them, ver. 25 And herein the word of God's prophets shall be fulfilled, ver 14 But, (3) Here is an intimation twice given that God would in the midst of wrath remember mercy, and not utterly destroy them, ver 10, 18

1 RUN ye to and fro through the streets of Jerusalem, and see now, and know, and seek in the
broad places thereof, [a] if ye can find a man, [b] if there
be *any* that executeth judgment, that seeketh the truth,
and I will pardon it
2 And though they say, The
LORD liveth, surely they swear falsly
3 O LORD,
are not thine eyes upon the truth? thou hast [d] stricken
them, but they have not grieved thou hast consumed
them, *but* [e] they have refused to receive correction [f] they
have made their faces harder than a rock, they have refused to return
4 Therefore I said, Surely these *are*
poor, they are foolish for [g] they know not the way of
the LORD, *nor* the judgment of their God.
5 I will
get me unto the great men, and will speak unto them,
for [h] they have known the way of the LORD, *and* the
judgment of their God but these have altogether [i] broken the yoke, *and* burst the bonds
6 Wherefore [k] a
lion out of the forest shall slay them, *and* a [l] wolf of the
‡ evenings shall spoil them, [m] a leopard shall watch over
their cities every one that goeth out thence shall be torn
in pieces because their transgressions are many, *and* their
backslidings are ‡ increased
7 ¶ How shall I pardon
thee for this? thy children have forsaken me, and [n] sworn
by *them that are* no gods when [o] I had fed them to the
full, they then [p] committed adultery, and assembled themselves by troops in the harlots houses
8 [q] They were
as fed horses in the morning every one neighed after his
neighbour's wife
9 [r] Shall I not visit for these *things*?
saith the LORD and shall not my soul be avenged on
such a nation as this?

a Ezek xxii 30
b Gen xviii 23 &c
Psal xii 1
c Chap iv 7
d Isa i 5 & ix 13
Chap ii 30
e Zeph iii 2
f Ezek iii 7 … Zech vii 12
g Chap viii 7
h Mic iii 1
i Psal ii 3
k Chap iv 7
l Psal civ 20
Hab i 8
‡ Or deserts
m Hos xiii 7
‡ Heb strong
n Josh xxiii 7
o Deut xxxii 15
p Chap … 9

v 1—9 God will ever be justified in his judgments and when he visits, verily there is a cause We have here,

1 Their many and aggravated sins

(1) All truth and honesty were banished. Search Jerusalem throughout, in all the places of concourse, and neither a magistrate could be found upright, nor a man faithful, such a universal corruption was spread through all ranks and degrees To spare Sodom ten righteous were required, to spare Jerusalem one would have sufficed, and is not found, at least no such was to be met in the places of public resort, where, if a few remained, they dared not appear

(2) They were false-hearted hypocrites Some indeed made profession of religion, and pretended a regard for truth, but they were perjured wretches, and faithless in all their vows of fidelity to God, whose eye was upon them, and from whom they could not be concealed, *v* 2, 3 *Note*, (1) Perjury is a crying sin, and there is an avenging God who hears (2) They who are insincere in their professions of Godliness, are more guilty than the openly abandoned

(3) They were obstinately hardened All God's visitations produced no humiliation they neither grieved for the sins that provoked him, nor sought to answer the end of his corrections; but daringly braved the divine vengeance, as neither ashamed of their wickedness nor afraid of the punishment, and insolently refused to return *Note*, When judgments have no effect, and men grow impudent in sin, their case appears desperate

(4) They were shamefully ignorant, *v* 4 *They knew not the way of the Lord, nor the judgment of their God* They understood neither his word, the manner of his worship, or the designs of his providences But the prophet was willing to hope these were foolish, because poor, and might have less opportunities of improvement yet he found the case no way mended with their betters *Note*, (1) Prevailing ignorance of the things of God cannot but be accompanied with abounding iniquity (2) Tho' high attainments of knowledge may not be in their power, all truths needful to salvation the poorest may learn So that they are without excuse for wilful ignorance is wilful sin

(5) The great had utterly cast off the divine government Among the princes, the priests, and the elders, at least, he expected wisdom and piety, and that they would pay attention to his word But just the reverse whatever their knowledge was, their practice was vowed ungodliness, breaking the yoke, and bursting the bonds of God's commands *Note*, In a corrupted state, the higher men's stations are, we may expect to find in them the greater abominations

(6) Their idolatries were infamous Forsaking God, they paid their worship to stocks and stones, and swore by them that were no gods Well might he therefore say, *How shall I pardon thee for this? v* 7

(7) They gave full scope to their bestial lusts, abused the plenty God bestowed to pamper their bodies, and, having made provision for the flesh, so impudent and barefaced were they in their indulgences, that in troops they assembled in the harlots houses, and, insatiable in their raging lusts, like fed horses in the morning, they neighed after their neighbour's wife, and added adultery to whoredom, to fill up the measure of their iniquities *Note*, They who would keep from grosser pollutions must bridle their appetites, and shun idleness If the fuel be prepared, the fire will quickly kindle

2 Their destruction is threatned by Nebuchadnezzar king of Babylon As a lion, irresistible in strength, as an evening wolf, fierce with hunger, and as a leopard, watching, darts on his prey, so irresistible, ravening, and swift, shall he come to execute God's judgments, to besiege their cities, and rend in pieces those who either come forth to oppose him, or seek to escape and this *because their transgressions are so many, and their backslidings so increased*

3 God appeals to them for the justice of this procedure *Shall I not visit for these things?* The honour of his government, as well as the holiness of his nature, requires that inquisition should be made, and judgment pass upon such offenders *And shall not my soul be avenged on such a nation as this?* His vindictive justice is essential to his nature, and national sins call for national judgments *Note*, Sin must be avenged, and visited either on the sinner's person or his surety

10 ¶ [s] Go ye up upon her walls, and destroy, [t] but
make not a full end take away her battlements, for
they *are* not the LORD's
11 For [u] the house of Israel
and the house of Judah have dealt very treacherously
against me, saith the LORD
12 [x] They have belied
the LORD, and said, [y] *It is* not he, neither shall evil
come upon us, neither shall we see sword nor famine
13 And the prophets shall become wind, and [z] the
word *is* not in them thus shall it be done unto them
14 Wherefore thus saith the LORD God of hosts,
Because ye speak this word, behold, [a] I will make my
words in thy mouth fire, and this people wood, and it
shall devour them
15 Lo, [b] I will bring a nation upon you from far, O house of Israel, saith the LORD
it *is* a mighty nation, it *is* an ancient nation, a nation
whose

s Chap xxxix 8
t Chap iv 27
u Chap iii 20
x 2 Chron. xxxvi 16
Chap iv 10.
y Isa xxviii. 15
z Chap xliii 2
a Chap i. 9.
b Deut xxviii 49
Isa v 26
Chap i 15 & vi 22

Before Christ 612

whole language thou knowest not, neither understandest
what they say 16 Their quiver *is* as an open sepul-
chre, they *are* all mighty men 17 And [c] they shall eat
up thine harvest, and thy bread, *which* thy sons and thy
daughters should eat they shall eat up thy flocks and
thine herds, they shall eat up thy vines and thy fig trees
they shall impoverish thy fenced cities, wherein thou
trustedst, with the sword 18 Nevertheless in those days,
saith the LORD, [d] I will not make a full end with you
19 ¶ And it shall come to pass when ye shall say,
[e] Wherefore doth the LORD our God all these *things*
unto us? then shalt thou answer them, Like as ye have
forsaken me, and served strange gods in your land, so
[f] shall ye serve strangers in a land *that is* not yours

c Lev xxvi 16 Deut xxviii 31, 33
d Chap iv 27
e Chap xiii 22 & xvi 10
f Deut xxviii 47, 48

v 10—19 The subject of these verses is nearly the same as the foregoing

1 The provocations they have given Israel and Judah, alike rebellious, have treacherously departed from God's ways and worship, *v* 11 fearless of God's warnings, yea daring to give the lie to his word in the mouth of his prophets, and vainly promising themselves peace and plenty as if the threatnings they denounced were melancholy fancies in their own brains, *v* 12 and would prove but as a puff of wind, and as if their own false prophets were rather to be regarded, retorting their denunciations upon them, *thus shall it be done unto them*, or *let it be done*, giving orders to punish the true prophets with the famine and the sword, for presuming to predict such judgments against them, *v* 13 *Note*, (1) It is at the bottom of the sinner's presumption and security, that he does not believe God is so holy as his word declares, and flatters himself there are some reserves of mercy, or that his faithful servants are too severe, and misrepresent his word (2) Many now scoff at the preaching of God's prophets as folly, and treat them as visionary enthusiasts, who will shortly find that what they despise as fictions, contrived to frighten the minds of the superstitious, are fearful realities

2 The punishment threatned for their impenitence That word of God's prophets they had despised should terribly be fulfilled as fire it should burn, and they be fuel to the flame, *v* 14 Those proud battlements, in which they relied, deserted of God their only sure defence, shall be easily thrown down by the besieging foe, *v* 10 From far, a mighty nation, an ancient nation, to whom they were utter strangers, marches at God's command against them, *v* 15 Their arrows devouring as the grave, and their warriors so mighty that they cannot stand before them, *v* 16 Their country shall be foraged, wasted, and plundered, their corn and cattle seized, and themselves and children left to pine with hunger, their cities ruined, and their garrisons slain with the sword, *v* 17 *Note*, (1) God will make sinners know at last whose word shall stand, his or theirs (2) Vain are all our confidences, when God hath forsaken us (3) The God of hosts hath all nations at his beck, and soon can make one sinful nation a scourge to its neighbour

3 In wrath God remembers mercy For the sake of the remnant according to the election of grace, a full end shall not be made of this sinful nation, *v* 18 *Note*, When God gives a commission to the sword, he prescribes the bounds, hitherto shalt thou come, and no further

4 God's justice will appear in his judgments Many of them quarrelling with their punishment would charge God foolishly, and, as if undeserving of this treatment, expostulate with him thereupon *wherefore doth the Lord our God* (to whom they hypocritically pleaded relation) *all these things unto us?* The reason is obvious, and the uprightness of his procedure clear *thou shalt answer them Like as ye have forsaken me*, my worship and service, *and served strange Gods in your land, so shall ye serve strangers*, the Chaldeans, *in a land that is not yours* and this a most just retaliation *Note*, (1) It is a sure sign of an unhumbled heart, when we murmur at punishment and find fault with the severity of our corrections (2) They who make themselves servants of sin shall, sooner or later, be made sick of the service

20 Declare this in the house of Jacob, and publish it
in Judah, saying, 21 Hear now this, O [g] foolish peo-
ple, and without † understanding, which have eyes and
see not, which have ears and hear not 22 [i] Fear ye
not me? saith the LORD will ye not tremble at my
presence, which have placed the sand *for* [k] the bound of
the sea, by a perpetual decree that it cannot pass it, and
though the waves thereof toss themselves, yet can they
not prevail, though they roar, yet can they not pass
over? 23 But this people hath a revolting and a re-
bellious heart they are revolted and gone 24 Neither
say they in their heart, Let us now fear the LORD our
God [l] that giveth rain, [m] both the former and the latter
in his season he reserveth unto us the appointed weeks
of the harvest

g Isa vi 9 Ezek xii 2 Mat xiii 14 John xii 40 Acts xxviii 26 Rom xi 8
† Heb Heart
i Rev xv 4
k Job xxxviii 10, 11 Ps civ 9
l Chap xiv 22
m Deut xi 14

v 20—24 When the prophet had to do with a people so obstinate and perverse, he had need cry aloud and spare not He charges them,

1 With their stupidity and sottishness They neither used their ears to attend to God's word nor their eyes to contemplate his works, but, as if blind and deaf, continued void of understanding *Note*, None so blind as those who will not see, or deaf as they who refuse to hear, and none so criminal as those that, in the midst of means and mercies, cause darkness rather than light

2 They were destitute of God's fear, notwithstanding the displays of majesty and mercy they beheld and experienced They saw the raging seas arise, and threaten to raise another deluge, yet, by his mighty power shut up as with gates of adamant, the proud waves are stayed, and their limits fixed by a perpetual decree, and *Fear ye not me? saith the Lord, will ye not tremble at my presence?* Surely his must prove them more senseless, perverse, and disobedient, than these foaming billows Yet, if his majesty moved them not, his mercy should engage them to fear the Lord and his goodness, who, with such constant providential care, causeth the rain to descend, *the former*, which in Judea was in part of October and November, after the sowing, and *the latter rain*, in part of March and April, *in his season*, as would be most conducive to produce a plenteous harvest, which he graciously bestowed on them Yet so ungrateful and insensible were they, that all this kindness wrought not on their obdurate souls, nor engaged them to say in their hearts, *Let us now fear the Lord our God* *Note*, (1) If the Lord put not his fear in our hearts, neither the works of his power nor the wonders of his providence will affect us yet will they leave us inexcusable (2) Where the fear of God is not, there must be confusion and every evil work

3 They were obstinately rebellious, and revolted from God their hearts were apostate from him and not for a season merely, but they went on in one continued course of iniquity, daily widening the breach, and filling up the measure of their iniquities *Note*, Such sots are we all by nature, so foolish, fearless, and revolted at enmity against God, and hating the restraints of his law, till he by his grace open our eyes, put his fear in our hearts, and reduce them to the obedience of Christ

Before Christ 612

25 ¶ [m] Your iniquities have turned away these *things*,
and your sins have withholden good *things* from you
26 For among my people are found wicked *men* [n] they
† lay wait as he that setteth snares, they set a trap, they
catch men 27 As a cage is full of birds, so *are* their
houses full of deceit therefore they are become great,
and waxen rich 28 They [o] are waxen fat, they shine
yea, [p] they overpass the deeds of the wicked [q] they
judge not the cause, the cause of the fatherless, [r] yet
they prosper and the right of the needy do they not
judge 29 [s] Shall I not visit for these *things?* saith the
LORD shall not my soul be avenged on such a nation
as this? 30 ¶ A wonderful and horrible thing is com-
mitted in the land. 31 [t] The prophets prophesy falsly,
and the ‡ priests bear rule by their means, and [u] my
people love *to have it* so and what will ye do in the end
thereof?

m Ps cvii 34 Isa lix 2
n Prov i 11 17
† Or pry, as fowlers lie in wait
o Deut xxxii 15
p Ezek xvi 49
q Isa i 23 Zech vii 10
r Job xii 6 Ps lxxiii 12
s Chap xiii 1 Ver 9
t Chap xiv 14 & xxiii 25 26 Ezek xiii 6
‡ Or princes
u Mic ii 6, 11

v 25—31 We have here,

1 The miseries their sins had already brought upon them *Your iniquities have turned away these things, and your sins have holden good things from you* The heavens had been shut up, the earth unfruitful, the seasons unkindly, and their harvests had failed *Note*, Lesser visitations, slighted, prepare the way for heavier judgments

2 Their provocations continued as bad as ever, yea grew worse and worse Their general character was wickedness, and that the more aggravated as being in profession God's people They were deceitful, treacherous, oppressive, covetous They had snares to entrap and destroy those who any way interfered with their interests, or were become the objects of their resentment for reproving them for their sins, *v* 26 As a cage with birds set for a decoy, that is filled with those that are caught, so are their houses filled with the gain of fraud and deceit Thus they become great, *v* 27 and, indulging their appetites out of their ill-gotten wealth, wax fat and shine *They overpass the deeds of the wicked*, are worse than the heathens around them, or, though pretending to religion, they exceed in iniquity the most abandoned profligates In vain the fatherless and needy cry for their assistance, to rescue them from oppression, or relieve them from their distresses, their ears are deaf to their cry, neither as advocates to them, or magistrates, do they regard right or justice, and yet, astonishing to tell! *they prosper*, *v* 28 Yet surely they fatten out for the slaughter But, above all other crimes, *a wonderful and horrible thing is committed in the land*, enough to make the ears of every one that hears thereof to tingle, and be amazed at the pitch of impiety to which they are arrived *The prophets prophesy falsly*, teaching divination and visions of

Before Christ 612.

peace for this devoted people, and, far from being discountenanced, *the priests*, or *princes* as the word signifies also, espouse them, and expose them against the true prophets as the tools of their ambition, that they may *bear rule by their means*, supporting themselves by a combination in iniquity, and *my people*, who should have espoused his cause against such a confederacy of iniquity, *love to have it so*, were well enough pleased with such priests as flattered them in their vices, and prophesied smooth things, and with rulers that took no care to execute the laws that should have restrained them. *Note*, (1.) An honest man, in this wicked world, is almost sure of being a prey; for, unable to speak his mind and act deceitfully, he cannot deal on even terms. (2.) We are here often struck with the view of prosperous wickedness, but let us not be staggered; mark the end of those men. (3.) Sin is a horrible thing, we need startle at it. (4.) They who pretend a commission from God, yet by their lies contradict his revealed word, are the most dangerous deceivers.

3. The consequences of these iniquities would be fatal. God will visit for their sins; his justice obliges that condign punishment be executed on such offenders; and *what will ye do in the end thereof?* What a state of misery and despair would they be driven to, when their country should be conquered, and themselves captives in Babylon? *Note*, An end will come of the longest life of prosperous wickedness; and it is an awful consideration what sinners will then do when they shall fall into the hands of the living God.

With mutual encouragements they quicken each other boldly to storm the place, *arise, let us go up at noon*, and, as if some delay had prevented their design from being immediately executed, they regret that the shadows of the evening are advancing, *v.* 4. yet resolved to carry their point, and confident of success, the time of Jerusalem's visitation being come, *v.* 6. they are too impatient to wait for the morning, and resolve that night to attempt the breach, *v.* 5. Some refer the words, *woe unto us*, &c. to the besieged, lamenting their desperate case, the day of their prosperity being at an end, and the dark night of their distress approaching. *Note*, (1.) When God's day of visitation is come, the sinner can be no longer safe. (2.) If they are so eager to storm the city and seize the wealth of Jerusalem, shall we shew less zeal and earnestness to enter the kingdom of heaven and obtain the unsearchable riches of glory? (3.) Nothing encourages the heart so much as confidence of success. And thus it is, in our spiritual warfare, that faith enables us to overcome. *Possunt quia posse videntur.*

4. The cause of all these judgments is their sins. Jerusalem was become a sink of wickedness; it flowed incessantly and abundantly, as the waters of a fountain; and all ranks and degrees of men were tainted, and particularly the whole city was a scene of oppression, where, like fishes in the sea, the great preyed upon the little; *violence and spoil is heard* in every corner, *and grief and wound*, the blood and the cries of the oppressed, are continually before God, calling for vengeance. *Note*, There is a day when the wrongs of the oppressed will be examined and avenged.

5. A fair admonition is once more given, if they have yet ears to hear. *Be thou instructed, O Jerusalem*, attend to understand and obey the calls to repentance, *lest my soul depart from thee*, or *be violently plucked away* from thee, his favour utterly departing from them, and his love to them turned into abhorrence, *lest I make thee desolate, a land not inhabited*. *Note*, (1.) God is unwilling to give up the sinner, and therefore he is patient, and pleads with him, that, though late, he may return. (2.) When all his offers of mercy are obstinately rejected, at last God will depart, and leave the sinner to his ruin, and then wo, wo unto him.

CHAP. VI.

In this chapter, therefore, we have, (1.) A prophecy of the invading of the land of Judah, and the besieging of Jerusalem by the Chaldean army, ver. 1—6. with the spoils they should make of the country, ver. 9. and the terror which all should be seized with on that occasion, ver. 22—26. (2.) An account of those sins of Judah and Jerusalem, which provoked God to bring this desolating judgment upon them. Their oppression, ver. 7. Their contempt of the word of God, ver. 10—12. Their worldliness, ver. 13. The treachery of their prophets, ver. 14. Their impudence in sin, ver. 15. Their obstinacy against reproofs, ver. 16, 19. Which made their sacrifices unacceptable to him, ver. 20. and for which he gave them up to ruin, ver. 21. He tried them first, ver. 27. And then rejected them as irreclaimable, ver. 28—30. (3.) Good counsel given them in the midst of all this, but in vain, ver. 8, 16, 17.

a Josh. xv. 63. Chap. i. 6.
b Chap. iv. 6.
† Or dwelling at home.
‡ Or pour out the engine of shot.
d Psal. lv. 9. 10, 11. Chap. xx. 8. Ezek. vii. 11, 23.
§ Heb. Corrected.
e Ezek. xxiii. 18.
|| Heb. be loosed, or disjointed.

1 O Ye children of Benjamin, ^a^ gather yourselves to
flee out of the midst of Jerusalem, and blow
the trumpet in Tekoa, and set up a sign of fire in Beth-
haccerem: for ^b^ evil appeareth out of the north, and great
destruction. 2 I have likened the daughter of Zion to
a † comely and delicate *woman*. 3 The shepherds with
their flocks shall come unto her; they shall pitch *their*
tents against her round about; they shall feed every one
in his place. 4 Prepare ye war against her; arise, and
let us go up at noon. Wo unto us, for the day goeth
away, for the shadows of the evening are stretched out.
5 Arise, and let us go by night, and let us destroy her
palaces. 6 ¶ For thus hath the LORD of hosts said,
Hew ye down trees, and ‡ cast a mount against Jerusa-
lem: this *is* the city to be visited; she *is* wholly oppression
in the midst of her. 7 ^c^ As a fountain casteth out her
waters, so she casteth out her wickedness: ^d^ violence and
spoil is heard in her; before me continually *is* grief and
wounds. 8 Be thou § instructed, O Jerusalem, lest ^e^ my
soul || depart from thee; lest I make thee desolate, a land
not inhabited.

v. 1—8. We have here,

1. An alarm spread of the approaching foe coming from the north, and spreading destruction before him. The trumpet is blown in Tekoa, the beacon lighted in Beth-haccerem, a place between Tekoa and Jerusalem, as a signal for their flight, if they hoped to escape, Jerusalem being ready to be besieged, *v.* 1.

2. Their weakness, and the formidable power of their foes, is described. The daughter of Zion is as helpless, and unable to make resistance, as a *comely and delicate woman*. Some instead of *woman* read *pasture*, in correspondence with the following similitude, where their invaders are compared to shepherds with their flocks, who would pitch their tents there, and eat up the land as easily, and make it bare, as the Ox licks up the grass of the field. *Note*, To have been brought up delicately makes every hardship more acutely felt.

3. In pursuance of God's commission their enemies hasten to the attack. *Prepare ye war against her*, and press the siege, *hew ye down trees, and cast a mount against Jerusalem*, to batter the walls, and, as soon as the breach is practicable, give the assault.

f 2 Kings xxiv. 16. & xxv. 4. & Chap. xvi. 16.
g Chap. vi. 25. Acts vii. 51.
h 2 Tim. iv. 3.
i Chap. xx. 9.
k Ezek. ix. 6.
l Deut. xxviii. 30. Chap. viii. 10.
m Isa. lvi. 11. Chap. viii. 10. Mic. iii. 5, 11.
n Chap. viii. 11. Ezek. xiii. 10.
|| Heb. bruise, or breach.
o Chap. iii. 3. & viii. 12.
p Isa. viii. 20. Chap. xviii. 15. Mal. iv. 4. Luke xvi. 29.
q Matt. xi. 29.
r Isa. xxi. 11. Ezek. iii. 17. Hab. ii. 1.
s Chap. xxii. 21. & xliv. 16.

9 ¶ Thus saith the LORD of hosts, ^f^ They shall
throughly glean the remnant of Israel as a vine: turn
back thine hand as a grape-gatherer into the baskets.
10 To whom shall I speak, and give warning, that they
may hear? behold, ^g^ their ear *is* uncircumcised, and they
cannot hearken: behold the word of the LORD is unto
them a reproach; ^h^ they have no delight in it. 11
Therefore ^i^ I am full of the fury of the LORD; I am
weary with holding in: I will pour it out ^k^ upon the
children abroad, and upon the assembly of young men
together: for even the husband with the wife shall be
taken, the aged with *him that is* full of days. 12 And
^l^ their houses shall be turned unto others, *with their* fields
and wives together: for I will stretch out my hand upon
the inhabitants of the land, saith the LORD. 13 For
from the least of them, even unto the greatest of them,
every one *is* given ^m^ to covetousness; and from the pro-
phet even unto the priest, every one dealeth falsly. 14
They have ^n^ healed also the || hurt *of the daughter* of my
people slightly, saying, Peace, peace; when *there is* no
peace. 15 ^o^ Were they ashamed when they had com-
mitted abomination? nay, they were not at all ashamed,
neither could they blush: therefore they shall fall among
them that fall: at the time *that* I visit them, they shall
be cast down, saith the LORD. 16 Thus saith the
LORD, Stand ye in the ways, and see, and ask for ^p^ the
old paths, where *is* the good way, and walk therein,
and ^q^ ye shall find rest for your souls. But they said,
We will not walk *therein*. 17 Also ^r^ I set watchmen
over you, *saying*, Hearken to the sound of the trumpet.
But they said, ^s^ We will not hearken.

v. 9—17. Farther iniquities are here discovered, and farther judgment denounced.

1. Their transgressions were multiplied.

(1.) They were deaf to all the warnings of the prophet. *To whom shall I speak and give warning, that they may hear?* intimating the universal disregard paid to his message. *Their ear is uncircumcised.* At first they would not hearken, and now they are left to the hardness of their hearts, *and they cannot hearken*. Nay, they counted God's word, that rebuked their sins, *a reproach* to them, and treated it, and those who delivered it, with insult and contempt. *They have no delight in it*, but the very contrary, a loathing, and aversion to it. *Note*, (1.) The fidelity of God's ministers, in rebuking men's sins, is often construed into personal abuse. (2.) We are not to wonder that the word of the gospel is looked upon as a reproach; it was so from the

Before Christ 612

beginning (3.) They who have no delight in the Bible, have no name in the book of life

[2] They were ſlaves to the love of money High and low, rich and poor, prieſt and prophet, all were given to covetouſneſs, and cared not by what falſhoods or means they enriched themſelves, ſo they could but ſecure the mammon of unrighteouſneſs *Note*, Nothing more fatally hardens the heart againſt God's word, than this rooted attachment to gain

[3] The prophets and prieſts, who by profeſſion and office ſhould have endeavoured to ſtop the torrent of ungodlineſs, contributed to make the diſeaſe more deſperate and incurable by their lying viſions, falſe gloſſes, and ſmooth diſcourſes, ſuited to lull the ſinner's conſcience into a fatal ſecurity, *crying, Peace, peace, when there is no peace* *Note*, There is no ſurer mark of a falſe prophet than this, that he avoids thoſe alarming expreſſions of God's word, that are ſuited to ſtartle the ſinner, that he is ſollicitous to ſoften what are counted harſh ſayings that it is his ſtudy not to offend, and his labour to lull thoſe to their reſt, who may have been made uneaſy by more faithful advocates for the truth

[4] They were ſhameleſs in their abominations The preachers of lies refuſed to bluſh, when never ſo clearly detected in their falſe doctrines and flattering divinations, and the people, alike hardened, neither were aſhamed of their ſins, nor afraid of the threatned puniſhments, *v* 15 *Note*, Thoſe faces that would not bluſh at rebuke, ſhall ſoon be pale as aſhes, when the terrors of God ſhall ſeize them

[5] The kindeſt admonitions of God had no influence on them he would have gathered them, but they would not *Thus ſaith the Lord, Stand ye in the way and ſee*, conſider your path, and whither it will lead you, to heaven or to hell, *and aſk for the old paths*, conſult your Bibles, enquire the way wherein the holy patriarchs walked *Where is the good way, the good old way* of truth and holineſs, which was revealed in the firſt promiſe, and which all God's ſaints have trod from the beginning *and ye ſhall find reſt unto your ſouls*, from all your fears, *but they ſaid, We will not walk therein*, as if determined to ruſh on their deſtruction Every method had God taken to deter and divert them from ſo fatal a reſolution *I ſet watchmen over you*, faithful miniſters of the ſanctuary, *ſaying, Hearken to the ſound of the trumpet*, bidding the voice of peace and mercy, or ſpreading the tremendous alarm of the guilt and puniſhment of ſin *But they ſaid, We will not hearken* reſiſting every method God had taken to ſave them, and, faithleſs and fearleſs of his judgments, perſiſting in their impenitence *Note*, (1) The importance of that eternity which depends thereon, ſhould engage us to a frequent and ſerious conſideration of our ways, *what we are doing, and whither we are going* (2) The paths of life and truth are eaſily found of thoſe who are at pains to enquire after them (3) The good way to heaven is Chriſt, his righteouſneſs and grace, and he is *the old way*, for from the beginning the goſpel was preached, and the ſaints of old were ſaved, even as we (4) They who are found in this way will obtain reſt to their ſouls, peace with God, internal conſolation, and comfortable confidence of arriving ſafe at their journey's end in heaven (5) God's faithful miniſters muſt lead men in this way, and cry aloud to invite ſinners to walk in it (6) They who will not be perſuaded by God's word, muſt be left to their own deluſions, and miſerable, eternally miſerable, will be the end of thoſe men

2 The terrible puniſhment of the Jewiſh people is foretold Becauſe they are thus obſtinate and hardned, the prophet declares, *I am full of the fury of the Lord*, the revelation made to him of the wrath ready to be revealed, was ſo awful, that it filled his heart with terrible apprehenſions for them, *I am weary with holding it*, as if unwilling to be the meſſenger of evil, he had refrained, till like a fire within him, it forced a paſſage, and he was conſtrained to ſpeak And fearful indeed are the devaſtations threatned, *I will pour out my fury upon* the little *children* playing in the ſtreets, *upon the aſſemblies of young men* aſſociated for mirth and pleaſure, *huſband and wife ſhall be taken* captives, and the moſt decrepid with age find no reverence, or pity, *v* 11 Their houſes are given to their enemies, with their fields, and what is ſtill more bitter, their wives are proſtituted to their luſts upon the whole land the hand of God's vengeance is ſtretched out, *v* 12 Then lying prophets ſhall then meet their doom, and *fall among them that fall*, in ſpite of all their vain confidence, *at the time that I viſit them ſhall they be caſt down, ſaith the Lord*, *v* 15 Thus ſhall their enemies plunder and deſtroy them, and be ſollicitous to leave none to eſcape, *they ſhall thoroughly glean the remnant of Iſrael as a vine*, as the poor after the vintage picked off every berry which was left *Turn back thine hand as a grape-gatherer into the baſkets*, till all the ſpoil is collected, and every Iſraelite led captive, *v* 9 *Note*, It is the moſt unpleaſing part of our office to be the meſſengers of evil, but it is abſolutely neceſſary that by the terrors of the Lord we ſhould perſuade men and however tremendous the ſubject, they who hear ought not to be diſpleaſed with the ſervants who faithfully report what they have received of the Lord

18 ¶ Therefore hear, ye nations, and know, O con-
gregation, what is among them 19 Hear, O earth,
behold, I will bring evil upon this people, even [u] the
fruit of their thoughts, becauſe they have not heark-
ned unto my words, nor to my law, but rejected it
20 [x] To what purpoſe cometh there to me incenſe [y] from
Sheba [z] and the ſweet cane from a far country? your
burnt-offerings *are* not acceptable, nor your ſacrifices
ſweet unto me 21 Therefore thus ſaith the LORD,
Behold, I will lay ſtumbling-blocks before this people,
and [a] the fathers and the ſons together ſhall fall upon
them the neighbour and his friend ſhall periſh
22 Thus ſaith the LORD, Behold, a people cometh
[a] from the north country, and a great nation ſhall be
raiſed from the ſides of the earth 23 They ſhall lay
hold on bow and ſpear they *are* cruel, and have no
mercy their voice roareth like the ſea, and they ride
upon horſes, ſet in array as men for war againſt thee,
O daughter of Zion 24 We have heard the fame
thereof our hands wax feeble [b] anguiſh hath taken
hold of us, *and* pain, as of a woman in travail 25
Go not forth into the field, nor walk by the way, for
the ſword of the enemy, *and* fear *is* on every ſide 26
¶ O daughter of my people, [c] gird *thee* with ſackcloth
and [d] wallow thyſelf in aſhes [d] make thee mourning *as*
for an only ſon, moſt bitter lamentation for the ſpoiler
ſhall ſuddenly come upon us 27 I have ſet thee *for*
a tower, *and* [e] a fortreſs among my people, that thou
mayeſt know and try their way 28 They *are* all ‡ grie-
vous revolters, [f] walking with ſlanders [g] *they are* braſs
and iron, [h] they are all corrupters 29 [i] The bellows
are burnt, the lead is conſumed of the fire, the founder
melteth in vain, for [k] the wicked are not plucked away
30 § Reprobate ſilver ſhall *men* call them becauſe the
LORD hath rejected them

v 18—30 We have here,

1 God's appeal to the whole world for the equity of his procedure When tidings of *what* was done *among them*, judgments ſo terrible and ſtrange, were reported, it might aſtoniſh them that God ſhould thus deal with his once ſo favoured people, but the wonder will ceaſe when their provocations are known Their ſufferings are the neceſſary *fruit of their thoughts*, evil, and only evil, and that continually, and the conſequence of their wicked ways, as diſobedient againſt all the warnings of God's prophets, and rebellious againſt all the reſtraints of his law *Note*, If men will not be *ruled* by God's word, they will juſtly be *ruined* by his wrath

2 The vanity of their pretended ſervices Their incenſe and perfumes, their offerings and ſacrifices, however rich, expenſive, and numerous, when brought with an hypocritical heart, as a means of purchaſing God's favour, with the hopes of expiating unrepented ſins, or to obtain a licence to abide in them, ſo far were they from being pleaſing and acceptable, they were his deteſtation and abhorrence, *v* 20

3 The deſtruction God would bring upon them Stumbling-blocks ſhould be ſet in their ways, their falſe prophets permitted to delude them, or the Chaldeans, by whom they ſhould be daſhed in pieces, both *father and ſon*, for ſin as together muſt ſuffer together, the *neighbour and his friend* for thoſe who have walked in evil fellowſhip, will be involved in the ſame calamity, *v* 21 From the north, a far diſtant country, the mighty enemies come, *v* 22 armed with bow and ſpear, fierce and cruel, they ſhew no mercy, their voice terrible as the roaring of the ſea, their cavalry ſwift and ſtrong, advancing in battle array *againſt thee, O daughter of Zion*

4 Terrible conſternation will ſeize the Jewiſh people at their approach Frightened at the very report, like a woman with child, that falls into travailing pangs, anguiſh will ſeize them, their hearts fail them, and their hands be feeble and incapable of reſiſtance, *v* 24 In terror they ſhut themſelves up within their city, not daring to ſtir, to till the ſoil, or carry on their huſbandry, or attempt to travel, *for the ſword of the enemy*, or *becauſe the enemy hath a ſword* ready drawn to ſlay, and *fear is on every ſide*, no place being ſafe *Note*, (1) The ſinner's terrors will ſeize him ſuddenly and ſeverely, as the pains of a travailing woman (2) When God ſends his panic into the heart, the mighty are feeble, and the brave turn coward

5 The prophet calls them to lamentation and bitter mourning, to lie in ſackcloth and aſhes, as one under the moſt afflicting anguiſh for the loſs of an only ſon, and this either as a token of repentance for their ſin, or as expreſſive of their deſperate ſorrows under their ſudden deſolations, *v* 26 *Note*, How much wiſer is it to prevent the judgment by ſpeedy humiliation, than by impenitence provoke the ſcourge, when our anguiſh will come too late to profit us?

Before Christ 612

u Iſa iii 11 Prov i 31
x Pſ l 8 &c Iſa i 11 Amos v 21 Mic vi 6 &c
y Iſa lx 6
a 2 Chron xxxvi 17
a Chap i 15 & x 22
b Chap iv 31 & xiii 21
c Chap iv 8
d Chap xxv 34 Mic i 10
e Zech xii 10
e Chap i 18 & xv 20
‡ Heb Revolters of revolters
f Chap ix 4
g Ezek xxii 18
h Iſa i 4
i Chap vi 29
k Ezek xxii 18
§ Or refuſe ſilver

6 God

Before Christ 600

6 God appoints the prophet to inspect their ways, and a sad report he makes of them *I have set thee for a tower*, to observe them, or *a trier*, to examine them, *and for a fortress among my people*, that as safe in the divine protection he might not fear their threatnings *that thou mayest know and try their way*, which the more it was searched into, the more would God's judgments appear righteous And what is the consequence of this inquisition? *They are grievous revolters*, or *revolters of revolters*, the most contumacious and stubborn transgressors *walking with slanders*, playing the hypocrite with God, or incessantly backbiting one another *They are brass and iron*, base and vile as these metals, having brasen fronts that cannot blush, and hearts steeled that are impenetrably hardened *They are all corrupters*, as those who adulterate metals, so they corrupt the doctrines of truth, or, in Satan's stead, turn tempters to each other *The bellows are burnt*, either the judgments they suffered had no effect on them, or the true prophets, who prophesied till they were hoarse with crying, could avail nothing, or the false prophets, who flattered them, are now consumed with them *The lead is consumed in the fire*, which was used in refining silver, but here was in vain or, *out of the fire it is perfect lead*, such are the people, without any thing precious or valuable in them, notwithstanding the furnace of affliction they had gone through *The founder melteth in vain*, all the prophet's labours were fruitless, and God's dispensations without effect *for the wicked are not plucked away* from their former abominations, but persist in them *Reprobate silver shall men call them*, mere dross, for *the Lord hath rejected them* from being his people, and given them up for a prey to their enemies *Note*, God tries every method with sinners, by calls of grace, and corrections of providence, and if, after all, they continue reprobate silver, their eternal ruin will lie at their own door

CHAP. VII

The prophet having in God's name reproved the people for their sins, and given them warning of the judgments of God that were coming upon them, in this chapter prosecutes the same intention for their humiliation and awakening 1 He shews them the vanity of trusting on their privileges and performances, ver 1—15 2 He minds them of the desolations of Shiloh, and foretels that such should be the desolations of Jerusalem, ver 12—16 3 God represents to the prophet their abominable idolatries, for which he was thus incensed against them, ver 17—20 4 He assures the people, that to obey is better than sacrifice, and that God would not accept the sacrifices of those that obstinately persisted in disobedience, ver 21—28 5 He threatens to lay the land utterly waste for their idolatry and impiety, and to multiply their slain as they had multiplied their sins, ver 29—34

1 THE word that came to Jeremiah from the
LORD, saying, 2 Stand in the gate of the
LORD's house, and proclaim there this word, and say,
Hear the word of the LORD, all *ye of* Judah that enter
in at these gates to worship the LORD 3 Thus saith
the LORD of hosts the God of Israel, Amend your
ways and your doings, and I will cause you to dwell in
this place 4 Trust ye not in lying words, saying,
The temple of the LORD, the temple of the LORD,
the temple of the LORD *are* these 5 For if ye
throughly amend your ways, and your doings, if ye
throughly execute judgment between a man and his
neighbour, 6 *If* ye oppress not the stranger, the fa-
therless, and the widow, and shed not innocent blood
in this place, neither walk after other gods to your hurt
7 Then will I cause you to dwell in this place, in the
land that I gave to your fathers for ever and ever 8
¶ Behold, ye trust in lying words that cannot profit
9 Will ye steal, murder, and commit adultery, and
swear falsely, and burn incense unto Baal, and walk af-
ter other gods whom ye know not, 10 And come and
stand before me in this house, which is called by my
name, and say, We are delivered to do all these abomi-
nations? 11 Is this house, which is called by my
name, become a den of robbers in your eyes? Behold,
even I have seen *it*, saith the LORD 12 But go ye
now unto my place, which *was* in Shiloh, where I set
my name at the first, and see what I did to it for the
wickedness of my people Israel 13 And now, because
ye have done all these works, saith the LORD, and I
spake unto you, rising up early and speaking, but ye
heard not, and I called you, but ye answered not
14 Therefore will I do unto *this* house which is called
by my name, wherein ye trust, and unto the place which
I gave to you, and to your fathers, as I have done to
Shiloh 15 And I will cast you out of my sight, as I
have cast out all your brethren, *even* the whole seed of
Ephraim

v 1—15 This chapter begins a new sermon and prophecy, designed, as the former, to lead the people to repentance

1 Directions are given what to speak, and where to deliver his message He must proclaim the word of the Lord, without adding thereto, or diminishing therefrom, and stand in the gate of the house of the Lord, the most frequented place, where those who came up to worship might hear, and probably was then one of the three great festivals, when the concourse was greatest *Note*, (1) A large auditory is desirable, where the words of truth are dispensed (2) We must not be afraid of being censured for extravagant zeal when in general the ministers of the sanctuary are careless, we cannot be faithful without being singular

2 The general contents of his discourse are, an exhortation to a repentance, with a gracious promise annexed *Thus saith the Lord of hosts*, at whose command and by whose authority he speaks, *the God of Israel* whom they, as his covenant people, are bound to obey, *Amend your ways, and your doings*, make a thorough change in them, for they are at present utterly perverse, *and I will cause you to dwell in this place*, to enjoy their land, and the temple service, and not remove into captivity, as would infallibly be the case if they continued impenitent

3 He specifies the particulars, which immediately, heartily, and thoroughly, must be amended, and they are summed up in two points, as being their grand evils, oppression and idolatry They must be just, their magistrates impartial, no allowed dishonesty permitted in their dealings, the fatherless and widows must not be injured, nor innocent blood any more defile the land, and all false gods must be utterly rejected and abhorred then God will make their abode in the good land given their fathers both safe and lasting, *v* 6, 7 *Note*, God only saith to the sinner, Do thyself no harm all that he requires of us is purely for our own good and happiness

4 He rebukes their vain confidence, and urges them no longer to trust in their formal duties and external privileges The false prophets magnified the outward service of the temple, as if in this all godliness consisted, and they readily embraced a religion that rested in mere externals of worship, and required no inward mortification of sin *The temple of the Lord* was ever in their mouths, their boast and confidence, and whilst thrice a year they attended there, they thought they fully satisfied their duty But alas! these were *lying words*, a delusive hope, that *could not profit* them, whilst they looked no further than the ritual service, and exercised no faith in Christ, which alone gave it any efficacy, and especially whilst all their sins continued unrepented of, and indulged *Will ye steal?* or, *ye do steal* He expostulates on their absurdity, and charges them with abomination They continued in murder, theft, perjury, adultery, idolatry, and yet dared appear before God in the temple, as if their sacrifices could atone for their crimes, and impudently affected still to pass for true servants and worshippers of God, saying in their words, or, which spoke as loud, in their actions, *we are delivered to do all these abominations*, either they thought themselves at liberty to sin, after they had appeared at the temple with their sacrifices, or, that having been delivered so long, they might go on still with impunity in their iniquities This with deepest indignation God beholds, and upbraids them with *Is this house, that is called by my name, become a den of robbers in your eyes?* as robbers take refuge in their den, so did they in the temple, thinking to cover their enormities with the cloak of ceremonies and sacrifices, but vain before God were these wretched coverings *Behold, I have seen it, saith the Lord*, their hypocrisy great as their impiety *Note*, (1) Many pride themselves in a *form of godliness*, who are strangers to the *power* of it, and whilst they boast of the *church*, and their attendance thrice in a year at the Lord's table, are in fact the farthest from the kingdom of God (2) To plead the sacrifice of Christ for sin, as a licence to continue in it, is the most detestable abuse of gospel grace (3) Few dare avow what notwithstanding their conduct evidently declares (4) The guise of godliness may pass upon men, but no hypocrisy can be concealed from the heart-searching God

5 He sets before them, for their admonition, and to shew the vanity of their hopes, the destruction of Israel, notwithstanding the tabernacle once pitched in Shiloh He bids them go thither, and read on the ruins of that once famed abode of God's ark, the insufficiency of that protection, when the wickedness of the worshippers, and of the priests, provoked God to wrath against them, *Josh* xviii 1 1 *Sam* iv 4—11 *Ps* lxxviii 60—67 and such would be their doom, since such had been their sins, *v* 13—15 With like abominations they had offended God, and equally deaf to the repeated admonitions of God's prophets had they been, *v* 13 therefore the temple and city of Jerusalem shall become as Shiloh, a desolation, *v* 14 and God will cast off the whole people of Judah, as he had already done by their brethren of Israel, who were gone long since into captivity, *v* 15 *Note*, (1) God's judgments on others are warnings to us

Before Christ 600.

us to avoid their ways, if we would escape their punishment (2) They who follow sinners examples will surely suffer with them (3) They who are cast off from God are truly miserable, and must, as the necessary consequence, be shortly cast down into hell

p Ex xxxii 10 Chap xi 14 & xiv 11 | q Chap xv 1 | r Chap. xliv 17, 19 | † Or, frame or workmanship of heaven | s 1 Cor x 22 | t Zeph i 3 | u Chap iv 4

16 Therefore p pray not thou for this people, neither lift up cry nor prayer for them, neither make intercession to me, for q I will not hear thee 17 ¶ Seest thou not what they do in the cities of Judah, and in the streets of Jerusalem? 18 r The children gather wood, and the fathers kindle the fire, and the women knead *their* dough to make cakes to the † queen of heaven, and to pour out drink-offerings unto other gods, that they may provoke me to anger 19 s Do they provoke me to anger? saith the LORD *do they* not *provoke* themselves to the confusion of their own faces? 20 Therefore thus saith the Lord GOD, Behold, mine anger and my fury shall be poured out upon this place, t upon man and upon beast, and upon the trees of the field, and upon the fruit of the ground, and u it shall burn, and shall not be quenched

v 16—20 Their own prayers and sacrifices, were so hypocritical and abominable, no good could be expected from them, but the prophet still continued their advocate, and his prayers were usually availing, but God will cut off from them every resource

1 He is forbid to pray for them Much as the prophet had their salvation at heart, God's decree is fixed, prayer cometh too late, *their ruin is determined*, v 16 *Note*, (1) They who preach to sinners must pray for them, yea, though they revile and persecute (2) In a desperate state is that people, concerning whom God refuses to be intreated, and shuts up the mouths of his prophets

2 God assigns the reason for his prohibition, their impudent iniquities, and incorrigible obstinacy Openly in the cities of Judah, yea, in the very streets of Jerusalem, under the prophet's eye, unawed by his presence, unaffected with his warnings, they performed their idolatrous rites, offering incense and drink-offerings to the queen of heaven, the moon, considered as a goddess, and to their other idols, and in the work all age and sexes joined, so universal was the corruption spread The very children gathered the wood, whilst their fathers kindled the fire, and the women kneaded the cakes, *to provoke* God *to anger*, v 17, 18 See how carefully idolaters initiated betimes their children in the service of their idol, shall we be less sollicitous to instruct ours in the knowledge of the living God? Could they so freely part with their bread and wine in these detestable rites, and shall not we more liberally in God's service break our bread to the hungry, and open our bottle to the thirsty?

3 He threatens them with the dire consequences of their conduct *Do they provoke me to anger?* No such perturbation, as we feel, enters [illegible] into the eternal mind Or doth he receive any damage by their wickedness? No as their goodness could not add to his self-sufficient bliss and happiness, neither can their wickedness take from it The hurt they do is only to themselves, bringing upon their own heads swift destruction *Therefore thus saith the Lord God, Behold, mine anger and my fury shall be poured out upon this place*, a deluge of wrath such as swept away the world of the ungodly, or which fell upon devoted Sodom The temple and city shall be utterly destroyed both man and beast be consumed, and the very trees and fruits of the ground devoured by the fire of divine wrath It shall burn with irresistible fury, *and shall not be quenched* And herein we have an awful representation of the punishment of all the wicked in hell, *who depart accursed into everlasting fire*

21 ¶ Thus saith the LORD of hosts the God of Israel, Put your burnt-offerings unto your sacrifices, and eat flesh 22 For I spake not unto your fathers, nor commanded them in the day that I brought them out of the land of Egypt, concerning burnt-offerings or sacrifices 23 But this thing commanded I them, saying Obey my voice, and I will be your God, and ye shall be my people and walk ye in all the ways that I have commanded you, that it may be well unto you 24 But they hearkened not, nor inclined their ear, but walked in the counsels *and* in the ‖ imagination of their evil heart, and went backward, and not forward 25 Since the day that your fathers came forth out of the land of Egypt unto this day, I have even sent unto you all my servants the prophets, daily rising up early, and sending *them* 26 Yet they hearkened not unto me, nor inclined their ear, but hardened their neck, they did worse than their fathers 27 Therefore thou shalt speak all these words unto them, but they will not hearken to thee thou shalt also call unto them, but they will not answer thee 28. But thou shalt say unto them, This *is* a nation, that obeyeth not the voice of the LORD their God, nor receiveth ‡ correction truth is perished, and is cut off from their mouth

Before Christ 600 | Ezek. ii 7 | ‡ Or instruction. Chap v 3

v 21—28 As they placed so much dependance on their sacrifices to procure their acceptance with God, God will have them know these are insignificant and vain, whilst they mistook their end, and perverted their institution *Put your burnt-offerings unto your sacrifices, and eat flesh*, either give over such vain oblations, and use them rather at your own tables, or add never so many or expensive offerings, and pretend never so religiously, to offer them before the Lord, they are utterly unacceptable, whilst the love and power of sin remains unsubdued in your hearts For,

1 Obedience, not sacrifice, is the great thing God requires The ten commandments were first delivered to their fathers in the wilderness, and though sacrifices were afterwards instituted, it was not for their own sake, but in order to lead them by faith to the great Antitype, whose atonement was therein represented, exclusive of which, they were utterly useless and unacceptable The principal part therefore of the Sinai covenant was, *Obey my voice*, and to this the promise was annexed, *I will be your God, and ye shall be my people* protecting them from their enemies, and preserving them in the possession of the promised land, and as long as they thus carefully walked in all God's ways, so long it should be well with them, and prosperity continually attend them

2 Disobedience to the moral law is their great offence, and this had been their case from their very coming out of Egypt to this day Their fathers and they had together rejected God's law, to walk after *the imaginations of their own evil hearts*; and, instead of advancing in the ways of holiness and happiness, turned back into the paths of sin and misery, v 24 and this in opposition to long and repeated warnings, brought them from those divinely-appointed ministers, whom God from time to time raised up to admonish them of the evil and danger of their ways, v 25 Instead of amending, every generation grew worse, and more hardened, till the measure of their iniquities now rose to the brim, v 26 Therefore the prophet is commanded to *speak all these words unto them*, those charges of their rebellion and obstinacy, and those warnings of their impending ruin Not that these would have any effect, God foretels him they would not hearken, nor answer to his calls *but*, to leave them inexcusable in their wickedness, *thou shalt say unto them*, *This is a nation that obeyeth not the voice of the Lord their God*, which relation aggravated their disobedience *nor receiveth correction*, they will not be taught by the word, nor reclaimed by the rod *truth is perished, and is cut off from their mouth*, they are false and faithless to God and man, and nothing but lies, insincerity, and hypocrisy, is to be found amongst them, and therefore nothing but ruin to be expected *Note*, We may not cease to admonish sinners, though we see no prospect of reclaiming them, we must speak, if but for a testimony against them

29 ¶ k Cut off thine hair, O *Jerusalem*, and cast *it* away, and take up a lamentation on high places, for the LORD hath rejected and forsaken the generation of his wrath 30 For the children of Judah have done evil in my sight, saith the LORD l they have set their abominations in the house which is called by my name, to pollute it 31 And they have built m the high places of Tophet, which *is* in the valley of the son of Hinnom, to burn their sons and their daughters in the fire, n which I commanded them not, neither came it † into my heart 32 ¶ Therefore behold, the days come, saith the LORD, that it shall no more be called Tophet, nor the valley of the son of Hinnom, but the valley of slaughter for they shall bury in Tophet, till there be no place 33 And p the carcases of this people shall be meat for the fowls of the heaven, and for the beasts of the earth, and none shall fray *them* away 34 Then q will I cause to cease from the cities of Judah, and from the streets of Jerusalem, the voice of mirth, and the voice of gladness, the voice of the bridegroom, and the voice of the bride for the land shall be desolate

k Job i 20 Isa xv 2 Chap xvi 6. Mic i 16 | l 2 Kings xxi 4 2 Chron xxxiii 5 Ezek vii 20 & viii 5 6 | m 2 Kings xxiii 10 Chap xix 6 | n Lev xviii 21 & xx 2 | † Heb Upon | o Chap xix 6 | p Deut xxviii 26 Ps lxxix 2 Chap. xvi 4 & xxxiv 20 | q Isa xxiv 7, 8 Chap xvi 9 & xxv 10 & xxxiii 11 Ezek xxvi 13 Hos ii 11 Rev xviii 23

v 29—34 Jerusalem, in the prospect of her approaching desolations, is called upon to cut off her hair, in token of deepest mourning, *Job* i 20 and on the high places, the scene of her abominations, to lift up an exceeding bitter cry, as rejected of God, devoted to wrath, and given up into the hands of her cruel enemies

1 Her

Before Christ 600

1 Her sin is exceeding sinful. *They have done evil in my sight, saith the Lord*, continued in a course of open and daring impiety, particularly their abominable idolatries provoked him, which to such an enormous height they had carried, that in God's own house they had dared to set up their images, and rear their altars, as if they designed on purpose to defile that holy place; and their sacrifices were as horrid and inhuman, as their deities were detestable. They *built the high places of Tophet*, where Moloch's hated image stood, and, deaf to the cries of nature, and the shrieks of murdered infants, their parents, lost to every feeling of natural affection, burnt their children in the fire. It is said, this was performed by heating the brazen idol red hot, and then the parent laid the child on his arms, whilst the priests beat drums to drown the horrid shrieks and cries: sacrifices which God never commanded, and such as he never thought of enjoining his worshippers. *Note*, When sin hath hardened the heart, it is amazing to what a pitch of barbarity and inhumanity men may go.

2 The vengeance denounced for this is exceeding terrible. Tophet, the scene of these abominations, shall shortly change its name for *the valley of slaughter*, or *of the slain*; for there shall multitudes fall by the sword, or be carried thither to be buried, in multitudes so great, that graves shall be wanting for them, v. 32. and the unburied corpses lie for meat to the fowls of heaven, and beasts of the earth, and not a man be left to fray them away, v. 33. Deserted now are the streets of Jerusalem; no voice of joy is heard, no congratulations of the bride or bridegroom; but either the sound of mournful lamentations, or the land so desolate, that none are left to weep, and more melancholy silence reigns. *Note*, God will soon change sinful mirth into everlasting mourning: we need rejoice with trembling.

CHAP. VIII.

The prophet proceeds in his chapter both to warn and to justify the displeasure of God against his people. 1. He represents the judgments coming so very terrible, that death, though dreadful, should be desired, ver. 1—3. 2. He aggravates the perfidy and wilfulness of the people, as what brought this ruin upon them, ver. 4—12. 3. He describes the great confusion and consternation that the whole land should be in upon the alarm of it, ver. 13—17. 4. The prophet is himself deeply affected with it, ver. 18—22.

1 AT that time, saith the LORD, they [a] shall bring out the bones of the kings of Judah, and the bones of his princes, and the bones of the priests, and the bones of the prophets, and the bones of the inhabitants of Jerusalem out of their graves: 2 And they shall spread them before the sun, and the moon, and all the host of heaven whom they have loved, and whom they have served, and after whom they have walked, and whom they have sought, and [b] whom they have worshipped: they shall not be gathered, nor be buried, [c] they shall be for dung upon the face of the earth. 3 And [d] death shall be chosen rather than life, by all the residue of them that remain of this evil family, which remain in all the places whither I have driven them, saith the LORD of hosts.

a Bar. ii. 24.

b 2 Kings xxiii. 5. 2 Chron. ...

c Chap. ix. 22.

d Rev. ix. 6.

v. 1—3. In the dreadful desolation here described, the [illegible] corpse [illegible] spoiled, [illegible] the [illegible] sufer not the dead to enjoy quiet repose.

1 The graves and sepulchres of Judah's kings and princes shall be opened, either through covetousness to search for treasures, or to shew insult even to the dead; or as a just judgment of God, [illegible] the bones of the kings, priests, prophets, and people, who had so rebelled against him, to be exposed with infamy before those luminaries of heaven whom they had *worshipped*, *loved*, *served*, and *sought*; they had walked in the most abominable idolatries, and kept them for their gods, and their favour was to be desired, and their blessing to be obtained for health and prosperity; ... now it appeared so, when they could not afford the least help, nor so much as cover their scattered bones, spread *for dung upon the face of the earth*, v. 1, 2. *Note*, In the day of judgment the sinner's [illegible] will be made [illegible] exposed, Isa. lxvi. 24.

Death, the most dreaded of human evils, now shall be courted, not that it [illegible] lost ought of its terror, but because life is become intolerable, not from a hope of happiness in the exchange, but from despair of [illegible] below. The survivors of *this evil family*, torn to so small a number will they be reduced, shall be so harassed and tormented in every place whither they are driven, that they shall look with envy on those who have perished by famine and the sword, and count their lot more eligible than their own, v. 3. *Note*, That cale is terrible indeed, when life becomes a burden, and the sinner is tempted to prefer strangling and death.

4 ¶ Moreover, thou shalt say unto them, Thus saith
the LORD, Shall they fall, and not arise? shall he
turn away, and not return? 5 Why *then* is this peo-
ple of Jerusalem slidden back, [e] by a perpetual back-
sliding? [f] they hold fast deceit, they refuse to return.
6 I hearkened and heard, *but* they spake not aright: no
man repented him of his wickedness, saying, What have
I done? every one turned to his course, as the horse
rusheth into the battle. 7 Yea, [g] the stork in the hea-
ven knoweth her appointed times, and the turtle, and
the crane, and the swallow observe the time of their
coming; but my people [h] know not the judgment of the
LORD. 8 How do ye say, We *are* wise, and [i] the
law of the LORD *is* with us? Lo, certainly [‖] in vain
made he *it*; the pen of the scribes *is* in vain. 9 [†] The
wise *men* are ashamed, they are dismayed and taken:
Lo, they have rejected the word of the LORD, and
[k] what wisdom *is* in them? 10 Therefore [l] will I give
their wives unto others, [m] *and* their fields to them that
shall inherit *them*: for [n] every one from the least even
unto the greatest is given to covetousness, from the pro-
phet even unto the priest every one dealeth falsly. 11.
For [o] they have healed the hurt of the daughter of my
people slightly, saying, [p] Peace, peace; when *there is* no
peace. 12 [q] Were they ashamed when they had com-
mitted abomination? nay, they were not at all ashamed,
neither could they blush: therefore shall they fall among
them that fall; in the time of their visitation they shall
be cast down, saith the LORD.

e Chap. vii. 24.

f Chap. ix. 6.

g Isa. i. 3.

h Chap. v. 4, 5. Luke xix. 42.

i Rom. ii. 17.

‖ Or, the false pen of the scribes worketh for falshood. Isa. x. 1.

† Or, Have they been ashamed, &c.

k Chap. vi. 15.

l Isa. viii. ...

m Deut. xxviii. 30. Chap. vi. 12.

n Am. v. 11. Zeph. i. 13.

o Isa. lvi. 11. Chap. vi. 13.

p Chap. vi. 14.

q Ezek. xiii. 10. Chap. iii. 3. & vi. 15.

v. 4—12. Never was people so infatuated to their ruin.

1 They persevered in their evil ways. In general, when a man falls, he feels immediately to recover himself, and if he lose his way, he is solicitous to return into the right path, v. 4. *Why then is this people of Jerusalem slidden back by a perpetual backsliding?* and instead of any desire to amend, *they hold fast deceit*, obstinate against every means of conviction, they refuse to return. *Note*, (1) They who backslide from God, wander endlessly and perpetually, unless his grace plucks them from ruin. (2) Nothing is so great a deceit as sin; it promises so much enjoyment and ever produces so much misery.

2 They disappointed God's expectations from them. He patiently waited and hearkened, if so be they might at last be prevailed upon to change their note, and learn the language of penitence: but not one *spake aright*, *nor repented of his wickedness*, reflecting with shame upon his conduct: but just the very reverse, they urged on their mad career in sin with such determined wayward obstinacy and self-will, *as the horse rusheth into the battle*. *Note*, (1) God is long-suffering to us-ward, not willing that any should perish, but that all should come unto repentance. (2) The first step to real penitence is serious reflection upon the evil of our past ways, *What have I done?* (3) The daring sinner that mocks at the terrors of the Lord, is chimerical, and headlong rushes into the depths of iniquity, will find them fearful realities, and that half was not told him.

3 They were more stupid and irrational than the fowls of heaven, whilst they made the highest pretensions to wisdom, v. 7—9. The birds of passage by instinct know the proper season for their coming and going, and how to direct their flight; but *my people know not the judgment of the Lord*; neither how to improve the calls of mercy in God's word, nor the corrections of affliction, nor his visitation on others; and yet they say, *We are wise, and the law of the Lord is with us*. How shameless their pretensions! when their whole conduct appeared so contradictory. In vain had they the law, and the pen of the scribes to write out copies or comments upon it, their exposition were false, or if right they paid no regard to them, it true. Then wise men themselves are confounded and dismayed: they could neither foresee nor avert: nor can it be wondered, when, *lo! they have rejected the word of the Lord*, sent by his prophets, and *what wisdom is in them*, when they reject the counsel of God, and refuse to be instructed? *Note*, (1) Many enjoy plenty of means, have Bibles and ministers, and yet are never the wiser for them. (2) Whatever pretences to wisdom they may make, who reject God's revealed word, they will be confounded in the day of judgment at their own egregious folly.

4 For their sins they shall suffer. Their sins are before charged on them, *chap.* vi. 13, 15. *Love of filthy lucre*, most scandalous in those who are to preach, and be examples to others of deadness to the world. *Infidelity*, their profession were false, and their doctrine diabolical, tending to lull the sinner to sleep into fatal security, instead of rousing him to a sense of his danger; and *hardened effrontery*, that knew not to blush, though convicted of their lies, and upbraided for their abomi-

Before Christ 600

us to avoid their ways, if we would escape their punishment (2.) They who follow sinners examples will surely suffer with them (3.) They who are cast off from God are truly miserable, and must, as the necessary consequence, be shortly cast down into hell

p Ex xxxii 10 Chap xi 14 & xiv 11 | Chap xv 1. r Chap xliv 17 19. † Or, frame, or work-manship of heaven. s 1 Cor x 22. Zeph i 3. u Chap iv 4.

16 Therefore ᵖ pray not thou for this people, neither lift up cry nor prayer for them, neither make intercession to me, for ᵠ I will not hear thee 17 ¶ Seest thou not what they do in the cities of Judah, and in the streets of Jerusalem? 18 ʳ The children gather wood, and the fathers kindle the fire, and the women knead *their* dough to make cakes to the † queen of heaven, and to pour out drink-offerings unto other gods, that they may provoke me to anger 19 ˢ Do they provoke me to anger? saith the LORD *do they* not *provoke* themselves to the confusion of their own faces? 20 Therefore thus saith the Lord GOD, Behold, mine anger, and my fury shall be poured out upon this place, ᵗ upon man and upon beast, and upon the trees of the field, and upon the fruit of the ground, and ᵘ it shall burn, and shall not be quenched

v 16—20 Their own prayers and services, were so hypocritical and abominable, no good could be expected from them, but the prophet still continued their advocate, and his prayers were usually availing, but God will cut off from them every resource

1 He is forbid to pray for them Much as the prophet had their salvation at heart, God's decree is fixed, prayer comes too late, their ruin is determined, v 16 *Note*, (1.) They who preach to sinners must pray for them, yea, though they revile and persecute (2.) In a desperate state is that people, concerning whom God refuses to be intreated, and shuts up the mouths of his prophets

2 God assigns the reason for his prohibition, their impudent iniquities, and incorrigible obstinacy Openly in the cities of Judah, yea, in the very streets of Jerusalem, under the prophet's eye, unawed by his presence, and unaffected with his warnings, they performed their idolatrous rites, offering their cakes and drink-offerings to the queen of heaven, the moon, consecrated for a goddess, and to their other idols, and in the work all ages and sexes joined, so universal was the corruption spread The very children gathered the wood, whilst their fathers kindled the fire, and the women kneaded the cakes, *to provoke* God *to anger*, v 17, 18 See how carefully idolaters initiated betimes their children in the service of their idols, shall we be less solicitous to instruct ours in the knowledge of the living God? Could they so freely part with their bread and wine in these detestable rites, and shall not we more liberally in God's service break our bread to the hungry, and open our bottle to the thirsty?

3 He threatens them with the dire consequences of this conduct *Do they provoke me to anger?* No such perturbation, as we feel, enters into the eternal mind Or doth he receive any damage by their wickedness? No as their goodness could not add to his full felicity and happiness, neither can their wickedness take from it The hurt they do is only to themselves, bringing upon their own heads swift destruction *Therefore thus saith the Lord God, Behold, mine anger and my fury shall be poured out upon this place*, a deluge of wrath such as swept away the world of the ungodly, or which fell upon devoted Sodom The temple and city shall be utterly destroyed, both man and beast be consumed, and the very trees and fruit of the ground devoured by the fire of divine wrath It shall burn with inextinguishable fury, *and shall not be quenched* And herein we have an awful representation of the punishment of all the wicked in hell, *who depart accursed into everlasting fire*

21 ¶ Thus saith the LORD of hosts the God of Israel, ˣ Put your burnt-offerings unto your sacrifices, and eat flesh 22 ʸ For I spake not unto your fathers, nor commanded them in the day that I brought them out of the land of Egypt, concerning burnt offerings or sacrifices 23 But this thing commanded I them, saying, Obey my voice, and ᶻ I will be your God, and ye shall be my people and ᵃ walk ye in all the ways that I have commanded you, that it may be well unto you 24 But they hearkened not, nor inclined their ear, but walked in the counsels *and* in the ‖ imagination of their evil heart, and ᵇ went backward, and not forward 25 Since the day that your fathers came forth out of the land of Egypt unto this day, I have even sent unto you all my servants the prophets, daily rising up early, and sending *them* 26 ᶜ Yet they hearkened not unto me, nor inclined their ear, but ᵈ hardened their neck, they did worse than their fathers. 27 Therefore ᵉ thou shalt speak all these words unto them, but they will not hearken to thee thou shalt also call unto them, but they will not answer thee 28 But thou shalt say unto them, This *is* a nation, that obeyeth not the voice of the LORD their God, nor receiveth ‡ correction truth is perished, and is cut off from their mouth

e Ezek ii 7. ‡ Or, instruction. Chap vi 8.

v 21—28 As they placed so much dependance on their sacrifices to procure their acceptance with God, God will have them know that they are insignificant and vain, whilst they mistook their end, and perverted their institution *Put your burnt-offerings unto your sacrifices, and eat flesh*, either give over such vain oblations, and use them rather at your own tables, or add never so many or expensive offerings, and pretend never so religiously to eat them before the Lord, they are utterly unacceptable, whilst the love and power of sin remains unsubdued in your hearts For,

1 Obedience, not sacrifice, is the great thing God requires The ten commandments were first delivered to their fathers in the wilderness, and though sacrifices were afterwards instituted, it was not for their own sake, but in order to lead them by faith to the great Antitype, whose atonement was therein represented, exclusive of which, they were utterly useless and unacceptable The principal part therefore of the Sinai covenant was, *Obey my voice*, and to this the promise was annexed, *I will be your God, and ye shall be my people*, protecting them from their enemies, and preserving them in the possession of the promised land, and as long as they thus carefully walked in all God's ways, so long it should be well with them, and prosperity continually attend them

2 Disobedience to the moral law is their great offence, and this has been their case from their very coming out of Egypt to this day Their fathers and they had together rejected God's law, to walk after *the imaginations of their own evil hearts*, and, instead of advancing in the ways of holiness and happiness, turned back into the paths of sin and misery, v 24 and this in opposition to long and repeated warnings, brought them from those divinely-appointed ministers, whom God from time to time raised up to admonish them of the evil and danger of their ways, v 25 Instead of amending, every generation grew worse, and more hardened, till the measure of their iniquities now rose to the brim, v 26 Therefore the prophet is commanded to *speak all these words unto them*, those charges of their rebellion and obstinacy, and those warnings of their impending ruin Not that these would have any effect God foretels him they would not hearken, nor answer to his calls *but*, to leave them inexcusable in their wickedness, *then shalt say unto them, This is a nation that obeyeth not the voice of the Lord their God*, which is an aggravated their disobedience, *nor receiveth correction*, they will not be taught by the word, nor reclaimed by the rod *truth is perished, and is cut off from their mouth*, they are false and faithless to God and man, and nothing but lies, insincerity, and hypocrisy, is to be found amongst them, and therefore nothing but ruin to be expected *Note*, We may not cease to admonish sinners, though we see no prospect of reclaiming them, we must speak, if but for a testimony against them

k Job i 20. Isa xv 2. Chap xvi 6. Mic i 16. l 2 Kings xxi 4. 2 Chron xxxiii 5. Ezek vii 20 & viii 5, 6. m 2 Kings xxiii 10. Chap xix 5. n Lev xviii 21 & xx 2. ‖ Heb up on. o Chap xix 6. p Deut xxviii 26. q Isa i 1. Chap xvi 9 & xxxiii 11. r Isa xxiv 7, 8. Chap xvi 9 & xxv 10. & xxxiii 11. Ezek xxvi 13. Hos ii 11. Rev xviii 23.

29 ¶ ᵏ Cut off thine hair, O *Jerusalem*, and cast *it* away, and take up a lamentation on high places, for the LORD hath rejected and forsaken the generation of his wrath 30 For the children of Judah have done evil in my sight, saith the LORD ˡ they have set their abominations in the house which is called by my name, to pollute it 31 And they have built ᵐ the high places of Tophet, which *is* in the valley of the son of Hinnom, to burn their sons and their daughters in the fire, ⁿ which I commanded them not, neither came it ‖ into my heart 32 ¶ Therefore behold, ᵒ the days come, saith the LORD, that it shall no more be called Tophet, nor the valley of the *son of Hinnom*, but the valley of slaughter for they shall bury in Tophet, till there be no place. 33 And ᵖ the carcases of this people shall be meat for the fowls of the heaven, and for the beasts of the earth, and none shall fray *them* away 34 Then ᵠ will I cause to cease from the cities of Judah, and from the streets of Jerusalem, the voice of mirth, and the voice of gladness, the voice of the bridegroom, and the voice of the bride for the land shall be desolate

v 29—34 Jerusalem, in the prospect of her approaching desolations, is called upon to cut off her hair, in token of deepest mourning, *Job* i 20 and on the high places, the scene of her abominations, to lift up an exceeding bitter cry, is rejected of God, devoted to wrath, and given up into the hands of her cruel enemies

I Her

Before Christ 600.

1 Her sin is exceeding sinful. They *have done evil in my sight, saith the Lord*, continued in a course of open and daring impiety: particularly their abominable idolatries provoked him, which to such an enormous height they had carried, that in *God's own house* they had dared to set up their images, and rear their altars, as if they designed on purpose to defile that holy place; and their sacrifices were as horrid and inhuman, as their deities were detestable. They *built the high places of Tophet*, where Moloch's hated image stood; and, deaf to the cries of nature, and the shrieks of murdered infants, there parents, lost to every feeling of natural affection, burnt their children in the fire. It is said, this was performed by heating the brazen idol red hot, and then the parent laid the child on his arms, whilst the priests beat drums to drown the horrid shrieks and cries: sacrifices which God never commanded, and such as he never thought of enjoining his worshippers. *Note*, When sin hath hardened the heart, it is amazing to what a pitch of barbarity and inhumanity men may go.

2 The vengeance denounced for this is exceeding terrible. Tophet, the scene of these abominations, shall shortly change its name for *the valley of slaughter*, or *of the slain*: for there shall multitudes fall by the sword, or be carried thither to be buried, multitudes so great, that graves shall be wanting for them, *v.* 32. and the unburied corpses lie for meat to the fowls of heaven, and beasts of the earth, and not a man be left to fray them away, *v.* 33. Deserted now are the streets of Jerusalem, no voice of joy is heard, no congratulations of the bride or bridegroom, but either the sound of mournful lamentations, or the land so desolate, that none are left to weep, and more melancholy silence reigns. *Note*, God will soon change sinful mirth into everlasting mourning: we need rejoice with trembling.

rible indeed, when life becomes a burden, and the sinner is tempted to prefer strangling and death.

CHAP. VIII.

The prophet proceeds in this chapter both to aggravate and to justify the [illegible] which God was bringing upon this people. 1. He represents the judgments coming so very terrible, that death, though dreadful, should be desired, ver. 1—3. *2. He aggravates the perverseness and wilfulness of the people, as what brought this ruin upon them,* ver. 4—12. *3. He describes the great confusion and consternation that the whole land should be in upon the alarm of it,* ver. 13—17. *4. The prophet is himself deeply affected with it,* ver. 18—22.

a 2 Kings xiii. —

1 AT that time, saith the LORD, they [a] shall bring
out the bones of the kings of Judah, and the
bones of his princes, and the bones of the priests, and
the bones of the prophets, and the bones of the inha-
bitants of Jerusalem out of their graves. 2 And they
shall spread them before the sun, and the moon, and
all the host of heaven, whom they have loved, and whom
they have served, and after whom they have walked,
and whom they have sought, and [b] whom they have
worshipped: they shall not be gathered, nor be buried,
[c] they shall be for dung upon the face of the earth. 3
And [d] death shall be chosen rather than life, by all the
residue of them that remain of this evil family, which
remain in all the places whither I have driven them,
saith the LORD of hosts.

b 2 Kings xxiii. 5. 2 Ch. [illegible] c Chap. ix. 22. & xvi. 4. d Rev. ix. 6.

v. 1—3. In the dreadful desolation before described, the unburied corpses lie exposed; here their savage invaders suffer not the dead to enjoy quiet repose.

1. The graves and sepulchres of Judah's kings and princes shall be opened, either through avarice, to search for treasures, or to shew insult even to their ashes, or as a just judgment of God, who suffered the bones of the king, priest, prophet, and people, who had [illegible] [illegible], to be exposed with [illegible] before those luminaries of heaven whom they had *worshipped*, *loved*, *served*, and *sought*: they had walked in the most abominable [illegible], and set up these for their gods, and their [illegible] to be defiled, and their bodies to be [illegible] [illegible] and [illegible] [illegible] the [illegible] [illegible] now [illegible] [illegible], when they could not afford the least help, nor so much as collect their scattered bones, *they shall be for dung upon the face of the earth*, *v.* 1, 2. *Note*, In the day of judgment the sinner's loathsome carcase will be more shamefully exposed, *Isa.* lxvi. 24.

Death, the most dreaded of human evils, now shall be courted, not that it hath lost ought of its horror, but because life is become intolerable: not from the hope of happiness in the exchange, but from despair of rest on this side below. The survivors of *this evil family* [illegible] [illegible] [illegible] [illegible] [illegible], shall be [illegible] [illegible] and tormented in every place whither they are driven, that they shall look with envy on those who have perished by famine and the sword, and count their lot more eligible than their own. *Note*, [illegible] [illegible] is ter-

4 ¶ Moreover, thou shalt say unto them, Thus saith
the LORD, Shall they fall, and not arise? shall he
turn away, and not return? 5 Why then is this peo-
ple of Jerusalem slidden back, [e] by a perpetual back-
sliding? [f] they hold fast deceit, they refuse to return.
6 I hearkned and heard, *but* they spake not aright: no
man repented him of his wickedness, saying, What have
I done? every one turned to his course, as the horse
rusheth into the battle. 7 Yea, [g] the stork in the hea-
ven knoweth her appointed times, and the turtle, and
the crane, and the swallow observe the time of their
coming; but my people [h] know not the judgment of the
LORD. 8 How do ye say, We *are* wise, and [i] the
law of the LORD *is* with us? Lo, certainly † in vain
made he *it*, the pen of the scribes *is* in vain. 9 ‡ The
wise *men* are ashamed, they are dismayed and taken:
Lo, they have rejected the word of the LORD, and
[k] what wisdom *is* in them? 10 Therefore [l] will I give
their wives unto others, [m] *and* their fields to them that
shall inherit *them*: for [n] every one from the least even
unto the greatest is given to covetousness, from the pro-
phet even unto the priest every one dealeth falsly. 11
For [o] they have healed the hurt of the daughter of my
people slightly, saying, [p] Peace, peace, when *there is* no
peace. 12 [q] Were they ashamed when they had com-
mitted abomination? nay, they were not at all ashamed,
neither could they blush: therefore shall they fall among
them that fall, in the time of their visitation they shall
be cast down, saith the LORD.

e Chap. v. 3. f Isa. xxvi. 3. Chap. ix. 6. g Isa. i. 3. h Chap. v. 4, 5. Luke xix. 42. i Rom. ii. 17. † Or, the false pen of the scribes worketh for falsehood. k Isa. x. 1. ‡ Or, Have they been ashamed, &c. Chap. vi. 15. l Isa. viii. 10. m Deut. xxviii. 30. Chap. vi. 12. Amos v. 11. Zeph. i. 13. n Isa. lvi. 11. Chap. vi. 13. o Chap. vi. 14. p Ezek. xiii. 10. q Chap. iii. 3. & vi. 15.

v. 4—12. Never was people so infatuated to their ruin.

1. They persevered in their evil ways. In general, when *man falls*, he *seeks immediately to recover himself*, and if he loses his way, he is sollicitous to return into the right path, *v.* 4. *Why then is this people of Jerusalem slidden back by a perpetual backsliding?* and instead of any desire to amend, *they hold fast deceit*, obstinate against every means of conviction, they refuse to return. *Note*, (1.) They who backslide from God, wander endlessly and perpetually, unless his grace plucks them from ruin. (2.) Nothing is so great a deceiver as sin; it promises so much enjoyment, and ever produces so much misery.

2. They disappointed God's expectations from them. He patiently waited and hearkned, if so be they might at last be prevailed upon to change their note, and learn the language of penitence; but not one *spake aright, nor repented of his wickedness*, reflecting with shame upon his conduct; but just the very reverse, they urged on their mad career in sin with such determined wayward[illegible] and fearlessness, *as the horse rusheth into the battle*. *Note*, (1.) God is long-suffering to us-ward, not willing that any should perish, but that all should come unto repentance. (2.) The first step to real penitence is serious reflection upon the evil of our past ways, *What have I done?* (3.) The daring sinner that mocks at the terrors of the Lord, as chimeras, and fearless rushes into the depths of iniquity, will find them fearful realities, and that half was not told him.

3. They were more stupid and irrational than the fowl of heaven, whilst they made the highest pretensions to wisdom, *v.* 7—9. The birds of passage by instinct know the proper season for their coming and going, and how to direct their flight; but *my people know not the judgment of the Lord*, neither how to improve the calls of mercy in God's word, nor the corrections of affliction, nor his visitations on others; and yet they say, *We are wise, and the law of the Lord is with us*. How shameless their pretensions! when their whole conduct appeared so contradictory. In vain had they the law, and the pen of the scribe to write out copies or comments upon it; their expositions were false, or at least they paid no regard to them, it [illegible]. Their wise men themselves are confounded at calamities they could neither foresee nor avert: nor can it be wondered, when, *lo! they have rejected the word of the Lord*, sent by his prophets; and *what wisdom is in them*, when they reject the counsel of God, and refuse to be instructed? *Note*, (1.) Many enjoy plenty of means, have Bibles and ministers, and yet are never the wiser for them. (2.) Whatever pretences to wisdom they may make, who reject God's revealed word, they will be confounded in the day of judgment at their own egregious folly.

4. For their sins they shall suffer. Their sins are before charged on them, *chap.* vi. 13—15. *Love of filthy lucre*, most scandalous in those who are to preach, and be examples to others of deadness to the world. *Insincerity*, their profession were false, and their doctrine dishonest, tending to lull the sinner's soul into fatal security, instead of rousing him to a sense of his danger, and *daring impudence*, that knew not to blush, though convicted of their lies, and upbraided for their

abomi-

Before Christ 600

abominations Therefore God's wrath is upon them, their wives shall be captives, and concubines to their enemies, their land possessed by aliens, and they in the time of visitation, when God makes inquisition for sin, shall fall with them that fall, cast down, and utterly consumed *Note*, (1) Companions in sin will fall together into the pit of destruction (2) They who have been instrumental to deceive others to their ruin, shall receive the greater damnation

13 ¶ I will surely consume them, saith the LORD,
ᵗ *there shall be* no grapes on the vine, nor figs on the fig-
tree, and the leaf shall fade, and *the things that* I have
given them shall pass away from them 14 Why do
we sit still? ˢ assemble yourselves, and let us enter into
the defenced cities, and let us be silent there for the
LORD our God hath put us to silence, and ᵗ given us
water of † gall to drink, because we have sinned against
the LORD 15 ᵘ We looked for peace, but no good
came and for a time of health, and behold trouble
16 The snorting of his horses was heard from Dan
the whole land trembled at the sound of the neighing
of his strong ones, for they are come and have de-
voured the land, and ‡ all that is in it, the city, and
those that dwell therein 17 For behold, I will send
serpents, cockatrices among you, which *will* ʸ not be
charmed, and they shall bite you, saith the LORD
18 ¶ *When* I would comfort myself against sorrow,
my heart *is* faint in me 19 Behold, the voice of the
cry of the daughter of my people, § because of them
that dwell in a far country *Is* not the LORD in
Zion? *is* not her king in her? why have ᶻ they pro-
voked me to anger with their graven images, *and* with
strange vanities? 20 ᵃ The harvest is past, the sum-
mer is ended, and we are not saved 21 For the
hurt of the daughter of my people am I hurt, I am
black astonishment hath taken hold on me 22 ᵇ *Is
there* no balm in Gilead? *is there* no physician there?
‖ why then is not the health of the daughter of my peo-
ple recovered?

ʳ Hos ii 9 Joel i 7 12 Luke xiii 6, &c
ˢ Chap iv 5
ᵗ Chap ix 15 & xxiii 15
† Or poison
ᵘ Chap xiv 19
ˣ Chap iv 15
‡ Heb The fulness thereof
ʸ Pf lviii 4 5 Eccles x 11
§ Or because of the country of them that are far off
ᶻ Isa i 4
ᵃ Ver 15
ᵇ Chap xlvi 11 & li 8
‖ Heb Why is no the cure or recovery of my people gone up?

v 13—22 Wicked men are plagued for their offences
1 God threatens utterly to consume them with famine and the sword Blasting and mildew shall strip their vines and fig-trees bare, and leave not a leaf thereon or their enemies would thus utterly consume their fruits, and rob them of all the providential gifts God had so richly bestowed on them in that land of plenty, *v* 13 and the Chaldeans with a mortal sting, as the [illegible] flying serpent in the wilderness, shall bite them with their invenomed fangs, and no charm be found to sooth their rage, or stop their ravages, *v* 17 *Note*, (1) It is just in God to take from us the mercies we have abused (2) When the worm in hell begins to gnaw the sinner's conscience, it never can be charmed to rest

2 Their complaints and distress are very bitter To sit still in the country must be their ruin, where famine wasted, and which would be first over-run by the invaders, therefore they resolve to enter the defenced cities, and *be silent there*, either hoping for protection, or rather intimating, that it were useless to complain when they despaired of redress, because their destruction was from *God*, who, *in just punishment for their sins*, which they are compelled to own, though they persisted in them, had given them the gall of affliction to drink And herein they seem rather to speak the language of indignation against God for their sufferings, than of humiliation for their sins, *v* 14 Their expectations of peace, with which the lying prophets had flattered them, and their own foolish hearts promised them, were now at an end Nothing but trouble and terror was before them, *v* 15 The very neighing of the numerous cavalry advancing from Dan made them tremble, whilst they beheld the cities and country wasted, and the inhabitants captives or slain *v* 16 *Note*, (1) Unhumbled sinners in sullen silence behold their ruin approach, without power to avoid it and without heart to deprecate the wrath they have provoked (2) When God sends his terrors before him, the stoutest tremble for fear (3) They who continue in their sins look for peace in vain, *for there is no peace, saith my God, [illegible]*

3 All their confidence had failed They buoyed themselves up with a vain hope that God, as king in Zion, would, notwithstanding all their provocations, not suffer the habitation of his holiness to be destroyed and they expostulate with him, as if he was unfaithful to his promises, or his power weakened, but God replies, to their confusion, *Why have they provoked me to [illegible] with their graven images?* Their destruction was their own seeking, they first rejected him for their God, before he forsook them as his people Their expectations from their [illegible] were disappointed also they continued to hope

they would come and force the Chaldeans to raise the siege, but *the harvest is past*, when they expected them, in April and May, *the summer is ended*, in July, and winter now approached, without the least prospect of deliverance, *and we are not saved*, so that they sunk into despair *Note*, (1) When the day of grace is over, nothing remains for the sinner, but a fearful looking-for of judgment (2) They who apostatize from God, can have no reasonable expectation of help and deliverance from him

4 The prophet bewails the miseries of his countrymen *When I would comfort myself against sorrow*, either by meditating on God's promises, or suggesting to himself arguments for hope and patience, *my heart is faint in me*, overcome with the views of the impending calamities, *v* 18 The cry of Zion's inhabitants rung doleful in his ears, groaning under the miseries they endured from the siege, or in their hard captivity, *v* 19 He felt his heart wounded through them, and was broken by the tender sympathy of their sufferings, black as mourners in deepest distress and overwhelmed with astonishment at the miseries he beheld, *v* 21 *Is there no balm in Gilead? is there no physician there?* either intimating the incurableness of their disease, and the death-stroke given to the kingdom, or as upbraiding them with their stupidity and obstinacy in refusing to be healed by the rich mercies of God, and rejecting the prophets that he had sent to them *Why then is not the health of my people recovered?* It was not for want of balm, or a physician, but purely owing to their wilful opposition to all the means and methods God had taken for their recovery *Note*, (1) A good man, a faithful minister, cannot but tenderly feel and lament for the miseries they see disobedient sinners pulling on their own heads (2) Sometimes even gracious souls find their anguish so great, that for a time they are dejected under it, and cannot take hold of the consolations of God's word (3) There is balm in Gilead, a cure for every sin-sick soul, even the blood of Jesus, and he is a physician, whose skill no spiritual disease, however inveterate, can baffle, and in his hands the most desperate case never miscarries

CHAP IX

In this chapter the prophet goes on faithfully to reprove sin, and to threaten God's judgments for it, and yet bitterly to lament both. He here, 1 expresseth his grief for the miseries of Judah and Jerusalem, and his detestation of their sins, which brought those miseries upon them, ver 1—11 2 He justifies God in the greatness of their destruction, ver 9, 12—16 3 He calls upon others to bewail their woeful case, ver 17—22 4 He shews them the folly of trusting in their own strength or wisdom, or the privileges of their circumcision, or any thing but God only, ver 23—26

1 ᵃ O H that my head were waters, and mine eyes a
fountain of tears, that I might weep day and
night for the slain of the daughter of my people!
2 Oh that I had in the wilderness a lodging place of
wayfaring men, that I might leave my people, and go
from them for ᶜ they *be* all adulterers, an assembly of
treacherous men 3 And they bend their tongues
like their bow *for* lies but they are not valiant for
the truth upon the earth, for ᵈ they proceed from evil
to evil, and ᵉ they know not me, saith the LORD
4 ᶠ Take ye heed every one of his ‡ neighbour and trust
ye not in any brother for every brother will utterly
supplant, and every neighbour will walk with slanders
5 And they will ‖ deceive every one his neighbour, and
will not speak the truth they have taught their tongue
to speak lies, *and* weary themselves to commit iniquity
6 Thine habitation *is* in the midst of deceit, through
deceit they refuse to know me, saith the LORD
7 Therefore thus saith the LORD of hosts, Be-
hold, I will melt them, and try them, for ʰ how shall
I do for the daughter of my people? 8 ⁱ Their tongue
is as an arrow shot out, it speaketh ᵏ deceit *one* speaketh
ˡ peaceably to his neighbour with his mouth, but in heart
he layeth § his wait 9 ¶ Shall I not visit them for
these *things*? saith the LORD shall not my soul be
avenged on such a nation as this? 10 For the moun-
tains will I take up a weeping and wailing, and for the
‖ habitations of the wilderness a lamentation, because they
are burnt up, so that none can pass through *them*, nei-
ther can *men* hear the voice of the cattle, both ⁿ the fowl
of the heavens and the beast are fled, they are gone
11 And I will make Jerusalem ᵒ heaps, *and* ᵖ a den of
dragons, and I will make the cities of Judah ¶ desolate,
without an inhabitant

ᵃ Isa xxii 4 Chap iv 19 & xiii 17 & xiv 17 Lam iii 48
ᶜ Chap v 7 8
ᵈ Isa lix 4 13 15
ᵉ 2 Tim iii 13
ᶠ Hos iv 3
‡ Or friend
ᵍ Chap xii 6 Mic vii 5 6
‖ Or mock, or beguile.
ʰ Hos xi 8
ⁱ Pf lxiv 3 Prov xx 14
ᵏ Pf xii & cxx
ˡ Pf xxviii 3 & lv
§ Or wait for him
ᵐ Chap v 9 29
‖ Or pastures
ⁿ Chap iv 25 & xii
ᵒ Isa xxv 2
ᵖ Chap x 22
¶ Heb desolation

[illegible] 1—11

Before Christ 600

v. 1—11. With bitter grief the prophet beheld the sins of his people, and the ruin they provoked.

1. He wishes that his head were waters, and his eyes a fountain of tears, that streams incessant might run down his cheeks for the miseries he foresaw, *v.* 1. Weary of dwelling amidst so polluted a people, and that he might give full vent to his sorrows, or be removed from the dreadful spectacle before him, he wishes for some desert lonely cave, preferring the company of the savages of the wood, to so wicked a nation, and safer amidst the lions of the forest, than his own treacherous and cruel countrymen. *Note,* (1.) A good man must be a patriot, and cannot unmoved behold the ruin of his country. (2.) In this vale of misery we may expect to have many a cause for weeping over our own sins, as well as others. They who suffer nothing to interrupt their carnal joy, may never hope to receive the blessedness promised to those that mourn. (3.) It is a dreadful symptom of the wickedness, and a sign of the approaching ruin of a people, when the souls of God's prophets, like Lot, are vexed with their abomination, and weary of dwelling in the midst of them.

2. The cause of these complaints is,

[1.] The sins of his people. They were all *adulterers,* corporally and spiritually, an assembly of *treacherous* men, apostates from God and his worship, *v.* 2. and false and faithless one to another, bending *their tongues like their bow for lies,* destitute of all zeal for truth, yea, rather opposing it with all their power, proceeding from evil to worse, instead of repenting and reforming, ignorant of God, and desiring to remain so, *v.* 3. Not a neighbour, no, not a brother could be trusted, so selfish and perfidious were they grown, *v.* 4. Lies were become familiar to their tongue, and slander the constant topic of their conversation, and no truth was to be expected from them. They stuck at no pains to compass their ends, *they weary themselves to commit iniquity,* so eagerly were they bent on it, *v.* 5. In the midst of such a people the prophet dwelt, and therefore need be on his guard against them, nor marvel if they acted deceitfully with him, when they acted hypocritically towards God, as the latter clause of *v.* 6. may be interpreted. Through the delusions of their false prophets they refused to receive the knowledge of God: no arrow was sharper than their bitter and lying words: and, whilst the guise of friendship and peace seemed to breathe in all their discourse, mischief was in their hearts, and they lay in wait to make a prey of those they had deluded. *Note,* (1.) Lewdness and lying are among the most deadly and prevailing iniquities. (2.) To be silent, and refuse to espouse the suffering cause of God and truth, is highly criminal. (3.) They who have accustomed themselves to a habit of lying, will not speak truth, even when they have no purpose or design to serve, but lye for lying sake. (4.) The service of sin is usually a wearisome task, and yet so enslaved are sinners to the love of it, that though the pain exceeds the pleasure, they pursue it yet again, and take more pains to go to hell, than was required to carry them to heaven. (5.) There is no stopping in the way of wickedness, every sin indulged opens a way for a greater. (6.) In a wicked and deceitful world we need be ever on our guard.

[2.] The sufferings of his people. They shall be put in the hottest furnace of affliction, to melt and try them, since all other methods have proved ineffectual, *v.* 7. The sword shall be bathed in blood, *v.* 8. the country wasted, the villages burnt, the lowing herds and bleating sheep no more be heard on the mountains, plundered and carried off by the Chaldean army, nor a living creature seen passing through the desolate land, even the wild beasts and the fowls of heaven shall desert it, unable to find food for their hunger, *v.* 10. except the dragons, who take up their abode in the ruined palaces of Jerusalem, and so utter will be the overthrow, that not an inhabitant shall remain in all the cities of Judah, *v.* 11. Thus will God visit for their iniquities, and his soul be avenged on such a people as this, *v.* 9. *Note,* (1.) In the severest of the afflictions God lays on his [illegible] land he intends to make the furnace fire which consumes the wicked, a means of purifying the remnant of his chosen, and separating them as silver from the dross. (2.) The iniquities of the people have often turned a fruitful land into barrenness. (3.) The prophet who beholds their desolation cannot withhold the tear of pity, yea, his eyes are fountains to bewail it: and when we look round upon the world that lies in wickedness, and see that great day of the perdition of ungodly men approach, need we not be more affected at a sight so unspeakably more terrible?

s Chap. xviii. 4. Hos. xiv. 9.
12 ¶ s Who *is* the wise man that may understand
this, and *who is he* to whom the mouth of the LORD
hath spoken, that he may declare it, for what the land
perisheth, *and* is burnt up like a wilderness that none
t Chap. iii. 24. † Heb. Stubbornness.
passeth through? 13 And the LORD saith, Because
they have forsaken my law which I set before them,
and have not obeyed my voice, neither walked therein;
14 t But have walked after the † imagination of their
own heart, and after Baalim, u which their fathers taught
them: 15 Therefore thus saith the LORD of hosts,
the God of Israel, Behold, I will feed them, *even* this
x Chap. viii. 14. & xxiii. 15. Lam. iii. 15, 19.
people, x with wormwood, and give them water of gall
y Lev. xxvi. 33. Deut. xxviii. 64.
to drink. 16 y I will scatter them also among the heathen,
whom neither they nor their fathers have known:
z Chap. xv. 4.
and I will send a sword after them, till I have consumed
a 2 Chron. xxxv. 25. Job iii. 8. Eccles. xii. 5.
them. 17 ¶ Thus saith the LORD of hosts, Consider
ye, and a call for the mourning women, that they may
come, and send for cunning *women,* that they may come:
b Ver. 1. Chap. xiv. 17.
18 And let them make haste, and take up a wailing
for us, b that our eyes may run down with tears, and
our eye-lids gush out with waters. 19 For a voice of
wailing is heard out of Zion, How are we spoiled! we
c Lev. xviii. 28. & xx. 22.
are greatly confounded, because c we have forsaken
the land, because d our dwellings have cast *us* out. 20
Yet hear the word of the LORD, O ye women, and
let your ear receive the word of his mouth, and teach
your daughters wailing, and every one her neighbour
lamentation. 21 For death is come up into our windows,
h Chap. vi. 11. Ezek. xxi.
and is entred into our palaces, to h cut off the
children from without, *and* the young men from the
e Chap. viii. 2.
streets. 22 Speak, Thus saith the LORD, Even e the
carcases of men shall fall as dung upon the open field,
and as the handful after the harvest-man, and none shall
gather *them.*

v. 12—22. If the people perish, it is not for want of awful and repeated warnings.

1. A summons is given to the wise men among them to understand and declare the cause of their calamities, *v.* 12. but as no such are found, the prophet himself is commissioned to proclaim both the reason of God's judgments and the terribleness of the vengeance he is about to execute. Their sin is apostacy from the worship and service of God commanded in the law, and disobedience against all the warnings and notices he had sent unto them, *v.* 13. in direct opposition to which, they followed the imaginations of their own wicked hearts, and served Baalim, a multitude of false gods, plunging into idolatry after their fathers example, and filling up the measure of their iniquities, *v.* 14. Most righteous therefore, and just as fearful, are God's judgments upon them. They shall be fed with bread of wormwood, and water of gall, the bitterest afflictions, *v.* 15. The sword and the famine shall devour them, and their carcases lie unburied on the plain as dung, or as a handful dropped after the harvest-man, which is not regarded or gathered up, *v.* 22. and if a few escape the general massacre, they shall be scattered in heathen lands, which their fathers never knew, and even there shall find no rest, the sword of vengeance still pursuing them till they are consumed, *v.* 16. *Note,* (1.) Every step of departure from God tends only to misery. (2.) Wherever the sinner flies, or is driven, the curse of God follows him closer than his shadow.

2. A summons is sent to the mourning women. It was customary among the Jews, as well as other nations, to hire such on the decease of their relations, who, by their cries, their doleful plaints, and melancholy ditties, awakened afresh the sorrows of the survivors. There would now be abundant occasion for them, when the multitude of deaths by famine and the sword should fill every house with lamentation, *v.* 17, 18. and cause not merely fictitious, but real anguish, when out of Zion the voice of wailing is heard, *How are we spoiled! we are greatly confounded,* at seeing their city stormed and taken, themselves captives, driven from their dwellings, and forced from their own, are led into a strange land, *v.* 19. Under such a dire calamity God calls on them, as most befitting their circumstances, to weep and wail. The word is addressed to the women, whose husbands probably had fallen in the siege, and the men being chiefly slain, none but they remained to lament the desolations. They are enjoined to teach their *daughters wailing, and every one her neighbour lamentation.* So universal would be the misery, that none would be exempted from feeling it, and therefore all are called to bewail it. *For death is come up into our windows,* like an enemy that scales the walls, though the gates are shut, *and is entered into our palaces:* the king on the throne, as well as the beggar on the dunghill, is exposed to the famine and the sword; and even the children in the street are murdered, and the young men, unable to make resistance, are slain by their cruel enemies, who have stormed the city, *v.* 21. *Note,* (1.) This is a vale of tears, where death continually spreads his ravages, and wakens up our sorrows. (2.) No palace can keep out this invader: kings and princes are dying worms. (3.) To grieve for the dead is natural, humane, pious, only let us not be swallowed up with immoderate sorrow. (4.) Many lament their losses and crosses bitterly, who never lament their sins, which are the occasion of them; and this is *the sorrow of the world that worketh death.*

23 ¶ Thus

Before Christ 600

23 ¶ Thus saith the LORD, [d] Let not the wise
man glory in his wisdom, neither let the mighty man
glory in his might, let not the rich man glory in his
riches 24 [e] But let him that glorieth, glory in this,
that he understandeth and knoweth me, that I *am* the
LORD [f] which exercise loving-kindness, judgment and
righteousness in the earth for [g] in these *things* I delight,
saith the LORD 25 ¶ Behold, the days come, saith
the LORD, that [h] I will punish all *them which are*
circumcised with the uncircumcised, 26 Egypt, and
Judah, and Edom, and the children of Ammon, and
Moab, and all *that are* ‖ in [i] the utmost corners, that
dwell in the wilderness for all *these* nations *are* uncir-
cumcised, and all the house of Israel *are* [k] uncircumcised
in the heart

d Ecclef ix 11 e 1 Cor i 31 2 Cor x 17 f Pf xxv 10 g Mic vii 18 h Rom ii 8—12 ‖ Heb Cut off into corners, or having the corners of their hair polled i Chap. xxv 23 & xlix 32 k Lev xxvi 41 Rom ii 28, 29

v 23—26 Having foretold their impending calamities, the prophet concludes with warning to them, not to have recourse to those vain confidences, which would prove refuge of lies, but to take that only method which remained of preventing their ruin, returning to the knowledge of God, and obedience to his will

1 He warns them against depending on their own wisdom, power, and wealth, to protect them, and directs them to the only sure refuge *Let not the wise man glory in his wisdom*, as if by his policies he could avert the storm *neither let the mighty man glory in his might*, which would afford no safety when fighting against God *Let not the rich man glory in his riches*, as if these could bribe the invaders, or hire auxiliaries to defend them, for vain would these things prove If therefore any man would have solid grounds for glorying, it must be *in this, that he understandeth and knoweth me*, the only object in whom a sinner can glory, *that I am the Lord*, the only hope, help, and Saviour of the guilty, *which exercise loving-kindness, judgment, and righteousness in the earth*, shewing mercy to the miserable, pardoning the sinful, strengthening the weak, just in all his providences, and righteous in all his ways, *for in these things I delight, saith the Lord* *Note*, (1.) Worldly supports are often a dangerous snare Wisdom, strength, and riches are apt to swell the heart with pride and self-importance, and then they prove our ruin (2.) Christ is our only glory In ourselves we have nothing but what we need be ashamed of, and renounce, in him there is all fulness (3.) What is God's delight, should be ours, and to be partakers of his compassions, to walk in his judgments, and be found in the practice of righteousness and true holiness, will be infinitely more profitable than the highest attainment of worldly wisdom, or the greatest possessions of worldly wealth

2 He warns them against trusting on their peculiar privileges, as promising themselves, because of the covenant of circumcision, that they should be preserved from evil, for this would stand them in no stead whilst their hearts were uncircumcised, and they continued devoted to the service not of the Lord, but of their lusts, therefore they would share with Egypt, and Edom, and the neighbouring uncircumcised nations, in their punishment, and find no distinction in the day when God went to judgment *Note*, Our partaking of the outward privileges and seals of the covenant will stand us in no stead, if we are destitute of the inward and spiritual grace, yea, will rather aggravate our guilt The *baptized*, unconverted, and unhumbled sinner will meet even a heavier doom than the *unbaptized* heathen

CHAP X.

Here we have, 1 A caution given the Jews not to learn the way of the heathen, ver 1, 2 Particularly their astrology and idolatry, which are brutish and foolish things, ver 3—5 and the worshippers of idols brutish, ver 8, 9 as will appear in the day of their visitation ver 14, 15 2 They are exhorted to adhere firmly to the God of Israel, for there is none like him, ver 6, 7 He is the true God, his power, and governs the world, ver 10—13 and his people are happy in him, ver 16 3 They are bid to expect distress, ver 17, 18 And that by a foreign enemy, which God would bring upon them for their sin, ver 20—22 4 This occasions the prophet's laments, ver 19 and prayers for the mitigation of it, ver 23—25

1 HEAR ye the word which the LORD speaketh
unto you, O house of Israel 2 Thus saith
the LORD, [a] Learn not the way of the heathen, and
be not dismayed at the signs of heaven, for the heathen
are dismayed at them 3 For the ‡ customs of the
people are vain for [b] *one* cutteth a tree out of the forest
(the work of the hands of the workman) with the axe
4 They deck it with silver and with gold, they fasten
it with nails and with hammers, that it move not 5

a Lev xviii 3 & xx 23 b Isa xliv 9, 14 ‡ Heb statutes or ordinances are vanity c Isa xl 19 & xliv 12

They *are* upright as the palm-tree, [d] but speak not
they must needs [e] be borne, because they cannot go
be not afraid of them, for [f] they cannot do evil, neither
also *is it* in them to do good 6 Forasmuch as [g] *there*
is none like unto thee, O LORD, thou *art* great, and
thy name *is* great in might 7 [h] Who would not fear
thee, O King of nations? for ‡ to thee doth it apper-
tain forasmuch as among all the wise *men* of the na-
tions, and in all their kingdoms *there is* none like unto
thee 8 But they are § altogether [i] brutish and fool-
ish the stock is a doctrine of vanities 9 Silver spread
into plates is brought from Tarshish, and [k] gold from
Uphaz, the work of the workman, and of the hands of
the founder blue and purple *is* their clothing they
are all the work of cunning *men* 10 But the LORD
is ‖ the true God, he *is* the living God, and ‡ an [l] ever-
lasting king at his wrath the earth shall tremble, and
the nations shall not abide his indignation 11 ‡ Thus
shall ye say unto them, [m] The gods that have not made
the heavens and the earth, *even* [n] they shall perish from
the earth, and from under these heavens 12 [o] He
hath made the earth by his power, he hath established
the world by his wisdom, and [p] hath stretched out the
heavens by his discretion 13 When [q] he uttereth his
voice *there is* § a multitude of waters in the heavens,
and he causeth the vapours to ascend from the ends of
the earth he maketh lightnings with rain, and bring-
eth forth the wind out of his treasures 14 Every man
is [r] brutish in *his* knowledge [s] every founder is con-
founded by the graven image for his molten image *is*
falshood, and *there is* no breath in them 15 They
are vanity, *and* the work of errors in the time of their
visitation they shall perish 16 [t] The portion of Jacob
is not like them for he *is* the former of all *things*, and
[u] Israel *is* the rod of his inheritance, the LORD of hosts
is his name

Before Christ 600

d Pf cxv 5 & cxxxv 16 e Isa xlvi 1, 7 f Isa xli 23 g Ex xv 11 Pf lxxxvi 8, 10 h Rev xv 4 ‡ Or it liketh thee § Heb In one, or at once i Pf cxv 8 Isa xli 29 Hab ii 18 Zech x 2 k Dan x 5 ‖ Heb The God of truth l Pf x 16 ‡ Heb King of eternity ‡ In the Chaldee tongue m Zeph ii 11 o Gen i 1, 6 Pf cxxxvi 5, 6 Chap li 15, &c p Job ix 8 Pf civ 2 Isa xl 22 q Job xxxviii 34 § Or noise r Pf xcvii 7 Chap li 17 s Isa xlii 17 & xliv 11 & xlv 16 t Chap li 19 Lam iii 24 u Pf lxxiv 2

v 1—16 As they were shortly to be carried captives to Babylon, a place most remarkably given to idolatry, superstition, and judicial astrology, need there was to guard them against the temptations to which they would be there exposed

1 They must not learn their ways, nor follow their works From the aspect of the heavens, from eclipses, and the conjunction of the planets, the astrologers pretended to foretel the fate of kingdoms, and the destiny of men; and their predictions, heard with superstitious awe, terrified the heathen but they must shew no regard to their prognostications, and much less pay divine honours to the sun, moon, and stars, as these men did, *v* 2 Nor must they join in their idolatry, and the *vain customs* or *ceremonies* of religion which they used A senseless log is the object of their adoration, cut from the wood, and squared by the carpenter, *v* 3 and however decked with gold and silver, and adorned with costliest robes of blue and purple, *v* 9 yet is unable to stand without being nailed and fastened, or to move without being carried It can neither hear the prayer of its votaries, or speak a word in answer to their requests Such *a doctrine of vanities is the stock*, *v* 8 *a work of errors and falshood*, that must deceive and disappoint those who are so infatuated as to expect ought from it unable alike to do good or evil, and therefore in no wise to be made the object either of fear or hope, *v* 5 *Brutish altogether and foolish* are the worshippers, *v* 8 and equally *brutish* the maker *in his knowledge*, who vainly conceits the work of his hands can be possessed of divinity, *v* 14 *Every founder is confounded*, who, after all his pains to make his god, can receive no benefit from him for how should they convey life, or any of the blessings of it, to others, who have *no breath in them*, to animate themselves *v* 14, yea, so far from helping others, that they are unable to help themselves, and *in the day of visitation*, these gods, who have made neither the heaven nor the earth, *shall perish*, with their senseless devotees, *v* 11

2 The prophet directs them to the only proper object of their worship, fear, and love and that is the glorious Jehovah, the only living and true God

\[1.\] *There is none like unto him* He is without a rival, and above all comparison none can either bestow such mercies, or inflict such miseries, as he *O Lord, thou art great*, transcendently great and glorious in his adorable perfections, and all his works of creation, providence, and grace; *and thy name is great*, exalted far above all blessing and praise *Who would not fear thee, O King of nations?* whose kingdom ruleth over all, the work of whose hands the whole creation is, and therefore by right should be universally feared and worshipped *for to thee doth it appertain*, and to thee alone to place that fear, and offer that worship elsewhere, argues both deep impiety, and senseless stupidity For none in wisdom none in power
among

Before Christ 6.0.

among earth's mightiest sons with him can be compared, v 7 *Note*, (1) God's eternal power and deity by the works of creation are so declared to all the world, as to leave idolaters without excuse (2) The more we contemplate the unsearchable greatness and glory of our God, the more we shall be filled with reverence and godly fear, and lost in wonder and adoration

[2] He is the only *true God*, and all pretenders to deity besides are false and counterfeit *He is the living God*, or *Gods*, the trinity in unity, having life in and of himself, whilst all creatures receive theirs from him, and idols are dead and inanimate He is *an everlasting king*, subsisting from all eternity, ruling over all, and of his dominion there is no end, whilst these are all the creatures of yesterday, and hourly running to decay *Note*, If God be our king, it behoves us to see that we approve ourselves faithful subjects, dependent on his protection, devoted to his service

[3] He is the Creator, Governor, and Judge of all *He hath made the earth by his power*, suspended in the vast expanse, and yet so firm that it cannot be moved from the place where God hath appointed it to perform its revolutions, and in the beautiful disposition of all things in it his infinite wisdom as well as power appears, *and hath stretched out the heavens by his discretion*, as a canopy over us, decked with those bright luminaries that peculiarly display his glory At his will, the whole machine is governed, he speaks, the heavens lour, the vapours rise, the lightnings flash, the thunders roll, the rain descends, the tempests roar, and all under his controul, v 13 When he cometh forth in judgment, *at his wrath the earth shall tremble*, afraid to meet the judge upon his throne, *and the nations shall not be able to abide his indignation*, if his wrath be kindled, yea, but a little, it will burn to the nethermost hell Most justly therefore doth he claim, and we are bound to pay our worship, adoration, and service to him, and him alone

[4] He is *the portion of Jacob*, and therefore they are under peculiar obligations to adore and serve him He has chosen and redeemed them, showered upon them his blessing on every side, and will be for ever their exceeding great reward *He is the former of all things*, and not like idol vanities, *and Israel is the rod of his inheritance*, separated for his peculiar people, *the Lord of hosts is his name*, his distinguished title, forasmuch as he doth whatsoever pleaseth him in the hosts of heaven, as well as among the inhabitants of the earth *Note*, (1) They who have God for their portion, cannot wish for more, for he is able to do for them exceeding abundantly above all they can ask or think (2) God's Israel are his inheritance, for they who chuse him for their God, in them he delights as his people, and his love and favour are better than the life itself

17 ¶ Gather up thy wares out of the land, O † in-
habitant of the fortress 18 For thus saith the LORD,
Behold, I will fling out the inhabitants of the land
at this once, and will distress them, that they may find
it so 19 ¶ Wo is me for my † hurt, my wound is
grievous but I said, Truly this *is* a grief, and I must
bear it 20 My tabernacle is spoiled, and all my
cords are broken my children are gone forth of me,
and they *are* not *there is* none to stretch forth my tent
any more, and to set up my curtains 21 For the
pastors are become brutish, and have not sought the
LORD therefore they shall not prosper, and all their
flocks shall be scattered 22 Behold, the noise of the
bruit is come, and a great commotion out of the north-
country, to make the cities of Judah desolate, *and* a
den of dragons 23 ¶ O LORD, I know that the
way of man *is* not in himself *it is* not in man that walk-
eth to direct his steps. 24 O LORD, correct me,
but with judgment, not in thine anger, lest thou ||
bring me to nothing 25 Pour out thy fury upon the
heathen that know thee not, and upon the families that
call not on thy name for they have eaten up Jacob,
and devoured him, and consumed him, and have made
his habitation desolate

v 17—25 We have here,

1 The threatened ruin of Judah and Jerusalem To secure their goods from the Chaldean army, the *Jews* are here represented as gathering them together, and conveying them to the fortress of Zion, but they will find it no place of safety As a stone out of a sling, so swiftly, so violently should they be cast out of their land and city, and sink into the depths of distress, *that they may find it so*, as the prophets have spoken, to whose word they refused to attend *Note*, They who have mocked at hell and damnation, as bugbears designed to awe the minds of the superstitious, will, to their cost, *find it so*, that these are dreadful realities.

2 A mournful lamentation is made over these evil times which some regard as the language of Zion bemoaning herself, but rather seems to be the words of the prophet affected at the view of their miseries, and sympathizing with them *Wo is me, for my hurt*, or *my breach*, when the walls of Jerusalem were battered down, the Chaldeans entered, and terribly massacred the inhabitants, *but I said, This is a grief, and I must bear it*, it was bitter indeed, but he desired to submit with patience *My tabernacle is spoiled*, both the city and temple, *and all my cords are broken*, so that the ruin is irreparable *My children are gone forth of me* into captivity, and none left to repair the desolation, v 20 And no marvel their affairs are so desperate, when *the pastors are become brutish*, the rulers in church and state, instead of attempting to prevent, hastened their ruin by their sin and folly, *they have not sought the Lord* in any of their distresses, but left him far above out of their sight, *therefore they shall not prosper*, no attempts to secure themselves shall succeed, *and all their flocks shall be scattered*, their enemies shall prevail, and that suddenly, *Behold, the noise of the bruit is come*, intelligence of the Chaldean army advancing, *a great commotion out of the north country*, from Babylon, *to make the cities of Judah desolate, and a den of dragons*, a righteous retaliation upon those who made them a *den of thieves* *Note*, (1) In our afflictions God permits us to complain, but he forbids us to murmur (2) When the pastors are brutish, no marvel the people are blind (3) They who live without prayer, and seek not to God for counsel and help, must needs err from the right way, and perish in their sins

Before Christ 608

3 Though the people have no ears to hear his preaching, God hath an ear to hear his prayer, and therefore to him the prophet looks up

(1) He acknowledges God's over-ruling providence and guidance, in all the affairs of men *O Lord, I know that the way of man is not in himself it is not in man that walketh to direct his steps*, a superior power controuls his thoughts and designs, and an unseen hand guides his steps, as was the case of Nebuchadnezzar in this invasion, and more generally may be applied to all mankind Whatever schemes we form, the event is not in our own power when we mean only to pursue our own purposes, God leads us insensibly to fulfil his designs, therefore amidst all our contrivances we must entirely refer ourselves to him for the success, conscious that we have no power of ourselves to help ourselves The Lord must dictate, guide, support, and prosper us, and then we shall walk aright

(2) In the name of the people, he entreats the removal or alleviation of their heavy judgments *O Lord, correct me*, for that they must expect, and acknowledge it to be their just desert, *but with judgment*, in measure, *not in thine anger*, as the wrath of an enemy, but in love, as the chastisement of a father, *least thou bring me to nothing*, for if his wrath be kindled, yea, but a little, who may abide it? *Note*, (1) Correction from God is kindness, and this rod, however grievous for the time to the flesh, we may not wish to have removed till it hath done its work (2) God's afflictions on his people are designed not *to bring them to nothing*, but to bring them to himself and to glory

(3) He beseeches God to remember their oppressors, and to recompence them according to the work of their hands *Pour out thy fury upon the heathen that know thee not*, God's own people are corrected in mercy, his enemies are to be destroyed in wrath, *and upon the families that call not upon the name of the Lord*, the nations of the ungodly, who neither know nor worship the true God, *for they have eaten up Jacob, and devoured him, and consumed him, and have made his habitation desolate*, which though God hath permitted as their just punishment, doth not at all lessen the guilt and malice of their persecutors *Note*, (1) Families who live without prayer, are to be accounted heathens (2) Ignorance of God is the inlet to all sin (3) When God hath corrected his people, he often turns the rod, and leaves on the instruments he employs the severest marks of his indignation

CHAP XI

In this chapter, 1 God, by the prophet, puts the people in mind of the covenant made with their fathers, and the condition of it, that they should be obedient to him, ver 1—7 2 He charges them with obstinately refusing to obey him, ver 8—10 3 He threatens them with utter ruin for their disobedience, especially for their idolatry, ver 11, 13 their idols shall not save them, ver 12 nor their prophets pray for them, ver 14 and justifies his proceedings against them, they having brought all this mischief upon themselves by their own wilfulness, ver 15—17 4 A conspiracy is formed against Jeremiah by the men of Anathoth, which God discovers to him, ver 18, 19 His prayer against them, ver 20 and a prediction of God's judgments upon them for it, ver. 21—23

1 THE word that came to Jeremiah from the
LORD, saying, 2 Hear ye the words of 6o8
this covenant, and speak unto the men of Judah, and
to the inhabitants of Jerusalem, 3 And say thou unto
them,

Before Christ 608

them, Thus saith the LORD God of Israel, [a] Cursed
be the man that obeyeth not the words of this cove-
nant, 4 [b] Which I commanded your fathers in the
day *that* I brought them forth out of the land of Egypt,
[c] from the iron furnace, saying, [d] Obey my voice, and
do them, according to all which I command you so
shall ye be my people, and I will be your God 5
That I may perform [e] the oath which I have sworn un-
to your fathers, [f] to give them a land flowing with milk
and honey, as *it is* this day Then answered I, and
said, † So be it, O LORD 6 Then the LORD
said unto me, Proclaim all these words in the cities of
Judah, and in the streets of Jerusalem, saying, Hear ye
the words of this covenant, [g] and do them 7 For I
earnestly protested unto your fathers, in the day *that* I
brought them up out of the land of Egypt, *even* unto
this day, [h] rising early and protesting, saying, Obey my
voice 8 [i] Yet they obeyed not, nor inclined their ear,
but [k] walked every one in the ‡ imagination of their
evil heart therefore I will bring upon them all the
words of this covenant, which I commanded *them* to do,
but they did *them* not 9 And the LORD said unto
me, A conspiracy is found among the men of Judah,
and among the inhabitants of Jerusalem 10 They are
turned back to the iniquities of their forefathers, which
refused to hear my words, and they went after other
gods to serve them the house of Israel and the house
of Judah have broken my covenant which I made with
their fathers.

a Deut xxvii 26 Gal iii 10 b Chap vii 23 c Deut iv 20 1 Kings viii 51 d Lev xxvi 3 12 e Deut vii 12 f Exod iii 8, 17 Lev xx 24 Deut vi 3 & xi 9 † Heb Amen Deut xxvii 26 1 Pf xv 5 h Chap vii 13, 25 i Chap vii 26 k Chap iii 17 & vii 24, & ix 14 ‡ Or stubbornness l Ezek xxii 25

v. 1—10 A new prophecy seems to begin at this chapter Jeremiah is sent of God again to this rebellious house of Judah

1 To remind them of the tenor of that covenant, by which they held the land of promise The great condition of which was their obedience, *v* 4 and this God earnestly pressed upon them as the one thing needful, charging their fathers to observe and do all his commandments, as the only means to secure his favour, and their relation to him, *v* 4 promising that, in consequence of this, they should possess the land of Canaan flowing with milk and honey, and this was farther enforced by the awful sanction of that terrible curse which would overtake the breakers of this covenant, *v* 3 God had not ceased from that day to continue his admonitions to them, and urge that fidelity to which they were so strictly obliged, *v* 7 And now this prophet must second those who went before in the same protestations and urgent calls to them, to hear and obey, *v* 6 which that they may do, he earnestly prays, *So be it, Lord!* ver 5 *Note*, (1) They who withdraw themselves from God's service, have no right to expect his protection (2) The condition of the legal covenant is obedience, and a curse is denounced on every transgression Blessed be God for a covenant of grace, established on better promises, and secured for ever by a better obedience than our own

2 To charge them with their gross violations of this covenant, by which they had forfeited all the blessings promised, and incurred all the penalties annexed to it, *They obeyed not*, neither they, nor their fathers, *nor inclined their ear* to the divinely commissioned messengers, that from time to time God sent to admonish them, *but walked every one in the imaginations of their evil heart*, without the least regard to God's law, therefore all the curses denounced against the disobedient lie at their door, *v* 8 and God saw their secret as well as their open wickedness A general conspiracy is formed among them, to discard God's worship and law, and to introduce the idols and customs of the heathens around them *The men of Judah, and inhabitants of Jerusalem*, city and country, high and low, are engaged in it, *v* 9 A little reformation had been made in the days of Josiah, but they quickly *turned back to the iniquities of their forefathers*, and sunk again into idolatry Israel first led the way, and Judah copied their abominations, so that the covenant God had made with their fathers was utterly broken, *v* 10 *Note*, (1) They who will not be ruled by God's law, must be destroyed under his curse (2) Though hand join in hand, the wicked shall not go unpunished

11 ¶ Therefore thus saith the LORD, Behold, I
will bring evil upon them, which they shall not be able
to † escape, and [n] though they shall cry unto me, I
will not hearken unto them 12 Then shall the cities
of Judah, and inhabitants of Jerusalem go, [o] and cry
unto the gods unto whom they offer incense, but they
shall not save them at all in the time of their ‡ trouble
13 For [p] *according* to the number of thy cities were thy
gods, O Judah; and *according* to the number of the
streets of Jerusalem, have ye set up altars to *that* ||
shameful thing, *even* altars to burn incense unto Baal
14 Therefore [p] pray not thou for this people, neither
lift up a cry or prayer for them for I will not hear
them in the time that they cry unto me for their trouble
15 [q] § What hath my beloved to do in mine house,
seeing she hath wrought lewdness with many? and the
holy flesh is passed from thee when thou dost evil,
then thou rejoicest. 16 The LORD called thy name,
A green olive-tree, fair *and* of goodly fruit with the
noise of a great tumult he hath kindled fire upon it,
and the branches of it are broken 17 For the LORD
of hosts, [s] that planted thee, hath pronounced evil a-
gainst thee, for the evil of the house of Israel, and of
the house of Judah, which they have done against them-
selves to provoke me to anger, in offering incense unto
Baal

† Heb to go forth of [n] Pf xviii 41 Prov i 28 Isa i 15 Chap xiv 12 Ezek viii 18 Mic iii 4 Zech vii 13 o Deut xxxii 37 ‡ Heb Evil m Chap ii 28 || Heb Shame Chap iii 24 Hos ix 10

Before Christ 608

p Exod xxxii 10 Chap vii 16 & xiv 11 1 John v 16 q Isa i 11, &c § Heb What is to my beloved in my house r Prov ii 14 s Exod xv 17 Isa v 2 Chap ii 21

v 11—17 The curse follows sin as close as the shadow does the body We have here,

1 Their miserable and helpless case *Therefore I will bring evil upon them*, the evil of punishment for the evil of sin, *which they shall not be able to escape*, neither their wisdom, nor might, nor riches, shall be able to avert the storm In vain will be their applications to God, he *will not* hear them, *v* 11 In vain their application to their idols, *they cannot help* them, *v* 12 Though so numberless, that not only every city, but every street had altars erected to *that shameful thing Baal*, ver 13 *Note*, (1) When wrath pursues the sinner, flight is vain (2) Prayer comes too late, when it is the time of judgment (3) Many cry to God to save them from their sufferings, who never lament the evil of the sins which procured them, and will may he therefore refuse to hear (4) All our idols and creature-dependances in a day of calamity, will be found miserable comforters (5) Sin is a shameful thing, and we must either take shame to ourselves now for it, or be put to everlasting shame in the day of visitation

2 The prophet is forbid to pray for them The decree was gone forth against them, and the prayers of good men now would be unavailable as their own, *v* 14 *Note*, They are desperate indeed that are beyond the reach of prayer

3 Their attendance at God's house could profit them nothing, when their hearts were so false and faithless with him. *What hath my beloved to do in mine house?* This title was given them for the fathers sake, *Rom* xi 28 but to what purpose did they keep up their attendance, *seeing she hath wrought lewdness with many*, committing such scandalous idolatry, as utterly separated them from all communion with God, and made their services barefaced hypocrisy, *and the holy flesh is passed from thee*, their sacrifices were no longer acceptable to God, and an end would quickly be put to them, when their temple was laid in ruins *when thou dost evil, then thou rejoicest*, and whilst this love of, and delight in iniquity remained, all services and sacrifices were but an abomination before God *Note*, They who trust on their external privileges, and outward attendance on the worship and ordinances of God, whilst their hearts are strangers to vital holiness, and enslaved by sin, will find themselves disowned of God, and all their dependance a delusion

4 The former favours they enjoyed, as they served but to aggravate their ingratitude, would be no security to them at present They were once indeed called *a green olive-tree, fair and of goodly fruit* God's blessing was upon them, and prosperity surrounded them on every side, but since they have changed their conduct, God hath changed his dispensations of providence towards them The Chaldeans, at his command, have kindled a fire, and burnt it, *and the branches*, their princes, priests, and great men, *are broken* and consumed, *v* 16 God hath *pronounced* sentence against them for their sins, especially their worship of Baal, which provoked his anger, and brought wrath upon their souls, and though he planted them, he will utterly root them up, *v* 17 *Note*, (1) They who sin against God, bring ruin upon their own soul (2) They who produce no fruits of holiness, like barren trees are only fit fuel for the flames

18 ¶ And the LORD hath given me knowledge
of it, and I know *it*, then thou shewedst me their do-
ings 19 But I *was* like a lamb, *or* an ox *that* is
brought to the slaughter, and I knew not that [t] they
had devised devices against me, *saying*, Let us destroy
‡ the tree with the fruit thereof, and [u] let us cut him off
from the land of the living, that his name may be no
more remembred 20 But, O LORD of hosts, that
judgest righteously, [x] that triest the reins and the heart,
let me see thy vengeance on them, for [y] unto thee have
I revealed my cause 21 Therefore thus saith the
LORD of the men of Anathoth, [z] that seek thy life,
saying, [a] Prophesy not in the name of the LORD, that
thou

t Chap xviii 18 ‡ Heb The stalk with his bread u Pf lxxxiii 4 x 1 Sam xvi 7 1 Chron xxviii 9 Pf vii 9 Chap xvii 10, & xx 12 Rev ii 23 y 1 Pet ii 23 z Chap xii 6 a Isa xxx 10 Amos ii 12 & vii 13 Mic ii 6

Before Christ 608

‡ Heb. Viſit upon them. b Ver. 19. Deut. xix. 4. Mat. 10. 2.

thou die not by our hand 22 Therefore thus ſaith
the LORD of hoſts, Behold, I will ‡ puniſh them, the
young men ſhall die by the ſword, their ſons and their
daughters ſhall die by famine 23 And b there ſhall
be no remnant of them, for I will bring evil upon the
men of Anathoth, *even* the year of their viſitation

v. 18—23 They who are ſent to bear witneſs againſt obſtinate ſinners, muſt, with Jeremiah, put their lives in their hand His fidelity here begins to expoſe him to the moſt imminent danger

1 A conſpiracy is formed againſt him, *v.* 19 by the men of Anathoth, his brethren, a city of prieſts, who ſhould have been foremoſt to ſupport him, but are ſo exaſperated at his ſharp reproofs, that nothing but his blood will ſatisfy them *Let us deſtroy the tree with the fruit thereof*, either the prophet and his family, or his prophecy some render the words, *Let us corrupt his bread with poiſon*, ſignifying the method they intended to take, in order to diſpatch him, and *let us cut him off from the land of the living, that his name be no more remembered*, and he and his prophecy buried in everlaſting oblivion *Note*, (1) It is no wonder to ſee wicked prieſts the bittereſt perſecutors of their faithful brethren, it was ever ſo of old (2) People take great pains to be rid of their troublers, but they muſt have God's permiſſion before any of their crafty deſigns can take place

2 God diſappoints their ſcheme, by informing the prophet of his danger, and ſetting him on his guard, *v.* 18 for he was *as a lamb or an ox that is brought to the ſlaughter*, without the leaſt ſuſpicion of their deſigns *Note*, (1) They who are conſcious of the integrity of their own conduct, are leaſt ready to entertain ſuſpicions of others (2) God preſerves us from many unforeſeen dangers, which we ſhould elſe have blindly ruſhed into (3) His prophets and faithful miniſters are his peculiar care

3 He lodges his appeal with God, the righteous judge, who knew his ſimplicity and their iniquity, therefore he prays, *Let me ſee thy vengeance on them*, not from a ſpirit of revenge, but from zeal for God's glory or it may be conſidered as prophetical of what would be their caſe, *for unto thee have I revealed my cauſe*, and therefore reſt ſatisfied in full confidence that juſtice will be done *Note*, (1) Whatever man doth againſt us, it is a comfort we have a righteous judge, who will vindicate thoſe that are oppreſſed with wrong (2) They who deviſe miſchief againſt others, will find the ſtone they have rolled return upon themſelves

4 Judgment is pronounced on the men of Anathoth They determined to ſilence the prophet at all hazards The provocation he had given them was *propheſying in the name of the Lord* without their licence, and in a way that reflected ſuch infamy upon their falſe doctrine and faithleſs conduct, and if they could not intimidate him from preaching, they reſolved to murder him, *v.* 21 therefore God denounces his judgments on the men of Anathoth Famine and the ſword ſhall ſlay them and their families, and not ſo much as a remnant ſhall eſcape the univerſal deſtruction *Note*, (1) No prohibition or threatning can ſtop the mouths of God's true miniſters, they are ready to ſuffer, but reſolved to cry aloud and ſpare not (2) The day of viſitation is at hand, when all the perſecutors of God's people, and eſpecially thoſe perfidious prieſts, who abuſe their power to ſuppreſs the teſtimony of God's few faithful ſervants, whoſe life and doctrine reflects upon their ignorance, errors, ſloth, and immoralities, ſhall receive their righteous doom

CHAP. XII.

In this chapter we have, 1 The prophet's humble complaint to God of the proſperity of the wicked, ver. 1, 2 and his appeal to God concerning his own integrity, ver. 3 with a prayer that God would for the ſake of the public puniſh the wicked, ver. 3, 4 2 God's rebuke to the prophet for his uneaſineſs at his preſent troubles, bidding him prepare for greater, ver. 5, 6 3 A ſad lamentation of the preſent deplorable ſtate of the Iſrael of God, ver. 7—13 4 An intimation of mercy to God's people in a denunciation of wrath againſt thoſe that afflicted them, but with a promiſe, that if they would at laſt join themſelves with the people of God, they ſhould come in ſharers with them in their privileges, ver. 14—17

a Ezra ix. 15. ‡ Or, reaſon the caſe with thee. b Job xxi. 6. &c. xxi. 7. Pſ. xxxvii. 1. 35. & lxxiii. 3. &c. Chap. v. 28. Hab. i. 4. Mal. iii. 15. c Iſa. xxix. 13. d Pſ. xvii. 3. & cxxxix. 1. e Chap. xi. 20. f Hoſ. iv. 3.

1 a RIghteous *art* thou, O LORD, when I plead
with thee *yet* let me ‡ talk with thee of *thy*
judgments, b Wherefore doth the way of the wicked
proſper? *wherefore* are all they happy that deal very
treacherouſly? 2 Thou haſt planted them, yea, they
have taken root they grow, yea, they bring forth
fruit, c thou *art* near in their mouth, and far from their
reins. 3 But thou, O LORD, d knoweſt me thou
haſt ſeen me, and e tried mine heart towards thee. pull
them out like ſheep for the ſlaughter, and prepare them
for the day of ſlaughter 4 How long ſhall f the land

Before Christ 608

g Pſ. cvii. 34. h Chap. iv. 25. & vii. 20. & xxiii. 10. i Joſh. iii. 15. 1 Chron. xii. 15. Chap. xlix. 19. & l. 44. k Chap. ix. 4. & xi. 21. ‡ Or, cried after thee fully. l Prov. xxvi. 25. ‖ Heb. Good things.

mourn, and the herbs of every field wither, g for the
wickedneſs of them that dwell therein? h the beaſts are
conſumed, and the birds, becauſe they ſaid, He ſhall
not ſee our laſt end 5 ¶ If thou haſt run with the
footmen, and they have wearied thee, then how canſt
thou contend with horſes? and if in the land of peace
wherein thou truſtedſt *they wearied thee*, then how wilt
thou do in i the ſwelling of Jordan? 6 For even k thy
brethren, and the houſe of thy father, even they have
dealt treacherouſly with thee, yea, they ‡ have called a
multitude after thee, l believe them not, though they
ſpeak ‖ fair words unto thee

v. 1—6 The proſperity of the wicked hath been a great temptation to more than one good man, *Pſal.* lxxiii Jeremiah is ſtaggered with it, and thus deſires to be reſolved concerning this point

1 He preſumes to plead with God, and talk with him of his judgments, deſiring to obtain information and have his own doubts ſilenced, fully perſuaded that God is righteous, though he ſees myſterious providences he cannot ſolve, *v.* 1 *Note*, (1) Though we may not find fault with God's diſpenſations, we may reaſon with him upon them, and enquire into the grounds of them, for our greater ſatisfaction (2) Tho' there may be dark providences we cannot underſtand, we muſt never quit this great and general truth, that *God is righteous*, and whatever he doth, is well done

2 The particular ſubject of his enquiry is, the proſperity of the wicked *Their way proſpers*, their malicious deſires take effect, their treachery and hypocriſy meet with ſucceſs, and *they are happy* to outward appearance, living at eaſe, and enjoying every earthly good *Thou haſt planted them*, as if they were God's peculiar care, *yea, they have taken root they grow, yea, they bring forth fruit*, their families increaſe, their wealth accumulates, and they ſeem fixed in their poſſeſſions, *thou art near in their mouth*, they make a profeſſion of godlineſs, and have the Lord's name often in their lips, but notwithſtanding he is *far from their reins*, they have no real inward faith, fear, or love of him *Note*, (1) Worldly proſperity is here frequently the lot of God's enemies, who in their life-time receive their good things (2) The language of piety is eaſily learnt, but God trieth the reins, and requireth truth in the inward parts, without which, all beſides is but ſounding braſs, and a tinkling cymbal

3 God knew his ſimplicity as well as their hypocriſy, that his heart was right towards him, and that in all the trials he had been expoſed to, he had approved his fidelity, *v.* 3 *Note*, (1) It is happy for us when we can appeal to God for our uprightneſs before him (2) God's judgment concerning us is not taken from our outward appearance, but from our hearts, *keep, therefore, thy heart with all diligence* (3) We may ſit eaſy under men's revilings, if we are conſcious of God's approbation of us

4 He deſires to ſee the ruin of theſe wicked ones, that as fattened for ſlaughter God would pull them out, and rid the land of that burden under which it groaned For their wickedneſs, the famine devoured, and even the beaſts and birds periſhed for want of ſuſtenance, *becauſe they ſaid, he ſhall not ſee our laſt end*, either God, whoſe judgments they mocked, or Jeremiah, whoſe prophecy they deſpiſed, and whom they reſolved to diſpatch, that he at leaſt ſhould not live to ſee the fulfilment of the threatenings he denounced againſt them *Note*, (1) Proſperous ſinners are only as the ox fattened for the ſlaughter (2) The earth groans under men's iniquities, but it ſhall ſhortly be relieved in their deſtruction

5 God anſwers his complaints, not indeed in a direct explication of his diſpenſations, but in an admonition deſigned for his own profiting *If thou haſt run with the footmen, and they have wearied thee, then how canſt thou contend with horſes?* If thou canſt not find out the devices of the men of Anathoth, how ſhould he fathom the ſecrets of God's providence ſo ſome interpret it or rather, if theſe conflicts with the men of Anathoth diſcouraged him, how would he be able to cope with the king, princes, and prieſts at Jeruſalem? *and if in the land of peace wherein thou truſtedſt*, in his own city, where he promiſed himſelf peace and ſafety, *they have wearied thee*, made ſuch an impreſſion on his ſpirits, *what wilt thou do in the ſwellings of Jordan?* when a flood of greater perſecution ſhould burſt forth upon him, and threaten to overwhelm him *For even thy brethren, the prieſts, the houſe of thy father*, to whom by blood he was ſo nearly connected, *even they have dealt treacherouſly with thee*, ſeeking to ſilence or deſtroy him *yea, they have called a multitude after thee*, raiſed a mob againſt him, and inſtigated them to inſult and hoot him as he paſſed, *believe them not though they ſpeak fair words unto thee*, they pretend to abhor perſecution, and to diſcountenance ſuch riotous proceedings, when in fact they are at the bottom of them, and when their words are ſmoother than oil, they have hearts full of rancorous enmity *Note*, (1) They who ſtand up for God and his truth, muſt prepare themſelves for the world's oppoſition (2) Our bit-

Before Christ 608

tereſt enemies are often our neareſt kinſmen, or our brethren in office (3) God prepares his ſervants by leſſer trials for greater ones (4) In our own ſtrength the leaſt temptation will weary us, in God's ſtrength, we ſhall be enabled to ſtem the ſwellings of Jordan

7 ¶ I have forſaken mine houſe, I have left mine
heritage, I have given † the dearly beloved of my ſoul
into the hands of her enemies 8 Mine heritage is unto
me as a lion in the foreſt, it ‡ crieth out againſt me
therefore have I hated it 9 Mine heritage *is* unto
me [m] *as* ‖ a ſpeckled bird, the birds round about *are*
againſt her, come ye, aſſemble all the beaſts of the
field, [n] come to devour 10 [o] Many paſtors have de-
ſtroyed my vineyard, [p] they have troden my portion
under foot, they have made my § pleaſant portion a de-
ſolate wilderneſs 11 They have made it deſolate, *and
being* deſolate it mourneth unto me, the whole land
is made deſolate, [q] becauſe no man layeth *it* to heart
12 The ſpoilers are come upon all high places through
the wilderneſs for the ſword of the LORD ſhall de-
vour from the *one* end of the land even to the *other* end
of the land no fleſh ſhall have peace 13 [r] They have
ſown wheat, but ſhall reap thorns they have put them-
ſelves to pain, *but* ſhall not profit and † they [s] ſhall
be aſhamed of your revenues, becauſe of the fierce anger
of the LORD

† Heb The love ‡ Heb Giveth out his voice [m] Luke xx 46. ‖ Heb A bird with talons [n] Rev xix 17 [o] Chap vi 3 [p] Iſa lxiii 18 § Heb Portion of deſire [q] Iſa xlii 25 [r] Lev xxvi 16 Deut xxviii 38 Mic vi 15 Hag i 6 † Or ye [s] Chap iii 25

v. 7—13 We have here,

1 God's dereliction of his people His temple he deſerts, his heritage he forſakes, the dearly-beloved of his ſoul he gives up into the hands of his enemies Once they bore theſe favoured titles, God delighted in them, ſeparated them for himſelf, and choſe them for a peculiar people, ſetting his love upon them, but their ingratitude drove him from them, and left them an eaſy prey to every invader, v 7 The people of his heritage were as lions in the foreſt, roaring againſt God in the perſons of his prophets, blaſpheming his name, and renouncing his government, and become cruel, blood thirſty and oppreſſive, *therefore have I hated it*, withdrawn every token of favour from them, and devoted them to deſtruction *Mine heritage is unto me as a ſpeckled bird*, a ſtrange bird, around which the reſt gather, and peck and perſecute it or, *a bird with talons*, ravenous, and ſprinkled with the blood of its prey *Note*, Wo unto the ſoul, to the people from whom God departs, they are on the verge of ruin

2 Their deſtruction by the Chaldeans *Come ye, aſſemble all ye beaſts of the field, come to devour*, the armies of Nebuchadnezzar, fierce and ſavage, are ſummoned to take the field, and conſume this devoted people, *Rev* xix 17, 18 and no ſooner is it ſpoken than done *Many paſtors*, the captains of the Chaldean hoſt, *have deſtroyed my vineyard, they have trodden my portion under foot, they have made my pleaſant land a wilderneſs*, once God regarded this place and people as his own, and delighted in it as his portion, but now univerſal deſolation reigns, the country is turned into a wilderneſs, the cities ſacked, burnt, and raſed from their foundations, the ſword devours from one end of the land to the other and whilſt this impenitent people layeth not their ſins to heart, the very earth mourns as more deeply affected than they, upbraiding their ingratitude and hardneſs of heart, v 11, 12 and all attempts to extricate themſelves are vain It is the *ſword of the Lord*, and *therefore no fleſh ſhall have peace*, though *they ſow wheat, they ſhall reap thorns*, literally a curſe being upon the ground for their ſins, and figuratively though they contrived to engage the Egyptians as their auxiliaries, they would prove a vexation to them, rather than aſſiſtance Their *pains* are ſpent to no *profit*, and ſhame and confuſion will cover them when they ſee all their ſchemes diſappointed, and their *revenues*, ſo lavishly ſpent to hire foreign aid, thrown away, *becauſe of the fierce anger of the Lord*, againſt which, all their policy and power were equally fruitleſs, and which was infinitely more to be feared than even the Chaldean army *Note*, (1) If we have God for our enemy, we can hope for no peace in time or eternity (2) Nothing can engage ſinners to lay to heart the evil of their ways, when God withdraws his ſpirit from them, even the heavieſt judgments then but harden and exaſperate (3) If God ſpared not his own *pleaſant land*, let no other guilty land hope to eſcape

14 ¶ Thus ſaith the LORD againſt all mine evil
neighbours, [t] that touch the inheritance which I have
cauſed my people Iſrael to inherit, Behold, I [u] will
pluck them out of their land, and pluck out the houſe
of Judah from among them 15 And it ſhall come to
paſs after that I have plucked them out, I will return,
and [x] have compaſſion on them, and will bring them
again every man to his heritage, and every man to his
land 16 And it ſhall come to paſs, if they will dili-
gently learn the ways of my people, to ſwear by my
name, The LORD liveth (as [y] they taught my people
to ſwear by Baal) then [z] ſhall they be built in the midſt
of my people 17 But [a] if they will not obey, I will
utterly pluck up, and deſtroy that nation, ſaith the
LORD

[t] Zech ii 8 [u] Deut xxx 3 Chap xii 3 [x] Ezek xxviii 25 [y] Num xxv. 1 &c [z] Zech i 10 Eph ii 18 [a] Iſa lx 12. Zech xiv 17 Luke xix. 27

Before Christ 608

v 14—17 Jeremiah's commiſſion extended not merely to his own people, but to the neighbouring nations

1 God threatens them with deſtruction for their unkindneſs to Iſrael They are called his *evil neighbours*, ſuch as the Moabites, Ammonites, Philiſtines, &c by their connections with whom God's people had been led into ſin and idolatry, and that is the greateſt evil that any can do us, *that touch the inheritance that I have cauſed my people Iſrael to inherit*, made inroads upon them, aſſiſted the Chaldeans to deſtroy them, and led away many captives for this God will viſit them *Behold, I will pluck them out of their land*, they too ſhall be utterly waſted and deſtroyed, *and pluck the houſe of Judah from among them*, who, when their ruin came, would be releaſed, and eſcape from their captivity *Note*, (1) It is a dangerous and irkſome ſtate to dwell in the midſt of *evil neighbours* (2) They who have been our tempters, are often made our tormentors (3) If judgment begin at the houſe of God, let not the ungodly and the ſinner think of eſcaping

2 God ſtill appears ready to have compaſſion on them, notwithſtanding his judgments againſt them Though caſt out, and captives, he *will bring them again every man to his heritage, and his own land*, on this condition, that forſaking their former idolatries, they *diligently learn the ways of my people*, to worſhip and ſerve the true God, *to ſwear by my name, The Lord liveth*, and renounce all idols, in oppoſition to their former wicked conduct, when *they taught my people to ſwear by Baal, then*, not only ſhall their captivity be turned, but *they ſhall be built in the midſt of my people*, become entitled to all the bleſſings and benefits of native Iſraelites, united with them in love, and admitted to the worſhip and ſervice of God's temple And this ſeems to look further than the converſion of many to the Jewiſh religion, who returned with them from Babylon, and had moſt eminently its accompliſhment when the Gentiles were gathered into the church, made fellow-heirs, and of the ſame body, and partakers of the promiſe in Chriſt by the goſpel, *Eph* xi 20, 21 when Jews and Gentiles became, without diſtinction, one fold under one ſhepherd *Note*, (1) The bittereſt enemies of God and his people may yet be reconciled, there is ever hope for the returning ſinner (2) They who learn the ways of God's people, will have their happy lot with them (3) They who would be proficients in the ſchool of Chriſt, muſt uſe all diligence, ſloth and ignorance are inſeparable

3 Judgment is denounced on thoſe who refuſed to obey the goſpel, and return to God *I will utterly pluck up and deſtroy that nation, ſaith the Lord* *Note*, There is but one alternative, either we muſt turn to God, and be made happy in everlaſting bleſſedneſs, or by departing from God, and continuing impenitent, go down into everlaſting burnings

CHAP XIII.

Still the prophet attempts to awaken this ſecure and ſtubborn people to repentance, by the conſideration of the judgments that were coming upon them He is to tell them, 1 By the ſign of a girdle ſpoiled, that their pride ſhould be ſtained, ver 1—11 2 *By the ſign of bottles filled with wine, that their counſels ſhould be blaſted, ver* 12—14 3 *In conſideration hereof he is to call them to repent and humble themſelves, ver* 15—21 4 *He is to convince them that for their obſtinacy the judgments of God are ſo prolonged, ver* 22—27

1 THUS ſaith the LORD unto me, Go, and 601.
get thee a linen girdle, and put it upon thy
loins, and put it not in water 2 So I got a girdle,
according to the word of the LORD, and put *it* on
my loins 3 And the word of the LORD came unto
me the ſecond time, ſaying, 4 Take the girdle that
thou haſt got, which *is* upon thy loins, and ariſe, go
to Euphrates, and hide it there in a hole of the rock
5 So I went and hid it by Euphrates, as the LORD
commanded me 6 And it came to paſs after many
days, that the LORD ſaid unto me, Ariſe, go to Eu-
phrates, and take the girdle from thence, which I com-
manded thee to hide there 7 Then I went to Eu-
phrates, and digged, and took the girdle from the
place where I had hid it; and behold, the girdle was
marred, [a] it was profitable for nothing 8 Then the
word

[a] Pſ xiv 3 Iſ l 4

Before Christ 602

word of the LORD came unto me, ſaying, 9 Thus
ſaith the LORD, After this manner [b] will I mar the
pride of Judah, and the great pride of Jeruſalem 10
This evil people which refuſe to hear my words, [c] which
walk in the † imagination of their heart, and walk after
other gods to ſerve them, and to worſhip them, ſhall
even be as this girdle, which is good for nothing 11
For as the girdle cleaveth to the loins of a man, ſo have
I cauſed to cleave unto me the whole houſe of Iſrael,
and the whole houſe of Judah, ſaith the LORD, that
they might be unto me for a people, and [d] for a name,
and for a praiſe, and for a glory [e] but they would not
hear

b Lev xxvi 19 Iſa i 11, 17 & xxiii 9
c Chap ix 8 14 & xi 8 & xvi 12 & xviii 12
† Or ſtubbornneſs.
d Chap xxxiii 9
e Pſ lxxxi 11 Chap vii 24

v 1—11 They who ſtopped their ears againſt the prophet's words, have now a ſign before their eyes, if any means might be found to faſten conviction upon their hearts We have,

1 The ſign *A linen girdle*, or ſaſh, which the prophet is commanded to procure and wear, and which would be the more taken notice of, as his rough garments were unuſed to be found with ſuch finery No water muſt touch it, but when worn a while, he muſt go to the river Euphrates, and hide it in a hole in the rock, where, by the riſing and falling of the river, it would wet and dry, and rot the ſooner After a while he is ſent to fetch it from thence, and found it ſpoiled and rotten, *v* 1—7 Interpreters are divided concerning this matter, whether it was only done in viſion, as *Ezek* viii 3 xi 24 or real The former ſeems more generally received, becauſe of the length of they way, and the time requi ed to be ſpent in the journey; when his preſence at home was ſo neceſſary, but I rather incline to the latter opinion It is expreſsly ſaid, *he did as the Lord commanded him*, it gave a ſignal proof of the prophet's obedience, was a reproof of the people's ſtubbornneſs, that refuſed to take a ſtep in God's ways, and pointed out the long journey they ſhould make over the Euphrates when carried captive to Babylon

2 The explanation God had choſen Iſrael, and *cauſed them to cleave to him*, as a girdle about the loins of a man, intimating how near and dear they were to him, brought into a ſtate of moſt intimate communion with him, permitted to enter into the courts of his houſe, favoured with his preſence, and engaged by innumerable favours to cleave to him in all fidelity and love That they might be to him *for a people*, a peculiar people, for *a name* renowned in the earth, and to ſhew forth his *praiſe* and *glory*, and thus, like the curious girdle of the ephod, be ornamental to their profeſſion, and an honour to their holy religion *But they would not hear*, and therefore he threatens to *mar the pride of Judah, and the great pride of Jeruſalem*, eſpecially elated with having the temple in the midſt of her, but the higher their pride roſe, the lower ſhould their fall be, *v* 9 Since they had corrupted their ways by wickedneſs, and refuſed to hear the words of God's prophets, following their own vain imaginations, and ſunk into abominable idolatries, God will utterly conſume them, and make them vile as that girdle of rags, *v* 10 *Note*, (1) The greater the mercies we enjoy, the greater are our obligations to be faithful (2) God's ſervice is the higheſt honour, and whilſt we are moſt ſollicitous to glorify him, we at the ſame time gain for ourſelves that great name which is worth our ambition (3) It is folly to pretend a relation to God as *his people*, if we are not to him *for a praiſe* (4.) They who have ſtrutted here in the high conceit of their own goodneſs and excellence, will find their ſhame moſt confounding when this their vaunted righteouſneſs ſhall appear in the preſence of God no better than filthy rags (5) Whatever we are proud of, whether parts, gifts, ſtation, wealth, power, God regards ſuch ſelf-complacence with abhorrence, and what turned angels into devils, will make men, who imitate their ſins, companions in their ſuffering

12 ¶ Therefore thou ſhalt ſpeak unto them this
word, Thus ſaith the LORD God of Iſrael, Every
bottle ſhall be filled with wine and they ſhall ſay unto
thee, Do we not certainly know, that every bottle
ſhall be filled with wine? 13 Then ſhalt thou ſay
unto them, Thus ſaith the LORD, Behold, I will fill
all the inhabitants of this land, even the kings that ſit
upon David's throne, and the prieſts, and the prophets,
and all the inhabitants of Jeruſalem [f] with drunkenneſs
14 And I will daſh them ‖ one againſt another, even
the fathers, and the ſons together, ſaith the LORD
I will not pity, nor ſpare, nor have mercy, ‡ but deſtroy
them 15 ¶ Hear ye, and give ear, [g] be not proud
for the LORD hath ſpoken 16 [h] Give glory to the
LORD your God before he cauſe [i] darkneſs, and before
your feet ſtumble upon the dark mountains, and
while ye [k] look for light, he turn it into [l] the ſhadow
of death, *and* make *it* groſs darkneſs 17. But if ye
will not hear it, my ſoul ſhall weep in ſecret places for
your pride, and [m] mine eyes ſhall weep ſore, and run
down with tears, becauſe the LORD's flock is carried
away captive. 18 Say unto the king, and to the
queen, Humble yourſelves, [n] ſit down, for your ‖ principalities
ſhall come down, *even* the crown of your glory
19 [o] The cities of the ſouth ſhall be ſhut up, and none
ſhall open *them*, Judah ſhall be carried away captive all
of it, it ſhall be wholly carried away captive 20 Lift
up your eyes, and behold them that come [p] from the
north where *is* the flock *that* was given thee, thy beautiful
flock? 21 What wilt thou ſay when he ſhall §
puniſh thee? (for [q] thou haſt taught them *to be* captains,
and as chief over thee) [r] ſhall not ſorrows take thee as a
woman in travail?

f Iſa li 17, 21 & lxiii 6 Chap xxv 27, & li 7
‖ Heb A man againſt his brother
‡ Heb from deſtroying them
g Iſa xxviii 22
h Joſh vii 19
i Iſa viii 22 Lam iii 2
k Iſa lix 9
l Pſ xliv 19

Before Christ 602

m Chap ix 1 Lam i 2, 16 & ii 18
n Iſa xlvii 1
‖ Or head-tires
o Deut xxviii 52
p Chap i 14 & vi 22,
§ Heb Viſit upon thee Chap xi 22
q 2 Kings xvi 7
r Chap vi 24

v 12—21 We have here,

1 Another judgment threatned, under the figure of bottles filled with wine They were filled with drunkenneſs, and they ſhall be filled with wrath not underſtanding the prophet's meaning, they ſeem to ridicule it, *Do we not certainly know that every bottle ſhall be filled with wine*, this is not ſuch a ſtrange thing that it need be uſhered in with ſuch pomp, as thus *ſaith the Lord God of Iſrael*, but let them attend the explanation, and it will be found momentous, for God threatens to fill all the inhabitants of the land, king, prieſts, prophets and people, high and low, *with drunkenneſs*, with a ſpirit of infatuation, which will have the ſame effect upon them as wine, their counſels ſhall be confounded, they ſhall ſtagger, be weak as a drunken man, and be made ſick with ſmiting, daſhed one againſt another with inteſtine quarrels, they ſhall help forward their own ruin, *even the fathers and the ſons together*, *I will not pity nor ſpare, nor have mercy, but deſtroy them* with an utter deſtruction *Note*, Drunkards are chief among thoſe whoſe damnation ſlumbereth not

2 An admonition given them of God, to humble themſelves before it was too late *Be not proud*, above being taught, or too ſtubborn to bend to reproof Yea, the king and queen are called upon to ſet their ſubjects the example, and *to ſit* down in the duſt, and there confeſſing their ſins, and acknowledging the juſtice of their ſufferings, to *give glory to God*, *before he* come forth in judgment, and *cauſe darkneſs*, giving them up to the Babyloniſh captivity, and *before your feet ſtumble upon the dark mountains*, or *of the twilight*, when in the evening they ſhould ſteal from the city in hopes of eſcaping, but ſhould be ſeized, or referring to the afflictions they ſhould ſuffer in the land of Babylon, whither they ſhould be carried priſoners, and *while ye look for light*, a gleam of proſperity, and aſſiſtance from their confederates, *he turn it into the ſhadow of death, and make it groſs darkneſs*, overwhelming them with their calamities and diſappointments, and ſinking them in deſpair For unleſs they prevented their doom by a timely repentance, it is determined *your principalities ſhall come down*, all the power and dignity in which they prided themſelves and confided, *even the crown of your glory*, plucked from the king's head with all the enſigns of royalty, and he, among the reſt, led into an inglorious captivity *Note*, (1) They who are too proud to bend, are not too high to be broken (2) If ſinners will not give God glory by their penitence, he will glorify himſelf in their perdition (3) There is no eſcaping God's judgments by attempting to fly from them, the only door of hope is in humiliation to fly to him (4) The vain hopes of ſinners will ſerve but to aggravate their miſery, and to increaſe their confuſion (5) It becomes thoſe who are moſt exalted to ſet the gracious example, kings are not too great to ſit in the duſt, when God calls to weeping and mourning for the ſins of the land

3 The prophet expreſſes the unſpeakable grief it would give him to ſee them reject the divine admonitions *If ye will not hear it*, and obey, *my ſoul ſhall weep in ſecret places for your pride*, to ſome lonely ſolitude he would retire, and pour out his grief before God, ſince it was vain to expoſtulate with them That pride and ſtubbornneſs they would not repent of, he with tears would bewail, and *weep ſore* for thoſe deſolations they would not believe, nor ſeek to avert, *becauſe the Lord's flock*, for ſuch they had once been, *is carried away captive*, and hereby God would be diſhonoured and blaſphemed, which eſpecially affected the prophet's heart *Note*, (1) They who know the terrors of the Lord themſelves, cannot but tremble for thoſe who appear inſenſible of their danger (2) The ſins of their people cauſe many an aching heart to God's miniſters, and they mourn ſore over thoſe they cannot mend

4 Their ruin was inevitable *Their cities* (which lay ſouth of Babylon) *ſhall be ſhut up*, either beſieged, or left without inhabitant, and their captivity be compleat In Jehoiakim's time ſome were carried away, but in Zedekiah's none ſhall be left, *v* 19 The terrible army of invaders is already in view, coming from the north. *Where is thy flock that was given thee, thy beautiful flock?* once ſo diſtinguiſhed with every mark of God's favour and regard, and the glory of the whole earth, now diſ-

Before Christ 608

terest enemies are often our nearest kinsmen, or our brethren in office (3) God prepares his servants by lesser trials for greater ones (4) In our own strength the least temptation will wear; us, in God's strength, we shall be enabled to stem the swellings of Jordan

7 ¶ I have forsaken mine house, I have left mine
heritage, I have given † the dearly beloved of my soul
into the hands of her enemies 8 Mine heritage is unto
me as a lion in the forest, it ‡ crieth out against me
therefore have I hated it 9 Mine heritage *is* unto
me [m] *as* || a speckled bird, the birds round about *are*
against her, come ye, assemble all the beasts of the
field, [n] come to devour 10 [o] Many pastors have de-
stroyed my vineyard, [p] they have troden my portion
under foot, they have made my § pleasant portion a de-
solate wilderness 11 They have made it desolate, *and*
being desolate it mourneth unto me, the whole land
is made desolate, [q] because no man layeth *it* to heart
12. The spoilers are come upon all high places through
the wilderness for the sword of the LORD shall de-
vour from the *one* end of the land even to the *other* end
of the land no flesh shall have peace 13 [r] They have
sown wheat, but shall reap thorns they have put them-
selves to pain, *but* shall not profit and † they [s] shall
be ashamed of your revenues, because of the fierce anger
of the LORD

† Heb The love ‡ Heb Crieth out his voice [m] Luke xx 10 || Heb A bird with talons [n] Rev xix 17 [o] Chap vi 3 [p] Isa lxiii 18 § Heb Portion of desire [q] Isa xlii 25 [r] Lev xxvi 16 Deut xxviii 38 Mic vi 15 Hag i 6 † Or ye [s] Chap iii 25

v 7—13 We have here,

1 God's dereliction of his people His temple he deserts, his heritage he forsakes, the dearly-beloved of his soul he gives up into the hands of his enemies Once they bore these favoured titles, God delighted in them, separated them for himself, and chose them for a peculiar people, setting his love upon them, but their ingratitude drove him from them, and left them an easy prey to every invader, *v* 7 The people of his heritage were as lions in the forest, roaring against God in the persons of his prophets, blaspheming his name, and renouncing his government, and become cruel, blood-thirsty and oppressive, *therefore have I hated it*, withdrawn every token of favour from them, and devoted them to destruction *Mine heritage is unto me as a speckled bird*, a strange bird, around which the rest gather, and peck and persecute it or, *a bird with talons*, ravenous, and sprinkled with the blood of its prey *Note*, Wo unto the soul, to the people from whom God departs, they are on the verge of ruin

2 Their destruction by the Chaldeans *Come ye, assemble all ye beasts of the field, come to devour*, the armies of Nebuchadnezzar, fierce and savage, are summoned to take the field, and consume this devoted people, *Rev* xix 17, 18 and no sooner is it spoken than done *Many pastors*, the captains of the Chaldean host, *have destroyed my vineyard, they have trodden my portion under foot, they have made my pleasant land a wilderness*, once God regarded this place and people as his own, and delighted in it as his portion, but now universal desolation reigns, the country is turned into a wilderness, the cities sacked, burnt, and rased from their foundations, the sword devours from one end of the land to the other and whilst this impenitent people layeth not their sins to heart, the very earth mourns as more deeply affected than they, upbraiding their ingratitude and hardness of heart, *v* 11, 12 and all attempts to extricate themselves are vain It is the *sword of the Lord*, and *therefore no flesh shall have peace*, though *they sow wheat, they shall reap thorns*, literally a curse being upon the ground for their sins, and figuratively though they continued to engage the Egyptians as their auxiliaries, they would prove a vexation to them, rather than assistance Their *pains* are spent to no *profit*, and shame and confusion will cover them when they see all their schemes disappointed, and their *revenues*, so lavishly spent to hire foreign aid, thrown away, *because of the fierce anger of the Lord*, against which, all their policy and power were equally fruitless, and which was infinitely more to be feared than even the Chaldean army *Note*, (1.) If we have God for our enemy, we can hope for no peace in time or eternity (2) Nothing can engage sinners to lay to heart the evil of their ways, when God withdraws his spirit from them, even the heaviest judgments then but harden and exasperate (3) If God spared not his own *pleasant land* let no other guilty land hope to escape

14 ¶ Thus saith the LORD against all mine evil
neighbours, [t] that touch the inheritance which I have
caused my people Israel to inherit, Behold, I [u] will
pluck them out of their land, and pluck out the house
of Judah from among them 15 And it shall come to
pass after that I have plucked them out, I will return,
and [x] have compassion on them, and will bring them
again every man to his heritage, and every man to his
land 16 And it shall come to pass, if they will dili-
gently learn the ways of my people, to swear by my
name, The LORD liveth (as [y] they taught my people
to swear by Baal) then [z] shall they be built in the midst
of my people 17 But [a] if they will not obey, I will
utterly pluck up, and destroy that nation, saith the
LORD

[t] Zech ii 8 [u] Deut xxx 3 Chap xxxii 37 [x] Ezek xxxvi 24

Before Christ 608

[y] Num xxv, &c [z] Zech i 10. Eph ii 18 [a] Isa lx 12. Zech xiv 17 Luke xix 27

v 14—17 Jeremiah's commission extended not merely to his own people, but to the neighbouring nations

1 God threatens them with destruction for their unkindness to Israel They are called his *evil neighbours*, such as the Moabites, Ammonites, Philistines, &c by their connections with whom God's people had been led into sin and idolatry, and that is the greatest evil that any can do us, *that touch the inheritance that I have caused my people Israel to inherit*, made inroads upon them, assisted the Chaldeans to destroy them, and led away many captives for this God will visit them *Behold, I will pluck them out of their land*, they too shall be utterly wasted and destroyed, *and pluck the house of Judah from among them*, who, when their time came, would be released, and escape from their captivity *Note*, (1) It is a dangerous and irksome state to dwell in the midst of *evil neighbours* (2) They who have been our tempters, are often made our tormentors (3) If judgment begin at the house of God, let not the ungodly and the sinner think of escaping

2 God still appears ready to have compassion on them, notwithstanding his judgments against them Though cast out, and captives, he *will bring them again every man to his heritage, and his own land*, on this condition, that forsaking their former idolatries, they *diligently learn the ways of my people*, to worship and serve the true God, *to swear by my name, The Lord liveth*, and renounce all idols, in opposition to their former wicked conduct, when *they taught my people to swear by Baal, then*, not only shall their captivity be turned, but *they shall be built in the midst of my people*, become entitled to all the blessings and benefits of native Israelites, united with them in love, and admitted to the worship and service of God's temple And this seems to look farther than the conversion of many to the Jewish religion, who returned with them from Babylon, and had most eminently its accomplishment when the Gentiles were gathered into the church, made fellow-heirs, and of the same body, and partakers of the promise in Christ by the gospel, *Eph* xi 20, 21. when Jews and Gentiles became, without distinction, one fold under one shepherd *Note*, (1) The bitterest enemies of God and his people may yet be reconciled, there is ever hope for the returning sinner (2) They who learn the ways of God's people, will have their happy lot with them (3) They who would be proficients in the school of Christ, must use all diligence, sloth and ignorance are inseparable

3 Judgment is denounced on those who refused to obey the gospel, and return to God *I will utterly pluck up and destroy that nation, saith the Lord* *Note*, There is but one alternative; either we must turn to God, and be made happy in everlasting blessedness, or by departing from God, and continuing impenitent, go down into everlasting burnings

CHAP XIII.

Still the prophet attempts to awaken this secure and stubborn people to repentance, by the consideration of the judgments that were coming upon them He is to tell them, 1 By the sign of a girdle spoiled, that their pride should be stained, ver 1—11 2 *By the sign of bottles filled with wine, that their counsels should be blasted,* ver 12—14 3 *In consideration hereof he is to call them to repent and humble themselves,* ver 15—21 4 *He is to convince them that for their obstinacy the judgments of God are so prolonged,* ver 22—27

1 THUS saith the LORD unto me, Go, and 601.
get thee a linen girdle, and put it upon thy
loins, and put it not in water 2 So I got a girdle,
according to the word of the LORD, and put *it* on
my loins 3 And the word of the LORD came unto
me the second time, saying, 4 Take the girdle that
thou hast got, which *is* upon thy loins, and arise, go
to Euphrates, and hide it there in a hole of the rock
5 So I went and hid it by Euphrates, as the LORD
commanded me 6 And it came to pass after many
days, that the LORD said unto me, Arise, go to Eu-
phrates, and take the girdle from thence, which I com-
manded thee to hide there 7 Then I went to Eu-
phrates, and digged, and took the girdle from the
place where I had hid it, and behold, the girdle was
marred, [a] it was profitable for nothing 8 Then the
word

[a] Isa xlv 9 ... [illegible]

Before Christ 602

word of the LORD came unto me, ſaying, 9 Thus
ſaith the LORD, After this manner [b] will I mar the
pride of Judah, and the great pride of Jeruſalem 10
This evil people which refuſe to hear my words, [c] which
walk in the † imagination of their heart, and walk after
other gods to ſerve them, and to worſhip them, ſhall
even be as this girdle, which is good for nothing 11
For as the girdle cleaveth to the loins of a man, ſo have
I cauſed to cleave unto me the whole houſe of Iſrael,
and the whole houſe of Judah, ſaith the LORD; that
they might be unto me for a people, and [d] for a name,
and for a praiſe, and for a glory [e] but they would not
hear

b Lev xxvi 19 Iſa ii 11, 17 & xxiii 9
c Chap ix 14 & xi 8 & xvi 12 & xviii 12
† Or ſtubbornneſs
d Chap xxxiii 9
e Pſ lxxxi 11 Chap vii 24

v 1—11 They who ſtopped their ears againſt the prophet's words, have now a ſign before their eyes, if any means might be found to faſten conviction upon their hearts We have,

1 The ſign *A linen girdle*, or ſaſh, which the prophet is commanded to procure and wear, and which would be the more taken notice of, as his rough garments were unuſed to be bound with ſuch finery No water muſt touch it, but when worn a while, he muſt go to the river Euphrates, and hide it in a hole in the rock, where, by the riſing and falling of the river, it would wet and dry, and rot the ſooner After a while he is ſent to fetch it from thence, and found it ſpoiled and rotten, *v* 1—7 Interpreters are divided concerning this matter, whether it was only done in viſion, as *Ezek* viii 3 xi 24 or real The former ſeems more generally received, becauſe of the length of the way, and the time required to be ſpent in the journey, when his preſence at home was ſo neceſſary, but I rather incline to the latter opinion It is expreſly ſaid, *he did as the Lord commanded him*, it gave a ſignal proof of the prophet's obedience, was a reproof of the people's ſtubbornneſs, that refuſed to take a ſtep in God's ways, and pointed out the long journey they ſhould make over the Euphrates when carried captive to Babylon

2 The explanation God had choſen Iſrael, and *cauſed them to cleave to him*, as a girdle about the loins of a man, intimating how near and dear they were to him, brought into a ſtate of moſt intimate communion with him, permitted to enter into the courts of his houſe, favoured with his preſence, and engaged by innumerable favours to cleave to him in all fidelity and love That they might be to him *for a people*, a peculiar people, *for a name* renowned in the earth, and to ſhew forth his *praiſe* and *glory*, and thus, like the curious girdle of the ephod, be ornamental to their profeſſion, and an honour to their holy religion *But they would not hear*, and therefore he threatens to *mar the pride of Judah, and the great pride of Jeruſalem*, eſpecially elated with having the temple in the midſt of her, but the higher their pride roſe, the lower ſhould their fall be, *v* 9 Since they had corrupted their ways by wickedneſs, and refuſed to hear the words of God's prophets, following their own vain imaginations, and ſunk into abominable idolatries, God will utterly conſume them, and make them vile as that girdle of rags, *v* 10 *Note*, (1) The greater the mercies we enjoy, the greater are our obligations to be faithful (2) God's ſervice is the higheſt honour, and whilſt we are moſt ſollicitous to glorify him, we at the ſame time gain for ourſelves that great name which is worth our ambition (3) It is folly to pretend a relation to God as *his people*, if we are not to him *for a praiſe* (4) They who have ſtrutted here in the high conceit of their own goodneſs and excellence, will find their ſhame moſt confounding when this their vaunted righteouſneſs ſhall appear in the preſence of God no better than filthy rags (5) Whatever we are proud of, whether parts, gifts, ſtation, wealth, power, God regards ſuch ſelf-complacence with abhorrence, and what turned angels into devils, will make men, who imitate their ſins, companions in their ſufferings

12 ¶ Therefore thou ſhalt ſpeak unto them this
word, Thus ſaith the LORD God of Iſrael, Every
bottle ſhall be filled with wine and they ſhall ſay unto
thee, Do we not certainly know, that every bottle
ſhall be filled with wine? 13 Then ſhalt thou ſay
unto them, Thus ſaith the LORD, Behold, I will fill
all the inhabitants of this land, even the kings that ſit
upon David's throne, and the prieſts, and the prophets,
and all the inhabitants of Jeruſalem [f] with drunkenneſs
14 And I will daſh them † one againſt another, even
the fathers, and the ſons together, ſaith the LORD
I will not pity, nor ſpare, nor have mercy, ‡ but deſtroy
them 15 ¶ Hear ye, and give ear, [g] be not proud
for the LORD hath ſpoken 16 [h] Give glory to the
LORD your God before he cauſe [i] darkneſs, and before
your feet ſtumble upon the dark mountains, and
while ye [k] look for light, he turn it into [l] the ſhadow
of death, *and* make *it* groſs darkneſs 17 But if ye

f Iſa li 17, 21 & lxiii 6 Chap xxv 27 & li 7
† Heb A man againſt his brother
‡ Heb from deſtroying them
g Iſa xxviii 22
h Joſh vii 19
i Iſa viii 22 Lam iii 2
k Iſa lix 9
l Pſ xliv 19

will not hear it, my ſoul ſhall weep in ſecret places for
your pride, and [m] mine eyes ſhall weep ſore, and run
down with tears, becauſe the LORD's flock is carried
away captive. 18 Say unto the king, and to the
queen, Humble yourſelves, [n] ſit down, for your ‖ principalities
ſhall come down, *even* the crown of your glory
19 [o] The cities of the ſouth ſhall be ſhut up, and none
ſhall open *them*, Judah ſhall be carried away captive all
of it, it ſhall be wholly carried away captive 20 Lift
up your eyes, and behold them that come [p] from the
north where *is* the flock *that* was given thee, thy beautiful
flock? 21 What wilt thou ſay when he ſhall §
puniſh thee? (for [q] thou haſt taught them *to be* captains,
and as chief over thee) [r] ſhall not ſorrows take thee as a
woman in travail?

Before Christ 602
m Chap ix 1 Lam i 2, 16 & ii 18
n Iſa xlvii 1
‖ Or head-tires
o Deut xxviii 52
p Chap i 14 & vi 22
§ Heb Viſit upon thee Chap xi 22
q 2 Kings xvi 7
r Chap vi 24

v 12—21 We have here,

1 Another judgment threatned, under the figure of bottles filled with wine They were filled with drunkenneſs, and they ſhall be filled with wrath not underſtanding the prophet's meaning, they ſeem to ridicule it, *Do we not certainly know that every bottle ſhall be filled with wine*, this is not ſuch a ſtrange thing that it need be uſhered in with ſuch pomp, as thus *ſaith the Lord God of Iſrael*, but let them attend the explanation, and it will be found momentous, for God threatens to fill all the inhabitants of the land, king, prieſts, prophets and people, high and low, *with drunkenneſs*, with a ſpirit of infatuation, which will have the ſame effect upon them as wine, their counſels ſhall be confounded, they ſhall ſtagger, be weak as a drunken man, and be made ſick with ſmiting, daſhed one againſt another with inteſtine quarrels, they ſhall help forward their own ruin, *even the fathers and the ſons together*, *I will not pity nor ſpare, nor have mercy, but deſtroy them* with an utter deſtruction *Note*, Drunkards are chief among thoſe whoſe damnation ſlumbereth not

2 An admonition given them of God, to humble themſelves before it was too late *Be not proud*, above being taught, or too ſtubborn to bend to reproof Yea, the king and queen are called upon to ſet their ſubjects the example, and *to ſit* down in the duſt, and there confeſſing their ſins, and acknowledging the juſtice of their ſufferings, to *give glory to God*, *before he* come forth in judgment, and *cauſe darkneſs*, giving them up to the Babyloniſh captivity, and *before your feet ſtumble upon the dark mountains*, or *of the twilight*, when in the evening they ſhould ſteal from the city in hopes of eſcaping, but ſhould be ſeized, or referring to the afflictions they ſhould ſuffer in the land of Babylon, whither they ſhould be carried priſoners, and *while ye look for light*, a gleam of proſperity, and aſſiſtance from their confederates, *he turn it into the ſhadow of death, and make it groſs darkneſs*, overwhelming them with their calamities and diſappointments, and ſinking them in deſpair For unleſs they prevented their doom by a timely repentance, it is determined *your principalities ſhall come down*, all the power and dignity in which they prided themſelves and confided, *even the crown of your glory*, plucked from the king's head with all the enſigns of royalty, and he, among the reſt, led into an inglorious captivity *Note*, (1) They who are too proud to bend, are not too high to be broken (2) If ſinners will not give God glory by their penitence, he will glorify himſelf in their perdition (3) There is no eſcaping God's judgments by attempting to fly from them, the only door of hope is in humiliation to fly to him (4) The vain hopes of ſinners will ſerve but to aggravate their miſery, and to increaſe their confuſion (5) It becomes thoſe who are moſt exalted to ſet the gracious example, kings are not too great to ſit in the duſt, when God calls to weeping and mourning for the ſins of the land

3 The prophet expreſſes the unſpeakable grief it would give him to ſee them reject the divine admonitions *If ye will not hear it*, and obey, *my ſoul ſhall weep in ſecret places for your pride*, to ſome lonely ſolitude he would retire, and pour out his griefs before God, ſince it was vain to expoſtulate with them That pride and ſtubbornneſs they would not repent of, he with tears would bewail, and *weep ſore* for thoſe deſolations they would not believe, nor ſeek to avert, *becauſe the Lord's flock*, for ſuch they had once been, *is carried away captive*, and hereby God would be diſhonoured and blaſphemed, which eſpecially affected the prophet's heart *Note*, (1) They who know the terrors of the Lord themſelves, cannot but tremble for thoſe who appear inſenſible of their danger (2) The ſins of their people cauſe many an aching heart to God's miniſters, and they mourn ſore over thoſe they cannot mend

4 Their ruin was inevitable *Their cities* (which lay ſouth of Babylon) *ſhall be ſhut up*, either beſieged, or left without inhabitant, and their captivity be compleat In Jehoiakim's time ſome were carried away, but in Zedekiah's none ſhall be left, *v* 19 The terrible army of invaders is already in view, coming from the north. *Where is thy flock that was given thee, thy beautiful flock?* once ſo diſtinguiſhed with every mark of God's favour and regard, and the glory of the whole earth, now diſperſed

I i

Before Chriſt 602

perſed and ſcattered, and their place is no more found *What wilt thou ſay when he ſhall puniſh thee?* how ſpeechleſs would they be found before God, when by the Chaldean ſword he ſhould ariſe to viſit their iniquities? *for thou haſt taught them to be captains, and as chief over thee*, having invited them into their country formerly, and thereby opened a door for their conqueſts, 2 *Kings* xvi 7 *Shall not ſorrows take thee as a woman in travail?* ſorrows, ſudden, terrible, and unavoidable, would then ſeize on this devoted Judea *Note*, (1) They who have the charge of others committed to them, parents, magiſtrates, and eſpecially miniſters, ſhould often think of the ſolemn account they muſt one day make before the great ſhepherd and biſhop of ſouls (2) They who have rejected God's admonitions will be ſpeechleſs in the day of their viſitation

22 ¶ And if thou ſay in thine heart, ^s Wherefore
come theſe things upon me? For the greatneſs of thine
iniquity are ^t thy ſkirts diſcovered, and thy heels † made
bare 23 Can the Ethiopian change his ſkin, or the
leopard his ſpots? *then* may ye alſo do good, that are
‡ accuſtomed to do evil 24 Therefore ^u will I ſcatter
them as ſtubble that paſſeth away by the wind of the
wilderneſs. 25 ^x This *is* thy lot, the portion of thy
meaſures from me, ſaith the LORD, becauſe thou haſt
forgotten me, and ^y truſted in falſhood 26 Therefore
^z will I diſcover thy ſkirts upon thy face, that thy ſhame
may appear 27 ^a I have ſeen thine adulteries, and thy
neighings, the lewdneſs of thy whoredom, *and* thine
abominations ^b on the hills in the fields wo unto thee,
^c O Jeruſalem, wilt thou not be made clean? § when
ſhall it once *be?*

^s Chap. v 19 & xvi 10. ^t Iſa xlvii 2 3 Ver 26. Nah iii 5 † Or ſhall be violently taken away ‡ Heb taught ^u Hoſ xiii 3 ^x Job xx 29 ^y Chap vii 4 ^z Lam i 8 Ezek xvi 37 & xxiii 29 Hoſ ii 10 ^a Chap v 8 ^b Iſa lxv 7 Chap ii 20 Ezek vi 13 ^c Chap iv 14 § Heb After when or how long yet

v 22—27 It is here foretold, as before, that captivity awaited them, when naked and barefoot they ſhould be led away, confounded and aſhamed before their conquerors, *v* 26 In this miſerable caſe,

1 They are repreſented as enquiring into the cauſe of their calamities *If thou ſay in thine heart*, for God knows what paſſes there, *Wherefore come theſe things upon me?* either quarrelling with their afflictions and fretting againſt the Lord, or driven by the ſeverity of their ſufferings penitently to enquire into their cauſe

2 God anſwers them, *For the greatneſs of thine iniquity are thy ſkirts diſcovered, and thy heels made bare* God had not laid on them more than they had deſerved, for their iniquities were great and numberleſs, and they utterly incorrigible the black *Ethiopian* as ſoon might *change his ſkin*, or *the leopard his ſpots*, as they be reclaimed from their abominations, which habit and cuſtom had ingrained, and made a ſecond nature, or learn that good which their prophets inculcated, *v* 23 God had been forgotten by them, and their confidence placed on *falſhood*, the broken reed of Egyptian aid, *v* 25 Their idolatries and adulteries had been multiplied on every hill, in every field, openly and without a bluſh, therefore they might eaſily perceive the cauſe of their ruin *Woe unto thee, O Jeruſalem* for theſe things they are ſcattered as ſtubble before the wind of the wilderneſs, the Chaldean army, *v* 24 and this is their lot, and the portion aſſigned them of God, in juſt judgment for ſuch impieties and impenitence, *v* 25 *Note*, (1) God never lays upon ſinners more than they deſerve, but in all his judgments will be juſtified (2) Every man by nature is born like the ſooty Ethiopian, black in original ſin, and by practice and habit the ſtain is ſtill deeper fixed in the ſoul Not all the waters of the ocean can change the hue, no labour or attempts of man to cleanſe himſelf are of any avail, the fountain of a Redeemer's blood alone can waſh this Ethiopian white, and change this leopard's ſpots (3) Inveterate habits are very difficultly conquered, but divine grace is all ſufficient

3 The prophet expoſtulates once more with them, dangerous as their caſe was, it might not be yet utterly deſperate, *wilt thou not be made clean?* ſhall no entreaty prevail, when the fountain is yet open, and God's patience waits, *when ſhall it once be?* ſurely it was now high time to bethink themſelves, when ruin was almoſt at the door *Note*, (1) The reaſon why ſinners periſh is becauſe they will not come to Chriſt that they might have life (2) We muſt be made clean, or we can never enter God's holy place in heaven (3) God waits long upon ſinners, and expoſtulates with them on their delays, and they who diſappoint his patience will be left without excuſe (4) Moſt men reſolve ſome time or other to repent, but, putting it off to a diſtant day, death ſurprizes them in their ſins

CHAP XIV

This chapter was penned upon occaſion of a great drought this judgment began in the latter end of Joſiah's reign, but, as it ſhould ſeem, continued in the beginning of Jehoiakim's Here is, (1) A melancholy deſcription of it, ver 1—7 (2) A prayer to God to put an end to it, and to return in mercy to their land, ver 7—9 (3) A ſevere threatening, that God would proceed in his controverſy, becauſe they proceeded in their iniquity, ver 10—12 (4) The prophet lays the blame on their falſe prophets, and the doom is paſſed both on the deceivers and the deceived, ver 13—16 (5) Directions given to the prophet to lament over them, and his continuing to intercede for them, ver 17—22

Before Chriſt 601

1 THE word of the LORD that came to Jeremiah 601
concerning † the dearth 2 Judah mourneth,
and the gates thereof languiſh, they are black unto the
ground, and the cry of Jeruſalem is gone up 3 And
their nobles have ſent their ‡ little ones to the waters,
they came to the pits, *and* found no water, they returned
with their veſſels empty they were aſhamed and confounded,
and ^a covered their heads 4 Becauſe the
ground is chapt, for there was no rain in the earth, ^b the
plowmen were aſhamed, they covered their heads. 5
Yea, the hind alſo calved in the field, and forſook *it*, becauſe
there was no graſs 6 And the wild aſſes did
ſtand in the high places, ^c they ſnuffed up the wind like
dragons their eyes did fail becauſe *there was* no graſs
7. ¶ O LORD, though our iniquities teſtify againſt us,
^d do thou *it* for thy name's ſake for our backſlidings are
many, we have ſinned againſt thee 8 O ^e the hope
of Iſrael, ^f the ſaviour thereof in time of trouble, why
ſhouldſt thou be as a ſtranger in the land, and as a wayfaring
man, ^g *that* turneth aſide to tarry for a night?
9 Why ſhouldſt thou be as a man aſtoniſhed, as a
mighty man ^h *that* cannot ſave? yet thou, O LORD,
art in the midſt of us, and we are called by thy name,
leave us not

† Heb The words of the dearth ‡ Heb. Or meaner ones. ^a 2 Sam xv 30. ^b Joel i 11 ^c Chap ii 24 ^d Pſ xxv 11. Iſa xlviii 11 ^e Chap xvii 13 ^f Pſ xlvi 1 ^g See 2 Chron. xxxiii 8 Pſ cxxxii. 14 ^h See Iſa lix. 1

v 1—9 The dearth, here at large deſcribed, had been before intimated It was the beginning of ſorrows, and a call to them, by repentance to prevent the greater judgments in ſtore We have here,

1 A moſt affecting deſcription, which God gives the prophet, of the diſtreſs this viſitation would bring upon the land, *v* 1. The voice of bitter mourning and the cry of anguiſh is heard throughout Judah and Jeruſalem The very *gates languiſh*, deſerted by thoſe who uſed to ſit in them, and every face gathers blackneſs, pining with famine, and bowed to the ground with weakneſs and deſpair, *v* 2 The nobles, as well as people, are involved in the calamity in vain their ſervants ſearch for water, the heavens give no ſhowers, the rivers are dry, they return with their veſſels empty, and, with their maſters, are overwhelmed with grief and ſhame at the diſappointment, *v* 3. Parched up for want of rain, the earth cleaves in wide fiſſures, impenetrable to the plough, and leaves the huſbandman confounded under the affliction, *v* 4 The very beaſts ſuffer the loving hind, now grown unnatural, abandons her young for want of nouriſhment to ſupply them, the wild aſſes on the mountains top, ſcorched with the heat, pant for breath, and ſnuff the wind, and *their eyes fail*, famiſhed, *becauſe there is no graſs*. *Note*, (1) The common bleſſings of life are uſually diſregarded. yet, if God *ſtays the bottles of heaven*, we ſhall quickly find a drop of water more valuable than mountains of gold (2) They that take no ſhame for their ſins juſtly provoke God to confound them with diſappointments (3) Many mourn over their miſeries, who ſhed no tears over the guilt which provokes them

2 The prophet addreſſes his importunate prayer to God in this their wretched ſituation, and herein ſets them an example to pray for themſelves, and in what manner

(1) He begins with deep and humbling acknowledgments of their guilt and ſinfulneſs, *O Lord, our iniquities teſtify againſt us*, too great to be palliated or excuſed, too public to be denied, *for our backſlidings are many, we have ſinned againſt thee*, in open violation of thy law, and in oppoſition to all the methods of thy grace, for which they ſtand convicted before God, and own the juſtice of his judgments *Note*, True penitents are liberal in ſelf-accuſation, and deſire never to cover their ſin, but to confeſs them in all their malignity

(2) He pleads earneſtly for mercy, though he acknowledges they deſerve puniſhment *do thou it for thy name's ſake*, this being the ſinner's prevailing plea, not his own deſerts, but that God would glorify the riches of his ſovereign grace and power in the ſalvation of the unworthy

(3) He fills his mouth with arguments, to enforce his petition, drawn from their relation to God, and his glory concerned in their ſuffering. *O the hope of Iſrael*, their only hope, who had in times paſt ſaved them notwithſtanding their provocation, and to whoſe endleſs mercy they had ſtill recourſe *the ſaviour thereof in time of trouble*, who had often heard and anſwered their cries and prayers in the day of their diſtreſs, and in whom they truſted that he would yet deliver them *why ſhouldſt thou be as a ſtranger in the land?* an unconcerned ſpectator of their miſeries, as not intereſted in them, *and as a wayfaring man, that turneth aſide to tarry for a night?* lodging at an inn, and departing without

Before Chriſt 601

out the leaſt connection formed with the people *Why ſhouldſt thou be as a man aſtoniſhed, as a mighty man that cannot ſave?* for ſuch reflections would be caſt upon him by the heathen, if he ſuffered his own people to become a prey to their enemies, as if he wanted wiſdom or power to deliver them *Yet thou, O Lord, art in the midſt of us*, no ſtranger among them, but had long dwelt in the temple at Jeruſalem, and therefore he begs that it may not now be forſaken, *and we are called by thy name*, in profeſſion, in outward covenant, the people of God, *leave us not*, for this is the conſummation of all miſery, to be deſerted by him is to be irrecoverably loſt and undone *Note*, (1) The moſt powerful arguments are thoſe drawn from God's own glory (2) They who fly to God as their alone hope and ſaviour in their deepeſt diſtreſs ſhall not periſh (3) If God ſeems to diſregard the afflictions of his people, they have only themſelves to blame for provoking him to leave them (4) They may ſeem deſerted for a while whom the Lord really loves, and he departs from them only to quicken their repentance, and awaken their importunity in prayer for his return

10 ¶ Thus ſaith the LORD unto this people, Thus
have [i] they loved to wander, they have not refrained
their feet, therefore the LORD doth not accept them,
[k] he will now remember their iniquity, and viſit their
ſins 11 Then ſaid the LORD unto me, [l] Pray not
for this people for *their* good 12 [m] When they faſt
I will not hear their cry, and [n] when they offer burnt-
offering and an oblation, I will not accept them but [o] I
will conſume them by the ſword, and by the famine,
and by the peſtilence 13 ¶ [p] Then ſaid I, Ah, LORD
GOD, behold, the prophets ſay unto them, Ye ſhall not
ſee the ſword, neither ſhall ye have famine, but I will
give you aſſured peace in this place 14 Then the
LORD ſaid unto me, [q] The prophets propheſy lies in
my name, [r] I ſent them not, neither have I commanded
them, neither ſpake unto them they propheſy unto you
a falſe viſion and divination, and a thing of nought, and
the deceit of their heart 15 Therefore thus ſaith the
LORD concerning the prophets that propheſy in my
name, and I ſent them not, yet they ſay, Sword and
famine ſhall not be in this land by ſword and famine
ſhall thoſe prophets be conſumed. 16 And the people
to whom they propheſy, ſhall be caſt out in the ſtreets
of Jeruſalem, becauſe of the famine, and the ſword, and
[s] they ſhall have none to bury them, their wives, nor
their ſons, nor their daughters for I will pour their
wickedneſs upon them

[i] Chap. ii. 23, &c. [k] Hoſ. viii. 13. & ix. 9. [l] Ex. xxxii. 10. Chap. vii. 16. & xi. 14. [m] Prov. i. 28. Iſa. i. 15. & lviii. 3. Chap. xi. 11. Ezek. viii. 18. Mic. iii. 4. [n] Chap. vi. 20. & vii. 21, 22. [o] Chap. ix. 16. Ezek. v. 12. [p] Chap. iv. 10. [q] Chap. xxiii. 10. [r] Chap. xxiii. 21. & xxvii. 15. & xxix. 8, 9. [s] Pſ. lxxix. 3.

v 10—16 If ought could have prevailed to obtain pardon or reſpite, it had been this interceſſion, but we find it in vain

1 God forbids him to pray for what he cannot grant, and he will not have the precious breath of prayer waſted, *v* 11 The meaſure of their iniquities was full, their ſentence paſſed *They have loved to wander*, have taken delight in ſin, and, notwithſtanding the repeated warnings, *they have not refrained their feet*, but continued to that hour obſtinately impenitent, *therefore the Lord doth not accept them* indeed it was impoſſible he ſhould *he will now remember their iniquity, and viſit their ſins*, to puniſh them In vain they faſted, prayed, ſacrificed, their ſervices were hypocritical, and, whilſt their iniquities were not put away, ſo far from being acceptable, they were an abomination Devoted therefore to deſtruction, he threatens, *I will conſume them by the ſword, and by the famine, and by the peſtilence*, his three ſore judgments *Note*, (1) Whilſt men continue determinately bent in the ways of ſin, nothing can prevent their approaching ruin (2) They who bring down God's wrath on their heads by their iniquities, will not be able to caſt their deſtruction on any fatal neceſſity they were under, but owe it to their own choice, *they have loved to wander* (3) All formal duties and devotions are but hypocriſy and a provocation, when offered by an unregenerate heart

2 The prophet, loth utterly to abandon his people, ſuggeſts that they had been deluded by the fair promiſes and confident aſſertions of the falſe prophets A poor excuſe, it muſt be owned, when they had before warning of their danger, and rules to judge them by, but it was the beſt he could make for them, and therefore pleads it in their behalf *Note*, When a caſe is really bad, charity will teach us to make the beſt of it

3 God over-rules his plea He diſclaims all thoſe prophets who pretended a commiſſion from him which he never gave Their divination is falſe, *a thing of nought*, *the deceit of their heart*, groundleſs, worthleſs, and deluſive, *v* 15 as will quickly appear, when the judgments of God ſhall begin with them, and that ſword and famine, which they ſo confidently pronounced would never come, ſhall conſume thoſe lying prophets, *v* 16 And thoſe who have been deceived by them muſt periſh with them by ſword and famine, together with their wives, their ſons and their daughters, and their corpſes lie unburied in the ſtreet of Jeruſalem, God being determined to bring the puniſhment of their wickedneſs in full meaſure upon them *Note*, (1) They who flatter ſinners to their ruin ſhall themſelves receive the greater damnation (2) It will be no excuſe for the deceived that they followed thoſe who pretended a miſſion from God, when they have their Bibles, and ſome few faithful miniſters who warn them of their deluſions (3) When ſinners ſuffer, they may look upon their wickedneſs as the cauſe of it And when the deceived and deceiver lie down in hell together, they will prove but miſerable comforters to each other

17 ¶ Therefore thou ſhalt ſay this word unto them,
[t] Let mine eyes run down with tears night and day, and
let them not ceaſe for the virgin daughter of my people
is broken with a great breach, with a very grievous blow
18 [u] If I go forth into the field, then behold the ſlain
with the ſword, and if I enter into the city, then behold
them that are ſick with famine, yea, both the prophet
and the prieſt go about into a land that they know not
19 Haſt thou utterly rejected Judah? hath thy ſoul
lothed Zion? why haſt thou ſmitten us, and *there is* no
healing for us? [x] we looked for peace, and *there is* no
good, and for the time of healing, and behold trouble
20 We acknowledge, O LORD, our wickedneſs, *and*
the iniquity of our fathers, for [y] we have ſinned againſt
thee 21 Do not abhor *us*, for thy name's ſake, do not
diſgrace the throne of thy glory [z] remember, [a] break
not thy covenant with us 22 Are there *any* among
[b] the vanities of the Gentiles that can cauſe rain? or can
the heavens give ſhowers? [c] *art* not thou he, O LORD
our God? therefore we will wait upon thee for thou
haſt made all theſe *things*

[t] Chap. ix. 1. & xiii. 17. Lam. i. 16. & ii. 18. [u] Ezek. vii. 15. [x] Chap. viii. 15. [y] Pſ. cvi. 6. Dan. ix. 8. [z] Pſ. lxxiv. 20. & cvi. 45. [a] Pſ. lxxxix. 39. [b] Deut. xxxii. 21. [c] Pſ. cxxxv. 7. & cxlvii. 8. Iſa. xxx. 23. Chap. v. 24. & x. 13. [d] Iſa. viii. 17.

v 17—22 The deſolations of Judah affect the prophet's heart, and he is permitted to lament them, and though diſcouraged from prayer, he doth not eſteem it an abſolute prohibition, therefore once more he intercedes in behalf of this guilty people

1 He weeps, with ceaſeleſs ſorrow, over the dreadful calamities of his people, and God enjoins him to inform them of the cauſe of his tears, if peradventure it might affect their hearts with ſome apprehenſion of their impending miſeries, *v* 17 Wherever he went, nothing but horrid ſcenes of devaſtation preſented themſelves to his view Without, the Chaldean ſword ſtrewed the ground with the corpſes of the ſlain, within the city famine raged, and every where the dying groans were heard of thoſe who periſhed for want of food, and both the prieſt and prophet, thoſe who had been the deceivers of the people, are ſharers in their ſufferings, dragged captives into a ſtrange land, or wandering as vagabonds Some underſtand this of the true prophets, ſuch as Ezekiel and Daniel, who were carried into Babylon with the reſt, and which would excite freſh grief to ſee the righteous involved with the wicked *Note*, Though we may not refuſe pronouncing the ſinner's doom, it ſhould appear we deſire not the woful day, and they, who will not hear our warnings, ſhould ſee our weeping over their loſt ſouls

2 Once more, he cannot keep ſilence he pours out his prayer, if there be but the *peradventure* of hope

(1) He humbly expoſtulates *Haſt thou utterly rejected Judah?* that once favoured family, that ſtock from which Shiloh comes, *hath thy ſoul lothed Zion?* that once loved name, where God delighted to dwell *why haſt thou ſmitten us, and there is no healing for us?* not merely with the rod of affliction, but with the ſword of judgment, whoſe wound is incurable Far other expectations had they entertained *we looked for peace*, ſuch was their fond hope, and ſo had their prophets flattered them, *and there is no good*, their affairs went from evil to worſe and *for a time of healing*, after the heavy chaſtiſement they had endured, *and behold trouble*, without proſpect of its end or abatement But will God be no more entreated?

(2) He confeſſes they deſerve all and more than all they have yet endured *We acknowledge, O Lord, our wickedneſs*, that it is great and aggravated, *and the iniquity of our fathers*, whoſe examples they imitated, and filled the meaſure of their iniquities, *for we have ſinned againſt thee*, and juſtly provoked his wrath and indignation againſt them They own their guilt, they caſt themſelves on his mercy, which,

3 The prophet, in their behalf, earneſtly begs, *Do not abhor us*, if not embraced with the wonted tokens of divine favour, yet let us not be treated with utter deteſtation, and ſuffered to be entirely rooted out, *for thy name's ſake*, for they have nothing but this to plead, his honour is concerned in their ruin, *do not diſgrace the throne of thy glory*, that temple where his honour dwelt; and if this was laid deſolate, the heathen would triumph as if their gods were greater than Jehovah, that ſit between the cherubims *Remember, break not thy covenant with us* Indeed the covenant was broken on their part; but, on their penitent return, they might ſtill plead his promiſe, and would prove his fidelity. *Note*, (1) The moſt prevailing plea in prayer is to be drawn from God's glory, as intereſted in our ſalvation (2) It is a

bitter

Before Chriſt 601

bitter grief to the faithful heart to ſee religion diſgraced, and God blaſphemed (3) We muſt plead God's covenant, not as doubting his fidelity to his promiſes, but for the encouragement of our own faith

4 He diſclaims all dependance upon idols, and looks to God alone for relief under the preſent diſtreſs by reaſon of the drought *Are there any among the vanities of the Gentiles that can cauſe rain?* No All theſe idols cannot produce one drop of dew *Or can the heavens give ſhowers?* No All ſecond cauſes only can act according to the will of the firſt mover Therefore they will look from theſe to him who alone bindeth up the waters in the thick cloud *Art not thou he, O Lord our God?* on whom our confidence is placed, and who alone canſt open the windows of heaven *Therefore we will wait upon thee*, till thou art pleaſed to anſwer our prayer, and cauſe the clouds to drop down from above *for thou haſt made all theſe things*, the heavens and earth, and all that in them is, even the rain hath a father, and the drops of dew are formed by him, and deſcend at his command *Note*, (1) We cannot place too little dependance on the creature, nor too much on the Creator (2) They who *wait upon* God muſt *wait for* him, and they who patiently continue ſo to do will not be diſappointed of their hope

CHAP XV

Notwithſtanding the prophet's prayer, (1) God abandons the people to ruin (2) The prophet himſelf complains to God of his continual ſtruggle with his perſecutors, ver 10 God aſſures him that he ſhall be taken under ſpecial protection, ver 11—14 He appeals to God concerning his ſincerity in the diſcharge of his prophetical office, and thinks it hard he ſhould not have more of the comfort of it, ver 15—18 Freſh ſecurity is given him that, if he continues faithful, God will continue his care and favour to him, ver 19—21

1 THEN ſaid the LORD unto me, [a] Though
[b] Moſes and [c] Samuel ſtood before me, *yet* my
mind *could* not *be* towards this people, caſt them out of
my ſight, and let them go forth 2 And it ſhall come
to paſs, if they ſay unto thee, Whither ſhall we go forth?
then thou ſhalt tell them, Thus ſaith the LORD, [d] Such
as *are for* death, to death, and ſuch as *are* for the ſword,
to the ſword, and ſuch as *are* for the famine, to the
famine, and ſuch as are for the captivity, to the captivity
3 And I will [e] appoint over them four kinds,
ſaith the LORD the ſword to ſlay, and the dogs to tear,
and [f] the fowls of the heaven, and the beaſts of the earth,
to devour and deſtroy 4 And I will cauſe them [g] to
be removed into all kingdoms of the earth, becauſe of
[h] Manaſſeh the ſon of Hezekiah king of Judah, for
that which he did in Jeruſalem 5 For [i] who ſhall have
pity upon thee, O Jeruſalem? or who ſhall bemone thee?
or who ſhall go aſide † to aſk how thou doſt? 6 [k] Thou
haſt forſaken me, ſaith the LORD, thou art gone backward
therefore will I ſtretch out my hand againſt thee,
and deſtroy thee, [l] I am weary with repenting 7 And
I will fan them with a fan in the gates ‡ of the land I
will bereave *them* of children, I will deſtroy my people,
ſith [m] they return not from their ways 8 Their widows
are increaſed to me above the ſand of the ſeas I have
brought upon them § againſt the mother of the young
men, a ſpoiler at noon-day I have cauſed *him* to fall
upon it ſuddenly, and terrors upon the city 9 [n] She
that hath born ſeven, languiſheth ſhe hath given up
the ghoſt, [o] her ſun is gone down while *it was* yet day
ſhe hath been aſhamed and confounded, and the reſidue
of them will I deliver to the ſword before their enemies,
ſaith the LORD

a Ezek xiv 14 &c b Exod xxxii 11 14 Pſ xcix 6 c 1 Sam vii 9 d Chap xliii 11 Ezek v 2 Zech xi 9 e Lev xxvi 16, &c f Chap vii 33 g Deut xxviii 25, Chap xxiv 9 Ezek xxiii 46 h 2 Kings xxi 11 & xxiii 26 & xxiv 3 i Iſa li 19 † Heb To aſk thy peace k Chap ii 13 19 l Hoſ xiii 14 ‡ Or of the earth Lev xxvi 33 m Iſa ix 13, Chap v 3 Amos iv 10, 11 § Or againſt the mother city a young man ſpoiling, or againſt the mother and the young men n 1 Sam ii 5 o Amos viii 9

v 1—9 When the meaſure of a nation's iniquities are full, then vengeance to the uttermoſt will overtake them, and all interceſſion for them is vain

1 The decree is gone forth, terrible, irreverſible The greateſt favourites of heaven, the mightieſt men in prayer, if they were again upon earth, could avail nothing They are abandoned to their fate, and doomed to deſtruction, *v* 1 And if, when their ruin was told them, they ſhould tauntingly ſay, *Whither ſhall we go forth?* the anſwer is ready According to the divine decree, ſome ſhould die by the ſword, by peſtilence, by famine, and their carcaſes unburied, *v* 3 be food for dogs and the fowls of heaven, and the remnant go into a miſerable captivity, *v* 4 not a friend ſhall remain to pity their deplorable caſe, or to teſtify the leaſt concern for them, *v* 5 God's patience at an end his hand ſtretched out to deſtroy them without ſparing, *v* 6 and they ſhall be diſtreſſed as chaff before the fan *a ſpoiler at noon day*, Nebuchadnezzar, with the Chaldean army, ſhall come upon them openly, ſuddenly conſume their men of war, increaſe the number of their widows, *v* 8 and leave the mothers childleſs, robbed of thoſe darlings which were as the light of their eyes, aſhamed, confounded, and deprived of that ſupport on which they truſted, part ſhall be ſlain with the famine, and the reſidue fall by the ſword of the enemy, when Jeruſalem ſhall be taken *Note*, (1) God's ſpirit will not always ſtrive, nor his patience wait for ſinners when their day of grace is trifled away, the day of recompence will overtake them (2) When the Lord begins, he will make an end Let us fear to provoke his indignation, leſt repentance ſhould come too late

2 The cauſe of theſe judgments is their ſins, paſt and preſent for God never ſmites without cauſe Their former iniquities under Manaſſeh, ſon of Hezekiah, his idolatry, murders, and abominations, aggravated by the conſideration how horridly he had degenerated from his pious father's ways, cried for vengeance, and the meaſure of the ſins of that generation was filled by the impenitence of the preſent They *forſook God*, went *backward*, apoſtate from his commands and ways and worſhip, and, notwithſtanding all the methods he had uſed to reclaim them both by his miniſters and his providences, *they returned not from their ways* And when ſinners perſiſt in their wickedneſs, and refuſe to hearken, they may be aſſured eternal perdition will be the conſequence

10 ¶ [p] Wo is me, my mother, that thou haſt born
me a man of ſtrife, and a man of contention to the
whole earth I have neither lent on uſury, nor men have
lent to me on uſury, *yet* every one of them doth curſe
me. 11 The LORD ſaid, Verily it ſhall be well with
thy remnant, verily [q] I will † cauſe the enemy to entreat
thee *well* in the time of evil, and in the time of affliction
12 Shall iron break the northern iron and the
ſteel? 13 [r] Thy ſubſtance and thy treaſures will I give
to the ſpoil without price, and *that* for all thy ſins, even
in all thy borders 14 And [s] I will make *thee* to paſs
with thine enemies into a land *which* thou knoweſt not
for [t] a fire is kindled in mine anger, *which* ſhall burn upon
you

p Job iii 1, &c Chap xx 14 q Chap xl 4 † Or intreat the enemy for thee r Chap xvii 3 s Chap xvi 13 t Deut xxxii 22

v 10—14 Jeremiah, returned from his public miniſtry, in private here pours out his complaints unto God

1 He bewails his unhappy caſe, perſecuted and reviled by his ungrateful countrymen, and this not without ſome appearance of impatience, as if angry with his mother for having born him ſo hard it is, under great provocations, to keep the heart quiet He complains he was *a man of ſtrife* not contentious in his own ſpirit, but abuſed for his faithfulneſs, and every occaſion taken to quarrel with him though he had given them not the leaſt cauſe he had *neither lent on uſury*, nor borrowed, had not entangled himſelf with ſecular affairs, but given himſelf up wholly to the work of his miniſtry, was engaged in no tranſactions and trade that could give occaſion to debate, or afford matter for litigious ſuits at law yet they *curſed him*, treated him with contempt or with abhorrence, pouring out curſes upon him for the fidelity he ſhewed in delivering the meſſages he received from God *Note*, (1) It is the lot of the faithful miniſters of God to meet with the baſeſt uſage, and the moſt ungrateful return for their labours (2) The goſpel teaches us to follow peace with all men, yet, through the perverſeneſs of the world, too commonly it happens, that when we ſpeak to them of peace they make them ready to battle (3) Deſirable as it is to live in friendſhip and quiet with thoſe around us, it muſt never be purchaſed by baſe compliances, or flattering them in their ſins (4) Miniſters of God muſt not entangle themſelves with the affairs of this world, the care of men's ſouls ought wholly to engroſs their time and thoughts

2 The Lord in mercy anſwers him with gracious aſſurances of his protection *Verily it ſhall be well with thy remnant* The words are in form of an oath, aſſuring him of God's bleſſing during the reſidue of his days whatever became of the people, he ſhould be preſerved Thoſe very enemies, that were the rod of God's indignation to his countrymen, ſhould ſhew him kindneſs and favour, as was fulfilled *chap* xxxix 11, 12 *Note*, (1) They who are faithful to God, he will be careful of them He hath in his hand the hearts of all men, and can raiſe us up friends where we leaſt expected them (2) The zealous miniſters of God have often found protection from thoſe who ſhew no concern about religion, when bitterly perſecuted by the falſe profeſſors of it

3 God threatens his enemies with ruin *Shall iron break the northern iron?* Either the Jews ſhould not be able to hurt him, who had been ſet, *chap* i 18 as an *iron pillar* againſt them, or rather, all their efforts to reſiſt the northern army of the Chaldeans ſhould be uſeleſs, their ſubſtance and treaſure ſhall fall an eaſy prey, in ſhameful captivity they ſhould be led to Babylon, and the heavy wrath of God purſue them, and this the juſt puniſhment of *their ſins*, aggravated and univerſal *in all their borders*, the corruption of their manners being general, and ſpread from one end of the land to the other

Before Christ 601.

15 ¶ O LORD, thou knoweſt, remember me, and
viſit me, and [u] revenge me of my perſecutors, take me
not away in thy long-ſuffering know that [x] for thy ſake
I have ſuffered rebuke 16 Thy words were found,
and I did [y] eat them, and thy word was unto me the joy
and rejoicing of mine heart, for † I am called by thy
name, O LORD God of hoſts 17 [z] I ſat not in the
aſſembly of the mockers, nor rejoiced I ſat alone be-
cauſe of thy hand for thou haſt filled me [a] with in-
dignation 18 Why is [b] my pain perpetual? and my
wound incurable, *which* refuſeth to be healed? wilt thou
be altogether unto me as [c] a liar, *and as* [d] waters *that* fail?
19 ¶ Therefore thus ſaith the LORD, [e] If thou return,
then will I bring thee again, *and* thou ſhalt ſtand before
me and if thou [f] take forth the precious from the vile,
[g] thou ſhalt be as my mouth let them return unto thee,
but return not thou unto them 20 And I will [h] make
thee unto this people a fenced braſen wall, and they ſhall
fight againſt thee, but [i] they ſhall not prevail againſt
thee, for I *am* with thee to ſave thee, and to deliver thee,
ſaith the LORD 21 And I will deliver thee out of the
hand of the wicked, and I will redeem thee out of the
hand of the terrible

u 2 Tim. iv 14. x Mat. v 10, 11. y Job xxiii 12. Ezek. iii 1, 3. Rev. x 9. † Heb. Thy name is called upon me. z Pſ. i 1 & xxvi 4, 5. a Mark iii 5. b Chap. xxx 15. c Chap. i 17—19. d Job vi 15 &c. e Zech. iii 7. f Ezek. xxii 26 & xliv 23. g 2 Cor. v 20. h Chap. i 18 & vi 27. Ezek. iii 9. i Pſ. cxxix 2. Chap. xx 11, 12.

v 15—21 We have here,

1 The prophet's earneſt application to God, appealing to him who ſearcheth the heart for his integrity, and intreating the fulfilment of his promiſes

(1) He prays, *O Lord, thou knoweſt* my innocence, my ſufferings, and the malice of my enemies, *remember me* for good, *and viſit me* with thy ſalvation, *and revenge me of my perſecutors* Perhaps this was his infirmity, or he deſired it for God's glory, in whoſe name he had ſpoken *take me not away in thy long-ſuffering*, give me my life for a prey, when they are cut off, or leave me not to their power and malice He acknowledges that to the long-ſuffering of God he muſt owe it, the beſt, in the rigour of juſtice, being obnoxious to God's wrath *Know*, acknowledge and make it evident to my enemies, by thy interpoſition on my behalf, *that for thy ſake I have ſuffered rebuke*, becauſe of his fidelity in diſcharging his office and when this is really the caſe, we may confidently expect God will plead our quarrel, and vindicate our integrity from all the revilings of men

(2) He pleads the diligence he uſed in executing his commiſſion, the delight he took in God's word, and his carefulneſs to keep himſelf from every ſinful compliance with them *Thy words were found, and I did eat them*, as a hungry man his food his ears were attentive to drink in what God delivered to him, he carefully thought over and digeſted the words in his mind, *and* his heart feaſted upon them *thy word was unto me the joy and rejoicing of my heart* either he hoped the terrible threatnings he brought would move the people to repentance, or the gracious aſſurance that God would ſupport him encouraged him, or, above all, amidſt the dark judgments the promiſes of the incarnation of the Meſſiah, and his great ſalvation, which mingled therewith, revived and comforted his ſoul *For I am called by thy name, O Lord of hoſts*, which he delighted in as his greateſt honour, though others perhaps turned it to his reproach *I ſat not in the aſſembly of mockers*, partaking with them in their ſins, or by ſilence conniving at their wickedneſs, or *with them that make merry*, levity being inconſiſtent with the ſeriouſneſs of his character, and the melancholy meſſage he bore, *and rejoiced not*, even partaking of any lawful recreation, which the dreadful evils he beheld approaching would not ſuffer him to taſte *I ſat alone*, meditating on his meſſage, and mourning over the people, becauſe of *thy hand*, which he ſaw lighting down upon the nation in vengeance, or becauſe of the ſpirit of prophecy which he felt, *for thou haſt filled me with indignation*, either the indignation of the people againſt him, or his diſpleaſure againſt them for their impenitence, or a ſenſe of the heavy wrath of God ready to overtake them *Note*, (1) The word of God is the ſweeteſt repaſt to the believer's ſoul, and thence he derives his moſt reviving draughts of conſolation (2) When we have work to do for God, we muſt not only forſake what is in itſelf ſinful, but forgo what to others might be innocent (3) There is a holy indignation without ſin, when miniſters grieve over the hardneſs of men's hearts

(3) He expoſtulates with God it ſeems with ſomething of a murmuring ſpirit *why is my pain perpetual?* which he ſuffered for the people's ſake in his own mind, or from their ill uſage *Why is my wound incurable, which refuſeth to be healed?* there appearing no hopes of a change for the better, or any end of their reproaches *Wilt thou be altogether unto me as a liar, and as waters that fail?* leaving him in their hands, though he had promiſed to deliver him, *chap* i 19 and giving his enemies occaſion to reproach his confidence? No God will not ſuffer him to be thus confounded, nor any that put their truſt in him Therefore,

2 God anſwers his prayer He had expreſſed ſome diſtruſt and impatience, *therefore*, ſays God, *if thou wilt return*, aſhamed of this impatience, and humbly confeſſing it, *then I will bring thee again* to peace of conſcience, and the exerciſe of the miniſtry with which God had entruſted him, *and thou ſhalt ſtand before me*, eſtabliſhed in his office as a prophet *and if thou take forth the precious from the vile*, ſpeaking comfort to God's people and terror to the impenitent, *thou ſhalt be as my mouth*, employed as God's mouth to the people *Let them return unto thee*, in penitence and obedience to thy word, *but return not thou unto them*, giving way in the leaſt, keeping back a ſyllable of the threatnings to be denounced againſt them, or making any compliance with them and then, if he approved himſelf thus faithful, God would fulfil to him his promiſe, *chap* i 18 making him *a brazen wall*, againſt which all the efforts of the princes ſhould be vain and impotent God's preſence ſhould comfort, his power ſupport him, and ſave him from his foes, however many or mighty, *v* 20, 21 *Note*, (1) If we would return to the enjoyment of comfort, we muſt be reſtored to the right ſpirit from which we have departed (2) They who miniſter before God muſt carefully divide the word of truth, giving to the faithful their portion of comfort, and to the ungodly faithful warnings of their danger (3) When we approve ourſelves faithful, we ſhall be ſupported againſt all oppoſition, God's ſtrength ſhall be made perfect in our weakneſs, and all our terrible foes ſhall be compelled to lick the duſt

CHAP XVI

In this chapter, (1) The greatneſs of the Jews calamity is illuſtrated by prohibitions given to the prophet, neither to ſet up a houſe of his own, ver 1—4 *nor to go into the houſe of mourning, ver* 5, 6, 7, *nor into the houſe of feaſting, ver* 8, 9 (2) *God is juſtified in theſe ſevere proceedings againſt them, by an account of their great wickedneſs, ver* 10—13 (3) *An intimation is given of mercy in reſerve, ver* 14, 15 *But,* (4) *They muſt firſt ſmart ſeverely, ver* 16—18 (5) *The prophet prays for and expreſſes his faith in the converſion of the Gentiles, ver* 19—21

1 THE word of the LORD came alſo unto me,
ſaying, 2 Thou ſhalt not take thee a wife,
neither ſhalt thou have ſons nor daughters in this place
3 For thus ſaith the LORD concerning the ſons and
concerning the daughters *that are* born in this place, and
concerning their mothers that bare them, and concerning
their fathers that begat them in this land, 4 [a] They
ſhall die of grievous deaths, [b] they ſhall not be lamented,
neither ſhall they be buried *but* they ſhall be as dung
upon the face of the earth, and they ſhall be conſumed
by the ſword, and by famine, and [c] their carcaſes ſhall
be meat for the fowls of heaven, and for the beaſts of the
earth 5 For thus ſaith the LORD, [d] Enter not into
the houſe of ‖ mourning, neither go to lament, nor be-
moan them for I have taken away my peace from this
people, ſaith the LORD, *even* loving-kindneſs and mer-
cies 6 Both the great and the ſmall ſhall die in this
land they ſhall not be buried, neither ſhall *men* lament
for them, nor [e] cut themſelves, nor [f] make themſelves
bald for them 7 Neither ſhall *men* ‖ tear *themſelves* for
them in mourning to comfort them for the dead, neither
ſhall *men* [g] give them the cup of conſolation to drink for
their father or for their mother 8 Thou ſhalt not alſo
go into the houſe of feaſting, to ſit with them to eat and
to drink 9 For thus ſaith the LORD of hoſts, the God
of Iſrael, Behold, [h] I will cauſe to ceaſe out of this place
in your eyes, and in your days, the voice of mirth, and
the voice of gladneſs, the voice of the bridegroom, and
the voice of the bride

a Chap. xv 2. b Chap. xxv 33. c Pſ. lxxix 2. Chap. vii 33 & xxxiv 20. d Ezek. xxiv 17, 22. ‖ Or mourning-feaſt. e Lev. xix 28. Deut. xiv 1. f Iſa. xxii 12. ‖ Or break bread for them. Deut. xxvi 14. Job xlii 11. Ezek. xxiv 17. g Prov. xxxi 6. h Iſa. xxiv 7, 8. Chap. vii 34 & xxv 10. Ezek. xxvi 13. Hoſ. ii 11. Rev. xviii 23.

v 1—9 Example is often more effectual than precept He, who was ſent to warn others of the deſtruction of the land, muſt by his conduct ſhew his aſſured conviction of the truth of what he preached They, who are urging men to look to the eternal world, muſt ſhew their own hearts fixed upon it, by their holy ſelf-denial and deadneſs to every thing on earth Three things are forbidden the prophet, and the reaſons for theſe prohibitions ſubjoined

1 He muſt not marry, nor have a family Not as if a life of celibacy were enjoined or deſirable, but becauſe of the diſtreſs coming upon the land, which would make a family a burden, and occaſion the bittereſt anguiſh from the grievous deaths of thoſe ſo near and dear to him. For God was about to pour down his judgments, to ſend forth death in all its terrors, armed with the famine, peſtilence, and ſword, and to cover the earth with carcaſes ſo numerous, that there ſhould not be graves to receive them, nor any to lament over or to bury them

Before Chriſt 601.

2 He muſt not go to the houſe of mourning, *v* 5 With friendly ſympathy he had, no doubt, been wont to weep with thoſe that wept, but now he muſt abſtain, and ſhew no uſual expreſſion of grief for his neareſt friend or relation, becauſe either the dead were removed from the evils to come, or rather as a ſign to them of the greatneſs of the approaching calamities, when death would make ſuch terrible devaſtation, that even the great ſhould lie unburied on the ground, and none be left to ſhew the laſt kind office to the corpſe, or to mourn over it God having removed his peace from the land, a conſumption utter and univerſal is decreed againſt it

3 He muſt not go to the houſe of feaſting, *v* 8 He had been accuſtomed, no doubt, to join with his friends when they made an entertainment, and innocently to partake of their repaſt, but now mirth was unſeaſonable, and when he foreſaw the terrible wrath of God impending, he wanted by his own conduct to awaken their concern The voice of mirth and bridal ſongs were about to ceaſe, and no voice to be heard but the ſhrieks of the miſerable and the groans of the dying

10 ¶ And it ſhall come to paſs when thou ſhalt ſhew
this people all theſe words, and they ſhall ſay unto thee,
i Chap v 19 & xiii 22 ⁱ Wherefore hath the LORD pronounced all this great
evil againſt us? or ᵏ what *is* our iniquity? or what *is* our
k Mal ii 17 ſin that we have committed againſt the LORD our God?
l Deut xxix 25 Chap xxii 9 11 Then ſhalt thou ſay unto them, Becauſe ˡ your fathers
have forſaken me, ſaith the LORD, and have walked
after other gods, and have ſerved them, and have worſhipped
them, and have forſaken me, and have not kept
m Chap vii 26 my law 12 And ᵐ ye have done worſe than your
n Chap xiii 10 fathers, (for behold, ⁿ ye walk every one after the ‖ imagination
‖ Or ſtubbornneſs of his evil heart, that they may not hearken unto
o Deut iv 27 & xxviii 64, 65 me) 13 Therefore will I ᵒ caſt you out of this land,
into a land that ye know not, *neither* ye nor your fathers,
and there ſhall ye ſerve other gods day and night, where
I will not ſhew you favour

v 10—13 We have here,

1 The inſolent and unhumbled challenge this hardened people ſhould make, beholding his conduct and hearing his warnings They would aſk, *Wherefore hath the Lord pronounced all this great evil againſt us?* as if they had never given him any provocation or, *What is our iniquity? or what is our ſin that we have committed againſt the Lord our God?* They pretend a claim to God, as their God, and would deny the charge the prophet continued to lay againſt them, ſo blind, hardened, and obſtinate, are ſinners in the error of their ways; and, inſtead of juſtifying God in his judgments, quarrel with his viſitations as unjuſt or ſevere

2 The prophet has his anſwer given him, and enough to ſilence their preſumption Their fathers iniquities, backſlidings, diſobedience, and idolatries, were great and ſhameful, *v* 11 but their own far exceeded inſtead of being warned by the judgments they ſuffered, or being led to repentance by God's patience, they had grown worſe and worſe, filling up what was lacking of the wickedneſs of their predeceſſors, more perverſely ſet on their own evil ways, and more reſolutely hardened againſt all the rebukes of God's prophets, *v* 12 therefore no wonder that, as the juſt puniſhment of their iniquities, God would caſt them out of that good land which they had defiled, ſend them far off into a miſerable captivity, make that idolatry which had been their ſin their grievous puniſhment, and withdraw from them every token of favour that might alleviate their miſeries

p Iſa xliii 18 Chap xxiii 7, 8 14 ¶ Therefore behold, the ᵖ days come, ſaith the
LORD, that it ſhall no more be ſaid, The LORD liveth
that brought up the children of Iſrael out of the land
of Egypt, 15 But, The LORD liveth that brought
up the children of Iſrael from the land of the north, and
q Chap xxiv 6 from all the lands whither he had driven them and ᑫ I
will bring them again into their land that I gave unto
their fathers 16 ¶ Behold, I will ſend for many
r Amos iv 2 Hab i 15 ʳ fiſhers, ſaith the LORD, and they ſhall fiſh them, and
after will I ſend for many hunters, and they ſhall hunt
them from every mountain, and from every hill, and
s Job xxxiv 21 Prov v 21 & xv 3 Chap xxxii 19 out of the holes of the rocks 17 For ˢ mine eyes *are*
upon all their ways they are not hid from my face,
neither is their iniquity hid from mine eyes 18 And
firſt I will recompenſe their iniquity, and their ſin double,
t Ezek xliii 7, 9 becauſe ᵗ they have defiled my land, they have filled
mine inheritance with the carcaſes of their deteſtable and
u Pſ xviii 2 abominable things 19 O LORD, ᵘ my ſtrength and
x Chap xvi Nah i 7 my fortreſs, and ˣ my refuge in the day of affliction,
y Mal i 11 Iſa xlv 14 ʸ the Gentiles ſhall come unto thee from the ends of the
earth, and ſhall ſay, Surely our fathers have inherited
lies, vanity, and *things* ᶻ wherein *there is* no profit 20
Shall a man make gods unto himſelf, and ᵃ they *are* no
a Chap ii 11 Gal iv 8 gods? 21 Therefore behold, I will this once cauſe them
to know, I will cauſe them to know mine hand, and my
b Chap xxxiii 2 might, and they ſhall know that ᵇ my name *is* the
LORD

v 14—21 In judgment God ſtill remembers mercy

1 He gives them hopes that a glorious day of deliverance ſhould come, ſo much greater than that of their redemption from Egypt, that in a meaſure it ſhould obliterate the mention of it, *v* 14, 15 And this was primarily fulfilled in the recovery of the Jews from Babylon, and the countries of the north whither they had been carried away captives, and may have reference to that more glorious expected event, when the Lord ſhall call them into his church from their preſent diſperſion

2 Before he ſhewed them this favour he would ſeverely viſit their iniquities As fiſhes taken in an evil net, and beaſts in the hunter's ſnare, ſo would God give them up to the Chaldeans to be taken and deſtroyed, who ſhould purſue them into all their lurking places, and drag them into captivity, *v* 16 Their evil ways, however ſecret, were not hid from God's eye he marked their impious rites and abominable idolatries, *the carcaſes of their deteſtable things*, offered to their idols, ſo many, and ſo univerſally practiſed through the land, that they had filled God's inheritance with their horrid profanations For this therefore he threatens to *recompenſe their ſin double*, not beyond what it deſerved, but double above all other viſitations he had brought upon them, or much more than they feared or apprehended *Note*, (1) No darkneſs can hide the ſinner from God's eye (2) Flight is in vain when he purſues no cave, no mountain, can then conceal the guilty from his judgment

3 The prophet is comforted not only in the proſpect that the puniſhment of his people, however ſevere, would have an end, but alſo with the foreſight of the converſion of the Gentiles, *O Lord, my ſtrength and fortreſs*, who had hitherto ſupported him amidſt all his infirmities, and againſt all his enemies, *and my refuge in the day of affliction*, who would preſerve him amidſt all the approaching evils *the Gentiles ſhall come unto thee from the ends of the earth*, either when the Jews returned from Babylon, and many proſelytes came up with them, or when the goſpel was preached, and the Gentiles became obedient to the faith, renouncing the idols of their fathers, convinced of their vanity and unprofitableneſs, *v* 19 and aſtoniſhed at their abſurdity, who ever could think thoſe to be gods which were the workmanſhip of their own hands, wood or ſtone, *v* 20 But now God will cauſe them to know better, making them, by his efficacious grace, acquainted with his own glorious perfections as the only living Jehovah, with the goſpel of his dear Son, and the way of life and ſalvation attainable through the Redeemer

Some chuſe rather to underſtand all this of the Jews, called Gentiles, becauſe of their imitation of their ſins, and now quitting with ſhame their idolatries, and returning to the one living and true God *Note*, (1) They who make God their refuge ſhall find ſupport under the heavieſt afflictions (2) When the ſinner, convinced and aſhamed of his folly, begins bitterly to reflect upon himſelf, then God will again reſtore him to his favour, and make him know once more the wonders of his grace

CHAP XVII

In this chapter, (1) God convicts the Jews of idolatry, and condemns them to captivity for it, ver 1—4 (2) *He ſhews them the folly of all their carnal confidences, and that this was one of the ſins upon which his controverſy with them was grounded,* ver 5—11 (3) *The prophet appeals to God on account of the malice of his enemies, committing himſelf to the divine protection, and begging of God to appear for him,* ver 12—18 (4) *God by the prophet warns the people to keep holy the ſabbath day, aſſuring them that, if they did, it ſhould be the lengthening out of their tranquillity, but if not, God would, by ſome deſolating judgment, aſſert the honour of his ſabbaths,* ver 19—27

a Job xix 24 1 THE ſin of Judah *is* written with ᵃ a pen of iron,
† Heb Nail *and* with the † point of a diamond, ᵇ *it is* graven
b Prov iii 3 upon the table of their heart, and upon the horns of your
‡ Or As they remember their children, ſo remember they their altars altars 2 ‡ Whilſt ᶜ their children remember their
c Chap vii 18 altars and ᵈ their groves by the green trees upon the high
d Judg iii 7 Iſa i 29 & xvii 8 hills 3 O my mountain in the field, ᵉ I will give thy
e Chap xv 13 ſubſtance, *and* all thy treaſures to the ſpoil, *and* thy high
places for ſin, throughout all thy borders 4 And thou,
§ Heb in thyſelf even § thyſelf ſhalt diſcontinue from thine heritage that
f Deut xxxii 22 Chap xv 14 I gave thee, and I will cauſe thee to ſerve thine enemies
in the land which thou knoweſt not for ye have kindled
ᶠ a fire in mine anger, *which* ſhall burn for ever

v 1—4 They ſeemed to wonder, *chap* xvi 10 what they had done to deſerve ſuch heavy judgments But ſurely their was cauſe abundant

Before Christ 601

1 *The sin of Judah is written with a pen of iron, with the point of a diamond*, deep, legible, and lasting are the characters; the love of their iniquities is *graven upon their hearts*, *the horns of the altars* of their idols, sprinkled with the blood of their sacrifices, proclaimed their guilt, and their very children, trained up in their idolatrous rites, were evidences against them, or, *as they remember their children*, so do they *their altars*, with the same fondness, and so strongly attached to their abominations. *Note*, The iniquity of sinners is written before God. If the blood of Jesus blot not out the deadly charge, woe unto them in the day when the judgment shall sit, and the books be opened.

2 The charge being proved, judgment is passed on them. The city and temple, called the mountain of the Lord's house, *Mic.* iv. 1. are devoted to the spoil, with all their treasures, for the sin of the people *throughout the land*. The sin was universal, and so would be the desolation. *And thou, even thyself*, or *in thee*, those who dwell in the land, or *through thyself*, the ruin is of thy own seeking, *shalt discontinue from thine heritage that I gave thee*, led captive into a strange land, and doomed to hard servitude under their tyrannical conquerors, and this through the fierce anger of the Lord kindled against them, and which would burn against the impenitent among them, not only all their days, but to eternity. *Note*, If sinners continue hardened under God's present judgments, they will find these but the beginning of sorrows, and the sparks of those everlasting burnings which are kindling for them.

5 ¶ Thus saith the LORD, Cursed *be* the man that
trusteth in man, and [g] maketh flesh his arm, and whose
heart departeth from the LORD. 6 For he shall be
[h] like the heath in the desart, and shall not see when good
cometh, but shall inhabit the parched places in the wil-
derness, *in* [i] a salt land, and not inhabited. 7 [k] Blessed
is the man that trusteth in the LORD, and whose hope
the LORD is. 8 For he shall be [l] as a tree planted by
the waters, and *that* spreadeth out her roots by the ri-
ver, and shall not see when heat cometh, but her leaf
shall be green, and shall not be careful in the year of
drought, [m] neither shall cease from yielding fruit. 9 ¶
The heart *is* deceitful above all *things*, and [n] desperately
wicked, who can know it? 10 [o] I the LORD search
the heart, *I* try the reins, [p] even to give every man ac-
cording to his ways, *and* according to the fruit of his
doings. 11 *As* the partridge sitteth *on eggs*, and hatch-
eth *them* not; *so* he that getteth riches, and not by right,
[q] shall leave them in the midst of his days, and [r] at his
end shall be a fool.

g Isa. xxx. 1. h Chap. xvii. 6. i Deut. xxix. 23. k Psal. ii. 12. & xxxiv. 8. & cxxv. 1. cxlvi. 5. Prov. xvi. 20. Isa. xxx. 18. l Psal. i. 3. m [illegible] n John xvi. 16. o Gen. vi. 5. 1 Sam. xvi. 7. 1 Chron. xxviii. 9. Psal. [illegible] Prov. xvi. 2. p Chap. xxxii. 19. Rom. ii. 6. Rev. ii. 23. q [illegible] r Luke xii. 20.

v. 5—11. The Jews often thought by their alliances with the neighbouring nations to gain protection against their invading enemies. This was both their sin, and a chief cause of their ruin.

1. The prophet denounces the curse of God against such as *trusted in man, and made flesh their arm, and whose heart departed from the Lord*, withdrawing their confidence from him, to place it on worms, which was to change a rock for a reed. Thus they trusted alternately on the Egyptians and Assyrians, *see chap.* xi. 36, 37. to their sad disappointment; or they placed such confidence in their relation after the flesh to Abraham, that they promised themselves security, notwithstanding their faithless departures from Abraham's God. But the consequences would be ruinous, *like the heath in the wilderness*, so desolate should they be made, and serve as fuel to the flames of God's wrath, and *see no good day*, or behold and pine away at the mercies others should receive, from which they would be excluded, and become as a land parched and uninhabited, their country a desert themselves destitute of every comfort. *Note*, (1.) God is the only worthy object of our faith and hope: human confidences may fail us, he never will. (2.) When we depend on our own doings and duties to recommend us to God's favour, instead of trusting on the divine righteousness and grace of Jesus, we shall by the issue be convinced of the vanity of our dependence.

2. As miserable as they are who depart from God, so blessed and happy are they, who, renouncing all other grounds of hope, rest their souls on God in Christ alone, *v.* 7. They shall be like the tree planted by the rivers, always flourishing, and fruitful, firm-rooted, and in the most scorching season watered [illegible]. Their profession shall be ornamented, their stability secured; in time of severest temptation they shall be kept from withering, and their fruits of holiness shall abound and abide, till grace ripen into glory.

3. The cause of all departure from God is here laid open. *The heart is deceitful above all things, and desperately wicked, who can know it?* Man's nature is fallen, *his heart* is radically corrupt, all its faculties perverted, and his whole mind and conscience defiled: *deceitful above all things*, put false glosses upon sin, that [illegible] and [illegible] delights

in the ways of indulgence, that are never found; buoys up the vain confidence of the sinner with hopes of impunity and peace, when God hath said, There is no peace: *and desperately wicked*; not only evil, but evil continually and incurably, desperately set upon it, without power to abstain from it, or ability to get rid of the bondage of corruption; nay, rather hugging the chains. *who can know it?* The more we know of ourselves, far from having fathomed the abyss of evil, we discover but the more clearly, that the depths of corruption are unfathomable; we can neither understand the number of our errors, nor promise ourselves for a moment security from the deepest and foulest falls. There is a mystery of iniquity within us, that none can know but God alone, and nothing can cure but his almighty grace; and therefore it were folly to depend on ourselves or others, in whose hearts such deceit and desperate wickedness are so deeply rooted. But *I the Lord search the heart*; its most secret purposes are known to him. *I try the reins*, and see the rising thought afar off: from him nothing is hid, nothing is secret; and thus all-seeing ought he to be, who is the final judge of all, and by whose decisions our eternal state must be determined, and every man receive judgment according to truth. *Note*, (1.) Nothing affords so humbling a consideration to us, as this striking view of our fallen nature; the pride of man must here for ever stand aghast and confounded. (2.) They who place confidence in their own hearts, in their resolutions and purposes, prove how ignorant they are of themselves, and predict only their own falls. (3.) Since at God's awful judgment we must shortly stand to receive our doom, it becomes us daily to be proving ourselves, and begging of God to discover to us our own hearts, that we may now so judge ourselves, as not then to be condemned of the Lord.

4. A heavy charge is laid against them for their covetousness and injustice. They would be rich, and stuck at no methods to succeed, right or wrong; but God will not suffer them to enjoy their ill-gotten gains. Though brooding over them, as a partridge on her nest, their riches, like her eggs addled or broken, should afford them no solid satisfaction; and in the midst of their days, when they thought their toils were over, and began to talk of enjoying themselves, they shall be cut off, and leave their wealth all behind, made monuments of the folly of trusting on uncertain riches more than in the living God; and these things are written for our admonition: may we hear and be wise.

12 ¶ A glorious high throne from the beginning, *is*
the place of our sanctuary. 13 O LORD, the hope
of Israel, [s] all that forsake thee shall be ashamed, *and*
they that depart from me shall be written in the earth,
because [t] they have forsaken the LORD, the fountain of
living waters. 14 Heal me, O LORD, and I shall
be healed; save me, and I shall be saved: for [u] thou
art my praise. 15 ¶ Behold, they say unto me,
[x] Where is the word of the LORD? let it come now.
16 As for me, [y] I have not hastned from *being* a pastor
[‖] to follow thee, neither have I desired the woful day,
thou knowest: that which came out of my lips was
right before thee. 17 Be not [z] a terror unto me, [a] thou
art my hope in the day of evil. 18 [b] Let them be
confounded that persecute me, but [c] let not me be con-
founded; let them be dismayed, but let not me be dis-
mayed: bring upon them the day of evil, [d] and ‡ de-
stroy them with double destruction.

s Psal. lxxiii. 27. Isa. i. 28. t Chap. ii. 13. u Deut. x. 21. x Isa. v. 19. Amos v. 18. 2 Pet. iii. 4. y Chap. i. 4, &c. ‖ Heb. After thee. z [illegible] a Psal. lxxxvi. 15. b Chap. xvii. 19. c Psal. xxxv. 4. & xl. 14. d Psal. xxv. 2. ‖ Chap. xi. 20. ‡ Heb. Break them with a double breach.

v. 12—18. We have the prophet here,

1. Acknowledging how well they deserved to be rejected, who were ungrateful to a God so great and gracious. *A glorious high throne from the beginning is the place of our sanctuary*: in the temple at Jerusalem God had erected his throne, there he manifested his presence, and thither, as to a sanctuary, the guilty might flee, and find an hiding place, even to the mercy-seat. *O God, the hope of Israel*, the never failing refuge of the faithful, in whom none ever trusted and were confounded: but *all that forsake thee*, basely withdraw their allegiance, turn aside unto idols, or place their dependence on an arm of flesh, they *shall be ashamed*, their confidences shall fail them, and their iniquities issue in their confusion. *They that depart from me*, and will not hear the warning of God in the mouth of his prophet, *shall be written in the earth*, numbered with transgressors, and trampled upon with contempt; or rather consigned to the grave, cut off in their iniquities, *because they have forsaken the Lord, the fountain of living waters*, the source of all blessedness; and they who depart from him court their own misery.

2. He prays for himself. *Heal me, O Lord*; for though a prophet, he found much infirmity [illegible] him, and the [illegible] of sin still rooted in his heart, the effects of which would prove mortal, without the powerful efficacy of divine grace: or he was broken hearted for the sins of the people, and in the view of the evil coming upon them. *Heal me, and I shall be healed; save me, and I shall be saved*: God's power [illegible] on this he placed his dependence, and with him [illegible]

Before Christ 601

humble prayer, in God's appointed way, sought the blessing he wanted; *for thou art my praise*, the object of it continually, who hitherto had given him abundant matter for his praises, and he trusted would continue to do so. *Note*, (1) Every blessing we need must be sought by the prayer of faith. (2) Sin is the soul's disease, and will be fatal unless healed by grace. The salvation of eternity must be begun on earth: they who would be saved in heaven, must now be saved from the power of evil.

3. He complains of their hardened infidelity. He faithfully delivered the message he received from God, and they treated it with contempt. *Where is the word of the Lord?* where are the threatned judgments? they saw no symptoms of their approach, and utterly disbelieved them; and therefore in defiance bid them come. *Let it come now*, as if they were above all fear, and dared the arm of omnipotence. *Note*, When sinners are thus incorrigible, their damnation slumbereth not.

4. Their ill usage and insolent treatment had not discouraged him from the faithful and diligent discharge of his office. *I have not hastened from being a pastor after thee*, following God's directions, notwithstanding every opposition; *neither have I desired the woeful day*, or wished to see the miseries he foretold; but prayed and preached with all his might, that by a timely repentance they might prevent the threatned judgments. And for this he could appeal to the heart-searching God, *Thou knowest it: that which came out of my lips was right before thee*: he spoke exactly according to God's word, with uprightness and simplicity, and was conscious of God's approbation of his conduct. *Note*, (1) Whatever treatment we meet with, we must patiently and boldly persist in the work of our ministry. (2) Many think the preachers of God's word delight in declaring the terrors of the Lord, but it is the most painful part of their office. (3) They who have the heart-searching God to appeal to, need not regard the revilings of men.

5. He begs God's protection and support, and that his enemies might be put to confusion. *Be not a terror to me*; not only do not confound me before them, but comfort me under their opposition; for more seems to be implied than is expressed. *Thou art my hope in the day of evil*, I disclaim all other dependance. *Let them be confounded*, convinced and penitent, or silenced by the infliction of the threatned vengeance; *but let not me be confounded* by their wickedness, or in the event proved to have spoken falsely. *Let them be dismayed*, with the sense of their danger; *but let not me be dismayed* by their revilings or persecutions. *Bring upon them the day of evil*, at which they scoff; since they will not be reformed, it is but just they should suffer for their impenitence: *and destroy them with a double destruction*; utterly, or beyond all their apprehensions; or by the Chaldeans first, and finally by the Romans. And this he prays, not out of revenge for a private injury done to him, but in zeal for God's glory dishonoured by them. *Note*, (1) There is enough in the best to terrify them, if God were strict to mark what is amiss. (2) When he is our hope, we need fear no evil. (3) If we are faithful, God will never suffer us to be confounded.

e Prov. viii 2, 3
19 ¶ Thus said the LORD unto me, Go and e stand
in the gate of the children of the people, whereby the
kings of Judah come in, and by the which they go out,
and in all the gates of Jerusalem; 20 And say unto
them, Hear ye the word of the LORD, ye kings of Ju-
dah, and all Judah, and all the inhabitants of Jerusa-
lem that enter in by these gates: 21 Thus saith the
f Num xv 32 &c. Neh xiii 19
LORD, f Take heed to yourselves, and bear no burden
on the sabbath day, nor bring *it* in by the gates of Je-
rusalem; 22 Neither carry forth a burden out of your
houses on the sabbath day, neither do ye any work, but
g Ex. xx 8 & xxiii 12 & xxxi 13 Ezek. xx
hallow ye the sabbath-day, as g I commanded your fa-
thers. 23 But h they obeyed not, neither inclined their
h Chap. xi
ear, but made their neck stiff, that they might not hear,
nor receive instruction. 24 And it shall come to pass,
if ye diligently hearken unto me, saith the LORD, to
bring in no burden through the gates of this city on
the sabbath day, but hallow the sabbath-day, to do no
i Chap. xxii 4
work therein; 25 i Then shall there enter into the
gates of this city, kings and princes sitting upon the
throne of David, riding in chariots, and on horses, they
and their princes, the men of Judah, and the inhabitants
of Jerusalem; and this city shall remain for ever. 26
k Chap. xxxii 44
And they shall come from the cities of Judah, and from
k the places about Jerusalem, and from the land of Ben-
jamin, and from the plain, and from the mountains,
and from the south, bringing burnt offerings, and sacri-
l Pf. l. 14 † Heb. Bringing praise or confession
fices, and meat-offerings, and incense, and l † bringing
sacrifices of praise unto the house of the LORD. 27
But if you will not hearken unto me to hallow the sab-
bath-day, and not to bear a burden, even entring in at
the gates of Jerusalem on the sabbath-day; then m will I
m Chap. lii 13 Amos ii 5
kindle a fire in the gates thereof, and it shall devour the
palaces of Jerusalem, and it shall not be quenched.

v. 19—27. This is a new discourse, the subject relates to the sanctification of the sabbath-day. We have,

1. The places where he must deliver it. In the gate of the king, that all the great men at the court might hear it, whose good example would be very influential, or their bad conduct productive of peculiar evil: and then in all the gates of Jerusalem, that all might hear, and none plead ignorance, from the least to the greatest, where the matter was of such universal concern.

2. The manner is prescribed in which the sabbath-day should be observed. *Thus saith the Lord*, whom all are bound to obey, and whose word whoever transgresses, doth it at his peril; *Take heed to yourselves*, where so much depended upon it, they had need be careful; or, *take heed to your souls*, for nothing is well done in God's sight, but what comes from the heart. They must *bear no burden*, be employed in no servile work of their ordinary calling, in husbandry, traffic, or merchandize; but *hallow the sabbath-day*, in the diligent and conscientious improvement of those sacred hours in every public and private means of grace, *as I commanded your fathers*. It was no new commandment, but enjoined from the day they were taken into covenant with God, on their deliverance from Egypt, though their fathers had rebelled and smarted for it, whose ill examples they must shun, and be admonished by their suffering, and not be, like them, untractable and disobedient.

3. The blessedness and benefit of observing the divine command would be very great to the nation, and to all who belonged thereunto. Their kings of the royal race of David should continue to reign in splendor, and they be happy under their mild government, *v.* 25. Their city and country should prosper exceedingly; religion flourish through the land, God's altar never want sacrifices, nor they the liberal offerings to bring, out of the abundance which God would bestow on them. *Note*, (1) True religion is the greatest friend to national happiness. (2) Nothing hath so immediate a tendency to promote godliness, as the conscientious observation of the sabbath-day.

4. Disobedience to this injunction would certainly be attended with the most fatal consequences. In just indignation for his slighted sabbaths, the fire of God's wrath would be kindled, nor ever be quenched, till the gates of Jerusalem are in flames by invading foes, the executioners of his vengeance, her palaces laid in smoky ruins, and utter desolations poured out upon all the cities of Judah. Let sabbath-breakers remember, and tremble at the fire of divine vengeance which they provoke.

CHAP. XVIII.

In this chapter we have, 1. God's ways of dealing with nations and kingdoms pointed out; that he can as easily do what he will with them, as the potter can with the clay, ver. 1—6. *But that he certainly will do what is just; nothing but impenitence will be a nation's ruin,* ver. 7—10. *2. The folly of the Jews demonstrated in departing from their God to idols, and so bringing ruin upon themselves, notwithstanding the fair warnings given them, and God's kind intentions towards them,* ver. 11—17. *3. The prophet's complaint to God of the ingratitude and malice of his enemies, and his prayers against them,* ver. 18—23.

1 THE word which came to Jeremiah from the
LORD, saying, 2 Arise, and go down to
the potter's house, and there I will cause thee to hear
my words. 3 Then I went down to the potter's house,
and behold, he wrought a work on the † wheels. 4 † Or frames, or seats
And the vessel that he made of clay was marred in the
hands of the potter, so he made it again another
vessel, a as seemed good to the potter to make *it*. 5 a Pf. cxv. Rom. ix 21
Then the word of the LORD came to me, saying,
6 O house of Israel, b cannot I do with you as this pot- b Isa. xlv 9 Wisd. xv 7 Rom. ix 20
ter? saith the LORD. Behold, c as the clay *is* in the
potter's hand, so *are* ye in mine hand, O house of c Isa. lxiv 8
Israel. 7 *At what* instant I shall speak concerning a
nation, and concerning a kingdom, to d pluck up, and d Chap. i
to pull down, and to destroy *it*; 8 e If that nation e Ezek. xviii 21 & xxxiii 11
against whom I have pronounced, turn from their evil,
f I will repent of the evil that I thought to do unto f Jonah iii 10
them. 9 And *at what* instant I shall speak concerning
a nation, and concerning a kingdom, to build and to
plant *it*; 10 If it do evil in my sight, that it obey
not my voice, then g I will repent of the good where- g 1 Sam. ii 30
with I said I would benefit them.

v. 1—10.

Before Christ 605

v. 1—10 God often teaches by similitudes to make the deeper impression, and that the truths may be the better remembered. We have,

1. The prophet sent to the potter's house, and informed, that God would there instruct him. Instantly obedient, he goes down, observes the workman turning the wheel, fashioning the vessels, marring and making them according to his pleasure.

2. God's application of the subject. Such absolute power as the potter hath over the clay, hath God over the sons of men. He hath the most incontestible right over us: it were arrogance in us to find fault with his procedure, and folly to oppose what we cannot prevent. According to the counsels of his own will he may dispose of nations and individuals, and none can say unto him, What dost thou? Submission absolute and entire to his will is our bounden duty: not that he exercises his power in any manner to the impeachment of his justice or mercy. He will be found righteous in all his ways, not only sovereignly great, but infinitely gracious. Even when his threatnings have gone forth against a nation, and their destruction approaches, if they repent and return, he will change the method of his dispensations towards them, remove their fears, and return to them in mercy. On the other hand, if he have spoken by way of promise, to crown a people with every national blessing, to enrich them with good, and prosper all their enterprizes; if they prove ungrateful for his favours, desert his service, and disobey his word, then he will turn the current of his kindness from them, and pour on them the wrath they have provoked. Note, (1.) All our miseries may be traced from our sins, whether private or public. (2.) God will make his glory to appear; and though he is absolutely sovereign none have a right to question him, he will vindicate his ways to man, and appear just when he judgeth.

11 ¶ Now therefore go to, speak to the men of Judah, and to the inhabitants of Jerusalem, saying, Thus
saith the LORD, Behold, I † frame evil against you,
and devise a device against you: [b] return ye now every
one from his evil way, and make your ways and your
doings good. 12 And they said, [i] There is no hope,
but we will walk after our own devices, and we will
every one do the imagination of his evil heart. 13
Therefore thus saith the LORD; [k] Ask ye now among
the heathen, who hath heard such things: the virgin of
Israel hath done [l] a very horrible thing. 14 Will *a
man leave* ‡ the snow of Lebanon, *which cometh* from the
rock of the field? *or* shall the cold flowing waters that
come from another place, be forsaken? 15 Because
[m] my people hath forgotten me, they have burnt incense
to vanity, and they have caused them to stumble in their
ways *from* [n] the ancient paths, to walk in paths, in a
way not cast up; 16 To make their land desolate,
and a perpetual hissing; every one that passeth thereby
shall be astonished, and wag his head. 17 [p] I will
scatter them [q] as with an east-wind before the enemy;
I will shew them the back and not the face in the day
of their calamity.

† Heb. Frame pot[ter] l[i]ke. b 2 Kings xvii. 13. Chap. vii. 3. & xxv. 5. & xxvi. 13. & xxxv. 15. i Chap. ii. [25]. k Chap. ii. 10. 1 Cor. v. 1. l Chap. v. 30. ‡ Or, my fields for a rock, or for the snow of Lebanon? Shall the running waters be forsaken for the strange cold waters? m Chap. ii. 13, 32. & iii. 21. & xiii. 25. & xv. 17. n Chap. vi. 16. p Chap. xix. 8. q [Chap.] xiii. 24. [r] Psal. xlviii. 7. [s] Chap. ii. 27. [t] Deut. xxxii. 35.

v. 11—17. The foregoing truths are here particularly applied to the Jewish nation. Here is,

1. The warning and admonition given to the Jewish people. Evil was on the wheel for them, though the execution was for a while suspended; and one more invitation given them, by their speedy and penitent return to prevent the impending ruin, v. 11. Note, God never strikes without warning: they who continue impenitent are inexcusable.

2. Their hardened rejection of the warning. *They said, There is no hope*; it nothing but putting from their sins would do, they resolved to abide the consequences. Let God do his worst, *we will walk after our own devices, and we will do every one the imagination of his evil heart.* Note, Sinners often do not express themselves with such effrontery in words, yet practically every sinner doth it in works, and these speak most strongly.

3. Their monstrous folly and wickedness upbraided. Among the vilest heathen nations were no abomination or insolence found equal to theirs: even the people of Nineveh repented at the preaching of Jonah; but, horrible to tell! Israel, that *virgin daughter*, that by her relation to God should have kept herself wholly for him, pure in his ways and worship, hath apostatized from him, hath forsaken the living God for dumb idols. *Will a man*, parched with thirst, *leave the snow water of Lebanon*, which cometh down melted in summer, *from the rock of the field? or shall the cold flowing waters that come from another place be forsaken* by the thirsty traveller? This would be folly unheard-of; yet more egregiously foolish were they, *because my people hath forgotten me*, the fountain of living waters, to drink at the broken cisterns of idolatries. *They have burnt incense to vanity*, to wretched deities, who could not profit them: or, *in vain they burn incense*, their services were an abomination whilst their sins remained: *and they have caused them to stumble in their ways*, their idols, or their false prophets, *from the ancient paths*, the way revealed of old in God's word, or *the paths of eternity*, which led to glory everlasting, *to walk in paths, in a way not cast up*, a road unknown to the saints of God, a way of wickedness and idolatry, in which they stumbled and fell into the pit of eternal misery; this being the certain and fatal consequence of their ways, *to make their land desolate*, ravaged by the enemy, and depopulated by famine and the sword; *a perpetual hissing*, every one who passed by expressing their abhorrence of such guilty conduct, *astonished* at the desolations they beheld, and *wagging their head*, deriding or upbraiding them. With blasts of displeasure, furious as *the east wind*, God will *scatter them before their enemies*, weak as stubble to resist their attacks, and *in the day of their calamity* turn a deaf ear to their cries, nor cast a look of compassion on their miseries. Note, (1.) Apostates deserve to be upbraided, and they will shortly awake to everlasting shame and contempt. (2.) They who persevere in the ways of sin, must expect no mercy in the day of judgment: God will then mock at their calamities, Prov. i. 26—28.

18 ¶ Then said they, [r] Come, and let us devise de-
vices against Jeremiah; for [s] the law shall not perish
from the priest, nor counsel from the wise, nor the
word from the prophet. Come, and let us smite him
† with the tongue, and let us not give heed to any of
his words. 19 Give heed to me, O LORD, and heark-
en to the voice of them that contend with me. 20
Shall evil be recompensed for good? for they have dig-
ged a pit for my soul. Remember that I stood before
thee to speak good for them, *and* [t] to turn away thy
wrath from them. 21 Therefore [u] deliver up their chil-
dren to the famine, and ‡ pour out their *blood* by the
force of the sword; and let their wives be bereaved of
their children, and *be* widows; and let their men be put
to death; *let* their young men *be* slain by the sword in
battle. 22 Let a cry be heard from their houses, when
thou shalt [x] bring a troop suddenly upon them: for [y] they
have digged a pit to take me, and hid snares for my
feet. 23 Yet, LORD, thou knowest all their counsel
against me § to slay *me*: [z] forgive not their iniquity,
[a] neither blot out their sin from thy sight, but let them
be overthrown before thee; deal *thus* with them in the
time of thine anger.

Before Christ 605

r Chap. xi. 19. s Lev. x. 11. Mal. ii. 7. John vii. 48. † Or, for the tongue. Chap. xxvi. 8, 9. t Psal. cv. 23. u Psal. cix. 10. ‡ Heb. Pour them out. x 2 Kings xxiv. 2. y Psal. lvii. 6. Ver. 20. § Heb. For death. z Psal. lix. 5. a Psal. cix. 14, 15.

v. 18—23. Behold the treatment the faithful ministers may expect from a disobedient and gainsaying people.

1. Enraged by his rebukes, they consult how to destroy him. To cover their malice, they pretend zeal for religion, and would brand him as a false prophet. *Then said they, Come, and let us devise devices against Jeremiah*, to get rid of him and his prophecies; *for the law shall not perish from the priest*, &c. Notwithstanding his predictions of the cessation of the temple service, of the infatuation of their counsels, and his warnings of the falsehood of their prophets, they flattered themselves their priesthood should continue, their rulers in church and state consult and secure their safety, and that they should see the fulfilment of the visions of peace with which their own prophets flattered them: therefore, said they, *Come, let us smite him with the tongue*, either accuse him as a lying prophet before the magistrates, to put him to death, v. 23; or load him with reproaches, and make him contemptible in the eyes of the people: *and let us not give heed to any of his words*, but treat him as a deceiver, who speaks not from the Lord, but out of his own heart. Note, (1.) The wicked world are in a confederacy against the true prophets, and none forward to shew their malice, than the false and faithless ministers who cannot bear their just rebuke. (2.) To cloak the malice of persecutors this was the old pretence, to represent the faithful and zealous ministers as men dangerous to the state, and not to be tolerated; or as deluders and enthusiasts, and to be trampled on. (3.) They who dare not encounter the lash of men's tongues, must never think of standing up for God. (4.) Rejection of the servant is an insult on the master. Little do the revilers of Christ's ministers think, that their reproaches light not so much on them as him.

2. He lodges his appeal with God, and begs his interposition on his behalf. He prayed God to take notice of their blasphemies and reproaches, v. 19, their ingratitude and cruelty, in returning him evil for good, and thirsting for his blood, when God, the searcher of hearts, knew how earnestly he had laboured, how fervently he had prayed, to avert the impending judgments from them, v. 20. Therefore in just indignation he imprecates upon them the vengeance they had provoked; that death in every tremendous shape might seize both young and old, and their widows, bereaved of husbands and children together, lament the fearful ravages they beheld; that shrieks and cries might

Before Christ 605

might fill the houses, when the enemy suddenly entering at the breach, massacred and plundered without pity or remorse for this would be but the just retaliation for the snares they laid to murder him, which, however secret, God knew and would avenge Their sin was now unpardonable, he that had often prayed for them, now abandons them to their ruin, not in a spirit of revenge desiring their misery, but in zeal for God's glory, to see that vindicated, waiting their final overthrow, and expecting and desiring God would *deal with them in the time of his anger* according to the denunciations which, as his prophet, he had delivered *Note*, (1) Jeremiah was a type of Jesus, thus basely reviled, ungratefully persecuted, and all his prayers returned with blasphemies (2) What Jeremiah spoke in the spirit of prophecy must not be pleaded as an example for our imitation We must pray for those that persecute us, if peradventure God may yet give them repentance (3) The persecutors of his prophets will find at last an avenging God, and woe to them against whom those abused ministers of grace stand up to bear witness in a judgment day

CHAP XIX

The ruin of Jerusalem and Judah is still the burden of the prophecy, and is prefigured by the breaking of a potter's vessel 1 In the presence of the elders, in the valley of Tophet, the approaching destruction, and the cause of it, is foretold, ver 1—9 2 The breaking of the vessel signified the irretrievableness of their case, ver 10—13 3 The same proclamation is repeated in the temple, ver 14, 15

1 THUS saith the LORD, Go and get a potter's earthen bottle, and *take* of the ancients of the people, and of the ancients of the priests, 2 And go forth unto the valley of the son of Hinnom, which *is* by the entry of † the east gate, and proclaim there the words that I shall tell thee 3 And say, Hear ye the word of the LORD, O kings of Judah, and inhabitants of Jerusalem, Thus saith the LORD of hosts, the God of Israel, Behold, I will bring evil upon this place, the which whosoever heareth, [a] his ears shall tingle 4 Because [b] they have forsaken me, and have ‡ estranged this place, and have burnt incense in it unto other gods, whom neither they nor their fathers have known, nor the kings of Judah, and have filled this place with the blood of innocents, 5 They have built also the high places of Baal, [c] to burn their sons with fire *for* burnt-offerings unto Baal, [d] which I commanded not, nor spake *it*, neither came *it* into my mind 6 Therefore behold, the days come, saith the LORD, that this place shall no more be called Tophet, nor the valley of the son of Hinnom, but the valley of slaughter 7 And I will make void the counsel of Judah and Jerusalem in this place, and I will cause them to fall by the sword before their enemies, and by the hands of them that seek their lives and [e] their carcases will I give to be meat for the fowls of the heaven, and for the beasts of the earth 8 And [f] I will make this city desolate, and an hissing, every one that passeth thereby shall be astonished and hiss, because of all the plagues thereof 9 And I will cause them [g] to eat the flesh of their sons, and the flesh of their daughters, and they shall eat every one the flesh of his friend in the siege and straitness, wherewith their enemies, and they that seek their lives, shall straiten them

† Heb The sun gate
a 1 Sam iii 11 2 Kings xxi 12
b Isa lxv 11 Chap ii 13, 17, 19 & xv 6 & xvii 13
‡ Or strangely abused
c Lev xviii 21
d Chap vii 31, 32 & xxxii 35
e Chap vii 33 & xvi 4 & xxxiv 20
f Chap xviii 16
g Lev xxvi 29 Deut xxviii 53 Lam iv 10

v 1—9 To awaken conviction in the hearts of a stupid people every method is tried, that they may be left at last utterly inexcusable

1 Jeremiah is ordered down to the valley of the son of Hinnom, the place where their most shocking idolatries were committed, and the destined spot of their terrible execution He is commanded to take an earthen pitcher, and, as witnesses of what he was about to do and say, to bring with him some of the ancients of the priests and people, for when God speaks by the meanest of his prophets, the greatest should not think themselves above attending their ministry

2 God will tell him there his message, which he must proclaim aloud as an herald, and the purport of it is most tremendous, which all are summoned to attend, from the greatest to the least, and enough it is to make *the ears of every one that heareth it to tingle*, as thunder-struck with the dreadful sound The sins charged upon them are most shocking and aggravated, apostasy from God, profanation of his temple, foul idolatry, barbarous cruelty, the inhuman sacrifice of infants to their abominable deities, yea, *even the burning their sons in the fire, as burnt-offerings unto Baal*, sacrifices abhorred of God, and such as he never thought of, nor expected from his worshippers For these abominations judgment is threatened proportionate to such atrocious guilt on that very spot the wrath of God should be executed upon them, and the valley acquire a new name no more called *Tophet*, from the drums that were beat to drown the cries of infants burning alive in sacrifice to Moloch, but *the valley of slaughter*, from the multitudes who should there be massacred by the Chaldeans Their counsels then should be made vain, which in that place they had taken to oppose their invaders, or to fly to their idols for relief in the day of their calamity, *v* 7 There they must fall by the sword of their merciless enemies, thirsting for their blood, their carcasses ignominiously exposed, and unburied, a prey *to the fowls of heaven, and the beasts of the earth* Such plagues and desolation shall come upon their city and country, that astonishment at the greatness of the calamity shall mix with indignation against their sins in every passer by, yea, to such straits should they be reduced in the siege, that famine should compel them to feed upon their dearest friends, and even their children, on their dead corpses, or murdered to satisfy their raging hunger, a scene of wretchedness that makes us shudder but to relate O sin! sin! what hast thou done!

Before Christ 605

10 Then shalt thou break [h] the bottle in the sight of the men that go with thee, 11 And shalt say unto them, Thus saith the LORD of hosts, [i] Even so will I break this people and this city, as *one* breaketh a potter's vessel that cannot be † made whole again, and they shall [k] bury *them* in Tophet, till *there be* no place to bury 12 Thus will I do unto this place, saith the LORD, and to the inhabitants thereof, and *even* make this city as Tophet 13 And the houses of Jerusalem, and the houses of the kings of Judah shall be defiled as the place of Tophet, because of all the houses upon whose [l] roofs they have burnt incense unto all the host of heaven, and [m] have poured out drink-offerings unto other gods 14 Then came Jeremiah from Tophet, whither the LORD had sent him to prophecy, and he stood in the court of the LORD's house, and said to all the people, 15 Thus saith the LORD of hosts, the God of Israel, Behold, I will bring upon this city and upon all her towns, all the evil that I have pronounced against it, because [n] they have hardned their necks, that they might not hear my words

h Ver 1
i Chap xxi 14 Lam iv 2
† Heb Healed
k Chap vii 32
l 2 Kings xxiii 12 Chap xxxii 29
m Chap vii 18
n Chap vii 26 & xvii 23

v 10—15 The judgment denounced is here,

1 Confirmed by a significant sign The earthen bottle in his hand is dashed in pieces on the ground, and the explication of it given, that so utter and irreparable should be their destruction The city and people should be broken like this vessel, and the spot whereon they stood be the place of execution, where so many should be slain, that graves should be wanting to bury them, yea, the city of Jerusalem should be as Tophet, and every house defiled with corpses of the slain, and rendered filthy and abominable as that detested place, because of the idolatries that had been practised therein, and the incense which on their roofs they had offered *to the hosts of heaven*

2 What he now spake in the presence of the ancients, in the valley of the son of Hinnom, he repeats solemnly in *the courts of the Lord's house* before all the people, that if they continue impenitent, they may be at least inexcusable All the denunciations of wrath God had spoken by Jeremiah were now ready to be executed on Jerusalem and all her towns, *because they had hardned their necks, that they might not hear my words* obstinately persisting in their iniquities, and deaf to all admonition *Note*, (1) Ministers must deliver their own souls, whether men will hear, or whether they will forbear (2) They who harden their hearts against God's warnings, must perish without remedy (3) In the day of judgment the damned will only have themselves to blame, and the sense of their wilfulness will aggravate their misery

CHAP XX

Such plain dealing as Jeremiah used in the foregoing chapter, one might easily foresee, if it did not convince and humble them, would provoke and exasperate them, and so it did, for here we find, 1 Jeremiah persecuted by Pashur, for preaching that sermon, ver 1, 2 2 Pashur threatened for so doing, and the word which Jeremiah had preached confirmed, ver 3—6 3 Jeremiah's complaining to God concerning ... to be a prophet, ver 7—10 ... God, and ... his appeal with him, ver 11 ... the day of his birth, ver 14—18 By which it appears he had

stil

Before Christ 605

and remainders of corruption in him still, and was a man subject to like passions as we are

1 NOW Pashur the son of [a] Immer the priest, who
was also chief governor in the house of the
LORD, heard that Jeremiah prophesied these things
2 Then Pashur [b] smote Jeremiah the prophet, and put
him in the stocks that *were* in the high gate of Ben-
jamin, which *was* by the house of the LORD 3
And it came to pass on the morrow, that Pashur
brought forth Jeremiah out of the stocks Then said
Jeremiah unto him, The LORD hath not called thy
name Pashur, but † Magor-missabib 4 For thus saith
the LORD, Behold I will make thee [c] a terror to thy-
self, and to all thy friends, and they shall fall by the
sword of their enemies, and thine eyes shall behold *it*,
and I will give all Judah into the hand of the king of
Babylon, and he shall carry them captive into Babylon,
and shall slay them with the sword 5 Moreover, [d] I
will deliver all the strength of this city, and all the
labours thereof, and all the precious things thereof,
and all the treasures of the kings of Judah will I give
into the hand of their enemies, which shall spoil
them, and take them, and carry them to Babylon
6 And thou Pashur, and all that dwell in thine house,
shall go into captivity, and thou shalt come to Baby-
lon, and there thou shalt die, and shalt be buried there,
thou and all thy friends, to whom thou hast prophe-
sied lies

a 1 Chron xxiv 14
b Mat xxi 35
† That is, Fear round about. c Chap vi 25 & xlvi 5 & xlix 29
d 2 Kings xx 17
e Isa xxxix 6

§ 1—6 They who will be zealous for God, and faithful to men's souls, must expect to be abused and insulted We have here,

1 The prophet smitten by Pashur, a priest, and a chief governor of the house of the Lord, perhaps the head of his course, *see 1 Chron* xxiv 14 or captain of the temple, *See Acts* iv 1 hearing the prophet's discourse, or being informed of it, tho' his sacred character should have been a protection, and his own station and profession restrained him from such violence, he fell into a rage, struck the prophet himself to silence him, or commanded some inferior officer to beat him, and, to add ignominy to the insult, he ordered him to be set in the stocks, or pillory, *at the high gate of Benjamin, which was by the house of the Lord*, that he might there be exposed, his person rendered contemptible, and his prophecies despised *Note*, (1) False prophets, and worldly minded priests have been ever the bitterest persecutors of God's faithful ministers (2) They who dare remonstrate against the iniquity of wicked priests, and an abandoned people, may not wonder if even the formalities of justice are not observed to oppress them

2 God's judgment upon the proud priest and persecutor, and the sentence on the land confirmed In silent suffering the prophet all night submitted to his ignominious confinement, but on the morrow, when brought forth for examination before the sanhedrim, or discharged because no real charge could be supported against him, he hath a revelation from God, which he denounces against this wicked man The Lord had changed his name from *Pashur* into *Magor-missabib*, *Terror round about*, importing the horror that would seize him and all his wicked adherents, when the Chaldean army should compass the city, and verify Jeremiah's prophecy His eyes should see his dearest friends and relations massacred, his country enslaved by the king of Babylon, the people slain or carried captive, the fortifications of Jerusalem razed to the ground, the treasures of the kings of Judah given for a prey to their invaders, and himself, with all his house, be led into slavery to Babylon, and die in that polluted land, with all his friends deceived by him, and to whom he had prophesied visions of peace *Note*, (1) God can soon make those who would frighten his prophets with menaces, a terror to themselves Let every persecutor tremble at Pashur's doom (2) They who think by stopping the mouths of God's prophets to procure themselves ease, but bind on their sentence, and hasten their doom

‖ Or, enticed. ‖ Chap i 6, 7.
f Or, It was in mine heart as a burning fire. g Job xxxii 18, 19.
h Psa xxxix 3.
i Psa xxxi 13.
k Job xix 19. Psa xli 9.

7 ¶ O LORD, thou hast ‖ deceived me, and I was
deceived thou art stronger than I, and hast prevailed
I am in derision daily, every one mocketh me 8 For
since I spake, I cried out, ᶠ I cried violence and spoil,
because the word of the LORD was made a reproach
unto me, and a derision daily 9 Then I said, I will
not make mention of him, nor speak any more in his
name But ‖ *his word* was in mine heart ᵍ as a burning
fire shut up in my bones, and ʰ I was weary with for-
bearing, and I could not *stay* 10 ¶ For ⁱ I heard the
defaming of many, fear on every side Report, *say they*,
and we will report it ᵏ All my familiars ˡ watched for
my halting, *saying*, Peradventure he will be enticed, and
we shall prevail against him, and we shall take our re-
venge on him 11 But ᵐ the LORD *is* with me as a
mighty terrible one therefore my persecutors shall
stumble, and ⁿ they shall not prevail, they shall be
greatly ashamed, for they shall not prosper, ᵒ *their*
everlasting confusion shall never be forgotten 12 But,
O LORD of hosts, ᵖ that triest the righteous, *and* seest
the reins and the heart, ᵠ let me see thy vengeance on
them for unto thee have I opened my cause 13
Sing unto the LORD, praise ye the LORD for he
hath delivered the soul of the poor from the hand of
evil doers.

Before Christ 605

l Chap i 19
m Chap xv 20 & xvii 18
n Chap xxiii 40
o Chap xi 20 & xvii 10
p Psa liv 10
q Psa xxxi 10 & cix 4

§ 7—13 Jeremiah, though a good man and a true prophet, appears here compassed with infirmities What he suffered seems to have exasperated his spirit, so that he spake unadvisedly with his lips

1 He is tempted to find fault with God *Thou hast deceived me and I was deceived*, either in not bringing the judgments God had sent him to foretel, or not protecting him from the insults of his enemies, as he had promised him, *chap* i 18, 19 But this was his impatience and bitterness God will ever be found true, and never deceive those who trust in him Or the words may be rendered in another manner, *Thou didst persuade me, and I was persuaded*, so *Gen* ix 27 when reluctant to take the prophetic office *thou art stronger than I, and hast prevailed*, silencing his pleas to be excused by unanswerable arguments, and injunctions not to be disobeyed and therefore since he was as it were pressed into the service, he was ready to think it hard in God, that he should leave him exposed to such ill-usage This was his infirmity

2 He complains of the affronts he met, and the injuries he received *I am in derision daily, every one mocketh me*, and nothing wounds a generous mind deeper than scorn But what hurt him more than any personal insults, was their contemptuous disregard of the word of God he preached They ridiculed the earnestness with which he delivered his message, and treated the charges he brought against them of violence and oppression, with derision at his preciseness, or the threatnings of the ravages their enemies should make, with contempt and disbelief He heard the vilest misrepresentations of his words and conduct, *v* 10 as seditious, false, and dangerous to the state, and his enemies stuck at no lies to blacken his character *Report, say they, and we will report it*, ready to spread the most malignant aspersions, and on the least shadow of offence to accuse him before the governors, and procure his condemnation For this purpose they set spies around him, who, under the guise of most cordial friendship, watched for his halting, in hopes that he would be taken in some or other of the snares they laid for him, give them a handle for accusation, and an opportunity to *revenge* themselves in his destruction for the threatnings he had denounced against them *Note*, (1) Ridicule and contempt are the common weapons of infidels and ungodly men against the preachers of the truth (2) It is grievous to a faithful soul to hear the word of God treated with levity and derision (3) The fairest professions often cloak the foulest designs (4) Neither the purest innocence, nor most consummate prudence, can protect us from malignant tongues, resolved to find or invent some cause of accusation

3 Discouraged with ill treatment he owns himself ready to give up his ministry Since he despaired of doing any good, he thought he might as well be silent, as exasperate them with fruitless rebukes *Note*, It is a most discouraging thing to the preachers of God's word, to see their labours in vain, and themselves rendered odious for their fidelity, but we must leave the event to God our duty is to persevere

4 He resolves, notwithstanding, to go on, and trust God in it, he was constrained to speak *the word of God was as a burning fire in his bones*, that must have vent or, *there was in mine heart as a burning fire*, such zeal for God, and love of men's souls, that he could not keep silence, and now he seems to triumph over his fears *The Lord is with me*, and therefore their malicious devices shall be disappointed, and return in vengeance on their own souls, for he is *as a mighty terrible one*, strong to save, and jealous to return the wrongs of his insulted ambassadors Therefore their persecutors will with shame and grief see their mischievous designs abortive, and *stumble* and fall into the pit they have digged, covered *as to an everlasting confusion, never to be forgotten* and such shall be the end of all the enemies of God's church and people *No weapon formed against them can prosper* and *every tongue that shall rise up in judgment against them he will condemn*

5 He appeals to the heart-searching God for the goodness of his cause, and, conscious of his integrity, expects to see justice done him on his enemies, and vengeance poured on their devoted heads *Note*, (1) It is a comfort to us, when, in the sight of that God who searcheth the reins, we can boldly appeal for our simplicity and sincerity (2) In all our sufferings, it is

Before Christ 605 a great relief to have a gracious God, into whose compassionate bosom we can pour out our complaints.

6 He rejoices in the confidence, that God will hear and grant his requests *Sing unto the Lord, praise ye the Lord*, the few faithful in Zion are called upon to join in his thanksgivings, *for he hath delivered the soul, or life of the poor, from the hand of evil doers*, he means himself, now rescued from the hands of Pashur, or, since he can by faith embrace God's promises, he exults in the performance of them as equally sure as if already fulfilled *Note*, They who trust on God, and are sincere before him, may rejoice always in the confidence that he will never leave nor forsake them

ᵛ Job iii 3 Chap xv 10 14 ¶ ᵛ Cursed *be* the day wherein I was born let not
the day wherein my mother bare me be blessed 15
Cursed *be* the man who brought tidings to my father,
saying, A man child is born unto thee, making him very
ᵃ Gen xix 25 glad 16 And let that man be as the cities ᵃ which the
ᵗ Job xv 21 LORD overthrew, and repented not and let him hear
ᵗ the cry in the morning, and the shouting at noon-tide
ᵘ Ibid iii 10 17 ᵘ Because he slew me not from the womb, or that my
mother might have been my grave, and her womb *to be*
ˣ Ibid v 20 always great *with me* 18 ˣ Wherefore came I forth out
of the womb to see labour and sorrow, that my days
should be consumed with shame?

v 14—18 Dire is the change between the notes of praise wherewith the former verses closed, and the melancholy sounds which here succeed Some have supposed, that this is here recorded as the humbling acknowledgment of what passed in his mind, during his confinement in the stocks, from which sad prevalence of impatience he was now recovered, but remembers to his shame how ill he had borne it He utters imprecations,

1 On the day of his birth, that ushered him into a world of misery Instead of celebrating its return with joy, he regards it as ominous, and brands it with a curse

2 On the messenger who carried the tidings to his father, and made him glad with the news that a son was born, he wishes that he might be destroyed as the inhabitants of Sodom, and be in perpetual terrors, as in the agonies of death, from some invading foe an imprecation shockingly severe and uncharitable Into such unbecoming extravagancies may passion, when prevailing, transport even good men, and leave them deep cause to repent their rashness

3 He wishes the messenger of his birth had been his murderer, or his mother's womb never released from its burden which must have been highly criminal to the one, and a perpetual and intolerable pain to the other wishes unn turn, as they were wicked and wilful

4 He expostulates with God *Why came I forth out of my mother's womb?* as if God had done him injustice in bringing him into the world, *that my days should be consumed with shame*, exposed to a continued series of insult, derision, and contempt, and herein he shewed much, very much of human infirmity, so weak are the best of men when left to themselves Let it serve to warn us against such a hasty spirit, that it is not only highly criminal before God, but makes us appear absurd and brutish, and must expose us to just censure from men

CHAP XXI

It is plain that the prophecies of this book are not placed in the same order that they were preached, for there are chapters after this which concern Jehoahaz, Jehoiakim, and Jeconiah, who all reigned before Zedekiah, in whose reign the prophecy of this chapter bears date Here is, 1 The message which Zedekiah sent to the prophet, to desire him to enquire of the Lord for them, ver 1, 2 *2 The answer which Jeremiah, in God's name, sent to that message, in which he, (1) Foretels the certain and inevitable ruin of the city, and the fruitlessness of their attempts for its preservation*, ver 3—7 *(2) He advises the people to go over to the king of Babylon*, ver 8—10 *(3) He advises the king and his family to repent and reform*, ver 11, 12 *and not to trust to the strength of their city and strong forts*, ver 13, 14

589 1 THE word which came unto Jeremiah from the
ᵃ Exod ix 28 LORD, when king Zedekiah ᵃ sent unto him
2 Chron xxxvi 12 Pashur the son of Melchiah, and Zephaniah the son of
† Or in treat Maaseiah the priest, saying, 2 † Enquire, I pray thee, of
the LORD for us, (for Nebuchadrezzar king of Baby-
lon maketh war against us) if so be that the LORD will
ᵇ Isa xlv 1, 2 deal with us according to all ᵇ his wondrous works, that
he may go up from us. 3 ¶ Then said Jeremiah unto
them, Thus shall ye say to Zedekiah, 4 Thus saith the
LORD God of Israel, Behold, I will turn back the wea-
pons of war that *are* in your hands, wherewith ye fight
against the king of Babylon, and *against* the Chaldeans
which besiege you without the walls, and I will assemble

them into the midst of this city 5 And I myself will Before Christ 589
fight against you ᶜ with an outstretched hand, and with ᶜ Exod vi 6
a strong arm, even in anger, and in fury, and in great
wrath 6 And I will smite the inhabitants of this city,
both man and beast they shall die of a great pestilence
7 And afterwards, saith the LORD, ᵈ I will deliver ᵈ Chap. xxxix 5 & lii 9
Zedekiah king of Judah, and his servants, and the
people, and *such as are* left in this city from the pesti-
lence, from the sword, and from the famine, into the
hand of Nebuchadrezzar king of Babylon, and into the
hand of their enemies, and into the hand of those that
seek their life, and he shall smite them with the edge of
the sword ᵉ he shall not spare them, neither have pity, ᵉ Ezek vii 5
nor have mercy

v 1—7 When the danger is distant, many affect to despise it who tremble at its approach, and instantly fly to those ministers in their distress, whose warnings in their prosperity they disregarded

1 Zedekiah is no sooner besieged by the Chaldeans, than he sends to consult with Jeremiah, under whose predictions he had refused to humble himself, 2 *Chron* xxxvi 12 and by the most honourable messengers entreats him *to enquire of the Lord* for them, and advise them how to get rid of their enemies, and raise the siege, thus magnifying his mercy, and adding to his former wondrous works, manifested to Hezekiah in the like distress, 2 *Chron* xxxii 20, 21 *Note*, (1) Many in trouble are willing enough to cry to God to ease them of their sufferings, who express little concern about their sins (2) They who have scorned the prayers of good men, in the day of evil will be glad of an interest in them (3) The gracious interpositions of God in behalf of the penitent and faithful, are no precedents to embolden the hope of the unhumbled

2 A tremendous answer is given to the enquiry from Israel's God, who tho' he disclaimed not the relation, and still had mercy in store for the nation, had decreed to give up the men of that wicked generation to deserved punishment Therefore he informs them, that all their efforts against their enemies would prove unsuccessful, and their city be taken by the Chaldeans, *v* 4 That resistance was vain, since God was their enemy, whose wrath burned like fire against them, and whose outstretched arm would destroy them with a terrible destruction The famine, pestilence, sword should consume them, and when at last the case proved desperate, and the few that remained with their king attempted to save themselves, they should be seized and massacred without remorse and pity, by their cruel enemies who sought their life, and having taken the city by storm, would glut their bloody revenge for their resistance *Note*, They who fight against God, rush on their own ruin, and there is no escape when the decree is gone forth, flight is then as fruitless as resistance

8 ¶ And unto this people thou shalt say, Thus saith
the LORD, Behold, I ᶠ set before you the way of life, ᶠ Deut xxx 19
and the way of death 9 ᵍ He that abideth in this city ᵍ Chap xxxviii 2
shall die by the sword, and by the famine, and by the
pestilence but he that goeth out, and falleth to the
Chaldeans that besiege you, he shall live, and ʰ his life ʰ Chap xxxix 18 & xlv 5
shall be unto him for a prey 10 For I have set my
face against this city for evil, and not for good, saith
the LORD, it shall be given into the hand of the king
of Babylon, and ⁱ he shall burn it with fire 11 ¶ And ⁱ 2 Chron xxxvi 19
touching the house of the king of Judah, *say*, Hear ye
the word of the LORD, 12 O house of David, thus
saith the LORD, ᵏ Execute judgment ˡ in the morning, ᵏ Chap xxii 3 Zech vii 9 ˡ Ps ci 8
and deliver *him that is* spoiled, out of the hand of the
oppressor, lest my fury go out like fire, and burn that
none can quench *it*, because of the evil of your doings
13 Behold, I *am* against thee, O † inhabitant of the † Heb Inhabitress
valley, *and* rock of the plain, saith the LORD, which
say, Who shall come down against us? or who shall
enter into our habitations? 14 But I will ‡ punish you ‡ Heb Visit upon
ᵐ according to the fruit of your doings, saith the LORD ᵐ Prov i 31 Isa iii 10, 11
and I will kindle a fire in the forest thereof, and ⁿ it shall ⁿ Chap lii 13
devour all things round about it

v 8—14 The messengers being dismissed with this rough reply, the prophet is sent to the people,

1 To admonish them of the only way which remained of saving their lives, by surrendering themselves up to the Chaldeans, as inevitable ruin would be the consequence of persisting to defend themselves; God's wrath bent, upon the city, the devouring fire ready to seize its palaces, and whoever abode in it being doomed to perish by the sword, the famine, and the pestilence A dreadful alternative! either an ignominious slavery, or a miserable death

Before Christ 609

2 To warn their king and princes, and call them to repentance at the peril of their souls In vain they boasted their descent from the house of David, who were so degenerate from his piety, they should, as his successors, discharge the duties of their high station, *execute judgment in the morning*, speedily, not spending their days in sloth and luxury, and *deliver the spoiled from the hand of the oppressor*, against whom he cried for justice this they had grievously neglected, and therefore God was about to visit them, nor should their greatness be any protection from the fire of his wrath One moment's respite is yet afforded them, one warning more given them, if so be by an immediate return, they may suspend, if not avert the descending blow *Note*, (1) They who are entrusted with the administration of justice, should be speedy as well as impartial in their decisions the delays of justice are almost as intolerable as oppression (2) Faithful prophets will not fear great men's faces, but plainly rebuke their sins (3) The sins of rulers will be most severely brought to account, as their influence and example are most pernicious

3 To confound the folly of the hopes they entertained They thought their city by situation, as well as art, impregnable, fortified by surrounding hills and craggy rocks, that rendered the approach of an enemy difficult, and therefore with confidence of safety defied all invaders, *who shall come down against us, who shall enter into our habitation*, but what defence is available when God saith, *Behold, I am against thee*, since his vengeance awoke to *punish them for the fruit of their doings*, their munition of rocks is levelled to the ground In righteous judgment the fire is kindled, and Jerusalem with all her palaces, like a forest, perishes in the flames. Wo to the sinner against whom this devouring fire of wrath is stirred up, who can dwell in everlasting burnings?

CHAP XXII

This chapter contains some warnings that in the preceding reigns God had given the kings of Judah 1 A message is sent to the royal family, as it should seem, in the reign of Jehoiakim, relating partly to Jehoahaz, who was carried away captive into Egypt, and partly to Jehoiakim who succeeded him, and was now upon the throne The king and princes are exhorted to execute judgment, and are assured that if they did so, the royal family should flourish, but otherwise it should be ruined, ver 1—10 *Jehoahaz is lamented*, ver 10—12 *Jehoiakim is reproved*, ver 13—19 2 *Another message sent them in the reign of Jehoiachin He is charged with an obstinate refusal to hear, threatened with destruction, and it is foretold that in him Solomon's house should fail*, ver 20—30

1 THUS saith the LORD, Go down to the house
of the king of Judah, and speak there this
word, 2 And say, Hear the word of the LORD, O
king of Judah, that sittest upon the throne of David,
thou, and thy servants, and thy people that enter in by
a Chap. xxi 12 these gates, 3 Thus saith the LORD, [a] Execute ye
judgment and righteousness, and deliver the spoiled out
of the hand of the oppressor and do no wrong, do no
violence to the stranger, the fatherless, nor the widow,
neither shed innocent blood in this place 4 For if ye do
b Chap xvii 25 † Heb. for David upon his throne. this thing indeed, [b] then shall there enter in by the gates
of this house, kings sitting † upon the throne of David,
riding in chariots, and on horses, he, and his servants,
c Isa i 20 d Heb vi 13 and his people 5 But [c] if ye will not hear these words,
[d] I swear by myself, saith the LORD, that this house
shall become a desolation 6 For thus saith the LORD
unto the king's house of Judah, Thou *art* Gilead unto
e Ps cvii 34 me, *and* the head of Lebanon *yet* surely [e] I will make
thee a wilderness, *and* cities *which* are not inhabited
f Chap xxi 14 7 And I will prepare destroyers against thee, every one
with his weapons, and they shall cut down [f] thy choice
cedars, and cast them into the fire 8 And many na-
g Deut xxix 24 1 Kings ix 8 tions shall pass by this city, and they shall say every man
to his neighbour, [g] Wherefore hath the LORD done
h 2 Chron xxxiv 25 thus unto this great city? 9 Then they shall answer,
[h] Because they have forsaken the covenant of the LORD
their God, and worshipped other gods, and served
them

v 1—9 Kings are God's vicegerents, accountable to him for their conduct, and when they abuse the power wherewith they are entrusted, or neglect the duties of their station, may expect his rebukes Jeremiah is here sent to the king of Judah Jehoiakim, the successor of David, and sitting on his throne, but grievously degenerated from his virtues He and his servants are summoned to attend

1 Their duty is set before them To administer judgment with impartiality, to vindicate the oppressed and injured, to do no wrong themselves, nor permit others to do it with impunity, to protect the stranger, the fatherless, and widow, and shed no innocent blood, either by lawless violence, or under the cloak of justice Very opposite to which had hitherto been their conduct, *v* 17

2 This would secure their prosperity, and entail a blessing upon their posterity, preserving long the crown of Judah to the royal race of David, and enabling them to live in splendor, answerable to their high dignity, *v* 4

3 On the contrary, if they persisted in their disobedience, by an oath, to make the sentence more awful and tremendous, God swears to make the house of the king of Judah a desolation, and that his kingdom should be involved in his ruin Though *thou art Gilead unto me, and the head of Lebanon*, full of riches, and strongly fortified, yet such ravages should be made in the land, that it should be wholly depopulated, and its fertile plains become an howling wilderness nor should instruments be wanting to execute the threatened vengeance, *I will prepare*, or *sanctify destroyers*, raise them up, and give them a commission of most righteous judgment In consequence of which, they shall as easily cut down and destroy the mighty men of Judah, as the cedars fall before the axe of the hewer, and are cast into the fire With astonishment the neighbouring nations behold the destruction, and enquire into the cause, that a people once so favoured of God, should now be so abandoned, and the answer is ready, because they have apostatized from God's worship, and sunk into foul idolatry *Note*, They who forsake God, are justly forsaken of him

10 ¶ [i] Weep ye not for the dead, neither bemoan him,
but weep sore for him [k] that goeth away for he shall re-
turn no more, nor see his native country 11 For
thus saith the LORD touching Shallum the son of Jo-
siah king of Judah, which reigned instead of Josiah his
father, which went forth out of this place, He shall not
return thither any more 12 But he shall die in the
place whither they have led him captive, and shall see
this land no more 13 ¶ [l] Wo unto him [m] that build-
eth his house by unrighteousness, and his chambers by
wrong, *that* useth his neighbours service without wages,
and [n] giveth him not for his work 14 That saith, I
will build me a wide house, and † large chambers, and
cutteth him out windows, and *it is* cieled with cedar,
and painted with vermillion 15 Shalt thou reign,
because thou closest *thyself* in cedar? [o] did not thy father
eat and drink, and do judgment and justice, *and* then *it
was* well with him? 16 He judged the cause of the
poor and needy, [p] then *it was* well *with him was* not
this to know me? saith the LORD 17 But thine
eyes and thine heart *are* not but for thy covetousness,
and for to shed innocent blood, and for oppression, and
for † violence to do *it* 18 Therefore thus saith the
LORD concerning Jehoiakim the son of Josiah king of
Judah, They shall not lament for him, *saying*, [q] Ah my
brother, or, ah sister they shall not lament for him,
saying, Ah lord, or ah his glory 19 [r] He shall be
buried with the burial of an ass, drawn and cast forth
beyond the gates of Jerusalem

i 2 Chron. xxxv 25
k 2 Kings xxiii 34 Ezek xix 4
l Ver 18
m Lev xix 13 Deut xxiv 14, 15 Mic iii 10 Hab ii 9
n Jam v 4
† Heb. thorough aired
o Ps cxxviii 2 Isa iii 10
p Prov xvi 12
† Or, incursion
q 1 Kings xiii 30
r 2 Chron. xxxvi 6 Chap xxxvi 30

v 10—19 Kings are not too high for God to humble, nor for his prophets to reprove We have here the sad doom of two read, who reigned successively in Judah, the sons of good Josiah, from whose steps they shamefully departed

1 Shallum, the same as Jehoahaz, the immediate successor of Josiah, 2 *Chron* xxxvi 1 After a short reign of three months, *see 2 Kings* xxiii 34 he was carried captive into Egypt, and from thence he must, by the divine decree, never return, but die in ignominy Him therefore the people are called upon to bewail, and rather weep over the captive son, than bedew with their tears the corpse of his pious father, who was at rest, and removed from beholding the evil to come *Note*, Dying saints may be justly envied, whilst living sinners are to be pitied

2 Jehoiakim, his successor, has not a more favourable judgment His sins were great, and though he now sat on the throne, the prophet faithfully dares to rebuke him *Proud*, and affecting to rival the greatness of his most illustrious predecessors, during the most flourishing state of their kingdom tho' himself no better than a viceroy, first to the king of Egypt, and then to the Babylonish monarch, he was building, or enlarging his palace, in the most magnificent taste, and with the most expensive decorations, and as the revenues of his kingdom probably were insufficient, he became *tyrannical and oppressive*, extorting money from his subjects, or constraining them to serve and supply him with materials, without paying them for their labour *Secure, and self-confident*, he promised himself many long years to enjoy his house of cedar, and that his pomp would

Before Chriſt 609

be his protection unjuſt and cruel withal, unlike his pious father, who lived in ſobriety and temperance, and adminiſtred juſtice with impartiality *Was not this to know me? ſaith the Lord*, it ſhewed true regard to God, and conſequently was attended with the divine bleſſing, *then it was well with him* But he with harpy talons ſtuck at no violence to gratify the inſatiate covetouſneſs of his heart, and ſhed the blood of the innocent, that he might ſeize their ſubſtance In conſequence of which his doom is read he ſhall die unlamented, neither his ſubjects nor relations ſhall expreſs the leaſt concern for his fate, his corpſe ſhall not have a tear dropped over it, and even want a grave *buried with the burial of an aſs, drawn* with ignominy, *and caſt forth beyond the gates of Jeruſalem*, which, though not obſerved in the hiſtory of the kings, was no doubt literally accompliſhed *Note*, (1) That great men ſhould dwell in palaces, is becoming, but when pride rears the ſtructure, condemnation lies againſt the ſoul (2) The chambers built by wrong will cry out for vengeance on the oppreſſor, and God will not let the defrauded labourer's complaint paſs by unheard (3) They who place dependance on proſperity and the enjoyment of the fruits of iniquity, will find their hopes terribly diſappointed (4) Covetouſneſs is the root of all evil from hence ſpring rapine, bloodſhed, and every evil work (5) The way to proſper is to know God, and ſerve him, whilſt deſtruction inevitable muſt be the portion of thoſe who forget and forſake him (6) It is an aggravation of ſin to have lived under pious parents, and in the face of their inſtructions and examples to prove rebellious (7) They who are lifted up the higheſt in pride, will ſhortly fall the loweſt in miſery

598
a 2 Kings xxiv 7
t Chap vi 17
u Ibid vii 23, &c
x Ibid xxiii 1
† Heb Inhabitreſs
y 2 Kings xxiv 6, 8 Chap xxxvii 1
z Cant viii 6 Hag ii 23
a 2 Kings xxiv 15
‡ Heb Lift up their mind
b Chap xlviii 38

20 ¶ Go up to Lebanon, and cry, and lift up thy
voice in Baſhan, and cry from the paſſages for all [s] thy
lovers are deſtroyed 21 I ſpake unto thee in thy pro-
ſperity, *but* [t] thou ſaidſt, I will not hear [u] this *hath been*
thy manner from thy youth, that thou obeyedſt not my
voice 22 The wind ſhall eat up all [x] thy paſtors, and
thy lovers ſhall go into captivity, ſurely then ſhalt thou
be aſhamed and confounded for all thy wickedneſs
23 O † inhabitant of Lebanon, that makeſt thy neſt in
the cedars, how gracious ſhalt thou be when pangs come
upon thee, the pain as of a woman in travail? 24 *As*
I live, ſaith the LORD, though [y] Coniah the ſon of Je-
hoiakim king of Judah were [z] the ſignet upon my right
hand, yet would I pluck thee thence, 25 And I will
give thee into the hand of them that ſeek thy life, and
into the hand *of them* whoſe face thou feareſt, even into
the hand of Nebuchadrezzar king of Babylon, and into
the hand of the Chaldeans 26 And [a] I will caſt thee
out, and thy mother that bare thee, into another coun-
try, where ye were not born, and there ſhall ye die
27 But to the land whereunto they ‡ deſire to return,
thither ſhall they not return 28 *Is* this man Coniah
a deſpiſed broken idol? *is he* [b] a veſſel wherein *is* no plea-
ſure? wherefore are they caſt out, he and his ſeed, and
are caſt into a land which they know not? 29 O
earth, earth, earth, hear the word of the LORD 30
Thus ſaith the LORD, Write ye this man childleſs, a
man *that* ſhall not proſper in his days for no man of his
ſeed ſhall proſper, ſitting upon the throne of David,
and ruling any more in Judah

v 20—30 We have line upon line, and warning upon warning, yet all inſufficient to alarm a ſtupid people

1 Their miſery and diſtreſs are painted in lively colours When their enemies were advancing, they are repreſented as running to the mountain-tops, and calling out for help to the neighbouring nations, but in vain, *for all thy lovers are deſtroyed*, and none willing to ſhew them the leaſt kindneſs in the day of their calamity They had been deaf to the warnings of the prophets, from the day they came out of Egypt, and diſobedient to the voice of God, vain of their proſperity, and confident they ſhould never be removed But now their deſolation approaches, when they ſhould *be confounded and aſhamed for all their wickedneſs*, destitute of help within, or of aſſiſtance from without, becauſe *the wind ſhall eat up all thy paſtors*, the governors in church and ſtate, kings, nobles, prieſts, and prophets, as weak to reſiſt the Chaldean hoſts, as ſtubble to oppoſe the furious whirlwind Though lofty in pride as Lebanon, and dwelling in houſes cieled with cedar, there would be no ſecurity, but be fuel for the devouring flames, whilſt from their enemies they might expect to find no favour, in the day when their deepeſt anguiſh ſhould ſeize them, as the pangs of a travailing woman,

2 The words, *How gracious ſhalt thou be*, may be rendered, *What favour wilt thou find?* and intimates the deſperateneſs of their caſe, which ſeems moſt agreeable to the context, though they may alſo be interpreted of the effects these judgments ſhould have upon them, when their diſtreſſes ſhould drive them in penitence to God, and they ſhould find mercy with him in the land of their captivity *Note*, (1) Proſperity is a dangerous ſtate they who live at eaſe too often care not to attend the warnings of God (2) Creature-dependance will fail in the day of calamity (3) It is well for us, if what we ſuffer brings us at laſt in pangs of real repentance to God

Before Chriſt 598

2 Their king's judgment is pronounced He is called *Coniah*, inſtead of *Jeconiah*, in contempt His name is ſhortned, intimating that his reign ſhould be cut ſhort, and his regal honour depart from him Doomed to a miſerable ſervitude, God threatens to give him up into the hands of the king of Babylon, whom he feared, and who ſought his life, with his mother and family, v 28 and pining in vain for the land of their nativity, they ſhould long drag their ignominious chain, and die in the place of their captivity His pious fathers had been as *a ſignet on God's right hand*, ſo dear to him, and valued by him, as the ring that bears the picture, or is the gift, of the perſon we love but his ill conduct had caſt him out of favour, and therefore God in high diſpleaſure threatens he will pluck him thence, and abandon him to ruin and this his determination is irrevocable, confirmed with an oath *As I live, ſaith the Lord*, who, ſince he can ſwear by no greater, ſwears by himſelf, v 24 *Note*, (1) They are undone for ever whom God abandons (2) The greateſt muſt not be too confident they know not what ſtrange calamities may await them

3 All who beheld this monarch fallen would tauntingly ſay, *Is this Coniah, a deſpiſed broken idol?* Yes ſo deſpicable is he grown, who late was idolized *Is he a veſſel wherein is no pleaſure?* he that was late the people's darling, is now diſregarded, and caſt by as a broken veſſel, led, with all that pertained to him, into a ſtrange land, there to ſuffer the puniſhment of his iniquities

4 The earth is ſummoned to mark his judgment either the people of Judea in particular, or of the world in general or, as if the clod under their feet would be more attentive than the hardened hearts of the men of that generation, it is called upon to hear the ſolemn ſentence *Thus ſaith the Lord, Write ye this man childleſs, a man that ſhall not proſper in his days*, after a ſhort reign of three months, he ſpent his whole life in captivity in Babylon *for no man of his ſeed ſhall proſper, ſitting on the throne of David, and ruling any more in Judah* In him ended the race of Judah's kings, and probably the line of Solomon was now extinct, Salathiel being ſuppoſed his adopted heir, to whom his pretenſions were bequeathed, and, though accounted his ſon, *Mat* i 12 was a deſcendant of Nathan, and the ſon of Neri, *Luke* iii 27

CHAP XXIII

In this chapter the prophet, in God's name, deals out his reproofs and threatnings, 1 Among the careleſs paſtors of the people, ver 1, 2 yet God promiſes to take care of the flock, ver 3—8 2 Among the wicked prophets and prieſts, whoſe ill character is here given at large, for which they muſt expect to be puniſhed, ver 9—32 3 Among the profane people, who ridiculed God's prophets, ver 33—40

a Chap x 21 & xii 10
Ezek xxxiv 2
b Ezek xxxiv 5
c Exod xxxii 34
d Chap xxxii 37
e Chap iii 15 Ezek xxxiv 11, &c
f Iſa iv 2 & xi 1 Chap xxxiii 14, 15 Dan ix 24 Zech iii 8 & vi 12 John i 45
g Iſa ix 6 h Pſ lxxii 2
i Deut xxxiii 28 Zech xiv 11
k Chap xxxiii 16 l 1 Cor i 30
m Chap xvi 14, 15
n Iſa xliii 5, 6

1 WO be unto [a] the paſtors that deſtroy and ſcatter
the ſheep of my paſture, ſaith the LORD
2 Therefore thus ſaith the LORD God of Iſrael againſt
the paſtors that feed my people, [b] Ye have ſcattered my
flock, and driven them away, and have not viſited
them, behold, I will viſit upon you the evil of your
doings, ſaith the LORD 3 And I will gather the
remnant of my flock, out of all countries whither I have
driven them, and will bring them again to their folds,
and they ſhall be fruitful and increaſe 4 And I will
ſet up ſhepherds over them, which ſhall feed them, and
they ſhall fear no more, nor be diſmayed, neither ſhall
they be lacking, ſaith the LORD 5 ¶ Behold, [f] the
days come, ſaith the LORD, that I will raiſe unto Da-
vid a righteous branch, and [g] a king ſhall reign and proſ-
per, and [h] ſhall execute judgment and juſtice in the earth
6 [i] In his days Judah ſhall be ſaved, and Iſrael ſhall dwell
ſafely [k] and this *is* his name whereby he ſhall be called,
[l] THE LORD OUR RIGHTEOUSNESS 7 There-
fore behold, [m] the days come, ſaith the LORD, that they
ſhall no more ſay, The LORD liveth which brought
up the children of Iſrael out of the land of Egypt 8
But, the LORD liveth, which brought up, and which
led the ſeed of the houſe of Iſrael out of the north coun-
try, and [n] from all the countries whither I had driven
them, and they ſhall dwell in their own land

v 1—8 The prophet's meſſage is a roll full of woe againſt a wicked nation, utterly corrupt both in its head and members

Before Christ 598.

1 He pronounces a woe on the *pastors* of Israel, their rulers in church and state, whose duty it was to have fed and protected the flock of God committed to their charge, but who had not only neglected to visit, and take care of the sheep, but had scattered and destroyed them by oppression and covetousness, by their bad examples leading them into sin, and thereby bringing ruin upon them, for these evils God would visit them with righteous judgment *Note*, They who have the rule over men's persons, and especially those who have the care of men's souls entrusted with them, should remember the awful charge, and what a solemn account they must one day make

2 He promises to take care of the flock they neglected

[1.] He will bring the scattered captives to their own land again, under the conduct of the shepherds Zerubbabel, Nehemiah, and others, raised up by his providence, men faithful in their office, under whose government they should increase in numbers, build again the waste places of Jerusalem and the cities of Judah, enjoy peace and prosperity, and no spoiler be permitted to devour them Some suppose this refers to gospel-times, when the elect of God should be gathered into his church, when under the ministry of the apostles and preachers the sheep of Christ should be fed with the rich doctrines of grace, filled with that divine faith which casteth out fear, and not one of the redeemed be ever suffered to perish, *John* x 28

[2.] God bids them expect with confidence the coming of the promised Messiah *Behold, the days come, saith the Lord*, swiftly advancing, and surely approaching, *that I will raise unto David a righteous branch*, by which name the Messiah is prefigured, *Isa* iv 2 *Zech* iii 8 *A branch*, because of his mean appearance, and the weakness of his incarnation, *a righteous branch*, perfectly so himself, and the author of all righteousness to others, and *raised unto David*, unto whom God had promised that from him the Messiah should descend, *and a king shall reign and prosper*, for mean as his appearance was, his throne was higher than the kings of the earth, established from eternity, continuing to eternity The kingdom he came to erect among men is an everlasting kingdom, victory and prosperity marked all his steps, the powers of sin and Satan were broken, and peace, love, and joy diffused in the hearts of all his redeemed people, *and he shall execute judgment and justice in the earth*, governing his people in righteousness, and executing judgment on their enemies *In his days Judah*, the chosen of God, *shall be saved* with an everlasting salvation, *and Israel*, the spiritual Israel, *shall dwell safely*, delivered from the power of Satan, the fears of guilt, the prevalence of corruption, enjoying the present favour of a covenant God, and expecting a rest eternal in the heavens *and this is the name whereby he shall be called, The Lord*, Jehovah, *our Righteousness*, by his obedience unto death, even the death of the cross, he hath brought in an everlasting righteousness, and all who by faith apprehend him, are made partakers of it, God imputes it to them, and regards them as complete in him A righteousness this, infinitely transcending all the righteousness of men or angels, as being the righteousness of Jehovah, and therefore, whoever make Jesus their refuge, and this righteousness their plea, can never enter into condemnation, but are entitled to the favour of God here, and to the inheritance of glory hereafter

3 The greatness of this salvation would so far obscure all the former deliverances God had wrought for his people, even their wondrous redemption from Egypt, that they should no more be mentioned And this must refer, not merely to their return from Babylon, but to their conversion under the preaching of the gospel, when multitudes were turned to the Lord, and may have yet a farther respect to the latter days, when the fulness of the Gentiles being come in, all Israel shall be saved, and literally be gathered, as many learned men suppose, to dwell in their own land, which hath never been the case with the ten tribes, since their first dispersion

9 ¶ Mine heart within me is broken, because of [a] the
prophets, [b] all my bones shake I am like a drunken man,
and like a man whom wine hath overcome, because of
the LORD, and because of the words of his holiness
10 For [c] the land is full of adulterers, for because of
‖ swearing the land mourneth [d] the pleasant places of
the wilderness are dried up, and their course is evil, and
their force *is* not right 11 For [e] both prophet and
priest are profane, yea, [f] in my house have I found their
wickedness, saith the LORD 12 [g] Wherefore their
way shall be unto them as slippery *ways* in the darkness
they shall be driven on and fall therein for I will
bring evil upon them, *even* the year of their visitation,
saith the LORD 13 And I have seen ‖ folly in the
prophets of Samaria, [h] they prophesied in Baal, and [i]
caused my people Israel to err 14. I have seen also in
the prophets of Jerusalem an horrible thing [k] they commit
adultery, and [l] walk in lies [m] they strengthen also the
hands of evil doers, that none doth return from his wic-
kedness they are all of them unto me [n] as Sodom, and
the inhabitants thereof as Gomorrah 15 Therefore
thus saith the LORD of hosts concerning the prophets,
Behold, I will feed them with wormwood, and make
them drink the water of gall for from the prophets of
Jerusalem is ‖ profaneness gone forth into all the land
16 Thus saith the LORD of hosts, [o] Hearken not unto
the words of the prophets that prophesy unto you, they
make you vain [p] they speak a vision of their own heart,
and not out of the mouth of the LORD 17 They
say still unto them that despise me, The LORD hath
said, [q] Ye shall have peace, and they say unto every one
that walketh after the § imagination of his own heart, [r]
No evil shall come upon you 18 For [s] who hath stood
in the ‖ counsel of the LORD, and hath perceived and
heard his word? who hath marked his word and heard
it? 19 Behold, [t] a whirlwind of the LORD is gone
forth in fury, even a grievous whirlwind, it shall fall
grievously upon the head of the wicked 20 [u] The
anger of the LORD shall not return, until he have
executed, and till he have performed the thoughts of
his heart in the latter days [w] ye shall consider it per-
fectly 21 [x] I have not sent these prophets, yet they
ran I have not spoken to them, yet they prophesied
22 But if they had stood in my counsel, and had caused
my people to hear my words, then they should have
turned them from their evil way, and from the evil of
their doings. 23 *Am* I a God at hand, saith the LORD,
and not a God afar off? 24. [y] Can any hide himself in
secret places, that I shall not see him? saith the LORD
[z] do not I fill heaven and earth? saith the LORD.
25 I have heard what the prophets said, that prophesy
lies in my name, saying, I have dreamed, I have dream-
ed 26 How long shall *this* be in the heart of the pro-
phets that prophesy lies? yea, *they are* prophets of the
deceit of their own heart, 27 [a] Which think to cause
my people to forget my name by their dreams which
they tell every man to his neighbour, [b] as their fathers
have forgotten my name, for Baal 28 The prophet
that hath a dream, let him tell a dream, and he that
hath my word, let him speak [c] my word [d] faithfully
what *is* the chaff to the wheat? saith the LORD 29
Is not my word like [e] as a fire? saith the LORD and
like a hammer [f] *that* breaketh [g] the rock in pieces? 30
Therefore behold, [h] I *am* against the prophets, saith the
LORD, that steal my words, every one from his neigh-
bour 31 Behold, I *am* against the prophets, saith the
LORD, that ‡ use their tongues, and say, He saith
32 Behold, I *am* against them that prophesy false dreams,
saith the LORD, and do tell them, and [i] cause my peo-
ple to err by their lies and [k] by their lightness, yet I sent
them not, nor commanded them therefore [l] they shall
not profit this people at all, saith the LORD

v. 9—32 When God comes to visit, none will suffer severer vengeance than those whose duty it was to have stood in the gap against the growing evils, but who basely joined in the general defection, and hardened and encouraged sinners by their smooth prophecies and ill example Against these the prophet is sent to denounce God's wrath

1 He appears deeply affected with what he saw, and the fearful message he was about to deliver *My heart within me is broken* with grief, because of the wickedness he beheld, and the ruin ready to ensue, *all my bones shake* with horror; *I am as a drunken man*, at a loss what to say or do, so confounded was he with the abominations he saw, *because of the Lord*, whose name was so dishonoured, *and because of the words of his holiness*, profanely abused by those who pretended to inspiration from him; or because of the dire judgments, which in righteous wrath he was sent to denounce against them *Note*, A true prophet grieves for the dishonour cast on God by men's wickedness, whilst he trembles at their approaching doom

2 He declares the dreadful state of the whole land *Full of adulterers*, corporally and spiritually, full of *swearers*, perjured or profane, who having cast off the fear of God, made no conscience of an oath For these things God had begun to visit them; *the land mourned* already with drought, the pastures failed, and famine devoured them, *and yet*, hardened in sin, *their course is evil*, they attend not to these warnings of God, but run to the same excess of evil, and will not be restrained, *and their force is not right*, their power and influence was exerted, not to suppress, but to encourage iniquity, *or their violence is not right*, full of rapine and injustice, as well as adultery and profaneness No marvel such a people are devoted to ruin

3 They

Marginal references: [a] Lam ii 1 ‖ Heb. ii [b] Chap v 7, & ix 2 ‖ Or, cursing [c] Chap ix 10 & xii 4 [d] Chap vi 13 Zeph iii 4 [e] Chap xi 15 Ezek viii 11 & xxiii 39 [f] Chap xx 6 & xiii 16 ‖ Or, an absurd thing [g] Chap ii 8 [h] Isa ix 16 [i] Chap xxix 23 [k] Ezek xiii 22 [l] Deut xxxii 32 Isa i 9, 10 [m] Chap viii 14 & ix 15 ‖ Or, hypocrisy [n] Mat vii 15 [o] Chap xiv 14 [p] Chap vi 14 & viii 11 Ezek xiii 10 Zech x 2 § Or, stubbornness [q] Mic iii 11 [r] Job xv 8 ‖ Or, secret [s] Chap xxv 32 & xxx 23 [t] Chap xxx 24 [u] Ezek ii 5 [w] Chap xiv 14 & xxvii 15 & xxix 9 [x] Psal cxxxix 7, &c Amos ix 2, 3 [y] 1 Kings viii 27 Psal cxxxix 7 [z] Acts xiii 8 [a] Judg iii 7 & viii 33 [b] 1 Pet iv 11 [c] 2 Cor ii 17 [d] Chap v 14 Luke xxiv 32 [e] 1 Cor ii 16 Heb iv 12 [f] 2 Cor x 4, 5 [g] Deut xviii 20 Chap xiv 14, 15 ‡ Or, smooth [h] Ver 16 [i] Zeph iii 4 [k] Lam ii 14

Before Christ 595

3. They who should have restrained them, are the ringleaders in sin *For both prophets and priests are profane* in their conversation and their lives, or *play the hypocrite*, pretending zeal for religion, and with the cloak of piety covering the foulest abominations *yea, in my house*, where most peculiarly God required purity, *have I found their wickedness, saith the Lord*, defiling the sacred place with their false doctrines, their flagrant immoralities, or idolatry, 1 Sam xi 22 The prophets of Israel had been bad, very bad, God had seen their wickedness and folly, prophesying in the name of Baal, and causing the people to err by their words, and debauching them by their ill examples but bad as the prophets of Samaria had been, the prophets of Jerusalem have equalled, yea, exceeded them in their abominations Horrible to tell! even in the face of God's temple *they commit adultery, and walk in lies*, reporting lying visions, making false pretences to prophecy, and turning the people from God to idols, hardening sinners in iniquity, crying peace, to lull their consciences asleep in fatal security, profaning God's name to vouch for their lies, v 17 and by their wicked deeds encouraging and emboldening others to sin *Note*, (1) No guilt so aggravated as theirs, who have not only their own blood, but the blood of lost souls lying upon them (2) Nothing so emboldens and hardens sinners, as when their teachers give them an occasion of offence by their ungodly conversation

4. An awful threatning is pronounced against them God regarded them as *the inhabitants of Sodom and Gomorrah*, their guilt so great, and crying to heaven for vengeance and swift it descends, *the Lord will bring evil upon them, even the year of their visitation* The time is fixed, the judgment ready to seize them, *their slippery ways* shall lead them into horrible *darkness*, they shall not be able to forsee nor avoid the ruin that approaches, *but be driven on* by irresistible violence, captivated by Satan and their own lusts, *and fall therein* from the depths of sin into the depths of misery, led into a miserable slavery, or perishing with famine and the sword, v 12 The bitterest and most poisonous cup of affliction, wormwood and gall, or *the juice of hemlock*, a cup of trembling, is mingled for them, to punish them for their horrid profaneness, the contagion of which had spread over the land Nothing being so dangerously infectious, and so fatally destructive, as the example of a debauched and abandoned ministry

5. God cautions the people to pay no regard to the lying suggestions of these false prophets, v 16 *They make you vain*, bolster you up in false hopes, speak the fancies of their own corrupted hearts, not the visions of inspiration, v 17 They cry peace to the wicked, to whom God hath said there is no peace, and promise them impunity when vengeance is ready to light upon them, v 17 Insulting and contradicting the prophets of the Lord, who affirmed God's wrath was ready to be revealed, they ridiculed their pretensions to prophesy, or boasting themselves of God's counsel, they vaunted their knowledge of his word and will, for who were so deep in his secrets as they? v 18 therefore, as the most effectual method of conviction, God will arise, *Behold, a whirlwind of the Lord is gone forth in fury*, the executioners of his judgments, the Chaldeans, with resistless violence are hasting to destroy, *even a grievous whirlwind, it shall fall grievously on the head of the wicked*, both on the deceived and the deceivers, but especially on the wicked prophets, nor depart from them till it hath answered God's decree and purpose, and extirpated them from the land, and conviction will come too late, when the sentence begins to be executed, they shall then see what they will not now believe, v 20 Or, *in the latter days*, may refer to the times of the gospel, or the final conversion of the Jews, when they shall consider all their past visitation, and be convinced and turned unto the Lord, tho' the former sense seems preferable, as more agreeable to the context God, by these his judgments, made it evident, that *he had not sent these prophets, yet they ran* without any commission from him, self-ordained, and pretending to prophesy when he had never taught them, but they palmed on the people the delusions of their corrupted hearts for his inspirations, v 21 and this was proved also from the effects of their ministry, for had they been sent of God, as they pretended, they would have made his word the standard of their preaching, and, as the blessed effect of their labours, would have beheld the conversion of men's souls turned by their preaching from the evil of their ways, the very reverse of which was evident, v 22 *Note*, (1) We need be often cautioned against false prophets, they are in every day more numerous than the true, and by authority and numbers seek to cast on them the brand of falshood, but by their fruits ye shall know them (2) No man may take on him the office of the ministry who is not called of God, and moved by the inspiration of the Holy Ghost They who profess they are, and yet are conscious of the falsehood of such declarations, God will not only disown, but severely punish (3) They who go forth in God's name and pretend to labour for him, yet see no effect of their ministry, and no one soul brought to a sense of sin and the knowledge of reconciliation by them, may justly suspect their doctrine is false, and themselves deluded

6. God expostulates with them on their folly and wickedness Do they think to deceive him by their lies? Can he, like man, a worm, only see the objects near him, and because afar off in heaven, is he unable to descry what passes here below, and in the hearts of men? Vain hope! to think of imposing on Omniscience, and evading his eye, who filleth heaven and earth with his presence The darkest recesses of the globe, or the darker devices of the human mind, are all naked and open to him, for there is no darkness, nor shadow of death, where any of the workers of wickedness can hide themselves, v 24 He heard and saw what these false prophets thought and spoke, he detected their impostures and lying dreams, which they reported as divine inspirations, and severely upbraids them with their hardened effrontery, *How long shall this be in the heart of the prophets that prophesy lies?* will they never have done with their lies? Or the words may be read, *How long* will they go on thus? *Is there any thing in the heart of the prophets that prophesy lies?* No, their mind and conscience is defiled, *yea, they are prophets of the deceit of their own hearts*, deceiving and being deceived, given up to their delusions to believe their own lie, and with most malignant intentions striving to debauch the minds of God's people to atheism and idolatry, as their fathers, by Baal's prophets, had been seduced before them, v 27 *Note*, (1) A sense of God's all-seeing eye is the great preservative from evil (2) They who would call off God's people, by pretences of new revelation, from the worship he hath prescribed, and the obedience he hath enjoined, evidently prove the falsehood of their pretensions

7. The prophet, in God's name, lays down the criterion to judge the false prophets and the true *He that hath a dream, let him tell his dream*, and the event will prove whether it comes from God or this is addressed to the false prophets, warning them not to call it a vision from God, but report what they dream *as a dream* *And he that hath my word*, a real and experimental knowledge of it, *let him speak my word faithfully*, without keeping back a tittle, however offensive or dangerous it may be to bear testimony to the truth *What is the chaff to the wheat, saith the Lord?* As different as these are, so different is the word of truth from the vain imaginations of the false prophets the one nutritive, substantial, weighty, the other light, vain, and delusive *Is not my word like fire, saith the Lord?* its operations quick, piercing, kindling a fire of conviction in the sinner's conscience, a fire of trial, separating the precious from the vile, a fire of love in the hearts of the faithful, *and like a hammer that breaketh the rock in pieces?* breaking the rocky heart of fallen man with deep contrition, and leading it to Christ, or stamping the hardened sinner to powder, denouncing upon him the vengeance of eternal punishment So effectual and mighty was the word in the mouth of the true prophets, whilst the preaching of the false prophets neither communicated light nor heat, was accompanied with no power, nor produced the least good effects on the people

8. God charges them with other notorious crimes *They steal my word, every one from his neighbour*, either the words of the true prophets, which they introduced the better to insinuate their falshoods, as if mimicking their language, they also partook of their inspiration or they prejudiced the people against them, and prevented them from paying regard to their admonitions and warnings They *use their tongues, and say, He saith*, pretending a divine commission, and taking the name of God in their mouths in vain, or *they smooth their tongues*, prophesy what will please and flatter men in their sins, and dare add God's sanction to their lies *They prophesy false dreams*, imposing the reveries of their own brain for inspiration, and *cause the people to err by their lies and by their lightness*, their false doctrines and evil examples encourage sinners in their wickedness, and for these things God threatens them with his vengeance *Behold, I am against the prophets*, three times he repeats it, to shew the certainty and terribleness of the wrath they had provoked He disowns the least connection with them, *I sent them not, neither commanded them*, they were lying boasters, who had no commission from him, *therefore they shall not profit this people at all*, but, the very reverse, shall bring down destruction on their heads as well as their own *Note*, None do more irreparable mischief in the church of God, than they who, pretending to be preachers of the truth, advance the doctrines of error, and beguile unstable souls

33. ¶ And when this people, or the prophet, or a
priest shall ask thee, saying, What *is* the burden of the
LORD? thou shalt then say unto them, What burden?
I will even forsake you, saith the LORD 34 And
as for the prophet, and the priest, and the people that
shall say, The burden of the LORD, I will even † punish that man and his house 35 Thus shall ye say
every one to his neighbour, and every one to his brother, What hath the LORD answered? and, What
hath the LORD spoken? 36 And the burden of the
LORD shall ye mention no more for every man's
word shall be his burden for ye have perverted the
words of the living God, of the LORD of hosts our

Before Christ 598

† Heb. visit upon.

God

Before Christ 598.

God. 37 Thus ſhalt thou ſay to the prophet, What
hath the LORD anſwered thee? and, What hath the
LORD ſpoken? 38 But ſince ye ſay, The burden of
the LORD; therefore thus ſaith the LORD, Becauſe
you ſay this word, The burden of the LORD, and I
have ſent unto you, ſaying, Ye ſhall not ſay, The bur-
den of the LORD: 39 Therefore behold, I, even I
will utterly forget you, and [e] I will forſake you, and the
city that I gave you and your fathers, *and* [f] *caſt you* out
of my preſence. 40 And I will bring [g] an everlaſting
reproach upon you, and a perpetual ſhame, which ſhall
not be forgotten.

e Ver. 33. f Chap. xv. 1. g Chap. xx. 11.

v. 33—40. It is evil indeed with any nation, when the moſt awful words of God are ſcoffed at, and made the object of ridicule.

1. The ſin here charged on the falſe prophets, prieſts, and people, is their horrid profaneneſs. Inſtead of humbly enquiring concerning God's mind and will, *v.* 35. they ſcoffingly repeated the prophet's words, and contemptuouſly enquired, *What is the burden of the Lord?* mocking the phraſe, as a cant term, becauſe the true prophets often made uſe of it, and deſpiſing the judgments which this word uſually imported; perverting thus *the words of the living God, of the Lord of hoſts our God*, contemning his power, and inſulting his majeſty; and though warned to deſiſt, they perſevered in their impious deriſion, *v.* 38. *Note*, (1.) It hath been the common effort of the wicked in all ages, to make God's word the butt of their wit, and by torturing ſome expreſſion to a ludicrous meaning, to turn the warnings of his miniſters into contempt. (2.) As long ago as Jeremiah, *the burden of the Lord* afforded matter of deriſion; he was one of thoſe preachers of hell and damnation which the men of that generation mocked at. Let ſuch ſinners then mock on, and fill up the meaſure of their iniquities. (3.) Wicked prophets and falſe preachers are uſually chief in this tranſgreſſion, and the great accuſers and revilers of the faithful; but that damnation they deride ſlumbereth not.

2. God declares his fixed purpoſe condignly to puniſh ſuch profaneneſs, *v.* 34. *Every man's word ſhall be his burden*, lay on him a load of guilt that, if unrepented of, ſhall ſink his ſoul into the depths of hell. *Behold, I, even I*, that living God, againſt whom ſuch wretches dare open their impious lips, *will utterly forget and forſake you*, and give you up to your terrible doom, without one kind remembrance to alleviate your miſery. The city God had given them and their fathers, ſhould be a prey for the Chaldean army, and they be led into a miſerable captivity; nor ſhould their ſhame and diſgrace come to an end. For a long while the whole nation ſhould ſuffer the marks of his fierce diſpleaſure, which to this day lies upon them, and the impenitent among them be ſentenced to everlaſting ſhame and contempt in the day of final recompence and perdition of ungodly men. *Note*, (1.) However men may mock at God's word, it will be ſeen at laſt whoſe word ſhall ſtand, his or theirs. (2.) The damnation ſinners deſpiſe, ſhall ſhortly and terribly come upon them, and their laugh of deriſion be turned into everlaſting weeping, and wailing, and gnaſhing of teeth.

CHAP. XXIV.

In the moſt deſolating judgments God knows how to ſeparate the precious from the vile. We have here, 1. A viſion of two baſkets of figs, one very good, and the other very bad, ver. 1, 2, 3. *2. The explication of this viſion, applying the good figs to thoſe that were already ſent into captivity for their good*, ver. 4—7. *The bad figs to thoſe that ſhould hereafter be ſent into captivity for their hurt*, ver. 8, 9, 10.

1 THE LORD ſhewed me, and behold, two baſ-
kets of figs *were* ſet before the temple of the
LORD, after that Nebuchadrezzar [a] king of Babylon
had carried away captive [b] Jeconiah the ſon of Jehoiakim
king of Judah, and the princes of Judah, with the
carpenters and ſmiths from Jeruſalem, and had brought
them to Babylon. 2 One baſket *had* [c] very good figs,
even like the figs *that are* firſt ripe: and the other baſ-
ket *had* [d] very naughty figs, which could not be eaten,
‡ they were ſo bad. 3 Then ſaid the LORD unto me,
What ſeeſt thou, Jeremiah? and I ſaid, Figs; the good
figs, very good; and the evil, very evil, that cannot
be eaten, they are ſo evil. 4 ¶ Again the word of
the LORD came unto me, ſaying, 5 Thus ſaith the
LORD the God of Iſrael, Like theſe good figs, ſo will
I acknowledge ‡ them that are carried away captive of
Judah, whom I have ſent out of this place into the
land of the Chaldeans [e] for *their* good. 6 For [f] I will
ſet mine eyes upon them for good, and [g] I will bring
them again to this land, and [h] I will build them, and not
pull *them* down; and I will plant them, and not pluck
them up. 7 And I will give them [i] an heart to know
me, that I *am* the LORD; and [k] they ſhall be my peo-
ple, and I will be their God: for they ſhall return unto
me with their whole heart. 8 ¶ And as [l] the evil figs,
which cannot be eaten, they are ſo evil; (ſurely thus
ſaith the LORD) ſo will I give Zedekiah the king of
Judah, and his princes, and the reſidue of Jeruſalem,
that remain in this land, and [m] them that dwell in the
land of Egypt: 9 And I will deliver them ‖ to be [n] re-
moved into all the kingdoms of the earth for *their* hurt,
[o] *to be* a reproach and a proverb, a taunt and [p] a curſe in
all places whither I ſhall drive them. 10 And [q] I will
ſend the ſword, the famine, and the peſtilence among
them, till they be conſumed from off the land, that I
gave unto them and to their fathers.

a 2 Kings xxiv. 12, &c. 2 Chron. xxxvi. 10. b Chap. xxii. 24. c Ver. 5. d Ver. 8. ‡ Heb. For badneſs. ‡ Heb. The captivity. e Rom. viii. 28. f Chap. xxxix. 12. g Chap. xii. 15. & xvi. 15. h Chap. xxxiii. 7. & xlii. 10. i Deut. xxx. 6. Chap. xxxii. 39. Ezek. xi. 19. & xxxvi. 26, 27. k Chap. xxx. 22. & xxxi. 33. & xxxii. 38. l Chap. xxix. 17. m Chap. xliii. & xliv. ‖ Heb. For removing, or vexation. n Deut. xxviii. 25, 37. 1 Kings ix. 7. 2 Chron. vii. 20. Chap. xv. 4. & xxix. 18. o Pſ. xliv. 14. p Chap. xxix. 18, 22. q Ibid. xxix. 17.

v. 1—10. Though in general the prophet's word was rejected by the people, yet there were ſome who heard it, and to whom it was a ſavour of life unto life. And tho' the nation's iniquities now being full, they fell into the promiſcuous ruin, yet even in their captivity God will take care of them, and make even this moſt afflictive providence work for their good.

1. The date of the viſion is in the beginning of Zedekiah's reign, when Nebuchadnezzar had carried away Jeconiah the king, and the princes of Judah, captives to Babylon, and with them the carpenters and ſmiths; either to employ them in his own works, or to deprive the captive land of their aſſiſtance in making fortifications and weapons of war.

2. The viſion itſelf conſiſted of two baſkets of figs, placed before the temple; the one, vile and naughty, that could not be eaten; the other, very good, *v.* 2, 3. The explication of which the Lord gives him, *v.* 5.

(1.) The good figs were the captives gone into Babylon: theſe God promiſes to regard, to cauſe their captivity to iſſue for their good; thoſe who were faithful ſhould be improved in the furnace of affliction, and thoſe who were otherwiſe till then, ſhould be, by grace, wrought upon and led to repentance by the viſitation. In conſequence of which, the eyes of his favour ſhould be upon them, they ſhould be again reſtored and firmly eſtabliſhed in their own land; and, better than all temporal good, the Lord engages to enrich them with enlarged ſpiritual underſtanding, and to beſtow on them the beſt of bleſſings, *I will give them a heart to know me, that I am the Lord*, by experience of his power, grace, and love exerted eminently for them, and exercised richly towards them; *and they ſhall be my people*, enjoying his protection, and taken into covenant with him, *and I will be their God*, their helper and defender, their portion, their exceeding great reward; *for they ſhall return unto me with their whole heart*, in ſimplicity and ſincerity, aſhamed of their backſliding, and unfeignedly penitent. *Note*, (1.) The ways of providence are myſterious; what ſeemed the greateſt affliction, proves often in its iſſue the moſt ſubſtantial bleſſing. (2.) God's hand is to be acknowledged in all our ſufferings, whatever inſtruments are employed; we muſt ſay, *I became dumb, and opened not my mouth, for it was thy doing*. (3.) If ever we come to the true knowledge of God, it muſt be wholly the gift of his grace; for without this, we can know nothing as we ought to know. (4.) Whatever our ſins and backſliding have been, whenever God gives us a heart to return unto him, we may be aſſured his arms are ſtill open to receive us. (5.) God ſays, *I will*, and *ye ſhall*; for the ſinner and backſlider are worſe than merely paſſive, they are reluctant; yea, the carnal mind is enmity againſt God; unleſs God therefore over-ruled our perverſeneſs and conquered our obſtinacy, we never ſhould be his people, nor he our God.

(2.) The evil figs repreſented the remnant which were left in Jeruſalem under Zedekiah, who, tho' they ſtood before the temple, yet were much worſe than their brethren that had gone into captivity; for not the greateſt ſinners are always the firſt to ſuffer. God permits them to ſtand to fill up the meaſure of their iniquities, whilſt he corrects his dear children with the ſcourges of paternal love: but their judgment advances; *ſurely, thus ſaith the Lord*, the decree is gone forth, and the execution of it ſure; Zedekiah and his princes, with the reſidue of Jeruſalem, are devoted to deſtruction; nor ſhould they, who fled to Egypt for ſhelter, be exempted, ſince thither the judgments of God ſhould follow them. *The ſword, the famine, the peſtilence*, ſhall conſume them, and thoſe who ſurvive, be doomed to a miſerable ſlavery, worſe than death, ſcattered into all lands *for their hurt*, where they ſhould have no means to adminiſter friendly conſolation to each other; and hardened, inſtead of repenting under their ſufferings, their yoke ſhould be made heavy, and their perſons deſpicable and odious; they ſhould be *a reproach, a proverb, a taunt, and a curſe in all places whither God would drive them*; and this ſeems to have a reference, not only to their deſolations under Nebuchadnezzar, but alſo to

Before Christ 598. look forward to their last more terrible destruction by the Romans, and the truth of the prediction appears verified this day in that unhappy people, who live under the evident curse of God, and the contempt of all nations whither they are scattered

CHAP XXV

This prophecy bears date some time before those prophecies in the foregoing chapters, for they are not placed in the exact order of time in which they were delivered. Here is, 1 A review of the prophecies that had been delivered to Judah and Jerusalem for many years last past, with the little success of them, ver 1—7 2 The destruction of Jerusalem by the king of Babylon, threatened for their contempt of God and their continuance in sin, ver 8—11 To which is annexed, a promise of their deliverance out of captivity, after seventy years, ver 12, 13, 14 3 A prediction of the devastation of divers other nations by Nebuchadrezzar, represented by a cup of fury put into their hands, ver 15—28 By a sword sent among them, ver 29—33 And a desolation made among the shepherds, and their flocks and pastures, ver 34—38

606 1 THE word that came to Jeremiah concerning all
the people of Judah, [a] in the fourth year of Jehoiakim the son of Josiah king of Judah, that *was* the
first year of Nebuchadrezzar king of Babylon 2 The
which Jeremiah the prophet spake unto all the people
of Judah, and to all the inhabitants of Jerusalem, saying,
3 [b] From the thirteenth year of Josiah the son of
Amon king of Judah, even unto this day (that *is* the
three and twentieth year) the word of the LORD hath
come unto me, and I have spoken unto you, rising early
and speaking, [c] but ye have not hearkned 4 And the
LORD hath sent unto you all his servants the prophets,
[d] rising early and sending *them*, but ye have not hearkened, nor inclined your ear to hear 5 They said, [e]
Turn ye again now every one from his evil way, and
from the evil of your doings, and [f] dwell in the land that
the LORD hath given unto you and to your fathers,
for ever and ever 6 And go not after other gods to
serve them, and to worship them, and provoke me not
to anger with the works of your hands, and I will do
you no hurt 7 Yet ye have not hearkened unto me,
saith the LORD, that ye might provoke me to anger
with the works of your hands, to your own hurt

a Chap xxxvi 1 b Chap i 2 From 629 to 606 c Chap xi 7, 8 & xiii 10, 11 & xvi 12 & xvii 23 & xviii 12 & xix 15 & xxii 21 d Chap vii 13, 25 & xxix 19 e 2 Kings xvii 13, Chap xviii 11 & xxxv 15 Jonah iii 8 f Isa xxxvii 27

v 1—7 This prophecy bears date in the first year of the reign of Nebuchadrezzar, and the fourth of Jehoiakim, and it is directed to the people in general, probably when assembled at Jerusalem on one of the three annual feasts If the princes will not hear, perhaps the people may, at least it will leave both inexcusable

1 The prophet reminds them how long and how earnestly God had been exhorting them, by his ministers and others, to turn from the evil of their ways Three and twenty years he had preached, from the 13th of Josiah, to the 4th of Jehoiakim, *rising early, and speaking* diligently, constantly, faithfully, whilst Micah, Nahum, and Habakkuk, had just preceded him, and Zephaniah was his contemporary, besides many others whom God in mercy had sent to warn them, unwilling they should perish, and accompanied his admonitions with the most gracious promises They are plainly told of their sins, and exhorted to repent of them, if they would return from their shameful idolatries, and from all their other evil works, then God's threatenings should not light upon them, but they should long and peaceably enjoy their good land *Note*, (1.) God will remember against the sinner all the means of grace he hath abused, to his greatest condemnation in the day of judgment (2) They who are sent on God's messages, need be earnest and diligent in delivering them, that they may at least be free from the blood of all men (3) God doth not strike without warning, but if we will not hear, we must perish

2 The prophet upbraids them with their impenitence and hardness of heart They *hearkened not, nor inclined their ear*, they would not so much as pay a moment's attention to the message, their heart was so averse to it, they resolved to abide *in their sins* and provocations, let the consequence be never so much to their hurt, and thus, as all impenitent sinners do, destroyed themselves

8 ¶ Therefore thus saith the LORD of hosts, Because ye have not heard my words, 9 Behold, I will
send and take [g] all the families of the north, saith the
LORD, and Nebuchadrezzar the king of Babylon [h] my
servant, and will bring them against this land, and against
the inhabitants thereof, and against all these nations round
about, and will utterly destroy them, and [i] make them an
astonishment and an hissing, and perpetual desolations.
10 Moreover, I will † take from them [k] the voice of
mirth, and the voice of gladness, the voice of the bridegroom, and the voice of the bride, the sound of the millstones, and the light of the candle 11 And this whole
land shall be a desolation, *and* an astonishment, and these
nations shall serve the king of Babylon seventy years
12 And [l] it shall come to pass when seventy years are
accomplished, *that* I will ‡ punish the king of Babylon,
and that nation, saith the LORD, for their iniquity, and
the land of the Chaldeans [m] and will make it perpetual
desolations 13 And I will bring upon that land all my
words which I have pronounced against it, *even* all *that*
is written in this book, which Jeremiah hath prophesied
against all the nations 14 For [n] many nations and [o]
great kings shall [p] serve themselves of them also and I
will [q] recompense them according to their deeds, and according to the works of their own hands

g Chap i 15 h Chap xxvii 6 & xliii 10 i Chap xviii 16

Before Christ 606. † Heb Cause to perish from them k Isa xxiv 7 Chap vii 34 & xvi 9 Ezek xxvi 13 Hos ii 11 Rev xviii 23 l 2 Chron xxxvi 21, 22 Ezra i 1 Chap xxix 10 Dan ix 2 ‡ Heb Visit upon m Isa xiii 19 & xiv 23 & xxi 1 Chap l 13, 23, 39, 40 & li 25 n Isa xiv 4 Chap l 9 & li 27 o Chap l 41 & li 27 p Chap xxvii 7 q Chap l 29 & li 24 Rev xviii 6

v 8—14 The judgment is pronounced on the rebellious people of Judah, and their destroyer shall not go unpunished

1 Judah shall be destroyed by the king of Babylon, God's servant in this behalf to execute vengeance on this devoted nation Around his standard the families of the north are summoned, his victorious army marches, and desolation marks their way, Judea falls, and all her neighbours, so far from affording her assistance, are involved in the general ruin, and so terrible the ravages, that they shall be *an astonishment and an hissing, and perpetual desolations* during seventy years the miseries should last, the voice of joy be never heard in the city, no nuptial songs, no sound of mirth, no provision should be left, nor candle burn in it, but melancholy silence reign, the land uncultivated, destitute of inhabitants, and swept with the besom of destruction *Note*, (1) They who will not be ruled by God's word, must be ruined (2) God often uses wicked instruments to chastise his own people, and they are made to do his work, when meaning only to aggrandise themselves

2 Babylon, the destroyer of others, shall herself also, after seventy years, be destroyed for her *iniquity*, her tyranny, pride, and cruelty to God's Israel, and the land of the Chaldeans shall be made *perpetual desolations*, when all the evil pronounced by Jeremiah, *chap* xlvi—li shall come upon them, and as she hath served herself of other nations, subduing and plundering them, God will recompense her in kind, and raise up many nations and great kings, the Medes, Persians, and their allies, to lay her waste, and enrich themselves with her spoils

Commentators differ in the date from whence these seventy years commence, some begin with the first of Nebuchadnezzar, others not till the captivity of Jehoiachin, eight years after Certain however it is, it was accomplished in its season, nor shall one jot or tittle ever pass from God's word, until the whole be fulfilled

15 ¶ For thus saith the LORD God of Israel unto
me, Take [r] the wine-cup of this fury at my hand, and
cause all the nations to whom I send thee to drink it
16 And [s] they shall drink, and be moved and [t] be mad,
because of the sword that I will send among them
17 Then took I the cup at the LORD's hand, and
made all the nations to drink, unto whom the LORD
had sent me 18 *To wit*, [u] Jerusalem, and the cities
of Judah, and the kings thereof, and the princes thereof, to make them a desolation, an astonishment, an
hissing, and a curse, (as *it is* this day) 19 [x] Pharaoh
king of Egypt, and his servants, and his princes, and
all his people, 20 And all the mingled people, and
all the kings of the land of Uz, [y] and all the kings of
the land of the Philistines, and Ashkelon, and Azzah,
and Ekron, and the remnant of Ashdod, 21 [a] Edom,
[b] and Moab, and the children of Ammon 22 And all
the kings of Tyrus, and all the kings of Zidon, and
the kings of the ‖ isles which *are* beyond the sea 23
[c] Dedan, and Tema, and Buz, and all ‡ *that are* in the
utmost corners, 24 And all the kings of Arabia, and
all the kings of [d] the mingled people that dwell in the
desert 25 And all the kings of Zimri, and all the
kings of [e] Elam, and all the kings of the Medes 26
And all the kings of the north, far and near, one with
another, and all the kingdoms of the world, which *are*
upon the face of the earth and [f] the king of Sheshach
shall drink after them 27 Therefore thou shalt say
unto them, Thus saith the LORD of hosts, the God of
Israel, [i] Drink ye, [k] and be drunken, and spew and fall,
and rise no more, because of the sword which I will
send

r Job xxi 20 Psal lxxv 8 Isa li 17 Rev xiv 10 s Ezek xxiii 34 Nah iii 11 t Chap li 7 u Isa li 17 x Chap xlvi 2 y Chap xlvii 1 & xlix 1 z Chap xlix 1 a Chap xlix 7 b Chap xlviii 1 ‖ Or, region by the sea side c Chap xlix 23 ‡ Heb cut off into corners, or, having the corners of the hair polled d Chap xlix 28 & l 37 e Chap xlix 34 f Chap li 41 i Hab ii 16 k Isa lxiii 6

Before Christ 606

kind among you 28 And it shall be, if they refuse
to take the cup at thine hand to drink, then shalt thou
say unto them, Thus saith the LORD of hosts, Ye
shall certainly drink 29 For lo, [l] I begin to bring evil
on the city [m] which is called by my name, and should ye
be utterly unpunished? Ye shall not be unpunished
for I will call for a sword upon all the inhabitants of the
earth, saith the LORD of hosts

l Chap xlix 12 Ezek ix 6 Luke xxiii 31 1 Pet iv 17
m Dan ix 18

v 15—29 Judgment here begins at the house of God, but it spreads far and near The neighbouring nations must drink of the same cup, and at last Babylon herself take it in turn

1 The judgment is represented under *a wine-cup of fury* The sins of all these nations had provoked God's wrath, and heavy it falls on them, like men intoxicated with liquor, without wisdom or might, they should become an easy conquest, and the sword of God devour them Nor would their reluctance to submit to their doom avail any thing, v 28 The prophet is commanded to make them drink, denouncing the judgments of God, that would quite overwhelm them and sink them into ruin, from which they should never, or at least not for a long while, recover *Note*, It is a fearful thing to fall into the hands of the living God then all resistance is vain

2 The nations who are the subjects of this prophecy, are, first Jerusalem and the cities of Judah their sins being most aggravated, they suffer first Egypt, on whom they placed dependence, next falls under the Babylonish yoke then all the mingled people, the bordering nations, some, as Tyre and Zidon, that had been their friends, others, as Moab and Edom, who had been the inveterate foes of Judah, but now sink in the promiscuous ruin far and wide the rapid conqueror spread his arms, even to all the kingdoms of the then known world, at least to the whole extent of that great monarchy, which was termed, from its vast territory, universal At last the lofty queen of nations herself must be laid in the dust, and the king of Sheshach, or Babylon, see *chap* li 41 must drink of the same cup, and perish as the kingdoms he had destroyed It is added, v 18 *as it is this day*, in a parenthesis probably that was inserted by Jeremiah, who lived to see the ruin of his country, or by him, whether Baruch or Ezra, who collected these prophecies when the event had verified the prediction

3 If God spares not his own people, let not the rest of the nations, of whom they have learnt idolatry, think to go unpunished His determination is fixed, and the accomplishment of it is inevitable *Note*, (1) When God arises to judge, the greatest nations are but as stubble before the whirlwind (2) Wherever sinners are, however many, however mighty, surely they shall not go unpunished

30 Therefore prophesy thou against them all these
words, and say unto them, [n] The LORD shall roar from
on high, and utter his voice from his holy habitation,
he shall mightily roar upon his habitation, he shall give
[o] a shout, as they that tread *the grapes*, against all the in-
habitants of the earth 31 A noise shall come *even* to
the ends of the earth, for the LORD hath a controversy
with the nations he will plead with all flesh, he will give
them that are wicked to the sword, saith the LORD
32 Thus saith the Lord of hosts, Behold, evil shall go
forth from nation to nation, and [p] a great whirlwind
shall be raised up from the coasts of the earth 33 And
the slain of the LORD shall be at that day from *one* end
of the earth even unto the *other* end of the earth [q] they
shall not be lamented, neither gathered, nor buried,
they shall be dung upon the ground. 34 ¶ [r] Howl,
ye shepherds, and cry, and wallow yourselves *in the ashes*,
ye principal of the flock for [†] the days of your slaugh-
ter, and of your dispersions, are accomplished, and ye
shall fall like a [‡] pleasant vessel 35 [s] And [§] the shep-
herds shall have no way to flee, nor the principal of the
flock to escape 36 A voice of the cry of the shepherds,
and an howling of the principal of the flock *shall be heard*
for the LORD hath spoiled their pasture 37 And the
peaceable habitations are cut down, [t] because of the fierce
anger of the LORD 38 [u] He hath forsaken his covert,
as the lion for their land is [‖] desolate because of the
fierceness of the oppressor, and because of his fierce
anger

n Isa xlii 13 Joel iii 16 Amos i 2
o Isa xvi 9 Chap xlviii 33
p Isa xxx 30 Chap xxiii 19 & xxx 23
q Chap xvi 4
r Chap iv 8 & vi 26
† Heb Your days for slaughter
‡ Heb a vessel of desire
s Amos ii 14
§ Heb Flight shall perish from the shepherds, and from, &c
t Isa xxiv
u Chap iv 7 & xlix 19
‖ Heb a wonder

v 30—38 The sword threatned is Nebuchadnezzar's, but the word is of God, who clothes him with all his power, and ensures to him the victory The terribleness of the judgment is here described

1 The tremendous voice of God shall be heard from on high in mighty thunderings He shall roar *upon his habitation*, the earth in general, or Jerusalem in particular, or *out of his habitation*, from the heavens, where he hath placed his radiant throne *He shall give a shout*, as when contending armies rush into the battle, and as those that tread the grapes at the vintage, and so loud the sound, the most distant realms shall hear, even to the ends of the earth

2 Righteous vengeance shall seize the wicked *The Lord hath a controversy with the nations* for their wickedness, and *he will plead with all flesh*, will bring them to his tribunal, *and he will give them that are wicked to the sword*, from nation to nation the judge shall go in circuit *A great whirlwind shall be raised up from the ends of the earth*, the Chaldean army first, then the Medes, afterwards the Greeks, and lastly the Romans, all God's executioners of vengeance, and those who fall by their arms are *the slain of the Lord*, from one end of the earth to the other, he marks the victims, and gives the sword its direction Unlamented they shall fall, v 33 for want of mourners, or because their friends and relations are so occupied with their own danger that they are insensible to every thing beside, unburied they shall lie as dung upon the earth, and no compassionate hand be found to gather the scattered corpses and hide them in a grave

3 The shepherds are called upon to howl for these horrible desolations either the kings of the earth in general, or the rulers of Judah in particular, to whom the words seem to be addressed *Wallow yourselves in the ashes, ye principal of the flock*, in the deepest agony, most bitter sorrow, and hopeless misery, *for the days of your slaughter and of your dispersions are accomplished*, like sheep before the wolf, torn, worried, and dispersed, *and ye shall fall like a pleasant vessel* irreparably broken in pieces Then flight will be vain, and all hope of escape desperate, v 35 See *chap* xxxix 4—6 Shrieks shall ascend on every side, the heart of the mightiest fail, ruin and desolation universal be spread around, and even *the peaceable habitations are cut down*, the palaces where peace and plenty reigned, or, as is common in the ravages of war, they who lived inoffensively, and never provoked the scourge, share in the general calamity of the land, *because of the fierce anger of the Lord*, the cause of all these fearful judgments *He hath forsaken his covert as a lion*, either God, going forth against the shepherds and their flocks to destroy them, or rather Nebuchadnezzar, roused up from Babylon, *and the land is desolate*, ravaged by his army, *because of the fierceness of the oppressor*, or *oppressing sword, and because of his fierce anger*, either the wrath of God or of the king of Babylon, rushing forth to the slaughter *Note*, (1) War is a dreadful scourge (2) The rulers, who were deepest in transgression, shall be chief in suffering (3) Wo unto the sinful soul against whom God rises up as an enemy May others judgments be our warnings, that we may hear and fear, and do no more wickedly

CHAP XXVI

As in the history of the Acts of the Apostles, *that of their preaching and that of their sufferings is interwoven, so it is in the account we have of the prophet Jeremiah, witness this chapter, where we are told, (1) How faithfully he preached,* ver 1—6 *(2) How spitefully he was persecuted for so doing,* ver 7—11 *(3) How bravely he stood to his doctrine in the face of his persecutors,* ver 12—15 *(4) How wonderfully he was protected by the prudence of the princes,* ver 16—19 *And tho' Urijah, another prophet, was about the same time put to death by Jehoiakim,* ver 20—23 *yet he escaped,* ver 24

610 ending 609 beginning

1 IN the beginning of the reign of Jehoiakim the
son of Josiah king of Judah, came this word from
the LORD, saying, 2 Thus saith the LORD, Stand
in the court of the LORD's house, and speak unto all
the cities of Judah, which come to worship in the
LORD's house, all the words that I command thee to
speak unto them, [a] diminish not a word 3 If so be
they will hearken, and turn every man from his evil way,
that I may [b] repent me of the evil which I purpose to
do unto them, because of the evil of their doings
4 And thou shalt say unto them, Thus saith the LORD,
If ye will not hearken to me to walk in my law, which
I have set before you, 5 To hearken to the words
of my servants the prophets, [c] whom I sent unto you,
both rising up early, and sending *them* (but ye have not
hearkened) 6 Then will I make this house like [d] Shi-
loh, and will make this city a curse to all the nations
of the earth

a Acts xx 27
b Chap xviii 8 Jonah iii 9
c Chap vii 13, 25 & xi 7 & xxv 3
d 1 Sam iv 12 Psal lxxviii 60 Chap vii 12, 14

v 1—6 They who would be faithful to God, in the discharge of their ministry, must set their faces like a flint, and be above the fear of man

1 Jeremiah is sent into the courts of the Lord's house, whither, on one of their solemn feasts, the people of the land were assembled out of the cities of Judah, and there, in the midst of that great congregation, he must deliver his message and, lest their greatness, their multitude, or their known enmity against

such

Before Christ 609

such faithful warnings, might daunt his courage, or warp him to palliate the severity of the threatning, he is charged not to *diminish a word* When we speak for God, we must neither be afraid nor ashamed to declare his whole counsel, and resolutely abide by the consequences

2 The purport of his discourse is to advise them of the danger of their sins, and the purpose of God to punish them, to exhort them to a speedy and unfeigned repentance, to assure them that then God would turn away his anger from them, but that, if they persisted in their impenitence, disobedience to his holy law, and disregard of his divinely appointed ministers, the consequences would be inevitably fatal, and their ruin ensue, Jerusalem and the temple, like Shiloh and the tabernacle there pitched of old, would be given into the hands of her enemies, and her judgment be so terrible, that it should be the deepest imprecation to say, *the Lord make thee like Jerusalem!* Now nothing here could give reasonable offence God graciously waited, he offered mercifully to receive them, they had only to return to him, and then the message breathed nothing but peace and pardon but they, who resolved to persist in their iniquities, could not bear to be told of the issue of them *Note*, (1) There is nothing in the most terrible denunciations of wrath to quarrel with, when the only end of these terrors of the Lord is to lead us to pardon and everlasting peace But, (2) If men will not be warned, they must be damned

7 So the priests, and the prophets, and all the people,
heard Jeremiah speaking these words in the house of the
LORD 8 ¶ Now it came to pass, when Jeremiah had
made an end of speaking all that the LORD had com-
manded *him* to speak unto all the people, that the priests,
and the prophets, and all the people took him, saying,
e Mat xxvi 66 Acts xxi 22
[e] Thou shalt surely die 9 Why hast thou prophesied
in the name of the LORD, saying, This house shall be
like Shiloh, and this city shall be desolate without an in-
habitant? and all the people were gathered against Jere-
miah, in the house of the LORD 10 ¶ When the
princes of Judah heard these things, then they came up
from the king's house unto the house of the LORD,
† Or at the door
and sat down † in the entry of the new gate of the
LORD's *house* 11 Then spake the priests, and the
prophets unto the princes, and to all the people, say-
‡ The judgment of death is for this man
ing, ‡ This man *is* worthy to die, for he hath prophe-
sied against this city, as ye have heard with your ears
12 ¶ Then spake Jeremiah unto all the princes, and
to all the people, saying, the LORD sent me to pro-
phesy against this house, and against this city, all the
f Chap vii 3
words that ye have heard 13 Therefore now [f] amend
g Ver 19
your ways, and your doings, and obey the voice of the
LORD your God, and [g] the LORD will repent him
of the evil that he hath pronounced against you 14
h Chap xxxviii 5
As for me, behold, [h] I *am* in your hand do with me
§ Heb It is good and right in your eyes
as § seemeth good and meet unto you 15 But know
ye for certain, that if ye put me to death, ye shall sure-
ly bring innocent blood upon yourselves, and upon this
city, and upon the inhabitants thereof for of a truth
i Ver 12
[i] the LORD hath sent me unto you, to speak all these
words in your ears

v 7—15 The plainest and most reasonable admonitions, delivered with the tenderest affection, and urged with the most solemn weight of God's authority, have no effect upon the hardened sinner but to exasperate his corruptions, as it here appears

1 Jeremiah is arrested for his preaching, and dragged before the magistrates, that he may be condemned and executed The ungodly priests and false prophets, that in all ages and places have been the bitterest enemies and persecutors of the few faithful, arose, exasperated at what they heard, and the people, at their instigation, readily followed them they seize the poor prophet, and threaten him with immediate death, either in the rage of pretended zeal, or by form of law, v 8 The charge against him is for falsehood, and blasphemous words spoken against that holy place, because in the name of the Lord he had said, *this house shall be like Shiloh, and this city shall be desolate without inhabitant* Such an uproar raised a vast tumult, and all the people ran together the tidings of which soon brought up the princes from the king's house into the temple, and before them as judges the criminal is produced, at *the entry of the new gate of the Lord's house*, where they sit to hear the cause The false prophets and priests, whose hand was ever first in the instigation of opposing the ministers of truth, stand forth to accuse him, not doubting but to gain the verdict in their favour, appealing for the truth of their charge to all the people who had heard Jeremiah's discourse, and demanding judgment against him as most worthy to die *Note*, They who will be zealous for God must sometimes put their lives in their hand How often since this have the true preachers of Christ been in danger by tumultuous mobs, instigated by apostate priests!

2 Jeremiah vindicates himself from the charge, not by denying it, but by maintaining the truth of what he had spoken The words were not his own God had sent him, and how could he then be silent? Besides, the threatnings only affected the impenitent So far therefore from desisting, he urges the admonition he had given, *Therefore now amend your ways and your doings, and obey the voice of the Lord your God*, who yet did not disclaim the relation, and was ready, instantly, on their repentance, to reverse the threatnings issued against them What was urged with so kind an intention surely deserved not punishment, but praise However, he submits to whatever sentence they thought fit to pronounce, but warns them of the danger of shedding the blood of an innocent man, which would cry for vengeance, and the still more atrocious guilt of slaying a prophet purely for delivering the words which *of a truth the Lord had sent him to speak*, who would not fail condignly to avenge such a flagrant insult upon himself, as well as such cruel injustice done to his servant *Note*, (1) To preach boldly, and suffer patiently for well-doing, is the true spirit of a Christian minister (2) We must abide by God's word, nor ever recede a step, though the greatest loss and damage, yea though death itself, threatens us for our fidelity

16 ¶ Then said the princes, and all the people unto
the priests, and to the prophets, This man *is* not worthy
to die for [k] he hath spoken to us in the name of the k Ver 12
LORD our God 17 Then rose up certain of the
elders of the land, and spake to all the assembly of the
people, saying, 18 [l] Micah the Morasthite prophesied l Mic i 1 about 713
in the days of Hezekiah king of Judah, and spake to all
the people of Judah, saying, Thus saith the LORD of
hosts, [m] Zion shall be plowed *like* a field, and Jerusalem m Mic iii 12
shall become heaps, and the mountain of the house, as
the high places of the forest 19 Did Hezekiah king
of Judah, and all Judah put him at all to death? did he
not fear the LORD, and besought † the LORD, and † Heb the face of the Lord
the LORD [n] repented him of the evil which he had pro- n Ver 13
nounced against them? Thus might we procure great
evil against our souls 20 And there was also a man
that prophesied in the name of the LORD, Urijah the
son of Shemaiah of Kirjath-jearim, who prophesied a-
gainst this city, and against this land, according to all
the words of Jeremiah 21 And when Jehoiakim the
king, with all his mighty men, and all the princes heard
his words, the king sought to put him to death, but
when Urijah heard it, he was afraid, and fled, and went
into Egypt 22 And Jehoiakim the king sent men into
Egypt, *namely*, Elnathan the son of Achbor, and *certain*
men with him into Egypt 23 And they fet forth Uri-
jah out of Egypt, and brought him unto Jehoiakim the
king, who [o] slew him with the sword, and cast his dead o Mat xxiii 34
body into the graves of ‡ the common people 24 Ne- ‡ Heb The sons of the people
vertheless the hand of [p] Ahikam the son of Shaphan was p 2 Kings xxii 12, 14 Chap xxxix 14 & xl 5
with Jeremiah, that they should not give him into the
hand of the people to put him to death.

v 16—24 God knoweth how to deliver his people out of temptation, and, when their case appears most desperate, to rescue them from the jaws of the lion

1 Jeremiah is acquitted, notwithstanding the malicious accusations of his enemies Such an evidence attended his defence, such a noble simplicity appeared in it, such approved fidelity, and God himself put such an awe upon the princes and people, that though they strangely hardened their hearts against the admonition given, yet they own God's authority, and dare not condemn the innocent prophet *Note*, There are many on whom the word of God hath so far an influence as to extort their assent to its truth, who nevertheless continue unhumbled in their sins.

2 Some of the court, from among the princes, and perhaps Ahikam after mentioned at their head, rose up in the prophet's defence, and, as a precedent, quoted the case of Micah, who a little before, in the days of Hezekiah, had prophesied as severe things as ever Jeremiah had done, *that Jerusalem should become heaps*, the city *ploughed as a field*, and the temple utterly demolished, v 18 yet so far were Hezekiah and his princes from condemning him to death for his fidelity, that they trembled at God's word, besought the Lord, repented of their evil deeds, and this was the lengthening of their prosperity, God accepting their repentance, and withholding the threatened judgment And such conduct, they insinuate, in the present case would be most fit and becoming, whereas to act otherwise in shedding innocent blood at the instigation of exasperated priests, incensed at having their pride, hypocrisy, and falsehood detected, would *procure great evil against their souls*, lay them under heavy guilt, and

Before Christ 598.

and expose them to God's awful vengeance *Note,* (1) The greatest men shew their wisdom in hearing and obeying the admonitions of God (2) The dreadful consequences of sin, if nothing else, should deter us from it, if we have little sense of its evil and malignity, the fear of evil at least should restrain us

3 Another instance is quoted of a prophet put to death in the present reign, which some suppose to be a case in point urged by Jeremiah's persecutors in reply to the former, and in order to obtain his condemnation Others, that it is the continuation of the same person's discourse, urging the guilt already brought upon the land by the murder of one prophet, and that to increase it, by a repetition of the like crime, could not but hasten their destruction Others suppose this story was added by Jeremiah himself, or whoever collected his prophecies, as an instance of God's extraordinary interposition in the present case, when so lately, in the same reign, another holy man Urijah, met his fate in the discharge of his office, and for the very same words Jeremiah had spoken Provoked by his preaching, the king and his nobles sought to slay him, and, to avoid it, the prophet either prudently absconded, or rather timorously deserted his post, for men of true grace may at times be overcome with fear, though usually little is to be got by flight, as in the present case Cowardice often exposes those to ruin whom courage might have extricated from danger The king sent after him to Egypt, whither he had fled, got him delivered up as a state-criminal, and slew him, probably with his own hand, at least commanded it to be done, and, to make the ignominy the greater, and his prophecies disregarded, *cast his dead body into the graves of the common people*

4 Notwithstanding all the pleas of his accusers, Ahikam, the son of Shaphan, 2 *Kings* xxii 12 a man who had lived under pious Josiah, a great man, yet a good man, and the prophet's friend, stood by him, and prevailed upon the princes not to deliver him into the hand of the enraged people, whom the priests had inflamed, and were ready to murder him, as soon as they could obtain permission *Note,* God hath in his hands the hearts of all men, and can raise us up friends, in the day of trial, where we least expected to find them

serve the king of Babylon 10 For [k] they prophesy a lie unto you, to remove you far from your land, and that I should drive you out, and ye should perish 11 But the nations that bring their neck under the yoke of the king of Babylon, and serve him, those will I let remain still in their own land, saith the LORD, and they shall till it, and dwell therein

k Ver 14 Chap xxiii 25 Lam ii 14

v 1—11 The date of this prophecy is in the beginning of the reign of Jehoiakim, then probably the yokes were made in token of Judah's subjection, which soon began, though only sent to the neighbouring nations several years after, in the reign of Zedekiah, when the time of their captivity drew nearer

1 The sign given is the making bonds and yokes, and the putting one on his own neck, in token of the bondage to which the people should be delivered, and thus he wore many years, as appears *chap* xxviii 1—10

2 He is commanded to send one of these to all the neighbouring nations, *v* 3 by the hand of the messengers who came to Jerusalem to congratulate Zedekiah on his accession, or to make a league with him to oppose the growing power of the king of Babylon, and, in case of invasion, to unite their forces A vain design! which God had determined to disappoint, and therefore they are enjoined to tell their masters from God, when they delivered the prophet's symbol of their captivity, that the *Lord of hosts,* at whose beck are the armies of heaven and earth, the *God of Israel,* in a covenant of peculiar grace, the great Creator of all, and who therefore had an absolute right to dispose of all the creatures of his hand, *v* 5 had given these lands, with all their produce, into the hand of Nebuchadnezzar king of Babylon, *his servant,* raised up to be his minister of wrath, *v* 6 and under his dominion they must continue, and under his son, and his son's son, see *chap* xxv 14, till the seventy years should be completed, during which the captivity should last, and then other mightier kings and nations should destroy this monarchy, and raise another on its ruins, *v* 7 Resistance to the divine decree would but aggravate their misery, and expose them to more horrid desolation, and various kinds of death, *v* 8 nor must they give heed to their diviners and sorcerers, who should flatter them with lying hopes, which would infallibly disappoint them, and, by encouraging them to resist, exasperate their conquerors more fearfully to destroy them, *v* 9, 10 whilst those who patiently submitted and surrendered themselves should find favour in the sight of their enemies, and be suffered quietly to remain under tribute, and not be carried away captive into a strange land *Note,* (1) The earth is the Lord's, and he doth as pleases him with it, and none have reason to murmur against his disposal of his own (2) The wicked frequently enjoy the greatest share of this world's good (3) To struggle against God's providence is to kick against the pricks, for when he judges he will overcome (4) Patience will lessen the burthens which perverseness but aggravates

CHAP XXVII

Since they will not submit to God's warnings, the prophet exhorts them to submit to his decree, and yield themselves up to the king of Babylon He gives this counsel in God's name to the kings of the neighbouring nations, assuring them that there was no remedy, but they must serve the king of Babylon, and yet in time there should be relief, for his dominion should last but seventy years, ver 1—11 (2) *To Zedekiah king of Judah* ver 12—14 *and to the priests and people, assuring them that the king of Babylon should succeed against them, and that a patient submission would be the only way to mitigate the calamity, and make it easy,* ver 12-22 *Thus the prophet, if they would but have hearkened to him, would have directed them in the paths of true policy, as well as of true piety*

1 IN the beginning of the reign of Jehoiakim the son of Josiah king of Judah, came this word unto
Jeremiah from the LORD, saying, 2 Thus [a] saith
the LORD to me, Make thee bonds and yokes, and
[b] put them upon thy neck, 3 And send them to the
king of Edom, and to the king of Moab, and to the
king of the Ammonites, and to the king of Tyrus, and
to the king of Zidon, by the hand of the messengers
which come to Jerusalem unto Zedekiah king of Judah,
4 And command them [c] to say unto their masters,
Thus saith the LORD of hosts, the God of Israel, thus
shall ye say unto your masters, 5 [d] I have made the
earth, the man and the beast that *are* upon the ground,
by my great power, and by my outstretched arm, and
[e] have given it unto whom it seemed meet unto me
6 And now I have given all these lands into the hand
of Nebuchadnezzar the king of Babylon [f] my servant,
and the beasts of the field have I given him also to serve
him 7 [g] And all nations shall serve him and his son,
and his son's son, until the very time of his land come,
[h] and *then* many nations and great kings shall serve themselves of him 8 And it shall come to pass, *that* the
nation and kingdom which will not serve the same Nebuchadnezzar the king of Babylon and that will not put
their neck under the yoke of the king of Babylon, that
nation will I punish, saith the LORD, with the sword,
and with the famine, and with the pestilence, until I
have consumed them by his hand 9 Therefore [i] hearken not ye to your prophets, nor to your diviners, nor
to your [j] dreamers, nor to your enchanters, nor to your
sorcerers, which speak unto you, saying, Ye shall not

a Or hath the Lord
b Chap xxviii 10, 12
c Or concerning their masters, saying
d Isa xlv 12
e Dan iv 17, 25, 32
f Chap xxv 9 Ezek xxix 18, 20
g 2 Chron xxxvi 20
h Chap xxv 14 Dan v
i Chap xxv
j Heb dreams

12 I spake also [l] to Zedekiah king of Judah, according to all these words, saying, Bring your necks under
the yoke of the king of Babylon, and serve him and his
people, and live 13 [m] Why will ye die, thou and
thy people, by the sword, by the famine, and by the
pestilence, as the LORD hath spoken against the nation
that will not serve the king of Babylon? 14 Therefore
hearken not unto the words of the prophets that speak
unto you, saying, Ye shall not serve the king of Babylon
for [n] they prophesy a lie unto you 15 For I have not
sent them, saith the LORD, yet they prophesy [o] a lie
in my name, that I might drive you out, and that ye
might perish, ye, and the prophets that prophesy unto
you 16 Also I spake to the priests, and to all this
people, saying, Thus saith the LORD, Hearken not to
the words of your prophets, that prophesy unto you,
saying, Behold [p] the vessels of the LORD's house shall
now shortly be brought again from Babylon, for they
prophesy a lie unto you 17 Hearken not unto them,
serve the king of Babylon and live wherefore should
this city be laid waste? 18 But [q] if they *be* prophets,
and if the word of the LORD be with them, let them
now make intercession to the LORD of hosts, that the
vessels *which are* left in the house of the LORD, and *in*
the house of the king of Judah, and at Jerusalem, go
not to Babylon 19 ¶ For thus saith the LORD of
hosts, [r] concerning the pillars, and concerning the sea,
and concerning the bases, and concerning the residue of
the vessels that remain in this city, 20 Which Nebuchadnezzar king of Babylon took not, when he carried
away [s] captive Jeconiah the son of Jehoiakim king of
Judah, from Jerusalem to Babylon, and all the [t] nobles of

l Chap xxxviii 17
m Ezek xviii 31
n Ver 10 Chap xiv 14 xxiii 21 & xxix 8, 9
o Heb In a lie, or lyingly
p Chap xxviii 3
q Ver 9, 14
r See 1 Kings vii 15 Chap lii 17 2 Kings xxv 13
s Chap xxiv 1
t Heb White ones 2 Kings xxv 13

Before Chriſt 596

of Judah and Jeruſalem 21 Yea, thus ſaith the LORD
of hoſts, the God of Iſrael, concerning the veſſels that
remain in the houſe of the LORD, and in the houſe of the
king of Judah, and of Jeruſalem, 22 They ſhall be
ᵗ carried to Babylon, and there ſhall they be until the
day that I ᵘ viſit them, ſaith the LORD then ˣ will I
bring them up, and reſtore them to this place

ᵗ 2 Kin xxv 13 2 Chron xxxvi 18 ᵘ 2 Chron xxxvi 21 Chap xxix 10 ˣ Ezra i 7, & vii 19

v 12—22 Jeruſalem was now tributary to the king of Babylon, but Zedekiah was meditating rebellion, and his falſe prophets encouraging him with hopes of ſucceſs, but the conſequence would be the completion of the nation's ruin

1 He addreſſes the king of Judah with earneſtneſs, beſeeching him, for his own and his people's ſake, patiently to ſubmit and live, ſince a revolt againſt the king of Babylon would certainly prove fatal in the iſſue, and expoſe them to all the miſeries of a ſiege and the maſſacre of a city taken by ſtorm, *v* 13 notwithſtanding the lies of the falſe prophets, who flattered him and the people to their ruin, and would themſelves fall under the judgment, *v* 14, 15 *Note*, (1) Rebellion againſt God will be attended with ſtill more fatal conſequences how much better is it to bow our necks to the eaſy yoke of Chriſt, and live? (2) They who embolden ſinners in their evil ways ſhall periſh with them, the deceived and the deceiver together

2 He gives the prieſts and people the ſame warning as he had given to their king, *v* 17 admoniſhing them of the folly of hearkening to the falſe prophets, *your prophets* he calls them, becauſe they choſe their lying viſions, and loved to have it ſo They told them that they ſhould be ſucceſsful in their revolt, *v* 16 and that the king of Babylon would ſoon be willing to purchaſe peace from them by the reſtoration of the ſacred veſſels which had been carried to Babylon, *v* 16 but, alas! they were only puſhing them to the precipice of deſtruction, bringing on the utter ruin of their city, and the demolition of the temple, when, as Nebuchadnezzar had before taken the veſſels of gold, *2 Kings* xxiv 13,—15 ſo far would he be from reſtoring them, that all the other veſſels, with the pillars, ſea, and baſes of braſs, ſhould follow them into Babylon, *v* 19, 20 Better therefore, far better were it, that they ſhould become interceſſors with God to prevent the impending judgments, and preſerve what was left, than flatter them with the deluſive hopes of the reſtoration of what had been carried away *Note*, (1) True prophets will be advocates before God in prayer for thoſe to whom they preach They who maintain no communion with God can have no commiſſion from him (2) The general ruin of ſinners ariſes from falſe hopes, with which their lying and lazy teachers flatter them, who cry peace when there is no peace

3 The prophecy concludes with a gleam of hope amidſt the darkneſs of this long captivity Though the veſſels of the Lord's houſe, and of the houſes of the kings and princes of Judah, ſhould be thus carried to Babylon, they ſhould not be loſt, but ſafely laid up againſt the time appointed of God, when, after the ſeventy years were fulfilled, they ſhould again be reſtored, which was marvellouſly fulfilled by Cyrus, *Ezra* i 7 *Note*, (1) In wrath God ſtill remembers mercy (2) If the time of the church's diſtreſs be long, we may not deſpair, *the viſion is for an appointed time, at the end it ſhall ſpeak bleſſed are all they that wait for it*

CHAP XXVIII

We have here, (1) Hananiah's falſe prophecy, in oppoſition to what Jeremiah had ſaid, who breaks the yoke which was on Jeremiah's neck, as a ſign of the looſing the yoke of the king of Babylon, ver 1—4 10, 11 (2) Jeremiah declares his wiſh it were true, but aſſures them it was falſe, ver 5—9 and reads the doom of the people, ver 12, 14 and of the prophet, ver 15, 17 which received a ſpeedy accompliſhment

595 1 AND it came to paſs the ſame year, in the begin
ning of the reign of Zedekiah king of Judah,
in the fourth year, *and* in the fifth month, *that* Hana-
niah the ſon of Azur the prophet, which *was* of Gibeon,
ſpake unto me in the houſe of the LORD, in the preſence
of the prieſts, and of all the people, ſaying, 2 Thus
ſpeaketh the LORD of hoſts, the God of Iſrael, ſaying,
ᵃ I have broken the yoke of the king of Babylon 3
ᵇ Within ‡ two full years will I bring again into this
place all the veſſels of the LORD's houſe, that Nebu-
chadnezzar king of Babylon took away from this place,
and carried them to Babylon 4 And ᶜ I will bring
again to this place, Jeconiah the ſon of Jehoiakim king
of Judah, with all the ‡ captives of Judah, that went
into Babylon, ſaith the LORD, for I will break the yoke
of the king of Babylon 5 ¶ Then the prophet Jere-
miah ſaid unto the prophet Hananiah in the preſence of
the prieſts, and in the preſence of all the people that
ſtood in the houſe of the LORD 6 Even the prophet
Jeremiah ſaid, ᵈ Amen the LORD do ſo, the LORD
perform thy words which thou haſt propheſied, to bring
again the veſſels of the LORD's houſe, and all that is
carried away captive, from Babylon into this place 7
Nevertheleſs, hear thou now this word that I ſpeak in
thine ears, and in the ears of all the people, 8 The
prophets that have been before me, and before thee of
old, propheſied both againſt many countries, and againſt
great kingdoms, of war, and of evil, and of peſtilence
9 ᵉ The prophet which propheſied of peace, when the
word of the prophet ſhall come to paſs, *then* ſhall the
prophet be known, that the LORD hath truly ſent
him

ᵃ Chap xxvii 12 ᵇ Chap xxvii 16 ‡ Heb Two years of days ᶜ Chap xxii 10 ‡ Heb Captivity ᵈ 1 Kin i 36 ᵉ Deut xviii 22

v 1—9 The date of this prophecy is the fourth of Zedekiah, called *the beginning* of his reign, or the former part, it continuing ſeven years longer, or becauſe in this year he paid a viſit to the king of Babylon, and received, as ſome ſuggeſt, a freſh inveſtiture of his dominions, with conſiderable additions of territory, *chap* li 59 or, as others, the fourth from the ſabbatical year, though the firſt ſenſe ſeems moſt natural

We have here the ſtruggle between a falſe and true prophet

1 Hananiah, the ſon of Azur, a falſe prophet, in the Lord's houſe, in the preſence of the prieſts and people, undertook to contradict all that Jeremiah had ſpoken, and, uſing the ſolemn preface of *Thus ſaith the Lord, the God of Iſrael*, as if he ſpoke by inſpiration from him, confidently aſſerts, both that the Babyloniſh yoke ſhould be broken, the veſſels of the ſanctuary reſtored, and the captive king Jeconiah, with all the priſoners, return from Babylon to Judea, and fixes the term, *within two full years* *Note*, The ſmooth tongues of lying prophets never ſpeak reproof, but flattery By this ye ſhall know them

2 Jeremiah heard him, and immediately replies Warm in his country's intereſt, he wiſhed nothing more ardently than its proſperity, and therefore adds his *Amen, the Lord do ſo, the Lord perform the words which thou haſt ſpoken*, as, if the Lord ſo pleaſed, he could be content to be counted a falſe prophet for the ſake of his brethren, ſo unjuſt were all their calumnies againſt him, as if he deſired the ruin of the nation Though ſome ſuppoſe he ſpoke theſe words ironically, fully ſure, as the next words ſhew, of the determined deſtruction coming upon them, and therefore appeals to the event to prove the falſehood of Hananiah's aſſertion He reminds him, before the people, how the prophets who were before their days ſpoke, all of whom, to a man, had denounced God's judgments againſt that and the neighbouring lands, ſuch as Iſaiah, Hoſea, Joel, Amos, Micah, Nahum, *v* 8 it was therefore rather a preſumption in Jeremiah's favour, who correſponded with them herein, that he had drank at the ſame fountain of inſpiration, whereas the prophet, which propheſieth of peace, as Hananiah had done, and unconditionally, without any calls to repentance, was much to be ſuſpected, that he ſought to pleaſe men, and at leaſt the event of the prediction ſhould be waited for ere his claim to a divine miſſion ſhould be admitted

10 ¶ Then Hananiah the prophet took ᶠ the yoke
from off the prophet Jeremiah's neck, and brake it
11 And Hananiah ſpake in the preſence of all the people,
ſaying, Thus ſaith the LORD, Even ſo ᵍ will I break
the yoke of Nebuchadnezzar king of Babylon from the
neck of all nations ʰ within the ſpace of two full years
And the prophet Jeremiah went his way 12 ¶ Then
the word of the LORD came unto Jeremiah *the prophet*
(after that Hananiah the prophet had broken the yoke
from off the neck of the prophet Jeremiah) ſaying, 13
Go, and tell Hananiah, ſaying, Thus ſaith the LORD,
Thou haſt broken the yokes of wood, but thou ſhalt
make ⁱ for them yokes of iron 14 For thus ſaith the
LORD of hoſts, the God of Iſrael, ᵏ I have put a yoke
of iron upon the neck of all theſe nations, that they may
ſerve Nebuchadnezzar king of Babylon, and they ſhall
ſerve him; ˡ and I have given him the beaſts of the field
alſo 15 ¶ Then ſaid the prophet Jeremiah unto Ha-
naniah the prophet, Hear now, Hananiah, ᵐ The LORD
hath not ſent thee, but thou makeſt this people to truſt
in a lie. 16 Therefore thus ſaith the LORD, Behold,
I will caſt thee from off the face of the earth this year
thou ſhalt die, becauſe ⁿ thou haſt taught ‡ rebellion
againſt the LORD 17 So Hananiah the prophet died
the ſame year, in the ſeventh month

ᶠ Chap xxvii 2 ᵍ Chap xxvii 7 ʰ Ver 3 ⁱ Ver … Ezek … 22 ᵏ Deut xxviii 48 Chap xxvii 4 ˡ Chap xxvii 6 ᵐ Chap xxix 31 ⁿ Deut xiii 5 Chap xxix 32 ‡ Heb Revolt

v 10—17 Irritated with ſuch a reply,

1 Hananiah tears the yoke which Jeremiah wore, in token of the ſubjection of the nation by Nebuchadnezzar and, plucking it from his neck, broke it in the preſence of all the people,

impiouſly

Before Christ 595

impiously and daringly adding this explication, which he prefaces with, *thus saith the Lord, so will I break the yoke of Nebuchadnezzar king of Babylon from the neck of all nations within the full years* *Note*, (1) Falsehood advanced with solemnity and confidence, often gains regard (2) Many dare affirm that to be God's truth, which shortly will be found a lie to their own damnation

2 *Jeremiah went his way*, disdaining to contend with him, or abhorring his profaneness, or withdrawing himself from the rage he saw kindling, or patiently sitting down under these reproaches, or to wait an answer from God

3 He is sent back with a fearful message Probably the same day, perhaps the same hour, whilst the people were yet assembled before the temple, and Hananiah triumphing, as if the day was his own, but short is the triumphing of the wicked So far should the nations be from breaking the yoke of the king of Babylon, as Hananiah had broken the yoke of wood, that it should grow more rigorous and severe, a yoke of iron, all efforts to shake it off would be fruitless, and all the foregoing prophecies, *chap* xxvii 6 be to a tittle fulfilled Such is the nation's doom But Hananiah hath a burden peculiarly his own, the punishment of his atrocious crimes He had pretended a commission from God, and with his name given sanction to his own lies, he had led the people with a delusive hope, to rush on their destruction, and above all, had *taught rebellion against God*, encouraging them to reject the warnings of the true prophets, and despise the divine admonitions, for which crimes he is doomed to death by the immediate judgment of God, within the course of that very year, which was within two months fulfilled, for he died in the seventh month, and this was the fifth and in his doom the people might have read the certainty of their own, and the truth of all Jeremiah had spoken, but their foolish hearts were darkened *Note*, (1) God will not suffer his prophets to be insulted with impunity (2) None may expect heavier judgment, than they who are hinderers of the word of God, and seek to prejudice men's minds against the faithful ministers of it (3) That sudden death is terrible indeed, which comes from God in a way of judgment

CHAP XXIX

We have here, 1 Jeremiah's letter to the captives, cautioning them to beware of the false prophets, to settle in Babylon, and patiently expect the expiration of the seventy years, denouncing death on two of their deceivers, ver 1—23 2 *Shemaiah's letter against Jeremiah*, ver 24—29 3 *A denunciation of God's wrath against him*, ver 30—32

597 1 NOW these *are* the words of the letter, that Jeremiah the prophet sent from Jerusalem unto
the residue of the elders which were carried away captives, and to the priests, and to the prophets, and to all
the people, whom Nebuchadnezzar had carried away
captive from Jerusalem to Babylon, 2 (After that
a 2 Kings xxiv 12 &c † Or chamberlains ᵃ Jeconiah the king, and the queen, and the † eunuchs,
the princes of Judah and Jerusalem, and the carpenters,
and the smiths were departed from Jerusalem) 3 By
the hand of Elasah the son of Shaphan, and Gemariah
the son of Hilkiah, (whom Zedekiah king of Judah
sent unto Babylon to Nebuchadnezzar king of Babylon)
saying, 4 Thus saith the LORD of hosts the God of
Israel unto all that are carried away captives, whom I
b Ver 28 have caused to be carried away from Jerusalem unto
Babylon, 5 ᵇ Build ye houses, and dwell *in them*, and
plant gardens, and eat the fruit of them 6 Take ye
wives, and beget sons and daughters, and take wives
for your sons, and give your daughters to husbands,
that they may bear sons and daughters, that ye may be
increased there, and not diminished 7 And seek the
c Ezra vi 10 1 Mac vii 33 1 Tim ii 2 peace of the city whither I have caused you to be carried
away captives, and ᶜ pray unto the LORD for it for in
the peace thereof shall ye have peace

v 1—7 We have here the letter of Jeremiah to the captives in Babylon, written by divine authority It is directed to the prophets, priests, and people carried away captive by Nebuchadnezzar, after Jeconiah had surrendered himself, whose case seemed most peculiarly miserable, and perhaps they envied their brethren who were left, though their own lot, if they knew how to improve it, was far more desirable The letter was sent by Zedekiah's messengers, who went with the tribute, or to cultivate the friendship of the king of Babylon, and the contents of it were designed to encourage their hope in God, to comfort them under their affliction, to exhort them patiently to wait God's appointed time, and prevent their being deluded by false prophets to expect a deliverance sooner than the expiration of the seventy years

Before Christ 597

1 He addresses them in God's name, and by his authority, *Thus saith the Lord of hosts*, able to save to the uttermost, and *the God of Israel*, who still acknowledged his relation to them, and had not cast them out of covenant though he had cast them out of their land this, though perplexed, they may not be in despair *I have caused you to be carried away from Jerusalem to Babylon*, God's hand was in it, without which, no human power could have prevailed against them *Note*, (1) Though God visit the iniquities of his people with a rod, and their sin with scourges, he is still their God, and will not take his loving-kindness utterly from them Let his Israel still hope in the Lord (2) The consideration from whose hand all our sufferings come, should silence every murmuring thought

2 He encourages them to sit down content in their present state, to wait patiently God's time of deliverance, and in the mean while settle themselves as comfortably as might be, to build, and plant, and marry, that they might not be diminished either in wealth or numbers, when they should return again unto their own land, *v* 5, 6 and intimates that God would give them a peaceable abode, and comfortable enjoyment of their possessions, even in the land of their captivity *Note*, Wherever we are cast by God's providence, or into whatever state of affliction, it is our wisdom not only to submit, but make the best of our situation, and live in hopes of better days

3 He exhorts them to be peaceable under the government of the king of Babylon, though a heathen, and an enemy to God, yet to shew all good fidelity, and so far from plotting against the state, in order to recover their liberty, to seek the prosperity of the country in which they were captives, and pray to God to preserve and increase it, for *in the peace thereof should they have peace* It was their interest to do so, seeing in every calamity of that land they would be involved, and in the prosperity of it find their advantage *Note*, If we must submit to the power of oppressors, and pray for the peace of the land of our captivity, how much more are we bound to be loyal subjects under the mildest government, and in this our land of liberty to seek and pray for the peace thereof?

8 ¶ For thus saith the LORD of hosts, the God of
Israel, Let not your prophets and your diviners that *be*
in the midst of you, ᵈ deceive you, neither hearken to d Chap xiv 14 & xxiii 21 & xxvii 15 Eph v 6
your dreams which ye cause to be dreamed 9 For
they prophesy falsly unto you in my name, ᵉ I have not
sent them, saith the LORD 10 ¶ For thus saith the e Chap xxvii 15
LORD, that ᶠ after seventy years be accomplished at Reckoning from 606
Babylon, ᵍ I will visit you, and perform my good word f 2 Chron xxxvi 21, 22 Ezra i 1 Chap xxv 12 & xxvii 22 Dan ix 2
towards you, in causing you to return to this place
11 For I know the thoughts that I think towards you,
saith the LORD, thoughts of peace, and not of evil,
to give you ‡ an expected end 12 ʰ Then shall ye call g Luke i 68 ‡ Heb. An end and expectation
upon me, and ye shall go and pray unto me, ⁱ and I will h Dan ix 3
hearken unto you 13 And ᵏ ye shall seek me, and find i Ps l 15
me, when ye shall search for me with all your heart 14 k Lev xxvi 39 40 Deut xxx 1 Ch l xxxii 7
And ᵐ I will be found of you, saith the LORD, and I m Deut iv 7 Ps xxxii 6 Isa lv 6
will turn away your captivity, and ⁿ I will gather you n Chap xxiii 3 Ezek xx 34 41 Chap xxiv 6 & xxxii 37
from all the nations, and from all the places whither I
have driven you, saith the LORD, and I will bring
you again into the place whence I caused you to be carried away captive

v 8—14 To engage them to patient waiting upon God,

1 He warns them to pay no regard to the false prophets, who promised them a speedy return to their own land, and thereby discouraged them from settling in Babylon Their dreams were the fancies of their own imagination, and never to be encouraged or listened to, since though they used the name of God, they lied, and never had a revelation from him, *v* 9, 10 *Note*, When people love to be deceived, they will readily find flatterers to their ruin

2 He assures them, though their prophets were false, God's promises would be found true, and accomplished in due season When the seventy years were ended, his purposes concerning them were all gracious, even their captivity was designed for their good, *chap* xxiv 5 and *the expected end* should assuredly come, only let them with patience wait for it, and in earnest prayer and supplication seek the fulfilment of the divine promises, searching *after God with all their heart*, in fervency and simplicity, and then he will assuredly be found of them in mercy, and turn their captivity into a blessed restoration unto their own land *Note*, (1) They who trust the promises of God, shall never be disappointed (2) As nothing can hasten any event one moment sooner than the divine decree hath fixed it, neither can any difficulties retard the execution of God's word when the appointed season comes (3) God's promises should excite, not supersede our prayers (4) They who search for God with all their heart, are sure to find him near to hear and answer them.

15 ¶ Be-

Before Christ 597

15 ¶ Because ye have said, The LORD hath raised
[p Chap xxviii 1 Ver xxiv 4] us up [p] prophets in Babylon 16 *Know* that thus saith
the LORD, of the king that sitteth upon the throne of
David, and of all the people that dwelleth in this city,
and of your brethren that are not gone forth with you in
to captivity, 17 Thus saith the LORD of hosts, Be-
[q Chap. xxiv 10] hold, I will send upon them, [q] the sword, the famine,
[r Ibid 8] and the pestilence, and will make them like vile [r] figs,
that cannot be eaten, they are so evil 18 And I will
persecute them with the sword, with the famine, and
[s Deut xxviii 25 2 Chron xxix 8] with the pestilence, and [s] will deliver them to be remov-
ed to all the kingdoms of the earth, † to be [t] a curse,
and an astonishment, and an hissing, and a reproach a-
[t Chap xv 4 & xxiv 9 & xxxiv 17] mong all the nations, whither I have driven them 19
Because they have not hearkened to my words, saith the
[† Heb For a curse] LORD, which [u] I sent unto them by my servants the
[t Chap xxv 18] prophets, rising up early, and sending *them*, but ye
[u Ibid xxv 4 & xxxii 33] would not hear, saith the LORD 20 ¶ Hear ye
therefore the word of the LORD, all ye of the capti-
vity, whom I have sent from Jerusalem to Babylon
21 Thus saith the LORD of hosts, the God of Israel,
of Ahab the son of Kolaiah, and of Zedekiah the son
of Maaseiah which prophesy a lie unto you in my name,
Behold, I will deliver them into the hand of Nebuchad-
rezzar king of Babylon, and he shall slay them before
[x Gen xlviii 20] your eyes 22 [x] And of them shall be taken up a curse
by all the captivity of Judah, which *are* in Babylon,
saying, The LORD make thee like Zedekiah, and like
Ahab, whom the king of Babylon roasted in the fire 23
[y Chap xxiii 14] Because [y] they have committed villany in Israel, and have
committed adultery with their neighbours wives, and
have spoken lying words in my name, which I have not
[z Prov v 21] commanded them, [z] even I know, and *am* a witness, saith
the LORD

v 15—23 Though there were some gracious souls among the captives, yet were there many who paid no regard to the words of Jeremiah, but hearkened to the false prophets, and received them as sent from God, and boasted they needed not look to Judea for advice, when they had prophets of their own in Babylon, on whom they might depend To these therefore the prophet addresses himself,

1 He warns them of the falshood of the declarations of these prophets They flattered the people with a speedy return to Judea, when, so far from it, the residue of those who were left in Jerusalem were doomed to the most grievous devastations by famine, pestilence, and the sword, and the few who survived, should be scattered into all kingdoms, and made the objects of derision, scorn, and detestation in every place, like vile figs unfit to be eaten, and cast as refuse on the dunghill, and this because of their impenitence and rejection of the repeated and earnest warnings which God, by his prophets, had vouchsafed them, as had been threatned before, *chap* xxiv *Note*, (1) They who flatter sinners with hopes contrary to God's word, are infallibly false prophets (2) When men make themselves vile by their sins, God, in just judgment, will make them viler in their sufferings

2 He denounces judgment on two of the false prophets, Ahab and Zedekiah, whose abominable lives, as well as atrocious lies, called for vengeance They were horrible adulterers, and yet dared to take God's name in their lips, and pretend he had sent them, when they knew he never commanded them, and under the cloak of profound hypocrisy practised every villany But though men might not discover their wickedness, God saw, and will recompense them according to their deeds Detected probably in some seditious practices, the king of Babylon would seize them, and burn them alive before their eyes for a terror to others A catastrophe so dreadful, that when any would wish the heaviest curse on their enemies, they should not be able to conceive a worse imprecation, *than the Lord make thee like Zedekiah, and like Ahab, whom the king of Babylon roasted in the fire* *Note*, (1) They who live in the practice of lewdness and adultery, and the like villany themselves, must needs belye their pretensions to a mission from God, and will have no boldness to rebuke the like practices in others (2) Secret as men's sins may be committed, the day is near when no darkness or shadow of death shall hide the workers of iniquity (3) Though wicked prophets and wicked men may escape the judgments of God in this life, there is a fire kindled for them where they must burn eternally, and none shall quench it

[596] [‖ Or dreamer] 24 ¶ *Thus* shalt thou also speak to Shemaiah the ‖
Nehelamite, saying, 25 Thus speaketh the LORD of
hosts, the God of Israel, saying, Because thou hast sent
[a 2 Kings xxv 18] letters in thy name unto all the people that *are* at Jerusa-
lem, and to [a] Zephaniah the son of Maaseiah the priest,
and to all the priests, saying, 26 The LORD hath
made thee priest in the stead of Jehoiada the priest,
that ye should be officers in the house of the LORD,
[b 2 Kings ix 11 Acts xxvi 24] for every man *that is* [b] mad, and maketh himself a prophet,
[c Chap xx 2] that thou shouldest [c] put him in prison and in the stocks
27 Now therefore why hast thou not reproved Jeremiah
[d Num iii 3 Ezra iii 8] of Anathoth, [d] which maketh himself a prophet to you?
[e Ver 5] 28 For therefore he sent unto us *in* Babylon, saying,
This *captivity is* long, [e] build ye houses and dwell *in them*,
and plant gardens, and eat the fruit of them 29 And
Zephaniah the priest read this letter in the ears of Jere-
miah the prophet 30 ¶ Then came the word of the
LORD unto Jeremiah, saying, 31 Send to all them
of the captivity, saying, Thus saith the LORD, con-
[f Ver 24] cerning Shemaiah [f] the Nehelamite, Because that Shema-
[g Chap xxviii 15] iah hath prophesied unto you, and [g] I sent him not, and
[Ver 9] he caused you to trust in a lie 32 Therefore thus
saith the LORD, Behold, I will punish Shemaiah the
Nehelamite and his seed he shall not have a man to
[h Ch p xx 6] dwell among this people, [h] neither shall he behold the
[i Ibid xxviii 16] good that I will do for my people, saith the LORD,
[‡ Heb revolt] because [i] he hath taught ‡ rebellion against the LORD

v 24—32 Whatever effect Jeremiah's letter had upon the people, we are not to wonder if the false prophets, whose lies he so faithfully rebuked, were exasperated We have here,

1 The endeavours used by one of these to get Jeremiah severely punished This was *Shemaiah, the Nehelamite*, or *the dreamer*, one of the lying prophets who deceived the people, and, in revenge for the reproofs contained in Jeremiah's letter, by the return of the messengers probably who had brought it, he writes in his own name, without consulting his brethren, to the people in general, and to Zephaniah in particular, who seems to have been in some chief station in the temple, well knowing that the church rulers bore no good will to the reforming prophets He suggests to him the necessity of exerting the authority with which he was invested *The Lord hath made thee priest, instead of Jehoiada the priest* Either he would insinuate, that he was, in zeal for God's glory, such another, or rather Jehoiada might be another name of Seraiah the high-priest, whose sagan or deputy he might be, or in some other chief office in the temple, *see chap* lii 24 He therefore, with the priests his brethren, should take cognizance of every enthusiastic fellow, *who is mad, and maketh himself a prophet* Such ill names do God's faithful ministers often bear, and to such insolent reproaches are they exposed, as if intruders into the sacred service, disturbed in mind, or under diabolical possession *That thou shouldst put him in prison, and in the stocks*, both to expose and punish such delinquents, of which number he affirms Jeremiah to be, and blames Zephaniah for not proceeding against him as a false prophet, *v* 27 the proof of which he supposes would be no longer doubted, when he repeated but one line of Jeremiah's letter, that *This captivity is long*, and that instead of hoping for a speedy restoration, the captives should settle themselves peaceably in Babylon, *v* 28 *Note*, (1) They who will be faithful to men's souls, must expect often to be treated as deceivers or madmen (2) Church power hath been often employed in tormenting her best friends (3) The accusation generally brought against the ministers of zeal are by their adversaries looked upon to carry evidence incontestable of their enthusiasm and delusion, yet when their words and preaching are calmly considered and examined, they contain nothing but the true sayings of God

2 Shemaiah's doom is read *Zephaniah read the letter in the ears of Jeremiah*, either privately out of kindness, to warn him of his enemies, for when known they are most easily guarded against, or to acquaint him with the charge before he proceeded to judgment upon the case And God gave Jeremiah an answer, which he is commanded to send to all those of the captivity, that they might be warned against the impostor, and mark his punishment for daring to pretend a divine mission, and *teaching rebellion against the Lord*, by dissuading the people from paying regard to his prophets Shemaiah shall not only perish himself, but his family be utterly cut off, his name be buried in oblivion, and none of his race ever see or taste of the goodness God hath still in store for his people *Note*, None perish under such aggravated guilt as those false teachers, at whose hand God will require the souls they have deceived and flattered to their ruin

CHAP XXX.

These two chapters, very different from the former, are wholly taken up with precious promises of a return out of captivity, and that typical of the glorious things reserved for the church in the days of the Messiah 1 *Notwithstanding their situation from a variety*

Before Christ 606

of circumſtances appeared deſperate, they ſhall be reſtored, ver 1—17 2 That at the return they ſhould enjoy ſingular bleſſings ſpiritual and temporal, ver 18—24

1 THE word that came to Jeremiah from the
LORD, ſaying, 2 Thus ſpeaketh the LORD
God of Iſrael, ſaying, Write thee all the words that I
have ſpoken unto thee in a book 3 For lo, the days
come, ſaith the LORD, [a] that I will bring again the
captivity of my people Iſrael and Judah, ſaith the LORD,
and I will cauſe them to return to the land that I gave to
their fathers, and they ſhall poſſeſs it 4 ¶ And theſe
are the words that the LORD ſpake concerning Iſrael,
and concerning Judah 5 For thus ſaith the LORD,
We have heard a voice of trembling, † of fear, and not
of peace 6 Aſk ye now, and ſee whether ‡ a man
doth travail with child? wherefore do I ſee every man
with his hands on his loins, [b] as a woman in travail, and
all faces are turned into paleneſs? 7 [c] Alas, for that
day *is* great, ſo that none *is* like it: it *is* even the time
of Jacob's trouble, but he ſhall be ſaved out of it 8
For it ſhall come to paſs in that day, ſaith the LORD
of hoſts, *that* I will break his yoke from off thy neck,
and will burſt thy bonds, and ſtrangers ſhall no more
ſerve themſelves of him 9 But they ſhall ſerve the
LORD their God, and David their king, [e] whom I will
raiſe up unto them

[a] Chap xxxii 44 & xxxiii 7 14 Ezek xxxix 25 Amos ix 14
† Or there is fear and no peace
‡ Heb a male
[b] Chap iv 31
[c] Joel ii 11 Amos v 18 Zeph i 14, &c
[e] Ezek xxxiv 23 & xxxvii 24 Hoſ iii 5 Acts ii 30

v 1—9 To perpetuate the memory of the great and gracious promiſes, God commands the prophet to write in a book *all the words* he had ſpoken to him, either all the preceding prophecies, or thoſe he had now ſpoken to him, relative to the enlargement of the Jews from their captivity, and the coming of the Meſſiah, and this to ſupport the faith and hope of the people of God, both of Iſrael and Judah

1 They are repreſented under the greateſt terror and diſtreſs It was a ſtrange ſight, but deſcriptive of the acuteneſs of their pains, to behold the men of war, like women in travail, with their hands on their loins, trembling, pallid, and crying out in their pangs, *Alas! for that day is great, ſo that none is like it*, ſo terrible and afflictive, and this may refer to the deſtruction of the Jews by the Chaldeans, or to their more terrible deſolations by the Romans and ſome ſuppoſe that it hath a farther reſpect even to the reign of Antichriſt, when the witneſſes ſhall be ſlain, and the church of Chriſt reduced to the moſt abject ſtate of wretchedneſs

2 The prophet muſt write a word of comfort for that gloomy and dark day *Though it is the time of Jacob's trouble, he ſhall be ſaved out of it*, God will ſtand by his ſuffering people, and reſcue them from the hands of their enemies *He will break their yoke*, deliver them from the Babyloniſh chains, or rather from their preſent ſtate of bondage, when ſtrangers in all nations whither they are diſperſed, *ſhall ſerve themſelves of them*, oppreſs and harraſs them as now or, beſt of all, from the bondage of ſin and Satan, their unbelief and impenitence, when they ſhall be turned unto the Lord, and *ſerve the Lord their God, and David their king*, which hath certainly a further view than to the reſtoration of the temple ſervice, and the governors of David's line, who preſided over them after the captivity in Babylon, even to the adored Meſſiah, David's Son, raiſed up to ſit on his throne, and David's Lord, whoſe divine character they ſhould acknowledge, ſubmit to his government, and join with his church in his worſhip, *whom I will raiſe up to them*, God, according to his promiſe, having conſtituted him to be a Prince and Saviour, to whom every knee muſt bow, and whom every tongue muſt confeſs *Note*, They who take Chriſt for their King, are bound to prove their profeſſions by their fidelity Loyalty conſiſts not in words but deeds.

10 ¶ Therefore [f] fear thou not, O my ſervant Jacob,
ſaith the LORD, neither be diſmayed, O Iſrael, for lo,
I will ſave thee from afar, and thy ſeed from the land of
their captivity, and Jacob ſhall return, and ſhall be in reſt
and quiet, [g] and none ſhall make *him* afraid 11 For I
am with thee, ſaith the LORD, to ſave thee [h] though
I make a full end of all nations whither I have ſcattered
thee, yet will I not make a full end of thee but I will
correct thee [i] in meaſure, and will not leave thee altoge-
ther unpuniſhed 12 For thus ſaith the LORD, [k] Thy
bruiſe *is* incurable, *and* thy wound *is* grievous. 13
There is none to plead thy cauſe, that thou mayeſt be
bound up [l] thou haſt no healing medicines 14 [m] All
thy lovers have forgotten thee they ſeek thee not, for I
have wounded thee with the wound [n] of an enemy, with
the chaſtiſement of a cruel one, for the multitude of

[f] Iſa xli 13 & xliii 5 & xliv 2 Chap xlvi 27
[g] Chap xxiii 28
[h] Amos ix 8
[i] Pſ vi 1 Iſa xxvii 8 Chap x 24 & xlvi 28
[k] Chap xv 18
[l] Chap viii 22
[m] Lam i 2
[n] Job xiii 24 & xix 11
[o] Job xxx 21

thine iniquity [p] *becauſe* thy ſins were increaſed 15 Why
[q] crieſt thou for thine affliction? thy ſorrow *is* incurable,
for the multitude of thine iniquity *becauſe* thy ſins were
increaſed, I have done theſe things unto thee 16
Therefore [r] all they that devour thee ſhall be devoured,
and all thine adverſaries, every one of them ſhall go into
captivity and they that ſpoil thee ſhall be a ſpoil, and
all that prey upon thee will I give for a prey 17 For
I will reſtore health unto thee, and I will heal thee of
thy wounds, ſaith the LORD, becauſe they called thee
an outcaſt, *ſaying*, [s] This *is* Zion, [t] whom no man ſeek-
eth after

Before Christ 606

[p] Chap v 6
[q] Ibid xv 18 Lam iii 39
[r] Ex xxiii 22 Iſa xxxiii 1 & xli 11 Chap x 25 Rev xiii 10
[s] Lam ii 15
[t] Ibid i 2

v 10—17 When God viſits his people, he ſtill in wrath remembers mercy

1 Their ſtate appears very deplorable, yea, to human view utterly deſperate *Their bruiſe incurable, their wound grievous*, ver 12 ſo that all reſtoration was deſpaired of, God himſelf ſeemed to be their enemy, their *cruel enemy*, ver 14 So ſevere, ſo long continued were the ſtrokes of his judgments upon them, they had not a friend in their troubles *to plead* for them, either with God or man, or ſo much as a kind hand ſtretched out to bind up their gaping wounds, or adminiſter *the healing medicine* of conſolation or advice, *v* 13 Their lovers, the neighbouring nations, who courted them in their proſperity, deſerted them in the day of their diſtreſs, *v* 14 and looked upon their caſe as deſperate, regarding Zion as *an outcaſt, whom no man ſeeketh after, abandoned to deſtruction*, all which extorted from them bitter complaints, *v* 15 not that they had any cauſe to charge God as ſevere, for becauſe of the multitude of their iniquities and their aggravated ſins, had theſe viſitations been ſent upon them, and their ſufferings were leſs than they deſerved, for however heavy the viſitation ſeemed to them, *God corrected them in meaſure*, and for their good, that he might *not leave them wholly unpuniſhed*, as a father chaſtiſing them, that they might be reformed, and not ruined *Note*, (1) If God's people ſin, they may not hope for impunity, the ſcourge ſhall ſurely come upon them, as well as others (2) In our ſufferings we are too apt to call the rod of a father *the chaſtiſements of a cruel one* (3) Sin hath a mortal ſting, none but God can heal the guilty ſoul (4) Whatever burden God lays upon us, we are bound to acknowledge it leſs than our iniquity hath deſerved (5) When the ſinner is reduced to the depths of ſelf-deſpair, then is the time when God magnifies the riches of his grace in his ſalvation

2 The Lord declares his purpoſe of mercy towards them Deſperate as their caſe ſeemed, both from their ſins and ſufferings, God bids them not *fear*, or *be diſmayed*, he owns them ſtill as his ſervants, *v* 10 and engages to ſave them, and when he will work, who ſhall let him? Though far diſperſed in diſtant lands, he will bring them back, and give them, for all the wars and tumults with which they had been harraſſed, peace and quiet in their own land, which ſeems more applicable to their laſt recovery, when they ſhall be gathered into the goſpel church, than to their return from Babylon, when their ſettlement met with many obſtructions As for their enemies, God threatens to deſtroy them utterly, *I will make a full end of all nations whither I have ſcattered thee, yet will I not make a full end of thee* the mightieſt monarchies are long ſince utterly ſubverted, and all other nations, among whom they had been captives, *devoured*, deſtroyed, and incorporated with their conquerors, *v* 16 but to this hour we ſee the people of the Jews as much a diſtinct and ſeparate people, as if they had been ſtill ſhut up from all other nations in their own land, preſerved for the promiſed mercy and notwithſtanding all their ſins and their calamities, God promiſes to pardon the one and heal the other, to *reſtore their health*, and *heal their wounds*, bringing them into a ſtate of temporal proſperity, and raiſing them from the power of corruption, converting their ſoul, and cauſing them to partake of all the bleſſings of his ſpiritual kingdom in Chriſt Jeſus. *Note*, (1) No ſinner's caſe is ſo far gone, as to be paſt the divine phyſician's cure (2) They who believe God's promiſes, will be delivered from diſtreſſing fear (3) The preſent ſtate of the Jewiſh people is a great and conſtant evidence of the inſpiration of the prophetic word

18 ¶ Thus ſaith the LORD, Behold, [u] I will bring
again the captivity of Jacob's tents, and [x] have mercy
on his dwelling places and the city ſhall be builded
upon her own heap, and the palace ſhall remain after
the manner thereof 19 And [y] out of them ſhall pro-
ceed thankſgiving, and the voice of them that make
merry and I will multiply them, and they ſhall not be
few, I will alſo glorify them, and they ſhall not be
ſmall 20 Their children alſo ſhall be as aforetime,
and their congregation ſhall be eſtabliſhed before me,
and I will puniſh all that oppreſs them 21 And their
‖ nobles ſhall be of themſelves, and [z] their governor
ſhall proceed from the midſt of them, and I will cauſe
him

[u] Ver 3.
[x] Pſ cii 13
[y] Iſa xxxv 10 & li 11.
‖ Heb Noble, or glorious One
[z] Gen xlix 10 Iſa ix 6

Before Christ 606.

him to draw near, and [a] he shall approach unto me
for who is this that engaged his heart to approach unto
me? saith the LORD 22 And [b] ye shall be my
people, and I will be your God 23 Behold, [c] the
whirlwind of the LORD goeth forth with fury, a ‡ con-
tinuing whirlwind, it shall || fall with pain upon the head
of the wicked 24 The fierce anger of the LORD
shall not return, until he have done it, and until he
have performed the intents of his heart [d] in the latter
days ye shall consider it

[a] Heb iv 14 [b] Chap xxiv 7 & xxx 1, 33 & xxxii 38 [c] Chap. xxiii 19 20. & xxv 32 ‡ Heb Cutting || Or remain [d] Gen xlix 1

v 18—24 The same subject is here pursued, and the promises here spoken have a twofold respect

1 To the return of the Jews from Babylon Then their city should be rebuilt on the same spot, the temple raised from its ashes, *v* 18 the sacred festivals be restored, their numbers be multiplied, their nation be respected, their children be playing in the streets in peace, their congregation at the temple undisturbed, their oppressors punished, their rulers, of themselves, not strangers, their governor one of their own nation, appointed of God, accepted of him, a pattern of devotion and piety to his subjects, *v* 21 The covenant of peculiarity shall be re-established, God their God, they his people, *v* 22 whilst all the wicked, who had persecuted them, shall be swept away as with a whirlwind, through *the fierce anger of the Lord*, that shall not return *until he hath done it*, fully established his people, and destroyed their foes

2 To their return to the church of God from their present dispersion, and this seems chiefly intended

(1) They shall be recovered from their captivity Some suppose literally that they shall be collected in Judea, and that the city of Jerusalem shall be rebuilt in all its former magnificence, however, they shall come into the church of Christ, the city of the living God, the spiritual Jerusalem, and the voice of thanksgiving for gospel-grace shall sound louder than the songs which accompanied the sacred festivals

(2) Their numbers will be great in the day of their conversion, and most glorious appearance will they make, when they shall be at once brought to the faith of the gospel, and *a nation be born in a day* At that day the children of the church shall be multiplied in a more astonishing manner than at the first preaching of the gospel, and no more persecuting powers remain to disturb the congregation of the faithful, *v* 20

(3) They will then be brought to know and acknowledge the true Messiah *His noble one, his glorious, or mighty one*, as the word may be rendered, *shall be of themselves*, and *their governour*, the Prince of Peace, able to save and to destroy, *shall proceed out of the midst of them*, rise up from the stock of Israel, *I will cause him to draw near, and he shall approach unto me* as mediator, appointed to be the surety and advocate of his people, and ever living in heaven to make intercession for them, in consequence of his having *engaged his heart* to God in the covenant of grace, *to draw near* to him by an obedience to death, even the death of the cross, in behalf of his people, who by sin were excluded from the divine favour and presence And this may well deserve a note of admiration, *Who is this?* This is Jesus, by whom lost souls are restored to the favour of the justly offended Jehovah, and he becomes *their God*, and they *his people*, which will be the case with the Jews at the latter day

(4) All the wicked will be cut off, they who will not submit to the Messiah's government, must perish under his wrath terrible and irresistible, which sinners will be made to feel, if not before, at least at the great day of his appearing and glory, and then it will be too late to consider when wrath comes upon them to the uttermost or, *in the latter days ye shall consider it*, shall see this prophecy accomplished, all the purposes of God's love to his people, and of wrath to his enemies, being fully performed

CHAP XXXI

This chapter is of the same nature with the former, and full of great and precious promises to the people of God 1 They shall be restored to peace and honour, joy and plenty, ver 1—14 Their sorrow for the loss of their children shall be at an end, ver 15, 16, 17 3 They shall repent of their sins, and God will graciously accept them, ver 18, 19, 20 4 They shall be increased, both in children and cattle, and not diminished as they had been, ver 21 30 5 God will renew his covenant with them, and enrich it with spiritual blessings, ver 31 34 6 These blessings shall be secured to those after them, even to the spiritual seed of Israel for ever, ver 35, 36 37 7 In confirmation of this, the city of Jerusalem shall be rebuilt, ver 38, 39, 40

1 [a] AT the same time, saith the LORD, will I be
[b] the God of all the families of Israel, and they
shall be my people 2 Thus saith the LORD, The
people *which were* left of the sword, [c] found grace in the
wilderness, *even* Israel, when [d] I went to cause him to
rest 3 The LORD hath appeared ‡ of old unto me,
‡ *saying*, Yea, I have loved thee [e] with an everlasting
love therefore with loving kindness [f] have I drawn
thee 4 Again [g] I will build thee, and thou shalt be
built, O virgin of Israel, thou shalt again be adorned
with thy [h] || tabrets, and shalt go forth in the dances of
them that make merry 5 [i] Thou shalt yet plant vines
upon the mountains of Samaria, the planters shall plant,
and shall § eat *them* as common things 6 For there
shall be a day, *that* [k] the watchmen upon the mount
Ephraim shall cry, [l] Arise ye, and let us go up to Zion
unto the LORD our God 7 For thus saith the
LORD, [m] Sing with gladness for Jacob, and shout a-
mong the chief of the nations publish ye, praise ye,
and say, O LORD, save thy people the remnant of
Israel 8 Behold, [n] I will bring them from the north
country, and gather them from the coasts of the earth,
and with them [o] the blind and the lame, the woman
with child, and her that travaileth with child together,
a great company shall return thither 9 [p] They shall
come with weeping, and [q] with † supplications will I
lead them I will cause them to walk by the rivers of
waters, [r] in a straight way wherein they shall not stum-
ble for I am a father to Israel, and Ephraim is [s] my
first born

[a] Chap xxx 24 [b] Chap iii 18 Acts iii 25 Rom xi 26 [c] Numb xiv 20 [d] Numb x 33. Deut i 33 Psal xcv 11 ‡ Heb From afar ‡ Or, say they [e] Mal i 2 [f] John vi 44 [g] Chap xxxiii 7 [h] Exod xv 20 Judg xi 34 || Or, timbrels [i] Isa lxv 21 § Heb Profane them [k] Isa lii 8 [l] Ibid ii 3 Mic iv 2 [m] Isa xii 6 [n] Chap iii 12, 18 [o] Isa xxxv 6 [p] Psal cxxvi 5 [q] Chap l 4 [r] Zech xii 10 † Or favours [s] Isa xxxv 8 & xliii 19 [t] Exod iv 22

v 1—9 The great mercy God had yet in store for his people is here at large declared for the support of their faith and hope

1 They shall all be his, and he will work for them a greater deliverance, than when he brought them out of Egypt *At the same time, in the latter days, will I be the God of all the families of Israel*, he will take them into covenant with him, after their long alienation from him, and all shall know him from the least to the greatest *and they shall be my people*, constrained by his grace, and devoting themselves to his service For as of old, the people that escaped the sword of Pharaoh in Egypt, *found grace in the wilderness*, being preserved and protected, *even Israel, when I went to cause them to rest* in Canaan, so now should they be preserved, and restored from their captive state to their own land But then the people might be apt to say, admitting his past deliverances, *The Lord hath appeared of old unto me*, but now we see none of his tokens, and therefore conclude ourselves rejected No, says God, *I have loved thee with an everlasting love*, which having subsisted from eternity, will endure to eternity, *therefore with loving-kindness have I drawn thee*, I have delivered thee out of thy former troubles, and will draw thee out of every pit *Note*, (1) Long afflictions are ready to breed despondence, but we should remember the past experience of God's people, and comfort our souls in hope (2) It is the abiding ground of consolation, that God's love is everlasting those who are once the objects of it, shall never be finally cast away (3) All our mercies in time or eternity flow from this everlasting love of God We have not chosen him, but he hath chosen us, called us by his grace, delivered us from the horrible pit of nature, constrained us by the cords of love to follow him, with the over-ruling energy of his grace hath overcome the strong bias of our corruptions, and drawn us from sin to holiness, from earth to heaven Lord, thus draw me, that I may run after thee

2 They shall be re-settled, and blest with plenty, either literally, when they should return from the captivity in Babylon, or spiritually, when, being converted to the Lord, Israel should be presented a chaste virgin to Christ, be built up on him the sure foundation, a glorious church, and filled with the abundance of spiritual joy, far exceeding the music and dances with which they celebrated the ceremonial festivals, *see Rev* xiv 2, 3 xix 7—9 In all their country, even Samaria, the seat of idolatry, gospel churches, represented by vines, should be planted, and enriched with numerous converts, from whom the planters, the ministers of the gospel, would receive the most abundant fruit

3 They shall with one heart, and in one place, unite in the worship of God The kingdoms of Israel and Judah shall be no more divided, but *there shall be a day*, the gospel-day, *that the watchmen upon mount Ephraim*, the ministers of the gospel, *shall cry, Arise ye, and let us go up to Zion unto the Lord our God* Though Ephraim was chief in the revolt from the house of David, and the worship at Jerusalem, now they shall be among the first to express their zeal for the worship and ordinances of the church of Christ, the spiritual Zion, and confess him to be their Lord and their God *Note*, They who were once chief rebels against God, when converted become his most zealous subjects and servants

4 The Gentiles are called upon to rejoice in the conversion of Israel, and to pray for their compleat salvation, *v* 7 for thus our praises for past mercies should ever quicken our

sup

Before Christ 606

supplications, and confirm our faith of greater yet in store for us

5 Notwithstanding all difficulties in the way, God will lead them safely home, either from Babylon, when no bodily infirmities should detain them, God being their strength and helper, or this may be interpreted spiritually of their recovery from the bondage of corruption, when God will lead the blind in a way they knew not, and make the lame man leap as an hart, when the travailing soul shall find rest from its pangs in Christ, and all the redeemed, a great company which no man can number, shall be brought into the church, *with weeping* for past offences, whilst they look upon him whom they have pierced, and *supplications* for present grace, which in the most abundant measure God will bestow, like *rivers of water*, to refresh them in their journey to glory, and he will make strait paths for their feet, that nothing may cause them to fall, whilst as a father with tenderest regard he watches over, and in his arms supports, the children of his grace, as Israel and Ephraim should be then accounted *Note*, (1) When God will work, all difficulties quickly vanish (2) We have a total impotence to take one step towards our own salvation, but when God calls, he will bestow the ability (3) All who return to God in truth, come to him with weeping and sorrow for past guilt, and supplication for present help (4) When we follow a divine call, we are sure of a divine protection, and shall find comfort in all the way (5) They who have God for their father, can want no manner of thing that is good

10 ¶ Hear the word of the LORD, O ye nations,
and declare *it* in the isles afar off, and say, He that
t Ex xxxiv scattered Israel [t] will gather him, and keep him, as a
shepherd *doth* his flock 11 For [u] the LORD hath re-
deemed Jacob, and ransomed him from the hand of
him [x] that *was* stronger than he 12 Therefore they
shall come and sing in the height of Zion, and shall
flow together to the goodness of the LORD, [y] for
wheat, and for wine, and for oil, and for the young
of the flock, and of the herd and their soul [z] shall be as
a watered garden, and they shall not sorrow any more
at all 13 Then [a] shall the virgin rejoice in the dance,
both young men and old together for I will turn their
mourning into joy, and [b] will comfort them, and make
them rejoice from their sorrow 14 And I will satiate
the soul of the priests with fatness, and [c] my people shall
be satisfied with my goodness, saith the LORD 15
¶ Thus saith the LORD, [d] A voice was heard in Ra-
mah, lamentation *and* bitter weeping Rachel weeping
for her children, refused to be comforted for her chil-
dren, because they *were* not 16 Thus saith the
LORD, [e] Refrain thy voice from weeping, and thine
eyes from tears for thy work shall be rewarded, saith
the LORD, and they shall come again from the land
of the enemy 17 And there is hope in thine end,
saith the LORD, that *thy* children shall come again to
their own border

v 10—17 The distant nations, and the isles afar off, are called upon to hear and observe the designs of mercy and grace which God hath towards his Israel

1 He will collect them from their dispersion, keep them as a shepherd his flock, and redeem them from the hand of all their mighty enemies, who had prevailed against them, *v* 10, 11 which was true of Israel after the flesh, when they were restored from Babylon, and will be still more eminently fulfilled, when they are brought in from their present state of captivity But it is also especially applicable to all the spiritual Israel of God, redeemed by the blood of Jesus, rescued from the power of sin and Satan, gathered in from the state of nature and corruption, in which they lay before dispersed amidst the world of the ungodly, and preserved and kept by the great shepherd of souls, out of whose hands none can pluck them

2 They shall be filled with plenty, joy, and gladness The returning captives with delight once more will stand on Zion's hill, adding his praise, *Ezra* iii 11 His goodness shall engage their heart to him, and all temporal good things shall abound they shall flourish as a watered garden, their sorrows be at an end the voice of joy again fill the streets of Jerusalem, and God's hand, seen in the salvation, shall turn their mourning and sorrow into overflowing joy and consolation, so that both priests and people shall be satiated with God's goodness, *v* 12—14 The souls of sinners, whether Jews or Gentiles, shall also experience this prophecy more gloriously fulfilled, when brought into the church of Christ, the spiritual Zion, their hearts shall be enlarged with love and praise, confirmed by the experience of divine goodness, and flowing together to Jesus, shall all be filled with good things, the heavenly bread of gospel grace, the word of life, the clear wine of the great and precious promises, whereby they become partakers of a divine nature, the oil of gladness, the unction from the holy One, and all the best of blessings he hath to bestow, making the soul *as a watered garden*, abounding in all the gifts and graces of the Spirit, in all the fruits of righteousness, the effects of which will be the exchange of all their mourning over their sins, corruptions, temptations, desertions, for joy in the sense of pardon, strength, and the light of God's countenance lifted up upon them, so that both ministers and people shall be satisfied with God's goodness, and as thus the tears at present are wiped away from their eyes, so shall they quickly go where *they shall not sorrow any more at all*, where every cause of it will be removed for ever, and their everlasting blessedness be compleat Hasten, Lord, this happy day!

3 The great cause of their grief would be removed Rachel, as if rising out of her grave, which lay between Ramah and Bethlehem, to bewail this catastrophe, personates the Jewish mothers with inconsolable anguish weeping over their children slain or gone into captivity, but the Lord silences her mourning with assurances, that she should not have borne these children in vain, since however now they seemed lost irrecoverably, he would bring them to their own border again, so that there was still hope in their end that it would be happy, and make the former days of sorrow forgotten This prophecy, we are assured had also a particular reference to the slaying the infants by Herod, *Mat* ii 16—18 the massacre reaching from Bethlehem to Ramah, and waking, as it were, Rachel that mother of Israel from her sepulchre, to lament the inhuman deed, and she is comforted with the assurance, that there is hope in their end, and a resurrection day these infants shall come from the land of death their enemy, to their own borders, the heavenly Canaan *Note*, (1) If we have hope in our end, we ought to be comforted under the troubles of the way (2) Parents are too apt to indulge inordinate sorrow for the death of their children, and refuse to be comforted, whereas, if they were gracious, they have cause to rejoice, and, if they died in infancy, have abundant reason to believe *there is hope in their end* we shall meet them in a better country

18 ¶ I have surely heard Ephraim bemoaning him-
self *thus*, [f] Thou hast chastised me, and I was chastised, f Ps xciv 12
as a bullock unaccustomed *to the yoke* [g] turn thou me, g Lam v 21
and I shall be turned, for thou *art* the LORD my God
19 Surely [h] after that I was turned, I repented, and h Deut xxx 2
after that I was † instructed, I smote upon *my* thigh I † Or knew
was ashamed, yea, even confounded, because [i] I did bear myself Luke xv 17
the reproach of my youth 20 [k] *Is* Ephraim my dear i Job xiii 26
son? *is he* a pleasant child? for since I spake against k Luke xv 3—
him, I do earnestly [l] remember him still therefore l Isa xlix 15
[m] my bowels ‡ are troubled for him [n] I will surely have m Isa lxiii 15 Hos xi
mercy upon him, saith the LORD 21 Set thee up 8 Luke xv 20
way-marks, make thee high heaps [o] set thine heart to- ‡ Heb
ward the high way, *even* the way *which* thou wentest Sound for him
turn again, O virgin of Israel, turn again to these thy
cities 22 ¶ How long wilt thou [p] go about, O thou n Hos xiv
backsliding daughter? for the LORD hath created a 4
new thing in the earth, [q] A woman shall compass § a o Chap l 5
man 23 Thus saith the LORD of hosts, the God p Chap ii 18 23, 36
of Israel, As yet they shall use this speech in the land q Isa vii 14 Mat i 18—20
of Judah and in the cities thereof, when I shall bring § Or, a mighty man
again their captivity, [r] The LORD bless thee, [s] O ha- r Ps cxxii 6, 7
bitation of justice, *and* mountain of holiness 24 s Isa lx 21
And there shall dwell in Judah itself, and in all the
cities thereof together, husbandmen, and they *that* go
forth with flocks 25 For [t] I have satiated the weary t Chap xxxiii 9
soul, and I have replenished every sorrowful soul 26 Mat v 4, 6 & xi 28
Upon this I awaked, and beheld; and my sleep was
sweet unto me

v 18—26 We have here,

1 Ephraim's repentance, representing the whole body of the Jewish people, and the figure of every awakened soul that returns to God He bemoans himself in the remembrance of his past iniquities, acknowledges the justice of the chastisement which his sins had provoked, reproaches his own stubbornness for struggling so long against God, *as a bullock unaccustomed to the yoke* He prays to the Lord for that converting grace which only can turn his perverse heart, and if God will work, then shall the happy change be wrought, and he be enabled by faith to rest upon God, and claim an interest in his regard, *for thou art the Lord my God* And when he can thus cast his burden upon the Lord, instantly the blessed effect appears *Surely after that I was turned, I repented*, the sense of the divine love, now more experimentally tasted, wrought a deeper sense of the evil and ingratitude of sin, and a greater abhorrence of it *and after that I was instructed*, in the knowledge of his own impurity and pollution, by the light of God's Spirit, and of the transcendent excellence and infinite grace of the neglected Saviour, *I smote upon*

Before Christ 606

upon my thigh, with holy indignation at his baſeneſs, ſtupidity, and perverſeneſs *I was aſhamed, yea, even confounded*, ſcarce able to look up to God from the conſciouſneſs of guilt, *because I did bear the reproach of my youth*, all his ſins, long ſince committed and forgotten, roſe up freſh to his memory, and from the earlieſt days of youth, gave him abundant cauſe for confuſion and ſelf-abhorrence *Note*, When a ſoul is by divine grace brought thus far, he is in the ſure road to glory

2 God's arms of love are open to receive the returning prodigal, with delight he bends over him, and pours out his paternal heart *Is Ephraim my dear ſon? is he a pleaſant child?* It expreſſes with a kind of ſurprize the joy God takes in ſeeing ſuch a change wrought upon a hardened ſinner, and intimates his readineſs to own the endeared relation of father, however unworthy the ſinner is to bear the name of child *a pleaſant child* too, for when the penitent returns to God, all his evil is forgiven and forgotten, and he becomes dear to God, as if he had never offended *For ſince I ſpake againſt him*, corrected him with ſome rebuke, and threatened him with more, *I do earneſtly remember him ſtill* with tender affection, *my bowels are troubled for him*, grieved for his afflictions, yearning over him in the duſt of humiliation *I will ſurely have mercy on him, ſaith the Lord*, pardon all that is paſt, reſtore him to what he hath loſt, beſtow new favours, and make him the object of eternal grace and mercy *Note*, (1) God's compaſſions to his undutiful children ſhould teach parents never to be inexorable, however offended (2) When the heavieſt afflictions for their ſins light on God's children, it is not becauſe he hath forgotten to be gracious, but that they have neglected to be dutiful, when they return to him, he will ſtill be found a father of mercies

3 The people of Iſrael, in the perſon of Ephraim, repentant and continuing mercy with God, are called to return to their own land *Set thee up way marks, make thee high heaps*, as a direction in the road, that they may not err, *ſet thine heart toward the highway, even the way that thou wenteſt* from Judea to Babylon, *turn again, O virgin of Iſrael, turn again to theſe thy cities*, which God now would reſtore to them *How long wilt thou go about, O thou backſliding daughter?* departing from God, and therefore wandering in endleſs mazes of error and miſery, *for the Lord hath created a new thing in the earth, a woman ſhall compaſs a man, a mighty one*, the Meſſiah, born of a virgin, by the immediate power of God, a ſtrange and unheard-of conception, to him the gathering of the people ſhall be, and they may be confident of their recovery, *when this breaker ſhall go up before them king at the head of them* *Note*, (1) The incarnation of Jeſus is the foundation of every bleſſing to God's Iſrael (2) Go about where we will, our ſouls never can find reſt, till we return from our backſliding, to the God from whom we have ſo greatly departed (3) We may expect many a difficulty in our path, when our faces are turned from the houſe of our priſon, towards God's Zion, and therefore need *ſet our heart towards it*, diſcouraged by no oppoſition

4 Great ſhall be the peace and proſperity of God's Iſrael Thoſe who behold them would admire them, and wiſh them the beſt of bleſſings, *The Lord bleſs thee, O habitation of juſtice, and mountain of holineſs*, for ſuch Jeruſalem ſhould become, and this, whatever reformation might be wrought by Nehemiah and Ezra, ſeems to have its full accompliſhment yet to come In conſequence of ſuch piety, great plenty ſhould be given them of all good things, their flocks ſhall abound, and a liberal proviſion be made to repleniſh and ſatisfy every weary and ſorrowful ſoul, and this is eſpecially to be referred to the ſpiritual Iſrael, to whom God will raiſe up paſtors after his own heart, under whoſe miniſtry they ſhall be abundantly repleniſhed, and their ſouls, weary and heavy laden with guilt and ſin, be refreſhed with a ſenſe of the love of Chriſt, and their ſorrows exchanged for joy and peace in believing

5 This viſion afforded the prophet great ſatisfaction and delight *Upon this I awaked*, perhaps with the tranſport of joy he felt at the revelation of theſe deſigns of grace to God's people, *and beheld*, for nothing fills a faithful miniſter's heart with greater pleaſure, than the proſpect of Chriſt's kingdom increaſing *and my ſleep was ſweet unto me*, peculiarly refreſhing and ſtrengthening *Note*, The mind much occupied on God, will often in ſleep find the communion ſtill maintained with him, and the very dreams holy and comforting

27 ¶ Behold, the days come, ſaith the LORD, that
[a] I will ſow the houſe of Iſrael, and the houſe of Judah
with the ſeed of man, and with the ſeed of beaſt 28
And it ſhall come to paſs, *that* like as I have watched
over them, [b] to pluck up, and to break down, and to
throw down, and to deſtroy, and to afflict, ſo will I
watch over them, [c] to build, and to plant, ſaith the
LORD 29 In thoſe days they ſhall ſay no more,
[d] The fathers have eaten a ſour grape, and the childrens
teeth are ſet on edge 30 But every one ſhall die for
his own iniquity, every man that eateth the ſour grape,
his teeth ſhall be ſet on edge 31 ¶ Behold, [e] the days
come, ſaith the LORD, that I will make a [c] new covenant with the houſe of Iſrael, and with the houſe of
Judah 32 [d] Not according to the covenant that I
made with their fathers in the day *that* I took them by
the hand, to bring them out of the land of Egypt
(which my covenant they brake, † although I was an
huſband unto them, ſaith the LORD) 33 [e] But this
ſhall be the covenant that I will make with the houſe of
Iſrael, After thoſe days, ſaith the LORD, [f] I will put
my law in their inward parts, and write it in their
hearts, and [g] will be their God, and they ſhall be my
people 34 And they ſhall teach no more every man
his neighbour, and every man his brother, ſaying, Know
the LORD for [h] they ſhall all know me, from the
leaſt of them unto the greateſt of them, ſaith the LORD
for [i] I will forgive their iniquity, and I will remember
their ſin no more

† Or, ſhould I have continued an huſband to them?

v 27—34 Farther diſcoveries of God's deſigns of grace towards his people are here made

1 They ſhall be multiplied exceedingly as a field ſown with ſeed, ſo ſhall both the men and cattle increaſe under the divine bleſſing, and inſtead of their former deſolations God promiſes to turn his hand, and to be as careful to protect and proſper them, as ever he had watched over them to afflict and deſtroy them, v 28 *Note*, They are truly ſafe and happy, who have God for their guardian

2 They ſhould no more be viſited for their fathers iniquities, and ſhould have no more reaſon to complain, that *the fathers have eaten a ſour grape, and the children's teeth are ſet on edge*, being puniſhed for the ſins of their anceſtors, particularly of Manaſſeh *but now every one ſhall die for his own iniquity*, for tho' the nation be no more expoſed to wrath as a body, ſinful individuals ſhould bear their own guilt *Every man that eateth the ſour grape, his teeth ſhall be ſet on edge*, and ſin, however tempting to the eye, will ever be found ſour in its effects, and produce much anguiſh to the ſoul, either in time or eternity

3 God will eſtabliſh his covenant with them the covenant of grace in Chriſt Jeſus, of which all the Iſrael of God are partakers, not of the Jews only, but of the Gentiles alſo, for ſo the apoſtle underſtands theſe words, *Heb* viii 8—12 This covenant is called *new*, not as in *ſubſtance* different from that made with the people when they came out of Egypt, but in the *form* in which it was exhibited Then it was delivered in type and figure, wrapped up under the veil of ceremonial rites and ſervices, whilſt now as with open face we behold the glory of God manifeſt in the face of Jeſus Chriſt, and in the goſpel ſee the cleareſt diſcoveries of his grace, though ſome ſuppoſe the Sinai covenant to be in ſubſtance different from the covenant of grace, as a covenant of peculiarity, and merely of a temporal nature The covenant made with them they quickly broke, by the moſt ungrateful departures from God, and ſetting up that hated thing idolatry, notwithſtanding all the diſtinguiſhing kindneſs of God to them as a tender huſband, patient under their provocations, and wooing them to return to him

4 The tenor of the covenant here promiſed is all mercy, and the bleſſings wholly ſpiritual, where God is all and in all He engages to write his law upon their hearts, and to enable them for the obedience he demands He *will be their God*, to bleſs them, and *they ſhall be his people*, conſtrained by his powerful grace, and engaged to give up themſelves to his government Abundance of divine knowledge ſhall then be diffuſed, and all the Iſrael of God be enriched with wiſdom and ſpiritual underſtanding and he concludes with the crowning bleſſing of all, *I will forgive their iniquity, and remember their ſin no more*, and every true Iſraelite is now entitled to theſe ineſtimable bleſſings

35 ¶ Thus ſaith the LORD, [k] which giveth the ſun
for a light by day, *and* the ordinances of the moon and
of the ſtars for a light by night, which divideth [l] the
ſea when the waves thereof roar, the LORD of hoſts
is his name 36 [m] If thoſe ordinances depart from before me, ſaith the LORD, *then* the ſeed of Iſrael alſo
ſhall ceaſe from being a nation before me for ever 37
Thus ſaith the LORD, If [n] heaven above can be meaſured, and the foundations of the earth ſearched out beneath, I will alſo caſt off all the ſeed of Iſrael, for all
that they have done, ſaith the LORD 38 ¶ Behold,
[o] the days come, ſaith the LORD, that the city ſhall be
built to the LORD [p] from the tower of Hananeel unto
the gate of the corner 39 And the meaſuring line
ſhall yet go forth over againſt it, upon the hill Gareb,
and ſhall compaſs about to Goath 40 And the whole
valley of the dead bodies, and of the aſhes, and all the
fields unto the brook of Kidron, [r] unto the corner of the
horſe-gate, toward the eaſt, *ſhall be* [s] holy unto the
LORD,

Before Christ 606

LORD, [i] it shall not be plucked up, nor thrown down any more for ever

[i] Mic. xvi 18

v 35—40 We have here,

1 The perpetuity of the church of Christ engaged for by him, whose omnipotence can ensure the fulfilment of the promises of his grace That Lord of hosts, whose power created, and whose arm upholds and guides the ordinances of heaven in regular succession, who first shut up the sea in bounds, and still, when it rages, causes the foaming billows to subside, who meted out the heavens, and laid the foundation of the deep, immense the space, unfathomable the abyss this mighty God declares, that sooner shall these heavenly orbs unruly leave their spheres, and the deep forsake its bed, to cover again the earth, than *Israel* cease to be a nation yea, sooner shall impossibilities be practicable, the immensity of space be measured, and *the foundations of the earth be searched out*, by what supported, and how it is hung in air, than the seed of Israel be cast off, so as to be utterly abandoned, notwithstanding *all they have done* All their iniquities and unbelief shall not prevent the covenant of grace from taking effect and this is equally true of all the Israel of God, who, notwithstanding all they have done, shall never perish, but have everlasting life, and in the worst of times a remnant, according to the election of grace, shall ever remain

2 The rebuilding and duration of the city of Jerusalem, the figure of the church Though it would quickly be laid in ruins, it should be raised again as large as ever, and *be holy unto the Lord*, no more polluted with idols, but wholly devoted to the worship and service of God *It shall not be plucked up, nor thrown down any more for ever*, which, if applied to the city of Jerusalem, can only signify that it should continue a long while, or, spoken of the church of Christ, shall be literally fulfilled, against which the gates of hell shall never prevail

CHAP XXXII

In this chapter, 1 Jeremiah is imprisoned for foretelling the destruction of Jerusalem, and the captivity of king Zedekiah, ver 1—5 *2 He buys some land, by God's appointment, as an assurance that in due time a happy end should be put to the present troubles,* ver 6—15 *3 He prays to God on this occasion,* ver 16—25 *4 God sends him a message to deliver to the people, (1) He must foretel the utter destruction of Judah and Jerusalem for their sins,* ver 26—35 *But, (2) At the same time assure them, that tho the destruction was total, it should not be final,* ver 36—44

589

1 THE word that came to Jeremiah from the
LORD [a] in the tenth year of Zedekiah king
of Judah, which *was* the eighteenth year of Nebuchad-
nezzar 2 For then the king of Babylon's army be-
sieged Jerusalem and Jeremiah the prophet [b] was shut
up in [c] the court of the prison, which *was* in the king
of Judah's house 3 For Zedekiah king of Judah had
shut him up, saying, [d] Wherefore dost thou prophesy,
and say, Thus saith the LORD, Behold, [e] I will give
this city into the hand of the king of Babylon, and he
shall take it 4 And Zedekiah king of Judah shall
not escape out of the hand of the Chaldeans, but shall
surely [f] be delivered into the hand of the king of Ba-
bylon, and shall speak with him mouth to mouth, and
his eyes shall behold his eyes 5 And he shall lead
Zedekiah to Babylon, and there shall he be until I
visit him, saith the LORD though ye fight with
the Chaldeans, [g] ye shall not prosper 6. ¶ And Jere-
miah said, The word of the LORD came unto me,
saying, 7 Behold, Hanameel the son of Shallum thine
uncle, shall come unto thee, saying, Buy thee my field
that *is* in Anathoth, for [h] the right of redemption *is* thine
to buy *it* 8 So Hanameel mine uncle's son came to
me in the court of the prison, according to the word of
the LORD, and said unto me, Buy my field, I pray
thee, that *is* in Anathoth, which *is* in the country of
Benjamin for the right of inheritance *is* thine, and the
redemption *is* thine, buy *it* for thyself then I knew
that this *was* the word of the LORD 9 And I
bought the field of Hanameel my uncle's son, that *was*
in Anathoth, and weighed him the money, *even* † seven-
teen shekels of silver 10 And I ‡ subscribed the evi-
dence, and sealed *it*, and took witnesses, and weighed
him the money in the balances 11 So I took the evi-
dence of the purchase, *both that which was* sealed *ac-
cording* to the law and custom, and *that which was* open.

[a] 2 Kings xxv 1, 2
[b] Mat v 12
[c] Neh iii 25 Chap xxxiii 1 & xxxvii 21 & xxxviii 6 xxxix 15
[d] Chap xxvi 29
[e] Chap xxxiv 2
[f] Chap xxxiv 3 & lii 9
[g] Prov xxi 30
[h] Lev xxv 24 25 Ruth iv 4
† Or, seven shekels and ten pieces of silver
‡ Heb Wrote in the book

12 And I gave the evidence of the purchase unto Ba-
ruch the son of Neriah, the son of Maaseiah, in the
sight of Hanameel my uncle's *son*, and in the presence of
the witnesses that subscribed the book of the purchase,
before all the Jews that sat in the court of the prison.
13 ¶ And I charged Baruch before them, saying, 14
Thus saith the LORD of hosts, the God of Israel, Take
these evidences, this evidence of the purchase, both *which*
is sealed, and this evidence *which is* open, and put them
in an earthen vessel, that they may continue many days
15 For thus saith the LORD of hosts, the God of Is-
rael, [k] Houses and fields, and vineyards shall be possessed
again in this land

Before Christ 589

[i] Ch. vii 2
[k] Ver 43

v 1—15 The fatal hour approached of Jerusalem's destruction, already the Chaldean army surrounded the walls, the prophecies of Jeremiah that were before despised, now we should have thought would carry conviction to every heart, and his advice be sought and followed implicitly in the present emergency How different the case!

1 Behold him a prisoner, shut up by the king's order in the court of the king's house, a place where probably the state-prisoners were kept The cause of his confinement was his declaration that Jerusalem should infallibly be taken, their desperate resistance against the besiegers be fruitless, and Zedekiah himself attempt to escape in vain he should be seized, delivered up to the victorious king of Babylon, see his indignation, and hear him pronounce judgment upon him, be led into an ignominious captivity, and there abide, till death came as a kind visitant to release him from his miseries This prophecy, so far from humbling, exasperated them against him, and lest by his preaching he should discourage the hearts of the people to surrender, they put him under this confinement, though not so rigorous but that he was allowed the air and company of his friends *Note*, (1) They who will go on God's messages must not be shocked at a prison (2) Nothing will convince hardened sinners even when God's judgments begin to operate, they flatter themselves they shall weather the storm

2 In the prison he becomes a purchaser Hanameel, his uncle's son, had a field to dispose of, and, as nearest of kin, the *right of redemption* was in Jeremiah The Lord let him know in the prison, that an offer of selling it would be made to him, as happened, *v* 8 and that it was his will he should buy the land, which was in the suburbs of Anathoth, a city of the priests, and which one of them might lawfully transfer to another, or some inheritance by the mother's side, which Hanameel had a right to part with The bargain is easily made, the money paid, the land conveyed with all the usual formalities, the deeds consigned to the care of Baruch, in the presence of the witnesses who subscribed them, to be set in an earthen vessel, and hid probably in the field for though the destruction of the city and country by the Chaldeans was certain, and therefore the money might appear lost, yet God assured him, on whose veracity he could depend, that the time would come, when every man's property would be restored, and houses, fields, and vineyards be bought and sold as usual and it was designed for an encouragement of the faith and hope of the people, when they saw the prophet himself acting in the full assurance of the truth he declared *Note*, When ministers shew themselves influenced by the word they preach, and fully persuaded of it, its effects will be more powerful on their hearers

16 ¶ Now when I had delivered the evidence of the
purchase unto Baruch the son of Neriah, I prayed unto
the LORD, saying, 17 Ah, LORD God, behold,
[l] thou hast made the heaven and the earth by thy great
power and stretched-out arm, *and* [m] there is nothing
‖ too hard for thee 18 Thou shewest [n] loving kind-
ness unto thousands, and recompensest the iniquity of the
fathers into the bosom of their children after them the
great, the mighty God, the LORD of hosts *is* his name
19 [o] Great in counsel, and mighty in work (for [p] thine
eyes *are* open upon all the ways of the sons of men,
[q] to give every one according to his ways, and according
to the fruit of his doings) 20 Which hast set signs
and wonders in the land of Egypt, *even* unto this day,
and in Israel, and amongst *other* men, and [r] hast made
thee a name, as at this day 21 And hast brought
forth thy people Israel out of the land of Egypt,
[s] with signs and with wonders, and with a strong
hand, and with a stretched out arm, and with great ter-
ror, 22 And hast given them this land which thou
didst swear to their fathers to give them, [u] a land flow-
ing with milk and honey 23 And they came in and
possessed it, [x] but they obeyed not thy voice, neither

[l] Gen i 1 Ps cxlvi 6 & Chap xxvii 5 & Job xlii.
[m] Ver 27 Luke i 37
‖ Or, hid from thee
[n] Ex xx 6 & xxxiv 7 Deut v 10.
[o] Isa ix. 6 & xxviii 29.
[p] Job xxxiv 21 Chap xvi 17 Prov v 21
[q] Chap xvii 10
[r] Ex ix 16 Isa lxiii 12 2 Sam vii 23
[s] Ex vi 6 1 Chron xvii 21
[t] Deut iv 34
[u] Ex iii 8
[x] Neh ix 26

Before Chriſt 589. walked in thy law, they have done nothing of all that
thou commandedſt them to do therefore thou haſt
cauſed all this evil to come upon them 24 Behold the
‡ Or engines of ſhot ‡ mounts, they are come unto the city to take it, and
the city is given into the hand of the Chaldeans that
fight againſt it, becauſe of the ſword, and of the famine,
and of the peſtilence, and what thou haſt ſpoken is
come to paſs, and behold, thou ſeeſt *it* 25 And thou
haſt ſaid unto me, O LORD God, Buy thee the field
§ Or though for money, and take witneſſes § for the city is given
into the hand of the Chaldeans.

v 16—25 Having tranſacted this buſineſs, and delivered the writings to Baruch's care, the prophet directs his prayer to God, grieved for the calamities impending, and in ſome perplexity how the deſolations ready to be accompliſhed on this people could correſpond with thoſe promiſes of their reſtoration

1 He adores the infinite perfections of God *his almighty power*, manifeſted in the amazing works of creation, which nothing can controul or reſiſt, *v* 17 *his boundleſs mercy*, ſhewing loving-kindneſs to thouſands *his inflexible juſtice*, in puniſhing ſin in thoſe who hate him, upon children's children, that copy after their fathers tranſgreſſions *his univerſal ſovereignty*, the great, the mighty God, the Lord of hoſts, who doth whatſoever pleaſeth him, and whom all the armies of heaven and earth obey, *v* 11 *his infinite wiſdom*, great in counſel, his deſigns planned with the moſt conſummate knowledge, and carried into execution with the moſt irreſiſtible energy *Omniſcient*, he beholds all the ways of the ſons of men, and knoweth every device of their hearts *the eternal judge*, who will in the day of recompenſe render to every man according to his works

2 He recounts the wonders he had wrought for his people of old, evident in the plagues of Egypt, their deliverance from thence, and in all the diſpenſations of his providence towards them from that day, bringing them into Canaan, according to the promiſe made to their fathers, as well as in what he did among the nations around them, in all which he got to himſelf great glory, and appeared worthy of their higheſt praiſe *Note*, The gracious dealings of God towards his people ſhould ever afford matter for our thanks, and encouragement to our faith

3 He laments their diſobedience, as the cauſe of all the miſeries to which they were now expoſed By a long train of rebellions they had brought their preſent evils upon themſelves, and the prophetic word, which they had diſregarded, began to receive its terrible accompliſhment Behold, the beſiegers compaſs the city, and raiſe their mounts and batteries againſt it; ſo that their caſe was deſperate, the city is given into the hands of the Chaldeans

4 He lays the doubts and perplexities of his mind before God *Thou haſt ſaid unto me*, in this ruinous ſituation of affairs, *Buy thee a field, and take witneſſes*, and this ſeemed ſtrange, when the land was devoted to deſtruction *Note*, (1) God's providences ſometimes appear to contradict his promiſes (2) When we have God's orders, we have nothing to do but obey, and truſt him with the iſſue (3) When we are in the dark concerning God's diſpenſations, we may humbly by prayer beg to be taught of God

26 ¶ Then came the word of the LORD unto Je-
ʸ Num xvi 22 remiah, ſaying, 27 Behold, I *am* the LORD, ʸ the
ᶻ Ver 17 God of all fleſh ᶻ Is there any thing too hard for me?
ᵃ Ver 3 28. Therefore thus ſaith the LORD, Behold, ᵃ I will
give this city into the hand of the Chaldeans, and into
the hand of Nebuchadrezzar king of Babylon, and he
ſhall take it 29 And the Chaldeans that fight againſt
ᵇ Chap. xxi 10 xxxvii 10 this city, ſhall come and ᵇ ſet fire on this city, and burn
it, with the houſes ᶜ upon whoſe roofs they have offered
ᶜ Chap xix 13 incenſe unto Baal, and poured out drink-offerings unto
other gods to provoke me to anger 30 For the
children of Iſrael, and the children of Judah have only
done evil before me from their youth for the children
of Iſrael have only provoked me to anger with the
work of their hands, ſaith the LORD 31 For this
† Heb for my anger city hath been to me, † *as* a provocation of mine anger,
and of my fury, from the day that they built it, even
unto this day; that I ſhould remove it from before my
face 32 Becauſe of all the evil of the children of
Iſrael, and of the children of Judah, which they have
ᵈ Iſa i 4—6 Dan ix 8 done to provoke me to anger, ᵈ they, their kings, their
princes, their prieſts, and their prophets, and the men
of Judah, and the inhabitants of Jeruſalem 33. And
ᵉ Chap ii 27 vii 24 they have turned unto me ᵉ the back, and not the face,
though I taught them, ᶠ riſing up early, and teaching
ᶠ Chap xxv 3 *them*, yet they have not hearkened to receive inſtruction
34 But they ſet their abominations in the houſe (which
is called by my name) to defile it 35. And they built Before Chriſt 589.
the high places of Baal, which *are* in the valley of the
ſon of Hinnom, to ᵍ cauſe their ſons and their daughters ᵍ Chap. vii 31 & xix. 5
to paſs through *the fire* unto ʰ Molech, which I com-
manded them not, neither came it into my mind, that ʰ Lev xviii 21 1 Kings xi 33
they ſhould do this abomination to cauſe Judah to ſin
36 And now therefore thus ſaith the LORD the God
of Iſrael concerning this city, whereof ye ſay, ⁱ It ſhall ⁱ Ver 24
be delivered into the hand of the king of Babylon, by
the ſword, and by the famine, and by the peſtilence
37 Behold, ᵏ I will gather them out of all countries whi- ᵏ Deut xxx 3 Chap xxiii 3 & xxix 14 & xxxi 10 Ezek xxxvi 24
ther I have driven them in mine anger and in my fury,
and in great wrath, and I will bring them again unto
this place, and I will cauſe ˡ them to dwell ſafely 38
And ᵐ they ſhall be my people, and I will be their God ˡ Chap xxxiii 16
39 And ⁿ I will give them one heart, ᵒ and one way, ᵐ Chap. xxiv 7 & xxx 22 & xxxi 33
that they may fear me ‡ for ever, for the good of them, ⁿ Ezek xi 19 & xxxvi 26
and of their children after them 40 And ᵖ I will make ᵒ Chap vi 16 Eph iv 3
an everlaſting covenant with them, that I will not turn ‡ Heb All days
away from them to do them good, but I will put my ᵖ Chap xxxi 31
fear in their hearts, that ᑫ they ſhall not depart from me ᑫ Pſ lxxx 18 Iſa lix 19
41 Yea, ʳ I will rejoice over them to do them good, and ʳ Deut xxx 9 Zeph iii 17
ˢ I will plant them in this land § aſſuredly, with my ˢ Chap xxiv 6 Amos ix 15
whole heart, and with my whole ſoul 42 For thus § Heb In truth and ſtability
ſaith the LORD, Like as I have brought all this great ᵗ Chap xxxiii 10
evil upon this people, ſo will I bring upon them all the ᵘ Chap xvii 26 & xxxiii 13
good that I have promiſed them 43 And fields ſhall ˣ Chap. xxxiii 7, 11
be bought in this land, whereof ye ſay, ᵗ *It is* deſolate
without man or beaſt, it is given into the hand of the
Chaldeans 44 Men ſhall buy fields for money, and
ſubſcribe evidences, and ſeal *them*, and take witneſſes ᵘ in
the land of Benjamin, and in the places about Jeruſa-
lem, and in the cities of Judah, and in the cities of the
mountains, and in the cities of the valley, and in the
cities of the ſouth for ˣ I will cauſe their captivity to
return, ſaith the LORD

v 26—44 We have here an immediate anſwer given to the prophet's prayer, and his mind fully ſatisfied The deſtruction wrought by the Chaldeans is perfectly conſiſtent with the promiſe, that the land ſhould be reinhabited, and fields and vineyards again be bought and ſold as before

1 The deſolations of the city and nation are determined by that almighty Jehovah, who is the *God of all fleſh*, weak and unable to reſiſt him, corrupt, and therefore provoking his wrath Nothing is *too hard* for him to do, he can ſave or deſtroy againſt all human probabilities This impregnable fortreſs, as it ſeems, muſt totter, ſince ſuch is his decree, before the arms of the Chaldean monarch, the city and temple be burnt with fire, with all the houſes where incenſe had been offered to Baal, and this the juſt judgment due to their aggravated provocations *From their youth*, the time when firſt they were formed into a people, or from the earlieſt infancy, corruption being in our nature from the womb, they had tranſgreſſed, and by their idolatries provoked God's anger, and ſeemed as if they ſtudied to offend him by their daring impiety, *v* 29, 30 Ever ſince the day Jeruſalem was built, either by the Jebuſites, or from the days of David, who ſo greatly beautified and enlarged it, the ſins of the inhabitants have been a continual provocation, for which the Lord had long ſince reſolved to remove them from before his face into a miſerable captivity, *v* 31 All orders and degrees of men were involved in the common guilt, from the loweſt to the king on the throne, and even the prieſts and prophets, who ſhould have been the reprovers of others by their word and example, were chief in the tranſgreſſion, *v*. 32 In vain God ſent them warning upon warning, they turned a deaf ear to his faithful prophets, and refuſed to bend either under the rebukes of his word, or the corrections of his providence, *v* 33 Nay, to ſuch a height of effrontery did they carry their impiety, that even in that temple built for his honour, they ſet up their hated idols, *v* 34 and with unnatural cruelty, as well as horrid profaneneſs, burnt even their children in the fire to Molech, or at leaſt cauſed them to paſs between the flames, as a luſtration and dedication to the idol's ſervice For ſuch ſins no marvel judgment came upon them to the uttermoſt, and that after the deſolating ſcourges of the ſword, the famine, and peſtilence had waſted them, the remnant was ſent into a miſerable captivity

2 Notwithſtanding, God hath mercy ſtill in ſtore Though the city is given up, and the land deſolate without man or beaſt, there ſhall be a door of hope opened, for in the worſt of time, we ſhould not deſpair Many great and precious promiſes are here delivered

[1] They ſhall return, after ſeventy years, from all the countries, whither in anger God had diſperſed them, and dwell in peace, under the divine protection, in their own land, acknowledged

Before Christ 589

knowleged again of God as his people, and professing their fidelity and allegiance to him as their God

[2] God will make with them *an everlasting covenant*, the tenor of which is most amazingly gracious, and which stands fast not only with them but with all the Israel of God (1) He promises to put *his fear into their hearts*, the principle of all true wisdom and godliness, *v* 39 *Note*, A heart to fear God must be his own gift (2) *He will give them one heart and one way*, a single eye to God's glory, fervent charity among themselves, one path of grace and holiness in which they should walk, and leave their blessing and good examples as the best inheritance to children's children *Note*, All who have truly given up their hearts to Christ, whatever lesser differences may subsist between them, will ever be united in love, and walk in one way of holiness as Christ also walked (3) *He will never turn away from doing them good* Whatever aspect his providences may have, all shall work together for their benefit, the riches of his grace shall minister a constant and abundant supply for their necessities, and, whilst he will never leave or forsake them, he will take care they shall never leave or forsake him, kept by his power, through faith, unto salvation *Note*, If the final perseverance of the saints depended on themselves, their stability would rest on a precarious foundation, but, blessed be God, it is in better hands the faithfulness of the promise secures, amidst all dangers and difficulties, the certainty of the event

[3] His temporal, as his spiritual mercies, shall be great God will plant them firmly in their own land, *his heart and soul* shall be, as it were, firmly engaged in it, such delight will he take *to do them good* And this shall be as surely accomplished, as *the evil* which he had brought upon them

[4] Then the whole country should be inhabited, property secure, estates valuable, and no land want a purchaser, so that Jeremiah may be at rest respecting that which he hath bought, and it is the earnest of what shall in that day be the case it will then be found that the money is not laid out unprofitably, when the Lord shall thus cause their captivity to return Some apply this spiritually to the deliverance from the bondage of corruption, and those purchased possessions provided for the redeemed in the heavenly Canaan

CHAP XXXIII.

The scope of this chapter is much the same with that of the foregoing It is here promised, 1 *That the city shall be rebuilt,* ver 1—6 2 *That the captives having their sins pardoned, shall be restored,* ver 7, 8 3 *That this shall redound very much to the glory of God,* ver 9 4 *That the country shall have both joy and plenty,* ver 10—14 5 *That a way shall be made for the coming of the Messiah,* ver 15, 16 6 *That the house of David, Levi, and Israel shall flourish again, and be established in the kingdom of Christ, a gospel ministry and the gospel church shall continue while the world stands,* ver 17—26

1 MOreover, the word of the LORD came unto
Jeremiah the second time, (while he was yet
[a] shut up in the court of the prison) saying, 2 Thus
saith the LORD, [b] the maker thereof, the LORD that
formed it, to establish it, the LORD *is* his name 3
[c] Call unto me, and I will answer thee, and [d] shew thee
great and † mighty things, which thou knowest not
4 For thus saith the LORD, the God of Israel, con-
cerning the houses of this city, and concerning the houses
of the kings of Judah, [e] *which are* thrown down by the
mounts, and by the sword 5 They come to fight with
the Chaldeans, but *it is* to fill them with the dead bodies
of men, whom I have slain in mine anger, and in my
fury, and for all whose wickedness I have hid my face
from this city 6 Behold, I will bring it health and
cure, and I will cure them, and [f] will reveal unto them
the abundance of peace and truth 7 And [g] I will
cause the captivity of Judah, and the captivity of Israel
to return, and [h] will build them as at the first 8 And
[i] I will cleanse them from all their iniquity, whereby
they have sinned against me, and [k] I will pardon all
their iniquities whereby they have sinned, and whereby
they have transgressed against me 9 ¶ And [l] it shall
be to me a name of joy, a praise and an honour before
all the nations of the earth, which shall hear all the good
that I do unto them and [m] they shall fear and tremble
for all the goodness, and for all the prosperity that I pro-
cure unto it

a Chap xxxii 2 b Isa xxxvii 26 c Ezek xxxvi 37 d Isa xlviii 6 † Or hidden e Chap xxxii 24 f Ps lxxxv 10 g Isa xi 12 Chap xxxii 44 Hos i 11 i Isa i 25 Chap xxiv 6 & xxxi 33 Mark xxxvi 25 Joel iii 21 Zech xiii 1 Heb ix 14 l Chap xxxi 34 Mic vii 18 m Chap xiii 11 Isa lx 5 Phil ii 12

v 1—9 Jeremiah still continued under confinement, but God's visits made the prophet's prison a more desirable place than the palace of Zedekiah The second time a message of peace is sent by him, to encourage the drooping hopes of the people ready to fall under their enemies, and sink into despair

1 The prophecy is from the Lord, whose power is able to accomplish all his promises, the maker and former of the earth, and all things therein, who first established, and when he pleases can rebuild, his Zion Jehovah is his name, self sufficient, and faithful to his word

2 Though God promises, the prophet must in prayer intercede for the fulfilment *Call upon me, and I will answer thee,* for promises do not supersede, but encourage our supplications, *and shew thee great and mighty things, which thou knowest not,* either the strange deliverance of the people from Babylon, when their situation seemed desperate, and an event no human foresight could discover, or the greater wonders of gospel-grace, of which this temporal redemption was the figure

3 Notwithstanding their present miseries, their houses, even those of their kings and nobles, battered down, their auxiliaries, or the besieged, slain under the ruins, or those which remained filled, through famine and pestilence, with the dead corpses of those who were slain in God's anger because of their wickedness yet deplorable as their situation is, it is not desperate *Behold, I will bring it health and cure,* restore their desolations, *I will reveal unto them the abundance of peace and truth, peace* to enjoy their blessings, and *truth,* the true worship of God and fidelity between man and man being restored *and I will cause the captivity of Judah and Israel to return,* many of the other tribes returning to Judea from Babylon, with those of Judah and Benjamin, *and I will cleanse them from all their iniquity,* the cause of their sufferings, both pardoning their guilt, and delivering them from the power of sin *And it shall be to me a name of joy, a praise, and an honour before all nations,* God would glorify himself in shewing them such mercy, which would be attended with the most blessed effects, their prosperity not breeding security and neglect of God, but engaging them more faithfully to serve him, and making them jealous of offending a God so gracious And this was still more eminently fulfilled by the coming of the Messiah, who, as the Sun of Righteousness, arose with *healing* in his wings, *Peace* was established by him between God and fallen man, and abundance of peace diffused in the sinner's conscience *Truth,* the only true way of approaching God, and walking so as to please him, was by him revealed, then the dreadful *captivity* of sin was loosed, and the souls of men delivered from the bondage of corruption In a dying Saviour's blood a fountain was opened, that *cleanseth* from all sin, and now rescued from the power, as well as guilt of their iniquities, the people of Jesus appear pleasing in his sight, an honour to their profession, and engaged by all the goodness they have tasted, with godly jealousy and fear to work out their salvation, diligent to please, and careful not to offend their merciful Saviour and reconciled God Blessed and happy are they who experience this great redemption, begun in present pardon, peace, grace and holiness, they shall see it shortly compleated in glory everlasting

10 Thus saith the LORD, Again there shall be
heard in this place ([n] which ye say *shall be* desolate with-
out man and without beast, *even* in the cities of Judah,
and in the streets of Jerusalem, *that are* desolate with-
out man and without inhabitant, and without beast)
11 [o] The voice of joy, and the voice of gladness, the
voice of the bridegroom and the voice of the bride, the
voice of them that shall say, [p] Praise the LORD of
hosts, for the LORD *is* good, for his mercy *endureth*
for ever, *and* of them that shall bring the sacrifice of
praise into the house of the LORD, for I will cause
to return the captivity of the land, as at the first, saith
the LORD 12 Thus saith the LORD of hosts,
Again in this place *which is* desolate without man and
without beast, and in all the cities thereof, shall be an
habitation of [r] shepherds causing *their* flocks to lie down
13 [s] In the cities of the mountains, in the cities of the
vale, and in the cities of the south, and in the land of
Benjamin, and in the places about Jerusalem, and in
the cities of Judah shall the flocks [t] pass again under the
hands of him that telleth *them*, saith the LORD 14
[u] Behold, the days come, saith the LORD, that I will
perform that good thing which I have promised unto
the house of Israel, and to the house of Judah 15
¶ In those days, and at that time will I cause [x] the Branch
of righteousness to grow up unto David, and [y] he shall
execute judgment and righteousness in the land 16 [z] In
those days shall Judah be saved, and Jerusalem shall dwell
safely and this *is the name* wherewith she shall be called,
The LORD our Righteousness.

n Chap xxxii 43 o Chap vii 34 Zech x p 1 Chron xvi 8, 34 2 Chron v 13 Psal cxxxvi 1 Isa xii 4 q Ver 7 r Chap xxxi 24 s Chap xvii 26 & xxxii 44 t Lev xxvii 32 u Chap xxiii 5 & xxxi 31 x Isa iv 2 & xi 1 Chap xxiii 5 Zech iii 8 & vi 12 y 1 Cor i 30 z Isa xl 1 Chap xxiii 6

v 10—16 We have here farther blessings promised to the people of God

Before Christ 589.

1 The voice of joy ſhall return to Zion The deſolations under which it had lain made many abandon themſelves to deſpair of ever ſeeing the country raiſed from its ruins, but God will again replenish Jeruſalem and the cities of Judah with multitudes of inhabitants, then the bridal ſongs ſhall be heard, and the more delightful ſounds of ſacred melody echo through the courts of the temple, when this freſh inſtance of his aſtoniſhing goodneſs would make them with ſacred rapture repeat the well known pſalm, where the burden of each verſe is, "For his mercy endureth for ever," and theſe moſt pleaſing ſacrifices of praiſe be offered without ceaſing This may alſo be referred to the times of the goſpel, the preaching of which would diffuſe the greateſt joy and gladneſs, and awaken the warmeſt praiſes for the infinite mercies of redeeming love, when all other ſacrifices ſhould ceaſe, but the ſpiritual ſacrifices of praiſe ſhall never ceaſe, begun in the church on earth, continued in heaven to eternity

2 Plenty ſhall fill their land The long deſerted fields ſhall now again be covered with bleating flocks, the ſhepherds in full ſecurity feeding them, and all the land over-ſpread with cattle, both mountains and vallies, *paſſing under the hands of him that telleth them*, that none may be lacking Myſtically this may be interpreted of the miniſters of Chriſt, *the ſhepherds*, and his redeemed people, *the flock* of his paſture, gathered out from all nations, vaſt in multitude, feeding ſecurely under the divine protection, known and numbered by him, and not one found wanting of all the Father hath given unto him

3 Greater than all temporal mercies, the divine Meſſiah is promiſed Long he had been expected as the hope of his Iſrael, and now the fulneſs of time approaches when he ſhall be revealed *In thoſe days, and at that time*, appointed in the eternal councils, *will I cauſe the Branch of Righteouſneſs to grow up unto David*, the Meſſiah, the great Author of all Righteouſneſs, and raiſed up to ſet on the throne of his father David, *and he ſhall execute judgment and righteouſneſs in the land*, all judgment being committed to him, and in righteouſneſs he will diſcharge the truſt committed to him, executing vengeance on the enemies of his people, vindicating them from wrong, and juſtifying them from every accuſation of ſin or Satan *In thoſe days ſhall Judah*, the choſen ſeed, *be ſaved* from wrath and hell, and all the powers of Satan, corruption, and the grave, with a certain and everlaſting ſalvation, *and Jeruſalem ſhall dwell ſafely*, delivered from the fear of every foe, and no more under condemnation, enjoying peace with God, and in their conſciences, which no enemy can diſturb or take away *and this is the name wherewith ſhe ſhall be called, The Lord our Righteouſneſs*, his church being joined to Chriſt in an everlaſting covenant, all things are hers, ſhe bears his name, his righteouſneſs is imputed to her, ſhe is made partaker of a divine nature, and ſtands compleat in him, righteous as he is righteous, 1 *John* iii 7

† Heb There ſhall not be cut off from David
ᵍ 2 Sam vii 16 1 Kings ii 4 Pſ lxxxix 29, 36
ʰ Iſa liv 9 Pſ lxxxix 37 Ver 25 Chap xxxi 36
ⁱ Iſa ix 6
ᵈ Gen xiii 16 & xv 5 & xxii 17 Chap xxxi 37
ᵉ Ver 20
ᶠ Ver 7 11

17 ¶ For thus ſaith the LORD, † David ſhall never
ᵍ want a man to ſit upon the throne of the houſe of Iſ-
rael 18 Neither ſhall the prieſts the Levites, want a
man before me to offer burnt-offerings, and to kindle
meat offerings, and to do ſacrifice continually 19 ¶
And the word of the LORD came unto Jeremiah,
ſaying, 20 Thus ſaith the LORD, ʰ If you can break
my covenant of the day, and my covenant of the night,
and that there ſhould not be day and night in their ſea-
ſon 21 *Then* may alſo my covenant be broken with
David my ſervant, ⁱ that he ſhould not have a ſon to
reign upon his throne, and with the Levites the prieſts,
my miniſters 22 As ᵈ the hoſt of heaven cannot be
numbred, neither the ſand of the ſea meaſured ſo will
I multiply the ſeed of David my ſervant, and the Le-
vites that miniſter unto me 23 Moreover, the word
of the LORD came to Jeremiah, ſaying, 24 Con-
ſidereſt thou not what this people have ſpoken, ſaying,
The two families which the LORD hath choſen, he
hath even caſt them off? thus they have deſpiſed my
people, that they ſhould be no more a nation before
them 25 Thus ſaith the LORD, ᵉ If my covenant
be not with day and night, *and if* I have not appointed
the ordinances of heaven and earth 26 Then will I
caſt away the ſeed of Jacob, and David my ſervant, *ſo*
that I will not take *any* of his ſeed *to be* rulers over the
ſeed of Abraham, Iſaac, and Jacob for ᶠ I will cauſe
their captivity to return, and have mercy on them

v 17—26 In the former verſe, the branch from the root of Jeſſe was promiſed Here the perpetuity of his kingdom is enſured

1 Chriſt's kingdom will be an everlaſting kingdom, for in him alone can the promiſe be fulfilled The houſe of David is long ſince extinct, or at leaſt his deſcendants are utterly unknown, and for near two thouſand years have been without the ſhadow of ſovereignty, but Jeſus reigns, and ſhall for ever ſit on the throne of glory, whilſt ſun and moon endureth, and ſooner ſhall the covenant of day and night be broken, than the covenant of redemption fail, which is eſtabliſhed with this Son of David

2 He will have an everlaſting prieſthood, v 18 of which the Aaronical prieſthood was typical This hath long ſince been aboliſhed, but Chriſt ever liveth to make interceſſion for us, and having offered one ſacrifice for ſin, is gone up into the preſence of God, to plead continually the efficacy of that oblation once offered, and in virtue thereof to obtain eternal redemption for his people, and this ſeems rather the ſenſe of the prophecy, than either the application of it to the Chriſtian miniſtry, or to believers in general, who are indeed a holy prieſthood ordained to offer up ſpiritual ſacrifices, and which will be continued to the end of time

3 God will multiply his ſeed beyond the ſtars of heaven, or the ſand of the ſea ſhore, v 22 *And the Levites that miniſter unto me*, the faithful ſo called, becauſe all of them are his miniſters, conſecrated for him, and offering continually before him, the ſacrifices of prayer and praiſe

4 His church ſhall never fail, or his redeemed people periſh During their captivity, many of the unbelieving Jews in deſpondence, or their enemies in triumph, were ready to conclude that the Lord had caſt off the two families he had choſen, the houſe of David and Aaron, or the two nations of Iſrael and Judah, *thus they have deſpiſed my people*, as if they were abandoned, and no more likely to be a nation, ſwallowed up by their conquerors, and ready to ſink into oblivion But ſooner ſhall the ſucceſſion of day and night be at an end, or the revolutions of the heavenly bodies be interrupted, than the ſeed of Jacob be caſt off, or a ruler of their own nation be wanting to reign over them, when God, as he hath declared, ſhall in mercy turn their captivity What God did in bringing his people from Babylon but imperfectly anſwers the greatneſs of this promiſe, and therefore we muſt look farther to the church of his redeemed, the Iſrael of God, who, whatever ſtate of ſufferings they may for a while be expoſed to, ſhall ſtill be preſerved under the government of Chriſt their king their captivity from the bondage of corruption God will cauſe to return, and though under Antichriſtian tyranny they may groan, God will break the yoke from off their necks, ſo that neither men nor devils ſhall ever be able to root out their memorial from the earth We ſee the church of Chriſt hath, in virtue of this promiſe, ſtood the fierceſt fires of perſecution during more than ſeventeen hundred years, and we may reſt aſſured ſhe will not only be preſerved to the end, and every member thereof, but that her latter end ſhall have great increaſe, and all her enemies be made her footſtool

CHAP XXXIV

In this chapter we have two meſſages which God ſent by Jeremiah (1) One to foretel the fate of Zedekiah king of Judah, that he ſhould fall into the hands of the king of Babylon, and live and die in captivity, ver 1—7 (2) *Another to read the doom both of prince and people for bringing back their ſervants into bondage, whom they had releaſed according to the law*, ver 8—11 *therefore God will bring the Chaldean army upon them again, when they began to hope they were got clear of them*, ver 12—22

ᵃ 2 Kings xxv 1 & Chap xxxix 1 & lii 4
† Heb The dominion of his hand
ᵇ Chap xxxii 3
ᶜ Chap xxxii 29 & xxxvii 10 & xxxix 8
ᵈ Chap xxxii 4
‡ Heb His mouth ſhall ſpeak to thy mouth
ᵉ 2 Chron xvi 14 & xxi 19
ᶠ Chap xxii 18

1 THE word which came unto Jeremiah from the
LORD, (ᵃ when Nebuchadnezzar king of Ba-
bylon, and all his army, and all the kingdoms of the earth
† of his dominion, and all the people fought againſt
Jeruſalem, and againſt all the cities thereof) ſaying,
2 Thus ſaith the LORD the God of Iſrael, Go, and
ſpeak to Zedekiah king of Judah, and tell him, Thus
ſaith the LORD, Behold, ᵇ I will give this city into the
hand of the king of Babylon, and ᶜ he ſhall burn it with
fire 3 And ᵈ thou ſhalt not eſcape out of his hand,
but ſhalt ſurely be taken, and delivered into his hand,
and thine eyes ſhall behold the eyes of the king of Ba-
bylon, and ‡ he ſhall ſpeak with thee mouth to mouth,
and thou ſhalt go to Babylon. 4 Yet hear the word
of the LORD, O Zedekiah king of Judah, Thus ſaith
the LORD of thee, Thou ſhalt not die by the ſword,
5 *But* thou ſhalt die in peace, and with ᵉ the burnings
of thy fathers the former kings which were before thee,
ſo ſhall they burn *odours* for thee, and ᶠ they will lament
thee, *ſaying*, Ah lord for I have pronounced the word,
ſaith the LORD 6 Then Jeremiah the prophet ſpake
all theſe words unto Zedekiah king of Judah in Jeruſalem,
7 When the king of Babylon's army fought againſt
Jeruſalem, and againſt all the cities of Judah that were
left, againſt Lachiſh, and againſt Azekah for theſe
defenced cities remained of the cities of Judah

Before Christ 605

v 1—7 This prophecy in its date precedes the former, being, it seems, the cause of Jeremiah's commitment to the court of the prison, *chap* xxxii 2—5 It was directed particularly to Zedekiah, and, though a king, the prophet faithfully delivered it, *v* 6 for they who will be true to their trust must not flatter nor fear the greatest Matters were now brought to a very desperate point but two cities, Azekah and Lachish, remained to Judah, and these, as well as Jerusalem, were now invested by the army of Nebuchadnezzar, *v* 7 yet Zedekiah and the people persisted in their obstinacy, and refused to surrender Hereupon,

1 Their doom is read Jerusalem should be burnt to the ground, himself made a prisoner, and, though attempting to escape, shall be seized and brought to the king of Babylon, and carried by him into a miserable captivity the just punishment of his rebellion against Nebuchadnezzar, and disobedience to the warnings of God

2 A gleam of mercy breaks through the gloom God assures him, and his word cannot fail, he shall not be put to death, but *die in peace*, on his bed, treated kindly by the king of Babylon, or, it may be, *in peace* with God, his sufferings in Babylon having been blessed to bring about his repentance, and, though a captive, he should be honourably interred, with the usual respect paid to the kings of Judah, and with the lamentations of the people, deeply afflicted with his loss *Note*, They who at last, though late, return to God, will find peace with him, and, however severe their afflictions may have been, they will have reason to bless God for them as their chief mercies The prison that leads to repentance is far preferable to the palace that is the scene of iniquity

8 ¶ *This is* the word that came unto Jeremiah from
† Heb c t. the LORD, after that the king Zedekiah had † made
a covenant with all the people which *were* at Jerusalem,
g Ex xxi 2 Deut xv 12 h Neh v 11 to proclaim g liberty unto them, 9 h That every man
should let his man servant, and every man his maid-
servant, *being* an Hebrew or an Hebrewess, go free,
that none should serve himself of them, *to wit*, of a Jew
his brother 10 Now when all the princes, and all
the people which had entred into the covenant, heard
that every one should let his man-servant, and every one
his maid servant go free, that none should serve them-
selves of them any more, then they obeyed and let *them*
599. go 11 But afterwards they turned and caused the ser-
vants and the handmaids, whom they had let go free,
to return, and brought them into subjection for servants
and for handmaids 12 ¶ Therefore the word of the
LORD came to Jeremiah from the LORD, saying,
13 Thus saith the LORD, the God of Israel, I made
a covenant with your fathers in the day that I brought
them forth out of the land of Egypt, out of the house
i Ex xxi 2 & xxiii 10 Deut xv 12 of bondmen, saying, 14 i At the end of seven years,
let ye go every man his brother an Hebrew, which
‡ Or hath sold himself ‡ hath been sold unto thee, and when he hath served
thee six years, thou shalt let him go free from thee but
your fathers hearkned not unto me, neither inclined their
§ Heb to day ear 15 And ye were § now turned, and had done right
in my sight, in proclaiming liberty every man to his
neighbour, and ye had made a covenant before me in
‖ Heb Upon which my name is called Chap vii 10 k Lev xix 12 the house ‖ which is called by my name 16 But ye
turned k and polluted my name, and caused every man
his servant, and every man his handmaid, whom he had
set at liberty at their pleasure, to return, and brought
them into subjection, to be unto you for servants and for
handmaids 17 Therefore thus saith the LORD, Ye
have not hearkned unto me in proclaiming liberty every
one to his brother, and every man to his neighbour
l Matt vii 2 Gal vi 7 Jam ii 13 behold, l I proclaim a liberty for you, saith the LORD,
to the sword, to the pestilence, and to the famine, and
† Heb for a removing m Deut xxviii 25, 64 Chap xxix 18 I will make you † to be m removed into all the kingdoms
of the earth 18 And I will give the men that have
transgressed my covenant, which have not performed the
words of the covenant which they had made before me,
n Gen xv 10 17 when n they cut the calf in twain, and passed between
the parts thereof, 19 The princes of Judah, and the
princes of Jerusalem, the eunuchs, and the priests, and
all the people of the land which passed between the parts
of the calf, 20 I will even give them into the hand of
their enemies, and into the hand of them that seek their
o Chap vii 33 & xvi 4 & xix 7 life, and o their dead bodies shall be for meat unto the
fowls of the heaven, and to the beasts of the earth
21 And Zedekiah king of Judah, and his princes, will
I give into the hand of their enemies, and into the hand
of them that seek their life, and into the hand of the
king of Babylon's army p which are gone up from you
Before Christ 605
22 q Behold I will command, saith the LORD, and cause
them to return to this city, and they shall fight against p Chap xxxvii 5, 11
it, and take it, and burn it with fire, and I will make q Chap xxxvii 8 10
the cities of Judah a desolation without an inhabitant

v 8—22 This prophecy was delivered during that interval when Nebuchadnezzar had raised the siege of Jerusalem to go to meet the army of Egypt which was advancing to relieve it

1 The occasion of the prophecy was their unjust and hypocritical conduct towards their servants The law had enjoined them every seventh year to release their brethren, who for poverty or debt had been sold for bondmen, in gratitude for their own deliverance from Egypt But this, amongst their other sins, their fathers had neglected, *v* 14 and they kept them still in servitude, notwithstanding the year of release was passed and, custom having authorised the evil, it was become general But, when the Chaldean army besieged the city, as the prophets no doubt had before rebuked them for such an avowed disobedience to the law, they now laid the matter to heart, convinced of the evil of the practice, and an edict was published by the king, princes, and people, for a general release, and, to confirm it, they made a solemn covenant in the temple to abide by God's law for the future, passing between the parts of the divided calf, as imprecating God's wrath, that they might be thus cut asunder, if they failed of performing their engagement In consequence of this, all their servants and handmaids were let free, as was right in God's sight, *v* 15 but when the siege was raised, and the storm seemed to be blown over, they again forced them to return to servitude, committing a most flagrant piece of injustice to them, playing a part most hypocritical and affronting to God, and justly bringing upon their heads the curse of a broken covenant *Note*, (1) The reformations which fear and danger make are seldom sincere or abiding (2) The most solemn bonds and vows will not long restrain those whose hearts are not right with God (3) If God's reprieves are abused, and made an encouragement to persist in the ways of wickedness, he will then proceed to execution, for none ever yet hardned their hearts against him and prospered

2 God pronounces judgment upon them for this treacherous dealing He dismisses them from his service and protection, *v* 17 devotes them to famine, pestilence, and the sword, the men who have transgressed the covenant shall be as the calf they divided, even the princes of Judah and Jerusalem, the eunuchs, the priests, and all the people of the Land, who had *so solemnly* sworn to observe it, *v* 18, 19 Given up into the hands of the Chaldeans, they are doomed to a miserable death, their carcases unburied, shall be cast as dung upon the earth, and be meat for the beasts and birds Nor may they think, because the king of Babylon is gone up from them, that they are safe He shall return instantly, besiege, storm, and burn Jerusalem, with all the other cities of Judah, spread desolation on the land, and leave it as an uninhabited wilderness, dragging Zedekiah and his princes, with the remnant that escape the sword, into an ignominious captivity, to know themselves the miseries of that servitude which they had made so heavy to their brethren *Note*, (1) The sinner's security is a sad presage of his destruction (2) Promising beginnings, to which the end does not correspond, only bring more aggravated guilt, and surer destruction Apostates, who were once professors, shall receive greater damnation

CHAP XXXV.

A variety of methods is tried to awaken the Jews to a sense of their sin, and to bring them to repentance and reformation (1) He sets before them the unshaken perseverance of the family of the Rechabites in their obedience to the commands of Jonadab their ancestor, ver 1—11 *(2) With this he aggravates their disobedience to God, and contempt of his precepts,* ver 12—15 *(3) He foretels the judgments of God upon the Jews for their impious disobedience,* ver 16, 17 *(4) He assures the Rechabites of the blessing of God upon them, for their pious obedience to their father,* ver 18, 19

1. THE word which came unto Jeremiah from the 606
LORD, in the days of Jehoiakim, the son of
Josiah king of Judah, saying, 2 Go unto the house
of a the Rechabites, and speak unto them, and bring a 2 Kings x. 15. 1 Chron. ii 55
them into the house of the LORD, into one of the cham-
bers, and give them wine to drink 3 Then I took
Jaazaniah, the son of Jeremiah, the son of Habaziniah,
and his brethren, and all his sons, and the whole house
of the Rechabites 4 And I brought them into the
house of the LORD, into the chamber of the sons of
Hanan, the son of Igdaliah a man of God, which *was*
by the chamber of the princes, which *was* above the
chamber of Maaseiah the son of Shallum, the keeper of
the door 5 And I set before the sons of the house
of the Rechabites pots full of wine, and cups, and I said
unto them, Drink ye wine. 6 But they said, We will

Before Chriſt 606 drink no wine for [c] Jonadab the ſon of Rechab our
father commanded us, ſaying, Ye ſhall drink no wine,
b 2 Kings x 15 *neither* ye, nor your ſons for ever 7 Neither ſhall ye
build houſe, nor ſow ſeed, nor plant vineyard, nor have
c Ex xx 12 Eph vi 2. *any* but all your days ye ſhall dwell in tents, [c] that ye
may live many days in the land where ye *be* ſtrangers
d Mal i 6 8 [d] Thus have we obeyed the voice of Jonadab the ſon
of Rechab our father, in all that he hath charged us, to
drink no wine all our days, we, our wives, our ſons, nor
our daughters, 9 Nor to build houſes for us to dwell
e 1 Tim vi 6 in [e] neither have we vineyard, nor field, nor ſeed 10
But we have dwelt in tents, and have obeyed, and done
according to all that Jonadab our father commanded us
11 But it came to paſs when Nebuchadnezzar king of
Babylon came up into the land, that we ſaid, Come,
and let us go to Jeruſalem for fear of the army of the
Chaldeans, and for fear of the army of the Syrians ſo
we dwell at Jeruſalem.

v 1—11 The date of this chapter ſeems to be about the fourth year of Jehoiakim, when, on account of his rebellion, Nebuchadnezzar invaded the land, and about ſeventeen years before the preceding prophecies were delivered

The Rechabites here mentioned were Kenites, of the poſterity of Hobab, Moſes's father-in-law, 1 *Chron* ii 55 *Judg* i 16 one family of which, denominated from Rechab their great progenitor, obſerved ſome peculiar rites, enjoined them by Jonadab, the ſon or lineal deſcendant of Rechab, a man famous for his piety in the days of Jehu, about 300 years before this time, 2 *Kings* x 15, 16

1. The injunctions Jonadab laid on them were, *to drink no wine*, and *dwell in tents*, having neither houſes nor land, nor vineyard, nor tillage, but to devote themſelves to a paſtoral life, remote from the buſy world, where corruption and vice moſt abound, and thereby be farther removed from temptation as they were *ſtrangers in the land*, they muſt be content with their lot, and deſire no great things, nor ſeek to accumulate wealth, which might provoke the envy of the people among whom they dwelt luxury alſo, the bane of body and ſoul, would thus be baniſhed from them, and, accuſtomed to hard fare, they would be the better able to meet the days of calamity, which the ſins of the land where they ſojourned were bringing upon them *Note*, (1) Though God hath not forbid us wine, temperance will dictate caution and ſelf-denial (2) It is deſirable to ſit looſe to this preſent world, and the leſs we have in it, generally, the leſs unwilling we ſhall be to part from it (3) They who are ſtrangers upon earth muſt never think of taking up their reſt below, but be ready, at a moment's warning, to put off this tabernacle

2 The Rechabites ſtrictly obſerved Jonadab's rule Men, women, and children, were all a family of Nazarites and tho' they were now obliged through neceſſity, by reaſon of the invaſion, to diſpenſe with one part of their father's injunctions, and had for ſafety retired to Jeruſalem, yet not with an intention to take up their abode there longer than the danger threatned and as for the other, they ſtill religiouſly obſerved it, and therefore, though urged by the prophet to drink, who had invited them together into one of the chambers of the temple, and ſet before them pot of wine, they abſolutely refuſed, and pleaded their father's order as the reaſon of their conduct *Note*, When there is a ſpirit of real ſobriety, the wine, even when it ſparkles, will have no influence, nor the ſollicitations of others be able to extort a compliance with the leaſt exceſs

12 ¶ Then came the word of the LORD unto Jere-
miah, ſaying, 13 Thus ſaith the LORD of hoſts, the
God of Iſrael, Go, and tell the men of Judah, and the
inhabitants of Jeruſalem, Will ye not receive inſtruction
to hearken to my words, ſaith the LORD 14 The
words of Jonadab the ſon of Rechab, that he commanded
his ſons not to drink wine, are performed; for unto this
day they drink none, but obey their father's command-
f 2 Chron xxxvi 15 ment [f] notwithſtanding I have ſpoken unto you, [g] riſing
g Chap vii 13 25 & xi 7 early, and ſpeaking, but ye hearkned not unto me
15 I have ſent alſo unto you all my ſervants the pro-
h Chap xviii 11 & xxv 5 phets, riſing up early and ſending *them*, ſaying, [h] Return
ye now every man from his evil way, and amend your
i Pſ xxxvii 27 Iſa i 19 doings, and go not after other gods to ſerve them, [i] and
ye ſhall dwell in the land, which I have given to you,
and to your fathers but ye have not inclined your ear,
nor hearkned unto me 16 Becauſe the ſons of Jonadab
the ſon of Rechab have performed the commandment
of their father, which he commanded them; but this
people hath not hearkned unto me 17 Therefore
thus ſaith the LORD God of hoſts, the God of Iſrael,
Behold, I will bring upon Judah, and upon all the in-
habitants of Jeruſalem, all the evil that I have pro- Before Chriſt 606
nounced againſt them becauſe [k] I have ſpoken unto
them, but they have not heard, and I have called unto k Prov i 24 Chap vii 13, 25
them, but they have not anſwered 18 ¶ And Jere-
miah ſaid unto the houſe of the Rechabites, Thus ſaith
the LORD of hoſts, the God of Iſrael, Becauſe ye have
obeyed the commandment of Jonadab your father, and
kept all his precepts, and done according to all that he
hath commanded you 19 Therefore thus ſaith the
LORD of hoſts, the God of Iſrael, † Jonadab the ſon of † Heb There ſhall not a man be cut off from Jonadab &
Rechab ſhall not want a man to ſtand before me for ever

v 12—19 It was not the prophet's intention to draw the Rechabites into a breach of their rule, but to ſet them forth as an example to Iſrael

1 The obedience of the Rechabites to their father ſerved to aggravate the rebellion of the Jews againſt the commands of God The commands of Jonadab, a mere man, were kept, the words of the eternal God diſregarded his injunctions, deſcending only by tradition, had more influence over his poſterity, than God's written laws, urged by a ſucceſſion of prophets daily inculcating their obſervance on the Jews It was a real piece of ſelf-denial the ſon of Rechab enjoined, in a matter before lawful, whereas what God had forbidden was highly criminal, and what he commanded would be their real comfort The Rechabites had no particular obligation to Jonadab to enforce their obedience, whilſt every thing Iſrael poſſeſſed in Canaan came from God's bounty, and was held on condition of their fidelity, ſo that both gratitude and duty ſhould have engaged them to obſerve God's commandments

2 The Jews are threatned for their diſobedience and baſe ingratitude The Rechabites ſhall riſe up in judgment and condemn them, and God will execute upon them all the threatnings he hath pronounced ſince they remained incorrigible, and would neither by admonitions nor corrections be warned and led unto repentance *Note*, Though vengeance is ſlow in coming, it is ſure to all that abide impenitent

3 The Rechabites are commended and rewarded for their dutiful obedience to their father Jonadab's commands *Jonadab the ſon of Rechab ſhall not want a man to ſtand before me for ever.* As long as Iſrael was a nation his poſterity ſhould continue in it, or perhaps to the end of time, the family, though now mixed with the Jews, being not extinct, or it may have reſpect to better days, when they ſhould be converted by the preaching of the goſpel, and, among other faithful ſouls, to the end of time *ſtand before the Lord*, to offer the ſpiritual ſacrifices of prayer and praiſe *Note*, Nothing entails more ſurely a bleſſing on children than their dutiful obſervance of their pious parents inſtructions

CHAP XXXVI

Here is another expedient tried to work upon this heedleſs and untoward people, but it is tried in vain (1) Baruch writes in a roll all Jeremiah's prophecies from his own mouth, ver 1—4. (2) He reads it publickly to the people, ver 5—10 and privately to the princes, ver 11—19 afterwards Jehudi reads it to the king, ver 20, 21 (3) The king burns it, and orders Jeremiah and Baruch to be proſecuted, ver 22—26 (4) Baruch writes in another roll all that was contained in the former, and adjoins the king's doom for burning the roll, ver 27—32

1 AND it came to paſs in the fourth year of Jehoi- 606
akim, the ſon of Joſiah king of Judah, *that* this
word came unto Jeremiah from the LORD, ſaying,
2 Take thee [a] a roll of a book, and [b] write therein all a Iſa viii 1
the words that I have ſpoken unto thee againſt Iſrael, and b Chap. xxx 2
againſt Judah, and againſt all the nations, from the day
I ſpake unto thee, [c] from the days of Joſiah, even unto c Chap xxv
this day 3 It may be that the houſe of Judah will hear 3
all the evil which I purpoſe to do unto them, that they
may return every man from his evil way, that I may for-
give their iniquity and their ſin 4 Then Jeremiah call-
ed Baruch the ſon of Neriah, and Baruch [d] wrote from d Ver 18 Chap xlv 1
the mouth of Jeremiah, all the words of the LORD,
which he had ſpoken unto him, upon a roll of a book
5 And Jeremiah commanded Baruch, ſaying, I *am* ſhut
up, I cannot go into the houſe of the LORD 6 There-
fore go thou and read in the roll, which thou haſt written
from my mouth, the words of the LORD, in the ears
of the people, in the LORD's houſe [e] upon the faſting- e Lev xvi 29 or xxiii
day and alſo thou ſhalt read them in the ears of all Judah, 27
that come out of their cities 7 It may be † they will
preſent their ſupplication before the LORD, and will re- † Heb Their ſupplication ſhall fall
turn every one from his evil way, for great *is* the anger
and fury that the LORD hath pronounced againſt this Chap xxxvii 20
people 8 And Baruch the ſon of Neriah did accord-
ing

Before Chriſt 606 ing to all that Jeremiah the prophet commanded him,
reading in the book the words of the LORD in the
LORD's houſe

v. 1—8 The date of this prophecy is the fourth year of Jehoiakim, about the ſame time the foregoing tranſaction happened

1 Jeremiah is ordered to take a roll of a book, ſo called becauſe they wrote on ſheets of vellum or parchment, which they rolled one over the other In this volume he muſt write all his ſermons and prophecies, delivered during a courſe of two and twenty years concerning Iſrael and Judah, and all the nations, that the people might hear once more a repetition of all the warnings and admonitions ſo ſolemnly given them, is the moſt likely method to work upon their obdurate hearts, when they heard the evil threatned, and be induced thereby to turn from the wickedneſs they had committed, which if they did, notwithſtanding all their provocations, God was ſtill ready to pardon all that was paſt Not that the expreſſion *it may be* implies any uncertainty in the divine preſcience; but the prophet muſt uſe the moſt probable means, and leave them at leaſt without excuſe, if they perſiſted in their ſins *Note*, (1) We have abundant cauſe to bleſs God for cauſing his word to be written, and not left to uncertain tradition (2) Nothing can work upon the ſinner's heart, if God's word doth not (3) The certain ruin ſin will bring upon us ſhould deter us from it (4) Whenever a ſinner by grace returns to God, all his iniquity, however great and aggravated, ſhall be forgiven him

2 Jeremiah inſtantly obeys, and employs Baruch as his amanuenſis, probably as the readier ſcribe, and being himſelf *ſhut up*, either confined by the king's order, or ſome indiſpoſition, from appearing at the temple Baruch muſt take the roll, and read all the contents of it in the Lord's houſe, when the people were aſſembled together *on the faſting-day*, mentioned *v* 9 or the great day of atonement, and alſo in the ears of all Judah, who came up out of their cities at the feaſt of tabernacles, or it may refer to the ſame time when, on occaſion of the faſt, they aſſembled at the temple *It may be they will preſent their ſupplication before the Lord*, affected with what they hear, and ſeek to him to avert the impending judgments, *and will return every man from his evil way*, turning to God ere the terrible threatnings pronounced take place. and Baruch failed not punctually to perform the prophet's orders *Note*, (1) Whenever the conſcience is awakened with a ſenſe of ſin, it will appear by an immediate application to God in prayer (2) The formalities of religion are often obſerved where the power of it is loſt, but this only more fatally deceives ſinners to their ruin

605. 9 And it came to paſs in the fifth year of Jehoiakim
the ſon of Joſiah king of Judah, in the ninth month,
f Ver 6 *that* they proclaimed f a faſt before the LORD to all the
people in Jeruſalem, and to all the people that came from
g Ver 8 the cities of Judah unto Jeruſalem 10 Then g read
Baruch in the book, the words of Jeremiah in the houſe
of the LORD, in the chamber of Gemariah, the ſon of
h Chap xxvi 10 Shaphan the ſcribe, in the higher court, h at the † entry
† Or door of the new gate of the LORD's houſe, in the ears of all
the people 11 ¶ When Michaiah the ſon of Gemariah
the ſon of Shaphan, had heard out of the book all
the words of the LORD, 12 Then he went down into
the king's houſe into the ſcribes chamber, and lo, all
the princes ſat there, *even* Eliſhama the ſcribe, and Delaiah
the ſon of Shemaiah, and Elnathan the ſon of Achbor,
and Gemariah the ſon of Shaphan, and Zedekiah
the ſon of Hananiah, and all the princes 13 Then
Michaiah declared unto them all the words that he had
heard when Baruch read the book in the ears of the people
14 Therefore all the princes ſent Jehudi the ſon
of Nethaniah, the ſon of Shelemiah, the ſon of Cuſhi,
unto Baruch, ſaying, Take in thine hand the roll wherein
thou haſt read in the ears of the people, and come
So Baruch the ſon of Neriah took the roll in his hand,
and came unto them 15 And they ſaid unto him, Sit
down now, and read it in our ears. So Baruch read *it*
in their ears 16 Now it came to paſs when they had
i Acts xxiv 25 heard all the words, they i were afraid, both one and
other, and ſaid unto Baruch, We will ſurely tell the king
of all theſe words 17 And they aſked Baruch, ſaying,
Tell us now, How didſt thou write all theſe words at his
mouth? 18 Then Baruch anſwered them, He pronounced
k Ver 4 all theſe words unto me with his mouth, k and
I wrote *them* with ink in the book 19 Then ſaid the
princes unto Baruch, Go hide thee, thou and Jeremiah,
and let no man know where ye *be*

v. 9—19 Some have ſuppoſed the faſting-day, *v* 6 was the ſame as *v* 9 and that the time, between the date of Jeremiah's being commanded to write and this reading, was employed in finiſhing the roll, for, if the ninth month refers not to Jehoiakim's reign but to the eccleſiaſtical year, his fifth year beginning in the ſeventh month, this might be only two months after Nor can it well be ſuppoſed but that, if it had been read ſome months before, *ſee* ver 1, 6 it would have come, ere this time, to the princes ears, otherwiſe this was the ſecond or third time of its being read, ſee *v* 6 line upon line and precept upon precept being needful for thoſe ſo dull of hearing We have, Before Chriſt 605

1 An extraordinary faſt proclaimed, on account, probably, of the threatned invaſion, *to all the people of Judah and Jeruſalem*, or, as the text ſeems to intimate, it was at their requeſt, *they proclaimed a faſt, even all the people*, &c *Note*, National faſts, without national reformation, will never turn away national judgments

2 Baruch, on that ſolemn occaſion, read out of the roll, at a window, or from a balcony, adjoining to Gemariah's chamber, in the audience of all the people who were in the court of the temple below

3 Michaiah, the ſon of Gemariah, who ſeems to have been affected with what he heard, ſoon carried the report to the king's houſe, where the princes were aſſembled, who ſeemed to have left the concerns of religion to the people, and to have been themſelves engaged in conſultation, for it courts to be godly is too commonly unfaſhionable Startled at the contents of the diſcourſe, he repeated them, and thereupon they deſire Baruch to attend them, and read over the words of the roll, with which he readily complied, not afraid of men's faces when God's word was to be delivered *Note*, (1) The diſcourſe that hath affected our own ſouls may often be profitably repeated for others good (2) They who are the faithful miniſters of Chriſt muſt be ready to bear their teſtimony, if called thereto, even before kings, and not be aſhamed

4 The princes appear greatly ſtruck with the words Baruch read, terrified at the threatned judgment, *both one and other*, good and bad, or *a man to his friend*, amazed, and looking at one another, as if enquiring what was to be done in the caſe Their general reſolution was to inform the king, to whoſe ill affections they were not ſtrangers, and therefore, thoſe who were gracious men at leaſt, juſtly apprehending he would be exaſperated, adviſed Baruch and Jeremiah to conceal themſelves, leſt, in his anger, he ſhould murder them But firſt, to gain the fulleſt ſatisfaction to themſelves, and to anſwer the enquiries the king might make, they enquire how he wrote theſe diſcourſes, and Baruch informs them Jeremiah pronounced, and he wrote from his mouth, which ſome regard as an idle queſtion, but ſeems to ariſe from a difficulty ſtarted, how Jeremiah could recollect ſo many diſcourſes, containing ſuch a variety of matter, the remembrance of which ſo exactly might give them a ſtronger conviction of the inſpiration under which he ſpoke

20 ¶ And they went in to the king into the court,
but they laid up the roll in the chamber of Eliſhama
the ſcribe, and told all the words in the ears of the king
21 So the king ſent Jehudi to fetch the roll, and he
took it out of Eliſhama the ſcribe's chamber, and Jehudi
read it in the ears of the king, and in the ears of
all the princes which ſtood beſide the king 22 Now
the king ſat l in the winter-houſe, in the ninth month, l Judg iii 20 Am iii. 15
and *there was a fire* on the hearth burning before him
23 And it came to paſs, *that* when Jehudi had read
three or four leaves, m he cut it with the penknife and m 2 Tim iv. 3
caſt *it* into the fire that *was* on the hearth, untill all the
roll was conſumed in the fire that was on the hearth
24. Yet they were not afraid, nor n rent their garments, n 2 Kings xxii 11.
neither the king, nor any of his ſervants that heard all
theſe words 25 Nevertheleſs Elnathan, and Delaiah,
and Gemariah had made interceſſion to the king, that
he would not burn the roll, but he would not hear them
26 But the king commanded Jerahmeel the ſon ‖ of ‖ Or of the king
Hammelech, and Seraiah the ſon of Azriel, and Shelemiah o 1 Kings xix 11
the ſon of Abdeel, o to take Baruch the ſcribe, and p Pſ cxxi 8
Jeremiah the prophet but p the LORD hid them 27 Chap i 19. Ver 19
¶ Then the word of the LORD came to Jeremiah (after
that the king had burnt the roll, and the words which
Baruch wrote at the mouth of Jeremiah) ſaying, 28
q Take thee again another roll, and write in it all the q Chap xxvii 13 14 2 Tim. ii 9
former words that were in the firſt roll, which Jehoiakim
the king of Judah hath burnt 29 And thou ſhalt ſay
to Jehoiakim king of Judah, Thus ſaith the LORD,
Thou haſt burnt this roll, ſaying, r Why haſt thou written r Chap xxxii 3.
therein, ſaying, The king of Babylon ſhall certainly
come and deſtroy this land, and ſhall cauſe to ceaſe from
thence man and beaſt? 30. Therefore thus ſaith the
LORD, of Jehoiakim king of Judah, s He ſhall have s Chap xxii 30
none to ſit upon the throne of David, and his dead body
ſhall t be caſt out in the day to the heat, and in the night t Chap xxii 19

Before Christ 605.

to the frost 31 And I will ‡ punish him and his
seed, and his servants, for their iniquity, and I will
bring upon them, and upon the inhabitants of Jerusalem,
and upon the men of Judah, all the evil that I have pro-
nounced against them, but they hearkened not 32 ¶
Then took Jeremiah another roll, and gave it to Baruch
the scribe the son of Neriah, ᵘ who wrote therein, from
the mouth of Jeremiah, all the words of the book which
Jehoiakim king of Judah had burnt in the fire, and there
were added besides unto them § many like words

‡ Heb Visit upon. ᵘ Ver 4, 18. § Heb Words as they.

v 20—32 Whilst Baruch was departed to secrete himself, the princes went into the court to the king, to inform him of what had passed, having carefully laid up the roll in Elishama's chamber, and he, curious to hear in full what they had summarily reported, immediately dispatched Jehudi for the roll, and bid him read it in his hearing, and before the princes who were with him Whereupon he gave an account,

1 Of Jehoiakim's daring impiety Two or three leaves were enough to enrage him, and, a fire being on the hearth before him, he cut the roll in pieces and burnt it, or Jehudi, who read it, did it at his command, he could not with patience hear such terrible denunciations obstinate in his sins, he would not bear to be rebuked, but vented the enmity of his heart against God and his prophets, and hoped to disappoint the predictions, or prevent the knowledge of them from spreading among the people *Note*, The despisers of God's word are among those who seem most surely given up to a reprobate mind

2 The princes who were present testified no horror or detestation at this shocking sight those who were in attendance on the king, not those who came up from Elishama's chamber, seem chiefly intended, at least these were deterred from expressing any becoming zeal for fear of offending three of them however, *v* 25 with humility interceded with the king not to burn the roll, but he was as deaf to their intreaties as to the prophet's warnings, *v* 25 *Note*, They who silently sit by, without testifying their abhorrence of the sins they see committed, are partakers in the guilt

3 Not content with having cut to pieces and burnt the roll, the king in his fury would probably have served the authors no better if he could have seized them, for which he issues immediate orders, *but the Lord hid them* whatever care they had taken to conceal themselves, it had been ineffectual, if the special providence of God had not watched over them and rescued them from the malice of this impious king *Note*, They who, for God's cause, boldly put their lives in their hand are often wonderfully protected by him, and saved from the fury of their persecutors

4 Jeremiah has a fresh order to write again the same words in another roll The burning the former can neither prevent the judgments approaching, nor destroy the word of God Jehoiakim was enraged to be told that his country should be destroyed, and left desolate without man and beast, and, not believing it himself, would have others regard it as a falsehood but it is a fact that will be shortly verified, and himself, his family, and servants, meet their deserved doom He shall be slain with the Chaldean sword, and his corps ignominiously exposed, be refused burial, and left to rot a putrid carcase on the earth, his seed be cut off, that none of his posterity should ever sit on the throne of David, his son Jeconiah, in three months, being dragged into captivity and written childless, and all the evils, threatned against Judah and Jerusalem terribly overtake them, according to the purport of the words written in the roll which was burnt Another is provided, the same words dictated by Jeremiah, and written by Baruch, with additions of many others like them So that, instead of disappointing the divine decrees, Jehoiakim only added fresh aggravations to his guilt, and drew heavier vengeance on his head *Note*, They who contend with God, and obstinately resist his counsel, only treasure up for themselves wrath against the day of wrath

CHAP XXXVII

In this chapter we have, (1) *A general idea of the ill character of Zedekiah's reign*, ver 1, 2 (2) *The message which he sent to Jeremiah to desire his prayers*, ver 3 (3) *The flattering hopes which the people had conceived, that the Chaldeans would quit the siege of Jerusalem*, ver 5 (4) *The assurance God gave them by Jeremiah (who was now at liberty*, ver 4) *that the Chaldean army should renew the siege and take the city*, ver 6—10 (5) *The imprisonment of Jeremiah, under pretence that he was a deserter*, ver 11—15 *The kindness which Zedekiah shewed him in his imprisonment*, ver 16—21

598.

1 AND ᵃ king Zedekiah the son of Josiah reigned
in stead of Coniah the son of Jehoiakim, whom
Nebuchadnezzar king of Babylon made king in the land
of Judah 2 ᵇ But neither he, ᶜ nor his servants, nor
the people of the land, did hearken unto the word of the

ᵃ 2 Kings xxiv 17. 2 Chron xxxvi 10. Chap xxii. 24. ᵇ 2 Chron. xxxvi 12, 14. ᶜ Prov xxix 12.

Before Christ 598.

LORD, which he spake by the prophet Jeremiah 3
And Zedekiah the king sent Jehucal the son of She-
lemiah, and ᵈ Zephaniah the son of Maaseiah the
priest, to the prophet Jeremiah, saying, ᵉ Pray now
unto the LORD our God for us 4 Now Jeremiah
came in and went out among the people for they had
not put him into prison 5 Then Pharaoh's army was
come forth out of Egypt and ᶠ when the Chaldeans that
besieged Jerusalem, heard tidings of them, they departed
from Jerusalem 6 ¶ Then came the word of the
LORD unto the prophet Jeremiah, saying, 7 Thus
saith the LORD, the God of Israel, Thus shall ye say
to the king of Judah, ᵍ that sent you unto me to enquire
of me, Behold, Pharaoh's army, which is come forth to
help you, ʰ shall return to Egypt into their own land
8 And ⁱ the Chaldeans shall come again, and fight a-
gainst this city, and take it, ᵏ and burn it with fire
9 Thus saith the LORD, Deceive not your † selves,
saying, The Chaldeans shall surely depart from us for
they shall not depart 10 For though ye had smitten
the whole army of the Chaldeans that fight against you,
and there remained *but* ‡ wounded men among them,
ˡ *yet* should they rise up every man in his tent, and burn
this city with fire

599. ᵈ Chap xxix 25. ᵉ Chap xxi. ᶠ Chap xxxiv. 21. ᵍ Chap xxi. ʰ Prov xxi 30. ⁱ Chap xxxiv 22. ᵏ Chap xxxiv 22. † Heb Souls. ‡ Heb Thrust through. ˡ Chap xliv 20.

v 1—10 When Nebuchadnezzar had slain Jehoiakim, and taken away Coniah his son, that shadow of royalty, he placed on the throne Zedekiah, a younger son of Josiah

1 His ill conduct is remarked, *v* 2 He copied too closely after his evil predecessors, and, though he saw in them the fatal consequences of slighting the word of God, he took not warning, neither he nor his courtiers paying any regard to the calls and admonitions delivered by Jeremiah

2 Though he neglected the prophet in his prosperity, when his distresses came upon him, he made application to him, earnestly intreating his prayers, for at that time the prophet enjoyed his liberty, and was not, as afterwards, shut up in prison, *v* 4 The Chaldeans, according to his prediction, had already begun the siege of Jerusalem, but, on hearing that an army of Egyptians were advancing to assist the Jews, though their king returned no more after his first defeat, 2 *Kings* xxiv 7. Nebuchadnezzar marched to give them battle. Zedekiah therefore begs the prophet to interest himself on their behalf, and pray the Lord to defeat the Chaldean army, and prevent their return to Jerusalem *Note*, (1) They who despise God's ministers when in health, and at their ease, are glad to fly to them and beg their prayers in the day of their calamity (2) Many, like Zedekiah, are very earnest to be delivered from their sufferings, who have no heart to part with their sins

3 Jeremiah answers not like a courtier, but, as a prophet, he tells them plainly, the Egyptians shall retreat or be defeated, the Chaldeans return to the siege, and never cease their attacks till they had taken the city and burnt it to the ground Therefore the hopes they entertained were groundless they deceived themselves, when they thought the Chaldeans would no more return, or not be able to succeed in their attempt, for, since God had decreed the fall of Jerusalem, though the Chaldeans had been smitten by them or their confederates, and none remained of their army but wounded men, such vigour would God put into them, that even they should rise up in their tents, whither they had been carried to be dressed, scale the walls, and burn the city with fire *Note*, (1) Sinners usually flatter themselves to their ruin, and easily believe the lie their corrupted hearts wish to be true (2) All human help is vain, when God is against us (3) When God hath work to do, he can make the weakest and most unlikely instruments effectual to accomplish his purpose

11 ¶ ᵐ And it came to pass that when the army of the
Chaldeans was † broken up from Jerusalem for fear of
Pharaoh's army, 12 Then Jeremiah went forth out
of Jerusalem to go into the land of Benjamin, ‡ to sepa-
rate himself thence in the midst of the people 13 And
when he was in the gate of Benjamin, a captain of the
ward *was* there, whose name was Irijah, the son of She-
lemiah, the son of Hananiah, and he took Jeremiah
the prophet, saying, Thou fallest away to the Chaldeans
14 Then said Jeremiah, ⁿ *It is* § false, I fall not away
to the Chaldeans but he hearkened not to him so
Irijah took Jeremiah, and brought him to the princes
15 Wherefore the princes were wroth with Jeremiah
and smote him, and ᵒ put him in prison in the house of
Jonathan the scribe, for they had made that the prison
16 ¶ When Jeremiah was entered ᵖ into the dungeon,
and into the § cabins, and Jeremiah had remained there
many

ᵐ Ver 5. † Heb Made to ascend. ‡ Or, to slip away from thence in the midst of the people. ⁿ Ps xxxv 11. § Heb Falsehood, or a lie. ᵒ Chap xxxviii 6. ᵖ Chap xxxviii 6. § Or, cells.

Before Christ 589

many days 17 Then Zedekiah the king sent and took
him out, and the king asked him secretly in his house,
and said, Is there *any* word from the LORD? and Jere-
miah said, There is for, said he, [q] thou shalt be deli-
vered into the hand of the king of Babylon 18 More-
over, Jeremiah said unto king Zedekiah, [r] What have
I offended against thee, or against thy servants, or against
this people, that ye have put me in prison? 19 Where
are now your prophets which prophesied unto you, say-
ing, The king of Babylon shall not come against you,
nor against this land? 20 Therefore hear now, I pray
thee, O my lord the king, let my supplication, I pray
thee, † be accepted before thee, that thou cause me not
to return to the house of Jonathan the scribe, lest I die
there 21 Then Zedekiah the king commanded that
they should commit Jeremiah [t] into the court of the pri-
son, and [u] that they should give him daily a piece of
bread out of the bakers street, until all the bread in the
city were spent Thus Jeremiah remained in the court
of the prison

[q] Chap xxi 7 & xxxiv 3 [r] Dan vi 22

[s] Chap xxvii 14

† Heb Fall before thee

[t] Chap xxxii 2 [u] Ps xxxiii 19 & xxxvii 19

v 11—21 Shortly after the message he had delivered, foreseeing the impending evils, *Jeremiah began to consult his own safety*, and to this end,

1 He attempted to retire from Jerusalem into Benjamin, perhaps to Anathoth, or some place of safety, *to separate himself* from a people doomed to destruction, or *to slip away thence in the midst of the people*, which probably he thought he might now do unperceived, when multitudes, who had flocked to Jerusalem on the invasion of the Chaldeans, were ready to take the opportunity of their departure, to return again into the country *Note*, When we have no call from God to stay, it is prudent to hide ourselves from the evils we foresee

2 He is arrested as a deserter, and imprisoned A captain, who kept ward at the gate of Benjamin, a descendant of Hananiah, probably the false prophet whose death Jeremiah had foretold, and who seems to have waited to do the prophet a mischief, seized him as he was passing through, and charged him with falling away to the Chaldeans an accusation false and malicious, and which Jeremiah, with all the confidence of conscious innocence, denied, but in vain, he would not let him go, but drew him before the magistrates, too ready to receive any *accusation against a man they hated*, they *condemn him* in a passion, without hearing his defence, and, after beating him, committed him to prison, thrusting him into the dungeon, the worst and most dismal cell of that dark and melancholy abode, where he continued many days *Note*, (1) The purest characters are often blackened with the vilest aspersions, and the best friends of the state reviled and accused as the enemies and betrayers of the nation (2) When prejudice and passion sit on the chair of magistracy, no justice can be hoped for (3) Every lie, however improbable, is easily believed against a man obnoxious for his piety and reproofs (4) It hath been the lot of the best of men to suffer for conscience sake We need not be ashamed of a prison, when such as Jeremiah and Paul have gone thither before us

3 When the Chaldean army returned, Zedekiah's fears drove him once more to seek the prophet's assistance but, being ashamed to have it known, he sent to him secretly from the miserable dungeon where he lay, and asked him if there was *any word from the Lord*? any new revelation made to him, or hope that the Chaldeans would raise the siege And the prophet, *not intimidated by all the rigors of a prison, nor fearing* what might be the consequences of his fidelity, plainly tell him *there is*, not a word of comfort, but of despair, *for, said he, thou shalt be delivered into the hand of the king of Babylon* And, seizing the moment when the king seemed affected with his message, he expostulates with him on the cruelty and injustice of the treatment he had suffered, merely for delivering the word he received from God, which the event had now verified, *v* 18 and upbraids him with the sin and folly of believing those false prophets who had flattered him and the people that the Chaldeans would no more return, when lo, their lies were now manifest to all men, and yet they were honoured and respected, whilst he was persecuted and perishing in a prison *Note*, (1) They who will not hearken to the voice of God's prophets, calling them to repentance, may in vain expect to hear from them messages of peace (2) They deserve to be upbraided with their folly who wilfully shut their eyes to their danger, and chuse their own delusions (3) No danger will discourage those who know the value of God's regard, their life is no longer dear to them, when it must be exposed for their fidelity to him

4 He prefers an earnest request to the king for his enlargement, who could not but be sensible of the injustice of his imprisonment, and such treatment as he had met must shortly, if continued, be his death He begs therefore, with great humility, that at least he may not be remanded to Jonathan's house *Note*, Though we must be ready to part with our lives when God calls, we are bound to use all prudent means for our preservation

5 The king grants his request, yea exceeds it He durst not discharge him, through fear of the princes, but he brings him into the court of the prison, where he was more at liberty, and enjoyed the air and gave orders, notwithstanding the scarcity of provisions, that every day, whilst any bread remained, he should have a loaf for his subsistence Thus his imprisonment really became his mercy, and he was protected both from the famine and the sword, to which those who were at large in the city were exposed *Note*, God can make the events which appeared *most afflictive turn out to us the most substantial blessings*

CHAP XXXVIII

In this chapter, just as in the former, 1 *Jeremiah, for his faithfulness, is put into the dungeon by the princes,* ver 1—6 2 *At the intercession of Ebed-melech the Ethiopian, by special order from the king, he is taken up out of the dungeon, and confined only to the court of the prison,* ver 7—13 3 *He has a private conference with the king upon the present juncture of affairs,* ver 14—23 4 *Care is taken to keep that conference private,* ver 24—28

1 THEN Shephatiah the son of Mattan, and Ge-
daliah the son of Pashur, and Jucal the son of
Shelemiah, and Pashur the son of Malchiah, heard the
words [a] that Jeremiah had spoken unto all the people,
saying, 2 Thus saith the LORD, [b] He that remain-
eth in this city shall die by the sword, by the famine,
and by the pestilence but he that goeth forth to the
Chaldeans shall live, for he shall have his life for a prey,
and shall live 3 Thus saith the LORD, [c] This city
shall surely be given into the hand of the king of Baby-
lon's army, which shall take it 4 Therefore the princes
said unto the king, We beseech thee, [d] let this man be
put to death for thus [e] he weakeneth the hands of the
men of war that remain in this city, and the hands of all
the people, in speaking such words unto them for [f] this
man seeketh not the † welfare of this people, but the
hurt 5 Then Zedekiah the king said, Behold, he *is*
in your hand for the king *is* not *he that* can do *any* thing
against you 6 [g] Then took they Jeremiah, and cast
him into the dungeon of Malchiah the son ‡ of Ham-
melech that *was* in the court of the prison and they let
down Jeremiah with cords And in the dungeon *there*
was no water, but mire so Jeremiah sunk in the mire
7 ¶ Now when [h] Ebed-melech [i] the Ethiopian, one of
the eunuchs which was in the king's house, heard that
they had put Jeremiah in the dungeon, (the king then
sitting in the gate of Benjamin) 8 Ebed-melech went
forth out of the king's house, and spake to the king,
saying, 9 My lord the king, these men have done evil
in all that they have done to Jeremiah the prophet,
whom they have cast into the dungeon, and he § is like
to die for hunger in the place where he is, for *there is*
no more bread in the city. 10 Then the king com-
manded Ebed-melech the Ethiopian, saying, Take from
hence thirty men with thee, and take up Jeremiah the
prophet out of the dungeon before he die 11 So
Ebed-melech took the men with him, and went into the
house of the king under the treasury, and took thence
old cast clouts, and old rotten rags, and let them down
by cords into the dungeon to Jeremiah 12 And Ebed-
melec the Ethiopian said unto Jeremiah, Put now *these*
old cast clouts, and rotten rags, under thine arm holes,
under the cords And Jeremiah did so 13 [k] So they
drew up Jeremiah with cords, and took him up out of
the dungeon, and Jeremiah remained [l] in the court of the
prison

[a] Chap xxi 8 [b] Chap xxi 9

[c] Chap xxxii 3

[d] Chap xxvi 11 [e] Job xi 15 [f] Acts xvi 20 & xxiv 5 † Heb Peace

[g] Chap xxxvii 21 ‡ Or of the king

[h] Chap xxxix 16 [i] Luke x 33, &c

§ Heb Will die

[k] Mat xxvi 13 [l] Chap xxxvii 21

v 1—13 *Jeremiah's troubles are not yet ended* We have here,

1 A fresh accusation brought against him by the princes Though he was a prisoner, many came to him, whom he failed not faithfully to admonish of the determined destruction of Jerusalem, and to counsel them, as the only way of securing their lives, to cast themselves on the mercy of the Chaldeans, who would certainly spare all those who surrendered, whilst they who persisted in a fruitless defence would miserably perish by famine, pestilence, and the sword Such discourse the princes regarded as highly treasonable, tending to weaken the hands of the people, and betray the city Him therefore would they have the king put him to death as a publick enemy, *who sought not*

Ss

the

Before Christ 589

the welfare of the people, but their hurt *Note,* (1) It is a mercy, in times of calamity, if but our lives are given us for a prey (2) The enemies of God's faithful miniſters often paint them as traitors, and troublers of the ſtate, when, in truth, all their warnings and advice are deſigned purely for the lengthening the nation's proſperity

2 Jeremiah is, by the king's permiſſion, put into the dungeon Unable to reſiſt the authority of the princes in the preſent diſtracted ſtate of things, or willing to gratify them, though at the expence of ſacrificing a man whom he knew to be innocent, and a prophet of the Lord, he is given up to their hands, and from them he muſt expect no mercy They drag the prophet from the court of the priſon unto another, over which Malchiah preſided, and, intending ſecretly to deſtroy him, which they dared not publickly do, they let him down with cords into a deep, a noiſome dungeon, where was *no water, but mire,* into which he ſunk, ſaith Joſephus, up to the neck, and there left him, not doubting but hunger, cold, the damp and loathſomeneſs of the place, would ſoon put an end to him, and then he would appear to have died a natural death Here he is ſuppoſed to have offered the prayer recorded *Lam* iii 55—57

3 God yet remembers him, and raiſes him up a friend at court, when his caſe appeared deſperate Ebed-melech, an Ethiopian by birth, but poſſeſſed of more humanity and piety than any native Iſraelite, a great man in office, yet a good man in the worſt times, and moſt corrupted court, not aſhamed to own the ſuffering cauſe of God and truth, no ſooner heard he the prophet's miſerable ſituation than he immediately ſought the king, who was now ſitting in the gate of Benjamin hearing cauſes, or holding ſome council of war or ſtate, and boldly, in the preſence of all his nobles, and many of the princes probably who were the authors of Jeremiah's ſuffering, charges them with a moſt unjuſt and cruel procedure, and the conſequence muſt neceſſarily be the prophet's death, famiſhed with hunger, unleſs ſpeedily relieved *Note,* Zeal for God makes men bold as lions

4 Zedekiah gives Ebed-melech orders immediately to draw the prophet from his dungeon, and a guard of ſoldiers to aſſiſt him, if any dared attempt to oppoſe his releaſe and, with the greateſt humanity and tenderneſs, he took care to bring ſome ſoft rags to put under Jeremiah's arms, that the cords which drew him up might not hurt him and now, once more brought forth from the dark and diſmal pit, he is reconveyed to *the court of the priſon* Probably Ebed-melech thought that ſafer for the prophet than his diſcharge, as he would be there ſheltered from danger, and fed from the king's ſtores *Note,* (1) When we dare be faithful, we ſhall often find more favour than we expected (2) The leaſt circumſtances that beſpeak the tenderneſs and humanity of a charitable heart ſhall be remembered and recompenſed at the reſurrection of the juſt

m Chap. xxxvi 37 14 ¶ Then [m] Zedekiah the king ſent and took Jere-
n 2 Kings xvi 18 miah the prophet unto him into [n] the † third entry that
† Or principal is in the houſe of the LORD, and the king ſaid unto
Jeremiah, I will aſk thee a thing hide nothing from me
15. Then Jeremiah ſaid unto Zedekiah, If I declare it
unto thee, wilt thou not ſurely put me to death? and
if I give thee counſel, wilt thou not hearken unto me?
16 So Zedekiah the king ſware ſecretly unto Jeremiah,
o Iſa lvii 16 ſaying, *As* the LORD liveth, [o] that made us this ſoul,
I will not put thee to death, neither will I give thee into
the hand of theſe men that ſeek thy life 17 Then ſaid
Jeremiah unto Zedekiah, Thus ſaith the LORD the God
of hoſts, the God of Iſrael, If thou wilt aſſuredly go
p Chap. xxxix 3 forth unto [p] the king of Babylon's princes, then thy ſoul
ſhall live, and this city ſhall not be burnt with fire, and
thou ſhalt live, and thine houſe 18 But if thou wilt
not go forth to the king of Babylon's princes, then ſhall
this city be given into the hand of the Chaldeans, and
they ſhall burn it with fire, and thou ſhalt not eſcape out
of their hand 19. And Zedekiah the king ſaid unto
Jeremiah, I am afraid of the Jews that are fallen to the
Chaldeans, leſt they deliver me into their hand, and they
mock me 20. But Jeremiah ſaid, They ſhall not deliver
thee obey, I beſeech thee, the voice of the LORD
which I ſpeak unto thee ſo it ſhall be well unto thee,
and thy ſoul ſhall live 21. But if thou refuſe to go
forth, this is the word that the LORD hath ſhewed me
q 2 Kings xxiv 15 22 And behold, all the women [q] that are left in the
king of Judah's houſe, *ſhall be* brought forth to the king
† Heb The men of thy peace of Babylon's princes, and thoſe *women* ſhall ſay, † Thy
friends have ſet thee on, and have prevailed againſt thee
thy feet are ſunk in the mire, *and* they are turned away
back 23 So they ſhall bring out all thy wives and
r Chap xxxix 6 [r] thy children to the Chaldeans, and thou ſhalt not eſcape
out of their hand, but ſhalt be taken by the hand of the

king of Babylon and thou ſhalt cauſe this city to be
burnt with fire 24 ¶ Then ſaid Zedekiah unto Jere-
miah, Let no man know of theſe words, and thou ſhalt
not die 25 But if the princes hear that I have talked
with thee, and they come unto thee, and ſay unto thee,
Declare unto us now what thou haſt ſaid unto the king,
hide it not from us, and we will not put thee to death;
alſo what the king ſaid unto thee. 26 Then thou ſhalt
ſay unto them, [s] I preſented my ſupplication before the s Chap xxxvii 20.
king, that he would not cauſe me to return to [t] Jona- t Chap xxxvii 15.
than's houſe to die there 27 Then came all the princes
unto Jeremiah, and aſked him, and he told them ac-
cording to all theſe words that the king had commanded
ſo they § left off ſpeaking with him, for the matter was § Heb *Were ſilent from him*
not perceived 28 So Jeremiah abode [u] in the court u Chap. xxxix 14.
of the priſon, until the day that Jeruſalem was taken,
and he was *there* when Jeruſalem was taken

v 14—28 Severe ſtruggles, no doubt, paſſed in the boſom of this unhappy monarch, halting between two opinions, divided between the fear of man and the fear of God, and perplexed with the warnings of conſcience and the ſtrivings of corruption

1 He ſeeks another interview with the prophet, appoints the place of meeting, for ſecrecy probably, at *the third entry* or gate, as it is ſuppoſed, of the aſcent that went up from the king's houſe to the temple, and, having ordered the prophet thither, he came to him, earneſtly deſiring him to tell him if he had any farther *word* from the Lord, in hopes, perhaps, there might be ſome comfort yet in ſtore for him Vain expectation! whilſt his heart continued impenitent and unhumbled

2 Before he anſwers the king's queſtion he begs a ſolemn aſſurance from him, that he will not put him to death for ſpeaking the truth, and, what was as much his concern as his own preſervation, that he would follow the advice he gave him, *v* 15 *Note,* (1) Readineſs to die in the cauſe of truth is not at all inconſiſtent with every prudent precaution to preſerve our lives (2) Miniſters have the moſt earneſt ſollicitude that ſinners ſhould hear and comply with the advice on which their life, their eternal life, depends

3 The king ſolemnly ſwears to ſave him harmleſs, *as the Lord liveth, who made us this ſoul,* may he take my life, if ever I attempt to deſtroy thee He will not himſelf put him to death, nor ſuffer the princes to hurt him As to obeying the advice, he is ſilent, deſigning to follow it only ſo far as it pleaſed him

4 Jeremiah fairly ſets before him the only ſtep which yet remained to be taken, in order to preſerve himſelf and the city By an immediate ſurrender, and caſting himſelf on the clemency of the king of Babylon, the city ſhould be preſerved from ruin, himſelf be permitted to live in peace, if not in ſplendor, and his family be preſerved but, if he refuſed, there was no hope, the Chaldeans would infallibly force their way into it, and burn the city with fire, and, though he might attempt to eſcape, he ſhould certainly be ſeized *Note,* There is but one way that ſinners can be ſafe, and that is by an entire ſubmiſſion to the righteouſneſs of God, and caſting their ſouls on the mercy of God revealed in the goſpel They who refuſe to do this muſt periſh

5 Zedekiah heſitates, and ſuggeſts his fears of the ignominy he ſhould be expoſed to, if the Chaldeans delivered him up to the Jews who had fallen to them, who would now treat him with contempt, or revenge themſelves on him for the threatnings he had uttered againſt them for deſerting him fears in themſelves indeed groundleſs, and eſpecially when, in obedience to a divine command, he caſt himſelf on the Lord's protection *Note,* (1) When our fooliſh reaſoning is heard, in oppoſition to God's word, we are ſure to act wrong (2) For fear of being laughed at, many dare not ſeek to be ſaved (3) Many terrify themſelves with groundleſs apprehenſions of danger, when the path of duty is the only path of ſafety

6 Jeremiah ſilences the objection with an aſſurance that his fears were without foundation *They will not deliver thee up,* but treat thee with reſpect and kindneſs *it ſhall be well with thee, and thy ſoul ſhall live* But, as each moment of delay was dangerous, he urges him to an immediate compliance with *the voice of God,* otherwiſe the reproach he feared would come more bitterly upon him from his own houſe, who would upbraid his folly for hearkening to the falſe prophets, thoſe pretended *friends,* but real enemies, *to his peace,* when he might have prevented their ruin and his own by hearkening to Jeremiah for the city ſhall be taken, his wives and children dragged forth to the tents of the Chaldeans, himſelf unable to eſcape, and made priſoner by the king of Babylon, and he will cauſe Jeruſalem to be burnt with fire through his folly and obſtinacy *Note,* (1) They who ſeek by ſin to avoid ſhame will but expoſe themſelves more bitterly to the reproach they deſire to ſhun (2) Wicked rulers are chargeable with all the evils they bring upon their unhappy ſubjects

7 They part hereupon, Zedekiah not being perſuaded to yield

Before Chriſt 588

yield to his advice, and, for the ſake of his reputation, willing to keep the ſubject of this conference a ſecret from the princes, who would probably hear of it, and be curious to know what paſſed he therefore confirms his promiſe of protecting him, if he concealed the converſation, but charges him not to divulge to them any thing he had ſaid, except his requeſt not to be ſent back again to Jonathan's houſe, to die there, which requeſt, no doubt, the prophet had made and when the princes came to Jeremiah, with this he eaſily put them off, and thus abode in ſafety in the court of the priſon, till Jeruſalem was taken *Note*, (1) Many teſtify greater concern for their worldly reputation, than for their ſalvation (2) We are not always obliged to tell all we know to every impertinent enquirer Tho' we muſt never utter an untruth, we may ſafely conceal what others have no right to know, and it would be dangerous to ourſelves to diſcover The wiſdom of the ſerpent is commendable, when joined to the harmleſneſs of the dove

CHAP XXXIX

We have here the verification of Jeremiah's predictions 1 Jeruſalem, after eighteen months ſiege, is taken by the Chaldean army, ver 1—3 2 Zedekiah attempting to make his eſcape, is ſeized and made a miſerable captive to the king of Babylon, ver 4—7 3 Jeruſalem is burnt to the ground, and the people carried captive, except the poor, ver 8—10 4 The Chaldeans are very kind to Jeremiah, and take particular care of him, ver 11—14 5 Ebedmelech too, for his kindneſs, is preſerved in this day of deſolation, ver 15—18

1 [a] IN the ninth year of Zedekiah king of Judah, in
the tenth month, came Nebuchadnezzar king of
Babylon, and all his army againſt Jeruſalem, and they
beſieged it 2 *And* in the eleventh year of Zedekiah,
in the fourth month, the ninth *day* of the month, the
city was broken up 3 And all [b] the princes of the king
of Babylon came in, and ſat in the middle gate, *even*
Nergal-ſharezer, Samgar nebo, Sarſechim, Rab ſaris,
Nergal-ſharezer, Rab mag, with all the reſidue of the
princes of the king of Babylon 4 And [c] it came to
paſs *that* when Zedekiah the king of Judah ſaw them,
and all the men of war, then they [d] fled, and went forth
out of the city by night, by the way of the king's garden,
by the gate betwixt the two walls, and he went
out the way of the plain 5 But the Chaldeans army
purſued after them, and overtook Zedekiah in the plains
of Jericho and [e] when they had taken him, they brought
him up to Nebuchadnezzar king of Babylon to Riblah
in the land of Hamath, where he † gave judgment upon
him 6 Then the king of Babylon ſlew the ſons of
Zedekiah in Riblah before his eyes alſo the king of
Babylon [f] ſlew all the nobles of Judah 7 Moreover,
he put out Zedekiah's eyes, and [g] bound him ‡ with
chains to carry him to Babylon. 8. ¶ [h] And the Chaldeans
burnt the king's houſe, and the houſes of the people
with fire, and brake down the walls of Jeruſalem. 9
Then Nebuzar-adan the ‖ captain of the guard carried
away captive into Babylon the remnant of the people
that remained in the city, and thoſe that fell away, that
fell to him, with the reſt of the people that remained
10 But Nebuzar adan the captain of the guard, [i] left
of the poor of the people which had nothing, in the land
of Judah, and gave them vineyards and § fields at the
ſame time

a 2 Kings xxv 1 Chap lii 4. — b Chap xxxviii 17 — c Chap lii 7 — d [illegible] — e Chap lii 9 — † Heb Spake with him judgments. f Chap lii 10. g Mat vii [illegible] ‡ Heb. With two brazen chains, or fetters h Chap. lii 13 ‖ Heb. Chief of the executioners or ſlaughter men Ver 11. i Chap xxx 17 § Heb In that day

v 1—10 At laſt the threatned judgment is executed Vengeance againſt ſinners, though ſlow, is ſure

1 The devoted city is taken by ſtorm, after ſuſtaining a ſiege of eighteen months, begun by the king in perſon, in the midſt of winter, and carried on with implacable reſentment for Zedekiah's perfidy and reſentment by his orders, Nebuchadnezzar himſelf having retired to Riblah, on what account is uncertain The names of the princes who took poſſeſſion of the middle gate, are recorded with their ſeveral offices, Samgarnebo, Rab ſaris, and Rab-mag being ſuppoſed not diſtinct perſons, but titles, the firſt ſignifying the ſtrict keeper of Nebo; the ſecond, the chief of the eunuchs, the laſt, the chief of the magicians Theſe, with their companions, ſat in the gate in triumph as victors, or to ſecure the entrance for their troops, till the city was thoroughly poſſeſſed and thus was fulfilled the prophecy, *chap* i 15

2 Zedekiah is ſeized Under covert of the night, in which the aſſault was made, when he found the city taken, he attempted to make his eſcape, and had got as far as the plains of Jericho, but his enemies being appriſed of his flight, quickly purſued and overtook him, brought him priſoner to Nebuchadnezzar at Riblah, where ſentence, grievous as death, is pronounced upon him his infant children are murdered before his eyes, the nobles of Judah ſlain, and then, as if to leave him all his miſerable days to reflect on this horrid ſpectacle, the laſt objects he ever ſhould behold, his eyes are put out, and, bound in fetters of braſs, he is led a wretched captive to Babylon, 2 *Kings* xxv 4 *Note*, (1) There is no flying from God (2) They who will not believe the warnings of God, muſt, in their ſufferings, be convinced of the truths they deſpiſed

3 Shortly after the city and temple were burnt, the walls raſed, the people carried away captives, and none left but the poor to till the ground and cultivate the vineyards, from whom the Chaldeans had nothing to fear, and who were probably put under a heavy tribute And this was a ſtrange alteration, and a juſt retaliation upon the cruel maſters who had ſo enſlaved their brethren, themſelves are now captives, whilſt their poor and oppreſſed ſervants are made proprietors of their eſtates So ſurely will it appear ſooner or later, that there is a righteous God which judgeth the earth

11 ¶ Now Nebuchadrezzar king of Babylon gave
charge [k] concerning Jeremiah to Nebuzar adan the captain
of the guard, ſaying, 12 Take him, and † look
well to him, and [l] do him no harm, but do unto him
even as he ſhall ſay unto thee 13 So Nebuzar adan
the captain of the guard ſent, and Nebuſhaſban, Rab-ſaris,
and Nergal-ſharezer, Rab mag, and all the king of
Babylon's princes 14 Even they ſent, and took Jeremiah
[m] out of the court of the priſon, and [n] committed
him unto Gedaliah [o] the ſon of Ahikam, the ſon of Shaphan,
that he ſhould carry him home ſo he dwelt among
the people 15 ¶ Now the word of the LORD came
unto Jeremiah, while he was ſhut up [p] in the court of
the priſon, ſaying, 16 Go and [q] ſpeak to Ebed-melech
the Ethiopian ſaying, Thus ſaith the LORD of hoſts
the God of Iſrael, Behold, I will bring my words upon
this city for evil, and not for good, and they ſhall be
accompliſhed in that day before thee 17 But [r] I will
deliver thee in that day, ſaith the LORD, and thou
ſhalt not be given into the hand of the men of whom
thou *art* afraid 18 For I will ſurely deliver thee, and
thou ſhalt not fall by the ſword, but [s] thy life ſhall be
for a prey unto thee, [t] becauſe thou haſt put thy truſt in
me ſaith the LORD

k Prov xi [illegible] † Heb Set thine eyes upon him l 1 Pet iii 13 2 Pet ii 9. — m Chap xxxviii 28 n Chap xl. [illegible] o Chap xxvi 24 p Chap xxxviii 13, [illegible] q Ibid 7—12 r 2 Pet ii 9. s Chap xxi 9 & xlv 5 t 1 Chron v 20. [illegible] xxxvii 40

v 11—18 They who entruſt them all with God, ſhall never have cauſe to regret the confidence they repoſe in him We have here,

1 The great care taken of Jeremiah, as God had promiſed him, *chap* xv 11 Even the king of Babylon, who no doubt had heard the prophecies he had delivered, the advice he had given, and his ſufferings on that account, intereſts himſelf for him, and charges Nebuzar-adan, the captain of the guard, either before the city was taken, or immediately thereupon, to uſe Jeremiah with particular kindneſs, releaſe him from his confinement, and not only ſave him from harm, but do for him whatever he ſhould requeſt, which orders he obeyed, as more fully appears in the next chapter *Note*, (1) They who ſuffer in our cauſe, are entitled to a ſuitable recompence (2,) Infidels and idolaters have often ſhewn more regard to God's ſervants than faithleſs profeſſors

2 Ebedmelech's kindneſs to the prophet is remembered and rewarded By an expreſs revelation from God, he is aſſured, though he ſhould ſee the calamities pronounced on the people executed, himſelf ſhould ſurvive them, and however much he feared for his ſafety, God will ſurely deliver him from the ſword of the Chaldeans, and give him *his life for a prey*, when all ſeemed devoted to death, and this becauſe *thou haſt put thy truſt in me, ſaith the Lord* *Note*, (1) Good men may have their fears in the day of danger But, (2) They who truſt on God, ſhall never be confounded

CHAP XL

The ſtory of the ſad remnant which is left, is of a piece with all that went before, though at firſt there were ſome hopeful proſpects of their well-doing, they ſoon appeared as obſtinate in ſin as ever, unhumbled and unreformed, till all the reſt of the judgments threatned in Deut xxviii *being brought upon them, that which completes the threatnings, was accompliſhed,* The Lord ſhall bring thee into Egypt again *In this chapter we have, 1 A more particular account of Jeremiah's diſcharge, and his ſettlement with Gedaliah,* ver 1—6 *2 The great reſort of the Jews that remained to Gedaliah, who was made their governor under the king of Babylon,*

and

Before Christ 588.

and the good posture they were in for a while under him, ver 7—
12 3 A treacherous design formed against Gedaliah, by Ishmael,
ver 13—16

1 THE word which came to Jeremiah from the
LORD, after that [a] Nebuzar-adan the captain of
the guard, had let him go from Ramah, when he had
taken him being bound in † chains among all that were
carried away captive of Jerusalem and Judah, *which*
were carried away captive unto Babylon 2 And the
captain of the guard took Jeremiah, and said unto him,
The LORD thy God hath pronounced this evil upon
this place 3 Now the LORD hath brought *it*, and
done according as he hath said, [b] because ye have sinned
against the LORD, and have not obeyed his voice,
therefore this thing is come upon you 4 And now,
behold, I loose thee this day from the chains which ‡
were upon thine hand if it seem good unto thee to come
with me into Babylon, come, and I will ‖ look well un-
to thee but if it seem ill unto thee to come with me
into Babylon, forbear behold, all the land *is* before
thee whither it seemeth good and convenient for thee
to go, thither go 5 Now while he was not yet gone
back, *he said*, Go back also to Gedaliah the son of Ahi-
kam the son of Shaphan, [c] whom the king of Babylon
hath made governor over the cities of Judah, and dwell
with him among the people or go wheresoever it seemeth
convenient unto thee to go So the captain of the guard
gave him victuals and a reward, and let him go 6
Then went Jeremiah unto Gedaliah the son of Ahikam
to Mizpah, and dwelt with him among the people *that*
were left in the land

a Chap xxxix 9
† Or manacles
b Deut xxix 24, 25 Chap 1 7
‡ Or are
‖ Heb Set mine eye upon thee Chap xxxix 12
c 2 Kings xxv 22, &c
d Mat vi 33

v 1—6 The chapter begins with, *The word which came to Jeremiah*, not that this chapter contains any prophecy, but it is a general title to all the following part of this book

The rendezvous of the captives, it seems, was appointed to be at Ramah, about seven miles from Jerusalem Thither, among others, Jeremiah was led, chained with the rest, probably through mistake of some inferior officer, who, after he had been discharged, *chap* xxxix 14 finding him at large, and not knowing the exemption granted him, joined him with his countrymen But Nebuzar-adan, on the review of the captives, immediately discovered, unbound, and discharged him with the greatest respect and kindness

1 Nebuzar-adan, though a heathen, could not but acknowledge the truth of Jeremiah's mission and prophecies now so exactly fulfilled, and, to the shame of those who rejected his warning, addresses the captives, reminding them of their sins and disobedience to the prophet's voice, which had provoked God's wrath, and brought this righteous judgment upon them

2 He gives him his choice Either to go to Babylon with him, and be treated with all kindness, and provided for to his heart's wish, or if he had rather stay in his native country, he was at his full liberty to chuse his abode, and perhaps to take possession of what estate in the country he pleased, the whole being at the disposal of the conqueror *Note*, They who sacrifice all for God, even in this life are often found no losers by their fidelity to him

3 Jeremiah appearing, it should seem, irresolute where to fix, Nebuzar-adan advised him to join Gedaliah, a prince of Judah, who seems early to have followed the prophet's advice, and fallen to the Chaldeans, and now as a reward was made governor of the land yet he would not prescribe to him, but left the matter to his own consideration, having supplied him with victuals, which, in the exhausted state of the country, were necessary for his present subsistence, and made him a handsome present beside, a noble instance of generosity in a heathen officer towards a holy prophet With his advice Jeremiah complied, and joined Gedaliah at Mizpah, rather chusing to sustain the hardship he might be exposed to in God's heritage, among his poor people, than dwell in affluence in the land of the heathen

7 ¶ [e] Now when all the captains of the forces which
were in the fields, *even* they and their men heard that
the king of Babylon had made Gedaliah the son of A-
hikam governor in the land, and had committed unto
him men, and women, and children, and of the poor
of the land, of them that were not carried away captive
to Babylon, 8 Then they came to Gedaliah to Miz-
pah, even Ishmael the son of Nethaniah, and Johanan
and Jonathan the sons of Kareah, and Seraiah the son
of Tanhumeth, and the sons of Ephai the Netophathite,
and Jezaniah the son of a Maachathite, they and their
men 9 And Gedaliah the son of Ahikam, the son of
Shaphan, sware unto them and to their men, saying,
Fear not to serve the Chaldeans dwell in the land, and
serve the king of Babylon, [f] and it shall be well with
you 10 As for me, Behold, I will dwell at Mizpah
† to serve the Chaldeans which will come unto us but
ye, gather ye wine, and summer-fruits, and oil, and
put *them* in your vessels, and dwell in your cities that ye
have taken 11 Likewise when all the Jews that *were*
in Moab, and among the Ammonites, and in Edom,
and that *were* in all the countries, heard that the king
of Babylon had left a remnant of Judah, and that he had
set over them Gedaliah the son of Ahikam the son of
Shaphan, 12 Even all the Jews returned out of all
places whither they were driven, and came to the land
of Judah, to Gedaliah unto Mizpah, and gathered wine
and summer fruits very much 13 ¶ Moreover Joha-
nan the son of Kareah, and all the captains of the forces
that *were* in the fields, came to Gedaliah to Mizpah,
14 And said unto him, Dost thou certainly know that
[g] Baalis the king of the Ammonites hath sent [h] Ishmael
the son of Nethaniah ‡ to slay thee? But Gedaliah the
son of Ahikam believed them not 15 Then Johanan
the son of Kareah spake to Gedaliah in Mizpah secretly,
saying, Let me go, I pray thee, and I will slay Ishmael
the son of Nethaniah, and no man shall know *it* where-
fore should he slay thee, that all the Jews *which are* ga-
thered unto thee should be scattered, and the remnant
of Judah perish? 16 But Gedaliah the son of Ahikam
said unto Johanan the son of Kareah, [i] Thou shalt not do
this thing, for thou speakest ‖ falsly of Ishmael

e 2 Kings xxv 23
Before Christ 588.
f Chap xxxviii 20.
† Heb To stand before
g Chap. [illegible]
h Ver [illegible]
‡ Heb To strike thee in soul
i 1 Cor. xiii 7
‖ Heb Falsehood or a lie

v 7—16 A sudden gleam of unexpected prosperity prepares but for the last stroke, which should ruin the miserable remnant which was left

1 Under Gedaliah's government, notwithstanding the late desolations, things seemed to wear a promising aspect The captains of the forces, who had not been able to throw themselves into the city during the siege, and had lurked in some retreat, or rather had escaped with the shattered remains of the soldiery, when Zedekiah was taken, came to Gedaliah to Mizpah, and as he had, it seems, full power left him from the king of Babylon to receive all who quietly submitted, he gave them a solemn oath of protection on condition of their fidelity, and assures them, that their fears were groundless of being delivered up to the Chaldeans, because they had been in arms against them, but if they now lived peaceably, they might live comfortably He himself would reside at Mizpah, and transact all the matters of tribute to be paid the Chaldeans, or *to stand before them*, to intercede for them if any enquiry was made after them, to convey to them any orders, and render homage on their behalf, whilst they had nothing to do but to occupy the land, to gather the vintage, the summer-fruits, and oil, lay up their winter store, and enjoy the plenty God had once more restored to them The rumour of this peaceful re-establishment of the government, under so good a man as Gedaliah, soon reached the neighbouring nations, and drew a vast concourse of Jews, who had taken refuge there, to return and submit to the Chaldean government, so that the country was again replenished with inhabitants, *and they gathered wine and summer-fruits very much* Thus once more they began to taste God's goodness, if that at last might lead them to repentance

2 A dark scheme appears framed to interrupt and destroy this short-lived prosperity Johanan, one of the captains who had returned, got intelligence of a plot contrived by Baalis, king of the Ammonites, the hereditary enemy of the Jews, and to be executed by Ishmael, who had undertaken to dispatch Gedaliah, envious probably at his advancement, and thinking himself, as of the seed royal, more fit to rule Of this Johanan informed the governor, and to prevent the threatened mischief, offered privately to dispatch Ishmael but Gedaliah, being a man of integrity himself, would not entertain a suspicion of Ishmael as capable of so base a deed, but rejects the intelligence as false, and forbids him to proceed a step farther in the affair *Note*, (1) Charity hopeth all things, thinketh no evil, and they who are conscious of their own simplicity, believe others guileless as themselves (2) No obligations can bind the swellings of ambition, such men would mount the throne over the corpse of those to whom they are even indebted for the very power of destroying them (3) It would be highly dangerous to kill by way of prevention, in such a case, no man's life would be safe from a malicious tongue (4) Though it were sinful to be suspicious, yet when advertised of our danger, it were wise to be on our guard

CHAP

Before Christ 588

CHAP XLI

It is a very tragical story that is related in this chapter, and shews, that evil pursues sinners The black cloud that was gathering in the foregoing chapter, here bursts in a dreadful storm 1 Gedaliah and all that were with him are barbarously slain by Ishmael, ver 1—3 2. A pit is filled with their dead bodies, ver 9 3 Some devout men that were going to Jerusalem are drawn in, and slain by Ishmael, ver 4—7 Only ten of them escaped, ver 8 4. Those that escaped the sword, are taken prisoners by Ishmael, and carried off towards the country of the Ammonites ver 10 5 By the conduct of Johanan, though the death of the slain is not revenged, yet the prisoners are recovered, and he now becomes their commander in chief, ver 11—16 6 His project is to carry them into the land of Egypt, ver 17, 18

a 2 Kings xxv 25 Chap xl 6, 8.
1 NOW it came to pass in the seventh month, [a] *that* Ishmael the son of Nethaniah the son of
Elishama of the seed royal, and the princes of the king,
even ten men with him, came unto Gedaliah the son of
b Ps xli 9 Ahikam to Mizpah, and there they [b] did eat bread to-
gether in Mizpah 2 Then arose Ishmael the son of
c 2 Kings xxv 25 Nethaniah, and the ten men that were with him, and [c]
smote Gedaliah the son of Ahikam the son of Shaphan
with the sword, and slew him, whom the king of Baby-
lon had made governor over the land 3 Ishmael also
slew all the Jews that were with him, *even* with Geda-
liah at Mizpah, and the Chaldeans that were found
there, *and* the men of war 4 And it came to pass
the second day after he had slain Gedaliah, and no man
knew *it*, 5 That there came certain from Shechem
from Shiloh, and from Samaria, *even* fourscore men
having their beards shaven, and their clothes rent, and
having cut themselves, with offerings and incense in
d 1 Sam i 7. their hand, to bring *them* to the house of the LORD
6 And Ishmael the son of Nethaniah went forth from
† Heb In going and weeping Mizpah to meet them, † weeping all along as he went
and it came to pass as he met them, he said unto them,
Come to Gedaliah the son of Ahikam 7 And it was
so when they came into the midst of the city, that Ish-
e 1 Macc vii 19 mael the son of Nethaniah slew them, [e] *and cast them*
into the midst of the pit, he, and the men that *were*
with him 8 But ten men were found among them
that said unto Ishmael, Slay us not for we have trea-
sures in the field, of wheat, and of barley, and of oil,
and of honey So he forbare, and slew them not among
their brethren 9 Now the pit wherein Ishmael had
‖ Or, near Gedaliah ‡ Heb By the hand of Gedaliah cast all the dead bodies of the men (‖ whom he had
slain ‡ because of Gedaliah) *was it*, [f] which Asa the king
f 1 Kings xv 22 2 Chron xvi 6 had made for fear of Baasha king of Israel, *and* Ish-
mael the son of Nethaniah filled it with *them that were*
slain 10 Then Ishmael carried away captive all the
g Chap xliii 6. residue of the people, that *were* in Mizpah, [g] *even* the
king's daughters, and all the people that remained in
Mizpah, whom Nebuzar-adan the captain of the guard
had committed to Gedaliah the son of Ahikam, and
Ishmael the son of Nethaniah carried them away captive,
and departed to go over to the Ammonites

v 1—10 A scene of more complicated villany and unprovoked barbarity can hardly be found than is here recorded

1 Gedaliah is assassinated Unsuspicious of Ishmael, and the princes with him, who came with a pretence of paying a visit of friendship, he kindly and generously entertained them, when, at a signal given, Ishmael, and the rest of the conspirators, suddenly rose on Gedaliah and slew him, nor sheathed their swords till they had in cold blood massacred all the men, both Jews and Chaldeans, which were in Mizpah And to this they seem to have been instigated by their revenge, because Gedaliah and the Jews had fallen to the Chaldeans, or by their envy, because Ishmael, of the seed royal, and the princes, could not bear to see Gedaliah preferred before them Such horrid work do the malignant tempers of fallen sinners make, when left without restraint

2 Not content with all the blood they had shed, their wanton cruelty seek new objects Fourscore men from Shechem, Samaria, and Shiloh, wholly ignorant of what had passed, were on their way to the temple at Jerusalem, with deepest signs of expressive woe to lament its desolations, and present, if but on the ruined altar, their oblations, so dear to them was the very dust thereof These with hypocritical tears, Ishmael went forth to meet, that he might decoy them to Mizpah, under pretence of an invitation from Gedaliah, as if he was yet alive, *v* 6 and they, unsuspicious of his design, went with him into the midst of the city, where they were instantly slain, and their bodies cast into one pit with those who fell with Gedaliah The pit was dug by Asa, when he fortified Mizpah against Baasha, 1 *Kings* xv 22 Ten men only escaped, by pleading the treasures they had concealed in the field, and covetousness prevailing over cruelty, they permitted them to live to discover them Whilst we read such scenes of horror, what reason have we to bless God for his restraining grace upon the hearts and hands of wicked men but for this the world would be an Aceldama, a field of blood

3 The bloody work being done, Ishmael attempts to secure the plunder and the prisoners, the king's daughters, and others, by a retreat to Baalis, king of the Ammonites, who seems to have instigated him to perpetrate this horrid deed

11 ¶ But when Johanan the son of Kareah, and [h] all [h] Chap xl 8
the captains of the forces that *were* with them, heard
of all the evil that Ishmael the son of Nethaniah had
done, 12 Then they took all the men, and went to
fight with Ishmael the son of Nethaniah, and found him
by [k] the great waters that *are* in Gibeon. 13 Now [k] 2 Sam ii 13
it came to pass, *that* when all the people which *were*
with Ishmael saw Johanan the son of Kareah, and all the
captains of the forces that *were* with him, then they were
glad 14 So all the people that Ishmael had carried
away captive from Mizpah, cast about and returned,
and went unto Johanan the son of Kareah 15 But
Ishmael the son of Nethaniah escaped from Johanan
with eight men, and went to the Ammonites 16
Then took Johanan the son of Kareah, and all the cap-
tains of the forces that *were* with him, all the remnant
of the people whom he had recovered from Ishmael the
son of Nethaniah, from Mizpah (after *that* he had slain
Gedaliah the son of Ahikam) *even* mighty men of war,
and the women and the children, and the eunuchs whom
he had brought again from Gibeon 17 And they de-
parted and dwelt in the habitation of [l] Chimham, which [l] 2 Sam xix 37, 38
is by Beth-lehem, to go to enter into Egypt 18 ‖ ‖ Heb from the face of
Because of the Chaldeans for they were afraid of them,
because Ishmael the son of Nethaniah had slain Geda-
liah the son of Ahikam, whom the king of Babylon
made governor in the land

v 11—18. A deed so atrocious could not be long concealed, and no sooner doth the report of it reach Johanan, than, fired with indignation, he collected all the forces he could muster, pursued the fugitives, and overtook them at the pool of Gibeon, which though not the direct road, they might have taken to prevent a pursuit, or get the treasures of the men whose lives they had spared, thus oftentimes we see men covetousness their destruction No sooner had Johanan and his troops appeared, than those with Ishmael immediately deserted him, and with difficulty he himself, with eight of the assassins, escaped to the land of Ammon perhaps now unwelcome guests, when stripped of that plunder the king of Ammon hoped to share Johanan with his forces, and those he had recovered, either through his own fiery spirit, or the just judgment of God upon the people, that would give them no rest till they were utterly consumed, resolved hereupon to depart into Egypt, either hoping that under the Egyptian government they should enjoy greater liberty, or, as was pretended, fearing the Chaldeans would punish them for the death of Gedaliah, though in fact they might rather have expected commendation from them, as his avengers The resolution however being taken, they left Mizpah, and pitched in the habitation of Chimham (so called, probably, as being given by David to that son of Barzillai) near Bethlehem, in the way that led to Egypt, ready to fly thither if any danger threatned them *Note*, Men's unbelieving fears often plunge them into the very miseries they dread

CHAP XLII

Johanan and the captains being strongly bent upon going into Egypt, had a great desire that God should direct them so to do, like Balaam, who, when he was determined to go curse Israel, asked God leave Here is, 1 The fair bargain that was made between Jeremiah and them about consulting God in this matter, ver 1—6 *2 The message at large which God sent them, in answer to their enquiry; in which, 1 They are encouraged to continue in the land of Judah, and assured, that if they did so, it should be well with them,* ver 7—12 *2 They are forbidden to go to Egypt, and plainly told that if they did, it would be their ruin,* ver 13—18 *3 They are charged with dissimulation in their asking what God's will was in this matter, and disobedience when they were told what it was, and sentence is passed upon them for it,* ver 19—22

Before Chriſt 588

1 THEN [a] all the captains of the forces, and Jo
hanan the ſon of Kareah, and Jezaniah the ſon
a Chap xl 8 of Hoſhaiah, and all the people from the leaſt even
unto the greateſt, came near, 2. And ſaid unto Jere-
miah the prophet, Let, we beſeech thee, our ſupplica-
† Heb Fall before thee tion † be accepted before thee, and [b] pray for us unto
b Iſa xxxvii 4 the LORD thy God, *even* for all this remnant, (for
we are left *but* a few of many, as thine eyes do behold
c Ezra viii 21 us) 3 That the LORD thy God may ſhew us [c] the
way wherein we may walk, and the thing that we may
do 4 Then Jeremiah the prophet ſaid unto them,
d 1 Sam xii 23 I have heard *you*, behold, I [d] will pray unto the LORD
your God according to your words, and it ſhall come
e 1 Kings xxii 14. to paſs, *that* [e] whatſoever thing the LORD ſhall anſwer
f 1 Sam iii 18 Acts xx 20. you, I will declare *it* unto you I will [f] keep nothing
back from you 5 Then they ſaid to Jeremiah, The
LORD be a true and faithful witneſs between us, if
we do not even according to all things for the which
g Deut v 28 Ver 20 Mat xv 8 the LORD thy God ſhall ſend thee to us 6 [g] Whether
h Deut vi 3 Chap. vii 23 *it be* good or whether *it be* evil, we will obey the voice
of the LORD our God, to whom we ſend thee [h] that
it may be well with us, when we obey the voice of the
LORD our God.

v 1—6 Jeremiah in all theſe changes had by divine Providence been preſerved perhaps he had retired to Anathoth, and thus eſcaped the maſſacre at Mizpah, and now joined Johanan's company Hereupon, in their preſent difficulties,

1 They unanimouſly reſolve to conſult him, and beg his prayers and advice With greateſt reſpect they approach him, deſire a favourable acceptance of their requeſt, and intreat him to pray for them, intimating how unworthy they thought themſelves to open their lips, and what a confidence they placed in his intereſt in the divine regard They were now reduced to a helpleſs few, as he ſaw, their condition truly deplorable, not knowing what to do, or whither to go, and therefore deſiring divine direction *Note*, In our difficulties and diſtreſs, our firſt recourſe ſhould be made to God in prayer, and if we have not a prophet's word to guide us, we may hope for God's good providence to direct us

2 Jeremiah readily undertakes the taſk The ſlights he had received did not abate his zeal and regard for the welfare of his countrymen His prayers ſhall be ever for them, and he promiſes faithfully to report what God ſhould reveal to him *Note*, (1) Miniſters ſhould be men of prayer, it is this muſt make way for the efficacy of their advice (2) It is required of ſuch to be faithful, delivering, without reſerve, the whole counſel of God

3 They ſolemnly engage to conform to God's will entirely without reſerve, and appeal to him for the uprightneſs of their intentions, profeſſing their full conviction that it never can be well with them, unleſs they are unfeignedly obedient a ſhocking piece of hypocriſy throughout, when they really meant nothing leſs *Note*, (1) They who would profit by a miniſter's prayers, muſt pay ſerious attention to his preaching (2) We never can be ſincere with God, if we do not obey his will ſo far as it is known to us (3) It can only then be ever well with us, when we are found following God in ſimplicity and truth

7 ¶ And it came to paſs after ten days, that the
word of the LORD came unto Jeremiah 8 Then
called he Johanan the ſon of Kareah, and all the cap-
tains of the forces which *were* with him, and all the
people from the leaſt even to the greateſt, 9 And
ſaid unto them, Thus ſaith the LORD the God of Iſ-
rael, unto whom ye ſent me to preſent your ſupplica-
tion before him, 10 If ye will ſtill abide in this land,
then will I build you, and not pull *you* down, and I will
i Ch xvi 45 plant you, and not pluck *you* up for [i] I repent me of
the evil that I have done unto you 11 Be not afraid of
the king of Babylon, of whom ye are afraid be not
k Rom viii 31 afraid of him, ſaith the LORD for [k] I *am* with you to
l Pſ cvi 46 ſave you, and to deliver you from his hand 12 And [l] I
will ſhew mercies unto you, that he may have mercy
upon you, and cauſe you to return to your own land
13. ¶ But if ye ſay, We will not dwell in this land,
m Chap xliv 16 [m] neither obey the voice of the LORD your God, 14
Saying, No, but we will go into the land of Egypt,
where we ſhall ſee no war, nor hear the ſound of the
trumpet, nor have hunger of bread, and there will we
dwell 15 (And now therefore hear the word of the
LORD, ye remnant of Judah, Thus ſaith the LORD
n Deut xvii 16 of hoſts, the God of Iſrael, If ye wholly [n] ſet your faces
to enter into Egypt, and go to ſojourn there) 16
Then it ſhall come to paſs, *that* [o] the ſword which ye
feared, ſhall overtake you there in the land of Egypt, o Ezek xi 8
and the famine whereof ye were afraid, ſhall follow cloſe
after you there in Egypt, and there ye ſhall die 17
[p] † So ſhall it be with all the men that ſet their faces to p Chap iv
go into Egypt to ſojourn there, they ſhall die by the † Heb So ſhall all the men be
ſword, by the famine, and by the peſtilence and [q] none
of them ſhall remain or eſcape from the evil that I will q Chap xliv 14 28
bring upon them 18 For thus ſaith the LORD of
hoſts, the God of Iſrael, As [r] mine anger and my fury r Chap vii 20.
hath been poured forth upon the inhabitants of Jeruſa
lem, ſo ſhall my fury be poured forth upon you, when
ye ſhall enter into Egypt and [s] ye ſhall be an execra s Chap xxiv 9
tion, and an aſtoniſhment, and a curſe, and a reproach
and ye ſhall ſee this place no more 19 ¶ The LORD t Ch ... 13
hath ſaid concerning you, O ye remnant of Judah Go
ye not into Egypt know certainly, [t] that I have ‡ ad
moniſhed you this day 20 For [u] ye § diſſembled in Deut iv 26
your hearts, when ye ſent me unto the LORD your ‡ Heb Teſtified againſt you
God, ſaying, [x] Pray for us unto the LORD our God, u Ezek xxxiii 31
and according unto all that the LORD our God ſhall
ſay, ſo declare unto us, and we will do *it* 21 And *now*
I have this day declared *it* to you, but ye have not obeyed
the voice of the LORD your God, nor any *thing* for the § Or ye have uſed deceit againſt your ſouls
which he hath ſent me unto you 22 Now therefore x Ver 2
know certainly, that [y] ye ſhall die by the ſword, by the y Ver 17
famine, and by the peſtilence, in the place whither ye
deſire ‖ to go, *and* to ſojourn ‖ Or to go to ſojourn.

v 7—22 God might well have refuſed to be enquired of by thoſe whoſe hypocriſy he well knew, but after ten days of ſuſpenſe he vouchſafes them an anſwer, which Jeremiah, in a public convocation of all the people from the leaſt unto the greateſt, faithfully delivers

1 God enjoins them to abide in the land where they were, nor think of going into Egypt, and, to engage them hereunto, he aſſures them of *his own compaſſion towards them*, that he *repented of the evil he had done unto them*, would change his providential diſpenſations towards them, and, inſtead of the deſtruction they apprehended, build and plant them in their own land Nor need they fear the king of Babylon, ſince God would ſhew them mercies, he ſhall be diſpoſed to do the ſame, God will reſtrain him, and ſave them from the revenge they feared he would take, and cauſe them peaceably and comfortably to poſſeſs the heritage of the Lord, with all who having taken ſhelter in the neighbouring countries, would return to join them *Note*, (1) God's mercy is the foundation of all our hopes and happineſs (2) He hath in his hands the hearts of kings, and can turn them according to his own will and wiſdom (3) They who carefully obey God's will, may humbly expect his bleſſing

2 He threatens them, in caſe of diſobedience, with the moſt terrible deſtruction If they refuſed to abide in Judea, and, contrary to this clear declaration of God's will, thought themſelves wiſer than him, and wilfully reſolved for Egypt, on the preſumption that there they ſhould ſee no war, or want of bread, he ſolemnly aſſures them, as many at leaſt as ſet their face to go into Egypt, and having the power might force the reluctant to join them, that thither God's wrath ſhould purſue them, the evils they feared terribly overtake them, the peſtilence, famine, and ſword deſtroy them, ſo that not one of them ſhould ſee their native land again, but all the ſtorms of vengeance, which ſo lately broke upon Jeruſalem, with redoubled fury ſhould be poured upon them, and they be made *an execration, an aſtoniſhment, a curſe, and a reproach*, to all who beheld their dire cataſtrophe *Note*, (1) They who think by ſin to eſcape ſuffering, are only ruſhing on the thick boſſes of God's buckler (2) The curſe of God follows ſinners cloſe as their ſhadow, they can no more fly from it, than from *themſelves* (3) They who have made themſelves vile by their ſin, God will make them viler by the judgments he will inflict upon them

3 The prophet reproaches them with their abominable hypocriſy, and, to leave them without excuſe, repeats the warning, *Go not into Egypt* They knew in their conſciences the diſſimulation they had uſed, and that before they enquired of God, they had taken their reſolution to go, and were reſolved to abide by it therefore, ſince they were obſtinately hardened, and refuſed to obey God's word, notwithſtanding the ſolemn appeal they had made to him of their ſincerity, their doom is unchangeably fixed; and in Egypt, where they chuſe to ſojourn, they ſhall die *by the ſword, by the famine*, and *by the peſtilence* *Note*, (1) Diſſemblers with God are ſure to bring fearful ruin on their own ſouls (2) If ſinners will not obey yet it becomes us to bear our teſtimony, and leave them at leaſt inexcuſable in their iniquity (3) The favourite ſchemes which

Before Christ 588. which the sinner forms to perpetuate his prosperity, or secure himself from harm, hurry him only the sooner to the precipice of ruin

CHAP XLIII

We have here, 1 The people's contempt of this message, they denied it to be the word of God, ver 1—3 and then made no difficulty of going into Egypt and forcing Jeremiah to go along with them, ver 4—7 2 God sends them another message, foretelling the king of Babylon's pursuit of them into Egypt, ver 8—13

1 AND it came to pass, *that* when Jeremiah had
made an end of speaking unto all the people,
all the words of the LORD their God, for which the
LORD their God had sent him to them, *even* all these
words, 2 Then spake [a] Azariah the son of Hoshaiah, (a Chap xlii 1)
and Johanan the son of Kareah, and all the proud men,
saying unto Jeremiah, Thou speakest falsly the LORD
our God hath not sent thee to say, Go not into Egypt
to sojourn there 3 But Baruch the son of Neriah set-
teth thee on against us, for to deliver us into the hand
of the Chaldeans, that they might put us to death, and
carry us away captives into Babylon 4 So Johanan
the son of Kareah, and all the captains of the forces,
and all the people, [b] obeyed not the voice of the LORD, (b Chap xlii 5 Ver)
to dwell in the land of Judah 5 But Johanan the son
of Kareah, and all the captains of the forces, took all
the remnant of Judah, that were returned from all na-
tions whither they had been driven, to dwell in the
land of Judah, 6 *Even* men, and women, and chil-
dren, and [c] the king's daughters, [d] and every person (c Chap. xli 10 d Chap. xxxix 9.)
that Nebuzaradan the captain of the guard had left
with Gedaliah the son of Ahikam the son of Shaphan,
and Jeremiah the prophet, and Baruch the son of Ne-
riah 7 So they came into the land of Egypt for
they obeyed not the voice of the LORD, thus came (e Ver 4 f Called Hanes. Isa xxx 4)
they, *even* to [f] Tahpanhes

v 1—7 To a message so plain there seemed no place for objection, but the devil will never fail to help sinners to an excuse for their infidelity and disobedience

1 They pretend Jeremiah imposed on them, and that this declaration was not from God Johanan and Azariah, with all *the proud men*, dare give the prophet the lie, and impute to Baruch's influence the answer he reported is from God, as if they two had formed a design to give them into the hands of the Chaldeans to destroy them: a suggestion not only utterly improbable, but most malicious, as well as ungrateful, when these very men had rather foregone all the comforts they might have enjoyed in Babylon, than desert their own country in its distressed situation *Note*, (1) Pride is among the most damning sins, the root of infidelity, and the sure road to hell (2) The truest friends of their country are often thus branded as the betrayers of it (3) They who are full of ill designs themselves, are the first to represent others in the same malignant colours The ministers of God, who labour purely for the good of men's souls, are thus usually calumniated, as meaning only to serve themselves, but their judgment is with their God

2 They march without delay for Egypt, resolved not to abide in Judea, as God enjoined them; and all the Jews who had returned thither in hopes of a peaceable habitation, are persuaded or compelled to accompany them, and, among the rest, Jeremiah and Baruch Tahpanhes, the royal residence, was the place whither they bent their course, and, as Egypt was then their ally, they probably met with a friendly reception *Note*, (1) Proud men hate contradiction, and will have their way if they cannot obtain consent, they will force compliance (2) They who go out of God's way, have only themselves to blame for the consequences

8 Then came the word of the LORD unto Jeremiah
in Tahpanhes, saying, 9 Take great stones in thine
hand, and hide them in the clay in the brick kiln,
which *is* at the entry of Pharaoh's house in Tahpanhes,
in the sight of the men of Judah 10 And say unto
them, Thus saith the LORD of hosts the God of Israel,
Behold, I will send and take Nebuchadrezzar the king
of Babylon [g] my servant, and will set his throne upon (g Chap. xxv 9 & xxvii 6)
these stones that I have hid, and he shall spread his royal
pavilion over them 11 And when he cometh [h] he shall (h Chap xlvi 13)
smite the land of Egypt, *and deliver* [i] such *as are* for (i Chap xv 2 Zech xi 9)
death, to death; and such *as are* for captivity, to capti-
vity; and such *as are* for the sword, to the sword. 12
And I will kindle a fire in [k] the houses of the gods of (Before Christ 588.)
Egypt, and he shall burn, and carry them away cap-
tives, and he shall array himself with the land of Egypt, (k Isa xix 1.)
as a shepherd putteth on his garment, and he shall go
forth from thence in peace 13 He shall break also
the † images of ‡ Beth shemesh, that *is* in the land of († Heb Statues, or standing images. ‡ Or the house of the sun.)
Egypt, and the houses of the gods of the Egyptians
shall he burn with fire

v 8—13 Though Jeremiah was now against his will in this strange land, God comforts him with the visits of his grace, and employs him to denounce his wrath since they have rejected him as their teacher, he must be their troubler They sought refuge in Egypt, hoping there to be protected from the Chaldeans, but thither shall the Chaldeans pursue them, and destroy both them, and the Egyptians who have received them

1 By a sign the destruction of Egypt is set forth God commands Jeremiah to take great stones, and hide them in the brick-kiln, which was not far from Pharaoh's house, in the sight of the men of Judah, who would observe the sign, and be inquisitive about the meaning

2 This is at large declared The king of Babylon, employed as God's servant, who had destroyed Jerusalem, shall prosecute his victories, and Egypt fall before him on these very stones should his throne be set, and his pavilion spread over it By famine, pestilence, and the sword, those doomed to death must fall, and others be led into a miserable captivity and so far from being able to defend their votaries, the numerous gods of Egypt shall not be able to defend themselves their temples with the idols burnt, and those of precious materials carried away among the spoils As easily as a shepherd puts on his coat, and so adorned, shall Nebuchadnezzar and his army return laden with the wealth of Egypt, and leave the country in peace, entirely subjected to his government *Note*, (1) It is dangerous admitting those into our friendship, whom God pursues as an enemy, lest we share in their plagues (2) God often makes one wicked nation a scourge to another, and whilst the conquerors mean nothing less, they are but the instruments his providence employs

CHAP XLIV

In this chapter we have, 1. An awakening sermon which Jeremiah preached to the Jews in Egypt, to reprove them for their idolatry, and to threaten the judgments of God against them for it, ver 1—14 2 The impudent and impious contempt which the people put upon this admonition, and their declared resolution to persist in their idolatries, ver 15—19 3 The sentence passed upon them for their obstinacy, that they should all be cut off, and perish in Egypt, except a very small number, and as a sign or earnest of it, the king of Egypt should shortly fall into the hands of the king of Babylon, and be unable any longer to protect them, ver 20—30

1 THE word that came to Jeremiah concerning 587
all the Jews which dwell in the land of Egypt,
which dwell at Migdol, and [a] at Tahpanhes, and at (a Chap xliii 7)
Noph, and in the country of Pathros, saying, 2 Thus
saith the LORD of hosts, the God of Israel, Ye have
seen all the evil that I have brought upon Jerusalem,
and upon all the cities of Judah; and behold, this day
they *are* a desolation, and no man dwelleth therein
3 Because of their wickedness which they have com-
mitted [b] to provoke me to anger, in that they went to (b Chap vii. 18)
burn incense, *and* to serve other gods whom they knew
not, *neither* they, you, nor your fathers 4 Howbeit,
[c] I sent unto you all my servants the prophets, rising (c 2 Chron xxxvi 15 Chap vii 25 & xxv 3 & xxvi 5 & xxix 19 & xxxii 33)
early and sending *them*, saying, O do not this abominable
thing that I hate 5 But they hearkned not, nor in-
clined their ear to turn from their wickedness, to burn
no incense unto other gods 6 Wherefore [d] my fury (d Chap xlii. 18)
and mine anger was poured forth, and was kindled in the
cities of Judah, and in the streets of Jerusalem, and they
are wasted *and* desolate, as at this day 7 Therefore
now thus saith the LORD, the God of hosts, the God
of Israel, Wherefore commit ye *this* great evil against
your souls, to cut off from you man and woman, child
and suckling † out of Judah, to leave you none to re- († Heb Out of the midst of Judah)
main, 8. In that [e] ye provoke me unto wrath with the (e Chap xxv 6)
works of your hands, burning incense unto other gods in
the land of Egypt, whither ye be gone to dwell, that ye
might cut yourselves off, and that ye might be [f] a curse, (f Chap xlii 18.)
and a reproach among all the nations of the earth?
9. Have ye forgotten the ‡ wickedness of your fathers, (‡ Heb. Wickednesses, or punishments.)
and

Before Christ 587

and the wickedness of the kings of Judah, and the wickedness of their wives, and your own wickedness, and the wickedness of your wives, which they have committed in the land of Judah, and in the streets of Jerusalem? 10 They are not § humbled *even* unto this day, neither have they feared nor walked in my law, nor in my statutes that I set before you, and before your fathers. 11 ¶ Therefore thus saith the LORD of hosts, the God of Israel, Behold, g I will set my face against you for evil, and to cut off all Judah. 12 And I will take the remnant of Judah, h that have set their faces to go into the land of Egypt to sojourn there, and they shall all be consumed, *and* fall in the land of Egypt: they shall even be consumed by the sword, *and* by the famine: they shall die, from the least even unto the greatest, by the sword, and by the famine: and i they shall be an execration, *and* an astonishment, and a curse, and a reproach. 13 For k I will punish them that dwell in the land of Egypt, as I have punished Jerusalem, by the sword, by the famine, and by the pestilence: 14 So that l none of the remnant of Judah which are gone into the land of Egypt to sojourn there, shall escape or remain, that they should return into the land of Judah, to the which they || have a desire to return to dwell there: for m none shall return but such as shall escape.

§ Heb. Contrite. Ps. li. 17. — g Lev. xvii. 10. Chap. xxi. 10. Amos ix. 4. — h Chap. xlii. 15. — i Chap. xlii. 18. — k Chap. xliii. 11. — l Chap. xlii. 17. — || Heb. Lift up their soul. — m Ver. 28.

v. 1—14. No sufferings will change the heart or conduct, till divine grace powerfully interposes. If any thing could have deterred a people from idolatry, we might well have thought what the Jews had suffered abundantly sufficient; yet here we behold them as mad upon their idols as ever. They were now dispersed in the several cities of Egypt, and Jeremiah is ordered,

1. To remind them of their past sins, in opposition to the most earnest admonitions, and the consequences they had beheld. They had seen their cities ruinous heaps, their fruitful country turned into a desert, without man or beast, v. 2. Their wickedness, especially their idolatries, were the cause of it; the folly as well as impiety of which, was amazing, v. 3. and this aggravated by the repeated admonitions they had rejected, and the earnest exhortations they had despised: when God sent by his prophets, saying, *O do not this abominable thing that I hate*, they turned a deaf ear, and persisted in their abominations; therefore was his wrath poured out upon them, and the desolations of the land, *as at that day*, stood a fearful warning against the like provocations. *Note*, (1.) Sin is the abominable thing God hates, and we cannot conceive or speak of it with sufficient detestation of its evil and malignity. (2.) The ministers of God, who warn others of the fearful consequences of sin, must do it with an earnestness and deep concern, such as the case demands. (3.) Judgments upon others should be our warnings: we are doubly culpable to sin not only against God's word, but against what our own eyes have seen.

2. He upbraids them with their present idolatries, burning incense to the gods of Egypt, bringing heavy guilt on their consciences, and assured destruction on body and soul, till they should be made a proverb of wickedness and wretchedness, and an execration among all nations. He upbraids them also with their forgetfulness of their father's wickedness, and their own, the cause of all the judgments under which they groaned: unaffected and unhumbled with which, to that very day they persisted in their disobedience to God's law, went on from evil to worse, to fill up the measure of their iniquities to the full. *Note*, (1.) When under judgments the heart grows harder, it is a dire symptom of a reprobate mind. (2.) They who sin against God, sin against their own souls, and bring upon themselves sure and swift destruction.

3. He denounces God's vengeance on them for these abominations. As many as set their faces to go into Egypt, and were the authors of that pernicious resolution, shall perish there without exception, from the least to the greatest, and by the very judgments they designed thereby to avoid, which God had brought on Jerusalem: nor should a man of them ever again return unto their own land, as they hoped and desired, when they thought they might do it with greater safety than at present, except the few that escaped out of the hands of Johanan. Or it intimates how much worse their condition would be in Egypt, than that of the captives in Babylon: some of these should come back again, but none shall return from Egypt. *Note*, (1.) They who will not be ruled by God's word, will be broken by his rod. (2.) They who will take their affairs out of God's hands, and think their own projects more to be depended on than God's promises and providence, will meet with sure disappointment.

15 ¶ Then all the men which knew that their wives had burnt incense unto other gods, and all the women that stood by, a great multitude, even all the people that dwelt in the land of Egypt, in Pathros, answered Jeremiah, saying, 16 *As for* the word that thou hast spoken unto us in the name of the LORD, n we will not hearken unto thee. 17 But we will certainly do o whatsoever thing goeth forth out of our own mouth, to burn incense p unto † the queen of heaven, and to pour out drink-offerings unto her, as we have done, we and our fathers, our kings and our princes, in the cities of Judah, and in the streets of Jerusalem: for *then* had we plenty of ‡ victuals, and were well, and saw no evil. 18 But since we left off to burn incense to the queen of heaven, and to pour out drink-offerings unto her, we have wanted all *things*, and have been consumed by the sword and by the famine. 19 And when q we burnt incense to the queen of heaven, and poured out drink-offerings unto her, did we make her cakes to worship her, and pour out drink-offerings unto her without our men?

Before Christ 587

n Chap. vi. 16, 17. — o Num. xxx. 12. Ver. 25. — p Chap. vii. 18. — † Or, frame of heaven. — ‡ Heb. Bread. — q Chap. vii. 18.

v. 15—19. Never surely appeared more daring effrontery, and hardened impenitence.

1. They avow their determined resolution to abide in their idolatries, and follow the devices of their own hearts. The women had been chiefly engaged in the idolatrous rites, and their husbands approve and vindicate their conduct. *Note*, Custom in sin makes men daring and impudent.

2. They support their determination by many pretended arguments. They had antiquity and ubiquity to recommend the practice: their fathers did so; their kings patronized it; they had numbers on their side; their whole land had made public profession of serving the queen of heaven, the moon, or the whole celestial host: nay, they affirm, that then they had plenty of all good things, and date all their miseries from their neglect of their idol's service. *Note*, (1.) Antiquity, authority, numbers, &c. are no arguments to vindicate any practice the word of God forbids. (2.) Such is the deceivableness of unrighteousness, that the very methods God takes to separate men from their sins, they urge as arguments to harden themselves therein.

3. The women regarding themselves as most aimed at by the prophet's rebuke, vindicate themselves by pleading their husbands countenance and approbation. Absurd pretence! as if that could authorise them to transgress God's law. *Note*, (1.) Disobedience is duty, when superiors enjoin or countenance what God forbids. (2.) It is grievous, when they who should assist each other in the way to heaven, are mutual tempters, and harden each other in their sins.

20 ¶ Then Jeremiah said unto all the people, to the men and to the women, and to all the people which had given him *that* answer, saying, 21 The incense that ye burnt in the cities of Judah, and in the streets of Jerusalem, ye and your fathers, your kings and your princes, and the people of the land, did not the LORD remember them, and came it *not* into his mind? 22 So that r the LORD could no longer bear, because of the evil of your doings, *and* because of the abominations which ye have committed; therefore is your land s a desolation, and an astonishment, and t a curse without an inhabitant, as at this day. 23 Because ye have burnt incense, and because ye have sinned against the LORD, and have not obeyed the voice of the LORD, nor walked in his law, nor in his statutes, nor in his testimonies; therefore this evil is happened unto you, as at this day. 24 Moreover, Jeremiah said unto all the people, and to all the women, Hear the word of the LORD, all Judah that *are* in the land of Egypt: 25 Thus saith the LORD of hosts, the God of Israel, saying, u Ye and your wives have both spoken with your mouths, and fulfilled with your hand, saying, We will surely perform our vows that we have vowed, to burn incense to the queen of heaven, and to pour out drink-offerings unto her: ye will surely accomplish your vows, and surely perform your vows. 26 Therefore hear ye the word of the LORD, all Judah that dwell in the land of Egypt, Behold, I have sworn by my great name, saith the LORD, that my name shall no more be named in the mouth of any man of Judah, in all the land of Egypt, saying, The LORD God liveth. 27 x Behold, I will watch over them for evil, and not for good, and all the men of Judah that *are* in the land of Egypt shall be consumed by the sword, and by the famine, until there be an end of them. 28. Yet a small number that escape

r 2 Chron. xxxvi. — s Ver. — t Ch. — u Ver. 15.

the

Before Christ 587

the sword, [y] shall return out of the land of Egypt into
the land of Judah, and all the remnant of Judah that
are gone into the land of Egypt to sojourn there, shall
know [z] whose words shall stand, † mine or theirs 29
¶ And this *shall be* a sign unto you, saith the LORD,
that I will punish you in this place, that ye may know
that my words shall surely stand against you for evil
30 Thus saith the LORD, Behold, [a] I will give Pha
raoh-hophra king of Egypt into the hand of his ene-
mies, and into the hand of them that seek his life, as
[b] I gave Zedekiah king of Judah into the hand of Ne
buchadrezzar king of Babylon his enemy, and that
sought his life

y Isa xxvii 13 Ver 14 · z Ps xxxiii 11 Ver 29 · † Heb. From me, or from them · a Chap xlvi Ezek xxix 3, &c · b Chap xxxix 5

v 20—30 The prophet is neither intimidated by their numbers, nor discouraged by their obstinacy If they will not reform, at least they shall hear their doom

1 He contradicts the false assertion they had made, that all their troubles arose from their neglecting the service of their idols, and shews them their real origin It is true, God did long bear with their provocations, in hopes they would repent, but he did not overlook or forget them no, he saw, and, unable longer to forbear, poured out his vengeance upon them for their wickedness, their idolatries, their rebellion, and disobedience to his warnings, for which their land was a desolation and themselves a curse at *that day*

2 God abandons them to the sin and ruin they have chosen, and this is addressed particularly to the women, who were chief in the transgression They had declared their determined purpose of persisting in their abominations, and fulfilling their vows to the queen of heaven, as if their being under a vow to do evil could lay them under an obligation to perform it therefore he gives them up to their own delusions, and since they said, Depart, he will depart, confirming it with an oath, to shew the immutability of his counsel He will take from them every remains of religion, they shall no more swear by his name either he will utterly consume all the Jews in Egypt by famine and the sword, and not leave a man to profane his holy name, or they shall sink into the idolatries of Egypt, incorporate with that nation, and forget the very mention of Israel's God A few indeed who, as Baruch, stood firm amidst the general apostacy, shall escape this destruction, and return again to their own land, and they shall see whose word shall stand, theirs, who promised the idolaters impunity, or his, who threatned them with ruin *Note*, (1) A greater curse cannot light upon the sinner, than to be given up of God to the devices of his own heart (2) However men flatter themselves, it will soon be proved whose word shall stand, God's or theirs

3 God gives them a sign of the certainty of the threatned judgments The king of Egypt, their protector, shall be shortly given into Nebuchadrezzar's hands, as Zedekiah had been, and, so far from defending them, should be ruined himself *Note*, They who for human confidences forsake the living God, shall find them no better than broken reeds

CHAP XLV.

This prophecy, with those that follow, were delivered a long while before the preceding Baruch, for his fidelity, is taken under God's especial protection, and here an encouragement is given to all God's faithful people to trust him in the most trying seasons We have here, 1 How he was frightened when he was brought into trouble for writing and reading Jeremiah's roll, ver 1—3 *2 How his fears were checked with a reproof for his great expectations, and silenced with a promise of preservation,* ver 4 5

606

1 THE word that Jeremiah the prophet spake un
to Baruch the son of Neriah, when he had
written these words in a book at the mouth of Jere-
miah, in the fourth year of Jehoiakim the son of Jo-
siah king of Judah, saying, 2 Thus saith the LORD
the God of Israel unto thee, O Baruch, 3 Thou didst
say, Wo is me now, for the LORD hath added grief
to my sorrow, I fainted in my sighing, and I find no
rest 4 ¶ [c] Thus shalt thou say unto him, The LORD
saith thus, Behold, *that* which I have built will I break
down, and that which I have planted I will pluck up,
even this whole land 5 And seekest thou great things
for thyself? seek *them* not for behold, [d] I will bring
evil upon all flesh, saith the LORD but thy life will
I give unto thee [e] for a prey in all places whither thou
goest

a Chap xxxvi 1, &c · b Chap xxxi 28 (?) · c Chap xxv 11 · d Chap xxi 9 & xxxix 18

v 1—5 Baruch had been the prophet Jeremiah's faithful assistant, *chap* xxxvi and hereby involved himself in trouble, and exposed himself to the fury of the enraged Jehoiakim We have,

1 The consternation God observes in him when the warrants were out for apprehending him *Wo is me now*, he looked upon himself as a dead man, *for the Lord hath added grief to my sorrow* After all the pains he had taken, and the reproaches he had endured, now his very life is in danger, and the anguish he felt on transcribing the dreadful doom of his people, is increased by his own sufferings *I fainted in my sighing*, unable to support the load of grief that oppressed him, *and I find no rest*, from his sorrows, or composure of mind under his troubles *Note*, (1) Our hearts are very unwilling to bear the cross (2) Many of our complaints arise more from our unbelieving fears, than our real danger (3) We should watch over the temper of our hearts, and the door of our lips, when tempted to impatience or despair under our sufferings, for God observes, and will reprove us for it

2 Jeremiah from God checks his aspiring thoughts, the disappointment of which seems to have been at the root of his complaints He was a man of abilities, a scribe to the prophet, and a follower of his piety, and he might hope this would recommend him to his countrymen, and enable him to rise to some distinguished post but it was absurd in him *to seek great things for himself*, when the whole nation was devoted to ruin, v 4, 5 *Note*, (1) If we had less expectations from the world, we should have less disappointments and cause to complain (2) Even good men are slow of heart to believe what Jesus hath spoken, *My kingdom is not of this world*, and have their hearts too much attached to worldly hopes and prospects

3 Though his hopes of greatness be blasted, his life is secured to him, and that is a distinguishing mercy, when death spreads around his universal ravages In all places, and amidst every danger, God promises to protect him, and with this he hath cause to be abundantly satisfied and thankful

CHAP XLVI

The ruin of the Jewish people was hastening, now the cup goes round to the neighbouring nations, beginning with Egypt, and at last ending with Babylon herself We have here, 1 The defeat of Pharaoh-necho, in the fourth year of Jehoiakim, ver 1—12 *2 The final conquest of Egypt some years after by Nebuchadnezzar,* ver 13—26 *3 A word of comfort to the Israel of God in the midst of those calamities,* ver 27, 28

Before Christ 606

1 THE word of the LORD which came to Je-
remiah the prophet, against the Gentiles, 2
Against Egypt, [a] against the army of Pharaoh necho
king of Egypt, which was by the river Euphrates in
Carchemish, [b] which Nebuchadnezzar king of Babylon
smote in the fourth year of Jehoiakim the son of Josiah
king of Judah 3 [c] Order ye the buckler and shield,
and draw near to battle 4 Harness the horses, and get
up, ye horsemen, and stand forth with *your* helmets, fur-
bish the spears, *and* put on the brigandines 5 Where-
fore have I seen them dismayed, *and* turned away back?
and their mighty ones are † beaten down, and are ‡ fled
apace, and look not back *for* fear *was* round about,
saith the LORD 6 § Let not the swift flee away,
[d] nor the mighty man escape they shall stumble, and
fall towards the north by the river Euphrates 7 Who
is this *that* cometh up as a flood, whose waters are
moved as the rivers? 8 Egypt riseth up like a flood
and *his* waters are moved like the rivers, and he saith,
I will go up, *and* will cover the earth, I will destroy
the city, and the inhabitants thereof 9 Come up, ye
horses, and rage, ye chariots, and let the mighty men
come forth, ‖ the Ethiopians, and † the Libyans that
handle the shield, and the Lydians [e] that handle *and*
bend the bow 10 For this *is* the day of the LORD
God of hosts, a day of vengeance, that he may avenge
him of his adversaries and the sword shall devour, and
[f] it shall be satiate, and made drunk with their blood
for the LORD God of hosts [g] hath a sacrifice in the
north-country by the river Euphrates 11 [h] Go up into
Gilead, and take balm, [i] O virgin, the daughter of E-
gypt in vain shalt thou use many medicines *for* thou
shalt not be cured. 12 The nations have heard of thy
shame, and thy cry hath filled the land for [k] the mighty
man hath stumbled against the mighty, *and* they are
fallen both together

a 2 Chron xxxv 20 · b 2 Kings xxiv 7 · c Chap li 11 Joel iii 9, &c · † Heb. broken in pieces · ‡ Heb. fled a flight · § Or, the swift shall not flee away Amos ii 14 · d Ps xxxiii 16 · ‖ Heb Cush · † Heb Put · e Isa lxvi 19 · f Isa xxxiv 5 · g Ezek xxxix 17 · h Chap viii 22 & li 8 · i Isa xlvii 1 · k Ver 6, 10

v 1—12 The prophecies following relate to the neighbouring nations of the Gentiles This describes the defeat of the Egyptians, who had often been the oppressors of God's Israel, and now their unprofitable allies, endeavouring to support them in

Before Christ 606

their rebellion againſt the king of Babylon, they bring his arms upon themſelves to their deſtruction

1 The Lord, ironically deriding their vain confidence and vaſt preparations, bids them collect their forces, fit on their armour, marſhal their hoſt, ruſh into the battle, vainly concluding the victory ſecure, and that the armies of Babylon, their cities and empire, would be utterly overwhelmed by their numerous forces, as the lands of Egypt were overflowed by the ſwellings of the Nile *Note*, They who are moſt ſelf-confident are uſually neareſt the precipice of ruin

2 He upbraids their cowardice and inglorious flight, when the army of the Chaldeans met them Where is now their boaſted valour, and great ſwelling words of vanity? See them broken, diſpirited, in panic fear, their mightieſt warriors turn their backs, and ſeek their ſafety in an ignominious flight, but ſeek it in vain, ſince God obſtructs their way, they cannot eſcape, their ſwifter purſuers are at their heels, they ſtumble near the Euphrates, to which they had advanced, and fall by the ſword of the Chaldeans, drunk with the blood of the ſlain, *for this is the day of the Lord of hoſts, a day of vengeance* for all the wrongs they have done his people, and for the late ſlaughter of Joſiah, and *a ſacrifice* to divine juſtice for all their abominations *Note*, (1) Sinners may expect a day of recompence (2) Flight is vain from the ſword of God's vengeance (3) One diſmaying impreſſion from God can make cowards of the braveſt Let not therefore the ſtrong man glory in his ſtrength

3 He declares their wound incurable In vain ſhould they attempt to repair their defeat, or to conceal their ſhame the nations around ſhall hear the cries of the wounded, and the groans of the dying, *the mighty have ſtumbled on the mighty*, heaps on heaps, pierced by the ſwords of their enemies, and no more ſhall they be able to make head againſt their foes, when, like a flood, they ſhall break in ſhortly upon them *Note*, They whom God conſigns to ruin ſtruggle in vain againſt their deſtiny

13 ¶ The word that the LORD ſpake to Jeremiah
the prophet, how Nebuchadrezzar king of Babylon
ſhould come *and* [l] ſmite the land of Egypt 14 Declare
ye in Egypt, and publiſh in Migdol, and publiſh in
Noph, and in Tahpanhes ſay ye, Stand faſt, and pre-
pare thee, for the ſword ſhall devour round about thee
15 Why are thy valiant *men* ſwept away? they ſtood
not, becauſe the LORD did drive them 16 He made
many to fall, yea, [m] one fell upon another, and they ſaid,
Ariſe, and let us go again to our own people, and to
the land of our nativity, from the oppreſſing ſword
17 They did cry there, Pharaoh king of Egypt *is but*
a noiſe, he hath paſſed the time appointed 18 *As* I
live, ſaith the King, [n] whoſe name *is* the LORD of hoſts,
Surely as Tabor *is* among the mountains, and as Car-
mel by the ſea, *ſo* ſhall he come 19 Oh thou daugh-
ter dwelling in Egypt, † furniſh thyſelf to go into cap-
tivity for Noph ſhall be waſte and deſolate without an
inhabitant 20 Egypt *is like* a very fair heifer, *but* de-
ſtruction cometh it cometh out of the north 21 Alſo
her hired men *are* in the midſt of her, like ‡ fatted bul-
locks, for they alſo are turned back, *and* are fled away
together, they did not ſtand, becauſe the day of their
calamity was come upon them, *and* the time of their
viſitation 22 The voice thereof ſhall go like a ſerpent,
for they ſhall march with an army, and come againſt
her with axes, as hewers of wood 23 They ſhall cut
down her foreſt, ſaith the LORD, though it cannot be
ſearched, becauſe they are more than the graſhoppers,
and *are* innumerable 24 The daughter of Egypt
ſhall be confounded, ſhe ſhall be delivered into the hand
of the people of the north. 25 The LORD of hoſts,
the God of Iſrael, ſaith, Behold I will puniſh the § mul-
titude of [o] No, and Pharaoh, and Egypt, [p] with their
gods, and their kings, even Pharaoh, and *all* them that
truſt in him 26 [q] And I will deliver them into the
hand of thoſe that ſeek their lives, and into the hand
of Nebuchadrezzar king of Babylon, and into the hand
of his ſervants and [r] afterwards it ſhall be inhabited, as
in the days of old, ſaith the LORD 27 ¶ But [s] fear
not thou, O my ſervant Jacob, and be not diſmayed,
O Iſrael, for behold, I will ſave thee from afar off, and
thy ſeed from the land of their captivity, and Jacob
[t] ſhall return, and be in reſt and at eaſe, and none ſhall
make *him* afraid 28 Fear thou not, O Jacob my ſer-
vant, ſaith the LORD, for I *am* with thee, for [u] I will
make a full end of all the nations whither I have driven
thee, but I will not make a full end of thee, [x] but cor-
rect thee in meaſure, yet will I ‖ not leave thee wholly
unpuniſhed

[l] Iſa xix 1 Ezek xxix & xxx & xxxii Fulfiled 572

[m] Ver 12

[n] Iſa xlvii 4 & xlviii 2 Chap xlviii 15

† Heb Make thee inſtruments of captivity

‡ Heb Bullocks of the ſtall

§ Or nourisher

[o] Ezek xxx 15 Nah iii 8

[p] Chap xliii 12 13 Ezek xxx 13

[q] Ezek xxxii 11 Ezek xxix 19

[r] Ezek xxix 13

[s] Iſa xli 13 & xliii 5 & xliv 2 Chap xxx 10

[t] Ezek xxxvii 21 Amos ix 14

[u] Chap x 24 & xxx 11

[x] Iſa lxxix 10 &c

‖ Or not utterly cut thee off

v 13—28 This begins a new prophecy The former regards the defeat of the Egyptians at Carchemiſh, this the deſtruction of their country ſome years after In thoſe very cities where the infatuated Jews ſought refuge, there muſt the land of Egypt's utter ruin be proclaimed We have here,

1 The alarm ſpread through the land, *v* 14 The ſword of the Chaldeans was making havock in the neighbouring countries, it is time for them therefore to prepare for war

2 Their auxiliaries deſert them, on the firſt defeat, finding themſelves unable to defend the frontiers, and not ſupported by Pharaoh as they expected God fought againſt them, deſtroyed and diſpirited them, ſo that they fled together in the day of their calamity willing therefore to have a pretext for retiring to their own countries, they cry out againſt Pharaoh, as having deceived and betrayed them he boaſted of certain victory, and the vaſt armies he could raiſe, and now they find it but mere empty noiſe, and boaſts without ability *Note*, (1) When God fights, reſiſtance is vain (2) They who deceive others with falſe hopes deſerve themſelves to be deceived in their expectations from them

3 Their ruin is determined by that eternal King whom all the hoſts of heaven and earth obey They are doomed to ſlaughter by the Chaldean ſword, as the trees of the foreſt fall before the hewer's axe, thick as the locuſts which once of old devoured the land, ſhall the ſoldiers of the king of Babylon cover the country, Egypt, like a heifer, ſo called perhaps in alluſion to the ox they worſhipped, muſt bend her fair neck to the yoke, and this daughter, living in eaſe and affluence, muſt prepare to go into captivity The deſtruction is ſure as the foundation of the mountains Tabor and Carmel, as it may be rendered, *ſurely as Tabor among the mountains, and Carmel, ſhall he go into the ſea*, ſo ſurely ſhall Pharaoh, and all *who truſt in him*, be overwhelmed in the abyſs of calamities, or, towering in pride as theſe mighty hills, the Babylonian conqueror ſhall advance, cut down his enemies, however many or mighty, with the falſe gods their confidence, *v* 25 and lay the country deſolate and waſte, depopulate the cities, and enſlave the inhabitants like the ſerpent wallowing in the duſt, and hiſſing, ſo low ſhould they be reduced, *v* 22 nor dare, for fear of offending, to make their complaints aloud though this may alſo be interpreted of the army of the Chaldeans, hiſſing as they marched, and breathing out threatnings againſt their Egyptian foes Thus compleat ſhould be their overthrow, for, tho' the arm employed is Nebuchadnezzar's, the puniſhment is from God, *v* 25 *Note*, (1) Whatever inſtruments are employed, God's hand ſhould be ſeen in every viſitation (2) They who truſt on any thing but God alone may expect diſappointment (3) When troubles threaten, it is a call to prepare for them

4 A gleam of hope cloſes the awful ſcene *Afterwards it ſhall be inhabited, as in the days of old, ſaith the Lord* Though it never after roſe to its priſtine ſplendor, it became a great and populous nation after forty years, *Ezek* xxix 13, 14 for God wounds and he heals

5 The people of God have a gracious promiſe to comfort them amidſt theſe deſolations, either the few faithful in Egypt or thoſe in Babylon, if Egypt ſhall return from their captivity, much more ſhall they The ſame aſſurance was given them before, *chap* xxx 11, 12 and this was in part fulfilled in their recovery from the Babyloniſh yoke, but ſhall be more eminently ſeen at the latter day for which purpoſe, amidſt all the changes of nations and fall of empires, they are to this day preſerved a diſtinct people, and may expect again to ſee reſt and eaſe in their own land

CHAP XLVII

This chapter reads the Philiſtines their doom, by the hand of Nebuchadrezzar It is ſhort, but terrible, and Tyre and Zidon, though they lay at ſome diſtance, come in ſharers with them in the deſtruction here threatened It is foretold, 1 that the forces of the northern crowns ſhould come upon them, to their great terror, ver 1—5 *2 That the war ſhould continue long, and their endeavours to put an end to it ſhould be in vain*, ver 6, 7

1 THE word of the LORD that came to Jeremiah
the prophet [a] againſt the Philiſtines, [b] before
that Pharaoh ſmote Gaza 2 Thus ſaith the LORD,
Behold, [c] waters riſe up [d] out of the north, and ſhall be
an overflowing flood, and ſhall overflow the land, and
‖ all that is therein, the city, and them that dwell there-
in then the men ſhall cry, and all the inhabitants of the
land ſhall howl 3 At [e] the noiſe of the ſtamping of
the hoofs of his ſtrong *horſes*, at the ruſhing of his cha-
riots, *and at* the rumbling of his wheels, the fathers ſhall
not look back to *their* children for feebleneſs of hands
4 Becauſe of the day that cometh to ſpoil all the Phi-
liſtines, *and* to cut off from [f] Tyrus and Zidon every
helper

[a] Ezek xxv 15 Zeph ii 4 5 Amos i 6, 7

‖ Heb the fulneſs thereof

[e] Chap viii 16 Nah iii 2

[f] Chap xxv 22

Before Christ 610

helper that remaineth for the LORD will spoil the
Philistines, the remnant of ‡ the country of Caphtor
5 Baldness is come upon Gaza, Ashkelon is cut off,
with the remnant of their valley how long wilt thou cut
thyself? 6 O thou sword of the LORD, how long
will it be ere thou be quiet? § put up thyself into thy
scabbard, rest and be still 7 ‖ How can it be quiet,
seeing the LORD hath given it a charge against Ashkelon,
and against the sea-shore, there hath he appointed
it

v 1—7 The Philistines had been the inveterate enemies of Israel they had received many a severe check in the days of David, but seem to have become a very powerful people, and were in peace and strongly fortified, when this prophecy was delivered, which was before Pharaoh smote Gaza, an event supposed to have happened during his expedition to Carchemish

1 The northern army of the Chaldeans is represented as a swelling flood, that bears down all opposition In terrors at their approach, the Philistines will howl, unable to resist the torrent, affrighted at the stamping of the horses and the rattling of the chariots, and flying as if death was at their heels, their fears should overcome the strongest natural affection, so that they should not *look back to their children*, and *through feebleness of hands* be unable to defend or carry them away It is the day of divine appointment for the destruction of the Philistines, and Tyre and Zidon must share the like fate, together *with the remnant of the country of Caphtor*, their near kin and neighbours Their cities are spoiled, their country plundered, their inhabitants destroyed, and Gaza and Ashkelon are described with signs of deepest woe, shaving off their hair, and cutting themselves, bemoaning these desolations *Note*, The strongest holds are no proof against the artillery of divine threatenings

2 The prophet, tenderly affected with the scene, cries out, *O sword of the Lord*, for though in the hand of Chaldeans, yet God put it there, *how long will it be ere thou be quiet?* and the dire contention cease, *put up thyself into thy scabbard, rest and be still* A good man prays thus for his bitterest enemies, and charity teaches us to beg that wars may cease in all the world, and a stop be put to the effusion of human gore so lavishly shed But when God hath a controversy, and his sword is drawn against a nation, *how can it be quiet*, till it hath executed vengeance on God's enemies, and accomplished his purposes towards a guilty people? *seeing he hath given it a charge against Ashkelon, and against the sea-shore*, the places above-mentioned, *there hath he appointed it* *Note*, Every thing here below is under the immediate government of God; even the ambition of princes, and the horrid ravages of war, are the instruments in his hands to execute the decrees of his providence on those nations whose provocations call for judgment

CHAP XLVIII

The doom of Moab is next read Here is, 1 The destruction foretold, that it should be great and general, should extend itself to all parts of the country, ver 1—6, 8 2 *The causes of this destruction assigned, it was sin that brought this ruin upon them, their pride and security, and carnal confidence*, ver 7, 11, 14, 29 *and their contempt of and enmity to God and his people*, ver 26, 27, 30 3 *A promise of the restoration of Moab*, ver 47

1 AGainst Moab thus saith the LORD of hosts, the
God of Israel, Wo unto Nebo, for it is spoiled
Kiriathaim is confounded *and* taken, ‖ Misgab is con-
founded and dismayed 2 *There shall be* no more praise
of Moab in Heshbon they have devised evil against it,
come and let us cut it off from *being* a nation, also thou
shalt be ‡ cut down, O Madmen, the sword shall pursue
thee 3 A voice of crying *shall be* from Horonaim,
spoiling and great destruction 4 Moab is destroyed,
her little ones have caused a cry to be heard 5 For
in the going up of Luhith, § continual weeping shall
go up for in the going down of Horonaim the enemies
have heard a cry of destruction 6 Flee, save your
lives, and be like ‖ the heath in the wilderness 7 ¶
For because thou hast trusted in thy works and in thy
treasures, thou shalt also be taken, and Chemosh shall
go forth into captivity *with* his priests and his princes
together 8 And the spoiler shall come upon every city,
and no city shall escape the valley also shall perish, and
the plain shall be destroyed, as the LORD hath spoken
9 Give wings unto Moab, that it may flee and get
away for the cities thereof shall be desolate, without
any to dwell therein 10 Cursed *be* he that doth the
work of the LORD ‖ deceitfully, and cursed *be* he that
keepeth back his sword from blood 11 ¶ Moab hath
been at ease from his youth, and he hath settled on his
lees, and hath not been emptied from vessel to vessel,
neither hath he gone into captivity therefore his taste
‡ remained in him, and his scent is not changed 12
Therefore behold the days come, saith the LORD, that
I will send unto him wanderers that shall cause him to
wander, and shall empty his vessels and break their bot-
tles 13 And Moab shall be ashamed of Chemosh,
as the house of Israel was ashamed of Bethel their con-
fidence.

v 1—13 We have here,

1 The destruction of Moab The Lord of Hosts, who hath all the armies of heaven and earth at his beck, sends forth spoilers, whose sword shall devour around, and pursue the fugitives, *v* 2 Desolation shall be spread on every side, every city be destroyed, *there shall be no more praise of Moab in Heshbon*, the place and people utterly ruined, every fruitful valley wasted, the land left without inhabitant, the princes and priests shall go into captivity, and with confusion they shall behold their idol Chemosh, their confidence, share their fate, unable as the Calf of Bethel to defend his votaries, *v* 7—13 In vain they cry *flee*, when flight is impossible, *v* 6 or perhaps this is the call of the prophet, ironically deriding their attempt to escape from city to city, when all must fall, and *no city escape* The city of Horonaim taken, echoes, and whilst the fugitives go weeping up the ascent to Luhith, the enemies hear their cry, and follow at their heels, *v* 5 Swift the destruction passes through as the bird cuts the air, and is on eagles wings they are hurried into captivity, *v* 9 *Moab*, throughout, *is destroyed*, and desolate, *as the heath in the wilderness*, not even the infants are spared, nor can their cries avail, *v* 4 The charge is given, and sealed with an anathema, *Cursed be he that doth the work of the Lord deceitfully, and cursed be he that keepeth back his sword from blood*, and no pleas of pity must be heard, when vengeance from God is to be executed *Note*, (1) When God's work is given us to do, of whatever kind, to act hypocritically, or negligently, will bring his curse upon our heads (2) The vain confidence of every sinner will as much disappoint their hopes in the day of trial, as Chemosh shamed his foolish votaries

2 The cause of this destruction is their pride and carnal security Like wine that hath not been emptied from vessel to vessel, Moab had been at ease from the days they were formed into a people, and had never known such captivities as Israel had undergone Strong as wine settled on its lees, filled with wealth, and confident with long prosperity, they defied danger, *trusting on their works*, their fortifications, or their idol-deities, the work of their own hands, and *in their treasures*, as if these were a sure defence, though the event must so fearfully disappoint their expectations, their works be demolished, their treasures and their gods together spoiled and carried off by the conquerors *Note*, (1) Worldly prosperity is a dangerous snare to the soul (2) God's enemies often enjoy here below that worldly ease and affluence to which his own people are strangers They have their good things here, and have nothing to hope for in eternity (3) Creature confidences in the day of evil prove utter vanity and vexation of spirit (4) The sinner's presumption is the prelude to his ruin.

14 ¶ How say ye, We *are* mighty and strong men
for the war? 15 Moab is spoiled and gone up *out of*
her cities, and ‡ his chosen young men are gone down to
the slaughter, saith the King, whose name *is* the LORD
of hosts 16 The calamity of Moab *is* near to come,
and his affliction hasteth fast 17 All ye that are about
him bemoan him, and all ye that know his name, say,
How is the strong staff broken, *and* the beautiful rod!
18 Thou daughter that dost inhabit Dibon, come down
from *thy* glory, and sit in thirst; for the spoiler of
Moab shall come upon thee, *and* he shall destroy thy
strong-holds 19 O ‡ inhabitant of Aroer, stand by the
way and espy, ask him that fleeth, and her that escap-
eth, *and* say, What is done? 20 Moab is confounded,
for it is broken down howl and cry, tell ye it in Ar-
non, that Moab is spoiled, 21 And judgment is come
upon the plain country; upon Holon, and upon Jah-
azah, and upon Mephaath, 22 And upon Dibon, and
upon Nebo, and upon Beth-diblathaim, 23 And upon
Kiriathaim, and upon Beth-gamul, and upon Beth-meon,
24 And upon Kerioth, and upon Bozrah, and upon
all the cities of the land of Moab, far or near. 25
The horn of Moab is cut off, and his arm is broken,
saith the LORD 26 ¶ Make ye him drunken for
he magnified *himself* against the LORD Moab also
shall wallow in his vomit, and he also shall be in derision
27 For was not Israel a derision unto thee? was he
found

Before Christ 599

t Chap ii 26
u Prov xxiv 17, 18
x Iſa ii 19
y Ibid xvi 6, &c
z Pſ xxxiii 11
|| Or thoſe on whom he ſtayeth do not right
a Chap l 36
b Iſa xv 5
c Ibid xvi 8, 9
d Ibid 10
Joel i 12
e Iſa xv 4
f Ibid 5, 6
§ Heb Deſolations
g Iſa xv 2, & xvi 12
h Ibid xv 5, & xvi 11
i Iſa xv 7
k Ibid 2
Chap xlviii 5
† Heb Diminiſhed
l Chap xxii 28
‡ Heb Neck
m Deut xxviii 49
Chap xlix 22 Dan vii 4 Hoſ viii 1
Hab i 8
n Chap. xlix 22
o Iſa xxiv 17, 18
p Amos v 19
q Num xxi 28
r Ibid 17
|| Heb The children of noiſe
s Num xxi 29
§ Heb In captivity
t Chap xlix 6, 39

found among thieves? for ſince thou ſpakeſt of him,
thou [u] ſkippedſt for joy 28 O ye that dwell in Moab,
leave the cities, and [x] dwell in the rock, and be like the
dove *that* maketh her neſt in the ſides of the hole's mouth
29 We have heard [y] the pride of Moab (he is exceeding
proud) his loftineſs, and his arrogancy, and his pride,
and the haughtineſs of his heart 30 I know his wrath,
ſaith the LORD, [z] but *it ſhall* not *be* ſo, || his lies ſhall
not ſo effect *it* 31 Therefore [a] will I howl for Moab,
and I will cry out for all Moab, *mine heart* ſhall mourn
for the men of Kir heres 32 [c] O vine of Sibmah, I
will weep for thee, with the weeping of Jazer, thy
plants are gone over the ſea, they reach *even* to the ſea
of Jazer, the ſpoiler is fallen upon thy ſummer fruits,
and upon thy vintage 33 And [d] joy and gladneſs is
taken from the plentiful field, and from the land of
Moab, and I have cauſed wine to fail from the wine-
preſſes, none ſhall tread with ſhouting, *their* ſhouting
ſhall be no ſhouting 34 [e] From the cry of Heſhbon
even unto Elealeh, *and even* unto Jahaz they have utter-
ed their voice, from Zoar *even* unto Horonaim, *as* an
heifer of three years old for the waters alſo of Nimrim
ſhall be § deſolate 35 Moreover, I will cauſe to ceaſe
in Moab, ſaith the LORD, [g] him that offereth in the high
places, and him that burneth incenſe to his gods 36
Therefore [h] mine heart ſhall ſound for Moab like pipes,
and mine heart ſhall ſound like pipes for the men of
Kir-heres becauſe [i] the riches *that* he hath gotten are
periſhed 37 For [k] every head *ſhall be* bald, and every
beard † clipt upon all the hands *ſhall be* cuttings, and
upon the loins ſackcloth 38 *There ſhall be* lamentation
generally upon all the houſe-tops of Moab, and in the
ſtreets thereof for I have broken Moab [l] like a veſſel,
wherein *is* no pleaſure, ſaith the LORD 39 They
ſhall howl, *ſaying*, How is it broken down! how hath
Moab turned the ‡ back with ſhame! ſo ſhall Moab be a
deriſion, and a diſmaying to all them about him 40
For thus ſaith the LORD, Behold, [m] he ſhall fly as an
eagle, and ſhall ſpread his wings over Moab 41 Keri-
oth is taken, and the ſtrong-holds are ſurpriſed, and [n] the
mighty men's hearts in Moab at that day ſhall be as
the heart of a woman in her pangs 42 And Moab
ſhall be deſtroyed from *being* a people, becauſe he hath
magnified *himſelf* againſt the LORD 43 [o] Fear, and
the pit, and the ſnare *ſhall be* upon thee, O inhabitant
of Moab, ſaith the LORD 44 [p] He that fleeth from
the fear, ſhall fall into the pit, and he that getteth up
out of the pit, ſhall be taken in the ſnare for I will
bring upon it, *even* upon Moab, the year of their viſi-
tation, ſaith the LORD 45 They that fled, ſtood
under the ſhadow of Heſhbon, becauſe of the force but
[q] a fire ſhall come forth out of Heſhbon, and a flame
from the midſt of Sihon, and [r] ſhall devour the corner
of Moab, and the crown of the head of || the tumultuous
ones 46 [s] Wo be unto thee, O Moab, the people of
Chemoſh periſheth for thy ſons are taken § captives,
and thy daughters captives 47 ¶ Yet [t] will I bring
again the captivity of Moab in the latter days, ſaith the
LORD Thus far *is* the judgment of Moab

v 14—47 The deſtruction of Moab is more largely painted, with the ſins, the cauſe of her calamities

1 The deſtruction is terrible, ſudden, univerſal, near, inescapable, drawn with the ſtrongeſt colours, if ſo be it might awaken a ſenſe of danger, and be the means of leading to repentance any of that devoted people They thought themſelves ſecure in their walled holds, able to repel any invader, *v* 14 but Moab is ſpoiled, her cities univerſally taken, *v* 20—24 Her people captives, the flower of her youth fallen by the ſword, ſent by that Lord of hoſts, whoſe power none can reſiſt, and from whoſe arm none can flee, *v* 15 near, even at the door, is the fearful judgment, *v* 16 and time it is for all around her to begin the lamentation over her, *How is the ſtrong ſtaff broken!* on which they truſted for ſupport, or that they had ſeen lifted up with terror *and the beautiful rod*, the kingdom once ſo ſplendid, is overturned; ſo poor and periſhing, are all human excellencies, *v* 17, Hurled from the ſummit of glory, her ſtrongeſt holds ſhall be laid in the duſt by the Chaldean ſpoiler, and the people reduced to the greateſt extremities, *v* 18 whilſt they who dwell in the utmoſt border, ſhall with ſollicitous concern enquire of the fugitives *What is done?* ver 19 and in anſwer hear, that all is in confuſion, their caſe deſperate, their fortreſs deſtroyed, their country waſted, their power broken, and for this they are called upon to *howl and cry*, ver 20, 25 Drunk with the cup of God's fury, Moab is become weak and ſick, *wallowing in his vomit*, a loathſome ſpectacle, a deriſion to the beholders, *v* 26, 39 Like a dove that flies to the clefts of the rock, the prophet calls on the inhabitants to quit their cities, and take refuge in ſome ſolitary cave, where they may be hid, *v* 28 With deepeſt ſighs of moſt expreſſive woe, the people are enjoined to lament their deſolations, *v* 37 and with ſympathetic tenderneſs the prophet mingles his tears with theirs, affected deeply with the terrible ſcene he beheld, *v* 31, 36 All gladneſs is baniſhed, their harveſt and vintage a prey to the ſpoiler, and nothing heard around but ſhrieks and groans, *v* 32, 34 The univerſal ruin ſpreading a univerſal lamentation, *v* 38 They can neither fly nor fight, for ſwift as an eagle darteth on his prey, the Babylonian conqueror advances, *v* 40 Their fortreſſes are ſeized, their mighty men ſunk under panic fear, *v* 41 every effort to eſcape fruitleſs they who attempt to avoid one evil, ſhall plunge into another, and ſince the judgment is from God, and the appointed time come, it is vain to hope for deliverance, *v* 43, 44 Even under the ſhadow of Heſhbon, where they hoped at leaſt to find ſome protection, the fire of the Chaldeans ſhall devour them, and *the crown of the head of the tumultuous ones*, their nobles and great men, who boaſted of their wealth and ſtrength, be laid low, *v* 45 Wo therefore to miſerable Moab, *the people of Chemoſh periſheth*, finding no protection from their God *Thy ſons are taken captives, and thy daughters captives*, and the land left deſolate without inhabitant, *v* 46

2 Their ſins are many and exceeding aggravated, and in theſe his judgments God is altogether righteous [1] *Inſufferable pride*, ver 29 where a variety of expreſſions are uſed to intimate in how many inſtances, and how deeply it appeared and wherever this ſpirit is found, there for ever the curſe of God will reſt [2] *Contempt of God*, ver 26 as if they were above his arm, and defied his threatnings [3] *Unkindneſs to God's people*, they mocked at their calamities, derided them when led captive, as if they had been thieves taken in the fact, and expreſſed a malicious pleaſure in their miſeries, *v* 27 *Note*, Nothing is more hateful to God than ſuch a diabolical temper and they who mock at the ſufferings of God's people, God will mock at them when their fear cometh [4] *Wrath and ſlander*, ver 30 They inſtigated probably the Chaldeans to extirpate the Jewiſh people, and by their lies ſought to exaſperate them, but ſaith God, *I know it*, and *it ſhall not be ſo* he ſees the devices of the crafty, will diſappoint the enemies of his church, and reckon with them for their malignity [5] *Their idolatry*, ver 35 Becauſe they burnt incenſe to their falſe gods, and preferred Chemoſh before the living Jehovah For theſe things God will viſit them, and be avenged of ſuch a nation as this

3 A gracious promiſe concludes the whole, and gives one ray of hope to prevent utter deſpair *Yet will I bring again the captivity of Moab in the latter days, ſaith the Lord*, which had a temporal accompliſhment, when, with the other captive nations, they were releaſed by Cyrus, and hath reſpect to thoſe more bleſſed days when Moab ſhould, with other Gentiles, ſubmit to the Meſſiah's kingdom, be delivered from the bondage of Satan, ſin, and death, and rejoice in that liberty wherewith Chriſt makes his people free

CHAP XLIX.

The cup of trembling ſtill goes round, and the nations muſt all drink of it, according to the inſtructions given to Jeremiah, chap xxv 15 This chapter puts it into the hands of, 1 *The Ammonites*, ver 1—6 2 *The Edomites*, ver 7—22 3 *The Syrians*, ver 23—27 4 *The Kedarens*, ver 28—33 5 *The Elamites*, ver 34—39

Before Christ 599

† Or Againſt
a Ezek xxi 28 & xxv 2
Amos i 13
Zeph ii 8, 9
|| Or Melchom
b Amos i 13
c Ibid 14
d Iſa xiv 2
Chap xxx 16
|| Or Melchom
e Chap xlviii 7
Amos i 15
§ Or thy valley floweth away
f Chap xxi 13

1 † CONcerning [a] the Ammonites, thus ſaith the
LORD, Hath Iſrael no ſons? hath he no heir?
why *then* doth || their king inherit Gad, and [b] his people
dwell in his cities? 2 Therefore behold, the days come,
ſaith the LORD, that I will cauſe an alarm of war to
be heard in [c] Rabbah of the Ammonites, and it ſhall be
a deſolate heap, and her daughters ſhall be burnt with
fire then ſhall Iſrael be heir unto them that were his
heirs, ſaith the LORD 3 Howl, O Heſhbon, for
Ai is ſpoiled cry, ye daughters of Rabbah, [d] gird ye
with ſackcloth lament and run to and fro by the
hedges, for || their king ſhall go into captivity, *and* his
[e] prieſts and his princes together. 4 Wherefore glorieſt
thou in the valleys, § thy flowing valley, O backſliding
daughter? [f] that truſted in her treaſures, *ſaying*, [g] Who
ſhall come unto me? 5 Behold, I will bring a fear
upon thee, ſaith the LORD God of hoſts, from all
thoſe that be about thee, and ye ſhall be driven out
every

Before Christ 599.

every man right forth, and none shall gather up him
that wandreth 6 And [h] afterward I will bring again
the captivity of the children of Ammon, saith the
LORD

v 1—6 The doom of the Ammonites is next read

1 The charges against them are, (1) *Illegal seizure of God's heritage* When the king of Assyria subdued and led captive the Gileadites, they immediately took possession of the territories as their own, as if there were no Israelites remaining to inherit the possessions of their brethren *Note*, They who are weak, will often be oppressed, but there is a day coming when judgment shall sit, and justice be impartially administred (2) *Apostacy from God*, ver 4 Lot, their father, had transmitted to them the worship of the true God, but they had quickly revolted to idols (3) *Their vain confidence*, they gloried in their vallies flowing with plenty, and in their treasures, as if by these secured they could defy their enemies, *v* 4 But they who depart from God, have little reason to promise themselves security and ease in their sins

2 Their judgment is pronounced The alarm of war is sounded, their invaders are sent from God to spoil and destroy, their cities are burnt with fire, their cries go up, in vain they fly for shelter *to the hedges*, their kings, priests, and princes together are seized, and led into captivity, *v* 3 and the remnant dispersed, and find no favour among the nations whither they wander, *v* 5 Then shall Israel obtain reprisals, seize their country, *and be heirs unto them that were his heirs*, which was fulfilled, 1 *Mac* v 6 and may perhaps have some respect to the days of the Messiah, *Isa* xi 14

3 A promise of restoration is added *Afterward I will bring again the captivity of Ammon*, temporally, restoring them again to their own land, or spiritually, at the coming of Christ, converting them, and bringing them into the glorious liberty of the sons of God

7 ¶ [i] Concerning Edom, thus saith the LORD of
hosts, *Is* wisdom no more in Teman? is counsel perish-
ed from the prudent? [k] is their wisdom vanished? 8
[l] Flee ye, † turn back, dwell deep, O inhabitants of
[m] Dedan, for I will bring the calamity of Esau upon him,
the time *that* I will visit him 9 If [n] grape gatherers
come to thee, would they not leave *some* gleaning
grapes? if thieves by night, they will destroy ‡ till they
have enough 10. But I have made [o] Esau bare, I have
uncovered his secret places, and he shall not be able to
hide himself his seed is spoiled, and his brethren and
his neighbours, [p] and he *is* not 11 Leave thy father-
less children, [q] I will preserve *them* alive, and let thy
widows trust in me 12 For thus saith the LORD,
Behold, [r] they whose judgment *was* not to drink of the
cup, have assuredly drunken, and *art* thou he *that*
shalt altogether go unpunished? thou shalt not go un-
punished, but thou shalt surely drink *of it* 13 For I
have sworn by myself, saith the LORD, that Bozrah
shall become a desolation, a reproach, a waste, and a
curse, and all the cities thereof shall be perpetual wastes
14 I have [s] heard a rumour from the LORD, and an
ambassador is sent unto the heathen, *saying*, Gather ye
together, and come against her, and rise up to the bat-
tle 15 For lo, I will make thee small among the
heathen, *and* despised among men 16 Thy terrible-
ness hath deceived thee, *and* the pride of thine heart, O
thou that dwellest in the clefts of the rock, that holdest
the height of the hill [t] though thou shouldst make thy
[u] nest as high as the eagle, I will bring thee down from
thence, saith the LORD. 17 Also Edom shall be a
desolation [x] every one that goeth by it shall be asto-
nished, and shall hiss at all the plagues thereof 18.
[y] As in the overthrow of Sodom and Gomorrah, and the
neighbour *cities* thereof, saith the LORD no man
shall abide there, neither shall a son of man dwell in
it 19 [z] Behold, he shall come up like a lion from [a] the
swelling of Jordan against the habitation of the strong
but I || will suddenly make him run away from her, and
who *is* a chosen *man that* I may appoint over her? for
[b] who *is* like me? and [c] who will § appoint me the time?
and who *is* that shepherd [d] that will stand before me?
20 Therefore hear the counsel of the LORD, that he
hath taken against Edom, and his purposes that he hath
purposed against the inhabitants of Teman surely [e] the
least of the flock shall draw them out; surely he shall
make their habitations desolate with them 21 The
earth is moved at the noise of their fall at the cry,
the noise thereof was heard in the † Red sea 22 Be-
hold, [f] he shall come up, and fly as the eagle, and spread
his wings over Bozrah and at that day shall the heart
of the mighty men of Edom be as the heart of a woman
in her pangs

v 7—22 Edom, in the day of Israel's calamity, cried, *Down with it, down with it, even to the ground*, Psal cxxxvii 7 the cup therefore is next put into her hand We have here,

1 The terrible destruction of the Edomites The calamity of Esau approaches, the day of their visitation, the inhabitants of Dedan are called upon to flee, and dwell deep beneath some rock or cave, to save their lives from the destroyer, *v* 8 The most careful grape-gatherers leave some berries, and the thieves, who break in at night, know when they have enough, and make off, *v* 9 but *Edom* is stripped *bare*, for can all his care to conceal his wealth, keep it from the spoiler, or the secret lurking places hide the fugitives his children are destroyed, and his neighbours, so far from helping, share his fate, *v* 10 so that in the day of his affliction, none of them are left to say, *Leave thy fatherless children, I will preserve them alive, and let thy widows trust in me*, though others consider these words as a gracious promise to a remnant of Edom who should be turned unto God, and his people, in every time of distress, may with comfort apply them to themselves, *v* 11 the less guilty nation than Edom have drank of the cup, therefore he may not expect to escape unpunished, *v* 12 By an oath, to confirm the immutability of his counsel, God hath sworn that Bozrah, the capital, and all the other cities, shall become a curse, a reproach, and perpetual desolation, *v* 13 lying in ruinous heaps, without inhabitant, as the cities of Sodom, *v* 18 At God's secret instigation, the Chaldeans, as if invited by an ambassador, come up as to certain victory, *v* 14 and depopulated and impoverished, the Edomites shall become a vile and despicable people, *v* 15 For though dwelling in fortresses, that appear impregnable as the craggy rock, God's almighty arm is able, and determined to bring them to the dust, *v* 16 With astonishment passengers behold, and hiss, insulting their fearful fall, *v* 17 As a lion driven from his covert on the banks of Jordan, by the rising flood, tears and devours the defenceless sheep, so shall the king of Babylon go up against the habitation of the strong, and Edom shall suddenly flee or it may be rendered, *I will cause him* (Nebuchadnezzar) *to run upon it suddenly*, and subdue the country, appointing a deputy over it, from among his captains, *for who is like me?* saith the Lord, able to execute all my purposes, *and who will appoint me the time* to dispute the battle, or retard the fulfilment of my decrees, *and who is that shepherd that will stand before me?* what king can defend his subjects against the power of the Almighty Jehovah? *v* 20 Therefore, since such is his decree to destroy Edom, the meanest soldier of the Chaldean army shall be sufficient to destroy the mightiest Edomite, and drag them from their lurking holes, *v* 20 Amazed at their fall, the earth trembles, or echoes, with the shout of the conquerors, and the cries of the vanquished, the sound of which reaches the distant shores, *v* 21

2 All their efforts to help themselves will be vain Their boasted wisdom now shall fail them, and all their schemes prove abortive, *v* 7 And their terribleness, *v* 16 their mighty armies, and strong fortresses, which in the pride of their heart they thought invincible, shall deceive them, when, swift as an eagle, the destroyer shall come up against them, and invest their capital Their terrible warriors, frighted, as a woman in the pangs of travail, should abandon themselves to despair, and fall an easy prey, *v* 22 or *thy terribleness*, which some render *thine idol*, hath vain protection in the day of their calamity *Note*, When God strikes, the strong men must bow themselves, for there is neither *counsel nor might against the Lord*

23 ¶ [g] Concerning Damascus Hamath is confound-
ed, and Arpad for they have heard evil tidings, they
are † faint-hearted, *there is* sorrow ‡ on the sea, it cannot
be quiet 24 Damascus is waxed feeble, *and* turneth
herself to flee, and fear hath seized on *her* [h] anguish
and sorrows have taken her as a woman in travail [i] 25
How is the city of praise not left, the city of my joy?
26 [k] Therefore her young men shall fall in her streets,
and all the men of war shall be cut off in that day, saith
the LORD of hosts 27 And [l] I will kindle a fire in
the wall of Damascus, and it shall consume the palaces
of Ben-hadad.

v 23—27 Syria, with Damascus the capital, and the other chief cities, next are brought to the bar, and doomed to a terrible overthrow No sooner are the tidings heard of the victorious armies of Babylon approaching, than instant confusion and terrors seize the inhabitants of the land The anguish spreads to the most distant border of the sea, or like its troubled waves, so restless are the inhabitants, and uneasy, *v* 23 Instead

82

Before Christ 599 of resistance, the citizens of Damascus, affrighted as a woman in the pangs of travail, place all their hopes in flight, *v* 24 *How is the city of praise*, so famous once, *not left* or spared, but ruined by the Chaldean enemy, *the city of my joy?* either the prophet admired its beauty, or her king lamented her ruins, *v* 25 her young men fallen, her warriors slain, her walls razed, her palaces burnt to the ground, *v* 26 God's wrath hath kindled the flames, and none can quench them *Note*, (1) They who place their joy in earthly comforts will be punished with greater bitterness in the loss of them (2) When God hath a controversy with a nation, he can easily dispirit the bravest, and make the strong men feeble

l Isa xxi 13, m Josh xi 10 Judg iv 2 28 ¶ l Concerning Kedar, and concerning the king-
doms of m Hazor, which Nebuchadnezzar king of Baby-
lon shall smite, thus saith the LORD, Arise ye, go up
to Kedar, and spoil the men of the east 29 Their
tents and their flocks shall they take away, they shall
take to themselves their curtains and all their vessels,
n Chap vi 25 and their camels, and they shall cry unto them, n Fear
o Ver 8 is on every side 30 ¶ o Flee, † get you far off, dwell
† Heb. Fly greatly deep, O ye inhabitants of Hazor, saith the LORD, for
Nebuchadnezzar king of Babylon hath taken counsel a-
gainst you, and hath conceived a purpose against you
‡ Or that is at ease Am vi 1 31 Arise, get you up unto the ‡ wealthy nation that
dwelleth without care, saith the LORD, which have
neither gates nor bars, *which* dwell alone 32 And
their camels shall be a booty, and the multitude of their
cattle a spoil, and I will scatter into all winds them
p Chap ix 26 & xxv 23 p *that are* in the utmost corners, and I will bring their
calamity from all sides thereof, saith the LORD 33
q Chap ix 11 & x 22 Mal i 3 And Hazor q shall be a dwelling for dragons, *and* a de-
solation for ever, there shall no man abide there, nor *any*
son of man dwell in it

v 28—33 Kedar was a son of Ishmael, his descendants settled in Arabia, Hazor or Petra was the capital, and had other tributary kingdoms under it, though some suppose that some of the Hazorites, who escaped in the days of Joshua, fled hither, and built a city of the same name with that they had deserted

Nebuchadnezzar is invited to come and spoil *this wealthy nation*, or rather *this nation living at ease, and dwelling without care*, in peace and security, unprepared to repel an invader, *that have neither gates nor bars*, not *dwelling* in cities, but *alone*, separate from other nations, and in tents, roving from place to place Their curtains, vessels, camels, and flocks, wherein their riches chiefly consisted, are given for a prey Unable to resist the arms of the conqueror, or countermine his purposes, they are called upon to flee, and, scattered on every side, their deserted country is ravaged, and their capital, in ruins, becomes no longer the abode of men, but of wild beasts for ever *Note*, (1) They who are most secure are not therefore most safe (2) The most inoffensive have no guard against the ravages of ambition and covetousness

598 r Chap xxv 25 34 ¶ The word of the LORD that came to Jeremiah
the prophet r against Elam, in the beginning of the reign
of Zedekiah, king of Judah, saying, 35 Thus saith
s Ps xlvi 9 the LORD of hosts, Behold, s I will break the bow of
Elam, the chief of their might 36 And upon Elam
will I bring the four winds, from the four quarters of
heaven, and will scatter them towards all those winds,
and there shall be no nation whither the outcasts of Elam
shall not come 37 For I will cause Elam to be dis-
mayed before their enemies, and before them that seek
their life and I will bring evil upon them, *even* my fierce
anger, saith the LORD, and I will send the sword after
them, till I have consumed them 38 And I will set my
throne in Elam, and will destroy from thence the king
and the princes, saith the LORD 39 ¶ But it shall
t Ver 6 Chap xlviii 47 come to pass in the latter days, *that* t I will bring again
the captivity of Elam, saith the LORD

v 34—39 Elam, concerned in this prophecy, which is dated in the beginning of Zedekiah's reign, is supposed not to be Persia at large, but a country nearer Judea, called Elymais, some of whose inhabitants served under Sennacherib, king of Assyria, at the siege of Jerusalem, *Isa* xxii 6 They were afterwards subdued by Nebuchadnezzar, and the kings of Babylon sometimes made it the seat of their residence, *Dan* viii 2

1 Universal destruction is threatened God undertakes to *break their bow*, and to disable *the chief of their might*, and then they must fall an easy prey *v* 35 By the Chaldean army they shall be dispersed into the four corners of the earth, as fugitives or captives, *v* 36 Terror shall seize them, the sword devour them, the wrath of God pursue them, and therein all evil is comprehended, *v* 37 nor shall the king and princes thereof escape, but fall in the promiscuous ruin, and the conqueror shall erect his throne in Elam, which may well be called the throne of God, by whose power and gift he obtained the dominion, *v* 38

2 A gracious promise is given them of restoration, which probably under Cyrus was accomplished in a measure, but more eminently was fulfilled when, by the preaching of the gospel, the Elamites, among other nations, were called into the church, and into the glorious liberty of the sons of God, *Acts* ii 9

CHAP L.

Babylon herself at last drinks of the cup Terrible is the vengeance denounced against her Many of the expressions in the Apocalypse are borrowed from hence, and the prophet might well have in his eye the destruction of Babylon mystical, and the deliverance of his people from her accursed yoke We have here, 1 *The ruin of Babylon*, ver 1—3 *and* 9—16 *and* 21—32 *and* 35—46 2 *The redemption of God's people*, ver 4—8 *and* 17—20 *and* 33, 34

1 THE word that the LORD spake a against Baby- 598 a Isa xiii 1 & xxi 1 & xlvii 1 Rev xviii 2
lon, *and* against the land of the Chaldeans by
Jeremiah the prophet 2 Declare ye among the na-
tions, and publish, and set up a standard, publish *and* b Rev xiv 8
conceal not say, b Babylon is taken, c Bel is confound- c Isa xlvi 1
ed, Merodach is broken in pieces, her idols are con- d Chap li 48
founded, her images are broken in pieces 3 For d out
of the north there cometh up a nation against her, which
shall make her land desolate, and none shall dwell therein
they shall remove, they shall depart both man and beast
4 ¶ e In those days, and in that time, saith the LORD, e Hos i 11
the children of Israel shall come, f they and the children f Hos i 11
of Judah together, g going and weeping, they shall go, g Ezra iii 12, 13 Ps cxxvi 5, 6 Chap xxxi 9 Zech xii 10
and seek the LORD their God 5 h They shall ask h Chap iii 16
the way to Zion with their faces thitherward, *saying*,
Come, and let us join ourselves to the LORD, i in a i Chap xxxi 31, &
perpetual covenant *that* shall not be forgotten 6 My
people hath been k lost sheep their shepherds have caused k Ps cxix 176 Isa liii 6 1 Pet ii 25
them to go astray, they have turned them away *on* the
mountains they have gone from mountain to hill, they
have forgotten their resting-place 7 All they that l Chap xl 3 Zech xi 5
found them have devoured them, and l their adversaries
said, m We offend not, because they have sinned against m Chap ii 3 Dan ix 16
the LORD, n the habitation of justice, even the LORD, n Ps xc 1 & xci 1
o the hope of their fathers 8 p Remove out of the o Ps xxii 4
midst of Babylon, and go forth out of the land of the p Isa xlviii 20 Chap li 6 45 Rev xviii 4
Chaldeans, and be as the he-goats before the flocks

v 1—8 We have here,

1 The destruction of Babylon foretold, with her idols And great joy would it administer, when these glad tidings were spread among the nations, that the rod of the oppressor was broken From the north the evil comes, from Media and Persia and by the northern princes shall Rome, the mystical Babylon, be destroyed, and the joyful cry go forth, *Babylon is fallen, is fallen*, Rev xiv 6—8

2. The people of God have a comfortable prospect opened before them they shall return to God and their own land Israel and Judah, now reunited, (many of the ten tribes joining with their brethren) *shall go weeping*, with penitential tears confessing their provocations, *and seek the Lord their God*, in faith trusting on the everlasting covenant, and still encouraged to make their humble supplications to him from whom they have so greatly departed for it is a sure symptom for good, when God bestows godly sorrow, and never can it be too late to return to him, when with weeping we seek his face Restored to God's favour, they are in the way to recover their lost inheritance, and, dismissed by Cyrus, enquire the way to Zion, steadfastly setting their faces thitherward, encouraging one another to come and renew their broken covenant, and henceforth approve themselves to God with more unshaken fidelity, *v* 5 And this is most applicable to all God's redeemed people, who, when rescued from the dominion of sin, with shame lament their past departures, with diligence enquire after God, and in all his holy ways desire to be found walking before him, bound to him in a covenant of everlasting love This may also particularly refer to the penitent return of the Jews at the last day

3 Their past miseries, here lamented, should quicken them to improve the moment of opportunity given them by Cyrus Like lost sheep they had long wandered, and those who should have led them aright contributed to their error thus exposed, they fell an easy prey to the devourers, who vindicated the cruelties they exercised upon them, as if it were no offence to punish those

Before Christ 595.

those severely who had transgressed so greatly against God and his worship, v 7 Therefore no sooner are they permitted to remove from Babylon, than they must eagerly seize the permission, and be as *the he-goat before the flocks*, each willing to lead the way, and encourage their brethren to follow them, v 8 And this is exceedingly applicable to the Jews in their present dispersion, who are wanderers in all lands; still deceived by their teachers, *forgetting their resting-place* Christ Jesus, and ready to follow every false pretender, a prey to all nations in which they are scattered, and many to this day think it no crime to plunder a Jew but the days will come when they shall be called home *to the Lord, the hope of their fathers* *Note*, (1) Opportunity is precious, and should be embraced (2) In promoting a good cause, it is well to be zealously affected, and among the first to lead the way

a Chap xxv 14

9 ¶ For lo, a I will raise and cause to come up against
Babylon, an assembly of great nations from the north-
country, and they shall set themselves in array against her,
from thence she shall be taken their arrows *shall be* as
of a mighty † expert man none shall return in vain
10 And Chaldea shall be a spoil a all that spoil her
shall be satisfied, saith the LORD 11 Because ye were
glad, because ye rejoiced, O ye destroyers of c mine he-
ritage, because ye are grown fat, f as the heifer at grass,
and ‡ bellow as bulls 12 Your mother shall be sore
confounded, she that bare you shall be ashamed behold,
the hindermost of the nations *shall be* a wilderness, a dry
land and a desert. 13 Because of the wrath of the
LORD, it shall not be inhabited, but x it shall be wholly
desolate y every one that goeth by Babylon shall be
astonished, and hiss at all her plagues 14 z Put your-
selves in array against Babylon round about all ye that
bend the bow, shoot at her, spare no arrows, for a she
hath sinned against the LORD. 15 Shout against her
round about she hath given her hand her foundations
are fallen, her walls are thrown down, for b it is the
vengeance of the LORD take vengeance upon her,
c as she hath done, do unto her 16 Cut off the sower
from Babylon, and him that handleth the § sickle in the
time of harvest for fear of the oppressing sword, they
shall turn every one to his people, and d they shall flee
every one to his own land 17 ¶ Israel *is* e a scattered
sheep, the lions have driven *him* away first f the king
of Assyria hath devoured him, and last g this Nebuchad-
rezzar king of Babylon hath broken his bones 18
Therefore thus saith the LORD of hosts, the God of Is-
rael, Behold, I will punish the king of Babylon and his
land, as I have punished the king of Assyria 19 And
h I will bring Israel again to his habitation, and he shall
feed on Carmel and Bashan, and his soul shall be satisfied
upon mount Ephraim and Gilead 20 In those days,
and in that time, saith the LORD, the iniquity of Israel
shall be sought for, and *there shall be* none, and the sins
of Judah, and i they shall not be found for k I will par-
don them whom I reserve

[Margin: † Or de-stroyer · Chap xxv 14 · c Isai xlvii 6 · Rev xviii · I Pet v · † Heb fat · ‡ Or neigh as steeds · x Chap xxv 12 · y Chap xlix 17 · z Chap li · a Rev xviii · b Chap li 6, 11 · c Ps cxxxvii 8 · Ver 29 · Rev xviii 6 · § Or scythe · d Isa xiii 14 · Chap li 9 · e Ver 6 · f 2 Kin xv 29, & xvii 6 · g 2 Kings xxiv 14 &c & xxv 7 &c · h Mic vii 14 · i Isa xliv · k Chap xxxi 34]

v 9—20 God's controversy with Babylon proceeds
1 She is given into the hands of the Medes and Persians At God's command their army assembles, and he directs their arrows to the mark, that none return in vain, v 9 Devoted to the spoil, Chaldea falls, v 10 depopulated and desolate, every one that passeth by shall hiss in derision and be astonished at her plagues, v 13 The mother-city Babylon shall be confounded and ashamed to find her helpless state, unable to make head against her besiegers, v 14 and forced to submit and yield her hand, v 15 She, who was once the golden head of nations, shall sink into the lowest place, and be a desert, barren and uninhabited, v 12 Her walls razed from the foundations, v 15 not so much as the dregs of the people left, and her auxiliaries fled for fear of the Persian sword

2 The cause of her fall is God's wrath and vengeance, provoked by the abuse of his people, for, though the Chaldeans were commissioned of God to afflict them for their sins, they meant only to gratify their own enmity and pride, and therefore exulted at their fall, fattened on their spoils, and bellowed as bulls with loud shouts, or *neighed as horses*, making their unhappy captives subservient to their brutal passions, v 11 *Note*, (1) Though God over-rules men's wickedness for purposes of his own glory, that doth not exculpate them (2) None may expect severer judgment from God than those who have persecuted God's people, and maliciously rejoiced at their fall

3 God promises mercifully to visit his people and punish their oppressors They had been as defenceless sheep worried by the lion the king of Assyria had [illegible] the ten tribes, and now Nebuchadnezzar had crushed the very bones of the other two But the king of Babylon shall be punished, as the king of Assyria had been, and righteous retaliation be rendered to their foes, v 15 whilst Israel shall be restored to their own habitation, and God will give them peace and plenty, and every temporal blessing, and, better than all the rest, pardon them freely, fully, and reserve them for an habitation in a better country, that is an heavenly, v 20 *Note*, (1) They who imitate others' sins may expect to share their plagues (2) When we return to God in penitence, we shall find him meeting us with pardon (3) Temporal mercies are doubly sweet when coming in a way of covenant love (4) When God pardons, he doth it abundantly, not only forgiving but forgetting, casting our sins as a stone into the mighty waters, that they may sink and never rise up again (5) God's people are *reserved* by him they are an election of grace, prepared and ordained unto glory

21 ¶ Go up against the land of † Merathaim, *even*
against it, and against the inhabitants of ‡ Pekod waste
and utterly destroy after them, saith the LORD, and
l do according to all that I have commanded thee
22 A sound of battle *is* in the land, and of great de-
struction 23 How is m the hammer of the whole earth
cut asunder and broken? how is n Babylon become a de-
solation among the nations? 24 I have laid a snare for
thee, and thou art also taken, O Babylon, and o thou
wast not aware thou art found, and also caught, be-
cause thou hast striven against the LORD 25 The
LORD hath opened his armoury, and hath brought
forth the weapons of his indignation for this *is* the
work of the LORD God of hosts, in the land of the
Chaldeans 26 Come against her p from § the utmost
border, open her store-houses ‖ cast her up as heaps,
and destroy her utterly let nothing of her be left 27
Slay all her q bullocks let them go down to the slaugh-
ter wo unto them, for their day is come, the time of
their visitation 28 The voice of them that flee, and
escape out of the land of Babylon, r to declare in Zion
the vengeance of the LORD our God, the vengeance
of his temple 29 Call together the archers against
Babylon all ye that bend the bow, camp against it
round about, let none thereof escape s recompense her
according to her work, according to all that she hath
done, do unto her for t she hath been proud against
the LORD, against the holy One of Israel 30 There-
fore u shall her young men fall in the streets, and all her
men of war shall be cut off in that day, saith the LORD
31 Behold, I *am* against thee, O *thou* ‖ most proud,
saith the LORD God of hosts, for thy day is come,
the time *that* I will visit thee 32 And the most proud
shall stumble and fall, and x none shall raise him up
and I will kindle a fire in his cities, and it shall devour
all round about him

[Margin: Before Christ 595 · † Or the rebels · ‡ Or visitation · l 2 Chron xxxvi 23 · Isa xliv 28 · m Isa xiv 6 · Chap li 20 · n Rev xviii 19 · o Chap li · p Isa xiii 5 · § Heb the end · ‖ Or tread her · q Isa xxxiv · r Chap li 10, 11 · s Ver 15 · Chap li 56 · Rev xviii 6 · t Rev xiii 6 · u Chap xlix 26 · ‖ Heb pride · x Rev xviii 21]

v 21—32 Babylon being doomed to ruin, we have here,

1 A commission given to Cyrus, his way pointed out, his conquest assured to him He is directed to march by the country of the Medes, and through Pekod in Assyria, beginning his conquest with these, and to execute exactly the instructions given him, for, though a mighty conqueror, he is but God's servant, *Isa* xliv 28 Great is the destruction he shall work, for the day of vengeance is come God's armoury is opened, he is furnished with weapons, both power and policy are given him from God Caught as a beast in a snare, by stratagem the city is taken, and ravage universal ensues, God having enjoined the conqueror of Babylon to retaliate the injuries she did to Zion none must escape, her mighty men, her bullocks, shall be slaughtered, her young men fall in the streets, and her riches be a prey to the captors the fire of God's wrath, thus kindled, shall burn till all the cities follow the fate of the capital and none be ever able to restore the ruined monarchy *Note*, the sinner, when rioting in plenty, is but as the ox fattening for the slaughter

2 God is most righteous in these his judgments, for the sins of Babylon are manifold (1) Her tyranny She had been *the hammer of the whole earth*, breaking in pieces all who opposed her; but now, astonishing to behold! she is herself *cut asunder and broken* (2) Her impious defiance of God *Thou hast striven against the Lord*, opposing his people and challenging him to vindicate their quarrel but wo to him that contendeth with his Maker (3) Her profanation of the temple, v 28 and the vessels of the sanctuary for, though God suffers for a while the enemies of his church to triumph, he will speedily avenge her wrongs (4) Her intolerable pride, [illegible] insolently even against the Lord himself, and thereby provoked his indignation

Before Christ 595

indignation *I am againſt thee, O thou moſt proud* and who can
ſtand, when God riſeth up as an enemy? *Note,* Unhumbled
pride will have a fall, often in this world, into abject wretched-
neſs, certainly in the next, into the belly of hell!

33 ¶ Thus ſaith the LORD of hoſts, The children
of Iſrael and the children of Judah *were* oppreſſed to-
gether, and all that took them captives held them faſt,
they refuſed to let them go 34 [y] Their redeemer *is*
ſtrong, the LORD of hoſts *is* his name, he ſhall
throughly plead their cauſe, [z] that he may give reſt to
the land, and diſquiet the inhabitants of Babylon 35
¶ A ſword *is* upon the Chaldeans, ſaith the LORD,
and upon the inhabitants of Babylon, and upon her
princes, and upon her wiſe *men* 36 A ſword *is* [a] upon
the † liars, and they ſhall dote, a ſword *is* upon her
mighty men, and they ſhall be diſmayed 37 A ſword
is upon their horſes, and upon their chariots, and upon
all the mingled people that *are* in the midſt of her, and
[b] they ſhall become as women a ſword *is* upon her
treaſures, and they ſhall be robbed 38 [c] A drought
is upon her waters, and they ſhall be dried up. for it *is*
the land of graven images, and they are mad upon *their*
‡ idols 39 Therefore [d] the wild beaſts of the deſert,
with the wild beaſts of the iſland, ſhall dwell *there,* and
the owls ſhall dwell therein and [e] it ſhall be no more
inhabited for ever neither ſhall it be dwelt in from
generation to generation 40 [f] As God overthrew So-
dom and Gomorrah, and the neighbour *cities* thereof,
ſaith the LORD *ſo* ſhall no man abide there, neither
ſhall any ſon of man dwell therein 41 Behold, a peo-
ple ſhall come from the north, and [g] a great nation,
and many kings ſhall be raiſed up from the coaſts of the
earth 42 They ſhall hold the bow and the lance
they [h] *are* cruel, and will not ſhew mercy [i] their voice
ſhall roar like the ſea, and they ſhall ride upon horſes,
every one put in aray like a man to the battle, againſt
thee, O daughter of Babylon 43 The king of Baby-
lon hath heard the report of them, and [k] his hands waxed
feeble [l] anguiſh took hold of him, *and* pangs as of a
woman in travail 44 Behold, he ſhall [m] come up like
a lion from the ſwelling of Jordan, unto the habitation
of the ſtrong but I will make them ſuddenly run away
from her and who *is* a choſen *man that* I may appoint
over her? for who *is* like me, and [n] who will appoint
me the time? and who *is* that ſhepherd that will ſtand
before me? 45 Therefore hear ye the counſel of the
LORD, that he hath taken againſt Babylon, and his
purpoſes that he hath purpoſed againſt the land of the
Chaldeans ſurely the leaſt of the flock ſhall draw them
out ſurely he ſhall make *their* habitation deſolate with
them 46 [o] At the noiſe of the taking of Babylon the
earth is moved, and the cry is heard among the na-
tions

y Rev xviii 8 z 2 Theſ i 6, 7 a Iſa xliv 25 Chap xlviii 30 † Heb Bars b Nah iii 13 c Iſa xliv 27 Chap li 32, 36 Rev xvi 12 ‡ Heb Terrors d Iſa xiii 21 22 & xxxiv 14 Chap li 37 Rev xviii 2 e Iſa xiii 20 Chap xxv 12 f Gen xix 25 Iſa xiii 19 Chap xlix 18 g Chap xxv 14 & li 27 Rev xvii 16 h Pſ cxxxvii 8 Iſa xiii 18 i Iſa v 30 k Iſa xiii 7 l Chap xlix 24 m Chap xlix 19, &c n Job xli 10 Chap xlix 19 o Chap xlix 21 Rev xviii 9

v 33—46 We have here,

1 The recovery of God's people from their ſtate of oppreſſion
Iſrael and Judah both groaned under the yoke, and their con-
querors refuſed to let them go but, when God determines their
deliverance, who can ſtay him? *Their Redeemer is ſtrong,* yet
almighty to ſave, *the Lord of hoſts is his name,* whom all the
armies of heaven and earth obey *He ſhall thoroughly plead their
cauſe,* avenge their wrongs, reſtore them to their own land, and
puniſh their oppreſſors And this is true of all the Iſrael of God,
whether under the ſpiritual bondage of ſin and Satan, or ſuffer-
ing under antichriſtian tyranny though their enemies refuſe to
let them go, the Lord is their avenger, to recompenſe tribulation
to them that trouble them, to break the bands of ſin and Satan,
and the power of their perſecutors, to ſet his people free, to
give them reſt ſpiritually on earth, and eternally with himſelf in
heaven Let them therefore truſt in the Lord, and rejoice in the
comfort of his aſſured ſalvation

2 The ruin of Babylon for her ſins; particularly her deten-
tion of God's Iſrael, and her abominable idolatries *They are
mad upon their idols,* ſo ſuperſtitiouſly devoted to them, or *their
terrors,* their images being frightful, and their worſhippers terri-
fied with fear of them And very applicable is this to the idola-
tries of Babylon myſtical, where image-worſhip ſo abounds
Upon this God's ſword is drawn, and terribly deſcends upon her
princes, her wiſe counſellors, her ſoothſayers, who deceived the
people with their lies, upon her mighty warriors, her cavalry,
her chariots, her auxiliaries, who ſhould through fear become
weak as women, upon her treaſures, devoted to the ſpoil, *v* 35,
37 *A drought* is ſent *upon her waters* in general, from whence
the land becomes barren, and famine enſues, or upon the river
that ran through Babylon in particular, the courſe of which was
turned, and the bed of it left dry opened a paſſage into the city,
v 38 So utterly ſhall this proud city be overthrown, that the
wild beaſts ſhall take up their abode in her ruinous palaces, and,
like the cities of Gomorrah, her deſolations ſhall be perpetual,
v 39, 40 From the north their merciless deſtroyers come,
compleatly armed, and ſpreading their terrors on every ſide.
Confounded at the report, the king of Babylon, like a travailing
woman, loſes all power of reſiſtance, and falls an eaſy prey
The very ſame expreſſions are uſed as *chap* xlix 22, 24 to ſhew
how exactly Babylon was to be puniſhed according to her
former treatment of Jeruſalem And as Nebuchadnezzar had
ſerved Edom, *chap* xlix 19—21 ſuch a lion ſhould Cyrus
prove to Chaldea, devouring and deſtroying all before him
And as Babylon of old, ſo ſhall Babylon myſtical be deſtroyed,
when the time fixed in God's eternal decree arrives, when the
ſaints of God will for ever triumph, and their enemies be eter-
nally tormented, *Rev* xiv 8 xviii 2—19

CHAP LI.

*This chapter is a continuation of the former prophecy againſt Babylon
1 Her ruin is at large ſet forth,* ver 1—58. *2 The ratifica-
tion of it by a ſign,* ver 59—64

1 THUS ſaith the LORD, Behold, I will raiſe
up againſt Babylon, and againſt them that dwell
in the † midſt of them that riſe up againſt me, [a] a deſtroy-
ing wind, 2 And will ſend unto Babylon [b] fanners,
that ſhall fan her, and ſhall empty her land for [c] in the
day of trouble they ſhall be againſt her round about
3 Againſt *him that* bendeth let the archer bend his
bow, and againſt *him that* lifteth himſelf up in his bri-
gandine, and ſpare ye not her young men, [d] deſtroy ye
utterly all her hoſt 4 Thus the ſlain ſhall fall in the
land of the Chaldeans, and *they that are* thruſt through
in her ſtreets 5 For Iſrael *hath* not *been* ‡ forſaken, nor
Judah of his God, of the LORD of hoſts, though
[e] their land was filled with ſin againſt the holy One of
Iſrael 6 [f] Flee out of the midſt of Babylon, and deli-
ver every man his ſoul be not cut off in her iniquity
for this *is* [g] the time of the LORD's vengeance [h] he
will render unto her a recompenſe 7 [i] Babylon *hath
been* a golden cup in the LORD's hand, that made all
the earth drunken [k] the nations have drunken of her
wine, therefore the nations are mad 8 [l] Babylon is
[m] ſuddenly fallen and deſtroyed [n] howl for her, [o] take
balm for her pain, if ſo be ſhe may be healed 9 We
would have healed Babylon, but ſhe is not healed for-
ſake her, and [p] let us go every one into his own country
for [q] her judgment reacheth unto heaven, and is lifted up
even to the ſkies 10 [r] The LORD hath brought
forth our righteouſneſs come and [s] let us declare in Zion
the work of the LORD our God 11 [t] Make bright
the arrows gather the ſhields [u] the LORD hath raiſed
up the ſpirit of the kings of the Medes for his device
is againſt Babylon, to deſtroy it, becauſe [x] it *is* the ven-
geance of the LORD, the vengeance of his temple
12 [y] Set up the ſtandard upon the walls of Babylon,
make the watch ſtrong, ſet up the watchmen, prepare
the ambuſhes for the LORD hath both deviſed and
done that which he ſpake againſt the inhabitants of Ba-
bylon 13 O thou that dwelleſt [z] upon many waters,
abundant in treaſures, thine end is come, *and* the mea-
ſure of thy covetouſneſs 14 The LORD of hoſts
[a] hath ſworn by himſelf, *ſaying,* Surely I will fill thee
with men, as with caterpillers, and they ſhall lift up
a ſhout againſt thee 15 [b] He hath made the earth by
his power, he hath eſtabliſhed the world by his wiſdom,
and [c] hath ſtretched out the heaven by his underſtanding
16 When he uttereth *his* voice, *there is* a § multitude of
waters in the heavens, and [d] he cauſeth the vapours to
aſcend from the ends of the earth, he maketh lightnings
with rain, and bringeth forth the wind out of his trea-
ſures 17 [e] Every man is ‖ brutiſh by *his* knowledge,
every founder is confounded by the graven image for
his molten image *is* falſhood, and *there is* no breath in
them 18 They *are* vanity, the work of errors [f] in
the time of their viſitation they ſhall periſh 19 [g] The
portion

Before Christ 595

† Heb Heart a Chap iv 11 b Chap xv 7 c Chap ii 14 d Chap l 21 † Heb Widowed e Chap xvi 18 f Chap l 8 Rev xviii 4 g Chap l 15 h Chap xxv 14 i Rev xvii 4 k Rev xiv 8 l Iſa xxi 9 Rev xiv 8 & xviii 2 m Chap l 46 n Rev xviii 9 o Chap xlvi 11 p Iſa xiii 14 q Rev xviii 5 r Pſ xxxvii 6 s Chap l 28 t Chap xlvi 4 u Iſa xiii 17 Ver 28 x Chap l 28 y Nah ii 1 & iii 14 z Rev xvii 1 a Heb by his ſoul b Gen i 1 Chap x 12 c Job ix 8 Pſ civ 2 Iſa xl 22 § Or noiſe d Pſ cxxxv 7 e Chap x 14 ‖ Or is more brutiſh than to know

Before Christ 595

portion of Jacob *is* not like them, for he *is* the former
of all things, and *Iſrael is* the rod of his inheritance
the LORD of hoſts *is* his name 20 [h] Thou *art* my
battle-ax *and* weapons of war for † with thee will I
break in pieces the nations, and with thee will I deſtroy
kingdoms 21 And with thee will I break in pieces
the horſe and his rider, and with thee will I break in
pieces the chariot and his rider 22 With thee alſo
will I break in pieces man and woman, and [i] with thee
will I break in pieces old and young, and with thee
will I break in pieces the young man and the maid
23 I will alſo break in pieces with thee the ſhepherd
and his flock, and with thee will I break in pieces the
huſbandman and his yoke of oxen, and with thee will I
break in pieces captains and rulers 24 And [k] I will
render unto Babylon, and to all the inhabitants of Chal-
dea, all their evil that they have done in Zion in your
ſight, ſaith the LORD 25 Behold, I *am* againſt
thee, [l] O deſtroying mountain, ſaith the LORD, which
deſtroyeſt all the earth, and I will ſtretch out mine
hand upon thee, and roll thee down from the rocks,
and will make thee [m] a burnt mountain 26 And they
ſhall not take of thee a ſtone for a corner, nor a ſtone
for foundations, but [n] thou ſhalt be ‡ deſolate for ever,
ſaith the LORD. 27, Set ye up a ſtandard in the land,
blow the trumpet among the nations, [o] prepare the nati-
ons againſt her, call together againſt her [p] the kingdoms
of Ararat, Minni, and Aſhchenaz, appoint a captain
againſt her, cauſe the horſes to come up as the rough
caterpillers 28 Prepare againſt her the nations with
the kings of the Medes, the captains thereof, and all
the rulers thereof, and all the land of his dominion
29 And the land ſhall tremble and ſorrow for every
purpoſe of the LORD ſhall be performed againſt Ba-
bylon, [q] to make the land of Babylon a deſolation with-
out an inhabitant 30 The mighty men of Babylon
have forborn to fight, they have remained in *their* holds,
[r] their might hath failed, [s] they became as women they
have burnt her dwelling-places, her bars are broken
31 [t] One poſt ſhall run to meet another, and one meſ-
ſenger to meet another, to ſhew the king of Babylon
that his city is taken at *one* end, 32 And that [u] the
paſſages are ſtopped, and the reeds they have burnt with
fire, and the men of war are affrighted 33 For thus
ſaith the LORD of hoſts the God of Iſrael, The daugh-
ter of Babylon *is* [x] like a threſhing-floor, § *it is* time to
threſh her yet a little while, and [y] the time of her har-
veſt ſhall come 34 Nebuchadnezzar the king of Ba-
bylon hath devoured me, [z] he hath cruſhed me, he hath
made me an empty veſſel, he hath ſwallowed me up
like a dragon, he hath filled his belly with my delicates,
he hath caſt me out 35 || The violence done to me
and to my † fleſh, [a] *be* upon Babylon, ſhall the ‡ inha-
bitant of Zion ſay, and my blood upon the inhabitants
of Chaldea, ſhall Jeruſalem ſay 36 Therefore thus ſaith
the LORD, Behold [b] I will plead thy cauſe, and take
vengeance for thee, [c] and I will dry up her ſea, and make
her ſprings dry 37 And [d] Babylon ſhall become heaps,
a dwelling-place for dragons, an aſtoniſhment, and an
hiſſing without an inhabitant 38 They ſhall roar to-
gether like lions they ſhall § yell as lions whelps 39
In their heat I will make their feaſts, and [e] I will make
them drunken, that they may rejoice and ſleep a per-
petual ſleep, and not wake, ſaith the LORD 40 I
will bring them down like lambs to the ſlaughter, like
rams with he-goats 41 How is [f] Sheſhach taken ! and
[g] how is the praiſe of the whole earth ſurpriſed ! how is
Babylon become an aſtoniſhment among the nations !
42 [h] The ſea is come up upon Babylon . ſhe is covered
with the multitude of the waves thereof. 43 Her ci-
ties are a deſolation, a dry land, and a wilderneſs, [i] a
land wherein no man dwelleth, neither doth *any* ſon of
man paſs thereby 44 And [k] I will puniſh Bel in Baby-
lon, and I will bring forth out of his mouth that which
he hath ſwallowed up, and and the nations ſhall not flow
together any more unto him, yea, the wall of Babylon
ſhall fall. 45 [l] My people, go ye out of the midſt of
her, and deliver ye every man his ſoul from the fierce
anger of the LORD. 46. And || leſt your heart faint,

h Iſa x. 5, 15 Chap l 23 † Or in, or by thee
i Chron. xxxvi 17 Ezek ix 6
k Chap l 15 Rev xvi. 6
l Iſa xiv 6 Zech. iv 7
m Rev viii 8.
n Chap l 4 ‡ Heb everlaſting deſolations
o Iſa xiii 3 Chap. xxv 14
p Chap l 41
q Chap l 39, 40
r Pſ lxxvi 5
s Chap l 37
t Ib 43
u Ib 38
x Iſa xxi 10, Mic iv 13
§ Or, in the time that he threſheth her Hab iii 12
y Iſa xvii 5 Joel iii 13 Rev xiv 15
z Chap l 17
|| Heb. My violence
† Or remainder
‡ Rev. xviii 6.
‡ Heb Inhabitreſs.
b Chap. l 34
c Ib 38
d Iſa xiii 22 Chap l 39 Rev xviii 2
§ Or ſhake themſelves
e Ver 57
f Chap xxv 26
g Iſa xiii 19
h Iſa viii 8
k Iſa xlvi 1 Chap l 2
l Ver 6 Chap. l. 8 Rev xviii 4
|| Or, let not

and ye fear for the rumour that ſhall be heard in the
land a rumour ſhall both come *one* year, and after that
in *another* year *ſhall come* a rumour, and violence in
the land, ruler againſt ruler 47 Therefore behold, the
days come, that [m] I will † do judgment upon the graven
images of Babylon, and her whole land ſhall be con-
founded, and all her ſlain ſhall fall in the midſt of her
48 Then [n] the heaven, and the earth, and all that *is*
therein, ſhall ſing for Babylon for [o] the ſpoilers ſhall
come unto her from the north, ſaith the LORD 49
‡ As Babylon *hath cauſed* the ſlain of Iſrael to fall ſo at
Babylon ſhall fall the ſlain of all the § earth 50 Ye that
have eſcaped the ſword, go away, ſtand not ſtill remem-
ber the LORD afar off, and let Jeruſalem come into
your mind 51 [p] We are confounded, becauſe we have
heard reproach, ſhame hath covered our faces for ſtran-
gers are come into the ſanctuaries of the LORD's houſe
52 Wherefore behold, the days come, ſaith the LORD,
that [q] I will do judgment upon her graven images, and
through all her land the wounded ſhall groan 53
[r] Though Babylon ſhould mount up to heaven, and
though ſhe ſhould fortify the height of her ſtrength, *yet*
from me ſhall ſpoilers come unto her, ſaith the LORD
54 A ſound of a cry *cometh* from Babylon, [s] and great
deſtruction from the land of the Chaldeans 55 Be-
cauſe the LORD hath ſpoiled Babylon, and deſtroyed
out of her the great voice, when her waves do roar like
great waters, a noiſe of their voice is uttered 56 Be-
cauſe the ſpoiler is come upon her, *even* upon Babylon,
and her mighty men are taken, every one of their bows
is broken, for the LORD God of recompenſes [t] ſhall
ſurely requite 57 And [u] I will make drunk her prin-
ces, and her wiſe *men*, her captains and her rulers, and
her mighty men , and they ſhall ſleep a perpetual ſleep,
and not wake, ſaith the King, whoſe name *is* the LORD
of hoſts 58 Thus ſaith the LORD of hoſts, § The
broad walls of Babylon ſhall be utterly || broken, and
her high gates ſhall be burnt with fire, and [x] the people
ſhall labour in vain, and the folk in the fire, and they
ſhall be weary

Before Christ 595
m Chap l 2. † Heb Viſit upon
n Iſa xliv 23 & xlix 13 Rev xviii 20
o Chap l 3
‡ Or both Babylon is to fall O ye ſlain of Iſrael, and with Babylon &
§ Or country
p Pſ cxxxvii 1 Lam ii 10
q Ver 47.
r Iſa xiv 12—15 Am ix 2 3 Obad 4.
s Chap l 22.
t 2 Theſ i 6
u Ver 39
§ Or, the walls of broad Babylon
|| Or made naked
x Hab ii 13

v 1—58 For the comfort of God's people, and the confuſion of his enemies, the deſtruction of this proud city is at large inſiſted on

1 God ſends forth and commiſſions the Medes and Perſians to deſtroy Babylon like a whirlwind they ſhall ſweep the earth, and ſcatter the Chaldeans as chaff, *v* 1, 2 murdering all who dared reſiſt them, without mercy or pity, *v* 3 The Perſian ſtandard is erected, and multitudes flock to it, thick as the caterpillars or locuſts cover the ground, *v* 27, 28 for when God hath work to do, inſtruments ſhall never be wanting

2 Notwithſtanding all the former might of this famed city, it ſhall now be weak, and unable to reſiſt Once God had clothed her with ſtrength, and as his battle-ax, *v* 20 ſent her to break in pieces the nations, their forces, and all their inhabitants ſmall and great, *v* 21—23 but now in vain they prepare their weapons of war, and furbiſh their armour, ruſty with long peace in vain they erect their ſtandard, and ſummon their ſoldiers to attend, to guard the walls, or prepare an ambuſh for their enemies, *v* 11, 12 Their courage is utterly failed, they are become as timorous as women, and fall without reſiſtance, *v* 29, 30 ſo eaſily can God, when he ſends his terrors forth, make cowards of the braveſt

3 The provocation Babylon had given was great her ſins cried to heaven for vengeance, *v* 9 (1) They have *riſen up againſt me*, *v* 1 in daring rebellion againſt God, and defiance of his power. (2) Babylon *is a golden cup, that made all the earth drunken*, *v* 7 ſhe hath been the head ſeat of idolatry, and the great temptreſs to all the nations over whom her power extended , by force or fraud engaging them to partake of her abominations, and, like her, become mad upon idols (3) Her incorrigibleneſs *We would have healed Babylon, but ſhe is not healed*, *v* 9 The faithful among the Jews that dwelt there would have turned them from their idolatries, but they were hardened in them Though this may alſo be underſtood of her auxiliary forces, who in vain attempted to reſcue her from ruin, her time to fall being come (4) Her covetouſneſs was inſatiable, *v* 13 graſping ſtill at farther conqueſts and ſpoil (5) Her tyranny over God's people As a dragon, Nebuchadnezzar had ſwallowed and devoured them , broke all their bones as a lion ; emptied them of all that was valuable , for which violence and bloodſhed, the inhabitants of Zion imprecate juſt vengeance upon their ravagers ; and theſe appeals of God's oppreſſed people ſhall not be long unanſwered

4 God in juſt judgment brings on Babylon the terrible ruin ſhe hath provoked by her ſin *againſt the holy One of Iſrael*, *v* 5

He

Before Christ 595

He will plead the cause of his distressed people, who seemed to be deserted and forsaken, and will take vengeance for them *v* 37 The time is fixed in the divine decree, *v* 6 when the wrongs of Zion shall be requited, *v* 24, 56 and God's people shall see the day, when Babylon shall fall as the slain of Israel, who fell by her sword, *v* 49 And this is the work of the Lord, and to be declared in Zion to his praise, vindicating his people's cause, *v* 10 and with a mighty and out-stretched arm punishing their foes He hath sworn their destruction, *v* 14 and is fully able to execute his threatnings, being the almighty Lord, the maker and governor of all, whom heaven and earth obey, and against whom the Babylonish idols can avail nothing, *v* 15—19 As he had before declared, *chap* x 12—16 where the very same expressions are used as here When this Lord of hosts arises, sure desolation marks his way *Babylon is fallen*, *v* 8 though now in all her pride since God hath pronounced her doom, it is as sure as if already executed The waters on which she dwelt shall afford her no defence, their course being diverted, and her rivers dried up by the besiegers, nor her treasures protect her, when her time is come, *v* 13 Though strong as a mountain, and late the destroyer of the nations, *v* 25 she is now made *a threshing-floor*, where all her inhabitants should be beaten in pieces, *v* 33 From year to year the rumour comes of the vast preparations made by the Persians, at last they approach, a battle ensues, the Babylonians are routed and driven within their walls, *v* 46 nor can these protect them Whilst there secure they revel, sudden their enemies enter through the bed of the river, and surprize them in their drunken feast Swift flies the dreadful news, messenger upon messenger informs the affrighted king that his city is taken, the passages seized, and resistance vain, *v* 31, 32 The houses are on fire, the bars of the gates broken, *v* 30 roaring at their impious carousal, and drunken, they are slain, and lie down to wake no more, *v* 38, 39 slaughtered as easily as sheep, *v* 40 deluged by the army of the Persians, breaking in like the waves of the sea, *v* 42 and utterly desolate, the land becomes a wilderness, the cities uninhabited, *v* 43 Their gods falling in the common ruin, and so far from helping their votaries, unable to defend themselves, *v* 44 yea, so entirely demolished shall these proud walls be, the wonder of the world, on which several chariots might drive abreast, that there should not be a stone left fit for any use, *v* 26 her gates burnt with fire, the very foundations razed, and every attempt to repair these desolations for ever fruitless, *v* 9, 26, 58

5 The people of God are warned to flee when they see the ruin approaching, that they may not be involved in it, nor overwhelmed with the terror of the destroying enemy, *v* 46 and gladly to accept the offer of liberty which Cyrus shall proclaim to them, *v* 45 They who had *escaped the sword of the Chaldeans*, reserved in mercy for such a time, must haste away to their own land They are called to *remember the Lord afar off*, in the land of their captivity, and to think of Jerusalem, the city of their solemnities, with eager longing to return thither, notwithstanding its present desolate state at which they were confounded, ashamed to think of their abominations, that had provoked God to give up his sanctuary to the profanation of the heathen But God now hath avenged their quarrel and his own, and condignly punished the Chaldeans and their gods, over whom Israel now may triumph, *v* 50—52 *Note*, (1) When we know the wrath of God is revealed against a world lying in wickedness, it is our wisdom to come out from among them, and be separate (2) In whatever state of affliction or distress we are, it is our duty, and will be our comfort to think upon God, and remember his faithfulness, mercy, and truth

6 According to their several interests those who hear of Babylon's fall will be greatly affected Some with astonishment and deep concern behold her sudden fall, *v* 41 and with an exceeding great and bitter cry bewail her desolations others shall rejoice in it, yea, *the very heaven and the earth shall sing*, *v* 48 giving praise to God for avenging the blood of his saints, and for the recovery of his people from captivity Throughout the whole description if we compare *Rev* xviii with this chapter, we shall see the strongest resemblance in the expression, and as now this proud city here devoted to ruin hath been for many ages desolate, according to the prophetic word, so surely shall Babylon mystical, the city of Rome, and the tyranny of popery, be destroyed, when God's time of vengeance comes

59 ¶ The word which Jeremiah the prophet com-
manded Seraiah the son of Neriah, the son of Maaseiah,
when he went ‖ with Zedekiah the king of Judah into
Babylon, in the fourth year of his reign and *this* Se-
raiah *was* † a quiet prince 60 So Jeremiah wrote in a
book all the evil that should come upon Babylon, *even*
all these words *that are* written against Babylon 61
And Jeremiah said to Seraiah, When thou comest to
Babylon, and shalt see, and shalt read all these words,
62 Then thou shalt say, O LORD, thou hast spoken
against this place, to cut it off, [y] that none shall remain
in it, neither man nor beast, but that [a] it shall be deso-
late for ever 63 And it shall be when thou hast
made an end of reading this book, *that* [z] thou shalt bind
a stone to it, and cast it into the midst of Euphrates
64 And thou shalt say, Thus shall Babylon sink, and
shall not rise from the evil that I will bring upon her
and they shall be weary Thus far *are* the words of
Jeremiah

‖ Or on the behalf of. † Heb. A prince of rest, or of Menucha

Before Christ 595

y Chap l ver 6. z Rev xviii 21

v 59—64 The prophecy concerning Babylon was long and terrible We have here,

1 A copy of it written and sent to the captive Jews in Babylon, by Seraiah, a quiet prince in those turbulent times, who was for peace, and it is spoken of to his honour He accompanied Zedekiah, as our version renders the words, or was sent *from Zedekiah*, as his ambassador to Nebuchadnezzar, in the fourth year of his reign, and sixty years before the destruction of Babylon

2 He is enjoined to read the words of the roll when he came to Babylon, in the presence of the captive Jews, for their encouragement, for however improbable the event, when they considered that vast city, so populous, and strongly fortified, the accomplishment of God's word was sure *Note*, The eye of faith staggers at no difficulties, if God hath promised, that is enough

3 He must make a solemn profession of his own faith in the truth of what he had read, that it would surely be fulfilled, *v* 62 and then in the presence of the people must tie a stone to the roll, and cast it into the river Euphrates, explaining the sign, that thus *should Babylon sink, and never rise up again*, wearied out with her plagues, exhausted, and unable to repair her desolations *Thus far are the words of Jeremiah*, not that this was the last of his prophecies, but that here the burden of Babylon ends With still greater magnificence is the fall of Babylon mystical represented, *Rev* xviii 21 and when God's final wrath is poured out upon the ungodly, their ruin will be irrecoverable and eternal

CHAP LII

The sad event here recorded we have had 2 Kings xxiv xxv *It shews the fulfilment of many of the foregoing prophecies, and well introduces the book of* Lamentations *We have*, 1 *The ill reign of Zedekiah*, ver 1—3 2 *The besieging and taking of Jerusalem by the Chaldeans*, ver 4—7 3 *The severe usage which Zedekiah and the princes met with*, ver 8—11 4 *The destruction of the city and temple*, ver 12—14 5 *The captivity of the people* ver 15, 16 *and the numbers of the captives*, ver 28—30 6 *The carrying off of the plunder of the temple*, ver 17—23 7 *The slaughter of the priests, and some other great men in cold blood*, ver 24—27 8 *The better days which king Jehoiachin lived to see, after the death of Nebuchadrezzar*, ver 31—34

1 [a] ZEdekiah *was* one and twenty years old when he 590
† began to reign, and he reigned eleven years a 2 Kings xxiv 18
in Jerusalem, and his mother's name *was* Hamutal the † Heb Reigned
daughter of Jeremiah of Libnah 2 And he did *that*
which was evil in the eyes of the LORD, [b] according to b 2 Kings xxiii 37
all that Jehoiakim had done 3 For through the anger
of the LORD it came to pass in Jerusalem and Judah,
till he had cast them out from his presence, that Zede-
kiah rebelled against the king of Babylon 4 ¶ And it 591
came to pass [c] in the ninth year of his reign, [d] in the tenth 590
month, in the tenth *day* of the month, *that* Nebuchad- c 2 Kings xxv 1
rezzar king of Babylon came, he and all his army against Chap xxxix 1
Jerusalem, and pitched against it, and built forts against d Zech viii
it round about 5 So the city was besieged unto the 19
eleventh year of king Zedekiah 6 And [e] in the fourth 588
month, in the ninth *day* of the month, [f] the famine was e Zech viii
sore in the city, so that there was no bread for the people 19
of the land 7 Then the city was broken up, and all f Chap xxxviii 9? 16
the men of war fled, and went forth out of the city [g] by g ... 14
night, by the way of the gate between the two walls,
which *was* by the king's garden, (now the Chaldeans
were by the city round about) and they went by the way
of the plain 8 ¶ But the army of the Chaldeans pur-
sued after the king, and [h] overtook Zedekiah in the plains h Chap xxxix 5
of Jericho, and all his army was scattered from him 9 Ezek xii 13
Then [i] they took the king, and carried him up unto the i Chap xxxii 4
king of Babylon to Riblah in the land of Hamath
where he gave judgment upon him 10 And the king
of Babylon slew the sons of Zedekiah before his eyes
he slew also all the princes of Judah in Riblah 11

Then

Before Christ 588

Then [k] he put out the eyes of Zedekiah, and the king of
Babylon bound him in chains, and carried him to
Babylon, and put him in ‡ priſon till the day of his
death.

k Ezek. xii 13 ‡ Heb. The houſe of the wards

v. 1—11 We are here told,

1 The cauſe of the ruin of Zedekiah and the people. It was their ſins that provoked God's *wrath* againſt them, and what particularly filled up the meaſure of their guilt, and haſtened their deſtruction, was his rebellion againſt the king of Babylon, in violation of the oath of God which was upon him; and this God permitted as a puniſhment for his former ſins, and as the means to haſten his ruin. *Note*, When ſinners wilfully depart from God, he gives them up to their own folly, and uſually nothing more is needful to puſh them on their deſtruction.

2 The inſtruments employed were the Chaldeans under Nebuchadnezzar, who, after a ſiege of about eighteen months, took the city by aſſault, the famine having diſabled the beſiegers, and the obſtinacy of the king and princes preventing a ſurrender.

3 Too late the king and the men of war who ſurvived, attempted to flee. Though covered by the *night*, they are quickly purſued and taken; for in vain is every effort the ſinner makes to elude his deſtiny. See the unhappy monarch dragged as a criminal before the Babyloniſh monarch, judgment paſſed on him, his ſons murdered before his eyes, his princes ſlain; and then, as if to fix upon his mind continually the memory of the ſhocking ſcene, his eyes put out, in chains carried to Babylon, and condemned in a priſon to languiſh out the remainder of his miſerable days. He would not be warned, therefore he muſt ſuffer for it.

12 ¶ Now [l] in the fifth month, in the tenth *day* of
the month ([m] which *was* the nineteenth year of Ne-
buchadrezzar king of Babylon) [n] came Nebuzar-adan †
captain of the guard, *which* ſerved the king of Babylon,
into Jeruſalem, 13 And burnt [p] the houſe of the
LORD, and the kings houſe, and all the houſes of Je-
ruſalem, and all the houſes of the great *men* burnt he with
fire 14 And all the army of the Chaldeans that *were*
with the captain of the guard, brake down all the walls
of Jeruſalem round about 15 Then Nebuzar-adan the
captain of the guard carried away captive *certain* of the
poor of the people, and the reſidue of the people, that
remained in the city, and thoſe that fell away, that fell
to the king of Babylon, and the reſt of the multitude
16 But Nebuzar-adan the captain of the guard, left *cer-
tain* of the poor of the land for the vine-dreſſers, and for
huſbandmen 17 [q] Alſo [r] the pillars of braſs that *were*
in the houſe of the LORD, and the baſes, and the braſen
ſea that *was* in the houſe of the LORD, the Chalde-
ans brake, and carried all the braſs of them to Babylon
18 [s] The caldrons alſo, and the ſhovels, and the ſnuffers,
and the ‡ bowls, and the ſpoons, and all the veſſels of braſs
wherewith they miniſtred, took they away 19 And
the baſons, and the ‖ fire pans, and the bowls, and the
caldrons, and the candleſticks, and the ſpoons, and the
cups, *that* which *was* of gold *in* gold, and *that* which
was of ſilver *in* ſilver, took the captain of the guard a-
way 20 The two pillars, one ſea, and twelve braſen
bulls that *were* under the baſes, which king Solomon
had made in the houſe of the LORD [t] the § braſs of all
theſe veſſels was without weight 21 And *concerning* [u]
the pillars, the height of one pillar *was* eighteen cubits,
and a † fillet of twelve cubits did compaſs it, and the
thickneſs thereof *was* four fingers *it was* hollow 22
And a chapiter of braſs *was* upon it, and the height
of one chapiter *was* five cubits, with net-work and
pomegranates upon the chapiters round about, all *of*
braſs the ſecond pillar alſo and the pomegranates *were*
like unto theſe 23 And there were ninety and ſix
pomegranates on a ſide, *and* [x] all the pomegranates upon
the net-work, *were* an hundred round about

‡ Or, baſons ‖ Or, cenſers

v. 12—23 A month after the taking the city, we have an account of its entire demolition by Nebuzar-adan, ſent for this purpoſe by Nebuchadnezzar: the temple is laid in aſhes, after being plundered of all its veſſels and all its braſs, the quantity of which was immenſe, and the particulars of it are mentioned, to ſhew the exact fulfilment of the prediction, *chap* xxvii 19. The palaces and houſes of Jeruſalem are burnt to the ground, the walls razed, and the reſidue of the people, who ſurvived the ſiege and famine, led captive with thoſe who had fallen to the Chaldeans. A melancholy ſcene! a warning to other nations how dangerous it is to provoke a jealous God.

24 ¶ And [y] the captain of the guard took Seraiah the
chief prieſt, and [z] Zephaniah the ſecond prieſt, and the
three keepers of the door 25 He took alſo out of the
city an eunuch, which had the charge of the men of war,
and [a] ſeven men of them that † were near the king's per-
ſon, which were found in the city, and ‡ the principal
ſcribe of the hoſt, who muſtered the people of the land,
and threeſcore men of the people of the land, *that were*
found in the midſt of the city 26 So Nebuzar-adan
the captain of the guard took them, and brought them
to the king of Babylon to Riblah 27 And the king
of Babylon ſmote them, and put them to death in Rib-
lah, in the land of Hamath Thus [b] Judah was carried
away captive out of his own land 28 This *is* the
people whom Nebuchadrezzar carried away captive, [c] in
the ſeventh year, [d] three thouſand Jews and three and
twenty 29 [e] In the eighteenth year of Nebuchadrez-
zar he carried away captive from Jeruſalem eight hund-
red thirty and two § perſons 30 [f] In the three and
twentieth year of Nebuchadrezzar, Nebuzar-adan the
captain of the guard carried away captive of the Jews
ſeven hundred forty and five perſons all the perſons
were four thouſand and ſix hundred

Before Christ 588. y 2 Kings xxv 18 z Chap xxi 1 & xxix 25 a 2 Kings xxv 19 † Heb Saw the King's face ‡ Or the ſcribe of the captain of the hoſt. b Deut xxviii 36 600 c 2 Kings xxiv 12 d 2 Kings xxiv 14 589 e Ver 12 § Heb Souls 584 f Chap xli 2

v. 24—30 When the ſword is drawn, it is not quickly ſheathed. We have here,

1 The dreadful execution of ſeventy-four of the principal men, who were brought up by Nebuzar-adan to the king of Babylon at Riblah. The account, 2 *Kings* xxv 18, 19 reckons them but ſeventy-two; ſome hence imagine that Jeremiah and Ebed-Melech were of the number who were taken, but afterwards releaſed, or two of leſs note than the reſt might not be there reckoned. All theſe were murdered in cold blood by Nebuchadnezzar's orders, as a puniſhment for their rebellion, and we muſt own this to be the juſt fate of traitors, whilſt we condemn the cruelty of the Chaldean king.

2 Their repeated captivities in the ſeventh, the nineteenth, and twenty-third years of Nebuchadnezzar. The two former we had an account of, 2 *Kings* xxiv 12 &c though the numbers conſiderably differ. Perhaps here the men of note are only mentioned, and officers; there the common people alſo; but the latter probably was the gleaning of the people after the death of Gedaliah, and the flight of Johanan. A number ſmall and inconſiderable, compared to the multitudes which once dwelt in the land, but by peſtilence, famine, and the ſword, they were thus miſerably reduced. Such ravages doth ſin make.

562

31 ¶ [g] And it came to paſs in the ſeven and thirtieth
year of the captivity of Jehoiachin king of Judah, in the
twelfth month, in the five and twentieth *day* of the
month, *that* Evil-merodach king of Babylon, in the *firſt*
year of his reign, [h] lifted up the head of Jehoiachin king
of Judah, and brought him forth out of priſon, 32
And ſpake † kindly unto him, and ſet his throne above
the throne of the kings that *were* with him in Babylon,
33 And changed his priſon garments and he [i] did con-
tinually eat bread before him all the days of his life 34
And *for* his diet, there was a continual diet given him
of the king of Babylon, ‖ every day a portion until the
day of his death, all the days of his life

g 2 Kings xxv 27, 28 h Gen xl 13 20 † Heb Good things with him i 2 Sam ix 13 Chap xv 11 ‖ Heb The matter of the day in his day

v. 31—34 The only difference between the account here given, and that, 2 *Kings* xxv is, that there Jehoiachin's deliverance from priſon is ſaid to be on the 27th day of the 12th month, here on the 25th: probably the orders were given this day, though not executed till two days after. The captive king experienced now a very happy change, releaſed from his priſon, arrayed in royal robes, inſtead of his priſon-garments, his throne exalted above his fellow-captive monarchs, treated with great affection and regard by the Babyloniſh emperor, admitted to a conſtant ſeat at his table, and nobly provided for all his days. Thus ſtrange are the changes of this ſhifting ſcene, proſperity and adverſity are often ſet over againſt each other, that in our higheſt eſtate we may never be confident, nor in the loweſt, deſpair. It was, no doubt, matter of inexpreſſible joy to this unhappy captive, after ſo long confinement, once more to taſte the ſweets of liberty. But how much greater the delight of the captive ſoul, when delivered from the bondage of corruption, exchanging his filthy priſon garments for the glorious robe of a Redeemer's righteouſneſs, fed at the table of the King of kings, yea, called to ſit down on his throne; and this rich proviſion, and theſe diſtinguiſhed honours, not only enduring to the day of his death, but to the ages of eternity.

THE EVANGELICAL EXPOSITOR; OR, A PRACTICAL COMMENT Upon the LAMENTATIONS of JEREMIAH.

THE penman of this book was Jeremiah, and fitly it follows his prophecy, expreſſing his feeling ſenſe of thoſe deſolations of his country he had foretold, and lived to ſee accompliſhed.

The compoſition is poetical and ſingular, each verſe in every chapter, except the fifth, beginning with a ſeveral letter of the alphabet, in order, once only the letter פ Pe *is ſet before* ע Ain, *chap* xi. 16 *In the third chapter, the alphabet is thrice repeated, every three verſes beginning with the ſame letter.*

Nothing can be conceived more tender, expreſſive, and affecting than the deſcriptions here given, nor are theſe Lamentations ſcarce now to be read, without mingling our tears with his. And how much more ſenſibly muſt they be touched with them, who were more immediately intereſted in the ſubject, and not only beheld theſe deſolations he lamented, but were themſelves a part of them?

The grand deſign of them is to lead the captives to repentance and humiliation for their ſins before God, and to inſpire them with ſome reviving hope amidſt all their ſorrows, that theſe deſolations would come to an end, and that returning to God, he would return unto them, put an end to their captivity, and wipe away all tears from their eyes

Before Christ 588

CHAP I

We have here the miſeries of Jeruſalem bitterly bewailed, and her preſent deplorable condition aggravated, by comparing it with her former proſperous ſtate; and all along ſin is acknowledged and complained of as the procuring cauſe of all theſe miſeries, and God is appealed to for juſtice againſt her enemies, and applied to for compaſſion towards them Here is, 1 A complaint made to God of their calamities, and his compaſſionate conſideration deſired, ver 1—11 2 The ſame complaint made to their friends, and their compaſſionate conſideration deſired, ver 12—17 3 An appeal to God and his righteouſneſs concerning it, ver 18—22 in which he is juſtified in their affliction, and is humbly ſolicited to juſtify himſelf in their deliverance

1. HOW doth the city ſit ſolitary, *that was* full
of people! [a] *how* is ſhe become as a widow!
ſhe *that was* great among the nations, [b] *and*
princeſs among the provinces, *how* is ſhe
become tributary! 2 She [c] weepeth ſore in the [d] night,
and her tears *are* on her cheeks [e] among all her lovers [f]
ſhe hath none to comfort *her*, all her friends have dealt
treacherouſly with her, they are become her enemies
3 Judah is gone into captivity, becauſe of affliction, †
and becauſe of great ſervitude [g] ſhe dwelleth among the
heathen, ſhe findeth no reſt all her perſecutors [h] over
took her between the ſtraits 4. The ways of Zion do
mourn, becauſe none come to the ſolemn feaſts all her
gates are deſolate her prieſts ſigh, her virgins are af-
flicted, and ſhe *is* in bitterneſs 5 Her adverſaries [i] are
the chief, her enemies proſper for the LORD hath af-
flicted her; [k] for the multitude of her tranſgreſſions, [l] her
children are gone into captivity before the enemy 6.
And from the daughter of Zion all her beauty is depart-
ed her princes are become like harts *that* find no pa-
ſture, and they are gone without ſtrength before the pur-
ſuer 7 Jeruſalem remembred in the days of her af-
fliction, and of her miſeries, all her ‡ pleaſant things
that ſhe had in the days of old, when her people fell into
the hand of the enemy, and none did help her, the ad-
verſaries ſaw her, *and* did mock at her ſabbaths 8 Je-
ruſalem hath grievouſly ſinned therefore ſhe is removed
all that honoured her, deſpiſe her, becauſe [m] they have
ſeen her nakedneſs yea, ſhe ſigheth, and turneth back-
ward 9 [n] Her filthineſs *is* in her ſkirts, [o] ſhe remem-
breth not her laſt end, therefore ſhe came down wonder-
fully [p] ſhe had no comforter O LORD, behold my
affliction for the enemy hath magnified *himſelf* 10
The adverſary hath ſpread out his hand upon all her
pleaſant things for ſhe hath ſeen *that* [q] the heathen en-
tred

[a] Iſa xlvii 7, 8. [b] Ezra iv 20 [c] Jer xiii. 17 [d] Job vii 3 Pſ vi 6 [e] Jer iv 30 & xxx 14 Ver 19. [f] Ver 9. 16 17 21 † Heb For the greatneſs of ſervitude [g] Chap ii 9 [h] Jer lii 8

Before Christ 588. [i] Deut xxviii 13, 44 [k] Jer xxx. 14 Dan. ix 11 [l] Jer lii 28 ‡ Or deſireable [m] Jer xiii 26 Ezek xvi 37 & xxiii 29 Hoſ ii 10 [n] Ezek xxiv 7 [o] Deut xxxii 29 [p] Ver 2, 17, 21 [q] Jer li 51

Before Chriſt 589

tred into her ſanctuary, whom thou didſt command *that*
ᵗ they ſhould not enter into thy congregation 11 All
her people ſigh, ˢ they ſeek bread, they have given their
pleaſant things for meat ‖ to relieve the ſoul ſee, O
LORD, and conſider, for I am become vile

ᵗ Deut xxiii 3 Neh xiii 1 ˢ Jer lii 6 ‖ Or to make the ſoul come again

v 1—11 With plaintive notes of woe the prophet's mournful muſe begins, and bids each reader drop the ſympathetic tear

1 He bewails the deſolations of Jeruſalem how changed from all her former glory, fallen into what an abyſs of wretchedneſs, amazed at what he beheld, and commiſerating her afflicted ſtate, he breaks forth, *How doth the city ſit ſolitary, that was full of people!* Silence reigns in the once-thronged ſtreets, and brooding over the ruins, with anguiſh too big for utterance, in melancholy ſolitude, Jeruſalem, as a diſconſolate widow, ſits on the ground, deſerted of God, her king a captive, her inhabitants dead with famine, peſtilence, or the ſword, or under the yoke of ſervitude in a ſtrange land A princeſs once among the nations, courted, reſpected, and obeyed, now bound with captive bands, an ignominious tributary to a heathen lord, *v* 2. No marvel tears inceſſant furrow her cheeks, and, as if too ſhort the day for ſorrow ſuch as hers, all night they flow, without a comforter, without a friend to pity her, and by partaking to alleviate her anguiſh Her lovers, who in the days of her proſperity with warm profeſſions teſtified their regard, deſert her in the day of her calamity, and her treacherous friends throw off the maſk, and act as open enemies *v* 2 Her children groan in ſervitude, ſubject to the caprice and tyranny of heathen maſters, and *finding no reſt* no end of toil, no peace of mind, no ſettled abode Hemmed in like a beaſt in the toils, her perſecutors have ſeized her, without the poſſibility of eſcape, *v* 3 *Her adverſaries are chief, her enemies proſper* and no marvel, ſince *the Lord hath afflicted her*, whoſe wrath is the cauſe of all her ſufferings, *v* 5 Like harts famiſhed for want of paſture, and weak as theſe timorous animals, her princes are unable to fight or fly, and fall an eaſy prey, *v* 6 deſpiſed now by thoſe who honoured her, ſtripped of all her wealth and ornaments, her nakedneſs appears, and confounded ſhe *ſighs and turns backward*, as if to hide her ſhame, *v* 8 Pining with famine, and ſunk in deſpondence, her people ſeek bread, and gladly part with all their jewels and pleaſant things to procure the ſmalleſt refreſhment ſo low are they reduced from that plenty in which they once rioted, and ſo grievouſly abuſed, *v* 11 *Note*, (1) They who wilfully depart from God, the ſoul's true reſt, may not hope to find reſt in any thing beſide (2) All afflictions are doubly heavy when we ſee them as coming from God, not in mercy, but in wrath (3) Men's ſins will ſurely bring them into ſtraits, when too late they will bewail their folly (4) Affluence abuſed is the ready way to pining want

Great were theſe miſeries under which the ſtate groaned, yet greater anguiſh to the gracious ſoul it was, to behold the ſacred ſervice of the temple interrupted Unfrequented now the ways of Zion mourn, her gates no longer thronged by thoſe who haſted to her ſolemn feaſts, are deſerted, deſolate *Her prieſts ſigh*, no ſacrifice bleeds, no incenſe ſmokes upon the altar, deſtitute of their portion, famiſhing through want *Her virgins are afflicted*, their ſongs of joy ſunk into mourning and woe, *and ſhe is in bitterneſs*, overwhelmed with anguiſh and diſtreſs, *v* 4 *Her beauty is departed*, not only her king and nobles captives, her country waſted, but, above all, the beautiful houſe of her ſanctuary in ruins, *v* 6 With ſacrilegious hands her enemies have ſeized all her pleaſant things, her ark, her altars, and thoſe who might not even enter the congregation, now riot in the very ſanctuary, plunder and ſpoil its ſacred treaſures, *v* 10 and, adding inſult to their ravages, mocked at their ſabbaths, or, as ſome think, in deriſion laid upon them that day heavier burdens, *v* 7 And what aggravated all, was the remembrance of the happy days of old, fled, to appearance for ever fled, and nothing now remaining but affliction and miſery, *v* 7 *Note*, (1) Nothing affects a good man's heart ſo deeply as the decay of vital godlineſs (2) To hear God diſhonoured, his worſhip and ordinances deſpiſed and ridiculed, is bitter to the faithful ſoul (3) The remembrance of the communion we have enjoyed with God, and the comforts we have taſted, ſerve but to aggravate our griefs, when by our unfaithfulneſs we have provoked God to withdraw, and leave us to our miſery

2 He laments over their ſins, the cauſe of theſe deſolations; for God is righteous in theſe his judgments *Her tranſgreſſions are multiplied*, *v* 5 and very grievous, *v* 8 numberleſs and aggravated *Her filthineſs is in her ſkirts*, open and avowed careleſs and ſecure, *ſhe remembreth not her laſt end*, nor conſiders in what miſery her iniquities will iſſue and having been moſt oppreſſive herſelf, the rich afflicting their poor brethren, and making their ſervitude heavy, *v* 3 juſtly therefore ſhe is devoted to the yoke, and her fall *wonderful*, *v* 9 as her provocation had exceeded *Note*, (1) Sin and ruin are inſeparable (2) No ſins are ſo aggravated as thoſe of God's profeſſing people,

3 Zion is introduced breaking forth into an earneſt cry to God under her ſufferings *O Lord, behold my afflictions*, with an eye of pity and compaſſion, ſince every other comforter is no more *ſee, O Lord, and conſider, for I am become vile*, reduced to the moſt abject miſery, and ready to ſink into deſpair, if thou doſt not interpoſe *Note*, (1) The only relief for the miſerable is earneſt application to the merciful God When all other's compaſſions fail, his fail not (2) If God afflicts his own people, it is in order to excite their more fervent applications to him, and make them know more of the wonders of his grace

Before Chriſt 588

12 ¶ *Is it* nothing to you, all ye that ‡ paſs by ? be
hold and ſee, ᶻ if there be any ſorrow like unto my ſor-
row, which is done unto me, wherewith the LORD hath
afflicted *me*, in the day of his fierce anger 13 From
above hath he ſent fire into my bones, and it prevaileth
againſt them he hath ſpread a net for my feet, he
hath turned me back he hath made me deſolate, *and*
faint all the day 14 ᵘ The yoke of my tranſgreſſions
is bound by his hand they are wreathed, *and* come up
upon my neck he hath made my ſtrength to fall, the
LORD hath delivered me into *their* hands, *from whom*
I am not able to riſe up 15 The LORD hath troden
under foot all my mighty *men* in the midſt of me he
hath called an aſſembly againſt me, to cruſh my young
men ˣ the LORD hath troden the virgin, the daughter
of Judah, *as* in a wine preſs 16 For theſe *things* I
weep, ʸ mine eye, mine eye runneth down with water,
becauſe the comforter that ſhould ‡ relieve my ſoul, is
far from me my children are deſolate, becauſe the enemy prevailed 17 ᵃ Zion ſpreadeth forth her hands,
and ᵃ *there is* none to comfort her the LORD hath
commanded concerning Jacob, *that* his adverſaries *ſhould*
be round about him Jeruſalem is as a menſtruous woman among them 18 ¶ The LORD ᵇ is righteous,
for I have ᶜ rebelled againſt his § commandment hear,
I pray you, all people, and behold my ſorrow my virgins and my young men are gone into captivity 19
I called for my lovers, *but* ᵈ they deceived me, my
prieſts and mine elders gave up the ghoſt in the city,
while they ſought their meat to relieve their ſouls 20
Behold, O LORD, for I *am* in diſtreſs, my ᵉ bowels
are troubled, mine heart is turned within me, for I
have grievouſly rebelled ᶠ abroad the ſword bereaveth,
at home *there is* death. 21 They have heard that I
ſigh, *there is* none to comfort me all mine enemies have
heard of my trouble, they are glad that thou haſt done
it thou wilt bring ᵍ the day *that* thou haſt called, and
they ſhall be ʰ like unto me 22 ⁱ Let all their wick-
edneſs come before thee and do unto them, as thou
haſt done unto me for all my tranſgreſſions for my
ſighs *are* many, and ᵏ my heart *is* faint

‡ Heb Paſs by the way ᶻ Dan ix 12 ᵘ Prov v 22 ˣ Iſa lxiii 3 ʸ Jer xiii 17 & xiv 17 Chap ii 18 ‡ Heb Bring back ᵃ Jer iv 31 ᵃ Ver 2 ᵇ Dan ix 7 ᶜ 1 Sam xii 14, 15 § Heb Mouth ᵈ Ver 2 Jer xxx 14 ᵉ Iſa xvi 11 Jer xlviii 36. Chap ii 11 Hoſ xi 8 ᶠ Deut xxxii 25 Ezek vii 15 ᵍ Iſa xiii &c Jer xlvi &c ʰ Jer l 49. ⁱ Pſ cix 15 ᵏ Chap v 17

v 12—22 The ſame complaints are here continued

1 She demands ſome compaſſion from the ſpectators of her miſery, in the view of the heavy hand of God upon her, whom ſhe acknowledges the author of her troubles *Is it nothing to you, all ye that paſs by?* can you unconcerned behold theſe deſolations, and not drop a tear over theſe ruins? *ſee if there be any ſorrow like unto my ſorrow*; ſo bitter and overwhelming How ready are we all in diſtreſs to think our own burden peculiarly heavy, when in fact we only ſhare the calamities common to men yet it muſt be owned her caſe was deplorable indeed In anger, in fierce anger, the Lord had afflicted her, a ſenſe of this added bitterneſs to every burden his fire is kindled in her palaces, or burns with fiercer flames within her guilty conſcience Entangled in his net ſhe could not flee, but falls backward, faint and unable to oppoſe the deſolations of her Chaldean foe, *v* 13. Under complicated judgments her yoke was made heavy, and her ſoul tranſgreſſions the cauſe of all; delivered into her enemy's hands, without the poſſibility of eſcaping, *v* 14 Her warriors, her valiant youth, and all her inhabitants, like grapes in the wine preſs, are trodden under foot by the Babyloniſh army, and their blood ſhed on every ſide, *v* 15 *Note*, Whatever judgments weigh us down, we may be aſſured, our tranſgreſſions have wreathed the yoke, and bound on the burden

2 She bewails with floods of tears her bitter anguiſh, and ſurely there is a cauſe for them *For theſe things I weep*, both for her ſin and for her ſufferings, and particularly, (1) *Becauſe the comforter that ſhould relieve my ſoul is far from me* When God departs, our miſery muſt needs be great all other afflictions are made light by the ſenſe of his preſence and love; but when the comforter, the only comforter of the faithful ſoul, is far from us, and nothing but wrath appears and deſpair, then

Before Christ 588

is our wretchedness compleat as it can be out of hell (2) Because her *children are desolate*, in captivity, v. 18 or *destroyed* by the sword of the merciless enemy, unable to comfort her, yea, their sad fate, is the cause of her torment (3) Because she could not find a friend In vain she spread forth her hands, intreating help, and pleading for compassion her lovers, who promised once so fair, deceived her, v 19 yea, shunned her, as if her touch communicated defilement, v 17 and none either cared or dared to interpose, when the destruction was by the divine decree, and her adversaries acted under his commission *Note*, (1) When God is our friend, we shall never want a comforter, if he is our enemy, none can comfort us (2) Creature-confidences are sure to fail us in the day of calamity (4) Because of the terrible famine *My priests and my elders gave up the ghost in the city, while they sought meat to relieve their souls*, and if these were perishing for want, how much more the common people? (5) Because of the desolations she beheld *Abroad the sword bereaveth, at home there is as death*, inevitable from the famine and the pestilence (6) Because of her insulting enemies They heard of her trouble, and with malicious pleasure rejoiced in it, v 21 and for these things her tears run down without intermission

3 She justifies God in these his judgments *The Lord is righteous*, however faithless her friends, or inhuman her foes, her sufferings were no more than she deserved *for I have rebelled, grievously rebelled against his commandments* *Note*, True penitents ever acknowledge the justice of God in punishing them, and never desire to excuse themselves, but speak of their sins with every aggravation

4 She presents her miserable case to the God of all mercy *Behold, O Lord, for I am in distress*, deeply afflicted, not only with her sufferings, but from a sense of her sins *my bowels are troubled, my heart is turned within me*, distracted and torn, uneasy and restless, and when the soul thus broken and contrite approaches God, he will not despise our prayer

5 She expects and intreats that God would visit her enemies *Thou wilt bring the day that thou hast called*, the time fixed in God's counsels for their punishment, *and they shall be like unto me*, in suffering, and as she believes this will come, she prays it may, *Let their wickedness come before thee*, be remembred and revenged *and do unto them as thou hast done unto me for all my transgressions*, is equally guilty, let them meet the same scourge, and heavy indeed that had been, as her anguish testified, *for my sighs are many, and my heart is faint* *Note*, (1) They who are alike guilty, may expect to be alike miserable (2) Though all private resentment is forbidden, we may pray to see God glorified in the ruin of his own and his people's enemies

CHAP II

The subject of this chapter is the same as the former 1 *Here is the anger of Zion's God taken notice of, as the cause of her calamities*, ver 1—9 2 *Here is the sorrow of Zion's children taken notice of, as the effect of her calamities*, ver 10—19 3 *The complaint is made to God, and the matter referred to his compassionate consideration*, ver 20—22 *The hand that wounded must make whole.*

1 HOW hath the LORD covered the daughter of
Zion with a cloud in his anger, *and* [a] cast down
from heaven unto the earth the beauty of Israel, and remembred
not [b] his footstool in the day of his anger?
2 The LORD hath swallowed up all the habitations
of Jacob, and [c] hath not pitied he hath thrown down
in his wrath the strong holds of the daughter of Judah
he hath brought *them* down to the ground, he hath
polluted the kingdom, and the princes thereof 3 He
hath cut off in [d] *his* fierce anger all the horn of Israel:
[e] he hath drawn back his right hand from before the enemy,
and [f] he burned against Jacob like a flaming fire
which devoureth round about 4 He hath bent his
bow like an enemy [g] he stood with his right hand as an
adversary, and slew all *that were* ‖ pleasant to the eye, in
the tabernacle of the daughter of Zion he poured out
his fury like fire 5 The LORD was [h] an enemy, he
hath swallowed up Israel, he hath swallowed up all her
palaces he hath destroyed his strong holds, and hath
increased in the daughter of Judah mourning and lamentation
6 And he hath violently [i] taken away his
† tabernacle, [k] as *if it were of* a garden, he hath destroyed
his places of the assembly [l] the LORD hath caused the
solemn feasts and sabbaths to be forgotten in Zion, and
hath despised in the indignation of his anger [m] the king
and the priest 7 The LORD hath cast off his altar,
he hath abhorred his sanctuary he hath § given up into
the hand of the enemy the walls of her palaces [n] they
have made a noise in the house of the LORD, as in the
day of a solemn feast 8 The LORD [o] hath purposed
to destroy the wall of the daughter of Zion [p] he hath
stretched out a line he hath not withdrawn his hand
from ‖ destroying therefore he made the rampart and
the wall to lament they languished together. 9 Her
gates are sunk into the ground he hath destroyed and
broken her bars [q] her king and her princes *are* among
the Gentiles the law *is no more*, [r] her prophets also find
no vision from the LORD

a Mat xi 23 b 1 Chron xxviii 2 Ps xcix 5 & cxxxii 7 c Ver 17 21 Chap iii 43 d Deut xxix 24 e Ps lxxiv 11 f Ps lxxxix 46 g Isa lxiii 10 ‖ Heb Desirable h Jer xxx 14 i Ps lxxx 12 & lxxxix 40 Isa v 5 † Or hedge k Isa i 8 l Chap i 4 Zeph iii 18 m Jer lii 9 § Heb Shut up

n Ps lxxiv 3, 4 o Isa v 5 Jer v 10 p 2 Kings xxi 13 Isa xxxiv 11 ‖ Heb Swallowing up q 2 Kings xxiv 15 & xxv 7 Chap iv 20 r Ps lxxiv 9 Ezek vii 26

v 1—9 The hand of God visible in their sufferings, and the sense of his displeasure so justly and highly provoked, peculiarly sharpen these lamentations

The Lord hath utterly ruined their civil and ecclesiastical polity, and destroyed their country A louring cloud big with wrath hangs over the daughter of Zion, and terrible darkness covers her all the beauty of Israel is tarnished, and from the highest pitch of excellence she falls into the abyss of wretchedness Even that temple, where God once chose to put his name, and that ark of the covenant, over which his presence visibly rested, are no more regarded by him, but given up to destruction, v 1 *The habitations of Jacob*, the land of Judea and Jerusalem, *the Lord hath swallowed up*, as a lion his prey, *and hath not pitied* *Their strong holds are thrown down in his wrath*, for if he is angry, yea but a little, who may abide it? They had polluted themselves by sin, therefore *he hath polluted the kingdom and the princes thereof*, giving them up into the hands of the heathen, v 2 All their strength is broken, their right hand disabled, or God's right hand, which had been their protection and defence, is withdrawn, and they become a prey to their enemies, for when God abandons a people, their ruin is sure Like a devouring fire his anger burns, and Jacob is devoured, v 3 As their enemy he stands, his arrows on the string pointed with death, his sword drawn and sharpened with fury, every pleasant object bleeds beneath the stroke, the princes, priests, and every endeared relation and even in the tabernacle his vengeance lighteth down, and it is utterly consumed, v 4 Before such an enemy what defence avails? her palaces, her fortresses, totter as in an earthquake, and disappear, whilst mournful lamentations rend the skies, and fill the devoted land of Judah, v 5 That temple, vast and magnificent, built for his honour, is torn up from its foundations, as easily and utterly as a tent in a garden is removed the places of assembly, the courts of the temple, or synagogues, are destroyed God abhorred their hypocritical services, and therefore dispersed their congregations Their solemn feasts and sabbaths are forgotten in Zion, none being left to celebrate them, no place for worship remaining Even the sacred characters of king and priest God hath despised in the indignation of his anger, because they have defiled their dignity by their iniquities, he hath destroyed both the kingdom and the priesthood the more sacred the character, the greater the profanation when such offend, v 6 *The Lord hath cast off his altar*, whilst they continued in their sins, the sacrifices and incense they offered were an abomination unto him *He hath abhorred the sanctuary*, and therefore devoted the walls to ruin, and in those sacred courts and temple, where Zion's songs were heard, there the Chaldeans shout, and riot, and blaspheme, v 7 Fixed is the purpose, deep the design; the line of destruction is marked out, and God's almighty hand never withdrawn till the desolations are completed, the wall and rampart levelled to the ground, v 8 Sunk are her gates, as if the earth had opened beneath them, her bars broken, *her king and princes* captive, *among the Gentiles the law is no more*, the sacred tables broken, the ordinances no longer observed, and none left to expound or hear these oracles of God They who neglect their Bibles, deserve to have them taken from them, and since they abhorred and persecuted their prophets when they had them, God punishes them in withdrawing his prophetic spirit from among them, and leaves them in darkness

10 The elders of the daughter of Zion sit upon the
ground [a] *and* keep silence they have [t] cast up dust upon
their heads they have girded themselves with sackcloth,
the virgins of Jerusalem hang down their heads to the
ground 11 [u] Mine eyes do fail with tears, [x] my bowels
are troubled, my liver is poured upon the earth, for
the destruction of the daughter of my people, because
[y] the children and the sucklings ‖ swoon in the streets
of the city. 12 They say to their mothers, Where *is*
corn and wine? when they swooned as the wounded in
the streets of the city, when their soul was poured out
into their mothers bosom 13 What thing shall I take
to witness for thee? what thing shall I liken to thee, O
daughter of Jerusalem? what shall I equal to thee, that
I may comfort thee, O virgin daughter of Zion? for
thy

s Job ii 13 t Job ii 12 u Chap i 16 x Chap i 20 y Ver 19 ‖ Or faint

Before Christ 588

thy breach *is* great like the sea who can heal thee?
14. [a] Thy prophets have seen vain and foolish things
for thee, and they have not discovered thine iniquity,
to turn away thy captivity, but have seen for thee false
burdens, and causes of banishment 15 All that pass
by [a] clap *their* hands at thee, they hiss and [b] wag their
head at the daughter of Jerusalem, *saying*, *Is* this the
city that *men* call [c] the perfection of beauty, the joy of
the whole earth? 16 [d] All thine enemies have opened
their mouth against thee they hiss and gnash the teeth,
they say, We have swallowed *her* up certainly this *is*
the day that we looked for we have found, we have
seen *it* 17 The LORD hath done *that* [e] which he had
devised he hath fulfilled his word that he had com-
manded in the days of old [f] he hath thrown down,
and hath not pitied and [g] he hath caused *thine* enemy
to rejoice over thee, he hath set up the horn of thine
adversaries 18 Their heart cried unto the LORD,
O wall of the daughter of Zion, [h] let tears run down
like a river day and night give thyself no rest, let not
the apple of thine eyes cease 19 Arise, cry out in the
night in the beginning of the watches [i] pour out thine
heart like water before the face of the LORD lift up
thy hands towards him, for the life of thy young child-
ren, [k] that faint for hunger in the top of every street
20 ¶ Behold, O LORD, and [l] consider to whom thou
hast done this [m] shall the women eat their fruit, *and*
children † of a span long? [n] shall the priest and the pro-
phet be slain in the sanctuary of the LORD? 21 The
young and the old lie on the ground in the streets, my
virgins and my young men are fallen by the sword thou
hast slain *them* in the day of thine anger, [o] thou hast
killed *and* not pitied 22 Thou hast called, as in a so-
lemn day, my terrors round about, so that in the day of
the LORD's anger none escaped nor remained those
that I have swaddled and brought up hath mine enemy
consumed

[a] Jer ii 8 & v 31 & xiv 14 & xxiii 16 & xxvii 14 & xxix 8, 9 Ezek xiii [illegible] a Ezek xxi 6 b 2 Kings xix 21 Ps xxii 7 c Ps xlviii 2 & l 2 d Chap ii 16 e Lev xxvi 16 & Deut xxviii 15 & f Ver 2 g Ps lxxxix 42 h Jer xiv 17 Chap i 16 i Ps lxii 8 k Ver 11 l Isa lxiv 9 m Lev xxvi 29 Deut xxviii 53 Jer xix 9 Chap iv 10 † Or, swaddled with their hands n Chap iv 16 o Ver 17 Chap iii 43

v 10—22 Nothing breathes here but lamentation, mourn-
ing, and woe

1 The mourners and their bitter anguish are described *The elders*, who in robes of state were seated on the throne of judgment, now sit on the ground with every expressive sign of sorrow, dust on their heads, and girt with sackcloth; the virgins of Jerusalem, so sprightly once and gay, with downcast eyes and melancholy looks bemoan their miseries, *v* 10 whilst the prophet himself, in deepest distress, wept till his eyes grew dim in their exhausted sockets, *his bowels troubled* with acutest pangs of grief, and all within him melted as it were through very anguish, for the destruction of the daughter of his people, *v* 2

2 Abundant cause appears for such bitter mourning

(1) The famine is very grievous The infants swoon thro' hunger, and cry to their tender mothers for bread, unable to relieve their wants, the fond parent sees them faint in the streets *as wounded*, or clasping them to their bosom they expire there, *v* 12 nay, more horrid still, driven by those cravings that silence even the strongest feelings of natural affection, the infant, murdered from the womb, is devoured by the famished mother, *v* 20 Well may we cry, in the view of such a scene, from *plague, pestilence, and famine, good Lord deliver us!*

(2) The sword of their enemies reeks with the blood of the slain no sacredness of place or character affords protection *The priest and prophet are slain in that sanctuary* whither they fled for refuge, *v* 20 neither young, nor old are spared, and even virgins bleed in the general massacre God's wrath had set their merciless enemies upon them *He* no more pitied them, and suffered their hearts to be steeled against every feeling of humanity, *v* 21 Thick as the crowded worshippers assembled in the days of their solemnities, now their terrible enemies, summoned of God, beset them round hemmed in on every side, *none escaped or remained*, but were slain or made captives; so that Zion, a childless widow, saw all her pains and care, bestowed on her helpless children, fruitless, nourished only as lambs for the slaughter and all this the Lord's doing, the effect of his fierce anger How then should we fear to provoke this jealous God

(3) Their prophets deluded them, *v* 14 Pretending to inspiration, they reported the dreams of their own foolish imaginations, alluring the people of peace, instead of rebuking them for their iniquity, flattering them in their sins, and hastening them to their ruin, *v* 14 *Note*, (1) No curse more heavy than to be given up to the delusion of lying prophets (2) They who prophesy smooth things, instead of shewing faithfulness to men's souls in rebuking their sins, evidence the falsehood of their pretended mission

(4) Their neighbours reproach, their enemies insult them As if well pleased with their fall, those that pass by hiss and wag the head, deriding their miseries, *Is this the city that men call the perfection of beauty? the joy of the whole earth?* Where now are these Jewish boasts?—With open mouths their enemies join the cry, blaspheming and reviling, *hissing* as serpents, and *gnashing their teeth*, in testimony of their abhorrence, *they say, we have swallowed her up*, delighted with the delicious repast, with the rich prey of Zion's palaces *Certainly this is the day we have looked for, we have found, we have seen it*, with malicious joy they triumph, and think they have prevailed to her everlasting destruction But let the enemies of God's church know, tho' sunk never so low, she will revive, and their triumphing will be short

(5) Their misery is unparalleled, their case to human view desperate, *v* 13 no nation ever suffered the like calamities, to seek, as a ground of comfort, for afflictions similar to those Zion had endured were vain *for thy breach is great like the sea*, which, when it overflows, with violence irresistible deluges the country *Who can heal thee?* no human wisdom or power can repair these desolations, *v* 13

(6) God himself appears their enemy *The Lord hath done that which he had devised*, his hand hath done it, his counsel planned the blow *he hath fulfilled his word, that he had commanded in the days of old*, for, when he gave them his holy law by Moses, he told them what would be the effects of their transgressions, *Lev* xxvi 17 *Deu* xxviii 20 which is now fulfilled *He hath thrown down, and hath not pitied*, sparing neither city nor temple *he hath caused the enemy to rejoice over thee*, giving Jerusalem for a prey to their teeth, *v* 17 and for these miseries no marvel if *their heart* in anguish *cried unto the Lord* in some the voice of mere nature, lamenting their sufferings, in others, it may be hoped also, the voice of grace bewailing their sins

3 They are exhorted, as the only means of redress, in deep humiliation to seek unto God He hath wounded, and he alone can heal *O wall of the daughter of Zion*, ye watchmen that stand thereon, and all others, *let tears* penitential *run down as a river day and night, give thyself no rest*, weep incessantly, *let not the apple of thine eye cease*, till thou hast found pardon and grace *Arise, cry out in the night*, importunate in prayer, and pleading hard with God for mercy, *in the beginning of the watches*, repeatedly and ceaseless till he vouchsafes an answer of peace, *pour out thine heart like water before the face of the Lord, lift up thine hands to him*, pour all thy griefs into his compassionate bosom, and urge every argument for pity, such as the infants groans expiring for hunger, *v* 19 *Behold, O Lord, and consider to whom thou hast done this*, to the seed of Abraham thy friend, the sons of Jacob thy chosen, the people thou didst separate for thine own *Note*, We can take no step so effectual to remove our miseries as spreading them in humble and fervent prayer before God None but he can help us, and none who ever truly sought him sought in vain

CHAP III

The scope of this chapter is the same with that of the two foregoing chapters, but the composition is somewhat different, that was in long verse, this in short, that in single alphabets, this in a treble one Here is, 1 A sad complaint of God's displeasure, and of the fruits of it, ver 1—20 2 *Words of comfort to God's people when they are in trouble and distress, ver* 21—36 3 *Duty prescribed in this afflicted state, ver* 37—41 4 *The complaint renewed, ver* 42—54 5 *Encouragement taken to hope in God, and continue waiting for his salvation, with an appeal to his justice against the persecutors of the church, ver* 55—63

1 I Am the man *that* hath seen affliction by the rod of
his wrath 2 He hath led me and brought *me*
into [a] darkness, but not *into* light 3 Surely against me
is he turned, he turneth his hand *against me* all the day
4 My flesh and my skin hath he made old, [b] he hath
broken my bones 5 He hath builded against me, and
compassed *me* with gall and travel 6 [c] He hath set
me in dark places, as *they that be* dead of old 7 [d] He
hath hedged me about, that I cannot get out he hath
made my chain heavy 8 Also when I cry and shout,
[e] he shutteth out my prayer 9 He hath inclosed my
ways with hewn stone he hath made my paths crooked
10 [f] He *was* unto me *as* a bear lying in wait, *and as* a
lion in secret places 11 He hath turned aside my ways,
and pulled me in pieces he hath made me desolate
12 He hath bent his bow, and [g] set me as a mark for
the arrow 13 [h] he hath caused the † arrows of his
quiver to enter into my reins 14 I was [i] a derision to
all my people, [k] *and* their song all the day 15 [l] He
hath filled me with ‡ bitterness, [m] he hath made me
drunken with wormwood 16 He hath also broken my
teeth with gravel stones, he hath § covered me with
ashes. 17 And thou hast removed my soul far off from

peace

a Ps lxxxviii 4 [illegible] b Isa xxxviii 13 Jer l 17 c Ps lxxxviii 5, 6 d Job iii 23 & xix 8 Hos ii 6 e Job xxx 20 Ver 44 f Isa xxxviii 13 Hos v 14 & xiii 7, 8 g Job vii 20 & xvi 12 h Job vi 4 † Heb sons i Jer xx 7 k Job xxx 9 l Jer ix 15 ‡ Heb bitternesses m Jer xxv 17, 18 § Or, rolled me in, &c

Before Christ 588

|| Heb. Good
† Or remember
n Jam iv 10
‡ Heb Bowed

peace I forgat || prosperity 18 And I said, My strength
and my hope is perished from the LORD, 19 † Re-
membring mine affliction and my misery, the wormwood
and the gall. 20 My soul hath *them* still in remem-
brance, n and is ‡ humbled in me

v 1—20 The prophet here mingles his lamentations over his own sufferings with those of the people, or he personates the church in general, and some, with good appearance of reason, suppose him herein a type of Christ

1 He laments over his afflictions as singularly heavy, embittered with a sense of God's wrath, *v* 1 for, though God chastises his own children ever in love, they are apt, especially when the rod lies heavy upon them, to think it is in anger

2 Darkness surrounded him he saw no light, no chearing beam of hope, no door of escape out of his miseries, and seemed as one already in the grave, *v* 6 which may refer to the dark dungeon in which he was shut up, or to the captivity of the people, wherein they thought themselves as buried among the heathen *Note*, (1) A child of light sometimes walks in darkness (2) We are too apt to be giving way to our unbelieving fears, and to think, when cast down, we are utterly cast off

3 God appears his enemy, *v* 3 He is the butt of all the arrows of his indignation, *v* 12, 13 So sorely was the land afflicted with all that variety of judgments which seemed as it were to exhaust God's quiver And herein the prophet seems not to speak of himself, but personates his people

4 God hath shut him up in the hand of his enemies, hedged him in with their forces, builded the mounts against him, and *compassed him with gall and travel*, *v* 5 every effort to disentangle himself riveted the chain but the faster, and made it the more heavy, *v* 7 His ways are *inclosed as with hewn stone*, he cannot break through, all his schemes are traversed, and *all his paths crooked*, the farther he advances the more he is bewildered, *v* 9 *Note*, Such will the crooked paths of sin be found, the farther we go in them the more miserable we shall grow

5 The Lord seemed to have made an utter end of him, emaciated through famine, his strength broken, *v* 4 As a lion and a bear waiting to seize their prey, so God watched over him for evil, *v* 10 He was filled with bitterness under the sense of what he felt, and with the apprehension of the greater evils he feared, and staggered as one drunk with affliction, *v* 15 covered with ashes, in the dust he lay, and eat worse than the bread of mourners, his teeth *broken with gravel-stones*, that were mingled with the meal, nay he hath *pulled me in pieces*, as one torn limb from limb Thus had God dispersed the Jews, and laid their land utterly *desolate*, *v* 11

6 The Lord refused to be intreated The loudest cries are in vain, he would neither hear the prophet's intercession nor the peoples prayer for themselves, and, when prayer fails of profiting, the case appears desperate indeed

7 He was a derision to all the people they mocked at and made merry with him, ridiculing his sorrows, and pleased with his sufferings, *v* 7 and to a generous spirit very hard is this to be born

8 He almost sunk into despair *Thou hast removed my soul far off from peace*, no prospect of it remained *I forgat prosperity*, never expecting its return *and I said, my strength and hope are perished from the Lord*, abandoned by him, and no more expecting help and support from him, and then despair was unavoidable so deeply are the faithful sometimes dejected and this arose from the view of his affliction and misery, which seemed more than he was able to bear, *v* 19

The Lord Jesus was emphatically this man of sorrows, destitute, afflicted, tormented, stricken, smitten of God, enduring all the wrath our iniquities deserved, derided in his agony, his soul in darkness and dereliction, and his misery compleat

• Ver 24
p Mal iii 6
q Zeph iii 5
r Ps xvi 5 & lxxiii 26 & cxix 57 Jer x 16
s Ver 21
t Ps xxxvii 7 Isa xxx 18
u Ps xxxix 9 Jer xv 17 Chap ii 10
‡ Or And
x Isa l 6 Mat v 39
y Ps xciv 14
z Ezek xxxiii 11
‖ Heb From his heart
* Ezek xviii 5

21 This I recall to my mind, therefore have I hope
22 ¶ p *It is of* the LORD's mercies that we are not
consumed, because his compassions fail not 23 q *They
are* new every morning great *is* thy faithfulness 24
r The LORD *is* my portion, saith my soul, s therefore
will I hope in him 25 The LORD *is* good unto them
that wait for him, to the soul *that* seeketh him. 26 *It
is* good that *a man* should both hope, and t quietly wait
for the salvation of the LORD 27. *It is* good for a man
that he bear the yoke in his youth 28 u He sitteth
alone, and keepeth silence, because he hath ‡ born *it*
upon him 29 He putteth his mouth in the dust, if so
be there may be hope 30 x He giveth *his* cheek to
him that smiteth him, he is filled full with reproach
31 For y the LORD will not cast off for ever 32 But
though he cause grief, yet will he have compassion ac-
cording to the multitude of his mercies 33 For z he
doth not afflict ‖ willingly, nor grieve the children of men
34 To crush under his feet all the prisoners of the earth,
35 To turn aside the right of a man before the face

§ of the most High, 36 To subvert a man in his cause,
|| the LORD approveth not

Before Christ 588

§ Or a superior
|| Heb The Lord doth not see Or, Doth not the Lord see?

v 21—36 At last a gleam of chearing hope breaks through the dreadful gloom *My soul hath them still in remembrance, and is humbled within me*, and real humiliation is the sure way to returning consolation or the words may be more truly rendered, *Thou wilt surely remember*, expressing his faith in God, notwithstanding all his sorrows, *for my soul meditates within me*, on thy grace, mercy, truth, and faithfulness, *this I recall to mind, therefore have I hope*, that still excludes despair A variety of reasons he suggests to encourage this hope, and comfort his heart in God

1 *It is of the Lord's mercies that we are not consumed*, as we have deserved to be It is mercy, infinite mercy, that spares any sinner for a moment we may wonder we are out of hell, and be ashamed to complain, when all temporal affliction is so much less than our iniquity deserves *His compassions fail not*, though sometimes they seem exhausted, and his loving-kindness quite gone for evermore, yet it is our infirmity when we fear it, and a little patience will prove it so, for *they are new every morning*, both temporal mercies, that every day fall thick around us as the drops of dew, and spiritual mercies in Christ Jesus, the source of which is inexhaustible

2 *Great is thy faithfulness* His truth eternally confirms what his mercy promises, and his everlasting covenant, well ordered in all things and sure, affords the most solid foundation for faith and hope in every time of need

3 *The Lord is my portion, saith my soul* Since God hath engaged to be such to his people, faith embraces the promise, and they who have an interest in his love and favour have all that heart can wish, and a possession which, when we are deprived of every earthly good, is enough to make us happy, and satisfy all our wishes *Therefore I hope in him*, when every other support fails And this hope will never make ashamed, for *the Lord is good to them that wait for him*, and will not disappoint their expectations, bestowing on them, according to their necessities, a rich supply for every want, *to the soul that seeketh him*, in earnest prayer and humble perseverance, in the use of those means of grace he hath appointed, for, though the answer may be delayed, the mercy is sure to be granted to all who *hope, and quietly wait for the salvation of the Lord*, not murmuring against God, but acquiescing in his holy will, patiently expecting his salvation, temporal, spiritual, and eternal, for it is *good* to do so, our highest interest as well as our bounden duty

4 Our very troubles are designed of God for our benefit *It is good for a man to bear the yoke in his youth* the yoke of afflictions, which serve to wean the mind from earthly vanities, and teach us to seek our better rest above, or the yoke of the commandments, Christ's easy yoke, which the sooner we take upon us, from the earliest days of youth, the pleasanter we shall find it though the former sense seems particularly here intended Such a one *sitteth alone*, retired to commune with God, to search out his own spirit, and to see and humble his soul under the cause of his afflictions, *and keepeth silence*, no murmuring word escapes him, he is dumb and openeth not his mouth, *because he hath born it upon him*, willingly yielding his neck to the yoke, or *because He* (God) *hath laid it on him*, and therefore this consideration silences every thought of discontent *He putteth his mouth in the dust*, confessing his vileness, and just desert of all his sufferings, and humbly bows before the chastening rod, *if so be there may be hope*, or *peradventure there is hope*, not as if doubting of the promises, but as confessing his own unworthiness to obtain the mercy he seeks Thus humbled, *he giveth his cheek to him that smiteth him*, can bear without resentment every indignity, *he is filled full with reproaches*, the lot of all who follow Christ, but never returns railing for railing, but contrariwise blessing, learning of him to be meek and lowly of heart Such is the spirit and temper of a real penitent, and the issue of such sufferings and submission cannot but be *good*, very good for us

5 *The Lord will not cast off for ever*, which is the great argument both for patience and repentance Though the faithful are cast down, they are not *cast off* their sufferings may be long, but they shall not be *for ever* His purposes of grace and love towards them are unchangeable, and in their lowest state they can still hope in his mercy Our heaviness indeed for a time may be great, through manifold temptations, *but, though he cause grief*, his chastisements all flow from his paternal heart towards us, and are designed to work Godly sorrow that leads to eternal salvation, and therefore, when the end of the affliction is answered, *he will yet have compassion according to the multitude of his mercies*, which are in Christ Jesus boundless and infinite, *for* with no other view doth he ever correct his dear children, *he doth not afflict willingly, nor grieve the children of men*, he takes no delight in our miseries, by our sins we provoke him, as a tender father, with reluctance to take the rod, but he feels for us when he chastises, and is grieved in our affliction, and gladly lays down the rod when it hath answered the end for which he sent it. Oh how great are the tender mercies of our God! How can we but kiss the rod of such a father!

6 Though he permits, for wise and holy ends, the oppression of the wicked, he is far from approving it *To crush under his*

feet

Before Christ 588

feet all the priſoners of the earth, as the Chaldeans trampled on his captive people, *to turn aſide the right of a man* by partial judgment, *before the face of the moſt high*, openly, in defiance of him whoſe vicegerents the judges of the earth are, *to ſubvert a man in his cauſe* by ſome clandeſtine and knaviſh arts, *the Lord approveth not*, he condemns all ſuch injuſtice, and will avenge it, or *doth he not ſee?* however ſecret the tranſaction, from his all-piercing eye it cannot be hid, and he will in no wiſe ſpare the guilty

b Pſ xxxiii 9 — 37 ¶ Who *is* he b *that* ſaith, and it cometh to paſs,
when the LORD commandeth it not? 38 Out of the
c Job ii 10 Iſ xlv 7 Am iii 6 — mouth of the moſt High proceedeth not c evil and good?
d Prov xix 3 — 39 d Wherefore doth a living man † complain, e a man
† Or murmur — for the puniſhment of his ſins? 40 Let us ſearch and
e Mic vii 9 — try our ways, and turn again to the LORD 41 f Let
f Pſ lxxxvi 4 — us lift up our heart with *our* hands unto God in the hea-
vens

v 37—41 They who truly know God and themſelves will find abundant arguments for ſubmiſſion to his will and pleaſure

1 He is the uncontroulable ſovereign *Who is he that ſaith, and it cometh to paſs, when the Lord commandeth it not?* His decrees are immutable, and all human ſchemes to defeat his eternal purpoſes fruitleſs *Out of the mouth of the moſt High proceedeth not evil and good?* Aſſuredly Every diſpenſation of his providence, proſperous or afflictive, is ordained by him, and nothing left to chance what therefore is his will ſhould be our delight, for all he doth is holy, juſt, and good

2 We have never reaſon to complain *Wherefore doth a living man complain?* a worm, whoſe breath is in his noſtrils, and in whoſe heart folly is bound up, a moſt incompetent judge of the diſpenſations of infinite wiſdom, a *living* man, whoſe life long ſince is forfeited to divine juſtice, and to whom it is an amazing act of mercy that he is out of hell, *a man for the puniſhment of his ſins?* how dare he complain, when all his ſufferings here are ſo much leſs than his deſerts Conſiderations these, which ſhould ever ſilence all repining, lead us to acknowledge God's mercy as well as juſtice in our ſevereſt afflictions, and thankfully to acquieſce in every diſpenſation

3 Our buſineſs, under every trouble, is to examine into the cauſe, and in deep humiliation return unto God *Let us ſearch and try our ways*, for, whilſt at all times ſelf-enquiry is needful, it is moſt peculiarly ſo under humbling providences, for verily there is a reaſon for them, a gracious God doth not willingly afflict The rule of judgment is the word of God, and prayer muſt direct us to the right application of it, that, under the influence of divine light, we may diſcover the true ſtate of our ſouls, *and turn again unto the Lord* in whatever way we may have departed from him, knowing that except we are converted we cannot be ſaved, and aſſured that, in all his dealings towards us, God's great deſign is to lead us to repentance Bleſſed and happy are they who learn to correſpond with him herein

4 In ſimplicity and Godly ſincerity we are called upon to devote and ſurrender ourſelves to God *Let us lift up our heart with our hands unto God in the heavens*, in prayer looking up to him whoſe glory is in the heavens, and whoſe throne ruleth over all, our hearts engaged, and unreſervedly offered on his altar, without which no ſervice of the lips is at all available, and, when we do ſo, this ſacrifice of a contrite ſpirit God will not deſpiſe, nor ever caſt out the prayer that cometh not out of feigned lips They who lift up their hearts to heaven in prayer ſhall ſhortly lift up their voices in heaven, amidſt the throng of glorified ſaints and angels, in everlaſting praiſe

g Chap ii 2, 17, 21 — 42 We have tranſgreſſed and have rebelled, thou
h ver 8 1 Cor iv — haſt not pardoned 43 Thou haſt covered with anger,
13 — and perſecuted us g thou haſt ſlain, thou haſt not pitied
k Chap ii 16 — 44 Thou haſt covered thyſelf with a cloud, that h *our*
l Iſ xxiv 17 — prayers ſhould not paſs through 45 Thou haſt made us
Jer xlviii 43 — i *as* the off-ſcouring and refuſe in the midſt of the people
m Jer iv 19 & ix 1 — 46 k All our enemies have opened their mouths againſt
& xiv 17 Chap i 16 — us 47 l Fear and a ſnare is come upon us, deſolation
n Pſ lxxvii 2 — and deſtruction 48 m Mine eye runneth down with
o Chap i 16 — rivers of water, for the deſtruction of the daughter of
† Or more than all — my people 49 n Mine eye trickleth down and ceaſeth
o Pſ xxxv 19 — not, without any intermiſſion 50 Till the LORD
p Jer 4 & xxxvii 16 — look down, and behold from heaven 51 Mine eye
q Dan vi 17 — affecteth mine heart, † becauſe of all the daughters of
r Pſ lxix 2 — my city 52 Mine enemies chaſed me ſore like a bird,
s Pſ xxxi 22 Iſ xxxviii 10 — o without cauſe 53 They have cut off my life in the
t John ii 24 — dungeon, and p caſt a ſtone upon me 54 q Waters
flowed over mine head, *then* r I ſaid, I am cut off

v 42—54 Nature will feel, and we are not forbid to mourn, though we are forbid to murmur

1 The prophet, in the name of all his people, with deep acknowledgment confeſſes their ſins, *We have tranſgreſſed and rebelled*, for ſin is rebellion againſt the majeſty of heaven, and ſinners the vileſt of traitors

2 He bewails their miſeries, ariſing from a ſenſe of God's diſpleaſure *Thou haſt not pardoned*, at leaſt no tokens of it appeared, whilſt their afflictions continued unremoved *thou haſt covered with anger and perſecuted us*, like a thick cloud it hung over them, and extinguiſhed for a while every ray of his light and comfort, whilſt, like a battering ſtorm, their troubles beat upon them inceſſantly *Thou haſt ſlain, and haſt not pitied*, given them up to the mercileſs ſword of the Chaldeans, nor could their cries reach his mercy-ſeat *Thou haſt covered thyſelf with a cloud, that our prayers ſhould not paſs through*, ſo apt are we, when we do not find an anſwer of mercy from God ſoon, to conclude that it is of no profit to pray, and are tempted to give up all hope

3 He laments the deriſion to which they were expoſed *Thou haſt made us as the off-ſcouring and refuſe in the midſt of the people*, to be trodden down by the heathen, *ſee* 1 *Cor* iv 13 and their enemies ſcoffed at their diſtreſs, a ſure ſymptom of a baſe mind, thus to inſult the miſerable

4 Their fears were great, their deſolations grievous taken in the ſnare of their foes, terrified with their threatnings their land and the cities of Judah utterly deſtroyed, and the people led into captivity, or ſlain with famine, peſtilence, and the ſword, v 47 Chaſed like a bird they fled before their foes, who *without a cauſe* perſecuted them, v 52 yet unable to eſcape, they ſeized them, and buried them alive in dungeons, or carried them to Babylon, which was the houſe of their priſon, and ſhut them up in captive bonds, as the dead, at the mouth of whoſe ſepulchre the ponderous ſtone is laid, v 53 *Waters* of affliction *flowed over mine head*, and, ſunk as it were in the abyſs of hopeleſs miſery, *then I ſaid, I am cut off*, ready to reſign themſelves to deſpair Note, Thoſe whom Satan hath caſt down by their ſins, he ſeeks to keep down by deſpair

5 In this ſtate of wretchedneſs the prophet, in the perſon of the church, and on her account, weeps bitterly *Mine eye runneth down with rivers of waters*, unutterable is his anguiſh for the deſtruction he beheld without intermiſſion *mine eye trickleth down*, and every ſcene of deſolation that preſented itſelf, pierced his heart with freſh anguiſh, and drew forth a new torrent of tears over the daughters of his people, or *more than all the daughters of my people* none, even of the tender ſex, were ſo deeply affected, and profuſe in tears, as the prophet, and thus he reſolved to continue weeping and praying, *till the Lord look down and behold from heaven*, and pitied, pardoned, and delivered them Note, (1) Let nothing drive us from waiting upon God (2) Our hearts will find no ſuch relief from their anguiſh, as by pouring out ſorrows into the boſom of a compaſſionate God. (3) If we continue inſtant and patient in prayer, we ſhall aſſuredly find at laſt an anſwer of peace

55 ¶ s I called upon thy name, O LORD, out of the — s Pſ cxxx 1. Jon ii 2, 3
low dungeon 56 Thou haſt heard my voice, hide
not thine ear at my breathing, at my cry 57 Thou — t Jam iv 8
dreweſt near in the day *that* I called upon thee thou
ſaidſt, Fear not 58 O LORD, u thou haſt plead- — u Jer li 36
ed the cauſes of my ſoul, thou haſt redeemed my life
59 O LORD, thou haſt ſeen my wrong, x judge thou — x Pſ xliii 1
my cauſe 60 Thou haſt ſeen all their vengeance, *and*
all their imaginations againſt me 61 Thou haſt heard
their reproach, O LORD, *and* all their imaginations
againſt me 62 The lips of thoſe that roſe up againſt
me, and their device againſt me all the day 63
Behold their ſitting down and their riſing up, y I *am* — y Ver 14
their muſic 64 z Render unto them a recompence, O — z Pſ xxviii. 4 2 Tim iv 14
LORD, according to the work of their hands 65 Give
them † ſorrow of heart, thy curſe unto them 66 Perſe- — † Or, obſtinacy of heart
cute and deſtroy them in anger, from under a the heavens — a Pſ viii 3.
of the LORD

v 55—66 Sad as their ſtate was, it was ſtill within the reach of prayer, and therefore,

1 The prophet cries unto God, *I called upon thy name, O Lord, out of the low dungeon*, which may refer to the prophet's own caſe, when ready to periſh in that miſerable ſituation, or may be his prayer for the people, reduced now to the deepeſt diſtreſs *Thou haſt heard my voice*, it is the expreſſion of his humble confidence, or the encouragement he drew from paſt experience, thou haſt heard, and wilt hear, the prayer of faith, therefore *hide not thine ear at my breathing, at my cry*, in the preſent calamity or it may be read, *Thou didſt not hide, &c* and ſo is a continuation of his grateful acknowledgment of paſt mercies *Thou dreweſt near in the day that I called upon thee*, manifeſting thy gracious preſence and ſupport *thou ſaidſt, Fear not*, and that encouraged my drooping heart *O Lord, thou haſt pleaded the cauſes of my ſoul, thou haſt redeemed my life*, reſcuing him from the inſtant death that threatned him in the dungeon, or delivering the people from their oppreſſions under the yoke of Egypt, Philiſtia, and other nations, and thus emboldened

Before Chriſt 588.

boldened his hope that the Lord would yet deliver them *Note*, (1) There is no priſon ſo deep, but prayer can find a ready way out of it to the throne of God (2) Paſt mercies ſhould encourage preſent hope (3) That is the effectual prayer, when the ſoul *breathes* forth its fervent deſires, and ſtill feels more than it can utter (4) They who by faith commit their ſouls to God, need fear no evil (5) If God hath redeemed our ſouls, then, however ſore beſet and thruſt at by our enemies, we ſhall never periſh

2 He refers his caſe and his people's unto the Lord God had ſeen the wrong his enemies had done him, their malicious deſigns, and their revengeful ſpirit, *v* 60 he had heard their reproaches and inſults, and how they daily made themſelves merry in deriding him, *v* 61—63 and therefore he appeals to him for judgment againſt them, *v* 59 not in a ſpirit of revenge, but that the juſtice of God may be ſeen in the righteous retaliation of their unprovoked malignity, *v* 64 *Give them ſorrow of heart, thy curſe unto them*, the heavieſt of all plagues, and the juſt deſert of their wickedneſs *Perſecute and deſtroy them in anger, from under the heavens of the Lord*, their deeds of darkneſs having made them unworthy the light of day *Note*, (1) Though fools ſtill mock on, and ſport at God's people, the day is near when their mirth will be turned into mourning (2) Wo to thoſe againſt whom God's oppreſſed people appeal to him for juſtice

CHAP IV

This chapter is another ſingle alphabet of Lamentations for the deſtruction of Jeruſalem, like thoſe in the two firſt chapters 1 The prophet here laments the injuries and indignities done to thoſe that uſed to be reſpected, ver 1, 2 2 *He laments the diſmal effects of the famine, which they were reduced to by the ſiege*, ver 3—10 3 *He laments the taking and ſacking of Jeruſalem*, ver 11, 12 4 *He acknowledges that the ſins of their leaders were the cauſe of all theſe calamities*, ver 13—16 5 *He gives up all as doomed to utter ruin, for their enemies were quite too hard for them*, ver 17—20 6 *He foretels the deſtruction of the Edomites, who triumphed in Jeruſalem's fall*, ver 21 7 *He foretels the return of the captivity of Zion at laſt*, ver 22

1 HOW is the gold become dim! *how* is the moſt fine gold changed! the ſtones of the ſanctuary are poured out [a] in the top of every ſtreet 2 The precious ſons of Zion, comparable to fine gold, how are they eſteemed [b] as earthen pitchers, the work of the hands of the potter! 3 Even the † ſea-monſters draw out the breaſt, they give ſuck to their young ones the daughter of my people *is become* cruel, [c] like the oſtriches in the wilderneſs 4 [d] The tongue of the ſucking child cleaveth to the roof of his mouth for thirſt: [e] the young children aſk bread, *and* no man breaketh *it* unto them 5 They that did feed delicately, are deſolate in the ſtreets *they that were* brought up ‡ in ſcarlet, [f] embrace dunghills 6 For the puniſhment of the iniquity of the daughter of my people, [g] is greater than the puniſhment of the ſin of Sodom, *that was* [h] overthrown as in a moment, and no hands ſtayed on her 7 Her Nazarites were purer than ſnow, they were whiter than milk, they were more ruddy in body than rubies, their poliſhing *was* of ſapphire 8 Their viſage is § blacker than a coal they are not known in the ſtreets their ſkin cleaveth to their bones it is withered, it is become like a ſtick 9 *They that be* ſlain with the ſword, are better than *they that be* ſlain with hunger for theſe ‖ pine away, ſtricken through for *want of* the fruits of the field 10 [i] The hands of the pitiful women have ſodden their own children, they were [k] their meat in the deſtruction of the daughter of my people 11 The LORD hath accompliſhed his fury, he hath poured out his fierce anger, and [l] hath kindled a fire in Zion, and it hath devoured the foundations thereof 12. The kings of the earth, and all the inhabitants of the world would not have believed, that the adverſary and the enemy ſhould have entered into the gates of Jeruſalem

[a] Chap ii 19
[b] Iſa xxx 14 Jer xix 11
† Or ſea calves
[c] Job xxxix 14, 16
[d] Pſ xxii 15
[e] Chap ii 11, 12
‡ Or upon
[f] Job xxiv 8
[g] Luke xii 48
[h] Gen xix 25
§ Heb. Darker than blackneſs
‖ Heb Flow out
[i] Chap ii 20.
[k] Deut xxviii 57 2 Kings vi 29
[l] Deut xxxii 22

v 1—12 Who can, unaffected, behold the deſolations here deſcribed?

1 The temple is laid in ruins; the gold tarniſhed, the ſtones of the demoliſhed ſanctuary ſcattered on every ſide Which may alſo be underſtood figuratively, as in the next verſe, of the precious ſons of Zion, the children of God, comparable to gold for their excellence, and living ſtones in the ſpiritual building the church, but now broken by the Chaldeans as an earthen pitcher, and lying ſlain in every ſtreet of the city

2 People of all ranks and ages periſh in the famine *The tongue of the ſucking child cleaves to the roof of his mouth for thirſt*, the famiſhed mothers breaſts are dry, and, unable to moiſten their lips, they ſeemed more cruel than the ſea monſters, or the oſtriches of the wilderneſs The weaned infant cried for bread, and the diſtreſſed parent hath it not to give, or, preſſed by inſufferable hunger, is deaf to his liſping, and cannot ſpare the leaſt morſel, *v* 3, 4 They who were uſed to every delicacy which affluence could procure, and *were brought up in ſcarlet*, or upon ſcarlet carpets ſpread under them, *now wander in the ſtreets, and rake the dunghill* for the vileſt ſcraps to appeaſe their raging appetite to ſuch diſtreſſes may the greateſt be reduced, *v* 5 Their Nazarites, who were ſeparated for God, and abſtained with niceſt care from every defilement, or her nobles, as ſome interpret it, that were ſo elegant and curious, white as ſnow, ruddy as rubies, and their ſkins ſmooth as poliſhed ſapphire, now, black with famine, grief, and melancholy, are ſo changed, that their viſage is no longer known, withered and deſtitute of all moiſture as a dry ſtick, *v* 7, 8 periſhing miſerably for want, a lingering death more terrible than the ſword, multitudes fall on every ſide, whilſt, driven by raging hunger, horrible to tell! even mothers murder their infants, and ravenouſly feed upon the ſodden corpſes, *v* 10

3 The cauſe of all is the ſin of Jeruſalem, provoking the fierce anger of the Lord, and now his fury poured out hath accompliſhed her ruin Greater than Sodom's puniſhment is hers, becauſe more aggravated her ſins that devoted city never ſlighted thoſe means Jeruſalem had enjoyed, therefore her overthrow, though terrible, was ſudden, whilſt, by a lingering death upon the rack, the deſtruction of Zion is compleated

4 They who behold theſe deſolations are aſtoniſhed So ſtrong the fortreſs, ſo numerous the forces, ſo highly honoured by the reſidence of the great God, ſo ſignally before reſcued by his interpoſition, the kings of the neighbouring nations never conceived it poſſible for the Chaldeans to have prevailed Nor could they, if Zion's defence had not firſt departed, and God been turned againſt her as an enemy, and then no marvel ruin terrible and remedileſs overtook her

13 ¶ [m] For the ſins of her prophets, *and* the iniquities of her prieſts, that have ſhed the blood of the juſt *in the midſt of her*. 14 They have wandered *as* blind *men* in the ſtreets, they have polluted themſelves with blood, † ſo that men could not touch their garments 15 They cried unto them, [n] Depart ye, ‡ *it is* unclean, depart, depart, touch not, when they fled away and wandred they ſaid among the heathen, They ſhall no more ſojourn *there* 16 The anger of the LORD hath divided them, he will no more regard them [o] they reſpected not the perſons of the prieſts, they favoured not the elders 17 As for us, [p] our eyes as yet failed for our vain help in our watching we have watched for a nation *that* could not ſave *us* 18 [q] They hunt our ſteps that we cannot go in our ſtreets our end is near, our days are fulfilled, for our end is come 19 Our perſecutors are [r] ſwifter than the eagles of the heaven they purſued us upon the mountains, they laid wait for us in the wilderneſs. 20 [s] The breath of our noſtrils, the anointed of the LORD [t] was taken in their pits, of whom we ſaid, Under his ſhadow we ſhall live among the heathen 21 [u] Rejoice and be glad, O daughter of Edom, that dwelleſt in the land of Uz, [x] the cup alſo ſhall paſs through unto thee thou ſhalt be drunken, and ſhalt make thyſelf naked 22 ¶ [y] § The puniſhment of thine iniquity is accompliſhed, O daughter of Zion, [z] he will no more carry thee away into captivity [a] he will viſit thine iniquity, O daughter of Edom, he will ‖ diſcover thy ſins

[m] Jer v 31, & xxiii 11
† Or and much as men could not but touch
[n] Is lii 11
‡ Or, polluted
[o] 2 Kings xxv 1
[p] 2 Kings xxiv 7 Iſa xxx 6, 7 Jer xxxvii 7 Ezek xxix 16
[q] 2 Kings xxv 4, 5
[r] Deut xxviii 49
[s] Gen ii 7 Chap ii 9
[t] Jer lii 8 Ezek xii 13, & xix 4, 8
[u] Eccleſ xi 9
[x] Jer xxv 15, 21
[y] Iſa xl 2
§ Or thine iniquity
[z] Ezek xxxvii 25
[a] Jer xxxv
‖ Or carry thee captive for thy ſins

v 13—22 We have here,

1 The principal cauſe of Jeruſalem's deſtruction *The ſins of her prophets and the iniquities of her prieſts*, who, whilſt by office and profeſſion they ſhould have reformed others, were the great example and encouragers of iniquity, and filled up faſt the meaſure of the national guilt *They ſhed the blood of the juſt*, being the firſt to perſecute God's faithful ones, eſpecially the true prophets, who remonſtrated againſt their wickedneſs *They wandered as blind men in the ſtreets*, pretending to lead others whilſt themſelves were bewildered in error, ignorance, and ſin, and, thus *polluted with blood*, every good man ſhunned their company as defiling, and cried unto all near them to beware of them, as if their touch or breath communicated infection, *depart ye, it is unclean, touch not* and in the lands whither they were carried captive theſe deſtroyers of their country were marked with a peculiar

Before Christ 588

culiar brand of infamy, *they said among the heathen, they shall no more sojourn there*, God having decreed, concerning these false teachers, that they should die in the land of their captivity, and never see or partake of the restoration God had promised to his people, v 15 Under God's peculiar wrath they were now divided and dispersed, and as he will no more regard them, neither shall they find any respect and favour from their heathen masters or the last words of v 16 may be interpreted as their sin, as well as punishment they had treated with contempt God's true and faithful ministers, and therefore they themselves justly receive the same *Note*, (1) Wicked priests and prophets, more than any others, conspire to hasten a nation's ruin (2) We cannot keep at too great a distance from their company whose evil communications tend to corrupt and destroy the soul

2 In the time of their calamity all help failed this unhappy people They expected assistance from the Egyptians, but in vain, eagerly they looked for their advancing to raise the siege, till their eyes failed, and too late they found their case desperate, and that their allies *could not save* them from the Chaldean army, v 17 their mounts were raised so high that they overlooked the walls, and if but a person appeared in the streets, they pursued him with their slings and arrows as a beast is hunted Their end *was near*, it now was evident they could not hold out long, the days appointed by the prophetic word were nearly expiring, and then the fearful *end* of Zion must *come*, v 19 Flight was useless, when, swifter than eagles, their persecutors pursued, nor could the mountain or wilderness afford a covert from their piercing eyes, v 19 nay even their king himself found no protection for his sacred person, and all their flattering hopes that under his protection they should be safe, amidst the surrounding heathen nations, now vanished as a dream they behold him seized, his eyes put out, and led away in brazen fetters a miserable captive, v 20 Some have applied this as if it had a reference to Christ, the anointed Saviour, seized by the hands of his enemies and slain, whilst his disheartened disciples, beholding the scene, were ready to abandon themselves to despair

3 A gracious promise closes the lamentation, so doleful and full of misery Edom had maliciously rejoiced at Zion's fall, and with pointed irony the prophet bids them continue their joy, but lets them know, the cup of vengeance which Jerusalem had tasted they must drink of, and sink down, as a drunken man overpowered with liquor, under the fury of the Lord, helpless be stripped of all their treasures and ornaments, and driven naked as slaves before their conquerors, and whilst Zion's punishment hath an end, and she is restored, no more to be a captive, the iniquity of Edom shall still be visited, and her sins discovered in the punishment inflicted on them And what is here said seems to look to future times, Edom being the figure of the antichristian powers, as Zion is of the church of God The Jews, after their return from Babylon, were, we know, led captive again, and are to this day in a state of bondage, but when Rome, the spiritual Edom, shall be destroyed, then shall the church be triumphant, and never know the yoke of captivity any more for ever

CHAP V.

This chapter, though it has the same number of verses with the first, second, and fourth, yet is not alphabetical as they were, but the scope of it is the same We have in it, 1 *A remonstrance of the present calamitous state of God's people in their captivity,* ver 1—16 2 *A protestation of their concern for God's sanctuary, as that which lay nearer their heart than any secular interest of their own,* ver 17, 18 3 *A humble supplication to God, and expostulation with him, for the returns of mercy,* ver 19—22.

1 REmember, O LORD, what is come upon us
a consider, and behold our reproach 2 Our
inheritance is turned to strangers, our houses to aliens
3 We are orphans and fatherless, our mothers *are* as
widows 4 We have drunken our water for money,
our wood is sold unto us 5 ‖ Our necks *are* under
persecution we labour, *and* have no rest 6 b We have
given the hand to the Egyptians, *and* to the Assyrians,
to be satisfied with bread 7 c Our fathers have sinned,
and *are* not, and we have born their iniquities 8 Ser-
vants have ruled over us *there is* none that doth deliver
us out of their hand 9 We gat our bread with *the peril*
of our lives, because of the sword ‡ of the wilderness
10 d Our skin was black like an oven, because of the
§ terrible famine 11 They ravished the women in
Zion, *and* the maids in the cities of Judah 12 Princes
are hanged up by their hand e the faces of elders were
not honoured 13 They took the young men ¶ to grind,
and the children fell under the wood 14 The elders
have ceased from the gate, the young men from their
musick 15 The joy of our heart is ceased, our dance
is turned into mourning 16. f † The crown is fallen
from our head wo unto us that we have sinned 17
For this g our heart is faint, h for these *things* our eyes
are dim 18. Because of i the mountain of Zion, which
is desolate, the foxes walk upon it

a Ps lxxix 10
‖ Heb On our necks are we persecuted
b Lam xxiv 2
c Jer xxxi 29. Ezek xviii 2
‡ Or in the pain
d Chap iv 8
§ Job xxx 30
‖ Heb terrors, or storms
e Isa xlvii 6
f Chap iv 16
¶ Or to carry the grist
f Ps lxxxix 39
† Heb. The crown of our head is fallen
g Chap i 22
h Ps vi 7
i Mic iii 12

v 1—18 The prophet, in the name of his afflicted people, presents their miserable case before the God of all mercy, intreating him to regard, consider, and remove the reproach under which they groan And no tear, no sigh of God's people, passes unnoticed

1 He spreads their present wretched state before God in a variety of particulars, wherein their grievous reproach appeared Deprived of the inheritance of their fathers, strangers have seized their estates, and dwell in the houses they had built, v 2 In a natural, political, and spiritual sense, they were become orphans and widows, the men slain with the sword, their king removed, and God himself had forsaken them, v 3 In their captivity they were not only destitute of the comforts of life, but the very necessaries were hardly to be procured by them, even their water and their wood were to be purchased at an exorbitant rate, v 4 Groaning under their heavy loads, scarce would their heathen masters allow them sleep, and probably forbid them the observance of their sabbaths, wearing them out with incessant toil, v 5 For a morsel of bread to relieve their hunger, they yielded their necks to bondage in Egypt and Assyria, v 6 The meanest among the nations whither they were dispersed tyrannized over them, and the cursed race of Ham, doomed to be the *servant of servants*, Gen ix 26, 27 is their master; to a state of such ignominy and wretched servitude were they reduced, and not a friend to interpose to mitigate their burdens, or deliver them from their bondage or their heathen masters suffered their very servants to insult them without check or rebuke, v 8 During the siege, when, driven by hunger, any ventured to go without the walls in quest of provision, *the sword of the wilderness*, or *of the plain*, the Chaldeans who guarded every avenue, exposed them to constant peril of their lives, v 9. Scorched up with famine, their shriveled skins looked black, as if burnt with fire, v 10 Sacrificed to brutal lust, their wives and virgins fell a prey to lawless ravishers, v 11. Their princes were hanged by their cruel conquerors, and perhaps, when dead, their bodies hung up *by the hand* and exposed The elders in age or office were insulted, and no respect paid to dignity or hoary locks, v 12 The young men are set *to grind*, or *carry the grist*, as if they were beasts of burden, and the very children sink under their loads of wood, unable to sustain them, v 13 The courts of justice are no more, the judges slain, or captives the voice of musick is silenced, their joy is fled, and all their gaiety exchanged for mourning, v 14, 15 The crown is fallen, their king a prisoner, their kingdom enslaved *Note*, This world is a scene of awful changes we must look to a better for everlasting crowns and uninterrupted joy

2 Their sins have provoked these judgments they own and lament it *Our fathers have sinned, and are not, and we have born their iniquities*, v 7 having added their own provocations to the past, till they had filled the measure of their sins *wo unto us*, v 16 our case is deplorable and pitiable, *that we have sinned*, and, having nothing to plead in vindication of themselves, they cast their souls upon the sovereign mercy and grace of God, acknowledging the justice of all they suffered, *for this our heart is faint*, both for their miseries and their sins, *for these things our eyes are dim* with weeping, *because of the mountain of Zion which is desolate*, the city and temple in ruins, *the foxes walk upon it*, without interruption, as in the desert *Note*, (1) Among the bitterest griefs, which affect the hearts of the faithful, are the desolations of Zion, the affliction of God's church and people (2) Sin is the root of all our sorrow, and more to be lamented than all the sufferings it occasions.

19 Thou, O LORD, k remainest for ever l thy
throne from generation to generation 20 Wherefore
dost thou forget us m for ever, *and* forsake us so long
time? 21 n Turn thou us unto thee, O LORD, and
we shall be turned o renew our days as of old 22
‖ But thou hast utterly rejected us, thou art very wroth
against us

k Ps ix 7, & x 16, & xxix 10, & cii 12, 27, & cxlv 13. Hab i 12
l Ps xlv 6
m Ps xiii 1
n Ps lxxx 3, 7, 19. Jer xxxi 18
o Hab iii 2
‖ Or, For wilt thou utterly reject us? wilt thou be, &c.

v 19—22 The people of God, for whom the prophet speaks,

1 Express their dependance upon God *Thou, O Lord, remainest for ever*, the same unchangeable Jehovah, faithful to all his promises, immutable in his decrees, and therefore his people may comfort themselves in the constancy of his regard, whatever troubles they are exposed to *thy throne from generation to generation* his dominion is eternal, and he who rules over all will over-rule every event for his people's good whilst Zion's God reigns his people need never despair

2 They

Before Christ 588

2 They expostulate with God on their unhappy case *Wherefore dost thou forget us for ever, and forsake us so long time?* It had been long, and they were ready to fear it would be for ever, yea every moment of his displeasure seemed an age to them, and their unbelief was ready often to suggest, *but thou hast utterly rejected us,* and there is no more hope, *thou art very wroth against us,* to consume us Or the words may be read, *For hast thou utterly rejected us? wilt thou be very wroth against us?* Humble expostulations are allowable we may reason with God concerning his judgments, though we may not quarrel with him on account of them

3 They pray *Turn thou us unto thee, and we shall be turned* Conscious of their sad departures from him, and their utter inability to help themselves, they look to him who alone can work the mighty change *Renew our days as of old* bring us to our former state of happiness, and enable us to imitate the examples of our pious ancestors This verse is repeated at last after the following one, v 22 by the Jewish rabbins, who would not have the book conclude with the last melancholy words *Note,* (1) No sinner would ever return from the evil of his way unless the effectual grace of God powerfully drew him (2) However dark the scene may close upon God's suffering saints on earth, let them commend their souls to him, and then they shall quickly wake up in glory, honour, and immortality

Before Christ 588

2

THE

THE

EVANGELICAL EXPOSITOR;

OR, A

PRACTICAL COMMENT

Upon the Book of the PROPHET

EZEKIEL.

WHEN *we entred upon the writings of the Prophets, which speak of the* things that should be hereafter, *methought we had the same call given us that St John had,* Rev iv 1 Come up hither, *but, when we enter upon the prophecy of this book, methinks we are called to* come up higher. *These waters of the sanctuary still grow deeper as they flow, so far from being fordable, that in some places they are scarce fathomable*

(1) *The penman of this prophecy was Ezekiel his name signifies* The strength of God, *or one* girt *or* strengthened of God. *Where he gives a commission he will give power to execute it Ezekiel's name was answered when God said,* I have made thy face strong against their faces.

(2) *Concerning the date of it, the place whence it is dated, and the time when The scene is laid in Babylon, when it was a* house of bondage *to the* Israel of God *there the prophecies of this book were preached, there they were written, when the prophet himself and the people to whom he prophesied were captives there. Ezekiel and Daniel are the only writing prophets of the Old Testament that lived and prophesied any where but in the land of Israel, except we add Jonah, who was sent to Nineveh to prophesy Ezekiel prophesied in the beginning of the captivity, Daniel in the latter end of it, it was an indication of God's good will to them, and his gracious designs concerning them in their affliction, that he raised up prophets among them, both to convince them when in the beginning of their troubles they were secure and unhumbled, which was Ezekiel's business, and to comfort them when in the latter end of their troubles they were dejected and discouraged If the Lord had been pleased to kill them, he would not have used such apt and proper means to cure them*

(3.) *Concerning the matter and scope of it,* 1 *There is much in it that is very mysterious, dark and hard to be understood, especially in the beginning and latter end of it, which therefore the Jewish rabbins forbad the reading of to their young men, till they came to be thirty years of age, lest by the difficulties they met with there they should be prejudiced against the Scriptures but if we read these difficult parts of Scripture with humility and reverence, and search them diligently, though we may not be able to unty all the knots we meet with, no more than we can solve all the phenomena in the book of nature, yet we may from them, as from the book of nature, gather a great deal for the confirming of our faith, and the encouraging of our hope in God* 2 *Though the visions here be intricate, such as an elephant may swim in, yet the sermons are mostly plain, such as a lamb may wade in, and the chief design of them is to* shew God's people their transgressions, *that in their captivity they might be repenting, and not repining* 3. *Tho' the reproofs here and the threatnings be very sharp and bold, yet, towards the close of the book, very comfortable assurances are given of great mercy God had in store for them, with particular reference to the Messiah's kingdom, to whom bore all the prophets witness The visions, which were the prophet's credentials, we have,* chap i—iii *the reproofs and threatnings,* chap iv—xxiv *and betwixt the comforts we have in the latter part of the book, we have messages sent to the nations that bordered upon the land of Israel, whose destruction is foretold* chap xxv—xxxv *to make way for the restoration of God's Israel, and the re-establishment of their city and temple, which are foretold* chap xxxvi. ad finem. *And those who would apply the comforts to themselves must apply the convictions to themselves.*

Before Christ 595

CHAP I

In this chapter we have, 1 The time when this prophecy was delivered, ver 1 the place where, ver 2 and the person by whom, ver 3 2 The introduction to it by a vision of the glory of God (1) The cherubim over which he appeared, ver 4—14 (2) The wheels that accompanied them, ver 15—26 (3) His glorious appearance on his throne, ver 26—28

NOW it came to pass in the thirtieth year,
in the fourth *month*, in the fifth *day* of the
month, (as I *was* among the captives [a] by
the river of Chebar) *that* [b] the heavens were
opened, and I saw visions of God 2 In the fifth *day*
of the month (which *was* the fifth year of [c] king Jehoi-
akin's captivity) 3 The word of the LORD came ex-
presly unto Ezekiel the priest, the son of Buzi, in the
land of the Chaldeans, by the river Chebar, and [d] the
hand of the LORD was there upon him

[a] Ver 3 Chap iii 15 [b] Isa ii 10 Acts vii 56 & x 11 Rev xix 11 [c] 2 Kings xxiv 12 [d] 1 Kings xviii 46 Chap iii 14, 22

v 1—3 We have here,

1 The date of the prophecy *In the thirtieth year*, as some suppose, of the prophet's life, when, according to custom, he entered on his priestly office, but others refer it to the æra commencing from Nabopolasser's reign, which was the twelfth of the captivity, reckoning from the third year of Jehoiakim, *and the fifth of Jehoiachin, or Coniah's captivity, in the fourth month, the fifth day of the month*, probably a sabbath day, when the prophet was employed in the blessed work of contemplation and prayer, for seven days after we find another vision of the same nature given him, *chap* iii 16 *Note*, They who seek to improve the sacred hours God hath separated for his own service, in waiting upon him, will find him often manifesting himself to them as he doth not unto the world

2 The place *among the captives by the river Chebar, in the land of the Chaldeans* In their afflicted state God thus shewed he had not forsaken them, but would encourage still their hope of mercy, and engage them to repent and turn to him The prophet shared in the common calamity, for in national judgments good and bad fall together but God knows how to comfort the hearts of his people with inward supports others partake not of, and usually his suffering saints have found in the day of their troubles more abundant consolations, 2 *Cor* i 5

3 The vision *The heavens were opened, and I saw the visions of God* some amazing displays of the divine glory appeared *And the word of the Lord came expresly unto Ezekiel the priest, the son of Buzi* The words translated *came expresly* are very emphatical in the original, implying the certainty, evidence, and clearness, of the prophetic word which God revealed to him *And the hand of the Lord was there upon him*, supporting him, that he might not be overpowered with the dazzling lustre, and strengthening him to go forth to deliver what was communicated to him *Note*, (1) They will be enabled to deliver their message with greatest boldness, who speak from the most assured conviction in their own souls (2) If God sends us forth in his ministry, we may expect his hand will be with us to strengthen us, and give demonstration and power to the word he puts into our mouth.

4 ¶ And I looked, and behold, a whirlwind came
out of the north, a great cloud, and a fire [†] infolding
itself, and a brightness *was* about it, and out of the midst
thereof as the colour of amber, out of the midst of the
fire 5 Also [e] out of the midst thereof *came* the likeness
of four living creatures And [f] this *was* their appearance
They had the likeness of a man 6 And [g] every one
had four faces, and [h] every one had four wings 7 And
their feet [i] *were* straight feet, and the sole of their feet
was like the sole of a calf's foot, and they sparkled [k] like
the colour of burnished brass 8 And *they had* the hands
of a man under their wings on their four sides, and they
four had their faces and their wings 9 [l] Their wings
were joined one to another, they turned not when they
went, they went every one straight forward 10 As
for [m] the likeness of their faces, they four [n] had the face
of a man, and the face of a lion on the right side, and
they four had [o] the face of an ox on the left side they
four also had the face of an eagle 11 Thus *were* their
faces and their wings *were* [‡] stretched upwards, *two*
wings of every one *were* joined one to another, and [r] two
covered their bodies 12 And [s] they went every one
straight forward [t] whither the spirit was to go, [u] they
went *and* they turned not when they went 13 As
for the likeness of the living creatures, their appearance
was like burning coals of fire, [x] *and* like the appearance
of lamps it went up and down among the living crea-
tures, and the fire was bright, and out of the fire went
forth lightning 14 And the living creatures ran, and
returned as the appearance of a flash of lightning

[†] Heb catching itself [e] Rev iv 6 &c [f] Chap x 8 & [g] Ver 10 Chap x 14, 21 [h] Isa vi 2 [i] Heb vii 23 [k] Rev i 15 [l] Ver 11, 12 [m] Rev iv [n] Num ii 10 [o] Num ii 3 [p] Num ii 18 Chap x 14 [q] Numb ii 25 [‡] Or divided above [r] Isa vi 2 [s] Ver 9 [t] Ver [u] Ver 17 [x] Rev iv

v 4—14 The introduction to these visions of God is very awful, tending to affect the prophet's mind with the highest reverence of that Jehovah whose minister he was, and to encourage the poor captives, whose glory seemed now departed from them but lo! their God is still in the midst of them

1 *Behold, a whirlwind out of the north, a great cloud*, the vehicle of this awful vision, *and a fire infolding itself*, a cheering fire to God's faithful people, a consuming fire to his foes, *and a brightness was about it*, the cloud was illuminated by the fire, an emblem of that irradiation which darted into the prophet's mind, *and out of the midst thereof as the colour of amber, out of the midst of the fire* Chasmal, translated *amber*, some render *a lively colour* others, *a coal exceedingly fired* others suppose Christ is meant, who is represented something similar thereunto, *Rev* i 15 iv 3 and hereunto I incline He it was who appeared to Moses in the bush, to Isaiah on his throne, and here to Ezekiel in the midst of the fire

2 *The likeness of four living creatures came out of the midst* of this vision, not real creatures, but emblematical representations, either of the angels who surround the throne of God, as some or rather of gospel ministers, see *Rev* iv 6—9, where the same emblematic figures appear They are *living creatures*, themselves quickened to spiritual life, lively in their ministrations, and the means of quickening others souls, *four*, as sent forth to the four quarters of the earth, to preach the gospel to every creature, *in the likeness of a man*, except in the following particulars

1 *They had four faces* (1) *The face of a man*, being taken from among men to minister in the things of God, with understanding to instruct the ignorant, and with the feelings of humanity to have compassion on the afflicted (2) *Of a lion*, to denote their courage and boldness in preaching the gospel amidst all opposition (3) *Of an ox*, to represent their indefatigable labour and patience (4) *Of an eagle*, signifying their piercing sight, and clear knowledge of the mysteries of God, and their soaring high in divine contemplation and holy affections

2 *Every one had* also *four wings*, v 6. From v 11—23 they seem to have had two more, as the seraphim in Isaiah, and the beasts in the revelations, four covered their bodies, and two were stretched upward, and these wings joined one to another, v 9 intimating, (1) The swiftness and diligence they use in executing God's will, and the work of their ministry (2) The concord and union which subsists among them, united in love, and fellow-labourers in the same gospel (3) The consciousness of their own infirmities, which makes them ashamed of their imperfect services, and count themselves unworthy to appear before God

3 *Their feet were straight feet*, ver 7, 9, 12 They walk uprightly before God, never turn aside to the crooked paths of error and immorality, they perseveringly go *forward*, undismayed by opposition, persecution, or temptation, and with a single eye to God's glory, *the sole of their feet was like the sole of a calf's feet*, one of the clean animals that divide the hoof, and intimates the purity of their conversation, or the firmness of their hearts in their ministry, *and they sparkled like the colour of burnished brass*, so beautiful upon the mountains are the feet of those that bring glad tidings of peace, and so bright the lustre of their holy examples

4 *They had the hands of a man under their wings on the four sides*, implying activity in executing what their wisdom and prudence directed, and many hands, because their work is vast and large, yet *under their wings*, not making ostentation of their labours, but ascribing the glory to him from whom all their strength is derived

5 They were under the guidance of the Holy Ghost *Whither the spirit was to go, they went* by him alone they are called to take the ministry upon them, *inwardly moved* by his powerful grace, by him they are supported in their labour, led into all truth, and readily disposed for every service which he is pleased to appoint them, nor can staggering at the difficulties nor can be *turned* back, by any fear of man, from delivering the message with which he hath sent them, like *coals of fire* they burn with divine zeal, v 13 and *as lamps* they shine bright themselves in the exercise of every divine grace, and hold forth the word of light to others, clear, distinct, enlightening, cheering, warming their souls *It went up and down among the living creatures*, the divine light and fire of zeal filled them; *bright*, shining on every side, and darting, like *lightning* to the ends of the earth so extensive, so powerful, so penetrating was the gospel word they preached and, when they had executed their ministry with the fervour and activity, they returned to give an account to their master, and to receive fresh orders from him, desiring to approve themselves to him in all things, and take no step but under his guidance and by his direction Let gospel ministers, looking on these cherubim, prove their own selves, and learn what they should be.

15 ¶

Before Christ 595.

15 ¶ Now as I beheld the living creatures, behold,
one wheel upon the earth by the living creatures, with
y Chap. x. 9, 10. his four faces. 16 y The appearance of the wheels,
and their work was like unto the colour of a beryl: and
they four had one likeness, and their appearance and their
work was as it were a wheel in the middle of a wheel.
17 When they went, they went upon their four sides:
and they returned not when they went. 18 As for their
z Rom. xi. 33. rings, they were z so high that they were dreadful, and
† Or, strakes. their † rings were full of eyes round about them four.
19 And when the living creatures went, the wheels
went by them: and when the living creatures were lift
a Ver. 12. up from the earth, the wheels were lift up. 20 a Whi-
thersoever the spirit was to go, they went, thither was
their spirit to go; and the wheels were lifted up over
‡ Or, of life. against them: for the spirit ‡ of the living creature was
b Ver. 19, 20. Chap. x. 17. in the wheels. 21 b When those went, these went, and
when those stood, these stood; and when those were lifted
up from the earth, the wheels were lifted up over against
§ Or, of life. them: for the spirit § of the living creature was in the
wheels. 22 And the likeness of the firmament upon
the heads of the living creature, was as the colour of the
terrible crystal, stretched forth over their heads above.
23 And under the firmament were their wings straight,
the one toward the other: every one had two, which
covered on this side, and every one had two, which co-
c Chap. x. 5. vered on that side, their bodies. 24 c And when they
d Chap. xliii. 2. went, I heard the noise of their wings, d like the noise
of great waters, as the voice of the Almighty, the voice
of speech as the noise of an host: when they stood, they
let down their wings. 25 And there was a voice from
the firmament, that was over their heads, when they stood,
and had let down their wings.

v. 15—25. The vision of the wheels follows that of the living creatures, which are variously interpreted. Some suppose them an emblem of the dispensations of providence, others of the word of God and the ministrations of it; but I rather follow those who interpret these wheels of the gospel churches, according to Rev. iv. where they are represented by four and twenty elders. But one wheel is mentioned, v. 15. for the church is one body, composed of innumerable believers, though it appears they were four, v. 16. and chap. x. 9. being collected from the four quarters of the world. The wheel may be considered as an emblem of perfection, for all the faithful are compleat in Christ; or it may represent the moveable state of the churches, or the different circumstances of prosperity and adversity to which they are alternately subject; or as composing a chariot with the Cherubim, 1 Chron. xxviii. 18. in which the Lord Jesus rides in majesty and glory, Cant. iii. 9. The wheels are by the living creatures, intimating that the several congregation of the faithful follow their ministers, who preside in their worship, stir up their souls to run the way of God's commandments, and direct and lead them aright. With his four faces, each wheel having four faces, one on each of the semicircles which composed it, being a wheel within a wheel, v. 16. not a smaller wheel in a larger, but two circles crossing each other at right angles, and forming one wheel or orb, as it is represented chap. x. 13. and these faces are the same with those of the Cherubim, signifying that there is the most exact resemblance between faithful pastors and their people, they having the like constancy in the profession they make, labouring in their sphere with equal diligence for God, and patiently bearing the same sufferings for the gospel's sake, endued, as spiritual men, with an enlightened understanding and knowledge of the mysteries of godliness, and tenderly compassionate to their brethren, bold as lion in the cause of God and truth, and soaring as the eagle above these sublunary things, having their affections fixed, not on things on earth, but things in heaven. Their appearance and work was like unto the colour of beryl, so excellent and precious are his people to the Lord, they are his jewels; and they four had one likeness, all true believers bearing the image of the same Lord, and perfectly resembling each other in their spirit and temper, they are all one in Christ Jesus; when they went they went upon their four sides, and they returned not when they went, being from their construction ready to turn to the four points, without wheeling about. The saints of God thus go still right on, and persevering advance towards their eternal home, v. 17. Their rings were high, for the church is visible, and lifted up above all the power of earth and hell; dreadful, the enemies of God's people shall be made to tremble before them; or they had fear, a reverential fear of God, shewn in his worship, and carefulness never to offend him; and they were full of eyes, clear-sighted in the knowledge of gospel truth, watchful over their own hearts, and jealous over each other. When the living creatures went the wheels went with them, the faithful joining with their ministers in the same worship, and followers of their good conversation in Christ; and when the living creatures were lift up from the earth, the wheels were lift up; for the lively frame of the minister's own soul, breathing in his discourses, hath the most immediate tendency to raise up the souls of his hearers to high and heavenly things. Whithersoever the spirit was to go, they went; under the guidance of God's Spirit they were led, and as he taught and directed, thither was their spirit to go, and the wheels were lift up over against them, close to the sides of the living creatures; for the spirit of the living creature was in the wheels; the same spirit actuating both ministers and people, giving them life and motion: and inseparably united, as animated by one soul, they went, or rested together. So intimate is the fellowship between a minister and his people, when he is active they will be lively; if he is indolent they will be ready to be infected thereby. Over the heads of the living creature was the likeness of a firmament, as the colour of the terrible chrystal, bright, dazzling, and transparent; for though the throne of Christ is above the firmament, he sees all things done on earth; his eyes look down upon his church and people, and they by faith are enabled through the gospel glass to look up to him, and behold his glory. Under the firmament their wings were strait, stretched upward, and touching each other, with two others covering each of their sides, v. 6, 11. and when they went, preaching the gospel, I heard the noise of their wings like the noise of great waters; so loud and extensive was the sound of their voice bearing the glad tidings of salvation to the distant Gentile lands, as the voice of the Almighty, awful, majestic, powerful; the voice of speech, for tho' the word is God's, the messengers are men; as the noise of a host, multitudes being employed in this ministry, and all uniting in one cry, warning every man, and teaching every man, that they may present every man perfect in Christ Jesus: and when they stood, they let down their wings, having finished the work on which they were sent, and waiting for fresh instructions, which they receive from Christ their Lord and Master, who speaks from the firmament over their heads, in his word, and by the secret influences of his Spirit, directing them whither to go, and what to speak; encouraging them to persist in their work on earth, or calling them to his rest in heaven.

26 ¶ e And above the firmament that was over their e Chap. x. 1.
heads, was the likeness of f a throne, as the appearance f Rev. iii. 21.
of a sapphire-stone: and upon the likeness of the throne
was the likeness as the appearance of g a man above upon g Isa. ix. 6.
it. 27 h And I saw as the colour of amber, as the h Chap. viii. 2.
appearance of fire round about within it, from the
appearance of his loins even upward, and from the
appearance of his loins even downward, I saw as it
were the appearance of fire, and it had brightness round
about. 28 i As the appearance of the bow that is in i Rev. iv. 3.
the cloud in the day of rain, so was the appearance of
the brightness round about. k This was the appearance k Chap. iii. 23. & viii. 4.
of the likeness of the glory of the LORD. And when I
saw it, l I fell upon my face, and I heard a voice of one l Chap. iii. 23. Dan. viii. 17. Rev. i. 17.
that spake.

v. 26—28. The most glorious part of the vision is yet to come. The living creatures were but the servants to prepare the way; here the Lord of life appears seated on his royal throne. Above the firmament was the likeness of a throne, the symbol of that universal dominion and eternal kingdom which, as God over all, the Lord Jesus essentially possesses, or which, as Mediator, he hath received: as the appearance of a sapphire-stone, very glorious; and upon the likeness of the throne was the likeness as the appearance of a man above upon it, even that divine Lord, who in the fulness of time condescended to appear in fashion as a man, and in the human form, before his incarnation, manifested himself to his people. He appeared as the colour of amber, as the appearance of fire round about within it, a fire of love to his people, a fire of wrath to his enemies: and this fire that appeared all over him had a brightness round about like the rainbow, v. 28. similar to which he is represented, Rev. x. 1. an emblem of the covenant of grace, in which Christ is the great author, purchaser, and bestower of every blessing. This was the appearance of the likeness of the glory of the Lord, of him who was the brightness of his Father's glory, and the express image of his person, and in whom dwelt all the fulness of the godhead bodily: and when I saw it, I fell upon my face, in humble adoration of this divine personage, and filled with reverence and godly fear: and I heard a voice of one that spake, with an articulate human voice, delivering to him the commission contained in the following chapter.

Before Christ 595.

CHAP. II.

We have here, Ezekiel's ordination to his office 1. He is commissioned to go as a prophet to the house of Israel, to deliver God's messages to them, ver 1—5 2 He is cautioned not to be afraid of them, ver 6 3 He is instructed what to say to them, which is signified by the vision of a roll, which he was ordered to eat, ver 7—10 and which, in the next chapter, we find he did eat

1 AND he said unto me, Son of man, stand upon
thy feet, and I will speak unto thee 2 And
a the spirit entred into me, when he spake unto me, and
set me upon my feet, that I heard him that spake unto
me 3 And he said unto me, Son of man, I send thee
to the children of Israel, to † a rebellious nation that hath
rebelled against me, b they and their fathers have transgressed
against me, *even* unto this very day 4 For
c *they are* ‡ impudent children and d stiff-hearted I do
send thee unto them, and thou shalt say unto them,
Thus saith the LORD God 5 e And they, whether
they will hear, or whether they will forbear, (for they
are a rebellious house) yet shall f know that there hath
been a prophet among them

a Chap. iii. 24. † Or, rebellious Gentiles. b Jer. iii. 25. c Chap. iii. 7. ‡ Heb. Hard of face. d Acts vii. 51. e Chap. iii. 11. f Chap. xxxiii. 33.

v 1—5 The divine person who appeared in the foregoing chapter, addresses the prophet by this title, *Son of man*, which may be considered as a humbling notice, lest he should be puffed up by the visions with which he was favoured, and the high commission bestowed on him, or rather as an honourable distinction, being the name the Son of God himself would bear in his incarnation, of whom the prophet is appointed to be the type and figure

1 He is commanded to arise and hear *Stand upon thy feet*, from his lowly prostration, *and I will speak unto thee*, which implied favour and encouragement, and all who humble their souls before God, may be assured they shall hear him speak to them in mercy And with this command there went forth power, *the spirit entered into me*, God's spirit strengthening him to stand up on his feet, and qualifying him with gifts and graces for the discharge of his high office Thus all our strength must come from Christ, he alone can enable us for that which he commands, and they who are sent by him, shall find his Spirit with them to the end of the world

2 His commission is given him *I send thee to the children of Israel*, though they had long since justly forfeited all title to his regard, *to a rebellious nation*, or *rebellious Gentiles*, for such they resembled in their idolatries hereditary transgressors, their fathers began the rebellion, and they had persisted in it to that day, *v* 3 by habit in sin become *impudent* and shameless, *stiff-hearted* and stubborn, that would not hear nor submit to rebuke to them he is sent, to speak in God's name, and by his authority, *v* 4 *and they, whether they will hear, or whether they will forbear, (for they are a rebellious house) yet shall know that there hath been a prophet among them* If they heard and repented, they would acknowledge and adore the goodness of God in sending them a prophet if they rejected him, they should prove the truth of his mission by the accomplishment of the judgments upon them which he pronounced, *v* 5 *Note*, (1) God's patience is wonderful, not willing that the most rebellious sinners should perish (2) They who persist in their iniquities, notwithstanding all the methods of providence and grace God hath used to recover them, will be left without excuse (3) None can speak with authority, who have not a divine commission (4) Whether sinners will hear or forbear, God will be glorified, and his faithful ministers be honourable and approved by him

6 ¶ And thou, son of man, g be not afraid of them,
neither be afraid of their words, though h ‖ briers and
thorns *be* with thee, and thou dost dwell among scorpions
i be not afraid of their words, nor be dismayed at
their looks, k though they *be* a rebellious house 7
And thou shalt speak my words unto them, whether
they will hear, or whether they will forbear, for they
are ‡ most rebellious 8 But thou, son of man, hear
what I say unto thee, Be not thou rebellious like that
rebellious house open thy mouth, and l eat that I give
thee 9 ¶ And when I looked, behold, an hand *was*
sent unto me, and lo, m a roll of a book *was* therein 10
And he spread it before me, and it *was* written within
and without, and *there was* written therein, lamentations,
and mourning, and wo

g Jer. i. 8. Luke xii. 4. h Mic. vii. 4. ‖ Or, rebels. i Chap. iii. 9. 1 Pet. iii. 14. k Jer. i. 17. Chap. iii. 9. ‡ Heb. Rebellion. l Rev. x. 9. m Chap. iii. 1.

v 6—10 Ezekiel was now appointed to his arduous office, and great courage it required to execute it with fidelity Therefore,

1 God charges him to be faithful, notwithstanding all the opposition he might expect His abode was among *briers and scorpions*, wicked men, persecutors, subtle, malignant, venomous, whose *words* would be bitter, and their *looks* malicious, frowning, fierce but he must not fear nor be dismayed at their threatenings, frowns, or ill usage, nor like them prove rebellious and turn away from God, but attentively hear, seriously digest, and boldly declare the message God would put into his mouth, *v* 8 *Note*, (1) God's faithful ministers may ever expect to meet with unreasonable and wicked men, but they must not fear their faces, nor be intimidated to keep back any thing of the whole counsel of God, how much soever they may be exposed thereby (2) Though those to whom we are sent are never so rebellious and perverse, we are bound at least to deliver our own souls by continuing to testify against them (3) They who are sent of God must carefully adhere to their instructions, and speak *his word* without adulteration, not conniving at men's sins, or, through fear of offending, softening the sharp rebuke, lest by such unfaithfulness they become partakers of their guilt and ruin

2 The roll, containing his message, is spread before him *When I looked, behold, an hand was sent unto me, and lo, a roll of a book was therein*, the hand of Christ who gave him his orders, and will support him in the discharge of his office *and he spread it before me*, that he might peruse the contents, and thro' divine illumination understand them *and it was written within and without*, on both sides of the parchment or vellum, denoting the multitude of matter it contained, *and* this too the most afflictive, for *there was written therein, lamentations, and mourning, and woe*, both with regard to the present wretched state of the Jews, so greatly to be bemoaned, and full of terrible threatnings of greater wrath and judgments ready to fall upon them for their impenitence *Note*, (1) They who bear God's message must carefully peruse their Bibles, that they may be sure to speak as the oracles of God (2) Impenitent sinners can expect to hear from God no word of comfort, but wrath to the uttermost

CHAP. III.

In this chapter we have the further preparation of the prophet for the work to which God called him 1 His eating of the roll, ver 1—3 2 Farther instructions and encouragements given him, ver 4—11 3 The mighty impulse he was under, with which he was carried to those that were to be his hearers, ver 12—15. 4 A further explication of his office and business as a prophet, under the similitude of a watchman, ver 16—21 5 The restraining and restoring of the prophet's liberty of speech, as God pleased, ver 22—27

1 MOreover he said unto me, Son of man, eat that
thou findest, a eat this roll, and go speak unto
the house of Israel 2 So I opened my mouth, and he
caused me to eat that roll 3 And he said unto me,
Son of man, b cause thy belly to eat, and fill thy bowels
with this roll that I give thee Then did I c eat *it*, and
it was in my mouth as honey for sweetness 4 ¶ And
he said unto me, Son of man, go, get thee unto the
house of Israel, and speak with my words unto them
5 For thou *art* not sent to a people ‖ of a strange speech,
and of an hard language, *but* to the house of Israel
6 Not to many people of a strange speech, and of an
hard language, whose words thou canst not understand
surely, e had I sent thee to them, they would have hearkened
unto thee 7 But the house of Israel will not
hearken unto thee, f for they will not hearken unto me
g for all the house of Israel *are* ‡ impudent and hard-hearted
8 Behold, I have made thy face strong against
their faces, and thy forehead strong against their foreheads
9 h As an adamant harder than flint have I
made thy forehead i fear them not, neither be dismayed
at their looks, though they *be* a rebellious house 10
Moreover, he said unto me, Son of man, all my words
that I shall speak unto thee, receive k in thine heart, and
hear with thine ears 11 And go, get thee to them of
the captivity, unto the children of thy people, and speak
unto them, and tell them, Thus saith the LORD God,
l whether they will hear, or whether they will forbear
12 Then m the spirit took me up, and I heard behind
me a voice of a great rushing, *saying*, Blessed *be* the glory
of the LORD from his place 13 *I heard* also the
noise of the wings of the living creatures that § touched
one another, and the noise of the wheels over against
them, and a noise of a great rushing 14 So the spirit
lifted me up, and took me away, and I went in bitterness,

a Chap. ii. 8, 9. b Rev. x. 9. c Jer. xv. 16. Rev. x. 10. d Ps. xix. 10. ‖ Heb. Deep of lip and heavy of language. e Matt. xi. 21, 23. f John xv. 20. g Chap. ii. 4. ‡ Heb. stiff of forehead and hard of heart. h Isa. l. 7. Jer. i. 18. Mic. iii. 8. i Jer. i. 8, 17. Chap. ii. 6. k Prov. ii. 1. l Chap. ii. 5. m Chap. viii. 3. 1 Kings xviii. 12. Acts viii. 39. § Heb. kissed.

Before Chriſt 595

ternefs, in ‖ the heat of my ſpirit, but [n] the hand of the
LORD was ſtrong upon me 15 ¶ Then I came to
them of the captivity at Tel-abib, that dwelt by the river
of Chebar, and [o] I ſat where they ſat, and remained there
aſtoniſhed among them ſeven days.

‖ Heb. Hot anger
n 2 Kings iii. 15 Chap viii 1
o Job ii 13

v 1—15 This is a continuation of the viſion of the foregoing chapter

1 The prophet eats the roll at the divine command, not literally, but figuratively he muſt read, mark, learn, and inwardly digeſt the prophetic word ſent him, filling his head with the knowledge, and his heart with the love of it, and not diſobedient to the heavenly viſion, he *opened his mouth*, and *the Lord cauſed him to eat the roll*, gave him underſtanding of his meſſage, and inclination and ability to diſcharge his office, and he found it in his mouth *as honey for ſweetneſs* whatever mourning and woe it contained to the impenitent, there were great and precious promiſes therein reſpecting Chriſt and his ſalvation, on which his ſoul fed with great delight *Note*, (1) God's word is the bread of life, every day to be fed upon by all his people, deeply to be received into the heart, and univerſally to be embraced and obeyed (2) They who miniſter to others in holy things, are eſpecially bound to meditate on their ſubject, and make ſolemn and ſerious preparation before they preſume to ſpeak God's word (3) All our ſufficiency is of God though we had the greateſt human ability, and the moſt intenſe application, unleſs he cauſeth us to eat the roll, and beſtows a ſpirit of wiſdom and underſtanding, we ſhall know nothing as we ought to know (4) They who make God's word their daily meditation, will find it ſweeter than honey or the honey-comb

2 He is ſent as before to the rebellious houſe of Iſrael When he had thoroughly learnt and digeſted the roll, he muſt go and faithfully deliver it, *v* 1 careful to ſpeak God's *words*, not his own, or the enticing words of man's wiſdom, but thoſe the Holy Ghoſt teacheth, *v* 4 *for thou art not ſent to a people of a ſtrange ſpeech, but to the houſe of Iſrael*, for whom he ought to have a tender concern, and from whom he might expect, as he ſpoke to them in their own tongue, and with the moſt convincing arguments, attention and obedience Or this is mentioned to upbraid their impenitence and obſtinacy in rejecting him, for had he been ſent to the moſt barbarous nations, whoſe language he could not underſtand, and muſt have ſpoken by an interpreter, yet would his preaching have been more effectual to them, than it will now be to his own countrymen, whoſe hardened hearts would be deaf to the plaineſt admonitions, and inattentive to the moſt awful warnings nor need the prophet marvel if they refuſed to hearken to him, when they had rejected God himſelf, *v* 7 Nevertheleſs he muſt go, and God engages to endue him with ſuch invincible courage and unſhaken intrepidity, that he ſhall be able to face, yea to confound the boldeſt, moſt impudent, and daring ſinners among them, and therefore whatever dangers threatned, he need not fear, or be diſmayed, *v* 8, 9 but go and utter *all God's words, receiving them into his own heart and ears*, without exception or diſputing againſt them, and delivering them without reſerve in God's name, *whether they will hear, or whether they will forbear*, *v* 10, 11 *Note*, (1) They who have the word of God clearly ſet before them, and wilfully reject the counſel of God againſt their own ſouls, are without excuſe (2) They who have impudent ſinners to deal with, need a forehead of adamant, not to be abaſhed or diſconcerted by their mockery or inſults (3) When we are called out to hard ſervices, we ſhall be furniſhed for our place and ſtation as our day is, our ſtrength ſhall be (4) Though we ſhould not ſee the happy fruit of our labours we could wiſh, we muſt not be diſcouraged from perſevering zeal in the diſcharge of our miniſtry

3 The Spirit of God with a holy violence ſets him on his work *He lifted me up, and took me away*, as Philip, *Acts* vi 39 carrying him thro the air from the place where he was, to another company of the captives ſeated at a diſtance on the ſame river Chebar, *and I heard behind me*, as he went, *a voice of a great ruſhing*, proceeding from the living creatures and the wheels, ſaying, *Bleſſed be the glory of God out of his place*, which may be conſidered as an aſcription of praiſe offered to God by all his redeemed, whether miniſters or people, proceeding from his church militant out of his temple on earth, or from his church triumphant out of heaven, on account of his glorious perfections, and all his righteous works and ways Or it may be a ſigh of lamentation after *the bleſſed glory of the Lord* removing *out of his place*, forſaking his temple *I heard alſo the noiſe of the wings of the living creatures*, who clapped them when they praiſed God, *that touched one another*, or, literally, *kiſſed a woman her ſiſter*, uniting in true love to God and one another, and joining in this doxology *and the noiſe of the wheels over againſt them*, actuated by the ſame ſpirit, and giving the ſame glory to God, and *a noiſe of a great ruſhing*, as before, *v* 12 *and I went in bitterneſs*, grieved at the people's wickedneſs, and affected with the doleful tidings he carried, *in the heat of my ſpirit*, moved with indignation, or fretting at the diſobedience

foretold, and reluctant to go on ſo unwelcome an errand *but the hand of the Lord was ſtrong upon me*, conſtraining him to the work, and mightily ſupporting him to go through with it *Then I came to them of the captivity at Tel-abib*, the Jews who were fixed there, *that dwelt by the river Chebar*, another colony on the ſame river, *and I ſat where they ſat*, attentive to their diſcourſe, or waiting the prophetic impulſe, *and remained there aſtoniſhed among them ſeven days*, as Job's friends, *Job* xi 13, overwhelmed with grief on beholding their miſery, or overpowered with the weight of the awful meſſage he brought them *Note*, (1) If God did not uſe a kind of holy violence with our reluctant hearts, we ſhould be ready at times to deſert our poſt (2) There may be many ſtruggles of fear and unbelief where grace reigns, and, though with trembling, we dare go at God's bidding (3) Nothing is more diſcouraging to a miniſter's ſpirit, than to ſee a hardened people unaffected under his diſcourſes (4) Great griefs are often ſilent, too big for utterance, and far beyond tears

16. And it came to paſs at the end of ſeven days,
that the word of the LORD came unto me, ſaying,
17. [p] Son of man, I have made thee [q] a watchman unto
the houſe of Iſrael therefore hear the word at my
mouth, and give them warning from me 18 When
I ſay unto the wicked, Thou ſhalt ſurely die, and thou
giveſt him not warning, nor ſpeakeſt to warn the wicked
from his wicked way, to ſave his life the ſame
wicked *man* ſhall die in his iniquity, but [r] his blood
will I require at thine hand 19 Yet if thou warn the
wicked, and he turn not from his wickedneſs, nor from
his wicked way, he ſhall die in his iniquity; [s] but thou
haſt delivered thy ſoul 20 Again, when [t] a righteous
man doth turn from his righteouſneſs, and commit iniquity,
and I lay [u] a ſtumbling-block before him, he ſhall
die because thou haſt not given him warning, he ſhall
die in his ſin, and his righteouſneſs which he hath done
ſhall not be remembred, but his blood will I require at
thine hand. 21 Nevertheleſs, if thou warn the righteous
man, that the righteous ſin not, and he doth not
ſin, [x] he ſhall ſurely live, becauſe he is warned alſo
thou haſt delivered thy ſoul.

p Chap xxxiii 7, &c
q Iſa lvi 8 & lxi 10 & lxii 6 Jer vi 17 Hoſ ix 8.
r Acts xx 26
s Iſa xlix 4, 5
t Chap. xviii 24 & xxxiii 12, 13
u 2 Theſ ii 11
x Prov xxviii 13

v 16—21 After ſeven days God ſends his word to him probably this was a ſabbath, and he will thus honour his day by eſpecial manifeſtations of himſelf

1 God tells him his office *Son of man, I have made thee a watchman unto the houſe of Iſrael*, to watch over their ſouls, to warn and guard them againſt their ſpiritual enemies, for which purpoſe, ſharp diſcernment, ſleepleſs vigilance, and courageous fidelity are needful *Note*, They whom God appoints for watchmen on the walls of his Zion, the church, muſt ſhun no toil, deſert their poſt for no danger, watch always, and pray for a better guard than their own, conſcious that without the divine benediction and care *the watchman waketh but in vain*

2 The duty of his office is ſet before him, the bleſſings of fidelity, and the curſe of unfaithfulneſs He muſt ſpeak according to the divine word communicated to him *Hear the word at my mouth, and give them warning from me*; and as the characters of men are different, he muſt diſtinguiſh between the precious and the vile, and give to each their due portion

[1] He muſt addreſs the wicked, to warn him of his danger, and lead him to repentance (1) Whilſt he perſiſts in his ſins he is a damned ſoul, and eternal death his portion (2) If he repents, and turns from his wickedneſs, *he ſhall ſave his life*, God being ready to pardon and receive every returning ſinner (3) Though the miniſter be negligent, that will be no excuſe, for the ſinner ſhall periſh in his iniquity Yet, (4) God will require at the watchman's hands the ſouls that were loſt through his careleſſneſs and unfaithfulneſs, and a terrible reckoning will this prove in a judgment day for all unfaithful and negligent miniſters (5) If they have been faithful, though unſucceſsful, God will approve their conduct, and they ſhall at leaſt deliver their own ſouls

[2] He muſt addreſs the righteous, either thoſe who are ſuch profeſſionally, or in ſincerity and truth (1) Some are only externally *righteous*, delivered from groſſer exceſſes, and obſervant of the forms of godlineſs merely Theſe eaſily *turn from their righteouſneſs, and commit iniquity* they have no inward principle to ſupport them in the time of temptation, and therefore apoſtatize from the little profeſſion they made In the way of ſuch God lays *ſtumbling-blocks*, to diſcover the ſecret wickedneſs that reigns within, placing them in ſuch circumſtances, and withholding his reſtraining grace, ſo that what is in their hearts breaks forth Theſe will die eternally, and all their good deeds and duties, on which they truſted, will ſtand them in no ſtead Of this he muſt admoniſh them, at the peril of his own ſoul, chargeable with their blood if he neglect his office; not that his neglect will be their exculpation; they ſhall notwithſtanding periſh in their apoſtacy (2) Some are righteous

Before Christ 595.

in sincerity and truth, justified by Christ Jesus, and sanctified by his spirit, yet these need warnings, not that they ever can or will perish, but that God, who hath ordained the end, hath also ordained the means, in the use of which their perseverance is secured These must be warned that they *sin not*, for in the most holy, corruption still wars, and they need continually to watch and pray against it, the effect of which will be, that he *sin* not, receiving and improving under the word of exhortation In this way *he shall surely live*, and finally be saved, the path of holiness being the way to glory The warning through divine grace will be made effectual, and the fidelity of the minister approved thus *he shall save his own soul, and those who hear him*, 1 Tim iv 6

y Chap i 3 Ver 14 z Chap viii 4 a Chap i 28 b Ibid i 28 c Ibid ii 2 d Ibid iv 8 e Ibid xxiv 27 Luke i 20, 22 † Heb A man reproving f Chap i 5 &c g Ibid xxiv 27 & xxxiii 22 h Ver 9, 26

22 ¶ And y the hand of the LORD was there upon
me, and he said unto me, Arise, go forth z into the plain,
and I will there talk with thee 23 Then I arose, and
went forth into the plain, and behold, a the glory of the
LORD stood there, as the glory which I saw by the river of Chebar, b and I fell on my face 24 Then c the
spirit entred into me, and set me upon my feet, and spake
with me, and said unto me, Go, shut thyself within thine
house 25 But thou, O son of man, behold, they d
shall put bands upon thee, and shall bind thee with them,
and thou shalt not go out among them 26 And e I
will make thy tongue cleave to the roof of thy mouth,
that thou shalt be dumb, and shalt not be to them † a
reprover, f for they *are* a rebellious house 27 g But
when I speak with thee, I will open thy mouth, and thou
shalt say unto them, Thus saith the LORD God, He
that heareth, let him hear, and he that forbeareth, let
him forbear h for they *are* a rebellious house

v 22—27 We have here a repetition of the former glorious vision made to the prophet in the plain, whither at the divine command he had gone forth, vouchsafed to him probably to confirm his faith, and overcome the reluctance he might feel, to undertake the prophetic office

1 He is commanded to go and shut himself up in his house, *v* 24 there to wait farther instructions from God, or, as withdrawing himself from a people unworthy of the divine notice, or as others with probability suggest, as a figure of Jerusalem closely besieged by the Chaldeans, so that none might go forth *Note*, (1) It is a heavy judgment on a people, when God shuts up and removes from them their faithful reprovers (2) Ministers have need of retirement, to learn of God themselves what they must declare unto others There is little prospect of profitable preaching, without previous meditation and prayer

2 He is warned of the insults they would put upon him *They shall put bands upon thee*, either as a disturber of the peace, as a false prophet, or a mad enthusiast, with all which characters the faithful and zealous ministers of God are often branded or this may be understood figuratively, either of the obstinate disobedience of the people which shut his mouth, or of the divine order to retire, which tied up his hands from labouring among them Therefore,

3 He must be silent, neither go among them, nor speak to them as a reprover, but leave them to their hard and impenitent hearts, as a *rebellious house*, till God shall take off the interdict, and having communicated to the prophet all his mind concerning them, shall open his mouth, and authorise and enable him to speak, whether they will *hear* and be reformed, or *forbear* at the peril of their eternal ruin God's mercy will thus be glorified in the salvation of the repentant sinner, or his justice in the damnation of the obstinately rebellious

CHAP IV

To shame the presumption of those who flattered themselves with a speedy return to Jerusalem, as the false prophets assured them, we have here, 1 Jerusalem besieged in a figure, and taken, ver 1—8 2 The raging famine typically represented by the prophet, ver 9—17

‡ Or, chief leaders § Or, a flat plate a Chap xvi 40

1 THOU also, son of man, take thee a tile, and
lay it before thee, and pourtray upon it the
city, *even* Jerusalem, 2 And lay siege against it, and
build a fort against it, and cast a mount against it set
the camp also against it, and set ‡ *battering* rams against
it round about 3 Moreover, take thou unto thee § an
iron pan, and set it *for* a wall of iron between thee and
the city, and set thy face against it, and it shall be besieged,
and thou shalt lay siege against it this *shall be*
a sign to the house of Israel 4 Lie thou also upon a
thy left side, and lay the iniquity of the house of Israel
upon it *according* to the number of the days that thou
shalt lie upon it, thou shalt bear their iniquity 5 For I
have laid upon thee the years of their iniquity, according
to the number of the days, ‖ three hundred and ninety
days so shalt thou bear the iniquity of the house of
Israel 6 And when thou hast accomplished them, lie
again on thy right side, and thou shalt bear the iniquity
of the house of Judah forty days I have appointed
thee § each day for a year 7 Therefore thou shalt set
thy face toward the siege of Jerusalem, and thine arm
shall be uncovered, and thou shalt prophesy against it
8 And behold, c I will lay bands upon thee, and thou
shalt not turn thee † from one side to another, till thou
hast ended the days of thy siege

Before Christ 594. ‖ Beginning 2 Kings xxi &c b Num xiv 34 § Heb A day for a year, a day for a year c Chap iii 25 † Heb From thy side to thy side

v 1—8 Whether the transactions mentioned in this chapter were done in reality or in vision only is dubious It is contended against the reality, that the position, *v* 4 without a miracle, could not be kept so long, and that the prophet is spoken of as sitting in his house before the expiration of the days Compare chap i 1, 2 viii 1 for from the fifth of the fourth month in the fifth year, to the fifth of the sixth month in the sixth year, are but four hundred and thirteen days, and seven of these must be at least deducted, *chap* iii 15 whilst three hundred and ninety, and forty, make four hundred and thirty days and as for the bread which the prophet is commanded to eat, it seems a severity and indecence which he could scarce be called to submit to Others, and those too of greatest weight, support the reality of the transaction, the things are spoken of as facts, by these he was to prophesy, *v* 7 when his lips were silent, he was to do this, *v* 12 in the sight of the people His situation or disagreeable diet being enjoined of God for purposes of his glory, he would be comfortably supported under it, and that he really used the bread spoken of *v* 9 his prayer *v* 14 strongly implies The days may be accounted for, by supposing an intercalated month that year, as was common, or that the forty days for Judah are included in the three hundred and ninety for Israel

1 On a tile he is commanded to pourtray the siege of Jerusalem, surrounded with mounts, bulwarks, and battering rams, and the iron pan set between him and the city, against which, as the representative of the Chaldean army he lays siege, signifies the strength of their works, as a wall of iron compassing the city, and the safety in which the besiegers lay being thus covered, and their fixed resolution to carry the place is implied by the prophet's face set against Jerusalem, and his arm made bare

2 He is ordered to lie on his left side three hundred and ninety days, and forty days on his right, or to accomplish the number of three hundred and ninety days for Israel, with forty for Judah, *bearing their iniquity*, the punishment of it, *a day for a year*, which years are reckoned from the revolt of Jeroboam to the destruction of the temple, and the forty years of Judah's peculiar iniquity are either the reign of Manasseh, or from the *thirteenth of Josiah, when Jeremiah began to prophesy* nothing contributing so much to a people's guilt and ruin, as the rejecting God's ministers, and the warnings he vouchsafes to them

3 Bound thus by the divine order as Ezekiel was, so should the Chaldean army be, not stir from the place till they had carried it, and the three hundred and ninety days, during which the prophet lay on his side, may signify the duration of the siege, for though it continued seventeen months in all, *2 Kings* xxv 1—4 yet if the interruption given to it by the Egyptians, *Jer* xxxvii 5 be deducted the close siege might not last more than those days

4 In this way Ezekiel must prophesy, *v* 7 not in words but by works, which speak strongest, and would leave them inexcusable if they refused to pay attention to them

d Hos ix 3 e Dan i 8 Acts x 14 f Exod xxii 31 Lev xi 40 & xvii 15 Deut xiv 21

9 ¶ Take thou also unto thee, wheat, and barley,
and beans, and lentiles, and millet, and fitches, and put
them in one vessel, and make thee bread thereof, *according*
to the number of the days that thou shalt lie upon
thy side three hundred and ninety days shalt thou eat
thereof 10 And thy meat which thou shalt eat *shall
be* by weight twenty shekels a day from time to time
shalt thou eat it 11 Thou shalt drink also water by
measure, the sixth part of an hin from time to time
shalt thou drink 12 And thou shalt eat it *as* barley-
cakes, and thou shalt bake it with dung that cometh
out of man in their sight 13 And the LORD said,
Even thus d shall the children of Israel eat their defiled
bread among the Gentiles, whither I will drive them
14 Then said I, Ah LORD God, behold, e my soul
hath not been polluted for from my youth up even
till now, have I not eaten of f that which dieth of itself,
or is torn in pieces, neither came there abominable flesh
into my mouth 15. Then he said unto me, Lo, I have
given

Before Christ 594

given thee cows dung for mans dung, and thou shalt
prepare thy bread therewith 16 Moreover, he said unto
me, Son of man, behold, I will break [g] the staff of bread
in Jerusalem, and they shall eat bread by weight, and
with care, and they shall drink water by measure, and
with astonishment 17 That they may [h] want bread and
water, and be astonished one with another, and [i] consumed away for their iniquity

g Lev xxvi 26 Ps cv 16 Isa iii 1 Chap iv 16 & xiv 13
h Lam iv 10
i Lev xxvi 39

v 9—17 To affect their minds with the terribleness of the famine, which would be the consequence of the siege, the prophet, during the three hundred and ninety days, must use the most wretched provision, and in the most scanty measure

1 His bread is ordered him of the vilest sort, *beans, lentils, millet, fitches,* mixed with *wheat and barley* To such distress would they be reduced, that the very provender for their cattle would be greedily devoured They who now live daintily, know not what straits they may be driven to ere they die

2 He is to be very sparing of this vile food, eating his bread by weight, and drinking water by measure, allowed but ten ounces of the former, and a pint of the latter each day, barely a sufficiency to keep him alive, a token of their great straits, and their obstinacy to hold out to the very last morsel, *Jer* xxxvii 21 *Note,* When God s glory requires it of us, we must not hesitate to endure any hardness, and deny ourselves the lawful comforts of life

3 He is to bake his bread with human ordure dried, in the sight of the people, that they might be affected with the grievousness of the famine, where fuel as well as food would be wanting, and no distinction be made between clean and unclean The prophet makes no objection to the wretchedness of the food, but apprehending ceremonial defilement would thence accrue to him, which, as a priest, he had ever carefully abstained from of every kind, *v* 14 he prays, if God pleases, for some mitigation in this point, and the Lord permits him to use *cow s dung instead of man's* *Note,* (1) The fear of sin affects the gracious soul more than any thing beside (2) God's condescension to the scruples of Ezekiel should teach us to use the like tenderness towards our brethren, and not to grieve their weak consciences

4 The intention of God's orders to Ezekiel is explained He is a sign unto them So sore shall be the famine during the siege of Jerusalem, that the little bread which remained should be used with the strictest *care,* in order to enable them the longer to hold out, yet, with *astonishment* they will find all their measures broken, their resistance fruitless, and their straits growing each day more desperate, *pining away in their iniquities,* and *astonished one with another,* unable to relieve or help each other, and shocked to behold the dire effects of famine, fatigue, and sickness, which made the besieged appear rather as spectres than men And at last delivered into the hands of the heathen, they should be compelled to eat the defiled bread of the Gentiles, as loathsome as the cakes the prophet baked Such are the sad effects of sin, and abused plenty thus justly ends in pining want

CHAP V

In this chapter we have a further and no less terrible denunciation of the judgments of God upon the Jewish nation, 1 *Represented by cutting, burning, and scattering of hair,* ver 1—4 2 *That sign is expounded and applied to Jerusalem,* (1) *Sin is charged upon her as the cause of this desolation, contempt of God's law,* ver 5—7 *and profanation of his sanctuary,* ver 11 (2) *Wrath is threatened, great wrath,* ver 8, 9, 10 *a variety of miseries,* ver 12, 16, 17 *such as should be then reproach and ruin,* ver 13—15

1 AND thou, son of man, take thee a sharp knife,
take thee a barbers rasor, and [a] cause *it* to pass
upon thine head, and upon thy beard, then take thee
balances to weigh, and divide the *hair* 2 [b] Thou shalt
burn with fire a third part in the midst of the city,
when [c] the days of the siege are fulfilled, and thou shalt
take a third part, *and* smite about it with a knife, and
a third part thou shalt scatter in the wind, and I will
draw out a sword after them 3 Thou shalt also take
thereof [e] a few in number, and bind them in thy [‖] skirts
4 Then take of them again, and cast them into the
midst of the fire, and burn them in the fire *for* [f] thereof shall a fire come forth into all the house of Israel

a Lev xxi 5 Chap xliv 20
b Ver 12
c Chap iv 1, 8
d Lev xxvi 33
e Jer xl 6 & lii 16
‖ Heb. Wings
f Chap xix 14

v 1—4 Jerusalem's ruin is here represented by another sign

1 The prophet must shave his head and beard, and carefully weigh and divide the hair into three parcels, one third must be burnt, another be cut in pieces, the other scattered in the wind, a few hairs excepted, which he must bind in his skirts, and then quickly take them thence, and burn them in the fire

2 The meaning of this is, that Jerusalem, which had been the head of the nation, and full of inhabitants, numerous as these hairs, must undergo the foulest disgrace, and be covered with bitterest grief, weighed in the balances of God s justice, the punishment suitable to their guilt is determined The city must be taken and burnt, one third of the inhabitants consumed in the flames, or by the famine, another slain with the sword during the siege, or attempting to escape, the other be dispersed into all the neighbouring countries, not only led captive into Chaldea, but flying for refuge to Egypt, Moab, and Ammon, whither the sword of the king of Babylon would pursue them A few under Gedaliah seemed reserved for mercy, but even among them the fire kindles, their ruler is slain, and this remnant miserably consumed, thus will God overcome when he judgeth If sinners will obstinately persist in their wickedness, utter destruction will infallibly overtake them

5 ¶ Thus saith the LORD God, This *is* Jerusalem
I have set it in the midst of the nations and countries *that are* round about her 6 And she hath changed
my judgments [g] into wickedness [h] more than the nations, g Jer ii 11 h Chap xvi 47
and my statutes more than the countries that *are* round
about her for they have refused my judgments and
my statutes, they have not walked in them 7 Therefore thus saith the LORD God, Because ye multiplied more than the nations that *are* round about you,
and have not walked in my statutes, neither have kept
my judgments, [i] neither have done according to the i Jer ii 10, 11
judgments of the nations that *are* round about you
8 Therefore thus saith the LORD God, Behold, [k] I, k Isa x 6
even I *am* against thee, and will execute judgments in
the midst of thee, in the sight of the nations 9 And
I will do in thee [l] that which I have not done, and where- l Lam iv 6
unto I will not do any more the like, because of all
thine abominations 10 Therefore the fathers shall eat
the sons in the midst of thee, and the sons [m] shall eat their m Lev xxvi 29 Deut xxviii 53 2 Kings vi 29 Jer xix 9 Lam ii 20 & iv 10 Baruch ii 3
fathers, and I will execute judgments in thee, and the
whole remnant of thee will I scatter into all the winds
11 Wherefore, *as* I live, saith the LORD God, Surely because thou hast defiled my sanctuary with all thy
detestable things, and with all thine abominations, therefore will I also diminish *thee,* [n] neither shall mine eye n Chap vii 4, 9 & viii 18
spare, neither will I have any pity 12 ¶ [o] A third o Jer xv 2 Ver 2
part of thee shall die with the pestilence, and with famine shall they be consumed in the midst of thee, and
a third part shall fall by the sword round about thee,
and [p] I will scatter a third part into all the winds, and p Chap vi 8
I will draw out a sword after them 13 [q] Thus shall q Lev xxvi 33
mine anger be accomplished, and I will cause my fury
to rest upon them, and [r] I will be comforted and [s] they r Isa i 24
shall know that I the LORD have spoken *it* in my s Deut xxxii 36 Isa i 24 t Chap vi 7, 10
zeal, when I have accomplished my fury in them 14
Moreover, I will make thee waste, and a reproach among the nations that *are* round about thee, in the sight
of all that pass by 15 So [u] it shall be a reproach and u Deut xxviii 37
a taunt, [x] an instruction and an astonishment unto the x 1 Cor x 11
nations that *are* round about thee, when I shall execute
judgments in thee in anger and in fury, and in furious
rebukes I the LORD have spoken *it* 16 When I
shall [y] send upon them the evil arrows of famine, which y Deut xxxii 23 24
shall be for *their* destruction, *and* which I will send to
destroy you, and I will increase the famine upon you,
and will break [z] your staff of bread 17 So will I send z Lev xxvi 26 Chap iv 16 & xiv 13
upon you famine and [a] evil beasts, and they shall bereave
thee, and pestilence and blood shall pass through thee,
and I will bring the sword upon thee I the LORD a Lev xxvi 22
have spoken *it*

v 5—17 The addition of the foregoing sign is here given at large, *This is Jerusalem* the name of the thing signified being given to the sign, as *this is my body*

1 Jerusalem was highly honoured, *v* 5 set in the midst of the nations, and exalted in privileges above them all, as a beacon on a hill, designed to diffuse the light of those divine oracles, which were intrusted to her For when God hath given distinguished mercies, he justly expects a suitable return

2 Her provocations were multiplied, great and aggravated *She hath changed my judgments into wickedness,* not only neglecting God's commands, and slighting his institutions, but introducing the idolatries and abomination of the heathen, and as if it was not enough to be like them, the profaneness and impiety of Israel were *more than the nations round about them,* yea,

they

Before Ch ist 594.

they did not according to the judgments of the nations round about them, they were more abandoned in wickedneſs, and ſhewed none of that reſpect for the true God which they paid to their idol deities And to ſuch a pitch of hardened inſolence and impudence in ſin were they grown, that in the very houſe erected for God's honour and worſhip, there did they ſet up their hated idols, and offered their deteſtable ſacrifices before them *Note*, (1) Many a comparatively virtuous heathen will riſe up and condemn the immoral lives of profeſſing chriſtians (2) When they who have been God's people by profeſſion, turn apoſtates, they uſually grow moſt abandoned

3 Her puniſhment ſhall be according to her ſins, terrible beyond what any nation before ever did, or ever ſhall again ſuffer, *v* 9 and public, in *the midſt of thee*, ver 8 that all around might behold God's righteous judgment, and be warned by her plagues

(1) God himſelf makes bare his holy arm *I, even I am againſt thee*, whatever inſtruments he employed, the deſtruction was from the Lord *in anger and fury, and furious rebukes*, as a man exaſperated with the moſt atrocious provocations, yea, all the fierceneſs of his wrath *ſhall be accompliſhed*, ver 13 ſo entire ſhall be their ruin, and his *fury ſhall reſt upon them* for a long ſeaſon, they ſhall lie under the marks of his fearful vengeance, and this without mercy or pity, *v* 11 Yea, ſo far from it, he will delight in their miſery, *I will be comforted*, ver 13 in thus eaſing himſelf of his enemies, under whom the very earth groaned, and in glorifying his juſtice and truth by the execution of theſe moſt righteous judgments And then at laſt when they feel, they will know the truth of his threatnings, and his jealouſy in vindicating his own glory, and the honour of his government *Note*, (1) Wo to the ſinner that provokes a jealous God When his wrath is kindled, yea but for a moment, who may abide it? (2) The miſery of the damned ſhall reſult to God's glory, and he will, without the leaſt impeachment of his mercy, delight in their torment, ſeeing it is the juſt reward of their deeds

(2) The particular judgments threatned are many and grievous (1) *Famine*, ſharp and deadly as a poiſoned arrow, *v* 16 ſo raging, that all natural affection ſhould be extinguiſhed thereby, and fathers eat their ſons, and ſons feed upon their murdered fathers (2) *Diſperſion*, the remnant which ſurvived the ſiege, ſhould be miſerably ſcattered in all lands, like Cain under a curſe, and vagabond in the earth (3) *Peſtilence*, which ſhould devour a third part, *v* 12 the uſual conſequence of famine (4) *The ſword*, which ſhould not only deſtroy a third part during the ſiege, but purſue the fugitives, and bring them at laſt to a miſerable end, *v* 12 (5) *Evil beaſts*, ver 17 not merely enemies, as ſavage as lions, but every furious beaſt of prey that ſhould break in upon them in herds, *bereave* them of their deareſt relatives, and devour thoſe who fled into the mountains and deſerts for ſhelter For as vain is it to fly from God's vengeance, as to reſiſt it

(3) Neighbouring nations would inſult their fall, reproach them for their wickedneſs, ridicule their vain confidence, and whilſt they were amazed and aſtoniſhed at the terribleneſs of the judgment, would receive *inſtruction*, and be warned of the dreadful danger of provoking ſuch a jealous God *Note*, When the judgments of God are ſeen in the earth, the inhabitants thereof ſhould learn righteouſneſs, and repent of thoſe ſins which they ſee productive of ſuch unutterable miſery in others

4 The veracity of God is engaged for executing the words of his threatnings *I, the Lord, have ſpoken it*, able to perform it, and who cannot lie, or repent, therefore the judgment is infallibly ſure to come And however, whilſt the threatned vengeance is diſtant, ſinners are apt to deſpiſe it, *when it is accompliſhed, they ſhall know* and feel the truth of thoſe threatnings, which they would not believe from the mouth of the prophet

CHAP VI

In this chapter we have, 1 The deſtruction of Iſrael and of their idols threatned, ver 1—7 2 *A promiſe of the gracious return of a remnant of them to God by true repentance*, ver 8—10 3 *Directions given to the prophet and other the Lord's ſervants, to lament both the iniquities and the calamities of Iſrael*, ver 11—14

1 AND the word of the LORD came unto me,
ſaying, 2 Son of man, ſet thy face towards
[a] the mountains of Iſrael, and propheſy againſt them. 3
And ſay, [b] Ye mountains of Iſrael, hear the word of the
LORD God, Thus ſaith the LORD God to the moun-
tains and to the hills, to the rivers and to the valleys, Be-
hold, I, *even* I will bring a ſword upon you, and [c] I will
deſtroy your high places 4 And your altars ſhall be
deſolate, and your † images ſhall be broken, and [d] I will
caſt down your ſlain *men* before your ‡ idols 5 And I
will ‖ lay the dead carcaſes of the children of Iſrael before
their idols, and [e] I will ſcatter your bones round about
your altars 6 In all your dwelling-places [f] the cities
ſhall be laid waſte, and the high places ſhall be deſo-
late, that your altars may be laid waſte and made de-
ſolate, and your idols may be broken and ceaſe, and
your images may be cut down, and your works may be
aboliſhed 7 And the ſlain ſhall fall in the midſt of you,
and [g] ye ſhall know that I *am* the LORD

a Chap xxxvi 1. b Mic vi 2. c Lev xxvi 30. † Or ſun-images Ver 6. d Lev xxvi 30. ‡ Heb Dunghill gods. ‖ Heb Give. e 2 Kings xxiii 16. f Jer ii 11. g Ver 13 Ch vii 4 &c.

v 1—7 We have here repeated denunciations of vengeance againſt a rebellious people

1 The prophet is commanded to *ſet his face towards the mountains of Iſrael, and propheſy againſt them*, againſt the whole land, and the inhabitants thereof, againſt the greateſt among them, particularly thoſe who had been the ringleaders in wickedneſs or the mountains are addreſſed, as if the rocks thereon were leſs obdurate, and the inanimate earth more ready to hear, than that ſtupid people, and againſt *the hills, the rivers, and the vallies* alſo, the eſpecial ſcenes of their idolatry, or as deſcriptive of the whole country againſt which judgment is denounced

2 Utter deſtruction is threatned both againſt the idols and their worſhippers, from God, for though the executioners of *his wrath* were the Chaldeans, the ſword in their hands was his So far from being able to protect their votaries, theſe mock deities would be unable to defend themſelves, their high places ſhould be deſtroyed, their altars deſolate, their images broken, and theſe *dunghill gods* (as the word for *idols*, ver 4. ſignifies) caſt into the duſt, their worſhippers ſhould ſhare their fate, ſlain before their idols, their dead corpſes ſhould be laid at their feet, and their bones ſcattered around theſe hateful altars, univerſal deſolation ſhould ſpread through the land, the cities be deſtroyed, every dwelling-place ruined, and thoſe high places and altars defiled by their abominations, be now more defiled with the blood and carcaſes of the ſlain, *and ye ſhall know that I am the Lord*, by terrible experience convinced of the difference between thoſe ſenſeleſs idols they ſerved, and that only living and true God whom they had ſlighted

8 ¶ [h] Yet will I leave a remnant, that ye may have
ſome that ſhall eſcape the ſword among the nations,
when ye ſhall be ſcattered through the countries 9
And they that eſcape of you ſhall remember me among
the nations, whither they ſhall be carried captives, becauſe
[i] I am broken with their whoriſh heart which hath de-
parted from me, [k] and with their eyes which go a whor-
ing after their idols. and [l] they ſhall lothe themſelves for
the evils which they have committed in all their abo-
minations 10 And they ſhall know that I *am* the
LORD, *and that* I have not ſaid [m] in vain that I would
do this evil unto them

h Chap xii 16. i Pſ lxxviii 40. k Num xv 39. l Lev xxvi 39. m Zech i 6.

v 8—10 When God executes judgment, he ſtill remembers mercy Though none ſhould be ſpared in Jeruſalem, a remnant of the diſperſed ſhall yet be reſcued from the devouring ſword

1 They ſhall *remember me* Either, [1] *The wrath of God*, viſible now in their ſufferings *among the nations whither they ſhall be carried captives*, would drive them to him, afflictions being often the moſt ſalutary means of recovering the backſliding ſoul or, [2] They would be drawn by *the tender mercies* of God they had ſlighted, who ſtill yearned over them, though ſo highly provoked by their ungrateful departures from him, and who was *broken with their whoriſh heart*, grieved to behold their ſpiritual adulteries, and attachment to their idols *Note*, Nothing wounds the awakened ſinner's conſcience more deeply, than a ſenſe of his baſe ingratitude, and his grieving the holy ſpirit of God

2 This will produce ſelf-loathing and genuine repentance *They ſhall lothe themſelves for the evils they have committed in all their abominations*, they will be brought, by remembring God, to a knowledge of their own abominations, will diſcover the malignity of their ſins, and the multitude of evils they had overlooked; and this will produce ſelf-abhorrence and ſelf loathing; even though God hath forgiven them, they never can forgive themſelves

3 They will then give glory to God *They ſhall know that I am the Lord*, acknowledging the truth of his word, the juſtice of their puniſhment, and the wonders of his grace, and this will be the caſe with every truly penitent ſoul

11 ¶ Thus ſaith the LORD God, [n] Smite with thine
hand, and ſtamp with thy foot, and ſay, [o] Alas, for all
the evil abominations of the houſe of Iſrael for they
ſhall fall by the ſword, by the famine, and by the pe
ſtilence. 12 He that is far off ſhall die of the peſtilence,
and he that is near ſhall fall by the ſword, and he that
remaineth and is beſieged ſhall die by the famine thus
will I accompliſh my fury upon them 13 Then [p] ſhall
ye know that I *am* the LORD, when their ſlain *men* ſhall
be among their idols round about their altars, [q] upon every

n Chap xxi 17. o Ibid Amos v 16. p Ver 7. q Jer ii 20.

Before Christ 594

high hill in all the tops of the mountains, and under
every green tree, and under every thick oak, the place
where they did offer sweet savour to all their idols 14
So will I stretch out my hand upon them, and make
the land desolate, yea, † more desolate than the wilder-
ness *towards* Diblath, in all their habitations, and they
shall know that I *am* the LORD

r Isa v 25
† Or desolate more than the wilderness

v 11—14 Since the Jews in general were too unaffected both with their sufferings and sins, the prophet is ordered,

1 To express the strongest sensations of grief and anguish for them, if it might contribute to awaken them from their insensibility, when they saw him so deeply affected on their account *Smite with thine hand, and stamp with thy foot, and say, Alas! for all the evil abominations of the house of Israel*, their sins were grievous, and their judgment would be terrible, devoted to famine, pestilence, and the sword *Note*, God's faithful ministers have the tenderest sensibility towards miserable sinners, and often weep over those who never shed a tear for themselves

2 To repeat the same awful warnings as he had done before, that they may have line upon line, and be assured of the certainty of the impending judgments in vain is flight when God pursues, *he that is far off shall die by the pestilence*, in vain is resistance, when the wrath of the Lord *he that is near*, and stands on his defence, *shall fall by the sword*, or perish by the famine in the straitness of the siege Since God's fury is provoked, he will accomplish their destruction Before those hated idols, in every place where they had offered incense unto them, shall their putrid corpses lie unburied, a manifest token of God's righteous vengeance, v 13 More desolate than the howling and barren wilderness towards Diblath, Deut viii 15 shall the whole land be made And since they refuse to fly to him, and prove his mercy God will force them to know him as the sin-avenging God, in the terrible judgments he will inflict upon them

CHAP VII

In this chapter the approaching ruin of the land of Israel is most particularly foretold, in affecting expressions often repeated, that if possible they might be awakened by repentance to prevent it The prophet must tell them, 1 *That it will be a complete destruction*, ver 1—6 2 *That it is near, even at the door*, ver 7—10 3 *That it is unavoidable*, ver 10—15 4 *That their strength and wealth should be no fence against it*, ver 16—19 5 *That the temple, in which they trusted, should itself be ruined*, ver 20—22 6 *That it should be an universal ruin, the sin that brought it having been universal*, ver 23—27

1 MOreover the word of the LORD came unto
me, saying, 2 Also thou son of man, thus
saith the LORD God unto the land of Israel, ᵃ An end,
the end is come upon the four corners of the land 3
Now *is* the end *come* upon thee, and I will send mine
anger upon thee, and ᵇ will judge thee according to thy
ways and will † recompense upon thee all thine abomi-
nations 4 And ᶜ mine eye shall not spare thee, neither
will I have pity but I will recompense thy ways upon
thee, and thine abominations shall be in the midst of
thee, and ᵈ ye shall know that I *am* the LORD 5
Thus saith the LORD God, An evil, an only evil,
behold, is come 6 An end is come, the end is come,
it ‡ watcheth for thee, behold, it is come 7 ᵉ The
morning is come upon thee, O thou that dwellest in the
land ᶠ the time is come, the day of trouble *is* near, and
not the || sounding again of the mountains 8 Now will
I shortly pour out my fury upon thee, and accomplish
mine anger upon thee and I will judge thee according
to thy ways, and will recompense thee for all thine
abominations 9 ʰ And mine eye shall not spare, neither
will I have pity I will recompense thee according to
thy ways, and thine abominations *that* are in the midst
of thee, and ye shall know that I *am* the LORD that
smiteth 10 Behold the day, behold, it is come, the
morning is gone forth, the rod hath blossomed, pride
hath budded 11 ⁱ Violence is risen up into a rod of
wickedness none of them *shall remain*, nor of their mul-
titude, nor of any § of theirs, ᵏ neither *shall there be* wail-
ing for them 12 The time is come, the day draweth
near, ˡ let not the buyer rejoice, nor the seller mourn
for wrath *is* upon all the multitude thereof 13 For
the seller shall not return to that which is sold, although
† they were yet alive for the vision *is* touching the
whole multitude thereof, *which* shall not return neither
shall any strengthen himself ‡ in the iniquity of his life
14 They have blown the trumpet, even to make all
ready, but none goeth to the battle for my wrath *is*
upon all the multitude thereof 15 ⁿ The sword *is*
without, and the pestilence and the famine within he
that *is* in the field shall die with the sword, and he that
is in the city, famine and pestilence shall devour him

Before Christ 594

‡ Or whose life is in his iniquity
ⁿ Deut xxxii 25 Lam i 20

v 1—15 Fair warning is here given to a careless people, and with great earnestness the prophet speaks, if so be he might awaken them from their lethargy

1 Their time of judgment is come, their end at hand, their destruction impending, and this is urged with a great variety of expressions, to shew the certainty, nearness, and terribleness of the calamity The whole land is doomed to ruin, v 2 *An evil*, such as was never heard of before approached, v 5 Their desolations watched for them, v 6 The dawn of their calamity was already broke upon them, *the day of trouble* swiftly advanced, not a mere sound, like the distant echo of a man's voice between the mountains, but a terrible shout of the Chaldean hosts already at the walls of the city, v 7 *Note*, (1) The end of all things is at hand, Are we ready? (2) Tho' God's patience bears long with sinners, he will surely visit them at the appointed time, and the evil of eternal vengeance will overtake them

2 Their destruction is from God's wrath, v 3 Their provocations had awakened *his fury*, and now in full vials he will *pour* it out on their devoted heads, and *accomplish* his anger, giving it full scope, v 8 and no pity or mercy shall mitigate the judgment, v 4, 9 and wo to those against whom God thus riseth up as an enemy

3 God herein acts with strictest justice The sentence passed on them would be in consequence of an impartial trial, and the righteous recompense of their great abominations, v 3 These being found in the midst of them unrepented of, wrath to the uttermost comes upon them, v 4 *The rod hath blossomed*, the rod of universal wickedness, and they gloried in it, *pride hath budded*, that sin peculiarly hateful to God, *and violence is risen up*, a scene of oppression and injustice appears, and the rod of upright government is turned into *a rod of wickedness*, to smite the innocent Though some understand these expressions as signifying the Chaldean monarch, the rod of God's anger swelling with pride, and ready to break in violently upon them as a flood, to punish them for their iniquities

4 The ruin coming upon them would be universal *None of them shall remain*, the whole nation utterly wasted by famine, pestilence, and the sword, princes and people shall fall together unlamented, none surviving to bemoan them, or the few who were left, wholly engrossed with care about themselves, v. 11 *The buyer should not rejoice, nor the seller mourn*, because both now would be on a level, alike captives, and removed from their own land, v 12 and no year of jubilee cause the possessions to revert to their former owners, *though they were yet alive*, ver 13 the whole multitude being doomed to a seventy years servitude in Babylon In vain on the approach of the enemy they blew *the trumpet* to oppose them, *but none goeth to the battle*, their courage is lost, *the wrath* of God upon them dispirits the bravest, and they fall an easy prey, v 14 The sword consumes without, the famine and pestilence within, and neither the city nor country can afford the least protection from these desolating judgments, v 15 and they who thought to strengthen themselves in their iniquity, and outbrave the threatened vengeance, now find themselves terribly disappointed, v 15 *Note*, (1) Multitudes are no protection from the wrath of God, sinners shall no more escape because they are many, than because they are mighty (2) They who strengthen themselves in wickedness, will find their rebel arm impotent and broken when God awakes to judgment

5 God's hand will be visible in their sufferings *And ye shall know that I am the Lord that smiteth* Though the Chaldean army be employed, they shall be convinced God's arm is made bare against them, and in their sufferings read his fearful indignation

16 ¶ But they that escape of them, shall escape, and
shall be on the mountains like doves of the valleys, all
of them mourning, every one for his iniquity 17
ᵖ All hands shall be feeble, and all knees shall † be weak
as water 18 They shall also ᵍ gird *themselves* with sack-
cloth, and horror shall cover them, and shame *shall be*
upon all faces, and baldness upon all their heads 19
They shall cast their silver in the streets, and their gold
shall be ‡ removed their silver and their gold shall not
be able to deliver them in the day of the wrath of the
LORD they shall not satisfy their souls, neither fill
their bowels because || it is the stumbling block of their
iniquity 20 ¶ As for ˢ the beauty of his ornament, he

ᵒ Prov x 11
ᵖ Isa xiii 7 Jer vi 24
† Heb Go into water
ᵍ Isa iii 24, & xv 2, 3 Jer xlviii 37 Amos viii 10
‡ Heb For a separation, or uncleanness
ʳ Prov xi 4 Zeph i 18 Ecclus v 8
|| Or their iniquity is their stumbling block
ˢ Jer vii 2

Before Christ 594

set it in majesty † but they made the images of their
abominations, *and* of their detestable things therein
therefore have I § set it far from them 21 And I will
give it into the hands of the strangers for a prey, and
to the wicked of the earth for a spoil, and they shall
pollute it 22 My face will I turn also from them,
and they shall pollute my secret *place* for † the robbers
shall enter into it and defile it.

† Jer vii 30 § Or made it unto them an unclean thing † Or burglars

v 16—22 We have here the miserable condition of the few who survive the ruin of their country

1 They are men of sorrows, and vagabonds in the earth On the solitary mountains, whither they have fled for refuge, like doves of the valley, they mourn *every one for his iniquity*, either for the punishment of it only, or with deep anguish bewailing their sins, which were the cause of their sufferings, *v* 16 weak as water to resist their enemies, *v* 17 and abandoning themselves to despair, in horrors of conscience, or terrified with continual fear, covered with shame and confusion because of their transgressions, or of their present wretched state, girt with sackcloth, and baldness on their heads, the expressive signs of deep unutterable anguish *Note*, (1) Sin and sorrow are inseparable (2) Our afflictions are then gracious, when they lead us to mourn for our iniquity (3) The sinner's confidence will end in despair and fruitless everlasting wailings

2 Their riches profit not in this day of wrath They had idolized the shining mammon, tho' it had been the *stumbling-block of their iniquity*, whilst they placed that affection and dependance upon their gold which they withdrew from God, but now they are made to know their folly and their sin, compelled to cast away their gold and silver as what would retard their flight, and unable with these to satisfy the cravings of hunger, or purchase a moment's rest or ease to their souls Some understand by the gold and silver their idols made of these precious metals, on which they trusted, but found their expectations from them terribly deceived *Note*, (1) Money is a dangerous snare, the inordinate love of it hath been the ruin of thousands (2) The greatest wealth can profit us nothing in a day of wrath, it cannot stay the arrests of death, or procure in hell a drop of water to cool a flaming tongue

3 Their temple is destroyed, magnificent and adorned as it had been, not merely by the immense profusion of gold, silver, and precious stones, bestowed on it, but infinitely more by the residence of the king of glory They had polluted it, and dared within these sacred walls to erect their detested idols, *therefore have I set it far from them*, removing them as captives into a distant land, and giving up the sanctuary to be trodden under foot by the heathen, to be polluted, profaned, plundered, and burnt, by the Chaldeans first, and afterwards by the Romans *My face also will I turn from them*, deserting the Jews in their distress, or not displeased with the ravages of their wicked enemies, but suffering them uncontrouled to spread havock and desolation on every side *Note*, They who forsake God may expect that he will forsake them in the day of their calamity

23 ¶ Make a chain for the land is full of [u] bloody
crimes, and the city is full of violence 24 Wherefore
I will bring the worst of the heathen, and they shall
possess their houses I will also make the pomp of the
strong to cease, and ‖ their holy places shall be defiled
25 ‡ Destruction cometh, and they shall seek peace,
and *there shall be* none 26 [x] Mischief shall come up-
on mischief, and rumour shall be upon rumour, then
[y] shall they seek a vision of the prophet but the law
shall perish from the priest, and counsel from the ancients
27 The king shall mourn, and the prince shall be cloath-
ed with desolation, and the hands of the people of the
land shall be troubled I will do unto them after their
way, [z] and § according to their deserts will I judge them,
and they shall know that I *am* the LORD

u 2 Kings xxi 16 ‖ Or they that sanctify them ‡ Heb Cutting off x Jer iv 20 y Chap vii ... Lam ii 9 z Mat vii § Heb With their judgments

v 23—27 We have here,

1 The charge laid against the Jewish people for which they are brought to God's bar *Make a chain* to bind the prisoner, and bring him before the judge, or to lead them into an ignominious captivity, *for the land is full of bloody crimes*, or *judgments of blood*, such crimes as by the law were capital, and called for the blood of the criminal, *the city is full of violence*, a scene of oppression, rapine, and injustice And when sin in a nation is thus triumphant, her destruction cannot be far distant

2 The sentence pronounced God threatens *to bring upon them the worst of the heathen*, the most savage and barbarous of the human species The noble, the rich, the proud oppressors, with all their pomp, must bow before them, and the fruits of their injustice be for a prey, *their holy places shall be defiled*, or *they that sanctify them*, their priests and Levites, slain, and lying in their blood Repeated rumours of the approaching enemy shall terrify them, *mischief upon mischief* shall overwhelm them, and destruction without remedy seize them at last no peace will be granted them by their exasperated foes, *v* 25 *They shall*, in their distress, *seek a vision of the prophet*, whom they before despised and rejected, *but* none shall be vouchsafed them, for *the law shall perish from the priest*, he shall neither be able to advise or comfort them, *and counsel shall perish from the ancients*, given up to infatuation, and become foolish in their imaginations so that they would be without resource *Then king shall mourn a prisoner, cloathed with desolation*, blind and in chains, *the hands of the people be troubled*, weak and unable to resist, God visiting now upon them their iniquities, and making them know his almighty power and vindictive wrath for God will make himself known, either in mercy to his people, or in vengeance to his enemies

Before Christ 594

CHAP VIII

The prophet here is brought in a vision to Jerusalem, that he might behold the sins which provoked these threatned judgments, ver 1—4 *and there he sees*, 1 *The image of jealousy set up at the gate of the temple*, ver 5, 6 2 *The elders of Israel worshipping all manner of images in a secret chamber*, ver 7—12 3 *The women weeping for Tammuz*, ver 13, 14 4 *The men worshipping the sun*, ver 15, 16 *And then appeals to him whether such a provoking people should have any pity shewed them*, ver 17, 18

1 AND it came to pass in the sixth year, in the
sixth *month*, in the fifth *day* of the month, *as*
I sat in mine house, and the elders of Judah [a] sat be-
fore me, that [b] the hand of the LORD God fell there
upon me 2 Then I beheld, and lo, a likeness [c] as the
appearance of fire from the appearance of his loins even
downward, fire and from his loins even upwards, as the
appearance of brightness, [d] as the colour of amber
3 And [e] he put forth the form of an hand, and took
me by a lock of mine head, and the spirit lift me up
between the earth and the heaven, and brought me in
the visions of God to Jerusalem, to the door of the inner
gate, that looketh toward the north, where *was* the seat
of [f] the image of jealousy, which provoketh to jealousy
4 And behold the glory of the God of Israel *was* there,
according to the vision that [g] I saw in the plain. 5
¶ Then said he unto me, Son of man, lift up thine eyes
now the way towards the north so I lift up mine eyes
the way towards the north, and behold, northward at
the gate of the altar, this image of jealousy in the entry
6 He said furthermore unto me, Son of man, seest thou
what they do? *even* the great abominations that the house
of Israel committeth here, that I should go far off from
my sanctuary, but turn thee yet again, *and* thou shalt
see greater abominations

a Chap xiv 1 b Chap i 3 c Chap i 27 d Chap i 4 e Dan v 5 f 2 Kings xxi 7 g Chap i ... & iii 22, 23

v 1—6 The days seem now to have been expired during which the prophet was to lie on his side, and a new vision is revealed to him, dated in the sixth year of Jehoiakin's captivity, about fourteen, or, if we suppose an intercalated month, about fifteen months after the former

1 He sat in his house, and the elders of Judah before him Probably it was a sabbath, and they were now assembled for the worship of God, or to consult the prophet in their present distressed circumstances, for affliction will often drive those to God's prophets who in their prosperity despised their admonitions

2 Then suddenly a divine extacy seized him, in the presence of the elders, and a glorious personage appeared, as fire from the loins downwards, and upwards bright and glistering The same probably as *chap* i 26, 27 even the Lord Jesus, clothed with majesty and glory, burning with love towards his people, and a consuming fire to his enemies

3 The prophet is caught away in vision to Jerusalem Swift as thought he passes through the air, and at the inner gate of the temple is set down to observe what are there transacted This seems to have been entirely visionary, and not any real or local removal of the prophet from Chaldea

4 He records what he saw there [1] He beheld the same glorious vision which had appeared to him before in the plain, *chap* iii 22, 23 God had not yet deserted his temple, though he was now about to do it, provoked by their daring profaneness, impiety, and base ingratitude [2] He beheld *the image of jealousy* set up close by the northern gate of the inner court, where stood the altar of burnt offering What the image was we are not told probably the idol Baal, 2 *Kings* xxi 7 But nothing could be conceived more affronting to God, nor could they have contrived a more effectual method to provoke the eyes of his jealousy Well therefore may he bid the prophet with wonder and detestation to behold these abominations, and upon the justice of his departure from a people so desperately wicked and greater abominations yet remained *Note*, (1) When we

Before Christ 594

set up the idols of pride, lust, and covetousness in our hearts, which should be the temple of the Holy Ghost, we become equally criminal with those who bowed to Baal (2) They who provoke God by their sins to depart from them, have only themselves to blame for the ruin which ensues

7. ¶ And he brought me to the door of the court,
and when I looked, behold, a hole in the wall 8
Then said he unto me, Son of man, dig now in the
wall and when I had digged in the wall, behold a door
9 And he said unto me, Go in, and behold the wicked
abominations that they do here 10 So I went in and
saw, and behold, every form of creeping things, and
abominable beasts, and all the † idols of the house of
Israel pourtrayed upon the wall round about 11 And
there stood before them seventy men of the ancients of
the house of Israel, and in the midst of them stood Jaazaniah the son of Shaphan, with every man his censer
in his hand, and a thick cloud of incense went up 12
Then said he unto me, Son of man, hast thou seen what
the ancients of the house of Israel do [h] in the dark,
every man in the chambers of his imagery, for they say,
[i] The LORD seeth us not, the LORD hath forsaken
the earth

† Or dunghill gods Chap vi 4
h John iii 20
i Psal x 11 Chap ix 9.

v 7—12 The farther the prophet goes the more his indignation is moved

1 He is led to the court of the priests, and behold a hole in the wall of one of the chambers, which he is commanded to enlarge, that he might see more distinctly what was done there, and when he had opened a passage he came to a door, at which he is bid to enter, and observe what passed within *Note*, (1) They who would know the mystery of iniquity within must dig deep into the hidden corners of their hearts (2) Hypocrites think often to hide their iniquities, but some unguarded place betrays their wickedness, and exposes their shame (3) Many make a fair shew in God's house in public, who, if followed to the secret chambers, would be found full of abominations

2 A scene of shocking wickedness is here laid open *Behold every form of creeping things, and abominable beasts* so immersed were they in idolatry, that even to the vilest reptiles, and the most odious and impure animals, they paid their adorations On the walls around were pourtrayed all the idols of Israel, and seventy elders, the whole great sanhedrim, and in the midst of them Jaazaniah the son of Shaphan, each with his censer, offered a cloud of incense to these hated deities, intimating how entirely the whole nation was infected with idolatry, when the great men, princes and priests together, were so devoted thereunto, and so liberal in their oblations *Note*, When they who should be examples to restrain others are themselves ringleaders in iniquity, the corruption of a nation must need become general

3 God bids him observe these abominations, done indeed *in the dark*, but what darkness or shadow of death can hide the workers of wickedness from his all-seeing eye? And *they say, the Lord seeth not, the Lord hath forsaken the earth*, as if he had deserted them, would pay no regard to them in their distress, and therefore they had recourse to the gods of the nations for help *Note*, (1) The heart of man is like these chambers of imagery, abominations pass there the sun would blush to behold (2) The day will come when the secrets of all hearts shall be revealed What a day of terror and confusion to the impenitent and unpardoned! (3) All sin is at bottom practical atheism (4) They who embolden themselves in iniquity by the flattering hope that the Lord hath forsaken the earth, shall find by the judgments he will inflict, how near he is to vindicate his injured honour

13 ¶ He said also unto me, Turn thee yet again,
and thou shalt see [k] greater abominations that they do
14 Then he brought me to the door of the gate of the
LORD's house, which *was* towards the north, and behold, there sat women weeping for Tammuz 15 ¶
Then said he unto me, Hast thou seen *this*, O son of
man? turn thee yet again, *and* thou shalt see greater
abominations than these 16 And he brought me into
the inner court of the LORD's house, and behold, at
the door of the temple of the LORD, between the porch
and the altar, *were* about [l] five and twenty men, with
their backs toward the temple of the LORD, and their
faces toward the east, and they worshipped [m] the sun
toward the east 17 ¶ Then he said unto me, Hast
thou seen *this*, O son of man? ‖ Is it a light thing to
the house of Judah, that they commit the abominations
which they commit here? for [n] they have filled the land
with violence, and have returned to provoke me to anger,
and lo, they put the branch to their nose 18 Therefore will I also deal in fury [o] mine eye shall not spare,
neither will I have pity and [p] though they cry in mine
ears with a loud voice, *yet* will I not hear them

k Turn ...
l Chap xi 1
m Deut iv 19 2 Kings xxiii 5, 11 Job xxxi 26 Jer xliv 17
‖ Or is there any thing lighter than to commit
n Mic vi 12
o Chap v 11 & vii 4, 9 & ix 10
p Prov i 28 Isa i 15 Jer xi 11 & xiv 12 Mic iii 4 Zech vii 13

v 13—18 Farther abominations pass in review before the prophet

1 At the north gate of the temple sat women weeping for Tammuz Probably the Adonis of the Grecians, beloved of Venus, according to the heathen fable, and slain by a wild boar In honour therefore of this goddess they observed the anniversary of his death with mourning and tears, and dared even in the gate of the Lord's house to appear celebrating the shameful service

2 In the inner court, the most sacred inclosure between the porch and the altar, where the priests ministred, there stood about five and twenty men, their backs turned to the temple, their faces to the east, adoring the rising sun

3 God bids the prophet observe with wonder what he saw, and appeals to him concerning the aggravated guilt of this abandoned people They made light of their dreadful provocations, and even *there*, in God's own house, performed their idolatrous rites *They filled the land* also *with violence*, and then *returned to provoke* God *to anger*, for, whilst such wickedness was committed, their very sacrifices must needs be an abomination and *lo they put the branch to their nose*, some nosegay perhaps of flowers, at which they smelled in honour of their idols, or, as some read the words, *they put the branch to their wrath*, or *his wrath*, adding fresh fuel to the fierceness of the divine wrath which burns against them *Therefore will I also deal in fury*, pouring on them the vengeance due to their iniquities, and judgment without mercy, which all their prayers and tears shall not be able to avert When sinners have turned their backs on God, it is but just for him to turn his back on them, and be deaf to their cries in the day of their calamity

CHAP IX

We have here, 1 The instruments that were to be employed in the destruction of the city, ver 1, 2 2 The removal of the Shechinah from the cherubim to the threshold of the temple, ver 3 3 Orders given to one of the persons employed to mark a remnant to be preserved from the common destruction, ver 3, 4 4 The warrant signed for the execution of the rest, and the execution begun accordingly, ver 5—7 5 The prophet's intercession for the mitigation of the sentence, which is denied, the decree being now gone forth, ver 8—10 6 The report made by him that marked the remnant of what he had done in that matter, ver 11

1 HE cried also in mine ears with a loud voice,
saying, Cause them that have charge over the
city to draw near, even every man *with* his destroying
weapon in his hand 2 And behold, six men came
from the way of the higher gate, which lieth toward the
north, and every man a slaughter weapon in his hand.
and [a] one man among them *was* clothed with linen,
with [b] a writer's inkhorn ‖ by his side, and they went in
and stood beside the brasen altar 3 And [c] the glory
of the God of Israel was gone up from the cherub whereupon he was, to the threshold of the house, and he called
to the man clothed with linen, which *had* the writer's
inkhorn by his side, 4 And the LORD said unto him,
Go through the midst of the city, through the midst
of Jerusalem, and set [d] a mark upon the foreheads of the
men that [e] sigh, and that cry for all the abominations
that be done in the midst thereof. 5 ¶ And to the
others he said in mine hearing, Go ye after him through
the city, and smite [f] let not your eye spare, neither
have ye pity 6 [g] Slay ‖ utterly old *and* young, both
maids and little children, and women, but come not
near any man upon whom *is* the mark, and [h] begin at
my sanctuary then they began at [i] the ancient men
which *were* before the house 7 And he said unto them,
[k] Defile the house, and fill the courts with the slain, go
ye forth, and they went forth and slew in the city

a Lev xvi 4 Chap x 2, 6, 7
b Mal iii 16
‖ Heb Upon his loins
c Chap iii 23 & viii 4 & x 4, 18 & xi 22, 23
d Ex xii 7 2 Cor i 22 Rev vii 3 & ix, 4 & xx 4
e 2 Pet ii 8.
f Ver 10
g 2 Chron xxxvi 17.
‖ Heb To destruction
h Jer xxv 29 1 Pet iv 17
i Chap viii 11 16
k 2 Chron xxxvi 17

v 1—7 We have heard the provocations of this people, and we see here their judgment lingereth not

1 A charge is given to the destroyers to approach, and instantly six warriors appear armed Their business is, as ministers of wrath, to destroy the city They come from the north, where the image of jealousy stood, from which quarter also their destruction advanced, *and they went in and stood beside the brasen altar*, waiting for orders, or intimating, that judgment would begin at the house of God, where the priests ministred whose hand had been chief in the transgression A seventh personage, differently clad, appears among them, armed not as a warrior,

but

Before Christ 594

but as a priest, *with a writer's inkhorn by his side*, and this seems to be no other than the great high-priest of our profession Christ Jesus, who, amidst all the judgments he sends on the earth, writes his own people in his book of life, and preserves them amidst the general desolations. *Note*, (1) God never wants ministers of wrath, when he hath vengeance to execute against sinners (2) They who have profaned the altar by their wickedness, justly fall as sacrifices before it (3) The people of God need not fear, whatever judgments are in the earth, their Lord and Saviour directs the sword, and will protect them from evil

2 God's glory, the Shechinah, removed from between the cherubims to the threshold of the house, as ready now to depart from the devoted temple, when he had given the last directions to separate the few precious from the vile And,

[1] *He called to the man clothed with linnen, &c* God's first care is for his own people; they were but few, yet precious in his sight They could not behold these abominations practised by their countrymen without the bitterest concern and anguish, which they testified publicly, and lamented before God in private On them therefore God commands a distinguishing mark to be set on the foreheads, that they might be known to belong to God, *See Rev* vii 3 in allusion to the marks on servants, or to the blood on the lintels of the Israelites in Egypt, to guard them from the destroying angel *Note*, (1) God's people cannot without the deepest concern behold a world lying in wickedness they remonstrate against the evil, and with tears before God and man lament over perishing souls (2) They who distinguish themselves by a concern for God's glory, he will distinguish them by a care for their safety (3) If we are sealed unto the day of redemption, we shall have nothing to fear in the day of calamity (4) The Lord Jesus knoweth those that are his, and not one of them shall be lost

[2] *To the others he said*, to the six destroyers, *Go ye after him through the city*, and slay with unrelenting severity both young and old, all of every age and sex, beginning at the sanctuary, the priests, who were chief in iniquity, must be the first and chief sufferers; and none must be spared, but those on whom is God's mark, these they may not touch, nor come near No sooner is the command issued, than the destroyers obey, beginning with those antients, the five and twenty, or the seventy which were before mentioned, profaning God's temple with their idolatries Nor need they fear to defile God's house with the blood of the slain, since they have his commission Because these antients have polluted it with their abominations, God will more pollute it with their dead carcases and when they have begun their bloody work in the sanctuary, they must finish it in the city by a general massacre, and it is done, *v* 7 *Note*, (1) They who persist in their impenitence, will die without mercy (2) The soul that hath God's mark of life can never perish (3) None in a judgment-day will meet so terrible a doom, as those who being appointed to admonish others, have seduced and destroyed the souls to whom they were ordained to minister

8 ¶ And it came to pass while they were slaying
them, and I was left, that I fell upon my face, and
cried, and said, [l] Ah, LORD God, wilt thou destroy
all the residue of Israel, in thy pouring out of thy fury
upon Jerusalem? 9 Then said he unto me, The ini-
quity of the house of Israel and Judah *is* [m] exceeding
great, and the land is [n] full of blood, and the city full
of † perverseness for they say, [o] The LORD hath for-
saken the earth, and the LORD seeth not 10 And as
for me also, [p] mine eye shall not spare, neither will I have
pity, *but* I will recompense their way upon their head
11 And behold, the man clothed with linen, which
had the inkhorn by his side, ‡ reported the matter, say-
ing, I have done as thou hast commanded me

l Chap xi 13
m Chap xi 25
n 2 Kings xxi 16
† Or, wresting of judgment
o Chap viii 12
p Chap v 11 & vii 4 & viii 18
‡ Heb Returned the word

v 8—11 We have here,

1 The prophet an intercessor in behalf of this miserable people Whilst the execution was performing, and the prophet alone in the temple, all who were there besides being slain, he fell upon his face in great humility, and *cried, and said, Ah, Lord God, wilt thou destroy all the residue of Israel, in thy pouring out of thy fury upon Jerusalem?* he dreaded a total excision, and fain would stay the avenging arm *Note*, A gracious soul cannot unmoved behold the miseries coming on the wicked, and fain would avert the dreadful storm by his prayer.

2 God cannot grant his request, their iniquities are such as admit of neither pardon nor reprieve their sins are most aggravated, their land full of blood, murders the most inhuman, and every atrocious crime prevailing, *the city is full of perverseness*, no justice or truth is regarded, and, atheistical in principles as practice, they blasphemously dared to deny the government of his providence, and flattered themselves with impunity in their iniquity therefore God threatens with unsparing hand to punish them, to shut up his compassions, and to refuse to be intreated by them or for them, bringing upon them the wrath they had so highly provoked and deserved *Note*, Though we may never cease to cry to God, there is a time when sinners are past the efficacy of prayer

Before Christ 594

3 The man clothed with linnen, &c reports, that the divine orders were accomplished, the people of God marked for life, the wicked destroyed The Lord Jesus hath thus finished the work God hath given him to do, his redeemed ones are secured from the power of the destroyer, their salvation is perfect and compleat, and wrath to the uttermost ready to be poured on the world of the ungodly

CHAP X

The same vision the prophet had seen, chap i *is here repeated, with a particular reference to the destruction of Jerusalem signified by* 1 *The scattering of the coals of fire upon the city, which were taken from between the cherubims*, ver 1—7 2 *The removal of the glory of God from the temple, and its being upon the wing to be gone*, ver 8—22 *When God goes out from a people, all judgments break in upon them*

1 THEN I looked, and behold, in [a] the firma-
ment that *was* above the head of the cherubims,
there appeared over them, as it were a sapphire-stone,
as the appearance of the likeness of a throne 2 And
he spake unto [b] the man clothed with the linen, and
said, Go in between the wheels, *even* under the cherub,
and fill † thine hand with coals of fire from between the
cherubims, and [c] scatter *them* over the city And he
went in in my sight 3 Now the cherubims stood on
the right side of the house, when the man went in, and
the cloud filled the inner court 4 [d] Then the glory of
the LORD † went up from the cherub, *and stood* over
the threshold of the house, and the house was filled with
the cloud, and the court was full of the brightness of the
LORD's glory 5 And [e] the sound of the cherubims
wings was heard, *even* to the utter court, as the voice of
the almighty God when he speaketh 6 And it came
to pass, *that* [f] when he had commanded the man clothed
with linen, saying, Take fire from between the wheels,
from between the cherubims; then he went in, and stood
beside the wheels 7 And *one* cherub § stretched forth
his hand from between the cherubims unto the fire that
was between the cherubims, and took *thereof*, and put
it into the hands of *him that was* clothed with linen
who took *it*, and went out

a Chap i 22, 26
b Chap ix 2
† Heb the hollow of thine hands
c Rev viii 5
d Ver 18 Chap i 28 & ix 3
† Heb was lifted up
e Chap i 24
f John xiv 31
§ Heb Sent forth

v 1—7 We have here a glorious appearance of the Divine Majesty, like that which the prophet saw, *chap* i A throne of dazzling brightness is set in the firmament above the cherubim, and God attending ministers stand ranged on the right side of the house, as expressive of their abhorrence of the image of jealousy that stood on the left

1 God departs from his holy place, *from the cherub*, where the Shechinah, the symbol of the divine presence, rested, *and stood over the threshold of the house*, is ready to depart, *and the house was filled with the cloud, and the court was full of the brightness of the Lord's glory*, see 1 Kings viii 11 The temple was in darkness, an emblem of the blindness of the Jews, and the court of the Gentiles illuminated, God having resolved to send to these the light of his gospel *And the sound of the cherubims wings was heard even to the utter court*, loud as the voice of mighty thunderings intimating their departure thence, or signifying the glorious voice of gospel grace, which, by the preaching of the apostles, should sound forth to the most distant nations

2 The city of Jerusalem is doomed to be burnt with fire, signified by the command to the man clad in linnen, &c to go in between the wheels under the cherub, and take thence burning coals, and scatter them on the city, and he immediately went in, *v* 7 when one of the cherub took off the coal, *chap* i 13 and put them in his hand, and he went forth strait to execute his commission, which intimates, (1) That the wrath of God against sin is most holy it is fire *from between the cherubims* (2) The Lord Jesus hath all judgment committed to him, and at his second coming to judge the world, shall burn up the earth, as then Jerusalem, with fire (3) The great quarrel of God against Jerusalem was especially their persecution of those ministers the cherubim represented

8 ¶ [g] And there appeared in the cherubims, the form
of a man's hand [h] under their wings 9 [i] And when I
looked, behold, the four wheels by the cherubims, one
wheel by one cherub, and another wheel by another
cherub and the appearance of the wheels *was* [k] as the
colour

g Chap i 8
h Chap i 8
i Chap i 15
k Chap i 16

Before Christ 594

colour of a beryl ſtone 10 And as for their appear-
ances they four had one likeneſs, as if a wheel had
been in the midſt of a wheel 11 [l] When they went,
they went upon their four ſides, they turned not as
they went, but to the place whither the head looked,
they followed it, they turned not as they went 12
And their whole body, and their backs, and their
hands, and their wings, and [m] the wheels were full of
eyes round about, even the wheels that they four had
13 As for the wheels, † it was cried unto them in my
hearing, O wheel 14 [n] And every one had four faces
the firſt face was the face of a cherub, and the ſecond
face was the face of a man, and the third the face of a
lion, and the fourth the face of an eagle 15 And
the cherubims were lifted up this is [o] the living creature
that I ſaw by the river of Chebar 16 [p] And when the
cherubims went, the wheels went by them and when
the cherubims lift up their wings, to mount up from
the earth, the ſame wheels alſo turned not from beſide
them 17 [q] When they ſtood, theſe ſtood, and when
they were lifted up, theſe lift up themſelves alſo for
the ſpirit ‡ of the living creature was in them 18 Then
[r] the glory of the LORD departed from off the threſhold
of the houſe, and ſtood over the cherubims 19 And
[s] the cherubims lift up their wings, and mounted up from
the earth in my ſight when they went out, the wheels
alſo were beſides them, and every one ſtood at the door of
the eaſt-gate of the LORD's houſe, and the glory of the
God of Iſrael was over them above 20 [t] This is the
living creature that I ſaw under the God of Iſrael, by
the river of Chebar, and I knew that they were the che-
rubims 21 Every one had four faces apiece, and every
one four wings, and the likeneſs of the hands of a man
was under their wings. 22 And the likeneſs of their
faces was the ſame faces which I ſaw by the river of
Chebar, their appearances and themſelves they went
every one ſtraight forward

l Chap. i. 17.
m Chap. i. 18.
† Or, they were called in my hearing, Wheel, or Galgal.
n Chap. i. 6, 10.
o Chap. i. 5.
p Chap. i. 19.
q Chap. i. 20, 21.
‡ Or of life.
r Ver. 4.
s Chap. xi. 22.
t Chap. i.

v 6—22 The particulars here recorded of this glorious viſion were before obſerved, chap i and with very little variation, except that the face of an ox there, is here called, v 14 the face of a cherub, which ſeems to intimate they were the ſame

They who interpret the cherubim of the angels, and the wheels of the divine providence, obſerve,

1 That this world, like theſe wheels, is in a ſtate of conſtant revolution, and though the diſpenſations of providence appear ſometimes intricate, as wheel within wheel, they all exactly correſpond, and tend to one great end, the glory of God

2 Nothing can interrupt the decrees of God whatever difficulties are in the way, the wheels go forward, and every obſtruction is born down, or removed

3 The angels are the miniſtring ſpirits, whoſe ſervice God is pleaſed to employ in his providential government of the world.

4 Whatever inſtruments he employs, the work is God's, whoſe Spirit is in the cherubim and the wheels, guides all their motions, and directs their ſteps There is no ſuch thing as chance or fortune in the world, the leaſt as well as the greateſt event is fixed by a divine unalterable decree, and brought to paſs by an irreſiſtible energy

The deſign of repeating this tranſcendently magnificent appearance here, ſeems to be in order to upbraid their wickedneſs and folly, who provoked this glorious God to depart from them, as he was now about to do He departs from the threſhold, aſcends his cherubic chariot, v 18 and upwards they mount, removing firſt to the outer gate of the Lord's houſe, then to a mountain on the eaſt, chap xi 23 and at laſt he utterly abandons the land Thus God at firſt cauſed his word to be preached to the Jews, and when they rejected his goſpel, he departed from them, and ſent his miniſters far off to the Gentiles

CHAP XI

This chapter concludes the prophet's viſion, in which he receives two meſſages 1 One of wrath againſt thoſe who continued ſtill at Jeruſalem, and were there in the height of preſumption, ver 1—13 *2 Another of comfort to thoſe who were carried captives into Babylon, and were there in the depth of deſpondency And as the former are aſſured that God has judgments in ſtore for them, notwithſtanding their preſent ſecurity, ſo the latter are aſſured, that God has mercy in ſtore for them, notwithſtanding their preſent diſtreſs,* ver 14—21 *And ſo the glory of God removes farther,* ver 22, 23 *The viſion diſappears,* ver 24 *and Ezekiel faithfully gives his hearers an account of it,* ver 25

Before Christ 594

1 MOreover, the ſpirit lift me up, and brought me
unto the eaſt gate of the LORD's houſe, which
looketh eaſtward and behold, at the door of the gate
[a] five and twenty men among whom I ſaw Jaazaniah
the ſon of Azur, and Pelatiah the ſon of Benaiah,
princes of the people 2 Then ſaid he unto me, Son
of man, theſe are the men that [b] deviſe † miſchief, and
give wicked counſel in this city 3 Which ſay, [c] It is
not near, let us build houſes [d] this city is the caldron,
and we be the fleſh 4 ¶ Therefore propheſy againſt
them, propheſy, O ſon of man 5 And [e] the ſpirit of
the LORD fell upon me, and ſaid unto me, Speak,
Thus ſaith the LORD, Thus have ye ſaid, O houſe of
Iſrael for I know the things that come into your mind,
every one of them 6 Ye have multiplied your ſlain
in this city, and ye have filled the ſtreets thereof with
the ſlain 7 Therefore thus ſaith the LORD God,
[f] Your ſlain whom ye have laid in the midſt of it, they
are the fleſh, and this city is the caldron but I will
bring you forth out of the midſt of it 8 Ye have
feared the ſword, and I will bring a ſword upon you,
ſaith the LORD God 9 And I will bring you out
of the midſt thereof, and deliver you into the hands of
ſtrangers, and will execute judgments among you 10
Ye ſhall fall by the ſword, I will judge you [g] in the
border of Iſrael, and [h] ye ſhall know that I am the LORD
11 This city ſhall not be your caldron, neither ſhall
ye be the fleſh in the midſt thereof; but I will judge
you in the border of Iſrael 12 And [i] ye ſhall know
that I am the LORD for ye have not walked in my
ſtatutes, neither executed my judgments, [k] but have done
after the manner of the heathen that are round about
you 13 ¶ And it came to paſs [l] when I propheſied,
that Pelatiah the ſon of Benaiah died then fell I down
upon my face, and cried with a loud voice, and ſaid,
[m] Ah, LORD God, wilt thou make a full end of the
remnant of Iſrael?

a Chap. viii. 16.
b Jer. xviii. 18.
† Or, vanity.
c Chap. xii. 22. Amos vi. 3. 2 Pet. iii.
d Jer. i. 13.
e Chap. ii.
f Chap. xxiv. 3, 6. Mic. iii.
g Jer. lii.
h Chap. v. 8. xiii. 9.
i Pſ. ix. 16. Ver. 10.
k Lev. xviii. 3. Deut. xii. 30.
l Hoſ. vi. 5.
m Chap. ix. 8.

v 1—13 The abominations which were done in the temple we have ſeen, and as great, it ſeems, prevailed in the courts of juſtice, as in the worſhip of the ſanctuary

1 Under the Spirit's conduct the prophet is led to the eaſt-gate of the Lord's houſe, where five and-twenty of the princes ſat, two of whom are mentioned by name, and theſe, though the ſame in number as thoſe, chap viii 16 are different, thoſe being prieſts between the porch and the altar, theſe, judges, or princes, ſitting in council, or preſiding in the courts of judicature, where they were chargeable with great abuſe They were abettors of wickedneſs *Theſe are the men that deviſe miſchief, or vanity,* contrived ſchemes for the defence of the city, and encouraged the people to rebel, in defiance of God's threatnings *and give wicked counſel in this city,* adviſing the perſecution of the prophets, and promiſing their countrymen all ſucceſs and ſecurity in their evil ways; denying the truth of God's warnings, and impiouſly declaring, *It is not near,* there was no danger from the Chaldean army; but that they may ſafely *build houſes,* and dwell in them peaceably, for *this city is the caldron, and we are the fleſh,* ridiculing what the prophet Jeremiah had ſpoken, chap i 13 or intimating, that no enemy would dare approach them, any more than a perſon would take with his hands the fleſh out of a boiling caldron *Note,* (1) The higher men are in office, the more criminal is their unfaithfulneſs. (2) Wicked counſellors hurry a deluded people to the precipice of ruin (3) They who put far from them the evil day, will find it terribly ſurprize them ere they are aware (4) Mockery at God's word will ſhortly end in miſery

2 He is commanded, and ſtrengthned by the Spirit of the Lord, to deliver with fidelity God's warnings to theſe wicked rulers *Propheſy againſt them, propheſy, O ſon of man* with boldneſs and zeal, for the greateſt are not too high or above divine rebuke nor can we do a greater act of kindneſs to ſinners, who are flattering themſelves to their ruin, than to undeceive them, and ſhew them the guilt and danger of their ſtate *And the Spirit of the Lord fell upon me, and ſaid unto me, Speak;* enabling him to open his mouth with undaunted courage, and not to fear the faces of the many or the mighty He muſt tell them,

[1] That God is privy to their devices, v 5 However ſecret their contrivances, or deep laid their ſchemes, he ſearcheth the heart, and nothing is hid from his all-ſeeing eye

[2] *Ye have multiplied the ſlain in the city,* by many inhuman murders, by the death of innocents, and the prophets of the Lord, and at their door lay all the blood which ſhould be ſhed during the ſiege In a ſenſe they little ſuſpected, that city ſhould be the caldron, and theſe dead corpſes the fleſh, the only inhabitants who ſhould remain in it, buried under the ruins

[3] God

Before Christ 594

[3] God will carry the survivors into captivity. Far from dwelling as they flattered themselves there safe as flesh in a caldron, v. 11. the Lord will drag them forth, and deliver them into the hands of the Chaldeans. *Note*, Every sinner is a self-deceiver: he cries peace to his soul, but it will shortly be found there is a lie in his right hand.

[4] By the sword they shall fall, not merely as warriors fighting during the siege, but as criminals brought to the bar of the king of Babylon, seized and bound. In Riblah, in *the border of Israel*, shall judgment pass on them, and they miserably perish under the hand of the executioner, *Jer.* lii. 9, 10.

[5] God will terribly make himself known to them by the judgments he executes. They would not acknowledge him as their Lord by obedience to his holy will, but cast off his government, and copied the manners of the heathen around them; therefore in the sufferings he will inflict they shall know him to be a jealous God, and prove the truth of his threatnings, the power of his wrath, and the severity of his justice.

3. An alarming providence confirms this awful warning. Pelatiah, the son of Benaiah, one of the five and twenty whom he saw at the gate, v. 1. dropped down dead as he uttered these words, an earnest of the fulfilment of this fearful prophecy. This seems to have been done in vision here, but no doubt happened at this very time, or when this prophecy was published. *Note*, God is pleased to make some present monuments of his judgments, when sudden death arrests the daring sinner in the midst of his profaneness and impiety.

4. The prophet, affected with this fearful stroke, deprecates the vengeance he saw ready to fall on the remnant of Israel. Though he denounced their doom, he did not desire the dreadful day, but wept, and prayed, and intreated, if so be the wrath might yet pass away.

14 Again the word of the LORD came unto me,
saying, 15 Son of man, thy brethren, *even* thy bre-
thren, the men of thy † kindred, and all the house of
Israel wholly *are* they, unto whom the inhabitants of
Jerusalem have said, [n] Get ye far from the LORD:
unto us is this land given in possession. 16 Therefore
say, Thus saith the LORD God, Although I have
cast them far off among the heathen, and although I
have scattered them among the countries, [o] yet will I
be to them as ‡ a little sanctuary in the countries where
they shall come. 17 Therefore say, Thus saith the
LORD God, [p] I will even gather you from the people,
and assemble you out of the countries where ye have
been scattered, and I will give you the land of Israel.
18 And they shall come thither, and they shall take
away [q] all the detestable things thereof, and all the abo-
minations thereof from thence. 19 And [r] I will give
them one heart, and I will put [s] a new spirit within you;
and I will take [t] the stony heart out of their flesh, and
will give them an heart of flesh: 20 [u] That they may
walk in my statutes, and keep mine ordinances, and do
them: and [x] they shall be my people, and I will be their
God. 21 But *as for them* whose heart walketh after
the heart of their detestable things, and their abomina-
tions, [y] I will recompense their way upon their own
heads, saith the LORD God.

† Or, redemption.
n Isa. lxvi. 5.
o Psal. xc. 1. & xci. 9. Isa. viii. 14.
‡ Or, a sanctuary for a little time.
p Jer. xxix. 14.
p Hos. i. 11.
q Hos. xiv. 8.
r Jer. xxxii. 39. Chap. xxxvi. 26.
s Psal. li. 10. Zech. vii. 12.
u Psal. cv. 45.
x Chap. xxxvii. 27.
y Chap. ix. 10.

v. 14—21. We have here,

1. The insults cast on the poor captives in Babylon by their proud brethren, who still continued in their own land: *They said, Get ye far from the Lord*, suggesting that as sinners above the rest they deserved to be cut off from the communion of the faithful, and to lose all their interest in the inheritance of the Lord, as forfeited: for *unto us is this land given for a possession*. The prophet therefore need not be affected for the destruction he saw coming on those who thus treated his *brethren*, the *men of his kindred*, or *redemption*, his nearest relations, who were captive with him, to whom the right of redemption of his lands belonged; and these in God's account, though slighted and trampled upon, are *the whole house of Israel*, the *good figs*, who for their benefit were sent into Babylon, whilst their revilers were the reprobate, the *evil figs*, to whom God disowned any relation. *Note*, They are often the severest censurers of others, whose own conduct will least bear examination.

2. The comfortable word the prophet is commanded to speak to them. God hath the most gracious designs towards them, and when their revilers are ruined, they shall be redeemed and saved.

[1] Though they want the temple, God will himself by his presence and love be a *little sanctuary* unto them, v. 16. and though he hath indeed dispersed them in the land of the heathen, where their condition seemed to be desperate, yet there he would visit them, and make them safe as under the horns of the altar, and happy in communion with him, as if they were in the courts of the Lord's house: or, *a sanctuary of a few*, the little remnant according to the election of grace: or, *for a little while*, during the seventy years captivity. *Note*, (1.) Whatever outward means of grace we are excluded from, God can abundantly make them up in divine communications. (2.) The way to the throne of God is in every place alike open, and we may assuredly find him near, whenever in fervent prayer we seek his face.

Before Christ 594

[2] God promises to bring them again to their own land, to collect them from their dispersion, and restore them to the possession of their lost inheritance, when the present occupants should utterly be consumed, v. 17.

[3] They shall not only be restored to their land, but, what is infinitely better, recovered from their backslidings, and renewed in the spirit of their minds. Their former detestable idolatries shall be wholly rooted out from amongst them, and the Lord in his rich grace assures them, he *will give them one heart*, single in its attachment to him and his worship, and faithfully devoted to his glory; and *put a new spirit within* them, giving them new affections, new desires, new purposes, new delight, new principles, new ends, that God may be glorified in them and by them. And *he will take away the stony heart out of their flesh*, the corrupt, hard, impenitent heart, that had before been stubborn and obstinate against God's word and warnings, *and will give them an heart of flesh*, tender, susceptible of the deepest impressions of shame and remorse for former unfaithfulness, and of love to God for his boundless mercies, now seen and felt with the most lively sensibility. Thus they shall be enabled for the practice of that obedience God enjoins, and in this way enjoy the comfort of that most blessed and endeared relation, *God their God*, and *they his people*, v. 20. And what is here spoken of them is true of all God's redeemed ones, whose hearts by nature are hard and stupid, but by the powerful energy of his Spirit are softened, and effectually converted to God, the whole man renewed after the image of Jesus, and the love of sin, of every idol, mortified within them. Where such a blessed change is wrought, it is the sure evidence of our relation to God, and the earnest of our return to the heavenly Canaan, whilst without it to hope for heaven would be the greatest delusion: there must be a meetness for it, ere we can truly expect an entrance into the inheritance among the saints in light.

3. A denunciation of wrath is pronounced on those who still dwelt in Jerusalem, and lived in their abominable idolatries. God will visit them according to their deeds, v. 21. By famine, pestilence, and the sword, they shall miserably perish. *Note*, Whilst the heart continues apostate from God, hell must be the sinner's doom.

22 ¶ [z] Then did the cherubims lift up their wings,
and the wheels beside them; and the glory of the God
of Israel *was* over them above. 23 And [a] the glory of
the LORD went up from the midst of the city, and
stood [b] upon the mountain, [c] which *is* on the east side
of the city. 24 ¶ Afterwards the spirit took me up,
and brought me in vision by the spirit of God into
Chaldea, to them of the captivity. So the vision that I
had seen went up from me. 25 Then I spake unto
them of the captivity [d] all the things that the LORD
had shewed me.

z Chap. x. 19.
a Chap. viii. 3.
b Zech. xiv. 4.
c Chap. xliii. 2.
d Acts xx. 20.

v. 22—25. The message being delivered to the prophet,

1. God departs, and abandons the city and temple to destruction. He went up in his cherubic chariot, and stood upon the mountain at the east of the city, supposed to be the Mount of Olives, either looking back with grief on those devoted walls, as in the days of his flesh he there wept over Jerusalem; or on that mount which had been the seat of idolatry and corruption, 2 *Kings* xxiii. 13. triumphing in the view of the destruction he was about to bring on the city. *Note*, Vengeance is God's strange work: he appears loth to strike; but when his abused patience is at an end, and the measure of the sinner's iniquity is full, God will delight in his torment.

2. The prophet is by the Spirit re-conveyed in vision to Chaldea, and thereupon the divine glory went up from him, and disappeared. He awaked from his extasy, and found himself in his own house among the captivity, and probably the elders of Judah still before him. *Note*, The saints of God, if at times favoured with some bright views of the divine glory, may expect them here below to be of no long continuance; but it is reserved for them in the happiness of the glorious world above, there to enjoy without interruption the beatific vision of God.

3. He immediately communicated to those of the captivity all the things he had seen and heard, as an encouragement to the poor captives to be thankful for their lot; and most probably notice was conveyed also to Jerusalem of the judgments threatened as a warning, which, if it led them not to return from their sins, might leave them inexcusable in their impenitence.

Before Christ 594

CHAP XII

The ruin of Jerusalem is the burden of this chapter 1 The prophet, by removing his stuff, and quitting his lodgings, must be a sign to set forth Zedekiah's flight out of Jerusalem in the utmost confusion, when the Chaldeans took the city, ver 1—16 2 The prophet, by eating his meat with trembling, must be a sign to set forth the famine in the city during the siege, and the consternation that the inhabitants should be in, ver 17—20, 3 A message is sent from God to assure the people that all these predictions should shortly be accomplished, and not be deferred, as they vainly hoped, ver 21—28

594 1 THE word of the LORD also came unto me,
saying, 2 Son of man, thou dwellest in the
a Chap ii 3 6 & iii 26 27 midst of a a rebellious house, which b have eyes to see,
and see not, they have ears to hear, and hear not c for
b Isa vi 9 & xlii 20 Jer v 21 Matt xiii 13 14 they are a rebellious house 3 Therefore thou son of
man, prepare thee † stuff for removing, and remove by
day in their sight, and thou shalt remove from thy place
c Chap ii 5 to another place in their sight, it may be they will con-
† Or instruments sider, though they be a rebellious house 4 Then shalt
thou bring forth thy stuff by day in their sight, as
d Jer xxxix 4 stuff for removing and thou shalt go forth d at even
in their sight, as ‡ they that go forth into captivity
‡ Heb The goings forth of captivity 5 Dig thou through the wall in their sight, and carry
out thereby 6 In their sight shalt thou bear it upon
thy shoulders, and carry it forth in the twilight thou
shalt cover thy face that thou see not the ground for I
e Chap xxiv 24 have set e thee for a sign unto the house of Israel 7 And
I did so as I was commanded I brought forth my stuff
§ Heb Digged for me, ver 5 by day, as stuff for captivity, and in the even I § digged
through the wall with mine hand, I brought it forth
in the twilight, and I bare it upon my shoulder in their
sight 8 ¶ And in the morning came the word of the
LORD unto me, saying, 9 Son of man, hath not the
house of Israel, the rebellious house, said unto thee,
What dost thou? 10 Say thou unto them, Thus saith
the LORD God, This burden concerneth the prince in
Jerusalem, and all the house of Israel that are among
f Ver 6 them 11 Say, f I am your sign like as I have done,
‖ Heb. by removing go into captivity so shall it be done unto them they shall ‖ remove and
go into captivity 12 And g the prince that is among
g Jer xxxix 4 them shall bear upon his shoulder in the twilight, and
shall go forth they shall dig through the wall to carry
out thereby he shall cover his face that he see not the
h Jer lii 9 ground with his eyes 13 My h net also will I spread
upon him, and he shall be taken in my snare, i and
i Chap xvii 20 I will bring him to Babylon to the land of the Chal-
deans, yet shall he not see it, though he shall die there
k 2 Kings xxv 4 14 And I will k scatter toward every wind all that are
round about him to help him, and all his bands, l and
l Chap v 2 12 I will draw out the sword after them 15 And m they
m Psal ix 16 Chap vi 7 shall know that I am the LORD, when I shall scatter
them among the nations, and disperse them in the
† Heb Men of number countries 16 But I will leave † a few men of them
from the sword, from the famine, and from the pestilence,
that they may declare all their abominations among the
heathen whither they come, and they shall know that
I am the LORD

v 1—16. Though many among the captives in Babylon profited under the visitation, yet multitudes were still hardened, flattered by their false prophets with hope of a speedy return to Jerusalem; and deaf to the admonitions of God's *messengers*, warning them to repent of their sins, and patiently submit to his will in bearing their appointed seventy years captivity They were a rebellious house, and would not see nor hear, and who so blind as those? To affect them therefore, not only by warnings but by the most expressive signs of the certain and terrible destruction of Jerusalem, the prophet is enjoined,

1 *To prepare his stuff for removing, his vessels of captivity*, as if going into a far country, and this openly in the sight of the people, *removing from place to place* as one unsettled, and seeking an abode in the twilight he must dig through the wall of his house, and carry out thereby his stuff, bearing it upon his own shoulders in a mournful habit, and with a dejected look, as one going into captivity, covering his face and stealing off in the dark, as one ashamed and afraid of discovery Thus he must be a sign to that rebellious house *It may be they will consider*, and, though not moved with what they heard, be affected with what they saw, *though they be a rebellious house* God thus tries every method with sinners, and ministers must not despair of repeating their labours with the most hardened and obstinate *it may be* they will repent and the most distant hope should encourage our perseverance in our work

2 The prophet instantly obeys, *v* 7 however laborious the work, or strange it might appear They who have God's commands must never hesitate We must be ready to do or suffer any thing for his glory and the good of men's souls, and count all our worldly stuff not worth a thought, if he calls us at any time to remove, knowing that we have in heaven a better and a more abiding substance

3 The Lord the next morning gives the prophet the explication of what he had enjoined, which he is to communicate to the people, who would naturally be inquisitive what he meant by this conduct, or perhaps they ridiculed him at his work, and, bantering cried, *What dost thou?* What is this strange fellow about? He must tell them, *this burden* of the prophetic word respected the prince Zedekiah and all the house of Israel Ezekiel is their sign herein, as he hath done, so shall they Their king, in whom they trusted, and by whose influence they hoped to be set at liberty and restored to their own country, so far from helping them, should be enslaved himself, and follow them to Babylon Pressed by the besiegers, and the city no longer tenable, by night he shall attempt to escape, breaking through the wall of the city for privacy, and carrying a bundle of his most valuable effects or provision with him, his face covered with *shame* at his miserable plight, or with a *mask* to prevent his being known but vain the attempt, God's net, the Chaldean army, should be spread over him, and he taken as a bird in a snare, led captive into Babylon, and dying there, yet doomed never to see the place, his eyes being put out, in just punishment of his perfidy, by the conqueror, *Jer* xxxix 7 His guards scattered, his forces fled, yet pursued by the sword, few shall be suffered to escape, and these dispersed in heathen lands, living monuments of divine vengeance, or perhaps there brought to repentance, acknowledging their abominations, and justifying God in his judgments Thus, saith he, *they shall know that I am the Lord*, omniscient, just, and almighty *Note*, God will make himself known, either in the terrors of his wrath to the impenitent, or in the riches of his grace to the humble

17 ¶ Moreover, the word of the LORD came to
me, saying, 18 Son of man, n eat thy bread with n Chap iv 16
quaking, and drink thy water with trembling and with
carefulness, 19 And say unto the people of the land,
Thus saith the LORD God, of the inhabitants of Jeru-
salem, and of the land of Israel, They shall eat their
bread with carefulness, and drink their water with asto-
nishment, o that her land may be desolate from † all o Psal cvii 34 Mic iii 12
that is therein, because of the violence of all them that † Heb. The fulness thereof
dwell therein 20 And the cities that are inhabited
shall be laid waste, and the land shall be desolate, and
ye shall know that I am the LORD

v 17—20 Ezekiel is still herein a sign unto them He must *eat his bread with trembling, and drink his water with fear and carefulness*, as if he was in danger of want, or expected it would be snatched from him, intimating the distress to which the inhabitants of Jerusalem should be reduced during the siege, terrified by their enemies without, dreading the ravages of famine within, and expecting shortly that both their bread and water would fail, and they miserably perish for want; the land being doomed to desolation universal, the cities wasted, the country ravaged, uncultivated, and destitute of man and beast, and this because of the *violence therein*, the bloodshed, oppression, and injustice exercised among them And these judgments would teach them that knowledge of God which in their prosperity they refused to learn *Note*, (1) They who abuse *fulness of bread* justly are punished with pining want (2) Those afflictions, on ourselves or others, are singular blessings to us, which lead us to a deeper knowledge of and acquaintance with God

21 ¶ And the word of the LORD came unto me,
saying, 22 Son of man, what is that proverb, that ye
have in the land of Israel, saying, p The days are pro- p Ver 27 Chap xi 3 Amos vi 3 2 Pet iii 4
longed, and every vision faileth? 23 Tell them there-
fore, Thus saith the LORD God, I will make this
proverb to cease, and they shall no more use it as a
proverb in Israel but say unto them, The days are at
hand, and the effect of every vision 24 For q there q Chap xiii 23
shall be no more any vain vision, nor flattering divina-
tion within the house of Israel 25 For I am the
LORD I will speak, and r the word that I shall speak r Isa lv 11 Dan ix 12 Zech i 6
shall come to pass it shall be no more prolonged for
in your days, O rebellious house, will I say the word,
and will perform it, saith the LORD God 26 ¶
Again the word of the LORD came to me, saying,
27 s Son of man, behold, they of the house of Israel say, s Ver 22 t 2 Pet iii 4
The vision that he seeth t is for many days to come, and

he

Before Christ 594.

he propheſieth of the times *that are* far off 28 Therefore
ſay unto them, Thus ſaith the LORD God, There
ſhall none of my words be prolonged any more, but
the word which I have ſpoken ſhall be done, ſaith the
LORD God

v 21—28 The awful warnings the prophet gave were too plain to be miſtaken, and the ſigns too forcible not to make ſome impreſſion Here we are told what methods they took to evade the conviction They affirmed that the time for the threatned judgments was prolonged, and would not yet arrive, ſo that they might hope for peace in their days, *v* 22 and that the prophetic viſion looked forward to ſome very diſtant ſeaſon, ſo that they need not diſturb themſelves about the event nay, ſome dared aſſert the evil never would come, *every viſion faileth, or periſheth* So apt are ſinners to abuſe God's patience, to harden their hearts becauſe judgment is not ſpeedily executed, and to flatter themſelves that the terrors of God are mere bugbears Nor did the falſe prophets fail to encourage the deluſion, *v* 24 ſo that the ſayings were induſtriouſly propagated, and became proverbial by frequent repetitions they began to believe their own lie Againſt this deceit the prophet ſets his face, and from God aſſures them their neglect of his judgments ſhall but haſten them

1 He will ſilence their falſe hopes, by bringing on them the threatned puniſhment, when every viſion ſhould take effect, their lying prophets be abaſhed, and their deluſive proverbs confounded, *v* 23, 24 *Note*, They who will not believe the warnings of God, will too late be terribly convinced by the infliction of his judgments

2 God will do this certainly and ſuddenly *I am the Lord*, whoſe truth is inviolable, his power almighty, his juſtice inexorable, and he will execute all his threatnings Since he hath ſpoken, it ſhall be done No longer reſpite ſhall be granted, but wrath to the uttermoſt come on the rebellious houſe of Iſrael, and that quickly, *the days are at hand*, even *in your days*, their eyes ſhould ſee the deſtruction within five or ſix years the whole ſhould be accompliſhed And the ſame aſſurance is repeated, *v* 28 to cut off all doubt of the event, ſince heaven and earth ſhall ſooner paſs away than one jot or tittle fail of God's word *Note*, It is the folly of ſinners, when they hear of death and judgment, to put far from them the evil day, and defer the great work of preparing for eternity to a more convenient ſeaſon when lo! their hour arrives, they bow, they fall, the grave receives them, a warning to others of the madneſs of procraſtination, and a loud call to-day, whilſt it is called to-day, to work out their ſalvation with fear and trembling.

CHAP XIII

None are more ſharply treated in Scripture than the falſe prophets They were the chief cauſes of the people's ruin The prophet here ſhews the ſin and puniſhment, 1 *Of the falſe prophets,* ver 1—16 2 *Of the falſe propheteſſes,* ver. 17—23

1 AND the word of the LORD came unto me,
ſaying, 2 Son of man, propheſy againſt the
prophets of Iſrael that propheſy, and ſay thou unto them
[a] that propheſy [b] out of their own hearts, Hear ye the
word of the LORD, 3 Thus ſaith the LORD God,
Wo unto the fooliſh prophets, that follow their own
ſpirit, † and have ſeen nothing. 4 O Iſrael, thy prophets
are [c] like the foxes in the deſerts 5 Ye [d] have
not gone up into the ‡ gaps, neither made up the hedge
for the houſe of Iſrael, to ſtand in the battle in the day
of the LORD 6 [e] They have ſeen vanity, and lying
divination, ſaying, The LORD ſaith, and the LORD
hath not ſent them, and they have made *others* to hope
that they would confirm the word 7 Have ye not
ſeen a vain viſion, and have ye not ſpoken a lying divination,
whereas ye ſay, The LORD ſaith *it*, albeit I have
not ſpoken? 8 Therefore thus ſaith the LORD God,
Becauſe ye have ſpoken vanity, and ſeen lies, therefore
behold I *am* againſt you, ſaith the LORD God 9 And
mine hand ſhall be upon the prophets that ſee vanity,
and that divine lies they ſhall not be in the § aſſembly
of my people, [f] neither ſhall they be written in the
writing of the houſe of Iſrael, neither ſhall they enter
into the land of Iſrael, and [g] ye ſhall know that I *am*
the LORD God

[a] Ver 17 [b] Jer xiv 14 & xxiii 16 † Or, and things which they have not ſeen [c] Cant ii 15 [d] Pſ cvi 23, 30 Chap xxii 30 ‡ Or breaches [e] Ver 23 Chap xii 24 § Or ſecret or counſel [f] Ezra ii 59, 62 Pſ lxix 28 [g] Chap xi 10, 12

v 1—9 The falſe prophets abounded, both in Judea and among the captives in Babylon, and by their flattering ſpeeches the hearts of the unwary people were beguiled againſt them therefore the prophet is ordered to direct his word They are called *the prophets of Iſrael* probably they arrogated that title to themſelves, and perſecuted the few faithful prophets becauſe they remonſtrated againſt and contradicted their falſehood and lies

1 A heavy charge is laid againſt them They were daring impoſtors, pretended a miſſion and inſtruction from God, when he never ſent them, forging viſions which they never ſaw, the mere contrivances of their own brain inſtead of being guided by the ſpirit of truth, they followed their own deceived hearts, and dared to advance that as the dictates of inſpiration which they knew to be a lie crafty and ravenous as the foxes of the deſert, they preyed on the deluded people, yet, wiſe as they accounted themſelves in their deceits, they were in fact *fooliſh prophets*, ſunk in ſpiritual ignorance and ſin, they uſed no efforts to prevent the impending judgments, *v* 5 nor ever ſtood up in the breach againſt the overflowings of ungodlineſs, with ſharp and faithful rebukes againſt the wicked, or fervent and *importunate prayer to God, in order to* avert his wrath, when he aroſe as an enemy againſt them Nay, they widened the gap they ſhould have made up, by baſely betraying men's ſouls, flattering them to their ruin, promiſing them peace, and with their ſolemn pretenſions and aſſeverations emboldening the people to *hope that the event would correſpond with their predictions*, hardening them in ſin, and haſtening their deſtruction. *Note*, (1) To pretend a miſſion from the Holy Ghoſt, when men are conſcious they never were *inwardly moved* by him, is daring blaſphemy and impiety (2) They who run, though God never ſent them, will ſhortly be ſtopped in their career, and periſh in their lie (3) A fooliſh prophet had never yet a miſſion from God they cannot be called who are not qualified (4) A greedy prophet ſhews who ſent him, not God but Mammon (5) They who ſtudy to pleaſe men's ears, inſtead of faithfully addreſſing their conſciences, are juſtly to be ſuſpected as deceivers

2 Vengeance is denounced againſt them, *v* 9 God is their enemy, and wo unto thoſe againſt whom he riſes up in anger. As they have juſtly forfeited them, they are for ever excluded from all the privileges of God's Iſrael, they ſhall either be cut off by death, or be excommunicated from the church, or, when the iſſue hath proved the falſehood of their predictions, they ſhall be confounded, and aſhamed to look thoſe in the face whom they have deluded they ſhall be no more conſulted, but abhorred as deceivers, ſhall die in a miſerable exile, and never be enrolled with the other captives when they return to their own land, excluded from their mercy, an earneſt of eternal excluſion from the heavenly Canaan And in theſe judgments, inflicted on the falſe prophets, God will make known the glory of his juſtice, holineſs, and truth

10 ¶ Becauſe, [h] even becauſe they have ſeduced my
people, ſaying, [i] Peace, and *there was* no peace, and
one built up † a wall, and lo, others [k] daubed it with
untempered *morter*. 11. Say unto them which daub *it*
with untempered *morter*, that it ſhall fall there ſhall
be [l] an overflowing ſhower, and ye, O great hailſtones,
ſhall fall, and a ſtormy wind ſhall rent *it* 12. Lo,
when the wall is fallen, ſhall it not be ſaid unto you,
Where *is* the daubing wherewith ye have daubed *it*?
13 Therefore thus ſaith the LORD God, I will even
rent *it* with a ſtormy wind in my fury and there ſhall
be an overflowing ſhower in mine anger, and great hailſtones
in *my* fury to conſume *it* 14 So will I break
down the wall that ye have daubed with untempered
morter, and bring it down to the ground, ſo that the
foundation thereof ſhall be diſcovered, and it ſhall fall,
and ye ſhall be conſumed in the midſt thereof and [m] ye
ſhall know that I *am* the LORD 15 Thus will I accompliſh
my wrath upon the wall, and upon them that
have daubed it with untempered *morter*, and will ſay unto
you, The wall *is* no *more*, neither they that daubed it,
16 *To wit*, the prophets of Iſrael, which propheſy concerning
Jeruſalem, and which ſee viſions [n] of peace for
her, and [o] *there is* no peace, ſaith the LORD God

[h] Gen xii 32 [i] Jer vi 14 & viii 11 † Or a ſlight wall [k] Chap xxii 28 [l] Iſa xxviii 2 Eccleſ xlix 9 [m] Ver 9, 21, 23 Chap xiv 8 [n] Jer vi 14 [o] Iſa lvii 21

v. 10—16. The falſe prophets are farther rebuked and threatened

1 They deceived the people They cried *peace*, as if God would give them deliverance from the Babyloniſh yoke, when *there was no peace*, no proſpect as yet of their return from captivity, or hope of their being able to ſupport themſelves in rebellion againſt the Chaldeans Thus *they ſeduced God's people*, thoſe who in profeſſion at leaſt were ſuch, and who had been ſeparated from other nations for his ſervice *One built up a wall*, pretending Jeruſalem was impregnable, and that the enemy ſhould never break through; and, this being found pleaſing to the people, *lo! others daubed it with untempered morter*, ſupporting with ſpecious arguments the aſſertion when, alas! their wall, however ſolid it appeared, was weak and tottering, and ready to fall before the firſt attacks of the beſiegers Such are the plauſible *errors* which hereticks introduce, and the ſmooth propheſies of miniſters who dare not honeſtly offend by their ſimplicity, but

Before Christ 594.

but court favour by flattering ſinners in their falſe hopes, the end of which will be the ruin of the deceived and the deceiver together

2 Judgment is paſſed upon them The Chaldean army, as an overflowing ſhower, as great hailſtones, and a ſtormy wind, ſhall overturn all their defences, and lay the walls of Jeruſalem in the duſt, armed with *the fury of God*, nothing can reſiſt the invaders, and then the vanity of theſe lying prophets will be ſeen, and the folly of thoſe who truſted in them manifeſt, when they who daubed the wall ſhall periſh under the ruins, *v* 14 *Note*, (1) The falſe refuges of the ſinner ſhall in the end prove his bane (2) When God is the enemy, reſiſtance is vain (3) They who deluded others to their deſtruction ſhall receive themſelves greater damnation

3 God ridicules their confidence, *v* 12 and triumphs in their fall *When the wall is fallen, it ſhall be ſaid unto you, Where is the daubing wherewith ye have daubed it?* Thoſe whom they had deceived would abuſe them for their falſe aſſurances, and the faithful, who diſregarded their predictions, mock at their calamities And it ſhall be then known and acknowledged that God is the Lord, when his word is thus verified, and his righteous judgments executed

17 ¶ Likewiſe thou, ſon of man, ſet thy face a-
p Ver 2 gainſt the daughters of thy people, which [p] propheſy out
of their own heart, and propheſy thou againſt them,
18 And ſay, Thus ſaith the LORD God, Wo to the
† Or elbows. *women* that ſew pillows to all † armholes, and make ker-
chiefs upon the head of every ſtature to hunt ſouls
Will ye hunt the ſouls of my people, and will ye ſave
the ſouls alive *that come* unto you? 19 And will ye
q Prov. xxviii 21 pollute me among my people [q] for handfuls of barley,
Mic iii 5 and for pieces of bread, to ſlay the ſouls that ſhould not
2 Pet. ii 3 die, and to ſave the ſouls alive that ſhould not live, by
your lying to my people that hear *your* lies? 20 Where-
fore thus ſaith the LORD God, Behold, I *am* againſt
‡ Or into gardens your pillows, wherewith ye there hunt the ſouls, ‡ to
make *them* fly, and I will tear them from your arms,
and will let the ſouls go, *even* the ſouls that ye hunt
to make *them* fly 21 Your kerchiefs alſo will I tear,
and deliver my people out of your hand, and they ſhall
r Ver 9. be no more in your hand to be hunted, and [r] ye ſhall
know that I *am* the LORD 22 Becauſe with lies ye
have made the heart of the righteous ſad, whom I have
s Jer xxiii 14 not made ſad, and [s] ſtrengthned the hands of the wicked,
§ Or that I ſhould ſave his life that he ſhould not return from his wicked way, § by
t 2 Pet ii 19 [t] promiſing him life 23 Therefore [u] ye ſhall ſee no
u Ver. 6, &c Chap. xii 24 Mic iii 6 more vanity, nor divine divinations, for I will deliver
x Ver 9 Chap xiv 8 & xv 7 my people out of your hand, [x] and ye ſhall know that
I *am* the LORD

v 17—23 As women, as well as men, had been favoured with divine revelation, there were ſuch now who pretended to inſpiration, and, actuated by the ſame evil ſpirit, joined the falſe prophets in their lies Againſt theſe the prophet is commanded to ſet his face Impudent ſinners need a bold reprover

1 The crimes of the falſe propheteſſes are charged upon them

(1) They publiſhed the fictitious viſions of their own hearts, yet ſolemnly avouched God's authority to give weight to their lies And too many hearkened to them, hoping or fearing according to their word *Note*, (1) Men eaſily believe what they wiſh true (2) When ſinners deſire to be flattered, and hate to be reproved, it is juſt in God to give them up to deluders

(2) They were vilely mercenary They meant to fleece the deluded people, and impiouſly proſtituted God's ſacred name to gain credit to their predictions even for a morſel of bread ready to tranſgreſs, and to invent a lying anſwer, ſuch as would pleaſe thoſe who conſulted them *Note*, (1) Nothing is more incompatible with a miſſion from God than the love of filthy lucre (2) Of all impiety that is chief, to abuſe the ſacred name of God and religion to ſerve worldly ends and purpoſes

(3) They uſed every art to enſnare men's ſouls, and hunt them into their net Sometimes ſoothing them with pleaſing dreams, *ſewing pillows to all arm holes*, or *elbows*, *and making kerchiefs upon the head of every ſtature*, intimating thereby how ſecurely they might reſt, and fear no enemy to ſtrip off their ornaments, engaging to ſave the ſouls alive whom God had doomed to die, and hardening thus the wicked in his impenitence *by promiſing him life*, when death temporal and eternal awaited him On the other hand, ſometimes they threatened, denouncing deſtruction on thoſe whom God had determined to ſave, and ſeeking to diſcourage the righteous, and *make their hearts ſad whom God had not made ſad* And this ſome refer particularly to the captives, whom they ſeverely cenſured for yielding to the Chaldeans, whilſt they promiſed thoſe who rebelled againſt Nebuchadnezzar all ſucceſs and proſperity *Note*, (1) Nothing ſtrengthens the hands of the wicked ſo much as to be bolſtered up with hopes that they may be ſaved though they perſiſt in their ſins (2) They who grieve the hearts of God's people, and ſeek to diſcourage them, ſhall ſeverely ſuffer for it

2 God threatens them with deſerved wrath He expoſtulates with them on the daring impiety of their conduct, *v* 18 and denounces a fearful wo upon them They ſhall be ſhortly ſilenced and confounded, when by the event their lies ſhould be detected; or they ſhould miſerably periſh in the ſiege, *v* 23 and God will reſcue his poor people whom they hunted into their toils, *tear off the pillows and kerchiefs*, diſcover their deluſions, expoſe them to contempt, and make them more abhorred than ever they had been loved or feared, and hereby he will not only deliver his people from their ſnares, but eminently magnify his own great name *Note*, (1) It is an unſpeakable mercy when God ſaves his people from thoſe who ſought to tyrannize over their conſciences (2) God will not ſuffer his choſen to be led away by the deluſions of falſe teachers, who, by preaching to them human ſufficiency, man's free will, univerſal ſalvation, &c puff them up in pride, and harden them in ſin, but will bring them to the knowledge of his bleſſed Self, comfort their dejected hearts with the views of his free grace and rich ſalvation, and, ſhedding abroad his love in their ſouls, make them both happy and holy.

CHAP XIV

1 *The elders of Iſrael come to him and enquire of the prophet, but becauſe hypocritical, they meet with a rebuke inſtead of acceptance*, ver 1—5 *and are called upon to repent and reform, elſe it is at their peril to enquire of God*, ver 6—11 2 *Though Noah, Daniel, and Job ſhould pray for this people, yet becauſe the decree is gone forth, their prayers ſhould not be anſwered*, ver 12—21 *And yet it is promiſed in the cloſe that a remnant ſhall eſcape*, ver 22, 23

1 THEN [a] came certain of the elders of Iſrael unto 593 a Chap xx 1
me, and ſat before me 2 And the word of
the LORD came unto me ſaying, 3 Son of man,
theſe men have ſet up their idols in their heart, and
put the ſtumbling-block of their iniquity before their
face [b] ſhould I be enquired of at all by them? 4 b 2 Kings iii 13.
Therefore ſpeak unto them, and ſay unto them, Thus
ſaith the LORD God, Every man of the houſe of Iſrael
that ſetteth up his idols in his heart, and putteth the
ſtumbling block of his iniquity before his face, and
cometh to the prophet, [c] I the LORD will anſwer him c 2 Theſſ ii 11
that cometh, according to the multitude of his idols,
5 That I may take the houſe of Iſrael in their own
heart, becauſe they are all eſtranged from me through
their idols 6 ¶ Therefore ſay unto the houſe of Iſrael,
Thus ſaith the LORD God, Repent and turn † *yourſelves* † Or others
from your idols, and turn away your faces from all your
abominations 7 For every one of the houſe of Iſrael,
or of the ſtranger that ſojourneth in Iſrael, which [d] ſepa- d Jer. ii 13
rateth himſelf from me, and ſetteth up his idols in his
heart, and putteth the ſtumbling block of his iniquity
before his face, and cometh to a prophet to enquire of
him concerning me I the LORD will anſwer him by
myſelf 8 And [e] I will ſet my face againſt that man, e Lev xvii 10 Chap xv 7
and will make him [f] a ſign and a proverb, and I will cut f Deut xxviii 37
him off from the midſt of my people, and [g] ye ſhall know Chap v 15
that I *am* the LORD 9 And if the prophet be de- g Chap vi 7
ceived when he has ſpoken a thing, [h] I the LORD have h 1 Kings xxii 23
deceived that prophet, and I will ſtretch out my hand Job xii 16
upon him, and will deſtroy him from the midſt of my Jer iv 10
people Iſrael. 10 And they ſhall bear the puniſhment 2 Theſſ ii 11
of their iniquity, the puniſhment of the prophet ſhall be
even as the puniſhment of him that ſeeketh *unto him*
11 That the houſe of Iſrael may go no more aſtray from
me, neither be polluted any more with all their tranſ-
greſſions [i] but that they may be my people, and I may i Chap xxxvii 23
be their God, ſaith the LORD God

v 1—11 We have here,

1 Certain of the elders of Iſrael waiting on the prophet with apparent concern about their ſouls, and ſollicitude to hear and receive his admonitions Whether they were of the captivity, or ſome who had come on buſineſs from Jeruſalem to Babylon, is uncertain *Note*, The face of devotion and ſeriouſneſs is often put on by thoſe, who are utterly deſtitute of the power of godlineſs

2 God let the prophet know what manner of men theſe were, whoſe heart ſo ill correſponded with their exteriors *They have ſet up their idols in their heart, or cauſed them to aſcend*

upon

Before Christ 593

upon their heart, their affections were placed upon them, their hearts the throne of idolatry, and though at a diſtance from their images, ſtill ſlaves to theſe vanities, ſuch an aſcendant had they over them. *They put the ſtumbling-block of their iniquity before their face*, and fall down to the ſtock and ſtone and ſhould ſuch dare enquire of God? what impious effrontery! what anſwer can be expected, but wrath to the uttermoſt. *Note*, (1) Heart idols are equally abominable with thoſe that are the work of men's hands, and covetouſneſs, ſelf-love, &c as much idolatry as the bowing down to gods of gold or ſilver. (2) They who put the ſtumbling-block of their iniquity before them, can expect nothing but to fall into the pit of deſtruction.

3 The Lord gives him an anſwer for them. With God there is no reſpect of perſons, whoever draws near to him in hypocriſy, ſhall bear his burden, and receive an anſwer *according to the multitude of his idols*, he will give them up to the deluſions they have choſen, and puniſh them according to their crimes. *That I may take the houſe of Iſrael in their own heart*, expoſing their ſin and folly, and bringing them to deſerved ſhame and puniſhment, *becauſe they are all eſtranged from me through their idols*, alienated from the ſervice and worſhip of God by their attachment to theſe abominations. *Note*, Our own hearts are our great plague and ſnare, they ſeduce us from God to indulge ſome favourite luſt, the idol within, and in ſpite of the remonſtrances of God's word, and our own conſciences, hurry us on to our ruin.

4 A ſolemn warning is given them to repent, on pain of eternal perdition, be they native Iſraelites, or ſojourners among them, they have the ſame call, they muſt turn from their idols, and from all their abominations, elſe, if they continued *to ſeparate themſelves* from God in this hated ſervice, and walked in theſe iniquities, God will ſpeak to them in terrible wrath, confound that daring impiety and hypocriſy which leads them to the prophet, pretending to conſult him, *v* 7 will make them ſpectacles of horror, cut them off by ſudden death, and by theſe monuments of vengeance teach others to tremble, and fear to offend that God who is a conſuming fire. *Note*, (1) The hypocrite ſhall be detected and confounded, often in this world, at fartheſt in a judgment day. (2) Of all ſinners, the hypocrites doom will be moſt terrible, *Mat* xxiv 51.

5 The doom of the falſe prophets is read. The deceiver and the deceived ſhall periſh together. Since the people chuſe their own deluſions, God will give up the prophets they conſulted to a lying ſpirit, 1 *Kings* xxii 22, 23 and in juſt judgment ſuffer them to be deceived by the devil. He will ſtretch out his avenging arm, and utterly deſtroy them from the midſt of the people, *v* 9 and both the falſe prophet, and they who ſeek to him, ſhall bear the puniſhment of their iniquity, dreadful as their aggravated provocations. Myſterious are the ways of God, and though we are often loſt in our enquiries why he permits the evil we ſee, the day will come when all his diſpenſations will be proved, beyond contradiction, to be altogether righteous and true.

6 The judgments executed on the wicked will be a warning to many of *the houſe of Iſrael, that they go no more aſtray*, beholding the dire effects which ariſe from ſuch departures from God, and made wiſe by the ſufferings of others. *neither be polluted with all their tranſgreſſions*, which would neceſſarily involve them in the ſame ruin, *but* on the contrary learn to love and ſerve the bleſſed God, *that they may be my people*, approving their fidelity, *and I may be their God, ſaith the Lord God*, bleſſing them with all good things here, and their portion and exceeding great reward hereafter. *Note*, (1) Others puniſhments ſhould deter us from their iniquities. (2) Sin defiles the ſoul, and renders it odious in the eyes of a holy God. (3) They who approve themſelves to God as his people, ſhall find the preſent and eternal advantages of his love and favour.

12 ¶ The word of the LORD came again to me,
ſaying, 13 Son of man, when the land ſinneth againſt
me by treſpaſſing grievouſly, then will I ſtretch out
mine hand upon it, and [k] will break the ſtaff of the bread
thereof, and will ſend famine upon it, and will cut off
man and beaſt from it. 14 [l] Though theſe three men,
Noah, Daniel, and Job were in it, they ſhould deliver
but their own ſouls [m] by their righteouſneſs, ſaith the
LORD God. 15 ¶ If I cauſe [n] noiſome beaſts to paſs
through the land, and they † ſpoil it, ſo that it be deſolate,
that no man may paſs through becauſe of the
beaſts: 16 *Though* theſe three men *were* ‡ in it, *as* I
live, ſaith the LORD God, they ſhall deliver neither
ſons nor daughters; they only ſhall be delivered, but
the land ſhall be deſolate. 17 ¶ Or *if* I bring [o] a ſword
upon that land, and ſay, Sword, go through the land;
ſo that I cut off man and beaſt from it: 18 Though
theſe three men *were* in it, *as* I live, ſaith the LORD
God, they ſhall deliver neither ſons nor daughters, but
they only ſhall be delivered themſelves. 19 ¶ Or *if* I
ſend a peſtilence into that land, and [p] pour out my fury
upon it in blood, to cut off from it man and beaſt: [p] Chap vii 8
20 Though Noah, Daniel, and Job *were* in it, *as* I
live, ſaith the LORD God, they ſhall deliver neither
ſon nor daughter; [q] they ſhall but deliver their own ſouls [q] Prov xi 4
by their righteouſneſs. 21 For thus ſaith the LORD
God, How much more when [r] I ſend my four ſore judgments [r] Chap v 17
upon Jeruſalem, the ſword, and the famine, and
the noiſome beaſt, and the peſtilence, to cut off from it
man and beaſt? 22 ¶ Yet behold, therein [s] ſhall be [s] Ibid 3
left a remnant that ſhall be brought forth, *both* ſons
and daughters: behold, they ſhall come forth unto you,
and ye ſhall ſee their way, and their doings: and ye ſhall
be comforted concerning the evil that I have brought upon
Jeruſalem, *even* concerning all that I have brought upon
it. 23 And they ſhall comfort you when ye ſee their
ways and their doings: and ye ſhall know that [t] I have [t] Jer xxii 8, 9
not done without cauſe, all that I have done in it, ſaith
the LORD God.

k Lev xxvi 26 Iſa iii 1 Chap iv 16 & v 16
l Jer xv 1 See Jer vii 16 & xi 14 & xiv 11
m Prov xi 4
n Lev xxvi 22 Chap v 17
† Or bereave
‡ Heb In the midſt of it
o Lev xxvi 25

v 12—23 We have here,

1 The heavy judgments threatned on a guilty land. When the meaſure of their ſins is full, wrath to the uttermoſt will overtake them. Four ſore plagues are here mentioned; *famine*, when the ſtaff of bread is broken, and man and beaſt periſh with hunger. *Wild beaſts*, ſo numerous and ravenous, that all travelling muſt be unſafe, and the land deſerted and deſolate. *The ſword*, commiſſioned of God to go through the land, and conſume what the famine hath left, for whatever hand wields the ſword, God gives it the direction, and appoints it where to fall. *Peſtilence*, that depopulates the country, and puts a taint in the blood incurably fatal. Theſe are the arrows bent againſt wicked nations, and when his own people offend, God will ſhake his ſcourge over them alſo.

2 All interceſſion is vain when the decree is gone forth. Though Noah, Job, and Daniel joined as advocates, their piety and prayers could be of no avail. They could not deliver a ſon or daughter, their own ſouls only ſhould be given them for a prey. The mention of Job, with Noah and Daniel, ſeems ſtrongly to prove that he really lived, and anſwered the character given him in the book which bears his name, eminent for patience as Noah for his integrity, when all fleſh had corrupted their ways, and Daniel, though a young man, had already appeared diſtinguiſhed by his wiſdom, humility, piety, zeal, and prayer. Perhaps ſome few remained who reſembled theſe holy men, and for their ſake a hope might be entertained, that Jeruſalem would yet be ſpared, as Sodom might have been, if but ten righteous had been found in it. Indeed if any thing could have averted the threatned wrath, theſe advocates had prevailed, but her time is come, the meaſure of her guilt is full, her ruin determined, and the wrath denounced inexorable. *Note*, (1) In the worſt of times, ſome few eminent ſaints are found. (2) Though they may not prevail to avert the ruin of their land, themſelves ſhall be ſaved amidſt the general deſolations, ſometimes exempted from the common calamity, and wonderfully preſerved: at leaſt, if they ſuffer with others, they ſhall enjoy divine conſolations, and whatever becomes of their bodies, their ſouls are ſafe for eternity.

3 A remnant is reſerved from the general ruin. *Brought forth* out of Jeruſalem to join their brethren in captivity, *and ye ſhall ſee their way and their doings*, either behold their penitent return to God, humbled and converted by the judgments they have ſuffered, or their hardened wickedneſs, which would convince the captives of the righteous judgment of God upon them, *and ye ſhall be comforted concerning all the evil I have brought upon Jeruſalem*, pleaſed to ſee the bleſſed effects wrought thereby, if it led the ſufferers to repentance, or ſatiſfied in the juſtice of God in his ſeverity upon ſuch tranſgreſſors. *and they ſhall comfort you, when ye ſee their way and their doings*, either it would delight them to ſee the gracious ſymptoms of their converſion, or if they perſiſted in their abominations, they would no longer grieve for their ſufferings, but juſtify God in them, *and ye ſhall know that I have not done without cauſe, all that I have done in it, ſaith the Lord*, but that the Lord in all his diſpenſations is righteous, juſt, and good. *Note*, (1) Nothing will hereafter be matter of greater thankfulneſs to God's people, than thoſe bittereſt afflictions here which have contributed to their ſoul good. (2) God will be glorified in all his works, and his ſaints will adore and delight in them, even the puniſhment of the wicked ſhall redound to his honour, and miniſter matter for their praiſes.

CHAP

Before Christ 593

CHAP XV

The destruction of Jerusalem is foretold, under the similitude of a vine cast into the fire We have, 1 The uselessness of a withered or barren vine, ver 1—5 2 The dreadful application of it to Jerusalem, ver 6—8

1 AND the word of the LORD came unto me,
saying, 2 Son of man, what is the vine tree
more than any tree, *or than* a branch which is among
the trees of the forest? 3 Shall wood be taken thereof
to do any work? or will *men* take a pin of it to hang
a John xv 6 any vessel thereon? 4 Behold, [a] it is cast into the fire
for fuel; the fire devoureth both the ends of it, and
† Heb Will it prosper? the midst of it is burnt † is it meet for *any* work? 5
Behold, when it was whole it was meet for no work
how much less shall it be meet yet for *any* work, when
the fire hath devoured it, and it is burned? 6 ¶
Therefore thus saith the LORD God, As the vine-
tree among the trees of the forest, which I have given
to the fire for fuel, so will I give the inhabitants of
b Lev xvii 10. Chap xiv 8 Jerusalem. 7 And [b] I will set my face against them,
they shall go out from *one* fire, [c] and *another* fire shall
c Isa xxiv 18 Amos v 19. devour them [d] and ye shall know that I *am* the LORD,
d Chap. vi 7 & vii 4 when I set my face against them 8 And I will make
the land desolate, because they have ‡ committed a tres-
‡ Heb. Trespassed a trespass pass, saith the LORD God

v 1—8 Jerusalem, in its beauty, was the joy of the whole earth, but now that sin hath defiled it, the flames are kindling to devour her palaces

1 She is compared to a wild and barren vine, the most unprofitable and useless tree in the forest, unfit for any work, and only suited for fuel to the fire And if when flourishing it was not fit for any service, how much less when reduced to ashes, *v* 5

2 The application of this similitude to Jerusalem follows, *v* 6 This city, with the inhabitants thereof, as the unprofitable vine, is doomed to the flames, because of their great provocations, *v* 8 God's wrath is kindled, and his face, as an implacable enemy, set against them, they were wholly unprofitable, brought him no glory yea, noxious as the plants of a wild vine, therefore their land shall be desolate, the fire devour them, and one calamity on another pursue them, till they are utterly consumed, and God terribly made known to them, in the judgments he would execute upon them *Note*, Wrath pursues sinners, till it is perfected in the everlasting burnings

CHAP XVI.

In this long discourse is set forth, 1 The despicable and deplorable beginnings of the Jewish church and nation, ver 3—5 2 The many honours and favours God had bestowed upon them, ver 6—14 3 Their treacherous and ungrateful departures from him to idolatry, represented by the most impudent whoredom, ver 15—34 4 A threatening of terrible judgments for this sin, ver 35—43 5 An aggravation both of their sin and of their punishment, by comparing them with Sodom and Samaria, ver 44—59 6 A promise of mercy to a penitent remnant, ver 60—63

1 AGAIN the word of the LORD came unto
me, saying, 2 Son of man, cause Jerusalem
to know her abominations, 3 And say, Thus saith
a Isa 10 [illegible] the LORD God unto Jerusalem, [a] Thy birth, and thy
nativity *is* of the land of Canaan, [b] thy father *was* an
b Ver 45 Amorite, and thy mother an Hittite 4 And *as for*
c Hos ii 3 thy nativity [c] in the day thou wast born, thy navel was
† Or when I looked upon thee not cut, neither wast thou washed in water † to supple
thee thou wast not salted at all, nor swaddled at all
5 None eye pitied thee, to do any of these unto thee,
to have compassion upon thee, but thou wast cast out
in the open field, to the lothing of thy person, in the
day that thou wast born

v 1—5 Ezekiel hath a commission here given him to prophecy against Jerusalem Abominations great and aggravated were in her, and he is to cause her to know them, it would leave her and the inhabitants inexcusable if they rejected the admonition And as nothing is more hateful than ingratitude, he must remind them of their base original and wretched state, when God was pleased to distinguish them with his favours, and upbraid them with their infamous unthankfulness

1 They were in their original vile and despicable *Thy birth, and thy nativity is of the land of Canaan* there Abraham sojourned, and the patriarchs and the Jewish nation seemed as if sprung from thence, whilst their descendants, in their temper and manners, copied too closely after the Canaanites, whose land they possessed *Thy father was an Amorite, and thy mother an Hittite*, not literally, for Abraham and Sarah were Chaldeans, but they were before their call idolaters like them, and by dwelling afterwards among them, were reckoned as natives of the soil, and in their practices the Jewish people imitated these wicked nations,

2 They were as a miserable helpless infant, abandoned the moment it was born, exposed in its blood without a friendly hand to wash, supple, or swaddle the wretched babe, or a compassionate eye to pity it nay, contrariwise, loathed and abhorred, which seems to refer to the state of the Jewish people in Egypt, where their infants were exposed, themselves hated, oppressed, and ready to perish, if God's compassions had not interposed to rescue them from instant destruction, and what is said of them, may be applied with a beautiful propriety to all the Israel of God By nature corrupt and born in sin, loathsome in the eyes of God, none able or willing to wash away their guilt, exposed to unavoidable ruin, helpless and hopeless but for the interposition of divine grace

6 ¶ And when I passed by thee, and saw thee † pol- † Or trodden under foot
luted in thine own blood, I said unto thee *when thou*
wast in thy blood, Live yea, [a] I said unto thee *when* d Gen xii 3
thou wast in thy blood, Live 7 [e] I have ‡ caused thee e Ex i 7
to multiply as the bud of the field, and thou hast in- ‡ Heb Made thee a million
creased and waxen great, and thou art come to || excel- || Heb Ornament of ornaments
lent ornaments *thy* breasts are fashioned, and thine hair
is grown, whereas thou *wast* naked and bare 8 Now
when I passed by thee, and looked upon thee, behold, § Heb Lives
thy time *was* the time of § love, and [f] I spread my skirt f Ruth iii 9
over thee, and covered thy nakedness yea, I sware un-
to thee, and entred into a covenant with thee, saith
the LORD God, and [g] thou becamest mine 9 Then g Ex xix 5
washed I thee with water yea, [h] I throughly washed h Heb ix. 14
away thy † blood from thee, and [i] I anointed thee with † Heb. Bloods
oil 10 I clothed thee also with broidered work, and i 1 John ii 20
shod thee with badgers skin, and I girded thee about
with fine linen, and I covered thee with silk 11 I
decked thee also with ornaments, and [k] I put bracelets k Gen xxiv 22, 47
upon thine hands, and [l] a chain upon thy neck 12 l Cant i 10
And I put a jewel on thy ‡ forehead, and ear-rings in ‡ Heb Nose
thine ears, and a beautiful crown upon thine head 13 Isa iii 21
Thus wast thou decked with gold and silver, and thy
raiment *was of* fine linen, and silk, and broidered work,
thou didst eat fine flour, and honey, and oil and thou
wast exceeding beautiful, and thou didst prosper into a
kingdom 14 And thy renown went forth among the
heathen for thy beauty for it *was* perfect through my
comeliness [m] which I had put upon thee, saith the LORD m 1 Cor iv 7
God

v 6—14 Eminently great and distinguished were the favours God shewed this forlorn infant, the figure of the Jewish nation

1 God rescued them from ruin He saw them lying in their blood, and said unto them, *Live*, delivering them from the bondage of Egypt when they were ready to perish, and the like he doth for all his spiritual Israel He *sees* their misery, guilt, and helplessness, *passes by* them, in consequence of his eternal counsels of grace, speaks the life-giving word, opens the fountain for sin and for uncleanness in a Saviour's side, washes them from all their defilement, implants the principle of spiritual life, which shall endure to eternity

2 He multiplied them, so that they grew up as an infant to woman's stature, and became marriageable, adorned them as a bride, with jewels, the spoil of the Egyptians, *v* 7 washed and anointed them, not only from the reproach of servitude, but arrayed them with gorgeous apparel, gave them abundance of good things, erected them into a great kingdom and set up his sanctuary among them, *v* 9—13 and this may be applied to the gifts and graces of God's Spirit, wherewith he beautifies the souls of the redeemed, and to the righteousness of the Redeemer, in which arrayed, his people appear glorious in the eyes of the holy God

3 He loved them, and espoused them to himself in an everlasting covenant *He spread his skirt over them*, their husband and protector, and as a wife of youth, so warmly and tenderly did he regard them so that *thy time was a time of love*, he not only dealt with them in a way of singular affection, but they also professed themselves wholly his, to love, enjoy, obey him And at Sinai the marriage-contract might be said to be signed, God there engaging to be their God, and they in return solemnly pledging their fidelity to him *Note*, (1) When God

hath

Before Christ 593

first manifests his grace to the miserable sinner, and plucking him as a brand from the belly of hell, shews him his deadly guilt cancelled by redeeming love, and heaven open to receive him; that *time* is emphatically *a time of love*, as God's people have proved by delightful experience (2) If God be ours in a covenant of promise, confirmed by an oath for our greater consolation, we are bound by every tie of love and duty to approve our fidelity before him (3) The soul that is sheltered under the skirt of divine protection, is safe from the fear of evil

4 As he made them great by his favour, he raised their fame high among the nations around them, v 14 They saw and admired their beauty, and in the happy days of David and Solomon, nothing seemed wanting to render the national happiness compleat, when without they were revered and honoured, and within enjoyed peace and plenty, the upright administration of justice, and the most abundant means of grace such *perfect comeliness* had *God put* on them *Note*, (1) Every true Israelite is perfect and compleat in the righteousness of his Redeemer (2) All his comeliness is from God's gift, and must be acknowledged to his glory we have nothing we have not received

15 ¶ But thou didst trust in thine own beauty, and
ⁿ playedst the harlot because of thy renown, and pour-
edst out thy fornications on every one that passed by
his it was 16 And ° of thy garments thou didst take,
and deckedst thy high places with divers colours, and
playedst the harlot thereupon *the like things* shall not
come, neither shall it be *so* 17 ᵖ Thou hast also taken
thy fair jewels of my gold and of my silver, which I
had given thee, and madest to thyself images † of men,
and didst commit whoredom with them 18 And
tookest thy broidered garments, and coveredst them
and thou hast set mine oil and mine incense before them
19 My meat also which I gave thee, fine flour, and
oil, and honey *wherewith* I fed thee, thou hast even
set it before them for ‡ a sweet savour and *thus* it was,
saith the LORD God 20 Moreover, ᑫ thou hast taken
thy sons and thy daughters, whom thou hast born unto
me, and these thou hast sacrificed unto them, to be de-
voured *is this* of thy whoredoms a small matter, 21
That thou hast slain my children, and delivered them
to cause them to pass through *the fire* for them? 22
And in all thy abominations and thy whoredoms thou
hast not remembered the days of thy youth, ʳ when thou
wast naked and bare, *and* ˢ wast polluted in thy blood
23 And it came to pass after all thy wickedness (ᵗ wo,
wo unto thee, saith the LORD God) 24 *That* ᵘ thou
hast also built unto thee ‖ an eminent place, and ˣ hast
made thee an high place in every street 25 Thou
hast built thy high place at every head of the way,
and hast made thy beauty to be abhorred, and hast
opened thy feet to every one that passed by, and mul-
tiplied thy whoredoms 26 Thou hast also committed
fornication ʸ with the Egyptians thy neighbours, great
of flesh, and ᶻ hast increased thy whoredoms, to provoke
me to anger 27 Behold therefore, I have stretched
out my hand over thee, and have diminished thine or-
dinary *food*, and delivered thee unto the will of them
that hate thee, ᵃ the daughters of the Philistines *which
are* ashamed of thy lewd way 28 ᵇ Thou hast played
the whore with the Assyrians, because thou wast unsa-
tiable yea, thou hast played the harlot with them,
and yet couldst not be satisfied 29 Thou hast more-
over multiplied thy fornication in the land of Canaan
ᶜ unto Chaldea, and yet thou wast not satisfied herewith.
30 How weak is thine heart, saith the LORD God,
seeing thou dost all these *things*, the work of an impe-
rious whorish woman? 31 In that ᵈ thou buildest thine
eminent place in the head of every way, and makest
thine high place in every street, and hast not been as an
harlot (in that thou scornest hire.) 32 *But as* a wife
that committeth adultery, *which* taketh strangers instead
of her husband 33 They give gifts to all whores, but
thou givest thy gifts to all thy lovers, and § hirest them
that they may come unto thee on every side for thy
whoredom 34 And the contrary is in thee from *other*
women in thy whoredoms, whereas none followeth thee
to commit whoredoms and in that thou givest a re-
ward, and no reward is given unto thee; therefore thou
art contrary.

ⁿ Isa i 21 & lvii 8 Jer ii 20 & iii 2, 6, 20 Chap xxiii 3 12
° 2 Kings xxiii 7 Chap vii 20 Hos ii 8
ᵖ Ex xxxii 2 4 2 Chron xxviii 24
† Heb Of a male
‡ Heb Or a savour of rest
ᑫ 2 Kings xvi 3 Ps cvi 37 Isa lvii 5 Chap xx 26 & xxxvii 23
ʳ Ver 7
ˢ Ver 6
ᵗ Isa iii 11.
ᵘ Ver 31
‖ Or brothel house
ˣ Isa xxxvii 5, 7 Jer ii 20
ʸ Isa xxx 2.
ᶻ Chap viii 10 14 & xxiii 1,,20
ᵃ 2 Chron xxviii 18 Ver 57
ᵇ 2 Kings xvi 10 2 Chron xxviii 23 Jer ii 18, 36 Chap xxiii 12, &c Hos v 13
ᶜ Chap xxiii 14
ᵈ Ver 24, 39
ᵉ Isa xxx 6 Hos viii 9
§ Heb Bribest

v 15—34 The peculiar favours which the Jewish people had received, exceedingly aggravated the guilt of their apostacy

1 They grew proud of their distinguished mercies, forgot their original meanness, v 22 trusted on their beauty, and forsook the rock of their salvation to *play the harlot* with dumb idols, v 15 *Note*, (1) The pride of beauty hath often proved the bane of its possessor (2) Forgetfulness of God and ourselves, is at the bottom of all our sinful departures from him

2 They ran into the grossest idolatry *Thou pouredst out thy fornications on every one that passed by, his it was* as a common strumpet prostitutes herself to every passenger, so ready were they to embrace every new deity that offered, *multiplying their whoredoms*, ver 25 beyond all other nations Lavish on these wretched paramours, their high places, like the harlot's bed, were decked with *diverse colours*, and the jewels God had given them employed to fashion and adorn their idols *The like things shall not come, neither shall it be so*, no such scandalous idolatry ever was, or shall be practised again, v 16, 17 Before the images, the work of their own hands, they lavished their incense and offerings, counting nothing too much to spend in the gratification of their lusts, v 18 *Thus it was, saith the Lord God*, open, avowed, and notorious, v 19 And as if all the rest had not been enough, their very children, those dearest gifts of God, shocking to relate, they had sacrificed to these hated deities inhuman, barbarous, unnatural, and robbing God of the property he claimed in them They are *my children*, saith he, v 21 not only as he had given them life and being, but as having adopted them in a peculiar covenant to be his people *Is this of thy whoredoms a small matter?* ver 20 Some, perhaps, affected to treat them as such, though so heinous and terrible, or the sense is, their other wickedness was great, but this the summit of iniquity With open effrontery, as a hardned whore, whose forehead is brass, and knows no shame, so had *they built an eminent place*, or a *brothel*, had set up their idol temples and altars in every street, and in the highway, sitting there as the harlot exposed, v 25 to inflame the passers by, and draw them in to commit adultery and idolatry, making their beauty abhorred of God and all good men, yea, of the very heathen, as a strumpet despicable and hated by those to whom she hath prostituted herself And her weakness herein appeared great as her wickedness, v 30 therefore a fearful wo is denounced against her, v 23 the dreadful effects of which will be seen in time and in eternity *Note*, (1) Our gold and silver are not our own, but God's, and to him we are accountable for the use we make of them (2) The lavishness of idolaters should shame the niggardliness of the worshippers of the true God (3) They who bring up their children in pride and vanity, and by their ill examples encourage them in sin, are more grievously guilty than even these idolaters the one only murdered their bodies, the others also murder their souls, and sacrifice them to devils (4) Many make light of sin now as a small matter, but the punishment of it will be found insupportably heavy (5) Wickedness and weakness are inseparably connected None but fools could barter the momentary pleasures of sin for the eternal torments of hell

3 There were peculiar circumstances attending their sins, which rendered them exceedingly aggravated

(1) Their insatiable lust after new gods, v 28. ever doting on the idols of those nations from whom they had suffered most grievously They committed fornication with the Egyptians, Assyrians, and Canaanites, and nothing seemed too far fetched, or too dearly bought, so great was their rage for idolatry, and after all they could *not be satisfied*, but still craved for more. *Note*, (1) Lawless lust is ever tormenting, craving, insatiate (2) They who forsake God can never find abiding satisfaction in any thing beside

(2) Their unhumbled obstinacy under the rebukes God had given them, v 27 His heavy hand had been again and again laid on them he would have brought them to repentance under his chastisements The famine wasted them, the Philistines ravaged their country, 2 *Chron* xxviii 18, 19 and even these idolaters were ashamed of the inconstancy of the Jewish people in so often changing their gods yet every correction left them still hardened, and they sinned yet more and more *Note*, When neither mercies draw, nor corrections bend, the case seems utterly desperate

(3) Their diversity from all other people, v 31—34 Other harlots prostituted themselves for hire, and gained something by their wickedness, but they, as a shameless adulteress, not for want, but merely for lewdness sake, not only courted but hired their lovers at a vast expence, contracting alliances with the Assyrians and Egyptians, 2 *Kings* xvi 8 *Isa* xxx 6, 7 soliciting their friendship, and hiring their gods for protectors

35 ¶ Wherefore, O ᶠ harlot, hear the word of the ᶠ Jer iii 1.
LORD 36 Thus saith the LORD God, Because
thy filthiness was poured out, and thy nakedness dis-
covered through thy whoredoms with thy lovers, and
with all the idols of thy abominations, and by the
blood

Before Christ 593

blood of thy children, which thou didst give unto
them, 37 Behold therefore, [g] I will gather all thy
lovers, with whom thou hast taken pleasure, and all
them that thou hast loved, with all *them* that thou hast
hated. I will even gather them round about against
thee, and will discover thy nakedness unto them, that
they may see all thy nakedness 38 And I will judge
thee, † as [h] women that break wedlock, and shed blood,
are judged, and I will give thee blood in [i] fury and
jealousy 39 And I will also give thee into their hand,
and they shall throw down [k] thine eminent place, and
shall break down thy high places they shall [l] strip thee
also of thy clothes, and shall take thy fair jewels, and
leave [m] thee naked and bare 40 They shall also bring
up a company against thee, and [n] they shall stone thee
with stones, and thrust thee through with their swords
41 And [o] they shall burn thine houses with fire, and
execute judgments upon thee in the sight of many wo-
men and I will cause thee to cease from playing the
harlot, and thou also shalt give no hire any more 42.
So [p] will I make my fury towards thee to rest, and my
jealousy shall depart from thee, and I will be quiet,
and will be no more angry 43 Because [q] thou hast not
remembred the days of thy youth, but hast fretted me
in all these *things*, behold therefore, [r] I also will recom-
pense thy way upon *thine* head, saith the LORD God,
and thou shalt not commit this lewdness, above all thine
abominations

v 35—43 It cannot be thought possible such a guilty land should long be spared God's justice requires vengeance to be executed on such a nation as this

1 Her crimes are recited, that God may appear righteous in his judgments Her filthy idolatries, the blood of murdered infants, her shameless lewdness, her base ingratitude, her long repeated provocations, which God speaks of as having grieved and *fretted* him to behold, *v* 43 these were her sins, too flagrant to be denied, and too hainous to admit of excuse

2 Sentence is pronounced upon her Murder and adultery were capital crimes, and therefore her judgment is an ignominious death Both those who loved and they who hated her will be spectators of her fall, yea, they shall be made the executioners of vengeance upon her, shall strip her of all her wealth and ornaments, and leave her naked to her shame, *v* 37 As a jealous husband, and as the avenger of blood, God will punish her, *v* 38 *she shall be stoned, and thrust through with swords*, when the Chaldean army battered down the walls of Jerusalem, massacred the inhabitants, destroyed the high places, and burnt the city with fire Thus God will recompense her according to her deserts, *v* 43 and make her a public example to *other women*, to the nations around, who, seeing her plagues, might be deterred from her sins, *v* 41 *Note*, (1) God justly makes those our tormentors to whom we have been tempters (2) Whatever sinners suffer, it is no more than their just desert (3) The judgments inflicted on others should warn us against their wicked ways.

3 When God hath destroyed their idolatry, then he will rest from his fury, his jealousy shall depart, and the effects of his anger be removed The captivity cured the Jews effectually of all inclination to idolatry, and then the controversy ceased, and God restored them again to their own land Though some understand this of their utter ruin and destruction, when they should no more be able to play the harlot, and when God, having executed his wrath upon them, he would rest satisfied in the righteous doom under which they perished, *v* 42 *Note*, Sin is at the root of all God's controversies with us when the cause is removed the effect will cease

44 ¶ Behold, every one that useth proverbs, shall
use *this* proverb against thee, saying, As *is* the mother,
so is her daughter 45 Thou *art* thy mother's daugh-
ter, that lotheth her husband and her children, and thou
art the sister of thy sisters, which lothed their husbands
and their children [s] your mother *was* an Hittite, and
your father an Amorite 46 And thine ‖ elder sister
is Samaria, she and her daughters that dwell at thy left
hand [t] and ‖ thy younger sister that dwelleth at thy
right hand, *is* Sodom and her daughters 47 Yet hast
thou not walked after their ways, nor done after their
abominations but as *if that were* a very little *thing*,
thou wast corrupted more than they in all thy ways
48 *As* I live, saith the LORD God, [u] Sodom thy sister
hath not done, she nor her daughters, as thou hast done,
thou and thy daughters 49 Behold, this was the ini-
quity of thy sister Sodom, pride, [x] fulness of bread, and
abundance of idleness was in her and in her daughters,
neither did she strengthen the hand of the poor and
needy 50 And they were haughty, and [y] committed
abomination before me therefore [z] I took them away
as I saw *good* 51 Neither hath Samaria committed half
of thy sins, but thou hast multiplied thine abominations
more than they, and [a] hast justified thy sisters in all thine
abominations which thou hast done 52 Thou also
which hast judged thy sisters, bear thine own shame for
thy sins that thou hast committed more abominable
than they they are more righteous than thou yea, be
thou confounded also, and bear thy shame, in that thou
hast justified thy sisters 53 [b] When I shall bring again
thy captivity, [c] the captivity of Sodom and her daugh-
ters, and the captivity of Samaria and her daughters,
then *will I bring again* the captivity of thy captives in
the midst of them 54 That thou mayst [d] bear thine
own shame, and mayst be confounded in all that thou hast
done, in that [e] thou art a comfort unto them 55 When
thy sisters, Sodom and her daughters, shall return to
their former estate, and Samaria and her daughters shall
return to their former estate, then thou and thy daugh-
ters shall return to your former estate 56 For thy
sister Sodom was not mentioned by thy mouth in the
day of thy ‖ pride 57 Before thy wickedness was dis-
covered, as at the time of *thy* [f] reproach of the daughters
of § Syria, and all *that are* round about her, [h] the
daughters of the Philistines, which † despise thee round
about 58 [h] Thou hast born thy lewdness, and thine a-
bominations, saith the LORD 59 For thus saith the
LORD God, I will even deal with thee as thou hast
done which hast despised the oath [i] in breaking the
covenant

Before Christ 593

v 44—59 The wickedness of the Jewish people is here further described by comparison with other nations

1 They were as bad as the Canaanites, whom the Lord had cast out before them They who use proverbs, shall say, *As is the mother, so is the daughter*, they exactly copied the manners of these nations, and seemed rather sprung from an Hittite and Amorite, than from Abraham and Sarah They bore the true character of an adultress, *lothing her husband and children*, so did they forsake God their husband for idols, and sacrifice their children to them, as the Canaanites had done before them, though so awfully warned against their wicked ways, *Lev* xviii 27, 28

2 They not only resembled, but exceeded the wickedness of Sodom and Samaria *Thou art the sister of thy sisters*, like them in all their abominations, apostate from God, and devoted to the most shocking idolatry Samaria, at *the left hand*, towards the north, is called the *elder*, or *greater sister*, because the metropolis of the ten tribes, whilst Jerusalem was only at the head of two and Sodom, *her younger sister*, because a smaller city, and lay at her right hand towards the south, with her *daughter* villages The sins of Sodom are particularly marked, *v* 49 Pride, gluttony, idleness, uncharitableness, oppression and Jerusalem had equalled, yea, exceeded them in all, not content to walk in their ways, she grew more corrupt and abominable in her doings, nor had her sister Samaria half her guilt, *v* 51 Her idols were more numerous, and her sins more aggravated by the means and mercies she had enjoyed She had judged them formerly, and severely censured and condemned them and their wickedness, 2 *Chron* xiii 8—10. but now her conduct justified and patronized all their iniquities, *v* 57 and comforted them with the plea, that the men of Judah were as bad, or worse than they, *v* 54 with shame and confusion therefore ought she to be covered, for her more grievous transgressions, either in repentance for them, or suffering the punishment due to them And another cause also for shame is suggested, *v* 56 *For thy sister Sodom was not mentioned by thy mouth in the day of thy pride*, in their prosperity they disdained the mention of the name of Sodom, or, they took no warning by her doom, to tremble for their own *Note*, (1) Pride is at the root of all sin (2) Excess and idleness are the fuel to vile affections (3) Let those who read Sodom's sins, tremble for themselves, least the abuse of their blessings should lead them into the same guilt and ruin (4) The advantages we enjoy are a great aggravation of our sins the same action is doubly guilty in those who sin against light and love (5) Sinners must be confounded, either with the shame of penitents here, or with the everlasting shame of reprobates in the day of visitation (6) Pride goeth before destruction, they who will not be warned must be ruined

3 Their judgments would be heavy, as those which fell on the devoted cities of Sodom and Samaria God had already in a measure humbled their pride, in the discovery of their wicked-

Before Christ 593

neſs, evident in the reproach and inſults they ſuffered from the Philiſtines and Syrians, 2 *Chron* xxviii 5 Thus they had begun to bear the puniſhment of their lewdneſs and abominations, *v* 50 and God will deal with them farther, as *they had done*, rejecting them for his people as they had rejected him for their God, deſpiſing the oath, and breaking the covenant they had made at Sinai They are doomed to a miſerable captivity, and Sodom and Samaria ſhall ſooner be reſtored than they for however the penitent remnant ſhould be recovered, the wicked would be utterly abandoned to ruin, *Jer* xxiv 9, 10 Though ſome underſtand this of the converſion of the Jews, when the fulneſs of the Gentiles is come in *Note*, (1) Sin and the curſe are inſeparable (2) They who make themſelves vile by their wickedneſs, God will make them viler ſtill by their ſufferings (3) Companions in ſin will ſhare the ſame fate, and periſh together (4) They who reject God, are juſtly rejected by him

60 ¶ Neverthele/s, I will remember my covenant
with thee in the days of thy youth, and [l] I will eſta-
bliſh unto thee an everlaſting covenant 61 Then
[i] thou ſhalt remember thy ways, and be aſhamed, when
thou ſhalt receive thy ſiſters, thine elder and thy
younger and I will give them unto thee for [m] daugh-
ters, [n] but not by thy covenant 62 And I will eſta-
bliſh my covenant with thee, and thou ſhalt know
that I *am* the LORD · 63 That thou mayſt re-
member and be confounded, and [o] never open thy
mouth any more becauſe of thy ſhame, when I am pa-
cified toward thee for all that thou haſt done, ſaith the
Lord GOD

[l] Jer. xxxii 40 &c. [i] Chap xx 43 [m] Ifa liv 1 & lx 4 Gal iv 26 &c [n] Jer xxxi 31 &c [o] Rom iii 19

v 60—63 The chapter cloſes with a gleam of hope, and mercy yet triumphs over judgment Though *they* were falſe and faithleſs, God is true, and his covenant of grace ſhall yet have its accompliſhment in the remnant reſerved by him in the days of the Meſſiah, to which the promiſe here hath an evident regard God will remember his covenant in rich mercy, and eſtabliſh it with them for ever in Chriſt Jeſus, the effects of which ſhould be,

1 Their deep and unfeigned humiliation Overcome with the ſenſe of his pardoning grace and love, they ſhall remember their ways, and be confounded for all their abominations, ſilenced, nor daring to complain of God's judgments, but acknowledging their deſerts, and the more firmly they are aſſured of his being pacified towards them, the more deeply ſhall they upbraid their own ingratitude againſt a God ſo gracious *Note*, (1) The great argument to engage us to evangelical repentance, is a ſenſe of God's reconciliation in Chriſt Jeſus None abhor themſelves ſo thoroughly, as thoſe who believe his love moſt aſſuredly (2) We are called upon ever to remember our ways, and be confounded, though God hath forgiven us, we ſhould never forgive ourſelves

2 He promiſes to bring the Gentiles into the communion of his church The heathen lands, once their ſiſters in iniquity, ſhall now be admitted with the Jews into the fellowſhip of the goſpel, to ſhare all the bleſſings and privileges thereof, and ſhall be received by them with warm affection *but not by thy covenant*, not by the Sinai covenant, not on condition of obſerving the ceremonial rites and inſtitutions, or not in virtue of their ſubmitting to the terms which the Jews, as conquerors, ſhould impoſe on them, who, under their carnal Meſſiah, flattered themſelves with extenſive empire no, but by the covenant of grace, in which there is no diſtinction between Jew or Gentile, both alike being called freely, and entitled to all the promiſed mercies through faith in the Redeemer.

3. God will herein make his glory eminently to appear *Thou ſhalt know that I am the Lord* he had often before threatned them to make himſelf known in judgment, now he will be known in mercy His faithfulneſs to his promiſes, and his rich grace, ſhall be manifeſted to them, and to their everlaſting comfort, in an everlaſting covenant eſtabliſhed in Chriſt Jeſus, they ſhall experience his everlaſting love

CHAP XVII

The perfidy of Zedekiah and the ruin of Judah, in conſequence of his rebellion, is the ſubject of this chapter, where God by the prophet, 1 *Threatens the ruin of him and his kingdom, by a parable of two eagles and a vine,* ver 1—10 *and the rendition of that parable,* ver 11—21 2 *He promiſeth hereafter to raiſe the royal family of Judah again in the Meſſiah and his kingdom,* ver 22—24

1 AND the word of the LORD came unto me,
ſaying, 2 Son of man, put forth a riddle,
and ſpeak a parable unto the houſe of Iſrael, 3 And
ſay, Thus ſaith the Lord GOD, A great eagle with
great wings, [a] long winged, full of feathers, which had
† divers colours, came unto Lebanon, and [b] took the
higheſt branch of the cedar 4 He cropt off the top
of his young twigs, and carried it into a land of traf-
fick, he ſet it in a city of merchants 5 [c] He took
alſo of the ſeed of the land, and ‡ planted it in a fruit-
ful field, he placed *it* by great waters, *and* ſet it *as* a
willow-tree 6 And [d] it grew and it became a ſpread-
ing vine of low ſtature, whoſe branches turned toward
him, and the roots thereof were under him ſo it be-
came a vine, and brought forth branches, and ſhot forth
ſprigs 7 There was alſo [e] another great eagle with
great wings, and many feathers, and behold, this vine
did bend her roots toward him, and ſhot forth her
branches toward him, that he might water it by the
furrows of her plantation 8 It was planted in a
good § ſoil by great waters, that it might bring forth
branches, and that it might bear fruit, that it might
be a goodly vine 9 Say thou, Thus ſaith the Lord
GOD, Shall it proſper? ſhall he not pull up the roots
thereof, and cut off the fruit thereof, that it wither?
it ſhall wither in all the leaves of her ſpring, even
without great power, or many people to pluck it up by
the roots thereof. 10 Yea behold, *being* planted, ſhall
it proſper? [f] ſhall it not utterly wither, when the eaſt-
wind toucheth it? it ſhall wither in the furrows where
it grew 11 Moreover, the word of the LORD came
unto me, ſaying, 12 [g] Say now to the rebellious houſe,
Know ye not what theſe *things mean*? tell *them*, Be-
hold, [h] the king of Babylon is come to Jeruſalem, and
hath taken the king thereof, and the princes thereof,
and led them with him to Babylon 13 And hath
taken of the king's ſeed, and made a covenant with
him, [i] and hath ‖ taken an oath of him he hath alſo
taken the mighty of the land 14 That the king-
dom might be baſe, that it might not lift itſelf up,
† *but* that by keeping of his covenant it might ſtand
15 But [k] he rebelled againſt him in ſending his am-
baſſadors into Egypt, [l] that they might give him horſes
and much people [m] ſhall he proſper? ſhall he eſcape
that doth ſuch *things*? or ſhall he break the covenant,
and be delivered? 16 *As* I live, ſaith the Lord GOD,
ſurely [n] in the place *where* the king *dwelleth* that made
him king, whoſe oath he deſpiſed, and whoſe covenant
he brake, *even* with him, in the midſt of Babylon he
ſhall die 17 Neither ſhall Pharaoh with *his* mighty
army and great company make for him in the war [o] by
caſting up mounts, and building forts to cut off many
perſons. 18 Seeing he deſpiſed the oath, by breaking
the covenant, (when lo, he had given his hand) and
hath done all theſe *things*, he ſhall not eſcape 19
Therefore thus ſaith the Lord GOD, *As* I live, ſurely
mine oath that he hath deſpiſed, and my covenant that
he hath broken, even it will I recompenſe upon his own
head 20 And I will [p] ſpread my net upon him, and
he ſhall be taken in my ſnare, and I will bring him to
Babylon, and will plead with him there for his treſpaſs
that he hath treſpaſſed againſt me 21 And [q] all his
fugitives with all his bands ſhall fall by the ſword, and
they that remain ſhall be ſcattered towards all winds
[r] and ye ſhall know that I the LORD have ſpoken *it*

[a] Mat xiii 1 [?] Dan iv 22 † Heb. Embroidering b 2 Kings xxiv 12 c 2 Kings xxiv 17 ‡ Heb Put it in a field of ſeed d Chap xix 11 e Ver 15 § Heb Field f Chap xix 12 Hoſ xiii 15 g Chap ii 3 h 2 Kings xxiv 12 & i 2 Chron xxxvi 13 ‖ Heb Brought him to an oath † Heb to keep his covenant, to ſtand to it k 2 Kings xxiv 20 l Iſa xxxi 1, 3 m Deut xvii 16 n Jer xxxii 5 & xxxix 7 Chap xii 13 o Jer xxxvii 7 Chap iv 2 p Chap xii 13 & xxxii 3 q Chap xii 14 r Chap v 13

v 1—21 We have here,

1 The riddle and parable Ezekiel is ordered to put forth to them, not that God would wrap up in obſcure expreſſions their approaching doom, but that, engaged by the method of propoſing it, they might pay greater attention to the warning

2 The explication of the riddle to the rebellious houſe of Judah, that they might not plead ignorance, but be left without excuſe

[1.] The great eagle, *v* 3 is Nebuchadnezzar, his *great and long wings* repreſent his vaſt dominions, and his coming to Lebanon, his invaſion of the land of Judea Jeconiah is the *higheſt branch* cropped by him; and the top of the young twigs, the princes of the land, and the ſeed-royal, which he carried into captivity to *a land of traffic*, to Babylon, the great mart and ſeat of the empire, *v* 4, 12 Zedekiah is *the ſeed of the land*, *v* 5 whom he *ſet with great circumſpection*, as the word ſignifies, in the fruitful field of Judea, having exacted from him an oath of allegiance, *v* 13 and thereupon appointed him king over much people, repreſented by *great waters*, having taken the mighty of the land as hoſtages for his fidelity, and that, weakened by their loſs, Zedekiah might be the leſs

Before Christ 593

inclined or able to rebel, v 14 and that though the kingdom ſtill remained, it might be baſe, reduced, and dependant upon the king of Babylon, and *by keeping of his covenant it might ſtand*, and flouriſh, though not in its former ſplendor, yet with comfort, peace, and dignity, as *a vine*, though *of a low ſtature*, whoſe branches turned towards Nebuchadnezzar, and the roots ſpread under him, ſafe and protected by his power, though ſubject to his diſpoſal and in this ſtate it *became a vine, and ſhot forth branches* The royal family increaſed, and for a while the people proſpered under Zedekiah's government, and might have grown greater, could they have been content with their ſtation *Note*, When by the providence of God we are reduced, it is our wiſdom, and will be our comfort, to ſubmit, and make the beſt improvement of our preſent ſtate, and then we ſhall find ſome good ariſing to us out of the evil

[2] The other great eagle, v 7 is the king of Egypt, with large and extenſive dominions, though not equal to the king of Babylon To him Zedekiah inclined, and though he was very flouriſhing in his preſent ſtate, under the dominion of Nebuchadnezzar, yet he could not bear his ſubjection, and turned his branches, ſent his ambaſſadors to Egypt, in order to obtain infantry and cavalry to ſupport him in the rebellion he meditated, and to *be watered by the furrows of her plantation*, as Egypt was by the Nile, hoping to be enriched and made great by this alliance with the Egyptians But they who are diſcontented with the ſtate Providence allots them, only plague themſelves by fighting againſt God, and aggravate the miſeries under which they are ſo impatient, as was Zedekiah's caſe For,

[3] God denounces his doom So far from being watered by Egypt, the vine ſhall wither in the furrows where it was planted, as a tree blaſted by the eaſt wind It ſhall be plucked up by the roots, and the fruit cut off, and this *without great power or many people*, any army being ſufficient to deſtroy that nation God hath devoted to ruin How can a wretch ſo perfidious, a covenant-breaker, hope to eſcape? v 15 By an oath, to ſhew the immutability of his counſel, God pronounces ſentence on the rebellious king, ungrateful to his benefactor, who left him a prince, when he might have bound him as a priſoner falſe to the oath of God, and faithleſs to his engagements, God will puniſh him for his perjury His Egyptian allies ſhall help in vain, v 17 and inſtead of ſuccouring Jeruſalem, ſhall be beaten themſelves Zedekiah's own forces, as cowards, ſhall flee, unable to ſtand in the day of battle, part ſlain with the ſword, and the ſhattered remains ſcattered to *the four winds*, v 21 Thus deſerted and helpleſs, he ſhall be taken in God's ſnare, delivered a priſoner to the victorious king of Babylon, whoſe covenant he broke, and die in captive bands in the land of Chaldea, the righteous vengeance due to his crimes and when this prediction ſhould be fulfilled, then at leaſt he ſhould be made to know that the Lord had ſpoken it, v 21 *Note*, (1) Oaths are ſacred things they who trifle with them, ſhall bear their judgment (2) Sinners will not now believe the threatnings of God againſt them, but the time will come, when they will be terribly convinced of their truth by fatal experience

22 ¶ Thus ſaith the Lord GOD, I will alſo take
of the higheſt branch of the high cedar, and will ſet
it, I will crop off from the top of his young twigs [a] a — a Iſa. xi 1 Jer xxiii 5 Zech. vi 8
tender one, and will plant *it* upon an high mountain
and eminent. 23 [b] In the mountain of the height of — b Pſ ii 6 Iſa ii 2, 3 Chap xx 40
Iſrael will I plant it and it ſhall bring forth boughs,
and bear fruit, [c] and be a goodly cedar and under it — c Mat xiii 32
ſhall dwell all fowl of every wing, in the ſhadow of — d Rev xi 15
the branches thereof ſhall they dwell. 24 And all
the trees of the field ſhall know that I the LORD
have brought down the high tree, have exalted the low
tree, have dried up the green tree, and have made the
dry tree to flouriſh [d] I the LORD have ſpoken, and
have done *it*.

v 22—24 In the midſt of the threatned deſolations we have a precious promiſe to ſupport the hopes of God's people, who might be ready to fear the royal line of David would be extinct, and the promiſe of the Meſſiah, who was to deſcend from him, be diſappointed

1 God will raiſe the tabernacle of David from its ruins out of the *cedar*, the Jewiſh nation, from the *higheſt branch*, the royal family of Judah, God will crop off a *tender* one, the Meſſiah, and *will plant it on a high mountain and eminent*, in the mount of God in glory, whither the Saviour aſcended after his reſurrection; or in his church on earth, the ſpiritual mount Zion, and from thence his boughs ſhall ſpread, fill the earth with fruit, and afford a ſafe ſhelter for fowl of every wing redeemed ſinners of all nations ſhall fly to him, and dwell under his ſhadow with delight, protected from every evil, and ſinging among the branches, happy in the experience of his love and favour Some apply this to Zerubbabel, in whom the line of David revived; but whatever reference it might have to him, we may venture to affirm, that a greater than Zerubbabel is here

Before Christ 593

2 God will be glorified in his work *As the trees of the field*, the nations of the earth, converted by the preaching of the goſpel, *ſhall know that I the Lord have brought down the high tree, have exalted the low tree, have dried up the green tree, and have made the dry tree to flouriſh*, which ſome interpret of the deſtruction of the Chaldean monarchy, and the reſtoration of the Jewiſh people others, of the ejection of the Jews, and the calling of the Gentiles, who ſeemed as a withered and dry tree, reſpecting all ſpiritual life and others, more generally, of the deſtruction of the kingdom of Satan, and the exaltation of the kingdom of Chriſt, which ſhall in the latter day ſpread univerſally, and endure to eternity *I the Lord have ſpoken, and have done it*, his word being as ſure as if it were already accompliſhed

CHAP XVIII

God will not only be juſt in all his dealings with men, but make his righteouſneſs appear We have here, 1 The corrupt proverb uſed by the profane Jews, ver 1—3 2 The reply given to it, in which God aſſerts in general his ſovereignty and juſtice ver 4 Pronounces a woe upon the wicked, ver 4, 20 and a bleſſing upon the righteous, ver 5—9 In particular, as to the caſe complained of, he aſſures us, (1) That it ſhall be ill with a wicked man, though he had a good father, ver 10—13 (2) That it ſhall be well with a good man, though he had a wicked father, ver 14—18 And therefore in this God is righteous, ver 19, 20 (3) That it ſhall be well with penitents, though they began never ſo ill, ver 21—23, 27, 28 (4) That it ſhall be ill with apoſtates, though they began never ſo well, ver 24, 26 And the uſe of all this is, (1) To clear the equity of all God's proceedings, ver 25, 29 (2) *To engage us to repent, and turn to God* ver 30—32 *And theſe are things which* belong to our *everlaſting* peace, *O that we may underſtand and regard them before they be* hid from our eyes!

1 THE word of the LORD came unto me again,
ſaying, 2 What mean ye, that ye uſe this
proverb concerning the land of Iſrael, ſaying, [a] The fa- — a Jer xxxi 29, Lam v 7
thers have eaten ſour grapes, and the children's teeth
are ſet on edge? 3 *As* I live, ſaith the Lord GOD,
ye ſhall not have *occaſion* any more to uſe this proverb
in Iſrael 4 Behold, all ſouls are mine, as the ſoul of
the father, ſo alſo the ſoul of the ſon is mine [b] the — b Rom vi 23
ſoul that ſinneth, it ſhall die 5 ¶ But if a man be
juſt, and [c] do † that which is lawful and right, 6 *And* — c Mic vi 8 † Heb judgment and juſtice
[d] hath not eaten upon the mountains, neither hath lift — d Chap xxii 9
up his eyes to the idols of the houſe of Iſrael, [e] neither — e Lev xviii 20 xx 10
hath defiled his neighbour's wife, neither hath come near
to [f] a menſtruous woman, 7 And hath not [g] oppreſſed — f Lev xviii 19 xx 18
any, *but* hath reſtored to the debtor [h] his pledge, hath — g Ex xxii 21 Lev xix 15 xxv 14
ſpoiled none by violence, hath [i] given his bread to the — h Ex xxii 26 Deut xxiv 12
hungry, and hath covered the naked with a garment, — i Deut xv 7 Iſa lviii 7 Mat xxv 35
8 He *that* hath not given forth [k] upon uſury, neither — k Ex xxii 25 Lev xxv 36 Deut xxiii 19 Neh v 7
hath taken any increaſe, *that* hath withdrawn his hand
from iniquity, hath executed true judgment between — l Zech viii 16
man and man 9 Hath walked in my ſtatutes, and
hath kept my judgments to deal truly, he *is* juſt, [m] he — m Hab ii 4
ſhall ſurely live, ſaith the Lord GOD

v 1—9 We have here,

1 The inſolent and impious proverb in uſe among the Jews, *The fathers have eaten ſour grapes, and the children's teeth are ſet on edge*, which implied a charge of injuſtice and cruelty in God, as if he puniſhed them for the ſins of their fathers, and they had themſelves done nothing to provoke the wrath under which they lay It was true indeed that, as a nation, their fathers ſins came into remembrance, but the abomination was theirs, that for them alone they ſuffered had they not copied after their forefathers wickedneſs they had never gone into captivity *Note*, When ſinners find fault with God, it is a ſure ſymptom their heart is yet hardened, and unhumbled under their ſufferings

2 The reproof God gives them hereupon *What mean ye, that ye uſe this proverb?* with ſuch a blaſphemous imputation God therefore will ſilence them, and ſwears by himſelf, they *ſhall* have occaſion to *uſe this proverb no more* He will inflict immediate judgment on the ſinners, and not defer it to another generation, and will make it manifeſt to themſelves and others, that their ſufferings are no more than their deſerts

3 He lays down the equitable method of his procedure He, as the eternal ſovereign, indeed is not bound to give us any account of his matters *All ſouls are his*, the work of his hands, accountable to him; and, as in mercy they have received their being from him, they may be aſſured he will do them no wrong

He

Before Christ 593

He waves however his right of ſovereignty, and eſtabliſhes a rule of judgment to which none can reaſonably object

(1) *The ſoul that ſinneth it ſhall die*, be expoſed to temporal judgments in this life, and his puniſhment not be deferred to another generation, which ſeems to be the meaning of the death here threatened, or he ſhall die eternally, ſeparated from the bliſsful preſence of God, and conſigned to the place of torment. Let impenitent ſinners hear and tremble

(2) *The juſt man ſhall live* and, that we may not miſtake, God gives his character in ſeveral particulars, both negatively and poſitively Happy for us will it be, if we can through grace call the character our own (1) He is no idolater, neither joins in the worſhip nor gives the leaſt countenance to the ſervice, hating both the idols and the things ſacrificed to them, never deigning to lift his eyes to the one, or to ſit down to feaſt on the other (2) He is no adulterer, nor lewd perſon, but poſſeſſes his veſſel in ſanctification and honour, neither by word or deed attempting the chaſtity of his neighbour's wife, nor in the time of her ſeparation approaching his own (3) He is not oppreſſive, by force or fraud depriving his neighbour of what is his juſt due, not taking advantage of his neceſſity, but reſtoring to the debtor his pledge when the redemption-money is paid, and, ſince the law had forbidden him to take uſury of his brethren, lending freely, hoping for nothing again (4) He is charitable to his power, feeding the hungry and cloathing the naked, willing to give, glad to diſtribute, and this not as depending on his works as meritorious, but actuated by a principle of love (5) He *withdraws his hand from iniquity*, will have no fellowſhip nor connection with wicked men or their deeds, and, if he hath been inadvertently drawn into evil, he haſtily returns, with grief and ſhame, to the right way (6) In all his dealings, either as a magiſtrate, a witneſs, a referee, or a man in buſineſs, he pays the ſtricteſt regard to truth and juſtice, and to his power deſires that every man may enjoy his right (7) To finiſh his character, he is not only juſt and merciful towards man, but pious towards God, *walking in God's ſtatutes*, making them the rule of his conduct, conſtant in his worſhip and ordinances, and *keeping God's judgments to deal truly*, never deviating from the line of juſtice God hath marked out *He is juſt* ſuch a converſation is an evidence to men of that righteouſneſs which by faith he poſſeſſes before God And *he ſhall ſurely live, ſaith the Lord God*, happy in the enjoyment of God's favour, exempted from the plagues which are the portion of the ungodly, and ſhall ſhortly live eternally with God in glory

† Or houſe-breaker n Numb. xxxv 31 — 10 ¶ If he beget a ſon *that is* a † robber, [n] a ſhed-
der of blood, and *that* doth the like to *any* one of theſe
things, 11 And that doth not any of thoſe *duties*, but
even hath eaten upon the mountains, and defiled his
neighbour's wife, 12 Hath oppreſſed the poor and
needy, hath ſpoiled by violence, hath not reſtored the
pledge, and hath lift up his eyes to the idols, hath com-
mitted abomination, 13 Hath given forth *upon* uſury,
and hath taken increaſe ſhall he then live? he ſhall not
o Ver 4 — live he hath done all theſe abominations, [o] he ſhall
p Lev xx 9 Chap iii 18 Acts xviii 6. — ſurely die, [p] his blood ſhall be upon him 14 ¶ Now
lo, *if* he beget a ſon that ſeeth all his father's ſins
which he hath done, and conſidereth, and doth not ſuch
like, 15 *That* hath not eaten upon the mountains,
neither hath lift up his eyes to the idols of the houſe of
Iſrael, hath not defiled his neighbour's wife, 16 Nei-
‡ Heb. Pledged the pledge, or taken to pledge — ther hath oppreſſed any, hath not ‡ withholden the
pledge, neither hath ſpoiled by violence, *but* hath given
his bread to the hungry, and hath covered the naked
with a garment, 17 *That* hath taken off his hand from
the poor, *that* hath not received uſury nor increaſe, hath
executed my judgments, hath walked in my ſtatutes,
he ſhall not die for the iniquity of his father, he ſhall
ſurely live 18 *As for* his father, becauſe he cruelly
oppreſſed, ſpoiled his brother by violence, and did *that*
which *is* not good among his people, lo, even he ſhall
q Ex xx 5 Deut v 9 — die in his iniquity 19 ¶ Yet ſay ye, Why? [q] doth
not the ſon bear the iniquity of the father? when the ſon
hath done that which is lawful and right, *and* hath kept
all my ſtatutes, and hath done them, he ſhall ſurely live
r Ver 4 s Deut xxiv 16 2 Kings xiv 6 2 Chron xxv 4 Jer xxxi 29 30 t Iſa iii 10 11 u Rom ii 9 — 20 [r] The ſoul that ſinneth, it ſhall die [s] the ſon ſhall
not bear the iniquity of the father, neither ſhall the father
bear the iniquity of the ſon; [t] the righteouſneſs of the
righteous ſhall be upon him, and [u] the wickedneſs of the
wicked ſhall be upon him.

v. 10—20 God, having laid down his method of procedure, applies it to particular caſes, demonſtrating the juſtice of his dealings, and the injuſtice of their cenſures

1 For the juſtice of his dealings he obſerves,

(1) That an ungodly ſon, though ſprung from a pious father, ſhall bear his own burden The caſe is not uncommon, for grace doth not run in the blood, nor is the moſt careful education always ſucceſsful the beſt of men have, to their grief, beheld the moſt ungodly children Dreadful are the ſins here ſuppoſed, and indeed uſually they grow moſt abandoned who ſin againſt the greateſt light and warnings This wicked ſon is deſcribed as the very reverſe to all goodneſs, a *robber*, a murderer, an idolater, an adulterer, an oppreſſor, an uſurer, in ſhort devoted to every abomination, the conſequence of which muſt be, *he ſhall not live* in the enjoyment of God's favour, or in peace in his poſſeſſions, he ſhall *ſurely die*, given up to the ſword of the enemy, or led captive, and, if he dies impenitent, conſigned to the eternal death of body and ſoul in hell, *his blood ſhall be upon him*, he hath only himſelf to blame for his deſtruction, his ſins the more aggravated and inexcuſable, and his miſery the more intolerable through the abuſe of the mercies he hath enjoyed

(2) The gracious ſon of a wicked father ſhall never fare the worſe for his deſcent from him And a happy thing it is when a child, inſtead of being influenced by his parent's ill example to imitate it, ſees, conſiders, and takes warning to ſhun thoſe vices to which they were addicted His character is the ſame deſcribed *v* 6 for all juſt men walk by the ſame rule, and mind the ſame things, and, being found in the ſame way, have the ſame bleſſed end, *he ſhall ſurely live*, and ſhall not die for his father's iniquity, but his graceleſs father, whoſe ways were perverſe before God, oppreſſive, unjuſt, and negligent of every good work, he ſhall bear his iniquity and periſh under it

2 Hence he infers the injuſtice of their cenſures *Yet ye ſay, Doth not the ſon bear the iniquity of the father?* No, in no wiſe He that doth *that which is lawful and right ſhall live*, but *the ſoul that ſinneth ſhall die*, whether father or ſon the ſon ſhall not be chargeable with his father's iniquity, nor the father, when he hath diſcharged his duty towards him, be anſwerable for the conduct of his ungodly ſon This is the ſettled rule of God's judgment *the righteouſneſs of the righteous ſhall be upon him*, he ſhall have the preſent and eternal comfort of well doing, *and the wickedneſs of the wicked ſhall be upon him*, cruſhing him down under temporal judgments, and ſinking him at laſt into the belly of hell

21 But [x] if the wicked will turn from all his ſins — x Chap xxxiii 12.
that he hath committed, and keep all my ſtatutes, and
do that which is lawful and right, he ſhall ſurely live,
he ſhall not die 22 All his tranſgreſſions that he hath
committed, [y] they ſhall not be mentioned unto him — y Heb. x 17
in his righteouſneſs that he hath done, he ſhall live
23 [z] Have I any pleaſure at all that the wicked ſhould — z Ver 32 Chap xxxiii 11 1 Tim ii 4 2 Pet iii 9
die? ſaith the LORD God *and* not that he ſhould
return from his ways and live? 24 ¶ But [a] when the
[b] righteous turneth away from his righteouſneſs, and — a Chap iii 20 1 Sam xv 11 b Matt xii 45 Luke xviii 9
[c] committeth iniquity, *and* doth according to all the abo-
minations that the wicked *man* doth ſhall he live? all
his righteouſneſs that he hath done ſhall not be men-
tioned, in his treſpaſs that he hath treſpaſſed, and in — c 2 Pet ii 20
his ſin that he hath ſinned, in them ſhall he die 25
¶ Yet ye ſay, [d] The way of the LORD is not equal — d Ver 29. Chap xxxiii 17 20.
Hear now, O houſe of Iſrael, [e] Is not my way equal? — e Gen xviii 25
[f] are not your ways unequal? 26 When a righteous — f Iſa i 4.
man turneth away from his righteouſneſs, and commit-
teth iniquity, and dieth in them; for his iniquity that
he hath done ſhall he die 27 Again, when the wick-
ed *man* turneth away from his wickedneſs that he hath
committed, and doth that which is lawful and right, he
ſhall ſave his ſoul alive 28 Becauſe [g] he conſidereth — g Ver 14.
and turneth away from all his tranſgreſſions that he hath
committed, he ſhall ſurely live, he ſhall not die 29
[h] Yet ſaith the houſe of Iſrael, The way of the LORD — h Ver 25
is not equal O houſe of Iſrael, are not my ways equal?
are not your ways unequal?

v. 21—29 The equity of the divine government is here further demonſtrated As God will not puniſh one man for the ſins of another, neither will he be rigorous to mark the tranſgreſſions of thoſe who return to him The finally impenitent only ſhall periſh

1 The ſinner that repents and turns to God ſhall ſurely live Not that of himſelf he is able to turn and change his own heart The work is God's to give repentance and this he doth, (1) By leading the ſinner to *conſider his ways*, *v* 28 giving him an enlightened knowledge of the evil and danger of ſin, and opening his eyes to a diſcovery of that guilt to which he was before a ſtranger; in conſequence of which, (2) He turns from ALL *his wickedneſs*, hating and forſaking it, and makes no allowed reſerve of the leaſt ſin (3) His obedience is ſincere and univerſal, *keeping all God's ſtatutes, and doing that which is*

lawful

Before Christ 593

lawful and right, according to his best knowledge of God's word, in simplicity and truth, though not in perfection And, when this is the case, he hath (4) an assured evidence of his pardon and acceptance with God, of which repentance indeed is not the cause but the effect His transgressions shall not only be forgiven but forgotten, not so much as *mentioned unto him*, to shame or upbraid him in the day of judgment (5) *He shall surely live, he shall not die* Which may be confined to that exemption from temporal calamities, which an external observance of the mosaical institutions seems to have secured, to which, rather than to real evangelical repentance, the context may then refer or we may interpret the life here promised of the enjoyment of God's love and favour both here and for ever, which are sure to all those who walk in righteousness and true holiness

2 God encourages sinners, from the views of his rich grace and mercy, to return to him *Have I any pleasure at all that the wicked should die? saith the Lord God?* No vengeance is his strange work, but mercy is his delight And though his justice is glorified in the punishment of the obstinately rebellious, yet he would rather glorify his grace in pardoning them, when *they turn from their ways and live* *Note*, The soul that perishes will have only himself to blame for his damnation

3 The righteous man who turns apostate will perish Not that one truly righteous ever will or can finally be cast away, but many who are professionally such, appear so before men, and count themselves righteous, do turn from their righteousness, cast off their profession, grow careless and outwardly profane and sensual, *commit iniquity* open and avowed, *according to all the abominations of the wicked*, joining with them, and in practice like them *Shall such live?* because of the former appearances of righteousness No Their good deeds, however many, will not be *mentioned* in their favour They turn back unto perdition, and die *in* their sins, v 24 and *for* them, v 26

4 God appeals to their consciences for the equity of his ways and the injustice of their reflections *Yet ye say the way of the Lord is not equal!* Impudently and blasphemously they dared arraign the divine justice at the bar of their partial self-love, though the procedure was so evidently equal and just nor could it possibly be otherwise, *the judge of all the earth* must needs *do right* The inequality therefore was in themselves, not in him he was righteous, but they had done wickedly, his judgments altogether just, their murmuring under them wicked as unreasonable

i Chap xviii 20 30 ⁱ Therefore I will judge you, O house of Israel,
every one according to his ways, saith the LORD God
k Matth iii 2 ᵏ repent, and turn † *yourselves* from all your transgres-
† Or others ver 3- sions, so iniquity shall not be your ruin 31 ¶ Cast
away from you all your transgressions, whereby ye have
l Jer xxxii 39 Chap xi 19 & xxxvi 26 transgressed, and make you a new heart, and a new
spirit, for why will ye die, O house of Israel? 32 For
m Lam iii 33 Chap xxxiii 11 2 Pet. iii 9 ᵐ I have no pleasure in the death of him that dieth,
saith the LORD God wherefore turn *yourselves*, and
live ye

v 30—32 The case being thus fairly stated, God's methods of procedure appear fully vindicated *I will judge you according to your ways*, giving to every man as his work is Yet, as their works and ways would so ill bear the severity of his enquiry, he lengthens their day of grace, and gives them yet space to repent, and an earnest invitation to engage them thereunto

1 He invites them to repent and live, *turning from all their transgressions* with shame and rooted aversion, and *casting* them *away*, with full purpose of heart never to return to them again And he calls on them *to make them a new heart and a new spirit*, thoroughly changed in all their tempers and dispositions, which though indeed their duty, yet God must give the power to enable them for what he doth command, *see chap* xi 19 and by his grace, preventing and following the word of exhortation he sends, it becomes effectual to the sinner's conversion

2 He enforces his invitation with various arguments [1] *So iniquity shall not be your ruin*, as otherwise it infallibly would be, for except we repent we must perish [2] God hath no delight in the sinner's death, and therefore expostulates, *Why will ye die, O house of Israel?* It is as pleasing to him to see the sinner turned from the evil of his ways, as it is unspeakably advantageous to ourselves They who refuse therefore to give him this satisfaction, sin against their own mercies, and die because they *will die* [3] Immortal life and glory are before us, if we truly turn to God *Turn yourselves, and live ye* And what can engage us, if these considerations are ineffectual

CHAP XIX

This chapter is a lamentation over the ruin of Judah and her kings of the illustrious house of David, ver 1. (1) The kingdom of Judah is here compared to a lioness, and the princes to lions, that were fierce and ravenous, but hunted down and taken in nets, ver 2—9 (2) The kingdom is compared to a vine, and the princes to branches, that had been strong and flourishing, but were now broken off and burnt, ver 10—14

1 MOreover, take thou up a lamentation for the
princes of Israel, 2 And say, What *is* thy
mother? A lioness she lay down among lions, she nou-
rished her whelps among young lions 3 And she
brought up ᵃ one of her whelps it became a young a 2 Chron. xxxvi 1
lion, and it learned to catch the prey, it devoured men
4 The nations also heard of him, he was taken in their
pit, and they ᵇ brought him with chains unto the land b 2 Kings xxiii 33 34
of Egypt 5 Now when she saw that she had waited, Jer xxii 11, 12
and her hope was lost, then she took ᶜ another of her
whelps, *and* made him a young lion 6 And ᵈ he went c 2 Kings xxiii 34
up and down among the lions, he became a young lion, d Jer xxii 13—17
and learned to catch the prey, *and* devoured men 7
And he knew their † desolate palaces, and ᵉ he laid waste † Or their widows
their cities, and the land was desolate, and the fulness e Jer xxii 17
thereof by the noise of his ᶠ roaring 8 ᵍ Then the f Prov xx 2
nations set against him on every side from the provinces, g 2 Kings xxiv 2
and spread their net over him he was taken in their pit
9 And ʰ they put him in ward in ‡ chains, and brought h 2 Chron xxxvi 6
him to the king of Babylon, they brought him into Jer xxii 18
holds, that his voice should no more be heard upon ‡ Or hooks
the mountains of Israel

v 1—9 We have here,

1 The prophet commanded to *take up a lamentation over the princes of Israel*, Jehoahaz, Jehoiakim, Jeconiah, and Zedekiah, whose mournful story would afford abundant matter for his grief *Note*, We should not only weep with those that weep, but over those also who never shed a tear for themselves

2 The Lord directs him what to say Under the figure of a lioness and her whelps he describes the kingdom and princes *The lioness, the mother*, is the tribe of Judah, ravening, fierce, full of rapine and injustice, *she lay down among lions*, joined in affinity with the neighbouring nations, and contracted alliances with them *She nourished her whelps among young lions*, brought up the young princes in principles of arbitrary power and oppression Jehoahaz, one of them, *became a young lion*, grown up, and seated on the throne of his father Josiah, *learned to catch the prey, and devoured men*, exercising the most tyrannical sway, and sparing neither the properties nor lives of his subjects, as his covetousness, his rage, or his caprice governed him *The nations also heard of him*, what oppression he used towards his people, and what designs he was forming to subdue his neighbours, and hereupon the Egyptians fell upon him, vanquished and led him away a prisoner into Egypt, where he died

Despairing of his return, the Jewish people advanced Jehoiakim to the throne, with the consent of Pharaoh, and he trod in the wicked steps of his predecessor, alike ravenous, arbitrary, and oppressive *He learned to catch the prey, he devoured men*, plundering his subjects and sacrificing their lives to his resentment *And he knew their desolate palaces*, ransacking them to discover the treasures concealed therein, or *he knew their widows*, when he had slain the husband he defiled their widows, and by his tyranny he drove his subjects from their cities, and made the land desolate through his roaring, neither their lives nor properties being any longer safe The nations hereupon collected under Nebuchadnezzar, surrounded him as a beast with toils, and he was taken prisoner as a lion in a pit, they bound him in chains and cast him into prison, where probably he quickly died, and was thrown on a dunghill, *see Jer* xxii 18, 19 and his roaring silenced, no more the terror of the mighty in the land of the living

10 ¶ Thy mother *is* ⁱ like a vine in thy ‖ blood, i Chap xvii 6
planted by the waters, she was fruitful, and full of ‖ Or quietness or likeness
branches by reason of many waters 11 And she had
strong rods, for the scepters of them that bear rule,
and her stature was exalted among the thick branches,
and she appeared in her height with the multitude of her
branches 12 But she was plucked up in fury, she was
cast down to the ground, and ᵏ the east-wind dried up k Chap xvii 10 Hos xiii 15
her fruit her strong rods were broken and withered, the
fire consumed them 13 And now she *is* planted in the
wilderness, in a dry and thirsty ground 14 And ˡ fire l Judg ix 15 Chap xvii 18
is gone out of a rod of her branches, *which* hath de-
voured her fruit, so that she hath ᵐ no strong rod *to be* m Jer lii 10
a scepter to rule ⁿ this *is* a lamentation, and shall be n Lam. iv 20
for a lamentation

v 10—14 The same persons, compared before to a lioness and her whelps, are here likened to a vine and its branches

1. *Thy mother*, the Jewish nation, *is like a vine in thy blood*, which,

Before Christ 593.

which, laid at the root, is said to contribute to its fertility, *planted by the waters*, enjoying the greatest advantages and privileges, *she was fruitful and full of branches by reason of many waters*, very rich and populous, *and she had strong rods for the scepters of them that bear rule*, many princes sprung from her, whose dignity was great, or the royal family was numerous, either of Joiakim or Zedekiah, to whom it may be referred, *and her stature was exalted among the thick branches*, the nation of the Jews was eminent and distinguished, *and appeared in her height with the multitude of her branches*, particularly in the glorious days of David and Solomon, when they were the admiration of the nations around them. But,

2. This vine *was plucked up in fury*. Having long provoked God by their sins, and Zedekiah by his rebellion filling up the measure of their iniquities, by the Chaldean army the country was utterly laid waste, the *strong rods broken, withered, burnt*, the king, princes, magistrates, slain or made captives. *And now she is planted in the wilderness, in a dry and thirsty ground*, carried to Babylon, where they suffered hard servitude: or this respects the remnant left in Judea, that by the ravages of the Chaldean army had been turned into a desert. *And a fire is gone out of a rod of her branches*: the rod is Zedekiah, and his rebellion the fire, *which hath devoured her fruit*, the people perishing by the famine, pestilence, and sword, during the siege of Jerusalem, *so that she hath no strong rod to be a scepter to rule*, Zedekiah being the last king of the house of David till the Messiah came. *This is a lamentation, and shall be for a lamentation*: the past desolations were grievous, but, instead of coming to an end, succeeding generations would have fresh cause to bemoan their miseries.

CHAP. XX.

In this chapter, 1. *The prophet is consulted by some of the elders of Israel*, ver. 1. 2. *He is instructed by God*, (1.) *To signify God's displeasure against them*, ver. 2, 3. *And*, (2.) *To shew them what just cause he had for that displeasure, by giving them a history of God's gracious dealings with their fathers, and their treacherous dealings with him*: [1.] *In Egypt*, ver. 1—9. [2.] *In the wilderness*, ver. 10—26. [3.] *In Canaan*, ver. 27—32. 3. *He must denounce the judgments of God against them*, ver. 33—36. 4. *He must tell them that God had mercy in store for them, that he would bring a remnant of them to repentance, re-establish them in their own land, and set up his sanctuary among them*, ver. 37—44. 5. *A word is dropped towards Jerusalem, which is explained in the next chapter*, ver. 45—49.

592
1 AND it came to pass in the seventh year, in
the fifth *month*, the tenth *day* of the month,
that [a] certain of the elders of Israel came to enquire of
the LORD, and sat before me. 2 Then came the
word of the LORD unto me, saying, 3 Son of man,
speak unto the elders of Israel, and say unto them, Thus
saith the LORD God, Are ye come to enquire of me?
as I live, saith the LORD God, [b] I will not be enquired
of by you. 4 [c] Wilt thou ‖ judge them, son of man,
wilt thou judge *them*? cause them to know the abominations of their fathers.

‖ Or plead for them.

v. 1—4. The date of this prophecy is in the seventh year of Jeconiah's captivity and Zedekiah's reign, the fifth month, the tenth day; and it was delivered on occasion of the elders of Israel, whether of the captivity, or from Jerusalem, coming to consult the prophet, as some suppose, from *v.* 32. whether they might not, to ingratiate themselves with their heathen masters, conform to their heathen worship: certain it is, whatever was the cause of their coming, their hearts were hypocritical, and the answer of God to them is full of wrath.

1. God refuses to be enquired of by them, *v.* 3. for they who draw near to God hypocritically, can expect no mercy at his hands; their very prayers will be turned into sin.

2. The prophet must arraign and condemn them; no more their advocate, but their accuser, and now constituted their judge to pronounce sentence upon them for all their own and their fathers abominations, *v.* 4.

5 ¶ And say unto them, Thus saith the LORD
God, In the day when [d] I chose Israel, and ‖ lifted up
mine hand unto the seed of the house of Jacob, and
made myself [e] known unto them in the land of Egypt,
when I lifted up mine hand unto them, saying, I *am*
the LORD your God; 6 In the day *that* I lifted up
mine hand unto them, to bring them forth of the land
of Egypt, into a land that I had espied for them, flowing with milk and honey, [f] which *is* the glory of all
lands: 7 Then said I unto them, Cast ye away every
man the abominations of his eyes, and defile not yourselves with the idols of Egypt: I *am* the LORD your
God. 8 But they rebelled against me, and would not
hearken unto me: they did not every man cast away
the abominations of their eyes, neither did they forsake
the idols of Egypt: then I said, I will pour out my fury
upon them, to accomplish my anger against them in the
midst of the land of Egypt. 9 [h] But I wrought for
my name's sake, that it should not be polluted before
the heathen, among whom they *were*, in whose sight I
made myself known unto them, in bringing them forth
out of the land of Egypt.

v. 5—9. God here begins to recapitulate the provocations of Israel; and they commenced from the day he began to form them into a people.

1. He reminds them of the wonders of his grace shown to them above all nations. *He chose* them for a peculiar people, in the time of their deepest affliction, and most abject wretchedness *in the land of Egypt, he made himself known to them*, by his name Jehovah, and the miracles he wrought for their deliverance; confirming his favour towards them by an oath, and assuring them of the inheritance he had provided for them in a *land flowing with milk and honey, the glory of all lands*, which he *espied for them*, singled out with peculiar care, as the happy spot appointed for their abode. *Note*, (1.) God's people do not chuse him, he chuses them. (2.) None truly know God, but those to whom he is pleased to reveal himself.

2. The commands he gave them were most reasonable and easy. They were enjoined to *cast away every man the abominations of his eyes, and not defile themselves with the idols of Egypt*. And this he enforces with the most cogent reason, *I am the Lord your God*, the only worthy object of worship, and to whom they were bound by unnumbered obligations.

3. They notwithstanding wilfully rebelled, and refused to hearken to God's commands, continuing in their abominations, and cleaving to the idols of Egypt, not deterred by all the plagues they beheld.

4. By his prophets he threatned to destroy them with the Egyptians. As they had joined in their idolatry, they deserved to share their ruin. But,

5. For his name's sake he wrought, that the heathen might not blaspheme, as if he was unfaithful to his promises, or unable to accomplish them. *Note*, All the arguments for God's favour towards us come not from our desert, but his sovereign grace, and the purposes of his own glory.

10 ¶ Wherefore [i] I caused them to go forth out
of the land of Egypt, and [k] brought them into the
wilderness. 11 And I gave them my statutes, and
† shewed them my judgments, [l] which *if* a man do, he
shall even live in them. 12 Moreover also, I gave
them [m] my sabbaths, to be a sign between me and
them, that they might know that I *am* the LORD that
sanctify them. 13 But [n] the house of Israel rebelled
against me in the wilderness: they walked not in my
statutes, and they despised my judgments, [o] which *if* a
man do, he shall even live in them; and my sabbaths
they greatly [p] polluted: then I said I would pour out
my fury upon them [q] in the wilderness to consume them.
14 [r] But I wrought for my name's sake, that it should
not be polluted before the heathen, in whose sight I
brought them out. 15 Yet also [s] I lifted up my hand
unto them in the wilderness, that I would not bring
them into the land which I had given *them*, flowing
with milk and honey, [t] which *is* the glory of all lands;
16 [u] Because they despised my judgments, and walked
not in my statutes, but polluted my sabbaths: for
their heart went after their idols. 17 Nevertheless,
mine eye spared them from destroying them, neither did
I make an end of them in the wilderness. 18 But I
said unto their children in the wilderness, Walk ye not
in the statutes of your fathers, neither observe their
judgments, nor defile yourselves with their idols: 19 I
am the LORD your God; [x] walk in my statutes, and
keep my judgments, and do them; 20 And [y] hallow
my sabbaths; and they shall be a sign between me and
you, that ye may know that I *am* the LORD your God.
21 Notwithstanding the [z] children rebelled against me:
they walked not in my statutes, neither kept my judgments to do them, [a] which *if* a man do, he shall even
live in them; they polluted my sabbaths: then I said I
would pour out my fury upon them, to accomplish my
anger against them in the wilderness. 22 [b] Nevertheless I withdrew mine hand, and [c] wrought for my
name's sake, that it should not be polluted in the sight
of

† Heb. Made them to know.

Before Christ 592.

of the heathen, in whoſe ſight I brought them forth
23 I lifted up mine hand unto them alſo in the wilder-
neſs, that [d] I would ſcatter them among the heathen,
and diſperſe them through the countries, 24 [e] Becauſe
they had not executed my judgments, but had deſpiſed
my ſtatutes, and had polluted my ſabbaths, and [f] their
eyes were after their fathers idols 25 Wherefore [g] I
gave them alſo ſtatutes *that were* not good, and judg-
ments whereby they ſhould not live 26 And I pol-
luted them in their own gifts, in that they cauſed to paſs
[i] through *the fire* all [i] that openeth the womb, that I
might make them deſolate, to the end that they might
know that I *am* the LORD

[d] Lev xxvi 33, Jer xv 4. [e] Ver 16 [f] Chap vi 9 [g] Pſ lxxxi 12. Ver 39 Rom i 24 [h] 2 Kings xvii 17 & xxi 6 2 Chron xxviii 3 xxxiii 6 Chap xvi 20 21 [i] Ex xiii 2

v 16—26 The mercies of God, and the ingratitude and diſobedience of the Jewiſh people, are here diſplayed

1 God's mercies towards them were amazingly great and ſingular He brought them forth from Egypt with a high hand, led them into the wilderneſs, where they lived by daily miracles, gave them his law, with the ſtatutes and judgments of his worſhip, by obſervance of which they might expect to live long and enjoy the promiſed inheritance, he gave them alſo his ſabbaths, the weekly ſabbath and the ſabbatical and jubilee years, a ſign of his favour towards them, a memorial of their deliverance from Egypt, a pledge of their entrance into the reſt of Canaan, and a figure of the eternal reſt which remained for the faithful in a better world thus God diſtinguiſhed them from all nations, and intended to make *them know that He the Lord ſanctified them*, theſe holy days, appointed for his immediate ſervice, having then, as they ſtill have, the moſt bleſſed influence upon the ſouls of thoſe who conſcientiouſly ſanctify their ſabbaths to keep them holy

2 Their ingratitude and undutifulneſs were moſt provoking *In the wilderneſs*, where they were ſurrounded with mercies and miracles, *they rebelled*, caſt off God's government, deſpiſed his ordinances, polluted his ſabbaths, and ſunk into idolatry, v 16

3 Offended with ſuch baſeneſs, God threatned utterly to conſume them in his fury, v 13 But for his own glory, that the heathen might not diſhonour his name, as if he was unable to bring his people into the land of Canaan, he reſolved to fulfil his promiſe yet, not to leave ſuch wickedneſs without a mark of his ſevere diſpleaſure, he ſware in his wrath, concerning the men of that generation, that they ſhould never enter into his reſt, v 15 and, in conſequence thereof, their carcaſes fell in the wilderneſs Let us therefore fear leſt, a promiſe being left us of entering into his reſt, any of us ſhould come ſhort of it, and periſh after the ſame example of unbelief and diſobedience

4 God did not make an utter end of them, but ſpared their children, and ſolemnly warned them, by their fathers ruin, againſt their ſins, not to walk *in their ſtatutes*, or copy their worſhip or manners, but to flee from idolatry, to know the Lord to be their God, to worſhip him according to his own preſcription, obſervant of his ſabbaths, and obedient to his laws *Note*, Children ſhould take warning by their parents ill example, and be more careful to abſtain from their ſins

5 *They notwithſtanding rebelled againſt God*, and trod in the ſteps of their ungodly fathers, ſabbath-breakers, diſobedient, idolaters, rejecting their own mercies, they provoked that wrath which would have deſtroyed them, had not God for his own glory reſtrained his arm, after making them feel ſome heavy ſtrokes of his diſpleaſure in the wilderneſs And though, according to his promiſe, he brought them into the land of Canaan, he foretold the fearful diſperſion to which at laſt they were doomed for their tranſgreſſions *Note*, (1) Sinners are ſelf-murderers they might have lived if they would have been obedient, but they prefer ſin and death (2) They who walk in the ways of their wicked anceſtors muſt expect their judgments

6 He gave them up to their own inventions, v 25 *Wherefore I gave them alſo ſtatutes that were not good, and judgments whereby they ſhould not live* He gave them up to the idolatrous cuſtoms of the nations, and ſuffered them to follow the vain traditions of their apoſtate forefathers Though ſome interpret this of the judgment he ſent upon them, others of the rites of the ceremonial law, on which depending for righteouſneſs, they became a ſtumbling block to them, inſtead of leading them to Chriſt *And I polluted them in their own gifts*, ſuffering them to offer ſacrifices to idols, even the inhuman oblations of the firſt-born to Molech, *to make them deſolate* thus weakened by their own more than ſavage conduct, they became an eaſier prey to their enemies *to the end that they might know that I am the Lord*, ſuſtain in the puniſhment inflicted upon them *Note*, (1) A greater curſe cannot fall upon the ſinner than to be left of God to the wickedneſs of his own heart (2) God will make himſelf known to ſinners if they will not receive him as their Lord and Saviour, they ſhall prove him to be God the avenger

Before Christ 591.

27 ¶ Therefore, ſon of man, ſpeak unto the houſe
of Iſrael, and ſay unto them, Thus ſaith the LORD God,
Yet in this your fathers have blaſphemed me, in that
they have † committed a treſpaſs againſt me 28 For
when I had brought them into the land, *for* the which
I lifted up mine hand to give it to them, then [k] they
ſaw every high hill, and all the thick trees, and they
offered there their ſacrifices, and there they preſented
the provocation of their offering there alſo they made
[l] their ſweet ſavour, and poured out there their drink-
offerings 29 Then I ‡ ſaid unto them, What *is* the
high place whereunto ye go? and the name thereof is
called Bamah unto this day 30 Wherefore ſay unto
the houſe of Iſrael, Thus ſaith the LORD God, Are ye
polluted after the manner of your fathers? and commit
ye whoredom after their abominations? 31 For when
ye offer your gifts, when [m] ye make your ſons to paſs
through the fire, ye pollute yourſelves with all your idols
even unto this day and [n] ſhall I be enquired of by you,
O houſe of Iſrael? *As* I live, ſaith the LORD God, I
will not be enquired of by you 32 And that which
cometh into your mind [o] ſhall not be at all, that ye ſay,
We will be as the heathen, as the families of the coun-
tries, to ſerve wood and ſtone

† Heb Treſpaſſed [k] Iſa lvii 5, &c [l] Chap xvi 19 ‡ Or told them what the high place was, or Bamah [m] Ver 26 [n] Ver 3 [o] Job v 1

v 27—32 Their provocations ceaſed not in the wilderneſs, but when they came into the land of Canaan the ſame abominations were practiſed

1 When God had fulfilled his promiſe to them, and brought them into the good land, they treſpaſſed yet more and more Inſtead of confining themſelves to God's altar, in conformity to the cuſtoms of the heathen, they choſe hills and groves for their places of worſhip, *and offered there their ſacrifices*, incenſe and libations, which, if offered to the God of Iſrael, were contrary to his precept but probably they rather there ſerved their idols, which made *the provocation of their offering* greater And, tho' warned of the folly and ſin of their idolatrous ſervices, when they had God's altar to go to, they perſiſted in their perverſeneſs, and the high places were to the laſt frequented *it is called Bamah to this day* So inveterately rooted is the love of ſin in the heart of the ſinner

2 Even after all the judgments executed upon them, the preſent generation committed the ſame abominations, polluting themſelves with idols, and cauſing their children to paſs through the fire to Molech, with the folly and wickedneſs of which God juſtly upbraids them, and how then could they dare enquire of him? or what anſwer of peace could they expect from him? he ſwears by himſelf, v 31 neither their perſons nor petitions ſhould be regarded, and their ſchemes of currying favour with their heathen maſters, by compliance with their worſhip, and incorporating with them by intermarriages, he will blaſt either they ſhall refuſe to admit them to join with them, or deſpiſe them for their perfidy *Note*, (1) Little is ever got by ſinful compliances the very enemies of religion will honour thoſe who ſhew ſteadineſs and integrity, whilſt they treat apoſtates with contempt (2) They who by irreligious profeſſion have once forfeited the world's favour, may deſpair of ever recovering it again

33 ¶ *As* I live, ſaith the LORD God, ſurely with
a mighty hand, and [p] with a ſtretched-out arm, and with
fury poured out, will I rule over you 34 And I will
bring you out from the people, and will gather you out
of the countries wherein ye are ſcattered, with a mighty
hand, and with a ſtretched out arm, and with fury poured
out. 35 And I will bring you into [q] the wilderneſs of
the people, and there will I plead with you face to face
36 Like as [r] I pleaded with your fathers in the wilder-
neſs of the land of Egypt, ſo will I plead with you, ſaith
the LORD God 37 And I will cauſe you [s] to paſs
under the rod, and I will bring you into the bond of the
covenant 38 And [t] I will purge out from among you
the rebels, and them that tranſgreſs againſt me I will
bring them forth out of the country where they ſojourn,
and [u] they ſhall not enter into the land of Iſrael, [x] and
ye ſhall know that I *am* the LORD. 39 [y] As for you,
O houſe of Iſrael, thus ſaith the LORD God, Go ye,
ſerve ye every one his idols, and hereafter *alſo*, if ye will
not hearken unto me but pollute ye my holy name no
more with your gifts, and with your idols 40 For [z] in
mine holy mountain, in the mountain of the height of
Iſrael, ſaith the LORD God, there ſhall all the houſe
of Iſrael, all of them in the land ſerve me there will I
accept them, and there will I require your offerings, and
the

[p] Jer xxi 5 [q] Chap xix 13 [r] 1 Cor x 5—10 [s] Lev xxvii 32 [t] Chap xxxiv 17, 20 Mat xxv 32 [u] Jer xliv 14 [x] Chap xiii 9 [y] Chap vi 7 Jud x 14 & xviii 13 [z] Amos iv 4 [a] Iſa ii 2, 3 Chap xvii 23 Mic iv 1

Before Chriſt 592

the † firſt-fruits of your oblations, with all your holy
things 41 I will accept you with your ‡ ſweet ſavour,
(† Or chief ‡ Heb. Sa: our of reſt) when I bring you out from the people, and gather you
out of the countries wherein ye have been ſcattered, and
I will be ſanctified in you before the heathen 42 And
(a Ver 44) [a] ye ſhall know that I *am* the LORD, when I ſhall
bring you into the land of Iſrael, into the country
for the which I lifted up mine hand to give it to
(b Chap xvi 63) your fathers 43 And there [b] ſhall ye remember your
ways, and all your doings wherein ye have been defiled,
(c Lev xxvi 39 Job xlii 6 Chap vi 9 Hoſ v 15 Zech xii 10) and ye ſhall [c] lothe yourſelves in your own ſight, for
all your evils that ye have committed 44 And [d] ye
ſhall know that I *am* the LORD, when I have wrought
with you for my name's ſake, not according to your
(d Ver 38) wicked ways, nor according to your corrupt doings, O
ye houſe of Iſrael, ſaith the Lord GOD.

v 33—44 Since they would not bow to the ſceptre of his righteous government, God here threatens,

1 To rule them with a rod of iron, diſappointing their ſchemes, and pouring out his fury upon them, *v* 33 They ſhall not be ſuffered to mingle with the heathen, whither they are ſcattered, but from thence will God collect them, when the Babylonians ſhall have ſubdued theſe nations, they ſhall be brought *into the wilderneſs of the people*, be carried captives into Chaldea, and there God will judge and puniſh them, as he had puniſhed their fathers in the wilderneſs, after they came out of Egypt *Note*, They ſtrive in vain, who ſeek to fruſtrate God's decrees

2 There is mercy in reſerve for a remnant, when the *rebels are purged out* by his judgments

[1] The rebels ſhall be for ever cut off from the congregation of the Lord, ſhall never more enter the land of Iſrael, *v* 38 given up to their idolatries, and totally excluded from God's worſhip, ſo that they *ſhall pollute his holy name no more*, by joining him with their idols, and at the ſame time that they pretended to honour him with their gifts, ſtill continuing in their idolatry *Note*, (1) The rebellious ſinner will be eternally ſeparated at laſt from the congregation of the juſt, and never enter the reſt of glory (2) That ſoul is completely miſerable whom God abandons (3) Pretences to religion, when the heart is enſlaved by idol luſts, do but add profaneneſs and hypocriſy to iniquity

[2] The choſen ſhall be ſeparated, and bleſſed with God's regard *They ſhall paſs under the rod*, viſited with corrections, and recovered in the furnace of affliction, or they ſhall be marked and diſtinguiſhed as God's people, as the ſhepherd marks the ſheep as they paſs under the rod They *ſhall be brought again into the bond of the covenant*, be acknowledged as God's peculiar people, be reſtored again from their diſperſion to their own land, *v* 41 and ſerve God in his Zion, his holy *mountain*, ver 40 Their oblations and their worſhip ſhall be accepted, repentance given them to acknowledge, bewail, and abhor themſelves for their former tranſgreſſions, God will be *ſanctified in them before the heathen*, who will confeſs his faithfulneſs to his promiſes, his power and grace diſplayed in their recovery, and they *ſhall know* that he is *the Lord*, by experience of theſe his diſpenſations of mercy towards them, wrought not for their ſakes, who deſerved nothing but to periſh in their iniquities, but for his own *name's ſake*, moſt eminently to diſplay his glory, as the promiſe-keeping and ſin-pardoning God, *v* 44 *Note*, (1) Afflictions are the moſt bleſſed means of good to God's people (2) They who are marked in God's eternal purpoſes, ſhall be preſerved for the heavenly inheritance, amidſt all the changes of this periſhing world (3) When God accepts our perſons in Chriſt Jeſus, then our poor and imperfect ſervices become a ſweet favour through the Beloved (4) The ſinner that returns to God and finds favour, ſees in the glaſs of God's love the baſeneſs, malignity, and ingratitude of ſin, and loaths himſelf for all his abominations (5) We never know God truly, till by experience coming to him as loſt ſinners, we prove the wonders of his pardoning love (6) All our ſalvation flows not from our deſerts, but God's rich mercy, and as he deſigns his own glory herein, to the praiſe of the glory of his grace it muſt be wholly aſcribed

45 ¶ Moreover, the word of the LORD came
(e Chap xxi 2) unto me, ſaying, 46 [e] Son of man, ſet thy face toward
the ſouth, and drop *thy word* toward the ſouth, and
propheſy againſt the foreſt of the ſouth-field; 47 And
ſay to the foreſt of the ſouth, Hear the word of the
LORD, Thus ſaith the Lord GOD, Behold, I will
(f Luke xxiii 31) kindle a fire in thee, and it ſhall devour [f] every green
tree in thee, and every dry tree the flaming flame
ſhall not be quenched, and all faces from the ſouth to
the north ſhall be burnt therein. 48 And all fleſh
ſhall ſee that I the LORD have kindled it it ſhall not
be quenched 49 Then ſaid I, Ah Lord GOD, they
(g Chap xvii 2) ſay of me, Doth he not ſpeak [g] parables?

v 45—49 This paragraph begins a new prophecy, and would moſt properly have begun the next chapter, the ſubject of both being the ſame, the threatned ruin of Judah and Jeruſalem

1 The foreſt of the ſouth field, towards which the prophet is commanded to ſet his face and drop his word, is the city of Jeruſalem, full of inhabitants, unfruitful as the trees of the wood, and the hearts of wicked men fierce and ravenous as the beaſts of the foreſt

2 God threatens to kindle a fire in it, a fire of wrath, and the conflagration ſhall be univerſal, devouring and deſtroying all ranks, young and old without diſtinction, from one end of the land to the other, and none can quench it, a deſtruction ſo terrible ſhall mark the finger of divine vengeance, and even the ſurrounding heathens ſhall acknowledge that this is God's doing, *v* 48

3 Ezekiel makes his complaint to God *Ah! Lord God, they ſay of me, Doth he not ſpeak parables?* they ſcoffed at the meſſage he brought them, as unintelligible, and counted it not worth their attention *Note*, They who have no inclination to profit by the word of God, will always have ſome fault to find with the delivery of it

CHAP XXI.

In this chapter we have, 1 An explication of the prophecy in the cloſe of the foregoing, which the people complained they could not underſtand, ver 1—5 *with directions to the prophet to ſhew himſelf deeply affected with it*, ver 6, 7 2 *A prediction of the ſword that was coming upon the land, by which all ſhould be laid waſte*, ver 8—17 3 *The king of Babylon's approach to Jeruſalem determined by divination*, ver 18—24 4 *Sentence paſſed upon Zedekiah king of Judah*, ver 25, 26, 27 5 *The deſtruction of the Ammonites by the ſword foretold*, ver 28—32

1 AND the word of the LORD came unto me,
(a Chap xx 46) ſaying, 2 [a] Son of man, ſet thy face toward
(b Deut xxxii 2 Amos vii 16 Micah ii 6, 11) Jeruſalem, and [b] drop *thy word* toward the holy places
and propheſy againſt the land of Iſrael, 3 And ſay
to the land of Iſrael, Thus ſaith the LORD, Be-
hold, I *am* againſt thee, and will draw forth my ſword
(c Chap xx 47) out of his ſheath, and will cut off from thee the
righteous and the wicked 4 Seeing then that I will
cut off from thee the righteous and the wicked, there-
fore ſhall my ſword go forth out of his ſheath againſt
all fleſh from the ſouth to the north 5 That all
fleſh may know that I the LORD have drawn forth
my ſword out of his ſheath it ſhall not return any
more 6 Sigh therefore, thou ſon of man, with the
breaking of *thy* loins, and with bitterneſs ſigh before
their eyes 7 And it ſhall be when they ſay unto
thee, Wherefore ſigheſt thou? that thou ſhalt anſwer,
For the tidings, becauſe it cometh and every heart
ſhall melt and all hands ſhall be feeble, and every
(† Heb Go into water) ſpirit ſhall faint, and all knees ſhall † be weak *as* water
behold, it cometh, and ſhall be brought to paſs, ſaith
the Lord GOD

v 1—7 That the people might be left without excuſe, we have here a clear expoſition of the parable foregoing

1 Againſt Jeruſalem is the prophetic word directed, the foreſt, where the fire of wrath is about to kindle, and *the holy places*, the temple and its courts, the profanations of which God will eſpecially avenge He is againſt them, and nothing then can protect them from ruin, he threatens to draw the ſword of judgment, and *cut off the righteous and the wicked*, who ſhare often together in national calamities, though God will abundantly make up to his faithful in inward conſolations, whatever outwardly they ſuffer in common with others *From ſouth to north* univerſal ruin is ſpread by the Chaldean army, and the ſword once drawn, is no more ſheathed till it hath made an utter end of them, agreeable to the foregoing parable, *chap* xx 47, 48

2 To affect them with a ſenſe of the terribleneſs of the threatned ruin, the prophet muſt himſelf appear deeply affected with it. He muſt ſigh with ſuch depth and bitterneſs before them, as if his heart was ready to break, and as the expreſſion of ſuch vaſt anguiſh would make them inquiſitive into the cauſe, he muſt tell them, it is *for the doleful tidings* he is ſent to deliver, the certain accompliſhment of which approached, when *every heart would melt*, &c their courage fail, and ſo diſpirited would they be, as neither to be able to fight or fly God hath ſpoken it, and not one jot or tittle ſhall fail, *v* 7 *Note*, (1) A miniſter who would affect others with what he ſpeaks, muſt

be

Before Christ 592.

be affected himself, and a tear dropt over a perishing soul is the most moving admonition. (2.) They who are never so stout-hearted against God's warnings now, will be overwhelmed with terror in the day of their calamity.

8 ¶ Again, the word of the LORD came unto me,
saying, 9 Son of man, prophesy and say, Thus saith
the LORD, Say, A sword, a sword is sharpened, and
also furbished: 10 It is sharpened to make a sore
slaughter; it is furbished that it may glitter: should we
then make mirth? it contemneth the rod of my son,
as every tree. 11 And he hath given it to be furbish-
ed, that it may be handled: the sword is sharpened, and
it is furbished, to give it into the hand of the slayer. 12
Cry and howl, son of man: for it shall be upon my
people, it shall be upon all the princes of Israel: ‡ ter-
rors, by reason of the sword, shall be upon my people:
smite therefore upon thy thigh. 13 Because it is a
trial, and what if the sword contemn even the rod? it
shall be no more, saith the Lord GOD. 14 Thou
therefore, son of man, prophesy, and smite thine || hands
together, and let the sword be doubled the third time,
the sword of the slain: it is the sword of the great men
that are slain, which entereth into their privy chambers.
15 I have set the § point of the sword against all their
gates, that their heart may faint, and their ruins be
multiplied: ah! it is made bright, it is † wrapt up for
the slaughter. 16 Go thee one way or other, either
on the right hand, ‡ or on the left, whithersoever thy face
is set. 17 I will also smite mine hands together, and
I will cause my fury to rest: I the LORD have said it.

v. 8—17. The sword drawn in the foregoing verses, is here sharpened to do terrible execution, glittering and bright, bearing down all before it. The scepter of Israel's king is unable to resist its fury, is a rotten stick, v. 10. or the words may be rendered, it is the rod of my son, the rod of Christ, executing judgment. It despiseth every tree, resistance is vain when he strikes, for when God contendeth, he will overcome.

1. It is put into the slayer's hand, v. 11. into the hands of Nebuchadnezzar, and directed against the princes and people of Israel, against all their gates, that their ruins may be multiplied, the city utterly demolished, and they, without power of resistance, faint and disheartened, v. 15. Whichever way the sword moves, to the right or left, it spreads havock round, v. 16. and the great men who fly in terrors to their secret chambers, find no protection from it, even there slain in their lurking-places, v. 14. And a severe trial it will prove to God's people, when they shall see it contemn even the rod, destroy the king, and put an end to the government of David's royal line. It shall be no more, saith the Lord God, none of David's family shall again wield the sceptre till the Messiah comes, v. 13. Note, (1.) No eminence of station can secure from God's judgment, nay, rather they who have by their ill examples contributed to the seduction of others, shall be most severely punished. (2.) Terrors will seize the guilty in the day of vengeance, from which they cannot flee. (3.) The strongest fortress hath no defence, when God is the assailant. (4.) The sword of judgment turns every way, let no sinner hope to escape from it.

2. The prophet is commanded to testify his bitter grief at these desolations, and to call on the people to join his lamentations. He must cry and howl, ver. 12. for the ravages he foretells; smiting his thigh, ver. 4. in the greatest agony, whilst the third time he redoubles the warning, a sword, a sword, ver. 8. and again, v. 14. which some refer to the three captivities of Jehoiakim, Jeconiah, and Zedekiah; others to the coming of the Chaldeans first, when they took Jerusalem; secondly, when Nebuzar-adan burnt it; and lastly, when in the twenty-third year of his reign, Nebuchadnezzar carried away the remnant of the people, Jer. lii. 5—30. Thus God will cause his fury to rest, when he hath executed vengeance on the devoted land, according to his faithful word, v. 17. and seeing this must shortly come to pass, the prophet expostulates with them on the unseasonableness of their present jollity: should we then make mirth? when a drawn sword hangs over our heads: rather in the dust of deepest humiliation, with bitter cries and tears should they seek to avert the impending blow. Note, (1.) They who declare the terrors of the Lord, must urge them vehemently, and redouble their warning. (2.) It is a heart-felt grief to God's ministers, to see sinners unconcerned about their approaching and endless misery. (3.) God's word will have its accomplishment, however now men slight and despise it.

18 ¶ The word of the LORD came unto me again,
saying, 19 Also thou son of man, appoint thee two
ways, that the sword of the king of Babylon may come:
both twain shall come forth out of one land: and choose
thou a place, choose it at the head of the way to the
city. 20 Appoint a way, that the sword may come to
Rabbath of the Ammonites, and to Judah in Jerusa-
lem the defenced. 21 For the king of Babylon stood
at the ‡ parting of the way, at the head of the two
ways, to use divination: he made his arrows bright, he
consulted with ‡ images, he looked in the liver. 22 At
his right hand was the divination for Jerusalem, to ap-
point || captains, to open the mouth in the slaughter, to
lift up the voice with shouting, to appoint battering
rams against the gates, to cast a mount, and to build a
fort. 23 And it shall be unto them as a false divination
in their sight, § to them that have sworn oaths: but he
will call to remembrance the iniquity, that they may be
taken. 24 Therefore thus saith the Lord GOD, Be-
cause ye have made your iniquity to be remembered, in
that your transgressions are discovered, so that in all your
doings your sins do appear; because, I say, that ye are
come to remembrance, ye shall be taken with the hand.
25 ¶ And thou profane wicked prince of Israel,
whose day is come, when iniquity shall have an end,
26 Thus saith the Lord GOD, Remove the diadem, and
take off the crown: this shall not be the same: exalt him
that is low, and abase him that is high. 27 † I will
overturn, overturn, overturn it: and it shall be no more,
until he come whose right it is; and I will give it him.

v. 18—27. The same subject is here farther pursued, and the sword brought to their walls.

1. He is commanded to describe on a tyle, or a table, two ways, leading from Babylon; the one to Rabbah, the capital of the Ammonites, the other to Jerusalem, the fortress and metropolis of Judah, v. 19, 20. Here, at the head of the way, he must represent Nebuchadnezzar halting, and though resolved to attack both places, uncertain with which to begin, using divination to determine his way, brightening the arrows on which it is supposed the names of the cities were engraven, and that the first that was drawn was to be first attacked, consulting the images, and looking into the liver, the methods used by the heathens to obtain direction, and enquire into the success of their enterprize. And all his divinations directed him to take the right-hand road which led to Jerusalem, to encamp around it, appoint the officers to direct the siege, raise up the hostile mounts, and batter the gates, till at the breach they might enter into the city. Note, (1.) The wisest men are often at a stand, it is not in man that walketh to direct his steps. (2.) Though many events appear to us merely fortuitous, yet even the lot comes forth according to God's disposal, and by his decree. (3.) Many are doing God's work, who are not at all sensible of him by whose hand they are guided.

2. Both prince and people draw their ruin upon their own heads.

[1.] The people, who despise the prophetic warnings, shall be seized and led captives. The Jews deemed the divination as vain, and not to be regarded, and the mention of it by the prophet disturbed not their security, though the oaths they had sworn and broken might justly alarm them with fears of an avenging God. Or perhaps they depended on the league made with Egypt, and confirmed by mutual oath for assistance. But he will call to remembrance the iniquity, the treachery and perjury of Zedekiah and the people, that they may be taken as birds in an evil net. Therefore thus saith the Lord, who is able to accomplish his purposes, and true to his word, because ye have made your iniquity to be remembered by new transgressions, adding to their past sins, in that your transgressions are discovered, their perfidious conduct exposed openly to the nations around, and to the king of Babylon, so that in all your doings, your sins do appear visible to every eye, because, I say, that they are come to remembrance before God and the king of Babylon, ye shall be taken with the hand, seized as a helpless bird in a net, and led captive for their iniquities. Note, (1.) Sinners flatter themselves often that the warnings of God are false divinations, but they will be found dreadful realities. (2.) The transgressions of the wicked will be discovered and punished, if not before, at the last in the great day of recompence.

[2.] The prince of Judah hath a peculiar burden laid on him, as the chief author of the nation's ruin. He is charged as profane and wicked, ver. 25. and who can but see so in the ingratitude, perjury, treachery, and rebellion of which he was guilty? and kings are not too high to be plainly told their sins and danger. His day is come to be destroyed, when iniquity shall have an end, when the measure shall be filled, and the punishment due to it inflicted. Thus saith the Lord God, remove the diadem, and take off the crown, degrade him from his dignity, and depose him from the throne of Judah; this shall not be the same, his kingdom shall not continue; exalt him that is low, Jehoiachin now a captive, Jer. lii. 31, 32. and abase him that is high, Zedekiah, the reigning monarch [illegible]

Before Christ 590

changes which the conqueror at his pleasure would make *I will overturn, overturn, overturn it*, certainly and utterly, *and it shall be no more* a kingdom under the rule of David's royal posterity, *until he come whose right it is*, the Messiah, raised up to sit on the throne of David his father, *Luke* i 32 *and I will give it him*, even a throne enduring as the days of eternity, and universal from pole to pole *Note*, (1) Profaneness and wickedness in a prince are doubly criminal, as the evil of his example is more extensively infectious (2) The day will come when all who do iniquity shall receive their righteous doom (3) Crowns are precarious possessions, the only unfading diadem must be sought in a better world (4) Pride will have a fall, whilst humility is the way to honour (5) The Lord Jesus is the rightful king and heir of all things, whatever enemies oppose his advancement, must finally be overthrown, and all his foes be made his footstool

28 ¶ And thou, son of man, prophesy, and say, Thus
saith the Lord GOD [e] concerning the Ammonites, and
concerning [f] their reproach even say thou, The sword,
the sword *is* drawn for the slaughter *it is* furbished, to
consume because of the glittering 29 Whiles [g] they
see vanity unto thee, whiles they divine a lie unto thee,
to bring thee upon the necks of *them that are* slain, of
the wicked, [i] whose day is come, when their iniquity
shall have an end 30 [u] Shall I cause *it* to return into
his sheath? I will judge thee in the place where thou
wast created, [x] in the land of thy nativity 31 And I
will pour out mine indignation upon thee, I will blow
against thee in the fire of my wrath, and deliver thee
into the hand of † brutish men, *and* skilful to destroy
32 Thou shalt be for fuel to the fire thy blood shall
be in the midst of the land, [y] thou shalt be no *more* remembered
for I the LORD have spoken *it*

v 28—32 Though Judah be first visited, let not Ammon think to escape

1 They had provoked God *by their reproach*, insulting over his Israel, as if he could not save them, *chap* xxv *Zeph* xi 8—10 whilst they flattered themselves now the king of Babylon was returned thither, that their gods would protect them, and their diviners and soothsayers confirmed them in their delusion *Note*, (1) God is jealous for his people, and will suffer no insult shewn them to go unpunished (2) Sinners usually flatter themselves into their ruin

2 God threatens to pour out his wrath upon them, *v* 31 The sword that was drawn against Judah is still unsheathed, *furbished for the slaughter*, and whetted *to consume* them, *to bring them on the necks of the slain, of the wicked*, they must perish by the same arm that slew the wicked Jews when their day was come, and their iniquities ripe for destruction, *v* 29 nor will the sword return to its scabbard, till it hath executed God's vengeance upon them *in the land of their nativity*, the place where they were settled ever since they were formed into a people, *v* 30 Fierce are the flames of wrath kindled against them, their appointed executioners savage in their tempers, and skilful to destroy, *v* 31 As fuel they must be consumed by the devouring fire of their enemies, and their blood be shed *in the midst of the land* whither the Chaldeans would penetrate, and the ruin they would make should never be repaired, *thou shalt be remembered no more, saith the Lord God*, all the traces of their nation being quite obliterated *Note*, (1) It is a fearful thing to fall into the hands of that God who is a consuming fire (2) Sinners are fuel for the flames of hell (3) They who promise themselves, because they have long been secure, they shall be always safe, will be dreadfully surprized when their unexpected ruin comes

CHAP XXII

Here are three several messages which God entrusts the prophet to deliver concerning Judah and Jerusalem 1 A catalogue of their sins is given, which had exposed them to shame, and for which God would bring them to ruin, ver 1—16 2 They are compared to dross, and as such condemned to the fire ver 17—22 3 All orders and degrees of men among them are here found guilty, and as none appeared as intercessors, they must all expect to share in the same punishment, ver 23—31

1 MOreover, the word of the LORD came unto
me, saying, 2 Now thou son of man, [a] wilt
thou ‖ judge, wilt thou judge [b] the ‖ bloody city? yea,
thou shalt shew her all her abominations 3 Then say
thou, Thus saith the Lord GOD, The city sheddeth
blood in the midst of it, that her time may come, and
maketh idols against herself, to defile herself 4 Thou
art become guilty in thy blood [c] that thou hast shed, and
hast defiled thyself in thine idols which thou hast made,
and thou hast caused thy days to draw near, and art
come *even* unto thy years, [d] therefore have I made thee
a reproach unto the heathen, and a mocking to all
countries 5 *Those that be* near, and *those that be* far
from thee, shall mock thee, *which art* ‖ infamous, *and*
much vexed 6 Behold, the princes of Israel, every one
were in thee to their § power to shed blood 7 In thee
have they [e] set light by father and mother in the
midst of thee have they dealt by † oppression with the
stranger in thee have they [f] vexed the fatherless and
the widow 8 Thou hast despised mine holy things,
and [g] hast profaned my sabbaths 9 In thee [h] are men
that carry tales to shed blood and in thee they eat upon
the mountains in the midst of thee they commit
lewdness 10 In thee have they [k] discovered their fathers
nakedness in thee have they humbled her that
was [l] set apart for pollution 11 And ‡ one hath committed
abomination [m] with his neighbour's wife, and
‖ another [n] hath lewdly defiled his daughter in law, and
another in thee hath humbled his [o] sister, his father's
daughter 12 In thee [p] have they taken gifts to shed
blood [q] thou hast taken usury and increase, and thou
hast greedily gained of thy neighbours by extortion, and
hast forgotten me, saith the Lord GOD 13 ¶ Behold
therefore, I have [r] smitten mine hand at thy dishonest
gain which thou hast made, [s] and at thy blood which
hath been in the midst of thee 14 Can thine heart
endure, or can thine hands be strong in the days that I
shall deal with thee? [t] I the LORD have spoken *it*, and
will do *it* 15 And [u] I will scatter thee among the
heathen, and disperse thee in the countries, and [x] will
consume thy filthiness out of thee 16 And thou shalt
§ take thine inheritance in thyself in the sight of the
heathen, and [y] thou shalt know that I *am* the LORD

v 1—16 Jerusalem, the bloody city, is here brought to the bar to be convicted and condemned and the prophet is constituted of God both her accuser and her judge

1 Her abominations are many, great, and aggravated, and they are *shewn* her to evince and manifest the justice of God in her destruction

(1) Murder The blood of innocents was shed *in the midst of her*, from assassinations, tyrannical abuse of power, or perversion of justice, the guilt of which cried aloud, *v* 4 The princes and magistrates, who should have avenged such crimes, were themselves the first to perpetrate them *to* the utmost of *their power*, ver 6 whilst talebearers sought to incense them by malicious reports and insinuations, and were chargeable with all the mischief which ensued, *v* 9 and perjured wretches or assassins, for money, were ready to swear away the life of the innocent, or murder in secret such as, by malice or revenge, were marked for their bloody knife, *v* 12

(2) Idolatry The sad effects of which were their pollution, *v* 4 and in consequence their destruction, *v* 3 And those who ran not to the grosser excesses, indulged themselves in eating on the mountains of the sacrifices, and thereby became partaker with the idolaters

(3) Disobedience to parents They *set light by father and mother*, despised their authority, disobeyed their commands, or mocked at their infirmities, and this is amongst the most atrocious crimes

(4) Oppression and deceit They took advantage of the ignorance or necessities of the stranger, vexed with exorbitant demands, or litigious suits, the fatherless and widow, who were unable to defend themselves, extorted usury from their brethren, and with greediness increased their gain to their neighbour's disadvantage, *v* 12

(5) The profanation of holy things, *v* 8 and particularly of the sabbath. They despised God's ordinances, either totally neglected the ceremonial rites and worship of the temple, or performed them in a careless perfunctory manner, and the sabbaths were no more observed than common days, and that generally opens a wide door to all ungodliness

(6) Lewdness of all sorts the most criminal and odious, open and barefaced, *v* 9 even incest, *v* 10 Ravishment, *even of her that was set apart for pollution*, with whom all commerce was particularly forbidden, *Lev* xx 11 Adultery, and the debauching even a daughter-in-law, and a sister, *v* 11 such horrid and shocking crimes were committed by them, and cried for vengeance

(7) At the root of all was their forgetfulness of God They left him [illegible] out of their sight, and then they feared to commit no wickedness

The charge being indisputable, the prophet, as judge, pronounces sentence on the criminal Her day is come, her measure of iniquity is full, she is ripe for vengeance, *v* 4 there-

Before Christ 592.

therefore God *hath made her a reproach to the heathen far and near*, *infamous* in their eyes, so vile and abandoned was her conduct, and *much vexed* with their derision and insults, yet no more than she most justly deserved. With indignation God smites his hand at her *dishonest gain* and *bloody* crimes, v. 13. and his fierce anger how can she sustain? when his terrible word shall receive its accomplishment, and his threatened wrath be poured out upon her, v. 14. In consequence of which, she will be *scattered among the heathen*, and miserably *dispersed in the countries*, till her filthiness was *consumed* by the destruction of the ringleaders in iniquity, and the recovery of a remnant brought to repentance in the furnace of affliction. And *thou shalt take thine inheritance in thyself*, rejected of God, and possessing nothing but a miserable being in want and wretchedness, *and thou shalt know that I am the Lord*, when these judgments are inflicted, and God's almighty power, impartial justice and inviolable truth hereby signally displayed, v. 16. *Note*, (1.) Though God bears long with sinners, he will not bear always. (2.) Reproach for God is honour and happiness; reproach for sin truly infamous, and the prelude to everlasting shame and contempt. (3.) The stoutest hearted sinners will tremble in a day of wrath. (4.) They who promise themselves impunity in their sins, in opposition to God's warnings, will find themselves terribly deceived. (5.) Sooner or later the soul will be made to know what a portion it hath lost by apostacy from God, and what wages it hath earned, even eternal death.

17 And the word of the LORD came unto me,
saying, 18 Son of man, ᵛ the house of Israel is to me
become dross: all they *are* brass, and tin, and iron, and
lead, in the midst of the furnace; they are *even* the ‖
dross of silver. 19 Therefore thus saith the Lord
GOD; Because ye are all become dross, behold therefore I will gather you into the midst of Jerusalem. 20
‡ *As* they gather silver, and brass, and iron, and lead,
and tin into the midst of the furnace, to blow the fire
upon it, to melt *it*; so will I gather *you* in mine anger,
and in my fury, and I will leave *you there*, and melt
you. 21 Yea, I will gather you, and blow upon you
in the fire of my wrath, and ye shall be melted in the
midst thereof. 22 As silver is melted in the midst of
the furnace, so shall ye be melted in the midst thereof;
and ye shall know that I the LORD have poured out
my fury upon you.

ᵛ Isa. i. 22. Jer. vi. 28. &c.
‖ Heb. Drosses.
‡ Heb. According to the gathering.

v. 17—22. They who have made themselves refuse and vile, must expect to be treated accordingly.

1. The whole house of Israel is become dross; once they were silver, but now wretchedly degenerated, despicable and useless as the scum of the furnace. Nothing precious remained in them, but like the baser metals they were as brass in impudence, as iron for hardness of heart, as tin for hypocrisy, and as lead for stupidity under all their warnings.

2. God threatens to gather them, as metals into the furnace, into Jerusalem, whither they would flee on the approach of the Chaldeans, silver, brass, iron, lead, and tin together; some gracious souls, represented by silver, being found among the rest who would be purified by that fire of affliction, which would consume the ungodly as dross. There God will blow upon them as a refiner, in wrath and anger melt them with his judgments, *and leave them there* under the dire tokens of his displeasure, devoted to famine, pestilence, and the sword during the siege, and made to acknowledge, in the judgments they felt, the heavy hand of God which was laid upon them. *Note*, In the day of judgment, the sinners of every character will be collected, and cast into the furnace of fire; and they who are once shut up there, will remain there to eternity.

23 ¶ And the word of the LORD came unto me,
saying, 24 Son of man, say unto her, Thou art the
land *that* is not cleansed, nor rained upon in the day
of indignation. 25 ᵃ *There is* a conspiracy of her pro-
phets in the midst thereof, like a roaring lion ravening
the prey; they have ᵇ devoured souls; ᶜ they have taken
the treasure and precious things; they have made her
many widows in the midst thereof. 26 Her priests
have † violated my law, and have profaned mine holy
things: they have ᵈ put no difference between the holy
and profane, neither have they shewed *difference* between
the unclean and the clean, and have hid their eyes from
my sabbaths, and I am profaned among them. 27
Her ᵉ princes in the midst thereof *are* like wolves ra-
vening the prey, to shed blood, *and* to destroy souls, to
get dishonest gain. 28 And ᶠ her prophets have daub-
ed them with untempered *morter*, ᵍ seeing vanity, and
divining lies unto them, ʰ saying, Thus saith the Lord
GOD, when the LORD hath not spoken. 29 ⁱ The
people of the land have used ‡ oppression, and exercised
robbery, and have vexed the poor and needy: yea, they
have oppressed the stranger wrongfully. 30 And ᵏ I
sought for a man amongst them, that should ˡ make up
the hedge, and ᵐ stand in the gap before me for the
land, that I should not destroy it: but I found none.
31 Therefore have I poured out mine indignation upon
them, I have consumed them with the fire of my
wrath: ⁿ their own way have I recompensed upon their
heads, saith the Lord GOD.

ᵃ Hos. vi. 9. ᵇ Mat. xxiii. 14. ᶜ Mic. iii. 11. Zeph. iii. 3. † Heb. Offered violence to. ᵈ Lev. x. 10. Jer. xv. 19. Chap. xliv. 23. ᵉ Mic. iii. 2, 3. ᶠ Chap. xiii. 10. ᵍ Ibid. xiii. 6. ʰ Ibid. xiii. 6, 7.
Before Christ 592. ⁱ Ver. 7. ‡ Or, deceit. ᵏ Jer. v. 1. ˡ Chap. xiii. 5. ᵐ Psal. cvi. 23. ⁿ Chap. ix. 10. & xi. 21. & xvi. 43.

v. 23—31. The various methods of divine providence and grace made no impression on the people of Israel. They were neither cleansed from their filthiness by the judgments they suffered, nor reformed by the warnings they received; like the parched ground not rained upon, so were their hearts hard and impenetrable; and whilst God withheld from them the dew of heaven to water the earth, in his indignation he sent a heavier judgment, withholding the dew of his heavenly influences, v. 24. All ranks and orders of men among them were advanced to the summit of wickedness.

1. The false prophets who should, by the office they pretended to assume, have stood in the gap, and by their prayers and labours sought to avert the impending judgments, instead of that, formed *a conspiracy* to persecute the true prophets, and flatter the people to their ruin. Like ravening lions *they devoured souls*, taking away the lives of the innocent, or by their false doctrines murdered immortal souls. *They have taken the treasure and precious things* of the innocent, destroyed by them, or of the deluded, who paid them well for their lying divinations of peace. *They have made her many widows in the midst thereof*, by the murders they have committed, or by their encouraging that rebellion in which so many perished. *Note*, Lying prophets who deceived sinners to their ruin, shall receive the heaviest strokes of vengeance.

2. The priests cordially joined with the false prophets in their wickedness. They *violated* God's *law*, perverting it in their explications, and contradicting it in their practice, so that instead of teaching others, their examples were the greatest encouragement to the wicked. They made no difference between *holy* and *profane*, paid no regard to the prescription of God, but lived at large, observing neither distinction of meats nor days; the sabbath to them was but as a common day; they admitted, indiscriminately, any into the courts of the temple, and out of it kept company with the ceremonially unclean, or the abandoned, without a word of rebuke. Thus God *was profaned among them*, his word abused, his ordinances slighted, his authority despised.

3. The princes, who as ministers of justice should have vindicated the oppressed, and exerted their power in the protection of injured innocence, were themselves *like wolves ravening the prey*, insidious, arbitrary, lawless, cruel; not only plundering the weak with impunity, and with dishonest gain grinding the faces of the poor, but even imbruing their hands in blood, as their rage, revenge, or covetousness led them, destroying the lives of those who had offended them, or on whose spoil they had fixed their greedy eye. And, shocking to relate! the infamous prophets, to curry favour with these wealthy patrons, flattered them in their wickedness, and *daubed them with untempered morter*, probably persuading them they did God service in persecuting the troublesome prophets, and the faithful who remonstrated against their sins, and vindicating their cruel deeds to others as wholsome severities. *Note*, (1.) The height of station aggravates the enormity of the offence. (2.) The daubing prophets at the elbows of the great, who prostitute the sacred office they pretend to bear, by mean compliances and infamous countenance given to their sins, shall shortly meet an avenging God.

4. The people naturally followed examples so pernicious; the system of corruption descended, and as each in an inferior station had power, he *used* it to *oppression*, and *exercised robbery*, vexing the poor by extortion, and treating the *stranger wrongfully*, whose ignorance laid him the more easily open to deceit and imposition.

5. So general and universal was the apostacy, that not a man was found among all these prophets, priests, princes, or people, who endeavoured to interpose *to make up the hedge*, or *stand in the gap* to avert by his prayers, his admonitions, or his labours, the impending wrath, and endeavour the reformation of the land. God sought for such, and sought in vain. *Note*, (1.) Sin makes the breach at which ruin enters. (2.) When none are found to pray or plead with God for the land, the case is desperate.

6. Because of these things, God's indignation is poured out; the fire kindles, the sinners are consumed together, and their own way recompensed on their heads. *Note*, However terrible the end of the ungodly may be, their sufferings shall be no more than their deserts.

CHAP.

Before Christ 592.

CHAP. XXIII.

This, as well as the sixteenth and twentieth chapters, is a history of the apostacies of God's people from him, and the aggravations of these apostacies under the similitude of corporal whoredom and adultery. Here is, 1. The apostacy of Israel and Samaria, ver. 1—8. And their ruin for it, ver. 9, 10. 2. The apostacy of Judah and Jerusalem, ver. 11—21. for which they shall likewise perish, ver. 22—35. 3. The joint-wickedness of both together, ver. 36—44. and the joint-ruin of them both, ver. 45—49.

1 THE word of the LORD came again unto me, saying, 2 Son of man, there were two women the daughters of one mother: 3 And they committed whoredoms in Egypt; they committed whoredoms in their youth: there were their breasts pressed, and there they bruised the teats of their virginity. 4 And the names of them *were* † Aholah the † elder, and § Aholibah her sister: and they were mine, and they bare sons and daughters. Thus *were* their names; Samaria *is* Aholah, and Jerusalem Aholibah. 5 And Aholah played the harlot when she was mine; and she doted on her lovers, on the Assyrians *her* neighbours, 6 *Which were* clothed with blue, captains and rulers, all of them desirable young men, horsemen riding upon horses. 7 Thus she committed her whoredoms with them, with all them *that were* ‖ the chosen men of Assyria, and with all on whom she doted, with all their idols she defiled herself. 8 Neither left she her whoredoms *brought* from Egypt: for in her youth they lay with her, and they bruised the breasts of her virginity, and poured their whoredom upon her. 9 Wherefore I have delivered her into the hand of her lovers, into the hand of the Assyrians, upon whom she doted. 10 These discovered her nakedness: they took her sons and her daughters, and slew her with the sword: and she became † famous among women; for they had executed judgment upon her.

v. 1—10. Israel and Judah, sister kingdoms, the daughters of one mother, sprung from the same origin-l stock, are here considered under the character of two infamous women, Aholah and Aholibah.

1. They were early debauched by idolatry; even in Egypt they began to transgress, and lost their virgin honour, *v.* 3.

2. Though they were God's espoused ones, and he was pleased to take them for his own, and to raise them up a numerous offspring; yet they treacherously departed from him, and played the harlot. *Aholah*, which is *Samaria*, signifies *her tabernacle*, she having first forsook God's tabernacle, and set up her own worship at Dan and Bethel. She is called the *elder*, or greater, the kingdom of Israel consisting of ten tribes. Though she had revolted from the royal house of David, God still owned her for his; but her abominable idolatries soon made a final separation. She *doated on her lovers*, particularly on *her Assyrian neighbours*, contracted alliances with them, admired their idols, their worship, and military forces, which were so richly dressed, and placed on them the dependance she withdrew from God, *v.* 7. Yet she persisted also in the worship of the gods of Egypt, the beginning of her apostacy, and served the calves in Bethel and Dan, as well as the newly-introduced deities of the Assyrians. *Note*, (1.) They who have been a professing people, when they apostatize, sink under the most aggravated guilt. (2.) Whatever we doat upon, becomes our idol; and God will not with impunity suffer us to give the honour, love, and homage due to him, unto another.

3. For their apostacy Samaria and Israel were destroyed. God made those on whom they had doated, and whose idols they served, the instruments of his vengeance, *v.* 9. They *discovered her nakedness*, stripped her of all her treasures, led her children captives, and utterly ruined the kingdom, executing God's judgments upon her; so that *she became famous among women*. Her crime and her dreadful end were the general subject of conversation in the neighbouring lands, and afforded an awful warning not to imitate her sin, lest the same plague should follow. *Note*, (1.) Those whom we have made our tempters, God in righteous judgment often makes our tormentors. (2.) They who render themselves famous by wickedness, will by God's vengeance be made monuments of wretchedness.

11 And when her sister Aholibah saw *this*, she was more corrupt in her inordinate love than she, and in her whoredoms more than her sister in *her* whoredoms. 12 She doted upon the Assyrians *her* neighbours, captains and rulers clothed most gorgeously, horsemen riding upon horses, all of them desirable young men. 13 Then I saw that she was defiled, *that* they *took* both one way, 14 And *that* she increased her whoredoms: for when she saw men pourtrayed upon the wall, the images of the Chaldeans pourtrayed with vermilion, 15 Girded with girdles upon their loins, exceeding in dyed attire upon their heads, all of them princes to look to, after the manner of the Babylonians of Chaldea, the land of their nativity: 16 And as soon as she saw them with her eyes, she doted upon them, and sent messengers unto them into Chaldea. 17 And the † Babylonians came to her into the bed of love, and they defiled her with their whoredom, and she was polluted with them, and her mind was ‡ alienated from them. 18 So she discovered her whoredoms, and discovered her nakedness: then my mind was alienated from her, like as my mind was alienated from her sister. 19 Yet she multiplied her whoredoms, in calling to remembrance the days of her youth, wherein she had played the harlot in the land of Egypt. 20 For she doted upon their paramours, whose flesh *is as* the flesh of asses, and whose issue *is like* the issue of horses. 21 Thus thou calledst to remembrance the lewdness of thy youth, in bruising thy teats by the Egyptians, for the paps of thy youth.

v. 11—21. Far from taking warning by Samaria's fate, Jerusalem not only copied but exceeded her abominations. She is called *Aholibah*, or, *my tabernacle is in her*, God having chosen Zion for his peculiar abode, and this exceedingly aggravated the guilt of her apostacy.

1. She took the same way to defile herself her sister had done, doating upon the Assyrians, admiring the dress and military appearance of their captains and soldiers, courting their alliance, depending on them for protection, increasing her idols beyond what Samaria had done, *v.* 14. falling in love with the very pictures of their deified heroes, who were pourtrayed in rich attire on the walls of their temples, *v.* 14, 15. and sending messengers to Chaldea to form a league, and adopt their idols and worship, *v.* 16. And no sooner had she taken the Babylonians to her adulterous bed, and defiled herself with their idols, than she *was alienated from them*, as lust and loathing often succeed each other. She rebelled under Jehoiakim and Zedekiah, 2 *Kings* xxiv. 1, 20. and cast off the alliance with Babylon, *v.* 17. and calling to mind with pleasure the idolatries of the Egyptians, *v.* 21. returned to play the harlot with them, *doating on these paramours*, as better suiting her insatiable lewdness, *v.* 20. openly *discovering her whoredoms and her nakedness*, as a brazen prostitute hardened against shame. *Note*, (1.) Inordinate appetites indulged only grow more fickle and craving. (2.) Long habit of sin gives effrontery to the lewd, and they dare avow and boast of what others blush to name, and tremble but to think of.

2. God saw and abhorred such shameless idolatry, and *his mind was alienated from her, as it was from her sister*. He cast off Judah also from her relation to him, and left her, as a wife divorced, to all the miseries which must ensue when his protection was withdrawn. *Note*, They who provoke God to cast them from his favour, have only themselves to blame for the miseries which follow.

22 ¶ Therefore, O Aholibah, thus saith the Lord GOD; Behold, I will raise up thy lovers against thee, from whom thy mind is alienated, and I will bring them against thee on every side; 23 The Babylonians, and all the Chaldeans, Pekod, and Shoa, and Koa, *and* all the Assyrians with them: all of them desirable young men, captains and rulers, great lords and renowned, all of them riding upon horses. 24 And they shall come against thee with chariots, waggons, and wheels, and with an assembly of people, *which* shall set against thee buckler and shield and helmet round about: and I will set judgment before them, and they shall judge thee according to their judgments. 25 And I will set my jealousy against thee, and they shall deal furiously with thee: they shall take away thy nose and thine ears; and thy remnant shall fall by the sword: they shall take thy sons and thy daughters; and thy residue shall be devoured by the fire. 26 They shall also strip thee out of thy clothes, and take away ‡ thy fair jewels. 27 Thus will I make thy lewdness to cease from thee, and thy whoredom *brought* from the land of Egypt: so that thou shalt not lift up thine eyes unto them, nor remember Egypt any more. 28 For thus saith the Lord GOD; [illegible] Behold,

Before Christ 593.

Behold, I will deliver thee into the hand *of them* whom thou hatest, into the hand *of them* from whom thy mind is alienated 29 And they shall deal with thee hatefully, and shall take away all thy labour, and shall leave thee naked and bare, and the nakedness of thy whoredoms shall be discovered, both thy lewdness and thy whoredoms 30 I will do these *things* unto thee, because thou hast gone a whoring after the heathen, *and* because thou art polluted with their idols 31 Thou hast walked in the way of thy sister, therefore will I give her cup into thine hand 32 Thus saith the Lord GOD, Thou shalt drink of thy sister's cup deep and large thou shalt be laughed to scorn, and had in derision, it containeth much 33 Thou shalt be filled with drunkenness and sorrow, with the cup of astonishment and desolation, with the cup of thy sister Samaria. 34 Thou shalt even drink it, and suck *it* out, and thou shalt break the sherds thereof, and pluck off thine own breasts for I have spoken *it*, saith the Lord GOD 35 Therefore thus saith the Lord GOD, Because thou hast forgotten me, and cast me behind thy back, therefore bear thou also thy lewdness, and thy whoredoms

v 22—35 We have here,

1 Judgment pronounced on Jerusalem for her crimes Those lovers on whom she doated are appointed to be her destroyers their armies, with a vast train of carriages, at God's command shall come up, besiege and destroy the cities, and lay waste the country, v 22—24 As a jealous husband, enraged with an adulterous wife, God will visit them in fury, the Chaldeans shall cut off *their nose and ears*, literally disfiguring them to render them loathsome, or destroying their king, princes, and priests, represented by these, and slay all the remnant of the people, except those who, stripped of all their ornaments, even to their cloaths, shall be driven, naked as slaves, into a miserable captivity, v 26 and the few houses in Jerusalem that have stood the fire unhurt, shall now be burnt with fire, v 25 Delivered into the hands of those they hated, and against whom they had rebelled, v 28 they may expect no favour or pity they will *deal hatefully* with them, treat them with rigour and severity, plunder all their possessions, leave them naked and bare, and in the greatness of their punishment the greatness of their crimes will appear, v 29

2 God's wrath evidently seen in their ruin will make their sufferings still more bitter Though he employs the Chaldeans as instruments, he says, v 30 *I will do these things unto thee*, and most righteous will he appear in his judgments their flagrant idolatries justify his severest strokes of vengeance, v 30 Since they walked in Samaria's ways, they deserve to drink of her cup full of fury, a cup of *drunkenness, sorrow, astonishment, and desolation*, the very dregs of which they must suck out, and, exposed to the scorn and derision of the nations around them, for madness and vexation at their wretched state, shall *pluck off their own breasts*, as men in a fit of rage and despair, v 31—34 Because they have *forgotten God*, which is the source of all their wickedness, and *cast him behind their backs*, despising his authority, and rejecting his government, he will lay upon them the punishment of their idolatries and lewdness, v 35 and make these to cease from among them, so that the remnant, who are brought through the fiery furnace, shall never return to idolatry again, v 27 as they never more did after the captivity *Note*, (1) They who share with the wicked in their sins, may expect to share with them in their plagues (2) The cup of drunkenness will ever prove a cup of sorrow (3) They who by lewdness have made themselves vile, justly deserve to have their whoredoms discovered, and to be made the derision of every beholder

36 ¶ The LORD said moreover unto me, Son of man, wilt thou judge Aholah and Aholibah? yea, declare unto them their abominations; 37 That they have committed adultery, and blood *is* in their hands, and with their idols have they committed adultery, and have also caused their sons whom they bare unto me, to pass for them through *the fire* to devour *them* 38 Moreover, this they have done unto me they have defiled my sanctuary in the same day, and have profaned my sabbaths 39 For when they had slain their children to their idols, then they came the same day into my sanctuary to profane it, and lo, thus have they done in the midst of mine house 40 And furthermore, that ye have sent for men to come from far, unto whom a messenger *was* sent, and lo, they came, for whom thou didst wash thyself, paintedst thy eyes, and deckedst thyself with ornaments, 41 And sattest upon a stately bed, and a table prepared before it, whereupon thou hast set mine incense and mine oil 42 And a voice of a multitude being at ease *was* with her, and with the men of the common sort *were* brought Sabeans from the wilderness, which put bracelets upon their hands, and beautiful crowns upon their heads 43 Then said I unto *her that was* old in adulteries, Will they now commit whoredoms with her, and she *with them*? 44 Yet they went in unto her, as they go in unto a woman that playeth the harlot so went they in unto Aholah and unto Aholibah the lewd women 45 ¶ And the righteous men, they shall judge them after the manner of adulteresses, and after the manner of women that shed blood, because they *are* adulteresses, and blood *is* in their hands 46 For thus saith the Lord GOD, I will bring up a company upon them, and will give them to be removed and spoiled 47 And the company shall stone them with stones, and dispatch them with their swords, they shall slay their sons and their daughters, and burn up their houses with fire 48 Thus will I cause lewdness to cease out of the land, that all women may be taught not to do after your lewdness 49 And they shall recompense your lewdness upon you, and ye shall bear the sins of your idols and ye shall know that I *am* the Lord GOD

v 36—49 After the account given of the wickedness of Judah and Israel, God appeals to the prophet, whether he ought any longer to plead for them, or whether he ought not in God's name to condemn them to the death they had deserved

1 He must *declare unto them their abominations*, and they were exceeding sinful

(1) Gross idolatry, which is spiritual adultery, the breach of the covenant between God and them, v 37

(2) The most unnatural murders, even the sacrificing their own children to Moloch, so besotted were they, and mad upon their idols, v 37

(3) Horrid profanation of God's sanctuary With the blood of innocents fresh upon them, that very day, with unhallowed feet and polluted lips, they dared appear before God in his temple, as if designing to affront him, or as if they thought with hypocritical services to impose upon him and this they did *in the midst of his house*, setting up their idols even there, or without shame daring to appear among the foremost worshippers

(4) They profaned the sabbath, not only by servile works, or taking their pleasures on that holy day, but by the worship of their idols, and the horrid sacrifices of their own children

(5) They courted the alliance of the heathen nations, the Egyptians, Assyrians, and Chaldeans; received their ambassadors in great state and splendor, as a harlot attires and paints herself to meet her paramour, made them a noble entertainment, used the sacred incense to perfume the room, and the oil to anoint them, as a mark of peculiar honour or perhaps, as some suspect, these were designed for the ambassadors' use, to be employed in their idols' service, v 41 A great concourse of people also assembled to grace their public entrance, *a multitude at ease*, who flattered themselves such great alliances must needs conduce to the security of the state And besides the Jewish populace, a number of Sabeans from the desert swelled the cavalcade, or of *drunkards*, as in the margin, to drink healths and huzza on this auspicious event, decked up with bracelets on their hands, and crowns upon their heads, that they might make the most splendid appearance, v 42 God in vain admonished them of the folly, sin, and danger of such connection they were *grown old in adultery*, and hardened against reproof The alliance was concluded, *they went in unto her*, as to a harlot Samaria first, and Jerusalem afterwards, *as lewd* and abandoned *women*, gladly received them, and joined in their idolatries, v 44 *Note*, (1) The affectation of being well with the great, hath been often a dangerous snare to men's souls (2) They who desert God for human confidences, however smiling their undertaking at first may appear, will find in the issue a lie in their right hand

2 He must denounce against them God's wrath *The righteous men, they shall judge them* which some understand of the prophets of God, who foretold their doom, and passed sentence upon them, though others more probably apply it to the Babylonians, who were comparatively *more righteous than they*, and were appointed of God as the executioners of his righteous vengeance Their crimes were capital, adultery and murder manifold, and their punishment accordingly, v 45 A company at God's command, the Chaldean army, shall come, and seize and spoil them, v 46 Some shall be stoned, slain with the engines that battered the city, others dispatched with the sword,

Before Christ 590.

sword, their sons and daughters murdered in their presence, their city and every house burnt with fire, v. 47. Thus by the utter ruin of the kingdom, the worship of idols should be utterly destroyed, and never more be restored, and all who beheld their ruin will be warned against their sins, v. 48. With such wrath and destruction should their lewdness be recompensed, and the burden of their guilt and punishment be heavily laid on them, so that if they will not be taught any other way, by their sufferings at least they shall be made to know that God is the Lord, true to his threatnings, and almighty to accomplish them, v. 49. *Note*, (1) Others falls should be our warning. (2) However sinners may flatter themselves, a day of recompence is near, when they will receive the wrath they have provoked.

CHAP. XXIV.

The design of this prophecy is to shew the certain ruin of Jerusalem. It was delivered the very day the king of Babylon began to prepare for the siege, ver. 2. 1. By the sign of flesh boiling in a pot is shewed, the miseries that Jerusalem should suffer during the siege, ver. 3—14. 2. By the sign of Ezekiel's not mourning for the death of his wife, is shewed, that the calamities coming upon Jerusalem were too great to be lamented, ver. 15—27.

590. 1 AGAIN in the ninth year, in the tenth month,
in the tenth *day* of the month, the word of the
LORD came unto me, saying, 2 Son of man, Write thee
the name of the day, *even* of this same day: the king of
Babylon set himself against Jerusalem [a] this same day.
3 And utter a parable unto the rebellious house, and
say unto them, Thus saith the Lord GOD, [b] Set on a
pot, set *it* on, and also pour water into it: 4 [c] Gather
the pieces thereof into it, *even* every good piece, the
thigh and the shoulder, fill *it* with the choice bones.
5 Take the choice of the flock, and [†] burn also the
bones under it, *and* make it boil well, and let them
seethe the bones of it therein. 6 ¶ Wherefore thus
saith the Lord GOD, Wo to the [d] bloody city, to the
pot whose scum *is* therein, and whose scum is not gone
out of it, bring it out piece by piece, [e] let no lot fall
upon it. 7 For her blood is in the midst of her, [f] she
set it upon the top of a rock, [g] she poured it not upon
the ground, to cover it with dust. 8 That it might
cause fury to come up to take vengeance, I have set her
blood upon the top of a rock, that it should not be co-
vered. 9 Therefore thus saith the Lord GOD, [h] Wo
to the bloody city, I will even make the pile for fire
great. 10 Heap on wood, kindle the fire, consume the
flesh, and spice it well, and let the bones be burnt. 11
Then set it empty upon the coals thereof, that the brass
of it may be hot, and may burn, and *that* the filthiness
of it may be molten in it, *that* the scum of it may be
consumed. 12 She hath wearied [†] *herself* with lies,
and her great scum went not forth out of her: her scum
shall be in the fire. 13 In thy filthiness *is* lewdness:
because I have [i] purged thee, and [k] thou wast not purg-
ed, [l] thou shalt not be purged from thy filthiness any
more, [m] till I have caused my fury to rest upon thee.
14 [n] I the LORD have spoken *it*, it shall come to
pass, and I will do *it*, I will not go back, [o] neither will
I spare, neither will I repent, according to thy ways,
and according to thy doings shall they judge thee, saith
the Lord GOD.

Margin: [a] Jer. lii. 4. [b] Jer. i. 13. Chap. xi. 3. [c] Mic. iii. 3. [†] Or, heap. [d] 2 Kings xxi. 16. Chap. xxii. [e] Chap. ix. 5, 6. [f] Isa. iii. 9. Ezek. xvii. 13. [h] Nah. iii. 1. Hab. ii. 12. [†] Or, herself. [i] 2 Chron. xxxvi. 15. [k] Jer. vi. 29. [m] Chap. v. 13. [n] 1 Sam. xv. 29. [o] Chap. v. 11.

v. 1—14. The king of Babylon was now gone forth with his army, his designs a secret probably to all, but God knew whither he could went, and what he was doing, and, the very day Jerusalem was invested, reveals it to the prophet, and bids him write it down, probably in some public register, that when the intelligence arrived, they might be confirmed in the divine authority by which he spake, since it was at a distance none could have conveyed the tidings, had they not come immediately from God: and hereby they might be assured of the fulfilment of all his other predictions, particularly the destruction of Jerusalem, which they still flattered themselves should not be taken. To undeceive them, though a rebellious house, God gives them,

1. A sign, *a boiling pot*, v. 3. *See Jer.* i. 13. filled with the best pieces of meat, v. 4. with the choicest bones from the prime of the flock, v. 5. and a fire continually fed, till the whole was thoroughly boiled together.

2. The explication of the sign, or parable. The pot is Jerusalem, *the bloody city*, on whom God denounces wo, v. 9.

the fire is God's wrath burning fierce and constant, the choice pieces are the great men of Jerusalem with their king, the bones, their strong warriors. These together must boil till their scum rises, intimating the wrath due to their provocations, and it is not *gone out*, they continuing impenitent under all their sufferings. Therefore God commands, *Bring it out piece by piece*, none of any age, sex, or station, must be spared: *let no lot fall upon it*, to save any from the general destruction. *Heap on wood, kindle the fire, consume the flesh*, thoroughly boil it down, denoting the intenseness and continuance of the miseries the besieged would undergo: *make it savoury*, that the Chaldeans may greedily devour the prey; and *let the bones be burnt*, the men of war destroyed: *then set it empty upon the coals thereof, that the brass of it may be hot and burn*, the city, after the siege, being by Nebuchadnezzar's order burnt to the ground.

3. The justice of God in this destruction of Jerusalem is manifested: it is the just reward of her crimes, so black and enormous. Because she hath shed openly and lavishly the blood of innocents, and far from desiring to conceal her guilt, on the top of the rock it stood proclaimed, as if daring divine vengeance. Probably on these eminencies they sacrificed their children, v. 7. therefore God heard the cry, and awaked to judgment, and in righteous retaliation will pour out their blood on the top of a rock, executing them publicly as malefactors. The *scum*, their filthy ways, *shall be consumed*, since instead of being led to repentance by what they had suffered, and the warnings God had given them, they harden their hearts like a pot which boils over, *their scum running over into the fire*, shall add fierceness to the flames, in which they will a terribly perish. With *lies*, with idol vanities, or the false hopes the prophets of Judah suggested, or the alliances she had formed, she had *wearied herself*, disappointed of all her expectations, v. 12. yet unhumbled still, and obstinately persisting in her sins. *In thy filthiness is lewdness*, a fixed and rooted delight in sin, and daring avowal of it, so that all the means used were ineffectual to reclaim her. *I have purged thee, and thou wast not purged*, therefore since the case was desperate, she is abandoned to ruin: she *shall not be purged from her filthiness any more*, no methods shall be used for her recovery, but God's fury shall rest upon her, v. 13. without pity, and without repentance, according to her deeds he will recompense her in judgment, and his decree gone forth is irreversible, *it shall surely come to pass*. *Note*, (1) Blood will cry for vengeance, and daring sinners shall one day be made a spectacle to angels and to men. (2) They who harden their hearts against the means God uses for their conversion, must perish without remedy. (3) It is most just to abandon those to their own lusts, who say unto the Almighty, Depart from us. (4) The truth of God is engaged for the punishment of sinners: unless he prove a liar, they must lie down in everlasting burnings.

15 ¶ Also the word of the LORD came unto me,
saying, 16 Son of man, behold, I take away from
thee [p] the desire of thine eyes with a stroke: yet neither
shalt thou mourn nor weep, neither shall thy tears run
down. 17 [†] Forbear to cry, make no mourning for
the dead, [q] bind the tire of thine head upon thee, and
put on thy shoes upon thy feet, and cover not *thy* [‡] lips,
and eat not the bread of men. 18 So I spake unto the
people in the morning, and at even my wife died, and
I did in the morning as I was commanded. 19 ¶ And
the people said unto me, Wilt thou not tell us what
these *things are* to us, that thou dost *so?* 20 Then I
answered them, The word of the LORD came unto me,
saying, 21 Speak unto the house of Israel, Thus saith
the Lord GOD, Behold, I will profane my sanctuary,
the excellency of your strength, the desire of your eyes,
and § that which your soul pitieth; and your sons and
your daughters whom ye have left shall fall by the sword.
22 And ye shall do as I have done: ye shall not cover
your lips, nor eat the bread of men. 23 And your tires
shall be upon your heads, and your shoes upon your feet:
ye shall not mourn nor weep, but ye shall pine away
for your iniquities, and mourn one towards another.
24 Thus [x] Ezekiel is unto you a sign: according to all
that he hath done shall ye do: [y] and when this cometh,
ye shall know that I *am* the Lord GOD. 25 Also
thou son of man, *shall it* not *be* in the day when I take
from them their strength, the joy of their glory, the de-
sire of their eyes, and ‖ that whereupon they set their
minds, their sons and their daughters, 26 *That* [a] he
that escapeth in that day shall come unto thee, to cause
thee to hear *it* with *thine* ears? 27 [b] In that day shall
thy mouth be opened to him which is escaped, and
thou shalt speak, and be no more dumb: and thou shalt

Before Christ 590.

be a sign unto them, and they shall know that I *am* the LORD.

v. 15—27. By another sign, that most nearly affected the prophet, the certain ruin of Jerusalem is foretold.

1. God will suddenly take from him the wife on whom he placed his fond affections, the desire of his eyes, with a stroke. *Note,* (1.) Those who are joined in marriage bonds should delight in each other, and study mutually to render themselves every day more amiable and desirable in each other's eyes. (2.) Death spares not the dearest relatives, and the suddenness of the stroke often renders the separation more grievous; but God's hand seen in the visitation, should reconcile us to his will: he gave, and when he pleases, may justly resume his own gifts.

2. Ezekiel is forbidden to shew any symptom of grief and mourning, such as were natural and usual on these melancholy occasions. His tears must neither flow, however bitter his inward anguish; nor must he make any change, as was usual in such a case, in his attire; nor *eat the bread of men,* such as was sent to mourners by their friends during their first pangs of sorrow, when they were supposed inattentive to the calls of nature.

3. The prophet is all obedience. He spake to the people in the morning concerning this melancholy event, and at even his prediction was verified, *his wife died* suddenly. The next morning he appeared as usual, without evincing one symptom of his bitter sorrow, since so the Lord had commanded him. *Note,* (1.) Submission to God's will, however bitter the affliction, is not only our duty, but should be our delight. (2.) They who are put in trust with the gospel, must shew a deadness to the world; not only to its inordinate cares, but must also moderate their sorrows, as examples to others of humble resignation.

4. Such a behaviour in the prophet naturally excited the people's enquiries into the cause; and suspecting it was with a view to them, they desired to be informed of the meaning of his conduct, and he is ordered fully to explain it to them. Ezekiel is a sign unto them: as God had done to him, so would he shortly deal with them, and cause them to act in like manner. Their sanctuary, once their glory and boast, *the desire of their eyes,* for though they had lost the power of godliness, they prized themselves in the temple, *the excellency of their strength,* on which they placed their chief confidence, and *that which their soul pitied,* they could not think of its desolations without being deeply affected; it *shall be profaned,* given into the hands of the heathen, and utterly demolished by them; and their sons and daughters, the joy of their hearts, who were left from the pestilence and famine, shall fall by the Chaldean sword, *v.* 21. And as Ezekiel had done, so should they do, shewing no token of grief, because so great it would overwhelm them, and be too big for utterance; or not daring to complain, for fear of provoking their conquerors; or when all were involved in the common calamity, none would remain exempted to lend the bread of mourners to their neighbours; nor could they make bare their feet, when forced to travel into a miserable captivity. Thus in silent anguish they should *pine away in their iniquities,* hardened in impenitence, and shut up in despair, and *mourn one toward another,* when they could privately meet together; not to bewail in penitence their sins, but to murmur and complain against God, and aggravate their miseries by their impatience under them. *Note,* (1.) Great griefs often stupify, and finding no vent in tears, pent up they overwhelm the soul. (2.) They who mourn only for their sufferings, but not for their sins, shew their hearts to be yet hardened.

5. The event would shortly verify the prophetic word. The tidings of the dreadful catastrophe of the Jews would reach Babylon; some miserable fugitive would report how terribly Jerusalem fell, *her strength* broken, her armies destroyed, her riches plundered; the temple, *the joy of their glory,* in which they placed especial confidence, destroyed; and their sons and daughters, on whom they had set their fond affections, the desire of their eyes, massacred by the Chaldean sword, *v.* 25. Then should the prophet's lips be opened, to converse with the messenger of these grievous tidings, and enquire into the particulars; and though from the time of this prophecy he *was dumb,* spoke no more to the Jews, but turned himself to other nations, then his tongue shall be loosed again, to address them, and urge the punishments inflicted on the rebellious, according to the sign given them, as argument for the repentance of the captives, who must *know and own* the truth and righteousness of God, manifested in the destruction of Jerusalem. *Note,* (1.) They who will not believe God's warnings, will at last be convinced of their truth by his judgments. (2.) When men set their minds on creature-comforts, God often punishes them in destroying their idols.

CHAP. XXV.

Judgment [illegible] at the house of God, but it does not end there: [illegible] been passed upon Judah, but the neighbouring nations are threatened. 1. The Ammonites, ver. 1—7. 2. The Moabites, ver. 8—11. 3. The Edomites, ver. 12—14. 4. The Philistines, ver. 15—17. That which [illegible] to the charge of each of them, is their barbarous and insolent carriage towards God's Israel, for none shall trample on God's people with impunity.

1 THE word of the LORD came again unto me,
saying, 2 Son of man, set thy face ᵃ against
the Ammonites, and prophesy against them; 3 And
say unto the Ammonites, Hear the word of the Lord
GOD; Thus saith the Lord GOD, ᵇ Because thou saidst,
Aha, against my sanctuary, when it was profaned; and
against the land of Israel, when it was desolate; and a-
gainst the house of Judah, when they went into capti-
vity; 4 Behold ᶜ therefore, I will deliver thee to the
† men of the east for a possession, and they shall set
their palaces in thee, and make their dwellings in thee:
they shall eat thy fruit, and they shall drink thy milk.
5 And I will make Rabbah ᵈ a stable for camels, and the
Ammonites a couching place for flocks: and ᵈ ye shall
know that I *am* the LORD. 6 For thus saith the
Lord GOD; Because thou ᵉ hast clapped *thine* hands,
and stamped with the feet, and ᶠ rejoiced in heart with
all thy despite against the land of Israel; 7 Behold,
therefore, I will stretch out mine hand upon thee, and
will deliver thee for a spoil to the heathen; and I will cut
thee off from the people, and I will cause thee to perish
out of the countries: I will destroy thee; and thou shalt
know that I *am* the LORD.

ᵃ Jer. xlix. 1, &c. Chap. xxi. 28. Amos i. 13. Zeph. ii. 9.
ᵇ Chap. xxvi. 2.
ᶜ Prov. xvii. 5.
† Heb. Children.
ᵈ Chap. xxiv. 24. & xxxv. 9.
ᵉ Job xxvii. 23. Lam. ii. 15. Zeph. ii. 15.
ᶠ Prov. xvii. 5. [illegible]

v. 1—7. The Ammonites, the implacable enemies of the Jewish people, are first to be reckoned with. The Lord Jehovah, the God of Israel, declares their provocations, and denounces their doom.

1. Their crime was, the malicious pleasure they took in seeing God's Israel ruined. They beheld with delight the profanations of the sanctuary, and exulted in the desolations and captivity of the people, expressing the rancour and despite of their hearts by their outward gestures, clapping their hands, leaping, and shouting for those miseries, which the least humanity would have taught them to pity. *Note,* (1.) The enmity of the natural heart against God's people is sure to express itself on their falls or misfortunes. (2.) God observes and will severely visit the malice and rancour shewn by the enemies of his Israel.

2. Their punishment for this insolent carriage will be their utter destruction. *The men of the east,* the Chaldeans, or the Arabians, who were in Nebuchadnezzar's army, and afterwards possessed the country, they shall seize their land for *a possession,* set up their palaces therein, and dwell there, feasting on their spoil, their fruits, and their milk, *v.* 4. Rabbah, the metropolis, shall be turned into *a stable for camels,* and the country feed the flocks of their conquerors, *v.* 5. God's stretched-out arm shall make an end of them, cut them off from being any longer a people, and cause them to perish from the earth, *v.* 6. and in this terrible destruction make his own great name known as the avenger of his people's wrongs.

8 ¶ Thus saith the Lord GOD; ᵍ Because that
Moab and Seir do say, Behold ʰ the house of Judah *is*
like unto all the heathen; 9 Therefore, behold, I
will open the ‖ side of Moab from the cities, from his
cities *which are* on his frontiers, the glory of the coun-
try Beth-jeshimoth, Baal-meon, and Kiriathaim, 10
Unto the men of the east ‡ with the Ammonites, and
will give them in possession, that the Ammonites may
not be remembered among the nations. 11 And I will
execute judgments upon Moab, and they shall know
that I *am* the LORD. 12 ¶ Thus saith the Lord
GOD, ⁱ Because that Edom hath dealt against the house
of Judah by taking vengeance, and hath greatly of-
fended, and revenged himself upon them; 13 There-
fore thus saith the Lord GOD, I will also stretch out
mine hand upon Edom, and will cut off man and beast
from it, and I will make it desolate from Teman; and
§ they of Dedan shall fall by the sword. 14 And ᵏ I
will lay my vengeance upon Edom by the hand of my
people Israel; and they shall do in Edom according to
mine anger, and according to my fury; and they shall
know my vengeance, saith the Lord GOD. 15 ¶
Thus saith the Lord GOD, ˡ Because ᵐ the Philistines
have dealt by revenge, and have taken vengeance with
a despiteful heart, to destroy *it* ‖ for the old hatred;

ᵍ Jer. xlviii. & xvi. [illegible]
ʰ [illegible] Kings [illegible]
‖ Heb. shoulder.
‡ Or, against the children of Ammon.
ⁱ Ps. cxxxvii. 7. Jer. xlix. 7, 8. Chap. xxxv. 2. Amos i. 11. Obad. 10, &c.
§ Or, they shall fall by the sword unto Dedan.
ᵏ Isa. xi. 14. [illegible]
ˡ Jer. xxv. 20. Amos i. 6.
ᵐ 2 Chron. xxviii. 18.
‖ Or, with perpetual hatred.

16 Therefore

Before Christ 588.

16 Therefore thus saith the Lord GOD, Behold, [a] I
will stretch out mine hand upon the Philistines, and I
will cut off the Cherethims, and [b] destroy the remnant
of the sea coast. 17 And I will execute great † ven-
geance upon them with furious rebukes; and they shall
know that I *am* the LORD, when I shall lay my ven-
geance upon them.

a Zeph. ii. 4, &c. Jer. xlvii. † Heb. Vengeances.

v. 8—17. These other guilty nations are called to God's bar, and hear their doom. Their crimes and their punishments are nearly similar.

1. The Moabites.

(1.) Their crime was, delight in the sins and sufferings of God's people. They say, *Behold the house of Judah is like unto all the heathen*; perfect apostates from their God, and wholly given to idolatry, and, as the consequence thereof, taken into the hands of the Babylonians, and no distinction subsisting between them and others, of which they used to boast. *Note*, (1.) Apostates from God's worship give the adversaries great occasion to blaspheme. (2.) Though the same event happens to the righteous and the wicked, yet God knows how to put a vast difference between them.

(2.) The punishment of Moab would be to become a prey to the same invaders as had destroyed the country of Ammon: their defences ruined, their country laid open, and their capital cities, their glory, demolished. Thus should they fall as the Ammonites their neighbours, whose name would be lost among the nations; and by these judgments God executes, his power, his wrath, and the truth of his threatnings would be known unto them.

2. The Idumites.

(1.) They not only, as their neighbours of Moab and Ammon, beheld and rejoiced in the fall of Judea, but they remembred the old grudge between Jacob and Esau, their subjection by David, and their chastisement by Amaziah, and now embraced the favourable moment to execute their cruel revenge upon the poor afflicted people, at which God is *highly* and justly *offended*, *v.* 12. *Note*, Whatever provocations we have received, it is highly criminal to entertain malice, or revenge ourselves: this is God's prerogative, *Vengeance is mine*.

(2.) God will punish them severely: from north to south the ravages of the Chaldeans shall spread, and man and beast be cut off by the out-stretched arm of the Lord; and when afterwards they returned from their captivity, and began to recover themselves, by the hand of *his people Israel* God will lay vengeance upon them, which was fulfilled under the Maccabees, 1 *Mac.* v. 3. and Hircanus, as Josephus relates, subdued and made them tributaries. Thus will the Lord pour out his anger and fury upon them, and make them know by what they feel, against what a God of omnipotence and justice they have offended.

3. The Philistines. Their sin and punishment is nearly similar. With a despiteful heart they seized this opportunity of taking vengeance for the old grudge they bore them: but they shall suffer for it, God's arm of vengeance shall espouse his people's quarrel, their mighty men shall perish, their maritime cities be destroyed, and with furious rebukes they shall be made to know, that Israel's God is above all gods, and be made to confess his righteous judgments.

CHAP. XXVI.

The city of Tyre, the famed mart of nations, and known throughout the world, is next brought to God's bar. We have here, 1. The sin charged upon Tyre, which was triumphing in the destruction of Jerusalem, ver. 2. 2. Its destruction foretold, (1.) The extremity of it, it should be utterly ruined, ver. 4—6, 12, 13, 14. (2.) The instruments of this destruction, many nations, ver. 3, particularly the king of Babylon, with his vast victorious army, ver. 7—11. (3.) The great surprize and alarm that this should give to the neighbouring nations, ver. 15—21.

1 AND it came to pass in the eleventh year, in the
first *day* of the month, *that* the word of the
LORD came unto me, saying, 2 Son of man, [i] be-
cause that Tyrus hath said against Jerusalem, [k] Aha, she
is broken *that was* the gates of the people: she is turn-
ed unto me, I shall be replenished *now* she is laid waste:
3 Therefore thus saith the Lord GOD, Behold, I *am*
against thee, O Tyrus, and will cause many nations to
come up against thee, as the sea causeth his waves to
come up. 4 And they shall destroy the walls of Tyrus,
and break down her towers: I will also scrape her dust
from her, and make her like the top of a rock. 5 It
shall be *a place for* the spreading of nets in the midst of
the sea: for I have spoken *it*, saith the Lord GOD: and
it shall become a spoil to the nations. 6 And her
daughters which *are* in the field shall be slain by the
sword; and [e] they shall know that I *am* the LORD. 7
¶ For thus saith the Lord GOD, Behold, I will bring
upon Tyrus Nebuchadrezzar king of Babylon, [f] a king
of kings, from the north, with horses, and with cha-
riots, and with horsemen, and companies, and much
people. 8 He shall slay with the sword thy daughters
in the field: and he shall make a fort against thee, and
† cast a mount against thee, and lift up the buckler a-
gainst thee. 9 And he shall set engines of war against
thy walls, and with his axes he shall break down thy
towers. 10 By reason of the abundance of his horses,
their dust shall cover thee: thy walls shall shake at the
noise of the horsemen, and of the wheels, and of the
chariots, when he shall enter into thy gates, ‡ as men
enter into a city wherein a breach is made. 11 With
the hoofs of his horses shall he tread down all thy streets:
he shall slay thy people by the sword, and thy § strong
garrisons shall go down to the ground. 12 And they
shall make a spoil of thy riches, and make a prey of thy
merchandise: and they shall break down thy walls, and
destroy || thy pleasant houses: and they shall lay thy
stones, and thy timber, and thy dust in the midst of the
water. 13 And I will cause the noise of [e] thy songs to
cease; and the sound of thy harps shall be no more heard.
14 And I will make thee like the top of a rock: thou
shalt be *a place* to spread nets upon; thou shalt be built
no more: for I the LORD have spoken *it*, saith the
Lord GOD.

i Ezek. xxiii. Jer. xxv. 22. & xlvii. 4. Amos i. 9. Zech. ix. 2. k Chap. xxv. 3.

Before Christ 588. e Chap. xxv. 5. f Ezra vii. 12. Dan. ii. 37. † Or, pour out the engine of shot. ‡ Heb. According to the enterings of a city broken up. § Or, pillars of thy strength. || Heb. houses of thy desire. e Isa. xxiv. 8. Chap. xxvi. 13.

v. 1—14. The same year Jerusalem was destroyed, was this prophecy delivered. We have,

1. The joy the Tyrians took in their ruin, and the hopes of advantage which they conceived would accrue to them from her fall. Jerusalem had been *the gates of the people*, much frequented, a place of great trade, but was now broken down; and they hoped all the traffic that had been carried on there, would be transferred to them, and that they should be replenished, both with people who might fly thither, or with captives, and the spoil sold by the conquerors. *Note*, It is very sinful to be pleased with the death or misfortunes of those who were our rivals in trade, or whose fall is our advantage; and the envy and covetousness which appear herein, God will assuredly remember and punish.

2. God threatens to visit Tyre for her iniquity. *I am against thee*, and he is more to be feared than innumerable hosts. At his beck, and under his guidance, the king of Babylon shall besiege the city with an immense army, raging like the waves of the sea: the dust raised by the multitude of his cavalry shall obscure the skies as a thick cloud, and his military engines shake down the walls, till at the breach his troops shall enter, and spread desolation on every side. *Her daughters shall be slain with the sword*, either the cities and people of the continent subject to Tyre, or so terrible should be the massacre when the city was taken, that not even the women will be spared: her *garrisons* beat *to the ground*, *the statues of her strength*, the images of her idols, on whom she placed her confidence, trodden under foot, the very pavement broken with the prancings of the horses, the rich merchandize becomes a prey to the besiegers, the walls razed, the whole city laid in ruins, the very dust swept off, and made bare as the top of a rock. Deserted now, no longer of mirth, no music, shall be heard any more in her, nor shall she ever be rebuilt, at least not on the same spot, or be restored to her former splendor, but remain a desart waste, as the top of a rock, a place for fishermen to dry their nets, which, according to the report of those who have been there, is to this day literally true of Tyre, since its final destruction. God hath spoken it, and therefore the fulfilment is sure, and in these judgments he will make himself terribly known to them.

15 ¶ Thus saith the Lord GOD to Tyrus; [f] Shall
not the isles shake at the sound of thy fall, when the
wounded cry, when the slaughter is made in the midst
of thee? 16 Then [g] all the princes of the sea shall
come down from their thrones, and lay away their
robes, and put off their broidered garments: they shall
clothe themselves with ‖ trembling; they shall sit upon
the ground, and shall tremble at *every* moment, and be
astonished at thee. 17 And [h] they shall take up a la-
mentation for thee, and say to thee, How art thou de-
stroyed, *that wast* inhabited ‡ of sea-faring men, the
renowned city which wast strong in the sea, she and her
inhabitants, which cause their terror *to be* on all that
haunt it? 18 Now shall the isles tremble in the day

f Chap. xxvii. 35. g Chap. xxxii. 10. ‖ Heb. tremblings. h Rev. xviii. 9. ‡ Heb. of the seas.

Before Christ 588

of thy fall, yea, the isles that are in the sea shall be
troubled at thy departure 19 For thus saith the Lord
k Rev xviii. 35 GOD, When I shall make thee a desolate city, like the
cities that are not inhabited, when I shall bring up the
deep upon thee, and great waters shall cover thee, 20
When I shall bring thee down with them that descend
into the pit, with the people of old time, and shall set
thee in the low parts of the earth, in places desolate of
old, with them that go down to the pit, that thou be
not inhabited, and I shall set glory in the land of the
l Chap xxvi 36 & xx 19 living 21 [l] I will make thee § a terror, and thou
shalt be no *more* though thou be sought for, [m] yet shalt
§ Heb Terrors thou never be found again, saith the Lord GOD

m Rev xviii 21

Ver 15—21 The dreadful ruin of Tyre is here farther described

1 The islands of the sea, terrified with her fall, will quake for fear, their princes descending from their thrones, with expressions of deepest sorrow shall mourn over her desolations, whilst they tremble in expectation of sharing her fate They shall take up their lamentation, astonished how such a glorious city could be destroyed, and weeping over the mighty fallen Once so *renowned* had Tyre been, *strong in the sea*, fortified by the waves as bulwarks, and filled with mariners, the most expert and bold, the terror of all that ploughed the main she reigned the unrivalled mistress of the ocean, but now was deserted and desolate, the people departed into captivity, the city, with its inhabitants, sunk under the waters, demolished by the army of the Chaldeans, rushing with resistless fury upon them, and bringing them down to the sides of the pit with those who have been long dead Yea, so total and entire shall be the overthrow, that scarce the vestiges shall remain where once it stood, and never again shall it be inhabited, at least not in the same spot, or with the same splendor So weak is human strength, so fading human greatness, so tottering the foundations of the strongest cities if we would dwell abidingly in safety, we must look above the earth for that better city whose maker and builder is God

The Lord will do this, v 19—21 *I will make thee a terror* his hand shall be visible in their ruin, and his design in her fall is to give her neighbours warning, that, terrified with her destruction, they may avoid her sin

3 The restoration of Israel, over whom she triumphed, shall aggravate the irreparable ruin of Tyre *I shall set glory in the land of the living*, in Israel, whither many souls, spiritually alive to God, should return from the captivity, and God will exalt and distinguish them with his love, favour, and protection *Note*, (1) The church of the redeemed is the land of the living, blessed and happy are they who have their portion therein (2) The souls alive to God by grace are assuredly designed for glory, for grace is glory begun (3) The joy and glory of the saints in heaven will aggravate the torments of the damned in hell, when they behold the bliss from which they are eternally excluded, and gnash with rage and despair

CHAP XXVII

In this chapter we have, 1 A large account of the dignity, wealth, and splendor of Tyre, ver 1—25 *which is designed to make its ruin the more lamentable 2 A prediction of its fall, and the consternation which all its neighbours shall thereby be put into,* ver 26—36 *And this is intended to stain the pride of all worldly glory, and by setting the one over against the other, to let us see the vanity and uncertainty of the riches, honours, and pleasures of the world, and what little reason we have to place our happiness in them, or to be confident of the continuance of them*

1 THE word of the LORD came again unto me,
saying, 2 Now thou son of man, take up a
a Chap xxvi 17 lamentation for Tyrus, 3 And say unto Tyrus, [a] O
thou that art situate at the entry of the sea, *which art*
b Isa xxiii [b] a merchant of the people for many isles, Thus saith
c Chap xxviii 12 the Lord GOD, O Tyrus, thou hast said, [c] I *am* of
‡ Heb Heart perfect beauty 4 Thy borders *are* in the ‡ midst of
the seas, thy builders have perfected thy beauty 5
‡ Heb Built They have ‡ made all thy *ship*-boards of fir trees of
Senir they have taken cedars from Lebanon, to make
masts for thee 6 *Of* the oaks of Bashan have they
§ Or, they have made thy hatches of ivory well trodden made thine oars § the company of the Ashurites have
made thy benches *of* ivory, *brought* out of the isles of
Chittim 7 Fine linen with broidered work from Egypt, was that which thou spreadest forth to be thy sail,
|| Or, purple and scarlet || blue and purple from the isles of Elishah was that
which covered thee 8 The inhabitants of Zidon and
Arvad were thy mariners thy wise *men*, O Tyrus, *that*
were in thee, were thy pilots 9 The ancients of Gebal, and the wise *men* thereof, were in thee thy † calkers,
† Heb Strengtheners or stoppers of chinks all the ships of the sea with their mariners were in thee
to occupy thy merchandise 10 They of Persia, and
of Lud, and of Phut were in thine army, thy men of
war they hanged the shield and helmet in thee, they
set forth thy comeliness 11 The men of Arvad with
thine army *were* upon thy walls round about, and the
Gammadims were in thy towers, they hanged their
shields upon thy walls round about they have made
thy beauty perfect 12 Tarshish *was* thy merchant by
reason of the multitude of all *kind of* riches, with silver,
iron, tin, and lead, they traded in thy fairs 13 Javan, Tubal, and Meshech, they *were* thy merchants,
they traded the persons of men, and vessels of brass, in
‡ Or merchandise thy ‡ market 14 They of the house of Togarmah
traded in thy fairs, with horses, and horsemen, and mules
15 The men of Dedan *were* thy merchants, many isles
were the merchandise of thine hand they brought thee
for a present, horns of ivory and ebony 16 § Syria
§ Heb Aram *was* thy merchant by reason of the multitude of || the
|| Heb Thy works wares of thy making they occupied in thy fairs with
emeralds, purple, and broidered work, and fine linen,
† Heb Chrysoprase and coral and † agate 17 Judah and the land of Israel, they *were* thy merchants they traded in thy market [d] wheat of [e] Minnith, and Pannag, and honey, and
d 1 Kings v 9 Ezra iii 7 Acts xii 20 oil, and ‡ balm 18 Damascus *was* thy merchant in the
e Judg xi 33 multitude of the wares of thy making, for the multitude of all riches in the wine of Helbon, and white
‡ Or rosin wool 19 Dan also and Javan going to and fro, occupied in thy fairs bright iron, cassia, and calamus were
in thy market 20 Dedan *was* thy merchant in § precious clothes for chariots 21 Arabia, and all the princes of [f] Kedar, they || occupied with thee in lambs, and
§ Heb Clothes of freedom f Isa lx 7 || Heb Were the merchants of thy hand rams, and goats in these *were they* thy merchants 22
The merchants of Sheba and Raamah, they *were* thy
merchants they occupied in thy fairs with chief of all
spices, and with all precious stones, and gold 23 [g] Haran, and Canneh, and [h] Eden, the merchants of Sheba,
g Gen xi 31 h 2 Kings xix 12 Ashur, *and* Chilmad *were* thy merchants 24 These
were thy merchants in † all sorts *of things* in blue
† Or excellent things ‡ clothes, and broidered work, and in chests of rich apparel, bound with cords, and made of cedar among thy
‡ Heb Foldings merchandise 25 [i] The ships of Tarshish did sing of
i Ps xlviii 7 Isa xxiii 14 thee in thy market, and thou wast replenished, and made
very glorious in the midst of the seas

v 1—25 Though Tyre was a heathen land, the prophet must make lamentation over it, for a gracious heart is filled with universal charity, and, touched with tender sympathy, laments over the miseries of the afflicted wherever they appear

We have,

1 The great prosperity of Tyre, which made her fall the more grievous

(1) She was most conveniently situated, *at the entry of the sea*, and surrounded by it, v 4 her harbour most commodious, and the grand mart of the world, whither all the produce of the east and west was brought and exchanged

(2) The city was most beautifully adorned with noble structures, where magnificence, elegance, and use contributed to *perfect her beauty*, ver 4

(3) Her fleets were numerous, admirably built and rigged, and some most superbly adorned, the very sails *fine linen embroidered from Egypt*, the pavilions covered *with purple and blue*, and the very benches inlaid *with ivory*, ver 6, 7

(4) Her ships were excellently *manned*, the *pilots* and chief officers Tyre supplied, v 8 the seamen, the adjacent country, and in her docks the wisest artificers were employed to refit and repair her navy

(5) The choicest soldiery were hired for her guard, *from* distant martial nations, v 10 furnished with weapons for war, which in time of peace were hung up in the armouries, ready to be used on any emergence, affording at once safety and ornament to the city, v 11 *Note*, The way to maintain a nation's peace is thus to be ever ready for war

(6) Her trade was vast and universal ships from every quarter of the globe crowded her harbour v 9 The nations, and the several commodities of their traffic, are mentioned, v 12—24 The countries of many of these are well-known, some utterly uncertain, and only afford the critics scope for conjecture, but of such immaterial points we may well be content to remain ignorant Observe, however, the vast advantages of trade, which an intercourse it opens, and brings in the produce of the most distant lands we enjoy as great plenty as if it had been the native growth of our own soil but still increasing wealth

in trading

Before Christ 588

increasing luxury usually rushes in, and the seeds of ruin are of en springing up in the midst of the greatest prosperity

2 Tyre prided herself on her beauty, and all nations praised and extolled her, *v* 3, 25 Thus is wealth often the food of vanity and they who abound in riches are cried up and praised The *great* are usually much more noticed and honoured than the *good*

26 ¶ Thy rowers have brought thee into great
waters [k] the east-wind hath broken thee in the † midst
of the seas 27 Thy [l] riches and thy fairs, thy mer-
chandise, thy mariners, and thy pilots, thy calkers, and
the occupiers of thy merchandise, and all thy men of
war that *are* in thee, ‡ and in all thy company which *is*
in the midst of thee, shall fall into the § midst of the
seas in the day of thy ruin 28 The ‖ suburbs shall
shake at the sound of the cry of thy pilots 29 And
all that handle the oar, the mariners, *and* all the pilots
of the sea, shall come down from their ships, they shall
stand upon the land, 30 And shall cause their voice
to be heard † against thee, and shall cry bitterly, and
shall [m] cast up dust upon their heads, they [n] shall wallow
themselves in the ashes 31 And they shall make them-
selves utterly bald for thee, and gird them with sack-
cloth, and they shall weep for thee with bitterness of
heart, *and* bitter wailing 32 And in their wailing they
shall take up a lamentation for thee, and lament over
thee, *saying*, [o] What *city is* like Tyrus, like the destroyed
in the midst of the sea? 33 When [p] thy wares went
forth out of the seas, thou filledst many people, thou
didst enrich the kings of the earth with the multitude
of thy riches, and of thy merchandise 34 In the time
when [q] thou shalt be broken by the seas in the depths
of the waters, thy merchandise and all thy company in
the midst of thee shall fall 35 All the inhabitants of
the isles shall be astonished at thee, and [r] their kings
shall be sore afraid, they shall be troubled in *their* coun-
tenance 36 The merchants among the people shall
hiss at thee, [s] thou shalt be ‡ a terror, [t] and ‖ never *shalt be*
any more

k Ps xlviii 7 † Heb Heart l Prov xi 4 Rev xviii 9, &c ‡ Or even with all § Heb heart ‖ Or waves, or beats † Or for or over thee Ver 31 Rev xviii 17 m Job ii 12 Rev xviii 19 n Esth iv 1, 3 Jer vi 26 o Rev xviii 18 p Rev xviii 12—19 q Chap xxvi 19 r Rev xviii 9 s Chap xxvi 21 ‡ Heb Terrors t Rev xviii 21 ‖ Heb Shalt not be for ever

v 26—36 The greatness of her wealth and excellence serves but to increase the misery of her fall Behold this proud city laid low in ruins a monument to other trading nations not to be secure in the day of prosperity

1 Like a rich vessel wrecked by the unskilfulness of the rowers, so was Tyre *brought into great waters*, exposed by some imprudent conduct of her governors to the resentment of the king of Babylon, *the east wind*, that dashed this gallant ship in pieces *in the midst of the seas*, and her merchandize, riches, inhabitants, soldiers and seamen, perished in the waters, *v* 27 Thus hath the unskilfulness of her pilots often ruined a nation

2 The dreadful cries of the sinking city shall reach *the suburbs*, the cities and villages on the continent, and the few who escape to the shore, as men from a shipwreck, *shall cause their voice to be heard against thee*, blaming the imprudent conduct of the pilots, who provoked the king of Babylon's resentment, or *for thee*, bewailing the desolations they beheld, with deepest expressions of anguish and vexation, *with dust on their heads, wallowing in ashes*, tearing off their hair, and weeping with bitterness and heart-felt grief, bemoaning in plaintive lamentations the dire catastrophe, once so great, so rich, a joyous city, replenishing with her merchandize the kings of the earth, now fallen into the lowest state of abject wretchedness, and, instead of the busy hum of crouded streets, solitude and silence reign throughout So awful a change can God in judgment quickly make, when he wrath rises against a guilty land

3 The utter ruin of this proud city shall fill some with terror and astonishment, *the kings of the* neighbouring *isles shall be sore afraid* If Tyre could not stand, which they deemed impregnable, how should they? Others shall hiss at her, mocking her vain confidence, and hoping, as she had done on the ruin of Jerusalem, that the trade of Tyre shall be transferred to their ports, and they shall be enriched thereby for, being thus fallen, *thou never shall be any more*, never rebuilt on the same spot, or rise to the same empire of the seas Some think this means no more than a long time, during seventy years, *see Isa* xxiii 15, 17 though the prophecy may respect her last destruction, since which to this day she hath lain in ruins The traffick and fall of the antichristian powers are described in expressions borrowed from this prophecy, *see Rev* xviii for their ruin shall as assuredly come in the season fixed by the divine decree

CHAP XXVIII

In this chapter we have, 1 A prediction of the fall of the king of Tyre in the destruction of that city, ver 1—10 2 A lamentation taken up for him, though he fall by his own iniquity, ver 11—19 3 A prophecy of the destruction of Zidon, which was in the neighbourhood of Tyre, ver 20—23 4 A promise of the restoration of God's Israel, though in the day of their calamity they were insulted over by their neighbours, ver 24, 25, 26

1 THE word of the LORD came again unto me,
saying, 2 Son of man, say unto the prince
of Tyrus, Thus saith the Lord GOD, [a] Because thine
heart *is* lifted up, and thou hast said, I *am* a god, [b] I sit
in the seat of God, [c] in the † midst of the seas; [d] yet
thou *art* a man, and not God, though thou set thine
heart as the heart of God 3 Behold, [e] thou *art* wiser
than Daniel, there is no secret that they can hide from
thee 4 With thy wisdom and with thine understand-
ing thou hast gotten thee riches, and hast gotten gold
and silver into thy treasures 5 [f] ‡ By thy great wis-
dom, *and* by thy traffick hast thou increased thy riches,
and thine heart is lifted up because of thy riches 6
Therefore thus saith the Lord GOD, Because [g] thou
hast set thine heart as the heart of God, 7 Behold
therefore, I will bring strangers upon thee, [h] the terrible
of the nations and they shall draw their swords against
the beauty of thy wisdom, and they shall defile thy
brightness 8 They shall bring thee down to the pit,
and thou shalt die the deaths of *them that are* slain in the
midst of the seas 9 Wilt thou yet say before him that
slayeth thee, I *am* God? but thou *shalt be* a man and no
God in the hand of him that § slayeth thee 10 Thou
[i] shalt die the deaths of the uncircumcised, by the hand
of strangers for I have spoken *it*, saith the Lord
GOD

a Prov xvi 18 b 2 Thess ii 4 c Chap xxvii 4 † Heb Heart d Isa xxxi 3 e Chap xiv 14 f Ps lxii 10 ‡ Heb By the greatness of thy wisdom g Ver 2 h Chap xxx 11 xxxi 12 &c i 1— § Or Wounded c Chap xxxi 18 &c

v 1—10 The prince of Tyre is next the subject of the prophetic word Distinct from the general ruin of his country, a particular warning is given to him

1 His pride was excessive *His heart was lifted up* in high conceit of his own excellence, as if he could rival the monarch of the universe he said, *I am a God*, boasted himself as a Deity, and perhaps expected divine honours should be paid him His throne seemed to be fixed firm as that of the Most High, and as glorious *in the midst of the seas*, which owned his sovereign sway But he is told, *Thou art man, and not God*, a poor, dependent, dying worm *though thou set thine heart as the heart of God*, thinking his wisdom and dominion great as those of the eternal Jehovah, and himself as worthy to be feared, obeyed, and worshipped Two things particularly he valued himself upon (1) His wisdom *Thou art wiser than Daniel*, in his own opinion at least The fame of Daniel had perhaps reached even to Tyre, as the most remarkable person for wisdom of all the wise men of the east but the king of Tyre fancied he far excelled him, and, with penetration approaching omniscience, would have it believed, *there was no secret could be hid from him* Thus often do we see knowledge puff up, and the most precious gifts of God perverted to his dishonour (2) His wealth By his wisdom he planned his schemes of traffick, and riches flowing in as a river upon him, every acquisition filled his mind with loftier imaginations of his own importance he ascribed his gains not to God's providence but his own prudence, and fancied himself thereby exalted above all danger The boast of Antichrist, 2 *Thess* ii 4 are expressed nearly in the same language, of whom the prince of Tyre is the type and figure

2 His doom is read He boasted himself a God, but he must die as a man The Chaldeans, *the terrible of the nations*, from a strange land shall come, and with drawn swords demolish the fort of Tyre, defile her beauty, and lay all her proud palaces in the dust, and this vain prince, far from finding respect shewn to that majesty he counted sacred, shall go to an ignominious grave, like those who are in a sea-fight slain and cast overboard without ceremony, a prey for fishes, *v* 8 and, worse still, he shall die under the curse of God, *the deaths of the uncircumcised*, eternally undone and lost And sure is the doom pronounced, since the God of truth hath spoken it, *v* 10

3 This will silence his arrogant pretensions Such vengeance executed upon him will prove his frailty and vanity, and his boast of godlike power and wisdom will vanish, when, in the hand of his murderers, he shall be found a weak and helpless worm *Note*, Death, at farthest, will make the proudest know they are but men

11 ¶ Moreover, the word of the LORD came unto
me, saying, 12 Son of man, [k] take up a lamentation
upon the king of Tyrus, and say unto him, Thus saith
the Lord GOD, Thou sealest up the sum full of wis-
dom and perfect in beauty 13 Thou hast been in
[l] Eden the garden of God, every precious stone *was* thy
covering,

k Chap xxvii 2 l Chap xxxi 8, 9

Before Christ 588

covering, the † sardius, topaz, and the diamond, the
‡ beryl, the onyx, and the jasper, the sapphire, the
§ emerald, and the carbuncle, and gold the workman-
ship of m thy tabrets and of thy pipes was prepared in
thee, in the day that thou wast created 14 Thou *art*
the anointed cherub that covereth and n I have set
thee *so*, thou wast upon the holy mountain of God,
thou hast walked up and down in the midst of the stones
of fire 15 Thou *wast* perfect in thy ways from the
day that thou wast created, till iniquity was found in
thee 16 By the multitude of thy merchandise they
have filled the midst of thee with violence, and thou hast
sinned therefore I will cast thee as profane out of the
mountain of God and I will destroy thee, O cover-
ing cherub, from the midst of the stones of fire 17
o Thine heart was lifted up because of thy beauty, thou
hast corrupted thy wisdom by reason of thy brightness
o I will cast thee to the ground, I will lay thee before
kings, that they may behold thee 18 Thou hast de-
filed thy sanctuaries by the multitude of thine iniquities,
by the iniquity of thy traffick, therefore will I bring
forth a fire from the midst of thee, it shall devour thee,
and I will bring thee to ashes upon the earth, in the
sight of all them that behold thee 19 All they that
know thee among the people, shall be astonished at thee
p thou shalt be ‖ a terror, and never *shalt* thou *be* any
more

† Or ruby ‡ Or chrysolite § Or chrysoprase m Chap xxvi 13. n Pl lxxv o Prov viii 13 oo Jam ii 6 p Chap xxvi 21 & xxvii 36 ‖ Heb terrors

v 11—19 We have here a lamentation over the prince of Tyrus

1 He was, to appearance, raised to the highest pitch of human prosperity *Thou sealest up the sum full of wisdom, and perfect in beauty*, compleat in every accomplishment of mind and person, and great as the wealth of this world could make him *Thou hast been in Eden the garden of God*, as happy, in appearance, as Adam in the delicious mansions prepared for him in the days of his innocence *Every precious stone* adorned him, studded his crown, and glittered on his royal robes The most curious and exquisite instruments of music were prepared to celebrate his birth or coronation day, *v* 13 *Thou art the anointed cherub that covereth*, alluding probably to the golden cherubim that covered the mercy-seat, or to that which guarded the tree of life in Eden, so beautiful he seemed, and so mighty to protect his people from every foe *And I have set thee so* to God he owed his advancement, and all the greatness he possessed *Thou wast upon the holy mount of God, thou hast walked up and down in the midst of the stones of fire*, adorned with jewels, as God's high-priest when he put on the precious breast-plate Which some interpret of Antichrist, assuming infallible wisdom, *v* 12 seated on high in the church of God, dressed in most costly apparel, *v* 13 pretending the authority of Christ to be the head and protector of the church, the mount of God, and usurping authority over the people of God, *the stones of fire*, who shine bright in all holy conversation

2 His iniquity brought him to destruction *Thou wast perfect in thy ways from the day that thou wast created*, prospered and wast successful, *till iniquity was found in thee* (1) There was *iniquity in traffick*, v 18 In *the multitude of merchandize* much fraud and violence was practised For very hard it is to be engaged in a multiplicity of business with clean hands the mystery of trade is too frequently a mystery of iniquity (2) He was proud and vain-glorious, *v* 17 *Thine heart was lifted up because of thy beauty*, and, gazing on his own excellencies, his wisdom became foolishness, for those who are proud of their attainments corrupt and spoil what otherwise would be praise-worthy (3) *Thou hast defiled thy sanctuaries* by idolatrous worship, or the lewd actions commonly practised there For which *multitude of iniquities* God threatens to destroy him, utterly to cast him down from his high estate, and cut him off from all his possessions as *profane*, having abused his station, he justly forfeits it in the dust the kings shall behold him lie, and take warning by his fall, or exult over him, *v* 17 A fire of divine wrath shall be kindled, consume his city to ashes, and himself in the midst of it, *v* 18 and the beholders, with terror and astonishment, shall wonder at his fearful fall, from which he shall never recover, *v* 19 All which is most applicable to *the man of sin*, whose coffers are filled with the gainful trade of purgatory, pardons and indulgences, proud of his dignity, corrupt in his worship, defiling the sanctuary with image-worship and superstition for which his day of ruin will come, when all his glory will be tarnished, when he shall be cast down with divine judgment, and at last doomed to the lake which burneth with fire for ever and ever *Note*, Let all the workers of iniquity tremble the same sins will assuredly produce the same destruction

q Chap vi 2 & xxv 2 Jer xxv 22

20 ¶ Again the word of the LORD came unto me,
saying, 21 Son of man, set thy face q against Zidon,
and prophesy against it, 22 And say, Thus saith the
Lord GOD, Behold I *am* against thee, O Zidon, and
r I will be glorified in the midst of thee and s they
shall know that I *am* the LORD, when I shall have
executed judgments in her, and shall be sanctified in
her 23 For I will send into her pestilence, and blood
into her streets, and the wounded shall be judged in the
midst of her by the sword upon her on every side, and
they shall know that I *am* the LORD 24 ¶ And there
shall be no more t a pricking brier unto the house of Israel,
nor *any* grieving thorn of all *that are* round about them
that despised them, and they shall know that I *am* the
Lord GOD 25 Thus saith the Lord GOD, When
u I shall have gathered the house of Israel from the people
among whom they are scattered, and shall be sanctified
in them in the sight of the heathen, then shall they dwell
in their land that I have given to my servant Jacob
26 And they shall dwell † safely therein, and shall build
houses, and x plant vineyards yea, they shall dwell with
confidence when I have executed judgments upon all those
that ‡ despise them round about them, and they shall know
that I *am* the LORD their God

Before Christ 588 r Ex xiv 4 Isa v 16 s Ps ix 16 & Isa xxiv 17, 18 t Num xxxiii 55 Josh xxiii 13 u Isa xi 12 Hos i 11 † Or with confidence x Jer xxxi 5 ‡ Or spoil

v 20—26 Two ways God will glorify himself

1 In the destruction of Zidon God is her enemy, will execute his judgments upon her, and be *sanctified*, make his holiness and justice appear in her ruin The depopulating scourge of pestilence shall be sent upon her, and the wounded shall fall on every side Thus will God make himself known in the vengeance he executes

2 In the restoration and prosperity of his Israel God will bring them again to their own land, and cause them to dwell safely the nations round, who despised and vexed them as briars and thorns, shall be no more, and he will *be sanctified among the heathen*, who will be made to own his hand evidently displayed in behalf of his own people and with comfort they shall know him to be the Lord, experiencing his mercy and proving his faithfulness And this restoration seems to look further than their return from Babylon, after which they were still frequently beset with enemies, and to have respect to their last recovery, when they shall be admitted into the church, and enter with the redeemed into that eternal rest where the wicked will cease from troubling, and every tear be for ever wiped from their eyes

CHAP XXIX

The four following chapters are concerning Egypt, which often proved a broken reed to the house of Israel 1 *The destruction of Pharaoh foretold, for his dealing deceitfully with Israel*, ver 1—7 2 *The desolation of the land of Egypt*, ver 8—12 3 *A promise of the restoration thereof in part after forty years*, ver 13—16 4 *The possession that should be given to Nebuchadnezzar of the land of Egypt*, ver 17—20 5 *A promise of mercy to Israel*, ver 21

1 IN the tenth year, in the tenth *month*, in the twelfth 589
day of the month, the word of the LORD came
unto me, saying, 2 Son of man, set thy face against
Pharaoh king of Egypt, and prophesy a against him,
and against all Egypt 3 Speak and say, Thus saith
the Lord GOD, b Behold, I *am* ‖ against thee, Pharaoh
king of Egypt, c the great dragon that lieth in the midst
of his rivers, which hath said, My river *is* mine own,
and I have made *it* for myself 4 But d I will put hooks
in thy jaws, and I will cause the fish of thy rivers to stick
unto thy scales, and I will bring thee up out of the midst
of thy rivers, and all the fish of thy rivers shall stick un-
to thy scales 5 And I will leave thee *thrown* into the
wilderness, thee and all the fish of thy rivers thou shalt
fall upon ‖ the open fields, thou shalt not be brought
together, nor gathered I have given thee for meat to
the beasts of the field, and to the fowls of the heaven
6 And all the inhabitants of Egypt f shall know that I
am the LORD, because they have been g a staff of reed
to the house of Israel 7 h When they took hold of
thee by thy hand, thou didst break, and rent all their
shoulder and when they leaned upon thee, thou brakest,
and madest all their loins to be at a stand.

a Isa xix 1 Jer xxv 19 & xlvi 2 b Jer xliv 30. ‖ Or above thee c Ps lxxiv 13, 14 Isa xxvii 1 & li 9 Chap xxxii 2 d Isa xxxvii 29 Chap xxxviii 4 e Ps lxxiv 14 ‖ Heb The face of the field f Isa ix 16 g 2 Kings xviii 21 Isa xxxvi 6 h Jer xxxvii 5 11

v 1—7 The date of this prophecy is observable It was just at the time when the Egyptian army was advancing to raise the siege of Jerusalem, and when the Jews confidently expected relief from their approach The vain hopes sinners entertain are often most sanguine when their ruin is nearest

Before Christ 589

The prophecy is directed against Egypt and her king, represented by a great dragon, or crocodile, lying in the river Nile We have here,

1 His pride *He lieth in the midst of his rivers*, secure, at ease, and rolling in wealth and pleasures, and hath said, *my river is my own, I have made it for myself*, as if he reigned independent of God, and owed to himself alone the monarchy he possessed Thus pride calls God's gifts our own, and, self-idolaters, we leave him far above out of our sight

2 The judgment executed on Pharaoh *I am against thee*, or *above thee*, able and determined to punish his arrogance God will put hooks in his jaws, and, with all the fish which stick to his scales, his numerous forces, will drag him out of his rivers, *v* 4 and in the wilderness give him, with all his army, for a prey *to the beasts of the earth and the fowls of heaven* Note, Pride is the prelude to destruction, and they who are most secure are usually most exposed

3 The provocation which most hastened the ruin of Egypt was her falsehood and deceitfulness with regard to the Jewish people Encouraged by the alliance with Pharaoh, Zedekiah rebelled against the king of Babylon, and now, when he looked for support from Egypt, the staff on which he leaned broke under him, to his vast disappointment and utter consternation, *rent his shoulder*, brought on him the Chaldean sword, *and made all his loins at a stand*, compelled to stand alone, and in the greatest amazement, conscious of his own inability to cope with Nebuchadnezzar's army It was folly indeed in Zedekiah to trust on such auxiliaries, but their perfidy in deceiving him was not the less criminal, and God will revenge such treachery

8 ¶ Therefore thus saith the Lord GOD, Behold,
I will bring a sword upon thee, and cut off man and
beast out of thee 9 And the land of Egypt shall be
desolate and waste, *and* they shall know that I *am* the
i Ch. 3 LORD, because he hath said, i The river *is* mine, and
I have made *it* 10 Behold therefore, I *am* against
thee, and against thy rivers, and I will make the land
† Heb. Wastes of waste of Egypt † utterly waste *and* desolate, k from the tower
of ‡ Syene even unto the border of Ethiopia 11 l No
k Chap. xxx 6 foot of man shall pass through it, nor foot of beast shall
‡ Heb. Seveneh pass through it, neither shall it be inhabited forty years
l Chap. xxxii 13 12 m And I will make the land of Egypt desolate in the
m Chap. xxx 7 midst of the countries *that are* desolate, and her cities
among the cities *that are* laid waste shall be desolate forty
years and I will scatter the Egyptians among the nations,
and will disperse them through the countries 13 ¶ Yet
n Isa. xix 23 Jer. xlvi 26 thus saith the Lord GOD, n At the end of forty years
will I gather the Egyptians from the people whither they
were scattered 14 And I will bring again the captivity
of Egypt, and will cause them to return *into* the land of
§ Or birth Pathros, into the land of their § habitation, and they shall
o Chap. xvii 6, 14 be there o a || base kingdom 15 It shall be the basest of
|| Heb. Low the kingdoms, neither shall it exalt itself any more above
the nations for I will diminish them, that they shall no
more rule over the nations 16 And it shall be no
more the confidence of the house of Israel, which bringeth
their iniquity to remembrance, when they shall look
after them but they shall know that I *am* the Lord
GOD.

v 8—16 We have here,

1 The terrible overthrow of Egypt foretold God will make them know by his judgments that he is the Lord, and prove the vanity of their insolent vaunt, *v* 9 The sword of the Chaldeans shall pass through the land, lay all waste before it, cut off man and beast from one end of Egypt to the other, *v* 10 and leave it depopulated, without trade, unfrequented and like a desert during forty years, *v* 11 the inhabitants in general being slain, or carried into captivity, *v* 12 We find, *v* 17 that in the 27th year of Jeconiah's captivity, Egypt was given to Nebuchadnezzar, and if we allow three years for completing the conquest, the forty years will end with the destruction of the Babylonian monarchy by Cyrus, when probably Egypt, as well as the other nations, recovered in great measure her liberty

2 The restoration of Egypt when the forty years were expired, not to her former grandeur and magnificence, but, tho' a kingdom, and flourishing under some of her monarchs, particularly the Ptolemies, yet by repeated conquests it still reduced to its present base and low estate under the Turks, to no more the mistress of nations, nor the stay of Israel, *to bring their iniquity to remembrance*, by their placing dependance upon Egypt and withdrawing their confidence from God Note, (1) God still in wrath remembers mercy (2) It is gracious and just in the Lord to remove those creature comforts and confidences which estranged our hearts from him

17 ¶ And it came to pass in the seven and twentieth Before Christ 572
year, in the first *month*, in the first *day* of the month, the
word of the LORD came unto me, saying, 18 Son
of man, Nebuchadrezzar king of Babylon caused his
army p to serve a great service against Tyrus every head p Jer. xxvii 6
was made bald, and every shoulder *was* peeled yet had
he no wages, nor his army for Tyrus, for the service that
he had served against it 19 Therefore thus saith the
Lord GOD, Behold, q I will give the land of Egypt q Dan. ii 21
unto Nebuchadrezzar king of Babylon, and he shall take
her multitude, and ‡ take her spoil, and take her prey, ‡ Heb. Spoil her spoil, and prey her prey
and it shall be the wages for his army 20 I have given
him the land of Egypt *for* his ‡ labour wherewith he ‡ Or, her work
served against it, because they wrought for me, saith r Ps. cxxxii 17
the Lord GOD 21 ¶ In that day r will I cause the
horn of the house of Israel to bud forth, and I will give
thee the opening of the mouth in the midst of them,
and they shall know that I *am* the LORD

v 17—21 This is the last of all Ezekiel's prophecies, and sixteen or seventeen years after the preceding, but all the prophecies concerning Egypt are laid together

1 In consideration of the hard service Nebuchadnezzar underwent before Tyre, *v* 18 the spoil of which so little repaid him for his pains, great part of their effects being removed, as history informs us, before the place was taken, Egypt is given him and his army for their wages, *v* 18 being before weakened by intestine divisions, it fell an easy prey to the conqueror As the vengeance executed on Tyre was by divine command, God will not suffer Nebuchadnezzar to work without a reward Note, (1) Even wicked men, when employed in God's service, find their account in it, they are paid in the good things of this life (2) Many who propose no other end but their own advantage, and perhaps the gratification of their ambition and covetousness, by the secret over-ruling power of God are made unwittingly subservient to his designs

2 A gracious promise is made to God's Israel *In that day will I cause the horn of the house of Israel to bud*, either at the day of Egypt's destruction, about which time Daniel and his fellows, Shadrach, Meshach, and Abednego, were so distinguished of God, and honoured by the king of Babylon, *see Dan.* i 3 xi 49 or shortly after, when Jehoiachim was enlarged from prison and honourably treated, *Jer.* lii 31, 32 or the time here spoken of may refer to the forty years, *v* 12 when the captivity of Israel as well as Egypt should end, and under Zerubbabel and others the nation should revive from its desolation. *And I will give thee the opening of the mouth in the midst of them*, when the fulfilment of the prophecies would give peculiar force to his exhortations, and embolden him in the work of the Lord For, though no more of his prophecies are recorded, no doubt he continued a faithful preacher to the people, which could not but prove a singular blessing to them For when God enlarges the hearts of his faithful servants, and enables them with boldness to speak, it is a gracious symptom of his purpose to make them see the travail of their souls in the salvation of those to whom they minister

CHAP. XXX

In this chapter we have, 1 A continuation of the prophecy against Egypt, in which is foretold the destruction of all her cities, and the several steps which the king of Babylon should take in pursuing on this destruction, ver 1—19 2 A repetition of a former prophecy against Egypt, just before the desolation of it began by their own ill conduct, which gradually weakened them and prepared the way for the king of Babylon, ver 20—26

1 THE word of the LORD came again unto me,
saying, 2 Son of man, prophesy and say,
Thus saith the Lord GOD, Howl ye, wo worth the
day 3 For the day *is* near, even the day of the
LORD *is* near, a cloudy day, it shall be the time of the
heathen 4 And the sword shall come upon Egypt,
and great ‡ pain shall be in Ethiopia, when the slain shall ‡ Or fear
fall in Egypt, and s they shall take away her multitude, s Chap. xxix 19
and her foundation shall be broken down 5 Ethiopia,
and ‡ Libya, and Lydia, t and all the mingled people, ‡ Heb. Phut
and Chub, and the § men of the land that is in league, t Jer. xxv 20
shall fall with them by the sword 6 Thus saith the § Heb. Children
LORD, They also that uphold Egypt shall fall, and the u Chap. xxix 10
pride of her power shall come down from the tower
of Syene shall they fall in it by the sword, saith the
Lord GOD 7 And x they shall be desolate in the x Chap. xxix 12
midst of the countries *that are* desolate, and her cities
shall be in the midst of the cities *that are* wasted 8

5 And

Before Christ 588

And they ſhall know that I *am* the LORD, when I have
ſet a fire in Egypt, and *when* [e] all her helpers ſhall be
|| deſtroyed 9 In that day [f] ſhall meſſengers go forth
from me in ſhips, to make [g] the careleſs Ethiopians
afraid, and great pain ſhall come upon them, as in the
day of Egypt for lo, it cometh 10 Thus ſaith the
LORD God, I will alſo make the multitude of Egypt
to ceaſe by the hand of Nebuchadrezzar king of Baby-
lon 11 He and his people with him, [h] the terrible
of the nations ſhall be brought to deſtroy the land and
they ſhall draw their ſwords againſt Egypt, and fill the
land with the ſlain 12 And [i] I will make the rivers
dry, and ſell the land into the hand of the wicked, and
I will make the land waſte, and all that is therein, by
the hand of ſtrangers I the LORD have ſpoken *it*
13 Thus ſaith the LORD God, I will alſo [k] deſtroy
the idols, and I will cauſe *their* † images to ceaſe out
of Noph and [l] there ſhall be no more a prince of the
land of Egypt, and I will put a fear *in the land of Egypt*
14 And I will make Pathros deſolate, and will ſet fire
in ‡ Zoan, [m] and will execute judgments in No 15
And I will pour my fury upon § Sin, the ſtrength of
Egypt, and I will cut off the multitude of No 16 And
I will ſet fire in Egypt, Sin ſhall have great pain, and No
ſhall be rent aſunder, and Noph *ſhall have* diſtreſſes daily
17 The young men of || Aven and of † Phi-beſeth,
ſhall fall by the ſword and theſe *cities* ſhall go into
captivity 18 [n] At Tehaphnehes alſo the day ſhall be
‡ darkned, when I ſhall break there the yokes of Egypt
and the pomp of her ſtrength ſhall ceaſe in her as for
her, a cloud ſhall cover her, and her daughters ſhall go
into captivity 19 Thus will I execute judgments in
Egypt and they ſhall know that I *am* the LORD

v 1—19 Fearful is the overthrow of the Egyptians here recorded

1 They are called to *howl*, and lament the dreadful day, big with wrath, and ſwift approaching, a day of darkneſs and gloominess, when every face ſhould gather blackneſs *It ſhall be the time of the heathen*, either the time to viſit the heathen nations of Egypt and Ethiopia, or the time of the Chaldean power *Note*, The ſinner's day, though long delayed, ſhall come at laſt, and then, too late, he will pour forth his remedileſs ſorrows

2 The threatned deſtruction ſhall utterly ruin both Egypt and her confederates The ſword of the victorious king of Babylon ſhall fill the land, from one end to the other, with the *carcaſes of the ſlain*, the cities ſhall be deſtroyed, *the images* broken, the country deſolate, terrors ſpread on every ſide, the beauty, ſtrength, and multitude of Egypt utterly waſted, and the dark cloud of abject wretchedneſs ſpread over them Thus ſhall a fierce and terrible enemy, *v* 11 from a ſtrange and diſtant land, *v* 12 *called* men, whom no laws of humanity or juſtice reſtrain, be let looſe upon them, and ravage without mercy The pride of Egypt, *v* 6 her *royal family*, ſhall be extinct, *v* 13 and no hopes remain from the riſing generation, *the young men being ſlain with the ſword*, *v* 17 *and the daughters gone into captivity* *v* 18 Nor ſhall her auxiliaries be able to give her the leaſt ſupport they ſhall fall with her, *v* 6 Ethiopia, Libya, Lydia, Chub, and all the *mingled people* of various nations, who are in league with Egypt, ſhall periſh And, whilſt many out of their countries, who ſojourned among the Egyptians, or were auxiliaries in their army, fall with them, *v* 5 the tidings of their deſtruction ſhall fly ſwift to the careleſs Ethiopians, and terrify them with the apprehenſions of ſharing Egypt's fate Nor is their apprehenſion groundleſs, for, *Lo! it cometh* *Note*, (1) Confederates in iniquity will periſh together (2) When we ſee our neighbour's houſe on fire, it is time to tremble for our own one ſinner's fall ſhould alarm the ſurvivors

3 God's hand is viſible in the judgment Whatever inſtrument he employs, the work is his own, *v* 10 His veracity is engaged for the fulfilment of the threatning, *v* 12 and, in the judgments he will execute, his power and faithfulneſs will appear, *and they ſhall know that he is the Lord* *Note*, (1) Whatever judgments are in the earth, God's hand is to be ſeen and acknowledged in them (2) One jot or tittle of God's word ſhall never fail

20 ¶ And it came to paſs in the eleventh year, in
the firſt *month*, in the ſeventh *day* of the month, *that*
the word of the LORD came unto me, ſaying, 21
Son of man, I have broken the arm of Pharaoh king
of Egypt; and lo, [o] it ſhall not be bound up to be
healed, to put a roller to bind it, to make it ſtrong to
hold the ſword 22 Therefore thus ſaith the LORD
God, Behold, I *am* againſt Pharaoh king of Egypt,
and will break his arms, the ſtrong, and *that which was*
broken, and I will cauſe the ſword to fall out of his
hand 23 And I will ſcatter the Egyptians among the
nations, and will diſperſe them through the countries
24 And I will ſtrengthen the arms of the king of Baby-
lon, and [q] put my ſword in his hand but I will break
Pharaoh's arms, and he ſhall groan before him with the
groanings of a deadly wounded *man* 25 But I will
ſtrengthen the arms of the king of Babylon, and the
arms of Pharaoh ſhall fall down, and [r] they ſhall know
that I *am* the LORD, when I ſhall put my ſword into
the hand of the king of Babylon, and he ſhall ſtretch
it out upon the land of Egypt 26 And I will ſcatter
the Egyptians among the nations, and diſperſe them
among the countries, and they ſhall know that I *am* the
LORD

v 20—26 The arms of the Egyptians, which had attempted to raiſe the ſiege of Jeruſalem, had been now forced to retire with ſhame to their own land, and, without making any farther efforts, left Jeruſalem to her fate, but their own ruin quickly followed It is foretold,

1 That Egypt ſhall be weakened by degrees and brought to deſtruction One arm of Pharaoh was already broken in the defeat received at Carchemiſh, *Jer* xlvi 2 and the conqueſt of a part of the Egyptian dominions, 2 *Kings* xxiv 7 and from this fatal ſtroke he never recovered, a ſecond blow would compleat his ruin His ſtrong arm, as well as that which was broken, God will break by the ſword of Nebuchadnezzar ſo that, unable to wield a ſword, groaning as a ſoldier deſperately wounded, he muſt fall His kingdom ſhall be vanquiſhed, his people diſperſed and led into captivity And in their ſufferings God afflicts, he will make them know that he is the Lord

2 That the king of Babylon ſhall grow ſtronger and ſtronger God will put a ſword into his hands, give him might to wield it, and ſubdue Egypt before him All power is given from above the ſtrength of the mightieſt is derived alone from the almighty God

CHAP XXXI

The prophecy of this, as of the two former chapters, is againſt Egypt, and deſigned to humble Pharaoh The prophet is here ordered, 1 To ſhew him that the king of Aſſyria had been like him in greatneſs, ver 3—9 And, 2 In pride and carnal ſecurity, ver 10 3 He is to relate to him the fall of the king of Aſſyria, what a noiſe it made among the nations, and what a warning it gave to all potent princes to take heed of pride, ver 11—17 4 He muſt leave the king of Egypt to apply all this to himſelf, to ſee his own face in the looking-glaſs of the king of Aſſyria's ſin, and to foreſee his own fall through the perſpective-glaſs of his ruin, ver 18

1 AND it came to paſs in the eleventh year, in the
third *month*, in the firſt *day* of the month, *that*
the word of the LORD came unto me, ſaying, 2 Son
of man, ſpeak unto Pharaoh king of Egypt, and to his
multitude, [a] Whom art thou like in thy greatneſs?
3 ¶ [b] Behold, the Aſſyrian *was* a cedar in Lebanon
‡ with fair branches, and with a ſhadowing ſhroud, and
of an high ſtature, and his top was among the thick
boughs 4 [c] The waters ‡ made him great, the deep
§ ſet him up on high, with her rivers running round
about his plants, and ſent out her little rivers unto all the
trees of the field 5 Therefore his height was exalted
above all the trees of the field, and his boughs were multi-
plied, and his branches became long becauſe of the mul-
titude of waters when || he ſhot forth 6 All [d] the fowls
of heaven made their neſts in his boughs, and under his
branches did all the beaſts of the field bring forth their
young, and under his ſhadow dwelt all great nations
7 Thus was he fair in his greatneſs, in the length of his
branches for his root was by great waters 8 The
cedars in [e] the garden of God could not hide him the
fir trees were not like his boughs, and the cheſnut trees
were not like his branches, nor any tree in the garden
of God was like unto him in his beauty 9 I have
made him fair by the multitude of his branches ſo that
all the trees of Eden, that *were* in the garden of God,
envied him

v 1—9 This prophecy bears date about five weeks before Jeruſalem was taken, when judgment, which had begun at the

a Ver 18. b Dan iv. 10 ‡ Heb fair of branches c Jer li. 36 Rev xvii 15 ‡ Or nouriſhed him § Or brought him up || Or it ſent them forth. d Dan iv 12 e Gen ii 8

Before Christ 588.

house of God, did not end there, but Egypt must also drink of the cup of trembling.

Pharaoh is bid to consult the records of time, and select the mightiest monarch that had gone before him, with whom to compare himself, even the Assyrian, who, notwithstanding all his ancient greatness, was now fallen. Nimrod had founded that monarchy, and the Babylonian empire had risen on its ruins. A warning to the greatest not to be high-minded, but fear.

The Assyrian monarch is compared to a tall and spreading cedar. His dignity most exalted, his dominions vastly extensive, and admirably governed, like the regular branches of a lofty tree, v. 7. No prince or potentate could vie with him of all the surrounding nations, v. 8. and they secretly envied his greatness, v. 9. the tribute which merit and prosperity usually must pay. Protected by his power, and safe under his government, multitudes from all nations chose to settle in his dominions, v. 6. Planted by the Divine Providence, v. 9. and watered with the abundance of temporal good things, he seemed sufficiently strong to resist every stormy blast, and *sent out little rivers to all the trees of the field*, all his subjects received abundant advantages from him. *Note*, They are truly great who employ their power and influence to promote the good of mankind.

f Dan. v. 20.

10 ¶ Therefore thus saith the LORD God, [f] Because thou hast lifted up thyself in height, and he hath
shot up his top among the thick boughs, and his heart
is lifted up in his height, 11 I have therefore delivered him into the hand of the mighty one of the heathen, [g] † he shall surely deal with him, I have driven
him out for his wickedness. 12 And strangers, [h] the
terrible of the nations, have cut him off, and have left
him: upon the mountains and in all the valleys his
branches are fallen, and his boughs are broken by all the
rivers of the land, and all the people of the earth are
gone down from his shadow, and have left him. 13
Upon his ruin shall the fowls of the heaven remain, and
all the beasts of the field shall be upon his branches:
14 To the end that none of all the trees by the waters
exalt themselves for their height, neither shoot up their
top among the thick boughs, neither their trees ‡ stand
up in their height, all that drink water: for [i] they are
delivered unto death, to the nether parts of the earth in
the midst of the children of men, with them that go
down to the pit. 15 Thus saith the LORD God, In
the day when he went down to the grave I caused a
mourning, I covered the deep for him, and I restrained
the floods thereof, and the great waters were stayed,
and I caused Lebanon § to mourn for him, and all the
trees of the field fainted for him. 16 I made the nations to shake at the sound of his fall, when I cast him down
to hell with them that descend into the pit: and all [k] the
trees of Eden, the choice and best of Lebanon, all that
drink water, [l] shall be comforted in the nether parts of the
earth. 17 They also went down into hell with him
unto *them that be* slain with the sword, and *they that were*
his arm *that* dwelt under his shadow in the midst of the
heathen. 18 ¶ [m] To whom art thou thus like in glory
and in greatness among the trees of Eden? yet shalt
thou be brought down with the trees of Eden unto
the nether parts of the earth: [n] thou shalt lie in the
midst of the uncircumcised, with *them that be* slain by
the sword. This *is* Pharaoh and all his multitude, saith
the LORD God.

g Judg. i. 7. Mat. vii. 2. † Or in doing he shall do unto him. h Chap. xxviii. 7. ‡ Or stand upon themselves for their height. i Chap. xxxii. ... § Heb. To be black. k Isa. xiv. 8. l Chap. xxxii. 31. m Ver. ... n Chap. xxviii. 10. & xxxii. 19, &c.

v. 10—18. The Assyrian monarch, whom Pharaoh resembled in greatness, he must resemble in his ruin.

1. They were both puffed up on their prosperity. *Thou hast lifted up thyself in height*, thou, O king of Egypt, or thou, O king of Assyria, for to either the words may be applied, and they are true of both, pride being the common snare which attends advancement, and few carry with them, into a superior sphere, the humble spirit of their former station.

2. They fall alike, as the just punishment of their pride and wickedness, v. 11.

(1.) The Assyrian by the hand of Nebuchadnezzar, *the mighty one of the heathen*, who in the beginning of his reign, in conjunction with Cyaxares king of the Medes, is said to have destroyed that monarchy, with Nineveh the capital, and transferred the seat of empire to Babylon. God had ordained his ruin, and therefore it must infallibly come to pass, v. 11. Already the mighty cedar is broken: the terrible army of Chaldeans and Medes have lopped all his branches, and left them withering on every mountain and valley, and by every river: the provinces of the empire dismembered, the cities and country subdued, so that, as birds from a falling tree, the several nations, who sought for shelter under the shadow of the Assyrian monarch, are fled, have deserted him in the day of his calamity, v. 12. His enemies, like birds and beasts of prey, feed upon him, or, literally, the fowls of heaven fall upon the carcases of the slain, or those who envied his greatness, v. 9. rejoice at his fall, v. 13. And herein God designed to warn proud monarchs of their danger, not to trust on their power or wealth, as if these could be their protection, but to remember they are mortal worms, and in an instant, when God strikes, numbered with the dead, v. 14. This the Assyrian monarch proved, and at his ruin a universal groan was given from all who were in league with him, as the forest echoes with the falling cedar, v. 16. a general stagnation of trade and commerce for a while prevailed, and, trembling for themselves, his allies fainted, conscious of their own inability to resist the conqueror of their mightier Assyrian friend, v. 15. whilst *the trees of Eden, the choice and best of Lebanon*, either the kingdoms subdued and ravaged by the Assyrian monarch in times past, or the nations in alliance with him, who shared his fearful destruction, v. 17. shall in their graves *be comforted* to see him brought as low as themselves, v. 16. *Note*, (1.) Wickedness is the cause of all our wretchedness. (2.) Pride will have a fall. (3.) They who are courted in prosperity will often be deserted in the day of calamity. (4.) The fall of great men usually involves multitudes in their ruin. (5.) God intends his providential strokes on others should be warnings to ourselves.

(2.) The Egyptian monarch may expect the same fate. Let him chuse the mightiest kingdoms with which to compare himself, nay were he even so great as the king of Assyria, it would not secure him from ruin: he should be brought to the same wretched state, lie down among the dead, yea *among the uncircumcised*, under the eternal wrath of God. *This is Pharaoh and his multitude*. Such shall be the end of all his greatness, grandeur, and numerous subjects. And thus *shall the wicked be turned into hell*, with *all the nations*, however many or mighty, *that forget God*.

CHAP. XXXII.

The destruction of Egypt is here represented under two similitudes. 1. The killing of a lion or whale, or some such devouring creature, ver. 1—16. 2. The funeral of a great commander or captain-general, ver. 17—32.

1 AND it came to pass in the twelfth year, in the
twelfth month, in the first *day* of the month,
that the word of the LORD came unto me, saying,
2 Son of man, take up a lamentation for Pharaoh king
of Egypt, and say unto him, [a] Thou art like a young
lion of the nations, [b] and thou *art* as a † whale in the
seas: and thou camest forth ‡ with thy rivers, and troubledst the waters with thy feet, and fouledst their rivers.
3 Thus saith the Lord GOD, I will therefore [c] spread
out my net over thee, with a company of many people,
and they shall bring thee up in my net. 4 Then [d] will
I leave thee upon the land, I will cast thee forth upon
the open field, and will cause [e] all the fowls of the heaven
to remain upon thee, and I will fill the beasts of the
whole earth with thee. 5 And I will lay thy flesh upon the mountains, and fill the valleys with thy height.
6 I will also water with thy blood the land wherein
thou swimmest, *even* to the mountains, and the rivers
shall be full of thee. 7 And when I shall § put thee
out, [f] I will cover the heaven, and make the stars
thereof dark; I will cover the sun with a cloud, and the
moon shall not give her light. 8 All the ‖ bright
lights of heaven will I make dark over thee, and set
darkness upon thy land, saith the Lord GOD. 9 I
will also ¦ vex the hearts of many people, when I shall
bring thy destruction among the nations, into the countries which thou hast not known. 10 Yea, I will make
many people amazed at thee, and their kings shall be
horribly afraid for thee, when I shall brandish my sword
before them; and [i] they shall tremble at *every* moment,
every man for his own life, in the day of thy fall. 11
¶ [l] For thus saith the Lord GOD, The sword of the
king of Babylon shall come upon thee. 12 By the
swords of the mighty [i] will I cause thy multitude to fall,
[k] the terrible of the nations all of them: and they shall
spoil the pomp of Egypt, and all the multitude thereof shall be destroyed. 13 I will destroy also all the
beasts thereof from beside the great waters; [l] neither
shall the foot of man trouble them any more, nor the
hoofs of beasts trouble them. 14 Then will I make
their waters deep, and cause their rivers to run like oil,

a Chap. xix. ... b Chap. xxix. 3. † Or, dragon. ‡ ... c Chap. xii. 13. ... d Chap. xxix. 5. e Rev. ... § Or, extinguish. f Isa. xiii. 10. Joel ii. 31. & iii. 15. Amos viii. 9. Mat. xxiv. 29. ‖ Heb. lights of the light in the heavens. ¦ Heb. Provoke to anger, or grief. i Chap. xxvi. 16. l Jer. xlvi. 26. i Chap. xxx. ... k Chap. xxviii. 7. l Chap. xxix. 11.

saith

Before Christ 587

‡ Heb. desolate from the fulness thereof.

faith the Lord GOD. 15 When I ſhall make the land
of Egypt deſolate, and the country ſhall be ‡ deſtitute
of that whereof it was full, when I ſhall ſmite all them
that dwell therein, then ſhall they know that I *am* the
LORD. 16 This *is* the lamentation wherewith they
ſhall lament her: the daughters of the nations ſhall lament
her: they ſhall lament for her, *even* for Egypt and for all
her multitude, ſaith the Lord GOD.

v. 1—16. Though Egypt was an idolatrous nation, and Pharaoh a wicked prince, the prophet muſt take up a lamentation over them. For the miniſters of God, when they can do no more, muſt weep over thoſe who, hardened in ſin, refuſe to ſhed a tear for themſelves.

1. The king of Egypt is compared to a lion, fierce, devouring, ravenous; to a whale, or crocodile *with his rivers*, a multitude of people, or *from his rivers*, ſallying forth in queſt of prey; and as this animal with his feet troubles the waters, ſo did he with his armies diſturb the tranquility of his neighbour. *Note*, Ambitious princes are the troublers of the earth, and the ſcourges of mankind.

2. His deſtruction is foretold. The ſame ſimilitude is continued; God, the author of his ruin, ſhall take him as a great fiſh in his net, with all his numerous forces, v. 3. and drag him to land, where, as a fiſh out of his element, he muſt periſh, and being caſt forth into the open field, become a prey for every fowl and every beaſt, v. 4. Yea, ſo immenſe will be the carnage, ſuch a torrent of blood be ſhed, that the vallies ſhall be filled with the corpſes of the ſlain, and the rivers ſwelled with human gore, hyperbolically ſpeaking, as high as the mountains, v. 5, 6. The ſword is God's, the executioners of vengeance the Chaldeans, v. 11. *Mighty*, men, *the terrible of the nations*, who ſhall *ſpoil the pomp*, plunder the wealth, and ſlay the multitude of the Egyptians, v. 12. Yea, the very cattle ſhall be deſtroyed, and the foot of man or beaſt ſhall no more diſturb the waters, ſo few ſhould remain, v. 13. The land throughout ſhall be deſolate, and all its plenty be at an end, v. 15. Even the luminaries of heaven, as if ſhocked to behold theſe ravages, ſhall be darkened and clothed in ſackcloth, v. 7, 8. And the once rapid rivers, as if congealed with grief, ſhall ſcarce flow, or with difficulty their heavy flood, v. 14.

3. The tidings of Pharaoh's fall with his multitudes, will alarm, amaze, and bitterly affect the nations. Not only the neighbours and allies would be vexed at their overthrow, lament them, and tremble at the judgments they beheld, v. 16, 17, 18. but even the remoteſt countries who had no connection with the Egyptians, v. 9. ſhall hear with aſtoniſhment the report, and dread every moment, leaſt that ſword of the Lord, brandiſhed before them by the king of Babylon, ſhould fall at laſt upon their heads. *Note*, (1.) When the ſword of judgment is brandiſhed before us, and we ſee others ſmitten, it is high time to tremble for ourſelves. (2.) Inſtead of being humbled by the viſitations of God before them, hardened ſinners murmur and fret againſt God.

4. The Lord will make himſelf as fully known by theſe ſtrokes of vengeance: the folly of pride and creature confidence will then appear, and God be found the only true abiding ſupport, and ſatiſfying portion.

‡ Ver. 10.

* Chap. xxxi. 18. Ver. 24, &c.

‖ Or, the ſword is laid.

† Ifa. i. 9, 10. Ver. 19.

* Ver. 21, 23.

‡ Or, dif-nay.

17 ¶ It came to paſs alſo in the twelfth year, in the
fifteenth *day* of the month, *that* the word of the LORD
came unto me, ſaying, 18 Son of man, wail for the
multitude of Egypt, and caſt them down, *even* her, and
the daughters of the famous nations, unto the nether
parts of the earth, with them that go down into the pit.
19 Whom doſt thou paſs in beauty? go down, and
be thou laid with the uncircumciſed. 20. They ſhall
fall in the midſt of *them that are* ſlain by the ſword: ‖
ſhe is delivered to the ſword: draw her, and all her multitudes.
21 The ſtrong among the mighty ſhall ſpeak
to him out of the midſt of hell with them that help
him: they are gone down, they lie uncircumciſed, ſlain
by the ſword. 22 Aſhur *is* there, and all her company:
his graves *are* about him: all of them ſlain, fallen
by the ſword. 23 Whoſe graves are ſet in the ſides of
the pit, and her company is round about her grave: all
of them ſlain, fallen by the ſword, which cauſed ‡ terror
in the land of the living. 24 There *is* Elam, and all
her multitude round about her grave, all of them ſlain,
fallen by the ſword, which are gone down uncircumciſed
into the nether parts of the earth, which cauſed their
terror in the land of the living; yet have they born their
ſhame with them that go down to the pit. 25 They
have ſet her a bed in the midſt of the ſlain with all her
multitude: her graves *are* round about him: all of them
uncircumciſed, ſlain by the ſword: though their terror
was cauſed in the land of the living, yet have they born
their ſhame with them that go down to the pit: he is put
in the midſt of *them that be* ſlain. 26 There *is* Meſhech,
Tubal, and all her multitude: her graves *are* round about
him: all of them uncircumciſed, ſlain by the ſword,
though they cauſed their terror in the land of the living.
27 And they ſhall not lie with the mighty, *that are*
fallen of the uncircumciſed, which are gone down to hell
with ‖ their weapons of war: and they have laid their
ſwords under their heads, but their iniquities ſhall be
upon their bones, though *they were* the terror of the
mighty in the land of the living. 28 Yea, thou ſhalt
be broken in the midſt of the uncircumciſed, and ſhalt
lie with *them that are* ſlain with the ſword. 29 There
is Edom, her kings and all her princes, which with
their might are § laid by *them that were* ſlain by the
ſword: they ſhall lie with the uncircumciſed, and with
them that go down to the pit. 30 There *be* the
princes of the north all of them, and all the Zidonians,
which are gone down with the ſlain, with their terror
they are aſhamed of their might, and they lie uncircumciſed
with *them that be* ſlain by the ſword, and bear their
ſhame with them that go down to the pit. 31 Pharaoh
ſhall ſee them, and ſhall be comforted over all his multitude,
even Pharaoh and all his army ſlain by the ſword,
ſaith the Lord GOD. 32 For I have cauſed my terror
in the land of the living: and he ſhall be laid in the
midſt of the uncircumciſed with *them that are* ſlain with
the ſword, *even* Pharaoh and all his multitude, ſaith the
Lord GOD.

Before Christ 587.

* Ver. 21.

‖ Heb. With weapons of their war.

§ Heb. Given or put.

* Chap. xxxviii. 6.

v. 17—32. About a fortnight after the former prophecy, was this delivered. It brings Pharaoh, with his multitude, to their graves, and the prophet muſt lament over them, or rather compoſe a funeral dirge to be ſung on this melancholy occaſion.

1. Egypt is brought to the grave, and received among the dead. The prophet is ordered to *caſt them down*, ver. 18. because divine power accompanied his prophetic word. Like other famous nations, ſhe muſt lie low, nor be exempted from the common fate of thoſe, whom in beauty ſhe rivalled, v. 19. She is delivered to the ſword, and dragged, as the corpſes of malefactors, in ignominy to the pit, v. 20. The mighty amongſt the dead are poetically repreſented as riſing to congratulate Pharaoh on his arrival, *Iſa.* xiv. 9. and admit him free of their dreary manſions, v. 21.

2. A variety of nations are mentioned who had gone down before him to the grave, and waited, in deriſion, to pay him mock honour, now become like one of them.

(1.) The Aſſyrian monarch, with his ſubjects, a vaſt congregation, once the terror of the living, now ſlain by the ſword, and their graves in rows placed round the ſepulchre of their king, v. 22, 23. *Note*, They who have been a terror to others, muſt themſelves fall before the King of Terrors.

(2.) The Perſians with their king next appear; they too had ruled a mighty noiſe in the world, but are now *gone down uncircumciſed*, unholy and profane, *into the nether parts of the earth*, ſlain by the ſword, and laid in an ignominious grave, v. 24, 25.

(3.) Meſhech and Tubal lie there, ſuppoſed to be the Scythian nation; not buried in ſtate as the mighty, but *with their ſwords under their heads*, as warriors, and *their iniquity ſhall be upon their bones*, dug out of their graves, and ignominiouſly expoſed, though once *the terror of the mighty in the land of the living*.

(4.) There lies Edom with her kings and princes. Their might unable to protect them, and forced to ſtoop to the devouring ſword. Though the circumciſed deſcendants of Abraham, yet being unlike him in their ſpirit and temper, they fall among the uncircumciſed. No outward privilege can protect thoſe, whoſe hearts are apoſtatized from God.

(5.) *The princes of the North, with the Zidonians*, notwithſtanding their maritime forces and ſtrong fortifications, are fallen, and their pride confounded in the duſt, v. 30.

Laſtly, Pharaoh with his multitude, ſlain by the ſword, ſhall make his grave with theſe, and ſhare that conſolation, if ſuch a wretched reflection can be ſuppoſed to adminiſter comfort, that he looks round and beholds other mighty monarchs as low and wretched as himſelf, v. 31, 32.

In all this deſcription of Egypt's fall, perhaps ſomething typical may be intended reſpecting the ruin of the antichriſtian foe, *Rev.* xi. 8. which may engage the prophet to dwell the longer upon it. And we may in general read and tremble, whilſt we ſee ſinners ſo many and mighty caſt down into the pit of deſtruction, and learn how fearful a thing it is to fall into the hands of the living God.

CHAP.

Before Christ 587

CHAP XXXIII

The prophet from speaking to other nations, returns to his own people 1 He must let them know what his office was that he was a watchman, and had received a charge concerning them, for which he was accountable, ver 1—9 2 He must let them know upon what terms they stand with God, that if a wicked man repent he shall not perish, but if a righteous man apostatize, he shall perish, ver 10—20 3 He must tell those who yet remained in the land of Israel, and flattered themselves that they should continue there, that their hopes would fail them, because they persisted in their sins, ver 21—29 4 Those are rebuked who attended Ezekiel's ministry, but were insincere in their professions of devotion, ver 30—33

1 AGAIN the word of the LORD came unto
me, saying, 2 Son of man, speak to the
children of thy people, and say unto them, When I
bring the sword upon a land, if the people of the land
take a man of their coasts, and set him for their [a] watch-
man 3 If when he seeth the sword come upon the
land, he blow the trumpet, and [b] warn the people, 4
Then † whosoever heareth the sound of the trumpet, and
taketh not warning, if the sword come, and take him
away, his blood shall be upon his own head 5 He
heard the sound of the trumpet, and took not warning,
[c] his blood shall be upon him but he that taketh warn-
ing, shall deliver his soul 6 But if the watchman see
the sword come, and blow not the trumpet, and the
people be not warned if the sword come and take
any person from among them, he is taken away in his
iniquity, but his blood will I require at the watchman's
hand 7 ¶ [d] So thou, O son of man, I have set thee a
watchman unto the house of Israel therefore thou shalt
hear the word [e] at my mouth, and [f] warn them from
me 8 When I say unto the wicked, O wicked *man*,
thou shalt surely die, if thou dost not speak to warn the
wicked from his way, that wicked *man* shall die in his
iniquity, but his blood will I require at thine hand
9 Nevertheless, if thou warn the wicked of his way
to turn from it if he do not turn from his way, he
shall die in his iniquity, but thou hast delivered thy
soul

[a] Chap iii 17 Heb xiii 17
[b] Col i 28
† Heb He that hearing heareth
[c] Acts xx 26
[d] Chap iii 17 &c
[e] 1 Pet iv 11
[f] Col i 28

v 1—9 Once more the prophet is sent to the rebellious house of Israel And we have here,

1 The office of a watchman described In times of danger and invasion, when the people set a watchman to descry the approaching enemy, his business is to wake, look out, and spread the alarm whenever he seeth *the sword coming*, in which case having discharged his trust, his own fidelity will be approved, and if others take warning they will be safe, if not, their blood will be on their own heads But if negligent, or asleep, the sword comes, and, for want of warning surprised, any soul perishes in his iniquity, then shall his blood be required at the watchman's hand, *v* 2—6 An awful charge! and well may they tremble for themselves who undertake to be watchmen to immortal souls against surrounding spiritual foes

2 God applies this to Ezekiel He is by divine commission appointed a watchman to the house of Israel, his business is attentively to hear, and faithfully to report the word of warning God shall deliver to him particularly he must say to the *wicked*, without distinction of persons, or fear of men's faces, *O wicked man, thou shalt surely die* Wherever unrepented iniquity is found, there the heavy wrath of God will lie, and neither the greatest will be spared, nor the meanest overlooked Death eternal will be the assured wages of sin, and wicked men are warned of this, that whilst there is yet hope they may fly from the wrath to come, to him who alone can, and will abundantly pardon If he neglected his duty, then the wicked should perish in his iniquity, for it will not excuse the careless sinner that he lived and died under a negligent pastor, when he had God's word in his hands, but his blood will God require at the prophet's hands, and terrible will be the cry of the blood of lost souls in the ear of unfaithful ministers in a judgment-day But if he was faithful, however obstinate the sinner might be, he would at least have the comfort of delivering his own soul, and though Israel be not gathered, he shall be glorious in the eyes of the Lord And this was not merely directed to him, but is also written for our instruction, and equally applicable to every one entrusted with the care of immortal souls, on whose fidelity so much depends, and whose unfaithfulness must be attended with such [illegible] guilt and misery

10 ¶ Therefore, O thou son of man, speak unto
the house of Israel, Thus ye speak, saying, If our trans-
gressions and our sins *be* upon us, and [g] we pine away
in them, how should we then live? 11 Say unto them,
As I live saith the Lord GOD, [h] I have no pleasure in
the death of the wicked, [i] but that the wicked turn from
his way and live turn ye, turn ye from your evil ways,
for [k] why will ye die, O house of Israel? 12 There-
fore, thou son of man, say unto the children of thy
people, [l] The righteousness of [m] the righteous shall not
deliver him in the day of his transgression as for the
wickedness of the wicked, he shall not fall thereby
in the day that he turneth from his wickedness, [n] neither
shall the righteous be able to live for *his righteousness* in
the day that he sinneth 13 When I shall say to the
righteous, *that* he shall surely live if he [o] trust to his
own righteousness, and commit iniquity, all his righte-
ousness shall not be remembred, but for his iniquity that
he hath committed, he shall die for it. 14 Again, when
I say unto the wicked, Thou shalt surely die if he turn
from his sin, and [p] do † that which is lawful and right,
15 *If* the wicked [q] restore the pledge, [r] give again that
he had robbed, walk in [s] the statutes of life without com-
mitting iniquity, he shall surely live, he shall no die
16 None of his sins that he hath committed, shall be
mentioned unto him he hath done that which is lawful
and right, he shall surely live 17 ¶ [t] Yet the children
of thy people say, The way of the LORD is not equal
but as for them, their way is not equal 18 [u] When
the righteous turneth from his righteousness, and com-
mitteth iniquity, he shall even die thereby 19 But
if the wicked turn from his wickedness, and do that
which is lawful and right, he shall live thereby 20 [x]
Yet ye say, The way of the LORD is not equal, O ye
house of Israel, [y] I will judge you every one after his
ways

Before Christ 587

[g] Chap xxiv 23
[h] 2 Sam xiv 14 Chap xviii 23 32 2 Pet iii 9
[i] Luke xv 20
[k] Chap xviii 31
[l] Chap iii 20 & xviii 24
[m] [illegible] xviii 9
[n] Heb x 38
[o] Luke xviii 9 Rom x 3
[p] [illegible]
† Heb Judgment and justice
[q] Chap xviii 7
[r] Exod xxii 1 4 Lev vi 4 Numb v 7
[s] Lev xviii 5 Chap xx 11, 13, 21
[t] Ver 20 Chap xviii 25 29
[u] 2 Pet ii 20 21
[x] Ver 17 Chap xviii 25 29
[y] Chap xviii 30 Mat xvi 27

v 10—20 The substance of these verses we had before, *chap* xviii 20 and we need repeatedly to have such important truths inculcated upon us

1 They quarrelled with God's dispensations of providence and grace, as if they were unjust and unequal, and would argue from the words with which the prophet concluded, *chap* xxiv 23 that it was in vain to call them to repentance and life, when their sins were bound upon them, and they must necessarily pine away in their iniquities, though the prophet had spoken conditionally of what would be their case, if they did not return to God, and with an express view to lead them to repentance *Note*, (1) They who chuse to err, will pervert the most glorious truths of God, that they may have a plea to harden themselves in iniquity (2) Many through despair of pardon rush presumptuously on their sins, and have their hearts hereby utterly hardened

2 God silences their *unjust reflections*

(1) Their despair had no foundation from God's word, but arose from their own wilfulness Far from delighting in the death of a sinner, vengeance is God's strange work He assures them, nay, by an oath confirms his word, that he had rather they would *turn and live*, nay, he warmly expostulates with them on the folly and perverseness of their conduct, and with repeated earnestness urges them to consider their ways, and turn from their iniquities that they may not die, as otherwise they infallibly must *Note*, (1) Sinners must repent, or perish (2) God is grieved, speaking after the manner of men, when they perversely reject the calls of his word (3) The damnation of the sinner lieth at his own door, in a day of judgment he will have only himself to blame

(2) Their charge upon God as dealing unequally, is refuted, they themselves being judges, for what can be so evidently equitable as his procedure? 1 *The righteous shall surely live*, ver 13 they who by the faith of Jesus, and by his spirit in them, are both accounted righteous before God, and really appear such before men but the most plausible professors, if they apostatize, will perish, and many such there ever were, and will be The grand source of their ruin is their pride, *they trust in their own righteousness*, the most fatal rock against which a soul can split, for the moment a sinner places confidence in his own doings and duties, and fancies himself strong enough to resist any temptation, he is already fallen This high conceit is his mortal sin, and the sure forerunner of his ruin puffed up with pride he falls into the snare of the devil, *commits iniquity*, lives and dies in the practice of it, and the consequence of this is, he perishes everlastingly all his pleas of former goodness will stand him in no stead at God's bar, he is found in unrepented guilt, and sinks under the curse into the belly of hell, and the more confident his former hopes were, and the

more

Before Christ 587.

more eminent his profeſſion, the more dreadful will his diſappointment be, and the more aggravated his guilt. Be not therefore high-minded, but fear. 2. *The wicked ſhall ſurely die*, ſuch is the decree of the unchangeable God; not that this terrible ſentence is deſigned to bar the door of hope againſt penitents, far from it; but to warn them of their danger, that they may eſcape from it. For, whenever a ſinner turns to God, however aggravated his guilt, and numberleſs or enormous his tranſgreſſions, he ſhall, through Jeſus, be accepted, and find that he can as eaſily pardon many tranſgreſſions as few; and for the encouragement of the trembling ſoul, God is pleaſed to aſſure us, his arms are open, and ſo far from upbraiding us with our rebellions, he will not ſo much as mention them in the day we return to him. The paſt ſhall all be cancelled, the preſent bleſſed change ſhall only be remembered, and in the way of truth and righteouſneſs, in which by divine grace we are enabled now to walk, we ſhall aſſuredly find eternal life.

The concluſion from the whole is clear. God's ways are equal, theirs unequal; he will not own therefore theſe unreaſonable and wicked men as his people, but turn them over to the prophet, *v.* 17. determined to *judge them according to their ways*; and however they diſpute againſt him, he will glorify his righteouſneſs in the deſtruction of the impenitent and apoſtates, and in the ſalvation of the penitent and faithful.

21 ¶ And it came to paſs in the twelfth year of [z] our
captivity, in the tenth *month*, in the fifth *day* of the
month, [a] *that* one that had eſcaped out of Jeruſalem,
came unto me, ſaying, [b] The city is ſmitten. 22 Now
[c] the hand of the LORD was upon me in the evening,
afore he that was eſcaped came; and had opened my
mouth, until he came to me in the morning; and my
mouth was opened, and I was no more [d] dumb. 23
Then the word of the LORD came unto me, ſaying,
24 Son of man, [e] they that inhabit thoſe waſtes of the
land of Iſrael, ſpeak, ſaying, [f] Abraham was one, and
he inherited the land: but we *are* many; the land is
given us for inheritance. 25 Wherefore ſay unto them,
Thus ſaith the Lord GOD, [g] Ye eat † with the blood,
and lift up your eyes toward your idols, and ſhed
blood: and ſhall ye poſſeſs the land? 26 Ye ſtand up-
on your ſword, ye work abomination, and ye defile every
one his neighbour's wife: and ſhall ye poſſeſs the land?
27 Say thou thus unto them, Thus ſaith the Lord
GOD, *As* I live, ſurely they that are in the waſtes ſhall
fall by the ſword, and him that is in the open field [i] will
I give to the beaſts ‡ to be devoured; and they that
be in the forts [k] and in the caves, ſhall die of the peſti-
lence. 28 For [l] I will lay the land || moſt deſolate, and
[m] the pomp of her ſtrength ſhall ceaſe; and the moun-
tains of Iſrael ſhall be deſolate, that none ſhall paſs
through. 29 [n] Then ſhall they know that I *am* the
LORD, when I have laid the land moſt deſolate, be-
cauſe of all their abominations which they have com-
mitted.

z Chap. i. 2. a Ibid. xxiv. 26. b 2 Kings xxv. 4. c Chap. i. 3. d Chap. iii. 26. & xxiv. 27. e Chap. ... f Iſa. li. 2. g Gen. ix. 4. Lev. iii. 17. & xvii. 10. & xix. 26. Deut. xii. 16. † Or, upon. h Chap. xxiii. 26. i Chap. xxxix. 4. ‡ Heb. to devour. k Judg. vi. 2. 1 Sam. xiii. 6. l Jer. xliv. 2. || Heb. Deſolation and deſolation. m Chap. vi. 2. & vii. 24. & xxiv. 21. n Ezek. ix. 16.

v. 21—29. Ezekiel had been informed, *chap.* xxiv. 26. that one of thoſe eſcaped out of the flames of Jeruſalem, ſhould give him an affecting narrative of the miſeries that devoted place had ſuffered, and lo! the meſſenger arrives. According to ſome, this was a year and four months after the fatal cataſtrophe, though others, by a different method of computation, ſuppoſe it only a month from the time of the deſtruction of Jeruſalem.

1. The prophet, the evening before the meſſenger arrived, by a divine impreſſion, being made acquainted with the ſad news he brought, *chap.* xxiv. 27. had begun anew, after a long ſilence, with earneſtneſs and zeal to addreſs his unhappy countrymen, taking occaſion from this ſad event to warn them of the dreadful conſequences of ſin, and call them to repentance.

2. After he had heard the particulars of the ſiege, and deſtruction of the city, with the ravages of the Chaldean army through the country, he hath a word from God ſent unto him, to be delivered to the miſerable remnant who inhabited the waſtes of Judea, and ſo far from being humbled with all the judgments they had ſeen, and the ſufferings they had felt, continued juſt as bad as ever: and theſe were either Johanan and his aſſociates, or ſome others who might ſtill have continued in Judea, after he and his company were departed into Egypt.

(1.) Their pride was inſufferable. Far from lamenting their ſins, which had cauſed the deſolations of the land, they count themſelves as high in God's favour as Abraham; yea, in ſome reſpect they think they exceed him, poſſeſſing their inheritance by a good title, and being many, to keep poſſeſſion of it against all oppoſers, *v.* 24.

(2.) Their other ſins were great and aggravated. [1.] *Ye eat with the blood*, contrary to the divine preſcription, Lev. xix.

26. or *upon the blood*, referring to the idolatrous practices of the heathen, who ſat down round the blood of the ſacrifices they had offered to devils, and fancied they held communion with them thereby. [2.] *Ye lift up your eyes towards your idols*, worſhipping their abominations. [3.] *Ye ſhed blood*, the blood of innocents. [4.] *Ye ſtand upon your ſword*, place confidence in an arm of fleſh. [5.] *Ye work abomination*, ſlaves to vile affections and unnatural luſts. [6.] *Ye defile every one his neighbour's wife*, which is juſtly reckoned among the moſt atrocious crimes.

(3.) The conſequence of ſuch wickedneſs could not but be fatal to them. *Shall ye poſſeſs the land?* ſuch miſcreants as the earth groaned to bear? No. The ſword of vengeance will purſue them in the waſte places; thoſe who are in the open fields the beaſts ſhall devour; and they who have fled to the forts and to the caves for ſhelter, ſhall die of the peſtilence, *v.* 27. One judgment ſhall follow upon another, till the land is compleatly deſolate, their remaining ſtrength they boaſted of is utterly ruined, and the very mountains waſted without flocks or herds feeding on them; nor ſhall a traveller paſs through the land, ſo uncultivated, ſo depopulated would it be, and filled with wild beaſts, *v.* 28. Such judgments would make them know an avenging *God*, who having ſworn to puniſh will execute his threatnings, and give them the juſt recompenſe their abominations deſerve, *v.* 29.

30 ¶ Alſo thou ſon of man, [o] the children of thy
people ſtill are talking [*] againſt thee by the walls, and
in the doors of the houſes, and ſpeak one to another,
every one to his brother, ſaying, Come, I pray you,
and hear what is the word that cometh forth from the
LORD. 31 And [p] they come unto thee as the people
cometh, and ‡ they ſit before thee *as* my people, and
they hear thy words, but they will not do them: [q] for
with their mouth they || ſhew much love, *but* their heart
goeth [r] after their covetouſneſs. 32 And lo, thou *art*
unto them as § a very lovely ſong of one that hath a
pleaſant voice, and can play well on an inſtrument: for
they hear thy words, but they do them not. 33 [s] And
when this cometh to paſs (lo it will come) then [t] ſhall
they know that a prophet hath been among them.

o 2 Chron. xxxvi. 16. * Or, of thee. p Chap. viii. 1. & xiv. 1. & xx. 1. ‡ Or, my people ſit before thee. q Pſ. lxxviii. 36, 37. Iſa. xxix. 13. || Heb. Make loves, or jeſts. r Luke xii. 14, 15. § Heb. A ſong of loves. s Jam. i. 22. t 1 Sam. iii. 20. Chap. ii. 5.

v. 30—33. The Jews which remained in the land were, we find, bad, very bad; nor were many of the captivity much better, as here evidently appears.

1. They were hypocritical mockers and revilers. They came with other worſhippers, and ſat, to appearance, gravely and attentively, as if deſirous to hear the prophetic word, and in their profeſſions before the prophet pretended much love; but their hearts were in the gall of bitterneſs and bond of iniquity; covetouſneſs reigned within; they were pleaſed with the prophet's manner, *his expreſſions and elocution* as a ſpeaker, but paid no regard to the matter. It was the amuſement of an hour; and when they were gone, they could readily join in the abuſe caſt upon him, and among their own party ridicule and revile the preacher, his doctrine, and his hearers. *Note*, (1.) Public perſons, eſpecially miniſters, will be the butt of obloquy. If they knew but half the evil ſaid of them, it might diſcourage them; but God knows their revilers, and will puniſh them. (2.) It is a ſerious matter to hear God's word; they who make a jeſt of things ſacred, will find by and by that God is not thus to be mocked. (3.) Many come to the ordinances in formality, and for faſhion ſake, who never ſo much as expect edification from them. (4.) We often ſee a ſmooth tongue cover a malignant heart: from the teeth outward, all a profeſſion of love and regard, but rancour and enmity rage within. (5.) Many take pleaſure in hearing the man and the miniſter, who pay no regard to the meſſage; and whilſt their ears are delighted, their hearts are untouched. (6.) Even among profeſſors of religion, covetouſneſs is a reigning ſin, and nothing more effectually quenches the good impreſſions of God's word than this.

2. God's word will ſtand when all contemners of it ſhall periſh together. *When this cometh to paſs (lo it will come)* however now ſcoffers deſpiſe the wrath of God, they will too late rue their folly; *then ſhall they know that a prophet hath been among them*, when the event verifies the prediction, and the threatned vengeance overtakes them.

CHAP. XXXIV.

The iniquities and calamities of God's Iſrael had been largely and pathetically lamented before. In this chapter the ſhepherds of Iſrael, their rulers both in the church and ſtate, are called to an account, as having been very much acceſſary to their ſin and ruin. 1. They are charged with negligence, unſkilfulneſs, and unfaithfulneſs in the management of public affairs, ver. 1, 6, 8. *2. They are diſplaced from their truſt for inſufficiency and treachery,* ver. 7, 10.

Before Christ 587

7, 10. 3 *God promises to take care of his flock though they did not*, ver. 11, 16 4 *A charge is exhibited against those of the flock that were fat and strong, for injuring the weak and feeble*, ver 17—22 5 *The Messiah is promised as the great and good shepherd of the sheep, who should redress all their grievances*, ver 23—31

1 AND the word of the LORD came unto me,
a Chap xxxiii 4 saying, 2 a Son of man, prophesy against b the
b Jer xxiii 1 shepherds of Israel, prophesy and say unto them, Thus
c Zech xi 16 saith the Lord GOD unto the shepherds, c Wo *be* to
d Rom xvi 18 the shepherds of Israel d that do feed themselves should
e John xxi 15 Acts xx 28 not the shepherds e feed the flocks? 3 f Ye eat the fat,
1 Pet v 2 and ye clothe you with the wool, ye kill them that
f Mic iii 2, 3 are fed *but* ye feed not the flock 4 g The diseased
g Ver 16 have ye not strengthened, neither have ye healed *that*
which was sick, neither have ye bound up *that which*
was broken, neither have ye brought again *that which*
was driven away, neither have ye sought *that which was*
h 1 Pet v 3 lost, but h with force and with cruelty have ye ruled
i Jer l 6 them 5 And i they were scattered † because *there is*
† Or without a shepherd no shepherd and they became meat to all the beasts
So ver 8 of the field, when they were scattered 6 My sheep
wandered through all the mountains, and upon every
k Ver 12 high hill yea, k my flock was scattered upon all the
face of the earth, and none did search or seek *after*
them

v 1—6 We have here,

1 A wo denounced against the shepherds of Israel, the princes and magistrates, or the priests and Levites, who were the great authors of Israel's ruin, and though their station was so high, and their profession so respectable, yet neither would screen them from severe rebuke, nor exempt them from God's fearful wrath Negligent pastors are the most criminal of all transgressors, and may expect the heaviest judgment

2 The sin charged upon them is enriching themselves at the expence of their neglected flocks, indifferent what became of the people committed to their charge, they never thought of feeding them, but of fattening themselves The *magistrates* took no pains to vindicate the oppressed, to relieve the poor, to bring back those who were fled to foreign lands, to suppress vice, or encourage religion the *ministers* intent only on their tythes and offerings, took no pains to seek the lost, to instruct the ignorant, recover the erroneous, warn the unruly, or comfort the feeble-minded, the souls of men seemed in no wise their concern With *force and cruelty*, both in church and state, *they ruled*, and used to the purposes of oppression the power committed to their trust for the protection and edification of God's people, so that they had really no shepherd, yea, worse than none for those who usurped the office were in fact ravening wolves Wo to the poor people that are in such a case!

7 ¶ Therefore, ye shepherds, hear the word of the
LORD, 8 *As* I live, saith the Lord GOD, surely
because my flock became a prey, and my flock became
meat to every beast of the field, because *there was* no
l Jer xxiii 2 shepherd, l neither did my shepherds search for my
flock, but the shepherds fed themselves, and fed not my
flock 9 Therefore, O ye shepherds, hear the word of
the LORD; 10 Thus saith the Lord GOD, Behold,
m Chap xiii 8 m I *am* against the shepherds, and n I will require my
n Ibid iii 18 Heb xiii 17 flock at their hand, and cause them to cease from feed-
ing the flock, neither shall the shepherds feed themselves
any more, for I will deliver my flock from their mouth,
that they may not be meat for them 11 ¶ For thus
saith the Lord GOD, Behold, I, *even* I, will both search
‖ Heb According to the seeking out, &c my sheep, and seek them out 12 ‖ As a shepherd
seeketh out his flock in the day that he is among his
sheep *that are* scattered; so will I seek out my sheep,
and will deliver them out of all places, where they have
o Joel ii 2 been scattered o in the cloudy and dark day. 13 And
p Jer xxiii 3 Chap xxviii 25 & xxxvii 21, 22 p I will bring them out from the people, and gather
them from the countries, and will bring them to their
own land, and feed them upon the mountains of Israel
by the rivers, and in all the inhabited places of the
q Ps xxiii 2 country 14 I will feed them q in a good pasture, and
upon the high mountains of Israel shall their fold be
there shall they lie in a good fold, and *in* a fat pasture
shall they feed upon the mountains of Israel. 15 I
will feed my flock, and I will cause them to lie down,
r Mic iv 6 Mat xviii 11 saith the Lord GOD 16 r I will seek *that which was*
lost, and bring again *that which was* driven away, and
will bind up *that which was* broken, and will strengthen
that which was sick: but I will destroy s the fat and the Before Christ 587
strong, I will feed them with judgment s Isa x 16 Amos iv

v 7—16 The careless shepherds are cited to God's bar God will punish them, and graciously rescue the flock they have abused

1 He will punish the shepherds for their neglect and rapaciousness, v 8 *God is against them*, and his wrath who can abide? He will call them to a severe account for the loss of every sheep of his flock that perished through their negligence Zedekiah, and the princes who rebelled, shall bear the guilt of all the innocent blood which was shed in consequence thereof And every lost soul shall cry for vengeance against the unfaithful minister who suffered him, unconcerned, to die in his iniquity God will turn them out of their office, and suffer them no more to fatten on the spoil. The king and princes of Judah shall be hurled from their high estate, and cast into the depths of abject wretchedness, and those priests and Levites who abused their sacred office, be degraded, v 10 *Note*, (1) Ministers can never too often reflect upon the solemn account they must one day make (2) God justly deprives oppressors of the power they abuse

2 God will himself take care of his own flock, none of his sheep shall perish Though their pastors are unfaithful, and neglect them, he will provide for them *Behold, I, even I the* Lord, able and willing to save them, I *will*, (1) *both search my sheep, and seek them out*, wherever they are dispersed through all the earth, not one shall be lost, v 11 He knoweth those that are his, and in his good time will bring them into his fold from their state of wandering, during the cloudy and dark day; and this was fulfilled primarily in the restoration of the Jews from their captivity, and is spiritually still fulfilling day by day, whilst by his word and grace he is gathering in his redeemed people from the earth, calling them out of darkness into his marvellous light, till he hath accomplished the number of his elect, and his eternal kingdom comes may my soul in that day be the object of his care! (2) He will *feed them upon the mountains of Israel*, and *cause them to lie down* in peace and safety, in a *good fold*, and a *fat pasture*, ver 14, 15 The Jews on their return to their own land, enjoyed abundance of blessings, and particularly the privileges of the sanctuary and ordinances of God's worship And in the church, the mount of God, do all believers find the rich pastures of grace, and the sweet waters of divine consolation inclosed as in a fold, under the protection of their Almighty shepherd, they are safe from all the powers of evil, and rest under his shadow with great delight happy the people that are in such a case! (3) He will not only recover them from their wanderings, but *heal* those that were hurt, during their state of departure from him, and *strengthen those that were sick* The awakened sinner feels his deadly wounds, his heart is broken with a sense of guilt, and weak he finds himself, and unable to resist his corruptions, but the Saviour who bought his sheep with his own blood, pours in his precious balm to asswage their pains, and cures the desperate. By his spirit he renews their minds, gives the medicine which heals their sickness, even his efficacious grace, which can save them from the bondage of corruption, and strengthens their weakness, that they may be enabled to walk and please God

3 It is repeated, to mark the certainty and terribleness of their destruction *I will destroy the fat and the strong*, for he who glorifies his mercy in the salvation of his people, will glorify his justice in the damnation of his and their enemies, *feeding them with judgment*, inflicting the righteous vengeance due to their iniquities

17 And *as for* you, O my flock, thus saith the
Lord GOD, t Behold, I judge between † cattle and t Chap xx 37, 38 Zech x 3 Mat xxv
cattle, between the rams and the ‖ he-goats, 18 *Seem-*
eth it a small thing unto you, to have eaten up the good
pasture, but ye must tread down with your feet the re-
sidue of your pastures? and to have drunk of the deep
waters, but ye must foul the residue with your feet?
19 And *as for* my flock, they eat that which ye have
trodden with your feet and they drink that which ye
have fouled with your feet 20 ¶ Therefore thus saith
the Lord GOD unto them, Behold, I, *even* I will judge
between the fat cattle, and between the lean cattle
21 Because ye have thrust with side, and with shoulder,
and pushed all the diseased with your horns, till ye have
scattered them abroad 22 Therefore will I save my
flock, and they shall no more be a prey, and I will judge
between cattle and cattle 23 And I will set up u one
shepherd over them, and he shall feed them, x *even*
my servant David, he shall feed them, and he shall
be their shepherd 24 And I the LORD will be
their God; and my servant David a prince among
them, I the LORD have spoken *it* 25 And I
will

Before Christ 587

will make with them a covenant of peace, and [a] will
cauſe the evil beaſts to ceaſe out of the land and [a] they
ſhall dwell ſafely in the wilderneſs, and ſleep in the
woods 26 And I will make them and the places round
about my hill, a bleſſing, and I will cauſe the ſhower
to come down in his ſeaſon there ſhall be [b] ſhowers of
bleſſing. 27 And [c] the tree of the field ſhall yield her
fruit, and the earth ſhall yield her increaſe, and they
ſhall be ſafe in their land, and ſhall know that I *am*
the LORD, when I have broken the bands of their
yoke, and delivered them out of the hand of thoſe that
ſerved themſelves of them 28 And they ſhall no
more be a prey to the heathen, neither ſhall the beaſts
of the land devour them, but [d] they ſhall dwell ſafely,
and none ſhall make *them* afraid 29 And I will raiſe
up for them [e] a plant † of renown, and they ſhall be
no more ‡ conſumed with hunger in the land, [f] neither
bear the ſhame of the heathen any more 30 Thus
ſhall they know that I the LORD their God *am* with
them, and *that* they, *even* the houſe of Iſrael, *are* my
people, ſaith the Lord GOD 31 And ye [g] my flock,
[h] the flock of my paſture, *are* men, *and* I *am* your God,
ſaith the Lord GOD

a Iſa xi 6–9 & xxxv 9 Hoſ ii 18 Jer xxiii 6
b Pſ lxviii 9
c Lev xxvi 4 Pſ lxxxv 12
d Jer xxx 10 & xlvi 27 Ver. 25
e Iſa xi 1 Jer xxiii 5
† Or for
‡ Heb taken away.
f Chap xxxvi 3, 6, 15
g John x 11
h Pſ c 3

v 17—31 The prophet turns from the ſhepherds to the flock, for they were of different kinds The church of profeſſors ever conſiſted of a mixed multitude, good and bad, but there is a diſcerning ſhepherd, the Lord Jeſus, here ſpoken of, who will ſhortly ſeparate the precious from the vile

1 A heavy charge is brought againſt ſome of the flock, the fat, the rams and he-goats, the wealthy who oppreſſed their neighbours, and, not content with the gains of extortion, embittered by their ill uſage the little which remained to the poor flock, as if they took a pleaſure in their diſtreſſes, v 18, 19 Nay, they not only trod down the paſtures, and fouled the waters, but *thruſt with the ſide and ſhoulder, and puſhed the diſeaſed with their horns*, adding affliction to the afflicted Many apply this to the Scribes and Phariſees, who devoured the poor, fouled the waters of truth by their traditions, and oppreſſed with their anathemas the poor of the flock, who confeſſed the Lord Jeſus Though it may be alſo generally applied to wicked men in every age, who have copied theſe deſtructive ways, and, tho' in profeſſion the flock of Chriſt, have ſhewn themſelves the moſt inveterate enemies of his faithful ſheep, but God will judge them, deliver his people from them now, and make an eternal ſeparation ſhortly between the precious and the vile

2 Rich conſolation is ſpoken to the faithful few God will ſave his flock, nor ſuffer them any more to be a prey to their enemies, particularly by raiſing up the promiſed Meſſiah, under whoſe protection his people ſhould dwell in ſafety

(1) His character and office are deſcribed *I will ſet up one ſhepherd over them* both Jew and Gentile under him ſhall become one fold, and by the divine appointment he is conſtituted the head over all things to his church, *and he ſhall feed them* by his word, his Spirit, his ordinances, his miniſters, *even my ſervant David*, ſo called as being David's promiſed ſeed, and God's *ſervant*, as employed by him in the work of the ſalvation of loſt ſouls *a plant of renown*, v 29 moſt tranſcendently glorious in his perſon and offices, and exalted in the preaching of his goſpel

(2) For his ſake *God will make with them a covenant of peace* Man is by nature in a ſtate of enmity with God, till Chriſt, our peace, brings us, who were far off, nigh unto God, then we become intereſted in the everlaſting covenant of grace, *God engages to be our God*, and *his ſervant David*, the Lord Jeſus, becomes our *prince* and ſaviour, to give repentance and remiſſion of ſins, and to reign over and protect his redeemed, v 24 and *Iſrael*, all true believers, ſhall be *his people*, to love, ſerve, and enjoy him to eternity, v 30

(3) Ineſtimably great and precious are the privileges to which the flock of God become entitled, in virtue of this covenant of peace Since *the Lord their God was with them*, v 30 their deliverance was ſure, and peace and plenty were now their happy portion *They ſhall be ſafe* under the divine protection, their ſpiritual enemies, *the evil beaſts*, v 25 ſubdued, and *cauſed to ceaſe out of the land* they ſhall be delivered from fear of evil; though in the midſt of ſnares and temptations, God will preſerve them, v 25, 28 and having broken the oppreſſors yoke, and reſcued them from thoſe who *ſerved themſelves of them*, he will make them *know he is the Lord*, by bleſſed experience of his almighty power, grace, and love, v 27 They ſhall want no manner of thing that is good, all ſpiritual bleſſings in Chriſt Jeſus ſhall ſurround them *I will make them and the places round about my hill, a bleſſing*, ſo eminently ſhall they be diſtinguiſhed with his favours, and all who ſee them will call them bleſſed, yea, they ſhall themſelves alſo be bleſſings to others *And I will cauſe the ſhower to come down in his ſeaſon*, the graces and conſolations of his Spirit, which the Redeemer ſhowers down upon the hearts of his people, according to their various neceſſities *There ſhall be ſhowers of bleſſing*, the greateſt abundance of the richeſt gifts of God, pardon, adoption, holineſs, glory, freely beſtowed upon the redeemed ſoul *and the tree of the field ſhall yield her fruit*, the fruits of righteouſneſs, which ſpring from theſe quickening ſhowers of grace *and the earth ſhall yield her increaſe*, in an abundance of converts raiſed up by the preaching of the goſpel *They ſhall be no more conſumed with hunger*, but be richly fed with that bread which cometh down from heaven, and giveth life unto the world *neither ſhall they bear the ſhame of the heathen any more*, God having appeared for them, and made it evident, by the diſpenſations of his providence and grace, that he is *their God*, v 31 their preſent portion, and exceeding great reward The Jews returned from captivity enjoyed literally many of theſe bleſſings outwardly, but they are moſt eminently fulfilled to the Iſrael of God in every age, who in Chriſt Jeſus are *bleſſed with all ſpiritual bleſſings in heavenly things*

CHAP XXXV

This chapter contains a prophecy of the deſtruction of Edom 1 Their ſin was malice to Iſrael, ver 5, 10, 13 *2 Their ruin is threatened for it God will be againſt them*, ver 3 *Their country ſhall be laid waſte*, ver 4 *depopulated, and made quite deſolate*, ver 6—9 *and left ſo, when other nations that had been waſted ſhould recover themſelves*, ver 14, 15

1 MOREOVER, the word of the LORD came
unto me, ſaying, 2 Son of man, ſet thy face
againſt mount Seir, and propheſy againſt it, 3 And
ſay unto it, Thus ſaith the Lord GOD, Behold, O
mount Seir, I *am* againſt thee, and I will ſtretch out
mine hand againſt thee, and I will make thee † moſt
deſolate 4 I will lay thy cities waſte, and thou ſhalt be
deſolate, and thou ſhalt [b] know that I *am* the LORD
5 Becauſe thou haſt had a ‡ perpetual hatred, and [c] haſt
§ ſhed *the blood of* the children of Iſrael by the force of
the ſword, in the time of their calamity, [d] in the time
that their iniquity *had* an end 6. Therefore, *as* I live,
ſaith the Lord GOD, I will prepare thee unto blood,
and blood ſhall purſue thee [e] ſith thou haſt not hated
blood, even blood ſhall purſue thee 7 Thus will I
make mount Seir moſt deſolate, and cut off from it him
that paſſeth out, and him that returneth 8 And I
will fill his mountains with his ſlain *men* in thy hills,
and in thy valleys, and in all thy rivers ſhall they fall
that are ſlain with the ſword 9 [f] I will make thee
perpetual deſolations, and thy cities ſhall not return,
and [g] ye ſhall know that I *am* the LORD

a Jer xlix 7, 8 Chap. xxv 12 Am i 11 Obad 10, &c
† Heb Deſolation and deſolation Ver 7
b Pſ ix 16
‡ Or hatred of old C. 10. xxv 15
c Pſ cxxxvii 7
§ Heb Poured out the children
d Chap xxi 25, 29 Dan ix 24
e Iſ lxiii 17 Mat vii 2.
f Jer xlix 13 Mal i 3, 4
g Iſ ix 16 Chap vi 7. & vii 4, 9

v 1—9 Mount Seir had before been arraigned and condemned a ſecond time, to ſhew the certainty and immutability of God's council, the prophet muſt repeat the charge and the judgment paſſed upon her Since *God was againſt her*, he muſt *ſet his face againſt her* too

1 The provocation given by the Edomites was, their enmity and ill behaviour towards God's Iſrael The hatred of Eſau againſt Jacob had been tranſmitted as a deadly feud to his poſterity, and now they had an opportunity to wreak their revenge upon the Jews, they failed not to improve it, and ſhed the blood of thoſe who fled in the day of their calamity, unable to reſiſt, when the meaſure of their iniquity was full, and their ruin completed, v 8 *Note*, (1) The quarrels of parents frequently deſcend to their children, and even national antipathies are often deeply rooted, but the moſt *perpetual hatred* is that which ever did and ever will ſubſiſt between the ſeed of the ſerpent and the ſeed of the woman (2) It is baſe and cruel to take advantage of the diſtreſs of others, to oppreſs them, and add to their affliction

2 The puniſhment denounced is the utter deſolation of their country, v 3 Since they had ſo laviſhly ſhed blood, God will give them blood to drink, v 6 The mountains ſhall be filled with the ſlain, and the ſword devour without mercy, v 8. ſo that on which ever ſide they turned, death met them Thus ſhould the country be made *perpetual deſolations*, and never more be reſtored to its former proſperity and in theſe judgments God will make himſelf known to them, as the avenger of his people's wrongs, and ſooner or later ſhall the revenge of the malicious be thus with fearful vengeance repaid

10 Becauſe thou haſt ſaid, Theſe two nations, and
theſe two countries ſhall be mine, and we will [h] poſſeſs
it, ‖ whereas [i] the LORD was there 11 Therefore,
as I live, ſaith the Lord GOD, I will even do [k] according
to thine anger, and according to thine envy which
thou haſt uſed out of thy hatred againſt them and I
will

h Pſ lxxxiii. 4, 12
‖ Or, though
i Pſ xlviii 3 & cxxxii 13, 14
k Mat. vii 2 Jam ii 13

Before Christ 587

will make myself known amongst them, when I have
judged thee 12 And thou shalt know that I *am* the
LORD, *and that* I have heard all thy blasphemies which
thou hast spoken against the mountains of Israel, say-
ing, They are laid desolate, they are given us ‡ to con-
sume 13 Thus with your mouth ye have § boasted
against me, and [l] have multiplied your words against
me: I have heard *them* 14 Thus saith the Lord
GOD, When the whole earth rejoiceth, I will make thee
desolate. 15 [m] As thou didst rejoice at the inheritance
of the house of Israel, because it was desolate, so will I
do unto thee thou shalt be desolate, O mount Seir,
and all Idumea, *even* all of it, and they shall know that
I *am* the LORD.

‡ Heb. To devour

§ Heb. Magnified

l 1 Sam. ii. 3

m Obad. 15

v. 10—15 We have here further instances of the wicked-ness of the Edomites

1 In their blasphemies both against God and his people *Thou hast said, These two nations and countries shall be mine*, they thought of seizing the land of Judah and Israel for their own, *whereas*, or *though, the Lord was there*, which shewed their profaneness and impiety, as if, notwithstanding his presence and protection, they could and would possess it. They concluded, because the land was desolate, that God had utterly abandoned his people, v. 12 but it was far otherwise, for every boast and insolent word uttered against them, the Lord regarded as a reproach cast upon himself, v. 13

2 They rejoiced to see the desolations of Israel, v. 15 their envy and hatred were thus gratified, and with a malicious pleasure they insulted over them

3 God remarked their wicked words he *heard*, and will avenge them, he will retaliate upon them all the anger, envy, and hatred they shewed to his people, and make them desolate as those over whom they rejoiced. Yea, when other nations shall see their miseries removed, Edom's desolations shall remain, or, as the words, v. 14 may be rendered, *The whole earth shall rejoice in the desolations which I shall make for thee*, pleased to behold their fall. And herein God will also glorify himself, and make his justice, power, and regard to his people, known in their enemies destruction, v. 11 *Note*, (1) Not an idle word escapes the divine cognizance, much less the hard speeches which profane and ungodly sinners utter against the Lord (2) They who maliciously rejoice in the death of others, by whom they hope to gain, may expect that others will express the same malicious pleasure over them, when the day of their fall arrives (3) God will order all the dispensations of his providence and grace in such a way, as to demonstrate his care and love for his own people

CHAP. XXXVI

There are two distinct prophecies in this chapter, 1 One that relates to the temporal estate of the Jews, wherein their present deplorable condition is described, and the triumphs of their neighbours in it, but it is promised, that their grievances should be all redressed, and they in due time settled again in their own land in the midst of peace and plenty, ver 1—15 2 Another that seems chiefly to concern their spiritual estate, wherein they are reminded of their former sins, and God's judgments upon them to humble them, ver 16—20 But it is promised, (1) That God would glorify himself in shewing mercy to them, ver 21—24 (2) That he would sanctify them, by giving them his grace, and fitting them for his service, and this for his own name's sake, and in answer to their prayers, ver 25—38

a Chap. vi. 2

b Chap. xxv. 3 & xxvi. 2

c Deut. xxxii. 13

† Chap. xxxv. 10

† Heb. Be cause for be cause

‡ Or, made to come up on the lip of the tongue

a Heb. ii. 3

b 1 Sam. ii. 15

§ Or, bottoms, or dales

i Chap. xxxviii. 19

k Ver. 3 Chap. xxxv. 10

1 ALSO thou son of man, prophesy unto [a] the
mountains of Israel, and say, Ye mountains of
Israel, hear the word of the LORD 2 Thus saith the
Lord GOD, Because [b] the enemy hath said against you,
Aha, [c] even the ancient high places [d] are ours in posses-
sion 3 Therefore prophesy and say, Thus saith the
Lord GOD, † Because they have made *you* desolate, and
swallowed you up on every side, that ye might be a pos-
session unto the residue of the heathen, and ye are ‡ ta-
ken up in the lips of talkers, and [e] *are* an infamy of the
people 4 Therefore ye mountains of Israel, hear the
word of the Lord GOD, Thus saith the Lord GOD to
the mountains, and to the hills, to the § rivers, and to
the valleys, to the desolate wastes, and to the cities *that*
are forsaken, which became a prey and derision to the
residue of the heathen that *are* round about 5 There-
fore thus saith the Lord GOD, [f] Surely in the fire of
my jealousy have I spoken against the residue of the hea-
then, and against all Idumea, [g] which have appointed
my land into their possession, with the joy of all *their*
heart, with despiteful minds to cast it out for a prey
6 Prophesy therefore concerning the land of Israel, and
say unto the mountains and to the hills, to the rivers and
to the valleys, Thus saith the Lord GOD, Behold, I
have spoken in my jealousy, and in my fury, because
[h] ye have borne the shame of the heathen 7 There-
fore thus saith the Lord GOD, I have lifted up mine
hand, surely the heathen that *are* about you, they shall
bear their shame 8 ¶ But ye, O mountains of Israel,
ye shall shoot forth your branches, and yield your fruit
to my people of Israel, for they are at hand to come
9 For behold, I *am* for you, and I will turn unto you,
and ye shall be tilled and sown 10 And [i] I will mul-
tiply men upon you, all the house of Israel, *even* all of
it, and the cities shall be inhabited, and the wastes shall
be builded 11 And I will multiply upon you man
and beast, and they shall increase and bring fruit, and
I will settle you after your old estates and will do bet-
ter *unto you* than at your beginnings, and [k] ye shall know
that I *am* the LORD 12 Yea, I will cause men to
walk upon you, *even* my people Israel, and [l] they shall
possess thee, and thou shalt be their inheritance, and
thou shalt no more henceforth [m] bereave them *of men*
13 Thus saith the Lord GOD, Because they say unto
you, [n] Thou *land* devourest up men, and hast bereaved
thy nations, 14 Therefore thou shalt devour men no
more, neither ‖ bereave thy nations any more, saith the
Lord GOD 15 [o] Neither will I cause *men* to hear in
thee the shame of the heathen any more, neither shalt
thou bear the reproach of the people any more, neither
shalt thou cause thy nations to fall any more, saith the
Lord GOD

Before Christ 587

h Ps. cxxiii. 3 Chap. xxxiv. 29

i Jer. xxxi.

k Chap. xxxvii. 6, 13

l Obad. 17

m Jer. xv. 7

n Num. xiii. 32

‖ Or, cause to fall

o Chap. xxxiv. 29

v. 1—15 The land of Israel was now desolate and depopulated, but God still thought upon the dust thereof We have,

1 His compassionate regard towards this miserable country It was become *a prey and derision to the residue of the heathen*, ver 4 Their neighbours insulted them, and every tongue, v. 3 was ready to spread their infamy v. 6 to upbraid them with their sins, and mock at their sufferings, whilst the nations around them, *the residue*, who had survived the judgments threatened, *chap* xxv xxvi each seized that part of Judea which bordered upon their own country, as their prey

2 His jealousy for his people Because with spiteful joy their enemies exulted in their miseries, and with daring intrusion entred the inheritance of the Lord, v. 5 *he hath spoken in the fire of his jealousy*, ver 5 *and in his fury*, ver 6 that he will severely avenge their wrongs, and cover with shame and confusion these inveterate and malicious foes, v. 7 *Note*, They who make God's people the subject of derision, will shortly be themselves exposed to everlasting shame and contempt

3 God gives his people assurance of a happy restoration, and plenty of all good things in their own land, and the time is at hand, v. 8 The mountains shall yield abundant fruit, tho' now uncultivated, they shall be tilled and sown, the cities that lie in ruins shall be replenished with inhabitants, v. 10 and *all the house of Israel, even all of it*, not the two tribes only, but the ten tribes who went before into captivity, *shall settle on their old estates*, and see their flocks and herds multiplying under the divine blessing, and God *will do better* for them than *at their beginnings*, particularly with regard to the spiritual blessings bestowed in the days of the Messiah, v. 11 Then should the mountains again become the abode of men, instead of wild beasts, which had dwelt therein the idolatries committed in them should cease, nor provoke God any more *to bereave them* of inhabitants, v. 12—14 and the reproach which had been laid on the mountains of Israel by the heathen, as if they had devoured all who dwelt in them, shall for ever be at an end, v. 15 Probably this prophecy looks to future times, and whatever fulfilment it received in the return of the Jews from Babylon, the perfect accomplishment of it is yet to come

16 ¶ Moreover, the word of the LORD came unto
me, saying, 17 Son of man, when the house of Israel
dwelt in their own land, [p] they defiled it by their own
way, and by their doings their way was before me as
the uncleanness of a removed woman 18 Wherefore
I poured my fury upon them [q] for the blood that they
had shed upon the land, and for their [r] idols *wherewith*
they had polluted it 19 And I scattered them among
the heathen, and they were dispersed through the coun-
tries according to their way, and according to their
doings I judged them 20 And when they entred un-
to the heathen whither they went, they [s] profaned my
holy

p Jer. ii. 7

q 2 Kings xxi. 16

r Chap. xxiii. 37

s Isai. lii. 5 Rom. ii. 24

Before Christ 587

holy name, when they ſaid to them, Theſe *are* the peo-
ple of the LORD, and are gone forth out of his land
21 ¶ But I had pity ^z for mine holy name, which the
houſe of Iſrael had profaned among the heathen whither
they went 22 Therefore ſay unto the houſe of Iſ-
rael, Thus ſaith the Lord GOD, I do not *this* ^a for your
ſakes, O houſe of Iſrael, but for mine holy name's ſake,
which ye have profaned among the heathen whither ye
went 23 And I will ſanctify my great name *which*
was profaned among the heathen, which ye have pro-
faned in the midſt of them, and the heathen ſhall know
that I *am* the LORD, ſaith the Lord GOD, when I
ſhall be ſanctified in you, before † their eyes 24 For
^w I will take you from among the heathen, and gather
you out of all countries, and will bring you into your
own land

^z Pſ cvi 8 Chap. xx 14
^a Pſ cxv 1 Ver 32
† O your
^w Chap xxiv 13 & xxxvii 21

v 16—24 The great end God propoſes is the advancement of his own glory, and therefore the unworthineſs of his people is no bar to their ſalvation, rather the more ſhall the riches of his grace be magnified

1 They had indeed forfeited all title to favour By their ſins they had diſhonoured God, and defiled the land ſo totally corrupted were they, that every thing they touched, like a woman in her ſeparation, became unclean, *v* 17 Murder and idolatry marked their way, and provoked God to pour out his fury upon them, *v* 18 and to ſcatter them for their abominations into heathen lands, *v* 19 Yet even there all their ſufferings were ſtill ineffectual, they ſinned yet more, and gave the adverſaries of the Lord occaſion to blaſpheme Their wicked lives brought a ſcandal on that name they profeſſed to reverence and ſerve, and the very heathen treated them with ſcorn *These are the people of the Lord* they mocked at their pretended relation to him, their conduct gave the lie to their profeſſions, or it implied an inſult on their God, as if, notwithſtanding all the Jewiſh boaſts, he were unable to ſave them from the hand of their enemies *Note*, The ſins of profeſſors are the greateſt ſcandal to religion, and give juſt occaſion to the adverſaries of the Lord to blaſpheme, but wo unto him by whom the offence cometh!

2 God will glorify his great name and the riches of his grace in their deliverance They had no reaſon to expect any thing from him but wrath to the uttermoſt, their provocations were ſo aggravated, but then the heathen would blaſpheme the more therefore, not for their ſake, but for his own glory, he will interpoſe, and gather them from among the nations, and bring them to their own land *Note*, Where ſin hath abounded, God is moſt exalted in mercy, cauſing his grace much more to abound

^x Iſa lii 15 Eph v 26 Heb x 22
^y Jer xxxii 39 Chap xi 19
^z Chap xi 20
^a Chap xxxvii 27
^b Rom xi 26
^c Pſ cv 16
^d Chap xxxiv 29
^e Chap xvi 61 63
^f Lev xxvi 39 Job xlii 6 Chap vi 9 & xx 43
^g Deut ix 5 Ver 22
^h Am ix 14, 15
^i Ver 9
^k Iſa li 3 Chap xxviii 13
^l Chap xvii 24 & xxii 14 & xxxvii 14
^m Mat vii 7

25 ¶ ^x Then will I ſprinkle clean water upon you,
and ye ſhall be clean from all your filthineſs, and from
all your idols will I cleanſe you 26 ^y A new heart
alſo will I give you, and a new ſpirit will I put within
you, and I will take away the ſtony heart out of your
fleſh, and I will give you an heart of fleſh 27 And I
will put my Spirit within you, and ^z cauſe you to walk
in my ſtatutes, and ye ſhall keep my judgments, and do
them 28 And ye ſhall dwell in the land that I gave
to your fathers, ^a and ye ſhall be my people, and I will
be your God 29 ^b I will alſo ſave you from all your
uncleanneſſes, ^c and I will call for the corn, and will in-
creaſe it, and ^d lay no famine upon you 30 And I
will multiply the fruit of the tree, and the increaſe of the
field, that ye ſhall receive no more reproach of famine
among the heathen 31 Then ^e ſhall ye remember
your own evil ways, and your doings that *were* not
good, and ^f ſhall lothe yourſelves in your own ſight, for
your iniquities and for your abominations 32 ^g Not
for your ſakes do I *this*, ſaith the Lord GOD, be it known
unto you be aſhamed and confounded for your own ways,
O houſe of Iſrael 33 Thus ſaith the Lord GOD, In the
day that I ſhall have cleanſed you from all your iniqui-
ties, ^h I will alſo cauſe *you* to dwell in the cities, and the
waſtes ſhall be builded 34 And the deſolate land
^i ſhall be tilled, whereas it lay deſolate in the ſight of
all that paſſed by 35 And they ſhall ſay, This land
that was deſolate, is become like the garden of ^k Eden,
and the waſte, and deſolate, and ruined cities *are become*
fenced, *and* are inhabited 36 Then the heathen that
are left round about you, ſhall know that I the LORD
build the ruined places, *and* plant *that that was* deſolate
^l I the LORD have ſpoken *it*, and I will do *it* 37
Thus ſaith the Lord GOD, I will yet for this be ^m en-
quired of by the houſe of Iſrael, to do *it* for them, I
will increaſe them with men like a flock 38 As † the
holy flock, as the flock of Jeruſalem in her ſolemn feaſts,
ſo ſhall the waſte cities be filled with flocks of men, and
they ſhall know that I *am* the LORD

† Heb The flock of holy things

v 25—38 Whatever accompliſhment this prophecy had in the return of the Jewiſh people from captivity, when they were for ever cured of all inclination to idolatry, it ſeems to have a more eſpecial regard to goſpel times We have here,

1 Many great and precious promiſes given to God's people (1) God will cleanſe them from all their ſins, *v* 25 by the blood of ſprinkling removing their guilt, and by the efficacy of his grace delivering them from the power of their iniquities (2) He will give them a new heart, *v* 26 a heart changed by his divine energy from its former ſtate of corruption, hardneſs, and unbelief, another ſpirit ſhall influence and guide them, the *ſtony heart*, inſenſible and obdurate, ſhall be taken away, and in its ſtead a *heart of fleſh* ſhall be given them, tender, and ſuſceptible of every gracious impreſſion (3) Having made new their hearts, he will make ſtrait paths for their feet, and enable them to walk therein, *v* 27 He will not only clearly point out the path of duty, but engage and conſtrain them to walk in it, and work in them to will and to do of his good pleaſure (4) He will take them into covenant with himſelf *Ye ſhall be my people, and I will be your God* He engages to make them ſuch as he would have them be, to work all for them and in them, and is himſelf the all-ſufficient portion of his people (5) He will give them plenty of all ſuch good things as they need, particularly, what the Jews counted the greateſt earthly bleſſing, they ſhall return to their own land, have abundance of corn and fruit, ſhall know no more famine as before, nor be reproached by the heathen, as forced to ſeek their bread from other countries, when, to the wonder and ſurprize of the ſurrounding nations, the land of Judea, lately ſo deſolate, ſhall be tilled, and become like the *garden of Eden* for fruitfulneſs, and the cities in ruins ſhall be fortified, and repleniſhed with inhabitants So ſoon can God's bleſſing make a barren land fruitful, as his curſe makes the fruitfulleſt land barren

Some interpreters ſuppoſe all theſe promiſes are yet to receive their accompliſhment in the recovery of the Jews from their preſent ſtate of diſperſion in the latter day

2 The effect of God's rich grace extended to them would be their unfeigned repentance *Then ſhall ye remember your own evil ways, and loath yourſelves in your own ſight for your iniquities, and for your abominations* Nothing brings the ſoul to true humiliation, and ſuch a ſenſe of the baſeneſs and ingratitude of ſin, as a view of God's pardoning love then we begin to loath ourſelves, ſin appears the abominable thing God hates, and therefore we hate it too every remembrance of the paſt covers us with genuine ſhame, and though God hath forgiven us we can never forgive ourſelves, for having ever offended a God ſo gracious

3 God intends his own glory in what he doth for them, they being utterly unworthy the leaſt regard, yet, though it is a matter of pure grace, he expects they ſhall ſeek it in the way of prayer, and be confounded for their former evil ways, *v* 32, 33 and he will give the anſwer of mercy, increaſing them as a flock, *the flock of Jeruſalem in her ſolemn feaſts*, immenſe numbers of ſheep being driven on that occaſion to Jeruſalem for ſacrifice, and vaſt multitudes of worſhippers aſſembled in the courts of the Lord's houſe, and ſo numerous and populous ſhould their deſolate land and cities become, ſince he hath ſpoken it, the accompliſhment is ſure *Note*, (1) Salvation is entirely of grace, our righteouſneſs and deſerts are utterly excluded, for indeed we have none, and God alone muſt be exalted in mercy (2) God's promiſes do not ſuperſede, but encourage our prayers They who reſtrain prayer before God, ſin againſt their own mercies (3) What God hath ſpoken is as good as done not one jot or tittle of his word ſhall ever fail

CHAP XXXVII

The reſtoration of the people of God is here preſented, 1 By a viſion of dry bones brought together, and raiſed to life, ver 1—14 2 By the coaliſion of two ſticks into one is ſhewn, the union of the two kingdoms of Iſrael and Judah at their return from captivity, ver 15—22 a type of the union of Jews and Gentiles in one church in the days of the Meſſiah, and ſo, 3 The prophet ſlides into a prediction of the kingdom of Chriſt, which ſhould be ſet up in the world, and of the glories and graces of that kingdom, ver 23—28

^a Chap i 3

1 ^a THE hand of the LORD was upon me, and
carried me out in the Spirit of the LORD,
and ſet me down in the midſt of the valley which *was*
full of bones, 2 And cauſed me to paſs by them round
about, and behold, *there were* very many in the open
valley, and lo, *they were* very dry 3 And he ſaid unto
me, Son of man, can theſe bones live? and I anſwered,
O Lord,

Before Chriſt 587 O Lord GOD, thou knoweſt 4 Again he ſaid unto
me, Propheſy † upon theſe bones, and ſay unto them,
† Or over O ye dry bones, hear the word of the LORD 5 Thus
b Ver 8, 10 ſaith the Lord GOD unto theſe bones, Behold, b I will
cauſe breath to enter into you, and ye ſhall live 6
And I will lay ſinews upon you, and will bring up fleſh
upon you, and cover you with ſkin, and put breath in
c Joel ii 27 & iii 17 you, and ye ſhall live, and c ye ſhall know that I *am*
the LORD 7 So I propheſied as I was commanded
d Acts ii 2 & xvi 26 and as I propheſied, there was a noiſe, and behold d a
ſhaking, and the bones came together, bone to his bone
8 And when I beheld, lo, the ſinews and the fleſh came
up upon them, and the ſkin covered them above, but
there was no breath in them 9 Then ſaid he unto me,
‡ Or breath, or ſpirit John iii 8 Acts ii 2 Propheſy unto the ‡ wind, propheſy, ſon of man, and
ſay to the wind, Thus ſaith the Lord GOD, e Come from
e Pſ civ 30 § Or ſpirit the four winds, O § breath, and breathe upon theſe ſlain,
that they may live 10 So I propheſied as he com-
manded me, and the breath came into them, and they
lived, and ſtood up upon their feet, an exceeding great
army 11 ¶ Then he ſaid unto me, Son of man, theſe
bones are the whole houſe of Iſrael behold, they ſay,
f Pſ cxli 7 g Iſa xlix 14 f Our bones are dried, and g our hope is loſt, we are cut
off for our parts 12 Therefore propheſy, and ſay un-
h Iſa xxvi 19 John v 25 28 to them, Thus ſaith the Lord GOD, Behold, h O my
people, I will open your graves, and cauſe you to come
up out of your graves, and bring you into the land of
Iſrael 13 And ye ſhall know that I *am* the LORD,
when I have opened your graves, O my people, and
i Chap xxxvi 27 brought you up out of your graves, 14 And i ſhall
put my Spirit in you, and ye ſhall live, and I ſhall place
you in your own land then ſhall ye know that I the
LORD have ſpoken *it*, and performed *it*, ſaith the
LORD

v 1—14 We have here,

1 The viſion Under the powerful impulſe of the Spirit, the prophet is carried into the valley full of dry bones, disjointed and ſcattered in confuſion an emblem of the Jewiſh people now captives in Babylon, ſo diſperſed that, to human view, their recovery was as much deſpaired of as the reſtoration of dry bones to life Therefore, when aſked, *Can theſe bones live?* he replies, *Thou knoweſt* Nothing ſhort of omnipotence can effect the amazing miracle *Note*, (1) Man's ſoul by nature is like theſe dry bones, totally void of all ſpiritual life, unable to exert one good deſire, or make the leaſt effort towards his recovery (2) God alone knows whom he deſigns for life, and whom he foreknew he predeſtinates to be conformed to the image of his ſon, quickning them from the death of ſin unto the life of righteouſneſs

2 The prophet is commanded to *propheſy upon* or *over theſe dry bones*, and to call on them to attend, *O ye dry bones, hear the word of the Lord* And ſince by a divine energy accompanying his word their reſtoration to life ſhould be accompliſhed, he is ordered, *v* 9 to pray unto the Spirit for his quickning influences, *Come, O breath, or ſpirit, and breathe upon theſe ſlain, that they may live* and, though the work might ſeem ſtrange and fruitleſs, the prophet obeyed, *v* 10 *Note*, (1) Though the ſinner's ſoul of himſelf be as incapable of receiving the goſpel call as dry bones of hearing our voice, yet muſt we ſpeak in dependance upon the Spirit, which God hath promiſed, to make the miniſtration of his own word effectual (2) Whilſt we are crying aloud to ſinners, we muſt be looking up to God, and pouring out our ſouls in prayer to him who quickneth the dead

3 A wonderful effect followed his propheſying, for they who go forth in dependance on the divine power ſhall ſee the wonders of God's grace A noiſe and ſhaking enſued, each bone joined his fellow, and fleſh and ſinews grew upon them, and, at the prophet's invocation, life entered into them, according to the promiſe, *v* 6 and they ſtood up, an exceeding great army, *v* 9, 10 Thus, by the proclamation of Cyrus, the captives were aſſembled, and, by the Divine Spirit animated, they were enabled to overcome all the difficulties in their way And we have here alſo a repreſentation, (1) Of our ſpiritual reſurrection from the death of ſin, by the preaching of the word a ſhaking is occaſioned among the ſouls dead in treſpaſſes and ſins, deep convictions make them tremble, and by the power of the Holy Ghoſt ſpiritual life is communicated (2) Of the reſurrection of the body in the laſt day, when all our ſcattered atoms ſhall be reunited, and the ſame body be raiſed by the power of God to life eternal

4 The application of the whole to the houſe of Iſrael They were theſe dry bones, reduced to the loweſt ſtate of abject miſery, and abandoning themſelves to deſpair But in the time of our deepeſt diſtreſs God will make his power and grace more eminently known, therefore the prophet is commanded to aſſure them, that God will deliver them from their captivity, which was like opening the graves to the dead, *v* 12 and give them life, in their reſtoration to the comfortable and peaceable poſſeſſion of their own land God hath ſpoken, and will perform it, they may confidently truſt him, for what he promiſes is as good as done *Note*, (1) In times of ſore temptation, and long continued diſtreſs, our faith is ready to faint, and unbelief to prevail (2) Though we may deſpair of ourſelves, our ſtate may not be deſperate, God can do for us more than we can think (3) The lower we are reduced, the more is the power and grace of God magnified in our recovery

15 ¶ The word of the LORD came again unto me,
ſaying, 16 Moreover, thou ſon of man, k take thee k Num xvii 2
one ſtick, and write upon it, For Judah, and for l the l 2 Chron xi 12, 13,
children of Iſrael his companions then take another 16
ſtick, and write upon it, For Joſeph the ſtick of
Ephraim, and *for* all the houſe of Iſrael, his compa-
nions 17 And m join them one to another into one m Jer l 4 Ver 22
ſtick, and they ſhall become one in thine hand 18 ¶ Hoſ i 11
And when the children of thy people ſhall ſpeak unto
thee, ſaying, Wilt thou not ſhew us what thou *meaneſt*
by theſe? 19 n Say unto them, Thus ſaith the Lord n Zech x 6
GOD, Behold, I will take the ſtick of Joſeph which *is*
in the hand of Ephraim, and the tribes of Iſrael his
fellows, and will put them with him, *even* with the ſtick
of Judah, and make them one ſtick, and they ſhall be
one in mine hand 20 ¶ And the ſticks whereon thou
writeſt, ſhall be in thine hand before their eyes 21
And ſay unto them, Thus ſaith the Lord GOD, Be-
hold, I will take the children of Iſrael from among the
heathen, whither they be gone, and will gather them
on every ſide, o and bring them into their own land o Ver 21
22 And p I will make them one nation in the land up- p Iſa xi 13
on the mountains of Iſrael, and q one king ſhall be king Jer iii 18 Hoſ i 11
to them all and they ſhall be no more two nations, q John x 16
neither ſhall they be divided into two kingdoms any more
at all 23 Neither ſhall they defile themſelves any
more with their idols, nor with their deteſtable things,
nor with any of their tranſgreſſions but I will ſave them
out of all their dwelling places, wherein they have ſin-
ned, and will cleanſe them ſo r ſhall they be my people, r Hoſ i 10
and I will be their God 24 And s David my ſervant s Iſa xl 11
ſhall be king over them and t they all ſhall have one Jer xxiii 5
ſhepherd they ſhall alſo walk in my judgments, and & xxx 9
obſerve my ſtatutes, and do them 25 And they ſhall Chap xxxiv 23, 24
dwell in the land that I have given unto Jacob my ſer- Luke i
vant, wherein your fathers have dwelt, and they ſhall 32
dwell therein, *even* they and their children, and their t Ver 22
childrens children u for ever, and my ſervant David *ſhall* John x 16
be their prince for ever 26 Moreover, I will make x a u Iſa lx 21
covenant of peace with them, it ſhall be an everlaſting Joel iii 20
covenant with them, and I will place them, and y mul- Amos ix 15
tiply them, and will ſet my z ſanctuary in the midſt of x Pſ lxxxix 3 Jer xxxii 40
them for evermore 27 a My tabernacle alſo ſhall be Chap xxxiv 25
with them yea, b I will be their God, and they ſhall y Chap xxxvi 37
be my people 28 And the heathen ſhall know that
c I the LORD do ſanctify Iſrael, when my ſanctuary ſhall a John i 14
be in the midſt of them for evermore b Chap xi 20 & xiv 11 & xxxvi 28 c Chap xx 12

v 15—28 For the encouragement of the faithful among the captives, great things are promiſed which God will do for them

1 The two kingdoms of Judah and Iſrael, ſo long ſeparated, and ſo often vexatious to each other, ſhall be reunited, and become one people and this is repreſented by the joining of two ſticks in the prophet's hand, on one of which was inſcribed the name of Judah and her companions, the tribe of Benjamin and thoſe of the other tribes who on the revolt cleaved to the houſe of David, on the other the name of Ephraim, and his companions the houſe of Iſrael, of which Samaria, which lay in the lot of Ephraim, was the capital The people who ſaw the ſign would naturally be inquiſitive, and deſire to know the meaning, *v* 18 and he muſt inform them, that as theſe ſticks became one in his hand, ſo ſhould they become one people in God's hand, *v* 19 no mutual jealouſies, no jarring diſcord, ſhall remain, but, returning together from their captivity, they ſhall become one nation, under one king which was primarily fulfilled on their return from Babylon, but ſeems principally to refer to goſpel times, when, under the king Meſſiah, Jews and Gentiles ſhall become one people, the partition wall being broken down, and they ſhall have one Lord, one faith, one baptiſm, and be one fold under one ſhepherd

2 All their idolatries ſhall be for ever done away, *v* 23 After their return from Babylon they never more relapſed God

hav n

Before Christ 587.

having ſaved them from the *places* of temptation, delivered them alſo from all inclination to their former abominations *Note*, (1) It is a ſingular mercy when God ſaves us from the places and perſons who have been a temptation to us, and by his gracious providence removes us from the evil (2) God will ſave his people from all their ſins, not only from their actual prevalence, yet he will mortify alſo their deſire after them, and indeed, unleſs the heart be cleanſed, it would ſignify little to have the temptation merely removed

3 They ſhall be taken into an everlaſting covenant of grace and peace with God, *v* 26 and he will effectually incline them to cleave to him *They ſhall be his people*, his grace will cauſe the glorious change, and *he will be their God*, to bleſs, preſerve, and protect them *David* the root from his ſtock, the Meſſiah, ſhall be their *king* and *ſhepherd*, to guard them from their enemies, to feed them under his care, making them obedient in all things to his bleſſed will, and engaging their fidelity to himſelf *Note*, (1) It is of God's grace, not our choice, by his power, not our own ability, that we become his people, and obedient to his holy will (2) The covenant of grace is everlaſting, they who are truly intereſted therein have their everlaſting happineſs ſecured

4 They ſhall for ever enjoy in peace the inheritance of their anceſtors, tranſmitting it to children's children, and ſhall be ſafe and happy under the rule of their anointed king Meſſiah, *v* 25 whoſe kingdom is an everlaſting kingdom, and his dominion that which never ſhall be deſtroyed And this ſeems to direct us, for the full accompliſhment of the prophecy, to future times, when this unhappy people, now ſo diſperſed, ſhall receive the Lord's Chriſt, and to the end of time enjoy the bleſſings of his government *Note*, Chriſt's ſubjects, the children of Zion, will be joyful in their king, ſince he for ever lives and reigns, they ſhall live and reign with him in glory everlaſting

5 God himſelf will dwell in the midſt of them They ſhall not only be increaſed and eſtabliſhed, but enjoy the ſpecial tokens of his preſence His ſanctuary and tabernacle, erected among them, ſhall never more be deſtroyed, Jeſus, the true tabernacle, in whom dwelt all the fulneſs of the Godhead bodily, ſhall be in the midſt of them, and in his church they ſhall ſee his glory, and maintain communion with him in the ordinances of his ſervice, and find, to their unſpeakable comfort, God to be their God, whilſt they ſhare in all the bleſſings of his people

6 God will be glorified among the heathen in ſuch his diſpenſations of mercy towards his Iſrael *They ſhall know* that he doth *ſanctify Iſrael*, by ſuch evident marks of his love, by ſuch powerful operations of his grace upon them, and by the erection of his ſanctuary among them for evermore *Note*, They who enjoy the privileges of the ſanctuary muſt ſhew the influence it hath upon them in the ſanctification of their hearts and lives

CHAP XXXVIII.

In this chapter we have intermixed, 1 The attempt that Gog and Magog ſhould make upon the land of Iſrael, and the vaſt army they ſhould bring into the field, ver 4—7 Their project and deſign in it, ver 8—13 God's hand in it, ver 4 2 The great terror that this ſhould ſtrike upon the land of Iſrael, ver 15, 16, 18—20 3 God's reſtraint upon theſe enemies, and his protection of his Iſrael, ver 2—4, 14 4 The defeat that ſhould be given to theſe enemies by the immediate hand of God, ver 21—23 Whatever enemy of Iſrael this primarily refers to, we are led by Rev xx 8 to look for a farther fulfilment of the prophecy in the latter day

1 AND the word of the LORD came unto me,
ſaying, 2 [a] Son of man, ſet thy face againſt
[b] Gog, the land of Magog, ‖ the chief prince of Meſhech
and Tubal, and propheſy againſt him, 3 And ſay,
Thus ſaith the Lord GOD, Behold, I *am* againſt thee,
O Gog, the chief prince of Meſhech and Tubal 4
And [c] I will turn thee ‖ back, and put hooks to thy
jaws, and I will bring thee forth, and all thine army,
horſes and horſemen, [d] all of them clothed with all ſorts
of armour, *even* a great company with bucklers and
ſhields, all of them handling ſwords 5 Perſia, Ethiopia,
and § Libya with them; all of them with ſhield
and helmet 6 Gomer and all his bands, the houſe
of Togarmah of the north-quarters, and all his bands,
and many people with thee 7 [e] Be thou prepared,
and prepare for thyſelf, thou and all thy company that
are aſſembled unto thee, and be thou a guard unto them
8 ¶ [f] After many days thou ſhalt be viſited in the
latter years thou ſhalt come into the land *that is* brought
back from the ſword, *and* [g] *is* gathered out of many
people againſt the mountains of Iſrael, which have been
always waſte but it is brought forth out of the nations,
and they ſhall dwell ſafely all of them 9 Thou ſhalt
aſcend and come like a ſtorm, thou ſhalt be like a cloud
to cover the land, thou and all thy bands, and [h] many
people with thee 10 Thus ſaith the Lord GOD, It
ſhall alſo come to paſs, *that* at the ſame time ſhall things
come into thy mind, and thou ſhalt ‖ think an evil
thought 11 And thou ſhalt ſay, I will go up to the
land of unwalled villages, I will [k] go to them that are at
reſt, that dwell † ſafely, all of them dwelling without
walls, and having neither bars nor gates, 12 ‡ To
[l] take a ſpoil, and to take a prey, to turn thine hand
upon the deſolate places *that are now* inhabited, [m] and
upon the people *that are* gathered out of the nations,
which have gotten cattle, and goods, that dwell in the
§ midſt of the land 13 Sheba and Dedan, and the
merchants of Tarſhiſh, with all the young lions thereof,
ſhall ſay unto thee, Art thou come to take a ſpoil? haſt
thou gathered thy company to take a prey? to carry away
ſilver and gold, to take away cattle and goods, to take
a great ſpoil?

v 1—13 Various have been the conjectures concerning Gog and Magog, the former the king, the latter probably the kingdom and as uncertain are the countries of Meſhech and Tubal Some ſuppoſe they have a particular reference to the ravages of Antiochus, and other enemies of Iſrael, after their return from their captivity, whilſt others interpret them of the later enemies of God's church, particularly of the Turks and Tartars Whoever they are, their attempts ſhall iſſue in their own confuſion, and God will glorify himſelf in judgment upon them

1 God reſolves to blaſt their enterprizes, great as their forces are, and terrible as their armament appears, and therefore his people need not fear, however threatening the danger *Note*, They who have an omnipotent God for them need not be concerned who are againſt them

2 The confederacy againſt God's Iſrael is ſtrong, and the army furniſhed with every weapon of war Perſia, Egypt, Libya, Gomer, are auxiliaries, under the conduct of Gog their mighty general, as their guard and leader, are bid ironically prepare for the battle, *v* 7 The armament is directed againſt the land of Iſrael, againſt thoſe who are *brought back from the ſword*, recovered from their diſperſion, and now dwelling ſafely, without fear of evil, without walls or gates, and therefore ſeem to be an eaſy prey to the invaders, *v* 11 Not doubting of his ſucceſs, the neighbouring nations of Sheba and Dedan, and the merchants of Tarſhiſh, ſhall congratulate Gog on his certain victory, *v* 13 or it may be envying him the ſpoil he is about to ſeize, or, as young lions, deſirous to ſhare it with him Like a riſing ſtorm, he threatens to ſweep all before him, *v* 9 and, ſure of his prey, thinks of nothing but reducing the land to the former deſolations from which it is now recovered, *v* 12 Such are the evil thoughts of this proud enemy, *v* 10 which God takes notice of, and will puniſh him for them *Note*, (1) The beginning of all evil is from within, *out of the heart proceed evil thoughts*, and they produce wicked works (2) They who are moſt confident of ſucceſs are often moſt fearfully diſappointed

3 Whatever ſucceſs may at firſt ſeem to follow the enemy, the fine will be fatal *after many days thou ſhalt be viſited* Thus Antiochus, though he prevailed ſo far, was at laſt brought low, and the Ottoman empire, that hath long riſen to ſuch a height of power, we expect alſo will be deſtroyed at the laſt

14 ¶ Therefore, ſon of man, propheſy and ſay unto
Gog, Thus ſaith the Lord GOD, [n] In that day when
my people of Iſrael dwelleth ſafely, ſhalt thou not know
it? 15 And thou ſhalt come from thy place out
of the north parts, thou and many people with thee,
all of them riding upon horſes, a great company, and a
mighty army 16 And thou ſhalt come up againſt my
people of Iſrael, as a cloud to cover the land, [p] it ſhall
be in the latter days, and I will bring thee againſt my
land, that the heathen may know me, when I ſhall be
ſanctified in thee, O Gog, before their eyes 17 Thus
ſaith the Lord GOD, *Art* thou he [q] of whom I have
ſpoken in old time ‖ by my ſervants the prophets of
Iſrael, which propheſied in thoſe days *many* years, that
I would bring thee againſt them? 18 And it ſhall
come to paſs at the ſame time, when Gog ſhall come
againſt the land of Iſrael, ſaith the Lord GOD, *that*
my fury ſhall come up in my face 19 For [r] in my
jealouſy, [s] *and* in the fire of my wrath have I ſpoken
[t] Surely in that day there ſhall be a great ſhaking in the
land of Iſrael 20 So that [u] the fiſhes of the ſea, and
the fowls of the heaven, and the beaſts of the field, and
all creeping things that creep upon the earth, and all the

men

a Chap xxxix 1 ‖ Or, prince of the chief
c 2 Kings xix 28 Chap xxix 4
d Chap xxiii 12 ‖ Chap xxxix 2 § Or, Phut
e Iſa viii 9, 10
f Iſa xxiv 22
h Rev xx 8
‖ Pſ xxxvi 4 ‖ Or, conceive a miſchievous purpoſe
k Jer xlix 31 † Or, confidently
‡ Heb To ſpoil a ſpoil and to prey a prey
l Iſa x 6
m Ver 8
§ Heb Navel

n Iſa iv 1
o Chap xxxix 2
p Ver 8
q Iſa xxx Mic v 5
‖ Heb By the hands of &c
r Chap xxxvi 5, 6
s Pſ lxxxix 46
t Rev xvi 18
u Hoſ iv 3

Before Christ 587.

men that are upon the face of the earth, shall shake at
my presence, and the mountains shall be thrown down,
and the † steep places shall fall, and every wall shall fall
to the ground 21 And I will call for a sword against
him throughout all my mountains, saith the Lord GOD
x every man's sword shall be against his brother. 22
And I will plead against him with pestilence, and with
blood, and y I will rain upon him, and upon his bands,
and upon the many people that are with him, an over-
flowing rain, and great hail-stones, fire and brimstone
23 Thus will I z magnify myself and sanctify myself,
and I will be known in the eyes of many nations, and
they shall know that I am the LORD

† Or towers or stairs. x Judg. vii 22. 2 Chron xx 23. y Isa xxx 30. Rev xvi 21. z Chap. xxxvi 23 & xxxvii 28.

v. 14—23 The prophecy is repeated to shew the certainty of the event

1 The enemy shall hear of the peace and plenty God's Israel enjoy, and how securely they dwell, and that shall induce him to come up, as secure of success, or *v.* 14 may signify the vanity of his attempt God will make him know no foe can disturb those whom he causeth to dwell in safety When God therefore brings him up, it is not for spoil, but to be himself for a prey, *that the heathen may know the jealousy of the Lord over his people*, and be confounded and in judgment he will be glorified in the destruction of his enemies and theirs *Note*, (1) All must contribute to advance the glory of the divine perfections, even the wicked shall cause his righteousness to be exalted in their sufferings (2) He who toucheth God's people touches the apple of his eye, and he will avenge their wrongs

2 God hath foretold the invasion of old time, that his people might not count it strange when it should come in *the latter days* Many things probably the prophets spoke which are not recorded and by another name the same enemy, here spoken of, may have been intended, as *Deut* xxxii 43 *Psal* ix 15 *Isa* xxvii 1 *Joel* iii 1 *Note*, Whatever troubles the church may fall into, there is effectual security given in the prophetic word for its perpetuity, and Christ's servants may triumph still in his sure salvation

3 The enemy shall be utterly destroyed and terrible is the scene of havock here described God's indignation rises at this insolent invader of his people, and flames of wrath flash from his eyes, in terrors at his frown the earth trembles, even the birds and beasts, as well as men, affrighted, quake, the mountains and precipices fall, and every fortress is laid in the dust the swords of this terrible host shall be turned against each other, pestilence shall devour them, and blood in rivers flow, a storm of vengeance shall descend from heaven upon them, as upon Sodom, hailstones, fire and brimstone, and rain, utter and fearful, shall overtake them *Note*, (1) They who have been a terror to others, God can easily make a terror to themselves (2) God cannot want instruments of vengeance the very sword of his enemies shall turn its point against them when he so ordains, and they shall become their own executioners

4 God will be glorified in the execution of these his judgments, and will display his power, justice, and truth, to the conviction of many nations, who shall be brought, by what they behold, to acknowledge him the only true God, and to ascribe to him the glory due unto his name

CHAP XXXIX

This chapter concludes the prophecy against Gog and Magog Here is, 1 An express prediction of their utter destruction, ver 1—7 *2 The vastness of that destruction shewn from the burning of their weapons*, ver 8—10 *The burying of their slain*, ver 11—16 *and the feasting of the fowls upon the dead bodies of those that were unburied*, ver 17—22 *3 God's gracious purposes to his Israel, in this and his other providences, are declared, and a promise of further mercy he had yet in store for them*, ver 23—29

1 THerefore, a thou son of man, prophesy against
Gog, and say, Thus saith the Lord GOD, Be-
hold, I am against thee, O Gog, the chief prince of
Meshech and Tubal 2 b And I will turn thee † back,
and ‡ leave but the sixth part of thee, c and will cause
thee to come up from the § north parts, and will bring
thee upon the mountains of Israel 3 And d I will
smite thy bow out of thy left hand, and will cause thine
arrows to fall out of thy right hand 4 Thou shalt fall
upon the mountains of Israel, thou and all thy bands,
and the people that is with thee e I will give thee unto
the ravenous birds of every || sort, and to the beasts of
the field to be devoured 5 Thou shalt fall upon the
† open field, for I have spoken it, saith the Lord GOD
6 And f I will send a fire on Magog, and among them
that dwell ‡ carelessly in the isles, and they shall know

a Chap xxxviii 2. b Chap xxxviii 4. † Or about. ‡ Or strike thee with six plagues, or draw thee back with an hook in thy teeth Chap xxxviii 4. c Chap xxxviii 15. § Heb sides of the north. d Ps lxxvi 3. e Chap xxxiii 27. || Heb Wing. † Heb face of the field. f Rev xx 9. ‡ Or confidently.

that I am the LORD 7 So will I make my holy name
known in the midst of my people Israel, and I will not
let them pollute my holy name any more, and the hea-
then shall g know that I am the LORD, the holy One in
Israel

g Chap xxxviii 16.

v. 1—7 When God begins he will make an end, his enemies shall feel his vengeance and perish utterly

1 He threatens the destruction of Gog and his army, and the desolation of his country His soldiers, for whom he drained his kingdom, and left but a sixth part behind him, shall be disabled from hurting God's people, and fall upon the mountains of Israel, a prey to every beast and bird, and, whilst the king with his army miserably perishes there, the fire of God, some consuming judgment, shall devour his country, and even the isles of his dominion, which promised themselves security from their situation, shall be consumed together for, when God riseth up to judgment, no place or person is privileged, or may hope for exemption *Note*, (1) The mightiest armies before God are as easily crushed as the moth (2) Whilst the ambitious unjustly labour to usurp the rights of others, God justly punishes them with the loss of what was their own

2 God will thus make himself known and glorious His people will prove his power, faithfulness, and grace, signally manifested on their behalf, and be engaged thereby, renouncing all their former idolatries, to cleave to him alone for nothing tends to separate the heart from sin so effectually as the right knowledge of God And his enemies the heathen shall know him too by these examples of his vengeance, shall fear to provoke his jealousy, nor dare any more to molest his people *Note*, The judgments of God on others should be our warnings

8 ¶ Behold, h it is come, and it is done, saith the
Lord GOD, this is the day whereof I have spoken 9
And they that dwell in the cities of Israel shall go forth,
and shall set on fire and burn the weapons, both the
shields and the bucklers, the bows and the arrows, and
the † hand-staves, and the spears, and they shall ‡ burn
them with fire seven years 10 So that they shall take
no wood out of the field, neither cut down any out of
the forests for they shall burn the weapons with fire,
and i they shall spoil those that spoiled them, and rob
those that robbed them, saith the Lord GOD 11 ¶
And it shall come to pass in that day, that I will give
unto Gog a place there of graves in Israel, the valley
of the passengers on the east of the sea, and § it shall stop
the noses of the passengers and there shall they bury Gog,
and all his multitude, and they shall call it, the valley
of || Hamon-gog, 12 And seven months shall the house
of Israel be burying of them, that they may cleanse the
land, 13 Yea, all the people of the land shall bury
them, and it shall be to them a renown, the day that I
shall be glorified, saith the Lord GOD 14 And they
shall sever out men † of continual employment, passing
through the land, to bury with the passengers those that
remain upon the face of the earth to cleanse it after the
end of seven months shall they search 15 And the
passengers that pass through the land, when any seeth a
man's bone, then shall he ‡ set up a sign by it, till the
buriers have buried it in the valley of Hamon-gog
16. And also the name of the city shall be § Hamonah
thus shall they cleanse the land 17 ¶ And thou son
of man, Thus saith the Lord GOD, Speak unto || every
feathered fowl, and to every beast of the field, k Assem-
ble yourselves and come, gather yourselves on every side
to my ‡ sacrifice that I do sacrifice for you, even a great
sacrifice upon the mountains of Israel, that ye may eat
flesh, and drink blood 18 Ye shall eat the flesh of the
mighty, and drink the blood of the princes of the earth,
of rams, of lambs, and of † goats, of bullocks, all
of them fatlings of Bashan, 19 And ye shall eat fat till
ye be full, and drink blood till ye be drunken, of my
sacrifice which I have sacrificed for you 20 Thus ye
shall be filled at my table with horses and chariots,
m with mighty men, and with all men of war, saith the
Lord GOD 21. And I will set my glory among the
heathen, and all the heathen shall see my judgment that
I have executed, and my hand that I have laid upon them
22 So the house of Israel shall know that I am the LORD
their God, from that day and forward

h Rev xxi 6. † Or javelins. ‡ Or make a fire of them. i Isa xiv 2. § Heb it shall stop the passengers. || That is, The multitude of Gog. † Heb. Of continuance. ‡ Heb. Build. § That is, The multitude. || Heb Fowl of every wing. k Isa xviii 6. ‡ Or slaughter. † Heb Great goats. l Deut xxxii 14. Ps xxii 12. m Rev xix 18.

v. 8—22 What God hath spoken is as sure as if it were already accomplished, whether it be promise or threatening *It*
is ... to each of them both present

Before Christ 587

By three things the dreadful deſtruction of the army of Gog is repreſented

1 By the vaſt quantity of weapons of war which, among other ſpoil, ſhould be collected, and furniſh the people of Iſrael with fuel during ſeven years, and every chip they burned, would ſerve to remind them of God's mercy, and to awaken their gratitude

2 By the length of time which it will take to bury the dead, and the numbers employed in the ſervice The whole houſe of Iſrael, aſſiſted by the paſſengers, who would willingly labour to remove ſo great a nuiſance, v 11 ſhall be no leſs than ſeven months employed in cleanſing the land, and collecting the bodies to their burying-place, *the valley of paſſengers, on the eaſt of the ſea*, of the dead ſea, or the ſea of Tiberias, a great thoroughfare from Syria to Egypt, which ſhall from this event, receive a new name, and be called the valley of *Hamon-gog*, and the city near thereunto *Hamonah*, alluding to the multitudes there buried And *it ſhall be a renown to Iſrael in that day, when God ſhall be glorified*, ſuch an aſtoniſhing inſtance of the divine interpoſition in their favour ſhall make them reſpected, and their humanity to the dead redound greatly to their honour And at the ſeventh month's end, when the multitudes that fell together are covered in the earth, certain perſon ſhall be appointed to go through the land, and bury the ſcattered corpſes, whilſt every traveller who paſſes by, when he ſees a bone, ſhall ſet up a mark for the notice of the ſearchers appointed, until the land be thoroughly cleanſed *Note*, (1) When our noſtrils are offended with the putrefaction of a corpſe, we ſhould remember the ſin which hath made theſe bodies ſo vile (2) They who have experienced great national mercies, ſhould unite in their labour to clear their land from every pollution of ſin, and to this every lover of his country will gladly lend a helping hand (3) To advance God's glory, is Iſrael's great renown

3 There will be enough for every bird and beaſt to feed upon, and they are commanded to come and devour the ſlain, ſacrificed to divine juſtice Corpſes enough there will be, not merely for a meal, but to fatten them, and this not only of the common ſoldiers, but of *the mighty*, and *the princes of the earth, with their horſes and chariots*, fallen in one promiſcuous ruin

Thus God will make the heathen to ſee and obſerve his judgments againſt the enemies of his people, and will advance his own great glory thereby whilſt the houſe of Iſrael ſhall exult in his ſalvation, and receive freſh confirmation of God's care and love, engaging their confidence in him *from that day forward*, even for ever Let God's Iſrael then to the end of time truſt in the Lord for ever, and be aſſured he will never diſappoint their expectations

23 ¶ And the heathen ſhall know that the houſe of
Iſrael went into captivity [n] for their iniquity becauſe
they treſpaſſed againſt me, therefore hid I my face from
them, and gave them into the hand of their enemies,
ſo fell they all by the ſword 24 According to their
uncleanneſs, and according to their tranſgreſſions have I
done unto them, and hid my face from them 25
Therefore thus ſaith the Lord GOD, Now will I bring
again the captivity of Jacob, and [o] have mercy upon the
whole houſe of Iſrael, and will be jealous for my holy
name 26 After that they have born their ſhame, and
all their treſpaſſes, whereby they have treſpaſſed againſt
me, when they dwelt ſafely in their land, and none made
them afraid 27 When I have brought them again
from the people, and gathered them out of their enemies
lands, and [p] am ſanctified in them in the ſight of many
nations, 28 Then ſhall they know that I *am* the
LORD their God, ‖ which cauſed them to be led into
captivity among the heathen but [q] I have gathered them
unto their own land, and have left none of them any
more there 29 Neither will I hide my face any more
from them for [r] I have poured out my Spirit upon the
houſe of Iſrael, ſaith the Lord GOD

n Dan ix 10 11
o Rom xi 2.
p Chap ... ‖ Heb. By my cauſing of them to be led ... q Chap ... r Joel ii 28 Acts ii ...

v 23—29 Much had the people of God ſuffered from the blaſphemies of their enemies, much under the heavy hand of God upon them in affliction, but now he will deliver them for ever out of all their troubles

1 The heathen ſhall be ſilenced, and convinced of God's deſigns in the ſufferings of his people They thought the captivity of Iſrael was owing to their weakneſs, or the inability of their God to protect them, but by this amazing exertion of divine power on their behalf, they ſhall ſee that the only cauſe of their ſuffering was their ſin, for which they were given into their enemies hand, v 23 and that God dealt with them according to their tranſgreſſions, in all the evil he brought upon them So that what he did was with a view to his own glory, viſiting their iniquity with a rod, yet, as he, the covenant ...ed, not taking his loving kindneſs from them, nor ſuffering his truth to fail, nor wanting power to recover and reſtore them to their former ſplendor, when they had ſmarted ſufficiently under his corrections

2 God's own people ſhall know his deſigns of grace towards them, notwithſtanding all they have ſuffered Jealous for his own honour, which the heathen had reproached, he will magnify himſelf in Iſrael's deliverance, v 25 and ſince *they have born their ſhame, and all their treſpaſſes*, a ſufficient meaſure of puniſhment for them, and teſtified unfeigned repentance for their provocations, aggravated by the mercies, peace, and comforts they had enjoyed, *when they dwelt ſafely in their land, and none made them afraid*, ver 26 Therefore he will now turn his hand, recover them from their diſperſion and bring them to their own land, and thereby God will *be ſanctified in the ſight of many nations*, who will own his diſpenſations toward his Iſrael to have been righteous, juſt, and good And they themſelves, whilſt they acknowledge God's juſtice in their ſufferings, ſhall experience his rich grace in their ſalvation, and know him to be *their God*, their covenant God, their God for ever and ever, v 28 for the light of his countenance ſhall no more be hid from them, the tokens of his favour be no more ſuſpended, but he will pour out his ſpirit upon them, that they ſhall not depart from him *Note*, (1) True penitents are willing to bear their ſhame, and own their ſufferings leſs than their iniquities deſerve (2) When by divine grace we return to God, he will return to us, and lift up again upon us the light of his countenance

CHAP. XL.

The nine following chapters are very myſterious They are full of difficulties, which the beſt commentators ſeem to have but unſatisfactorily explained, and many have entirely paſſed them over in ſilence Till the event ſhall have explained the prophecy, it is, perhaps, wiſeſt to be content to be ignorant The matter here is not at all eſſential to our ſalvation, the things neceſſary thereunto are written as with a ſun-beam It ſeems, however, very evident, that no material city or temple can be here intended, the dimenſions being ſo vaſt, the circumference of the walls of this new Jeruſalem exceeding the compaſs of the whole land of Canaan, nor doth the deſcription of the ſtructure or ſituation correſpond with the temple built by Solomon or Zerubbabel, chap xlv 2 xlv 1—5 *Some imagine the city ſpoken of*, Rev xx *is the ſame with this here deſcribed, but though ſome of the expreſſions there uſed ſeem to be borrowed from hence, there is a very great difference both with reſpect to the gates, and the compaſs of the walls, and beſides, no temple was there It is probable therefore, that the whole of this prophecy muſt be underſtood figuratively, either of the goſpel-church, particularly in the latter day, when her glory ſhall appear brighteſt, and an immenſe acceſſion of converts be made of ſuch as ſhall be ſaved, or of the ſtate of glory, when all the redeemed ſhall come to the eternal temple, where they ſhall ſerve God day and night, and go out no more.*

In this chapter we have, 1 A general account of this viſion of the temple and city, ver 1—4 2 *A particular account of it, in which a deſcription is given*, (1) *Of the outſide wall*, ver 5 (2) *Of the eaſt gate*, ver 6—19 (3) *Of the north gate*, ver 20—23 (4) *Of the ſouth gate*, ver 24—31 *and the chambers and other appurtenances belonging to theſe gates* (5) *Of the inner court, both towards the eaſt and towards the ſouth*, ver 32—38 (6) *Of the tables*, ver 39—43 (7) *Of the lodgings for the ſingers and the prieſts*, ver 44—47 (8) *Of the porch of the houſe*, ver 48, 49

573

1 IN the five and twentieth year of [a] our captivity, in
the beginning of the year, in the tenth *day* of the
month, in the fourteenth year after that [b] the city was
ſmitten, in the ſelf ſame day [c] the hand of the LORD
was upon me, and brought me thither 2 In the viſions
of God brought he me into the land of Iſrael, and ſet
me upon [d] a very high mountain, ‖ by which *was* as the
frame of [e] a city on the ſouth 3 And he brought me
thither, and behold, *there was* a man, whoſe appearance
was [f] like the appearance of braſs, with a line of flax in
his hand, [g] and a meaſuring reed, and he ſtood in the
gate 4 And the man ſaid unto me, Son of man, behold
with thine eyes, and hear with thine ears, and ſet
thine heart upon all that I ſhall ſhew thee, for to the
intent that I might ſhew *them* unto thee, *art* thou
brought hither declare all that thou ſeeſt to the houſe
of Iſrael

a Chap i 2.
b Ibid. xxxiii 21
c Ibid i 3
d Iſ ii 2 Rev xxi 10 ‖ Or upon which
e Gal iv ...
f Rev ...
g Ibid ... ... xi 1 ... xx 5

v 1—4 The date of the prophecy is in the twenty fifth year of the captivity of Jeconiah, in the tenth day of the beginning of the year which was reckoned in two different ways the civil year began at the autumnal equinox, and then this tenth day muſt have been the ... day of atonement the eccleſiaſtical year commenced from the vernal equinox, and then the day falls on the tenth of Niſan, anſwering to part of our March

Before Christ 574 and April, when the paſchal lamb was ſeparated from the flock, in order to be ſlain on the fourteenth

The ſcene is laid in the land of Judea, and in viſion the prophet is ſet on a very high mountain, and there was, as it were, *the frame of a city*, ſull in his view. There appeared to him in the gate, a glorious perſonage, the Lord Jeſus Chriſt, the maker and builder of this city of God, his church. His figure was bright and gliſtering as burniſhed braſs, and in his hand he bore a meaſuring reed and line, and addreſſing the prophet, bid him carefully behold, attentively hear, with fixed thoughtfulneſs weigh, and with fidelity deliver to the houſe of Iſrael, what was about to be revealed to him. *Note*, (1) The miniſters of God muſt themſelves carefully read, mark, learn, and inwardly digeſt the word of truth, that they may be enabled truly to declare it to others (2) We muſt be ourſelves divinely taught by the Lord Jeſus, before we can poſſibly teach others

5 And behold, a wall on the outſide of the houſe round
about, and in the man's hand a meaſuring reed of ſix
cubits *long*, by the cubit, and an hand-breadth so he
measured the breadth of the building one reed and the
height one reed 6 ¶ Then came he unto the gate
which looketh toward the eaſt, and went up the ſtairs
thereof, and meaſured the threſhold of the gate, *which*
was one reed broad, and the other threſhold of the *gate*,
which was one reed broad 7 And *every* little chamber
was one reed long, and one reed broad, and between
the little chambers *were* five cubits, and the threſhold of
the gate, by the porch of the gate within *was* one reed
8 He meaſured alſo the porch of the gate within, one
reed 9 Then meaſured he the porch of the gate,
eight cubits, and the poſts thereof two cubits, and the
porch of the gate *was* inward 10 And the little
chambers of the gate eaſt-ward, *were* three on this ſide,
and three on that ſide, they three *were* of one meaſure,
and the poſts had one meaſure on this ſide, and on that
ſide 11 And he meaſured the breadth of the entry
of the gate ten cubits, *and* the length of the gate thirteen cubits 12 The † ſpace alſo before the little
chambers *was* one cubit *on this ſide*, and the ſpace *was*
one cubit on that ſide, and the little chambers *were* ſix
cubits on this ſide, and ſix cubits on that ſide 13 He
meaſured then the gate from the roof of *one* little chamber to the roof of another the breadth *was* five and
twenty cubits, door againſt door 14 He made alſo
poſts of threeſcore cubits, even unto the poſt of the
court round about the gate 15 And from the face
of the gate of the entrance, unto the face of the porch
of the inner gate, *were* fifty cubits 16 And *there*
were ‖ narrow windows to the little chambers, and to
their poſts within the gate round about, and likewiſe to
the § arches and windows *were* round about ‖ inward
and upon *each* poſt *were* palm-trees 17 Then brought
he me into the outward court, and lo, *there were* chambers, and a pavement made for the court round about
thirty chambers *were* upon the pavement 18 And
the pavement by the ſide of the gates, over againſt the
length of the gates, *was* the lower pavement 19 Then
he meaſured the breadth from the forefront of the lower
gate, unto the forefront of the inner court ‖ without,
an hundred cubits eaſt-ward and north-ward. 20 ¶
And the gate of the outer court that looked toward the
north, he meaſured the length thereof, and the breadth
thereof 21 And the little chambers thereof *were* three
on this ſide, and three on that ſide, and the poſts thereof, and the arches thereof were after the meaſure of
the firſt gate the length thereof *was* fifty cubits, and
the breadth five and twenty cubits 22 And their
windows, and their arches, and their palm-trees, *were*
after the meaſure of the gate that looketh towards the
eaſt, and they went up unto it by ſeven ſteps, and the
arches thereof *were* before them 23 And the gate of
the inner court *was* over againſt the gate toward the
north, and toward the eaſt, and he meaſured from gate
to gate an hundred cubits 24 ¶ After that, he
brought me toward the ſouth, and behold, a gate toward the ſouth, and he meaſured the poſts thereof, and
the arches thereof, according to theſe meaſures 25
And *there were* windows in it, and in the arches thereof
round about, like thoſe windows, the length *was* fifty
cubits, and the breadth five and twenty cubits 26
And *there were* ſeven ſteps to go up to it, and the
arches thereof *were* before them, and it had palm-trees,
one on this ſide, and another on that ſide, upon the
poſts thereof

Heb ... Mat vi 33 or John x 7 † Heb Whoſe face was the way toward the eaſt So Ver 20 ... † Heb Limit or bound ... ‖ Heb Shut or cloſed § Heb Or galleries or arches Ver 21 30 ‖ Or within ... Rev xi 2 ... ‖ Or from without ... Ver 16 ... Ch lxxxiv

v 5—26 The meaſuring reed in the hand of the glorious perſon before mentioned was ſix cubits long, exceeding the common cubit by a hand's breadth

The outer wall is firſt meaſured, three yards and an half high, and of the ſame width The church is a ſacred incloſure, and ſafely protected by the power and love of him, who is as a wall of fire round about his people

In this wall were three gates, at the eaſt, the north, and ſouth, typical, it may be, of Jeſus the way to God, no man coming to the Father but by him The aſcent to the gates was by ſeven ſteps, intimating, that when we go to the temple, we ſhould lift up our hearts to God The *little chambers* adjoining to the gate, ſhould teach all true worſhippers, eſpecially miniſters, to ſeek no great things here below, and they were *many*, for in our father's houſe are many manſions Each chamber had windows, for all believers enjoy the light of the divine word the windows were *narrow*, the meaſure of our knowledge here below being at the beſt imperfect The different *courts* may intimate the different eſtates of God's people, ſome of whom maintain more intimate communion with him than others The *poſts*, with palm-trees engraven on them, repreſent the ſtrength and flouriſhing condition of the ſaints of God, never overwhelmed with the heavieſt afflictions, and triumphing over all their foes The *glittering pavement*, ver 17 may teach us where all the glories of this preſent world ſhould be put, even under our feet

27 And *there was* a gate in the inner court toward
the ſouth, and he meaſured from gate to gate toward
the ſouth an hundred cubits 28 And he brought me
to the inner court by the ſouth gate, and he meaſured
the ſouth gate according to theſe meaſures 29 And
the little chambers thereof, and the poſts thereof, and
the arches thereof according to theſe meaſures, and *there*
were windows in it, and in the arches thereof round about
it was fifty cubits long, and five and twenty cubits
broad 30 And the arches round about *were* five and
twenty cubits long, and five cubits † broad 31 And
the arches thereof *were* toward the utter court, and
palm-trees *were* upon the poſts thereof, and the going
up to it *had* eight ſteps 32 ¶ And he brought me
into the inner court toward the eaſt, and he meaſured
the gate according to theſe meaſures 33 And the little
chambers thereof, and the poſts thereof, and the arches
thereof *were* according to theſe meaſures, and *there were*
windows therein, and in the arches thereof round about,
it was fifty cubits long, and five and twenty cubits
broad 34 And the arches thereof *were* toward the
outward court, and palm-trees *were* upon the poſts
thereof on this ſide, and on that ſide, and the going up
to it *had* eight ſteps 35 ¶ And he brought me to
the north gate, and meaſured *it* according to theſe meaſures 36 The little chambers thereof, the poſts
thereof, and the arches thereof, and the windows to it
round about the length *was* fifty cubits, and the
breadth five and twenty cubits 37 And the poſts
thereof *were* toward the utter court, and palm-trees *were*
upon the poſts thereof, on this ſide, and on that ſide,
and the going up to it *had* eight ſteps 38 And the
chambers and the entries thereof *were* by the poſts of
the gates, where they waſhed the burnt offering

v 27—38 *The inner court* here deſcribed appears exactly ſimilar with the outer, for though ſome Chriſtians are much more advanced than others, yet all bear the ſame image of Chriſt, differing only as brethren of ſeveral ſtatures By *eight ſteps* was the aſcent into this court, the nearer we approach to God, the more ſhall we be raiſed above the world, and the things of it

39 ¶ And in the porch of the gate *were* two tables
on this ſide, and two tables on that ſide, to ſlay thereon
the burnt offering, and the ſin-offering, and the treſpaſs-offering 40 And at the ſide without, as one goeth up to the entry of the north-gate, *were* two tables,
and on the other ſide, which *was* at the porch of the
gate, *were* two tables 41 Four tables *were* on this
ſide, and four tables on that ſide, by the ſide of the
gate, eight tables, whereupon they ſlew *their ſacrifices*
42 And the four tables *were* of hewn ſtone for the
burnt

Before Christ 574

burnt-offering, of a cubit and an half long, and a cubit and an half broad, and one cubit high: whereupon also they laid the instruments wherewith they slew the burnt-offering and the sacrifice. 43 And within *were* hooks, an hand broad, fastned round about: and upon the tables *was* the flesh of the offering. 44 ¶ And without the inner gate *were* the chambers of [x] the singers in the inner court, which *was* at the side of the north-gate; and their prospect *was* toward the south: one at the side of the east-gate, *having* the prospect toward the north. 45 And he said unto me, This chamber whose prospect *is* toward the south, *is* for the priests, [y] the keepers of the † charge of the house. 46 And the chamber whose prospect *is* toward the north, *is* for the priests, [z] the keepers of the charge of the altar: these *are* the sons of [b] Zadok among the sons of Levi, which come near to the LORD to minister unto him. 47 So he measured the court, an hundred cubits long, and an hundred cubits broad, four square; and the altar *that was* before the house. 48 ¶ And he brought me to the porch of the house, and measured *each* post of the porch, five cubits on this side, and five cubits on that side: and the breadth of the gate *was* three cubits on this side, and three cubits on that side. 49 The length of the porch *was* twenty cubits, and the breadth eleven cubits, and *he brought me* by the steps whereby they went up to it: and *there were* [c] pillars by the posts, one on this side, and another on that side.

x 1 Chron. vi. 31. Col. iii. 16. — y Num. iii. 28, 32, 38. — † Or, ward, or ordinance. Ver. 45. — z Lev. vi. 12, 13. — b 1 Kings ii. 35. — c 1 Kings vii. 21. Rev. iii. 12.

37—49 We have here notice taken,

1. Of the tables, to slay and prepare the sacrifices for the altar. Before we draw near to God, we should prepare our offering, and not be rash with our lips, to utter any thing before God.

2. The chambers, some for the singers, others for the priests, who had the care of the house and the altar. They who serve at the temple, deserve a provision there.

3. The altar in the inner court represents the Lord Jesus, and as it stood in the center against the three gates, all the worshippers in the most distant court could look to it: for him in all our worship we must ever keep in view, by whom alone we have access unto God.

4. Before the temple was a porch, with pillars, probably like *Jachin* and *Boaz*, intimating the stability and beauty of the gospel-church.

CHAP. XLI.

An account was given of the porch of the house in the close of the foregoing chapter, this brings us to the temple itself, the description of which creates much difficulty to the critical expositors, and occasions differences among them. Those must consult them, who are nice in their inquiries into the meaning of the particulars of this delineation, it shall suffice us to observe, 1. The dimensions of the house, the posts of it, ver. 1. the door, ver. 2. the wall and the side chambers, ver. 5, 6. the foundations and wall of the chambers, and their doors, ver. 8—11. the house itself, ver. 13. 2. The dimensions of the oracle, or most holy place, ver. 3, 4. 3. An account of another building over against the separate place, ver. 12—15. 4. The manner of the building of the house, ver. 7, 16, 17. 5. The ornaments of the house, ver. 18, 19, 20. 6. The altar of incense, and the table, ver. 22. 7. The doors between the temple and the oracle, ver. 23, 26. There is so much difference both in the terms and in the rules of architecture between one age and another, one place and another, that it ought not to be any stumbling-block to us, that there is so much in these descriptions dark and hard to be understood, about the meaning of which the learned are not agreed. To one not skilled in mathematics the mathematical description of a modern structure would be scarce intelligible, and yet to a common carpenter or mason among the Jews at that time, we may suppose all this in the literal sense of it was easy enough.

1 AFterward he brought me to the temple, and measured the posts, six cubits broad on the one side, and six cubits broad on the other side, *which was* the breadth of the [a] tabernacle. 2 And the breadth of [b] the † door *was* ten cubits, and the sides of the door *were* five cubits on the one side, and five cubits on the other side: and he measured the length thereof forty cubits, and the breadth twenty cubits. 3 Then went he inward, and measured the post of the door two cubits, and the door six cubits, and the breadth of the door seven cubits. 4 So he measured the length thereof twenty cubits, and the breadth twenty cubits before the temple: and he said unto me, This *is* the most holy *place*. 5 After, he measured the wall of the house six cubits, and the breadth of [d] *every* side chamber four cubits round about the house on every side. 6 And the side-chambers *were* three, ‡ one over another, and || thirty in order, and they entred into the wall which *was* of the house for the side chambers, round about, that they might § have hold, but they had not hold in the wall of the house. 7 [e] And || *there was* an enlarging, and a winding about still upward to the side-chambers: for the winding about of the house went still upward round about the house: therefore the breadth of the house *was still* upward, and [f] so increased *from* the lowest *chamber* to the highest by the midst. 8 I saw also the height of the house round about: the foundations of the side chambers *were* [g] a full reed of six great cubits. 9 The thickness of the wall which *was* for the side chamber without, *was* five cubits, and *that* which *was* left, *was* the place of the side chambers that *were* within. 10 And between the chambers *was* the wideness of twenty cubits round about the house on every side. 11 And the doors of the side-chambers *were* toward the *place that was* left, one door toward the north, and another door toward the south, and the breadth of the place *that was* left, *was* five cubits round about.

a Ex. xxvi. — b 1 Kings vi. — † Or, entrance. — d 1 Kings vi. 5. — ‡ Heb. side chamber over side-chamber. — || Or, three and thirty times, or feet. — § Heb. be holden. — e 1 Kings vi. 8. — || Heb. it was made broader, and went round. — f Eph. iv. 15. Heb. vi. 1. 2 Pet. iii. 18. — g Chap. xl. 5.

v. 1—11 The prophet is at last brought to the temple. So they who commit themselves to the divine guidance, shall be brought to his eternal presence in the better temple above.

The door was as wide as the whole tabernacle of Moses, the gospel opening a great door, and effectual, and the numbers admitted into the christian church vastly exceeding those who ever joined in the Jewish worship.

The chambers in the sides of the temple increased a cubit in breadth each story, which was taken out of the thickness of the wall. The higher we build for glory, the more enlarged should be our hearts with faith, and love, and heavenly-mindedness.

12 Now the building that *was* before the separate place, at the end toward the west, *was* seventy cubits broad, and the wall of the building *was* five cubits thick round about, and the length thereof ninety cubits. 13 So he measured the house, an hundred cubits long, and the separate place, and the building, with the walls thereof, an hundred cubits long. 14 Also the breadth of the face of the house, and of the separate place toward the east, an hundred cubits. 15 And he measured the length of the building over-against the separate place which *was* behind it, and [h] the † galleries thereof on the one side, and on the other side, an hundred cubits, with the inner temple, and the porches of the court. 16 The door posts, and [i] the narrow windows, and the galleries round about on their three stories, over against the door ‡ cieled with wood round about, || and from the ground up to the windows, and the windows *were* covered. 17 To that above the door, even unto the inner house and without, and by all the wall round about within and without, by § measure. 18 And *it was* made with cherubims and [k] palm-trees, so that a palm-tree *was* between a cherub and a cherub, and *every* cherub had two faces. 19 So that [l] the face of a man [m] *was* toward the palm-tree on the one side, and the face of a young lion toward the palm tree on the other side: *it was* made through all the house round about. 20 From the ground unto above the door *were* cherubims and palm-trees made, and *on* the wall of the temple. 21 The ‡ posts of the temple *were* squared, *and* the face of the sanctuary; the appearance *of the one* as the appearance *of the other*. 22 [n] The altar of wood *was* three cubits high, and the length thereof two cubits, and the corners thereof, and the length thereof, and the walls thereof *were* of wood: and he said unto me, This *is* [o] the table that *is* before the LORD. 23 And the temple and the sanctuary had two doors. 24 And the doors had two leaves *apiece*, two turning leaves; two *leaves* for the one door, and two leaves for the other *door*. 25 And *there were* made on them, on [p] the doors of the temple, cherubims, and palm trees, like as *were* made upon the walls; *there were* thick planks upon the face of the porch without. 26 And *there were* [q] narrow windows and palm trees on the one side, and on the other side,

h Cant. iii. 5. — † Or, several walks, or walks with pillars. Chap. xl. 16. — ‡ Heb. cieling of wood. — || Or, and the ground unto the windows. — § Heb. measures. — k 1 Kings vi. 29. Rev. vii. 9. — l Chap. i. 10. — m Heb. iii. 13. 1 Pet. ii. 12. — ‡ Heb. post. — n John iv. 23. — o Mal. i. 7, 12. — p John x. 7. 1 Cor. xvi. 9. — q John i. 18. Heb. x. 19.

Before Christ 574

side, on the sides of the porch, and *upon* the side-cham
bers of the house, and thick planks

v 12—26 In neither of the other two temples do we find any thing that answers this building, which stood in a court by itself

The temple itself was adorned with cherubims and palm-trees, alternately, being carved on the wall, only two of the cherub's faces appeared Every priest who looked thereon, might learn what his duty required of him, to join the wisdom of the man to the courage of the lion and then he stood between two palm-trees, the ensigns of triumph, assured of victory over all the powers of wickedness

The altar here was of wood, and no mention of the gold wherewith it was overlaid in the other temples, perhaps to intimate that no more material fire or incense would be made use of, but the more grateful fire of love, and incense of prayer and praise And it is called a table, *v* 22 the great sacrifice being once offered, we have only now to feast thereupon, and eat that flesh and drink that blood, which gives immortal life to the souls

CHAP XLII

The chapter continues and concludes the measuring of this mystical temple, of which it is very hard to understand the architecture, and yet more hard to comprehend the mystical meaning Here is, 1 A description of the chambers that were about the courts, their situation and structure, ver 1—13 and the uses for which they were designed, ver 13, 14 2 A survey of the whole compass of ground, which was taken up with the house, and the courts belonging to it, ver 15—20.

a Rev xi 1.

1 THEN he brought me forth into [a] the utter
court, the way toward the north, and he
brought me into the chamber that *was* over against the
separate place, and which *was* before the building to-
ward the north 2 Before the length of an hundred
cubits *was* the north-door, and the breadth *was* fifty
cubits 3 Over against the twenty *cubits*, which *were*
for the inner court, and over against the pavement
which *was* for the utter court, *was* gallery against gal-
lery in three *stories* 4. And before the chambers *was* a
walk of ten cubits breadth inward, a way of one cubit,
and their doors toward the north 5 Now the upper
chambers *were* shorter for the galleries were [b] higher
than these, ‖ than the lower, and than the middlemost
of the building 6 For they *were* in three *stories*, but
had not pillars as the pillars of the courts therefore *the*
building was straitned more than the lowest, and the
middlemost from the ground 7 And [c] the wall that
was without over against the chambers, towards the
utter court on the forepart of the chambers, the length
thereof *was* fifty cubits 8 For the length of the
chambers that *were* in the utter court *was* fifty cubits
and lo, before the temple *were* an hundred cubits 9
And † from under these chambers *was* ‖ the entry on
the east side, § as one goeth into them from the utter
court 10 The chambers *were* in the thickness of the
wall of the court toward the east, over against the sepa-
rate place, and over against the building 11 And
the way before them *was* like the appearance of the
chambers which *were* towards the north, as long as
they, *and* as broad as they, and all their goings out
were both according to their fashions, and according
to their doors 12 And according to the doors of the
chambers that *were* toward the south, *was* a door in the
head of the way, *even* the way directly before the wall
toward the east, as one entreth into them 13 ¶ Then
said he unto me, The north-chambers, *and* the south-
chambers, which *are* before the separate place, they *be*
holy chambers, where the priests that approach unto the
LORD [d] shall eat the most holy things there shall they
lay the most holy things, and the meat-offering, and
the sin-offering, and the trespass-offering, for the place
is holy 14 When the priests enter therein, then shall
they not go out of the holy *place* into the utter court,
but there they shall lay their [e] garments, wherein they
minister, for they *are* holy and shall put on other gar-
ments, and shall approach to *those things* which *are* for
the people.

b 1 Cor xv 41 42
‖ Or and the building consisted of the lower and the middlemost
c Job i 10 Ps xxxiv 7 Isa xxvi 1 & ix 18 Zech ii 5
† Or from the place
‖ Or he that brought me
§ Or as he came
d Lev vi 16 26 ... vii 6 ... Num xviii 9 10
e Isa lxi 10

v 1—14 We have here,

1 The chambers about the temple Probably designed for the retirement of the holy worshippers, where they might be alone for prayer and meditation they who would find comfort in public ordinances, must maintain communion with God in private The chambers were many, for in the heavenly temple there are many mansions They had galleries before them, where they who lodged there might meet and converse together about the things of God, the great privilege, duty, and delight of God's people

2 These chambers, many of them at least, were appropriated for the use of the priests, and were the places where they deposited the holy things, and their sacred vestments They who have the charge of the sanctuary must reside upon the spot, and God hath made a provision for them, that they might wait on him without distraction.

15 Now when he had made an end of measuring
the inner house, he brought me forth toward the gate
whose prospect *is* toward the east, and measured it round
about. 16 He measured the east † side with the mea-
suring-reed, five hundred reeds, with the measuring-
reed round about 17 He measured the north-side five
hundred reeds, with the measuring-reed round about.
18 He measured the south-side five hundred reeds, with
the measuring reed 19 ¶ He turned about to the
west side, *and* measured five hundred reeds, with the
measuring-reed 20 He measured it by the four sides
it had a wall round about, [g] five hundred *reeds* long, and
five hundred broad, to make a separation between the
sanctuary and the profane place

† Heb Wind
g Chap. xlv 2

v 15—20 The ground on which this temple and its courts stood, is computed to be about eight miles in circumference, intimating the vast extent of the church of Christ in the times of the gospel, and particularly when the fulness of the Gentiles is come in A wall of separation divided the sanctuary from the profane place, to signify the present exclusion of all those from the blessings and benefits of Christ's church and kingdom, who continue unhumbled in their sins, and to prefigure the eternal separation of the world that lieth in wickedness, from the presence of God in glory

CHAP XLIII.

The prophet having given us a view of this mystical temple, comes now to describe the worship that should be performed in it In this chapter we have, 1 The glory of God filling the temple, ver 1—6 2 A promise given of the continuance of God's presence with his people, upon condition of their return to and continuance in his instituted worship, and the renunciation of idolatry, ver 7—12. 3 A description of the altar of burnt-offerings, ver 13—17 4 Directions given for the consecration of that altar, ver 18—27 And Ezekiel seems here to stand between God and Israel, as Moses did, when the sanctuary was first set up

1 AFterward he brought me to the gate, *even* the
gate that looketh toward the east 2 [a] And
behold, the glory of the God of Israel came from the
way of the east and [b] his voice *was* like a noise of many
waters, and the earth shined with his glory 3 And *it*
was [c] according to the appearance of the vision which I
saw, *even* according to the vision that I saw, when I
came † to [d] destroy the city and the visions *were* like
the vision that I saw by the river Chebar and I fell
upon my face 4 And the glory of the LORD came
into the house by the way of the gate, whose prospect
is toward the east 5 So the Spirit took me up,
and brought me into the inner court, and behold, [e] the
glory of the LORD filled the house 6 And I heard
him speaking unto me out of the house, and the man
stood by me

a Chap xi 23
b Rev i 15 & xiv 2 & xix 6
c Chap i 4 & viii 4
† Or when I prophesied that the city should be destroyed
d Jer i 10
e 1 Kings viii 10 11 Chap xliv 4

v 1—6 The temple was great and glorious, but infinitely greater the glory of the divine inhabitant who condescended there to take up his abode

1 The same bright vision that had before been seen by the prophet, again appears from the east It was the *glory of the God of Israel*, like many waters his voice was heard far off, his gospel having spread into distant lands, *and the earth shined with his glory*, his church, as the moon, reflecting the lustre she hath borrowed from him the sun of righteousness

2 This glory of God filled the house, and when the prophet in humble adoration had fallen prostrate on the earth, the Spirit took him up, and brought him to the inner court, to behold God's glory, and receive his instructions, and

Before Christ 574. the man, Christ Jesus, *stood* by him, for through him alone can we hold communion with God, or hear his voice with comfort.

7 ¶ And he said unto me, Son of man, the place of my throne, and the place of the soles of my feet, where I will dwell in the midst of the children of Israel for ever, and my holy name shall the house of Israel no more defile, *neither* they, nor their kings, by their whoredom, nor by the carcases of their kings in their high places. 8 In their setting of their threshold by my thresholds, and their posts by my posts, and the wall between me and them, they have even defiled my holy name by their abominations that they have committed: wherefore I have consumed them in mine anger. 9 Now let them put away their whoredom, and the carcases of their kings far from me, and I will dwell in the midst of them for ever. 10 ¶ Thou son of man, shew the house to the house of Israel, that they may be ashamed of their iniquities, and let them measure the pattern. 11 And if they be ashamed of all that they have done, shew them the form of the house, and the fashion thereof, and the goings out thereof, and the comings in thereof, and all the forms thereof, and all the ordinances thereof, and all the forms thereof, and all the laws thereof: and write *it* in their sight, that they may keep the whole form thereof, and all the ordinances thereof, and do them. 12 This *is* the law of the house; upon the top of the mountain, the whole limit thereof round about *shall be* most holy. Behold, this *is* the law of the house.

Ver. 7—12. God having taken possession of his temple, admonishes them of the obligations lying upon them, to be more faithful to him than they had ever yet been.

1. They had formerly grievously offended, and had been deservedly punished. They and their kings had been gross idolaters, and worshipped on the high places, ver. 7. They had corrupted the service of the sanctuary by their own inventions, had even dared to erect their idols and altars in that sacred place, and by such abominations had provoked God's wrath and indignation against them, ver. 8. *Note*, They who thus [illegible] depart from God, provoke him to take up the scourge and plague them for their offences.

2. He calls on them to repent, and graciously promises to make them much as he would have them be. They must *put away their whoredoms*, their idolatrous services, and the *carcases of their kings*, which some suggest were buried in or near the house of God, or rather the idols themselves are meant, as loathsome in God's sight as a putrid corpse in ours; and in order to induce them hereunto, the prophet must shew them *the house*, that a sense of the mercy God had in store for them, may work upon their hearts, and his goodness lead them to repentance, ver. 10; and if they expressed shame and contrition in the view of their past conduct, then he must go further, and give them a more distinct view of the glorious fabric, and all its parts, and give them in writing all the ordinances thereof, that they may keep them and do them, ver. 11. And whilst God is thus using the strongest motives, he promises to make them effectual. *They shall defile my name no more*, yea, he will engage their hearts to his blessed self, and, in consequence thereof, *dwell in the midst of them for ever*, as their God. *Note*, (1.) If the goodness of God doth not lead sinners to repentance, nothing else can ever produce it. (2.) When we begin to return to God, every step we take will give us fresh reason for deeper humiliation and self-loathing. (3.) They who are restored to God's favour, will above all things desire henceforth to walk in his way. (4.) The work of the sinner's salvation is from God alone, it is an act of his sovereign grace, and wholly effected by his divine power.

3. The law of God's house is declared, ver. 12: not only the sanctuary, but the whole mountain is now most holy; no veil in the gospel church excludes the believer, but *through the blood of Jesus we have boldness to enter into the holiest*, Heb. x. 19; and are called upon as his disciples to *perfect holiness in the fear of God*.

13 ¶ And these *are* the measures of the altar after the cubits: The cubit *is* a cubit and an hand breadth; even the bottom *shall be* a cubit, and the breadth a cubit, and the border thereof by the edge thereof round about *shall be* a span: and this *shall be* the higher place of the altar. 14 And from the bottom *upon* the ground, *even* to the lower settle, *shall be* two cubits, and the breadth one cubit; and from the lesser settle, *even* to the greater settle, *shall be* four cubits, and the breadth one cubit. 15 So the altar *shall be* four cubits; and from the altar and upward *shall be* four horns. 16 And the altar *shall be* twelve *cubits* long, twelve broad, square in the four squares thereof. 17 And the settle *shall be* fourteen *cubits* long, and fourteen broad in the four squares thereof; and the border about it *shall be* half a cubit; and the bottom thereof *shall be* a cubit about; and his stairs shall look toward the east. 18 ¶ And he said unto me, Son of man, Thus saith the Lord GOD, These *are* the ordinances of the altar, in the day when they shall make it, to offer burnt offerings thereon, and to sprinkle blood thereon. 19 And thou shalt give to the priests the Levites that be of the seed of Zadok, which approach unto me, to minister unto me, saith the Lord GOD, a young bullock for a sin-offering. 20 And thou shalt take of the blood thereof, and put *it* on the four horns of it, and on the four corners of the settle, and upon the border round about: thus shalt thou cleanse and purge it. 21 Thou shalt take the bullock also of the sin offering, and he shall burn it in the appointed place of the house, without the sanctuary. 22 And on the second day thou shalt offer a kid of the goats without blemish for a sin-offering; and they shall cleanse the altar, as they did cleanse *it* with the bullock. 23 When thou hast made an end of cleansing *it*, thou shalt offer a young bullock without blemish, and a ram out of the flock without blemish. 24 And thou shalt offer them before the LORD, and the priests shall cast salt upon them, and they shall offer them up *for* a burnt offering unto the LORD. 25 Seven days shalt thou prepare every day a goat *for* a sin-offering: they shall also prepare a young bullock, and a ram out of the flock, without blemish. 26 Seven days shall they purge the altar and purify it; and they shall consecrate themselves. 27 And when these days are expired, it shall be, *that* upon the eighth day, and *so* forward, the priests shall make your burnt offerings upon the altar, and your peace offerings; and I will accept you, saith the Lord GOD.

Ver. 13—27. We have here,

1. *The altar*, typical of the Lord Jesus, through whom all our services find acceptance with God, and the sinner that flies to the horns of this altar, shall find a sure refuge from fear of evil.

2. The consecration of the altar, and the service to be performed on it, which God promised to accept. Christ, by offering his own blood in the atonement, hath consecrated himself as the altar, and every believer is now a spiritual priest, ordained to offer spiritual sacrifices thereon, acceptable and well-pleasing to God through him.

CHAP. XLIV.

In this chapter we have, 1. The appropriating of the east gate of the temple to the prince, ver. 1—3. 2. A reproof sent to the house of Israel for their former profanations of God's sanctuary, with a charge to them to be more strict for the future, ver. 4—9. 3. The degradation of the Levites that had formerly been guilty of idolatry, and the establishment of the priesthood in the family of Zadok, which had kept their integrity, ver. 10—16. 4. Divers laws and ordinances concerning the priests, ver. 17—31.

1 THEN he brought me back the way of the gate of the outward sanctuary which looketh toward the east; and it *was* shut. 2 Then said the LORD unto me, This gate shall be shut, it shall not be opened, and no man shall enter in by it, because the LORD the God of Israel hath entered in by it, therefore it shall be shut. 3 *It is* for the prince; the prince, he shall sit in it to eat bread before the LORD; he shall enter in by the way of the porch of *that* gate, and shall go out by the way of the same.

Ver. 1—3. The prophet, following his heavenly guide, returns to the east gate, which, in honour of him, whose glory entered the temple thereat, was kept shut ever after, only the prince was admitted to eat his part of the peace offerings, in the porch, and to go in and out *by the way of the porch of that gate*: which some interpreters suppose, is the mystical sense to signify the blessed Virgin, the mother of [illegible] other, that the report that the [illegible] of [illegible] that [illegible] and by reason of him, till Christ the

Marginal notes (left): 1 Chron. xxviii. 2. — Lev. xxvi. 30. Jer. xvi. 18. 2 Kings xxi. 4, 5. & xxiii. 11, 12. Chap. viii. 3. & xxiii. 39. & xliv. 7. — † Or, *for there was but a wall between me and them.* — † Or, *sum, number.* — 1 Chron. xxviii. 11. 1 Pet. ii. 4, 5. — Heb. xiii. 10. 1 Pet. ii. 5. — † Chap. xl. 5. & xli. 8. — † Heb. *bosom.* — Heb. *lip.*

Marginal notes (right): Before Christ 574. — § Heb. *Harel*, i. e. *The mountain of God.* † Heb. *Ariel*, i. e. *The lion of God.* Isa. xxix. 1. — Exod. xx. 26. — Chap. xliii. 15. — Ex. xxix. 10. Lev. viii. 14, 15. — Lev. iv. 21. — Heb. ix. 24. — Heb. xiii. 11. — Lev. ii. 13. Mark ix. 49, 50. & vii. — Exod. xxix. 35. Lev. viii. 33. — † Heb. *fill their hand.* — Lev. ix. 1. — § Or, *thank-offerings.* — Ephes. i. 6. — 1 Tim. vi. 15. — Chap. xlvi.

Before Christ 574

prince entring himſelf, hath opened a way for all believers Others interpret it of the church of Chriſt upon earth, ſhut againſt all profane and impenitent ſinners, and only open to thoſe, who by the faith of Jeſus become one with him, and ſo have *boldneſs to enter into the holieſt of all*

4 ¶ Then brought he me the way of the north gate
c Chap iii 23 & xliii 5 — before the houſe, and I looked, and ᶜ behold, the glory
of the LORD filled the houſe of the LORD, and I
fell upon my face 5 And the LORD ſaid unto me,
d Chap xl 4 — ᵈ Son of man, † mark well, and behold with thine eyes,
† Heb Set thine heart — and hear with thine ears all that I ſay unto thee concerning
all the ordinances of the houſe of the LORD,
and all the laws thereof, and mark well the entring in
of the houſe, with every going forth of the ſanctuary
e Chap ii 5 — 6 ᵉ And thou ſhalt ſay to the rebellious, *even* to the
houſe of Iſrael, Thus ſaith the Lord GOD, O ye
f Chap xlv 9 1 Pet iv 3 — houſe of Iſrael, ᶠ let it ſuffice you of all your abominations,
g Chap xliii 8 — 7 ᵍ In that ye have brought *into my ſanctuary* ‡
‡ Heb Children of a ſtranger — ſtrangers ʰ uncircumciſed in heart, and uncircumciſed in
h Lev xxvi 41 Deut x 16 Jer iv 4 Rom ii 29 — fleſh, to be in my ſanctuary to pollute it, *even* my
houſe, when ye offer my bread, the fat and the blood,
and they have broken my covenant, becauſe of all your
abominations 8 And ye have not kept the charge of
mine holy things but ye have ſet keepers of my §
§ Heb Ward or ordinance, ver 14, 16 — charge in my ſanctuary for yourſelves 9 ¶ Thus ſaith
i Pſ 1 16 — the Lord GOD, ⁱ No ſtranger uncircumciſed in heart,
nor uncircumciſed in fleſh, ſhall enter into my ſanctuary,
of any ſtranger that *is* among the children of
Iſrael

v 4—9 Once more we have the prophet proſtrate, adoring the great God, whoſe glory he beheld Deep views of the divine Majeſty will ever produce the moſt abaſing apprehenſions of ourſelves

1 The prophet is charged to take notice of what he ſaw, and attend to what was told him, for they whom God employs, muſt carefully obſerve his orders, and be firſt taught themſelves of him, before they can be effectual teachers of others

2 He is commanded, [1] To deliver the meſſage God gave him to the houſe of Iſrael, that rebellious houſe, to convince them of their ſins Their abominations were great, and it was high time for them to amend they had introduced into the ſanctuary the uncircumciſed and the profane, to the defilement of that holy place, and the great diſhonour of God, and inſtead of chuſing the moſt able, zealous, and godly miniſters from among the prieſts and Levites, *ye have ſet keepers in my ſanctuary for yourſelves*, ſuch as ſtudied to pleaſe, not profit them, and would flatter them in their ſins, inſtead of teſtifying againſt them *Note*, (1) They who begin to taſte any thing of the bitterneſs of ſin, will reflect with grief on every moment of the time paſt when they walked therein (2) It is a high profanation of Chriſt's table, when perſons profane and immoral are admitted thereunto, and he will reſent the provocation (3) They who chuſe flattering prieſts will periſh in their own deluſions [2] To point out to them the path of duty *No ſtranger, uncircumciſed in heart or fleſh, may enter the ſanctuary*, and happy would it be for the church of Chriſt if theſe directions were more carefully obſerved, and none admitted to partake of her moſt ſacred ordinances, much leſs entruſted with the miniſtry, who have not given ſome ſatiſfactory evidence by their principles and practice, that they are partakers of the grace of God in truth

k 2 Kings xxiii 8 2 Chron xxix 4, 5 Chap xlviii 11 — 10 ᵏ And the Levites that are gone away far from
me, when Iſrael went aſtray, which went aſtray away
from me after their idols, they ſhall even bear their iniquity
11 Yet they ſhall be miniſters in my ſanctuary,
having charge at the gates of the houſe, and miniſtring
to the houſe they ſhall ſlay the burnt-offering,
and the ſacrifice for the people, and they ſhall ſtand before
l 2 Kings xvi 10 — them to miniſter unto them 12 Becauſe ˡ they
‖ Heb Were for a ſtumbling block of iniquity unto, &c — miniſtred unto them before their idols, and ‖ cauſed the
houſe of Iſrael to fall into iniquity, therefore have I
lift up mine hand againſt them, ſaith the Lord GOD,
m 2 Kings xxiii 9 — and they ſhall bear their iniquity 13 ᵐ And they ſhall
not come near unto me to do the office of a prieſt unto
‖ Heb Holineſs of holineſſes, or holineſs — me, nor to come near to any of my ‖ holy things in
the moſt holy *place* but they ſhall bear their ſhame,
and their abominations which they have committed
14 But I will make them keepers of the charge of the
houſe for all the ſervice thereof, and for all that ſhall
n Chap xl 46 & xliii 19 — be done therein 15 ¶ ⁿ But the prieſts the Levites,
the ſons of Zadok, that kept the charge of my ſanctuary,
when the children of Iſrael went aſtray from
me, they ſhall come near to me to miniſter unto me,
and they ſhall ſtand before me to offer unto me the fat
and the blood, ſaith the Lord GOD 16 They ſhall
enter into my ſanctuary, and they ſhall come near to ᵒ — o Chap xli 22
my table, to miniſter unto me, and they ſhall keep my
charge

v 10—16 The Lord is here taking account of his ſervants

1 The unfaithful are degraded they had betrayed their truſt, and as a miniſter's ill example hath ever the moſt pernicious effects, their idolatry had emboldened the people in their iniquities, therefore God will ſuffer them no more to miniſter as formerly before him yet not utterly to exclude them, and ſink them in deſpair, as if reprobate, and as if no place was left for repentance, they are ſtill to be employed in the more ſervile offices, and to partake in the proviſion of God's houſe, bearing their ſhame, though not utterly caſt away *Note*, (1) The church will never recover her primitive beauty, till her primitive diſcipline is reſtored (2) Though open offenders muſt be put to ſhame, too much ſeverity and rigour may drive thoſe to deſpair whom we ſhould deſire to lead to repentance

2 The faithful are diſtinguiſhed *The ſons of Zadok*, who in the general apoſtacy maintained their integrity, are confirmed in their office, and in the high honour of drawing near to God in his moſt ſolemn ſervices Fidelity ſhall never loſe its reward, and they who know the happineſs of communion with God, deſire no higher honour or greater reward than to be eſtabliſhed his ſervants for ever, and preſerved in a conſtant ſtate of nearneſs to his bleſſed ſelf

17 ¶ And it ſhall come to paſs, *that* when they en-
ter in at the gates of the inner court, ᵖ they ſhall be — p Ex xxviii 39, 40 & xxxix 27
clothed with linen garments, and no wool ſhall come
upon them, whilſt they miniſter in the gates of the in-
ner-court, and within 18 ᑫ They ſhall have linen — q Ex xxxix 28
bonnets upon their heads, and ſhall have linen breeches
upon their loins they ſhall not gird *themſelves* † with — † Heb In, or with ſweat
any thing that cauſeth ſweat 19 And when they go
forth into the utter court, *even* into the utter-court to
the people, ʳ they ſhall put off their garments wherein — r Chap xlii 14
they miniſtred, and lay them in the holy chambers, and
they ſhall put on other garments, and they ſhall not ˢ — s Chap xlvi 20 Ex xxix 37 & xxx 29
ſanctify the people with their garments 20 ᵗ Neither — t Lev xxi 5
ſhall they ſhave their heads, ᵘ nor ſuffer their locks to — u Num vi 5
grow long, they ſhall only poll their heads 21 ˣ Nei- — x Lev x 9
ther ſhall any prieſt drink wine, when they enter into
the inner-court 22 Neither ſhall they take for their
wives ʸ a widow, or her that is ‡ put away but they — y Lev xxi 7, 13
ſhall take maidens of the ſeed of the houſe of Iſrael, or — ‡ Heb Thruſt forth
a widow § that had a prieſt before 23 And ᶻ they — § Heb From a prieſt
ſhall teach my people *the difference* between the holy — z Lev x 10, 11 Chap xxii 26 Mal ii 7
and profane, and cauſe men to diſcern between the un-
clean and the clean 24 And ᵃ in controverſy they ſhall — a Deut xvii 8, 9 2 Chron xix 8, 10
ſtand in judgment, *and* they ſhall judge it according to
my judgments and they ſhall keep my laws and my
ſtatutes, in all mine aſſemblies, and they ſhall hallow my
ſabbaths 25 And they ſhall come at no ᵇ dead perſon — b Lev xxi 1, 2, 11
to defile themſelves but for father, or for mother, or
for ſon, or for daughter, for brother, or for ſiſter, that
hath had no huſband, they may defile themſelves 26
And ᶜ after he is cleanſed, they ſhall reckon unto him — c Num vi 10 & xix 11
ſeven days 27 And in the day that he goeth into the
ſanctuary unto the inner-court to miniſter in the ſanc-
tuary, he ſhall offer his ſin-offering, ſaith the Lord GOD
28 And it ſhall be unto them for an inheritance, I ᵈ — d Num xviii 20 Deut x 9 & xviii 1, 2 Joſh xiii 14, 33
am their inheritance and ye ſhall give them no poſſeſſion
in Iſrael, I *am* their poſſeſſion 29 They ſhall eat the
meat offering, and the ſin-offering, and the treſpaſs-of-
fering, and every ‖ dedicate thing in Iſrael ſhall be — ‖ Or devoted
theirs. 30 And ᵉ the ‡ firſt of all the firſt-fruits of all — e Ex xiii 2 & xxii 29 Num iii 13
things, and every oblation of all of every ſort of your — ‡ Or chief
oblations ſhall be the prieſts ye ᶠ ſhall alſo give unto — f Num xv 20 Neh x 37
the prieſts the firſt of your dough, that he may cauſe the
bleſſing to reſt in thine houſe 31 The prieſts ſhall not
eat of any thing that is ᵍ dead of itſelf, or torn, whether — g Ex xxii 31 Lev xxii 8
it be fowl or beaſt

v 17—31 The faithful who are appointed to miniſter before God, have here directions given them

1 Concerning their clothes They muſt wear linen garment when they are employed in their miniſtry, that they might not ſweat, and put them off when they have finiſhed the ſervice *and not ſanctify the people with their garments*, that the

teach

Before Christ 574.

touch of them communicated any holineſs, or leaſt any ſuperſtitious conceit might be entertained thereof by the people The miniſters of Chriſt, above all others, are eſpecially called upon to keep their garments clean from every ſpot, for on them every eye will be fixed

2 Concerning their hair They muſt not be on the one hand ſhaved, as the prieſts of Egypt, nor on the other effeminately affect long hair, but have their heads polled The Romiſh prieſts chuſe to copy after their heathen predeceſſors

3 Concerning their drink No wine muſt enter their lips when they went in to miniſter *Note*, Nothing can be conceived in a chriſtian miniſter more ſcandalouſly infamous than intemperance

4 Concerning their marriages They may not take for a wife a woman divorced, leaſt her ſuſpicious character bring a diſhonour upon her huſband, nor a *widow*, unleſs it be a prieſt's widow, but a maiden of the houſe of Iſrael *Note*, (1) It is a mark of the antichriſtian church to forbid marriage to the clergy (2) Miniſters above all others, for the honour of their high office, need be eſpecially careful whom they chuſe for their yoke fellow

5 Concerning the exerciſe of their miniſtry [1] They muſt teach the people *the difference between the holy and profane, between the clean and unclean* and this with regard to perſons, principles, and practices, pointing out the evil as to be avoided, and the good to be embraced and followed [2] In appeals made to them, they muſt judge impartially according to God's word [3] In their aſſemblies they muſt be directed in their worſhip and diſcipline by his laws and ſtatutes, and *hallow God's ſabbaths*, both in private and public, and exhort others to do the ſame

6 Concerning their mourning They may not come near a dead corpſe, which would make them ceremonially unclean, and prevent them from approaching the ſanctuary only for thoſe neareſt relations ſpecified v 25 they may defile themſelves but before they return to their ſacred ſervices again they muſt be cleanſed by a ſin-offering Though miniſters are not forbidden to ſorrow as men, they muſt be examples of reſignation, and ſee that their grief does not break in upon the duties of their office

7 Concerning their maintenance They had no inheritance in Iſrael, but their proviſion aroſe from the altar they ſerved God was their poſſeſſion, whoſe favour is the richeſt portion, and whilſt they exerted themſelves in his ſervice, the piety of the people would procure them plenty of all needful things, ſo that they ſhould not be reduced to eat what died of itſelf, or was torn, and in return, the bleſſing of God's miniſters reſting upon them, would amply compenſate the people for what they employed in his ſervice and their maintenance *Note*, God's miniſters have a right to live by the altars they ſerve, and it is the intereſt, as well as duty of the people, to take care of them, for the bleſſing of God in anſwer to their prayers ſhall be an abundant recompenſe

CHAP XLV

In this chapter is farther repreſented to the prophet in viſion, 1 The diviſion of the holy land So much for the temple and the prieſts that attended the ſervice of it, ver 1—4 So much for the Levites, ver 5 So much for the city, ver 6 So much for the prince, and the reſidue to the people, ver 7, 8 2 The ordinances of juſtice that were given both to prince and people, ver 9—12 3 The oblations they were to offer, and the prince's part in theſe oblations, ver 13—17 Particularly in the beginning of the year, ver 18—20 and in the paſſover, and the feaſt of tabernacles, ver 21—25 And all this ſeems to point at the new church-ſtate that ſhould be ſet up under the goſpel, which both for extent and purity ſhall far exceed that of the Old Teſtament

1 MOREOVER, when ye ſhall ‖ divide by lot
the land for inheritance, ye ſhall ᵃ offer an obla-
tion unto the LORD, † an holy portion of the land
the length *ſhall be* the length of five and twenty thou-
ſand *reeds*, and the breadth *ſhall be* ten thouſand this
ſhall be holy in all the borders thereof round about 2
Of this there ſhall be for the ſanctuary ᵇ five hundred
in length, with five hundred *in breadth*, ſquare round
about; and fifty cubits round about for the § ſuburbs
thereof 3 And of this meaſure ſhalt thou meaſure the
length of five and twenty thouſand, and the breadth of
ten thouſand and in it ſhall be the ſanctuary, *and* the
moſt holy *place* 4 The holy *portion* of the land ſhall
be for the prieſts the miniſters of the ſanctuary, which
ſhall come near to miniſter unto the LORD, and it ſhall
be a place for their houſes, and an holy place for the
ſanctuary 5 And the five and twenty thouſand of
length, and the ten thouſand of breadth, ſhall alſo the
Levites, the miniſters of the houſe have for themſelves,
for a poſſeſſion for ᶜ twenty chambers 6 ¶ And ye
ſhall appoint the poſſeſſion of the city five thouſand broad,
and five and twenty thouſand long over againſt the ob-
lation of the holy *portion* it ſhall be for the whole houſe
of Iſrael 7 ¶ And *a portion ſhall be* for ᵈ the prince on
the one ſide, and on the other ſide of the oblation of
the holy *portion*, and of the poſſeſſion of the city, before
the oblation of the holy *portion*, and before the poſſeſ-
ſion of the city, ᵉ from the weſt-ſide weſtward, and from
the eaſt-ſide eaſtward and the length *ſhall be* over againſt
one of the portions, from the weſt border unto the eaſt-
border. 8 In the land ſhall be his poſſeſſion in Iſrael,
and ᶠ my princes ſhall no more oppreſs my people, and
the reſt of the land ſhall they give to the houſe of Iſrael
according to their tribes

‖ Heb [illegible] ‖ Heb cauſe to fall ᵃ Chap [illegible] † Heb holineſs ᵇ Chap xlii 20 § Or void places ᶜ Chap xl 17 ᵈ Iſa [illegible] 6 & [illegible] 12 ᵉ Pſ lxxii 8 ᶠ Chap xlvi 18

v 1—8 The diviſion of the land here directed, is very different from that made by Moſes and Joſhua, and the extent of the country divided vaſtly exceeds that ancient inheritance of God's Iſrael, the land of Canaan this therefore moſt fitly may be referred to the kingdom of Chriſt, and his church, enlarged by the vaſt acceſſion of converts, both of Jews and Gentiles

1 The firſt portion is for God, his ſanctuary in the midſt, and around it the abode of the prieſts and Levites, with the land appropriated for their uſe, and this is conſidered as *an oblation unto the Lord*, for what is done to them for his ſake, he accepts as done unto himſelf Their reſidence is near the ſanctuary, for there muſt their conſtant attendance be A non-reſident miniſter of Chriſt, is a contradiction in terms

2 The next portion is for the city, where the whole houſe of Iſrael, at leaſt ſome of every tribe, dwelt a figure of the Iſrael of God, united in one communion, and become one fold under one ſhepherd

3 The portion of the prince is allotted him without the admeaſurement is not mentioned, but enough to maintain his dignity, and prevent the oppreſſion of the people which ſome interpret of the prince Meſſiah, whoſe dominion ſhall extend eaſt and weſt, and who around his church and people, is a guard to protect them from the inroads of every enemy

4 The reſt of the land is appointed for the tribes to inhabit, who, under the government of their prince Meſſiah, ſhall be ſafe and happy

9 ¶ Thus ſaith the Lord GOD, ᵍ Let it ſuffice you,
O princes of Iſrael remove violence and ſpoil, and exe-
cute judgment and juſtice, and take away your ‡ exac-
tions from my people, ſaith the Lord GOD 10 Ye
ſhall have ʰ juſt balances, and a juſt ephah, and a juſt
bath 11 The ephah and the bath ſhall be of one mea-
ſure, that the bath may contain the tenth part of an
homer, and the ephah the tenth part of an homer the
meaſure thereof ſhall be after the homer 12 And ⁱ
the ſhekel *ſhall be* twenty gerahs twenty ſhekels, five
and twenty ſhekels, fifteen ſhekels ſhall be your
manah

ᵍ Chap xliv 6 [illegible] ‡ Or expulſions ʰ Lev xix 35, 36 Prov xi 1 ⁱ Ex xxx 13 Lev xxvii 25 Num iii 47

v 9—12 We have here,

1 An injunction laid on the princes to avoid all oppreſſion, and miniſter true judgment to the people, it being high time to put an end to the paſt ſcene of extortion and violence Princes muſt remember they are but men, and accountable to him from whom they have received their power, the abuſe of which will in the end prove fatally ruinous to themſelves

2 The people muſt exerciſe uprightneſs in their dealings among themſelves, conſcientiouſly exact in their coins, weights, and meaſure True piety towards God, will ever produce honeſty towards men

13 This *is* the oblation that ye ſhall offer, the ſixth
part of an ephah of an homer of wheat, and ye ſhall give
the ſixth part of an ephah of an homer of barley 14
Concerning the ordinance of oil, the bath of oil, *ye ſhall
offer* the tenth part of a bath out of the cor, *which is* an
homer of ten baths, for ten baths *are* an homer 15
And one ‖ lamb out of the flock, out of two hundred,
out of the fat paſtures of Iſrael, for a meat offering,
and for a burnt offering, and for ‡ peace-offerings, to
make reconciliation for them, ſaith the Lord GOD 16
All the people of the land § ſhall *give* this oblation ‖ for
the prince in Iſrael 17 And it ſhall be the prince's part
to give burnt offerings, and meat-offerings, and drink-
offerings, in the feaſts, and in the new-moons, and in
the ſabbaths, in all ſolemnities of the houſe of Iſrael
he ſhall prepare ᵏ the ſin offering, and the meat offering,
and the burnt offering, and the peace offerings, to make
recon-

‖ Or kid ‡ Or thank-offerings Ver 17 § Heb ſhall be for ‖ Or with ᵏ [illegible] Chr [illegible] 24 [illegible] 13

Before Christ 574

reconciliation for the house of Israel 18 Thus saith
the Lord GOD, In the first *month*, in the first *day* of
the month, thou shalt take a young bullock without
l Lev. xvi. 16 blemish, and l cleanse the sanctuary 19 And the priest
shall take of the blood of the sin offering, and put *it*
upon the posts of the house, and upon the four corners
of the settle of the altar, and upon the posts of the gate
of the inner court 20 And so thou shalt do the se-
venth *day* of the month, for every one that erreth, and
for *him that is* simple so shall ye reconcile the house
m Lev. xxiii. 5. Num. ix. 3. & xxviii. 16. Deut. xvi. 1 21 m In the first *month*, in the fourteenth day of the
month, ye shall have the passover, a feast of seven days,
unleavened bread shall be eaten 22 And upon that
day shall the prince prepare for himself, and for all the
n Lev. iv. 3 people of the land, n a bullock *for* a sin-offering 23
And seven days of the feast he shall prepare a burnt
o Isa. liii. 9. 2 Cor. v. 21 offering to the LORD, seven bullocks, and seven rams o
without blemish, daily the seven days, and a kid of the
goats daily *for* a sin offering 24 And he shall prepare
a meat offering of an ephah for a bullock, and an ephah
for a ram, and an hin of oil for an ephah 25 In the
seventh *month*, in the fifteenth day of the month shall
p Lev. xxiii. 34. Num. xxix. 12. Deut. xvi. 13 he do the like in the p feast of the seven days, according
to the sin-offering, according to the burnt offering, and
according to the meat-offering, and according to the
oil

v 13—25 Particular directions are laid down for the ser-
vice of God

1 Respecting the oblations to be offered by all the people of the land of their corn a sixtieth part, of their wine the hundredth, of their lambs one in two hundred, but from the fattest pastures, must be offered, *for the prince in Israel*, or *to the prince of Israel*, the Lord Jesus, to whose honour these were devoted for the maintenance of his ministers, and for the more immediate service of his church, and for whose sake they are accepted, *v* 17 *Note*, (1.) They who enjoy the blessings of God's providence, are bound to honour him with a part of their abundance (2.) Our oblations, prayers, and praises are then accepted, when the atoning blood of the Lamb hath made the reconciliation, and opened us a way to the throne of God

2 Respecting their solemnities, which differed exceedingly from the Mosaical institutions, and intimated a change in that dispensation

(1.) On the first day of the year the sanctuary was to be cleansed by the blood of a sin-offering, and the same ceremony was repeated on the seventh day for him that had *erred* and was *simple* Even since man on earth hath need of cleansing continually, the purest societies of christians must ever apply to the atoning blood, and we are bound every year, yea every day, to beg the forgiveness of our negligences and ignorances, which, without the all-powerful intercession and oblation of the great high priest of our profession, Jesus Christ, must eternally destroy us

(2.) On the fourteenth of Nisan the passover is to be kept, with the seven days of unleavened bread, and a bullock each day, offered for a sin-offering, *v* 22 prepared by the prince, with its meat and drink offering, besides a kid of the goats each day for a sin-offering, and seven bullocks and rams for a burnt-offering All which are typical of the Lord Jesus, who hath prepared himself a sacrifice for us, and is our passover, by whose blood we have received the atonement, to whom we must have an eye in all our approaches to God, and on whom by faith we must feast to the strengthening and refreshing of our souls

(3.) On the seventh month, the fifteenth day, the feast of tabernacles ordered to be observed seven days, with the same sacrifices as before All pointing to the great Redeemer, and directing us to him, in and through whom alone all our services are accepted of God

CHAP XLVI

In this chapter we have, 1 Some farther rules given, both to the priests and to the people, relating to their worship, ver 1—15 *2 A law concerning the prince's disposal of his inheritance,* ver 16—18 *3 A description of the places provided for the boiling of the sacrifices, and the baking of the meat-offerings,* ver 19—24

1 THUS saith the Lord GOD, The gate of the
inner court that looketh toward the east, shall
be shut the six working days but on the sabbath it
shall be opened, and in the day of the new moon it
q Chap. xliv. 3 shall be opened 2 And q the prince shall enter by
the way of the porch of *that* gate without, and shall
stand by the post of the gate, and the priests shall pre-
pare his burnt offering, and his peace offerings, and he
shall worship at the threshold of the gate then he shall
go forth, but the gate shall not be shut until the even-
ing 3 Likewise the people of the land shall worship
at the door of this gate before the LORD, in the sab-
baths, and in the new-moons 4 And the burnt-of-
fering that the prince shall offer unto the LORD in the
sabbath-day, *shall be* six lambs without blemish, and a
ram without blemish 5 And the meat-offering *shall be*
an ephah for a ram, and the meat-offering for the lambs,
† as he shall be able to give, and an hin of oil to an † Heb. the gift of his hand
ephah 6 And in the day of the new moon *it shall be*
a young bullock without blemish, and six lambs, and a
ram they shall be without blemish 7 And he shall
prepare a meat offering, an ephah for a bullock, and an
ephah for a ram and for the lambs according as his
hand shall attain unto, and an hin of oil to an ephah
8 And when the prince shall enter, he shall go in by
the way of the porch of *that* gate, and he shall go
forth by the way thereof 9 ¶ But when the people
of the land shall come before the LORD *in the solemn*
feasts, he that entreth in by the way of the north-gate to
worship, shall go out by the way of the south gate and
he that entreth by the way of the south-gate, shall go
forth by the way of the north-gate he shall not return
by the way of the gate whereby he came in, but shall
go forth over against it 10 And the prince in the
midst of them, when they go in, shall go in, and
when they go forth, shall go forth 11 And in the
feasts, and in the solemnities, the meat-offering shall be
an ephah to a bullock, and an ephah to a ram, and to
the lambs as he is able to give, and an hin of oil to an
ephah 12 Now when the prince shall prepare a volun
tary burnt-offering, or peace offerings, voluntarily unto
the LORD, *one* shall then open him the gate that look-
eth toward the east, and he shall prepare his burnt-of-
fering, and his peace offerings, as he did on the sab
bath-day then he shall go forth, and after his going
forth, *one* shall shut the gate 13 b Thou shalt daily b Exod. xxix. 38. Num. xxviii. 3
prepare a burnt offering unto the LORD, *of* a lamb ‡ of ‡ Heb. a son of his year
the first year without blemish thou shalt prepare it §
every morning 14 And thou shalt prepare a meat-of- § Heb. Morning by morning
fering for it every morning, the sixth part of an ephah,
and the third part of an hin of oil, to temper with the
fine flour, a meat-offering continually, by a perpetual
ordinance unto the LORD 15 Thus shall they pre-
pare the lamb, and the meat offering, and the oil, every
morning, *for* a continual burnt-offering

v 1—15 The rules here prescribed for the place and manner of God's worship, like the preceding solemnities, differed far from those prescribed by the law of Moses

1 The east-gate, that at other times was always shut, *chap* xliv 2 on the sabbaths, the new-moons, and when the prince offered a voluntary sacrifice, was to be opened for him though in form he must not go through it into the inner-court, but stand in the porch, by the post of the door, from whence he might see the priests offering the sacrifices he brought By the north and south gates the people were to enter the courts of the house, observing always to return by the gate opposite that by which they came in and on the sabbaths and new-moon they were to attend the prince at the east-gate, who should be in the midst of them, their leader and example in the holy service *Note*, (1.) It is the greatest glory of a prince to be a pattern to his people of true piety (2.) They who are the highest on earth, when they know themselves, will think themselves honoured in the meanest place of the church of God (3.) With Christ our king at our head, we may boldly draw near to the throne of God, and be assured of gracious acceptance in his sight (4.) When we set our heart towards the heavenly temple, we may not look back, but still forgetting the things which are behind, must press forward to those that are before

2 The sacrifices the prince must provide, are a daily burnt-offering of a lamb, on the sabbath six lambs and a ram, on the new moons an ox was moreover added all of them without blemish, with their several meat and drink offerings, some of these as much larger than was ordered by the law of Moses, whilst those for the lambs are left to his ability, *v* 5 Our offering at God's altar must be proportioned to the prosperity with which he hath blessed us Where he hath given much of them, he expecteth the more

16 ¶ Thus saith the Lord GOD, If the prince
give a gift unto any of his sons, the inheritance thereof
shall be his sons, it *shall be* their possession by inheritance

17 But

Before Christ 574

17 But if he give a gift of his inheritance to one of
his servants, then it shall be his to [c] the year of liberty;
after, it shall return to the prince but his inheritance
shall be his sons for them 18 Moreover, [d] the prince
shall not take of the people's inheritance, by oppression
to thrust them out of their possession; *but* he shall give
his sons inheritance out of his own possession that
my people be not scattered every man from his pos-
session

c Lev. xxv 10
d Chap. xlv 8

v. 16—18 If a prince wanted to leave an inheritance to any of his children, he is permitted to settle a part of his possessions upon him, and it would continue to his descendants for ever; but if he made a gift of land to any of his servants, it must revert to his family again at the year of Jubilee These gifts must be out of his own patrimony, and not the fruits of oppression, or the plunder of his people Kings must by their mild and equitable rule gain the love of their subjects; this will prove their greatest riches, for then they will be ready to sacrifice their lives and fortunes in his service

19 ¶ After, he brought me through the entry, which
was at the side of the gate, into the holy chambers of
the priests, which looked toward the north and behold,
there *was* a place on the two sides west-ward 20 Then
said he unto me, This *is* the place where the priests shall
boil the trespass-offering, and the sin offering, where they
shall bake the meat-offering that they bear *them* not
out into the utter court, [e] to sanctify the people 21
Then he brought me forth into the utter court, and
caused me to pass by the four corners of the court, and
behold, † in every corner of the court *there was* a court
22 In the four corners of the court *there were* courts
‡ joined of forty *cubits* long, and thirty broad these
four § corners *were* of one measure 23 And *there was*
a row *of building* round about in them, round about
them four and *it was* made with boiling-places under the
rows round about 24 Then said he unto me, These
are the places of them that boil, where the ministers of
the house shall boil the sacrifice of the people.

e Chap. xliv 19
† Heb. A court in a corner of a court, and a court in a corner of a court
‡ Or made with chimneys
§ Heb. Cornered

v. 19—24 The altar being so liberally as above supplied with sacrifices, part of which belonged to the priests, and were to be eaten in the holy place, there were boilers and ovens near their chambers, where they prepared these holy things, none of which might be carried out *into the outer court, to sanctify the people*, who might fancy, that partaking of these holy things would recommend them to God's favour, or that but touching them communicated virtue Such superstitious conceits the ministers of the sanctuary must never countenance

CHAP XLVII

In this chapter we have, 1 The vision of the holy waters, their rise, extent depth, and healing virtue, the plenty of fish in them, and an account of the trees growing on the banks of them, ver 1—12 2 An appointment of the borders of the land of Canaan, which was to be divided by lot to the tribes of Israel, and the strangers that sojourned among them, ver 13—23

1 AFTERWARD he brought me again unto the
door of the house, and behold, [a] water issued
out from under the threshold of the house eastward
for the fore-front of the house *stood* toward the east,
and the waters came down from under from the
right side of the house, at the south side of [b] the altar
2 Then brought he me out of the way of the gate
northward, and led me about the way without unto
the utter gate by the way that looketh eastward, and
behold, there ran out waters on the right side 3 And
when the man that had the line in his hand, went forth
eastward, he measured a thousand cubits, and he
brought me through the waters the ‖ waters *were* [c] to
the ancles 4 Again he measured a thousand, and
brought me through the waters, the waters *were* to the
knees again he measured a thousand, and brought me
through, the waters *were* to the loins 5 Afterward he
measured a thousand, *and it was* a river that I could not
pass over for the waters were risen, [d] waters ‡ to swim
in, a river that could not be passed over 6 ¶ And he
said unto me, Son of man, hast thou seen *this?* then he
brought me, and caused me to return to the brink of
the river 7 Now when I had returned, behold, at the
§ bank of the river *were* very many [e] trees on the one side
and on the other 8 Then said he unto me, These
waters issue out towards the east country, and go down
into the ‖ desart, and go into the sea *which being* brought
forth into the sea, the waters shall be healed 9 And
it shall come to pass, *that* every thing that liveth, which
moveth, whithersoever the † rivers shall come, shall live
and there shall be a very great multitude of fish, because
these waters shall come thither for they shall be healed,
and every thing shall live whither the river cometh
10 And it shall come to pass, *that* [f] the fishers shall
stand upon it, from En-gedi even unto En-eglaim;
they shall be a *place* to spread forth nets, their fish shall
be according to their kinds as the fish of [g] the great sea,
exceeding many. 11 [h] But the miry places thereof,
and the marshes thereof, ‡ shall not be healed, they
shall be given to salt 12 And by the river upon the
bank thereof on this side and on that side, shall § grow
all trees for meat, [i] whose leaf shall not fade, neither
shall the fruit thereof be consumed it shall bring forth
[k] ‖ new fruit according to his months, because their wa-
ters they issued out of the sanctuary, and the fruit
thereof shall be for meat, and the leaf thereof for
[l] medicine.

a Joel iii 18 Zech xiv 8 & xiv 8 Rev xxii 1
b Heb xiii 10
‖ Heb. Waters of the ancles
c Prov iv 18 Mat v 3
d Rom xi
‡ Heb. of swimming
Before Christ 574
§ Heb. Lip.
e Rev xxii 2
‖ Or plain Deut iii 17 & iv 49 Josh iii 16
† Heb. Two rivers
f Mat iv 19 & xiii 47
g Num xxxiv 6 Chap xlviii 28
h Rev xxii 8
‡ Or and that which shall not be healed
§ Heb. Come up
i Job viii 16 Psal i 3 Jer xvii 8
k Gal v 22 or Rev xxii 2
‖ Or principal
† Heb. for bruises and sores
l Rev xxii 2

v. 1—12 These waters of the sanctuary are usually supposed to signify the gospel of Jesus, the blessed effects and glorious extent of it being hereby represented There was nothing like these streams flowing from the material temple at Jerusalem, and therefore it is evident the vision must be taken in a mystical sense

1 The fountain-head was in the sanctuary, and from the threshold of the house the waters issued In the temple did Christ and his apostles daily teach, and from thence did the word of the Lord go forth into the Gentile lands; and he himself is both the temple and the door, from which these living waters flow, and who gives them their quickening power and efficacy

2 The course of the river was eastward, and then, either by dividing its streams, or by winding round, it turned west into the sea, either the Dead Sea, the Lake of Sodom, or the Mediterranean The gospel, which began to be preached at first in Galilee, and spread afterwards chiefly through the countries that lay east of Judea, went forth in process of time into all lands, even to the ends of the earth

3 The waters as they ran grew wider and deeper the prophet and his divinely-appointed guide crossing it thrice, at the distance of a thousand cubits each from the fountain-head, found the river swoln from their ankles to their knees, then risen to their loins; and when the fourth time they would have crossed the waters, they were no longer fordable, *v.* 5 And this may refer, [1] To the spreading of the gospel in the world from small beginnings the church of God hath increased exceedingly, and shall go on still enlarging, till the whole earth shall be covered with the knowledge of the Lord, as the waters cover the sea [2] To the truths of God, which the farther we search, the deeper we shall find them Some things are plain and obvious, and reach but to the ankles; in others, more difficult, experience and enquiry will lead us farther up to the loins, whilst in some, the farther we go, the more we are lost, and can only stand on the river's brink, and cry with Paul, *O the depth!* Rom xi 33 [3] To the work of grace in a believer's soul, which by continual accession of light and love from the great fountain-head, increases with the increase of God, till we come to the perfect man, to the measure of the stature of the fulness of Christ

4 Wherever these streams went forth, their wondrous virtue appeared even the waters of Sodom were *healed*, *v.* 8 For such is the mighty efficacy of the Saviour's grace, that it reaches to the most desperate the vilest may find pardon through his blood, and renovation by the power of his Spirit to the uttermost his salvation extends, and none are beyond it, who do not wilfully reject it *And whithersoever these rivers came, they* communicated life, *v.* 9 Such is the quickening influence which attends the gospel of Jesus wherever it is preached, dead sinners live; and, like a well-watered tree, the souls of believers are green and flourishing but the obstinate and impenitent are left to their misery, as *the marshes and miry places*, *v.* 11 abandoned to eternal ruin

5 Vast shoals of fish shall live in this river, and the fishermen cast in their nets, and dry them on the banks thereof intimating the multitude of converts that by the preaching of the gospel shall be called into the church of Christ, and the diligence and laboriousness of the ministers of Christ, as well as the success of their ministrations, for their labour shall not be in vain in the Lord

6 On the banks every useful tree for food or physic grew, their leaf never fading, their fruit ever abounding, See *Rev* xxii

Before Christ 574.

xxii 2 These represent the souls of the faithful, the trees of righteousness, the planting of the Lord, deriving from Jesus their life and vigour, watered every moment by his grace, green in their professions, in every good work bringing forth fruit to the glory of God, pouring the balm of friendly advice and consolation into the hearts of the tempted and afflicted, and persevering in every labour of love, till their life of grace on earth shall be exchanged for the eternal life of glory in heaven

13 ¶ Thus saith the Lord GOD, This *shall be*
the border, whereby ye shall inherit the land, accord-
ing to the twelve tribes of Israel ⁿ Joseph *shall have*
two portions 14 And ye shall inherit it, one as well
as another *concerning* the which ° I † lifted up mine hand
to give it unto your fathers, and this land shall fall
unto you for inheritance 15 And this *shall be* the
border of the land toward the north side from the
great sea, the way of Hethlon, as men go to Zedad,
16 Hamath, Berothah, Sibraim, which *is* between the
border of Damascus, and the border of Hamath, ‡ Ha-
zar-hatticon, which *is* by the coast of Hauran 17 And
the border from the sea, shall be ° Hazar-enan, the
border of Damascus, and the north northward, and
the border of Hamath and *this is* the north-side
18 And the east side ye shall measure § from Hauran,
and from Damascus, and from Gilead, and from the
land of Israel *by* Jordan, from the border unto the
east sea and *this is* the east side 19 And the south-
side southward from Tamar, *even* to ᵖ the waters of
‖ strife *in* Kadesh, the † river, to the great sea and *this*
is the south-side ‡ southward 20 The west-side also
shall be the great sea from the border, till a man come
over against Hamath this *is* the west-side 21 So
shall ye divide this land unto you, according to the
tribes of Israel 22 ¶ And it shall come to pass, *that*
ye shall divide it by lot for an inheritance unto you,
and to the strangers that sojourn among you, which
shall beget children among you and ᑫ they shall be
unto you as born in the country among the children of
Israel, they shall have inheritance with you among the
tribes of Israel 23 And it shall come to pass, *that* in
what tribe the stranger sojourneth, there shall ye give
him his inheritance, saith the Lord GOD

ⁿ Gen xlviii 5 1 Chron v 1 Chap xlviii 4 5
° Gen xii 7 & xiii 15 & xvii 8 & xxvi 3 & xxviii 13
† Or sware
‡ Or the middle village
° Chap xlviii 1
§ Heb From between
ᵖ Num xx 13 14
‖ Or Meribah
† Or valley
‡ Or toward Teman
ᑫ Rom iii 29 & x 12 Gal iii 28 Eph iii 6

ᵜ 13—23 The borders of the land here marked out are considerably larger than those described by Moses and Joshua, or than the country possessed by the Israelites after their return from the Babylonish captivity, and shews this must be understood typically of the church of Christ, and the true Israel of God, which, under the gospel dispensation, should have a great increase

Joseph hath two portions, to complete the number of the twelve tribes, Levi being taken to attend the sanctuary, and having a portion adjoining thereunto They are to divide the land into twelve equal shares, *See Rev* vii 4—8 which was not the case at the first division of the country, when the greater tribes had more, and the smaller less But now in the church of Christ believers are all one, entitled to the same privileges, and sharing alike the same grace and glory, and this in virtue of the everlasting covenant, confirmed by an oath, and sure to all the spiritual seed

Here also the strangers are allowed to inherit among native Israelites which before was forbidden, for now the middle wall of partition is taken down, and the Gentiles made fellow heirs and of the same body, members of Christ, and inheritors of the kingdom of God

CHAP XLVIII

1 The particular directions given for the distribution of the land, of which we had the metes and bounds assigned in the foregoing chapter 1 The portion of the twelve tribes, seven to the north of the sanctuary, ver 1—7, and five to the south, ver 23—29 2 The allotment of land for the sanctuary, and the priests, ver 8—11 for the Levites, ver 12—14 for the city, ver 15—20 and for the prince, ver 21, 22 Much of this we had before, chap xlv 1—8 3 A plan of the city, its gates, and the new name given to it, ver 30—35 which seals up and concludes the vision and prophecy of this book

1 NOW these *are* the names of the tribes, ᵃ from
the north end to the coast of the way of
Hethlon, as one goeth to Hamath, Hazar-enan, the
border of Damascus northward, to the coast of Ha-
math (for these are his sides east *and* west) † a *portion*
for ᵇ Dan 2 And by the border of Dan, from the
east-side unto the west side, a *portion* for Asher 3
And by the border of Asher, from the east-side even
unto the west-side, a *portion* for Naphtali 4 And by
the border of Naphtali, from the east side unto the
west-side, a *portion* for Manasseh 5 And by the bor-
der of Manasseh, from the east-side unto the west-
side, a *portion* for Ephraim 6 And by the border
of Ephraim, from the east-side even unto the west side,
a *portion* for Reuben 7 And by the border of Reu-
ben, from the east-side unto the west-side, a *portion*
for Judah 8 ¶ And by the border of Judah, from
the east-side unto the west-side, shall be ᶜ the offering
which ye shall offer of five and twenty thousand *reeds*
in breadth, and *in* length as one of the *other* parts,
from the east-side unto the west side, and the sanctu-
ary shall be ᵈ in the midst of it 9 The oblation that
ye shall offer unto the LORD, *shall be* of five and
twenty thousand in length, and of ten thousand in
breadth 10 And for them, *even* for the priests, shall
be *this* holy oblation, toward the north, five and
twenty thousand *in length*, and toward the west ten
thousand in breadth, and toward the east ten thou-
sand in breadth, and toward the south five and twenty
thousand in length, and the sanctuary of the LORD
shall be in the midst thereof 11 ᵉ ‡ *It shall be* for the
priests *that are* sanctified, of the sons of Zadok, which
have kept my § charge, which went not astray when
the children of Israel went astray ᶠ as the Levites went
astray 12 And *this* oblation of the land that is of-
fered, shall be unto them a thing most holy by the
border of the Levites 13 And over against the bor-
der of the priests, the Levites *shall have* five and twenty
thousand in length, and ten thousand in breadth all
the length *shall be* five and twenty thousand, and the
breadth ten thousand 14 And ᵍ they shall not sell of
it, neither exchange, nor alienate the first-fruits of the
land for *it is* holy unto the LORD 15 ¶ And
the five thousand *that are* left in the breadth over
against the five and twenty thousand, shall be a pro-
fane *place* for the city, for dwelling and for suburbs,
and the city shall be in the midst thereof 16 And
these *shall be* the measures thereof, the north-side four
thousand and five hundred, and the south-side four
thousand and five hundred, and on the east-side four
thousand and five hundred, and the west side four thou-
sand and five hundred 17 And the suburbs of the
city shall be toward the north two hundred and fifty,
and toward the south two hundred and fifty, and to-
ward the east two hundred and fifty, and toward the
west two hundred and fifty 18 And the residue in
length over against the oblation of the holy *portion*,
shall be ten thousand east-ward, and ten thousand west-
ward and it shall be over against the oblation of the
holy *portion*, and the increase thereof ʰ shall be for food
unto them that serve the city 19 And they that
serve the city, shall serve it out of all the tribes of Israel
20 All ⁱ the oblation *shall be* five and twenty thousand,
by five and twenty thousand ye shall offer the holy
oblation four-square, with the possession of the city
21 ¶ And the residue *shall be* for the prince on the
one side, and on the other of the holy oblation, and
of the possession of the city over against the five and
twenty thousand, of the oblation toward the east-border,
and west-ward over against the five and twenty thou-
sand toward the west-border, over against the portions
for the prince, and it shall be the holy oblation, and
the sanctuary of the house *shall be* in the midst thereof
22 Moreover, from the possession of the Levites, and
from the possession of the city, *being* in the midst *of*
that which is the prince's, between the border of Judah
and the border of Benjamin, shall be for the prince
23 As for the rest of the tribes, from the east-side
unto the west side, Benjamin *shall have* ‖ a *portion* 24
And by the border of Benjamin, from the east side unto
the west-side, Simeon *shall have* ‖ a *portion* 25 And by
the border of Simeon, from the east side unto the west
side, Issachar a *portion* 26 And by the border of
Issachar,

ᵃ Chap xlvii 15
† Heb One portion
ᵇ Josh xix 40 &c
ᶜ Chap xlv 1
ᵈ Ver 21
ᵉ Chap xliv 15
‡ Or The sanctified portion shall be for the priests
§ Or ordinance
ᶠ Chap xliv 10
ᵍ Exod xxii 29
ʰ Deut xviii 4 Chap xliv 30
ⁱ Chap xlv 1
‖ Heb One portion

Before Christ 574

Issachar, from the east-side unto the west side, Zebu-
lun a *portion* 27 And by the border of Zebulun,
from the east-side unto the west side, Gad a *portion*
28 And by the border of Gad, at the south-side
south-ward, the border shall be even from Tamar *unto*
the waters of ‡ strife *in* Kadesh, *and* to the river [h] toward
the great sea 29 This *is* the land which ye shall divide
by lot unto the tribes of Israel for inheritance, and these
are their portions, saith the Lord GOD

‡ Heb Meribah Kadesh. h Chap. xlvii 19

v 1—29 The division of the land, and the position of the several tribes, are very different from what had ever been the case, either under Joshua, or after the Babylonish captivity

1 Dan, the last provided for, *Josh* xix 40 is here the first, for under the gospel so it often happens, *Matth* xix 30 and the chief of sinners become the chief of saints

2 The tribes lay contiguous in a row, mutual supports to each other, signifying the union maintained in the church of Christ between the members, and the mutual assistance each communicates and receives, for the strengthening and comfort of the whole body

3 The sanctuary with the Levites lay in the midst, seven tribes were to the north, five to the south of it, thus they might more conveniently meet together, and maintain communion with each other

4 The priests portion was round the temple, that they might be at hand continually, and as they were liberally provided for by the oblations, they were the more obliged to attend at the altar *Note*, It is the worst of sacrilege when priests fatten on the spoils of that altar, at which they never serve

5 The lands of the priests were unalienable, and might neither be sold nor exchanged What is dedicated to God's service may no more be diverted to other purposes

6 The city is four-square, and the suburbs equally extending on every side, called the *profane* place, being, in comparison with the sanctuary, *common* for all the people of the several tribes This city represents the gospel-church, in which the faithful are joined together under the government of their great king, Jesus, and safe under his protection, no enemy can approach to hurt them

7 There shall be a number selected out of all the tribes to serve the city, intimating the duty of those who are magistrates, or ministers, or private Christians, to lay out themselves for the advancement of Christ's church and kingdom in the world

8 The prince's lot is suited to his high dignity, *v* 21 near the sanctuary, as designed to be the protector of religion, and the example of true godliness to his subjects Christ is the church's prince, her defence, and glory

9 Judah and Benjamin lay on each side the sanctuary, as the most honourable place They who kept their integrity, and stood faithful when others apostatized, shall receive the reward of their fidelity

30 ¶ And these *are* the goings out of the city on
the north-side, four thousand and five hundred measures
31 And the gates of the city *shall be* after the names
of the tribes of Israel, three gates north-ward, one gate
of Reuben, one gate of Judah, one gate of Levi 32
And at the east-side four thousand and five hundred
and three gates, and one gate of Joseph, one gate of
Benjamin, one gate of Dan 33 And at the south side
four thousand and five hundred measures and three
gates, one gate of Simeon, one gate of Issachar, one
gate of Zebulun 34 At the west-side four thousand
and five hundred, *with* their three gates, one gate of
Gad, one gate of Asher, one gate of Naphtali 35 *It
was* round about eighteen thousand *measures* [m] and the
name of the city from that day *shall be*, ‡ [n] The LORD
is there

i Rev xxi 12 &c.

m Jer xxxiii 16. ‡ Heb Jehovah Shammah Ex xvii 15 Judg vi 24. n Zech ii 10 Rev vii 15 & xxi 3 & xxii 3

v 30—35 The immense extent of this city, computed by some at 32,000 miles, evidently shews it must be mystically taken, as that glorious church into which all nations should flow together The twelve gates bearing the names of the twelve tribes, intimate the freedom of access which all believers have through Jesus, the door into the city of God none are excluded, who do not exclude themselves The name the city bears is *Jehovah Shammah*, God in a peculiar manner manifesting his presence in the midst of his church and people here below, preserving them from all their foes he is near to hear and grant all their petitions; comforting them with a sense of his love, and dwelling in their hearts, now become the habitation of God through the Spirit And this also will be the consummation of the eternal bliss and glory, that *God is there*, shining on his chosen with the unclouded beams of everlasting consolation Blessed and happy they, who are called to enter by the gates into the city, and enjoy that unutterable felicity of being for ever with the Lord

THE

THE

EVANGELICAL EXPOSITOR;

OR, A

PRACTICAL COMMENT

Upon the Book of the PROPHET

DANIEL.

TO comfort the distressed people of Israel during their sad captivity, God was pleased to raise them up prophets in Babylon. Daniel, the author of the following book, was probably of the seed-royal, or at least of noble blood, and eminent, as we find in his cotemporary Ezekiel, for his distinguished wisdom, as well as singular piety. In his prophecies the precise time of the Messiah's coming is so expresly fixed, that the Jews, unwilling to submit to the evidence, degrade him from the rank of prophets, and, making a distinction between the influence of the Holy Spirit and the gift of prophecy, admit that he wrote under the former, though they will not allow him the latter. But he is expresly stiled a prophet, Matth. xxiv. 15. *and may justly claim a place among the chief of them, his predictions being so distinct and particular, and the events described so momentous, respecting the great monarchies that should successively arise, with a particular regard to the Messiah and his kingdom, which at last should be set up in the world, and endure to the end of time.*

This book is written partly in Hebrew, and partly in Chaldee. The story of Bel and the Dragon, and Susannah and the Elders, that are extant in the Greek of Theodotion, and in the Vulgate Latin version, and by them annexed to this book, as a part of it, are evidently apocryphal and spurious.

Before Christ 60[illegible]

CHAP. I.

This chapter gives us a more particular account of the beginning of Daniel's life, his original, and education, than we have of any other of the prophets. We have here, 1. Jehoiakim's first captivity, ver. 1, 2. *in which Daniel, with others of the seed royal, was carried to Babylon. 2. The choice made of Daniel, and some other young men, to be brought up in the Chaldean literature, that they might be fitted to serve the government, and the provision made for them,* ver. 3—7. *3. Their pious refusal to eat the portion of the king's meat, and their determining to live upon pulse and water, which, having tried it, the master of the eunuchs allowed them to do, finding that it agreed very well with them,* ver. 8—16. *4. Their wonderful improvement above all their fellows in wisdom and knowledge,* ver. 17—21.

a 2 Kings xxiv. 1. 2 Chron. xxxvi. 6. Jer. xxxvii. 35. b Judg. ii. 14. c Gen. x. 10. d 2 Chron. xxxvi. 7. e 2 Kings xx. 17, 18. Isa. xxxix. 7.

1 IN the third year of the reign of Jehoiakim king
of Judah, [a] came Nebuchadnezzar king of Babylon
unto Jerusalem, and besieged it.
2 And [b] the LORD gave Jehoiakim king of Judah into
his hand, with part of the vessels of the house of
GOD, which he carried into [c] the land of Shinar, to the
house of his god, and [d] he brought the vessels into the
treasure house of his god.
3 ¶ And the king spake
unto Ashpenaz the master of his eunuchs, that he should
bring [e] *certain* of the children of Israel, [f] and of the

5

king's seed, and of the princes;
4 Children [g] in whom
was no blemish, but well favoured, and skilful in all
wisdom, and cunning in knowledge, and understanding
science, and [h] such as *had* ability in them to stand in
the king's palace, and [i] whom they might teach the
learning and the tongue of the Chaldeans.
5 And the
king appointed them a daily provision of the king's
meat, and of the wine which he drank: so nourishing
them [k] three years, that at the end thereof [l] they might
stand before the king.
6 Now among these were of
the children of Judah, Daniel, Hananiah, Mishael, and
Azariah:
7 Unto whom the prince of the eunuchs
[m] gave names: [n] for he gave unto Daniel *the name* of
Belteshazzar; and to Hananiah, of Shadrach; and to
Mishael, of Meshach; and to Azariah, of Abed-nego.

Before Christ [illegible]

Ver. 1—7. God had threatned Hezekiah to punish him for his pride, that the treasures in which he gloried, should be plundered by the king to whose ambassadors he had vainly shewed them, and his children led into captivity, *Isa.* xxxix. 6, 7. The fulfilment of that prophecy is here recorded. In the third of Jehoiakim, which was the first year of Nebuchadnezzar, that conqueror invaded Judea, and besieged and took Jerusalem; yet, not determining entirely to subvert the government, he left the king in possession of his royal dignity, though a tributary, and contented himself with the plunder of a part of the

vessels

Before Christ 606

vessels of the sanctuary, as a trophy of his victory, and to be placed in the temple of his god, as a tribute of thankfulness for his success. So much more devotion and gratitude do idolaters often shew to their false gods, than the professors of his religion pay to the only living and true Jehovah. He chose also the most promising and ingenious youths, that were of royal or noble extraction, to be trained up in his court, and qualified for offices of trust and government under him. Thus whilst he rendered them useful ministers of state, they served also as hostages for the fidelity of their parents. We may observe,

1. The directions given for the choice of these youths, which shewed the consummate wisdom and policy of the monarch. They must be without deformity, *well-favoured*, the lovely countenance bespeaking often the sweet disposition of the mind. They must be *young*, that they might more readily incorporate with the people among whom they were captives, and learn their manners and language: and *persons of genius* and learning, well skilled in all the knowledge that was proper for their years and station, and likely to improve under the tuition of their Chaldean masters.

2. The care taken of their maintenance and education. Three years they were liberally maintained at the king's expence, and under the most accomplished masters, that they might become acquainted with the language, laws, arts, and learning of the Chaldeans; and, at the expiration of this time, be qualified to appear before the king, and fill that department most suited to their genius and capacity. *Note*, (1.) The good education of youth is a public concern. (2.) They who wish to serve their generation, must spend their earlier days not in idleness or pleasure, but study: if that season be lost, it is afterwards scarcely to be redeemed.

3. Among these youths four are particularly mentioned, as rendering themselves most remarkable in the succeeding history. Their names were, Daniel, which signifies, *God is my judge*; Hananiah, *God is gracious to me*; Mishael, *asked of God*; and Azariah, *God is my help*. These the prince of the eunuchs changed into other names, either to shew his authority over them, or to intimate that they were now naturalized, and become Chaldeans; or in honour of the gods of Babylon, instead of the God of Israel, whose name they bore, and hoping perhaps the more easily to seduce them to the worship of the idols after whom they were now called. Thus Daniel is named Belteshazzar, or *Bel's treasurer*; Hananiah, Shadrach, *the messenger of the sun*; Mishael, Meshach, or *of Sehach*, the name of one of their gods or goddesses; Azariah, Abed-nego, *the servant of Nego*, perhaps the same idol mentioned *Isa.* xlvi. 1. But tho' their names were changed, their hearts were the same; and, far from serving these idols, they approved themselves the servants of the true God.

8 ¶ But Daniel purposed in his heart, that he
[e] would not defile himself with the portion of the king's
meat, nor with the wine which he drank: therefore he
requested of the prince of the eunuchs, that he might
not defile himself. 9 Now [f] GOD had brought Da-
niel into favour and tender love with the prince of the
eunuchs. 10 And the prince of the eunuchs said unto
Daniel, [g] I fear my lord the king, who hath appointed
your meat, and your drink: for why should he see your
faces worse liking than the children which *are* of your
† sort? then shall ye make *me* [r] endanger my head to
the king. 11 Then said Daniel to ‡ Melzar, whom
the prince of the eunuchs had set over Daniel, Hana-
niah, Mishael, and Azariah, 12 Prove thy servants, I
beseech thee, [s] ten days; and let them give us [t] pulse to
eat, and water to drink. 13 Then let our countenances
be looked upon before thee, and the countenance of the
children that eat of the portion of the king's meat:
and as thou seest, deal with thy servants. 14 So he
consented to them in this matter, and proved them ten
days. 15 And at the end of ten days, their counte-
nances appeared fairer and fatter in flesh, than all the
children which did eat the portion of the king's meat.
16 Thus Melzar took away the portion of their meat,
and the wine that they should drink; and gave them
pulse.

e Lev. xi. … Deut. xxxii. 38. Ezek. iv. 13. … f Gen. xxxix. 21. Psal. cvi. 46. … q John … † Or, term, or, continuance. r P… xxv. 5. ‡ Or, the steward. s Rom. iv. 15. t Deut. viii.

v. 8—16. We have here,

1. Daniel a favourite with the prince of the eunuchs. His own amiable qualities no doubt deserved regard; but the singular affection he found from this heathen master was from God, who hath in his hand the hearts of all men. If we find favour therefore with those from whom perhaps we least expected it, let us acknowledge this to be the gift of God.

2. He is scrupulously careful to maintain a conscience void of offence. The king had allowed him and his companions a liberal maintenance; but they feared to defile themselves with the meat and wine of the king, either as being such food as was forbidden by their law, or as having been offered in sacrifice to idols, or blessed in their name: they rather therefore chose to live upon the plainest and coarsest diet, than on these dainties; and Daniel, as their spokesman, intercedes for them with the prince of the eunuchs, that they might be excused from using the king's provision, and be permitted to live on pulse and water, hard fare for the sons of princes! *Note*, (1.) They who would preserve their souls from sin, must keep a strict guard over their sensual appetites. (2.) The poorest repast eaten with a good conscience, is a more delicious morsel, than all the dainties of the luxurious. (3.) They who have a sense of the evil of sin, will think no suffering or self-denial hard, in order to escape from it. (4.) Humble entreaty will prevail on those, whom obstinate refusal would but have exasperated; as was the case here; for,

3. The prince of the eunuchs, after some objections, consents. He was fearful, lest such spare diet should make these young princes look worse than their fellows; the consequence of which would perhaps be the anger of the king, and might cost him his head. But as Daniel and his companions desire only ten days trial by way of experiment, he is satisfied to wait that time, and compare them with the others: or else Melzar, the officer to whose care they were entrusted, and to whom Daniel addressed anew his request, grants them this liberty, perhaps with the connivance of his superior; and the event approved the experiment; for at the expiration of the ten days, these were fairer and fatter than the others, who had feasted on the king's dainties. *Note*, (1.) An abstemious diet is the best friend to health. (2.) Let the poor, who are reduced to pulse and water, remember, that God's blessing can make these preferable to a stalled ox. (3.) Whatever we deny ourselves for God's glory, shall, in the issue, prove our greatest gain.

17 ¶ As for these four children, [u] GOD gave them
[x] knowledge and skill in all learning and wisdom: and
Daniel [y] had understanding in all visions and dreams.
18 Now, [z] at the end of the days that the king had
said he should bring them in, then the prince of the
eunuchs brought them in before Nebuchadnezzar.
19 And the king communed with them; and among
them all was found none like Daniel, Hananiah, Mi-
shael, and Azariah: therefore [a] stood they before the
king. 20 [b] And in all matters of wisdom *and* under-
standing that the king enquired of them, he found
them ten times better than all the magicians *and* astro-
nomers that *were* in all his realm. 21 And [c] Daniel
continued *even* unto the first year of king Cyrus.

u Jam. i. 17. x Acts vii. 22. y Num. xii. 6. 2 Chron. xxvi. 5. Chap. x. 1. 603. z Ver. 5. a Gen. xli. 46. b 1 Kings x. 1. c Chap. vi. 28. & x. 1.

v. 17—21. We are here told,

1. The great progress in learning these gracious youths made under the divine blessing. They minded their business, and God eminently blessed them, giving them singular skill and knowledge; and Daniel in particular was endued with *understanding in all visions and dreams*, which he was enabled to interpret, not by any pretended rules of art, but by divine inspiration; and in these also God was pleased to make known unto him future events.

2. The king highly honoured them at the expiration of the three years. When he came to examine into the proficiency of these students, he found none to be compared with those four: he therefore took them into his service, and dignified them with a seat at his council-board. And he had abundant reason to approve the choice he had made of them; for *in all matters of wisdom and understanding*, respecting the conduct of affairs private or public, they *were ten times better* than the wisest and most experienced of his counsellors, and the most celebrated of the magicians. From this time till the first year of Cyrus, Daniel continued at court and in favour, and lived to see that happy event, the restoration of his people to their own land. *Note*, (1.) They who singly make God's glory their aim, most effectually consult their own honour and happiness. (2.) Wisdom is not always confined to age: when God teaches, he can give to youth more understanding than the ancients.

CHAP. II.

It was said, chap. i. 17. that Daniel had understanding in dreams; and here we have an early and eminent instance of it, which soon made him famous in the court of Babylon. We have, 1. The great perplexity that Nebuchadnezzar was put into by a dream which he had forgot, and his command to the magicians to tell him what it was, which they could not, ver. 1—11. 2. Orders given to destroy them all, and Daniel and his fellows among the rest, ver. 12—15. 3. The discovery of this secret to him in answer to prayer, and the thanksgiving he offered up to God thereupon, ver. 16—23. 4. His admission to the king, and the discovery he made to him, both of his dream, and of the interpretation of it, ver. 24—45. 5. The great honour which Nebuchadnezzar

buchadnezzar put upon Daniel, in recompence for this, and the preferment of his companions with him, ver. 46—49.

1 AND in the ſecond year of the reign of Nebu-
chadnezzar, Nebuchadnezzar dreamed dreams,
ᵃ wherewith his ſpirit was troubled, and his ſleep brake
from him. 2 Then the king commanded to call the
magicians, and the aſtrologers, and the ſorcerers, and
the Chaldeans, for to ſhew the king his dreams. So
they came, and ſtood before the king. 3 And the
king ſaid unto them, I have dreamed a dream, and
my ſpirit was troubled to know the dream. 4 Then
ſpake the Chaldeans to the king in Syriac, ᵇ O king,
live for ever: ᶜ tell thy ſervants the dream, and we will
ſhew the interpretation. 5 The king anſwered and
ſaid to the Chaldeans, The thing is gone from me: if
ye will not make known unto me the dream, with the
interpretation thereof, ye ſhall be ᵈ cut in pieces, and
your houſes ſhall be made a dunghil. 6 But if ye
ſhew the dream, and the interpretation thereof, ye ſhall
receive of me gifts, ᵉ and rewards, and great honour:
therefore ſhew me the dream, and the interpretation
thereof. 7 They anſwered again and ſaid, Let the
king tell his ſervants the dream, and we will ſhew the
interpretation of it. 8 The king anſwered and ſaid,
I know of certainty, that ye would † gain the time, be-
cauſe ye ſee the thing *is* gone from me. 9 But if ye
will not make known unto me the dream, ᶠ *there is but*
one decree for you: for ye have prepared lying and
corrupt words to ſpeak before me, till the time be
changed: therefore tell me the dream, and I ſhall know
that ye can ſhew me the interpretation thereof. 10 ¶
The Chaldeans anſwered before the king, and ſaid, There
is not a man upon the earth that can ſhew the king's
matter: therefore *there is* no king, lord, nor ruler, *that*
aſked ſuch things at any magician, or aſtrologer, or
Chaldean. 11 And *it is* a rare thing that the king re-
quireth, and there is none other that can ſhew it before
the king, ᵍ except the gods, whoſe dwelling is not with
fleſh. 12 For this cauſe the king was angry and very
furious, and commanded to deſtroy all the wiſe-*men* of
Babylon. 13 And the decree went forth, that the wiſe-
men ſhould be ſlain; and they ſought Daniel and his
fellows to be ſlain.

v. 1—13. The date of this prophecy is ſaid to be in the ſecond year of Nebuchadnezzar's reign; but as it appears Daniel was carried captive in the firſt, and continued three years under the tuition of the Chaldean ſages, this creates a difficulty, which interpreters have variouſly ſolved. The moſt probable way of accounting for it ſeems to be, that this year was the fourth from his being aſſociated with his father in the empire, and the ſecond from his death, when he reigned alone; or, *the ſecond year in the reign of Nebuchadnezzar*, commencing from the time Daniel was appointed to ſome employment about the king. We have here,

1. The troubled dreams of this mighty monarch. Whilſt his meaneſt ſubjects ſlept undiſturbed, his agitated mind was harraſſed with ſtrange imaginations, and the deep impreſſions made by them dwelt upon his ſpirit, occaſioned vaſt perplexity in his thoughts, and drove ſleep from his eyelids. *Note*, We are apt to envy thoſe who roll in affluence, and live in all the pomp of earthly grandeur; but we know not the pangs they often feel, and their ſleepleſs hours, becauſe of fear in the night.

2. His magicians and aſtrologers are ſummoned to ſhew the dream, and the interpretation thereof; for though the painful impreſſion of it remained, the particulars were gone from his memory. They inſtantly attend his orders, with warmeſt wiſhes for his proſperity expreſs their high reſpect for the king, and requeſting the recital of the dream, confidently promiſe the interpretation thereof. They ſpoke in the Syriac or Chaldee tongue, which was then the ſame, however different ſince; and to the eighth chapter this language is uſed, that the Chaldeans might read, and be convinced of the folly of their idolatry, and turned to the true God. The requeſt of the magicians ſeemed highly reaſonable; but the king, unable to grant it, inſiſted upon their telling him the dream itſelf, on penalty of their utter deſtruction if they failed, and with promiſe of the greateſt reward and honour if they could gratify him herein. In vain they remonſtrated the impoſſibility and unreaſonableneſs of the demand; *impoſſible*, becauſe, as they confeſs, none but the *gods, who have not their dwelling with fleſh*, were capable of ſuch knowledge. They admit the divine omniſcience, though, blindly erring, they aſcribe that which alone belongs to the one infi-

nite and eternal Jehovah, to their many fictitious deities. *Unreaſonable*, becauſe never king before required ſuch a thing from any magician or ſoothſayer. But their remonſtrances exaſperate, inſtead of convincing this deſpotic monarch; for arbitrary power is deaf to reaſon. He upbraids them, as if they had combined to impoſe upon him, and meant only to gain time, till either he ſhould loſe the deſire of knowing the dream, or be unable to recollect, if what they ſhould advance was true; or till his threatning to puniſh them ſhould be changed: he therefore inſiſts on the immediate ſatisfaction of his deſire, perſuaded that, could they tell the dream, they could not fail of giving the true interpretation alſo. The magicians repeat their remonſtrances, and the king grows more furious; for where paſſion rages, and obſtinacy in the wrong refuſes to hear the voice of truth, reaſon, however mildly urged, inſtead of ſoothing, but exaſperates; and where power is with the oppreſſors, what they cannot ſupport with equity, they will puſh on with fury. The magicians and wiſe men are therefore doomed to die without exception; and Daniel and his fellows, though entirely ignorant of the whole tranſaction, are ſought for among the reſt to be ſlain. We may obſerve here, (1.) What a miſery it is to live under an arbitrary government, where neither law nor reaſon avail any thing againſt the deſpotic will of a mercileſs tyrant. (2.) Though theſe magicians were now about to ſuffer unjuſtly, yet God was righteous, in permitting thoſe to be puniſhed for what they really never pretended to do, in return for their daring to impoſe on others, by pretending to that which they knew themſelves unable to perform.

14 ¶ ʰ Then Daniel anſwered with counſel and wiſ-
dom to Arioch the † captain of the king's guard, which
was gone forth to ſlay the wiſe *men* of Babylon: 15 He
anſwered and ſaid to Arioch the king's captain, Why
is the decree *ſo* haſty from the king? Then Arioch
made the thing known to Daniel. 16 Then Daniel
went in, and ⁱ deſired of the king that he would give
him time, and ᵏ that he would ſhew the king the inter-
pretation. 17 Then Daniel went ˡ to his houſe, and
made the thing ᵐ known to Hananiah, Miſhael, and
Azariah, his companions: 18 ⁿ That they would deſire
mercies of the GOD of heaven concerning this ſecret;
that Daniel and his fellows ſhould not periſh ᵒ with the
reſt of the wiſe *men* of Babylon. 19 ¶ Then was the
ſecret revealed unto Daniel ᵖ in a night viſion. Then
Daniel bleſſed the GOD of heaven. 20 Daniel an-
ſwered and ſaid, ᵠ Bleſſed be the name of GOD for
ever and ever: for wiſdom and might are his: 21 And
he changeth ʳ the times and the ſeaſons: ˢ he removeth
kings, and ſetteth up kings: ᵗ he giveth wiſdom unto
the wiſe, and knowledge to them that know under-
ſtanding. 22 ᵘ He revealeth the deep and ſecret things:
ˣ he knoweth what *is* in the darkneſs, and ʸ the light
dwelleth with him. 23 I thank thee, and praiſe thee,
O thou God of my fathers, who haſt given me wiſdom
and might, and ᶻ haſt made known unto me now what
we deſired of thee: for thou haſt *now* made known unto
us the king's matter.

v. 14—23. When tyrants reign, they will not want inſtruments to execute their unjuſt decrees. Already was Arioch gone forth for this bloody work, and Daniel, among the reſt, appointed to the ſlaughter: but God had otherwiſe ordained; and now when deſtruction ſeemed moſt fearfully to hang over him and his companions, all things were working together for their more diſtinguiſhed honour and advancement. So little can we judge of good or evil by outward appearances.

Daniel, though before this ſo famed for his ſkill, and acknowledged by the king to be ten times wiſer than all his ſages, had not been conſulted or thought of; for paſſion excludes all deliberate reflection; but his prudence and prayer now warded off the fatal blow that threatened ſo much miſchief.

1. He mildly interrogates the captain on the reaſon of this haſty decree; and when he learnt the cauſe, he *went in*, or *up* unto the king, and humbly begs a ſhort reſpite, undertaking to give the king all the ſatisfaction he deſired; and now ſenſible of his haſtineſs, or rather wrought upon by the inviſible hand of him who hath the hearts of kings at his diſpoſal, the requeſt is granted, and the execution ſtayed.

2. No ſooner is Daniel retired than he hath recourſe in prayer to the God of heaven, who alone could reveal the ſecret; and he engages his three faithful companions to join in their ſupplications for the ſame mercy, in which they were alike intereſted with himſelf, ſince, ſhould the king's decree be put in force, they muſt periſh with the magicians. *Note*, (1.) In every emergence prayer ſhould be our firſt recourſe. (2.) It is good to have praying friends, and our duty to deſire, as well as our high privilege to enjoy, an intereſt in their ſupplications.
(3.) All

Before Christ 603.

(3) All our hopes of an answer from God arise from faith in his promised mercies, and they who thus draw near to him, ſhall never be diſappointed.

3. God heard and anſwered their requeſts. He revealed the ſecret to Daniel in a *night-viſion*: either the following night he dreamed the ſame dream Nebuchadnezzar had forgotten, or God revealed it to him, with the interpretation thereof, immediately after the prayer he had offered. So effectual is the fervent prayer of the righteous, God will ſhew them ſecret things, which others cannot attain to.

4. No ſooner is the mercy granted, than his grateful heart overflows with deep acknowledgments. They who pray in faith, are ſure to praiſe with joyful lips. He adores and *bleſſes* God's great and glorious *name for ever and ever*, ſo worthy to be praiſed, and to be had in everlaſting remembrance. (1) He aſcribes to him all *wiſdom and might*, *wiſdom* infinite to deſign, and *power* infinite to execute all his purpoſes. (2) He acknowledges him as the ſovereign diſpoſer of all perſons and things. *He changeth the times and ſeaſons*, all the revolutions of ſtates and kingdoms are his work, as much as the various ſeaſons of the year. No chance or uncertainty is left in any of the things beneath the ſun, but all are fixed and come to paſs, according to his eternal counſels. *He removeth kings, and ſetteth up kings*; for he is King of kings, and they and their kingdoms ſtand or fall at his pleaſure. (3) He is the giver of all wiſdom, the greateſt politicians and the wiſeſt ſtateſmen are wholly indebted to him for the abilities which they poſſeſs, *for he giveth wiſdom to the wiſe, and knowledge to them that know underſtanding*, and where the moſt enlarged minds muſt come ſhort, and all human ſcience be at a ſtand, *he revealeth the deep and ſecret things*, the myſteries of grace, and ſecrets of providence, particularly the dream of the king, which none but he could ever declare, for *he knoweth what is in darkneſs*, the inmoſt receſſes of men's hearts, the ſchemes laid with deepeſt ſecrecy, and the dreams of darkneſs, even thoſe that when men awake are fled from their memory, *and the light dwelleth with him*, no darkneſs conceals from his all-ſeeing eye, and all divine illumination flows from him, as rays from the ſun. (4) He particularly adores him for the revelation he had now given him of this dream. *I thank and praiſe thee, O thou God of my fathers, who haſt given me wiſdom*, to underſtand this ſecret, *and might*, or courage, to go in to the king during his fury, *and haſt made known unto me now what we deſired of thee*, the revelation and interpretation of the king's dream, which they had ſought with their united prayers, *for thou haſt made known unto us the king's matter*, or *word*. *Note*, (1) Whatever God beſtows upon us, to his glory muſt it be aſcribed. (2) True humility will make us willing to communicate with our brethren the honour God puts upon us, and to aſcribe our mercies to the efficacy of their prayers, as much as of our own.

24 ¶ Therefore Daniel went in unto Arioch, whom
the king had ordained to deſtroy the wiſe-*men* of Baby-
lon: he went and ſaid thus unto him, Deſtroy not the
wiſe-*men* of Babylon: bring me in before the king, and
I will ſhew unto the king the interpretation. 25 Then
Arioch brought in Daniel before the king in haſte, and
ſaid thus unto him, I have found a man of [a] the captives
of Judah, that will make known unto the king the in-
terpretation. 26 The king anſwered and ſaid to Da-
niel, whoſe name *was* Belteſhazzar, Art thou able to
make known unto me the dream which I have ſeen, and
the interpretation thereof? 27 Daniel anſwered in the
preſence of the king, and ſaid, The ſecret which the king
hath demanded, cannot the wiſe *men*, the aſtrologers,
the magicians, the ſoothſayers, ſhew unto the king; 28
But there is [c] a God in heaven [d] that revealeth ſecrets,
and † maketh known to the king Nebuchadnezzar,
[e] what ſhall be in the latter days. Thy dream, and the
viſions of thy head upon thy bed, are theſe; 29 (As
for thee, O king, thy thoughts came into *thy mind*, upon
thy bed, what ſhould come to paſs hereafter: and [f] he
that revealeth ſecrets, maketh known unto thee what
ſhall come to paſs. 30 [g] But as for me, this ſecret is
not revealed to me, for *any* wiſdom that I have more
than any living, but ‡ for *their* ſakes that ſhall make
known the interpretation to the king, and [h] that thou
mighteſt know the thoughts of thy heart.

† Chald. Hath made known.

‡ Or, for the intent that the interpretation may be made known to the king.

℣. 24—30. No ſooner had Daniel returned due thanks to that God who had ſo graciouſly anſwered his prayer, than in haſte he applies to Arioch to be introduced to the king, and by giving him the ſatisfaction he deſired with regard to his dream, to prevent the execution of the raſh ſentence he had pronounced againſt his ſages. Arioch is eager to bring him to the preſence of the monarch, well-knowing how acceptable the ſervice would be, and, courtier-like, inſinuates, as if he had *ſought* for an *interpreter*, when he really only ſought for Daniel as his *executioner*. So ready are the crafty at improving incidents to their own advantage, where, inſtead of juſtly claiming merit, they really deſerved rebuke.

1. The king haſtily interrogates Daniel on the matter, *Art thou able to make known unto me the dream, and the interpretation of the matter?* which may expreſs either his doubt of his ability, where all the wiſe men of the court had before confeſſed their ignorance, or his admiration at the amazing underſtanding of ſo young a man, or his eagerneſs to hear the particulars of that dream which had ſo deeply affected him.

2. Daniel's anſwer is moſt noble, ſpirited, and pious.

(1) He ſeeks to cover the magicians with confuſion, and to convince the king of the vanity of truſting on ſuch wretched guides: they deſerved not indeed to be deſtroyed, but ought to be deſpiſed. This ſecret baffled all their rules of art, and ſhewed how ill-grounded were their pretences to occult ſcience, and the folly of depending upon them. *Note*, The experience of diſappointment ſhould wean us from creature-confidences.

(2) He would direct the king to the only proper object of his worſhip and truſt, even *the God of heaven, who revealeth ſecrets*, ſecrets which all the pretended deities of the Chaldeans could never teach their worſhippers, and which human reaſon never could diſcover.

(3) He declares the matter in queſtion to be highly momentous, that the king's dream was from God, and the ſubject of it relative to the greateſt events of futurity, the exaltation and demolition of the ſucceſſive monarchies of the world, till in the latter day that kingdom ſhould be erected that ſhall never be deſtroyed. It ſhould ſeem as if the king, ℣. 29 was muſing upon the fate of the monarchy himſelf had erected, when God in viſion ſhewed him the things that ſhould afterwards come to paſs.

(4) He humbly diſclaims all merit, and deſires that this diſcovery may not be aſcribed to any ſuperior ſagacity in him, but that the praiſe may be aſcribed purely to God, who revealed this ſecret to him, *for their ſakes that ſhall make known the interpretation to the king*, even for the ſake of all the Jewiſh people, as well as himſelf and his companions, that they might obtain favour in the ſight of the king, whoſe ſervants and captives they were, and for the king's ſake alſo, *that thou mighteſt know the thoughts of thy heart*, which he was ſo anxious to do, and in which the Lord condeſcended to gratify him. *Note*, (1) Diſtinguiſhed abilities never appear ſo admirable, as when accompanied by diſtinguiſhed humility. (2) A gracious ſoul deſires to diſclaim all merit, and to aſcribe to God's free grace all the excellence which is in him, and all the good done by him. (3) The humble are ever ready to think, that what God doth for them and by them, is more for others ſakes than for their own.

31 ¶ Thou, O king, ſaweſt, and behold, a great
image: this great image, whoſe brightneſs *was* excel-
lent, ſtood before thee, and the form thereof *was* terri-
ble. 32 [l] This image's head *was* of fine gold, his
breaſt and his arms of ſilver, his belly and his ‖ thighs
of braſs, 33 His legs of iron, his feet part of iron,
and part of clay. 34 Thou ſaweſt till that [m] a ſtone
was cut out ‡ [n] without hands, which ſmote the image
upon his feet *that were* of iron and clay, and brake them
to pieces. 35 Then was the iron, the clay, the braſs,
the ſilver, and the gold [o] broken to pieces together, and
became [n] like the chaff of the ſummer threſhing-floors,
and the wind carried them away, [o] that no place was
found for them: and the ſtone that ſmote the image
[p] became a great mountain, and [q] filled the whole earth.
36 ¶ This *is* the dream; and we will tell the inter-
pretation thereof before the king. 37 [r] Thou, O king,
art a king of kings: for [s] the God of heaven hath given
thee a kingdom, power, and ſtrength, and glory. 38
[t] And wherefoever the children of men dwell, the beaſts
of the field, and the fowls of the heaven hath he given
into thine hand, and hath made thee ruler over them all:
thou *art* this head of gold. 39 And [u] after thee ſhall
ariſe another kingdom [x] inferior to thee, and another
[y] third kingdom of braſs, [z] which ſhall bear rule over
all the earth. 40 And [a] the fourth kingdom [b] ſhall be
ſtrong as iron: foraſmuch as iron breaketh in pieces,
and ſubdueth all *things*: and as iron that breaketh all
theſe, ſhall it break in pieces, and bruiſe. 41 And
whereas [c] thou ſaweſt the feet and toes, part of potters
clay, and part of iron: the kingdom ſhall be divided,
but there ſhall be in it of the ſtrength of the iron, for-
aſmuch as thou ſaweſt the iron mixed with miry clay.
42 And *as* the toes of the feet *were* part of iron, and
part of clay, *ſo* the kingdom ſhall be partly ſtrong, and

‖ Or, ſides.

‡ Or, which was not in hands.

partly

Before Christ 603

§ Or, fragile.

partly § broken 43 And whereas thou sawest iron
mixed with miry clay, they shall mingle themselves with
the seed of men but they shall not cleave one to an-
other, even as iron is not mixed with clay 44 And
in the days of these kings shall [d] the God of heaven set
up a kingdom, [e] which shall never be destroyed and
the kingdom shall not be left to other people, *but* [f] it
shall break in pieces, and consume all these kingdoms,
and it shall stand for ever 45 Forasmuch as thou saw-
est that [g] the stone was [h] cut out of the mountain with-
out hands, and that it brake in pieces the iron, the brass,
the clay, the silver, and the gold, the great God hath
made known to the king what shall come to pass here-
after and the dream *is* certain, and the interpretation
thereof sure

d Ver 28 e Chap iv 3, 34 & vi 26 & vii 14, 27 Mic iv 7 Luke i 33 John xii 34 f Pf ii 9 Isa lx 12 1 Cor xv 24 g Isa xxviii 16 h Ver 35

v 31—45 Having prefaced his discourse with such piety and humility, he proceeds to the point, to the king's entire satisfaction We have,

1 The dream An image, in a human form, stood before the king, the sculpture admirable, the lustre uncommon the form tremendous, either its countenance breathed fury, or its Colossian size struck the beholders with fear and awe The head was gold, the breast and arms silver, the belly and thighs brass, the legs iron, the feet part of iron, part of clay Thus stood the mighty image, till, by an unseen hand, a stone, hewn from the mountain, smote the feet, and sudden the image fell, dashed in pieces with the stroke, and beaten to dust as *the chaff of the summer threshing-floors*, whilst the stone, that smote the statue, swelled into a mountain, so vast and huge that it filled the whole earth

2 The interpretation In speaking of which he joins his companions with himself, v 36 to do them honour, and because it was given in answer to their prayers

[1] The image represented the successive monarchies of the world 1 *The head of gold* was the Chaldean monarchy, over which Nebuchadnezzar then presided, his dominion was vast, and he ruled with most despotic sway, the lives and properties of his subjects being at his disposal but all his power, greatness, and glory, were derived from above, though he was *a king of kings*, he was but the minister of *the God of heaven*, who had *given* into his hand the kingdoms of the world, and to whom he was accountable, and of this the highest of the sons of men should be ever reminded This monarchy was to be transmitted to his son Evilmerodach, and his son's son Belshazzar, till the expiration of the seventy years prophesied of by Jeremiah, xxv 9—11 xxvii 5—7 2 *The breast and arms of silver* signified the kingdom of the Medes and Persians, *inferior* to the former, as silver is less precious than gold, for, though at first their dominions were as extensive, they quickly declined from the summit of grandeur This monarchy was founded by Cyrus, whose father was a Persian, his mother a Mede, the *two arms* that met in him, and lasted, according to the computation of some, 130 years, though others extend it to 204 years 3 The third kingdom, represented by the belly and thighs of brass, was the Grecian monarchy under Alexander, who subdued the last Medo-Persian king Darius Codomannus, and bore *rule over all the earth*, weeping, it is said, that he had not more worlds to conquer After his decease his dominions were divided, and chiefly possessed by two of his successors, whose descendants, the Seleucidæ and Lagidæ, who reigned in Egypt and Syria, are the thighs of brass 4 The fourth monarchy is the Roman, signified by the legs of iron, and the feet of iron and clay Strong as iron, their armies broke in pieces the Grecian empire, and subdued most of the nations in the then known world, and the Jewish people especially felt their terrible fury but, in process of time, this monarchy declined from its former splendor, and became broken and divided into ten different kingdoms by the irruption of the Goths and Vandals, like the feet and toes, part of iron and clay, some of these states, that rose out of the ruins of the empire, retaining much of the strength of the iron, whilst others were weak as miry clay and though *they shall mingle themselves with the seed of men*, the barbarous nations which broke in upon them, or endeavour to cement the divided kingdoms by intermarriages and alliances, yet the attempt will be as fruitless as to mix iron and clay together, the jarring interests and ambition of the several states preventing their cordial union, and inducing them to weaken and destroy each other

[2] The stone, hewn out of the mountain without hands, prefigured the kingdom of the divine Messiah, not supported by human power, or promoted by human policy, but by the invisible agency of the eternal Spirit established beyond the malice of every enemy, and enduring for ever and ever The God of heaven himself more immediately sets up this kingdom, of which his own Son is the glorious head It rose in the days of those kings who reigned during the last monarchy, Christ being born under the reign of Augustus and as it then began to spread, and hath continued to this day, so shall it be still wider and farther extended, till all the opposing powers of earth are broken, and every enemy shall bow before it A kingdom this, which shall not, as the former monarchies, be transferred from one people to another, but shall endure not only through the days of time, but be coeval with the ages of eternity

Thus having declared the dream, with the interpretation, to the fullest satisfaction of the king, he closes with an assurance of the divine original of the dream, as coming from that great God who only can foresee and foretel future events, and compared with whom the gods of the nations are less than nothing and vanity His word is truth, and therefore the events here predicted will assuredly be fulfilled in their season *The dream is certain, and the interpretation sure*

Before Christ 603

46 ¶ Then the king Nebuchadnezzar fell upon his
face, and [i] worshipped Daniel, and commanded that
they should offer an oblation, [k] and sweet odours unto
him 47 The king answered unto Daniel, and said,
Of a truth *it is*, that [l] your God *is* a God of gods, and
a Lord of kings, and [m] a revealer of secrets, seeing thou
couldst reveal this secret 48 Then the king made Da-
niel [n] a great man, and [o] gave him many great gifts,
and made him ruler over the whole province of Babylon,
[p] and chief of the governors over all the wise *men* of Ba-
bylon 49 Then Daniel requested of the king, and [q] he
set Shadrach, Meshach, and Abed-nego over the affairs
of the province of Babylon but Daniel *sat* in the gate
of the king

i Acts x 25 & xiv 13 k Ezra vi 10 l Deut x 17 m Ver 28 n 1 Sam xxv 2 o Ver 6 p Chap iv 9 & v 11 q Chap iii 12

v 46—49 We have here,

1 This mighty king prostrate before the prophet He was overwhelmed with wonder and awe at what he heard, and as if a divinity had spoken, (for no other, he supposes, could reveal such hidden things of futurity) he falls down to worship his captive, and commands divine honours to be paid him, which, though no doubt Daniel utterly rejected, sufficiently testified the high apprehensions the king entertained of his surpassing excellence

2 He ascribes the highest honour to the God of Daniel, acknowledging his incomparable glory and greatness, as the *God of Gods*, infinitely superior to all others, *the Lord of kings*, setting them up and removing them at his pleasure, and *a revealer of secrets* which none besides could ever have known

3 He advanced Daniel to the highest post of honour, loaded him with gifts, made him governor of Babylon the metropolis of the empire, placed him at the head of all the wise men, and kept him in his court, probably as his prime minister Nor were his companions forgotten, but, at his request, they were raised to the dignity of chief rulers in the province of Babylon *Note*, (1) They, whom the providence of God advances, should not forget their old friends (2) It is a supreme blessing and happiness for any nation, when men of eminent abilities, joined with distinguished piety, are put in trust with the administration of affairs

CHAP III

High places are slippery places, and kings favours a precarious possession Those who were lately in the highest honour are here fallen into the deepest disgrace, and yet, in the issue, good is brought out of the evil, God more highly glorified, and they more eminently distinguished hereby 1 Nebuchadnezzar erects and dedicates a golden image, requiring all his subjects to fall down and worship it, which is generally complied with, ver 1—7 *2 Information is given against the Jewish princes for refusing to worship it,* ver 8—12 *3 They constantly persist in their refusal, notwithstanding the king's menaces,* ver 13—18 *4 They are cast into the fiery furnace for their refusal,* ver 19—23 *5 They are miraculously preserved,* ver 24—27 *6 The king gives honour to God thereupon, and shews favour to those faithful witnesses,* ver 28, 29, 30 *To this story the Apostle alludes,* Heb xi 34

1 NEbuchadnezzar the king made [a] an image of
gold, whose height *was* threescore cubits, *and*
the breadth thereof six cubits he set it up in the plain
of Dura, in the province of Babylon 2 Then Nebu-
chadnezzar the king sent to gather together the princes,
the governors, and the captains, the judges, the trea-
surers, the counsellers, the sheriffs, and all the rulers of
the provinces, to come to the dedication of the image
which Nebuchadnezzar the king had set up 3 [b] Then
the princes, the governors, and captains, the judges, the
treasurers, the counsellers, the sheriffs, and all the rulers
of the provinces were gathered together unto the dedi-
cation of the image that Nebuchadnezzar the king had
set up. and they stood before the image that Nebuchad-
nezzar had set up. 4 Then an herald cried aloud, to
you it is commanded, [d] O people, nations, and lan-
guages, 5 *That* at what time ye hear the sound of the

a Chap ii 31 b Prov i c Chap iv 1 & vi 25

cornet,

Before Christ 587

cornet, flute, harp, sackbut, psaltery, † dulcimer, and
all kinds of music, ye fall down and worship the golden
image that Nebuchadnezzar the king hath set up 6.
And [e] whoso falleth not down and worshippeth, shall
[f] the same hour be [g] cast into the midst of a burning fiery
furnace 7 Therefore at that time, when all the people
heard the sound of the cornet, flute, harp, sackbut, psal-
tery, and all kinds of music, all the people, the nations,
and the languages, fell down *and* worshipped the golden
image that Nebuchadnezzar the king had set up

† Chald Symphony. e Rev xiii 15. f Rom iii. g Jer xxix 22.

v 1—7 The king had lately made a noble confession of the glory of Daniel's God, but the conviction is soon forgotten, and his attachment to idolatry prevail and, as we too often see the dog return to his vomit again,

1 He erects a golden image of immense size, thirty yards high or upwards At what time, or on what occasion, this was done, is not said probably not long after the events recorded in the former chapter, and perhaps, as some have suggested, in order to clear himself from the imputation of Judaism, which, on the advancement of Daniel and his companions, might have been whispered by the envious courtiers Though I rather incline to think he intended it as an image of himself, and in the pride of his heart affecting divine honours, would establish this impious worship whilst he was alive, in order the better to perpetuate it when he should be dead

2 A general summons is sent to all the magistrates, governors, and officers, civil, military, and religious, throughout this vast empire, to attend the dedication of this image, who instantly assembled, ready to obey the king's injunction

3 A proclamation is made to all the vast assembly of the king's pleasure, that the moment they heard the burst of instruments of musick collected on that occasion, to celebrate the praises of their deity, they should unanimously prostrate themselves before him, on penalty, in case of refusal, of being cast into a burning fiery furnace Thus hath the Devil prepared every engine to seduce or compel the sinner into his service, both the soft blandishments of sense to allure, and fearful punishments threatened to extort a compliance

4 All testified a ready submission No sooner was the signal given than the adoring assembly is prostrate on the plain When it is dangerous to be singular, and pleasure invites, few will hesitate about the consequences of yielding to the temptation

8 ¶ Wherefore at that time certain Chaldeans came
near and accused the Jews 9 They spake and said to
the king Nebuchadnezzar, [h] O king, live for ever. 10
Thou, O king, hast made a decree, that every man that
shall hear the sound of the cornet, flute, harp, sackbut,
psaltery, and dulcimer, and all kinds of music, shall fall
down and worship the golden image 11 And whoso
falleth not down and worshippeth, *that* he should be cast
into the midst of a burning fiery furnace 12 [i] There
are certain Jews whom thou hast set over the affairs of the
province of Babylon, Shadrach, Meshach, and Abed-
nego these men, O king, ‖ have not regarded thee,
they serve not thy gods, nor worship the golden image
which thou hast set up 13 ¶ Then Nebuchadnezzar
in *his* rage and fury commanded to bring Shadrach,
Meshach, and Abed-nego then [k] they brought these
men before the king. 14 Nebuchadnezzar spake and
said unto them, *Is it* † true, O Shadrach, Meshach, and
Abed nego? do not ye serve [l] my gods, nor worship
the golden image which I have set up? 15 Now if ye
be ready, that at what time ye hear the sound of the
cornet, flute, harp, sackbut, psaltery, and dulcimer,
and all kinds of music, ye fall down and worship the
image which I have made, *well* but if ye worship not,
ye shall be cast the same hour into the midst of a burning
fiery furnace, [m] and who *is* that God that shall deliver
you out of my hands? 16 Shadrach, Meshach, and
Abed nego answered and said to the king, O Nebu-
chadnezzar, [n] we *are* not careful to answer thee in [o] this
matter 17 If it be *so*, our God, whom we serve, is able
to deliver us from the burning fiery furnace, and he will
deliver *us* out of thine hand, O king 18 But if not,
be it known unto thee, O king, that [p] we will not serve
thy gods, nor worship the golden image which thou hast
set up

h Chap ii 4. v 10. & vi 6, 21. i Chap ii 49. ‖ Chald Have set no regard upon thee. k Ver 13. † Or of purpose. l Ver 1. Chap iv 4. m Ex v 2. 2 Kin xviii 35. n Pe xii 1. o Ex v 2. p Mat x 19. Luke xii 11. Acts iv 19. v 29.

v 8—18 We have here,

1 The malicious accusation brought against Shadrach, Meshach, and Abednego, for disobedience to the king's command They had attended at his summons but, instead of complying with such gross idolatry, resolved to endure any torments rather than commit so great a crime Many had, no doubt, envied their advancement, and gladly embraced this occasion to ruin them They therefore, with warmest wishes for his prosperity, address the king as his most faithful and loyal subjects, who had the honour of his government most at heart, remind him of the decree he had issued, and inform him of the disregard paid to it by these three men, a crime, they insinuate, aggravated by their ingratitude herein shewn for the favours they had received, in being raised from captives to the highest posts of the state, and which, should they be overlooked in this their contempt of the king's commands, would reflect dishonour on his government, be of the worst consequence to the kingdom, and have a bad influence on the people Daniel is not mentioned it should seem he was absent, or too high in the king's favour to be meddled with

2 The king, exasperated at the information, in a rage commands these men to be seized, and dragged into his presence With fury sparkling in his eyes, and terror in his voice, he demands of them in answer to the accusation, whether it was *true*, or, as the words may be rendered, *Is it of purpose* that you have done this, contumaciously, in defiance of my authority and contempt of my Gods? Once more he offers to prove them, if they will now comply to worship the golden image, all shall be well, if not, the furnace is ready, and they shall instantly be cast into the flames, from which he defies their God to save them, v 15 A dire alternative! to bow or burn How thankful ought we to be that we are not driven to this trying proof of our constancy, and that the fires, once kindled by popish idolaters in this land for the like purpose, are now extinguished

3 With unshaken fortitude and sedateness of mind, they mildly unite in their reply, not reproaching him as tyrannical, but meekly resigning themselves up to God in the way of duty, and with deliberate courage determined to abide by their resolution, whatever the consequence might be They seek no evasion, ask for no respite, for, where duty is plain, to deliberate is sinful, and to parley the prelude of compliance with the temptation *O Nebuchadnezzar, we are not careful to answer thee in this matter* Carnal reason indeed might have suggested a thousand palliatives to excuse the sin, but, when God's commandment was to express, these gracious souls could not hesitate a moment whether they should obey God or man They want no time to word their answer They cannot, dare not, do it Their lives were dear to them, but death, with all its terrors, cannot shake their steady souls they are content by faith to commit their lives to his care who gave them, and can preserve them, if he pleases, in the burning fiery furnace, or deliver them from it However, whether God was pleased miraculously to interpose for them or not, their purpose is fixed, they will not serve his gods nor worship his image *Note*, (1) In the way of duty we must never be *careful* about consequences (2) If we have true faith in God, it will cast out enslaving fear, and enable us in the day of trial to commit our all into his hand, confident that he will support us under our sufferings, or deliver us out of them (3) The way to be ready for the severest conflicts is daily to deny ourselves They who first refused to eat of the king's meat were now enabled to refuse to worship his god.

19 ¶ Then was Nebuchadnezzar [r] full of fury, and
the form of his visage was changed against Shadrach,
Meshach, and Abed-nego *therefore* he spake and [s] com-
manded that they should heat the furnace one seven
times more than it was wont to be heat 20 And he
commanded the † most mighty men that *were* in his
army, to bind Shadrach, Meshach, and Abed-nego, *and*
to cast *them* into the burning fiery furnace 21 Then
these men were bound in their ‡ coats, their hosen, and
their § hats, and their *other* garments, and were cast in-
to the midst of the burning fiery furnace 22 There-
fore because the king's commandment was urgent, and
the furnace exceeding hot, the ‖ flame of the fire [t] slew
those men that took up Shadrach, Meshach, and Abed-
nego 23 And these three men, Shadrach, Meshach,
and Abed nego, [u] fell down bound into the midst of the
burning fiery furnace 24 Then Nebuchadnezzar the
king was astonished, and rose up in haste, *and* spake and
said unto his ‖ counsellors, did not we cast three men
bound into the midst of the fire? They answered and
said unto the king, True, O king 25 He answered
and said, Lo, I see four men loose, walking in the midst
of the fire, and [x] they have no hurt, and the form of the
fourth is like [y] the son of God 26 ¶ Then Nebu-
chadnezzar came near to the mouth of the burning fiery
furnace, *and* spake and said, Shadrach, Meshach, and
Abed-nego, ye servants of the most high God, [z] come
forth, and come *hither* Then Shadrach, Meshach, and
Abed-nego came forth of the midst of the fire 27
And the princes, governors, and captains, and the king's

r Acts vii. 54. s Prov xxi. 24. † Chald Mighty of strength. ‡ Or mantles. § Or turbants. ‖ Or spark. t Prov xxi 18. u Ps xxxiv 19. Chap vi 16. ‖ Or governors. x Ps xci 3. Isa xliii 2. Heb xi 34. y Job i 6. Ps xxx v 7. Ver 28. Heb i 14. z Isa xxviii 16. & lii 12. 1 Pet i 7.

Before Christ 587

counsellors, being gathered together, saw [a] these men, [b] upon whose bodies the fire had no power, [c] nor was an hair of their head singed, neither were their coats changed, nor the smell of fire had passed on them.

[a] Isa xxvi 21 [b] Heb xi 34 [c] Ma x 30

v 19—27 An answer so firm, and yet withal so sedate, might have been expected to have wrought some relentings on the tyrant's mind, especially after the confessions himself had made of the glory of that God to whom they so faithfully adhered but we see it was quite otherwise

1 The monarch, exasperated, with fury in his looks, like a fiend of darkness, as if the furnace should be the emblem of the rage with which his bosom burned, commanded it to be heated seven times hotter than usual, which, if his passion would have admitted of deliberation, he must have seen would be a favour, instead of an aggravation of the punishment, and serve but the sooner to dispatch these martyrs for the truth but God over-ruled the tyrant's rage to make his own glory more illustrious in their deliverance In haste they are hurried to the flames, caught up, as they stood, in their cloaths, bound by the mightiest men of Nebuchadnezzar's army, and instantly cast into the fiery furnace, which, being so intensely heated, and the urgency of the king's command hurrying the men who bore them too near the mouth, the flame instantly slew them A righteous judgment, it should seem, upon them who were the ready instruments of this tyrant's cruelty, and probably the very persons who had lodged the accusation against these children of the Most High *Note*, (1) Could men see their own countenances, when rage foams in their lips and flashes from their eyes, they would startle at themselves as devils in a human form (2) Terrible was this furnace we cannot look into it without horror yet here a moment would end the martyrs sufferings but there is a fiercer fire kindled for sinners in hell, that tortures eternally, where death brings no relief, but the smoak of the torment ascendeth for ever and ever, and they have no rest day nor night (3) Persecutors of God's people may expect He will avenge their wrongs

2 God is pleased astonishingly to interpose for the rescue of his faithful servants Struck with terror and astonishment at the death of his mighty warriors, the king hastily arose, and how great his surprize, when, in the midst of that furnace where the objects of his rage had fallen bound, he beholds four persons loose, walking unhurt in the midst of the flames! He calls his counsellors, asks them concerning the order for the execution of these men, and they declare it was punctually executed He looks attentively on the sight three of the persons are well known to him, the fourth he conceived to be like some heavenly messenger, a *son of God*, either one of the angelic host, *or*, which he might have heard from Daniel, that *uncreated* angel of the covenant the Lord Christ, who had of old so often appeared to his people in a human form Approaching then the mouth of the furnace, with high respect he now addresses those servants *of the most high God*, whom he had treated so cruelly, and invites them by name to come forth nor did they delay to obey him, and, to the astonishment of all those princes and governours who surrounded the king, walked out of the midst of the fire, with not a hair singed, *nor so much as the smell of fire* issuing from them or their garments *Note*, (1) The afflictions into which God's people are cast resemble this furnace far from being able to hurt them, they only consume *the cords of corruption* which fettered them, and set them more at liberty to walk with God and the presence of Jesus in the midst of them not only prevents their trials from being painful, but enables them to count them all joy (2) They who are enabled confidently to trust in God often experience wonderful deliverances (3) God will make those proud men, who have persecuted his people, bow at their feet and know that he hath loved them (4) Every redeemed sinner comes into the presence of the eternal King, as these three worthies, *a brand plucked out of the burning*

28 *Then* Nebuchadnezzar spake, and said, Blessed *be*
the God of Shadrach, Meshach, and Abed-nego, who
hath sent his angel, and [d] delivered his servants that
trusted in him, and have changed the king's word, and
[e] yielded their bodies, [f] that they might not serve nor
worship any god, except their own God 29 [g] Therefore
I make a decree, That every people, nation, and
language, which speak [h] any thing amiss against the
God of Shadrach, Meshach, and Abednego, shall be
[i] cut in pieces, and their houses shall be made a dunghill,
[k] because there is no other god that can deliver after this
sort 30 Then the king promoted Shadrach, Meshach,
and Abed-nego, in the province of Babylon

[d] … [e] … [f] … [g] Chap iv … Ch … [h] … Chald … [i] Chald … made pieces Chap ii 5 [k] Chap vi 27

v 28—30 Struck with deep conviction by what he had beheld,

1 This mighty monarch adores the power and grace of that glorious God, whose wondrous interposition appeared in the deliverance of these his faithful servants. It now was evident, that no other god could deliver as he had done, and that his care and kindness never deserted those who steadily adhered to him in the hour of trial Thus can God change the voice even of persecutors, and learn blasphemers to bless and praise

Before Christ 587

2 He commends the courage and constancy of these three worthies, that dared contradict a king armed with fury, and, with a noble contempt of life, resolved to cleave to their own God, in the face of a fiery furnace, committing themselves with unshaken confidence into his hands *Note*, (1) A steady adherence to the cause of God and truth will often extort approbation even from enemies, whilst they who meanly desert their principles will only render themselves despicable even in the eyes of those who seduced them (2) When sin or death must be the alternative, we may emphatically say *to die is gain* (3) They who are enabled to trust God, will assuredly prove true to him

3 He issues an edict, forbidding, on the severest penalties, any of his subjects to speak *any thing amiss of the God of Shadrach, Meshach, and Abednego* As the Chaldeans had taken the Jews captives, they probably thought and spoke contemptuously and blasphemously of their God, which must have grieved exceedingly the faithful in Babylon but now, though they are not converts to his worship, they are taught to think highly of his glory, since, by the confession of their king, none of their gods, not even their admired Bel, could deliver after this manner *Note*, It is a mercy when the lips of adversaries are sealed up with conviction, though their hearts may be as far as ever from true conversion

4 He highly promoted these three men in the province of Babylon so that they received a present reward of their fidelity For sometimes God gives in this world, to those who dare hazard all for his sake, *an hundred fold, and in the world to come life everlasting*

CHAP IV.

The penman of this chapter is Nebuchadnezzar himself, but Daniel, a prophet by inspiration, inserts it in his history, and so it is become a part of sacred writ, and a very observable part Here is, 1 The preface to his narrative, wherein he acknowledges God's dominion over him, ver 1, 2, 3 2 The narrative itself, wherein he relates, (1) His dream, which puzzled the magicians, ver 1—18 (2) The interpretation of it by Daniel, who shewed him that it prognosticated his own fall, and therefore advised him to repent, ver. 19—27 (3) The accomplishment of it in his running stark mad for seven years, and then recovering the use of his reason again, ver 28—36 (4) The conclusion of the narrative, with an humble acknowledgment and adoration of God as Lord of all, ver 37 This was extorted from him by the over-ruling power of that God who hath all men's hearts in his hand, and stands upon record a lasting proof of God's supremacy, a monument of his glory, a trophy of his victory, and a warning to all not to think of prospering, while they lift up or harden their hearts against God

1 NEbuchadnezzar the king, [a] unto all people, nations,
and languages, that dwell in all the earth,
Peace be multiplied unto you 2 ¶ I thought it good
to shew the signs and wonders [b] that the high God hath
wrought toward me 3 [c] How great *are* his signs! and
how mighty *are* his wonders! his kingdom *is* [d] an everlasting
kingdom, and his dominion *is* from generation to
generation

[a] Chap iii 4 & vi 25 ¶ Chald It was seemly before me. [b] Chap iii 26. [c] Chap vi 27 Rom xi 33 [d] Ver 34 Chap ii 44 & vi 26

v 1—3 The introduction to this edict begins not with pompous titles, as was the usual stile of eastern monarchs, but with that simplicity and humility which afflictions had taught the royal penman, *Nebuchadnezzar the king*

It is directed to *all people, &c that dwell on the earth*, who, whilst he published his own shame, might admire and adore the greatness and the grace of God herein displayed And he adds his cordial salutation, *Peace be multiplied unto you*

The design of the writing is to acquaint them with the signs and wonders God had wrought towards him The world in general had heard, no doubt, of the strange event which had befallen him, his dream, his madness, and recovery here he gives them an account of it from his own pen, content to bear his reproach, so that God may be glorified thereby *Note*, What God hath done *against* us as the effect of our sins, as well as what he hath done *for* us in mercy, should be mentioned to his glory, and for our own humiliation

In the contemplation of what had passed, he breaks forth into admiration of God's wondrous works, *How great are his signs! and how mighty are his wonders!* the more he reviewed the scene, the more he was lost in amaze, convinced by fullest experience, his pride is mortified, he feels himself a worm, the creature of a day, he foresees his own monarchy hastening to ruin, but he beholds a kingdom about to be erected, which should be eternal, and humbly acknowledges God's incontestable right to the universal sovereignty and everlasting dominion

Before Christ 570.

4 I Nebuchadnezzar was at rest in mine house, [e] and
flourishing in my palace 5 I saw a dream which
made me afraid, and the thoughts upon my bed, and
the visions of my head [f] troubled me 6 Therefore
made I a decree to bring in all the wise-*men* of Babylon
before me, that they might make known unto me the in-
terpretation of the dream 7 Then came in the magi-
cians, the astrologers, the Chaldeans, and the sooth-
sayers and I told the dream before them, [g] but they
did not make known unto me the interpretation thereof
8 ¶ But at the last Daniel came in before me ([h] whose
name *was* Belteshazzar, according to the name of my
God, [i] and in whom *is* the spirit of the holy gods) and
before him I told the dream, *saying*, 9 O Belteshazzar,
[k] master of the magicians, because I know that the spirit
of the holy gods *is* in thee, and no secret troubleth thee,
tell me the visions of my dream that I have seen, and
the interpretation thereof 10 Thus *were* the visions of
mine head in my bed, I saw, and behold, a tree in the
midst of the earth, and the height thereof [m] *was* great 11
The tree grew, and was strong, and [n] the height thereof
reached unto heaven, and the sight thereof to the end of
all the earth 12 The leaves thereof *were* fair, and the
fruit thereof much, and in it *was* meat for all [o] the
beasts of the field had shadow under it, and the fowls
of the heaven dwelt in the boughs thereof, and all flesh
was fed of it 13 I saw in the visions of my head upon
my bed, and behold, [p] a watcher, and [q] an holy one
came down from heaven 14 He cried † aloud, and
said thus, Hew down the tree, and cut off his branches,
shake off his leaves, and scatter his fruit, let the beasts
[r] get away from under it, and the fowls from his bran-
ches 15 Nevertheless, leave the stump of his roots in
the earth, even with a band of iron and brass, in the
tender grass of the field, and let it be wet with the dew
of heaven, and let his portion *be* with the beasts in the
grass of the earth 16 Let his heart be changed from
man's, and let a beast's heart be given unto him, and
let seven [s] times pass over him 17 This matter *is* [t] by
the decree of the watchers, and the demand by the word
of the holy ones [u] to the intent that the living may
know, that [x] the most High ruleth in the kingdom of
men, and giveth it to whomsoever he will, and setteth
up over it [y] the basest of men 18 This dream I king
Nebuchadnezzar have seen now thou, O Belteshazzar,
declare the interpretation thereof, forasmuch as all the
wise *men* of my kingdom are not able to make known unto
me the interpretation but thou art able, for the spirit
of the holy gods *is* in thee 19 ¶ Then Daniel (whose
name *was* Belteshazzar) [a] was astonished for one hour,
and his thoughts [b] troubled him the king spake, and
said, Belteshazzar, let not the dream, or the interpreta-
tion thereof trouble thee Belteshazzar answered and
said, My lord, [c] the dream *be* to them that hate thee,
and the interpretation thereof to thine enemies 20 [d]
The tree that thou sawest, which grew, and was strong,
whose height reached unto the heaven, and the sight
thereof to all the earth, 21 Whose leaves *were* fair,
and the fruit thereof much, and in it *was* meat for all,
under which the beasts of the field dwelt, and upon
whose branches the fowls of the heaven had their habi-
tation 22 [e] It *is* thou, O king, that art grown, and
become strong for thy greatness is grown, and reacheth
unto heaven, and thy dominion to the end of the earth
23 And whereas [f] the king saw a watcher, and an holy
one coming down from heaven, and saying, Hew the
tree down, and destroy it, yet leave the stump of the
roots thereof in the earth, even with a band of iron and
brass in the tender grass of the field, and let it be wet
with the dew of heaven, and [g] *let* his portion *be* with the
beasts of the field, till seven times pass over him, 24
This *is* the interpretation, O king, and this *is* the decree
of the most High, which is come upon my lord the
king 25 That they shall [h] drive thee from men, and
thy dwelling shall be with the beasts of the field, and
they shall make thee [i] to eat grass as oxen, and they shall
wet thee with the dew of heaven, and seven times shall
pass over thee, till [k] thou know that the most High
ruleth in the kingdom of men, and [l] giveth it to whom-
soever he will 26 And whereas they commanded to
leave the stump of the tree-roots, thy kingdom shall be
sure unto thee, after that thou shalt have known that [m]
the heavens do rule 27 Wherefore, O king, let my
counsel be acceptable unto thee, and break off thy sins
by righteousness, and thine iniquities by shewing mercy
to the poor, [n] if it may be ‡ a lengthening of thy tran-
quillity

e Job xx 5. f Chap i 1. g Chap ii 4 Isa xliv 25. h Chap i 7. i Isa lxiii 11 Chap. ii 11 &c. k Chap. ii 48. & v 11. m Ezek. xxxi 3 Ps xxxvii 35. n Chap ii 37. o Matt xiii 32. p Ezek xxxi 6. q Psal ciii 20. r Ver. 17 23. s Chap viii 13. Jude 14. † Chald With might. t Ezek xxxi 12 &c. u Chap xi 13. & xii 7. x 1 Kings xxi 10. y Psal ix 16. Chap. v 21. a Psal lxxxvii 8. b Ver. 7. a Job xviii 20. b Jer iv 19. c Jer xxx 7. d Ver 10, &c. e 2 Sam xii 7. Chap ii 38. f Ver 17. g Chap v 21. h Chap v 21, &c. i Psal cvi 20. k Psal lxxxiii 18. l Jer xxvii 5. m Matt xxi 25 Luke xv 18, 21. n 1 Kings xxi 29 Psal xli &c. Isa lviii 7 &c. ‡ Or, an healing of thine error.

v 4—27 Returned victorious from his wars, a conquered world at his feet, the mighty Nebuchadnezzar after all his toils sets himself down to rest in his palace, *flourishing* in health of body and vigour of mind, crowned with glory and affluence, and no enemy able to trouble his repose Then, when most he seemed secure, God's secret hand dashed all his joys, and one dream filled him with terror and dismay so easily can God disturb the joyous sinner, and in a moment, even in the midst of his worldly comforts, make him feel the beginning of sorrows

1 He summoned his magicians and astrologers to attend repeated his dream, and demanded the interpretation But though they had boasted, *chap* ii 4, 7 that they wanted nothing more than to hear it, in order to explain it, now their rules of art or magic failed them, and they are obliged to confess their ignorance

2 When none besides could give the king any satisfaction, at last Daniel appears, whether sent for expressly, or of his own accord coming in at this juncture, is not said He is called Belteshazzar, from Bel, the god of the Chaldeans, and the king, who had before experienced his superior wisdom, addresses him with high respect, as the *master of the magicians*, not as being of their number but excelling them in knowledge, or as appointed their president, *chap* ii 48 but that for which he most admired him was, that the *spirit of the holy gods* was in him either he speaks as a heathen, who believed a multitude of gods, or perhaps he might have learned from the Jews the knowledge of the Elohim, the three Persons in one Godhead, and concluded from what he had experienced before, that under the teaching of God's spirit, every secret could by him be easily interpreted

3 He declares to him the dream which troubled him He beheld a lofty and spreading tree, which reached to the heavens, and was visible to the ends of the earth, the *leaves*, or *branches* beautiful, and laden with fruit, affording shelter and food to all the beasts of the earth, and the fowls of heaven When lo! *a watcher, and an holy one* came down from heaven, and published aloud the decree of the most High, that the tree must be cut down, its branches broken, its fruit destroyed, and all the beasts and fowls are bid to depart from under it Yet is it not to be rooted up, but the stump must be left encircled with a band of iron, and this the holy messenger explains of a man, who should be degraded into a brute, exposed to the dew of heaven, and dwell among the beasts during seven years, and this is by the immutable *decree of the watchers, and the demand of the holy ones*, and the end purposed in this whole transaction is to magnify the most High, to make his universal power and sovereignty known, who at his pleasure can humble the greatest, and exalt the meanest of the sons of men Such was the dream, which since the magicians cannot interpret, he looks to Daniel to explain, confident that he is able to unfold the secret

4 Daniel, at his command, addresses himself to the task assigned him

(1) He appeared at first exceedingly affected with what he heard, *astonished for one hour*, ver 19 at the heavy judgment contained in the vision *Note*, The minister of God beholds, with deepest concern, the miseries impending over the heads of the wicked, who seem unconcerned and unaffected with any sense of their own danger

(2) He introduces with a most respectful compliment the unpleasing interpretation The king had observed his amazement, and bid him not fear to disclose the secret, v 19 desiring, however terrible, to know the truth and Daniel, not as a courtier, who meant to flatter, but as one who really wished the prosperity of his prince, intimates how desirous he was, if God so pleased, that the dire contents of this vision had rather respected the king's enemies than himself *Note*, When we are constrained to be the messengers of evil to sinners, we must do it in such a way as to evidence we have not desired the woeful day, and wish the evil averted

(3) He declares plainly the purport of the dream, [1] The tree represents this mighty monarch, *It is thou, O king*, whose conquests had spread on every side, whose growing greatness all admired, under whose government the nations enjoyed protection, and by him were rendered rich and flourishing Thus should the kings of the earth be the fathers of their people, protecting them from oppression, and seeking to promote their wealth and prosperity and they are great indeed who thus improve their divinely delegated power [2] His doom is read, which his pride had provoked, v 23—25 The watcher and the holy one coming down from heaven, is usually interpreted

of

Before Christ 570 of the holy angels, whose ministry God employs in executing the decrees of his providence, and who approve and applaud them as altogether righteous, v 17 or perhaps it may signify that *watcher* over his Israel, that *holy One*, the uncreated Angel of the covenant, to whom all judgment is committed, and who in the government of the world fulfills the eternal counsels of *the holy Ones*, the persons of the undivided Godhead, the *watchers* over their peculiar people

To vast prosperity was Nebuchadnezzar advanced, but the command is, *Hew down the tree*, and then his greatness and glory would all be laid in the dust, so vain and transitory is all human grandeur, which one blast of the breath of God's displeasure destroys in a moment Fallen from his high estate, and struck with madness, he shall be driven from the abode of men, and make his dwelling seven years with the beasts, himself a brute in human shape, and eating grass like the ox *Note*, Among the most deplorable of all judgments is madness, may we never by our pride, and the abuse of our reason, provoke God to deprive us of it!

The judgment is heavy, yet doth God in the midst of wrath remember mercy Though cut down, he is not utterly destroyed, though bound as a madman with a band of iron, the root remains, and recovery is not impossible God's design in the visitation, however severe, is gracious, even to humble his pride, and make him and all men know God's power, and own his sovereignty, who rules over all, and doth according to the counsel of his own will. And when it shall be thus made manifest that *the heavens do rule*, even the God whose throne is there, then shall his senses return, he shall again resume the reins of empire, and give to the most High the glory due unto his name

5 The prophet finishes his discourse with a word of faithful and seasonable advice He introduces it with great submission, and begs a kind reception from the king of what was meant purely for his good *Note*, We must court sinners to secure their own mercies His sins were the cause of the threatned judgments, these therefore he exhorts him without delay to forsake As his despotic power had probably been in many instances abused, to the purposes of injustice and oppression, he urges him to the practice of righteousness, and shewing mercy to the poor, many of whom groaned probably under captive bonds, and cried for deliverance And this he presses as a means, at least, of lengthening his tranquility, though it might not be able to avert the threatned judgment *Note*, Without repentance and amendment, there can be no hope of pardon and salvation

569 28. ¶ All *this* came upon the king Nebuchadnezzar
29 At the end of twelve months he walked in the pa-
o Prov xvi 18 lace of the kingdom of Babylon 30 The king o spake
p Gen x 10 and said, Is not this great Babylon that p I have built for
the house of the kingdom, by the might of my power,
q Hab i 16 q and for the honour of my majesty? 31 r While the
r Luke xii 20 word *was* in the king's mouth, there fell a voice from
s 1 Sam xiii 13 heaven, *saying*, O king Nebuchadnezzar, s to thee it is
spoken, The kingdom is departed from thee 32 And
t Ver 25 t they shall drive thee from men, and thy dwelling *shall*
be with the beasts of the field: they shall make thee to
eat grass as oxen, and seven times shall pass over thee,
until thou know that the most High ruleth in the kingdom of men, and giveth it to whomsoever he will
u Job xx 5 33 u The same hour was the thing fulfilled upon Nebuchadnezzar, and he was driven from men, and did
eat grass as oxen, and his body was wet with the dew
of heaven, till his hairs were grown like eagles *feathers*,
and his nails like birds *claws*

v 28—33 We find it was not long ere the divine decree took place, and behold here its exact accomplishment

1 One year God's patience waited, for he is long suffering, even towards the most obstinate offenders, but still the monarch's heart remained unchanged Walking on the roof of his palace, or on the terrace of those amazing hanging gardens, which overlooked the city, his eyes beheld with conscious pride the glorious prospect full in his view, and whilst his bosom glowed with self-importance, his tongue betrayed the language of his heart The king spake and said, either to his nobles around him, or some foreigners whom he took with him, to survey the vast metropolis, or in a secret whisper of self-applause, *Is not this great Babylon that I have built?* &c He ascribes the whole to his own power and might, and forgets the God who had given him the ability No marvel therefore, that the end he proposed was neither God's glory, nor his people's good, but *the honour of his own majesty* Such self-seekers are all proud men let us beware of contemplating with self-complacency any thing we have done, lest God behold the robbery of his glory, and smite us for our pride, as he did Nebuchadnezzar

2 Instantly as the words dropped from his lips, a voice from heaven pronounced his doom, that he is deposed from his dignity, and the prophecy before spoken, immediately to take place, Before Christ 569
and this is no sooner spoken than done On a sudden his reason is lost, degenerated into a brute in human shape, he is driven from his palace, and herds with the beasts of the forest, feeding with them upon grass as the ox, his body exposed to all the inclemencies of the sky, his hair grown like eagles feathers, and his nails like birds claws *Note*, God can soon humble the proudest, and make those who were the envy and admiration of mankind, despicable as the worm that crawls.

34 And x at the end of the days, I Nebuchadnezzar 562 x Ver 16.
y lift up mine eyes unto heaven, and mine understanding y Ps xxv 1
returned unto me, and I blessed the most High, and I
praised and honoured him z that liveth for ever, whose z Chap xii 7 Rev iv 10.
dominion *is* a an everlasting dominion, and his kingdom
is from generation to generation 35 And b all the in- a Ps x 16 Chap ii 44 & vii 14 Mic iv 7 Luke i 33
habitants of the earth *are* reputed as nothing and he
doth according to his will in the army of heaven, and
among the inhabitants of the earth and none can stay b Isa xl 15, 17
his hand, or say unto him, c What dost thou? 36 At c Job ix 12 Isa xlv 9.
the same time my reason returned unto me, and for
the glory of my kingdom, mine honour d and bright- d Chap iv 30
ness returned unto me, and my counsellors and my
lords sought unto me, and I was established in my kingdom, and excellent majesty was added unto me 37
Now I Nebuchadnezzar praise and extol and honour the
King of heaven, all whose works e *are* truth, and his e Rev xv 3.
ways judgment, and f those that walk in pride he is able f Exod xviii 11 Chap v 20.
to abase.

v 34—37 The prophecy of his humiliation we have seen fulfilled, and may expect in its season to hear of his restoration

1 At the end of the seven years he *lifted up* his *eyes to heaven*, not merely as a man rescued from the herd of brutes, but as a humbled sinner looking to a pardoning God The return of reason itself had not been a blessing, if grace had not opened the eyes of his mind to a discovery of his provocations of the justice of his sufferings, and the glory of the divine majesty. To bring him to this, was the purpose of God's heavy hand upon him, and then even his madness was his mercy he had never truly *come to himself* if he had not been thus *beside himself* Thus God sometimes seems to work by contraries, and when, like the patriarch, we may think all *these things are against me*, they are then working together for our good

2 The first exercise of his enlightned mind is adoration *I blessed the most High*, &c *Note*, They who live in the habitual neglect of prayer and praise, however wise they may be reputed among men, act more madly than he that eateth straw like the ox He acknowledges now the eternal dominion and sovereignty of God, who for ever lives, for ever reigns, for his kingdom is from everlasting to everlasting Before him all nations are as nothing, and the greatest of men, in comparison with him, insignificant as the drop of the bucket, or the dust of the balance His kingdom is universal; angels as well as men acknowledge him their Lord, the creatures of his pleasure, and wholly subject to his controul His power is irresistible, his arm omnipotent, whatever he wills is done, nor dare any arraign his proceedings, or challenge an account of any of his matters Not that he ever doth, or can do wrong, *his ways are judgment*, perfectly righteous and wise, and *his works truth*, fulfilling with nicest exactness whatever he hath spoken in his word, *and those who walk in pride he is able to abase*, an eminent instance of which Nebuchadnezzar acknowledged himself to be, and wishes other proud men to be warned by his example, *whilst he extols and praises the King of heaven*, who in wrath had still remembered mercy

3 With his returning reason his majestic countenance returned He appeared in his former brightness and glory, his lords received him again as their sovereign, probably acquainted by Daniel with the dream, and the expected recovery of their king Once more he resumed the reins of government, and under the divine benediction *excellent majesty was added* unto him, he grew more respected than ever and his latter end was greater than his beginning He did not however long survive this wondrous change, but, I would hope, continued in the same blessed sentiments, and died a monument of sovereign grace

CHAP V

The destruction of the kingdom of Babylon had been long and often foretold when it was at a distance In this chapter we have it accomplished, and a prediction of it the very same night that it happened We must know, that about two years before this Cyrus king of Persia, a growing monarch, came against Babylon with a great army, Belshazzar the reigning monarch met him, fought him, and was routed by him in a pitched battle He and his scattered

Before Christ 563

tered forces retired into the city, where Cyrus besieged him. They were very secure, because the river Euphrates was their bulwark, and they had twenty years provisions in the city, but in the second year of the siege he took it, as is here related. We have in this chapter, 1. The riotous, idolatrous, and sacrilegious feast which Belshazzar made, ver. 1—4. 2. The alarm given him in the midst of his jollity by a hand writing on the wall, which none of his wise men could read or tell him the meaning of, ver. 5—9. 3. The interpretation of the mystical character, by Daniel, ver. 10—28. 4. The immediate accomplishment of the interpretation in the slaying of the king and seizing of the kingdom, ver. 30, 31.

529 1 BELSHAZZAR the king made a great feast to a thousand of his lords, and drank wine before the thousand. 2 Belshazzar, whiles he tasted the wine, commanded to bring the golden and silver vessels, which his † father Nebuchadnezzar had ‡ taken out of the temple which *was* in Jerusalem, that the king and his princes, his wives and his concubines might drink therein. 3 Then they brought the golden vessels that were taken out of the temple of the house of GOD, which *was* at Jerusalem, and the king and his princes, his wives and his concubines drank in them. 4 They drank wine, and praised the gods of gold, and of silver, of brass, of iron, of wood, and of stone. 5 ¶ In the same hour came forth fingers of a man's hand, and wrote over against the candlestick upon the plaister of the wall of the king's palace, and the king saw the part of the hand that wrote. 6 Then the king's ‖ countenance was changed, and his thoughts troubled him, so that the § joints of his loins were loosed, and his knees smote one against another. 7 The king cried † aloud to bring in the astrologers, the Chaldeans, and the soothsayers. *And* the king spake and said to the wise *men* of Babylon, Whosoever shall read this writing, and shew me the interpretation thereof, shall be clothed with ‡ scarlet, and *have* a chain of gold about his neck, and shall be the third ruler in the kingdom. 8 Then came in all the king's wise-*men*, but they could not read the writing, nor make known to the king the interpretation thereof. 9 Then was king Belshazzar greatly troubled, and his countenance was changed in him, and his lords were astonished.

v. 1—9 Belshazzar, the subject of this chapter, was the grandson of Nebuchadnezzar, *Jer.* xxvii. 7. whose monarchy, according to the term fixed in the prophetic word, was now hasting to ruin. We have here,

1. An account of his impiety and profaneness. Unaffected with the perilousness of his case, though a victorious army was at the gates of Babylon, on some returning solemnity in honour of his gods, or to celebrate his birth-day, he invites all the great men of his court, or officers of his army, to partake of a grand entertainment he had provided, and graciously condescends to make one at the festal board, and *drank wine before them*. In the midst of mirth and jollity, the sacred vessels of the temple occurred to him, and in a frolick, or to express his contempt of Israel's God, and to do honour to his own, he commands them to be brought, and all present drunk out of them, and praised their idol gods, who had given them these spoils of their enemies: probably the report of the deliverance of Israel from Babylon might now be propagated, the seventy years being just at an end, some say that very night they expired, and this might be done in defiance of Israel's God, and in ridicule of the prophetic word. *Note*, (1.) Drunkenness is the door to every abomination. (2.) They are hastening apace to ruin, who can make a jest of things sacred. (3.) The joyous sinner in the midst of his carousals is a most pitiable object, dancing and singing on the brink of the gulph where the worm dieth not, and the fire is not quenched.

2. A sudden event terribly interrupts their impious joys. In the midst of their carousal, a hand appears over against the candlestick, and writes upon the plaister of the wall. Struck with terror at the sight, Belshazzar's countenance changed, his pallid cheeks, his quivering lips, his trembling knees, his [illegible] frame, bespoke the horror of his soul, and conscious guilt [illegible] dire forebodings of the dreadful doom hereby portended. In haste he calls aloud to bring the wisest of his Chaldean sages, and promises the highest reward to the man who can read and interpret the writing, but in vain; for though the words were *Chaldee*, the manner or form of writing was such as utterly baffled their skill, or by a divine judgment, to make the skill of Daniel more illustrious, God confounded their understandings, and this increased the more the anxiety of the monarch, and filled his lords with consternation and astonishment. *Note*, (1.) The most daring sinner God can reach, one touch of his hand, yea, *their own thoughts* let loose upon them, are enough to make them a terror to themselves. (2.) Shall an unknown writing thus trouble the conscience of Belshazzar, and shall not all the curses so plainly written in the book of God, affect the careless and impenitent?

Before Christ 519

10 ¶ *Now* the queen, by reason of the words of the king and his lords, came into the banquet-house, *and* the queen spake and said, O king, live for ever: let not thy thoughts trouble thee, nor let thy countenance be changed. 11 There is a man in thy kingdom, in whom *is* the spirit of the holy gods, and in the days of thy † father, light and understanding and wisdom like the wisdom of the gods, was found in him, whom the king Nebuchadnezzar thy father, the king, *I say*, thy father made master of the magicians, astrologers, Chaldeans, *and* soothsayers, 12 Forasmuch as an excellent spirit, and knowledge, and understanding, interpreting of dreams, and shewing of hard sentences, and dissolving of ‡ doubts were found in the same Daniel, whom the king named Belteshazzar: now let Daniel be called, and he will shew the interpretation. 13 Then was Daniel brought in before the king, *and* the king spake and said unto Daniel, *Art* thou that Daniel, which *art* of the children of the captivity of Judah, whom the king my father brought out of Jewry? 14 I have even heard of thee, that the spirit of the gods *is* in thee, and *that* light, and understanding, and excellent wisdom is found in thee. 15 And now the wise *men*, the astrologers have been brought in before me, that they should read this writing, and make known unto me the interpretation thereof: but they could not shew the interpretation of the thing. 16 And I have heard of thee, that thou canst ‖ make interpretations, and dissolve doubts: now if thou canst read the writing, and make known to me the interpretation thereof, thou shalt be clothed with scarlet, and *have* a chain of gold about thy neck, and shalt be the third ruler in the kingdom. 17 ¶ Then Daniel answered and said before the king, Let thy gifts be to thyself, and give thy rewards to another, yet I will read the writing unto the king, and make known to him the interpretation. 18 O thou king, the most high GOD gave Nebuchadnezzar thy father a kingdom, and majesty, and glory, and honour. 19 And for the majesty that he gave him, all people, nations, and languages, trembled and feared before him: whom he would he slew, and whom he would he kept alive, and whom he would he set up, and whom he would he put down. 20 But when his heart was lifted up, and his mind hardened § in pride, he was † deposed from his kingly throne, and they took his glory from him. 21 And he was driven from the sons of men, and his heart was made like the beasts, and his dwelling *was* with the wild asses: they fed him with grass like oxen, and his body was wet with the dew of heaven, till he knew that the most high GOD ruled in the kingdom of men, and *that* he appointeth over it whomsoever he will. 22 And thou his son, O Belshazzar, hast not humbled thine heart, though thou knewest all this: 23 But hast lifted up thyself against the LORD of heaven, and they have brought the vessels of his house before thee, and thou and thy lords, thy wives and thy concubines have drunk wine in them, and thou hast praised the gods of silver and gold, of brass, iron, wood, and stone, which see not, nor hear, nor know: and the GOD in whose hand thy breath *is*, and whose *are* all thy ways, hast thou not glorified. 24 Then was the part of the hand sent from him, and this writing was written. 25 ¶ And this *is* the writing that was written, MENE, MENE, TEKEL, UPHARSIN. 26 This *is* the interpretation of the thing: MENE, God hath numbered thy kingdom, and finished it. 27 TEKEL, thou art weighed in the balances, and art found wanting. 28 PERES, thy kingdom is divided, and given to the Medes and Persians. 29 Then commanded Belshazzar, and they clothed Daniel with scarlet, and *put* a chain of gold about his neck, and made a proclamation concerning him, that he should be the third ruler in the kingdom.

v. 10—29 In this state of dismay and confusion we have

1. The advice of the queen, who had not been [illegible]

Before Christ 539.

the feast, but, on hearing what had passed, had come to the banqueting-house. She is supposed to be not the wife of Belshazzar, but of his father Evilmerodach, called by Herodotus Nitocris, and greatly famed for her prudence: though others think her to be Amytis, the grandmother of the king, and wife of Nebuchadnezzar. It appears she was well acquainted with the transactions of former time, and knew the abilities of Daniel, and therefore is bold to say, though the wise men of Babylon were at a stand, that the king need not fear but an interpreter could be found. Probably Daniel's interest had long since declined at court, and he seems now to have lived in obscurity among the rest of his captive countrymen. So ready often, in a new reign, are the best and most faithful of the ancient counsellors to be thrown by and neglected. But the high character the queen gives of this now forgotten sage could not but excite a desire to have him called. She speaks of him as something more than human, possessed of wisdom, approaching omniscience, and penetration so deep, that no secrets or difficulties whatever puzzled him, and by experience the king Nebuchadnezzar had proved him to be possessed of a spirit far excelling all the magicians and astrologers of his kingdom. In consequence of which, he had advanced him to be master of all the sages, and named him Belteshazzar, in honour of his god. The queen desires therefore he may be sent for, and doubts not but he will give the king full satisfaction.

2. Daniel is instantly summoned, and appears before the king, unknown to him by person, as appears by Belshazzar's question, *v.* 13. But having heard such high encomiums of his wisdom, he is desirous to try whether he can read and interpret the writing, of which the magicians confess their ignorance, and promises him the same rewards as he had offered to them, if he could clearly explain the matter: even that he should be arrayed in richest robes of honour, and promoted to the third place for dignity in his kingdom.

3. Daniel undertakes to read and interpret the writing, but prefaces his discourse with some striking remarks and admonitions.

(1.) The proffered gifts he nobly disdains, as the reward of his interpretation; he neither wanted nor sought them. At his age, advancement would be but a burden, and when the whole government was so quickly to be overturned, such honours were not worth acceptance. Yet he will freely satisfy the king, if that can be called satisfaction, which, instead of relieving his fears, must increase his distress. *Note,* A sense of the near approaching end of all things should make us sit loose to the trifles of this changing and perishing world.

(2.) He recounts God's dispensations towards his father, or, as is most commonly supposed, his grandfather, Nebuchadnezzar, it being not unusual in scripture to term a more remote ancestor father. By the providence and gift of the most high God, from whom all good things come, and to whose blessing all our prosperity ought ever to be ascribed, Nebuchadnezzar had acquired such dominion, honour, and authority, as perhaps no prince before had ever attained to: so irresistible his power, that none dared contend with him, and trembling at his feet, all nations bowed before him. His government despotic, his authority absolute, the liberty and property, the life or death of all his subjects hung on his breath; his will was law, his orders obeyed without remonstrance or hesitation: a dangerous power to be vested in the bosom of a fallen creature, a curse upon the land where such arbitrary monarchs rule. Abusing his authority, Nebuchadnezzar had acted with that tyranny and oppression which lawless power, directed by caprice, naturally produced; and hardened in pride, he not only behaved unjust to man, but insolent towards the most high, ascribing to his own prowess his successes, and affecting independence of every superior. For these things the God of heaven hurled him from his throne, and degraded him not merely to the lowest state of human meanness, but to a level with the brute creation, to be the companion of *wild asses,* ver. 21. justly depriving him of the reason he had abused, and for his savageness and oppression, sending him to dwell with the beasts he chose to imitate; till humbled in the dust, he was brought to acknowledge the government of the most High, and own himself the subject of his pleasure.

(3.) He arraigns Belshazzar for his crimes, aggravated by the neglect of all the warnings God had given him in his father's case. He knew all that had passed, yet nevertheless,

[1.] He *had not humbled his heart,* ver. 22. but continued impenitent in the same pride and rebellion against God. *Note,* It is an aggravation of children's sins, if instead of being admonished by their fathers' miseries, they persist to follow their destructive ways.

[2.] He had exceeded in impiety his ungodly sire. *Thou hast lifted up thyself against,* or *above the Lord of heaven,* with more daring blasphemy, defying his power and dishonouring his name, as if he were his superior, and shewing the contempt in which he held him, by his horrid profanation of the vessels of the temple, while he praised his idol gods, senseless as the vessels from which he poured out the libation to them.

[3.] *The God in whose hand thy breath is, and whose are all thy ways, hast thou not glorified,* a charge, before which who need not tremble! our breath is from him, it is momentarily preserved by him, our ways under his controul, every event at his disposal. To glorify him is the great end of our being, our duty, and should be our delight; but we have failed and gone astray every one in his own way, casting off his government, and negligent of his glory. The Lord humble us for this, that we may not meet Belshazzar's doom.

Before Christ 538.

4. Having thus proved his crimes, Daniel pronounces his doom, according to the tenor of the writing on the wall, the explication of which he had demanded. Then when his iniquity was at the height, at this impious feast, came this hand from God, and wrote these words, MENE MENE, TEKEL UPHARSIN. The words are Chaldee, and signify, *He hath numbered, he hath numbered, he hath weighed, and they divide;* the several particulars of which he explains.

MENE, *God hath numbered thy kingdom,* and *finished it;* the term of the monarchy is expiring, its ruin is near, and the word is repeated to shew its certainty.

TEKEL, *Thou art weighed in the balances, and found wanting;* God, who weighs in the balances of exact justice the actions and characters of men, pronounces him worthless and reprobate.

PERES, the singular of Pharsin, (*U* being the copulative) *And thy kingdom is divided, and given to the Medes and Persians;* such is the irreversible decree of the Almighty; and Belshazzar, convinced in his conscience that Daniel had spoken the truth, though so fearful the sentence, immediately confers on him the promised reward. Withering honours! the pageantry of an hour, and all this world's honours viewed in their true light, are no better.

The sinner and the hypocrite's doom is like Belshazzar's. At death their days are numbered; in judgment they will be weighed in the balance of God's holy law, and found wanting; and then be given up to the devil and his angels, to be tormented to eternity.

30 ¶ [h] In that night was Belshazzar the king of the Chaldeans slain. h Ver. 1, 2.
31 And [i] Darius the Median took the kingdom, *being* † about threescore and two years old. i Chap. ix. 1. † Chal. The son of, &c.

v. 30, 31. The writing is scarce sooner interpreted than verified. That very night the city was taken, and Belshazzar slain: taking advantage of this debauch of the king, history informs us, that Cyrus entered the city by the bed of the river, the waters of which he had cut off; and the guards being fast asleep, and overcome with wine, made no resistance; so that all the gates being opened, Gadates and Gobryas, two great men, who being ill used by Belshazzar, had revolted to Cyrus, went directly to the palace, and slew the king with all his attendants. Thus ended the Babylonish empire; and Darius the Mede, called also Cyaxares, the uncle of Cyrus, ascended the throne, the first king of the second monarchy. He was sixty-two years old, and consequently was born the year Jechoniah was carried captive, 2 *Kings* xxiv. 12. God so ordering, that at the very time his people were sent into Babylon, their deliverer should be provided. Cyrus reigned in conjunction with his uncle, though being the younger, he is not mentioned; and after two years succeeded him in the sole government of the empire, concerning whom so many prophecies had gone before, all which we find he most exactly fulfilled. Thus though God visit his people for their sin, he will not be wroth for ever; and in the darkest day of affliction there is still hope in the end.

CHAP. VI.

It is a very observable and improvable story that we have in this chapter, how Daniel, by faith, stopped the mouths of lions, *and so obtained a good report,* Heb. xi. 33. *The three children were cast into the fiery furnace for not committing a known sin, Daniel was cast into the lions den for not omitting a known duty, and God's miraculous delivering both them and him is left upon record for the encouragement of his servants in all ages, to be resolute and constant both in their abhorrence of that which is evil, and in their adherence to that which is good, whatever it cost them. In this chapter we have,* 1. *Daniel's preferment in the court of Darius,* ver. 1—3. 2. *The envy and malice of his enemies,* ver. 4, 5. 3. *The decree they obtained against prayer for thirty days,* ver. 6—9. 4. *Daniel's constancy in prayer notwithstanding,* ver. 10. 5. *Information given against him for it, and the casting of him into the den of lions,* ver. 11—17. 6. *His miraculous preservation and deliverance out of it,* ver. 18—23. 7. *The casting of his accusers into the den, and their destruction there,* ver. 24. 8. *The decree which Darius made upon this occasion in honour of the God of Daniel, and the prosperity of Daniel afterwards,* ver. 25—28.

1 IT pleased Darius to set [a] over the kingdom an hundred and twenty princes, which should be a Esth. i. 1.

Before Christ 538

over the whole kingdom, 2 And over these, three
presidents (of whom Daniel *was* first) that the princes
might give accounts unto them, and the king should
have no damage 3 Then this Daniel was preferred
above the presidents and princes, [b] because an excellent
spirit *was* in him, and the king thought to set him
over the whole realm 4 ¶ Then [c] the presidents and
princes sought to find occasion against Daniel concern-
ing the kingdom, [d] but they could find none occasion
nor fault forasmuch as he *was* faithful, [e] neither was
there any error or fault found in him 5 Then said
these men, We shall not find any occasion against this
Daniel, except we find *it* against him concerning [f] the
law of his God

[b] Chap. v 12. [c] Eccles. iv 4. [d] 1 Pet. ii 12. [e] 1 Sam. xviii 14. [f] Ezek. iii 8.

v 1—5 Daniel had been highly advanced by Belshazzar, and on a reverse of government he might have expected a reverse of station, but it happened quite otherwise

1 He is preferred to the first post in the kingdom by the new emperor Darius, who probably had heard of his predictions and uncommon wisdom, and was glad to have so great a man to employ under him In the new distribution of the empire into one hundred and twenty provinces, under the care of so many princes, three presidents were appointed to inspect the conduct of these governors, and their accounts of these Daniel was chief His excellent spirit was his commendation to Darius, and so well satisfied was he of his abilities and integrity, that he meditated his farther advancement, designing as viceroy to set him over the whole realm Daniel must now be very aged, it being above seventy years since he was carried captive to Babylon, but his natural force, it seems, was not abated, and his experience was increased It was a proof of the wisdom of Darius to make such a choice, and it was a noble testimony to the uprightness of the minister, that no *fault was to be found in him*, *v* 4 Happy the nation blessed with such wise princes, and upright ministers

2 His greatness naturally provoked the envy of the courtiers, who, though his merit stood confessed, could not bear to see a foreigner, a *Jew*, a captive, thus preferred before them Thus will superior excellence, however spotless the character, awaken the malignant passions of the corrupted heart They eyed him with malicious acuteness, and hoped, but hoped in vain, to find some flaw in his management, which might afford a handle for accusation Despairing at last of being able to attack him on account of his civil conduct, they can think of no method of ruining him, unless it be on account of his religion *Note*, (1) It is an honourable testimony when even enemies own our integrity, and, except concerning the law of our God, have no evil thing justly to say of us (2) The more the eyes of malignant observers are fixed upon us, the more careful should we be in the minutest particulars to walk circumspectly, and cut off occasion from those that desire occasion against us (3) Our fidelity to God will often expose us to the persecution of the world, but when we thus suffer, we need be neither afraid nor ashamed

6 Then these presidents and princes † assembled to-
gether to the king, and said thus unto him, [g] King Da-
rius, live for ever 7 [h] All the presidents of the king-
dom, the governors, and the princes, the counsellors,
and the captains, have consulted together to establish
a royal statute, and to make a firm decree, that who-
soever shall ask a petition of any god or man for thirty
days, save of thee, O king, he shall be cast into the
den of lions 8 Now, O king, establish the decree,
and sign the writing, that it be not changed, according
to the law of the Medes and Persians, [i] which † altereth
not 9 Wherefore [k] king Darius signed the writing
and the decree 10 ¶ Now when Daniel knew that
the writing was signed, he went into his house, and [l]
his windows being open in his chamber [m] toward Jerusa-
lem, he kneeled upon his knees [n] three times a day, [o]
and prayed, and gave thanks before his God, [p] as he did
aforetime

† Or came tumultuously. [g] Neh. ii 3. Ver. 21. Chap. ii 4. [i] Esth. viii 8. † Chald. passeth not. [k] Ps. cxviii 9. [l] Mat. x 32. [m] 1 Kings viii 47, 48. [n] Ps. lv 17. Acts ii 2. [o] Acts ii 1. [o] Phil. iv 6. [p] Rev. ii 13.

v 6—10 Since there was no probability of finding matter of accusation against Daniel, but on account of his religion, and no law then in being seems to have restrained him from worshipping God in his own way, they craftily contrive a new one to ensnare him

1 They make a solemn application to Darius for his approbation of a new edict, which seemed indeed to contain in it an uncommon respect for the king, but was really big with evil. They came in a body, and pretended it was the unanimous suffrage, after mature deliberation of *all the presidents*, &c though probably many of the princes excepted to it, and *all* the presidents were but two, for Daniel, their chief, certainly consented not to it But if the concurrence had been never so general, the matter of the request was utterly wrong, that *no man should ask a petition of God or man, save of the king, for thirty days*, on penalty of being cast into *the lions den* Had it only forbid religious worship for so long a time, it had been highly impious, but to extend the prohibition to all civil requests between man and man, must have been to the highest degree inconvenient, absurd, and unreasonable yet as it seemed to put such distinguished honour on the king, and set him in a sort even above the gods, this court to his pride blinded his reason, and he consents and seals the decree, then become unalterable by the law of the Medes and Persians *Note*, (1) The malicious care not what mischief is done, so their vile spirit be gratified, let dearest friends suffer, so the object of their enmity be but ruined (2) It is the unhappiness of kings, that they can hardly know the truth, and compassed with flatterers, often are accessary to evils they never meant (3) Pride is our weak side, when that is attacked by flattery, we had need double our guard

2 Daniel persisted in his stated practice of devotion Though he knew the decree was signed, and the penalty so fearful, he went as usual *to his house, and prayed and gave thanks unto his God upon his knees three times a day*, turning his face towards the temple, though in ruins, and hoping God would remember its desolations, 1 *Kings* viii 48, 49 nor did he seek concealment, his windows were open Whatever precautions or excuses cowardly fear and selfish prudence might have dictated, he dared not submit to any thing which might dishonour God, disgrace his profession, or discourage his people any suffering, or death itself in his eyes were preferable to but the appearance of unfaithfulness *Note*, (1) In time of danger to be ashamed of Christ, or afraid to suffer for him, is the sure way to be disowned by him in the day of his appearing (2) What lukewarm christians so carefully inculcate under the specious name of prudence, is for the most part base selfishness, and a treacherous betraying the cause of God and truth (3) A gracious soul cannot live a day without prayer and praise, and though he never kneels or sings to be seen or heard of men, he is never ashamed to be known to do so (4) Thrice a day Daniel prayed, notwithstanding all his occupations and engagements, can we then have a plea for a less frequent attendance on the throne of grace?

11 Then these men † assembled, and found Daniel
praying and making supplication before his God 12
Then they came near, and spake before the king, con-
cerning the king's decree, Hast thou not signed a de-
cree, that every man that shall ask *a petition* of any God
or man within thirty days, save of thee, O king, shall
be cast into the den of lions? The king answered and
said, The thing *is* true, according to the law of the
Medes and Persians, which altereth not 13 Then an-
swered they and said before the king, That Daniel [q]
which *is* of the children of the captivity of Judah, [r] re-
gardeth not thee, O king, nor the decree that thou hast
signed, but maketh his petition three times a day 14
Then the king when he heard *these* words, [s] was sore
displeased with himself, and set *his* heart on Daniel to
deliver him and he laboured till the going down of the
sun to deliver him 15 Then these men assembled unto
the king, and said unto the king, Know, O king, that
the law of the Medes and Persians *is*, that no decree nor
statute which the king establisheth may be changed
16 Then the king commanded, and they brought
Daniel, and cast *him* into the den of lions *now* the
king spake and said unto Daniel, Thy God whom thou
[t] servest continually, he will deliver thee 17 And [u] a
stone was brought and laid upon the mouth of the den,
and the king sealed it with his own signet, and with the
signet of his lords, that the purpose might not be
changed concerning Daniel

† Or came tumultuously. [q] Chap. i 6. [r] Chap. iii 12. [s] Mark vi 26. [t] Acts xxvii 23. [u] Lam. iii 53. Mat. xxvii 66.

v 11—17 The snare was so laid, that it could not but succeed Accordingly we have here,

1 Daniel discovered acting in disobedience to the law They knew probably his stated hours of devotion, and assembling tumultuously, as the word signifies, broke in upon him in the very act of prayer

2 Without delay an impeachment is laid against him before the king After having gained a recognition of the edict on which it was founded, they bring their accusation, and not content with the proof of the fact, they seek by the manner of their charge to exasperate the king against him They call Daniel *one of the captivity of Judah*, as if the despicable condition of his people, from among whom he had been preferred to such high honour, aggravated the crime of disobedience with ingratitude, and they intimate that he did this in proud contempt of the king's authority, *He regardeth not thee, O king, nor the*

de- cree

Before Christ 537

decree that thou hast signed, and thus is conscientious adherence to God in the way of duty still frequently branded as obstinacy and contempt of authority, but *we believe that thou shalt come to judge the world*

3 Too late the king perceived the fatal tendency of this impious edict, and the malicious intent of those who proposed it, and *sore displeased* at himself for what he had done, *set his heart to deliver Daniel* from the penalty he had incurred, and laboured all day by every means to persuade his accusers to drop the prosecution, but in vain His enemies insist the law must have its course, according to the fundamental maxim of their government, *v* 18 and, though with deep reluctance, Darius is compelled to order the execution of this venerable saint, this aged sage, this upright minister, for no real crime, but for doing that which was his highest honour, and worthy the greatest commendation To make sure work, that no escape should be practicable, a ponderous stone is laid on the den's mouth, and as if the king's signet thereon afforded not sufficient security, the lords added theirs also, to prevent all possibility of collusion Thus the precautions taken to secure the body of Jesus rendered his resurrection more undeniable and notorious, so easily can God take the wise and make ous in their own craftiness

4 The king encourages Daniel to trust in God *Thy God whom thou servest continually, he will deliver thee*, since for no crime, but purely for fidelity to his God he suffered, he was as able now to deliver him from the lions, as he had saved his servants of old from the devouring fire *Note*, Let us but be faithful, and then we may safely trust our all with God

18 ¶ Then the king went to his palace, and passed
the night fasting neither were instruments of music
brought before him, and his sleep went from him 19
Then the king arose very early in the morning, and
went in haste unto the den of lions 20 And when he
came to the den, he cried with a lamentable voice unto
Daniel, *and* the king spake and said to Daniel, O
Daniel, servant of the living GOD, [x] is thy GOD, whom
thou servest continually, able to deliver thee from the
lions? 21 Then said Daniel unto the king, [y] O king,
live for ever 22 [z] My GOD hath sent his angel, [a] and
hath shut the lions mouths that they have not hurt me
forasmuch as [b] before him innocency was found in me,
and also [c] before thee, O king, have I done no hurt
23 Then was the king exceeding glad for him, and
commanded that they should take Daniel up out of the
den So Daniel was taken up out of the den, and no
manner of hurt was found upon him, [d] because he be-
lieved in his GOD 24 ¶ And the king commanded,
and they brought [e] those men which had accused Daniel,
and they cast *them* into the den of lions, them, [f] their
children, and their wives; and the lions had the mastery
over them, and brake all their bones in pieces or ever
they came at the bottom of the den

x Chap iii 15, 17
y Ibid ii.4
z Ps xci 11 Chap iii 28
a Heb xi 33
b Rev xiv 5
c Acts xxiv 16
d Heb xi 33
e Deut xix 19 Esth vii 10
f Deut xxiv 16 2 Kings xiv 6

v 18—24 We are told,

1 The melancholy night Darius passed He returned to his palace, overwhelmed with grief, vexation, and self-reproach his appetite was gone, his ears incapable of relishing one cheerful note, fasting he passed the night, and sleepless waited in suspense the return of day—a troubled conscience puts a thorn even in a downy pillow

2 At early dawn he springs from his bed, and eager to know what he dreaded to ask, with a lamentable voice addresses the faithful sufferer, *O Daniel, servant*, &c which some make his question as fluctuating between hope and despair, but seems rather expressive of his astonishment and admiration, when, on the nearer approach to the den, and hearing his voice, he perceived Daniel was yet alive

3 Daniel addressing the king, recounts his miraculous deliverance He does not upbraid Darius with giving him up into the hand of his enemies, but expresses his warmest wishes for his prosperity, *O king, live for ever* *My God*, in whom I trusted, *hath sent his angel, and stopped the lions mouths that they have not hurt me*, and herein God bore testimony to his innocence Nor could the king in conscience imagine that Daniel designed him either injury or affront in what he had done *Note*, God will stand by his faithful people in the hour of temptation; and though their souls may be among lions, he can not only keep them safe, but make their consolations abound Daniel in the den, with the presence of that heavenly visitant, was happier far than Darius in his palace

4 Daniel is immediately discharged The king, transported with joy, orders him to be taken out of the den, and not a blemish was found on him, so carefully had that God, in whom he believed, preserved him nor shall any who boldly trust in him have ever reason to be ashamed of their confidence

5 Daniel's persecutors are justly consigned to that den from which he is delivered Darius was now fully assured that it was of mere malice they had accused him, and will avenge the innocent blood they meant to shed, and by a fearful example of severity, to deter others from the like conspiracies, their wives and children share their fate when, lo! these ravening lions, who mildly crouched at the prophet's feet, with open mouths seized these miscreants as they fell, and broke all their bones ere they touched the bottom of the den *Note*, God's justice in this world is sometimes eminently seen in suffering the malicious to fall into the pit they have digged for others

25 ¶ [g] Then king Darius wrote unto all people, na-
tions and languages, that dwell in all the earth, Peace
be multiplied unto you 26 [h] I make a decree, that
in every dominion of my kingdom men tremble and fear
before the GOD of Daniel for [i] he *is* the living GOD,
and [k] stedfast for ever, [l] and his kingdom *that* which
shall not be destroyed, and his dominion *shall be even*
unto the end 27 [m] He delivereth and rescueth, [n] and
he worketh signs and wonders in heaven and in earth, who
hath delivered Daniel from the † power of the lions
28 [o] So this Daniel prospered in the reign of Darius,
and in the reign of [p] Cyrus the Persian.

g Chap iv 1,
h Ibid iii 29
i Ibid iv 34
k Jam i 17
l Chap. ii 44 & iv 3, 34 & vii 14 27 Luke i
m 2 Cor i 10
n Chap iv 3
† Heb Hand
o Heb xi
p Chap i 21

v 25—28 Darius, exceedingly affected with the miracle,

1 Issues an edict throughout his kingdom, enjoining the highest reverence and veneration for Daniel's God, that in all provinces of his empire men should *fear and tremble* before him, *for he is the living God*, self-existent, the author of life to all his creatures, *and stedfast for ever*, himself unchangeable and everlasting, his decrees immutable, his promises inviolable, *and his kingdom that which shall not be destroyed, and his dominion shall be even unto the end*, unlike the kingdoms of the world, it can neither be shaken by external violence, nor is subject to internal decay, but enduring as the days of eternity *He delivereth and rescueth* his faithful from the deepest afflictions, *and he worketh signs and wonders in heaven and in earth*, controuling at his pleasure the course of nature, an eminent instance of which had now appeared, *who hath delivered Daniel from the power of the lions*

2 Daniel is restored to all his former honours and dignity, and during his whole reign continued greatly in favour with the king, and his successor Cyrus shewed him the same respect So wonderfully can God over-rule the events which seemed most grievous for our good, and make, if he pleases, a prison like Joseph's, or a den of lions as Daniel's, the means of our greatest prosperity

CHAP VII

The six former chapters of this book were historical, we now enter, with fear and trembling, upon the six latter, which are prophetical, wherein are many things dark, and hard to be understood, which we dare not positively determine the sense of, and yet many things plain and profitable, which I trust God will enable us to improve In this chapter we have, 1 Daniel's vision of the four beasts, ver 1, 8 2 His vision of God's throne of government and judgment, ver 9, 14 3 The interpretation of these visions given him by an angel, ver 15—28 Whether those visions look as far forward as the end of time, or whether they were to have a speedy accomplishment, is hard to say, nor are the most judicious interpreters agreed concerning it

555

1 IN the first year of Belshazzar king of Babylon,
[a] Daniel † had a dream, and visions of his head
upon his bed then he [b] wrote the dream, *and* told the
sum of the ‡ matters 2 Daniel spake, and said, I saw
in my vision by night, and behold, the four winds of the
heaven strove upon the great sea 3 And four great
beasts [c] came up from the sea, divers one from another
4 The first *was* [d] like a lion, and had eagle's wings
and I beheld till the wings thereof were pluckt, § and it
was lifted up from the earth, and [e] made stand upon the
feet as a man, and a man's heart was given to it 5
And behold, another beast, [f] a second, like to a bear,
and ‖ it raised itself up on one side, and [g] *it had* three
ribs in the mouth of it, between the teeth of it and
they said thus unto it, Arise, devour much flesh 6
After this, I beheld, and lo, [h] another like a leopard,
which had upon the back of it four wings of a fowl, the
beast had also four heads, and dominion was given to it
7 After this, I saw, in the night visions, and behold,
[i] a fourth beast, dreadful and terrible, and strong ex-
ceedingly, and it had great iron teeth [k] it devoured
and brake in pieces, and stamped the residue with the
feet of it, and it *was* divers from all the beasts that *were*
before

a Am ii
† Chald saw
b Rom xv 4
‡ Or words
c Rev xiii 1
d Jer iv 7 13 & xlix 19 Ezek xvii 3 Hab i 8
§ Or wherewith
e Ezek i 5
f Chap ii 39
‖ Or it raised up one dominion
g Chap viii 4
h Chap ii 39
i Chap ii 40
k Matt 38

Before Christ 555

before it, [l] and it had ten horns 8 I considered the
horns, and behold, [m] there came up among them an
other little horn, before whom there were three of the
first horns pluckt up by the roots and behold, in this
horn *were* eyes like [n] the eyes of man, and [o] a mouth
speaking great things

l Rev xiii 1. m Ver 21 Chap viii 9. n Rev ix 7. o Ver 25 2 Thes ii 4 Rev xiii 5

v 1—8 The date of this vision is in the first year of Belshazzar It was revealed to Daniel on his bed in a dream, and when he awoke he wrote it down, and communicated it to his brethren whom it so nearly concerned They were about to be delivered from their long captivity, but must not expect uninterrupted tranquility, as they perhaps flattered themselves, in the land to which they were about to return

In the vision he observed,

1 The four winds strove upon the great sea, and the effect of such a furious storm must needs be the most violent agitation This sea is the world with its inhabitants, the winds the monarchs of the earth contending for mastery, and filling it with violence and confusion

2 From this foaming ocean came up four great beasts, in figure different from each other, representing the four great monarchies, and the different genius of the people by whom they were erected

[1] *The first was like a lion*, which was the Babylonish monarchy, strong and despotic *and had eagle's wings*, intimating the rapidity of Nebuchadnezzar's conquests, but the wings were soon plucked, *the which it was lift up from the earth*, for under his successors the empire began to be diminished and weakened, they lost their courage and intrepidity, and the lion's heart was changed into a man's

2 *The second beast was like unto a bear*, representing the Medo Persian monarchy, fierce and savage, *and it raised itself up on one side*, on the side of Persia, from whence Cyrus the conqueror came, *and it had three ribs in the mouth of it, between the teeth of it*, so many dismembered provinces, probably of the Babylonish empire, which it first devoured, *and they said thus unto it, Arise, devour much flesh*, either the generals of the Persian army encouraged their troops to lay their enemies, or these are the orders of the Divine Providence to Cyrus, sending him to devour the spoils of the conquered Chaldeans

3 The third beast, that next arose, was *like a leopard*, prefiguring the Grecian monarchy under Alexander, agile, crafty, spotted, a compound of vices and virtues, or this may refer to the motley people of this vast empire *It had upon the back of it four wings like a fowl*, so swift were his marches, so rapid his conquests *The beast also had four heads*, the empire, on Alexander's decease, being divided into four parts Macedonia fell to Antipater, or, as others, to Cassander, Asia to Antigonus, or, as some say, to Lysimachus, Syria to Seleucus, and Egypt to Ptolemy *And dominion was given to it* God's hand being strongly evident in the successes of the Grecian conqueror

4 The fourth beast differed from all the rest, *being dreadful and terrible, and strong exceedingly*, which most interpret of the Roman empire, *and it had great iron teeth*, devouring, breaking in pieces, and stamping down all who stood in its way, as the Roman generals and armies did, till they had erected universal monarchy *And it had ten horns*, the empire, on its decline, being divided into so many kingdoms The *little horn*, v 8 is by the best interpreters supposed to be the antichristian power, which rose from small beginnings, and from an ecclesiastic the bishop of Rome became a temporal prince, and seized on considerable territories, dispossessing three of the other horns *And in this horn were eyes like the eyes of a man*, intimating the vigilance and craft of the Romish court and emissaries, *and a mouth speaking proud things*, boasting of infallibility, power to remit sin, and other such like proud blasphemies Some interpret this of the kingdom of Syria, and the little horn of Antiochus, but the former sense is preferable, and more agreeable to the vision, as that kingdom rather belonged to the vision of the third beast

9 ¶ [p] I beheld till the thrones were cast down, and
[q] the ancient of days did sit, [r] whose garment *was* white
as snow, and the hair of his head like the pure wool
his throne *was like* the fiery flame, [s] *and* his wheels *as*
burning fire 10 [t] A fiery stream issued and came
forth from before him [u] thousand thousands ministred
unto him, and ten thousand times ten thousand stood
before him the judgment was set, and [x] the books were
opened 11 I beheld then, because of the voice of the
great words which the horn spake I beheld, *even* till
the beast was slain, and his body destroyed, and given
[y] to the burning flame 12 As concerning [z] the rest
of the beasts, they had their dominion taken away yet
their lives were prolonged for a season and time 13 I
saw in the night visions, and behold, [a] *one* like the son
of man came with the clouds of heaven, and came to the
ancient of days, and they brought him near before him

p Rev xx 4. q Ver 13, 22. r Ps civ 2 Rev i 14. s Ezek i 15, 16. t Ps l 3 & xcvii 3 Isa xxx 33. u 1 Kings xxii 19 Ps lxviii 17 Rev v 11. x Rev xx 4, 12. y 2 Thes ii 8 Rev xix 20. z Ver 4, &c. a Ezek i 26 Rev i 7, 13 & xiv, 14

14. [b] And there was given him dominion and glory,
and a kingdom, [c] that all people, nations, and languages
should serve him his dominion *is* [d] an everlasting dominion,
which shall not pass away, and his kingdom *that*
which shall not be destroyed

b Ps ii 6, 7, 8 & cx 1, 2. c Chap iii 4. d Ps cxlv 13 Chap ii 44 Mic iv 7 Luke i 33 John xii 34. Heb xii 28

v 9—14 Very glorious things are here recorded, for the comfort of the people of God under all the persecutions they may be called to suffer in this wicked world

1 An awful judge makes his appearance *I beheld till the thrones were cast down*, all these monarchies successively overturned or it may be read *till the thrones were set up*, the thrones of judgment, the thrones of God and the Lamb and this may point either at his providential judgments on all the enemies of his church in this world, or his final and eternal judgment at the great day of his appearing and glory *And the ancient of days did sit*, God the Father, the Judge of all his garment *was white as snow*, denoting his perfect righteousness, and that his bosom is the seat of justice, *and the hair of his head like pure wool*, venerable and majestic *his throne was as the fiery flame, and his wheels as burning fire*, so piercing his scrutiny, so swift the execution of his sentence, and so terrible his wrath *a fiery stream issued and came forth before him*, to consume his adversaries, *thousand thousands ministred unto him*, angels and archangels, *and ten thousand times ten thousand stood before him*, waiting from his lips their eternal doom *The judgment was set* the court ready to hear and determine, *and the books were opened*, the book of revelation, the book of omniscience, the book of conscience, in allusion to proceedings in courts of human judicature

2 The prisoner at the bar is condemned and executed *I beheld then, because of the voice of the great words which the horn spake*, his pride and blasphemies being proved, and condign punishment decreed, *I beheld, even till the beast was slain*, which some interpret of the fall of the Syrian empire after Antiochus, but much better may be applied to the Romish power, both pagan and papal, *and his body destroyed, and given to the burning flame*, Rome the seat of the antichristian tyranny, being, very probably, doomed, as Sodom, to be devoured with fire from heaven, and the beast and the false prophet will together at last be cast into the burning lake See Rev xvii xviii xix *As concerning the rest of the beasts*, the other three monarchies, *they had their dominion taken away*, successively giving place to each other, *yet their lives were prolonged for a season and a time*, tho' the sovereign power departed from them, they each continued in being as a people, whereas, when judgment passes on the fourth, he will perish at once and utterly

3 The kingdom of the Messiah is to be set up on the ruin of his enemies *I saw in the night-visions, and behold one like the son of man*, like the sons of men in his incarnation, but more than man in the glory of his divine person, *came in the clouds of heaven*, with great majesty, to take possession of his kingdom, *and came to the ancient of days*, his eternal Father, either at his ascension, or rather it refers to the future day of his glory, when he shall take to himself his great power and reign, *and they brought him near before him, and there was given him dominion, and power, and glory, and a kingdom*, his mediatorial kingdom, which, as the man Christ Jesus, he receives from his Father, and this kingdom, we doubt not, will be more eminent and extensive upon earth hereafter than it hath ever yet been, so *that all people, nations, and languages, shall serve him*, in the obedient to the faith, and become his loyal subjects and, as his kingdom will be universal in its extent, it will, for the comfort of God's people, be eternal in duration, for *his dominion is an everlasting dominion, and his kingdom that which shall not be destroyed* Blessed and happy are they who have their lot and portion among the favoured subjects of this divine Redeemer!

15 ¶ I Daniel [e] was grieved in my spirit in the midst
of *my* body, and the visions of my head troubled me
16 I came near unto one of them that stood by, and
[d] asked him the truth of all this so he told me, and
[e] made me know the interpretation of the things 17
These great beasts, which are four, *are* four kings,
which shall arise out of the earth 18 But [f] the saints
of the [‖] most High shall take the kingdom, and possess
the kingdom for ever, even for ever and ever 19
Then I would know the truth of the fourth beast, which
was divers from all the others, exceeding dreadful, whose
teeth *were of* iron, and his nails *of* brass, *which* devoured,
brake in pieces, and stamped the residue with his feet
20 And of the ten horns that *were* in his head, and *of*
the other which came up, and before whom three fell,
even *of* that horn that had eyes, and a mouth that spake
very great things, [g] whose look *was* more stout than his
fellows 21 I beheld, and [h] the same horn made war
with the saints, and prevailed against them, 22 Until
the ancient of days came, and [i] judgment was given to
the saints of the most High, and [k] the time came that

c Ver 28 Chap viii 27 & x 8, 16. d Prov ii 2. e Rev i 1. f Isa lx 13 Ver 22 Rev v 10. ‖ Chald High ones, i e things, or places. g Chap viii 10 & xi 37. h Chap vii 25, 21 & xi 31 Rev xi 7 xiii 7 & xvii 14. i Ver 18 1 Cor vi 2 Rev i 6 & v 10 & xx 4. k Isa lxii 4

Before Christ 555

the ſaints poſſeſſed the kingdom 23 Thus he ſaid,
The fourth beaſt ſhall be [l] the fourth kingdom upon earth,
which ſhall be divers from all kingdoms, and [m] ſhall
devour the whole earth, and ſhall tread it down, and
break it in pieces 24 And [n] the ten horns out of this
kingdom *are* ten kings *that* ſhall ariſe and another ſhall
ariſe after them, and he ſhall be divers from the firſt,
and he ſhall ſubdue three kings 25 And [o] he ſhall
ſpeak *great* words againſt the moſt High, and ſhall wear
out the ſaints of the moſt High, [p] and think to change
times and laws and they ſhall be given into his hand,
[q] until a time and times, and the dividing of time
26 [r] But the judgment ſhall ſit, and they ſhall take
away his dominion, to conſume, and to deſtroy *it* unto
the end 27 And [s] the kingdom and dominion, and
the greatneſs of the kingdom under the whole heaven,
ſhall be given to the people of the ſaints of the moſt High,
whoſe kingdom *is* an everlaſting kingdom, [t] and all
‡ dominions ſhall ſerve and obey him 28 Hitherto *is*
the end of the matter As for me Daniel, [u] my cogitations
much troubled me, and my countenance changed
in me but [x] I kept the matter in my heart

l Chap ii 40 Luke ii 1 m Chap xii 7 Mat. xxiv 28 n Ver 7, 8 Rev xvii 12 o Iſa xxxvii 23 Chap. viii 24, 25, & xi 28, 30, 31, 36 1 Mac i 46. Rev xiii 5, 6 p Chap ii 21 q Chap xii 7 Rev xii 14 r Ver x 22 s Luke i 33 John xii 34 t Iſa lx 12 ‡ Or rulers u Ver 15 x Luke ii 51

v 15—28 The viſions ſo affected the prophet that his mind was much troubled, and, earneſtly deſirous to be informed of the meaning of what he ſaw, he enquires of one of the celeſtial attendants on the throne concerning them, who readily relieved him from his ſuſpence, and explained the particulars of his prophetic dream *Note*, (1) When we are ignorant, we ſhould never be aſhamed to enquire of thoſe who can teach us (2) The truths of God ſhould engage our diligent attention, and what we read or hear we ſhould, by prayer and meditation, endeavour fully to underſtand

The interpretation given is,

1 That the four beaſts are four kings, or kingdoms, which ſhould ariſe out of the earth, and, ſpringing from the duſt, ſhould return thither again but a fifth ſhould ſucceed them, of heavenly original, and endure for ever and ever, as he more fully afterwards explains

2 As Daniel was moſt ſollicitous to have a fuller explication of the meaning of the fourth beaſt, which ſeemed the fierceſt of them all, and of the ten horns, and the little horn that ſprung up afterwards, that had eyes, and a mouth that ſpake great things, and *his look more ſtout than his fellows*, which made war againſt the ſaints of the moſt High, and prevailed, till the Ancient of days came, vindicated their cauſe, and ſlew their adverſary, *v* 21 the angel informs him, that this terrible beaſt is the fourth kingdom, concerning the meaning of which interpreters are divided, ſome ſuppoſing it the kingdom of the Seleucidæ, others the Turkiſh empire, but I moſt incline to thoſe who think it the Roman monarchy, pagan and papal, to which the characters given ſeem moſt exactly to agree It was diverſe from all the other kingdoms in its form of government, it trod down and devoured the whole earth, by long and bloody wars ſubduing the nations which refuſed to ſubmit The ten horns are ten kings, or kingdoms, which roſe on the decline of the empire, when the Huns, Goths, Alans, and other northern nations, ſucceſſively diſmembered the empire, and erected theſe ten ſeparate kingdoms which though learned interpreters reckon differently, in the grand points they agree, that theſe ten kingdoms were erected by them, and here repreſented by the ten horns The little horn they ſuppoſe the papal power, riſing to its height after this diviſion of the empire, *ſpeaking great things*, pretending to be Chriſt's vicar upon earth, and aſſuming the incommunicable prerogatives of the moſt High, and *his look more ſtout than his fellows*, the head of that power aſſuming authority, not only over all his fellow biſhops, but over all kings and princes He is diverſe from the other monarchs, having the eccleſiaſtical as well as civil dominion, and ruling over the conſciences as well as perſons of his ſubjects *He ſhall ſubdue three kings*, which Mr *Mede* reckons were the kingdoms of the Greeks, Lombards, and Franks Sir Iſaac Newton ſuppoſes them to be the kingdom of the Lombards, the exarchate of Ravenna, and the dukedom of Rome The biſhop of Clogher interprets them of the Campagnia of Rome, the exarchate of Ravenna, and the region of Pentapolis, which are called St Peter's patrimony, and under the civil juriſdiction of the biſhop of Rome *And he ſhall ſpeak great words againſt the moſt High*, the words of blaſphemy, affecting ſuch authority and ſpiritual power as if he was God upon earth, and the rival of the eternal Majeſty By wars and perſecutions, and inquiſitorial dungeons, he *ſhall wear out the ſaints of the moſt High*, endeavouring to weary out their patience and bring them under his yoke, *and he ſhall think to change the times and laws*, affecting to depoſe and ſet up kings at his pleaſure, to alter the conſtitution of kingdoms, conſecrating particular times and ſeaſons, diſpenſing with the laws of God and man, and binding his own upon the conſciences of men *and they ſhall be given into his hand*, he ſhall for a while ſucceed in his uſurpations, *until a time and times, and the dividing of time*, three years and a half, the ſame with the 1260 days, and the forty-two months, *Rev* xi 2, 3 xii 14 xiii 5 during which the tyranny of Antichriſt ſhall prevail But God will at laſt judge this perſecuting power, and utterly deſtroy it, ſetting up on its ruins the kingdom of his Chriſt, whoſe people ſhall then for ever reign with him, enjoying freely all privileges and ordinances, without diſturbance, and ſeeing all their enemies made their footſtool And this ſome refer to a temporal reign of the ſaints upon earth, under Chriſt their head, others to the reign of grace in the ſouls of the redeemed of the Lord, and the univerſal ſpread of the goſpel in the world at the latter day, others to the kingdom of the Redeemer in heaven, when, after the laſt judgment, his ſaints ſhall reign with him in glory everlaſting In whichever ſenſe it be taken, the proſpect is truly glorious, and ſuited to ſupport the faith, the patience, and conſtancy of his people, who may be aſſured, in the darkeſt times, that the enemy ſhall not be able finally to prevail

3 Daniel appears much impreſſed and affected with what had been told him his very look was altered by it, but he kept the matter in his heart, pondering thereupon, and ſeeking thoroughly to underſtand the meaning, that he might tranſmit the viſion, with the interpretation, to ſucceeding generations *Note*, It is good thus to ſtore up in our hearts the bleſſed words of truth we hear, ready to produce them, on every proper occaſion, for the edification and comfort of our brethren

CHAP VIII.

In this chapter we have, 1 *The viſion of the ram, and the he-goat, and the little horn that ſhould fight and prevail againſt the people of God for a certain limited time*, ver 1—14 2 *The interpretation of this viſion by an angel*, ver 15—27

1 IN the third year of the reign of king Belſhazzar,
a viſion appeared unto me, *even unto* me Daniel,
after that which appeared unto me [a] at the firſt 2 And
I ſaw in a viſion (and it came to paſs when I ſaw, that
[b] I *was* at Shuſhan *in* the palace, which *is* in the province
of Elam) and I ſaw in a viſion, and I was by the
river of Ulai 3 Then I lifted up mine eyes, and ſaw,
and behold, there ſtood before the river, [c] a ram which
had two horns, and the two horns *were* high but one
was higher than the other, and the higher came up laſt
4 I ſaw the ram [d] puſhing weſt-ward, and north-ward,
and ſouth-ward ſo that no beaſt might ſtand before
him, neither *was there any* that could deliver out of his
hand, but [e] he did according to his will, and became
great. 5 And as I was conſidering, behold, [f] an he-goat
came from the weſt, on the face of the whole earth,
and † touched not the ground and the goat *had* ‡ a
notable horn between his eyes 6 And he came to the
ram that had two horns, which I had ſeen ſtanding before
the river, and ran unto him in the fury of his power
7 And I ſaw him come cloſe unto the ram, and
[g] he was moved with choler againſt him, and ſmote the
ram, and brake his two horns, and [h] there was no power
in the ram to ſtand before him, but he caſt him down to
the ground, and ſtamped upon him and there was none
that could deliver the ram out of his hand 8 Therefore
the he-goat waxed very great, and [i] when he was
ſtrong, the great horn was broken and for it came up
four notable ones, [k] towards the four winds of heaven
9 And [l] out of one of them came forth a little horn,
which waxed exceeding great, [m] toward the ſouth, and
toward the eaſt, and toward [n] the pleaſant *land* 10
[o] And it waxed great, *even* § to the hoſt of heaven,
[p] and it caſt down *ſome* of the hoſt, and of the ſtars to
the ground, and ſtamped upon them 11 Yea, [q] he
magnified *himſelf* even ‖ to [r] the prince of the hoſt, and
[s] by him [t] the daily *ſacrifice* was taken away, and the
place of his ſanctuary was caſt down 12 And ¶ an hoſt
was given *him* againſt the daily *ſacrifice* [u] by reaſon of
tranſgreſſion, and it [x] caſt down the truth to the ground,
and it practiſed [y] and proſpered 13 ¶ Then I heard
[z] one ſaint ſpeaking, and another ſaint ſaid unto ‖ that
certain *ſaint* which ſpake, How long *ſhall be* the viſion
concerning the daily *ſacrifice*, and [a] the tranſgreſſion of
deſolation, to give both the ſanctuary and the hoſt to be
trodden under foot? 14 And he ſaid unto me, Unto
two thouſand and three hundred days, then ſhall the
ſanctuary be ‖ cleanſed

Before Christ 555 a Chap vii 1 b Eſth viii 3 c Chap viii 20 d Chap viii 5 e Chap v 19 & xi 3 f Ver 21 † Or none touched him in the earth ‡ Heb A horn of ſight g Prov v 4 h Num xiv 9 i Chap xi 31 k Chap xi 4 l Chap xi 21 & xi 21 m Chap xi 25 n Pſ xlviii 2 Ezek xx 6, 15 Chap xi 16 41 45 o Chap xi 28 § Or againſt p Rev xii 4 q Jer xlviii 26 42 Ver 25 Chap xi 36 ‖ Or againſt r Joſh v 14 s Chap xi 31 & xii 11 1 Mac i 44—64 t Exod xxix 38 Num xxviii 3 ¶ Or the hoſt was given over for the tranſgreſſion againſt the daily ſacrifice u 1 Mac i 11, &c 2 Mac iv 13—17 x Iſa lix 14 y Jer xii 1 z Chap iv 13 1 Pet i 12 ‖ Heb Palmoni, or the numberer of ſecrets, or the wonderful numberer a Iſa ix 6 Chap xi 31 & xii 11 1 Mac i 54 ‖ Heb Juſtified

v 1—14

Before Christ 551

v 1—14 This ſecond viſion is dated in the third year of Belſhazzar's reign The ſcene is laid in Shuſhan, which was one of the royal palaces of the kings of Perſia by the river Ulai Daniel was now in Babylon, but he ſeemed to be there, near the monarch whom the viſion chiefly concerned

1 He ſaw *a ram*, the emblem of the ſecond monarchy, having two very high horns, the nations of Medes and Perſians, and one horn, which roſe the laſt, *was higher than the other*, the Perſians under Cyrus taking the lead, though at firſt inferior to the Medes This animal ſeemed to puſh furiouſly, weſtward, northward, and ſouthward, extending his conqueſts on every ſide, none of the nations being able to ſtand before him, ſo that he did as he pleaſed, and *became great*, roſe to univerſal empire But ſuch is the periſhing nature of all ſublunary things, that the ſeeds of corruption and ruin are ripening when a nation's outward proſperity ſeems moſt eſtabliſhed for,

2 *A he-goat* attacks and overcomes the *ram* This repreſents the Grecian monarchy under Alexander he came from *the weſt*, from Macedon, *on the face of the whole earth*, ſweeping it with his victorious arms, and weeping, it is ſaid, that he had not another world to conquer *and he touched not the ground*, ſo rapid were his marches, that he rather ſeemed to fly than walk *and the goat had a notable horn between his eyes*, deſcriptive of Alexander, the firſt founder of the monarchy, ſo eminent a conqueror, ſo ſagacious a general, and attended by his father's wiſeſt counſellers *He came to the ram with two horns*, the Perſian monarch Darius Codomannus, then in poſſeſſion of the kingdom, *and ran unto him in the fury of his power*, eager to engage, and furious in the attack he made, highly exaſperated by the meſſage of contempt Darius had ſent him, he came *cloſe to the ram*, joined battle with him and *ſmote him* in three general engagements, at the Granicus, at Iſſus, and Arbela, *and brake his two horns*, overthrew his armies, and so entirely deſtroyed the force of the Perſian empire, that *there was no power in the ram to ſtand before him, but he caſt him to the ground and ſtamped upon him*, quite ſubdued the whole kingdom of Perſia, *and there was none that could deliver the ram out of his hand*, his allies all falling with him Thus *the he-goat waxed very great*, the Grecian monarchy being eſtabliſhed through the greateſt part of the then known world

3 In this flouriſhing ſtate of the new empire, a ſudden ſtroke divides it into four parts *The great horn was broken* Alexander, at thirty two or three years of age, was cut off ſuddenly, by a drunken debauch, as ſome ſay, or by poiſon, as others, *and for it*, in his room, *came up four notable ones*, his four captains, who divided his dominions among them, *ſee chap* vii 6 *toward the four winds*, Syria lying eaſtward, Macedonia to the weſt, leſſer Aſia to the north, and Egypt to the ſouth *Note*, Many take great pains, whilſt others reap the fruit of their labours

4 The principal thing intended in the viſion, as what more immediately concerned the Jewiſh people, is *the little horn* coming out of one of theſe kingdoms, Antiochus Epiphanes, the king of Syria, who had been a hoſtage at Rome, and, making his eſcape, ſeized the throne, in prejudice of his elder brother's ſon He *waxed exceeding great toward the ſouth*, ſubduing part of Egypt, and, but for the interpoſition of the Romans, would have vanquiſhed the whole, *and toward the eaſt*, invading Armenia and Perſia, with the countries beyond the Euphrates, *ſee* 1 *Mac* iii 31 vi 42 *and toward the pleaſant land* of Judea, which he ravaged, *and it waxed great, even to the hoſt of heaven*, the people of God, his church militant on earth, *and it caſt down ſome of the hoſt, and of the ſtars, to the ground, and ſtamped on them*, perſecuting ſome of them unto death, even the moſt eminent, as Eleazar and the ſeven brethren, 2 *Mac* vi 7 and prevailing on others, by threatnings, tortures, or flatteries, to renounce their holy profeſſion *Yea, he magnified himſelf to the prince of the hoſt*, diſpoſſeſſing Onias the high-prieſt of his dignity, or rather affronting God himſelf, their King, by his blaſphemies, profaning his temple, and aboliſhing his worſhip, *and by him the daily ſacrifice was taken away*, the altar being deſtroyed, *and the place of his ſanctuary was caſt down*, though the temple was not demoliſhed, it was ſo profaned and plundered that the ſervice utterly ceaſed, 1 *Mac* i 22 iii 45—52 *And an hoſt was given him againſt the daily ſacrifice*, a watch being ſet to prevent it, or a number of apoſtates joining him to aboliſh the worſhip of God or it may be rendered, *the hoſt was delivered* into his hands, *becauſe of tranſgreſſion againſt the daily ſacrifice*, God puniſhing the Jewiſh people for their ſins, and giving them into the hands of this enemy, ſo that he *caſt the truth to the ground*, deſtroying all the ſacred writings he could ſeize; and he *practiſed and proſpered*, being the rod of God's indignation *Note*, (1) If God's people ſuffer, their ſins are ſurely the cauſe (2) The wicked perſecutor can have no power but what the Lord permits, and therefore we are to acknowledge God's hand in all the church's calamities (3) They who ſlight or abuſe the privileges of the ſanctuary, which they enjoy, juſtly deſerve to be deprived of them

5 The time limited for the continuation of this tyranny is intimated *Then I heard one ſaint ſpeaking*, the ſubject of his diſcourſe being probably this viſion, *and another ſaint ſaid unto that certain ſaint that ſpake*, or, *to Palmoni that ſpake*, to him *who hath all ſecrets numbered*, is the word, as by ſome tranſlated, the Lord Jeſus, to whom we muſt apply if we would know the mind of God The queſtion put was, *how long the daily ſacrifice ſhould be interrupted, the tranſgreſſion of deſolation*, the image of Jupiter, ſtand in the holy place, *the ſanctuary and hoſt be trodden under foot?* The anſwer is, *unto* 2300 *days*, being ſix years, three months, and eighteen days, which ſome compute from the 15th of the month Ciſleu, in the 145th year of the Seleucidæ, when the abomination was ſet up, 1 *Mac* i 57, to the victory obtained by Judas Maccabeus over Nicanor, Antiochus's general, on the 13th of Adar, 151, which is juſt 2300 Others begin from the defection of Menelaus in 141 to the purifying the altar by Judas Maccabeus on the 25th of Ciſleu, 148 *ſee* 1 *Mac* iv 52 The time of the ſufferings of God's people may be long, and the trial ſevere, but the iſſue is certain, they ſhall have peace at the laſt let them only with faith and patience wait for it

Before Christ 551

15 ¶ And it came to paſs when I, *even* I Daniel,
had ſeen the viſion, and [a] ſought for the meaning, then [a] 1 Pet i. 10
behold, there ſtood before me as the appearance of a
man 16 And I heard a man's voice [c] between *the* [c] Chap xii 6 7
banks of Ulai, which called, and ſaid, [d] Gabriel, make [d] Chap. ix 21 Luke i 19, 20
this *man* to underſtand the viſion 17 So he came
near where I ſtood and when he came, I was afraid,
and [e] fell upon my face but he ſaid unto me, Under- [e] Ezek i 28 Rev i. 17
ſtand, O ſon of man, for at the time of the end *ſhall be*
the viſion 18 [f] Now as he was ſpeaking with me, [f] Chap x 9 10 Luke ix 32
I was in a deep ſleep on my face toward the ground
but [g] he touched me, and ſet me upright 19 And [g] Ezek ii 2
he ſaid, Behold, I will make thee know what ſhall be
in the laſt end of the indignation for [h] at the time ap- [h] Chap ix 27 & xi 35, 36 & xii 7
pointed the end *ſhall be* 20 [i] The ram which thou [i] Ver 3
ſaweſt having two horns, *are* the kings of Media and
Perſia 21 And [k] the rough goat *is* the king of Grecia, [k] Ver 5
and the great horn that *is* between his eyes, [l] is the [l] Chap xi 3.
firſt king 22 [m] Now that being broken, whereas four [m] Chap xi. 4
ſtood up for it, [n] four kingdoms ſhall ſtand up out [n] Mat xiii. 25
of the nation, but not in his power 23 And in the
latter time of their kingdom, [o] when the tranſgreſſors [o] 2 Mac iv 11, &c & v 15
are come to the full, a king [p] of fierce countenance,
and underſtanding dark ſentences, ſhall ſtand up 24 [p] Deu xxviii 50
And his power ſhall be mighty, [q] but not by his own [q] Rev xvii 13 17
power and he ſhall deſtroy wonderfully, [r] and ſhall [r] Chap xi 36
proſper and practiſe, and ſhall deſtroy the mighty and
† the holy people 25 And through his policy alſo he † Heb The people of the holy ones
ſhall cauſe craft to proſper in his hand, and [s] he ſhall
magnify *himſelf* in his heart, [t] and by peace ſhall deſtroy [s] 2 Mac ix. 7, 8 11
many he ſhall alſo ſtand up againſt the prince of princes, [t] Chap. xi. 21
but [u] he ſhall be broken without hand 26 And the [u] 1 Mac vi 8 2 Mac ix 9 Acts xii 23
viſion of the evening and the morning, which was told,
[x] is true, [y] wherefore ſhut thou up the viſion, for it *ſhall* [x] Rom iii 4 [y] Iſa viii 16 Rev xxii 10
be for many days 27 [z] And I Daniel fainted and was [z] Chap vii 15, 28 & x 8 16
ſick *certain* days, afterward I roſe up, [a] and did the king's [a] Chap vi 3
buſineſs, and I was aſtoniſhed at the viſion, but none
underſtood *it*

v 15—27 The viſion he had ſeen excited in the prophet a great deſire to know the meaning of it, and whilſt in his own mind he pondered what he had ſeen and heard, God graciouſly orders one of his angels to explain the particulars to him *Note*, When, in God's appointed ways, we are earneſtly deſirous to know his mind and will, he will enlighten our minds, and lead us in the right way We have,

1 The deep impreſſion made on Daniel by the approach of the heavenly meſſenger Overpowered with his glory, he trembled, and fell at his feet as in a ſwoon, and *a deep ſleep came* upon him, *v* 18 The ſpirit is ſometimes willing, when the fleſh is weak

2 The angel gently raiſe him from the duſt, and *ſets him* on his feet, bidding him attend to and underſtand the explication he was about to give concerning *what ſhall be in the laſt end of the indignation, for at the time of the end ſhall be the viſion*, or *the end of the viſion is for a time*, fixed by the divine decree, when the troubles of God's people ſhould ceaſe, and his indignation be removed from them, *at the time appointed* *Note*, All the ſufferings of God's people have their bounds and limits, and by faith and patience they ſhall be enabled with comfort to ſee their end

3 He gives the interpretation of the viſion, mentioned before, *v* 3—14 *The ram* repreſents *the kings of Media and Perſia*, the he-goat the Grecian empire the great horn Alexander, the four horns the captains who divided his dominion, who were not at all equal to him in power and greatneſs On the decline of the Grecian empire, a king would ariſe in the kingdom of Syria, whoſe character and exploits are more largely inſiſted up-
on

Before Christ 553

on, as they more nearly concerned the people of Israel, whose *transgressions being come to the full*, God would raise up this scourge to punish them. He is represented as *a king of fierce countenance*, savage and brutish, neither fearing God or man, *and understanding dark sentences*, crafty, politic, and of consummate dissimulation, *and his power shall be mighty*, raised to the throne of Syria, *but not by his own power*, being supported by Eumenes king of Pergamus, and Attalus his brother, in his usurpation, *he shall destroy wonderfully*, making a dreadful havoc among *the mighty*, the Egyptians, whom he invaded, and *the holy people* the Jews, who were such by profession, whom he harrassed dreadfully, and God suffers him to *prosper and practise*. Craft is his grand engine, and by policy he shall succeed: thus he robbed his nephew of his kingdom, and under pretence of friendship seized upon Egypt: *and he shall magnify himself in his heart*, be filled with pride on his success; *and by peace shall destroy many*, under the cloak of treaties and specious professions, he shall encroach on his neighbours, as he did in Egypt and Judea, or *in peace*, surprizing them by an unprepared and unexpected attack in the midst of profound security. *And he shall stand up against the Prince of princes*, the most high God, erecting an idol in his temple, and putting a stop to his worship; *but he shall be broken without hand*, not by any outward enemy, but by the secret hand of God, who struck him with a disease in his bowels, and in his body the worms bred so fast, that his flesh rotted on him, and the stench was intolerable, 1 *Mac* vi 8. 2 *Mac* ix 5—9 so that he died a dreadful monument of divine vengeance, confessing, it is said, the judgment of God, and owning himself vanquished. *And the vision of the evening and of the morning*, the 2300 days, *v* 14 *is true*, so long the sanctuary shall be defiled: *wherefore shut thou up the vision* from the Chaldeans, whose ruin approached, or the Persian, whose destruction would in its season follow, *for it shall be for many days*, it being upwards of three hundred years from the time of the prophecy, to the death of Antiochus. *Note*, (1.) Whatever God decrees, though the fulfilment be distant, it is sure. (2.) They who magnify themselves against God, shall by death be made to know they are but men.

Lastly, The vision left a deep impression upon him. He *fainted* on the view of the terrible sufferings his people were to endure, and *he was sick certain days*, could not recover from the distress into which the vision had thrown him. *Afterwards I rose up*, from his bed, to which he had been confined, *and did the king's business*, according to the duty of his place; *and I was astonished at the vision*, at the awful contents of it, *but none understood it*, he either kept the whole quite a secret, or if he told the vision, he mentioned not the interpretation, shutting it up as he was commanded. *Note*, (1.) The distress of God's people cannot but deeply affect every gracious soul. (2.) Our grief must never be so inordinate as to disable us from the duties of our station.

CHAP. IX.

In this chapter we have, 1. Daniel's prayer for the restoration of the Jews who were in captivity, in which he confesseth sin, acknowledgeth the justice of God in their calamities, but pleads God's promises of mercy which he had yet in store for them, ver. 1—19. *2. An immediate answer sent him by an angel, in which, (1.) He is assured of the discharge of the Jews out of their captivity presently*, ver. 20—23. *and is informed concerning the redemption of the world by Jesus Christ, of which that was a type, what should be the nature of it, and when it should be accomplished*, ver. 24—27. *And it is the clearest prophecy of the Messiah in all the Old* Testament.

538 a Chap. v. 31. & vi. 28. b 2 Chron. xxxvi. 21. Jer. xxv. 12. & xxix. 10. c Pf. cii. 1. & cxxxi. Chap. vi. 10.

1 IN the first year of [a] Darius the son of Ahasuerus,
of the seed of the Medes, which was made king
over the realm of the Chaldeans, 2 In the first year
of his reign, I Daniel understood by books the number
of the years, whereof the word of the LORD came to
[b] Jeremiah the prophet, that he would accomplish seven-
ty years in the desolations of Jerusalem. 3 ¶ And I
set my face unto the Lord GOD, [c] to seek by prayer
and supplications, with fasting, and sackcloth, and
ashes.

v. 1—3. The date of this prophecy is in the first year of Darius, when the seventy years of the Jewish captivity ended, reckoning from the third of Jehoiakim.

1. Daniel had been diligently searching the Scriptures, and out of the book of Jeremiah understood that the time was at hand for the accomplishment of God's promise, in the restoration of his people. *Note*, They who diligently search the Scriptures will find there what will amply compensate their pains.

2. He became an earnest intercessor for the accomplishment of the promised mercy. In fasting and sackcloth he deeply humbled himself, under a sense of the sins which had provoked God's displeasure, and as a mourner over the desolations of Zion, and with faith and importunity *set his face* to the Lord, *to seek by prayer and supplications* the hastening their deliverance in his good time. *Note*, (1.) What God promises should be the matter of our prayers. (2.) They who have the interests of God's church at heart, cannot but be deeply affected with its desolations, and earnest supplicants that God would *revive his work in the midst of the years*.

Before Christ 538.

4 And I prayed unto the LORD my God, and made
my confession, and said, O [d] Lord, the great and dread-
ful God, keeping the covenant, [e] and mercy to them
that love him, and to them that keep his command-
ments. 5 [f] We have sinned, and have committed
iniquity, and have done wickedly, and have rebelled,
even by departing from thy precepts, and from thy
judgments: 6 [g] Neither have we hearkned unto thy
servants the prophets, which spake in thy name, to our
kings, our princes, and our fathers, and to all the peo-
ple of the land. 7 O Lord, [h] righteousness † belong-
eth unto thee, but unto us [i] confusion of faces, as at
this day; to the men of Judah, and to the inhabitants
of Jerusalem, and unto all Israel *that are* near, and *that
are* far off, through all the countries whither thou hast
driven them, because of their trespass that they have
trespassed against thee. 8 O Lord, [k] to us *belongeth*
confusion of face, to our kings, to our princes, and to
our fathers, because we have sinned against thee. 9
[l] To the Lord our God *belong* mercies and forgivenesses,
though we have rebelled against him. 10 Neither
have we obeyed the voice of the LORD our God, to
walk in his laws which he set before us by his servants
the prophets. 11 Yea, [m] all Israel have transgressed
thy law, even by departing, that they might not obey
thy voice; therefore the curse is poured upon us, and
the oath [n] that *is* written in the law of Moses the servant
of God, because we have sinned against him. 12 And
[o] he hath confirmed his words which he spake against us,
and against our judges that judged us, by bringing up-
on us a great evil: [p] for under the whole heaven hath
not been done, as hath been done upon Jerusalem.
13 [q] As *it is* written in the law of Moses, all this evil
is come upon us: [r] yet made we not our prayer before
the LORD our God, that we might turn from our
iniquities, and understand thy truth. 14 Therefore
hath the LORD [s] watched upon the evil, and brought
it upon us: for [t] the LORD our God *is* righteous in all
his works which he doth: for we obeyed not his voice.
15 And now, O LORD our God, [u] that hast brought
thy people forth out of the land of Egypt with a mighty
hand, and hast gotten thee [x] renown as at this day;
[y] we have sinned, we have done wickedly. 16 ¶ O
LORD, [z] according to all thy righteousness, I beseech
thee, let thine anger and thy fury be turned away from
thy city Jerusalem, [a] thy holy mountain: because for
our sins, [b] and for the iniquities of our fathers, [c] Je-
rusalem and thy people [d] *are become* a reproach to all
that are about us. 17 Now therefore, O our God,
hear the prayer of thy servant, and his supplications,
[e] and cause thy face to shine upon thy sanctuary [f] *that is*
desolate, [g] for the LORD's sake. 18 [h] O my God,
incline thine ear, and hear; open thine eyes, [i] and be-
hold our desolations, and the city [k] which is called by
thy name: for we do not present our supplications before
thee [l] for our righteousnesses, but for thy great mercies.
19 O LORD hear, O LORD forgive, O LORD
hearken and do; defer not, [m] for thine own sake, O
my God: for thy city and thy people are called by thy
name.

d Deut. vii. 9. Neh. i. 5. & ix. 32. e Exod. xx. 6. f 1 Kings viii. 47, 48. Pf. cvi. 6. Isa. lxiv. 5, 6, &c. Baruch i. 17. g 2 Chron. xxxvi. 15, 16. h Pf. li. 4. † Or, thou hast, &c. i Rom. vi. 21. k Ezra ix. 6. Bar. i. 15. l Neh. ix. 17. Psalm cxxx. 4, 7. m Isa. i. 3, 6. n Lev. xxvi. 14, &c. Deut. xxvii. 15, &c. and xxviii. 15, &c. & xxix. 20, &c. & xxx. 17, 18. & xxxi. 17, &c. & xxxii. 19, &c. Lam. i. 17. o Zech. i. 6. p Lam. i. 12. & ii. 13. Ezek. v. 9. Amos iii. 2. q Ver. 11. r Hos. vii. 7. s Jer. xxxi. 28. & xliv. 27. t Neh. ix. 33. u Exod. vi. 6. & xxxii. 11. 1 Kings viii. 51. Neh. i. 10. Jer. xxxii. 20. y Ver. 5. z 1 Sam. xii. 7. Pf. xxxi. 1. & lxxi. 2. a Mic. vi. 5. Zech. viii. 3. b Exod. xx. 5. c Lam. ii. 15, 16. d Pf. xliv. 14. & lxxix. 4. e Num. vi. 25. Pf. lxxx. 3, 7, 19. f Lam. v. 18. g John xvi. 24. h Isa. xxxvii. 17. i Exod. iii. 7. k Jer. xxv. 29. l Isa. lxiv. xxv. 12. m Pf. lxxix. 9.

v. 4—19. We have here Daniel's effectual fervent prayer.

1. He opens with a most reverential address *to the great and dreadful God*, terrible to the sinner, and a consuming fire, yet *full of mercy* towards those who love and serve him, and *faithful* to all the promises of that everlasting covenant he hath established with them, *v.* 4.

2. He makes his humble confession of sin, the cause of all their sufferings. They had provoked God by every possible aggravation of their iniquities, they had rebelled against him, rejected his government, broken all his precepts, positive and moral, and from the king upon the throne, to the meanest of the people, notwithstanding their peculiar obligation, all had joined in the revolt, and were alike deaf to the admonitions of God's prophets, the corrections of his providences, and the threat-

Before Christ 538.

threatnings of his word; and this is repeatedly acknowledged, v. 9—11, 14. as the burden which lay on the prophet's heart, as it ever will on all true penitents, when they begin in simplicity and godly sincerity to return to God.

3. He justifies God in the punishments inflicted upon them. God was righteous, and they could not in the least except to his dispensations; heavy as his hand was upon them in all the countries of their dispersion, it was less than their iniquities deserved; and with *confusion of face* they must bow into the dust, and kiss the rod that smote them; *all from the king to the beggar*, must own in the acknowledgment of God's justice, and take deepest shame to themselves for their provocations, for they had the fairest notice of the consequences of their iniquities; nor could God, consistent with the honour of his government, overlook such flagrant offences: the curse under which they groaned had been foretold by Moses, and God's faithfulness was glorified in the infliction of it upon them, v. 11. Their sufferings were singular as their crime, enough it might be thought to have long since bowed the most obdurate heart; but they had continued incorrigibly impenitent, never thought of returning to God; nay, they did not so much as direct one prayer to him to sanctify their afflictions, or to remove his terrible indignation from them. No marvel therefore that he still *watched over them for evil*. *Note*, (1.) In all our sufferings, however severe, we must own God is righteous, and take to ourselves deserved shame. (2.) If sinners continue incorrigible, God's wrath will abide upon them. (3.) In our anguish our first recourse should be to God *in prayer*.

4. Though the iniquities of the people were so incontestibly evident and aggravated, the prophet still had recourse to the divine mercy, v. 9. it was God's distinguished glory, that to him belonged *mercies and forgivenesses*; his patience infinite, his compassions boundless; and this is the only hope of the miserable sinner, else he must for ever despair. Wondrous had been the instances of the divine interposition in time past; the fame of his delivering his people from Egypt, was to that day heard to his glory: what he had done before, therefore, the prophet hopes he will do again, and by delivering them now from Babylon, exalt yet more abundantly his own great name, and once more magnify his power and grace towards them, *Jer.* xvi. 14. As if to excite the Divine commiseration, he spreads their present wretchedness before him; they were become the contempt of the heathen, and a reproach to the neighbouring nations; their holy city of Jerusalem laid in ruins, and that once glorious sanctuary, their boast and honour, now desolate and profaned. *Note*, (1.) They who have made themselves wicked, may expect that God will make them vile. (2.) Nothing afflicts the gracious heart so much as the desolations of the sanctuary, and the triumphs of the wicked over it.

5. He concludes with importunate supplications, urged with the greatest vehemence and most engaging pleas. He founds all his hopes upon the covenant relation God yet stood in towards them, *O our God*, and therefore is emboldened to ask, [1.] The forgiveness of their sins, the cause of their calamities; and this is the sinner's first concern, the pardon of his guilt being more desirable than the removal of all his afflictions. [2.] He begs that he would turn away his wrath from Jerusalem, under the dire tokens of which the city at present lay, and *cause his face to shine upon the desolate sanctuary*, restoring it from the ruins, setting up again his worship there, and favouring them once more with a sense of his gracious presence in the midst of them. [3.] He entreats that the Lord would not defer their deliverance and recovery. They seemed at the last gasp, and the time of the promise was now come, so that he could with faith plead for a present and immediate answer of peace; and he urges this his request,

(1.) With an absolute renunciation of any trust and dependance on themselves, as deserving the least notice or regard, v. 18. and this every humbled sinner who approaches God unfeignedly doth.

(2.) With an entire dependance on God, drawing their pleas for mercy from the consideration of his own glory. It must be *for his own sake*, not theirs, v. 19. to magnify the riches of his grace; *for the Lord's sake*, v. 17. the Lord Jesus, the sinner's atonement, righteousness and advocate, in and thro' whom alone any covenant mercies can be bestowed. *His righteousness*, v. 16. would be herein displayed, when he should execute vengeance on their cruel enemies, and prove his faithfulness to his promises; and *his mercy*, v. 18. would in the most eminent manner be evidenced, when thus exercised towards objects so utterly unworthy, and withal so exceedingly miserable. And finally, the sanctuary was his own, v. 17. and *the city and people called by his name*, v. 19. He had an interest therefore in their recovery and restoration, and they had, by virtue of their relation to him, a peculiar claim upon him, to help them, even for his own glory, the most effectual plea we can make in any of our prayers.

20 ¶ And [n] whiles I was speaking, and praying, and confessing [o] my sin, and the sin of my people Israel, and presenting my supplication before the LORD my God, for the holy mountain of my God; 21 Yea, whiles I was speaking in prayer, even the man [p] Gabriel, whom I had seen in the vision at the beginning, being caused to fly † swiftly, [q] touched me [r] about the time of the evening oblation. 22 And [s] he informed *me*, and talked with me, and said, O Daniel, I am now come forth to give thee skill and understanding. 23 [t] At the beginning of thy supplications the commandment came forth, and I am come to shew *thee*; for [u] thou *art* ‡ greatly beloved: therefore understand the matter, and consider the vision. 24 Seventy weeks are determined upon thy people, and upon thy holy city, to § finish the transgression, and to || make an end of sins, and [x] to make reconciliation for iniquity, and [y] to bring in everlasting righteousness, and [z] to seal up the vision and ¶ prophecy, and [a] to anoint the most Holy. 25 [b] Know therefore and understand, *that* [c] from the going forth of the commandment to ‡ restore and to build Jerusalem, unto the Messiah [d] the Prince, *shall be* seven weeks, and threescore and two weeks: the street shall be built again, and the § wall, [e] even in troublous times. 26 And after threescore and two weeks [f] shall Messiah be cut off, [g] but not for himself: and the people of the prince that shall come, shall [h] destroy the city, and the sanctuary; and [i] the end thereof *shall be* [k] with a flood, and unto the end of the war desolations are determined. 27 (And [l] he shall confirm || the covenant with many for one week: and in the midst of the week he shall cause the sacrifice and the oblation to cease, and ¶ for the overspreading of [m] abominations, he shall make *it* desolate, even until [n] the consummation, and that determined shall be poured upon the ‡ desolate.

Marginal notes: n Isa. lxv. 24. Acts iv. 31. — o Ezek. vi. 9. — p Chap. viii. 16. — † Heb. With weariness, or flight. — q Chap. viii. 18. & x. 10, 16. — r 1 Kings xviii. 36. — s Chap. x. 14. — t Chap. x. 12. — u Chap. x. 11, 19. — ‡ Heb. A man of desires. — § Or, restrain. — || Or, seal up. Lam. iv. 22. — x Isa. liii. 10. 2 Cor. v. 21. — y Isa. li. 6, 8. Jer. xxiii. 6. Heb. ix. 12. — z Mat. xi. 13. — ¶ Heb. Prophet. — a Luke i. 35. John iii. 34. Heb. ix. 14. — b Mat. xxiv. 15. — c Ezra vii. 11. See Or. Neh. ii. 18. — ‡ Or, build again, &c. — d Isa. lv. 4. — § Or, breach, or ditch. — e Neh. iv. 8, &c. — f Isa. liii. 8. Mat. ix. 2. — g 2 Cor. v. 21. — h Mat. xxii. 7. Luke xix. 44. — i Mat. xxiv. 14. — k Isa. viii. 7, 8. Chap. xi. 22. Nah. i. 8. — l Rom. v. 15. — || Or, a. — ¶ Or, upon the battlements shall be the idols of the desolator. — m Mat. xxiv. 15. Mark xiii. 14. Luke xxi. 20. — n Isa. x. 22, 23. & xxviii. 22. Chap. xi. 36. Luke xxi. 24. Rom. xi. 26. — ‡ Or, desolator.

v. 20—27. Very memorable is the answer here given to the prophet's prayer, and it contains one of the most remarkable prophecies of the Messiah which is to be found in the book of God. We have,

1. The time when this answer was given him, whilst *he was speaking and praying*, confessing his own sins and those of his people, and making supplication before God for pardon, and the restoration of God's sanctuary. The hour he had chosen for these devotions, was that of the evening oblation, when the lamb was offered, which prefigured him who should appear *in the end of the world to take away sin by the sacrifice of himself*, and for whose sake this revelation was now made to the prophet. *Note*, (1.) God is pleased some times to return immediate and sensible answers to the prayers of his faithful people. (2.) Daniel, though so distinguished a saint, does not approach God, but with the humiliation of a sinner; the best of men are no better. Woe to those whose pride leads them to entertain higher conceits of their attainment.

2. The messenger is an angel, *Gabriel the mighty One of God*, appearing in a human form, the same Daniel had seen before, *chap.* viii. 16. He came with haste to deliver the message on which he was sent from on high, *and touched* him to engage his attention, and give him an intimation to desist from prayer, and hearken to what he was about to deliver, talking familiarly with him, as a man with his friend, v. 22. He informs Daniel, that the moment he began to seek the Lord, *the commandment came forth*, either from the Lord, dispatching him on his errand, or at that very time the proclamation for the Jews release was signed by Cyrus. He lets him know how highly he was regarded of God, *Thou art greatly beloved*, or *art desires*, exceeding amiable in the eyes of God and all his saints: and as the Lord intended to reveal to him his secrets, he must attend to, *and consider the following vision*. *Note*, (1.) Angels, though great in power and might, are but the servants of God's pleasure, and ministers to the heirs of salvation. (2.) God's saints are greatly beloved by him, and he makes them know it by the visits of his grace, not to raise in them a conceit of themselves, but to humble them under a sense of their unworthiness, and engage a large return of love and gratitude. (3.) They who would understand the things of God, must consider them attentively and seriously.

3. The message which he brought. *Seventy weeks* of years, as they are generally interpreted, containing 490 years, *are determined upon thy people, and the holy city*; so long God had decreed their polity should last, or the most remarkable events concerning them should fall within that space of time; *to finish the transgression, and to make an end of sins, and to make reconciliation for iniquity, and to bring in everlasting righteousness, and to seal up the vision and prophecy, and to anoint the most Holy*. These are the grand matters which shall be transacted within that period by the Messiah, the hope of Israel. He came *to finish transgression*, by taking upon himself the iniquities of his people, and thereby compleatly satisfying the justice of God on their behalf, that so he might be reconciled to them, no sin be any longer imputed to them, no condemnation ever more be suffered to light upon them, but that their redemption should be perfect and eternal, obtained by the oblation of his body once for all, *and to bring in everlasting righteousness*, or *the righteousness of ages*.

Before Christ 538

ages, that divine righteouſneſs, which in his own perſon, by his obedience to death, even the death of the croſs, he ſhould work out for his people, which ſhould be *brought in* for their uſe and benefit, imputed to them as their own, and in virtue of which, the redeemed in all ages ſtand juſtified before God, and are enabled to claim the reward of eternal life, which God hath promiſed to perfect obedience *and to ſeal up the viſion and propheſy*, which ſhould receive their full accompliſhment in Chriſt Jeſus, *and to anoint the moſt Holy*, the Meſſiah, moſt holy both in his divine and human nature, and appointed to, and qualified for the office of mediator by that oil of gladneſs, the gift of the Spirit, which the Father without meaſure imparted to him. Though this may alſo be applied to the people of God, who have an unction from the Holy One, and are ſanctified by his ſpirit, which in the days of the Meſſiah ſhould be poured out in the moſt abundant manner. *Know therefore and underſtand, that from the time of the going forth of the commandment to reſtore and to build Jeruſalem, unto Meſſiah the Prince, ſhall be ſeven weeks, and threeſcore and two weeks* this is the period fixed, from whence the ſeventy weeks are to be dated, which ſome ſuppoſe commenced from that very day of Cyrus's proclamation, and exactly ended at Chriſt's death, but in order to make the intermediate time correſpond herewith, they allow but 130 years to the Perſian monarchy, which, according to the beſt hiſtorians, continued more than two hundred others, and which ſeems the more approved way of computing theſe weeks, ſuppoſe the commencement of them not to be from Cyrus's permiſſion of the Jews to return, but from the edict of Artaxerxes, in his ſeventh year, *Ezra* vii 8—12 or from that given to Nehemiah, in the twentieth year of his reign, *Neh.* ii 1—8 wherein expreſs mention is made of rebuilding Jeruſalem, and this will make the expiration of the ſixty-nine weeks, or 483 years, fall juſt at the year thirty-three, being generally ſuppoſed the year of Chriſt's death. The dividing of the weeks into different periods of ſeven, threeſcore and two, and one, ſeems to have reſpect to the different events, peculiar to theſe ſeveral ſpaces of time. The firſt ſeven weeks, or forty-nine years, includes the troubleſome times when the city was rebuilding, during which Sanballat, Tobiah, and Geſhem, ſo oppoſed the work. And the like oppoſition may they expect who zealouſly ſtand up in every age to build the walls of Chriſt's church, but againſt them no enemy ſhall finally prevail. *And after threeſcore and two weeks ſhall Meſſiah be cut off*, at the expiration of 483 years, *but not for himſelf*, but for the ſins of his people, which were laid upon him. *and the people of the prince that ſhall come, ſhall deſtroy the city and the ſanctuary*, as the Roman emperor did with his armies, *and the end thereof ſhall be with a flood*, ſo irreſiſtibly ſhould they ſweep the land, *and unto the end of the war deſolations are determined*, from the beginning of the war to the end, God had in righteous judgment given the Jewiſh people up to be conſumed. *And he ſhall confirm the covenant with many for one week* which, as ſome ſuppoſe, refers to Meſſiah the Prince, confirming the covenant of grace, and by his own oblation of himſelf putting a period to the ceremonial ſervices, but rather reſpects the prince of the Romans, who ſhould come, having for that purpoſe made peace with other nations, as he did, in order to be more diſengaged to wreak his vengeance on the Jews. *and in the midſt of the week he ſhall cauſe the ſacrifice and the oblation to ceaſe*, thro' the ſtraitneſs of the ſiege, the famine which prevailed, and the tumults which were in the city, before it was taken they had ceaſed to offer the daily ſacrifice, *for the overſpreading of abominations*, for the wickedneſs of the Jewiſh people, who had filled up the meaſure of their iniquities, *he ſhall make it deſolate*, God giving the land into the hand of the Romans. ſome read the word, *upon the wing*, or battlement, *ſhall be the idols of the deſolator*, the Roman enſign, with their idols thereon pourtrayed, ſhould be fixed on the walls, or in the ſanctuary, *even until the conſummation, and that determined ſhall be poured upon the deſolate*, either theſe armies with their abominations ſhould beſiege the city, till the determined conſumption ſhould be made, and the land utterly deſolate, or their deſolation ſhould remain till the time prefixed in the Divine decree, when the fulneſs of the Gentiles ſhould come in, *Luke* xxi 24. Some render the words, *upon the deſolator*, meaning the Roman, who ſhould themſelves be at laſt cut off, and then the deſolations of Zion ſhall ceaſe.

This laſt week, according to the interpretation given, is ſeparated from the reſt, and the events contained in it, through the forbearance of God, deferred for a time, till about thirty years after the expiration of the ſixty-nine weeks. On the whole, we have here an unanſwerable argument againſt the Jews, who reject the true Meſſiah, it being evident, according to theſe prophecies, that he muſt have appeared many hundred years ago, and all the things predicted of him, exactly correſponding with our adored Lord appearing in the fleſh, we are aſſured that this is he that ſhould come, nor look for another.

CHAP. X.

This chapter and the two next (which conclude this book) make up one entire viſion and propheſy, which was communicated to Daniel for the uſe of the church, not by ſigns and figures as before, chap vii *and* viii *but by expreſs words, and this was about two years after the viſion in the foregoing chapter. This chapter ſhews us,* 1 *Daniel's ſolemn faſting and humiliation,* ver 1—3. 2 *A glorious appearance of the Son of God, and the deep impreſſion it made upon him,* ver 4—9. 3 *The encouragement that was given him to expect ſuch a diſcovery of future events, as ſhould be ſatisfactory and uſeful both to others and to himſelf, and that he ſhould be enabled both to underſtand the meaning of this diſcovery, though difficult, and to bear up under the luſtre of it, though* dazzling *and* dreadful, *ver* 10—21.

Before Christ 534

1 IN the third year of Cyrus, king of Perſia, a a Mat. xii.
thing was revealed unto Daniel, (b whoſe name 17.
was called Belteſhazzar) and c the thing *was* true, but b Chap. i. 7.
the time appointed *was* long, and d he underſtood the c Chap. viii. 26. Rev. xix. 9.
thing, and had underſtanding of the viſion. 2 In thoſe
days I Daniel was e mourning three † full weeks. 3 I ate d Chap. i. 17.
no ‡ pleaſant bread, f neither came fleſh nor wine in my e Jer. ix. 1.
mouth, neither did I anoint myſelf at all, till three † Heb. Weeks of days.
whole weeks were fulfilled. 4 And in the four and
twentieth day of the firſt month, as I was by the ſide of ‡ Heb. Bread of deſires.
the great river, which *is* g Hiddekel. 5 Then I lift
up mine eyes, and looked, and behold, h a certain man f Mat. vi. 17.
clothed in linen, whoſe loins *were* i girded with k fine g Gen. ii. 14.
gold of Uphaz. 6 His body alſo *was* like the beryl, h John v.
and l his face as the appearance of lightning, m and his 13. Chap. xii. 6.
eyes as lamps of fire, and his arms, n and his feet like in
colour to poliſhed braſs, o and the voice of his words
like the voice of a multitude. 7 And I Daniel p alone p Mat. xvii.
ſaw the viſion, for the men that were with me ſaw not
the viſion. but a great quaking fell upon them, ſo that
they q fled to hide themſelves. 8 Therefore I was left
alone, and ſaw this great viſion, r and there remained no
ſtrength in me. for § my comelineſs was turned in me
into corruption, and I retained no ſtrength. 9 Yet q Gen. iii. 10.
heard I the voice of his words. and s when I heard the r Chap. viii. 27.
voice of his words, then was I in a deep ſleep on my face, s Chap. viii. 18. § Or, vigour.
and my face toward the ground.

v 1—9 In the third year of Cyrus, this laſt of Daniel's prophecies bears date. He was now a very aged man, and high in God's favour, who revealed to him another ſcene of events, which would certainly come to paſs in their appointed ſeaſon, though the time was long, at the diſtance of three hundred years. and this viſion was not couched under any emblematical figures, as the former, but in direct words declared, ſo that he had a clear underſtanding of the facts related, and of the things that ſhould come to paſs.

We have an account,

1 Of the ſituation in which the prophet was when this viſion appeared to him. He had been *mourning three full weeks*, and *ate no pleaſant bread*, what he uſed was coarſe as well as ſcanty, he neither taſted *fleſh* nor *wine*, nor *anointed himſelf* during the whole time, but ſpent it in deep humiliation of ſoul and body before the Lord. The cauſe, ſome ſuggeſt, was the wickedneſs of the Jews he had foreſeen in cutting off the Meſſiah, and the deſolations which would follow it, as others, the backwardneſs of many in Babylon to return to Jeruſalem, or the obſtruction and difficulties they met with who were returned to Judea. But whatever was the cauſe, it ſhewed the mortified ſpirit of this holy ſaint of God, and the concern he bore towards his people.

2 A glorious perſonage appears to him. he was by the river Hiddekel, with others probably aſſembled for the purpoſes of devotion, when lifting up his eyes, he ſaw *a man*, the man Chriſt Jeſus, who in the fulneſs of time ſhould become incarnate. he was clothed in ſacerdotal garments of linen, as the great high prieſt of our profeſſion, in ſpotleſs innocence, girt with a girdle of the *gold of Uphaz*, intimating his own excellence and perfection, and his readineſs to fulfil the work which was given him to do. *his body was like the beryl*, beautiful and poliſhed, his countenance bright *as the lightning*, and full of awful majeſty, *and his eyes ſhone as lamps of fire*, piercing into the ſecrets of the ſoul, and ſpeaking terror to his enemies. *His arms and feet like poliſhed braſs*, denoted his almighty power and ſtability to uphold his church and people, and tread down their foes, *and his voice like the voice of a multitude*, loud and heard afar off, the voice of his judgments, and eſpecially of his goſpel. Juſt in the ſame manner he afterwards appeared to John, *Rev.* i 13—15.

3 This glorious perſon was viſible to him, but not to thoſe who were with him, yet they heard and ſaw enough to fill them with deep conſternation, *ſo that they fled to hide themſelves*, whilſt Daniel remained alone before the Lord, and overwhelmed with the brightneſs of his glory, he fell into a ſwoon at his feet, pale as death, and his ſtrength utterly gone, ſo unable are the beſt of men, in this frail ſtate of mortality, to bear the diſcoveries

Before Christ 534

vetics of the Divine glory yet, though prostrate on the ground, and his bodily senses locked up in sleep, he heard *the voice of his words*, the Lord having other ways of conveying his mind to us than through the organs of sense, he can speak immediately to the soul

10 ¶ And [u] behold, an hand touched me, which set
me upon my knees, and *upon* the palms of my hands
11 And he said unto me, O Daniel, [x] a man greatly
beloved, understand the words that I speak unto thee,
and stand upright for unto thee am I now sent And
when he had spoken this word unto me, I stood tremb
ling 12 Then said he unto me, [y] Fear not, Daniel
for from the first day that thou didst set thine heart to
understand, and to chasten thyself before thy God, [z] thy
words were heard, and I am come for thy words 13
But [a] the prince of the kingdom of Persia [b] withstood me
one and twenty days but lo, [c] Michael † one of the
chief princes came to help me, and I remained there with
the kings of Persia 14 Now I am come to make thee
understand what shall befal thy people [d] in the latter
days for [e] yet the vision *is* for *many* days 15 And
when he had spoken such words unto me, [f] I set my face
toward the ground, and I became dumb 16 And be-
hold, *one* like the similitude of the sons of men [g] touched
my lips then I opened my mouth, and spake, and said
unto him that stood before me, O my lord, by the vi-
sion [h] my sorrows are turned upon me, and I have re-
tained no strength 17 For how can ‡ the servant of
this my lord, talk with § this my lord? for as for me,
straight way there remained no strength in me, neither
is there breath left in me 18 Then there came [i] again
and touched me, *one* like the appearance of a man, and
he strengthned me 19 And said, [k] O man greatly be-
loved, fear not, peace *be* unto thee, be strong, yea, be
strong And when he had spoken unto me, I was
strengthned, and said, Let my lord speak, for thou
hast strengthned me 20 Then said he, Knowest thou
wherefore I come unto thee? and now will I re-
turn to fight [l] with the prince of Persia and when
I am gone forth, lo, the prince of Grecia shall come
21 But I will shew thee *that which is* noted in the scrip-
ture of truth and *there is* none that ‖ holdeth with me
in these things, [m] but Michael your prince

u Chap ix 21 Rev i 13 · x Chap ix 23 · y Jol n iv 18 Rev i 17 · z Chap ix 4, &c · a Ver 20 · b Eph vi 12 · c Ver 21 Chap xii 1 Jude 9 Rev xii 7 · † Or, the first · d Gen xlix 1 Chap ii 28 · e Chap viii 26 Hab ii 3 · f Ver 9 · g Isa vi 7 Jer i 9 · h Ver 8 · ‡ Or, this servant of my lord · § Or, that my lord · i Chap viii 18 · k Ver 11 · l Ver 13 · ‖ Heb strengtheneth himself · m Ver 13 Jude 9 Rev xii 7

v 10—21 From this debilitated state of body, the prophet is by degrees restored, and raised up to hear the words of the vision

1 *An hand touched me*, not the hand of Christ, but one of his ministring servants in a human form, *v* 16 and *raised him upon his hands and knees*, then bid him stand upright, which he did, though still *trembling*, *v* 11 Thus the Lord raises up dejected souls from the depths of despair, a beam of hope and comfort first breaks in improving the little strength God bestows, they begin to stand up, yet notwithstanding, their fears and doubts for a while still keep them trembling

2 The angel kindly encourages him he assures him of God's great regard to him, *v* 11 bids him not fear, *v* 12 but receive with attention what he was about to declare to him, *v* 11 for God had heard his supplications from the moment he began to speak, had respect unto his humiliations, and had sent on purpose to inform him of what should befal his people *in the latter days*, in the days of Antiochus and the prophecy extends also to more distant events, even to the reign of Antichrist, the resurrection of the dead, and the end of time, *for the vision is for many days* The angel farther informs him, that he was detained in the court of Persia one and twenty days, the time of Daniel's mourning, to counteract the devices of the prince of the kingdom of Persia, either Cambyses, or rather an evil angel, who had been endeavouring at the court of Persia to do some mischief to the people of God, but the enemy was disappointed, for Michael, a chief archangel, or rather the prince of angels, the Lord Jesus, came to Gabriel's help, strengthened him to disappoint the designs that were forming, for which end he had abode so long with the king and nobles of Persia *Note*, (1) A sense of God's love to our souls, is the grand barrier against terrifying fears (2) The moment God's people begin to speak, his ear is attentive to their prayers, and ready to grant their petition (3) Whatever plots devils or men form against Christ's people, he is able to baffle their attempt, and save his chosen from the power of evil (4) Though we need not pry curiously into the nature and employment of angels, much less pay them adoration, we may be thankful to the prince who employs them, for unnumbered kind offices we owe them, when ourselves were not apprehensive of the least danger

3 The prophet, though raised upon his feet, with downcast eyes, dumb with amazement and reverential awe, stood statue-like and motionless at these words, till the same kind hand that raised him from the dust, touched his lips, and gave him liberty of speech when, with deepest respect addressing the heavenly messenger, the prophet owns his terrors, and acknowledges their cause The vision had overpowered him, conscious of his own defilement and impurity, for saith he *How can the servant of this my lord*, I who am but dust and ashes, *talk with this*, or, *that my lord*, the glorious personage who had appeared to him, and probably still was near him no marvel his strength failed him, and that his breath even now scarce sufficed to tell his fears, *v* 17 *Note*, (1) A sense of the infinite distance between a holy God and a sinful worm, should justly overwhelm us with reverential awe, and make us own when we approach him, how unable we are *to order our speech, by reason of darkness* (2) Till God, by the effectual hand of his grace, touch our lips and loose the string of our tongue, we can neither speak of him nor to him aright

4 To remove all his fears, the third time the angelic messenger drew near, and by a touch communicated strength, both to the prophet's body and mind, that he might be capable of conversing with him, and attending to the message he was sent to bring him To remove all his fears, the angel repeats the assurances of God's love encourages him to resume his wonted peace, wishes him all prosperity in body and soul, bids him be strong in the Lord and the power of his might, and cast away every distressing apprehension, since God so highly regarded him Power accompanied his word, and Daniel, now sensible of an increase of strength, and acknowledging the favour, is ready, with deepest respect, to hear whatever his honoured visitant shall say *Note*, (1) God speaks peace to the troubled consciences of his people, and by his spirit seals the word in their hearts (2) Though we of ourselves are weak as infancy, we can do all things through Christ strengthening us

5 He gives him in general a hint of what he more fully explains afterwards *Then said he, Knowest thou wherefore I am come unto thee?* it was, as he had told him, in answer to his prayers, and to inform him concerning his people, *v* 12, 14 *and now will I return to fight with the prince of Persia*, to continue to baffle his malice against the people of God *and when I am gone forth*, having finished his work successfully, *lo! the prince of Grecia shall come*, under the Grecian monarchy, which should succeed the Persian, the same evil spirit would seek to raise up a spirit of persecution against the Jewish people, especially by means of Antiochus *But I will shew thee that which is noted in the scripture of truth*, in the decrees of God, concerning these future events *and there is none that holdeth with me in these things, but Michael your prince*, even Christ, the prince and head of his church, by whose upholding strength the ministry of his servants becomes effectual, and who will be the everlasting protector and defender of his people, from all the malice and enmity of earth or hell

CHAP XI

The angel Gabriel in this chapter performs his promise Here is a prediction, 1 Of the setting up of the Grecian upon the ruins of the Persian monarchy, ver 1—4 2 Of the affairs of the two kingdoms of Egypt and Syria, with reference to each other, ver 5—20 3 Of the rise of Antiochus Epiphanes, and his actions and successes, ver 21—29 4 Of the great mischief he should do to the Jewish church and nation, and his contempt of all religion, ver 30—39 5 Of his ruin at last, in the heat of his pursuit, ver 40—45

1 ALSO I, [a] in the first year of [b] Darius the Mede,
even I stood to confirm and to strengthen
him

a Chap ix 1 · b Ibid v 31

v 1 The first verse properly belongs to the foregoing chapter, and declares how instrumental Gabriel had been already in furthering the restoration of the Jewish people *he stood to confirm and strengthen Darius*, as soon as he had ascended the throne, in conjunction with Cyrus, in his purpose of releasing the captive Jews, when probably many opposed it God's people have friends they often little think of, and more and mightier are with them, than can be against them.

2 And now will I shew thee the truth, Behold,
there shall stand up yet three kings in Persia, and the
fourth shall be far richer than *they* all and by his
strength [c] through his riches he shall stir up all against
the realm of Grecia 3 And [d] a mighty king shall stand
up, that shall rule with great dominion, and do ac-
cording to his will 4 And when he shall stand up,
[e] his kingdom shall be broken, and shall be divided to-
ward the four winds of heaven, [f] and not to his poste-
rity,

c Chap viii 6, 7 · d Chap viii 5 · e Chap viii 7, 8 · f Ibid iv 8

Before Christ 534.

rity, [g] nor according to his dominion which he ruled:
for his kingdom shall be pluckt up, even for others be-
sides those.

[g] Chap viii 22

v 2—4 The angel, as he had promised, here leads the prophet into futurity.

1 He begins with the Persian monarchy, which had just arisen: three others should succeed Darius, then on the throne; Cyrus, his son Cambyses, and Darius Hystaspes; a fourth, richer than all the rest, should arise, Xerxes, who by his strength and riches should stir up all his own provinces and confederates, to raise an army the most numerous that probably was ever assembled, in order to invade the Grecian territories. Of which expedition heathen historians are full, and of his shameful defeat.

2 He passes on to the Grecian monarchy: to avenge this attack, a mighty king should arise, even Alexander; and having subdued the Persian empire, should set up his own despotic throne, and govern with absolute sway: but his kingdom must be quickly broken and divided, not among his posterity, none of whom succeeded him, but among others, his four great generals; who neither ruled such extensive dominions, nor with so absolute a sway as Alexander had done. So poor and transitory are human possessions: he that layeth up riches, cannot tell who shall gather them.

5 ¶ And the king of the south shall be strong, and
one of his princes, and he shall be strong above him,
and have dominion: his dominion *shall be* a great do-
minion. 6 And in the end of years they shall † join
themselves together; for the king's daughter of the south
shall come to the king of the north to make an agree-
ment: but she shall not retain the power of the arm,
neither shall he stand, nor his arm; but she shall be given
up, and they that brought her, and ‡ he that begat her,
and he that strengthned her in *these* times. 7 But
out of a branch of her root shall *one* stand up in his §
estate, which shall come with an army, and shall enter
into the fortress of the king of the north, and shall
deal against them, and shall prevail: 8 And shall also
carry captives into Egypt [h] their gods, with their princes,
and with || their precious vessels of silver and of gold; and
he shall continue *more* years than the king of the north.
9 So the king of the south shall come into *his* king-
dom, and shall return into his own land. 10 But his
sons † shall be stirred up, and shall assemble a multi-
tude of great forces: and *one* shall certainly come, [i] and
overflow, and pass through: then shall he ‡ return,
and be stirred up, [k] *even* to his fortress. 11 And the
king of the south shall be moved with choler, and shall
come forth and fight with him, *even* with the king of
the north: and he shall set forth a great multitude, but
the multitude shall be given into his hand. 12 *And*
when he hath taken away the multitude, [l] his heart
shall be lifted up; and he shall cast down *many* ten thou-
sands: but he shall not be strengthned *by it*. 13 For
the king of the north shall return, and shall set forth a
multitude greater than the former, and shall certainly come
(§ after certain years) with a great army and with much
riches. 14 And in those times there shall many stand
up against the king of the south: also || the robbers of
thy people shall exalt themselves to establish the vision;
but they shall fall. 15 So the king of the north shall
come, and cast up a mount, [m] and take the most fenced
cities: and the arms of the south shall not withstand,
neither his chosen people, neither *shall there be any*
strength to withstand. 16 But he that cometh against
him, [n] shall do according to his own will, and none
shall stand before him: and he shall stand in the † glo-
rious land, which by his hand shall be consumed. 17
He shall also set his face to enter with the strength of
his whole kingdom, and ‡ upright ones with him:
thus shall he do; and he shall give him the daughter
of women corrupting her: but she shall not stand *on*
his side, neither be for him. 18 After this shall he
turn his face unto the isles, and shall take many:
but a prince for his own behalf shall cause § the re-
proach offered by him to cease; without his own re-
proach he shall cause *it* [o] to turn upon him. 19 Then
he shall turn his face towards the fort of his own
land: but he shall stumble and fall, [p] and not be
found. 20 Then shall stand up in his || estate ‡ a raiser
of taxes *in* the glory of the kingdom: but within
few days he shall be destroyed, neither in ‡ anger, nor
in battle.

† Heb. Associate themselves

‡ Or, whom she brought forth

§ Or, place, or office.

[h] Isa xxxvii 19 & xlvi 1

|| Heb. Vessels of their desire

† Or, shall war

[i] Isa viii 8 Chap ix 26

‡ Or, be stirred up again

[k] Ver 7

[l] Chap viii 5

§ Heb. At the end of times even years

|| Heb. the children of robbers

[m] Jer v 13

[n] Chap viii 4

† Heb. land of ornament

[o] Chap. viii 9 Ver 41, 45

‡ Or, much uprightness, or, equal conditions

§ Heb. his reproach

[p] Job xx 8

|| Or, place, Ver 21

‡ Heb. One that causeth an exactor to pass over

‡ Heb. Angers.

v 5—20. The angel proceeds with the account of those events in two of these divided kingdoms, with which the people of the Jews were more nearly concerned. He foretels,

1 That two kingdoms shall arise. *The king of the south*, Ptolemy Lagus, *shall be strong*, reigning over Egypt, Libya, Cyrene, Ethiopia, Arabia, Phœnicia, Cœlo-Syria, Cyprus, several islands in the Ægean sea, and divers cities in Greece; *and one of his princes*, of Alexander's captains, Seleucus Nicanor, or the conqueror, the king of Syria, *shall be strong above him*, being the most powerful of the successors of Alexander, and possessing the largest dominions. By these two kingdoms the Jewish people were by turns miserably harrassed.

2 An attempt should be made, after some years, to unite these kingdoms by marriage: Antiochus Theos, the third king of Syria, marrying Berenice, the daughter of Ptolemy Philadelphus, in order thereby to put an end to the wars, wherewith the two kingdoms had been harrassed; but the design would prove abortive; *she shall not retain the power of the arm*: on the death of her father, Antiochus dismissed Berenice, and took his former wife Laodice, whom he had divorced; *neither shall he stand, nor his arm*, Laodice getting Antiochus poisoned, and Berenice, with all her Egyptian attendants, and her infant son, *whom she brought forth*, as it is in the margin, instead of *him that begat her*, being given up to Callinicus, Laodice's son, were murdered, *and he that strengthned her in these times*, her brother, who set out to her assistance, came too late.

3 A war hereupon will ensue. A branch from the same root, Ptolemy Evergetes, Berenice's brother, to revenge his sister's death, shall invade Syria, defeat Callinicus, seize his fortresses, plunder his country, and return laden with prisoners and spoil into Egypt; whither he was recalled by a sedition, which prevented him from entirely subduing the kingdom of the Seleucidæ. He should continue longer than the king of the north, surviving him, as Dr Prideaux remarks, about four years.

4 The sons of Seleucus Callinicus, Ceraunus and Antiochus, shall raise a vast army to recover what their father had lost: and *one* of them, Antiochus, whose brother was murdered or poisoned, having now the sole command, marched his army against the king of Egypt, bearing down at first all before him, overrunning Cœlo-Syria, and part of Arabia, and laying siege to the fortress of Raphia on his return, *v* 10. There the king of Egypt, exasperated by his ravages, met him with his army. The forces of both the combatants, according to Polybius, were prodigious, and a bloody battle was fought, in which the army of Antiochus was utterly routed, and vast multitudes slain and taken prisoners, *v* 11. Elated with this victory, the Egyptian monarch's heart was filled with pride, and forcing his way into the temple, he offered sacrifice in the holiest of all for his success. But though he had cast down so many thousands, he was not *strengthened by it*, neglecting to improve his advantages, and returning in security to the enjoyment of his pleasures, *v* 12. Dying about fourteen years after, Antiochus took advantage of the minority of his infant son Ptolemy Epiphanes, and raising a larger army than before, and collecting vast wealth, invaded the kingdom of Egypt, *v* 13. and was seconded in the attempt by many powerful allies: among the rest a lawless band of Jewish banditti, taking advantage of the feeble state of Egypt, *sought to establish the vision*, and help forward its accomplishment by their inroads, *but they shall fall*. Some interpret this of the apostates, who had joined the king of Egypt, but were cut off by Antiochus when he took Jerusalem, *v* 14. Advancing with his army, the king of Syria besieged and took the fenced cities of Phœnicia and Cœlo Syria; and after defeating Scopas, the Egyptian general, Ptolemy was unable to make head against him, *v* 15. But at his will the conqueror ravaged the country without opposition, and the Jews voluntarily submitting, *he stood in the glorious land*, which his numerous forces eat up and *consumed*; or, *by his hand it was perfected*, they being taken under his protection, and on account of their ready surrender, obtaining many privileges, *v* 16. Pushing on his ambitious design, he purposed entring Egypt with all his forces, among which were many Jews, the upright ones: and under a pretence of alliance, giving his beautiful daughter Cleopatra in marriage to Ptolemy, he thought by corrupting her to induce her to betray her husband; but his politick deceived him, for she took part with her husband, and disappointed his hopes, *v* 17. Hereupon he turned his arms to the isles in the Ægean sea, many of which he took. But the Romans, whom he insulted by invading their allies, and treating their ambassadors with contempt, stopped his career, and after many shameful defeats, obliged him to quit Lesser Asia, pay all the expences of the war, and give his own son for an hostage. Thus the reproach he had cast on them, was turned upon himself, *v* 18. Returning now to his own land, probably to Antioch, his capital, he set himself to collect the money, stipulated by treaty to be paid to the Romans; in order to which, he attempted to rob
the

Before Christ 534

the temple of Jupiter at Elymais but the people, exaſperated, roſe and ſlew him, *v* 19 His ſon Philopator ſucceeded him, *a raiſer of taxes*, obliged to oppreſs his people to levy the tribute impoſed on his father by the Romans His reign laſted not many years, and he fell not *in anger or in battle*, but by poiſon, thro' the treachery of Heliodorus his treaſurer, *v* 20 So paſſing are the kingdoms of this world, bleſſed be God for that which never fadeth away, where no wars diſturb, nor enemies enter, but an eternal reſt remaineth for the people of God

21 And in his eſtate [q] ſhall ſtand up a vile perſon, to
whom they ſhall not give the honour of the kingdom
but he ſhall come in peaceably, and [r] obtain the kingdom by flatteries 22 And [s] with the arms of a flood
ſhall [t] they be overflown from before him, and ſhall be
broken, [u] yea, alſo the prince of the covenant 23
And after the league *made* with him, he ſhall work deceitfully, for he ſhall come up, and ſhall become ſtrong (171)
with a ſmall people 24 He ſhall enter † peaceably
even upon the fatteſt places of the province, and he
ſhall do *that* which his fathers have not done, nor his
fathers fathers, [x] he ſhall ſcatter among them the prey
and ſpoil, and riches *yea*, and he ſhall [y] forecaſt his devices againſt the ſtrong holds, even for a time 25 (170)
And he ſhall ſtir up his power and his courage againſt
the king of the ſouth with a great army, and the king
of the ſouth ſhall be ſtirred up to battle with a very
great and mighty army, but he ſhall not ſtand for
they ſhall forecaſt devices againſt him 26 Yea, they
that feed of the portion of his meat, ſhall deſtroy him,
and his army ſhall overflow and many ſhall fall down
ſlain 27 And both theſe kings hearts *ſhall be* to do
miſchief, and they ſhall [z] ſpeak lies at one table, [a] but
it ſhall not proſper for [b] yet the end *ſhall be* at the (168)
time appointed 28 Then ſhall he return into his land
with great riches, and [c] his heart *ſhall be* againſt the
holy covenant and he ſhall do *exploits*, and return to
his own land. 29 At the time appointed he ſhall return, and come toward the ſouth, but it ſhall not be
[d] as the former, or [e] as the latter 30 ¶ For [f] the ſhips
of Chittim ſhall come againſt him therefore he ſhall be
grieved and return, and have indignation [g] againſt the
holy covenant ſo ſhall he do, he ſhall even return,
[h] and have intelligence with them that forſake the holy
covenant 31 And arms ſhall ſtand on his part, and
[i] they ſhall pollute the ſanctuary of ſtrength, and ſhall
take away the daily *ſacrifice*, [k] and they ſhall place the
abomination that ‡ maketh deſolate 32 [l] And ſuch as
do wickedly againſt the covenant, ſhall he corrupt by
flatteries but [m] the people that do know their God,
ſhall be ſtrong, and do *exploits* 33 And [n] they that
underſtand among the people, ſhall inſtruct many yet
they ſhall fall by the ſword, and by flame, by captivity and by ſpoil *many* days 34 Now when they
ſhall fall, [o] they ſhall be holpen with a little help [p] but
many ſhall cleave to them with flatteries 35 And
ſome of them of underſtanding ſhall fall, [q] to try them,
and to purge, and to make *them* white, [r] *even* to the
time of the end [s] becauſe *it is* yet for a time appointed 36 And the king ſhall do according to his
will, and he ſhall exalt himſelf, [t] and magnify himſelf
above every god, [u] and ſhall ſpeak marvellous things
[x] againſt the God of gods, and ſhall proſper [y] till the indignation be accompliſhed for that that is determined,
ſhall be done 37 Neither ſhall he regard the god of
his fathers, [z] nor the deſire of women, [a] nor regard any
god for he ſhall magnify himſelf above all. 38 But
in his eſtate ſhall he honour the God of § forces and a
god whom his fathers knew not, ſhall he honour with
gold and ſilver, and with precious ſtones, and pleaſant
things 39 Thus ſhall he do in the ‖ moſt ſtrong holds
with a ſtrange god, whom he ſhall acknowledge *and*
increaſe with glory and he ſhall cauſe them to rule
over many, and ſhall divide the land for † gain 40 And
at the time of the end ſhall the king of the ſouth puſh
at him, and the king of the north ſhall come againſt
him like a whirlwind, with chariots, [c] and with horſemen,
and with many ſhips, and he ſhall enter into the countries, [d] and ſhall overflow and paſs over 41 He ſhall
enter alſo into the ‡ glorious land, and many *countries*
ſhall be overthrown but theſe ſhall eſcape out of his
hand, [e] *even* Edom, and Moab, and the chief of the children of Ammon 42 He ſhall ſtretch forth his hand
alſo upon the countries, and the land of Egypt ſhall
not eſcape 43 But he ſhall have power over the treaſures of gold, and of ſilver, and over all the precious
things of Egypt and the Libyans, and the Ethiopians
ſhall be at his ſteps 44 But tidings out of the eaſt, and
out of the north ſhall trouble him therefore he ſhall
go forth with great fury to deſtroy, and utterly to
make away many 45 And he ſhall plant the tabernacles of his palace between the ſeas in [f] the § glorious
holy mountain, [g] yet he ſhall come to his end, [h] and
none ſhall help him

Before Christ 534

[e] Iſa xi. 14.

[f] Pſ xlviii. 2. Ver 16, 41

§ Heb Mountain of delight of holineſs

[g] 1 Mac vi. 8—16 or Rev xx. 20.

[h] Pſ I 22

v 21—45 We have here a long prophecy concerning Antiochus Epiphanes, the ſucceſſor of Seleucus Philopater, and the inveterate perſecutor of the Jewiſh people

1 He is deſcribed *as a vile perſon* He had been a hoſtage at Rome, and by his immoralities, debaucheries, and extravagancies, had rendered himſelf deſpicable, and gained the title of *Epimanes the madman*, though on his coming to the crown he aſſumed that of *Epiphanes the illuſtrious*.

2 By fraud he gained the crown of Syria none ever thought of advancing him to the throne, but pretending only to take the adminiſtration, on the death of his brother, till his brother's ſon, who was an hoſtage at Rome, ſhould return to his kingdom, he met with no oppoſition But when he had once ſeized the reins, he reſolved to keep them by flatteries and preſents he won the nobles and citizens to eſpouſe his cauſe, and prevailed on Eumenes, the king of Pergamus, and Attalus, to aſſiſt him againſt the uſurper Heliodorus, *v* 1 whom he utterly routed with his forces, and entering Judea, depoſed Onias the prieſt, *the prince of the covenant*, though others think this refers to Demetrius, the lawful heir of Syria, to whom he was under an engagement to reſign the kingdom, *v* 22 but by his cunning got him detained at Rome, till, with a ſmall body of adherents, he poſſeſſed himſelf of all the fortreſſes and principal cities of Syria, and, by his munificence, ſtrongly attached his followers to his intereſts, *v* 23, 24 Some however ſuppoſe this refers to Ptolemy Philometor, whoſe friend and guardian he pretended to be, and entering Egypt with a ſmall but faithful band, he ſeized the ſtrong-holds of Egypt, and thus got the power of the kingdom into his hands This was his firſt expedition into Egypt, 1 *Mac* i 18 he afterwards entered it in a more hoſtile way, 2 *Mac* v 1 defeated Ptolemy, who oppoſed him, and over-ran the country, the king of Egypt being betrayed by his courtiers and generals, *v* 26 On this a treaty of peace was ſet on foot, and both the kings meeting at one table, either as friends at an entertainment, or in conſultation, as if deſigning to eſtabliſh firm peace and amity, endeavoured to impoſe on each other, neither intending to obſerve the terms of their agreement, and at the time appointed by the Divine Providence, the war broke out afreſh, *v* 27

In his return from Egypt, laden with ſpoils, he took Jeruſalem in his way, and hating the Jews for their covenant-relation to God, *v* 28 and being provoked by ſome commotions in his abſence, he maſſacred eighty thouſand, men, women, and children, and as many more he led captive or ſold, entered the temple, plundered it of all its veſſels, and adding theſe to the ſpoils of Egypt, arrived at Antioch, 2 *Mac* v 5—21 *Note*, The peculiarities of God's people, and his diſtinguiſhing love to them, provoke the world's hatred againſt them

A third war with Egypt enſued Antiochus again invaded the land, but his ſucceſs was not at all anſwerable to his former expeditions, *v* 29 The Romans eſpouſing the cauſe of Ptolemy, ſent their ambaſſadors, commanding him to retire, on peril of their declaring war againſt him, which, though reluctantly, he was obliged to do, and not being able to accompliſh his deſigns upon Egypt, reſolved to wreak his vengeance on the Jews, as he did moſt inhumanly, being aſſiſted by many apoſtates, who had forſaken the God of Iſrael, ſuch as Jaſon, Menelaus, and others, *See* 1 *Mac* i 11—15 *Note*, Apoſtates from the truth are uſually the bittereſt perſecutors Having the power in his hand, and armies at his beck, he entered the ſanctuary, polluted it with every abomination, prohibited the daily ſacrifice, ſet up an idol in the temple, and dedicated it to Jupiter Olympius, 2 *Mac*, vi 2

To court the favour of the tyrant, many of the wicked Jews conſented to abandon their profeſſion of the true religion, and worſhipped idols, *v* 32 For they whoſe lives are wrong, muſt needs be deſtitute of true principles, and ready to embrace any religion which promiſes them moſt advantage But the faithful were alike proof againſt flattery and threatening, and dared endure the ſevereſt torments, 1 *Mac* i 63—66 2 *Mac* vii Whilſt compelled by deſpair, ſome took to arms, and, under their valiant leader Judas Maccabæus, did great exploits, *v* 32 In ſuch days of general apoſtacy, they who knew God, by their inſtructions, and their example of patient ſufferings,

Before Chriſt 534

zealouſly inſtructed their brethren, but they were perſecuted to death, ſome ſlain with the ſword, others burnt, others enſlaved, and their ſubſtance plundered This perſecution laſted during three years and a half, *v* 33 when the noble effort of the Maccabees obtained a little reſpite, *v* 34 with whom many of the apoſtate Jews joined, when they appeared victorious, but they received the puniſhment of their perfidy, *See* 2 *Mac* xii 40 To try the faith and patience of the ſaints, and to brighten their crown, ſome of them alſo were ſuffered to *fall* into great affliction, 1 *Mac* i 60, 61 for this furnace is often needful for God's deareſt children, and they are brought to it to purge away their remaining droſs but however great the ſufferings of the faithful may be, there is *a time appointed* for their end, *v* 35

The following verſes many good interpreters ſuppoſe to refer not to Antiochus, but to the Romans, particularly to the power of the papal Antichriſt, of which Antiochus was the figure Thus the pope aſſumes deſpotic power, *v* 36 diſpenſing with the laws of God and man, depoſing princes, &c and exalteth himſelf *above every God*, either angels or civil magiſtrates, *See* 2 *Theſ* ii 4 ſpeaking great ſwelling words of blaſphemy, and proſpering till the period of his uſurpations ſhall end, *See Rev* xi 2, 3 xiii 5 forbidding marriage, *v* 37 and ſhewing an utter diſregard of God and his ordinances, ſetting up *Mahuzzim*, departed ſaints and angels, as guardians and protectors, and worſhipping them, *v* 38 paying adoration to a breaden god, or conſecrated wafer, with great pageantry of worſhip, erecting the images of *Mahuzzim* in the temples, and the people aſcribe divine honours to them, and take them for patrons, as St George for England, &c and the pope makes gain of their ſuperſtition, *v* 39 From the ſouth and north, at the time appointed, the Turks and Saracens came, and ſpread deſolation over part of this antichriſtian empire, *v* 40 The *glorious land* of Judea alſo fell into their poſſeſſion, with many other countries, *Moab and Edom, with Ammon*, only *eſcape*, ſuppoſed to ſignify Arabia, which is ſtill independent of the Turkiſh government, *v* 41 Egypt, with its treaſures, are poſſeſſed by them, *v* 42, 43 and the Libyans and Ethiopians at their command, till in future times ſome powers from the eaſt and north ſhall ſpread an alarm in the Ottoman empire, and the Turks ſhall aſſemble their forces, *v* 44, 45 and pitch their tents in the land of Judea, where they ſhall utterly be deſtroyed, *See Ezek* xxxviii xxix In this way many interpret the prophecy, but I rather incline to thoſe who refer the whole to Antiochus, whoſe pride, inſolence, and blaſphemies were notorious He regarded no God, ſet himſelf above them, introduced new deities, in his brutal executions made no diſtinction of age or ſex, but murdered women and infants In the fortreſs of the temple he erected the ſtrange god Jupiter, honoured him with gold and ſilver, cauſed his prieſts to bear rule, and gave them a rich revenue out of the land, *v* 39 doing juſt as he pleaſed, till he time appointed of God came to ſtop his mad career

On ſome attack of Ptolemy, *v* 40 Antiochus once more with fury marched againſt him, ſweeping the countries which lay in his way, particularly the land of Judea, whilſt Moab, Idom, and Ammon eſcaped his ravages, *v* 40 Egypt was plundered, the treaſures carried off, and the Libyans and Aſſyrians favoured the invaſion But in the midſt of his ſucceſſes, the tidings of the revolt of the Perſians and Parthians, *v* 44 called him back to Syria, and in rage at the diſappointment, and the embarraſſment of his affairs, to which the Jews had contributed, he threatened to exterminate them, but when he thought of gratifying his full revenge, God ſmote him, *See chap* viii 25 and he died miſerably, *v* 45 So will God in the time of need interpoſe for his people, and, however their enemies may ſeem for a while to prevail, they ſhall be rooted out at laſt

CHAP XII

After the prediction of the troubles of the Jews under Antiochus, prefiguring the troubles of the Christian church under the antichriſtian power, we have here, 1 *Comforts for the ſupport of God's people in thoſe times of trouble,* ver 1—4 2 *A conference between Chriſt and an angel, concerning the time of the continuance of theſe events,* ver 5—7 3 *Daniel's enquiry for his own ſatiſfaction,* ver 8 *and the anſwer he received to that enquiry,* ver 9—13

1 AND at that time ſhall [a] Michael ſtand up, the
great prince which ſtandeth for the children of
thy people, [b] and there ſhall be a time of trouble, ſuch
as never was ſince there was a nation, *even* to that ſame
time and at that time thy people ſhall be delivered,
[c] every one *that ſhall be* found written in [d] the book 2
And many of [e] them that ſleep in the duſt of the earth
ſhall awake, [f] ſome to everlaſting life, and ſome to ſhame,
[g] *and* everlaſting contempt 3 And [h] they that be
‡ wiſe, [i] ſhall ſhine as the brightneſs of the firmament,
and [k] they that turn many to righteouſneſs, [l] as the ſtars
for ever and ever 4 [m] But thou, O Daniel, [n] ſhut up
the words, and ſeal the book, *even* to the time of the
end many ſhall run to and fro, and [o] knowledge ſhall
be increaſed

a Chap x 13, 21 b Jer xxx 7 Mat xxiv 21 Rev xvi 18 c Rev xiii 8 d Ex xxxii 32 Pſ lvi 8 Ezek xiii 9 Luke x 20 Phil iv 3 Rev iii 5 & xiii 8 e Ezek xxxvii 12 f Mat xxv 46 John v 28, 29 Acts xxiv 15 g Iſ lxvi 24 Rom ix 21 h Chap xi 33, 35 ‡ Or teachers i Prov iv 18 Wiſd iii 7 Mat xiii 43 k Jam v 20 l 1 Cor xv 41 m Chap viii 26 Ver 9 n Rev x 4 & xxii 10 o Iſ xxix 18 Hoſ vi 3

v 1—4 When the troubles of God's people are at their height, the power and grace of their Redeemer ſhall be the more magnified in their deliverance

1 Chriſt, *the great Prince*, ſhall ſtand up in the time of great tribulation, either to ſave the Jews from the perſecutions of Antiochus, or to ſave his church from the antichriſtian tyranny, or at the great day, when he ſhall come to compleat the redemption of his people, and to execute final vengeance on their enemies, when all that are written among the righteous, and found in the book of life of the Lamb, ſhall be delivered from the power of evil for ever

2 In this great day of the appearing of our God and Saviour, an awful diſtinction will be made between the perſons who ſhall awake from the duſt of death, ſome of them ariſing to *everlaſting life*, while others, who died impenitent, ſhall awake to *ſhame and everlaſting contempt*, which would be a glorious encouragement for the ſufferers under the perſecution of Antiochus, *See Heb* xi 35 as it is to all the ſuffering ſaints of God to the end of time

3 The reward of the faithful will then be great *The wiſe*, who know and believe in Jeſus to the ſaving of their ſouls, deep read in their own ſinful ſtate, and the ſufficiency of the Redeemer's blood and righteouſneſs, theſe ſhall ſhine as *the brightneſs of the firmament*, perfectly holy, and happy, and glorious as their Lord, *and they that turn many to righteouſneſs*, the miniſters of the goſpel, and others who laboured for this bleſſed purpoſe, to bring men to the knowledge of a Redeemer's righteouſneſs, as the alone ground of their acceptance with God, and to convert their ſouls to the love and practice of holineſs, they ſhall ſhine *as the ſtars for ever and ever*, with undiminiſhed luſtre through the ages of eternity A powerful engagement this, to thoſe who are put in truſt with the goſpel, to labour with fidelity and zeal in the bleſſed cauſe, when every ſoul converted by their miniſtry ſhall add a jewel to their crown

4 Daniel is commanded to *ſeal up the book unto the time of the end*, either he was to keep the viſion ſecret, or it would not be underſtood or regarded till the times of trial came, which were at a diſtance, or it intimates the darkneſs and obſcurity of the book, till the accompliſhment of the events ſhould diſcover the meaning of the prophetic word *Many ſhall run to and fro*, at the end of time, when the things here ſpoken of begin to be fulfilled, earneſtly ſearching into this ſealed book *and knowledge ſhall be increaſed*, light will then be caſt on the prophecies, ſo that the diligent enquirer ſhall be able to underſtand them more fully than they had ever been underſtood before *Note*, (1) They who would draw knowledge from the deep well of prophetic truth, muſt diligently examine and compare ſpiritual things with ſpiritual, and in prayer fervently aſk divine illumination (2) However dark and obſcure the prophecies may now be, the time will come, when they will be clear as if written with a ſun-beam

5 ¶ Then I Daniel looked, and behold, there ſtood
other two, the one on this ſide of the bank of the river,
and the other on that ſide of the † bank of [p] the river
6 And *one* ſaid to [q] the man clothed in linen, which
was † upon the waters of the river, [r] How long *ſhall it*
be to the end of theſe wonders? 7 And I heard the
man clothed in linen, which *was* upon the waters of the
river, when [s] he held up his right hand, and his left
hand unto heaven, and ſware by him [t] that liveth for
ever, [u] that *it ſhall be* for a time, times, and an half
and [x] when he ſhall have accompliſhed to ſcatter the
power of the holy people, all theſe *things* ſhall be finiſh-
ed 8 And I heard, but [y] I underſtood not then ſaid
I, O my Lord, what *ſhall be* the § end of theſe *things*?
9 And he ſaid, Go thy way, Daniel for the words *are*
cloſed up, and ſealed [z] till the time of the end 10
[a] Many ſhall be purified, and made white, and tried
[b] but the wicked ſhall do wickedly and none of the
wicked ſhall underſtand, but [c] the wiſe ſhall underſtand,
11 And from the time *that* [d] the daily *ſacrifice* ſhall be
taken away, and ‖ the abomination that maketh deſo-
late ſet up, *there ſhall be* a thouſand two hundred and
ninety days. 12 Bleſſed *is* he that waiteth, and com-
eth to the thouſand three hundred and five and thirty
days 13 But go thou thy way till the end *be* ¶ for
[e] thou ſhalt reſt, and [f] ſtand in thy lot [g] at the end of
the days

† Heb Lip p Chap x 4 q Chap x 5 † Or from above r Chap viii 13 s Rev x 5, 6 t Chap iv 34 u Chap vii 25 & xi 1 Rev xi 14 x Rev x 7 y Chap vii 28 § Or laſt z Ver 4 a Chap xi 35 Zech xiii 9 b 1 Sam xxiv 13 Hoſ xiv 9 Rev xxii 11 c Chap xi 33, 35 d Chap viii 11 & xi 31 ‖ Heb ſet up the abomination ¶ Or and thou ſhalt reſt e Iſ lvii 2 f Pſ i 5 g 1 Cor xv 23

v 5—13 The myſterious things before ſpoken naturally excited in the prophet's mind the deſire to know *when the end* of

Before Christ 534.

of these things *should be*, and *what* would be the sign of their conclusion.

1. *How long shall it be to the end of these wonders?* This question is put by one of the angels who stood by the river, in the prophet's hearing, to the glorious personage who stood upon, or *above*, the waters of the river, the Lord Jesus, described before, *chap.* x. 5. Daniel probably feared to be too inquisitive, and though he wished to know, yet dared not ask. The answer is ushered in with great solemnity. Lifting up his hands to heaven, the great High-priest of our profession, by a solemn oath, *v.* 7. for the confirmation of the faith of his servant, (*See Rev.* x. 5, 6.) declares that the troubles will continue *for a time, times, and half*; *and when he shall have accomplished to scatter the power of the holy people, all these things shall be finished.* This some explain of the conclusion of the troubles under Antiochus, who for three years and a half held Jerusalem, and quite dispersed and broke the Jewish people. Others apply it to the reign and fall of Antichrist, where the same numbers are used, *Rev.* xi. 2, 3. xii. 6—14. when the dispersion of the Jews shall end, and they shall be gathered out of all lands; which blessed event may the Lord hasten in his time!

2. *What shall the end of these things be?* Encouraged by what he had heard of Christ's condescension in answering the former question, and not understanding the meaning of what he heard, Daniel himself is emboldened to ask, *what* events would more distinctly mark the conclusion of these troubles; or, as the words may be rendered, *what is the last of these things?* *Note*, (1.) Through the darkness of their minds the greatest saints are often at a loss in their enquiries, and humbly own their ignorance. (2.) We have one to apply to under all our doubts and difficulties, who is able to solve them. (3.) When we see the prevalence of iniquity, and the triumphs of the ungodly, we are ready in amaze to cry, What will be the end of these things? as if the cause of Christ was utterly overwhelmed; but it shall prevail at last over all opposition.

The answer Christ gives to the prophet's enquiry is very gracious. He shall know as much as he needs, and is bid to be content about the rest. *Go thy way, Daniel*, be satisfied with what thou hast heard, and prepare for eternity; *for the words are closed up, and sealed unto the end of time*, will continue till then dark and obscure, when time would interpret the vision. *Many shall be purified, and made white, and tried*, by their afflictions, and come like silver from the furnace: *but the wicked shall do wickedly*, persisting in their impenitence, and given up to judicial blindness of heart. *None of the wicked shall understand*, neither the word nor providences of God; *but the wise shall understand* both, and improve thereby. *And*, as to the immediate solution of the question, he gives him some dates by which it might be known: *from the time that the daily sacrifice shall be taken away, and the abomination which maketh desolate, there shall be a thousand two hundred and ninety days*; which some refer to what Antiochus did, and confine the prophecy to the Jewish people. Others suppose it to refer to Antichrist, the antitype, who, in opposition to the one sacrifice of Christ, hath set up the merits of man, established the worship of saints and images, and other abominations. The length of this state of trouble is declared to be *a thousand two hundred and ninety days*. *See Rev.* xiii. 5. The days here added to the number there given are, as some think, the space allotted for the conversion of the Jews. *Blessed is he that waiteth, and cometh to the thousand three hundred and five and thirty days*, at the end of which all the enemies of Christ and his people will, it is supposed, be utterly destroyed, and times of the greatest happiness and joy succeed. The period of these events indeed still remains a secret; but of this the people of God may be sure, that the end of all the sufferings of his church is fixed; that we are called with patience to wait for the blessed day; and that our happiness will then be compleat and everlasting.

The conclusion of our Lord's answer is a word of comfort, particularly addressed to Daniel himself. *Go thy way till the end be*, prepare for death, and wait for the resurrection morn; *for thou shalt rest*, dying in the Lord, and delivered for ever from all the burdens of mortality; *and stand in thy lot at the end of the days*, raised to a glorious inheritance at the last, and put in possession of that eternal kingdom God hath prepared for those who are faithful unto death. *Note*, (1.) Whilst God continues us upon earth, our business is to be found in the work he hath given us to do, waiting for our dismission, and ever ready to receive it with joy. (2.) A child of God, like Noah's dove, must not expect his rest in this tempestuous world; but when his head rests upon a pillow of dust, then shall his soul find rest in the Saviour's bosom. (3.) Whatever our lot or portion may be in this world, we have an inheritance before us incorruptible, undefiled, which fadeth not away, the believing prospect of which will effectually support us under all the trials of life, and carry us triumphant through all the terrors of death. (4.) We know, (for every believer hath the infallible promise of the unchangeable God to support his confidence,) to our everlasting comfort we know, the day is near, when Jesus shall appear, and then shall we appear with him in glory. Even so, Amen! come, Lord Jesus, come quickly!

THE

THE

EVANGELICAL EXPOSITOR;

OR, A

PRACTICAL COMMENT

Upon the PROPHECY of

HOSEA.

THE twelve minor prophets, are so called, not from any inferiority in their inspiration, or as if their writings were of less value and authority than those of their brethren, but because their prophecies were shorter, and contained in a less volume

Hosea is the first of them, as they stand in the order of our Bibles, though not the oldest, Jonah, Joel, and Amos, being thought to have prophesied before him His stile is concise and sententious, in some places very obscure, in others clear and pathetic He chiefly addressed himself to the ten tribes, exhorting, admonishing, rebuking, warning them, and foretelling the dire consequences of their impenitence He lived very long, and saw the accomplishment of his own prophecies in the ruin and captivity of Israel, for not one jot or tittle shall ever fail of the divine word till all be fulfilled

CHAP I

Before Christ 786

The mind of God is revealed to his prophet, and by him to the people, in the three first chapters by signs and types, but afterwards by discourse In this chapter we have, 1 The general title of the whole book, ver 1 2 Some particular instructions he was ordered to give to the people of God (1) He must convince them of their sin in going a whoring from God, by marrying a wife of whoredoms, ver 2, 3 (2) He must foretel the ruin coming upon them for their sin in the names of his sons, which signified God's disowning and abandoning them, ver 4, 5, 6, 8, 9 (3) He must speak comfortably to the kingdom of Judah, which still retained the pure worship of God, and assure them of the salvation of the Lord, ver 7 (4) He must give an intimation of the great mercy God had in store both for Israel and Judah, in the latter days, ver 10, 11 for in this prophecy many precious promises of mercy are mixed with the threatnings of wrath

a 2 Pet i 21
† i e A Saviour

1 THE word of the LORD that [a] came unto
† Hosea, the son of Beeri, in the days of Uzziah, Jotham, Ahaz, *and* Hezekiah, kings
of Judah, and in the days of Jeroboam the son of Joash
king of Israel

1 The prophet opens with an account of his name and parentage He was called *Hosea*, the same as Jesus or Joshua, *a Saviour*, the great business of his ministry being to promote the salvation of his people His father's name is mentioned, but of what tribe or place he was, is not said

He prophesied during the reigns of four kings of Judah, and their cotemporaries, who ruled in Israel, though but one of them is mentioned Their lives were so bad perhaps, that their very names were odious

b Chap iii 1

2 The beginning of the word of the LORD by
Hosea And the LORD said to Hosea, [b] Go, take unto
thee a wife of whoredoms, and children of whoredoms
for [c] the land hath committed great whoredom, *departing*
from the LORD
3 So he went and took † Gomer the
daughter of ‡ Diblaim, which conceived and bare him a
son
4 And the LORD said unto him, Call his name
|| Jezreel, for yet a little *while*, and [d] I will § avenge the
blood of Jezreel upon the house of Jehu, and will cause
to cease the kingdom of the house of Israel
5 And it
shall come to pass at that day, that [e] I will break the
bow of Israel in the valley of Jezreel
6 ¶ And she
conceived again, and bare a daughter, and *God* said unto him, Call her name ¶ Lo-ruhamah for I will no
more have mercy upon the house of Israel, ‡ but I will
[f] utterly take them away
7 But I will have mercy upon the house of Judah, and [g] will save them by the
LORD their God, [h] and will not save them by bow, nor
by sword, nor by battle, by horses, nor by horsemen.

Before Christ 786

c Pf lxxiii 27 Ezek xxiii 3 &c
† i e Consummation or consumption
‡ i e Cakes of figs
|| i e The seed, or scattering of God
d 2 Kings x, 11 17
§ Heb Visit
e 2 Kings xv 29
¶ i e Not having obtained mercy
‡ Or that I should altogether pardon them
f 2 Kings xv 23
g Jer xxiii 6
h Zech iv 6 &c ix 10

2—7 The first revelation of God's will to Hosea, was a fearful threatning against a rebellious people, under the figure of a man taking a *wife of whoredoms*, whom the prophet personates, to convince them of their abominations, and of the just judgment of God coming upon them

Some indeed have supposed, that Hosea literally did this which is here spoken, and married a woman of infamous conduct, Gomer, a noted strumpet, the daughter of Diblaim, by whom he had the children after mentioned but it can hardly be supposed the Lord would command him to do an action which must make him scandalous in the eyes of the people, and especially when he would be so unqualified thereby to reprove their whoredom The sense therefore above given seems much more eligible, which would fully answer the intention of rebuking

Before Christ 786

buking their wickedneſs, who ſhould have been a holy people, but had turned from God to idols, a ſin more deteſtable and odious, than if a woman ſhould treacherouſly depart from her huſband's bed, commit adultery, and bring a ſpurious brood into his family In the names of the children born of this adultereſs, the prophet is commiſſioned to foretel the approaching ruin of that devoted people

1 In the name of the firſt ſon, who is called Jezreel, God ſhews Jeroboam the deſtruction determined againſt his family, and the cauſe of it *Jezreel* ſignifies *the ſeed of God*, or *ſcattered of God*, and this is explained *for yet a little while*, in a few years, under his ſon Jechoniah, *and I will avenge the blood of Jezreel upon the houſe of Jehu*, the blood of Ahab, and his ſons and kinsfolks, which Jehu ſhed, for tho' the action was right, and God commended it, 2 *Kings* x 30 yet the temper with which Jehu did it was evil, intending not God's glory, but the gratification of his own pride, ambition, and cruelty, as afterwards evidently appeared, for tho he pretended zeal for God, when he ſeized the throne, he ſtill kept the calves in Dan and Bethel Thus many of the good works of pride and ſelf-righteouſneſs become evil from the temper with which they are done, and bring down a curſe inſtead of a bleſſing *And I will cauſe to ceaſe the kingdom of the houſe of Iſrael*, in the family of Jehu, as was ſoon fulfilled, 2 *Kings* xv 8—10 Or this may relate to the deſtruction of the ten tribes by Salmaneſer, 2 *Kings* xvii 6—23 *And it ſhall come to paſs in that day, that I will break the bow of Iſrael in the valley of Jezreel*, which refers to Menachem's ſlaughter of Shallum, 2 *Kings* xv 14—16 or to ſome battle fought there with Salmaneſer, before he ſubdued the country, 2 *Kings* xvii 6 *Note*, They who depart from God, weaken their own arms, and ſin brings certain ruin in its train

2 In the name of the ſecond child, Lo-ruhamah, God foretels his entire rejection of the whole nation The word ſignifies *not having obtained mercy*, 1 *Pet* xi 10 intimating, as the prophet from God explains it, that God would have no more mercy on the Iſraelites, but would *utterly take them away*, as was done by the king of Aſſyria, 2 *Kings* xvii Wo to the ſinner with whom God's mercies are at an end !

3 A promiſe of mercy is made to the houſe of Judah, that had preſerved the true worſhip of God, for he hath ever a choſen remnant, who, when others apoſtatiſe, ſtill approve their fidelity *I will have mercy upon the houſe of Judah, and will ſave them by the Lord their God*, not by any human power or weapons, which may refer to the deliverance of the Jews from Sennacherib's army, 2 *Kings* xix 35 or perhaps to the greater ſalvation which the Lord Jeſus ſhould accompliſh, ſubduing all the ſpiritual foes of his people, and by his own arm making them more than conquerors *Note*, (1) All our ſalvation comes not from any merit in us, but the mere mercy of our God (2) They who cleave to God as their God, ſhall find he will own them in the day of trouble, and interpoſe for their reſcue (3) Thoſe whom God *will* ſave, not all the wicked on earth, nor all the devils in hell ſhall be able to deſtroy

8 ¶ Now when ſhe had weaned Lo-ruhamah, ſhe
conceived and bare a ſon 9 Then ſaid *God*, Call his
name † Lo-ammi for [i] ye *are* not my people, and I
will not be your *God*. 10 ¶ Yet [k] the number of the
children of Iſrael ſhall be as the ſand of the ſea, which
cannot be meaſured nor numbered, [l] and it ſhall come to
paſs, *that* ‡ in the place where it was ſaid unto them,
[m] Ye *are* not my people, *there* it ſhall be ſaid unto them,
Ye are the ſons of the living God 11. [n] Then ſhall the
children of Judah, and the children of Iſrael be gathered
together, and appoint themſelves one head, and they
ſhall come up out of the land § for great *ſhall be* the
day of Jezreel

† i e Not my people
i 1 Kings xvii 6 18
k Gen. xxxii 12
l Rom ix 25 26 1 Pet ii 10
‡ Or inſtead of that
m Chap. ii 23
n Iſa xi 12 Jer iii 18 Ezek xxxiv 23 & xxxvii 16 22
§ Or, though great has been

v 8—11 The decree gone forth againſt this wicked nation is here confirmed in the name of a ſon, the third child, called Lo-ammi, after Lo-ruhamah was *weaned*, which may ſignify the patience of God for a while bearing with them, or that full captivity, when many of Gilead and Galilee were carried away by Tiglath-pileſer, 2 *Kings* xv 29

1 God rejects Iſrael from being his people, as the name *Lo-Ammi* ſignifies, *ye are not my people*, having caſt off my government and worſhip *and I will not be your God*, to bleſs, protect, and ſave you *Note*, (1) They who revolt from God, are juſtly rejected by him (2) Many claim a relation to God in name, whoſe works deny him, and whom he will therefore diſown

2 In wrath God remembers mercy, and a gracious promiſe is made of their reſtoration He that wounds will heal *Yet the number of the children of Iſrael ſhall be as the ſand of the ſea, which cannot be meaſured nor numbered*; which prophecy, whatever primary reſpect it might have to the return of the Iſraelites from their captivity with their brethren, or whatever ground of comfort it might afford to the pious captives there, yet we are aſſured, *Rom* ix 25—26 was to have its glorious accompliſhment, when Jews and Gentiles ſhould be converted to the faith of Chriſt, as was eminently the caſe, when by the preaching of the goſpel at the firſt, multitudes were added to the church, and daily we obſerve the innumerable hoſt increaſing, till the fulneſs of the Gentiles ſhall be come in at the laſt day, and *ſo all Iſrael ſhall be ſaved* *And it ſhall come to paſs, that in the place where it was ſaid unto them, Ye are not my people, there it ſhall be ſaid unto them, Ye are the ſons of the living God*, adopted into the family, and admitted to all the great and diſtinguiſhed privileges of the children of God *Then ſhall the children of Judah and the children of Iſrael be gathered together*, which ſome interpret of the union of theſe divided kingdoms, on their return from Babylon; but rather reſpects the times of the goſpel, when Galileans, Samaritans, and Jews, converted by the preaching of Chriſt and his apoſtles, were joined in one Chriſtian church, and the Gentiles afterwards incorporated therein And ſome alſo ſuppoſe particular reſpect is had to the times when the Jews ſhall be collected from their preſent diſperſion, and be univerſally turned to the Lord, *and appoint themſelves one head*, the Divine Meſſiah, to whom they ſhall be gathered at the laſt, willingly ſubmitting themſelves to his bleſſed government *and they ſhall come up out of the land*, or *the earth*, collected from all parts of it, or as experiencing a kind of reſurrection *from the ſtate* of miſery, like death, in which they lay, *for great ſhall be the day of Jezreel*, after all the affliction they have endured, their latter end ſhall be full of glory, and *Jezreel, the ſeed of God*, the faithful, ſhall be ſaved with an everlaſting ſalvation *Note*, (1) Every believer is diſtinguiſhed with the eminent dignity of being a child of the living God, and however he may be deſpiſed of men, is glorious in the eyes of the Moſt High and Moſt Holy, and ſhall be acknowledged by him in the laſt great day (2) The people of God have Chriſt for their living head, deriving from him all vital influence, yielding themſelves up to him, to be directed and governed, and through him maintaining mutual communion with each other, being all *one* in Chriſt Jeſus (3) They who have Chriſt for their head, *muſt come up from the earth*, and ſet their affections on things above, where Chriſt ſitteth at the right hand of God

CHAP II

The ſcope of this chapter ſeems to be much the ſame with that of the foregoing As there, ſo here, 1 God by the prophet diſcovers and charges ſin home upon them particularly their idolatry, and forgetting God, and their obligations to him, ver 1, 2, 5, 8 2 *He threatens to take away from them that plenty of all good things with which they had ſerved their idols, and to abandon them to ruin without remedy*, ver 3, 4, 6, 7, 9—13 3 *Yet he promiſeth at laſt to return in ways of mercy to them for his own ſake*, ver 14 *to reſtore them to their former plenty*, ver 15 *to cure them of their inclination to idolatry*, ver 16, 17 *to renew his covenant with them*, ver 18—20 *and to bleſs them with all good things*, ver. 21—23

1 SAY ye unto your brethren, ‖ Ammi, and to your
ſiſters, ‡ Ruhamah 2 Plead with your mother,
plead for [a] ſhe *is* not my wife, neither *am* I her huſ
band let her therefore put away [b] her whoredoms out
of her ſight, and her adulteries from between her breaſts,
3 Leſt I ſtrip her naked and ſet her [c] as in the day that
ſhe was born, and make her as a wilderneſs, and ſet her
like a dry land, and ſlay her with thirſt 4 And I will
not have mercy upon her children, for they *be* the chil-
dren of whoredoms. 5 For [d] their mother hath played
the harlot ſhe that conceived them hath done ſhame-
fully for ſhe ſaid, [e] I will go after my lovers [f] that give
me my bread, and my water, my wool and my flax,
mine oil and my § drink

‖ i e My people
‡ i e Having obtained mercy
a Iſa l 1
b Ezek xvi 25
c Hoſ 4
d Ibid 15
e Jer xliv 17
f Ver 12
§ Heb Drinks

v 1—5 The firſt words of this chapter may be either taken in connection with the latter part of the preceding, as ſpeaking comfort to the people of God, thoſe faithful ones, who, having choſen Chriſt for their head, are reſtored to God's favour, acknowledged by him, as *Ammi my people*, and *Ruhamah, having obtained mercy* or they have reſpect to thoſe Jewiſh converts, who in the times of the goſpel being turned to Chriſt Jeſus, and become the children of God by faith in him, are exhorted to rebuke and expoſtulate with their mother, the Jewiſh church, for her rejection of the true Meſſiah

1 God threatens utterly to ſeparate himſelf from her *She is not my wife*, hath behaved unworthy of that relation *ſhe hath played the harlot*, *v* 5 hath broken the marriage-covenant, caſting off all obedience, and committing ſpiritual adultery againſt the Lord *She that conceived them hath done ſhamefully*, leaving dumb idols, and going a whoring after ſtocks and ſtones or, *ſhe hath made aſhamed*, has been a ſcandal to her huſband and her family, and therefore he will no more own her *neither am I her huſband*, to protect, cheriſh, or provide for her he thruſts her out, gives her a divorce, and ſeparates her from all the ho-

Before Christ 786

nour and comfort of the relation in which she stood *Note*, (1) They who treacherously depart from God, will provoke him to depart from them, and wo unto the soul that is in such a case (2) Sin is not only the abominable thing God hates, but the *shameful* thing that will sooner or later cover the sinner with everlasting confusion and contempt

2 He invites her to repent and return Though offended, he was not inexorable, *Let her therefore put her whoredoms out of her sight, and her adulteries from between her breasts* as these were the occasion of the fatal separation between God and them, when the cause was removed, the effect would cease *Note*, (1) God delighteth not in the death of a sinner, but rather that he should return and live (2) They who would truly return to God, must not only put away the grosser acts of sin, but seek to root out of their bosoms the love of it, that they may be pure within

3 The consequences of her impenitence, if persisted in, would be fatal God waits upon sinners long, but if they will not turn, he whets his sword as he here threatens, *lest I strip her naked, and set her as in the day that she was born*, alluding to the wretched state of a new-born infant So destitute and miserable were they when first God took them for his people in Egypt, *Ezek* xvi 4 and to a like state of wretchedness should they be reduced *and make her a wilderness, and set her as a dry land, and slay her with thirst*, he will bring them into circumstances as deplorable as their fathers in the wilderness, or utterly destroy and ruin their nation, as the carcases of those who fell in that barren land And *I will not have mercy on her children*, but the curse shall fatally rest upon them, as it doth to this day for the rejection of the Messiah, *for they are children of whoredoms*, imitating the ill example of their parents, and therefore sharing their punishment

4 He upbraids her ingratitude and folly She *played the harlot*, committing idolatry, that shameful thing, *for she said, I will go after my lovers*, her idols, on which she doated, and to whom she ascribed all the good things she enjoyed, *that gave me my bread*, &c robbing God of the glory of his gifts, and giving this honour unto stocks and stones, or the hosts of heaven, *Jer* xliv 17, 18 *Note*, (1) The folly, as well as baseness of sin, is prodigious (2) They who make their belly their God, and the delights of sense their happiness, are in the broad way of ruin (3) Worldly prosperity and abundance have been the fatal snare by which many an immortal soul hath been ruined

r Job iii 23 & xix 8 Lam iii 7, 9
† Heb Wall a wall
h Jer ii 36
i Ezek xvi 8
k Job xx x 2 &c
‡ Heb New wine
§ Or, wherewith they made Baal
l Isa xlvi 6 Ezek xxiii 29
‖ Or, take away
m Ezek xvi 37 & xxiii 29
† Heb Folly or villany
n Ver 5
o Ps lxxx 12, 13 Isa v 5

6 ¶ Therefore behold, [g] I will hedge up thy way with
thorns, and † make a wall, that she shall not find her
paths 7 And she shall follow after her lovers, [h] but she
shall not overtake them, and she shall seek them, but
shall not find *them* then shall she say, I will go and re-
turn to [i] my first husband, for [k] then *was* it better with
me than now 8 For she did not know that I gave her
corn, and ‡ wine, and oil, and multiplied her silver and
gold, § *which* they prepared for Baal 9 Therefore will
I return and [l] take away my corn in the time thereof, and
my wine in the season thereof, and will ‖ recover my wool
and my flax *given* to cover her nakedness 10 And
now [m] will I discover her † lewdness in the sight of her
lovers, and none shall deliver her out of mine hand
11 I will also cause all her mirth to cease, her feast
days, her new moons, and her sabbaths, and all her
solemn feasts 12 And I will destroy her vines, and
her fig trees, whereof she hath said, [n] These *are* my re-
wards that my lovers have given me and [o] I will
make them a forest, and the beasts of the field shall
eat them 13 And I will visit upon her the days of
Baalim, wherein she burnt incense to them, and she
decked herself with her ear-rings and her jewels, and
she went after her lovers, and forgat me, saith the
LORD

v 6—13 They who go on obstinately in their evil ways, may assuredly expect that vengeance, though slow, will surely overtake them Thus God threatens the Israelites,

1 He will compass them with troubles, out of which they shall see no way to escape *I will hedge up thy way with thorns, and make a wall that she shall not find her paths*, as when they were besieged, however much they desired it, *v* 7 they could neither go to seek help from their allies, nor visit their idols at Dan and Bethel Or else this implies, that all their endeavours to extricate themselves from their troubles would but the more involve and torment them, and their pretended friends prove to them no better than a broken reed *Note*, (1) They who depart from God, will find the curse pursue them as close as their shadow, and the more they persist in their froward ways, the more miseries they shall find in them (2) When God arrests the sinner by the afflictions of his providence, it is to convince him of the evil of his pursuits and to turn him back from ruin

2 These troubles shall have a blessed effect, on many of them at least, *then shall they say*, when every other hope proves desperate, *I will go and return to my first husband*, the Lord God of Israel, *for then it was better with me than it is now* Note, (1) It is well if despair of creature-comforts and confidences drives the sinner to God, and even then he will not cast him out (2) Whoever hath once tasted the blessedness of God's service, and hath unfaithfully departed from it, will find by the longest experience, that none of the pleasures of sin are to be compared with a sense of God's love, and the testimony of a good conscience (3) Returning backsliders, who do their first works, shall be restored again to their first love

Before Christ 785

3 Because they had abused the plenty God had given them, unless they repented thus and returned to him, he threatens them with famine, poverty, and nakedness More stupid than the ox that knows his owner, they did not acknowledge God the author of the mercies so liberally bestowed on them, but dishonoured him by lavishing their riches on their hated idols, *v* 8 Most justly therefore he threatens to resume the gifts they thus abused, and make them know by the miseries he will inflict, the wickedness and ingratitude of their conduct *Note*, They who profusely spend their substance in pride, luxury, gaming, and the service of diverse lusts and pleasures, are as criminal as if they *prepared it for Baal*

[1] God will take from them their corn and wine, and make them know want and hunger Their harvest shall become a heap of chaff, and their vintage disappoint their expectations And those vines and fig-trees shall be destroyed by their invaders, or by inclement seasons, which they regarded as the gifts of their idols, *v* 15 He calls them *my corn*, *my wine*, for we are but stewards, the property is still in him, by whatever title we hold our creature-comforts, to him we must be accountable for them To abuse them is the sure way to provoke God to deprive us of them in time, or worse, to punish us for our unfaithfulness in eternity

[2] He will strip them naked to their shame *Now will I discover her lewdness in the sight of her lovers*, when scattered among the nations, who shall treat them with insult and contempt, as an infamous strumpet, *and none shall deliver her out of my hands*, neither the idols, nor the allies in whom they trusted *Note*, None can save that soul which God determines to destroy

[3] God will turn her mirth into mourning Though they had forsaken the temple at Jerusalem, they still kept up the days of feasting, not in honour of God, but of their calves, and turned these sacred seasons into times of carnal merriment and riot, utterly perverting the holy design of their institution But now when famine had cut off all their provisions, or their victorious enemies had ravaged their country, and led them captive into a strange land, these solemnities must cease of course, and they be sunk in misery and mourning *Note*, (1) Holy days and seasons, by unholy men perverted, are often turned into an occasion of more than ordinary drunkenness, lewdness, and riot (2) When we abuse God's institutions, it is just with him to rob those of the form, who have lost the power of godliness

4 All this misery coming upon them, was owing to their idolatry and apostacy from God *I will visit upon her the days of Baalim* punishing them for their long course of idolatry from the days of the Judges, ever since which they had *burnt incense* to one deity or another, and decked themselves in their best attire on their holy days, to do honour to these dunghill-gods, *and forgat me, saith the Lord*, which is the origin and aggravation of all their other sin *Note*, Forgetfulness of God is at the bottom of all our sins, and the chief of them

14 ¶ † Therefore behold, [p] I will allure her, and
bring her into the wilderness, and speak † comfortably
unto her. 15 And I will give her her vineyards from
thence, and [q] the valley of Achor for a door of hope,
and she shall sing there, [r] as in the days of her youth,
and as in the day when she came up out of the land of
Egypt 16 And it shall be at that day, saith the
LORD, *that* thou shalt call me § Ishi, and shalt call
me no more ‖ Baali 17 For [s] I will take away the
names of Baalim out of her mouth, and they shall no
more be remembered by their name 18 And in that
day will I make [t] a covenant for them with the beasts
of the field, and with the fowls of heaven, and *with* the
creeping things of the ground and [u] I will break the
bow, and the sword, and the battle out of the earth,
and will make them to [x] lie down safely 19 And I
will betroth thee unto me for ever, yea, I will betroth
thee unto me in righteousness, and in judgment, and in
loving-kindness, and in mercies 20 I will even be-
troth thee unto me in faithfulness, and [y] thou shalt
know the LORD 21 And it shall come to pass in
that day, I will hear, saith the LORD, [z] I will hear the
heavens, and they shall hear the earth, 22 And the
earth

† Or, nevertheless
p Cant i 4 John vi 44
† Heb To her heart
q Josh vii 26
r Jer ii 2 Ezek xvi 22, 60
§ i e My husband Ver 10
‖ i e My lord
s Ex xxiii 13 Josh xxiii 7 Ps xvi 4 Zech xiii
t Job v 23 Isa xi 6 Ezek xxxiv 25
u Ps xlvi 9 Isa ii 4 Ezek xxxix 9 Zech ix 10
x Lev xxvi 5 Jer xxiii 6
y Jer xxxi 33, 34 John xvii 3
z Zech viii 12

Before Christ 786

a Chap i 4 b Jer xxxi 27 Zech. x 9 c Chap i 6 d Chap i 10 Zech xiii 9 Rom ix 26 1 Pet ii 10.

earth shall hear the corn, and the wine, and the oil, and [a] they shall hear Jezreel 23 And [b] I will sow her unto me in the earth, and [c] I will have mercy upon her that had not obtained mercy, and I [d] will say to *them which were* not my people, Thou *art* my people, and they shall say, *Thou art* my GOD

v 14—23 The threatnings in the foregoing verses were not more tremendous, than the promises in these are reviving. When we might have expected, from the conclusion of the last verse, to have heard the most fearful curses reiterated, as the just vengeance of their idolatry and forgetfulness of God, amazing inference! *Therefore*, says God, *will I allure her*, as if to magnify the triumphs of his grace or it intimates his boundless patience, determined to try every method before he abandoned them to ruin Some render the word, *Nevertheless* all these provocations shall not stay the current of my mercy Where sin hath abounded, there shall grace much more abound, and appear to be *free grace indeed!*

1 God will revive and comfort them, *v* 14, 15 The allusion is to the bringing them out of Egypt, through the wilderness, into the land flowing with milk and honey, which they entered through the valley of Achor And with like mercy will he again visit them, either by his gospel calling many of them into the church of the Redeemer at the first, or finally by recovering them from their present dispersion, and converting them to the faith of Christ in the last day *I will allure her* with the kindest words of tender affection, by the great and gracious promises of his word, and the sweetly constraining influences of his Spirit, *and bring her into the wilderness*, either separating them from the rest of the world for himself, or by the afflictive dispensations of his providences humbling their souls, or convincing them of their misery and guilt, in order to lead them more earnestly to seek the riches of his grace, *and speak comfortably unto her*, encouraging the dejected hearts of his poor people, burdened with guilt and heavy laden with trouble, and shewing them, in Christ Jesus, that peace, pardon, and plenteous redemption, which miserable sinners so exceedingly need, and which are to them tidings of great joy *and I will give her vineyards from thence*, either the abundance of temporal blessings which they had lost, or rather the graces and consolations of his Spirit, which are more refreshing than wine to the weary, *and the valley of Achor*, where Achan was stoned, *for a door of hope*, this being their first entrance into the promised land, and the pledge of their possessing the rest Thus, when God converts the souls of his people to himself, the accursed thing sin is put away, a door of hope is opened to them after their darkness and distress, and, in the present grace they receive, they have the pledge of that eternal glory which is prepared for them *and she shall sing there as in the days of her youth, as in the day when she came up out of Egypt*, when they beheld the Egyptians dead on the sea-shore, so shall the people of God rejoice in the complete victory of their Redeemer, and triumph in the God of their salvation, happy in the present possession of his love, and the assured prospect of eternal blessedness *Note*, (1) Nothing hath so powerful an effect upon the sinner's conscience as the alluring promises of gospel grace (2) A soul brought into the wilderness of conviction is ready to fear that destruction is before him, but the gate of life lies in this valley of the shadow of death

2 God will cleanse them from all their idols They shall not only no more worship Baal, but not even take his name in their lips *And it shall be in that day, saith the Lord*, when the Jews shall be turned to him, *thou shalt call me Ishi*, *my husband*, by faith embracing the Lord Jesus as the blessed bridegroom of their souls, *and shalt call me no more Baali*, which signifies *my husband* also, or *my Lord*, but was a name which had been so much abused in worshipping their idols, that the very mention of it should be abhorred, and the memory of it stamped with oblivion, *for I will take away the names of Baalim out of her mouth, and they shall no more be remembered by their name*, idolatry of every kind being utterly abolished; as will be fully accomplished in the latter day, when every idol, papal as well as pagan, shall fall for ever *Note*, (1) The endearing relation God is pleased to assume, as the husband of his people, should engage our warmest affection and most unshaken fidelity (2) It is a sure symptom of God's gracious designs towards the sinner's soul, when he separates him from his beloved idols and lusts (3) When a thing, innocent in itself, is abused to the purposes of superstition and idolatry, it should from thenceforth be avoided

3 God will be their protector from every foe, whether the savages of the forest, or the more dangerous savages, wicked men, or fiends of darkness The beasts of the earth, as bound by a covenant, shall no more hurt nor destroy God's redeemed people, and all their brutal persecutors, with the old lion their ruler, shall be for ever disabled from hurting them Then war shall cease in all the earth, and, quiet from fear of evil, they shall *lie down safely*, under the guardian care of their almighty Lord and Saviour *Note*, (1) When God is our friend, who can harm us? (2) Whether we lie down on bed of sleep, or in the dust of death, alike serene we may quietly repose on Jesus, and be assured that under his wings we must be safe

4 God will anew take them into a covenant of marriage, notwithstanding their former divorce *I will betroth thee unto me for ever*, which may refer to the Jews in particular, who at last shall be brought again into the visible church of the redeemed, or may be applied to every particular believer, whether Jew or Gentile, who have not chosen Christ, but he hath chosen them, and by his grace engages them to choose him as their Lord and husband, and to cleave to him in love and faithfulness And this endeared relation shall subsist *for ever*, *the gifts and callings of God being without repentance*, they cannot be cast away, because he cannot change *Yea I will betroth thee unto me in righteousness*, dealing with them in the most assured sincerity, or adorning them with the spotless robes of righteousness, which he their Redeemer hath wrought out for them as their wedding-garment, arrayed in which they are all fair in his eyes, *and in judgment*, in such a way as is most perfectly consistent with his justice, though they are in themselves polluted, and deserve his wrath instead of his love, *and in loving-kindnesses*, to shew them his warmest regard; *and in mercies*, bestowing on them every blessing a sinful soul can need, and this purely flowing not from any merit in them but from his undeserved favour, *and in faithfulness*, engaging to fulfil every promise of the covenant to them; and not only true to his part of the contract, but keeping them also faithful to theirs, *and thou shalt know the Lord*, his excellence and glory, such a knowledge as shall effectually engage their love and duty to him, and secure to them, as the consequence, eternal life Blessed and happy is the soul that is in such a case!

5 God will enrich them with the blessings of the basket and the store, or perhaps the better spiritual blessings of grace are represented by the corn and wine They had before, *v* 12, been threatned with the destruction of their worldly comforts; but now, being restored to God's favour, they shall regain the creature good they had forfeited and this is represented by a beautiful figure, wherein the prayers of the whole creation, which groans under the curse of sin, are represented as ascending into the ears of the Lord of sabaoth *I will hear the heavens*, or *answer* their cry, desiring permission to drop down the dew, without which they are as brass over the sinner's head, *and the heavens shall hear the earth*, gasping for want of rain *and the earth shall hear the corn, and the wine, and the oil*, withering for drought; *and they shall hear Jezreel*, furnishing an abundant supply for the famished people And thus doth the a w o heavenly influences descend on the thirsty soul, and under the dispensation of the word and ordinances of Christ such quickening, comforting, and strengthening grace is dispensed, that God's chosen grow up, and bring forth the abundant fruits of righteousness and true holiness

6 God will greatly increase the number of his Israel *I will sow her unto me in the earth*, either the dispersed Israelites, that had been scattered in all lands, and in their days of captivity seemed buried as seed beneath the clods of the valley, but shall at last spring up more numerous than ever, or, by the preaching of the word of gospel grace, this divine seed should be sown, from whence a glorious harvest should be gathered of *Israelites indeed*, of true believers, *the seed of God*, as the word *Jezreel* signifies

7 God will reverse the sentence pronounced upon them, and change their ominous names *They shall no more be called Lo-ammi and Lo-ruhamah*, *for I will have mercy on her that had not obtained mercy*, both Jews and Gentiles, to whom the apostle expressly applies this promise, *Rom* ix 25 *and I will say to them which were not my people*, the Gentiles before the gospel came unto them, and the Jews who for a while are cut off from their relation to God till the fulness of the Gentiles is come in, *Thou art my people*, restored and recovered, through Jesus Christ, to his love and protection, *and they shall say, Thou art my God*, enabled by faith to embrace the promises, and to approve their fidelity to him *Note*, (1) The salvation of the sinner is an act of God's infinite mercy (2) None are so bad as to be beyond the reach of this mercy whilst on this side eternity, and therefore never to be despaired of (3) The richest of all mercies is to have God for our own God, every possible blessing is comprehended in that relation (4) They who can truly claim a covenant relation to God will own, it is all for themselves, that they owe it to the election of grace; for we had never chosen him, if he had not first chosen us

CHAP III

In this chapter we have, 1 The bad character which the people of Israel now had, they were as is said of the Athenians, Acts xvii 16 *wholly given to idolatry*, ver 1 2 *The low condition which they should be reduced to by their apostasy, and other instances of God's controversy with them*, ver 2, 3, 4 3 *The blessed reformation that should at length be wrought upon them in the latter days*, ver 5

Before Chriſt 785.

1 THEN ſaid the LORD unto me, [a] Go yet,
love a woman (beloved of *her* friend, yet an
adultereſs) according to the love of the LORD toward
the children of Iſrael, who look to other gods, and love
flagons of † wine. 2 So I bought her to me for fifteen
pieces of ſilver, and *for* an homer of barley, and an half-
homer of barley 3 And I ſaid unto her, Thou ſhalt
[b] abide for me many days, thou ſhalt not play the harlot,
and thou ſhalt not be for *another* man, ſo *will* I alſo *be*
for thee 4 For the children of Iſrael ſhall abide many
days [c] without a king, and without a prince, and with-
out a ſacrifice, and ‡ without an image, and without an
ephod, and *without* [d] teraphim 5 Afterward ſhall the
children of Iſrael return, and ſeek the LORD their God,
and [e] David their king, and ſhall fear the LORD, and
his goodneſs [f] in the latter days

[a] Chap i 2. † Heb Grapes. [b] Deut. xxi 13 [c] Chap x 3 ‡ Heb A ſtanding, or ſtatue [d] Judg xvii 5 [e] Jer xxx 9 Ezek xxxiv 23 & xxxvii 24 [f] Iſa ii 2 Mic iv 1

v 1—5 The prophet ſtill perſonates the character of a man who had betrothed a woman and loved her, though an adultereſs, and her affections placed upon another, and this in order to reproach the baſeneſs and ingratitude of the people of Iſrael, who had thus treacherouſly departed from God

1 The prophet repreſents their baſeneſs and ingratitude, and God's amazing love to them, notwithſtanding they had played the harlot and gone after idols, looking to them for help and comfort, delighting in drunkenneſs and intemperance, and the better pleaſed with their abominable deities becauſe their feaſts were thus celebrated *Note*, A drunkard will ever pay his adorations where there are *flagons of wine* Such infamous conduct might well provoke God's abhorrence, yet, aſtoniſhing to tell! he was ſtill Iſrael's *friend*, and loved her, though *an adultereſs* *Note*, The ſoul which is brought to a real ſight of his own vileneſs ſtands amazed at God's grace, that he ſhould ever reſpect a wretch, where there was nothing to engage his love, but every thing to excite his loathing

2 He deſcribes the gracious methods God took to bring them home to himſelf By the price the prophet pays for this adultereſs, *v* 2 is repreſented the vileneſs and worthleſſneſs of that ſinful people It was but half as much as was paid for a ſlave, *Exod.* xxi 32 and the barley may ſignify the wretched ſtate to which, during their captivity, the Iſraelites ſhould be reduced *So I bought her*, &c *and I ſaid unto her, Thou ſhalt abide for me many days*, as a widow in ſolitude, and lamenting their paſt ill conduct *and thou ſhalt not be for another man*, not commit adultery any more, *ſo will I alſo be for thee*, after proper trial and correction God will again own the relation of an huſband *Note*, (1) Though God has deſigns of grace towards a ſinful ſoul, he is often pleaſed to leave us for a while under deep convictions and ſad apprehenſions of our ſtate, the more to endear the mercy when he receives us into the boſom of his love (2) When God ſeparates a ſinner for himſelf, from the moment his grace is revealed to him, the ſinner begins to ſeparate himſelf from his iniquities (3) God waits to be gracious when we deſire to return and be for him alone, he is ready to receive us, and engages to be *ours* for ever

The parable is particularly applied to the people of Iſrael

[1] They ſhall be left deſolate as a widow *They ſhall abide many days without a king, and without a prince*, &c which hath been the caſe with the ten tribes ſince their captivity by Salmanezer, and is at preſent the ſtate of the whole Jewiſh nation, and hath been theſe ſeventeen hundred years They are without any form of civil government, have *no ſacrifice*; are without an *image*, being entirely cured of idolatry, *without an ephod*, their prieſthood is no more, nor have they any method of enquiring at God's mouth as formerly, *and without teraphim* which ſome ſuppoſe to be the ſame as *Urim and Thummim*, and render it, *without manifeſtations*, though others ſay they were little images, which they conſulted about future events, of which no methods they ſhould take, during their diſperſion, whether lawful or unlawful, would inform them and woful is the ſtate of that people thus cut off from all communion with God

[2] They ſhall at laſt be received again as a wife *Afterwards*, when the days of their ſeparation are ended, *ſhall the children of Iſrael return* from their long apoſtacy, *and ſeek the Lord their God, and David their king*, the rejected Meſſiah, whom they will then receive for their Lord and King, earneſtly ſollicting to be admitted into his church, *and ſhall fear the Lord and his goodneſs in the latter days*, with filial fear of offending any more a God ſo gracious Which prophecy, whatever reference it may have to thoſe Jews who were converted by the firſt preaching of the goſpel, ſeems to look to ſome glorious future day for its full accompliſhment *Note*, (1) They who would return to God and find mercy, muſt diligently ſeek him through the Son of his love (2) If Chriſt be our king, we muſt prove our loyalty by our fidelity (3) A ſenſe of God's goodneſs, and of the baſeneſs of ingratitude, more powerfully reſtrains a faithful ſoul from offending than any ſervile fears of wrath

Before Chriſt 870.

CHAP IV.

The prophet here in God's name arraigns a ſinful nation 1 *He ſhews them the grounds of God's controverſy with them, a general prevalence of vice and profaneneſs*, ver 1, 2 *Ignorance and forgetfulneſs of God*, ver 6, 7 *Worldly-mindedneſs in their prieſts*, ver 8 *Drunkenneſs and uncleanneſs*, ver 11 *Uſing divination and witchcraft*, ver 12 *Offering ſacrifice in high places*, ver 13 *Whoredoms*, ver 14, 18 *And bribery among magiſtrates*, ver 18 2 *He ſhews them what would be the conſequences of God's controverſy, God would puniſh them for theſe things*, ver 9 *The whole land be laid waſte*, ver 3 *All ſorts of people cut off*, ver 5 *Their honour loſt*, ver 7 *Their creature comforts rendered unſatiſfying*, ver 10 *and themſelves made aſhamed*, ver 19 *And, which is the ſoreſt judgment of all, they ſhould be let alone in their ſins*, ver. 17 *they ſhall not reprove one another*, ver 4 *God will not puniſh them*, ver 14 *Nay, he will let them proſper*, ver 16 3 *He gives warning to Judah not to tread in the ſteps of Iſrael, becauſe they ſaw their ſteps went down to hell*, ver 15

1 HEAR the word of the LORD, ye children of
Iſrael for the LORD hath [a] a controverſy with
the inhabitants of the land, becauſe *there is* no truth, nor
mercy, [b] nor knowledge of God in the land 2 By
ſwearing, and lying, and killing, and ſtealing, and com-
mitting adultery, they break out, and † blood toucheth
blood 3 Therefore [c] ſhall the land mourn, and every
one that dwelleth therein ſhall languiſh with the beaſts
of the field, and with the fowls of heaven, yea, the fiſhes
of the ſea alſo ſhall be taken away 4 Yet [d] let no man
ſtrive, nor reprove another for thy people *are* [e] as they
that ſtrive with the prieſt 5 Therefore ſhalt thou fall
in the day, and the prophet alſo ſhall fall with thee in
the night, and I will ‡ deſtroy thy mother

[a] Iſa i 18. & iii 13 Jer xxv 31 Chap xii 2. Mic vi 2 [b] Jer iv 22. † Heb Bloods [c] Jer iv 28 & xii 4 Zeph i 3 [d] Gen xix 9 Mat vii 6 [e] Deut xvii 12 ‡ Heb Cut off.

v 1—5 Iſrael's ſins are the cauſe of all her miſeries

1 The prophet in God's name ſummons the people to attend the charge he is about to lay againſt them *Hear the word of the Lord, ye children of Iſrael for the Lord hath a controverſy with the inhabitants of the land* Sin was the high offence, the cauſe of all their miſeries and ours, and in God's own people it is more exceeding ſinful

2 Their indictment charges them with many high crimes and miſdemeanors, for one of a thouſand of which they cannot anſwer him *There is no truth* hypocritical towards God, and faithleſs towards men, their profeſſions were deceit, and their promiſes falſehood *nor mercy*, for where honeſty is baniſhed, charity cannot ſubſiſt They paid no regard to the diſtreſſes of the indigent, and, wrapped up in themſelves, with unfeeling diſregard beheld the miſeries of others *Nor knowledge of God in the land* they deſired not to know him, their hearts were averſe from his teachings, and this wilful ignorance was at once the cauſe and aggravation of their other ſins *By ſwearing* they increaſed their load of guilt, wantonly profane, and taking God's name in vain *and lying*, they added perjury to profaneneſs, and in their ordinary converſation copied cloſely after their father the Devil, who was a liar from the beginning *And* by a complication of all the moſt enormous crimes filled up the meaſure of their iniquities, *by killing, and ſtealing, and committing adultery, they break out*, with lawleſs violence, unreſtrained by the laws of God or man, as a torrent, that ſweeps away every mound and deluges the country *And blood toucheth blood*, ſo vaſt is the effuſion of it, occaſioned by the frequency of murders, or the dreadful maſſacres of the ſucceſſive kings, each graſping at the crown over the corpſe of his predeceſſor, 2 *Kings* xv 8—30

3 An awful ſentence is paſſed upon them for ſuch ſins, where-ever they are found, are ſure to meet a juſt recompenſe of reward *Therefore ſhall the land mourn*, laid waſte and deſolate with famine and the ſword, *and every one that dwelleth therein ſhall languiſh, with the beaſts of the field and the fowls of heaven*, pining for want, or conſumed with war and peſtilence, *yea the fiſhes of the ſea ſhall be taken away*, that no food may remain to ſatisfy their hunger *Note*, God can quickly conſume a ſinful land he hath only to withdraw his mercies, and we periſh immediately

4 Their caſe is deſperate *Yet let no man ſtrive, nor reprove another* either theſe are the words of the incorrigible people, ſilencing their reprovers, or of God to the prophet, enjoining him and other good men to deſiſt from their labours, and abandon them to ruin *for thy people are as they that ſtrive with the prieſt*, they are ſo impudent in ſin, that they would fly in the face even of the prieſts of God who admoniſhed them, or all were become ſo bad, that, if a prieſt dared reprove them, they retorted on him, Phyſician heal thyſelf *Therefore ſhalt thou fall in the day*, the day of vengeance approaching, or *to-day*, immediately the wrath ſhall go forth, *and the prophet alſo*, the falſe prophets who deceived them with lying divinations, *ſhall fall in the night of deep adverſity*, which approaches, *and I will deſtroy*

Before Christ 780

thy mother, either Samaria the metropolis, or the nation in general, for both are doomed to utter ruin. *Note*, (1) They who are deaf to rebuke are on the precipice of ruin. (2) We are bound not to suffer ſin upon our brethren, without friendly admonition, but when we perceive them exaſperated, inſtead of humbled, ſilence becomes duty. (3) When ſinners ſtrive with their faithful miniſters, and refuſe to hear, their blood is on their own heads. (4) They who have contributed to ſeduce others ſhall meet the heavieſt vengeance in the day of recompenſe.

6 ¶ [f] My people are † deſtroyed for lack of know-
ledge: [g] becauſe thou haſt rejected knowledge, I will alſo
reject thee, that thou ſhalt be no prieſt to me: ſeeing
thou haſt forgotten the law of thy God, I will alſo for-
get thy children. 7 [h] As they were increaſed, ſo they
ſinned againſt me: [i] *therefore* will I change their glory
into ſhame. 8 They eat up the ſin of my people, and
they ‡ ſet their heart on their iniquity. 9 And there
ſhall be [k] like people, like prieſt: and I will puniſh them
for their ways, and § reward them their doings. 10
For [l] they ſhall eat, and not have enough: they ſhall
commit whoredom, and ſhall not increaſe: becauſe they
have left off to take heed to the LORD. 11 Whore-
dom, and [m] wine, and new wine take away the heart.

f Iſa v 13. † Heb cut off. g 1 Sam ii 30. h Ch ix 15. Pſal ... 29. i ... k Iſa xxiv. § Heb cauſe to return. l Lev xxvi 26. Prov ... m ... Luke xxiii.

v 6—11. The ſin and puniſhment of the ungodly prieſts correſpond with each other.

1 They rejected the knowledge of God, and ſuffered the people to periſh for lack of it. And though this will be no excuſe for the people, who choſe darkneſs rather than light, yet will the blood be required at the negligent watchman's hands. *I will alſo reject thee, that thou ſhalt be no prieſt to me*, cut off from the office and benefit of the prieſthood. *Note*, (1) Ignorance in prieſts is doubly ſcandalous, and wilful ignorance the more exceſſive criminal, as thereby not only their own ſouls but the ſouls of others are deſtroyed. (2) Ignorance in the people is ſo far from being the mother of devotion, that it is the forerunner of deſtruction. (3) Though, in ſuch careleſs days as ours, men unqualified by ignorance, and ſcandalous by immoralities, are too often permitted to call themſelves miniſters of God, he will with abhorrence reject their pretentions, and in the great day drive them from his throne with a *Depart, accurſed, I never knew you*.

2 They *forgat the law of God*, v 6, took no pains to remember it themſelves or inculcate it upon others; therefore God threatens, *I alſo will forget thy children*, the children of the prieſts, who ſhould be degraded, and not ſucceed their fathers in the prieſthood, or the people, whom they ſhould have regarded and taught as their ſpiritual fathers; but becauſe they had neglected them God will diſown them. Wicked parents thus bring a curſe upon their own offspring.

3 The abuſe of their bleſſings ſhall prove their bane. *As they were increaſed* in numbers, wealth, and power, *ſo they ſinned againſt me* with more daring profaneneſs and inſolent ingratitude; *therefore will I change their glory into ſhame*, when, led into a wretched captivity, they ſhould be ſtripped of all their poſſeſſions and honours, and mingle with the ignominious herd.

4 They were luxurious. *They eat up the ſin of my people*, feaſting on the ſin-offerings; and, whilſt they were careleſs about inſtructing the people concerning the nature and deſign of the ſacrifices, they fattened themſelves upon the choiceſt part of them; *they ſet their heart on their iniquity*, wholly given up to the indulgence of their appetites, or *lifted up their ſoul* thereunto, well pleaſed the people ſhould continue to ſin, becauſe they would multiply the ſacrifices, and provide food for their gluttony. *And there ſhall be like people, like prieſt*, equally ignorant, intemperate, and profane; for when prieſts ſhew ſuch ill examples, no marvel a general profligacy of manners enſues. *And I will puniſh them for their ways*: they who were companions in ſin ſhall ſuffer together, *and reward them their doings*, pouring out that vengeance upon them which they have provoked. *For they ſhall eat, and not have enough*, either their inſatiable appetite ſhould ever be craving, and find no ſatisfaction, or during the famine, or in captivity, they ſhould know the pinching of hunger, and pine away for very want of ſuſtenance.

5 They committed whoredom, and thought to have a numerous iſſue by theſe unlawful means; but they *ſhall not increaſe*, God will diſappoint their deſires, or ſlay their children: *becauſe they have left off to take heed to the Lord*; apoſtate from his ſervice, and open violaters of his law. *Note*, (1) When God is diſregarded, men ſtick at no abominations. (2) God's curſe will blaſt all unlawful ways of increaſe.

6 They had given their hearts to wine and women. *Whoredom and wine, and new wine, take away the heart*, utterly eſtrange it from God, or ſuch ſin ſtupifies the conſcience, and rob men of their reaſon, ſo that they act as if infatuated. Thus doth the curſe ever follow the ſin, cloſe as the ſhadow doth the body.

12 ¶ My people aſk counſel at their ſtocks, and
their ſtaff declareth unto them: for [n] the ſpirit of whore-
doms hath cauſed *them* to err, and they have gone a
whoring from under their God. 13 [o] They ſacrifice
upon the tops of the mountains, and burn incenſe upon
the hills under oaks and poplars, and elms, becauſe the
ſhadow thereof *is* good: [p] therefore your daughters ſhall
commit whoredom, and your ſpouſes ſhall commit adul-
tery. 14 † I will not puniſh your daughters when they
commit whoredom, nor your ſpouſes when they commit
adultery: for themſelves are ſeparated with whores, and
they ſacrifice with harlots: therefore the people *that* doth
not underſtand ſhall fall. 15 ¶ Though thou Iſrael
play the harlot, *yet* let not Judah offend; and come not
ye [q] unto Gilgal, neither go ye up to [r] Beth-aven, [s] nor
[t] ſwear, The LORD liveth. 16 For Iſrael [u] ſlideth
back, as a backſliding heifer: now the LORD will feed
them as a lamb in a large place. 17 Ephraim *is* joined
to idols: [x] let him alone. 18 Their drink is ‡ ſour:
they have committed whoredom continually: [y] her § rulers
with ſhame do love, Give ye. 19 The wind hath
bound her up in her wings, and [z] they ſhall be aſhamed
becauſe of their ſacrifices.

Before Christ 780

n Iſa xliv 20. Chap v 4. o Iſa i 29. & lvii 5, 7. Ezek vi 13. & xx 28. p Am vii 17. Rom i 28. † Or ſhall I not, &c. q Chap ix 15. & xii 11. Am iv 4. & v 5. r 1 Kin xii 29. Chap x 5. Am v 5. s Zeph i 5. t Am viii 14. u Zech vii 11. x Mat xv 14. ‡ Heb Gone. y Mic vii 3. § Heb Shields. Pſ xlvii 9. z Jer ii 26.

v 12—19. The prophet goes on to charge upon the people of Iſrael thoſe atrocious crimes which cried for vengeance.

1 Their ſins were,

[1] Idolatry. *The ſpirit of whoredoms hath cauſed them to err*: their hearts were violently bent upon their idols, with ſuch raging deſires as the lewd ſeek the embraces of an harlot; and ſo aſtoniſhingly beſotted, that they leave the living God, who would have been their huſband, father, friend, almighty to help, all-wiſe to direct them, to *aſk counſel at their ſtocks*, as if the log they had ſquared and planed could teach them; *and their ſtaff declareth unto them*, either ſome little image engraved on them, to which they paid their devotions, or they uſed the divinations of the heathen, *ſee Ezek* xxi 21, and by the falling of their ſtaff took directions for their conduct. To theſe ſenſeleſs idols they offered their ſacrifices and incenſe, *on the tops of mountains, under oaks and poplars, and elms, becauſe the ſhadow thereof is good*, copying the manners of their heathen neighbours, and chuſing the ſame places for the ſcene of their impure rites and ceremonies.

[2] Adultery. *They are ſeparated with whores, and ſacrifice with harlots*, the worſhip of their gods being celebrated with ſuch abominations, and this *continually*, v 18: theſe crimes were their habitual practice.

[3] Bribery, and perverſion of juſtice. *Her rulers with ſhame do love, Give ye*. Nothing could be obtained of them without a fee, who ſhould have adminiſtered juſtice freely, and gain, not right, ſwayed their deciſions.

[4] They obſtinately perſiſted in their wicked ways, v 16. *Iſrael ſlideth back, as a backſliding heifer*, or refractory, that no fence can keep in, or that will not ſuffer the yoke, and, when goaded to draw, goes backward. So had they been, refuſing to be reſtrained by God's law, or kicking againſt the pricks of the prophetic warnings and afflictive providences; and ſo wedded were they to their *idols*, v 17. Sins theſe, which, where-ever they are found, will aſſuredly, as here, provoke God's wrath and indignation againſt the guilty ſoul: for *the people that doth not underſtand* the danger and evil of their ways, *ſhall fall*, v 14, and periſh in their iniquities.

2 God threatens them with a variety of evils, as the righteous puniſhment of their tranſgreſſions.

[1] *Your daughters ſhall commit whoredom, and your ſpouſes ſhall commit adultery*, led by the bad example of their huſbands and fathers, and permitted with impunity to do ſo, v 14, as a puniſhment for the like crimes, which they had committed.

[2] They ſhall be given as ſheep to the ſlaughter. *The Lord will feed them as a lamb in a large place*, and their proſperity ſhall haſten their perdition; or as one lamb, ſeparated from the flock and in a deſert, falls a prey to the devouring wolves, ſo ſhould they be given up to the hand of the Aſſyrians, and diſperſed in their vaſt empire.

[3] God will abandon them to their own heart, v 17; and a heavier curſe cannot fall upon the ſinner, than when God withdraws all his grace, and ſaith, *Let him alone*, let my Spirit no more ſtrive, nor miniſters rebuke, nor conſcience check, nor providences reſtrain, nor mercies affect him: then his doom is fixed.

[4] God will make their ſin their puniſhment, as the drunkard often proves. *Their drink is ſour*, their ſtomachs overcharged, and ſickneſs like death ſeizing them, till *every table is filled with vomit*.

[5] They ſhall be hurried away captives. *The wind hath bound her up in her wings*: the Aſſyrians, like a whirlwind, ſhall carry all before them; and then, too late, *they ſhall be aſhamed of their ſacrifices*, when their folly, in truſting to idols and departing from God, will be made manifeſt.

Before Christ 780

3. Judah is admonished to take warning by Israel's sin *Tho' thou Israel play the harlot, yet let not Judah offend* Some interpreters suppose this is rather a caution to Israel, among all their other sins, not to draw their brethren of the house of Judah to offend with them, which would aggravate their guilt I rather incline to suppose it addressed to Judah, who might be tempted to join with the house of Israel in idolatry, which would be more criminal in them, who had the temple in the midst of them, and had not yet apostatised from God, and therefore they are forbidden to meet the Israelites in their places of idolatrous worship, *Come not ye unto Gilgal*, the chief scene of their wickedness, *see chap. ix 15 xi 11* *neither go ye up to Bethaven* once the name was *Bethel*, the house of God, but, since the golden calf hath been erected there, it is *Bethaven*, a house of iniquity, and to be shunned as the plague *nor swear, The Lord liveth*, profanely, or falsely, or thoughtlessly taking this awful name into their lips *Note*, (1) The more advantages we enjoy to know God, and the more obligations we are under to cleave to him, the more will every departure from him bring aggravated guilt (2) They who would abstain from sin must shun the company of evil men, and never venture into the places of temptation when we are out of the path of duty we may not expect protection (3) They who shew no sacred reverence for God's name, evidently declare the profaneness and impiety of their hearts

CHAP V

The scope of this chapter is the same with the foregoing, to aggravate the sin both of Israel and Judah, and to denounce the judgments of God against them 1 *They are called to hearken to the charge*, ver 1, 8 2 *They are accused of many sins, which are here aggravated* [1] *Persecution*, ver 1, 2 [2] *Spiritual whoredom*, ver 3, 4 [3] *Pride*, ver 5 [4] *Apostasy from God*, ver 7 [5] *The tyranny of the princes, and the tameness of the people in submitting to it*, ver 10, 11 3 *They are threatened with God's displeasure for these sins, he knows all their wickedness*, ver 3 *and makes known his wrath against them for it*, ver 9 (1) *They shall fall in their iniquity*, ver 5 (2) *God will forsake them*, ver 6 (3) *Their portions shall be devoured*, ver 7 (4) *God will rebuke them and pour out his wrath upon them*, ver 9, 10 (5) *They shall be oppressed*, ver 11 (6) *God will be as a moth to them in secret*, ver 12 *and as a lion in public judgments*, ver 14 4 *They are blamed for the wrong course they took under their afflictions*, ver 13 5 *It is intimated that they shall at length take a right course*, ver 15

a Chap iv 6 1 HEAR ye this, a O priests, and hearken, ye
house of Israel, and give ye ear, O house of the
king, for judgment *is* toward you, because ye have
been a snare on Mizpeh, and a net spread upon Tabor
b Ps xxix 15 2 And the revolters are b profound to make slaughter, †
† Or, and, &c though I *have been* ‡ a rebuker of them all 3 c I
‡ Heb A correction know Ephraim, and Israel is not hid from me for now,
c Am iii 2 O Ephraim, thou committest whoredom, *and* Israel is
§ Heb Give defiled 4 They will not § frame their doings to turn
d Chap iv 12 unto their God. for d the spirit of whoredoms *is* in the
midst of them, and they have not known the LORD
e Chap vii 10 5 And e the pride of Israel doth testify to his face
therefore shall Israel and Ephraim fall in their iniquity
f Prov i 28 Isa i 15 Jer xi 11 Ezek viii 18 Mic iii 4 John vii 34 Judah also shall fall with them 6 f They shall go with
their flocks, and with their herds to seek the LORD
but they shall not find *him*, he hath withdrawn himself
g Mal ii 11 from them 7 g They have dealt treacherously against
h Zech xi 8 the LORD for they have begotten strange children
now shall h a month devour them with their portions

v 1—7 Again the prophet returns to the charge, and cites the king, priests, and people of Israel, to hear their accusation and doom from God, who knew all their wickedness, however hypocritically covered, or committed in secret *Note*, (1) No sinner is so great as to be above God's judgments, or so mean as to be overlooked by him (2) God knoweth the hidden things of darkness, nor can the shadow of death hide the workers of iniquity

1 He charges a variety of crimes upon them [1] They studied to draw their neighbours to join in their idolatries *Ye have been a snare on Mizpah, and a net spread upon Tabor*, two mountains where probably their idol altars stood near the borders of Judah, as snares set by hunters to entrap their game Some have suggested, that here Jeroboam placed spies to see who went up to Jerusalem at the solemn feasts, that they might be prosecuted for it on their return *Note*, They who under the cloak of friendship would entice us into sin, are our most mortal enemies [2] *The revolters are profound to make slaughter*; apostates being the bitterest persecutors, they who had themselves revolted from God, laid snares to murder those who refused to comply with their wicked ways or, as the words may be interpreted, they offered vast sacrifices with a shew of devotion, to provide noble entertainments, in order to seduce the unwary to join with them, *though I have been a rebuker of them all*, God by his prophet had awfully and repeatedly warned them of their wickedness, yet they still persisted in it, and this greatly aggravated their guilt [3] They committed whoredom *the spirit of whoredom* possessed their hearts, and the acts of it defiled their bodies, this God saw, who searcheth the heart, and whose eye no deeds of darkness, however secretly committed, can escape Let guilty sinners know it and tremble [4] They were wilfully ignorant, and obstinately perverse *They will not frame their doings to turn unto their God*, utterly averse to all the means and methods which might lead to their conversion, *and they have not known the Lord*, for indeed they desired not the knowledge of his ways [5] *The pride of Israel doth testify to his face*, so open, avowed, and notorious, they were grown insolent in sin, and past shame, as their very looks declared [6] They *dealt treacherously against the Lord*, as a wife that leaves her husband for another *they have begotten strange children*, intermingling in marriages with the heathen, or bringing up their children in the same idolatries they themselves committed, and dreadful is that parent's guilt, whose children's murdered souls, destroyed by his example, or bad instructions, shall cry for vengeance against him

2 He pronounces sentence upon them *Judgment is toward you*, *v* 1 God is ready to call them to his bar, and make them know his terrible wrath *They shall fall in their iniquity*, under the load of unrepented guilt *and Judah shall fall with them*, who copying their wicked ways, shall partake of their ruin, led captive with them into the same strange land So surely shall companions in sin suffer together, and they who persist in their iniquities, shall in them assuredly perish nor shall their forced return to God in the day of their distress, stand them in any stead Though they *go with their flocks and their herds to seek the Lord*, their hearts being unhumbled, and their prayers merely extorted by the apprehension of danger, God will pay no regard to them, *they shall not find him*, so as to obtain any favour or protection, *he hath withdrawn himself from them*, and left them to their deserved ruin There is a time when God will be no more entreated, and they who will not know the day of their visitation, shall be disregarded when they cry in the day of their calamity and *now* their swift destruction approaches, *a month shall devour them with their portions*, they, and all they possess, shall be shortly ruined Or this may refer to their new-moons and sacrifices, on which they trusted, but so far from being of use to them, their hypocritical services added but to their guilt, and hastened the wrath of God upon them *Note*, (1) The sinner's day is near, when vengeance will overtake him (2) They who take up with their portion in this world, will find to their sorrow how wretched a choice they have made

8 i Blow ye the cornet in Gibeah, *and* the trumpet i Chap viii 1
in Ramah cry aloud *at* k Beth aven after thee, O k Chap iv 15
Benjamin 9 Ephraim shall be desolate in the day of
rebuke among the tribes of Israel have I made known
that which shall surely be 10 The princes of Judah
were like them that l remove the bound *therefore* I will l Deut xix 14
pour out my wrath upon them like water 11 Ephraim
is oppressed, *and* broken in judgment because he will-
ingly walked after m the commandment 12 Therefore m 1 Kings xii 28
will I *be* unto Ephraim n as a moth and to the house of n Job xiii 28 Isa l 9
Judah as ‖ rottenness 13 When Ephraim saw his sick- ‖ Heb A worm
ness, and Judah *saw* his wound, then o went Ephraim to o 2 Kings xv 19
the Assyrian, and sent to p king † Jareb yet could he Chap vii 11 & xii 1
not heal you, nor cure you of your wound 14 For p Chap x 6
q I *will be* unto Ephraim as a lion, and as a young lion to † Or, of Jareb
the house of Judah I, *even* I will tear and go away, q Lam iii 10
I will take away, *and* none shall rescue *him* 15 ¶ I
will go *and* return to my place, till r they § acknowledge r Lev xxvi 40 Jer xxix 12 Ezek vi 9 & xx 43 & xxxvi 31
their offence, and seek my face s in their affliction they § Heb Be guilty
will seek me early s Ps lxxviii 34

v 8—15 The judgment was denounced, and lo! it is even now at the door

1 The alarm is sounded *Blow ye the cornet in Gibeah, and the trumpet in Ramah*, the frontier towns of Judah, to let them know the approach of the enemy *cry aloud at Beth-aven after thee, O Benjamin*, the enemy is on thy back, and ready to advance from the conquest of Israel to invade Judea When our neighbour's house is on fire, it is high time to look to our own The ruin of those who are cut off in their sins, should be a warning to the survivors

2 The destruction of Ephraim had been long foretold *Ephraim shall be desolate in the day of rebuke*, led captive by Salmaneser *among the tribes of Israel have I made known that which shall surely be*, the prophets repeatedly gave them notice of what would be the consequence of their sins, but they rejected their admonitions, and disbelieved their prophecies, and therefore

were

Before Christ 780.

were without excuſe *Note*, Sinners turn a deaf ear to the denunciations of God's wrath, and would fain treat them as mere chimæras, but they will find them terrible realities, and things *that ſhall ſurely be*

3. The princes of Judah took no warning by their neighbours fall, but equalled them in iniquity, and therefore muſt periſh together with them *The princes of Judah were like them that remove the land mark*, paid no regard to property, but oppreſſed their inferiors, and ſeized their poſſeſſions or figuratively taken, they refuſed to be kept within any bounds by God's law, and broke through every reſtraint *therefore I will pour out my wrath upon them like water*, which, as the deluge, ſhall ſweep them away *Note*, They who abuſe their power to oppreſſion, ſhall be made to know there is a judge above, the patron of the injured, and the avenger of their wrongs

4 Ephraim's ſin and ruin are again mentioned [1] Their ſin They *willingly walked after the commandment*, obeying the orders of Jeroboam and his idolatrous ſucceſſors, who enjoined the worſhip of the calves and far from oppoſing theſe impious commands, the people, very well pleaſed with the idolatrous worſhip, readily complied with them For this God threatens, [2] To puniſh them *Ephraim is oppreſſed, and broken in judgment*, this was a part of their immediate ſufferings, being ruled by tyrants, and broken with the oppreſſion and injuſtice of their princes and magiſtrates, and this was a juſt *judgment* upon them They who willingly became ſlaves to their princes humour, deſerved the galling yoke laid upon them Servility invites the exerciſe of tyranny *Therefore will I be unto Ephraim as a moth*, ſilently, and by degrees weakening them, and bringing them to deſtruction *and to the houſe of Judah as rottenneſs* in the bones, that ſpreads and deſtroys the ſubſtance, or a worm, that eats into the heart of the tree, and it withers away *Note*, Vengeance comes ſlowly, that ſinners may have ſpace to repent, but if they neglect the warnings given them, they are ſure to be undone at the laſt

5 The methods they took to help their weakneſs were ſinful, and proved ineffectual *When Ephraim ſaw his ſickneſs, and Judah his wound, then went Ephraim to the Aſſyrian, and ſent to king Jareb*, probably the ſame with Pul, or Tiglath-pileſer, ſee 2 *Kings* xv 19 xvi 7 xvii 3 *yet could he not heal you, nor cure you of your wound*, on the contrary, he increaſed inſtead of relieving their malady, and helped forward their ruin, 2 *Kings* xv 29 2 *Chron* xxviii 20 So ſurely will they, who fly to creature dependances, and forſake God, find them miſerable comforters, and rue their fooliſh choice And thus alſo, when a ſoul, under conviction of ſins, flies to his ſorrows, repentance, prayers, duties, for help, inſtead of Chriſt, he will find, inſtead of growing better, the evil will but be exaſperated

6 Provoked by ſuch conduct, God threatens them with heavier judgments, before he was but as a moth, but now *I will be unto Ephraim as a lion, and as a young lion to the houſe of Judah*, devouring and deſtroying them by his judgments, and by the ſword of the Aſſyrians *I, even I will tear and go away* as a lion, fearleſs of being purſued, *I will take away*, as that ravenous beaſt drags the prey to his den, *and none ſhall reſcue him*, thoſe who ſurvived of the people of Judah and Iſrael, ſhould be carried captives, and none be able to releaſe them from this afflictive diſpenſation, till he ſhould return in mercy unto them *I will go and return to my place*, abandoning them for a ſeaſon to their miſeries, *till* his chaſtiſements had humbled their ſtubborn hearts, and *they acknowledge their offence*, taking ſhame for their abominations, and confeſſing the juſtice of their puniſhment, *and ſeek my face* for pardon and reſtoration *for in their affliction*, brought to a ſenſe of their ſin, by the ſufferings they endure, *they will ſeek me early*, with fervent importunity, riſing up betimes, and crying for mercy, and then there is hope their miſeries may come to an end *Note*, (1) When lighter chaſtiſements are ineffectual, God will make ſinners feel his heavy hand (2) If he departs from the ſoul, then nothing but miſery is left behind him (3) Though God ſometimes appears utterly to forſake his people, he waits only for their humiliations and prayers, in order to return and be gracious unto them (4) True penitents are always liberal in acknowledgments and ſelf-reproaches (5) The afflictions, however ſevere, that drive the ſinner to ſeek God's face, are in reality the greateſt mercies

CHAP VI

Some among the people are really penitent, and we have, 1 Their reſolution to return unto God, in which they encourage their brethren to join them, ver 1—3 2 Many who made a fair profeſſion, proved hypocritical, they ſhall be ſeverely puniſhed, ver 4—11

1 [a] COME, and let us return unto the LORD
for [b] he hath torn, and he will heal us; he
hath ſmitten, and will he bind us up 2 [c] After two
days will he revive us, in the third day he will raiſe us
up, and we ſhall live in his ſight 3 Then † ſhall we
know, [d] *if* we follow on to know the LORD his going forth is prepared as the morning; and [e] he ſhall come unto us [f] as the rain, as the latter *and* former rain unto the earth

a Chap v 15
b Deut xxxii 39
1 Sam ii 6
Job v 18
† Or, we ſhall know, we ſhall follow on &c
d Mat xiii 12
e Pſ lxxii 6
f Job xxix 23

v. 1—3 Their prayers promiſed a ſpeedy return to God, in the cloſe of the laſt chapter, and therefore the prophet, with the faithful ſouls among them, is repreſented exciting and encouraging them to put in execution the gracious purpoſes they had formed, for good deſires ſhould never be ſuffered to cool

1 The matter of their exhortation is, *Come, and let us return unto the Lord*, from whom we have ſo greatly departed, renouncing now all other confidences and idol worſhip, and depending on him alone for help

2 The motives on which they preſs ſuch a return, are many and powerful

(1) They are aſſured of his help and healing They had felt by dire experience his power to deſtroy, *v* 1 and the ſame hand was as able to ſave them, and would aſſuredly be ſtretched out to raiſe them from their depreſſed and wretched ſtate *After two days will he revive us, in the third day will he raiſe us up, and we ſhall live in his ſight*, though we lie as dead corpſes in our graves during the captivity, he will not ſuffer us utterly to periſh, but after a ſhort time will reſtore us again to our own land, and give us again a ſenſe of his favour, and the light of his countenance And this may refer to their reſtoration from the Babyloniſh captivity, or look forward perhaps to their recovery from their preſent diſperſion Some have ſuppoſed theſe words to relate to Chriſt riſing on the third day from the dead, in whom alſo his people are riſen, by virtue of their union with him But though this be a great and glorious truth, I doubt much whether it be referred to in this prophecy *Note*, (1) If we are torn and ſmitten, whatever be the inſtrument, God's hand is to be acknowledged (2) Whatever the hurt of the ſinner may be, however deep the wounds of his conſcience, they are not paſt the divine phyſician's cure (3) Nothing is ſo encouraging a ground to return to God, as a believing view of the riches of his grace in Chriſt Jeſus

(2) They ſhall have their knowledge of God increaſed *Then ſhall we know, if we follow on to know the Lord*, or, as the words may be rendered, *we ſhall know, we ſhall follow on to know the Lord*, ſhall know his power, grace, and love, and encouraged by what we have attained, ſhall be reaching after greater meaſures of divine knowledge *Note*, (1) The moſt deſirable of all attainments, is the knowledge of God, for with this eternal life is inſeparably connected, *John* xvii 3 (2) They who have any true knowledge of God, deſire by prayer, the word, and ordinances, to increaſe it yet more abundantly, till they come where they ſhall know even as they are known

(3) They ſhall enjoy the richeſt conſolations *His going forth is prepared as the morning*, though God had left them to a dark night of affliction, like the returning ſun, he was ready to ariſe upon them with healing in his wings, and ſure as the return of the morning, and cheering as the light of day, would be the return of his favour and grace to them, whenever they truly ſought him *and he ſhall come unto us as the rain, as the latter and former rain unto the earth*, in the abundance of his bleſſings, as theſe ſeaſonable ſhowers cauſed the barns to be filled with corn, and their vats to overflow with wine and oil And theſe promiſes, whatever particular reſpect they had to the recovery of the Jews from Babylon, ſeem to look forward to the Meſſiah's days, the glorious ſun of righteouſneſs, whoſe bleſſed goſpel, like the dew of heaven, ſhould drop upon the ſoul of ſinners, and fill the face of the world with fruit

4 ¶ [g] O Ephraim, what ſhall I do unto thee? O Ju-
dah, what ſhall I do unto thee? For your ‖ goodneſs
is [h] as a morning cloud, and as the early dew it goeth
away 5 Therefore [i] have I hewed *them* by the pro
phets I have ſlain them by the words of my mouth,
‖ and thy judgments *are as* the light *that* goeth forth
6 For [k] I deſired mercy, and [l] not ſacrifice, and the
knowledge of God, more than burnt-offerings 7 But
they § like men [m] have tranſgreſſed the covenant there
have they dealt treacherouſly againſt me 8 [n] Gilead *is*
a city of them that work iniquity, *and is* ‖ polluted with
blood 9 And as troops of robbers wait for a man, *ſo*
the company of prieſts murder in the way ‖ by conſent
for they commit lewdneſs 10 I have ſeen an horrible
thing in the houſe of Iſrael there *is* the whoredom of
Ephraim, Iſrael is defiled 11 ‖ Alſo, O Judah, he hath
ſet [p] an harveſt for thee, when I returned the captivity
of my people

g Chap xi 8
‖ Or, mercy or kindneſs
h Chap xiii 3
i 1 Kings xix 17 Jer xxiii 29
2 Cor x 4, 5
‖ Or, that thy judgments might be &c
k 1 Sam xv 22 Eccl v 1 Mat ix 13 & xii 7
l Pſ l 8 Prov xxi 3 Iſa i 11
§ Or, like Adam Job xxxi 33
m Chap viii 1
n Chap xii 11
‖ Or, conſpiracy for blood
o Jer v 9
Jer xxxi 25
‖ Or, to Shechem
‖ Or, ſet, &c
p Jer xxxi
§ Or, Joel iii 13

v 4—11 There appeared promiſing hopes that a reconciliation would be effected but we have here,

1 Their hypocriſy, and the concern God expreſſed thereat *O Ephraim, &c O Judah, what ſhall I do unto thee?* what could

Before Chr. 780

be done that he had not done to reclaim them; and though it had been hitherto ineffectual, he speaks with reluctance, as yet unwilling to give them up, though they had so justly deserved it, *for your goodness is as a morning cloud, and as the early dew it goeth away*, so short-lived was the reformation under Jehu, and in the days of Hezekiah and Josiah. *Note*, (1.) God's compassions to sinners is amazing, and his patience and dealings with them must leave them without excuse. (2.) Many begin well, and for a while make a fair religious profession, whose goodness hath no more abidance than the morning cloud, and vanishes as the early dew before the sun of persecution, or the blasts of temptation.

2. God had severely rebuked them for their unfaithfulness. *Therefore have I hewed them by the prophets*, sharply reproving their hypocrisy, and cutting them to the heart with denunciations of wrath. *I have slain them by the words of my mouth*, devoting them to death, and then it is as sure as if every word was a drawn sword, *and thy judgments are as the light that goeth forth*. God's warnings were clear and plain, and the afflictions they suffered evidently came from his hand, so that their impenitence was inexcusable, and all that came upon them must needs appear altogether righteous and just. *Note*, (1.) The hearts of sinners are hard as the rock, and knotty as the rigid oak; God's ministers must therefore use the sharp two-edged sword, and hew them by the terrors of the Lord, and with the remonstrances of their baseness and ingratitude. (2.) The threatenings God pronounces against the ungodly, if they do not repent, are sure to be executed; they are already as dead men.

3. He tells them what he required of them. *For I desired mercy, not sacrifice; and the knowledge of God more than burnt-offerings*; for these had in themselves no intrinsic value, their only use was to point out the necessity of an atonement, and to lead them to a Saviour; and when they rested in the form of godliness, whilst they neglected the power of it, the most expensive sacrifices were of no avail. The thing God required was their hearts, not their beasts; that they should know, acknowledge, worship and serve him as their Lord and God, and exercise *mercy*, *chesed*, rendered *goodness*, ver. 4. comprehending the whole scope of practical godliness, and proceeding from the divine principle of the love of God and man in the heart; and this must ever be remembered, since without it all professions of religion are but an empty name.

4. They shamefully *transgressed the covenant like Adam* the first sinner, or *like men*, the wicked ones in the old world, or the multitude of the ungodly who still abound; *there have they dealt treacherously against me*, even in the very sacrifices they offered, and their other religious acts, they played the hypocrite, their hearts were wrong, and their very services therefore an abomination. And this was evident from their practice, *Gilead is a city of them that work iniquity*, the whole country was given up to it, or that particular city Ramoth-Gilead, inhabited by priests and Levites, whose wickedness was more criminal, and the influence of their bad examples more extensively fatal; for none do such irreparable hurt to men's souls, or wound the cause of God so deeply, as profligate worldly idolatrous priests, *and is polluted with blood*, for ungodly priests are the bitterest persecutors. Probably, this being a city of refuge, a bribe would protect wilful murderers, and for filthy lucre the innocent were delivered into the hands of the avenger of blood. Nor is it a wonder to see them kill men's bodies, when we daily see the more criminal face of men's souls. *And as troops of robbers wait for a man, so the company of priests murder in the way by consent*: the general body of them was corrupt, and they connived at and upheld each other in their wicked ways, and were ever ready to assist each other to persecute or oppress those against whom they bore enmity: or they murder *in the way to Shechem*, lying in wait for those poor Israelites who turned their back on the calves, and went up to Jerusalem to worship. *They commit lewdness*, or *enormity*, the most atrocious crimes, with deep contrivance, as the word signifies. *I have seen an horrible thing in the house of Israel; there is the whoredom of Ephraim*, corporal and spiritual, *Israel is defiled*, the whole nation addicted to idolatry and lewdness. *Also, O Judah, he hath set an harvest for thee*, the time fixed, and thou art ripe for ruin: or the words may be rendered in another sense, and then the prophecy closes with a promise of mercy. *But, O Judah, he hath set an harvest for thee*, God hath joy in store for thee, *when I returned*, or *return*, *the captivity of my people* from Babylon, which would occasion great gladness through all the tribes. *Note*, (1.) Sin is a horrible thing; it should shock us wherever we see it committed. (2.) God's grace triumphs over the provocations of his people, and when we deserve punishment, his thoughts towards us are thoughts of peace and not of evil.

CHAP. VII.

In this chapter, the heavy accusation drawn up against Israel for their wickedness, and their stupid contempt of God's favours, ver. 1, 2. Their particular sins. (1.) Of the court, the king, princes, &c. ver. 3—7. (2.) Of the country. Ephraim is charged with conforming to the nations, ver. 8. senselessness and stupidity under the judgments of God, ver. 9—11. ingratitude to God for his mercies, ver. 13. incorrigibleness under his judgments, ver. 14. contempt of God, ver. 15. and hypocrisy in their pretences to return to him, ver. 16. They are also threatened with a severe chastisement, which shall humble them, ver. 12. and if that prevail not, then with an utter destruction, ver. 13. particularly their princes, ver. 16.

Before Chr. 780

1 WHEN I † would have healed Israel, then the
iniquity of Ephraim was discovered, and the
‡ wickedness of Samaria: for they commit falshood:
and the thief cometh in, *and* the troop of robbers ||
spoileth without. 2 And they consider not in their
hearts, *that* I remember all their wickedness: § now [b]
their own doings have beset them about; they are before
my face. 3 They make the king glad with their wick-
edness, and the princes [c] with their lies. 4 They *are*
all adulterers, as an oven heated by the baker, *who*
ceaseth from † raising after he hath kneaded the dough,
until it be leavened. 5 In the day of our king, the
princes have made *him* sick [d] ‡ with bottles of wine; he
stretched out his hand with scorners. 6 For [e] they
have made ready their heart like an oven, whiles they
lie in wait: their baker sleepeth all the night; in the
morning it burneth as a flaming fire. 7 They are all
hot as an oven, and have devoured their judges; [f] all
their kings are fallen; [g] *there is* none among them that
calleth unto me.

a Jer. li. 9. † Or, did heal. ‡ Or, evils. || Heb. spoileth. § Or, their own doings &c. b Prov. v. 22. c Rom. i. † Or, waking. d Isa. xxviii. 1. ‡ Or, with heat through wine. e Mic. vii. 2. f 2 Kings xv. 10, 14, &c. g Isa. lxiv. 7.

v. 1—7. We have here,

1. What God had done for his people. *I would have healed*, or *I healed Israel*, restoring their civil state under Jeroboam the son of Joash to a flourishing condition, 2 *Kings* xiv. 25, 26, or under Jehu, destroying the worship of Baal, 2 *Kings* x. 25—30. and thus by his mercies he called upon them to forsake all their idolatries, and turn to him with their whole hearts.

2. They refused to be healed, *when* God had dealt with them in so much mercy, *then the iniquity of Ephraim was discovered*, and *the wickedness of Samaria*, the golden calves, were still kept, and their idolatries grew more open and infamous, and with them a train of iniquities entered.

[1.] *They commit falshood* in their transactions with men, perfidious and deceiving, and in their professions to God hypocritical.

[2.] They were a set of banditti, *the thief cometh in, and the troop of robbers spoileth without*, some interpret this of the judgment of God upon them, who, for their perfidy to each other, were given up to be devoured one of another.

[3.] They left God far above out of their sight. *They consider not in their hearts that I remember all their wickedness*, either careless about it, or infidel, as if God did not see, or would not punish them, though he is the jealous God, who will in no wise spare the guilty, and from whom nothing is hid, nothing is secret. *Now their own doings have beset them about*, their sins are open, multiplied, notorious, which every observer may discover, and much more God's all-seeing eye, *they are before my face*: some understand this of the punishment their sins should bring upon them, as when Samaria was besieged, then it would be past doubt that God observed, and would punish them for their iniquities. *Note*, (1.) Every sin has for its root infidelity. We promise ourselves impunity in our disregard of God's threatenings, and then dare to offend. (2.) Sooner or later God will convince the sinner that he remembers his ways.

[4.] *They make the king glad with their wickedness, and the princes with their lies.* The people readily conformed to their ordinances, and worshipped the calves, whilst the priests flattered them with assurances, that God was as well served at Dan or Bethel, as at Jerusalem: or, to curry favour, they were ever ready to blacken those whom the princes disliked, and with lying praises to cry up their favourites.

[5.] *They are all adulterers*, king, princes, priests, and people, both corporally and spiritually inflamed with lust, as an oven heated by the baker, ver. 4—7, who waiteth till his dough is leavened, and the oven thoroughly heated, and then puts in the loaves: so do these adulterers entertain their corrupt desires, and contrive how to gratify them: and when their schemes are ripe, *they lie in wait*, ver. 6. to perpetrate their wickedness. *Note*, They who thus burn in their lust, may expect shortly to burn in hell.

[6.] They were given up to drunkenness and revelling. *In the day of our king*, his birth-day, or the anniversary of his coronation, or some festival instituted by him, then they caroused without restraint, *the princes have made him sick with bottles of wine*, for this is one of the curses attendant upon drunkenness: *he stretched out his hand with scorners*, they grew daring over their cups, and with the king at their head made a jest of religion, and blasphemed the most High; for when men are intoxicated with liquor, they stick at no impiety or wickedness.

They

Before Christ 780

They have made their hearts like an oven, their drunkenness hath set fire to their lusts, *they lie in wait* to seize their prey. As the baker kindles the fire, and sleeping till morning finds his oven hot, so burned their lewd hearts, every one neighing after his neighbour's wife, *Jer.* v. 8. *Note*, Drunkenness is not only highly criminal in itself, but it is the door at which every enormity enters uncontrouled.

[7.] They *have devoured their judges, hot as an oven* in wrath against them, and killing those magistrates who attempted to punish them for their crimes. *All their kings are fallen*, they were regicides, and joined with successive usurpers, to murder one monarch after another.

[8.] They were sunk in hardened stupidity. *There is none among them that calleth unto me*, neither the ravages committed at home, nor the inroads of their enemies from abroad, nor any of the distresses in which they were involved, turned their thoughts to God, or brought them to their knees. *Note*, They who live without prayer, must continue hardened, and perish in their sins.

8 Ephraim, he hath [h] mixed himself among the people, Ephraim is a cake not turned. 9 [i] Strangers have devoured his strength, and he knoweth it not: yea, gray hairs are † here and there upon him, yet he knoweth not. 10 And [k] the pride of Israel testifieth to his face, and [l] they do not return to the LORD their God, nor seek him for all this. 11 ¶ Ephraim also is like a silly dove without heart: [m] they call to Egypt, they go to Assyria. 12 When they shall go, [n] I will spread my net upon them, I will bring them down as the fowls of the heaven, I will chastise them as their congregation hath heard. 13 Wo unto them, for they have fled from me: destruction unto them, because they have transgressed against me: though [o] I have redeemed them, yet they have spoken lies against me. 14 And [p] they have not cried unto me with their heart, when they howled upon their beds: they assemble themselves for corn and wine, *and* they rebel against me. 15 Though I have bound, [q] *and* strengthened their arms, yet do they imagine mischief against me. 16 [r] They return, *but* not to the most High: [s] they are like a deceitful bow: their princes shall fall by the sword for [t] the rage of their tongue: this *shall be* their derision in the land of Egypt.

h Ps. cvi. 35. i 2 Kings xiii. 7. † Heb. sprinkled. k Chap. v. 5. l Isa. ix. 13. m 2 Kings xvii. 4. & Chap. v. 13. & xii. 1. & n Ezek. xii. 13. o Exod. xiv. ... p Ps. lxxviii. 36. Jer. iii. 10. Zech. vii. 5. q 2 Kings xiv. 25. r Chap. xi. 7. s Ps. lxxviii. 57. t Dan. vii. 25. ... 9.

v. 8—16. The sins and punishments of Israel are here interwoven.

1. They were mingled among the heathen, *v.* 8. either by intermarriages contrary to God's law, or by their alliances with them, and sollicitations of assistance from them; or worst of all, by learning their idolatries, and conforming to their customs. *Ephraim is a cake not turned*, burnt on one side, and dough on the other, and therefore unfit for use: the mixture of heathen superstition destroyed all the acceptableness of their worship to God. *Note*, (1.) Bad company is ever corrupting; they who mingle with such, will grow like them. (2.) Many professors are made up of inconsistences, and *like a cake not turned*, are ever swinging to extremes.

2. They were insensible of the decays under which they were hasting to dissolution. *Strangers have devoured his strength*, See 2 *Kings* xiii. 7. xv. 19, 20, 29. *and he knoweth it not*, is not sensible of the loss sustained; *yea, grey hairs are here and there upon him*, the speaking symptoms of old age and death approaching, *yet he knoweth it not*, is not aware of his danger, nor sensible how near he is to the precipice of ruin. *Note*, Declensions in religion, like these grey hairs, steal insensibly on many, and though others perceive them distinctly, the backslider himself is not aware of them.

3. They were proud and unhumbled, all the mortifying providences they had undergone did not bring down their high thoughts of themselves, nor engage their penitent return to God. Notwithstanding their growing weakness and hastening ruin, *they do not return to the Lord their God, nor seek him for all this*; and this is the worst symptom of a sinner's case, when he still *restrains prayer before God*.

4. They were *like a silly dove without heart*, both foolish and timorous, and instead of seeking to God in their distress, *they call to Egypt* for assistance, 2 *Kings* xvii. 4. *They go to Assyria* for help, the people who had ever been the implacable enemies of their nation, and waited only an opportunity to devour them. So senseless is the sinner, and courts those as his best friends who are his tempters and destroyers; but God will make them rue their folly; *when they shall go, I will spread my net upon them*, and bring them into difficulties inextricable; *I will bring them down as the fowls of heaven* from the height of pride, *I will chastise them as their congregation hath heard*, sending upon them the judgments which they had heard so often read in his word, *Lev.* xxvi. *Deut.* xxviii. *Note*, (1.) They who leave the good ways of God, will soon find themselves intangled in misery. (2.) Pride must come down in humiliation, or be cast down by divine judgments. (3.) We should well observe the warnings of God's word, for not one jot or tittle of it shall fail.

5. They were revolters, rebellious, hypocritical, and ungrateful, notwithstanding all that God had done for them. *Wo unto them!* they rush on their own ruin, *for they have fled from me*, rejected his service, deserted his worship, and placed no dependance upon him; following their calves, and seeking to their neighbours in time of trouble, instead of God. *Destruction unto them*, sure and inevitable, *because they have transgressed against me*, violating his laws by the most atrocious crimes, and these aggravated by all the wondrous mercies they had received at God's hands; *though I have redeemed them* of old so often, and of late so eminently out of the hands of their enemies, 2 *Kings* xiv. 25. *yet have they spoken lies against me*, setting up their idols, or hypocritically pretending reformation, or denying his word in the mouth of his prophets, or atheistically disbelieving his being or his providence. *And they have not cried unto me with their heart*, even when their sufferings extorted prayers from their lips, *when they howled upon their beds* under God's heavy hand, or in their idol temples the beds of their adultery. They wanted to be rid of their sufferings, not of their sins, and then their loudest roarings were no better than the howlings of dogs, for no prayer can be acceptable to God, whilst unrepented iniquities are still embraced. *They assemble themselves for corn and wine*, these were the grand objects of their desires, they sought no spiritual blessings, but only asked meat for their lust; no marvel therefore such supplications were rejected. *And they rebel against me*, rejecting his government, and seeking to dethrone him, in order to exalt their idols in his seat. *Though I have bound and strengthened their arms*, healing their breaches under Joash and Jeroboam, *yet they imagine mischief against me*, persecuting his prophets, who rebuked them in God's name for their sins, or giving to their idols the honour of their successes, and charging God as the author of all their evils; with basest ingratitude thus requiting him. *They return*, they make a shew of doing so, as in the times of Jehu, *but not to the most High*, they quickly relapsed into idolatry, or *not on high*, their affections are not led up to high and heavenly things, but grovel still on earth; *they are like a deceitful bow*, whose arrow misses the mark, or breaks in the archer's hand as he draws the string; so did they disappoint the expectations which their professions had raised. Therefore *their princes shall fall by the sword* of the Assyrians, or of conspirators, *for the rage of their tongue*, their blasphemies against God, and reviling of his prophet: *this shall be their derision in the land of Egypt*, who will mock at their calamities, instead of bringing them assistance. *Note*, (1.) The sinner's tongue shall at last fall upon him. (2.) They who by their wickedness bring themselves into trouble, instead of pity justly meet with derision.

CHAP. VIII.

This chapter, as that before, divides itself into the sins and punishments of Israel. 1. *The sins of Israel is here set forth*, (1.) *In many general expressions*, ver. 1, 3, 12, 14. (2.) *In many particular instances, setting up kings without God*, ver. 4. *and setting up idols against God*, ver. 4, 5, 6, 11. *and courting alliances with the neighbour nations*, ver. 8, 9, 10. (3.) *In the aggravation of it, that they still kept up a profession of religion, and relation to God*, ver. 2, 13, 14. 2. *The punishment of Israel is pointed out. God would bring an enemy upon them*, ver. 1, 3. *All their projects should be blasted*, ver. 7. *Their confidence in idols and foreign alliances should disappoint them*, ver. 6, 8, 10. *Their strength at home should fail them*, ver. 14. *their sacrifices should have no reckoning made of them, and their sins should have a reckoning made for them*, ver. 13.

Before Christ 780

1 [a] SET the trumpet to [‖] thy mouth: *he shall come* [b] as an eagle against the house of the LORD, because [c] they have transgressed my covenant, and trespassed against my law. 2 Israel shall [d] cry unto me, My God, [e] we know thee. 3 Israel hath cast off *the thing that is* good: the enemy shall pursue him. 4 They have set up kings, but not by me: they have made princes, and I knew *it* not: [f] of their silver and their gold have they made them idols, that they may be cut off. 5 ¶ Thy calf, O Samaria, hath cast *thee* off; mine anger is kindled against them: [g] how long *will it be* ere they attain to innocency? 6 For from Israel *was* it also; the workman made it; therefore it *is* not God: but the calf of Samaria shall be broken in pieces. 7 For [h] they have sown the wind, and they shall reap the whirlwind: it hath no [‖] stalk: the bud shall yield no meal: if so be it yield, the strangers shall swallow it up.

a Chap. v. 8. ‖ Heb. The roof of thy mouth. b Deut. xxviii. 49. Jer. iv. 13. Hab. i. 8. c Chap. vi. 7. d Ps. lxxviii. 34. e Tit. i. 16. f Chap. ii. 8. & xiii. 2. g Jer. xiii. 27. h Chap. x. 13. ‖ Or, standing corn.

v. 1—7. The

Before Christ 760.

v. 1—7. The prophet is here commanded to spread the alarm, *Set the trumpet to thy mouth*, and deliver at least his own soul, if he may not save theirs.

1. He charges them in general as rebels and traitors against the Lord their king, *they have transgressed my covenant, and trespassed against my law*, by a variety of crimes, in direct violation of it, and by a general apostacy of heart from God, and disregard of his worship and service. *Israel hath cast off the thing that is good, or him that is good*, even God; justly therefore are they rejected by him.

2. *Because* of this, *the enemy shall pursue him*, ver. 3. Salmaneser, the Assyrian king, *as an eagle he shall come against the house of the Lord*, so they called themselves, and thought their relation to him as his family would be their protection; but when they had turned out such undutiful and rebellious children, God gave them into the enemy's hand, and swift as an eagle hasteth to her prey, should he seize their country, and spread desolation on every side. *Note*, No external relation to God can profit us, if our hearts are alienated from him.

3. In their distress they will plead for help, as God's people. *Israel shall cry unto me*, but in vain, *My God, we know thee*, claiming an interest in him, and professing to know him as the true God; but their professions are hypocritical, and therefore their prayers are rejected.

4. Several particular crimes are charged upon them. (1.) *They have set up kings, but not by me*; they took the government out of his hands, when he was their king, revolted from the house of David, and set up Jeroboam: and about this time several had mounted the throne successively by the murder of their predecessors, 2 *Kings* xv. 8. and herein the people had not consulted God at all, but followed their own humour, and gratified their own passions; *they have made princes, and I knew it not*, without his approbation or consent, affecting independance, and shewing an utter disregard to God's honour and pleasure: and they may not hope to prosper who thus take their affairs into their own hands, and leave God far above out of their sight. (2.) They not only made themselves kings, but gods also, *of their silver and their gold have they made them idols*, and to this day the covetous do the same, *that they may be cut off* by their enemies, the Assyrians, when their gods of gold could yield them no assistance. *Thy calf, O Samaria, hath cast thee off*, was the cause of their being rejected of God, and given to the sword and to captivity, or *hath deserted thee*, failed their hopes in the day of trouble, and was seized among other spoils, and carried away by the king of Assyria. Probably when Samaria became the capital, another calf might be erected there, or one of those from Dan or Bethel was removed thither. *Mine anger is kindled against them*, the idolaters, who worshipped the work of their own hands. *From Israel was it also*, erected with the approbation of the people, and molten out of their treasures; *the workman made it, therefore it is not God*, a most conclusive and unrefragable argument; *but the calf*, or *for the calf, of Samaria shall be broken to pieces*, a sure proof of its vanity; so far from helping them, it could not rescue itself from the hands of the enemy.

5. The prophet expostulates with them on their folly and obstinacy. *How long will it be ere they attain unto innocency?* leaving these wretched dependencies, and returning to the pure worship of God, nor any longer provoke the fierce anger of the Lord. *Note*, It is the grief of ministers to behold the perverseness of sinners, and they cannot but warmly remonstrate against their provocations.

6. He warns them of the fatal issue of their ways. *For they have sown the wind*, in the fruitless labour of their idolatrous worship, and their expectation of help from their allies, *and they shall reap the whirlwind*, they shall not merely be disappointed of their harvest, but reap their own destruction, swept away by the Assyrian army, as by a resistless whirlwind: *it hath no stalk*, their seed produces nothing, *the bud shall yield no meal*, withered with blasting and mildew; *and if so be it yield, the strangers shall swallow it up*; so far would it be from a blessing to them, that they prospered and grew wealthy in their sinful and idolatrous courses, their riches would be a temptation to their enemies to come and plunder them. And thus will every sinner and hypocrite's hope perish; they will reap as they sow, and find by dire experience that the wages of sin is death.

f Jer. xxii. 28. & xlviii. 38. g Hos. v. 13. & vii. 11. h Jer. ii. 24. i Ezek. xvi. 33, 34. k Heb. Loves. l Chap. x. 10. m 2 Kings xvii. 3. n Isa. x. 8. Dan. ii. 37. o Chap. xii. 11. p Deut. iv. 6, 8. q Jer. vii. 21. Zech. vii. 6. r Chap. ix. 4.

8 Israel is swallowed up: now shall they be among
the Gentiles, f as a vessel wherein *is* no pleasure. 9 For
they are gone up to Assyria, a wild ass alone by himself:
Ephraim k hath hired | lovers. 10 Yea, though they
have hired among the nations, now l will I gather them,
and | they shall sorrow a little for the burden of m the
king of princes. 11 Because Ephraim hath made many
altars to sin, altars shall be unto him to sin. 12 I have
written to him the great things of my law, *but* they were
counted as a strange thing. 13 q They sacrifice flesh |
for the sacrifices of mine offerings, and eat *it*; *but* r the
LORD accepteth them not; now will he remember
their iniquity, and visit their sins: r they shall return to
Egypt. 14 For Israel hath forgotten s his maker, and
buildeth temples; and Judah hath multiplied fenced cities:
but I will send t a fire upon his cities, and it shall
devour the palaces thereof.

Before Christ 760.

r Deut. xxviii. 68. Chap. ix. 3. & xi. 5. s Isa. xxix. 23. Eph. ii. 10. t Jer. li. 13.

v. 8—14. They who forsake God, forsake their own mercies.

1. Israel's ruin is foretold. *Israel is swallowed up*, their whole country shall be devoured, and themselves led captive by the Assyrians: *now shall they be among the Gentiles, as a vessel wherein is no pleasure*, dispersed, contemptible, and mean. They had profaned the crown of their glory, and therefore justly were trodden under foot. *Note*, They who dishonour their holy profession, deserve to be made despicable.

2. The cause of their desolations is their departure from God. *For they are gone up to Assyria*, to engage their assistance, 2 *Kings* xv. 19. *a wild ass alone by himself*, so obstinate, untractable, and headstrong were they in their ways, or such they should become when carried captive, they should experience every hardship in a strange land. *Ephraim hath hired lovers*, by expensive presents endeavouring to purchase the friendship of the neighbouring nations, thus deserting God, and changing a rock for a reed. *Note*, The sinner is as foolish as he is wicked, and instead of the happiness he expects, really courts his own ruin.

3. Their lovers whom they courted will prove their destroyers. *Though they have hired among the nations, now will I gather them*, either their enemies against them, or themselves into the midst of their besieged cities, *as sheaves to the floor*, Mic. iv. 8. *and they shall sorrow a little for the burden of the king of princes*, the tribute imposed upon them by the king of Assyria, which is the prelude to greater evils approaching, and which should bring more bitter sorrows along with them. God thus gives warning before he strikes, and brings sinners first into lesser troubles, to see if that will lead them to repentance, before he pours out the vials of his wrath.

4. Their multiplied temples, altars, and sacrifices, shall stand them in no stead. *Because Ephraim hath made many altars to sin*, to offer sin-offerings upon them with great shew of devotion, *altars shall be unto him for sin*, so far from expiating his crimes, the very altars would aggravate them, as being reared contrary to the divine prescription, *Deut.* xii. 3—5. and dedicated to the honour of the calves, and other idols. *I have written to him the great things of my law*, wherein all the great things which pertain unto life and godliness were clearly set forth, what God required of them, in what manner he would be worshipped and served, what sacrifices should be offered, and where; and what was the great end of the sacrifices, even to lead them to that atoning blood that should be shed in the fulness of time; *but they were counted as a strange thing*, they paid no regard to the institutions of God; and after long disuse, counted the prophets who would bring them back to the true worship and service of God, as setters forth of strange doctrines. *They sacrifice flesh for the sacrifices of mine offerings, and eat it*; instead of offering it to God, they feasted upon it themselves, and made their devotions minister to their luxury; no marvel therefore *the Lord accepteth them not*, neither them nor their offerings; *now will he remember their iniquities, and visit their sins*; so far from pardoning them, that the very sacrifices of atonement which they offered, should only add to their iniquities: *they shall return into Egypt*, whither many fled on the Assyrian invasion, and miserably perished, *chap.* ix. 3, 6. or their captivity in Babylon should be as another Egyptian bondage. *For Israel hath forgotten his maker*, his worship and ways, *and buildeth temples* to idols, *and Judah hath multiplied fenced cities*, placing their confidence on these feeble bulwarks, instead of the arm of Omnipotence; *but I will send a fire upon his cities, and it shall devour the palaces thereof*, which we see fearfully accomplished, *Jer.* lii. *Note*, (1.) God's own word, not our fancies, must be the directory of our worship. (2.) The law of God contains great things to the enlightened mind, even the way to pardon, peace, life, and glory everlasting. If the things contained therein, to any appear strange and unaccountable, it is owing to the corruption, blindness, and ignorance of their fallen minds. (3.) Let not that which God hath written for our learning, be suffered to become strange through our neglect. (4.) Sacrifices for sin, whilst the love of it is unmortified, are abominable; they who think by their duties thus to commute for their iniquities, will find the works in which they chiefly trusted, turned into sin. (5.) They who think to fence against God's judgments, only build Babel walls.

CHAP. IX.

In this chapter, 1. God threatens to deprive this degenerate people of all their worldly enjoyments, because they had forgot it to whom they owed them, so that they should have no comfort either in receiving them themselves, or offering them to God, ver. 1—9. 2. He dooms them to utter ruin, for their own sins and the sins of their prophets,

Before Christ 760

prophets, ver 6—8 3 *He upbraids them with the wickedness of their fathers before them, in whose steps they trod*, ver 9, 10 4 *He threatens them with the destruction of their children, and the rooting out of their posterity*, ver 11—17

1 REjoice not, O Israel, for joy, as *other* people for
thou hast gone a whoring from thy God, thou
hast loved [a] a reward | upon every corn-floor 2 [b] The
floor and the ‡ wine press shall not feed them, and the
new wine shall fail in her 3 They shall not dwell in
the LORD's land, but [c] Ephraim shall return to Egypt,
and [d] they shall eat unclean *things* in Assyria 4 [e] They
shall not offer wine-*offerings* to the LORD, [f] neither shall
they be pleasing unto him [g] their sacrifices *shall be* un-
to them as the bread of mourners all that eat thereof
shall be polluted for their bread for their soul shall
not come into the house of the LORD 5 What will
ye do in the solemn day, and in the day of the feast of
the LORD? 6 For lo, they are gone, because of
destruction Egypt shall gather them up, Memphis
shall bury them § the pleasant *places* for their silver,
[h] nettles shall possess them thorns *shall be* in their ta-
bernacles

a Jer xliv 17 | Or, in b Chap ii 9 ‡ Or Wine-fat c Chap viii 13, & xi 5 d Ezek iv 13 Dan i 8 e Chap vi 6 f Jer vi 20 g Deut xxvi 14 § Heb The desire h Isa xxxi 13 & xxxiv 13, Chap x 8.

v 1—6 Israel's guilt and ruin are still the burden of the prophetic word

1 They are forbidden to *rejoice as other people* Though now perhaps their affairs might be flourishing, as under Jeroboam, or their harvest plenteous, yet, whilst their sins were so many, they ought to weep and lament, for judgment hung over their heads *Note*, The joys of the impenitent sinner are as unseemly as songs of mirth in the mouth of a dying malefactor

2 Their iniquities, which witnessed against them, should damp their mirth, and bring them to mourning *For thou hast gone a whoring from thy God*, committing spiritual adultery with stocks and stones *thou hast loved a reward upon every corn-floor*, prostituting themselves, as an harlot for hire, to their idols, regarding their corn and wine as their gifts, *See chap* xi 5, 12 and offering their tithes and first fruits at their idol shrines, instead of the sanctuary at Jerusalem *Note*, (1) They who place their affections on earthly goods, commit the same spiritual adultery, as if they worshipped an idol (2) Many spend freely on their lusts, what they would greatly grudge to employ in the service of God

3 Wrath is gone forth against them for their wickedness

(1) Their earthly goods shall perish Their land shall be cursed with barrenness, *the floor and the wine-press shall not feed them, and the new wine shall fail in her*, blasting, mildew, or the ravages of an enemy, shall rob them of their abused blessings, and leave them pining for want so poor and perishing a possession is every earthly good

(2) *They shall not dwell in the Lord's land* since they have broken the covenant on which they held possession, he, as proprietor, will resume the grant, and send them into a miserable captivity *They shall return to Egypt*, as fugitives and vagabonds flying from the sword of the Assyrian *and they shall eat unclean things in Assyria*, led captives thither, and driven through hunger to eat food forbidden by the law, and such as was unfit for men to eat, as the prodigal's husks *Note*, They who will not be governed by God's laws, shall not dwell in his land *The wicked shall be cast into hell, with all the nations that forget God*

(3) In their dispersion they should be deprived of the possibility of keeping up any profession of religion, and have neither altar nor sacrifice *They shall not offer wine-offerings to the Lord*, much less any other oblations *neither shall their sacrifices be pleasing unto him*, if they had power to offer them, their impenitence and hypocrisy would render them an abomination *Their sacrifices shall be unto them as the bread of mourners*, instead of purging them from their sins, *all that eat thereof shall be polluted*, See Deut xxvi 14 *for their bread for their soul*, either the common bread, that which fed them, or the *Minchah*, the portion of bread or flower which accompanied the sin-offerings, *shall not come into the house of the Lord*, that glorious temple being destroyed, nor, if it stood, would their oblations be accepted *What will ye do in the solemn day, and in the day of the feast of the Lord?* the sabbaths, new moons, &c when groaning under their burdens, they should neither have sacrifice to slay, nor altar to offer them, nor permission to observe these solemn seasons *Note*, They who slight and abuse the means of grace they enjoy, shall know, by dire experience in their loss, the value of the mercies they disregarded

(4) They and their land shall be utterly destroyed *For lo, they are gone, because of destruction*, thinking to find refuge in Egypt from the sword of the Assyrians, but they are mistaken *Egypt shall gather them up, Memphis shall bury them*; one of the chief cities whither they fled, and probably died with the pestilence, or through want *The pleasant places for their silver, nettles shall possess them thorns shall be in their tabernacles* so utterly shall all their cities be demolished, and their land be desolate without inhabitant *Note*, There is no escaping from God the sinner may fly to him, and find mercy, to attempt to fly from him is madness, and must end in misery

Before Christ 760

7 The days of visitation are come, the days of re-
compense are come, Israel shall know *it* the prophet
is a fool, [i] the | spiritual man *is* mad, for the mul-
titude of thine iniquity, and the great hatred 8 [k] The
watchman of Ephraim *was* with my God *but* the pro-
phet *is* a snare of a fowler in all his ways, *and* hatred in
the house of his God 9 [l] They have deeply corrupted
themselves, as in the days of [m] Gibeah [n] *therefore* [o] he will
remember their iniquity, he will visit their sins 10 I
found Israel like grapes in the wilderness I saw your
fathers [o] as the first ripe in the fig-tree at her first time
but [p] they went to Baal peor, and [q] separated themselves
unto [r] that shame, and *their* abominations were accord-
ing as they loved

i Mic ii 11 Zeph iii 4 | Heb Man of the Spirit k 1 Sam ix 17 l Isa xxxi 6, Chap x 9 m Judg xix 22 n Chap viii 13 o Isa xxviii 4 Mic vii 1 p Num xxv 3 q Chap iv 14 r Jer xi 13

v 7—10 To awaken their consciences God threatens them,

1 With the speedy execution of his judgments *The days of visitation are come, the days of recompense are come*, they are surely coming, and near, even at the door *Israel shall know it*, by dire experience, and feel the wrath they would not believe or fear *Note*, A day of recompense for sinners is at hand, when God will visit upon them all their iniquities

2 They would then change their sentiments, both concerning the false prophets and the true They said in the days of their prosperity, concerning the true prophets who warned them of these judgments, *The prophet is a fool, the spiritual man is mad*; treating their persons with contempt, and their preaching as madness but now it will appear that the false prophets in whom they trusted, who prophesied to them of peace, were the fools, their pretences to spirituality and inspiration, mere phrensies of the brain, and their promise of prosperity to a wicked people, direct madness, and to these delusions they were given up, *for the multitude of their iniquities, and for their great hatred*, they hated God, his word, his ministers, and therefore he justly left them to themselves, to fill up the measure of their iniquities, and hasten their own destruction *The watchman of Ephraim was with my God*, was formerly on the Lord's side, and received directions from him, and should be so now, but *the prophet*, the false prophet, *is a snare of a fowler in all his ways*, leading the people wrong by his example and his preaching, *and hatred in the house of his God* his lies being detected, he becomes execrable even at Beth-el or, his hatred is bitter against those who cleave to the true worship of God, whom nevertheless the deceiver calls *his God*, and pretends inspiration from him *Note*, (1) It is no new thing for the true prophets to be branded as fools or madmen (2) They who hate the truth, are justly given up to strong delusions to believe a lie (3) Hatred and contempt of God's faithful ministers will be shortly severely punished

3 Their iniquities shall be discovered and recompensed *They have deeply corrupted themselves*, not only the false prophets, but the people in general, *as in the days of Gibeah*, See Judg xix advanced to the highest pitch of lewdness, cruelty, and contempt of God, *therefore he will remember their iniquity, he will visit their sins*, taking exemplary vengeance on them, as of old on that devoted city *I found Israel like grapes in the wilderness* took delight in them there, as a traveller who had found such refreshment in a barren place *I saw your fathers as the first ripe in the fig tree at her first time*, pleased with their flourishing estate, delighting in them as his chosen, showering down upon them his blessing, and watching over them with constant care, which aggravated the baseness of their ingratitude, when *they went unto Baal-peor*, See Numb xxv *and separated themselves unto that shame*; joining in the obscene rites with which the idol was worshipped *and their abominations were according as they loved*, the daughters of Moab, whose embraces they sought, drew them into this abominable idolatry. *Note*, (1) The sinner's iniquity will certainly sooner or later prove his shame (2) When the inordinate love of women rages in the heart, to please them the infatuated slave sticks at no abomination

11 *As for* Ephraim, their glory shall fly away like a
bird, from the birth, and from the womb, and from the
conception 12 [s] Though they bring up their children,
yet will I bereave them, *that there shall* not *be* a man
left yea, wo also to them when I depart from them
13 Ephraim, [t] as I saw Tyrus, *is* planted in a pleasant
place but Ephraim shall bring forth his children to the
murderer 14 Give them, O LORD what wilt thou
give? give them [u] a | miscarrying womb, and dry
breasts 15 All their wickedness [x] *is* in Gilgal, for
there

s Job xxvii 14 t Ezek xxvi & xxvii & xxviii u Luke xxiii 29 | Heb That casteth the fruit x Chap iv 15 & xii 11

Before Christ 760

y Isa i 23
z Job xviii 16
† Heb The desires
a 2 Chron xxxvi 16

there I hated them for the wickedness of their doings
I will drive them out of mine house, I will love them
no more y all their princes *are* revolters 16 Ephraim
is smitten, z their root is dried up, they shall bear no
fruit yea, though they bring forth, yet will I slay *even*
† the beloved *fruit* of their womb 17 My God will
cast them away, a because they did not hearken unto him
and they shall be wanderers among the nations

v 11—17 The wrath of God is revealed from heaven against all ungodliness and unrighteousness of men, and here we see it fearfully lighting upon the transgressors

God threatens them with a variety of miseries

1 Death shall spread its ravages among them, and their children shall perish before their eyes, some dying in the cradle, others carried *from the womb* to the grave, others perishing even *from the conception* And though some should be spared to grow up, yet, by the sword, the famine, or pestilence, they would be consumed, or carried captives, *till not a man be left* *yea, wo also to them, when I depart from them*, for this is the heaviest of judgments the sinner is wretched indeed whom God abandons At present indeed these judgments seemed to be far away, Ephraim, as Tyre, was in prosperity, well fortified, and replenished with inhabitants, v 13, but *the murderer*, the Assyrian army, shall devour his children Already *Ephraim is smitten*, v 16 with tokens of God's displeasure, and soon shall be utterly destroyed *Their root is dried up, they shall bear no fruit*, like a tree withered and blasted *yea, though they bring forth*, a few of them at least, *yet will I slay even the beloved fruit of their womb*, so that when the prophet would intercede for them, he could not but think the barren womb a blessing *Give them, O Lord what wilt thou give? give them a miscarrying womb, and dry breasts* better far have no children, than only to bring them up for the slaughter *Note* (1) Death makes no distinction, nor pays regard to infants cries or parents tears (2) The children parents most doat upon, are often snatched from their arms, to teach them the folly and sin of creature-idolatry (3) Those who are written childless need not murmur, the crosses children occasion to us, often more than counterbalance all the comfort of them

2 In hatred God will cast them off, and cast them out They had given him indeed abundant provocation to do so *All their wickedness is in Gilgal*, which was become the chief place of their idolatrous worship, and from thence it spread through the land *There I hated them* for their abominations, profaning that place where once God's tabernacle had been pitched *For the wickedness of their doings I will drive them out of my house*, from the place where he had settled them in Canaan, the type and figure of his church, expulsion from the one implying they were excommunicate from the other *I will love them no more*, at least, for a long while they shall not enjoy any tokens of his favour and regard *All their princes are revolters*, they, who should have restrained the people's wickedness, were chief in the transgression, and emboldened them in sin by their evil examples No wonder therefore that *my God will cast them away*, as reprobate, and thrust them from his presence as abominable, *because they did not hearken unto him*, rejecting the commands of his law, and the warnings of his prophets *and they shall be wanderers among the nations*, dispersed into all lands, and, like Cain, vagabonds in the earth, as was the case in their first captivity, and is awfully verified in their posterity to this day *Note*, (1) Of all miseries none can be greater than to be hated of God, and they who persist in malicious wickedness may assuredly expect it (2) It is a distinguishing mercy to the few faithful, that when others are abandoned and forsaken, they can still say, *My God*

CHAP X

In this chapter, 1 The people of Israel are charged with gross corruptions in the worship of God, and are threatened with the destruction of their images and altars, ver 1, 2, 5, 6, 8 2 They are charged with corruptions in the administration of the civil government, and are threatened with the ruin of it, ver 3, 4, 7 3 They are charged with imitating the sins of their fathers, and with security in their own sins, and are threatened with humbling judgments, ver 9—11 4 They are earnestly invited to repent and reform, and are threatened with ruin if they did not, ver 12—15

Before Christ 740

a Nahum ii 2
‖ Or a vine emptying the fruit which it giveth
b Chap viii 11 & xii 11
‡ Or, he hath divided their heart
§ Heb behead
c Ver 7
Chap iii 4 & xi 5 Micah iv 9

1 ISRAEL a *is* ‖ an empty vine, he bringeth forth
fruit unto himself according to the multitude
of his fruit, b he hath increased the altars, according to
the goodness of his land, they have made goodly images
2 ‡ Their heart is divided, now shall they be
found faulty he shall § break down their altars he
shall spoil their images 3 For now they shall say,
c We have no king, because we feared not the LORD,
what then should a king do to us? 4 They have

d Deut xxix 18 Amos v 7 & vi 12 Acts viii 23 Heb xii 15
‖ Or Chemarim, Zeph i 4
e 1 Sam iv 21, 22
f Chap v 13
g Chap xi 6
h Ver 3
i Deut ix 21
k Chap iv 6
l Isa ii 19 Luke xxiii 30 Rev vi 16 & ix 6

spoken words, swearing falsly in making a covenant
thus judgment springeth up d as hemlock in the furrows
of the field 5 The inhabitants of Samaria shall fear
because of the calves of Beth aven for the people
thereof shall mourn over it, and ‖ the priests thereof
that rejoiced on it, e for the glory thereof, because it
is departed from it 6 It shall be also carried unto
Assyria *for* a present to f king Jareb Ephraim shall
receive shame, and Israel shall be ashamed g of his own
counsel 7 *As for* Samaria, h her king is cut off as
the foam upon the water 8 The high places also of
Aven, i the sin of Israel shall be destroyed k the thorn
and the thistle shall come up on their altars, and l they
shall say to the mountains, Cover us, and to the hills,
Fall on us

v 1—8, Still the sins of the people, and the judgments of God, are the burden of the prophecy

1 Their sins are charged upon them

[1] They are destitute of all goodness *Israel is an empty vine*, of no profit to the owner *he bringeth forth fruit unto himself*, he thinks not of advancing God's glory, but his own, and his earthly good things are spent not in God's service, but consumed on his lusts, or in the worship of idols, and perhaps he is therefore an *empty vine*, being thus impoverished and exhausted

[2] They are devoted to idolatry *According to the multitude of his fruit*, as his riches increased, *he hath increased the altars*, &c turning thus God's gifts against him, and abusing his blessings to the vilest purposes *Note*, We too often see an increase of wealth abused to the increase of wickedness, instead of being employed as a more enlarged opportunity put into men's hands of serving God's cause, and doing good in their generation

[3] *Their heart is divided*, among themselves factions rage, and sects dispute about the preference of idols or rather, their heart is divided between God and the calves *Now shall they be found faulty*, this halting between both being highly criminal, for a divided heart God abhors or, *they shall be desolated*, with his judgments

[4] *They have spoken words, swearing falsly in making a covenant*, perjured and prophane, making no conscience of oaths or leagues, and on the very seat of judgment, injustice and oppression sat enthroned *Thus judgment*, which should have been administred with impartiality as a medicine, through false witnesses, and a corrupt magistracy, *springeth up as hemlock in the furrows of the field*, baleful and poisonous, perverted to the greater loss or ruin of the injured and God will visit for these things, and avenge the quarrel of those who are oppressed with wrong

2 Their punishments are denounced

[1] *They shall say, We have no king*, as bad as none, when justice was so ill administered, or really without a king, through the frequent assassinations of their monarchs, or having none able to protect them from their enemies, or, as at the last, when they and their king together were led captives into Assyria *because we feared not the Lord*, which was the source of all their miseries, *what then should a king do to us?* if they had one, he could afford them no protection from the judgments of the eternal King which they had provoked *As for Samaria*, the metropolis of Israel, *her king is cut off as the foam upon the water* In prophetic language, what shall be, is spoken or is already done, Hoshea, the last king, being doomed to fall, weak as the froth which flies on the surface, and easily broken as the bubbles before the Assyrian army

[2] Their idols shall be destroyed, and be as little able to help them as their king *He shall break down their altars, he shall spoil their images* the Assyrian monarch shall do it, the rod of God's indignation *The inhabitants of Samaria shall fear because of the calves of Beth-aven*, for them, lest they should be seized by the enemy, or for themselves, as if now they were taken the land would be left defenceless *for the people thereof shall mourn over it*, of Beth-aven, or the worshippers of the calves in general shall lament their loss, *and the priests thereof that rejoiced on it*, who shall grieve, as particularly interested, *for the glory thereof, because it is departed from it*, and no more surrounded with crouds of worshippers or the glory of Beth-aven is now departed, their calf being gone *It shall also be carried unto Assyria for a present to king Jareb*, as a trophy of victory over Samaria and her god *Ephraim shall receive shame*, when they see their idols demolished, and their folly in trusting them manifested *and Israel shall be ashamed of his own counsel*, in paying divine worship to such vanities *The high places also of Aven*, of iniquity, the scenes where their idolatries were committed, *the sin of Israel shall be destroyed the thorn and the thistle shall come up on their altars*, being left in ruin, and unfrequented, *and* in their bitter distress *they*, the people who were wont to worship there, *shall say to the mountains, Cover us, and to the hills, Fall on us*, as it seeking even under them a cover from their miseries, and desiring to be hid from the wrath of God *Note*,

Before Christ 740

(1) When we make any creature our idol, God juſtly breaks it down, and leaves us to mourn our folly (2) When the day of vengeance comes, in vain doth the ſinner cry to rocks and mountains to hide him from the wrath of the Lamb

9 ᵐ O Iſrael, thou haſt ſinned from the days of Gi-
beah there they ſtood the battle in Gibeah againſt the
children of iniquity ⁿ did not overtake them 10 *It*
is in my deſire that I ſhould chaſtiſe them and ° the
people ſhall be gathered againſt them, † when they ſhall
bind themſelves in their two furrows 11 And Eph-
raim *is as* an heifer *that is* taught, *and* loveth to tread
out *the corn*, but I paſſed over upon ‡ her fair neck
I will make Ephraim to ride Judah ſhall plow, *and*
Jacob ſhall break his clods 12 ᵖ Sow to yourſelves
in righteouſneſs, reap in mercy ᵠ break up your fal-
low ground for ʳ *it is* time to ſeek the LORD, till
he come and rain righteouſneſs upon you 13 ˢ Ye
have plowed wickedneſs, ye have reaped iniquity, ye
have eaten the fruit of lies becauſe thou didſt truſt
in thy way, ᵗ in the multitude of thy mighty men 14
Therefore ſhall a tumult ariſe among thy people, and
ᵘ all thy fortreſſes ſhall be ſpoiled, as Shalman ſpoiled
ˣ Beth arbel in the day of battle the mother was daſhed
in pieces upon *her* children 15 So ſhall Beth-el do
unto you, becauſe of § your great wickedneſs in a morn-
ing ʸ ſhall the king of Iſrael utterly be cut off

m Chap. ix 9. n Judg. xx 47. o Jer. xvi 16 Chap. x 10. † Or, When I ſhall bind them for their two tranſgreſſions, or in their two habitations. ‡ Heb. The beauty of her neck. p Prov. xi 18. q Jer. iv 3. r Is. lv 6. Job iv 8. Prov. xxii 8. Gal. vi 8. t Pſ. xxxiii 16. u Chap. xiii 16. x 2 Kings xviii 34 & xix 13. § Heb. The evil of your evil. y 2 Kings xvii 6.

ᵐ 9—15 The prophet here,

1 Reminds them of their wickedneſs, committed in a conſtant ſeries from the days of their predeceſſors *From the days of Gibeah*, when the Levite's concubine was ſo atrociouſly abuſed, *thou haſt ſinned*, continued in the practice of ſuch abominations, or, *more then the day of Gibeah*, exceeding them in iniquity *there they ſtood*, with daring effrontery, on their defence *The battle in Gibeah againſt the children of iniquity did not overtake them* in the two firſt engagements they were victorious, and at laſt ſix hundred men made their eſcape but as the ſin of Iſrael now exceeded theirs, the battle ſhould overtake them, notwithſtanding their preſent proſperity in iniquity

2 God will viſit them *It is my deſire that I ſhould chaſtiſe them* on this he determined, and would take delight in their ſufferings *and the people ſhall be gathered againſt them*, as Iſrael was of old againſt Benjamin, *when they ſhall bind themſelves in their two furrows*, fortified with a double intrenchment or, *they ſhall bind them*, their enemies ſhall yoke them as oxen, to plow their ground or, *when I ſhall bind them for their two tranſgreſſions*, their forſaking God for idols, and their corporal and ſpiritual adultery *And Ephraim is an heifer that is taught* to plow, and bear the yoke, to ſubmit to God's commands, but with reluctance yielded her neck *and loveth* rather *to tread out the corn*, where ſhe can eat to the full, than labour in the furrows of obedience *but I paſſed over upon her fair neck*, put a yoke upon it *I will make Ephraim to ride*, or *cauſe to ride on Ephraim*, the Aſſyrians ſhall have dominion over them *Judah ſhall plow, and Jacob ſhall break the clods*, being brought into bondage by their conquerors Some give a very different ſenſe of the words, as ſpeaking the kind care of God in teaching his people, and the gentle methods he took to engage their obedience, as one ſtrokes the heifer's neck to encourage her, and bring her to the yoke He laid then his inſtitutions upon them, and ſet them to their work, that they might bring forth fruit abundantly to his glory and their own comfort And to this ſenſe the following words ſeem applicable, which contain,

3 An exhortation to righteouſneſs, prayer, and penitence *Sow to yourſelves in righteouſneſs*, walk in all holy converſation and godlineſs, in the practice of every good word and work, which will bring their own reward *reap in mercy*, everlaſting life being the reward, not of debt, but of grace *break up your fallow ground*, for ſuch is the heart of man, being naturally hard, unprofitable for any good fruit, over-run with the briars and thorns of corrupt affections, and needs continually to be broken up by a humbling conviction of our ſinfulneſs, guilt, and miſery, that the ſeed of divine grace may ſpread and grow, and bring forth abundantly *for it is time to ſeek the Lord*, whoſe bleſſing alone can proſper the ſeed ſown, *till he come and rain righteouſneſs upon you*, give us that righteouſneſs which he demands of us, for without him we have no power to produce it And this ſome apply to Chriſt, who ſhould come *as the rain*, Pſ lxxii 6 and bring in that *everlaſting righteouſneſs*, in which all his redeemed people ſhould find acceptance with God *Ye have plowed wickedneſs*, toiled hard in the ſervice of ſin, and an Egyptian taſk-maſter had they found it *Ye have reaped iniquity*, a plenteous harveſt of evil, both of guilt and puniſhment *ye have eaten the fruit of lies*, diſappointed in their expectations, and finding nothing of that ſweetneſs and ſatiſfaction they promiſed themſelves, *becauſe thou didſt truſt in thy way*, on idol confidences, or heathen alliances, *and in the multitude of thy mighty men*, their own armies and garriſons, which were poor defences againſt the wrath of God which they had provoked, and thus will all the confidences and comforts of the ſinner aſſuredly diſappoint his hopes

4 An utter deſtruction awaits them *Therefore*, becauſe of their ſins and vain confidences, *ſhall a tumult ariſe among thy people*, from inſurrections at home, and the invaſion of the Aſſyrian army *and all the fortreſſes ſhall be ſpoiled*, ſo that they ſhould find no place of refuge, *as Shalman*, (the ſame probably as Salmaneſer), *ſpoiled Beth-arbel in the day of battle*, a well-known tranſaction in that day, when the place was ſacked, the people moſt inhumanly maſſacred, *the mother was daſhed in pieces with her children*, and ſuch would be their caſe, *ſo ſhall Beth-el do unto you, becauſe of your great wickedneſs*, particularly their idolatry committed at Beth-el, which would bring down the like fearful vengeance upon them Or, *ſo will he do unto you, O Beth-el*, commit the ſame ravages in this chief ſeat of idolatry *In a morning ſhall the king of Iſrael be utterly cut off*, certainly and ſpeedily as the morning returns, or, when they think the day of proſperity and liberty is dawning upon them, then ſhall their king Hoſhea be cut off, and all the nation periſh with him *Note*, Whatever miſeries we feel or fear, whether national or perſonal, reſpecting our bodies or our ſouls, they all ſpring from the ſame cauſe, ſin, ſin is the deadly root of bitterneſs

CHAP XI.

In this chapter we have, 1 The great goodneſs God had ſhewn his people Iſrael, ver 1, 3 4 2 Their ungrateful carriage towards him notwithſtanding, ver 2, 3, 4, 7, 12 3 Threatenings of wrath againſt them for their ingratitude and treachery, ver 5, 6 4 Mercy remembred in the midſt of wrath, ver 8, 9 5 Promiſe of what God would yet do for them, ver 10, 11 6 An honourable character given of Judah, ver 12

1 ᵃ WHEN Iſrael *was* a child, then I loved him,
and ᵇ called my ſon out of Egypt. 2 ᶜ *As*
they called them, ſo they went from them they ſacri-
ficed unto Baalim, and burnt incenſe to graven images
3 ᵈ I taught Ephraim alſo to go, taking them † by
their arms, but they knew not that I healed them 4
ᵉ I drew them with cords of a man, with bands of love,
and I was to them as they that ‡ take off the yoke on
their jaws, and I laid meat unto them 5 ¶ He ſhall
not return into the land of Egypt, but the Aſſyrian
ſhall be his king, becauſe they refuſed to return 6
And the ſword ſhall abide on his cities, and ſhall con-
ſume his branches, and devour *them*, ᵍ becauſe of their
own counſels 7 And my people are bent to back-
ſliding from me ʰ though they called them to the moſt
High, § none at all would exalt *him*

a Ezek. xvi 6 &c. b Mat. ii 15. c 2 Chron. xxxvi 15, 16. d Ex. xix 4. Deut. xxxii 10 &c. † Or, on his arms. e Can. i 4. ‡ Heb. Lift up. f 2 Kings xvii 13. g Chap. x 6. h Ver. 2. Chap. vii 16. § Heb. Together they exalted not.

ᵛ 1—7 God puts the people of Iſrael in mind,

1 Of the *grace* and mercy he had ſhewn them *When Iſrael was a child, then I loved him*, in their weak and helpleſs ſtate, when firſt God took them for a people; *and called my ſon out of Egypt*, from the houſe of their priſon and prophetically this declares what ſhould be the caſe with Chriſt, God's own incarnate Son, to whom, Mat xi 15 the words are expreſsly applied, and in and through whom the people of God have obtained a deliverance from the bondage of guilt and corruption, infinitely more intolerable than that of Egypt *I taught Ephraim alſo to go*, with all the tenderneſs and care of the fondeſt mother, *taking them by the arms*, giving them his holy law to direct them, and by a pillar and cloud guiding their marches in the trackleſs wilderneſs And thus God ſtill upholds his choſen, teaching them by his word and ſpirit, carrying them through their trials and temptations, ſtrengthening their ſouls for his work and ſervice, and ſuffering none to pluck them out of his hand *I healed them* of their diſeaſes and plagues, as he doth the ſouls of his people, when wounded by ſin, or pining with ſpiritual decay. *I drew them with cords of a man, with bands of love*, by every endearing motive, and the powerfully conſtraining influence of his love ſhed abroad in their heart, by which God ſtill draws his people, not only perſuading, but obliging them with pleading conſtraint to come unto him *I was to them as they that take off the yoke on their jaws*, as the huſbandman unmuzzles the ox, or looſes the yoke from its neck, ſo had God delivered them from the ſervitude of Egypt, as he doth his people in general from the bondage of corruption *and I laid meat unto them*, the manna and quails wherewith he fed them in the wilderneſs, the emblems of the better ſpiritual bread that cometh down from heaven, with which God ſtrengthens and comforts his redeemed people in their way through this deſart world to the land of eternal reſt

2 Of the baſe *ingratitude* with which they had requited him *As they*, the prophets of the Lord, *called them* to their duty, and to return from their ſinful backſlidings, *ſo they*, *went from them*

Before Christ 740.

them the more importunately they were ſollicited, the more obſtinate and refractory they grew *They ſacrificed to Baalim, and burnt incenſe to graven images*, the abominable thing againſt which they were ſo particularly warned All God's kindneſs was thrown away upon them *they knew not that I healed them*, but aſcribe to their idols all their mercies *and my people are bent to backſliding from me*, both under a conſtant propenſity to depart from him, and wilfully ſet upon their abominations, though *his people*, which relation aggravated their guilt exceedingly *They refuſed to return*, v 5 whether courted or threatned, they perſiſted in evil *though they called them to the moſt High*, to leave their idols, and return to the worſhip of the true God, *none at all would exalt him*, give him the glory due unto his name, or *lift up* their prayers to him for mercy, or their hearts from earthly vanities to high and heavenly things *Note*, (1) Such is the natural heart of man, ever prone to evil, perverſe and obſtinate, and the beſt have much to lament over the remainder of this inbred corruption (2) Much pains are often ſpent to little purpoſe by God's faithful miniſters, yet, though ſinners will not hear, God is thereby glorified in leaving them without excuſe

3 Heavy wrath is denounced againſt them *He ſhall not return into the land of Egypt, but the Aſſyrian ſhall be his king*, whoſe yoke would be ſo much heavier, that they would wiſh rather for the taſk-maſters of Egypt again or ſo ſtraitly ſhould they be beſieged, or ſo far carried away captives, that they would be able to ſend no ambaſſadors to Egypt for aſſiſtance *And the ſword ſhall abide on all their cities*, the deſtruction ſhall be long-continued, as well as univerſal, *and ſhall conſume his branches, and devour them*, the villages and country round, or the inhabitants thereof, *becauſe of their own counſels*, which were their ruin *Note*, Sinners have none to blame but themſelves they chuſe thoſe ways which neceſſarily lead to their own perdition

l Jer ix 7 Chap vi 4 ††† Or might or could I &c k Gen xiv 8 & xix 24, 25 Deut xxix 23 Amos iv 11 l Iſa lxiii 15 Jer xxxi 20 m Pſ lxxviii 38 n Num xxiii 19 Iſa lv 8, 9 Mal iii 6 o Chap iii 5 p Iſa xxxi 4 Joel iii 16 Amos i 2 q Pſ ii 11 r Iſa lx 8 s 2 Sam xxiii 3 ‡ Or with the moſt holy

8 l How ††† ſhall I give thee up, Ephraim? *how* ſhall
I deliver thee, Iſrael? how ſhall I make thee as k Ad-
mah? *how* ſhall I ſet thee as Zeboim? l mine heart is
turned within me, my repentings are kindled together
9 m I will not execute the fierceneſs of mine anger, I
will not return to deſtroy Ephraim, n for I *am* God, and
not man, the holy One in the midſt of thee, and I will
not enter into the city 10 o They ſhall walk after the
LORD p he ſhall roar like a lion when he ſhall roar,
then the children ſhall tremble from the weſt 11 They
ſhall q tremble as a bird out of Egypt, and r as a dove
out of the land of Aſſyria and I will place them in their
houſes, ſaith the LORD 12 Ephraim compaſſeth me
about with lies, and the houſe of Iſrael with deceit but
Judah yet s ruleth with God, and is faithful ‡ with the
ſaints

v 8—12 We have here,

1 The reluctance gracious God expreſſes in giving up the once choſen people of Iſrael to ruin *How ſhall I give thee up, Ephraim?* &c. Juſtice might well plead for their total excìſion, and that, like the cities which were conſumed with fire, *Deut* xxix 23 Iſrael ſhould be given up to the ſame terrible vengeance, but mercy pleads for ſome mitigation or reſpite, if not for pardon, and God, as a father, with bowels of tendereſt compaſſion, appears moſt backward to ruin even this rebellious ſon, and mercy prevails *mine heart is turned within me, my repentings are kindled together*, not that God's mind is capable of change, or that he knows repentance with regard to any of the diſpenſations of his providence or grace, but he ſpeaks after the manner of men, and will change his manner of acting towards them, as we do when we alter our mind, and repent of our purpoſes And moſt aſtoniſhing do theſe compaſſions of our God appear! Oh that the ungrateful ſinner would for a moment pauſe, and think of them ſurely they muſt ſoften his obdurate heart

Some give the words a different ſenſe, *How might I give thee up?* &c how juſt would it be to do ſo? not the ſins of Sodom and her daughter cities were greater but, to magnify his grace to Iſrael, though he ſpared not the one, he will have mercy on the other Thus every redeemed ſoul is juſtly in himſelf deſerved to periſh as thoſe who are cut off in their iniquity, but ſovereign grace will be magnified in them

2 God's determination to ſpare them *I will not execute the fierceneſs of mine anger*, in blotting out their name from under heaven, *I will not return to deſtroy Ephraim*, though I viſit them in a little wrath, *I will not enter into the city*, though Jeruſalem, Samaria, and the other cities, he waſte for a time, their deſolation ſhall not be perpetual, as thoſe of Admah and Zeboim *for I am God, and not man* human compaſſions indeed would long ago have failed, but the divine are everlaſting or, though man is fickle and changeable, God is faithful, and true to his covenant, and will perform it notwithſtanding all their provocation *The holy One in the midſt of thee* Chriſt is his people's protector for his life, who ſtands in the midſt of them to plead for them they are ſpared, and, though they deſerve puniſhment, through him they obtain mercy *They ſhall walk after the Lord*, the Meſſiah their Saviour, their Leader and Commander, the Captain of their ſalvation, being effectually drawn to him by the great and precious promiſe of his goſpel *He ſhall roar like a lion*, his word ſhall be heard far and near *when he ſhall roar, then the children ſhall tremble from the weſt*, the children of God, whoſe hearts ſhall be deeply affected with the preaching of the goſpel and this may reſpect the Gentiles, as well as the Jews, the goſpel having chiefly ſpread that way hitherto *They ſhall tremble as a bird out of Egypt, and as a dove out of the land of Aſſyria*, flying ſwiftly, as the timorous dove when purſued by a bird of prey, to the covert of redeeming grace *and I will place them in their houſes, ſaith the Lord*, in the church of God below, and ſhortly in the eternal manſions of glory above *Note*, (1) When we are moſt diſcouraged with the ſenſe of our own deſerts, we ſhould ſtill remember with whom we have to do *he is God, and not man*, and as his majeſty is, ſo is his mercy (2) The trembling of the ſinner is uſually the firſt ſymptom of his return to God (3) When Chriſt is our captain, and we walk after him, we cannot fail of victory over every foe

3 A heavy complaint ſtill lies againſt Ephraim *He compaſſeth me about with lies, and the houſe of Iſrael with deceit* This ſeems to be a new diſcourſe, and moſt properly ſhould begin the next chapter Their ſervices were hypocritical, and their profeſſion deceitful, and therefore an abhorrence in the ſight of the heart-ſearching God

4 Judah is highly commended *Judah yet ruleth with God* The two tribes ſubmitted to that *Theocracy* God had eſtabliſhed among them, and their kings ruled according to God's law, and received their directions from him in their emergencies, which was their trueſt honour and higheſt dignity *and is faithful with the ſaints*, cleaving to the worſhip of the ſanctuary, and treading in the ſteps of their pious progenitors, and, while they do ſo, they may aſſuredly expect God will be faithful to his promiſes, and preſerve them to his everlaſting kingdom *Note*, (1) They who make God their king ſhall be exalted to reign with him (2) The faithful will be rewarded with manſions in glory, when the hypocrite and unbeliever ſhall receive their portion in everlaſting burnings

CHAP XII

In this chapter we have, 1 *A high charge drawn up both againſt Iſrael and Judah for their ſins, which were the ground of God's controverſy with them*, ver 1, 2 *Particularly the ſin of fraud and injuſtice which Ephraim juſtifies himſelf in*, ver 8 *And the ſin of idolatry*, ver 11 *by which God is provoked to contend with them*, ver 14 2 *The aggravations of their ſins are the honour God put upon their father Jacob*, ver 3—5 *The advancement of them into a people from low and mean beginnings*, ver 12, 13 *And the proviſion he had made for their ſpiritual welfare by the prophets he ſent them*, ver 10 3 *A call to the unconverted to turn to God*, ver 6 4 *An intimation of mercy that God had in ſtore for them*, ver 9

a 2 Kings xvii 4 Chap v 13 & vii 11 b Iſa xxx 6 & lvii 9 c Chap iv 1 Mic vi 2 d Prov xii 14 e Gen xxv 26 f Gen xxxii 24, &c ‡ Heb Was a prince or behaved himſelf princely g Gen xxviii 12, 19 & xxxv 9, 10 h Exod iii 15 i Chap xiv 1 Mic vi 8

1 EPhraim feedeth on wind, and followeth after the 725
eaſt-wind he daily increaſeth lies and deſolation,
and a they do make a covenant with the Aſſyrians, b and
oil is carried into Egypt 2 c The LORD hath alſo a
controverſy with Judah, and will puniſh Jacob according
to his ways, d according to his doings will he recom-
penſe him 3 ¶ He took his brother e by the heel in
the womb, and by his ſtrength f he ‡ had power with
God 4 Yea, he had power over the angel, and pre-
vailed he wept and made ſupplication unto him he
found him g *in* Beth-el, and there he ſpake with us 5
Even the LORD God of hoſts, the LORD *is* his h me-
morial 6 Therefore i turn thou to thy God keep
mercy and judgment, and wait on thy God continually

v 1—6 We have here,

1 The folly of *Ephraim*, *he feedeth on wind, and followeth after the eaſt-wind*, entertaining fallacious hopes, and counting his idol, or his heathen neighbours, for aſſiſtance, a labour as vain as purſuing the wind *he daily increaſeth lies and deſolation*, his ſtrange gods and foreign alliances, which will prove *a lie in his right hand*, and bring ruin upon him *and they do make a covenant with Aſſyria*, 2 *Kings* xvii 19 thinking to ſecure their ſafety thereby, *and oil is carried into Egypt*, to purchaſe their favour and help, but neither ſhall be of any ſervice to them, but will help to impoveriſh them and haſten their deſtruction *Note*, They who truſt on creature confidences will find them not only deceitful, but ruinous

2 *The Lord hath alſo a controverſy with Judah*, who now began to degenerate and fall into idolatry, *and therefore he will puniſh Jacob according to his ways, according to his doings will he recompenſe him*, diſcovering his ſins and taking vengeance for them

3 Their degeneracy from the piety of their forefather was a great aggravation of their guilt *He, Jacob, took his brother by*

he

Before Christ 725

the heel, ſo ſoon did he begin to ſtruggle for the birthright, whilſt they had bowed down their necks to idols, and ſubjected themſelves to the heathen, *and by his ſtrength he had power with God, yea he had power over the angel, and prevailed*, when he wreſtled with him in the way, Gen xxxii 24 The Son of God in human form coming to prove his faith and conſtancy, and ſtrengthening him for the conflict *he wept and made ſupplication unto him*, and thus prevailed, theſe being the moſt potent arms we can uſe to obtain every bleſſing from the Angel of the covenant, whoſe eternal power and Godhead here appear, being the object of the patriarch's adoration and prayers His faithleſs ſeed had given up the ſtruggle, and, having revolted from God's worſhip, had forfeited all intereſt in him, and communion with him, as all muſt do who live a prayerleſs life *He found him at Bethel*, both before and after this, Gen xxviii 19 xxxv 9 and there renewed the covenant with him, and in him with his poſterity, *there he ſpake with us* but they had apoſtatized, and turned Bethel, *the houſe of God*, into Bethaven, *the houſe of iniquity*, and therefore had juſtly forfeited the promiſed mercies And this perſon, with whom Jacob wreſtled, and who ſpake to him, was the true Jehovah, *even the Lord God of hoſts, the Lord Jehovah is his memorial*, his name, expreſſive of his ſelf-exiſtence, eternity, and immutability, who ſhould by right be worſhipped, adored and ſerved by all, and by them eſpecially to whom he had appeared ſo gracious Their neglect of him therefore and diſobedience were the more criminal

4 They are exhorted yet to return to God *Therefore turn thou to thy God*, to this glorious Jehovah, from whom they had ſo greatly departed, and, whenever they did ſo, they would prove his covenant mercies ſtill ſure to them, and he will own his relation to them as their God *Keep mercy and judgment*, the two grand pillars of vital Godlineſs, comprehending every act of kindneſs to men's bodies or ſouls, and that integrity and uprightneſs which in every word and deed ſhould be obſerved, *and wait on thy God continually*, in every appointed means of grace, for thoſe ſupports of his Spirit which alone can enable us for the exerciſe of charity and juſtice to men, and that unreſerved obedience and reſignation we owe to his bleſſed Self

7 ¶ *He is* † a merchant, [k] the balances of deceit *are*
in his hand he loveth to ‡ oppreſs 8 And Ephraim
ſaid, [l] Yet I am become rich, I have found me out ſub-
ſtance § *in* all my labours they ſhall find none iniquity
in me, that *were* ſin 9 And [m] I, *that am* the LORD
thy God from the land of Egypt, [n] will yet make thee
to dwell in tabernacles, as in the days of the ſolemn feaſt
10 ‖ I have alſo ſpoken by the prophets, and I have
multiplied viſions, and uſed ſimilitudes, by the miniſtry
of the prophets 11 [o] *Is there* iniquity in Gilead? ſure-
ly they are vanity, they ſacrifice bullocks [p] in Gilgal,
yea, [q] their altars *are* as heaps in the furrows of the fields
12 And [r] Jacob fled into the country of Syria, and
[s] Iſrael ſerved for a wife, and for a wife he kept *ſheep*
13 And [t] by a prophet the LORD brought Iſrael out
of Egypt, and by a prophet was he preſerved 14 E-
phraim provoked *him* to anger moſt bitterly, therefore
[u] ſhall he leave his blood upon him and [x] his reproach
ſhall his Lord return unto him

† Or Canaan Ezek xvi 3 k Prov xi 1 ‡ Or deceive l Rev iii 17 § Or all my labours ſuffice me not, he ſhall have puniſhment of iniquity in whom is ſin m Chap xii 9 n Lev xxiii 42 ‖ Or I will ſpeak o Chap vi 8 p Chap iv 15 Amos iv 4 q Chap viii 11 r Gen xxviii 5 s Gen xxix 20 t Exod xii 50 u Ezek xviii 13 x Dan xi 18

v 7—14 In theſe words there is a change of perſon from Judah to Ephraim

1 Ephraim is charged with deceit in trade *He is a merchant*, or *a Canaanite*, more like ſuch a one than a deſcendant from Iſrael, *the balances of deceit are in his hand*, impoſing by falſe weights and meaſures on thoſe with whom he dealt *he loveth to oppreſs*, takes delight in ſuch wickedneſs, and pleaſes himſelf with the thought of his own ingenuity *Note*, Fraudulent tradeſmen are the vileſt of robbers

2 Ephraim vindicates himſelf from the accuſation *Yet I am become rich, I have found me out ſubſtance*, as if his ſucceſs juſtified the means by which he acquired his riches, and that his proſperity, notwithſtanding the warnings of the prophets, ſecured his impunity *In all my labours they ſhall find none iniquity in me, that were ſin*, none ſuch as deſerved that name, ſo fair and upright they pretended their dealings had been, and that, if their trade was ſubmitted to ſevereſt ſcrutiny, it would ſtand the teſt, whilſt to their own labour, not God's bleſſing, they impiouſly aſcribe their gain *Note*, (1) A carnal heart regards his riches as his moſt ſubſtantial good (2) Many pride themſelves on their fair character among men, who in the day of God will be found very different from what they appear (3) Self-deceivers will not call their iniquity ſin it is the way of trade, every body does ſo one could not live without it theſe are plauſible excuſes, but God is not mocked All unrighteouſneſs is ſin, and the wages of it death eternal

3 Idolatry is charged upon them *Is there iniquity in Gilead?* in that pleaſant land, in a city of prieſts, a city of refuge too? *ſurely they are vanity* the inhabitants, like the other Iſraelites, are devoted to idolatry, *they ſacrifice bullocks in Gilgal*, to their idols, *yea their altars are as heaps in the furrows of the field*, ſo thick they ſtood, or, as ſome ſuppoſe, ſo ſhould they be beaten in pieces, and become a heap of rubbiſh

4 Notwithſtanding theſe provocations God gives ſome intimations of mercy in ſtore for them *And I, that am the Lord thy God*, ſtill owning the relation, *from the land of Egypt*, from that time having taken them for his people, *will yet make thee to dwell in tabernacles, as in the days of the ſolemn feaſt*, which might refer to their return from Babylon, or rather reſpects the times of the goſpel, when the converted Jews ſhould rejoice in Chriſt Jeſus, and have a place in his church perhaps it may alſo look forward to their expected day of grace *I have alſo ſpoken to the prophets* in time paſt, or *I will ſpeak*, ſending forth paſtors and teachers to preach his goſpel, *and I have multiplied*, or *will multiply, viſions*, I have done ſo, and will again under the goſpel diſpenſation, *and* I have *uſed*, or *will uſe, ſimilitudes*, as was the caſe in the Jewiſh church, where the whole ſervice was figurative, and was eſpecially fulfilled in the parables which Chriſt ſo frequently delivered *Note*, The Lord hath uſed every gracious method to communicate to us the meſſages of his grace, if, after all, we continue wilfully ignorant, ſin lieth at our door

5 What God had done for their forefathers was a ſtrong proof of his kindneſs to them, and ſerved to ſhew their ingratitude *And Jacob fled into the country of Syria*, to Laban, *and Iſrael ſerved for a wife* ſeven years, *and*, being then deceived by Laban, who gave him Leah inſtead of Rachel, on receiving her alſo the following week, *for a wife he kept ſheep*, ſeven years more, which is inſtanced both as a proof of the meanneſs of their original, for *a Syrian ready to periſh was their father*, and as a mark of God's favour to them, in raiſing them from ſo low a beginning to be a mighty nation, and reflected highly on their ingratitude *And by a prophet God brought Iſrael out of Egypt, and by a prophet was he preſerved*, by Moſes, who was the figure of Chriſt, the great Redeemer and Saviour, the Deliverer of his people from the bondage of ſin, ſatan, death, and hell Now God having ſo wonderfully dealt with them, and ſaved them from their enemies, they were bound by every tie of love and duty to ſerve him, but they made the baſeſt returns when they rebelled againſt him, and rejected his prophets, to one of whom they had ſuch unſpeakable obligations *Note*, All God's goodneſs to the ſinner will be remembered at the laſt, to convince him of his ingratitude and leave him without excuſe

6 They having made the moſt baſe returns to God for his kindneſs, he is juſtly provoked to puniſh them ſeverely *Ephraim provoked him to anger moſt bitterly* by his ſins, and eſpecially idolatry *therefore ſhall he leave his blood upon him*, either the innocent blood ſhed by him ſhall be required of him, or *his own blood ſhall be poured upon him*, ſhed by the ſword of vengeance for all his crying ſins, *and his reproach ſhall the Lord return upon him*, the reproaches caſt upon God by his idolatry, and on the prophets who teſtified againſt it, ſhall return into his own boſom, when he ſhall be a poor, wretched, deſpicable captive in a ſtrange land *Note*, The ſinner ſhall ſurely bear the ſhame of his iniquities, either in time covered with penitent confuſion, or in eternity with everlaſting contempt

CHAP XIII

1 *The people of Iſrael are reproved and threatened for their idolatry*, ver 1—4 2 *They are reproved and threatened for their wantonneſs, pride, and luxury, and other abuſes of their wealth and proſperity*, ver 5—8 3 *The ruin that is coming upon them, for theſe and their other ſins, is foretold as very terrible*, ver 12, 13, 15, 16 4 *Thoſe that yet retain a reſpect for their God are encouraged to hope that he will yet appear for their relief, though their kings and princes, and all their other ſupports, fail them*, ver 9, 10, 11, 14 *Note*, *Far better is it to bear the rebuke of ſin now, and repent of it, than eternally to periſh under it*

1 WHEN Ephraim ſpake † trembling, he exalt-
ed himſelf in Iſrael; but when he offended in
Baal, he died 2 And now [a] they ‡ ſin more and more,
and [b] have made them molten images of their ſilver,
and idols according to their own underſtanding, all of it
the work of the craftſmen they ſay of them, Let § the
men that ſacrifice, [c] kiſs the calves 3 Therefore they
ſhall be [d] as the morning cloud, and as the early dew that
paſſeth away, [e] as the chaff *that* is driven with the whirlwind
out of the floor, and as the ſmoke out of the chimney

† Or there was trembling a 2 Kin iii 13 ‡ Heb Add to ſin b Chap ii 8 & viii 4 § Or the ſacrifices of men c 1 Kin xix 18 d Chap vi 4 e Dan ii 35

v 1—3 The ſin which above all others filled up the meaſure of Iſrael's crimes was their idolatry, and this is here eſpecially reproved

1 It had been the bane of their proſperity, and the cauſe of all their miſeries *When Ephraim ſpake trembling*, with deep veneration towards the Divine Majeſty, and with filial fear before him, *he exalted himſelf in Iſrael*, grew diſtinguiſhed and great among the tribes; or *when he ſpake there was trembling*, all heard him with reſpect and honour, *but when he offended in Baal, he died*, they went apace to ruin, and at laſt periſhed as a nation for their idolatry *Note*, A Godlineſs is the honour and ſtability

Before Christ 7[25]

lity of a nation, so is sin the shame, and, sooner or later, will be the ruin of any people

2 They had multiplied their abominations *And now they sin more and more*, having once offended in Baal, they grew worse and worse, *and have made them molten images of their silver, and idols according to their own understanding, all of it the work of the craftsmen*, miserable gods! which silver could make, and craftsmen did *They say of them, Let the men that sacrifice kiss the calves*, in token of religious adoration, when they brought their offerings, or, as some read the words, *Let those that sacrifice a man kiss the calves*, as if they offered human sacrifices to these hated idols

3 God's wrath is denounced upon them for their idolatries *Therefore they shall be as the morning cloud*, that vanishes before the sun, *and as the early dew that passeth away, as the chaff that is driven with the whirlwind out of the floor*, light, worthless, and weak, *and as the smoke out of the chimney*, that is scattered as it rises So easily, speedily, and universally, would their ruin come upon them by the army of the Assyrians

4 Yet I *am* the LORD thy God from the land of
Egypt, and thou shalt know no God but me for *there
is* no saviour beside me 5 ¶ I did know thee in the
wilderness, in the land of † great drought 6 According to their pasture, so were they filled they were
filled, and their heart was exalted therefore have they
forgotten me 7. Therefore I will be unto them as a
lion, as a leopard by the way will I observe them 8
I will meet them as a bear *that is* bereaved *of her whelps*,
and will rent the caul of their heart, and there will I devour them like a lion † the wild beasts shall tear them

v 4—8 We may observe here,

1 The obligations God had laid upon them *Yet, notwithstanding their provocations, I am the Lord their God from the land of Egypt*, from the day he took them from thence he declared his regard to them, and to this day was ready to own the relation on their penitent return to him *And thou shalt know no God but me* they ought to have known no other, and would find by experience none but he able to save them, *for there is no saviour besides me* on whatever else they placed their confidence, they would be assuredly disappointed *I did know thee in the wilderness*, when reduced to the greatest distress, *in the land of great drought*, where every necessary of life was wanting, yet he liberally provided for them, brought water from the rock, rained manna from heaven, and fed them by daily miracles

2 Their ingratitude to God for these Mercies *According to their pasture, so were they filled* they rioted in luxury when he brought them into Canaan *they were filled* with the plenty there provided for them, *and their heart was exalted*, their sensuality made them proud and secure *therefore have they forgotten me*. *Note*, Worldly prosperity is very apt to seduce the heart from God, and such is our vileness, that the mercies which should excite our love, and quicken our thankfulness, too often make us forget the giver in the gift, and abuse in pride and luxury the blessings he bestows

3 The wrath denounced against them for their baseness *Therefore I will be unto them as a lion*, &c By all these beasts of prey the Lord designs to shew the severity of his vengeance, and the terrible ravages which shall be made amongst them with the lion's strength, the lynx or leopard's eye, and the fury of a bear bereaved of her whelps, shall the Assyrians, the beasts he sends among them, mark them out for the slaughter, rush on them, unable to resist, and tear them in pieces without remorse or pity. So fearful a thing it is to fall into the hands of the living God, if his wrath be kindled yea but a little Sinner, how can thine heart endure when God shall thus deal with thee?

9 ¶ O Israel, thou hast destroyed thyself, but in
me *is* thine help 10 I will be thy king where *is
any other* that may save thee in all thy cities? and thy
judges of whom thou saidst, Give me a king and princes?
11 I gave thee a king in mine anger, and took *him*
away in my wrath 12 The iniquity of Ephraim *is*
bound up his sin *is* hid. 13 The sorrows of a travailing woman shall come upon him, he *is* an unwise son,
for he should not stay long in *the place of* the breaking
forth of children 14 I will ransom them from the
power of the grave I will redeem them from death
O death, I will be thy plagues, O grave, I will be
thy destruction. repentance shall be hid from mine eyes
15 ¶ Though he be fruitful among *his* brethren, an
east-wind shall come, the wind of the LORD shall come
up from the wilderness, and his spring shall become dry,
and his fountain shall be dried up, he shall spoil the
treasure of all † pleasant vessels 16 Samaria shall
become desolate, for she hath rebelled against her God
they shall fall by the sword, their infants shall be dashed
in pieces, and their women with child shall be ript up

v 9—16 The prophet pathetically laments the miseries of his people, *O Israel, thou hast destroyed thyself* their sins were the cause of all the threatned judgments, and they had only themselves to blame for their sufferings And this is most applicable to every fallen creature, who by his sins hath most justly provoked God's wrath and indignation against him, and must perish eternally if sovereign grace do not interpose *But in me is thy help* desperate as their case appeared, God was still able and willing to save them when they truly turned to him The most guilty need not despair of pardon, nor the most helpless of deliverance, since God hath laid help on one mighty to save Though in and of ourselves not a ray of hope appears, nor the least ability remains of working out our own salvation, they who look to him shall hear his atoning blood speak peace to their consciences, and find his almighty grace effectual to subdue the power of their corruptions

1 The first step which led to their destruction was casting off the divine government and asking a king *And where is thy king now, that he may save thee in all thy cities?* Unable to protect them, he is a captive himself So foolish as well as sinful an exchange had they made, when God had said, *I will be thy king*, whom they rejected *And where are thy judges, of whom thou saidst, Give me a king and princes?* They are now no longer able to support the sinking state *I gave them a king in mine anger*, for God sometimes is pleased to gratify the desires of the wicked, and make the thing they ask their heaviest curse and plague, *and I took him away in my wrath*, either Saul, or, as the words may be rendered, *I will take him away*, that is Hoshea, the last king of Israel, with whom the whole nation was destroyed, or carried into captivity Thus God *in wrath* takes away what he gave *in anger*, and leaves us to mourn in bitterness our perverseness and folly

2 Their other sins were many, and ready to be produced against them *The iniquity of Ephraim is bound up, his sin is hid* The sinner himself is little apprized of the black catalogue of sins ready to be produced against him, but they are all upon record, treasured up against the day of wrath *The sorrows of a travailing woman shall come upon him*, distress and anguish the most agonizing and painful *He is an unwise son*, that will neither learn of God's word nor be taught by his judgments, *for he should not stay long in the place of the breaking forth of children*. He considers not how to extricate himself from his troubles, or by repentance to prevent them, struggling no more than a stillborn child Or the words may be rendered, *For he will not stay the time for the breaking forth of children* they would not wait for the Messiah, who should bring many sons unto glory, but turned from him to serve idols and thus were cut off in their sins, because they *rebelled against* their *God*, v 16

3 Their judgment is threatned *Though he be fruitful among his brethren*, as the name Ephraim signifies, increased in numbers, and abounding in wealth and honour, *an east-wind shall come*, the army of the Assyrian marching rapidly and irresistibly, *the wind of the Lord*, as being sent and commissioned by him, *shall come up from the wilderness*, hot and scorching, as it sometimes blows in the sandy desarts, *and his spring shall become dry, and his fountain shall be dried up*, their country laid utterly desolate, *and he shall spoil the treasure of all pleasant places*, the Assyrian monarch shall seize all their richest and most valuable possessions *Samaria shall become desolate*, her palaces laid in the dust, her houses without inhabitants, *for she hath rebelled against her God* by her idolatries and other sins *They shall fall by the sword of the enemy, their children shall be dashed to pieces, and their women with child shall be ripped up* such inhuman massacres should the Assyrians commit, in revenge of their perfidy, and the long siege they sustained With horror, whilst we read, let it be remembered, *such is man* and nothing but the restraints of grace prevent the world from being an Aceldama, a field of blood

4 One gracious promise serves to brighten up this dark scene Though they had rejected God's government and worship, yet still says he, *I will be their king*, to rescue and save them from the hand of their enemies *I will ransom them from the power of the grave*, not merely from their state of captivity, in which they seemed as buried, but these promises look forward to the great salvation of Jesus, who gave his life a ransom for many, *I will redeem them from death*, raising their souls from the death of sin to a life of righteousness, in virtue of the price he hath paid for his people, and at the last day coming to bring their bodies forth from their graves, fashioned like to his glorious body *O death, I will be thy plagues, O grave, I will be thy destruction* Death is already a vanquished foe, through the resurrection of Jesus, and shortly it will be entirely swallowed up in victory, when its very being shall be destroyed, and the grave no more devour, because *there shall be no more death* Well may the Apostle triumph in the prospect, and every faithful soul exult in this glorious hope! *Repentance shall be hid from mine eyes* the decree is gone forth, the promise is unchangeable, the victory is sure for with God there is no variableness or shadow of turning Therefore we may confidently *trust, and not be afraid*

CHAP

Before Christ 725.

CHAP. XIV.

The strain of this chapter differs much from that of the foregoing chapters. Those were generally made up of reproofs for sin and threatenings of wrath, but this is made up of exhortations to repentance and promises of mercy, and with these the prophet closes; for all the foregoing convictions and terrors he had spoken were designed to prepare and make way for these. He wounds that he may heal, the Spirit convinceth that he may comfort. We have here, 1. Directions in repenting, what to do and what to say, ver. 1—3. 2. Encouragement to repent, taken from God's readiness to receive the returning sinner, ver. 4, 5; and the comforts he has prepared for them, ver. 5—7. 3. A solemn recommendation of these things to our serious thoughts, ver. 9.

1 O Israel, return unto the LORD thy God; [b] for
thou hast fallen by thine iniquity. 2 [c] Take
with you words, and turn to the LORD; say unto him,
[d] Take away all iniquity, and † receive *us* graciously:
so will we render the calves of our lips. 3 [f] Ashur
shall not save us; we will not ride upon horses, neither
will we say any more to the work of our hands,
Ye are our gods: for in thee the fatherless findeth
mercy.

v. 1—3. A door of hope is here opened for God's people. He is not inexorable; he waiteth to be gracious.

1. They are called upon and enjoined to come to him. *O Israel, return unto the Lord*, who is still ready to receive the perishing sinner, to pardon and save him; and, though so long rejected, will not refuse to be called *thy God*: *for thou hast fallen by thine iniquity*, which then, now, and ever, was, is, and will be the cause of all our miseries; but when we see, feel, and lament it, and turn to God, then shall not iniquity be our destruction.

2. Words are suggested to them, suitable to their state and condition. *Take with you words, and turn unto the Lord; say unto him, Take away all iniquity*; this being the first great want of the sinner's soul. His guilt lies upon him as a heavy burden, which he longs to have removed; his corruption the inward sore of him; and he is without power to help himself. Earnestly therefore he prays for a sense of God's pardoning love, to deliver him from the condemnation of sin, of *all* sin, as blotted out through the blood of Jesus; and for power against iniquity, against *every iniquity*, that it may be mortified and subdued by divine grace: *and receive us graciously*, for we have no desert to plead, but the very reverse; or *receive good*, accept us and our services as well pleasing in Christ Jesus; or *give good*, every blessing which we need, and the ability for that goodness thou dost enjoin; for from him alone cometh every good and perfect gift, whilst *in our flesh there dwelleth no good thing*: *so will we render the calves of our lips*, those sacrifices of praise *which shall please the Lord better than a bullock that hath horns and hoofs*. *Ashur shall not save us, we will not ride upon horses*, seeking to Assyria or Egypt for help; *neither will we say any more to the work of our hands, Ye are our gods*; their idols being renounced and abhorred; and thus the returning sinner, who in simplicity approaches a pardoning God, feels his heart constrained to part with every idol, to renounce his most easily besetting sin, to disclaim all dependence upon his own doings and duties, and every trust upon creature help, that he may solely rest on the blood, the righteousness, the Spirit of a Redeemer, and expect his whole salvation from the sovereign grace of God. *For in thee the fatherless findeth mercy*. It is God's great honour and glory, that he doth not despise nor reject the prayer of the poor destitute: nay, though our distresses arise from our own folly and perverseness, he will not therefore cast us out, but the more magnify the wonders of his mercy in the depth of our misery, and in the view of our utter unworthiness.

4 ¶ I will heal their backsliding, I will love them [h]
freely: for mine anger is turned away from him. 5 [i] I
will be as the dew unto Israel: [k] he shall grow as the
lily, and ‖ cast forth his roots as Lebanon. 6 His
branches shall spread, and [l] his beauty shall be as the
olive tree, [m] and his smell as Lebanon. 7 They [n] that
dwell under his shadow shall return; they shall revive *as*
the corn, and ‖ grow as the vine: the § scent thereof *shall*
be as the wine of Lebanon.

v. 4—7. Great and precious are the promises here recorded, in answer to the prayer of real penitence. God assures them,

1. Of the removal of that wrath they dreaded: *mine anger is turned away from him*. There is no wrath in God against the sinner that returns to him through Jesus Christ, and pleads the full atonement and perfect righteousness of his divine substitute.

2. *I will love them freely*. Sin, the cause of his displeasure, being through the Redeemer forgiven and blotted out, he can, consistently with his own glory, *love them*, and he will *love them freely*, not in consideration of any desert in them, for they have none, but according to the good pleasure of his own will. The only reason which we can assign for his favour to us is, that *he hath mercy because he will have mercy*.

3. *I will heal their backsliding*. Recover them from their sinful departures, apply the suitable medicines of grace to their wounds, and deliver them from the power of *all* that iniquity against which they pray.

4. He will quicken, comfort, stablish, strengthen, settle them. *I will be as the dew to Israel*, refreshing the parched ground; and so doth his word and Spirit revive the drooping heart of the poor dejected sinner. *He shall grow as the lily*, in the beauty of a gracious profession, and the unsullied exemplariness of a good conversation, *and cast forth his roots as Lebanon*, firm rooted on the rock Christ, enabled to withstand every stormy blast of temptation, and never to be plucked up by the united force of earth or hell. In the believer the purity of the lily and the strength of the cedar are united. *His branches shall spread*, the gospel church being enlarged with converts, and each redeemed soul increasing in the knowledge and love of God, *and*, abounding in every good word and work, *his beauty shall be as the olive-tree*, whose leaves are ever green; so pleasing and persevering in the beauty of holiness shall God's people appear, *and his smell as Lebanon*, the graces he exercises, and the acceptable sacrifices he offers, fragrant as the odoriferous trees that grew on that famed mountain. *They that dwell under his shadow shall return*, under the shadow of Jesus, that covers the faithful from the scorching heat of a fiery law, and refreshes the soul of the weary; and to him shall they continually return for shelter and consolation; *they shall revive as the corn*, that in the spring vegetates strongly after the nipping blasts of winter's cold, so believers rise from their afflictions and temptations, fairer and stronger than before, *and grow as the vine*, supported by the divine power, and fruitful in all good works, to the praise and glory of God; *and the scent thereof shall be as the wine of Lebanon*, diffusing their fragrance, and by their examples and gracious discourse serving as cordials to revive the dejected and disconsolate.

8 Ephraim *shall say*, What have I to do any more with
idols? [o] I have heard *him*, and observed him: I *am* like
a green fir tree. [p] From me *is* thy fruit found. 9 Who
is wise, and he shall understand these *things*? prudent,
and he shall know them? for [r] the ways of the LORD
are right, and the just shall walk in them: but the transgressors
shall fall therein.

v. 8—9. We have here,

1. Penitent Ephraim's final determination. *Ephraim shall say, What have I to do any more with idols?* with abhorrence casting them away, and purposing in the strength of divine grace to return to them no more. Thus doth the converted soul renounce, with detestation, his once most beloved sins, and this for ever; not that we can fulfil the least of these resolutions in our own strength: no. It is God that promises he will make Ephraim speak thus, and he will give him the ability to perform his purposes.

2. God's gracious regard towards him. *I have heard him, and observed him*, heard his prayers, and seen his tears, and noted all the gracious purposes his heart hath formed; for God delights to behold the returning prodigal, and looks with tenderest compassion and warmest affection on him that is poor and of a contrite spirit, ready to answer and relieve all his complaints.

3. The Lord will bless, protect, and save him. *I am like a green fir-tree*. Under the shadow of Jesus his people sit with great delight, safe from the sultry beam of day, and protected from storm and rain, from every spiritual enemy, and from the power of evil; and the leaves are ever green, Christ being the same yesterday, to-day, and for ever, ever living to make intercession for them. *From me is thy fruit found*, all our spiritual blessings being derived from him, and all our fruits of grace springing from the supplies ministered by him the living root, and are therefore to be ascribed entirely to his praise and glory.

4. The prophet closes with recommending these words to our most serious attention. *Who is wise, and he shall understand these things? prudent, and he shall know them?* Such will be inquisitive into the mind of God, and, searching the Scriptures daily, shall be enlightened with the knowledge of the truth: *for the ways of the Lord are right*, all his dispensations of providence and grace being conformable to the strictest rules of eternal justice; and the more they are truly understood, the more shall we acknowledge them to be so; *and the just shall walk in them*, obedient to his will, submissive to his providence: *but the transgressors shall fall therein*, the same word, which is a savour of life unto life to some, will prove the savour of death unto death to others, through their disobedience to God's word, or their abuse of the most glorious truths contained therein; the same doctrines of gospel grace affording the sweetest consolation, and suggesting to the faithful the strongest argument for all holy conversation, whilst the hypocrite and apostate suck from them deadly poison, and make that which should have been for their help an occasion of falling.

THE

EVANGELICAL EXPOSITOR;

OR, A

PRACTICAL COMMENT

Upon the PROPHECY of

J O E L.

WE are altogether uncertain concerning the time when this prophet prophesied: it is probable he was cotemporary with Amos, as he speaks of the same judgments of locusts, and drought, and fire, that Amos laments, which is an intimation that they appeared about the same time, Amos in Israel, and Joel in Judah. Hosea and Obadiah prophesied about the same time, and it appears that Amos prophesied in the days of Jeroboam the second king of Israel, Amos vii 10. *God sent variety of prophets, that they might strengthen the hands one of another, and out of the mouth of two or three witnesses every word might be established. In this prophecy,* 1 *The desolation made by hosts of noxious insects is described,* chap i *and part of* chap ii 2 *The people are hereupon called to repentance,* chap ii 3. *Promises are made of the return of mercy upon their repentance,* chap ii *and promises of the pouring out the Spirit in the latter days.* 4 *The cause of God's people is pleaded against their enemies, whom God would in due time reckon with,* chap, iii *and glorious things are spoken of the Gospel Jerusalem, and of the prosperity and perpetuity of it*

CHAP I

This chapter is a description of a lamentable devastation made in Judea by locusts and caterpillars some think the prophet speaks of it as a thing to come, and gives warning of it beforehand, as usually the prophets did, others think it was now present, and his business is to affect the people with it, and awaken them by it to repentance 1 It is spoken of as a judgment which had no precedent in former ages ver 1—7 2 *All sorts of people sharing in the calamity are called upon to lament it,* ver 8—13 3 *They are directed to look up to God in their lamentations, and to humble themselves before him,* ver 14—20

Before Christ 800.

1 THE word of the LORD that [a] came to
Joel the son of Pethuel 2 Hear this, ye
old men, and give ear all ye inhabitants of the
land Hath this been in your days, or even in the days
of your fathers? 3 [b] Tell ye your children of it, and
let your children tell their children, and their children
another generation 4 [c] That which the palmer worm
hath left, hath the locust eaten, and that which the
locust hath left, hath the canker worm eaten, and that
which the canker worm hath left, hath the caterpillar
eaten 5 Awake ye drunkards, and weep, and howl
all ye drinkers of wine, because of the new wine, for it
is cut off from your mouth 6 For a nation is come
up upon my land, strong, and without number, [d] whose
teeth are the teeth of a lion, and he hath the cheek teeth
of a great lion 7 He hath laid my vine waste, and
[e] barked my fig tree he hath made it clean bare, and
cast it away, the branches thereof are made white

v 1—7 The prophet opens his discourse,

1 With an address to all the inhabitants of Judea, old and young, whose attention he demands to the message he was about to deliver a message of judgment, such as the oldest could not remember, nor the tradition of former ages produce, and which ought to be handed down to the latest posterity, *v* 3 that, warned by the sufferings of their forefathers, they may avoid their sins

2 The judgment itself is an invasion from a terrible enemy And is by many applied to the Assyrians, who ravaged and desolated the country, but may literally be better referred to the armies of locusts and other insects, which, in swarms succeeding each other, devoured all the fruits of the earth, and left the whole land barren as the scorched desert Despicable as they might seem apart, their multitudes made them formidable nor the ravages of the lions from the forest could be more fatal not only the vine leaves are eaten up, but the very fig-trees are barked and destroyed by them *Note*, God never wants instruments of vengeance the most insignificant insect can in his hand be made the severest scourge, and a locust terrible as a lion

3 The *drunkards* are admonished to lament the judgment, which their sins had provoked, and by which they would be particularly affected, *because the new wine is cut off from their mouths* And justly doth God punish those who abused his favours, by depriving them of their good things, and leaving them in want and wretchedness to lament their folly

8 ¶ Lament like a virgin girded with sackcloth for
the husband of her youth 9 [f] The meat offering, and
the drink offering, is cut off from the house of the
LORD, the priests the LORD's ministers mourn
10. The field is wasted, [g] the land mourneth, for the

corn

Before Christ 800.

corn is wasted the new wine is † dried up, the oil lan-
guisheth 11 Be ye ashamed, O ye husbandmen, howl,
O ye vine-dressers, for the wheat and for the barley,
because the harvest of the field is perished 12 The
vine is dried up, and the fig-tree languisheth, the pome-
granate-tree, the palm tree also, and the apple-tree, *even*
all the trees of the field are withered because [h] joy is
withered away from the sons of men 13 Gird your-
selves, and lament, ye priests howl, ye ministers of the
altar come, lie all night in sackcloth, ye ministers of
my God for the [i] meat offering and the drink-offering
is withholden from the house of your God

† Or, ashamed. — Jer. xlviii. 33.

v 8—13 The whole nation, deeply affected with the calamity, is called upon to mourn in sackcloth, as a virgin that is robbed of her betrothed spouse, on whom her warmest affections were fixed, and whose loss fills her heart with bitterest anguish *Note*, They who are wedded to worldly comforts find it death to part from them

The corn, wine, and oil, are perished, the trees stripped of leaves and fruit, and withered away, the very earth looks dark, and *mourneth* over the desolations, *because joy is withered away from the sons of men*, the songs of harvest and the shouting of the vintage are silent, and nothing is heard but howling and groans Particularly,

1 The husbandmen and vine-dressers are called to bewail the dreadful devastations their labours are ruined, their hopes disappointed, themselves and families left to pine in want and perish by famine

2 The priests of the sanctuary are commanded to join the general cry, and mourn over the deserted altars, where no sacrifice smoaked, no oblation was presented They are called *ministers of the altar*, as bound to a constant attendance there, and *ministers of my God*, this being their distinguished honour, and the motive to their indefatigable labour They would now be peculiar sufferers, and be destitute of that maintenance with which the altar used to supply them, but a nobler concern must fill their minds, and grief to see God's worship neglected must swallow up every other concern that is merely their own *Note*, A true minister of God hath his glory more at heart than every other consideration compared with this, he counts not even his own life dear unto himself

14 ¶ [k] Sanctify ye a fast, call [l] a † solemn assembly,
gather the elders, *and* all the inhabitants of the land *into*
the house of the LORD your God, and cry unto the
LORD 15 [m] Alas for the day! for [n] the day of the
LORD is at hand, and as a destruction from the Al-
mighty shall it come 16 Is not the meat cut off be-
fore our eyes, *yea*, [o] joy and gladness from the house
of our God? 17 The † seed is rotten under their clods,
the garners are laid desolate, the barns are broken down,
for the corn is withered 18 How do the beasts groan!
the herds of cattle are perplexed, because they have no
pasture, yea, the flocks of sheep are made desolate
19 [p] O LORD, to thee will I cry for [q] the fire hath
devoured the § pastures of the wilderness, and the flame
hath burnt all the trees of the field 20 The beasts
of the field [r] cry also unto thee for the rivers of waters
are dried up, and the fire hath devoured the pastures
of the wilderness

k Chap. ii. 15. — l Lev. xxiii. 36. — † Or, day of restraint. — m Jer. xxx. 7. — n Isa. xiii. 6. — o Deut. xii. 7. — † Heb. Grains. — p Psal. l. 15. — q Jer. ix. 10. — § Or, habitations. — r Psal. civ. 21.

v 14—20 To avert the heavy wrath upon them, the prophet points out to them the properest means to be pursued As their sufferings came from God's displeasure, to remove this must be their first concern

1 Let a solemn fast be proclaimed A day of deep humiliation sanctified and set apart, that with united supplications they might surround the throne of grace, and whilst, by a strict abstinence from meat and drink, they acknowledged themselves unworthy of every mercy, and, prostrate in the court of the Lord's house, confessed the justice of the judgments he had inflicted, they might with prayers and tears cry unto a pardoning God, that sin, the cause of their calamity, being forgiven, their sufferings, the due effects thereof, might be removed *Note*, (1) National judgments call for national humiliation (2) When we are found in God's appointed ways, we may humbly hope he will meet us in mercy (3) Affliction then answers the end for which it was sent, when it brings us to our knees, and raises the cry of fervent importunate prayer

2 Abundant reason there is for this humiliation

[1] What they suffered already was grievous If they looked into their garners, they were empty, if to God's house, no sacrifice or oblation was seen, if to the country, desolate it mourned, the seed under the clods rotten, and the very beasts groan, *perplexed* for want of food, and pining away *Note*, (1) How terrible is famine how thankful ought we to be for the plenty we have so long enjoyed, and how should we fear to provoke God, by our abuse of his mercies, to withhold them! (2) The very earth mourns, the very beasts groan under men's sins, and shall we ourselves be the only insensible beings in the whole creation?

[2] What they feared was yet more terrible *for the day of the Lord is at hand* What they felt was but the beginning of sorrows, *and* a foretaste of the greater evil approaching, *as destruction from the Almighty it shall come*, which may refer to the ruin of the nation at first by the Chaldeans, or afterwards by the Romans, sent of God to punish them for their iniquities, whose arm of omnipotence is irresistible And more generally this may be applied to every sinner, whose judgment advances, whose damnation slumbereth not, whose everlasting destruction is at the door unless he repents without delay, he perishes eternally Well may we therefore cry, *Alas for the day!*

3 The prophet urges them hereunto by the examples before them

[1] His own *O Lord, to thee will I cry* as deeply affected with their sins and their sufferings, he earnestly addresses his prayer to God, to him who wounds, and alone is able to heal, the fire of whose wrath, whatever instruments were employed, had consumed them, and he only, who had kindled, could quench it *Note*, They who call others to fasting and prayer, must themselves lead the way in the fervency of their own devotions

[2] Of the beasts *The beasts of the field cry unto thee also* with sounds inarticulate indeed, but which the Lord can hear and pity They are parched with thirst and famished with hunger; *for the rivers of water are dried up, and the fire hath devoured the pastures of the wilderness*, scorched up with the excessive drought *Note*, The very lowing of the oxen, yea the ravens cries, shall rise up in judgment to reproach the stupidity of the sinner who restrains prayer before God

CHAP II

In this chapter we have, 1 *A further description of that terrible desolation which should be made*, ver 1—11 2 *A solemn call to the people, to return and repent, to fast and pray, and seek unto God for mercy, with directions how to do this aright*, ver 12—17 3 *A promise that, upon their repentance, God would remove the judgment, and restore unto them plenty of all good things*, ver 18—27 4 *A prediction of the setting up of the kingdom of the Messiah in the world, by the pouring out of the Spirit in the latter days*, ver 28—32

1 BLOW ye the † trumpet in Zion, and sound an
alarm in my holy mountain let all the inhabit-
ants of the land tremble for [a] the day of the LORD
cometh, for *it is* nigh at hand, 2 [b] A day of darkness
and of gloominess, a day of clouds and of thick dark-
ness, as the morning spread upon the mountains [c] a
great people and a strong, [d] there hath not been ever
the like, neither shall be any more after it, *even* to the
years ‖ of many generations 3 [e] A fire devoureth be-
fore them, and behind them a flame burneth the land
is as [f] the garden of Eden before them, [g] and behind
them a desolate wilderness, yea, and nothing shall escape
them 4 [h] The appearance of them *is* as the appear-
ance of horses, and as horsemen, so shall they run 5
[i] Like the noise of chariots on the tops of mountains
shall they leap, like the noise of a flame of fire that
devoureth the stubble, as a strong people set in battle
array 6 Before their face the people shall be much
pained [k] all faces shall gather § blackness 7 They
shall run like mighty men they shall climb the wall like
men of war, and [l] they shall march every one on his
ways, and they shall not break their ranks 8 Neither
shall one thrust another, they shall walk every one in
his path and *when* they fall upon the ‖ sword, they shall
not be wounded 9 They shall run to and fro in the
city they shall run upon the wall, they shall climb up
upon the houses they shall enter in at the windows like
a thief, 10 The earth shall quake before them, the
heavens shall tremble, [m] the sun and the moon shall be
dark, and the stars shall withdraw their shining, 11
And [n] the LORD shall utter his voice before his army
for his camp *is* very great for [o] he *is* strong that exe-
cuteth his word, for [p] the day of the LORD *is* great
and very terrible, and who can abide it?

† Or, cornet. — a Chap. i. 15. — Zeph. i. 14, 15. — b Amos v. 18. — d Chap. i. 14. — ‖ Heb. of generation and generation. — f Gen. ii. 8. — k Nah. ii. 10. — § Heb. a pot. — l Prov. xxx. 27. — ‖ Or, dart. — m Isa. xiii. 10. — Matt. xxiv. 29. — n Chap. iii. 16. — o Rev. xviii. 8. — p Jer. xxx. 7. — Amos v. 18. — Zeph. i. 15.

v 1—11 The heavy judgment coming upon the people of Israel is here set forth

1 The alarm is spread *Blow ye the trumpet in Zion, and sound an alarm in my holy mountain*, to give notice of the invading foe, and to prepare them for the approaching danger This was

the

Before Christ 800

the priest's office, who, as the watchman upon Zion's walls, must warn sinners of the wrath of God ready to light upon them, and urge them, whilst there is hope, to flee from it. The judgments at the door should make the people tremble, and the fatal day is nigh, fixed in the divine decree, to punish the transgressors, *a day of darkness*, &c. when the very sun should be obscured with clouds of locusts, or, as these phrases may signify, the deepest calamities would overtake them, *as the morning spread upon the mountains*, coming suddenly, and spreading universally and irresistibly, or the air should be so darkened with the swarms of insects, that at mid-day the light should not exceed the dawning of the morning.

2. The army is marshalled in battle array, *v.* 2. *A great people and a strong*, supplying by multitude what they singly want in might, nor were there ever before, nor shall there be hereafter, such ravages committed by them in Judea. As they advanced they swept the land as with the besom of destruction, and behind them the country looked black and barren as if fire had devoured it, so that what was as the garden of Eden before them quickly appeared as *a desolate wilderness*, nothing escaping their devouring jaws. Swift and bold as horses, they rushed on, and, as rattling chariots over the rugged mountains, the sound was heard afar off, leaping as they advanced, and terrible as the roaring of devouring fire, that spreads resistless on every side, marching firm, embodied in exact battalion, as soldiers keep their rank, *v.* 7, 8. In vain against them the sword is drawn, they elude the stroke, or those that fall are not found wanting, so vast is their multitude. Not only the country is devoured by them, but the cities are covered, the houses are filled with them, *v.* 9. and these were the forerunners and emblems of the Chaldean armies, that should in like manner spread desolations on every side, destroy the country, sack the cities, plunder and captivate the inhabitants, and leave Judea a wilderness, without man or beast. *Note*, (1.) There is no fence against God's judgments. (2.) The sound of them in our ears should be to us loud calls to repentance.

3. Great would be the terror spread through the land by these invaders. The people, seized with pangs as a woman in travel, would be in the deepest consternation, and every face *gather blackness*, livid as the corpse from which the spirit is fled. The very earth *shall quake before them, the heavens tremble*, and the luminaries thereof *be darkened*, *v.* 10. obscured by the locusts, or, figuratively, it bespeaks the deep distress of the inhabitants, from the king upon the throne to the lowest of the people. And well may they indeed tremble who see thus the wrath of God revealed against them. For,

4. This is his doing. It is *his army*, that marches under his direction, and animated by his voice, who, as their captain, leads them on to victory. Too numerous to be opposed, too strong to be resisted, since they are sent to execute his word. *For the day of the Lord is great, and very terrible, and who can abide it?* *Note*, The impenitent sinner must needs perish, unable to oppose the arm of Omnipotence, or bear up under the strokes of his fierce anger.

12 ¶ Therefore also now, saith the LORD, turn
ye *even* to me with all your heart, and with fasting,
and with weeping, and with mourning. 13 And rent
your heart and not your garments, and turn unto the
LORD your God for he *is* gracious and merciful,
slow to anger, and of great kindness, and repenteth
him of the evil. 14 Who knoweth *if* he will return
and repent, and leave a blessing behind him, *even* a
meat-offering, and a drink-offering unto the LORD
your God? 15 ¶ Blow the trumpet in Zion, sanc-
tify a fast, call a solemn assembly. 16 Gather the peo-
ple, sanctify the congregation, assemble the elders,
gather the children, and those that suck the breasts:
let the bridegroom go forth of his chamber, and the
bride out of her closet. 17 Let the priests, the ministers
of the LORD, weep between the porch and the altar,
and let them say, Spare thy people, O LORD, and
give not thine heritage to reproach, that the heathen
should rule over them: wherefore should they say
among the people, Where *is* their God? 18 ¶ Then
will the LORD be jealous for his land, and pity his
people. 19 Yea, the LORD will answer and say unto
his people, Behold, I will send you corn, and wine,
and oil, and ye shall be satisfied therewith: and I will
no more make you a reproach among the heathen.
20 But I will remove far off from you the northern
army, and will drive him into a land barren and deso-
late, with his face toward the east sea, and his hinder
part toward the utmost sea, and his stink shall come
up, and his ill savour shall come up, because he hath
done great things.

v. 12—20. To oppose these desolating judgments, when they come, were vain, to avert them, before they arrived, was yet possible, and the way is here prescribed.

1. By a penitent return to God.

[1.] Let a solemn fast be proclaimed, *see ch.* i. 14. and all summoned to appear before God, from the highest to the lowest, from the hoary head to the babe that sucks the breast, the universal judgment called for deep and universal abasement: nor must the bridegroom or bride be absent. In public calamities all private joys must be swallowed up.

[2.] Let the priests, with deepest mourning and most fervent supplications, pour forth their complaints to God, and, standing between the porch and the altar, on which now no sacrifices smoaked, with tears of heartfelt woe cry unto God, if mercy yet is to be found, *Spare thy people, O Lord*: they plead their relation which, though an aggravation of their sin, yet ministers a ground for hope, that yet the Lord would not utterly cast them off, *and give not thine heritage to reproach*, by driving them into strange countries to seek for food, or suffering them, thus impoverished, to fall an easy prey into the hands of their enemies, *that the heathen should rule over them*. *Wherefore should they say among the people, Where is their God?* Not only their lives and characters but God's glory was concerned, and for his own great name's sake, though they deserved no favour, they might plead for his interposition. *Note*, (1.) The ministers of God must themselves be deeply affected, if they would affect the hearts of their people. (2.) Mercy is all a miserable sinner can ask at God's hand. (3.) Our most powerful plea in prayer are to be drawn from God's own glory, as interested in our salvation.

[3.] Let the people join their ministers with prayers and tears, and heartfelt humiliation, *v.* 12, 13. and, without which every outward expression of distress is but hypocrisy, *turn ye to the Lord their God* in simplicity and truth, deeply convinced of the evil of their sins, and truly abhorring themselves in the view of them, putting away the accursed thing, and cleaving to the Lord with full purpose of heart, through his grace, to approve henceforward their unshaken fidelity to him. In this way, sinners as we are, a door of hope will yet be opened for us.

2. The most powerful arguments are suggested to engage them hereunto. He is called *the Lord your God*, who hath not disclaimed yet his relation to them, *for he is gracious and merciful*, and though highly provoked, he is not inexorable, he delights not in the death of a sinner, *slow to anger*, unwilling, even after repeated offences, to destroy the guilty, waiting with astonishing patience, *and of great kindness*, ready to receive him the moment he relents and returns, *and repenteth him of the evil*, changing the afflictive dispensations of his providence towards the penitent, and, instead of wrath, thinketh upon mercy. And surely nothing can break the obdurate heart, if such tender pity and undeserved compassion lead us not to repentance. *Who knoweth if he will return and repent*, averting the heavy temporal calamities threatened, of which they might entertain good hope if they truly turned to him, *and leave a blessing behind him*, not as departing from them, but as coming to their rescue, and staying the ravages of the locusts, *even a meat-offering and a drink-offering for the Lord our God*, for their desire were more intent on having God's altar supplied than their own tables covered, and this was a gracious evidence of the truth of their repentance.

3. God gives them the strongest assurance, he will hear their prayer, and will both help them and glorify himself. He will *be jealous for the land*, for his great name sake, and *will pity his people* in their deep distress. The plenty shall be restored, their reproach be removed, *v.* 18. and the arid wilderness destroyed, and cast in heaps into the sea, filling the air with the stench of their putrid carcases, *because he hath done great things*, because of the mischief they have occasioned, or, *for he will do great things*, God will make bare his arm for their rescue, and do for his people the great things promised in this and the following verses. Some apply this to the destruction of Sennacherib's army, and probably the locusts, both in their invasion and destruction were a figure of the Assyrians. *Note*, God will assuredly hear when his people cry, and their enemies and his shall know the fierceness of his wrath.

21 ¶ Fear not, O land, be glad, and rejoice: for
the LORD will do great things. 22 Be not afraid, ye
beasts of the field: for the pastures of the wilderness
do spring, for the tree beareth her fruit, the fig tree
and the vine do yield their strength. 23 Be glad then,
ye children of Zion, and rejoice in the LORD your
God: for he hath given you ‖ the former rain ‖ mode-
rately, and he will cause to come down for you the
rain, the former rain and the latter rain in the first *month*.
24 And the floors shall be full of wheat, and the fats
shall overflow with wine and oil. 25 And I will re-
store to you the years that the locust hath eaten, the
canker

Before Christ 800

canker worm, and the caterpillar, and the palmer worm, my great army which I sent among you. 26 And ye shall eat in plenty, and be satisfied, and praise the name of the LORD your God, that hath dealt wondrously with you: and my people shall never be ashamed. 27 And [a] ye shall know that I *am* in the midst of Israel, and *that* I *am* the LORD your God, and none else: and my people shall never be ashamed.

[a] Chap. iii. 17.

v. 21—27. Many great and precious promises are here added for the comfort and joy of the people of God.

1. Their *fears* shall be all removed. The Lord will do great things for them, rescuing them wonderfully from the evils of every enemy, whether the locusts or Chaldeans; as he will also save the souls of his people in Christ Jesus from every spiritual foe, and deliver them from the fears of guilt, and the powers of corruption.

2. Their joys shall be restored. *Their temporal comforts shall abound*; the devastations of the locusts shall be repaired, v. 25; the pastures which had been devoured shall spring afresh, watered with the dew of heaven, v. 22. The rain, moderately descending in its season, shall fertilize the soil, and cause their corn, their vines, their olive and fig-trees, to shoot vigorously, and bring forth fruit abundantly, v. 22, 23; so that their granaries should be filled, and their fats overflow, v. 24. And what is far better than even their restored plenty, he will give them *spiritual consolation*, and the sanctified enjoyment of their comforts. They shall *rejoice in the Lord their God*, ascribing to him the praise of all their mercies, and happy in a sense of his love and favour, v. 26. By experience now they shall be brought to know God's gracious presence in the midst of them, and that he alone is God, even *their God, and none else*; all idols being utterly rejected by them, and his great name alone adored and exalted. And this will be most eminently the case, when that *teacher of righteousness*, (as the words, v. 23. may be rendered, instead of *the former rain moderately*,) which God would send, even the divine Messiah, should come, and by his own obedience unto death work out, and in his gospel direct us to, that one divine and everlasting righteousness, which is the grand source of every believer's joy, and will be to all eternity.

3. *They shall never be ashamed*, never have cause to be so, through want of food, as before: or rather, the Lord their confidence will never disappoint their hope; he will be their rock and refuge in every time of need; they shall experience his constant and uninterrupted favour in time, and in the day of his appearing and glory, stand forth before him with great boldness, assured of his everlasting love.

4. The very beasts that groaned and cried to God, shall have the cause of their fears and cries removed. *The pastures of the wilderness do spring*; even to them hath God respect, for his mercies are over all his works, *Jonah* iv. 11.

28 ¶ [b] And it shall come to pass afterward, *that* I
will pour out my spirit upon all flesh; and your sons
and your daughters shall prophesy, your old men shall
dream dreams, your young men shall see visions: 29
And [c] also upon the servants, and upon the handmaids
in those days, will I pour out my spirit. 30 And [t] I
will shew wonders in the heavens, and in the earth, blood
and fire and pillars of smoke. 31 [t] The sun shall be
turned into darkness, and the moon into blood, before
the great and the terrible day of the LORD come. 32
And it shall come to pass, *that* [u] whosoever shall call on
the name of the LORD shall be delivered: for [x] in
mount Zion and in Jerusalem shall be deliverance, as
the LORD hath said, and in the remnant whom the
LORD shall call.

[b] Isa. xliv. 3. Ezek. xxxix. 29. Acts ii. 17. ... Matt. xxiv. 29. ... Luke xxi. ... Rom. x. 13. ... Obad. 17.

v. 28—32. The promises here evidently look forward to the times of the gospel; and in all the former troubles of the people of God, the prospect of these blessed days was a great support under their affliction.

1. There shall be a most plenteous effusion of the Spirit, upon the apostles at the day of Pentecost, to which the prophecy is expressly applied, *Acts* ii. 16, 17. and afterward *upon all flesh*, Gentiles as well as Jews, who should be made partakers of the Holy Ghost, both of his miraculous powers, as well as the ordinary gifts and graces he bestows; the latter of which still continue, though the former have ceased; yet perhaps not for ever. Old and young, persons of both sexes, should share partakers of the blessing; and even the meanest servants and handmaidens, not be excluded from these unspeakable gifts. Thus they should be enabled to prophecy, either to foretell things to come, as Agabus, the daughters of Philip, and others, *Acts* xi. 28. xiii. 1. xxi. 9, 10. or to speak the truths of God to the edification of others, or to join in his praises with

enlarged hearts; in all which senses the word prophecy is used.

2. A scene of dreadful prodigies shall follow, v. 30, 31. which had their primary accomplishment in the dreadful ravages of the Roman army in Judea, and the strange sights and appearances in the air, which ushered in the destruction of Jerusalem, and will also precede the final coming of the eternal Judge, and usher in *that great and terrible day of the Lord*. Happy would it be for the sinner, if the tremendous views of that awful day should approach might alarm his conscience, and awaken his concern, to fly to the bosom of Jesus for shelter from the wrath to come, that he may be hid there in the day of the Lord's fierce anger.

3. The faithful in that great day are secured from fear of evil. *It shall come to pass, that whosoever shall call on the name of the Lord shall be delivered*, as those were who believed in Jesus, and fled to Pella on the approaching siege of Jerusalem. And more generally this must be extended to all Christ's redeemed people, who in him are sure to find present and everlasting salvation from all the great enemies of their souls; and waiting upon him by faith in constant prayer, obtain from him help in every time of need. *For in mount Zion, and in Jerusalem* in the gospel church, *shall be deliverance, as the Lord hath said*, who is faithful to all his promises, and neither can nor will ever leave or forsake his people; *and in the remnant whom the Lord shall call*, no one of whom shall ever perish; for whom he hath effectually called, he will powerfully keep, and none shall ever pluck them out of his hands. Blessed and happy are they who have a part in this salvation, may my lot be with them!

CHAP. III.

The gracious promise which closed the foregoing chapter is here enlarged upon. Here is a prediction, 1. Of God's reckoning with the enemies of his people for all the injuries that they had done them, ver. 1—8. 2. Of God's judging all nations when the measure of their iniquity is full, and appearing publicly to the everlasting confusion of all impenitent sinners, and the everlasting comfort of all his faithful servants, ver. 9—17. 3. Of the provision God has made for the refreshment of his people, for their safety and purity, when their enemies shall be made desolate, ver. 18—21. These promises were not of private interpretation only, but were written for our learning, that we through patience and comfort of this scripture might have hope.

1 FOR behold, in those days, and in that time when
I shall bring again the captivity of Judah and
Jerusalem, 2 I will also gather all nations, and will
bring them down [a] into the valley of Jehoshaphat, and
will plead with them there for my people, and *for* my
heritage Israel, whom they have scattered among the
nations, and parted my land. 3 And they have cast
lots for my people; and have given a boy for an harlot,
and sold a girl for wine, that they might drink. 4
Yea, and what have ye to do [b] with me, O Tyre and
Zidon, and all the coasts of Palestine? Will ye render
me a recompense? And if ye recompense me, [c] swiftly
and speedily will I return your recompense upon your
own head; 5 Because ye have taken my silver and my
gold, and have carried into your temples my goodly
[‖] pleasant things: 6 The children also of Judah, and
the children of Jerusalem have ye sold unto [§] the Grecians,
that ye might remove them far from their border.
7 Behold, I will raise them out of the place whither ye
have sold them, and [d] will return your recompense upon
your own head: 8 And I will [e] sell your sons and your
daughters into the hand of the children of Judah, and
they shall sell them to the Sabeans, to a people far off:
for the LORD hath spoken *it*.

[a] 2 Chron. xx. 26. Ver. 12. Zech. xiv. 4. Rev. xvi. 16.
[b] Acts ix. 4.
[c] Luke xviii. 8.
[‖] Heb. Desirable.
[§] Heb. The sons of the Grecians.
[d] Ver. 4. Rev. xiii. 10.
[e] 1 Kings xx... 13. Ver. 6.

v. 1—8. The sufferings of God's people, and the destruction of their enemies, have their appointed periods.

1. *In those days* of the Messiah, *I will bring again the captivity of Judah and Jerusalem*, many of them by the preaching of the gospel being called into the glorious liberty of the sons of God, from the bondage of corruption, more intolerable than that of Egypt or Chaldea. Perhaps also this may have respect to their recovery from their present dispersion.

2. Their enemies shall be reckoned with, v. 2. which some apply to Sennacherib and the Assyrians, and suppose the days spoken of to refer to the recovery of the dispersed Jews, who had fled or been taken prisoners on that invasion. Others apply it to the Romans and neighbouring nations, who had severely wasted God's heritage: and some imagine they see in this prophecy the destruction of the Turkish and papal powers, as

4 I

sembled

Before Chriſt 800

ſembled to make war againſt the Saints of the moſt High, after all their former perſecutions of them, whoſe quarrel God will now ſignally eſpouſe, and avenge their wrongs

3 The charges lying againſt theſe enemies of his people are, for their cruelty, robbery, inſult, and oppreſſion They *ſcattered them among the nations*, ſeized and ſold them for ſlaves, particularly *to the Grecians*, v 6 removing them far from their own land, which they *parted* among themſelves, either thus parcelled it out to his ſoldiers, or the neighbouring nations each ſeized that portion which lay contiguous to them *and they have caſt lots for my people*, in ſuch vaſt numbers were they taken captive, and their value ſo ſmall, that their conquerors *gave a boy* for the hire of *an harlot, and a girl for wine, that they might drink* Thus in drinking and whoring they ſquandered the prey they had taken, the common vices of perſecutors *God's gold and ſilver* they had *plundered*, what he had given to his people, and regarded ſtill as his own and his *pleaſant things*, perhaps the veſſels or treaſures of his ſanctuary, they had carried to the temple of their idols, adding ſacrilege and impiety to robbery Well may God therefore expoſtulate with them, *What have you to do with me, O Tyre and Zidon, and all the coaſts of Paleſtine?* which may be put for all the enemies of Chriſt's church and people in every age *What have you to do with me?* how dare you diſtreſs my people, what provocation have they given? *will you render me a recompenſe?* Have they done you any injury, which you would thus retaliate? no they were *quiet in the land*, and had never juſtly offended them *Note*, (1) No ſweetneſs of temper, or inoffenſiveneſs of diſpoſition, can ſoften the enmity of the wicked (2) We muſt not think it ſtrange if we receive the greateſt unkindneſs from thoſe whom we have ever ſtudied to oblige

4 God threatens them to return their wickedneſs into their own boſom *If ye recompenſe me*, pretending to retaliate wrongs they had received from God's people, *I will ſwiftly and ſpeedily return your recompenſe upon your own head*, and give tribulation to thoſe that troubled them Whilſt God recovered his own children from the places whither they had diſperſed and ſold them, he will ſell the children of theſe his enemies into the hands of the men of Judah, and they, in juſt retaliation of the wrongs they have received, ſhall ſell them *to the Sabeans, to a people far off* And for this the veracity of God is engaged, *the mouth of the Lord hath ſpoken it* the accompliſhment of which prophecy ſome refer to the days of the Maccabees, others, to the future deſtruction of the perſecuting powers of Popery or Mahomediſm certain however it is, that all the enemies of Chriſt's church and people ſhall at the laſt be made their footſtool

f Iſa viii 9, 10 † Heb. Sanctify g Iſa ii 4 Mic iv 3 ‡ Or ſcythes h Zech xii 8. § Or, The Lord ſhall bring down i Ver 2 k Mat xiii 39 Rev xiv 15, 19 l Chron xx 1 ‖ Or threſhing m Chap ii 10, 31 n Jer xxv 30 Chap ii 11 Amos i 2 o Iſa li 6 † Heb. Place of repair or harbour p Chap ii 6 q Dan xi 45 r Iſa xxxv 8 Zech xiv 21 Rev xxi 2

9 ¶ f Proclaim ye this among the Gentiles † pre-
pare war, wake up the mighty men, let all the men of
war draw near, let them come up 10 g Beat your
plow ſhares into ſwords, and your ‡ pruning hooks into
ſpears h let the weak ſay, *I am* ſtrong 11 Aſſemble
yourſelves, and come, all ye heathen, and gather your
ſelves together round about thither § cauſe thy mighty
ones to come down, O LORD 12 Let the heathen be
wakened, and come up to i the valley of Jehoſhaphat
for there will I ſit to judge all the heathen round about
13 k Put ye in the ſickle, for the harveſt is ripe, come,
get ye down, for the preſs is full, the fats overflow, for
their wickedneſs *is* great 14 l Multitudes, multitudes
in the valley of ‖ deciſion for the day of the LORD
is near in the valley of deciſion 15 m The ſun and the
moon ſhall be darkned, and the ſtars ſhall withdraw
their ſhining 16 The LORD alſo ſhall n roar out of
Zion, and utter his voice from Jeruſalem, and the hea
vens and the earth ſhall ſhake, but the LORD *will be*
the † hope of his people, and the ſtrength of the chil-
dren of Iſrael 17 So p ſhall ye know that I *am* the
LORD your God dwelling in Zion, q my holy moun
tain then ſhall Jeruſalem be holy, and r there ſhall no
ſtrangers paſs through her any more

v 9—17 Commentators greatly differ about the times referred to in the prophecy Some ſuppoſe it fulfilled in the deſtruction of Sennacherib, or the Aſſyrians, or Antiochus others, that it looks forward to more diſtant ages, and foretel the ruin of all the antichriſtian perſecuting powers, whether pagan, papal, or Mahometan, and many expreſſions in the *Revelations*, which ſeem to ſpeak of that event, are borrowed from hence Some ſtill carry the accompliſhment farther, and read in it the great day of final judgment, when the wicked ſhall be caſt into hell, and the ſaints of God ſhall receive the kingdom of their Father

1 A defiance is ſent to all God's enemies Let them collect their force muſter their armies, furniſh themſelves with weapons, encourage each other for the conflict, v 10 unite their aſſembled legions, haſten to the field of battle, v 11 rouſe up their courage, and ſtand in array *Multitudes, multitudes*, innumerable the hoſt in the *valley of deciſion*, the ſame as *the valley of Jehoſhaphat*, which may not mark any particular place, but the end for which they are aſſembled, *Jehoſhaphat* ſignifying *the judgment of the Lord*, who will there plead with, condemn, and deſtroy his enemies, and *the day is near*, v 14

They who refer this to the ſlaughter of the antichriſtian powers, *Rev* xvi 14, 16 xix 18—21 ſuppoſe they will in the latter day be gathered together in the land of Judea, to make war on the ſaints of the moſt High, and by ſome eminent ſtroke of vengeance from God be utterly conſumed

Applying it to the day of judgment, we may learn, (1) That it is near, uncertain when, but ſurely approaching highly therefore doth it concern us to be always ready (2) That day will fix our final ſtate, whether for happineſs or miſery eternal, according to the unerring deciſions of the God of truth and judgment

2 At the prophet's prayer the executioners of vengeance appear *Cauſe thy mighty ones to come down, O Lord*, either the holy angels, or the Chriſtian princes under Chriſt their leader, going down to the valley of deciſion, to join battle with their foes *Put ye in the ſickle, for the harveſt is ripe, come, get ye down, for the preſs is full, the fats overflow*, their enemies are ripe for judgment, *See Rev* xiv 18—20 xix 15—20 and the reaſon is given, *becauſe their wickedneſs is great*

3 To the impenitent ſinner, or antichriſtian foe, that day will be full of horror *The ſun and the moon ſhall be darkned, and the ſtars ſhall withdraw their ſhining* as will be literally the caſe in the great day of judgment, when theſe luminaries ſhall be extinguiſhed Or figuratively it refers to the kings and princes of the earth, who ſhall be caſt down before the armies of the living God *When the Lord ſhall roar out of Zion, and utter his voice from Jeruſalem*, appearing on the behalf of his church and people, and ſpreading terror and diſmay among their enemies *and the heavens and earth ſhall ſhake*, the mightieſt will tremble before him, or as at the day of final judgment it will be ſeen, when the heavens being on fire ſhall be diſſolved, and the earth ſhall be burnt up Woe to the wicked, who then ſhall find no ſhelter, no rock to hide, no mountain to cover their guilty heads

4 The people of God will triumph and rejoice, for *the Lord ſhall be the hope of his people*, he that had ever been the object of their hope and truſt, will not then diſappoint them, but will be their *refuge* in this day of evil *and the ſtrength of the children of Iſrael*, ſupporting them through all their conflicts, and crowning them at laſt with victory *So ſhall ye know that I am the Lord your God*, by happy experience of his power and grace, *dwelling in Zion my holy mountain*, in the midſt of the church of his redeemed *Then ſhall Jeruſalem be holy*, or holineſs, all the ſaints of God at the laſt ſhall be made perfect, as their Father which is in heaven is perfect *and there ſhall no ſtranger paſs through her any more*, no enemy being left to hurt them, no hypocrite or ungodly perſons being any longer found among them

s Amos ix 13 † Heb Go t Exod xlvii 1 Zech xiv 8 Rev xxii 1 u Num xxv 1 Mic vi 5 x Iſa xix 1, &c y Obad 10 z Ther f ‡ Or a ſtable § Or even I the Lord that dwelleth in Zion a Ver 17 Rev xxi 3

18 ¶ And it ſhall come to paſs in that day, *that* the
mountains s ſhall drop down new wine, and the hills
ſhall flow with milk, and all the rivers of Judah ſhall
† flow with waters, and t a fountain ſhall come forth of
the houſe of the LORD, and ſhall water u the valley of
Shittim 19 x Egypt ſhall be a deſolation, y and Edom
ſhall be a deſolate wilderneſs, z for the violence *againſt*
the children of Judah, becauſe they have ſhed innocent
blood in their land 20 But Judah ſhall ‡ dwell for
ever, and Jeruſalem from generation to generation 21
For I will cleanſe their blood *that* I have not cleanſed,
§ for a the LORD dwelleth in Zion

v 18—21 Theſe great and precious promiſes conclude the prophecy, which, whatever reſpect they may have to the Jews, ſeem chiefly to look to the times of goſpel grace, or final glory

1 There ſhall be the moſt abundant plenty, v 18 either of temporal good things, or rather of ſpiritual bleſſings, diffuſed among the faithful The *wine* and *milk* of goſpel grace ſhall flow down like torrents from the hills, refreſhing, ſtrengthening, comforting the members of Chriſt's church, and from him, the everflowing, overflowing fountain, ſhall the healing ſtream go forth, watering *the valley of Shittim*, a barren valley beyond Jordan, which may ſignify the Gentile world, and intimate the fruitfulneſs which this watering of the ſanctuary ſhould produce, and the extent of the Redeemer's grace, even to the moſt diſtant corners of the earth

2 The inveterate enemies of the church ſhall be deſtroyed, v 19 *Egypt* and *Edom* had often ſhewn their implacable hatred againſt Judah, and ſhed innocent blood in the land, but

they

Before Christ 800.

they ſhall now be made perpetual deſolations. And theſe nations are the figures of the preſent perſecutors of God's people, particularly of *Rome*, called Egypt myſtically, *Rev.* xi. 8. and red with the blood of ſaints and martyrs; but blood ſhall now be given her to drink, together with all the other perſecuting powers, pagan or Mahometan, who will periſh together. Or if this be applied to the laſt great day, then death, ſin, and Satan, the moſt mortal foes of the redeemed, ſhall be deſtroyed together and for ever.

3 The people of God ſhall from thenceforth enjoy undiſturbed repoſe. *Judah ſhall dwell for ever, and Jeruſalem from generation to generation*; to the end of time the church of Chriſt ſhall be preſerved ſafe from all the attacks of the gates of hell, or in the eternal ſtate of bliſs, the redeemed ſhall dwell ſafely in manſions of glory. *For I will cleanſe their blood that I have not cleanſed*, pardoning all their guilt, ſaving them from the power of all their ſins; and, at the laſt, deſtroying the very being of ſin in them: *for the Lord dwelleth in Zion*, and therefore his people may comfortably and confidently expect to be made partakers of the fulneſs of this his great ſalvation.

THE EVANGELICAL EXPOSITOR;

OR, A

PRACTICAL COMMENT

Upon the PROPHECY of

A M O S.

THOUGH this prophet appeared a little before Isaiah, yet he was not, as some have imagined, that Amos who was the father of Isaiah, (Isa i 1) *for in the Hebrew their names are very different, and their families too of a different character, for Isaiah was a courtier, Amos a herdsman Amos signifies a* burden, *his word was the* burden of the Lord *He was (as most think) of Judah, yet prophesied chiefly against Israel, and at Bethel,* chap vii 13 *He begins with threatnings against the neighbour-nations that were enemies to Israel,* chap i *and* ii *Then calls Israel to account, and judgeth them for their idolatry, their unworthy walking under the favours God had bestowed upon them, and their incorrigibleness under his judgments,* chap iii *and* iv *He calls them to repentance,* chap v *rejecting their hypocritical sacrifices, unless they did repent He foretels the desolations that were coming upon them, notwithstanding their security,* chap vi. *some particular judgments,* chap vii *particularly on Amaziah, and after other reproofs and threatnings,* chap viii *and* ix *concludes with a promise of the setting up of the Messiah's kingdom, and the happiness of God's spiritual Israel therein, just as the prophecy of Joel concluded*

Before Christ 787

CHAP I

In this chapter we have, 1 *The general title of this prophecy,* ver 1 *with the general scope of it,* ver 2 2 *God's particular controversy with Syria,* ver 3—5 *with Palestine,* ver 6-8 *with Tyre,* ver 9, 10 *with Edom,* ver 11, 12 *and with Ammon,* ver 13—15 *for their cruelty to his people, and the many injuries they had done them*

1 THE words of † Amos, [a] who was among the herdsmen of Tekoa, which he saw concerning Israel, [b] in the days of Uzziah king of Judah, and in the days of Jeroboam the son of Joash king of Israel, two years before [c] the earthquake

Ver 1 The prophecy opens with an account of the writer Amos, an inhabitant of Tekoa, in the tribe of Judah, *a herdsman,* not brought up in the school of the prophets, nor probably furnished with human literature, but God can make the foolish things of the world to confound the wise, and when he speaks, *who can but prophesy?* chap iii 8

The ten tribes of Israel are chiefly the subject of the prophetic word which God revealed to Amos, and he saw the things he declares with the same evidence and clearness, as if they had been presented before his bodily eyes

The prophecy is dated in the reigns of Uzziah and Jeroboam the second, *two years before the earthquake,* a very remarkable event, which happened in Uzziah's reign, probably at the beginning of it Compare 2 Kin xv 1 *with* 2 Kin xiv 23

2 And he said, [d] The LORD will roar from Zion, and utter his voice from Jerusalem and the habitations
of the shepherds shall mourn, and the top of Carmel
shall wither 3 Thus saith the LORD, For three
transgressions of [e] Damascus, and for four I will not
‖ turn away *the punishment* thereof [f] because they have
threshed Gilead with threshing instruments of iron 4
But [g] I will send a fire into the house of Hazael, which
shall devour the palaces of Ben-hadad 5 I will break
also the bar of Damascus, and cut off the inhabitant
from ‡ the plain of Aven, and him that holdeth the
sceptre from § the house of Eden and [h] the people of
Syria shall go into captivity unto Kir, saith the LORD
6 ¶ Thus saith the LORD, For three transgressions of
[i] Gaza, and for four I will not turn away *the punishment*
thereof because [k] they carried away captive the whole
captivity, to deliver *them* up to Edom 7 But [l] I will
send a fire on the wall of Gaza, which shall devour the
palaces thereof 8 And I will cut off the inhabitant
[m] from Ashdod, and him that holdeth the sceptre from
Ashkelon, and I will turn mine hand against Ekron,
and the remnant of the Philistines shall perish, saith the
Lord GOD 9 ¶ Thus saith the LORD, For three
transgressions of [n] Tyrus, and for four I will not turn
away *the punishment* thereof because they delivered up
the whole captivity to Edom, and remembred not [o] the
brotherly covenant 10 But I will send a fire on the
wall of Tyrus, which shall devour the palaces thereof
11 ¶ Thus saith the LORD, For three transgressions
of [p] Edom, and for four I will not turn away *the punishment* thereof because he did pursue [q] his brother with

Zech xiv 5

Before Christ 787

r Obad ix 10.
s Jer xlix 1 Ezek xxv 2 Zeph ii 9
t 2 Sam xi 1
† Or divided the mountains
u 2 Sam xii 26
x Jer xlix 3

the ſword, and did caſt off all pity, and his anger did
tear perpetually, and kept his wrath for ever 12 But
r I will ſend a fire upon Teman, which ſhall devour the
palaces of Bozrah 13 ¶ Thus ſaith the LORD, For
three tranſgreſſions of s the children of Ammon, and for
four I will not turn away *the puniſhment* thereof because
t they have † ript up the women with child of Gilead,
that they might enlarge their border 14 But I will
kindle a fire in the wall of u Rabbah, and it ſhall devour
the palaces thereof, with ſhouting in the day of battle,
with a tempeſt in the day of the whirlwind 15 And x
their king ſhall go into captivity, he and his princes together, ſaith the LORD

v. 2—15 The general tenor of the propheſy before us is intimated in theſe firſt words of it *The Lord will roar from Zion, and utter his voice from Jeruſalem*, loud and terrible as the lion roars, or as the voice of mighty thunderings From between the cherubims, his ſeat of judgment, he denounces his wrath on the enemies of his people, *the paſtures of the ſhepherds ſhall mourn*, terrified with the ſound, *and the top of Carmel ſhall wither*, ſcorched with the flaſhing lightnings, or, as is interpreted *chap* iv 7 conſumed with *drought*

The *charge* and *ſentence* againſt theſe nations are nearly the ſame Their multiplied iniquities and idolatries, ſignified by *three* and *four tranſgreſſions*, and above all their perſecution and oppreſſion of God's heritage, cried for vengeance againſt them, and God, as the prophet declares, had fixed their doom, for he ſpake not of himſelf, but *thus ſaith the Lord*, able to execute all the threatnings of his word, and ſolemnly engaging to do ſo, *I will not turn away the puniſhment thereof*, the ſentence is gone forth, irreverſible, immutable

1 Damaſcus, the capital of Syria, is brought to the bar, beſides the general charge of multiplied tranſgreſſions, her peculiar iniquity was, that *they have threſhed Gilead with threſhing inſtruments of iron*, ſo terribly had Hazael ravaged that part of the country, 2 *Kings* x 32, 33 xiii 3—7 The wrath of God therefore, as devouring fire, ſhall conſume the royal palaces and temples of Syria, and the invading enemy beſieging and forcing their way into Damaſcus, the ſeat of empire, they ſhall cut off *the inhabitants from the plain of Aven*, a delightful valley near it, the ſcene of their idolatry, *and him that holdeth the ſceptre from the houſe of Eden*, ſome pleaſure houſe probably of the kings of Syria, and the people of *Syria ſhall go into captivity to Kir, ſaith the Lord*, one tittle of whoſe word ſhall never fail See the accompliſhment of the propheſy, 2 *Kings* xvi 19

2 Gaza, a chief city of the Philiſtines, is next found guilty and puniſhed *Becauſe they carried away captive the whole captivity, to deliver them up to Edom*, the event referred to ſeems to be that, 2 *Chron* xxi 17 when they ravaged and plundered the country, and ſeized all Jehoram's family except one ſon, and all his ſubſtance, for which the chief cities of Philiſtia, with the nobles and inhabitants, are doomed to deſtruction, and *the remnant of them ſhall periſh*, God will leave them neither root nor branch and ſuch will at laſt be the fate of all the enemies and perſecutors of God's people

3 Tyre, like the other neighbours of Iſrael, notwithſtanding *the brotherly covenant* which had ſubſiſted of old between Solomon and Hiram, ſpared them not in the day of their calamity, but *delivered up the whole captivity to Edom*, either ſuch as they had ſeized in ſome inroad into the country, or thoſe who had fled to Tyre for ſhelter from the invaſion of their enemies, theſe they delivered up, or ſold for ſlaves to their implacable enemies the Edomites but the proud wall and palaces of Tyre ſhall be overthrown in juſt vengeance for ſuch unkindneſs, as was done by Nebuchadnezzar after a thirteen years ſiege *Note*, Unkindneſs is doubly grating from thoſe, of whom we had juſt reaſon to expect every act of friendſhip

4 Edom, with hereditary hatred, perſecuted the ſeed of Jacob, and though brethren in blood, yet in enmity moſt inveterate they *purſued them with the ſword*, Numb xx 19 2 *Chron* xxviii 17 and were ever ready to do them all poſſible miſchief, but it ſhall be returned upon their own head, and their cities and palaces ſhall be deſtroyed, as was done by Nebuchadnezzar, and afterward more terribly by the Maccabees, 1 *Macc* v 28 *Note*, (1) The enmity which ariſes between neareſt relations, hath uſually peculiar malignity (2) Such enmity is exceeding ſinful, and will provoke exemplary vengeance againſt the offenders and the implacable

5 The children of Ammon, with Rabbah their capital, are devoted to ruin, and their king and princes doomed to ignominious captivity their judgment ſhall be ſevere, ſudden, and irreſiſtible, *v.* 14 their crimes were atrocious, *they have ripped up the women with child of Gilead, that they might enlarge their border*, with moſt inhuman cruelty maſſacring the inhabitants, without pity, remorſe, or diſtinction of age, ſex, or condition *Note*, (1) Covetouſneſs and cruelty are twin ſiſters, and the inordinate love of money is often ſeen to harden the heart againſt all the feelings of humanity (2) It is righteous in God

to give thoſe to the ſpoil, whoſe ſubſtance was the gain of oppreſſion and injuſtice

CHAP II

In this chapter we have, 1 God's controverſy with Moab, ver 1—3 2 His quarrel with Judah, ver 4, 5 3 His charge againſt Iſrael, to which all that goes before is but an introduction Obſerve, (1) The ſins they are charged with injuſtice, oppreſſion, whoredom, ver 6—8 (2) The aggravations of theſe ſins, the temporal and ſpiritual mercies God had beſtowed upon them, for which they had made him ſuch ungrateful returns, ver 9—12 (3) God's complaint of them for their ſins, ver 13 and his threatenings of their ruin, and their utter inability to prevent it, ver 14—16

Before Christ 787

a Iſa xv 1 Jer xlviii 1 Ezek xxv 8 Zeph ii 8
b 2 Kings iii 27
c Num xxiv 17
d Iſa xxviii 15 Jer xvi 19, 20 Rom i 25
e Jer li 13
f Chap viii 6
† Or young woman
g Exod xxii 26
‡ Or ſuch as they have fined or mulcted

1 THUS ſaith the LORD, for three tranſgreſſions
of a Moab, and for four I will not turn away
the puniſhment thereof because b he burnt the bones of
the king of Edom into lime 2 But I will ſend a fire
upon Moab, and it ſhall devour the palaces of Kirioth, and Moab ſhall die with tumult, with ſhouting,
and with the ſound of the trumpet 3 And I will cut
off c the judge from the midſt thereof, and will ſlay all
the princes thereof with him, ſaith the LORD 4
¶ Thus ſaith the LORD, for three tranſgreſſions of
Judah, and for four I will not turn away *the puniſhment*
thereof because they have deſpiſed the law of the
LORD, and have not kept his commandments, d and
their lies cauſed them to err, after the which their fathers
have walked 5 But I will ſend a fire upon Judah,
and e it ſhall devour the palaces of Jeruſalem 6 ¶ Thus
ſaith the LORD, For three tranſgreſſions of Iſrael,
and for four I will not turn away *the puniſhment* thereof
becauſe f they ſold the righteous for ſilver, and the poor
for a pair of ſhoes 7 That pant after the duſt of the
earth on the head of the poor, and turn aſide the way
of the meek and a man and his father will go in unto
the *ſame* † maid, to profane my holy name 8 And
they lay *themſelves* down upon clothes g laid to pledge,
by every altar, and they drink the wine of ‡ the condemned *in* the houſe of their god

v. 1—8 God's controverſy ſtill proceeds,

1 With Moab Their multiplied tranſgreſſions called for vengeance, and one peculiarly heinous is noted *Becauſe he burnt the bones of the king of Edom into lime*, probably in revenge, for the diſtreſs to which the king of Edom had reduced him, 2 *Kings* iii 26—27 he ſome time after ſeized the perſon of the king of Edom, and burnt him alive, or having ravaged the country, dug up his bones out of his grave, and burnt them to lime, for which inhumanity God threatens to puniſh him with an invading foe, who with all the horrid din of war ſhould ſeize his cities and palaces, murder the inhabitants, and cut off all the princes and judges of Moab, which was done by Nebuchadnezzar a few years after the deſtruction of Jeruſalem

2 Judah is brought to the bar alike with heathen nations, and therefore alike in puniſhment Many were her tranſgreſſions but the root of all, and the moſt criminal, is her revolt from God, that God the nations around her never knew *they deſpiſed God's law, and kept not his commandments*, rejecting his worſhip, and diſobedient to his holy will, *and their lies cauſed them to err*, their idols, their falſe prophets, the lying vanities on which they truſted, and the lying viſions in which they believed, their fathers had done before them, the meaſure of whoſe iniquities they filled up Juſtly therefore is the fire of wrath kindled, and ready to devour the palaces of Jeruſalem, *ſee* Jer li 13 *Note*, If other ſinners muſt periſh, apoſtates ſurely will fall under double vengeance

3 Iſrael brings up the rear, laſt in judgment, not leaſt in puniſhment The crimes of this people were peculiarly aggravated by their relation to God, and therefore are more particularly inſiſted upon

(1) Their perverſion of juſtice, before their corrupt judges, the bribe, not the truth, carried the cauſe, and the meaneſt ſatisfaction influenced their deciſion, *v* 6

(2) Their oppreſſion of the poor, the very pittance they poſſeſſed, their rulers, as greedy cormorants, panted after, or they wanted to drag them through the duſt, to gratify their pride and cruelty, and becauſe they were *meek* and patient, the more inſolently they trampled upon, or plundered them, which was a great aggravation of the wickedneſs

(3) Their abominable impurities, even inceſt itſelf, *v* 7 for where the reins are once caſt upon the neck of brutiſh appetite, men are hurried into exceſſes that at firſt they would have ſtartled at with horror and ſuch wickedneſs in God's profeſſing

people,

Before Christ 787

people, could not but greatly profane his holy name, and give abundant cause to the enemies of the Lord to blaspheme

4 Their impiety and idolatry They lay themselves down upon clothes laid to pledge by every altar, which, according to the law, should have been restored before sun-setting, Exod xxii 26 but they carried them into their idol-temples, and either slept there on them all night, in honour of their deities, or regaled themselves there on the sacrifices they had offered, whilst the poor were pining in want and nakedness, *and they drink the wine of the condemned in the house of their God*, as if their idolatry could atone for their injustice, and the price of blood would be an acceptable offering For such transgressions, no marvel God threatens, *I will not turn away the punishment thereof*, ver 4

9 ¶ Yet destroyed I [h] the Amorite before them, [i]
whose height *was* like the height of the cedars, and he
was strong as the oaks, yet I [k] destroyed his fruit from
above, and his roots from beneath. 10 Also [l] I brought
you up from the land of Egypt, and led you forty
years through the wilderness, to possess the land of the
Amorite. 11 And I raised up of your sons for pro-
phets, and of your young men for [m] Nazarites *Is it*
not even thus, O ye children of Israel? saith the
LORD 12 But ye gave the Nazarites wine to drink,
and commanded the prophets, [n] saying, Prophesy not
13 Behold, † I [o] am pressed under you, as a cart *is*
pressed *that is* full of sheaves 14 Therefore [p] the flight
shall perish from the swift, and [q] the strong shall not
strengthen his force, neither shall the mighty deliver
‡ himself 15 Neither shall he stand that handleth
the bow, and *he that is* swift of foot shall not deliver
himself, [r] neither shall he that rideth the horse deliver
himself 16 And *he that is* ‖ courageous among the
mighty shall flee away naked in that day, saith the
LORD

h Num xxi 24 Deut ii 31 Josh xxiv 8
i Num xiii 28 32, 33
k Isa v 24 Mal iv 1
l Exod xii 51 Mic vi 4
m Num vi 2
n Isa xxx 10 Jer xi 21 Chap vii 12, 13 Mic ii 6
† Or I will press your place, as a cart full of sheaves presseth
o Isa xxx 16
p Chap ix 1
q Ps lxxxiii 5
‡ Heb His soul, or life
r Ps xxxiii 17
‖ Heb Strong of his heart

v 9—16 The besetting crimes of Israel was among their blackest crimes

1 God reminds them of what he had done for them He had destroyed the Amorites before them, though so warlike and mighty a people, had cut them off root and branch, and given them their land for a possession, *v* 9 He had brought them marvellously from the iron bondage in Egypt, had led and fed them in the wilderness by continual miracles, *v* 10 He had honoured them with peculiar marks of favour, raising up *their sons for prophets*, from Moses to that time, and *their young men for Nazarites*, as Samson, Samuel, and others, whose holy abstinence and self-denial should have taught them to imitate such gracious examples *Is it not thus, O ye children of Israel, saith the Lord?* The facts were notorious beyond contradiction *Note*, (1) Faithful ministers are the greatest blessings to a nation, and not to have profited by their labours, will one day bring a heavy reckoning (2) When in the heat of youth the power of divine grace is seen effectually restraining the corrupt appetite, and purifying the heart, such examples are peculiarly striking

2 He upbraids them with what they had done against him They *gave the Nazarites wine to drink*, enticing or threatening them into a compliance, and *commanded the prophets, saying, Prophesy not*, whilst the people turned a deaf ear to them, the rulers and priests persecuted, and endeavoured to silence them, chap vii 12, 13 These, and the like abominations, were as a heavy burden which the Lord was weary to bear *I am pressed under you, as a cart is pressed that is full of sheaves*, though some read this as a threatening, *I will press your place as a cart full of sheaves presseth*, intimating the distress which should be brought upon them in the siege of Samaria *Note*, (1) The devil and his agents are very busy to draw off the minds of young men from divine things, and they triumph if they can succeed in the debauch of a Nazarite (2) They who hate the truth, and exert their power to suppress it, shall shortly answer for it at their peril (3) Though God's patience bear long with sinners, he will not bear always, the day of recompense will come, when he *will ease him of his adversaries*, Isa i 24

3 Judgment is pronounced upon them for their sins He will load *them* with his wrath, who have burdened *him* with their iniquities The Assyrian, the rod of his anger, shall come, and flight or resistance will be alike in vain the mighty shall fall, and the swift be overtaken by their swifter pursuers The most courageous warriors shall flee naked, casting away their armour, and consulting only how they may escape, and this is confirmed by *thus saith the Lord*, whose denunciations shall have a sure accomplishment *Note*, The sinner in the day of God will find his case desperate, unable to endure, or escape from the wrath he hath provoked

Before Christ 787

CHAP. III.

The Israelites are warned, 1 Of the judgments of God denounced against them, that they might be hereby awakened out of their security, ver 1—8 2 Of the sins that were found among them, for which God was provoked thus to threaten, thus to punish, that they might justify God in his controversy with them, and unless they repented and reformed, might expect no other but that God should proceed in his controversy, ver 9—15

1 HEAR this word that the LORD hath spoken
against you, O children of Israel, against the
whole family which I brought up from the land of
Egypt, saying, 2 [a] You only have I known of all the
families of the earth [b] therefore I will punish you for
all your iniquities 3 Can two walk together, except
they be agreed? 4 Will a lion roar in the forest,
when he hath no prey? will a young lion † cry out of
his den, if he have taken nothing? 5 Can a bird fall
in a snare upon the earth where no gin *is* for him?
shall *one* take up a snare from the earth, and have taken
nothing at all? 6 Shall a trumpet be blown in the
city, and the people ‡ not be afraid? [c] shall there be
evil in a city, and the LORD hath not done *it*? 7
Surely the Lord GOD will do nothing, but [d] he reveal-
eth his secret unto his servants the prophets 8 [e] The
lion hath roared, who will not fear? the Lord GOD
hath spoken, [f] who can but prophesy?

a Deut vii 6 & x 15
b Dan ix 12 Matt xi 22 Luke xii 47 Rom ii 9 1 Pet iv 17
† Heb Give forth his voice
‡ Or run together
c Isa xlv 7
d Gen vi 13 & xviii 17 Ps xxv 14 John xv 15
e Chap i 2
f Acts iv 20 & v 20, 29

v 1—8 The prophet solemnly awakens the attention of this stupid people, and calls on them to *hear* and tremble at *the word which the Lord hath spoken against them*

1 Their ingratitude will provoke him to punish them Of all families of the earth, they had been distinguished by his peculiar favour, though so few when they went into Egypt, yet he had multiplied them exceedingly, and brought them up from thence with a high hand, and *therefore* their rebellion against him was the more criminal, and would bring a heavier judgment on their heads *Note*, None perish under deeper guilt, than those who have abused distinguishing means and mercies

2 In their state of apostacy, no communion can subsist between him and them *Can two walk together, except they be agreed?* There must be reconciliation before there could be any renewed fellowship, and as they obstinately rejected every call to repent, the enmity must subsist, and their ruin be the consequence *Note*, God is ready to be reconciled to sinners, but if they reject his mercy, they may expect his wrath

3 The judgments God threatened were not pretended, but real, nor should they be removed from them till they were effectually humbled by them *Will the lion roar in the forest when he hath no prey?* &c No they only roar in sight of their prey, or when they have seized it *Can a bird fall in a snare upon the earth where no gin is for him?* No God had really spread the snare of affliction for them, nor would take it up fruitless, they would assuredly be snared and taken, nor would the visitation be removed, till the end for which it was sent should be answered, *v* 5 *Note*, (1) The terrors of the Lord are not phantoms raised to frighten the weak, the ignorant, or superstitious, but awful realities that must shortly come to pass (2) The sinner's transgression will assuredly bring him into the snare of guilt and misery, and nothing but God's rich grace, bringing him to real repentance, can deliver him out of it

4 The warnings they received ought justly to alarm them, and in the sufferings they were about to feel, God's hand would visibly appear *Shall a trumpet be blown in the city, and the people not be afraid?* of the approaching foe, or *run together*, to consider how to avert the storm Thus God, by his prophets, had spread the alarm, and it was at their peril if they disregarded them *Shall there be evil in a city, and the Lord hath not done it?* No all affliction comes from him, and without him not a hair of our head falls *Surely the Lord God will do nothing, but he revealeth his secret unto his servants the prophets*, that before he strikes, they may give fair warning to the guilty, and exhort them by a speedy humiliation to avert the impending wrath *The lion hath roared, who will not fear?* The Lord hath denounced his vengeance against the impenitent, and abundant cause there is they should tremble before him *The Lord hath spoken, who can but prophesy?* Who, that hath the glory of God and the good of men's souls at heart, can refrain from speaking, when God stirs up his mind with holy zeal, and shews him the dreadful danger about which sinners appear so fearfully unconcerned! *Note*, (1) In all our trials and troubles, God's hand is to be acknowledged it must silence every murmur, when we know he hath done it (2) God is very gracious, he never strikes, till having warned in vain the sinner prove incorrigible (3) Necessity is laid upon those, whose spirit God inwardly

moves

Before Christ 787

moves with affecting views of the miseries of a world that lieth in wickedness, to labour, if possible, to pluck these brands from the burning.

9 ¶ Publish in the palaces at Ashdod, and in the
palaces in the land of Egypt, and say, Assemble your-
selves upon the mountains of Samaria, and behold the
great tumults in the midst thereof, and the † oppressed
in the midst thereof. 10 For [g] they know not to do
right, saith the LORD, who store up violence and †
robbery in their palaces. 11 Therefore thus saith the
Lord GOD, [h] An adversary *there shall be* even round
about the land, and he shall bring down thy strength
from thee, and thy palaces shall be spoiled. 12 Thus
saith the LORD, As the shepherd ‖ taketh out of the
mouth of the lion two legs, or a piece of an ear, so
shall the children of Israel be taken out that dwell in
Samaria, in the corner of a bed, and § in Damascus *in*
a couch. 13 Hear ye and testify in the house of Ja-
cob, saith the Lord GOD, the God of hosts. 14
That in the day that I shall ‡ visit the transgressions of
Israel upon him, I will also visit the altars of Beth-el,
and the horns of the altar shall be cut off, and fall to
the ground. 15 And I will smite [i] the winter-house
with the summer-house, and [k] the houses of ivory shall
perish, and the great houses shall have an end, saith the
LORD.

† Or, oppressions. g Jer. iv. 22. † Or, spoil. h 2 Kings xvi. 6. ‖ Heb. Delivereth. § Or, on the bed's feet. ‡ Or, punish Israel for. i Judg. iii. 20. Jer. xxxvi. 22. k 1 Kings xxii. 39.

v. 9—15. The neighbouring nations, the princes of Philistia and Egypt, are summoned to hear the trial of Israel, that they may bear witness to the righteousness of the Lord, and in their punishments be themselves admonished, v. 9. We have,

1. The crimes of which Israel is found guilty. (1.) *Behold the great tumults in the midst thereof*, the outrages committed in lawless riot, and passed off with impunity. (2.) Behold *the oppressed in the midst thereof*: injustice, oppression, rapine, and violence fill every street, and the injured groan without redress, *for they know not to do right*, they had no desire to do it, or by so long a course of wickedness their very judgment was perverted, and their reason blinded: *they store up violence and robbery in their palaces*, thus heaping up wrath against the day of wrath. *Note*, Sin is of that bewitching nature, that by long practice it gains, as it were, a sanction in the mind, and the conscience utterly defiled yields consent and approbation.

2. The sentence pronounced upon Israel is terrible. *An adversary*, the Assyrian king, shall be raised up, that shall demolish their fortresses, and plunder their palaces of their ill-gotten wealth, v. 11. The inhabitants shall be massacred and devoured as a helpless sheep in a lion's mouth; a wretched remnant only shall escape, like the *two legs, or piece of an ear*, which the shepherd rescues from his consuming jaws: a few out of Samaria, *in the corner of a bed*, so poor that they have only part of a bed to lie on, or who ran thither to hide themselves, *and in Damascus in a couch*, a mere handful, who fled thither when Samaria was taken, or when this city fell likewise, some few of them narrowly escaped, v. 12. This sentence God's prophets and priests are called upon faithfully to deliver to *the house of Jacob*, ver. 13. and to assure them the day will come, when *he will visit their transgressions* with deserved vengeance; when their idolatrous *altars at Beth-el* should fall, and *the horns of them be cut off*, nor afford the least refuge to those who fled thither, their idol confidences utterly failing them. Their houses filled with oppression shall also be laid in the dust; their winter and summer-houses, many of them curiously adorned with ivory, and the structure superb and magnificent, shall be plundered and demolished by the invading foe. *Note*, (1.) Great houses afford no protection against God's judgments; rather when built by unrighteousness, maintained by oppression, or abused by pride and luxury, they provoke them more speedily and fearfully. (2.) They who make any creature their idol, will sooner or later be convinced of the folly and misery of their dependance thereon.

CHAP. IV.

In this chapter, 1. The oppressors of Israel are threatned, ver. 1—3. 2. The idolaters are given up to their own hearts lusts, ver. 4, 5. 3. All their sins are aggravated by their incorrigibleness, and refusal to return and reform, notwithstanding the various rebukes of providence they had been under, ver. 6—11. 4. They are invited yet at length to humble themselves before God, since it is impossible for them to make their part good against him, ver. 12, 13.

1 HEAR this word, ye [a] kine of Bashan, that *are*
in the mountain of Samaria, [b] which oppress
the poor, which crush the needy, which say to their
masters, Bring, and let us drink. 2 [c] The Lord GOD
hath sworn by his holiness, that lo, the days shall come
upon you, that he will take you away [d] with hooks, and
your posterity with fish-hooks. 3 And [e] ye shall go
out at the breaches, every *cow at that which is* before
her, and ye shall cast ‖ *them* into the palace, saith the
LORD. 4 ¶ Come to Beth-el and transgress, at
Gilgal multiply transgression; and bring your [f] sacrifices
every morning, *and* [g] your tithes after † three years.
5 [h] And ‖ offer a sacrifice of thanksgiving with leaven,
and proclaim *and* publish the free offerings: for § this
liketh you, O ye children of Israel, saith the Lord
GOD.

a Psal. xxii. 12. Ezek. xxxix. 18. b Ch. iii. 9. c Psal. lxxxix. 35. d Jer. xvi. 16. Hab. i. 15. e Ezek. xii. 5, 12. ‖ Or, ye shall cast away yourselves into the palace, or fort. f Ch. v. 21. & xii. 11. Chap. v. 5. g Deut. xiv. 28. † Heb. three years of days. h Lev. vii. 13. & xxiii. 17. ‖ Heb. Offer by burning. § Heb. So ye love.

v. 1—5. God's controversy against the oppressors and idolaters is here continued.

1. The oppressors are convicted, and their punishment read. Like kine of Bashan they were strong, wanton, unruly, breaking down the fence of justice, and treading the weak under their feet; they fattened on the mountains of Samaria, *oppressing the poor, and crushing the needy*, by an enormous load of taxes, or the perversion of justice, or with a hard hand extorting such rents from their indigent tenants, as left them scarce a sufficiency to live; *which say to their masters, Bring, and let us drink*, which may be the words of the magistrates encouraging the masters of the poor to find some accusation against them, and for an entertainment they would decide the cause in their favour; or of one oppressive lord to another, willing to feast with him on the spoils of oppression. But God will not suffer such deeds to pass with impunity. *He hath sworn by his holiness*, and irrevocable is the decree: they shall be taken and destroyed as easily and irresistibly as the fish which is caught by the hook; and they and their posterity who should survive the slaughter made by the Assyrians, shall be sold for captives, and carried, as fish out of their element, into a strange land. Their city walls being beat down by a besieging army, at the breaches some would attempt to escape, whilst others *cast themselves into the palace or citadel*, or lodged their substance there, but in vain; the fugitives will be pursued, and the high fortress laid low, even to the dust. *Note*, (1.) God will one day appear the patron of the injured, and avenge their wrongs. (2.) The fruits of oppression are often made the food of intemperance, and thus doubly aggravate the sinner's guilt. (3.) What is got by wickedness often perishes strangely, and every observer may see the finger of God in the visitation.

2. The idolaters are abandoned to their own devices, and a heavier curse cannot be laid upon them. Ironically speaking, God bids them go on to *multiply their transgressions* at Beth-el and Gilgal, to bring their daily sacrifices, and offer their tythes at their idol-temples and altars, instead of the sanctuary at Jerusalem; and mimicking the worship of his temple, he saith, *offer your sacrifice of thanksgiving with leaven* to your idols, Lev. vii. 13. and out of ostentation of piety, or inviting others to the feast, *publish and proclaim the free offerings, for this liketh you, O ye children of Israel*. They took a pleasure and pride in their idolatrous services: justly therefore doth God give them up to their own inventions, to fill up the measure of their iniquities.

6 ¶ And I also have given you cleanness of teeth in
all your cities, and want of bread in all your places,
[i] yet have ye not returned unto me, saith the LORD.
7 And also I have withholden the rain from you, when
there were yet three months to the harvest, and I caused
it to rain upon one city, and caused it not to rain upon
another city: one piece was rained upon, and the piece
whereupon it rained not, withered. 8 So two *or* three
cities wandred unto one city to drink water, but they
were not satisfied, yet have ye not returned unto me,
saith the LORD. 9 [l] I have smitten you with blasting
and mildew; ‖ when your gardens, and your vineyards,
and your fig-trees, and your olive-trees increased, [m] the
palmer-worm devoured *them*: yet have ye not returned
unto me, saith the LORD. 10 I have sent among
you the pestilence ‖ after the manner of Egypt: your
young men have I slain with the sword, ‖ and have taken
away your horses, and I have made the stink of your
camps to come up unto your nostrils: yet have ye not
returned unto me, saith the LORD. 11 I have over-
thrown *some* of you, as [n] God overthrew Sodom and Go-
morrah, and ye were as a firebrand plucked out of the
burning: yet have ye not returned unto me, saith
the LORD. 12 Therefore [o] thus will I do unto thee,
O Israel: *and* because I will do this unto thee, [p] prepare
to meet thy God, O Israel. 13 For lo, he that form-
eth

i Jer. v. 3. k Deut. xxviii. 23. Hag. ii. 17. ‖ Or, when the multitude of your gardens, &c. the palmer-worm, &c. l Joel i. 4. & ii. 25. ‖ Or, in the way. ‖ Heb. With the captivity of your horses. m Gen. xix. 24, 25. Isa. xiii. 19. Jer. xlix. 18. n Zech. iii. 2. Jude 23. o Ch. v. 4. p Ezek. xiii. 5. & xxii. 30. Luke xiv. 31, 32.

Before Christ 787

eth the mountains, and createth the § wind, and [s] declareth unto man what *is* his thought, [t] that maketh the morning darkness, and [u] treadeth upon the high places of the earth, the LORD, [x] the God of hosts *is* his name.

§ Or spirit. s Dan. ii. 28. t Chap. viii. 9. u Deut. xxxii. 13. & xxxiii. 29. Mic. i. 3. x Chap. v. 8. & ix. 6.

v. 6—13. The incorrigibleness of this people left them wholly inexcusable in their sins. God had tried repeatedly, by his visitations to bend their stubborn hearts, ready to receive them if they humbled their souls, waiting with long patience, and loth to abandon them to ruin; but neither mercies nor judgments had any effect. Five times he complains, *yet have ye not returned unto me, saith the Lord.* We have here,

1. An account of the methods God had taken, by lesser judgments, to bring them to repentance.

[1.] He had visited them with famine in all their cities, 2 *Kings* viii. 1. *I have given you cleanness of teeth,* there being no provision left, not even bread to chew, and satisfy the cravings of hunger: yet this was ineffectual, they repented not.

[2.] He sent a drought upon the land, and with-held the rain *when there were yet three months to the harvest,* the time when it usually fell, and without it the corn was scorched up and withered away: but that they might observe, that this was not a thing merely *accidental,* or owing to any influence of secondary causes, but by Divine direction, as a judgment on them, *he caused it to rain on one city, and not on another,* and gave the clouds their commission to water *one piece,* of the land, whilst the other which lay contiguous, was scorched up with heat and drought: and probably this distinction was observable, the idolaters being punished, and the few faithful men thus distinguished. In this distress, *two or three cities wandered into one city, to drink water, but they were not satisfied,* there being none, or but little to spare from their own wants, and even this produced no change.

[3.] Blasting and mildew next destroyed their corn and wine, and the palmer-worm devoured all their trees and herbage; yet they persisted in impenitence, and turned not to him that smote them.

[4.] The pestilence succeeded. They fell by a sudden stroke, like the first-born of Egypt, and God slew them in numbers with the sword of an enemy; or *in the way of Egypt,* as they went thither for food, some fell by the pestilence, and others, who went in companies, were intercepted and slain by their enemies, and their corpses left unburied, filling the air with noisome effluvia: yet notwithstanding, the survivors repented not.

[5.] By fire from heaven God overthrew some of them like Sodom and Gomorrah, as monuments of vengeance, and a warning to the rest who were spared, as brands *plucked out of the burning;* yet all their judgments left them as they found them, hardened in sin; and till God is pleased to bestow his effectual grace, all outward means and methods to bend the sinner's heart will be fruitless.

2. Since all hath proved hitherto ineffectual, by the divinely appointed Messiah God will nevertheless bring salvation unto them, and cause his grace to triumph over their guilt and corruption. *Thus saith the Lord, I will do unto thee, O Israel,* notwithstanding all these provocations; or because nothing else can avail with them, I will do as I have promised, sending the divine Messiah who shall turn away ungodliness from Jacob: *and because I will do this unto thee,* let such an act of astonishing mercy and grace melt and bend thy stubborn neck, and *prepare to meet thy God, O Israel,* to receive him with readiness, submission, and delight, who cometh with tidings of salvation. *For lo, he that formeth the mountains,* the great Creator of all, and who can make every mountain of difficulty a plain before his people; *and createth the wind,* holding these turbulent servants under his command; *and declareth unto man what is his thought,* being the searcher of hearts, and revealing unto men, by his prophets, his own purposes concerning them, which are thoughts *of peace, and not of evil; that maketh the morning darkness,* changing prosperity into adversity, or the *darkness morning,* sending Christ, the day-star, to arise, *and treadeth upon the high places of the earth,* exalted above all, and treading down the proudest of his foes, *the Lord,* Jehovah, *the God of hosts is his name,* to whom all must bow, and humble their souls at his feet.

The words are generally understood in a quite different sense, as a threatening of more terrible judgment, since the former visitations were ineffectual. They must now prepare to meet an offended God, coming forth to execute vengeance; and how would they be able to stand when he appeared, whose power was irresistible as his wrath was intolerable? It is our wisdom to prepare to meet God as our God, by faith, penitence, and prayer, before we are summoned to appear at his bar in an hour of death, or at the day of judgment.

CHAP. V.

The scope of this chapter is to prosecute the exhortation given to Israel in the close of the former, to prepare to meet his God; he here tells them, 1. *What preparation they must make; they must seek to the Lord, and not to their idols,* ver. 4—8. *they must seek the good and love it,* ver. 14, 15. 2. *Why they must make this preparation.* (1.) *Because of the present deplorable condition they were in,* ver. 1—3. (2.) *Because it was sin that brought them into this condition,* ver. 7, 10, 11, 12. (3.) *Because this would be their happiness, and God would be found of them,* ver. 8, 9, 14. (4.) *Because without it he would bring utter ruin upon them,* ver. 5, 6, 13, 16, 17. *And* (5.) *All their confidences would fail them:* [1.] *Their profane contempt and defiance of God's judgments would not secure them,* ver. 18—20. [2.] *Their external services would not avail to turn away the wrath of God,* ver. 21—24. [3.] *Their long possession of their idol gods, and course of holy duties, would not be their protection, while they kept to their idolatrous customs,* ver. 25—27. *They have no force or way left to save themselves, but by repentance and reformation.*

1 HEAR ye this word which I take up against
you, [a] *even* a lamentation, O house of Israel. 2
The virgin of Israel is fallen; she shall no more rise:
she is forsaken upon her land; *there is* none to raise her
up. 3 For thus saith the Lord GOD; The city that
went out *by* a thousand, shall leave an hundred, and that
which went forth *by* an hundred, shall leave ten, to the
house of Israel.

a Ezek. xix. 1. b 2 Kings xvii. 6.

v. 1—3. The prophet cannot but be himself affected with the miseries he foresees coming upon the people; whilst therefore he demands of them attention to the doleful tidings, he laments in elegiac strains of woe the virgin of Israel fallen, as if she was already a dead corpse, since God had pronounced her doom.

1. Her ruin is irrecoverable. She is not only *fallen,* but fallen *to rise no more,* having never been a kingdom since the ten tribes were carried captive by Salmaneser. *She is forsaken upon her land,* both of God, her allies, and her own people, *there is none to raise her up,* either able or willing to help her; for those whom God will destroy, none can save.

2. The inhabitants shall be diminished, and brought very low. Before the final vengeance overtook them, a variety of calamities had reduced their numbers; so that the city which could formerly muster a thousand men, could on the invasion raise but an hundred; and the village that had an hundred inhabitants was reduced to ten: or these numbers only remained after the campaign, but one in ten escaping the ravages of war.

4 ¶ For thus saith the LORD unto the house of
Israel, [c] Seek ye me, and ye shall live. 5 But seek not
[d] Beth-el, nor enter into Gilgal, and pass not to [e] Beer-
sheba: for Gilgal shall surely go into captivity, and [f]
Beth-el shall come to nought. 6 Seek the LORD,
and ye shall live; lest he break out like fire in the house
of Joseph, and devour *it,* and *there be* none to quench *it*
in Beth-el. 7 Ye who turn judgment to wormwood,
and leave off righteousness in the earth, 8 *Seek him*
that maketh [h] the seven stars and Orion, and turneth
the shadow of death into the morning, and maketh the
day dark with night: [i] that calleth for the waters of the
sea, and poureth them out upon the face of the earth:
[k] the LORD *is* his name: 9 That strengtheneth the
‡ spoiled against the strong, so that the spoiled shall
come against the fortress. 10 [l] They hate him that re-
buketh in the gate, and they abhor him that speaketh
uprightly. 11 Forasmuch therefore as your treading *is*
upon the poor, and ye take from him burdens of wheat:
[m] ye have built houses of hewn stone, but ye shall not
dwell in them; ye have planted ‡ pleasant vineyards, but
ye shall not drink wine of them. 12 For I know your
manifold transgressions, and your mighty sins: they af-
flict the just, they take a bribe, and [n] they turn aside
the poor in the gate *from their right.* 13 Therefore the
prudent [o] shall keep silence in that time; for it *is* an evil
time. 14 [p] Seek good, and not evil, that ye may live:
and so the LORD, the God of hosts, shall be with you,
as ye have spoken. 15 Hate the evil, and love the
good, and establish judgment in the gate: [q] it may be
that the LORD God of hosts will be gracious unto the
remnant of Joseph.

c Jer. xxix. 13. d Chap. iv. 4. e Chap. viii. 14. f Hos. iv. 15. g Chap. vi. 12. h Job ix. 9. & xxxviii. 31. i Chap. ix. 6. k Psal. lxxxiii. 18. ‡ Heb. Spoil. l 1 Kings xxii. 8. Isa. xxix. 21. Wisd. ii. 12. Rev. xi. 10. m Deut. xxviii. 30. Zeph. i. 13. Hag. i. 6. ‡ Heb. Vineyards of desire. n Chap. ii. 7. o Chap. vi. 10. p Isa. i. 16, 17. q Joel ii. 14.

v. 4—15. The blessing of obedience, and the miseries of sin, are topics we should often dwell upon, that we may choose the one and avoid the other.

1. The sins of Israel are brought to their remembrance, that they might repent and amend the evil of their ways. In general, *v.* 12. God charges them with *manifold transgressions and mighty sins,* he knew them, however secretly committed, and

Before Christ 787

now produces them for their conviction *Note*, The sinner that is brought to a true knowledge of his state, stands amazed at the *multitude* of his transgressions, by thought, word, and deed committed against the divine Majesty, and is shocked at the flagrant enormities that cry for vengeance against him

[1.] They were *idolaters*, flying to Beth-el and Gilgal, where their idols were, instead of having recourse to God at his temple

[2.] They practised the most flagrant *injustice*, *ye turn judgment to wormwood*, acting in direct opposition thereto, *and leave off righteousness in the earth*, having not the least regard for it, but trampling it under foot

[3.] They were *oppressors* of the poor, not only plundering them of *burdens of wheat*, their very gleaning, or the fruit gotten by hard labour, but also *trod* them under foot, *v.* 11 Imperious, insolent, and cruel to them, they *afflicted the just*, perhaps hated them, because they were so, and took every opportunity to harass and torment them *They take a bribe*, and *they turn aside the poor in the gate from their right*, be the right of the cause never so clear, the bribe carries it against law and equity, and they who cannot fee them, may not expect redress of the most flagrant injustice

[4.] They were *malicious persecutors* of God's faithful ministers and people *They hate him that rebuketh in the gate*, the ministers and prophets, who openly preached against their iniquities, *and they abhor him that speaketh uprightly*, the conversation, yea, the very person of such is their abhorrence, as they are a constant and living reproof to their iniquities And in those evil days, when the enmity of the wicked is so avowed, *the prudent shall keep silence at that time*, ver. 13 When a man will be made an offender for a word, it is as dangerous to complain, as fruitless to reprove *Note*, Good men are often driven to unwilling silence, though it is a pain and grief to them

2. Their punishment is foretold, except they repent The head quarters of their idolatry, Beth-el and Gilgal, shall come to nought, and the inhabitants go into captivity, *v.* 5 A fire shall devour the house of Joseph, it shall consume the whole nation, and *none* of their idols at *Beth-el* shall be able to *quench it*, *v.* 6 so little protection can any creature afford us in the day of wrath Though by the fruits of oppression they reared magnificent abodes for themselves, they shall not be suffered to dwell in them, nor eat the fruits of the pleasant vineyards they had planted, *v.* 11 by death cut off, or by captivity removed far away *Note*, What is not honestly got, is not likely to be long enjoyed

3. To prevent this threatned vengeance, they are exhorted speedily to seek the Lord for pardon and grace, in order that their hearts and lives may be reformed and changed *Seek ye me, saith the Lord*, my mercy and favour, and return to my worship and service, and *ye shall live*, notwithstanding all that is past, their guilt shall be forgiven, and their forfeited lives restored, they shall be suffered still to dwell in their own land, and what is far better, as partakers of God's grace shall live *spiritually* his people on earth, and *eternally* with him in heaven But they must renounce their idolatries at Beth-el and Gilgal, for whilst these remained, no mercy could be hoped for and what wretched vanities were these, compared with him, whom they were exhorted to seek, and to whose favour they were invited, he *maketh the seven stars*, called the Pleiades, and *Orion*, another constellation, with all the heavenly hosts, *and turneth the shadow of death into the morning, and maketh the day dark with night*, directing the constant revolutions of day and night, or as he pleases, able to turn the deepest night of distress into the day of exultation and joy, or the meridian brightness of prosperity into the darkness of most abject wretchedness, *that calleth for the waters of the sea, and poureth them out upon the face of the earth*, as in the deluge, to punish an ungodly world, or by exhalations from the great abyss of waters, replenishes the clouds, that drop down the rain to water the earth, *the Lord is his name*, Jehovah, the self-sufficient, all-sufficient God *That strengtheneth the spoiled against the strong*, enabling them to stand against their oppressors, yea, though vanquished before, raising them above their conquerors, *so that the spoiled shall come against the fortress*, besiege and take it However desperate therefore their national affairs might appear, if God became their friend, they might be easily retrieved if then they would be delivered from danger, they must return to God, and the paths of duty *Seek good and not evil*, putting away all your abominations, and desiring henceforward to know God's holy will, and walk in all his holy ways, *that ye may live*, as God had promised, *v.* 4 *and so the Lord the God of hosts shall be with you, as ye have spoken*, as once they boasted he was, or as now they prayed he might be, and his approving presence is better than life itself *Hate the evil*, not only because it is hurtful to your souls, but because it is so offensive and odious to the holy God, *and love the good*, God himself, his people, his ways, his worship, delighting in the Lord, and in every good word and work which may advance his glory *and*, particularly, what they had hitherto so neglected, *establish judgment in the gate*, that justice may be administred to all impartially, freely, speedily, *it may be that the Lord will be gracious unto the remnant of Joseph*, though reduced to a few, this conduct would be the means of restoring their prosperity, at least the remnant of the truly faithful souls should find favour and grace in the eyes of the Lord *Note*, The way of duty is the path of safety, and God hath never yet failed those who seek him

16 Therefore the LORD the God of hosts, the
Lord saith thus, Wailing *shall be* in all streets, and they
shall say in all the high ways, Alas, alas and they
shall call the husbandman to mourning, and [r] such as [r] Jer ix 17
are skilful of lamentation, to wailing 17 And in all
vineyards *shall be* wailing for [s] I will pass through thee, [s] Exod xii 12
saith the LORD 18 [t] Wo unto you that desire the [t] Isa v 19 Jer xvii 15 & xxx 7 Joel ii 2 Zeph i 15 2 Pet iii 4
day of the LORD to what end *is* it for you? the day
of the LORD *is* darkness, and not light 19 [u] As if a [u] Jer xlviii 44
man did flee from a lion, and a bear met him, or went
into the house, and leaned his hand on the wall, and a
serpent bit him 20 *Shall* not the day of the LORD
be darkness, and not light? even very dark, and no
brightness in it?

v. 16—20 This clause is connected not with the words immediately preceding, but with the foregoing part of the chapter, and declares what would be the case, if neither judgments, mercies, nor exhortations wrought upon them

1. Such calamities were coming upon them, as would raise a bitter and universal mourning Their streets should echo with wailing, and their highways resound with lamentations, even the husbandman and the vine-dresser shall leave their employments, to join the general cry, Alas! alas! Whilst those, whose profession it had been to awaken the sorrows of others, shall now with no fictitious notes of woe pour forth their anguish, and raise the melancholy sound, *for I will pass through thee, saith the Lord*, with such fearful vengeance and desolations, as when of old the destroying angel passed through the land of Egypt

2. The scoffers are particularly and severely rebuked Many of the profane and ungodly mocked at the warnings given, and with daring insolence and hardened infidelity bid the day come, as if they neither believed nor feared it Therefore *wo unto you that desire the day of the Lord*, it would come faster than they were aware, *to what end is it for you?* it would make them wish a thousand times their impious speeches unsaid, *for the day of the Lord is darkness, and not light*, a terrible day for them And it is repeated, *v.* 20 to affect them with a sense of their danger, *even very dark, and no brightness in it*, when the hopes with which these sinners, and all who are like them, flattered themselves, shall be lost in black unfathomable despair No door of escape shall then be open, it shall be *as if a man fled from a lion, and a bear met him*, such a multitude of dire calamities should surround them, *or went into a house, and leaned on the wall, and a serpent bit him*, for no place in a day of wrath can afford the impenitent sinner shelter or support Perhaps some wished for these troublesome times that were threatned, hoping to make their own advantage of them, but, to their cost, they would find themselves dreadfully involved in the common calamity

21 ¶ [x] I hate, I despise your feast days, and [y] I will [x] Prov xxi 27 Isa i 11 Jer vi 20
not ‖ smell in your solemn assemblies 22 Though ye [y] Lev xxvi 31
offer me burnt-offerings, and your meat offerings, [z] I will ‖ Or smell your holy days
not accept *them* neither will I regard the ‡ peace-offer- [z] Isa lxvi 3
ings of your fat beasts 23 Take thou away from me ‡ Or thank offering.
the noise of thy songs, for I will not hear the melody of
thy viols 24 But let judgment ‖ run down as waters, ‖ Heb Roll.
and righteousness as a mighty stream 25 [a] Have ye [a] Acts vii 42 Isa xliii 23.
offered unto me sacrifices and offerings in the wilderness
forty years, O house of Israel? 26 But ye have born
§ the tabernacle of your Moloch and Chiun your ima- § Or Siccuth your king
ges, the star of your god, which ye made to yourselves [b] 1 Kings xi 33
27 Therefore will I cause [c] you to go into captivity be- [c] Ibid xvii 6 Acts vii 43
yond Damascus, saith the LORD, whose name *is* the
God of hosts

v. 21—27 Amidst abounding ungodliness, they flattered themselves the form of godliness they observed would preserve them from ruin, but they are wofully mistaken

1. Their sacrifices and service, so far from being pleasing to God, were his abomination, and their sacred songs grated harsh discord in his ears Not only they were performed contrary to his institution, at Beth-el instead of Jerusalem, but also their allowed iniquity and barefaced hypocrisy made them doubly displeasing and loathsome in his sight *Note*, (1.) Formality and hypocrisy are more odious to God than open profaneness, these shall receive greater damnation (2.) Many flatter themselves their duties and devotions will carry them to heaven, when their pride and vain confidence in these things only the more certainly lead them down to hell.

Before Christ 787

2 What God required of them was righteouſneſs and judgment, without which no ſacrifices could avail *Let judgment run down as waters*, freely, copiouſly, without interruption, *and righteouſneſs as a mighty ſtream*, bearing down before it ungodlineſs and wrong,

3 To idols, not to God, had their ſacrifices been offered *Have ye offered unto me ſacrifices and offerings in the wilderneſs forty years?* No The greateſt part of the time none were offered, and, of the few ſacrifices they did bring, the golden calf had a chief ſhare ſo ſoon idolatry began, and had continued ever ſince among them. *Ye have born the tabernacle of Moloch*, little ſhrines, or ſmall images of that hated idol, probably the ſun, in honour of whom they burnt their children in the fire, *and Chiun*, the ſame as *Remphan*, *Acts* vii 43 probably the planet Saturn, *your images*, *the ſtar of your god*, *which ye made to yourſelves*, the worſhip of the heavenly hoſt being the moſt ancient idolatry, which they ſeem to have adopted, worſhipping and ſerving the creature inſtead of the Creator

4 For theſe things they are doomed to an ignominious captivity *Therefore I will cauſe you to go into captivity beyond Damaſcus*, into a more diſtant and ſtrange land, even *beyond Babylon*, as Stephen quotes it, *Acts* vii 43 as far as Halah and Habor, cities of the Medes, and the infallible certainty of the prediction is confirmed by thus *ſaith the Lord*, *whoſe name is the God of hoſts* almighty to execute, and true to accompliſh, the threatenings of his word

CHAP VI

In this chapter we have, 1 *A ſinful people ſtudying to* put a ſlight *upon God's threatenings*, *and to make them appear* trivial, *confiding in their privileges and preeminences above other nations*, ver 2, 3 *and their power*, ver 13 *and wholly addicted to their pleaſures*, ver 3—6 2 *A* ſerious prophet *ſtudying to* put a weight *upon God's threatenings*, *and to make them appear* terrible, *by ſetting forth the ſeverity of theſe judgments that were coming upon theſe ſenſualiſts*, ver 7 *God's abhorring them*, *and abandoning them and theirs to death*, ver 8—11 *and bringing utter deſolation upon them*, ver 12—14

a Luke xii 19, 20. † Or rich. Luke vi 24 or ſecure b Ex xix 5 c Jer ii 10 Nah iii 8 d Iſa x 9 e 2 Chron xxvi 6 f Ezek xii 27 Mat xxiv 48 g Chap v 18 h Pſ x 11 ... ‡ Or abound with ſuperfluities i Iſa v 12 k 1 Chron xxiii 5 l Gen xxxvii 25 m Jer xxx 7 ∥ Or breach

1 WO to them *that are* † at eaſe in Zion, and
truſt in the mountain of Samaria, *which are*
named [b] chief of the nations to whom the houſe of Iſrael
came 2 [c] Paſs ye unto Calneh, and ſee, and from
thence go ye to Hemath the great then go down to
[e] Gath of the Philiſtines *be they* better than theſe kingdoms?
or their border greater than your border? 3
Ye [f] that put far away [g] the evil day, and cauſe [h] the
ſeat of violence to come near, 4 That lie upon beds
of ivory, and ‡ ſtretch themſelves upon their couches,
and eat the lambs out of the flocks and the calves out
of the midſt of the ſtall, 5 [i] That § chant to the ſound
of the viol, *and* invent to themſelves inſtruments of
muſic, [k] like David, 6 That drink wine in bowls,
and anoint themſelves with the chief ointments but
[l] they are not grieved for [m] the ∥ affliction of Joſeph
7 ¶ Therefore now ſhall they go captive with the firſt
that go captive, and the banquet of them that ſtretched
themſelves ſhall be removed

v 1— When ſinners are moſt ſecure, and at eaſe, then will the terrible woes of God ſuddenly ſurprize them We have here,

1 A deſcription of their pride, ſecurity, and ſenſuality

[1] They were puffed up with confidence on their wealth and fortreſſes, and conceited they would be their defence from the judgments threatened *They are at eaſe in Zion*, wallowing in affluence *and truſt in the mountain of Samaria*, the city by art and nature being ſtrongly fortified, *which are named the chief of the nations*, the principal perſons of Judah and Iſrael, who dwelt in Zion and Samaria, *to whom the houſe of Iſrael came*, for judgment, or theſe cities were the capitals of the two nations, and thither the people reſorted Yet, illuſtrious and great as Zion and Samaria were, they need not look far to find other places diſtinguiſhed in the annals of fame, but now reduced to ruin, ſuch as Calneh, *Gen* x 10 Hemath and Gath, *Kings* xvii 17 chief cities of kingdoms greater than Iſrael and Judah, and their territories more extenſive, *ver* 2 and if they fell from their towering height of pride, let not Zion and Samaria be ſecure *Note*, (1) Greatneſs is too apt to beget pride (2) Others falls ſhould be our warning

[2] They promiſed themſelves impunity in their iniquities *They put far away the evil day*, keeping it out of their thoughts, leſt it ſhould damp their joys, or flattering themſelves with long years of indulgence, unaffected with judgment which appeared so diſtant, or perhaps never would come, *and cauſe the ſeat of violence to come near*, acting with injuſtice and oppreſſion, on the preſumption of not being called to account for their tranſgreſſions Thus the hope of impunity emboldens ſinners to commit iniquity

[3] They ſunk into ſenſuality, and abuſed their abundance to miniſter to their indolence, luxury, and carnal delights *They lie upon beds of ivory*, &c not that any of theſe things in themſelves are evil, or, temperately uſed, are forbidden, the ſin was placing their affections on theſe things, abuſing them to intemperance, ſquandering their time and wealth, which ſhould be otherwiſe employed, and racking their inventions for new amuſements, a conduct peculiarly unſeaſonable when the miſeries of the land called for mourning and humiliation, *but they are not grieved for the affliction of Joſeph*, either for the breaches the nation had ſuſtained, or the greater evils threatned, or they did not ſympathize with thoſe of their brethren who were in trouble, too intent upon their own pleaſures to care about others pains *Note*, (1) They who live in a round of diſſipation and amuſements are as effectually alienated from God as if they were ſunk in groſſer exceſſes (2) When pleaſure is made the grand purſuit and happineſs, every thought and object are ſhunned which would intrude ſerious reflection

2 For theſe things God denounces a woe againſt them, v 7. *Therefore now ſhall they go captive with the firſt that go captive, and the banquet of them that ſtretched themſelves ſhall be removed* they ſhall experience an awful change The chief in ſin ſhall be the firſt in ſuffering, their palaces ſhall be turned into houſes of bondage, their indolence into hard ſervitude, their bowls of wine and fatted calves ſhall be exchanged for bread and water, from beds of ivory they ſhall be reduced to lye on the cold earth, and their muſic ſhall be loſt in groans.

8 [n] The Lord GOD hath ſworn by himſelf, ſaith
the LORD, the God of hoſts, I abhor the excellency
of Jacob, and hate his palaces therefore will I deliver
up the city, with † all that is therein 9 And it ſhall
come to paſs, that [o] if there remain ten in one houſe,
that they ſhall die 10 And a man's uncle ſhall take
him up, and he [p] that burneth him, to bring out the
bones out of the houſe, and ſhall ſay unto him that *is*
by the ſides of the houſe, *Is there* yet *any* with thee?
and he ſhall ſay, No then ſhall he ſay, [q] Hold thy
tongue, for ‡ we may not make mention of the name
of the LORD 11 For behold, the LORD commandeth,
and he will ſmite the great houſe with § breaches,
and the little houſe with clefts 12 ¶ Shall horſes run
upon the rock? will *one* plow *there* with oxen? for [s] ye
have turned judgment into gall, and the fruit of righteouſneſs
into hemlock 13 Ye which rejoice in a thing
of nought, which ſay, [t] Have we not taken to us horns
by our own ſtrength? 14 But behold, [u] I will raiſe up
againſt you a nation, O houſe of Iſrael, ſaith the LORD,
the God of hoſts, and they ſhall afflict you from the
entering in of Hemath, unto the ∥ river of the wilderneſs

n Jer li 14 Heb vi 13, 17 † Heb. The fulneſs thereof o Chap v 3 p 1 Sam xxxi 12 q Chap v 13 ‡ Or they will not, or have not § Or droppings r Chap ii 5 s Hoſ x 4 Chap v 7 t Dan iv 30 u Jer v 15 ∥ Or valley

v 8—14 As the ſins of Iſrael cried for vengeance, we here find it bound upon them by the tremendous oath of God that cannot lie And wo unto the ſinner concerning whom he ſhall thus ſwear in wrath to pour forth upon him the fierceneſs of his indignation

1 He declares his abhorrence of them, and his determined purpoſe to deliver them into the hand of their enemies Their *excellency*, their cities, fortreſſes, and treaſures, on which they prided themſelves, and their *palaces*, built by unrighteouſneſs, are hateful, and under a curſe, doomed to be the prey of an invading foe, when their capital, with all therein, ſhould be beſieged and taken *Note*, They who are the objects of God's hatred are miſerable indeed!

2 The peſtilence or famine ſhall devour thoſe that the ſword hath ſpared If ten men eſcape in one houſe, *they ſhall all die*, and a man's neareſt relation be obliged to do the laſt offices to the dead corpſe, the mortality being ſo univerſal *And when he that burneth* goes round to bring out *the bones* of the dead, to ſuch ſkeletons were they probably reduced who died by famine, and ſhall aſk of the laſt ſurvivor that is in the houſe, *Is there yet any with thee? he ſhall ſay, No* Then he without ſhall reply, *Hold thy tongue, for we may not make mention of the name of the Lord* Either this is the language of their impenitence, diſcouraging all humbling applications to God, or of their deſpair, as if their caſe was hopeleſs, and it was in vain to pray, or of their repentance, forbidding the ſurvivor to murmur, ſince all their ſufferings were no more than their ſins had juſtly provoked

3 Their houſes ſhall be deſtroyed *He will ſmite the great houſe with breaches, and the little houſe with clefts*, neither rich nor poor ſhall eſcape ſince both are involved in guilt, he commands execution to paſs on them alike, for he is no reſpecter of perſons

4 All methods that could be taken for their good would be utterly fruitleſs, as if one ſhould attempt to plow and harrow a rock,

Before Christ 787

rock, so hardened and impenetrable were their hearts, *v.* 12. The past labours of the prophets had been ineffectual, and their future ones promised no better ſucceſs; *for they* perſiſted in their wicked ways, *ye have turned judgment into gall, and the fruit of righteouſneſs into hemlock*: inſtead of rendering juſtice to the injured, they but aggravated their oppreſſion by their unrighteous deciſions, under the formalities of law. *Ye which rejoice in a thing of nought*, in their idols, their wealth, their power, which, againſt God's judgments, would afford no more protection than a ſtraw againſt the ſtroke of the battle-ax; *which ſay, Have we not taken to us horns by our own ſtrength?* have we not obtained victory over our enemies by our own arm, and are we not able in ſelf-ſufficiency to ſtand our ground againſt every foe? Such was the language of their proud hearts, and they dared utter theſe vain boaſtings, to God's great diſhonour. *Note*, (1.) Proſperity neceſſarily increaſes the pride of thoſe who forget God. (2.) They who flatter themſelves with the conceit of their own goodneſs, and the ſtrength of their own reſolutions, *rejoice in a thing of nought*.

5. Their whole land ſhall be ſubdued and deſtroyed. *The Lord God of hoſts*, againſt whom they had behaved ſo exceeding proudly, he that hath the armies of heaven and earth at his command, will ſend *a nation* againſt them, the Aſſyrians, *to afflict them* with all the miſeries of a deſtructive war, and at laſt to carry them captive into a ſtrange land, *from the entering in of Hemath unto the river of the wilderneſs*, from one end of Iſrael to the other, 2 *Kings* xiv. 25. for when God begins he will make an end, and he never wants inſtruments of vengeance to execute his righteous decrees.

CHAP. VII.

In this chapter we have, 1. Iſrael threatened with leſſer judgments, but reprieved, and the judgments turned away at the prayer of Amos, ver. 1—6. 2. God's patience is at length worn out by their obſtinacy, and they are ſentenced to utter ruin, ver. 7—9. 3. Amaziah informs againſt Amos, ver. 10, 11. and doth what he can to rid the country of him as a public nuiſance, ver. 12, 13. 4. Amos juſtifies himſelf in what he did as a prophet, ver. 14, 15. and denounceth the judgments of God againſt his perſecutor, ver. 16, 17.

1 THUS hath the Lord GOD ſhewed unto me,
and behold, [a] he formed † graſhoppers in the
beginning of the ſhooting up of the latter growth, and
lo *it was* the latter growth after the king's mowings.
2 And it came to paſs, *that* when they had made an
end of eating the graſs of the land, then I ſaid, O Lord
GOD, forgive, I beſeech thee, [b] ‡ by whom ſhall Jacob
ariſe? for he *is* ſmall. 3 [c] The LORD repented for
this: It ſhall not be, ſaith the LORD. 4 ¶ Thus hath
the Lord GOD ſhewed unto me, and behold, the Lord
GOD called to contend by fire, and it devoured the
great deep, and did eat up a part. 5 Then ſaid I, O
Lord GOD, [d] ceaſe, I beſeech thee, [e] by whom ſhall
Jacob ariſe? for he *is* ſmall. 6 The LORD repented
for this: This alſo ſhall not be, ſaith the Lord GOD.
7 ¶ Thus he ſhewed me, and behold, the LORD ſtood
upon a wall *made* by a plumb-line, with a plumb-line in
his hand. 8 And the LORD ſaid unto me, Amos,
what ſeeſt thou? And I ſaid, A plumb-line. Then ſaid
the LORD, Behold, [f] I will ſet a plumb-line in the
midſt of my people Iſrael, [g] I will not again paſs by
them any more. 9 And [h] the high places of Iſaac ſhall
be deſolate, and the ſanctuaries of Iſrael ſhall be laid
waſte, and [i] I will riſe againſt the houſe of Jeroboam
with the ſword.

a Chap. iv. 9. † Or, green worms. b Iſa. li. 19. ‡ Or, who of, or, for Jacob ſhall ſtand. c Jonah iii. 10. d Ex. xxxii. 11. e Ver. 2. f Kings [illegible] Chap. viii. h [illegible] i [illegible] 1 Kings xv. 10.

v. 1—9. The prophet ſpoke before what he heard from God in words; here he relates what was revealed to him in viſion; and both confirming the ſame event, the ruin of a rebellious people. We have,

1. The judgment of graſhoppers or locuſts, which are removed at the prophet's interceſſion. They were *formed* in the viſion by God's hand, and commiſſioned to devour the after-graſs, after the firſt mowing. Some underſtand this figuratively of the Aſſyrian army, which, under Pul their king, plundered the country, 2 *Kings* xv. 19. after it had begun to revive a little under Jeroboam, 2 *Kings* xiv. 25. from the ravages it had before ſuffered, *ſee* 2 *Kings* xiii. 3—22. Affected with the melancholy ſcene, the prophet becomes an earneſt advocate for the miſerable land: *then I ſaid, O Lord, forgive, I beſeech thee*. Sin was the cauſe of all their ſuffering, and the removal of that was the great object of the prophet's prayer. *Ceaſe, I beſeech thee*, the unequal controverſy, which muſt elſe quickly conſume this ſinful people, unable to ſtand before God's judgments: and

he enforces his plea by their relation to him as the ſeed of Jacob, the low eſtate of miſery to which they were already reduced, and the abſolute deſpair into which they muſt fall, unleſs he was pleaſed graciouſly to pity, pardon, and ſave them. *By whom ſhall Jacob ariſe, for he is ſmall?* The Lord heard and was intreated, he *repented for this*, removed this afflictive diſpenſation of his providence at the prophet's inſtance. *It ſhall not be, ſaith the Lord*, either the locuſts, or the Aſſyrian army, ſhall not be permitted utterly to deſtroy the land, *See* 2 *Kings* xv. 19, 20. *Note*, (1.) Whilſt we declare to ſinners the judgments they provoke, every true prophet cannot but be an earneſt advocate to avert them, ſo far is he from deſiring the woful day. (2.) Sin is the cauſe of every human miſery, and the pardon of that is to be ſought in the firſt place, in order to open the door for every other mercy. (3.) The low and afflicted ſtate of the church is a powerful argument to plead for preſent help. (4.) Powerfully effectual and mightily availing is the fervent prayer of a righteous man. Such advocates with God are the greateſt bleſſings to their country.

2. Another judgment by fire ſucceeds, and this alſo is extinguiſhed at the prophet's prayer. *The Lord called to contend by fire*, and ready at his commands the elements obey him: *it devoured the great deep*, it ſeemed to dry up the ocean, *and did eat up a part* of the earth, which may refer either to ſome remarkable viſitation of lightening, conſuming part of their country, or to the intenſe heat of the ſun, occaſioning a drought through the land, and conſuming them by famine; or figuratively deſcribes the devaſtations of the Aſſyrian army under Tiglath Pileſer, 2 *Kings* xv. 29. and the captivity of a part of the land. Hereupon the prophet repeats his former requeſt, and again ſucceeds in preventing their final ruin. *Note*, (1.) God hath many arrows in his quiver, and when one judgment doth not humble a ſinful ſoul, he will ſend another. (2.) God is not unwilling to multiply his pardons, if we are not weary in waiting upon him with our prayers.

3. In a third viſion their final ruin is predicted, for reprieves are not pardons; and they whom neither mercies nor judgments effectually work upon, may expect to be at laſt utterly abandoned of God. *And he ſhewed me, and behold the Lord ſtood upon a wall made by a plumb-line*: the Jewiſh ſtate was like a wall of adamant, ſtrong, and raiſed by the divine architect ſtrait and regular; and now he came, *with a plumb-line in his hand*, to diſcover their crookedneſs, who had ſo departed from the line of duty and his pure worſhip. On the proof therefore of their incorrigible perverſeneſs, he now reſolves to paſs by *them no more*, and therefore the *prophet may no more intercede for them*. Their doom is fixed; their high places ſhall be deſtroyed, their idol-temples demoliſhed, notwithſtanding the holy progenitors from whom they deſcended, which they might flatter themſelves would be their protection; and the houſe of Jeroboam, the great author of their apoſtacy from God, ſhall be cut off, as was ſhortly after accompliſhed by Shallum, 2 *Kings* xv. 10. *Note*, (1.) No outward privileges will protect apoſtates from ruin. (2.) Walls of adamant are no defence againſt God's judgments. (3.) In all God's viſitations he acts with ſtricteſt juſtice, ſo that they who ſuffer have not the ſhadow of complaint. (4.) Though God bears long with ſinners, he will not bear always: vengeance, though ſlow, is ſure.

10 ¶ Then Amaziah [k] the prieſt of Beth-el ſent to
[l] Jeroboam king of Iſrael, ſaying, Amos hath [m] conſpired
againſt thee in the midſt of the houſe of Iſrael:
the land is not able to bear all his words. 11 For
thus Amos ſaith, [n] Jeroboam ſhall die by the ſword, and
Iſrael ſhall ſurely be led away captive out of their own
land. 12 Alſo Amaziah ſaid unto Amos, O thou ſeer,
go, flee thee away into the land of Judah, and there eat
bread, and propheſy there: 13 But [o] propheſy not
again any more at Beth-el: for [p] it *is* the king's chapel,
and it *is* the ‡ king's court. 14 ¶ Then anſwered
Amos, and ſaid to Amaziah, I *was* no prophet, neither
was I [q] a prophet's ſon; [r] but I *was* an herdman, and a
gatherer of § ſycomore-fruit. 15 And the LORD took
me as I followed the flock, and the LORD ſaid unto
me, Go, propheſy unto my people Iſrael. 16 ¶ Now
therefore hear thou the word of the LORD: thou ſayeſt,
Propheſy not againſt Iſrael, and [t] drop not *thy word*
againſt the houſe of Iſaac. 17 [u] Therefore thus ſaith
the LORD; [x] Thy wife ſhall be an harlot in the city,
and thy ſons and thy daughters ſhall fall by the ſword,
and thy land ſhall be divided by line; and thou ſhalt
die in a polluted land: and [y] Iſrael ſhall ſurely go into
captivity forth of his land.

k 1 Kings xii. 32. Jer. xx. 1, 2. l 2 Kings xiv. 23. m Jer. xxvi. 8. n Ver. 9. Chap. ii. 12. p 1 Kings xii. 32. ‡ Heb. Houſe of the kingdom. q 1 Kings xx. 35. r Chap. i. 1. Zech. xiii. 5. § Or, wild figs. s Chap. ii. 12. Ver. 13. Mic. ii. 6. t Ezek. xxi. 2. u Jer. xxviii. 12. Chap. xxix. 21, 25. x Hoſ. iv. 13. y 2 Kings xv. 29. & xvii. 6.

v. 10—17. From the kindneſs which the prophet had ſhewn by his interceſſion in behalf of the land, and the manifeſt deſign of all the judgments threatened, which was to lead them to repentance, we might have expected the moſt grateful returns:

would

Before Christ 787

would have been made to their affectionate friend, and faithful reprover; but let not the best of men be surprized at the basest ingratitude they meet with.

1 Amaziah, the *priest* of Bethel, or *prince*, the chief ruler perhaps both in ecclesiastical and civil affairs, could not bear the threatnings of the prophet, and therefore transmits to court an accusation against him as a traitor against the nation, as one that sowed sedition among the people, and spirited them up to murder the king, so that if timely care was not taken, the land would not be able *to bear his words*: either they would breed a revolt, or the country was so exasperated against him, that he would insinuate nothing could be more popular act than to silence or punish him. *For thus Amos saith, Jeroboam shall die by the sword, and Israel shall surely be led away captive out of their own land*; which was partly false, and partly true. Israel's ruin indeed the prophet foretold, but Amaziah suppresses the circumstances of Amos's intercession, and his declarations that their repentance would prevent the judgment. As for Jeroboam's death, the prophet said no such thing: the threatning was against his house, not himself, *v.* 9. but this was easily perverted. *Note*, (1.) Apostate priests are the bitterest persecutors of the true prophets. (2.) It is a common method with designing men to represent the faithful as seditious, and troublers of the land, tho' in fact they are the best friends of it. (3.) They who bear testimony for God against men's sins, may expect to meet with the most malicious insinuations against them, and to have their words often tortured to a meaning of which they never dreamt.

2. Amaziah endeavours to drive Amos out of the country. What answer he received from court is not said; it should seem not one so favourable as he expected, and therefore to be rid of him at any rate, by pretending regard for his safety, which he insinuates would be in danger, he advises him to quit Bethel, and fly to Judah, where he would be better received and rewarded; judging from his own case that Amos prophesied for bread, *v.* 12. which at Bethel he would never get. Besides, the place was improper; it was *the king's chapel*, and *court*, where his plain speaking could not fail of being disagreeable; court-preaching requiring soft words, and smooth prophecies: nor could he think of making converts there, where the torrent ran so strong against him, and would the more endanger his safety, the more he attempted to oppose it. *Note*, (1.) False and faithless prophets measure the faithful by themselves, and think their only motives are that filthy lucre and worldly esteem which they adore. (2.) A zealous active minister is a burdensome stone in the eyes of the lazy and negligent, especially when he happens to be in a public situation, where his conduct more glaringly reflects on theirs, and therefore by fair means or foul they will strive to get rid of him.

3. Amos answers this wicked priest with the steadiness which became his office, and as one not to be intimidated by danger from the discharge of his duty. As for himself, he was not descended from a prophet, or bred up in their schools, but was *an herdsman, and a gatherer of sycamore-fruit*, to serve his family or cattle; and from this employment the Lord called him to *go and prophesy unto Israel*. His divine mission therefore authorized him; he durst not desert his post, since he was sent thither of God; and as he had been accustomed to hard fare, he was the better prepared to meet with any hardships in the course of his ministry, though they who dared oppose and oppress him should suffer for it; and Amaziah, who had forbid him to prophesy, among the first. *His wife* shall become *an harlot*, and her wickedness reflect infamy on him: his children *shall fall by the sword* of an enemy, and his eyes shall behold it; his estate shall be divided among the conquerors, and himself survive these miseries, to die a wretched captive in a polluted land: *and Israel shall surely go into captivity forth of his land*, as he would see fatally verified. *Note*, (1.) God often chuses weak and unlikely instruments; but whom he sends he will both qualify them for their office, and strengthen them to discharge it faithfully. (2.) Persecutors of God's prophets shall shortly meet their fearful doom. (3.) It is in vain to attempt silencing those whom God hath commanded to speak. (4.) God's word will surely take place, whatever opposition sinners may make against it.

CHAP. VIII.

Sinful times are here attended with sorrowful times, so necessary is the connection between them. It is threatned again and again that their laughter shall be turned into mourning. 1. By the vision of a basket of summer-fruit is signified the hastning on of their ruin, ver. 1—3. *2. Oppressors are here called to an account for their cheating of the poor, and their destruction is foretold,* ver. 4—10. *3. A famine of the word of God is here made the punishment of a people that go a whoring after other gods,* ver. 11—14.

1 THUS hath the Lord GOD shewed unto me,
and behold, a basket of summer-fruit. 2 And
he said, Amos, what seest thou? and I said, A basket
of summer-fruit. Then said the LORD unto me,
a The end is come upon my people of Israel, b I will not
again pass by them any more. 3 And c the songs of
the temple † shall be howlings in that day, saith the
Lord GOD: there shall be many dead bodies in every
place, d they shall cast *them* forth with silence.

a Ezek. vii. 2, 6. b Chap. vii. 8. c Chap. v. 23. † Heb. Shall howl. d Chap. vi. 9, 10.

v. 1—3. The prophet is called upon to attend to another vision, and lo! a basket of summer-fruit stood before him, an emblem of that people ripe for destruction, and ready to be devoured by their enemies.

1. Their end is come; they have been suffered like fruit to grow till they were fully ripe, and now are to be spared no longer. God's patience is wearied out, and their ruin resolved. Though God bears long, the impenitent sinner's fate will come at last.

2. Their ruin will be terrible. *The songs of the temple shall be howlings in that day, saith the Lord God*; the places where their idols praises resounded, now shall be filled with shrieks and groans; and *there shall be many dead bodies in every place*, slain by the sword, the famine, or the pestilence: *they shall cast them forth in silence*, without any funeral solemnity, or expression of grief, as if the dead were happier than the living; or sullenly submitting, because they cannot help themselves; or bidding others *be silent*, and not take the least notice of what might otherwise the besieged, or encourage their enemies. *Note*, (1.) Sinful mirth will end in bitter mourning. (2.) God's judgments do often but harden the hearts of the impenitent.

4 ¶ Hear this, O ye that e swallow up the needy,
even to make the poor of the land to fail, 5 Saying,
f when will the new-moon be gone, that we may sell
corn? g and the sabbath, that we may set forth wheat,
h making the ephah small, and the shekel great, and
† falsifying the balances by deceit? 6 That i we may
buy the poor for silver, and the needy for a pair of shoes,
yea, and sell the refuse of the wheat? 7 k The LORD
hath sworn by the excellency of Jacob, Surely I will
never forget any of their works. 8 l Shall not the land
tremble for this, and every one mourn that dwelleth
therein? and it shall rise up wholly as a flood; and it
shall be cast out and drowned, m as *by* the flood of
Egypt. 9 And it shall come to pass in that day, saith
the Lord GOD, that n I will cause the sun to go down
at noon, and I will darken the earth in the clear day.
10 And o I will turn your feasts into mourning, and all
your songs into lamentation; and p I will bring up sack-
cloth upon all loins, and baldness upon every head; and
q I will make it as the mourning of an only *son*, and the
end thereof as a bitter day.

e Psal. xiv. 4. Prov. xxx. 14. f Mal. i. 13. g Neh. xiii. 15, 16. h Mic. vi. 10. † Heb. Perverting the balances of deceit. i Hos. xii. 7. Chap. ii. 6. k Chap. vi. 8. l Hos. iv. 3. m Chap. ix. 5. n Job v. 14. Isa. xiii. 10. & lix. 9, 10. Jer. xv. 9. o Tobit ii. 6. p Isa. xv. 2, 3. Jer. xlviii. 37. Ezek. vii. 18. q Jer. vi. 26. Zech. xii. 10.

v. 4—10. A people whose iniquities were so flagrant may expect the judgment they have provoked.

1. Their sins were heinous. *They swallow up the needy*, by oppression and injustice, *even to make the poor of the land to fail*, starving them for want of necessary food. So addicted were they to covetousness, that, though they kept up the form of religion, they were tired and weary of the service, longing for the sacred hours of the sabbath and new moons to be gone, that they might resume their work and merchandize, which met with this unwelcome interruption, *v.* 5. nor did they make any conscience how they got their wealth, so they did but get it. They sold by a small measure, *making the ephah small*; but, when they received money, they would use their own weights, *making the shekel great*, refusing to take it unless it weighed more than it ought; and falsified *the balances by deceit*, that so the scale might always hang in their favour; and by such fraudulent practices they so impoverished their poor neighbours, that they were forced to sell themselves to their oppressive masters, they *buy the poor for silver, and the needy for a pair of shoes*, to such necessities were they reduced; *yea, and sell the refuse of the wheat*, making them take the corn that was not fit for bread, and exacting their own price for it. *Note*, (1.) Covetousness is destitute of all bowels and mercies. (2.) To a worldly man the sabbath is an irksome day; and, when he is employed in religious duties, his heart goeth after his covetousness, and even on his knees the thoughts of business thrust out the thoughts of God. (3.) He who is destitute of true piety can never be an honest man.

2. Their ruin is sure and terrible, confirmed by the oath of the unchangeable God, who saith, *Surely I will never forget any of their works*, but remember them in terrible judgment: they shewed no mercy, and they shall find none. And woe to the miserable sinner that is under such a curse! *Shall not the land tremble for this?* as weary to bear such miscreants upon it, and ready to swallow them up by an earthquake, *for the* * * *and every one mourn that dwelleth therein*, shocked at the inhumanity, or confounded at the judgments sent upon the transgressors.

it

it shall rise up wholly as a flood, the calamity overwhelming the land, as Egypt was covered with the overflowing of the Nile, *v* 9. *And it shall come to pass in that day, saith the Lord God, that I will cause the sun to go down at noon, and I will darken the earth in the clear day*: in the midst of their prosperity their whole kingdom, with the princes and nobles, shall be destroyed suddenly and unexpectedly, or when these oppressors were in the midst of life and prosperity, death should at a stroke close their eyes in darkness, and send them to the grave. *And I will turn your feasts into mourning, and all your songs into lamentation*, when their temples destroyed, their country desolate, themselves captives, every sound of joy would be banished, and with every expressive sign of bitter woe they would bewail their hopeless miseries, as *the mourning of an only son, and the end thereof as a bitter day*, no prospect remaining of the removal of these calamities. *Note*, (1.) Riches got by rapine, will in the end bring ruin. (2.) They who will not tremble for the sins of the land, shall be made to tremble when the threatned judgment comes. (3.) However high the oppressor may be seated, the flood of God's wrath shall overwhelm him. (4.) The sinner's mirth will end in mourning, and God sometimes is pleased to arrest him in the midst of his career of prosperity, and by a sudden stroke to send him into darkness.

11 Behold, the days come, saith the Lord GOD,
that I will send a famine in the land, not a famine of
bread, nor a thirst for water, but of hearing the words
of the LORD: 12 And they shall wander from sea to
sea, and from the north even to the east, they shall run
to and fro to seek the word of the LORD, and shall
not find *it*. 13 In that day shall the fair virgins and
young men faint for thirst. 14 They that swear by
the sin of Samaria, and say, Thy god, O Dan, liveth;
and, The manner of Beer-sheba liveth; even they
shall fall, and never rise up again.

v. 11—14. We have had before heavy temporal judgments denounced, but here,

1. A spiritual judgment is threatned, *a famine not of bread nor of water, but of hearing the words of the Lord*, from the time of their last captivity, no more prophets shall appear to them, having rejected God and his Christ, in vain will they seek for prophets of their own, *v.* 12. and pine away in their iniquities, *v.* 13. rejected and destitute, as they are this day. *Note*, (1.) The word of God is the food of immortal souls; they must perish from whom it is withdrawn. (2.) They who have abused the means of grace they have enjoyed, are justly punished by having them removed. (3.) Among the heaviest curses of God upon a people or nation, is the taking from them the light of truth, and abandoning them to the blindness and hardness of their own hearts.

2. The ringleaders in idolatry are doomed to destruction. *They that swear by the sin of Samaria*, impious and profane, glorying in their shame, and swearing by their idols which they should have detested, *and say, Thy god, O Dan, liveth, and the manner of Beer-sheba liveth*, making their adjurations by the hated deities there placed, and the worship performed to them, *even they shall fall, and never rise up again*, driven into a captivity from which they never have returned, and it is to be feared, perishing there also eternally in their impenitence.

CHAP. IX.

In this chapter we have, 1. Judgments threatned, which the sinners shall not escape, ver. 1—4, which an Almighty power shall inflict, ver. 5, 6. which this sinful people have deserved, ver. 7, 8. and yet it shall not be an utter ruin, ver. 8. for a remnant shall escape, ver. 9. but the wicked shall perish, ver. 10. 2. Mercy promised, which was to be bestowed in the latter days, ver. 11—15. as appears by the application of it to the days of the Messiah, Acts xv. 16. And with these comfortable promises, after all the foregoing rebukes and threatnings, the book concludes.

1 I Saw the LORD standing upon the altar, and he
said, Smite the lintel of the door, that the posts
may shake: and cut them in the head, all of them; and
I will slay the last of them with the sword: he that
fleeth of them, shall not flee away, and he that escapeth
of them, shall not be delivered. 2 Though they dig
into hell, thence shall mine hand take them; though
they climb up to heaven, thence will I bring them
down. 3 And though they hide themselves in the top
of Carmel, I will search and take them out thence; and
though they be hid from my sight in the bottom of the
sea, thence will I command the serpent, and he shall
bite them. 4 And though they go into captivity before
their enemies, thence will I command the sword,
and it shall slay them: and I will set mine eyes upon
them for evil, and not for good. 5 And the Lord
GOD of hosts *is* he that toucheth the land, and it shall
melt, and all that dwell therein shall mourn, and it
shall rise up wholly like a flood, and shall be drowned
as *by* the flood of Egypt. 6 *It is* he that buildeth his
stories in the heaven, and hath founded his troop in
the earth; he that calleth for the waters of the sea, and
poureth them out upon the face of the earth: the
LORD *is* his name. 7 *Are* ye not as children of the
Ethiopians unto me, O children of Israel? saith the
LORD. Have not I brought up Israel out of the land
of Egypt? and the Philistines from Caphtor, and the
Syrians from Kir? 8 Behold, the eyes of the Lord
GOD *are* upon the sinful kingdom, and I will destroy
it from off the face of the earth; saving that I will not
utterly destroy the house of Jacob, saith the LORD. 9
For lo, I will command, and I will sift the house of
Israel among all nations, like as *corn* is sifted in a sieve,
yet shall not the least § grain fall upon the earth. 10
All the sinners of my people shall die by the sword,
which say, The evil shall not overtake nor prevent us.

v. 1—10. The judgments of God against a people devoted to destruction are here fearfully declared.

1. The awful command for the execution of these criminals is issued. *I saw the Lord standing upon the altar* at Bethel probably, as about to stamp it into powder, and destroy the idols with their worshippers, *and he said, Smite the lintel of the door, that the posts may shake*, intimating the demolition of the idol temples, *and cut them in the head all of them, and I will slay the last of them with the sword*, the king, princes, priests and people that committed idolatry there.

2. All attempts to escape from God's avenging arm will be fruitless: they shall be arrested in their flight, and no place afford them protection in this day of wrath. Could they dig into hell, it would not conceal them, or could they climb the heights of heaven, thence would he drag them down, *v.* 3. The caves or thickets of Carmel could not hide them from his all-piercing eye, nor the depths of the sea cover them, God has even there his instruments of vengeance, *v.* 3. Nay, when in a miserable captivity they might have hoped the vengeance of God would rest, the sword should still pursue them, and make them exchange a wretched life for a more tormenting death. *Note*, When God is against us it matters not who are for us, they can afford us neither help nor hope.

3. He that pronounces their doom is fully able to execute his threatnings. *The Lord God of hosts is he that toucheth the land, and it shall melt*; a touch, a frown from him can dissolve the earth, or deluge it with waters, *and all that dwell therein shall mourn* in bitterness the loss of all their substance, and whatever is dear to them besides, swallowed up in the flood of his judgments, *v.* 6. *It is he*, that great Creator of all, *who buildeth his stories in the heaven*, like a stately palace reared by his power and supported by his providence, *and hath founded his troop in the earth*, all things here below being the instruments of his pleasure, and ready to execute his command: *he that calleth for the waters of the sea, and poureth them out upon the earth*, to descend in tempests from the clouds, or burst from the bosom of the deep to punish guilty mortals, *the Lord of hosts is his name*, able to perform all the purposes of his will. As happy and safe as it is to have him our friend, so miserable and fatal must it be to have him our enemy.

4. Their iniquities had cut them off from their former honourable relation to this Almighty God. They were become, by their sins, black as Ethiopians, and would be regarded no more by him than these heathen; nor should they count upon the mercies God had shewed in bringing them from Egypt, as if these were so peculiarly distinguishing, or ensured his future favour, for he had brought *the Philistines from Caphtor*, the place of their nativity, or whither they had been carried captive; and *the Syrians from Kir*, the land of their captivity, 2 Kings xvi. 19. yet neither of these nations shared his favour, nor would escape at last his judgments. *For behold, the eyes of the Lord God are upon the sinful kingdom*, on every guilty land, especially on Israel, whose guilt was most aggravated, *and I will destroy it from off the face of the earth*, as was done by Salmaneser. *Note*, When profession degenerates, and in spirit depart from God, their privileges will stand them in no stead, but rather aggravate their guilt beyond that of the vilest heathen.

5. A remnant of Israel, even those who have preserved their fidelity, shall be preserved amidst the general ruin. *I will not utterly destroy the house of Jacob, saith the Lord*, his eye beholds the men that sigh, and cry for all the abominations of the land, and they shall be hid in the day of his fierce anger. *For lo, I will command*, by his over-ruling providence, *and I will sift the house of Israel among all nations, as corn is sifted in a sieve*, all the affliction coming upon them shall be so ordered as to separate the precious from the vile: *yet shall not the least grain fall upon the*

Before Christ 787

the earth, or *the leaſt ſtone*, not one of the faithful ſhall periſh, but *all the ſinners of my people ſhall die by the ſword, which ſay, The evil ſhall not overtake nor prevent us*, ſo daring in wickedneſs were they grown, but ſhall find, to their everlaſting confuſion, the vanity of their impious boaſts *Note*, (1) Though God's ſpiritual Iſrael are ſcattered in the world that lieth in wickedneſs, not one of them ſhall periſh, and the afflictions they meet with ſhall but ſerve to ſeparate them for God, and cleanſe them from the chaff of corruption, that they may be pure in heart (2) When the ſinner moſt confidently flatters himſelf with aſſurances of impunity, there is a lie in his right hand, and vengeance is at his heels

11 ¶ In that day [s] will I raiſe up the tabernacle of
David that is fallen, and † cloſe up the breaches thereof,
and I will raiſe up his ruins, and I will build it as in
the days of old 12 [t] That they may poſſeſs the rem-
nant of [u] Edom, and of all the heathen, ‡ which are
called by my name, ſaith the LORD that doth this
13 Behold, the days come, ſaith the LORD, that [x] the
plowmen ſhall overtake the reaper, and the treader of
grapes him that ſoweth ſeed, and [y] the mountains ſhall
drop ‖ ſweet wine, and all the hills ſhall melt 14
And [z] I will bring again the captivity of my people of
Iſrael, and [a] they ſhall build the waſte cities, and inhabit
them, and they ſhall plant vineyards, and drink the wine
thereof, they ſhall alſo make gardens, and eat the fruit
of them 15 And I will plant them upon their land,
and [b] they ſhall no more be pulled up out of their land
which I have given them, ſaith the LORD thy God

[s] Acts xv 16 17 † Heb Hedge, or wall [t] Obad 19 [u] Num xxiv 18 ‡ Heb. Upon whom my name is called [x] Lev xxvi 5 [y] Joel iii 18 ‖ Or new wine [z] Ezek xxxvii 21 Hoſ i 11 [a] Iſa lxv 21 [b] Joel iii 20

v 11—15 With one bright beam of hope the prophecy cloſes, and in the promiſed Meſſiah, ſtill a glorious proſpect remains of Iſrael's reſtoration, for to him bear all the prophets witneſs

1 In the Meſſiah ſhall the glory of David's throne be reſtored *In that day will I raiſe up the tabernacle of David that is fallen, and cloſe up the breaches thereof, and I will raiſe up his ruins, and I will build it as in the days of old*, to what event this refers, we can have no doubt, having an infallible interpreter for our guide, *Acts* xv. 16 When Chriſt came into the world, the church, the ſpiritual kingdom of our David, was fallen as low as the royal family from whence the Redeemer ſprung, but in and by him the breaches were repaired, the goſpel of the kingdom was preached at his command, and religion revived its drooping head, and ſhone more glorioully than in the brighteſt days of old Nor was the church now confined to one nation or people, but Gentiles, as well as Jews, became the happy ſubjects of Chriſt's government A remnant of Edom, and from the lands of the heathen ſhall now become the church's poſſeſſion, and be called by the name of Chriſt, admitted into the fellowſhip and privileges of the goſpel, *ſaith the Lord who doth this*, whoſe power and grace can and will accompliſh what he hath promiſed, and bleſſed be his name for what we have ſeen of the fulfilment hereof, and ſhall ſee daily, till the fulneſs of the Gentiles be come in, and all the Iſrael of God be finally ſaved

2 The moſt abundant meaſure of ſpiritual bleſſings will then be diffuſed, ſignified by images of the moſt amazing plenty, the harveſt and vintage being ſo vaſt, that it ſhould continue till ſeed time again, and the very mountains, as if diſſolved, pour down ſtreams of wine, and milk, and honey, the gifts, the graces, and conſolations of the holy ghoſt in the times of the goſpel, being beſtowed in a more eminent and extenſive manner than ever before

3 The captivity of God's Iſrael will then be for ever at an end, they ſhall be delivered from the bondage of corruption into the glorious liberty of the ſons of God, and help to build the walls of the ſpiritual temple, enjoying, as members of the church of Chriſt, that peace, proſperity, and plenty of heavenly bleſſings, which would be better than the fruit of gardens or vineyards, *v* 14 Though ſome ſuppoſe this literally will be fulfilled, and that the Jews, when converted to Chriſt in the latter day, will be *planted in their own land*, and enjoy all that outward proſperity here deſcribed

4 This happy eſtate of God's Iſrael ſhall never more be interrupted *They ſhall no more be pulled up out of their land which I have given them, ſaith the Lord thy God*, he will preſerve them alike from the power of their corruptions within, as well as from their ſpiritual enemies without, none of whom ſhall ever pluck the weakeſt believer out of his hands, God, their God, their covenant God, ſhall fulfill his promiſes, and ſecure their ſtability for ever, till the bleſſed day comes, that they ſhall be taken out of the reach of every foe, and be brought to the heavenly Canaan, to the manſions of eternal reſt and glory, provided for them before the foundations of the world

THE EVANGELICAL EXPOSITOR; OR, A PRACTICAL COMMENT Upon the PROPHECY of OBADIAH.

VARIOUS have been the conjectures concerning Obadiah, who or from whence he was, but they are wholly uncertain. At what time he wrote is also dubious, some making him cotemporary with Hosea, Joel, and Amos, whilst others place him later, with Jeremiah and Ezekiel. His name signifies a Servant of the LORD, *and his prophecy is concerning Edom, a nation nearly allied to the Jews, but deriving from Esau their fathers hereditary enmity against them, and their ruin is the burden of this little volume.*

CHAP. I.

Before Christ 587.

We have, after the preface, ver. 1. [1.] Threatnings against Edom. (1.) That their pride should be humbled, ver. 2—4. (2.) Their wealth plundered, ver. 5—7. (3.) Their wisdom infatuated, ver. 8, 9. (4.) Their spiteful carriage towards God's Israel avenged, ver. 10—16. [2.] Gracious promises to Israel, that they shall be victorious over the Edomites, ver. 17—20. And that the kingdom of the Messiah shall be set up, by the bringing in the great salvation, ver. 21.

1 THE vision of † Obadiah. Thus saith the
Lord GOD, ᵃ concerning Edom, ᵇ we have
heard a rumour from the LORD, and an
ambassador is sent among the heathen, A-
rise ye, and let us rise up against her in battle. 2 Be-
hold, I have made thee small among the heathen: thou
art greatly despised. 3 ¶ The pride of thine heart hath
deceived thee, thou that dwellest in the clefts of ᶜ the
rock, whose habitation *is* high; ᵈ that saith in his heart,
Who shall bring me down to the ground? 4 ᵉ Though
thou exalt *thyself* as the eagle, and though thou set thy
nest among the stars, thence will I bring thee down,
saith the LORD. 5 ᶠ If thieves came to thee, if rob-
bers by night (how art thou cut off!) would they not
have stolen till they had enough? if the grape gatherers
came to thee, ᵍ would they not leave ‡ *some* grapes? 6
How are *the things* of Esau searched out! *how* are his hid
things sought up? 7 All the men of thy confederacy
have brought thee *even* to the border: the men ‖ that
were at peace with thee have deceived thee, *and* prevailed
against thee; § *they that eat* thy bread, have laid a wound
under thee: *there is* none understanding † in him. 8 ʰ
Shall I not in that day, saith the LORD, even destroy
the wise *men* out of Edom, and understanding out of the
mount of Esau? 9 And thy mighty men, O Teman,
shall be dismayed, to the end that every one of the mount
of Esau may be cut off by slaughter.

v. 1—9. *The vision of Obadiah concerning Edom,* the inveterate enemy of God's people of old, and probably the type and figure of all the Antichristian foes, whether Papal, Pagan, or Mahometan, which, like these of old, shall utterly be destroyed at the last.

1. An ambassador is sent among the heathen, to gather them together to battle against Idumea, either the prophet, or some other minister of providence, or a herald dispatched by Nebuchadnezzar to summon his warriors to assemble, and his confederates to come to his assistance, *See Jer.* xlix. 15. for when God hath work to do, he hath in his hands instruments ever ready.

2. Edom shall be ruined, and all her confidences shall fail, for God is her enemy. Her heathen neighbours shall treat her as little and contemptible, *v.* 3. and though she flatters herself they have the same high opinion of her she hath of herself, *her pride hath deceived her,* ver. 3. as it generally does those who fancy others value them as much as they do themselves. She thought, because her situation was strong amidst high rocks, where nature, as well as art, contributed to her security, that she could there defy the impotent attack of all her foes, *v.* 3. Thus sinners, secure in self-confidence, despise the wrath which is ready to overtake them: but though she were as high as the rock or the eagle's nest, yea, though her battlements reached to the stars, *thence will I bring thee down, saith the Lord,* before whose judgment the proudest sinner cannot stand. Her wealth shall become a prey to her enemies, and the ravagers of the Chaldeans shall utterly spoil the country. Though robbers by night plunder an house, they leave something behind, and the most careful grape-gatherers cannot glean every cluster; but these shall ransack every secret place, and spare nothing, leaving the land bare as a rock, *v.* 5, 6. Do the Edomites place dependance on their allies? they will disappoint their expectations: though they received their ambassador with respect, and attended them to their borders, or joined their forces as auxiliaries, and marched to the borders of Edom as if to fight their enemies, receiving subsidies and provisions from the Edomites, and pretending firm attachment to their cause, yet will they betray it, desert to their invaders, and turn their arms against those who hired them; who, whilst they leaned on them for support, feel from their pretended friendly arm, a secret mortal wound, *v.* 7. Not all the wisdom of their wise men, nor the courage

Before Christ 587

of their warriors, will then be able to avail them God hath infatuated the counſels of the one, and panic fear ſeizes the others, doomed to the ſlaughter, ſo that not a man of them ſhall eſcape Thus when God contends he will ſurely overcome our wiſdom will prove folly, our ſtrength weakneſs, our confidence deluſion, when he is our foe

ᶦ Gen xxvii 41 Pſ cxxxvii 7 Ezek xxv 12 & xxxv 5 Am i 11 ᵏ Ezek xxxv 9 Mal i 4 ˡ Jer li 9, 11 † Or his ſubſtance. ᵐ Joel iii 3 ⁿ Pſ l 18 ᵒ Job xxxi 29 ‡ Heb Magnified thy mouth ᵖ Pſ cxxxvii 7 § Or forces ‖ Or ſhut up. ᑫ Ezek xxxv 15 Jam ii 13 ʳ Jer xxv 29 & xlix 12 Joel iii 17 ˢ 1 Pet iv 17 † Or ſup up

10 ¶ ᶦ For *thy* violence againſt thy brother Jacob,
ſhame ſhall cover thee, and ᵏ thou ſhalt be cut off for
ever 11 In the day that thou ſtoodeſt on the other
ſide, in the day that ˡ the ſtrangers carried away captive
† his forces, and foreigners entred into his gates, and
ᵐ caſt lots upon Jeruſalem, even thou ⁿ *waſt* as one of
them 12 But thou ſhouldſt not have looked on the
day of thy brother, in the day that he became a ſtranger,
ᵒ neither ſhouldſt thou have rejoiced over the children of
Judah in the day of their deſtruction, neither ſhouldſt
thou have ‡ ſpoken proudly in the day of diſtreſs
13 ᵖ Thou ſhouldſt not have entred into the gate of my
people in the day of their calamity, yea, thou ſhouldſt
not have looked on their affliction in the day of their
calamity, nor have laid *hands* on their § ſubſtance in
the day of their calamity 14 Neither ſhouldſt thou
have ſtood in the croſs-way, to cut off thoſe of his that
did eſcape, neither ſhouldſt thou have ‖ delivered up
thoſe of his that did remain in the day of diſtreſs
15 For the day of the LORD *is* near upon all the
heathen ᑫ as thou haſt done, it ſhall be done unto thee,
thy reward ſhall return upon thine own head 16 For
ʳ as ye have drunk upon my holy mountain, *ſo* ſhall all
the heathen drink continually, ˢ yea, they ſhall drink,
and they ſhall † ſwallow down, and they ſhall be as
though they had not been

v 10—16 If Edom's doom be heavy, her ſins have provoked it, and, amidſt all the other iniquities of that devoted people, none come deeper into the account than their *violence againſt* their *brother Jacob*, whoſe relation to them by blood, and the peculiar favour God had ſhewn him, ſhou'd have engaged their affection and aſſiſtance in the day of calamity but too often we ſee neareſt relations ſhew us the leaſt regard

1 They had, with moſt malicious enmity, rejoiced in the ruin of Iſrael, and in a variety of inſtances helped forward their diſtreſs God tells them what *they ſhould not have done*, and therein upbraids them with what *they had done* Inſtead of affording the Jews a friendly hand, or at leaſt commiſerating their calamity, and dropping a tear of tender compaſſion over their afflictions, they ſtood *on the other ſide*, not merely unconcerned ſpectators, but pleaſed with the ſcene, and helping forward the ruin of Jeruſalem, when the Chaldeans entered the city, led the inhabitants captive, and divided the ſpoil, *v* 11 nay, they inſulted the unhappy ſufferers, and mocked at their diſtreſs, *v* 12 Eager to plunder, they ruſhed with the beſiegers into the city, and pillaged whatever they laid their hands upon, *v* 13 and with ſavage inhumanity ſtood in the croſs-way to ſeize the few who eſcaped from the Chaldean ſword, and murdered them in cold blood, or delivered them up to their cruel enemies, *v* 15 For ſuch atrocious wickedneſs,

2 Vengeance, ſuch as their crimes deſerved, deſcends upon them *The day of the Lord*, that great and terrible day of wrath, approaches, when he will recompenſe the wickedneſs of the heathen, and Edom ſhall drink deep of the cup of his indignation Since judgment had begun at the houſe of God, Edom may not think to eſcape *As thou haſt done, it ſhall be done unto thee*, when other heathen nations are deſtroyed, Edom ſhall fall in the general ruin, and, whilſt the Jews only were captives

for a while, and would be again reſtored, and preſerved ſtill as a people, the Edomites ſhame would be *continual*, they *ſhall be cut off for ever, and be as though they had not been*, their nation extirpated, and not a trace of them remain And thus ſhall the enemies of Chriſt and his church be at laſt deſtroyed for ever, and every antichriſtian foe ſhall be caſt as a millſtone into the ſea and ſink, and never riſe up again, *Rev* xviii 21 *So let all thine enemies periſh, O Lord!*

† Or they that eſcape † Or it ſhall be holy ᵗ Iſa xiv 1 Am ix 11 ᵘ Iſa x 17 Zech xii 6 ˣ Am ix 12 ʸ 1 Kings xvii 9 § Or, ſhall poſſeſs that of the Canaanites, which are in Sepharad ᶻ 1 Tim iv 16 ᵃ Pſ xxii 28 Dan ii 44 Zech xiv 9 Luke i 33 Rev xi 15

17 ¶ But upon mount Zion ſhall be † deliverance,
and † there ſhall be holineſs, and ᵗ the houſe of Jacob
ſhall poſſeſs their poſſeſſions 18 And ᵘ the houſe of
Jacob ſhall be a fire, and the houſe of Joſeph a flame,
and the houſe of Eſau for ſtubble, and they ſhall kindle
in them, and devour them, and there ſhall not be *any*
remaining of the houſe of Eſau, for the LORD hath
ſpoken *it* 19 And *they of* the ſouth ˣ ſhall poſſeſs the
mount of Eſau, and *they of* the plain, the Philiſtines
and they ſhall poſſeſs the fields of Ephraim, and the
fields of Samaria, and Benjamin *ſhall poſſeſs* Gilead 20
And the captivity of this hoſt of the children of Iſrael
ſhall poſſeſs that of the Canaanites, *even* ʸ unto Zarephath,
and the captivity of Jeruſalem, § which *is* in Sepharad,
ſhall poſſeſs the cities of the ſouth 21 And ᶻ ſaviours
ſhall come upon mount Zion to judge the mount of Eſau,
and ᵃ the kingdom ſhall be the LORD's

v 17—21 The ſame cloud, which looked ſo dark and terrible towards the Egyptians, afforded brightneſs and comfort to Iſrael's camp Thus the deſtruction of the church's enemies, before threatned, is accompanied with great and precious promiſes to her friends, in which, to the lateſt ages, they may rejoice

1 *Upon mount Zion there ſhall be deliverance* God will raiſe up a deliverer for them in diſtreſs, as Cyrus, and afterwards Judas Maccabeus, but a greater deliverance than theſe is ſurely here intended, even that which Jeſus hath obtained for us, people from the bondage of Satan, ſin, and death

2 *And there ſhall be holineſs*, in the goſpel church, in conſequence of the deliverance obtained for them all Chriſt's redeemed people ſhall partake of the ſanctifying influences of his Spirit, and be made pure within, this being a diſtinguiſhed part of the ſalvation he hath wrought, that we ſhould be delivered from the power as well as puniſhment of our ſins

3 The church of the redeemed ſhall be extended far and wide *The houſe of Jacob ſhall poſſeſs their poſſeſſions*, as was ſpiritually the caſe when, by the preaching of the miniſters of the goſpel, the Gentiles gave themſelves up unto the Lord then, like fire, the word of God ſpread on every ſide, the hearts of ſinners were pierced, and their moſt beloved ſins conſumed, *v* 18 the borders of the church were then greatly enlarged, and they ſhall continue to be ſo, till at laſt they ſhall ſpread from pole to pole, when *the ſaviours*, thoſe who publiſh the glad tidings of ſalvation, ſhall go forth, clothed with divine energy, convincing men of ſin, and turning them unto the Lord, and then the kingdoms of the world ſhall become the kingdoms of the Lord and his Chriſt

Some ſuppoſe a more literal accompliſhment of the prophecy, when in the laſt days the Jews ſhall be converted, and return to their own land, their borders be greatly enlarged, and, judgment being executed upon all the perſecuting power, papal, pagan, or Mahometan, Chriſt ſhall reign on mount Zion, and *over his ancients glorious* This however at leaſt we are ſure of, that the day of the Lord will come, *which ſhall burn as an oven*, *when all the proud* perſecutors, *and all who do wickedly, ſhall be conſumed* together, and God's deſpiſed and perſecuted people ſhall reign with Jeſus their king in glory everlaſting

THE

EVANGELICAL EXPOSITOR;

OR, A

PRACTICAL COMMENT

Upon the PROPHECY of

JONAH.

THIS book of Jonah, though it be placed here in the midst of the prophetical books of Scripture, yet is rather a history than a prophecy, one line of prediction there is in it, Yet forty days and Nineveh shall be overthrown, *the rest of the book is a narrative of the preface to, and the consequences of, that prediction. In the midst of the obscure prophecies before and after this book, wherein are many things dark and hard to be understood, which are puzzling to the learned, and are* strong meat for strong men, *comes in this plain and pleasant story, which is entertaining to the weakest, and* milk for babes *Probably Jonah was himself the penman of this book, and he, as Moses and other inspired penmen, records his own faults, which is an evidence that in these writings they designed God's glory, and not their own We read of this same Jonah,* 2 Kings, xiv 25 *where we find that he was of Gath-hepher in Galilee, a city that belongs to the tribe of Zebulun, in a remote corner of the land of Israel for the Spirit, which like the wind* blows where it listeth, *will as easily find out Jonah in Galilee, as Isaiah at Jerusalem We find also that he was a messenger of mercy to Israel in the reign of Jeroboam the second, for the success of his arms, in the* restoring of the coast of Israel, *is said to be* according to the word of the Lord, which he spake by the hand of his servant Jonah the prophet. *Those prophecies were not committed to writing, but this against Nineveh was, chiefly for the sake of the story that depends upon it, and that is recorded chiefly for the sake of Christ, of whom Jonah was a type It contains also very remarkable instances of human infirmity in Jonah, and of God's mercy, both in pardoning* repenting *sinners, witness Nineveh, and in bearing with* repining *saints, witness Jonah*

Before Christ 862

CHAP I

In this chapter we have, 1 A command given to Jonah to go preach at Nineveh, ver. 1, 2 2 *Jonah's disobedience to that command,* ver 3 3 *The pursuit and arrest of him for it by a storm,* ver 4—6 4 *The discovery made that his disobedience was the cause thereof,* ver 7—10 5 *The casting of him into the sea, for the stilling of the waves,* ver 11—16 6 *The miraculous preservation of his life in the belly of a fish,* ver 17.

† or Amittai. a 2 Kings xiv 25. Mat. xii 39 [remaining marginal references illegible]

1 NOW the word of the LORD came unto
Jonah [a] the son of ‡ Amittai, saying,
2 Arise, go to Nineveh [b] that great city,
and cry against it, for [c] their wickedness
is come up before me 3 But Jonah rose up [d] to flee
unto Tarshish from the presence of the LORD, and
went down to [e] Joppa, and he found a ship going to
Tarshish so he paid the fare thereof, and went down
into it to go with them unto Tarshish, [f] from the presence of the LORD

v 1—3 We have here,

1 The prophet's name and parentage Jonah, *a dove*, God's prophets being harmless as them, and, like the dove of Noah, bringing the olive-branch of peace, the tidings of mercy and salvation to perishing sinners his father's name is Amittai, *my truth*, for prophets must be sons of truth, faithful to their office, and steady to maintain the truths of God

Before Christ 862

2 His mission *The word of the Lord came to him*, bidding him *arise, and go to Nineveh, that great city*, the metropolis of the Assyrian empire, where wickedness abounded, as in great cities it usually doth, the multitudes of sinners serving to embolden and stimulate each other to commit iniquity It was now ripe for vengeance, and he must go and cry aloud in the streets, to give the inhabitants warning of their approaching doom, unless they repented

3 His disobedience. He rose up to flee *from the presence of the Lord*, from the land of Judea, where God in an especial manner appeared between the cherubims, *to Tarshish*, either Tarsus in Cilicia, or *the sea*, determined to ship himself in the first vessel, and fly any whither rather than go to Nineveh Either he dreaded the dangers of the service, or rather, as he suggests, *chap* iv 2 he knew God's compassions, that the Ninevites would be forgiven, and himself be counted a false prophet A ship was ready to sail as soon as he arrived at Joppa, and he instantly paid the fare and embarked Providence seemed to concur with his desires but the *ready* way is not always the *right* way, and they who flee from duty, whatever present relief they may gain, are only treasuring up for themselves greater sorrow

Before Christ 862.

4 ¶ But the LORD sent out a great wind into the
sea, and there was a mighty tempest in the sea, so that
the ship was like to be broken 5 Then the mariners
z Acts xxvii 18, 19
were afraid, and cried every man unto his god, z and cast
forth the wares that *were* in the ship, into the sea, to
lighten *it* of them but Jonah was gone down into the
sides of the ship, and he lay, and was fast asleep 6 So
h Rom xiii 11
the ship master came to him, and said unto him, h What
meanest thou, O sleeper? arise, call upon thy GOD,
i Joel ii 14
i if so be that GOD will think upon us, that we perish
not 7 And they said every one to his fellow, Come,
and let us cast lots, that we may know for whose cause
k Prov xvi 33
this evil *is* upon us So k they cast lots, and the lot fell
upon Jonah 8 Then said they unto him, Tell us, we
pray thee, for whose cause this evil *is* upon us what *is*
thine occupation? and whence comest thou? what *is* thy
country? and of what people *art* thou? 9 And he
l Acts xxvii 23
said unto them, I *am* an Hebrew, and l I fear the LORD
the GOD of heaven, which hath made the sea and the
† Heb With great fear
dry land 10 Then were the men † exceedingly afraid,
and said unto him, Why hast thou done this? (for the
men knew that he fled from the presence of the LORD,
because he had told them)

v 4--10 They who think to fly from God will soon perceive the folly of the attempt

1 God sends a mighty tempest on the ship in which the prophet sailed, so that it seemed ready, each moment to founder Such storm doth sin raise in the conscience, and the poor soul in despondence is ready to give himself up for lost, little suspecting that the very tempest, which he imagines will be his ruin, is only designed to drive him to the haven of rest

2 Jonah alone seemed unconcerned about the danger The mariners, affrighted, ran to their prayers, and cried to their idols for help for the imminent views of death will sometimes bring those to their knees who never thought of bowing them before, and, life being dearer to them than all besides, they readily part with their merchandize, and cast it into the sea, to lighten the ship Worldly goods are nothing worth when death stares men in the face what folly then, for the sake of them, to make shipwreck of faith and a good conscience, and lose an immortal soul, *infinitely more precious than the dying body!* When will men be wise? The roaring billows, that terrified the heathen seamen, served but to rock Jonah asleep he, of all that company, appeared the only person insensible, though none had so much cause to be alarmed into such stupefaction doth sin sometimes lull the conscience of the backslider he hath lost all apprehension of danger, and even the judgments, which make others tremble, he passes over unaffected From such blindness and hardness of heart good Lord deliver us!

3 The ship-master rouses him from his slumbers, and upbraids him with his insensibility *What meanest thou, O sleeper?* Strange, that a prophet of the Lord should need reproof even from the mouth of a heathen! *Arise, call upon thy God* delay is ruinous when danger urges They had cried to their gods in vain, perhaps his was more able to help them, *if so be that God will think upon us, that we perish not*, as, without immediate help they knew they must *Note*, (1) Even gracious souls need sometimes to be quickened, and stirred up from their sleepy frame of spirit to cry unto God (2) No danger is so great, but, if God think upon us, he is able to save us to the uttermost

4 The storm increasing, notwithstanding all their endeavours and prayers, they began to suspect that there might be among them some atrocious sinner, on whose account the divine displeasure pursued them, and, as was usual with the heathens, they resolved to enquire which of them it was, and to refer the decision to the lot, and so God ordered it, that the lot fell upon Jonah, v 7 Thus is the iniquity of the sinner often found out by means he never suspected, and when he thought himself most secure and concealed from detection

5 They hereupon strictly interrogate the prophet The lot had fixed this as the man, and he is called upon to acknowledge his crime, that they might know *for whose cause*, or *for what cause, this evil was upon them* what he had done to provoke God, what was his occupation whence he came, and to what country he belonged *Note*, In order to get our troubles removed, we must search diligently into our sins, which are the cause of them

6 Jonah, without reserve, makes confession of his crime, and probably, now convicted in his own conscience, desired to take to himself all the shame and punishment which he felt he had deserved He declares himself by nation and religion a Hebrew, which was an aggravation of his guilt, his *occupation* was that of a prophet of the Most High, *I fear the Lord*, Jehovah, *the God of heaven, which hath made the sea and the dry land*, which, though it added to his sin, yet he owns to God's glory, and in order to the instruction of the heathen mariners, who blindly worshipped gods many, instead of the one true and living Jehovah His *crime* he owns *he told them that he fled from the presence of the Lord*, rebellious to his command, and running from his duty, for which this judgment was sent *Note*, When we have sinned, nothing remains but to justify God in his judgments, and with penitence to bow into the dust

7 The seamen appear exceedingly affected with his narrative Probably they had heard what the God of the Hebrews had done of old, and this increased their terrors With just upbraidings therefore of the prophet, who by his wickedness had brought them into this imminent danger, they expostulate with him, *Why hast thou done this?* why didst thou so foolishly attempt to fly and why embark with us, to involve us with thyself in danger? *Note*, (1) They who profess religion, and act unsuitably, deserve to be reproached (2) None know how extensive and dangerous the consequence of but one sin may be

11 ¶ Then said they unto him, What shall we do
unto thee, that the sea may be † calm unto us? (for the
† Heb Be silent from us
sea ‡ wrought and was tempestuous) 12 And he said
‡ Or grew more and more tempestuous
unto them, Take me up, and cast me forth into the sea,
so shall the sea be calm unto you for I know that for
my sake this great tempest *is* upon you 13 Never-
§ Heb Digged
theless the men § rowed hard to bring *it* to the land,
m Prov xxi 30
m but they could not, for the sea wrought, and was
tempestuous against them 14 Wherefore they cried
unto the LORD, and said, We beseech thee, O LORD,
we beseech thee, let us not perish for this man's life,
n Ps cxv
and lay not upon us innocent blood for n thou, O
LORD, hast done as it pleased thee 15 So they took
o Ps lxxxix
up Jonah, and cast him forth into the sea, and o the sea
‖ Heb Stood
‖ ceased from her raging 16 Then p the men feared
p Mark iv 41
the LORD exceedingly, and † offered a sacrifice unto
† Heb Sacrificed a sacrifice
the LORD, and ‡ made vows 17 ¶ Now the LORD
‡ Heb Vowed vows
had prepared a great fish to swallow up Jonah, and
q Matt xii 40 Luke xi 30
q Jonah was in the § belly of the fish three days and three
§ Heb Bowels
nights

v 11—17 The criminal is detected by his own confession, the question is, what is to be done with him?

1 They refer the matter to himself Since he was a prophet of the God of the Hebrews, he best could inform them what was the likeliest means to appease his anger, and thereby obtain deliverance from the storm, which raged more furiously than ever *Note*, When by our sins we have raised a storm of wrath around us, it highly imports us to enquire how it may be appeased

2 Jonah pronounces his own doom, v 12 He well knew himself to be the troubler, and that, till he was cast into the sea, *there could be no hope of the storm's abating*, and therefore he bids them throw him overboard he would not be his own destroyer, yet, conscious he deserved to die, he offers himself for execution, and chuses rather himself to perish, than involve the innocent in destruction *Note*, (1) They who truly know the evil of sin, and are deeply humbled under it, are ready to submit to any shame or suffering, whereby God may be glorified, and reparation be made to the injured (2) When sin hath raised a storm, we may never hope for peace till the accursed thing is removed

3 Very unwilling to execute this grievous sentence, the mariners rowed hard for land, but the more they strove the more the sea wrought, and was tempestuous, so that despair took place *in every countenance*, and nothing remained but this last experiment, with which they felt the more reluctance to comply on account of the noble simplicity and deep humiliation which now probably appeared in the penitent prophet *Note*, (1) When a gracious man, overtaken with a fault, with frank acknowledgement takes shame to himself, he is entitled to our greatest compassion, nor should we ever by severity aggravate his distress (2) There is no striving against God counsels his will must be done

4 Before they execute the dread decree, they present their importunate supplications to God, that he would not impute to them innocent blood, nor cause them to perish for taking away this man's life, when they had desired to know his will, and acted now, according to the best of their light, in conformity thereto, it appearing to be his pleasure that Jonah should be cast into the sea *Note*, (1) In all our emergencies we must have recourse to God in prayer (2) When we follow, according to our best knowledge, under the guidance of Divine Providence, what appears to be God['s] will, we are bound with full heart [illegible] to trust him with the issue

5 Jonah is cast into the sea, and, to the astonishment of the mariners, instantly the storm ceased *They feared the Lord exceedingly*, amazed at the sudden change and filled with thankfulness, offered an immediate *sacrifice* of praise and thanksgiving, and *made vows* of future oblation whenever they should reach the shore Thus sometimes our greatest loss proves our greatest gain The acquaintance they hereby gained with Israel's God
imply

Before Christ 862

amply compensated for the damage they had sustained by the storm

6 By a miracle the prophet's life is preserved God, who designed not to destroy but save him, had prepared a fish, *a whale* our Lord calls it, *Matth* xii 40 which swallowed him live, and by almighty power he was preserved three days and three nights, at least part of three days, unhurt in the fish's stomach, a monument of divine mercy, and an illustrious type of him, who, when he had given his life a ransom for others, lay so long in the grave, and rose again the third day, *Matth* xii 40

CHAP II

Afflictions often prove the best physic for the soul Jonah is now brought home to God, and cries after him In his prayer we have, 1 The great distress and danger he was in, ver 2, 3, 5, 6 2 The despair he was thereby almost reduced to, ver 4 3 The encouragement he took in this deplorable condition, ver 4, 7 4 The assurance he had of God's favour to him, ver 6, 7 5 The warning he gives to others, ver 8 6 The praise of all is given to God, ver 9 7 Jonah's deliverance out of the belly of the fish, ver 10

a Ps cxxx 1
b Ps cxx 1
† Or out of the
c Ps lxv 2
‡ Or the grave
§ Heb Heart
d Ps xlii 7
e Ps xxxi 22
f 2 Chron vi 38
g Ps lxix 1
Lam iii 54
|| Heb Cuttings off of
h Ps xvi 10
† Or the pit
i Ps xxxi 6
k Ps l 14, 23
Hos xiv 2
Heb xiii 15
l Ps iii 8

1 THEN Jonah [a] prayed unto the LORD his God
out of the fish's belly, 2 And said, I [b] cried
by reason of mine affliction unto the LORD, and [c] he
heard me, out of the belly of ‡ hell cried I, *and* thou
heardest my voice 3 For thou hadst cast me into the
deep, in the § midst of the seas, and the floods com-
passed me about, [d] all thy billows and thy waves passed
over me 4 [e] Then I said, I am cast out of thy sight,
yet I will [f] look again toward thy holy temple 5 [g] The
waters compassed me round about, *even* to the soul
the depth closed me round about, the weeds were wrapt
about my head 6 I went down to the || bottoms of the
mountains, the earth with her bars *was* about me for
ever yet hast thou brought up my life [h] from † cor-
ruption, O LORD my God 7 When my soul fainted
within me, I remembered the LORD, and my prayer
came in unto thee, into thine holy temple 8 They
that observe [i] lying vanities forsake their own mercy
9 But I will sacrifice unto thee with the voice of [k] thanks-
giving, I will pay *that* that I have vowed [l] salvation *is*
of the LORD.

v 1—9 Never, to appearance, was situation more desperate than when Jonah was cast into the stormy ocean, unless it were when he descended into the fish's belly yet even in the lowest state of misery God can save, and Jonah now is as safe in the monster's stomach as if he were on dry land, and finds both power to pray, and fervent desires after the Lord his God, who thus plainly shewed him he had not abandoned him to destruction, and thereby engaged him to exercise faith in his pardoning grace and preserving providence *Note*, (1) No place can separate the soul from communion with God, wherever we are, the way to a throne of grace is open (2) Our encouragement to draw near to God is the humble persuasion that he is our God, reconciled to us, and willing to hear and help us in every time of need

1 He cried and was heard *I cried by reason of mine affliction* This was the blessed means of driving him to God *Out of the belly of hell cried I*, out of the belly of the fish, where he seemed buried as in his grave *and thou heardest my voice*, for no prayer of faith returns without an answer of peace

2 He describes his distressed situation, sunk in the deep, *buried in the midst of the seas, compassed with the floods*, and all the waves and billows running over him And this was God's doing, *v* 3 His life appeared in the most imminent danger he was inclosed with waters, and his head wrapped with sea-weeds, *v* 5 *he went down to the bottoms of the mountains*, when the hill ascended, and *the bars of the earth*, so deep he sunk, appeared to be about him for ever his state helpless and hopeless To such distress are God's dearest children sometimes reduced, to shew them more eminently the power and grace of God engaged for their deliverance

3 His heart began to fail him God's displeasure, seen in his wretched case, discouraged him, and he feared that he was abandoned, and *cast out of God's sight*, as he knew he had justly deserved to be Thus, when outward trials oppress them, God's people are sometimes sore beset with inward fears, and unbelief, as if God had utterly forsaken them, and hid his face in displeasure

4 His heart is encouraged notwithstanding to trust still in God and, in the exercise of faith, he directs his prayer to heaven from whence alone his help could come When his soul fainted, he *remembered God*, thought upon his power to save, reflected on the riches of his grace, and his own past experience, and thus his hopes revived, his fears were silenced And in the same way must every child of God overcome his unbelieving fears, remembering his power and love, who hath engaged to save to the uttermost all that trust in him

5 His prayer was answered, it entered into the holy temple above, and God in mercy regarded his suffering servant, which gratefully acknowledges to the glory of the Lord his God *Yet hast thou brought up my life from corruption*, either this he said in the fish's belly, and it speaks the language of his faith, assured God would interpose to save him, or when he afterwards was cast on the land, and wrote down this prayer and complaint, he added this to the praise of the glory of God, and for the confirmation and encouragement of others in the like case, that they might see, that none ever trusted God, and were confounded

6 He gives a warning to others of the vanity of idols, and declares the blessedness of dependance upon God *They that observe lying vanities, forsake their own mercy* no idols can save after this sort Perhaps he intended also herein to reflect upon his own folly in flying from God, whose work would have been its own reward, whilst misery is the sure attendant on every departure from him

7 He solemnly engages to offer the grateful sacrifice of praise, and to discharge the vow he had made in trouble, which might be some sacrifice which he would offer at the temple at Jerusalem, or his resolution to go without delay to Nineveh, in obedience to God's command *Note*, (1) Thanksgiving and praise are the tribute we owe, and should without ceasing pay to the God of our mercies (2) Every gracious soul, when he rises from his falls, sets himself with redoubled earnestness to the work and service of God

8 He concludes with ascribing glory to God *Salvation is of the Lord*, and from him alone the temporal, spiritual, and eternal salvation of his people is to be expected, even from his power and love, and to be acknowledged to his glory And they who depend on him for all shall find, by blessed experience, that he hath never failed them who trust him

10 ¶ And the LORD spake unto the fish, and [a] it
vomited out Jonah upon the dry land

a Chap i 17 Hos vi 2 Mat xii 40

v 10 In answer to his prayer, he is discharged from his prison He who commanded the fish to receive him, now obliges him to disgorge his prey, and once more the prophet is safe on shore, as one raised from the dead Thus God restores the poor sinner, when he is often ready to despair of himself, and raises him from the death of sin to the life of righteousness Jonah's deliverance was also the type of the resurrection of Jesus, and is a pledge of ours When we see what God hath done for him, we need not think it incredible he should raise our bodies from the dust.

CHAP III

In this chapter we have, 1 Jonah's mission renewed, and the command a second time given him to go preach at Nineveh, ver 1, 2 2 Jonah's message faithfully delivered, ver 3, 4 3 The repentance and reformation of the Ninevites thereupon, ver 5—9 4 God's gracious revocation of the sentence, and the prevention of the threatned ruin, ver 10

1 AND the word of the LORD came unto Jonah
the second time, saying, 2 Arise, go unto Ni-
neveh that great city, and preach unto it the preaching
[a] that I bid thee 3 So Jonah arose and went unto Ni-
neveh according to the word of the LORD (now Ni-
neveh was || an exceeding great city of three days jour-
ney) 4 And Jonah began to enter into the city a
day's journey, and he cried, and said, [b] Yet forty days
and Nineveh shall be overthrown

a Jer i 17
|| Heb A great city of God So Gen xxx 8 Ps xxxvi 6 & lxxx 10
b Ver 10 2 Kings xx 1, 6 Jer xviii 8

v 1—4 No more disobedient to the heavenly vision, we now find Jonah ready to go and serve God, though he might justly have dismissed him from his service, employs him again

1 God sends him the second time to Nineveh, commanding him to preach what he had before ordered him, and herein he gave him a fresh token of his reconciliation and regard, and put him once more on the proof of his fidelity

2 Jonah instantly proceeds on his journey, no longer deterred by any consideration his affliction had effectually wrought upon him, and his ready obedience shewed the truth of his repentance Boldly therefore he delivered his message, going on to the streets of that vast city, which, by historians, is said to have been sixty miles in compass, and crying aloud, God's herald, *Yet forty days, and Nineveh shall be overthrown*, by some immediate stroke of divine vengeance, and most probably he informed them that their sins were the cause of this terrible judgment denounced against them the time is short, yet it is suffi-

Before Christ 862. the mercy that they have this space allotted them to repent *one day's journey* he advanced with this awful warning, and waited the returning day to proceed farther through the city *Note*, (1) God's servants must apply themselves to his work according to his word, however dangerous or difficult the service may appear (2) God's messages to his prophets cannot alter, the impenitent sinner must perish, but those who return to him shall find mercy (3) They who carry God's warnings to a careless world must cry aloud, and by their earnestness shew how deeply they are affected with the dangers they foretel (4) Great and wicked cities have need to tremble, an offended God can at his pleasure instantly swallow them up, or devour them as Sodom with fire from heaven (5) What sinner would not tremble, if assured that forty days should bring him to the grave? and yet he sits unconcerned, though uncertain whether so many hours or minutes are allotted him

c Matt. xii. 41. Luke xi. 32. 5 ¶ So the people of Nineveh c believed GOD, and
proclaimed a fast, and put on sackcloth, from the great-
est of them even to the least of them 6 For word
came unto the king of Nineveh, and he arose from his
throne, and he laid his robe from him, and covered *him*
d Job ii. 8. with sackcloth, and d sat in ashes 7 And he caused *it*
to be proclaimed, and published through Nineveh (by
† Heb. Caused men. e Joel ii. 12, &c. the decree of the king and his † nobles) saying, e Let
neither man nor beast, herd nor flock, taste any thing,
let them not feed, nor drink water 8 But let man and
beast be covered with sackcloth, and cry mightily unto
GOD yea, let them turn every one from his evil way,
f Isa. lix. 6. and from f the violence that *is* in their hands 9 g Who
g Joel ii. 14. can tell *if* GOD will turn and repent, and turn away
from his fierce anger, that we perish not? 10 ¶ And
h Jer. xviii. 8. Amos vii. 3, 6. h GOD saw their works, that they turned from their
evil way, and GOD repented of the evil that he had said
that he would do unto them, and he did *it* not

v 5—10 One day's preaching effectually wrought upon the Ninevites, and rendered it unnecessary for the prophet to proceed any further Astonishing to tell! they repented at the preaching of Jonah, whilst Israel, under so many prophets, so long rising up and speaking to them, repented not Therefore shall these Ninevites rise up in the judgment, and condemn them with all others, who enjoying richer means of grace, continue hardened and impenitent under them

1 They *believed God* Such divine power and efficacious grace accompanied the prophet's word, that conviction seized their consciences, and they instantly began to consider how they might avert their impending doom, and obtain mercy with this offended God *Note*, It is a blessed symptom for good when the sinner attends to God's word, and receives it as true, bowing in deep conviction under the charge laid against him

2 A general fast is immediately proclaimed and observed Tidings of this dreadful sentence were quickly carried to the palace, and far from representing the prophet as a madman, or disturber of the peace, the nobles and people received him as an ambassador from God, and reported his message with deep seriousness to their king, probably Pul, 2 *Kings* xv 19 whereupon he rose from his throne, deeply affected with the prophet's word, and laying aside the ensigns of royalty, *covered himself with sackcloth, and sat in ashes* a noble example for his people's imitation, and a becoming expression of his own unfeigned humiliation And all the people at his command, from the greatest to the least, copied after their royal master, and lay in sackcloth, deprecating that vengeance which all had provoked, and which was ready to confound them together According to the decree of the king and his nobles, a fast is kept most strict and solemn, nor man nor beast may taste ought, not so much as water, but, covered with sackcloth, they are enjoined to cry mightily to God, even the beasts, for lack of food, would lift up their inarticulate voices and men, women, and children must unite in their prayers for mercy, if yet mercy may be found Nor are they merely to make profession of penitence, but instantly must mend their lives, without which, their prayers would be but hypocrisy *let them turn every one from his evil way*, whatever his peculiar sin hath been, *and* especially *from the violence that is in their hands*, fraud and oppression being then reigning iniquities And when this is done, *Who can tell if God will turn and repent, and turn away from his fierce anger, that we perish not?* The wrath was great, their provocations aggravated, their judgment just, but God is not inexorable, there is yet hope, and that should encourage and hasten their repentance *Note*, (1) The higher our station is, the more exemplary should be our conduct (2) The way not to perish under the sword of God's judgments, is to bow under the rod of his admonition (3) Fervent prayer is mighty effectual; as long as a sinner is stirred up to cry to God, there is yet hope (4) In times of national distress, all must unite, to deprecate the wrath which is threatened (5) They who fast for sin, must turn from the practice and love of it, else the mere afflicting the body availeth

not (6) The greater encouragement to the sinner to turn to God is, that there is not only a peradventure of mercy, but an assurance of it confirmed by the unchangeable oath of the God who cannot lie

3 *God saw their works*, and heard their prayers, he observed their faith in his word, and the change wrought amongst them, he compassionated their distress, he reversed his threatnings, and extended to them the mercy they so earnestly besought He delighteth not in the death of any sinner, it is only by their own wilful impenitence that they bring down his wrath upon them

CHAP IV

Here is, 1 *Jonah's repining at God's mercy to Nineveh*, ver 1, 2, 3 2 *The gentle reproof God gave him for it*, ver 4 3 *Jonah's discontent at the withering of the gourd, and his justifying of himself in that discontent*, ver 5—9 4 *God's improving of it for his conviction, that he ought not to be angry at the sparing of Nineveh*, ver 10, 11 *Man's badness and God's goodness serve here for a foil to each other, that the former may appear the more exceeding sinful, and the latter the more exceeding gracious*

1 BUT a it displeased Jonah exceedingly, and he was a Matt. xx. 15.
very angry 2 And he prayed unto the LORD,
and said, I pray thee, O LORD, *was* not this my say-
ing, when I was yet in my country? Therefore b I fled b Ch. i. 3.
before unto Tarshish for I knew that c thou *art* a gra- c Exod. xxxiv. 6. Psal. lxxxvi. 5. Joel ii. 13.
cious God, and merciful, slow to anger, and of great
kindness, and repentest thee of the evil 3 Therefore
now, O LORD, d take, I beseech thee, my life from d 1 Kings xix. 4.
me, for e *it is* better for me to die than to live 4 e Ver. 8.
¶ Then said the LORD, f † Doest thou well to be f Matt. xx. 15. † Or, Art thou greatly angry?
angry?

v 1—4 Never was perverseness more strange and unaccountable than here appears in this angry prophet

1 He is exceedingly displeased at the Ninevites repentance, and the mercy extended to them, which one should have thought would have been the very joy of his heart Perhaps he had imbibed the common Jewish prejudice against the heathen, and was unwilling the crumbs of mercy should be cast to these dogs Probably also he esteemed this a deep reflection upon Israel, that heathens should repent so readily, and they continue obdurate But what seems most to have touched him, was his own reputation, lest he should be counted a false prophet So apt are we to be selfish, and more concerned about the vain world's opinion, than about God's glory, and the good of men's souls

2 He dares expostulate with God on the subject It is said he prayed, *v.* 2 but very unlike was this prayer from what he had so lately offered up to God He begins with justifying himself to God for his flight to Tarshish, insolently intimating that he was then in the right, having foreseen this would be the consequence, because, as he suggests, he knew God's gracious character, and his readiness to receive and pardon returning sinners a most amazing cause and for his displeasure So ready are passionate people to suggest the most absurd reasons to justify their anger And now in a passion he is tired of life, and wants God instantly to dispatch him, as if it was *better for him to die than to live*, and bear the reproach of a false prophet a temper indeed very unfit for a dying man, but those who are blinded by their passions are destitute of reflection, and usually deaf to advice

3 God justly rebukes him for his impatience and causeless perverseness *Doest thou well to be angry?* what a mild rebuke for so great a provocation! If God be thus gentle, much more ought we to be so, and use that soft answer which turneth away wrath or, *is doing good displeasing to thee*, which should have been his delight? Surely never was greater forbearance, instead of striking him dead in judgment, as he deserved, the Lord kindly seeks to soften his resentment, and bring him to a better mind What miserable, eternally miserable souls had many been, if God had given them their wishes, and sent that death they impatiently invoked

5 So Jonah went out of the city, and sat on the
east-side of the city, and there made him a booth, and
sat under it in the shadow, till he might see what would
become of the city 6 And the LORD God prepared
a § gourd, and made *it* to come over Jonah, that it § Or, palmcrist.
might be a shadow over his head, to deliver him from
his grief So Jonah ‡ was exceeding glad of the gourd. ‡ Heb. Rejoiced with great joy.
7 But God prepared a worm when the morning rose
the next day, and it smote the gourd that it withered
8 And it came to pass when the sun did arise, that God
prepared ‖ a vehement east wind, and the sun beat upon ‖ Or, silent, or deaf.
the

Before Christ 862

the head of Jonah, that he fainted, and [g] wished in
himself to die, and said, *It is* better for me to die than
to live 9 And God said to Jonah, † Dost thou well
to be angry for the gourd? And he said, ‡ I do well to
be angry *even* unto death 10 Then said the LORD,
Thou hast had pity on the gourd for the which thou
hast not laboured, neither madest it grow, which § came
up in a night, and perished in a night 11 And should
not I spare Nineveh [h] that great city, wherein are more
than sixscore thousand persons, [i] that cannot discern between their right hand and their left hand, and *also* much
cattle?

g Ver 3
† Or, Art thou greatly angry?
‡ Or, I am greatly angry?
§ Heb Was the son of the night.
h Chap 1 2 & iii 3
i Deut 1 39

v 5—11 The beginning of strife is usually like the letting-out of water, passion having once taken the reins, goes from evil to worse

1 Jonah retires in sullen silence, and waits without the city, to see what would become of it; having made him a booth with boughs of trees, to shelter him from the sun and rain Probably he thought, if the greater judgments were removed, *some* lesser ones might be inflicted, and save his credit as a prophet, or he might presume the repentance of the Ninevites would be of no long continuance, and then their ruin would return upon them

2 Though in his present spirit he little deserved any favour from God, yet he who is good to the evil and unthankful, thought upon him in his incommodious habitation, and caused *a gourd*, or, as others interpret it, a tree called the *Ricinus*, or *Palma Christi*, to spring up suddenly, and spread its shadow over him, *to deliver him from his grief* probably the heat of the sun was very troublesome, and added to his other vexations *Note*, (1) They who vex themselves with imaginary ills, are often suffered to feel real misery (2) Though we are often froward children, God is a tender father, and pities us even when we deserve punishment

3 Jonah was *exceedingly glad* of this gourd, *he rejoiced with a great joy*, as the words may be rendered, excessive in his gladness, as he had been in his anger So easily do hot and hasty spirits run to extremes, and they who vex themselves about the loss of worldly trifles, are usually as easily and as much elated with their gain

4 God smote the gourd by a worm he had prepared next morning, and left Jonah as much exposed as ever, and, to make him feel more sensibly the loss, he sent a vehement east-wind, which with the hot sun-beams beat upon him, so that he was quite overpowered, and ready to die with the heat, from which he had no shelter So quickly fading are all our earthly comforts, which God pleases to send a worm to our gourd, and when we are most happy in them, perhaps even then the instruments are at work to destroy them In all sublunary goods therefore we should rejoice as if we rejoiced not, that we may be ready to bless God when he takes away, as well as when he gives

Before Christ 862

5 Jonah relapses into his former fretfulness, and with impatient discontent at the loss of the gourd, again wishes for death, as a deliverance from his misery, *v* 8 Thus inordinate affection lays a foundation for inordinate affliction

6 God expostulates with him on his sin and folly *Dost thou well to be angry for the gourd?* *Note*, It becomes us in all our losses and crosses to check our inordinate discontent and anger, and ask, *Do I well to be angry?* so long, so often, on such frivolous occasions? One moment's reflection should shame and silence us

7 Far from standing abashed at this reproof, he daringly vindicates his perverseness *I do well to be angry even unto death* Thus do ungoverned passions bear down reason and conscience, and, deaf to conviction, men vindicate the most glaring absurdity and guilt Nay, self-murderers, many fret themselves into diseases of body, as well as bring sin upon their souls, and will indulge their fretfulness and rage, though death be the consequence

8 God applies to him for his conviction the case of this gourd, about which he so vexed himself If he was so concerned about a poor shrub, the growth of a night, the creature of a day, which he had used no pains to plant or water, with much more pity might God well regard the vast city of Nineveh, where, besides the other inhabitants, were more than six score thousand infants, unable to distinguish good from evil, besides *much cattle* The animal life was far preferable to the vegetable, and much more immortal souls to both, and here were thousands, and such as never by actual transgression had offended Arguments which should for ever silence his discontent, and lead him to adore the transcendent mercy and righteousness of God We may reasonably hope the prophet was convinced, and humbled to the dust, and that he left us this faithful record of his sin and folly, that we might be warned against the like perverseness, or be encouraged to repent of it, and find mercy.

THE EVANGELICAL EXPOSITOR; OR, A PRACTICAL COMMENT Upon the PROPHECY of MICAH.

WE shall have some account of this prophet in the first verse of the book of his prophecy, and therefore shall here only observe, that being contemporary with the prophet Isaiah (only that he began to prophesy a little after him) there is a near resemblance between that prophet's prophecy and this, and there is a prediction of the advancement and establishment of the gospel-church, which both of them have, almost in the same words, that out of the mouth of two such witnesses so great a word might be established. Compare Isa. ii. 2, 3. *with* Micah iv. 1, 2. *Isaiah's prophecy is said to be concerning Judah and Jerusalem, but Micah's concerning Samaria and Jerusalem; for though this prophecy be dated only by the reigns of the kings of Judah, yet it refers to the kingdom of Israel, the approaching ruin of which, in the captivity of the ten tribes, he plainly* foretels, *and sadly* laments. *The scope of the whole is,* 1. *To convince sinners of their sins, by setting them in order before them, charging both Israel and Judah with idolatry, covetousness, oppression, contempt of the word of God, and their rulers especially, both in church and state, with the abuse of their power: and also by shewing them the judgments of God ready to break in upon them for their sins.* 2. *To comfort God's people with promises of mercy and deliverance, especially with an assurance of the coming of the Messiah, and of the grace of the gospel through him. It is remarkable concerning this prophecy, and confirms its authority, that we find two quotations out of it, made publicly upon very solemn occasions, and both referring to very great events.* (1.) *One is, a prediction of the destruction of Jerusalem,* chap. iii. 12. *which we find quoted in the Old Testament, by the* Elders of the land, *Jer.* xxvi. 17, 18. *in justification of Jeremiah, when he foretold the judgments of God coming upon Jerusalem, and to stay the proceedings of the court against him. Micah (say they) foretold, that* Zion should be plowed as a field, *and Hezekiah did not put him to death, why then should we punish Jeremiah for saying the same?* (2.) *Another is, a prediction of the birth of Christ,* chap. v. 2. *which we find quoted in the New Testament, by the* chief priests and scribes of the people, *in answer to Herod's enquiry,* where Christ should be born? *Matt.* ii. 5, 6. *for still we find, that to him bear all the prophets witness.*

Before Christ 750.

CHAP. I.

In this chapter we have, 1. *The title of the book,* ver. 1. *and a preface demanding attention,* ver. 2. 2. *Warning given of desolating judgments hastening upon the kingdoms of Israel and Judah,* ver. 3, 4. *for their sins,* ver. 5. 3. *The particulars of the destruction,* ver. 6, 7. 4. *The greatness of it illustrated,* (1.) *By the prophet's sorrow for it,* ver. 8, 9. *and* (2.) *by the general sorrow that should be for it,* ver. 10–16.

a 2 Pet. i. 21. b Jer. xxvi. 18. c Amos i. 1. ‖ Deut. xxxii. 1. Isa. i. 2. ‖ Heb. Hear, ye people, all of them. e Ps. l. 7. f Ps. xxvi. 21.

1 THE word of the LORD that came to
a Micah the Morasthite in the days of Jotham, Ahaz, *and* Hezekiah, kings of Judah, c which he saw concerning Samaria
and Jerusalem. 2 d ‖ Hear, all ye people; hearken, O
earth, and all that therein is; and let the Lord GOD
be witness against you, the LORD from his holy temple.
3 For behold, f the LORD cometh forth out of
g his place, and will come down, and tread upon h the
high places of the earth. 4 And i the mountains shall
be molten under him, and the valleys shall be cleft
as wax before the fire, *and* as the waters *that are* poured
down ‖ a steep place. 5 For the transgression of Jacob
is all this, and for the sins of the house of Israel.
What *is* the transgression of Jacob? k *is it* not Samaria?
and what *are* the high places of Judah? l *are they*
not Jerusalem? 6 Therefore I will make Samaria m as
an heap of the field, *and* as plantings of a vineyard,
and I will pour down the stones thereof into the valley,
and I will discover the foundations thereof. 7 And
n all the graven images thereof shall be beaten to pieces,
and all the hires thereof shall be burnt with the fire,
and all the idols thereof will I lay desolate: for she gathered
it of the hire of an harlot, and they shall return
to the hire of an harlot.

Before Christ 750.

g Psal. cxv. 3. h Deut. xxxii. 13. & xxxiii. 29. Amos iv. 13. i Judg. v. 5. Isa. lxiv. 1. 2. Amos ix. 5. Hab. iii. 6. 10. ‖ Heb. A descent. k Hos. viii. 5. l 2 Kings xvi. 11, 12. 2 Chron. xxviii. 24. m Chap. iii. 12. n Isa. xxvi. 9.

Before Christ 750

v 1—7 Micah, or Micaiah, the author of this prophecy, was a Morasthite, so named from the place of his nativity He lived under the best and worst of Judah's princes, and in all times of prosperity or adversity faithfully declared the word which God gave him concerning Samaria and Jerusalem, the capitals of the two kingdoms, the judgments which were ready to light upon them being the great burden of this prophecy

1 A solemn call is given to pay deep attention to the word about to be delivered *Hear, all ye people* of Judah and Israel, *hearken, O earth, and all that therein is*, if these refuse to listen, the very inanimate earth, trembling before the Lord, shall condemn their insensibility and hardness of heart *and let the Lord God be witness against you*, if ye disregard or despise these warnings, that I have faithfully delivered my message, and that your blood is on your own heads, even *the Lord from his holy temple* in heaven, from whence he beholds the inhabitants of the world, and from thence sends down his judgments on those who are disobedient to his word *Note*, They who turn a deaf ear to the admonitions of God's ministers, shall shortly be terribly convinced by experience of the threatenings they would not believe

2 The desolating judgments of God are foretold, which were ready to overtake them The Lord cloathed with vengeance descends to destroy them under his feet their strongest fortresses are trod into the dust, and the high places of their idols demolished Their princes and great men, with all their lofty looks, are brought low, and *the valleys cleft*, the lowest of the people sharing in the general calamity, and all unable to resist his arm, as wax melts *before the fire*, or to bear up against his judgments, that as a torrent spread desolation on every side Samaria, the capital, shall then be laid in ruins, and be made as the furrows of the field, razed from the foundations, and scarce one stone left upon another, v 6 which, as Josephus relates, was fully accomplished by Hircanus *Note*, When God rises to judgment, no place can protect the guilty

3 The cause of all their miseries is their sin, and if it be asked, *What is the transgression of Jacob?* the crime peculiarly provoking, *Is it not Samaria?* the calf, and idolatry there committed *And what are the high places of Judah? are they not Jerusalem?* set up there with most impious effrontery against God's temple, yea, in the very courts of the sanctuary an altar is reared to idols, 2 Kings xvi 10—18 *Note*, (1) Sin is at the bottom of all suffering (2) Great cities and persons, whose bad conduct and example spread the contagion of iniquity, shall be first and deepest in punishment

4 The demolition of their idols, as well as themselves, is threatned They shall be broken in pieces by the Assyrians, and made utterly desolate Such as were not worth carrying away for a spoil, shall be stripped of their ornaments, and left as naked logs, *and all the hires thereof shall be burnt with fire*, their palaces and substance, which they esteemed the gifts of their idols, and the hire of their idolatry and as what *they gathered of the hire of an harlot, shall return to the hire of an harlot*, be given to their idolatrous enemies, who would regard the spoil as the reward sent by their gods, and spend it in their service Or the sense may be, that their wealth, which was as ill-gotten as the money earned by prostitution, would be, like it, under the curse of God, and quickly consumed *Note*, The wages got by sin will be ever cursed with a curse, and such gain cannot prosper

8 Therefore ᵉ I will wail and howl, ᶠ I will go stript
and naked ᵍ I will make a wailing like the dragons, and
mourning as the owls 9 For ‖ her wound *is* incurable,
for ʰ it is come unto Judah he is come unto the
gate of my people, *even* to Jerusalem 10 ¶ ⁱ Declare
ye *it* not at Gath, weep ye not at all in the house of
‡ Aphrah ᵏ roll thyself in the dust 11 Pass ye away,
thou § inhabitant of Saphir, ˡ having thy shame naked,
the inhabitant of ‖ Zaanan came not forth in the mourning
of ‡ Beth-ezel, he shall receive of you his standing
12 For the inhabitant of Maroth waited carefully for
good, but ᵐ evil came down from the LORD unto the
gate of Jerusalem 13 O thou inhabitant of Lachish,
bind the chariot to the swift beast she *is* the beginning
of the sin to the daughter of Zion for the transgressions
of Israel were found in thee 14 Therefore shalt thou
give presents to Moresheth-gath the houses of † Achzib
shall be a lie to the kings of Israel 15 Yet will I
bring an heir unto thee, O inhabitant of Mareshah § he
shall come unto Adullam the glory of Israel 16 ʸ Make
thee bald, and poll thee for thy delicate children, enlarge
thy baldness as the eagle, for they are gone into
captivity from thee

v 8—16 We have here,

1 The prophet deeply lamenting the desolations he beheld approaching, wailing as a dragon, and mourning as an owl, because *the wound is incurable*, the decree being gone forth against Israel, and their impenitence obstinate and determined, and now the Assyrian army is at the very gate of Jerusalem *Note*, True prophets are themselves sore afflicted at the view of the threatnings they are obliged to declare, and so far from taking a delight in these sad messages of woe, they weep over sinners whilst they warn them

2 Other cities are called upon to join the prophet's mourning, but withal are admonished *not to declare it in Gath*, nor weep so as to let the Philistines see their grief, who would triumph with malicious pleasure in their calamities, and every gracious soul wishes to conceal the sins or sorrows of God's people, at which the wicked would rejoice In silent grief they are commanded *to roll themselves in the dust, in the house of Aphrah*, the *house of dust*, all their cities being reduced to ruinous heaps *The inhabitant of Saphir*, or *fair*, as the name imports, fair and beautiful, must now go *naked* into captivity, stripped of all their wealth and riches *The inhabitant of Zaanan*, once numerous as a flock, *came not forth in the mourning of Beth-ezel*, to condole with her, or to help her, being too much engaged with their own miseries, for *he shall receive of you his standing*, the enemy encamping near them, and making them pay dear for the resistance their city made against him, v 11 *The inhabitant of Maroth waited carefully for good*, hoping at last to see some stop put to the ravages of the Assyrians, *but* were quite in despair, when the *evil came down from the Lord unto the gate of Jerusalem*, and they beheld the enemy preparing to besiege it, v 12 Lachish is now bid to flee, or rather ironically her attempts to do so are derided, she being doomed with the rest to captivity *She is the beginning of sin to the daughter of Zion* lying contiguous to Israel, this city became first infected, and the idolatry the inhabitants had learned, spread through the land of Judah, and therefore, as ringleaders in sin, they justly deserve severest judgment, the iniquities of the land lying chiefly at their door, v 13 In vain by presents would they court the Philistines of *Moresheth-gath* to assist them, though they promised them fair, they would fail them in the day of trial *The houses of Achzib shall be a lie to the kings of Israel*, as the name Achzib signifies, v 14 Mareshah also shall be a prey, God will bring *an heir* to her, one who should seize the country, as if it were his by inheritance *He shall come unto Adullam the glory of Israel*, shall seize this fortress on which they trusted, or *even to the glory of Israel*, to Jerusalem itself, v. 15 *Make thee bald, and poll thee for thy delicate children*, which seems addressed to the land in general *enlarge thy baldness as the eagle*, shew every expressive sign of woe, *for they are gone into captivity from thee* The prophet speaks of it as already done, for what God decrees is as sure to come to pass, as if it were that moment accomplished

CHAP II

In this chapter we have, 1 The sins with which the people of Israel are charged, covetousness and oppression, fraudulent and violent practices, ver 1, 2 Dealing barbarously, even with women and children, and other harmless people, ver 8, 9 Opposition of God's prophets, ver 6, 7 and delighting in false prophets, ver 11 2 The judgments with which they are threatned, that they should be humbled, impoverished, ver 3, 4, 5 and banished, ver 10 3 Gracious promises of comfort for them in the Messiah, ver 12, 13 And this is the sum and scope of most of the chapters of this and other prophecies

1 WO to them ᵃ that devise iniquity, and ᵇ work 730
evil upon their beds when the morning is
light, they practise it, because it is in the power of their
hand 2 And ᶜ they covet fields, and take *them* by violence,
and houses, and take *them* away so they ‡ oppress
a man and his house, even a man and his heritage
3 Therefore thus saith the LORD, Behold, against this
family do I devise an evil, from which ye shall not remove
your necks, neither shall ye go haughtily ᵈ for
this time *is* evil 4 ¶ In that day shall *one* take up a
parable against you, and lament with ‡ a doleful lamentation,
and say, We be utterly spoiled ᵉ he hath
changed the portion of my people how hath he removed
it from me? § turning away, he hath divided
our fields 5 Therefore thou shalt have none that
shall ᶠ cast a cord by lot in the congregation of the
LORD

v 1—5 It is true both of nations and individuals, that they would never have been sufferers, if they had not first been sinners

1 The sins of this people are brought to light With deep contrivance, even on their beds, they planned their wicked designs, and having, in the day cast their greedy eyes on some field or house which lay convenient for them, they devised how

Before Chriſt 750.

to diſpoſſeſs the owner, and, like Ahab, ſeize the heritage and, eager to put their ſchemes in execution, no ſooner does the morning break, than they are in haſte to be at their evil work, and having the power in their hands, ſtick at no oppreſſion, fraud, or injuſtice, to accompliſh their deſigns, careleſs about the miſeries they may entail upon the unhappy families of thoſe who fall the victims of their covetouſneſs *Note*, (1) Where inordinate love of gain poſſeſſes the heart, the very feelings of humanity are often baniſhed (2) The more deſign and deliberation there is in ſin, the more exceeding ſinful it becomes (3) They who abuſe their power to oppreſſion, will find a greater than they to eſpouſe the cauſe of the injured

2 God threatens them with condign puniſhment They flattered themſelves they could as eaſily eſcape the curſe, as they had broken the commands of God, and *haughtily* looked down on their inferiors, and deſpiſed the warnings of the prophets, but God will *deviſe an evil* againſt them, the Aſſyrian invaſion, from which they cannot *remove their necks*, and in this time of evil, diſtreſs, and perplexity, the lofty looks of the proud ſhall be brought low, for pride will ſurely ſooner or later have a fall, *v* 3 To ſuch miſery would they be then reduced, that they would be a proverb in the mouth of every beholder, inſulted by their enemies, and by their friends bitterly lamented, the general cry will be, *We are utterly ſpoiled*, their perſons captives, their ſubſtance plundered, their land poſſeſſed by ſtrangers, their *portion changed*, and given into the hands of the heathen *Turning away, he hath divided our fields*, either God in anger hath turned from them, and given them up to the ſpoil, or the Aſſyrian conqueror, before he retired, divided their land among others, ſo that now they ſhould neither have the country to divide, as in the days of Joſhua, nor people to inhabit it, nor a *congregation of the Lord*, wherein to caſt the lot before him *Note*, (1) What is got by fraud, will uſually be no abiding poſſeſſion (2) There is a righteous God, who will ſhortly deal with proud oppreſſors according to their deſerts

† Or pro pheſy ye not, let them pro pheſy
‡ Iſa xxx 10 Am vii 16
‡ Or ſhort ned
§ Heb Yeſ terday
‖ Or wives
h Heb iv 9
i Jer iii 2
† Or walk with the wind and lie falſely

6 † ᵍ Propheſy ye not, *ſay they to them that* prophe-
ſy they ſhall not propheſy to them, *that* they ſhall not
take ſhame 7 ¶ O *thou that art* named the houſe of
Jacob, is the ſpirit of the LORD ‡ ſtraitned? *are* theſe
his doings? do not my words do good to him that
walketh uprightly? 8 Even § of late my people is
riſen up as an enemy ye pull off the robe with the gar-
ment from them that paſs by ſecurely, as men averſe
from war 9 The ‖ women of my people have ye caſt
out from their pleaſant houſes, from their children have
ye taken away my glory for ever 10 Ariſe ye, and
depart, for this *is* not *your* ʰ reſt becauſe ⁱ it is polluted,
it ſhall deſtroy *you* even with a ſore deſtruction 11 If
a man † walking in the ſpirit and falſhood, do lie, *ſaying*,
I will propheſy unto thee of wine, and of ſtrong drink,
he ſhall even be the prophet of this people

v 6—11 They who chuſe their own deluſions, are juſtly given up to them The ſins and puniſhments of this people exactly correſpond

1 Their perſecution of the prophets is puniſhed by depriving them of theſe faithful miniſters, and abandoning them to their own inventions *Propheſy not, ſay they to them that propheſy*, they could not bear their harſh admonitions, nor patiently hear the judgments they denounced, and therefore enjoined them ſilence Thus they who will not be reformed, hate to be reproved, and ſtill ſeek to ſilence the faithful miniſters who will not ſuffer them to go on quietly in their iniquities, but denounce thoſe terrors of the Lord which diſturb their repoſe Some read the word, *Propheſy not*, is addreſſed to the true prophets but *propheſy ye*, the falſe prophets, who flattered them in their iniquities ſuch teachers they choſe, as with lies and falſhood lulled them aſleep, promiſing them peace, though they added drunkenneſs to thirſt, the companions or encouragers of their wickedneſs, and though they abuſed their bleſſings ſo vilely, propheſying *of wine and ſtrong drink*, the beſt news in a drunkard's ears, *he ſhall be the prophet of this people* For ſuch abominable conduct God expoſtulates with them, *O thou that art named the houſe of Jacob*, glorying in their deſcent from this patriarch, *is the Spirit of the Lord ſtraitned?* will their prohibition ſtop God's Spirit? and when he ſpeaks, can the prophets forbear? Or will they limit him to viſions of peace, and reſtrain him from foretelling the judgments they provoked? *Are theſe his doings?* does ſuch conduct become the houſe of Jacob or, is this like God's people? or, doth God delight in vengeance? No they forced him to this ſtrange work *Do not my words*, ſaith he, *do good to him that walketh uprightly?* If they enjoy not the bleſſing, they have only themſelves to blame, who by their impenitence put good things from them For theſe things therefore God gives them up to their own deluſions, and bid his prophets be ſilent *They ſhall not propheſy to them, that they ſhall not take ſhame*, either that the prophet may not expoſe themſelves to the inſults they had met with, or that they ſhould reprove the people no more, who, as they had choſen, *v* 11 lying prophets as their ſin, ſhall be curſt with them as their plague, and a heavier one cannot light upon them *Note*, (1) They who are vile themſelves, chuſe thoſe for teachers who moſt reſemble them, and from whom they leaſt fear reproof (2) None hate God's word, but thoſe who walk contrary thereto the upright delight in it, and adore the juſtice of the wrath therein revealed, as well as the riches of the grace (3) Many are happy when their miniſters who diſturbed them are removed or ſilenced, not knowing the wrath and reprobacy which is herein contained

Before Chriſt 730.

2 Their oppreſſion ſhall be puniſhed with captivity *Even of late my people is riſen up as an enemy*, as when the Iſraelites fell upon their brethren, 2 *Chron* xxviii 6 or they grew more and more oppreſſive *Ye pull off the robe with the garment*, ſtripping the poor quite naked, and this without the leaſt provocation, *from thoſe who paſs by ſecurely*, little ſuſpecting ſuch violence, *as men averſe from war*, peaceable themſelves, they thought to paſs unmoleſted Nay, to ſuch a pitch of inhumanity they advanced, that they ſpared not helpleſs women and children, plundering their pleaſant houſes and *from their defenceleſs children have ye taken away my glory for ever*, enſlaving them, and ſelling them to the heathen, thus depriving them of all the bleſſings of God's worſhip for ever, and robbing him of his glory But God will give them according to their deeds the oppreſſors ſhall in their turn be oppreſſed *Ariſe ye, and depart*, prepare for captivity, *for this is not your reſt* you flattered yourſelves with an abiding manſion here, but God hath decreed the contrary *Becauſe it is polluted, it ſhall deſtroy you even with a ſore deſtruction*, the land ſhall ſhake them out, as the Canaanites of old, and the Chaldean ſword ſhall ſpread dreadful ravages among them, the juſt puniſhment of their cruelty and oppreſſion *Note*, (1) To oppreſs the fatherleſs and widows is peculiarly criminal, and God will ſurely be the avenger of their wrongs (2) This world is not our reſt, we muſt not think of it here below *it is polluted*, and every thing around us is ready to communicate defilement We muſt *ariſe and depart*, weaned from it in affection, and paſſing through it as a pilgrim through a ſtrange land, careful to avoid the pollutions that are in it, and haſtening on to our only true reſt, which is above with God in glory

12 ¶ I will ſurely aſſemble, O Jacob, all of thee
I will ſurely ᵏ gather the remnant of Iſrael, I will put
them together as the ſheep of Bozrah, as the flock in
the midſt of their fold they ſhall make great noiſe by
reaſon of *the multitude of* men 13 ˡ The breaker is
come up before them, they have broken up, and ᵐ have
paſſed through the gate, and are gone out by it, and
ⁿ their king ſhall paſs before them, and ᵒ the LORD on
the head of them

k ch iv 6
l Dan ii 35
m I ii 10
n Hoſ iii 5
o Iſa lii 12

v 12, 13 God ſtill in judgment remembers mercy The chapter cloſes with a gracious promiſe of the adored Meſſiah

The Lord will aſſemble the ſcattered remnant of his people, and unite them in one glorious fold, where they ſhall together rejoice aloud under their divine Shepherd's care, which was accompliſhed when by the preaching of the goſpel God's ſpiritual Iſrael were called into his church, and rejoiced in his ſalvation *The breaker is gone up before them*, Chriſt Jeſus, who hath born down all oppoſition from ſin and Satan, and opened a way for his ranſomed to paſs over, eſpecially by his reſurrection and aſcenſion, leading their captivity captive *they have broken up, and have paſſed through the gate, and are gone out by it*, made more than conquerors through his grace, and enabled triumphant to paſs through the gate of death *and their king ſhall paſs before them, and the Lord on the head of them*, Jeſus the captain of their ſalvation leading the way, opening the kingdom of heaven to all believers, and bringing many ſons unto glory, even all that the Father hath given him, that hoſt which no man can number

Some ſuppoſe this to be ſtill a continued threatening, that they ſhall be aſſembled as ſheep for the ſlaughter, and cry out in their diſtreſs, whilſt the Aſſyrians, with their king at their head, under the divine guidance, ſhall enter by the breach into the city, and lead forth the people with their king captives to Babylon, and this ſenſe is very ſuitable to the foregoing verſe

CHAP III

It is needful with ſome ſinners to rebuke them ſharply, nor muſt the prophet of the Lord fear the faces or frowns of men 1 He reproves and threatens the oppreſſing princes, ver 1—4 and falſe and flattering prophets, ver 5—8 2 He gives them their deſerts, as acting in conjunction for the ruin of the kingdom, of which they ſhould ſee the ruins, ver 9—12

AND

Before Christ 710.

1 AND I said, Hear, I pray you, O heads of Ja-
cob, and ye princes of the house of Israel, [a] *Is*
it not for you to know judgment? 2 Who hate the
good, and love the evil, who pluck off their skin from
off them, and their flesh from off their bones 3 Who
also [b] eat the flesh of my people, and flay their skin
from off them, and they break their bones, and chop
them in pieces, as for the pot, and [c] as flesh within the
caldron 4 Then [d] shall they cry unto the LORD,
but he will not hear them he will even hide his face
from them at that time, as they have behaved themselves
ill in their doings 5 ¶ Thus saith the LORD [e] con-
cerning the prophets that make my people err, that
[f] bite with their teeth, and cry, Peace and [g] he that
putteth not into their mouths, they even prepare war
against him 6 [h] Therefore night *shall be* unto you
that ye shall not have a vision, and it shall be dark unto
you, that ye shall not divine, and the sun shall go down
over the prophets, and the day shall be dark over them
7 Then shall the seers be ashamed, and the diviners
confounded yea, they shall all cover their † lips, for
there is no answer of God

[a] Jer v 4, 5. [b] Ps xiv 4. [c] Ezek xi. [d] Ps xviii 41 Prov i 28 Ezek viii 18 Zech vii 13 [e] Is lvi 10, 11 Ezek xiii [f] Chap iii 11 Mat vii [g] Ezek xiii 18 [h] Isa viii Ezek xiii 23 Zech xiii 4. † Heb upper lips

v 1—7 The higher the station, the more sacred the office, the more dangerously influential will be an ill example, and the more aggravated is every transgression The princes and priests, who should have been the support of religion, are chief in sin, and shall be chief in suffering

1 The princes are arraigned and condemned With great boldness the prophet charges their crimes upon their consciences, and bids them hear what the prince of the kings of the earth hath decreed concerning them The duty of their station, as magistrates, required that they should be wise to know and impartial to administer justice but the very reverse had their conduct been They *hate the good*, the righteous man and his causes, *and love the evil*, approving the wicked, and countenancing them, or they hated goodness itself, and delighted in wickedness and oppression, like wild beasts tearing the flock of God's pasture, fleecing them to the very skin by their exactions and rapine, yea, to the very marrow they devoured them, breaking their bones, and chopping them *as for the pot* For which barbarity and rapaciousness God threatens to cast out their prayer in the day of distress, and turn a deaf ear to their cries, as they have done to the cries of the oppressed And just will be the retaliation

2 The false prophets are next convicted, and their doom is read They caused the people to err by their lies, crying *peace*, when God had said there is no peace they *bite with the teeth*, either gnash upon the true prophets for their reproofs, or so long as the people fed them well, they flattered them in their sins *and he that putteth not into their mouths, they even prepare war against him*, denounce God's judgments against him, or stir up his neighbours or the princes to persecute him For which wickedness they shall be brought into the *night* of dark and dismal calamities, and be for ever silenced, experience giving the lie to their divinations, or *because of divination* shall these evils come upon them, all their prosperity shall be at an end, *their sun shall set*, and darkness and dismay surround them *confounded* and *ashamed*, they shall no more dare open their lips, for now it shall be evident to all, that they never had an *answer from God*, tho' they made use of his sacred name to preface their pretended revelations Let those who usurp the office of God's ministers without a divine call remember the day is near when their sin and shame shall be made manifest to all

8 ¶ But truly I am [i] full of power by the Spirit of
the LORD, and of judgment, and of might, [k] to de-
clare unto Jacob his transgression, and to Israel his sin
9 [l] Hear this, I pray you, ye heads of the house of Ja-
cob, and princes of the house of Israel, that abhor judg-
ment, and pervert all equity 10 [m] They build up
Zion [n] with ‡ blood, and Jerusalem with iniquity 11
[o] The heads thereof judge for reward, and [p] the priests
thereof teach for hire, and the prophets thereof divine
for money [q] yet will they lean upon the LORD, † and
say, *Is* not the LORD among us? none evil can come
upon us 12 Therefore shall Zion for your sake [r] be
plowed *as* a field, and [s] Jerusalem shall become heaps,
and the mountain of the house as the high places of the
forest

[i] Job xxxii 18 [k] Isa lviii 1 [l] Ver 1 [m] Jer xxii 13, Hab ii 12. [n] Ezek xxii 27 Zeph iii 3 ‡ Heb. bloods [o] Isa i 23 Hos iv 18 Chap vii 3 [p] Jer vi 13 [q] Isa xlviii 2 Jer vii 4 Rom ii 17 † Heb. saying [r] Jer xxvi 18 Chap i 6 [s] Mat xxiv 2

v 8—12 In opposition to the character of the false prophets Micah declares,

1 Whence he received his commission, and how he discharged it *The Spirit of the Lord* had called him, and furnished him with gifts and graces for the work of his ministry, therefore he could say, *truly I am full of power* he speaks with confidence, for he knew he said no more than the truth *and of judgment and of might*, he feared neither the many nor the mighty, he delivered his message with dignity, as one having authority with zeal for God's glory and the good of men's souls, and with *judgment*, discretion guiding his zeal, and his discernment was clear, both to distinguish truth from falsehood, and to know how to speak a word in season, therefore, being thus qualified for his ministry, he boldly declared *to Jacob his transgression, and to Israel his sin*, whether they would hear or whether they would forbear *Note*, (1) Those whom God calls into the ministry he qualifies for it (2) They who go to bear testimony against a sinful people, need much courage and fidelity to discharge their trust

2 Being thus sent on God's errand, he, without respect of persons, delivers his message, and calls upon the heads of Jacob, and the princes, priests, and prophets, who had been the ringleaders in sin, to hear God's righteous judgments The princes, as magistrates, abhorred justice, and perverted the law to oppression, the highest bribe with them ever carried the cause, and nothing could be transacted without a fee They sucked the very blood of the poor, or murdered the innocent to seize their goods and then built them stately palaces at Jerusalem, or ornamented the temple, with the wages of their iniquity The priests, equally mercenary, and lovers of filthy lucre, *taught for hire*, not for God's glory, or the good of men's souls, and, if they were well paid, they readily suited their doctrine to the palate of their hearers The prophets also *divined for money*, the who enquired of them were sure to hear good news, if they paid them well and yet, notwithstanding these abominations, *they lean upon the Lord, and say, Is not the Lord among us?* Because they had the temple and the outward ordinances, they flattered themselves they had God's favour and presence among them, and therefore *none evil can come upon us*, as if their external privileges would be their protection but they were fatally deceived, as all will be who rest on the form, whilst they deny the power of godliness *Therefore shall Zion for your sake be plowed as a field*, &c Their sins had provoked God to send utter destruction on the temple and city in which they placed their confidence, not a stone shall be left on another, but the whole be reduced to a ruinous heap, which was in great measure done by the Chaldeans, and most literally fulfilled by the Romans *Note*, (1) Ministers must know no respect of persons, when they speak in God's name, but rebuke the greatest with all authority (2) Nothing is so opposite to the character of Christ's ambassadors, as that of serving for hire and loving *filthy lucre* (3) Outward privileges abused aggravate the guilt and hasten the ruin of sinners, whilst they are placing their confidence in them (4) The sins of the great bring down those judgments that overwhelm their whole country with desolation

CHAP IV.

The ruin of the Jewish church and people was above foretold The promises of the establishment of the gospel church in its stead are here revealed 1 *It shall be advanced and enlarged by the accession of the nations to it*, ver 1, 2 2 *It shall be protected in tranquillity and peace*, ver 3, 4 3 *It shall be kept close and constant, and faithful to God*, ver 5 4 *Under Christ's government all its grievances should be redressed*, ver 6, 7 5 *It shall have an ample and flourishing dominion*, ver 8 6 *Its troubles shall be brought to a happy issue*, ver 9, 10 7 *Its enemies shall be disquieted, nay destroyed, in and by their attempts against it*, ver 11—13

1 BUT [a] in the last days it shall come to pass, *that*
[b] the mountain of the house of the LORD shall
be established in the top of the mountains, and it shall
be exalted above the hills, and people shall [c] flow unto
it 2 And [d] many nations shall come and say, [e] Come
and let us go up to the mountain of the LORD, and
to the house of the God of Jacob, and he will teach us
of his ways, and we will walk in his paths for the law
shall go forth of Zion, and the word of the LORD
[f] from Jerusalem 3 ¶ And [g] he shall judge among
many people, and [h] rebuke strong nations afar off, and
[i] they shall beat their swords into plow shares, and their
spears into ‡ pruning hooks nation shall not lift up a
sword against nation, neither shall they learn war any
more 4 But [k] they shall sit every man under his vine,
and under his fig tree, and none shall make *them* afraid
for the mouth of the LORD of hosts hath spoken *it*
5 For [l] all people will walk every one in the name
of his god, and [m] we will walk in the name of the
LORD our God for ever and ever 6 In that day,
saith the LORD, [n] will I assemble her that halteth, and
I will gather her *that is* driven out, and her that I have
afflicted 7 And I will make her [o] that halted, a rem-
nant,

Before Christ 710

[a] Isa ii 2, &c Ezek xvii 22, 23 [b] Ps lxviii 15, 16 [c] Isa lx 8 [d] Ps lxxii 8 Dan vii 14 [e] Jer xxxi 6 & l 5 Zech viii 21, 22 [f] Luke xxiv 47 [g] Ps ix 6 [h] John xvi 8, 9 [i] Isa xlvi 9 Hos ii 18 Zech ix 10 ‡ Or scythes [k] 1 Kings iv 25 Zech iii 10 [l] Jer ii 11 [m] Zech x 12 [n] Ezek xxxiv 16 [o] Zeph iii 19

94

Before Christ 710.

ſ Dan vii 14 Luke i 33

nant, and her *that was* caſt far off, a ſtrong nation, and
ſ the LORD ſhall reign over them in mount Zion,
from henceforth even for ever

v 1—7 After the deſolations before deſcribed, never could a more welcome *But* come in, than begins the preſent chapter, where, according to the riches of God's grace, the former melancholy ſcene changes, and the goſpel-church, a brighter phoenix, riſes from the aſhes of Zion

1 The church of Chriſt ſhall be firmly eſtabliſhed, and gloriouſly exalted *In the laſt days*, the days of the Meſſiah, *it ſhall come to paſs, that the mountain of the Lord's houſe ſhall be eſtabliſhed in the top of the mountains, and it ſhall be exalted above the hills*, fixed on a baſis immoveable, againſt which the gates of hell cannot prevail, raiſed high above all the power of its enemies, and conſpicuous as a city ſet on an hill And this had its primary accompliſhment when Chriſt and his apoſtles firſt erected this glorious fabric, and ſhall more eminently be fulfilled when, in the latter day, the kingdoms of the world will become the kingdoms of the Lord and of his Chriſt

2 Vaſt multitudes of converts *ſhall flow into it*, numerous as the drops which mighty rivers pour into the ocean, *and many nations*, at leaſt great numbers out of them, *ſhall come and ſay, Come and let us go up to the mountain of the Lord, to the houſe of the God of Jacob*, encouraging each other eagerly to preſs into the church, *and he*, Chriſt the head of his church, *will teach us his ways*, by his word and Spirit, *and we will walk in his paths*, ſupported by his grace, and ſtrengthened to follow him *for the law ſhall go forth out of Zion*, the law of the Spirit of life in Chriſt Jeſus, *and the word of the Lord from Jeruſalem*, the goſpel there began to be firſt preached, and from thence the healing waters of the ſanctuary have flowed into all lands, and through mercy into our own And they who have an enlightened mind will value the ineſtimable bleſſing

3 The power which will accompany the preaching of the goſpel ſhall effectually change men's hearts, and bring them to mutual love and peace *He ſhall judge among many people, and rebuke ſtrong nations afar off*, convincing the Gentiles of their ſin, and the judgment of God againſt it, and bringing them to repentance and faith, in conſequence of which, *ſwords* ſhall be turned *into plow-ſhares*, all quarrels and animoſities ceaſe, the proud and paſſionate ſpirits of men be made humble and peaceable, and wars be for ever at an end, whilſt each, ſitting in comfort under his own vine and fig-tree, ſhall be quiet from fear of evil, which, ſo far as the goſpel now prevails, will be the ſpirit of every converted ſoul, and it ſhall univerſally be diffuſed in the laſt days, when this happy ſtate of things ſhall more gloriouſly appear *for the mouth of the Lord hath ſpoken it*, and therefore, however unlikely it may ſeem, it ſhall be fulfilled at the appointed time

4 There will then be the greateſt conſtancy among Chriſtians in their holy profeſſion *For all people will walk every one in the name of his god* This is uſually the caſe, *Jer* ii 11 or this will be the caſe till the Meſſiah ſhall convert them to himſelf *And we will walk in the name of the Lord our God for ever and ever*, with unſhaken fidelity and unremitting ardor, ſuch being the full purpoſe of every gracious ſoul

5 Though the ſouls of ſinners are like a poor flock before devouring wolves, worried, torn, ſcattered, and maimed, God will collect them, heal their wounds, ſtrengthen their weakneſs, recover them from their wanderings afar off, and bring them into his fold And this ſome particularly refer to the Jews, who ſhall be recovered from their preſent diſperſion at laſt, and, after all their afflictions, become a great and glorious people to the Lord

6 The Lord ſhall then reign in his church for ever and ever He hath begun to ſet up his kingdom already in the world, but hereafter he will more eminently diſplay his power and grace, when, the fulneſs of the Gentiles being come in, and Iſrael reſtored, *He ſhall reign in mount Zion and over his ancients glorіouſly*

8 ¶ And thou, O tower of the flock, the ſtronghold
of the daughter of Zion, unto thee ſhall it come, even
the firſt dominion, the kingdom ſhall come to the daugh-
ter of Jeruſalem 9 Now why doſt thou cry out aloud?
q *is there* no king in thee? is thy counſellor periſhed?
for pangs have taken thee as a woman in travail 10
Be in pain, and labour to bring forth, O daughter of
Zion, like a woman in travail for now ſhalt thou go
forth out of the city, and r thou ſhalt dwell in the field,
and thou ſhalt go *even* to Babylon, there ſhalt thou be
delivered there the LORD ſhall redeem thee from the
hand of thine enemies 11 ¶ Now alſo many nations
are gathered againſt thee, that ſay, Let her be defiled,
and let our eye look upon Zion 12 But they know
not the thoughts of the LORD, neither underſtand they
his counſel for he ſhall gather them as the ſheaves into
the floor 13 Ariſe and s threſh, O daughter of Zion

q Jer viii 19 Hoſ iii 3 & x 3

r Hoſ ii 14

s Iſa xli 15 16 Jer li 33

for I will make thine horn iron, and I will make thy
hoofs braſs, and thou ſhalt beat in pieces many people
and I will t conſecrate their gain unto the LORD, and
their ſubſtance unto u the Lord of the whole earth

Before Christ 710.

t Lev xxvii 27 Joſh vi 19

u Zech iv 14 & vi 5

v 8—13 The words, *O tower of the flock, Migdal-Eder*, are left by many untranſlated, as the name of a place near Bethlehem, *Gen*, xxxv 19—21 Others ſuppoſe them put for Jeruſalem, the ſtronghold of the daughter of Zion Whilſt others, and with reaſon, conjecture this to be one of the titles of the Meſſiah, *the tower* of his redeemed *flock, and the ſtronghold of his church* And,

1 It is here promiſed that in him the kingdom of David, which was fallen, ſhould revive in all its ſplendor, according to the *firſt dominion, the kingdom ſhall come to the daughter of Jeruſalem* There the goſpel of the kingdom began to be preached, many Jews were admitted members of it, and the apoſtles, who were of the ſtock of Iſrael, were the chief perſons in it perhaps alſo particular reſpect may be had to Chriſt's coming to them at the time of their laſt converſion, when the kingdom of the Meſſiah ſhall moſt eminently come to them

2 The temporal deliverances God will work for his Iſrael, are the figure and earneſt of the ſpiritual redemption he hath in ſtore for them

1 They are repreſented as in a ſtate of great diſtreſs, crying aloud as a travailing woman in pangs, their king no more, *their counſellors periſhed*, caſt out of their cities, and dwelling in the fields, led captive to Babylon, and ſerving their Chaldean maſters So low are God's people ſometimes reduced

2 God will deliver them from thence Cyrus is his appointed inſtrument, raiſed up to reſcue them from the houſe of their priſon The figure of that greater Redeemer, who came to preach deliverance to captive ſouls from the bondage of corruption, and to bring them into the glorious liberty of the ſons of God

3 When new troubles ariſe, new helpers ſhall be given them The church militant may expect little reſt here below *Now alſo*, after their reſtoration from Babylon, *many nations ſhall be gathered againſt thee*, as particularly was the caſe in the days of the Maccabees, *that ſay, Let her be defiled, and let our eye look upon Zion*, pleaſed with the thoughts of her ruin, and hoping to behold it *but they know not the thoughts of the Lord, neither underſtand they his counſel*, which were the very oppoſite to theirs, for, whilſt they deſigned the deſtruction of Zion, he intends to overrule their aſſembling to their own confuſion and perdition *for he ſhall gather them as ſheaves into the floor*, ripe for ruin, and then the daughter of Zion ſhall be ſtrengthened to *ariſe* and *threſh*, puſhing her enemies as with *horns of iron*, treading them under foot as with *hoofs of braſs*, and beating them in pieces *And I will conſecrate their gain unto the Lord, and their ſubſtance unto the Lord of the whole earth* The ſpoil, which was gotten by the Lord's power, ought juſtly to be devoted to his honour and ſervice All our gains are from him, and ſhould be employed for him

This prophecy, ſome ſuppoſe, literally was accompliſhed in the victories of the Maccabees over Antiochus and the neighbouring nations Whilſt others ſuppoſe it to refer to the ſpiritual conqueſts of the Redeemer And ſome imagine it relates to the deſtruction of the antichriſtian powers in the latter days, when the kingdom of Jeſus ſhall be triumphantly ſet up, and all his foes be made his footſtool

CHAP V

In this chapter we have, 1 *A prediction of the troubles and diſtreſſes of the Jewiſh nation,* ver 1 2 *A promiſe of the Meſſiah, and of his kingdom, to ſupport the people of God in theſe troubles* (1) *Of the birth of the Meſſiah,* ver 2, 3 (2) *Of his advancement,* ver 4 (3) *Of his protection of his people, and his victory over their enemies,* ver 5, 6 (4) *Of the great increaſe of the church, and the bleſſings that ſhall come to the world by it,* ver 7 (5) *Of the deſtruction of the enemies of the church, whether theſe without, or thoſe within,* ver 8—15

1. NOW gather thyſelf in troops, O daughter of
troops he hath laid ſiege againſt us they ſhall
ſmite the judge of Iſrael with a rod upon the cheek
2 But thou, a Beth-lehem b Ephratah, *though* thou be
little among c the thouſands of Judah, *yet* out of thee
ſhall he come forth unto me, *that is* to be ruler in Iſrael
d whoſe goings forth *have been* from of old, ‖ from ever-
laſting 3 Therefore will he give them up, until the
time *that* e ſhe which travaileth hath brought forth
then f the remnant of his brethren ſhall return unto the
children of Iſrael 4 ¶ And he ſhall ſtand and † feed
in the ſtrength of the LORD, in the majeſty of the
name of the LORD his God, and they ſhall abide for
now ſhall g he be great unto the ends of the earth

a Mat ii 6 Joh vii 42

b Gen xxxv 19 Pſ cxxxii 6

c 1 Sam xxiii 23

d Prov viii 22 23

‖ Heb From the days of eternity

e Iſa vii 14

f Joh x 16

† Or rule

g Iſa lii 13 &c.

5 And

Before Christ 710

5 And this *man* [h] shall be the peace when [i] the Assy-
rian shall come into our land and when he shall
tread in our palaces, then shall we raise against him
seven shepherds, and eight § principal men 6 And
they shall || waste the land of Assyria with the sword,
and the land of Nimrod † in the entrances thereof
thus [k] shall he deliver *us* from the Assyrian, when he
cometh into our land, and when he treadeth within our
borders

h Eph. ii 14 i Rev. xiii 7 § Heb Princes of men. || Heb Eat up † Or with her own naked swords k Luke i 71

v 1—6 We have here,

1 Troublous times coming upon Zion *Now gather thyself in troops, O daughter of troops*, which seems addressed to the Chaldeans *he hath laid siege against us*, the king of Babylon, with his army *they shall smite the judge of Israel with a rod upon his cheek*, Zedekiah and the princes being most ignominiously and cruelly treated by Nebuchadnezzar, and his sons slain before his eyes

2 The Messiah is promised, the grand support of his Israel in every time of their distress the hopes of his appearing may well keep them from sinking into despair, and engage them to wait patiently for him *But thou, Bethlehem Ephratah*, though *thou be little among the thousands of Judah, yet out of thee shall he come forth unto me, that is to be ruler in Israel, whose goings forth have been of old, from everlasting* St Matthew has left us no doubt concerning whom these words are spoken they relate to Christ, and of him the ancient Jewish interpreters understood them (1) They fix the place of his nativity at Bethlehem (2) They describe the office of the Messiah to be *a ruler* in Israel, not indeed over Israel after the flesh, but over his spiritual subjects, the children of Abraham by faith (3) They assert his eternal Godhead *from everlasting* are *his goings forth* Tho', as man, he came forth from the lineage of David, and out of the city of Bethlehem, as God he is from everlasting to everlasting, *without beginning of days or end of life*

3 Before his appearing in the flesh the Jews shall go through much tribulation *Therefore, or notwithstanding, will he give them up*, for a while, to be harassed by their enemies, *until the time that she which travaileth hath brought forth*, which many interpreters refer to the blessed virgin, the mother of Christ, of whom the long expected Saviour, in the fulness of time, should be born for the consolation of Israel Or these words may relate to Christ's rejection of the Jewish nation for a while, for their unbelief, until the church, the spiritual Zion, hath brought forth the fulness of the Gentiles *then the remnant of his brethren*, the Jewish people, *shall return to the children of Israel*, and be admitted into the church of the redeemed Or this may comprehend the Gentiles also, whom Christ is not ashamed to call his brethren, *Heb* ii 11 who with the Jews will become at last one fold under one shepherd

4 The people of Christ shall then be safe and happy under his blessed government *He shall stand and feed in the strength of the Lord*, clothed with divine power, able to protect the sheep of his pasture, and ever watching over them with kind sollicitude, providing for their wants, and ministring to them out of his fulness, *in the majesty of the name of the Lord his God*, being himself, in his nature and perfections, very God, and also, as Mediator, invested with a delegated power over all in heaven and earth, *and* therefore *they shall abide* for ever the objects of his love, and under his care, none being able to separate them from him, and in their affections and fidelity firmly united to him, or *they shall sit* under his shadow, quiet and safe from fear of evil *for now shall he be great unto the ends of the earth*, when, his gospel being spread abroad, all flesh shall see his glory, and the nations be gathered unto him *And this man shall be the peace man* is not in the original *this shall be the peace*, this Messiah, who by the blood of his cross shall make peace with God on the behalf of perishing sinners, and by his grace shall preserve his people from all the enemies of their souls, *when the Assyrian shall come into our land*, as he delivered them from Sennacherib's invasion, so will he still protect his redeemed from the power of the wicked *and when he shall tread in our palaces*, and seems ready to swallow up the people of God, *then shall we raise against him seven shepherds, and eight principal men* the Lord, their protector, hath instruments ready to employ in the service of his people, and for the destruction of their enemies *and they shall waste the land of Assyria with the sword, and the land of Nimrod in the entrances thereof thus shall he deliver us from the Assyrian, when he cometh into our land, and when he treadeth within our borders* And the destruction of these inveterate enemies of the church of old, seems to prefigure the conquests of the gospel, before which Satan and the powers of darkness fell as lightning from heaven, and may be considered as having respect also to the final destruction of Christ's enemies, when the pagan, papal, and Mahometan powers, which last now possess these countries, shall at last be destroyed *Note*, (1) Christ's people need not fear, though surrounded with enemies, assaulted by temptations, and beset with corruptions, *he will be their peace when the Assyrian cometh into the land* (2) All the church's foes shall shortly be made her footstool, and little faith and patience will issue in eternal triumph

7 And the remnant of Jacob shall be in the midst
of many people, [l] as a dew from the LORD, as the
showers upon the grass, that tarrieth not for man, nor
waiteth for the sons of men 8 ¶ And the remnant of
Jacob shall be among the Gentiles in the midst of many
people, [m] as a lion among the beasts of the forest, as a
young lion among the flocks of † sheep who, if he go
through, both treadeth down, and teareth in pieces, and
none can deliver 9 Thine hand shall be lift up upon
their adversaries, and all thine enemies shall be cut off
10 And it shall come to pass in that day, saith the
LORD, that [n] I will cut off thy horses out of the midst
of thee, and I will destroy thy chariots 11 And [o] I
will cut off the cities of thy land, and throw down all
thy strong-holds 12 And I will cut off witchcrafts
out of thine hand, and thou shalt have no *more* sooth-
sayers 13 Thy graven images also will I cut off, and
thy ‡ standing images out of the midst of thee, and thou
shalt no more worship the work of thine hands 14
And I will pluck up thy groves out of the midst of
thee so will I destroy thy || cities 15 And [p] I will
execute vengeance in anger, and fury upon the heathen,
such as they have not heard

Before Christ 710 l Psal. cx 3 1 Cor iii 6 m 2 Cor x 4, 5 1 John v 4, 5 † Or goats n Zech ix 10 o Ezek xxxviii 11 ‡ Or statues || Or enemies p 2 Thess i 8, Psal. cxxxix 7

v 7—15 A glorious remnant of Jacob, according to the election of grace, shall be saved, blessed themselves, and a blessing unto others And this remnant may be understood, either of those who were the first preachers of the gospel, whose word distilled as the dew, and who vanquished the superstition and idolatry of the Gentile world, or of the redeemed people in general, who are but a remnant, compared with those that perish

1 They shall be *as the dew in the midst of many people*, numerous as dew-drops, of heavenly extraction, fruitful in good works, and blessings to all around them, *as the showers upon the grass, that tarrieth not for man, nor waiteth for the sons of men*, and so free, bounteous, and unsought are the gifts of God's grace, preventing our desires, and above all our deserts

2 *They shall be as a lion among the beasts of the forest*, so courageous and strong, and before them their enemies shall be as a flock of helpless sheep, unable to make the least resistance, *v* 8 and fall an easy prey to their arms Thus shall it be at the last with all who persist in their enmity against Christ and his church, they shall perish together

3 They shall cease from all human confidences, nor any longer need them, when all their foes are fallen *Their horses and chariots* for war shall be destroyed, as useless, and the fortifications of *their cities*, and their *strong holds* be demolished and a mercy it is when these vain confidences are taken from us, which were a temptation to us to trust on them more than God *Their witchcraft* and unlawful arts of divination shall be cut off, and never more regarded, *v* 12 Every monument of idolatry shall be utterly abolished, their images and groves cast down, and *the cities* where idolatry prevailed, or the temples large as cities, dedicated to their idols, destroyed, or as in the margin, *thy enemies*, both within and without

4 Vengeance shall then light on every disobedient sinner, *such as they have not heard*, so terrible, or *which have not heard*, refused to receive the Lord Christ, and disregarded his salvation, for which, judgment shall come upon them to the uttermost

CHAP VI

The prophet here is again a reprover 1 God enters an action against his people for their base ingratitude, and the ill returns they had made for his favours, ver 1—5 *2 He shews the wrong course they took under conviction, and the frivolous proposals they made in answer to his charge, and what course they should have taken, ver* 6—8 *3 He calls upon them to hear the voice of his judgment, and points out their sins, the occasion of his controversy with them, ver* 9 *their injustice, ver* 10—15 *and their idolatry, ver* 16 *for both which ruin was coming upon them*

1 HEAR ye [a] now what the LORD saith, Arise,
contend thou || before the mountains, [b] and let
the hills hear thy voice 2 [c] Hear ye, O mountains,
[d] the LORD's controversy, and ye strong foundations
of the earth for [e] the LORD hath a controversy with
his people, and he will plead with Israel 3 O my
people, [f] what have I done unto thee, and wherein have
I wearied thee? testify against me 4 For [g] I brought
thee up out of the land of Egypt, and redeemed thee
out of the house of servants, and I sent before thee
Moses, Aaron, and Miriam 5 O my people, re-
member now what [h] Balak king of Moab consulted,
and what Balaam the son of Beor answered him from [i]
Shittim

a Heb. iv 4 || Or with b [illegible] Mic i 2 c Isa i 2 d [illegible] e Isa i 18 & v 3, 4 & liii 26 Hos iv 1 f Jer ii 5, 31 g Exod xii 51 & xiv 30 Amos ii 10 h Numb xxii 5, 6 & xxiii 7 Deut xxiii 4 Josh xxiv 9 Rev ii 14 i Numb xxv 1, &c

Before Christ 710

Shittim unto Gilgal, that ye may know the righteousness
of the LORD

v 1—5 This chapter begins a new subject

1 The prophet is summoned to arise, and *contend before the mountains*, he must cry so loud, that the hills may echo again, publickly to expose the shame of Israel, and call even these inanimate creatures, the very foundations of the earth, to witness against the stupidity and insensibility of this people, who, when God spoke, turned a deaf ear to his admonitions *Note*, They who plead earnestly for God, must cry aloud, though mockers revile the vehemence of their discourse

2 The cause of this earnestness is the *controversy* God hath against *his people*, whose sins are great and aggravated, and call for vengeance upon them Though they are called Israel, their relation to God serves to aggravate their offence none sin so heinously as God's own people, every wilful transgression of theirs is against light and love

3 He expostulates with them on their base ingratitude He challenges them to shew if he had ever done ought to provoke their ill usage, or been a severe master to them, in the services he had enjoined them, v 3 He reminds them of the repeated and inestimable favours he had showered upon them, bringing them from their bondage in Egypt, raising them up divinely appointed leaders, guiding them safe through the wilderness, baffling the devices of Balak, and compelling Balaam, the prophet he had sent for to curse Israel, to answer him with blessings instead of curses upon their heads, *from Shittim to Gilgal* he brought them into the promised land, notwithstanding the whoredoms they had committed with the Moabites, and all this was done *that ye may know the righteousness of the Lord*, the faithfulness of God to his promises, his goodness to them, and the justice of his present controversy against them, for the base returns they had made Whenever he pleads against us, surely there is a cause

k Ps xv 1 & xxiv 3 John vi 28
l Isa i 11
m Ps l 9 & li 16 Isa i 11
n Deut x 12 Hos xii 6
o Gen xviii 19 Isa i 17
p Col iii 12
† Heb Humble thyself to walk
q Rom xi 20 1 Pet v 6

6 ¶ k Wherewith shall I come before the LORD,
and bow myself before the high God? shall I come
before him l with burnt offerings, with calves of a year
old? 7 m Will the LORD be pleased with thousands
of rams, *or* with ten thousands of rivers of oil? shall I
give my first-born *for* my transgression, the fruit of my
body *for* the sin of my soul? 8 He hath n shewed thee,
O man, what *is* good, and what doth the LORD re-
quire of thee, but o to do justly, and p to love mercy,
and to † walk q humbly with thy God?

v 6—8 Some suppose these are the words of God's Israel, desiring to make up the controversy by a penitent return, and enquiring the way, but rather they are the words of Balak to Balaam, sollicitous to gain, at any rate, an interest in God to curse Israel, though at the expence of the sacrifice of his first-born, an oblation, which it cannot be supposed the Israelites, under a penitential sense of sin, would ever have thought of offering, but very suitable to the ideas of a heathen

1 He suggests his readiness to offer the most expensive sacrifices, even *thousands of rams*, or *ten thousands of rivers of oil*, speaking hyperbolically, nay, if a more precious oblation was needful to make the atonement, even the fruit of his body, his first-born son shall bleed and this may be applied to the awakened sinner seeking reconciliation with God, trembling before his majesty, enquiring of his ministers what I must do to be saved, brought into the dust of humiliation, sollicitous to avert his displeasure and obtain his favour, burthened with sin upon his conscience, to be relieved from which, he could willingly part with the dearest thing he possesses, not that aught we can do could ever satisfy offended Justice The blood of all mankind had never been able to make satisfaction for the least sin, the blood of Jesus alone is the effectual propitiation

2 Balaam answers his enquiry *He hath shewed thee, O man, what is good*, not external offerings, but moral duties are what he prescribes, *and what doth the Lord require of thee, but to do justly*, administring impartial justice to his subjects, and seeing that none be oppressed with wrong, *to love mercy*, delighting in all acts of kindness and benevolence towards the distressed and indigent, *and to walk humbly with thy God*, acknowledging his own insignificance, and ascribing to God the glory due unto his name

If we consider this as an answer given to a guilty conscience seeking reconciliation, we have, (1) The object of faith proposed in the word *thy God*, in Christ Jesus he become such to the believing sinner, who, through the blood and righteousness of the Redeemer, is entitled to an interest in his favour and regard (2) The duty God requires of those who truly turn to him, is not any outward thing merely, but the heart devoted to his will and service, and what he commands is not only *good* and right in itself, but good for us, conducing to our happiness, as well as his glory And this is, [1] *To do justice*, rendering to all their due, and injuring none in body, soul, goods, or fame. [2] *To love mercy*, not only extending relief to the necessitous, and pardoning every offence, but delighting to be employed in doing good, and counting the service its own reward And, [3] *To walk humbly with God*, conscious of the poverty and imperfection of our best services, submissive to his government, and resigned to his providences

Before Christ 710

† Or the name shall see that which is
‡ Or is there yet unto every man an house of the wicked &c
| Heb measure of leanness Amos viii 5
r Prov xi 1 & xx 10, 23
§ Or shall I be pure with &c
s Hos xii 7
t Jer v 27, 28
u Ibid ix 8
x Lev xxvi 26 Hos iv 10
y Deut xxviii 38, 39 Amos v 11 Zeph i 13 Hag i 6
z 1 Kings xvi 25, 26 Hos v 11
a 1 Kings xvi 30 &c
† Or astonishment

9 The LORD's voice crieth unto the city, and †
the man of wisdom shall see thy name hear ye the rod,
and who hath appointed it 10 ¶ ‡ *Are there* yet the
treasures of wickedness in the house of the wicked, and
the | scant measure r *that is* abominable? 11 § Shall I
count *them* pure with s the wicked balances, and with
the bag of deceitful weights? 12 For t the rich men
thereof are full of violence, and the inhabitants thereof
have spoken lies, and their tongue *is* u deceitful in their
mouth 13 Therefore also will I make *thee* sick in
smiting thee, in making *thee* desolate because of thy sins
14 x Thou shalt eat, but not be satisfied, and thy cast
ing down *shall be* in the midst of thee, and thou shalt
take hold, but shalt not deliver and *that* which thou
deliverest will I give up to the sword 15 Thou shalt
y sow, but thou shalt not reap thou shalt tread the
olives, but thou shalt not anoint thee with oil and
sweet wine, but shalt not drink wine 16 ¶ For the
statutes of z Omri are kept, and all the works of the
house of a Ahab, and ye walk in their counsels, that I
should make thee a † desolation, and the inhabitants
thereof an hissing, therefore ye shall bear the reproach
of my people

v 9—16 Their ingratitude being too plain, God's controversy proceeds against them

1 They are commanded to hearken *The Lord's voice crieth unto the city*, unto the capital, where wickedness most abounded, or to every city in the land *and the man of wisdom shall see thy name*, adore his perfections legible in his providences, and the judgments he executes on the earth, this being the highest point of wisdom, to know God, and observe his agency in every dispensation *Hear ye the rod*, the warnings God gives in his word and providences, which the man of heavenly wisdom bids us remark, *and* see God's hand in the stroke, who *hath appointed it*, in time, measure, and duration, according to the good pleasure of his will *Note*, (1) The voice of God's true ministers is the voice of God, and to be heard with reverence and submission (2) Every providence has a tongue, if we have but ears to attend the message it brings (3) When we consider God hath appointed the rod, it becomes us to bow down in silent resignation, sollicitous only to answer the end for which our afflictions are sent

2 A charge of fraud and violence is brought against them, for which God will not hold them guiltless By scanty measures, and false weights, they increased their treasures, and the rich by violence and oppression filled their houses with spoil, of which, after all the warnings given them, they had not *yet* made restitution And the inhabitants of inferior station copying after their wealthier neighbours, by lies and deceit imposed on the unwary who dealt with them, and made no scruple of falsehood, in order to make the greater gain of their wares and as they robbed one another, they robbed God also of his glory by foul idolatry *The statutes of Omri are kept, and all the works of the house of Ahab*, the same abominations were practised, as these wicked kings had enjoined, nor would its being the statute law of their kingdom be any exculpation of the crime no authority can supersede the divine commands

3 For these things God will judge them *Therefore I will make thee sick in smiting thee*, with sore judgments, which should lay waste their kingdom, and make them desolate, *because of their sins* *Thou shalt eat, and not be satisfied*, either wanting food, or the curse of God being upon their provision *and thy casting down shall be in the midst of thee*, intestine discords should render them an easy conquest for the invading foe; their attempts to rescue their friends and families from captivity shall be fruitless or if they preserved a part, another enemy should quickly consume it, v 14 Their corn, wine, and oil should fail them, blasted, and never coming to maturity, or spoiled and devoured by the enemy, v 15 Thus they shall be made a *desolation*, Samaria, their capital, being destroyed by Salmaneser, *and the inhabitants thereof an hissing*, the whole land going into captivity, and treated with scorn and derision by their insulting conqueror, *therefore shall ye bear the reproach of my people*, the wrath threatned against them in the law if they proved rebellious, or the reproach due to the oppressors for their cruelty and injustice to God's people *Note*, (1) When God will visit, he can put a spirit of discord into a land, and make a sinful people their own executioners (2) None deserve severer reproach than those who, by their iniquitous conduct, bring a dishonour upon the religious profession they made

Before Chriſt 710.

CHAP VII.

In this chapter, 1 The prophet, in the name of the church, ſadly laments the woful decay of religion, and the deluge of impiety and immorality which overwhelmed the nation, and bore down the fences of all that is juſt and ſacred, ver 1—6 *2 The prophet, for the ſake of the church, preſcribes comforts, and counſels them what to do* (1) *They muſt have an eye to God,* ver 7 (2) *They muſt courageouſly bear up againſt the inſolences of the enemy,* ver 8—10 (3) *They muſt patiently lie down under the rebukes of their God,* ver 9 (4) *They muſt expect that the trouble would continue long, and endeavour to make the beſt of it,* ver 11—13 (5) *They muſt encourage themſelves with God's promiſes, in anſwer to the prophet's prayers,* ver 14, 15 (6) *They muſt foreſee the fall of their triumphant enemies,* ver 16, 17 (7) *They muſt themſelves triumph in the mercy and faithfulneſs of God,* ver 18—20 *and with that comfortable word the prophecy concludes*

1 WO is me, for I am as † when they have ga-
thered the ſummer-fruits, as the grape-glean-
ings of the vintage *there is* no cluſter to eat [a] my ſoul
deſired the firſt-ripe fruit 2 [b] The ‡ good *man* is pe-
riſhed out of the earth and *there is* none upright among
men they all lie in wait for blood they hunt every
man his brother with a net 3 ¶ That they may [c] do
evil with both hands earneſtly, [d] the prince aſketh, and
the judge *aſketh* for a reward and the great *man* he ut-
tereth ‖ his miſchievous deſire ſo they wrap it up 4
The beſt of them [e] *is* as a brier the moſt upright *is*
ſharper than a thorn-hedge the day of thy watchmen
and the viſitation cometh, now ſhall be their perplexity
5 ¶ [g] Truſt ye not in a friend, put ye not confidence in
a guide keep the doors of thy mouth from her that
lieth in thy boſom 6 For [h] the ſon diſhonoureth the
father, the daughter riſeth up againſt her mother, the
daughter-in-law againſt her mother-in law, a man's ene-
mies *are* the men of his own houſe

† Heb The gatherings of ſummer. a Iſa xxviii 4 Hoſ ix 10. b Pſ xii 1 Iſa lvii 1. ‡ Or godly, or merciful. c Jer iii 5. d Hoſ iv 18. ‖ Heb The miſchief of his ſoul. f Ezek ii 6. g Jer ix 4. h Ezek xxii 7 Mat x 21, 36 Luke xii 53 & xxi 16.

v 1—6 Like righteous Lot, the prophet here bewails his unhappy fate, compelled to dwell among ſuch an abandoned people, for a gracious heart is pained to behold the overflowings of ungodlineſs

1 He was ſingular and ſolitary, and ſcarce could find a gracious companion amidſt the thouſands of his countrymen ſo few good men remained, as the berries which hung on the vine after the gleanings There *is no cluſter to eat,* no ſociety of upright men to join with, *my ſoul deſired the firſt ripe fruit,* longed for the converſe of ſuch as had the firſt fruits of the ſpirit, as the holy men of old, but there were none remaining *The good man is periſhed out of the earth, and there is none upright among men,* at leaſt the prophet could not find them, but, like Elijah, thought he was left alone *Note,* It is a ſad ſymptom of a nation's ruin when good men are taken away, and they who riſe up in their places appear *utterly degenerate from their piety*

2 They ſtick at nothing to get wealth, lying *in wait for blood,* that they may ſeize the ſpoil of the innocent, and like wild beaſts, hunting their very brethren into their toil, that they may plunder and oppreſs them With *both hands* earneſtly they ſet themſelves to the practice of wickedneſs, and even the magiſtrates and princes are chief in the tranſgreſſion Judging for reward, money, not juſtice, ever carrying the cauſe before them *and the great man he uttereth his miſchievous deſire, ſo they wrap it up,* or *twiſt it together,* emboldened by the known corruption of the judge he is not afraid to appear openly in a bad cauſe, and having the prince on his ſide, they make the cords of iniquity ſtrong, or *they perplex it,* rendering the matter ſo intricate, that the truth cannot be eaſily unravelled *The beſt of them,* and bad indeed is that beſt, *is as a brier,* miſchievous and hurtful, *and the moſt upright is ſharper than a thorn-hedge,* they who have any tranſactions with them are ſure to be ſcratched and torn, and for ſuch abomination God will viſit them, *the day of thy watchmen and the viſitation cometh,* the day the true prophet predicted, and the time when judgment ſhould paſs on the wicked watchmen in church and ſtate, *now ſhall be their perplexity,* unable to extricate themſelves from the troubles in which they were involved

3 All good faith was loſt among them, no ſuch thing as a friend was to be met with, and no confidence to be put in any who pretended to be a guide in church or ſtate, nay, the very wife of their boſom was not to be truſted, being in thoſe degenerate days baſe enough to betray the ſecrets of her huſband, v 5

4 All reverence of parents was baniſhed, *the ſon diſhonoureth the father,* ſpeaking contemptibly of him, behaving diſreſpectful and diſobedient, *and the daughter riſeth up againſt her mother,* with rudeneſs unbecoming her ſex, as well as her relation *the daughter in law againſt her mother-in law,* *and a man's enemies are thoſe of his own houſe,* his children, his ſervants, who ſhould be moſt ſollicitous to advance his intereſt, conſpiring to ruin him *Note,* Nothing ſhews an abandoned heart more ſtrongly, than contempt of parental authority

7 Therefore I will [i] look unto the LORD I will
wait for the God of my ſalvation [k] my God will hear
me 8 ¶ [l] Rejoice not againſt me, O mine enemy
[m] When I fall, I ſhall ariſe when I ſit in darkneſs, the
LORD *ſhall be* a light unto me 9 [n] I will bear the
indignation of the LORD, becauſe I have ſinned againſt
him, until he plead my cauſe, and execute judgment for
me he will bring me forth to the light, *and* I ſhall be-
hold his righteouſneſs 10 † Then *ſhe that is* mine
enemy ſhall ſee *it,* and ſhame ſhall cover her which ſaid
unto me, [o] Where is the LORD thy God [p] mine [q] eyes
ſhall behold her now ſhall ſhe be troden down as the
mire of the ſtreets. 11 *In* the day that [q] thy walls are
to be built, *in* that day ſhall the decree be far removed
12 *In* that day *alſo* [r] he ſhall come even to thee from
Aſſyria, and *from* the fortified cities, and from the for-
treſs even to the river, and [s] from ſea to ſea, and *from*
mountain to mountain 13 ‡ Notwithſtanding the land
ſhall be [t] deſolate, becauſe of them that dwell therein, [u]
for the fruit of their doings

i Heb xii 2. k Pſ iv 3. l Lam iv 21. m Pſ xxxvii 24 Prov xxiv 16. n Lam iii 39. † Or and thou wilt ſee her that is mine enemy, and cover her with ſhame. o Pſ xlii 3, 10 & lxxix 10 & cxv 2 Joel ii 17. p Pſ lviii 10 Mic iv 11. q Amos ix 11 &c. r Iſa xix 23 &c. s Iſa lx 4 & lxviii 5. ‡ Or after that it hath been. t Jer ix 6. u Chap iii 12. Jer xxi 14.

v 7—13 In theſe calamitous times the prophet looks upward, thence comes his hope *I will look unto the Lord,* ſince no dependance was to be placed on man, *I will wait for the God of my ſalvation,* for the performance of his promiſes, the removal of the preſent diſtreſſes or for Chriſt's appearing, whoſe incarnation the good men of old ſo earneſtly deſired, *my God will hear me,* and anſwer my prayers, of which alſo all his people may be confident, when they wait upon him faithfully and patiently Having thus caſt his care upon God, the prophet, in the perſon of his people,

1 Profeſſes his confidence in God *Rejoice not againſt me, O mine enemy,* though caſt down, God's people were not deſtroyed, and ſhort would be the triumphing of their enemies, *when I fall, I ſhall ariſe,* ſtrengthened with divine power, *when I ſit in darkneſs,* diſconſolate, dejected, *the Lord ſhall be a light unto me,* reviving, comforting, and quickening me, and bringing me out of all my afflictions, and thus at all times ought the redeemed of the Lord to ſtay themſelves upon him

2 He humbly bows before the chaſtning rod, and owns the righteouſneſs of the ſufferings brought upon the land *I will bear the indignation of the Lord* with patient ſubmiſſion, *becauſe I have ſinned againſt him,* and therefore ſhould not dare murmur againſt God's righteous judgments, for all true penitents lay their mouths in the duſt whatever indignation is upon them, their ſins have deſerved it, and they will juſtify God in his judgments, and ſo doing they may hope for God's appearing on their behalf, *until he plead my cauſe,* as he aſſuredly will in due time, *and execute judgment for me,* pouring down vengeance on all the oppreſſors of his people, *and he will bring me forth to the light,* eſpouſe their quarrel, and reſcuing them from their calamities, making his favour towards them openly appear, *and I ſhall behold his righteouſneſs,* his juſtice in puniſhing their wicked enemies, his grace in ſuccouring his afflicted people, his faithfulneſs in accompliſhing his promiſes, for they who humbly ſubmit themſelves to God and caſt their care upon him, ſhall ever find he careth for them

3 Their enemies, covered with confuſion, ſhall behold this ſalvation, ſo unlike what they looked for, v 10 They once tauntingly aſked, *Where is the Lord thy God?* and now they are anſwered, Lo! this is our God, and we have waited for him *mine eyes ſhall behold her,* their enemies, reduced to the loweſt ſtate of abject wretchedneſs, *now ſhall ſhe be troden down as the mire in the ſtreets* which was fulfilled in the conqueſt of Babylon by the Perſians, and ſhall be proved true in the deſtruction of all the foes of God's ſpiritual Iſrael *In the day that thy walls are to be built,* the walls of Jeruſalem, after their return from Babylon, *in that day ſhall the decree be far removed* which obſtructed the building for a while *In that day alſo he ſhall come unto thee,* multitudes of the Jews returning to Jeruſalem *from Aſſyria, and from the fortified cities,* where they had been captives, and from all places whither they had been diſperſed and fled for ſhelter And in a ſpiritual ſenſe this may be applied to the building the walls of the ſpiritual Zion, into which, from all parts, multitudes of converts ſhall flock together *Notwithſtanding the land ſhall be deſolate, for the cauſe of them that dwell therein, for the fruit of their doings,* theſe gracious prophecies ſhall not ſuperſede the divine threatnings going before, ſo as to embolden the impenitent with hopes of impunity, nor, on the other hand, ſhall all the ſins and ſufferings of the people change theſe deſigns of mercy, which, *notwithſtanding* the diſtreſs to which they ſhall be firſt reduced, ſhall be brought to paſs in their ſeaſon

Before Christ 710

14 ¶ ‖ Feed thy people with thy rod, the flock of
thine heritage, which dwell solitarily *in* the wood, in
(‖ Or rule) the midst of Carmel let them feed *in* Bashan and Gi-
lead, as in the days of old 15 According to the days
of thy coming out of the land of Egypt will I shew
(x Isa xxvi 11) unto him marvellous things 16 ¶ [x] The nations shall
see, and be confounded at all their might [y] they shall
(y Job xxi 5) lay their hand upon *their* mouth, their ears shall be deaf
(z Ps lxxii 9 Isa xlix 23 a Ps xviii 45) 17 They shall lick [z] the dust like a serpent, [a] they shall
move out of their holes like ‡ worms of the earth they
(‡ Or creeping things) shall be afraid of the LORD our God, and shall fear
(b Exod xxxiv 6) because of thee 18 Who *is* a God like unto thee, [b]
that pardoneth iniquity, and passeth by the transgression
(c Ps ciii 9 Isa lvii 16 Jer iii 5) of the remnant of his heritage? [c] he retaineth not his
anger for ever, because he delighteth *in* mercy 19 He
will turn again, he will have compassion upon us he
will subdue our iniquities and thou wilt cast all their
(d Luke i 72, 73) sins into the depths of the sea 20 [d] Thou wilt perform
the truth to Jacob, *and* the mercy to Abraham, which
(e Heb vi 17, 18) thou hast [e] sworn unto our fathers from the days of
old

v 14—20 We have here,

1 The prophet's prayer on the behalf of his people *Feed thy people with thy rod*, directing them in their way, and bringing them into green pastures, *the flock of thine heritage*, whom he hath chosen for his own, and therefore is peculiarly engaged for their preservation and safety, *which dwell solitarily in the wood*, separated from the rest of mankind by the distinguishing grace of God, and even in their captivity unmixed with the nations, *in the midst of Carmel*, scattered in Assyria, as sheep upon a mountain without a shepherd *let them feed in Bashan and Gilead, as in the days of old*, in the richest pastures, abounding in all blessings spiritual and temporal; as will be the case when they shall be gathered from their dispersion into the gospel-church, and made one fold under one shepherd

2 God is pleased graciously to answer the prophet's prayer *According to the days of thy coming out of the land of Egypt, will I shew unto him marvellous things*, as wonderful should be their deliverance from Babylon, as from Egypt, and more amazing his work of redemption by Jesus Christ, rescuing his people from their spiritual enemies, and eclipsing all the former manifestations of his power and grace exerted on their behalf Then insulting foes shall then be confounded, silent with shame, and stopping their ears, as unwilling to hear the wonders of God's love towards his people, *v* 16 Yea, the curse of the serpent shall be upon them, *Gen* iii 14 trodden into the dust, and prostrate before those whom once they trampled upon like *worms of the earth*, scarce daring to lift their heads from their lurking places, for fear of *the Lord our God*, whose judgments are upon them, and *because of thee*, whom they have abused, but now behold triumphant over them And so low shall every enemy of Christ's church and people be brought at last

3 With wonder, love, and praise the prophet beholds what God is about to do for his church *Who is a god like unto thee?* none can be found like him for the perfections of his nature, and the works of his providence and grace, especially *that pardoneth iniquity, and passeth by the transgression of the remnant of his heritage*, this being God's distinguishing glory, that he is a pardoning God, and this above all things raises the admiration, and engages the affections of the miserable sinner *he retaineth not his anger for ever*, though for a time, by our unfaithfulness, we provoke him to visit our iniquities with the rod, and our sin with scourges, he is not implacable nor inexorable, but ready to receive the returning soul, *because he delighteth in mercy*, and waits to be gracious, more ready to pardon than we to pray, and willing to give exceeding abundantly beyond all we can ask or think *He will turn again*, though he withdraws for a little moment his loving-kindness in displeasure, and turns away his face from us, *he will have compassion upon us*, mourning his absence, and seeking his return, he will lift up again the light of his countenance, removing our sorrows, and speaking peace to our troubled souls *he will subdue our iniquities*, delivering us from the power as well as punishment of them, breaking the yoke of corruption, and putting our inbred enemies under our feet His grace shall overcome our depravity, and sin shall not have any longer the dominion over us, which a soul who hath tasted the bitterness of sin, looks upon as the most inestimable blessing *and thou wilt cast all their sins into the depths of the sea*, they shall be not only forgiven but forgotten, so totally done away in the blood of a Redeemer, that they shall never be remembered against us, and not one of all the numerous host ever rise up again to distress, or to destroy us *Thou wilt perform the truth to Jacob, and the mercy to Abraham*, the everlasting covenant of grace shall stand fast to all their seed, and the faithfulness of God is engaged for the fulfilment of it, *which thou hast sworn unto our fathers from the days of old*, that by two immutable things, in which it is impossible that God should lie, we might have strong consolation who have fled for refuge, to lay hold of the hope set before us And for this, for ever and for ever praise the Lord, O my soul!

THE

EVANGELICAL EXPOSITOR;

OR, A

PRACTICAL COMMENT

Upon the PROPHECY of

N A H U M.

THE name of this prophet signifies a comforter, for it was a charge given to all the prophets, Comfort ye, comfort, ye my people, *and even this prophet, tho' wholly taken up in foretelling the destruction of Nineveh, which speaks terror to the Assyrians, yet even in that is a comforter to the ten tribes of Israel, who, it is probable, were now lately carried captives into Assyria It is very uncertain at what time he lived and prophesied, but most probable that he lived in the time of Hezekiah, and prophesied against Nineveh, after the captivity of Israel by the king of Assyria, which was in the ninth year of Hezekiah, and before Sennacherib's invading Judah, which was in the fourteenth year of Hezekiah, for to that attempt, and his defeat, it is suppos'd the first chapter hath reference, and, it is probable, was delivered a little before it, for the encouragement of God's people in that day of treading down and perplexity*

CHAP I

Before Christ 713

In this chapter we have, 1 The inscription of the book, ver 1 2 A magnificent display of the glory of God, in a mixture of wrath against the wicked, and mercy towards his people, and the discovery of his majesty and power in both, ver 2—8 3 A particular application of this to the destruction of Sennacherib and his army, when they besieged Jerusalem which was a very memorable instance of the power both of God's justice and of his mercy, and spoke abundance of terror to his enemies, and encouragement to his faithful servants, ver 9—16

a Zeph ii 13
‡ i e The comforter, or consolation

1 THE burden of [a] Nineveh The book of
the vision of ‡ Nahum the Elkoshite

1 At the preaching of Jonah the Ninevites repented, and were spared, but, returning as the dog to their vomit again, Nahum is sent about an hundred years after to pronounce their doom, and bind the heavy burden of God's wrath upon them

His prophecy is called *The book of the vision of Nahum* it was what God revealed to him, and he wrote in a book, and sent probably to Nineveh The prophet is called the Elkoshite, either from the name of his father, or the place of his birth, there being a village in Galilee, as Jerom reports, called *Helkesi*

† Or the Lord is a jealous God, and a revenger, &c
b Exod xx 5 & xxxiv 14
c Deut xxxii 35
d Exod xxxiv 6 7
e Hab iii 5
f Psal cvi 9 Isa l 2

2 † God *is* [b] jealous, and [c] the LORD revengeth,
the LORD revengeth and *is* furious, the LORD will
take vengeance on his adversaries, and he reserveth
wrath for his enemies 3 The LORD *is* [d] slow to
anger, and great in power, and will not at all acquit *the*
wicked the LORD *hath* his way in the whirlwind, and
in the storm, and in the clouds *are* the dust of his feet
4 [f] He rebuketh the sea, and maketh it dry, and drieth
up all the rivers Bashan languisheth, and Carmel, and
the flower of Lebanon languisheth 5 The mountains
quake at him, and the hills melt, and the earth is burnt
at his presence, yea, the world, and all that dwell there-
in 6 Who can stand before his indignation ? and [h]
who can ‡ abide in the fierceness of his anger ? his fury
is poured out like fire, and the rocks are thrown down
by him 7 The LORD *is* good, || a strong-hold in the
day of trouble, and [i] he knoweth them that trust in
him 8 But [k] with an over-running flood he will make
an utter end of the place thereof, and darkness shall
pursue his enemies

Before Christ 713
g Psal xcvii 5 Mic i 4
h Mal iii 2
‡ Heb stand up
|| Or strength
i Psal i 6 2 Tim ii 19
k Dan ix 26 & xi 10, 22, 40

ver 2—8 Like the pillar of the cloud and fire, the description of the divine perfection and glory speaks terror to the church's foes, and comfort to her friends wrath most fearful and mercy most adorable are here revealed To Nineveh God makes himself known

1 As the *jealous* God, who revengeth the indignities put upon him *The Lord is jealous* of his own honour, and will not suffer his glory to be given to idols, nor tamely see his people insulted He *revengeth*, thrice it is repeated, to shew the certainty and fearfulness of his vengeance He is *furious*, or *master of wrath*, hath it under command, can restrain or let it loose at his pleasure, and this without that perturbation which ever accompanies it in our minds *he reserveth wrath for his enemies*, though spared long by his patience, there is wrath in store for the impenitent, and, though *slow to anger*, *he will not at all acquit the wicked*, who, in opposition to all his warnings, persist in their rebellion against him they will at last be condemned and executed

2 His *power is great*, so, as our fallible is he is angry, yet but a little, who may abide it ? All the elements wait his orders, the wind and storm fulfil his word, and *the clouds are the dust of his feet* on these he cometh forth to judgment, and desolation marks his way, ver 3 At his rebuke the sea, the rivers, are dried, as when of old he opened a way through

Before Christ 713

them for his redeemed to pass over, and the most fruitful spots, as Bashan and Carmel, languish when he is pleased to restrain the dew of heaven, v. 4. His earthquakes shake the tottering mountains and trembling hills, or the mightiest nations, such as the Assyrian, compared to these for strength, are cast down before his indignation. *At his presence the earth is burnt up,* with the parching sun-beams, or forked lightnings, *yea the world, and all that dwell therein,* as it will be at last in the universal conflagration, 2 *Pet.* iii. 10. Before such *indignation,* such devouring *fire,* who can stand, when even the massy rocks are *thrown down* as stubble before him. So weak, so easily ruined, are the greatest kingdoms, and the most hardened and daring sinners. We may well say of such an omnipotent God, that it is good to have him for our friend, but terrible to meet him as an enemy.

3. His mercy to his people is great as his wrath towards his enemies. *The Lord is good* in himself, and in all the dispensations of his providence and grace, *a strong hold in the day of trouble,* as Hezekiah found when he was invaded by Sennacherib, and as the redeemed will ever prove him to be amidst all the trials and temptations with which they are exercised. *he knoweth them that trust in him,* renouncing every other confidence, and staying themselves on him alone; these he knows, approves, delights in, and will protect and preserve them from the power of evil. *But with an overflowing flood will he make an utter end of the place thereof,* of Nineveh; his judgments, like a deluge, shall overwhelm the city and destroy it; *and darkness shall pursue his enemies,* the darkness of affliction and trouble here below, and hereafter they shall be driven into eternal darkness, where there is weeping and wailing and gnashing of teeth.

9 What do ye imagine against the LORD? he will
make an utter end: affliction shall not rise up the second
time. 10 For while *they be* folden together *as* thorns,
and while they are drunken *as* drunkards, they shall
be devoured as stubble fully dry. 11 ¹ There is *one*
come out of thee, that imagineth evil against the
LORD, † a wicked counsellor. 12 Thus saith the
LORD, Though *they be* quiet, and likewise many, ⁿ yet
thus shall they be ‡ cut down, when he shall pass
through. Though I have afflicted thee, I will afflict thee
no more. 13 For now will I break his yoke from off
thee, and will burst thy bonds in sunder. 14 And the
LORD hath given a commandment concerning thee,
that no more of thy name be sown: out of the house
of thy gods will I cut off the graven image, and the
molten image; I will make thy grave; for thou art vile.
15 Behold, ᵒ upon the mountains the feet of him that
bringeth good tidings, that publisheth peace! O Judah,
‖ keep thy solemn feasts, perform thy vows: for § the
wicked shall no more pass through thee; he is utterly
cut off.

¹ Chap. iii. 11. ᵐ 2 Kings xviii. 13. † Heb. A counsellor of Belial. ⁿ 2 Kings xix. 35. ‡ Heb. Shorn. ᵒ Isa. lii. 7. Rom. x. 15. ‖ Heb. Feast. § Heb. Belial.

v. 9—15. It is generally thought these verses refer to the destruction of the Assyrian army under Sennacherib.

1. The Lord mocks at their impotent designs. *What do ye imagine against the Lord?* how vain the counsel, how fruitless the attempt! *There is one come out of thee,* Sennacherib, *that imagineth mischief against the Lord,* to plunder his temple, and captivate his people, *a wicked counsellor,* who by Rabshakeh advised the people to despair of God's help, abandon their king, and submit to his yoke, 2 *Kings* xviii. 29—31. but their politics are as unavailing as their power.

2. He threatens them with *utter* ruin. He will make an end of them at once, and there will be no need to repeat the blow, so compleat shall be their ruin, both of the army at first, and afterward of Nineveh itself, *v.* 9. Unprofitable as thorns, and like them bound up ready for the burning, and *drunken as drunkards,* incapable of making resistance, *they shall be devoured as stubble fully dry,* in which the fire rages, and quickly and irrecoverably it is consumed. *Thus saith the Lord,* whose word is faithful, *though they be quiet,* secure of success, *and likewise many,* and therefore fearing no opposition, *yet thus shall they be cut down, when he shall pass through,* even the destroying angel, who in one night slew a hundred fourscore and five thousand, 2 *Kings* xix. 35. so often do we see sinners cut off in the midst of their carnal security. Nor shall the king escape. *the Lord hath given a commandment concerning thee, that no more of thy name be sown,* his fame and glory should be spread no further, but, returning with ignominy to his own land, he should perish miserably by the hands of his own children. *Out of the house of thy gods will I cut off the graven image and the molten image,* perhaps the temple where he was slain was demolished, as defiled with blood, or this would be the case when the capital should fall into the enemies hand. *I will make thy grave, for thou art vile,* which refers either to Sennacherib himself, brought thus ignominiously to the dust, because of his violence and wickedness; or to Nineveh, whose inhabitants should be buried in the ruin of the city, because of their iniquities. *Note,* They who make themselves in God's sight vile by their sins, shall shortly be made *an abhorring unto all flesh.*

3. God will save his own people out of all their troubles. *Though I have afflicted thee, I will afflict thee no more,* that is to say, no more by Sennacherib, or his successors in Nineveh, to whom they had been tributary; from their bondage God's people shall be set free, the figure of that more glorious liberty into which Jesus, our Redeemer, hath brought the sons of God, *v.* 13. Then shall the glad tidings be diffused through the land, of Sennacherib's army fallen, or of Nineveh destroyed, and *peace* return after the ravages of war. Judah now may resume the interrupted service of the sanctuary, which during this invasion was impracticable to many of the people, and must *perform her vows* made in the day of distress, and now piously and thankfully to be paid to God for her deliverance. Nor is this only a present mercy, but it is farther promised, that *the wicked shall no more pass through thee, he is utterly cut off,* no more should they be invaded by them, but the race of Sennacherib, and Nineveh, the seat of empire, should be utterly cut off and destroyed. *Note,* (1.) The gospel proclaims the glad tidings of pardon and peace by Jesus Christ, and of victory over all our spiritual foes, and beautiful upon the mountains are their feet who publish these tidings of joy. (2.) Every mercy we receive from God should be an engagement to our fidelity, and zeal in his worship and service.

CHAP. II.

We have here, 1. The approach of the enemy that should besiege Nineveh, and the terror of his military preparations, ver. 1—5. 2. The taking the city, ver. 6. 3. The captivity of the queen, the flight of the inhabitants, the seizing of all its wealth, and the mighty consternation it should be in, ver. 7—10. 4. And all this because of their sin against God, and God's appearing against them, ver. 11—13.

1 † HE that dasheth in pieces is come up before
thy face: ᵃ keep the munition, watch the way,
make *thy* loins strong, fortify *thy* power mightily. 2
For ᵇ the LORD hath turned away ‡ the excellency of
Jacob, as ‡ the excellency of Israel: for ᶜ the emptiers
have emptied them out, and marred their vine-branches.
3 The shield of his mighty men is made red, the valiant
men *are* in scarlet: the chariots *shall be* with ‖ flaming
torches in the day of his preparation, and the fir trees
shall be terribly shaken. 4 The chariots shall rage in
the streets, they shall justle one against another in the
broad ways: § they shall seem like torches, they shall run
like the lightnings. 5 He shall recount his worthies:
they shall stumble in their walk; they shall make haste
to the wall thereof, and the ‡ defence shall be prepared.
6 The gates of the rivers shall be opened, and the palace
shall be dissolved. 7 And ‡ Huzzab shall be ‖ led
away captive, she shall be brought up, and her maids
shall lead *her* as with the voice of doves, tabring upon
their breasts. 8 But Nineveh *is* of old like a pool of
water: yet they shall flee away. Stand, stand, *shall they
cry*; but none shall § look back. 9 Take ye the spoil
of silver, take the spoil of gold: for *there is* none end
of the store, *and* glory out of all the † pleasant furniture.
10 She is empty, and void, and waste: and ᵈ the heart
melteth, and ᵉ the knees smite together, and much pain
is in all loins, *and* ᶠ the faces of them all gather blackness.

† Or, the disperser, or, hammer. ᵃ Jer. li. 11. ᵇ Isa. x. 12. ‡ Or, the pride. ᶜ Ps. lxxx. 12. ‖ Or, fiery torches. § Heb. Their show. ‡ Heb. Covering, or coverer. ‡ Or, that which was established. ‖ Or, discovered. § Or, cause them to turn. ‡ Or, and their infinite store. † Heb. Vessels of desire. ᵈ Isa. xiii. 7, 8. ᵉ Dan. v. 6. ᶠ Joel ii. 6.

v. 1—10. Nineveh is doomed to fall, and lo! her enemies approach. *He that dasheth in pieces is come up before thy face,* Nabopolassar the Babylonian, with Cyaxares the Mede, *Tobit* xiv. 15. The Ninevites are ironically called to *keep the munition,* to guard the walls, to *watch the way* to the avenues of the city, to *make their loins strong,* and *fortify their power mightily,* to do their utmost to ward off the blow, but all their efforts will be vain, since their ruin is decreed.

1. The cause of it, among other provocations, is their ill usage of God's Israel. *The Lord hath turned away the excellency of Jacob as the excellency of Israel,* hath humbled and brought them low, and hath employed the Assyrian as his instrument; but they gratified their pride, covetousness, and ambition herein, *for the emptiers have emptied them out, and marred their vine branches,* plundering and destroying the country, and leading many of the people into captivity.

2. The terrible destruction coming upon Nineveh, for this and all her other sins, is described. The shields of the enemy are prepared, glittering with burnished brass, or red with the blood of the slain. *The valiant men in scarlet,* magnificently arrayed,

Before Christ 713

arrayed; *their chariots*, when preparing for the ſiege, ſhall ſhine *with flaming torches*, to direct their way by night, or ſet fire to the city. *The fir-trees*, the mighty men of Nineveh, *ſhall be terribly ſhaken*, quaking for fear, whilſt *the chariots* of the enemy *rage in the ſtreets*, approaching the gates, or entered into the city, ſo eager to advance, that they ſhall *juſtle one againſt another*, devouring as *torches* of fire, and ſwift as *lightning*, ver. 4. *He ſhall recount his worthies*, chuſing out the mighty men to ſtorm the place, and in haſte to obey, they ſhall ſtumble, though inſtantly recovering themſelves, and mounting the breach, under the cover of *the defence* which *is prepared*, ver. 5. Or this may be underſtood of the king of Nineveh muſtering his forces, manning the walls, and preparing to ſuſtain the ſiege, though his warriors *ſhall ſtumble in their walk*, and fall; at laſt the beſiegers ſhall enter *at the gates of the rivers*, either forced or betrayed into their hands, and then *the palace ſhall be diſſolved*, both the temples of the idols, and the houſes of their princes ſhall be laid in ruins, *and Huzzab ſhall be led away captive*, which ſome interpret of the queen, others of the king, compared to a woman for his effeminacy; or perhaps it may ſignify Nineveh itſelf, which before *ſat as a queen*, but is now hurled from her dignity, and lamented by her maids of honour, her inhabitants, who, whilſt they are repreſented ſupporting her fainting under her calamities, utter their doleful moans, and beat their breaſts for grief and anguiſh, v. 7. Thus, though of old this mighty city was like *a pool of water*, full of wealth and inhabitants, and tranquil and at eaſe, *yet they ſhall flee away*, like waters when the dam is broken down, and as weak before their enemies; in vain ſome gallant chief ſhould cry, *Stand, ſtand*, panic fear hath ſeized them, and none dares even look behind him. The beſiegers now are called to ſeize *the ſpoil of ſilver, gold*, and rich furniture, immenſe, invaluable; and thoroughly is the city ranſacked, and left *empty, void*, and *waſte*, without inhabitant, a heap of ruins; none of that populous place dare reſiſt, their hearts are melted, their knees knock againſt each other, they are like women in travail, and their countenances darkned like the livid faces of the dead.

11 Where *is* the dwelling of the lions, and the feed-
ing-place of the young lions? where the lion, *even* the
old lion walked, *and* the lion's whelp, and none made
g Ezek. xix. 2. *them* afraid. 12 The lion did tear in pieces [g] enough
for his whelps, and ſtrangled for his lioneſſes, and filled
his holes with prey, and his dens with ravin. 13 Be-
hold, I *am* againſt thee, ſaith the LORD of hoſts, and
I will burn her chariots in the ſmoke, and the ſword
ſhall devour thy young lions, and I will cut off thy prey
h 2 Kings xix. 9. from the earth, and the voice of [h] thy meſſengers ſhall
no more be heard.

V. 11—13. They who inſulted over the calamities of others, juſtly deſerve retaliation in the day of their diſtreſs.

1. Nineveh is triumphed over by her enemies. Like a lion in time paſt had the king of this ſtrong city ravened uncontrouled, and filled his young lions with food, and the den with prey, *and ſtrangled for his lioneſſes*, his wives and concubines, who ſhared the ſpoils of the conquered nations, whilſt none dared withſtand or oppoſe him: but where is his dwelling now? it is deſolate and ruined. *Note*, Wealth gotten by violence is a precarious tenure, a ſhort-lived poſſeſſion.

2. God is her enemy, therefore ſhe muſt fall. *Behold, I am againſt thee*, and his wrath is more terrible than innumerable foes; he *will burn her chariots in the ſmoke* of the city in flames round them, *and the ſword ſhall devour the young lions*, the inhabitants thereof, their children, enriched by rapine and ſpoil; *I will cut off thy prey from the earth*, deſtroying all their ſubſtance which they had collected, *and the voice of thy meſſengers ſhall be no more heard*, demanding tribute, menacing the poor ſubjected nations, or like Rabſhekah, uttering their blaſphemies againſt God. *Note*, (1.) God will ſhortly ſilence the tongue of the blaſphemer. (2.) They who, to raiſe wealth for their children, ſtick at no fraud or injuſtice, are in righteous judgment deprived of them.

CHAP. III.

This chapter concludes the burden of Nineveh. 1. The ſins of that great city are charged upon it, murder, ver. 1. whoredom and witchcraft, ver. 4. and a general extent of wickedneſs, ver. 19. 2. Judgments are threatned againſt it, blood for blood, ver. 2, 3. and ſhame for ſhameful ſins, ver. 5, 6, 7. 3. Inſtances are given of the like deſolations brought upon other places for the like ſins, ver. 8—11. 4. The overthrow of all thoſe things which they put their confidence in, is foretold, ver. 12—19.

a Ezek. xxiv. 6, 9. Hab. ii. 12. † Heb. City of bloods. 1 WO to [a] the † bloody city, it *is* all full of lies
and robbery, the prey departeth not. 2 The
noiſe of a whip, and the noiſe of the rattling of the
wheels, and of the prancing of horſes, and of the jump-
ing chariots. 3 The horſemen lifted up both ‡ the
bright ſword, and the glittering ſpear, and *there is* a mul-
titude of ſlain, and a great number of carcaſes, and
there is none end of their corpſes; they ſtumble upon
their corpſes: 4 Becauſe of the multitude of the whore-
doms of the well-favoured harlot, [b] the miſtreſs of witch-
crafts, that ſelleth nations through her whoredoms, and
families through her witchcrafts. 5 Behold, I *am* a-
gainſt thee, ſaith the LORD of hoſts, and [c] I will diſ-
cover thy ſkirts upon thy face, [d] and I will ſhew the na-
tions thy nakedneſs, and the kingdoms thy ſhame. 6
And I will caſt abominable filth upon thee, and make
thee vile, and will ſet thee as a gazing-ſtock. 7 And it
ſhall come to paſs, *that* all they that look upon thee,
ſhall flee from thee, and ſay, Nineveh is laid waſte, [e]
who will bemoan her? whence ſhall I ſeek comforters
for thee?

‡ Heb. The flame of the ſword, and the lightning of the ſpear.
b Iſa. xlvii. 9, 12. Rev. xviii. 2, 3.
c Iſa. xlvii. 2, 3. Jer. xiii. 22, 26. Ezek. xvi. 37.
d Hab. ii. 16.
e Jer. xv. 5.

V. 1—7. Where ſin unrepented is found, there all the terrible woes of God are written againſt the guilty ſoul.

1. The ſins of Nineveh are charged upon her. It is *a bloody city*: innocent blood was ſhed there with impunity, or by the unjuſt wars her ambition waged againſt her neighbours; *full of lies*, where no honeſty, truth, or fidelity was to be found; and *of robbery*, each preying on his neighbour, or on the nations around them; *the prey departeth not*, they never deſiſt from plundering, nor think of making reſtitution to the injured. *her whoredoms* were multiplied, both carnal and ſpiritual: her idolatries notorious, their lewdneſs infamous; like a well-favoured harlot ſhe enticed the nations to learn her ways, and, being a *miſtreſs of witchcrafts*, bound them as with magic ſpell to ſell themſelves to work wickedneſs, and, having brought them firſt under corporal bondage, afterwards enſlaved their ſouls. *Note*, The charms of a harlot are like the ſpells of witchcraft, and iſſue in the deſtruction of body and ſoul.

2. Her judgment is read. The noiſe of the invading foe is heard, *the whip* of the charioteer, the *rattling of the wheels*, the *prancing of the horſes*, the *jumping of the chariots*, ſound terrible: *the bright ſword* is unſheathed, the *glittering ſpear* is brandiſhed, and ſo innumerable the multitude of the ſlain, that the very ſtreets and ways are obſtructed by them, and men *ſtumble* over them, v. 3. Since God is her foe, ſhe ſhall be ſtripped naked to her ſhame, deprived of all her wealth and power, expoſed as a ſtrumpet to the deriſion of thoſe ſhe had ſeduced, carted as a whore, and daubed with *abominable filth* and dung, *made vile* and contemptible, *a gazing-ſtock* of public reproach and infamy; every paſſenger, inſtead of affording the leaſt kindneſs or compaſſion, ſhall ſhun her with abhorrence, *and ſay, Nineveh is laid waſte*, pleaſed to proclaim the tidings, or aſtoniſhed at the fearful change; *who ſhall bemoan her?* ſhe deſerves no pity, that ſhewed none: *whence ſhall I ſeek comforters for thee?* the calamity is too great to admit of conſolation, nor can any be found to diſcharge this friendly office to a city ſo univerſally deteſted. *Note*, (1.) They who in the day of their proſperity treated others with inſolence, may expect, when they fall, to be trampled upon by every foot. (2.) The beſt-favoured harlot will ſhortly be a foul hag, hated and ſhunned by her former deareſt paramours.

8 [f] Art thou better than ‖ populous [g] No, that was
ſituate among the rivers, *that had* the waters round about
it, whoſe rampart *was* the ſea, *and* her wall *was* from
the ſea? 9 Ethiopia and Egypt *were* her ſtrength, and
it was infinite; Put and Lubim were thy helpers. 10
Yet *was* ſhe carried away, ſhe went into captivity: [h] her
young children alſo were daſhed in pieces [i] at the top
of all the ſtreets: and they caſt lots for her honourable
men, and all her great men were bound in chains. 11
Thou ſhalt alſo be [k] drunken: thou ſhalt be hid, thou
alſo ſhalt ſeek ſtrength becauſe of the enemy. 12 All
thy ſtrongholds *ſhall be like* [l] fig-trees with the firſt ripe
figs: if they be ſhaken they ſhall even fall into the
mouth of the eater. 13 Behold, [m] thy people in the
midſt of thee *are* women: the gates of thy land ſhall be
ſet wide open unto thine enemies, the fire ſhall devour
thy bars. 14 Draw thee waters for the ſiege, [n] fortify
thy ſtrongholds: go into clay, and tread the morter,
make ſtrong the brick-kiln. 15 There ſhall the fire
devour thee; the ſword ſhall cut thee off, it ſhall eat
thee up like the canker-worm: make thyſelf many as
the canker-worm, make thyſelf many as the locuſts.
16 Thou haſt multiplied thy merchants above the ſtars
of heaven: the canker-worm ‖ ſpoileth and flieth away.
17. [o] Thy crowned *are* as the locuſts, and thy captains

f Amos vi. 2.
‖ Heb. No Amon.
g Jer. xlvi. 25, 26. Ezek. xxx. 14—16.
h Pſ. cxxxvii. 9. Iſa. xiii. 16. Hoſ. xiii. 16.
i Lam. ii. 19.
k Jer. xxv. 17. Chap. i. 10.
l Rev. vi. 13.
m Iſa. iii. 25. & ii. 30.
n Chap. ii. 1.
‖ Or ſpreadeth himſelf.
o Rev. ix. 7.

Before Christ 713

p Ex xv 16 Ps lxvi 6
§ Or valiant ones
q 1 Kings xxii 17
r Lam ii 15

as the great graſhoppers, which camp in the hedges in
the cold day, *but* when the ſun ariſeth they flee away,
and their place is not known where they *are* 18 [p] Thy
ſhepherds ſlumber, O king of Aſſyria thy § nobles
ſhall dwell *in the duſt* [q] thy people is ſcattered upon the
mountains, and no man gathereth *them* 19 *There is*
no healing of thy bruiſe thy wound is grievous [r] all
that hear the bruit of thee ſhall clap the hands over thee,
for upon whom hath not thy wickedneſs paſſed continually?

v 8—19 All the vain confidences of Nineveh are here deſtroyed She thought herſelf ſafe becauſe of her greatneſs, but vain is her preſumption *Art thou better than populous No?* which ſome ſuppoſe to be Thebes, others Memphis, others Alexandria, a city vaſt and full of inhabitants, fortified by art and nature, and ſituate in a place almoſt inacceſſible to an enemy, *v* 8 ſupported by all the united forces of Egypt and Ethiopia, whoſe armies were immenſe, and helped by her confederates of Libya and Mauritania yet with all theſe advantages No was deſtroyed, probably by Sennacherib, the inhabitants carried captives, the infants daſhed in pieces againſt the ſtones by the inhuman ſoldiers, her honourable men divided by lot as ſlaves among the conquerors, and her nobles bound in chains And if ſuch a city fell ſo fearfully, the men of Nineveh ought not to be thus ſecure the ſame treatment awaited them

1 Their forces ſhall be diſpirited, weakened, and deſtroyed, ſtaggering like drunkards, effeminate, and terrified as women, *v* 13 flying to hide themſelves, and ſeeking in vain help from others againſt their enemies for, when God diſpirits the hoſt, the braveſt turn cowards

2 Their fortreſſes ſhall ſtand them in no ſtead Though they take every precaution to repair the walls, to lay in proviſion, to place numerous garriſons therein, and aſſemble their whole force in order to oppoſe the invaders, *v* 14, 15 yet *their ſtrongholds* ſhall fall as eaſily before the beſiegers as a *ripe fig* when the tree is ſhaken, *v* 12 her gates ſhall be ſet wide open, the fire ſhall devour the bars, *v* 13 and with the ſword ſhall their enemies conſume, as the canker-worm, all the inhabitants of their cities, though numerous as the ſwarms of locuſts, *v* 15

3 Their friends ſhall deſert them The merchants, that once crouded the ſtreets of Nineveh, and enriched themſelves with the traffick there carried on, will no ſooner behold the ſtorm approaching, than with their wealth they will forſake the devoted city, and *fly away as the canker-worm* when the field is eaten up, and their auxiliaries and tributary kings, who in the days of peace camped around them, and promiſed them aſſiſtance, no ſooner feel the ſcorching ſun of danger, than like locuſts, they take their flight and are heard of no more

4 Their princes and officers, the ſhepherds who ſhould defend the flock, *ſlumber*, enervated with ſloth and luxury, and aſleep when they ſhould be at their poſts, or they ſleep the ſleep of death, and are laid with *the nobles in the duſt*, whilſt the people, as ſheep without a ſhepherd, are ſcattered, and fall an eaſy prey to the enemy

5 Their caſe is deſperate Their *bruiſe* incurable, their *wound grievous*, the city and empire fall together at a blow, never to be reſtored again With triumph ſhall the oppreſſed nations *clap their hands* at the ſound of their fall, *for upon whom hath not thy wickedneſs paſſed continually?* having been oppreſſed, harraſſed, and plundered by the Aſſyrians they will rejoice to ſee their deſtroyers deſtroyed Let proud oppreſſors and hardened ſinners tremble their day ſhall come to fall, and heaven and earth ſhall exult in their deſtruction

THE

THE EVANGELICAL EXPOSITOR; OR, A PRACTICAL COMMENT Upon the PROPHECY of HABAKKUK.

THE time of Habakkuk's prophesying is not said: the most probable conjecture is that he lived in the reign of king Manasseh, when wickedness abounded, and destruction was hastening on, destruction by the Chaldeans, whom this prophet mentions as the instruments of God's judgments, and Manasseh was himself carried to Babylon, as an earnest of what should come afterwards. The mention made of Habakkuk in the apocryphal book of Bel and the Dragon, and what the rabbins say of his being the son of the Shunamite, are mere Jewish fables. The prophecy of this book is a mixture of the prophet's addresses to God in the people's name, and to the people in God's name: for it is the office of the prophets to carry messages both ways. And we have in it a lively representation of the intercourse and communion that there is between a gracious God and a gracious soul. The whole particularly refers to the invasion of the land of Judah by the Chaldeans, who spoiled the people of God, as a just punishment of the spoil they had been guilty of among themselves: but it is of general use, especially to help us through that great temptation with which good men have in all ages been exercised, arising from the power and prosperity of the wicked, and the sufferings of the righteous by it.

Before Christ 690

CHAP. I.

In this chapter, 1. The prophet complains to God of the violence done by the abuse of the sword of justice *among his own people, and the hardships thereby put upon many good people,* ver. 1—4. 2. *God by him foretels the punishment of that abuse of power by the* sword of war, *and the desolations which the army of the Chaldeans should make upon them,* ver. 5—11. 3. *Then the prophet complains of that too, and is grieved that the Chaldeans prevail so far,* ver. 12—17.

1 THE burden which ‡ Habakkuk the pro-
phet did [a] see. 2. O LORD, how long
shall I cry, and thou wilt not hear! *even*
[b] cry out unto thee *of* violence, and thou
wilt not save! 3 Why dost thou shew me iniquity, and
cause *me* to behold grievance? for spoiling and violence
are ‖ before me: and there are *that* raise up strife and
contention. 4 Therefore the law is § slacked, and
judgment doth never go forth: for [c] the wicked doth
compass about the righteous; therefore ‖ wrong judg-
ment proceedeth.

‡ i.e. An embracer, or the embracer. a Isa. i. 1. b Jer. xx. 8. ‖ Or, against. § Or, intermitted. c Job xxi. 7. Jer. xii. 1. ‖ Or, wrested.

v. 1—4. This prophecy is called a burden, as it contains a heavy threatning of wrath for provoking iniquities.

1. The prophet bewails the miserable state of the land, where violence raged, iniquity reigned with impunity, rapine and injustice appeared without a veil, and whilst families and neighbours were set at variance by those who *raise up strife and contention*, the kingdom was torn with intestine divisions, fomented by the wicked, who loved to fish in these troubled waters. *The law is slacked*, hath lost all its vigour, *and judgment doth never go forth* against the offenders, who are emboldened to commit every crime by this neglect: but, though the guilty escape, the innocent are persecuted, *for the wicked doth compass about the righteous*, confederate to oppress the few faithful, and pervert justice, *therefore wrong judgment proceedeth*, the just are condemned, whilst the criminals are acquitted. And when wickedness is thus prevalent in a nation, ruin cannot be far off.

2. The prophet bewails his own unhappy fate, condemned to dwell in the sight of such abominations, which grieved his righteous soul, *v.* 3. and though an importunate advocate with God, no answer was given him. *O Lord, how long shall I cry, and thou wilt not hear? even cry unto thee of violence, and thou wilt not save!* notwithstanding all his prayer, no stop was put to the abounding ungodliness, and on this account he expostulates, lest it should seem as if the Lord had forsaken the earth, when wickedness thus prospered. *Note*, (1.) When we can do no more for sinners, it becomes us still to pray for them. (2.) Gracious souls, whilst they are in the world, must bear this burden, of seeing and hearing abominations that grieve their spirits: but yet a little while they shall be released, and go where the wicked cease from troubling. (3.) It hath been a trial to many a good man's faith to behold prosperous iniquity; but we shall shortly see God justified in all his works and ways.

5. ¶ [a] Behold ye among the heathen, and regard, and
wonder marvellously: for I will work a work in your
days, *which* ye will not believe though it be told *you*.
6 For lo, [e] I raise up the Chaldeans, *that* bitter and
hasty nation, which shall march through the ‡ breadth
of the land, to possess the dwelling-places *that are* not
theirs.

a Isa. xxix. 14. Acts xiii. 41. e 2 Chron. xxxvi. 6. ‡ Heb. Breadths.

Before Chriſt 690

theirs 7 They are terrible and dreadful ‡ their judg-
ment and their dignity ſhall proceed of themſelves 8
Their horſes alſo are ſwifter than the leopards, and are
more fierce than [f] the evening wolves and their horſe-
men ſhall ſpread themſelves, and their horſemen ſhall come
from far, [g] they ſhall fly as the eagle *that* haſteth to eat
9 They ſhall come all for violence § their faces ſhall
ſup up *as* the eaſt-wind, and they ſhall gather the cap-
tivity as the ſand 10 And they ſhall ſcoff at the
kings, and the princes *ſhall be* a ſcorn unto them they
ſhall deride every ſtrong hold, for they ſhall heap duſt
and take it 11 Then ſhall *his* mind change, and he
ſhall paſs over, and offend, [h] *imputing* this his power un-
to his god

‡ Or from them ſhall proceed the judgment of theſe and the captivity of theſe
f Jer v 6 Zeph iii 3
g Jer iv 13
§ Heb The oppoſition of their faces toward the eaſt
h Dan v 4

v 5—11 Though God bears long with the veſſels of wrath fitted for deſtruction, he will not bear always

1 He gives them notice of a terrible judgment ready to deſcend upon them *Behold ye among the heathen, and regard,* ſee what fearful work God is doing among them, and Iſrael's turn would ſhortly come, *and wonder marvellouſly,* aſtoniſhed at the deſolations which are wrought in the earth *for I will work a work in your days, which ye will not believe though it be told you,* which was the deſtruction of the Jewiſh nation, with their cities, and the temple at Jeruſalem, which the Chaldeans, under the divine direction, would accompliſh, and this within the preſent age, ſo that many then alive ſhould ſee what the people of the Jews in general, notwithſtanding all the prophetic warnings, treated as utterly incredible The Apoſtle applies this to the deſpiſers of Chriſt and his goſpel, whoſe deſtruction, terrible and ſure, approaches, notwithſtanding their inſenſibility and preſumption

2 He deſcribes the dreadful ravages the Chaldeans ſhould make among them Raiſed up at God's call, and ſent to execute his vengeance, they ſhall come to ſeize by conqueſt the dwelling-places which are not theirs and, among other victims to their ambition, Judea ſhall be ſubdued by them They are deſcribed as a *bitter and haſty nation,* cruel and merciless in their diſpoſitions, inveterate in their enmities, and rapid in executing their enterprizes *they are terrible and dreadful,* the fame of their victories is ſpread, and their fierce look injects diſmay into their enemies *their judgment and their dignity ſhall proceed of themſelves,* their will is their rule, imperious in their commands, and ſtrangers to the laws of clemency, equity, and humanity *Their cavalry, ſwifter than the leopards,* and *fiercer than evening wolves,* ſhall charge, purſue, and bear down all oppoſition, plundering and devouring the country, ſpreading themſelves on every ſide, and haſting from their own diſtant land with ſuch velocity as the eagle darteth on his prey, *v* 8 *They ſhall come all for violence,* purely to ravage and ſpoil *their faces ſhall ſup up as the eaſt-wind,* blaſting all before them, leaving the land bare, or *their faces ſhall look towards the eaſt,* deſigning to tranſfer their ſpoil and captives thither, which they collect innumerable *as the ſand, v* 9 *They ſhall ſcoff at the kings* of Judah, with their nobles and confederates, *deriding every ſtrong hold,* as unable to reſiſt their victorious arms *for they ſhall heap duſt and take it,* ſo eaſily will their mounts be raiſed by their numerous pioneers *Then ſhall his mind change* the king of Babylon, grown haughty by ſucceſs, ſhall meditate new conqueſts, and *he ſhall paſs over* all bounds of reaſon and equity, *and ſhall offend* by new acts of cruelty and injuſtice, *imputing this his power unto his god,* aſcribing his ſucceſs to his idol deities Though ſome underſtand the words in a different ſenſe, as predicting Nebuchadnezzar's puniſhment *His mind ſhall change* from a man to a beaſt, and *he ſhall paſs over* from the ſociety of men to dwell in the deſert, *and be puniſhed* for his pride and wickedneſs, for making *this his power his god,* as if he were a divinity, and poſſeſſed omnipotence *Note,* (1) It is a fearful thing to fall into the hands of deſpotic tyrants (2) Succeſs often miniſters fuel for pride, and many by proſperity have their *minds changed* for the worſe

12 ¶ [i] *Art* thou not from everlaſting, O LORD my
God, mine holy One? we ſhall not die O LORD,
[k] thou haſt ordained them for judgment, and O † mighty
God, thou haſt eſtabliſhed them for correction 13
[l] *Thou art* of purer eyes than to behold evil, and canſt
not look on ‡ iniquity wherefore lookeſt thou upon
them [m] that deal treacherouſly, *and* holdeſt thy tongue
when the wicked devoureth *the man that is* more righte-
ous than he? 14 And makeſt men as the fiſhes of the
ſea, as the § creeping things *that have* no ruler over them?
15 [n] They take up all of them with the angle they
catch them in their net, and gather them in their drag,
therefore they rejoice and are glad 16 Therefore [o] they
ſacrifice unto their net, and burn incenſe unto their drag
becauſe by them their portion *is* fat, and their meat
‖ plenteous 17 Shall they therefore empty their net,
and not ſpare continually to ſlay the nations?

i Lam v 19
k 2 Kings xix 25 Iſa x 5—7
† Heb Rock Deut xxxii 4
l Pſ v 5
‡ Or grievance
m Iſa xxi 2
§ Or moving
n Amos iv 2
o Iſa x 13 & xxxvii 24, 25
‖ Heb fat

v 12—17 The judgments ready to come upon the people diſtreſſed the prophet, as their ſins had done before, ſeeing the righteous, as well as the wicked, would be involved therein, he therefore flies to God in prayer, and expoſtulates with him on theſe afflictive diſpenſations, that he may obtain an anſwer to ſatisfy his own mind, and thoſe who, like him, approved ſtill their fidelity to God

1 He profeſſeth his own unſhaken faith in God, under every circumſtance of diſtreſs and difficulty *Art thou not from everlaſting?* thou art the ſame unchangeable Jehovah, whoſe covenant ſtands faſt, and is like his nature, everlaſting, *O Lord, my God,* in whoſe favour he had an aſſured intereſt, *mine holy One,* whoſe diſpenſations, however dark to us, are perfectly righteous and true, who is *holy* eſſentially, and the author of all holineſs to others, *we ſhall not die,* however threatning the judgments, the nation ſhall not utterly be extirpated, the covenant of the eternal God forbids it and hence every believer muſt draw his conſolation, and derive ſupport to his faith when ſhaken by temptation His life is bound up with that of the eternal God, *becauſe,* ſays Jeſus, *I live, ye ſhall live alſo*; though the Chaldeans threatned high, they were but inſtruments in God's hand *O Lord, thou haſt ordained them for judgment,* to puniſh the wicked, *O mighty God,* whoſe power can over-rule all the purpoſes of men, *thou haſt eſtabliſhed them for correction,* to chaſten thy children for good, that they may not be delivered unto death, this being the gracious deſign of God in all the afflictions he ſends upon his choſen, and which ſhould be their comfort under them *Thou art of purer eyes than to behold evil, and canſt not look upon iniquity,* not that God's eye is not in every place, but he doth not approve of wickedneſs, it is his abhorrence, nor can he ſee the afflictions of his people, and the iniquity of their oppreſſors, with connivance or ſatisfaction, and to theſe principles he reſolved to adhere, however appearances might ſeem to contradict them *Note,* (1) Sound and well-eſtabliſhed principles are the great ſupport in time of trial (2) God's permiſſion of wickedneſs doth not imply his approbation, nor is the evil he ſuffers his people to undergo any mark of his diſpleaſure, but contrariwiſe, becauſe they are ſons, he chaſtiſeth them with the rod of men

2 He begs a ſolution of his difficulties under the preſent diſtreſsful ſcene before him, when piety was oppreſſed, and wickedneſs triumphant *wherefore lookeſt thou upon them that deal treacherouſly,* giving them ſucceſs in their perfidious deſigns, *and holdeſt thy tongue when the wicked devoureth the man that is more righteous than he?* as the Chaldeans did the Jews, and God's ſilence diſtreſſed the prophet and other good men, how to reconcile this with their general principles *And makeſt men as the fiſhes of the ſea,* ſeeming to ſhew no more care towards men in general, and his own people in particular, than over the fiſhes, where the weaker are a prey to the ſtrong, and whoever will may take them in their net, *as the creeping things that have no ruler over them,* to protect and defend them Thus helpleſs were they before their enemies, as if God had forſaken the earth, and left the good a prey to the wicked and the weak a ſpoil to the ſtrong, to be caught as eaſily as fiſh *with the angle,* and by a variety of means, by the net or drag, to be ſeized and deſtroyed without concern yea, to be a ſport and paſtime to their murderers, as fiſhermen *rejoice and are glad* when their net is filled, *v* 15 *Therefore they ſacrifice to their own net, and burn incenſe to their own drag,* applaud themſelves in their own contrivances, and the ſucceſs of them, *becauſe by them their portion is fat, and their meat plenteous,* they thus enlarged their wealth, and were enabled to live more luxuriouſly, and this was their happineſs *Shall they therefore empty their net, and not ſpare continually to ſlay the nations?* ſhall they go on ſucceſsfully from nation to nation, murdering and plundering at their pleaſure? Will a righteous God permit this? he leaves the matter with the Lord, and in faith and hope is emboldened to expect his interpoſition *Note,* (1) Whatever difficulties occur in the divine providence, we muſt caſt our care upon God, and wait patiently for his ſalvation (2) Ambitious princes make no more account of men than of fiſhes, and rejoice in battles gained at the expence of multitudes of lives, but God will reckon ſuch conquerors as the moſt bloody murderers of mankind

CHAP. II

The anſwer given to the prophet's prayer is, 1 That after God hath ſerved his own purpoſes by the prevailing power of the Chaldeans, has tried the faith and patience of his people, and diſtinguiſhed between the hypocrites and the ſincere among them, he will reckon with the Chaldeans for their inſatiable thirſt after dominion and wealth, for which they themſelves ſhould at length be made a prey, ver 2—8 2 *That not they only, but all other ſinners like them, ſhould periſh under a divine woe* (1) *Thoſe that are greedy of wealth and honours,* ver 9—11 (2) *Thoſe that are injurious and oppreſſive, and raiſe eſtates by wrong and rapine,* ver 12—14 (3) *Thoſe that promote drunkenneſs, that they may expoſe their neighbours to ſhame,* ver 15—17 (4) *Thoſe that worſhip idols,* ver 18—20.

2 1 I

Before Chriſt 690

1 I WILL [a] ſtand upon my watch, and ſet me upon
the tower, and [b] will watch to ſee what he will ſay
unto me, and what I ſhall anſwer † when I am re-
proved 2 And the LORD anſwered me, and ſaid,
[c] Write the viſion, and make *it* plain upon tables, that
he may run that readeth it 3 For [d] the viſion *is* yet
for an appointed time, but at the end it ſhall ſpeak, and
not lye though it tarry, wait for it, becauſe it will
[e] ſurely come, it will not tarry 4 Behold, his ſoul
which is lifted up, is not upright in him but [f] the juſt
ſhall live by his faith

a Iſa xxi 8, 11. b Pſ lxxxv 8. † Or in me. ‡ Heb Upon my reproof, or arguing. c Iſ viii 1. d xxx 8. Dan x 14. e Heb x 37. f John iii 36. Rom i 17. Gal iii 11. Heb x 38.

v 1—4 We have here,

1 The prophet waiting in faith for an anſwer to his prayer *I will ſtand upon my watch, and ſet me upon my tower*, as a watchman waiting for intelligence, *and will watch to ſee what he will ſay to me*, with regard to the requeſts he had made, and the difficulties he was under, *and what I ſhall anſwer when I am reproved*, either for the boldneſs of his expoſtulations, or how he ſhould ſilence the objections of others, who might, from theſe melancholy appearances, argue againſt the providence of God *Note*, (1) When we are in perplexity, and know not how to reconcile God's providences with his promiſes, we muſt go up to the tower of prayer and meditation and ſtand our ground there by faith againſt the aſſaults of temptation, looking to God for an anſwer of peace (2) When we have been with God in prayer, conſulting his word, or reflecting on his diſpenſations, we muſt obſerve what God *ſpeaks unto us* by any of theſe means, for our conviction, direction, encouragement, or conſolation

2 God anſwers him in mercy, and ſhews him the deſtruction of theſe mercileſs ravagers for he never diſappoints the expectations of his waiting people For the comfort of the faithful he is commanded to *write the viſion*, that it may be preſerved, and handed down, unadulterated by tradition; *and make it plain upon tables*, which were then uſed for writing, and covered with wax, on which the letters were impreſſed, and this was to be done very plainly, and hung up in ſome conſpicuous place, *that he may run that readeth it*, ſo legible that it might be eaſily read even by the moſt curſory look, or as one ran by it and but turned his head that way And ſuch ſhould our preaching be, that the meaneſt capacities might comprehend it, never wiſhing to be admired as orators, but uſing all plainneſs of ſpeech, that God's word may be underſtood *For the viſion is yet for an appointed time* though it be diſtant, the day of its accompliſhment is fixed and ſure *at the end it ſhall ſpeak, and not lie*; the Lord will not diſappoint the faith and patience of his people, or *He will ſpeak*, who is the faithful and true witneſs, the prophet come to lead us into all truth *Though it*, the promiſe, or *He*, the Meſſiah, *tarry long*, or at leaſt ſeem to do ſo to thoſe who longed for his appearing, *wait for it*, or *Him*, the fulfilment of the promiſe, or the coming of the Lord; *becauſe it will ſurely come, and not tarry* a moment beyond the time fixed in God's eternal counſels, or, *for he that cometh will come*, as the Apoſtle quotes the words, *Heb* x 37 applying them to the Lord Jeſus, the great hope of his people, on whom they are called to ſtay themſelves under every afflictive diſpenſation And herein the truth of grace is to be proved *Behold his ſoul, which is lifted up, is not upright in him* they who deſpiſe the viſion, or diſtruſt the promiſe, and, inſtead of waiting upon God, endeavour to ſhift for themſelves, depending on their own devices, they ſhew the unſoundneſs of their hearts *But the juſt ſhall live by faith* they who truſted God, even in the midſt of their calamities, ſhould be preſerved, and, in their captivity, the expectation of the Meſſiah ſhould ſupport them, and by faith in him their eternal life ſhould be ſecured The words are quoted thrice by the Apoſtle as a proof of the great doctrine of juſtification by faith only, and they teach us, (1) That no man is juſt, or juſtified before God, by any doings or duties of his own, but by faith in Jeſus (2) That all true believers ſhall live, kept by faith unto ſalvation, notwithſtanding every effort of their ſpiritual enemies (3) The meritorious cauſe of our life of grace or glory is not our faith, conſidered as our own act, but the object of it, Chriſt Jeſus, his blood and righteouſneſs alone

5 ¶ † Yea alſo, becauſe he tranſgreſſeth by wine,
he is a proud man, neither keepeth at home, who en-
largeth his deſire [g] as hell, and *is* as death, and cannot
be ſatisfied, but [h] gathereth unto him all nations, and
heapeth unto him all people 6 Shall not all theſe take
up a parable againſt him, and a taunting proverb againſt
him, and ſay, ‡ Woe to him that increaſeth *that which*
is not his how long? and to him [i] that ladeth himſelf
with thick clay 7 Shall they not riſe up ſuddenly that
ſhall bite thee, and awake that ſhall vex thee, and thou
ſhalt be for booties unto them? 8 [k] Becauſe thou haſt
ſpoiled many nations, all the remnant of the people ſhall
ſpoil thee [l] becauſe of men's § blood, and *for* the vio-
lence of the land, of the city, and of all that dwell
therein 9 ¶ Wo to him [m] that ‖ coveteth an evil co
vetouſneſs to his houſe, that he may ſet his neſt on high,
that he may be delivered from the power of evil 10
Thou haſt conſulted ſhame to thy houſe, by cutting off
many people, and haſt ſinned *againſt* thy ſoul 11 For
[n] the ſtone ſhall cry out of the wall, and the † beam out
of the timber ſhall ‡ anſwer it 12 ¶ Wo to him that
buildeth a town [o] with blood, and ſtabliſheth a city by
iniquity 13 Behold, *is it* not of the LORD of hoſts,
that [p] the people ſhall labour in the very fire, and the
people ſhall weary themſelves § for very vanity? 14
For [q] the earth ſhall be filled with the knowledge of the
glory of the LORD, as the waters cover the ſea

† Or, How much more. g Prov xxvii 20. Iſa v 14. ‡ Or, Ho, he. i Tim vi 9, 10. k Iſa xxxiii 1. l ver 17. § Heb bloods. m Jer xxii 13. ‖ Or, gaineth an evil gain. n Luke xix 40. † Or, piece, or faſtening. ‡ Or, witneſs againſt it. o Jer xxii 13. Ezek xxiv 9. Mic iii 10. p Jer li 58. § Or, in vain. q Iſa xi 9.

v 5—14 Some commentators, ſuppoſing from the foregoing verſes, which refer to goſpel times, that theſe words go on to deſcribe the character of the ſucceeding enemies of the church, apply them to the Roman people, and eſpecially their emperors, to whom no doubt they are very applicable, but I rather incline, with the generality, to refer the prophecy to Nebuchadnezzar and his ſucceſſors in the Babylonian monarchy

1 Moſt heavy accuſations are laid againſt this enemy of God's people drunkenneſs and ſenſuality, impious pride, even to expect adoration, covetouſneſs inſatiable, *v* 5 injuſtice and oppreſſion, *v* 6 the blood of innocents, ambition, that knew no bounds, *v* 9 theſe and the like were the crimes with which he ſtood chargeable before God Therefore,

2 Repeated woes are denounced upon him, and, when he is fallen, he will be juſtly inſulted by thoſe nations over whom he lorded it before *Shall not all theſe take up a parable againſt him, and a taunting proverb*, pleaſed to behold his diſgrace, and deriding his pride and preſumption, and ſay, Wo, wo, wo, unto him

1 *Wo to him that increaſeth that which is not his*, oppreſſing and plundering to increaſe his wealth *how long* ſhall iniquity thus prevail, and the unrighteous proſper? *and to him that ladeth himſelf with thick clay*, the riches of the world being no better, and they who lade themſelves with theſe by catching care and injuſtice, bring a heavy burden upon their ſouls, which will ſink them into perdition and deſtruction *Shall not they riſe up ſuddenly that ſhall bite thee, and awake that ſhall vex thee?* certainly they ſhall the Perſians and the Medes will ſpoil him of the thick clay on which he doated; *and thou ſhalt be for booties unto them* As he had ſpoiled others, ſo ſhall they ſpoil him, the juſt retaliation for the innocent *blood* he had ſhed, the *violence* he had committed, and the cities he had deſtroyed, whoſe inhabitants he plundered, *v* 8 God keeps a ſtrict account, and in the dreadful day of judgment the black catalogue will be produced againſt the proud oppreſſor and daring ſinner to his everlaſting confuſion

2 *Wo to him that coveteth an evil covetouſneſs to his houſe*, inſatiable after wealth, and ever graſping at more, for covetouſneſs brings its own curſe along with it, and cannot be ſatisfied, robbing men of all the comforts in their families they otherwiſe might have enjoyed *that he may ſet his neſt on high*, raiſe his family above dependence, and advance them higher in the world, *that he may be delivered from the power of evil*, ſecured from the power of his enemies, and from want, the great evil he dreads, though, alas! theſe are vain pretexts to gloſs over his covetouſneſs, and his defences but feeble againſt the evils he fears *Thou haſt conſulted ſhame to thy houſe, by cutting off many people*, fixing, by ſuch unjuſt and cruel conduct, a mark of indelible infamy on his family, *and haſt ſinned againſt thy ſoul*, expoſing it to God's wrath and damnation *for the ſtone ſhall cry out of the wall*, if other witneſſes of his guilt are wanting, and his frauds and deceits have been ſo cunningly d[illegible] to eſcape the eye of men, *and the beam out of the timber ſhall anſwer it*, calling for vengeance upon the head of the unjuſt and the oppreſſor

3 *Wo to him that buildeth a town with blood, and eſtabliſheth a city by iniquity*, as Nebuchadnezzar had built or adorned Babylon with the ſpoils of conquered nations, *Dan* iv 33 *Behold, is it not of the Lord of hoſts, that the people ſhall labour in the very fire, and the people ſhall weary themſelves for very vanity?* So fruitleſs will be all the endeavours of the Babylonians to preſerve themſelves from their enemies *For the earth ſhall be filled with the knowledge of the glory of the Lord, as the waters cover the ſea* when in the fall of Babylon God will be glorified, and the fame of his judgments ſpread into all lands And this verſe ſeems to look forward alſo to greater events than the fall of Babylon, even to the times of the goſpel, when the kingdom of darkneſs ſhall fall before the word of Jeſus, and the knowledge of his glory be diffuſed, till at laſt, by his power and grace, the *very ends of the earth ſhall remember themſelves and be turned to the Lord, and all fleſh ſhall ſee the ſalvation of our God*

15 ¶ Wo unto him that giveth his neighbour drink
that putteſt thy ‖ bottle to *him*, and makeſt *him* drunk-
en alſo, that thou [r] mayſt look on their nakedneſs 16
Thou art filled ‡ with ſhame for glory [s] drink thou
alſo,

† Or, poiſon. r Gen ix 22. ‡ Or, more with ſhame than with glory. s Jer xxv 26, & li 57.

Before Christ 690.

also, and let thy foreskin be uncovered the cup of the
LORD's right hand shall be turned unto thee, and shame-
ful spuing *shall be* on thy glory 17 For the violence of
Lebanon shall cover thee and the spoil of beasts *which*
made them afraid ᵗ because of men's blood, and for the
violence of the land, of the city, and all that dwell there-
in 18 ¶ What profiteth the graven image, that the
maker thereof hath graven it, the molten image, and ᵘ a
teacher of lies, that † the maker of his work trusteth
therein to make *him* ˣ dumb idols ? 19 Wo unto him
that saith to the wood, Awake, to the dumb stone,
Arise, it shall teach, behold, it *is* laid over with gold
and silver, and *there is* no breath at all in the midst of
it 20 But ʸ the LORD *is* in his holy temple ‡ let
all the earth keep silence before him.

ᵗ Ver 8 ᵘ Jer x 8, 14 Zech x 2 † Heb The fashioner of his fashion ˣ 1 Cor xii 2 ʸ Ps xi 4 ‡ Heb Be silent all the earth before him Zeph i 7 Zech ii 13

v 15—20 The former verses cried out of oppression and wrong, for which the woes were there denounced, here we have two other causes for them, drunkenness and idolatry

1 Drunkenness *Wo unto him that giveth his neighbour drink*, as Belshazzar did, when he made a feast for his thousand lords, Dan v 1 *that puttest thy bottle to him*, urging him to drink, *and makest him drunken also* Such are factors for hell, and enemies to mankind, and tho' it may be called hospitality, good cheer, and giving them a hearty welcome, thus to make the glass circulate, it is indeed among the most deadly wickednesses, and will provoke the heaviest wrath of God Wo unto the drunkards, from the palace to the cottage ! wrath is gone forth against them *that thou mayst look on their nakedness*, draw out their secrets, or expose them to ridicule, or induce them to some foolish or indiscreet act or bargain, this being the malignant view for which men often ply their neighbours with liquor, but God will be the avenger of all such *Thou art filled with shame for glory*, God will render such persons vile and abhorred *drink thou also, and let thy foreskin be uncovered*, a cup of wrath is put into his hands, *the cup of the Lord's right hand is turned unto thee* The same vengeance which the Chaldeans had executed upon others, shall return upon their own heads, when they should be stripped naked to their shame, *and*, like drunkards, *shameful spewing shall be on thy glory*, they shall be rendered contemptible and loathsome, and all their riches and greatness be spoiled and defiled *The violence of Lebanon shall cover thee*, either the same destruction as they had made in the temple of God; or this should rise up in judgment against them, or they should be hunted down as wild beasts in Lebanon *the spoil of beasts which made them afraid*, once the terror of the country, but now destroyed, and this for the reason alledged before, *because of men's blood, and for the violence of the land, and of the city, and of all that dwell therein*

Many apply this to Babylon mystical, the great whore that maketh all nations drunk with the wine of her fornication, whose end will be according to her works, *See Rev* xviii 3—6

2 Idolatry Babylon was full of idols, but all the gold and silver lavished upon them, or the curious sculpture, profited the maker nothing at all Though they cried before them, *Arise to help us*, and expected from them directions in their emergencies, yet it was folly, nay madness, to expect a dumb stone, a lifeless log, to teach, or awake to succour them Such expectations could only be raised by the great *teacher of lies*, whom these idols effectually serve, and nothing but woe can be the consequence of trusting on these lying vanities Babylon mystical, the church of Rome, copies close after her pattern in ancient days, and hath multiplied her images of gold and silver, of the Trinity, the Saviour, the Virgin Mary, of saints and angels, crowding their churches with them, where miserable devotees are seen continually kneeling before the breathless image or dumb stone Their crafty priests indeed represent these as *laymen's books*, but God regards them with abomination, as *teachers of lies* *But the Lord is in his holy temple*, not in idols of wood, or stone, or gold, but in heaven, beholding the hearts and ways of all the children of men, and in his church, where his special presence abides, comforting his people, and protecting them from their enemies *Let all the earth keep silence before him*, paying him the worship due unto his name with reverence and godly fear, and never more ascribing his honour to graven images

CHAP. III.

[illegible] prophet [illegible] 1 He considers the works of God to [illegible] his people [illegible] ver 2 2 He calls to [illegible] which the church formerly had of God, [illegible] when he [illegible] of Egypt [illegible] to Canaan, ver 3—15 [illegible] the present troubles of the [illegible] hopes that the [illegible] though all [illegible] ver 16—19

1 A Prayer of Habakkuk the prophet ᵃ upon Sig-
gionoth 2 O LORD, I have heard thy † speech,
and was afraid O LORD, ‡ revive thy work in the
midst of the years, in the midst of the years make known,
in wrath remember mercy

Before Christ 690. ᵃ Ps vii 1 † Heb Report, or hearing ‡ Or, preserve alive

v 1, 2 This chapter is called *a prayer of Habakkuk the prophet*, it is drawn up like David's psalms, and suited for the service of the sanctuary, to be sung *upon Sigionoth*, probably the musical instrument which accompanied it

1 The prophet acknowledges the notices of his will, which God had given him, and the impression they made upon him *O Lord, I have heard thy speech, and was afraid*, because of the sad tidings concerning the desolations of his people, which affected him exceedingly

2 He cries on their behalf, that God would manifest his favour to them in the time of their distress *O Lord, revive thy work in the midst of the years*, give the people some tokens of regard before the captivity ends, or revive the work of grace among them, which cannot but comfort and support them *In the midst of the years make known* thy power, providence, and love *in wrath remember mercy*, and shew them some signs of reconciliation, that they may not sink into despair *Note*, (1) The work of grace in a believer's heart sometimes appears decaying, his spirit lifeless, and he feels abundant cause to cry, *Revive thy work, O Lord !* (2) When we are stirred up to cry to God, whatever wrath our souls appear to be under, there is then good hope of mercy in store for us

3 ᵇ God came from † Teman, and the holy One from
mount Paran Selah His glory covered the heavens,
and the earth was full of his praise 4 And *his* bright-
ness was as the light, he had ‡ horns *coming* out of his
hand, and there *was* the hiding of his power 5 ᶜ Be-
fore him went the pestilence, and § burning coals went
forth at his feet 6 He stood and measured the earth
he beheld, and drove asunder the nations, and the ever-
lasting mountains were scattered, the perpetual hills did
bow his ways *are* everlasting 7 I saw the tents of
‖ Cushan | in affliction *and* the curtains of ᵈ the land
of Midian did tremble 8 Was the LORD displeased
ᵉ against the rivers ? *was* thine anger against the rivers ?
was thy wrath against the sea, that ᶠ thou didst ride up-
on thine horses, *and* ‡ thy chariots of salvation ? 9 Thy
bow was made quite naked, *according* to the oaths of the
tribes, *even thy* word Selah ᵍ Thou didst cleave § the
earth with rivers 10 ʰ The mountains saw thee, *and*
they trembled the overflowing of the water passed by
the deep uttered his voice, *and* lift up his hands on high
11 The sun *and* moon ⁱ stood still in their habitation
‖ at the light of thine ᵏ arrows they went, *and* at the
shining of thy glittering spear 12 Thou didst march
through the land in indignation, thou didst thresh the
heathen in anger 13 Thou wentest forth for the sal-
vation of thy people, *even* for salvation with thine a-
nointed ˡ thou woundedst the head out of the house of
the wicked, by discovering the foundation unto the neck
Selah 14 ᵐ Thou didst strike through with his staves
the head of his villages they ‖ came out as a whirlwind
to scatter me their rejoicing *was* as to ⁿ devour the poor
secretly 15 ᵒ Thou didst walk through the sea with
thine horses, *through* the § heap of great waters

v 3—15 The prophet, as the encouragement of his faith, remembers the days of old, and mentions the past deliverances God had wrought for his people, as a plea for present help

1 He had appeared to them on Sinai, with most magnificent displays of his greatness and glory He was seen as marching in majesty from Seir, from Teman and Paran, whilst the heavens shone with his brightness, and earth rang with his praise, or *was full of his light*, ver 3 as the sun he shone, *he had horns*, or *beams, coming out of his hand*, or *sides*, begirt around with irradiation *and there was the hiding of his power*, a little of his glory appeared, the far greater part was hid, for *the greatness of his power who can manifest it?*

2 He sent his messengers before him, to prepare the way of his people *Before him went the pestilence, and burning coals went forth at his feet*, when Egypt felt his plagues, or when the Canaanites were by his judgments consumed and wasted, in order to their final destruction *He stood and measured the earth*, dividing the land of Canaan among the tribes, and with a look expelled the inhabitants The mighty sons of Anak, strong as the *everlasting mountains, were scattered and broken*, and all the nobles and princes of the land, who thought their possessions sure as *the perpetual hills, did bow* before the God of Israel for *his ways are everlasting*, nor can any of the sons of men stand be-

Before Christ 690.

his decrees of old in his arm. With panic fears the neighbouring nations of Midian and Cushan, v. 7. beheld and trembled, lest on them also the desolations should extend: so easily can God dismay the mightiest.

3. When the Red Sea was divided, and Jordan driven back, it seemed as if the very rivers affrighted fled from his displeasure, whilst, as the captain of Israel's host, he rode triumphant through the parted waters, and led them on horses and chariots of salvation, v. 8. walking securely along through the bed of the Red Sea, v. 15. The overflowing streams, Josh. iii. 15. *passed by*, retiring on either side: *the deep uttered his voice, and lift up his hands on high*, roaring as it fled, and heaping up on either side a watery wall, that reached to the skies.

4. His rivers cleaved the earth, v. 9. when in the barren wilderness the stony rock at his command poured forth a torrent of waters, following Israel's camp through all their journeys in that dry and barren land.

5. To give Israel an opportunity to destroy their enemies, *the sun and the moon stood still in their habitation*, Josh. x. 12. *At the light of thine arrows they went, and at the shining of thy glittering spear*, God himself fought for them, and directed them in the pursuit of their routed foes. *Thy bow was made quite naked*, to consume their enemies, *according to the oaths of the tribes, even thy word*, having sworn to their fathers to give them this land for an heritage. From one end of Canaan to the other did the Lord, as the leader of Israel's army, *march in indignation* against the wickedness of the inhabitants, and *threshed them in anger*, as corn in the floor, v. 12. *Thou wentest forth for the salvation of thy people, even for salvation with thine anointed*, assisting and strengthening his divinely appointed generals, Moses, Aaron, and Joshua: *thou woundedst the head out of the houses of the wicked*, the princes of Canaan, *by discovering the foundation*, utterly destroying their cities and the inhabitants, *unto the neck*, the whole body politic, with all the members of it, being cut in pieces. *Thou didst strike through with his staves the head of his villages*, turning their own arms against them, and ruining the country throughout. *Their rejoicing was as to devour the poor secretly*, they were confident of victory over God's poor people, or this was part of their crimes which provoked these judgments of God against them.

Some suppose the whole of this section refers to the coming of the Lord Jesus Christ in the flesh, his erection of his spiritual kingdom in the world, the subdual of sin, Satan, death, and hell before him, and especially his coming at the latter day for the destruction of the antichristian powers, of all which, his appearances for his people in time past no doubt were typical, and we may, in every time of our distress and trouble, as confidently hope to see this great salvation of God, as ever Israel experienced his salvation from their enemies of old.

16 p When I heard, my belly trembled; my lips
quivered at the voice: rottenness entered into my bones,
and I trembled in myself, || that I might rest in the
day of trouble: when he cometh up unto the people, he
will † invade them with his troops. 17 ¶ Although
the fig tree shall not blossom, neither *shall* fruit *be* in
the vines, the labour of the olive shall § fail, and the
field, shall yield no meat, the flock shall be cut off from
the fold, and *there shall be* no herd in the stalls: 18
q Yet I will rejoice in the LORD, I will joy in the God
of my salvation. 19. The Lord GOD *is* r my strength,
and he will s make my feet like t hinds *feet*, and he will
make me to walk upon mine high places. To the
chief singer on my || stringed instruments.

p Ver. 2. Ps. cxix. 120. Jer. xx. 9. ... || Or ...

† Or, cut them in pieces. § Heb. Lie. q Job xiii. 15. r Ps. xxvii. 1. Isa. xii. 2. s 2 Sam. xxii. 34. Ps. xviii. 33. t Deut. ... || Heb. Neginoth. Ps. iv. title.

V. 16—19. The tidings of distress which the prophet heard concerning the people of God, though there was hope in the end, affected him deeply.

1. *When I heard, my belly trembled, my lips quivered at the voice*, overpowered with fear and dismay: *rottenness entered into my bones*, his whole frame seemed as dissolved. *I trembled in myself*, at the desolations he beheld, *that I might rest*, or, *notwithstanding I shall rest in the day of trouble*, be safe under the divine protection, and delivered from the evil, though he plainly foresaw, that *when he cometh up unto the people*, when the Chaldeans with their king come up, *he will invade them*, or *cut them in pieces with his troops*. Note, (1.) Holy souls tremble at God's word, and with awful apprehensions look forward to the wrath ready to be revealed from heaven. (2.) God's people are enabled to exercise faith in him in the worst of times, and they shall be hid in the day of his fierce anger.

2. Notwithstanding every discouraging circumstance, his faith triumphs in the God of his salvation. He supposes the worst of calamities that can happen, that drought, blasting mildew, or the ravages of an enemy, destroy their vines, fig-trees, and olives, that pestilence and famine devour the cattle, so that the barren fields are quite forsaken, v. 18. *Yet I will rejoice in the Lord, I will joy in the God of my salvation*. And thus can a faithful soul under the loss of every earthly comfort rejoice in Christ Jesus, in the present experience of his grace, and the assured expectation of his glory, a joy which the world can neither give nor take away. *The Lord God is my strength*, when every other help fails, and upheld by his everlasting arms, our present and eternal salvation is secured to us, he will bring us safe through all our trials, and none shall pluck us out of his hand: *and he will make my feet like hinds feet*, firm, and swift to run the way of his commandments, amidst every difficulty and danger: *and he will make me to walk upon my high places*, victorious over every foe, as every believer shall shortly be, when he cometh to the mount of God in glory. Thus ends the prophet's prayer, with assured faith, and joyful hope; and he hath left it upon record, directed *to the chief singer on the stringed instruments*, to teach God's people in all their trials never to cease from prayer and praise, but, rejoicing in hope, to expect with humble confidence the final, full, and eternal salvation of God.

THE EVANGELICAL EXPOSITOR; OR, A PRACTICAL COMMENT Upon the PROPHECY of ZEPHANIAH.

THIS prophet is placed last, as he was last in time of all the minor prophets before the captivity, and not long before Jeremiah, who lived at the time of the captivity. He foretels the general destruction of Judah and Jerusalem by the Chaldeans, and sets their sins in order before them, which had provoked God to bring their ruin upon them, calls them to repentance, threatens the neighbour nations with the like destructions, and gives encouraging promises of their joyful return out of captivity in due time, which have a reference to the grace of the gospel.

Before Christ 612.

CHAP. I.

After the title of the book, ver. 1. here is, 1. A threatning of the destruction of Judah and Jerusalem, an utter destruction by the Chaldeans, ver. 2—4. 2. A charge against them for their gross sins, which provoked God to bring that destruction upon them, ver. 5, 6. and so he goes on in the rest of the chapter, setting both the judgments before them, that they might prevent them or prepare for them, and the sins that destroy them, that they might judge themselves, and justify God in what was brought upon them. (1.) They must hold their peace, because they had greatly sinned, ver. 7—9. But (2.) They shall howl because the trouble will be great. The day of the Lord is near, and it will be a terrible day, ver. 10—18.

a 2 Pet. i. 21.

1 THE word of the LORD [a] which came unto Zephaniah the son of Cushi, the son of
Gedaliah, the son of Amariah, the son of
Hizkiah, in the days of Josiah, the son of
Amon king of Judah. 2 † I will utterly consume all
things from off the land, saith the LORD. 3 [b] I will
consume man and beast; I will consume the fowls of
the heaven, and the fishes of the sea, and the ‡ stum-
bling-block with the wicked, and I will cut off man
from off the land, saith the LORD. 4 I will also
stretch out mine hand upon Judah, and upon all the
inhabitants of Jerusalem, and I will cut off the rem-
nant of Baal from this place, *and* the name of the
Chemarims with the priests; 5 And them [c] that wor-
ship the host of heaven upon the house-tops, and them
that worship, *and* [d] that swear § by the LORD, and that
swear [e] by Malcham; 6 And [f] them that are turned back
from the LORD, and *those* that have not sought the
LORD, nor enquired for him.

† Heb. By taking away I will make an end. b Hos. iv. 3. ‡ Ezek. xiv. 3. ‡ Or, idols. c 2 Kings xxiii. 5. Hos. x. 5. 2 Kings xxiii. 12. Jer. xix. 13. d Isa. xlviii. 1. Hos. iv. 15. § Or, to the LORD. e Josh. xxiii. 7. 1 Kings xi. 33. f Isa. i. 4. Jer. xv. 6.

V. 1—6. We have,

1. An account of the penman of this prophecy, Zephaniah, whose pedigree for four generations back is mentioned, probably as one of distinguished note, and some have thought him of the blood-royal, and a descendant from Hezekiah, king of Judah, the same word in the original as Hizkiah. He lived in the best times, even in the reforming reign of Josiah; and yet we find the people at bottom, many of them at least, notwithstanding their apparent change, continued bad, very bad, or quickly relapsed, and departed from their promising beginnings. Of so short continuance are the effects we ought by the most zealous reformers among a backsliding people. *The word of the Lord came* to the prophet, for he spake not in his own name, but as the Spirit gave him utterance.

Before Christ 612.

2. The burden of his prophecy is the approaching destruction of the land of Judea, and all things therein, both man and beast.

(1.) *I will consume and cut off man from off the land, saith the Lord*; even the good men that yet remain will be involved in the national calamity. But *the wicked* are especially intended against them the Lord will *stretch out his hand*, in wrath to smite and consume them from the earth, with their *stumbling-blocks*, those hated idols, which was their mortal sin. *I will cut off the remnant of Baal from this place*, those who, notwithstanding all Josiah's care, still continued the worship of Baal: *and the name of the Chemarims with the priests*. The Chemarims were *idolatrous priests*, as the word is translated, 2 Kings xxiii. 5. so called either from the black garments they wore, or from their faces blackened with the smoke of the fire where they sacrificed. These should be cut off, yea their very name buried in oblivion, or mentioned with detestation. And those who on house-tops worship the host of heaven, shall share the same fate, with all those who *swear by the Lord, or to the Lord and Malcham*, or *Moloch*, seeking to reconcile the inconsistent service of both, and pretending to worship them together, irreconcileable as that must for ever be: *and them that are turned back from the Lord*, apostate from the profession they once made: *and those that have not sought the Lord, nor enquired for him*; careless and prayerless sinners, who never troubled themselves about God, his worship, or service; these will he destroy together. *Note*, (1.) The prayerless soul is a lost soul. (2.) They who seek to reconcile their religion with the way of the world, and would serve God and Mammon too, just perish with the devil's desire. If they swear by Malcham, conform to the maxims, customs, or vanities of the world, they may serve God in form as much as they please, but they will be numbered with the transgressors.

Before Christ 612.

(2) *I will conſume the beaſts, the fowls of the heaven, and the fiſhes of the ſea*, being deſigned for man's comfort, they are involved in his puniſhment, when by ſin he forfeits all his mercies

7 ᵏ Hold thy peace at the preſence of the Lord
GOD for the day of the LORD *is* at hand for ˡ the
LORD hath prepared a ſacrifice, he hath † bid his
gueſts 8 And it ſhall come to paſs in the day of the
LORD's ſacrifice, that I will puniſh the princes, and
ᵐ the king's children, and all *ſuch as are* clothed with
ſtrange apparel 9 In the ſame day alſo will I puniſh
all thoſe that leap on the threſhold, which fill their
maſters houſes with violence and deceit 10 And it
ſhall come to paſs in that day, ſaith the LORD, *that*
there ſhall be the noiſe of a cry from the fiſh-gate, and
an howling from the ſecond, and a great craſhing from
the hills 11 Howl, ye inhabitants of Makteſh, for
all the merchant-people are cut down all they that bear
ſilver are cut off 12 And it ſhall come to paſs at that
time, *that* I will ⁿ ſearch Jeruſalem with candles, and
puniſh the men ᵒ *that are* ‡ ſettled on their lees, ᵖ that
ſay in their heart, The LORD will not do good, neither
will he do evil 13 Therefore their goods ſhall become
a booty, and their houſes a deſolation they ſhall alſo
build houſes, ᑫ but not inhabit *them*, and they ſhall plant
vineyards, but not drink the wine thereof

k Hab ii 20. Zech ii 13. l Iſa xxxiv 6 Jer xlvi 10. Ezek. xxxix 17 Rev xix 17. † Heb ſanctified, or prepared. m Jer xxxix 6. n Obad 6. o Jer xlviii 11. ‡ Heb Curded, or thickened. p Pſ xciv 7. q Deut xxviii 30. Am v 11.

v 7—13 The day of vengeance approaches, and the nation, as a ſacrifice to divine juſtice, is ready to be offered up, and *the Lord hath bid his gueſts*, the Chaldeans, or the fowls of the heaven, to feed upon the carcaſes of the ſlain

1 Thoſe are deſcribed who are devoted to deſtruction

(1) *The princes and king's children*, for judgment begins with the higheſt, *and all ſuch as are clothed with ſtrange apparel*, either the veſtments in which they worſhipped their idols, or they affected in their dreſs to imitate their heathen neighbours in finery and extravagance, and their cloaths proclaimed the pride and vanity of their hearts

(2) The oppreſſors, *who leap on the threſhold*, who daringly thruſt themſelves in at their neighbour's door, and ſeize what comes to hand, *filling their maſters houſes with violence and deceit*, who ſet them on this wickedneſs, and protect them from juſtice and puniſhment

(3) *The rich merchants, and all they that bear ſilver*, having plenty of money to trade, and buy and ſell, and get gain

(4) *All that are ſettled upon their lees*, living in pleaſure, affluence, eaſe, and carnal ſecurity, and this begetting infidelity; *that ſay in their heart*, though, like many other practical atheiſts, they dare not openly avow their ſentiments, *The Lord will not do good, neither will he do evil*, denying his providential government of the world, and that neither his ſervice would be attended with reward, nor ſin with any puniſhment, leaving him out of their ſight, and intimating in fact that there was no God And as it is ſo much for their intereſt there ſhould be none, ſenſualiſts would fain perſuade themſelves there is none but ſuch is theſe God will aſſuredly detect and puniſh *I will ſearch Jeruſalem with candles*, that none may be able to hide themſelves, and *puniſh* them with judgment from which none ſhall be able to eſcape *Note*, Many are driven to the dreadful and deceitful refuge of infidelity, that they may ſilence conſcience thereby, and enjoy their guilty pleaſures undiſturbed

2 Their cry will be terrible when the ſtroke of vengeance deſcends *In that day, ſaith the Lord, there ſhall be the noiſe of a cry from the fiſh-gate*, of the miſerable inhabitants flying before their Chaldean purſuers, *and a great craſhing from the hills*, either of the enemy ſhouting and ruſhing on to the ſlaughter, or of the houſes of the nobles, built on the higheſt part of Zion and Moriah, now plundered and beat to the ground *Howl, ye inhabitants of Makteſh*, a ſtreet of Jeruſalem, into which the enemy broke, or it is put for the whole body of the people howling over their deſolations *Their merchants are cut down*, and their ſubſtance a ſpoil to the Chaldeans yea, *their gods are become a booty*, ſo far from being able to help them, unable to deliver themſelves *Their houſes*, which they built, flattering themſelves with a long abode in them, *are become a deſolation*, and *the vineyards* they planted, afford their produce not to them, but to their conquerors

3 The prophet, with all other who are like him, are commanded to *hold their peace at the preſence of the Lord God*, not daring to diſpute againſt his righteous judgments, nor ſuffered to open their mouths to pray for a people devoted to deſtruction

14 The great day of the LORD *is* near, *it is* near,
and haſteth greatly, *even* the voice of the day of the
LORD the mighty man ſhall cry there bitterly 15
That day *is* ʳ a day of wrath, a day of trouble and di-
ſtreſs, a day of waſteneſs and deſolation, a day of dark-
neſs and gloomineſs, a day of clouds and thick darkneſs
16 A day of the trumpet and alarm againſt the fenced
cities, and againſt the high towers 17 And I will
bring diſtreſs upon men, that they ſhall walk like ˢ blind
men, becauſe they have ſinned againſt the LORD and
their blood ſhall be poured out as duſt, and their fleſh
as the dung 18 ᵗ Neither their ſilver nor their gold
ſhall be able to deliver them in the day of the LORD's
wrath, but the whole land ſhall be ᵘ devoured by the fire
of his jealouſy for he ſhall make even a ſpeedy rid-
dance of all them that dwell in the land

r Iſa xxii 5. Jer xxx 7. Am v 18. Before Christ 612. s Deut xxviii 28. t Prov xi 4. Ezek vii 19. u Chap iii 8.

v 14—18 If any thing can alarm the ſinners in Zion, the prophet's awful warnings muſt ſurely do it

1 *The great day of the Lord*, when he will take vengeance on the Jews by the ſword of the Chaldeans, *is near, it is near, and haſteth greatly*, but a moment remains to fly from this devouring fire It is madneſs for the ſinner to *ſlumber*, whoſe *damnation ſlumbereth not*

2 This will be a day of terror and diſmay *The voice of the day of the Lord* will ſtrike a panic into the boldeſt, *the mighty man ſhall cry there bitterly*, like women quite diſpirited, and wringing their hands when they ſhould graſp the ſword *That day is a day of wrath*, of the wrath of God, and of the fury of the Chaldeans, his inſtruments of vengeance *a day of trouble and diſtreſs*, to the miſerable inhabitants, *of waſteneſs and deſolation* to the whole land, to Jeruſalem, the temple, and all the cities thereof *a day of darkneſs and gloomineſs, a day of clouds and thick darkneſs*, without a gleam of hope, and big with deſpair *A day of the trumpet and alarm againſt the fenced cities, and againſt the high towers*, ſpreading horror and diſmay on every ſide *And I will bring diſtreſs upon men*, perplexed, and not knowing which way to turn, *that they ſhall walk like blind men*, ruſhing upon their own ruin

3 Deſtruction univerſal and unavoidable will enſue *Their blood ſhall be poured out as duſt*, ſo profuſely, ſo diſregarded, *and their fleſh as the dung*, their carcaſes left unburied on the earth *Neither their ſilver nor their gold ſhall be able to deliver them in the day of the Lord's wrath* for in that day they profit not *but the whole land ſhall be devoured by the fire of his jealouſy*, ſo furious, ſo implacable, nothing can ſtay the raging flames *for he ſhall make even a ſpeedy riddance of all them that dwell in the land*, and leave them neither root nor branch *Note*, It is a fearful thing indeed to fall into the hands of a jealous God

4 Sin, ſin, that accurſed thing, is the cauſe of all this miſery *Becauſe they have ſinned againſt the Lord*, this is the provocation, and the ſting of every affliction it is this which puts the worm that never dies into the conſcience, and kindles the flames that never can be quenched O ſin, ſin, what haſt thou done?

CHAP II

In this chapter we have, 1 *An earneſt exhortation to the nation of the Jews to repent and turn to God before the judgments threatened came*, ver 1—3 2 *A denunciation of the judgments of God againſt diverſe of the neighbour nations that had aſſiſted or rejoiced in the calamity of Iſrael* (1) *The Philiſtines*, ver 1—7 (2) *The Moabites and Ammonites*, ver 8—11 (3) *The Ethiopians and Aſſyrians*, ver 12—15

1 † GAther yourſelves together, yea, gather toge-
ther, O nation not ‡ deſired 2 Before
ᵃ the decree bring forth, *before* the day paſs as the chaff,
before the fierce anger of the LORD come upon you,
before the day of the LORD's anger come upon you
3 Seek ye the LORD, all ye ᵇ meek of the earth
which have wrought his judgment, ſeek righteouſneſs,
ſeek meekneſs ᶜ it may be, ye ſhall be hid in the day
of the LORD's anger

† Or examine. ‡ Or deſirous. a 2 Kings xxiii 27. b Pſ cxlix 4 Mat v 5. c Joel ii 14. Amos v 15. Jonah iii 9.

v 1—3 God warns before he ſtrikes, that ſinners may have time to return, and prevent the threatened judgments

1 A ſummons is ſent to this people *Gather yourſelves together, yea, gather together*, to faſt and pray, and humble your ſouls, or *ſearch yourſelves*, examine your ways, that you may diſcover your ſins, and turn unto the Lord, *O nation not deſired*, or *deſirous* after God and his favour, negligent and careleſs, or not pleaſing to him, but odious through the multitude of their provocations

2 They are urged inſtantly to lay their caſe to heart, *before the decree bring forth*, and be put in execution, *before the day paſs as the chaff*, when they ſhould be driven into captivity, unable to withſtand their fate, as chaff before the whirlwind, *before the fierce anger of the Lord, the day of the Lord's anger come upon you*, terrible beyond expreſſion Delays are dangerous where eternity is at ſtake, and the wrath of God threatned

Before Chriſt 612

we need be quickened to ſeize the preſent moment, and to-day, whilſt it is called to-day, not to harden our hearts.

3. The few gracious ſouls among them are addreſſed, whatever others do, to make their calling and election ſure. *Seek ye the Lord, all ye meek of the earth*: this is the character of God's people; they are meek and lowly of heart, patient under the provocations of men, and ſubmiſſive under the afflictive providences of God; *which have wrought his judgment*, obedient to his laws, obſervant of his worſhip. Such as theſe, who will receive the word of exhortation, are enjoined to ſeek the Lord by prayer and ſupplication with thankſgiving. *Seek righteouſneſs, ſeek meekneſs*, a greater increaſe of grace, that they may be more holy and exemplary; for none who know themſelves can reſt in any preſent attainments, conſcious how ſhort they come at the beſt, and therefore *ſo getting the things that are behind, they reach to thoſe which are before, preſſing to the mark for the prize of their high calling in Chriſt Jeſus.*

4. There is hope that ſuch may eſcape the general deſolations, and, by a peculiar interpoſition of Divine Providence, be hid *in the day of the Lord's anger*, and not periſh with their ungodly countrymen: but, whether involved in temporal calamities or not with others, *it* not only *may be*, but it certainly *ſhall be*, that ſuch ſhall be hid in the great day of his wrath.

d Jer. xlvii. 4, 5. Ezek. xxv. 15. Amos i. 6. Zech. ix. 5. e Ezek. xxv. 16. f Joſh. xiii. 3.

4 ¶ For [d] Gaza ſhall be forſaken, and Aſhkelon a
deſolation: they ſhall drive out Aſhdod at the noon-
day, and Ekron ſhall be rooted up. 5 Wo unto [e] the
inhabitants of the ſea-coaſts, the nation of the Chere-
thites; the word of the LORD *is* againſt you; [f] O
Canaan, the land of the Philiſtines, I will even deſtroy
thee, that there ſhall be no inhabitant. 6 And the
ſea-coaſt ſhall be dwellings *and* cottages for ſhepherds,
and folds for flocks. 7 And the coaſt ſhall be for
the remnant of the houſe of Judah; they ſhall feed
thereupon; in the houſes of Aſhkelon ſhall they lie down
in the evening: † for the LORD their God ſhall viſit
them, and turn away their captivity.

† Or, when.

v. 4—7. The neighbouring nations are here called to the bar, and their doom read. Though judgment begins at the houſe of God, it will not end there. The Philiſtines were the antient enemies of Iſrael, and would rejoice at their fall; but they are deſtined to the ſame deſtruction.

1. They ſhall be extirpated as uſurpers, their land lying within the bounds of the country given to Iſrael, *Joſh.* xiii. 3. God pronounces a woe againſt them, with their neighbours the Cherethites, unleſs this be ſuppoſed another name for the Philiſtines. Their capital cities are devoted to ruin: they muſt fall ſince *God's word is againſt them*, whoſe purpoſes and decrees are irreſiſtible. Their deſtruction will be univerſal, not an inhabitant ſhall be left, *v.* 5. and their ſea-coaſt, where their cities once ſtood full of inhabitants, ſhall only now afford a few miſerable cottages, where ſhepherds watch and fold their flocks.

2. Judah ſhall poſſeſs the land, repair and inhabit their cities in peace, *when the Lord ſhall viſit them, and turn away their captivity*, which was fulfilled after their return from Babylon, in the days of the Maccabees.

g Jer. xlviii. 27. h Jer. xlix. 1. i Iſa. xv. 1. Jer. xlviii. 1. Ezek. xxv. 9. Amos ii. 1. k Amos i. 13. l Gen. xix. 25. Deut. xxix. 23. m Iſa. xvi. 6. Jer. xlviii. 29. ‡ Heb. Make lean.

8 ¶ I have heard [g] the reproach of Moab, and the
revilings of the children of Ammon, whereby they have
reproached my people, and [h] magnified *themſelves* againſt
their border. 9 Therefore *as* I live, ſaith the LORD
of hoſts, the God of Iſrael, Surely [i] Moab ſhall be as
Sodom, and [k] the children of Ammon as Gomorrah,
[l] *even* the breeding of nettles, and ſalt-pits, and a per-
petual deſolation: the reſidue of my people ſhall ſpoil
them, and the remnant of my people ſhall poſſeſs them.
10 This ſhall they have [m] for their pride, becauſe they
have reproached and magnified *themſelves* againſt the
people of the LORD of hoſts. 11 The LORD *will be*
terrible unto them: for he will ‡ famiſh all the gods of
the earth; and *men* ſhall worſhip him, every one from
his place, *even* all the iſles of the heathen.

v. 8—11. Moab and Ammon, the children of Lot, are joined together, alike in ſin and in ſuffering.

1. Their ſin is, (1.) Reproach and reviling of God's people, inſulting them in the day of their calamity, and probably helping forward their ruin; and they *magnified themſelves againſt their border*, ſeizing what lay contiguous to their country: but God *heard*, and noted their words and works, and will recompenſe them. (2.) *Their pride*. Puffed up with ſelf-conceit, they looked on the people of the Lord of hoſts as contemptible, and thereby deſpiſed their religion and their God. *Note*, Pride is the firſt-born of hell, and in God's ſight moſt odious.

2. Their judgment is the ſame, condemned to an overthrow, terrible as that of Sodom and Gomorrah; their country ſhall become barren and uncultivated as a wilderneſs, and Iſrael, whom they have inſulted, ſhall, after their return from Babylon, ſpoil them, and poſſeſs the country, after it had begun to revive from the deſolations of Nebuchadnezzar: and this is confirmed by the oath of the Lord of hoſts, none of whoſe words ſhall fail. *Note*, They who have trampled on others, in juſt judgment are brought under the feet of thoſe whom they thus inſulted.

3. A gracious promiſe, which reſpects the times of the goſpel, cloſes the burden of Moab and Ammon. God will not only be terrible to them, but he will *famiſh* or bring *leanneſs upon all the gods of the earth*, when idolatry before the power of the goſpel of Jeſus ſhould be deſtroyed; *and men ſhall worſhip him, every one from his place*, or *in his place*, without going up to Jeruſalem, the ſpiritual ſacrifices of prayer and praiſe being acceptable now in every place; *even all the iſles of the heathen*; and, bleſſed be God, we ſee the promiſe fulfilled graciouſly to us in this land.

n Iſa. xviii. 1. & xx. 4. Ezek. xxx. 9. o Iſa. x. 12. Ezek. xxxi. 3. Nah. i. 8. & ii. 10. & iii. 15. p Iſa. xxxiv. 11, 14. † Or, pelican. q Amos ix. 1. ‡ Or, When he hath uncovered. r Iſa. xlvii. 8. Rev. xviii. 7. s Job xxvii. 23. Lam. ii. 15. Ezek. xxvii. 36.

12 ¶ Ye [n] Ethiopians alſo, *ye ſhall be* ſlain by my
ſword. 13 And he will ſtretch out his hand againſt
the north, and [o] deſtroy Aſſyria, and will make Nine-
veh a deſolation, *and* dry like a wilderneſs. 14 And
flocks ſhall lie down in the midſt of her, all the beaſts
of the nations: both [p] the † cormorant and the bittern
ſhall lodge in the upper [q] lintels of it; *their* voice ſhall
ſing in the windows; deſolation *ſhall be* in the threſholds:
‡ for he ſhall uncover the cedar-work. 15 This *is*
the rejoicing city that dwelt careleſly, that ſaid in her
heart, [r] I *am*, and *there is* none beſide me: how is
ſhe become a deſolation, a place for beaſts to lie down
in! every one that paſſeth by her, [s] ſhall hiſs, *and* wag
his hand.

v. 12—15. The inhabitants of Arabia, or Ethiopia, and the Aſſyrians, with Nineveh their capital, are devoted to deſtruction, which was brought upon them by Nebuchadnezzar. And we have,

1. The ſtate of proſperity and ſecurity in which Nineveh had been. *This is the rejoicing city that dwelt careleſly*, mirth and jollity once rang through her palaces, and, fearleſs of danger, no melancholy thought interrupted the jocund hours: *that ſaid in her heart, I am, and there is none beſide me*, none to be compared to me for wealth, ſtrength, and beauty. But when ſelf-complacence ſwells the boſom of the proud, and ſecurity lulls the ſinner to his deceitful reſt, ruin hangs over him, wrath is at his heels.

2. The miſerable ſituation to which Nineveh ſhall be reduced. Turned to a heap of ruins, theſe proud palaces ſhall become the den of wild beaſts, and the abode of every rueful ominous bird. The deſcription, *v.* 14. is inimitably beautiful, and which a comment can but debaſe. It expreſſes the utter deſolation which would enſue, and every paſſenger who beheld the ſcene, whilſt they wonder at the fearful change, will *hiſs and wag* the hand, inſulting over her fall, who ſo often inſulted over others.

CHAP. III.

We now return to Jeruſalem, and muſt again hear what God has to ſay to her, 1. *By way of reproof and threatening, for the abundance of wickedneſs that was found in her, ver.* 1—7. 2. *By way of promiſe of mercy, which God had yet in reſerve for them.* (1.) *That he would bring in a glorious work of reformation among them, cleanſe them from their ſins, and bring them home to himſelf, ver.* 8—13. (2.) *That he would bring about a glorious work of ſalvation for them, when he had thus prepared them for it, ver.* 14—20. *Thus the* Redeemer ſhall come *to Zion, and to ſhew his own way, ſhall* turn away ungodlineſs from Jacob. *Theſe promiſes were to have their full accompliſhment in goſpel times and goſpel graces.*

† Or, gluttonous. ‡ Or, Inſtruction. a Ezek. xxii. 27. Mic. iii. 9, 10. b Hab. i. 8. c Jer. xxiii. 11, 32. Hoſ. ix. 7. d Ezek. xxii. 26. Mal. ii. 8. e Deut. xxxii. 4. f Ver. 15, 17. § Heb. Morning by morning. g Jer. iii. 3. & vi. 15. & viii. 12. ‖ Or, corners.

1. WO to † her that is filthy and polluted, to the
oppreſſing city! 2 She obeyed not the voice;
ſhe received not ‡ correction; ſhe truſted not in the
LORD; ſhe drew not near to her God. 3 [a] Her
princes within her *are* roaring lions; her judges *are*
[b] evening wolves; they gnaw not the bones till the mor-
row. 4 Her prophets *are* light *and* treacherous per-
ſons: her prieſts have polluted the ſanctuary, they have
done [d] violence to the law. 5 [e] The juſt LORD *is* [f] in
the midſt thereof; he will not do iniquity: § every
morning doth he bring his judgment to light, he faileth
not; but [g] the unjuſt knoweth no ſhame. 6 I have cut
off the nations: their ‖ towers are deſolate; I made their
ſtreets waſte, that none paſſeth by: their cities are de-
ſtroyed,

Before Christ 612 stroyed, so that there is no man, that there is none inha-
bitant 7 I said, Surely thou wilt fear me thou wilt
receive instruction, so their dwelling should not be cut
off, howsoever I punished them but they rose early,
and corrupted all their doings

v 1–7 Jerusalem again is the burden of this prophecy where God might justly have expected all obedience, there nothing is found but abomination

1 The whole city is full of wickedness *Wo to her that is filthy and polluted* with complicated sins, *to the oppressing city*, where lawless violence prevailed *She obeyed not the voice*, disobedient to God's will, and paying no regard to his law *She received not correction*, neither the admonitions of the prophets, nor the rod of afflictive providences, produced any good effect *She trusted not in the Lord*, but in her idols and heathen allies *She drew not near to her God*, breaking the covenant, forsaking the God of her mercies, and restraining prayer before him, which same particularly apply to the Pharisees in the days of Christ, who were full of uncleanness, trusted in themselves, and came not to Jesus for pardon, righteousness, and salvation

2 The leading men are chief in transgression The nobles and judges are rapacious and cruel as roaring lions and evening wolves, when driven by hunger they sally forth in search of prey, *they gnaw not the bones till the morrow*, or *in the morning*, eating up on the spot even the very bones of the prey which falls into their hands *Her prophets are light and treacherous*, their vain conduct gave the lie to their pretensions, and their word tended to betray the interests of religion, and to ruin the souls of men *Note*, Levity in a prophet must render him a discredit to his profession *Her priests* were faithless, *they polluted the sanctuary* by their sins, which they should have adorned by the purity of their lives and *did violence to the law*, perverted it by false glosses, or contradicted what it taught by their bad examples these therefore shall receive greater damnation

3 Their sins were aggravated by many considerations

(1) God's presence was eminently with them *The just Lord is in the midst of thee*, his Shechinah dwelt among them, he beheld all their ways, which could not but provoke the eyes of his holiness *He will not do iniquity*, nor can he suffer it in others with impunity *Every morning doth he bring his judgment to light*, sending his prophets to warn men of the evil and danger of their ways *He faileth not*, with long patience and constant admonitions to call them to repentance *but the unjust knoweth no shame*, never blushing at their guilt or their ingratitude, and they who are past shame, are past cure

(2) He had executed judgments on other nations, that they might take warning, destroying their cities, and leaving their land desolate without inhabitants, v 6 *I said, Surely thou wilt fear me*, affected with the sufferings of others, and not daring to provoke a jealous God *Thou wilt receive instruction*, by their [illegible], *so their dwelling should not be cut off, howsoever I punished them*, his visitations being designed to rescue them from destruction, if they heard *the rod, and who had appointed it* But,

(3) *They rose early, and corrupted all their doings*, grew worse and worse, filling up the measure of their iniquities, and wilfully rushed on their ruin *Note*, Damned souls will to eternity have only their own obstinacy and folly to blame *How oft would I have gathered you, and ye would not!*

Mic vii 7 8 ¶ Therefore wait ye upon me, saith the LORD,
until the day that I rise up to the prey for my deter-
Joel iii 2 mination *is* to gather the nations, that I may assemble
the kingdoms to pour upon them mine indignation, *even*
Chap i 18 all my fierce anger for all the earth shall be devoured
with the fire of my jealousy 9 For then will I turn to
Isa xix 18 the people a pure † language, that they may all call
† Heb lip upon the name of the LORD, to serve him with one
‡ Heb shoulder ‡ consent 10 From beyond the rivers of Ethiopia,
Ps lxviii 31 my suppliants, *even the* daughter of my dispersed, shall
Isa xviii 7 Acts viii 27 bring mine offering 11 In that day shalt thou not be
ashamed for all thy doings, wherein thou hast trans-
gressed against me for then I will take away out of
Jer vii 4 the midst of thee them that rejoice in thy pride, and
§ Heb In my holy mountain thou shalt no more be haughty § because of my holy
mountain 12 I will also leave in the midst of thee an
Isa xiv 32 Zech xi 11 afflicted and poor people, and they shall trust in the name
of the LORD 13 The remnant of Israel shall not do
1 John iii 9 iniquity, nor speak lies neither shall a deceitful tongue
Rev xiv 5 be found in their mouth for they shall feed and lie
down, and none shall make *them* afraid

v 8–13 Amidst all the desolations determined, the prospect of the days of the Messiah gave some reviving hopes to the faithful, who are commanded to wait still upon God, and expect his salvation

1 He will rise up to avenge himself, and seize the prey,

for which purpose he assembles the nations of the ungodly, to pour out upon them his wrath, who refuse to submit to the proffers of his grace, and obey not his gospel Or the sense may be, He will assemble the kingdoms, the Roman army collected from them, *to pour upon them*, the Jewish people, *mine indignation*, for rejecting their Messiah, and their whole country shall be devoured *with the fire of my jealousy*

2 He will set up and establish the gospel kingdom throughout the world, and bring the nations to the obedience of the faith *For then will I turn to the people a pure language*, the converting grace of God effectually changing the conversation; so that renewed souls speak a different language from what they used to do, telling now of the things which God hath done for their souls, and with one mind and one mouth glorifying him and the faithful among all nations shall have one common tongue, and join in the same blessed service of prayer and praise, *calling upon the name of the Lord, and serving him with one consent* And thus God's dispersed people, now brought to humble supplicants, from Egypt and all the places of their dispersion, shall come bringing their *offering*, even their bodies, souls, and spirits, a living sacrifice to God, v 10 Prayer being the immediate voice of the humbled sinner, and every true supplicant, not only in words but in deed, presents himself to God, to glorify him, not only in his lips but in his life In that day their shame shall be done away, their sins being forgiven, and the power of them subdued The proud and self-righteous, the hypocrites, such as were the Scribes and Pharisees, who trust in their services at the temple, and on their works and doings, shall then be destroyed, v 11 Nothing being more offensive to God, than that high conceit which such miserable sinners entertain of their own formal services and imperfect duties *I will also leave in the midst of thee an afflicted and poor people*, as when the Chaldeans carried all the nobles captives, and left the poor of the land for husbandmen and vine dressers And a poor afflicted people are God's redeemed, afflicted with temptations, corruption, persecution, poor, generally in worldly goods, always in spirit, sensible of their own wants and wretchedness, and begging at the door of mercy for the bread of life *and they shall trust in the name of the Lord*, in his blood and righteousness, as the only ground of their acceptance before God *The remnant of Israel*, these poor afflicted ones, *shall not do iniquity*, but by the effectual grace of God shall be enabled to walk in all holy conversation and godliness, *nor speak lies*, truth stamping all their words, and faithful to the doctrines of the gospel, holding the truth in the light and love of it *neither shall a deceitful tongue be found in their mouth*, *so they shall feed*, as the sheep of Christ's pasture, on the ordinances, *and lie down* in peace under the protection of their great Shepherd, *and none shall make them afraid*, none of their enemies, spiritual or temporal, shall be able to terrify or to destroy them, for their heart standeth fast, and trusteth in the Lord

14 ¶ Sing, O daughter of Zion, shout, O Israel, Isa xii 6 & liv 1 Zech ix 9
be glad and rejoice with all the heart, O daughter of
Jerusalem 15 The LORD hath taken away thy
judgments, he hath cast out thine enemy the King of
Israel, *even* the LORD *is* in the midst of thee thou Ver 5, 17
shalt not see evil any more 16 In that day it shall
be said to Jerusalem, Fear thou not *and to* Zion, Let Heb xii 12
not thine hands be † slack 17 The LORD thy God † Or faint
in the midst of thee *is* mighty, he will save, he will Jer xxxii 41
rejoice over thee with joy he will ‡ rest in his love, ‡ Heb. Be silent
he will joy over thee with singing 18 I will gather
them that are sorrowful for the solemn assembly, *who* Lam i 4
are of thee, *to whom* § the reproach of it *was* a burden § Heb The burden upon it was reproach
19 Behold, at that time I will undo all that afflict thee,
and I will save her that halteth, and gather her that was Joel iii 2
driven out, and I will ‖ get them praise and fame in Ezek xxxiv 16 Mic iv 6
every land, ¶ where they have been put to shame 20 ‖ Heb set them for a praise Isa lx 18
At that time will I bring you *again*, even in the time
that I gather you for I will make you a name, and ¶ Heb Of their shame
a praise among all people of the earth, when I turn back Isa xi 12 Ezek xxxvii 21
your captivity before your eyes, saith the LORD

v 14–20 The promises here made seem to have particular respect to the recovery of God's dispersed Israel in the last days, for though they had some fulfilment in their deliverance from Babylon, yet after that they saw evil again, and are now lying under the longest and heaviest of all their afflictions, but when God shall fulfil the word, they *shall see evil no more*, ver 15.

Zion is called upon to rejoice and shout for joy in the prospect of her approaching glorious redemption, v 14 and she is enjoined no longer to fear or be dispirited in the view of the greatness or number of her foes, v 16 because God promises,

1 To remove all *judgments* from her, all temporal judgments, such as exile, dispersion, poverty, contempt; all spiritual judgments, such as blindness, unbelief, and hardness of heart All her *enemies shall be cast out*, that now possess the land of Israel

Before Christ 612

Iſrael, and *he will undo all that afflict them* Though weak, feeble, and halting, their *captivity ſhall be brought back*, ver 20 never to be repeated, *for thou ſhalt ſee evil no more*, their troubles now being for ever at an end

2 God promiſes to be in the midſt of them, as *their king*, Meſſiah, to ſave them from the power of all evil, as *their God*, ver 17 in a covenant of everlaſting love, and who will never leave nor forſake them He is *mighty*, yea, Almighty, able to ſave to the uttermoſt, and to fulfil all the pomiſes of his word in ſpite of whatever oppoſition may be raiſed from Satan, ſin, death, or hell, and willing as he is able, *he will ſave* his people in time and in eternity *He will rejoice over thee with joy and ſinging*, the converſion of ſinners being the delight of the Redeemer, and he ſees then in them *the travail of his ſoul, and is ſatisfied* *He will reſt in his love*, unchangeably the ſame, no cloud ſhall ever hide from them again the bright beams of his countenance, and he will himſelf feel complacence in the expreſſions of his favour vouchſafed to his dear people

3 They ſhall again enjoy the ordinances which have been ſo long interrupted, and after which they mourned during their diſperſion *I will gather them that are ſorrowful for the ſolemn aſſembly*, who weep over the deſolations of Zion, *who are of thee*,

4

the true children of the Jeruſalem which is above, the mother of us all, *to whom the reproach of it was a burden*, deeply affected with the inſults of their enemies, which was the caſe of the pious Jews in Babylon, who were, in God's appointed time, reſtored to their temple and worſhip at Jeruſalem The Jews in their preſent diſperſion lament alſo the ſad interruption of the ſervice of the ſanctuary, and thoſe who are converted from among them long for the day of their brethren's reſtoration, when they may be gathered either into the church of Chriſt, or, as ſome ſuppoſe, be collected together in their own land, and ſerve God literally in his holy mountain at Jeruſalem, and their reproach be for ever rolled away

4 They ſhall become honourable and reſpected, as they have been contemned and deſpiſed *I will get them praiſe and fame in every land where they have been put to ſhame*, for their rejection of the Meſſiah, but now being turned unto the Lord, all chriſtian lands will praiſe them for their obedience to the faith, and the fame of their converſion will ſpread a general joy, they ſhall then be *a name and a praiſe among all people of the earth*, for which happy event all gracious ſouls ſhould unite their fervent ſupplications, that the Lord would be pleaſed to haſten it in his time

THE

THE

EVANGELICAL EXPOSITOR;

OR, A

PRACTICAL COMMENT

Upon the PROPHECY of

HAGGAI.

THE three last of the prophets were raised up of God, after the return of the Jews from Babylon. Haggai and Zechariah appeared much about the same time, eighteen years after, when the building of the temple was both retarded by its enemies, and neglected by its friends, Ezra v 1 *to reprove them for their remissness, and to encourage them to revive that good work when it had stood still for some time, and to go on with it vigorously, notwithstanding the opposition they met with in it Haggai began two months before Zechariah, who was raised up to second him, that out of the mouth of two witnesses the word might be established but Zechariah continued longer at the work, for all Haggai's prophecies that are recorded, were delivered within four months, in the second year of Darius, between the beginning of the sixth month, and the end of the ninth but we have Zechariah's prophecies dated above two years after,* Zech vii 1 *They both prophesied of Christ, Haggai speaks of him as the Glory of the latter House, Zechariah as the Man the Branch as they saw the day approaching, they sought thus to raise the expectations of Israel, and prepare them for his reception*

CHAP I

Before Christ 5 0

In this chapter we have, 1 A reproof of the Jews for their dilatoriness and slothfulness in building the temple, with an exhortation to resume that good work, and to prosecute it in good earnest, ver 1—11 *2 The good success of this sermon, appearing in the people's return and close application to that work, wherein the prophet in God's name animated and encouraged them, assuring them that God was with them,* ver 12—15

1 [a] IN the second year of Darius the king, in the sixth
month, in the first day of the month, [b] came the
word of the LORD by † Haggai the prophet
unto [c] Zerubbabel the son of Shealtiel [d] governor
of Judah, and to Joshua the son of Josedech the high
priest, saying, 2 Thus speaketh the LORD of hosts,
saying, This people say, The time is not come, the time
that the LORD's house should be built 3 Then came
the word of the LORD by Haggai the prophet, saying,
4 [e] *Is it* time for you, O ye, to dwell in your cieled
houses, and this house *lie* waste? 5 Now therefore
thus saith the LORD of hosts, ‡ Consider your ways
6 Ye have [f] sown much, and bring in little ye eat,
but ye have not enough ye drink, but ye are not filled
with drink ye clothe you, but there is none warm and
[g] he that earneth wages, earneth wages *to put it* into a
bag || with holes 7 ¶ Thus saith the LORD of hosts,
[h] Consider your ways 8 Go up to the mountain, and
bring wood, and build the house, and I will take plea-
sure in it, and I will be glorified, saith the LORD. 9.
Ye looked for much, and lo *it came* to little and when
ye brought *it* home, [i] I did § blow upon it why? saith
the LORD of hosts, because of mine house that *is* waste,
and ye run every man unto his own house 10 There-
fore [k] the heaven over you is stayed from dew, and the
earth is stayed *from* her fruit 11 And I [l] called for a
drought upon the land, and upon the mountains, and upon
the corn, and upon the new wine, and upon the oil, and
upon *that* which the ground bringeth forth, and upon men,
and upon cattle, and [m] upon all the labour of the hands

a Ezra iv 24 & v 1 / ch i 1 b 2 Pet i 21 † i e The ... of the Lord, or my faith c 1 Chron. iii 17, 19 d Ezra i 8 & ii 63 e 2 Sam vii 2 Ps cxxxii 3, &c ‡ Heb Set your heart upon f Deut xxviii 38 Hos iv 10 Mic vi 14 15 Chap. ii 16 g Zech viii [illegible] || Heb pierced through h Lam iii 40 Ver 5 2 Cor xiii 5

Before Christ 5 0 i Chap ii 17 § Or blow it away k Lev xxvi 19 Deut xxviii 23 1 Kings viii 1 m Chap ii 17

v 1—11 The date of this prophecy is in the second year of Darius the king, in the sixth month, the first day of the month Not Darius the Mede, but probably Darius Hystaspes, who came to the throne about fifteen years after the proclamation of Cyrus *The word of the Lord* which was sent to Haggai, he is commanded to deliver *to Zerubbabel the son of Shealtiel*, or Salathiel, his nephew, it should seem, 1 *Chron* iii 17—19 at least his adopted son and successor in the government, *and to Joshua the son of Josedech the high priest*, these being the chief persons in church and state, on whom it was especially incumbent to stir up the people to their duty

1 They are charged with great negligence and remissness in the work of God *This people*, who have so lately enjoyed such distinguished favour from God, *say*, *The time is not come, the time that the Lord's house should be built*, they had begun the foundations immediately on their return from Babylon, but the building had been interrupted through the misrepresentations of their enemies at the Persian court, and though for a season they had liberty to proceed, they seem to have been too indifferent about it, and were ready to suggest arguments to encourage themselves in their negligence, either they were too poor as yet to proceed in it, or the late unseasonable years were interpreted as a providen-

Before Christ 520

til intimation, that it was not yet proper to carry on the work, and therefore they deferred it to a more convenient season. So often are we ready to put off what is present duty to some future time, and in excuse to pretend a providential interposition, when in truth we only follow our own inclinations.

2. For this lukewarmness and carelessness, God's displeasure had already appeared against them. The wants of which they complained had their origin from hence, nor would they be relieved till this matter was rectified. Their land was under a curse, and though *they sowed much*, they *reaped little*, they had neither meat, drink, nor cloths sufficient to support and keep them warm, or what they had, God permitted them to have no comfort in it, and the money they gained was quickly lost, as if they had put it into a bag with holes, v. 6. The drought had parched up their land, and disappointed their expectations of plenty, v. 10, 11. and what they gathered into their storehouses, *God blew upon it*, ver. 9. and it wasted insensibly, or *blew it away* as stubble, by some providential judgments: and the reason he informs them, *because of mine house that is waste, and ye run every man unto his own house*, diligent and active in seeking their own interests, and promoting their own advantage, and unconcerned about the house of God and the glory of his name. *Note*, (1.) They who look for much from creature-comforts, must prepare for disappointment. (2.) In our common blessings we are as much dependant upon God's ceaseless providential care, as if we were fed daily by miracles. (3.) If God blows upon our possessions, we shall pine in the midst of plenty, and his wrath will embitter every comfort. (2.) They who seek first the kingdom of God, and his righteousness, consult best for both worlds, and happiness in time, as well as eternity, arising only from his favour and blessing.

3. He expostulates with them hereupon. *Is it time for you, O ye*, who can find no time to serve God, nor build his house, *to dwell in your cieled houses?* Theirs were completely finished and furnished, whilst his lay waste. So often do professors *all seek their own things, and not those which be Jesus Christ's*, but great is their guilt.

4. He endeavours to rouse them from their lethargy, and to set them to work. *Consider your ways*, what miseries they have already brought upon you, the baseness and ingratitude of such conduct, and what will be the end of these things. *Consider your ways*, that, convinced of their evil, you may amend them without delay, and begin instantly the neglected work of God's temple. *Go up to the mountain, and bring wood* from Lebanon, *and build the house, and I will take pleasure in it*, accept their labours and the sacrifices there offered, *and I will be glorified, saith the Lord*, in the work of your hands, the worship there performed should redound to his praise. *Note*, (1.) The first step to all godliness is serious consideration, and this preparation of the heart is from the Lord. (2.) They who consider their ways to any good purpose, must shew it by immediate reformation of what is wrong. (3.) Whenever we return unto God, and his neglected service, he will still be found gracious, he will take pleasure in us, and be glorified in mercy.

n Ezra v. 2. — 12 ¶ [n] Then Zerubbabel the son of Shealtiel, and
Joshua the son of Josedech the high priest, with all the
remnant of the people, obeyed the voice of the LORD
their God, and the words of Haggai the prophet, (as
the LORD their God had sent him) and the people did
fear before the LORD. 13 Then spake Haggai the
LORD's messenger, in the LORD's message unto the
o 2 Chron. xv. 2. Rom. viii. 31. — people, saying, [o] I am with you, saith the LORD. 14
p 1 Pet. i. 3. q Chap. i. 1. — And the LORD [p] stirred up the spirit of Zerubbabel
the son of Shealtiel, [q] governor of Judah, and the spirit
of Joshua the son of Josedech the high priest, and the
spirit of all the remnant of the people; and they came
r Ezra v. 2. — and [r] did work in the house of the LORD of hosts their
God, 15 In the four and twentieth day of the sixth
month, in the second year of Darius the king.

v. 12—15. We have here an account of the happy success with which the prophet's admonition was attended.

1. They obeyed instantly the voice of the Lord their God. Zerubbabel and Joshua led the way, and the people cheerfully followed their good examples, *fearing before the Lord*, under a sense of his displeasure visible in their past visitations, and justly apprehensive lest they should provoke heavier judgments. *They came and did work in the house of the Lord of hosts their God* within three weeks after the warning they had received, v. 15. the intermediate time probably being spent in providing the materials, and for the sudden alteration they stood indebted to God's rich grace, who stirred up their spirits, v. 14. inclining and encouraging them to the undertaking. *Note*, (1.) The word in the mouth of God's ministers is the voice of God, and must be respected accordingly. (2.) Holy fear is a blessed principle of action. (3.) When we see how negligent we have been, the consideration should quicken us to double diligence, that we may redeem the time. (4.) Whatever good is in us, or done by us, we owe it entirely to God's free grace, from whom alone all holy desires, and all just works do proceed.

Before Christ 520

2. God hereupon sends his prophet to them, with a new message of encouragement. *I am with you, saith the Lord*, to pardon your past neglect, to assist you in your present labours, to protect you from your enemies, and to crown your work with success. *Note*, If God says, *I am with you*, that is enough, we need not wish for more; his presence includes all blessedness.

CHAP. II.

In this chapter we have three sermons preached by the prophet Haggai, for the encouragement of those that were forward to build the temple. In the first, he assures the builders that the glory of this house should exceed that of Solomon's, in which he has an eye to the coming of Christ, ver. 1—9. In the second he assures them, that though their delay to build the temple had retarded the prosperous progress of their other affairs, yet now they had set about it in good earnest God would bless them, and give them success, ver. 10—19. In the third, he assures Zerubbabel, that as a reward of his faith, zeal and activity herein, he should be a favourite of heaven, and one of the ancestors of Messiah the prince, whose kingdom should be set up on the ruins of all opposing powers, ver. 20—23.

1 IN the seventh month, in the one and twentieth day
of the month, came the word of the LORD † † Heb. By the hand. See Chap. i. 1.
by the prophet Haggai, saying, 2 Speak now to Ze-
rubbabel the son of Shealtiel governor of Judah, and to
Joshua the son of Josedech the high priest, and to the
residue of the people, saying, 3 [a] Who is left among a Ezra iii. 12.
you that saw this house in her first glory? and how do
ye see it now? [b] is it not in your eyes in comparison of b Zech. iv. 10.
it, as nothing? 4 Yet now [c] be strong, O Zerubba- c Ibid. 1 Chr. xxviii. 20.
bel, saith the LORD; and be strong, O Joshua son of
Josedech the high priest; and be strong, all ye people
of the land, saith the LORD, and work: for [d] I am d Chap. i. 13.
with you, saith the LORD of hosts; 5 *According to*
the word that I covenanted with you when ye came out
of Egypt, so [e] my spirit remaineth among you: fear ye e Isa. lxiii. 11.
not. 6 For thus saith the LORD of hosts, [f] Yet once, f Ver. 21. Heb. xii. 26.
it is a little while, and [g] I will shake the heavens, and g Joel iii. 16.
the earth, and the sea, and the dry land; 7 And I
will shake all nations, and [h] the desire of all nations shall h Gen. xlix. 10.
come, and I will [i] fill this house with glory, saith the i Mal. iii. 1.
LORD of hosts. 8 The silver is mine, and the gold
is mine, saith the LORD of hosts. 9 The glory of this
latter house shall be greater than of the former, saith
the LORD of hosts: and in this place will I give peace,
saith the LORD of hosts.

v. 1—9. Having set themselves heartily to their work, God encourages them by a second message, about a month after the former, to proceed in the building. Some, probably who had seen the former temple, which had been destroyed about seventy years, beheld with grief the present structure, so little comparable to that for magnificence, and perhaps discouraged the hearts of the builders, suggesting what an insignificant house this would be; but God bid the prophet say, *Be strong, O Zerubbabel and Joshua, and all ye people of the land, and work*, nor be disheartened at any obstacles. And he suggests, for this purpose, the most reviving grounds of encouragement.

1. God will be with them with his special presence, and the comforts of his spirit, according to his covenant when he brought them out of Egypt, and took them for his own, therefore they *need not fear*, success should crown their labours; or as some read the words, *I am with you, with the Word*, the Lord Jesus, the essential word, *with whom I covenanted*, he being the covenant Head and fulfiller, and through him all the blessings of it shall be secured to them, and his spirit of wisdom and might should be their guide, to their safety and consolation; and if he be with us, then shall we be strong.

2. In this temple shall the Messiah incarnate appear, and give it far greater glory than ever Solomon's temple could boast of. *Yet once, it is a little while* before this shall come to pass; for though the coming of Christ was distant five hundred years, it was a little while in God's sight, or compared with the time since the first promise had been given; and *yet once* may have reference to God's appearance on Sinai, when he revealed himself in such tremendous majesty, shaking the heavens and the earth, as now should again be done. Before the coming of Christ, the nations and all their rulers had been shaken in pieces as by an earthquake, through the prevalence of the Roman arms; and when Christ appeared, his gospel made a shaking among the nations, awakening the consciences of men, and changing their natures, destroying and silencing the oracles of the heathen, and abolishing the whole ceremonial institution, Heb. xii. 26. *And the desire*

Before Chriſt 5-0

ſire of all nations ſhall come, He, whoſe ſalvation is to extend to all nations, the deſirable object which every miſerable ſinner ſo greatly needs, and whom all ſhould long for as their only hope and refuge, *and I will fill this houſe with glory, ſaith the Lord*, by the preſence of the incarnate Jehovah, which ſhould far exceed in glory the Shechinah of old It is true they might ſay, that their treaſures were utterly inſufficient to adorn the temple, as it had been overlaid by Solomon with gold, but God anticipates the objection *The ſilver and the gold is mine*, theſe were his own before Solomon beſtowed them on his building, and he could, if he had pleaſed, have given them enough to have done likewiſe, but his glory was not by theſe exalted *Far greater ſhould be the glory of this latter houſe, than of the former*, though neither ark, nor Shechinah, nor Urim and Thummim, nor celeſtial fire were there, the fullneſs of the Godhead bodily reſident in Jeſus ſhould far ſurpaſs all theſe, and the miracles he wrought, and the goſpel he declared, far exalted the latter houſe above the former *and in this place will I give peace, ſaith the Lord God*, not temporal peace, for under the ſecond temple the Jews enjoyed little of that, but ſpiritual peace, which Jeſus the Prince of Peace came to purchaſe, preach, and communicate to all his redeemed people

10 ¶ In the four and twentieth *day* of the ninth
month, in the ſecond year of Darius, came the word of
the LORD by Haggai the prophet, ſaying, 11 Thus
k Lev x 11 ſaith the LORD of hoſts, k Aſk now the prieſts *con-*
Deut xxxiii 10 Mal ii 7 *cerning* the law, ſaying, 12 If one bear holy fleſh in
the ſkirt of his garment, and with his ſkirt do touch
bread, or pottage, or wine, or oil, or any meat, ſhall
it be holy? And the prieſts anſwered and ſaid, No
l Num xix 11 22 13 Then ſaid Haggai, l If *one that is* unclean by a dead
body, touch any of theſe, ſhall it be unclean? And
the prieſts anſwered and ſaid, It ſhall be unclean 14
m Tit i 15 Then anſwered Haggai, and ſaid, m So *is* this people, and
ſo *is* the nation before me, ſaith the LORD, and ſo *is*
every work of their hands, and that which they offer
there *is* unclean 15 And now, I pray you, conſider
from this day and upward, from before a ſtone was laid
upon a ſtone in the temple of the LORD 16 Since
n Chap i 6 thoſe *days* were, n when *one* came to an heap of twenty
Zech viii 10 *meaſures*, there were *but* ten when one came to the
preſs fat, for to draw out fifty *veſſels* out of the preſs,
o Deut there were *but* twenty 17 ¶ o I ſmote you p with blaſt-
xxviii 22 ing, and with mildew, and with hail, q in all the labours
1 King viii 37 Chap i 6 of your hands, r yet ye *turned* not to me, ſaith the LORD
p Amos iv 9 18 Conſider now from this day, and upward, from the
four and twentieth day of the ninth *month*, *even* from
q Chap i 11 the day that the foundation of the LORD's temple was
r Amos iv 8 laid, conſider *it* 19 s *Is* the ſeed yet in the barn? yea
s Zech viii 12 as yet the vine, and the fig-tree, and the pomegranate,
t Mal iii 10 Mat vi 33 and the olive-tree hath not brought forth t from this
day will I bleſs *you*

v 10—19 This diſcourſe was delivered above two months after the former, and is deſigned,

1 To humble them under a ſenſe of their pollution and ſinfulneſs, and in order hereunto the prophet is ſent to enquire of the prieſts, not ſo much for his information as their conviction He puts two queſtions to them concerning the law, of which they were the expounders, (1) Whether a perſon carrying holy fleſh in his garment, ſanctified by the touch of it any common meat, to which they anſwered, No, for though the garment muſt be waſhed before it could be employed in common uſes, *Lev* vi 27 yet it communicated no virtue to what it touched (2) Whether if a perſon unclean touched any of theſe, it ſhould be unclean, they ſaid, *It ſhall be unclean*, Num xix 22 ſo much more eaſily is pollution communicated than purity Then anſwered Haggai, applying the caſe to the prieſts and people, *So is this nation before me, ſaith the Lord*, their ritual devotions and ſervices, like the garment carrying holy fleſh, could not ſanctify, whilſt their hearts being unclean, every thing they touched received defilement, and eſpecially, as ſeems to be the intention of the prophet to ſhew, was this the caſe with them whilſt they neglected the building God's houſe, and this they are called upon to *conſider*, and lay to heart, that in their reflections on the paſt, they might lie low before God, *from this day upward, even from before a ſtone was laid upon a ſtone in the temple of the Lord*, from that day, when they left off the work about ſeventeen years ago, they had been under the conſtant marks of God's diſpleaſure, the ſure proof of their ſins Their harveſt had failed their expectations, the heap of corn which ſhould have yielded twenty meaſures, when it came to be threſhed gave but ten, and when from the quantity of grapes he put into the preſs, the vine-dreſſer hoped to draw out fifty meaſures, *there were but twenty*, ver 16 Blaſting, mildew and hail, deſtroyed the fruits of the earth, *yet ye turned not unto me, ſaith the Lord*, continued unhumbled under thoſe providences, and reſumed not the work of the ſanctuary all which they ſhould remember, and humble their ſouls before the Lord

2 To encourage them, he bids them obſerve from the day forward, that they began to return to God, and ſet themſelves heartily to his neglected ſervice, what a bleſſed alteration would appear *Is the ſeed yet in the barn?* No they had juſt ſown it, and it was not yet come up, and uncertain what harveſt it would produce, their fruit trees, it being winter, were now empty, but ſaith God, *from this day will I bleſs you*, with plenty of all good things, and to their full conviction demonſtrate how much they conſulted even their own advantage in returning to his work and ſervice *Note*, They who faithfully apply themſelves to God's work, ſhall aſſuredly find his bleſſing, ſometimes in providential gifts of this world's goods, always in the comfort he will beſtow upon their ſouls

20 ¶ And again the word of the LORD came unto
Haggai in the four and twentieth *day* of the month,
ſaying, 21 Speak to Zerubbabel, u governor of Ju- u Chap i 14
dah, ſaying, x I will ſhake the heavens and the earth, x Ver 6, 7 Heb. xii 26
22 And y I will overthrow the throne of kingdoms, and y Mat xxiv 7
I will deſtroy the ſtrength of the kingdoms of the
heathen, and z I will overthrow the chariots, and thoſe z Mic v 10. Zech iv 6 & x 10.
that ride in them, and the horſes and their riders ſhall
come down, every one by the ſword of his brother.
23 In that day, ſaith the LORD of hoſts, will I take
thee, O Zerubbabel my ſervant, the ſon of Shealtiel,
ſaith the LORD, and a will make thee as a ſignet for a Cant viii 6 Ecclus xlix 11
b I have choſen thee, ſaith the LORD of hoſts b Iſa. xlii 1.

v 20—23 The ſame day in which Haggai had delivered this meſſage to the people in general, he is ſent to Zerubbabel in particular, with encouragement to him under the difficulties of his office, and the dangers to which he ſaw himſelf and the nation expoſed from their weakneſs, and the powerful nations around them

1 He may expect to ſee ſtrange revolutions, like the ſhakings of heaven and earth *The throne of kingdoms*, the Perſian monarchy, would be overthrown, and *the kingdoms of the heathen* be deſtroyed, with their chariots and horſemen, *every one by the ſword of his brother*, which may include the ſucceſſive monarchies, the Grecian and Roman, and be extended to all the enemies of Chriſt's church and people to the end of time

2 Zerubbabel ſhall be protected and defended in the midſt of theſe commotions, or the promiſe reſpects his glorious deſcendant the Meſſiah, of whom he was the figure He is emphatically the *ſervant* of the Lord, raiſed up to do his pleaſure *I will make thee as a ſignet, for I have choſen thee, ſaith the Lord of hoſts*, he is the elect of God, in whom his ſoul delighteth, precious as a ſignet, and entruſted with all power in heaven and in earth, who is himſelf ſealed as the Head of his redeemed people, and he in like manner ſealeth them unto the day of redemption

THE

THE EVANGELICAL EXPOSITOR; OR, A PRACTICAL COMMENT Upon the PROPHECY of ZECHARIAH.

THIS prophet was collegue with the prophet Haggai, and began to propheſy ſome time after him, but he continued longer, ſoared higher in viſions and revelations, and wrote more than he had done He begins with a plain practical ſermon, expreſſive of that which was the ſcope of his propheſying in the five firſt verſes, but afterwards, to the end of chap. vi *he relates the viſions he ſaw, and the inſtructions he received immediately from heaven by them At* chap vii *from an enquiry made by the Jews concerning faſting, he takes occaſion to ſhew them the duty of their preſent day, and to encourage them to hope for God's favour, to the end of* chap. viii *After which there are two ſermons, which are both called* burdens of the word of the Lord, *one begins with* chap ix *the other with* chap xii *which probably were preached ſome time after, the ſcope of which is to reprove for ſin and threaten God's judgments againſt the impenitent, and to encourage thoſe that feared God with aſſurances of mercy God had in ſtore for his church, and eſpecially of the coming of the Meſſiah and the ſitting up of his kingdom in the world.*

Before Christ 520

CHAP I

In this chapter, after the introduction, ver 1 *we have,* 1 *An awakening call to a ſinful people to repent of their ſins and return to God,* ver 2—6 2 *Great encouragement given to hope for mercy* (1) *By the viſion of the horſes,* ver 7—11 (2) *By the prayer of the angel for Jeruſalem, and the anſwer to it,* ver 12—17 (3) *By the viſion of the four carpenters that were employed to cut off the four horns, with which Judah and Jeruſalem were ſcattered,* ver 18—21

520
a Ezra iv 24 Hag i 1
b 2 Pet i 21
c Ezra v 1
‖ i e The Lord remembers
d Dan ix 22
† Heb With displeaſure
e Jer xxv 5 & xxxv 15 Mal iii 7 Jam iv 8
f Iſa xxxi 6 Jer iii 12 & xviii 11 Ezek xviii 30 Hoſ xiv 1
g Dan ix 12
§ Or overtake
h Lam i 18

1 IN the eighth month, [a] in the ſecond year of Da-
rius, [b] came the word of the LORD [c] unto ‖ Ze-
chariah the ſon of Barachiah, the ſon of Iddo the
prophet, ſaying, 2 [d] The LORD hath been
† ſore diſpleaſed with your fathers 3 Therefore ſay
thou unto them, Thus ſaith the LORD of hoſts, [e] Turn
ye unto me, ſaith the LORD of hoſts, and I will turn
unto you, ſaith the LORD of hoſts 4 Be ye not as
your fathers, unto whom the former prophets have cried,
ſaying, Thus ſaith the LORD of hoſts, [f] Turn ye now
from your evil ways, and *from* your evil doings but they
did not hear, nor hearken unto me, ſaith the LORD
5 Your fathers, where *are* they? and the prophets, do
they live for ever? 6 But my words and my ſtatutes,
which I commanded my ſervants the prophets, [g] did
they not § take hold of your fathers? and they returned
and ſaid, [h] Like as the LORD of hoſts thought to do
unto us, according to our ways, and according to our
doings, ſo hath he dealt with us.

v 1—6 The prophet Zechariah received his commiſſion from God, and began to ſpeak about two months after Haggai He is called the ſon of Barachiah, and the ſame, as ſome ſuppoſe, whom our Lord mentions, *Matth* xxiii 35 as ſlain between the porch and the altar, *the ſon of Iddo, the prophet*, which may refer to Zechariah, and not his grandfather, or he might be a prophet alſo He begins his diſcourſe,

Before Christ 520.

1 With reminding them of the ſins and provocations of their forefathers, with whom God was ſore diſpleaſed, and whom he had ſeverely puniſhed, whoſe ſufferings ſhould be a warning to them, *v* 2

2 With exhorting the people to turn unto God, and gives them the moſt gracious encouragement to do ſo, for he *will turn unto you*, and thrice he adds, *thus ſaith the Lord of hoſts*, to give weight and authority to the admonition, and engage their faith in the certainty of his promiſed mercy Conſcious guilt makes the heart fearful, and the ſinner, who ſees his iniquities in their true colours, can ſcarce be perſuaded that God can and will receive one ſo unworthy into his favour

3 He reminds them of the ſins of their forefathers, which had provoked God, and bids them take warning by their ſufferings, and not imitate their bad examples, *v* 2 *Be ye not as your fathers*, treading in their ſteps, who, though repeatedly, fervently, and for a long ſeaſon, called upon by the former prophets to repent, turned a deaf ear to God's word and hardened their hearts, and *where are they?* They went captives into a ſtrange land, and many of them no doubt were cut off in their iniquities, and were gone to receive the juſt reward of their deeds And the prophets are dead alſo; but their words ſurvived them, and overtook the ſinners againſt whom they were denounced; and this in ſo evident a manner, that when the threatned judgments came, too late, in their accompliſhment, their forefathers, in a miſerable captivity, felt that righteous venge-

Before Chriſt 520

vengeance they would not believe till it took hold upon them *Note*, (1) The example of parents is no plea for following their ways, when contrary to God's word (2) We ſhould often think of thoſe who are gone before, *where are they?* gone to bliſs or miſery eternal, and we are haſtening after them whither then are we going? (3) God's miniſters are dying men we ſhould improve the ſeaſon they are ſpared to labour among us whilſt each of them, conſidering their own mortality, ſhould ſpeak as a dying man to dying men, and deliver at leaſt their own ſouls (4) Though the denunciations of wrath do not immediately take place againſt the ſinner, being in much patience delayed, yet, if he perſiſts in impenitence, they will *take hold* of him at laſt, and too late, in the belly of hell, he will feel that wrath from which he would not be perſuaded to flee

519

7 ¶ Upon the four and twentieth day of the ele-
venth month, which *is* the month Sebat, in the ſecond
year of Darius, came the word of the LORD unto
Zechariah the ſon of Barachiah, the ſon of Iddo the pro-
phet, ſaying, 8 I ſaw by night, and behold, [i] a man
riding upon a red horſe, and he ſtood among the myrtle-
trees that *were* in the bottom, and behind him *were there*
[k] red horſes † ſpeckled and white 9 Then ſaid I, O
my lord, what *are* theſe? And the angel that talked
with me, ſaid unto me, I will ſhew thee what theſe *be*
10 And the man that ſtood among the myrtle trees
anſwered and ſaid, Theſe *are they* whom [l] the LORD
hath ſent to walk to and fro through the earth 11
And they anſwered the angel of the LORD that ſtood
among the myrtle-trees, and ſaid, We have walked to
and fro through the earth, and behold, all the earth
[m] ſitteth ſtill, and is at reſt 12 ¶ Then the angel of
the LORD anſwered and ſaid, [n] O LORD of hoſts,
how long wilt thou not have mercy on Jeruſalem, and
on the cities of Judah, againſt which thou haſt had in-
dignation [o] theſe threeſcore and ten years? 13 And
the LORD anſwered the angel that talked with me,
with good words, *and* comfortable words 14 So the
angel that communed with me, ſaid unto me, Cry thou,
ſaying, Thus ſaith the LORD of hoſts, I am [p] jea-
lous for Jeruſalem and for Zion with a great jealouſy
15 And I am very ſore diſpleaſed with the heathen
[q] *that are* at eaſe for [r] I was but a little diſpleaſed,
and they helped forward the affliction 16 Therefore
thus ſaith the LORD, [s] I am returned to Jeruſalem
with mercies my houſe ſhall be built in it, ſaith the
LORD of hoſts, and a line ſhall be ſtretched forth upon
Jeruſalem 17 Cry yet, ſaying, Thus ſaith the LORD
of hoſts, my cities through proſperity ſhall yet be ſpread
abroad, and the LORD ſhall yet comfort Zion, and
[t] ſhall yet chooſe Jeruſalem

[i] Rev. vi. 2. Rev. i. 13. [k] Chap. vi. † Or bay [l] Heb. i. [m] Chap. vi. [n] Rev. vi. 10 [o] Dan. ix. 2. Chap. vii. 5 [p] Chap. viii. [q] Ver. 11. Pſalm. 6. [s] Chap. viii. [t] Iſa. xiv. 1. Chap. ii. 12.

v 7—17 The viſion here recorded was given to the prophet about three months after the former diſcourſe was delivered, and is deſigned for the encouragement of the people who had turned unto God, and diligently employed themſelves in rebuilding his holy temple We have

1 The viſion, *v* 8 *The grove of myrtles in the bottom* fitly repreſented the ſtate of the Jewiſh church, ſunk very low in the deep gloom of afflictions and want, and ſurrounded by the hills of the neighbouring nations, far greater than they It may ſignify alſo the church militant in general, which through much tribulation enters into the kingdom of God, the members of which, though low, are cloſely united, and their graces breathe fragrance before God In the midſt of them Jeſus appears, become *man* for us men and for our ſalvation, and going forth to fight our battles, conquering and to conquer, and *riding upon a red horſe* is the Captain of ſalvation, who by his own blood is to redeem his people, and by his power tread down his enemies, till their blood reaches to the horſes bridles, *Rev* xiv 20 Behind him ſtood marſhalled the armies of heaven, his miniſtring ſpirits, on horſes of different colours, according to the various ſervices in which they are employed, for judgment or for mercy

2 The prophet, filled with admiration at what he beheld, preſumes with deep reſpect to aſk, *O my Lord, what are theſe?* And the angel, he that is the head of all principalities and powers, even *the man that ſtood among the myrtle-trees*, is graciouſly pleaſed to inform him *Theſe are they whom the Lord hath ſent to walk to and fro in the earth*, to execute his commands, and miniſter to the heirs of ſalvation So kind and condeſcending is Jeſus to the humble enquirer after divine knowledge, that cry, *What I know not teach thou me* theſe he will guide into all truth

3 He hears the report theſe miniſtring ſpirits make to their King and Lord They had diſcharged their commiſſion, and report, that *the earth ſitteth ſtill, and is at reſt*, undiſturbed by wars, as was the caſe in the reign of Darius, ſecure and at eaſe, whilſt the poor people of God are under affliction and perpetual alarms Thus ſtill a careleſs world ſleeps on but they will ſhortly be fearfully rouſed from this fatal lethargy

4 The Angel, the Lord Jeſus hereupon becomes an advocate for his redeemed, and cries for mercy now at laſt upon them, after the long time God hath afflicted them, during ſeventy years, which, if computed from the burning of the temple, were juſt now completed ſo long had they ſuffered the marks of God's indignation, and now he begs that he will ſay, *It is enough* It is well for the church we have ſuch an advocate with the Father and in all times of trouble we ſhould remember this for our ſupport

5 An anſwer of peace is given to this Saviour's prayer *The Lord anſwered the angel with good words, and comfortable words*, for him the Father heareth always and if he undertake our cauſe, it ſhall not miſcarry

6 He communicates this anſwer to the prophet, to be proclaimed to his people for their comfort and encouragement *Thus ſaith the Lord of hoſts, I am jealous for Jeruſalem and for Zion with a great jealouſy* on their behalf, to repair their wrongs, and zealous to promote their happineſs Their enemies, who now ſit at eaſe, are the objects of his wrath he ſent them to correct his people in a little *diſpleaſure*, *and they helped forward the affliction*, exceeding their orders in cruelty and inhumanity, and inſulted over the miſeries of their unhappy captives but God will avenge their quarrel Whilſt on the other hand the prophet muſt proclaim aloud, *Thus ſaith the Lord, I am returned to Jeruſalem with mercies* the temple ſhall be built, Jeruſalem be raiſed from its ruins, and plenty and proſperity once more dwell in the cities of Judah *And the Lord ſhall yet comfort Zion*, after the days of her mourning, *and ſhall yet chuſe Jeruſalem*, for his bleſt abode which was literally fulfilled in the days of Zerubbabel and of the Maccabees, but moſt eminently when the Meſſiah appeared in the midſt of her, and his goſpel went forth through all the cities of the land

18 ¶ Then lift I up mine eyes, and ſaw, and be-
hold, four horns 19 And I ſaid unto the angel that
talked with me, What *be* theſe? And he anſwered me,
[u] Theſe *are* the horns which have ſcattered Judah, Iſrael,
and Jeruſalem 20 And the LORD ſhewed me four
carpenters 21 Then ſaid I, What came theſe to do?
And he ſpake, ſaying, Theſe *are* the horns which have
ſcattered Judah, ſo that no man did lift up his head
but [x] theſe are come to fray them, to caſt out the horns
of the Gentiles, which lift up *their* horn over the land
of Judah to ſcatter it

[u] Lam. ii. 3. & v. 3. or Dan. vii. 3. [x] Obad. 21

v 18—21 We have here a ſecond viſion to the ſame purpoſe as the former, comforting the people of Iſrael againſt their mighty foes

1 The prophet ſaw four horns, and, aſking an explanation of them, is informed, that *theſe are the horns which have ſcattered Judah, Iſrael, and Jeruſalem*, the various nations that at different times harraſſed and diſperſed them, *ſo that no man did lift up his head*, ſo oppreſſed and diſpirited they were, and brought ſo low Some refer theſe horns to the Samaritans, Arabians, Ammonites, and Philiſtines, who gave them ſuch hindrance in the building the temple and city And all who ſet about this bleſſed work may expect to be puſhed at by many a horn

2 The Lord ſhewed him *four carpenters*, or *ſmiths*, 1 *Sam* xiii 19 Theſe he had not ſeen Our fear of danger ſo engages us, that we often overlook the help provided for us And he tells him what theſe came to do, *v* 20 *to fray them, to caſt out the horns of the Gentiles* And theſe may be interpreted of the ſeveral monarchies which have riſen up to deſtroy each other, or of the angels whom God ſends to execute his judgments, or of the four great promoters of God's work, Zerubbabel, Joſhua, Ezra, and Nehemiah, or perhaps of the miniſters of the goſpel, who go forth and are ſtrengthened for carrying on the work of God in the midſt of all oppoſition *Note*, Whatever enemies are againſt us, we have greater friends for us and, though ſore thruſt at that we ſhould fall, in the Lord is our help, who will break all the horns of the ungodly

CHAP II

In this chapter we have, 1 *Another of the prophet's viſions*, ver 1, 2 2 *A ſermon upon it* (1) *By way of explanation of the viſion, ſhewing it to be a prediction of the repleniſhing of Jeruſalem, and of its ſafety and honour*, ver 3, 5 (2) *By way of application Here is*, 1 *A uſe of exhortation to the Jews that were yet in Babylon, preſſing them to haſten their return to their own land*, ver 6—9 2 *A uſe of conſolation to thoſe that were returned, in reference to the many difficulties they had to ſtruggle with*, ver 10, 11 3 *A uſe of caution to all not to preſcribe to God, or limit him, but patiently to wait for him*, ver 13

Before Christ 519.

1 I LIFT up mine eyes again, and looked, and be-
hold, ᵃ a man with a measuring line in his hand
2 Then said I, Whither goest thou? And he said un-
to me, ᵇ To measure Jerusalem to see what *is* the breadth
thereof, and what *is* the length thereof 3 And be-
hold, the angel that talked with me went forth, and an-
other angel went out to meet him, 4 And said unto
him, Run, speak to this young man, saying, Jerusalem
shall be inhabited *as* towns without walls for the multi-
tude of men and cattle therein 5 For I, saith the
LORD, will be unto her ᶜ a wall of fire round about,
ᵈ and will be the glory in the midst of her

v 1—5 The prophet had declared that *a line should be stretched forth upon Jerusalem*, and now in vision it is done And more seems intended than the mere rebuilding this city, even the erection of that glorious church, which the Redeemer of men should, in the fulness of time, come to establish in the earth

1 The vision he beholds is *a man with a measuring-line in his hand*, the same person as before, the Lord Jesus going forth according to the eternal decrees, to mark out the bounds of his church, and by his word and Spirit to build up the walls, that it may be a glorious church, in doctrine, discipline, and all holy conversation

2 The prophet, desirous to be informed concerning what he saw, asks, *Whither goest thou?* and he tells him, *to measure Jerusalem, &c* Then going forth, another angel meets him, and desires him to go back and inform the young man, for such, tho' a prophet, it seems Zechariah was, concerning the meaning of the vision that *Jerusalem shall be inhabited as towns without walls*, intimating its safety, security, and populousness, replenished with men and beasts in multitudes, protected as with a wall of fire, and filled with the glory of the Lord, *v* 5 which, though in a sense literally applicable to this city, is much rather to be considered as descriptive of the church of Christ, when all nations should flow into it, safe under the care of Jesus, as if surrounded by a wall of fire, his people shall dwell in peace, and in his ordinances he will manifest to them his presence, and be in the midst of their assemblies their glory and defence

6 ¶ Ho, ho, *come forth*, and ᵉ flee from the land of
the north, saith the LORD for I have spread you a-
broad as the four winds of the heaven, saith the LORD
7 ᶠ Deliver thyself, O Zion, that dwellest *with* the
daughter of Babylon 8 For thus saith the LORD of
hosts, After the glory hath he sent me unto the nations
which spoiled you, for he that ᵍ toucheth you, toucheth
the apple of his eye 9 For behold, I will shake mine
hand upon them, and ʰ they shall be a spoil to their ser-
vants and ⁱ ye shall know that the LORD of hosts hath
sent me

v 6—9 Though a general permission had been given to all the Jewish captives to return to their own land, many, discouraged by the difficulties they apprehended in resettling, and who had perhaps well provided for themselves in the land of their captivity, took no advantage of the proclamation of Cyrus, but sat down content in that strange land To rebuke their backwardness, and to quicken their return, God sends a summons to them in all places of their dispersion *Ho, ho, come forth* And such is the kind voice of gospel-grace, when miserable sinners are hugging their chains, and sleep in the prison of their iniquities

1 They are commanded to *flee* as for their lives, and escape without delay from the house of their prison, no longer dwelling *with the daughter of Babylon*, but coming to Zion, now prepared for their reception, *v* 7 *Note*, All things are ready, if we are ready Jesus calls, our duty, our interest, is to obey if we reject his word, and continue willing slaves of sin, our blood will be upon our own heads

2 Their apprehensions of the difficulties and dangers they may meet with are silenced nay, where they were they would be much more exposed, *for thus saith the Lord of hosts, After the glory* promised, *v* 5 and the glorious beginnings which had appeared, *hath he sent me unto the nations that spoiled you*, the Chaldeans, to avenge the wrongs they had suffered from them, *for he that toucheth you, toucheth the apple of his eye*, so tender, so careful, is God of his dear people, and so quick in his resentments of every offence given to them *For behold, I will shake my hand upon them*, the Babylonians, *and they shall be a spoil to their servants*, being destroyed by the Persians under Darius, against whom they had revolted, and should the Jews stay there, they would then suffer for their folly *And ye shall know that the Lord of hosts hath sent me*, when the prophecy receive its accomplishment *Note*, (1) Every child of God is dear to him, as if they were his very eye, and he will suffer no injury to be done them with impunity (2) All Christ's enemies shall fall before him he will perfect, what he hath begun, the work of his pro-

ple's salvation and therein his glory shall appear, and his divine mission be fully evidenced

10 ¶ ᵏ Sing and rejoice, O daughter of Zion for
lo, I come, and ˡ I will dwell in the midst of thee,
saith the LORD 11 And ᵐ many nations shall be
joined to the LORD ⁿ in that day, and shall be ᵒ my
people and I will dwell in the midst of thee, and
ᵖ thou shalt know that the LORD of hosts hath sent me
unto thee. 12 And the LORD shall inherit Judah his
portion in the holy land, ᑫ and shall choose Jerusalem
again 13 ʳ Be silent, O all flesh, before the LORD
for he is raised up ˢ out of † his holy habitation

v 10—13 The church and the people of God are called to sing and rejoice on the appearing of the great Redeemer

1 They shall have his presence in the midst of them *For lo I come*, not only as incarnate, but in the preaching of his gospel to the end of time, *and I will dwell in the midst of thee, saith the Lord*, in his special presence accompanying his ordinances, *and thou shalt know that the Lord of hosts hath sent me unto thee*, by experience of his power and grace upon each of their hearts

2 Great accessions from all nations shall be made to the church *Many nations shall be joined to the Lord in that day*, the Gentiles being called into the fellowship of the gospel, and obedient to the faith, *and* thus shall be entitled to all the blessings of the covenant of grace, they *shall be my people*, to serve and enjoy me

3 The Jewish people shall be restored to their own land *The Lord shall inherit Judah his portion in the holy land, and shall chuse Jerusalem again*, either they shall be converted and brought into the church, which is *the holy land*, or literally, as many suppose, shall at the time of their recovery at last be put in possession of Judea, rebuild Jerusalem, and as the redeemed of Jesus worship the Lord in the beauty of holiness

4 Silence is proclaimed through the earth to *all flesh* Either they are enjoined to behold with astonishment this wonderful work of the recovery of Israel, or this is addressed to the enemies of God's church and people, who will be confounded and for ever silenced in the dust, when, *raised up from his holy habitation*, the Lord shall come to vindicate their wrongs, and execute judgment on the ungodly

CHAP III

Here is, 1 *A vision relating to Joshua, as the representative of the church in his time* (1) *He is accused by Satan, but is brought off by Christ*, ver 1 2 (2) *He appears in filthy garments, but has them changed*, ver 3, 4, 5 (3) *He is assured of being established in his office, if he carry himself well*, ver 6, 7 2 *A sermon relating to Christ the* Branch, *who should be endued with all perfections for his undertaking, should be carried triumphantly through it, and by whom we should have pardon and peace*, ver 8, 10

1 AND he shewed me ᵃ Joshua the high-priest,
standing before ᵇ the angel of the LORD, ᶜ and
‖ Satan standing at his right hand ‡ to resist him 2
And the LORD said unto Satan, ᵈ The LORD rebuke
thee, O Satan, even the LORD ᵉ that hath chosen Jeru
salem, rebuke thee ᶠ *is* not this a brand plucked out of
the fire? 3 Now Joshua was clothed with ᵍ filthy gar-
ments, and stood before the angel 4 And he answered
and spake unto those that stood before him, saying, Take
away the filthy garments from him And unto him he
said, Behold, I have caused ʰ thine iniquity to pass from
thee, and I will clothe thee with ⁱ change of raiment
5 And I said, Let them ᵏ set a fair mitre upon his head
So they set a fair mitre upon his head and clothed him
with garments and the angel of the LORD stood by
6 And the angel of the LORD protested unto Joshua,
saying, 7 Thus saith the LORD of hosts, If thou
wilt walk in my ways, and if thou wilt keep my § charge,
then thou shalt also judge my house, and shalt also keep
my courts, and I will give thee ‖ places to walk among
these that stand by

v 1—7 Joshua the high-priest is here in vision shewed to Zechariah as standing before the Lord, the angel of the covenant, and he appears the representative of the priesthood and people to whom he ministered, who were defiled with guilt, and enslaved by corruption, from both of which God here in the person of Joshua promises to deliver them

1 He appears as a criminal before his great judge, and his accuser lays heavy charges against him, but he is acquitted

Before Christ 519

He stood before the angel of the Lord, and Satan at his right hand to resist him, to oppose him in his work, and raise difficulties to discourage him, and to more effectually urge the accusations of guilt he laid against him But *the Lord* Jesus Christ is his advocate, his pleads his cause and *said unto Satan, the Lord rebuke thee, Satan* Which may be considered as the Redeemer's prayer to his Father, to confound and silence this malicious adversary, or as his declaration what should be, *the Lord shall rebuke thee*, and avenge this enmity against his people, *for he hath chosen Jerusalem*, and therefore every tongue that riseth in judgment against her he will condemn, no charge can lie against God's elect *Is not this a brand pluckt out of the fire?* as Joshua and the people had been out of their captivity, and as all the people of God are when called out of a state of sin and guilt, in which they were exposed to the wrath of God, and fit fuel for the flames of hell, but, being now rescued by sovereign grace, in vain doth the enemy of souls attempt to kindle that fire which the blood of Jesus hath extinguished *Note*, (1) None ever stood up zealously for God, but whose right hand Satan did not place himself as an adversary (2) There is enough in the best of men to afford ground for accusation, if we had not a better righteousness than our own to plead in arrest of judgment (3) They who put their cause in Christ's hands need not fear the accuser of the brethren, they shall be justified from all things (4) The best way of answering the Devil's accusations is by looking up to God in prayer, and saying, *the Lord rebuke thee, Satan* (5) Every child of God is *a brand pluckt from the fire* How often have we stood on the brink of everlasting burnings, and lo! Jesus rescued us from ruin (6) The Lord's past mercies, which we have experienced, are an earnest of his present care they shall never be burnt, whom he hath once pluckt from the fire

2 He appears in filthy garments, as one polluted, and no doubt, as a sinful man, he had abundant cause to confess his shame Some suggest this was on account of the strange wives the priests had taken, and some of them his own sons, *Ezra* x 18 but he seems rather to represent the state of the people in general, whose best righteousness was but as *filthy rags*, *Isa* lxiv 6 but the Lord takes care for his cleansing *The angel* looked on him not with anger but compassion, and commanded his attendant ministers to strip off *the filthy garments*, the meaning of which he explains to his comfort, *Behold, I have caused thy iniquity to pass from thee*, the guilt of it is pardoned, the power of it subdued God sanctifies by his Spirit all those whom Jesus hath washed from their sins by his blood, and thus prepares them as a holy priesthood *And I will clothe thee with change of raiment*, that he might appear lovely, as before loathsome And thus doth Jesus array all his people in that divine righteousness which is without spot, and adorn them with those graces of his Spirit which make them all-glorious within and this is the Lord's doing, and marvellous in our eyes Arrayed in priestly robes, Joshua now looks great, for, at the Lord's command, the sacerdotal mitre is set on his head, and the priestly garments for beauty and glory are put upon him and though, from his former pollution, he might fear he should be turned out of his office, he is solemnly confirmed in it, *v* 6 *The angel of the Lord protested unto Joshua, saying, thus saith the Lord of hosts, If thou wilt walk in my ways*, in all the paths of righteousness and truth prescribed in God's word, *and if thou wilt keep my charge*, faithful in his sacerdotal office, vigilant, active, laborious, *then thou shalt also judge my house, and shalt also keep my courts*, presiding over the temple and its service, and enjoying all the honours and advantages resulting from that high station, *and I will give thee places to walk among those that stand by*, highly respected by his fellow ministers in the temple, or made a companion of glorified saints and angels at last, as the reward of his fidelity *Note*, (1) The ministers of God have a solemn trust committed to them, and they must look well how they discharge it (2) They who are faithful to Jesus shall be exalted in his better temple, and made to walk with him in white in glory everlasting, *for they are worthy*

8 Hear now, O Joshua the high-priest, thou and thy fellows that sit before thee for [l] they *are* men [‖] wondred at for behold, I will bring forth [m] my servant [n] the BRANCH 9 For behold, the stone that I have laid before Joshua [o] upon one stone *shall be* [p] seven eyes, behold, I will engrave the graving thereof, saith the LORD of hosts, and [q] I will remove the iniquity of that land in one day 10 [r] In that day, saith the LORD of hosts, [s] shall ye call every man his neighbour under the vine and under the fig tree

v 8—10 The priesthood of Joshua was typical of Christ, the great high-priest of our profession, and from him derived all its efficacy To him therefore Joshua and his fellows are directed to look *Hear now, O Joshua, thou and thy fellows that sit before thee, for they are men wondered at* for their singularity, or their strange deliverance from captivity, or *men of a sign*, types of the priesthood of Jesus *Note*, Christ's redeemed ones are men *wondered at* by others for their holy ways, which appear strange to a carnal world, and they are wonders to themselves, when they reflect on God's astonishing grace, and what he hath done for their souls

The promise given to them is the sending the expected Messiah, who is here described,

1 As *the Branch Behold I will bring forth my servant the Branch*, the Branch from the root of Jesse, who should be born in the fulness of time, weak to outward view as a tender rod, yet filling the world with fruit God's *servant*, who should fulfil all his pleasure, and perfect the work of salvation whereunto God had appointed him

2 As the *stone*, the precious corner-stone of the spiritual temple, and the rock of offence to all who stumble at the word It is *laid before Joshua*, that he may build thereon, as the only sure foundation of the sinner's hope *Upon one stone shall be seven eyes*, denoting either the perfection of his wisdom and the fulness of his grace to discover and supply all the wants of his people, or this may refer to the eyes of all believers, which are directed to him, that out of his fulness they may receive grace for grace, *behold, I will engrave the graving thereof, saith the Lord of hosts*, alluding probably to the engraving and polishing the corners of the temple, and may signify that Christ should be adorned with all gifts and graces for the discharge of his office as Mediator, or it may refer to the prints of the instruments in his flesh by which he suffered, or perhaps to his exaltation after his resurrection, when he was crowned with glory and honour

3 He shall save his people by one oblation of himself once offered *I will remove the iniquity of that land in one day*, even in that day when Jesus on the cross cried, It is finished, and gave up the ghost, compleating the work of atonement, and securing the eternal redemption of his people

4 In consequence of this, his people shall enjoy great peace of conscience, and rejoice together in the salvation of God *In that day* of gospel grace, *shall ye call every man his neighbour under his vine and under his fig tree* For, when iniquity is taken away, the soul sits happy under the shadow of Jesus, and invites all around to come and taste how good the Lord is, to join in his ordinances, and maintain sweet communion with him and with each other, a foretaste of that blessed state, *where the peace of God, which passeth all understanding, shall keep our hearts and minds*

CHAP IV

In this chapter we have, 1 The awakening of the prophet to observe the vision, ver 1 2 The vision itself, of a candlestick with seven lamps, which were supplied with oil, and kept burning immediately from two olive trees that grew by it, one on either side, ver 2, 3 3 The general encouragement hereby intended to be given to the builders of the temple to go on in that good work, assuring them that it should be brought to perfection at last, ver 4—10 4 The particular explication of the vision for the illustration of these assurances, ver 11—14

1 AND [a] the angel that talked with me, came again and waked me, as a man that is wakened out of his sleep, 2 And said unto me, What seest thou? And I said, I have looked, and behold, [b] a candlestick all *of* gold, [‖] with a bowl upon the top of it, [c] and his seven lamps thereon, and [‖] seven pipes to the seven lamps, which *were* upon the top thereof 3 And [d] two olive-trees by it, one upon the right *side* of the bowl, and the other upon the left *side* thereof 4 So I answered and spake to the angel that talked with me, saying, What *are* these, my lord? 5 Then the angel that talked with me answered, and said unto me, Knowest thou not what these be? And I said, No, my lord 6 Then he answered and spake unto me, saying, This *is* the word of the LORD unto Zerubbabel, saying, [e] Not by [§] might, nor by power, but by my spirit saith the LORD of hosts 7 Who *art* thou, [f] O great mountain? before Zerubbabel *thou shalt become* a plain, and he shall bring forth the head-stone thereof [g] with shoutings, *crying*, Grace, grace unto it 8 Moreover the word of the LORD came unto me, saying, 9 The hands of Zerubbabel [h] have laid the foundation of this house, his hands shall also [i] finish it, and [k] thou shalt know that [l] the LORD of hosts hath sent me unto you 10 For who hath despised the day of [m] small things? [‖] for they shall rejoice, and shall see the [¶] plummet in the hand of Zerubbabel *with* those seven, [n] they *are* the eyes of the LORD, which run to and fro through the whole earth,

[l] Ps lxxi 7 Isa viii 18 [‖] Heb Of wonder [m] Isa xlii 1 & lii 13 Ezek xxxiv [n] Isa iv 2 ... Jer xxiii 5 & xxxiii 15 Luke i 78 [o] Ps cxviii 22 Isa xxviii 16 [p] Chap iii 9 [q] Jer l 20 Mic vii 18 [r] Chap iv [s] Mic iv 4 [a] Chap ii 3 [b] Ex xxv 31 [‖] Heb With her bowl [c] Rev iv 5 [‖] Or seven several pipes to the lamps [d] Ver 11 Rev xi 4 [e] Hos i 7 [§] Or army [f] Jer li 25 Matt xxi 21 [g] Ezra iii 11 13 [h] Ezra iii 10 [i] Ezra vi 15 Heb xii 2 [k] Chap ii 9, 11 & vi 15 [l] Isa xlviii 16 Chap ii 8 [m] Hag ii 3 [‖] Or since the seven eyes of the LORD shall rejoice [¶] Heb Stone of tin [n] 2 Chron xvi 9 Prov xv 3 Chap iii 9

Before Christ 519

2. 1—10 Our prophet probably with the glorious visions he had seen, his spirits failed him, and he sunk down in sleep, *See Dan* viii 8 but he is awakened and strengthened by the Lord Jesus, to behold other visions and revelations of the Lord

1 On his awaking a question is put to him, *What seest thou?* And he looked, *and behold a candlestick of gold*, &c like, in some respects, to that in the temple of old, the figure of the church of Christ, *of gold*, denoting its excellence and purity, *the bowl upon the top of it* full of oil implies that fulness of grace in Jesus, out of whom all we do receive, *the seven lamps* may signify all believers in general, or the ministers of the gospel particularly, who are burning and shining lights, and being once kindled by the fire of divine grace, never more are extinguished, but are fed with constant supplies of oil from *the two olive trees*, Christ and the Comforter, through *the seven pipes*, the various means of prayer, the word, meditation, sacraments, &c which Christ hath instituted as channels of conveying to us the constant influences of his grace

2 The prophet humbly enquires into the meaning of what he saw *What are these, my Lord?* And the angel, to reprove his dullness, or quicken his attention, answers, *Knowest thou not what these be?* He replies, with a humble confession of his ignorance, *No, my Lord* very graciously therefore this angel condescends to explain the vision to him, *This is the word of the Lord to Zerubbabel*, an illustration of what God had spoken to him before, *saying, Not by might, nor by power, but by my spirit, saith the Lord of hosts* As the lamps were supplied with oil, without any human assistance from the olive-trees, that poured the oil into the bowl, which thence was communicated to them through the seven golden pipes, so should Zerubbabel be supplied with strength from on high, for the work in which he is engaged and thus is every faithful soul made more than conqueror, not through any human sufficiency, but by the power of divine grace alone

It is promised here concerning Zerubbabel,

1 That he shall overcome all difficulties in his way *Who art thou, O great mountain? Before Zerubbabel thou shalt become a plain* Whatever opposition he met from the Persian monarchy, or from Sanballat and the Samaritans, it should be easily surmounted *Note*, In the eye of sense mountains unpassable obstruct the way to glory, but faith looks up to Jesus, the great Zerubbabel, and as he hath put all enemies under his own feet, so will he put them under ours, and thus the mountain become a plain

2 He shall see the completion of the work he hath begun *He shall bring forth the head-stone thereof with shoutings, crying, Grace, grace unto it*, rejoicing and praising God for the ability he hath supplied for finishing his temple And herein, (1) He is a type of Christ, who on the cross exulting cried, It is finished, or it may refer to the day when he shall rejoice over all his redeemed in glory *with joy and singing*, Zeph iii 17 (2) Of every believer, who, when God shall have finished his work, and brought him happily to the end of his labours, shall stand forth before his throne, ascribing the whole of his salvation to sovereign, rich, and boundless grace, and join his voice with ten thousand times ten thousand others, thus sing, *Grace, grace unto it*

3 Zerubbabel shall hereby be fully convinced, with all the Jews, of the divine mission of the prophet, ver 9 or rather this may be referred to Christ, who will make his people know by blessed experience, when he hath completed the work of grace in their hearts, that he is indeed the Saviour of the world, and that *him hath God the Father sent*

4 The enemies of Judah shall be confounded, and those, among themselves, who at first were disheartened, shall rejoice, when they see the work brought to so happy an issue *For who hath despised the day of small things?* Sanballat, and many even of the Jews, despised the mean beginnings of the temple, but they shall quickly change their mind *for they*, the Jews, who at first despaired of being able to finish the work, *shall rejoice, and shall see the plummet in the hand of Zerubbabel*, the building rising fast and beautiful under his direction, *with those seven, they are the eyes of the Lord, which run to and fro through the whole earth*, supported by the divine providence, and instructed by divine wisdom, he shall be enabled to complete the glorious work *Note*, (1) The work of God in the soul begins with a *day of small things*, the light but glimmering, the graces weak, yet these are not to be *despised*, for in the end they shall have great increase (2) Instead of being discouraged, because our labours have but little success, we must be thankful for that little, and trust in him who giveth the increase (3) It is a great joy to all faithful people to see ministers and magistrates exerting themselves in the cause of God and truth (4) They who are under the guidance of *these seven eyes* of God's providence and grace need never despair, whatever difficulties are in their way

11 ¶ Then answered I, and said unto him, What
are these * two olive trees, upon the right *side* of the can-
dlestick, and upon the left *side* thereof? 12 And I
answered again, and said unto him, What *be these* two
olive branches which ‡ through the two golden pipes
‡ empty the golden *oil* out of themselves? 13 And
he answered me, and said, Knowest thou not what these
be? And I said, No, my lord 14 Then said he,
[b] These *are* the two § anointed ones, that stand by [q] the
LORD of the whole earth

* Ver 3
‡ Heb By the hand of
‡ Or empty out of themselves gold into the gold
[b] Rev xi 4
§ Sons of oil
[q] Josh iii 11, Chap vi 5

℣ 11—14 Since he had found such favour in the eyes of the Lord, the prophet continues his enquiries, not to gratify his curiosity, but to furnish himself with matter for the good of his people

1 He begs information concerning the two olive-trees, and what the two branches signify that emptied their oil into the golden bowl through the two golden pipes, and, being interrogated as before, *Knowest thou not what these be?* he again acknowledges his ignorance

2 He is told what the olive-trees and branches signify *These are the two anointed ones*, or *the sons of oil*, which some interpret of the gifts and graces of the Spirit, some of Christ and the Holy Ghost, others of Christ in his two natures, or in his offices of priest and king, from whom the golden oil of grace is poured forth, *that stand before the Lord of the whole earth*, God the Father, who governs the affairs of the world and the church in and by his Son, to whom all power is committed, and by the Holy Ghost, which proceeds from them both, and is the quickening Spirit in the hearts of all the faithful.

CHAP V

Let the sinners in Zion be afraid though God speaks peace to his people, his wrath is revealed from heaven against the ungodly, for, 1 God will reckon severely with those particular persons among them that continued wicked and profane, they shall lie under the curse, which the prophet sees in a flying roll, ver 1—4 2 *If the body of the nation hereafter degenerate, it shall be carried off, and hurried away with a swift destruction, under the pressing weight of divine wrath, represented by a* talent of lead *upon the* mouth of an ephah, *carried upon the wing to the land of Shinar*, ver 5—11

1 THEN I turned, and lift up mine eyes and
looked, and behold, a flying roll 2 And he
said unto me, What seest thou? And I answered, I see
a flying roll, the length thereof *is* twenty cubits, and the
breadth thereof ten cubits 3 Then said he unto me,
This *is* the curse that goeth over the face of the whole
earth for † every one [a] that stealeth shall be cut off *as*
on this side, according to it and [b] every one that swear-
eth shall be cut off *as* on that side, according to it 4
I will bring it forth, saith the LORD of hosts, and it
shall enter into the house of the thief, and into the house
of [c] him that sweareth falsly by my name and it shall
remain in the midst of his house, and [d] shall consume it,
with the timber thereof, and the stones thereof

† Or every one of this people that stealeth holdeth himself guiltless, as it doth
[a] Exod xx 15
[b] Ex xx 7
Ver 4
[c] Chap viii 17
[d] Lev xiv 45

℣ 1—4 A new vision here appears, big with terrible judgment against the wicked

1 The prophet, looking upwards, beheld *a flying roll*, and, being asked what he saw, describes a strange sight, a roll of vast length appeared expanded in the air, and carried by the wind

2 This is explained to him by the angel, as containing *the curse*, the long catalogue of lamentation, mourning, and woe, which are the wages of sin, *that goeth forth over the whole earth*, either the world in general, where all have sinned and come short of the glory of God, or over the whole land of Israel, which seems principally intended *Note*, Sinners, whose eyes are blinded by the god of this world, see no danger, and walk on fearless and secure, but the enlightened mind, that looks into God's word, beholds with trembling the wrath which hangs over their devoted heads, and wonders at their insensibility

3 The crimes particularly here charged upon them are *theft* and *perjury* The curse lies against *every one that stealeth*, whether robbing God, *Mal* iii 8 or man, their parents or others, whether in the lesser acts of fraud, imposition, deceit, and knavery, or the more atrocious deed of open violence, *and every one that sweareth*, profanely, rashly, passionately, thoughtlessly, falsely, *shall be cut off*, God will not hold them guiltless, wrath is upon them

4 God will himself certainly execute the curse denounced on their crimes *I will bring it forth, saith the Lord of hosts* It shall not only cut off the sinners themselves, and destroy both soul and body in hell, but it shall entail ruin upon their whole house and family and like the plague of leprosy prove incurable, till the whole be utterly demolished and laid in ruins

5 ¶ Then the angel [e] that talked with me, went
forth, and said unto me, Lift up now thine eyes, and
see what *is* this that goeth forth 6 And I said, What
is it? And he said, This *is* [f] an ephah that goeth forth

[e] Chap ii 3 &c
[f] Mat xiii 33

He

Before Christ 519

He said moreover, This is their † resemblance through
all the earth 7 And behold there was lift up a talent
of lead and this is [k] a woman that sitteth in the midst
of the ephah 8 And he said, This is [h] wickedness,
and he cast it into the midst of the ephah, and he cast
the weight of lead upon the mouth thereof 9 Then
lift I up mine eyes, and looked, and behold, there came
out two women, and the wind was in their wings, (for
[i] they had wings like the wings of a stork) and they lift
up the ephah between the earth and the heaven 10
Then said I to the angel that talked with me, Whither
do these bear the ephah? 11 And he said unto me,
To [k] build it an house in [l] the land of ‡ Shinar, and it
shall be established, and set there upon her own base

† Or eye. f Rev. xvii. g 2 Thess. ii. i 1 Pet. i. k Jer. xxix. 5. l Gen. x. 10. ‡ i.e. Snakar, Babylon.

v. 5—11 Another vision succeeds, dark and hard to be understood The prophet is commanded to look up, and say what he saw, but, through the distance, or dimness of his sight, he does not distinctly perceive the object, and asks *what it is*, and is answered

1 It *is an ephah*, a measure containing about seven gallons, and seems to signify the measure of the iniquity of the Jewish people And *he said moreover, This is their resemblance in all the earth*, or *their eye*, throughout Judea, or through all the countries where they were dispersed their wickedness abounded, and especially in the times of Christ the measure of their sins was filled fast

2 *A woman* appears, *sitting in the midst of the ephah*, the representative of the sinners among them, and a lively figure of her who afterwards should arise, *the mother of harlots* And he said, *This is wickedness*, intimating the exceeding sinfulness of their iniquity, who, being professors of godliness, had so grievously degenerated

3 A talent of lead is cast as a cover on the mouth of the ephah, to shew how impossible it would be to escape from the wrath they had provoked, and how insupportable the load would be on the impenitent

4 Two women came forth, with wings like a stork, and, lifting up the ephah, with the wind in their wings swiftly conveyed it to the land of Shinar, or Babylon, where they built it an house, and set it upon its base And these seem to represent the Roman armies, swiftly marching to the destruction of Jerusalem, and carrying the Jewish nation into a more dreadful captivity, and of much longer continuance, than they had endured in Babylon and to this day we see them sunk under this load Some refer this to Antichrist, and his destruction and it may well be applied to the eternal perdition of all ungodly men, who, when the measure of their iniquity is full, will be caught away from the earth, under their load of guilt, and cast down into Shinar, into the everlasting burnings, where is weeping and wailing and gnashing of teeth

CHAP VI

Here is, 1 God, as king of nations, ruling the world by the ministry of angels, in the vision of the four chariots, ver 1—8 2 God, as king of saints, ruling the church by the mediation of Christ, in the figure of Joshua the high-priest crowned, the ceremony performed, and then explained concerning Christ, ver 9—15

1 AND I turned, and lift up mine eyes, and looked, and behold, there came four [a] chariots out
from between two mountains, and the mountains *were*
mountains of [b] brass 2 In the first chariot *were* [c] red
horses, and in the second chariot [d] black horses 3 And
in the third chariot [e] white horses, and in the fourth
chariot grisled and ‖ bay horses 4 Then I answered,
and [f] said unto the angel that talked with me, What
are these, my lord? 5 And the angel answered, and
said unto me, These *are* the four [g] ‡ spirits of the heavens, which go forth from [h] standing before the LORD
of all the earth 6 The black horses, which *are* therein,
go forth into the north country, and the white go forth
after them, and the grisled go forth toward the south-country
7 And the bay went forth, and sought to go,
that they might walk to and fro through the earth and
he said, Get ye hence, [i] walk to and fro through the
earth So they walked to and fro through the earth
8 Then cried he upon me, and spake unto me, saying,
Behold, these that go toward the north-country have
[k] quieted my spirit in the north-country

a Rev. vi. 11. ... b Prov. xix. ... c Chap. i. 8. Rev. vi. 4. d Rev. vi. 5. e Rev. vi. 2. ‖ Or strong. ... f Chap. v. ... g 1 Pet. i. 12. ‡ Or winds. ... h 1 Kings xxii. 19. ... Luke i. 19. i Chap. i. ... k 1 Sam. xii. 14.

v. 1—8 The vision of this chapter is of very difficult interpretation The chariots coming from between the brazen mountains are supposed to represent either,

1 The apostles and ministers of the gospel, going forth into all lands according to God's eternal counsels, signified by the mountains of brass The different colours of the horses may denote their various messages of wrath or mercy, their ministry is accompanied with the powerful operations of the Spirit, compared to the wind, which acts invisibly, yet irresistibly, and they are sent from Christ, the Lord of the whole earth, to the different parts of the world, and by their labours sinners are brought back to God's favour, and his wrath is turned away, *his spirit quieted* towards them Or,

2 These signify the angelic hosts, *the spirits of the heavens*, coming forth from the mount of God into the earth, as executioners of God's decrees, and instruments of wrath or mercy according as God is pleased to send them, and when they have gone to and fro, and accomplished their ministry, God is well pleased, and his Spirit quieted and refreshed Or,

3 These are the four monarchies, called *the winds of the heavens*, Dan vii 2 The Babylonian is represented by the red horses, the Persian by the black, the Grecian by the white, and the Roman by the grisled and bay horses, who walked to and fro in the earth, or through the land of Judea, and subdued it And a peculiar notice is taken of those who went forth into the north-country, *they have quieted my spirit*, having avenged on the Babylonians the violence they had used towards God's captive Israel Or,

4 They refer to the dispensations of Divine Providence in general, which proceed according to God's eternal counsels, and are fixed as brazen mountains, against which it is vain to struggle His chariots run at his will, chariots of love to his friends, to whom all things work together for good, chariots of war to his enemies, whom he treads under his horses feet from him the ministers of Providence take their directions, and each in his sphere accomplishes the work which is given him to do, and God is well pleased in beholding the counsels of his own will fulfilled by them

9 ¶ And the word of the LORD came unto me,
saying, 10 Take of *them* of the captivity, *even* of Heldai, of Tobijah, and of Jedaiah, which are come from
Babylon, and come thou the same day, and go into the
house of Josiah the son of Zephaniah, 11 Then take
silver and gold, and make [l] crowns, and set *them* upon
the head of Joshua, the son of Josedech the high-priest,
12 And speak unto him, saying, Thus speaketh the
LORD of hosts, saying, Behold, [m] the man whose name
is [n] the BRANCH, and he shall † grow up out of his
place, and [o] he shall build the temple of the LORD
13 Even he shall build the temple of the LORD, and
[p] he shall bear the glory, and shall sit and rule upon his
throne, and [q] he shall be a priest upon his throne, and
the counsel of peace shall be between them both 14
And the crowns shall be to [r] Helem, and to Tobijah,
and to Jedaiah, and to Hen the son of Zephaniah,
[s] for a memorial in the temple of the LORD 15 And
[t] they *that are* far off shall come and build in the temple
of the LORD, and [u] ye shall know that the LORD
of hosts hath sent me unto you And *this* shall come to
pass, if ye will diligently obey the voice of the LORD
your God

l Cant. iii. 11. Chap. iii. 5. Rev. xix. 12. m John i. 45. n Chap. iii. 8. † Or branch up from under him. o Mat. xvi. 18. p Isa. xxii. 24. q Psal. cx. 4. Heb. iii. 1. r Ver. 10. s 1 Sam. ii. 30. Mark xiv. 9. t Isa. lx. 10. u Chap. ii. 9. & iv. 9.

v. 9—15 Before God taught the people by vision, here by type and figure

1 Joshua the high-priest is crowned by Zechariah with crowns of gold and silver, made of the offerings which Heldai, Tobijah, and Jedaiah brought from Babylon, and in their presence They who came not yet up to the temple sent their presents thither, and with their purse endeavoured to compensate for their absence The crowns on Joshua were designed to intimate the union of the kingly and sacerdotal office in him whom he prefigured, and whose name he bore

2 A prophecy, founded on this figure, is delivered to Joshua *Thus speaketh the Lord of hosts, saying, Behold the man whose name is the Branch*, the divine Messiah, *and he shall grow up out of his place*, from Bethlehem-Ephratah, the city appointed for the place of his birth, *and he shall build the temple of the Lord*, the gospel-church, of which he is the great architect, and by his power alone it is raised up and established, *even he shall build the temple of the Lord*, to God hath he decreed, *and he shall bear the glory*, to him the entire glory of it shall be ascribed, and every member of that church will with delight cast down his golden crown at his feet, and own that he, who alone hath won it, deserves to wear it for ever, *and he shall sit and rule upon his throne, and he shall be a priest upon his throne*, having all power delivered to him, and able to save to the uttermost in virtue of the oblation once offered as a priest, God hath highly exalted him, and as he ever lives to plead the redemption he hath obtained for his people, so, in their glorious King, he reigns to apply it effectually to them *and the counsel of peace shall be between them both*, either between Jehovah and the man, the Branch, or be-

Before Chriſt 519

tween the kingly and ſacerdotal offices of Chriſt, or *the counſel of peace* is the goſpel, preached to both Jew and Gentile, and uniting them together in love *And the crowns ſhall be to Helem, and to Tobijah, and to Hen the ſon of Zephaniah, for a memorial in the temple of the Lord*, either for a conſtant teſtimony of the generous liberality of theſe good men, or to put the people in mind of him who ſhould come, and to whom the crowns particularly referred *And they that are afar off ſhall come*, either the Jews yet in Babylon, or the Gentiles, *Eph* ii 12, 13 who ſhould be called by grace into the participation of all the privileges of the goſpel, *and build in the temple of the Lord*, as workers together helping forward the work of God, and by their labours bringing ſouls to Jeſus Chriſt, as lively ſtones to be built up on him, the One great and glorious foundation, *and ye ſhall know that the Lord of hoſts hath ſent me unto you*, the accompliſhment of the prophecy would be a proof of his divine miſſion *And this ſhall come to paſs, if ye will diligently obey the voice of the Lord your God*, not that their obedience was the condition on which the fulfilment of theſe promiſes depended, but as many as proved faithful and obedient, would be convinced of the prophet's divine authority, or if they uſed their diligence in building the temple, God would take care they ſhould not want every needful aſſiſtance *Note*, When we are enabled to improve the talent we are entruſted with, then God giveth more grace

CHAP VII

In this chapter we have, 1 A caſe of conſcience propoſed to the prophet by the children of the captivity concerning faſting, ver 1—3 2 The anſwer to his queſtion, which is given in this and the next chapter In this chapter, (1) The prophet ſharply reproves them for the miſmanagement of their faſts, ver 4—7 (2) He exhorts them to reform their lives which would be the beſt way of faſting, and to take heed of thoſe ſins which brought thoſe judgments upon them, which they kept theſe faſts in memory of, ver 8—14

518 1 AND it came to paſs in the fourth year of king
Darius, *that* the word of the LORD came unto
Zechariah in the fourth *day* of the ninth month, *even* in
Chiſleu, 2 When [a] they had ſent unto the houſe of
God, Sherezer, and Regem melech, and their men to
† pray before the LORD, 3 *And* to ſpeak unto [b] the
prieſts which *were* in the houſe of the LORD of hoſts,
and to the prophets, ſaying, Should I weep in [c] the fifth
month, [d] ſeparating myſelf, as I have done theſe ſo many
years? 4 ¶ Then came the word of the LORD of
hoſts unto me, ſaying, 5 Speak unto all the people of
the land, and to the prieſts, ſaying, When ye [e] faſted
and mourned in the fifth and [f] ſeventh *month*, [g] even
thoſe ſeventy years, did ye at all faſt [h] unto me, *even*
to me? 6 And when ye did eat, and when ye did
drink, [i] did not ye eat *for yourſelves*, and drink *for yourſelves*?
7 ‖ *Should ye* not *hear* the words which the
LORD hath cried by the former prophets, when Jeruſalem
was inhabited, and in proſperity, and the cities
thereof round about her, when *men* inhabited the ſouth
and the plain?

[a] Mal ii 7
† Heb Intreat the face of the Lord
[b] Deut xxxiii 10
[c] Jer lii 12 Chap viii 19
[d] 1 Cor vii 5
[e] Iſa lviii 5
[f] 2 Kings xxv 25 Chap viii 19
[g] Chap i 12
[h] Rom xiv 6
[i] 1 Cor x 31
‖ Or, are not theſe the words

v 1—7 Though we have nothing here recorded of the prophet for two years, we are aſſured he was well employed, *Ezra* vi 14 but he had no commiſſion to publiſh his diſcourſes, till on the preſent occaſion We have,

1 The queſtion propoſed concerning faſting *Sherezer and Regem-melech*, perſons of ſome note, *with their men*, are commiſſioned in the name of the people to *go up to the houſe of God*, either from Babylon, or from thoſe who were ſituated in the country of Judea, at a diſtance from Jeruſalem, to whom, in *v* 5 the anſwer ſeems to be directed Their buſineſs at the temple was *to pray before the Lord*, as the greateſt of men ſhould count it their honour to do, *and to ſpeak to the prieſts which were in the houſe of the Lord of hoſts*, whoſe office and buſineſs it is to explain the will of God, and the people, even the chief of them, ſhould with reverence and attention hear the law at their mouth, for they who are ſincere in their prayers, will be ſerious in their enquiries to know God's mind, that they may do it, *and to the prophets*, whom God had then in mercy raiſed up to them, *ſaying, ſhould I weep in the fifth month*, on the day when the temple was burnt by the Chaldeans, *ſeparating myſelf* for faſting and prayer, *as I have done theſe ſo many years*? during their captivity, and ſince their return, which now they doubted whether it were proper for them to continue, their temple being in great forwardneſs, and a proſpect of its happy re-eſtabliſhment before them *Note*, (1) In caſes of conſcience God's miniſter ſhould be conſulted (2) When God afflicts, he calls to weeping and faſting to be ſtupid, or unconcerned, would be to deſpiſe the chaſtening of the Almighty, and provoke a heavier ſcourge

2 Zechariah hath an anſwer given him for them, and it is a ſharp reproof for their hypocriſy and diſobedience They had faſted indeed, *in the fifth and ſeventh month*, in memory of the burning the temple, and the murder of Gedaliah, but their faſts were mere ceremonious duties, without any real humiliation of ſoul *did ye at all faſt unto me, even to me?* Their eye was not ſingle, they did not propoſe God's glory as their end, and therefore their ſervices could not be acceptable, however long they had continued them, in mentioning which, they ſeem tacitly to upbraid God with not taking notice of them, and to value themſelves on their performances but their faſts were no more pleaſing than their common meals, or their feſtivals, in which *they eat and drink for themſelves*, not giving him thanks, or doing him honour, or deſigning, in the uſe of his creatures, to glorify him, but to indulge themſelves *Should ye not hear the words which the Lord hath cried by the former prophets, when Jeruſalem was inhabited, and in proſperity, and the cities thereof round about her, when men inhabited the ſouth and the plain?* This was what they ſhould have done, which would have prevented the deſolations, and in their faſts theſe ſcriptures ſhould have been attended to, both as a matter of humiliation, and as a warning againſt the iniquities which had provoked God to deſtroy the land But this they had neglected, and it is then to no purpoſe to faſt, whilſt our hearts continue unhumbled for the ſins which are the cauſe of our calamities

Before Chriſt 518

8 ¶ And the word of the LORD came unto Zechariah,
ſaying, 9 Thus ſpeaketh the LORD of hoſts,
ſaying, [k] Execute true judgment, and ſhew mercy and
compaſſion every man to his brother 10 And [l] oppreſs
not the widow, nor the fatherleſs, the ſtranger,
nor the poor, and [m] let none of you imagine evil againſt
his brother in your heart 11 But they refuſed to
hearken, [n] and † pulled away the ſhoulder, and [o] ſtopped
their ears, that they ſhould not hear 12 Yea,
[p] they made their hearts *as* an adamant-ſtone, leſt they
ſhould hear the law, and the words which the LORD
of hoſts hath ſent in his ſpirit by the former prophets
therefore [q] came a great wrath from the LORD of hoſts
13 Therefore it is come to paſs *that*, as he cried, and
they would not hear, [r] ſo they cried, and I would not
hear, ſaith the LORD of hoſts 14 But I ſcattered
them with a whirlwind among all the nations whom they
knew not thus the land was deſolate after them, that
no man paſſed through nor returned for they laid [s] the
‡ pleaſant land deſolate

[k] Iſa lviii 6 Mic vi 8 Chap viii 16 Matt xxiii 23
[l] Exod xxii 21 Deut xxiv 17 Iſa i 23 Jer v 28
[m] Chap viii 17
[n] Neh ix 29 Heb Chap vi 16
† Heb they gave a backſliding ſhoulder
[o] Acts vii 57
[p] Jer xvii 1 Ezek xi 19
[q] Dan ix 11, 12
[r] Prov i 24—28 Iſa i 15 Jer xi 11 & xiv 12 Mic iii 4
[s] Dan viii 9
‡ Heb land of deſire

v 8—14 The examples they had ſeen, and the words of the preceding prophets, ſhould have been warnings to them

1 The prophet puts them in mind what had been the ſubject of the former prophets diſcourſes *Thus ſpeaketh the Lord of hoſts, ſaying, execute true judgment*, impartially adminiſtring juſtice without reſpect of perſons, *and ſhew mercy and compaſſion every man to his brother*, under all his wants of body or ſoul, aſſiſting him with our advice, our purſe, our perſon, and our prayers, forgiving every provocation, and bearing his infirmities *And oppreſs not the widow, nor the fatherleſs, the ſtranger, nor the poor*, whoſe helpleſs ſtate ſhould plead for them, *and let none of you imagine evil againſt his brother in your heart*, neither harbour a deſign of miſchief, nor entertain an evil ſurmiſe concerning them

2 He reminds them of the diſobedience of their fathers *They refuſed to hearken, and pulled away the ſhoulder*, diſobedient and refractory againſt all the warnings given them, *and ſtopped their ears, that they ſhould not hear*, nor deigning ſo much as to hearken to God's meſſages *Yea, they made their hearts as an adamant ſtone*, impenetrable to conviction, neither regarding the law of Moſes, nor the words of his divinely commiſſioned meſſengers the prophets

3 For theſe things *came a great wrath* upon them, *from the Lord of hoſts*, and ſince they would not hear his calls, God refuſed to hear their cries in the day of their calamity, ſcattered them among the nations, laid their pleaſant land deſolate, a righteous judgment upon them for their obſtinacy, impenitence, and hardneſs of heart *Note*, (1) They who in proſperity ſet at nought God's threatenings, will cry too late for mercy, when it is the time of judgment (2) Sinners have only themſelves to blame for their eternal ruin

CHAP VIII

The work of miniſters is rightly to divide the word of truth, and to give every one their portion Whilſt the hypocrites are rebuked, the faithful muſt be encouraged Here are two meſſages 1 the firſt ver 1 God promiſeth that Jeruſalem ſhall be reſtored, reformed, repleniſhed, ver 2—8 That the country ſhall be rich, their national affairs ſucceſsful, their reputation retrieved, and their ſtate

Before Christ 518.

in all respects the reverse of what it had been, ver. 9—15. And then exhorts them to reform what was amiss among them, that they might be ready for these favours designed for them, ver. 16, 17. In the latter of these messages, ver. 18. he promiseth that their fasts should be superseded by the return of mercy, ver. 19. And that thereupon they should be replenished, enriched, and strengthened by the accession of foreigners to them, ver. 20—23.

1 AGAIN the word of the LORD of hosts came
to me, saying, 2 Thus saith the LORD of
hosts, [a] I was jealous for Zion with great jealousy, and
I was jealous for her [b] with great fury. 3 Thus saith
the LORD, I am returned unto Zion, and [c] will dwell
in the midst of Jerusalem, and Jerusalem [d] shall be called
a city of truth, and the mountain of the LORD of
hosts, the holy mountain. 4 Thus saith the LORD
of hosts, [e] There shall yet old men and old women dwell
in the streets of Jerusalem, and every man with his staff
in his hand † for very age. 5 And the streets of the
city shall be full of boys and girls playing in the streets
thereof. 6 Thus saith the LORD of hosts, If it be ‡
marvellous in the eyes of the remnant of this people in
these days, [f] should it also be marvellous in mine eyes?
saith the LORD of hosts. 7 Thus saith the LORD of
hosts, Behold, [g] I will save my people from the east coun-
try, and from ‖ the west country; 8. And [h] I will bring
them, and they shall dwell in the midst of Jerusalem,
and they shall be my people, and [i] I will be their God in
truth and in righteousness.

v. 1—8. God keepeth not his anger for ever, he will return and be gracious.

1. He will be *jealous for Zion with great jealousy*, concerned to vindicate her honour, and avenge her wrongs, *and* therefore *with great fury* shall his vengeance light on her enemies.

2. He will *return to Zion*: he speaks of it as already done, since his promise is sure, *and dwell in the midst of Jerusalem*, manifesting his gracious presence to them at the temple, and meeting them in his ordinances; and this was most eminently fulfilled, when *the word was made flesh, and dwelt among them*.

3. He will work a glorious change on the place and people. *Jerusalem shall be a city of truth*, eminent for integrity and honesty; *the mountain of the Lord of hosts*, where he condescends to take up his abode, *the holy mountain*, cleared from all idolatry, and pure before God. The church of Christ *is the pillar and ground of truth*; in it all truth of doctrine and uprightness of conversation are found; it is firm as the everlasting mountains, and cannot be shaken; and on the heart of every living member thereof there is written, *Holiness to the Lord*.

4. He will give them long life, peace, and prosperity. No diseases shall sweep them off, nor war spread its ravages among them; but in the streets shall vigorous old age appear, and tho' time hath impaired much of nature's strength, the staff shall still support the hoary head; whilst the rising generation, numerous and healthful, shall in youthful exercises and innocent sport, mix in the streets, secure from fear of evil. In the church are found fathers in Christ, young men and children, a multitude of converts, each adorning their place and station, and ripening for glory.

5. He will save the dispersed of Israel from Babylon and Egypt, and bring them back to their own land; and, better than all their other mercies, he will take them again into the covenant, and engage their hearts unto himself. *They shall be my people*, engaged, inclined, and enabled to be so, by his preventing and effectual grace; *and I will be their God in truth and in righteousness*, faithful to all his promises. And this seems to have a regard to all the Israel of God, who shall be called and converted unto him, be received into the arms of his love, by his grace effectually engaged in his service, and through the everlasting righteousness of Jesus, and according to the unchangeable promises of the everlasting covenant, God will be their God, to bless, preserve, and keep them, their portion and exceeding great reward in time and in eternity.

6. However incredible this may seem, and marvellous, with God all things are possible; and therefore strange as it is, it will be found true, for not one jot or tittle shall fail of all his promises. If we can believe, we shall see the salvation of God.

9 ¶ Thus saith the LORD of hosts, [k] Let your
hands be strong, ye that hear in these days these words
by the mouth of [l] the prophets, which *were* in the day
that the foundation of the house of the LORD of hosts
was laid, that the temple might be built. 10 For be-
fore these days † there was no [m] hire for man, nor any
hire for beast; neither *was* [n] *there any* peace to him that
went out, or came in, because of the affliction: for I set
all men, every one against his neighbour. 11 But now
I *will* not *be* unto the residue of this people, as in the
former days, saith the LORD of hosts. 12 For [o] the
seed *shall be* prosperous; the vine shall give her fruit, and
the ground shall give her increase, and the heavens shall
give their dew; and I will cause the remnant of this peo-
ple to possess [p] all these *things*. 13 And it shall come
to pass, *that* as ye were [q] a curse among the heathen, O
house of Judah, and house of Israel; so will I save you,
and ye shall be [r] a blessing: fear not, *but* let your hands
be strong. 14 For thus saith the LORD of hosts, As
I thought to punish you, [s] when your fathers provoked
me to wrath, saith the LORD of hosts, and I repented
not: 15 So again have I thought in these days to do
well unto Jerusalem, and to the house of Judah: fear ye
not. 16 ¶ [t] These *are* the things that ye shall do; [u]
Speak ye every man the truth to his neighbour; [x] † exe-
cute the judgment of truth and peace in your gates: 17
And [y] let none of you imagine evil in your hearts a-
gainst his neighbour; [z] and love no false oath: for all
these *are things* that I hate, saith the LORD.

v. 9—17. We have here,

1. The great encouragements given to the people who, attentive to the voice of God's prophets, laboured zealously to further the work of the temple; for they who are faithful to him, may expect comfort from him. They had laboured under many difficulties during the time when God's house was neglected; there was *no hire for man or beasts*, trade was dead, and the produce of the earth so little, that few hands were needed to reap and gather it. Their enemies on every side made incroads upon them, and robbers in their own country made travelling dangerous, and no man's property was secure; and an evil spirit of dissension and strife was sown among themselves, so that every one seemed *set against his neighbour*; but now God will change his manner of acting towards them. Their ground shall produce abundantly, and enriched with all manner of store, they shall possess their good things undisturbed, *v.* 12. Instead of that reproach they had suffered among the heathen, now God will save them in so distinguished a manner, that all who beheld them would acknowledge them to be the blessed of the Lord, and their example and labours would make them a blessing to all around them. As surely as he had threatened to punish their fathers, and had done it, as they had seen, so surely now will he *do well* unto them, for his gifts and calling are without repentance. They may therefore confidently hope to see the fulfilment of all his promises, and should neither fear the multitude of their enemies, nor the difficulties in their way, but *be strong* in the assurance of divine support; and this is the powerful argument to engage all believers to work out their own salvation, because it is God who worketh in them to will and to do of his good pleasure.

2. Their duty is set before them, the same which the prophets had inculcated upon their disobedient fathers of old. *Speak ye every man the truth to his neighbour*, in simplicity, putting away falshood, deceit, and all prevarication; *execute the judgment of truth and peace in your gates*: let justice be impartially administered, and seek to heal all differences. *And let none of you imagine evil in your hearts against his neighbour*, nor entertain an ill wish, nor harbour an ill surmise against any of them; *and love no false oath*, but abhor and discountenance every thing which may lead thereunto: *for all these are things that I hate, saith the Lord*, and therefore we should hate them also.

18. ¶ And the word of the LORD of hosts came
unto me, saying, 19 Thus saith the LORD of hosts,
The fast of [a] the fourth *month*, and the fast of [b] the fifth,
and the fast of [c] the seventh, and the fast of [d] the tenth,
shall be to the house of Judah [e] joy and gladness, and
cheerful ‖ feasts; [f] therefore love the truth and peace.
20 Thus saith the LORD of hosts, *It shall* yet *come to
pass*, that there shall come people, and the inhabitants
of many cities: 21 And the inhabitants of one *city* shall
go to another, saying, [g] Let us go ‖ speedily to ‖ pray
before the LORD, and to seek the LORD of hosts: I
will go also. 22 Yea, [h] many people and strong nations
shall come to seek the LORD of hosts in Jerusalem, and
to pray before the LORD. 23 Thus saith the LORD
of hosts, In those days *it shall come to pass*, that ten men
shall take hold out of all languages of the nations, even
shall take hold of the skirt of him that is a Jew, saying,
We will go with you: for we have heard [i] *that* God *is*
with you.

v. 18—23. They had put a question to their prophet, *chap.* vii. 3. concerning their fasts, and it is here fully answered.

1. A happy period is put to their fasts, and they shall be turned into days of festivity. They observed the fast of the

Before Christ 518

fourth month, in memory of the taking Jerusalem, of the fifth, because then the temple was burnt, of the seventh, on account of Gedaliah's murder, of the tenth, because then Nebuchadnezzar began the siege but now, when God will restore Jerusalem, and rear up again his temple, the memory of these melancholy scenes of desolation shall be lost in the joy and gladness arising from their present happy estate *Therefore love truth and peace*, let this be the grateful return you make for the divine mercies bestowed upon you

2 God promises to enlarge them abundantly with multitudes of proselytes, or this hath rather a more immediate reference to the times of the gospel, when the Gentiles should come into the church of Christ *The inhabitants of many cities*, among whom the apostles and others preached, shall become obedient to the faith, and sollicitous for the salvation of others, each shall say to his neighbour, Come, and *let us go speedily to pray before the Lord*, no longer lying down in their former state of blindness and guilt, but, without delay, seeking *the Lord of hosts* whilst yet he may be found, and in fervent and importunate prayer, the language of every truly converted soul, eager to obtain mercy and acceptance before him *I will go also*, shall one say to another, glad to join the happy company, and hasting to the courts of Zion Multitudes out of all nations shall assemble for this blessed purpose, and then the name of the Jew shall be no longer hated or despised, but *ten men out of all languages*, many converted by the preaching of the Apostles, and other ministers of Christ, *shall take hold of the skirt of him that is a Jew*, the first preachers of the gospel being chiefly of that nation, *saying, we will go with you, for we have heard that God is with you*, the divine Redeemer being of the stock of Israel after the flesh, to whom it was promised of old the gathering of the people should be, and to whom the ministers of truth desire to lead the souls who are under their care *Note*, (1) Every truly converted soul will immediately be found upon his knees, seeking the Lord (2) They who have themselves tasted that the Lord is gracious, cannot but be sollicitous that other should come and partake of their mercies (3) A gracious purpose should be executed *speedily*, delays are dangerous

CHAP IX

Here is, 1 A prophecy against the Jews unrighteous neighbours, the Syrians, Tyrians, Philistines, and others, ver 1—6 with an intimation of mercy to some of them in their conversion, ver 7 a promise of mercy to God's people in their protection, ver 8 2 A prophecy of their righteous king, the Messiah, and his coming, with a description of him, ver 9 and of his kingdom, the nature and extent of it, ver 10 3 An account of the great redemption he hath obtained for his people, and the blessings thence arising, for which they must be glad, ver 11—17

587
1 THE burden of the word of the LORD in the
a Amos i 3 land of Hadrach, and [a] Damascus *shall be* the
rest thereof when the eyes of man, as of all the tribes
b 2 Chron xx 12 of Israel [b] *shall be* toward the LORD 2 And Hamath
c Obad 20 also shall border thereby, Tyrus and [c] Zidon, though
d Ezek xxviii 3, &c it be very [d] wise 3 And Tyrus did build herself a
e Job xxvii 16 strong hold, and [e] heaped up silver as the dust, and fine
f Isa xxiii 1 gold as the mire of the streets 4 Behold, [f] the LORD
will cast her out, and he will smite her power in the sea,
g Jer xlvii 5, Zeph ii 4 and she shall be devoured with fire 5 [g] Ashkelon shall
see *it*, and fear, Gaza also *shall see it*, and be very sorrowful,
and Ekron for her expectation shall be ashamed,
and the king shall perish from Gaza, and Ashkelon
h Amos i 8 shall not be inhabited 6 And a bastard shall dwell [h]
in Ashdod, and I will cut off the pride of the Philistines
‡ Heb Bloods 7 And I will take away his ‡ blood out of his
mouth, and his abominations from between his teeth,
but he that remaineth, even he *shall be* for our God,
i Gal iii 28 and he shall be as a governor in Judah, and [i] Ekron as
k Ps xxxiv 7, Chap ii 5 a Jebusite 8 And [k] I will encamp about mine house
because of the army, because of him that passeth by, and
l Isa lx 18, Ezek xxviii 24 because of him that returneth, and [l] no oppressor shall
m 2 Chron xvi 9, Ps xxxiv 15 pass through them any more for now [m] have I seen with
mine eyes

v 1—8 When God comes with blessing to his people, he will execute vengeance on their enemies

1 The neighbouring nations, who had been such oppressors of Israel, shall be punished

(1) Syria and Damascus come first under judgment, on them shall *rest* the wrath of God, which *burdens* intolerable, and this on account of their ill usage of God's people, whose eyes, as the eyes of one man, are *toward the Lord*, crying for help against their enemies *Hamath*, who borders thereby, shall meet the same fate, 2 Some apply the word to a quite different sense, and suppose they speak not wrath but mercy That *the word of the Lord* is his gospel, which shall rest in Damascus, and many of the inhabitants, as the Israel of God, shall look towards the Lord, and this was fulfilled when St Paul was near Damascus, brought to the knowledge of Jesus, and immediately preached him in the synagogues

Before Christ 587

(2) Tyre and Zidon, though supported by every human advantage, *very wise, very strong, and fortified, and very rich*, shall fall, God will cast her out, destroy her power in the sea where she reigned queen of the ocean, and *she shall be devoured with fire* *Note*, There is neither counsel nor might against the Lord

(3) The cities of the Philistines, Ashkelon, Gaza, and Ekron, shall be terrified at their neighbours ruin, *ashamed* of the confidence they reposed in Tyre, the *king of Gaza* shall *perish*, *Ashkelon* shall become desolate and uninhabited, and *a bastard shall dwell in Ashdod*, which was fulfilled when Alexander destroyed all these places, and captivated the inhabitants, and afterwards the Jews, under the Maccabees, seized many of them, and subdued great part of these countries

2 A remnant of these shall be saved Their bloody enmity against God's people, and their abominable idolatries shall be removved, *but he that remaineth, even he shall be for our God*, saved by his grace, and converted by the preaching of the gospel, *and he shall be as a governor in Judah*, dear to God, and honourable as the chiefs of Judah, *and Ekron as a Jebusite*, or inhabitant of Jebus, that is Jerusalem, the middle wall of partition being broken down, and no difference any longer subsisting between Jew and Gentile, but all be admitted into the church, and heirs together of the grace of life

3 God's care over his own people will eminently appear *I will encamp about mine house because of the army, because of him that passeth by, and because of him that returneth*, which literally refers to the protection God gave them against the army of the Greeks under Alexander who, amidst his other ravages, favoured the Jews And spiritually it speaks God's watchfulness over his chosen, who, amidst all the legions of hell, and the powers of earth combined against them, are and shall be for ever preserved, *and no oppressor shall pass through them any more*, which cannot so well be understood of the Jewish people, since many enemies afterwards oppressed them, but is gloriously verified respecting the Israel of God, who being justified from all things by the blood and righteousness of Jesus, shall never enter into condemnation, or be brought again under the yoke of bondage *for now have I seen with mine eyes*, which expresses his watchfulness over his people, and his delight in them, so that they are safe from all the powers of evil

9 ¶ [n] Rejoice greatly, O daughter of Zion, shout, n Isa lxii 11, Chap ii 10, Matt xxi 5, John xii 15
O daughter of Jerusalem behold, thy king cometh
unto thee he *is* just, and having salvation, lowly, and
riding upon an ass, and upon a colt the foal of an ass
10 And I will [o] cut off the chariot from Ephraim, and o Hos i 7, &c
the horse from Jerusalem, and the battle-bow shall be
cut off, and [p] he shall speak peace unto the heathen p Eph ii 14, 2 Cor v 19
and his dominion *shall be* [q] from sea *even* to sea, and from q Ps lxxii 8
the river *even* to the ends of the earth 11 As for thee
also, ‡ by the blood of thy covenant, I have sent forth ‡ Or, whose covenant is by blood
thy [r] prisoners out of the pit, wherein *is* no water. r Exod xxiv 8, Heb xiii 20, Isa li 14

v 9—11 The former verse directed us to the salvation of the great Redeemer, here he appears in great humility, yet bringing joy to all his saints

1 The *word* Messiah appears, and the prophet cries, *Behold him* that the eye of faith might be directed forward to that blessed time, which was now fast approaching *thy king cometh unto thee*, the long-expected son of David, to sit on his father's throne, *he is just*, in himself perfectly righteous, and administring the kingdom of his grace with the highest justice, *and having salvation*, the author and finisher of it, procuring it by his blood and righteousness, and ascending to his throne to apply it to his people's hearts, and make them partakers of it in time and in eternity *lowly*, humbling himself to so as takes to the form of a servant, and to the death of a slave, or *poor* and *afflicted*, as he appeared during all the days of his sojourning here below *and riding upon an ass, and upon a colt the foal of an ass*, or even upon a colt, for thus our Lord made his entry into Jerusalem, *Mat* xxi 4, 5 amidst the Hosannah's of the multitude

2 He will erect a glorious kingdom in the world, not by weapons of war, or outward force, but by the preaching of his gospel, bowing the hearts of men to submit to his easy yoke, and under his government they shall be safe, nor need the chariot, horse, or battle bow to defend them And the heathen shall share the blessings of his government, for to them *he will speak peace*, sending to them his gospel of peace, and causing them to enjoy in their soul the peace of God which passeth all understanding, and making them men of peace and quiet in the land, *and his dominion shall be from sea even to sea, and from the river even to the ends of the earth*, reaching as peace of time from pole to pole, especially in the last days, when all nations shall hear his gospel, and become obedient to the faith

3. The great deliverance to be wrought for the church is ascribed to the *blood* of the everlasting *covenant*, the blood of Jesus, which he shed upon the cross it is called *thy covenant*, the church's, because the blessings and benefits of it are her's, thro' Christ, who is the great Covenant-head to his people, and this blood was prefigured in all the sacrifices which the Jews offered of old By virtue of this, *I have sent forth thy prisoners*, for the redeemed by nature are in the same state of guilt and corruption as others, concluded *under sin*, till through the efficacy of atoning blood they are called by divine grace, and quickened by the holy ghost to come forth *out of the pit, wherein is no water*, where they must be sure to perish miserably, unless relieved And all who are brought out from thence look back with wonder, love, and praise, when they consider the horrible pit from which the Lord hath drawn them Therefore,

4. They are commanded to rejoice in the view of all these inestimable blessings, yea, to rejoice greatly, *v* 9 as well it becomes those to do who have seen the King in his beauty, and are made partakers of his great salvation

12 ¶ Turn ye to the strong hold, ye prisoners of
hope, even to day do I declare, *that* I will render double
unto thee 13 When I have bent Judah for me, filled
the bow with Ephraim, and raised up thy sons, O
Zion, against thy sons, O Greece, and made thee as
the sword of a mighty man 14 And the LORD shall
be seen over them and his arrow shall go forth as the
lightning and the Lord GOD shall blow the trumpet,
and shall go with whirlwinds of the south. 15 The
LORD of hosts shall defend them, and they shall de
vour and subdue with sling-stones, and they shall drink,
and make a noise as through wine, and they shall be
filled like bowls, *and* as the corners of the altar 16
And the LORD their God shall save them in that day
as the flock of his people, for *they shall be as* the stones
of a crown, lifted up as an ensign upon his land 17
For how great *is* his goodness, and how great *is* his
beauty! corn shall make the young men § cheerful, and
new wine the maids

v 12—17 The promises here delivered seem not so much to belong to any happy state of the Jewish affairs, as to the times of the gospel, at least then they shall most eminently receive their accomplishment

1. Sinners are invited to turn to *the strong hold* Christ Jesus, who alone is able to protect them from the assaults of their spiritual enemies Satan, sin, and death, to save them from the wrath of God, the curse of a broken law, and to supply all their wants out of his fulness They are called *prisoners of hope*, by nature enslaved by corruption, and condemned by guilt; their state in themselves desperate, and every effort to escape fruitless yet in the gospel, hope beams into the prison, Jesus hath opened the doors, by his blood having obtained redemption from all sins, by his righteousness having purchased eternal glory, by his grace calling the prisoners forth, and enabling them to turn, and *turn* to him, by faith quitting all other dependencies, and resting their whole salvation on him alone

2. They are assured of all protection and favour *To day do I declare that I will render double unto thee*, twice as much as they hoped for, comforts far exceeding all their afflictions, and blessings double to any their fathers had experienced the spiritual blessings in Christ Jesus in heavenly things being unspeakably superior to the greatest temporal prosperity and earthly good things

3. They shall be victorious under the divine guidance over every enemy, and be defended by almighty power *When I have bent Judah for me, filled the bow with Ephraim*, or filled the hand with the bow, strengthened their arms to bend it, and put the mighty weapons into their hands, the spiritual weapons of the gospel, with which the Apostles went forth, shooting the arrows of conviction into the stoutest hearts of sinners, and bringing them to the obedience of Christ, *and raised up thy sons, O Zion, against thy sons, O Greece*, the wise disputers of this world, for which Greece was famed, as the seat of human literature and science, but all this proud wisdom should be humbled before the gospel-word, and the wise made willing to become fools that they may be wise, *and made thee as the sword of a mighty man*, so piercing and sharp is the word of God in the mouths of his ministers, when accompanied by the demonstration of the spirit *And the Lord shall be seen over them*, as when on the day of pentecost the fiery tongues descended upon the apostles, or in the constant supports of grace and courage he ministered unto them, and still doth minister to all his servants, evidently manifesting the divine power which makes their labours effectual, *and his arrow shall go forth as the lightning*, swift shall his gospel spread, and fill the world with its light and glory *and the Lord God shall blow the trumpet*, his ministers shall sound a terrible alarm in the ears of impenitent sinners, *and shall go with whirlwinds of the south*, executing judgment on all who obey not his word, or the *trumpet* is like the jubilee trumpet, a proclamation of pardon, peace, and liberty, and *the whirlwinds*, the irresistible energy of the word preached, bearing down all opposition before it in the sinner's heart *The Lord of hosts shall defend them* from every foe, *and they shall devour and subdue with sling-stones*, though they seem as unequal to contend with their enemies respecting wisdom and power, as David to cope with Goliath, yet like him, these weak things shall confound the mighty, and bring the most self-righteous and stout hearted sinner to bow in the dust, and accept the grace of the gospel, *they shall drink* deep at the fountain of truth, and of the consolations of the spirit, *and make a noise as through wine*, full of joy and thankfulness, and songs of praise, *and they shall be filled* with the love of God, and a sense of the efficacy of the atonement of Jesus, *as bowls* with the blood of the sacrifices, and *as the corners of the altar* on which it was sprinkled, as our consciences are with the blood of Christ, sealing our pardon and peace *And the Lord God shall save them in that day as the flock of his people*, either the ministers above spoken of, whom the Lord sends to fight his battles, or rather those who are subdued by the sword of the spirit, and now numbered with such as bear Christ's easy yoke, and share in the blessings of his people, whom like a shepherd he feeds, watches over, and protects from every evil *for they shall be as the stones of a crown*, so precious in God's sight, the jewels that shall glitter in the Redeemer's crown to all eternity, *lifted up as an ensign upon the land*, trophies of the victories of Jesus, and a monument of his grace for ever and ever

Some refer these promises to the [illegible] after the flesh which under the Maccabees they were victorious over Antiochus and their other foes, but the sense given seems far preferable, and gives a nobler view of the prophecy

4. The Redeemed shall be filled with wonder, love, and praise *For how great is his goodness*, in thus laying us living, dying for us, and bestowing upon us the riches of his grace and the abundance of his blessings, *and how great is his beauty?* In every redeemed sinner's eye he is beyond compare, *the chiefest of ten thousand, and altogether lovely corn shall make the young men cheerful, and new wine the maids*, the faithful in Christ Jesus shall be vigorous, active, lively, going forth, as refreshed with corn and wine, singing in the good ways of God, and *fruitful*, as it is by some translated, in every good word and work

CHAP X

The scope of this chapter is much the same with that of the preceding Now, 1 They are here directed to eye the great God in all events, and, both in the evils they suffered, and the comforts they desired, to acknowledge his hand, ver 1—4 2 *They are encouraged to expect strength and success from him, in all their struggles with their enemies, and to hope that the issue would be glorious at last*, ver 5—12

1 ASK ye of the LORD rain in the time of
the latter rain, *so* the LORD shall make
bright clouds, and give them showers of rain, to
every one grass in the field 2 For the idols have
spoken vanity, and the diviners have seen a lie, and
have told false dreams, they comfort in vain there-
fore they went their way as a flock, they were troubled,
because *there was* no shepherd 3 Mine anger was kind-
led against the shepherds, and I punished the goats
for the LORD of hosts hath visited his flock the house
of Judah, and hath made them as his goodly horse in
the battle 4 Out of him came forth the corner, out
of him the nail, out of him the battle bow, out of him
every § oppressor together

v 1—4 God is now returning in mercy to his people, and therefore,

1. They are directed to apply to him for the rain in its season, on which the fruitfulness of their land depended In Judea the rain fell periodically, the former rain in autumn, about seed time, the latter in March, April, and May, for whence to September they had scarce any, and if these failed, the harvest necessarily suffered Now God promises to hear their prayers, to send his clouds, and by watering their lands seasonably, to give them plenty of the fruit of the earth The common blessings of providence are to be humbly sought, not looked upon as things of course, but as rich gifts of grace, and this may be referred mystically to the influences of God's spirit, by which our souls are alone quickened to bring forth fruit unto God, and therefore we must ask the holy spirit from God, in continual and importunate prayer

2. None of the idols of the heathen, or those their fathers worshipped, could give rain, their false prophets and diviners, who pretended to consult them, and return answers from them as oracles, were liars, they told false dreams, *and comforted in vain*, following these wicked shepherds, they had now

suffered

Before Christ 587

astray as a flock, and for this their shepherds in church and state, who had deluded them, were cut off in anger and none left, and *the goats*, the princes and priests, that, instead of going before the flock aright, misled and misused them, God had *punished* severely By these examples they should therefore be warned, and cease from idolatry, worshipping and serving God alone Especially,

3 Seeing God had now done such great things for them, visiting them with his favour as *his flock* recovered from their dispersion and captivity, and *hath made them as his goodly horse in the battle*, beautiful, strong, and formidable *Out of him went forth the corner*, he laid the foundation of their restoration, *out of him the nail*, which fastened them together, *out of him the battle bow*, all their military power was derived from him, *out of him every oppressor*, or *exactor*, either those enemies which had oppressed them did it by his permission, or the word may be taken in correspondence with the rest, that all the might they had, or should be endued with, to make any of the neighbouring nations tributary to them, must be from his gift alone

Some apply this to the Messiah, the Corner-stone, the nail fastened in a sure place, the battle bow to subdue all the enemies of his people, and assign this as the reason why God will visit them, and strengthen them, seeing he gives them him, he will with him freely give them every other blessing

5 ¶ And they shall be as [m] mighty men, which [n]
tread down *their enemies* in the mire of the streets in the
battle, and they shall fight, [o] because the LORD *is* with
them, and † the riders on horses shall be confounded 6
And I will strengthen the house of Judah, and I will
save the house of Joseph, [p] and I will bring them again
to place them, for [q] I have mercy upon them and they
shall be as though I had not cast them off for I *am*
the LORD their God, and will hear them 7 And
they of Ephraim shall be like a mighty man, and their
heart [r] shall rejoice as through wine yea, their children
shall see *it*, and be glad, their heart shall rejoice in the
LORD 8 [s] I will ‡ hiss for them, and gather them,
for I have redeemed them and [t] they shall increase as
they have increased 9 And I will [u] sow them among
the people and they shall remember me in far countries, and they shall live with their children, and turn
again 10 [x] I will bring them again also out of the land
of Egypt, and gather them out of Assyria, and I [y] will
bring them into the land of Gilead and Lebanon, and
[z] *place* shall not be found for them 11 [a] And he shall
pass through the sea with affliction, and [b] shall smite
the waves in the sea, and all the deeps of the river shall
dry up and the pride of Assyria shall be brought
down, and [c] the sceptre of Egypt shall depart away
12 And I will [d] strengthen them in the LORD, and
[e] they shall walk up and down in his name, saith the
LORD

m Gen xlix 24
n Ps xviii 42
o Rom viii 31
† Or, they shall make the riders on horses ashamed
p Jer iii 18 & xxiii 8
q Hos i 7
r Eph v 18
s Mat xi 28 John x 3, 4
‡ Or, whistle Isa v 26 & vii 18
t Isa xlix 19
u Hos ii 23
x Isa xi 11
y Chap xi 1, 2
z Isa xlix 19
a Ibid xi 15 16
b Rev xvi 12
c Ezek xxx 13
d John xv 5
e Mic iv 5

v 5—12 The promises contained in these verses certainly look farther than the establishment of Israel after their first captivity, and either appertain to the gospel-church in general, or have special reference to the Jewish people in the last days, when they shall be turned to the Lord

1 As applicable to the Israel of God in general *Because the Lord is with them*, with the preachers of his gospel, and the faithful in Christ Jesus, they shall be *as mighty men*, ver 5, 7 strengthened by grace to fight the Lord's battles against all their enemies, within and without, and the strongest shall fall before them, 5 They shall be *saved* with an everlasting salvation through the mercy of God, and live safely and comfortably in the church of the redeemed, being released from the bondage of corruption They shall be as the natural branches of the true olive, and God will be their covenant God, ready to *hear* and answer all their prayers, v 6 He will fill them with spiritual joy, as men rejoice through new wine, and their blessings shall descend to children's children, who shall behold their fathers mercies, partake of them, and rejoice in the same salvation, for Christ's church shall never fail, but continue through all ages, v 7 His gospel, as the shepherd's whistle, shall effectually gather them out of all lands, from the captivity of sin, much more hard and sore than that of Egypt or Assyria, v 10 for Jesus hath redeemed them by his most precious blood from every enemy, and great shall be their multitude, far exceeding that of Israel, when increased as the sand of the sea shore, v 8 See Hos i 10 *God will sow them among the people*, as his precious seed in all lands, and the most *distant countries* shall *remember* him, and turning to the Lord, shall live with their children the life of grace and glory, v 9 They shall possess the good land where all spiritual blessings abound, and place shall scarce be found for the multitude of converts, *and not one of them shall be left*, not one of the redeemed shall be finally lost, v 9 Through many tribulations indeed they must enter into the kingdom of God, but he will open a way for them through all their difficulties, and cause their strongest and most inveterate foes to fall before them, v 11 In the Lord is their strength, therefore they must prevail, *and they shall walk up and down in his name*, going forth in his might, and making mention of his righteousness only, walking by faith, and safely kept by the power of God unto salvation

Before Christ 587

2 These promises may also be particularly applied to Israel, when they shall be recovered from their present dispersion in the latter day, when God will convert their hearts to himself, increasing them more than ever, will strengthen them against all their foes, and probably make them his chief instruments in the ruin of the Antichristian foe, after whose fall, it is supposed by many good interpreters, that they will dwell long and happily in their own land of Judea, and being now become the people of Jesus, shall glory in his name as much as they have before blasphemed it

CHAP XI.

Though many of the Jewish nation received the Lord's Christ, far the most rejected him, for which their doom is here denounced We have, 1 A prediction of the destruction itself that should come upon the Jewish nation, ver 1—3 2 The putting of it into the hands of the Messiah (1) He is charged with the custody of that flock, ver 4—6 (2) He undertakes it, and bears rule in it, ver 7, 8 (3) Finding it perverse, he gives it up, ver 9 Breaks his shepherd's staff, ver 10, 11 Resents the indignities done him, and he contempt put upon him, ver 12, 13 And then breaks his other staff, ver 14 (4) He turns them over into the hands of foolish shepherds, who, instead of preventing, shall complete their ruin, and both the blind leaders and the blind followers shall fall together into the ditch, ver 15—17

1. OPEN thy doors, O Lebanon, [a] that the fire may
devour thy cedars 2 Howl, fir-tree, for the
cedar is fallen, because the mighty are spoiled howl, O
ye oaks of Bashan, [b] for † the forest of the vintage is
come down 3 ¶ *There is* a voice of the howling of
the shepherds, for their glory is spoiled, a voice of the
roaring of young lions, for the pride of Jordan is spoiled

a Luke xix 43, 44
b Isa xxxii 19
† Or, the defenced forest

v 1—3 The destruction of the Jewish temple and nation is here foretold

1 They are devoted to ruin *Open thy doors, O Lebanon, that the fire may devour thy cedars*, which may be understood of the temple, in building which, much cedar of Lebanon was employed, or of the gates of Jerusalem, both of them being forced open, and burnt by the Roman soldiers The *fir-tree* and the *cedar*, *the mighty* men of war, the princes and rulers, are doomed to fall, and given up to the spoil, and this being fixed in the divine decree, is spoken of as already done The *oaks of Bashan*, the mightiest, are now hewn down, and the *forest of the vineyard*, or *the fortified forest*, Jerusalem, strong and filled with inhabitants, is destroyed, *their glory is spoiled*, their treasures plundered, *the pride of Jordan is spoiled*, the whole land of Judea wasted, in which the lions, who infested the banks of this river, the emblems of the princes and judges who oppressed and harassed the poor people

2 This will make an howling among *the shepherds*, the great men of the nation, who will with bitterest grief behold these desolations, and be themselves terribly involved in them They who roared over their prey, and were the terrors of others, have now in just judgment their terrors turned upon them *Note*, In a day of recompence, wicked and careless shepherds in church and state, will meet the heaviest doom

4 Thus saith the LORD my God, [c] Feed the flock
of the slaughter 5 [f] Whose possessors slay them, and
[g] hold themselves not guilty and they that [f] sell them,
[g] say, Blessed *be* the LORD, for I am rich and their
own shepherds pity them not 6 For [h] I will no more
pity the inhabitants of the land, saith the LORD but
lo, I will deliver the men, every one to his neighbour's
hand, and into the hand of his king, and they shall
smite the land, and out of their hand I will not deliver
them. 7 And I will feed the flock of slaughter, *even* [k]
you, O † poor of the flock and I took unto me two
staves, the one I called [l] Beauty, and the other I called
‖ Bands, and I fed the flock 8 Three shepherds also I
cut off [m] in one month, and my soul ‖ lothed them, and
their soul also abhorred me 9 Then said I, I will not
feed you [n] that that dieth, let it die and that that is to
be cut off, let it be cut off, and let the rest eat every
one the flesh of § another, 10 ¶ And I took my staff,

c Rev xviii 9
d Acts xx 29
e Jer iii 15 & 1 7 John xvi 2
f 2 Pet ii 3
g Deut xxix 19 Hos xii 8 Mic iii 11
h James ii 13
i John x 12
k Ver 11 Mat xi 5
† Or, verily the poor
‖ Or, Binders
‖ Heb was straitened for them
¶ Heb of his fellow, or neighbour

Before Christ 587

even Beauty, and [o] cut it asunder, that I might break
my covenant which I had made with all the people
11 And it was broken in that day and ‖ so [p] the poor
of the flock that waited upon me, knew that it *was* the
word of the LORD 12 And I said unto them, if ye
think good, give *me* my price, and if not, forbear So
[q] they weighed for my price thirty *pieces* of silver 13
And the LORD said unto me, Cast it unto [r] the potter
a goodly price that I was prised at of them And I took
the thirty *pieces* of silver, and cast them to the potter in
the house of the LORD 14 Then I cut asunder mine
other staff, *even* Bands, that [s] I might break the brother
hood between Judah and Israel

Rom xi 9. ‖ Or the poor of the flock, &c knew certainly. p Zeph iii 12. q Matt xxvi 15. r Matt xxvii 9. s Rom xi 20.

℣ 4—14 The people of the Jews are called *the flock of the slaughter*, as being so severely treated by their shepherds, or as devoted to the sword The prophet, as the type of Christ, is commanded to feed them, ministring his gospel among them, that the remnant of the poor among them might be fed with the word of God, whilst others ripened for destruction We have,

1 An account of their miserable plight *Their possessors*, who, as good shepherds in church or state, should have taken all care of them, *slay them*, their priests, scribes, and pharisees, by false doctrines destroyed their souls *and hold themselves not guilty*, blinded by pride in their errors, *and they who sell them say, blessed be the Lord, for I am rich* making long prayers, though laden with the spoils of widows houses, and valuing themselves on their external piety and goodness, when their burnt-offerings were robbery, and their hearts abominable, shewing no pity towards the souls of the people And sad is that church's case, where such careless, selfish, covetous pastors rule

2 For this God gives them up to destruction *I will no more spare the inhabitants of the land*, who were involved in the general guilt, and doomed to sink in one promiscuous ruin Their own intestine divisions will pave the way, and the Roman emperor, the king they chose, *John* xix 15 shall complete their desolations

3 Before their judgment comes, Christ undertakes to *feed the flock of slaughter, the poor of the flock*, the chosen remnant among them, chiefly poor people, who were made partakers of the Saviour's grace, and all the blessings of his gospel, whilst the rulers and great men in general rejected the counsel of the Lord against their own souls, and hereby filled up the measure of their iniquities To execute his pastoral office the great Shepherd takes two staves, the one he calls *Beauty*, the other *Bands*, concerning the meaning of which there is great diversity of opinions the most probable seem to be, either that these signify the gospel, and the ordinances thereof, whereby the members of the church are united together, or they refer to the different persons of the flock, some of whom would walk before the Lord in the beauty of holiness, whilst others continued under the power of sin, and were doomed to the bands of captivity, or these may denote the beauty of the service of the sanctuary, and the bands of civil government among them and he *fed the flock*, as he had undertaken to do *Three shepherds also he cut off in one month*, which may refer to the punishment of the wicked shepherds in general, or to the princes, priests, and prophets, or the three sects of Pharisees, Sadducees, and Herodians, or perhaps it may relate to some singular judgment on three notorious offenders, of whom we have no record remaining

4 For their obstinacy and impenitence the Jews in general are rejected *My soul loathed them, and their soul also abhorred me*, they could not bear his high pretensions as the Messiah, nor endure his sharp rebukes and whilst the sinner persists in his enmity against God, he must be an abomination in his sight *Then said I, I will not feed you*, will take no more care of them, nor continue his gospel any longer among them *that that dieth, let it die, and that that is cut off, let it be cut off* he devotes them to the ruin they have provoked, and consigns them over to the pestilence and the sword *and let the rest eat every one the flesh of another*, through the severity of famine, or the rancour of their mutual animosities *And*, in token of this utter rejection of them, *I took my staff, even Beauty, and cut it asunder*, to signify the ceasing of his pastoral office, and his abandoning them to destruction, the *covenant* of peculiarity being henceforth *broken* and abolished, *and it was broken in that day*, when Christ rejected them, *see Matth* xxi 43 or when he died, and this was evident when shortly after Jerusalem and the temple were destroyed *and the poor of the flock that waited on me*, the disciples of Christ who attended his ministry, and were generally of the poorer sort, the kingdom of God being chiefly composed of such, *knew that it was the word of the Lord*, it being mixed with *faith* in their hearts, and they fully trusted that every tittle would come to pass as Jesus had spoken

5 We have a particular instance of their contempt of Christ *I said unto them, Give me my price, and if not, forbear*, discharge me, if you like not my service, or, if you think me worth nothing, pay me nothing *So they weighed for my price thirty pieces of silver*, the price of a servant, *Exod* xxi 32 *a goodly price*, saith he ironically, *that I was valued at of them* with disdain therefore he casts it *to the potter, in the house of the Lord* To what this refers we cannot be at a loss, *see Matth* xxvii 9, 10 this being the price for which Judas sold his master, and with this sum, which in remorse the traitor had cast down in the temple, the chief priests bought the potter's field, a waste ground where clay had been dug, to bury strangers in

6 Their whole civil state and polity is hereupon dissolved *Then I cut asunder my other staff, even Bands, that I might break the brotherhood between Judah and Israel*, a spirit of dissension being sowed among them, which hastened their destruction, and, when destroyed by the Romans, they were separated and dispersed as captives into all lands Thus, when ungodliness abounds, the bonds of civil society are loosed, and such a wicked people hasten their own dissolution

15 ¶ And the LORD said unto me, Take unto thee
yet the instruments of [t] a foolish shepherd 16 For lo,
I will raise up [u] a shepherd in the land, [x] *which* shall not
visit *those that be* cut off, neither shall seek the young
one, nor heal *that that* is broken, nor † feed that that
standeth still but he shall eat the flesh of the fat, and
tear their claws in pieces 17 [y] Wo to the idol shep-
herd that leaveth the flock the sword *shall be* upon his
arm, and upon his right eye his arm shall be clean dried
up, and his right eye shall be utterly darkned

℣ 15—17 Having rejected the good Shepherd Christ Jesus, the Jewish people are given up to wicked and foolish shepherds, whom the prophet is here commanded to personate, such as were the scribes and pharisees, who deceived and deluded the people with false expositions and vain hopes, preying upon them instead of feeding them, and, far from seeking to save that which was lost, or healing the wounded, they neglected their charge, or made their proselytes sevenfold more the children of hell than they were before, for which, heavy curses are denounced upon them and the character and woes belong to others besides them, who in the Christian church pretending to feed the flock of the Lord, in reality betray and destroy them We may read here,

1 The character of every foolish idol-shepherd (1) *He leaveth the flock*, he neglects the duty of his ministry, resides not among the people committed to his care, and for some poor pittance gets a hireling to supply his place (2) *He doth not visit those that be cut off*, takes no pains to recover lost souls, nor ever goes round his parish or district to admonish and exhort the people (3) He doth not *seek the young ones*, by catechising and early instruction desiring to bring them up in the nurture and admonition of the Lord (4) *He doth not heal that which is broken*, but, if a poor sinner applies to him under conviction of sin, with a bleeding heart, he is a physician of no value, he knows not what advice to give, and wickedly and ignorantly heals the hurt slightly, crying peace, peace, when there is no peace, thus making the evil worse (5) *He doth not feed that which standeth still*, and through weakness and hunger is ready to faint, the famished flock look up and are not fed, the husks of dry morality, or the hemlock of false doctrine, such as human dignity and freewill, justification by works, and self-righteous endeavours, are laid before them to their ruin (6) *He eats the flesh of the fat, and tears their claws in pieces* [illegible] the work of the ministry, yet [illegible] in exacting the wages of it, and in luxury and ease devours the flesh as well as the fleece of the poor flock

2 The curse is sure and heavy upon him *His arm shall be dried up, and his right eye darkned*, judicial blindness shall seal him up under wrath, his power to oppress the flock shall be destroyed, and *the sword* of wrath overtake him *Wo therefore to the idol shepherd*

CHAP XII

In this chapter God promises, 1 That the attempts of the church's enemies against her shall be to their own ruin, ver 2, 3, 4, 6 2 *That the endeavours of the church's friends for her good shall be successful*, ver 5 3 *That God will protect and strengthen the meanest and weakest that belong to his church, and work salvation for them*, ver 7, 8 4 *That as a preparation for all this mercy and a pledge of it, he will pour upon them a spirit of prayer and repentance, the products of which shall be universal and very particular*, ver 9—14

1 THE burden of the word of the LORD for
Israel, saith the LORD, which stretcheth forth
the heavens, and layeth the foundation of the earth, and
formeth the spirit of man within him 2 Behold,
I will make Jerusalem a cup of trembling unto all
the people round about, when they shall be in the siege
both

Before Christ 587

Before Christ 587

both against Judah *and* against Jerusalem 3 ¶ And
[e] in that day will I make Jerusalem [f] a burdensome stone
for all people all that burden themselves with it shall be
cut in pieces, though all the people of the earth be ga-
thered together against it 4 In that day, saith the
LORD, [g] I will smite every horse with astonishment,
and his rider with madness, and I will open mine eyes
upon the house of Judah, and will smite every horse of
the people with blindness 5 And the governors of
Judah shall say in their heart, ‡ The inhabitants of Jeru-
salem *shall be* my strength in the LORD of hosts their
God 6 ¶ In that day will I make the governors of
Judah [h] like a hearth of fire among the wood, and like
a torch of fire in a sheaf, and they shall devour all the
people round about, on the right hand and on the left
and Jerusalem shall be inhabited again in her own place,
even in Jerusalem 7 The LORD also shall save the
tents of Judah first, that the glory of the house of David,
and the glory of the inhabitants of Jerusalem, [i] do not
magnify *themselves* against Judah 8 In that day [k] shall
the LORD defend the inhabitants of Jerusalem, and [l] he
that is § feeble among them at that day shall be as David,
and the house of David *shall be* as ‖ God, as the angel
of the LORD before them

e Ver 4 6, 8 9 11 f Dan ii 35 Mat xxi 44. g Psal lxvi 6 Ezek xxxviii 4. ‡ Or there is strength to me and to the inhabitants &c h Obad 18 i 1 Cor i 31 k Chap ii 5 l Joel iii 10 § Heb Fallen ‖ Elohim, or angels.

v 1—8 The promises contained in this chapter refer either to the church of God in general, or the Jewish people in particular, when in the last days God shall bring them into his fold The prophecy is called a burden, because it is filled with terror to Israel's enemies, and it is prefaced with an awful description of him who undertakes to accomplish his own word, *He stretcheth forth the heavens, and layeth the foundation of the earth*, the Creator, Governor, and Upholder of all things, who *formeth the spirit of man within him*, the God of the spirits of all flesh, who hath the sovereign dominion over them, and influences them according to his own will, encouraging the hearts of his people, and injecting terrors into his enemies God promises,

1 To make the efforts of all the enemies of his church issue in their confusion They who persecute God's people, and lay siege against them, shall have a cup of trembling put into their hands, *v* 2 Be their foes never so many, never so mighty, spiritual or temporal, instead of prevailing against the redeemed, they shall pull down ruin upon their own heads, as a burdensome stone, which crushes the man who attempts to lift it up, *v* 3 God's eyes of love and favour are upon them, therefore their foes shall be smitten with blindness, astonishment, and madness, and baffled in all their enterprises, *v* 4 whilst the governors of the church, the ministers of Christ, by the gospel-word they preach, like a devouring fire and a torch in a sheaf, shall bear down all before them, and none shall be able to resist the wisdom and spirit by which they speak, *v* 6

They who apply this to the Jewish people, refer the prophecy either to the times of the Maccabees, or rather suppose it hath respect to their future greatness, and that when they are returned to settle in their own land, the Mahometan powers will go up to besiege them, whose armies chiefly consist of cavalry, and shall fall on the mountains of Israel, defeated and destroyed by the Jewish forces

2 God will establish his church, and build it up great and glorious, *v* 6 defending every member thereof with his everlasting arms of love and power, *v* 8 On him the governors of Judah shall place their confidence, he being the strength of the inhabitants of Jerusalem, the bulwark of the country, and not any human supports, with which, as fortifications, they may be surrounded, *v* 5 The meanest, who dwell in tents, he will save, and none of the more distinguished and honourable members must arrogate to themselves any part in the salvation, and *magnify* themselves over their brethren, as if they owed to them their protection and support, when the whole is from God, and all alike debtors to sovereign grace, *v* 7, by which the weakest believer *shall be as David*, able to cope with their mightiest foes, *and the house of David*, the spiritual descendants of Jesus, David's son, a royal generation, they *shall be as God*, strong as the arm of omnipotence, *as the angel of the Lord before them*, all Christ's power being engaged for them, and they interested in it, he is their strength and their Redeemer

Some understand this as literally to have its accomplishment, when Jerusalem shall be built on the very spot where it stood of old, and be again inhabited, *even in Jerusalem* on which occasion the eastern antichristian powers shall assemble against it, and God will save them, both in the country and city, in some most distinguished manner, so that his arm shall be visible, and the glory ascribed to him alone The former sense I should prefer

9 ¶ And it shall come to pass in that day, *that* [m] I
will seek to destroy all the nations that come against

m Hag ii 22

Jerusalem 10 And [n] I will pour upon the house of
David, and upon the inhabitants of Jerusalem, the spirit
of grace and of supplications, and they shall [o] look up-
on me whom they have pierced, and they shall mourn
for him [p] as one mourneth for *his* only *son*, and shall be
in bitterness for him, as one that is in bitterness for *his*
first-born 11 In that day shall there be a great [q] mourn-
ing in Jerusalem, as the mourning of [r] Hadadrimmon in
[s] the valley of Megiddon 12 And [t] the land shall mourn,
† every family apart, the family of the house of David
apart, and their wives [u] apart the family of the house
of [x] Nathan apart, and their wives apart 13 The
family of the house of Levi apart, and their wives apart
the family ‡ of [y] Shimei apart, and their wives apart
14 All the families that remain, every family apart,
and their wives apart.

Before Christ 587

n Joel ii 28 o John xix 34 37 Rev i 7 p Jer vi 26 Amos viii 10 q Acts ii 37 r 2 Kings xxiii 29 2 Chron xxxv 22—25 s Ezek [illegible] t Mat xxiv 30 Rev i 7 † Heb. families families u 1 Cor vii. 5 x 2 Sam v 14 ‡ Or Simeon, as LXX &c y 1 Chron. iv 19

v 9—14 To apply these great things to the days of the Maccabees seems to enervate the prophecy, a greater than they is surely here intended

1 All enemies of Christ's church and people shall be destroyed, as before was promised

2 A spirit of grace, and supplications, and mourning shall be poured forth upon all the people of God

[1] *A spirit of grace*, the Spirit of God shall be given to them, as a quickening, illuminating, converting, sanctifying, comforting Spirit, the author of every divine and gracious temper in them, and witnessing to his own blessed work in the hearts of the redeemed

[2] *A spirit of supplications*, for every gracious soul immediately is brought to his knees, and lives in an habitual course of waiting upon God, his soul can no more live without prayer than his body without breath he is stirred up to the exercise of prayer, and assisted in the act by that Spirit of adoption which enables him to cry Abba, father, and help his infirmities, and, in answer to his supplication, grace upon grace is bestowed, by which means he increaseth with the increase of God

[3] A spirit of mourning *They shall look upon me whom they have pierced, and mourn, see John* xix 37 Their eye shall be directed in prayer to Christ, through whom alone the sinner hath access to God, and the view of a crucified Jesus will melt their heart and make their eyes overflow When we consider that he was wounded for our transgressions, that our sins were the nails, the spear that pierced the body of the Saviour, this will produce that godly sorrow which worketh repentance unto salvation never to be repented of, which nothing but faith, beholding the evil of sin as placed before the cross, can ever beget in us and this mourning will be heart-felt and bitter, like that of a parent for his first-born son, or like the several mournings of Israel for Benjamin at the rock Rimmon, *Judg* xx 47 and for Josiah in the valley of Megiddon, where that pious king was slain, 2 *Kings* xxiii 29 And this will be the case with every individual believer, with every family, with every society of real Christians, the highest in rank, and the honest by office, *v* 12, 13 shall herein set the example, and all shall concur in lamenting their sin and wickedness, and looking to Jesus for pardon and peace

They who refer this to the people of the Jews particularly, suppose that at their conversion, which will be general and sudden, this shall be fulfilled, when, the vail being taken from their hearts, they shall behold that Messiah whom they crucified, and, returning to him with weeping and supplication, shall testify their unfeigned remorse and sorrow for that black deed Perhaps also their lost genealogies may be then restored, and, literally taken, the several families apart shall each lament over their crucified Lord

CHAP XIII

In this chapter we have, 1 Some further promises relating to gospel-times, here is a promise of the remission of sins, ver 1 *and of the reformation of manners,* ver 2 *and particularly of the convicting and silencing of false prophets,* ver 2—6 2 *A clear prediction of the sufferings of Christ, and the dispersion of his disciples thereupon,* ver 7 *and of the destruction of the greater part of the Jewish nation not long after,* ver 8 *and of the purifying of a remnant of them, a peculiar people to God,* ver 9

1 IN that day there shall be [a] a fountain [b] opened to
the house of David, and to the inhabitants of Je-
rusalem, [c] for sin, and for † uncleanness 2 ¶ And it
shall come to pass in that day, saith the LORD of hosts,
that I will [d] cut off the names of the idols out of the land,
and they shall no more be remembred and also I will
cause [e] the prophets and the unclean spirit to pass out
of the land 3 And it shall come to pass, *that* when
any

a John xix 34 b Chap xii 1 Rev i 5 [illegible]

Before Christ 587

any shall yet prophesy, then [f] his father and his mother,
that begat him, shall say unto him, Thou shalt not live,
for thou speakest [g] lies in the name of the LORD and
his father and his mother, that begat him, shall thrust
him through when he prophesieth 4 And it shall come
to pass in that day, *that* [h] the prophets shall be ashamed
every one of his vision, when he hath prophesied nei-
ther shall they [i] wear ‡ a rough garment to deceive 5
But he shall say, [k] I *am* no prophet, I *am* an husband-
man, for man taught me to keep cattle from my youth
6 And *one* shall say unto him, What *are* these [l] wounds
in thine hands? Then he shall answer, *Those* with which
I was wounded *in* the house of my friends

f Deut xiii 6, 8. g 1 Tim iv. h Mic iii 6, 7. i 2 Kings i 8. Mat iii 4. ‡ Heb A garment of hair. k Amos vii 14. l 1 Kings xviii 28.

v 1—6 The subject of the former chapter is here continued, and the great blessings arising from the gospel of Jesus are set forth

1 The guilt of sin shall be done away through his atoning blood *In that day* of the crucifixion of Jesus, *there shall be a fountain opened to the house of David and to the inhabitants of Jerusalem*, to all sinners of every rank and degree, *for sin and for uncleanness*, for all need this cleansing, being defiled with guilt, and altogether as an unclean thing before the God of purity, nor can any thing wash out the stains but *this fountain opened*, where there is all fulness of merit, and to which all are freely invited, that they may wash and be clean They who neglect so great a salvation, ignorant of their pollution, or too proud, like Naaman, to stoop to this humbling method of salvation, must perish in their sins

2 Idolatry shall be rooted out, and the names of their idols be never again mentioned as objects of worship which was the case with the Jews after their return from captivity But the promise seems here to look further either to the destruction of the idols of paganism, which fell before the gospel, or to the rooting out the image-worship that remains in the antichristian church

3 The false prophets shall deceive no more *I will cause the prophets, and the unclean spirit*, by which they were actuated, *to pass out of the land*, so that when any pretender to prophecy shall arise, his nearest relatives, *Deut* xiii 6, 11 shall seize, accuse, and execute judgment upon him, *v* 3 yea, so ashamed shall they themselves be of their former pretensions, that they shall strip off the *rough garments* which they had worn out of seeming sanctity and austerity, and *say, I am no prophet, I am an husbandman*, and from my youth was bred to this occupation, unwilling to own he was ever engaged in any other, *v* 5 and when questioned concerning *the wounds in his hands*, he will reply, to evade the truth, that they were wounds received in the house of his friends, not as the rebuke for assuming the prophetical character, as they really were, but correction he received for some neglect in his secular business, *v* 6 *Note*, (1) Our dearest relations, who would turn us away from God, must be rejected with abhorrence (2) Pretenders to godliness will sooner or later be detected, the demure look and rough garment of the hypocrite will not always deceive (3) Parents must use the rod of correction, these wounds shew the truest affection to their children

Some suppose the last verse refers to Christ, upbraided by the Jews as a false prophet, and from the wounds in his hand they suggest he suffered justly as a deceiver To which he replies, that he was so treated indeed among those who should have been his friends, but that the wounds were not for any crime he had done, but in consequence of the satisfaction he had undertaken to make to divine justice as the surety of his people, as is implied in the following verse

7 ¶ Awake, O sword, against my [m] shepherd, and
against the man [n] *that is* my fellow, saith the LORD
of hosts [o] smite the shepherd, and the sheep shall be
scattered and I will turn mine hand upon [p] the little
ones. 8 And it shall come to pass, *that* in all the land,
saith the LORD, [q] two parts therein shall be cut off, *and*
die, but [r] the third shall be left therein 9 And I will
bring the third part through the fire, and will [s] refine
them as silver is refined, and will try them as gold is
tried [t] they shall call on my name, and I will hear
them [u] I will say, It *is* my people, and they shall say,
The LORD *is* [x] my God

m Heb xiii 20. n John x 30. o Mat xxvi 31. Mark xiv 27. p Luke xii 32. q Ezek v 2, 12. r Rom xi 5. s 1 Pet i 6, 7. t Psal l 15. u Hos ii 23. x John xx 28.

v 7—9 That the Messiah should be cut off was before prophesied we have here the execution of that decree

1 God the Father commissions the sword of justice to pierce the Redeemer *Awake my sword against my shepherd, even against the man that is my fellow, saith the Lord of hosts* In essential dignity he was God's fellow, and counted it no robbery to be equal with God, in office he was God's shepherd, appointed to be the great covenant head of his redeemed flock, who should lay down his life for his sheep This sword our sins had provoked, it had long slumbered, but now awakes, according to the eternal purpose, against the Son of God, since upon him are laid the iniquities of us all he who bears our sins must carry our sorrows

2 The sheep hereupon are scattered Which the great shepherd himself quotes, *Matth* xxvi 31 as fulfilled on that dismal night when he was apprehended, and all his disciples forsook him and fled But he promises soon to recover them *I will turn mine hand upon the little ones* They were now like children, timorous, affrighted, and weak, but soon were brought back, and endued with power from on high, so that they went forth bold champions in his cause, and God mightily supported them, and gave them wonderful success in their labours

3 The impenitent Jews shall perish, but a remnant shall be saved, two parts being cut off during their war with the Romans A *third*, the remnant according to the election of grace shall escape, as through the fire, getting out of Jerusalem to Pella before the Romans formed the siege and these, refined in the furnace of affliction, and proved faithful, shall be a people for God, calling upon his name, and answered in all their requests, he will own the relation they claim to him as their God, and give them every blessing they can ask or need Some refer this to the world and church in general, one third of which will scarcely be found faithful amidst the far more numerous herd of professors, the hypocrites, formalists, and self-righteous *Note*, (1) Those whom God saves he first refines in the furnace of affliction They who were never thus exercised have reason to fear they are bastards, and not sons (2) They are gracious troubles which serve to purge us from the remaining dross of corruption (3) God's people are all confessors in prayer, and they find their diligence of being so employed, in the answers of grace and peace he bestows (4) They who have taken the Lord for their God, will never have cause to repent their choice

CHAP XIV

To what time the day here spoken of belongs is dubious, whether to the times of the gospel dispensation or the great day of the Lord Judgment and mercy are here mingled 1 *The gates of hell are here threatening the church*, ver 1 2 *and yet not prevailing* 2 *The power of heaven appears here for the church, and against the enemies of it*, ver 3, 4, 5 3 *The events concerning the church are here represented as mixed*, ver 6, 7 *but issuing well at last* 4 *The spreading of the means of knowledge is here foretold, and the setting up of the gospel kingdom in the world*, ver 8, 9 *which shall be the enlargement and establishment of another Jerusalem*, ver 10, 11 5 *Those shall be reckoned with that fought against Jerusalem*, ver 12—15 *and those that were left God's worship there*, ver 17—19 6 *It is promised that there shall be great resort to the church, and great purity and piety in it*, ver 16, 20, 21

1 BEhold, [a] the day of the LORD cometh, and thy
spoil shall be divided in the midst of thee 2
For [b] I will gather all nations against Jerusalem to battle,
and the city shall be taken, and [c] the houses rifled, and
the women ravished, and [d] half of the city shall go forth
into captivity, and [e] the residue of the people shall not
be cut off from the city 3 Then shall the LORD
[f] go forth, and fight against those nations, as when he
fought in the day of battle. 4 ¶ And his feet shall
stand in that day upon [g] the mount of Olives, which *is*
before Jerusalem on the east, and the mount of Olives
shall cleave in the midst thereof toward the east, and to-
ward the west, *and* [h] *there shall be* a very great valley,
and half of the mountain shall remove toward the north,
and half of it toward the south 5 And ye shall flee *to*
the valley of the mountains for the valley of the moun-
tains shall reach unto Azal yea, ye shall flee like as ye
fled from before [i] the earthquake in the days of Uzziah
king of Judah and [k] the LORD my God shall come,
and all the saints with thee 6 And it shall come to pass
in that day, *that* the light shall not be clear, *nor* dark
7 ‖ But it shall be [l] one day [m] which shall be known to
the LORD, not day, nor night but it shall come to pass,
that at [n] evening-time it shall be light

a Acts ii 20. b Ezek xxxviii 4. 5, 6 Dan. xii 1. c Isa xiii 16. d Rev xi 7. e Chap xiii 8. f 1 Chr xxxviii 23. Rev xix 14, &c. g Acts i 12. h Joel iii 12, 14. i Amos i 1. k Mat xxiv 30, 31. Jude 14. ‖ Or the day shall be one. l Rev xxii 5. m Mat xxiv 36. n Isa xxx 26. Acts ii 17. Rev xxi. 23

v 1—7 We have here,

1 *A day of judgment*, *v* 1, 2 which may refer to the taking Jerusalem by the Romans, when all the brutal rage of war was let loose, and half the people carried into captivity, a remnant being left, even those who, according to the divine warning, had before saved themselves by flight Or this may better be ascribed to the prevalence of the power of antichrist over the church for a while, so that few faithful at all be left

Before Christ 587

2 *A day of mercy*, when Chriſt ſhall go forth to fight his people's battles, to deſtroy their deſtroyers, *v* 3 *And his feet ſhall ſtand in that day upon the mount of olives*, as when he aſcended up from thence, and quickly after made a way for the Gentile world to draw near unto God, ſignified by the dividing aſunder the mountain, and opening a great valley between, in which Jews and Gentiles ſhould aſſemble together and incorporate, eager to be admitted into the church, which ſhall now be exceedingly enlarged, *v* 5 flying thither with as much ſpeed as thoſe in the days of Joſiah fled from the earthquake, and there God's preſence in the midſt of his ſaints ſhall eminently appear

Some refer this to the ſecond coming of Chriſt, when they ſuppoſe he ſhall deſcend on that very ſpot from which he aſcended; that the valley ſhall be the place where the dead ſhall be raiſed and aſſembled, many of whom will then be fleeing to the mountains to cover them from the preſence of the Judge, now appearing with ten thouſands of his ſaints, and be more terrified at his coming than thoſe were who fled from the earthquake in Uzziah's days, which threatned to ſwallow them up It muſt be confeſſed this prophecy is of very difficult interpretation However we may learn, (1) That the Lord Jeſus will come to judge the world, and that it highly imports us to be ready to meet him (2) That it will be too late then to flee from his wrath, if we have not before betaken ourſelves to the refuge of his mercy (3) That they will then be truly happy who can ſay, *My God ſhall come*, for he will be moſt welcome to all who have an intereſt in his love and favour

3 *It ſhall come to paſs in that day, that the light ſhall not be clear, nor dark* Which may refer either to the imperfect attainments of Chriſt's ſaints upon earth, compared with what they expect hereafter, or to the diſpenſations of God's providence towards his church, over which there ſhall hang clouds of trouble whilſt in this militant ſtate below *But it ſhall be one day*, a ſhort time that this will be the caſe, *which will be known unto the Lord*, who takes notice of his people under all their remaining infirmities and troubles, and hath appointed their end *At evening-time it ſhall be light* when the day of time ſhall come to its period, and eternity open to view, then all ſhall be light to God's people for ever, when their faith and patience ſhall be crowned with glory, their ſun ſhall no more go down, nor their moon withdraw itſelf and therefore in our preſent darkneſs and troubles we ſhould wait ſtill upon God, and hope for a happy iſſue at laſt out of all

Some refer this to the ſpiritual reign of Chriſt, when his goſpel ſhall be ſpread abroad in the latter day, and the darkneſs of Mahomediſm, paganiſm, and popery, be utterly diſpelled

8 And it ſhall be in that day, *that* [o] living waters
ſhall go out from Jeruſalem half of them toward the
† former ſea, and half of them toward the hinder ſea
in ſummer and in winter ſhall it be 9 And the
LORD ſhall be [p] king over all the earth in that day
ſhall there be one LORD, and his name one 10 All
the land ſhall be turned [q] as a plain from Geba to Rimmon,
ſouth of Jeruſalem and it ſhall be lifted up, and
[r] inhabited in her place from Benjamin's gate unto the
place of the firſt gate, unto the corner gate, and *from*
the tower of Hananeel unto the king's wine preſſes
11 And *men* ſhall dwell in it, and [t] there ſhall be no
more utter deſtruction, [u] but Jeruſalem ‡ ſhall be ſafely
inhabited 12 ¶ And this ſhall be the plague wherewith
the LORD will ſmite all the people that have fought
againſt Jeruſalem [x] Their fleſh ſhall conſume away while
they ſtand upon their feet, and [y] their eyes ſhall conſume
away in their holes, and [z] their tongue ſhall conſume away
in their mouth 13 (And it ſhall come to paſs in that
day, *that* [a] a great tumult from the LORD ſhall be
among them, and they ſhall lay hold every one on the
hand of his neighbour, and [b] his hand ſhall riſe up
againſt the hand of his neighbour 14 And Judah alſo
ſhall fight § at Jeruſalem, and the wealth of all the
heathen round about ſhall be gathered together, gold,
and ſilver, and apparel in great abundance) 15 And
[c] ſo ſhall be the plague of the horſe, of the mule, of the
camel, and of the aſs, and of all the beaſts that ſhall be
in theſe tents, as this plague

o Ezek xlvii 1 Joel iii 18 Rev xxii 1 † Or eaſtern Joel ii 20 p Hoſ i 11 1 Tim vi 15 q Iſa xl 4 Chap iv 7 r Chap xii 6 s Neh iii 1 Jer xxxi 38 t Rev xxii 3 u Jer xxiii 6 ‡ Or ſhall abide Ver 10 x Acts xii 23 y Acts xiii 11 z Rev xvi Luke xxi 24 a 1 Sam xiv 15, 20 b Zech xxxviii 21 § Or againſt c Luke xxxix 10 17, & d Ver 12

v 8—15 Farther bleſſings are here promiſed to God Iſrael

1 *Living waters ſhall go out from Jeruſalem*, even the goſpel, which began to be preached at Jeruſalem, and went forth, from eaſt to weſt, into all parts of the world, and will continue to the end of time to flow, till the earth ſhall be covered with the knowledge of the Lord as the waters cover the ſea

2 Chriſt will erect an univerſal kingdom in the earth All competitors will at laſt be deſtroyed *there ſhall be one Lord* owned and acknowledged through the whole world, *and his name one*, every diſtinction of party, and difference of opinion and worſhip, will be laid aſide, and all with one heart and one mouth ſhall unite in prayer and praiſe before him

3 The church ſhall be glorious, abundantly repleniſhed, and the abode of peace for ever *All the land ſhall be turned as a plain*, every mountain and hill laid low, *from Geba to Rimmon*, all oppoſition deſtroyed, and Jeruſalem, the goſpel-church, *lifted up* as a beacon on an hill, whither all the converts ſhall flock together, ſo that it ſhall be filled with inhabitants from one end to the other, *v* 11 Wars ſhall then ceaſe, no civil diſcords nor eccleſiaſtical anathemas ſhall diſturb the peace of God's people, they ſhall dwell in ſafety, and none evermore make them afraid

4 The enemies of the church ſhall be utterly cut off Their once-pampered *fleſh* ſhall be emaciated, and conſume away, their *eyes*, full of covetouſneſs, envy, laſciviouſneſs, ſhall rot in their ſockets, and their *tongues*, defiled with blaſphemy, reproach, and falſhood, ſhall periſh God will put his terrors in the midſt of them, and in their confuſion every man's ſword ſhall be againſt his fellow, ſo that they ſhall be their own executioners, *ſee Rev* xvii 16 the ſaints of God, who go forth to fight, will have nothing to do but to gather the immenſity of rich ſpoils, *v* 14 and the very beaſts of theſe ſinners ſhall ſhare their plagues, and be deſtroyed with them, 15 All which ſeems much more applicable to the deſtruction of the antichriſtian powers than to the diſſenſions and deſtruction of Jeruſalem, to which it is by ſome referred

16 ¶ And it ſhall come to paſs, *that* every one *that*
is left of all the nations which came againſt Jeruſalem,
ſhall even [e] go up from year to year to worſhip the King
the LORD of hoſts, and to keep [f] the feaſt of tabernacles
17 And it ſhall be, *that* [g] whoſo will not come
up of *all* the families of the earth unto Jeruſalem, to
worſhip the King the LORD of hoſts, even upon them
[h] ſhall be no rain 18 And if the family of Egypt go
not up, and come not, [i] that have no *rain* there ſhall
be the plague wherewith the LORD will ſmite the heathen
that come not up to keep the feaſt of tabernacles
19 This ſhall be the † puniſhment of Egypt, and the
puniſhment of all nations that come not up to keep the
feaſt of tabernacles 20 ¶ In that day ſhall [k] there be
upon the ‡ bells of the horſes, [l] HOLINESS UNTO
THE LORD, and the pots in the LORD's houſe
ſhall be like the bowls before the altar 21 Yea, every
pot in Jeruſalem and in Judah ſhall be Holineſs unto
the LORD of hoſts and all they that ſacrifice, ſhall
come and take of them, and ſeethe therein and in that
day [m] there ſhall be no more the § Canaanite in the houſe
of the LORD of hoſts

e Iſa lxvi 23 f Lev xxiii 34 g Hoſ ix 4 John vii h Iſa lx 12 h Deut xxviii 24 i Ezek 10 † Or ſin k Iſa xxiii 18 ‡ Or bridles l Exod xxviii 36 m Iſa xxxv 8 § Joel iii 17 Rev xxi 27 & xxii 15 § Zech xiv 3 Rev xxii 3 &c

v 16—21 The deſtruction of the wicked ſhall bring a great acceſſion of converts to the church

1 A remnant, according to the election of grace, who have dwelt among the enemies of Chriſt, ſhall now be brought home to him, and with his people *go up from year to year to worſhip the King the Lord of hoſts, and to keep the feaſt of tabernacles* not that theſe Jewiſh feſtivals will be then obſerved, but Chriſt's redeemed will, with ſuch joy as they teſtified on this occaſion, commemorate his wonderful deliverance of them from the bondage of ſin and Satan, and be ceaſeleſs in their ſupplications to him that he would perfect their redemption, and bring them into the heavenly Canaan, the final and eternal reſt which remaineth for the people of God

2 Thoſe who refuſe or neglect this holy worſhip ſhall be puniſhed with famine, either, literally, for want of rain the earth ſhall give them no food, or, ſpiritually, they ſhall be deſtitute of the heavenly influences of grace, and deprived of the goſpel, given up to the curſe of barrenneſs, and periſhing in their iniquities And if Egypt, which owes its fertility to the overflowing of the Nile more than to the clouds, be found among thoſe who are culpable, her puniſhment ſhall be the ſame He, who prevents the rain from falling on others, will prevent the Nile from overflowing them, and give them the ſame curſe of barrenneſs and famine *Note*, (1) Though ſome ſinners may think their ſituation will be a protection to them from the threatned evils, they will find God's arm can as eaſily reach them as others (2) They who live in neglect of God's worſhip will ſurely die under his curſe

3 When the wicked are conſumed, the church ſhall appear glorious in the beauty of holineſs Upon the very *bells of their horſes* ſhall be engraven, as on the high-prieſt's mitre, *Holineſs to the Lord*, the people of Jeſus being an holy prieſthood, their profeſſion being public, their converſation exemplary, and in all their actions, civil as well as religious, one uniform tenor

of

Before Christ 587

of holiness will appear. *And the pots in the Lord's house*, which the priests used in their apartments, *shall be as the bowls before the altar*, consecrated to God, and employed in a holy manner, God's spiritual priests making even their common meals a sacrifice, by their prayers, thanksgiving, and gracious use of God's creatures, whether they eat or drink doing all to the glory of God. *And every pot in Jerusalem and in Judah shall be holiness unto the Lord of hosts*, consecrated to his glory, as the vessels of the sanctuary. *And all they that sacrifice shall come and take of them and seethe therein*, the ceremonial distinction between one vessel and another no longer subsisting, and the real holiness of heart and life in every member of the church rendering their offerings acceptable, through Jesus Christ, in every place. *And in that day there shall be no more the Canaanite in the house of the Lord of hosts*, the church being thoroughly purged of all the ungodly and profane. Whether this state of perfection and purity shall ever be seen in the church of Christ under the sun, many doubt, yet certain at least it is, such will be the case in that eternal world to which we are going, for *there nothing shall* ever *enter that defileth, or maketh unclean.*

Before Christ 587

THE

EVANGELICAL EXPOSITOR;

OR, A

PRACTICAL COMMENT

Upon the PROPHECY of

MALACHI.

MALACHI was probably the last of the prophets, though he gives us no date of his Prophecy, as most of the others had done. In him prophecy ceased for the space of about four hundred Years, till the appearing of the Great Prophet, who should come into the world. We have, 1. His name, Malachi, but no account of his country or parentage. Malachi signifies my angel; *which has given occasion for a conjecture, that this prophet was indeed an angel from heaven, and not a man, as that,* Judges ii. 1. *But there is no just ground for the conjecture: prophets were* messengers, *God's messengers, this prophet was so, his name is the very same with that which we find in the original,* chap. iii. 1. *for* my messenger; *and perhaps from that word he might (though probably he had another name) be called Malachi. 2. The scope of the prophecy. Haggai and Zechariah were sent to reprove the people for delaying to build the temple; Malachi was sent to reprove them for the neglect of it when it was built, and for their profanation of the temple-service; for from idolatry and superstition they run into the other extreme of impiety and irreligion; and the sins he witnesseth against are the same that we find complained of in Nehemiah's time, with whom, it is probable, he was contemporary. And now prophecy was to cease, he speaks more clearly of the Messiah as nigh at hand, than any other of the prophets had done; and concludes with a direction to the people of God, to keep in remembrance the law of Moses, while they were in expectation of the gospel of Christ.*

CHAP. I.

Before Christ [illegible]

This prophet is sent, first to convince, and then to comfort. He opens the wound, and then applies the healing balm. He reproves the Jews, 1. For their ingratitude to God, in return for the favours he had shewn them, ver. 1—5. 2. For their negligence and remissness in observing his institutions, of which the priests were particularly culpable, ver. 6—14.

1 THE burden of the word of the LORD to
Israel by ‖ Malachi. 2 [a] I have loved
you, saith the LORD. Yet ye say, Where-
in hast thou loved us? was not Esau Ja-
cob's brother? saith the LORD: yet [b] I loved Jacob,
3 And [c] I hated Esau, and laid his mountains, and his
heritage waste, for the dragons of the wilderness. 4
Whereas Edom saith, We are impoverished, [d] but we
will return and build the desolate places; thus saith the
LORD of hosts, They shall build, but I will throw
down; and they shall call them, The border of wicked-
ness, and the people against whom the LORD hath in-
dignation for ever. 5 And your eyes shall see, and ye
shall say, [e] The LORD will be magnified ‖ from the
border of Israel.

‖ i. e. My angel or messenger.
a Deut. vii. 8.
b Rom. ix. 13.
c Jer. xlix. 18. Ezek. xxxv. 9. Obad. 10, &c.
d Isa. ix. 10.
e Psal. xxxv. 27.
‖ Heb. from upon.

Ver. 1—5. The word of the Lord to Israel is called a *burden*; it contains sharp rebukes, and bound upon the impenitent a load of wrath, which would sink them into the belly of hell. The charge against Israel here advanced is their ingratitude. God asserts his love to them from the days of old. *I have loved you, saith the Lord*; but they seemed insensible of the mercy, and unaffected with it. *Yet ye say, Wherein hast thou loved us?* as if the instances of his regard were so slight and so few, that they had little or no obligations to him. To convince them of their baseness, he proves, by the distinguishing favours shewn them, the love he had towards them.

Before Christ [illegible]

1. He had preferred Jacob, though the younger brother, to Esau, and entailed upon him the covenant of promise. *Was not Esau Jacob's brother?* and, as his elder, should have succeeded to the birthright; but God, who acts according to the counsel of his own will, had been pleased, to shew his sovereignty, to chuse the younger, and reject the first-born. *Yet I loved Jacob*, chose him when yet unborn, not only to be the father of God's peculiar people, but personally, as an elect vessel: *and I hated Esau*, so far at least as to deprive him of the birthright and blessing; and, left destitute of divine grace, his profaneness fitted him as a vessel of wrath for destruction.

2. Their posterity were deeply affected by this original difference God had made between their great progenitors. *I laid his mountains and his heritage waste for the dragons of the wilderness*, as was done by the Chaldeans: and though Judea was also desolated by them, yet there was a distinguishing difference, the ruin of the one were for a while only, of the other, perpetual. For though the Idumites attempt to repair their breaches, God will disappoint their endeavours. *They shall build, but I will throw down.* God was against them, and who ever

hardened

Before Christ 400.

hardened their hearts against him, and prospered? *and they shall call them the border of wickedness*, their sins shall be notorious, and read in their sufferings; *the people against whom the Lord hath indignation for ever.* God's people provoke him, and he visits their iniquities with a rod; but his enemies provoke him, and their scourge is a scorpion, and his wrath against them is for ever wrath to come. *And your eyes shall see* the desolations of Edom, and the distinction made between them and Israel, *and ye shall say, The Lord will be magnified from the border of Israel*; he intends his own glory in these distinguishing mercies shewn them, and justly deserves and demands their praises; not to have offered them must prove their base ingratitude.

f Ex. xx. 12. Eph. vi. 2. g Luke vi. 46. h Hos. v. 1. i Hos. xii. 8.

6 ¶ f A son honoureth *his* father, and a servant his
master: g if then I *be* a father, where *is* mine honour?
and if I *be* a master, where *is* my fear? saith the LORD
of hosts unto you, h O priests, that despise my name?
and ye say, i Wherein have we despised thy name? 7
Ye offer polluted bread upon mine altar; and ye say,
Wherein have we polluted thee? In that ye say, The
table of the LORD *is* contemptible. 8 And k if ye
offer the blind for sacrifice, *is it* not evil? and if ye
offer the lame and sick, *is it* not evil? offer it now
unto thy governor; will he be pleased with thee, or ac-
cept thy person? saith the LORD of hosts. 9 And
now l I pray you, beseech God that he will be gracious
unto us: this hath been by your means: m will he regard
your persons? saith the LORD of hosts. 10 Who
is there even among you that would shut the doors *for
nought*? neither do ye kindle *fire* on mine altar for nought.
n I have no pleasure in you, saith the LORD of hosts,
neither will I accept an offering at your hand. 11 For
from the rising of the sun even unto the going down of
the same, my name *shall be* great among the Gentiles,
and p in every place q incense *shall be* offered unto my
name, and a pure offering: for r my name *shall be* great
among the heathen, saith the LORD of hosts. 12 ¶
But ye have profaned it, in that ye say, The table of the
LORD *is* s polluted; and the fruit thereof, *even* his
meat *is* contemptible. 13 Ye said also, Behold, t what
a weariness *is it*! and ye have snuffed at it, saith the
LORD of hosts; and u ye brought *that which was* torn,
and the lame, and the sick; thus ye brought an offer-
ing: should I accept this of your hands? saith the
LORD. 14 But cursed *be* x the deceiver, which hath
in his flock a male, and voweth and sacrificeth unto the
LORD a corrupt thing: for y I *am* a great King, saith
the LORD of hosts, and my name *is* dreadful among
the heathen.

k Lev. xxii. 22. Deut. xv. 21. Ver. 14. l Isa. xlvi. 12. m 1 Sam. ii. 30. n Isa. i. 11. Jer. vi. 20. Amos v. 21. o Ps. cxiii. 3. Isa. lix. 19. p John iv. 21. 1 Tim. ii. 8. q Rev. viii. 3. r Isa. lxvi. 19, 20. s Dan. v. 3, 4. t Amos viii. 5. u Ver. 8. x Acts v. 1, 2. Ver. 8. y Ps. xlvii. 2. 1 Tim. vi. 15.

v. 6—14. The bad example of the priests being of most pernicious consequence to the people, God sends to them a severe rebuke.

1. God tells them what he might justly have expected from them. *A son honoureth his father, and a servant his master*; at least, all admit that this ought to be, and they are accounted, unnatural, undutiful, and wicked, who act otherwise. *If then I be a father, where is mine honour? and if I be a master, where is my fear?* If reverence, respect, and fear be paid to an earthly parent or master, how much more due are they to our Father and Master in heaven? and to rob him of this his honour, how much more criminal?

2. He charges them with the insolent contempt with which they had treated him. *They despised his name*, paid no regard to his honour, and neglected his worship and service, *and profaned it*, *v.* 12. by their irreverent use of it, and perverting it to serve their own pride, covetousness, and luxury, bringing the highest reproach upon it by their whole conduct; for nothing so deeply dishonours God, as the bad lives of those who call themselves his ministers. And yet with daring effrontery they deny the charge. *Ye say, Wherein have we despised thee?* either they were so *ignorant* of the divine law, as to think they had observed it, or so *atheistical*, as to imagine God could not detect them. Thus hardened sinners justify themselves in evil, and say, like the adulteress, *I have done no wickedness*; but God will reprove them, and set in order the things they have done.

(1.) *Ye offer polluted bread upon mine altar*; either the shew-bread, or the meat offering, which accompanied the daily sacrifice, was made of the refuse of the wheat, or of flower damaged and unfit for use: *and yet ye say, Wherein have we polluted thee?* as if there was no harm in what they had done; and this attempt to vindicate themselves was an aggravation of their sin.

(2.) *Ye say, The table of the Lord is contemptible*; perhaps not publicly, but among themselves, they treated the divine institutions with ridicule; and though it was for their interest to keep up the form of religion, they talked of it as a mere juggle, designed to keep the vulgar in awe: or if they said not so much, their conduct spoke aloud their sentiments. They paid no veneration to the sanctuary, or its ordinances. *Ye say, The table of the Lord is polluted, and the fruit thereof, even his meat, is contemptible*; as if it was no better than any other table: their own were better served than his; and the fat and the blood, which were the Lord's portion, were in their eyes contemptible, and very little deserving so many laws concerning them.

(3.) They offered the blind and the lame, *v.* 8. and the torn and the sick, *v.* 13. for sacrifices to God, such as they would not have dared to have presented to their governor, because he would have esteemed it an affront. And is *not* this *evil*? contrary to God's express command, and a designed insult. *Note*, They who think God will be satisfied with careless, cold, negligent, hasty prayers, the labour of the lips or the book, when all the life of devotion, of faith and love is wanting, are but offering the blind and lame for sacrifice, and their services will be accounted but an abomination.

(4.) They were perfectly mercenaries, and served merely for hire. They would not shut a door of the temple, nor kindle a fire there, unless they were well paid: the work of the sanctuary was no delight to them, the wages was all they looked at. *Note*, Though God would have us live by the altar we serve, yet to have an eye to this, as the inducement to undertake the ministry, is in God's sight most abominable, and such hirelings will be abhorred and disowned by the great *Bishop of souls*.

(5.) The service they were obliged to be employed in was *a weariness* to them. They were always complaining of the *hard duty*, *v.* 13. to be so constant in attendance on the temple, so strict in the observance of the forms and ordinances prescribed, they thought quite tiresome, and *snuffed at it* with discontent and reluctance, dragging themselves to the task, and hurrying it over as fast as possible. Would to God these had been the only ministers of the sanctuary on whom these things were chargeable.

3. He expostulates with them on this conduct of theirs. *Should I accept this at your hands?* can such sacrifices and services be pleasing? No, saith God, *I have no pleasure in you, neither will I accept an offering at your hands*, since they had made themselves vile; and *this* had been by *their means*, with their connivance and encouragement, that such despicable sacrifices were offered. *Shall I regard your persons? saith the Lord of hosts*. It was impossible he should, and therefore their prayers, which the prophet ironically calls them to offer, *v.* 9. must needs be unavailing and rejected. *Note*, If our persons are not accepted of God through the blood of atonement, all our prayers must needs be fruitless.

Some understand *v.* 9. as containing a serious exhortation to the priests, who had been the chief authors of all the evil, to repent of their sins, and cry to God for mercy on the behalf of themselves and the people, and not to flatter them with vain hopes, that God accepted their persons more than others, seeing the holiness of their office aggravated their sins, and would increase their punishment.

4. Since they thus dishonoured God, he will glorify himself, rejecting them, and turning to the Gentiles, setting up his church *from the rising of the sun even unto the going down of the same*. *My name*, saith he, *shall be great among the Gentiles*; they shall render him that glory of which Israel had robbed him: *and in every place incense shall be offered to my name*, the incense of prayer and praise, arising from all the worshipping assemblies of true believers, who are consecrated spiritual priests, to offer spiritual sacrifices acceptable to God through Jesus Christ, *and a pure offering*, even themselves, their bodies, souls, and spirits, a living sacrifice; *for my name shall be great among the heathen*: it is repeated to assure them of the certainty of the event, and that when the time came that the Gentiles should be fellow-heirs, and of the same body, they might remember that the mouth of the Lord had spoken it.

5. A curse is pronounced on these careless and wicked priests, and on all others who are deceivers like them. *Cursed be the deceiver, which hath in his flock a male, and voweth and sacrificeth unto the Lord a corrupt thing*. Though they might think thus to satisfy their consciences, and the corrupt priests, indulgent of their faults, flattered them it would be accepted, they were both deceivers and deceived. God is not to be thus mocked; they would put a cheat upon him, but in fact deceived themselves, and brought wrath upon their souls. He will be served with the best, or not at all: to attempt to put him off with the refuse, is increasing our provocation; *For I am a great King, saith the Lord of hosts*, and therefore to be honoured according to his excellent greatness; *and my name is dreadful among the heathen*, the judgments he had executed upon them made it so, and their more provoking wickedness would bring down still heavier vengeance upon their head.

Before Christ 400

CHAP II

Further charges are here laid against the priests 1 *They profaned the ordinance of the ministry, their sin is aggravated, and they are severely threatened for it,* ver 1, 9 2 *The ordinance of marriage was profaned both by priests and people, in marrying strangers,* ver 10, 12 *treating their wives unkindly,* ver 13 *putting them away,* ver 16 *and herein dealing treacherously,* ver 10, 14, 15 *And that which was at the bottom of this, and other instances of profaneness, was downright atheism, thinking God altogether such a one as themselves, which was in effect to say, there is no God,* ver 17 *And these reproofs to them are warnings to us*

1 AND now, [a] O ye priests, this commandment *is*
for you 2 [b] If ye will not hear, and if ye will
not lay *it* to heart, to [c] give glory unto my name, saith
the LORD of hosts, I will even send a curse upon
you, and I will curse your blessings yea, I have cursed
them already, because ye do not lay *it* to heart 3 Be-
hold, [d] I will corrupt your seed, [e] and spread dung upon
your faces, *even* the dung of your solemn feasts, and
† *one* shall take you away with it 4 And ye shall know
that I have sent this commandment unto you, that my
covenant might be with Levi, saith the LORD of hosts
5 [f] My covenant was with him of life and peace, and I
gave them to him ‡ *for* [g] the fear wherewith he feared
me, and was afraid before my name 6 [h] The law of
truth was in his mouth, and [i] iniquity was not found in
his lips he walked with me in peace and equity, and
did [k] turn many away from iniquity 7 For the priests
lips should keep knowledge, and they should seek the
law at his mouth for [m] he *is* the messenger of the
LORD of hosts. 8 But ye are departed out of the
way ye [n] have caused many to § stumble at the law
[o] ye have corrupted the covenant of Levi, saith the
LORD of hosts 9 [p] Therefore have I also made you
contemptible and base before all the people, according
as ye have not kept my ways, but have ‖ been partial
in the law

[a] Chap i 6 [b] Lev xxvi 14 &c Deut xxviii 15 &c [c] Josh vii 19 [d] Acts xi 28 [e] 1 Sam ii 30 † Or, it shall take you away to it [f] Num xxv 12 ‡ Or, and [g] Ex xxxii 26 Num xxv 11 Deut xxxiii 8, 9 [h] Deu xxxiii 10 [i] Rev xiv 5 [k] Jer xxiii 22 Dan xii 3 [l] Lev x 11 Deut xvii 9, 10 Ezra vii 10 Jer xviii 18 Hag ii 11, 12 [m] Gal iv 14. 2 Cor v 20 [n] 1 Sam ii 17 Jer xviii 15 § Or, fall in the law [o] Neh xiii 29 [p] 1 Sam ii 30 ‖ Heb Accepted faces Mic iii 5

v 1—9 This word of God is particularly directed to the priests *And now, O ye priests, this commandment is for you*, and they were bound deeply to consider the divine rebuke here given them The prophet shews,

1 What was their *duty*, *v* 7 *The priests lips should keep knowledge*, their mind should be stored with divine wisdom, wise expositors of the law of God, ready to answer every case proposed to them, and diligent to preach and inculcate the truths of God *and they*, the people, *should seek the law at his mouth*, teachable and inquisitive, desiring to know the mind of the Lord, humble hearers, and ready to follow his will, so far as it is made known to them *for he is the messenger of the Lord of hosts*, distinguished with this high honour, and employed in this high office, to carry God's messages to men, and, as an ambassador, to transact the great concerns which belong to the eternal world Such therefore were bound by every obligation to walk worthy their high vocation and calling

2 What had been their *practice*, the very contrary to all this *But ye are departed out of the way*, in principle and practice utterly apostatized from God *ye have caused many to stumble at the law*, corrupted by their false doctrines, and emboldened by their ill examples, for nothing tends to make men infidels and libertines, so much as the wicked, careless, and worldly lives of those who pretend to be God's ministers *Ye have corrupted the covenant of Levi*; defeated the great end and intention of it, as if the priesthood, instead of being instituted in order to lead sinners to a pardoning God, and make them holy and happy, was designed merely to enrich the priests, and fatten them with the spoils of the altar *Ye have not kept my ways*, neither the commandments moral or ceremonial *but have been partial in the law*, in their observance of it, or *accepted persons in the law*, giving wrong judgments in favour of some, and to the prejudice of others

3 Their sins were greatly aggravated by the consideration of the peculiar honour God had put upon them in this covenant of priesthood established with their fathers, and by their degeneracy from their pious example. *My covenant was with Levi*, God took that tribe into a peculiar relation, to attend solely on his worship, a covenant *of life and peace*, containing a promise of long life and prosperity to themselves here, and of endless life and peace hereafter, if they proved faithful And also their ministration were intended to be *life* to the guilty sinner, whose iniquity, which called for death, should be removed by faith in the blood of the sacrifices offered, and *peace* with an offended God be restored to their troubled consciences *And I gave them* *to him*, the blessings of life and peace, *for the fear wherewith he feared me*, he rewarded the zeal of Levi, *Exod* xxxii 26 and the boldness of Phinehas, *Num* xxv 11, 12 with the settlement of the priesthood in that tribe and family Or it may be read, *I gave them to him, and the fear wherewith he feared me*, this being, as every other grace, the gift of God *and he was afraid before my name*, continuing faithful in God's service, jealous of offending, approving himself in all simplicity before him *The law of truth was in his mouth*, he always spoke according to the oracles of God, *and iniquity was not found in his lips*, he never perverted the truth to flatter the great, nor concealed what would be offensive in order to please men, but plainly, freely, and fully, in all cases declared the word of God, and, in matters of judicature, decided with strictest impartiality, without respect of persons *He walked with me in peace and equity*, his life adorned his doctrine, he was himself a man of peace, and the peace-maker among others; of unimpeached integrity, as ministers should be, an example to the flock in every good word and work *and did turn many away from iniquity*, his life gave weight to his preaching, and God bestowed success on his labours, so that they were effectual to the converting many sinners from the evil of their ways and every faithful preacher of God's word may expect to see such fruit of their ministry, when they thus walk and speak, and as the blessed issue of such a conversation, after having turned many to righteousness, will bless God in eternity for ever having heard and known them, they shall shine as the stars in the firmament for ever and ever Such godly priests as are here described had there been of old in the Jewish church, and to have been descended from, and inherited the covenant of priesthood, yet to have degenerated from their examples, and betrayed the trust delivered down to them, was the aggravated crime of that generation

Some apply this to Christ of whom indeed the Levitical priesthood was a type and figure, and in whom most eminently these things were fulfilled With him the everlasting covenant *of life and peace* was established, who is the purchaser of both for his people, and they are given into his hands to be distributed to the members of his body mystical, and he hath obtained this life and peace for them, because he *feared*, humbled himself to obey the precept, and submitted to the penalty of the law for us *In his mouth the law of truth*, the gospel of our salvation, was found, in his lips was no guile, perfectly spotless in all his conversation, and turning many from iniquity, even all who ever shall be saved

4 Judgment is denounced upon them They had already begun to feel God's displeasure, and to the uttermost it shall light upon them [1] They had begun to feel God's wrath *I have already cursed your blessings*, they had no comfort in their work, nor any enjoyment of their wages, all their temporal blessings were embittered, and nothing prospered in their hands *because ye do not lay it to heart*, to repent of your sins, and glorify God in your ministry *Therefore have I also made you contemptible*, since they had made themselves vile, God justly exposed them *before all the people*, and returned upon their own heads the contempt they had shown of his service Nor can there be conceived a more infamous and despicable character than that of a profane, wicked, and negligent priest [2] What they had felt, if they continued impenitent, was but the prelude to greater evils in store for them *If ye will not hear these warnings, and if ye will not lay it to heart, to give glory unto my name, saith the Lord of hosts*, by an immediate return to him with broken hearts, and desire of ministring henceforth to God's glory, *I will even send a curse upon you*, even that wrath which shall burn like fire *and I will curse your blessings*, their benedictions on the people shall be turned into curses, and their worldly good things be imbittered with the sense of his displeasure, or destroyed *Behold, I will corrupt your seed*, that it shall rot under the clod, and famine be the consequence, *and spread dung upon your faces, even the dung of your solemn feasts*, so far should these be from pleasing God, that he would treat them with the utmost contempt and aversion, as if the dung of the beasts they brought were cast into their faces *and one shall take you away*, either the Romans, or any other person would count them fit only for the dunghil, or the devil, the sinner's tormentor, shall seize them, and drag them with him into the pit of destruction *Note*, (1) They who rest on the external performances of religion, so far from pleasing God, will find that their dependance on these will render them abominable in his sight (2) The day is coming, when God will take away all the wicked from the earth, and deliver them over to the tormentor

10 [q] Have we not all one father? [r] hath not one God
created us? why do we [s] deal treacherously every man
against his brother, by profaning the covenant of our
fathers? 11 ¶ Judah hath dealt treacherously, and
an abomination is committed in Israel and in Jerusalem
for Judah hath profaned [t] the holiness of the LORD
which he loved, and [u] hath married the daughter of a
strange god 12 The LORD will cut off the man

[q] 1 Cor viii 6 Eph iv 6 [r] Job xxxi 15 [s] Jer ix 4 ... [t] Ezr ix 2 ... Jer ii 3 ... Acts ... [u] Ezra x 2 Neh xiii 23

Before Christ 400.

that doth this † the master and the scholar out of the
tabernacles of Jacob, [x] and him that offereth an offering
unto the LORD of hosts. 13 And [y] this have ye
done ‡ again, [z] covering the altar of the LORD with
tears, with weeping, and with crying out, insomuch
that he regardeth not the offering any more, or re-
ceiveth *it* with good will at your hand. 14 ¶ Yet ye
say, Wherefore? Because the LORD hath been witness
between thee and [a] the wife of thy youth, against whom
thou hast dealt treacherously: [b] yet *is* she thy compa-
nion, and the wife of thy covenant. 15 And [c] did he
not make one? yet had he the residue of the Spirit.
and wherefore one? that he might seek [d] a § godly seed.
therefore take heed to your spirit, and let none deal
treacherously against the wife of his youth. 16 For
[e] the LORD the God of Israel saith, ‖ that he hateth
putting away: for *one* covereth violence with his gar-
ment, saith the LORD of hosts: therefore take heed to
your spirit, that you deal not treacherously. 17 ¶ [f] Ye
have wearied the LORD with your words: yet ye say,
Wherein have we wearied *him*? When ye say, Every
one that doth evil, *is* good in the sight of the LORD,
and he delighteth in them; or, [g] where *is* the God of
judgment?

† Or, him that waketh, and him that answereth. x Neh. xiii. 28. y Ezra x. 2. ‡ Or, in the second place. z 1 Sam. i. 6, 10. a Prov. v. 18. b Prov. ii. 17. c Mat. xix. 4. d Ezra ix. 2. 1 Cor. vii. 14. § Heb. A seed of God. e Deut. xxiv. 1. Mat. v. 31. & xix. 9. ‖ Or, if he hate her, put her away. f Isa. xliii. 24. Chap. iii. 13, &c. g [illegible]

v. 10—17. As corrupt principles naturally lead to corrupt practices, so on the other hand, the love of sin, and the service of it, harden the heart in infidelity and atheism.

1. Their practices were very bad. In general they *dealt treacherously every man against his brother*, perverting justice, and having respect to persons, and in all their dealings full of dishonesty; thus *profaning the covenant of their fathers*, wherein such injustice and fraud were forbidden, and which was peculiarly criminal in them, who had *one father*, were brethren in a peculiar sense, as sprung from Abraham, and *one God* their Creator, not merely as men, but who had formed them in a covenant of peculiarity as a people for himself. But of all their other treacherous dealings, that which especially is here brought to account, is their violation of God's covenant with regard to their marriages, both taking wives of the heathen, which had been so expressly forbidden, *Exod.* xxxiv. 15. and abusing and divorcing those of their own nation.

(1.) They took wives of the heathen, called here, *the daughters of a strange god*, trained in their worship and service, as a child in the family, and this was *to profane the holiness of the Lord which he loved*. They were set apart for a peculiar people, dedicated to God, and to be observant of his holy law, and he then loved and delighted in them, when they approved their fidelity to him; but by these strange marriages they *profaned* their covenant of separation, and became an *abomination* in the sight of God, *v.* 11. for which he threatens *to cut them off*, both *master and scholar*, or, as in the margin, *both him that waketh*, the magistrates and elders, whose office it was to call and excite the people to their duty; *and him that answereth*, the people in general, who should be obedient to their admonitions, as a servant to his master's call. These God will destroy together, *and him that offereth an offering unto the Lord of hosts*, the priests who should be found guilty of the like crime, as many of them were, *Ezra* x. 18, 44. *Note*, (1.) They who profess the faith of Jesus, should no more be yoked now with unbelievers, than these with the *daughters of a strange god*; and ministers especially should shun so unequal a connection. (2.) Nothing more fatally endangers the soul, and exposes it to everlasting perdition, than rashly taking those to be our wives or husbands, who are dead in trespasses and sin. The daughter of a strange god will much sooner make a convert of her husband to idolatry, to the ways of sin and this world, than he can ever hope to bring her to the knowledge and worship of Jesus.

(2.) *This have ye done again*, or in *the second place*, abused and divorced the wives of their own nation, probably to make room for their foreigners, so that they *covered the altar of the Lord with tears, with weeping, and with crying*, complaining of the ill usage of their husbands: *insomuch that he regardeth not the offering any more, or receiveth it with good will at your hand*. These tears stood on the altar as a memorial against them, and all their offerings were but hypocritical, whilst they persisted in such wickedness. *Yet ye say, Wherefore?* why should not God accept our offerings? The reason is obvious, *because the Lord hath been witness* of those plighted vows which were exchanged *between thee and the wife of thy youth, against whom thou hast dealt treacherously*, divorcing her, or marrying others to vex her; and he will be an awful avenger of this breach of contract, aggravated as the sin is by various considerations. She is a *wife of youth*; placed her affections upon thee in those best days of youth and beauty, and therefore not afterwards to be neglected or abhorred. *She is thy companion*, hath been the partner of all thy cares and griefs, and borne an equal share in them: *and the wife of thy covenant*, bound to her by every sacred tie, till death shall part; and therefore it would be most cruel, base, ungrateful, and unjust, to treat her with falshood, or break the marriage-bond. *And did not he make one?* When the great Creator formed us, did it not evidently appear, that he intended one man should have but one wife, in the case of our first parents; *yet had he the residue of the Spirit*, and could as easily have formed many Eves as one. *And wherefore one?* The reason is, *that he might seek a godly seed*, or *a seed of God*, a noble and legitimate offspring, a seed to serve him, which is the great end of marriage; not to gratify men's lawless lusts and appetites, but to beget children, who may be brought up in the nurture and admonition of the Lord. *Therefore take heed to your spirit*, keep your hearts, keep your eye, keep every wandering desire in subjection, which would lead you after forbidden objects: *and let none deal treacherously with the wife of his youth*, but be constant, faithful, affectionate, and cleave to her alone: *for the Lord the God of Israel saith, that he hateth putting away*; and though permitted for the hardness of their hearts, to prevent worse consequences, it was displeasing to God, and contrary to his original institution; and therefore the author of such separation will be abhorred of God. *For one covereth violence with his garment*, and thinks, by pretending the permission of the law, he can cover the violence done his wife by the divorce; or he grieves, vexes, and ill uses her in private, and in public casts his garment over her, as if he would protect and cherish her; but God sees, and will punish the unfaithful. *Therefore take heed to your spirit, that you deal not treacherously*; and great need there is that we, whose hearts are by nature so corrupt, should take heed to them; especially in this estate we need watch against every alienation of affection and unkindness, for if but once a breach be made, the mischief is often afterwards irreparable.

2. Their principles were corrupt, and their words corresponded with their works. *Ye have wearied the Lord with your words*, speaking perversely, and vindicating themselves in their wickedness, which was highly provoking. *Yet ye say, Wherein have we wearied him?* denying the charge, and maintaining their innocence, which aggravated their crime. *When ye say, Every one that doth evil is good in the sight of the Lord, and he delighteth in them*; observing the prosperity of the wicked, they concluded God approved and rewarded him, which cast the most blasphemous imputation on the holiness of God. *Or where is the God of judgment?* why doth he not appear to punish sin as he hath threatned? They infer from his patience, that he hath forsaken the earth, and that let men live as they list, they have nothing to fear. Such infidel scoffers there were of old, that said, *Where is the promise of his coming?* and such there still are, who put far away the evil day, and say, *Tush, God careth not for it*; but they will be terribly undeceived when this God of judgment shortly appears to punish ungodly sinners, among their other crimes, *for all the hard speeches they have spoken against him*, Jude 15.

CHAP. III.

In this chapter we have, 1. A promise of the coming of the Messiah, and of his forerunner, who will speak comfort to his church and people, and terror to the wicked, ver. 1—6. 2. A reproof of the Jews for corrupting God's ordinances, and sacrilegiously robbing him of his dues; with a charge to them to amend this matter, and a promise, that if they did, God would return in mercy to them, ver. 7—12. 3. A description of the wickedness of the wicked that speak against God, ver. 13—15. And of the righteousness of the righteous that speak for him, with the precious promises made to them, ver. 16—18.

1 BEhold, [a] I will send my messenger, and he shall
[b] prepare the way before me: and the LORD
whom ye seek, shall suddenly [c] come to his [d] temple,
[e] even † the messenger of the covenant, whom ye delight
in: behold, he shall come, saith the LORD of hosts.
2 But who may abide [f] the day of his coming? and
who shall stand when he appeareth? for [g] he *is* like a
refiner's fire, and like fullers sope. 3 And [h] he shall sit
as a refiner and purifier of silver: and he shall purify
the sons of Levi, and purge them as gold and silver,
that they may offer unto the LORD an offering in
righteousness. 4 Then shall [i] the offering of Judah
and Jerusalem be pleasant unto the LORD, as in the
days of old, and as in ‡ former years. 5 And [k] I will
come near to you to judgment, and I will be a swift wit-
ness against the sorcerers, and against the adulterers, [l] and
against false swearers, and against those that § oppress
the hireling in *his* wages, the widow and the fatherless,
and that turn aside the stranger *from his right*, and fear
not me, saith the Lord of hosts. 6 For I *am* the LORD,

a Mat. xi. 10. Mar. i. 2. Luke i. 76. & vii. 27. b Isa. xl. 3. c Mat. xxi. 12. d [illegible] e Isa. lxiii. 9. † Or, the prince. Dan. ix. 25. f Chap. iv. 1. Rev. vi. 16, 17. g Isa. iv. 4. Mat. iii. 11, 12. h Isa. [illegible] i Chap. i. 11. Heb. xiii. 15. ‡ Or, ancient. k 2 Thess. i. 7, 8. l Jam. v. 4, 12. § Or, defraud.

I change

Before Christ 400

[m] I change not [n] therefore ye sons of Jacob are not
consumed

m Num xxiii 19 Rom xi 29 Jam i 17
n Lam iii 22, 23

v 1—5 If the words of the conclusion of the foregoing chapter be considered, as they are by some, as the scoff of the infidel, who, because the Messiah's appearing was long delayed, concluded he would never come, the opening of this chapter contains a full answer to such a suggestion

1 The harbinger of the Messiah approaches *Behold, I will send my messenger, and he shall prepare the way before me* Of whom this is spoken we can not be in doubt, *Mat* xi 10 *Mark* i 2 John the Baptist being sent to point out the Lamb of God, and, by preaching repentance, to lead them to him who alone can give remission of sins

2 The Lord of life and glory shall immediately follow his herald and forerunner *The Lord, whom ye seek*, the long-expected Messiah, to whom the eyes of Israel were directed, *shall suddenly come to his temple*, and by his presence fulfil the prophecy of Haggai, putting the most distinguished honour on that holy place *Even the messenger of the covenant* of grace, who, as the great prophet sent from God, publishes and explains the tenor of that covenant more clearly and distinctly than it was ever done before, *whom ye delight in*, they in general pleased themselves with the expectation of him, though they entirely mistook the nature of his office, but many there were also among them, who waited for him as a spiritual Messiah, coming to save his people from their sins *He shall come, saith the Lord of hosts*, whose promise is faithful, and the accomplishment of it, in the fulness of time, sure

3 The great end of his coming is declared Many wished for his appearing, who little understood the design of it, therefore is the question asked, *But who may abide the day of his coming?* who will be able to bear the doctrine he advances, concerning his own deity, the purpose of his coming to die for sinners, the nature of his kingdom, &c or his sharp and piercing rebukes against the characters of the men of that generation, held in highest admiration, *and who shall stand when he appeareth?* before the piercing energy of his word, which intimates how few would be able to endure or receive the truths he taught *for he is like a refiner's fire*, by his word separating the precious from the vile, distinguishing the true sense of God's word from the adulterating glosses of the scribes, and purifying his own people who received him, whilst the wicked, who rejected him, are cast away as dross *and like fullers soap*, which cleanses the garment from spots, so shall he cleanse his people from their sins

Some shall be happy partakers of his grace On them *he shall sit as a refiner and purifier of silver*, by the various methods he uses, he will purge away the dross of guilt and corruption from their souls, sitting by, to see every means of grace made effectual, and every providence sanctified, never putting them in any furnace of affliction or temptation, but he himself regulates the fire, and takes care they shall be in it no longer, nor feel it fiercer, than he will enable them to bear, and shall ultimately be for their good *And he shall purify the sons of Levi*, not merely those Jews who were of that family, or the apostles and ministers of the gospel but all his people, who are consecrated to be priests unto God, and, by the imputation of his blood and righteousness, are prepared to stand before God without spot or blemish *and purge them as gold and silver, that they may offer unto the Lord an offering in righteousness*, even themselves a living sacrifice, and the well-pleasing oblation of prayer and praise, and all their works and labours of love, accepted now in Jesus Christ *Then shall the offering of Judah and Jerusalem be pleasant unto the Lord, as in the days of old, and as in former years*, like the offering of Abel, the sacrifice of Abraham, or the burnt-offering of Aaron, which the heavenly fire devoured Justified by the blood and righteousness, and sanctified by the Spirit of Jesus, all the services of his people shall be a sweet-smelling savour

To some to judgment he will come into the world, a savour of death unto them, as of life unto others Their characters are declared they are *sorcerers*, who used enchantment and divination, *adulterers*, wallowing in the lusts of uncleanness, *false swearers*, who profaned God's name, and called him to witness to a lie, *oppressors of the hireling*, defrauding him of his wages, *of the widow and fatherless*, taking advantage of their helplessness to plunder and devour them, *and turn aside the stranger from his right*, because ignorant of the law, or through the partiality of the judges *and*, worst of all, they *fear not me, saith the Lord of hosts*, nor obey his gospel For all which things Christ threatens to be a swift witness against them, and will bring their sins to light, however secretly committed, and execute just judgment in consequence upon them, and that quickly, as he did, shortly after his appearing in the flesh, in the destruction of Jerusalem, and as he will do in the great day of perdition of all the ungodly

4 He ratifies the immutable purpose of his word *I am the Lord*, Jehovah, self-existent, self-sufficient, able to save or destroy to the uttermost *I change not*, his decrees of wrath against the impenitent will never alter to eternity, and his promises of mercy to his people never fail *therefore ye sons of Jacob are not consumed*, as he had hitherto kept them as a people, in virtue of the covenant of peculiarity which subsisted notwithstanding their provocations, much more shall the spiritual sons of Jacob, in consequence of the everlasting covenant of grace, be preserved, and every child of God, through the unchangeable love of God, be kept from perishing eternally not one of them shall be lost

Before Christ 400

7 ¶ Even [o] from the days of your fathers ye are
gone away from mine ordinances, and have not kept
them [p] return unto me, and I will return unto you,
saith the LORD of hosts but [q] ye said, Wherein
shall we return? 8 ¶ Will a man rob † God? yet
ye have robbed me, but ye say, Wherein have we
robbed thee? [r] In tithes and offerings 9 Ye *are* cursed
with a curse for ye have robbed me, *even* this whole
nation 10 [s] Bring ye all the tithes into [t] the store
house, that there may be meat in mine house, and prove
me now herewith, saith the LORD of hosts, if I will
not open you [t] the windows of heaven, and [u] pour you
out a blessing, [x] that *there shall* not *be room* enough *to*
receive it 11 And I will rebuke the devourer for
your sakes, and he shall not destroy the fruits of your
ground, neither shall your vine cast her fruits be
fore the time in the field, saith the LORD of
hosts 12 And all nations shall call [y] you blessed
for ye shall be a delightsome land, saith the LORD
of hosts

o Acts vii 51
p Zech i 3
q Rom x 21
† Or the gods Gen xlv 22
r Neh xiii 10.
s Prov iii 9, 10
t 1 Chron xxvi 20 Neh x 38 &c xiii 12
t Gen vii 11 2 Kings vii 2
u 2 Chron xxxi 10
x ...
y Deut xxviii 3

v 7—12 We have here,

1 The charge drawn up against the Jewish people, of long-continued iniquities From *the days of their fathers* the apostacy began, they had forsaken *God's ordinances*, and had *not kept them*, yet he, patient and gracious, invited them to return, with the kindest assurances of forgiveness and acceptance *Return unto me, and I will return unto you*, but they, instead of obeying, in the pride and stubbornness of their hearts replied, *Wherein shall we return?* as if they had done nothing amiss, and needed no repentance, or were displeased at the gracious invitation, because it implied a rebuke God therefore lays their crimes to their conscience *Will a man rob God?* or *the gods*, even a heathen would not act thus towards his idols or *the judges*, none could think with impunity thus to treat a magistrate, how daring the attempt then, and how insolent the provocation, to rob God of his honour, glory, and service, as they had done, *yet ye have robbed me* *Note*, Robbers of God are the worst of robbers All they persist in maintaining their innocence, and impudently challenge him to prove the accusation *Wherein have we robbed thee?* The proof is evident, *in tithes and offerings* they robbed God's altar of his due, and his ministers of their maintenance, making no conscience or defrauding them of their appointed portion, or giving them the worst, when the best should have been brought, as if the blind and lame were good enough for an offering This was the sin of *the whole nation*, and the universality of the crime was an aggravation of it, therefore *ye are cursed with a curse*, with barrenness, want, and locusts which devoured their labours So little is got by robbing God, for they who think they shall grow the richer by their fraudulent dealings with God's priests will find the curse of God, like a canker-worm, devouring their substance

2 They are warned to amend their ways And the gracious invitation still abides the same, *Return unto me, and I will return unto you* And they would find themselves abundant gainers by rendering to him his due, *Bring ye all the tithes into the store house*, all, conscientiously scrupulous that nothing in quantity or quality be kept back *that there may be meat in my house* for God's altar should be served before our own tables and the support of his worship and service should be dearer to us, than any secular concern more immediately our own, and such honesty will be found the best policy as it will procure God's blessing *And prove me now herewith, saith the Lord of hosts*, if they should not find abundantly their advantage in so doing They who dare trust God, will be convinced by experience, that their dues paid to the altar, or their charity to the poor, shall never impoverish but enrich them Prove me, *if I will not open you the windows of heaven*, which had been shut up, and send the needful refreshing rain, *and pour you out a blessing*, such abundant fruitfulness, and plenty of all good things *so that ye shall not be sufficient*, there shall be more than there are hands to reap and gather, barns to fill, or vessels to receive *and I will rebuke the devourer for your sake*, the locust and caterpillar shall no more *destroy the fruit of your ground*, *neither shall the vine*, through drought, blasting, or hurricane, *cast her fruits before the time in the field* *And all nations*, who before reproached them with their want and poverty, *shall call you blessed*, beholding the evident care and kindness of God toward them, *for ye shall be a delightsome land, saith the Lord of hosts*,

Before Christ 400.

hosts, where plenty reigns, and over which God continually watches with his peculiar love and favour, and these indeed make the *truly delightſome land*

13 ¶ [a] Your words have been [a] ſtout againſt me, ſaith
the LORD yet ye ſay, What have we ſpoken *ſo much*
againſt thee? 14 Ye have ſaid, It *is* vain to ſerve
God and what profit *is it*, that we have kept his ordi-
nance, and that we have walked † mournfully before
the LORD of hoſts? 15 ‡ And now [b] we call the
proud happy ‖ yea, [c] they that work wickedneſs are §
ſet up, yea, [d] *they that* tempt God, are even delivered.
16 ¶ Then they that feared the LORD, [e] ſpake often
one to another, and [f] the LORD hearkned, and heard
it, and [g] a book of remembrance was written before him
for them that feared the LORD, and that thought upon
his name 17 And [h] they ſhall be mine, ſaith the
LORD of hoſts, in that day when I make up [i] my †
jewels, and [k] I will ſpare them as a man ſpareth his own
ſon that ſerveth him 18 Then ſhall ye ‡ return, [l] and
diſcern between the righteous and the wicked; between
him that ſerveth God, and him that ſerveth him not

[a] Chap. ii. 17. [a] Job xxi. 14, 15. Zeph. i. 12. † Heb. In black. ‡ Or therefore now, &c. [b] Chap. ii. 17. ‖ Or ſeeing, or becauſe. [c] Pſ. xii. 8. § Heb. Built. [d] Pſ. lxxiii. 12. [e] Pſ. lxvi. 16. Heb. iii. 13. [f] Pſ. cxxxix. 4. [g] Pſ. lvi. 8. [h] Exod. xix. 5. Pſ. cxxxv. 4. Tit. ii. 14. [i] Iſa. lxii. 3. † Or ſpecial treaſure. [k] Pſ. ciii. 13. ‡ Or be converted. [l] Ps. i. 3. Dan. xii. 2.

v. 13—18 The eyes of the Lord are in every place, beholding the evil and the good He obſerves the characters of men, and they will be puniſhed or rewarded accordingly

1 He obſerved among the Jews ſome who, with daring inſolence, arraigned the diſpenſations of his providence and grace, and revolted from his worſhip and ordinances *Your words have been ſtout againſt me, ſaith the Lord yet ye ſay, what have we ſpoken ſo much againſt thee?* as if they had been clear from blame, or ſ[illegible] an inadvertent word had dropped from them, it was not a matter that deſerved ſuch ſharp admonition So ready are ſinners to extenuate their faults, and becauſe they have no ſenſe of the evil of ſin themſelves, they think God ſevere in his rebukes, yet ſurely they had provoked him moſt highly *Ye have ſaid, it is vain to ſerve God*, ſince there is nothing to be got by his ſervice, but the wicked often fare better than the righteous, *and what profit is it that we have kept his ordinance*, except in the [illegible] [illegible]tion of his worſhip and ceremonies, *and that we have walked mournfully before the Lord of hoſts*, in the habit of penitents Perhaps reference is here had to the Sadducees, who denied a future ſtate, and the Phariſees, who, though rigidly ſcrupulous in the form of godlineſs, did it merely for worldly ends, and looked upon it as a burdenſome taſk But their evil report will be confuted by the experience of every gracious ſoul, who will find God's ways both pleaſant and profitable, and count God's ſervice perfect freedom, and its own reward *And now we call the proud happy*, they judged of happineſs by outward wealth and ſplendor, and ſince *they that work wickedneſs are ſet up, yea, they that tempt God are delivered*, for ſuch they beheld who proſpered in iniquity, and though their preſumptuous ſins ſeemed to cry for vengeance, no evil came upon them, therefore they were ready to conclude, that there was neither a providence here, nor a judgment to come, and that thoſe were the happieſt who gratified every deſire of the fleſh and of the mind And theſe were the hard ſpeeches God heard, which he will confute and confound when the wrath, which purſues the moſt proſperous ſinner, ſhall quickly overtake him

2 He heard with pleaſure the gracious converſation of a remnant who feared and ſerved him We have,

[1] Their character (1) *They feared the Lord*, reverenced his authority, ſubmitted to his providential will without murmuring, were jealous of offending, and perſevered with conſtancy in his holy worſhip and ways (2) *They thought upon his name*, remembered him, his word, his promiſes, and meditated thereon, ſupporting their faith in theſe trying days, with the conſideration of his adorable perfections, maintaining ſtill their communion with him (3) *They ſpake often one to another*, the more iniquity abounded, the more they ſtirred each other up to love and to good works, whilſt others ſpake ſo much againſt God, they made bold profeſſion of his religion, and encouraged each other with zeal to appear in his cauſe, when their neighbours had renounced all religious worſhip and converſation, they aſſembled to talk of God's goodneſs, and to unite in prayer and praiſe at a throne of grace May we, who live in theſe ungodly days, be enabled to go and do likewiſe

[2] The honour God put upon them (1) *The Lord hearkened and heard it*, was preſent in their private aſſemblies, and where two or three met together for theſe gracious purpoſes, he was in the midſt of them, teſtifying his approbation of their conduct, by the comfort, ſtrength, and encouragement he beſtowed upon them (2) *A book of remembrance was written before him*, he entered every gracious word into the records of eternity, they were indelible from his all comprehenſive mind, and treaſured up for their comfort unto the great day, when they ſhall come into remembrance, and be recompenſed at the reſurrection of the juſt (3) *They ſhall be mine, ſaith the Lord of hoſts, in that day when I make up my jewels*, delivered from the flames of Jeruſalem, in which the others fell, or in general this is ſpoken of all God's ſaints, who are *jewels* dear and precious to him, glittering with divine graces, and intended to deck the crown of the eternal King, they are *mine*, ſaith God, he hath a peculiar property in his people, and regards them as a man doth his own things, with eſpecial affection *The day* referred to, is that of the appearing of the great God and Saviour Jeſus Chriſt, who ſhall ſeparate between the precious and the vile, and when the wicked are made as the dung, the righteous ſhall ſhine forth as the ſun in the kingdom of their father he will *make them up*, collecting them together into his glorious treaſury in heaven, and there ſhall they be ever with the Lord (4) *I will ſpare them, as a man ſpareth his own ſon that ſerveth him*, they ſhall continually experience from God a father's love ſince they ſhew themſelves in ſpirit and temper his dutiful children, he will overlook their infirmities, will forgive their offences, tenderneſs ſhall ſoften all his rebukes, whilſt every feeble effort to pleaſe him, though but like the liſpings of a child, ſhall be accepted, and they ſhall be owned as the bleſſed children of their father at the laſt day (5) He will put ſuch a diſtinguiſhing difference between them and others, that all ſhall in time and eternity take knowledge of them, and own they are the bleſſed of the Lord *Then ſhall ye*, who have ſpoken ſo ſtoutly againſt the Lord, and the unprofitableneſs of his ſervice, *return*, or *be converted*, ſhall change your ſentiments and language, *and ſhall diſcern* by the ſequel, the difference God makes between the *righteous and the wicked, between him that ſerveth God, and him that ſerveth him not*, and this was evident at the deſtruction of Jeruſalem, out of which the people of God had eſcaped before the ſiege, and ſhall be abundantly manifeſt in the judgment day The real characters of men are now difficult to be diſcerned, the veil of hypocriſy, our prejudices, and the weakneſs of our underſtandings, make us often miſtake, and count them gracious whom God will diſown, and thoſe reprobate whom he hath choſen, but every man's true ſtate will then appear *the righteous* in Chriſt Jeſus, through his blood and ſpirit, who have loved and ſerved him, will then be without ſpot before the throne of God, and go with him into eternal glory, whilſt the wicked, *who lived in impenitence or hypocriſy*, ſhall be ſeen and abhorred of all, and go away into the everlaſting fire prepared for the devil and his angels Reader, *Judge nothing before the time* concerning the characters of others, but *judge thyſelf*, that thou mayeſt not be judged of the Lord

CHAP IV

We have here the proper inſtructions given us (very proper to cloſe the canon of the Old Teſtament with) 1 *Concerning the ſtate of recompence and retribution that is before us, the miſery of the wicked, and the happineſs of the righteous in that ſtate*, ver 1, 2, 3 2 *A call to be ready for it, by attention to the calls and teachings of God's word and miniſters*, ver 4—6

1 FOR behold, [a] the day cometh that ſhall burn
as an oven, and all the proud, yea, and all that
do wickedly ſhall be [b] ſtubble, and the day that cometh
ſhall burn them up, ſaith the LORD of hoſts, that
it ſhall [c] leave them neither root nor branch 2 ¶ But
unto you that fear my name, ſhall [d] the ſun of righteouſ-
neſs ariſe with [e] healing in [f] his ‖ wings, and [g] ye ſhall
go forth, and grow up as calves of the ſtall 3 And
[h] ye ſhall tread down the wicked, for they ſhall be aſhes
under the ſoles of your feet, in the day that I ſhall do
this, ſaith the LORD of hoſts

[a] Chap. iii. 2. 2 Theſ. i. 7, 8. 2 Pet. iii. 7. [b] Obad. 18. [c] Amos ii. 9. [d] Luke i. 78. Eph. v. 14. 2 Pet. i. 19. Rev. ii. 28. [e] Pſ. ciii. 3. Iſa. liii. 5. Hoſ. xiv. 4. Matt. iv. 23. [f] Pſ. cxxxix. 9. ‖ Or rays. [g] John xv. [h] Pſ. xl. 4.

v. 1—3 The coming of Chriſt here ſpoken of for the deſtruction of Jeruſalem and the wicked Jews, is the type and figure of his appearing at the laſt for the perdition of the ungodly, and the day of their final judgment, will be the day of the ſaints final recompenſe

1 The Lord Jeſus will be a conſuming fire to the wicked *Behold*, with ſurprize and terror, *the day cometh*, the evil day, which the tranſgreſſor put far away, *that ſhall burn as an oven*, when the wrath of God ſhall be revealed, and the fire be kindled around the devoted city, *and all the proud*, the ſcribes and Phariſees who rejected the Lord Jeſus, *and all that do wickedly*, the apoſtate Jewiſh people, *ſhall be as ſtubble* to the devouring flame, *and the day that cometh ſhall burn them up, ſaith the Lord of hoſts, that it ſhall leave them neither root nor branch*, the whole nation being deſtroyed, and the city and temple burnt and raſed to their foundations

Thus in the great day of the wrath of the Lamb, he ſhall be revealed from heaven in flaming fire, taking vengeance on *the proud*, the ſelf-righteous and unhumbled ſinner, who truſted for ſalvation on his own doings and duties, *and on all that do wickedly*, the careleſs and profane, who know not God and obey not his goſpel, they ſhall be veſſels of wrath fitted for deſtruction, as fuel for the flames, and caſt together into the everlaſting burnings of hell, where their worm never dies, and their fire is not quenched

Before Christ 400

2 He will be a reviving sun to his people *Unto you that fear my name, shall the sun of righteousness arise with healing in his wings*, he led his people out of Jerusalem to Pella, when it was ready to be destroyed, and more generally on all his people he thus *arises*, when first he calls them out of darkness into his marvellous light, he is their sun, the fountain of all spiritual light and life, by his bright beams they are quickened, bring forth fruit abundantly, rejoice before him, and walk in the light of truth, which leads to the mansions of glory He is the *sun of righteousness*, shining without spot himself, the author of everlasting righteousness to his people, and the powerful and effectual agent, who by his mighty working transforms them into his own image of righteousness and true holiness *in his wings*, his rays of light and grace, there is *healing*, our spiritual diseases are cured, the native darkness of the mind removed, and our sin-sick souls restored to health and strength, by the genial influences of his reviving beams And in the resurrection morn with brighter glories shall our sun appear, and shine for ever upon his redeemed people

3 In consequence of this, *ye shall go forth*, either out of Jerusalem to Pella, where the Christians found a place of refuge, or rather, ye shall go forth to walk in the light of the Lord, rejoicing in his salvation, steadily advancing in the path of grace and glory, and running with delight the way of God's commandments, *and grow up as calves of the stall*, fat and well liking, so replenished shall they be with the influences of God's spirit, and fed with the bread of life, strengthening and increasing with the increase of God *And ye shall tread down the wicked, for they shall be as ashes under the soles of your feet, in the day that I shall do this, saith the Lord of hosts*, the wicked Jews, who persecuted them, shall now be burnt with their cities, and trod into the dust Thus when the conquests of the Redeemer shall be completed, and death itself destroyed, then shall the wicked be brought low, and every foe that troubled God's saints be trodden under foot, while the triumphs of the redeemed will be everlasting, and when the smoak of the sinner's torment ascends, they will cry, Hallelujah

[i] Exod xx 3 &c [k] Deut iv 10 [l] Ps cxlvii 19

4 ¶ Remember ye [i] the law of Moses my servant,
which I commanded unto him [k] in Horeb for all Israel,
with [l] the statutes and judgments 5 ¶ Behold, I will send
you [m] Elijah the prophet, before the coming of the great
and dreadful day of the LORD 6 And [n] he shall turn
the heart of the fathers † to the children, and the heart
of the children to their fathers, lest I come and [o] smite ‡
the earth with a curse

4

Before Christ 400

[m] Mat xi 14 & xvii 12 Mark ix 11 Luke i 17 [n] Ecclus xlviii 10 † Or with [o] Mat xxiv 24 ‡ Or the land

v 4—6 The canon of the Old Testament here receives a solemn close The Jewish people are to expect no more prophets till the great forerunner of the Messiah appears, and therefore,

1 They must keep steadfast to the law and the testimony, and be guided only by God's past revealed will *Remember ye the law of my servant Moses, which I commanded unto him in Horeb, with the statutes and judgments*, moral and ceremonial, all which would have a direct tendency to lead them to Christ, for which purpose the law was their schoolmaster, and which must now be their only rule, in contradistinction to the corrupt glosses which their teachers shortly after began to put upon it *Note*, The word of God alone, exclusive of all traditions and human expositions, must be our rule, the labours of others may assist our enquiries after truth, but after all, we must call no man master, one is our master, even Christ, and he hath promised we shall be taught of him, and by prayer and meditation on his word, humbly desiring to know his mind, he will lead us in to all truth

2 They must live in the constant expectation of the Messiah, and his forerunner John the Baptist *Behold, I will send you Elijah the prophet*, one in the spirit and power of Elijah, *Luke* i 17 one in zeal, courage to rebuke sin, piety and austerity of manners resembling him, *Mat* xi 14 *before the coming of the great and terrible day of the Lord*, when, for the rejection of the true Messiah, wrath to the uttermost should be poured out upon their land, and their city and temple utterly destroyed, *Acts* ii 20 *He shall turn the heart of the fathers to the children, and the heart of the children to their fathers*, or of the fathers *with* the children, both one and the other by his preaching shall be turned to Christ, and directed to the Lamb of God, which is come to take away the sin of the world, *least I come and smite the earth with a curse*, which would be the certain consequence of their rejecting the Lord's Christ, and visibly remains upon the Jewish people to this day

THE

Evangelical Expositor:

OR, A

COMMENTARY

ON THE

NEW TESTAMENT.

WITH

PRACTICAL OBSERVATIONS.

PREFACE.

THE sum and substance of all the scriptures is Jesus Christ. Him we have seen as the great object of faith and hope proposed in the Old Testament, and the great subject of all the foregoing prophecies. In the New we behold him in the fulness of time appearing, accomplishing all the things written concerning himself, putting a period to the former shadowy and typical dispensation, and establishing that church which is to endure to the end of time.

Between these inspired writings certain books are often inserted in our Bibles, called Apocryphal, or hidden, books not only destitute of divine authority, but of any authority, and which with holy indignation a gracious spirit grieves to behold intruded between the sacred volumes of God's word, and stamped with a kind of Reverence by their situation there, though some of them are evidently infamous forgeries. Not one of them but contains evident falsehoods, and many of the stories are as absurd, ridiculous, false, and fabulous, as any of the most lying Romances, or heathen mythologies. It is to be lamented, as one of the things our pious reformers left unfinished, that these unhallowed books should still remain in our Kalendar, as first lessons for near two months of the year, among which, not to mention the ridiculously absurd and lying stories of Bel and the Dragon, or Susannah and the Elders, even in the best of them, the book of Wisdom, and the Ecclesiasticus, besides a multitude of palpable falsehoods, there are advanced many wicked and false doctrines, which a Christian cannot but regard with abhorrence, and which to hear read in the house of God, sounds still more shocking. As in the book of Wisdom, chap. iii. 13—18. where the marriage-bed is condemned as sinful, and bastards excluded from salvation. Chap. vii. 25. the Divine Logos is spoken of as a vapour. Chap. viii. 20. The transmigration of souls into good or bad bodies, according to their deserts, is intimated, with other follies and falsities, too many to be recapitulated. And in the book of Ecclesiasticus, the Divine Logos is said to be created, according to the Arian heresy, chap. xxiv. 9. Honouring parents, and giving alms, are said to make atonement for sin, chap. iii. 3—30. And chap. xii. 4, 5. the writer dissuades from helping sinners, or charitably relieving the ungodly, doctrines diametrically opposite to the most glorious truths of God's word. Besides a number of other mistakes and untruths, which justly should expunge them from a place between the two sacred volumes, and consign them at least to the shelf, among other legends of antiquity, or the libraries of heathenism. Nor need any minister of our church count himself at all bound to the use of them, because they stand in the Kalendar, nor should there be any objection to the Liturgy in general, since by the preface to the Homilies we are enjoined to consider the first lessons to be read, and to change them for any other out of the New Testament, which we shall judge more to edification, with a commendation on such diligence.

The book now before us, called the New Testament, contains,

1. The four Gospels, in which we have an account of the appearing of the Messiah's harbinger John the Baptist, with the promise of which the Old Testament closed. And shortly after Christ himself is manifested in the flesh, the history of whose life, from his miraculous conception to his death upon the cross, is contained in these four volumes: a multitude of his miracles are recorded, the sermons he preached, the doctrines he maintained, the persecutions he endured, and the fulfilment of all the prophecies concerning his incarnation, descent, the place of his nativity, the nature of his office, &c. Finally, after seeing the Saviour dying upon a cross and laid in his grave, we are told of his glorious resurrection, confirmed by incontestible evidence, and his ascension to the right hand of God, whereby he compleated the glorious work he had undertaken, and obtained eternal redemption for us.

2. The Acts of the Apostles. The book opens with an account of the ascension of our Lord, and the qualifications he shortly after bestowed on the apostles, by the gift of the Holy Ghost on the day of Pentecost, to fulfil the commission he had before given them to preach the gospel to every creature: in consequence of which we are informed they went forth spreading the gospel, working miracles, suffering a variety of persecutions, yet seeing the success of their labours in every place, forming churches not only in Judea, but more abundantly in the Gentile world, the wall of partition being now broken down: and especially we have an account of the labours of Paul, the great apostle of the Gentiles, witnessing to small and great the glorious truths he once persecuted, and now as zealously espoused, even to prison and to death.

3 The Epistles, *occasioned many of them by disputes which early arose in the Christian church, and thereby occasioned the great and distinguishing doctrines of Christianity to be more distinctly, explicitly, and fully committed to writing, and the various duties thence depending, personal or relative, to God or man, to be urged upon the faithful from right principles, and from those strongest motives which the truths of Christianity furnished Such good hath accrued to us from the unhappy divisions which we lament whilst we read some of the epistles.*

4 The Revelation of St John, *which closes the canon of Scripture, and is prophetical of those great events which should happen in the world, and particularly as they respect the church of Christ to the end of time, wherein are many things dark indeed and hard to be understood, the fulfilment of which will be the surest key to the events predicted and, till then, our search after the meaning of them should be attended with humble diffidence and reverential awe, praying that God* would accomplish the number of his elect and hasten his kingdom, *when all that is now mysterious will be unfolded.*

THE

EVANGELICAL EXPOSITOR;

OR, A

PRACTICAL COMMENT

Upon the GOSPEL according to

St. MATTHEW.

WE *have now before us*, 1. The New Testament of our Lord and Saviour Jesus Christ, *so this second part of the Holy Bible is intitled*, The New Covenant, *so it might as well be rendered; the word signifies both. But when it is (as here) spoken of as Christ's act and deed, it is most properly rendered a Testament, for he is the Testator, and it becomes of force* by his death, *Heb* iv 16, 17 *nor is there, as in covenants, a previous treaty between the parties, but what is granted, is owing to the will, the free-will, the good-will of the Testator Jesus Christ This is called a New Testament, to distinguish it from that which was given by Moses, and was now antiquated, and to signify that it should be always new, and should never wax old and grow out of date*

2 *We have before us* the four gospels. *Gospel signifies good news or glad tidings, and this history of Christ's coming* into the world to save sinners, *is without doubt the best news that ever came from heaven to earth, the angel gave it this title*, Luke ii 10 Εὐαγγελίζομαι ὑμῖν, I bring you good tidings, *I bring the gospel to you And the prophet foretold it*, Isa lii. 7 ——lxi 1 *where it is said, that in the days of the Messiah* good tidings *should be preached Gospel is an old Saxon word, it is God's spell or word. The whole New Testament is the gospel St Paul calls it his gospel, because he was one of the preachers of it O that we may each of us make it ours, by our cordial acceptance of it, and subjection to it! But the four books which contain the history of the Redeemer, we commonly call the four gospels, and the inspired penmen of them the Evangelists, not* exclusively, *for all the preachers of the gospel are Evangelists, but* by way of Eminence.

3 *We have before us* the Gospel according to St Matthew *The penman was by birth a Jew, by calling a publican, till Christ commanded his attendance, and then he left* the receipt of custom *to follow him, and was one of those that accompanied him* all the time that the Lord Jesus went in and out, beginning from the baptism of John, unto the day that he was taken up, *Acts* i 21, 22. *and was therefore a competent witness of what he has here recorded He is said to have written this history about eight years after Christ's ascension Many of the ancients say he wrote it in the Hebrew or Syriac language, but the tradition is sufficiently disproved by Dr. Whitby, doubtless it was written in Greek, as the other parts of the New Testament were, not in that language which was peculiar to the Jews, whose church and state were near a period, but that which was common to the world, and in which the knowledge of Christ would be most effectually transmitted to the nations of the earth, yet it is probable there might be an edition of it in Hebrew, published by St Matthew himself, at the same time that he wrote it in Greek, the former for the Jews, the latter for the Gentiles, when he left Judea to go and preach among the Gentiles. Let us bless God that we have it, and have it in a language we understand.*

CHAP I

This Evangelist begins with the account of Christ's pedigree and birth, his ancestors from whom he descended, and the manner of his entry into the world, to make it appear that he was indeed the Messiah promised, for it was foretold that he should be the son of David, and should be born of a virgin, *and that he was so is very plainly shewn, for here is, 1 His pedigree from Abraham, in forty-two generations, three fourteens, ver 1—17 2 An account of the circumstances of his birth, so far as was requisite to shew that he was* born of a virgin, *ver* 18—25

1 THE book of [a] the generation of Jesus
Christ, the son of David, the son of Abra-
ham 2 [b] Abraham begat Isaac, and [c]
Isaac begat Jacob, and [d] Jacob begat Judas
and his brethren 3 And [e] Judas begat Pharez and
Zara of Thamar, and [f] Pharez begat Esrom, and Esrom
begat Aram 4 And Aram begat Aminadab, and A-
minadab begat Naasson, and Naasson begat Salmon
5 And Salmon begat Booz of Rachab, and Booz begat
Obed of Ruth, and Obed begat Jesse 6 And Jesse
begat David the king, and [g] David the king begat So-
lomon of her *that had been the wife* of Urias 7 And
Solomon begat Roboam, and Roboam begat Abia,
and Abia begat Asa 8 And Asa begat Josaphat, and
Josaphat begat Joram, and [h] Joram begat Ozias 9
And Ozias begat Joatham, and Joatham begat Achaz,
and Achaz begat Ezekias 10 And Ezekias begat
Manasses, and Manasses begat Amon, and Amon begat
Josias 11 And [i] Josias begat Jechonias and his bre-
thren, about the time they were carried away to Baby-
lon 12 And after they were brought to Babylon, Je-
chonias begat Salathiel, and [k] Salathiel begat Zorobabel
13 And Zorobabel begat Abiud, and Abiud begat E-
liakim, and Eliakim begat Azor 14 And Azor be-
gat Sadoc, and Sadoc begat Achim, and Achim begat
Eliud 15 And Eliud begat Eleazar, and Eleazar
begat Matthan, and Matthan begat Jacob 16 And
Jacob begat Joseph the husband of Mary, of whom was
born Jesus, who is called Christ 17 So all the gene-
rations from Abraham to David, *are* fourteen genera-
tions and from David until the carrying away into
Babylon, *are* fourteen generations and from the carry-
ing away into Babylon unto Christ, *are* fourteen gene-
rations

[a] Gen xii 3 xxii 18 compared with Gal iii 16 & Psalm [illegible] 11 [illegible] with Acts xiii 23 Jer xxiii 5 Chap xxi [illegible] Luke i 32 [b] Gen xxi 2 [c] Ibid xxv 26 [d] Ibid xxix 35 [e] Ibid xxxviii 27 [f] Ruth iv 18 1 Chron ii 5 9—15 [g] 1 Chron iii 9—15 [h] Three others intervened See 1 Chron iii 11 12 [i] Jehoiakim intervened 1 Chron iii 15 16 and some read Josias begat Jakim and Jakim begat Jeconias [k] 1 Chron iii 19 Ezra iii 2 Neh xii 1

ver 1—17 As the Old Testament opened with the generation of the heaven and the earth, the New begins with the generation of Him who, in the fulness of time, became incarnate for man's redemption from the curse he had brought upon himself, and under which the whole creation groaned. We have here his genealogy from authentic records, to prove the accomplishment of the prophecies which went before concerning him, as sprung, according to the flesh, from David and Abraham, *Gen* xii 3 2 *Sam* vii 12 for which purpose these genealogical tables are produced, abundantly sufficient for the conviction of the Jews in that day, that Jesus was descended from these patriarchs, whatever cavils have since been raised, or difficulties started against them.

In this genealogy we may observe, (1) That the line of descent is not drawn through the first born, but in many, as Abraham, Jacob, Judah, David, &c from the younger sons. (2) That of the four women mentioned, we have two Gentiles and two adulteresses, who would seem to add no honour to their descendants but herein we have an intimation, that Christ's salvation was not designed to be confined to the Jewish people, but to be extended to the Gentiles also and that the most guilty need not despair, when they see that our Lord, in taking *the form of sinful flesh*, humbles himself to derive his descent from such as these. (3) In the genealogy there are several persons passed over, for which reason it is difficult, and of little import to resolve, and the Evangelist is [illegible], though the distance of three generations, is said to be the son of his remote ancestor, as in the case of Ozias, or [illegible] some suppose of Jeshebo. (4) The generations are divided into three fourteens, not that there were no more persons really in the descent, but that the evangelist thought fit to mention no more. In the first, we see the family of David rising to the throne; in the second, a race of kings descend from him; in the last, the royal family declined even to a poor carpenter. So fading is the world's prospects. Yet then, when to human view all prospect of the kingdom being restored to David's house seemed desperate, Jesus arose to sit on his father's throne, *Luke* i 32 when God promises, we never need despair (5) Jesus is called *Christ*, ver 16 or *Messiah*, the anointed One, uniting in his person the threefold offices, to which men were anointed under the law, of prophet, priest, and king, and all his followers are called *Christians*, an honourable title, and most applicable to those who have indeed received *an unction from the holy One*, and are consecrated to God *as kings and priests*, to reign at last with their exalted head.

18 ¶ Now [l] the birth of Jesus Christ was on this wise
† When as his mother Mary was espoused to Joseph,
before they came together, [m] she was found with child
of the holy Ghost 19 Then Joseph her husband being
a just man, and not willing to [n] make her a public ex-
ample, was minded to put her away privily 20 But
while he thought on these things, behold, the angel of
the LORD appeared unto him in a dream, saying,
Joseph, thou son of David, fear not to take unto thee
Mary thy wife for that which is ‡ conceived in her
is of the holy Ghost 21 And she shall bring forth a
son, and thou shalt call his name [o] Jesus for he shall
save his people from their sins 22 (Now all this was
done, that it might be fulfilled which was spoken of the
LORD by the prophet, saying, 23 [p] Behold, a virgin
shall be with child, and shall bring forth a son, and they
shall call his name Emmanuel, which, being interpreted,
is, God with us) 24 Then Joseph being raised from
sleep, did as the angel of the LORD had bidden him,
and took unto him his wife 25 And he knew her not,
till she had brought forth her first-born son, and he
called his name Jesus

[l] Luke i 27 † Then a year before the common account called Anno Domini [m] Luke i 35 [n] Deut xxiv 1 ‡ Gr Begotten [o] Luke i 31 & ii 21 Acts iv 12 & v 31 & xiii 23 [p] Isa vii 14

ver 18—25 The account of the birth of Jesus follows his genealogy. And we have here,

1 His miraculous conception, ver 18 His mother Mary had been betrothed to Joseph, but before the marriage was consummated she was found with child, through the wondrous operation of the Holy Ghost, who formed Christ's human nature, that it might be pure from every spot of that corruption that naturally descends with his being to every son of Adam, and that he might thus be a Lamb without blemish, fit for God's altar.

2 Joseph's prudent resolve, ver 19 Probably Mary herself communicated to him the circumstances of her case, and though a thousand suggestions might rise up to question her veracity, and to take her to his bed in such a situation he could not think of, being *a just man*, yet was he unwilling withal *to make her a public example*, and have her punished with death as an adulteress her artless story and unaffected simplicity, though strange the relation, might well have caused him to hesitate, and where the shadow of a doubt remained, a just man will ever lean to the side of mercy and charity, therefore he resolved *to put her away privily*, as little as possible to wound her character, whilst duty bids him preserve his own. *Note*, (1) Tho' apparently the greatest injuries may be done us, it is wise to suppress rash anger, and deliberate before we punish. (2) In very dark cases, where any circumstances appear that will admit of a favourable interpretation, charity, which thinketh no evil, will gladly entertain them.

3 The Lord relieves Joseph from his perplexity while he deliberates what was fit to be done for God's glory and his own peace, in Mary's case, the angel of the Lord in a dream directs him how to act. For when we are in doubt, yet in simplicity desire to know and follow God's will, we shall be directed, if not by an angel or a dream, yet by some word of God, or intimation of providence. Joseph is now diverted from his purpose, and bid, without hesitation, take to him his wife, since her conception is not the fruit of adultery, but of the Holy Ghost and the angel calls him *Joseph, thou son of David*, to lead his thoughts from this extraordinary circumstance to the Messiah who should descend from him, assuring him withal, that this child now conceived is designed to be the very person, as the name given him imports, he shall be called *Jesus*, or the Saviour, this being the great end of his appearing, *to save his people from their sins*, from the punishment and the power of them. *Note*, They to whom Jesus is a Saviour, are hereby distinguished they are saved not only from guilt, but from corruption, every one who nameth the name of Christ, must depart from iniquity, or they are none of his, yet from him alone it cometh that they are enabled so to do.

4 The accomplishment of the scriptures herein is observed by the Evangelist. The prophecy of Isaiah, *chap* vii 14 had foretold, *a virgin shall conceive, and bring forth a son, and his name be called Immanuel*, which was now fulfilled, Mary being that virgin, and God himself become incarnate in her womb and thus uniting in his own person the two natures, the divine and human, Jesus was enabled to execute the office of a Saviour, having a body to offer for the sins of men, and infinite

value to enhance the sacrifice, arising from the dignity of his person, by which means God became reconciled to us, and we who were far off, were brought nigh unto God. How mysterious this union! Let us wonder, love and adore!

5. Joseph no sooner awaked, than he obeyed the heavenly vision, which carried undoubted evidence to his mind of its original, and publickly celebrated his marriage, though he knew not Mary as a wife, at least not till after the birth of Jesus: whether afterwards he did or no, is not said, and immaterial for us to know; this holy abstinence of Joseph was sufficient to shew, the child Jesus was the virgin's son, and in obedience to the angel's command, he called his name Jesus. *Note*, (1.) When God commands, we must obey without hesitation. (2.) Since Jesus is now come into the world, we are called upon to accept of his salvation; for if we neglect or despise it, *how shall we escape?*

CHAP. II.

In this chapter we have the history of our Saviour's infancy, where we find, 1. The wise men's solicitous enquiry after Christ, ver. 1—8. 2. Their devout attendance on him, when they found out where he was, ver. 9—12. 3. Christ's flight into Egypt to avoid the cruelty of Herod, ver. 13—15. 4. The barbarous murder of the infants of Bethlehem, ver. 16—18. 5. Christ's return out of Egypt into the land of Israel again, ver. 19—23.

The fourth year before the common account called Anno Domini. a Luke ii. 4, 7. b Isa. lx. 3. c Gen. xxv. 6. d Num. xxiv. 17.

1 NOW when [a] Jesus was born in Bethlehem of
Judea, in the days of Herod the king, behold,
[b] there came wise-men [c] from the east to Jerusalem, 2
Saying, Where is he that is born king of the Jews?
for we have seen [d] his star in the east, and are come to
worship him. 3 When Herod the king had heard
these things, he was troubled, and all Jerusalem with
him. 4 And when he had gathered all the chief priests
and scribes of the people together, he demanded of them
where Christ should be born. 5 And they said unto
him, In Bethlehem of Judea: for thus it is written by
the prophet, 6 And [e] thou Bethlehem *in* the land of
Judah, art not the least among the princes of Judah:
for out of thee shall come a Governor that shall † rule
my people Israel. 7 Then Herod, when he had pri-
vily called the wise-men, enquired of them diligently
what time the star appeared. 8 And he sent them to
Bethlehem, and said, Go and search diligently for the
young child, and when you have found *him*, bring me
word again,[f] that I may come and worship him also.

e Mic. v. 2. John vii. 42. † Or, Feed. Isa. xl. 11. f [illegible] Ver. 16.

v. 1—8. Though the birth of Jesus, the King of kings, was ushered into the world with none of those rejoicings that usually attend the nativity of the princes of the earth, we have some instances of very distinguished notice paid to the infant Saviour.

1. Wise men came from the east, led by the observance of an extraordinary star which appeared in the heavens; who they were, and from whence they came, we are not clearly told; the most approved opinion seems to be that they were of the Persian Magi, among whom some tradition seems to have obtained of a great prince at that time about to come into the world, which might arise from Balaam's prophecy, or from their acquaintance with the Jewish scriptures, which, during the captivity, were probably brought among them: and this expectation, Tacitus observes, was spread through the east. As these Magi were much conversant in astronomy, the uncommon luminous phenomenon, a meteor, or star, which they observed over Judea, might have led them thither, concluding this was the signal of his appearing, as they might be assured also by a divine impulse on their minds. They were Gentiles, it is certain, and this was a happy presage of their future conversion; and their wisdom most eminently appeared in coming to him, the knowledge of whom alone could make them wise unto salvation. The highest attainments in science without this wisdom, are no better than splendid ignorance.

2. They directed their journey to Jerusalem the capital, naturally concluding there to meet with all needful information. *Herod* at that time reigned in Judea, an Idomite, set up by the Romans, under whose power the Jews were, the sceptre being now departed from Shiloh; and to him it should seem they applied themselves, enquiring after the child who was born King of the Jews, concerning which they speak with greatest confidence; and having seen his star in the east, the intimation of his birth, were come to worship him; either to pay him their civil homage, or to offer divine adoration. *Note*, (1.) They who know the value of Christ's favour, will stick at no pains in following him whithersoever he calls them. (2.) Jesus is truly the object worthy of our adoration, even in his lowest humiliation; the Babe in the manger is still the mighty God, the everlasting Father, the Prince of peace.

3. This enquiry of the wise men exceedingly affected Herod. He could be no stranger to the prophecies concerning the Messiah, and the time of the accomplishment of them was confessedly now at hand. He was troubled therefore least his own throne should be shaken, and all the people who heard the story, seem alike disturbed, fearing the tumults which they might suppose would be the consequence of a struggle for the crown, as they had in general no notion of the Messiah as a spiritual Saviour, but as a mighty prince and conqueror. *Note*, Worldly hearts are ever afraid, lest the spreading of the kingdom of Jesus should clash with their interests.

4. To give them a resolution of the question, and perhaps to gain particular information himself, for purposes his mind already harboured, he called a council of the chief priests, those most distinguished for station and abilities, and the scribes learned in the law, and most conversant with the prophecies, that he might have their concurring sentiments concerning the place where *the Christ*, the Messiah should be born. And thus, by divine providence, this wicked king, who consulted them with the vilest design, is made the instrument of obtaining a distinguished suffrage, even from the wisest of the Jewish nation, to the place of the Messiah's birth, and where the babe Jesus actually was born.

5. They are unanimous in their opinion, for the prophet Micah hath expresly determined the place to be Bethlehem of Judea, *chap.* v. 2. and they cite the prophecy, in sense the same with the original, though with some variation in the expression. Thence the ruler and governor of his Israel should arise, and who is and ever will be the Lord of the redeemed, reigning in their hearts, and bringing them into subjection to his blessed self.

6. Herod hereupon dismisses the wise men in search of this child, after examining them in private with greatest accuracy concerning the time when the star appeared, and having concerted in his own mind the bloody project of cutting off him, whom he eyed already with jealousy as the rival of his throne; and therefore he strictly charges them, after having made diligent search at Bethlehem, to return, and acquaint him with the place of his abode, hypocritically pretending a desire to pay his worship to the young child, born, and destined of God to such distinguished honour. So often hath the mask of religion concealed the foulest designs.

None of his courtiers were sent with these strangers; perhaps he was afraid to awaken the suspicion of the parents of Jesus, his ambition and cruelty being fully known; or so God, in his over-ruling providence, ordered it, who taketh the wise in their own craftiness, and can divert the enemies of his people from using the most obvious means which they seem to have in their power to distress or destroy them.

9 ¶ When they had heard the king, they departed;
and lo, the star which they saw in the east, went before
them, till it came and stood over where the young child
was. 10 [g] When they saw the star, they rejoiced with g Psal. cv. 3.
exceeding great joy. 11 ¶ And when they were come
into the house, they saw the young child with Mary his
mother, and fell down, and worshipped him: and when
they had opened their treasures, [h] they presented unto h Psal. lxxii. 10. Isa. lx. 6.
him gifts, gold, and frankincense, and myrrh. 12
And being warned of God [i] in a dream, that they should i Chap. i. 20.
not return to Herod, they departed into their own coun-
try another way.

v. 9—12. With attention and respect the wise men received their directions, and departed in search of the King of the Jews. And,

1. We find them happily conducted to the spot where he is. The star which they had seen at Christ's birth, afterwards disappeared, at least, if as some suggest, it led them to the borders of Judea, it then left them, but now returned, hanging low in the sky, and moving on before them till it stood over the house where Jesus was: for before this, it seems, his parents had changed the place of his birth in a stable, for a more commodious abode. The return of the star, as it promised them a happy issue of their journey, rejoiced them exceedingly; and under its guidance being led to the house, they entered without farther enquiry: and finding the child with his virgin mother, they immediately prostrated themselves before him, worshipping him as their God, or honouring him as their King. And according to the eastern custom, of making presents to their monarchs when they make their addresses to them, they opened their treasures, and presented him gold, frankincense, and myrrh, *Isa.* lx. 6. and this also providentially supplied Joseph and Mary with a sufficiency for the long journey they were quickly after called to undertake. *Note*, (1.) When we are found in the way of duty, using the means God hath given us, we shall not be left without a guide. (2.) The word of God, and the ministry of it, is now this star to lead us to Jesus; and blessed and happy are they who follow its direction. (3.) When for a while we have been left in the darkness of affliction, temptation, or desertion, with double joy we behold the re-appearing of the day star

to our benighted ſouls, and rejoice with exceeding great joy (4) Jeſus is the object of our adorations, to him every knee muſt bow (5) The Lord by ſtrange and unexpected ways often ſupplies the wants of his people, they who truſt him, will aſſuredly own that he hath never failed them in time of need

2 To prevent their return to Jeruſalem according to Herod's deſire, God, by a dream, which carried its own evidence that it came from him, probably the very day or night after their arrival at Bethlehem, warned them not to go back to Herod, and accordingly they immediately departed into their own country another way So eaſily can God blaſt the malicious deſigns of the ungodly

13 And when they were departed, behold, the angel
of the LORD appeared to Joſeph in a dream, ſaying,
Ariſe, and take the young child, and his mother, and
flee into Egypt, and be thou there until I bring thee
k Rev xii 4 word for k Herod will ſeek the young child to deſtroy
him 14 When he aroſe, he took the young child
l Mat x 23. and his mother by night, and l departed into Egypt
15 And was there until the death of Herod that it
might be fulfilled which was ſpoken of the LORD by
m Hoſ xi 1. the prophet, ſaying, m Out of Egypt have I called my
ſon.

v 13—15 No ſooner were the wiſe men departed, than God, who knew the cruel intentions of Herod, takes care of the ſafety of the child Jeſus

1 The Lord in a dream appriſes Joſeph of the danger to which the young child was expoſed, and bids him, without delay, ſecure the babe with his mother, in Egypt, from the fury of this bloody king, and expect further directions there Immediately, that very night he aroſe and fled with his family to this appointed place of refuge, and there continued till the death of Herod, which ſoon followed the maſſacre of the infants *Note*, (1) The place where God's people ſuffered the bitterest perſecution, affords an aſylum for his ſon ſo eaſily can he, who hath in his hands the hearts of all men, make our once inveterate enemies our firmeſt friends (2) God's commands the faithful heart obeys without heſitation or delay having committed our all to him, we muſt be ſafe under his guidance

2 Particular notice is taken of the fulfilling of the ſcripture herein, *out of Egypt have I called my ſon*, Hoſ xi 1 which whatever reference it hath to Iſrael as a people, had now its moſt direct accompliſhment in the flight of Jeſus thither, and his return from thence

16 ¶ Then Herod when he ſaw that he was mocked
of the wiſe-men, was exceeding wroth, and ſent forth
n Chap x 34 and n ſlew all the children that were in Bethlehem, and
in all the coaſts thereof, from two years old and under,
according to the time which he had diligently enquired
of the wiſe men. 17 Then was fulfilled that which was
o Jer xxxi 15 ſpoken by Jeremy the prophet, ſaying, 18 o In Rama
was there a voice heard, lamentation and weeping, and
great mourning, Rachael weeping *for* her children, and
would not be comforted, becauſe they are not

v 16—18 We are told here, as we might have expected, from the character of this wicked prince,

1 The fury he was in at being diſappointed of the wiſe-men He waited from day to day, in expectation of receiving intelligence from them, but hearing at laſt they were gone home another way, his jealouſy was more inflamed againſt his ſuppoſed rival, and his wrath more exaſperated

2 The politic, but inhuman contrivance he formed to rid himſelf of his fears He ſlew all the male children under two years of age, in all Bethlehem, and the territory belonging to it, being ſatisfied, from the information he had received of the wiſe men, that the infant king could not exceed that age, and therefore muſt periſh in this general maſſacre An inſtance of barbarity, which, though moſt agreeable to the character of that ſavage monarch, who had with his own hand ſlain his own children, we cannot read without horror, ſo that Auguſtus might well ſay, *it was better to be Herod's ſwine, than his ſon* The firſt crown of martyrdom for Jeſus was won by these infant ſufferers, and the honour to which they are advanced, infinitely repays the torments they endured

3 The fulfillment of the ſcripture herein is again obſerved, and to this event, no doubt, the prophet had immediate regard, *Jer* xxxi 15 For though we ſee it fulfilled in a meaſure, when the ſword of the Chaldeans, and the captivity of the Jews which enſued, awakened Rachel, as it were, from her grave, which was near Bethlehem, to lament her children deſtroyed, or led to Babylon; yet, in a peculiarly ſtriking manner may this tender mother's griefs be now ſaid to overflow, when ſo many of her daughters rived with inconſolable anguiſh for their infants torn from their boſom, and writhing on the ſpear of inhuman murderers *Note*, Though God forbids us not with acuteſt anguiſh to bewail the ravages death makes in our families, inconſolable grief is ſinful Chriſtians muſt never ſorrow as if they had no hope, or as if their comforts were all bound up in a dying worm

19 ¶ But when Herod was dead, behold, an angel
of the Lord appeareth in a dream to Joſeph in Egypt,
20 Saying, Ariſe, and take the young child, and his
mother, and go into the land of Iſrael p for they are p Exo. iv 19
dead which ſought the young child's life 21 And he
aroſe, and took the young child and his mother, and
came into the land of Iſrael 22 But when he heard
that Archelaus did reign in Judea, in the room of his
father Herod, he was afraid to go thither q notwith- q P. [illegible]
ſtanding being warned of God in a dream, he turned
aſide into the parts of Galilee 23 And he came and
dwelt in a city called Nazareth, that it might be fulfil-
led which was ſpoken by the prophets, r He ſhall be r Judg xiii 5 Iſa xi 1
called a Nazarene

v 19—23 The ſojourning of our Lord in Egypt was but ſhort Quickly after the maſſacre of the infants, Herod was ſtruck with a mortal diſeaſe, loathſome and incurable, that made him a ſpectacle to others, a torment to himſelf So ſoon can God humble proud tyrants, and make them feel that wrath they would not fear Hereupon,

1 The Lord ſent his angel, who informed Joſeph in a dream, of Herod's death, and bids him ariſe, ſince he may now ſafely return to the land of Iſrael They who are driven far from the ordinances of God, and his people, wiſh to be no longer abſent from them than neceſſity obliges them

2 Joſeph is all obedience cheerful readineſs in following God's direction, being the ſure effect of real devotedneſs to his will He returns with the child and his mother to the land of Iſrael, but hearing that Archelaus, a ſon of Herod's, and an inheritor of his brutal temper reigned in Judea, he was juſtly afraid of ſettling under his juriſdiction, and in this emergence again the Lord ſignifies his pleaſure to him by his angel, and points him out a place of ſafety, in the obſcure retreat of Nazareth, a little town in Galilee, then under the government of Antipas, another of Herod's children, but a man of a milder temper than his brother *Note*, (1) They who are willing to follow the path of duty, if they knew it, ſhall be directed aright (2) No danger muſt deter us when we have God's call to go, but we muſt not willingly ruſh into temptation (3) God will find a quiet reſting-place for his people ſometimes under the ſun, but aſſuredly above it

3 This was done alſo, that the ſcripture might be fulfilled, which ſaid, *He ſhall be called a Nazarene*, either this refers to *Iſa* xi 1 where Chriſt is called a branch, *netzer*, out of the root of Jeſſe, the city Nazareth deriving its name from this word or to *Judg* xiii 5 Samſon being the type of the great Nazarite and Saviour Jeſus Or rather in general, the prophecies which foretold his mean appearance, and the contempt and reproach he ſhould be expoſed to, were thus fulfilled, Nazareth being a deſpicable place, and his very coming from thence was urged by his enemies as an argument againſt his miſſion, *can any good thing come out of* ſo mean and contemptible a place as *Nazareth?* *Note*, They who are followers of Jeſus of Nazareth, muſt not be aſhamed of his reproach, nor of any opprobrious names with which his enemies and theirs may ſeek to render them odious or deſpicable The diſciple is then but as his Lord

CHAP III

In this chapter we have, 1 *The life, doctrine, and baptiſm of John,* ver 1—12 2 *Jeſus baptiſed of him,* ver 13—17

1 IN thoſe days came a John the Baptiſt, preaching b in a Mark i, Luke iii 2
the wilderneſs of Judea, 2 And ſaying, c Repent
ye, d for the kingdom of heaven is at hand 3 For this b Joſh xv 61
is he that was ſpoken of by the prophet Eſaias, ſaying, c Chap iv. 17
e The voice of one crying in the wilderneſs, prepare ye d Dan ii.44
the way of the Lord, make his paths ſtraight. 4 e Iſa xl 3, Mark i 3, Luke iii 4, John i 23
And the ſame John f had his raiment of camel's hair,
and a leathern girdle about his loins, and his meat
was locuſts and wild honey. 5 Then went out to him f 2 Kin i 8, Zech xiii. 4
Jeruſalem, and g all Judea, and all the region round a-
bout Jordan, 6 And were baptized of him in Jordan, g Luke xvi 16
h confeſſing their ſins h Mal iv 6

v. 1—6 Prophecy under the Old Teſtament cloſed with the promiſe of the coming of Elijah, that is, of one in his ſpirit and temper, and here we find that prophecy accompliſhed in John the Baptiſt, ſo called from the ordinance of baptiſm he admini-

adminiſtred to his diſciples, who appeared *in thoſe days*, not immediately after the events related in the preceding chapter, but at about twenty-ſeven or twenty-eight years diſtance, during which time we never but once hear any thing of our bleſſed Lord, who lived in obſcurity, and not improbably maintained himſelf by manual labour. We have,

1. The place where John opened his miniſtry, in the wilderneſs of Judea, not a place literally uninhabited, but not ſo populous as the other parts of the country. *See Joſh.* xv. 61, 62.

2. The doctrine he preached. *Repentance*, a change of mind and principles, and of manners and practice, in both which reſpects the Jewiſh people were exceedingly corrupt; and this he urges on that evangelical conſideration, that *the kingdom of heaven is at hand*, the kingdom of the Meſſiah, the goſpel diſpenſation, which affords the ſtrongeſt engagements to draw the minds of ſinners to return to God, from the views of the riches of his grace therein revealed. *Note*, (1.) It is a ſenſe of God's pardoning love revealed in the goſpel, that alone can work the effectual repentance unto ſalvation never to be repented of. (2.) The *kingdom of Jeſus is the kingdom of heaven*, for all who are now partakers of his grace, are heirs of his glory, and ſure to reign with him for ever. (3.) All the members of Chriſt's kingdom are real penitents, whoſe minds and hearts are changed by grace, and their lives renewed in holineſs.

3. Herein John fulfilled the prophecy delivered concerning him, *Iſa.* xl. 3, 4. *The voice of one crying*, loud as the ox bellows, intimating the fervour and vehemence with which John preached, *Prepare ye the way of the Lord, make his paths ſtraight*. As the harbinger, or herald, he goes before to clear the way for the King of Glory, preaching that repentance which was ſo peculiarly needful at a time when the traditions of men had made God's word of no effect, and the corruption of the general practice was the natural effect of their corrupt principles, and pointing them from their ſinful courſes to him who was *the way, the truth, and the life*, by whom alone they could be ſaved. *Note*, (1.) The ways of ſin are crooked ways, that lead down to death and hell. (2.) Nothing can ſave us from them, but repentance towards God, and faith in our Lord Jeſus Chriſt.

4. His garb and diet were auſtere, as his word was ſtartling. He ſeemed an uncouth courtier to prepare the way of the eternal King. A rough garment, girt with a leathern girdle, was his cloathing, as being the promiſed Elias, *See* 2 *Kings* i. 8. and his meat was plain and abſtemious, ſuch as the wilderneſs afforded, locuſts and wild honey. *Note*, They who preach mortification and repentance to others, ſhould themſelves ſhow a becoming indifference to this world, and the gratifications of it.

5. A numerous auditory attended his miniſtry, ſtruck by the ſingularity of his appearance and manners, and, above all, by the power of the word he preached. Multitudes from Jeruſalem, Judea, and the country beyond Jordan, reſorted to him, a general expectation of the Meſſiah being now raiſed through the land; and ſo far were many affected with his diſcourſes, that they made profeſſion of repentance, confeſſed their ſins, and were baptized in Jordan. But among a multitude of profeſſors, the ſequel ſhewed there were few real penitents. Uncommon zeal and ſtriking delivery will often collect an audience, and excite curioſity; but divine grace alone can effect converſion.

It hath been a much-diſputed point, reſpecting the manner of adminiſtring the ordinance of baptiſm, whether by immerſion or ſprinkling; and where the form is reſted upon, inſtead of the power of godlineſs, there is room open for abundant debate. I muſt confeſs, for my own part, I ſee no reaſon to ſuppoſe ſuch immenſe multitudes were all dipped in Jordan, nor how it would be practicable to provide dipping garments for them: nor does the word βαπτιζω (baptizo) convey the ſame meaning as βαπτω (bapto), but rather ſeem to intimate ſprinkling or pouring water upon them; and the baptiſm of the Holy Ghoſt, which this baptiſm of John's prefigured, would lead us ſtrongly to that meaning of the word. But whilſt we ſhould avoid all rigid cenſures on thoſe who differ from us in these ceremonials, and ſee that in whatever manner baptiſm be adminiſtered, we do not reſt upon the ordinance, it is an eſſential concern, that our ſouls be really partakers of the thing ſignified, even ſprinkled with the blood of Jeſus, and ſaved by the waſhing of regeneration and the renewing of the Holy Ghoſt.

i Chap. xii. 34. Luke iii. 7. — 7 ¶ But when he ſaw many of the Phariſees and Sadducees come to his baptiſm, he ſaid unto them, [i] O generation of vipers, who hath warned you to flee from

k Rom. v. 9. — [k] the wrath to come? 8 Bring forth therefore fruits meet for repentance. 9 And think not to ſay within

l John viii. 33. — yourſelves, [l] We have Abraham to *our* father: for I ſay unto you, that God is able of theſe ſtones to raiſe up children unto Abraham. 10 And now alſo the ax is

m Ch. vii. 19. John xv. 6. — laid unto the root of the trees: therefore [m] every tree which bringeth not forth good *fruit*, is hewn down and

n Acts i. 5. — caſt into the fire. 11 [n] I indeed baptize you with water unto repentance, but he that cometh after me, is mightier than I, whoſe ſhoes I am not worthy to bear:

o Iſ. iv. 4. Mal. iii. 2. — [o] he ſhall baptize you with the Holy Ghoſt, and *with* fire. 12 [p] Whoſe fan *is* in his hand, and he will throughly purge his floor, and gather his wheat into the garner; but [q] he will burn up the chaff with unquenchable fire.

p Mal. iii. 3.

q Mal. iv. 1.

ℶ 7—12. The Phariſees and Sadducees were men of very different characters; the one pretended uncommon ſanctity, and were rigid obſervers of the rituals of religion, deriving their name from that *ſeparation of themſelves from other men* in which they gloried. The Sadducees, on the other hand, ſo denominated from their maſter Sadok, were the very reverſe, avowedly infidel in their principles, and, it is to be feared, as licentious in their practice. *Yet many of both theſe ſects*, either ſtruck with John's preaching, or more probably to gain the higher veneration with the people, who were ſtrongly engaged in John's favour as a prophet ſent from God, applied to him for baptiſm; and to them he here *addreſſes his diſcourſe*.

1. He opens with a moſt ſevere reproof, and mortifying appellation. *O generation of vipers*, ſpecious, yet venomous as a ſerpent, *who hath warned you to flee from the wrath to come?* either from their temporal calamities which were approaching, and then repentance might have averted; or from the eternal ruin they had provoked by their pride, hypocriſy, infidelity, and wickedneſs. *Note*, (1.) To flee from the wrath to come, is every ſinner's great concern; but none will take the warning, till they ſee and feel the imminence of their danger. (2.) Miniſters muſt deal plainly and freely with men's conſciences; nor muſt the ſelf-righteous formaliſt be addreſſed with leſs ſeverity than the abandoned ſinner.

2. He admoniſhes them of their duty. *Bring forth therefore fruits meet for repentance*, without which all the water in the river would never profit them any thing; for all who are baptized unto repentance muſt ſee, that in all humility and lowlineſs of mind, in all patience and perſeverance in well-doing, in all holy converſation and godlineſs, they prove the truth of the grace which is in them, elſe ſhall the baptized ſinner be as the heathen man and the publican.

3. He cautions them againſt truſting on their external privileges, on which he knew they depended for acceptance before God. Becauſe they were Abraham's children they flattered themſelves with ſafety, and thought repentance in their caſe unneceſſary: but John would undeceive them; and pointing probably to thoſe ſtones which Joſhua ſet up in Jordan, *Joſh.* iv. 20. aſſured them God could from theſe raiſe up children to Abraham, and needed not his deſcendants after the fleſh to compoſe his church. *Note*, (1.) Many flatter themſelves, that their being members of the viſible church, and having partaken of baptiſm and the Lord's ſupper, will ſtand them in ſtead in the day of God, who will find themſelves woefully diſappointed. (2.) Miniſters muſt lay open thoſe refuges of lies to which the ſelf-righteous and the ſinner betake themſelves, and rouſe thoſe to a ſenſe of their danger, who rock themſelves aſleep in vain imaginations. (3.) The nearer we are related to great and good men, ſo far from being a protection to us, it will but aggravate our guilt if we degenerate from their piety.

4. He gives them fair warning. The time was ſhort ere judgment would begin at the houſe of God: the ax was now laid to the root of the tree, by the preaching of the goſpel; and their laſt moment of probation expiring. If they rejected the counſel of God, and refuſed to repent and amend their ways, then they were marked for ruin, as trees that bear no fruit, fit only for fuel. The temporal judgments of God ſhall conſume them with their city, or, worſe, the eternal wrath of God ſhall overwhelm them in hell. *Note*, The day of grace is a precious ſeaſon not to be trifled with; our eternity of happineſs or miſery depends on our neglect or improvement of it.

5. He directs them to that glorious perſonage whoſe forerunner he was, acknowledging his preeminence in all things. He could indeed call them to repentance, and adminiſter baptiſm to thoſe who made profeſſion of it; but a greater than himſelf muſt give the grace to repent, concerning whom he owns he was not worthy to perform the meaneſt offices to him, even to carry his ſhoes after him: ſo lowly are the ſaints of God in their own eyes. *He ſhall baptize you with the Holy Ghoſt, and with fire*, either at the day of Pentecoſt, *Acts* ii. 3. or his influences, like fire, ſhould purify, warm, and enliven their ſouls. Or, as ſome ſuggeſt, this baptiſm may refer to the judgments he would pour out on the impenitent, when having, like the huſbandman, ſeparated the wheat, his people, from the chaff of hypocrites and unfaithful profeſſors, he would burn up the latter with unquenchable fire. *Note*, (1.) The operations of *God's Spirit in the believer's heart*, like fire, illuminate his underſtanding, conſume his vile affections, and raiſe him, as the flame mounts upwards, to high and heavenly things. (2.) The church is Chriſt's floor; in it there is a mixt multitude of good and bad, *faithful and hypocrites*, as the chaff and wheat lying together: but the day is near when the ſeparation ſhall be made, ſometimes even here by the divine word and providences,

aſſuredly

assuredly at Christ's appearing, when the eternal state of men shall be determined The redeemed then shall be gathered as the wheat into God's garner in heaven, separated from all chaff for ever, and not a grain lost, and the impenitent and reprobate be consigned to the everlasting burnings

13 ᵗ Then cometh Jesus ˢ from Galilee to Jordan
unto John to be baptized of him 14 But John forbad him, saying, I have need to be baptized of thee,
and comest thou to me 15 And Jesus answering,
said unto him, Suffer *it to be so* now for thus it becometh us to fulfil all righteousness Then he suffered
him 16 And Jesus, when he was baptized, went up
straightway out of the water and lo, the heavens were
opened unto him, and he saw ᵗ the Spirit of God descending like a dove, and lighting upon him 17 And
ᵘ lo, a voice from heaven, saying, ˣ This is my beloved
Son, in whom I am well pleased

ʳ Mark i 9 Luke iii 21 ˢ Chap ii 22 ᵗ Isa xi 2 ᵘ John xii 28 ˣ Ps ii 7 Isa xlii 1 Chap xvii 5 Eph i 6 2 Pet i 17

v 13—17 Christ, who had hitherto lived in obscurity, began now to enter upon his glorious work, and, in order thereto, comes to John to be baptized, whose preaching had raised men's expectations concerning the glorious person of whom he spake Not that Christ needed this baptism, but he would shew his approbation of it, as well as receive that public testimony that John on this occasion was appointed to bear to him

1 John, who knew Jesus by divine revelation, *John* i 33 appears unwilling to admit his master to the ordinance of baptism which he administred He who had no sin, could surely need no repentance Besides counting himself unworthy of pouring water upon him, from whom himself needed the greater baptism of the Spirit, he would humbly have excused himself from the office *I have need to be baptized of thee, and comest thou to me?* *Note*, (1) The most holy souls are ever the most humble (2) Christ's condescensions are so amazing, that our faith sometimes is ready to stagger at the view of them (3) The greatest saints and prophets have need of the baptism of Jesus, both of the sprinkling of his blood to cleanse their consciences, and of the influences of his Spirit to purify their hearts, and they are always most sensible of their wants (4) They who preach repentance to others, had need be deeply concerned to be baptized with the Holy Ghost themselves, lest, after having been the means of saving others, they themselves should be cast away

2 The Lord over-rules John's objection In his present state of humiliation it became him to submit to this among other divine institutions, that he might in all things be a pattern of righteousness, and therefore John must for the present comply Nor does he any longer hesitate, but admitted him to baptism accordingly, fully satisfied in the will and wisdom of his Lord *Note*, (1) It is becoming to countenance and encourage every good work, and those who may be higher in wisdom and grace than their teachers, are bound nevertheless to attend their ministry, and set an example to others (2) Christ fulfilled all righteousness, ceremonial as well as moral, and by his obedience is become the end of the law for righteousness to every one that believeth (3) There are often reasons for the divine procedure, concerning which we must be content to be ignorant *Thou knowest it not now, but thou shalt know hereafter*

3 God is pleased to bear a signal attestation to the glory of the Redeemer on this occasion Immediately as he went up from the river's bank, or *from the water*, where he had been baptized, *the heavens were opened*, a chasm being made in the firmament, as if the everlasting doors were wide unfolded, and John, as well as Jesus, beheld the visible descent of the Holy Ghost upon him, in a hovering dove like motion, and it rested upon or over his head He being constituted the great prophet of his people, as the man Christ Jesus, had the Spirit without measure bestowed upon him, to enable him for the discharge of his office, and in him, as the head of his church, all fulness dwells, that he may from thence communicate both gifts and graces to his members according to their wants And besides the visible appearance here described, an audible voice was heard from the excellent Glory, *This is my beloved Son, in whom I am well pleased* God's *Son*, not by creation as angels, or by adoption as the saints, but by a filiation peculiar to himself, being self-existent and eternal as the Father, yet standing in this relation towards him *Beloved*, because the express image of his person; and being now become incarnate for our redemption, according to the eternal counsels, therefore God the Father delighted in him, expressing his entire satisfaction in his undertaking *in whom I am well pleased*; which he never could say of any of the sons of men beside, all having sinned and come short of the glory of God Jesus alone is the one glorious character on which God can look with approbation, whose righteousness is perfect, and for whose sake it is, as having made the atonement, that any of the sons of men can find acceptance before God Because he is well pleased with Jesus, he hath now opened the kingdom of heaven to all believers in him, and whosoever cometh to God by him shall be in no wise cast out

Thus, whilst every other character, considered in itself, from the first man to the last, must be God's abhorrence, since altogether born in sin, we may notwithstanding be sure of acceptance in this beloved, and shall be regarded as complete in him, when we by faith receive him as God hath set him forth to us, as our wisdom, righteousness, sanctification, and redemption, our all in all

CHAP IV

When Jesus entered upon his ministry, John is scarce heard of again, as the stars disappear when the sun arises We have in this chapter, 1 The temptation Christ underwent, the triple assault the tempter made upon him, and the repulse he gave to each assault, ver 1—11 2 The teaching work he undertook, the places he preached in, ver 12—16 and the subject he preached on, ver 17 3 His calling of disciples, Peter and Andrew, James and John, ver 18—22 4 His curing of diseases, ver 23, 24 and the great resort of people to him, both to be taught and to be healed

1 THEN was ᵃ Jesus led up of ᵇ the Spirit into
the wilderness, ᶜ to be tempted of the devil 2
And when he had ᵈ fasted forty days and forty nights, he
was afterwards an hungred 3 And when the tempter
came to him, he said, If thou be the Son of God, command that these stones be made bread 4 But he answered and said, It is written, ᵉ Man shall not live by
bread alone, but by every word that proceedeth out of
the mouth of God 5 Then the devil taketh him up
into ᶠ the holy city, and setteth him on a pinnacle of the
temple, 6 And saith unto him, If thou be the Son
of God, cast thyself down for it is written, ᵍ He shall
give his angels charge concerning thee, and in their
hands they shall bear thee up, lest at any time thou dash
thy foot against a stone 7 Jesus said unto him, ʰ It is
written again, ⁱ Thou shalt not tempt the Lord thy God
8 Again, the devil taketh him up into an exceeding
high mountain, and sheweth him all the kingdoms of
the world, and the glory of them 9 And saith unto
him, All these things will I give thee, if thou wilt fall
down and worship me 10 Then saith Jesus unto him,
Get thee hence, Satan for it is written, ᵏ Thou shalt
worship the Lord thy God, and him only shalt thou
serve 11 ˡ Then the devil leaveth him, and behold,
ᵐ angels came and ministred unto him

ᵃ Mark i 12 Luke iv 1 ᵇ 1 Kings xviii 12 ᶜ Heb iv 15 ᵈ Exod xxxiv 28 1 Kings xix 8 ᵉ Deut viii 3 ᶠ Neh xi 1 Isa lii 1 Chap xxvii 53 ᵍ Ps xci 11 ʰ Eph vi 17 ⁱ Deut vi 16 ᵏ Deut vi 13 & x 20 ˡ Jam iv 7 ᵐ Heb i 14

v 1—11 Jesus being now prepared for the battle, enters the lists against the great enemy of souls, whose kingdom he came to destroy We have,

1 The time of this conflict *Then*, immediately after he had received the attestation of God to his Sonship, and the fulness of the Spirit for the exercise of his office as Mediator *Note*, (1) Before God calls us into temptation, he will furnish us with spiritual strength (2) Great manifestations are often the prelude to our severest conflicts (3) The confidence of our adoption of God will be the most effectual shield to quench all the fiery darts of the wicked one

2 The place *In the wilderness*, far from the abode of men, amidst lonely wastes, where only the savages of the forest roamed, to give the enemy every advantage against him, and therein more gloriously to display his own power and all-sufficiency The first man fell in a paradise of delights, the second man stood unmoved against every blast of temptation, firm as the rocks of the wilderness, his present dreary dwelling

3 The preparatives to the combat *He was led up of the Spirit*, by a divine impulse on his mind, into the higher, more mountainous, and uninhabited part of the country, and this with design to meet the tempter, and defeat all his wiles And hereunto he condescended, (1) That feeling what sore temptations mean, he might be a compassionate high priest, having been tempted in all points as we are, only without sin (2) To encourage us to trust him in every time of need He who defeated that enemy once himself, can by the same strength make us more than conquerors Forty days, like Moses in the mount, he continued there alone, and without sustenance, at last he felt all those acute cravings of hunger which, as man, he was subject to in common with us, and which gave the enemy another advantage against him, and rendered the Redeemer's triumphs more illustrious The first representative of mankind, when wallowing in plenty, was tempted by one forbidden tree, the last covenant head of his people, though famishing for want, is deaf to every sollicitation of the wicked one

4 The temptations themselves, a threefold cord, and yet broken with ease The design of them was to shake Christ's confidence in God, and lead him to some dishonourable step,
which,

which, had it been possible, must have utterly unqualified him for the work of redemption

(1) In the first temptation the devil sought to lead him to a distrust of God's providential care and goodness, and, in order thereto, *the tempter came to him* He had by his secret suggestions, during the forty days before, sought to disturb the mind of Jesus, but in vain, now therefore he assumes a visible form, not such a fearful figure as our early misguided apprehensions suggest, and our delusive prints hold him forth, but some pleasing human shape, or perhaps transformed into an angel of light The tempter well knew the circumstances of our Lord, and directs his assault where the weakest side appeared he hoped the cravings of hunger might lead him to some undue means of relief Thus vigilant and crafty is the wily adversary to suit his temptation to our situation and condition, and particularly in want and distress, to suggest some sinful expedient to extricate ourselves from our troubles, without waiting God's leisure, or consulting his will He often says, Better steal than starve, though God says, 'Tis better die than sin He prefaces his temptation with a sly insinuation; *If thou be the Son of God*, as if he doubted the fact, though so lately the voice from heaven had affirmed it, and he desired to shake the faith of Jesus, suggesting, that if this really were the case, it was inconceivable that God would leave such a one to starve in the wilderness Or, *seeing thou art the Son of God*, he admits the fact, and wishes to see a present exertion of his divine power in a miracle so necessary for his own support, *command that these stones be made bread* Note, (1) The great battery of the devil is raised against our faith, for if the foundation of our confidence be shaken, the superstructure must needs totter He is ever striking at this to make the children of God doubt their adoption, and, in order thereto, he urges against them sometimes their outward distresses, sometimes their inward weakness and infirmities, as if both the one and the other were inconsistent with the relation they claim (2) If once the enemy can engage us to entertain hard thoughts of God, then he is sure to prevail

Christ repels the assaults of the wicked one with the shield of faith, and the sword of the Spirit, which is the word of God, and therein teaches us how to ward off the like temptations *He answered and said, It is written, Man shall not live by bread alone, but by every word that proceedeth out of the mouth of God* The Lord hath other ways of supporting men's bodies than by bread merely, and therefore it was not so absolutely necessary for his sustenance, but that he could be supported without it, nor would he at Satan's instigation do that which might look like distrust of his Father's care, doubt of his word, or suspicion of his relation to him Note, (1) The written word is the only rule of our faith and practice if Christ himself adhered to that alone, let no pretences of the Spirit's superior teaching lead us off from this sure guide (2) God's time is the best time, and *he that believeth will not make haste*, will take no rash step for his own relief under his trials, but patiently expect the salvation of God

(2) The first attack being repelled, a second is prepared since he cannot lead the Saviour to distrust or despair, he will try to puff him up with presumption So unwearied is the tempter, and often changing his wiles, according to our circumstances, from one extreme to the other

He taketh him up, by divine permission, with the consent of Jesus, who suffered the devil to have such power over his body, and to carry him, *into the holy city*, Jerusalem, so called from the peculiar privileges it enjoyed of God's worship and ordinances, *and set him upon a pinnacle or wing of the temple*, one of the battlements probably, which was of an immense height And since Jesus had expressed such confidence in his Father, and unshaken dependance on his word, he grounds thereon his temptation *If thou be the Son of God, cast thyself down*, and give an incontestible proof of it to the priests and people worshipping below, who will no doubt receive thee as the Messiah, when thus coming as if immediately from heaven into the temple nor will there be any danger in the experiment, since *it is written*, and therein thou art fully satisfied, *He shall give his angels*, &c The application of which words to Christ was right, but a part of the text is artfully suppressed, *in all thy ways*, for out of the way of duty we may never hope for protection And it is misapplied, being designed not to tempt men to rush into temptation, presuming upon the divine care, but to engage the faithful to trust God in time of trial, assured of divine support From all which we may observe, (1.) That one grand engine of the tempter is, to make our heads giddy by setting us up on high The pinnacle of the temple is a dangerous exaltation Those who are eminent in station, fortune, or reputation, advanced to dignities in church or state, or distinguished with abilities, *gifts*, graces, or even success in their ministry, need to tremble for themselves, and the higher they stand, to cleave the faster to Jesus their temple, lest their exaltation prove their destruction (2) Though the devil can tempt, he cannot compel Sin is our own act, and without our consent the most dire temptations fasten not the least evil on our conscience Should we be tempted to the greatest crimes, to self-murder, or blasphemy, the Son of God was himself thus tempted, yet without sin (3) Scriptures may be suggested by the enemy to the minds of God's people, much to their distress and discouragement on the one hand, or, on the other, to lull their consciences in fatal security, therefore we must search the scriptures diligently, that we may know what is God's mind therein, and be kept from those dangerous errors and delusions, which often the scriptures are vouched to patronize (4) We must never separate the means from the end, nor expect out of God's way the protection of his providence and grace Though Jesus is a Saviour to the uttermost, we may not sin that grace may abound, and predestination to life eternal necessarily includes the diligent improvement of all the means needful to make our election sure

The same word of truth supplies our Lord with a full confutation of Satan's sophistry; for in the scriptures there is an answer ready for every case, and we can be in no circumstance or temptation, but that word will afford us direction, strength, and comfort *It is written again, Thou shalt not tempt the Lord thy God* The tempter had said, *It is written*, but the scripture cannot contradict itself, and therefore to know the mind of God, we must compare spiritual things with spiritual, and not mutilate the word of truth, nor apply it contrary to the intention of the Spirit To trust God is duty, to tempt him is sinful Christ needed no confirmation of what he was already assured, nor was he called unnecessarily to make an experiment of God's power in such a miraculous preservation

(3) Once more, though baffled, the enemy returns to the charge, and summoning up all his force in one blow, by the most glaring display of this world's glory tempts our Lord to the horrid crime of idolatry The forest of our temptations is sometimes reserved for the last, that God's power and grace may be more gloriously displayed, and the devil's malice most bitterly disappointed

Again the devil taketh him up, probably transported him thro' the air, *into an exceeding high mountain*, that the fictitious scene he was about to display might appear real, *and there he sheweth him all the kingdoms of the world, and the glory of them* Whatever grandeur, wealth, pleasure, reigned in them, were set before him in the most enlivened colours, to catch his fancy, and engage his admiration and all these he proffers to bestow on him, on one condition, which thousands, without any such reward, were daily doing, *if thou wilt fall down and worship me.* A proposal so horrid, as would not bear a thought, and is rejected with detestation *Get thee hence, Satan*, such insolence provoked the Saviour's righteous indignation, and he drives the tempter from his presence, unable to endure such a daring attempt upon the majesty of Jehovah, the only object of worship, *for it is written, Thou shalt worship the Lord thy God, and him only shalt thou serve* Note, (1) The minds of God's greatest saints may be sometimes harrassed with the most blasphemous suggestions, and they should not count this as if some strange thing happened unto them (2) The glory of the world is the grand snare the enemy lays for men's souls, and it looks very desirable to the eye of sense, but faith sees through the delusion, beholds vanity stamped on every thing beneath the sun, and scorns *all this* which Satan offers as dung and loss, compared with the excellency of the knowledge of Christ, and the glories of his grace (3) Some temptations come under the guise of plausibility and harmlessness, and require recollection before we can discover the craft of the devil, others bring the brand of hell in their forehead, and would bear men down merely with the weight of the present advantage thence accruing these must not be parlyed with a moment, but rejected with abhorrence (4) God is alone the object of worship, and whatever else be made the idol of our adoration, whether the horrid forms of monsters in a pagod, or the images of saints, and virgins, and crucifixes in a popish chapel, it is no better than falling down to the devil

5 Satan, now vanquished and unable to resist the commanding word of Jesus, quits the field He found him more than man, *invulnerable in every part*, and feels himself a vanquished foe Thus shall the sons of God through this great Captain of their salvation tread Satan under their feet, enabled to wrestle with spiritual wickednesses, and to prevail against the power of darkness Though hard the conflict, the victory is sure to all who stand fast, strong in the Lord, and in the power of his might

6 The angels, the attendant servants of *Jesus*, now visibly appeared, and ministred unto him They had beheld, as spectators, the conflict and triumphs of the Lord, and now congratulate his victory, and supply him with those needful refreshments which his exhausted body craved *Note*, (1) Christ alone obtained the victory for us, his own arm hath brought salvation unto him (2) Angels minister to the heirs of salvation; we need not fear therefore what devils can do against us (3) Though our relief be for a while delayed, it shall assuredly come at last *Trust in the Lord* therefore, *and verily thou shalt be fed* (4) Our Master was himself tempted, that he might feel for us, and supply us with all needful supports, when we are in like manner sore thrust at that we should fall

m Mark i 14 Luke iv 31 John iv 43 12 ¶ m Now when Jeſus had heard that John was
caſt into priſon, he departed into Galilee 13 And
leaving Nazareth, he came and dwelt in Capernaum
which is upon the ſea-coaſt, in the borders of Zabulon
and Nephthalim 14 That it might be fulfilled which
n Iſa ix 1, 2 was ſpoken by Eſaias the prophet, ſaying, 15 n The
land of Zabulon, and the land of Nephthalim, *by* the way
of the ſea beyond Jordan, Galilee of the Gentiles 16
The people which ſat in darkneſs ſaw great light and
to them which ſat in the region and ſhadow of death,
light is ſprung up 17 ¶ From that time Jeſus began
o Chap iii 2 to preach, and to ſay, o Repent, for the kingdom of
heaven is at hand

v 12—17 Chriſt now, having entered upon his miniſtry, began to publiſh the glad tidings of that ſalvation he came to procure Many events are recorded which intervened between his temptations on the mount and his abode at Capernaum theſe we ſhall meet with in the other evangeliſts Matthew haſtens forward to the time when John was caſt into priſon, on which occaſion Jeſus departed from Nazareth to Galilee, and fixed his abode at Capernaum, a city in the tribe of Nephthali, bordering on Zebulon, ſituate on the ſea of Tiberias, called elſewhere the lake of Genneſareth The men of Nazareth had rejected him, *Luke* iv 29 and therefore God juſtly leaves them to themſelves, and ſends his Son and his goſpel to a place that will more cheerfully welcome them

1 Special notice is here taken of the fulfilment of the Scripture in this removal of our Lord, as Iſaias had before of old propheſied, *that the people* in theſe regions of Zebulon and Nephthali, called *Galilee of the Gentiles* from the intermixture of a multitude of ſtrangers of other nations among the Jews, *which ſat in darkneſs*, in ſpiritual darkneſs and ignorance, *ſaw a great light*, Chriſt the ſun of righteouſneſs ariſing with healing in his wings, and bringing life into light and liberty to thoſe *who ſat in the region and ſhadow of death*, dead in treſpaſſes and ſins till quickened by the effectual power of this Saviour's grace, and enlightened by the glorious goſpel he preached *Note*, (1) They who are deſtitute of the knowledge of Chriſt are in darkneſs reſpecting all the things that make for their everlaſting peace, and near the borders of eternal death (2) Chriſt is to the ſoul what the ſun is to the world, yea more, for he is not only the author of light, but gives the faculty of viſion alſo, without which the light would ſhine in darkneſs, and the darkneſs never comprehend it (3) The way in which ſpiritual light is diffuſed is by the preaching of the goſpel, where this is not truly miniſtred, darkneſs muſt needs reign uncontrouled

2 We are told what was the ſubject of his miniſtry from the time he began to open his commiſſion, *Repent ye, for the kingdom of heaven is at hand*, the ſame words and the ſame ſubject on which John his harbinger had preached before for in the great eſſential doctrines all faithful miniſters of the goſpel perfectly agree Jeſus preached repentance, not only as what *we muſt do*, but *what he would give*, without which in vain were every call to repent

p Mark i 16 Luke v 2 18 ¶ And p Jeſus walking by the ſea of Galilee,
ſaw two brethren, Simon, called Peter, and Andrew
his brother, caſting a net into the ſea (for they were
fiſhers) 19 And he ſaith unto them, Follow me, and
q 1 Kings xix 19, 20 I will make you fiſhers of men 20 And q they ſtraight-
way left *their* nets and followed him 21 And r going
r Mark i 19 from thence, he ſaw other two brethren, James *the ſon*
of Zebedee, and John his brother, in a ſhip with Ze-
bedee their father, mending their nets and he called
s Chap x 37 Mark x 28 Luke xiv 33 them 22 And they immediately s left the ſhip and
their father, and followed him

v 18—22 Chriſt being now about to erect his kingdom in the world, he is pleaſed to make choice of certain perſons to be the conſtant attendants of his miniſtry and ſpectators of his miracles, that they might afterwards go forth to tell of the things they had heard and ſeen, and ſpread the goſpel of their maſter to the ends of the earth

1 The perſons he made choice of were ſuch as to human view were very unfit inſtruments for the work, but the more evident would it be that the power was of God, and not of them, when afterwards they appeared ſo mighty in word and deed They were by occupation fiſhermen, whom Jeſus, as he walked by the ſea-ſhore, ſaw employed in their honeſt and laborious vocation the firſt two were caſting a net into the ſea, brethren by blood as well as buſineſs, their names Simon and Andrew, men unlettered, unknown, and unnoticed, the next two were of the like employment, and with their father Zebedee mending their nets *Note*, (1) Not only to the poor was the goſpel preached by our Lord, but from them the great pillars of the church were taken let them therefore never be deſpiſed (2) It is happy in a family when brethren in blood are brethren in the Lord, and heirs together of the grace of life

(3) Induſtry is highly commendable, and Jeſus wills that all his ſervants ſhould be found well employed idleneſs is the ſure characteriſtic of Satan's ſervice

2 They had it ſeems before, *ſee John* i 37 become acquainted with Chriſt, but now they are called to conſtant attendance upon him, *Follow me*, and, by an image taken from their preſent employment, he lets them know the more honourable ſervice for which he deſigned them, *I will make you fiſhers of men*, the inſtruments of gathering ſouls by the goſpel into his church And what he calls them to he will qualify them for in following him they ſhall learn a wiſdom which the ſchools can never teach them *Note*, (1) Unleſs miniſters have a divine call, as well as a human ordination, they will run without being ſent, and can expect no bleſſing in their work (2) None can truly preach Chriſt who have not firſt faithfully followed him (3) If in our ordinary vocations diligence is neceſſary, how much more needful is it that fiſhers of men ſhould be indefatigable and laborious, when the gain of immortal ſouls will ſo amply repay their toil

3 Theſe diſciples immediately obeyed the call, quitting their employment, and leaving their deareſt relatives, to devote and attach themſelves entirely to their divine Lord and Maſter, ſuch power had his conſtraining word, and ſo readily and chearfully did they follow him *Note*, (1) When Chriſt effectually calls a ſinner, ſuch power accompanies his word as draws the heart by irreſiſtible bonds of love unto his bleſſed Self (2) There are ſeaſons when, for the ſake of Chriſt, we muſt be ready to part with all (3) Thoſe who are employed in the miniſtry have eſpecial need to detach themſelves from worldly concerns, that they may give themſelves wholly up to their awful truſt and charge

23 ¶ And Jeſus went about all Galilee, t teaching in t Chap ix 35
their ſynagogues, and preaching the goſpel of the king-
dom, and healing all manner of ſickneſs and all manner
of diſeaſe among the people 24 And his fame went
throughout all Syria and they brought unto him all
ſick people that were taken with divers diſeaſes and tor-
ments, and thoſe which were poſſeſſed with devils, and
thoſe which were lunatic, and thoſe that had the palſy,
and he healed them 25 And u there followed him u Mark iii 7
great multitudes of people from Galilee, and *from* Deca-
polis, and *from* Jeruſalem, and *from* Judea, and *from* be-
yond Jordan

v 23—25 We have here,

1 Chriſt's labours as a preacher All Galilee heard his teaching, he appeared publicly in their ſynagogues, and publiſhed *the goſpel of the kingdom*, the glad tidings of ſalvation, exhorting his hearers to that repentance and newneſs of life which became thoſe who had received the grace of God in truth

2 His cures as a phyſician, wrought in confirmation of his doctrine He did good to men's bodies as well as ſouls, and by a word healed *all manner of ſickneſs and diſeaſes* among the people, however violent, inveterate, or of long ſtanding the incurables of other phyſicians went from him reſtored to perfect health and ſoundneſs Nor did he merely relieve the moſt tormenting diſorders of the body, but the more deplorable ones of the mind, the lunatic recovered the perfect exerciſe of his reaſon, and the poſſeſſed, whoſe bodies by divine permiſſion Satan's legions had ſeized and miſerably harraſſed, were ſet free, and the foul fiends ejected No painful operations, no tedious courſe of medicine almoſt as bad as the malady, were employed a word, a touch, compleated the cure, and all was *freely* done, without money and without price The moſt wretched, the pooreſt, never applied in vain No marvel that his fame ſpread through the adjacent coaſts of Syria, and that multitudes of patients ſought this great phyſician's help His cures beſpoke his character, and vouched for his miſſion, they were innumerable, public, immediate, perfect, ſuch as none could diſpute or gainſay, his very enemies being judges And they repreſent the more noble cures of men's ſouls by divine grace from all the diſeaſes of ſin, wherein we ſee the Saviour's power ſtill diſplayed

3 His popularity ariſing from both An immenſe auditory, from all the parts, near and diſtant, aſſembled, curious to hear, or deſirous to be healed, or convinced by his preaching and miracles, or enviouſly waiting for an opportunity to deſtroy him *Note*, (1) The preachers of the goſpel will generally be popular, their meſſage engages the attention of an auditory (2) Multitudes hear the goſpel, but few receive it to the ſaving of their ſouls

CHAP V

This chapter, with the two following, contains our Saviour's ſermon on the mount, the deſign of which ſeems to be not only to reſcue the law from the corrupt gloſſes of the elders, but, by opening its ſpirituality, to ſhew the neceſſity of a better righteouſneſs than our own, in order to our acceptance with God After the preparatory circumſtances, ver 1, 2 He ſhews, 1 Wherein true bleſſedneſs conſiſts, ver 3—12 2 Preſcribes the ſtanding rules of his diſciples duty, ver 13—20 3 Gives the true expoſition of God's law, in oppoſition to the corrupt gloſſes of the Scribes and Phariſees, ver 21—48

1 AND ſeeing the multitudes, he went up into a
mountain and when he was ſet, his diſciples
came unto him 2 And [a] he opened his mouth, and
taught them, ſaying,

a Prov viii 1 2 6

v 1, 2 Among the multitudes who followed him, many profeſſed themſelves his diſciples For their ſakes therefore eſpecially, as well as for the improvement of all who attended him, he took the preſent opportunity to lay open to them at large the doctrines of truth For the convenience of being heard, he went up to a mountain, where, ſurrounded by his diſciples, and ſeated amidſt the attentive throng, *He opened his mouth, and taught them*, whilſt they hung upon his lips, and in ſilence, with their eyes fixed on him, drank in the ſacred truths he uttered *Note*, It is enlivening and encouraging to the miniſters of the goſpel to behold a numerous and attentive auditory, and that is ſacred fire, which not the deſire of being popular, but the hope of being extenſively uſeful, kindles in their heart, and gives energy and warmth to their diſcourſe

3 ¶ [b] Bleſſed *are* the poor in ſpirit for theirs is the
kingdom of heaven 4 [c] Bleſſed *are* they that mourn
[d] for they ſhall be comforted 5 [e] Bleſſed *are* the meek
[f] for they ſhall inherit the earth 6 [g] Bleſſed *are* they
which do hunger and thirſt after righteouſneſs for [h] they
ſhall be filled 7 Bleſſed *are* the merciful [i] for they
ſhall obtain mercy 8 [k] Bleſſed *are* the pure in heart
[l] for they ſhall ſee God 9 [m] Bleſſed *are* the peace-
makers for they ſhall be called the children of God
10 [n] Bleſſed *are* they which are perſecuted for righteouſ-
neſs ſake [o] for theirs is the kingdom of heaven 11
[p] Bleſſed are ye when men ſhall revile you, and perſecute
you, and [q] ſhall ſay all manner of evil againſt you falſly
for my ſake 12 [r] Rejoice and be exceeding glad for
great *is* your reward in heaven for [s] ſo perſecuted they
the prophets which were before you

b Iſ lvii 15 Prov xvi 19 Iſa lvii 15 & lxvi 1 c Iſa lxi 2, 3 Luke vi 21 d Iſa xxxv 10, Rev vii 17 e 1 Pet iii 4 f Pſ xxxvii 11 g Pſ xlii 2 & lxiii 1 h Iſa lv 1 Luke i 53 John vi 35 & vii 37 i Pſ xxxvii 26 Chap vi 14 2 Tim i 16 Heb vi 10 k Pſ xxiv 4 l Iſa xxxiii 17 1 John iii 2, 3 m 1 Cor xiii 12 Heb xii 14 n 2 Tim iii 12 o 1 Thes i 5 p Luke vi 22 q 1 Pet iv 14 r Luke vi 23 Acts v 41 & xvi 25 Col i 24 s 2 Chron xxxvi 16 Chap xxiii 34 37 Acts vii 52 1 Thes ii 15

v 3—12 To be happy is the univerſal deſire, but, whilſt all purſue this as their aim, few, very few, attain the accompliſhment of their wiſhes and the reaſon is evident they miſtake both wherein man's true happineſs conſiſts, and the means which lead to it, conſequently are ever bewildered in a fruitleſs ſearch, and tormented with continual diſappointment To divert us from our wrong purſuits, to inform us what is our true good, and to direct us to the attainment of real bleſſedneſs, is the gracious deſign of our adored Lord Yet to many the doctrines he advances will appear paradoxical and ſtrange, tho, bleſſed be his name, every enlightened and converted ſoul will own, that, however ſtrange they ſeem to others, they are found by his happy experience to be indeed the true ſayings of God

In eight characters Chriſt ſhews wherein true bleſſedneſs conſiſts, and pronounces on each, *Bleſſed are ye* at preſent they are the truly happy ſouls on earth, and their reward awaiteth them eternally in heaven O may this bleſſedneſs be mine!

The firſt beatitude

Bleſſed are the poor in ſpirit, for theirs is the kingdom of heaven Wherein then doth this *poverty of ſpirit* conſiſt? I anſwer, (1) In a deep and humbling ſenſe of our own ſpiritual wants and wretchedneſs, which brings off the ſinner from every dependance upon his own goodneſs for acceptance with God, and his own abilities to walk and pleaſe him, to a conſtant renunciation of himſelf, to a repoſe of his confidence on the blood and righteouſneſs of Jeſus alone as his title to God's regard, and on the grace of Jeſus for all ſufficiency to think or act aright (2) In an entire reſignation of ourſelves to God, and contentment with our lot, ſitting looſe to the world and all the things of it, in poverty chearful, our minds conformed to our condition, in proſperity humble, condeſcending, kind, and ſympathizing with the neceſſitous (3) In low thoughts of ourſelves, our abilities, attainments, and poſſeſſions of whatever kind, in honour preferring others to ourſelves, the laſt and leaſt in our own opinion, and ſeeing much, very much, to humble us in the view of our miſimprovement of thoſe bleſſings which God hath beſtowed on us, and in which he hath made us to differ from others Now ſuch as theſe are bleſſed in the preſent ſatisfaction ariſing from the exerciſe of ſuch a ſpirit and temper, and in a happy freedom from the murmurs, repinings, diſcontent, and mortifications, which make the proud and diſcontented perpetually uneaſy They are bleſſed with the experience of God's love and favour, who looks with delight and approbation on him that is poor and of a contrite ſpirit, and, as the ſummit of all felicity, *theirs is the kingdom of heaven*, the riches of the kingdom of grace below, and all the unſearchable riches of Chriſt and glory above, are their aſſured and eternal portion

The ſecond beatitude

Bleſſed are they that mourn We are apt to count mourners miſerable, and to judge of happineſs by the ſmiles of the countenance, but Chriſt teaches us a different leſſon Not that all who mourn are bleſſed there is the mourning of *diſcontent*, the ſorrow of the world that worketh death, the inconſolable tears of thoſe who lament like Micah after their idols, and the melancholy of deſpair, theſe bring a curſe and torment inſtead of a bleſſing The mourning here commended is, (1) A penitential mourning over ſin, in the views of our baſe ingratitude, a mourning after God, under darkneſs and deſertion, a mourning over the diſhonour brought upon him by the impieties of the wicked and the unfaithfulneſs of his people, a mourning over the diſtreſſes of the miſerable, and eſpecially a mourning over loſt ſouls, which makes our tears like thoſe of Jeſus flow, whilſt we are pouring forth before God our fervent prayers on their behalf Theſe are bleſſed the tears ſhed for ſin have a ſweetneſs unutterable, a ſacred pleaſure mingles *with them, to* which all the noiſy mirth of fools, excluſive of the heavineſs which ſucceeds, is not to be compared, and they are the ſeed of eternal joy, for *they ſhall be comforted*, here below, in a ſenſe of God's love ſhed abroad in their hearts, in the conſolations ariſing from a ſenſe of pardoning love, in the ſacred delight of beholding ſinners turned from the evil of their ways, and hereafter in the eternal fruition of God, and the inconceivable bleſſedneſs thence ariſing, when every tear ſhall be wiped from our eyes, and we ſhall drink of pure, unſullied, and eternal pleaſures as out of a river

The third beatitude

Bleſſed are the meek *Reſpecting God*, ſubmiſſive to his word and providences, never replying againſt the one, or murmuring againſt the other *reſpecting man*, mild, inoffenſive, eaſy to be intreated, unmoved with provocation, forbearing and forgiving, reſenting no injuries, actuated by no private revenge, in patience and peace poſſeſſing their ſouls, yet not mean-ſpirited, cowardly, and tame, through fear of man, but, whilſt in their own cauſe gentle as the lamb, in the cauſe of God and truth bold as lions, zealous to maintain the rights of others, whilſt they recede from their own, and ſteady patrons of the injured and the abſent They are bleſſed, they are, like their Lord, happy in themſelves, beloved of all who know the value of ſuch a ſpirit, and dear in the ſight of God *They ſhall inherit the earth*, ſhall have as much of this preſent world as is for their good, but above all, and what ſeems here chiefly intended, they ſhall have a part in that better *new earth* wherein dwelleth righteouſneſs, and be counted inheritors among the ſaints in light

The fourth beatitude

Bleſſed are thoſe who hunger and thirſt after righteouſneſs The righteouſneſs here ſpoken of as the object of deſire is, (1) *The imputed righteouſneſs* of Jeſus Chriſt, which the guilty ſinner, who feels his ſpiritual nakedneſs, eagerly longs for, as the famiſhed cries for food, or the parched throat craves the cooling draught, aſſured without it he muſt periſh (2) *The implanted righteouſneſs* which the Spirit of Jeſus communicates and for this the poor and helpleſs ſinner hungers more than for his daily bread, inaſmuch as the life and health of his ſoul are infinitely preferable to the life and health of his body Theſe *are bleſſed* ſouls, for every ſuch deſire is in a meaſure the proof of our poſſeſſing the righteouſneſs after which we pant, and *they ſhall be filled* out of the fulneſs of Jeſus, who hath enough of both to ſupply all their wants, to make them completely righteous in himſelf here, and to fill them with joy and peace in believing, and hereafter to perfect them in holineſs, and bring them to happineſs eternal

The fifth beatitude

Bleſſed are the merciful This is the moſt amiable character of God, and herein his people reſemble him (1) Mercy is *their temper*, they have a heart that can be touched with human wretchedneſs, and though they may not have it always in their power to relieve, they are ever tenderly compaſſionate towards the diſtreſſes of the miſerable (2) Mercy *is their practice* ſo far as their power extends they are ready to ſhew mercy, yea, they take delight therein, and count this work its own reward They are merciful *to men's ſouls*, pitying and inſtructing the ignorant, warning the unruly, comforting the feeble mind, helping the weak, and labouring to ſnatch the wicked as brands from the burning They are merciful *to men's bodies*, relieving the neceſſities of the poor, the friendleſs, and the deſtitute, they are eyes to the blind, feet to the lame, phyſicians to the ſick, ſupport to the aged and infirm; ready to aſſiſt with their advice, their purſe, or influence, according to the various diſtreſſes of thoſe who apply to them yea, diligent to diſcover thoſe objects of modeſt worth and neglected indigence that are aſhamed or backward to apply for relief They are merciful even *to the brute beaſts* not only their ſervants and labourers are never vexed with unreaſonable burdens, their very cattle ſhare their clemency, and own the kind and tender maſter This is bleſſedneſs They who are thus like God in ſpirit,

will

will taste something of divine felicity, and of all the joys beneath the sun none will be found comparable with the exalted pleasure of doing good And *they shall obtain mercy* such merciful ones plead no merit the more they are enabled to do, the less opinion they entertain of their deserts, as every advance in grace brings proportionably greater light, and therewith greater humility They cast themselves therefore wholly on the mercy of God in Jesus Christ, and they shall find mercy of the Lord in the great day, and more they need not wish for, since his mercy includes eternal life and glory

The sixth beatitude

Blessed are the pure in heart, who by faith are cleansed from all allowed hypocrisy, covetousness, pride, and sensuality, jealous to keep themselves unspotted from the world, maintaining undefiled religion, in simplicity and godly sincerity walking with God, and desiring, as the summit of their happiness, to be perfect as their Father which is in heaven is perfect They are blessed in the present paths of pleasantness and peace in which they go, and *they shall see God* as the consummation of all felicity, be with him where he is, be like him as he is, and from the light of his countenance, and the constant effusions of his love, drink in blessedness unutterable and eternal

The seventh beatitude

Blessed are the peace-makers, men of peace themselves, and desirous to cultivate the like disposition among others, following it with all men as far as is consistent with truth and purity, averse to all disputes and angry contentions, softening the spirits of the exasperated, and kindly interposing, though sometimes at the expence of much ill-will, to repair the breaches, and heal the divisions, which the fiery and self-willed spirits of others have occasioned the first to forgive, the last to be offended, and where others prepare themselves for battle, still ready, though injured, to seek reconciliation Such men shall be *blessed* in their deed they shall be accounted faithful subjects of the Prince of peace, and *be called the children of God*, who is the God of peace, and if children, then heirs, heirs of God, and joint-heirs with Christ, appointed to reign with him in glory everlasting

The eighth beatitude

Blessed are they that are persecuted for righteousness sake All who follow Christ must expect his cross, and every godly man, as long as a child of wickedness is in the world, must suffer persecution of one kind or other where power is with oppressors, there it will reach to fines, imprisonment, and even death itself, where milder governments give protection from grosser injuries, there the lower methods of reviling, calumny, falsehood, insult, ridicule, and vile misrepresentations, will be the lot of Christ's disciples Various pretexts indeed are commonly used to give a specious colouring to this conduct in lands professing godliness, as if it was not righteousness men persecuted, but what they are pleased to call enthusiasm, or to stamp with some other opprobrious name but, whatever occasional offences may have been given, the ground and root of the malignity shewn against the people of God is their profession of the doctrines of the divine righteousness, which the proud and wise men must ever scoff at, and the practice of experimental godliness, which is equally reproving and offensive to the formal and profane on which accounts therefore, now and ever, the few faithful must expect to follow Jesus bearing his reproach But, however they are regarded among men, they are pronounced blessed by the author of all blessing, and *theirs is the kingdom of heaven* Nor need any now marvel at these things among us, when, among God's professing people of old, *the prophets* were so *persecuted* before us, Jeremiah, Isaiah, Elijah, &c and therefore we are commanded to *rejoice and be exceeding glad* to be numbered among such worthies, and expect that *great reward* in glory which God hath promised to those who, by patient continuance in well doing, seek with them glory, honour, and immortality

t Mark ix 50 Luke xiv 34
u Prov iv 18, Phil ii 15
x Mark iv 21 Luke viii 16 & xi 33
y 1 Pet ii 12
z 1 Cor xiv 25

13 Ye are the salt of the earth t but if the salt have
lost his savour, wherewith shall it be salted? It is thence-
forth good for nothing, but to be cast out, and to be
trodden under foot of men 14 u Ye are the light of
the world A city that is set on a hill cannot be hid
15 x Neither do men light a candle, and put it under
a bushel but on a candlestick, and it giveth light unto
all that are in the house. 16 Let your light so shine
before men, y that they may see your good works, and
z glorify your Father which is in heaven

v 13—16 These words are directed to the disciples in general, and to the apostles and ministers of Christ in particular, and their character is set forth under two similitudes.

1. As the *salt of the earth.* Their lives and conversations must be exemplary, not only free from taint themselves, that is, from the allowed practice of sin, but endeavouring to preserve others from the putrefaction of it, seasoning the earth with the doctrines of the gospel, diffusing the *savour of the knowledge of Christ* in every place, and thus becoming blessings to mankind But, should they depart from the truth, disgrace their character, degenerate into lukewarmness and indifference, or apostatize to erroneous principles and licentious practices, their state, if not utterly desperate, is seldom ever retrieved, like stars they fall to rise no more though their profession may continue, their savour is lost, they become insipid and tasteless, and are doomed *to be cast out and trodden under foot of men* as worthless and contemptible, expelled from the communion of the saints below, and everlastingly excluded from the assembly of the blessed above

2 As *the light of the world*, to spread the bright truths of salvation among benighted mortals, and point out to them the path which leads to eternal day, especially to lead sinners to Christ the light of life and in so doing they would be distinguished as *a city set on a hill*, and needed peculiar circumspection whilst so many eyes would be fixed upon them Every minister, every christian, stands on an eminence, more is expected from them than from others, and many watch for their halting as candles are lighted not to be covered, but to be set *on a candlestick, and give light to all in the house*, so were they endued with gifts and graces to illuminate the church of Christ, and diffuse the gospel word around, *neither* through fear or shame concealing ought of the whole counsel of God, and in their lives, as well as lips, must their light shine, in every work of faith and labour of love which may be profitable to men's bodies or souls, that, whilst others are stirred up to holy emulation thereby, abundant praise also may redound to God, who is then eminently glorified when his people bring forth much fruit

17 ¶ Think not that I am come to destroy the law
or the prophets a I am not come to destroy, but to ful- a Rom iii 31 & x 4 Gal iii 24
fil 18 For verily I say unto you, b Till heaven and
earth pass, one jot or one tittle shall in no wise pass from b Luke xvi 17
the law, till all be fulfilled 19 c Whosoever therefore
shall break one of these least commandments, and shall c Jam ii 10
teach men so, he shall be called the least in the kingdom
of heaven but whosoever shall do and teach *them*, the
same shall be called great in the kingdom of heaven
20 For I say unto you, That except your righteousness
shall exceed d *the righteousness* of the scribes and Phari- d Chap. xxiii 23, &c Rom ix 31 & x 3
sees, ye shall in no case enter into the kingdom of hea-
ven

v 17—20 As the former verses seemed particularly addressed to his disciples, our Lord here more generally directs his discourse to the multitude

1 He obviates the prejudices he knew many would entertain, and confutes the objections his enemies would make, as if he was about to abrogate the law, and introduce a new system, when in fact he only meant to rescue the oracles of God from the corrupt glosses the false teachers had put on them

[1.] He is not come to destroy the law and the prophets, as some of them might think, but to fulfil them To fulfil the *moral law*, by his own perfect obedience, the *ceremonial*, by answering in his own person, and oblation of himself, all the types and figures, the *prophets*, by accomplishing all their predictions, yea, and so far from loosening the obligations to obedience, he came, in perfect correspondence with God's ministers before him, to enforce them, and to vindicate the everlasting rule of moral righteousness from the mistakes and adulterations of the Scribes and Pharisees, to explain its spirituality and extent, and from right principles to urge the practice of true holiness.

[2.] He asserts the perpetuity and eternal obligation of the moral law whilst heaven and earth endures, not a tittle shall pass from it unaccomplished, nor the least of its commands ever be abolished It is the transcript of God's holiness, he can require nothing less, the least failure is eternally mortal, and though we are relieved by the blood and righteousness of our divine Substitute from the condemning power of the law, our duty still remains the same, and we are as much as ever bound to regard this as the one unerring rule of obedience Whoever therefore dares avowedly to transgress the least command, and *teach others to do so*, by his example or his preaching, as if it might be done with impunity, which was the case with many of the rabbi's of that day, he shall be rejected of God as least esteemed and worthless, and have no part in the kingdom of heaven, whilst they who, by the purity of their doctrine and the exemplariness of their conduct, enforce the necessity of obedience to every command, accounting none too trivial to be observed, they shall be esteemed and honoured of God as faithful here, and exalted to eternal glory hereafter *Note*, (1) The least sin hath eternal death for its wages (2) They who extenuate the evil of sin, and promise transgressors impunity, will be reckoned with as the most daring rebels against God's government

2. He professes it his purpose to enforce a righteousness beyond that of their most admired characters the Scribes and Pharisees, who were thought even to go to works of supererogation, and yet, what perhaps they would hear with astonishment, he assures his hearers their righteousness must exceed the righteousness of the

the Scribes and Pharisees, or they may never hope to enter the kingdom of heaven. The most extensive pharisaical righteousness of doctrinal orthodoxy, scrupulous exactness in the forms of religion, abstinence from grosser vices, accompanied with whatever alms, or fastings, or prayers, comes infinitely short of the spirituality of God's law; a perfect righteousness is required, which can alone be found in the adored Jesus, and that everlasting righteousness he was ordained to *bring in*, which faith embraces, and working by love, its genuine fruit, enables the redeemed to act on principles a Pharisee never knew; it purifies the heart, engages the soul to an universal delight in the law of God after the inward man, and begets the desire of unreserved obedience thereunto. And though in many things we all offend, yet are our persons and services then acceptable to God in Jesus Christ, whilst all the duties of the formal and self-righteous, when strained to the highest pitch, are only a greater abomination in the sight of God.

† O, To them. e Ex. xx. 13. f Le. xxiv. 21. g 1 John iii. 15. ‡ i. e. Empty. Jam. ii. 20. h Job xlii. 8. 1 Tim. ii. 8. i Job xx. i. Luke xii. 58. k Ps. xxxi. Isa. lv. 6. l John xv. m Chap. xviii. 34.

21 Ye have heard that it was said † by them of old
time, e Thou shalt not kill; and f whosoever shall kill,
shall be in danger of the judgment. 22 But I say unto you, that g whosoever is angry with his brother without a cause, shall be in danger of the judgment: and
whosoever shall say to his brother, ‡ Raca, shall be in
danger of the council: but whosoever shall say, Thou
fool, shall be in danger of hell-fire. 23 Therefore if
thou bring thy gift to the altar, and there rememberest
that thy brother hath ought against thee; 24 h Leave
there thy gift before the altar, and go thy way; first be
reconciled to thy brother, and then come and offer thy
gift. 25 i Agree with thine adversary quickly, k whilst
thou art in the way with him; lest at any time the adversary deliver thee to l the judge, and the judge deliver
thee to m the officer, and thou be cast into prison.
26 Verily I say unto thee, Thou shalt by no means
come out thence, till thou hast paid the uttermost farthing.

v. 21—26. Our Lord here gives a spiritual exposition of part of the moral law, and very different from that of their pharisaical teachers.

1. He begins with the sixth commandment. *Ye have heard*, out of the law read in the synagogue every sabbath-day, *that it was said by them of old time*, by the ancients, the elders who expounded the law, or *to the ancients* their forefathers, *thou shalt not kill*; and, confining the command merely to the act of murder, they taught, that only such as had been thus capitally criminal were liable to the sword of justice either of God or man, excluding all inferior deeds of the like tendency from being accounted breaches of the law. But Christ teaches them far otherwise. *I say unto you*, and he speaks as having authority, *that* not only you are forbidden to murder yourselves, or any other person, directly or indirectly, but whosoever entertains rash and causeless anger, or harbours a malicious wish or design against any man, though it never be executed, is liable to God's judgment, and criminal at his bar, as a murderer in his heart. If the evil within break forth in opprobrious or contemptuous language, such as, *Thou empty fellow*, it deserves the cognizance of the Sanhedrim; but if it proceeds yet farther, to bitter reviling and rash censures, to say, *Thou fool*, thou vile reprobate, such a breach of the law shall be punished with hell-fire. This should (1.) awaken in our minds a deep sense of our guilt and sin, and humble us before God in the review of our past transgressions; well may we cry, on the rehearsal of this law, *Lord have mercy upon us*. (2.) It should make us more watchful over our hearts, to suppress the rising of anger on trivial provocations, the inadvertencies or mistakes of others, or our own groundless surmises; yet, though the provocation be great, and the cause of anger just, we must see that it be not excessive, vehement, hurtful, or abiding. Our lips should be under the like restraint, that nothing hasty, perverse, spiteful, contemptible, reproachful, insolent, abusive, or malignant, proceed out of our mouth. The right government of the tongue is the sure proof of grace in the heart.

2. He recommends the exercise of that christian love and peace which is the fulfilling of the law; and if offences come, as they will in this corrupted state, we should be ever ready to confess our fault, ask pardon, make restitution, and seek reconciliation, and that,

[1.] Because till then we can offer to God no acceptable service, for all our worship and duties without charity are nothing worth. If therefore we have done an injury to any man, such as the breaches of the commandment above remarked, before we presume to offer our gift at God's altar, our praises, prayers, or whatever religious service we propose, we must reflect wherein and how much we have offended, and seek immediate reconciliation, since hatred and uncharitableness would make our best works an abomination, and love is better than all burnt-offerings. Should our brother continue inexorable, and refuse all the submissions we were ready to make, we may not then be restrained from drawing near to God, and may humbly expect that forgiveness from him which we cannot obtain from man.

[2.] Because, till this is done, the wrath of God abideth on us. For as it would be highly prudent for the debtor to seek to accomodate matters with his creditor before a suit commences, lest he should be summoned before the civil magistrate, and, the proof being clear, he should be consigned to the officer and cast into prison, without the possibility of deliverance, much more should the guilty sinner solicitously desire reconciliation with God and man, lest, dying in hatred and uncharitableness, his iniquities should witness against him at God's bar, and he should perish everlastingly. God is every sinner's *adversary*: our eternity depends on being at peace with him; therefore we need be anxious about it: the moment of time which is hurrying by is the space allotted us to agree with him; therefore every delay is highly dangerous: if we die in unpardoned sin, we have nothing to expect but a fearful judgment, where we are sure to be cast, the officers of vengeance are ready to execute the sentence, and the prison of hell is prepared to receive the condemned soul, where in everlasting burnings the guilty must be for ever paying, yet be never able to discharge the debt they owe to inexorable justice.

27 ¶ Ye have heard that it was said by them of old
time, n Thou shalt not commit adultery: 28 But I say
unto you, That o whosoever looketh on a woman to lust
after her, hath committed adultery with her already in his
heart. 29 And p if thy right eye offend thee, q pluck
it out, and cast *it* from thee: for *it* is profitable for
thee that one of thy members should perish, and not
that thy whole body should be cast into hell. 30 And
if thy right hand offend thee, cut it off, and cast *it*
from thee: for it is profitable for thee that one of thy
members should perish, and not that thy whole body
should be cast into hell. 31 It hath been said, Whosoever shall put away his wife, let him give her a writing of divorcement: 32 But I say unto you, That
s whosoever shall put away his wife, saving for the cause
of fornication, causeth her to commit adultery: and
whosoever shall marry her that is divorced, committeth
adultery.

n Ex. xx. 14. Deut. v. 18. o Job xxxi. 1. Prov. vi. 25. p Chap. xviii. 8. Luke ix. 43—47. q Chap. xix. 12. Rom. viii. 13. Col. iii. 5. r Deut. xxiv. 1. s Chap. xix. 9. Luke xvi. 18. Rom. vii. 3. 1 Cor. vii. 10, 11.

v. 27—32. The seventh commandment is here expounded by the same infallible interpreter: and well may we say, in the view of the spirituality of the law, *Thy commandment is exceeding broad*. The commandment delivered *to the ancients* at mount Sinai said, *Thou shalt not commit adultery*; and the pharisaical expositors had confined the breach of it literally to this grossest act of lewdness, excluding all the lower degrees of impurity, in thought, word, or deed: but Christ gives a very different extent to the command, to confound their proud claims who dared to boast they were *no adulterers*, Luke xviii. 11.

1. Every unchaste desire in the heart is adultery in the sight of God. The eye, the hand, the feet, the tongue, that by amorous glances, wanton dalliance, or impure discourse, tend to kindle the unhallowed fire of lust, or blow it up into a flame, and every contrivance to gratify this impurity of heart, though it be never brought to effect, involve the conscience in the same horrid guilt.

2. We are commanded therefore to cut off the right hand and pluck out the right eye, which would lead us to offend; not literally indeed to maim or mutilate our bodies, though that, if commanded, should be readily complied with rather than commit sin; but figuratively it signifies, however near and dear to us the sin may be, by long habit become incorporated as it were with our very frame, and hard to part with as these most useful members of our bodies, yet must it be torn away and cast from us with abhorrence. The *heart* must be kept with all diligence, no lewd vain thoughts harboured, especially when alone, solitude being often a great temptation to impurity. *The eyes* must be restrained from gazing on a tempting object, and kept as under a covenant from looking on a maid: yea, every object which would awaken evil desire must be shunned, lascivious representations on the stage, impure pictures, books of amours, lewd plays, *&c.* not to forget curious, expensive, and indecent dress, that exposes the person with a design to catch the wandering eye, and at once declares the spirit of the temptress, whilst it is a net to ensnare unstable souls. *The hand*, the foot, that can convey the silent innuendo, must be restrained from every motion of evil, *since he that toucheth her shall not be innocent*. *The tongue* must be rather plucked out than utter corrupt communication, or be suffered, by discourse grossly impure, or more dangerously and wittily lascivious, in sly insinuations and double meanings, to breathe the poison into the ears of the unwary. As the grand means to restrain these evils, every approach to them must be guarded by daily abstinence and self-denial, making no provision for the flesh to fulfil the lusts thereof.

3 A powerful argument is used to enforce this Raging appetite will not be conquered by any thing short of the terrors of the Lord The damnation of hell is the wages of uncleanness, and they who burn with impure desires must lie down in everlasting burnings, where the worm dieth not and the fire is not quenched, and dearly do men purchase carnal delights at this price of eternal misery The sentence is repeated, because men are very unwilling to believe what sounds so terrible in their ears, but the decree is fixed and immutable those who refuse to fear it now must feel it for ever Better therefore, far better, is it to suffer the present crucifixion of vile affections, than indulge them at the penalty of never-ending torments

4 All divorce is unlawful, except in the case of adultery The Jews indeed, for the hardness of their hearts, were permitted to put away their wives by a public instrument before witnesses, but this was contrary to the original institution of marriage, and therefore our Lord utterly condemns all separation, except in case of a breach of the matrimonial bond and should the person divorced marry again, she would commit adultery, as well as he who should take her to wife, and the crimes of both would also lie at the door of him who put her away, for they who lead others into sin shall be chargeable with all the guilt they bring upon them

33 ¶ Again ye have heard that it hath been said by
them of old time, ' Thou shalt not forswear thyself, but
shalt perform unto the Lord thine oaths 34 But I say
unto you, [t] Swear not at all, neither by heaven, [x] for
it is God's throne 35 Nor by the earth, for it is his
footstool neither by Jerusalem, [y] for it is the city of
the great King 36 Neither shalt thou swear by thy
head, because thou canst not make one hair white or
black 37 But [z] let your communication be, Yea, yea,
Nay, nay for whatsoever is more than these, cometh
of evil

[s] Exod xx 7 Lev xix 12 Deut xxiii 21 23 [t] Jam v 12 [x] Isa lxvi 1 Chap xxiii 22 [y] Ps xlviii 2 [z] 2 Cor i [?] Jam v [?]

v 33—37 The third commandment forbad perjury, and enjoined the performance of the vows which were made unto the Lord, or to men under the sanction of an oath in his name and hereunto the scribes restricted the commandment, accounting oaths in common allowable, if true, reckoning it no sin to swear by the creatures, and that such oaths laid them under no obligation to fulfil them but Christ would give them a better exposition

I say unto you, Swear not at all Not that every oath is unlawful, since in matters of controversy, before a judge, an oath for confirmation is an end of all strife, and on solemn occasions such appeals to God are high acts of religious worship, *see 2 Cor* i 23 but all rash swearing, on trivial occasions, in common discourse, is forbidden, with all unnecessary multiplication of oaths, under which this land groans God's sacred name must never be taken in the lips thoughtlessly, irreverently, wantonly, nor may we use any creature to swear by, neither heaven nor earth, nor the temple, nor our heads, our lives, our souls, much less the idols of heathenism, such as Jupiter, or the like, this being equally criminal as to swear by the name of God himself *Therefore our communication must be, Yea, yea, Nay, nay*, simply affirming or denying, without oath or imprecation *for whatsoever is more than these cometh of evil*, or *from the evil one* the devil, or from the fountain of evil in the corrupted heart Where more than simple affirmation or denial is thought to be necessary, there is implied a suspicion of veracity, which every rash oath for confirmation will serve but to increase, for they who make no conscience of an oath cannot be supposed to make conscience of a lie

38 ¶ Ye have heard that it hath been said, [a] An eye
for an eye, and a tooth for a tooth 39 But I say unto
you, [b] that ye resist not evil but whosoever shall smite
thee on thy right cheek, [c] turn to him the other also
40 And if any man will sue thee at the law, and take
away thy coat, let him have thy cloke also 41 And
whosoever shall compel thee to go a mile, go with him
twain 42 Give to him that asketh of thee, and [d] from
him that would borrow of thee, turn not thou away

[a] Exod xxi 24 Lev xxiv 20 Deut xix 21 [b] Prov xx 22 xxiv 29 Rom xii 17 19 1 Cor vi 7 1 Thess v 15 1 Pet iii 9 [c] Isa l 6 Lam iii 30 [d] Luke vi 30 Deut xv 7 [?] Luke vi 35

v 38—42 The law of retaliation, *Exod* xxi 24 which permitted the magistrate to execute a punishment of the same kind as the injury, or, as some suppose, to fix a mulct upon the offender equivalent to the harm done, had been grievously abused to extortion, and pleaded in vindication of private revenge Christ therefore teaches his disciples of what spirit they should be Magistracy is God's institution, and the punishment of men's crimes righteous and just, but all private revenge is forbidden It is true indeed that self-preservation, the care of our families, the honour of God, and the good of society, may often make the redress of injuries not only lawful, but necessary, but in innumerable instances our duty is meekly and silently to bear and forbear

1 If a man strike us on the right cheek, or otherwise injure our person, or treat us with indignity, we may not render evil for evil, and by a return of the blow inflame the quarrel, but put up with it, or, if it be needful, put the case into the hand of the civil magistrate and though our patience may be counted pusillanimity, and our forbearing may expose us to fresh insults, as if in fact we turned the other cheek, yet it is infinitely better, for conscience sake towards God, thus to suffer, than to maintain our character or gratify our revenge by a challenge or a fray, which must provoke his wrath and end in our perdition

2 In cases of injury to our property, whether by litigious, malicious, and false prosecutions, or in private disputes, though our coat were taken from us, it were better for peace sake to give our inner garment too, than fly to the law for redress for, if the matter of injury be small, which we may sustain without hurting our families, it is not only the most pious, but most prudent also, to sit down with the first loss, since the expences of the suit often exceed the value of what we may recover

3 If we are compelled by force to accompany a person a mile, rather than struggle or contend it is better to go two And thus in all other cases of affronts and injuries the like rule holds Hard tasks indeed for flesh and blood! but let it be remembered, *Flesh and blood cannot inherit the kingdom of God*

4 We must not only revenge no injuries, but do every kindness in our power to our neighbour, ready to relieve the wants of every real object of charity which presents itself to us, according to our abilities, and freely lending, without interest, to the industrious, but necessitous a small sum to help such a one in his trade, without any real loss to ourselves, may be of vast service to him And in the manner also of exercising our bounty we never should appear reluctant, frowning, or giving as if it was extorted from us, but be happy to have it in our power to relieve the wants of our poor petitioners

43 ¶ Ye have heard that it hath been said, [e] Thou
shalt love thy neighbour, and [f] hate thine enemy 44
But I say unto you, [g] Love your enemies, [h] bless them
that curse you, do good to them that hate you, and
[k] pray for them which despitefully use you, and persecute
you 45 [l] That ye may be the children of your Father
which is in heaven, for he maketh his sun to rise on the
evil and on the good, and sendeth rain on the just and
on the unjust 46 For [m] if ye love them which love
you, what reward have ye? do not even the publicans
the same? 47 And if ye salute your brethren only,
what do you more *than others*? do not even the publicans
so? 48 [n] Be ye therefore perfect, even as your Father
which is in heaven is perfect

[e] Lev xix 18 [f] Deut vii 1, 2 Ps cxxxix 21 22 [g] Luke vi 27 [h] Rom xii 14 1 Cor iv 12 [i] Rom xii 20 [k] Luke xxiii 34 Acts vii 60 [l] Luke vi 35 [m] Luke vi 32 [n] Lev xx 7 [?] Job ii Col i [?]

v 43—48 The whole law being fulfilled in one word, *Thou shalt love thy neighbour as thyself*, this is here insisted upon, and who that neighbour is, declared

The Jewish expositors had vilely corrupted this divine precept by the addition they had made to it, *Thou shalt hate thine enemy* And, as they confined their neighbour to those merely of their own religion and nation, they interpreted this as a command to hate all mankind beside, in direct opposition to the letter of God's law, *Exod* xxiii 4, 5 *Deut* xxiii 7 But Christ teaches us very differently

1 He recommends universal charity *I say unto you, Love your enemies* We cannot place confidence or take complacence in them or their evil ways, but we must bear all good-will towards them, remark with satisfaction whatever is commendable in them, and sincerely desire their present and eternal happiness, returning their curses with blessings, shewing every act of kindness to their bodies and souls who express the bitterest enmity against us, and, if they will suffer us to do no more, at least praying for those who despitefully use and persecute us such being the treatment the true disciples of Jesus may expect, and such the gracious returns they are bound to make And this is the distinguishing spirit of Christianity, and what nothing but the grace of Jesus can produce

2 He enforces his command with these strong arguments

[1] In so doing we shall resemble our Father which is in heaven, and prove our adoption of him, who, in the distribution of his providential mercies, causes his sun to rise and his rain to fall indiscriminately upon the evil and the good *Note*, (1) Our commonest though most unnoticed blessings are those for which we are most deeply indebted to God (2) No man's state is to be known by any outward gifts of Providence, the just and unjust share them alike (3) If God thus sets us the example, we must diligently copy it

[2] We must shew the distinguishing spirit of our profession, and adorn it If we only loved them who love us, or paid civility and respect to our brethren alone, what thanks would be due, where the obligation was reciprocal, and where even publicans would rival us We must do more than others, if we profess more, not confining our regard to our nearest friends or relations, to those of our own party or nation, but opening our hearts

hearts wide as the world, and doing good to all, even to the evil and unthankful

[3] Our eye must be fixed not on the attainments of others, but on that perfection which is in our Father, and to be perfect like him should be our holy ambition, not that we shall be able absolutely to attain thereunto, but after this we must reach, and take up with nothing short of it And as this must be our study, labour, and prayer in general, so particularly in this love towards our enemies should we desire to resemble him, which is a temper truly divine and Godlike

CHAP VI

Christ having in the former chapter armed his disciples against the corrupt doctrines and opinions of the Scribes and Pharisees, next rebukes the corrupt practices of which they were notoriously guilty, hypocrisy and worldly-mindedness, sins which, of all others, the professors of religion need to guard against, as most easily besetting them who have escaped the grosser pollutions that are in the world, through lust We are here cautioned, 1 Against hypocrisy, we must not be as the hypocrites are, nor do as the hypocrites do [1] In giving of alms, ver 1—4 [2] In prayer, ver 5—8 We are here taught what to pray for, and how to pray, ver 9—13 and to forgive, ver 14, 15 [3] In fasting, ver 16—18 2 Against worldly-mindedness (1) In covetousness, which is the destroying sin of hypocrites, ver 19—24 (2) In our cares, which is the disquieting sin of many gracious souls, ver 25—34

1 TAKE heed that ye do not your alms before men, to be seen of them otherwise ye have no reward of your Father which is in heaven 2 Therefore

[a] when thou dost *thine* alms, do not sound a trumpet before thee, as the hypocrites do, in the synagogues, and in the streets, that they may have glory of men Verily I say unto you, they have their reward 3 But when thou dost alms, let not thy left hand know what thy right hand doth 4 That thine alms may be in secret, and thy Father which seeth in secret, [b] himself shall reward thee openly

a Rom xii 8

b Luke xiv 14

v 1—4 Having before rescued the law from the false expositions of the Pharisees, our Lord here shews the true religion of the heart, as expressed in the three great duties of alms, prayer, and fasting, in which these deluded teachers gloried, but erred exceedingly in the performance of them

1 Our Lord cautions us against all ostentatious shew in bestowing our alms *Take heed that ye do not your alms before men, to be seen of them* hypocrisy is a subtle sin, and where we are least apprehensive of danger, is ever ready to insinuate itself, yet the fear of being wrong, must not keep us from doing right Alms-giving is every christian's bounden duty, and though not to be trusted upon as our righteousness before God, nor done to engage the applause of men, must nevertheless, according to our ability, be practised for God's glory, and the assistance of our brethren and God, who is not unrighteous, will remember and reward *the works of faith and labours of love*

He describes the methods the hypocrites used to proclaim their own goodness, and solicit the estimation of others They *sound a trumpet*, either literally to gather the poor to their doors, or they gave their alms in the most public manner, on purpose that they might be seen and admired

3 They had the reward they sought, and all they had to expect, the ignorant blessed their liberality, and praised their charity Note, The hypocrite's portion is all in hand, and hereafter he hath nothing to hope for

4 Christ gives direction concerning the proper way of doing our alms *Let not thy left hand know what thy right hand doth*, the expression is proverbial, and intimate the secrecy we should use, never designedly letting others know our alms-deeds, nor desirous they should be acquainted with them And with regard to ourselves, we should forget them, and never dwell upon them even in our thoughts, to flatter our own vain-glory and self conceit

5 Such good deeds as these flowing from faith, which worketh by love, shall not fail of their reward, secret as they are, He that seeth in secret will record them, and when we have forgotten them, and would be ashamed to hear them mentioned, he will remember and recompence them openly, before men and angels, at the resurrection of the just

5 And when thou prayest, thou shalt not be as the hypocrites *are* for they love to pray standing in the synagogues, and in the corners of the streets, that they may be seen of men Verily, I say unto you, they have their reward 6 But thou, when thou prayest,

[c] enter into thy closet, and when thou hast shut thy door, pray to thy Father which is in secret, and thy Father which seeth in secret, shall reward thee openly

c 2 Kings iv 33 [illegible]

7 But when ye pray, [d] use not vain repetitions, [e] as the heathen do for they think that they shall be heard for their much speaking 8 Be not ye therefore like unto them for your Father knoweth what things ye have need of, before ye ask him

d Ecclus v 14 &c vii 14

e 1 Kings xviii 26, 29

v 5—8 Prayer next comes to be considered It were an open declaration of impiety, irreligion, and atheism, to live without some acknowledgment of God's goodness, and profession of dependence on his care at least, none who bear the name of Christian can be supposed to live without prayer, any more than the body can live without breath We have here two grand directions concerning this most necessary duty

1 That it be not performed hypocritically, *to be seen of men* The Pharisees chose the synagogues and the corners of the street for the places of their devotions, that men's eyes might be upon them, *standing* up, that they might be more conspicuous, and *loving* the work, merely for the sake of the reward they proposed to themselves, which they received, and a miserable reward it was, to be applauded of poor mortals like themselves, when they were abhorred of the great and holy God Our Lord teaches his disciples to pray in a different manner, public places are unfit for private prayer We must retire thereto from the observation of men as much as may be, not only to avoid ostentation, but in order to be alone with God, removed from all interruption that would distract our thoughts, and out of the hearing of others, that we may freely speak before our Father which is in secret, to whom alone it should be our desire to approve ourselves, comparatively indifferent what men may think or say of us, if he regard us with paternal love, and expecting from him the answer of our petitions, which he promises to bestow For he *who seeth in secret*, though invisible to us, is yet present with us, and acquainted with our inmost soul, and will *reward* us openly, answering our requests in present blessings, owning us at the great day of his appearing and glory, and bestowing the promised eternal reward, [illegible] not indeed of debt, but of grace

2 That we use not *vain repetitions, as the heathens do, who think that they shall be heard for their much speaking*, not that repetitions, or much speaking in prayer are condemned, seeing the same petitions may be often repeated, and speak thus the deepest sensibility of our wants, and the greatest importunity of desire, *Mat* xxvi 44 *Dan* ix 18 *Ps* cxxxvi and also when our wants are many and great on particular occasions, and our spirit at liberty, we are never restrained from pouring out all our requests into the bosom of our omniscient God and Father, *Luke* vi 12 The practice condemned is, (1) *The vain babblings* of those who pray by rote, like parrots, as they tell their beads, repeating so many Ave Marias, or Pater Nosters, and constantly, without life or spirituality, going over the same dull round of words, like a mill horse with his bells, pleased with the tinkling of his own unmeaning music (2) *The much speaking*, which arises from an affectation of prolixity, especially in social prayer, where instead of speaking to God, men love to hear the sound of their own voice, and wish others to admire their gifts, their fluency, their fervency, and zeal, making a vast parade of words, adoration, thanksgivings, requests, intercessions, &c like Baal's priests, from morning to noon, crying, O Baal, hear us such lip-labour is not only lost labour, but worse, an abomination unto the Lord, and to be avoided by all his spiritual worshippers For our *Father*, which is in heaven, *knoweth what things we have need of before we ask him*, therefore does not want to be particularly informed, as if he were ignorant, nor is to be prevailed upon merely by our cries But as our Father, he expects to be called upon, and is ever ready to hear and answer us, omniscient, he knows our necessities, and all-sufficient, he will relieve them, even when we through our blindness know not what to ask, or through our ignorance ask amiss, yea, sometimes cannot ask at all, overwhelmed with distress, and speaking only in tears and groans which cannot be uttered, *Rom* viii 27

9 After this manner therefore pray ye [f] Our Father

[g] which art in heaven, [h] Hallowed be thy name 10

[i] Thy kingdom come [k] Thy will be done in earth [l] as

it is in heaven 11 [m] Give us this day our daily bread

12 And forgive us our debts, [n] as we forgive our

debtors 13 And [o] lead us not into temptation, but

deliver us from evil [p] for thine is the kingdom, and

[q] the power, and [r] the glory, for ever Amen 14 For

[s] if ye forgive men their trespasses, your heavenly Father

will also forgive you 15 But [t] if ye forgive not men

their trespasses, neither will your Father forgive your

trespasses

f Luke xi 2 [illegible]

[illegible]

v 9—15 Having condemned the prayer of formality and pride, our Lord here suggests both matter and words for our use

The prayer before us may be considered both as a form, and as a directory. It is concise, yet comprehensive, containing our chief wants in a few words; not that we are always bound to the use of it, or should regard it as more sacred than other prayers of the scripture; but being in frequent use, we need be well acquainted with its meaning, that when we repeat it, *we may pray with the spirit, and with the understanding also*.

We have,

1. The preface. *Our Father which art in heaven.* The great object of prayer is God alone; the encouraging motives to approach him are, that he is *our Father*, our reconciled God and Father in Christ Jesus, from whose paternal heart we may expect the tenderest compassions and most gracious attention; and as he is *in heaven*, adored by saints and angels, who knows our necessities better than we can express them, and hath all power to supply them exceeding abundantly above all that we can ask or think; so that we may come to him in faith, nothing doubting. As *our* common Father also, we are taught the spirit of love and charity, which should breathe in all our prayers, and profess ourselves hereby one of those many brethren whom, through Christ Jesus, he is bringing to glory, and for whom, as they for us, we are mutual advocates.

2. The petitions. They are six in number; the first three more immediately relate to God's glory, the last to our own wants.

[1.] *Hallowed be thy Name.* The *name* of God comprehends his being, perfections, and all the manifestations he hath made of himself in his works and word. That it may be *hallowed*, or *sanctified*, signifies our ascription of praise to him, according to his excellent greatness; and our desire, that he may be ever more and more exalted that we ourselves, and all others, may believe in him, love him, fear and serve him as we ought to do, and in our lips and lives shew forth his glory, and that since all good is from him, all may be ascribed to him.

[2.] *Thy kingdom come.* The kingdom of the Messiah seems principally here intended, which was now ready to appear; and being once set up in the world, we are required to pray for its enlargement and final consummation. As a *kingdom of grace*, we beg it may be erected in our own hearts more and more, till every thought be brought into the obedience of Christ; that it may diffuse its benign influence far and wide, and the light of the gospel-word, and the power of the gospel-grace cover the earth as the waters cover the sea; that God may thus accomplish the number of his elect, and hasten that eternal *kingdom of glory*, when all his saints collected round his throne shall, to eternity, adore him, enjoy his favour, and be made for ever happy in his service.

[3.] *Thy will be done in earth, as it is in heaven.* God is glorified, and his kingdom comes when his will is made ours; his preceptive will obeyed, his providential will acquiesced in. Thus we pray, that without dispute, we may receive the revelation he hath given us, believe in the Lord Jesus Christ, receive him as our king, and approve ourselves obedient subjects to his government in all things; never murmuring against his commands as severe, or his prohibitions as grievous, but counting his will to be always holy, just, and good. We pray for resignation to all his afflictive dispensations, contentment in every station, submission under every burden, and a heart to bless him, not only when he gives, but when he takes away; in short, that we may be as the clay in the hands of the potter, to be, act, and suffer, according to the good pleasure of his will; and this cheerfully, universally, continually, as the spirits of just men made perfect and the spotless angels fulfil his will in heaven. *Note*, (1.) It is mockery of God to pray that his will may be done, and daily live in allowed opposition to it. (2.) None may hope to serve God in heaven, who have not on earth made his glory their end, his word their rule, his will their delight.

[4.] *Give us this day our daily bread*; either for our souls, the bread of life, that we may be strengthened in the inner man, and increase with the increase of God; or for our bodies, the food which is convenient for us, not delicacies, but necessaries; not such as pampered appetite craves, but what used with temperance and sobriety may best fit us for the work of our station, and God's service. We ask *our* own bread, not what we have a right to, for all is God's gift, but what is honestly come by, neither the bread of idleness nor deceit; we are taught to ask *daily* for it, as acknowledging our dependance upon God for all we have and enjoy, and for *this day* only, not excluding a provident care, but as mindful of our jeopardy every hour, and dead to corroding sollicitude and perplexing suggestions about futurity, and content to trust him for the morrow, in the use of the same means we employ to-day. And this we beg for others as well as ourselves, that they and we may praise God together, who filleth our hearts with food and gladness. Thus all repining, envy, and discontent, will be excluded; content with our allotted portion, we shall wish for nothing more.

[5.] *And forgive us our debts, as we forgive our debtors.* Our debts are our sins; having failed in the debt of duty, we become liable to the debt of punishment. These sins are innumerable, great, and aggravated; and we have nothing to pay, unable to make the least satisfaction for them to divine justice: they are daily increasing, and if God deals with us according to our deserts, we are undone for ever. Therefore we cry, *forgive*, which intimates the deep and humble sense we have of our miserable and insolvent state, and our hope in the mercy of God, through Jesus Christ, for pardon. However numberless, great, and aggravated our sins may be, they are not beyond the blood of atonement, and God's boundless grace: he can pardon even beyond all that we can ask. A plea also is put into our mouths, not as meritorious, but as an argument founded on God's promise, *v.* 14. and an encouragement to our own souls to hope in his mercy, *as we forgive our debtors*; for if we do so, how much more shall the Father of mercies forgive us? Whilst on the other hand, we may not dare to hope, or pray for pardon, if we can retain allowed malice against one creature upon earth, and do not *from the heart* forgive our brother his trespasses. Though the offences or injuries done us may have been never so great, we are called upon to pardon them fully, freely, without reserve or upbraiding; yea, to forget them as though they had never been; and how reasonable the injunction, when none can ever have offended us, as we have provoked God; since he therefore for Christ's sake hath forgiven us, so ought we to forgive one another. To pray this petition with rancour, resentment, or ill-will abiding on the heart, would be to imprecate a curse upon our souls, instead of obtaining a blessing.

[6.] *Lead us not into temptation, but deliver us from evil*; conscious of our own weakness, we beg to be kept from the power of temptation, or to be supported under our trials that we may not fall. Not that God can be tempted with evil, or tempteth any man; but if he with-holds his grace, our own corrupted hearts naturally rush into the snare, and our adversary, the devil, is ever going about seeking whom he may devour; from his power, *that wicked one*, the author of all evil, we pray to be delivered; so that if assaulted, we may not be overcome by him: and from all the evil with which we are compassed on every side, from the evil world with all its snares, from evil men with all their wiles, or violence; from our own evil hearts with all their traitor lusts; from the evil of sin and punishment, in time or in eternity.

3. The doxology, and conclusion. *For thine is the kingdom, and the power, and the glory, for ever and ever. Amen.* Which may be considered as a solemn ascription of praise to God; as an act of faith in his power and grace; and a plea to enforce our petitions in which God's own glory is so greatly concerned. All praise and honour are in the highest to be ascribed to him, whilst after all we must own he is far exalted above all blessing and praise. His power is able to supply all our wants, we may therefore confidently trust him; since his is the kingdom, we may expect protection, and his own glory engages him to grant the requests which his word and spirit teach us to ask. We may therefore well add our warm Amen, earnest that our requests may be answered, and God therein glorified, in faith resting assured that it will be so, and therefore rising from our knees rejoicing in hope of the glory of God.

16 ¶ Moreover, [x] when ye fast, be not as the hypo- x Isa lviii. 5. Joel ii. 13.
crites of a sad countenance: for they disfigure their faces,
that they may appear unto men to fast. Verily, I say
unto you, they have their reward. 17 But thou when
thou fastest, anoint thy head, and wash thy face; 18
That thou appear not unto men to fast, but unto thy
Father which is in secret: and thy Father which seeth in
secret, shall reward thee openly.

v. 16—18. Having given directions for alms-giving and prayer, our Lord proceeds to fasting, a needful, though much neglected duty. This flesh needs the curb of constant mortification, and our sins call for such humiliation. We are here,

1. Cautioned against the hypocritical shew of the Pharisees. They made a vast parade of mortification, outwardly disfiguring their faces, and putting on an affected rueful countenance, pretending that deep contrition of soul which they never felt, that men might admire the austerity of their lives, and reverence them for their extraordinary sanctity; and so far they had their reward. They were highly esteemed among men, but how poor a consideration this, when, for their hypocrisy, they were an abomination in the sight of God. *Note*, Many who have denied the cravings of the body, have fallen victims to the pride of their heart.

2. We are directed how to fast. As the humiliation is before God, we must studiously avoid all external shew, appear in dress and countenance as on other days, dead to men's applause or censure; desiring only God's acceptance and regard in Christ Jesus, which in this way we are sure to find, and our Father which seeth in secret shall reward us openly.

19 ¶ [y] Lay not up for yourselves treasures upon earth, y Prov. xxiii. 4. Luke xii. 33, &c. 1 Tim. vi. 9, 17. Heb. xiii. 5. James v. 1. 1 Tim. vi. 19.
where moth and rust doth corrupt, and where thieves
break through and steal. 20 But lay up for yourselves
treasures in heaven, where neither moth nor rust doth
corrupt,

corrupt, and where thieves do not break through nor
steal 21 For where your treasure is, there will your
heart be also 22. [a] The light of the body is the eye
if therefore thine eye be single, thy whole body shall
be full of light 23 But if thine eye be evil, thy whole
body shall be full of darkness If therefore the light
that is in thee be darkness, how great is that darkness!
24 ¶ [b] No man can serve two masters for either he
will hate the one, and love the other, or else he will
hold to the one, and despise the other [c] Ye cannot
serve God and mammon

[a] Luke xi 34. [b] Luke xvi 13. [c] Jam iv 4. 1 John ii 15.

v 19—24 No sin is so besetting and dangerous to the professors of religion as worldly-mindedness, and where it prevails, there is no surer proof of the hypocrisy of the heart Against this, therefore, our Lord especially warns his disciples

1 He cautions them against laying up *their treasures upon earth* Nothing under the sun should be regarded by us as our portion, nor ought we, with increasing eagerness, to be still grasping at more, and continually adding to our stores, we must neither take up our rest in these things, nor depend upon them as substantial and abiding good, for a thousand accidents may deprive us of all The moth may corrupt our garments, the rust, blasting, mildew, or vermin destroy our corn, and thieves rob us of that gold and silver we treasured up with so much care It were folly therefore to count these our treasures

2 He tells us how we may secure a better, and a more enduring substance *Lay up for yourselves treasures in heaven* in the way of God's grace seek to secure the riches of his glory, especially by a right employment of this world's wealth, make to yourselves friends of the mammon of unrighteousness, send your wealth before you in works of charity, and then you will find it again with abundant interest laid up in that sure place, where it will be exposed neither to corruption nor violence

3 He enforces his advice by that weighty argument, that *where your treasure is, there will your heart be also*, if it be on earth, our minds will be earthly, sensual, if in heaven, our hearts will be drawn up to high and heavenly things, for as the needle follows the magnet, so do our affections pursue what we count our treasure Where this is, thither are our desires drawn out, our hopes and fears, joys and sorrows, are all influenced hereby When God is made our portion, then on him will our souls be fixed

4 According to a man's spirit and temper, so will his conduct be *The light of the body is the eye if therefore thine eye be single*, which was a common and well-known phrase for a liberal temper, *then thy whole body will be full of light*, the actions will all correspond with the principle, and the whole conversation will abound with good to the glory of God, *but if thine eye be evil*, if a sordid temper governs thee, *thy whole body will be full of darkness*, all the faculties will be enslaved by it, the whole conduct influenced by it, to use mean, avaricious, and base ways to gratify such a spirit *If therefore the light that is in thee be darkness, how great is that darkness!* if covetousness extinguish every generous and noble sentiment in the soul, what a train of vile and unbecoming deeds will follow, whilst every consideration is absorbed in that one of gain, greedily sought by any means, lawful or unlawful, and the consequence must needs be, that such a one will sink into eternal darkness and misery Such seems to be the sense of the words, which most exactly corresponds with the context Some by *the eye* understand the *practical judgment*, according as that is endued with just discernment, or is erroneous and corrupt, so will the corresponding practice be good or evil; and this particularly will appear in the preference given to heavenly or earthly treasures

5 We must make our choice which world we will have, and which master we will serve, the commands of both being incompatible There is no dividing the heart, God will have all or none, but the hypocrite wants to secure both worlds together, and to serve God just so far as consists with his interest and convenience, *but no man can serve two masters*, whose commands are contradictory, and never were two masters more opposite than *God and mammon* God demands the heart, enjoins contentment, honesty, charity, deadness to this world, and bids his servants forego their ease, their gain, their honour, their esteem among men, to seek in the first place his kingdom and righteousness *Mammon* commends the glittering stores of this vain world, bids his servants eat, drink, and be merry; pursue their worldly interests, honours, and esteem, mind chiefly themselves, live *for* themselves, spend *on* themselves; and by every means secure wealth, as the principal thing, and man's chief good Thus opposite are these masters, the service of the one must be attended with abhorrence of the other; we are called upon to make our choice, and let us remember eternity depend upon it

25 ¶ Therefore I say unto you, [d] Take no thought
for your life, what ye shall eat, or what ye shall drink;
nor yet for your body, what ye shall put on Is not
the life more than meat, and the body than raiment?
26 Behold the fowls of the air for they sow not, neither
do they reap, nor gather into barns, [e] yet your
heavenly Father feedeth them Are ye not much better
than they? 27 Which of you by taking thought
can add one cubit unto his stature? 28 And why take
ye thought for raiment? Consider the lilies of the field
how they grow, they toil not, neither do they spin
29 And yet I say unto you, that even Solomon in all
his glory, was not arrayed like one of these 30
Wherefore if God so clothe the grass of the field, which
to day is, and to morrow is cast into the oven, *shall he*
not much more *clothe* you, [f] O ye of little faith? 31
Therefore take no thought, saying, What shall we eat?
or what shall we drink? or wherewithal shall we be
clothed? 32 (For after all these things do the Gentiles
seek) for [g] your heavenly Father knoweth that ye
have need of all these things 33 But [h] seek ye first the
kingdom of God, and his righteousness, and all these
things shall be added unto you 34 [i] Take therefore
no thought for the morrow for the morrow shall take
thought for the things of itself Sufficient unto the day
is the evil thereof

[d] Luke xii 22. Phil iv 6. 1 Pet v 7. [e] Job xxxviii 41. Psal cxlvii 9. [f] Chap xiv 31. [g] 1 Pet v 7. [h] 1 Kings iii 11 &c. Prov. xiv 9. [i] Mark x 30. 1 Tim iv 8. Heb xiii 5. Ver 11.

v 25—34 Many think themselves far removed from covetousness, whose hearts, notwithstanding, are overcharged with the cares of this life, and though not sordidly avaricious, evidently shew their affections more set on things on earth, than the things in heaven We have therefore,

1 An admonition against all inordinate anxiety about a worldly provision *Take no thought*, &c There is a thoughtfulness and care needful and commendable, Prov xxvii 23 Our families cannot be otherwise provided for, nor the duties of our station discharged, but the caution here given, is levelled against tormenting sollicitude, and unbelieving distrust of God's providence, which is dishonourable to him, as distressing to ourselves Our life is in his hands, and whilst we are employing the appointed means in dependance upon his blessing, we must with satisfaction cast our care upon him, to give us sickness or health, comforts or crosses, want or abundance, as he pleases, and when we do so, we have his promise to assure us we shall have just that which is good for us.

2 Christ enforces his admonition by several considerations, which, if we seriously thought upon, would ever furnish us with abundant arguments to silence all disquieting carefulness

[1] If God gives the greater blessings, will he withhold the less? *Is not the life more than meat, and the body than raiment?* If God hath freely given us the life without our thought or care, and hitherto hath preserved them amidst innumerable dangers, can it be supposed he will suffer us to perish for lack of food or raiment?

[2] *Behold the fowls of the air*, numerous and voracious as they are, without any care of their own, by the Divine Providence, a daily provision is made for them, *though they sow not, nor reap, nor gather into barns* And if God thus provides for them, *are ye not much better than they?* more excellent in nature, and therefore much more the objects of his care can *the heir of heaven* be famished, when *the fowls of heaven* are fed

[3] Unprofitable, as well as unnecessary, are all our anxious cares *Which of you, by taking thought, can add one cubit unto his stature, or age?* Will our sollicitude add to our height, or will our thoughtfulness lengthen our lives a year, a month, a day, an hour, beyond the boundary decreed? How vain and foolish then to disquiet ourselves about other things equally out of our power? We are called upon here to make a virtue of necessity, and submit quietly to the determinations of providence

[4] To silence our carefulness about raiment, Christ points to the flowers which were probably near him, and made the application more beautifully striking *Consider the lilies of the field*, that grow without care or culture, without toil or labour yet even *Solomon* on his throne, adorned with richest robes, *in all his glory, was not arrayed like one of these* *Wherefore, if God so clothe the grass of the field*, which is so worthless, fading, and transitory, *which to-day is* in such beauty, and *to morrow is cast into the oven* to burn, *shall he not much more clothe you, O ye of little faith?* *Note*, (1) All our anxiety about worldly things arises from unbelief (2) It is the height of folly and vanity to be proud of fine cloaths, when every flower of the field must far outshine us (3) Every object around us, if our mind be rightly disposed, will afford us arguments for faith, and quiet dependance on God's care

[5] Such anxiety is heathenish, and utterly unbecoming those who have the light of revelation Gentiles indeed, who have no knowledge of a particular providence, may be concerned after these things, and imagine they must get them merely by their own care and labour, but it is a shame for Christians, who are better taught, not to shew the excellence of their principles by the

the nobler practice of deadness to the world and confidence in God

[6.] *Our heavenly Father knoweth we have need of all these things*, and therefore we may confidently expect the supply of every want He hath a father's bowels to feel for us, we have a sure interest in him, he knows our wants, and, be they never so *many or great, he can abundantly relieve them* His care for us makes our carefulness for ourselves needless

3 Christ directs us to the proper object of our cares *Seek ye first the kingdom of God and his righteousness* Religion is our great business to be a living member of Christ's church is infinitely more our concern than how our bodies shall be fed, and *his righteousness*, which is our title to the kingdom, is the robe we should be more sollicitous to put on than any other raiment and with this divine righteousness inherent purity must be sought with diligence, in the use of every means of grace, and in the *first* place counting all dung and loss, compared with the great concerns of our souls and the eternal world, which should in a measure swallow up all other considerations Indeed the trifles of time will sit light upon those who have the glories of eternity in view Besides, this is the way to secure all the rest of our wants, for he who is able abundantly to supply them is pleased to assure us, that then *all these things shall be added unto us*, they shall be thrown in *as over and above* all the spiritual blessings Oh that we were but wise to know our true interests! we should find by experience nothing was ever lost by faith unfeigned, and diligent caring for the soul

4 As the conclusion of the matter, we are, without sollicitude about futurity, to cast our care upon God, who will care for us *Take no thought for the morrow*, which doth not forbid prudent foresight, or enjoin an absolute disregard about our business or our families, but all perplexing anxiety, all disquieting fears about what may never happen, or, if it doth, may give us no such trouble as we apprehend, and all unbelieving distrust of God Our business is to mind present duty, and leave events to God *To-morrow shall take thought for the things of itself* it is folly to be disquieted about what may never come to pass Who knows whether to-morrow belongs to time or to eternity And if it returns, He, who supplied our wants to-day, will supply our wants to-morrow *Sufficient for the day is the evil thereof* we need not anticipate our troubles, or torment ourselves with imaginary ills each day has sufficient, without borrowing to-morrow's burden to increase the load and which not all our previous cares and fears will make the lighter It is God's curse on the wicked world, that they are self-tormentors, whilst they who live by faith may always rejoice in hope

CHAP VII

This chapter continues and concludes Christ's sermon on the mount We have, 1 Some rules concerning censure and reproof, ver 1—6 2 *Encouragements given us to pray to God for what we need*, ver 7—11 3 *The necessity of strictness in conversation urged upon us*, ver 13, 14 4 *A caution given us to take heed of false prophets*, ver 15,—20 5 *The conclusion of the sermon*, ver 21—27 6 *The impression which Christ's doctrine made upon his hearers*, ver 28, 29

a Luke vi 37, &c Rom ii 1 & xiv 4, 10 Jam ii 13 & iv 11 12
b Mark iv 24
c Luke vi 41, &c
d Prov ix 7 8 & xxiii 9 Chap xv 26 Acts xiii 45 46

1. [a] JUdge not, that ye be not judged 2 For with
what judgment ye judge, ye shall be judged
And [b] with what measure you mete, it shall be measured
to you again 3 And [c] why beholdest thou the mote
that is in thy brother's eye, but considerest not the beam
that is in thine own eye? 4 Or how wilt thou say
to thy brother, Let me pull out the mote out of thine
eye, and behold, a beam *is* in thine own eye? 5 Thou
hypocrite, first cast out the beam out of thine own eye,
and then shalt thou see clearly to cast out the mote out
of thy brother's eye 6 ¶ [d] Give not that which *is*
holy unto the dogs, neither cast ye your pearls before
swine, lest they trample them under their feet, and turn
again and rent you

v 1—6 The proud and self-righteous are ever most censorious Against such is this reproof levelled

1 Our Lord forbids all rash judgment, unreasonable jealousies, evil surmising, and rigid censures *Judge not*, uncharitably, unmercifully, under a spirit of revenge or prejudice, decide not concerning a man's spiritual state from some single act or circumstance, nor pretend to know his heart, much less to determine concerning his everlasting state to his own master he standeth or falleth This precept doth not forbid the judgment of the civil magistrate, nor our forming conclusions of others state as well as our own, agreeably to the word of God, for, though our own judgment may be fallible, his must be according to truth

The prohibition is enforced by a weighty reason *Judge not, that ye be not judged*. Our charity and mercifulness to others will be the means of securing the like favourable judgment to ourselves, whilst a spirit of censoriousness will provoke the resentment and ill-will of others, and be returned generally in as liberal abuse beside, what is infinitely more to be feared, God will give judgment without mercy to those who shewed no mercy, and with rigour of severest justice will call those to his bar who dared usurp his throne, and sit as self-authorised judges of their brethren

2 He gives us some rules about reproof, not forbidding the kind jealousy of love, but condemning the magisterial rebukes of self-sufficient pride Before we look at others faults, we should well consider if there be not greater in ourselves For how unseasonable and unjust would it be with malignant eye to mark, aggravate, and with severity condemn, the infirmities and follies of others, the mote which is in their eye, whilst we extenuate, excuse, or justify, what is far more culpable, the beam which is in our own? or with what face of hardened effrontery can we dare set up for reformers of them, whilst greater evils, unredressed, lie at our own door? This is the grossest hypocrisy, and such pretended zeal against sin but a greater abomination in God's sight, who trieth the heart Before we presume to correct others, we should therefore reform the evils in ourselves, lest they should retort, Physician heal thyself, and our admonition, though just in itself, be rejected with contempt

3 Christ forbids not only uncharitable censures and magisterial rebukes, but imprudent and unseasonable reproofs *Give not that which is holy to dogs, neither cast ye your pearls before swine* Where men discover their profaneness and impiety, professedly infidel, or avowed enemies to the truths of God, who despise instruction, and are but more exasperated by admonition, there it would be folly, and abuse of things sacred, to persist in rebuking them, and we can only expect insult and harm to ourselves without any profit to them or glory to God but, whilst prudence is enjoined, we must take care not to make our caution an excuse for our cowardice, not to think men such till we have found them so, nor be afraid of any consequences, when duty calls us, even in the face of persecutors, to bear a faithful testimony to the truths of God

7 ¶ [e] Ask, and it shall be given you seek, and ye e Mark xi 24
shall find knock, and it shall be opened unto you Chap xxi 22 Luke xi 9, &c
8 For [f] every one that asketh, receiveth and he that John xiv 13 & xv 7
seeketh, findeth and to him that knocketh, it shall be Jam i 5, 6
opened 9 Or what man is there of you, whom if his f Prov viii 17 Jer
son ask bread, will he give him a stone? 10 Or if he xxix 12
ask a fish, will he give him a serpent? 11 If ye then,
being evil, know how to give good gifts unto your
children, how much more shall your Father, which is in
heaven, give good things to them that ask him?

v 7—11 Prayer is the means appointed of God to obtain of him the supply of every want, spiritual and temporal, and therefore,

1 The command given is, *Ask, seek, knock*, implying the fervour, diligence, constancy, and importunity, which must be used, if we would obtain the relief of our necessities, and a deep and humbling sense of our wants, and faith in God's promises, will engage us so to do, without which there can be no availing prayer

2 A gracious promise is annexed They who thus pray shall surely speed God will hear and answer them according to their various wants Every petitioner, without respect of persons, that thus in faith draws near unto God, *receives* an answer of peace, *finds* acceptance and favour with him, hath the door of mercy *opened*, and is welcome to enter and freely take out of God's fulness whatever blessing he needs *Note*, They who refuse or neglect to ask, deserve to want The prayerless soul will be left inexcusable

3 As an engagement to pray with assurance of being heard, our Lord enforces his command by an argument drawn from the compassions of our earthly parents Evil as we are by nature, scarce one can be found so unnatural as to be deaf to the cries of his own flesh and blood, much less inhumanly to give his children things noxious, instead of the food they crave If then, in such corrupted creatures as we are, such compassion and regard are found towards our offspring, much more will the Father of mercies graciously hear and grant the petition of his dear children who wait upon him his love, his power, are infinitely greater than ours, and therefore they shall want no manner of thing that is good Their own requests perhaps may be sometimes improper, unnecessary, unseasonable, and their prayers he will best answer by kind denials, whilst all that his wisdom and goodness sees fit shall be given them, in such manner and measure as shall be most for their benefit and his own glory

12 ¶ Therefore all things [g] whatsoever ye would that g Luke vi 31
men should do to you, do ye even so to them [h] for h Rom xiii 8
this is the law and the prophets 13 [i] Enter ye in at i Luke xiii 24
the strait gate for wide *is* the gate, and broad *is* the
way, that leadeth to destruction, and many there be
which go in thereat 14 Because strait *is* the gate,
and

and narrow *is* the way which leadeth unto life, and few there be that find it

v 12—14 We have here,

1 The conclusion and sum of the foregoing commands, the golden rule, universally applicable in all cases To do unto our neighbours as, according to reason and religion, we might expect they should do for us, *if our situations were reversed* to do them no injury, to give them every assistance in our power, to deal with them in uprightness and integrity without making the least advantage of their ignorance or necessities And this doctrine both the law and the prophets inculcate, and in this one word the commands of both, respecting our duty towards our neighbour, are summed up The rule is short, and easy to be remembered, but how wide and difficult the practice!

2 Christ urges us to all diligence *in securing eternal life*, and points out the only way thereto *Strive to enter in at the strait gate* The gate is Christ, his blood and righteousness it is *strait*, as it admits none of the trappings of pride and self-righteousness, and calls us to part from all our most beloved sins, to deny ourselves, take up our cross, and follow Christ And as this will require much labour, prayer, and self-denial, Christ urges the necessity of striving to enter in

[1] Because of the ruin and danger which attend the ways of sin, in which the multitude walks unconcerned, *for wide is the gate, and broad is the way, that leadeth to destruction* There no restraint withholds the unbridled appetite, here pleasure, riches, honour, spread their lure, there all may find the gratification of their darling passion, or are engaged so to hope by that wily tempter, who welcomes all with fairest promises of joy and happiness, *and many there be which go in thereat*, naturally disposed to follow the bent of their fallen minds, and walking every one in his own way To swim therefore against the stream of inbred corruption, and the tide of custom too, is difficult but let us remember that the end is destruction, that these paths lead down to hell, that, whether they be those of carelessness and neglect about the soul, open immorality, or self-righteous hypocrisy, all tend to eternal misery, and meet in the place of torment

2 *Because strait is the gate, and narrow is the way, which leadeth unto life, and few there be that find it* There we must stoop low, our pride be mortified, all self-dependance be renounced, there the restraints of God's law hedge up the way, and leave us the narrow path of holiness only to walk in, there our very nature must be changed, our inveterate evil habits subdued, our corruptions mortified, there we must expect to meet with many trials, afflictions, and temptations, from inbred evil and outward enemies, there every inch must be won with perpetual war against sin, earth, and hell, and every step must be taken with watchful care, since dangers and snares lie at the right hand and at the left no marvel then *there be few that find it*, comparatively few at least, a remnant, a little flock, according to the election of grace When therefore the difficulties are so great, the diligence should be proportionable, and since there are but few saved, we should strive to be of that number, and the issue will repay our pains *eternal life* will infinitely more than compensate for all the struggles of the way

15 ¶ [k] Beware of false prophets, [l] which come to
you in sheep's clothing, but [m] inwardly they are raven-
ing wolves 16 [n] Ye shall know them by their fruits
[o] Do men gather grapes of thorns, or figs of thistles?
17 Even so [p] every good tree bringeth forth good fruit
but a corrupt tree bringeth forth evil fruit 18 A good
tree cannot bring forth evil fruit neither *can* a corrupt
tree bring forth good fruit 19 [q] Every tree that bring-
eth not forth good fruit, is hewn down, and cast into
the fire 20 Wherefore by their fruits ye shall know
them.

k Deut xiii 1 Jer xxiii 16 Chap xxiv 11 2 Pet ii 1 1 John iv 1 ... 4 2 Cor xi ... Chap xii 33 Luke vi 44 Chap xii 33 ... John xv 2 6

v 15—20 False Christs and false prophets would shortly arise, and false teachers were already abundantly numerous Against these the Lord therefore cautions his disciples, and sets down marks whereby they may be distinguished

1 Our Lord describes them as *wolves in sheep's clothing*, such as the Pharisees and Scribes were, who with exterior marks of sanctity, and austerity in their manners and garb, were inwardly full of enmity against the doctrines of grace and true holiness, and in their spirit hypocritical, proud, and covetous And probably our Lord hath respect to the false apostles, the judaizing teachers, and all that should ever afterwards appear in the church, preaching the abominable doctrines of man's self-sufficiency, free-will to good, justification by works, and the like, *grievous wolves*, Acts xx 29 whom pride, not godliness, Rom xvi 18 hath drawn into the ministry Beware of them

2 He lays down the rule by which we must prove all who pretend a mission from him *Ye shall know them by their fruits*, just as easily as a tree is known They who are evil can no more preach the truth, and live it too, than a thorn can bear grapes And, on the other hand, where the soul is right with God, there the fruits of truth and holiness naturally and necessarily are produced Two ways the prophet may be known

[1] By his life Is his conduct exemplary, self-denying, humble, meek, zealous, doth the love of God and of men's souls appear to influence and actuate him in all his works and ways, at least in the *general* temper of his mind, and tendency of his conversation, is this manifested? these are good fruits of a good tree But is he worldly-minded, proud, sensual, indolent, more willing to fleece than to feed the flock, rigid in exacting the wages, but unwilling to be employed in the work of the ministry encouraging instead of reproving sinners by his example, conforming to the ways of a wicked world, instead of being transformed in the spirit of his mind? these are evident proofs of the falsehood of such a prophet's pretensions

[2] By his doctrine, which seems chiefly intended here for false prophet may with the veil of hypocrisy cover his iniquities so as to appear righteous unto men But are his doctrines according to truth, and drawn from the sacred fountain? doth he preach the dignity or the desperate wickedness of the human nature? the freedom of man's will, or his utter impotence to every good thought, desire, or work doth he declare the damnable nature of sin, the utter guilt of every man by nature and practice, and the wrath of God revealed from heaven against all unrighteousness, or encourage the false hopes of sinners by smooth prophecies, and soften the harsh terms of hell and damnation, that he may not offend the ear with such inharmonious sounds? doth he exalt the divine Redeemer, his person, his offices, his blood, his righteousness, or slightly pass over these glorious subjects, for dry ethics, and lectures on morality? doth he enforce religion as an experimental thing, as the work of God's Spirit in the heart, purifying the inner man, or doth he dwell on mere external forms and duties, as silent about divine agency as if he knew not whether there were any Holy Ghost? doth he offend sinners by the freedom of his rebukes, and the formal and self-righteous by his scrutinizing detection of their hypocrisy, or doth he study to please men, and, like the false prophets of old, secure the good word of the deluded and misguided world? by these and the like fruits shall they be known *Try therefore the spirits, whether they be of God, for many false prophets are gone out into the world*, 1 John iv 1

3 He declares the terrible end of these wolves in sheep's clothing As the barren tree is only fit fuel for the flames, so are these marked for ruin, the axe of death shall shortly be laid to their root, and ruin eternal be their portion Beware therefore of false prophets, lest, deluded by them, you partake of their plagues

21 ¶ Not every one that saith unto me, [r] Lord,
Lord, shall enter into the kingdom of heaven, but he
that doth the will of my Father which is in heaven
22 Many will say to me in that day, Lord, Lord,
have we not prophesied in thy name? and in thy name
have cast out devils? and in thy name done many won-
derful works? 23 And then will I profess unto them,
[t] I never knew you [u] depart from me, ye that work
iniquity 24 Therefore [x] whosoever heareth these say-
ings of mine, and doth them, I will liken him unto a
wise man, which built his house upon [y] a rock 25
And the rain descended, and the floods came, and the
winds blew, and beat upon that house and it fell not,
for it was founded upon a rock 26 And every one
that heareth these sayings of mine, and doth them not,
shall be likened unto a foolish man, which built his
house upon the sand 27 And the rain descended, and
the floods came, and the winds blew, and beat upon
that house and it fell, and great was the fall of it
28 And it came to pass, when Jesus had ended these
sayings, [z] the people were astonished at his doctrine
29 For he taught them as one having authority, and
not as the scribes

r Hos viii 2 Luke vi 46 & xiii 25 Rom ii 13 · s Numb xxiv 4 John xi 51 1 Cor xiii · t Chap xxv 12 Luke xiii 27 u Ps v 5 Chap xxv 41 x Luke vi 47 ... 11 · z Chap xiii 54 Mark i 22 Luke iv 32 John vii 46

v 21—29 We have here the conclusion of this awakening discourse, and the deep impression it made on the hearers

1 Our Lord shews that no profession of religion destitute of the power of godliness, will stand a man in any stead at the judgment-day

(1) It is not saying, but doing must prove our calling and election of God *Not every one that saith unto me, Lord, Lord*, in boasting profession and noisy devotion, *shall enter into the kingdom of heaven*, be enrolled as living members of his church, or be admitted inheritors of his glory, *but he that doth the will of my Father which is in heaven*, who truly believes on him whom God hath sent, takes him for his Lord and Master, not merely in word and tongue, but in deed and in truth; obedient to his commands, following him in righteousness and true holiness, desirous to do his will on earth as he hopes shortly to do his will in heaven Reader, is this character thine?

[2] Many

[2.] Many in the day of Christ will appear to have deluded themselves with false hopes, whose pleas will then be fearfully silenced. *Many will say to me in that great day* of judgment, *Lord, Lord, have we not prophesied in thy name*? Many of those who may have filled the highest stations of the church on earth, have been to appearance the most zealous preachers, or public professors in it, yet proved no better than Balaam or Caiaphas; yea, *and in thy name have cast out devils*, as Judas, and many others no doubt, *and in thy name done many wonderful works*? even working the most astonishing miracles: and yet Christ declares, *Then will I profess unto them, I never knew you*, never called or owned you for my servants; *depart from me, all ye that work iniquity*. Notwithstanding all your pleas, your hearts have been false and faithless, and your professions utterly unsound, and therefore your portion must be to depart accursed with the Devil and his angels. Learn hence these awful truths. (1.) That a man may be a professor, a minister, yea distinguished with gifts and successful in his labours, and yet be finally cast away; may be the instrument of saving others, and perish himself; may cast out devils from the hearts of others, and harbour them in his own. (2.) Names may pass upon men, but God searcheth the heart. There are secret sins to be found in many, under the cloke of most glaring profession, and they shall receive greater damnation. (3.) In the day of judgment, terrible will be the disappointment of those, who [illegible] then lives long were working, as they thought, for life, were esteemed as patterns of piety, and cried up as the excellent of the earth, and yet will be found not only to have deceived others, but to have deluded themselves, falling from the height of self-righteous hopes into the depths of endless despair, and from the gates of heaven driven into the belly of hell. Let every man prove well his own work, and judge himself, that he may be found sincere and without offence at the day of Christ.

2. He enforces the truths he had delivered by an apposite parable of a wise and foolish builder, describing the different foundations they laid, and the different issue of their labours.

[1.] The wise builder, his labours, and success, are described. 1. His character is given; *he heareth these sayings of mine, and doth them*. Herein is seen the man that hath wisdom. He receives the truth in the love of it, obeys the precepts, is influenced by the gospel as a living principle of action, and seeks conformity in heart and life to his divine Lord and Master. 2. *He builds upon a rock*, on Jesus Christ, the only sure and safe foundation, depending on his blood and righteousness alone for pardon and acceptance: and under the teachings of his word and Spirit, and the supports of his grace, the glorious superstructure rises of righteousness and true holiness. As he builds for eternity, he is zealous in labouring to make his calling and election sure, and in every good word and work seeks to approve himself to the great master. 3. His work stands against every storm. He may expect and will meet with many a severe blast; the *rain* of temptation, the *floods* of corruption within, the overflowings of ungodliness without, the *wind* of persecution, all may unite their fury against him, to move him from his stedfastness, to shake his confidence in Christ, to discourage or seduce him from the good ways of the Lord; but in vain: the gates of hell can never prevail against the work of a believer. He shall be made to stand in the day of evil, in the hour of death he shall be supported, his work shall stand the fiery trial, and in the day of judgment he shall be approved and rewarded by the Lord of life and glory.

[2.] The foolish builder, and his sad end, are set forth for our warning. 1. His character is, that *he heareth these sayings of Christ, and doth them not*. He makes profession of religion, and attends upon the ordinances, but goes no further; the doctrines of the gospel have no deep effect upon his heart, nor an universal and abiding influence on his conduct. 2. He builds *upon the sand*, leaving Christ, to rest upon something in himself, and looking for acceptance, in whole or in part, on account of some external things wherein he differs from others, whether moral duties, alms, honesty, and the like, or on the form of godliness, baptism, prayers, frequenting the house and table of the Lord, &c. or if he hath a speculative knowledge of the truth, and knows the vanity of these things, he rests on that knowledge, without any experimental possession of the blessings of the gospel, and then it profiteth him nothing; or, if his notions are yet more spiritualized, he rests on his inward feelings, or supposed gifts and graces, his confidence, depending upon what he calls *the Christ within*, which is but a more refined self-righteousness, and a more subtle delusion: and therefore, when the time of trial comes, his house will fall, and crush him under its ruins. If persecution arises for the word's sake, such are quickly offended; in times of affliction and trouble their hopes cannot support and comfort them; and in death they utterly fail; at least, if the hypocrite's hope stand out to the last, they die with him, deluded and despair from that moment seize him, and too late he discovers the fatal mistake, when it is irremediable, and his eternal state is determined.

3. Great was the impression made by this discourse of our Lord on his audience: they were as men thunderstruck, astonished with the uncommon power, weight, and energy, which attended his preaching. They admired the dignity with which he spake, addressing them in his own name as one invested with authority: and his sentiments were new, as well as weighty, utterly unlike the flat and spiritless comments of the scribes, who servilely adhered to the traditions and decisions of their rabbi's. And yet, alas! the impression soon wore off from many, from the most of them. So easy, so common, is it to hear with admiration the eloquent or powerful preachers of the gospel, to feel a transient glow, and notwithstanding to continue in ignorance, unbelief, under the power of sin, and perish everlastingly.

CHAP. VIII.

In this chapter we have, 1. *Christ's cleansing of a leper*, ver. 1—4. 2. *His curing a palsy and fever*, ver. 5—1[illegible]. 3. *His conversation with two that had a mind to follow him*, ver. 19—22. 4. *[illegible] controlling of the tempest*, ver. 23—27. 5. *His casting out devils*, ver. 28—34.

1 WHEN he was come down from the mountain, great multitudes followed him. 2 [a] And behold, there came [b] a leper, and worshipped him, saying, Lord, if thou wilt, thou canst make me clean. 3 And Jesus put forth *his* hand and touched him, saying, I will, be thou clean. And immediately his leprosy was cleansed. 4 And Jesus saith unto him, [c] See thou tell no man, but go thy way, shew thyself to the priest, and offer the gift [d] that Moses commanded, for a testimony unto them.

a Mark i. 40. Luke v. 12.
b Lev. xiii. 40.
c Chap. [illegible] Mark [illegible]
d Lev. xiv. 4.

v. 1—4. Struck with the power of his word, the multitude who had heard Christ preach, followed him when he came down from the mount; and lo! a fresh occasion offers to raise their admiration, and confirm their faith in him as a teacher sent from God; for they who follow on to know the Lord, shall see fresh manifestations of his power, grace, and glory, every step they advance. We have,

1. A miserable leper's address to our Lord. The leprosy was esteemed by the Jews a disease immediately sent from God, incurable by human art, (2 *Kings* v. 7.) so defiling, as to exclude the unhappy object not only from the sanctuary, but, for the most part, from human converse and society; a lively figure of the fallen sinner, covered with guilt, full of corruption, excluded from God's presence, cut off from the communion of the saints, incurable by any human means, himself unclean, and communicating defilement to all around him. Yet, deplorable as the case appears, blessed be God, it is not desperate; there is balm in Gilead, and a physician there. *Behold, there came a leper*, who had himself perhaps heard our Lord preach, or [illegible] by the fame of his wondrous works, *and worshipped him*, either with deepest respect as a prophet, or enlightened with the knowledge of his divine character, and paying him due adoration, *saying, Lord, if thou wilt, thou canst make me clean*. He doubted not his power and all-sufficiency, and therefore cast himself on his mercy for a cure. And herein he is the emblem of the awakened sinner, brought to a sight of his native misery. (1.) He casts himself down at the feet of Jesus in prayer, laying his guilty and polluted soul before him. (2.) He looks up to him as able to save to the uttermost, nor dares distrust that his blood and righteousness can justify the most guilty, and his grace renew the vilest heart: but often he hesitates in the view of his own unworthiness, and fears whether the Lord will have respect to one so utterly unworthy. (3.) However, as he sees no hope any where else, he presents his desperate case, assured he must perish, unless the Lord hath respect to him. But none ever yet perished at the feet of Jesus: for,

2. *Jesus put forth his hand and touched him, saying, I will, be thou clean: and immediately his leprosy was cleansed*. Such power accompanied his word and touch, as instantly effected the cure. And with like words of grace doth Jesus speak to every poor sinner who applies to him. His answer is ever, *I will*: he is ready as able to pardon and save the miserable and the desperate who come to him. *Be thou clean*; thy guilt is cancelled, thy soul is delivered from the bondage of corruption, my blood, my grace are sufficient for thee, and freely extended to thee: and by faith his word is realized to the soul; the leprosy [illegible] off, guilt no more terrifies the conscience, nor hath corruption any longer dominion over the heart.

3. Our Lord charges him not to divulge the means of his cure, but to go immediately to the priest, obtain their acknowledgment of his being healed, and offer the sacrifices prescribed. And this he did for the man's sake, lest out of envy the priests should refuse to pronounce him clean; and that [illegible] might be a testimony of the fact to all, when it should be more publicly known how the cure was wrought, [illegible] to cut off occasion from those who desired to represent our Lord as a breaker of Moses's laws, and thereby to prejudice the people against him. *Note*, Every soul cleansed by [illegible] will [illegible]

to offer the grateful sacrifice not only of his lips, but of his heart, to God, and will seek to approve himself, to his Redeemer's glory, a living testimony of his power and grace

g Luke vii 1 5 ¶ [g] And when Jesus was entred into Capernaum,
there came unto him a centurion, beseeching him,
6 And saying, Lord, my servant lieth at home sick of
the palsy, grievously tormented 7 And Jesus said, I
will come and heal him 8 The centurion answered
h Luke xv 19 and said, Lord, [h] I am not worthy that thou shouldst
i Psal cvii 20 come under my roof but [i] speak the word only, and
my servant shall be healed 9 For I am a man under
authority, having soldiers under me and I say to this
man, Go, and he goeth and to another, Come, and he
cometh and to my servant, Do this, and he doth it
10 When Jesus heard *it*, he marvelled, and said to them
that followed, Verily I say unto you, I have not found
so great faith, no not in Israel 11 And I say unto
Gen xxviii 14 Mal i 11 Luke xiii 29 you, that [h] many shall come from the east and west, and
shall sit down with Abraham, and Isaac, and Jacob, in
the kingdom of heaven 12 But [i] the children of the
k chap xxii 13 xxv 30 kingdom shall be cast out [k] into outer darkness there
shall be weeping and gnashing of teeth 13 And Jesus
l chap ix 29 said unto the centurion, Go thy way, and [l] as thou hast
believed, so be it done unto thee And his servant was
healed in the self-same hour.

v 5—13 Capernaum was the place where our Lord had fixed his abode, and whither he returned after his journey thro' Galilee and there we are told,

1 The application made to him by a Roman centurion, the captain of a troop consisting of an hundred men *A soldier*, from whom religion is least expected, but there are some faithful in all professions *a man of rank*, few of whom were numbered among the followers of Jesus *not many such are called*, blessed be God, it is not said, *not any*, *a Gentile* too, and for a Gentile, for Christ came a light to lighten the Gentiles, as well as to be the glory of his people Israel After sending messengers to beg the help of Jesus, (*Luke* vii 2) he came himself, a humble supplicant on the behalf of his sick servant, afflicted *with the palsy, and grievously tormented*, commending his miserable case to the compassions of Jesus And herein he shewed, (1) His high respect for the Lord Jesus, and his dependance upon him (2) His great humanity towards his sick servant, not turning him out of doors because unable to work, but tenderly taking care of him, and seeking every means for his relief a noble example, and which should also be an encouragement to servants to discharge their station with fidelity and honesty, as this will naturally endear them to their masters, *see Luke* vii 2

2 The answer Christ gave to his request *I will come and heal him* Though a poor servant, diseased, a Gentile also, Jesus is no respecter of persons, and his ministers herein must resemble him, ready on the first application to visit the meanest of their flock

3 The deep humility and distinguished faith expressed by the centurion *Lord, I am not worthy that thou shouldst come under my roof*, so lowly were the thoughts he entertained of himself, so high his estimation of the dignity of the Redeemer A gracious soul ever acknowledges himself thus less than the least of all God's mercies Nor does he think Christ's presence necessary, so full was his confidence in the power of Jesus, that he is assured a single word will be sufficient to effect the cure, the most inveterate disease being entirely under the command of Jesus, and coming and going at his bidding for if he, who was but an inferior officer, met with with such ready obedience from his soldiers and servants, much more would a word from him, who had no superior, be obeyed Learn hence, (1) The character of a good servant, he obeys his master without answering again or hesitating (2) The nature of diseases, they are Christ's servants, they come and go only as he orders, and execute that commission he gives them (3) The duty of every Christian is to be obedient in all things, to do what Jesus pleases to command, and chearfully to suffer what he ordains

4 The high approbation of the centurion expressed by our Lord on this occasion *When Jesus heard it he marvelled*, not that he was surprized as with an unexpected thing, since this faith was his own gift, but he expressed himself as admiring what was so excellent and uncommon, that it might be more remarked by others, saying to his followers, *Verily, I say unto you, I have not found so great faith, no not in Israel*, none of that generation had given such proof of faith as this Gentile *Note*, The attainments of those who have enjoyed less means than others will condemn the unprofitableness, and rise up in judgment against the slothfulness and carelessness of such as, blessed with every advantage for their soul, have abused or neglected them

5 Christ takes occasion from hence to foretel the calling of the Gentiles, and rejection of the Jews for their unbelief Tho' the Jews, prejudiced to their nation, could not bear the thoughts that the heathen should share in the common salvation, our Lord assures them, that from all lands multitudes should be gathered unto him, and admitted to the same privileges, and have a place in the same kingdom as the most distinguished patriarchs whilst, to their greater astonishment, they who boasted themselves as, exclusive of all others, the children of the kingdom, will, so far from having any part or lot in it, *be cast into outer darkness*, as guests excluded from the bridal feast, and thrust out, *where shall be weeping and gnashing of teeth*, the expressive signs of most poignant anguish, which will especially be the case with damned souls in the place of torment *Note*, (1) We shall see many in the kingdom of heaven, whom we least expected to find there, and multitudes cast out, of whom we had the most confident expectations (2) It will profit a man nothing at the day of judgment to have been a professed member of Christ's kingdom, and a nominal child of God, if he is not possessed of the spirit of adoption, and hath not approved his fidelity as a loyal subject (3) The torments of hell should be often remembered, to quicken us with greater diligence in fleeing from the wrath to come

6 The servant is cured *Jesus said unto the centurion, Go thy way, and as thou hast believed, so be it done unto thee* With a double grace the favour is conferred, his faith approved, whilst his request is granted, for instantly the cure was wrought, *his servant was healed in the self-same hour* He that said, Let there be light, and there was light, *need* but say, and *it is done*, in every other case What confidence then should we repose in this almighty Saviour, and never in our deepest afflictions distrust his power or love!

14 ¶ And [m] when Jesus was come into Peter's house, m Mark i 29 Luke iv 38
he saw his wife's mother laid, and sick of a fever. 15
And he touched her hand, and the fever left her and
she arose, and ministred unto them 16 [n] When the n Mark i 32 Luke iv 40
even was come, they brought unto him many that were
possessed with devils and he cast out the spirits with
his word, and healed all that were sick 17 That it
might be fulfilled which was spoken by Esaias the pro-
phet, saying, [o] Himself took our infirmities, and bare *our* o Isa liii 4 1 Pet ii 24
sicknesses

v 14—17 The great Physician is continually manifesting his healing power We have,

1 Another cure wrought by him on Peter's wife's mother, who lay ill of a fever in Peter's house He was married we find, in opposition to the popish celibacy His care of his aged relations bespoke his gracious spirit Jesus, who will never fail to repay the entertainment given him in our houses, or in our hearts, by a touch rebuked the disorder, and instantly every symptom vanished, and her strength was perfectly restored, so that she was able to wait upon him and the guests, as an evidence of her cure, and a testimony of her gratitude *Note*, They whom Christ heals, are bound to employ the strength and health he gives in his blessed service

2 At even, it being a sabbath-day, (*See Mark* i 21) and their days being reckoned from one sun-setting to the other, the people thronged the door with their sick, and those possessed of devils, Satan being at that time permitted to exercise uncommon dominion over men's bodies, that the power of Jesus might more eminently appear But whatever the diseases were, or however strong the possession of these unclean spirits, one word of Jesus effectually drove them out, and healed every disease

3 The fulfilment of the scripture herein is observed, to the prophecy, *Isa* liii 4 not only includes Christ's suffering the punishment due to our sins, 1 *Pet* ii 24 but also his sympathizing tenderness towards us under the diseases that are the fruits of sin, and his gracious power exerted to deliver us from them

18. ¶ Now when Jesus saw great multitudes about
him, he gave commandment to depart unto the other
side 19 And [p] a certain scribe came, and said unto p Luke ix 57
him, Master, I will follow thee whithersoever thou go-
est 20 And Jesus saith unto him, The foxes have
holes, and the birds of the air *have* nests, but the Son
of man hath not where to lay *his* head 21 And [q] an- q Luke ix 59
other of his disciples said unto him, Lord, [r] suffer me r Lev xxi 11, 12
first to go and bury my father 22 But Jesus said
unto him, Follow me, and [r] let the dead bury their Num vi 6, 7
dead

v 18—22 Great multitudes being some time after (*see Mark* iv 35) collected together, more from curiosity or secular view, it is probable, than desirous of his divine instructions, our Lord commanded his disciples to remove to the other side of the lake, to avoid the croud, to enjoy some needful retirement, to prove their obedience, or to spread the gospel in other places, whither those who were hearty in his cause would follow him, and the rest give it up Hereupon we are informed of a conversation which passed with two persons who seemed desirous to join him

1 One of them was a scribe, who seemed to express great forwardness, zeal, and resolution to follow Christ where-ever he went, but his warmth soon cooled, when he understood that he must expect none of those worldly advantages with which he flattered himself from being an apostle of Jesus, since, instead of earthly grandeur and the conveniences of life, the Messiah, the Son of man, was more destitute even than the birds or foxes, and had not a place of his own to repose his weary head, or refresh himself with the sleep he now wanted after his toils *Note*, (1) Sudden starts of zeal, and hasty resolutions, are far from being the best evidences of faithful adherence to Christ (2) Many are willing to follow Christ if they can get by him, who quickly cool in their ardour, when their worldly interest, character, or ease, must be denied for his sake (3) The poverty of the Lord Jesus, and his wants, should teach us in every state therewith to be content

2 Another man, who had professed himself a disciple, and might be perhaps an appointed evangelist, wanted at this time to be excused from attending his master His plea was plausible his father was either aged and sick, and he desired to stay with him till he should have discharged the last offices to him, or rather he was now dead, and wished to wait upon him to his grave before he went with Jesus, but Christ will not admit the excuse he must leave all, and come, there were enough dead in trespasses and sins, who might take care of the corpse and the funeral, whilst a more urgent and nobler employment called for his services, even to follow Jesus and preach the gospel *Note*, (1) Worldly engagements, even about necessary things in our families, are apt to prove a great hindrance to our following Christ (2) They who want an excuse for declining duty will easily find it (3) There are times when God's service may demand our attendance, and engage us to leave father, mother, house, and all, and he is not worthy of Christ who can set any thing in competition with him

t Mark iv 35 Luke viii 22 23 ¶ And [t] when he was entred into a ship, his dis-
ciples followed him 24 And behold, [u] there arose a
u Isa liv 11 great tempest in the sea, insomuch that the ship was
covered with the waves but he was asleep 25 And
his disciples came to him, and awoke him, saying,
Lord, save us we perish 26 And he saith unto
them, Why are ye fearful, O ye of little faith? Then
x Ps cvii 13 he arose and [x] rebuked the winds and the sea, and there
was a great calm 27 But the men marvelled, saying,
y Ps lxv 7 & lxxxix & cvii 29 What manner of man is this, that [y] even the winds and
the sea obey him!

v 23—27 Christ having issued his orders to cross the lake, his chosen disciples immediately obeyed and launched forth, for no dangers or difficulties will deter those from following Jesus, who know the blessedness of his service Since their master was with them, they counted, no doubt, they were perfectly safe, but for the trial of their faith, and the manifestation of his glory, we find them plunged into the greatest danger and distress

1 No sooner were they got to sea, than a violent hurricane overtook them The waves like mountains rolled, broke over them with dreadful roar, and their boat, filled almost with water, was ready instantly to founder in the deep whilst Jesus, as if unconcerned and unacquainted with the danger, wearied with his labours, sweetly slept *Note*, (1) They who follow Christ will meet with many a storm (2) Christ often seems to disregard his people when their dangers seem most imminent (3) The temptations permitted to overtake the faithful are designed not to harm them, but to exercise, strengthen, and brighten their graces

2 With deep distress the affrighted disciples ran to their Lord, and with their cries awoke him, saying *Lord, save us, we perish*, their case was desperate if he did not immediately interpose *Note*, (1) Awakened consciences feel their perilous condition, and see their inevitable destruction, without divine grace and help (2) Prayer will be then fervent and importunate, when the deep sensibility of danger raises the cry (3) They who come to Jesus must exercise faith in his sufficiency to save, though utterly despairing of help in themselves (4) Even doubts and fears will sometimes mingle with the prayer of faith

3 Jesus with calmness and majestic dignity arose, rebukes their fears, then bids the storm be still, and suddenly the foaming billows subside, the winds are hushed, the troubled waters now are smooth, and not a breath of air dimples the polished surface *Note*, (1) In the stormy seasons of temptation, many a fear distresses the faithful heart (2) Those may have true faith who have but *little faith* (3) The weakness of our faith, and the prevalence of our fears deserve rebuke, as they reflect dishonour upon the faithfulness, power, and grace of Jesus *Why are ye fearful?* (4) Though the storm of temptation be never so violent, no sinner that cleaves to Jesus shall ever perish (5) Where the distress of the soul hath been peculiarly deep, and the trials uncommonly severe, there usually the strongest consolations, and the most delightful sensations follow, of joy and peace in believing

4 The effect produced by the miracle was the astonishment of the mariners, or disciples who were in the ship, or of both Never was such an amazing change known before, and this naturally leads them to express their admiration of this wonderful person, whom even winds and waves obeyed *Note*, They who have experienced the power of a Saviour's grace, in circumstances where every prospect seemed covered with darkness and despair, cannot but wonder and adore

28 ¶ [z] And when he was come to the other side, z Mark v 1 Luke viii 26.
into the country of the Gergesenes, there met him two
possessed with devils, coming out of the tombs, exceed-
ing fierce, so that no man might pass by that way 29.
And behold, they cried out, saying, What have we to
do with thee, Jesus thou Son of God? art thou come
hither to torment us [a] before the time? 30 And there was a 2 Pet ii 4 Jude 6
a good way off from them an herd of many swine feeding
31 So the devils besought him, saying, If thou cast
us out, suffer us to go away into the herd of swine.
32 And he said unto them, Go And when they were
come out, they went into the herd of swine and be-
hold, the whole herd of swine ran violently down a
steep place into the sea, and perished in the waters
33 And they that kept them fled, and went their ways
into the city, and told every thing, and what was be-
fallen to the possessed of the devils 34 And behold,
the whole city came out to meet Jesus, and when they
saw him, [b] they besought him that he would depart out b Deut v 25 Luke v 8 Acts xvi 39
of their coasts

v 28—34 Continued miracles of mercy mark every step of the divine Redeemer

The country of the Gergesenes, here mentioned, bordered on the side of the lake which they had crossed, and they were no sooner arrived, than a fresh occasion offers to display the power and grace of Jesus

1 Two miserable objects met him, *possessed of devils, coming out of the tombs*, the place where they took up their residence, driven thither by the wicked spirits who actuated them, to make their abode the more dreary and dismal, or to confirm the notion of spirits haunting these melancholy places, or by solitude to increase their ferocity, and render them more mischievous, for they were *exceeding fierce, so that no man durst pass that way* for fear of them *Note*, When anger, malice, and revenge dwell in the bosom, there Satan's power reigns, and men then turn worse than savages to their kind

2 The devils address the Lord, as trembling at his presence, and fearful of being dispossessed *What have we to do with thee, Jesus, thou Son of God?* They well knew his power and godhead, and their hopeless state he never came to be a Saviour unto them, but their destroyer, and all their desire is, that he would let them alone, at least in the heathen world, if he drove them from Judea, and not come thither *to torment them before the time* Torment eternal they expected, they were persuaded he would be their terrible judge, and they ask only a momentary respite before the last and dreadful day, when their misery will be complete *Note*, (1) The devils know and tremble (2) They who say to Jesus and his servants, What have we to do with thee? depart from us, and reject the counsel of God against their own souls, must perish with fiends of darkness

3 Being unable to keep possession of the bodies of men, they desire to enter into a herd of swine that fed there, for even over these they could have no power without divine permission, and this they besought, either from their innate pleasure in mischief, or rather from a crafty design to make Christ an unwelcome guest in that country, and Jesus, from whom none of their wiles could be hid, permitted it, perhaps because these swine belonged to the Jews, who kept them for food in defiance of God's laws, or for covetousness, to make merchandize of them and he would thus punish their owners Or he designed hereby to manifest his own divine power, to prove the reality of the miracle, and confound the Sadducean doctrine, which denied the existence of spirits good or evil No sooner had these fiends obtained their request, than they flew as to their prey, and all the herd of swine madly rushed down a precipice into the sea, and were choaked, to the great terror of those that kept them, who fled, and filled the city and country with the report And so grieved were they at their loss, and affrighted with the apprehensions of greater judgment, that, instead of adoring him for the miracle he had wrought on the two possessed persons, or welcoming him to their country, they besought him to depart, like many other worldlings, who love their swine better than their souls We may observe here, (1) The restraint laid upon these spirits of wickedness they cannot touch a swine without permission, and however malignant and fierce the devil

is

is, Jeſus holds his chain, and in all his temptations ſaith, Hitherto mayſt thou go, and no further (2) Where Satan rules in the children of diſobedience, he fails not to drive them into many fooliſh and hurtful luſts, which neceſſarily drown both body and ſoul in perdition (3) By nothing doth the god of this world hold firmer poſſeſſion of men's hearts againſt Chriſt, than by ſuggeſting the loſſes and croſſes to which his ſervice may expoſe them, and bewitching them with the love of gain in preference to the love of God

CHAP IX.

We have in this chapter remarkable inſtances of the power and pity of the Lord Jeſus, ſufficient to convince us that he is both able to ſave to the uttermoſt all that come to God by him, and as willing as he is able His power and pity appear here in the good offices he did, 1 To the bodies of people, in curing the palſy, ver 2—8 Raiſing to life the ruler's daughter, and healing the bloody Iſſue, ver 18—26 Giving ſight to two blind men, ver 27—31 Caſting the devil out of one poſſeſſed, ver 32—34 and healing all manner of ſickneſs, ver 35 2 To the ſouls of people In forgiving ſins, ver 2 Calling Matthew, and converſing freely with publicans and ſinners, ver 9—13 Conſidering the frame of his diſciples, with reference to the duty of faſting, ver 14—17 Preaching the goſpel, and in compaſſion to the multitude providing preachers for them, ver 35—38

1 AND he entred into a ſhip, and paſſed over, and
came into [a] his own city 2 [b] And behold,
they brought to him a man ſick of the palſy, lying on
a bed [c] And Jeſus ſeeing their faith, ſaid unto the ſick
of the palſy, Son, be of good cheer, [d] thy ſins be for-
given thee 3 And behold, certain of the ſcribes ſaid
within themſelves, This man blaſphemeth 4 And
[e] Jeſus knowing their thoughts, ſaid, Wherefore think
ye evil in your hearts? 5 For whether is eaſier to ſay,
Thy ſins be forgiven thee? or to ſay, Ariſe and walk?
6 But that ye may know that [f] the Son of man hath
power on earth to forgive ſins (then ſaith he to
the ſick of the palſy) Ariſe, take up thy bed, and go
unto thine houſe 7 And he aroſe, and departed to
his houſe 8 But when the multitude ſaw it, they mar-
velled, and glorified God, which had given ſuch power
unto men

a Chap iv 13. b Mark ii 3. Luke v 18. c Chap viii 10. d Isa [illegible] e Chap [illegible] 25. f John x [illegible] Acts v 31

v 1—8 Jeſus will not abide where he is an unwelcome gueſt, but wo to thoſe who bid him depart, for nothing but wrath and miſery are left behind him Leaving the country of the Gergeſenes, he returned to Capernaum, the uſual place of his reſidence, where we find him curing a poor paralytic, for his work was ever to be doing good

1 His friends brought him to Jeſus, unable himſelf to ſtand or walk they had compaſſion for their brother, and counted no pains too great to obtain his cure, and they were perſuaded the Lord both could and would relieve him from his miſery *Note*, Thoſe of our dear friends and relatives, who are themſelves benumbed in ſpirit as with the palſy, and cannot come to Chriſt, we muſt carry in the arms of prayer and love, and ſpread their caſe before him perhaps in ſo doing we may ſave a ſoul from death

2 Chriſt kindly received them *ſeeing their faith*, either of thoſe who brought him, or of the ſick man alſo, and to revive the heart of the poor afflicted patient, more diſtreſſed probably by his ſins than his ſufferings, Jeſus ſaith, *Son, be of good cheer, thy ſins be forgiven thee* *Note*, (1) Sin is the bittereſt of all our burdens, the ſting of ſickneſs and death itſelf is taken out when our iniquity is pardoned (2) They who come to Chriſt are called upon to be of good cheer, no poor beggar ever went from his door with a denial (3) God ſometimes ſeverely afflicts his deareſt children, they muſt not queſtion their adoption becauſe of their ſufferings, but ſhould rather conclude, that God then dealeth with them as ſons, *Heb* xii 5

3 The Scribes, who were the doctors of the law, and expounded it to the people, highly offended with what Jeſus had ſaid, though they did not ſpeak their ſentiments, yet in their hearts regarded him as a blaſphemer, for preſuming by his own authority to forgive ſin, which is the prerogative of God alone, and contains a ſtrong argument for his divinity, in which light theſe men evidently regarded his declaration *Note*, Many among us are like theſe ſcribes, though they will not ſay it is blaſphemy, in ſeem to pardon our ſin, they are ready to brand thoſe as blaſphemers, who ſay they have the pardon Jeſus pronounces

4 To give them a proof of his divinity, and confute their vain imagination, Jeſus lets them know he perceived their thoughts *Wherefore think ye evil in your hearts* conſidering him as a blaſphemer, *For whether is eaſier to ſay, Thy ſins be forgiven thee? or to ſay, Ariſe and walk* He that by his own power could effect the one, evidently proved he had a right to pronounce the other *Note*, Our hearts are naked and open before the Lord, and he obſerves and is diſpleaſed at every evil thought which riſes or lodges there

5 He demonſtrates the power he had to forgive ſin, by removing that diſeaſe which was the puniſhment of it, and bids the paralytic *ariſe* before them all, and, as a proof of his health and ſtrength being perfectly reſtored, to *take up* that *bed*, on which as a cripple he lay, and *go unto his houſe* And lo! to the aſtoniſhment of the multitude, who glorified God for ſo great a miracle, and to the confuſion of theſe murmurers, the man inſtantly aroſe, took up his bed, and departed, cured of every infirmity *Note*, (1) Though we have no ſtrength of ourſelves to help ourſelves, when Jeſus ſpeaks to the paralytic ſoul, power accompanies his word, and enables us for that which he commands (2) The mercies ſhown to others demand our praiſes, and for every good gift beſtowed on the ſons of men, God is to be glorified

9 ¶ And as Jeſus paſſed forth from thence, [g] he ſaw
a man, named Matthew, ſitting at the receipt of cuſ-
tom And he ſaith unto him, Follow me And he aroſe
and followed him 10 ¶ And it came to paſs, as Jeſus
ſat at meat in the houſe, behold, many publicans and
ſinners came and ſat down with him and his diſciples
11 And when the Phariſees ſaw *it*, they ſaid unto
his diſciples, [h] Why eateth your Maſter with publicans
and ſinners? 12 But when Jeſus heard *that*, he ſaid
unto them, They that be whole need not a phyſician,
but they that are ſick 13 But go ye, and learn what
that meaneth, [i] I will have mercy, and not ſacrifice
For I am not come to call the righteous, [k] but ſinners
to repentance

g Mark ii 14 Luke v 27. h Gen xliii 32. Iſa lxv 5. Chap xi 19. Acts x 28. i 1 Sam xv 22. Prov xxi 3. Hoſ vi 6. Mic vi 6 &c. k Luke xix 10. Rom v 6, 8. 1 Tim i 15

v 9—13 The publicans were thoſe who farmed or collected the cuſtoms impoſed by the Romans, and were not only therefore odious to the Jews, who abhorred this mark of ſervitude, but were alſo for the moſt part men of infamous conduct, who enriched themſelves by exaction, being ſure of having the government on their ſide Hence publicans and ſinners are ſo often uſed to include the moſt guilty and abandoned characters, yet ſuch as theſe Jeſus came to ſave, and out of them was pleaſed to chuſe one of his moſt eminent diſciples, an Apoſtle and Evangeliſt, the penman of this goſpel We have,

1 His call His name is Matthew, *the gift of God*, which ſome ſuppoſe was given him by our Lord on this occaſion, when before he was known by that of Levi, as the other evangeliſts call him, though it was common for the ſame perſon to have two names He was ſitting at the receipt of cuſtom, in the office where it was to be paid, and perhaps little thought of following Chriſt but the Lord is often ſtrangely found of them who ſought him not, and prevents us with the bleſſings of his grace, that to his glory it may be for ever acknowledged he hath choſen us, not we him One word effectually wrought upon the publican's heart he ſaid, *Follow me*, *and* immediately *he aroſe and followed him* Power accompanies the word of Jeſus, when he calls a ſoul unto himſelf, which bears down all objections, and out of the moſt enſnaring engagements of this world ſome are made monuments of grace, for nothing is too hard for God

2 Having taſted the grace of Jeſus himſelf, he is ſollicitous his brethren by profeſſion ſhould be acquainted with him alſo, and for this purpoſe made a feaſt for Jeſus and his diſciples, to which many publicans and ſinners were invited nor did the Lord diſdain their company, but gladly ſat down with them *Note*, (1) They who have truly experienced the Redeemer's grace, from that moment begin to labour, that all who are near and dear to them may partake of their bleſſing (2) Where the heart is open to Chriſt, there all who are his diſciples will be welcome for his ſake

3 The Phariſees with malignant eye marked the condeſcenſions of Jeſus, and wanted to caſt a reflection upon his character, and prejudice his diſciples againſt him *Why eateth your Maſter with publicans and ſinners?* Theſe proud and ſelf-righteous creatures thought it infamous to be ſeen in ſuch company, and would inſinuate, that our Lord was like the men with whom he had ſat down to meat *Note*, (1) The ſelf-righteous formaliſts are ever the moſt rapid cenſurers of others conduct (2) The nobleſt acts of charity are liable to the baſeſt miſrepreſentations

4 Chriſt vindicates himſelf from their inſinuations He overheard their whiſpers, or his diſciples, weak themſelves, carried the queſtion to him, that they might be furniſhed with an anſwer, for to him in all our difficulties we muſt have recourſe, and he gives them an abundant vindication of his conduct *They that be whole need not a phyſician, but they that are ſick* He came into the world as the great phyſician of ſin-ſick ſouls, ſinners are his unhappy patients, who groan under their ſpiritual maladies, incurable but for his healing grace and they who

feel

feel their miseries and fly to him, he is ever ready to relieve; but the wilfully ignorant, and the self-righteous, who know nothing of their deep corruption, guilt, and sinfulness, and conceit themselves whole; these, as they experience no want of him, and will not come to him that they may have life, are lost to perish in their blindness and their pride. *But go ye*, saith he, *and learn what that meaneth*, Hos. vi. 6. *I will have mercy, and not sacrifice*; that is, in a comparative sense, acts of kindness and charity to men's bodies or souls are much more acceptable to God, than all the formalities of ritual devotion; and therefore Christ intimates, that his conversing with sinners for their good, was, according to the word of truth, far more pleasing to God, than their scrupulous adherence to the tradition of the elders. *For I am not come to call the righteous, but sinners to repentance*; this being the very end of his mission, he was fully justified in receiving them into his company, that he might acquaint them with his salvation. Had man been righteous, he never had needed a Redeemer; and they who fancy they are such, have nothing to do with him who came only to seek and save that which is lost. The Saviour's errand is to sinners, the vilest of sinners, to invite them to return to God, with promises of pardon purchased by his blood, and to call them in virtue thereof to repent and turn from all their abominations. And to this a sense of his love engages them, and for this his grace enables them; whilst they who vainly conceit that they are righteous, and need no repentance, are left to perish in their own deceivings.

14 ¶ Then came to him the disciples of John, say-
l Mark ii. 18. Luke v. 33. ing, l Why do m we and the Pharisees fast often, but
thy disciples fast not? 15 And Jesus said unto them,
m Prov. xx. 6. Can n the children of the bride-chamber mourn, as long
as the bridegroom is with them? But the day will come,
n John iii. 29. when o the bridegroom shall be taken from them, and
o Acts i. 9. p then shall they fast. 16 No man putteth a piece of
p Acts xiii. 3. new cloth unto an old garment. For that which is put
in to fill it up, taketh from the garment, and the rent
is made worse. 17 Neither do men put new wine into
old bottles. Else the bottles break, and the wine runneth out, and the bottles perish. But they put new wine
into new bottles, and both are preserved.

v. 14—17. Our Lord was ever beset by insidious foes, yet his wisdom enabled him to confute and confound all their malicious designs. We have here,

1. The question addressed to Jesus by some of John's disciples. *Why do we and the disciples of the Pharisees fast often, but thy disciples fast not?* and herein they would insinuate, that they were not so strict and holy in their religious profession as they ought to be. It appears from *Luke* v. 33. that they were set on by the Pharisees, who joined them; for designing and wicked men study how to set good men at variance, and are happy if they can suggest any cause of discord between them. They seem to take a pride in proclaiming the frequency of their own fasts, and to look down upon the disciples of Jesus as far their inferiors in this respect; and this leaven of self complacence effectually destroyed what otherwise might be laudable in their practice. *Note*, (1.) In the externals of devotion and mortification, formal professors often go farther than true converts; being under a spirit of bondage, they rest upon their austerities, which in fact are not *of any value* in the sight of God, *but are to the satisfying of the flesh*, Col. ii. 23. (2.) They who boast of their own good works, evidently shew their religion is vain.

2. Christ vindicates his disciples by an appeal to themselves. *Can the children of the bride-chamber mourn, as long as the bridegroom is with them?* On such seasons of festivity fasting would be unseasonable. Christ was this heavenly bridegroom, as John had called him, *John* iii. 29. he came now openly to espouse his church, whom he had loved from eternity. His disciples were the children of the bride-chamber, who, whilst their Lord was with them, could not but rejoice; but the time would come, when *the bridegroom* should be *taken from them, and then shall they fast*: besides, at present they were but young disciples, and therefore to be inured by degrees to harder services. As improper would it be to lay upon them at present their austerities, as to put a piece of new cloth on an old garment, which would soon make a worse hole than that which it covered; or new wine, which ferments most, into old bottles, which, being made of leather or skins, would by long use grow weak, and be liable to burst; *but new wine must be put into new bottles*, and then *both are preserved*. There must be a proper consideration had of the persons and their measure of grace: children and babes in Christ must not be set upon the services which require peculiar intenseness of mind, or the severest acts of self-denial; but gently led, as Jacob's cattle, *Gen.* xxxiii. 13. lest by being over driven they should be destroyed.

q Mark v. 22. Luke viii. 41. 18 ¶ q While he spake these things unto them, be-
hold, there came a certain ruler, and worshipped him,
saying, My daughter is even now dead: but come and
r John xi. 25. lay thy hand upon her, and r she shall live. 19 And
Jesus arose and followed him, and *so did* his disciples.
20 ¶ (And behold a woman which was diseased with
s Lev. xv. 19. &c. s an issue of blood twelve years, came behind *him*, and
touched the hem of his garment. 21 For she said
within herself, If I may but touch his garment, I shall
be whole. 22 But Jesus turned him about, and when
t Luke vii. 50. & viii. 48. & xvii. 19. & xviii. 42. he saw her, he said, Daughter, be of good comfort, t thy
faith hath made thee whole. And the woman was made
whole from that hour.) 23 And when Jesus came into the ruler's house, and saw u the minstrels, and the
u 2 Chron. xxxv. 25. people making a noise, 24 He said unto them, x Give
x Acts xx. 10. place, for the maid is not dead, but sleepeth. And they
laughed him to scorn. 25 But when the people were
put forth, he went in, and took her by the hand, and
the maid arose. 26 And the fame hereof went abroad
into all that land.

v. 18—26. While Jesus was vindicating the conduct of his disciples from the cavils of those who found fault with them, an agreeable avocation calls him from this unpleasing work of disputation.

1. A ruler of the synagogue, a man of rank and importance, applies to Jesus on the behalf of his daughter, who was either now in the very agony of death, as the other evangelists say, or by this time, as he concludes, actually dead. He therefore with deepest humility begs him to come to his house, and lay his hand upon her, persuaded that Jesus could easily restore her, desperate as the case appeared. Though few, very few, in his station respected Christ, he was one of those singularly favoured, to whom it was given to believe on his name. *Note*, (1.) Christ has disciples of every rank; and though in general to the poor the gospel is preached, yet some, though not many, mighty, and noble are called. (2.) The breaches in our family should drive us to the Lord, if not to restore the dead to life, at least to sanctify the providence as a means of quickening our own souls.

2. Christ immediately complies with his request; for he is more willing to give, than we to ask, and none seek him in vain; and his disciples followed him, desirous to behold a fresh instance of the divine power of their Lord.

3. In the way he heals a poor woman afflicted with a disease of long standing, that weakened her in body, rendered her ceremonially unclean, and impoverished her in seeking a cure, without obtaining any relief from the physicians. As her disorder was of such a nature that she might be ashamed to mention it, and by the law should have kept her from mingling in society with others, she came behind our Lord, and touched the hem of his garment, persuaded that there was such a plenitude of healing virtue in Jesus, that if she but touched his garment she should certainly be cured. Nor was she disappointed of her hope, she immediately felt herself perfectly well; but must not steal off unnoticed. Though others observed her not, Jesus, who had brought her thither, knew what was done, and for his own glory and her comfort addresses her with kind encouragement, saying, *Daughter, be of good comfort, thy faith hath made thee whole*. *Note*, (1.) The poor sinner who comes to Christ, ashamed, confounded, and distressed, shall be sent from him rejoicing. (2.) They who honour Christ by believing in his name, he will honour, approving and rewarding the faith which he bestows.

4. He is pleased to raise from the dead the ruler's daughter. At his arrival he found the house filled with mourners and minstrels, as was usual on those occasions, with melancholy notes of woe, exciting greater grief and wailing; but he bad them cease their lamentations, and leave the room, since they would find the damsel not as they supposed dead and past hope, but as one asleep, whom he would soon awake; though they assured him she was dead, and supposing the case desperate, treated what he said with utter contempt. But he quickly convinced them of their folly and wickedness herein; for having ordered them to be put out of the house, or room, as unworthy to be spectators of his miracles who thus derided him, in the presence of the father and mother, and three of his disciples, he went in, took her by the hand, and at his word she instantly arose, alive and well as if she had indeed awaked from a refreshing sleep. *Note*, (1.) Death is but a longer night, and sleep its [illegible] mysteries. They who die in the Lord, are said to sleep in Jesus; for though dead to us, they live to him, and only wait for the resurrection morn to wake up to eternal life and day, when sleep and death shall be no more. (2.) When our dear relatives go before us to their bed of dust, though nature cannot but feel the pangs of parting, we sorrow not as those who have no hope. If they fall asleep in Christ, we shall wake up together shortly never to part again. (3.) Many scoff at Christ's word, and because they cannot comprehend them, treat them as foolishness, though they will be found the wisdom of God. (4.) He that by a touch, a word, raised the dead body, doth this

by his word and spirit raise our souls from the death of sin unto the life of righteousness We are wholly passive, nor can perform the least act of spiritual life, till he hath first quickened us

5 The fame of this amazing miracle soon spread throughout that land, the certainty of the fact being put beyond doubt by the multitude of those who had been fully convinced of the damsel's death

27 ¶ And when Jesus departed thence, two blind
men followed him, crying and saying, Thou son of
David, have mercy on us 28 And when he was come
into the house, the blind men came to him and Jesus
saith unto them, believe ye that I am able to do this?
They said unto him, Yea, Lord 29 Then touched he
their eyes, saying, According to your faith be it unto
you 30 And their eyes were opened, and Jesus straitly
charged them, saying, [y] See that no man know *it*. 31
[z] But they, when they were departed, spread abroad his
fame in all that country 32 ¶ [a] As they went out,
behold, they brought to him a dumb man possessed with
a devil 33 And when the devil was cast out, the
dumb spake and the multitudes marvelled, saying, It
was never so seen in Israel 34 But the Pharisees said,
[b] He casteth out the devils through the prince of the
devils

y Chap viii 4 & xii 10 & xvii 9. z Mark vii 36. a Luke xi 14.

b Chap xii 24 Mark iii 2

v 27—34 Miracle upon miracle confirmed our Lord's divine mission, and left those inexcusable who, in the face of such evidence, rejected him

1 We find him, immediately after raising Jairus's daughter, giving sight to two blind men

[1] They followed him with importunate cries, hearing of his fame, and hoping for a cure He who gave life to the dead, could surely give sight to the blind Their address shewed their persuasion, that Jesus was the true Messiah, the promised Son of David, and all their prayers centered in one point, *have mercy on us* All the sinner needs is comprehended in this one word, and all he can hope for, or ask, is free, unmerited grace Being in the same distress, they joined their mutual supplications, fellow-sufferers should be joint petitioners and though their request was not, as usual, immediately granted, they did not desist, but with persevering earnestness followed him through the street, and then into the house If the Lord Jesus for a while seem to disregard our prayers, it must not be interpreted a denial of our requests, but as designed to quicken our importunity, and to make the mercy sought more valued by us We shall assuredly succeed, if we faint not

[2] In answer to the question of our Lord, they make a noble confession of their faith Jesus asked them, *Believe ye that I am able to do this?* to open your eyes, and by my own divine power to cure your blindness, *they said unto him, yea, Lord*, we are fully persuaded of it *Note*, (1) They who have true faith, never desist till they have obtained the blessing (2) In all our trials, the full and fixed persuasion of Christ's power to save us out of them, must be as an anchor to our souls amidst the storm (3) Christ requires open profession of our faith, that we may give him the glory due unto his name

[3] Hereupon he grants their request *He touched their eyes, saying, According to your faith be it unto you And their eyes were opened* He knew their sincerity, and he designed to express his approbation of their faith in conferring the cure Whoever still comes to him with their wants, will find the same language from Jesus, *according to our faith*, the blessings of the gospel become possessed by us Whatever we want, faith may ever draw it out of his fulness, and whenever we fail of strength or comfort, we may be assured it is owing to our unbelief

[4] He strictly charges them to conceal the miracle he had wrought for them Either he shunned all appearance of seeking popular applause, or he knew the more his fame spread, the more his enemies would be exasperated or perhaps he did it to prevent the Jews, or his own disciples, too much disposed to expect in their Messiah a temporal prince, from crowding around him, or attempting, by insurrections, to set him on the throne of Israel

[5] They, notwithstanding, *spread abroad his fame*, so full of gratitude, they could not conceal the favour; and though their disobedience was not commendable, their motive no doubt pleaded their excuse Well meant zeal, though sometimes imprudently exerted, should not meet a harsh censure

2 He cures a dumb man possessed of a devil His friends brought him to Jesus as a truly pitiable object, just as the blind men, who were healed, went out, for Christ's door was open to all the miserable, and he was never weary in doing good The favour is no sooner asked than granted, the devil is dispossessed, and the dumb man speaks freely as ever *Note*, They who live in the neglect of prayer and praise and godly conversation, are under the possession of this spirit of dumbness, but when the grace of Jesus touches the heart, the tongue of the dumb will instantly sing, speaking his praises, and telling what great things God hath done for his soul

3 These miracles had a very different effect on the spectators *The multitudes marvelled*, and owned, to the glory of Jesus, that never had such miracles been seen before in Israel, so many, so immediate, and performed with such divine authority But the malignant Pharisees, determined to find fault, though unable to deny the facts, imputed these miracles to diabolical agency, as if Christ was in league with the devil They who are bent against conviction, will always have something to object, and the more they are pressed with the evidence of the truth, the more enraged, inveterate, and blasphemous is their abuse

35 And [c] Jesus went about all the cities and villages,
[d] teaching in their synagogues and preaching the gospel
of the kingdom, and healing every sickness, and every
disease among the people 36 ¶ [e] But when he saw the
multitudes, he was moved with compassion on them,
because they fainted, and were † scattered abroad, [f] as
sheep having no shepherd 37 Then saith he unto his
disciples, [g] The harvest truly *is* plenteous, but the labourers
are few 38 [h] Pray ye therefore, [i] the Lord of
the harvest, that he will send forth labourers into his
harvest

c Mark vi 6 Luke xiii 22 d Chap iv 23 e Mark vi 34 † Gr Cast down f Num xxvii 17 1 Kings xxii 17 g Jer v 6 Chap x 6 Luke x 2 John iv 35 h 2 Thes iii 1 i Chap x 1 Eph iv 11

v 35—38 Christ did not long fix his abode at one place We have an account,

1 Of his journies, preaching, and cures, through all the cities and villages of Galilee He taught publickly in the synagogues the doctrines of the gospel, and the nature, blessings, and privileges of that kingdom he came to erect, and in confirmation of his mission in every place performed the most miraculous cures on the bodies of all the diseased who applied to him, as his word was designed to heal the greater maladies of their souls

2 Of the compassion he expressed towards the multitudes who followed him It grieved him to see the darkness, ignorance and carelessness which every where appeared, *they fainted*, perishing through lack of knowledge, instead of the bread of life and truth, fed with the miserable husks of Pharisaical traditions, and misled in the most essential truths of God's word, through the adulterations with which their scribes had corrupted it, *and they were scattered abroad, as sheep without a shepherd*, exposed to the great destroyer of souls, and destitute of every faithful guide to bring them to the fold of God they who should have directed them aright, contributed to increase their errors, or by total negligence abandoned them to ruin Our Lord therefore stirs up his disciples to pray, that since the harvest is so plenteous, and multitudes of immortal souls willing to hear the good word of God, and so few to labour for their conversion, to gather them into God's church the great Lord of the harvest would send forth labourers qualified for their work, and bless them with success *Note*, (1) They who know the value of their own souls, cannot but feel with Jesus, the tenderest compassion for those who live in ignorance, error and sin, and pity them the more because they appear so insensible, and to have no pity on themselves (2) The neglect of ministers is an awful judgment upon the people, and must be attended with aggravated guilt and ruin on their own souls (3) When multitudes appear attentive, and willing to hear the gospel, it is a grief to see them deprived of the means, and a double obligation is laid on the few faithful to exert themselves (4) The grievous neglect of men's souls we see should excite our fervent prayers to God, that he would revive his work in the midst of the years, and send forth faithful shepherds to feed and guide his flock (5) Christ must appoint his own servants, he is the Lord of the harvest, none can call or qualify for the office but himself, and whom he sends he will support and bless, their labour shall not be in vain in the Lord They who see no gracious fruits of their ministry, may justly conclude the Lord of the harvest never sent them (6) All Christ's servants are *labourers*, there are no loiterers who are of his appointing Diligence, fidelity, and zeal mark their ministrations

CHAP X

In answer to the prayers enjoined in the former chapter for faithful labourers, we have, 1 The general commission that was given them, ver 1 2 The names of the persons to whom this commission was given, ver 2—4 3 The instructions that were given them, which are very full and particular, (1) Concerning the services they were to do, ver 5—15 (2) Concerning the sufferings they were to undergo, with the counsel given, and support promised to them, ver 16—42 And these things, though primarily intended for direction to the apostles then, are of use to all Christ's ministers, with whom he is, and will be always to the end of the world

Mark iii. 13. Luke vi. 13.

1 AND [a] when he had called unto him his twelve
disciples, he gave them power *against* unclean
spirits, to cast them out, and to heal all manner of sick-
ness, and all manner of disease 2 Now the Names
of the twelve apostles are these, The first, Simon, who
is called Peter, and Andrew his brother, James *the son*
of Zebedee, and John his brother, 3 Philip and Bar-
tholomew, Thomas, and Matthew the publican, James
the son of Alpheus, and Lebbeus, whose surname was
Thaddeus, 4 Simon the Canaanite, and Judas Isca-
riot, who also betrayed him

v. 1—4 Those whom our Lord intended to be his ministers and ambassadors, he had before called to be his attendants, that they might learn from his divine instructions the truths they must preach to others, and imitate his bright example which they beheld None can possibly be fit for the ministry, or be called of God to take that office upon them, who have not first been taught of Christ by communion with him, and acquaintance with his word, the blessed truths they are to declare to others, and been furnished with gifts as well as graces for that arduous employment It is the scandal of any church, and must be the ruin of the people's souls, when such are sent forth as ministers who are themselves ignorant, careless, and unacquainted with the glorious truths of God, and merely take up the ministry as a maintenance, and they who read them shall share their guilt

1 Christ *called them unto him* in private, from the rest of the disciples, and with their commission to preach his gospel, invested them with authority over the unclean spirits and diseases of every kind, that by their miracles they might confirm their mission *Note*, (1) A particular call is needful for the ministry, besides the general one to be Christ's disciple, and we must see this clear, before we presume to it (2) The great design of the gospel-ministry is to oppose and destroy Satan's power over the hearts of men Though bodily possessions may be less frequent, his empire over men's souls is still mighty, and nothing but the power of the gospel can effectually cast out the unclean spirit from the fallen heart (3) In the grace of Jesus there is a cure for every sickness, none of our spiritual maladies are so inveterate, but there is in his word medicine that can heal the sickness

2 The number and names of the apostles are recorded They were twelve in number, according to the tribes of Israel, to whom they were sent They are mentioned in pairs, being sent forth by two and two, as mutual helps to each other, and some of them were brethren in blood, as well as apostleship, and happy it is where relations are thus, by grace, doubly united Peter is placed first, not as invested with superior power over his fellow-labourers, but as among those who were first called, and appeared ever most zealous in the cause Matthew, the writer of this gospel, humbly sets Thomas before himself, though the other evangelists place him after Matthew, and he adds his former occupation, *the publican*, as a foil to set off the distinguished grace of Jesus to him, and to keep him lowly in his own eyes, remembering from whence he was taken Simon, another of the same name with Peter, is distinguished from him, by being called the *Canaanite*, either from his city, Cana of Galilee, or, as the name signifies, he was of the *zealots*, *Luke* vi 15 a sect among the Jews, who in imitation of Phinehas, out of pretended zeal for God's glory, executed vengeance on offenders, without any process before the magistrates Judas the traitor is the last The purest society will have some such among them he is called *Iscariot*, concerning which there are many conjectures, the most probable seems to be, that it was given him from the place of his nativity, and to distinguish him from the other Judas or Jude, the brother of James

5 [b] These twelve Jesus sent forth and commanded
them, saying, Go not into the way of the Gentiles, and
into *any* city of the Samaritans enter ye not 6 But go
rather to [c] the lost sheep of the house of Israel. 7 And
as ye go, preach, saying, The kingdom of heaven is at
hand 8 Heal the sick, cleanse the lepers, raise the
dead, cast out devils freely ye have received, [f] freely
give 9 Provide neither gold nor silver, nor brass, in
your purses 10 Nor scrip for your journey, neither
two coats, neither shoes, nor yet staves (for [g] the work-
man is worthy of his meat) 11 And into whatsoever
city or town ye shall enter, enquire who in it is worthy,
and there abide till ye go thence 12 And when ye
come into an house, salute it 13 And [h] if the house
be worthy, let your peace come upon it but if it be
not worthy, [i] let your peace return to you 14 And
whosoever shall not receive you, nor hear your words
when ye depart out of that house, or city, [k] shake off the
dust of your feet 15 Verily I say unto you, [l] It shall
be more tolerable for the land of Sodom and Gomorrah
in the day of judgment, than for that city.

v. 5—15 Christ having given the apostles their commission, directs them how to discharge it aright

1 Their ministry must be confined to the lost sheep of the house of Israel alone, and therefore they are forbidden to enter any city of the Gentiles or Samaritans The covenant of peculiarity was not yet dissolved, and for the fathers sake the Jews were beloved It was needful therefore that to them the Gospel should first be preached, that the elect of God among them might be gathered in, and the rest left inexcusable in their infidelity

2 The subject of their preaching must be the same that John at first, and Jesus himself had inculcated, *that the kingdom of heaven was at hand*, and therefore urging all men to repent and turn to God, as became the true members of the Messiah's kingdom *Note*, (1) Truth is uniform Novel doctrines carry their own confutation along with them (2) The nearness of Christ's coming in his kingdom should quicken our diligence to prepare to meet him

3 They are directed to work miracles in confirmation of their mission, and to engage the readier attention to their doctrine in the name of Jesus they shall be enabled to heal the sick, cleanse the lepers, raise even the dead, and cast out devils from the possessed, evidences these of divine power, which none who were not wilfully obstinate, could withstand, and for these acts of benevolence to men's bodies or souls, they must neither desire nor receive the least reward, shewing their disinterested zeal and charity, and giving as freely as they had received *Note*, Nothing more evidently characterises the faithful ministers of Christ, than their disinterested labours, not seeking gain for themselves, but the good of mankind

4 They need not be at all sollicitous about a provision for their journey, nor should they take either money in their purse, or meat in their scrip, or change of garments, or any other than the cloaths they had on, the sandals on their feet, and the staff in their hands he who employed them in their work, will take care they shall not want Though they may not desire to enrich themselves by their labours, they justly deserved their maintenance *Note*, Though ministers must not seek filthy lucre, they have a right to a subsistence, and they who preach the gospel shall live by the gospel

5 As they were going into places where they were utterly unknown, their first enquiry must be who *was worthy* in the place, not of the gospel or the grace of God, but who was most noted for hospitality, and the entertainment of strangers, and abide in their house during their stay, if they found a welcome In which case, entering with kindest wishes of every temporal, spiritual, and eternal blessing, they should salute the master and his houshold, and if they received a courteous and hearty entertainment, then all the blessings they wished for should descend upon that house but if their salute was returned with coldness or incivility, then their good wishes should not be lost, but instead of descending on that family, should return with blessings upon their own souls But wo to that house or city that should, by their unkind behaviour, compel them to depart! They are commanded to shake off the dust of their feet against them, either as testifying their abhorrence of their wickedness in thrusting the gospel from them, or as a testimony against them in the day of judgment, at which awful season even Sodom and Gomorrah would not meet with so heavy a doom, as these who rejected the counsel of God against their own souls *Note*, (1) Though in the sight of God all are upon a level, and can plead no desert before him, yet respecting men some have more worthy characters, and are of a more generous spirit than others (2) Religion is never a plea for rudeness or morosity to be courteous is a gospel-duty (3) No good wishes are ever lost, the prayer offered for the evil and unthankful will bring a blessing to us, if they procure none for them (4) Nothing is lost by being employed in God's service, and the support of the gospel, no money laid out in any way will bring richer returns than this (5) They who reject God's minister reject him, whose ambassadors they are, so he will interpret it, and avenge their quarrel (6) When any place or people slight the gospel, justly doth God take it from them (7) There is a day of judgment at hand, when among the various degrees of punishment which will be inflicted on sinners, none will endure so heavy vengeance as those against whom the dust of a slighted and rejected gospel shall rise up for a testimony

16 ¶ [m] Behold, I send you forth as sheep in the
midst of wolves [n] be ye therefore wise as serpents, and
harmless as doves 17 But beware of men, for [o] they
will deliver you up to the councils, and they will [p] scourge
you in their synagogues 18 And [q] ye shall be brought
before governors and kings for my sake, [r] for a testimony
against them and the Gentiles 19. But when they deli-
ver you up, [s] take no thought how or what ye shall
speak,

speak, for it shall be given you in that same hour what
ye shall speak 20 For it is not ye that speak, but
the spirit of your Father which speaketh in you 21
And the brother shall deliver up the brother to death,
and the father the child and the children shall rise up
against *their* parents, and cause them to be put to death
22 And ye shall be hated of all men for my name's
sake but he that endureth to the end, shall be saved
23 But when they persecute you in this city, flee ye
into another for verily I say unto you, Ye shall not
have gone over the cities of Israel, till the Son of man
be come 24 The disciple is not above *his* master, nor
the servant above his lord 25 It is enough for the
disciple that he be as his master, and the servant as his
lord if they have called the master of the house Beel-
zebub, how much more *shall they call* them of his house-
hold 26 Fear them not therefore for there is no-
thing covered, that shall not be revealed, and hid, that
shall not be known 27 What I tell you in darkness,
that speak ye in light and what ye hear in the ear, *that*
preach ye upon the house-tops 28 And fear not
them which kill the body, but are not able to kill the
soul but rather fear him which is able to destroy both
soul and body in hell 29 Are not two sparrows sold
for a farthing and one of them shall not fall on the
ground without your Father 30 But the very hairs
of your head are all numbered 31 Fear ye not there-
fore, ye are of more value than many sparrows 32
Whosoever therefore shall confess me before men, him
will I confess also before my Father which is in heaven
33 But whosoever shall deny me before men, him
will I also deny before my Father which is in heaven
34 Think not that I am come to send peace on earth
I came not to send peace, but a sword 35 For I am
come to set a man at variance against his father, and
the daughter against her mother, and the daughter-in-
law against her mother-in-law 36 And a man's foes
shall be they of his own houshold 37 He that loveth
father and mother more than me, is not worthy of me
and he that loveth son or daughter more than me, is
not worthy of me 38 And he that taketh not his
cross, and followeth after me, is not worthy of me
39 He that findeth his life shall lose it and he that
loseth his life for my sake, shall find it 40 ¶ He that
receiveth you, receiveth me, and he that receiveth me,
receiveth him that sent me 41 He that receiveth a
prophet in the name of a prophet, shall receive a pro-
phet's reward, and he that receiveth a righteous man in
the name of a righteous man, shall receive a righteous
man's reward 42 And whosoever shall give to drink
unto one of these little ones, a cup of cold water only
in the name of a disciple, verily I say unto you, he shall
in no wise lose his reward

V 16—42 As they were now beginning the work of their ministry, our Lord informs them of the trouble and persecution to which they will be hereafter exposed in the exercise of their office, that when they came, they might not think some strange thing had happened unto them as they might otherwise do, if their heads were filled with the hopes of a temporal kingdom And that they may not be at a loss in these seasons of trial, they have here gracious encouragements to support them, and directions for their conduct in such emergencies

1 They must expect to meet with many difficulties and much suffering They were harmless and defenceless as sheep, and were going forth into a world where they would be worried by wicked men, fierce and savage as wolves for Christ's name sake, and for their fidelity to him, they would be *hated*, the natural heart being full of enmity against God and his image, and this being at the root of all persecution, with whatever specious pretence the wicked seek to cloak their enmity They would be *arraigned* as criminals, and brought to the bar, the arm of justice which should be stretched forth to protect the innocent, having in all ages, through false misrepresentations and partial judges, been made the means of the most cruel oppressions of God's people They would be exposed to *suffer in their persons, even unto death*, so bitter will the inveterate malice of their enemies go not content with scourging them, and putting them to shame, ver 17 they will persecute some even unto blood, and with all the ignominy of a public execution take away their lives To give a pretext for such cruelties, they will be *branded with every opprobrious name*, ver 25 and *their characters be blackened*, as if they were very fiends of hell This being the art of persecutors in every age to misrepresent the people of God, and dress them up in the most odious colours, the more easily to destroy them So far, therefore, from that outward peace and prosperity which the Jews fancied would attend the Messiah's kingdom, they must look for the sword of persecution, and a state of constant variance and warfare with the world which lieth in wickedness, v 34, 35 That gospel of peace, which in itself breathes such charity and good-will to men, through the perverseness of the natural heart, would give occasion to the most implacable feuds, difference of religion being the ground of the most cruel persecutions Now these things they are warned of, that they *may count the cost*, and knowing the consequences, their choice may be deliberate and fixed These trials also would be the more severe, considering the persons from whom they would come, from *men*, ver 17 even those of their own nation, *from the very persons to whom* they preached, and for whose souls they laboured From *all men*, men of all ranks and degrees, and from the world in general which lieth in wickedness, few of whom would receive their testimony, and the rest would be not only hardened, but exasperated against them *From the great men*, the kings and governors of the earth, who would employ their power in oppressing and opposing them, for the gospel seldom meets with friends among the great Yea, from those *who make a shew of religion*, even in the synagogues they would find the most inveterate foes, v 17 who would even count God honoured in the punishment they inflicted on them, and place their bitterest malice to the score of zeal for his glory and such persecutors on principle are the worst of persecutors And finally, what would be of all others the most irksome to be born, *from their nearest and dearest relations* the most inveterate enmity may be expected The nearest ties of blood shall be dissolved, even brothers shall lose all fraternal affection, yea, parents turn unnatural to their own offspring, and children forget all duty and regard, v 21 Even daughters shall rise up against their mothers, and the daughter-in-law, who before lived peaceably with her mother-in-law, will now entertain the deadliest animosity, inflamed with blind zeal and bigotry, as if from the moment their dearest relatives embraced the gospel of Jesus, no affection or respect was henceforward due to them, no measures to be kept with them, but that with implacable enmity they must be persecuted, accused, or murdered, *so that a man's bitterest foes shall be those of his own houshold*, and this hath been grievously verified by the experience of past ages, and more or less, as our good conversation in Christ exhibits the stronger contrast to the ways of a world which lieth in wickedness, will be the case to the end of time

2 Christ gives them counsel and encouragement how to bear up under these heavy trials His counsel is,

(1) *Be wise as serpents* When we have crafty enemies to deal with, we are bound to use every prudential means for our own preservation, and as far as may be to counteract their mischievous designs, nor unnecessarily expose ourselves to danger

(2) *Be harmless as doves*, give no needless provocation, shew no rancour or ill will in return for any injuries, manifest that genuine simplicity and harmlessness of conduct, which may cut off occasion from those who seek occasion, and then the subtlety of the serpent is laudable, when thus joined with the innocence of the dove

(3) *Beware of men* Be cautious whom you trust, and with whom you are connected In this false and wicked world, we must not hastily believe every word, or be open to every plausible professor prudent reserve often keeps us from fruitless repentance

(4) *When they persecute you in one city, flee into another* In cases where life is in danger, or virulent opposition prevents all opportunity of exercising our ministry, then to flee is duty, provided no unlawful means are used to escape, and that we follow the leadings of providence, not deserting our post through fear, but maintaining our zeal and integrity unshaken

(5) *Fear not them who can kill the body, but are not able to kill the soul*, this mortal life is the utmost to which their rage can extend, *but rather fear him which is able to destroy both soul and body in hell* The soul is the valuable part of man, the body is but dust, and however great the terrors of persecutors may be, the terrors of the Lord are greater, the everlasting burnings of hell, the wrath of the eternal God, and the sufferings both of soul and body in torment, without measure and without end, must be remembered as an antidote against the fear of man, when he comes armed with every instrument of torture, rack, gibbet, fire or sword How much better is it bravely to endure a momentary pang, and in an instant be gone beyond all the malice of persecutors, than by base compliance provoke God, from whose hands none can deliver us, and whose wrath will be for ever wrath to come?

(6) *What I tell you in darkness, that speak ye in light* Let nothing intimidate you from a bold and open profession and ministration of the gospel, *and what ye hear in the ear*, of my secrets communicated to you as your friend, or master, this being the custom of the Jewish doctors to whisper in their disciples ears, *that preach ye upon the house-tops*, which being low and flat roofed, a person might be heard in the street, from them di-

stinctly, and this intimates, that in the most public places of concourse, they must deliver their message without fear or shame Christ's gospel seeks no covert, nor must his ministers conceal any thing from their hearers of the whole counsel of God

The encouragement proposed to them boldly to endure hardness as good soldiers of Jesus Christ, is great as the dangers they had to grapple with were intimidating

1 *Verily I say unto you, ye shall not have gone over*, or *finished*, *the cities of Israel, till the Son of man be come* Before they could have finished their testimony, they would see the kingdom of heaven, which they preached, come with power, when, after the resurrection and ascension of Jesus, and the effusion of the Holy Ghost upon them, they should be endued with greater powers, and see the most wonderful effects of their ministry, the prospect of which should quicken them in their present labours

2 They need not be under any concern about *what they should say* when brought before their superiors, and accused by their enemies, *for it shall be given you in the same hour what ye shall speak*, being under a divine guidance they should never be at a loss, but should be enabled to vindicate the truth with the most powerful arguments, and to deliver themselves with greatest propriety, to the astonishment of their adversaries, endued with wisdom and power more than human, which the most subtle of their foes shall not be able either to gainsay or resist, *for it is not ye that speak, but the spirit of your father which speaketh in*, or *by, you*, and when on emergencies we are suddenly called forth to speak for Christ, if his glory be our single aim, we shall still find the same teaching and strength, and may comfortably trust him for assistance

3 Their very sufferings should tend to propagate the gospel they preached, and be *for a testimony against Jews and Gentiles*, before whose tribunal, when brought as criminals, they would have a more public opportunity of bearing witness to the glorious truths of God, and if they sealed them with their blood, as martyrs, this would be a stronger confirmation of the truth of their mission, and leave those who rejected their testimony inexcusable

4 *He that endureth to the end shall be saved* These light afflictions are but for a moment, their end is near, death at the worst shall put a period to them, a little patience and perseverance will make them more than conquerors, and *the far more exceeding and eternal weight of glory* will infinitely overpay all the sufferings of this present time

5 They could never be treated worse than their master had been before them Whatever persecution or reproach they might endure, He, who was so greatly their superior, had suffered the same They had called him *Beelzebub*, a devil, the prince of the devils, and treated him with every imaginable ignominy, and this contradiction of sinners he patiently endured Having therefore so glorious an example before them, they might well be content to bear his reproach, and count it their honour to be made like their Lord and Master Who of us should start at shame, insult, or suffering, when we look to Jesus, and see what he endured?

6 *There is nothing covered that shall not be revealed, nor hid that shall not be known* However their enemies might seek to suppress the word of truth, it should blaze forth in spite of all opposition, and their characters, though blackened by the most malignant calumnies, should quickly be vindicated, their innocence proved, their integrity vindicated either in this world, or at furthest at that great day, when every man's work shall be tried of what sort it is, and they be declared faithful, and exalted to glory in the sight of men and angels Little need we then regard the revilings of men, when our judgment is with our God, and he shall soon bring forth *our righteousness as the light*

7 They shall be under the peculiar care of providence, and therefore might comfortably and confidently trust, and not be afraid If a sparrow falls not to the ground, poor and worthless as it is, without the cognizance, and only according to the will of the eternal God, whose providence extends to the very least and lowest creatures he hath made, and who hath left nothing to chance or contingency, but hath enrolled in his eternal decrees every event the most minute, as well as the most important, which cannot but come to pass according to the counsel of his will nay, if the very hairs of their head are numbered, and not one of them can fall unknown or unnoticed, how little need they fear death or danger, their enemies, however inveterate, can have no power over them, except it be given them from above, and they may be assured the least evil cannot reach them without the divine permission They are of *more value than many sparrows*, and therefore not only as men, but as disciples dear to Jesus, may expect his peculiar care and protection *Note*, True faith in God's providence will silence all our fears, and shew them as fruitless as they are sinful, *since the counsel of the Lord that shall stand*

8 According as they are faithful, they will be owned or rejected by Jesus, at the great day of his appearing and glory *Whosoever therefore shall confess me before men, him will I confess also before my Father which is in heaven* Whatever reproach or danger a bold and open profession of Jesus may expose us to, it will redound to our distinguished honour in the day of Christ, when the great Judge and Lord of all shall testify his approbation of our conduct before men and angels, and present us before the throne of God, as proved and found faithful, and who shall therefore be advanced to glory, honour, and immortality *But whosoever shall deny me before men, him will I also deny before my Father which is in heaven*, whoever through coward fear, or shame, starts back in the day of trial, and hides or denies his profession before men, he shall be disowned by me in the great day, rejected with abhorrence, and exposed to everlasting shame and contempt for such base apostacy Every motive, therefore, of fear or hope, urges us to be faithful

9 Whatever their losses may be for Christ, they shall be abundantly gainers in the end It is true they may be called upon to part with every thing near and dear to them, and must love the Lord Jesus and his service above all besides, ready to sacrifice every thing for him when it stands in competition with his glory Neither father, mother, son, or daughter, must rival him in our hearts, nay, our very lives must not be dear unto us, when for his sake called to lay them down Whatever cross the Lord Jesus calls us to endure, whatever commands he is pleased to lay upon us, we are no *worthy* of a name among his disciples, unless we chearfully take it up, and obediently follow him and indeed in so doing, we most effectually consult our own advantage and safety *For he that findeth his life*, preserving it at the expence of some base compliance, or unfaithful conduct, *shall lose it*, all the comforts of it shall be embittered to him here, and he shall perish eternally, so that in the issue he shall see his folly great as his sin whilst *he that loseth his life for my sake*, ready to lay it down when called for, rather than take one step out of the path of duty, *he shall find it* at the resurrection of the just, with most ample compensation for all his losses, in the eternal blessedness of body and soul with God in glory

Lastly, Though they would find many enemies, they would meet also with faithful friends, whom, for their kindness to his disciples, he would abundantly reward He would regard every instance of respect and affection shewn to them as done to himself, and God the Father will assuredly repay it Whoever therefore received their word, or the word of those who should succeed them, and shewed kindness to their persons as the ministers and prophets of the Lord, *he shall receive a prophet's reward*, blessed by his labours, and sharing with him in the promise of eternal happiness And in like manner, *he that receiveth a righteous man in the name of a righteous man*, loving and kind to him, not for any worldly, personal, or private considerations, but purely on account of him whose image he bears, *he shall receive a righteous man's reward*, partaking with him that life and glory which is the gift of God in Jesus Christ, the reward, not of debt, but of grace Nay, the very least and most inconsiderable favours shewn to the very meanest disciple, if but *a cup of cold water*, shall be remembered and recompensed at the resurrection of the just Considerations these, admirably suited to comfort them under all their trials and afflictions, and embolden them with fidelity to persevere And we are alike interested in these things, and should be comforted and encouraged under all our troubles for the gospel's sake, with the same reviving expectations

CHAP XI

In this chapter we have, 1 The unwearied diligence of our Lord in preaching the gospel, ver 1 2 His discourse with the disciple of John concerning his being the Messiah, ver 2—6 3 The honourable testimony that Christ bore to John Baptist, ver 7—15 4 The sad account he gives of that generation in general, and especially of some particular places, with reference to the success, both of John's ministry, and of his own, ver 16—24 5 His thanksgiving to his Father for the wise and gracious method he had taken in revealing the great mysteries of the gospel, ver 25, 26 6 His gracious call and invitation to poor sinners to come to him, and to be ruled and taught and saved by him, ver 27—30

1 AND it came to pass, when Jesus had made an
end of commanding his twelve disciples, he de-
parted thence to teach and to preach in their cities 2
ᵃ Now when John had heard in the prison the works of
Christ, he sent two of his disciples, 3 And said unto
him, ᵇ Art thou he that should come, or do we look for
another? 4 Jesus answered and said unto them, Go,
and shew John again those things which ye do hear and
see 5 ᶜ The blind receive their sight, and the lame
walk, the lepers are cleansed, and the deaf hear, the
dead are raised up, and ᵈ the poor have the gospel preach-
ed to them. 6 And ᵉ blessed is he whosoever shall not
be ᶠ offended in me

v. 1—6. Having finished his instructions to his disciples whom he sent forth, he did not devolve the work to them and sit down idle himself, but *departed thence to teach and preach in their cities*; and in this blessed work the disciples sent from John found him employed. We are told,

1. Where John was, *in prison*, for his fidelity in reproving Herod the king. Such reward may the zealous ministers of God sometimes expect to meet. But the fame of Jesus reached him even there: and now, no doubt, with joy he heard of his labours and success. If we are disabled, it is still a most reviving cordial to hear that the work of God prospers.

2. The question he put to Jesus by the disciples whom he sent. *Art thou he that should come, or do we look for another?* art thou the promised Messiah, or no? Some have supposed John was himself in doubt, and either discouraged by his long confinement, or, like the rest of his countrymen, prepossessed with the notions of a temporal Messiah; though it seems much more reasonable, from the testimony John had born to him, to suppose, that not for his own sake he sent this message, but for the sake of his disciples, who though they had cleaved to John hitherto, yet, he being shortly to leave them and to be cut off, he introduces them to Jesus, that they might receive from him the fullest conviction of his character, and henceforward commence his disciples. *Note*, (1.) God will not leave his people destitute: if one able minister is removed, another is raised up. (2.) It is the duty of faithful ministers to lead their hearers off from all attachment to men, even themselves, and to direct them simply to Jesus. (3.) Where the matters of our eternal salvation are concerned, it becomes us to be inquisitive, and to see that our faith be built on sure grounds.

3. The answer Christ returned to their enquiries. He refers them to the facts which they beheld, as the most satisfactory proof of his being that Messiah which should come into the world. *The blind receive their sight, the lame walk*, &c. full evidences these of a divine mission, and a clear fulfilment of the prophecies which went before concerning him, *Isa.* xxxv. 6. lxi. 1. *and the poor have the gospel preached unto them*, those whom the Scribes and Pharisees despised, he received kindly, and acquainted them with the glad tidings of his grace, which many of them willingly received: or *the poor preach the gospel*, mean and illiterate men are endued with great gifts and abilities to propagate the doctrines of the gospel: *and blessed is he whosoever shall not be offended in me*, not prejudiced against him because of his poverty, the meanness of his station, and the despicable followers which attended him; but, looking above all these things, beholds in his works and words his divine character, and gives him the glory due unto his name. *Note*, (1.) Many treat the poor with contempt, but Christ hath taught us a different lesson; of such his church is chiefly composed, and this adds abundant honour to them. (2.) There are many things in Christ's character and gospel which minister occasion of offence to the proud and self-righteous; but faith admires the condescensions of Jesus, and adores him for that at which others stumble and fall.

a Luke vii. 24. 7 ¶ a And as they departed, Jesus began to say un-
to the multitudes concerning John, What went ye out
b Eph. iv. 14. into the wilderness to see? b A reed shaken with the
wind? 8 But what went ye out for to see? A man
clothed in soft raiment? Behold, they that wear soft
clothing are in kings houses. 9 But what went ye out
for to see? A prophet? yea, I say unto you, and more
than a prophet. 10 For this is he of whom it is writ-
c Mal. iii. 1. Mark i. 2. ten, c Behold, I send my messenger before thy face,
which shall prepare thy way before thee. 11 Verily
I say unto you, among them that are born of women,
d Luke i. 15. d there hath not risen a greater than John the Baptist:
notwithstanding, he that is least in the kingdom of hea-
ven is greater than he. 12 And from the days of John
e Chap. iii. 5. Luke xvi. 24. the Baptist, until now, e the kingdom of heaven suffer-
eth violence, and the violent take it by force. 13 For
all the prophets and the law prophesied until John.
f Mal. iv. 5. Ch. xvii. 12. Luke i. 17. 14 And, if ye will receive *it*, f this is Elias which was
for to come. 15 g He that hath ears to hear, let him
g Chap. xiii. 9. 43. Mark iv. 9. 23. & vii. 16. Rev. ii. 7. 11. 17. 29. hear.

v. 7—15. When John's disciples were gone, Jesus took this opportunity of paying a high encomium on his character and ministry. He would not say it in their hearing, lest it should seem flattery, nor would have it reported to John, for he well knew how ill the best can bear even deserved praise.

1. He addresses a question to the multitude around him, many of whom had been John's hearers. *What went ye out into the wilderness to see? A reed shaken with the wind?* Was it mere curiosity, or did you suppose him a man unsteady and wavering? It was John's honour that he was uniform and steady in his preaching and labour: and an intimation is contained in the question, that they who had gone so far to hear him should well consider what he had said, and enquire what profit they got by their attendance. *Note*, Many go a great way to hear ministers from curiosity, who soon forget all they hear, as a dream. *But what went ye out for to see? A man clothed in soft raiment?* No. His garb bespoke his deadness to the world. He neither spoke nor dressed like a courtier. His reproofs were plain and rough as his appearance: the case of those to whom he addressed himself required it. *Behold, they that wear soft clothing, and live delicately, are in kings houses*; and he was utterly unlike those: his manners austere, his conduct steady. *Note*, (1.) In the work of the ministry unshaken resolution is needful, which is alike unmoved by frowns or smiles. (2.) They who have heard and seen God's ministers should often enquire what they have gained thereby, or what end they purposed by their attendance. (3.) Our dress should be according to our station. It is no evil in those who are in kings courts to put on soft cloathing, though it would be sinful in others to imitate them in expensive finery, which they can neither afford, and which is unbecoming their situation or character in life.

2. He tells them plainly the distinguished honour of this eminent teacher. *But what went ye out for to see? a prophet? yea, I say unto you, and more than a prophet.* In general all held John for a prophet, and yet they understood not that peculiar distinction he enjoyed above all who went before him.

[1.] He was the person foretold, *Mal.* iii. 1. as the forerunner of the Messiah, who should more immediately prepare his way, and usher him into the world. The other prophets saw him at a distance, and only spoke of him as to appear in the fulness of time. John beheld him face to face, and pointed him out as present. *Behold the Lamb of God.*

[2.] *Among them that are born of women, there hath not risen a greater than John the Baptist.* Not only his miraculous birth, his being filled with the Holy Ghost from his mother's womb, his exemplary life, rendered him singular; but, above all, the clear revelation he had of the Messiah, his baptising him in Jordan, seeing the heavens opened and the Holy Ghost descending upon him, and the testimony he bore to him on that occasion, these made John far superior to all his predecessors. *Nevertheless, he that is least in the kingdom of God is greater than he*, the least of the ministers and apostles of Christ, or the meanest believer in him, would in clearness of gospel light, and knowledge of Jesus, be able to see farther, and to speak more distinctly, of his obedience, righteousness, sufferings, death, of his grace and glory, of the spiritual nature of his kingdom, than even the most eminent saints and prophets of old. *Note*, (1.) True greatness is not to be measured by outward splendor, but by the gifts and graces of God's Spirit, and the manifestation which Jesus makes of himself to the soul. (2.) If we enjoy greater advantages than others, our condemnation will be the greater if we do not profit under them.

[3.] By John the gospel of the kingdom began to be preached, and God owned his ministry with eminent success; for *from the days of John the Baptist until now*, a space of little more than two years, *the kingdom of heaven suffereth violence, and the violent take it by force*, the publicans and harlots, who by the Scribes and Pharisees would be reckoned intruders, convinced now of their guilt, and turned to the Lord, eagerly pressed for a place in the Messiah's kingdom; and multitudes of others, awakened to a discovery of their sin and danger, eagerly embraced the declarations of grace, and with a holy violence strove to enter in at the strait gate. *Note*, (1.) Wherever divine grace hath quickened the soul, there salvation will be made the great concern, and eager diligence used to make our calling and election sure. (2.) It is a distinguished honour conferred on any minister of the gospel, when God is pleased to make him eminently instrumental in calling sinners to flee from the wrath to come. (3.) Sluggish and negligent triflers in religion may never hope for admission into the kingdom of God.

[4.] In the ministry of John the Old-Testament dispensation closed, and the new began. *For all the prophets and the law prophesied until John*, in types and predictions they pointed to the future Messiah, all the ritual service of the temple being designed to direct the worshippers to him, and, viewed in this light, it appears truly glorious; but now he was come, in whom all these were to be fulfilled. *And if ye will receive it*, and can credit my assertion, *this is Elias which was for to come*, not Elijah personally, but he who was spoken of, *Mal.* iv. 5. and who came in the spirit and power of Elijah, like him in dress and manners, and imitating his zeal. *He that hath ears to hear, let him hear*, which intimates that these were things that deserved attentively to be weighed, and, though dark and difficult to be believed, were truths of great importance. *Note*, (1.) The word of God must be examined with serious concern: it is not a slight and cursory perusal which will be sufficient to let us into the meaning; deep meditation, fervent prayer, and comparing spiritual things with spiritual, being necessary to a right understanding of the mysteries of grace. (2.) It is not hearing, but *receiving* the truth in the light and love of it, which can make us wise unto salvation.

16 ¶ But h whereunto shall I liken this generation? h Luke vii. 31.
It is like unto children sitting in the markets, and calling

p 1 Cor xii 6, 7 unto their fellows, 17 And ſaying, p We have piped
unto you, and ye have not danced we have mourned
q Chap iii 4 Luke i 15 unto you, and ye have not lamented 18 For q John
came neither eating nor drinking, and they ſay, He hath
r Chap ix 11 a devil 19 r The ſon of man came eating and drink-
ing, and they ſay, Behold, a man gluttonous, and a
wine bibber, a friend of publicans and ſinners but wiſ-
s Luke x 13 dom is juſtified of her children 20 ¶ s Then began
t Ezek iii 7 he to t upbraid the cities wherein moſt of his mighty
works were done, becauſe they repented not 21 Wo
unto thee Chorazin, wo unto thee Bethſaida for if the
mighty works which were done in you, had been done
in Tyre and Sidon, they would have repented long ago
u Jonah iii 7 8 u in ſackcloth and aſhes 22 But I ſay unto you, x It
x Chap x 15 Ver 24 ſhall be more tolerable for Tyre and Sidon at the day
of judgment than for you 23 And thou Capernaum,
y Iſa xiv 13 Jer li 53 y which art exalted unto heaven, ſhalt be brought down
to hell for if the mighty works which have been done
in thee, had been done in Sodom, it would have re-
mained until this day 24 But I ſay unto you, that
z Lam iv 6 Luke x 12. z it ſhall be more tolerable for the land of Sodom in the
day of judgment than for thee

v 16—24 Having ſpoken of the excellence of John's miniſtry, he cannot but reflect upon the inexcuſable perverſeneſs and ſtubbornneſs of that generation, which had for the moſt part continued in their impenitence, notwithſtanding John's preaching, and in oppoſition to all the miracles and means of grace which they had enjoyed under his own miniſtry and that of his apoſtles For which an awful reckoning remained

1 He is at a loſs for a ſimilitude whereunto he ſhall liken the men of that generation, they acted ſo contradictorily and abſurdly, like ſullen and froward children, that, when their playfellows uſe every little art to engage them, mimicking a wedding or a funeral, and inviting them to dance with them, or in mournful reſponſes to anſwer them, moroſe and ill-natured they will join in neither Such was the temper of the Scribes and Phariſees, with their diſciples, reſpecting the miniſtry of Chriſt and his forerunner. They uſed different means, but neither could prevail *John* called to mourning, preaching repentance and humiliation, and in his own abſtemious and ſelf-denying conduct ſet them an example of mortification, and, ſo far from being affected thereby, they treated him as melancholy, and poſſeſſed by a devil *The Son of man*, with the ſweeteſt muſick of goſpel grace, ſought to engage their minds, and by every kind word and deed endeavoured to inſinuate himſelf into their affections, free and open in his manners, affable to all, joining with them in partaking the innocent refreſhments of nature, and ready to converſe with the chief of ſinners for their good, and immediately they brand him as *a glutton, a wine-bibber, a friend of publicans and ſinners*, an encourager and a partaker with them in their immoralities *But wiſdom is juſtified of her children* They who are by grace made acquainted with the truth, will approve all the means and methods which God is pleaſed to uſe, though others reject and deſpiſe them or *Chriſt*, the *wiſdom* of God, will be acquitted of all their malicious accuſations of wicked men, by all who truly become the children of God, and are enlightened to know his true character They will admire and adore him for what others revile and malign him *Note*, (1) There is nothing ſo abſurd or contradictory that the enemies of the goſpel will not ſay and do, in order to vent their malice againſt the miniſters and truths of God (2) God uſes every means with ſinners, declaring the terrors of his law and the comforts of his goſpel, ſending them, by turns, mercies and judgments, and all to work on their obdurate hearts, or to leave them inexcuſable in their impenitence (3) Different miniſters have different manners of addreſs, and are more particularly ſuited to the diſpoſitions and tempers of ſome than of others ſome are ſtruck with a Boanerges, ſome melted under a Barnabas, a ſon of conſolation; ſome are affected with the more auſtere manners of a John, others engaged by the ſweetneſs and affability of Jeſus Every one hath his gift, and all for the edification of the body of Chriſt (4) The moſt powerful and engaging miniſtrations are not always crowned with ſucceſs but, when we have diſcharged our ſouls, and men refuſe to hear the voice of truth, of reaſon, of conſcience, neither drawn by the bonds of love, nor driven to God by all the terrors of wrath to come, then their blood is on their own heads, we are free (5) The greateſt, the beſt of men, yea he that was more than man, have been reviled as mad or libertines, as preaching doctrines of deſpair or licentiouſneſs Let it not ſeem ſtrange if the ſame things be ſaid of us, and if what is our higheſt honour in God's ſight be made matter of ſevereſt reproach He is near who will juſtify us (6) Though the goſpel and the miniſters of it in general be ſlighted and reviled of men to ſome their word will be a ſavour of life, and they will juſtify God in all his ways, being themſelves living inſtances of the efficacy of the methods he hath taken to bring poor ſinners to himſelf

2 As he had reproached the obſtinacy of that generation in general, he particularly upbraids the cities *wherein moſt of his mighty works were done, becauſe they repented not*, for to lead them thereunto was the great end of all his miracles and preaching, but it had been in vain and how ſhall they eſcape who neglect ſo great a ſalvation? they muſt needs periſh who reject the only remedy that can cure them and ſuch wilful obſtinacy muſt bring down greater damnation *Note*, God is pleaſed to diſpenſe the means of grace, as well as the gifts of providence, *ſovereignly* Why one place ſhould enjoy them, whilſt another, leſs guilty, is abandoned to darkneſs and ignorance, can only be reſolved into the divine pleaſure *Even ſo, Father, for ſo it ſeemed good in thy ſight*

Two inſtances are particularly brought of cities who had enjoyed the greateſt means and mercies, and yet were more hardened than even the vileſt of the heathen

1 *Wo unto thee Chorazin, wo unto thee Bethſaida*, places in Galilee peculiarly favoured with Chriſt's miracles and teaching, and yet the generality of the inhabitants perſiſted in their impenitence, though, had the like mighty works been done even in *Tyre and Sidon*, abandoned to wickedneſs as they were, it is to human appearance highly probable that, like Nineveh of old, they would *have repented in ſackcloth and aſhes*, and humbled themſelves to prevent the impending ruin Therefore at the judgment-day their doom ſhall be more tolerable than that of thoſe cities which, by rejecting the goſpel, fall under the moſt aggravated guilt *Note*, An awful day is near, when the eternal ſtates of all muſt be determined, when all the means of grace and mercies we have enjoyed muſt be accounted for, and none will receive ſo great damnation as thoſe who have abuſed them, and, in oppoſition to the cleareſt light of the goſpel, have perſiſted in the darkneſs of error and ſin

2 Capernaum with peculiar emphaſis is threatened *Thou*, moſt dignified by the reſidence of Jeſus, and diſtinguiſhed with ſingular advantages above all other cities, *which art exalted to heaven* in outward privileges, *ſhalt be brought down to hell*, falling the deeper into eternal miſery from the heights of abuſed mercy Even Sodom's doom will be more tolerable than hers, for, if the like miracles and long-continued miniſtry of Jeſus had been vouchſafed to that city, it ſeems highly probable ten righteous at leaſt would have been found, and the threatened ruin averted but, if Sodom was not ſpared with leſs guilt, Capernaum, with greater, muſt needs ſink under more aggravated ruin *Note*, Many of this day ſeldom think of the ineſtimable talent committed to them in the oracles of God and the goſpel of his Son, but for theſe things a ſolemn account muſt ſoon be given, and wo to the ſinner whoſe profiting at that day ſhall not appear

25 ¶ a At that time Jeſus anſwered and ſaid, I thank a Luke x 21
thee, O Father, Lord of heaven and earth, becauſe b thou b Iſa xxix
haſt hid theſe things from the wiſe and prudent, and c haſt 14 & xliv
revealed them unto babes 26 Even ſo, Father, for ſo 18 2 Cor iii 14
it ſeemed good in thy ſight 27 d All things are deli- c Pſ viii 1 Cor i 2
vered unto me of my Father and no man knoweth the d Chap.
Son but the Father e neither knoweth any man the xxviii 18 John xvi
Father, ſave the Son, and he to whomſoever the Son e John i
will reveal *him* 28 ¶ Come unto me, all f ye that & x 15
labour and are heavy laden, and I will give you reſt f Jer xxxi
29 Take my yoke upon you, and g learn of me, for 25 Luke
h I am meek and lowly in heart and i ye ſhall find reſt xv 17 & xxiii 1, Rom viii
unto your ſouls 30 For k my yoke is eaſy, and my & 1 Pet ii. 21
burden is light h Zech ix 9 Phil ii 3 i Jer vi 16 k [illegible]

v 25—30 Though in general the perverſeneſs of the many afforded the moſt melancholy proſpect of their deſtruction, yet did not the goſpel word return in vain There was ſtill a remnant, according to the election of grace, who heard and believed

1 Our bleſſed Lord here offers up his thanks to God the Father for the children he had given him, though few, and in the eyes of men deſpicable, poor, and illiterate, yet precious to Jeſus, and the travail of his ſoul

[1] He addreſſes God as His *Father*, in whoſe love he had the moſt aſſured intereſt, and as *the Lord of heaven and earth*, the ſovereign diſpoſer of all things, able to do whatever he pleaſed, according to the counſels of his own will *Note*, Prayer is then a pleaſing ſervice, when we can call God Father, approach him with confidence, and, perſuaded of his all-ſufficiency to ſupply our wants, can quietly caſt our care upon him

[2] He adores his ſovereignty in being pleaſed to hide the glorious truths of goſpel-grace from the wiſe and prudent, and revealing them to ſuch as, comparatively ſpeaking, reſpecting natural abilities, learning and human accompliſhments, were vaſtly their inferiors, but if God is pleaſed to chuſe theſe babes, Jeſus, acquieſcing in his Father's holy will, approves of and delights in it *Note*, (1) It is a mortifying truth, and of hardeſt digeſtion to the proud heart of man, that thoſe whom the world admire as great, learned, and wiſe, the deepeſt ſcholar, the moſt profound ſtateſmen, the moſt reverend doctors, and acute metaphyſicians,

physicians, are not merely on a level with the meanest clown, respecting the knowledge that maketh wise unto salvation, but for the most part farther removed from it, and, according to God's all-wise decrees, eternally excluded, given up to learned ignorance, and left to the spiritual blindness of their fallen hearts (2.) Those whom God chuses for his people are usually such as man despises, poor in every sense, in station, abilities, human literature, and all that a foolish world admires Some few indeed are found of the wise, mighty, and noble, but not *many*, enough to shew what God could do, if he pleased, while we are humbly to acquiesce in what he hath done Yet this will ever be, as it was from the beginning, a stone of stumbling and rock of offence. *Have any of the rulers and Pharisees believed?* (3.) Whatever difference is made between one and another is purely owing to God's sovereign will and pleasure, and not to any thing foreseen in them, or done, or to be done, by them, and therefore, in all God's dispensations of providence or grace, if a curious enquirer, or disputer of this world, enquires into the reasons why and wherefore God thus acts, we have but one to give, *Even so, Father, for so it seemed good in thy sight* They who are dissatisfied with this reason, must close their Bibles, and expatiate in the boundless regions of scepticism and infidelity in search of a better

2 Christ invites those babes, whom the Father hath given him, to come unto him, with kindest assurances both of his power and willingness to help and save them

[1.] He declares the plenitude of power with which he is invested for the comfort of all who should apply to him for refuge *All things are delivered unto me of my Father* As Mediator he hath received a delegated authority, distinct from that which he essentially possesses as God over all, blessed for ever The work of reconciliation, and all the blessings of grace and glory, are lodged in his hands *And no man knoweth the Son but the Father, neither knoweth any man the Father save the Son, and he to whomsoever the Son will reveal him* It is not the effort of man's skill and labour, but a divine revelation which alone can make known to us the true character of God, his triune existence and perfections, together with the designs of his grace according to the tenor of the everlasting covenant And as there is a mutual consciousness between the divine Persons in the undivided Godhead, He, who from eternity lay in the bosom of the Father, is alone able to make him known, and to communicate his eternal counsels to us, being invested with his mediatorial character for this very purpose *Note*, (1.) There is no true knowledge of God, or intercourse to be maintained with him, but in and by Jesus Christ (2.) To those, whom Christ takes for his disciples, he *manifests himself as he doth not unto the world*, John xiv 22.

[2.] He declares his readiness to receive every poor sinner who comes to him weary and heavy laden, and invites them to lay down their burdens of sin and sorrow at his feet, that they may find rest unto their souls (1.) The persons invited are *all that labour and are heavy laden*, those who are convinced of their guilt and danger, feel the insupportable burden of sin, and are weary, not merely of the burdensome rites of the ceremonial law, but of the bondage of corruption And *all*, without distinction of nation, or difference in the measure of their guilt and sinfulness, are invited Jesus rejects none because of the depth of their miseries, who do not themselves reject his mercies (2.) The invitation is, *Come to me*, willing to receive, and able to relieve, all the wants of the miserable and the desperate, who by faith cast their care upon me, renouncing every other hope and dependance, placing their trust on me alone as their Saviour to the uttermost, and taking me henceforward for their Lord and Master (3.) The promise made to such is, *I will give you rest*, pardon and peace of conscience to silence the accusations of guilt, power against sin to deliver you from the wearisome bondage of corruption, setting the soul at liberty from all terrifying fears, and enabling you on sure foundations to expect a part in the eternal rest which remaineth for the people of God (4.) The dutiful returns for such mercies are here prescribed *Take my yoke upon you* We must receive Christ in all his offices, as the King to rule in and over us, as well as the Prophet to teach, and the Priest to atone for us Obedience to his gospel must follow faith in his promises, and he asks nothing from us but that we should copy his example and be like him, that we may be meet for the enjoyment of him *Learn of me, for I am meek and lowly in heart*, tempers which must ever characterise the disciples of Jesus, in opposition to that pride, perverseness, passion, and self-will, which are natural to the fallen mind He was *meek* under every provocation, patient towards the dulness of his scholars, *lowly in heart*, condescending to the meanest, and submitting for our sakes to every abasement, and when we learn to be like him we *shall find rest to our souls*, such divine dispositions will bring a present heaven to the soul, and enable us to enter into rest here below, happy in communion with Jesus, and stamped with his image Nor may we think his *yoke* implies any thing grievous No *His yoke is easy, and his burden light* his service is perfect freedom Even the afflictions, temptations, and difficulties we may meet, are to be counted all joy, since so sure will be the assistance of his grace, so abundant his consolations, and so blessed the issue, that we have reason continually to go on our way rejoicing, and to own to his eternal praise, and for the encouragement of others, *that his ways are ways of pleasantness, and all his paths are peace*

CHAP XII

In this chapter we have, 1 Christ's clearing of the law of the fourth commandment concerning the sabbath-day, and vindicating it from some superstitious notions advanced by the Jewish teachers, shewing that works of necessity and mercy are to be done on that day, ver 1—13 2 *The prudence, humility, and self denial of our Lord Jesus in working his miracles*, ver 14—22 3 *Christ's answer to the blasphemous cavils and calumnies of the Scribes and Pharisees, who imputed his casting out devils to a compact with the devil*, ver 22—38 4 *Christ's reply to a tempting demand of the Scribes and Pharisees, challenging him to shew them a sign from heaven*, ver 38—45 5 *Christ's judgment about his kindred and relations*, ver 46 ad finem

1 [a] AT that time Jesus went on the sabbath-day a Mark ii
through the corn, and his disciples were an 23 Luke vi 1
hungred, and [b] began to pluck the ears of corn, and to b Deut
eat. 2 But when the Pharisees saw *it*, they said unto xxiii 25
him, Behold, thy disciples do that which is not lawful
to do upon the sabbath-day 3 But he said unto them,
Have ye not read what David did when he was an hun-
gred, and they that were with him, 4 [c] How he en- c 1 Sam
tred into the house of God, and did eat the shew-bread, xxi 6
which was not lawful for him to eat, neither for them
which were with him, [d] but only for the priests? 5 Or d Ex xxix
have ye not read [e] in the law, how that on the sabbath- 33 Lev
days the priests in the temple profane the sabbath, and xxiv 9 e Numb
are blameless? 6 But I say unto you, that in this place xxviii 9
[f] is *one* greater than the temple 7 But if ye had known f Mal iii 1
what this meaneth, [g] I will have mercy, and not sacri- g Hos vi 6
fice, ye would not have condemned the guiltless 8 Chap ix 13
For the Son of man is Lord even of the sabbath-day.
9 [h] And when he was departed thence, he went into h Mark iii
their synagogue 10, ¶ And behold, there was a man 1 Luke vi
which had *his* hand withered and they asked him, say- 6.
ing, [i] Is it lawful to heal on the sabbath days? that they i Luke xiii
might accuse him 11 And he said unto them, What 14 — xiv
man shall there be among you that shall have one sheep, 3 John ix.
and if it fall into a pit on the sabbath-day, will he not 16
lay hold on it, and lift *it* out? 12 How much then is
a man better than a sheep? wherefore it is lawful to do
well on the sabbath-days 13. Then saith he to the man,
[k] Stretch forth thine hand and he stretched *it* forth, k 1 Kings
and *it* was restored whole, like as the other xiii 6

v 1—13 Those who are most corrupt in their morals, sometimes think to atone for the defect, by their rigid zeal for the rituals of religion; as was the case of the Pharisees, who, whilst they lowered the other commands to the mere letter, stretched the strict observation of the sabbatical rest to an extreme that was never designed Which false explication our Lord confutes, and shews that works of mercy and charity may be practised consistent with the most religious observance of the sabbath-day

1 The occasion given for this discourse arose from the invidious reflections of the Pharisees on the disciples of Jesus for rubbing the ears of corn in their hand on the sabbath-day, as they passed through the fields, and eating them, being hungry This the Pharisees observed, and mentioned to Jesus as a thing unlawful to be done on the sabbath-day The law had allowed the gathering such ears of corn, *Deut* xxiii 25 but they regard the bodily labour of rubbing them in their hands as a transgression of the rest enjoined, according to the traditions of the elders *Note*, (1.) Christ's disciples were inured to want and coarse fare we must not count it hard, if God in his providence at any time brings us into the like straits, and causes us to know what it is to be hungry (2.) The most innocent actions are liable to the most perverse interpretations from those who wait for an opportunity to find fault

2 Christ vindicates the practice of his disciples by allowed precedents or unanswerable arguments.

[1.] By allowed precedents

(1.) In the case of David and his men, who, being pressed with hunger, was, with the high-priest's consent, permitted to eat the shew-bread, which none ordinarily might do but the priests alone And if it was adjudged lawful to dispense with a positive institution of God to satisfy David's hunger, it surely could not be thought sinful, in like circumstances, to dispense merely with the traditions of the elders *Note*, Where life itself is in danger through hunger, necessity, if it does not justify, should at least be admitted as the excuse for deviating from the ordinary rule of justice *See Prov* vi 30

(2.) In

(2.) In the case of the priests, who were obliged to do much servile work on the sabbath-day, such as slaying, flaming, and cutting up the beasts for sacrifice, &c. and yet none could conceive this a transgression of the commandment; and how much less the merely rubbing out a few ears of corn in their hands for necessary food. But it might be objected they were not priests, nor was this the temple-service had a particular dispensation; therefore,

[2.] He adds arguments to the examples he produced.

(1.) *I say unto you, that in this place is one greater than the temple.* And if the priests were blameless in their service, much more were the disciples of Jesus allowed to satisfy their hunger when attending on their master, who was the Lord of the temple, in dignity and holiness infinitely greater, having all the fulness of the Godhead bodily, and from him alone that fabric derived all the sanctity it possessed.

[2.] *If ye had known what this meaneth, I will have mercy, and not sacrifice,* Hos. vi. 6. *ye would not have condemned the guiltless.* They were ignorant of those Scriptures they pretended to urge; for, if they had understood them, they would have observed, that the great commandment of charity was vastly superior to mere ritual observances, and therefore would never have condemned the disciples for thus satisfying the cravings of hunger on the sabbath-day. *Note,* Ignorance of God's word is generally the cause of rash censures on our brethren, and this is especially culpable in those who pretend to teach others.

[3.] *The Son of man is Lord even of the sabbath-day.* He who enjoined the rest, and prescribed the rule on mount Sinai, must needs know what obedience himself required, and best interpret his own mind, and be fully authorised to make any alteration he should think fit. Thus now, though the commandment of observing a seventh day still is in force, he hath transferred it from the last to the first day of the week, called from him *the Lord's day.*

3. By the cure of a paralytic man in the synagogue on a sabbath day some time after, he took occasion further to vindicate works of mercy and charity as most lawful and acceptable to God on that day.

[1.] The person on whom the cure was wrought had *a withered arm,* so that he was disabled from labour; yet, though unable to work, whilst he could walk, he failed not to be at the place of worship. And in the way of duty we may hope for a blessing.

[2.] The Pharisees, ever on the watch, suspecting Jesus would cure him, questioned him concerning his thoughts of the lawfulness of healing on the sabbath day, which their doctors, except in cases of extremity, had forbidden; and their design herein was *to accuse him,* either to the Sanhedrim, if he acted contrary to their determinations, as a sabbath-breaker; or to the people, if he declared it unlawful, and contradicted his own vindication of his disciples.

[3.] Christ answers them by an appeal to their own conduct. If one of their sheep fell into a pit, none scrupled to draw it out on the sabbath day: how much then was a man better than a sheep, and his distresses rather to be relieved. No doubt therefore could be made but that it was lawful to do good on the sabbath day.

[4.] Without delay, and, for ought appears, without waiting for a request from the poor patient, who might, from the temper of these men, be discouraged from making application, *Jesus bids him stretch out his hand,* and power accompanied the command; *He stretched it forth, and,* to the astonishment of the beholders, *it was restored whole as the other.* *Note,* Like this withered arm are our souls, impotent of themselves to every thing that is good; and yet the calls to believe and obey, notwithstanding our inability for both, are neither absurd nor unreasonable, since Christ hath promised to accompany his word with the efficacy of his Spirit, and enable his chosen for that which he commands.

14 ¶ Then the Pharisees went out, and held a coun-
cil against him, how they might destroy him. 15 But
when Jesus knew *it,* he withdrew himself from thence:
and great multitudes followed him, and he healed them
all. 16 And charged them that they should not make
him known: 17 That it might be fulfilled which was
spoken by Esaias the prophet, saying, 18 Behold,
my servant whom I have chosen, my beloved in whom
my soul is well pleased: I will put my spirit upon him,
and he shall shew judgment to the Gentiles. 19 He
shall not strive, nor cry, neither shall any man hear his
voice in the streets. 20 A bruised reed shall he not
break, and smoking flax shall he not quench, till he send
forth judgment unto victory. 21 And in his name shall
the Gentiles trust.

14—21. Exasperated, instead of convinced by his preaching and miracles, we are told here,

1. The malicious designs of the Pharisees. They met in consultation, determined some way or other to put an end to his obnoxious discourses and his life together, for which this last pretended breach of the sabbath might afford them a handle, cloaking with zeal for religion the blackest crimes of hell.

2. Christ hereupon chose to retire, and avoid the danger he foresaw, his hour not being yet come: but still he was attended, even in his retirement, by multitudes, to whom he continued his accustomed mercies, healing all their infirmities; but *charged them that they should not make him known:* not desiring fame from his miracles, and now particularly willing to be concealed from the malice of his persecutors. *Note,* God's approbation, not man's applause, is what we should covet.

3. The fulfilment of the Scripture herein is observed, *Isa.* xlii. 1—4. *Behold,* with wonder and astonishment, *my servant,* so low he humbled himself, who counted it no robbery to be equal with God, *whom I have chosen,* designed for the office of Mediator, and now qualified for the work of redemption, *my beloved, in whom I am well pleased,* from eternity the object of his complacence, and in his person, office, and character as the Messiah, God the Father delighted, and by repeated declarations from heaven expressed his approbation of his Son. *I will put my spirit upon him,* anointing him with the oil of gladness above his fellows, bestowing such a plenitude of gifts and graces upon him as may enable him gloriously to discharge and accomplish his arduous undertaking; *and he shall shew judgment to the Gentiles,* preaching to them that gospel wherein God's righteousness is revealed, and his eternal determinations concerning sinful men is made known. *He shall not strive,* with noise and ostentation setting up his kingdom, *neither shall any man hear his voice in the streets,* contentious or clamorous against his opposers. *A bruised reed shall he not break,* the broken-hearted, weak, and trembling sinner he will bind up and strengthen, *and smoaking flax shall he not quench,* those who have but the beginnings of spiritual life, in whom the graces are feeble, and much darkness and infirmity remains, he will quicken, and blow the smoaking flax into a flame, *till he sends forth judgment unto victory,* by the power of his gospel dispelling the darkness of error, delivering the soul from the bondage of corruption, and causing his grace to reign through righteousness unto eternal life, perfecting in the hearts of his people the salvation he hath begun. *And in his name shall the Gentiles trust,* the heathen nations shall become obedient to the faith, be incorporated with his chosen people, and place all their hopes of salvation on the blood and righteousness alone of this divine Redeemer.

22 ¶ Then was brought unto him one possessed
with a devil, blind and dumb: and he healed him, in-
somuch that the blind and dumb both spake and saw.
23 And all the people were amazed, and said, Is not
this the Son of David? 24 But when the Pharisees
heard *it,* they said, This *fellow* doth not cast out de-
vils, but by Beelzebub the prince of the devils. 25
And Jesus knew their thoughts, and said unto them,
Every kingdom divided against itself, is brought to de-
solation: and every city or house divided against itself,
shall not stand: 26 And if Satan cast out Satan, he
is divided against himself; how shall then his kingdom
stand? 27 And if I by Beelzebub cast out devils, by
whom do your children cast *them* out? therefore they
shall be your judges. 28 But if I cast out devils by
the Spirit of God, then the kingdom of God is come
unto you. 29 Or else how can one enter into a strong
man's house, and spoil his goods, except he first bind
the strong man? and then he will spoil his house. 30
He that is not with me, is against me: and he that ga-
thereth not with me, scattereth abroad. 31 ¶ Where-
fore I say unto you, All manner of sin and blasphemy
shall be forgiven unto men: but the blasphemy *against*
the *holy* Ghost shall not be forgiven unto men. 32 And
whosoever speaketh a word against the Son of man, it
shall be forgiven him: but whosoever speaketh against
the holy Ghost, it shall not be forgiven him, neither in
this world, neither in the *world* to come. 33 Either
make the tree good, and his fruit good; or else make
the tree corrupt, and his fruit corrupt: for the tree is
known by *his* fruit. 34 O generation of vipers, how
can ye, being evil, speak good things? for out of the
abundance of the heart the mouth speaketh. 35 A good
man out of the good treasure of the heart bringeth forth
good things: and an evil man out of the evil treasure
bringeth forth evil things. 36 But I say unto you,
that every idle word that men shall speak, they shall
give account thereof in the day of judgment. 37 For
by thy words thou shalt be justified, and by thy words
thou shalt be condemned.

22—37 Christ had before shewn his power over Satan's kingdom, dispossessing him from the bodies as well as souls of many We have here,

1 Another instance of his curing one possessed by a devil, a man *blind and dumb* through the power of this wicked spirit, The emblem of the sinner, whose eyes the god of this world hath blinded, and whose lips are sealed up from prayer and praise, and all conversation to the use of edifying One word of Jesus restored his lost senses, his sight and speech were perfectly recovered

2 The people admired the astonishing efficacy of the word of Jesus, and reasonably concluded, *Is not this the son of David?* the promised Messiah? but the Pharisees, when they heard it, stung with envy, and obstinately hardened against conviction, with blasphemous cavil and abusive insult replied, *This fellow doth not cast out devils but by Beelzebub the prince of the devils* The fact they could not deny, but imputed the miracle to a compact with the devil To such miserable shifts are they driven, who, determined in infidelity, refuse to submit to the evidence of truth

3 Christ refutes so base an accusation He knew their malicious designs, and heard their words of blasphemy, and therefore he at large vindicates himself Their assertion was absurd, and self-contradictory It is an allowed maxim, that every kingdom, city, or family, divided against itself, must hasten its own dissolution impossible therefore would it be for Satan to think of supporting his dominion by those means which naturally must subvert it, the miracles of Christ being wrought in confirmation of those doctrines of truth and holiness which directly tend to destroy the works of the devil, *v* 25, 26 Add to this, that among themselves they admitted some exorcists did cast out devils by the power of God, *Acts* xix 9 *Mark* ix 38 Why then should they not by parity of reason admit that his miracles evidenced a divine power? therefore these men should rise up in judgment and condemn them for this partiality and blasphemy It being then incontestibly apparent that Christ's miracles were effected by the Spirit of God, he urges this as a proof that *the kingdom of God*, of the Messiah promised to bruise the serpent's head, was actually now *come unto* them for, if this had not been the case, how could it be possible that he should thus dispossess the devil from the bodies and souls of men? This wicked spirit, as a strong man armed, will keep fast hold of his prey and guard his house Nothing but a superior power can bind his arms, and rescue his prisoners from him, which Jesus had done, and therefore proved that he received no assistance from him, but was his superior and conqueror Besides, the very nature of their kingdoms being directly opposite, there can be no fellowship, yea there is implacable enmity, between them, and all who league with the one are regarded as rebels against the other so that they who gather not to Christ as their shepherd, and list under his banners as their king, are *scattered*, exposed to his wrath, and devoted to destruction So far therefore from a confederacy between Christ and Satan, there is open war between them, and not even a neutrality permitted *Note*, (1) Divisions are the surest way to destruction in church and state (2) The devil hath a potent kingdom erected in the world, and he will do his utmost to support it but Christ is come to destroy his dominion, and will finally prevail (3) They who are under the influence of prejudice will blame that very conduct in those they dislike, which they approve in those they love (4) The destruction of Satan's power in the soul is the work of the Spirit of God, and whenever that is evidently seen, there the kingdom of God is assuredly come (5) Coldness and indifference in the cause of Christ will be regarded as enmity against him we must be hearty in his service, or we shall be dealt with as traitors

4 From what hath been observed he takes occasion to caution his hearers against that unpardonable crime, *blasphemy against the Holy Ghost* All other sins, however deep, multiplied, or aggravated, may be forgiven, Christ's blood being a sufficient atonement for them, and whosoever pleads it in faith will find pardon, even those who reviled or crucified him, *but whosoever speaketh against the Holy Ghost it shall not be forgiven, neither in this world, nor in the world to come* And this *blasphemy* is not any denial of his divine Person, or opposition to his work through ignorance, nor any resistance against the ministry of his word, nor wilful sin committed against his light and warnings, but "a wilful and despiteful rejection of the Spirit of grace, the "imputing his miraculous operations and illuminations to diabolical agency, the contradicting and denying the doctrines "he reveals, and this through obstinate malice, in opposition "to a man's own light and conscience" This is a direct sin against our remedy, and must needs be attended with inevitable perdition

5 Christ addresses the Pharisees, convicting them of the wickedness of their hearts by the malice which appeared in their lips It was as absurd for them, who committed such blasphemies, to pretend to sanctity, as to expect good fruit from an evil tree For, as a man's heart is to be discerned by his words and actions, it plainly appeared, by what they spoke out of the *abundance of their hearts*, that they were *a generation of vipers*, thrusting out their invenomed tongues against Christ and blaspheming him, the natural effect of the *evil* which dwelt within them *A good man out of the good treasure of his heart*, replenished with divine grace, *bringeth forth good things*, such as are for the use of edifying, and for the glory of God *But an evil man*, whose spirit is unrenewed, *out of the evil treasure* of corruption which is natural to him, *bringeth forth evil*, in the corrupt communication which proceeds out of his mouth, and the polluted streams in his life and conversation, which break forth from the inexhausted source within And if not an idle word passes without the divine notice, but we must answer for it in a judgment day, how much more terrible must be the blasphemer's guilt? With what circumspection then should we keep the door of our lips, when our eternal state is to be determined thereby, and our words must all be produced at the bar of God as evidences of our justification or condemnation, and sentence proceed accordingly? We may learn hence, (1) That, unless the heart be renewed by the power of God's Spirit, nothing but evil, and that continually, can proceed out of it (2) Our words are the index of our minds, and by our general course of communication our state Godward may be easily discovered (3) The solemn account that we must one day make for every word that is in our tongue should be ever on our mind, to restrain all idle, vain, impertinent discourse, as well as what is more immediately noxious How much hath every man to lament on this behalf!

38 ¶ [h] Then certain of the scribes and of the Pharisees
answered, saying, Master, we would see a sign from thee
39 But he answered and said to them, An evil and [i] adulterous generation seeketh after a sign, and there shall no
sign be given to it but the sign of the prophet Jonas
40 For as [k] Jonas was three days and three nights in the
whale's belly so shall the Son of man be three days and
three nights in the heart of the earth 41 The men of
Nineveh [l] shall rise in judgment with this generation,
and shall condemn it [m] because they repented at the
preaching of Jonas, and behold a greater than Jonas *is*
here 42 The queen of the south shall rise up in the
judgment with this generation, and shall condemn it
for [n] she came from the uttermost parts of the earth to
hear the wisdom of Solomon, and behold a greater than
Solomon *is* here 43 [o] When the unclean spirit is gone
out of a man, [p] he walketh through dry places, seeking
rest, and findeth none 44 Then he saith, I will return
into my house, from whence I came out and when he
is come, he findeth *it* empty, swept, and garnished
45 Then goeth he, and taketh with himself seven other
spirits more wicked than himself, and they enter in and
dwell there and [q] the last state of that man is worse
than the first Even so shall it be also unto this wicked
generation

[h] Chap xvi 1 Mark viii 11 Luke xi 16, 29 1 Cor i 22
[i] Isa lvii 3
[k] Jonah i 17
[l] Jer iii 11 Ezek xvi 51 Rom ii 27
[m] Jonah iii 5
[n] 1 Kings x 1 2 Chron ix 1
[o] Luke xi 24
[p] Job i 7 1 Pet v 8
[q] Heb vi 4 & x 26 2 Pet ii 20

v 38—45 Though what our Lord had said was sufficient to convince every impartial hearer, certain scribes and Pharisees pretended they were not yet satisfied of his divine mission, and though they address him with respect, calling him *Master*, it seems to be done hypocritically, for they demand *a sign from heaven*, perhaps such as of old appeared on mount Sinai, intimating that, notwithstanding his other miracles, without this they should not acknowledge him as the Messiah a demand unreasonable and insolent, and which our Lord justly denies They who are dissatisfied with the evidence of truth he hath been pleased to give, notwithstanding what they may pretend, would never be convinced by any other

1 He brands them as *an evil and adulterous generation*, degenerate from the piety of their forefathers, and chargeable with the most criminal apostacy from God, literally and spiritually committing adultery against him

2 He rejects their demand No sign shall be given them, such as they required, *from heaven*, but one should be given them *from the earth* in his resurrection, which had been prefigured by Jonas the prophet, who, after being *three days and three nights in the whale's belly*, was cast alive on dry land *so shall the Son of man be three days and three nights in the heart of the earth*, that is, part of three natural days, as the Jews computed their times for so long he lay in the grave, reckoning Friday, before sun-setting, as one, Saturday two, and Sunday, after sun-set, when the third day commenced, as three, our Lord then rising from the dead and if this did not convince them, nothing would *Note*, The resurrection of Jesus is the great hinge on which our everlasting salvation turns, and the grand sign confirming all the rest, and they who refuse the evidence with which this is attended, and ask for more, we may be fully sure desire no sign to confirm their faith, but a plea for their infidelity

3 He warns them of the consequences which would attend the wilfulness and wickedness of the men of that generation

The men of Nineveh shall rise up as witnesses to condemn them, for they, though heathens, repented at the preaching of Jonas for one day only but Christ had wrought manifold miracles, had long and earnestly preached the gospel of the kingdom, and shortly was to rise from the dead, in all which he was far superior to Jonas If therefore they rejected him, far greater would be their condemnation than that which was threatned against the men of Nineveh, and their speedy repentance shall rise up to condemn the unbelief and impenitence of the men of that generation

In like manner shall *the queen of the south*, who came from far on the report of Solomon's wisdom, condemn these despisers of Christ and his gospel She, though a Gentile, no sooner heard the wise king than she owned the truth of the report concerning him but, when *a greater than Solomon was there*, even Jesus, in whom dwelt all the treasures of wisdom and knowledge, the men of that generation refused to receive his word, or believe in him, and therefore how aggravated will be their condemnation! They who have enjoyed and abused the greatest means and mercies shall sink under heavier guilt, and receive greater damnation

4 He describes their character, as willing slaves of Satan They were like one possessed of the devil, who goeth for a while out, to return with double violence He is called an *unclean spirit* having lost all purity himself, he ceases not to tempt men to all manner of uncleanness *He walketh in dry places*, like a melancholy person, *seeking rest, and findeth none*, being miserable when he is no longer in mischief, and therefore, taking seven other spirits worse than himself, he returns to his former abode, and finds the sinner's heart ready to entertain them, as a house swept and garnished to receive its guests, and there they fix their stay, so that *the last state of that man is worse than the first*, more wicked than before *even so shall it be also unto this wicked generation* The Devil, who by Christ's preaching and miracles for a while retired from Judea into the Gentile world, afterwards, when the gospel spread among the heathen, returned with sevenfold power to the Jews, who readily received him, and with all malice and wickedness persecuted the ministers of Christ, which brought upon that devoted people final destruction

q Mark iii 31 Luke viii 20. 46 ¶ While he yet talked to the people, [q] behold,
r Chap xiii 55 his mother and [r] his brethren stood without, desiring to
speak with him 47 Then one said unto him, Behold,
thy mother and thy brethren stand without, desiring to
speak with thee 48 But he answered and said unto
s Deut xxxiii 9 him that told him, [s] Who is my mother? And who are
my brethren? 49 And he stretched forth his hand towards his disciples, and said, Behold my mother, and
t John xv 14 my brethren 50 For [t] whosoever shall do the will of
my Father which is in heaven, the same is my brother,
and sister, and mother.

v 46—50 Whilst Christ continued his discourses, which bore so hard upon the Pharisees, we are told,

1 That his mother and brethren stood without apprehensive perhaps of his danger to which he would be exposed thereby, they desired to speak to him, and warn him against giving such offensive and plain rebukes. Whether these were his brethren by the same mother Mary, or by a former wife of Joseph's, or his cousin-germans as many suppose, is not a matter at all material Hereupon one of his auditors immediately informed him of their request *Note*, (1) Near relations, by their fears for us, often lay hindrances in our way (2) Danger must not deter us from fidelity in the way of our duty

2 Christ replies, in answer to the message, *Who is my mother, and who are my brethren?* not as contemning parental authority, or disregarding the ties of blood, but intimating that the address was unseasonable, and, when God's glory was concerned, no natural or civil respects were to be attended We are bound to love them much, but to love God more yea, and the union which divine grace makes betwixt kindred souls is in many respects stronger than the bonds of blood *He stretched forth his hand to his disciples, and said, Behold my mother and my brethren*, so affectionately did he regard them *for whosoever shall do the will of my Father which is in heaven*, attentive to the gospel, and obedient to the faith, *the same is my brother, and sister, and mother*, so near and dear to him *Note*, (1) The mark of discipleship to Jesus is obedience to the revealed word and will of God (2) However despised we may be, or rejected of men, it is sufficient honour to be esteemed the brethren of Jesus (3) They who resemble Christ in spirit, temper, and disposition, and have the blessed image of that one Father, even God, stamped upon them, will be acknowledged by the Lord of life and glory in the day of his appearing, and admitted, as heirs of God and joint heirs with Christ, to share with him the eternal inheritance

CHAP XIII

In this chapter we have, 1 The parable of the sower, with its explication, and the reason why Christ chose this method of teaching, ver 1—23 2 Of the tares, ver 24—30 3 Of the grain of mustard-seed, ver 31, 32 4 Of the leaven, ver 33 5 The parable of the tares explained, with a further reason for Christ's using parables, ver 34—43 6 The parable of the hid treasure, the pearl of great price, and of the net, ver 44—50 7 The application to his disciples, under the parable of the good householder, ver 51, 52 8 The contempt put upon Christ by his countrymen, ver 53—58

1 THE same day went Jesus out of the house, and
sat by the sea-side 2 And [a] great multitudes a Mark iv 1. Luke viii 4
were gathered together unto him, so that he went into a
ship, and sat, and the whole multitude stood on the shore
3 And he spake many things unto them in parables,
saying, Behold a sower went forth to sow 4 And when
he sowed, some *seeds* fell by the way-side, and the fowls
came and devoured them up 5 Some fell upon stony
places, where they had not much earth and forthwith
they sprung up, because they had no deepness of earth
6 And when the sun was up, they were scorched, and,
because they had not root, they withered away 7 And
some fell among thorns. and the thorns sprung up and
choked them 8 But other fell into good ground, and
brought forth fruit, some an hundred-fold, some sixty-
fold, some thirty-fold 9 [b] Who hath ears to hear, let b Chap xi 15
him hear 10 And the disciples came, and said unto
him, Why speakest thou unto them in parables? 11.
He answered and said unto them, Because [c] it is given c Chap xi 25 & xvi 17 1 Cor ii 10
unto you to know the mysteries of the kingdom of hea-
ven, but to them it is not given. 12 For [d] whosoever
hath, to him shall be given, and he shall have more d Chap xxv 29
abundance. but whosoever hath not, from him shall be
taken away even that he hath 13 Therefore speak I
to them in parables because they, seeing, see not and
hearing, they hear not, neither do they understand 14
And in them is fulfilled the prophecy of Esaias, which
saith, [e] By hearing ye shall hear, and shall not under- e Isa vi 9
stand. and seeing ye shall see, and shall not perceive
15 For this people's heart is waxed gross, and [f] their f Heb v 11
ears are dull of hearing, and their eyes they have closed,
lest at any time they should see with *their* eyes, and hear
with *their* ears, and should understand with *their* heart,
and should be converted, and I should heal them 16
But [g] blessed *are* your eyes, for they see, and your ears, g Chap xvi 17 Luke x 23
for they hear 17 For verily I say unto you, that [h] many
prophets and righteous men have desired to see those h Heb xi 13 1 Pet i 10
things which ye see, and have not seen *them* and to
hear those things which ye hear, and have not heard
them 18 [i] Hear ye therefore the parable of the sower i Mark iv 13 Luke viii 11
19 When any one heareth the word of the kingdom,
and understandeth *it* not, then cometh the wicked one,
and catcheth away that which was sown in his heart
this is he which received seed by the way-side 20 But
he that received the seed into stony places, the same is
he that heareth the word, and [k] anon with joy receiveth k Isa lviii 2 Ezek xxxiii 31 32
it 21 Yet hath he not root in himself, but [l] dureth l Mark iv 20 John v 35 Heb vi 4 Gal v 7
for a while for when tribulation or persecution ariseth
because of the word, [m] by and by he is offended 22 m Chap xi 6
He also that received seed [n] among the thorns, is he that n Jer iv 3
heareth the word and the care of this world, and [o] the o Chap xix 23 1 Tim vi 9
deceitfulness of riches choke the word, and he becometh
unfruitful. 23 But he that received seed into the good
ground, is he that heareth the word, and understandeth
it, [p] which also beareth fruit, and bringeth forth [q] some p John xv 5 q 1 Cor xii 11
an hundred fold, some sixty, some thirty

v 1—23 With indefatigable diligence did the great prophet of his people labour to inculcate the doctrine of his gospel *The same day went Jesus out of the house, and sat by the sea-side*, his auditory being too great for a house to contain them, and there, ascending a ship for his pulpit, whilst the attentive multitude crouded the shore, he spake *many things unto them in parables*, more, probably, than are here recorded, and he chose this method for reasons given, *v* 13, 35 *Note*, (1) In preaching the gospel we are called to be instant in season and out of season no time nor place is unsuitable to speak a word for Christ and

for

for immortal ſouls (2.) Where Chriſt is preached there ſhould we with delight attend: his preſence and bleſſing on the ſea-ſhore are better than all the magnificence of Solomon's temple without him.

1. The parable with which Chriſt opens his diſcourſe is that of a ſower, ſowing his ſeed, with the various ſoils on which it fell, and the conſequences thereof. By familiar and well-known objects Chriſt would thus convey more pleaſingly his divine inſtructions, and teach them to ſpiritualize their daily labours, and to draw from them profitable meditation. The explication of the parable Chriſt is pleaſed himſelf to give, and we cannot err when following an infallible interpreter. The *ſeed* is *the word of the kingdom*, the goſpel; *the ſower* is the Lord Jeſus, with all his divinely appointed miniſters; and he alſo by his Spirit quickens the ſeed ſown, that it may bring forth fruit in the hearts of his people. *The field is the world* in general; and the ſeveral ſorts of ground here mentioned, on which the ſeed falls, repreſent the different tempers of thoſe to whom the goſpel is preached, and the effects thereby produced upon them; and we may obſerve but one ſort in four brought forth any laſting fruit: for, though the ſame word of truth is preached to multitudes, it becomes an incorruptible ſeed but to a few. An awful warning to all to take heed how they hear: for many are called, but few choſen.

[1.] Some are like the way-ſide, where the ſeed, falling on the hard ground, not broken up, is expoſed to the birds and devoured. This repreſents the caſe of thoſe who are careleſs, negligent, and inattentive hearers, on whom the word of God makes no impreſſion: they *underſtand it not*, being under the darkneſs of their fallen mind, and their hearts hardened. *The wicked one*, the devil, ever watchful to prevent all good from entering, no ſooner obſerves ſuch a one in the way of the goſpel than he ſeeks to divert him from it, and catches away the word from his heart as it falls, diſtracting his attention by ſome objects around him, or ſuggeſting ſome idle, vain, worldly, or trifling thoughts, ſo that the word of God is immediately effaced from the memory, and becomes utterly unprofitable.

[2.] Others are like the ſtony ground, on which whatever is ſown ſprings up quickly, the earth being ſhallow; but, unable to bear the ſcorching ſun, for want of root, it withers away. Such are they who attend the miniſtry of the word, and, ſtruck at firſt greatly with what they hear, give an immediate aſſent to its truth, and inſtantly commence profeſſors; but the root of the matter is not in them, they are not brought to a deep and humbling ſenſe of the ſinfulneſs of their nature, they do not ſee the utter impotence of their hearts to all good, they are not humbled to an univerſal renunciation of themſelves, nor led to Chriſt alone for pardon, righteouſneſs, grace, and glory: but, whilſt ſome lively impreſſion or ſudden flaſh of joy ſucceeds their hearing, they are ready to conclude the work is done, when it is not even yet begun; their hearts continue unhumbled and unholy, they are not partakers of the grace of God in truth, nor influenced by the divine principle of faith which worketh by love; they have never truly counted the coſt, and therefore, when they are called to painful ſelf-denial for Chriſt's ſake, to endure reproach, the loſs of friends or fortune, or the ſevereſt ſufferings which invenomed perſecutors may inflict, then they ſhrink from the croſs, diſhonour their profeſſion, comply with the world, are offended, and walk no more with Jeſus. May we never be numbered among ſuch apoſtates from the truth!

[3.] Another ſort of hearers are compared to the ſeed ſown among thorns. These go farther than the former: they take up and continue a fair profeſſion, are attendants on the word and ordinances, and in appearance Chriſtians altogether; but inſenſibly the cares of the world, a too great anxiety about a proviſion for themſelves or families, an inordinate love of money, and too eager a purſuit after it, theſe, under many a ſpecious cloak of prudent care and becoming induſtry, ſeduce the affections to gold from God, and inſenſibly, like the thorns, eat out the life and ſpirit of that godlineſs they once ſeemed poſſeſſed of; the heart grows cold, eternal things loſe their importance, the vanities of time appear more ſignificant; and though the profeſſion of religion and the form of duties may ſtill be carried on, it is mere huſk, no ſubſtantial fruit of grace is produced: the word is choked, and the ſoul drowned in perdition and deſtruction. How many thus have fallen! May we be warned of the imminent danger, and fear for ourſelves, leſt this evil world ſteal away our hearts from God.

[4.] Though others were unfruitful, one ſort of hearers are mentioned, who, like the good ground, repaid the huſbandman's toils. Their hearts by divine grace were opened to receive the ſeed of the goſpel, and, watered by the dews of heavenly influence, it grew, and brought forth fruit abundantly. They are deſcribed not merely as hearing the word, but *underſtanding* it, the eyes of their mind being enlightened, and they receive the truth not only in the light but in the love of it. In their heart the ſeed takes root, and brings forth the genuine fruits of righteouſneſs and true holineſs; and this variouſly, according to the meaſure of the gift of Chriſt: for though the quality of the fruit be the ſame in all, wrought by that one and the ſelf-ſame Spirit, yet in ſome theſe fruits are more eminent and abundant than in others. May Jeſus give us then the hearing ear and underſtanding heart, that our profiting may appear; and may we ſeek to abide and abound in every fruit of grace, which by Jeſus Chriſt are to the praiſe and glory of God!

2. Chriſt reſolves the queſtion addreſſed to him by his diſciples, *v.* 10. why he ſpoke to the people by parables. In general ſuch was the good pleaſure of his will. With regard to thoſe who were his diſciples, he intended to ſtir up their enquiries after the explication of what they heard; and it was their peculiar mercy that to them *it was given to know the myſteries of the kingdom*, he being ready to lead them into the knowledge of all truth; but to others it was *not given*. God is ſovereign in the diſpenſations of his grace, and is pleaſed to withhold from ſome what he beſtows on others; and where none have any claim upon him, he may, no doubt, do what he will with his own, *v.* 11. Where he hath been pleaſed to give a ſpiritual underſtanding, and the influences of his Spirit, there he will continue to work, and perfect that which he begins, increaſing his gifts of wiſdom and grace: but where there is no ſpiritual knowledge of Chriſt, no experience of his grace, no deſire to profit by his word, there he will take away the external gifts, the means of grace, or miniſtry of the goſpel, which ſuch perſons before enjoyed, and leave them to the blindneſs they have choſen, *v.* 12. And this he aſſigns as the reaſon why he ſpake to them in parables, without expounding them to the multitude as he did to his own diſciples. He deſigned to leave thoſe who wilfully had rejected the light of his miracles and doctrines to the blindneſs and impenitence of their own hearts. *They* did not chuſe to ſee or underſtand, and therefore he decrees in juſt judgment that they ſhall not, *v.* 13. And herein the prophecy of Iſaiah, *ch.* vi. *v.* 9, 10. was fulfilled. The Jews were now given up to that judicial blindneſs he had foretold. In the midſt of the glorious light of the goſpel, and in the face of the aſtoniſhing miracles wherewith Jeſus as the Meſſiah had confirmed his miſſion, they obſtinately ſtopped their ears, and cloſed their eyes, as if they were afraid the force of conviction and the ſtrong evidence of truth ſhould overpower them, and neceſſitate them to ſubmit to the Saviour's doctrine, and yield up their hearts and ways to his government; which they being reſolved not to do, his Spirit will no longer ſtrive with them, and they are left to the ignorance and impenitence of their hearts, *v.* 14, 15. But towards thoſe whom he had choſen for diſciples, God had the moſt gracious deſigns: he had given them the ſeeing eye and the hearing ear, and bleſſed them with the underſtanding thoſe myſteries of his grace which were hid from other's eyes, *v.* 16. yea, they enjoyed transcendent favours beyond all the prophets and righteous men which had gone before them; for, earneſtly as they longed for the appearing of the Meſſiah, and to behold him incarnate, they ſaw his day but at a diſtance, and chiefly beheld the great things of his kingdom wrapped up in types and figures, whilſt his preſent diſciples beheld him face to face, ſaw his miracles, and from his own mouth more diſtinctly were informed of thoſe truths which the others ſaw only through a glaſs darkly, *v.* 16. *Note*, (1.) Why God is pleaſed to give the knowledge of his truth to one, and withhold it from another, can only be reſolved into the good pleaſure of his own will. (2.) All our wiſdom in divine things is the gift of God: till he opens the eyes of our minds, the wiſeſt of men are in groſs darkneſs. (3.) Many enjoy the means of grace whoſe hearts only grow more hard and inſenſible under them. They hate the light, and therefore are juſtly abandoned to the darkneſs they have choſen. (4.) The greateſt of all bleſſings is the knowledge of Jeſus, for him to know is everlaſting life. (5.) If we are diſtinguiſhed by peculiar circumſtances of the divine regard, the ſtronger obligation is laid upon us to be thankful, and to walk in the light as children of the light.

24 ¶ Another parable put he forth unto them, ſaying,
The kingdom of heaven is likened unto [a] a man which ver. 37
ſowed good ſeed in his field: 25 But while men ſlept,
his enemy came and ſowed tares among the wheat, and
went his way. 26 But when the blade was ſprung up,
and brought forth fruit, then appeared the tares alſo. 27
So the ſervants of the houſholder came and ſaid unto him,
Sir, Didſt thou not ſow good ſeed in thy field? from
whence then hath it tares? 28 He ſaid unto them, An
enemy hath done this. The ſervants ſaid unto him, Wilt
thou then that we go and gather them up? 29 But he
ſaid, Nay; leſt while ye gather up the tares, ye root up
alſo the wheat with them. 30 Let both grow together
until the harveſt: and in the time of harveſt I will ſay to
the reapers, Gather ye together firſt the tares, and bind
them in bundles to burn them: but [b] gather the wheat into Chap. iii. 12
my barn. 31 ¶ Another parable put he forth unto them,
ſaying, [c] The kingdom of heaven is like to a grain of Mark iv. 31 Luke xiii. 19
muſtard-ſeed, which a man took and ſowed in his field:
32 Which indeed is the leaſt of all ſeeds: but when it
is grown, it is the greateſt among herbs, and [d] becometh a

tree so that the birds of the air come and lodge in the
branches thereof 33 ¶ [x] Another parable spake he unto
them, The kingdom of heaven is like unto leaven, which
a woman took and [y] hid in three † measures of meal, [z] till
the whole was leavened 34 All these things spake Jesus
unto the multitude in parables, and without a parable
spake he not unto them 35 That it might be fulfilled
which was spoken by the prophet, saying, [a] I will open my
mouth in parables, I will utter things [b] which have been
kept secret from the foundation of the world 36 Then
Jesus sent the multitude away, and went into the house
and his disciples came unto him, saying, [c] Declare unto us
the parable of the tares of the field 37 He answered
and said unto them, He that soweth the good seed, is the
Son of man 38 The field is the world the good seed
are the children of the kingdom but the tares are [d] the
children of the wicked one 39 The enemy that sowed
them is the devil [e] the harvest is the end of the world
and the reapers are the angels 40 As therefore the tares
are gathered and burnt in the fire, so shall it be in the end
of this world 41 The Son of man shall send forth his
angels, and they shall gather out of his kingdom all
‡ things that offend, and them which do iniquity, 42
And [f] shall cast them into a furnace of fire [g] there shall
be wailing and gnashing of teeth 43 [h] Then shall the
righteous shine forth as the sun, in the kingdom of their
Father [i] Who hath ears to hear, let him hear

[x] Luke xiii 20
[y] Ps xxix 11
† This measure contained nearly a peck and an half
[z] 1 Cor v 7
[a] Ps lxxviii 2
[b] Rom xvi 25 1 Cor ii 7 Eph iii 9 Col i 26
[c] Ezek xxxvi 37 Jam i 5
[d] John viii 44 Acts xiii 10 1 John iii 8
[e] Joel iii 13 Rev xiv 15
‡ Or Scandals Rom xvi 17 2 Pet ii 1
[f] Chap iii 12 Rev xix 20
[g] Chap viii 12
[h] Dan xii 3 1 Cor xv 42
[i] Chap xi 15

v 24—43 Our Lord further continues his discourse to the people in parables, chusing in this manner to wrap up the doctrines he inculcated, according to the prophecy, (*Ps* lxxviii 2) and whilst he thus opened a door for enquiry to his disciples, to whom he afterwards explained the meaning of the figures he used, and informed them of the secrets of wisdom couched under their parables, he left the multitude, who shewed no sollicitude to be informed of their meaning, to their ignorance, v 34, 35 Three parables are here delivered, one of which is afterwards particularly explained by our Lord in private to his disciples, who desired to be informed of its design, v 36 We have,

1 The parable of the tares, which is the representation of the visible church in particular, as the former related to the world in general

(1) The sower of *the good seed* is *the Son of man*, who by himself, and the ministers he hath appointed, sows the seed of eternal life in the hearts of his people, and causes it to take root, and bring forth fruit all that is good in man entirely proceeds from him

(2) *The field is the world*, through which the gospel is spread, and particularly the visible church, where the word is preached, and Christ's servants, under him the great husbandman, continually labour to break up the fallow ground, and cast in the living seed

(3) *The good seed are the children of the kingdom*, those who by faith embrace the doctrines of the gospel, and in all holy conversation and godliness adorn it

(4) *The tares are the children of the wicked one*, all hypocrites and careless professors, who, though they have a name to live in the visible church, are really dead in trespasses and sins; under the influence of the devil, resembling him in their spirit and tempers, and a trouble and vexation to the children of God among whom they associate

(5) *The enemy that sowed them is the devil*, that spirit of wickedness, whose unwearied labours are employed to corrupt and destroy the souls of men, and who watches day and night to take advantage against the church of Christ and whilst we are off our guard, or lulled by outward prosperity into a state of security, he insinuates his pernicious errors in doctrine and practice, seducing unstable souls and for a while the mischief is not discovered, so artful are his wiles, like the villain who sowed tares, and slipped away unnoticed under the covert of the night But though at first the secret wickedness, which lurked under the cloke of plausible profession, is not perceived, in a little while the difference between the wheat and tares becomes very visible The exercise of grace in the one appears evident in the spirituality of their tempers, the simplicity of their hearts, and the purity of their manners, whilst observation and experience discovers the unfaithfulness of the tares, and a day of trial shews their real character With grief and surprize the faithful ministers and servants of Jesus behold the errors and immoralities among the professors of godliness, and carry their sorrowful enquiries to their Lord, v 27 for they who have a zeal for him, cannot but be affected with every thing in his church which reflects dishonour upon his holy religion, v 27 He informs them whence these tares sprung He marked his enemy in all his ways, but for his own more abundant glory permitted his malicious attempts, v 28 He does not reflect upon his servants, as if negligence were to be charged on them, nor will he grant their request, of immediately eradicating these pernicious inmates There would be danger, if it was left to us, lest our undistinguishing eye might class among the hypocrites some who were sincere, or, too rigid or hasty in our judgments, should count those tares, whom the Lord knew to be the true seed, for his all-seeing eye alone can discern the true characters of men They are therefore permitted to grow together, the day of separation will come, when the distinction between tares and wheat will be evident And from hence we should learn, (1) That as long as Christ has a church, the devil will still be seeking to disturb the peace, or corrupt the purity of the professing members of it, notwithstanding the care of the most vigilant pastors, and the administration of the strictest discipline (2) We should be very cautious of pronouncing rash and hasty censures on the characters of others God only knoweth the heart, and it is better that many criminals should escape, than one righteous person be condemned

(6) *The harvest is the end of the world, the reapers are the angels*, they shall go forth, and make the awful separation *All that offend and do iniquity*, whose pernicious doctrines, or immoral conduct, have been a scandal to the religion they professed, shall be gathered out, and, like tares, bound in bundles for the burning The distinction between the *righteous and* the wicked shall then be too evident to admit of a mistake, and the separation between them shall be perfect and everlasting For,

(7) *They shall cast them*, the tares, *into a furnace of fire*, the fire prepared for the devil and his angels, the place of torment appointed for all the ungodly, where they shall burn, and none shall quench them, their pangs intolerable and eternal, under *the wrath of God, which is for ever wrath to come*, where every expression of acutest anguish and black despair shall prove how fearful a thing it is to fall into the hands of the living God Lord, gather not my soul with these sinners!

(8) *The wheat* shall be gathered into God's *barn* The righteous being proved and found faithful, shall be collected in one glorious company, and *shine forth as the sun*, arrayed in robes of spotless purity, and clothed with honour and immortality; admitted into their Father's kingdom, and sitting down on the throne of their Lord, to reign with him for ever and ever The prospect of such a glorious state before us should deeply engage our attention, *he* therefore *that hath ears to hear, let him hear*

2 The parable *of the grain of mustard-seed*, which from one of the smallest seeds, grows, in the eastern countries, into the greatest of herbs, so that, like a spreading tree, the birds find shelter in its branches And such is,

(1) The work of God in a redeemed soul The beginnings are often small, and scarce perceptible, but, watered with divine influences, the seed of eternal life springs up, and amidst all the *stormy blasts of temptation, corruption, persecution*, affliction, to which it is exposed, increaseth with the increase of God

(2) Such also was the Messiah's kingdom at the first Christ and his disciples seemed little, mean, and despicable, but their word took deep root, abundant converts were made, the gospel spread on every side, and filled the face of the world with fruit and, like the enlarging circle in the water, the church of Christ shall go on increasing, till the kingdoms of the world become the kingdom of the Lord, and all the fowls of the air, both Jews and Gentiles, be converted, and flock together into it Hasten, O Lord, this happy day!

3 The parable of the *leaven* As a little of this diffuses itself gradually through the whole mass of meal with which it is mingled, so doth the gospel word, when quickened by divine grace, powerfully diffuse its *energy through* all *the faculties* of the soul, and over all the members of the body, sanctifying the whole, communicating throughout a sweet savour of Christ, and working a blessed and universal change into his image and likeness, and spreading far and wide among all nations, the word of truth shall continue its mighty operations, till all nations shall be brought to the obedience of the faith *Note*, (1) Divine grace works often imperceptibly, but irresistibly (2) Where the leaven of truth is hid in the heart, there its influence will infallibly appear, there will be a sweet savour of Christ in all we speak or do

44 ¶ Again, the kingdom of heaven is like unto
[k] treasure hid in a field the which when a man hath
found, he hideth, and for joy thereof goeth and [l] selleth
all that he hath, and [m] buyeth that field 45 ¶ Again,
the kingdom of heaven is like unto a merchant-man,
seeking goodly pearls 46 Who when he had found
[n] one pearl of great price, he went and sold all that he
had, and bought it 47 ¶ Again, the kingdom of
heaven is like unto a net that was cast into the sea, and
[o] gathered of every kind 48 Which when it was full,
they drew to shore, and sat down, and gathered the good
into vessels, but cast the bad away 49 So shall it be

[k] Prov ii 4
[l] Phil iii 8
[m] Isa lv 1 Rev iii 18
[n] 1 Cor vi 9 Rev ii 18
[o] Chap xxii 10

at the end of the world the angels shall come forth,
ᵒ Chap xxv and ᵖ sever the wicked from among the just, 50 And
ᵖ Ver 42 ᑫ shall cast them into the furnace of fire, there shall be
wailing and gnashing of teeth 51 Jesus saith unto
them, Have ye understood all these things? They say
unto him, Yea, Lord 52 Then said he unto them,
Therefore every scribe which is instructed unto the kingdom of heaven, is like unto a man that is an housholder,
ʳ Cant vii 13 which bringeth forth out of his treasure ʳ things new
and old

v 44—52 Four other parables conclude our blessed Lord's discourse

1 *The treasure hid in the field*, which is Christ himself, and the great and precious promises that are in him The field is the scripture, wherein *He* is revealed to us, in whom are hid all the treasures of wisdom and knowledge, and from whom the most inestimable riches to a sinner, of pardon, peace, righteousness, and grace, are to be derived These are *hid* from us though we have the scriptures before us, we cannot look farther than the surface of them, till God imparts the spiritual understanding, and enables us to dig deep in the precious mine When we have found the treasure, we must *hide* it in our hearts, and nothing can equal the *joy* with which a poor sinner discovers the riches of the grace revealed in Jesus Christ for the sake of this we shall be ready to part with all besides, and count an interest in his love and favour the most invaluable treasure

2 The parable of the pearl of great price is much of the same import with the foregoing The *merchant* is the convinced sinner, seeking after Christ and his salvation, *the pearl of great price*, an object indeed deserving our most eager pursuit Shall merchants compass sea and land for one poor jewel, and shall we not be more assiduous in securing an interest in Jesus, and the possession of all the jewels of grace and glory? He *finds* it, as all who truly seek the Saviour assuredly will, and then with cheerfulness sells all to become possessor of it, content to quit the world, with all its riches, honours, pleasures, his sins, with all their allurements, yea, and to part with his own righteousness too, that he may be found in Christ, a partaker of his redemption, and that, stript of all beside, Christ may be to him all and in all

3 The parable of *the net cast into the sea*, with the explication annexed The *net* is the gospel preached to every creature, the ministers of Christ are the fishermen, who cast it into the *sea*, the world by it a multitude of souls are inclosed, and brought into the visible church When it is *full*, in the latter days, and all, both Jews and Gentiles, are gathered into it, then cometh the end, when the net shall be drawn to shore, in the great day of final separation, and the contents of it be examined The *good fish*, the *just*, who in Christ Jesus are justified from all things, and found faithful, shall be gathered into the vessels of glory prepared for their reception, whilst the angels, the ministers employed in this service, shall separate the *bad*, *the wicked*, from among them, and cast them away as vile and reprobate into the everlasting burnings *Note*, (1) Many who have had a place in the gospel church, will at the last day be rejected by the great head of the church, as hypocrites and unfaithful (2) They who live in wickedness, have nothing to expect but an eternity of woe (3) The consideration of the dreadful end of those who perish, should awaken our greater sollicitude to make our calling and election sure

4 The parable of the housholder aptly finishes, as the practical improvement of the whole Our Lord, *v* 51 had interrogated them on their proficiency, whether they had understood the meaning of the parables he had uttered, and as they had replied in the affirmative, he directs them to the proper use of the knowledge which they possessed They were to be evangelical *scribes*, to preach the everlasting gospel, as the scribes in their days expounded the law and herein they were to resemble an *housholder*, who having made a liberal provision for the family under his care, brings forth out of his storehouse *things new and old*, as each is best suited to their wants The family under our care is the church of Christ, that particular part of it to which we are ordained to minister Our treasure is the word of truth, and Christ especially therein revealed, with an experimental knowledge of him in all his offices, of the riches of his salvation, and the obligation to love and serve him thence arising These we must set before the people, drawn from the sacred storehouses of the Old and New Testament, inculcating anew ancient truths; adding to old experiences, new observation, and providing thus a supply of spiritual food, suited to every state, condition, and circumstance of the people whom we serve And this wisdom, this ability to minister, no attainments of science, no researches of philosophy, no force of genius can bestow it is the gift of the great Master of the family, the Lord Jesus, and they who would savingly teach others the doctrines of the kingdom, must be themselves first taught of him.

53 ¶ And it came to pass that when Jesus had finished these parables, he departed thence 54 ˢ And when ˢ Mark vi 1 Luke iv. 16
he was come into his own country, he taught them in
their synagogue, insomuch that they were astonished,
and said, Whence hath this man this wisdom, and these
mighty works? 55 ᵗ Is not this ᵘ the carpenter's son? is ᵗ Is xlix 7 ᵘ John vi 42
not his mother called Mary? and his brethren, James,
and Joses, and Simon, and Judas? 56 And his sisters,
are they not all with us? Whence then hath this man all
these things? 57 And ˣ they were offended in him ˣ Is liii 3 Chap xi 6
But Jesus said unto them, A prophet is not without
honour, save in his own country, and in his own house
58 And ʸ he did not many mighty works there, because ʸ Mark vi 5
of their unbelief

v 53—58 When Jesus had finished this discourse, he returned to his own city Nazareth, where he had before been so contumeliously treated, and where he again met the like contempt

1 Though they could not help being astonished at the wisdom and authority with which he spoke in their synagogue, and the mighty works he performed, yet their questions shew the prejudices they entertained against him They knew his parentage and education he had not been brought up under their admired doctors, and his father was of no higher rank than a carpenter his mother Mary, a woman of no account, and his brethren and sisters mean, low, and illiterate people and at this they stumbled, despised his person, and slighted his ministry

2 Christ gently rebukes their unreasonable prejudices, and punishes them for their low thoughts of him They acted according to vulgar prepossessions, which lead us to pay little reverence and respect to those with whom we have been familiar; and if they rise to superior excellence, and above their former station, they are envied Therefore, since they despised and rejected him, refused to believe his doctrine, and submit to the evidence of his miracles, he *did not many mighty works there*, not for want of power, but in just judgment, leaving them to their unbelief and hardness of heart *Note*, (1) Prejudices entertained against ministers is a great obstruction to our profiting by their labours (2) We owe it to our unbelief, that we see and experience no more of the mighty works of Jesus

CHAP XIV.

John Baptist had said concerning Christ, He must increase, but I must decrease, John iii 30 The morning-star is here disappearing, and the sun of righteousness rising to his meridian lustre Here is, 1 The martyrdom of John, his imprisonment for his faithfulness to Herod, ver 1—5 And the beheading of him to please Herodias, ver 6—12 2 The miracles of Christ (1) His feeding five thousand men, that came to him to be taught, with five loaves and two fishes, ver 13—21 (2) Christ's walking on the water to his disciples in a storm, ver 22—33 (3) His healing the sick with the touch of the hem of his garment, ver 34—36

1 AT that time ᵃ Herod the tetrarch heard of the ᵃ Mark vi 14 Luke ix 7
fame of Jesus, 2 And said unto his servants,
This is John the baptist, ᵇ he is risen from the dead, and ᵇ Luke xv 5
therefore mighty works do shew forth themselves in
him 3 ¶ For Herod had laid hold on John, and
bound him, and put *him* in prison for Herodias's sake,
his brother Philip's wife 4 For John said unto him,
ᶜ It is not lawful for thee to have her 5 And when he ᶜ Lev xviii 16 & xx 21
would have put him to death, he feared the multitude,
because ᵈ they counted him as a prophet 6 But when ᵈ Chap xxi. 26 Luke xx 6
Herod's birth-day was kept, the daughter of Herodias
danced before them, and pleased Herod 7 Whereupon ᵉ he promised with an oath to give her whatsoever ᵉ Jer xli 1 Esther v. 6
she would ask 8 And she, being before instructed of
her mother, said, Give me here John baptist's head in a
charger. 9 And the king was sorry: nevertheless for
the oath's sake, and them which sat with him at meat,
he commanded *it* to be given *her* 10 And he sent
and beheaded John in the prison 11 And his head
was brought in a charger, and given to the damsel
and she brought *it* to her mother 12 And his disciples
came, and took up the body and buried it, and went
and told Jesus

v 1—12 John, the harbinger of Jesus, had lately finished his glorious race, and won the crown of martyrdom We have in these verses an account of that bloody scene, and the occasion

occasion of its being here introduced is intimated, v 2 The fame of Jesus and his miracles began to be noised, and no sooner did they reach Herod's ears, than his guilty conscience betrayed his fears, and instantly suggested, that this was John whom he had beheaded, but now raised from the dead, and endued with more extraordinary powers to vindicate his injured character, and perhaps avenge himself on his persecutors *Note*, (1) On this side hell, the greatest torment is a guilty conscience (2) Persecutors will find they in vain seek to be rid of their troublers though one be slain or removed, God will raise up fresh witnesses to the truth (3) Many under the horrors of conscience, like the devils, tremble, yet continue impenitent Convictions are not conversion

In the story of John's sufferings we are told,

1 The occasion of them and this was, his fidelity and zeal in reproving Herod for his flagitious enormities, and especially for his adultery and incest with Herodias, his brother Philip's wife, whom he had inveigled away from her own husband, and though he was alive, and had children by her, yet had Herod publicly married her, and continued to cohabit with her This atrocious crime John plainly and faithfully charged upon his conscience, as utterly unlawful, and sure to bring down the wrath of God upon him Though a king, John feared not to discharge his commission As the greatest monarchs have no prerogative to break God's laws, his ministers must boldly vindicate his honour, and, without respect of persons, declare his wrath against the mightiest transgressors

2 For this John was imprisoned Instigated by Herodias, who meditated revenge, as well as to gratify his own resentments, Herod had seized, bound, and cast him into prison They who will be zealous against sin, must prepare to suffer Faithful rebukes, however kindly meant, will be often resented as affronts, and expose us to the vengeance of an enraged persecutor, but when we have a good cause, and a good conscience, we need not fear bonds or imprisonment

3 Herod would have dispatched him out of hand, and rid himself of this troubler, but his fears prevailed over his resentment, and for a while restrained him from the bloody deed John's character as a prophet had procured him such general veneration, that to murder him outright might provoke some popular insurrection, and endanger his own person and government *Note*, (1) None are greater slaves to fear, than they who affect to tyrannize with despotic sway (2) The fear of man often restrains those who have cast off all fear of God

4 At last the barbarous deed is contrived and executed, and, after a tedious confinement, the faithful martyr is by death released, and goes where the wicked cease from troubling It appears probable, that the whole plot was concerted by Herodias, whose unrelenting malice could not rest whilst John was yet alive, and that Herod was privy to the design; the circumstances being contrived merely to blind the populace However, whether he knew it, or rashly involved himself by his oath, Herod is without excuse The time chosen for the execution of the design was Herod's birth-day, and the instrument was Salome, the daughter of Herodias To grace the festival, she condescended to appear before the august assembly, and danced so exquisitely, that Herod in a transport of delight swore to gratify her in whatever request she should make At her mother's instigation she demands the head of John the Baptist, who thought hereby at once to get rid of his reproofs, and glut her revenge Struck with this bloody request, at least appearing to be so, Herod expressed great sorrow and reluctance to comply with it The injustice, cruelty, and infamy of such an action cried aloud Nevertheless, pretending conscience, as if a rash oath could oblige him to commit so wicked a deed, and out of respect to those around him, who being witnesses to the oath approved the performance of it, and probably were glad to get rid of so troublesome a reprover, he gives orders for John's execution in the prison, and instantly, without form or process, sends one of his savage instruments to bring the head of the holy Baptist in a charger The bloody dish is delivered to Salome, and she presents it to her mother, a feast for her cruel revenge, whilst with malicious delight she beholds that tongue for ever silent, that had so deeply wounded her repose *Note*, (1) Seasons of carnal mirth and jollity are usually attended with much mischief, Feasting and dancing are pleasing to the flesh; but they are pernicious to the spirit, and often productive of fatal consequences (2) Rash oaths involve the conscience in dreadful dilemmas, where guilt is sure to fasten on either side yet, when we have sworn to do evil, that oath is more safely broken than kept Our obligation to keep God's laws cannot be superseded by any other we chuse to lay ourselves under (3) The bosom, that should be the seat of tenderness, when fired with lust and revenge, becomes the most barbarous and savage (4) The bad example of parents are fatally pernicious We quickly learn the evil to which the bias of corrupt nature leans so strongly (5) Many are made sorry by their sins, who never have godly sorrow for them Though scourged by their consciences, their love of evil bears down their convictions (6) The triumphing of the wicked is short; God will soon require at their hand the innocent blood they have shed

5 The disciples of John hearing the sad catastrophe, came to pay their last kind offices to their master's corpse, and testify their affection and respect by attending it to the grave, and then went and informed Jesus of the event, on whose ministry probably they had attended since John's imprisonment and if they were drawn nearer to him by their former master's removal, they were in the issue gainers by their loss *Note*, (1) As the dust of his saints is precious to the Lord, so should their very corpses be to us, for the sake of the spirit which dwelt in them (2) We must carry all our griefs to Jesus, and be confident he will alleviate the sorrows we pour into his compassionate bosom (3) Whatever human helps, friends, or ministers, we may be deprived of, we may not despond, our Master in heaven ever lives, and if we are driven nearer to him, he can more than compensate our losses

13 ¶ [f] When Jesus heard *of it*, [g] he departed thence [f] Mark v. 32. Luke 9. 10
by ship into a desart place, apart and when the people [g] Chap. xii. 15. & xv.
had heard *thereof*, they followed him on foot out of the
cities 14 And Jesus went forth, and saw a great mul- [h] Chap. ix. 36.
titude, and [h] was moved with compassion toward them,
and he healed their sick 15 And when it was evening,
his disciples came to him, saying, This is a desart place,
and the time is now past, send the multitude away, that
they may go into the villages, and buy themselves vic-
tuals. 16 But Jesus said unto them, They need not
depart, give ye them to eat 17 And they say unto
him, [i] We have here but five loaves, and two fishes [i] Num. xi. 22. 2 Kings iv. 43.
18 He said, Bring them hither to me. 19 And he
commanded the multitude to sit down on the grass, and
took the five loaves, and the two fishes, and looking up
to heaven, [k] he blessed, and brake, and gave the loaves [k] Chap. xv. 36. & xxvi. 26. Rom. xiv. 6.
to *his* disciples, and [l] the disciples to the multitude 20. [l] Chap. xv. 45.
And they did all eat, and were filled and they took up
of the fragments that remained, twelve baskets full. 21
And they that had eaten were about five thousand men,
beside women and children.

v 13—21 To shelter himself from the jealousy of a cruel tyrant, as well as to give some rest to his disciples, returned from their travels and preaching, our Lord withdrew into a desart place His hour was not yet come; nor was he called to expose himself to Herod's enmity, and therefore he took this prudential step, teaching us by his example, though always to be prepared for suffering in the way of duty, not rashly or needlessly to court persecution Hereupon we are told,

1 That the multitude, who had heard of his departure, immediately followed him on foot, so eager were they to attend his ministry Though there might be danger in cleaving to a man so obnoxious, and they must go many a weary step to attend him, nothing discouraged them They who have a relish for the gospel, will follow it in all its removes, and stick at no pains to enjoy the sincere milk of the word nor will persecution abate their ardor, but increase it

2 The sight of so many poor souls awakened the compassions of Jesus, and though he came thither for retirement, he gladly chose to forego his own ease to do them good He would not suffer them to come so far in vain, and therefore *went forth*, pitying their sad case, destitute of food for their bodies, many sick and weak, and, worst of all, their souls perishing for lack of knowledge and therefore he undertakes the relief of all their necessities, healing their sick, instructing them in the doctrines of his kingdom, and designing, ere they parted, to spread a table for them in the wilderness With like compassions should we regard the souls and bodies of men, and then shall we readily lay out ourselves, and chearfully spend and be spent in their service

3 The disciples, ignorant of the intentions of their Master, and foreseeing the inconveniences which must arise from detaining so vast a multitude there, where no refreshment could be procured, desired their Lord to dismiss the congregation, the day beginning to decline, But he, who knew his own intentions, to try their faith, bids them communicate their little stock of provisions to the people The disciples reasonably object the insufficiency of their slender store, amounting to no more than five loaves and two fishes, which, though they were ready to part with, would not be tasted among such a multitude Yet Jesus bad them bring them to him, and trust his power. *Note*, (1) In following Christ we may be reduced to the greatest strait, but in the way of duty we must trust, and not be afraid (2) They who have Christ, have all, and abound, his presence and love can abundantly compensate every loss, and enable us to be content even to be hungry, and in need of daily food (3) Christ and his disciples lived on coarse and scanty fare, to teach us abstinence and the mortification of our sensual appetite (4) Though we have but little, we should be ready, when duty calls, to give of that little

4 Our Lord distributes the provision Having commanded the multitude to sit down, where the grass was their carpet, he craved a blessing on the meal, and breaking the bread, gave it to his *disciples*, who waited on the multitude, as they sat in ranks opposite each other, and with astonishment beheld the meat grow under their hands, and increase as it descended *Note*, (1) Christ himself is the living bread, which faith daily feeds upon, in him there is enough for all, and to spare (2) We should never sit down to our meals without asking God's blessing It is among the surest marks of an irreligious family, or an irreligious heart, wherever this is neglected, We who are fed by his bounty, are surely bound at least to acknowledge the favour (3) When we charitably break our bread to the hungry, we shall find no diminution of our store

5 There was enough, and more than enough for all *They did all eat, and were filled*, five thousand men, besides women and children and, instead of suffering any loss, the disciples, on collecting the fragments, find that they far exceed the original food, amounting to *twelve baskets full*. *Note*, (1) The blessing of God can multiply a little into abundance, and none are paid with so good interest, as those who in charity lend unto the Lord (2) Though we have plenty, it must not therefore tempt us to waste Since we cannot make one bit of bread, and multitudes of God's poor may want it, every crumb should be carefully collected The truly liberal will be the best oeconomists

22. ¶ And straightway Jesus constrained his disciples
to get into a ship, and to go before him unto the other
m Mark vi. 46 &c. side, while he sent the multitudes away 23 m And
when he had sent the multitudes away, he went up into
n John vi. 16 &c. a mountain apart to pray, and n when the evening was
come, he was there alone 24 But the ship was now in
o Isa liv. 11 the midst of the sea, o tossed with waves for the wind
p [illegible] was contrary 25 And p in the fourth watch of the
q Job ix. 8 night, Jesus went unto them q walking on the sea 26
And when the disciples saw him walking on the sea, they
were troubled, saying, It is a spirit, and they cried out
for fear. 27 But straightway Jesus spake unto them,
saying, Be of good cheer, it is I, be not afraid 28
And Peter answered him and said, Lord, if it be thou,
bid me come unto thee on the water 29 And he said,
Come. And when Peter was come down out of the
ship, he walked on the water to go to Jesus 30 But
r Acts xiv. 2. when he saw r the wind boistrous, he was afraid. and
beginning to sink, he cried, saying, Lord, save me 31
s Ps. xviii. 6 And immediately s Jesus stretched forth *his* hand, and
caught him, and said unto him, O thou of little faith,
wherefore didst thou doubt? 32. And when they were
come into the ship, the wind ceased 33 Then they
that were in the ship came and worshipped him, saying,
t Ps. ii. 7 Chap. xvi. 16 John i. 49 Of a truth t thou art the Son of God

v 22—33 Miracle succeeds to miracle he had just preserved the multitude from being famished, and now he saves his disciples *from foundering in the storm* The Lord *is ever a* very present help in trouble We are told,

1 The constraint he put upon his disciples, ordering them to embark whilst he dismissed the multitude There appeared in the people present a deep conviction of his being the Messiah, and, *according to their prejudices*, they now thought of proclaiming him king, which opportunity his disciples were ready eagerly to embrace but they mistook the nature of his kingdom, and for a while entertained the false notions of their countrymen *Note*, The disciples of Christ are ever too apt to look *for a temporal instead of a spiritual kingdom*

2 When he had sent away his disciples, though reluctant, and dismissed the people, he retired for prayer and communion with God, and in that pleasing work continued till night drew on *Note*, They who are much in public ministrations, *need also be much in prayer and converse with God* They will be most fervent in their discourses, who come from their knees into their pulpits

3 His disciples, who had embarked at his command, were now in imminent danger All was smooth when they set sail; but now when they were far from land the storm arose, and the wind blew directly against them Thus in the way of duty we may meet with sore temptations, and be sometimes at our wits end All things may seem to be against us, and the dispensations of providence and grace dark and gloomy as this tempestuous night, and yet even then are all things *working* together for our good If we steadily hold on our course, and walk by faith, not by sight, we shall arrive safe at the shore of eternal rest

4 In the time of need Jesus approaches them at the morning watch, walking on the stormy waves, and thereby shewing them his power to save them, and his attention to them in the hour of danger But they not knowing him, and observing something moving on the waters, concluded it an apparition, or some evil spirit, and supposing it foreboded some mischief to them, *cried out for fear* but Jesus immediately undeceived them, and with his well-known voice endeavours to quiet their apprehensions of danger *Be of good cheer, be undismayed, it is I*, your master and Lord, *be not afraid*, whilst I am so nigh, and able to save you *Note*, (1) Christ is nearer us when we are in trouble, than we are aware of, and when we seem abandoned by him, his right hand is under us, to keep us from sinking (2) When the soul is in distress, we are ready to interpret even the appearances in our favour as ominous, and to start from our approaching mercies (3) If Christ speaks comfort to our hearts, we need not then be afraid of any danger or distress, for he through all can make us more than conquerors

5. Their fears being somewhat quieted, Peter, impatient to be at his Master's feet, and ever the foremost to express his fidelity and zeal, begs leave, if it was the Lord indeed, his doubts not being entirely removed, that he would command him to come down, and enable him to go *to him on the waters* Tho' eager to go, he dares not without a warrant, but if Jesus bids him, neither winds nor waves dismay him The Lord grants his request, and, at once to convince him of his weakness, and confirm his faith, permits him to come *Note*, (1) They who love the Lord Jesus Christ in sincerity, will, at his bidding, go through fire or water (2) Though no dangers must deter us in the way of duty, we may not wilfully run into them without a divine call (3) Christ knows our hearts, and though he sees much infirmity mingled with our warmest profession, he knows how to pity and pardon the one, whilst he kindly accepts the other

6. Peter no sooner receives permission, than immediately he boldly casts himself into the deep, and, by faith upheld, walks on the foaming billows But when he felt the stormy wind, and observed the boisterous waves, his faith staggered, his fears prevailed, and he began to sink Ready to perish, he instantly and eagerly cries, *Lord, save me*, and in the last extremity stretches the arms of faith and prayer towards the almighty Saviour *Note*, (1) Whilst we walk by faith, not by sight, we shall stand firm amidst the storms of this tumultuous world (2) The strongest believers are sometimes shaken, and, to humble and beat down all self-confidence, the Saviour is pleased to withhold his grace, and then they instantly feel how weak they are (3) *We may never expect perfect deliverance from our fears*, till we are perfected in love, and that is reserved for the happiness of a better world (4) We cannot but stagger, the moment we take our eye off from Christ and his promises, to look at the difficulties and dangers before us, and our own inability to surmount them. (5) Though Christ permits true believers sometimes to begin to sink, he will not suffer them to be drowned, but means only to magnify his power and grace towards them, and to excite their gratitude and love in the more abundant experience of his salvation (6) *Times of danger should be times of prayer*, and *Jesus never yet failed the poor* sinner, who, sensible of his inevitable ruin without him, thus ardently cried, *Lord, save me*

7 The prayer is scarce sooner uttered than answered; the almighty hand of Jesus stretched out, snatched him from the jaws of death, *and raising him up, he rebukes his weak and* wavering faith, that, after experiencing so much of his Lord's power, could yet distrust him *Note*, (1) Many a time may every faithful soul remember the occasion, when he was ready to give up all for lost, and seemed sinking into eternal death, and then did Jesus snatch us as brands from the burning (2) All our disquieting fears arise from our unbelief, and should drive us more to our knees, that the cause of them may be removed by the increase of our faith. (3) Little faith, though it may leave us in a fright, will never leave us finally to fall None can sink who have ever taken hold on Christ (4) When we dishonour our Lord by distrusting his power and love, we deserve to be upbraided for it.

8 On the coming of Jesus into the ship with Peter, the storm instantly ceased, the waves subsided, and, struck with astonishment, all who were in the ship fell at his feet, acknowledging his divine power and godhead in the wonders they had seen, and adoring him for the mercies they had received *Note*, (1) When Christ comes to visit the troubled soul, then the winds of distress and temptation are hushed, and the tempest of doubts and fears is calmed (2) Experience of the Redeemer's grace and power should confirm our faith, and excite our adoration, and this is the blessed end for which he permits his people to be exercised, that he may more abundantly display his own glory in their salvation

34 ¶ u And when they were gone over, they came u Mark vi. 53
into the land of Gennesaret 35 And when the men
of that place had knowledge of him, they sent out into all
that country round about, and brought unto him all that
were diseased, 36 And besought him that they might
only

only touch the hem of his garment and ˣ as many as
touched were made perfectly whole

ˣ Chap ix 20 Mark vi 56 Luke vi 19 Acts xix

v 34—36 The storm being over, and their ship arrived safe to port, they disembarked in the fruitful land of Gennesaret, and thus shall the saints of God at last, when all the tempests of life are blown over, reach that land, where there is undisturbed repose, and pleasures for evermore

No sooner is it known that Jesus is there, than we are told, the eagerness with which the people of that country crouded round him, spreading the glad tidings through the neighbourhood, and bringing all their diseased to Jesus, the great and general physician And such was their faith in his sufficiency to heal all their maladies, that they *besought him*, if but to *touch the hem of his garment*, persuaded such virtue resided in him, that nothing more was needful to their cure nor were they disappointed in their confidence or application He granted their request, and as many as touched him immediately were made perfectly whole *Note*, (1) Christ's visits are precious, we should improve them with diligence (2) If we have found him a Saviour unto us, it becomes us to spread the glad tidings, and invite others to come and share our blessings (3) There is no disease of our souls, but Jesus hath healing for it If we perish, it is because we will not come to him that we may have life (4) They who in faith and humility approach the Saviour, are sure never to go disappointed away.

CHAP XV

In this chapter we have, 1 Christ's discourse with the scribes and Pharisees about human traditions and injunctions, ver 1—9 2 His discourse with the multitude, and with his disciples, concerning the things that defile a man, ver 10—20 3 His casting the devil out of the woman of Canaan's daughter, ver 21—28 4 His healing of all that were brought to him, ver 29—31 5 His feeding four thousand men with seven loaves and a few little fishes, ver 32—39

ᵃ Mark vii 1 — 1 THEN ᵃ came to Jesus scribes and Pharisees,
which were of Jerusalem, saying, 2 Why do
ᵇ Col ii 8 — thy disciples transgress ᵇ the tradition of the elders ? for
they wash not their hands when they eat bread 3 But
he answered and said unto them, Why do you also
transgress the commandment of God by your tradition ?
ᶜ Ex xx 12 Deut v 16 — 4 For God commanded, saying, ᶜ Honour thy father
ᵈ Ex xxi 17 Lev xx 9 Prov xx 20 & xxx 17 — and mother and, ᵈ He that curseth father or mother,
let him die the death 5 But ye say, Whosoever shall
say to *his* father or *his* mother, *It is* a gift by whatsoever thou mightest be profited by me, 6 And honour
ᵉ Prov i 25 — not his father or his mother, *he shall be free*. ᵉ Thus
have ye made the commandment of God of none effect
ᶠ Isa xxix 13 Ezek xxxiii 31 — by your tradition 7 Ye hypocrites, well did Esaias
prophesy of you, saying, 8 ᶠ This people draweth nigh
unto me with their mouth, and honoureth me with their
lips but their heart is far from me 9 But in vain
ᵍ Col ii 18 — do they worship me, ᵍ teaching *for doctrines* the commandments of men

v 1—9 Since the purity of the Redeemer's conduct was such that his most inveterate enemies could not convince him of sin, the scribes and Pharisees endeavoured, if they could not prove him guilty of a breach of God's law, to accuse him at least as a breaker of the canons of their church

1 The accusation laid against him is for permitting his disciples "to transgress the tradition of the elders, and eat bread "with unwashen hands" which to them appeared highly criminal, who, having lost the spirit and power of godliness, were wholly engrossed with the form, and spent their zeal in practising and enforcing the vain superstitions of their own invention as the most essential parts of religion And similar hereunto we still too frequently see the most rigid and superstitious observers of the form of godliness the greatest enemies to the power of it, and the most inveterate persecutors of the spiritually minded

2 Christ answers their accusation, vindicates his disciples, and rebukes their hypocrisy

[1] He vindicates his disciples, by shewing the folly and wickedness of the traditions on which they grounded their charge, and recriminates by a juster accusation of their conduct who made void the commandments of God by their traditions In proof of which he produces the fifth commandment, where the duty of children towards their parents is enjoined, and in the honour we must pay to them there is included the relief of their wants, in case of need and to this law God hath annexed the most awful sanction The transgressor who curses, or but *speaks contemptibly* of, his father or mother, is doomed to death, *Exod* xxi 17 But their false casuistry had provided an evasion, to avoid ministring to the necessities of their parents, and their tradition asserted, that however urgent these might be, if they *vowed to employ in sacred uses*, what should have been given to relieve their parents wants, or rather, as Dr Gill interprets the passage, vowed that what they had should be *as Corban*, as if dedicated to the sanctuary, and should not be given to their parents use, they were then supposed to be bound by their vow, and though the things were not employed in sacred uses, they thought themselves authorized under this pretence to withhold from their father or mother the relief they ought to have afforded them a tradition as absurd as impious, and utterly overturning the law of God *Note*, (1) Many who are flaming in zeal for trifling human ceremonies, disregard and violate the most essential precepts of charity, and the most evident commands of God's law (2) Tradition has been ever a treacherous guide, therefore neither antiquity nor authority must weigh a rush with us against the revealed truths of God's word

[2] He rebukes their hypocrisy He knew their hearts, and therefore there was no rashness nor uncharitableness in the charge laid against them and he brings his reproof from Isaiah, for what the prophet spake as the character of the men of his day, had also a further view to the generation then present, who exactly answered the description, and they are indeed equally applicable to the state of all hypocrites and formal professors to the end of time They made an outward shew of religion, and, so far as lip-service and external worship went, pretended to honour God, but their hearts, without which he *is pleased with no services*, were far estranged from him and whilst they appeared to pay the highest respect to God, they set up their traditions and human inventions, *many of them in direct opposition to God's law*, and this rendered all their worship and apparent devotion vain, useless, and rejected *Note*, (1) Hypocrisy is among the most common and fatal sins, and though men may not discover it in us, from God it cannot be hid (2) God's first requirement of us is our heart, if this be alienated from him, nothing we can offer him beside will meet with any acceptance

10 ¶ ʰ And he called the multitude, and said unto — ʰ Mark vii 14
them, Hear and understand. 11 ⁱ Not that which goeth — ⁱ Acts x 15 Rom xiv 14 1 Tim iv 4 Tit i 15
into the mouth defileth a man, but that which cometh
out of the mouth, this defileth a man 12 Then came
his disciples, and said unto him, Knowest thou that the
Pharisees were offended after they heard this saying ?
13 But he answered and said, ᵏ Every plant which my — ᵏ John xv 2
heavenly Father hath not planted, shall be rooted up
14 Let them alone ˡ they be blind leaders of the blind — ˡ Is ix 16
And if the blind lead the blind, ᵐ both shall fall into the — ᵐ Also in Chap xi 16
ditch 15 Then answered Peter, and said unto him,
Declare unto us this parable 16 And Jesus said, Are — ⁿ 1 Cor iii 6
ye also ⁿ yet without understanding ? 17 Do not ye — Rev iii 17
yet understand, that whatsoever entreth in at the mouth,
goeth into the belly, and is cast out into the draught ? — ° Jam i 15 9 Heb v 12
18 But ° those things which proceed out of the mouth, — ° Jam iii 6
come forth from the heart, and they defile the man
19 For ᵖ out of the heart proceed evil thoughts, murders, adulteries, fornications, thefts, false witness, blasphemies 20 These are the things which defile a — ᵖ Gen vi 5 & viii 21 Prov vi 14 Jer xvii 9
man but to eat with unwashen hands, defileth not a
man

v 10—20 Having vindicated his disciples, and rebuked the hypocrisy of the Pharisees, he endeavours to set the multitude in general right in a matter of such importance, which had been *so grievously mistaken* And for this purpose he calls them unto him, as they probably had withdrawn whilst the Pharisees had talked with him, and bids them hear and understand, for it requires much attention and careful examination before we can emancipate ourselves from the fetters of long-rooted error, and the prejudices of education

1 He lays down this grand axiom, that all defilement comes from within It was a superstitious tradition which the Pharisees inculcated, that the meat eaten with unwashen hands communicated pollution to the soul, whereas nothing can defile that but sin, which taking its rise in the heart, issues forth at the mouth And herein he levelled a tacit rebuke against these cavillers, who, whilst they contended for cleanness and purity, betrayed the venom and malignity of their own hearts The severest censurers of others are usually thus found most culpable themselves Whilst they pretend to pluck the mote from their brother's eye, they discover not the beam which is in their own

2 *When they were retired into a house, the disciples*, aware of the great offence this declaration gave to the Pharisees, expressed their concern about it, as if the observation had been better suppressed, and might prejudice and exasperate them against him *Note*, (1) Truth, however offensive, must be spoken, and the woe lies not against those who give the offence, but against those who take it (2) We are too apt to

fear for others, and to fear, leaſt ſome of the audience ſhould be diſguſted with plain dealing But they who would convert men's ſouls, muſt often be content to offend nice ears

3 In anſwer to their ſuggeſtion, Jeſus vindicates what he had ſpoken, as proper and neceſſary As theſe men, and their traditions, were not thoſe heavenly plants, which God the Father had planted, they are thus, by the piercing word of truth, diſcovered, detected, and rooted up If they are offended, the diſciples need not regard it, for high as their character was among the people, they were in fact no better than *blind leaders of the blind*, ignorant themſelves of ſaving truth, and miſleading thoſe who blindly and implicitly obeyed their dictates And the neceſſary conſequence of this was, that they muſt periſh together, and fall into the pit of eternal miſery *Note*, (1) However plauſible men's profeſſions may be, and however admired their characters, if they are not the planting of God, and experimentally partakers of the quickening influences of his ſpirit, their ruin is as ſure as that of impenitent publicans and harlots (2) Pride and blindneſs of heart are inſeparable companions, and none are ſo far from the light of truth, as thoſe who, filled with the conceit of their own wiſdom and abilities, vainly boaſt how clear they ſee (3) The deceived and the deceiver will periſh together, and they who chuſe their own deluſions, have themſelves only to blame for the ruin which enſues

4 Peter, in the name of the diſciples, not underſtanding the meaning of the parable, or ſtill biaſſed by the prejudices of education, deſires his maſter to explain himſelf more diſtinctly on this point. and though their backwardneſs to underſtand was culpable, their deſire to be informed was commendable It is always good to be inquiſitive about the great concerns of our ſouls, and Chriſt is willing to teach thoſe who deſire to learn, whilſt the wilfully ignorant, the ſelf-ſufficient, and the proud, are juſtly left to their darkneſs and ruin.

5 Chriſt rebukes the dulneſs of their capacity, yet graciouſly condeſcends to give a farther explication of what he had advanced *Are ye alſo yet without underſtanding?* They had enjoyed many and long opportunities for profiting under him, and it was a ſhame in a matter ſo plain, they ſhould be yet ſo ignorant Chriſt juſtly expects our means and mercies ſhould produce a proportionate advancement in grace and knowledge Nothing could be more evident than that the meat, of whatever ſort it were, which entered at the mouth, and merely paſſed through the body, could communicate no moral defilement to the ſoul But the heart being the ſource and fountain of all ſpiritual impurity, what flowed from thence alone communicated in God's ſight defilement to the man and the corrupt and impure ſtreams which flow from thence he enumerates, a dreadful catalogue, but the natural produce of every fallen ſpirit (1) *Evil thoughts*, ſuch as lewd deſires, infidel reaſonings, covetous wiſhes, malicious purpoſes, fraudulent deſigns, which never appeared in words or actions, but were naked and open before God, and brought guilt upon the ſoul (2) *Murders*, not only the effuſion of human blood, but every word of anger, every act of violence, every expreſſion of malice, hatred, or revenge. (3) *Adulteries*, *fornications*, with all the various ſteps and contrivances which have a tendency to lead men to theſe horrid deeds (4) *Thefts*, whether committed by force or fraud (5) *Falſe witneſs* in perjuries, lies, deceit, and miſrepreſentation (6) *Blaſphemies*, againſt God or man. Theſe are the great violations of God's law, the things which involve the conſcience in guilt, and make us loathſome in the eyes of divine purity whilſt to eat with unwaſhen hands communicates no defilement to the ſoul, nor in the leaſt renders any man a ſinner before God

q Mark vii. 24. 21 ¶ q Then Jeſus went thence, and departed into the
coaſts of Tyre and Sidon 22 And behold, a woman of
Canaan came out of the ſame coaſts, and cried unto him,
ſaying, Have mercy on me, O Lord, thou Son of David, my daughter is grievouſly vexed with a devil 23.
r Pſal. xxii. 2. Jer. xiv. 9. Lam. iii. 8. But r he anſwered her not a word And his diſciples
came and beſought him, ſaying, Send her away, for ſhe
crieth after us 24 But he anſwered and ſaid, I am not
s Chap. x. 6. Rom. xv. 8. ſent, but unto s the loſt ſheep of the houſe of Iſrael
t Gen. xxxii. 26. 25 Then came ſhe and t worſhipped him, ſaying, Lord,
u Chap. vii. 6. help me 26 But he anſwered and ſaid, u It is not meet
to take the children's bread, and caſt it to the dogs
x Pſal. lxxiii. 22. Prov. xxx. 2. 27 And ſhe ſaid, x Truth, Lord yet the dogs eat of the
crumbs which fall from their maſter's table 28 y Then
y [illegible] 26. Jeſus anſwered and ſaid unto her, O woman, great is
thy faith be it unto thee even as thou wilt And her
daughter was made whole from that very hour

v. 21—28 Departing from the country of Genneſaret, our Lord viſited the coaſts of Tyre and Sidon He had a peculiar object in his view, and by one act of favour to the poor Gentiles, would intimate the mercy he had in ſtore for them We have,

1 The application made to him by a poor woman of that country, a Canaanite; perhaps a deſcendant of that accurſed race, but ſelected as a monument of mercy Having heard the fame of Jeſus, ſhe ſeized the preſent moment to prefer her requeſt Her caſe was very afflictive, her daughter was *grievouſly vexed with a devil*, poſſeſſed and tormented by him, and therefore ſhe earneſtly cries, *Have mercy on me, O Lord, thou Son of David* She profeſſes her faith in him, as the true Meſſiah, expreſſes her confidence of his power to help her, and conſcious of her own unworthineſs to receive any favour from him, caſts herſelf entirely on his mercy *Note*, (1) To ſee a child under the power of diſeaſe, is deeply felt by every tender parent, but to behold them under the power of ſin and Satan, is far more grievous (2) When we can do no more for our unhappy offſpring, we muſt continue in prayer to preſent their miſerable ſtate to Jeſus, if ſo be, he may interpoſe to heal them (3) The mercies ſhewn to our children are favours done to ourſelves, and ſhould be ſo acknowledged (4) All that a ſinner hath to aſk of the Saviour is mere mercy, we have no claim upon him, and can only caſt ourſelves at his feet, to do with us, and by us, according to the riches of his grace

2 Her application at firſt appears to be utterly diſregarded, and Jeſus condeſcended to make no reply, not that he meant to deny her requeſt, but to exerciſe her faith, and quicken her importunity His diſciples, who had never ſeen before their maſter deaf to the intreaties of the miſerable, intereſted themſelves in her behalf, and not merely to be rid of her cries, but probably affected with her deep diſtreſs, wiſhed her requeſt granted, and that ſhe were diſmiſſed in peace, but his anſwer, *v.* 24 ſeemed to carry a ſtill more unfavourable aſpect, as if his miniſtry and miracles were to be confined to Iſrael alone Nay, when the poor petitioner, notwithſtanding all diſcouragement, approaching nearer, fell down at his feet, importunately reiterating her requeſt, ſhe apparently meets with ſtill a rougher reception, ſeems to be ſpurned away as a dog, and excluded from the participation of mercies which were confined to God's covenant people, as if all out of the pale of peculiarity deſerved to be treated as impure animals, and rejected by the faithful *Note*, (1) We muſt not conclude our requeſts are refuſed, becauſe they are not immediately granted, nor that though the Saviour ſeems to frown, he forbids further intreaty, it is to exerciſe our faith, and quicken our prayers (2) Gracious ſouls are ever ready advocates and interceſſors for the miſerable (3) If the Lord write bitter things againſt us, it is to humble our ſouls before him, and make us ſee how vile and unworthy we are of any favour at his hands

3 Not diſmayed by this repulſe, nor driven to quit her hold, her faith cleaves to him, and her ſoul bows down before him Far from being offended at being treated as a dog, or ſinking into deſpair at Chriſt's reply, her anſwer expreſſed the deep humility and unſhaken dependance of her heart upon him "*Truth, Lord*, ſhe replied, I own the charge, more vile and "worthleſs than I am no dog can be, a ſinner, a Gentile, un-"deſerving of any favour yet, as a dog, regard me" (ſo gracefully and powerfully doth ſhe improve that for her plea, which ſeemed to convey the greateſt diſcouragement,) "they "are permitted, under their maſter's table, to pick up the "crumbs that fall, I aſk no more Whilſt happier Iſraelites "enjoy the abundance of thy miracles, let one crumb fall on "me, a poor Canaanite; no loſs to them, to me a mercy ſo "unſpeakable" *Note*, (1) Nothing muſt ever drive us from Chriſt, the more we are diſtreſſed, the more ſhould we cleave to him If we periſh, we periſh, let it be at leaſt at the feet of Jeſus, and there none ever yet were finally caſt away (2) We can never have too lowly thoughts of ourſelves, the worſt we can ſay of ourſelves, or others can ſay of us, is nothing ſo bad as God ſees in us (3) Active faith lays hold even on the hand that ſeems ſtretched out to deſtroy "though "thou ſlay me, yet will I truſt in thee" And this is indeed the the triumph of faith

4 As if amazed and overcome by faith ſo diſtinguiſhed, Jeſus grants her requeſt, and diſmiſſes her with the higheſt marks of his approbation To her utmoſt wiſhes he extends the favour, and inſtantly her daughter was made whole *Note*, (1) Nothing is ſo pleaſing and honourable to Jeſus, as great faith in his power and love (2) There is no mercy that we can aſk, believing, which Jeſus will ever refuſe us, whether it be pardon, grace, or glory, it ſhall aſſuredly be given us

29 And Jeſus departed z from thence, and came nigh z Mark vii. 31.
unto the ſea of Galilee, and went up into a mountain,
and ſat down there 30 And great multitudes came
unto him, having with them thoſe that were lame, blind,
dumb, maimed, and many others, and caſt them down
at Jeſus feet, and a he healed them 31 Inſomuch that a Iſa. xxxv. 5, 6. Chap. xi. 5.
the multitude wondered, when they ſaw the dumb to
ſpeak, the maimed to be whole, the lame to walk, and
the blind to ſee and they glorified the God of Iſrael
32 ¶ b Then Jeſus called his diſciples unto him, and ſaid, b Mark viii. 1.
I have compaſſion on the multitude, becauſe they con-

tinue with me now three days, and have nothing to eat
and I will not send them away fasting, lest they faint by
c Numb xi 22 2 Kings iv 43 the way 33 And his disciples say unto him, c Whence
should we have so much bread in the wilderness, as to fill
so great a multitude? 34 And Jesus saith unto them,
How many loaves have ye? and they said, Seven, and a
few little fishes 35 And he commanded the multitude
to sit down on the ground 36 And he took the seven
d Chap xiv 19 Rom xiv 6 loaves and the fishes, and d gave thanks, and brake *them*,
and gave to his disciples, and the disciples to the multitude
37 And they did all eat, and were filled and
they took up of the broken meat that was left, seven
baskets full 38 And they that did eat, were four thousand
men, beside women and children. 39 And he
sent away the multitude, and took ship, and came into
the coasts of Magdala

v 29—39 Having finished the work which he went thither to do, Jesus returned again to the coasts of Galilee and seating himself on a rising ground, as the great and universal physician, appeared ready to receive and relieve every miserable patient whatever his disease might be, without money, and without price We have an account,

1 Of the multitudes who came to him, bringing the afflicted with various maladies, and casting them down at his feet And his compassions were so great, his power so effectual, that he healed them all *Note*, (1) The diseases of our bodies drive us instantly to the physician, though his art is uncertain, shall not the more dangerous diseases of our souls drive us to Jesus, whose medicines of grace are infallible? (2) The world is full of sickness and pain because full of sin, if the cause be once removed through the blood, the righteousness, the Spirit of Jesus, the effects will quickly for ever cease, and the inhabitants above shall never more say *I am sick*

2 These wonders of power and grace deeply affected the beholders Amazed to hear the dumb to speak, to see the lame walk, the blind restored to sight, and every malady removed with a word, *they glorified the God of Israel* for sending the promised Messiah, for such these words bespoke him, whom they now beheld *Note*, Every mercy demands a tribute of praise, and if the removal of bodily complaints excited such wonder and thankfulness, how much more should we admire the riches of the gift, and adore the God of our salvation, if our souls have experienced the power of his healing grace, if our once blind eyes see the light of truth, if our ears, once deaf, are open to the gospel's joyful sound, if our once lame feet are strengthened to run the way of his commandments For these unutterable blessings, praise the Lord, O my soul

3 A singular miracle is wrought, wherein all partook, similar to what he had done before, *chap* xiv with this little variation, that here *four thousand, besides women and children* are fed with *seven loaves and a few little fishes* there, *five thousand men, besides women and children*, were fed *with five loaves*

[1] The circumstances of the people here assembled, moved the compassion of Jesus So eager were they to attend on his ministry, and to behold his miracles, that for three days successively they continued with him, and if they brought any little provision with them, it was ere this consumed, so that they had now nothing to eat, and as many of them came from far, and could not soon get a supply of food, to send them away thus fasting might expose them to faint by the way through weakness, and to perish with hunger Calling his disciples, therefore, he acquainted them with his gracious design of feeding them there, but they forgetting what they had so lately seen, *chap* xiv 21 objected to the possibility of providing meat for such a multitude in that wilderness, and especially when by his question he seemed to intend supplying the table out of their scanty store, which appeared so insufficient, being no more than seven loaves, and a few small fishes *Note*, (1) They who know the sweetness of the gospel word, will undergo weariness and hunger, rather than be deprived of it (2) It is through our forgetfulness of the past interpositions we have experienced, that under new difficulties we fall into fresh perplexity

[2] Having commanded them to sit down, he took the loaves and fishes as before, and thanking God for the provision, he divided the bread and fishes among the disciples, that they should distribute them to the multitude and lo from any lack, when all had eaten and were filled, seven baskets full of fragments still remained The provision indeed was somewhat more, the company fewer, and the fragments less than in the former instance, but the miracle was the same in one case as the other; and the wondrous enlargement of the food evidenced the same divine creative power *Note*, We stand astonished at this relation but is not every corn that is cast into the earth as marvellously increased at the harvest? yet who thinks of the wonder working hand of him, by whose daily bread we are continually fed?

[3] Having liberally satisfied his guests, he dismissed them to their own homes Thither duty called them, we cannot always be in attendance on the sanctuary, it is not proper we should be As for himself and his disciples, they took ship, and came into the coasts of Magdala His work was to be going about doing good, and in every place he left behind him abundant marks of his transcendent power, grace, and love

CHAP XVI

None of Christ's miracles are recorded in this chapter, but four of his discourses Here is, 1 *A conference with the Pharisees, who challenged him to shew them a sign from heaven, ver* 1—4 2 *Another with his disciples about the leaven of the Pharisees, ver* 5—12 3 *Another with them concerning himself, as the Christ, and concerning his church built upon him, ver* 13—20 4 *Another concerning his sufferings for them and theirs for him, ver* 21—28 *And all these are written for our learning*

1 a THE Pharisees also with the Sadducees, came, a Chap xii 38 Luke xii 54 1 Cor i 22
and tempting, desired him that he would shew
them a sign from heaven 2 He answered and said unto
them, When it is evening, ye say, *It will be* fair weather
for the sky is red 3 And in the morning, *It will be* foul
weather to day for the sky is red and lowring O ye
hypocrites, ye can discern the face of the sky, but can ye
not *discern* the signs of the times? 4 b A wicked and b Chap xii 39
adulterous generation seeketh after a sign, and there shall
no sign be given unto it, but the sign of the prophet
Jonas And he left them and departed

v 1—4 However opposite in their tenets the Pharisees and Sadducees were, in their enmity against Christ and his gospel they perfectly agreed

1 They came in concert, with a view to tempt and entangle him, and, pretending dissatisfaction with the miracles he wrought, desired a proof of the divine mission he assumed, by some sign from heaven, such as appeared when the law was given on Sinai Not indeed that they wished to be convinced, but merely sought some refuge for their infidelity *Note*, They who, after all the miracles Jesus hath wrought, desire farther evidence of his character, evidently shew they determine not to receive him, and if never so many signs or wonders were granted them, yet would they not believe in him

2 Christ justly refuses to gratify their vain curiosity, and unreasonable request There was evidence sufficient before them, if they chose to see, and they did not want natural sagacity to judge of it From observing the appearances of the sky they determined what weather would follow If the sky was red at evening, they presumed, by observation and experience, the following day would be fair but, if in the morning the sky appeared red and lowring, then it would be wet or windy and from great probability drew these conclusions But how glaringly did they play the hypocrite, when, pretending the highest veneration for Moses and the prophets, though they could judge of the weather by the appearances of the sky, they could not discern *the signs of the times*, so clearly and distinctly revealed in the sacred writings, could neither see the present exact fulfilment of all the prophecies concerning the Messiah, nor the ruin coming upon themselves for rejecting him and therefore, since they were a wicked and adulterous generation, wilfully blind to the evidence of truth, no other sign shall be given them than the miracles they had already rejected, except his resurrection from the dead after three days, prefigured by the abode of the prophet Jonas in the whale's belly And with this he left them, as incorrigible sinners, with whom it was in vain to remonstrate, and crossed the lake to another part of the country *Note*, (1) Many are wise enough in human concerns, yea deeply skilled in the mysteries of science, who yet are stark blind with regard to their souls (2) They who by their obstinacy and infidelity provoke Christ to depart from them, are justly given up to perdition

5 ¶ c And when his disciples were come to the other c Mark viii 14
side, they had forgotten to take bread. 6 Then Jesus
said unto them, d Take heed and beware of the leaven
of the Pharisees, and of the Sadducees 7 And they
reasoned among themselves, saying, *It is* because we have
taken no bread 8 *Which* when Jesus perceived, he said
unto them, O ye of little faith, why reason ye among
yourselves, because ye have brought no bread? 9 e Do e Chap xiv 17 John vi 9
ye not yet understand, neither remember the five loaves
of the five thousand, and how many baskets ye took up?
10 f Neither the seven loaves of the four thousand, and
how many baskets ye took up? 11 How is it that ye
do not understand, that I spake *it* not to you concerning
bread, that ye should beware of the leaven of the Pharisees,
and of the Sadducees? 12. Then understood they

how

how that he bad *them* not beware of the leaven of bread, but of the doctrine of the Pharisees, and of the Sadducees

v 5—12 Departing in haste, the disciples had forgotten to take with them provisions as usual and thereupon from temporal things he takes occasion to introduce spiritual instructions

1 He cautions them to beware of the leaven of the Pharisees and of the Sadducees, of their principles and doctrines, which would spread their pernicious influences through the whole man

2 They mistook his meaning, and, taking his words literally, they concluded privately among themselves that it was intended as a rebuke for their carelessness, or a caution not to make use of the bread of the Pharisees and Sadducees, nor so much as to eat with them

3 He reproves them for the sinful distrust of their hearts, and the dulness of their apprehensions It was a proof of the weakness of their faith, after the miracles they had so lately seen, to harbour a moment's distrust about a provision, which their master could so easily supply and it shewed their stupidity, not to understand, after what had passed, that it could not be of bread literally that he spoke, but of something spiritual and figurative, of much greater moment than bread merely *Note*, (1) Christ is displeased with his people when they harbour worldly fears, and are disturbed about the meat that perisheth It is a proof of little faith indeed, to suppose that those who have a promise of heaven for their home should want bread by the way (2) If we remembered better the past experience of God's care, it would administer an argument to silence our present distrusts and perplexities

4 At last they comprehend his meaning, that he spake not of the bread but of the doctrines of these sects, cautioning them against the false traditions, pride, and self-righteousness of the Pharisees, and against the infidelity and licentious principles of the Sadducees, both fatally dangerous against which we have alike need to be on our guard. *Take heed and beware* of them

13 ¶ When Jesus came into the coasts of Cesarea
Philippi, he asked his disciples, saying, [g] Whom do men
say that I, the Son of man, am? 14 And they said,
Some *say that thou art* John the Baptist, some Elias, and
others Jeremias, or one of the prophets 15 He saith
unto them, But whom say ye that I am? 16 And Simon Peter answered and said, [h] Thou art Christ, the Son
of the living God 17 And Jesus answered and said
unto him, Blessed art thou, Simon Bar-jona for flesh
and blood hath not revealed *it* unto thee, [i] but my Father
which is in heaven 18 And I say also unto thee, that
thou art Peter, and upon [k] this rock I will build my
church and the gates of hell shall not prevail against it
19 And [l] I will give unto thee the keys of the kingdom of heaven and whatsoever thou shalt bind on earth,
shall be bound in heaven and whatsoever thou shalt loose
on earth, shall be loosed in heaven 20 [m] Then charged
he his disciples that they should tell no man that he was
Jesus the Christ

[g] Mark viii 27 Luke ix 18
[h] John vi 69 & xi 27 Acts viii 37 John iv 15 & v 5
[i] Chap xi 27 1 Cor ii 10 Gal i 16
[k] Ver 10 1 Cor iii 11 1 Pet ii 6.
[l] Chap xviii 18 John xx 23
[m] Chap xvii 9.

v 13—20 Being now in the remotest part of the country, our Lord took occasion in private conference to enquire into the opinions entertained concerning himself by the people in general, and by his disciples in particular Not that he was ignorant of either, but he meant to lead them to an open confession of their faith in him

1 He asks concerning the general opinion which the people formed of him, who appeared under the name of *the Son of man*, the humble title he assumed when he emptied himself, and was made in the likeness of sinful flesh Or it may be read, *Whom do men say that I am? The son of man?* Do they acknowledge my character and mission as the Messiah or, What do they think of me?

2 The disciples, who had heard the different sentiments of the multitude, informed him that there was a variety of conjecture formed concerning him, some supposing him John the Baptist risen from the dead, others Elias, prophesied of by Malachi, others Jeremias, or one of the ancient prophets sent to reform the guilty age opinions which shewed the honourable sentiments the common people entertained of him, yet far short of the truth The meanness of his birth, relations, dress, and followers, seem to have quite excluded the notion of his true character as the Messiah, whom their prejudices had always represented as to come with all the pomp of majesty, and the glory of a conquering hero

3 He questions them concerning their own sentiments of him They had been better taught, and therefore should have higher notions of his true character, and, being shortly to become teachers of others, they were peculiarly called upon to entertain right apprehensions of this important truth themselves *Note*, We must know Jesus ourselves, his person and offices, or it is impossible we should truly be his ministers to others

4 Peter, according to his usual zeal and forwardness, in the name of the rest, and as their spokesman, nobly replies, *Thou art Christ, the Son of the living God* They understood his real character, they truly believed in him as the divine Messiah, the anointed prophet, priest, and king of his people, and were ready to confess him not merely as Son of man, but as the co-equal Son of God

5 Christ expresses his high commendation of this truly apostolic confession It was a distinguished blessing which Peter possessed thus to know the Lord's Christ, and what neither sprung from his birth, education, or his own reasoning, but from divine revelation So noble and open a profession of his faith shewed him to be what his name imported, a rock and hereupon Christ adds, *Upon this rock will I build my church*; which some apply personally to Peter, and may in a sound sense be admitted, as one of those apostles on whom, as the foundation, the church is said to be built, being raised chiefly by their ministry, *Eph* ii 20 *Rev* xxi 14 Nor can this at all countenance the absurd pretensions of the bishops of Rome, who are neither his successors in office or doctrine Indeed nothing can more evidence the weakness of their claims than such perverted scriptures, wrested and pressed into the service But by the rock more probably is meant Christ himself, who in speaking pointed to his own person, and being evidently the rock on which Peter himself built, the true foundation, other than which can no man lay, 1 *Cor* iii 11 Hereon he is pleased to raise the glorious superstructure of his church the work and the glory of it are all his own, and on his power, love, and faithfulness, its stability rests nor shall the gates of hell ever prevail against it, neither the power nor policy of Satan or his instruments shall be able to destroy the church, nor shall death or the grave finally detain one member of it, but they shall be triumphant at last, and see every foe made their footstool *Note*, (1) Nothing is so acceptable to Jesus as a bold profession of our confidence in him (2) They are truly blessed who savingly know the Son of God (3) All we know of God and his Christ is from his own revelation and unless he himself is pleased to teach us, we know nothing as we ought to know (4) The church of Christ is his own planting and building, and every member of it is fixed on that rock of ages against which no foe can prevail the crafts and assaults of Satan, the malice of men, the open attacks of persecutors, and the secret machinations of heretics and hypocrites, are alike impotent against those who are kept by the power of God through faith unto salvation

6 Having engaged to erect his church, Christ provides for the government of it, and commits to Peter and the other apostles the keys, the ensigns of authority, empowering him and them in his name, *see John* xx 23 to declare what was lawful and unlawful, to charge sin upon men's consciences, and absolve them on their humiliation, to pronounce spiritual censures or loose men from them, and what they did upon earth in his name, and according to his will and word, he engages to ratify in heaven And this is particularly addressed to Peter here, as being ordained to be the first preacher of the gospel both to the Jews and Gentiles, and as the honour conferred upon him for the glorious confession he had made

7 He strictly charges his disciples at present to conceal what they knew of his divine person and character and this for many reasons, because his hour was not yet come, and such declarations would exasperate the Pharisees to destroy him, alarm the government, and occasion an insurrection among the people, big with the hopes of a temporal Messiah, besides that they were to be better furnished, after his resurrection, with greater abilities for their work, and fuller evidence of the truth in their own souls, and for the conviction of others

21 ¶ From that time forth began Jesus to [n] shew
unto his disciples, how that he must go unto Jerusalem,
and suffer many things of the elders and chief priests,
and scribes, and be killed, and be raised again the third
day 22 Then Peter took him, and began to rebuke
him, saying, ¶ | Be it far from thee, Lord this shall not
be unto thee 23 But he turned, and said unto Peter,
[o] Get thee behind me, Satan, thou art an offence unto
me for thou savourest not the things that be of God,
but those that be of men

[n] Chap xx 17 Mark viii 31 Luke ix 22
| Or, Pity thyself
[o] 2 Sam xix 22

v 21—23 To check the aspiring hopes which his own disciples foolishly entertained concerning the nature of his kingdom, he begins to inform them of the sufferings he must undergo and *from that time*, when their faith appeared established in him, inculcated this mortifying lesson, as they were able to bear it Christ's method is to let us into the knowledge of his truth by degrees it would utterly have staggered us, if we had known at first all the discouragements we should afterwards meet with

1 He foretels his sufferings and death, (strange tidings to their ears) the scene of which would be in Jerusalem, the holy city, and the instruments the most admired characters, the elders, chief-priests, and scribes, who by their office and profession should have been the first to receive and honour him as the Messiah

Messiah but withal he informs them, to support their hopes, that the third day he should rise again And all this *must* be So God had decreed in his eternal counsels and no other way could the salvation of his people be secured

2 Peter, still the foremost to speak, though now as faulty as he had been before commendable, could not bear to hear of his death and sufferings, and therefore had the boldness to take him aside and expostulate with him, expressing his displeasure at what he had heard, his abhorrence of the thought of it, and his presumption that it was impossible the Messiah should thus suffer, and the Son of the living God be put to death *Note*, (1) Our hearts ill bear commendation; like Peter, we are too apt to presume upon it (2) How intricate soever God's ways may appear, and his dispensations however painful to us, it is not for us to question the rectitude of his procedure, or pretend to be wiser than he submission and silence are our bounden duty (3) Our corrupt nature ever shrinks from the cross with abhorrence Had Christ thus started back from it, what had become of us?

3 With a sharp rebuke the Lord testifies his displeasure against Peter *He turned*, with sternness in his look, *and said unto Peter*, in the hearing of the twelve, *Get thee behind me, Satan*, be gone thou speakest under his influence and this pretended kindness implies real enmity *Thou art an offence*, or *hindrance, to me*, opposing the great end for which I came into the world *for thou savourest not the things that be of God*, dost not relish the contrivance of infinite wisdom, for the manifestation of his own glory, and the redemption of sinners, by my sufferings, *but those that be of men*, expecting in the Messiah a temporal monarch, and influenced by the hopes of worldly wealth, power, and honour *Note*, (1) Left but for a moment to ourselves, however high our attainments have been, we must instantly sink under the power of Satan (2) We may find often as dangerous snares in the false kindness of our friends as in the avowed enmity of our foes (3) Whoever on any pretence would dissuade us from the path of duty, we must reject the advice with abhorrence, and rebuke them with severity. (4) Maxims of carnal policy, and desire of earthly ease and honour, are strangely apt to insinuate themselves even into good men, and disincline them from taking up that cross which God hath appointed them We have need of constant jealousy over our hearts, lest, imitating Peter's conduct, we should meet with his rebuke.

p Mark viii 34 Luke ix 23
q Chap x 38 Acts xiv 22 1 Thes iii 3 2 Tim iii 12
r Luke xvii 33 John xii 25
s Ps xlix 7, 8
t Chap xxvi 64 Dan vii 10 Chap xxv 31 Jude 14
x Prov xxiv 12 Jer xvii 10 2 Cor v 10
y Mark ix 1 Luke ix 27

24. ¶ [p] Then said Jesus unto his disciples, If any man
will come after me, let him deny himself, and [q] take up
his cross, and follow me 25 For [r] whosoever will save
his life, shall lose it · and whosoever will lose his life for
my sake, shall find it 26 For what is a man profited,
if he shall gain the whole world, and lose his own soul?
or [s] what shall a man give in exchange for his soul?
27 For [t] the Son of man shall come in the glory of his
Father, [u] with his angels, and then [x] he shall reward
every man according to his works 28 Verily I say
unto you, [y] There be some standing here, which shall
not taste of death, till they see the Son of man coming
in his kingdom

v 24—28 As he had foretold them of the sufferings himself must endure, he forewarns them also to expect the like treatment, and advertises them that only thus bearing his cross they could be truly his disciples

1 He plainly sets before them the terms of discipleship; very different from what their national prejudices suggested. *If any man will come after me*, a volunteer in my service, and chusing it with all the trials which for my sake he may be exposed to endure, *let him deny himself*, his own will and wisdom, his pride and self-righteousness, his carnal lusts and appetites, his worldly honour, ease, and advantage, and whatever else would tend to clog, retard, or turn him back from my service, *and* let him *take up his cross*, cheerfully submitting to every providential affliction, and ready to expose himself in the way of duty to persecutions, losses, reproaches, sufferings, yea, even to death itself, if need be, for my sake, and the open and avowed profession of my name *and* let him *follow me* in all humility, patience, faith, perseverance, stedfast and unmoveable in the work of the Lord, whether to do or suffer according to his holy will Hard terms for flesh and blood! Indeed we must have more than human ability, or they would be impracticable *Note*, (1) Self-denial is the first lesson of Christ's school (2) There never yet was a Christian without his cross Far therefore from being discouraged by what we suffer, we should rather conclude our real discipleship from this conformity to our Lord (3) It becomes us however to take care the cross we bear is the cross of Christ, and not what our own wilfulness or sins have brought upon us

2 Christ suggests the most powerful arguments to engage us with steadiness and cheerfulness to embrace his proposal

[1] An eternity of happiness or misery depends on our present choice and conduct. Whoever, by base and sinful compliances with a world that lieth in wickedness, would screen himself from sufferings and death, takes the direct method to destroy for ever the life he thus seeks to preserve Whilst he who with unshaken fidelity, for the sake of Christ and his gospel, is ready to endure the loss of all things, and even of life itself, rather than dishonour his profession, or betray the cause in which he is engaged, this man shall in eternity be unspeakably a gainer, and effectually secure the life he thus bravely dares to part with We must therefore weigh time against eternity, and, under the influences of realizing faith, shall not hesitate a moment, whether we shall suffer with Christ that we may reign with him, or, prolonging a momentary existence by our cowardice, perish everlastingly

[2] Our immortal souls are at stake, infinitely more valuable than ten thousand worlds Admit that we should, by complying with the world, gain all that it hath to bestow, wallow in its wealth, riot in its pleasures, or rise to the pinnacle of earthly grandeur, yet, if this be purchased by the loss of our souls for ever, driven from the presence of God, and consigned to everlasting torment, how inconceivably foolish will this bargain appear shortly, and how irreparable the damage? since, had a man millions of gold and silver, yea worlds unnumbered, to bestow, they would in God's account be lighter on the balances than vanity itself, yea, would be less than nothing, if proffered in exchange to redeem but one soul from death eternal *Note*, (1) The value of the soul and the vanity of the world should be the subjects of our frequent meditation (2) How many thousands are daily bartering their souls for the most miserable pittance of this world's honours, gain, and pleasures! and yet so hath the god of this world blinded them, that they will not see the folly, the madness of their pursuits (3) A soul lost, is lost for ever, there is no redemption in the grave (4) There is but one sufficient price to redeem the soul from death, and that is the blood of Christ, and all other things in God's account are as dung and dross

[3] The rewards of eternal glory will infinitely compensate all the sufferings of this present time This is a perishing world, the end of all things is at hand, the Judge is at the door; the Son of man shall come in all the glory of divinity, with his angelic guards around his throne of judgment, and then will he dispense his rewards according to men's works, when the faithful shall receive the eternal glory, honour, and immortality, he hath promised, and the wicked, the worldling and apostates, the wages of their iniquity in eternal torment *Note*, To live under the constant expectation of this great day, is the best means of strengthening us against every trial we may be called to encounter

[4] As an especial argument to secure their fidelity, Christ assures them, that some there present, before their death, should see the glory of the Messiah's kingdom begun, in his resurrection from the dead, the out-pouring of his Spirit in the day of Pentecost, the spreading of his gospel, and the destruction of the Jewish state and nation, their bitterest persecutors, which would be an emblem of the final perdition of all ungodly men in the judgment-day

CHAP XVII.

In this chapter we have, 1 Christ in his pomp and glory transfigured, ver 1—13 *2 Christ in his power and grace casting the devil out of a child*, ver 14—21 *And, 3 Christ in his poverty and great humiliation, (1) Foretelling his own sufferings*, ver 22, 23 *(2) Paying tribute*, ver 24—27

1 AND [a] after six days, Jesus taketh Peter, James
and John his brother, and bringeth them up
into an high mountain apart, 2 And was transfigured
before them, and [b] his face did shine as the sun, and his
raiment was white as the light 3 And behold, there
appeared unto them Moses and Elias talking with him
4 Then answered Peter, and said unto Jesus, Lord, it
is good for us to be here if thou wilt, let us make here
three tabernacles; one for thee, and one for Moses, and
one for Elias 5 While he yet spake, behold, a bright
cloud overshadowed them and [c] behold, a voice out of
the cloud, which said, [d] This is my beloved Son, [e] in
whom I am well pleased; [f] hear ye him 6 And when
the disciples heard *it*, they fell on their face, and were
sore afraid. 7 And Jesus came and [g] touched them,
and said, Arise, and be not afraid 8 And when they
had lift up their eyes, they saw no man, save Jesus only
9 And as they came down from the mountain, [h] Jesus
charged them, saying, Tell the vision to no man, until
the Son of man be risen again from the dead 10 And
his disciples asked him, saying, [i] Why then say the scribes,
that Elias must first come? 11. And Jesus answered
and said unto them, Elias truly shall first come, and [k] restore

a Mark ix 2 Luke ix 28
b Ex xxxiv 29, 35 2 Pet i 1
c 2 Pet i 17
d Chap iii 17
e Isa xlii 1
f Deut xviii 15, 18, 19
g Dan viii 18 x 18
h Chap xvi 20
i Mal iv 5
k Luke i 17

2

ſtore all things 12 But I ſay unto you, that Elias is
l Chap xiv 10 come already, and they knew him not, l but have done
m Chap xvi 21 unto him whatſoever they liſted m likewiſe ſhall alſo
the Son of man ſuffer of them 13 Then the diſciples
underſtood that he ſpake unto them of John the Bap-
tiſt

v 1—13 As Chriſt had ſo lately ſpoken of the Son of man's coming in his kingdom, he here gives them a glimpſe of his glory on the mount of transfiguration We are told,

1 When and where this happened, and who were the ſpectators It was *ſix* days after the former diſcourſe above recorded, or, according to St Luke, about *eight*, he taking in the day the diſcourſe paſſed, and that on which the transfiguration happened, and the other evangeliſts only mentioning the intervening ſpace of time The place was the top of a mountain apart, whither he had retired for prayer, with three of his diſciples, Peter, James, and John, whom he was pleaſed to favour with the glorious viſion, the lively impreſſion of which dwelt long after on their minds *See* 2 *Pet* i 16, 17

2 The manner of his transfiguration As he was praying, *Luke* ix 29 the glory of the divinity burſt forth, and he who bore the form of a ſervant ſuddenly appeared in the form of God, *Phil* ii 6 His face, as the ſun ſhining in its ſtrength, dazzled the beholders with its tranſcendent luſtre, and ſuch bright beams darted from his glorified body, that, ſurrounded with irradiation, his very raiment glittered, and became white as the light An awful pleaſing ſight! Happy the favoured ſouls who then beheld him! and yet far happier they who ſhall with open face behold him on the mount of God, and be changed into the ſame image, faſhioned like to his glorious body

3 The attendants who waited on him, Moſes and Elias They too appeared in glory Known probably to the diſciples by immediate revelation, or by the converſation they heard, which, we are told, *Luke* ix 31, reſpected Chriſt's ſufferings and death at Jeruſalem

4 Overwhelmed with wonder and delight, Peter, the ready ſpokeſman for his brethren, expreſſes the exulting rapture of his heart, and wiſhes for the continuance of the glorious viſion Fain would he forever there fix his body, and with a mixture of commendable piety and inconſiderate weakneſs, propoſes to make three booths, where Chriſt with his celeſtial viſitants might dwell, ſcarce knowing what he ſaid through the tranſport of his mind *Note*, (1) They who have ever known experimentally the ſweetneſs of communion with Jeſus, and have by faith beheld ſome of his glory, long to maintain the delightful intercourſe, for it is good to be with him (2) The place to enjoy Chriſt's viſits is not in the buſy world, or gay circle, but in retirement, meditation, and prayer in this mount of the Lord he may ſtill be ſeen (3) Though in ſome happy moments we ſeem for a while upon the glorious hill, we have now no abiding tabernacle there, and quickly the bright viſion is removed! Bleſſed be God however, we look for a houſe not made with hands, eternal in the heavens, and there we ſhall be ever with the Lord

5 A bright cloud, at the inſtant Peter ſpoke, overſhadowed them, the emblem of the Divine Preſence, and from the excellent glory iſſued forth the voice of God the Father proclaiming the dignity, excellence, and acceptableneſs of his dear Son Jeſus, and enjoining on them ſolemn attention to all his words *This is my beloved Son, in whom I am well pleaſed, hear ye him* Where we may obſerve, (1) That this was a repetition of what had been declared at Chriſt's baptiſm, containing the grand truth on which our everlaſting hopes depend, that God is well pleaſed with the undertaking of Jeſus, and is in him reconciling ſinners to himſelf, ſatisfied with his ſubſtitution on their behalf, and therefore not imputing their treſpaſſes unto them (2) There never hath appeared but one Perſon under the ſun concerning whom God could ſay, In him I am well pleaſed, and that was his own Son Him therefore we muſt hear, ſince only by and through him can God be well pleaſed with us his blood, his righteouſneſs, muſt be alone our truſt, his word of goſpel-grace our conſtant rule, his will our duty and delight Lord, ſpeak thou to my heart, that I may thus hear thee!

6 Terrified with the appearance of the Divine Majeſty, and trembling at the voice of God, the diſciples proſtrated themſelves on the earth in ſilent adoration, conſcious of their own vileneſs, and afraid to lift up their eyes before the holy Lord God But Jeſus kindly approached and quieted their fears, encouraged them to riſe, and bid them not be afraid, the voice they had heard was not that of an angry God, but of the Father of mercies, not ſpeaking out of the thick darkneſs, as on mount Sinai, the demands of a perfect law, but out of the bright cloud of goſpel light and love, publiſhing ſalvation, and pointing them to a Redeemer *Note*, (1) Conſciouſneſs of guilt muſt ever make us dread to appear before a jealous God It is in Chriſt's righteouſneſs alone we can with boldneſs approach his throne (2) Jeſus is the comforter of his afflicted people, and when we are diſmayed under what we feel or fear, and ready to ſink down in deſpair, his words of conſolation revive our drooping heads, and embolden us to look up

7 Riſing at the command of Jeſus, when they looked round the viſion had diſappeared, and Moſes and Elias were gone Jeſus however ſtill remained with them in his uſual form as before his transfiguration *Note*, If Chriſt remain with us, we can eaſily reſt content with the loſs of any thing beſides

8 He charged them, as they came down from the mount, to make no notice of the viſion they had ſeen, but reſerve it till his reſurrection from the dead, when that would add credibility to their report, which now, conſidering the ſtate of ſufferings which was before him, might be diſbelieved and rejected

9 A difficulty aroſe in the diſciples mind. revolving what had paſſed, the ſhort ſtay Elias made, and the injunctions of ſecreſy laid upon them, why it ſhould be ſo often inculcated by the ſcribes that Elias muſt firſt come, publickly uſhering in the appearing of the Meſſiah, and this queſtion they begged their maſter to reſolve which he doth to their full ſatisfaction He tells them, it was true that Elias muſt be the forerunner of the Meſſiah, as was propheſied, *Mal* iv 5, 6 and by his preaching *reſtore all things*, preach the doctrines of repentance, and direct the people to him who comes to make all things new But this had already been fulfilled, there had appeared one in the *ſpirit* and power of Elias, whom they knew not, as the perſon meant by the prophecy, and him the Scribes and Phariſees in general had rejected, and treated with contempt, and Herod had murdered him And as they had perſecuted to death the meſſenger, ſo would they deal by the maſter, that *Son of man*, whoſe way he was ſent to prepare, who would ſuffer the like indignities, cruelty, and death itſelf by their hands *Note*, (1) When we do not thoroughly underſtand any paſſage of ſcripture, we muſt go to Chriſt on our knees, and ſhall find prayer the beſt means of arriving at the truth (2) If we are treated with inſult and cruelty by the world, let it not be thought ſtrange we are compaſſed with a great cloud of witneſſes who have trod the way before us

Laſtly, The diſciples now underſtood clearly what he meant, and that John the Baptiſt was the perſon to whom he pointed, and from the fulfilment of the prophecy in him, they received a freſh confirmation of their faith in Jeſus, as the Chriſt

14 ¶ n And when they were come to the multitude, n Mark ix
there came to him a *certain* man kneeling down to him, 14 Luke ix.
and ſaying, 15 Lord, have mercy on my ſon, for he 37
is lunatic, and ſore vexed for oft-times he falleth into
the fire, and oft into the water 16 And I brought him
to thy diſciples, and they could not cure him 17 Then
Jeſus anſwered and ſaid, O faithleſs and perverſe gene-
ration, how long ſhall I be with you? how long ſhall I
ſuffer you? bring him hither to me 18 And Jeſus re-
buked the devil, and he departed out of him and the
child was cured from that very hour 19 Then came
the diſciples to Jeſus apart, and ſaid, Why could not we
caſt him out? 20 And Jeſus ſaid unto them, Becauſe
of your unbelief for verily I ſay unto you, o if ye have o Chap. xxi
faith as a grain of muſtard ſeed, ye ſhall ſay unto this 21 Mark
mountain, Remove hence to yonder place, and it ſhall xi 23 Luke xvii 6
remove, and nothing ſhall be impoſſible unto you 21 1 Co xiii 2
Howbeit this kind goeth not out, but by prayer and
faſting

v 14—21 The next day, when Jeſus, with the three diſciples, returned from the mountain, to the reſt of their company and the people who waited for him, he found his preſence greatly needed, and opportunely arrived to give a freſh diſplay of his power and mercy

1 An afflicted father addreſſes him on his knees, in behalf of his only ſon, poſſeſſed with a devil, a lunatic, and frequently ſeized with epileptic fits, in which he fell into the fire or water, which ever he chanced to be near, to the great hazard of his life In the abſence of Chriſt he had applied in vain to the diſciples, who were unable to caſt him out, ſo that unleſs he could help, the caſe was deſperate *Note*, (1) Tender parents ſuffer in every pang which their children feel (2) Under all their diſeaſes of body or ſoul, we muſt carry our children's miſeries to Jeſus, and at leaſt commend them in prayer to him, when every other means and method fail

2 Chriſt compaſſionates the caſe, and bids the patient be brought to him, but directs a ſharp rebuke to that perverſe and faithleſs generation the Scribes and Phariſees, and people who probably inſulted the diſciples on their failure in attempting the cure, and imagined this was a caſe which would baffle the maſter's ſkill Juſtly he upbraids them with their unbelief and hardneſs of heart, after all the miracles he had wrought before them, and well might he refuſe any longer to bear with their perverſeneſs Yet his patience waits, and he will give them freſh inſtances of his power, that at leaſt they may be inexcuſable in their rejecting him *Note*, (1) Nothing is ſo provoking to the Redeemer, as the perverſeneſs and unbelief of thoſe, to whom he hath long vouchſafed the means of grace (2) Men's wickedneſs will not prevent the exerciſe of Chriſt's goodneſs

 and

and if this leads them not to repentance, it will heap up wrath upon them against the day of wrath

3 Jesus, with a word, dispossessed the devil, and the child immediately received a perfect cure Before his authoritative command, Satan fell a vanquished foe, and by the word of Jesus, the sword of the spirit, and the shield of faith, shall we still triumph over the powers of darkness, and see the arch-enemy of our souls bruised under our feet

4 The disciples took the first opportunity, when alone, to enquire of their master why they had failed in attempting the cure, and dispossessing the evil spirit, being concerned perhaps for their reputation among the people, or fearful lest they had provoked the Lord to withdraw that miraculous power he had once bestowed on them *Note*, When we see ourselves baffled in contending with the powers of evil, it becomes us seriously to enquire how we came to fail, and by what means the fault may be amended

5 Christ gives them a full answer it was *their unbelief* which prevented the cure Whilst the multitude in general were *utterly* faithless, *they* were culpable in a *lesser measure*, for, though they were not utterly destitute of faith, they had at this time failed in the exercise of it For else, the least measure of this miraculous faith, possessed and exerted, was sufficient to remove the mountain now before them, and to do whatever else, however to human view impossible, should be needful to confirm the truth of their mission, to promote the glory of God and the good of mankind but this faith must be the fruit of earnest prayer and fasting, the means appointed of God for the obtaining it Some refer the words, *this kind*, not to faith, but to the devils, supposing some more difficult to be dispossessed than others, and considering this as another reason why they could not succeed but the former sense appears preferable *Note*, (1) Whenever we fail in duty, and are foiled in temptation, to this we must ever ascribe it, It is *because of our unbelief* (2) Though we may not be classed with unbelievers, yet have we daily cause to lament the weakness of our faith (3) The faith of miracles is ceased, we cannot now say to this mountain, Remove but it is as great an instance of divine power, and requires as real an exercise of divine faith, to remove the mountains of guilt and corruption And, blessed be the Lord, this faith remaineth in all the elect people of God

p Chap xvi 21 & xx 18 Mark ix 31 Luke ix 44 Acts ii 23
22 ¶ p And while they abode in Galilee, Jesus said
unto them, q The Son of man shall be betrayed into
the hands of men 23 And they shall kill him, and
the third day he shall be raised again And they were
exceeding sorry

v 22, 23 While they were journeying through Galilee, in their return to Capernaum, we are told,

1 That Jesus again took occasion to remind his disciples of the sufferings to which, according to the eternal counsels of God, he must be delivered up, through the treachery and malice of wicked men, who, thirsting for his blood, would murder him by the most cruel and ignominious death, *see Luke* xxiv 7 But for their comfort he added, on the third day he should rise again

2 His disciples appeared exceeding sorry, and deeply affected with what he told them They did not understand what his rising again meant, and then all the rest appeared dark and dismal, and utterly contradictory to those opinions of the Messiah which they had entertained *Note*, Through the darkness of our mind we suffer, needlessly, many a gloomy hour under afflictive providences We do not look to their end, or understand how all these things are working together for our good if we did, we should be always rejoicing

r Mark ix 33 † A coin worth fifteen pence Ex xxx 13 & xxxviii 26
24 ¶ And when r they were come to Capernaum,
they that received tribute-*money* came to Peter, and
said, Doth not your master pay tribute? 25 He saith,
Yes And when he was come into the house, Jesus pre-
vented him, saying, What thinkest thou, Simon? of
whom do the kings of the earth take custom or tribute?
of their own children, or of strangers? 26 Peter saith
unto him, Of strangers Jesus saith unto him, Then
are the children free 27 Notwithstanding, lest we
should offend them, go thou to the sea, and cast an hook,
and take up the fish that first cometh up and when thou
hast opened his mouth, thou shalt find ‡ a piece of money
that take, and s give unto them, for me and thee

‡ Gr A stater which was worth 2s 6d
s Rom xiii

v 24—27, The tribute mentioned here was the half shekel, about fifteen pence in value, which every Jew, above twenty years of age, paid annually to the temple for the maintenance of the service

1 The collectors of this tax applied to Peter, at whose house, probably, Jesus dwelt when at Capernaum, *Matt* viii 14 to know if his Master did not pay the usual tribute And Peter, not doubting his Master was inclined to comply with the established law, answered in the affirmative

2 Jesus prevented him, as he came to speak to him of the matter, with a question, which shewed his omniscience as acquainted with the purpose of his coming, and the right he had to exemption, had he chosen to plead his privilege *Of whom do the kings of the earth take custom, or tribute, of their own children, or of strangers?* their subjects, or foreigners who trade in their country? The answer was obvious and Peter instantly replied, Such taxes could be exacted from none but strangers, since to tax their own children would be absurd and useless *Then*, said Jesus, *are the children free*, and consequently I, who am the Son of God, for the service of whose temple this is levied, am excused from the payment of it Nevertheless he waves his right, though so poor as to be unable, without a miracle, to furnish the pittance demanded, and, to avoid the appearance of offence to those who, not knowing his character, might be led to esteem him, if he had refused to pay, a despiser of the temple, and thereby might be prejudiced against his doctrine, he orders Peter to go to the sea, and, baiting his hook, to take up the first fish which came to it, in the mouth of which he would find a stater, a piece of money of the value of a Jewish shekel, which would just suffice to pay for both, and remove all occasion of offence We may learn hence, (1) The divine perfections which shone forth in Jesus during his humiliation All creatures are under his controul, and subservient to his pleasure he appears acquainted with all that passes in the heart of man and in the depths of the sea thus, even when in the form of a man, shewing still his divine power and Godhead (2) If Christ paid tribute, and submitted to the powers in church and state, who can plead a right to exemption? (3) In many cases it is a Christian's duty to wave his title to what may be strictly his due, and even to suffer in his secular interests, rather than give offence, or prejudice any against the gospel We shall in the end be no losers by such self-denial (4) When Christ would work a miracle, Peter must use the appointed means, for it is in the way of diligence in duty, not in sloth, that we can expect a divine interposition in our behalf (5) When Christ could have furnished all his wants for ever, he chose just a sufficiency for the present emergence, and depended for a subsistence afterwards in the ordinary way, to teach us, if we have enough for to-day, to trust God for the morrow

CHAP XVIII

We have here, 1 Instructions concerning humility, ver 1—6 2 Concerning offences in general, ver 7 particularly offences given, (1) By us to ourselves, ver 8, 9 (2) By us to others, ver 10—14 (3) By others to us, which are of two sorts, [1] Scandalous sins, that are to be reproved, ver 15—20 [2] Personal wrongs, that are to be forgiven, ver 21—35 See how practical Christ's preaching was he could have revealed mysteries, but he pressed plain duties, especially those that are most displeasing to flesh and blood

a Mark ix 33 Luke ix 46 & xxii 24
1 a AT the same time came the disciples unto Jesus,
saying, Who is the greatest in the kingdom
of heaven? 2 And Jesus called a little child unto him,
and set him in the midst of them, 3 And said, Verily
I say unto you, Except ye be converted, and b become
as little children, ye shall not enter into the kingdom
of heaven 4 c Whosoever therefore shall humble him-
self as this little child, the same is greatest in the
kingdom of heaven 5 And d whoso shall receive one
such little child in my name, receiveth me 6 But
e whoso shall offend one of these little ones which believe
in me, it were better for him that a millstone were hanged
about his neck, and *that* he were drowned in the depth
of the sea

b 1 Cor xiv 20 c Chap xx 27 1 Pet v 5 d Chap x 42 e Mark ix 42 Luke xvii 1

v 1—7 The disciples, deeply tinctured with Jewish prejudices, entertained very false conceptions of the Messiah's kingdom, and had, in the way to Capernaum, been disputing which of them should have the precedence in it Jesus, who knew what had been the subject of their contention, now asked them concerning it And, after some silence and shame at being discovered, *see Mark* ix 33, 34 they,

1 Propose to him the question in dispute, which of them should be promoted to the first post of honour in his kingdom, for each had formed some pretence to this distinguished place And so ready are we all to be partial in our own favour, instead of being humbly content, in the views of our real deserts, to sit down with the least and the lowest

2 By an apposite emblem Christ seeks to rebuke their vanity, and teach them what spirit they should put on He took a little child and set him in the midst of them, that they might look and learn whilst he commented on the case assuring them, that such was the nature of his kingdom, that none could enter therein, or partake of its honours and privileges, unless their heart were converted, and turned from the affectation of earthly grandeur and greatness, and, like little children, they become dead to the

con-

contentions of ambition, and the vain desires of outward wealth and eminence. Whilst the way to secure the most honourable place among his members upon earth, and the highest throne next his own in glory, was by sinking lowest in their own apprehensions of themselves, and, instead of affecting magisterial dominion over others, becoming humble, teachable, and ready to sit down at the feet of the meanest. Hard lessons these for human pride! *Note*, (1.) Besides our first general conversion from a state of nature to a state of grace, we need conversion daily from the errors and evils that still would be cleaving to us, and therefore must continually pray, Turn thou us, and so shall we be turned. (2.) The way to honour is humility. The lowliest souls are dearest to the Lord, they most resemble him. Whilst pride made angels devils, defaced God's image from the human soul, drove man from paradise, and bars the gate against his return.

3. Christ expresses his high regard and tender concern for those who in this childlike spirit are his disciples indeed. Whosoever shall shew them the least kindness, for the sake of their relation to him, he will regard it as if the favour had been shewn to his own person. Whilst to offend one of these, to persecute or oppress them, to take advantage of their simplicity or meekness to trample on them, or of their weakness to endeavour to deceive or discourage them, the most dreadful of judgments will be the punishment of such an offender: and better were it for him to have come to the most fearful death by the hands of the public executioner, even to be thrown into the sea with a milstone about his neck, than with such guilt to fall into the hands of an avenging God, under whose wrath he must perish, both body and soul, in hell. *Note*, (1.) Christ has the tenderest care for his poor people; and a cup of cold water given to the meanest in his name shall not lose its reward. (2.) It is a fearful thing to fall into the hands of a jealous God. They who now oppress and oppose the meek disciples of Jesus little think against whom they offend, and the vengeance which awaits them.

f 1 Cor xi 19 7 ¶ Wo unto the world because of offences! for [f] it
g Chap xxvi 24 must needs be that offences come; but [g] wo to that man
h Chap v 29 30 by whom the offence cometh! 8 Wherefore [h] if thy
Mark ix 43 hand or thy foot offend thee, cut them off, and cast *them*
from thee: it is better for thee to enter into life halt or
maimed, rather than, having two hands or two feet, to
be cast into everlasting fire. 9 And if thine eye offend
thee, pluck it out, and cast *it* from thee: it is better for
thee to enter into life with one eye, rather than, having
i Rom xiv 3 10, 21 two eyes, to be cast into hell-fire. 10 [i] Take heed that
k Pf xxxiv 7 Heb i ye despise not one of these little ones; for I say unto you,
14 that in heaven [k] their angels do always [l] behold the face
l ... 19 of my Father which is in heaven. 11 For [m] the Son of
m Luke ix 56 man is come to save that which was lost. 12 How
Luke xix 10 think ye? [n] if a man have an hundred sheep, and [o] one
n Luke xv 4 of them be gone astray, doth he not leave the ninety and
o Ifa liii 6 nine, and goeth into the mountains, and [p] seeketh that
Jer l 6 which is gone astray? 13 And if so be that he find it,
p Ezek xxxiv 16. verily I say unto you, he rejoiceth more of that *sheep*,
than of the ninety and nine which went not astray.
14 Even so it is not the will of your Father which is in
heaven, that one of these little ones should perish.

v. 7—14. We have here the wo denounced against the world because of offences. Under which are comprehended whatever hath a tendency to seduce or affright the soul from the good way of the Lord, or to discourage and grieve the hearts of the righteous.

1. That there will be offences is certain. Considering the craft, malice, and vigilance of Satan, the perverseness of ungodly men and their rooted enmity to the gospel, and, above all, the deep and desperate native wickedness of every human heart, it is morally impossible offences should not come; and God, for wise ends, hath decreed to permit them: but this will in no wise extenuate the guilt of those by whom the offence cometh, nor abate the severity of their judgment. *Note*, (1.) We are travelling a dangerous road: this world is full of evil, of snares and stumbling-blocks; the multitude lieth in wickedness; and many who pretend to know the path of safety only lie in wait to deceive. We need be jealous of our going, cleave to God's word alone, and neither be offended with the enmity of those that are without, nor the hypocrisy and falls of those that are professors within, remembering *the foundation of God standeth sure. He knoweth those that are his*, and will keep them, that *nothing shall offend them*, Pf cxix 165. (2.) Though the deceived and the deceiver perish together, yet will *they* lie down under aggravated guilt who have been Satan's instruments to lead others into error or sin. Their blood will be upon the heads of their seducers.

2. Whatever may be occasion of offence to ourselves or others, however near and dear to us it may be, we must part with it. The body of sin must be crucified. And though it may be as painful to mortify particular corruptions as to suffer the amputation of a hand or a foot, unrelenting severity is needful, where our own souls or others are in danger. And however acute the pain, or however sensibly felt the loss may be, it is better, infinitely better to endure the momentary pang of present self-denial, that we may escape eternal misery, and secure a life of never-ending glory, than for a transitory indulgence of appetite, and the sensual enjoyments of an hour, to be cast into devouring fire, and dwell in everlasting burnings. *Note*, (1.) In this state of corruption, not only the grosser pollutions that are in the world through lust must be abhorred, but every word, every action, be avoided, which may tend in the remotest way to inflame our own passions or ensnare others. (2.) It is of absolute necessity that we should often in temptation look at the burnings of hell, and gain from thence arguments to start from the most pleasurable sins. (3.) They only who have begun the life of grace know experimentally what is meant by these severe operations of self-denial.

3. A particular caution is given to beware of despising the least of Christ's little ones, the weakest of his disciples. We may not be indifferent about our carriage towards them, careless of what may offend them, must not treat them with contempt, as if regardless of their welfare, or slighting their weakness or infirmities, nor do ought to distress, discourage, ensnare, or lead them into sin; but we should shew our tenderness towards them, and our jealousy for them, by every expression of kindness in word or deed, and by a careful avoiding whatever may grieve or hurt them.

4. He enforces his discourse by several cogent arguments.

[1.] Because the meanest heir of salvation is attended by angelic ministers. And if those glorious spirits, who in heaven behold the face of God, and stand around his throne, the ready servants of his will, do not disdain to wait upon these little ones, much less should we think them beneath our regard; and may justly dread, if we should treat them ill, these guardian spirits would be our accusers, and be employed as executioners of the divine displeasure against us.

[2.] Because it is the very purpose of Christ's coming to seek and save lost souls. And if, on this transcendently gracious design, he condescended to stoop so low, the least of those for whom he became incarnate have hereby an unutterable dignity and value conferred upon them, and therefore should neither be despised nor offended, for this he must highly resent. *Note*, (1.) Our souls are lost, eternally lost, without Christ Jesus. (2.) Salvation is purely of grace. When we were without help or hope, he died for the ungodly. (3.) They who are purchased by the blood of Christ should be precious in our eyes. If he did so much to save them, surely we should be peculiarly careful to do nothing to offend them.

[3.] Because it is God's will and pleasure that not one of these little ones perish. And we are bound to correspond with him herein, and according to our ability to help forward the purposes of his grace, and put no stumbling-blocks in their way. Our Lord illustrates this by a parable, and appeals to them as judges of the case. Suppose a man possessed of a hundred sheep, and one be strayed from the flock, his sollicitude is greater in searching after it, and his joy more sensible on finding it, than he feels about all the rest which went not astray. And such concern hath God for the wandering children of his grace, recovering them and rejoicing over them: and, as he hath in his eternal counsels determined their salvation, he cannot but be highly displeased with all who attempt to obstruct it, or are careless about advancing it, and regards such conduct as an avowed opposition, or criminal disregard, of his holy will and pleasure. *Note*, (1.) God's people are his flock, and though sometimes they wander from him in the wilderness of sin, he will not suffer them to perish, but graciously is pleased to pursue them with mercy, and bring them back to the fold again. (2.) Though none can frustrate the purposes of God's love towards his redeemed, yet every obstruction laid in their way he will highly resent. (3.) Since all true believers, of whatever state or condition, have one common Father, they should love as brethren, honour and esteem each other as members of the same family, avoid every occasion of grieving one another, and study every means of advancing their mutual good.

15 ¶ Moreover, [q] if thy brother shall trespass against q Lev xix
thee, go and tell him his fault between thee and him 17 Luke
alone: if he shall hear thee, thou hast gained thy brother. xvii 3
16 But if he will not hear *thee, then* take with thee one or
two more, that [r] in the mouth of two or three witnesses r Numb xxxv 30
every word may be established. 17 And if he shall neg- Deut xix
lect to hear them, tell it unto the church; but if he neglect 15 John viii 17
to hear the church, let him be unto thee [s] as an heathen 2 Cor xiii 1 s Rom xvi
man, and a publican. 18 Verily I say unto you, 17 1 Cor
[t] Whatsoever ye shall bind on earth, shall be bound in v 11 2 Thef iii 6
heaven: and whatsoever ye shall loose on earth, shall be t Chap xvi
loosed in heaven. 19 Again I say unto you, that if two 19 John xx 23
of you shall agree on earth as touching any thing that u Jam v 16.
they shall ask, [u] it shall be done for them of my Father 1 John iii 22 & v 14.
which

which is in heaven 20 For where two or three are
gathered together in my name, there am I in the midst
of them

v 15—20 As we must be careful not to give offence, as careful should we be to shew all Christian tenderness and charity when we are justly offended Since in this frail and corrupted state even good men are but men, and liable to fall, transgressing the precepts of prudence, justice, or charity, we are therefore here directed in such cases how to behave towards them

1 If brother, *a professing member of our most holy faith*, act unsuitable thereunto, and do us an injury, or give us cause of complaint against him, we must first give him a private and kind admonition of his fault, and mildly argue the case, *desiring to bring him to repentance and amendment, more sollicitous for his good, than the redress of our own wrongs* We may not in this case, through fear of offending on the one hand, be silent, and suffer sin upon our brother without rebuke, nor, *on the other, give way to our anger or revenge*, and by a public reproof expose him to others, which, however true the charge, would serve not to recover, but exasperate him the more In this way of mild and secret admonition we may hope for *success*, and if he *express his sorrow, and desire reconciliation*, then the rebuke will be esteemed a kindness, the friendship more strongly cemented, our brother recovered, and the offence forgiven and forgotten

2 *If this method of reproof prove abortive*, and he is obstinate against conviction, and displeased instead of humbling himself, then take two or three faithful impartial Christian brethren, and in their presence let the matter be discussed, that they *may hear and judge*, and add their weight to bring the party offending to due submission and reparation of the injury Or if their sentiments be disregarded also, they will be evidences before the church of the steps which have been taken, and ready *to confirm the truth of the just accusation of the injured person*

3 If every other method prove ineffectual, then the matter should be laid before the church, the society of faithful people among whom such a one associates, that he may have a public admonition *for his offence*, and be called upon to repent and amend of the evil he hath done

4 If he still remains incorrigible, and persists in his iniquity, then he is to be excluded from the communion of the faithful, and no more connection and familiarity is to be maintained with him, for the charity which teaches us to forgive our enemies, forbids us not to be on our guard against those who have used us ill, and refuse to repair the injury From the whole we may learn, (1) Under every injury received, to guard our own hearts against passion or revenge this wrath of man worketh not the righteousness of God (2) Never to speak of another's faults behind his back, till we have in love and the spirit of meekness first admonished him to his face (3) To be ready under every provocation to forgive and forget, the moment real repentance appears in our brother (4) Not to endeavour to form a party in our favour, but in cases of offence, real or supposed, where the sentiments of brethren may differ about the facts, to let some common impartial friends hear and judge, before the matter be mentioned in public, or but whispered to others

5 Christ delegates authority to his church thus to censure offenders, and ratifies the sentence that shall be pronounced in correspondence with this his revealed word So that those who for their notorious evils are excluded from the society of the faithful now, shall be written among the reprobates, and for ever banished from the presence of God, unless they repent of their transgressions, and then they are again to be received into the bosom of the church, and all that is past to be entirely forgiven The absolution pronounced on them by the minister of God on earth shall be ratified in heaven, and the correction having become effectual, the broken-hearted penitent is to be comforted, and restored to his former place, both in the church of God, and in our brotherly affection and regard

6 For their encouragement in every religious concern, and especially with regard to the recovery of those who are fallen into sin, that they may be restored, our Lord declares the mighty efficacy of united prayer Whatever, according to the divine will, two or three faithful souls shall meet together with joint supplications to beg at God's hands, he will assuredly hear and grant their request For wherever the smallest number of real believers assemble in Christ's name, depending on his promises, and desiring above all things the advancement of his glory, there will he ever be quickening their prayers, strengthening their faith, enlivening their hopes, and comforting their hearts, and when he is one of the company, their supplications must be effectual, for him the Father heareth always, and what an encouragement is this to social prayer!

21 ¶ Then came Peter to him, and said, Lord, how
oft shall my brother sin against me, and I forgive him?
* till seven times? 22 Jesus saith unto him, I say not
unto thee, Until seven times ʸ but, until seventy times
seven 23 ¶ Therefore is the kingdom of heaven lik-
ened unto a certain king which would take account of
his servants 24 And when he had begun to reckon,
one was brought unto him, which owed him ten thou-
sand † talents 25 But forasmuch as he had not to
pay, his lord commanded him to be sold, and his wife,
and * children, and all that he had, and payment to be
made 26 The servant therefore fell down, and wor-
shipped him, saying, Lord, have patience with me, and
I will pay thee all 27 Then the lord of that servant
was moved with compassion, and loosed him, and for-
gave him the debt 28 But the same servant went out,
and found one of his fellow servants, which owed him
‡ an hundred pence and he laid hands on him, and
took *him* by the throat, saying, Pay me that thou owest
29 And his fellow-servant fell down at his feet, and
besought him, saying, Have patience with me, and I
will pay thee all 30 And he would not but went
and cast him into prison, till he should pay the debt
31 So when his fellow-servants saw what was done, they
were very sorry, and came and told unto their lord all
that was done 32 Then his lord, after that he had
called him, said unto him, O thou wicked servant, I
forgave thee all that debt, because thou desiredst me
33 Shouldst not thou also have had compassion on thy
fellow-servant, even as I had pity on thee? 34 And
his lord was wroth, and delivered him to the tormentors,
till he should pay all that was due unto him 35 * So
likewise shall my heavenly Father do also unto you, if
ye from your hearts forgive not every one his brother
their trespasses

v 21—35 As our Lord had just given directions concerning the charitable conduct to be observed towards offenders, Peter, desirous to know how far this forgiveness of personal injuries extended, proposed to his Master the question, Whether, if the offence was repeated seven times, the forgiveness must be as often granted on the repentance of the offender? He concluded this a great stretch of charity, but our Lord's answer shewed him how limited were his apprehensions *I say not unto thee, Until seven times but, until seventy times seven* intimating, that we must make no limitation to our forgiveness, but be always and in all cases ready to grant it, whenever the offender *repents*, *imitating the divine compassions, which know no bounds, nor end* And to enforce and elucidate this, he introduces a parable, wherein the godlike charity appears most eminent, and the guilt and danger of the opposite conduct is drawn *in striking colours*

The parable represents,

1 The noble clemency of a great lord, who looking into his affairs, and revising his own accounts, (which it were well if every great man did) found, among other debtors, one who owed him an immense sum, the least part of which he was unable to discharge In consequence whereof, in course of law, he gave orders that himself and family should be sold for slaves, and all he had disposed of for his use But, terrified at the sentence, though just, the poor debtor intreats a respite, with many fair promises of payment, when, moved with his distress, the compassionate master generously and freely forgave him all, and delivered him at once from his terrors and his debt And this may be applied to the case between God and the sinner (1) We are deeply in arrear to him every sin is a debt, and we are overwhelmed with it we possess a sinful nature, and our thoughts, words, and deeds have been so perverse before God, so often and so greatly have we offended, that no computation can reach the number of our transgressions, nor can we conceive the greatness of our guilt or provocations (2) The misery of our case, and what renders it most deplorable, yea, desperate, is, that we have nothing to pay Could we render by a perfect obedience the present debt of duty, this would make no compensation for past iniquity, but indeed, our nature being corrupt, we are so far from paying for the past offences, that we are daily, hourly increasing the immense arrears (3) God keeps an account of all not a word is in our tongue, nor a thought in our hearts, but he knoweth it all together, so that we can no more conceal our transgressions from him, than we can cancel them (4) If the divine law takes its course, the consequence must be, that we should be sold to suffer for our iniquities, and in the place of torment, in body and soul continue *satisfying the justice of God to eternity* (5) The discovery of this dreadful situation made to the sinner's soul by the preaching of the word to his conscience, or some awakening providence, fills him with terror, and sets him a crying for mercy But usually at first the cries of the awakened conscience are for a respite, with many promises of amendment, which the sinner foolishly thinks will be accepted in payment And he does not see his own utter insolvency, but thinks, though

the ignorance and self-righteousness of his heart, that he can make God some payment, till by and by the trial convinces him his best is bad, and self-despair strips him naked at the feet of the cross of Christ (6.) God's infinite compassions extend through the Redeemer to the most guilty and desperate He freely and fully forgives all that is past not that he doth it without a satisfaction made to his justice, this the Son of his love, incarnate, and dying under the guilt of our sins, hath paid, but the mercy of pardon, reconciliation, and deliverance from the bondage of guilt and corruption, is to us freely given, to the praise of the glory of his grace, without money and without price

2 We are told the unsuitable conduct this much obliged servant shewed respecting a fellow-servant of his, who owed him a trifling debt He no sooner obtained his own pardon and liberty, than he went out, seized and throttled him, till he was almost choaked, and with menaces and insolence demanded instant payment, or threatened him with a prison In vain his poor brother begged a respite, and, in the very words himself had used, desired only time, and the debt should be paid, he was deaf to intreaty, and thrust him into a jail a piece of cruelty and oppression, that the other servants beheld with grief and indignation, and failed not to acquaint their lord with this inhuman behaviour *Note*, (1.) Many professors, who presume upon God's forgiveness, shew, by their covetousness and rigorous censures of others, the hypocrisy of their hearts, and the vanity of their hopes (2.) Offences done to us, compared with those we have committed against God, are so trivial, that we should be ashamed to show rigour in exacting reparation (3.) Pride and passion render men unmerciful though they know a prison pays no debts, they take delight in this gratifying their insolence or revenge (4.) The debtor may not complain, though he be dealt with rigorously, humble in treaty becomes his condition, especially when he suffers only the fruits of his folly or extravagance (5.) A compassionate heart feels for the distresses of others, and, if it can afford no other relief to them, carries the case of the oppressor and the oppressed to God in prayer, and his ears are open thereunto, he will answer in mercy and judgment (6.) It is especially grievous to a gracious soul, to see in professors of religion a spirit of bitterness and unmercifulness, and he laments it before the Lord

3 Just resentment fired the master's heart on hearing these tidings, and instantly citing this hardened wretch before him, he charges him with his wickedness, and upbraids him with his cruelty and ingratitude for all the mercies he had so lately received, expostulating with him on the case, and leaving him without excuse In wrath he bids him therefore instantly be seized, and delivered to the tormentors, to be confined in prison, and suffer the most rigorous punishment, till all the former debt should be paid

Some have urged this circumstance as an argument, that God really pardons sin, and leaves us on our good behaviour for the future, but if we transgress, then he revive the past But as God's *gifts and callings are without repentance*, and we are assured that he *remembers no more* the iniquities he once forgave, (*Heb* viii 12.) we must understand the forgiveness here (if we suppose the parable is in every particular to be applied to the sinner's case) to be the presumption the person entertained on the view of the gospel offers, that he was pardoned, when in fact he was not Or if we suppose it a real act of forgiveness to a child of God, his being delivered to the tormentor for his after sin and ingratitude, may well refer to the temporal calamities that God is often pleased to inflict on his people for their offences, visiting their iniquities with the rod, and their sin with scourges though his loving-kindness he doth not take from them, nor suffer his truth to fail But, after all, I am much more inclined to think, that the scope of the parable is principally to be attended to, without a strict application of it in every particular to God's dealing with sinners, and then we shall see nothing can be more suited to enforce mutual forgiveness, since without it we may not hope ourselves to be forgiven of God And thus,

The general design of the parable is explained, *v.* 35. God will deal with us as we deal with our brethren, and if we shew an implacable and unforgiving spirit, whatever hopes of pardon we may entertain, they are delusive, his wrath hangs over us, and in the great day of account we shall be delivered to the tormentors. Most bounden are we therefore to forgive every injury, nor ever harbour the least wish or desire of revenge, so we expect greater mercy and forgiveness from God, than ever can come from us, and therefore a sense of his pardoning love should kindle ours.

CHAP. XIX.

In this chapter we have, 1. Christ changing his quarters, leaving Galilee, and coming into the coasts of Judea, ver. 1, 2. 2. His dispute with the Pharisees about divorce, and his discourse with his disciples upon occasion of it, ver. 3—12. 3. The kind entertainment he gave to some little children which were brought to him, ver. 13—15. 4. *An account of what passed between Christ and a hopeful young gentleman that applied himself to him,* ver. 16—22. 5. *His discourse with his disciples upon that occasion concerning the difficulty of the salvation of those that have much in the world, and the certain recompence of those that have left all for Christ,* ver. 23—30.

1 AND it came to pass, that [a] when Jesus had fi- [a Mark x 1]
nished these sayings, he departed from Galilee,
and came into the coasts of Judea, beyond Jordan 2
And [b] great multitudes followed him, and he healed [b Chap xii 15]
them there 3 ¶ The Pharisees also came unto him,
tempting him, and saying unto him, Is it lawful for a
man to put away his wife for every cause? 4 And he
answered and said unto them, Have ye not read, that [c] he [c Gen i 27 & v 2 Mal ii 15]
which made *them* at the beginning, made them male and
female? 5 And said, For this cause [d] shall a man leave [d Gen ii 24 Mark x 7 Eph v 31]
father and mother, and shall cleave to his wife and
[e] they twain shall be one flesh 6 Wherefore they are [e 1 Cor vi 16 & vii 2]
no more twain, but one flesh What therefore God hath
joined together, let no man put asunder 7 They say
unto him, [f] Why did Moses then command to give a [f Deut xxiv 1 Chap v 31]
writing of divorcement, and to put her away? 8 He
saith unto them, Moses, because of the hardness of your
hearts, suffered you to put away your wives but from
the beginning it was not so 9 And I say unto you,
[g] Whosoever shall put away his wife, except *it be* for for- [g Chap v 32 Mark x 11 Luke xvi 18 1 Cor vii 11]
nication, and shall marry another, committeth adultery
and whoso marrieth her which is put away, doth com-
mit adultery 10 ¶ His disciples say unto him, If the
case of the man be so with *his* wife, it is not good to
marry 11 But he said unto them, All men cannot [h 1 Cor vii 2, 7, 9]
receive this saying, save *they* to whom it is given 12
For there are some eunuchs, which were so born from
their mothers womb and there are some eunuchs, which
were made eunuchs of men and there be eunuchs,
[i] which have made themselves eunuchs for the kingdom [i 1 Cor vii 32, 34]
of heaven's sake He that is able to receive *it*, let him
receive *it*

V. 1—12 Having finished his ministry in Galilee, Christ departed to return no more, till after his resurrection, unless for one passing visit, (*Luke* xvii 11.) When God's ministers have done their work in a place, Providence directs their removal, and till they have, none of their enemies in earth or hell can displace them Christ was now advancing towards Jerusalem, the scene of his sufferings, and in his way took that part of Judea, where John had chiefly exercised his ministry, *beyond*, or, as it may be rendered, *on this side Jordan*, and, as was usual in every place through which he passed, great multitudes resorted to him, and, according to his wonted compassions, he healed them of all their diseases, in confirmation of the doctrine which he taught

His ever inveterate enemies the Pharisees failed not to attend him here also, using all their wiles to draw him into a snare, that they might prejudice the people against him For which end we have here,

1 The insidious question they proposed to him concerning divorces *Whether it was lawful for a man to put away his wife for every cause?* a question much debated in their schools, and through the abuse of the permission granted in the law of Moses, they had done it on the most frivolous pretences The Pharisees hoped therefore either to have matter of accusation against him, if he condemned divorces, as an opposer to the law of Moses, or, if he allowed them thus generally, they would have treated him as licentious, the more serious Jews condemning those divorces which were made on trifling provocation.

2 In answer, Christ refers them to the original institution of marriage, as the best solution of the difficulty they proposed Let them consider that, and they might resolve their own question It would appear from thence, that such arbitrary divorces were directly repugnant to the nature of the matrimonial bond In the very creation of the first man and woman, the indissoluble union between them might be collected Adam had none but Eve, nor could divorce her for another, when no other woman then subsisted The bond of this relation the nearest, God ordained, that even a father or mother must be left for the sake of a wife not that marriage vacates the obligation lying upon us to help and relieve them, No but if all admit, that the reciprocal relation between parent and child may not be broken, much less can the nearer connection of man and wife be dissolved They *are one flesh*, near to each other as the members of the same body which no one ever thought of parting with, but cherishes with tenderest care Those therefore whom God hath thus indissolubly joined, it would be highly criminal and presumptuous in man to separate

3 The Pharisees start an objection to this interpretation of scripture, and flatter themselves they have Moses on their side, *v.* 7 *Why then did Moses, &c* very ready to seize the shadow of a plea, and by representing Christ as an enemy to the institutions of Moses, to render him suspected, and prejudice the people against him Thus do wicked men endeavour to pervert the blessed scriptures, and make them militate against themselves

4 Christ answers their objection, and in a way that did not a little reflect on their ill tempers and conduct What they suppose a *command*, our Lord says was merely a *toleration*, and permitted as a judicial and political law, to prevent the greater evils which must ensue, such being their *hardness of heart*, that, rather than their helpless wives should be cruelly treated, perhaps murdered to be rid of them, such being their malignity and obduracy, God was pleased for their sakes to dispense with his positive law, though *from the beginning it was not so* Nor in the gospel state should this be any longer suffered, Christ being come to restore this ordinance to its primitive institution, and to take away the hardness of men's hearts, therefore henceforward no divorces would be allowed of, save in the case of unfaithfulness to the marriage-bed and whosoever on any other cause should divorce his wife, and marry another, would be guilty of adultery, as he would be also who married her thus divorced

5 The disciples, on hearing this determination of their Master, could not help, when they were alone, suggesting their apprehensions of the unhappiness of the married state, if divorces were so strictly prohibited, and that the experiment would be so dangerous, that it amounted to an injunction of celibacy So apt are men to seek liberty for the indulgence of appetite, and to argue against the best institutions, because of some inconveniences which may arise from them If we possess the spirit of Christianity, of meekness, patience, and love, we shall learn to bear each other's burdens, compassionate each other's infirmities, and be thankful for the comforts we enjoy, which far exceed the inconveniencies divorce can be supposed to remedy

6 Christ replies to their suggestion, that their reasoning in one view was right, and that a single state is preferable for those who have the gift of continence, especially in days of persecution and distress, and where the cares of a family, and the incumbrances thereto annexed, would make it more difficult for the first preachers of the gospel to be travelling from place to place, or take up too much of their time and thoughts, instead of better things But there are few, very few comparatively, who are possessed of this gift, and therefore marriage, with all its crosses, is far the most preferable, and to be chosen as a matter of duty, and when entered upon in the fear and love of God, the comforts of that relation will be found to overpay us for all the crosses But some there are from the birth by natural constitution formed for celibacy, strangers to the desire of women, some by the wickedness of men are incapacitated for the marriage state, and some, seeing powerful reasons to determine their choice, for the sake of greater usefulness in the service of Jesus Christ, have such particular supplies of divine grace given them, as to be able to forego the delights of wedlock, and may laudably purpose to live a single life, though not under any vows, if afterwards they should see cause to change their sentiments, nor as any thing meritorious, as the papists suggest, but purely, that being disengaged from the cares of life, they may be enabled to employ themselves more entirely in the work of God, than otherwise they could *He that is able to receive it, let him receive it*

k Mark x 13 Luke xviii 15 — 13 ¶ k Then were there brought unto him little chil-
dren, that he should put *his* hands on them, and pray
and the disciples rebuked them 14 But Jesus said,
Suffer little children, and forbid them not to come unto
l Chap xviii 3 1 Cor xiv 20 — me for l of such is the kingdom of heaven 15 And
he laid *his* hands on them, and departed thence.

v. 13—15 We have seen multitudes of others making their application to Christ, here we behold some pious parents bringing their children to crave his divine benediction

1 They brought their infants, that Jesus might lay his hands upon them, and pray for them, in faith expecting that he could impart to them spiritual blessings, and that his prayers would be attended with gracious effect. *Note*, They who have tasted the grace of Jesus themselves, cannot but earnestly desire, that all theirs may share with them the inestimable mercy, and therefore fail not to present their little ones to him for his blessing

2 The disciples, apprehensive lest such a precedent would induce others to bring their children, and thereby occasion their Master much trouble, or supposing it beneath him to take notice of infants, or useless to bring them to him, rebuked those who brought the children, and wanted to prevent their application But,

3 Christ expressed his displeasure against his disciples for obstructing so charitable a work, and bids them suffer these babes to be brought, seeing *of such is the kingdom of heaven* Not only like these in spirit and temper should the members of his church be, but also that they, as well as grown persons, are capable of becoming subjects of the gospel kingdom, and of having an interest in its spiritual blessings and privileges and if so, then there seems no reason why they may not by baptism be admitted into the visible communion of the faithful *And he laid his hands on them*, and blessed them, (*Mark* x 16) Tho' they cannot stretch out their infant hands to him in faith and prayer, he can confer on them his gifts of grace, and prepare them for his eternal kingdom Thus having confirmed the privileges of the lambs of his flock, *he departed thence*

16 ¶ m And behold, one came and said unto him, m Mark x 17 Luke xviii 18
Good master, what good thing shall I do that I may have
eternal life? 17. And he said unto him, Why callest
thou me good? *there is* none good but one, *that is* God
but n if thou wilt enter into life, keep the command- n Gal iii 12
ments 18 He saith unto him, Which? Jesus said,
o Thou shalt do no murder, Thou shalt not commit o Ex xx 13. Deut v 17
adultery, Thou shalt not steal, Thou shalt not bear false
witness 19 p Honour thy father and *thy* mother and p Chap xv 4
q Thou shalt love thy neighbour as thyself 20 The q Lev xix 18 Chap. xxii 39 Rom xiii 8, 9 Gal v 14
young man said unto him, All these things have I kept
from my youth up what lack I yet? 21 Jesus said
unto him, If thou wilt be perfect, r go *and* sell that
thou hast, and give to the poor, and thou shalt have r Luke xii 33, & xvi 9. Acts ii 45 1 Tim vi 18, 19
treasure in heaven and come *and* follow me 22 But
when the young man heard that saying, he went away
sorrowful for he had great possessions.

v. 16—22 We have here a conference between a promising young man, who came with a question of the last importance, and our blessed Lord, whose answer is designed for his conviction and humiliation, in order to lead him to a better righteousness than his own, for the obtaining that eternal life which he enquired after

1 His address was most respectful, and his enquiry of the last consequence Though Christ appeared outwardly mean and despicable, and he himself was a person of distinction, yet he humbly knelt before him, and with a title of uncommon veneration addressed him, desiring to be informed by him, as a prophet sent from God, by what works of righteousness he might assuredly obtain that eternal life he seemed above all things solicitous to secure *Note*, (1) Eternal life is the grand object, and most deserving our first concern (2) Youth and riches are dangerous snares, that too frequently divert the mind from the consideration of another world, but the more rare, the more commendable it is, when we see any person possessed of both, seeking in the first place the kingdom of God (3) They who would learn the way to eternal life, must be daily coming to Christ on their knees

2 *Our Lord replies both to his address and question* As the young ruler regarded him as a mere man, the title of *Good*, in that emphatical sense, was misapplied, since no creature is absolutely and perfectly good, but God alone As to the question, according to the views wherewith he came, expecting to obtain life by obedience to the law as a covenant of works, there was but one way *If thou wilt enter into life, keep the commandments*, perfectly, universally, perpetually Nothing short of this can secure a title to eternal life under the law, where every defect, failure, or omission, immediately incurs the penalty of the curse denounced, *Deut* vi 25 In which answer Christ appears designing to lead him to a view of the impossibility of obtaining righteousness and life eternal by any doings and duties of his own, and, by unhinging him from an opinion of his own goodness and abilities, to shew him the necessity of a better righteousness than his own for his title to life and glory *Note*, (1) There is no absolute goodness in man, all we have at best is imperfect (2) There was once a way to life by personal perfect obedience, but since the first man's sin none ever went that way, he only excepted, who was more than man

3 *Willing to know what these commandments were*, and conceiving his abilities and inclinations equal to the task, the young ruler begs a distinct enumeration of them, and Jesus, to convince him how mistaken an idea he had formed of himself, instances only in the duties of the second table, which he had probably learnt by heart, and which, if rightly understood, would minister to him abundant matter for humiliation, and shew him the impossibility of obtaining eternal life by his own obedience

4 Ignorant of the spirituality of the law, and judging according to the *wretched literal comments of the scribes*, he thought he might safely vouch for his obedience From his youth up he had escaped from the grosser pollutions that are in the world, and made conscience of his ways He was no adulterer, thief, murderer, or perjured person; and having kept all these commandments, as he supposed, desired, with some shew of self-complacence, to know what farther was required, as if he only wanted to be informed, and was ready to obey *Note*, (1)

Pride

Pride on our duties is as damnable as the indulgence of our ſins (2) It may appear a ſtrange, but it is a true aſſertion, that the faireſt characters in the eyes of the world are uſually the fartheſt from the kingdom of God (3) We may be fully aſſured we know neither God's law nor our own hearts, when we preſume to ſay of the leaſt of his commandments, All theſe have I kept from my youth (4) A humbling ſight of our ſins, not a vain conceit of ourſelves, is the firſt ſtep to the kingdom of God

5 To convince him how miſtaken his apprehenſions were of his own goodneſs, Chriſt puts him upon giving a proof of obedience to that leading precept of the law, and only true principle of duty, *Thou ſhalt love thy neighbour as thyſelf*, and he would preſently ſee how much he lacked of the attainments he boaſted He wiſhed to be *perfect*, if he would be, as one ſtep towards it, let him ſell all his poſſeſſions, diſtribute them to the poor, have his affections taken off from earthly things, commence a conſtant attendant on Jeſus, take up his croſs, and follow his footſteps, and then he would ſecure the treaſures of eternity, and be in the way to that eternal life he ſought *Note*, (1) A holy deadneſs to the world is at all times the duty of Chriſt's diſciples; and there may be occaſions ſtill, where literally we muſt be ready to part with all for his ſake (2) Covetouſneſs and inordinate love of the world are often ſeen in the faireſt profeſſors, and are among the ſaddeſt ſymptoms of the inſincerity and hypocriſy of their hearts (3) They who leave all for Chriſt, will be no looſers in the end, the treaſures of eternity will prove an ample recompenſe

6 Unable to bear theſe hard ſayings, and not at all inclined to part from his great poſſeſſions, though eternal life was at ſtake, the young man thought the way too narrow, yet, grieved to find he had not reached the perfection he fancied in himſelf, and loth to quit Chriſt and eternal life, *he went away ſorrowful*, unwilling to loſe the hopes of heaven, and yet reſolved not to part with his great poſſeſſions on earth *Note*, (1) Riches are the rock on which innumerable ſouls are ſhipwrecked, and drowned thereby in perdition and deſtruction (2) The more we have of this world, in general the cloſer our affections cleave to it, and increaſing wealth brings uſually an increaſe of ſnares (3) Many are ſorry to part with Chriſt, and ſubmit with reluctance to the yoke of ſin and the world, who yet periſh under the bondage of corruption

23 ¶ Then ſaid Jeſus unto his diſciples, Verily I ſay
unto you, that [a] a rich man ſhall hardly enter into the
kingdom of heaven 24 And again I ſay unto you,
[t] It is eaſier for a camel to go through the eye of a
needle, than for a rich man to enter into the kingdom
of God 25. When his diſciples heard *it*, they were
exceedingly amazed, ſaying, Who then can be ſaved?
26 But Jeſus beheld them, and ſaid unto them, With
men this is impoſſible, [u] but with God all things are
poſſible 27 ¶ Then anſwered Peter, and ſaid unto
him, Behold, [x] we have forſaken all, and followed thee,
what ſhall we have therefore? 28. And Jeſus ſaid
unto them, Verily I ſay unto you, that ye which have
followed me [y] in the regeneration, when the Son of man
ſhall ſit in the throne of his glory, [z] ye alſo ſhall ſit upon
twelve thrones, [a] judging the twelve tribes of Iſrael
29 And every one that hath forſaken houſes, or bre-
thren, or ſiſters, or father, or mother, or wife, or
children, or lands for my name's ſake, ſhall receive an
hundred-fold, and ſhall inherit everlaſting life 30
But [b] many *that are* firſt ſhall be laſt; and the laſt *ſhall
be* firſt

[a] Mark x 24 1 Cor i 26 1 Tim vi 9 10
[t] Jer xiii 23 Luke xviii. 25
[u] Jer xxxii 17 Zech viii 6 Luke i 37 & xviii 27
[x] Deut xxxiii 9 Chap iv 20
[y] Heb ix 10 or Acts iii 21 2 Pet. iii 13
[z] Luke xxii 28—30 2 Tim ii 12
[a] 1 Cor vi 2, 3
[b] Chap. xx 16 Luke xiii 30

v 23—30 On occaſion of ſo promiſing a youth's departure from him, through inordinate attachment to worldly wealth, our Lord, directing his diſcourſe to his diſciples,

1 Obſerves the vaſt obſtructions which riches lay in the way of men's ſalvation A rich man, whoſe heart is engaged with the care and love of his ſubſtance, can hardly ever become a ſubject of Chriſt's kingdom upon earth, or an inheritor of his kingdom in heaven Things in their nature the moſt impracticable may be expected to happen, even, according to the proverbial expreſſion, for a camel to go through a needle's eye, ſooner than for a man, whoſe heart is attached to his wealth, and ſeeks his happineſs therein, to become a real diſciple of Jeſus, and an inheritor of glory *Note*, (1) The immenſe difficulties riches put in our way to heaven ſhould make us thankful in a low condition, that God hath not expoſed us to this temptation, ſhould ſuppreſs every riſing of envy againſt our wealthy neighbours, and quench every inordinate deſire of abundance (2) They who are rich, have more duties to diſcharge; more ſins to beſet them; more temptations to ſtruggle with, more ſelf-denial to exerciſe; and a larger account of talents to ſettle than others; and therefore great grace is needful to ſanctify great poſſeſſions.

2 The diſciples expreſs their aſtoniſhment at their Maſter's aſſertion, and if the caſe ſtood thus, according to their miſtaken ideas of the Meſſiah's kingdom, they do not conceive it poſſible to be ſupported, if all the rich and great are excluded, who uſually ſway the world or if they underſtood him of the heavenly kingdom, they are ready to conclude, that few or any would ever attain thereunto, as many are poſſeſſed of wealth, and almoſt all deſire it *Note*, The wonder is, conſidering the difficulties in the way of ſalvation, not that ſo *few* are ſaved, but that *any* obtain it The more the hindrances are, the greater diligence we need uſe to ſurmount them

3 Chriſt with concern obſerving their ſurprize and conſternation, replied, that indeed with men, conſidering their native corruption and worldly-mindedneſs, ſalvation was utterly out of their reach, they being unable to effect the needful change in their own hearts, or in each other's, more than human ſufficiency was requiſite This is the work of God, impoſſibilities with us are poſſible with him almighty grace can ſubdue the moſt inveterate corruptions, ſpiritualize the affections of the moſt worldly-minded, and enable the rich as well as the poor to overcome the temptations of their perilous ſtate, and ſhew themſelves rich in faith, and heirs of the kingdom None therefore are to be deſpaired of, when God will work, who can let it?——Some refer this to the Meſſiah's kingdom upon earth, as if the anſwer implied, that though it appeared ſo impracticable to them to ſet up this kingdom, in oppoſition to all the wealth and greatneſs of the world, yet ſuch ſupports ſhould be miniſtered to them, poor and inconſiderable as they were, as ſhould enable them to withſtand all their enemies, and make their labours ſucceſsful

4 Peter, in the name of his brethren, thought this no unfavourable ſeaſon to enquire what they ſhould get, ſince they had left all and followed him It is true their all was not much, but ſuch as it was, it was equally dear to them as if they had poſſeſſed greater wealth *Note*, (1) If our ſpirit be right, tho' our loſs for Chriſt exceed not the widow's mite, he will accept it as if we had left greater poſſeſſions (2) Though it is not the mere motive of advantage that influences the faithful, we may notwithſtanding with comfort look to the great recompenſe of reward

5 Chriſt engages, that they who forſake all for him ſhall be no looſers in the iſſue *They who have followed him in the regeneration*, ſhall be honoured with the moſt eminent ſeats in his kingdom, and *ſit upon twelve thrones, judging the twelve tribes of Iſrael*

In the regeneration, refers either to the preſent ſtate of the diſciples who had followed Chriſt, and may ſpiritually deſcribe the change which had paſſed on their ſouls by the renewing power of divine grace Or this may ſignify their attendance upon him, and devoting themſelves to his ſervice in ſetting up that kingdom which was deſigned to effect a glorious reformation in the world This phraſe may likewiſe be connected with the latter part of the clauſe, *when the Son of man ſhall ſit in the throne of his glory, in the regeneration*, and then it hath reſpect to the future ſtate of the Redeemer's exaltation, when, after his aſcenſion from the dead, they ſhould be endued with power from on high, the former Moſaical diſpenſation ſhould be aboliſhed, and they commiſſioned to preach the goſpel, and erect the Chriſtian church, in which *old* things, the Jewiſh ceremonials, would paſs away, and all things become new; new ordinances be adminiſtered, and new hearts and minds be given to the converts

Their ſitting on thrones, &c may imply either the dignity of their apoſtleſhip, to which they ſhould be advanced, to charge the Jews with their crimes, eſpecially their rejection of the Meſſiah, and to denounce the vengeance ready to be executed upon them, which, in conſequence of their predictions, they ſhould ſee accompliſhed Or this refers to their diſtinguiſhed place of honour, when in the great day of the Redeemer's appearing and glory, they ſhould be admitted to ſit down as aſſeſſors with him, on thrones around his own, approving and applauding his judgment, diſpenſed according to the word they preached, and afterwards ſhall in the eternal world reign with Chriſt in glory everlaſting

And whilſt he thus promiſed the twelve this diſtinguiſhed honour, he added alſo, for the encouragement of all who ſhould tread in their ſteps to the end of time, that the like rewards ſhould be the portion of the faithful It is ſuppoſed, that for Chriſt's ſake all his true diſciples would be called upon to make very painful ſacrifices, and often be forced to loſe the affection of neareſt and deareſt relations, be ſeparated from the greateſt comforts of life, and deprived of all they poſſeſſed but he engages to indemnify them for their loſſes, ſometimes in *kind*, by his providence ſo ordering events, as that they ſhall in preſent advantages receive *a hundred fold*, or at leaſt always *in comfort* ſhall have an abundant recompenſe, enjoying clearer and brighter manifeſtations of God's love and favour; and, for temporal loſſes, finding their ſouls enriched by ſpiritual graces, beſides the glorious hope of *eternal life* in the world to come, ſecured by the faithfulneſs of the true witneſs, and the unchangeable promiſes of God, which muſt needs infinitely overpay us for all the croſſes and loſſes of this tranſitory world We may learn from

the

the whole of this discourse, (1) To expect, if we are Christ's disciples, many a cross, and to be ready to part with whatever stands in competition with his honour and interest (2) To be thankful if we are not called to those severer exercises of discipleship which others before us have endured (3) To keep the promises in our eye when the day of trial comes, and then we shall think nothing too hard to suffer, or too dear to lose A sense of the Redeemer's present love, and a prospect of the glory which shall be revealed, will make every present affliction light, and cause us to rejoice in the midst of our sorrows (4) The time we must suffer for Christ is momentary, but our reign with him shall be eternal

6 He adds, by way of obviating any mistake which might arise, as if eternal life was the reward of merit, not of grace, or as if priority of calling gave precedence in his kingdom, that *many who were first shall be last, and the last first* Many of the Jews who were first called refusing the invitation, and many Gentiles through grace, though last invited, eagerly embracing the gospel, and also of those, both of the Jews and Gentiles, many who were truly and effectually called and converted at first, would be outstripped in attainments, and excelled in spirituality, zeal, and fidelity, by those who in order of time should afterwards come in, and be exalted to higher honours in his kingdom, which he elucidates by a parable in the succeeding chapter *Note*, If we are called late, we must work the faster, and give the greater diligence to redeem the time

CHAP XX

Here are four things in this chapter 1 *The parable of the labourers in the vineyard*, ver 1—16 2 *A prediction of Christ's approaching sufferings*, ver 17—19 3 *The petition of two of the disciples, by their mother, reproved*, ver 20—28 4 *The petition of the two blind men granted, and their eyes opened*, ver 29—34

a Isa v 1 Chap xxi 33 b 1 Kin xviii 12 2 Tim iii 15 c Isa lxi 10 2 Pet i 5 † i e Seven pence half penny

1 FOR a the kingdom of heaven is like unto a man
that is an housholder, which went out b early in the
morning to hire c labourers into his vineyard 2 And
when he had agreed with the labourers for † a penny a day,
he sent them into his vineyard 3 And he went out about
the third hour, and saw others standing idle in the market-
place 4 And said unto them, Go ye also into the vine-
yard, and whatsoever is right, I will give you And they
went their way 5 Again he went out about the sixth
and ninth hour, and did likewise 6 And about the
eleventh hour he went out, and found others standing idle,
and saith unto them, Why stand ye here all the day idle?
7 They say unto him, Because no man hath hired us
He saith unto them, *Go ye also into the vineyard, and
whatsoever is right, that shall ye receive* 8 So when
even was come, the lord of the vineyard saith unto his
steward, Call the labourers, and give them *their* hire, be-
ginning from the last unto the first 9 And when they
came that *were hired* about the eleventh hour, d they re-
ceived every man a penny 10 But when the first came,
they supposed that they should have received more, and
they likewise received every man a penny 11 And when
they had received *it*, they murmured against the good man
of the house, 12 Saying, These last have wrought but
one hour, and thou hast made them equal unto us, which
have born the burden and heat of the day 13 But he
answered one of them and said, Friend, e I do thee no
wrong didst not thou agree with me for a penny? 14
Take *that* thine is, and go thy way I will give unto this
last, even as unto thee 15 f Is it not lawful for me to
do what I will with mine own? is thine eye evil because
I am good? 16 g So the last shall be first, and the first
last for h many be called, but few chosen

d Rom [illegible] e Rom [illegible] f Rom [illegible] g Chap xix 30 h Chap xxii 14

¶ 1—16 This parable is a comment on the text which concluded the foregoing chapter, and represents to us the gospel dispensation, and this with particular application to the Jews and Gentiles, the former of whom were ever for excluding the latter from all the blessings of the Messiah's kingdom, and could never endure the thoughts of the heathen being admitted to equal privileges with themselves But so God had ordained, and though for their fathers' sakes the first offers of the gospel were to be made to them, yet the Gentiles were shortly to be admitted fellow heirs, and of the same body More generally the parable may also represent to us the sovereignty of God in the dispensation of his gifts of grace and glory As he is debtor to none he may do what he will with his own, may bestow his blessings at what time, measure, manner, as he pleases, and reward according to the good pleasure of his will

1 We have an account in this parable of the agreement made with the labourers by the master of the vineyard *The vineyard* may represent the church, *the master*, the Lord Jesus, *the labourers*, as many as the Lord our God shall call, *the market-place*, the world, that lieth in wickedness, where, till he comes to hire us, we are idle, unemployed, or worse, employed in mischief, serving divers lusts and pleasures, and doing no work God is pleased with, or that can bring any revenue of glory to him Our work for which we are engaged is caring for the soul, and in this service our own benefit, as well as God's glory, is consulted, for indeed, *if we be righteous, what do we unto him?* yet God is pleased to hire us to labour for ourselves, and, as the reward of grace, to promise us the wages of spiritual and eternal blessings, signified by the Roman penny, about seven pence halfpenny in value, the usual hire of a day-labourer The *day* of life is our working season, a short moment, in which we have much to do, and therefore are called to do it with our might, before the night cometh when no man can work And if the burden be heavy, or the heat intense, the time is short, the shadows of the evening are hasting on, and the night of death will dismiss us to our eternal rest The different hours may represent, (1) The calling of Jews and Gentiles, the *early* morning call may point to the ministry of Christ, the third hour, to that of the Apostles sent to the lost sheep of the house of Israel, the sixth and ninth hours may refer to their preaching still to those of Judea only, and to the dispersed among the Gentiles for a time, till at the eleventh hour the call was enlarged to the heathen world, to those who had never heard the glad tidings of salvation before, and then readily accepted the invitation of entering into the vineyard of Jesus (2) The different ages of those who are effectually called of the Lord Some are brought home to him in childhood, as Timothy From early youth, like good Josiah, their heart is tender, and grace begins its blessed work, engaging them to give themselves up to the service of their Redeemer Others at different periods are called to Jesus, received by grace, in the very prime of life, from their gay pursuits, or as they are first entering on the world, brought out of it to follow Christ Some are stopped, after a long career in evil, and in their declining years mercifully constrained to bow to the Redeemer and a few, even at the eleventh hour, bending to the grave under decrepit age, are made signal monuments of divine mercy and sovereignty, and proofs of his ability to save to the uttermost No bonds of custom in sin, no fetters of worldly connections, no length of time, or depth of corruption, prevent the efficacy of God's grace towards his chosen It is happy for those who begin soonest, but it is never too late Whilst the day lasts, the call still is, *Whosoever will, let him come*, but we may not trifle with the moment of opportunity eternity is at stake, and therefore to-day, whilst it is called to-day, we must embrace the gracious invitation

2 The evening came, the labourers were called, their wages paid, and each received a penny The evening is the end of time, when the great account will be settled, and all, both Jews and Gentiles, will appear at the judgment-seat of Christ, the great *steward*, to receive according to the things they have done in the body He is represented beginning with the last, and giving to each the same reward, for as the wages is not of debt, but of grace, in heaven (as some conceive) all shall enjoy the same perfect measure of glory, at least, every vessel, if there be a diversity of capacities, shall be full

3 They who had entered the vineyard first, seeing the rest thus recompensed, supposed their labours entitled them to more than their agreement, and therefore were disappointed when they received no more than a penny, and began to murmur and complain, as if an injustice had been done them in making those their equals in the wages, who had so much later in the day entered upon the work And this represents the case of the Jews, who, because they were the ancient people of God, were first called, and had enjoyed peculiar privileges beyond any other nation, would fain have monopolized the advantages of the Messiah's kingdom, or at least have possessed its chief honours and could not endure the thought that the Gentiles should be made their equals, and share the same grace and glory with them

4 The master of the vineyard silences the murmurers, addressing himself to one of them, *saying, Friend, I do thee no wrong, &c* There could be no injustice done him, as he had the full sum agreed for, and therefore he ought to be content He had a right to dispose of his own money as he pleased, and if he chose to give unto the last a penny as well as to the first it were wicked and envious to repine against the gracious giver And all this is true, not only with regard to the Jews and Gentiles, but generally with regard to all mankind in general (1) God, who is justice itself, neither can nor will do wrong to any (2) His gifts of providence and grace are his own, and as none have a title to either, though they on whom he is pleased to bestow them have reason to be thankful, they from whom he withholds them have no just cause to complain (3) If we can claim any thing from God as our own, it is only in virtue of his gracious promise, not on account of our desert (4)

We

We are too apt to be making comparisons between ourselves and others, and, partial in our own favour, are ready to think, that kindnesses shewn to others, are injustice done to ourselves (5) Envy makes us self-tormentors, and is at once our sin and our curse

5 The text of the discourse concludes it, being the point which was to be proved, *so the first shall be last, and the last first* Many Gentiles should far outshine the Jewish converts who were first admitted into the church, and many rising disciples would be found, who in knowledge, grace, and holiness would overtake and exceed those who were in Christ before them *For*, not those who are foremost in profession are always first in the race, but contrariwise, *many* who *are called* into the outward communion of the church, are never effectually converted and turned to God, and it will be found at last, that there are *but few*, comparatively speaking, *chosen* to eternal life and glory an assertion most alarming, and which should awaken all our sollicitude to make our calling and election sure, that we may be of that few

17 ¶ And Jesus going up to Jerusalem, took the
twelve disciples apart in the way, [l] and said unto them,
18 Behold, we go up to Jerusalem, and the Son of man
shall be betrayed unto the chief priests, and unto the
scribes, and they shall condemn him to death 19 And
[k] shall deliver him to the Gentiles to mock and to
scourge and to crucify *him* and the third day he shall
rise again.

l Chap xvi 21 Mark x 32 Luke xviii 31 k Chap xxvii 2 Acts iv 27

v 17—19 To prepare them for that scene of distress and sufferings on which he was about to enter, he once more took his disciples apart, as they went up together to Jerusalem, and repeated what he said before, *chap*. xvi 21 xvii 22, 23 informing them now more particularly concerning the manner of his sufferings and death, which he had foretold That he should not only be betrayed into his enemies hands, but persecuted with unrelenting malice, and by a most unrighteous sentence condemned to die That he should be delivered to the Gentiles, the Romans, who alone had then the power of life and death in Judea, and, after enduring the most shocking and barbarous indignities, should suffer death upon a cross Tidings that no doubt filled them with horror and dismay but he adds, for their comfort and support, that on the third day he should rise again *Note*, In all the troubles we feel or fear, it is a comfort to look forward to a resurrection day, when they will all be for ever at an end

20 ¶ [l] Then came to him the mother of [m] Zebedee's
children, with her sons, worshipping *him*, and desiring a
certain thing of him. 21 And he said unto her, What
wilt thou? She saith unto him, [n] Grant that these my
two sons may sit, the one on thy right hand, and the
other on the left in thy kingdom 22. But Jesus an-
swered and said, [o] Ye know not what ye ask Are ye
able to drink of [p] the cup that I shall drink of, and to
be baptized with the baptism that I am baptized with?
They say unto him, [q] We are able 23 And he saith
unto them, [r] Ye shall drink indeed of my cup, and be
baptized with the baptism that I am baptized with but
to sit on my right hand, and on my left, is not mine to
give, [†] but *it shall be given to them* for whom it is pre-
pared of my Father 24 And when the ten heard *it*,
[s] they were moved with indignation against the two bre-
thren 25 But Jesus called them unto him, and said,
Ye know that the princes of the Gentiles exercise domi-
nion over them, and they that are great exercise autho-
rity upon them 26 But it shall not be so among
you but whosoever will be great among you, let him
be your minister 27 And whosoever will be chief
among you, [t] let him be your servant 28. [u] Even as
[x] the Son of man came not to be ministred unto, but
to minister, and [y] to give his life a ransom [z] for
many

l Mark x 35 m Chap iv 21 n Jer xlv 5. o Jam iv 3 p Chap. xxvi 39, 42 q Chap xxvi 56 r Acts xii 2 † Or Save to them for Chap xxv 34 John xvii — Rev — 10 17 [illegible] 5 12 [illegible] Luke xxii 24 &c t Rom. xv 2 [illegible] 19 u John xiii 13 [illegible] Luke xxii 27 [illegible]

v 20—28 Far from being cured of their national prejudices by all the sufferings our Lord had foretold them he should endure, they concluded these would be only the prelude to the more glorious manifestation of his power at his rising again And therefore,

1 Two of the disciples, James and John, the sons of Zebedee, with their mother Salome, who is supposed to have been nearly related to Joseph, and might therefore hope to have a strong interest in Jesus, came to their Master, and through her preferring their request, with deep respect she besought him to grant her a favour, and being ordered to name it, she desired him to confer on her two sons the first honours of that kingdom which they shortly expected would appear.

2 Pitying their ignorance and weakness, instead of upbraiding their pride and folly, our Lord turned to the two disciples, and gently admonishes them, saying, *Ye know not what ye ask* Your notions of the nature of my kingdom are utterly mistaken it is not an earthly throne to which I shall be exalted, and as mistaken are you in the means of attaining the honours you seek You are not aware of the sufferings and trials that must be endured by all those who would come to reign with me Through much tribulation lies the entrance into heaven, and can you, think ye, drink of my bitter cup, or bear to be baptized in blood, as I must shortly be? Such sufferings as these they were not prepared for their ambition looked so high, that they saw not the dangers which were before them, nor knew what manner of spirit they were of *Note*, (1) They who would reign with Christ, must first suffer with him, and every Christian should well count the cost, before he begins to take up his cross (2) In all our sufferings it should sweeten our cup to think that Christ hath drank of it before us, and all the bitterness of sin he hath taken away

3 Their self-confidence is a natural consequence of their pride, and therefore they without hesitation boldly engage for their own ability and fidelity; though, alas! they were sad strangers to themselves, and knew not what they said *Note*, Young converts are often very forward, till sad experience hath taught them their own weakness

4 Christ replies, and assures them they shall suffer for him, and in a manner they probably at that time little apprehended But though they did so, still he left their request in suspense The honour they sought was to be disposed of according to God's eternal counsels, and not to be given, *save to them for whom it is prepared of my Father* In the distribution of spiritual, temporal, and eternal blessings, all are dispensed according to the plan laid down in the eternal mind, and concerted in the everlasting covenant of grace nothing can be added thereto, or diminished therefrom

5 The same ambitious spirit which spake in the request of John and James, equally appeared in the indignation of the other ten against them, who each thought himself as much entitled to the superiority which they desired They did not grieve for the sin of their brethren, but were angry at what they conceived an affront to them, and whilst they violently condemned their ambition, like many others, were blind to the same spirit in themselves *Note*, Desire of preeminence is among the most fruitful sources of disputes among brethren Instead of being in his own eyes the last and the least, each is for assuming a superiority, which the proud heart of his fellow is very unwilling to admit

6 To silence the dispute, and strike at the root of the evil, Jesus with the greatest tenderness called them to him, and, to beat down that spirit of ambition, so evil in itself, and so peculiarly unbecoming their holy and humble profession, he endeavours to undeceive them respecting the nature of his kingdom, which was purely spiritual The kings and princes of the Gentiles indeed thirsted after dominion and despotic sway, and the more potent exercised unbounded authority over their weaker vassals and subjects, but utterly unlike them must their conduct be Their greatness must consist not in lording it over God's heritage, but in their abounding labours, not in aspiring desires to rule, but in humble endeavours to promote the salvation of men's souls The only laudable ambition Jesus can approve, is the holy strife who shall be most condescending, and the first in every work and labour of love to serve the meanest who bear the Christian name Nor did he, their Master, recommend ought to them, of which himself had not set them an eminent example, who came not to take state upon himself, and be served with earthly pomp and grandeur, but humbled himself to the lowest offices in the service of men's souls and bodies, and, after living the life of a servant, was about to die the death of a slave, that by the sacrifice of himself he might give *a ransom for many*, even for all those whom the Father had given him, in whose stead he was about to suffer, in order to redeem them from the guilt and power of their sins, and from the wrath of God which they had provoked, and having him therefore for such a pattern of humility, they were peculiarly obliged to copy after it *Note*, (1) The affectation of earthly pomp and splendor is utterly unbecoming those who pretend to be the ministers of the meek and humble Jesus (2) The church of Christ hath never suffered greater injuries than from the tyranny and oppression of those, who professing to be the successors of the Apostles, seem to have inherited nothing from them, but that lordly, ambitious, and domineering spirit for which Jesus so justly reprimanded them (3) The only allowable ambition among the ministers of Christ is, who shall be most humble and serviceable to their brethren, and herein most conformed to their blessed Master's image (4) The life which the Lord Jesus laid down, was the price of our redemption; and being accepted of God as complete and full, the redemption obtained by it was eternal those therefore for whom he died can never more suffer under the sins for which he paid a ransom

29 And as they departed from Jericho, a great mul-
titude followed him 30 ¶ [b] And behold, two [c] blind
men sitting by the way-side, when they heard that Jesus
passed by, [d] cried out, saying, Have mercy on us, O
Lord, thou son of David 31 And the multitude re-
buked them, because they should hold their peace but
[e] they cried the more, saying, Have mercy on us, O
Lord, thou son of David 32 And Jesus stood still,
and called them, and said, [f] What will ye that I shall do
unto you? 33 They say unto him, [g] Lord, that our
eyes may be opened. 34 So Jesus had compassion on
them, and touched their eyes and immediately [h] their
eyes received sight, and they followed him

[a] Mark x 46 Luke xviii 35
[b] Chap ix 27
[c] Isa lix 10
[d] Mat xviii 30
[e] Luke xvii 2
[f] Chap. vi 7
[g] Isa xxxv 5
[h] Luke i 79

v 29—34 Advancing still towards Jerusalem, Jesus and his disciples passed through Jericho, attended as usual by a vast multitude, whom curiosity to hear or see his miracles, desire to learn, or want of his healing influence, had drawn together, when behold a wondrous instance of his power and compassion appears

1 Two blind men, beggars, sit by the way-side, and hearing from some of the multitude, that the famed prophet of Nazareth, who had wrought so many miracles, was passing by, they immediately concluded it a most providential circumstance, and with united and loud supplications cried out incessantly, *Have mercy on us, O Lord, thou son of David* Note, (1) In these blind beggars we may behold a lively emblem of our souls Our understanding is darkness, and we utterly destitute of all good, perishing inevitably in want and wretchedness, unless the divine mercy respect our misery and relieve us (2) They who feel their real state, will cry after Jesus, the only hope of the miserable and the destitute (3) Providential opportunities should be improved, if we neglect them now, they never may return

2 They made so loud a noise, and cried so vehemently, that the multitude rebuked them as troublesome, and bad them be silent But this only made them redouble their prayers, saying, *Have mercy on us, O Lord, thou son of David* Thou, who art so able to help us, whose tender mercies have been so often extended to others, let our pitiable case engage thy notice, and move thy wonted compassions And herein they have set us a noble example, (1) Of fervent prayer Their wants were great, they felt them with deep sensibility, therefore they cried so loud, so persevering So should we do We may meet with many discouragements in seeking Christ, but these, instead of silencing our prayer, should quicken our importunity (2) Of confident faith They were fully persuaded, that what they asked, he was willing and able to grant them His power as the Lord, his office as the Son of David, emboldened their trust in his mercy It is by faith we must thus in every distress honour Jesus by casting our care upon him, pleading his name as the ground of our confidence (3) Of deep humility They ask for mercy alone, referring themselves entirely to him for the manner in which he pleases to dispense it to them We have no merit, can claim nothing at God's hands, deserve nothing but wrath and hell all our hope is in his boundless grace, to supply all our poverty and wretchedness, to pardon our guilt, and bestow the gifts of his Spirit to deliver us from the power of our sin This mercy grant, O Son of David!

3 Christ, who had heard their cries, and knew what rebukes they had met with, stood and called them to him, for he delights to revive the spirit of the contrite, and to relieve the wants of the miserable He bids them therefore prefer their request, intimating his readiness to grant the mercy they had so importunately sought *Note*, The promises of Christ give an unlimited scope to our prayers we can ask nothing really good for us, which Jesus is not willing to bestow

4 The poor blind men have a ready answer, *Lord, that our eyes may be opened* They ask not for silver or gold, but for a boon far more difficult to be granted, which yet they are assured he can easily bestow We have need to prefer the same prayer every day, and would to God we were more deeply affected with our spiritual blindness, that our applications might be more frequent and fervent

5 Their cure is immediate The compassions of Jesus left them not in suspense he touched their eyes, a flood of day instantly broke upon them, and joining the company, they joyfully followed him, testifying their gratitude, love and praise *Note*, They who are enlightened by the Redeemer's grace, will from that moment cleave to him in his holy ways, and gratefully labour to advance his glory

CHAP XXI

The death and resurrection of Jesus Christ are the two grand hinges upon which our salvation turns, and therefore the history of his sufferings, even unto death, and his rising again, is more particularly recorded by all the Evangelists than any other part of his story We have here, 1 The public entry which he made into Jerusalem, upon the first day of the passion-week, ver 1—11 2 *The authority he exercised there, in cleansing the temple, and driving out of it the buyers and sellers,* ver 12—16 3 *The emblem he gave of the state of the Jewish church, in cursing the barren fig-tree, and his discourse with his disciples thereupon,* ver 17—22 4 *His justifying his own authority, by appealing to the baptism of John,* ver 23—27 5 *His shaming the infidelity and obstinacy of the chief priests and elders, with the repentance of the publicans, illustrated by the parable of the two sons,* ver 29—32 6 *His reading the doom of the Jewish church for its unfruitfulness, in the parable of the vineyard let out to unthankful husbandmen,* ver 33—46

1 AND [a] when they drew nigh unto Jerusalem, and
were come to Bethphage, unto the mount of
Olives, then sent Jesus two disciples, 2 Saying unto
them, Go into the village over-against you, and straight-
way ye shall find an ass tied, and a colt with her loose
them, and bring *them* unto me 3 And if any man say
ought unto you, ye shall say, The Lord hath need of
them, and straightway he will send them 4 All this
was done, that it might be fulfilled which was spoken by
the prophet, saying, 5 [b] Tell ye the daughter of Sion,
Behold, [c] thy king cometh unto thee, meek, and sitting
upon an ass, and a colt the foal of an ass. 6 And the
disciples went, and did as Jesus commanded them, 7
And brought the ass and the colt, and [d] put on them
their clothes, and they set *him* thereon 8 And a very
great multitude spread their garments in the way, [e] o-
thers cut down branches from the trees, and strewed *them*
in the way 9 And the multitudes that went before,
and that followed, cried, saying, [f] Hosanna to the son of
David [g] Blessed is he that cometh in the name of the
Lord, Hosanna in the highest 10 And when he was
come into Jerusalem, all the city was moved, saying,
Who is this? 11 And the multitude said, This is Je-
sus [h] the prophet of Nazareth of Galilee

[a] Mark xi 1 Luke xix 29
[b] Isa lxii 11 Zech ix 9 John xii 15
[c] Cant iii 11
[d] 2 Kings ix 13
[e] 1 Mac xiii 51 Mac x 7 John xii 13
[f] Psal cxviii 25
[g] Ibid 26 Chap xx 29
[h] Chap ...

v 1—11 Being about to offer himself as the true paschal Lamb for the sins of his people, our blessed Lord determined to make his triumphant entry first into Jerusalem, as a prelude to those more exalted honours, to which on his resurrection from the dead he should be advanced We are told on his approaching the suburbs, where he halted,

1 The preparations he ordered to be made We find no heralds sent to clear the way, no guards surround his glittering car, no music fills the air with harmony, no officers of state with gorgeous robes attend their mighty sovereign The lowly Jesus despised this pageantry, it fitted not his state of humiliation, and therefore, though he could in an instant have commanded down cherubic legions to attend his steps, and made the clouds his chariots, he chose his poor disciples to be with him, and seated on an ass's colt, nor even that his own, determines thus to make his public entry Yet even here he takes occasion to display his divine omniscience, and influence over the spirits of men, sending his disciples to the village over-against them, directing them where to find the ass tied with her foal, assuring them, that if any man offered to question them for loosing the ass, it would be sufficient to say their Master wanted them, and he would immediately let them go

2 The fulfilment of the scripture herein is particularly remarked Long before had the prophets Isaiah and Zechariah predicted this event, *Tell ye the daughter of Zion* glad tidings of great joy *Behold*, admire and adore him, *thy king*, the long-expected Messiah, *cometh unto thee*, bringing salvation, *meek* as a lamb, to bear every indignity for Zion's sake and gentle to rule with a sceptre of love in the hearts of his people, *sitting upon an ass, and a colt the foal of an ass*, like one of the ancient judges of Israel, and in such humility as was best suited to the character he bore *Note*, Christ is Zion's king his happy subjects may well rejoice in his power and love, but let his enemies tremble, though he comes now like a lamb, he will shortly roar against them as a lion

3 The disciples having obeyed their Master's orders, and brought the ass with her colt, they spread their garments on them, and seated him thereon, and with every expression of exultation and joy, which this poor and, to human view, despicable multitude could shew, they ushered him into the city, spreading their garments instead of carpets on the ground, or hanging them by the way-side, cutting down boughs of trees, and strewing them by the road, carrying palm-branches in their hands, (*John* xii 13) as in the feast of tabernacles, and uttering with loud Hosannahs their triumphant songs of praise, welcoming their adored Messiah, the Son of David, who came with divine authority from on high, wishing him all prosperity, honour, happiness, and glory, praying for the appearing of his kingdom, and that his throne might be exalted over all, and calling on the heavenly hosts to join in their blessings, praise, and adoration *Note*, (1) The coming of Jesus into the sinner's

heart

heart is still matter of greater exultation, and deserves louder shouts of praise (2) They who have tasted the preciousness of a Redeemer's grace in their own souls cannot but long to see his kingdom established in the hearts of others, and fervently pray for its more abundant manifestation in the world

5 Such an uncommon scene excited great emotion in the inhabitants of Jerusalem, according as they were differently affected with wonder, envy, contempt, or exultation; and the general enquiry was, *Who is this?* that comes with such a train and such acclamations To which the multitude replied, *This is Jesus, the prophet of Nazareth of Galilee*, whose doctrines and miracles have rendered him so famed, and confirmed his divine mission *Note*, (1) Christ is often little known where the greatest profession of his religion is made (2) The poor despised multitude judge righter concerning Jesus, his character, and gospel, than the wise and noble, who often affect to despise them

12 ¶ ^i And Jesus went into the temple of God, and — i Mark xi 11 Luke xix 45 John ii 15
cast out all them that sold and bought in the temple, and
overthrew the tables of the money-changers, and the
seats of them that sold doves, 13 And said unto them,
It is written, ^k My house shall be called the house of — k Isa lvi 7
prayer, ^l but ye have made it a den of thieves 14 And — l Jer vii 11
the blind and the lame came to him in the temple, and
he healed them 15 And when the chief priests and
scribes saw the wonderful things that he did, and the
children crying in the temple, and saying, Hosanna to
the Son of David, they were sore displeased, 16 And
said unto him, Hearest thou what these say? And Jesus
saith unto them, Yea, have ye never read, ^m Out of the — m Psal viii 2
mouth of babes and sucklings thou hast perfected praise?
17 ¶ And he left them, and went out of the city into
Bethany, and he lodged there

v 12—17 The son of God the King in Zion, regards his temple as his palace, and thitherward directs his steps

1 He purges it of intruders, the buyers and sellers, who in the courts carried on their traffic, exchanging bills to purchase sheep and doves for sacrifice, or money to pay the annual half shekel, and under pretence that this was in order to further the temple service, the priests, through avarice, connived at it, enriching themselves by the extortion practised on these occasions But the Lord overthrew their stalls, and drove them out before him, confounded and unable to bear his frowns, or resist his arm, vindicating his conduct, and condemning their wickedness by a quotation from *Isa* lvi 7 and *Jer* vii 11 saying, *It is written, My house shall be called a house of prayer*, to which men should resort, and where God had promised to hear their supplications, *but ye have made it a den of thieves*, perverting it to the vilest purposes, dishonouring God, and plundering the people *Note*, (1) The vilest corruptions have been introduced into the church by those who, making advantage the end of their profession, counterfeit godliness in order to make gain (2) The eyes of his peculiar jealousy are upon his church, and nothing can more offend the blessed head of it, than to behold an avaricious spirit in those who, by their very calling, profess themselves crucified to the world

2 When he had ejected the intruders, he sat as a King upon his throne to dispense his royal favours, healing the blind and lame who came to him in the temple, and thither the spiritually blind and lame are invited still to come to him, and by his word and spirit he continues to manifest there his healing power and grace

3 He rebukes the envy of the chief priests and scribes They could not bear to see such incontestible miracles wrought by him, and when the very children, struck with the works of Jesus, joined their feeble voices to the acclamations of the multitude, and cried, *Hosanna to the Son of David*, they were stung with malignant envy, and intimated to Jesus, that to hear without silencing such silly little creatures, proved him weakly vain and ostentatious But Jesus vindicates these infant praises he heard, he approved their lispings, and had these cavillers known the scripture, they might have herein observed their fulfilment, where it was written, *Out of the mouth of babes and sucklings thou hast ordained strength*, Psal viii 2 God's strength was now made perfect in their weakness, and the Messiah's praise advanced by these feeble instruments, to the confusion and condemnation of those who rejected and denied him *Note*, (1) Greatness and goodness are ever the objects of envy, and the proud cannot bear to hear the tribute of commendation payed to superior excellence (2) It is happy when children learn betimes to lisp the Redeemer's praise Though education cannot bestow grace, yet example and instruction in the way of godliness, are means we may humbly hope God will effectually bless (3) The prayers and services of little children are pleasing to the dear Saviour, and he will graciously accept their feeble efforts to express their gratitude

4 Leaving them to reflect on what had passed, he departed to Bethany where he lodged, about two miles from Jerusalem, thus for a while withdrawing himself from their malice and fury, and depriving them of the blessing of his presence, which they had so justly forfeited

18 ^n Now in the morning as he returned into the city, — n Mark xi 12
he hungred 19 And when he saw † a fig tree in the — † Gr one fig tree
way, he came to it, and ^o found nothing thereon, but — o Luke xiii 6
leaves only, and said unto it, Let no fruit grow on thee — Rev iii
henceforward for ever And presently the fig-tree withered away 20 And when the disciples saw *it*, they
marvelled, saying, How soon is the fig-tree withered away? 21 Jesus answered and said unto them, Verily
I say unto you, ^p If ye have faith and ^q doubt not, ye — p Chap xvii 20 Luke xvii 6
shall not only do this *which is done* to the fig-tree, but — q James i 6
also if ye shall say unto this mountain, Be thou removed,
and be thou cast into the sea it shall be done 22
And ^r all things whatsoever ye shall ask in prayer, be- — r Chap vii 7 John xiv 13 & xv 7 & xvi 23 1 John v 14
lieving, ye shall receive

v 18—22 In the morning early Jesus returned to Jerusalem, and having probably come out fasting, he was hungry, being, as man, subject to all our sinless infirmities And seeing a fig-tree remarkably flourishing, he made up to it, expecting to have found fruit, but found nothing but leaves, on which denouncing a curse upon it for its barrenness, the tree immediately began to wither And herein Christ seems to have particularly in his view the Jewish people, of which this fig-tree was a lively emblem They were, in their profession of religion, zealous and plausible, but barren of all true fruits of righteousness, and therefore were now given up to the curse, to be destroyed without remedy *Note*, (1) Christ requires of his disciples not merely leaves of profession, but the fruit of grace, tho too many deceive his expectations, and rest in the form, whilst they continue strangers to the power of godliness (2) The curse will light upon the barren trees often in this world the hypocrite's hope perisheth, they discover their insincerity, and wither in the eyes of man, but at farthest, the day of recompence will blast their confidences

The disciples the next morning passing with their master the same way, *Mark* xi 20 observed with wonder how soon the fig-tree was withered away which Jesus had cursed the preceding day and so terrible are his comminations, and sure to light down upon the devoted sinner's head In answer to which observation, Jesus replied, that this was little, compared with the power they should be endued with, if they exercised unshaken and unwavering faith in God, not hesitating, or reasoning how the miracle could be performed, but trusting God's power and promises, in which case they would be enabled, not merely to dry up a fig-tree with a word, but to say *to this mountain*, on which they now stood, *be thou removed, and cast into the sea*, and *it shall be done* Such astonishing miracles should they be enabled to work, and whatever other thing they should find needful in the execution of their ministry, for the honour of God and the furtherance of his gospel, they need only ask it in prayer, nothing doubting, and it should assuredly be granted them *Note*, The prayer of faith is sure to prevail, to this God denies nothing If ever we want, are unhappy, or in distress, to this source it may be traced, to the distrust of his promises, his power, or his love

23 ¶ ^s And when he was come into the temple, the — s Mark xi 27 Luke xx 1
chief priests and the elders of the people came unto him
as he was teaching, and said, ^t By what authority dost — t Exod ii 14 Acts iv 7
thou these things? and who gave thee this authority?
24 And Jesus answered and said unto them, I also will
ask you one thing, which if ye tell me, I in like wise will
tell you by what authority I do these things 25 ^u The — u Prov xxvi 26
baptism of John, whence was it? from heaven, or of
men? And they reasoned with themselves, saying, If we
shall say, From heaven, he will say unto us, Why did
ye not then believe him? 26 But if we shall say, Of
men, we fear the people, for all hold John as a prophet 27 And they answered Jesus, and said, ^x We — x Job v 13
cannot tell And he said unto them, Neither tell I you
by what authority I do these things

v 23—27 We have here,

1 The insolent demand made upon our Lord, and the interruption given him in his blessed work, by the chief priests and elders, the rulers in church and state, who, unable any longer to contain, and filled with indignation at what they had seen and heard the preceding day, insisted upon his producing authority for what he did, and shewing the commission under which he acted, presuming that his answer would infallibly lay him open to some accusation, which they had so long wished to find against him *Note*, When we are faithfully labouring for Christ, we need not wonder, if Satan and his instruments labour to interrupt us

2 Christ

2 Christ answers their demand by another He knew how to confound them, whilst they thought to silence him, and is ready out of their own mouths to condemn them *The baptism of John, was it of heaven, or of men?* Was he commissioned from heaven, or went forth at his own will, or under merely human authority? The question was short, but the dilemma to which it reduced them, was inextricable They plainly saw, if they should say, John acted under a divine commission, then Christ would have an immediate proof of his own, and they would be inexcusable for not receiving him as the Messiah, to whom John bore witness On the other hand, their own honour, lives, and safety, were at stake, the people being fully persuaded of John's prophetic character, which should they deny, they justly apprehended least they should be stoned like blasphemers, and therefore, contrary to their own convictions, they chose to confess ignorance, and tell a lie, rather than own the divine mission of the messenger, which would, in its consequence, involve the divine authority of Jesus But if they thus wilfully chose to appear ignorant in one case, our Lord was fully vindicated in refusing to give them further satisfaction about himself, seeing it was in vain to talk with those, who had first resolved not to be convinced *Note*, (1) Worldly minds are unspeakably more influenced by the fear of men, than by the fear of God (2) Many are more afraid of shame than sin, and therefore hesitate not at a lie concerning their thoughts and apprehensions, their affections and intentions, their remembering or forgetting things, &c because they flatter themselves nobody can disprove them but there is a searcher of hearts, from whom no secrets are hid (3) If men wilfully shut their eyes against the truth, it is in vain to reason with them any farther

28 ¶ But what think you? A certain man had two
sons, and he came to the first, and said, Son, go work
to day in my vineyard 29 He answered and said, I will
not but afterward he repented, and went 30 And
he came to the second, and said likewise And he an-
y Chap xxiii 3 swered and said, [y] *I go*, sir, and went not 31 Whe-
ther of them twain did the will of his father? They say
z Luke vii 29, 30 unto him, The first Jesus saith unto them, [z] Verily
I say unto you, that the publicans and the harlots go in-
a Chap iii 8 to the kingdom of God before you. 32 For [a] John
came unto you in the way of righteousness, and ye be-
b Luke iii 12 lieved him not: [b] but the publicans and the harlots be-
c [illegible] lieved him And [c] ye, when ye had seen *it*, repented
not afterward, that ye might believe him

v 28—32 Having silenced their cavils, he makes an attack upon their conscience, in a parable, with an application to them

1 We have the parable itself A certain man had two sons, whom he sent into his vineyard to work the one appeared at first refractory, undutiful, and refused to obey his father's commands, but afterward, reflecting on his ill conduct, he was sorry, repented, and went to his work the other no sooner was bid to go than with profound respect he promised immediate obedience, but never went The question which did his father's will was too evident to admit of hesitation, and they allow the penitent to be the dutiful son *Note*, (1) God is our father, he commands his children to serve and glorify him, by our relation to him obedience is our duty, and should be our delight The day of life is the day of labour, and should therefore diligently be improved by us But, (2) Such is our vile nature, that we are rebellious children, refuse to hearken, yea, dare to say, *We will not* serve him, but our own lusts and pleasures, and insolently turn from him, every one in his own way (3) Whenever by divine grace we are led to repent and return, God in Christ is graciously pleased to receive us, to forgive our wickedness and insolence, again he permits us to be employed in his service, and restores us to his regard (4) Whilst some prove better than they promise, others prove the very contrary, make fair professions of love to Christ and his service, but never go further, Christians in word and in tongue, but not in deed and in truth

2 Christ applies the parable to those who were before him, the primary scope of which is to shew, that publicans and harlots, repenting, would enter the kingdom sooner than they, and probably he hath an eye here unto the Gentiles, who would repent and be converted by the gospel, when the Jewish nation, for their impenitence and unbelief, would be rejected And this had evidently appeared in the effect of John's ministry, who came *in the way of righteousness*, his life remarkably exemplary, his doctrine directly tending to lead men to repentance, and faith in the Messiah, whereby he proved his mission from God but notwithstanding *ye believed him not* though you pretend such respect for God, as the second son did for his father, you did not receive John's testimony, nor believe the doctrines he preached, but *the publicans and harlots believed him*, were convinced of their guilt and danger, received his testimony concerning Jesus, repented and were baptized *and*, notwithstanding these remarkable fruits of his ministry, which served to evidence the divine power and authority which accompanied his word, *ye, when ye had seen it, repented not afterward, that ye might believe him*, but continued obstinately hardened against every method of conviction *Note*, (1) The success of our ministry is one of the best testimonials of our mission from God (2) Formal professors are much more difficultly wrought upon, and seldomer converted, than careless sinners Strictness in the ceremonials of religion, and the pride of duties trusted upon for righteousness, are among the strongest holds of Satan in the human heart (3) Wherever the gospel comes in power, converting publicans and harlots, there will it leave those inexcusable who, beholding its efficacy on others, still contradict, and blaspheme, and reject the counsel of God against their own souls

33 ¶ Hear [d] another parable There was a certain d Mark xii 1 Luke xx 9
housholder [e] which planted a vineyard, and hedged it e Psal lxxx 9 Cant viii 11
round about, and digged a wine press in it, and built a Isa v 1 Jer ii 21
tower, and let it out to husbandmen, and went into a far
country 34 And when the time of the fruit drew near,
he sent his servants to the husbandmen, that they might
receive the fruits of it 35 And the husbandmen took
his servants, [f] and beat one, and killed another, and f 2 Chron xxxvi 16
stoned another 36 Again he sent other servants, more Neh ix 26
than the first and they did unto them likewise 37 Chap xxiii 34
But last of all he sent unto them his son, saying, They Acts vii 52
will reverence my son 38 But, when the husbandmen 1 Thess ii 15 Heb xi
saw the son, they said among themselves, [g] This is the 36 &c
heir, [h] come, let us kill him, and let us seize on his in- g Heb i 2
heritance 39 And they caught *him*, and [i] cast him h Chap xxvi & xxvii
out of the vineyard, and slew *him* 40 When the Lord 1
therefore of the vineyard cometh, what will he do unto i Heb xiii
those husbandmen? 41 They say unto him, He will 12
miserably destroy those wicked men, and [k] will let out *his*
vineyard unto other husbandmen, which shall render him k Acts xiii 46 & xv
the fruits in their seasons 42 Jesus saith unto them, 6
Did ye never read in the scriptures, [l] The stone which
the builders rejected, the same is become the head of the l Psal cxviii
corner this is the Lord's doing, and it is marvellous 22 Acts iv
in our eyes? 43 Therefore say I unto you, [m] The 11 1 Pet ii
kingdom of God shall be taken from you, and given to m Chap viii
a nation bringing forth the fruits thereof 44 And 12
[n] whosoever shall fall on this stone, shall be broken but
[o] on whomsoever it shall fall, it will grind him to pow- n Isa viii 14 15
der 45 And when the chief priests and Pharisees had Rom ix 33 o Isa lx 12
heard his parables, they perceived that he spake of them Dan ii 44
46 But when they sought to lay hands on him, they
feared the multitude, because [p] they took him for a pro- p Luke vii
phet 16 John vii 40

v 33—46 Another parable, nearly of the same import as the former, is here delivered We have,

1 The privileges which the Jewish church had long enjoyed, represented by a vineyard let out to husbandmen They had been planted in a pleasant land, fenced round by God's peculiar care, blessed with the means of grace, in the midst of them he had set up his altar, manifested his presence, deposited his lively oracles, instituted divine ordinances, appointed a holy ministry nothing that could conduce to their fruitfulness or defence was lacking and therefore, having settled their constitution at Sinai, or at the dedication of the temple, retiring between the cherubim, he committed to the chief priests and elders the care of his church, for the edification of which they were required, as husbandmen in a vineyard, to labour *Note*, (1) Christ's church is his vineyard, and under his especial care, whilst the world in general lieth in wickedness (2) Ministers in the church must *labour* in the word and doctrine a life of ease, indolence, and self-gratification, is inconsistent with this sacred employment

2 Enjoying such means and mercies, God justly expected their profiting should appear, and sent accordingly his prophets to remind them of their obligations, and stir them up and direct them to the discharge of them, that they might, in the fruits of grace and righteousness, render that tribute to God which was so much his due

3 The baseness and cruelty of the husbandmen to these divine messengers was astonishing They abused, insulted, and persecuted the prophets, and even went so far as to imbrue their hands in their blood, *Jer* xx 2 *Neh* ix 26 *2 Chron* xxiv 21 and when the Lord, in his patience and pity, sent others in succession, to see if at last some change might be wrought, the rising generation repeated all the wickedness of their forefathers *Note*, (1) It hath been the lot of all God's faithful ministers from the beginning to suffer persecution, and none have been deeper in this transgression than those who by office and profession filled the most distinguished places in his church (2)

God .

God's patience with sinners is astonishing Though provoked and insulted in the person of his ambassadors, he still sends them with proffers of peace and pardon

4 When, in infinite condescension and love, God sent to them his Son, to whom they might well be expected to pay reverence and attention and from whose ministry and miracles at least, if they rejected others, some blessed change might have been hoped for, so far were they from receiving and submitting to him, that, to fill up the measure of their iniquities, they immediately began to plot against him, and what these husbandmen had done they were now about to repeat, to cast him out and slay him, as if, when they had crucified him without the walls of Jerusalem, they might then lord it without controul in the church, and, by the murder of the heir, seize the inheritance without opposition

5 Christ appeals to them for what they thought must be the consequence, when the Lord of the vineyard came, for come he surely will, to reckon with the persecutors of his prophets and the murderers of his Son And they, not yet understanding the meaning couched under these parabolic expressions, readily replied, no doubt the case of these wicked husbandmen will be terrible, they have nothing to expect but condign punishment for their crimes, and that the vineyard should be committed to more trusty servants Thus unwittingly pronouncing their own doom, and justifying God's procedure in rejecting them, and calling the Gentiles into his church, who would render him more abundant honour, love, and service *Note*, (1) Even those who perish shall be made to confess God's righteousness, and shall out of their own mouths be condemned (2) The end of all the ungodly, and of the persecutors of Christ and his people, is to be miserably destroyed under the consuming wrath of an offended God

6 When, on our Lord's intimating their concern in this parable, they had testified their abhorrence of the thought he suggested of murdering God's son, *Luke* xx 16—19 he assures them this would infallibly be the case and they had, no doubt, often read the scripture which foretold it, *Ps* cxviii 22 *The stone* was himself, the rock on which his church should be built up, *the builders* were the chief priests and elders, who rejected him, and *refused* to own him as the Messiah, yet, notwithstanding their malice and infidelity, he must become *the headstone of the corner*, exalted to be the head of all principalities and powers, and of his church in particular, both of Jews and Gentiles united in one glorious body And *this is the Lord's doing*, who, in his predeterminate counsel and foreknowledge, permitted and over-ruled their wickedness for good, and would, at his resurrection and ascension, thus advance his son Jesus, and give him a name above every name, and *it is marvellous in our eyes*, the obduracy of the Jews, the calling of the Gentiles, the rejection of the Messiah and his exaltation, are all marvellously ordered to advance the divine glory, to pour confusion on the enemies of the Redeemer, and effectually to secure the salvation of his peculiar people

7 Christ particularly addressing himself to the chief priests, elders, and people before him, makes a direct application of all he had spoken to their case The gospel they had rejected should shortly be taken from them, and they abandoned of God, because of their infidelity and impenitence, whilst this word of salvation should be sent to the Gentiles, who would thankfully embrace it, be admitted into the Messiah's kingdom, and approve themselves faithful subjects of it in all holy conversation and godliness Whosoever therefore among them, offended at the humiliation of Jesus, through ignorance or prejudice rejected him as the Messiah, *shall be broken*, as a man that stumbles against a stone but whosoever, in his state of exaltation, obstinately persist in their malice against him, shall be crushed in pieces by him as under the fall of a mighty rock *Note*, They who will not bow to the sceptre of a Redeemer's grace, must miserably perish under the iron rod of his judgment

Lastly, The chief priests and pharisees could not mistake his meaning they plainly perceived the drift of his parables and discourse, and saw it expressly levelled against them, out of their own mouths drawing their condemnation, and confirming the sentence of wrath and reprobacy against them, but so hardened were they, that, instead of instantly humbling their souls that they might avert the threatened vengeance, they were so enraged that they would instantly have laid violent hands upon him, and probably have murdered him on the spot, but the fear of the people restrained them, who, taking Jesus for a prophet, would at present have interposed for his rescue they were therefore constrained to defer their revenge to a more convenient season *Note*, (1) The word of God is powerful and penetrating, and conscience will make the application, Thou art the man (2) They who are not corrected by reproof, must be exasperated thereby (3) It is a mercy that God hath many ways of restraining men's wickedness, though they have cast off his fear he can bind them with human fetters, when they refuse to be governed by his divine law

CHAP XXII

This chapter is a continuation of Christ's discourses in the temple, two or three days before he died his discourses then are largely recorded, as being of special weight and consequence In this chapter we have, 1 Instructions given, by the parable of the marriage-supper, concerning the rejection of the Jews and the calling of the Gentiles, ver 1—10 *and, by the doom of the guest that had not the wedding-garment, the danger of hypocrisy in the profession of Christianity,* ver 11—14 2 *Disputes with the Pharisees, Sadducees, and scribes, who opposed Christ* (1) *Concerning paying tribute to Cesar,* ver 15—22 (2) *Concerning the resurrection of the dead and the future state,* ver 23—33 (3) *Concerning the great commandment of the law,* ver 34—40 (4) *Concerning the relation of the Messiah to David,* ver 41—46

1 AND Jesus answered and spake unto them again
by parables, and said, 2 [a] The kingdom of [a] Luke xiv 16
heaven is like unto a certain king, [b] which made a mar- [b] Rev xix 7, 9
riage for his son, 3 And [c] sent forth his servants to call [c] Prov ix 3, &c
them that were bidden to the wedding and they would
not come 4 Again, he sent forth other servants, say-
ing, Tell them which are bidden, Behold, I have pre-
pared my dinner [d] my oxen and *my* fatlings *are* killed, [d] Prov ix 2
and all things *are* ready [e] come unto the marriage [e] Rev xxii 17
5 But they [f] made light of *it*, and went their ways, [f] Heb ii 3
[g] one to his farm, another to his merchandise 6 And [g] 1 Tim vi 9, 10
the remnant took his servants, and [h] entreated *them* spite- [h] 2 Chron xxxvi 16
fully, and slew *them* 7 But when the king heard *there-* Chap xxi 35
of, he was wroth and [i] he sent forth his armies, and
destroyed those murderers, and burnt up their city 8 [i] Dan ix 26. Luke xix. 27, 43
Then saith he to his servants, The wedding is ready, but
they which were bidden [k] were not worthy 9 Go ye [k] Acts xiii 46
therefore [l] into the high-ways, and [m] as many as ye shall [l] Prov i 20
find, bid to the marriage 10 So those servants went [m] Mar xvi 15
out into the *high* ways, and [n] gathered together all, as [n] Chap xiii 47
many as they found, both bad and good and the wed-
ding was furnished with guests 11 ¶ And when the
king came in to see the guests, he saw there a man
[o] which had not on a wedding-garment 12 And he [o] Zech iii 3, 4 Luke xv 22 Rev iii 18 & xix 8
saith unto him, Friend, how camest thou in hither, not
having a wedding garment? and he was speechless 13
Then said the king to the servants, Bind him hand and
foot, and take him away, and [p] cast *him* into outer dark- [p] Chap viii 12 & xiii 42 & xxiv 51 & xxv 30
ness there shall be weeping and gnashing of teeth. 14
[q] For many are called, but few *are* chosen [q] Chap xix 30 & xx 16.

v 1—14 This parable is in import much the same as the foregoing, shewing the rejection of the Jewish people for their obstinate infidelity, and the calling of the Gentiles consequent thereupon

The gospel dispensation is compared to a magnificent entertainment made by a king on the marriage of his son, which represents the rich provision made for poor sinners, and the gracious invitation sent to them by the great bridegroom of his church, Christ Jesus, the son of the eternal King We have,

1 The rich provision made on this occasion The oxen and fatlings are killed, with all that vast abundance which became the royal table, signifying those spiritual blessings which a poor and perishing sinner needs, such as the pardon of sin, acceptance with God as righteous, a sense of his love, the comforts and graces of the Holy Ghost, spiritual supports to carry him through the journey of time, and the glorious hope of the enjoyment of God in eternity And these afford the richest feast for a sinful soul

2 The repeated calls sent to those who had been invited, urging their attendance Thus in particular the Lord sent out the seventy disciples to call the Jewish people, and, when they refused to hearken, he again, after his resurrection, sent forth his apostles and evangelists, with greater vehemence to urge their coming, having now perfected the redemption of his people by the one oblation of himself, and fully obtained for them all spiritual blessings in heavenly things He invited them therefore once more to join themselves to the Lord, and take him as their covenant head and glorious bridegroom And thus in general, by his ministers to the end of time, doth the Lord send forth his gracious invitations to miserable sinners, entreating them to come and secure their own happiness, be reconciled to God, and partake of the gospel feast, where all things are ready which they can wish or need; where Jesus is ready to receive them, the Father to pardon and bless them, the Spirit to comfort and strengthen them Well therefore may we with earnestness beseech men, as they value all that is dear to them, *Come unto the marriage*

3 The folly and wickedness of those who were invited appear in striking colours, at first in a careless and insolent refusal of the favour done them, and afterwards, when expostulated with, and again intreated to comply, by a contemptuous treatment of the message, and a more cruel treatment of the messengers some slighted and despised the offer, preferring their worldly avocations, and pretending more necessary engagements, whilst others, provoked with the importunity of the servants, not only insulted and reviled them, but even in a rage imbrued their hands in their blood Thus it happened to the first preachers of the gospel the Jewish people slighted their admonitions, and, instead of hearkning to the word of salvation, were the bitter persecutors and murderers of those who preached it Nor were they singular herein The same invitation hath ever since, to this very day, met with very much of the like treatment Many continue to make light of Christ, negligent about the concerns of their immortal souls, their pleasures, their gains, their worldly engagement, occupy all their hearts, and they have neither leisure nor inclination to mind the concerns of religion They are engrossed with the cares of life, and anxious about so many other things, that, they pretend, they cannot attend to the one thing needful Thus thousands turn their backs on Christ; their farm and their merchandise occupy them wholly, and the calls of the gospel find no entrance into their deaf ears Whilst others, exasperated at being disturbed in their sinful pursuits by the zealous ministers of God, hate and revile them, and would, but for human restraints, renew the former persecutions They who preach the gospel must expect to suffer for it

4 The offended monarch, in righteous wrath, to vindicate his honour and avenge his servants wrongs, sent forth his armies, destroyed these murderers, and burnt up their cities The Roman armies, at God's command, thus destroyed the Jewish nation and burnt up Jerusalem, as the punishment due to them for rejecting and murdering their Messiah and his ministers And the like vengeance awaits all that obey not the gospel, and persecute the preachers of it wrath will shortly come upon them to the uttermost

5 The calling of the Gentiles was a consequence of the rejection of the Jews God's feast shall not be prepared in vain When they who were first bidden therefore by their refusal were judged unworthy a place in his kingdom, he sent forth his servants into the heathen world, with a general invitation, to preach the gospel to every creature Which commission they readily executed, inviting all of every rank and station, and sinners of every degree, to come to Jesus Christ, with assurances of a ready welcome from him And thus the Christian church was filled with an innumerable multitude of converts, some really and truly turned to God, others but false-hearted and hypocritical professors *Note*, (1) Christ will have a church and people in the world, however many reject his gospel (2) The invitation is general God indeed knoweth those that are his we do not, therefore must preach the gospel to every creature (3) Under the dispensation of grace by Jesus Christ, all petty distinctions between one sinner and another are in a manner abolished, as the least sinner must eternally perish without it, the greatest have a full and free redemption offered in him No man perishes through the greatness of his sins, but through his unbelief and neglect of the gospel (4) The visible church is a mixt multitude, and will continue so till the great day of separation we may expect to find in it bad, as well as good

6 The discovery, conviction, and condemnation of hypocrites in the church is represented by the king's visit to his guests; where observing one without a wedding-garment, (which probably might be provided for the guests on these occasions, and therefore the neglect was criminal, especially if he preferred his rags before the bright garments which lay ready for him) He addressed him with a startling enquiry how he dared intrude himself there without the wedding-garment and, speechless at the question, his silence confessed his guilt Shackled therefore as a malefactor, the king commands him to be dragged from the room illuminated for the bridal feast, and thrust into the darkness without, to bewail, with unavailing expressions of bitter anguish, his presumption, sin, and folly Where we may observe, (1) The particular notice the Lord takes of those who profess to believe in him he trieth the heart. Hypocrisy may deceive men, but not God The day will come when the false-hearted shall be detected, either by sifting providences in this world, or at the appearing of the King upon his throne. May we now so judge ourselves, that we may not then be judged of the Lord! (2) The wedding-garment here seems to be the righteousness of our Redeemer, provided for us to put on And it is our sin, and will be our ruin, that through ignorance we know not the want of it, or through pride reject it, and dare to appear before God in the filthy rags of our own righteousness, which cannot cover our shame. (3) They must needs be speechless in the day of God, who in profession have joined in the outward ordinances, whilst their faith hath never put on Christ, nor their hearts been conformed to his image (4) Hypocrites in the church will receive the sorest damnation in eternal torments, doomed to suffer agonies unutterable and inconceivable, and filled with the most excruciating rage, horror, and despair

7 The parable concludes with the repetition of the observation Christ had made before, that *many are called, but few chosen* An alarming notice, to examine ourselves whether we be in the faith, how we came in to the Lord's table, what garments we are cloathed with, and how we can bear the master's piercing eye

15, ¶ r Then went the Pharisees, and s took counsel r Mark xii 13 Luke xx 20
how they might intangle him in *his* talk 16 And they
sent out unto him their disciples, with the Herodians, s Mic ii 1
saying, t Master, we know that thou art true, and teach- t Ps xii 2
est the way of God in truth, neither carest thou for any
man, for thou regardest not the person of men. 17
Tell us therefore, What thinkest thou? Is it lawful to
give tribute unto Cesar, or not? 18. But Jesus perceived their wickedness, and said, Why tempt ye me,
ye hypocrites? 19 Shew me the tribute-money And
they brought unto him † a penny 20 And he saith † In value seven pence halfpenny Chap xx 2
unto them, Whose *is* this image and superscription?
21 They say unto him, Cesar's Then saith he unto
them, u Render therefore unto Cesar, the things which u Chap. xvii 25 Rom xiii 7
are Cesar's and unto God, the things that are God's
22 When they had heard *these words*, they marvelled,
and left him, and went their way

v 15—22 Ceaseless in their designs of malice, the Pharisees, associated with the Herodians, endeavoured to entangle him in his talk, and by some captious subject of dispute to draw from him some expression whereon to found an accusation against him So little can the purest innocence, or the most faultless integrity, screen us from the malevolence of wicked men

The Herodians are thought to be a sect of the Jews who were the partizans of Herod, and were zealous for the Roman government and the payment of the tribute, whilst the Pharisees and the rest of the nation abhorred the yoke, and hardly could brook this ignominious badge of servitude They were therefore proper instruments on the present occasion

1 The question they put to our Lord was whether it was *lawful to pay tribute to Cesar, or not* And they concluded this would necessarily involve him in a dilemma Should he deny the lawfulness of paying tribute, straitway the Herodians would accuse him to the government as a rebel and incendiary should he affirm it, the Pharisees thought he would immediately exasperate the people, and give them the wished-for opportunity, to destroy him *Note*, It hath been the old practice of Satan's emissaries to lay snares for God's servants, and, by catching an unguarded expression, by wilful mistake or designed misrepresentation to blacken and abuse them But there is one who heareth and judgeth

2 To cover this insidious design, they use the deepest expressions of respect As if, conscientiously disposed to follow the path of duty, and highly venerating Christ's wisdom and piety, they desired his directions for their conduct, persuaded that, being a teacher come from God, no frowns nor fear of man would sway his determinations *Note*, (1) The fairest professions often cloke the foulest designs (2) The character of Christ should be the pattern for all his ministers Faithful and true to God themselves, no fear nor flattery must tempt them to conceal any thing of the whole counsel of God from others, but, regardless of men's persons, with zeal and simplicity they must discharge their commission, and speak the truth as it is in Jesus

3 Christ baffles their craft and disappoints their designs He knew the secret wickedness they meditated, and by his question, which shewed his knowledge of their hearts, reproved their hypocrisy *Why tempt ye me, ye hypocrites? shew me the tribute-money* Out of their own mouths he would silence them, and answer them with their own confessions for, producing to him *a penny*, a silver Roman coin, he demanded whose image and superscription it bore and, they replying *Cesar's*, he answered, *Render therefore unto Cesar the things that are Cesar's* As the coining money was the royal prerogative, the circulation of such coin implied subjection to the person whose image it bore there could be no doubt therefore but that, if Cesar's money was regarded as the current coin of the land, there could be no unlawfulness in rendering him the tribute which bore his image, in return for the protection and administration of the civil government, which they received from him And this interfered not with their religious duties they must *render also unto God the things which are God's* Thus neither could the civil government have cause to be offended, nor the Pharisees be able to accuse him without condemning themselves *Note*, (1) When we have to deal with crafty adversaries, we need be wise as serpents, whilst we are harmless as doves (2) The mask of hypocrites, however naturally painted, cannot impose upon him who trieth the heart Their hope of concealment is delusion; and whilst they tempt him they destroy themselves (3) Captious questions should have

have a cautious answer, that, if possible, they who came to ensnare us may be confounded themselves. (4) It is reasonable we should pay tribute to the government from which we receive protection. Christ's servants must on principle be loyal subjects. But, though Cesar has our tribute, God must have our hearts. (5) We must submit to every ordinance of man for the Lord's sake; but, if human injunctions contradict divine commands, God must be obeyed, and we must be content to suffer.

4 Though confounded with his reply, they could not but admire his wisdom, and, defeated in their purpose, they retired with shame as baffled foes, unable to find the least ground for accusation against him. May the Lord ever endue his ministers with the like wisdom, and enable them to disappoint the malice of those who lie in wait for an occasion against them!

x Mark xii 18 Luke xx 27 y Acts xxiii 8 z Deu xxv 5 a Tob iii 8

23 ¶ x The same day came to him the Sadducees,
y which say that there is no resurrection, and asked him,
24 Saying, Master, z Moses said, If a man die, having
no children, his brother shall marry his wife, and raise
up seed unto his brother 25 a Now there were with
us seven brethren, and the first, when he had married
a wife, deceased, and, having no issue, left his wife unto
his brother 26 Likewise the second also, and the third,
unto the seventh 27 And last of all the woman died
also 28 Therefore, in the resurrection, whose wife
shall she be of the seven? for they all had her 29 Je-
sus answered and said unto them, Ye do err, b not know-
ing the scriptures, c nor the power of God 30 For in
the resurrection they neither marry nor are given in mar-
riage, d but are as the angels of God in heaven 31
But, as touching the resurrection of the dead, have ye
not read that which was spoken unto you by God, say-
ing, 32 e I am the God of Abraham, and the God of
Isaac, and the God of Jacob? God is not the God of
the dead, but of the living 33 And when the multi-
tude heard this, they were astonished at his doctrine

b Job xix 25, 26 Ezek xxxvii 5—10 Dan xii 2 c Acts xxvi 8 d 1 John iii 2 e Exod iii 6, 15 Acts vii 32 Heb. xi 16

v 23—33 The Pharisees and Herodians being foiled, the Sadducees next resolved to take the field of controversy against him. They utterly denied a future state, the existence of angels or spirits, and the resurrection of the dead, and thought they could propose a question to our Lord which it would puzzle him to decide.

1 They stated a case, (whether real or imaginary was not material) founded on the Mosaical institutions concerning the widow of a man who died childless, whose brother, according to the law, *Deut* xxv 5, was obliged to marry her, and raise up an heir to the inheritance of the deceased. The question they proposed therefore was, if a woman successively married seven brothers, and, having no children by either, at last died herself, whose wife she shall be at the resurrection, since all could claim the same title to her. They thought thus to lead our Lord to join them in denying a resurrection, or to reduce him to own his ignorance, or to make a decision they could prove to be absurd, and unsupported by reason or Scripture.

2 Christ rectifies their mistake, reproves their ignorance, and shews their objection against a resurrection to be fallacious: they erred, *not knowing the scriptures, nor the power of God*. The Scriptures declare there shall be a resurrection, *Job* xix 26 *Ezek* xxxvii *Dan* xii 2. and though the collection of the scattered atoms of the human body appears never so difficult, it *is not beyond the almighty power of God to effect*. Besides, their ideas of a future state were false and carnal. There will be no occasion there for marriage, to perpetuate inheritances, or to keep up a succession of names, or to minister to our comforts or alleviate our cares, but all will be in heaven as the angels of God, perfectly pure and spiritual, and happy as those glorious ministers which surround the throne of God. But our Lord rests not in confuting their mistakes: he supports the truth by unanswerable arguments, drawn even from the Pentateuch, the sacred authority of which books they themselves admitted. Now, concerning the resurrection of the dead, they must needs remember what God himself declared at that memorable occasion when he appeared to Moses in the burning bush, *Exod* iii 6 where he said, *I am the God of Abraham, Isaac, and Jacob*, tho' these patriarchs were long since dead. He saith not *I was*, but *I am*, he standing toward them still in the same relation; and as his being their God implies some peculiarly great and glorious advantages thence accruing, but these holy men, during all their lives, were strangers and pilgrims in the earth, exercised with various troubles and afflictions, therefore it follows there must be a future state, where their eternal reward awaits them. Besides, *God is not the God of the dead, but of the living*. Had these patriarchs ceased to be when their bodies died, God could not with any propriety be said to continue in the same covenant-relation to them as before. His being *their God* proves them still alive, and the existence therefore of their souls as immortal is evident. But he was not only the God of their souls, but of the men in their whole persons. As therefore their souls now live, their bodies will be quickened also, else would he be still the God of the dead: the resurrection of the body, as well as the immortality of the soul, therefore is here supposed, and the argument conclusive against the tenets of the Sadducees. *Note*, (1) The cause of all our grand errors is the ignorance of the Scriptures. (2) Many things to the eye of sense impossible, the eye of faith, that looks to the promises and power of God sees not only possible, but sure and certain. (3) They who have the Lord for their God need not wish for more: he will be their eternal portion and exceeding great reward.

3 The Sadducees were silenced, the multitude astonished; they had never before heard the eternal happiness of the righteous, the immortality of the soul, and the resurrection from the dead, so nobly defended and proved.

f Mark xii 28 Luke x 25

34 ¶ f But when the Pharisees had heard that he had
put the Sadducees to silence, they were gathered together
35 Then one of them *which was* a lawyer, asked *him* a
question, tempting him, and saying, 36 Master, which
is the great commandment in the law? 37 Jesus said
unto him, g Thou shalt love the Lord thy God with all
thy heart, and with all thy soul, and with all thy mind
38 This is the first and great commandment 39 And
the second *is* like unto it, h Thou shalt love thy neigh-
bour as thyself 40 i On these two commandments
hang all the law and the prophets

g Deut vi 5 & x 12 & xxx 6 Luke x 27 h Lev xix 18 Rom xiii 9 Gal v 14 1 Tim i 5 Jam ii 8 i Chap vii 12

v 34—40 The Pharisees here again return to the charge, and, grieved probably he should be able to silence those whom they could not, consulted together how to put a stop to his increasing reputation, which so eclipsed their own. They who greatly shine, must expect to be greatly envied. They resolved once more to try their skill, and by a question, which had afforded much disputation among themselves, endeavour, if they can, to draw something from him of which they still hoped to make their advantage.

1 The question was, *which is the great commandment of the law?* some esteeming it to be circumcision, others the observation of the sabbath, others the wearing the phylacteries. And should he determine the question in favour of any one party of disputants, the rest would probably have been offended with the decision.

2. His answer carries evidence and conviction along with it. The first and great commandment is the perfect love of God, and the next the loving our neighbour as ourselves; these two commandments comprise the whole moral law, with all the duties enforced by the prophets, and to be obedient to them, this divine principle of love can alone engage us. These commandments still continue in full force, and in the practical exercise of those consists all vital religion: for though we are not under the law, that we should expect life from our obedience, nor capable of discharging perfectly these just and holy precepts, yet are we bound to set them before us as our rule of duty, and by the gospel-faith, which worketh by love, shall be enabled in a measure to walk as Christ also walked, humbly following, though unable to attain unto the perfection of his bright example. *Note*, (1) We must love the Lord our God. We must first believe that he is *our God*, our reconciled God in Jesus Christ, and then love will be the immediate effect: this will produce a hearty obedience to his commands, and unreserved submission to his providence. The love of God will make us count none of his commandments grievous, and reckon every dispensation righteous, just, and good. (2) The love of our neighbours follows. They must be dear to us as we are to ourselves: their persons, property, characters, be regarded as our own, and we should be ready in every good word and work to do them service, wish them every blessing, and desire to act towards them, in every situation, as we could reasonably expect they should behave to us, if they were in our circumstances. The more we appear under the influence of these divine precepts, the more we shall shew of the spirit and power of true Christianity.

41. ¶ k While the Pharisees were gathered together,
Jesus asked them, 42 Saying, What think ye of Christ?
whose Son is he? They say unto him, *The son* of David
43 He saith unto them, How then doth David l in spi-
rit call him Lord, saying, 44 m The LORD said unto
my Lord, Sit thou on my right hand, till I make thine
enemies thy footstool? 45 n If David then call him
Lord, how is he his son. 46 And no man was able
to answer him a word, neither durst any man (from that
day forth) ask him any more questions

k Mark xii 35 Luke xx 41 l 2 Sam xxiii 2 m Ps cx 1 Acts ii 34 Heb i 13 & x 12, 13 n Rev xxii 16

v 41—46 Having thus silenced all his opponents, our Lord is now pleased to put a question in turn to those who had so often tempted him. And he did it when they were gathered together

together, to consult how to ensnare him, that his triumph over them might be more distinguished

1 The question seemed so plain that a child might answer it *What think ye of Christ? whose Son is he?* And they have their reply ready, little imagining in what difficulties it would involve them *They say unto him, The Son of David* So far they were right, the Scripture had thus determined, *Ps* lxxxix 35, 36 *Isa* ix 7 xi 1 It is a question we should be seriously concerned to answer, What we think of his person, offices, undertaking, and whether he is a *Christ* to us, a Saviour to the uttermost

2 From their answer our Lord proposes to them another question of more difficult solution How is the Messiah's being David's Son reconcileable with his being David's Lord? for such the psalmist acknowledges him, when, speaking under divine inspiration, *Ps* cx 1 he saith, *The Lord*, God the Father, *said unto my Lord*, the divine Messiah, *Sit thou at my right hand*, exalted to the throne of the Majesty in the heavens, *till I make thine enemies thy footstool*, for so long will he reign till every foe is destroyed, and the kingdoms of the world become the kingdoms of the Lord and of his Christ *If David then call him Lord*, acknowledging him his superior, and a divine person, *how is he his Son?* and to descend from him as man?

3 This question quite puzzled them They seem to have been ignorant of the divine character of the Messiah, they regarded him as a mere man, and understood not the union of God and man in one Christ, or, if they knew it, they were not willing to acknowledge his Deity, and chose to be silent, rather than reply Perceiving now how unequal a match they all together were for his superior wisdom, they durst not encounter him with any more ensnaring questions, and avoided any farther disputes which they found must issue in their shame *Note*, Many are silenced, without being convinced, have their arguments confuted, while their hearts still remain unconverted

CHAP XXIII

Christ here, 1 cautions his disciples against the pride and hypocrisy of the Scribes and Pharisees, ver 1—12 2 *He denounces woes against them for their sins*, ver 13—33 3 *He foretels the ruin of Jerusalem*, ver 34—39

1 THEN spake Jesus to the multitude, and to his
disciples, 2 Saying, The Scribes and the Pha-
risees sit in Moses seat 3. All therefore whatsoever they
bid you observe, *that* observe and do; but do not ye after
their works for [a] they say, and do not 4 For [b] they
bind heavy burdens, and grievous to be born, and lay
them on mens shoulders, but they themselves will not
move them with one of their fingers 5. But [c] all their
works they do for to be seen of men [d] they make broad
their phylacteries, and enlarge the borders of their gar-
ments, 6 [e] And love the uppermost rooms at feasts,
and the chief seats in the synagogues, 7 And greetings
in the markets, and to be called of men, Rabbi, Rabbi
8 [f] But be not ye called Rabbi for one is your Master,
even Christ, and all ye are brethren 9 And call no man
your Father upon the earth for [g] one is your Father
which is in heaven 10 Neither be ye called masters
for one is your Master, *even* Christ 11 [h] But he that
is greatest among you, shall be your servant 12 [i] And
whosoever shall exalt himself, shall be abased, and he
that shall humble himself, shall be exalted.

[a] Rom ii 21 [b] Isa x 1 Luke xi 46 Acts xv 10. Gal vi 13 [c] Chap vi 1 2 5, 16 [d] Numb xv 38 Deut vi 8 & xxii 12 Prov iii 3 [e] Mark xii 38, 39 Luke xi 43 & xx 46 3 John 9 [f] Jam iii 1 2 Cor i 24 1 Pet v 3 [g] Mal i 6 [h] Chap xx 26 27 [i] Prov xxix 23 Luke xiv 11 & xviii 14 Jam iv 6 1 Pet v 5

v 1—12 Among all the Jewish sects the Pharisees maintained the most distinguished rank, for their reputed wisdom and piety, their specious appearance of religion, and external attention to the forms of godliness, obtained them so high a character, that it was usually said, if but two men reached heaven, one of them would be a Pharisee Yet none ever fell under more censures from Christ than these reputed patterns of sanctity, because indeed they were the most inveterate enemies of him and his gospel as those of a like stamp ever have been and will be to the end of time Their religion was outside, their hearts enmity against God, filled with pride, self-righteousness, love of esteem, worldly-mindedness, and hatred to the power of internal vital godliness Whom the world therefore admired as the best sort of people in it, God abhorred as the worst, as the farthest from his kingdom and righteousness And the case is the same to this very day Against these whited sepulchres Christ therefore cautions his disciples

1 He honours the office they bore as expositors of the law, who sat in Moses's seat, and read and interpreted in the synagogues the sacred oracles to the people And so far as they spake agreeably to the Scriptures they were to be attended to, and their word to be observed and done *Note*, (1) The most sacred and honourable offices in the church have often been filled by the worst of men Yet ought not this to bring any dishonour upon the ministry itself, or prejudice us against the order, that many, who are a scandal to the name they bear, have thrust themselves into it (2) When wicked men preach sound truth, their word is to be received, whilst their works are abhorred Though example is most forcible to persuade and it can hardly be expected that they should convince others, who do not themselves appear to believe the very doctrines they preach

2 He brands the men who lived so unsuitably to the word they taught, and cautions the people to beware of imitating them *Do not after their works for they say, and do not* They boasted indeed of the purity of their morals, as well as the orthodoxy of their sentiments, but the one was as corrupt as the other was culpable Several things our Lord charges upon them

[1] Their hypocrisy They were very strict preachers of the law, and rigid in enforcing the additions made by their vain traditions, laying upon men's consciences burdens intolerable, whilst they themselves dispensed with their own observance of them, and their practice gave the lie to their preaching *Note*, Many preachers pretend the greatest zeal for morality, whose lives shew the laxest morals, and who must therefore be damned upon their own shewing

[2] Their formality, and desire of human applause Their religion consisted of outside, and to make a fair shew before men was their great ambition Instead of internal spirituality, and meditation on God's word, *they made broad their phylacteries*, which were scrolls of parchment, on which select portions of the law were written, sewed up in the skin of a clean beast, and hung at their arms and over their foreheads, and by their uncommon breadth they meant to insinuate their uncommon zeal for the law *And they enlarge the borders of their garments*, not only conforming to the precept, *Numb* xv 38—40 but affecting, by the width of their fringes, to shew their distinguished sanctity, and observance of the command So true it is still, that the most zealous contenders for the *form* of godliness are often the greatest strangers to the *power* of it, and the loudest devotees but mere sounding brass and tinkling cymbals

[3] Their pride and affectation of preeminence They coveted always the most distinguished place at an entertainment, and even in the synagogues, where they assembled for religious worship, the same desire of precedency appeared in their choice of the chief seats, as if their business there was more to make a figure themselves, than to pay their humble adorations In like manner they affected sounding titles of respect, and, when they appeared in public, they loved to have deep homage paid them, and to be addressed with, Rabbi, Rabbi! that others might hear and observe their importance and dignity *Note*, (1) There is no harm in receiving or giving titles of honour to whom honour is due but to take a pleasure in hearing the sound, to be puffed up with the title, and to be offended at the omission of it, these mark detestable pride (2) Nothing can shew a stronger tincture of Pharisaism than coming to God's house to seek our own glory, and to be more anxious in what pew we are placed than with what spirit we worship

3 He forbids his disciples to challenge for themselves, or ascribe to others, any such pompous names as the Scribes assumed They must not be called *Rabbi*, affecting human honour, or any title importing dominion over the faith or consciences of their brethren nor must they be stiled *Master*, as if upon their own authority they sat up for guides and leaders, but must own *one Master* only, that is *Christ*, whose word alone must be their rule, whilst they, as brethren, arrogated no supremacy over each other, alike submissive to their common head Nor may they give flattering titles to any, calling *no man Father upon the earth* Not that this forbids us honouring our natural parents, or those who have begotten us in the gospel, or paying due reverence to age or dignity, but we must regard no man as the founder of our religion, or as the head of the church, to whom, in matters of conscience, we owe implicit obedience, this being the sole prerogative of our God and Father, whose throne is in the heavens but if any man among them excelled in gifts or graces, or was esteemed and preferred to a more honourable place in the church than others, far from being puffed up with his eminence, he is required to be the more condescending and laborious, employing himself the more zealously and humbly for the benefit of his fellow Christians And our Lord subjoins the most forcible argument to support what he had advanced *Whosoever shall exalt himself*, grow proud, imperious, and assuming over his brethren, *shall be abased*, either in penitent humiliation, when brought to a sight of his sin, in this world, or be covered with confusion in the more awful day of Christ's appearing whilst *he that humbleth himself* in every work and labour of love, and in a lowly sense of his own deep unworthiness, *he shall be exalted* in the eyes of God and all good men, and that both now and for ever

13 ¶ But [k] wo unto you, Scribes and Pharisees, hy-
pocrites for ye shut up the kingdom of heaven against
men for ye neither go in yourselves, neither suffer ye
them that are entring to go in 14 Wo unto you,
Scribes and Pharisees, hypocrites, for [l] ye devour widows
houses,

[k] Luke xi 52 [l] Mark xii 40 Luke xx 47 2 Tim iii 6 Tit i 11

houſes, and for a pretence make long prayer, therefore
ye ſhall receive the greater damnation 15 Wo unto
you, ſcribes and Phariſees, hypocrites, for ye compaſs
ſea and land to make one proſelyte, and when he is made,
ye make him twofold more the child of hell than your-
ſelves 16 Wo unto you, ye [m] blind guides, which ſay,
[n] Whoſoever ſhall ſwear by the temple, it is nothing
but whoſoever ſhall ſwear by the gold of the temple, he
is a debtor 17. Ye fools, and blind: for whether is
greater, the gold, [o] or the temple that ſanctifieth the
gold? 18 And whoſoever ſhall ſwear by the altar, it
is nothing but whoſoever ſweareth by the gift that is
upon it, he is † guilty. 19 Ye fools, and blind for
whether is greater, the gift, [p] or the altar that ſanctifieth
the gift 20. Whoſo therefore ſhall ſwear by the altar,
ſweareth by it, and by all things thereon. 21 And
whoſo ſhall ſwear by the temple, ſweareth by it, and by
him [q] that dwelleth therein 22 And he that ſhall
ſwear by heaven, ſweareth by [r] the throne of God, and
by him that ſitteth thereon 23 Wo unto you, ſcribes
and Phariſees, hypocrites, for [s] ye pay tythe of mint,
and aniſe, and cummin, [t] and have omitted the weightier
matters of the law, judgment, mercy, and faith theſe
ought ye to have done, and not to leave the other un-
done 24 Ye blind guides, which ſtrain at a gnat, and
ſwallow a camel 25 Wo unto you, ſcribes and Pha-
riſees, hypocrites, for [u] ye make clean the outſide of
the cup and of the platter, but within they are full of
extortion and exceſs 26 Thou blind Phariſee, cleanſe
firſt that *which is* within the cup and platter, [x] that the
outſide of them may be clean alſo 27 [y] Wo unto you,
ſcribes and Phariſees, hypocrites for ye are like unto
whited ſepulchres, which indeed appear beautiful out-
ward, but are within full of dead men's bones, and of
all uncleanneſs 28 Even ſo ye alſo outwardly appear
righteous unto men, but within ye are full of hypocriſy
and iniquity 29 [z] Wo unto you, ſcribes and Phari-
ſees, hypocrites, becauſe ye build the tombs of the pro-
phets, and garniſh the ſepulchres of the righteous, 30
And ſay, If we had been in the days of our fathers, we
would not have been partakers with them in the blood
of the prophets. 31. Wherefore [a] ye be witneſſes unto
yourſelves, that [b] ye are the children of them which
killed the prophets 32 [c] Fill ye up then the meaſure
of your fathers. 33. Ye ſerpents, [d] ye generation of
vipers, how can ye eſcape the damnation of hell?

[m] Chap. xv 14 [n] Chap. v 33, 34 [o] Ex. xxx 29 † Or a debtor, or bound [p] Ex. xxix 37 [q] 1 Kings viii 13 2 Chron. vi. 2 [r] Chap. v 34 Acts vii 49 [s] Luke xi 42 & xviii 12 [t] 1 Sam. xv 22 Hoſ. vi 6 Mic. vi 8 Chap. ix 13, & xii 7 [u] Mark vii 4 Luke xi 39 [x] Tit. i 15 [y] Luke xi 44 [z] Luke xi 47 [a] Pſ. lxiv 8 [b] Acts vii 51, 52 1 Theſ. ii 15 [c] 1 Theſ. ii 16 [d] Chap. iii 7 & xii 34.

v 13—33 Like Ezekiel's bitter roll, we have here repeated fearful woes, like ſo many bolts of thunder levelled againſt theſe proud ſelf-righteous Phariſees The general charge againſt them is their being *hypocrites*, proved in a variety of particulars, and this being the character God eſpecially abhors, we ſhould be the more jealous over our own ſouls, that this rank weed of bitterneſs ſpring not up under the profeſſion of godlineſs, and mar the whole

1 Pretending to be teachers of the law, and poſſeſſed of the key of knowledge, inſtead of explaining the ſpiritual meaning of all the typical rites, as pointing to Chriſt, or the purport of the prophecies which related to him, they ſtudiouſly ſought to pervert both, commenting upon them in ſuch a way as moſt entirely to overturn the true nature of the Meſſiah's office and kingdom, and led the people to reſt on the ſhadows inſtead of the ſubſtance Invenomed enemies to the goſpel, they turned a deaf ear to all Chriſt advanced in proof of his own divine character and miſſion, and not only rejected him themſelves, but uſed their utmoſt efforts, employing all their influence, their examples, and their cunning, to prejudice the people againſt him and his goſpel, reviling his perſon, doctrine, and miracles, and thundering out their anathemas againſt thoſe who ſhould profeſs to receive him as the Meſſiah

2 They made the cloke of religion ſubſervient to the baſeſt purpoſes of gain and avarice; inſinuating themſelves into the confidence of helpleſs widows, on whom, by their long prayers and affected ſhew of devotion, they impoſed, and who ſuppoſing their piety great as the appearances of it, entruſted them with the management of their affairs, and were directed by their advice, by which means, taking advantage of their ſuperſtition and credulity, they fleeced them of their ſubſtance, and enriched themſelves with the ſpoil of the moſt cruel inhumanity, as well as baſeſt injuſtice; for which, though they might eſcape the *cenſures of men, God, the all-ſeeing Judge*, would ſurely give them *greater damnation* in the day of recompenſe *Note*, (1) The vileſt wickedneſs may ſometimes be ſo ſhaded by craft, as to elude the eye of human obſervation. (2) The appearance of godlineſs put on to cover worldly deſigns, is in God's account the moſt atrocious of crimes (3) Long prayers are not always culpable, it is only when they are *for a pretence*, that they become an abomination (4) There are degrees of miſery in hell ſome ſhall receive greater damnation than others, and the moſt dreadful vengeance of all ſhall light on the hypocrite's head

3 They exerted the greateſt zeal to make proſelytes from the Gentiles, in order to heighten their own reputation, and ſtrengthen their party, and ſtuck at no pains to ſucceed in their attempts, which, when they had done, they abuſed the aſcendancy they obtained over the conſciences of their converts to inſtil the moſt virulent prejudices into them againſt Chriſt and his goſpel, making them more bigotted than themſelves to the vain traditions of the elders, and more bitter perſecutors, even than their maſters, of the diſciples of Jeſus, *See* Acts xiii 45 xiv 2—19 xvii 5 xviii 6 Thus their pretended converſion ſerved to render them but *twofold more the children of hell than themſelves* *Note*, (1) Every impenitent ſinner and hypocrite is a child of hell, of his father the devil, and doomed to dwell with him eternally But of theſe ſome ſhew greater malignity againſt Chriſt and his goſpel than others, and theſe are ſuch uſually as fancy themſelves converted, and are the ſtricteſt obſervers of the forms and ceremonies of religion (2) The induſtry theſe Phariſees uſed to gain *proſelytes* in ſo bad a cauſe, ſhould condemn our negligence and want of zeal, who take ſo little pains to make converts to Chriſt and his goſpel

4 They were *blind guides*, erring through greedineſs after gain, and deceiving others, miſleading them into the moſt dangerous errors reſpecting the obligation of oaths, diſtinguiſhing between the temple and the gold, the altar and the gift, as if they might ſwear by the former, and break the oath with impunity, but an oath by the latter was conſcientiouſly obligatory and the reaſon was clear, becauſe theſe blind guides made gain of the gold vowed to the temple ſervice, and of the gifts offered on the altar But how abſurd and fooliſh this diſtinction? the temple which ſanctified the gold, and the altar which ſanctified the gift, muſt needs be more holy than the gold and gift which received all their ſanctity from being offered there the oath made by the temple and altar ſhould therefore rather be thought more binding, than that made by the gold or the gift Indeed theſe kinds of oaths were in themſelves evil and profane, but if a man once made them, he was bound to fulfil them An oath by the altar included all the gifts thereon, as alſo to ſwear by the temple, or by heaven, implied an appeal to him who dwelleth there, manifeſting his preſence between the cherubims, or *ſitting on his throne moſt high*; and *therefore every breach of* ſuch oath was direct perjury *Note*, (1) It is a dreadful thing for the poor people, when they who undertake to ſhew them the way to heaven are blind and ignorant; and it is ſtill more terrible for the blind guides themſelves, who will periſh under the guilt of thoſe ſouls they have miſled and ruined (2) Oaths are ſacred, they are an appeal to the heart-ſearching God by him alone we may ſwear, but if any profanely ſwear by other things, their profaneneſs will be no plea for their perjury, they are ſtill in conſcience bound to fulfil their oath as to the Lord

5 They were ſcrupulous about trifles, and negligent of the eſſential duties of religion They were moſt exact in the payment of their tythes, even to the ſmall herbs of their garden, to the mint, and aniſe, and cummin, but they *omitted the weightier matters of the law*, ſuch as *judgment*, the due adminiſtration of juſtice, and protecting the weak and helpleſs againſt their oppreſſors, *mercy*, the kind relief they ſhould have ſhown to the diſtreſſed, and *faith*, a dependance upon God's care and love, and the grateful return due in conſequence thereof Theſe they ſhould have practiſed, as the moſt important and momentous, whilſt matters comparatively trivial deſerved but a ſubordinate regard but they were ſuch *blind guides*, corrupt in practice as well as doctrine, *they ſtrained at a gnat, or ſtrained out a gnat* from their liquors, as if it would choak them, pretended ſuch a ſcrupulous attention to avoid the leaſt ſin, and practiſe the niceſt morality, whilſt they could *ſwallow a camel*, making no conſcience in ſecret of the moſt enormous crimes, to gratify their pride, their covetouſneſs, and their malice, *See* ver 14 *chap* xxvii 6 *John* xviii 28 *Note*, (1) The payment of our tythes to the uttermoſt farthing Chriſt commands, *This ſhould ye have done* They who are unjuſt to God's miniſters in withholding their dues, are worſe than even theſe Phariſees (2) The practice of one duty can never be pleaded as a compenſation for the neglect of another, and much leſs can obſervances merely ceremonial excuſe the neglect of thoſe weightier moral precepts, *judgment, mercy*, and *faith* (3) Many pretend a ſcrupulous conſcience in trifles, who, when any thing important to them is at ſtake, heſitate not at committing the moſt flagrant immoralities

6 Their religion conſiſted in mere externals, whilſt their *hearts continued utterly corrupt and defiled* They were very curious about waſhing their cups and platters, and placed much purity in this, whilſt they cared little by what oppreſſion they got the proviſion they eat out of them at leaſt, their inward

together to consult how to ensnare him, that his triumph over them might be more distinguished

1 The question seemed so plain that a child might answer it *What think ye of Christ? whose Son is he?* And they have their reply ready, little imagining in what difficulties it would involve them *They say unto him, The Son of David* So far they were right, the Scripture had thus determined, *Ps* lxxxix 35, 36 *Isa* ix 7 xi 1 It is a question we should be seriously concerned to answer, What we think of his person, offices, undertaking, and whether he is a *Christ* to us, a Saviour to the uttermost

2 From their answer our Lord proposes to them another question of more difficult solution How is the Messiah's being David's Son reconcileable with his being David's Lord? for such the psalmist acknowledges him, when, speaking under divine inspiration, *Ps* cx 1 he saith, *The Lord*, God the Father, *said unto my Lord*, the divine Messiah, *Sit thou at my right hand*, exalted to the throne of the Majesty in the heavens, *till I make thine enemies thy footstool*, for so long will he reign till every foe is destroyed, and the kingdoms of the world become the kingdoms of the Lord and of his Christ *If David then call him Lord*, acknowledging him his superior, and a divine person, *how is he his Son?* and to descend from him as man?

3 This question quite puzzled them They seem to have been ignorant of the divine character of the Messiah, they regarded him as a mere man, and understood not the union of God and man in one Christ, or, if they knew it, they were not willing to acknowledge his Deity, and chose to be silent, rather than reply Perceiving now how unequal a match they all together were for his superior wisdom, they durst not encounter him with any more ensnaring questions, and avoided any farther disputes which they found must issue in their shame *Note*, Many are silenced, without being convinced, have their arguments confuted, while their hearts still remain unconverted

CHAP XXIII

Christ here, 1 cautions his disciples against the pride and hypocrisy of the Scribes and Pharisees, ver 1—12 2 *He denounces woes against them for their sins*, ver 13—33 3 *He foretels the ruin of Jerusalem*, ver 34—39

1 THEN spake Jesus to the multitude, and to his
disciples, 2 Saying, The Scribes and the Pha-
risees sit in Moses seat 3 All therefore whatsoever they
bid you observe, *that* observe and do; but do not ye after
their works for [a] they say, and do not 4 For [b] they
bind heavy burdens, and grievous to be born, and lay
them on mens shoulders, but they themselves will not
move them with one of their fingers 5. But [c] all their
works they do for to be seen of men [d] they make broad
their phylacteries, and enlarge the borders of their gar-
ments, 6 [e] And love the uppermost rooms at feasts,
and the chief seats in the synagogues, 7 And greetings
in the markets, and to be called of men, Rabbi, Rabbi
8 [f] But be not ye called Rabbi for one is your Master,
even Christ, and all ye are brethren 9 And call no man
your Father upon the earth for [g] one is your Father
which is in heaven 10 Neither be ye called masters
for one is your Master, *even* Christ 11 [h] But he that
is greatest among you, shall be your servant 12 [i] And
whosoever shall exalt himself, shall be abased; and he
that shall humble himself, shall be exalted.

[a] Rom ii 19 [b] Isa x 1 Luke xi 46 Acts xv 10 Gal vi 13 [c] Chap vi 1, 2 5, 16 [d] Numb xv 38 Deut vi 8 & xxii 12 Prov iii 3 [e] Mark xii 38 39 Luke xi 43 & xx 46 3 John 9 [f] Jam iii 1 2 Cor i 24 1 Pet v 3 [g] Mal i 6 [h] Ch xx 26 27 [i] Prov xxix 23 Luke xiv 11 & xviii 14 Jam iv 6 1 Pet v 5

v. 1—12 Among all the Jewish sects the Pharisees maintained the most distinguished rank, for their reputed wisdom and piety, their specious appearance of religion, and external attention to the forms of godliness, obtained them so high a character, that it was usually said, if but two men reached heaven, one of them would be a Pharisee Yet none ever fell under more censures from Christ than these reputed patterns of sanctity, because indeed they were the most inveterate enemies of him and his gospel as those of a like stamp ever have been and will be to the end of time Their religion was outside, their hearts enmity against God, filled with pride, self-righteousness, love of esteem, worldly-mindedness, and hatred to the power of internal vital godliness Whom the world therefore admired as the best sort of people in it, God abhorred as the worst, as the furthest from his kingdom and righteousness And the case is the same to this very day Against these whited sepulchres Christ therefore cautions his disciples

1 He honours the office they bore as expositors of the law, who sat in Moses's seat, and read and interpreted in the synagogues the sacred oracles to the people And so far as they spake agreeably to the Scriptures they were to be attended to and their word to be observed and done *Note*, (1) The most sacred and honourable offices in the church have often been filled by the worst of men Yet ought not this to bring any dishonour upon the ministry itself, or prejudice us against the order, that many, who are a scandal to the name they bear, have thrust themselves into it (2) When wicked men preach sound truth, their word is to be received, whilst their works are abhorred Though example is most forcible to persuade and it can hardly be expected that they should convince others, who do not themselves appear to believe the very doctrines they preach

2 He brands the men who lived so unsuitably to the word they taught, and cautions the people to beware of imitating them *Do not after their works for they say, and do not* They boasted indeed of the purity of their morals, as well as the orthodoxy of their sentiments, but the one was as corrupt as the other was culpable Several things our Lord charges upon them

[1] Their hypocrisy They were very strict preachers of the law, and rigid in enforcing the additions made by their vain traditions, laying upon men's consciences burdens intolerable, whilst they themselves dispensed with their own observance of them, and their practice gave the lie to their preaching *Note*, Many preachers pretend the greatest zeal for morality, whose lives shew the laxest morals, and who must therefore be damned upon their own shewing

[2] Their formality, and desire of human applause Their religion consisted of outside, and to make a fair shew before men was their great ambition Instead of internal spirituality, and meditation on God's word, *they made broad their phylacteries*, which were scrolls of parchment, on which select portions of the law were written, sewed up in the skin of a clean beast, and hung at their arms and over their foreheads, and by their uncommon breadth they meant to insinuate their uncommon zeal for the law *And they enlarge the borders of their garments*, not only conforming to the precept, *Numb* xv 38—40 but affecting, by the width of their fringes, to shew their distinguished sanctity, and observance of the command So true it is still, that the most zealous contenders for the *form* of godliness are often the greatest strangers to the *power* of it, and the loudest devotees but mere sounding brass and tinkling cymbals

[3] Their pride and affectation of preeminence They coveted always the most distinguished place at an entertainment, and even in the synagogues, where they assembled for religious worship, the same desire of precedency appeared in their choice of the chief seats, as if their business there was more to make a figure themselves, than to pay their humble adorations In like manner they affected sounding titles of respect, and, when they appeared in public, they loved to have deep homage paid them, and to be addressed with, Rabbi, Rabbi! that others might hear and observe their importance and dignity *Note*, (1) There is no harm in receiving or giving titles of honour to whom honour is due but to take a pleasure in hearing the sound, to be puffed up with the title, and to be offended at the omission of it, these mark detestable pride (2) Nothing can shew a stronger tincture of Pharisaism than coming to God's house to seek our own glory, and to be more anxious in what pew we are placed than with what spirit we worship

3 He forbids his disciples to challenge for themselves, or ascribe to others, any such pompous names as the Scribes assumed They must not be called *Rabbi*, affecting human honour, or any title importing dominion over the faith or consciences of their brethren nor must they be stiled *Master*, as if upon their own authority they sit up for guides and leaders, but must own *one Master* only, that is *Christ*, whose word alone must be their rule, whilst they, as brethren, arrogated no supremacy over each other, alike submissive to their common head Nor may they give flattering titles to any, calling *no man Father upon the earth* Not that this forbids us honouring our natural parents, or those who have begotten us in the gospel, or paying due reverence to age or dignity, but we must regard no man as the founder of our religion, or as the head of the church, to whom, in matters of conscience, we owe implicit obedience, this being the sole prerogative of our God and Father, whose throne is in the heavens but if any man among them excelled in gifts or graces, or was esteemed and preferred to a more honourable place in the church than others, far from being puffed up with his eminence, he is required to be the more condescending and laborious, employing himself the more zealously and humbly for the benefit of his fellow Christians And our Lord subjoins the most forcible argument to support what he had advanced *Whosoever shall exalt himself*, grow proud, imperious, and assuming over his brethren, *shall be abased*, either in penitent humiliation, when brought to a sight of his sin, in this world, or be covered with confusion in the more awful day of Christ's appearing whilst *he that humbleth himself* in every work and labour of love, and in a lowly sense of his own deep unworthiness, *he shall be exalted* in the eyes of God and all good men, and that both now and for ever

13 ¶ But [k] wo unto you, Scribes and Pharisees, hy-
pocrites for ye shut up the kingdom of heaven against
men for ye neither go in yourselves, neither suffer ye
them that are entring to go in 14 Wo unto you,
Scribes and Pharisees, hypocrites, for [l] ye devour widows
houses,

[k] Luke xi 52 [l] Mark xii 40 Luke xx 47 2 Tim iii 6 Tit i 11

houses, and for a pretence make long prayer, therefore
ye shall receive the greater damnation 15 Wo unto
you, scribes and Pharisees, hypocrites; for ye compass
sea and land to make one proselyte, and when he is made,
ye make him twofold more the child of hell than your-
selves 16 Wo unto you, ye [m] blind guides, which say,
[n] Whosoever shall swear by the temple, it is nothing
but whosoever shall swear by the gold of the temple, he
is a debtor 17 Ye fools, and blind for whether is
greater, the gold, [o] or the temple that sanctifieth the
gold? 18 And whosoever shall swear by the altar, it
is nothing: but whosoever sweareth by the gift that is
upon it, he is † guilty 19 Ye fools, and blind for
whether *is* greater, the gift, [p] or the altar that sanctifieth
the gift 20 Whoso therefore shall swear by the altar,
sweareth by it, and by all things thereon 21 And
whoso shall swear by the temple, sweareth by it, and by
him [q] that dwelleth therein 22 And he that shall
swear by heaven, sweareth by [r] the throne of God, and
by him that sitteth thereon. 23 Wo unto you, scribes
and Pharisees, hypocrites, for [s] ye pay tythe of mint,
and anise, and cummin, [t] and have omitted the weightier
matters of the law, judgment, mercy, and faith these
ought ye to have done, and not to leave the other un-
done 24 Ye blind guides, which strain at a gnat, and
swallow a camel 25 Wo unto you, scribes and Pha-
risees, hypocrites, for [u] ye make clean the outside of
the cup and of the platter, but within they are full of
extortion and excess 26 Thou blind Pharisee, cleanse
first that *which is* within the cup and platter, [x] that the
outside of them may be clean also 27 [y] Wo unto you,
scribes and Pharisees, hypocrites for ye are like unto
whited sepulchres, which indeed appear beautiful out-
ward, but are within full of dead men's bones, and of
all uncleanness 28 Even so ye also outwardly appear
righteous unto men, but within ye are full of hypocrisy
and iniquity 29 [z] Wo unto you, scribes and Phari-
sees, hypocrites, because ye build the tombs of the pro-
phets, and garnish the sepulchres of the righteous, 30
And say, If we had been in the days of our fathers, we
would not have been partakers with them in the blood
of the prophets 31 Wherefore [a] ye be witnesses unto
yourselves, that [b] ye are the children of them which
killed the prophets. 32 [c] Fill ye up then the measure
of your fathers. 33. Ye serpents, [d] ye generation of
vipers, how can ye escape the damnation of hell?

m Chap. xv. 14. n Chap. v. 33, 34. o Ex. xxx. 29. † Or, a debtor, or bound. p Ex. xxix. 37. q 1 Kings viii. 13. 2 Chron. vi. 2. r Chap. v. 34. Acts vii. 49. s Luke xi. 42. & xviii. 12. t 1 Sam. xv. 22. Hos. vi. 6. Mic. vi. 8. Chap. ix. 13. & xii. 7. u Mark vii. 4. Luke xi. 39. x Tit. i. 15. y Luke xi. 44. z Luke xi. 47. a Ps. lxiv. 8. b Acts vii. 51, 52. 1 Thess. ii. 15. c 1 Thess. ii. 16. d Chap. iii. 7. & xii. 34.

v. 13—33 Like Ezekiel's bitter roll, we have here repeated fearful woes, like so many bolts of thunder levelled against these proud self-righteous Pharisees The general charge against them is their being *hypocrites*, proved in a variety of particulars, and this being the character God especially abhors, we should be the more jealous over our own souls, that this rank weed of bitterness spring not up under the profession of godliness, and mar the whole.

1 Pretending to be teachers of the law, and possessed of the key of knowledge, instead of explaining the spiritual meaning of all the typical rites, as pointing to Christ, or the purport of the prophecies which related to him, they studiously sought to pervert both, commenting upon them in such a way as most entirely to overturn the true nature of the Messiah's office and kingdom, and led the people to rest on the shadows instead of the substance Invenomed enemies to the gospel, they turned a deaf ear to all Christ advanced in proof of his own divine character and mission, and not only rejected him themselves, but used their utmost efforts, employing all their influence, their examples, and their cunning, to prejudice the people against him and his gospel, reviling his person, doctrine, and miracles, and thundering out their anathemas against those who should profess to receive him as the Messiah.

2 They made the cloke of religion subservient to the basest purposes of gain and avarice; insinuating themselves into the confidence of helpless widows, on whom, by their long prayers and affected shew of devotion, they imposed, and who supposing their piety great as the appearances of it, entrusted them with the management of their affairs, and were directed by their advice, by which means, taking advantage of their superstition and credulity, they fleeced them of their substance, and enriched themselves with the spoil of the most cruel inhumanity, as well as basest injustice; for which, though they might escape the *censures of men, God,* the all-seeing Judge, would surely give them *greater damnation* in the day of recompense *Note,* (1) The vilest wickedness may sometimes be so shaded by craft, as to elude the eye of human observation (2) The appearance of godliness put on to cover worldly designs, is in God's account the most atrocious of crimes (3) Long prayers are not always culpable, it is only when they are *for a pretence,* that they become an abomination (4) There are degrees of misery in hell some shall receive greater damnation than others, and the most dreadful vengeance of all shall light on the hypocrite's head

3 They exerted the greatest zeal to make proselytes from the Gentiles, in order to heighten their own reputation, and strengthen their party, and stuck at no pains to succeed in their attempts, which, when they had done, they abused the ascendancy they obtained over the consciences of their converts to instil the most virulent prejudices into them against Christ and his gospel, making them more bigotted than themselves to the vain traditions of the elders, and more bitter persecutors, even than their masters, of the disciples of Jesus, *See Acts* xiii 45 xiv 2—19 xvii 5 xviii 6 Thus their pretended conversion served to render them but *twofold more the children of hell than themselves* *Note,* (1) Every impenitent sinner and hypocrite is a child of hell, of his father the devil, and doomed to dwell with him eternally But of these some shew greater malignity against Christ and his gospel than others, and these are such usually as they themselves converted, and are the strictest observers of the forms and ceremonies of religion (2) The industry these Pharisees used to gain proselytes in so bad a cause, should condemn our negligence and want of zeal, who take so little pains to make converts to Christ and his gospel

4 They were *blind guides,* erring through greediness after gain and deceiving others, misleading them into the most dangerous errors respecting the obligation of oaths, distinguishing between the temple and the gold, the altar and the gift, as if they might swear by the former, and break the oath with impunity, but an oath by the latter was conscientiously obligatory and the reason was clear, because these blind guides made gain of the gold vowed to the temple service, and of the gifts offered on the altar But how absurd and foolish this distinction? the temple which sanctified the gold, and the altar which sanctified the gift, must needs be more holy than the gold and gift, which received all their sanctity from being offered there the oath made by the temple and altar should therefore rather be thought more binding, than that made by the gold or the gift Indeed these kinds of oaths were in themselves evil and profane, but if a man once made them, he was bound to fulfil them An oath by the altar included all the gifts thereon, as also to swear by the temple, or by heaven, implied an appeal to him who dwelleth there, manifesting his presence between the cherubims, or sitting on his throne most high, and therefore every breach of such oath was direct perjury *Note,* (1) It is a dreadful thing for the poor people, when they who undertake to shew them the way to heaven are blind and ignorant, and it is still more terrible for the blind guides themselves, who will perish under the guilt of those souls they have misled and ruined (2) Oaths are sacred, they are an appeal to the heart-searching God by him alone we may swear, but if any profanely swear by other things, their profaneness will be no plea for their perjury, they are still in conscience bound to fulfil their oath as to the Lord

5 They were scrupulous about trifles, and negligent of the essential duties of religion They were most exact in the payment of their tythe, even to the small herbs of their garden, to the mint, and anise, and cummin, but they *omitted the weightier matters of the law,* such as *judgment,* the due administration of justice, and protecting the weak and helpless against their oppressors, *mercy,* the kind relief they should have shown to the distressed, and *faith,* a dependance upon God's care and love, and the grateful return due in consequence thereof These they should have practised, as the most important and momentous; whilst matters comparatively trivial deserved but a subordinate regard but they were such *blind guides,* corrupt in practice as well as doctrine, *they strained at a gnat,* or *strained out a gnat* from their liquors, as if it would choak them, pretended such a scrupulous attention to avoid the least sin, and practise the nicest morality, whilst they could *swallow a camel,* making no conscience in secret of the most enormous crimes, to gratify their pride, their covetousness, and their malice, *See* ver 14 *chap* xxvii. 6 *John* xviii 28 *Note,* (1) The payment of our tythes to the uttermost farthing Christ commands, *This should ye have done* They who are unjust to God's ministers in withholding their dues, are worse than even these Pharisees (2) The practice of one duty can never be pleaded as a compensation for the neglect of another, and much less can observances merely ceremonial excuse the neglect of those weightier moral precepts, *judgment, mercy,* and *faith* (3) Many pretend a scrupulous conscience in trifles, who, when any thing important to them is at stake, hesitate not at committing the most flagrant immoralities

6 Their religion consisted in mere externals, whilst their hearts *continued utterly corrupt and defiled* They were very curious about washing their cups and platters, and placed much purity in this, whilst they cared little by what oppression they got the provision they eat out of them at least, their inward

parts were very wickedneſs, whatever ſpecious cloke they threw over their ways Juſtly therefore doth Jeſus upbraid them, *Thou blind Phariſee!* dark to the pollution of thy ſoul, cleanſe firſt thy inmoſt thoughts, principles, and deſigns; begin within, be pure in heart, and then you may with conſiſtence contend for an exact conformity to the external rites and ceremonies enjoined by the law But in their preſent ſtate they were the very reverſe of real purity, like whited ſepulchres, garniſhed and glittering without, but within full of pollution and putrefaction, the lively emblem of their hypocriſy and iniquity, lurking under the ſplendid guiſe of uncommon piety *Note*, (1) Our hearts are our grand concern, all our ſervices in religion will be acceptable or abominable, as they are truly purified by the blood of Jeſus, or left polluted with native guilt and corruption (2) They who have never ſeen, felt, and lamented the plague of their own hearts, muſt neceſſarily be blind to all ſpiritual concerns, ſince here all vital godlineſs begins (3) The world abounds with whited ſepulchres, we need be warned of them, leſt miſtaking ſhew for reality, we eſteem thoſe patterns of piety, who are in fact but ſinks of pollution, full of pride, worldly-mindedneſs, and enmity to the power of experimental religion

7 They pretended a high veneration for the prophets of old, and, in honour of their memories, built ſumptuous monuments for them, and kept them with the niceſt care They made great profeſſions of the reſpect they would have paid them, had they been ſo happy as to have lived in their days, and condemned bitterly the wickedneſs of their forefathers in perſecuting and murdering them, proteſting againſt ſuch violence, and that they would have never joined in ſhedding ſuch innocent blood Thus by their own confeſſion they allowed themſelves the deſcendants of thoſe who had murdered the prophets, and how much of their ſpirit they had imbibed, their behaviour towards John the Baptiſt, and their paſt and preſent malicious deſigns againſt Jeſus, plainly evidenced Therefore he juſtly abandons them to the ruin they have deſerved, leaving them to fill up the meaſure of their iniquities, by crucifying him, the Lord of life and glory, and perſecuting even to death his apoſtles and miniſters, till wrath ſhould come upon them to the uttermoſt *Ye ſerpents*, ſubtle and poiſonous, *ye generation of vipers*, fierce and malignant, *how can ye eſcape the damnation of hell?* In their preſent temper and conduct, it was impoſſible but that the eternal wrath of God muſt abide upon them *Note*, (1) Many pretend reſpect for paſt reformers and good men, who perſecute with greateſt virulence thoſe who tread in their ſteps (2) The deceitfulneſs of the heart is great we are ſtrangely apt to flatter ourſelves, how well we ſhould have done and acted if we had been in other perſons circumſtances Many think the hard-hearted Jews, who left the Son of God to lie in a manger, who heard his doctrine, and ſaw his miracles, and yet crucified him, were ſinners of a peculiar dye, and had they lived then, they ſhould have welcomed him with rapture to their houſes and their hearts, who yet treat his word, his miniſters, his people, with the ſame contempt and enmity (3) God's patience waits long with offenders, but their meaſure of ſin will be full, and then ſhall wrath come upon them to the uttermoſt (4) The damnation of hell is to be freely denounced againſt the impenitent and hypocrites, how unwilling ſoever they may be to hear it, or ready to mock at theſe terrors of the Lord

34 ¶ [a] Wherefore behold, I ſend unto you prophets, [a Luke xi 49]
and wiſe men, and ſcribes, and [f] *ſome* of them ye ſhall [f Acts vii 59 & xii 2]
kill and crucify, and [g] *ſome* of them ſhall ye ſcourge in [g Chap x 17 Acts xxii 19 2 Cor xi 24, 25]
your ſynagogues, and [h] perſecute *them* from city to city [h Acts viii 1]
35 That upon you may come all the righteous blood
ſhed upon the earth, from [i] the blood of righteous Abel [i Gen iv 8]
unto [k] the blood of Zacharias ſon of Barachias, whom [k 2 Chron xxiv 21]
ye ſlew between the temple and the altar 36 Verily I [l Luke xiii 34]
ſay unto you, All theſe things ſhall come upon this ge- [m 2 Chron xxxvi 15 Neh ix 26]
neration 37 [l] O Jeruſalem, Jeruſalem, [m] thou that [n 2 Eſd i 30]
killeſt the prophets, and ſtoneſt them which are ſent un- [o Pſ xvii 8 & xci 4]
to thee, how often would [n] I have gathered thy children [p Pſ lxxxi 11]
together even as a hen gathereth her chickens [o] under [q Pſ cxviii 26 Chap xxi 9]
her wings, and [p] ye would not! 38 Behold, your houſe
is left unto you deſolate 39 For I ſay unto you, Ye
ſhall not ſee me henceforth, till ye ſhall ſay, [q] Bleſſed *is*
he that cometh in the name of the Lord

v 34—39 Their fathers they allowed had perſecuted and ſlain the prophets of the Lord, and they would ſoon prove themſelves genuine deſcendants from them

1 Chriſt foretells what would be their behaviour towards his Apoſtles and Evangeliſts Once more he would give them a trial, by ſending to them his miniſters, inveſted with divine authority from him their God and King, who in gifts and grace ſhould be no way inferior to the prophets, wiſe men, and ſcribes who went before them But inſtead of obedience to their word, or reſpect for their perſons, they would juſt do as their fathers before them, or worſe, perſecuting them from city to city, ſcourging them in their ſynagogues, and putting them to the moſt ignominious and cruel deaths *See Acts* vii 59 xii 2. v 10 xxvi 11

2 The meaſure of all their fathers ſins, which thus they imitated, approved, and exceeded, being full, God would not fail to require at their hands all the blood which had been ſhed for righteouſneſs ſake, from the blood of righteous Abel, the firſt martyr, to the blood of Zechariah, the ſon of Barachiah, or Jehoiada, *See 2 Chron* xxiv 20, 21 whom they ſlew between the porch and the altar, and was the laſt martyr for the truth recorded in the Old Teſtament On this generation Chriſt aſſures them ſhall *all theſe things come*, all the heavy wrath threatened for their forefathers guilt and their own *Note*, (1) Every inſult and injury ſhewn to God's righteous ones, ſhall, ſooner or later, be ſeverely avenged (2) The nearer judgments approach, the louder they call for repentance

3 Chriſt pathetically laments over the wickedneſs of Jeruſalem, and denounces her doom

[1] He laments over her wickedneſs, upbraiding her with ingratitude and impenitence under all the means and mercies ſhe had enjoyed *Thou that killeſt the prophets, and ſtoneſt them which are ſent unto thee*, as blaſphemers Such had been, and would be again her practice, and the great truths of God have been often thus loaded with the ſevereſt cenſures, and the moſt faithful and zealous advocates for them perſecuted under the ſpecious pretence of vindicating God's honour, and puniſhing thoſe whom theſe pretended zealots are pleaſed to brand as enthuſiaſts or heretics Yet, ſays Chriſt, *How often would I have gathered thy children together, even as a hen gathereth her chickens under her wings, and ye would not* As man, and a miniſter of the circumciſion, Chriſt peculiarly regarded Iſrael for their fathers ſake, he wiſhed therefore to engage them to attend his miniſtry, that by acknowledging him as the Meſſiah, they might at leaſt prevent the doom with which their rejecting him would be attended But *ye*, the Scribes and Phariſees, who prejudiced the people againſt him *would not*, effectually preventing the people from receiving Chriſt as the Meſſiah, to do which they in general ſeem to have been diſpoſed, and thus theſe falſe guides brought ruin upon themſelves and their deluded followers *Note*, (1) They who have fled to Chriſt for refuge, will find a ſure covert from the ſtorm of divine wrath, whilſt all who refuſe his ſalvation will be left expoſed to deſerved vengeance (2) Chriſt will viſit for all the means and mercies men have abuſed, and a deſpiſed and rejected goſpel will bring down the heavieſt condemnation

[2] He reads her doom *Your houſe is left unto you deſolate* God was now about to abandon them as incorrigible, to leave his temple, and his preſence withdrawn, the gold became dim, the fine gold was changed Nothing but deſolation remained within thoſe once ſacred walls, when the divine inhabitant was fled, nor would it be long ere one ſtone ſhould not be left on another When God departed, their glory and defence forſook them their city and nation with their temple were now devoted to utter deſtruction

4 He takes his ſad farewel of that temple he never more would enter, nor would they ever ſee him after his departure to heaven, till that great day of his appearing and glory, when too late they would be convinced of his being the Meſſiah, and be glad to join in thoſe aſcriptions of praiſe to him, at which they had been ſo enraged Some ſuppoſe this refers to the converſion of the Jews in the latter day, when they ſhall welcome that Redeemer their fathers crucified with hoſannas, bleſſing, and praiſe *Note*, (1) The day is near when every eye ſhall behold the once crucified Jeſus on a throne of judgment, and then wo to thoſe who pierced him! (2) They who will not ſee, are juſtly given up to the blindneſs of their hearts, and ſince they would not bow to the ſceptre of a Redeemer's grace, they muſt periſh under the rod of his judgment (3) If we welcome Jeſus now to our hearts, and he is pleaſed to make them his temple, and by his Spirit to take up his reſidence therein, then ſhall the day of his appearing and glory be our exceeding great joy, and we ſhall riſe up to welcome and call him bleſſed *who cometh in the name of the Lord*, to be glorified in his ſaints, and admired of all that believe

CHAP XXIV

In this chapter we have, 1 The prophecy of the deſtruction of Jeruſalem, and the utter ruin of the Jewiſh church and nation, which was now haſtening on, and was completed about forty years after, the prefaces to that deſtruction, and conſequences of it, yet looking further to Chriſt's coming at the end of time, and the conſummation of all things, of which that was a type and figure, ver 1—31 2 *The practical application of this prophecy for the awakening and quickening of his diſciples to prepare for theſe great and awful things,* ver 32—51

1 [a] AND Jeſus went out, and departed from the [a Mark xiii 1 Luke xxi 5]
temple, and his diſciples came to *him* for to
ſhew him the buildings of the temple 2. And Jeſus
ſaid

said unto them, See ye not all these things? verily I say
unto you, [b] There shall not be left here one stone upon
another, that shall not be thrown down.

v. 1, 2. Having foretold the desolations of Zion, Christ took his last farewel of the temple's devoted walls, and went out to return no more. On his departing we are told the conversation that passed between Jesus and his disciples. They were astonished probably at his prediction, perhaps incredulous of its fulfilment, and begged him a moment to behold the magnificent structure, and view the strength and beauty of the fabric. Tinctured with national prejudices, they seem to have been over-pleased with the outward glory of the building, and thought with regret of its desolations; but Christ, so far from reversing the sentence, more awfully confirms it, decreeing its utter and irrecoverable ruin, so that not even one stone should be left upon another; which, by the concurring testimony of historians, was literally fulfilled, and the very ground ploughed up where the temple stood. *Note*, We are too apt to look upon outward grandeur with the eye of sense, and to be influenced by the pomp and glory of the world; but the eye of faith sees the vanity of every thing below the sun, and looks above it for all that is truly great, and permanently glorious.

3 ¶ And as he sat upon the mount of Olives, the
disciples came unto him privately, saying, [c] Tell us,
when shall these things be? and what *shall be* the sign
of thy coming, and of the end of the world? 4 And
Jesus answered and said unto them, [d] Take heed that no
man deceive you. 5 For [e] many shall come in my
name, saying, I am Christ; and [f] shall deceive many.
6 And ye shall hear of wars, and rumours of wars: see
that ye be not troubled: for all *these things* must come
to pass, but the end is not yet. 7 For [g] nation shall
rise against nation, and kingdom against kingdom: and
there shall be [h] famines, and pestilences, and earthquakes
in divers places. 8 All these *are* the beginning of sorrows.
9 [i] Then shall they deliver you up to be afflicted, and
shall kill you: and [k] ye shall be hated of all nations for
my name's sake. 10 And then [l] shall many be offended,
and [m] shall betray one another, and shall hate one
another. 11 [n] And many false prophets shall rise, [o] and
shall deceive many. 12 And because iniquity shall
abound, the love of many shall wax cold. 13 [p] But he
that shall endure unto the end, the same shall be saved.
14 And [q] this gospel of the kingdom shall be preached
in all the world, for a witness unto all nations; and then
shall the end come. 15 When ye therefore shall see
the abomination of desolation, [r] spoken of by Daniel the
prophet, stand in the holy place, ([s] whoso readeth, let
him understand) 16 Then let them which be in Judea,
[t] flee into the mountains. 17 Let him which is on the
house-top, not come down to take any thing out of his
house: 18 Neither let him which is in the field return
back to take his clothes. 19 And [u] wo unto them that
are with child, and to them that give suck in those days.
20 But pray ye that your flight be not in the winter,
neither on the sabbath-day. 21 For [x] then shall be
great tribulation, such as was not since the beginning of
the world to this time, no, nor ever shall be. 22 And
except those days should be shortned, there should no
flesh be saved: [y] but for the elect's sake those days shall
be shortned. 23 Then if any man shall say unto you,
Lo, here *is* Christ, or there; believe *it* not. 24 For
there shall arise false christs, and [a] false prophets, and
[b] shall shew great signs and wonders; insomuch that ([c] if
it were possible) they shall deceive the very elect. 25
Behold, I have told you before. 26 Wherefore, if they
shall say unto you, Behold, he is in the desart, go not
forth: Behold, *he is* in the secret chambers, believe *it*
not. 27 [d] For as the lightning cometh out of the east,
and shineth even unto the west; so shall also the coming
of the Son of man be. 28 For [e] wheresoever the car-
case is, there will the eagles be gathered together. 29
¶ Immediately after the tribulation of those days, [f] shall
the sun be darkned, and the moon shall not give her
light, and the stars shall fall from heaven, and the pow-
ers of the heavens shall be shaken: 30 And [g] then
shall appear the sign of the Son of man in heaven: and
[h] then shall all the tribes of the earth mourn, and [i] they
shall see the Son of man coming in the clouds of hea-
ven, with power and [k] great glory. 31. And [l] he shall
send his angels with a great sound of a trumpet, and
they shall gather together his elect from the four winds,
from one end of heaven to the other.

v. 3—31. Ascending the mount of Olives, opposite to which the temple stood full in view, the disciples, as he sat there, came privately unto him, saying, *Tell us, when shall these things be?* the destruction of the city and temple: *and what shall be the sign of thy coming, and of the end of the world?* According to their rooted prejudices they seem still to have expected him to appear as a glorious temporal Messiah; and by his coming, meant not his appearing in the day of judgment; or, *by the end of the world*, the final consummation of all things; but rather, the end of the present age, and the period of the Jewish economy; supposing it probable, that the destruction of the temple would pave the way for the erection of another far more magnificent, when in all the pomp of earthly majesty he would appear, and they should be highly advanced in that universal kingdom they expected him to establish. They were very sollicitous therefore to be informed of the signs which should usher him to the throne; and Jesus, to caution them against delusion, to rectify their mistakes, and to confirm them in the faith when they should see the predictions accomplished, answers their questions.

1. He cautions his disciples against deceivers. Having rejected the true Messiah, yet impatient for the temporal deliverance they expected from him, the Jews were open to receive every pretender who set up in his name; and to the false Christs and false prophets who should arise, were they justly to be given up, who so obstinately and wickedly had rejected the true. They must pay no regard to the pretensions of these deluders, and turn a deaf ear to their emissaries, who say, Christ is in the desert, or hid in some secret chamber, and ready to appear. Nor are they to be believed, though they may do strange feats, and pretend to work miracles, which will impose upon the credulous. So powerfully indeed will the great seducer play off his illusions, that nothing but God's effectual grace and everlasting promises could preserve even the elect from being deceived: but Christ, who had chosen, would keep them; and therefore they must remember these cautions now given them in the day of temptation, (v. 25.) which would set them on their guard, and preserve them from seduction. *Note*, (1.) The devil and his instruments may do strange things to support the credit of his falling cause, and lying wonders may be wrought that may stagger the incautious; but whatever would draw us from Christ must be rejected with abhorrence. (2.) It is the comfort of Christ's real disciples, that it is not possible they should be fatally or finally deceived. (3.) Novel pretensions and opinions in matters of religion are ever to be suspected: there cannot be a new, or another gospel. (4.) We are kept by the power of God unto salvation, yet are warned to be on our guard, as if we were to keep ourselves. He who hath ordained the end, hath also appointed the means.

2. Wars and rumours of wars will precede the threatned destruction. By insurrections and seditions against the Roman government in Judea, thousands miserably perished; whilst intestine commotions and slaughters among themselves prepared the way for their final destruction, when, on their last revolt, the Romans marched their armies to besiege and utterly ruin their city and nation. Yet Christ warns his disciples not to be discouraged by these things, so as to discontinue their preaching, or be terrified in their minds; *for these things must first come to pass, but the end is not yet*; the Jews shall be spared a little longer, to experience other judgments. *Note*, (1.) The ravages of war make dreadful work; we cannot but tremble at the alarm; though where the heart is fixed on the rock of ages, we shall not be troubled. Nature will shudder, but faith can raise us above our fears. (2.) God's decrees are unchangeable. What he hath ordained, must come to pass; and this should quiet our minds, and silence our murmurings: we know he doth all things well.

3. Another sign he gives them of the approaching desolation. *Nation shall rise up against nation, &c.* great commotions being in the Roman empire between the contenders for sovereignty; and there shall be *famines, and pestilences, and earthquakes in divers places*; all which came to pass before the destruction of Jerusalem, and are called *the beginnings of sorrows*, being but the prelude to the pangs in which she should expire; as all the temporal judgments which light upon the heads of sinners, are but the beginnings of sorrows, inconceivably bitter as they are endless.

4. He bids them expect a fiery persecution. Far from standing high in that earthly kingdom with which they flattered themselves, nothing but bonds, imprisonment, and death in all its most terrible forms, awaited them, hated both of Jews and Gentiles for the sake of Christ, and his gospel which they preached. And these trying seasons would have awful effects on many who before professed the faith of Jesus, but now, when the cross lay so heavy, would be offended, and apostatize: for suffering times are the test for hypocrites, whose fair profession then is quickly blasted. They studiously seek occasions to quar-

rel with religion, and then revolt from it, content to be Chriſtians only as long as it coſts them neither the loſs of eaſe, intereſt, or honour; and as apoſtates uſually turn the bittereſt perſecutors, by ſuch falſe brethren they ſhould be betrayed, and hated with uncommon malignity. Through the concurrence of ſuch unfaithfulneſs amongſt profeſſors, ſuch enmity in their perſecutors, and ſuch deluding and ſeducing teachers as would ariſe, *iniquity* would peculiarly *abound*, and, as the conſequences of it, *the love of many* ſhould *wax cold*. Though perſecution would make the flame burn fiercer in ſome, many would be glad to ſeek a ſhelter from the ſtorm by concealing their profeſſion, or falling into decays, into ſects and parties, loſe the vital warmth and power of godlineſs, at leaſt for a time. For ſouls truly alive to God may under temptation ſuffer much, and, like trees in winter, it cannot be known whether they will ever ſpring again; but where there is ſtill grace in the heart, there will be a revival, and a return to their firſt love. But for the comfort of thoſe who approve themſelves faithful in theſe trying times, *they* ſhall be ſaved. The remnant according to the election of grace ſhall not periſh in the furnace of adverſity, but either comfortably ſurvive their troubles in this world, or have a more abundant recompenſe in that which is eternal.

5. Notwithſtanding all their ſufferings, *this goſpel of the kingdom*, that points the way to the kingdom of grace and of glory, *ſhall be preached in all the world*, to which their very perſecutions eminently contributed, (*Acts* viii. 1—4.) the apoſtles and others carrying the glad tidings into all the kingdoms under the Roman empire, and probably beyond its limits, (*Col.* i. 6, 23.) *for a witneſs to all nations*, of pardon and peace to thoſe who believed, and as a teſtimony againſt thoſe who perſiſted in their infidelity. And all this was done within forty years after our Lord's aſcenſion, and before Jeruſalem was deſtroyed, and is mentioned as the laſt ſign of its approaching ruin.

6. Having foretold the ſigns of the times, our Lord proceeds to inform them of the immediate cauſes of the deſtruction, and to direct them how to act when the deſolation came up as a flood. They *would ſee the abomination of deſolation*, the Roman armies compaſſing their city and the holy place, with ſtandards flying, on which they bore the images of their gods ſo hateful to the Jewiſh nation; and then whoſoever read the prophet Daniel, would ſee by the event his prediction verified. When this was the caſe, then it was high time for them to flee, and leave the devoted city and country; betaking themſelves to the mountains for concealment from the ravages of the invaders. And when the danger was ſo near and urgent, not a moment was to be loſt: they muſt not go into their houſe, if walking on its roof, to pack up their goods, nor return from the field to carry off their cloaths; but, as they were, inſtantly flee for their lives to ſome place of ſafety, as we are told the Chriſtians immediately did to Pella, on the approach of the Roman army. In this ſeaſon of diſtreſs ſome will be found in circumſtances peculiarly melancholy and grievous; even *ſuch as are with child, and give ſuck*, whoſe flight will be hereby greatly retarded, and it will be more difficult for them to eſcape. Alſo they had need pray, *that their flight might not be in the winter*, when the inclemency of the weather and depth of the roads would increaſe their calamity; *nor on the ſabbath-day*, when many, who ſtill were attached to the rigid obſervance of that day, would be ſcrupulous of travelling, or when the Jews would prevent their journey as contrary to the law. But flee they muſt, for in the city Jeruſalem during the ſiege there would be ſuch a ſcene of miſery, horror, and diſtreſs, as never before was known, nor ever ſhall be, till the time of the conſummation of all things; ſo that ſhould theſe calamities continue, not one of the Jewiſh nation would be left. But God having yet a remnant among them, according to the *election of grace*, and from the deſcendants of thoſe who ſhould eſcape the ſword, deſigning in ſome future day to raiſe up a people for himſelf, he therefore hath ſhortened theſe calamitous days, not dealing with them in that rigour they deſerved, but for his elect's ſake ſparing them from an utter extirpation. *Note*, (1.) In days of tribulation, when God opens a door of eſcape, we muſt thankfully embrace the opportunity. Though we may never fly from duty, we muſt not expoſe ourſelves to unneceſſary danger. (2.) Delays are dangerous; eſpecially where our ſouls are at ſtake. The preſent moment only is allotted us to flee for refuge to the mountain of a Saviour's grace. (3.) At the worſt of times, and in the worſt of places, God hath a few, and for their ſakes he is graciouſly pleaſed to ſhorten the days of calamity. The men of this wicked world little think how much they are indebted to thoſe whom they often deſpiſe and abhor.

7. He adds a repeated caution againſt deceivers, whoſe fallacious promiſes in theſe calamitous times would be more eaſily credited; and pretending to come as the Meſſiah to reſcue the Jewiſh nation from the Roman yoke, would find many ready to receive them, and willing to be deluded with the leaſt ſhadow of hope: and their pretended ſigns and wonders would have a great effect on multitudes; but they muſt remember this warning, and reject all theſe impoſtors.

8. He aſſures them the ruin of Jeruſalem and the Jewiſh nation ſhould be ſudden, irreſiſtible, and awful, as when the blaſt of lightning darts from the cloud. And as eagles by their quick ſcent diſcover and ſeize the carcaſe, ſo ſhould the Romans, bearing the figure of eagles on their ſtandards, ſurround the city as a corpſe to be devoured by them, and through the land hunt out, ſeize, and deſtroy this devoted people.

Some ſuppoſe there is a reference here to the ſwift ſpreading of the goſpel through the world, as a light from heaven illuminating the earth, breaking through the clouds of darkneſs and ſuperſtition, ſeen far and wide, attended with moſt amazing ſucceſs, when innumerable converts eagerly flocked to Chriſt, as eagles to the carcaſe, which was indeed the caſe, but the former ſenſe ſeems to be principally intended.

9. The utter ruin of the eccleſiaſtical and civil ſtate of the Jewiſh nation will then *immediately* enſue. All their glory will depart, all their temple ſervice ceaſe, their entire diſperſion be accompliſhed; metaphorically repreſented by a total dire eclipſe of all the luminaries of heaven, and by a diſſolution of the very frame of nature. Then will the Meſſiah, whom they have rejected, appear to execute the threatned vengeance upon them; and all their tribes with deepeſt anguiſh and diſtreſs will too late mourn their infidelity, and feel the weight of that blood they imprecated on their heads.

Laſtly, On this final ruin of Jeruſalem, the angels of the churches, Chriſt's miniſters, ſhall blow the goſpel-trumpet, and ſpread its awful pleaſing ſound throughout the earth, which, accompanied with the demonſtration of the Spirit and power, will be made effectual to the converſion of all the elect of God thro' the whole earth: and this goſpel will continue to be preached till the end of time, when he ſhall have accompliſhed their number; and then ſhall he be revealed from heaven at the day of final judgment, of which this is the type and figure.

Though to this ſingle event of the deſtruction of the Jewiſh people and nation, I incline to think this prophecy moſt immediately applicable; yet probably there is alſo contained in it a ſtrong reference to the more awful appearance of the great Judge of quick and dead in the laſt day, whoſe coming will be uſhered in with the ſame ſigns of wars, peſtilence, famine, and earthquakes; whoſe goſpel will be firſt ſpread through all lands; and whoſe appearance will be ſudden, unexpected, and terrible as the lightning; and then ſhall all thoſe things literally come to paſs, which are here recorded. Before the brightneſs of his preſence ſhall the ſun and moon be darkened, the ſtars fall from their ſpheres, the elements melt, the heavens be wrapped together as a ſcroll, and the earth be conſumed. With horror the guilty world, ſtartled from their ſlumbers and ſecurity, will behold the terrible Judge ſeated on his throne, ſurrounded by angelic hoſts, the miniſters of flame, who wait his orders, and execute his ſentence. Too late with tears of anguiſh and deſpair they will bewail their inevitable miſery, who had ever before refuſed to mourn in penitence their provocations. With power irreſiſtible, and glory inconceivable, ſhall the Son of man be revealed in clouds burning with vengeance againſt his foes, bright with refreſhing beams of chearing light to gladden the hearts of his redeemed. Then every eye ſhall ſee him, and from his lips expect their irrevocable doom. Awakened from the duſt by the laſt trumpet's blaſt, around his throne ſhall his elect be gathered, conducted by miniſtring angels, whilſt every boſom glows with hope, delight, and joy unſpeakable and full of glory; and welcomed by their Lord, as thoſe his grace hath choſen, his power hath preſerved, their eternal bliſs ſhall be ſecured; whilſt they in wonder, love, and adoration bow before him, with thankfulneſs unutterable own the ſovereign favour, and aſcribe to him alone the everlaſting praiſe. Thruſt from his preſence, ſpeechleſs with guilt, covered with ſhame, the unbelievers, the impenitent, the hypocrite, ſhall then be conſigned to their manſions of eternal horror, torment, and deſpair, and find the juſt but terrible reward of their deeds. Conſider, ſinful ſoul, ere that day comes, *who can dwell with devouring fire? who can dwell in everlaſting burnings?*

32 [m] Now learn a parable of the fig-tree. When his [m Mark xiii. 28. Luke xxi. 29.]
branch is yet tender, and putteth forth leaves, ye know
that ſummer *is* nigh: 33. So likewiſe ye, when ye ſhall
ſee all theſe things, know [n] that † it is near, *even* at the [n James v. 9. † Or, He.]
doors. 34. Verily I ſay unto you, [o] This generation [o Chap. xvi. 28.]
ſhall not paſs, till all theſe things be fulfilled. 35.
[p] Heaven and earth ſhall paſs away, but my words ſhall [p Chap. v. 18. Iſa. li. 6.]
not paſs away. 36. ¶ But of that day and hour know- [Chap. 18. 11.]
eth no man, no, not the angels of heaven, [q] but my Father only. 37. But as the days of Noe *were*, ſo ſhall [q Zech. xiv. 7. Acts i. 7.]
alſo the coming of the Son of man be. 38. [r] For as in [r Gen. vi. 3, &c. & vii. 5.]
the days that were before the flood, they were eating [Luke xvii. 26. 1 Pet. iii. 20.]
and drinking, marrying and giving in marriage, until
the day that Noe entred into the ark, 39. And knew not
until the flood came, and took them all away; [s] ſo ſhall [s 1 Theſ. v. 3.]
alſo the coming of the Son of man be. 40. [t] Then [t Luke xvii. 36, &c.]
ſhall two be in the field, the one ſhall be taken, and the
other left. 41. Two *women ſhall be* grinding at the mill,
the

the one ſhall be taken, and the other left 42 ¶
u Watch therefore, for ye know not what hour your Lord
doth come 43 x But know this, that if the good man
of the houſe had known in what watch the thief would
come, he would have watched, and would not have ſuf
fered his houſe to be broken up. 44 y Therefore be ye
alſo ready for in ſuch an hour as you think not, the
Son of man cometh. 45 Who then is a faithful and
wiſe ſervant, whom his Lord hath made ruler over his
houſhold, z to give them meat in due ſeaſon? 46
a Bleſſed is that ſervant, whom his Lord when he com-
eth, ſhall find ſo doing 47 Verily I ſay unto you, that
b he ſhall make him ruler over all his goods 48 c But
and if that evil ſervant ſhall ſay in his heart, My Lord
delayeth his coming, 49 d And ſhall begin to ſmite *his*
fellow-ſervants, and to eat and drink with the drunken
50 The Lord of that ſervant ſhall come in a day when
he looketh not for him, and in an hour that he is not
aware of, 51 And ſhall cut him aſunder, and appoint
him his portion with the hypocrites e there ſhall be
weeping and gnaſhing of teeth.

u Chap xxv 13, Mark xiii 33, Luke xxi 36 x Luke xii 39 &c 1 Theſ v 2 2 Pet iii 10 Rev iii 3 & xvi 15 y 1 Theſ v 6 Pet iv 7 z John xxi 15 Acts xx 28 a Rev xvi 15 b Chap xxv 21 c Wiſd ii 1—9 d 1 Pet v 3 e Chap viii 12 & xxii 13

v 32—51 As the events predicted would ſpeedily have their accompliſhment, they muſt prepare for them

1 They may judge of the approach of Jeruſalem's ruin by the ſigns mentioned, as eaſily and as ſurely as they would conclude ſummer at hand, when the fig-tree begins to bud, and put forth leaves The things Chriſt had ſpoken would certainly and ſpeedily have their fulfilment heaven and earth ſhould paſs, ſooner than one jot or tittle of his word could fail, and they of that generation would behold it, though the very day or hour fixed in the divine decree for Jeruſalem's fall, no man nor angel knew, that being a ſecret in the divine boſom

Many underſtand the laſt verſe as a tranſition to what relates to the final judgment. It is fixed in the divine mind, it cometh certainly, the time is ſhort, the hour unknown, that we might be always ready, leſt that day ſhould come upon us unawares

2 He deſcribes the ſenſuality and ſecurity in which the Jewiſh people would be ſurprized Like the men of the old world, who ſlighted Noah's warnings, perſiſted in the ſervice of their luſts and pleaſures, and, drowned in carnal gratifications, would not believe the threatned judgments, till wrath came upon them, and the flood ſwept them away In ſuch a ſtate of falſe peace and worldly purſuits would the Jews be found when their deſtroyers came, notwithſtanding all the warnings of Chriſt and his apoſtles, and then, by wondrous turns of providence, where two perſons were found at the ſame employments in the field, or at the mill, one ſhall be taken, either a captive, or ſlain, and the other ſhall be left, eſcaping from the hands of the enemy

And this will eſpecially be the caſe with the world of the ungodly before the great day of the Lord comes They will be ſurprized in the midſt of ſenſual and earthly gratifications, refuſing to hear the voice of God's miniſters calling them to repentance, he will give them up to the ſpirit of ſlumber Their indulgencies drive them to infidelity, and their unbelief hardens them in their ſins, ſo reciprocally do the love of pleaſure and infidelity operate Thus they will put far away the evil day, though they only impoſe upon themſelves, and will be more terribly ſurprized with its ſudden arrival and then an awful and eternal ſeparation ſhall be made between the children of men who were before of the ſame occupation, engaged in the ſame labours, dwelling perhaps under one roof, or partners of the ſame bed; but of whom one was taken by ſovereign diſtinguiſhing grace, and called by the goſpel to be a ſervant of Jeſus, and the other left a ſlave of corruption Theſe ſhall now be for ever ſeparated; the one caught up to the Saviour's boſom, the other left to the eternal miſery and ruin he hath choſen What thankfulneſs then do all who are taken owe to *him*, who, when others ſo near, ſo like themſelves periſh, is pleaſed to ſave them with an everlaſting ſalvation!

3 He admoniſhes them in the view of theſe things to be always ready, faithfully diſcharging their truſt, and, as uncertain of the time, ever wakeful and watchful, that when theſe judgments come, they may be found on their guard And what is here ſaid, was not peculiarly directed to them, but is ſpoken to all, who being in jeopardy every hour, and not knowing whether the very next they may not be called to meet their Lord by death, or at the throne of judgment, have continual need to be expecting and preparing for their great change. Two things we know That Chriſt will come, but when is uncertain, and therefore left uncertain, that we might be always ready, unleſs we act more fooliſhly reſpecting our ſouls, than any man of common prudence does with regard to his perſon or ſubſtance; for if he be admoniſhed of danger from the approach of a thief by night, he will watch to prevent the robber's entrance and how much more then are we called to watch, that we may not be ſurprized at midnight with the coming of the great Judge, and periſh in a fatal ſecurity, body and ſoul for ever Our Lord enforces this great duty of watchfulneſs by the caſe of a maſter and his two ſervants, the one negligent, the other diligent and watchful, recommending it to us to copy the example of the wiſe and faithful ſervant, that we may receive his reward, and eſcape the miſery which neglect and careleſſneſs about the concerns of our ſouls muſt neceſſarily be attended with

[1] The wiſe and faithful ſervant repreſents every gracious ſoul, and eſpecially the miniſters of Chriſt, who are ſent by him, the great ruler of his family the church, to ſerve in their ſeveral departments, according to their ſeveral capacities Their buſineſs is to *ſerve*, not themſelves, but the heirs of ſalvation, for whom they are appointed to labour, ſtudying to render them every kind office, and to give them that meat of the ſound, ſavoury, and ſtrengthening doctrines of truth, which they need, and this regularly in due ſeaſon, and as ſhall beſt ſuit the ſtate of every one of their people Herein the faithful miniſter muſt approve, (1) His *wiſdom*, in ſtudying and conſulting their wants, and how to ſupply them (2) His *faithfulneſs*, in diſcharging his truſt, with a conſtant regard to his maſter's honour, and an eye to the real good of thoſe committed to his care, willing to approve himſelf to their conſciences, and, when both cannot be done, more ſollicitous to profit than to pleaſe them (3) His *diligence*, always employed in the bleſſed work, that when his maſter comes, he may be *found ſo doing*. *Note*, Love of idleneſs and eaſe in a miniſter is doubly criminal Where ſuch a faithful ſervant thus labours, he ſhall not loſe his reward The bleſſing of Jeſus ſhall reſt upon him in life, in death, for ever he will have the comfort of his work when he lives, will feel ſatisfaction in it when he dies, and the bleſſing ſhall follow him into the eternal world, where he ſhall be advanced to the higheſt honours, and ſhine forth in the kingdom of Jeſus, as the ſun for ever and ever May ſuch a proſpect animate our zeal, and quicken our diligence

[2] The very reverſe is the conduct and end of the wicked ſervant, under which character every miniſter and profeſſor of religion is repreſented, whoſe practice and principles contradict his pretenſions (1) His *practice* is deſcribed as bad, very bad, quarrelſome, inſolent, and oppreſſive to his fellow-ſervants, and abuſing the power he is entruſted with over them Inſtead of ſtudying their good, and labouring for their ſervice, he is wholly taken up with the indulgence of his own appetites If he can find good eating and drinking for himſelf, he cares nothing how his maſter's intereſts fare, and his company are thoſe with whom he can feaſt to the full, in luxury, exceſs, and drunkenneſs *Note*, The Lord obſerves the conduct of thoſe who call themſelves his miniſters and ſervants He marks their pride and inſolence, ſmiting with words of reproach, or, under pretence of vindicating their maſter's honour, abuſing with the exerciſe of oppreſſive authority their more faithful fellow-ſervants, uſually becauſe they are faithful The Lord ſees their carnal lives, their unbecoming aſſociates, their compliances with a world lying in wickedneſs, and their partaking in other men's ſins, perhaps loſt in exceſs themſelves *Miniſters!* yet, horrid to tell, drunkards, or companions with them! Will he not viſit for theſe things?—(2) His *principles* are as infidel, as his practice is immoral Far from living in a conſtant expectation of his Maſter's coming, he puts far off the evil day, and flatters himſelf there is no danger yet And thus his heart is emboldened to live after the faſhion of the world, and to neglect the awful charge committed to him *Note*, There is much more infidelity both in miniſters and people profeſſing godlineſs, than they themſelves are aware of; yet many a man would be ſhocked and affronted to be charged as an infidel, whoſe practice, notwithſtanding, every day evidences the infidelity of his heart, and demonſtrates, that it is impoſſible he can believe the ſolemn account he muſt ſhortly make, when he ſo ſeldom, or ſo careleſsly thinks of it, and takes ſo little pains to prepare for it —(3) His *doom* is fearful Surprized by his Maſter's coming in death or judgment, his negligence and guilt will ſtare him in the face, when it is too late for repentance or amendment He ſhall be cut off from all his ſenſual purſuits, in the midſt of his iniquities; and, ſeparated for ever from the Lord, his portion ſhall be appointed him with hypocrites in the deepeſt abyſs of miſery, where eternal weeping and gnaſhing of teeth beſpeak the unutterable torments of the damned Let every careleſs ſinner, and, above all, every negligent, faithleſs, worldly-minded miniſter, read this awful ſentence and tremble, whilſt yet there is hope They ſhall aſſuredly receive greater damnation than any others, who, under the guiſe of a pretended commiſſion from Chriſt, have deluded and deſtroyed the people committed to their charge, and by their errors, negligence, or ill examples, lie down with the blood of loſt ſouls upon their heads crying for vengeance

CHAP XXV

The necessity of preparing to meet the Lord in judgment, is enforced, 1 In the parable of the ten virgins, ver 1—13 2 In the parable of the three servants, ver 14—30 3 In a more plain description of the process of the last judgment, ver 31—46 and these are things of awful consideration because of everlasting concern to every one of us

1 THEN shall the kingdom of heaven be likened
unto ten [a] virgins, which took their lamps, and
went forth to meet [b] the bridegroom 2 [c] And five of
them were wise, and five *were* foolish 3 They that
were foolish took their lamps, and took no oil with
them 4 But the wise [d] took oil in their vessels with
their lamps 5 While the bridegroom tarried, [e] they
all slumbered and slept 6 And [f] at midnight, there
was [g] a cry made, Behold, the bridegroom cometh, go
ye out to meet him 7 Then all those virgins arose, [h]
and trimmed their lamps 8 And the foolish said unto
the wise, Give us of your oil; [i] for our lamps are † gone
out 9 But the wise answered, saying, *Not so*, lest
there be not enough for us and you but go ye rather
to [k] them that sell, and buy for yourselves 10 And
while they went to buy, the bridegroom came, and they
that were ready went in with him to the marriage, and [l]
the door was shut 11 Afterward came also the other
virgins, saying, [m] Lord, Lord, open to us 12 But he
answered and said, Verily I say unto you, [n] I know you
not 13 [o] Watch therefore, for ye know neither the
day, nor the hour wherein the Son of man cometh

a Ps xlv 14 Rev xxi 2, 9
b Eph v 31, 32 Rev xix 7
c Chap xiii 47 & xxii 10
d Zech iv 2, 3 John i 16.
e Chap xxvi 43 Jam i 2
f Mark xiii 35, Luke xii 20
g Chap xxiv 31 1 Thes iv 16
h Luke xii 35 2 Pet iii 14
i Job viii 13 14 & xviii 5, 6 & xxi 17
† Or going out Job xi 20
k Isa lv 1
l Luke xiii 25
m Chap vii 21 22
n Chap vii 23
o Chap xxiv 42 1 Cor xvi 13 1 Thes v 6 1 Pet v 8 Rev xvi

v 1—13 Though this parable, as connected with the former chapter, may have a particular reference to the destruction of the Jewish people, who had slighted the gospel salvation, and neglected their day of grace, yet it may well be understood as of more general import, and including a warning and caution to men in every age and place

The parable itself is taken from a common custom in those days, when the bridegroom used to go in the evening attended by his friends, to the house of the bride, who, on hearing of his approach, went out with lights, accompanied by a number of virgins, her companions, to welcome his arrival, and conduct him to the entertainment provided on that occasion, and such shall be the state of the gospel church at the coming of Christ, as we see here represented We have,

1 The persons here spoken of, *the virgins, who went out with their lamps to meet the Bridegroom* The *Bridegroom* is the Lord Jesus, who condescends to call his church his spouse, and to honour every member of it with that near and exalted relation *The virgins* are those professors of religion, who appear desirous to present themselves to Christ, in the comeliness, beauty, and simplicity, which his righteousness and grace puts upon them, they *go forth to meet him*, found in his ways and ordinances here on earth, expecting his coming from heaven, and if they are *his* indeed, loving and looking for the day of his appearing

2 The characters of the virgins They were very different, as their actions shewed *Five of them were wise*, and as an evidence of their foresight and prudence, they took care to be well provided with oil, that they might have enough, if they should tarry long in waiting These represent the faithful souls made wise unto salvation, whose hearts are truly supplied with the oil of divine grace, and have not only the light of profession, but the real experimental knowledge of Jesus Christ, possess a living principle, and partake of a divine nature, but *five were foolish*, who, though in appearance associated with the others, were unacquainted with the life-giving truths of the gospel, professors, but not possessors of the grace which is in Jesus Christ, shining to others in a name to live, but really dead and dark in their own souls they have lamps, but *no oil with them*, destitute of spiritual life, careful only to make a fair shew in the flesh, and recommend themselves to their neighbours as Christians, without a single eye to Christ, and a real desire in simplicity and godly sincerity to approve themselves to him And they are foolish indeed, who thus deceiving others, most fatally deceive and destroy their own souls

3 The Bridegroom not coming so soon as they expected, *they all slumbered and slept*, but as their state was different when awake, it was different also when asleep Indeed *the wise*, the faithful souls, through the abiding corruption of their nature, worldly avocations, removal from the gospel, and the communication of lively christians, slothfulness, or neglect of spiritual exercises, the power and prevalence of temptation, outward cares and affliction, connection with others lifeless or careless in their walk, through these and the like causes, even once vigorous christians grow sometimes into a lifeless state of soul the love of Christ, and of their brethren, waxes cold, indifference to the concerns of eternity succeeds, and though they lament it, the sorrow is not deep or lasting, notwithstanding the root of the matter is in them, and afflictions, the word, and renewed breathings of the divine spirit, will yet revive the dying flame The *foolish*, satisfied in external profession, sleep the sleep of death, sunk in carnal security, and utterly resting upon the form of godliness

4 At midnight, the cry of the Bridegroom's approach startled them from their slumbers, and instantly they were summoned to meet him with their lamps Thus suddenly surprized are we often by death, and even gracious souls start at the summons, not expecting it so near, and conscious of their own unfaithfulness whilst horror seizes the hypocrite and the sinner, and they awake to meet their inevitable doom But doth our Lord delay? Is this moment yet our own? Awake then thou that sleepest, prevent this dire alarm.

5 Instantly they arose, and began to trim their lamps The wise found much to do, and blushed to be thus overtaken, but their oil soon revived the expiring flame, their faith and love regained their exercise, and welcoming their Redeemer, they confidently expected to be found of him in peace The foolish too essayed to prepare, but alas! too late their lamps were gone out, and no oil to be procured in vain they seek to beg from their companions, or buy from others, they have lost the moment which cannot be regained Thus even in this world the lamp of profession is often extinguished, and the unfaithfulness of the heart appears though if the hypocrite's hope burns to his last hour, in death it expires then he will know the value of what he hath lost, when it cannot be regained none will then be found able to impart of their grace, what the best possess being barely sufficient for themselves Whilst there is life indeed, the market is still open to the latest moment, they who come to Christ may buy pardon, grace, and peace, without money and without price but when death closes the scene, the lamp of hope is for ever extinguished, and as the tree falleth, it must lie

6 Whilst the foolish virgins went to buy, the Bridegroom came Many on their death-beds express deep concern for their neglected souls, and think by some extraordinary acts of devotion and charity, still to purchase heaven, mistaking the market and spending their labours on that which satisfieth not Christ alone can save a sinking soul, and to the last, they who come humbly to him, never find it too late—*They that were ready went in with him to the marriage*, all who are found cloathed in his righteousness, and shining in the graces of his spirit, are admitted to his eternal presence, and sit down with him in glory *and* then *the door was shut*, they who are entered into the rest of the blessed, go out no more, and they who are once excluded, can never more gain admission the great gulph is fixed, and despair hath for ever barred the door of hope Too late *the foolish virgins came*, importunately craving admittance, for in death and judgment they will often learn to pray and cry who never prayed before, but all entrance is refused to them, and the Bridegroom utterly disowns them, *verily I say unto you, I know you not*, and wo to that sinful soul thus abandoned of God to his misery, and doomed never to enter into his rest

7 The inference from the whole is, *Watch therefore*, the concerns of our souls are infinitely momentous, and will not admit of being trifled with, the time is short, eternity depends upon our improvement of it We know neither the day nor the hour when we shall be summoned away, the sleeping virgins had a midnight call, and why not you or I? Watch therefore, that you may be always ready to go forth with joy to meet the Lord

14 ¶ For *the kingdom of heaven is* as a [p] man traveling
into a far country, who called his own servants, and de-
livered unto them his goods 15 [q] And unto one he
gave five † talents, to another two, and to another one,
to every man according to his several ability, and
straightway took his journey. 16 Then he that had
received the five talents, went and [r] traded with the
same, and made *them* other five talents 17 And like-
wise he that *had received* two, he also gained other two
18 But he that had received one, went and digged in
the earth, and hid his lord's money 19 After a long
time the lord of those servants cometh, and [s] reckoneth
with them 20 And so he that had received five ta-
lents, came and brought other five talents, saying, Lord,
thou deliveredst unto me five talents behold, [t] I have
gained beside them five talents more 21 His lord
said unto him, Well done, thou good and faithful ser-
vant, thou hast been faithful over a few things, [u] I will
make thee ruler over many things enter thou into [x] the
joy of thy lord 22 He also that had received two ta-
lents, came and said, Lord, thou deliveredst unto me
two

p Luke xix 12
q Rom xii 6 1 Cor xii 11 Eph iv 11
† A talent ... Chap xviii 24
r 1 Pet iv 10
s Rom xiv 12
t Jam ii 18
u ...
x ...

two talents b hold, I have gained other two talents beſides them 23 His lord ſaid unto him, y Well done, y Ver. 21. 1 Pet. i. 7
good and faithful ſervant, thou haſt been faithful over a few things, I will make thee ruler over many things
enter thou into the joy of thy lord 24 Then he which
had received the one talent, came and ſaid, Lord, z I z Ezek. x. 25.
knew thee that thou art an hard man, reaping where
thou haſt not ſown, and gathering where thou haſt not
ſtrawed 25 And I was afraid, and went and hid thy
talent in the earth : lo, there thou haſt *that is* thine
26 His lord anſwered and ſaid unto him, Thou wicked
and ſlothful ſervant, thou kneweſt that I reap where I
ſowed not, and gather where I have not ſtrawed 27
Thou oughteſt therefore to have put my money to the
exchangers, and then at my coming I ſhould have received mine own with uſury 28 Take therefore the talent
from him, and give it unto him which hath ten talents
29 a For unto every one that hath ſhall be given, and he a Ch. p. xi. 12. Mark iv. 25. Luke viii. 18.
ſhall have abundance : but from him that hath not ſhall
be taken away, even that which he hath. 30 And caſt
ye the unprofitable ſervant b into outer darkneſs there b Chap. viii. 12. & xxiv. 51.
ſhall be weeping and gnaſhing of teeth

v. 14—30 As a farther illuſtration of the method in which the Lord will deal with the viſible members of his church, the following parable is delivered Chriſt is the great Maſter and Lord of all, we are all his ſervants in profeſſion, and they eſpecially, who are put in truſt with the goſpel : our great buſineſs therefore here below is, to make our profiting appear to the glory of our Lord We are told,

1 The truſt committed to theſe ſervants during their maſter's abſence To one he gave five talents, to another two, to another one, to the leaſt a very conſiderable ſum, a ſingle talent of ſilver amounting by the loweſt computation to upwards of 353 *l* and theſe talents may refer either, (1) To the gifts he beſtowed on his diſciples after his aſcenſion, qualifying them with extraordinary miraculous powers, and furniſhing them with ability for the diſcharge of the arduous truſt committed to them, whilſt he went up to heaven, being in the fulneſs of time again to return, and call his ſervants to account for the improvement of that which he had committed to their care (2) The talents may refer in general to all the gifts of nature or providence, of which we are poſſeſſed, and which are lent us of the Lord, purely to ſerve the purpoſes of his glory, and promote the intereſts of his kingdom, and for them we muſt be accountable to him in the great day of his appearing Some have more than others, God being ſovereign in his bounty, and as we deſerve nothing from him, it is a mercy that we ſhould be entruſted with the leaſt talent They, who by their ſtation, abilities, or poſſeſſions, are entruſted with much, whoſe capital is large, and influence moſt extenſive, have the more to anſwer for, and need give the greater diligence : but all have ſomething, the meaneſt have one immortal ſoul to care for, infinitely more precious than millions of ſilver or gold

2 The improvement each made of the talents committed to them Two of them immediately ſet themſelves to work, and by their diligence doubled their capital Thus faithful miniſters and chriſtians laying out themſelves in the Redeemer's work and ſervice, ſee the moſt abundant bleſſing attending their labours of love Their own ſouls are enriched with knowledge and grace, whilſt they are ſerving others, the church is edified and increaſed, and immortal ſouls are gained for Chriſt, in his account the richeſt treaſure —One of the ſervants, and he that had leaſt, was negligent and careleſs, inſtead of making uſe of his talent, he went and hid it in the earth : repreſenting herein the character of thoſe, whether miniſters, or profeſſors of religion, who make no improvement of their natural abilities, or providential endowments, but are ſo buried in earthly-mindedneſs, and attention to this world's purſuits, that they have neither inclination nor leiſure to ſerve the intereſts of Chriſt and or ſoul

3 After a long time the maſter of theſe ſervants came to reckon with them : for though the Lord Jeſus waits long, he will aſſuredly come at laſt, and we muſt at his tribunal, every one of us, render up our account Oh! that it might be with joy, and not with ſorrow.

(1) The faithful ſervants with readineſs appeared, and gave up their accounts, highly to their maſter's ſatisfaction, who failed not abundantly to reward their diligence He that had five talents, had gained other five : he that two, had doubled them, both therefore are received with the ſame token of approbation, and partake of the ſame rewards Thus in the day of Chriſt, the faithful miniſters and diſciples of Jeſus acknowledging the truſt committed to them as a matter of grace, will produce full evidence of their diligence and profiting, and whether it be leſs or more of the gifts of nature or providence which they have poſſeſſed, their Lord will graciouſly accept the improvement they have made, will commend their fidelity, and abundantly reward them, exalting them to a throne of glory in his eternal kingdom, and admitting them into the participation of thoſe unſpeakable and never-ending joys which are at his right hand for evermore : a reward indeed infinitely exceeding all their ſervices But as it was through grace they received their talents, through grace alone were enabled to improve them; ſo it is of grace, not of debt, they receive the recompenſe ſo far beyond all they could deſire or deſerve

(2) The ſlothful ſervant next appears, and fain would excuſe his own negligence by the moſt unjuſt reflection upon his gracious Maſter, pretending apprehenſions of his auſterity, and rigorous exactions, as if he expected to reap where he had neither manured the ſoil, nor ſown the ſeed : producing therefore the talent, and pleading fear, he hopes his Lord will be ſatisfied with his own, and not diſapprove his care of hiding it, that he might reſtore it entire at his return Such are the ſentiments, pleas, and excuſes of the falſe and faithleſs diſciple [1] He hath hard thoughts of God, and thinks his demands too rigorous and ſevere, deſirous to lay the blame of his ſins on him rather than himſelf [2] He is under the bondage of fear, the little he affects to do proceeds from a ſlaviſh principle, and where this reigns, no acceptable ſervice can be rendered to God [3] He depends for his acceptance with God on a negative religion, and thinks it very ſufficient if he can plead he hath done no harm, hath not been ſo bad as others, nor indulged in thoſe exceſſes which they fell into, though he can produce neither the works of faith, or labours of love [4] He preſumes on the validity of his plea, and ſees not that there is a lie in his right hand

(3) Convicted out of his own mouth, judgment is pronounced on him His ſloth and wickedneſs were evident, and to be idle in the ſervice of God is highly criminal His very excuſe ſhewed ſelf-contradiction, ſince if he had ſo auſtere a perſon to deal with, at leaſt he ſhould have given the money into a banker's hands, where it would have been equally ſafe, and bore lawful intereſt *Note*, The ſinner's excuſes in the day of judgment will but prove his guilt more evident : if God was the hard maſter he pretends, he ought to have been at more pains to pleaſe him, and more diligent to improve the meaſure of gifts or grace, however ſmall, which was vouchſafed him Juſtly therefore doth ſentence proceed, *take the talent from him*, for they who uſe not the gifts, means, and mercies, temporal or ſpiritual, which they enjoy, deſerve to forfeit them, *and give it unto him which hath ten talents* God thus graciouſly rewarding the fidelity and diligence of his ſervants with an increaſe of bleſſings, adding to the ſtore they have improved, whilſt he often ſtrips off even the profeſſion of the hypocrites, and deprives them of the common gifts of nature, providence, or goſpel-privileges which they before enjoyed Nor doth the unprofitable ſervant's puniſhment reſt in the mere loſs of what he poſſeſſed, but in the ſufferings to which he ſhall be doomed, when caſt *into the outer darkneſs, where there ſhall be weeping and gnaſhing of teeth* *Note*, (1) Hell is the place of the ſinner's torment, and the miſeries of that diſmal manſion the direſt expreſſions of human agony and diſtreſs can but faintly repreſent (2) If the ſlothful and unprofitable meet ſo fearful a doom, where will the extravagant and abandoned appear, who have ſquandered inſtead of hiding the talent, and abuſed it to the moſt immediate diſhonour and injury of the maſter who intruſted them therewith ?

31 ¶ When c the Son of man ſhall come in his glory, c Zech. xiv. 5. Chap. xvi. 27. 1 Theſ. iv. 16. 2 Theſ. i. 7. Jude 14. Rev. i. 7.
and all the holy angels with him, then ſhall he ſit upon
the throne of his glory 32 And d before him ſhall be d Rom. xiv. 10. 2 Cor. v. 10. Rev. i. 7. & xx. 12.
gathered all nations, and e he ſhall ſeparate them one
from another, as a ſhepherd divideth his ſheep from
the goats 33 And he ſhall ſet the ſheep on his right e Ezek. xxxiv. 17. Chap. xiii. 49.
hand, but the goats on the left 34 Then ſhall the
King ſay unto them on his right hand, Come, ye bleſſed
of my Father, inherit the kingdom f prepared for you f Chap. xx. 23. Mark x. 40. Heb. xi. 16.
from the foundation of the world 35 g For I was an
hungred, and ye gave me meat I was thirſty, and ye g Iſa. lviii. 7. Ezek. xviii. 7. Jam. i. 27.
gave me drink h I was a ſtranger, and ye took me in
36 i Naked, and ye clothed me I was ſick, and ye
viſited me k I was in priſon, and ye came unto me h Heb. xiii. 2.
37 Then ſhall the righteous anſwer him, ſaying, Lord, i Jam. ii. 15, 16.
when ſaw we thee an hungred, and fed *thee*? or thirſty,
and gave *thee* drink ? 38 When ſaw we thee a ſtranger, k 2 Tim. i. 16.
and took *thee* in? or naked, and clothed *thee*? 39 Or l Prov. xix. 17. Chap. x. 42. Heb. vi. 10.
when ſaw we thee ſick, or in priſon, and came unto
thee? 40 And the King ſhall anſwer, and ſay unto
them, Verily I ſay unto you, l Inaſmuch as ye have done m Chap. vii. 23.
it unto one of the leaſt of theſe my brethren, ye have n Pr. ix. 17.
done *it* unto me 41 Then ſhall he ſay alſo unto them o Mark ix. 44, 46, 48.
on the left hand, n Depart from me, ye o curſed, into p Amos vi. 6. Jam. ii. 15, 16. 1 John iii. 17.
everlaſting fire, prepared for the devil and his angels
42 p For I was an hungred, and ye gave me no meat

I was thirſty, and ye gave me no drink · 43. I was a
ſtranger, and ye took me not in naked, and ye clothed
me not ſick, and in priſon, and ye viſited me not
44 Then ſhall they alſo anſwer him, ſaying, Lord,
when ſaw we thee an hungred, or athirſt, or a ſtranger,
or naked, or ſick, or in priſon, and did not miniſter
unto thee? 45 Then ſhall he anſwer them ſaying,
Verily I ſay unto you, [q] Inaſmuch as ye did *it* not to
one of the leaſt of theſe, ye did *it* not to me 46 And
[r] theſe ſhall go away into everlaſting puniſhment but
the righteous into life eternal.

[q] Prov xiv 31 & xvii 5 Zech ii 8 Acts ix 5.
[r] Dan xii 2 John v 29. Rev xiv 11 & xx 10

v 31—46 Without a parable, our Lord proceeds in theſe verſes to give a delineation of that awful proceſs, which will be obſerved in the great day of final judgment may it awaken our minds to prepare for it! We have,

1 The majeſty of the eternal Judge diſplayed *The Son of man*, the incarnate Jeſus, who once ſuffered on a croſs, and is now exalted to the crown, all power being given him in heaven and in earth, at his bar ſhall the nations be aſſembled, and every individual *of the ſons of Adam muſt then appear before him*, to receive, according to the deciſions of his juſtice, everlaſting happineſs, or eternal torment In the glory of eſſential deity, with the peculiar dignity of Mediator, ſhall he be revealed, the myriads of bright angelic hoſts ſhall grace his train, and ſtand the ready miniſters to execute his orders whilſt ſeated on a throne of glory, brighter than the ſun when he goeth forth in his ſtrength, every eye ſhall ſee him, and from his lips expect their irrevocable doom Shall I be there? my ſoul, tremble at the thought, and give all diligence to be found of him in peace

2 The all diſcerning eye of Jeſus, incapable of miſtaking the true characters of men, ſhall now make the final ſeparation His ſheep, who in faith unfeigned, and love without diſſimulation, followed him the true ſhepherd, ſhall, in diſtinguiſhed honour, be placed high at his right hand whilſt *the goats*, the hypocrites and impenitent, whoſe hearts remain uncleanſed from their native filthineſs, who lived and died in ſin unpardoned, ſhall be degraded to the left with ſhame, the prelude to their approaching fearful ſentence Reader, conſider, where ſhall thy place be?

3 The faithful ſhall be received with the moſt endearing welcome *Then*, when he ſhall have made the ſeparation, and no one ſpot remains among the glorious hoſt, addreſſing himſelf with every endearment of voice and aſpect, *the King*, whoſe word is with power, and his ſentence unchangeable, he *ſhall ſay unto them*, *Come*, ye, the everlaſting objects of my love, whom by grace I have choſen and called, and who have followed me in the regeneration, come, to be for ever with me, to behold and partake of my glory, *ye bleſſed children of my Father*, honoured with this diſtinguiſhed title, though deſpiſed, abhorred of men, precious to the God of heaven, bleſſed with his preſent and eternal favour; come, *inherit the kingdom*, as joint-heirs with me, a kingdom that cannot be moved, eternal in the heavens, compared with which, all earthly grandeur vaniſhes, as the glow-worm before the meridian ſun, a kingdom of never-fading glory, *prepared* by the power and grace of the Almighty, on purpoſe to crown the felicity of his choſen, and this *from the foundation of the world* From eternity the plan was laid, in the creation the deſign appeared, and now the thrones are ready to receive you, that you may reign with me for ever and ever With what rapture and delight, with what joy unſpeakable and full of glory will the redeemed hear this addreſs from the mouth of their adored Judge, of their beloved Lord! Oh that my lot may be amongſt theſe ſaints in light!

4 Chriſt mentions the evidences of their relation to him as his people, clearly ſhewn in the regard paid for his ſake, to their brethren in affliction and diſtreſs the deſtitute, hungry, and naked their hands were open to relieve, the ſick were cheered by their preſence and ſweet counſel, and all the horrors of a priſon kept them not from viſiting the faithful there confined for the teſtimony of Jeſus Chriſt, ſupporting their wants, and not aſhamed of their bonds Works of genuine charity theſe, which though in no wiſe meritorious, or challenging a reward at his hands, Jeſus remembers, and in the riches of his grace is pleaſed to mention to their honour, as undoubted tokens of their faith unfeigned Surprized to hear their Lord make mention of their poor inſignificant ſervices, and with deep humility conſcious how little they deſerved it at his hands, the righteous were ready to queſtion and diſclaim the works attributed to them They never ſaw, at leaſt the moſt of them, their Lord in the fleſh, and cannot hear, without ſome confuſion, his declarations with regard to their duties, when they ever bluſhed to think how defective they had been but the king from his throne ſhall anſwer, with ſtrongeſt aſſurances of his kind reſentment of their conduct, that he regards what they did for the meaneſt of his diſciples, whom in his infinite condeſcenſion he is pleaſed to call *my brethren*, is done unto himſelf He interprets our practice by our principles, it is not ſo much the duty, as the ſpirit in which it is performed, that he reſpects. The leaſt deed of charity, even a cup of cold water, when beſtowed with a deſire to his glory, and proceeding from love to him, ſhall be remembered with diſtinguiſhed honour And in the leaſt of his poor people Jeſus is ſtill preſent with us, and what we beſtow to relieve their wants, will be equally acceptable to him, as if we had viſited him in the days of his fleſh, and miniſtred to him of our ſubſtance What an engagement and encouragement this, to every work and labour of love

5 Sentence is paſſed on thoſe at the left hand With terror in his voice, and frowns of terrible ire, the Judge ſhall pronounce the unchangeable decree *Depart from me, ye* objects of my abhorrence, whoſe guilt and impenitence provoke my indignation, be for ever baniſhed from my preſence, and therewith from all bliſs, and eaſe, and happineſs for ever *Depart, ye curſed*, on whom my wrath eternally abides, and all the penalties of a broken law, vengeance ſhall purſue you to the bottomleſs pit, thither muſt ye be driven, *into everlaſting fire*, to dwell in flames that never can be quenched, where an agonizing body adds to the miſery of the tortured ſoul, and as intolerable as the torment is, ſo eternal is the ſuffering, no ray of hope ſhall ever chear the horrid gloom · there is neither proſpect of an end, nor remiſſion of the torture, but black deſpair adds bitterneſs inexpreſſible to every pang the damned feel and this not originally deſigned for you, but *prepared for the devil and his angels*, whom ye have choſen to imitate, his ſervice to obey, his works to follow, and therefore with him muſt ſuffer, alike in ſin, alike in puniſhment With ſuch companions to ſpend eternity, how terrible! In ſuch torments to lie down, how intolerable! Oh ſin, ſin, what haſt thou done!

6 The reaſon for the ſentence is given, and the criminal's plea over-ruled The inſtances of their guilt are produced, drawn from the omiſſions of thoſe duties which the righteous practiſed, the ſure evidences of the want of that faith which worketh by love Engroſſed with ſelfiſh conſiderations, negligent and at eaſe, they cared not for the diſtreſſes of the miſerable, nor ſought to alleviate them, were unconcerned what the faithful ſuffered for their maſter's ſake, and if at any time humanity, ſenſibility to diſtreſs, oſtentation, or ſelf-complacence opened their purſes to the relief of indigence, their gifts never flowed from the divine principle of love to Jeſus and his brethren, nor were directed to his glory alone, therefore they were as reprobate ſilver They object indeed to the charge, and becauſe they never ſaw Chriſt in the fleſh, preſume they cannot be accuſed of thus neglecting him, but the plea is frivolous Chriſt is one with every member of his church, ſuffers in them and with them, and every inſult, ſlight, or neglect ſhewn to them, he reckons done to himſelf And this ſhould comfort the deſpiſed and ſuffering ſervants of Jeſus, he feels and takes a part in all their troubles, and let thoſe who treat them with indignity, tremble They may pretend indeed, they mean to diſcountenance and diſcourage a deluded ſect, to ridicule or oppreſs a company of enthuſiaſtic religioniſts, and the like, but men need well conſider what they do, and whether they act clearly on the authority of their bibles, and under the influence of fervent charity, leaſt a perſecuted Jeſus ſhould riſe up terribly to avenge his own and his people's wrongs If the doom of the negligent, the unmerciful, and uncharitable be ſo dreadful, what will be the caſe with the unjuſt, and the perſecutors of God's people?

7 The ſentence is no ſooner pronounced than executed *Theſe ſhall go away into everlaſting puniſhment*, there is no appeal from Chriſt's bar, nor eſcape from his judgment the doom is irrevocable, the execution immediate Driven from his preſence, they are caſt into the burning lake, and the ſmoke of their torment aſcendeth up for ever and ever *But the righteous*, who in their Redeemer were found complete, and in their characters by his grace approved as faithful, ſhall go *into life eternal*, to the enjoyment of God in his kingdom of glory, to partake of all the bleſſedneſs which the boundleſs love and power of an all-ſufficient God can beſtow on his moſt favoured children, their holineſs and happineſs perfected, and their bliſs ſecured to eternity

CHAP XXVI

The croſs of Chriſt is the Chriſtian's glory We here ſee him entering on the ſcene of his ſufferings We have, 1 The preface to them [1] The previous notice given by him of them to his diſciples, ver 1, 2 [2] *The ruler's conſpiracy againſt him*, ver 3—5 [3] *The anointing of his head at a ſupper in Bethany*, ver 6—13 [4] *Judas's bargain with the prieſts to betray him*, ver 14—16 [5] *Chriſt's eating the paſſover with his diſciples*, ver 17—25 [6] *His inſtituting the Lord's ſupper, and his diſcourſe with his diſciples after it*, ver 26—35 2. *His entrance upon them, and ſome of the particulars of them* (1) *His agony in the garden*, ver 36—46 (2) *The ſeizing of him by the officers, with Judas's help*, ver 47—56 (3) *His arraignment before the chief prieſt and his condemnation in his court*, ver 57—68 (4) *Peter's denying him*, ver 69—75

1 AND it came to pass, when Jesus had finished all
these sayings, he said unto his disciples, 2 Ye
know that [a] after two days is *the feast of* the passover, and
the Son of man is betrayed to be crucified 3 [b] Then as-
sembled together the chief priests, and the scribes, and
the elders of the people, unto the palace of the high
priest, who was called Caiaphas, 4 And consulted that
they might take Jesus by subtilty, and kill *him* 5 But
they said, Not on the feast-*day*, [c] lest there be an uproar
among the people.

[a] Mark xiv 1 Luke xxii 1 John xiii 1
[b] Psal ii 2 John xi 47 Acts iv 25—27
[c] John xiii 29

v 1—5 The time was now at hand fixed in the eternal counsels, when Messiah, the prince, should be cut off for the sins of his people

1 He gives his disciples notice of his betrayal and approaching crucifixion, that they might be the less surprized He had finished his discourse on the sufferings they might expect, and their encouragement to bear up under them, and now he was going himself to set them the bright example they should copy The views of a suffering Christ should support every suffering christian Within two days the dreadful plot should be executed, and it is as sure as if already done, that he *is betrayed to be crucified*

2 Just at this time the chief priests, scribes, and elders, the members of the Sanhedrim, and the men of highest authority among the Jews, exasperated now beyond measure, and resolved upon the death of Jesus, assembled to consult upon the properest means of accomplishing their bloody purpose The high priest's palace was the place where these conspirators met, and having weighed the dangers of an uproar which might ensue, if on the feast-day they should attempt to arrest him amidst the concourse of people who attended him, they resolved, if possible, to watch their opportunity to seize him privately, and either thus make away with him, or get him condemned by the Roman governor, and execute him as a malefactor, on account of crimes they were ready to lay to his charge *Note*, The fear of man often restrains those from wickedness, who are unawed by any fear of God

6 ¶ [d] Now when Jesus was in Bethany, in the house
of Simon the leper 7 There came unto him a woman
having an alabaster-box of very precious ointment, and
poured *it* on his head, as he sat at *meat* 8 But when
his disciples saw *it*, they had indignation, saying, To what
purpose *is* this waste? 9 For this ointment might have
been sold for much, and given to the poor. 10 When
Jesus understood *it*, he said unto them, Why trouble ye
the woman? for she hath wrought a good work upon
me 11 [e] For ye have the poor always with you, [f] but
me ye have not always 12 For in that she hath pour-
ed this ointment on my body, she did *it* for my burial
13 Verily I say unto you, Wheresoever this gospel shall
be preached in the whole world, *there* shall also this that
this woman hath done, be told for a memorial of her

[d] Mark xiv 3 Luke vii 37 John xii 3
[e] Deut xv 11 John xii 8
[f] Chap xxviii 20 John xiii 33

v 6—13 Jesus, though he spent the day at Jerusalem, retired at even to Bethany, a village at a little distance from thence, and was now in the house of Simon the leper, one of those probably who had experienced his healing power, and had become his faithful disciple We are told,

1 The singular mark of respect shewn him by a gracious woman who was present when they sat at meat She poured upon his head a box of precious ointment, as the profession of her faith in him as the Messiah, the anointed of God, and as a token of her love to him, as her adored Lord and Saviour

Some have imagined that this occurrence is the same with that related, *John* xii 1 and they reconcile the accounts by supposing, that this woman, there said to be Mary, Lazarus's sister, who with his family, were invited to the entertainment, might not only anoint our Saviour's head, but his feet also, though one of the evangelists mentions the one, and the other the other, and that this, though here introduced, was done six days before Others suppose they are two distinct occurrences, differing in time, place, and manner, and this to me seems most probable

2 The offence the disciples took at the matter They among themselves censured the action as an unnecessary waste of what might have been more profitably employed, if the money, so valuable a box of ointment would bring, had been given to the poor, and perhaps meant tacitly to blame their master for permitting this to be done, and not discountenancing the woman *Note*, (1) Charity bids us put the best construction on what is dubious, and we should be very careful how we censure those of over-doing or as guilty of imprudence, who go farther than we dare or care to do Probably the fault we complain of will be found more justly retorted, and that not their intemperate rashness, but our lukewarmness and want of zeal and love for Jesus is to be blamed (2) That is never waste which is employed for Christ and his service

3 Christ rebukes his disciples, and vindicates this gracious woman He knew their murmurs, and expostulates with them on the unjustness of their indignation, *why trouble ye the woman* by such harsh judging, and unkind sentiments of her conduct? The work was both suitable and seasonable, deserving commendation, not censure Among the poor, for whom they expressed such jealousy, they would always find objects to exercise their charity, but his bodily presence with them was short, and therefore this act of respect was not only pleasing to him but had a particular view which they knew not it was intended for his burial, as an embalming of his body though now alive, which she would not have an opportunity to do when he was dead, and this she did either by revelation, or the Holy Ghost directed her to the action for this end So far therefore from its turning to her reproach, it should be mentioned to her perpetual honour, as the evidence of her genuine faith and love, wherever the gospel should be preached in the whole world *Note*, (1) If we knew the principles and motives on which others act, we should often see abundant reason to approve that conduct which now we condemn (2) It is a real grief to a gracious soul to be censured for well-doing, especially by those whose approbation he had reason to expect, but our judgment is with the Lord, and our reward with our God (3) We never need want opportunities of doing good, if we have hearts to do it, objects of distress every where abound (4) Those who honour Jesus he will honour A name in his records, or the book of life of the Lamb, secures immortal fame and glory

14 ¶ Then [g] one of the twelve, called [h] Judas Iscariot,
went unto the chief priests, 15 And said *unto them*,
[i] What will you give me, and I will deliver him unto
you? And they covenanted with him [k] for thirty pieces
of silver 16 And from that time he sought opportu-
nity to betray him

[g] Mark xiv 10 Luke xxii 3
[h] Chap x 4
[i] 1 Tim vi 10
[k] Zech xi 12 Chap xxvii 3

v 14—16 The traitor Judas provoked with the vindication of the woman, and vexed at the reproof which he peculiarly felt, as having been the chief murmurer and instigator of the rest, given up now to the devil's power, presently arose full of malice and resentment, and went directly to the chief priests, who wanted, but could not hope to find, so fit an instrument for their hellish purpose We may not startle that one of the twelve was a traitor, or had a devil where shall we find, among professors in general, so small a proportion of hypocrites and apostates? We have,

1 The offer he made *What will ye give me, and I will deliver him unto you?* This was the very thing they desired, they dared not seize him openly, nothing therefore could be more opportune than to have a traitor among his followers, who could introduce them secretly, that they might arrest him without an uproar The love of money, backed by resentment at a supposed affront, hurried him on, and though conscious of his master's innocence, he does not presume to vindicate his own baseness, by pretending the discovery of any crime, or daring to appear as an evidence against him, yet resolved to ruin him, he proposes this villainous treachery *Note*, (1) Many want only opportunity and temptation, to shew the baseness and hypocrisy of their hearts (2) None wound the cause so deep as those, who from apostles turn apostates, and employ their bitter enmity against the gospel they once preached and espoused (3) When the heart is bent on mischief, the devil will suggest the means (4) The love of money is the fatal bait by which thousands have perished, and for gold have basely sold their God

2 The chief priests eagerly embraced the offer, and immediately the bargain is struck for thirty shekels of silver, in value about three pound fifteen shillings, which was by law the price of a slave (*Exod* xxi 32) *the goodly price he was valued at by them*, *Zech* xi 13 *Note*, (1) They who sell themselves to work wickedness, often find the wages wretched as the service is vile (2) Many cry out against the falsehood of this traitor, yet by crafty bargain, and inordinate profit on their goods, how often have they lied, deceived, defrauded, and sold their master for less than thirty pieces of silver?

3 From that time Judas *sought opportunity to betray him*, that acquainting them with his retirement, they might seize him in the absence of the multitude The way of sin is headlong, one crime draws on another, the conscience is hardened by the repetition of guilt, and onward the miserable slave of Satan is hurried to the precipice of eternal ruin

17 ¶ [l] Now [m] the first *day* of the *feast of* unleavened
bread, the disciples came to Jesus, saying unto him,
Where wilt thou that we prepare for thee to eat the pass-
over? 18 And he said, Go into the city to such a man,
and say unto him, The master saith, My time is at hand,
I will keep the passover at thy house with my disciples
19. And the disciples did as Jesus had appointed them,
and

[l] Mark xiv 12 Luke xxii 7
[m] Exod xii 6 18

and they made ready the passover 20 Now when the
even was come, he sat down with the twelve 21 And
as they did eat, he said, Verily I say unto you, that ⁿ one
of you shall betray me. 22 And they were exceeding
sorrowful, and began every one of them to say unto him,
Lord, is it I? 23 And he answered and said, ᵒ He that
dippeth his hand with me in the dish, the same shall be-
tray me 24 The Son of man goeth as it is written of
him but wo unto that man by whom the Son of man is
betrayed it had been good for that man if he had not
been born 25 Then Judas, which betrayed him, ᵖ an-
swered and said, Master, is it I? He said unto him, Thou
hast said

ⁿ John xiii. 21. ᵒ Luke xxii. 21. ᵖ John xiii. 26.

v. 17—25 We have here our Lord's celebration of his last passover

1 The preparation for that solemnity *The first day of the feast of unleavened bread*, when the paschal Lamb was to be killed and eaten in the evening, the disciples presuming their Master would keep the passover at Jerusalem, though they knew of no house ready for his and their reception, asked him *where* they must prepare the paschal supper? and Christ, at the same time that he gave them a striking proof of his omniscience, directs them to a person who, on delivering the message he gave them, would shew them the place they sought *Say unto him*, who was probably a disciple, and well knew Jesus, *the Master saith, My time is at hand*, the time of his departure, *I will keep the passover at thy house with my disciples*, this was hereafter the last kind office he would be able to shew him The disciples, without hesitation, obeyed, found all things as he had said, prepared the passover, and at even when he came, the twelve sat down with him at the table *Note*, (1) Christ must send to prepare himself a welcome in our hearts, when he saith, *I will*, the work is done (2) When we follow Christ in his commands, he will make us feast with him in his comforts

2 During the supper, he took occasion to inform them of a circumstance which many of them would be shocked to hear, and this was, that one of them *should betray him* He well knew the traitor and the plot, and gave them this notice for the confirmation of their faith, when the thing should come to pass Exceedingly distressed at the thought that he should be betrayed, and more that one of them should be so perfidious, with anxious sollicitude the eleven began severally to ask him, *Lord, is it I?* each perhaps trembling at the deceitfulness and treachery of their hearts, or rather grieved at the suspicion, and conscious of their innocence, desired to clear themselves from such an imputation Just then, it seems, Judas stretched out his hand to dip the bread into the dish, and by this circumstance Christ pointed out the traitor, *he that dippeth his hand with me in the dish, the same shall betray me*, which he mentions, to make the perfidy appear more base, and to shew the fulfilment of the scripture, whilst he adds a terrible commination, if any thing might startle the hardened conscience of this apostate The Son of man must indeed, according to the determinate counsel and foreknowledge of God, be thus betrayed, but wo to the traitor; *it had been good for that man if he had not been born*, a convincing proof of the eternal misery of every damned soul With impudent effrontery, unabashed, though conscious of his guilt, Judas, who had been silent before, perceiving himself pointed at, endeavoured to brave it out, either fancying that Christ could not know of his guilt, or would not directly charge him with it, and therefore said, *Lord, is it I? He said unto him, Thou hast said* The reply is express he was the man *Note*, (1) True humility will ever make us jealous over these vile hearts, we know not to what we may be tempted, nor how weak we are to resist, nothing is too bad for the best to do if left one moment to themselves, therefore we should *never be high-minded, but fear* (2) The more nearly we have been connected with Jesus, in the participation of his ordinances, the more aggravated will be the guilt of unfaithfulness (3) Men may put a bold face upon a bad cause, and they may indeed escape the judgment of men, but God trieth the heart

26 ¶ ᵠ And as they were eating, ʳ Jesus took bread,
and ‡ blessed *it*, and brake *it*, and gave *it* to the disciples,
and said, Take, eat, this is my body 27 And he took
the cup, and gave thanks, and gave *it* to them, saying, ˢ
Drink ye all of it 28 For this is my blood of ᵗ the
New Testament, which is shed ᵘ for many for the remis-
sion of sins 29 But I say unto you, ʷ I will not drink
henceforth of this fruit of the vine, ˣ until that day when
I drink it new with you in my Father's kingdom 30
And when they had sung an ‖ hymn, they went out
into the mount of Olives

ᵠ Mark xiv. 22. Luke xxii. 19. ʳ 1 Cor. xi. 24. ‡ Many Greek copies have, *gave thanks*. ˢ Mark xiv. 23. 1 Cor. xi. 25. ᵗ Jer. xxxi. 31. ᵘ Chap. xx. 28. Rom. v. 15. ʷ Luke xxii. 18. ˣ Acts x. 41. ‖ Or, Psalm. Some think Psalms 113—118.

v. 26—30 All Jewish ordinances were now about to be abrogated and among them the passover In its room Christ here institutes the great gospel ordinance, called from hence, *the Lord's supper*, where he is held forth as our passover, the Lamb slain from the foundation of the world, and we are invited to come and feast thereon The paschal supper being ended,

1 Our Lord took bread which lay by him, and blessing it, brake, and gave to his disciples, commanding them to eat, and explaining the import of what he did, saying, *this is my body*, the representation of the sacrifice I am about to suffer for your redemption, when my body shall be thus broken on the tree, the constant memorial of which shall thus be observed in my church to all ages, as the passover perpetuated the memory of Israel's deliverance from Egypt

The doctrine of transubstantiation raised from hence is too absurd to need confutation, and not only gives the lie to our senses, and contradicts the very nature of a sacrament, but would make Christ eat his own flesh and blood

2 He took the cup, and with thanksgiving and prayer having consecrated the wine, gave it to them, and commanded them all to drink of it, as the representation and memorial of that blood which he was now just ready to shed; to confirm and establish the New Testament, or Covenant, and to procure for them all spiritual blessings, especially that chief of all, the remission of sins, and for as many also, as afterwards trusting on his atonement, should plead the redemption hereby purchased for them, from sin and guilt for ever

3 He takes a solemn farewell No more would he ever drink of this passover cup the very ordinance itself was henceforth abolished, to give place to this new institution in the gospel church No more would they enjoy this free and familiar converse with him, till the day, the glorious day arrived, when admitted to his eternal kingdom, they should partake of those unutterable joys (signified by *the new wine*) which are at his right hand for evermore *Note*, A dying saint with delight takes his farewel of all the comforts he ever enjoyed here below, sweet as ordinances, the word, communion with God were to his soul, he is going where, instead of the drops he tasted here below, he shall be admitted to drink of the living streams of eternal consolations, that flow uninterrupted, ever new, from the throne of God

4 They closed the solemnity with a hymn, and never is the song of praise more suitable than on such an occasion Hereupon departing from the house, he retired, by moonlight, to the mount of Olives, the place appointed for the scene of his agonizing sorrows

31 Then saith Jesus unto them, ʸ All ye shall be ᶻ of-
fended because of me this night for it is written, ᵇ I
will smite the shepherd, and the sheep of the flock shall
be scattered abroad 32 But after I am risen again, ᶜ I
will go before you into Galilee 33 Peter answered and
said unto him, ᵈ Though all men shall be offended be-
cause of thee, *yet* will I never be offended 34 Jesus
said unto him, ᵉ Verily I say unto thee, that this night
before the cock crow, thou shalt deny me thrice 35
Peter said unto him, Though I should die with thee, yet
will I not deny thee Likewise also said all the dis-
ciples

ʸ Mark xiv. 27. John xvi. 32. ᶻ Chap. xi. 6. ᵇ Zech. xiii. 7. ᶜ Chap. xxviii. 7. 10. ᵈ 2 Kings viii. 13. ᵉ John xiii. 38. 1 Cor. x. 12.

v. 31—35 In their way to the mount of Olives, we are told,

1 The prediction of his sufferings, and of their flight, which Christ delivered to his disciples He foretels them of the offence they would take at the treatment he must meet that very night insomuch that every one of them would desert him, and fulfil the scripture, *Zech* xiii 7 but though he should be smitten, and die, as it was prophesied of him, yet he should rise again, and come to them, recover them from their fright and dispersion, and go before them into Galilee, where they would meet him to their unspeakable comfort *Note*, (1) We know not our own weakness till the trying hour comes, and by our falls we are convinced (2) We are never safe, and must never be secure The sweetest seasons of communion with Christ are sometime succeeded with the sorest temptations (3) The Lord is very pitiful, he knoweth our weakness, and doth not cast us off, though for our cowardice and unfaithfulness we so often deserve it he turns again, and restores the fallen, by his grace bringing them back to his blessed fold

2 Peter, unable to bear such a reflection, with presumptuous confidence *engages for his own fidelity*, though all the rest should fly He not only trusted on his own resolutions, but intimates a strong conceit of his superior courage *Note*, A haughty spirit is sure to fall We have lost our footing the moment we begin to think any thing is of ourselves; and if Jesus hath any love to our souls, he will let us feel, by sad experience, our own weakness and corruption

3 Christ warns him of the delusion he was under, in this self-confidence of boasting, and assures him, that all his vaunted courage would quickly fail him Yea, that he should not only forsake, but disown him, repeatedly disown him, and that during the present night, before the crowing of the cock announced the approaching return of day And thus he solemnly

con

confirms, *Verily I say unto thee* He knew Peter better than Peter knew himself *Note*, The forwardest to boast are usually the first and foulest in their falls

4 Peter still persists in his vain confidence, though warned by him who could not err, and with increasing vehemence, unable to bear the suspicion of denying his Master, solemnly affirms that he will sooner die than be guilty of such baseness And all the disciples joined his assertion, unwilling to be outdone by Peter, and equally confident of their own zeal for their Lord *Note*, (1) When death and danger are at a distance it is easy to boast great things, but, when they come, how many stagger! (2) It is among the follies bound up in the human heart, that we are all apt to think more highly of ourselves than we ought to think, and sad experience is in general needful to bring us to a more humbling view of our weakness and wickedness.

36. ¶ [f] Then cometh Jesus with them unto a place
called Gethsemane, and saith unto the disciples, Sit ye
here, while I go and pray yonder 37 And he took
with him Peter, and the two sons of Zebedee, and began
to be sorrowful, and [g] very heavy 38. Then saith he
unto them, [h] My soul is exceeding sorrowful, even unto
death tarry ye here, and watch with me [i] 39 And [k] he
went a little farther, and fell on his face, and [k] prayed,
saying, [l] O my Father, if it be possible, let [m] this cup
pass from me nevertheless, [n] not as I will, but as thou
wilt 40 And he cometh unto the disciples and findeth
them [o] asleep, and saith unto Peter, What, could ye not
watch with me one hour? 41 [p] Watch and pray, that
ye enter not into temptation the spirit indeed *is* willing,
[q] but the flesh *is* weak 42 He went away again the
second time, and prayed, saying, O my Father, if this
cup may not pass away from me, except I drink it, [r] thy
will be done 43 And he came and found them asleep
again [s] for their eyes were heavy 44. And he left
them, and went away again, and prayed the third time,
saying the same words 45 Then cometh he to his disciples,
and saith unto them, Sleep on now, and take
your rest, behold, the hour is at hand, and the Son of
man is betrayed into the hands of sinners 46 Rise,
let us be going behold, he is at hand that doth betray
me.

f Mark xiv ... Luke xxii 39. John xviii 1 — g ... xvi 14 John xii 27 — h Psal. vi 3 ... 3 — k Heb v 7 — l John xii ... — m Chap xx ... — n John vi 38 — o Ver 5 Chap xxv 5 — p ... Eph vi 18 — q ... Rom ... Gal v 17 — r Chap vi ... — s ...

v 36—46 With sacred reverence we are here called to approach the scene of the Redeemer's agony The storm of divine vengeance now arose, to discharge all its fury on him who bore our sins and carried our sorrows

1 The place whither he retired was called Gethsemane, *an olive-press*, for there it pleased the Lord to bruise him and put him to grief The companions he took with him were his disciples, all but Judas, and, leaving the others at a distance, with an injunction to sit there, He, with Peter, James, and John, retired into some more secluded part of the garden to pray They who had seen his transfiguration are chosen to be witnesses of his deepest humiliation

2 There his agony began the sorrows of death compassed him about, and distress and consternation unutterable seized upon his soul The words in the original are most emphatical, expressive of the heaviest load of grief, perplexity, dejection, and anguish No outward cause appeared, the conflict was internal the powers of darkness now rallied their once-defeated forces, and summoned up all their fury for this decisive blow The wrath of an offended God, due to the sins of millions of mankind, all centred now on their Redeemer, and weighed him down under the intolerable burden Death, with all its horrors of ignominy, shame, and torture, stood before him, and, worse than ten thousand deaths of the body, the pains of hell gat hold upon his soul, the wages of our iniquities

3 In this distress he acquaints his disciples with the sorrows of his soul, that even now pressed him down to the gates of death, and only would end entirely with his expiring breath sorrows such as mortal never knew before, and perhaps beyond what even the damned ever felt He enjoins them to tarry there and *watch* with him observe his agony, and be on their guard against their own approaching temptations

4 He humbly applies to him, whose terrors he suffered with a troubled mind Being truly man, as well as God, he could not but wish for relief from pain, from pain so agonising, and therefore poured out strong crying and tears, *Heb* v 7 He went a little farther, that alone he might tread the winepress of the wrath of God, and there falling on his face, under a load of guilt and misery to the humanity insupportable, he poured out his complaints before his Father, *O my Father*, for with unshaken faith he still looked through the dark cloud, *if it be possible, let this cup pass from me*, if, consistent with the glory of the divine perfections and the redemption of his people, these torments may be alleviated or removed, his nature craves relief *nevertheless*, if all I suffer is needful to glorify thee and to secure their salvation, I am all resignation, I bow my neck, and say, *Not as I will, but as thou wilt*, his human will, with perfect acquiescence, submits to the divine *Note*, (1) In all our sorrows it is good to make God our refuge, and in prayer to pour out our griefs into his compassionate bosom (2) Humble desire to be delivered from our sufferings is perfectly consistent with the most unfeigned resignation under them (3) Whether our troubles are removed or not, it is a sure token for good when we can say, *Not my will but thine be done.*

5 Arising from the earth, he returned to his three disciples, and lo! astonishing to tell, whilst their master was agonizing they were asleep Oppressed with grief, their senses were stupefied and their eyes closed so weak and wretched is man, left for a moment to himself But Christ rouses them from their slumbers, and gently chides their disobedience to his commands, and inattention to his sufferings, and, directing his discourse to Peter, who lately appeared so forward in his professions of fidelity and zeal, he said, *What!* is it possible! asleep! and I overwhelmed with anguish *Could not ye*, from whom I had such expectations, and whose plighted vows of constancy till death promised other conduct, *could ye not watch with me one hour?* so short the space, so little difficult the command *Watch and pray*, you have need to be awake, if not to sympathize and join with me, at least to guard yourselves, *that ye enter not into temptation*, and by this sloth and drowsiness be exposed to fall more easily, when the approaching hour of your temptation comes Yet, whilst he thus gently rebukes and admonishes, he also pities and kindly excuses them, *the spirit truly is willing*, he knew their hearts were really attached to him, their love without dissimulation, and that their desire was to serve him, *but the flesh is weak*, the corruptible body weighed down the soul, and the remaining corruption and indwelling evil hindred them from doing the things which they would, and he knew whereof they were made, forgave, and cast the mantle of love over the failings he could not but condemn *Note*, (1) Slothfulness, and neglect of prayer, in time of temptation, are the sure forerunners of a fall We need always watch, but, when we are forewarned of danger near, we should double our guard, and be more importunate at a throne of grace (2) Whilst we dwell in these bodies of flesh and corruption we shall find sad warrings within, and they whose souls are most sincere and sensible will groan most, being burdened with this body of sin and death, and long to get rid of it (3) We have a compassionate High-priest, who can be touched with the feeling of our infirmities, and will not withdraw his love from us when we fall under temptation, but in mercy will restore our souls to paths of righteousness for his name's sake

6 Our Lord again retires, repeats his fervent supplications, and submits to all his Father's will Again he returns, and finds his disciples sleeping, their heavy eyelids were involuntarily closed, and all his remonstrances were ineffectual to keep them awake and watchful The third time he withdraws, redoubles his prayers, renews his self-resignation, and is heard though the cup may not pass from him, he is strengthened to bear the load, and patiently to yield up his soul to God Coming to his disciples, still they sleep, and now he consigns them to their repose, if they can or dare any longer indulge themselves when his foes and theirs are now at hand It is high time to awake when the traitor is so near *Arise, let us be going*, not to flee from the sufferings before him, but to meet them since the hour, fixed in the divine decree, is come, Jesus is prepared, and resigns himself into the hands of his enemies *Note*, (1) Though we have not an immediate answer, we must pray and not faint (2) Repetition of the same requests in prayer is often far removed from the *vain repetitions* which our Lord condemns Reiterated cries in the same words bespeak the warmest importunity of desire (3) When calls and warnings rouse us not from spiritual slumbers, it is a mercy if Jesus sends heavier judgments, or corrections, to rouse our sluggish souls

47 ¶ [t] And while he yet spake, lo, [u] Judas, one of
the twelve, came, and with him [x] a great multitude, with
swords and staves, from the chief priests and elders of the
people 48 Now he that betrayed him gave them a sign,
saying, Whomsoever I shall kiss, that same is he, hold
him fast 49 And forthwith he came to Jesus, and said,
Hail, master, [y] and kissed him 50. And Jesus said unto
him, † Friend, wherefore art thou come? Then came
they and laid hands on Jesus, and [z] took him. 51 And
behold, [a] one of them which were with Jesus stretched
out his hand, and drew his sword, and struck a servant
of the high priest's, and smote off his ear 52 Then said
Jesus unto him, [b] Put up again thy sword into his place
for [c] all they that take the sword shall perish with the
sword 53 Thinkest thou that I cannot now pray to
my Father, and he shall presently give me more than
twelve legions of angels? 54 But how then shall the
scriptures be fulfilled, [e] that thus it must be? 55 In
that

t Mark xiv. 43 Luke xxii 47 John xviii 3 — u Acts i 16 — x Psal. iii ... — y 2 Sam. xx 9 ... — † Or Companion Psal. xli 9 ... Acts iv 25 — z Lam. iv 20. Acts ii. 23 — a John xviii 10 — b Rom xii 19 2 Cor x ... — c Gen ix 6 Rev xiii 10 — d 2 Kings vi 17 — e Psal. xxii ... Isa liii 7 Dan ix 26 Acts xxvi 22

that ſame hour ſaid Jeſus to the multitudes, Are ye come
out as againſt a thief, with ſwords and ſtaves for to take
me? I ſat daily with you teaching in the temple, and
ye laid no hold on me 56 But all this was done,
[r] that the ſcriptures of the prophets might be fulfilled
[s] Then all the diſciples forſook him and fled

[r] Lam iv 20 [s] Ver 31

v 47—56 As the words dropped from his lips, his enemies appear to ſeize him

1 Judas, who knew the place of his Maſter's retirement, led the way, one of the twelve, and lately dipping his hand with him in the ſame diſh, now the guide to this ſavage band, compoſed of Roman ſoldiers and the ſervants and officers of the chief prieſts, armed with ſwords and ſtaves, and under their authority pretending to ſeize Jeſus as a criminal Thus, whilſt good men often ſleep, unapprized of danger, the wicked are awake, and plotting their deſtruction It is well for us that one is our Guardian who neither ſlumbers nor ſleeps

2 He had given them a ſignal before they ſet out, leſt in the night they ſhould miſtake, by the glimmering of torches, the perſon of Jeſus, and this was, that whomſoever he ſhould kiſs, that was he, whom they ſhould ſeize and bind Accordingly, with the moſt hardened impudence, he no ſooner deſcried his well known Maſter's face, than he approached with the deepeſt profeſſions of reſpect and warmeſt good wiſhes, and with a kiſs executed his traiterous deſign Well knowing his villany, Jeſus rebukes his baſeneſs, and with the piercing title of *Friend*, that ſhould have ſpoken ten thouſand daggers to his heart, replies, *Wherefore art thou come?* how durſt thou be preſent? What loſt to all ſhame? adding ſuch impudence to foul ingratitude? *Note*, The bittereſt enmity lurks often under the moſt plauſible profeſſions and apparent civilities

3 Chriſt is immediately arreſted and bound as a malefactor He quietly yielded up himſelf now his hour was come, and as a criminal ſubmitted to the arreſts of divine judgment for our tranſgreſſions Though wicked men indeed meant only to gratify their malice, they fulfilled *the determinate counſel of God*, Acts ii 23

4 Peter, fired with zeal at what he ſaw, inſtantly drew his ſword, and, attempting a reſcue, ſtruck at one of the high-prieſt's ſervants, who probably appeared very active on that occaſion, and cut off his ear His zeal in itſelf was commendable, but this exertion of it was neither enjoined, nor diſcreet, and therefore,

5 Chriſt rebuked him for his raſhneſs, and bid him ſheath his ſword, *for they that take the ſword ſhall periſh with the ſword* Reſiſtance at preſent only expoſed them to uſeleſs danger, but, ere long, they would ſee thoſe who arreſted their Maſter fall by the ſword of the Romans, or in ſome civil tumult as their own executioners As for them, the weapons of their warfare were not carnal, but ſpiritual, patience and prayer were their beſt defence Beſides, Chriſt neither needed their help nor choſe to be reſcued, if he had, effectual ſuccours were even now at hand, more than twelve legions of angels, upwards of ſeventy thouſand, were ready to appear, one of the leaſt of whom could deſtroy a world He had only to aſk his Father, and theſe miniſters of flame would attend his orders, *but how then ſhould the ſcriptures be fulfilled, that thus it muſt be?* and their accompliſhment, wherein alſo was involved the ſalvation of his people, was far dearer to him than his own ſafety *It muſt be* that he ſhould ſuffer, that he might redeem, and therefore he willingly reſigned himſelf as a lamb to the ſlaughter, *Iſa* liii 7 *Note*, (1) God wants not our ſervices we miſtake, when we think our feeble arm of importance to his cauſe (2) Chriſt' ſufferings were voluntary he might, whenever he pleaſed, have been releaſed, but his love to ſinful ſouls bound him ſtronger than the cords of his perſecutors (3) Surrounded as the people of God are with enemies, ſtill more and mightier are thoſe which are for them than all who can be againſt them, the innumerable company of angels is their guard, and miniſter to the heirs of ſalvation

6 Chriſt turns from his diſciples to the multitude, and mildly expoſtulates with them on their preſent conduct What uſe was there in all this armed hoſt? had he behaved as a deſperate villain, who needed ſuch force to overcome him? or had he fled from public juſtice, that at midnight, in this clandeſtine manner, they ſought to arreſt him? The gentleneſs and innocence of all his conduct confuted the one, and his public daily appearance in the temple the other but the Scripture muſt be fulfilled, and God's eternal counſel thus receive their accompliſhment *Note*, They who are the moſt inveterate enemies of Chriſt and his church, are only inſtruments in God's hand, whoſe very wickedneſs he over rules to bring about the counſel of his own will

7 His diſciples hereupon ſhamefully deſerted him, and fled Seeing him paſſively ſubmit, fearing leſt Peter's raſh action ſhould exaſperate the guard, and that they ſhould be murdered, or ſeized with their Maſter, each endeavoured to ſhift for himſelf, and left him alone to bear his burden Their baſeneſs and ingratitude herein were highly criminal but thus it became him to *tread the winepreſs alone*

57 ¶ [h] And they that had laid hold on Jeſus led *him*
away to Caiaphas the high-prieſt, [i] where the ſcribes and
the elders were aſſembled 58 But Peter followed him
afar off unto the high-prieſt's palace, and went in, and
ſat with the ſervants to ſee the end 59 Now the chief
prieſts and elders, and all the council, [k] ſought falſe witneſs
againſt Jeſus to put him to death, 60 But found
none yea, though many falſe witneſſes came, yet found
they none At the laſt came two falſe witneſſes, 61
And ſaid, This *fellow* ſaid, [l] I am able to deſtroy the
temple of God, and to build it in three days 62 And
the high-prieſt aroſe, and ſaid unto him, Anſwereſt thou
nothing? what *is it which* theſe witneſs againſt thee?
63 But Jeſus [m] held his peace And the high-prieſt
anſwered and ſaid unto him, [n] I adjure thee by the living
God, that thou tell us whether thou be the Chriſt the
Son of God. 64 Jeſus ſaith unto him, Thou haſt ſaid
nevertheleſs I ſay unto you, [o] Hereafter ſhall ye ſee the
Son of man ſitting on the right hand of power, and
[p] coming in the clouds of heaven 65 [q] Then the high-prieſt
rent his clothes, ſaying, He hath ſpoken blaſphemy,
what further need have we of witneſſes? behold, now
ye have heard his blaſphemy 66. What think ye?
They anſwered and ſaid, [r] He is guilty of death 67
[s] Then did they ſpit in his face, and buffeted him, and
[t] others ſmote *him* with † the palms of their hands,
68 Saying, Propheſy unto us, thou Chriſt, Who is he
that ſmote thee?

[h] Mark xiv 53 Luke xxii 54 John xviii 12 [i] Pſalm xxii 16 [k] Pſ xxvii 12 & xxxv 11 [l] Chap xxvii 40 John ii 19 [m] Pſ xxxviii 13 Iſa liii 7 Chap xxvii 12, 14 [n] Lev v 1 [o] Dan vii 13 Chap xvi 27 & xxiv 30 Rom xiv 10 [p] Pſ cx 1 Rev i 7 [q] 2 Kings xviii 37 [r] Lev xxiv 16 John xix 7 [s] Iſa l 6 Chap xxvii 30 [t] John xviii 22 † Or rods

v 57—68 Our Lord, being ſeized as a malefactor, is dragged before the rulers, and his proceſs begun

1 His judges were his inveterate perſecutors, the chief prieſts, ſcribes, and elders, who, though in the dead of night, waked to do him miſchief, and were now aſſembled at the palace of Caiaphas the high-prieſt Before this confederacy of treacherous men was he preſented as a criminal, whilſt they ſat in judgment upon him The lamb of God, now about to be offered for the ſins of the world, was thus preſented to the prieſt, *ſee Lev* xvii 5 before he bled on the altar

2 Peter, whoſe fright began a little to abate, ſollicitous about his maſter's fate, followed at a diſtance the croud, and, mingling with the ſervants in the hall, thought he might, unnoticed there, hear the iſſue of the trial, and ſee whether Chriſt would deliver himſelf by ſome miraculous act of power, or what puniſhment they would inflict upon him Thus, without a call, having thruſt himſelf into temptation, he could not expect divine ſupport, and his cowardly hypocriſy, of appearing among the croud as one of thoſe who had been employed to ſeize the priſoner, foreboded no good For they who are aſhamed to be known as Chriſt's diſciples, if brought to the trial, will, like Peter, ſolemnly diſown him

3 Having brought Chriſt to their bar, and previouſly determined his condemnation, the queſtion was, where to procure evidence to furniſh them with a pretext for putting him to death, nothing leſs than his blood being able to ſatisfy his mercileſs and unjuſt judges but though they endeavoured to procure accuſations, and ſuborn witneſſes againſt him, yet the falſhoods they advanced were ſo palpable and inconſiſtent, that they carried their own confutation, and even before ſuch partial judges could not furniſh the ſhadow of a crime At laſt two falſe witneſſes appeared, and with virulence and inſolence alledged they had heard him ſay, *I am able to deſtroy the temple of God, and to build it in three days* He had ſaid no ſuch thing His words were, *Deſtroy ye this temple*, not that *made with hands*, as they added, *Mark* xiv 58 but the temple of his body, *John* ii 21 and his raiſing it up referred to his own reſurrection, not the rebuilding of the material houſe of God But by ſuch a falſe quotation they meant to accuſe him as an enemy to the holy place, and a blaſphemer againſt God, as well as one that dealt in magic, from his preſuming to ſay he could raiſe ſuch a building in three days A far-fetched accuſation indeed! and too weak to ſupport the bloody ſentence they deſired to ground thereon *Note*, If falſe witneſſes roſe up againſt the innocent Jeſus, laying to his charge things he knew not of, let it not appear ſtrange if we meet with the like injurious treatment The diſciple is not above his Maſter

4 Unable longer to retain his rage, the high-prieſt in a fury roſe, vexed to be able to produce no more plauſible an accuſation, and out of all patience to behold the meekneſs and ſilence of Jeſus, *dumb as the ſheep before her ſhearers*, *Iſa* liii 7 he bids him make his defence inſtantly, if he had ought to ſay why ſentence ſhould not paſs upon him But Jeſus held his peace He knew their deſigns, and that the cleareſt evidence of innocence would weigh nothing before ſuch judges The high-prieſt hereupon adjures and commands him upon oath to anſwer whether he were indeed the Meſſiah, God's eternal Son, or not, that from his own mouth they might obtain a charge againſt him which they ſought for from other witneſſes in vain *Note*,

The

The silence of Jesus should teach us meekness before our bitterest persecutors.

5. To this solemn interrogatory Jesus makes a direct reply. He was apprised of their captious design; but his hour was come, therefore he professes himself to be that very Messiah concerning whom the high-priest spoke, though he knew the disdain with which they would treat his claim: *nevertheless* he made it before them all. And since they would admit no present proof of it, he would give them one *hereafter*, which should astonish them, *Ye shall see the Son of man sitting at the right hand of power, and coming in the clouds of heaven.* Which would be fulfilled in the effusion of his Spirit after his ascension, in the ruin of their state and nation, and most eminently in the great day of his appearing and glory, when they, who now sat as his judges, must stand as criminals at his bar, and perish under his righteous vengeance. *Note*, Impenitent sinners will one day be convinced, when it is too late, of the eternal ruin they have brought upon their heads by rejecting the Lord's Christ.

6. Pretending to be shocked at such blasphemy, in token of his abhorrence, the high-priest rent his clothes, and, appealing to the council for the evidence of the crime, now clear from the confession of Jesus, presumes further witnesses to be needless; and all concurred in the opinion that he deserved to die as a blasphemer, for arrogating to himself divine power and honours. Thus was he condemned, though innocent, that we might be acquitted, though guilty.

7. No sooner was he thus unjustly condemned, than they began to treat him with all manner of indignities: some of the company, or the officers and servants, *spat on his face*, in token of detestation and contempt; beat and buffeted him with the palms of their hands, or with rods; and in ridicule of his prophetic character, having blindfolded his eyes, bid him tell who smote him. To such insult and suffering did the holy Jesus submit for our sakes: he hid not his face from shame and spitting, that our faces might not be covered with everlasting shame and contempt; he was bruised for our iniquities, that we might not be crushed for ever under the wrath of God. If we then, for his sake, are rendered contemptible, ridiculed and mocked by wicked men, let it be remembered how much more he bore for us; and let us never be ashamed of his reproach.

69 ¶ [u] Now Peter [x] sat without in the palace: and
a damsel came unto him, saying, Thou also wast with
Jesus of Galilee. 70 But he denied before them all,
saying, I know not what thou sayest. 71 And when he
was gone out into the porch, another *maid* saw him, and
said unto them that were there, This *fellow* was also
with Jesus of Nazareth. 72 And again he denied with
an oath, [y] I do not know the man. 73 And after a
while came unto him they that stood by, and said to
Peter, Surely thou also art *one* of them; for [z] thy speech
bewrayeth thee. 74 Then began he to curse and to
swear, *saying*, I know not the man. And immediately
the cock crew. 75 And Peter remembered the words
of Jesus, which said unto him, Before the cock crow,
thou shalt deny me thrice. And he went out, and [c] wept
bitterly.

u Mark xiv. 66. Luke xxii. 55. John xviii. 16, 17, 25. x Pf. li. 1. & cxix. 115. y Chap. xxvi. 70. Ver. 58. z Luke xxii. 59. a Ver. 34. b Psal. vii. 16. c Zech. xii. 10. 2 Cor. vii. 11.

v. 69—75. We have here the memorable event of Peter's fall and recovery: A warning to us never to be self-confident, lest we should fall like him; nor, when fallen, however foully, to despair, since the same door of hope is open for us.

1. His sin, with all the aggravations of it, is faithfully recorded, and blessed be God for the simplicity of the sacred historians. Had they, in their account of God's saints, like the historians of human biographers, blazoned the excellencies and concealed the faults and infirmities of their worthies, how many a dear child of God would have wrote bitter things against his soul! Whilst his Master was suffering within, Peter sat with the servants without. In bad company no good can ever be expected; in the devil's palace we must not hope for protection; and, if we will associate with the crowd of his servants, the consequence naturally follows, we must be like them, or be laughed at. (1.) The temptation came first from one of the servant-maids; for the weakest instrument in the devil's hands can do much mischief. She shrewdly suspected, perhaps by Peter's melancholy look, that he was a disciple of Jesus, or she had seen him formerly among Christ's attendants, and therefore charged him with her suspicions. Peter, quite disconcerted, shuffled out an answer, false, as he knew, and faithless, pretending not to understand her, and before them all denying the charge. *Note*, Many, who would hesitate at a direct lie, stick not at an evasion, and will pretend not to understand what is said, when, in truth, it is because they are ashamed of their profession, and dare not avow their knowledge of Christ; which is most base, cowardly, and criminal. (2.) The second temptation quickly followed, and from a similar quarter. With infinite contempt of Peter's appearance, another maid-servant came up to him as he stood in the porch, perhaps meaning to steal off for fear of further discovery, and, looking in his face, perfectly recollected his person among the followers of Jesus, and confidently asserted before those who stood by, that this fellow was certainly a disciple of Jesus the Nazarene; as if it was a reproach to admit such a fellow into their company. With such contempt and insolence are the disciples of Jesus often treated by those who know *them* not, because they knew *him* not. To silence such a suspicion, he solemnly denies even his knowledge of the person of Jesus, as if he had never seen him; and, to gain credit, backs his assertion with an oath; a shrewd proof of the falsehood he urged: for they justly are to be suspected of making no conscience of a lie, who make none of rash oaths. (3.) A little while after, one who, perhaps excited by what had been suggested, marked Peter more narrowly, and was convinced by his provincial dialect and accent that he must be a Galilean, concluded certainly he was a follower of Jesus, and asserted it to his face before the company, with this evident proof, *thy speech bewrayeth thee*. Quite in a consternation, and not knowing what to say or do, he thought with a resolute air to carry it off; and, as in a passion at being suspected of such a thing, he began to curse and to swear, affirming with most horrid imprecations, that he never had the least knowledge or acquaintance with *the man* they mentioned, nor had ever before in his life seen him. He could not indeed have taken a more effectual way to prove he did not belong to Jesus; his disciples never used such language. *Note*, (1.) One lie generally paves the way for another, and then perjury becomes needful to support the falsehood. So dreadfully connected are the links of sin. (2.) A real disciple of Jesus may ever be known by his discourse; his speech will indeed bewray him. (3.) Whilst we look at such a fearful fall, we should tremble for ourselves, and dread the first step of deviation from the path of truth, lest with Peter we should be hurried down the precipice.

2. His recovery affords us as amazing an instance of divine grace as his fall hath done of human weakness and corruption. *Immediately*, as he spake, *the cock crew*; a sound in Peter's ears more terrible than the burst of loudest thunders: it instantly recalled to his memory what Jesus had foretold, and he had most guiltily accomplished; his baseness, ingratitude, profaneness, perjury, all stared him in the face, and overwhelmed him with confusion. Unable to stay there a moment longer, *he went out* to give vent, in some retired corner, to the bursting anguish of his soul; and with tears of bitterest sorrow and unfeigned repentance bewailed his sin, and found mercy with a pardoning God. *Note*, (1.) Nothing so deeply affects the truly gracious heart as the sense of his ingratitude, and base returns for all the love of Jesus to his sinful soul. (2.) They who have never wept with Peter over their sins, it is to be feared have never felt their bitterness. (3.) It is never too late to return to God. None perish merely because of the greatness of their sins, but through their impenitence and unbelief.

CHAP. XXVII.

We have in this chapter the affecting story of the sufferings and death of our Saviour Christ, which are the only foundation of every fallen sinner's hope. We have here, 1. The delivering of him to Pilate, ver. 1, 2. *2. The despair of Judas,* ver. 3—10. *3. The arraignment and trial of Christ before Pilate,* ver. 11—14. *4. The clamours of the people against him,* ver. 15—25. *5. Sentence passed and executed upon him,* ver. 26—33. *6. The indignities done him, and reproaches cast upon him,* ver. 34—44. *7. Many remarkable signs attended his death,* ver. 45—56. *8. His burial, and the watch set on his grave,* ver. 57—66.

1 WHEN the morning was come, [a] all the chief
priests and elders of the people [b] took counsel
against Jesus to put him to death: 2 And when they
had bound him, [c] they led *him* away, and delivered him
to Pontius Pilate the governor. 3 ¶ Then Judas, which
had betrayed him, when he saw that he was condemned,
[d] repented himself, and brought again [e] the thirty pieces
of silver to the chief-priests and elders, 4 Saying, I
have sinned, in that I have betrayed the innocent blood.
And they said, What *is that* to us? see thou *to that*.
5 And he cast down the pieces of silver in the temple,
and departed, and went and [f] hanged himself. 6 And
the chief priests took the silver pieces, and said, It is not
lawful for to put them into the treasury, because it is the
price of blood. 7 And they took counsel, and bought
with them the potters field, to bury strangers in. 8
Wherefore that field was called, [g] The field of blood,
unto this day. 9 (Then was fulfilled [h] that which was
spoken by Jeremy the prophet, saying, And they took
the thirty pieces of silver, the price of him that was valued,
† whom they of the children of Israel did value;
10 And gave them for the potters field, as the Lord
appointed me.)

a Mark xv. 1. Luke xxiii. 1. John xviii. 28. b Pf. ii. 2. Acts iv. 26. c Isa. liii. 8. d 2 Cor. vii. 10. e Chap. xxvi. 15. f Acts i. 18. g Acts i. 19. h Zech. xi. 12. † Or, Whom they bought of the children, &c.

v 1—10 Though they had condemned the innocent Jeſus as worthy of death, they had not in their hands the power of capital puniſhments, and therefore muſt have him ſentenced by the Roman governor before they could proceed to execution, the ſceptre being now departed from Judah, and the country become a Roman province Hereupon we are told,

1 On a ſecond counſel held in the morning, in order effectually to get their bloody purpoſes executed of putting him to death, they determined to accuſe him before Pilate, at that time the Roman preſident, as an infamous malefactor and incendiary; and accordingly, binding him as a criminal, they led him ignominiouſly through the ſtreets, from the houſe of Caiaphas to the governor's palace, and delivered him up, that ſentence might be pronounced upon him, and that he might die the death of the croſs, unwittingly fulfilling the predictions of Jeſus, *chap* xx 19

2 Remorſe had by this time ſeized on the conſcience of Judas When he ſaw that Jeſus was condemned, and ready to be executed, filled with horror, and agitated with ſelf-indignation, anguiſh, and deſpair, he ran to the temple, and there, in one of the chambers to which the council ſeems to have been adjourned, he brought the hated price of his wickedneſs, the thirty pieces of ſilver, and, publickly acknowledging the atrocious crime he had committed in betraying innocent blood, would have returned their wages of unrighteouſneſs But they, inſtead of being ſtruck with conviction, treated his confeſſion with contempt He had anſwered their ends, and as to the means employed, or the guilt he had incurred, they cared not about it, as if it was nothing to them that they had bribed him to commit the villainy, and were that moment perſecuting to death the innocent perſon he had betrayed Made deſperate by ſuch neglect, and the unavailableneſs of this attempt to ſtop the proſecution of Jeſus, his life became a burden, and the devil urged him to put an end to it Caſting down the abhorred ſilver in the temple before them, and, flying to ſome ſolitude, he immediately hung himſelf, by ſelf-murder finiſhing the meaſure of his iniquities *Note*, (1) The time will come when the ſweeteſt ſins will be turned into the poiſon of aſps (2) There is no repentance without reſtitution of ill-gotten gain, and taking ſhame to ourſelves before the accomplices of our guilt (3) When wicked men can bring the profeſſors of religion to join them, indifferent to the remorſe they afterwards behold in them, they only mock at the calamity, and at firſt the cauſe of it (4) The love of money hath been the fatal ſnare to many a ſoul for this they have plunged themſelves into the gulph of perdition (5) Deſpair is among the greateſt crimes, and often ends in ſelf murder, a remedy ſtill worſe than the diſeaſe For the deepeſt guilt there is mercy to be hoped but, when men fly from God to the devil for eaſe, they are undone for ever

3 The money being left, they conſulted how to diſpoſe of it Pretending conſcience, they would not put it into the temple treaſury, though probably it was taken from thence, becauſe it was the price of blood, and therefore, with the ſhew of great piety and humanity, laid it out to purchaſe a ſmall piece of ground which had been dug up by a potter, and was of little value, to bury ſtrangers or proſelytes whereby they perpetuated their own infamy, the people, who knew what money made the purchaſe, calling it juſtly Aceldama, or the field of blood And herein they exactly fulfilled what the prophet had foretold, *Zech* xi 12, 13 The words are ſaid to be in Jeremy, though only found in Zechariah concerning which there are many ways ſuggeſted to ſolve the difficulty The moſt probable ſeems to be, either that, in the diviſion of the ſacred books, the laſt volume began with Jeremiah, and therefore, though containing all the later prophets, bore his name, or that Jeremiah had ſo propheſied firſt, but had not committed it to writing, and Zechariah confirmed and wrote it in his prophecy The words, as they ſtand in the prophet, are, *They weighed for my price thirty pieces of ſilver And the Lord ſaid unto me, Caſt it to the potter, a goodly price that I was prized at of them And I took the thirty pieces of ſilver and caſt them to the potter in the houſe of the Lord* Thus did they, who rejected the Meſſiah, fulfill all the prophecies concerning him *Note*, (1) They who are bitter perſecutors of God's people, ſtill ſtudy to maintain the character of piety and humanity among men (2) Chriſt's blood hath provided a reſting-place for poor ſinners after death And though he was treated with ſuch contempt, and his price ſo low, we ſee in his humiliation peculiar glory, and the deeper his abaſement was, it renders him in the eyes of all that believe more precious

11 [i] And Jeſus ſtood before the governor, and the
governor aſked him, ſaying, Art thou the king of the
Jews? And Jeſus ſaid unto him, [k] Thou ſayeſt 12
And when he was accuſed of the chief prieſts and elders,
[l] he anſwered nothing. 13 Then ſaith Pilate unto him,
[m] Heareſt thou not how many things they witneſs againſt
thee? 14 And he anſwered him to never a word, in-
ſomuch that the governor marvelled greatly 15 Now
at *that* feaſt the governor was wont to releaſe unto the
people a priſoner, whom they would 16 And they had
then [n] a notable priſoner, called Barabbas 17 There-
fore, when they were gathered together, Pilate ſaid unto
them, Whom will ye that I releaſe unto you? Barabbas,
or Jeſus, which is called Chriſt? 18 For he knew that
[o] for envy they had delivered him 19 ¶ When he
was ſet down on the judgment-ſeat, his wife ſent unto
him, ſaying, Have thou nothing to do with that juſt man
for [p] I have ſuffered many things this day in [q] a dream
becauſe of him 20 [r] But the chief prieſts and elders
perſuaded the multitude that they ſhould aſk Barabbas,
and deſtroy Jeſus 21 The governor anſwered and ſaid
unto them, Whether of the twain will ye that I releaſe
unto you? They ſaid, Barabbas 22 Pilate ſaith unto
them, What ſhall I do then with Jeſus, which is called
Chriſt? They all ſay unto him, Let him be crucified
23 And the governor ſaid, Why, what evil hath he
done? But they cried out the more, ſaying, Let him be
crucified 24 ¶ When Pilate ſaw that he could prevail
nothing, but that rather a tumult was made, [s] he took
water, and waſhed his hands before the multitude, ſay-
ing, I am innocent of the blood of this juſt perſon ſee
ye *to it* 25 Then anſwered all the people, and ſaid,
[t] His blood *be* on us, and on our children

i Mark xv 2 Luke xxiii 3 John xviii 33
k John xviii 37 1 Tim vi 13
l Chap xxvi 63
m Chap xxvi 62
n Luke xxiii 19 John xviii 40
o Acts iii 13
p Dan ii 1, &c
q Job xxxiii 15, 16
r Acts iii 14
s Deut xxi 6
t Acts v 28

v 11—25 Behold the Son of God a priſoner at a human bar, and He, to whom every knee muſt bow, and meet him as their eternal Judge, now appears as a criminal before Pilate having condeſcended to bear our ſins, he ſubmits to ſuffer in our ſtead as a tranſgreſſor We have,

1 The charge laid againſt him Knowing the jealouſy of the Roman government, the chief prieſts, his accuſers, had ſuggeſted that, in aſſuming the character of the Meſſiah, he meant to raiſe an inſurrection, and make himſelf a king Pilate therefore interrogated him on this head, whether he preſumed to arrogate the title of *King of the Jews?* and Jeſus acknowledged the charge, though he aſſumed no ſuch temporal dominion as they ſuggeſted, his kingdom was not of this world *ſee John* xviii 36 The chief prieſts and elders were hereupon very loud and clamorous in their accuſations, as if he was a perverter of the people, a ſower of ſedition, forbidding to give tribute to Ceſar, and affecting the ſovereignty of the country To all which Jeſus, with aſtoniſhing patience, made no reply What they ſaid was indeed notoriouſly falſe, as themſelves knew but he wanted not to defend himſelf, his hour was come, and he ſtood prepared to anſwer the demands of divine juſtice, and to bear our ſins in his own body on the tree Therefore, when Pilate urged him to reply to the charges, and clear himſelf of theſe accuſations, he obſerved a profound ſilence, to the great aſtoniſhment of the governor, who could not account for ſo unuſual a behaviour in a perſon whoſe life was at ſtake, and depended on that moment *Note*, (1) It hath been uſual with the enemies of the ſervants of Jeſus to dreſs them up ſo as to render them ſuſpected by the civil government, and to inſinuate ill deſigns againſt the ſtate, in order the more eaſily to oppreſs them (2) Silence is often the beſt anſwer to the accuſations of malice, and when we know our defence is ſure to be over-ruled, it is fruitleſs to contend

2 Pilate, convinced of the innocence of Jeſus, and well knowing the motive of the virulence ſhewn againſt him by the chief prieſts, who were ſtung with envy at the excellence of his character, and the high reputation he held with many, which eclipſed their own, wiſhed for a pretext to releaſe him And hereunto he was yet more induced by a meſſage from his wife, who juſt at that time, whilſt the trial was going on, ſent to entreat him to do nothing againſt that *juſt man* before him for ſhe had that morning been terrified by a very uncommon dream concerning him, which bore ſtrong marks of a divine original, and therefore conjured him to diſcharge the priſoner, leſt he ſhould bring down the wrath of God upon himſelf and family by condemning the innocent Therefore, as it was an eſtabliſhed cuſtom at that feaſt to gratify the people with the releaſe of any priſoner whom they choſe, Pilate thought he could not fail of ſucceeding by propoſing to the people their choice, whether of Barabbas or Jeſus The infamous character of Barabbas, who for ſedition and murder, and other villainies, was held in greateſt deteſtation, left him no room to doubt that the people would prefer Jeſus, whom they had ſo lately uſhered with hoſannas into the city, and whoſe excellencies all muſt have ſeen *Note*, (1) God hath acceſs to the ſpirit, and can ſpeak to our ſouls when our ſenſes are locked up in deep repoſe (2) Sinners have ſometimes ſolemn warnings, but they are too apt to ſlight the heavenly admonition (3) The nearer and dearer any perſon is to us, the more are we obliged to watch over them for good

3 The multitude, inſtigated by the craft of their wily prieſts, who repreſented Jeſus in every black and diabolical colour, engaged them to prefer Barabbas before him, and, to the aſtoniſhment of Pilate, they demanded the murderer, and rejected the Lord of life and glory and, not content with this, when the

governor, willing to releaſe Jeſus, enquired of them what they wiſhed he ſhould do with him whom many regarded as the Chriſt, or Meſſiah, they with one conſent cried out, *Let him be crucified*, a death the moſt painful, ignominious, and accurſed Shocked at ſuch a demand, Pilate remonſtrates with them on the injuſtice and cruelty of ſuch an action, *Why, what evil hath he done?* On ſevereſt ſcrutiny, his judge could ſee no fault in him, his adverſaries prove none, nor did even the traitor ſuggeſt the ſhadow of a crime A glorious teſtimony of the avowed innocence of Jeſus But notwithſtanding, this tumultuous aſſembly, wrought up to a pitch of fury by their malignant prieſts and rulers, with louder cries demanded his crucifixion, determined to extort the governor's conſent, and bear down reaſon and juſtice with rage and clamour *Note*, (1) How little dependence is to be placed on popular applauſe They who one day cried, Hoſanna to the Son of David, now cry, Crucify him, crucify him (2) The unſpotted innocency of the Lamb of God evidently ſhews, that he bore not his own ſins, but the ſins of others he voluntarily ſubmitted to die as a criminal, that he, though juſt, might ſuffer the puniſhment due to the unjuſt, and thereby bring us unto God

4 Pilate, unable to prevail with them, and not having reſolution to deny their requeſt, ſo importunately and clamorouſly urged, for fear of an uproar, yet conſcious of the innocence of Jeſus, and ſhocked at the thought of murdering a juſt man, bethought himſelf of a miſerable expedient to pacify his conſcience without diſobliging the people and therefore, though yielding to their importunity, he proteſts againſt the fact, and, taking water before them all, he waſhed his hands, that by this ſignificative action he might appear clear from all the guilt which ſhould enſue, declaring himſelf innocent of this righteous blood, and therefore, ſince they compelled him to condemn the innocent, he lays it wholly upon them to anſwer for the crime before God and the world An abſurd procedure indeed in a judge, whom nothing ſhould awe from the adminiſtration of impartial juſtice And it but the more aggravated his guilt, thus avowedly to act againſt his own conſcience, and to do the very thing againſt which he proteſted But ſuch contradictions muſt follow, where men's convictions are ſtrong, but their corruptions ſtronger

5 They heſitate not to ſubject themſelves to all the conſequences which might enſue, and, ſince Pilate ſeemed ſcrupulous, they are very ready to quiet his conſcience by ſolemnly transferring all the guilt upon their own, madly imprecating on themſelves, and their lateſt poſterity, the vengeance, if any were due, *His blood be on us, and on our children* So daring do preſumptuous ſinners grow ſo little are they apprehenſive of the conſequences of their impiety But theſe murderers ſoon found the vengeance they imprecated terribly lighting on their devoted heads in the utter deſtruction of themſelves and families, ſuch multitudes being crucified by Titus during the ſiege, that the croſſes ſtood ſo thick around the walls, that there was no more room for them, five hundred in a day thus miſerably expiring And to this hour the effects of that imprecation are viſible upon this miſerable people, and will be, till, returning to the Lord whom they once rejected, the wrath ſhall be removed, and their iniquity be forgiven

u Mark xv 15 Luke xxiii 24 26 ¶ [u] Then releaſed he Barabbas unto them and
when he had ſcourged Jeſus, he delivered him to be cru-
x John xix 1 cified 27 [x] Then the ſoldiers of the governor took
† Or, Governor's houſe Jeſus into the † common hall, and gathered unto him
the whole band of *ſoldiers* 28 And they ſtripped him,
y Luke xxiii 11 and [y] put on him a ſcarlet robe 29 ¶ And when they
had platted a crown of thorns, they put *it* upon his head,
and a reed in his right hand and they bowed the knee
before him, and mocked him, ſaying, Hail, King of the
z Iſa l 6 Chap. xxvi 67 Jews 30 And [z] they ſpit upon him, and took the
reed, and ſmote him on the head. 31 And after that
they had mocked him, they took the robe off from him,
a Chap. xxi 39 Heb xiii 12 and put his own raiment on him, and [a] led him away to
crucify him 32 And as they came out, they found a
man of Cyrene, Simon by name him they compelled
to bear his croſs

v 26—32 The matter being thus determined

1 Pilate, having releaſed Barabbas, that moſt infamous criminal, delivered Jeſus over to their will, having firſt ſcourged him ſeverely, in hopes of moving their compaſſion, *John* xix 1 but finding it all ineffectual, and that they were bent on his deſtruction, he appoints his immediate execution on the croſs, as they inſiſted And herein we may obſerve, (1) The fulfilment of the Scriptures, *Pſ* cxxix 3 *Iſa* l 6 liii 5 where theſe ſtripes had been foretold (2) In the releaſe of Barabbas we have an emblem of our own deliverance through Jeſus Chriſt As guilty are we as this notorious priſoner we have robbed God of his glory, and often laboured to murder our own and others ſouls For which we muſt all have periſhed without hope, had not our divine Subſtitute yielded up himſelf that we might go free, and that the chief of ſinners might find in him plenteous redemption (3) Bloody as the ſtripes of Jeſus appear, we need bleſs God for them, ſince by theſe ſtripes we are healed

2 Being delivered into the hands of the inhuman ſoldiers, they dragged him into the common hall, and, to make themſelves merry in his miſeries, and in the view of the character he aſſumed as a king, they ſtripped off his cloaths, arrayed him in a ſcarlet robe in mockery, and platting a crown of thorns, in deriſion placed it on his head, giving him a reed, or hollow cane, for a ſceptre, and, gathering the whole band round him, they, with inſulting homage bowed the knee, and addreſſed him with the deriding title of King of the Jews, whilſt ſome ſpit in his face in contempt of his majeſty, and others ſnatched the cane out of his hand and ſmote him on the head, that the thorns might wound the deeper his ſacred temples With horror, indignation, and aſtoniſhment, whilſt we reflect on their wickedneſs, let ſome meaſure thereof be transferred to our own They were but the inſtruments, we the cauſe, of all his torment And when we ſee the innocent Lamb of God ſubmitting to theſe indignities, and look on that face, marred more than any man's, defiled with ſpitting, black with buffetings, and dyed with blood ſtreaming from his temples, what emotions of love and gratitude ſhould glow in our boſom towards him who endured ſuch things for us, that we might not be the mockery of devils, the ſcorn of angels, and abhorred of God?

3 Glutted with cruelty, and ſatiated with ſuch inhuman mirth, they ſtripped off his robes of mock majeſty, and put on him again his own ſeamleſs garment, the perquiſite of thoſe who ſhould be more immediately employed in his execution Then, binding his croſs upon him, *John* xix 17 they led him, as a lamb to the ſlaughter, a ſpectacle through the city, to ſuffer without the gate But, it ſeems, wearied out with his ſufferings, his ſtrength failed him, and they were obliged to releaſe him of his load, leſt they ſhould be diſappointed of their cruelty in nailing him alive to the tree Seizing on one who was paſſing by, known probably to have been a diſciple of Jeſus, and therefore treated with ſuch indignity, they compel him to bear the croſs after Chriſt to the place of execution *Note*, Every faithful ſoul muſt expect his croſs, and be content to go to Jeſus without the camp, *bearing his reproach*

33 [b] And when they were come unto a place called b Mark xv 22 Luke xxiii 33
Golgotha, that is to ſay, a place of a ſkull, 34 ¶ John xix 17.
[c] They gave him vinegar to drink mingled with gall c Pſ lxix
and when he had taſted *thereof*, he would not drink 35 21
And they crucified him, and parted his garments, caſt-
ing lots that it might be fulfilled which was ſpoken by
the prophet, [d] They parted my garments among them, d Pſ xxii
and upon my veſture did they caſt lots 36 And ſit- 18
ting down, they watched him there 37 And ſet up
over his head, his accuſation written, THIS IS JESUS
THE KING OF THE JEWS 38 Then were there
[e] two thieves crucified with him one on the right hand, e Iſa liii 12
and another on the left 39 ¶ And they that paſſed by
reviled him, [f] wagging their heads, 40 And ſaying, f Pſ xxii 7. & cix 25
[g] Thou that deſtroyeſt the temple, and buildeſt *it* in three Lam ii 15
days, ſave thyſelf [h] if thou be the ſon of God, come g Chap. xxvi
down from the croſs 41 Likewiſe alſo the chief prieſts 61 John ii 19
mocking him, with the ſcribes and elders, ſaid, 42 h Chap. xxvi.
He ſaved others, himſelf he cannot ſave If he be the 63
King of Iſrael, let him now come down from the croſs,
and we will believe him. 43 [i] He truſted in God, let i Pſ xxii 8
him deliver him now, if he will have him for he ſaid, Wiſd ii 18
[k] I am the Son of God 44 [l] The thieves alſo which k Chap. xxvi. 64
were crucified with him, caſt the ſame in his teeth 45 l Luke xxiii 39, &c
Now [m] from the ſixth hour there was darkneſs over all m Amos viii. 9
the ‖ land unto the ninth hour 46 And about the ‖ Or Earth.
ninth hour Jeſus [n] cried with a loud voice, ſaying, Eli, n Heb v 7.
Eli, lama ſabachthani? that is to ſay, [o] My God, my o Pſ xxii 1
God, why haſt thou forſaken me? 47 Some of them
that ſtood there, when they heard that, ſaid, This man
calleth for Elias 48 And ſtraightway one of them
ran, and took a ſpunge, and [p] filled *it* with vinegar, and p Pſ lxix.
put *it* on a reed, and gave him to drink 49 The reſt 21
ſaid, Let be, let us ſee whether Elias will come to ſave
him

v 33—49 We have here an account of the crucifixion of Jeſus

1 The place where he ſuffered was called *Golgotha*, ſignifying the place of a ſkull, either from the form of the hill, or becauſe the malefactors executed there, were buried on the ſpot Where death therefore erected his trophies, there Chriſt, who taſted death for every man, erected his croſs, that he might in triumph look down upon his vanquiſhed foe, as it was ſaid, O death, I will be thy deſtruction

2 Before

2 Before they nailed him to the tree, they offered him a bitter cup of vinegar mingled with gall, instead of the potion usually given to malefactors to stupify their sense of pain, striving thus by every malicious contrivance to sharpen his sufferings, and make his death peculiarly bitter. He tasted it, but refused to drink. He wanted not to prolong his life, nor would do ought to discompose his mind, prepared to feel every misery before him, and desiring not to be excused the sensation of any one painful pang he must endure. The gall of that cup our sins supplied, had he not atoned for them, we must eternally have drank to the dregs the cup of bitterness and trembling.

3 *They crucified him*, which was done by stretching the arms on the wood as it lay upon the ground, and nailing them, then they fastened the feet to a piece of wood fixed to the body of the cross, and lifting it up, stuck it fast in a hole prepared to receive it, the shock of which dislocated the bones of the criminal, and there hanging upon the nails, in convulsions and torments inexpressible, he expired. Thus did the Son of God humble himself to death, even the death of the cross. Whilst angels with wonder and amaze behold him, what sentiments of transcendent admiration and love should glow in our bosoms, when we see him dying on the accursed tree, for us men and for our salvation?

4 As he was hung up naked to bear our shame, who by sin had lost the robe of innocence, the executioners divided his garments as their fee, and whilst they sat down and watched him, that no rescue might be attempted, should the people now relent, they cast lots for his outer garment, which was without seam, and must have been spoiled if cut to pieces, thus in the most exact manner fulfilling the prophetic word, *Psal.* xxii. 18. *They parted my garments among them, and upon my vesture did they cast lots.*

5 On the cross a tablet was hung, importing the crime for which he suffered, as was usual on these occasions. But this bespoke his honour, rather than reproach. *This is Jesus the King of the Jews.* Such indeed he really was, and whatever intention they had who wrote it, God designed even here that a testimony should be born to his Messiah.

6 Two thieves were crucified with him, and he placed in the midst, as if to stamp the most indelible infamy upon him, as the vilest of all malefactors. *Thus was he numbered with transgressors, and with the wicked in his death.* Though he had done no violence, yet, bearing the sins of many, divine justice treated him as a criminal, and he died under the curse of our iniquities.

7 On the cross he endured the greatest contradiction of sinners against himself.

[1.] From the common people, and passengers who went by as he hung on the tree. Unmoved at his sufferings, unaffected with the astonishing patience wherewith he bore them, they vented their blasphemies against him, wagging their heads, as insulting over his miseries, (*Psal.* xxii. 8.) and triumphing in his torments, upbraiding him with his pretended ability of destroying the temple, and raising it in three days, and bidding him now put forth some of that power of which he boasted, in coming down from the cross to which he was nailed, and thus at least prove the truth of the high pretensions he made, as being the Son of God. *Note*, (1.) When a man is run down, and cast out by the great and the rulers, every one is ready to join in the cry. (2.) If Christ was thus reviled and ridiculed, let us not think it strange, if the mouth of the ungodly be opened upon us in bitter words.

[2.] *From the chief priests, scribes, and elders.* They came to feast their eyes with this sight of misery, and, instead of being at their devotions in the temple, (*Lev.* xxiii. 7.) meanly mixed with the rabble around the cross, to gratify their malice, and spit their venom, mocking at him, and saying, *He saved others, himself he cannot save.* His present state they suggest evidently proved the delusion of the miracles to which he pretended, and the impossibility of his being the Saviour of the world, whereas in fact, the very reason why he cannot save himself, is because it would not then be possible for him to save others, since on his sufferings their salvation depended. As he assumed the honour of Israel's King, they upbraid him with his arrogance, and bid him exert his authority, and loose himself from the cross, then they protest they will believe in him, though, after what he had done, this was a mere subterfuge to their infidelity. Had he complied with their proposals, they would instantly have found new objections, and would suppose some trick had been played, that he had never been nailed to the tree, as they afterwards evaded the evidence of his resurrection, by the absurd pretence that his disciples stole away the body by night. Because Jesus had professed such unshaken confidence in God, and claimed so near a relation to the Most High, they now bid him put it to the proof, intimating, that God's not delivering him in his distress, shewed him a deceiver, and whilst they thus vilified him in the eyes of the people, they hurled a fiery arrow against the faith of the Redeemer, to terrify his innocent soul, as if there was no hope for him in his God, (*Psal.* xxii. 8.) Unmoved the Saviour heard in silence their blasphemies, and persisted patiently in accomplishing his own glorious work. *Note*, (1.) Jesus became a king by suffering the cross, he went from thence to reign. Let us not forget then the way to his kingdom, if we suffer with him, we shall also reign with him. (2.) Many pretend want of evidence as a reason for their unbelief, but were Christ to indulge them with the grant of what themselves propose, they would be as far from faith in him as ever. The fault is in the heart: they who believe not Moses and the prophets, will be proof against every other method of conviction.

[3.] From the thieves who were crucified with him. Some suppose, that only one of them reviled him, (*See Luke* xxiii. 39.) and say this is a Hebrew way of speaking, as if they were afraid of ascribing too much to the sovereign grace of God herein displayed. But I own I see no reason for doubting, that both at first joined in the same blasphemy and abuse, though one of them, struck with the behaviour of Jesus, and convinced of his own wickedness in this, as well as all his former conduct, afterwards cast his eyes of faith on the expiring Saviour; and if so, this tended only to make the triumphs of boundless mercy, and the riches of the redemption of Jesus, appear the more illustrious in his salvation.

8 A dreadful darkness now came on over all the land. The sun miraculously withdrew his light, as if terrified to behold his Maker's agony, and testifying his abhorrence of such transcendently atrocious wickedness, affording an emblem of the judicial blindness to which this devoted people were now abandoned. It might be intended also to represent the dreadful conflict with the rulers of the darkness of this world, which Jesus maintained on the cross, when by dying he destroyed him that had the power of death, that is the devil. And this eclipse of the great luminary of heaven was also but a faint image of the darker eclipse in the Redeemer's soul, when every cheering beam of consolation was withdrawn, the light of his Father's countenance withheld, and a sense of this dereliction, arising from the wrath of an offended God, compleated the measure of his sufferings. Three such hours had never passed since *darkness was upon the face of the deep.*

9 After a long and silent conflict, about the ninth hour, his agony being now at the summit, with a loud but lamentable voice Jesus cried, *Eli, Eli, lama sabachthani? My God, my God, why hast thou forsaken me?* Strange accents from him whom God had repeatedly owned for his beloved Son, and in whom he had testified himself so well pleased! We never hear one complaint from these sacred lips of all his inhuman treatment, or bodily torment; what he then felt was infinitely more insupportable, and extorted this exceeding bitter cry. Not that the hypostatic union was dissolved, or that there was any real abatement of the Father's love towards him, never did he as Mediator appear more amiable than now, when by the eternal Spirit he offered himself without spot unto God. But since he took upon himself all the sins of his people, he was given for a while into the enemy's hands, and all the powers of hell let loose upon him, every divine support was withdrawn, and the terrors of wrath due from an offended God seized on his soul, and sunk him in the lowest deeps. Despair excepted, I question much, whether the spirits of the damned have felt the wrath of God in this its utmost depth of bitterness: yet, though forsaken, firm and unshaken Jesus hangs fast on God, and in this deepest dereliction still can say, *My God.*

Lastly, The by-standers, whether wilfully or ignorantly mistaking his words, said he *called for Elias*, as if he wanted his help, and that it was too late for him *to cry now.* And hereupon one ran and filled a spunge with vinegar, and with a cane lifted it to his lips, which might be a suggestion of compassion, since his pains must have created intolerable thirst, though usually it is supposed to be done to mock and teaze him, and add to his anguish, whilst the rest deriding said, *Let be*, let him alone, *let us see whether Elias will come to save him*, since he is to be the forerunner of the Messiah, but no such help they presume will be afforded him, alike abandoned by heaven and earth.

50 ¶ Jesus, when he had cried again with a loud
voice, yielded up the ghost. 51 And behold the
vail of the temple was rent in twain, from the top to the
bottom, and the earth did quake, and the rocks rent,
52 And the graves were opened, and many bodies of
saints which slept, arose, 53 And came out of the
graves after his resurrection, and went into the holy city,
and appeared unto many. 54 Now when the centurion,
and they that were with him, watching Jesus, saw the
earthquake, and those things that were done, they feared
greatly, saying, Truly this was the Son of God. 55
And many women were there (beholding afar off)
which followed Jesus from Galilee, ministring unto
him. 56 Among which was Mary Magdalene, and
Mary the mother of James and Joses, and the mother
of Zebedee's children.

v. 50—56

v 50—56 The conflict is now over, the victory compleat, sin atoned for, Satan's head bruised, justice satisfied, death vanquished, hell shut up, the kingdom of heaven opened for all believers, and all this by the death of Jesus here recorded, concerning which we are told,

1 The manner in which he expired Having finished the work the Father had given him to do, *he cried*, not as a dying man, exhausted and spent, but *with a loud voice*, the shout of victory over all his conquered foes, and thus in his full strength *yielded up the ghost*, freely resigned his soul into his Father's hands, and his body to death, the threatened wages of sin, which he had consented to bear Thus fell the spiritual Sampson, *spoiling principalities and powers, and triumphing over them* on his cross Thus died the great Redeemer, just at the time when the evening sacrifice of the lamb was slain, the figure of him who in the evening of the world appeared to take away sin by the sacrifice of himself

2 The miracles which attended his death

[1] *Behold, the vail of the temple was rent in twain*, which separated the holy of holies from the outer tabernacle, where the table of incense stood, and the golden candlestick, and this at the very time probably when the priests were there ministring, and burning the sacred incense before it Whereby was signified, (1) The abolition of the Mosaical services, the darkness of that dispensation being now removed, and its mysteries unvailed, so that with open face we now behold the glory of the Lord (2) The demolition of the partition wall between Jews and Gentiles, who are alike called into the fellowship of the gospel, and partakers of the same privileges (3) The free access which every sinner hath to God, so that he may now come boldly to a throne of grace, and, when death shall rend the vail of flesh, to a throne of glory, *by that new and living way which Jesus hath consecrated for us through the vail, that is to say, his flesh*, Heb iv 16 x 19, 20

[2] *The earth did quake, and the rocks were rent* by it, marks of God's wrath against these murderers, and of that fury he would pour out upon them, when their rocky hearts should be broken in pieces Hereby also was figured the destruction of Satan's kingdom, and the wondrous changes now about to be wrought in the world, when the most stout-hearted sinners should tremble before the Lord, and feel their souls rent with deepest conviction when led to look up to a crucified Jesus

[3] *The graves were opened*, immediately by the earthquake, *and many bodies of the saints which slept, arose, and came out of the graves after his resurrection, and went into the holy city, and appeared unto many* a glorious proof of Christ's victory over death and the grave, and an assurance to all his saints of a joyful resurrection

Who these saints were, whether the patriarchs, or such as had seen Christ in the flesh, whether they kept their bodies, and ascended with their Lord into glory, or afterwards returned into the state of the dead, to whom they appeared, what they said or did, these and the like enquiries, being matters of mere curiosity, the Holy Ghost hath not thought fit to reveal to us All that is needful for us to know, is told us, and herein we should thankfully acquiesce, not coveting *to be wise above what is written*

3 The effect which the death of Christ and subsequent miracles had on the centurion and soldiers who kept guard at the place of execution Though soldiers, savage and cruel, heathens, and strangers to the true God, yet, the very persons who had treated Jesus with such indignity, had dragged him to that place, and nailed him to the tree, these strange sights, the darkness, earthquake, and expiring cry of the Redeemer, filled them with consternation Their stout hearts trembled for fear, lest they should be swallowed up in righteous vengeance, and these amazing effects of divine power and interposition extorted from them that noble testimony to the Saviour's divine mission and character, *Truly this was the Son of God*

4 To the honour of the weaker sex, mention is made of several women, and three of their names are recorded, who, though the disciples in general had forsaken their Master, and fled, continued their attendance in his last moments, and having followed *Jesus out of Galilee*, and ministred to him of their substance, now stood afar off, perhaps not daring to approach nearer, and with broken heart and floods of tears beheld and lamented their dying Lord, unable to minister to him either help or comfort *Note*, (1) The longer and the further we have followed Christ, the more should it engage us to cleave to him, even to the end (2) They who love the Lord Jesus in their heart, will be happy to employ their substance in his service

57 [a] When the even was come, there came a rich
man of Arimathea, named Joseph, who also himself was
Jesus's disciple 58 He went to Pilate, and begged
the body of Jesus Then Pilate commanded the body to
be delivered 59 And when Joseph had taken the body, he wrapped it in a clean linen cloth, 60 And laid
it [b] in his own new tomb, which he had hewn out in
the rock and he rolled a great stone to the door of the
sepulchre, and departed 61 And there was Mary
Magdalene, and the other Mary, sitting over-against the
sepulchre 62 ¶ Now the next day that followed the
day of the preparation, the chief priests and Pharisees
came together unto Pilate, 63 Saying, Sir, We remember that that deceiver said, while he was yet alive,
[a] After three days I will rise again 64 [a] Command
therefore that the sepulchre be made sure until the third
day, lest his disciples come by night, and steal him
away, and say unto the people, He is risen from the
dead so the last error shall be worse than the first
65 Pilate said unto them, Ye have a † watch, go your
way, make *it* as sure as you can 66 So they went and
made the sepulchre sure, [b] sealing the stone, and setting a
watch

[a] Mark xv 42 Luke xxiii 50 John xix 38

[b] Isa liii 9

[a] Chap. xvi 21 & xvii 23 & xx 19

[a] Chap. xii 8 (?)

† Or guard

[b] Dan vi 17

v 57—66 It was foretold, that the Messiah should make *his grave with the wicked, and with the rich in his death*, and we here see it fulfilled in the honourable interment given him by Joseph of Arimathea, after he had died as a malefactor, and suffered in our stead the wages of sin Several circumstances concerning this burial are here taken notice of

1 The time The evening of the day on which he suffered, which was Friday, some time before the Jewish sabbath commenced

2 The person who charged himself with the care of the burial Joseph of Arimathea, a man of wealth and distinction, one of the Sanhedrim, and a secret disciple of Jesus, though through fear he had not publicly avowed it, but now, when Christ seemed deserted of all, he dared step forth, boldly went in to Pilate, and begged the corpse, that he might inter it with due respect, which was granted immediately, and an order sent to deliver the body to him *Note*, (1) There are more secret disciples than we are often aware of (2) The possession of worldly wealth and honour is usually a grievous check to the faithful and open profession of Jesus and his cause (3) In times of trial, when the boldest are ready to shrink, we sometimes see those who were scarce numbered among disciples before, come forth with unexpected courage and fidelity, and make a noble confession before many witnesses

3 The manner of it He took down the body from the cross, and wrapped it in clean linnen, according to the custom of the Jews, and he himself attended, and performed these last kind offices to his dead Master

4 The place where Joseph laid the corpse *In his own new tomb, hewn out in a rock*, and closed with *a great stone* at the mouth, which when Joseph had done, he departed in silent sorrow to bewail his loss So Divine providence ordered the circumstances, that none having lain there before, there could be no doubt, when Christ rose, concerning the person, and the solid rock out of which the sepulchre was hewn, prevented the possibility of suspicion of any secret access to the body, except by the entrance, and that was sufficiently guarded *Note*, (1) He who when alive had not a house to cover his head, when dead, wanted a grave so destitute was the Lord of glory, who then after him dares complain? (2) Since Jesus hath lain in the grave, he hath perfumed the noisome abode, and in this bed of dust, as the phœnix in her fabled nest, we now lie down, only to rise in brighter array, and take our flight to mansions of eternal glory

5 The care Christ's enemies took to have the sepulchre secured The chief priests and Pharisees, who were such scrupulous observers of the sabbath, had not patience to wait the evening till it was over, but assembled, and went in a body to Pilate, to petition him for a guard, in order to secure the body against the following day, because they suggest, that Jesus, *that deceiver*, (so do they call him who is the truth itself) had *said, while he was yet alive*, so that they admit he was now certainly dead, *After three days I will rise again* We find not indeed he had ever expressly said so to them, and if they founded their suggestion upon what they had heard, (*John* ii 19) then their own barefaced wickedness was yet more evident, since on this very passage, which they applied to the temple, they formed great part of their accusation against him Pretending therefore to fear, *lest his disciples should come by night, and steal him away, and say he is risen*, they desire to be furnished with a band of soldiers, to prevent all such attempts, lest, if such a trick should be played, the *consequences of this last error*, in not properly guarding the sepulchre, *should be worse than the first*, in suffering him to preach and live so long, for should this be once believed, the character of Jesus would then be established, and his doctrines spread with greater rapidity than ever Pilate readily gratified them in granting their request, though no doubt he regarded their fears as absurd and ridiculous, and presumed they had little now to apprehend from a dead man They had a body of soldiers in the tower of Antonia, for the service of the temple, and he permits them to detach what number they pleased to guard the sepulchre, and to use every other method to make the

the place as sure as they could. Nor did they fail to take every step to prevent the possibility of an imposture, setting a guard of soldiers, in whom they could confide, to watch the body that night, and *sealing the stone* with the public seal, either of Pilate or the Sanhedrim, that none might presume to enter, till the next day they should return themselves, and producing the dead corpse undeceive the people, and detect the impostor. Thus by the gracious providence of God was every circumstance so ordered, respecting the resurrection of Jesus, that our faith in that grand event might have the most unshaken grounds of evidence indisputable, and be more strongly confirmed by all the methods his enemies took to guard the body from the possibility of being clandestinely removed. Indeed it can scarce be supposed, that his disciples, who all so basely forsook him and fled when he was alive, would ever return to steal him away when he was dead: and they could have no end to answer by it, for to endeavour, by saying he was risen, to impose on the people, would be inconceivable madness and folly in them, since they must thereby expose themselves to every suffering for their testimony, and be of all men the most miserable in this world, conscious of dying with a lye in their right hand, and having no hope in the next. But had they desired or designed to execute such a scheme, they must have been now effectually prevented. In the face of a body of armed soldiers, placed as centinels on the sepulchre, and whose lives depended upon their watchfulness, to suppose they would ever have attempted to break the public seal, roll back a ponderous stone, descend into the tomb, and carry off the body by stealth, is an absurdity too glaring to be conceived. So far as human, or diabolical power could go, Christ's enemies went; but counsel and might are alike vain against the Lord. They who oppose his kingdom, will find their attempts not only baffled, but turned to their own confusion; their guilt but the more aggravated, and their eternal ruin more dreadful.

CHAP. XXVIII.

We left the Lord of life the prisoner of death. The third day arrives; death's bands are loosed; he leads his captivity captive. The Lord is risen indeed. We have here some of the evidences of that signal event. 1. The testimony of the angel, ver. 1—8. *2. His appearance himself to the women*, ver. 9, 10. *3. The confession of the adversaries that were upon the guard*, ver. 11—15. *4. Christ's appearance to the disciples in Galilee, and the commission he gave them*, ver. 16—20.

1 [a] IN the end of the sabbath, as it began to dawn
towards the first *day* of the week, came Mary
Magdalene, and [b] the other Mary, to see the sepulchre.
2 And behold, there † was a great earthquake; for the
angel of the Lord descended from heaven, and came
and rolled back the stone from the door, and sat upon
it. 3 [c] His countenance was like lightning, and his
raiment white as snow. 4 And [d] for fear of him the
keepers did shake, and became as dead men. 5 And
the angel answered and said unto the women, Fear not
ye: for I know that ye seek Jesus which was crucified.
6 He is not here: for he is risen, [e] as he said. Come,
see the place where the Lord lay. 7 And go quickly,
and tell his disciples that he is risen from the dead;
and behold, [f] he goeth before you into Galilee, there
[g] shall ye see him, lo, I have told you. 8 And they
departed quickly from the sepulchre [h] with fear, and
great joy, and did run to bring his disciples word. 9
¶ And as they went to tell his disciples, behold, Jesus
met them, saying, All hail. And they came and
[i] held him by the feet, and worshipped him. 10 Then
said Jesus unto them, Be not afraid: go tell [k] my brethren,
that [l] they go into Galilee, and there shall they
see me.

[a] Mark xvi. 2. Luke xxiv. 1. John xx. 1. [b] Chap. xxvii. 56. † Or had been. [c] Dan. x. 6. [d] Psal. cxlix. 6. Isa. xxxiii. 14. [e] Chap. xii. 40. & xvi. 21. & xvii. 23. & xx. 19. [f] Chap. xxvi. 32. Ver. 10. [g] Acts i. 3. & x. 41. [h] Psal. ii. 11. [i] Cant. iii. 4. [k] John xx. 17. Heb. ii. 11. [l] Ver. 7.

v. 1—10. The resurrection of Jesus being the grand hinge on which our hope of salvation turns, it must afford the most singular satisfaction to observe the amazing force of evidence wherewith this glorious event is attested. Had he still lain in the grave, and had death maintained his dominion over him, our faith had been vain, and we must have perished in our sins: but, glory be to God, he hath raised up Jesus from the dead, and hath thereby begotten us to a new and lively hope. Some testimonies of this fact are here produced; many more will be found in the other Evangelists. We have,

1. The visit made to the sepulchre by those holy women who had attended Jesus to the cross and to the grave, even Mary Magdalene, and Mary the mother of James; and they came now to see the sepulchre, as it was, as they left it, bringing spices to embalm the body; this was *in the end of the sabbath, as it began to dawn towards the first day of the week*. Christ had lain in the grave part of our Friday, all Saturday, which was the Jewish sabbath, and on the Sunday morning, the third day, very early, probably about four o'clock, he arose, after dwelling among the dead about six and thirty hours; long enough to shew his death real, yet not so long as that his body should see corruption, *Psal.* xvi. 10.

2. As they went, and talked about the difficulty of removing the stone at the mouth of the sepulchre, which seems to have been more ponderous than they could roll away, *behold!* to their astonishment, *there was a great earthquake*, which, had the guards indeed slept, must needs have roused them; *for the angel of the Lord descended from heaven*, as the officer of the Most High, sent to release from the arrests of death the body of the Redeemer: the immense debt of our sins being now paid and cancelled, and the justice of God satisfied, the surety by right became entitled to his discharge. Therefore he *came and rolled back the stone from the door*, thus opening the prison, whilst Jesus, as our representative, arose for our justification, as he had been delivered for our offences; *and* the angel *sat upon it*, defying all the powers of earth or hell to roll it on again; waiting there to welcome the poor women who were on their way, and striking terror and dismay into the stout-hearted soldiers. *His countenance was* bright *as the lightning, and his raiment white as snow*, the emblem of purity and victory. Trembling in every limb, the guards shook like the earth which rocked under their feet, and, pale as death, with haste fled from the tremendous presence of this angelic minister.

The other Evangelists mention two angels: one sat on the stone without, and invited and led the women into the sepulchre, where they found another; the one of which stood at the feet, and the other at the head of the grave, where the body had lain.

3. The women being come to the sepulchre, were at first affrighted at the sight, (*Mark* xvi. 5.) but the angel kindly accosting them, endeavoured to silence their fears. *Fear not ye*; whatever terrors seize the sinners in Zion, the redeemed of the Lord need not tremble; *for I know that ye seek Jesus that was crucified*, and they who seek a crucified Jesus, have nothing to fear, have every thing to hope: none ever sought his face in vain. *He is not here*, that you should any longer bedew his corpse with tears: no; *he is risen* for your everlasting comfort, *as he said* he should, on the third day. Then graciously inviting them to *come and see the place where the Lord lay*, that they might be convinced he was not there, he probably led the way into the sepulchre, whither they followed him, and saw the other angel, mentioned *John* xx. 12. And hereupon the angel dismisses them with a message to the disconsolate disciples; *Go quickly, and* be the messengers of this glad news; *tell his disciples*, now dejected and despairing, *he is risen from the dead*, to their surprize and joy; *and behold*, for the confirmation of your own faith and theirs, *he goeth before you into Galilee*, where you and they must follow him, and *there shall ye see him*, converse with him, and receive the fullest assurance of his resurrection. *Lo! I have told you*; remember to deliver these tidings, and be assured of the truth of what I have spoken.

4. Agitated with surprize and joy at what they had seen and heard, and eager to communicate the glad news, they ran to the disciples; and in the way Jesus himself met them, and with kindest salutation accosted them, *All hail*, all peace, happiness, and joy be with you! With lowliest reverence they cast themselves instantly at his feet, and in a transport of love embraced them, adoring him as their risen Lord and Saviour. Then Jesus, further to confirm their hearts, and remove every fear, bids them *not be afraid*; they need apprehend neither danger nor delusion, but must deliver the message his angel had put into their mouths: *Go tell my brethren*, by such an endearing name was he pleased to distinguish his disciples, *that they go into Galilee, and there shall they see me*. *Note*, (1.) Christ is not ashamed to call his servants brethren; yea, though their unfaithfulness hath made them unworthy of such a relation, he will not disown them. (2.) Faith in a risen Redeemer effectually silences a sinner's fears: in him we see the great salvation accomplished, and are filled with joy and peace in believing.

11. ¶ Now when they were going, behold, some of
the watch came into the city, and shewed unto the chief
priests all the things that were done. 12 And when
they were assembled with the elders, and had taken
counsel, they gave large money unto the soldiers, 13
Saying, Say ye, His disciples came by night, and stole
him away while we slept. 14 And if this come to the
governor's ears, we will persuade him, and [m] secure you.
15 [n] So they took the money, and did as they were
taught: and this saying is commonly reported among
the Jews until this day.

[m] Acts xii. 19. [n] Tit. i. 10.

v. 11—15. The resurrection of Jesus is proved by a cloud of unexceptionable witnesses; among whom his very enemies held a distinguished place.

1 The guard who had fled, had juſt reached the city as the women were on their return thither, and ſome of them, probably the officers who commanded the detachment, went directly to the chief prieſts, and to their aſtoniſhment related all that had paſſed, the earthquake, the deſcent of the angel, the removal of the ſtone, and the riſing of Jeſus, and if any thing could ever have ſhocked their obdurate hearts, one ſhould conceive the report of ſuch inconteſtible eye-witneſſes of the fact would have convinced them of their wickedneſs, and turned them to the Lord But they were determined in impenitence and unbelief, and therefore given up to a reprobate mind Hereupon,

2 The chief prieſts and elders conſulted together, and reſolved to ſupport what they had done at all events, and therefore to invent the moſt plauſible pretext to evade the evidence of the reſurrection of Jeſus, knowing the powerful effects of money, and how ready men are to ſell the truth, nay, their very ſouls for it, they bribed high all the guard to tell a lie as abſurd as wicked, that *his diſciples came by night, and ſtole him away while they ſlept* And as the men might juſtly apprehend ſuch a confeſſed criminal neglect in them, as ſleeping upon guard, might be attended with rigorous puniſhment if it came to the governor's ears, the rulers engage to interpoſe their influence, and to ſave them harmleſs But the whole contrivance was ſo barefaced a ſham, that it carried its own confutation, except to ſuch as choſe their own deluſions Can it be conceived, that where the truſt was ſo important, and death the penalty of neglect, that a centinel would ſleep? But if one man may be ſuppoſed to be overtaken, would a whole band of men be all aſleep at once? If they had been ſo, would thoſe timid diſciples, who had fled at the firſt approach of danger, when their Maſter was alive, now dare ruſh into the jaws of death, to reſcue his corpſe? Could ſuch a number of them as was requiſite to roll away the ſtone, and remove the body, have been able to accompliſh ſuch a thing without waking one of the numerous hoſt that lay around the tomb? and if they ſlept, how could they poſſibly know that his diſciples came and ſtole him away? Nay, their very living to ſupport the falſhood, was a full proof againſt them, for, had they ſlept as they pretended, theſe very prieſts had been the firſt to have had them put to death for their neglect, inſtead of intereſting themſelves to ſcreen them from puniſhment

3 The bribe extorted from the heathen ſoldiers an eaſy compliance *they took the money*, and ſaid *and did as they were taught* And this ſenſeleſs ſtory being induſtriouſly propagated by the prieſts, was readily followed by thoſe who wiſhed to be deceived, and continued long after to be commonly reported among the Jews, to render the diſciples odious, and prevent the effects of their miniſtry *Note*, (1) Money is the grand bait for the groſſeſt crimes the raging love of that once rooted in the heart, ſwallows up every conſideration of truth, honeſty, and juſtice (2) No outward evidence is ſufficient to overcome the infidelity of the heart, without the powerful operations of the Holy Ghoſt Were we to chuſe what proofs we would, greater could not be given than theſe men beheld, and yet not one of them was converted No ſigns or wonders will convince thoſe who reject the goſpel (3) A malicious lye once raiſed, in its conſequences is often fatally extenſive, but wo to the author!

16 ¶ Then the eleven diſciples went away into Gali-
lee, into a mountain, [o] where Jeſus had appointed them
17 And when they ſaw him, they worſhipped him
but ſome doubted 18 And Jeſus came, and ſpake
unto them, ſaying, [p] All power is given unto me in hea-
ven and in earth 19 ¶ [q] Go ye therefore and † teach
[r] all nations, baptizing them in the name of the Father,
and of the Son, and of the Holy Ghoſt 20 Teach-
ing them to [s] obſerve all things whatſoever I have com-
manded you and lo, I am with you alway, even unto
the end of the world. Amen

o Chap xxvi 32 Ver 7, 10

p Chap xi 27 John xiii 3 Heb ii 8 1 Pet iii 22 Rev i 18 & xix 16.

q Mark xvi 15

† Or Make diſciples of, Acts xiv 21

r Rom x 18 Col i 23

s Acts ii 42

v 16—20 According to the directions of their Maſter, the eleven Apoſtles went into Galilee to the mountain appointed, having ſummoned a general meeting of all the diſciples, whoſe number amounted to above five hundred There Jeſus again appeared unto them, and, fully convinced now of his being the Son of God, they paid him divine adoration But *ſome* among them ſtill *doubted*, weak and wavering, and ſcarce able to credit the teſtimony of their ſenſes ſo very ſlow of heart were they to believe, and ſo little diſpoſed to be credulous in a matter of ſuch infinite importance But Jeſus ſoon removed all their doubts, converſing familiarly with them, and giving them the moſt indubitable proofs of the identity of his perſon, and the certainty of his reſurrection Hereupon, as he was now about to take his farewel of earth, he inveſts them with his authority, ſends them out under his influence, directs them in their work, and aſſures them of his bleſſing on their labours

1 He aſſerts the authority with which he is inveſted, and in virtue of which he puts them in truſt with his goſpel *All power is given unto me in heaven and in earth* As Mediator, he had received the univerſal ſovereignty, angels, principalities, and powers above were made ſubject unto him, and on earth all things and perſons were put under his government, which was a moſt encouraging conſideration to them who were about to go forth in his name, ſince his ſupport would make them more than conquerors *Note*, When we are diſcouraged with the view of our own weakneſs and inſufficiency, we ſhould look by faith to the all-ſufficiency of Jeſus, and be comforted

2 He gives them a commiſſion out of the plenitude of his power *Go ye therefore, and* all who ſhall in ſucceeding ages be put in truſt with the ſame goſpel, *teach all nations*, for all reſpect of perſons and people is now at an end the ſalvation purchaſed is a common ſalvation, and whoſoever will, let him come They are to carry the glad tidings into all lands, and make diſciples every where, *baptizing them*, and then houſhold who ſhould be converted by their miniſtry, *in the name of the Father, and of the Son, and of the Holy Ghoſt*, admitting them by this rite into the viſible communion of the church, on the profeſſion of their faith in the eternal Father, Son, and Spirit, the one God, to whoſe worſhip and ſervice they are hereby dedicated *teaching them to obſerve all things whatſoever I have commanded you*, declaring to them the riches of the grace, and the extent of the privileges of the goſpel, with all the mighty obligations to obedience, reſulting from faith, which worketh by love, enjoining the word of Jeſus as the only rule of duty, to which nothing is to be added, and from whence nothing muſt be diminiſhed, and urging the diſciples to adorn the doctrine they profeſs by that conſcientious obſervance of all thoſe moral duties and poſitive ordinances which may prove the truth of the grace which is in them, bring glory to God, and credit to their holy religion

3 He aſſures them of his conſtant ſpiritual preſence, to teach, comfort, and proſper them in all their labours of love *Lo! I am with you*, be aſſured of it, as the moſt undoubted truth, though my bodily preſence be removed, my Spirit ſhall abundantly ſupply that loſs, in all difficulties and dangers I will ſupport you, in all emergences I will direct you, I will give you ſucceſs in all your labours, and conſolation in all your ſufferings, and that *alway, even to the end of the world* Not only all your days ſhall you find me near to help you, but to the end of time your ſucceſſors in the miniſtry ſhall experience my continual ſupport and bleſſing, in the preaching that goſpel you deliver unto them *Amen* Verily I ſay unto you, who am the faithful and true witneſs, I will fulfill my promiſes Or this may be the Evangeliſt's word, expreſſing his own, and the church's faith and prayer, that ſo it *may be*, and ſo we believe it *ſhall be* What Chriſt hath promiſed, we may confidently expect to receive, and pray in faith, nothing doubting

THE

THE

EVANGELICAL EXPOSITOR;

OR, A

PRACTICAL COMMENT

Upon the GOSPEL according to

St. MARK.

WE have heard the evidence given in by the first witness to the doctrine and miracles of our Lord Jesus, and now here is another witness produced, who calls for our attention The second living creature *saith,* Come and see, *Rev* vi 3 *The author of this Epistle is Mark whether the same person mentioned* Acts xv. 37, 38 *or him whom Peter calls his son,* 1 Pet v 13 *is uncertain He was not of the number of the apostles, but might probably be one of the seventy His gospel is shorter than that of Matthew, containing much the same matter, with many additional circumstances. Thus out of the mouth of two or three witnesses is every word established*

CHAP I

Mark's narrative takes not rise so early as those of Matthew and Luke do, from the birth of our Saviour, but from John's baptism, from which he presently passeth to Christ's public ministry Accordingly in this chapter we have, 1 *The office of John Baptist illustrated by the prophecy of him,* ver 1—3 *and the history of him,* ver 4—8 2 *Christ's baptism, and his being owned from heaven,* ver 9—11 3 *His temptation,* ver 12, 13 4 *His preaching,* ver 14, 15, 21, 22, 38, 39 5 *His calling disciples,* ver 16—20 6 *His praying,* ver 35 7 *His working miracles* (1) *His rebuking an unclean spirit,* ver 23—28 (2) *His curing Peter's mother-in-law that was ill of a fever,* ver 29—31 (3) *His healing all that came to him,* ver 32, 34, 35 (4) *His cleansing a leper,* ver 40—45

1 THE beginning of the gospel of Jesus
Christ [a] the Son of God, 2. As it is writ-
ten in the prophets, [b] Behold, I send my
messenger before thy face, which shall
prepare thy way before thee 3 [c] The voice of one
crying in the wilderness, Prepare ye the way of the Lord,
make his paths straight 4 [d] John did baptize in the
wilderness, and preach the baptism of repentance, | for
the remission of sins. 5 [e] And there went out unto him
all the land of Judea, and they of Jerusalem, and were
all baptized of him in the river of Jordan, confessing
their sins 6 And John was clothed [f] with camel's hair,
and [g] with a girdle of a skin about his loins and he
did eat [h] locusts and wild honey 7 And preached,
saying, [i] There cometh one mightier than I after me,
the latchet of whose shoes I am not worthy to stoop
down and unloose 8 [k] I indeed have baptized you
with water but he shall baptize you [l] with the Holy
Ghost

a Ps ii 6 Mat iii 17 & xvi 16 & xxvi 64 b Mal iii 1 Mat xi 10. c Isa xl 3 Mat iii 3 Luke iii 4 John i 23 d Mat iii 1 Luke iii 3 John iii 23 | Or Unto e Mat iii 5 f Zech xiii 4 g 2 Kings i 8 h Lev xi 22 i Mat iii 11 Luke iii 16 John i 27 k Acts i 5 & xix 4 l Isa xliv 3 Joel ii 28 Acts ii 4 & xi 15, 16

4

v 1—8 St Mark commences his history with the account of John's baptism, the messenger sent before the Messiah, according to the ancient prophecies, to prepare his way Isaiah and Malachi had both spoken of him, *Isa* xl 3 *Mal* iii 1 and agreeable thereunto John commenced his ministry in the wilderness, calling the people to repentance, and faith in the promised Messiah, in order that they might obtain remission of their sins

1 John's preaching *was the beginning of the gospel of Jesus Christ the Son of God* Not that the gospel then first began to be published, for it had been the subject of the ministry of all the prophets, and in the promise of the Seed of the woman had been preached to the first man immediately after his fall but the gospel dispensation, in opposition to the law, began more immediately from the baptism of John, whose office it was particularly to point the people to the Lamb of God, now made manifest in the flesh to take away the sin of the world This was the glad news John declared, *the gospel of Jesus Christ,* who is both the *Author* and *Subject* of it, and, as *the Son of God,* endued with all-sufficiency for the great work of man's salvation, which he came to accomplish To him the Baptist bore witness, acknowledging his surpassing dignity, and confessed his own unworthiness to be employed in the meanest offices by his Lord, and whilst, in consequence of his preaching, and the people's profession of repentance, he admitted them to baptism in token of the forgiveness of their sins, he bad them expect a more efficacious baptism than this of water, even of the Holy Ghost, which the Messiah, to whom he directed them, should shed on them abundantly, to cleanse them from all their iniquities

2 His appearance was singular, as that of the ancient prophets, and his dress and diet bespoke his mortified spirit and deadness to the world A rough camel's hair garment, tied with a leathern girdle, defended him from the cold, and locusts and wild honey, such as the wilderness afforded, satisfied his hunger *Note,* They who preach the gospel must learn to endure hardness, and be ready, whenever duty calls, to forego any of the delights of sense for the sake of the service in which they are engaged

3 Mul-

3 Multitudes attended him, and appeared deeply affected with John's discourses, confessing their sins, and desiring to be admitted to his baptism. The word of the gospel is powerful. The doctrines of repentance and faith, when urged upon the heart, awaken the conscience: and all who truly preach Jesus Christ will assuredly see the success of their ministrations. They who have never known themselves instrumental to the convincing and converting one sinner, have demonstrative evidence before them, that they are not the messengers of Christ, and do not preach his truth.

m Mat. iii. 13. Luke iii. 21.
n Isa. xi. 2.
o Ps. ii. 7. Isa. xlii. 1. Chap. ix. 7. 2 Pet. i. 17.
p Mat. iv. 1. Luke iv. 1.
q Ex. xxxiv. 28. 1 Kings xix. 8.
r Job v. 23.
s Heb. i. 14.

9 [m] And it came to pass in those days, that Jesus came from Nazareth of Galilee, and was baptized of John in Jordan. 10 And straightway coming up out of the water, he saw the heavens opened, and [n] the Spirit like a dove descending upon him: 11 And there came a voice from heaven, *saying*, [o] Thou art my beloved Son, in whom I am well pleased. 12 [p] And immediately the Spirit driveth him into the wilderness. 13 And he was there in the wilderness [q] forty days tempted of Satan, and [r] was with the wild beasts, and [s] the angels ministred unto him.

v. 9—13. The account of Christ's ministry and temptations St. Matthew hath recorded more at large, *ch.* iii. iv.

1 He was baptised of John in Jordan. Not that he had any sins to confess, though in *the likeness of sinful flesh*, but he would comply with every instituted ordinance of God: and now also he was eminently to be pointed out as the Messiah, and to enter upon his mission. Accordingly the heavens were opened, the Holy Ghost visibly descended upon him, and God himself by an audible voice bore testimony to him as his Son, and declared his perfect satisfaction in the undertaking in which he was engaged. *Note*, (1.) If God is ever well-pleased with us, it can only be in and through his dear Son. (2.) Whenever we are truly baptised into Christ, the Spirit of God will as really be communicated to us as it visibly descended upon him.

2 He immediately entred upon his temptation, led by the Holy Spirit from the brink of Jordan into the howling wilderness, to make his abode with beasts, whilst Satan sharpened every poisoned arrow in his quiver against him, but, to his bitter disappointment, though in this lonely desart, he found all his arts foiled by this second Adam, which even in Eden he had practised with such success upon the first. Thus forty days Christ bore with all the tempter's malice, and baffled all his wiles, till Satan, despairing, at last quitted the field, unable to make the least impression: and then the angelic hosts, who had with admiration beheld the dreadful conflict, appeared to congratulate the Saviour's victory, and to minister to his hunger. *Note*, (1.) Every converted soul must prepare for temptation. (2.) Solitude often proves a dangerous snare. (3.) Christ knows what sore temptations mean. He tenderly compassionates his suffering people, and is near to succour and defend them. (4.) The angels minister to the heirs of salvation: yea, the Lord upon their right hand is their defence, and keepeth them, that the wicked one toucheth them not.

t Mat. iv. 12.
u Mat. iv. 23.
w Gal. iv. 4. Eph. i. 10.
x Dan. ii. 44.
y Mat. iii. 2. iv. 17.
z Mat. iv. 18.
a 1 Kings xix. 19.
b Mat. iv. 21.
c Mat. iv. 22.
d Luke iv. 31.
e Chap. ii.
f Mat. vii. 29.

14 [t] Now after that John was put in prison, Jesus came into Galilee, preaching the gospel of the kingdom of God, 15 And saying, [w] The time is fulfilled, and [x] the kingdom of God is at hand: [y] repent ye, and believe the gospel. 16 [z] Now, as he walked by the sea of Galilee, he saw Simon, and Andrew his brother, casting a net into the sea: (for they were fishers.) 17 And Jesus said unto them, Come ye after me, and I will make you to become fishers of men. 18 And [a] straightway they forsook their nets, and followed him. 19 And when he had gone a little further thence, he saw James *the son* of Zebedee, and John his brother, who also were in the ship, mending their nets. 20 And straightway he called them: and they left [b] their father Zebedee in the ship, with the hired servants, and went after him. 21 And [c] they went into Capernaum, and straightway on the sabbath day he entred into the synagogue, and taught. 22 And [d] they were astonished at his doctrine: for [e] he taught them as one that had authority, and not as the scribes.

v. 14—22. When John's ministry was finished by his imprisonment, Christ came into Galilee, and there,

1 He preached *the gospel of the kingdom of God*, inviting all his countrymen to come and partake of the inestimable blessings of that dispensation of grace which he was commissioned to publish, *the time* being *fulfilled* which had been marked out for the appearing of the Messiah by the prophets, and decreed in the counsels of God; and therefore, as his kingdom was immediately to be erected, he exhorted all his hearers to *repent, and believe the gospel*; to discover, acknowledge, and bewail their offences against God's holy law, to renounce their vain confidences in themselves, to change their mistaken sentiments concerning the nature of the Messiah's kingdom, and, instantly turning to him, to receive the glad tidings he brought of the salvation he came to procure for them, even pardon, peace, righteousness, and eternal life, the gift of God through the sacrifice and obedience to death of his Son. *Note*, (1.) The gospel will be glad tidings to none who do not see and feel their misery and guilt, and, instead of flattering themselves in their own eyes, now change their minds, and stand convinced of their lost estate. (2.) Faith in the gospel word entitles us to claim the fulfilment of all the promises: nor is it any presumption, rejecting all confidence in ourselves, to be confident of the Saviour's love and faithfulness.

2 He called four of his disciples to a more constant attendance upon him, that they might be better qualified for the work in which he designed to employ them. (1.) They were *fishers*, for the kingdom of Jesus was not to be erected by the wisdom of men, but by the power of God. (2.) He found them at *their vocation*. Honest industry in his sight is highly commendable. (3.) They were two pair of *brethren*: and that is an additional happiness, when they, who are so near to each other in blood, are united together in one Lord. (4.) They *left all* to follow Christ. When he calls we must count nothing too dear to part with for his sake.

3 With these disciples, his attendants, he entred into Capernaum, and on the sabbath preached in the synagogue, to the astonishment of the auditory; such a divine power and authority attended his teaching, as the people had never found under their scribes and rabbies. *Note*, The gospel word is mighty and powerful. No marvel then if the preachers of it are distinguished from the insipid doctors of moral virtue, philosophical disquisitions, or empty formality.

23 [f] And there was in their synagogue a man † with an unclean spirit, and he cried out, 24 Saying, Let us alone; [g] what have we to do with thee, thou Jesus of Nazareth? Art thou come to destroy us? [h] I know thee who thou art, [i] the Holy One of God. 25 And Jesus rebuked him, saying, Hold thy peace, and come out of him. 26 And when the unclean spirit [k] had torn him, and cried with a loud voice, he came out of him. 27 And they were all amazed, insomuch that they questioned among themselves, saying, What thing is this? What new doctrine *is* this? for with authority commandeth he even the unclean spirits, and they do obey him. 28 And immediately his fame spread abroad throughout all the region round about Galilee.

f Luke iv. 33.
† Gr. In.
g Mat. viii. 29.
h Jam. ii. 19.
i Dan. ix. 24. Luke i. 35.
k Chap. ix. 20.

v. 23—28. Christ confirmed his mission by his miracles. And, to give the greater weight to his discourse, we find him here,

1 Casting out a devil from one possessed. He is called *an unclean spirit*, for he is such in his own nature, by his suggestions he defiles the consciences of men, and, by the temptations he presents before them, seduces them into all impurity of body and soul. Dreading the presence and power of Jesus, *he cried out*, using the man's organs of speech, *saying, let us alone, what have we to do with thee?* They knew themselves unable to contend, and therefore tremble at the thought of being dispossessed of their prey: but, to do him all the mischief in their power, this fiend seems in reproach to call him *Jesus of Nazareth*: and though he adds, *I know thee who thou art, the holy One of God*, there was probably the most malicious design couched under that fair confession, even to raise a suspicion of confederacy between Jesus and Satan. Christ therefore silences him, disdaining to receive a testimony from him, and disappointing his malicious designs: with a sharp rebuke he bids him instantly quit his prey, and leave the body which he had possessed: and, though furious at being dispossessed, with a fearful outcry, as if he would have rent the man in pieces, or designing to terrify the spectators, he departs, compelled, though with reluctance, to yield to the commanding voice of Jesus. *Note*, (1.) Though such possessions may not now be found, how many, under the influence of *an unclean spirit*, are still led captive by the devil at his will! (2.) The grace of Jesus is still the same, and he can and doth subdue the strongest power of Satan in the sinner's heart. (3.) Many a poor soul, when Christ first approaches him with the gospel word, is grievously harrassed, and cries out, as if his misery was now greater than ever before; but these terrors are the forerunners of peace and joy in believing.

2 The people were all amazed at what they heard and saw, and could not help saying one to another, *What thing is this?* Never was such astonishing power before exerted! *What new doctrine is this?* delivered with such majesty, and confirmed by such miracles. He acts not as exorcists, by charms and invocations, but *with authority commandeth he even the unclean spirits, and they obey him*, unable to make the least resistance. Hereupon the fame of his preaching and miracles began to be exceedingly spread through all the region round about Galilee. *Note*, Christ's doctrine was not new, but the old doctrine which had

had been from the beginning, but had for a long time been so forgotten and neglected, that it appeared now quite uncommon As in these days, the doctrines of the gospel are by many called new doctrines, because, alas! we have for a long season in general so grievously departed from them

l Mat viii 14 Luke iv 38 29 l And forthwith, when they were come out of the
synagogue, they entred into the house of Simon and
Andrew, with James and John 30 But Simon's wife's
mother lay sick of a fever, and anon they tell him of
her 31 And he came and took her by the hand, and
lift her up, and immediately the fever left her, and she
m Mat viii 16 Luke iv 40 ministred unto them 32 m And at even, when the sun
did set, they brought unto him all that were diseased,
n Gen xlix 10 and them that were possessed with devils 33 And n all
the city was gathered together at the door 34 And he
o Isa liii 4 healed many that were o sick of divers diseases, and cast
p Acts xvi 17 18 out many devils, and p suffered not the devils † to speak,
† Or to say they knew him because they knew him. 35 And q in the morning,
q Luke iv 42 rising up a great while before day, he went out, and departed into a solitary place, and there prayed 36 And
Simon, and they that were with him, followed after him
37 And when they had found him, they said unto him,
All men seek for thee 38 And he said unto them,
Let us go into the next towns, that I may preach there
r Isa lxi 1 also r for therefore came I forth 39 And he preached
in their synagogues throughout all Galilee, and cast out
devils.

v 29—39 Wherever Jesus went he left the glorious marks of his power and grace

1 Soon after he had retired from the synagogue to Simon's house to take some refreshment, some of the company informed him of the illness of Peter's mother, confined to her bed with a fever Immediately he arose, went to her bed-side, lifted her up, and instantly the fever left her The cure was perfect, not so much as any weakness remained, but she immediately rose, and waited on Jesus and the guests *Note*, When we have experienced the Redeemer's healing grace, it becomes us to shew our gratitude by immediately employing the strength he hath given us in his service

2 A multitude of other cures were wrought by him the same day For no sooner was the sabbath ended (before which they might scruple to carry the sick to him) than the door was crouded with patients, and not one went away without a cure, and many devils were ejected by his word, whom he permitted not *to say that they knew him* (as the words may best be rendered) not chusing to have them speak ought concerning him, lest it should give occasion to suggest there was a confederacy between him and them

3 After some needful repose, very early in the morning, long before break of day, he retired to a solitary place, that he might, uninterrupted, enjoy sweet communion with his Father in secret, and pour out his soul in prayer before him *Note*, (1) Early rising is as profitable to the soul as the body, whilst sloth is alike hurtful to both (2) When our spirits are most fresh and vigorous, it is then the properest time to retire for prayer and communion with God

4 Peter and his companions no sooner missed him in the morning than they sought him out, and desired him to return to Capernaum, there being so great enquiries made after him But Christ could not confine himself there, the rest of the country must share his ministrations, being sent for this purpose to go about preaching and working miracles through the whole land and accordingly he did so, his disciples attending him in his travels, hearing his divine teaching, and beholding the wonders of his power and love

s Mat viii 2 Luke v 12 t Lev xiii 46 Chron xxvi 21 40 And there came s a leper to him, beseeching
him, and kneeling down to him, and saying unto him,
If thou wilt, thou canst make me clean. 41 And Jesus,
moved with compassion, put forth *his* hand, and touched
him, and saith unto him, I will, be thou clean 42 And
as soon as he had spoken, immediately the leprosy departed from him, and he was cleansed 43 And he
straitly charged him, and forthwith sent him away, 44
u Chap v 43 And saith unto him, u See thou say nothing to any man
x Lev xiv 4 10 but go thy way, shew thyself to the priest, and offer for
thy cleansing those things x which Moses commanded for
a testimony unto them 45 But he went out, and began to publish *it* much, and to blaze abroad the matter,
insomuch that Jesus could no more openly enter into the
city, but was without in desert places and they came
to him from every quarter

v 40—45 This miracle was before recorded, *Matt* viii 2 We are taught by it,

1 What we are poor, defiled, loathsome sinners, under the incurable disease of a corrupted nature, and desperate, unless the great Physician of souls exert his healing power on our behalf

2 Whither we must go to Jesus, bowed down under the sense of our vileness, and unworthiness to approach him, yet casting ourselves at his feet as alone able to relieve us from our misery, and with a humble persuasion he will not spurn us from him, but that he is willing as well as able to help and heal us

3 Christ never rejects the souls of the miserable that fly to him his bowels of compassion yearn over them, the hand of his grace is sure to be stretched out towards them And though we often come trembling, between fear and hope whether he will receive, pardon, help, and save us, he is pleased to remove our doubts, and saith to our souls, *I will*, and power instantly accompanies his promise

4 To those whom Christ cures he gives a strict charge, and they must carefully obey his injunctions, and especially beware not to return unto folly, lest a worse thing happen unto them, but daily they are called to present themselves, body, soul, and spirit, before the great High-priest of their profession, that he, who hath made them clean, may keep them clean

5 They who have tasted the love of Jesus delight to spread the savour of his name, and to testify their gratitude towards him both with their lips and in their lives

CHAP II

In this chapter we have, 1 *Christ's healing a man that was sick of a palsy*, ver 1—12 2 *His calling Matthew from the receipt of custom, and his eating upon that occasion with publicans and sinners, and justifying himself in so doing*, ver 13—17 3 *His justifying his disciples in not fasting so much as those of the Pharisees did*, ver 18—22 4 *His justifying them in plucking the ears of corn on the sabbath-day*, ver 23—28 *All which passages we had before*, Mat ix *and* xii

1. AND again a he entred into Capernaum, after a Mat ix 1 Luke v 18
some days, and it was noised that he was in the
house 2 And straightway many b were gathered toge- b Gen xlix 10
ther, insomuch that there was no room to receive *them*,
no not so much as about the door. and c he preached c Luke iv 18
the word unto them 3 And they come unto him,
bringing one sick of the palsy, which was born of four,
4 And when they could not come nigh unto him for the
press, they uncovered the roof where he was. and when
they had broken *it* up, they let down the bed wherein
the sick of the palsy lay 5 When Jesus saw their faith,
he said unto the sick of the palsy, Son, d thy sins be d Ps ciii 3
forgiven thee 6 But there were certain of the scribes Isa xxxiii 24
sitting there, and reasoning in their hearts, 7 Why 1 John
doth this man thus speak blasphemies? e who can for- ii 12
give sins but God only? 8 And immediately, when e Job xiv 4 Isa xliii 25
f Jesus perceived in his spirit that they so reasoned with- f Ps cxxxix
in themselves, he said unto them, Why reason ye these 2 John ii
things in your hearts? 9 Whether is it easier to say to 24 & vi 64.
the sick of the palsy, Thy sins be forgiven thee or to
say, Arise, and take up thy bed and walk? 10. But
that ye may know that g the Son of man hath power on g John xvii
earth to forgive sins, (he saith to the sick of the palsy) 2
11 I say unto thee, Arise, and take up thy bed, and
go thy way into thine house 12 And immediately he
arose, took up the bed, and went forth before them all,
insomuch that they were all amazed, and glorified God,
saying, We never saw it on this fashion

v 1—12 No sooner had our Lord returned to Capernaum, from his journey through the villages of Galilee, than the rumour of it quickly spread through the place, and, eager to improve the precious opportunity of his presence, such multitudes assembled at the house, that there was no coming even to the door, so thick was the crowd And a blessed sight it is to behold such numbers flocking to the Saviour

1 He preached unto them Some might have thought the time, the place, improper for a sermon There were synagogues, what need of preaching in a house, or at the window? Perhaps to teach us, that no time or place is improper to speak a word for God and for immortal souls

2 During Christ's preaching, or in some interval of his discourses, the friends of a poor paralytic man, sollicitous to present his pitiable case before him, would fain have pressed through the crowd, but, finding the attempt impracticable, they carried him up to the top of the house where Jesus was, and, breaking up a part of the flat roof, let down the sick man on his bed before him *Note*, They who truly seek the Lord, will be discouraged by no difficulties from coming to him

5 Struck

3 Struck with such an instance of their faith, the compassionate Jesus kindly accosts the afflicted patient, and seals the pardon of his sins as the introduction to his cure This being the cause of every sickness and disease, the bitterness of them is past, when the sin that occasioned them is forgiven

4 The Scribes and Pharisees who were present, regarded it as errant blasphemy in a mere man, as they regarded Jesus, to assume the incommunicable prerogative of God, in thus by his own authority presuming to forgive sin He knew their secret reasonings, and in his answer gave them a proof of his divinity, as the searcher of hearts To shew them, therefore, he possessed the power he assumed, he bids the man arise and walk, and appeals to themselves for the conclusion, whether he who could thus sovereignly, in an instant, remove the effects of sin, could not as easily remit the guilt of it *Note, The man* Christ Jesus is also *very God*, able to forgive and to save to the uttermost every poor sinner that comes to him

4 *The paralytic man received his cure the moment* Jesus commanded him to arise, and to the astonishment of all, he was so perfectly restored to health and strength, as to carry home the bed on which he had been brought Such unprecedented cures extorted acknowledgments from every beholder, *that the like was never seen before in Israel*

h Prov i 20. Mat xiii 9 — 13 And he went forth again [h] by the sea-side, and
all the multitude resorted unto him, and he taught
i Mat ix 9, &c Luke v 27 — them 14 [i] And as he passed by, he saw Levi *the son*
of Alpheus sitting at the receipt of custom, and said
unto him, Follow me And he arose and followed him
15 And it came to pass, that as Jesus sat at meat in his
house, many publicans and sinners sat also together with
Jesus and his disciples *for there were many*, and they
followed him 16 And when the Scribes and Pharisees saw him eat with publicans and sinners, they said
k Gen xxxix 3— Isa lxv 5 Acts x 28 — unto his disciples, [k] How is it that he eateth and drinketh
with publicans and sinners? 17 When Jesus heard *it*,
he saith unto them, They that are whole, have no need
l Luke xviii 10—14 & xix 10 Rom v 6, 8 1 Tim i 15 — of the physician, but they that are sick [l] I came not to
call the righteous, but sinners to repentance

v 13—17 Having departed from the house to the sea-side, thither the multitude followed him, and he preached to them the gospel After which,

1 He called Levi, or Matthew, a publican, who was sitting in his office receiving the customs, and such power accompanied his word, that instantly he left his gainful possession, and followed Jesus as his disciple *Note*, (1) Nothing is too difficult for Almighty grace, they who seem most deeply involved in the world, and sunk in guilt and corruption, are often snatched in sovereign love, as brands from the burning (2) If Christ did not first seek us, we should never have sought him

2 Levi, in tender regard for his brother publicans, longed to make them acquainted with Jesus, whose grace he himself had so richly tasted, and therefore invited them to his house, where Jesus disdained not to sit among them infamous in general as their characters were, he joined them not as an associate, but, as the great physician of souls, visited them as diseased patients *Note*, They who have tasted the grace of the Redeemer themselves, cannot but be sollicitous that their friends and neighbours should partake with them

3 Christ vindicates his conduct from the censorious cavils of the Pharisees He despised *not the poor sinner's souls*, but as this was the very end of his coming to call such to repentance, he was unaffected with the reviling of those who conceited themselves righteous, and yet were much farther from the kingdom of heaven, than the very sinners whom they despised *Note*, (1) *The best deeds are often most basely misrepresented* by the invenomed tongue of malice (2) None have ought to do with Christ but sin-sick souls, who feel themselves lost without him, the proud and self-righteous are left to perish in the delusions they have chosen

m Mat ix 14 Luke v 33 — 18 [m] And the disciples of John, and of [n] the Pharisees used to fast, and they come and [o] say unto him,
n Luke xviii 12 — Why do the disciples of John, and of the Pharisees
o Isa xx 6 — fast, but thy disciples fast not? 19 And Jesus said
p John iii 29 — unto them, Can [p] the children of the bride-chamber fast
while the bridegroom is with them? as long as they
have the bridegroom with them, they cannot fast 20
q Acts i 9 — But the days will come when [q] the bridegroom shall be
r Acts xiii 3 — taken away from them, and [r] then shall they fast in
† Or raw, or unwrought — those days 21 No man also seweth a piece of † new
cloth on an old garment else the new piece that filled
it up taketh away from the old, and the rent is made
worse 22 And no man putteth new wine into old
bottles, else the new wine doth burst the bottles, and
the wine is spilled, and the bottles will be marred but
new wine must be put into new bottles 23 [s] And it — s Mat xii 1 Luke vi 1
came to pass that he went through the corn-fields on the
sabbath day, and his disciples began as they went [t] to — t Deut xxiii 25
pluck the ears of corn 24 And the Pharisees said unto him, Behold, why do they on the sabbath-day that
which is not lawful? 25 And he said unto them,
Have ye never read [u] what David did, when he had — u 1 Sam xxi 6
need, and was an hungred, he and they that were with
him? 26 *How he went into the house of God in the*
days of Abiathar the high priest, and did eat the shew-
bread, [x] which is not lawful to eat, but for the priests, — x Exod xxix 33 Luke xxiv 9
and gave also to them which were with him? 27 And
he said unto them, The sabbath was made for man,
and not man for the sabbath 28 Therefore the Son
of man is Lord also of the sabbath

v 18—28 Christ having justified his own conduct from the censure of Pharisaical pride, justifies also his disciples for not observing unnecessary austerities, and vindicates them for plucking the ears of corn on the sabbath-day to satisfy their hunger

1 The disciples of John, who, after their master's example, fasted often, and the Pharisees, who placed great dependance on this bodily exercise, express their wonder that Jesus enjoined *no such rigid rules on his disciples as they practised* So ready are those who fancy their own strictness meritorious, to censure all who come short of their standard of excellence Christ answers their question, and vindicates his disciples, they were but beginners, and it was improper to put them on the more *difficult exercises of self denial, least they should be discouraged thereby*, and contract a disgust to the service Besides, during his presence with them, like a newly married bride, it became them to rejoice it would be time enough when he should be taken from them, to mourn and fast Thus should we learn not to exact too much from *young converts*, and the lambs of the flock, and especially in fasting we should consider the great end and use of it, and that of itself, it is no farther good, than these are obtained

2 The Pharisees soon seized another occasion of offence, from the disciples plucking the ears of corn on the sabbath-day, as they passed through the fields Rigidly scrupulous, as many others like them still are, about the form of godliness, and severe in judging all who do not coincide with them, yet blind to the deep-rooted evil and abominations of their hearts Christ vindicates them by a precedent the Pharisees will not dispute, and reasons with them by arguments they cannot disprove David had done what seemed a much more exceptionable thing *in eating the shew-bread*, and Abiathar, who succeeded his father soon after as high-priest, had consented to it, because ceremonial observances must give way to the great law of charity and self-preservation Besides, the very institution of the sabbath was designed for man's benefit, to give rest to his body, and time to spend *in the immediate service of God*, and caring for his soul, and therefore doth not require him to abstain from what is more immediately necessary for the support and preservation of his life the provision for which was a law of nature, and subsisted previous to the institution of the sabbath The Messiah, therefore, who can best interpret his own laws, and is Lord of the sabbath, has an undoubted right to permit this liberty to his disciples, as such refreshment of their bodies will enable them more effectually to discharge the duties of the holy day *Note*, (1) Our sabbaths should be our delight, and therefore must not, by unreasonable strictness, be made a burden (2) Though we are allowed to eat and drink, as shall best enable us for the service of the sabbath, it is a gross violation of the day, by indulging our appetite to stupify our faculties, and render body and soul utterly unfit for the exercises of devotion

CHAP III

In this chapter we have, 1 Christ's healing a man that had a withered hand on the sabbath-day, and the combination of his enemies against him for it, ver 1—6 *2 The universal resort of people to him from all parts to be healed, and the relief they all found with him, ver* 7—12 *3 His ordaining his twelve apostles to be attendants on him, and the preachers of his gospel, ver* 13—21 *4 His answer to the blasphemous cavil of the scribes, who imputed his power to cast out devils, to a confederacy with the prince of the devils, ver* 22—30 *5 His owning his disciples for his nearest and dearest relations, ver* 31—35

1. AND [a] he entered again into the synagogue, and — a Mark xii 9 Luke vi 6
there was a man there which had a withered
hand 2 And they watched him, [b] whether he would — b Luke xiii 14 & xiv 3 John ix 16
heal him on the sabbath-day, that they might accuse
him 3 And he saith unto the man which had the — ‖ Or, Arise, or stand up in the midst
withered hand, ‖ Stand forth 4 And he saith unto
them,

them, Is it lawful to do good on the sabbath-days, or
to do evil? to save life, or to kill? but they held their
peace 5 And when he had looked round about on
them with anger, being grieved for the ‡ hardness of
their hearts, he saith unto him, [c] Stretch forth thine
hand And he stretched *it* out and his hand was re-
stored whole as the other 6 [d] And the Pharisees went
forth, and straightway took counsel with [e] the Herodians
against him, how they might destroy him 7 But
Jesus [f] withdrew himself with his disciples to the sea
and a great multitude from Galilee followed him, and
from Judea, 8 And from Jerusalem, and from Idu-
mea, and from beyond Jordan, and they about Tyre
and Sidon, a great multitude, when they had heard
what great things he did, came unto him 9 And he
spake to his disciples, that a small ship should wait on
him, because of the multitude, lest they should throng
him 10 For he had healed many, insomuch that they
pressed upon him for to touch him, as many as had
‖ plagues 11 And unclean spirits, when they saw him,
fell down before him, and cried, saying, [g] Thou art the
Son of God 12 And [h] he straitly charged them, that
they should not make him known.

‡ Or blindness
c 1 Kings xiii 6
d Mat xii 14, &c
e Mat xxii 16
f Mat, x 23
‖ Or Chastisements or corrections Heb xii 6
g Luke iv 41
h Chap i

v 1—12 We see here Christ dispensing his miraculous cures

1 In the synagogue, on the sabbath-day, he healed a man who had a withered hand He knew the malignity of his enemies, and that from such a deed of mercy they would seek to raise an accusation against him as a sabbath-breaker He therefore first put a question to them for their determination, whether it was lawful on the sabbath-day to do an act of mercy, or to do evil, by neglecting it? to contribute to man's health and ease, or to let him languish, perhaps die, for want of assistance? The question answered itself, but they resolved not to admit the conviction, and in sullen silence held their peace With indignation looking round upon them, grieved and displeased at their wilful obstinacy and hardness of heart, Jesus will not suffer their malevolence to prevent his works of grace, therefore in the face of the congregation he bids the lame man stretch out his hand, and instantly it was restored to perfect strength and soundness *Note*, (1) Deeds of mercy and charity are ever pleasing to God, and no day unseasonable for them (2) They who are obstinate in error and unbelief, will be convinced by no arguments (3) Jesus looks still with indignation upon the hard-hearted sinner, and if he doth not now tremble under his frowns, he must quickly be consumed under his wrath (4) It is a grief to the Saviour, and all who are his people, when they behold men wilfully sinning against their own mercies (5) If people will be offended at our well-doing, we must not be concerned about their censures (6) He who bids us stretch out the arms of faith and prayer, must himself minister the ability In vain are gospel calls, without the effectual power of gospel-grace

2 By the sea-side, whither he withdrew to shelter himself from the malice of his exasperated foes, who were now consulting his destruction, he liberally dispensed his cures to the multitudes, who resorted to him for healing from all the regions round about, till at last he was constrained to go into a boat, and put off a little from the shore such crowds of diseased persons thronging upon him, in the confidence that could they but touch him, it would be sufficient to heal them of the most inveterate plagues Even the devils, who dwelt in many, whose bodies they had possessed, no sooner saw him, than they were forced to prostrate themselves before him, confessed his divine power and godhead, and owned him as the Messiah But, to avoid the least appearance of receiving a testimony from them of his mission and character, lest his enemies should suggest there was a confederacy between him and them, he sealed up their lips in silence, and left his own works to speak his glory, enjoining the same silence on all whom he had healed *Note*, (1) It is grievous to think, that men should ever deny that divinity of our Lord, which even devils confessed (2) We never should seek the applause of men, it is enough that our works testify for us

13 [i] And he goeth up into a mountain, and [k] calleth
unto him whom he would and [l] they came unto him
14 And [m] he ordained twelve, that they should be with
him, and that he might send them forth to preach
15 And to have power to heal sicknesses, and to cast
out devils 16 And Simon he surnamed Peter 17
And James *the son* of Zebedee, and John the brother of
James (and he surnamed them Boanerges, which is [n] the
sons of thunder) 18 And Andrew, and Philip, and
Bartholomew, and Matthew, and Thomas, and James
the son of Alpheus, and Thaddeus, and Simon the Ca-
naanite, 19 And Judas Iscariot, which also betrayed
him and they went into an house 20 And the mul-
titude cometh together again, [o] so that they could not
so much as eat bread 21. And when his friends heard
of it, they went out to lay hold of him for they said,
[p] He is beside himself

i Mat x 1 Luke vi 12
k John xv 16 Acts i 2
l John xv ...
m Heb v ...
n Isa lviii 1
o Chap vi 31
p 2 Kings ix 11 Acts xxvi 24 2 Cor v 13

2

v 13—21 We have here,

1 The ordination of the twelve apostles Going up into a mountain, he called to him, as the sovereign dispenser of his own gifts, whom he would from among his professed disciples, and they immediately came to him Twelve of them he selected to be his constant attendants, to be witnesses of his doctrine, life, and miracles, and to preach his gospel Their names we had before, but the title given to the sons of Zebedee Mark particularly mentions they were called *Boanerges*, sons of thunder, either from the loudness of their voice, the vehemence of their address, or the powerful energy which should accompany their preaching John, whose epistles breathe nothing but love, was one of them, and it would seem thereby to be intimated, that nothing acts so powerfully and forcibly upon the sinner's heart, as the doctrines of the rich love and free grace of God in Jesus Christ These twelve the Lord was pleased to invest with miraculous powers, to heal sicknesses, and cast out devils, in confirmation of the doctrines they were to teach And having thus appointed them their office, Christ retired with them into an house for refreshment, and they henceforward attended him as his peculiar family, and continued in the greatest intimacy with him during his abode upon earth *Note*, The Saviour's choice is sovereign, and none but those whom he particularly calls, can be empowered to go forth in his name

2 No sooner was he known to be in the house at Capernaum, than the multitude assembled, eager to hear him, and tho' he and his disciples had scarce time for necessary refreshment, yet he is ready to instruct them Such incessant labours, without respite, excited the concern of some of his friends, who could not help thinking his zeal carried him too far, and that he would *faint* with fatigue and want of repose They came therefore to persuade him to desist for a while, lest he should impair his health by such uninterrupted toils Perhaps some might think his intellects disturbed, and would fain constrain him to come in and rest himself *Note*, (1) Faithful ministers will sometimes find as great trials from the mistaken affection of their friends, as from the avowed opposition of their enemies (2) Fervent zeal is often branded with madness by those who never felt the love of immortal souls, *but if we be beside ourselves, it is to God*, 2 Cor v 13

22 ¶ [q] And the scribes which came down from Je-
rusalem, said, [r] He hath Beelzebub, and by the prince
of the devils casteth he out devils 23 And he called
them unto him, and said unto them in parables, How
can Satan cast out Satan? 24 And if a kingdom be
divided against itself, that kingdom cannot stand 25
And if a house be divided against itself, that house can-
not stand 26 And if Satan rise up against himself,
and be divided, he cannot stand, but hath an end
27 [s] No man can enter into a strong man's house, and
spoil his goods, except he will first bind the strong
man, and then he will spoil his house 28 Verily I
say unto you, All sins shall be forgiven unto the sons of
men, and [t] blasphemies wherewith soever they shall blas-
pheme 29 But [u] he that shall blaspheme against the
Holy Ghost, hath never forgiveness, but is in danger of
eternal damnation 30 Because they said, He hath an
unclean spirit

q Mat xii 24 &c Luke xi 15 &c
r Mat ix 34 John viii 48 5
s Isa xlix 24 John xvi 11
t 1 Tim i 13 16
u 1 Sam ii 25 Heb vi 6 & x 26 1 John v 16.

v 22—30 That he did cast out devils from them that were possessed, was evident To evade the force of the miracles therefore, we have here,

1 The vile railed by the Scribes and Pharisees who came down from Jerusalem They pretended he was in compact with Beelzebub, the prince of the devils, and derived the power from him

2 Christ confutes their suggestion, and solemnly warns them of the unpardonable guilt they brought hereby upon their souls It was as absurd and self-contradictory to suppose, that Satan would cast out Satan, to confirm doctrines directly tending to destroy his power over the souls of men, as to suppose that a kingdom, or a house, divided against itself, can stand, or be established by intestine factions and civil wars The power which Jesus exerted over the fiends of darkness, was like that which the conqueror exercises over the vanquished, when he enters the fortress, binds the prisoner, and spoils his substance Satan never would quit his hold, unless compelled Evident therefore it was, that Christ came not as his associate, but as

his

his destroyer To impute, therefore, his miracles to diabolical agency, was such wilful obstinacy and blasphemy against the Holy Ghost, by whose powerful operations these miracles were wrought, that though all other sin might be forgiven, this was eternally unpardonable, and would expose them to everlasting destruction, as no other means of conviction or recovery would be ever afforded them

31 ¶ [x] There came then his brethren and his mother,
and standing without, sent unto him, calling him 32
And the multitude sat about him, and they said unto
him, Behold, thy mother and thy brethren without seek
for thee 33 And he answered them, saying, [y] Who is
my mother, or my brethren? 34 And he looked
round about on them which sat about him, and said,
Behold, my mother and my brethren 35 For [z] who-
soever shall do the will of God, the same is my brother,
and my sister, and mother

x Mat xii 46 Luke viii 19
y Mat xii 48 9
z John xv 14

v 31—35 Perhaps these were the friends, v 20, 21 who wanted to lay hold on him, or they got his mother and brethren to join them, and perceiving him still go on discoursing, made another effort to call him off Though the crowd sat so thick around him that they could not come near him, they conveyed to him however, by some of the multitude, their desire to speak with him, but he was too well employed to be diverted from it, and therefore, instead of paying any regard to his mother or brethren in this case, he turned to those around him, professing a regard for them like that due to a mother or brethren, and declaring those to be his nearest and dearest relations who truly believed, and heartily obeyed the revealed will of God *Note*, (1) How great is the folly, as well idolatry of the Romish church in worshipping the virgin, as if she could command her son now he is in heaven, when even in the days of his flesh she was judged so unfit to advise him? (2) When we are engaged in the work of Jesus, and in the way of duty, nothing must divert us from the service

CHAP IV

In this chapter we have, 1 The parable of the seed, and the four sorts of ground, ver 1—9 with the exposition of it, ver 10—20 and the application of it, ver 21—25 2 The parable of the seed growing gradually, but insensibly, ver 26—29 3 The parable of the grain of mustard seed, and a general account of Christ's parables, ver 30—34 4 The miracle of Christ's suddenstilling a storm at sea, ver 35—41

1 [a] AND he began again to teach by the sea-side and
there was gathered unto him a great multitude,
so that he entred into a ship, and sat in the sea and the
whole multitude was by the sea, on the land 2 And he
taught them many things by parables, and said unto them
in his doctrine, 3 Hearken, Behold, there went out a
sower to sow 4 And it came to pass as he sowed, some
fell by the way side, and the fowls of the air came and
devoured it up 5 And some fell on stony ground,
where it had not much earth, and immediately it sprang
up, because it had no depth of earth 6 But when the
sun was up, it was scorched, and because it had no root,
it withered away 7 And some fell among thorns, and
the thorns grew up and choked it, and it yielded no
fruit 8 And other fell on good ground, and [b] did yield
fruit that sprang up, and increased, and brought forth
some thirty, and some sixty, and some an hundred 9
And he said unto them, [c] He that hath ears to hear, let
him hear 10 And when he was alone, they that were a-
bout him with the twelve, asked of him the parable
11 And he said unto them, [d] Unto you it is given to
know the mystery of the kingdom of God but unto
them that are without, all *these* things are done in para-
bles 12 [e] That seeing they may see, and not perceive,
and hearing they may hear, and not understand, lest at
any time they should be converted, and *their* sins should
be forgiven them 13 And he said unto them, Know
ye not this parable? and how then will you know all
parables? 14 ¶ [f] The sower soweth the word 15
And these are they by the way side, where the word is
sown but when they have heard, Satan cometh imme-
diately, and taketh away the word that was sown in their
hearts 16 And these are they likewise which are sown
on stony ground, who when they have heard the word, [g]
immediately receive it with gladness 17 And have
no root in themselves, [h] and so endure but for a time
afterward when affliction or persecution ariseth for the
word's sake, [i] immediately they are offended 18 And
these are they which are sown [k] among the thorns such
as hear the word, 19 And [l] the cares of this world,
and the deceitfulness of riches, and the lusts of other
things entring in, choke the word, and it becometh un-
fruitful 20 And these are they which are sown on
good ground, such as hear the word, and receive *it*, [m]
and bring forth fruit, some thirty fold, some sixty, and
some an hundred

a Mat xiii 1 &c Luke viii 4, &c
b John xv 5 Col i 6
c Mat xi 15
d Mat xiii 11 &c
e Isa vi 9 John xii 40 Acts xxviii 26 Rom xi 8
f Mat xiii 19 Luke viii 11
g Isa lviii 2 Ezek xxxiii 31 Chap vi 20 John v 35
h Mat vii 26
i Mat xi 6
k Jer iv 3
l Mat xix 23 1 Tim vi 9 2 Tim iv 10
m John xv 16

v 1—20 For the convenience of being heard by the vast multitudes who attended him, our Lord again returns to the sea-shore, and entring into a boat, sat down and taught this great and attentive congregation Preaching to them the doctrines of truth under parables drawn from familiar objects We have,

1 The parable of the sower, which represents the different effects of the gospel-word upon the hearts of men, *Mat* xiii 3 He commands attention, v 3 for all who would understand must give diligence, and well consider what they hear The parable itself was plain, but even the twelve were dull of apprehension, and understood it not, but when they were retired with the rest of the disciples, they desired of Jesus the explanation of it to which he graciously condescends, informing them of the distinguished grace bestowed on them, whilst others were left to the blindness of their hearts, yet wondering withal at them wanting an explanation of what was so plain, v 13 *Note*, (1) The human understanding is strangely dark in spiritual concerns the plainest truths of God's word to the natural man are utterly unintelligible (2) It is a distinguishing act of grace when God is pleased to remove the vail from the heart, and opens the understanding to understand the scriptures (3) The more we are acquainted with our own stupid ignorance in the things of God, the more thankful shall we be for divine teaching

2 The explication Christ gives is this *The seed is the word of God*, himself, and all his faithful labourers, are the sowers The hearers are the soil, to many of them the word preached doth not profit, not being mixed with faith, but few, comparatively speaking, effectually receive it, so as to profit thereby Some are careless and inattentive, the seed sown doth not at all abide upon their hearts, Satan, by some vanity, amusement, or avocation, instantly snatches it away Others for a moment hear it with joy, their passions are affected, but their hearts are unchanged, therefore, no sooner is the impression worn off, than they are like blasted corn which withers away Some are so engrossed with the riches and cares of the world, the eager pursuits of its honours, pleasures, or esteem, that these, by degrees, eat out the life of their profession, carnalize their souls, and make them earthly, sensual Thus for the perishing trifles of time, they lose all the glories of eternity A few, amidst the general apostacy, with patient perseverance endure, bring forth the gracious fruits of faith and holiness, in measure according as God is pleased to dispense to every man his gift.

21 ¶ And he said unto them, [o] Is a candle brought
to be put under a bushel, or under a bed? and not to be
set on a candlestick? 22 For [p] there is nothing hid
which shall not be manifested neither was any thing
kept secret, but that it should come abroad, 23 [q] If
any man have ears to hear, let him hear 24 And he
said unto them, Take heed what you hear [r] with what
measure ye mete, it shall be measured to you and unto
you that hear shall more be given 25 [s] For he that
hath, to him shall be given and he that hath not, from
him shall be taken even that which he hath 26 ¶ And
he said, [t] So is the kingdom of God, as if a man should
cast seed into the ground, 27 And should sleep, and
rise night and day, and the seed should spring and grow
up, he knoweth not how 28 For the earth bringeth
forth fruit of herself, first the blade, then the ear, after
that the full corn in the ear 29 But when the fruit is
[||] brought forth, immediately he putteth in the sickle,
because the harvest is come 30 ¶ And he said, [u]
Whereunto shall we liken the kingdom of God? or with
what comparison shall we compare it? 31 *It is* like a
grain of mustard-seed, which when it is sown in the
earth, is less than all the seeds that be in the earth 32
But when it is sown, [x] it groweth up, and becometh
greater than all herbs, and shooteth out great branches,
so that the fowls of the air may lodge under the shadow
of it 33 [y] And with many such parables spake he the
word unto them as they were able to hear *it* 34 But
[z] without a parable spake he not unto them, and when
they were alone, he expounded all things to his disciples

o Mat v 15 Luke viii 16 & xi 33
p Job xii 22 Mat x 26 Luke xii 2
q Mat xi 15
r Mat vii 2 Luke vi 38
s Mat xiii 12 Luke viii 18 & xix 26 John xv 2 Rev xxii 11
t Mat xiii 24
|| Or, ripe
u Mat xiii 31 Luke xiii 18
x Psal lxxx 8—11 Prov iv 18
y Mat xiii 34 John xvi 12
z Ver 11

v 21—34

v 21—34 Our Lord proceeds to teach them under other parabolic representations

1 By the use we make of a candle when lighted up, Christ informs them what he justly expected of them, even to shine as lights in the world, communicating to others the truths they in secret learnt of him, and keeping back nothing of the whole counsel of God Whatever gifts of nature or grace we enjoy, they are to be employed for God's glory and the good of mankind, and not through love of ease, or false shame, concealed or neglected It is not enough that we walk in the light ourselves, we must let our light also shine before men

2 He warns them of the danger of negligence in improving the means and mercies they enjoyed They are called upon to hear, and to take heed what they hear, that they may not let the word slip, nor be deluded, but by a careful use of their measure of the gift of grace to increase their store, God being ready to communicate more abundant knowledge to such attentive hearers, and to give farther assistances of spiritual light and strength to those who employ aright in the service of Christ and immortal souls the portion they have received, whilst he punishes the negligent and inattentive, by withdrawing from them the privileges wherewith he had favoured them

3 He describes the progress of his gospel in the world, and of the seed of divine grace in the heart, by the growth of corn which, though unseen for a while, and covered with earth, shoots up, increases insensibly till the harvest, and then produces the ripe ear Thus the ministry of Jesus at first was scarce perceived, but the seed he sowed afterwards sprang up, continues through his word and spirit still to grow, and shall shortly fill the face of the whole world with fruit And so also in every heart, where the seed of eternal life is sown by any minister of God, it grows without his care, when perhaps he is removed far away, or sleeps in death, it is watered with the dew of heavenly influences, and though the manner of the spirit's operation in the divine change which is wrought is mysterious, as the manner how the corn vegetates, yet the effects are visible, the soul is renewed day by day, the seed of grace, from small beginnings, shoots insensibly upwards till the time of harvest, when the ripe corn is gathered in, and perfected in holiness the saints of God enter their eternal rest Lord, quicken this seed sown in our souls day by day!

4 Much to the same purpose as the former, is the parable of the grain of mustard-seed, and represents, (1) The progress of the gospel, which, from the smallest beginnings of the ministry of twelve poor fishermen, hath spread through the earth, and shall in due time reach from pole to pole, when all the kingdoms of the world shall become the kingdoms of the Lord and his Christ (2) The work of grace upon the heart At first, like a grain of mustard-seed, it is scarce perceptible, but increasing with the increase of God, the herb grows into a tree, and meet to be transplanted among the cedars of glorified saints in the paradise of God

5 He added many other like parables, that by line upon line, in this familiar manner, he might communicate spiritual truths under material objects, and without a parable spake he not unto them They who desired to understand might easily do it, and where difficulties arose, he was always ready, when alone, to explain them to the disciples, whilst those who superficially heard, neglected and forgot the word preached, were justly left in their native blindness and ignorance

a Mat viii 18 —27 Luke viii 22

35 [a] And the same day when the even was come,
he saith unto them, Let us pass over unto the other
side 36 And when they had sent away the multi-
tude, they took him even as he was in the ship, and
there were also with him other little ships 37 And
[b] there arose a great storm of wind, and the waves beat
into the ship, so that it was now full 38 And he was
in the hinder part of the ship, [c] asleep on a pillow and
they awake him, and say unto him, Master, carest thou
not that we perish? 39 And he arose, and [d] rebuk-
ed the wind, and said unto the sea, Peace, be still and
the wind ceased, and there was a great calm 40 And
he said unto them, Why are ye so fearful? how is it
that you have no faith? 41 And they feared exceed-
ingly, and said one to another, What manner of man
is this, that even [e] the wind and the sea obey him?

b Isa liv 11.

c Ps x 1 Isa xiv 15

d Ps cvi 9

e Ps lxv 7 & lxxxix 9 & cvii 29

v 35—41 No sooner had Christ finished his discourse, and dismissed the people, than he bids the disciples cross the lake, having work that calls him to the other side Jesus was never weary in well-doing, neither should we

1 The disciples, without hesitation, obey, ready to follow their master wherever he led them, and accordingly they set sail in the same vessel which had been his pulpit, and a number of other boats accompanied them For though the multitude departed, those whose hearts were affected with what they had heard, chose to cleave to the Lord, and follow him whithersoever he went, by land or by water *Note*, (1) They who are Christ's disciples indeed, will never leave nor forsake him, whatever dangers may threaten (2) If Christ be with us, we may boldly launch forth, his presence and blessing will be our support and comfort

2 A dreadful and sudden storm brought them into the most imminent danger, and, covered with waves, and full almost of water, the boat was ready to founder *Note*, The church, and every faithful soul in it, hath at times been brought into the most perilous circumstances, nothing hath kept either from sinking but this, that Christ was there

3 He slept securely in the stern on a pillow, tired with the labours of the day the storm that drove the disciples to their wits end, seemed but to rock him faster to repose *Note*, When we are in our deepest distresses, Christ sometimes appears to disregard our danger, as if he slept, inattentive to our cries, but he sees, he hears, and will be found a very present help in trouble

4 The disciples in a fright awake him with their cries, *Master, carest thou not that we perish?* art thou indifferent about our danger, and wilt thou suffer us to be drowned? Their application to him bespoke their faith, but their address breathed the language of impatience and dishonourable fear Such a mixture of grace and corruption often appears in the best of men

5 The Lord, whom winds and waves obey, arose, and at his commanding word, *Peace, be still*, the billows in a moment ceased to roar, the swelling sea subsided, the winds were hushed, not a breath of air dimpled the ocean, not a whisper broke the solemn silence When our unruly passions are like *the troubled sea which cannot rest*, Isa lvii 20 the voice of Jesus, heard by faith, subdues their violence, and calms their rage — Under deep afflictions and temptations, when we are ready to abandon ourselves to despair, he silences our fears, and stills our griefs, speaking that inward peace to the conscience, that in the midst of sorrows can make us rejoice with joy unspeakable and full of glory

6 He rebukes their unbelieving fears *Why are ye so fearful?* so unnecessarily, so inordinately fearful? *How is it that ye have no faith?* not in exercise at least, though they had faith in him in general, in this particular their fears prevailed How often do we under our trials deserve the same rebuke?

7 The miracle filled the mariners with most reverential fear of the majesty in which Jesus now appeared, and with amazement they observed to each other, that he must be surely more than man, whom stormy winds and raging waves so instantly obey

CHAP V.

In this chapter we have, 1 *Christ's casting the legion of devils out of the man possessed, and suffering them to enter into the swine,* ver 1—20 *Christ's healing the woman with the bloody issue in the way as he was going to raise Jairus's daughter to life,* ver 21—43 *These three miracles we had the story of before,* Mat viii 28, &c *and* Mat ix 18, &c *but more fully related here*

1 [a] AND they came over unto the other side of the a Mat viii 28 Luke viii 26
sea, into the country of the Gadarenes. 2
And when he was come out of the ship, immediately
there met him out of the tombs, a man with an un-
clean spirit, 3 Who had *his* dwelling among the
tombs, and no man could bind him, no not with
chains 4 Because that he had been often bound with
fetters and chains, and the chains had been plucked a-
sunder by him, and the fetters broken in pieces neither
could any man tame him 5 And always night and
day he was in the mountains, and in the tombs, crying
and cutting himself with stones 6 But when he saw
Jesus afar off, he ran and worshipped him, 7 And
cried with a loud voice, and said, What have I to do
with thee, Jesus, thou Son of the most high God? I
adjure thee by God, [b] that thou torment me not 8 b 2 Pet ii 4 Jude 6
(For he said unto him, Come out of the man, thou un-
clean spirit) 9 And he asked him, What *is* thy
name? And he answered, saying, My name *is* Legion
for we are many 10 And he besought him much,
that he would not send them away out of the country
11 Now there was there nigh unto the mountains, a
great herd of swine feeding 12 And all the devils be-
sought him, saying, Send us into the swine, that we
may enter into them 13 And forthwith Jesus gave
them leave And the unclean spirits went out, and
entred into the swine, and the herd ran violently down
a steep place into the sea, (they were about two thou-
sand) and were choked in the sea 14 And they that
fed

ted the swine fled, and told *it* in the city, and in the
country And they went out to see what it was that
was done 15 And they come to Jesus, and see him
that was possessed with the devil, and had the legion,
sitting, and clothed, and in his right mind, and they
were afraid 16 And they that saw *it*, told them how
it befel to him that was possessed with the devil, and
also concerning the swine 17 And [c] they began to
c Deut v 25 Luke v 8 Acts xvi 39 pray him to depart out of their coasts 18 And when
he was come into the ship, he that had been possessed
d Luke viii 38 with the devil, [d] prayed him that he might be with him
19 Howbeit, Jesus suffered him not, but saith unto
him, Go home to thy friends, and tell them how great
things the Lord hath done for thee, and hath had com-
passion on thee 20 And he departed, and began to
publish in Decapolis, how great things Jesus had done
for him and all men did marvel

v 1—20 What a miserable creature is man, when left to the power of the devil! What a mercy that Jesus is come to destroy the works of the devil, and to take the prey from the mighty An eminent instance of this here appears We have,

1 The wretched case of a poor demoniack, driven by an unclean spirit, to dwell among the tombs, a terror to himself, and to all who approached him, so raging, that none could sooth him, so strong, no fetters could bind him Though it had been often attempted, he broke the bands in sunder, and fled, living in the mountains, and in the tombs, uttering horrid yellings, and cutting himself with the sharp stones, till the blood gushed out *Note*, (1) We have here a lively emblem of the natural man, his mind and conscience are defiled, his passions drive him furiously on, and will be restrained by no fetters of God's law, under the power of Satan he is hurried to the excess of riot, madly wounding his own soul by sin, and dangerous to all around him, insensible to every fearful consequence, and wilful in disobedience (2) Solitude gives peculiar advantage to the temptations of *an unclean spirit*

2 No sooner was Jesus disembarked, than the man in whom the devil was, ran and worshipped him the wicked spirit being awed by his presence, or his power was now suspended Matthew says there were two, perhaps Mark mentions one only, as being the more fierce, and to him the Lord directed his discourse

3 On beholding so pitiable an object, Jesus bid the unclean spirit depart, nor could his expostulation or intreaty prevail, though in the greatest dread and horror the devil addressed him, acknowledging his divine power and glory, importunately begging, since he could have no interest in him, he might have nothing to do with him, and that he would not send him into the place of torment, and compel him to retire from the world to the prison of hell before the day of final judgment *Note*, (1) The confession of the devil was orthodox, but it is not a form of sound words, but the work of the Holy Ghost upon the heart, that can avail to our salvation (2) When Christ comes to visit our souls, he casts out the unclean spirit, gives a new heart, and puts a right spirit within us

4 To shew his own power over the fiends of darkness, Christ demanded the name of this evil spirit, and was answered, *My name is legion, for we are many* A legion of Roman soldiers some reckon at six thousand, whilst others increase it to more than twelve, and this intimates the immense numbers of these fallen spirits which war against the souls of men, their vast power, regular order, and unanimity what need then have we, who wrestle with these principalities and powers, to put on the whole armour of God, and to be continually looking up for the strength of our God, that we may be able to stand in the evil day

5 Since they must quit their present hold, the devil earnestly besought him not to expel them from that heathen country, as he dispossessed them from Judea And there being a herd of swine feeding near the place, they desired permission to enter those unclean animal hoping, by destroying them, to prejudice the people against Jesus, and to gratify their own delight in mischief, and for wise and just reason Christ permitted their request, when instantly the devils seized the whole herd, about two thousand, and filling them with madness, hurried them down a precipice into the lake, where they perished in the waters

6 The keepers, who fled affrighted, spread through all the country the amazing story of the cure of the demoniack, and the destruction of the swine On which a vast concourse of people assembled to see this strange sight, and, to their great surprize, found the man who had been possessed, and a terror to the country, now peaceably sitting at the feet of Jesus, clothed, and in the perfect exercise of his reason and they who had been eye-witnesses of the cure, reported all the circumstance concerning the recovery of the man, and the destruction of the swine Hereupon afraid, lest Jesus should punish them yet more condignly if he tarried there, and more concerned for their temporal than eternal interests, they intreated him to depart out of the country And since they thus sinned against their own mercies, Jesus abandons them to the delusions they had chosen

7 Though his countrymen rejected Christ, the poor man who was cured, would fain have followed him, but Jesus bid him rather return, and bear testimony to the miracle of grace he had experienced, and awaken thereby the concern of his friends to seek after the Lord, who had done so great things for him Accordingly the man obeyed his command, and transported with gratitude, published every where in that country what Jesus had done for him, to the great astonishment of all who heard the story *Note*, (1) They who know the blessing of Christ's presence, long to be ever near him, and cannot but lament if their lot be cast among the tents of Kedar, where no gospel hath no place (2) They who are restored by Jesus to their right mind, from that moment begin to live to his glory, and to speak his praises (3) What the Lord doth for the faithful soul are great things indeed, for which we can never enough adore and thank him

21 And when Jesus was passed over again by ship
unto the other side, much people gathered unto him,
and he was nigh unto the sea 22 [e] And behold, e Matt ix 18 Luke viii 41
there cometh one of the rulers of the synagogue, Jairus
by name, and when he saw him, he fell at his feet,
23 And besought him greatly, saying, My little
daughter lieth [f] at the point of death, *I pray thee* come f Matt ix
and lay thy hands on her, that she may be healed, and
[g] she shall live 24 And *Jesus* went with him, and g John xi 25
much people followed him, and thronged him 25
And a certain woman which had [h] an issue of blood h Lev xv 19, &c.
twelve years, 26 And had suffered many things of
many physicians, and had spent all that she had, and
was nothing bettered, but rather grew worse, 27 When
she had heard of Jesus, came in the press behind, and
touched his garment 28 For she said, If I may touch
but his clothes, I shall be whole 29 And straightway
the fountain of her blood was dried up and she felt in
her body that she was healed of that plague 30
And Jesus immediately knowing in himself, that [i] virtue i Luke vi 19
had gone out of him, turned him about in the press,
and said, Who touched my clothes? 31 And his dis-
ciples said unto him, Thou seest the multitude throng-
ing thee, and sayest thou, Who touched me? 32 And
he looked round about to see her that had done this
thing 33 But the woman fearing and trembling,
knowing what was done in her, came and fell down be-
fore him, and told him all the truth 34 And he said
unto her, Daughter, [k] thy faith hath † made thee k Matt ix 22 Chap x 52
whole go in peace, and be whole of thy plague † Gr Saved thee Acts xiv 9

v 21—34 Since the Gadarenes rejected him, Christ crosses the lake to Capernaum, where he expected a more welcome reception Hereupon,

1 A ruler of the synagogue, with deepest respect, made his application to him, in behalf of his little daughter, who lay a dying when he came out from his house, and was even then dead, yet such was his faith in the power of Jesus, that he was persuaded, desperate as the case appeared, he could still restore her to life and health *Note*, The state of the sinner dead in trespasses and sins, is to human view irrecoverably desperate, but nothing is impossible with God

2 As Jesus went with the ruler, a poor diseased woman stole a cure Her malady discouraged her from making an open application to Jesus, and her faith persuaded her it was needless, the very touch of his garment's hem, in her apprehension, sufficient for her cure, even though her disorder had baffled the physician's skill, and under their hand her pockets had not only been emptied, but her complaints aggravated Nor was she mistaken, for no sooner had she through the crowd got near enough to touch his garment, than immediately on so doing, her disease was removed, she felt her health perfectly restored, and was retiring with wonder and thankfulness But Jesus, who perceived the virtue which had gone out of him, for the manifestation of his own glory, and the confirmation of the poor patient's faith, turning himself, demanded who touched him? which the disciples answered with a kind of surprize and rudeness, as if, considering the crowd, such a question was very strange But Jesus overlooked their frowardness, and casting his eye round to discover the person he meant, the poor woman, conscious of what had passed, and trembling, lest the Lord should be displeased at the manner in which she had surreptitiously obtained her cure, came and fell at his feet, declaring all that had passed Whereupon, far from being angry, Jesus encouraged and comforted her, making honourable mention of her faith, and dismissed her not only with a cure, but with his peace and benediction, which was infinitely better

Note,

Note, (1) We are generally driven to Christ by mere necessity, having in vain tried all other methods, and convinced at last that he must save us freely, or we must perish (2) All our spiritual diseases can only be removed by the touch of faith, till virtue come out of Christ, we can have no health in ourselves (3) Where he works, a universal blessed change appears in all the tempers of the mind, and in the whole outward conduct and conversation (4) When we are discouraged with fear, at the feet of Jesus we should lay our burdens, and he will speak peace to our troubled souls

l Luke viii. 49. 35 [l] While he yet spake, there came from the ruler
of the synagogue's *house*, *certain* which said, Thy daughter is dead, why troublest thou the Master any further?
36 As soon as Jesus heard the word that was spoken,
he saith unto the ruler of the synagogue, Be not afraid,
only believe 37 And he suffered no man to follow
him, save Peter, and James, and John the brother of
James 38 And he cometh to the house of the ruler
of the synagogue, and seeth the tumult, and them that
wept and wailed greatly 39. And when he was come
in, he saith unto them, Why make ye this ado, and
m John xi. 11. weep? the damsel is not dead, [m] but sleepeth 40 And
n Acts ix. 40. they laughed him to scorn But [n] when he had put them
all out, he taketh the father and the mother of the
damsel, and them that were with him, and entreth in
where the damsel was lying 41 And he took the damsel by the hand, and said unto her, Talitha cumi, which
is being interpreted, Damsel (I say unto thee) arise 42
And straightway the damsel arose, and walked, for she
was *of the age* of twelve years and they were astonished
o Matt. ix. 30. Luke v. 14. with a great astonishment 43 And [o] he charged them
straitly, that no man should know it and commanded
that something should be given her to eat

v 35—43 A discouraging message met the afflicted Jairus as Jesus was now on the way with him Tidings were brought that his daughter was dead, and his friends conclude it was in vain to trouble Christ any farther, supposing that though he cured the sick, to raise the dead was beyond his power But,

1 Our Lord encourages the distressed parent, bids him not to give way to despondence, but *only believe*, and he should still see that death, as well as disease, was under his controul *Note*, Faith is the great preservative from all our fears when those who are nearest and dearest to us are removed, we have a ground of abiding consolation, that we shall meet them at the resurrection of the just

2 When he came to the house, he suffered none to enter with him but Peter, James, and John, enough to be witnesses of the miracle, with the father and mother of the child and rebuking the excessive lamentations of those who were within, he assured them there was no real cause for them, as the damsel was not irrecoverable, as they apprehended, but though sleeping in the arms of death, he would awake her But they, fully assured of her death, treated with derision this suggestion Unworthy, therefore, to be witnesses of his wondrous power and grace, he put them all out, and permitting only his three disciples, and the parents of the damsel, to be with him, he went in where the child lay, took her by the hand, and bid her rise, when instantly her spirit returned, she rose, being about twelve years old, and, to the exceeding amazement of her parents, walked about in perfect health, and to shew she still retained her former animal life, and that her appetite was restored with her health, he bid them give her something to eat *Note*, (1) We are dead in trespasses and sins, as this child, till by the gospel word awakened Jesus imparts the effectual power, and enables us to rise at his command to newness of life (2) When Christ gives spiritual life, it must be daily fed in the use of those means of grace, whereby he continues to minister strength and nourishment to the soul

3 He gave them all a strict charge not to divulge this miracle He knew how his growing fame would exasperate his enemies, and as his hour was not yet come, he used every prudent means to preserve his life, till he had finished the work which was given him to do

CHAP VI

*He*re, 1 *Christ contemned by his countrymen*, ver 1—6 2 *The power he gave his apostles over unclean spirits*, ver 7—13 3 *A strange notion which Herod and others had of Christ, upon which occasion, we have the story of the martyrdom of John Baptist*, ver 14—29 4 *Christ's retirement into a desert place with his disciples, the crowds that followed him thither to receive instruction from him, and his feeding five thousand of them with five loaves and two fishes*, ver 30—44 5 *Christ's walking upon the sea to his disciples, and the abundance of cures he wrought on the other side the water*, ver 45—56

1 [a] AND he went out from thence, and came into a Matt. xiii. 54. Luke iv. 16.
his own country, and his disciples follow him
2 And when the sabbath-day was come, he began to
teach in the synagogue and many hearing *him*, [b] were b Matt. vii. 28. Ch. i. 22. Luke iv. 32.
astonished, saying, From whence hath this man these
things? and what wisdom *is* this which is given unto
him, that even such mighty works are wrought by his
hands? 3 [c] Is not this the carpenter, the son of Mary, c Luke iii. 23. John vi. 42.
the brother of James and Joses, and of Juda, and Simon?
and are not his sisters here with us? and [d] they were d Matt. xi. 6.
offended at him 4 But Jesus said unto them, [e] A pro- e Matt. xiii. 57. John iv. 44.
phet is not without honour but in his own country, and
among his own kin, and in his own house. 5 And [f]
he could there do no mighty work, save that he laid f Matt. xiii. 58. Gen. xix. 22.
his hands upon a few sick folk, and healed *them* 6
And he marvelled because of their unbelief [g] And he g Matt. ix. 35. Luke xiii. 22.
went round about the villages, teaching

v 1—6 From Capernaum our Lord visited the place of his education, Nazareth, accompanied by his disciples And there, as was his custom,

1 On the sabbath-day he entred into the synagogue, and from the law and the prophets preached the things concerning himself with such dignity and elocution, as quite amazed his countrymen He had been bred among them, a carpenter by trade, without any education, his family and relations were all persons of mean and low circumstances, how he should be able to discourse with such readiness, and perform such miraculous works, they could not conceive, and yet their prejudices against him, on account of his low birth and education, prevailed over their admiration, and notwithstanding all the wonders they beheld, they disdained to be followers of a person so mean and despicable in their account *Note*, (1) The humiliation of Jesus, at which they were offended, should make him the dearer to us (2) If the Lord, in our nature, submitted to earn with the labour of his hands the bread he eat, let it teach us how commendable is industry, and never to despise any man because he is poor

2 To rebuke their folly, and punish their unbelief, he reminds them how they verified that proverbial saying, *A prophet is not without honour but in his own country, and among his own kin, and in his own house*; people ordinarily paying more respect to strangers and persons unknown, than to those with whom having been indulged in familiarity, they are ready to treat them with contempt Therefore, except healing a few sick folk, he refused to exercise his power and grace among them Their unbelief bound up, as it were, the hands of his omnipotence, and marvelling at it, he left them, in just judgment, to the perverseness and impenitence of their hearts, carrying the glad tidings of salvation from them to the other villages of Galilee, where greater respect would be payed to his person and ministry

7 ¶ [h] And he calleth unto him the twelve, and began h Matt. x. 1. Luke ix. 1.
to send them forth by two and two, and gave them
power *over* unclean spirits, 8 And commanded them
that they should take nothing for *their* journey, save a
staff only no scrip, no bread, no money in *their* purse
9 But *be* [i] shod with sandals and not put on two coats i Acts xii. 8.
10 And he said unto them, In what place soever ye
enter into an house, there abide till ye depart from that
place 11 And whosoever shall not receive you, nor
hear you, when ye depart thence, [k] shake off the dust k Matt. x. 14. Acts xiii. 51.
under your feet, for a testimony against them Verily I
say unto you, [l] It shall be more tolerable for Sodom and l Matt. x. 15.
Gomorrha in the day of judgment than for that city
12 And they went out, and preached that men should
repent 13 And [m] they cast out many devils, and [n] a m Matt. x. 1.
nointed with oil many that were sick, and healed *them* n James v. 14.

v 7—13 The twelve having now for a while attended their master, are here,

1 Sent forth to preach what they had learned of him, and endued with power to work miracles, and cast out devils, in confirmation of the doctrine they taught For their mutual comfort and support, they were joined in pairs, and forbid to cumber themselves with cloaths or provisions, but must set off just as they were, with only their stick in their hand, the cloaths on their backs, and the sandals on their feet, trusting upon divine providence for a supply of their wants during their travel Their message would deserve and procure them a welcome Wherever therefore they came, and were received into a house, there they must fix their quarters till they removed to another city or village But if in any place they were refused a hospitable

hospitable entertainment, and no attention was paid to their preaching, they are commanded immediately to depart, shaking off the dust of their feet, in testimony of abhorrence of their wickedness and infidelity, and not Sodom or Gomorrha in the day of Judgment will meet so severe a doom as that city *Note*, (1) They who reject the calls of the gospel, perish under the most accumulated guilt (2) The ministers of Christ are worthy of their maintenance, and since they have renounced the world for the service of men's souls, it becomes those to whom they minister liberally to supply their wants, that they may be wholly without care, to give themselves up to the word of God and to prayer

2 The apostles went, in obedience to their master's orders, preaching the doctrine of repentance, and calling men to turn unto the Lord, and receive his Messiah, whose kingdom was ready to appear And in confirmation of their divine authority, they cast out devils, and miraculously healed the sick, by anointing them with oil in the name of the Lord, in token of their being restored to health *Note*, The great end of the ministry is the conversion of men's souls They who have not this in view, and do not see any fruit of their labours, may justly suspect they run without being sent

14 ° And king Herod heard *of him*, (for his name
o Mat xiv 1 Luke ix 7 — was spread abroad) and he said, That [p] John the Baptist
was risen from the dead, and therefore mighty works do
shew forth themselves in him 15 [q] Others said, That
it is Elias And others said, That it is a prophet, or
as one of the prophets 16. But when Herod heard
thereof, he said, It is John whom I beheaded, he is
risen from the dead 17 For Herod himself had sent
forth and laid hold upon John, and bound him in prison
for Herodias sake, his brother Philip's wife, for he had
married her 18 For John had said unto Herod, [r] It
is not lawful for thee to have thy brother's wife 19
Therefore Herodias had † a quarrel against him, and
would have killed him, but she could not 20 For
Herod feared John, knowing that he was a just man
and an holy, and ‡ observed him, and when he heard
him, he did many things, and [s] heard him gladly
21 And when a convenient day was come that Herod
on his birth day made a supper to his lords, high captains, and chief estates of Galilee 22 And when the
daughter of the said Herodias came in, and danced,
and pleased Herod, and them that sat with him, the
king said unto the damsel, Ask of me whatsoever thou
wilt, and I will give *it* thee 23 And [t] he sware unto
her, Whatsoever thou shalt ask of me, I will give *it*
thee, unto the half of my kingdom 24 And she went
forth, and said unto her mother, What shall I ask?
And she said, The head of John the Baptist 25 And
she came in straightway with haste unto the king, and
asked, saying, I will that thou give me by and by in a
charger, the head of John the Baptist 26 And the
king was exceeding sorry, *yet* for his oath's sake, and
for their sakes which sat with him, he would not reject
her 27 And immediately the king sent an executioner, and commanded his head to be brought and he
went and beheaded him in the prison, 28 And brought
his head in a charger, and gave it to the damsel and
the damsel gave it to her mother 29 And when his
disciples heard *of it*, they came and took up his corps,
and laid it in a tomb

† Or, an inward grudge ‡ Or, saved him

v 14—20 The fame of Jesus had by this time reached the ears of Herod His guilty conscience suggested to him that John, whom he had murdered, was now risen from the dead, and invested with greater powers than before, perhaps to avenge his blood upon the head of his murderer Others thought him to be Elijah, the forerunner of the Messiah, others one of the ancient prophets revived, others a new prophet sent of God, like those of old, but all mistook his true character, and knew him not as the Saviour of the world Herod, haunted with the ghosts of his injustice and cruelty, persisted in the conviction, that this was surely John the Baptist, whom he had beheaded The narrative of which bloody transaction is related in nearly the same words as before, *Mat* xiv To what was there said, we may here further observe,

1 How far a man may go in his convictions, without being ever effectually wrought upon Herod was in his conscience persuaded that John was a *just man, and a holy*, his whole demeanor shewed the Baptist to be such, and commanded veneration And so far many go, as to be convinced of the integrity of God's ministers, and reverence their character; to *observe* them, to attend their ministry with seriousness and constancy, to do many things that are right through their preaching, yea, to take delight in their discourses, and to feel a transient joy whilst sitting under them and yet like Herod, may never be divorced from their darling sins, nor their hearts at all effectually changed

2 How commendable is fidelity! All the respect and kindness of Herod did not make John the least indulgent to his sins; he told him plainly, though a king, the guilt and danger of his state, and charged upon his conscience his lewdness, adultery, and incest in marrying his brother's wife and such should we be, imitating this holy plainness and simplicity, neither moved by caresses, nor deterred by fear, but approving ourselves to every man's conscience in the sight of God

3 They who will be thus faithful, may expect to be often severely treated The hearts of sinners will be exasperated, and malice will drive them, like Herodias, to contrive some mischief against their reprovers, and thus to revenge the honest rebukes, which they regard as premeditated affronts

30 And the apostles gathered themselves together unto Jesus, and told him all things, both what they had
done, and what they had taught 31 And he said
unto them, Come ye yourselves apart into a desert
place, and rest a while for [u] there were many coming
and going, and they had no leisure so much as to eat
32 And [x] they departed into a desert place by ship privately 33 And the people saw them departing and
many knew him, and ran a foot thither out of all cities,
and outwent them, and came together unto him 34
And Jesus when he came out, saw much people, and
[y] was moved with compassion towards them, [z] because
they were as sheep not having a shepherd and he began to teach them many things 35 And when the
day was now far spent, his disciples came unto him, and
said, This is a desert place, and now the time *is* far
passed 36 Send them away, that they may go into
the country round about, and into the villages, and
buy themselves bread for they have nothing to eat
37 He answered and said unto them, [a] Give ye them to
eat And they say unto him, [b] Shall we go and buy two
hundred ‖ penny-worth of bread, and give them to
eat? 38 He saith unto them, How many loaves have
ye? go and see And when they knew, they say, Five,
and two fishes. 39 And he commanded them to make
all sit down by companies upon the green grass 40
And they sat down in ranks by hundreds and by fifties
41 And when he had taken the five loaves, and the
two fishes, he looked up to heaven, and [c] blessed, and
brake the loaves, and gave *them* to his disciples, [d] to set
before them, and the two fishes divided he among them
all 42. And they did all eat, and were filled 43
And they took up twelve baskets full of the fragments,
and of the fishes 44 And they that did eat of the
loaves, were about five thousand men

u Chap iii. 20 x Mat xiv 13 Luke ix 10 y Mat ix 36 z 1 Kings xxii 17 Ezek xxxiv 5 a John vi 5, &c b Num xi 22 2 Kings iv 43 ‖ A Roman penny, Seven pence Half-penny Mat xviii 28 c Mat xv 36 & xxvi 26 Rom xiv 6 d Mat xxiv 45

v 30—44 The apostles having executed the commission with which their master had entrusted them, return to give him an account of their ministry and success And blessed and happy are they who can give up this account to him with joy!

Satisfied in their report, and well pleased with their service, our Lord,

1 Testifies his tenderness and regard for them, by calling them into a retirement, where they might repose themselves a while after their labours For where they were, such crowds were perpetually coming and going, desirous to hear, or wanting to be healed, that they had no leisure even to eat their necessary food *Note*, (1) In these frail bodies at present, the most ardent spirits must yield to some repose and relaxation, it is reserved for the felicity of a better world, to serve God day and night without ceasing (2) Our rest must be but *for a while*, just enough to strengthen us to return with fresh vigour to the work of the Lord

2 He shews his compassions to the multitude who followed them For though they withdrew privately, and coasted the lake in a boat, to a desert place near the city of Bethsaida, yet many watched the course they steered, and were so eager after the company and teaching of Jesus, that they ran thither than the boat went, and were on the spot when he arrived, ready to receive him Jesus, on disembarking, beheld them with compassion, knowing how destitute they were of faithful guides, and neglected as sheep without a shepherd, and therefore well pleased to be interrupted and deprived of his purposed retirement, he instantly set himself to instruct them in the things pertaining to his kingdom, and their own everlasting peace, in which delightful work, and in healing their sick, he continued till evening drew on. *Note*, (1) They who have a true relish for

for the gospel of Jesus, will take many a weary step for the sake of attending that ministry, where it is dispensed with power (2) It is a peculiar pleasure to preach to those, who appear a-thirst for the word of truth

3 He not only fed their souls with the heavenly manna of his doctrine, but their bodies by miraculous food The disciples, as the day drew to a close, reminded him how far the people were from any inhabited place, and that the night would soon come on; it would be necessary, therefore, they suggest, to dismiss the multitude, that they might get some refreshment after fasting so long But He, to prove their faith, bid them provide for them the necessary repast In a surprize, they look not to his power, but to their own inability Where should they get bread, or money to buy it, when two hundred pennyworth would not be sufficient to give a morsel to each? Perceiving they had no notion whence the supply should come, he enquired what store of provision they had with them? they told him only five barley loaves, and two fishes, a quantity utterly insufficient to satisfy such a multitude Commanding them to be brought, Jesus took the loaves, and having disposed the people in ranks, a hundred in depth, and fifty in length, he gave thanks, brake, and gave to his disciples, who waited on the guests, and far from want, there appeared enough and to spare they not only made a hearty meal, but left fragments sufficient to fill twelve baskets, which Christ commanded to be collected with care, not only to supply their future wants, but to make the miracle appear more illustrious *Note*, (1) They who love the word, will for the sake of it sometimes forego their necessary food (2) Barley loaves, with Christ's blessing, afford a sweeter feast than the richest delicacies without it (3) Christ's disciples must be content with, and thankful for coarse fare (4) Waste, even of crumbs of barley bread, is sinful, no fragments are to be lost, when there are so many who want them

c Mat xiv 22 John vi 17
45 c And straightway he constrained his disciples to
get into the ship, and to go to the other side before un-
to Bethsaida, while he sent away the people. 46 And
when he had sent them away, he departed into a moun-
tain to pray 47. And when even was come, the ship
was in the midst of the sea, and he alone on the land
48 And he saw them f toiling in rowing (for the wind
was contrary unto them) and g about the fourth watch
of the night he cometh unto them, h walking upon the
sea, and i would have passed by them. 49. But when
they saw him walking upon the sea, they supposed it had
been a spirit, and cried out 50 (For they all saw him,
and were troubled) And immediately he talked with
them, and saith unto them, Be of good cheer, it is I,
be not afraid 51 And he went up unto them into
the ship, and the wind ceased and they were sore a-
mazed in themselves beyond measure, and wondred
52 For they considered not *the miracle* of the loaves,
for their heart was † hardned 53 k And when they
had passed over, they came into the land of Gennesaret,
and drew to the shore 54 And when they were come
out of the ship, straightway they knew him, 55. And
ran through that whole region round about, and began
to carry about in beds those that were sick, where they
heard he was 56 And whithersoever he entred, into
villages, or cities, or country, they laid the sick in the
streets, and besought him l that they might touch, if
it were but the border of his garment and m as many
as touched him, were made whole

f Isa liv 11
g Psal xlvi 1
h Job ix 8
i Luke xxiv 28
† Or Darkened Chap iii 5 & viii 17 & xvi 14
k Mat xiv 34
l Chap v 27
m Chap iii 10 Luke vi 19 Acts xix 12

v 45—56 The entertainment being finished, Christ bid his disciples first embark, and cross the lake, which they did with reluctance, thinking this a good opportunity for him to declare himself, and set up, as they expected, his temporal kingdom But he, dismissing the multitude, retired into a mountain, as he was wont, to spend some time in prayer, to teach us the necessity of keeping up private communion with God, as the best means of enabling us to go comfortably through our public ministrations Mean time we are told,

1 The distress of the disciples The wind was tempestuous, and directly a-head, so that though they pulled hard, they got no way, and had advanced in many hours not above thirty furlongs We may expect in Christ's service to meet with difficulties, but if we patiently persevere, all will be well

2 After exercising their faith and patience till the morning watch, at last Christ came to them, walking upon the waters, and seemed as though he would have passed them, but they all discovered something walking on the water, and supposing it an apparition, shrieked out, exceedingly affrighted, till his well known voice stilled their fears, saying, *Be of good cheer, it is I, be not afraid*, and entring the boat, instantly the wind and waves subsided, to the exceeding astonishment of the apostles, who, forgetting the miracle of the loaves which they had just seen, were so dull and stupid in their hearts, as to be surprized at this new manifestation of their Master's divine power, though they were daily eye witnesses to his stupendous miracles *Note*, (1) If Christ's people toil hard through a night of temptation, or desertion, the morning will come, a little faith and patience shall bring them to the light of peace and joy (2) Our fancies raise a thousand unnecessary fears, and in our distress we often suspect that Christ is passing from us, when he is really coming to us (3) It is then comfortable with the troubled soul when Jesus reveals himself, and saith with the voice of love, *It is I, be of good cheer* Lord, speak thou to my soul, and it shall rest from all its fears!

3 No sooner had they reached the shore, near Capernaum, than immediately the rumour of his arrival spread on every side, and vast multitudes crowded around him, bringing the sick and diseased, in every city, town, or village that he passed, they were laid on beds in the streets, and besought him, that they might touch, if but the border of his garment, and as many as touched him were perfectly cured, whatever was their malady O Jesus, enable me to touch thee with my trembling hand of faith, and heal thou my sin-sick soul!

CHAP VII

In this chapter we have, 1 Christ's dispute with the scribes and Pharisees about eating meat with unwashen hands, ver 1—13 The needful instructions he gave to the people upon that occasion, and these further explained to his disciples, ver 14—23 2 His curing the woman of Canaan's daughter that was possessed, ver 24—30 3 The relief of a man that was deaf, and had an impediment in his speech, ver 31—37

1 a THEN came together unto him the Pharisees,
and certain of the scribes, which came from
Jerusalem 2 And when they saw some of his disciples
eat bread with defiled (that is to say, with unwashen)
hands, they found fault 3 For the Pharisees, and all
the Jews, except they wash *their* hands † oft, eat not,
b holding the tradition of the elders 4 And *when they
come* from the market, except they wash, they eat not.
And many other things there be, which they have re-
ceived to hold, *as* the washing of cups and pots, bra-
sen vessels, and of ‡ tables 5 Then the Pharisees
and scribes asked him, b Why walk not thy disciples ac-
cording to the tradition of the elders, but eat bread with
unwashen hands? 6 He answered and said unto them,
Well hath Esaias prophesied of you hypocrites, as it is
written, c This people honoureth me with *their* lips, but
their heart is far from me 7 Howbeit, in vain do
they worship me, d teaching for doctrines the command
ments of men 8 For laying aside the commandment
of God, ye hold the tradition of men, as the washing of
pots and cups and many other such like things ye do
9 And he said unto them, e Full well ye § reject the
commandment of God, that ye may keep your own tra-
dition 10 For Moses said, f Honour thy father and
thy mother and, g Whoso curseth father or mother, let
him die the death 11 But ye say, If a man shall say
to his father or mother, *It is* ‖ Corban, that is to say, a
gift, by whatsoever thou mightest be profited by me
he shall be free 12 And ye suffer him no more to do
ought for his father or his mother 13 Making the
word of God of none effect through your tradition, which
ye have delivered and many such like things do ye
14 ¶ h And when he had called all the people unto
him, he said unto them, Hearken unto me every one of
you, and understand 15 i There is nothing from with-
out a man that entring into him can defile him but
the things which come out of him, those are they that
defile the man 16 k If any man have ears to hear, let
him hear 17. And when he was entred into the house
from the people, his disciples asked him concerning the
parable 18 And he saith unto them, Are ye so with-
out understanding also? Do ye not perceive, that what-
soever thing from without entreth into the man, it can-
not defile him, 19 Because it entreth not into his
heart, but into the belly, and goeth out into the draught,
purging all meats? 20. And he said, l That which
cometh out of the man, that defileth the man 21 For
from within, m out of the heart of men, proceed evil
thoughts, adulteries, fornications, murders, 22 Thefts,
† covet-

a Mat xv 1
† Or With the fist
‡ Or beds
b Col ii 8
c Isa xxix 13
d Col ii 18—22
e Prov i 25
§ Or frustrate
f Ex xx 12 Deut v 16
g Ex xxi 17 Lev xx 9 Prov xx 20 & xxx 17
‖ See Mat xv 5
h Mat xv 10
i Acts x 15 Rom xiv 14 1 Tim iv 4 Tit i 15
k Mat xi 15 & xiii 9
l Jam iii 6
m Gen vi 5 & viii 21 Prov vi 14 Jer

† Or, Covetousnesses, wickednesses

† covetouſneſs, wickedneſs, deceit, laſciviouſneſs, an evil eye, blaſphemy, pride, fooliſhneſs 23 All theſe evil things come from within, and defile the man

v 1—23 The Scribes and Phariſees could not bear to ſee the poor people follow Jeſus, though to be cured, yet they could take a long journey purely to cavil with him

1 They found fault with his diſciples for eating with unwaſhen hands, contrary to the tradition of the elders, and complained to Chriſt of their criminal neglect, for ſo they eſteemed it, being ſuperſtitiouſly ſcrupulous to waſh before they ſat down to meat, when they returned from market, and on a variety of other occaſions, pretending great carefulneſs to avoid defilement And for the ſame purpoſe they waſhed alſo their pots, cups, braſen veſſels, and tables, or beds, leſt by the touch of any impure perſon they ſhould have contracted pollution, and fancying much religion conſiſted in theſe abſurd traditions, they were ready to condemn every deviation from them with greater ſeverity, than even the breaches of God's written law

2 Chriſt vindicates his diſciples, and reproves the hypocriſy and wickedneſs of their accuſers They truly fulfilled the prophecy of Iſaiah, apoſtate in heart from God, whilſt they pretended to honour him with the lip and the knee in much apparent devotion They ſtamped human traditions with divine authority, impoſed them as obligatory on men's conſciences, and not only laid great ſtreſs upon the obſervance of theſe ſuperſtitious waſhings, but really ſubverted the plaineſt and weightieſt commands of the law, when they ſtood in competition with their traditions A more flagrant evidence of which cannot be conceived, than our Lord here produces againſt them The tradition of the elders had eſtabliſhed it as a rule, that if a man ſwore by *Corban*, by the gold of the temple, or that he would devote ſuch a thing to the treaſury of the temple, or would regard it as a devoted thing, and not part with it on any occaſion, he was bound to fulfil his vow And though the commandment of God had ſo expreſsly provided for the honour and ſupport of parents, laying an awful curſe upon the undutiful ſon that ſpoke or acted contemptuouſly againſt them, yet they held he was bound by his vow, and diſpenſed with from obſerving the evident commands of God, and the plaineſt dictates of duty and gratitude, ſo that he might ſafely withhold the leaſt relief from his parents, however indigent, infirm, or aged, yea, was conſcientiouſly obliged to do ſo a tradition ſo iniquitous and ſhocking, as moſt directly violated the word of God, and made it of no effect Yet this, and many other things as impious, did the Phariſees impoſe on their diſciples, and, under the maſk of pretended ſanctity, and reverence for the temple, ſapped the very foundations of true religion

3 To prevent the people from being impoſed upon by theſe blind guides, he demands their attention to his diſcourſe, as being a matter of higheſt importance, for if their principles were right, a correſpondent practice would follow This great axiom therefore Chriſt lays down, that nothing without a man, which he touches or eats, any farther than it hath a bad influence upon his heart, can render him in God's ſight morally unclean, but that all impurity comes from within and the evil thoughts and deſires which are expreſſed in words and actions, theſe are what defile the man, and render him odious in the ſight of God, and this he bids them carefully remark and remember The diſciples, far from being yet emancipated from the vulgar opinions concerning the things by which a perſon was defiled, when they were alone, deſired our Lord to explain his laſt obſervation to them, which appeared to them hard to be underſtood With an air of ſurprize at their dulneſs, our Lord reproves their ſtupidity if others were in the dark, they at leaſt ſhould have underſtood him However, he is pleaſed to explain his meaning, ſo as to prevent the poſſibility of miſtake Two things he lays down, and ſupports with the cleareſt arguments (1) That whatever meats a man may eat, as they do not enter into his heart, which is the ſource of all moral purity or pollution, but merely paſs through the body, therefore without intemperance they can communicate no defilement before God (2) That the origin of all evil, and the cauſe of all uncleanneſs, is from within, whence proceeds all that train of evils before obſerved, *Mat* xv 19 to which others are here added, *covetouſneſſes*, the unſatisfied cravings of the heart after worldly things, *wickedneſs*, the contrivances of malice, and delight in miſchief, *deceit*, in words or deeds, to conceal the deſigns of iniquity, *laſciviouſneſs*, the impure imaginations, dalliance, or diſcourſe, which the lewd indulge, though deterred from groſſer acts of impurity, *an evil eye*, envying the enjoyment of others, or coveting what they poſſeſs, *pride*, the high conceit, the lofty look, the contemptuous or inſolent carriage of the ſwelling heart, *fooliſhneſs*, the boaſts of vanity, the ebullition of folly, the raſhneſs of inconſiderate cenſure, and the [illegible] of imprudence Theſe, and theſe alone, are the defiling things that ſpring from the fountain head of evil in the fallen ſpirit and render the ſoul vile in itſelf, and abominable in the eyes of God

24 ¶ n And from thence he aroſe, and went into the borders of Tyre and Sidon, and entred into an houſe, and would have no man know *it*, but he could not be hid 25 For a certain woman, whoſe young daughter had an unclean ſpirit, heard of him, and came and fell at his feet 26 (The woman was a † Greek, a Syrophenician by nation) and ſhe beſought him that he would caſt forth the devil out of her daughter 27 But Jeſus ſaid unto her, Let the children firſt be filled for o it is not meet to take the children's bread, and to caſt *it* unto the dogs 28 And ſhe anſwered and ſaid unto him, Yes, Lord yet the dogs under the table eat of the children's crumbs 29 And he ſaid unto her, For this ſaying, t go thy way, the devil is gone out of thy daughter 30 And when ſhe was come to her houſe, ſhe found the devil gone out, and her daughter laid upon the bed

n Mat xv 21

† Or, Gentile

v 24—30 We have here one ſhort excurſion of the divine Redeemer into the coaſts of the Gentiles, an earneſt of the gracious deſigns he had in ſtore for them But, that he might not offend the Jews, to whom he was particularly ſent, he choſe not to appear in public, and therefore entred into a houſe but, tho' he would have no man know it, his fame was too much ſpread abroad to admit of his concealment And we have,

1 The application of a poor Gentile to him in behalf of her daughter who was poſſeſſed Falling at his feet, ſhe earneſtly importuned him to caſt out the devil from her child At firſt her addreſs met with ſuch diſcouragement as Jeſus was very unuſed to give to poor petitioners Compared with the choſen people of Iſrael, he ſpeaks as if the Gentiles were but as dogs, to whom the children's meat (the miracles he wrought) muſt not be thrown, at leaſt, not till the children firſt be filled Far from deſiſting on ſuch a repulſe, ſhe wonderfully turns the apparent refuſal into an argument for granting the favour ſhe aſked, and deſired, as a dog, only to have one crumb, one miracle, among the multitudes that every day were ſo abundantly diſpenſed to the Jewiſh children Note, (1) They who have children poſſeſſed with unclean ſpirits, cannot but earneſtly preſent their ſad caſe before the Lord, who alone can cure them (2) A poor ſupplicant at the feet of Jeſus may confidently hope amidſt every diſcouragement for an anſwer of peace at the laſt If Jeſus delays, it is to exerciſe their faith, and prove their perſeverance

2 The cure is wrought Pleaſed with the poor Gentile's addreſs, and admiring her faith, he grants her requeſt *The devil is gone out of thy daughter*, as ſhe found to her unſpeakable comfort, when, depending on the accompliſhment of the word of Jeſus, ſhe returned to her houſe So ſure is the prayer of faith to prevail

31 ¶ And again p departing from the coaſts of Tyre and Sidon, he came unto the ſea of Galilee through the midſt of the coaſts of Decapolis 32 And q they bring unto him one that was deaf, and had an impediment in his ſpeech and they beſeech him to put his hand upon him 33 And r he took him aſide from the multitude, and put his fingers into his ears, and he ſpit, and touched his tongue 34 And s looking up to heaven, t he ſighed, and ſaith unto him, Ephphatha, that is, Be opened 35 And ſtraightway u his ears were opened, and the ſtring of his tongue was looſed, and he ſpake plain 36 And x he charged them that they ſhould tell no man but the more he charged them, ſo much the more a great deal they publiſhed *it*, 37 And were beyond meaſure aſtoniſhed, ſaying, He hath done all things well he maketh both the deaf to hear, and the dumb to ſpeak

p Mat xv 29
q Mat ix 32 Luke xi 14
r Chap viii 23
s John xi 41 & xvii 1
t John xi 33 38 Iſa xxxv 6
x Chap v 43

v 31—37 Jeſus was never weary of the delightful work of going about doing good On his return from the Gentile coaſt into the region of Decapolis, a new object of mercy is preſented before him

1 The caſe was affective the poor patient was deaf, and either quite dumb, or not able to ſpeak without much difficulty the emblem of the miſerable ſinner, whoſe ears are cloſed to all the ſweet ſounds of goſpel-grace, and unaffected with the thunders of Sinai, his lips ſealed up, unable to ſpeak the language of prayer or praiſe, or to communicate in converſation grace to the hearers

2 The cure was ſingular not by a word merely, as Jeſus uſually wrought his miracles, but taking the poor man aſide, he *put his fingers into his ears, and ſpit, and touched his tongue*, not as cauſes that could contribute to his cure, but to ſhew he was not bound to any method of procedure Then *looking up to heaven, he ſighed*, in compaſſion to the human miſeries, or grieved

for

for the hardneſs of their hearts, who, after ſo many miracles, believed not on him, *and* then *ſaith unto him, Ephphatha*, that is in the Chaldee dialect, *Be opened*, and inſtantly the cure was wrought, he heard diſtinctly and ſpake plainly And thus by the commanding voice of his Spirit he ſaith to the ſpiritually deaf and dumb, Be opened, and the ears are unſtopped, the tongue is looſed, they know the joyful ſound of goſpel-grace, and ſpeak aloud the praiſes of their Redeemer

3 To avoid all appearances of vain glory, and not to exaſperate his malicious enemies, he gave the people a charge to conceal the miracle, but they could not be ſilent, nay, rather the more they publiſhed it, that ſuch modeſt excellence might be known, and all with aſtoniſhment heard the report, and from ſuch repeated inſtances were compelled to acknowledge to his honour, that all his works beſpoke the glory of his character, full of power and grace, without the leaſt tincture of oſtentation *He hath done all things well he maketh both the deaf to hear, and the dumb to ſpeak* Is not this then the Chriſt? *See Iſa* xxxv 5, 6

CHAP VIII

In this chapter we have, 1 Chriſt's miraculous feeding four thouſand with ſeven loaves and a few ſmall fiſhes, ver 1—9 2 *His refuſing to give the Phariſees a ſign from heaven*, ver 10—13 3 *His cautioning his diſciples to take heed of the leaven of Phariſaiſm and Herodianiſm*, ver 14—21 4 *His giving ſight to a blind man at Bethſaida*, ver 22—26 5 *Peter's confeſſion of him*, ver 27—30 6 *The notice he gave his diſciples of his own approaching ſufferings*, ver 31—33 *and the warning he gave them to prepare for ſufferings likewiſe*, ver 34—38

a Mat xv 32 1 [a] IN thoſe days the multitude being very great, and
having nothing to eat, Jeſus called his diſciples
b Mat ix 36 unto him, and ſaith unto them, 2 [b] I have compaſſion
c Pſ xxxiv 10 on the multitude, [c] becauſe they have now been with
me three days, and have nothing to eat 3 And if
I ſend them away faſting to their own houſes, they will
faint by the way for divers of them came from far
d Num xi 21 2 Kings iv 43 4 And his diſciples anſwered him, [d] From whence can
a man ſatisfy theſe men with bread here in the wilderneſs?
5 And he aſked them, How many loaves have
ye? And they ſaid, Seven 6 And he commanded
the people to ſit down on the ground and he took the
e Mat xxvi 26 Chap vi 41 Rom xiv 6 ſeven loaves, and [e] gave thanks, and brake, and gave
to his diſciples to ſet before *them* and [f] they did ſet
them before the people 7 And they had a few ſmall
f Mat xxiv 45 fiſhes and he bleſſed, and commanded to ſet them alſo
before *them* 8 So they did eat, and were filled and
they took up of the broken meat that was left, ſeven
baſkets 9 And they that had eaten were about four
thouſand, and he ſent them away

v 1—9 The compaſſions of Jeſus flow without ceaſing towards the wretched and indigent Vaſt multitudes followed him, and, ſo eager were the people to attend him, that neither toil nor hunger diſcouraged them He therefore who graciouſly fed their ſouls with his heavenly doctrine, here again is pleaſed by a miracle to feed their famiſhed bodies We have ſeen it recorded in nearly the ſame words, *Mat* xv 32 and may learn, (1) To count nothing *hard in the way of duty*, whilſt we are following Chriſt (2) To truſt him with our bodies as well as ſouls, and verily we ſhall be fed (3) Not to be diſcouraged if we do not ſometimes ſee any immediate proſpect of relief under our difficulties the Lord can open an unexpected door of deliverance for us

10 ¶ And ſtraitway he entred into a ſhip with his
diſciples, and came into the parts of Dalmanutha 11
And the Phariſees came forth, and began to queſtion
g Mat xii 38 xvi 1 with him, [g] ſeeking of him a ſign from heaven, tempting
him 12 And he ſighed deeply in his ſpirit, and
h John iv 48 1 Cor i 22 ſaith, [h] Why doth this generation ſeek after a ſign? verily
I ſay unto you, [i] There ſhall no ſign be given to
i Mat xvi 4 this generation 13 And he left them, and entring into
the ſhip again, departed to the other ſide 14 ¶
k Mat xvi 5, 6 [k] Now *the diſciples* had forgotten to take bread, neither
had they in the ſhip with them more than one loaf 15
l Luke xii 1 And he charged them, ſaying, [l] Take heed, beware of
the leaven of the Phariſees, and *of* the leaven of Herod
16 And they reaſoned among themſelves, ſaying, *It is*
becauſe we have no bread 17 And when Jeſus knew
it, he ſaith unto them, Why reaſon ye, becauſe ye have
m Chap vi 52 no bread? [m] perceive ye not yet, neither underſtand?
have ye your heart yet hardened? 18 Having eyes,
ſee ye not? and having ears, hear ye not? and do ye
not remember? 19 [n] When I brake the five loaves n Chap vi 43
among five thouſand, how many baſkets full of fragments
took ye up? They ſay unto him, Twelve 20
[o] And when the ſeven among four thouſand, how many o Ver 8
baſkets full of fragments took ye up? And they ſaid,
Seven 21 And he ſaid unto them, [p] How is it that p Mat xvi 11
ye do not underſtand?

v 10—21 Dalmanutha was a place not far from Magdala, *Mat* xv 39 thither our Lord bent his courſe

1 The Phariſees there met him, and cavilling as uſual, demanded a ſign from heaven, as if all his other miracles did not ſufficiently prove his divine miſſion not that they deſired to be convinced, but ſought a pretence for their infidelity Therefore,

2 Chriſt refuſed to grant their requeſt Not that he could not work the miracle they ſought, but becauſe he knew the wickedneſs of their intentions in aſking it, and therefore *ſighing deeply*, as grieved for the hardneſs of their hearts, he expoſtulates with them on the unreaſonableneſs of their infidelity, when ſuch amazing ſigns had been given them for their conviction already, and denying their requeſt, he abandons them to their ruin *Note*, They who will not ſubmit to the evidence of the ſcriptures, are juſtly given up to the blindneſs of their minds, and left to periſh in their unbelief

3 On this he took occaſion, as they were croſſing the lake, to caution his diſciples againſt the leaven of the Phariſees and of Herod, which they, having forgotten to take ſcarce any bread with them, interpreted literally as a rebuke for their careleſſneſs, and an admonition not to apply to the Phariſees for relief, or to eat of their bread And whilſt they were caſting the blame of their negligence upon each other, Jeſus, who perceived their folly and ſtupidity, ſharply rebuked them for their uneaſineſs in this matter, as arguing great unbelief of his power, which they had ſeen ſo wonderfully and lately exerted, whereof he reminds them, and therefore it was ſtrange they ſhould be ſo ſenſeleſs, and their hearts yet hardened, as not to perceive, that he meant not his diſcourſe concerning bread literally, which he could ſo eaſily ſupply, but of the doctrines of the Phariſees and Herod, which were to be ſhunned as dangerouſly pernicious *Note*, (1) It is amazing to think of the hardneſs of our hearts, that, after multiplied experience of God's goodneſs, we are apt again to diſtruſt his care the moment new difficulties ariſe (2) The more we know and underſtand what Chriſt is, and hath done for his people, the more will our hearts be engaged to truſt him in every emergence

22 ¶ And he cometh to Bethſaida, and they bring a
blind man unto him, and beſought him [q] to touch him q Chap v 23
23 And he took the blind man by the hand, and [r] led r Ver 1
him out of the town, and when he had [s] ſpit on his s John ix 6 Rev iii 18
eyes, and put his hands upon him, he aſked him if he
ſaw ought 24 And he looked up, and ſaid, I ſee men
as trees walking 25 After that he put *his* hands again
upon his eyes, and made him look up and he was reſtored,
and [t] ſaw every man clearly 26 And he ſent t Prov iv 18
him away to his houſe, ſaying, Neither go into the
town, [u] nor tell *it* to any in the town u Ver 1 Luke xiv 42

v 22—26 This miracle is related by Mark alone, and is probably ſelected from the innumerable multitude of others, becauſe ſome circumſtances in it are ſingular

1 The application was made to Jeſus by the poor blind man's friends, who led him to the Saviour, deſiring that he would touch him, perſuaded that this would effectually work the cure *Note*, In our prayers we ſhould not ceaſe to pray for poor blind ſouls, intreating the Lord to open the eyes of their mind

2 *He took the blind man by the hand, and led him out of* the town, chuſing to heal him ſecretly, and perhaps in juſt judgment upon the place, where ſo many miracles had been wrought, and yet they continued in their infidelity

3 He healed him, and this he did not by a word, but in an unuſual manner, and gradually He ſpat on his eyes, and aſking what he ſaw, ſome glimmerings of light broke in upon him, and he beheld *men as trees walking*, his viſion being yet indiſtinct and confuſed, but when Jeſus had put his hands upon his eyes, and bid him look up again, then he ſaw every object clearly Thus often is he pleaſed to work in the heart at firſt the light, like the dawning day, breaks upon the ſoul, and ſome glimmerings of ſpiritual things are perceived, of the danger and guilt of ſin, the neceſſity of caring for the ſoul, the want of a Redeemer, &c. Afterwards our views enlarge, we gain deeper diſcoveries of our own corruption, and Chriſt's all-ſufficiency, till at laſt we come to the perfect day in glory, and know even as we are known

4 He charges the man not to return to Bethſaida, not acquaint any one there with his cure their obſtinate impenitence under the miracles they had ſeen rendered them unworthy of

any more of those mighty works They who slight their own mercies, justly forfeit them

27 ¶ [x] And Jesus went out, and his disciples, into the towns of Cesarea-Philippi and by the way he asked his disciples, saying unto them, Whom do men say that I am? 28 And they answered, [y] John the Baptist but some *say*, Elias, and others, One of the prophets 29 And he saith unto them, But whom say ye that I am? And Peter answereth and saith unto him, [z] Thou art the Christ 30 And [a] he charged them that they should tell no man of him 31 And [b] he began to teach them, that the Son of man must suffer many things, and be rejected of the elders, and of the chief priests, and scribes, and be killed, and after three days rise again 32 And he spake that saying openly And [c] Peter took him, and began to rebuke him 33 But when he had turned about, and looked on his disciples, he rebuked Peter, saying, [d] Get thee behind me, Satan for thou savourest not the things that be of God, but the things that be of men 34 ¶ And when he had called the people unto him, with his disciples also, [e] he said unto them, Whosoever will come after me, let him deny himself, and [f] take up his cross, and follow me 35 For whosoever will save his life, shall lose it, but whosoever shall lose his life for my sake and the gospel's, the same shall save it 36 For what shall it profit a man, if he shall gain the whole world, and lose his own soul? 37 Or [h] what shall a man give in exchange for his soul? 38 [i] Whosoever therefore shall be ashamed of me, and of my words, in this adulterous and sinful generation, of him also shall the Son of man be ashamed when [k] he cometh in the glory of his Father, [l] with the holy angels

v 27—38 In their journey to the towns of Cesarea Philippi, we are told,

1 The enquiry of Christ concerning the opinion which the people entertained of him, and what were the sentiments of the Apostles in particular They inform him of the general veneration in which he was held, though men's opinions concerning him were divided; some supposing him the Baptist risen from the dead, others, Elias, others, one of the former prophets returned With regard to themselves, Peter, in the name of the rest, professes their faith in him as a much greater character, even that of the divine Messiah Hereupon Jesus commanded them to keep this for the present secret, the time being not yet come for declaring in such express terms his pretensions, lest the people, prepossessed with the notions of a temporal Messiah, should be excited to an insurrection or his enemies be exasperated to cut him off immediately, before he had finished his work For though nothing happens but by the divine decree, in time and manner fixed from eternity, and no man dies before his appointed hour, yet he who hath ordained the end, hath ordained the means most proper to accomplish the counsels of his own will

2 Christ hereupon informs them more freely and openly than he had done before, concerning the sufferings he must endure, to wean them from those vain imaginations concerning the temporal kingdom they expected, and to prepare them for so afflictive an event Peter, heart-struck at the mention, he could not bear to hear of his Master's death, when he had just entertained the most sanguine hopes of his greatness, and therefore taking him aside, expressed his astonishment that he should talk in such a manner for which Peter got a severe and just rebuke before his fellow-disciples, to check their aspiring views, as well as his own Christ tells him, he acted as his bitterest enemy in opposing his suffering Satan could do no worse and he shewed an utter want of discernment concerning the nature of the Messiah's kingdom, and the great ends which God designed to accomplish by that death he was about to undergo In truth, Peter's eyes were so fixed on temporal grandeur, that he could relish nothing which seemed to contradict his aspiring views *Note*, (1) In true disciples there may be found what calls for sharp rebuke (2) The cross is ever displeasing to our fallen nature, and we are too apt, like Peter, to be seeking for ourselves ease or greatness hence in suffering time so many are offended

3 He takes occasion hereupon to declare the terms of discipleship, and to suggest arguments to engage his faithful followers to meet courageously the persecution they must expect in his service Self-denial, resolution to take up the cross, and conformity to the pattern of a suffering Saviour, are absolutely required of every follower of Jesus nor must we count our life dear to us, when his service requires us to part with them Not that our sufferings, or even death itself, will be our loss, no they will prove our greatest gain, and we shall find in life eternal an abundant recompence Whilst if through fear or dread of suffering in his world, we save our lives by base compliances, our loss will be irreparable and eternal, we shall perish without remedy, and the gain of ten thousand worlds will never counterval the loss of an immortal soul and as sure as ever we are ashamed of the cause of Jesus and disown him by our unfaithfulness, so surely may we expect to be disowned by him in the great day of his appearing and glory let us therefore count the cost, and with full purpose of heart cleave unto the Lord

CHAP IX

In this chapter we have, 1 Christ's transfiguration upon the mount, ver 1—13 2 His casting the devil out of a child, when the disciples could not do it, ver 14—29 3 His prediction of his own sufferings and death, ver 30—32 4 The check he gave to his disciples for disputing who should be greatest, ver 33—37 And to John, for rebuking one who cast out devils in Christ's name, and did not follow with them, ver 38—41 5 Christ's discourse with his disciples of the danger of offending one of his little ones, ver 42 and of indulging that in ourselves which is an offence, and an occasion of sin to us, ver 43—50 most of which passages we had before, Mat xvii and xviii

1 AND he said unto them, [a] Verily I say unto you, that there be some of them that stand here, which shall not taste of death, [b] till they have seen the kingdom of God come with power 2 ¶ And [c] after six days Jesus taketh with him Peter, and James, and John, and leadeth them up into an high mountain apart by themselves and he was transfigured before them 3 And his raiment became shining, [e] exceeding white as snow, so as no fuller on earth can white them 4 And there appeared unto them Elias, with Moses and they were talking with Jesus 5 And Peter answered and said to Jesus, Master, it is good for us to be here and let us make three tabernacles, one for thee, and one for Moses, and one for Elias 6 For he wist not what to say, for they were sore afraid 7 And there was a cloud that overshadowed them and [f] a voice came out of the cloud, saying, [g] This is my beloved Son [h] hear him 8 And suddenly when they had looked round about, they saw no man any more, save Jesus only with themselves 9 And as they came down from the mountain, [i] he charged them that they should tell no man what things they had seen, till the Son of man were risen from the dead 10 And they kept that saying with themselves, questioning one with another what the rising from the dead should mean 11 ¶ And they asked him, saying, Why say the scribes that [k] Elias must first come? 12 And he answered and told them, Elias verily cometh first, and restoreth all things, and [l] how it is written of the Son of man, that he must suffer many things, and be set at nought 13 But I say unto you, that [m] Elias is indeed come, and [n] they have done unto him whatsoever they listed, as it is written of him

v 1—13 The first verse of this chapter should properly, as in *Matthew*, have closed the preceding, as it is the conclusion of that discourse, and an argument to engage the fidelity of his disciples, from the view of the nearness of the Messiah's coming, with power and glory, to punish the persecutors of his people by the destruction of the Jewish state and nation, and, by the mighty effusion of his Spirit, to erect his church in the world, and bless the labours of his faithful ministers with the most astonishing success, and these events some of those then present should live to see

Six days after the former discourse we have an account,

1 Of his transfiguration on the mount, in presence of three of his disciples, *See Mat* xvii This glimpse of his glory would serve to prevent the *offence of the cross*, and enable them, when they reflected on what they now saw and heard, to stand fast, unmoved under all the discouragements which their faith might afterwards encounter

2 Of the discourse which passed between Christ and his disciples as they came down from the mountain However desirous Peter was of dwelling there, the glorious scene was transient, like those bright seasons of heavenly consolation we sometimes enjoy below, and though we say it is *good for us* to be here, he who knows best, will not have us now live by sight, but by faith Christ, as they went, particularly charged them to take no notice of what they had seen and heard, at least, not till after his resurrection from the dead, when this vision would gain the more ready credence, and serve to prove his divine glory even in the midst of his humiliation What the

resurrection from the dead should mean, they were at a loss to conceive, whether it was to be taken literally, or to be applied metaphorically to his exaltation from his present state of poverty and indigence, to the throne of that glorious temporal kingdom which their prejudices still expected. And as they had been taught by their scribes, that Elias was to prepare the way for the Messiah's coming and kingdom, they enquired of him whether there was any real ground for such an expectation, especially as Elias had made so short a stay with them on the mount, and had not appeared at all in public. Christ clears up their doubts. The person spoken of by the prophet Malachi, was not to be Elias personally, according to the traditions taught by the scribes, but one in his spirit and power, and he had already appeared, and been rejected, plainly pointing them to John the Baptist, in whom the prophecy was fulfilled. And the same inspired writings that foretold the coming of John, predicted also the sufferings and indignities the Messiah should suffer, these therefore also they may assuredly expect to see accomplished in their season.

o Mat. xvii. 14. Luke ix. 37. 14 ¶ o And when he came to *his* disciples, he saw a
great multitude about them, and the scribes question-
ing with them. 15 And straightway all the people,
when they beheld him, were greatly amazed, and run-
ning to him, saluted him. 16 And he asked the
scribes, What question ye with them? 17 And one
of the multitude answered and said, Master, I have
brought unto thee my son, which hath a dumb spirit;
18 And wheresoever he taketh him, he teareth him:
and he foameth, and gnasheth with his teeth, and pineth
away: and I spake to thy disciples, that they should cast
him out, and they could not. 19 He answered him,
and saith, O faithless generation, how long shall I be
with you? how long shall I suffer you? bring him unto
p Chap. i. 26. Rev. xi. 12. me. 20 And they brought him unto him: and p when
he saw him, straightway the spirit tare him, and he fell
on the ground, and wallowed foaming. 21 And he
asked his father, How long is it ago since this came un-
to him? And he said, Of a child. 22 And oft-times
it hath cast him into the fire, and into the waters to
destroy him: but if thou canst do any thing, have com-
passion on us, and help us. 23 Jesus said unto him,
q Chap. xi. 23. Luke xvii. 6. q If thou canst believe, all things *are* possible to him that
believeth. 24 And straightway the father of the child
cried out, and said with tears, Lord, I believe; help
thou mine unbelief. 25 When Jesus saw that the peo-
ple came running together, he rebuked the foul spirit,
saying unto him, Thou dumb and deaf spirit, I charge
thee, Come out of him, and enter no more into him.
26 And *the spirit* cried, and rent him sore, and came
out of him; and he was as one dead, insomuch that
many said, He is dead. 27 But Jesus took him by
the hand, and lifted him up, and he arose. 28 And
when he was come into the house, his disciples asked
him privately, Why could not we cast him out? 29
And he said unto them, This kind can come forth by
nothing, but by fasting and prayer.

v. 14—29. At the return of Jesus with his three disciples from the mount, he found their companions in no small perplexity.

1. The cause of it was, their being unable to heal a child possessed of a devil, who was brought to them for cure during their master's absence: whereupon the Scribes triumphed over them, and probably were now disputing against them concerning their Master's doctrine and miracles, and the authority they pretended to derive from him. In this juncture Jesus himself appeared; and struck with surprize at his critical arrival, the people with eagerness ran to him, congratulating him on his return, and giving him a hearty welcome. *Note*, (1.) They who have ever tasted the sweetness of communion with Jesus, cannot but mourn his absence, and welcome his return. (2.) When we are most at a loss what to say or do, the Lord then appears peculiarly gracious in coming to our help, and ordering our goings.

2. Addressing himself to the Scribes on the cause of the dispute, they dared not to answer him; but the father of the child represented the piteous case, and the unsuccessfulness of his application to the disciples. His child was possessed of a *dumb spirit*, under whose malicious influence he was often thrown into terrible convulsions, foaming at the mouth, gnashing his teeth, and pining away under the frequent and violent returns of these diabolical agitations. And he had brought him to the disciples, who had attempted to cure him in vain.

3. With a sharp rebuke to the malicious Scribes, and all others who had joined them in their dispute with the disciples, (among whom, probably, the father of the child might be included, on being disappointed in his application) he brands them as a *faithless generation*, wilfully blind to all the stupendous evidences of his power which he had shown, a people who wearied out his patience; but he would give them, notwithstanding, a fresh evidence of that divine mission they disputed, and therefore bids the father bring the child to him. If they will not believe, they shall, at least, be left without excuse.

4. No sooner was the lad brought within sight of Jesus, than the spirit, enraged at being about to be dispossessed, threw him to the ground in the most violent agonies, as if he would have torn him in pieces, and there he lay wallowing and foaming. To make the cure appear more singular, Jesus hereupon asked, How long he had been thus afflicted? The father answered, from his very infancy; and representing the imminent dangers to which he was frequently exposed, of being drowned or burnt, by this malicious spirit, who had oft cast him into the fire and into the water, he importunately begs, if this be not a case beyond the power of Jesus, that he would compassionate a parent as well as child so distressed, and help them out of their miseries. *Note*, (1.) In our first approaches to Christ, young converts often meet the most violent conflicts. (2.) The possession of inveterate corruption is from the womb, and nothing but the almighty grace of Jesus can cure the deeply-rooted evil. (3.) Sometimes we doubt Christ's power, sometimes his willingness to help us, and both shew the unbelief of our hearts.

5. In answer to his suggestion, Christ replied, *If thou canst believe, all things are possible*, &c. He had said, *If thou canst do*, as if he suspected Christ's want of power, therefore he retorts upon him, and bids him suspect his want of faith; yet to encourage his trust, assures him, that this and every other case is possible, when the application is made in faith. With eagerness and tears, between fear and hope, the afflicted father cried out, *Lord, I believe* thy all-sufficiency, and grieving over the hardness and infidelity of my heart, beg thee to *help mine unbelief*, and enable me confidently to trust thee. *Note*, (1.) If ever we come short of any of our requests, we may assuredly impute it to our unbelief. (2.) It is a sure sign of some faith when a man is convinced of, and really cries to be delivered from, the unbelief of his heart. (3.) The strongest in faith need every day to pray for the pardon of their remaining unbelief, and an increase of this most necessary grace.

6. Christ performs the wondrous cure. The people came running to see how the affair would end, and whether Jesus or Satan prevailed; when with a voice of authority our Lord bids the foul fiend, who had made the child dumb and deaf, to depart, and never more return to him: nor dared the devil disobey, though with the deepest reluctance and most violent struggles quitting his hold, insomuch that the lad lay breathless and motionless, so that many verily thought him dead. But Jesus stretching out his hand, lifted him up, and immediately he arose perfectly well. *Note*, (1.) After Christ hath begun his work upon the heart in seasons of sore temptation, the soul, to human view, may appear as if utterly lost, but Jesus causes it again to revive, and restores us from our falls. (2.) Where he hath once dispossessed the enemy, he will effectually prevent his return; those whom he will save, shall never perish.

7. When the disciples enquired privately why they had miscarried, our Lord lets them know it was through want of this kind of faith, and their having neglected the instituted means for obtaining it, prayer and fasting. *Note*, If we neglect the means, our graces will necessarily decay and languish.

30 ¶ r And they departed thence, and passed through r Mat. xvii. 22. Luke ix. 44.
Galilee; and he would not that any man should know
it. 31 For he taught his disciples, and said unto them,
s The Son of man is delivered into the hands of men, s Chap. x. 33. Luke xxii. 44.
and they shall kill him; and after that he is killed, he
shall rise the third day. 32 But they understood not
that saying, and were afraid to ask him. 33 ¶ t And t Mat. xviii. 1. Luke ix. 46.
he came to Capernaum; and being in the house, he asked
them, What was it that ye disputed among yourselves
by the way? 34 But they held their peace: for by
the way u they had disputed among themselves, who u Luke xxii. 24.
should be the greatest. 35 And he sat down, and called
the twelve, and saith unto them, x If any man desire to x Chap. x. 43.
be first, *the same* shall be last of all, and servant of all.
36 And he took a child, and set him in the midst of
them: and when he had taken him in his arms, he said
unto them, 37 y Whosoever shall receive one of such y Mat. x. 42. Luke x. 16.
children in my name, receiveth me: and z whosoever
shall receive me, receiveth not me, but him that sent z John v. & xii. 44. & xiv. 21.
me. 38 ¶ a And John answered him, saying, Master, a Luke ix. 49.
we saw one casting out devils in thy name, and he fol-
loweth not us; and b we forbad him, because he fol- b Num. xi. 28.
loweth not us. 39 But Jesus said, Forbid him not:
for c there is no man which shall do a miracle in my c 1 Cor. xii. 3.
name,

d Mat xii 30 Phil i 18

name, that can lightly ſpeak evil of me 40 For [d] he
that is not againſt us, is on our part

v 30—40 Being in haſte to go towards Jeruſalem, and deſigning to be alone with his diſciples, he travelled through Galilee with all ſecreſy, to prevent any interruption from the people aſſembling around him And by the way, we are told,

1 The repeated notices he gave to his diſciples of his approaching ſufferings, death, and reſurrection, but they underſtood not his meaning, clear as the words were Their prejudices concerning his temporal kingdom, ſpread a vail over their hearts, and they were aſhamed and afraid to aſk him, leſt they ſhould meet with a rebuke for their dulneſs *Note*, Many live and die in ignorance, becauſe they are aſhamed to own it, and to enquire of thoſe who would inſtruct them

2 He reproves them for their pride and affectation of ſuperiority He knew the ſubject of their diſputes in the way had been, who ſhould poſſeſs the firſt honours in his kingdom, but he put a queſtion, as if he wanted to be informed concerning it, to which, aſhamed of what had paſſed, they returned no anſwer But Jeſus, to ſhew them that he knew the ſecrets of all hearts, and to check theſe moſt unbecoming deſires of temporal grandeur, aſſured them, that this ambitious affectation of pre-eminence, would be puniſhed with the loweſt degradation whilſt the ſureſt way to riſe, would be by entertaining the lowlieſt thoughts of themſelves, and ſtudying how to be moſt ſerviceable to the meaneſt of his diſciples And to impreſs what he had ſpoken the more deeply, he took a little child into his arms, whoſe humility, teachableneſs, and unambitious ſimplicity they ought to imitate, aſſuring them, that whoever ſhewed regard to the loweſt of his people, becauſe of ſuch a ſpirit in them, for the ſake of their reſembling and relation to him, he would regard it as done to himſelf, yea, God the Father, who ſent him, would requite it *Note*, (1) Chriſt obſerves, and is diſpleaſed with the angry diſputes of his diſciples, and will call them to account for them (2) Nothing is ſo contrary to the ſpirit of chriſtianity, as the affectation of pre-eminence

3 He checks the jealouſy and raſhneſs of the beloved diſciple John in his travels, when he was ſent forth with his fellow-labourers to preach the goſpel, had ſeen a man caſting out devils in Chriſt's name, perhaps one of the Baptiſt's diſciples, who, though a believer in Jeſus as the Meſſiah, had not conſtantly attended him as they had done, nor been inveſted with any particular commiſſion from him Jealous therefore for their Maſter's honour, or perhaps rather for their own, unwilling others ſhould ſhare theſe miraculous powers with them, they had forbad him, becauſe he had not been a profeſſed diſciple, or inveſted with any ſuch commiſſion as they had received But Jeſus ſaid, *Forbid him not* One who had ſuch faith in his name would not eaſily be brought to ſay or do any thing diſhonourable to his cauſe Such an one ought rather to be countenanced than diſcouraged, and, as he took not part with the enemy, but rather the contrary, he was to be regarded as a friend *Note*, (1) Partial to our own opinion and party, we are apt to monopolize Chriſt, and to think our cauſe is ſo much his, that all who *follow not with us* are to be regarded *as ſeparated from him* but there may be a great diverſity of opinions in leſſer matters among thoſe who together hold the head, and therefore we ſhould bear and forbear, think and let think, without raſh and rigid cenſures of thoſe who differ from us (2) Wherever real good is done, where Chriſt is preached and ſouls reſcued from the power of Satan, though we may count the methods purſued irregular and unauthoriſed, we muſt leave every man to ſtand or fall to his own Maſter, and beware how we oppoſe what is attended with a bleſſing from God (3) Where nothing appears contradictory to the faith of the goſpel, charity ever bids us hope the beſt

e Mat x 42 Heb vi 10
f Mat xviii 6 Luke xvii 2
g Mat v 29
† Or cauſe thee to offend Ver 45, 47
h Iſa lxvi 24 Judith xvi 17

41. [e] For whoſoever ſhall give you a cup of water to
drink, in my name, becauſe ye belong to Chriſt, verily
I ſay unto you, he ſhall not loſe his reward 42 And
[f] whoſoever ſhall offend one of *theſe* little ones that believe
in me, it is better for him that a milſtone were hanged
about his neck, and he were caſt into the ſea. 43 [g] And
if thy hand † offend thee, cut it off it is better for thee
to enter into life maimed, than, having two hands, to
go into hell, into the fire that never ſhall be quenched
44 [h] Where their worm dieth not, and the fire is not
quenched 45. And if thy foot offend thee, cut it off
it is better for thee to enter halt into life, than, having
two feet, to be caſt into hell, into the fire that never
ſhall be quenched 46 Where their worm dieth not,
and the fire is not quenched 47. And if thine eye
offend thee, pluck it out it is better for thee to enter
into the kingdom of God with one eye, than, having
two eyes, to be caſt into hell fire 48 Where their
worm dieth not and the fire is not quenched 49 For
every one ſhall be ſalted with fire, and [i] every ſacrifice
ſhall be ſalted with ſalt 50 [k] Salt *is* good [l] but if the
ſalt have loſt his ſaltneſs, wherewith will you ſeaſon it?
Have ſalt in yourſelves, and [m] have peace one with another

i Lev ii 13 Ezek xliii 24
k Col iv 6
l Mat v 13 Luke xiv 34
m Pſ xxxiv 14 Rom xii 18 Heb xii 14

v 41—50 Chriſt will not ſuffer the leaſt kindneſs done to his pooreſt diſciples to be unrewarded, nor the leaſt offence given to them to go unpuniſhed The heavieſt of all judgments hangs over that guilty head that ſhall hinder, diſcourage, or grieve the weak, or do ought to turn them back from Chriſt And therefore, if any corruption in our hearts, or allurement from the world, or darling idol, would ſeduce us from the path of duty, and lead us and others into ſin, though they were near and dear to us as a hand, a foot, or an eye, they muſt be cut off without pity Eternity is at ſtake, and as a life of everlaſting glory will amply repay us for every ſuch ſacrifice we make, ſo will the endleſs torments in hell make us rue the indulgence of our ſins, when, for a momentary gratification, we ſhould be doomed to endure the gnawings of a guilty conſcience filled with the wrath of God, and the intolerable agonies of burning unquenchable and eternal For as, under the law, every burnt-offering was ſalted before it was laid on the altar, where the fire never went out, ſo every apoſtate ſhall fall a ſacrifice to divine juſtice, and be caſt into the fire of hell, preſerved by the power of God from an extinction of their being, to ſuffer that wrath of God which is for ever wrath to come And, on the other hand, the ſoul which is ſeaſoned with divine grace, and offered daily a living ſacrifice to God, ſhall be preſerved incorruptible, ſeparated from the taint of this world's pollutions, and kept by the power of God through faith unto ſalvation For, as *ſalt is good* to preſerve meat from putrefaction, and render it ſavoury, ſo doth the grace of God preſerve the ſoul from the corruption of ſin, and renders thoſe who poſſeſs this ineſtimable gift bleſſings to others, by ſpreading the ſweet ſavour of Chriſt in the world *But if the ſalt have loſt its ſaltneſs*, and they, whoſe hearts, lips, and lives, ſhould be ſeaſoned with this ſalt of grace, prove deſtitute of it, and apoſtatize from their profeſſion, their fall is uſually irrecoverable, and their ruin inevitable Therefore ſee that ye *have ſalt in yourſelves*, the life of grace in your ſouls, ſubduing the corruptions within, and ſhewing itſelf in a ſavoury converſation, in every good word and work that may miniſter edification to others, *and have peace one with another*, united in cloſeſt bonds of love and fellowſhip, laying aſide all diſputes and envyings, and concurring to promote and propagate the goſpel through the world *Note*, (1) The terrors and eternity of hell torments, if really believed, will be a powerful check to the raging paſſions of the ſoul (2) They who have the ſalt of grace muſt ſhew it in their lips and in their lives, and, where this is really found, ſuch ſhall never ſee corruption

CHAP X

In this chapter we have, 1 Chriſt's diſpute with the Phariſees concerning divorce, ver 1—12 2 The kind entertainment he gave to the little children that were brought to him to be bleſſed, ver 13—16 3 His trial of the rich man that enquired what he muſt do to get to heaven, ver 17—22 4 His diſcourſe with his diſciples upon that occaſion concerning the peril of riches, ver 23—27 and the advantage of being impoveriſhed for his ſake, ver 28—31 5 The repeated notice he gave his diſciples of his ſufferings and death approaching, ver 32—34 6 The counſel he gave to James and John, to think of ſuffering with him rather than of reigning with him, ver 35—45 7 The cure of Bartimeus, a poor blind man, ver 46—52 All which paſſages of ſtory we had the ſubſtance of before, Matt xix *and* xx

1 AND [a] he aroſe from thence, and cometh into
the coaſts of Judea, by the farther ſide of Jordan
and the people reſort unto him again, and, as he
was wont, he taught them again 2 ¶ And the Phariſees
came to him, and aſked him, Is it lawful for a man
to put away his wife? tempting him 3 And he anſwered
and ſaid unto them, What did Moſes command
you? 4 And they ſaid, [b] Moſes ſuffered to write a bill
of divorcement, and to put her away 5 And Jeſus
anſwered and ſaid unto them, For the hardneſs of your
heart he wrote you this precept 6 But from the beginning
of the creation, [c] God made them male and female
7 For this cauſe [d] ſhall a man leave his father and mother,
and cleave to his wife, 8 And [e] they twain ſhall
be one fleſh ſo then they are no more twain, but one
fleſh 9 What therefore God hath joined together,
let not man put aſunder 10 And in the houſe his diſciples
aſked him again of the ſame matter 11 And
he ſaith unto them, [f] Whoſoever ſhall put away his wife,
and marry another, committeth adultery againſt her
12 And

a Mat xix 1
b Deut xxiv 1 Mat v 31
c Gen i 27 & v 2 Mal ii 15
d Gen ii 24
e 1 Cor vi 16 Eph v 31
f Mat v 32 & xix 9 Luke xvi 18 1 Cor vii 10

12 And if a woman ſhall put away her huſband, and
be married to another, ſhe committeth adultery

v 1—12 Wherever our Lord journeys, we find him employed in the bleſſed work of preaching the word, to teach us to be inſtant in ſeaſon and out of ſeaſon Multitudes ſtill followed him, ſome to hear, ſome to be healed, and ſome with a malignant purpoſe to entangle him in his talk, and raiſe ſome matter of accuſation againſt him Of this number were the Phariſees, who, by an enſnaring queſtion concerning divorce, endeavoured to lead him into a dilemma, either of contradicting Moſes, or being expoſed to the cenſure of a man of looſe morals He aſked them what Moſes had commanded? They anſwered, that in many caſes he had permitted divorce Our Lord replies, that it was no more than a *permiſſion*, granted merely becauſe of the hardneſs of their hearts and their cruel diſpoſition, as a law of the ſtate to prevent worſe conſequences, but at the beginning it was not ſo the very creation of one man and one woman, and but one, intimated the inſeparable union between them, the ſettling the law of marriage, Gen ii 24 declared it, ſince, for the ſake of this relation, a man muſt quit even the deareſt ties of nature, and prefer his wife to father and mother and the connection ariſing from the marriage-bond is ſo cloſe, that, as Adam and Eve were one fleſh, her body being formed from his, ſo muſt every huſband and wife reckon themſelves *as no more twain, but one fleſh* Whom God therefore hath thus indiſſolubly joined together, it would be the higheſt preſumption in man to ſeparate

The diſciples, who had been uſed, according to the generally received opinion among the Jews, to think divorces lawful, deſired in private farther information on this point And our Lord informs them there was but one lawful cauſe for divorce, and, except in the caſe of adultery, whatever man or woman divorced their partner, and married again, would themſelves be adulterers, and expoſed the injured party to the like crime *Note*, It becomes us firſt well to weigh the caſe before we take a companion for our lives when once the choice is made, mutual kindneſs and forbearance, and deſire to pleaſe, ſhould every day endear the relation, and remove whatever might occaſion a wiſh of ſeparation

g Mat xix 13 Luke xviii 15

13 ¶ g And they brought young children to him,
that he ſhould touch them, and *his* diſciples rebuked
thoſe that brought *them* 14 But when Jeſus ſaw *it*,
he was much diſpleaſed, and ſaid unto them, Suffer the
little children to come unto me, and forbid them not

h Mat xviii 3 1 Cor xiv 20 1 Pet ii 2

i Iſa xl 11

for h of ſuch is the kingdom of God 15 Verily I ſay
unto you, Whoſoever ſhall not receive the kingdom of
God as a little child, he ſhall not enter therein 16
And i he took them up in his arms, put his hands upon
them, and bleſſed them

v 13—16 Chriſt Jeſus hath a tenderneſs for the lambs of his flock he doth not refuſe the requeſt of thoſe pious parents who preſent their babes to him before they can liſp his praiſes The diſciples here indeed oppoſed their application, but Jeſus encouraged it, took up the infants in his arms, laid his hands upon them, and bleſſed them And, if they were capable of receiving the ſpiritual bleſſings of his kingdom, what ſhould hinder their being admitted by baptiſm into the viſible communion of his church? Of ſuch he declares the kingdom of God conſiſted, as well as of grown perſons, who in humility, teachableneſs, and dependence upon their Father's care, muſt become as little children, without which they never can partake of the privileges of this kingdom Lord give me then this ſpirit of a child, that I may be enabled to cry, Abba, Father!

k Mat xix 16 Luke xviii 18

17 ¶ k And when he was gone forth into the way,
there came one running, and kneeled to him, and aſked
him, Good Maſter, what ſhall I do that I may inherit
eternal life? 18 And Jeſus ſaid unto him, Why calleſt
thou me good? *There is* none good, but one, *that is*

l Ex xx 13 Deut v 17

m Chap vii 10

God 19 Thou knoweſt the commandments, l Do not
commit adultery, Do not kill, Do not ſteal, Do not bear
falſe witneſs, Defraud not, m Honour thy father and mo-
ther 20 And he anſwered and ſaid unto him, Maſter,

n Phil iii 6

n all theſe have I obſerved from my youth 21 Then
Jeſus, beholding him, loved him, and ſaid unto him, One

o Luke xii 33 & xvi 9 Act iv 34 1 Tim vi 18 19

p 2 Tim iv 10

thing thou lackeſt go thy way, o ſell whatſoever thou
haſt, and give to the poor, and thou ſhalt have treaſure
in heaven, and come, take up thy croſs, and follow me
22 And he was ſad at that ſaying, and p went away
grieved for he had great poſſeſſions 23 ¶ And Jeſus
looked round about, and ſaith unto his diſciples, How
hardly ſhall they that have riches enter into the kingdom
of God! 24 And the diſciples were aſtoniſhed at his
words But Jeſus anſwered again, and ſaith unto them,

q Job xxxi 24 Pſal lii 7 & lxii 10 1 Tim vi 17

r Jer xxxii 17

s Gen xxxix 1 Chap i 18

t Mat xix 27 Luke xviii 28

u Deut xxxiii 9

x 2 Chron xxv 9 Luke xviii 29 30

y Mat xix 30 & xx 16 Luke xiii 30

Children, q how hard is it for them that truſt in riches
to enter into the kingdom of God! 25 It is eaſier
for a camel to go through the eye of a needle, than for
a rich man to enter into the kingdom of God 26 And
they were aſtoniſhed out of meaſure, ſaying among them-
ſelves, Who then can be ſaved? 27 And Jeſus, look-
ing upon them, ſaith, With men *it is* impoſſible, but
not with God for r with God all things are poſſible
28 ¶ s Then Peter began to ſay unto him, Lo, t we
have left all, and have followed thee 29 And Jeſus
anſwered and ſaid, Verily I ſay unto you, there is no man
that hath left houſe, or brethren, or ſiſters, or father,
or mother, or wife, or children, or lands, for my ſake
and the goſpel's, 30 But x he ſhall receive an hundred
fold now in this time, houſes, and brethren, and ſiſters,
and mothers, and children, and lands, with perſecutions,
and in the world to come eternal life 31 But y many
that are firſt, ſhall be laſt and the laſt, firſt

v 17—31 We have here,

1 The young ruler's application to Chriſt, and ſorrowful departure from him, which we conſidered, *Mat* xix 16 His addreſs was moſt reſpectful and his queſtion infinitely important, eternal life being our great concern, and to ſecure that the one thing needful and, where the value of an immortal ſoul is felt, we cannot but be ſollicitous in our applications to Jeſus, who is the way, the truth, and the life Our Lord perceived the error under which he laboured, and, rebuking him for giving the title of *good* to any perſon whom he regarded as a mere man, deſired to diſcover to him the inſufficiency of his own righteouſneſs, and his inability to keep the law, by a perfect obedience to which eternal life alone could be ſecured and as the precepts of the ſecond table our Lord ſets before him the path of duty Ignorant of the ſpiritual extent of the commandments, he conceives he may venture to ſay he hath kept all theſe from his youth, becauſe he hath eſcaped the groſſer violations of them So apt are we to flatter ourſelves in our own eyes that we are righteous, when indeed it is our ignorance that hides from us our ſinfulneſs Something amiable in him attracted the regards of Jeſus, and, looking upon him with compaſſion, he would fain humble thoſe high thoughts of himſelf which he had entertained and, to bring him to the teſt, he bids him give one proof of his obedience and charity, by ſelling all his poſſeſſions, diſtributing them to the poor, truſting on the promiſe of a more enduring ſubſtance in heaven, and then let him take up his croſs and follow a ſuffering Saviour, and this would infallibly bring him to the eternal life he ſought But, alas! theſe were too hard ſayings for ſo rich a man to comply with he went away ſorely chagrined at the propoſal, and, if ſuch was the only alternative, he rather choſe to part with eternal life than his great poſſeſſions *Note*, (1) The only proper uſe of worldly wealth is to do good with it Though we may not be commanded to ſell all literally, we muſt remember we are really no more than ſtewards, and that a ſolemn account will ſhortly be required concerning every penny we have poſſeſſed (2) Great riches often prove a great ſnare How many by theſe have loſt eternal life? (3) A man may be poſſeſſed of a thouſand amiable qualities, and yet be utterly deſtitute of true grace

2 Chriſt obſerves, to the aſtoniſhment of the diſciples, the difficulty of their ſalvation who have the abundance of this world, and whoſe hearts, in conſequence thereof, are engaged to truſt on their riches and when, by the impracticability of a camel's going through a needle's eye, he intimated the immenſe obſtructions there were in the way of a rich man's ſalvation, the diſciples, above meaſure aſtoniſhed, concluded the impoſſibility of any man's being ſaved, ſince ſuch as were not rich in general wiſhed to be ſo, and they were conſcious to themſelves how much their own hearts were ſet on temporal grandeur Jeſus, looking with compaſſion upon them, to relieve in ſome meaſure their anxiety, bid them conſider that, though ſuch a change of heart as was needful to every mortified diſciple of his was beyond the power of man, it was not beyond the power of God, who can give the moſt wealthy the deepeſt poverty of ſpirit, and enable thoſe, who have the greateſt obſtructions in their way to glory, to ſurmount them

3 They who leave all for Chriſt ſhall be no loſers thereby Peter mentions with ſome ſatisfaction, that, though their poſſeſſions and connections were not great, they had given them up to follow him And Chriſt aſſures him that what they or any other ſhould part with for his ſake, would prove in the iſſue to be their unſpeakable gain whether a man quitted his home, his ſubſtance, his relations, or friends, or whatever elſe was dear to him, for the ſake of faithful adherence to Chriſt and his goſpel, he ſhould find his richeſt advantage in it, in preſent comfort, and ſometimes in kind, the Lord would give him an hundred fold, *with perſecutions*, which all who will live godly in Chriſt Jeſus muſt expect as long as they are in the body, and in the world to come an eternal life of happineſs and glory *But many that are firſt* in profeſſion will be outſtripped in zeal

and

and fidelity by others, who will be called after them, as to come in *last* in the race whilst *the last*, who seemed farthest from the kingdom of heaven, and latest embraced the offers of the gospel, by their diligence will often first reach the goal, *see* 1 *Cor* xv 10 *Note*, (1) The nearest and dearest relations must not weigh with us, when set in competition with our profession of Christ, and the service of his gospel (2) Till we come to heaven, however prosperous our circumstances may be, we are to expect the cross, it is only then that we shall have finished our warfare, and entered into our eternal rest

32 ¶ [r] And they were in the way going up to Jeru-
salem and Jesus went before them, and they were a-
mazed, and as they followed, they were afraid And
he took again the twelve, and [s] began to tell them what
things should happen unto him, 33 *Saying*, Behold,
we go up to Jerusalem, and the Son of man shall be de-
livered unto the chief priests, and unto the scribes and
they shall condemn him to death, and [t] shall deliver him
to the Gentiles, 34 And they shall mock him, and
shall scourge him, and shall spit upon him, and shall kill
him and the third day he shall rise again 35 ¶ [c] And
James and John the sons of Zebedee come unto him,
saying, Master, we would that thou shouldest do for us
whatsoever we shall desire 36 And he said unto them,
[d] What would ye that I should do for you? 37 They
said unto him, [e] Grant unto us that we may sit, one on
thy right hand, and the other on thy left hand, in thy
glory 38 But Jesus said unto them, [f] Ye know not
what ye ask can ye drink of the [g] cup that I drink of?
and be baptized with the baptism that I am baptized
with? 39 And they said unto him, [h] we can And
Jesus said unto them, [i] Ye shall indeed drink of the cup
that I drink of, and with the baptism that I am bap-
tized withal, shall ye be baptized 40 But to sit on
my right hand, and on my left hand, is not mine to give,
‡ but *it shall be given* to them for whom it is prepared
41 And when the ten heard *it*, [k] they began to be
much displeased with James and John 42 But Jesus
called them to him, and saith unto them, Ye know that
they which are accounted to rule over the Gentiles, exer-
cise lordship over them, and their great ones exercise
authority upon them 43 But so shall it not be among
you but whosoever will be great among you, [l] shall be
your minister 44 And whosoever of you will be the
chiefest, shall be servant of all 45 For even [m] the Son
of man came not to be ministred unto, but to minister,
and [n] to give his life a ransom [o] for many

[r] Mat xx 17 Luke xviii 31 [s] Chap viii 31 & ix 31 [b] Chap ix 31 Luke ix 22 [c] Mat xx 20 [d] Esth v 3 [e] Jer xlv 5 [f] Jam iv 3 [g] Chap xiv 36 [h] Chap xiv 31 [i] Acts xii 2 ‡ Or Save to them for whom &c Mat xx 23 John xvii 2 [k] Mat xx 24 [l] 1 Cor ix 19 &c [m] Luke xxii 27 [n] Isa liii 10 Dan ix 26 [o] Tim ii 6 Tit ii 14 Mat xx 28

v 32—45 The nearer Christ drew to the scene of his sufferings, the plainer he warns his disciples of them, that they might be the less surprized at them when they came

1 He here appears eagerly hastening to face his enemies, whilst his disciples, considering what he had suggested would happen to him at Jerusalem, were amazed at his resolution and followed him trembling, apprehensive, probably, lest they might be involved in his troubles To prepare them for this distressing event, Christ again called them, and told them distinctly all that would befall him, that, when it came to pass, they might remember that he suffered nothing of which he was not apprized, and to which he did not voluntarily submit adding, after all his indignities and death, that he should rise again, and that, if they understood it, would have been a sufficient support against all their fears

2 He rebukes the pride and ambition of the disciples, which all these warnings could not cure Two of them wanted to be prime ministers in his kingdom, and, through their mother, wished to have a general promise granted them of bestowing on them a request they were about to make, which proved to be no less than securing the two most honourable places next the throne, when Christ should, as they expected, set up his earthly reign But, as they mistook the nature of the Messiah's kingdom, which called them to suffer, not to bear rule, so also was their desire impossible to be granted, it being unalterably fixed by the eternal decree of God on whom the honour of glory should be bestowed The ten, as culpable as the two petitioners, and equally ambitious of the places they sought, were exceedingly displeased at their affecting the precedency, to which they thought themselves equally entitled But Jesus, to silence both parties, lets them know, that the kingdom he was about to erect was not to be governed as earthly monarchies, where the rulers exercised despotic sway but, on the contrary, he would be the greatest in the Messiah's kingdom, who was in his own eyes most abased, and most ready in every work and labour of love to serve the meanest disciple, for herein he nearest resembled his Master, who came with deepest humility as a servant, and was to die upon a cross as a slave, paying down the ransom for the sins of many, whom he intended to bring in this way unto glory

46 ¶ [p] And they came to Jericho and as he went
out of Jericho with his disciples, and a great number of
people, [q] blind Bartimeus, the son of Timeus, sat by
the high-way-side, begging 47 And when he heard
that it was Jesus of Nazareth, he began to cry out, and
say, Jesus, thou son of David, have mercy on me 48
And many charged him that he should hold his peace
but [r] he cried the more a great deal, Thou son of David,
have mercy on me 49 And Jesus stood still, and com-
manded him to be called and they call the blind man,
saying unto him, Be of good comfort, rise, he calleth
thee 50 And he, casting away his garment, rose, and
came to Jesus 51 And Jesus answered and said unto
him, What wilt thou that I should do unto thee? The
blind man said unto him, † Lord, [s] that I might receive
my sight 52 And Jesus said unto him, Go thy way,
[u] thy faith hath ‡ made thee whole And immediately
[x] he received his sight, and followed Jesus in the way

[p] Mat xx 29 Luke xviii 35 [q] Isa lix 10 [r] Luke xviii 39 [s] Mat vii 7 † Or Rabboni John xx 16 Isa xxxv 5 [u] Chap v 34 ‡ Or Saved thee [x] Luke i 79

v 46—52 In Matthew we were told of two blind men, here but of one, perhaps he was the most remarkable, as the son of Timeus He sat begging by the way-side, and no sooner heard of Jesus passing by, than, crying incessantly, he would not be silenced till Jesus stood and called him, when, eager to be led to him, he threw off his upper garment, and, coming before the Saviour, presented his request and received his cure In him we see, (1) An emblem of the sinner's misery, poor, blind, and destitute And a happy thing it is when, brought to a sense of this misery, he is found at the way-side of ordinances, crying after Jesus (2) The blind and lame are among the truest objects of charity, and to their cries we must never be deaf (3) The calls of Jesus are our encouragement to come to him, and they are so general, free, and full, that, whenever a poor, guilty, corrupted creature feels his wants, we may safely say to such a one, *He calleth thee* (4) When we are coming to Christ, whatever would prove a hindrance, like this garment, should be cast off, particularly that robe of self-righteousness and self-sufficiency which sticks so close to us (5) None truly cry to him, and go away without relief If we have faith in his power and love, we shall assuredly see the salvation of God (6) When Christ enlightens the eyes of our minds, it is in order that we should henceforth keep him ever in view, and follow him in all his holy ways

CHAP XI

We have here, 1 *Christ's riding in triumph into Jerusalem,* ver 1—11 2 *His cursing the barren fig-tree,* ver 12, 13, 14 3 *His driving those out of the temple that turned it into an exchange,* ver 15—19 4 *His discourse with his disciples concerning the power of faith and efficacy of prayer, on occasion of the withering of the fig tree he cursed,* ver 20—26 5 *His reply to those who questioned his authority,* ver 27—33

1 [a] AND when they came nigh to Jerusalem, unto
Bethphage, and Bethany, at the mount of
Olives, he sendeth forth two of his disciples, 2 And
saith unto them, Go your way into the village over
against you, and as soon as ye be entred into it, ye
shall find a colt tied, whereon never man sat, loose him,
and bring *him* 3 And if any man say unto you, Why
do ye this? say ye that the Lord hath need of him; and
straightway he will send him hither 4 And they went
their way, and found the colt tied by the door without,
in a place where two ways met and they loose him.
5 And certain of them that stood there said unto them,
What do ye loosing the colt? 6 And they said unto
them even as Jesus had commanded and they let them
go 7 And they brought the colt to Jesus, and [b] cast
their garments on him; [c] and he sat upon him 8 And
many spread their garments in the way and [d] others cut
down branches off the trees, and strawed *them* in the way
9 And they that went before, and they that followed,
cried, saying, [e] Hosanna, [f] blessed *is* he that cometh in
the name of the Lord 10 Blessed *be* [g] the kingdom
of our father David, that cometh in the name of the
Lord, Hosanna in the highest 11 And [h] Jesus entred
into Jerusalem, and into the temple; and when he had
looked round about upon all things, and now the even
tide was come, he went out unto Bethany with the
twelve

[a] Mat xxi 1 Luke xix 29 John xii 12 [b] 2 Kings ix 13 [c] Zech ix 9 [d] Lev xxiii 40 1 Mac xiii 51 John xii 13 [e] Psal cxviii 25 [f] Psal cxviii 26 Mat xxiii 39 [g] Luke i 32 [h] Mat xxi 12

v 1—11 The last week of the life of Jesus now is come, and we see him here entring Jerusalem in triumph, so little terrified with the fears of his enemies, or cast down by the sufferings he was about to undergo

1 He enters Jerusalem amidst the hosannas of the people He ordered his disciples, when he drew near the city, to bring an ass's colt from the opposite village, directing them to the spot, and delivering a message from him, if any questioned them for what they did Accordingly they went as Jesus had commanded them, and, when the owners of the colt demanded why they loosed him, they told them *the Lord hath need of him*, and they contentedly let him go Seated on this mean animal did Jesus enter the city, whilst, to express their gladness, his poor followers spread their garments in the way, and cut down branches from the trees as at the feast of tabernacles, surrounding him with hosannas, wishing prosperity to the long-expected Messiah, now bringing salvation to his people, praying that his reign may be long and happy who comes to sit on his father David's throne, invested with divine authority, calling on the angels to join their praises, and begging God to pour down the best of blessings on the Messiah and his people

2 He went directly to the temple that was his palace he aimed not at a temporal but spiritual dominion After looking round him to observe what was done there, and spy out the abuses which called for his correction, and, as appears from *Mat* xxi 12, 13 casting out those who trafficked there, he retired in the evening to Bethany with the twelve, the place he chose for his abode *Note*, The eye of Jesus is upon his temple, to see what the priests do there, it is upon the living temple of his people's heart, observing every rising thought of evil How watchful then need we be!

l Mat xxi 18 12 ¶ [l] And on the morrow, when they were come
from Bethany, he was hungry 13 And seeing a fig-
tree afar off, having leaves, he came, if haply he might
k 2 Tim iii 5 Rev iii 1 find any thing thereon and, when he came to it, [k] he
found nothing but leaves, for the time of figs was not
yet 14 And Jesus answered and said unto it, No man
eat fruit of thee hereafter for ever And his disciples
l Mat xxi 12 Luke xix 45 John ii 14 heard *it* 15 ¶ [l] And they come to Jerusalem and
Jesus went into the temple, and began to cast out them
that sold and bought in the temple, and overthrew the
tables of the money-changers, and the seats of them that
sold doves, 16 And would not suffer that any man
should carry any vessel through the temple 17 And
m Isa lvi 7 he taught, saying unto them, Is it not written, [m] My
house shall be called of all nations the house of prayer?
n Jer vii 11 but [n] ye have made it a den of thieves 18 And the
scribes and chief priests heard *it*, and sought how they
o Chap i 22 Luke iv 32 might destroy him for they feared him, because [o] all
the people was astonished at his doctrine 19 And when
p Mat xxi 19 even was come, he went out of the city 20 ¶ [p] And
in the morning, as they passed by, they saw the fig-
tree dried up from the roots 21 And Peter, calling
to remembrance, saith unto him, Master, behold, the
q Heb vi 8 fig tree, [q] which thou cursedst, is withered away 22
And Jesus, answering, saith unto them, Have faith in
God 23 For verily I say unto you, that whosoever
shall say unto this mountain, Be thou removed, and
r Jam i 6 be thou cast into the sea, and [r] shall not doubt in his
s Mat xvii 20 Luke xvii 6 heart, but [s] shall believe that those things which he
saith shall come to pass, he shall have whatsoever he
t Mat vii 7 John xv 7 xvi 24 1 John v 14 saith 24 Therefore I say unto you, [t] What things
soever ye desire when ye pray, believe that ye receive
them, and ye shall have *them* 25 And when ye stand,
u Mat vi 14 Col iii 13 praying, [u] forgive, if ye have ought against any that
your Father also, which is in heaven, may forgive you
x Mat xviii 35 your trespasses 26 [x] But, if you do not forgive, nei-
ther will your Father, which is in heaven, forgive your
trespasses

v 12—26 We have here,

1 The cursing of the barren fig-tree, the type of the destruction of the Jewish nation Our Lord, on his return from Bethany to the temple in the morning, being hungry, seeing a very flourishing fig-tree, came, expecting to find some figs thereon; *for the time of figs was not yet*, or, *it was not a season of figs*, it was a bad year but that tree promised better than others, or *the time of figs*, when they should be gathered in, *was not yet*, and therefore he might expect fruit on the tree, but, finding none, he cursed the tree in the hearing of his disciples, who took particular notice of it For the curse of the Lord are fearful, and never fall in vain

2 He purges the temple of the buyers and sellers, who had made that sacred place a house of merchandize It appears from *Mat* xxi 12 he had done the same the preceding day, but, probably supported and encouraged by the priests, the traders had returned to their former traffick the next day, and were thus again expelled And, to vindicate his procedure, he quoted the words of the prophet, *Isa* lvi 6, 7 where God, speaking of the sons of the stranger, the proselytes, undertakes to welcome them to his house, which should be a house of prayer to all nations But the court, which was appropriated to the service of the Gentiles, they had profaned by turning it into a market, and made it by their knavery and extortion a den of thieves

3 The priests and scribes, incensed at what they saw and heard, especially those severe rebukes which reflected so deeply on their characters, were bitterly exasperated, and being determined to murder him, sought only how they might do it without exposing themselves to the fury of the populace, for they were afraid openly to use violence, the people in general expressing such a veneration for Christ's person, and such respect and reverence for his doctrine *Note*, Envy and malice naturally lead to murder, and it is only the fear of men that in a multitude of instances deters the wicked from the very act

4 In the evening they returned to Bethany, and next morning, in their way to the city, the disciples took notice with surprize of the withering of the fig-tree, and Peter, pointing to the tree, observed to his Master how it was withered away in consequence of the curse he had pronounced upon it And from thence Christ took occasion to encourage them confidently to exercise faith in God at all times, and especially in the exertion of the miraculous powers with which he had furnished them, they should find nothing impossible, not even to remove the mountain on which they stood, and cast it into the sea, if they had an unshaken trust in the divine power and promises, and looked up to God, nothing doubting for whatever they should ask in prayer, which should be for his glory to give, and they were warranted from his word to expect, should certainly be given them And on this occasion, as what would be essential to their obtaining an answer to their prayers, he inculcates fervent charity and mutual forgiveness when they stood praying for forgiveness, they must be ready to grant that pardon to others which they themselves sought at God's hand But if, under the spirit of uncharitableness, they refused to forgive their brother his trespasses, their prayers would be in vain, and they may never hope for the pardon themselves sought at the hands of their heavenly Father *Note*, (1) Faith is the conquering grace that overcomes the world, and bears down all obstacles before it If at any time we are terrified by guilt, or enslaved by corruption, it is through our want of *faith in God* (2) Nothing can be a more powerful argument to engage our charity and forgiveness towards others, than what arises from our own prayers

27 ¶ And they come again to Jerusalem and [y] as y Mat xxi 23 Luke xx 1
he was walking in the temple, there come to him the
chief priests, and the scribes, and the elders, 28 And
say unto him, [z] by what authority dost thou these things? z Exod ii 14 Acts iv 7
And who gave thee this authority to do these things?
29 And Jesus answered and said unto them, I will also
ask of you one question, and answer me, and I will tell
you by what authority I do these things 30 [a] The a Prov xxvi 5
baptism of John, was it from heaven, or of men? an-
swer me 31 And they reasoned with themselves, say-
ing, It we shall say, From heaven, he will say, [b] Why b Ch. i 4 Mat iii
then did ye not believe him? 32 But if we shall say,
Of men, they feared the people for [c] all men counted c Mat xiv 5
John, that he was a prophet indeed 33 And they
answered and said unto Jesus, [d] We cannot tell And d Jer v
Jesus, answering, said unto them, Neither do I tell you
by what authority I do these things

v 27—33 Vexed at the heart to behold the respect paid to Jesus, and impatient to revenge his rebukes, which they construed into reproaches, we have here,

1 The demand of the high-priests and elders, challenging Christ to produce his authority for what he had said and done the preceding days, as if he had been lord and master of the temple

2 He answers their question by another By what authority did John preach and baptise? give me a direct reply The answer was easy, but the difficulties in which on either side it involved them were great They saw that to confess his mission divine, was to own all that Jesus claimed, John having born testimony to him, to deny that the Baptist was sent of God, and to brand him as a pretender and impostor, would instantly enrage the people to rise up, perhaps, and stone them, all men in general being persuaded of John's prophetic character therefore, after reasoning on the matter, they are forced to conceal under the truth they dared not own, and to pretend ignorance of what they knew, as the only way to evade the answer Christ demanded of them He therefore was fully justified in refusing them further information, when it evidently appeared they sought not conviction of the truth, but merely his destruction *Note*, (1)

It

It is a mercy to be able to put to silence the ignorance of foolish men, and at least to confound those who refuse to be convinced (2) They who wilfully chuse to be ignorant are justly abandoned to judicial blindness

CHAP XII

In this chapter we have, 1 *The parable of the vineyard let out to unthankful husbandmen, representing the sin and ruin of the Jewish church,* ver 1—12 2 *Christ's silencing those who thought to ensnare him with a question about paying tribute to Cesar,* ver 13—17 3 *His silencing the Sadducees, who attempted to perplex the doctrine of the resurrection,* ver 18—27 4 *His conference with a scribe about the first and great command of the law,* ver 28—34 5 *His puzzling the scribes with a question about Christ's being the Son of David,* ver 35, 36, 37 6 *The caution he gave the people to take heed of the scribes,* ver 38, 39, 40 7 *His commendation of the poor widow that cast her two mites into the treasury,* ver 41—44

1 [a] AND he began to speak unto them by parables
[b] A *certain* man planted a vineyard, and set an
hedge about it, and digged *a place for* the wine fat, and
built a tower, and let it out to husbandmen, and went
into a far country 2 And at the season [c] he sent to the
husbandmen a servant, that he might receive from the
husbandmen of the fruit of the vineyard 3 [d] And they
caught *him*, and beat him, and sent *him* away empty
4 [d] And again he sent unto them another servant, and
at him they cast stones, and wounded *him* in the head,
and sent *him* away shamefully handled 5 And again
he sent another, and him they killed and many others,
beating some, and killing some 6 Having yet there-
fore one son, his well-beloved, he sent him also last unto
them, saying, They will reverence my son 7 But those
husbandmen said amongst themselves, This is the heir,
[f] come, let us kill him, and the inheritance shall be ours
8 And they took him, and killed *him*, and [g] cast *him*
out of the vineyard 9 What shall therefore the Lord
of the vineyard do? he will come and destroy the hus-
bandmen, and [h] will give the vineyard unto others
10 And have ye not read this scripture? [i] The stone
which the builders rejected is become the head of the
corner 11 This was the Lord's doing, and it is mar-
vellous in our eyes 12 And [k] they sought to lay hold
on him, but feared the people, for they knew that he
had spoken the parable against them and they left him,
and went their way

a Mat xxi 33 Luke xx 9
b Psal lxxx 8 Cant viii 11 Isa v 1 Jer ii 21
c 2 Chron xxxvi 15
d 2 Chron xxxvi 16 Neh ix 26 Mat xxiii 34, 37 Acts vii 52 1 Thess ii 15 Heb xi 36 &c
e Heb i 2
f Chap xiv 1
g Heb xiii 12
h Rom xi 11
i Psal cxviii 22
k Chap xi 18

v 1—12 Since they had thus wickedly rejected their Messiah, he here in parable sets forth before them the guilt and ruin coming upon them in consequence thereof The parable of the vineyard we had before, *Matt* xxi 33 The scope and design of it is to upbraid them with their continual rejection and persecution of God's prophets from the days of their forefathers to that hour, the measure of whose guilt they were now about to fill up in the murder of the Son of God, and thus they would bring down the temporal and eternal wrath of God upon their devoted heads, who, instead of the Jewish people, would admit the Gentiles in their stead, and, in spite of all their envy and enmity, erect his glorious church on that one foundation and chief corner-stone the Messiah, whom they rejected, and hereby make his marvellous power and grace evident to all The parable was too plain for them to mistake the meaning, the chief priests and elders perceived it was levelled at them, and, enraged beyond measure at such boldness, though they dared not apprehend him publickly, they consulted how they could privately get him into their power and cut him off *Note,* (1) God expects from those who are placed in his vineyard the church, that they should render him the tribute of love and duty for which they stand so highly indebted (2) In all ages the true ministers of Christ have met with the cruellest usage, and usually their bitterest persecutors have been those who have pretended a divine commission, and to be labourers in God's vineyard (3) God will have a church and people in the world, whatever opposition may be formed against them (4) It is a truly marvellous thing in the eyes of a gracious soul, when he observes the operations of divine grace in himself, and how the Lord sets up his kingdom within him, in spite of all the opposition from Satan and indwelling sin (5) They who refuse to be convinced by the truth of God's word, are generally exasperated both against the minister and his message, and thus what was sent as *a savour of life unto life*, to them becomes *a savour of death unto death*

13 ¶ [l] And they send unto him certain of the Pha-
risees, and of the Herodians, to catch him in *his* words
14 And when they were come, they say unto him,
[m] Master, we know that thou art true, and carest for no
man for thou regardest not the person of men, but
teachest the way of God in truth Is it lawful to give
tribute to Cesar, or not? 15 Shall we give, or shall
we not give? But he, knowing their hypocrisy, said
unto them, Why tempt ye me? bring me † a penny,
that I may see *it* 16 And they brought *it* and he
saith unto them, Whose *is* this image and superscription?
And they said unto him, Cesar's 17 And Jesus, an-
swering, said unto them, [n] Render to Cesar the things
that are Cesar's, and to God the things that are God's.
And they marvelled at him

l Mat xxii 15 Luke xx 20
m Psal xii 2
† A small coin worth sevenpence-halfpenny Mat xviii 28
n Rom xiii 7

v 13—17 We have here a new attempt made by the Pharisees and Herodians, bitter enemies to each other, but close leagued against Christ They wanted to catch up something which might serve to accuse him, and they thought they had a question which would not fail either to render him obnoxious to the civil powers, or to blast his reputation with the people, should he enforce subjection to the Roman yoke, which they so abhorred Pretending therefore great respect to Christ, as a person of unspotted integrity, and above the fear of men, they bring to him a case of conscience, as if they wished to be guided by his superior judgment The question was whether it was lawful to pay tribute to Cesar or not? He saw their hypocrisy, and confounds their devices, bidding them produce the tribute-money, and tell him whose image or superscription it bore On their saying, *Cesar's*, he then bid them render to Cesar his own By admitting the currency of his coin, they owned their subjection to him, and were bound to pay the tribute required in return for the protection they enjoyed, whilst God's right over them remained unalienably the same in all religious concerns he was alone the Lord of their conscience, and to all his commands unreserved submission must be paid an answer so wise, so convincing and unexceptionable, as even astonished his very enemies *Note,* (1) The sects most bitter against each other will readily unite to oppose the power of true Christianity (2) The professions of false friends are usually most specious, when their designs are most malignant (3) It is a dangerous thing for ministers to interfere about civil rights, their business is to teach subjection to the powers that are (4) Hypocrisy, however artful the veil, cannot be concealed from the knowledge of him who trieth the reins and the heart

18 ¶ [o] Then come unto him the Sadducees, [p] which
say there is no resurrection, and they asked him, saying,
19 Master, [q] Moses wrote unto us, If a man's brother
die, and leave his wife behind him, and leave no child-
ren, that his brother should take his wife, and raise up
seed unto his brother 20 [r] Now there were seven bre-
thren and the first took a wife, and dying left no seed
21 And the second took her, and died, neither left he
any seed and the third likewise 22 And the seven
had her, and left no seed last of all the woman died
also 23 In the resurrection therefore, when they shall
rise, whose wife shall she be of them? for the seven had
her to wife 24 And Jesus, answering, said unto them,
Do ye not therefore err, [s] because ye know not the scrip-
tures, [t] neither the power of God? 25 For, when they
shall rise from the dead, they neither marry nor are given
in marriage but [u] are as the angels which are in heaven
26 And as touching the dead, that they rise have ye
not read in the book of Moses, how in the bush God
spake unto him, saying, [x] I *am* the God of Abraham,
and the God of Isaac, and the God of Jacob? 27 He
is not the God of the dead, but the God of the living
ye therefore do greatly err.

o Mat xxii 23 Luke xx 27
p Acts xxiii 8
q Deut xxv 5
r Tob iii 8
s John xx 9 Luke xxiv 45 Dan xii 2
t Acts xxvi 8
u 1 Cor xv 42, 49
x Exod iii 6 Acts vii 32 Heb xi 16

v 18—27 The Sadducees, the free-thinkers and reasoners of the age, came next, fraught with wisdom and sophistry, and thought that, though others had been unequal to the task, they were able to propose a question which the wisdom of Jesus would find it hard to answer But they were deceived to their cost, their ignorance exposed, their error detected, and that resurrection they denied proved by the clearest evidence of Moses, whose authority they admitted, *see Matt* xxii 23 *Note,* (1) Many infidels pretend a reverence for the Scriptures, in order the more artfully to introduce their suggestions, to shake our faith and destroy their credit (2) It is impossible but they should err, not knowing the Scriptures, who, instead of submitting their fallen reason to God's word, insist that even the doctrines of revelation shall be first cited to this fallacious tribunal, and be admitted only so far as they are pleased to stamp them as rational, but, if found incomprehensible, they reject them as absurd

y Mat xxii 35 Luke x 25

28 ¶ y And one of the ſcribes came, and, having heard them reaſoning together, and perceiving that he had anſwered them well, aſked him, Which is the firſt commandment of all? 29 And Jeſus anſwered him, The firſt of all the commandments *is*, z Hear, O Iſrael, The Lord our God is one Lord 30 And a thou ſhalt love the Lord thy God with all thy heart, and with all thy ſoul, and with all thy mind, and with all thy ſtrength this is the firſt commandment 31 And the ſecond *is* like, *namely* this, b Thou ſhalt love thy neighbour as thyſelf there is none other commandment greater than theſe 32 And the ſcribe ſaid unto him, Well, Maſter, thou haſt ſaid the truth for c there is one God, and there is none other but he 33 And to love him with all the heart, and with all the underſtanding, and with all the ſoul, and with all the ſtrength, and to love *his* neighbour as himſelf, d is more than all whole-burnt-offerings and ſacrifices 34 And when Jeſus ſaw that he anſwered diſcreetly, he ſaid unto him, Thou art not far from the kingdom of God And no man after that durſt aſk him any queſtion

z Deut vi 4 a Deut vi 5 & x 12 & xxx 6 b Lev xix 18 Rom xiii 9 Gal v 14 1 Tim i 5 Jam ii 8 c Deut iv 39 Iſa xlv 6 14 d Hoſ vi 6

v 28—34 Struck with the force of our Lord's reaſoning, one of the ſcribes, who were of the ſect of the Phariſees, acknowledged he had *anſwered well*, yet, willing to try his judgment farther, he propoſes,

1 An important queſtion for his ſolution *which is the firſt commandment of all?* the greateſt, moſt neceſſary to be obſerved, and moſt influential over the whole tenor of our conduct

2 Chriſt fully anſwers him The firſt and great commandment is *the love of God* He, who is God alone, demands and deſerves the whole heart and mind, and ſoul and ſtrength and in this one word is comprehended the principle of all holy obedience, and that which neceſſarily engages in his worſhip and ſervice the whole body, ſoul, and ſpirit, and without this love nothing acceptable to him can be performed The ſecond commandment is of a like comprehenſive nature, enjoining us *to love our neighbour as ourſelves*, fervently and unfeignedly, behaving towards him with ſuch juſtice and mercy as we, if our circumſtances were reverſed, might juſtly deſire and expect from him Theſe two comprehend every ſuppoſable duty towards God and man, and there can be no greater commandment, ſince in theſe the whole law is fulfilled

3 The ſcribe confeſſes the juſtneſs of our Lord's anſwer, convinced of its admirable propriety and wiſdom, and adds his teſtimony to the truth of his obſervations, that there is one only living and true God, and that to love, worſhip, and ſerve him with the moſt active powers of our ſouls, and to exerciſe this divine charity to our neighbour, is in God's account far more acceptable than the moſt expenſive ſervices, or all the ritual obſervances

4 Chriſt approves the judicious remarks he made he ſhewed himſelf a man of underſtanding, unbiaſſed by the generally received traditions, and, as his mind appeared ingenuous and open to conviction, he was not far from the kingdom of God In ſuch a ſpirit if he had examined the prophets, and weighed, under the divine benediction, the evidence of Chriſt's miſſion and miracles, he would be led into the truth, and become a member of the Meſſiah's kingdom

5 From this time all the captious cavillers were ſilenced Such conſummate wiſdom appeared in him, that none durſt any more encounter him *Note*, (1) They who improve the light God hath given them will receive an increaſe of it, and be led into all truth (2) Many a man goes to the borders of the truth, *not far from the kingdom of God*, and yet never enters into it, almoſt but not altogether a Chriſtian

e Mat xxii 41 Luke xx 41 f 2 Sam xxiii 2 g Pſ cx 1 Acts ii 34 Heb i 13 [illegible] Rev xxii 16 i Mat xxiii 1 Luke xx 46 k Luke xi 43 l John [illegible] m Mat xxiii 14 Tit i 11

35 ¶ e And Jeſus anſwered and ſaid, while he taught in the temple, How ſay the ſcribes that Chriſt is the ſon of David? 36 For David himſelf ſaid f by the Holy Ghoſt, g The LORD ſaid unto my Lord, Sit thou on my right hand, till I make thine enemies thy footſtool 37 David therefore himſelf calleth him Lord, and whence is he *then* his Son? And the common people heard him gladly 38 ¶ And he ſaid unto them in his doctrine, i Beware of the ſcribes, which love to go in long clothing, and k *love* ſalutations in the market-places, 39 l And the chief ſeats in the ſynagogues, and the uppermoſt rooms at feaſts 40 m Which devour widows houſes, and for a pretence make long prayers theſe ſhall receive greater damnation

35—40 They had frequently endeavoured to puzzle him with queſtions captious and difficult Our Lord now poſes them with a queſtion, which, as expoſitors of the Scripture, the ſcribes ſhould have thoroughly underſtood

1 The queſtion was, How the Meſſiah, whom they all admitted to be David's ſon, could at the ſame time be David's Lord, as he expreſsly calls him, *Pſ* cx 1 This was a myſtery to the ſcribes not underſtanding the twofold nature of the Meſſiah as God and man, they could not anſwer the queſtion Hereupon the common people, convinced how far Jeſus in wiſdom ſurpaſſed all their teachers, hearkened with delight to his divine diſcourſes *Note*, (1) A babe in Chriſt underſtands more of the myſteries of godlineſs than the wiſeſt unenlightened ſcribe (2) Popularity, and the approbation of the vulgar, is often caſt as a reproach on the miniſters of the goſpel by thoſe who envy them, as the ſcribes of old did their Maſter

2 He takes occaſion to caution the people from being deceived by the ſanctified appearance of their falſe teachers, whilſt in fact they were ſlaves to pride and worldly-mindedneſs They wore particular garments, long and trailing on the ground, or with fringes of extraordinary breadth, as a token of ſuperior piety, and made long prayers that they might appear men of extraordinary devotion, but all they did was hypocritical and deſigning, in order to gain the ſeat of preeminence and publick ſalutations of high reſpect, and as a cloak under which to worm themſelves into the confidence of widows whom they plundered to enrich themſelves for which abominations they would bring down the heavieſt wrath of God upon their ſouls *Note*, (1) Inordinate deſire of human reſpect and honour is the ſure ſymptom of a proud, worldly, and unmortified heart (2) Hypocriſy is among the moſt common and moſt crying ſins Beware of it

41 ¶ And n Jeſus ſat over againſt the treaſury, and beheld how the people caſt money into o the treaſury and many that were rich caſt in much 42 And there came a certain poor widow, and ſhe threw in two mites, which make a farthing 43 And he called unto him his diſciples, and ſaith unto them, Verily I ſay unto you, that p this poor widow hath caſt more in, than all they which have caſt into the treaſury. 44 For all *they* did caſt in of their abundance but ſhe of her want did caſt in all that ſhe had, *even* all her living

n Luke xxi 1 o 2 Kings xii 9 p 2 Cor viii 12

v 41—44 For the maintenance of the temple-worſhip and ſacrifices, there were coffers placed in the court for the reception of the free-will offerings of the people Our Lord, being ſeated near the treaſury, where theſe ſtood, obſerved the people who caſt in their money Many of the rich gave much, as became them, but, among the reſt, a poor widow came and caſt in two mites Highly applauding the deed, our Lord pointed her out to his diſciples, as having preſented a richer and more acceptable offering than thoſe who out of their abundance had given more liberally They had enough left ſtill to ſupply their wants, but ſhe, out of love to the ſervice, threw in her little all, truſting on the divine providence for her future ſuſtenance *Note*, (1) Almſgiving is a moſt needful duty, and our Lord expects, according to our abilities, that we ſhould be ready to diſtribute, willing to communicate but he looks not merely at the gift, but the ſpirit and temper of the giver, for that alone ſtamps the offering with its value in his account (2) None can be ſuppoſed poorer than this widow, yet ſhe gave If we have but little, that muſt be no excuſe, we muſt give our diligence to *give of that little*, and then it is accepted *according to that a man hath, and not according to that he hath not* (3) A truly gracious and charitable ſoul will ſometimes ſtraiten himſelf to ſupply other's more urgent wants, willing not only *to his power*, but *above his power*, to aſſiſt them

CHAP XIII

Chriſt foretels the deſtruction of the city and temple, the figure of the day of final recompenſe, warning all men to watch leſt they be ſurprized unawares by judgments in this world, or the ſudden appearing of the Son of man

1 AND a as he went out of the temple, one of his diſciples ſaith unto him, Maſter, ſee what manner of ſtones, and what buildings *are here* 2 And Jeſus anſwering ſaid unto him, Seeſt thou theſe great buildings? b there ſhall not be left one ſtone upon another, that ſhall not be thrown down 3 And as he ſat upon the mount of Olives, over againſt the temple, Peter, and James, and John, and Andrew, aſked him privately, 4 Tell us, when ſhall theſe things be? and what *ſhall be* the ſign when all theſe things ſhall be fulfilled?

a Mat xxiv 1 Luke xxi 5 b [illegible]

v 1—4 Departing now from the temple to return no more, one of his diſciples, pleaſed with the beauty of that ſtupendous fabric, could not help obſerving to him, of what maſſy ſtone it was built, and how magnificently adorned But Chriſt aſſures him, admirable as it appeared, and ſtrong as it ſtood, the day

day was near when it ſhould be ſo utterly raſed from the foundations, that one ſtone ſhould not be left upon another Struck with ſo ſad a proſpect, four of the diſciples came privately to him, as he ſat in the mount of Olives, deſiring to be informed when theſe awful predictions would come to paſs, and what would be the ſigns of their approaching fulfilment

5 And Jeſus anſwering them, began to ſay, [a] Take
heed leſt any man deceive you 6 For [d] many ſhall
come in my name, ſaying, I am *Chriſt* and [e] ſhall de-
ceive many 7 And when ye ſhall hear of wars, and
rumours of wars, be ye not troubled for *ſuch things*
muſt needs be, but the end *ſhall* not *be* yet 8 For
[f] nation ſhall riſe againſt nation, and kingdom againſt
kingdom and there ſhall be earthquakes in *divers* places,
and there ſhall be [g] famines and troubles theſe *are* the
beginnings of † ſorrows 9 ¶ But take heed to your-
ſelves for [h] they ſhall deliver you up to councils, and
in the ſynagogues ye ſhall be beaten, and ye ſhall be
brought before rulers and kings for my ſake, for a teſti-
mony againſt them 10 And [k] the goſpel muſt firſt
be publiſhed among all nations 11 But [l] when they
ſhall lead *you*, and deliver you up, take no thought be-
forehand what ye ſhall ſpeak, neither do ye premeditate
but whatſoever ſhall be given you in that hour, that
ſpeak ye for it is not ye that ſpeak, but the Holy
Ghoſt 12 Now [m] the brother ſhall betray the brother
to death, and the father the ſon and children ſhall riſe
up againſt *their* parents, and ſhall cauſe them to be put
to death 13 And ye ſhall be hated of all men for my
name's ſake but [n] he that ſhall endure unto the end,
the ſame ſhall be ſaved

v 5—13 In anſwering the queſtion their curioſity raiſed, Chriſt gives them ſome cautions for the direction of their conſcience, it being infinitely more their concern to be always ready to meet the approaching calamities, than to know the preciſe time of their arrival

1 He cautions them againſt the falſe Chriſts which ſhould ariſe, and ſeduce many of the Jews, who were ready to run after every impoſtor, whilſt they had rejected the true Meſſiah

2 He warns them not to be diſcouraged with the wars and commotions, the famines, earthquakes, and peſtilence, which would ravage the earth, theſe being but the beginning of ſorrows, *the end is not yet* and what is here ſpoken with an immediate reference to the Jewiſh ſtate and nation, ſeems alſo to have a view to the like calamities which will be the ſigns and preſages of the final diſſolution of all things But amidſt the wreck of nature, and the flames of a diſſolving world, the ſoul that is ſtayed upon Chriſt need not be troubled, his ſafety is ſecured by the everlaſting promiſes of the unchanging Jehovah

3 He bids them prepare for perſecutions, and exhorts them to bear up courageouſly under them Far from poſſeſſing that earthly greatneſs and reſpect with which they flattered themſelves, they muſt expect the very reverſe, they will *be hated of all men* for his ſake in enmity to Jeſus and his goſpel, the world in general would combine againſt them yea, even *their neareſt relations* would prove falſe and faithleſs, and become the bittereſt enemies, and breaking the ſtrongeſt ties of nature, perſecute them even to death They would be dragged before the rulers, civil and eccleſiaſtical, and puniſhed as heretical and ſeditious yea, even before the heathen kings and magiſtrates they would be accuſed, and called to ſeal the teſtimony they bore, with their blood But diſtreſſing as theſe things might appear, they have abundant reaſon to truſt and not be afraid Jeſus aſſures them he will ſtand by them When called to anſwer before the tribunals of the Mightieſt, they need not diſtreſs themſelves about what they ſhall ſay, a divine revelation ſhall be given to them, and they ſhall be directed in the propereſt manner to reply to every charge, yea, their very trial before the kings and rulers ſhall prove a teſtimony againſt them, they will thereby have an opportunity of preaching the goſpel to thoſe who might never elſe have heard it And whatever attempts are made to ſuppreſs and ſilence them, they ſhall prove abortive, Chriſt will cauſe his goſpel to be preached and ſpread, in defiance of oppoſition, into all lands, and either ſhelter them from the malice of their perſecutors, or reward their fidelity unto death with the crown of everlaſting life and glory conſiderations, ſufficient to make them welcome the croſs, whilſt ſuch a crown was in view *Note*, (1) Sufferings for Chriſt ſtumble many we need to take heed that we be not thereby offended (2) The image of Jeſus, as it muſt reprove the world, will ever procure the hatred of men againſt thoſe who poſſeſs it (3) The ſpirit of bigotry and enmity, which is in the natural heart, againſt Chriſt and his people, ſometimes breaks through the ſtrongeſt ties of blood, makes children rebellious, and parents unnatural, even to with the death of thoſe they are moſt bound to love and cheriſh (4) Wherever the goſpel is preached, if it be not received, it will at leaſt riſe up for a teſtimony againſt all who neglect or reject ſo great a ſalvation (4) When we are called to ſtand forth for Chriſt, we may ſtill confidently expect to be ſupported by him, and to be taught by his ſpirit how to ſpeak and act for his glory (5) All ſufferings, and even death itſelf, will be regarded as light afflictions that are but for a moment, by thoſe whoſe faith realizes to their minds, the far more exceeding and eternal weight of glory

14 ¶ [o] But when ye ſhall ſee the abomination of deſo-
lation, [p] ſpoken of by Daniel the prophet, ſtanding
where it ought not, ([q] let him that readeth, underſtand)
then let them that be in Judea [r] flee to the mountains
15 And let him that is on the houſe-top, not go down
into the houſe, neither enter therein, to take any thing
out of his houſe 16 And let him that is in the field,
not turn back again for to take up his garment 17
But [s] wo to them that are with child, and to them that
give ſuck in thoſe days 18 And pray ye that your
flight be not in the winter. 19 For [t] in thoſe days
ſhall be affliction, ſuch as was not from the beginning of
the creation which God created, unto this time, neither
ſhall be 20 And except that the Lord had ſhortned
thoſe days, no fleſh ſhould be ſaved but [u] for the elect's
ſake, whom he hath choſen, he hath ſhortned the days
21 And then [x] if any man ſhall ſay to you, Lo, here
is Chriſt, or lo, *he is* there believe *him* not 22 For
falſe Chriſts, and [y] falſe prophets ſhall riſe, and ſhall [z]
ſhew ſigns and wonders, to ſeduce, [a] if *it were* poſſible,
even the elect 23 But [b] take ye heed behold, I have
foretold you all things

v 14—23 Two things the diſciples are here taught,

1 To ſecure their lives by flight, when the Roman army, *the abomination of deſolation*, appears before Jeruſalem No moment muſt be loſt, no attempt made to ſave any thing, they muſt ſeek their ſafety in inſtant flight Thoſe who are heavy with child, or have babes at their breaſts, will be in that day moſt peculiarly miſerable, as leſs able to fly, or to bear the hardſhips which they muſt undergo, and if this flight were in winter, the inclemency of the ſeaſon would make the ſituation of the fugitives more deplorable, therefore they need pray that it may not be ſo But whenever the time comes, ſuch a ſcene of affliction, miſery, and deſolation, will appear, as never was from the creation before, and never will be again to the end of time They who read the hiſtory of Joſephus, may ſee this prophecy awfully fulfilled Indeed it is marvellous that any inhabitant of Judea ſurvived this dire cataſtrophe, nothing but the moſt gracious interpoſition of divine providence could have prevented their utter extirpation But God having ſtill a remnant among the Jewiſh people, and deſigns of grace towards ſome, who, in diſtant ages ſhould deſcend from them, for the ſake of theſe *his elect*, will ſhorten the days of affliction, and pluck ſome as brands from the burning *Note*, Many who abhor and perſecute God's people, know not how much they are indebted to them and their prayers

2 To take care of their ſouls Seducers will abound in thoſe evil days, and with large promiſes of procuring them relief from the impending calamities, will perſuade many to join them, giving themſelves out for the Meſſiah, or pretending to have found him, and with lying wonders and falſe miracles, will not only impoſe upon the credulous, but would, *if it were poſſible*, deceive the very elect Chriſt warns them, therefore, againſt impoſtures, which he ſo plainly foretels *Note*, It is a moſt comfortable conſideration, that in ſpite of Satan's wiles, and all the cunning craftineſs of men who lie in wait to deceive, God's choſen cannot be ſeduced They have an infallible teſt, his written word, to prove the ſpirits whether they are of God, and he will enlighten their minds, and lead them into all truth

24 ¶ [c] But in thoſe days, after that tribulation, [d] the
ſun ſhall be darkned, and the moon ſhall not give her
light 25 And the ſtars of heaven ſhall fall, and the
powers that *are* in heaven ſhall be ſhaken 26 And
[e] then ſhall they ſee the Son of man coming in the
clouds, with great power and [f] glory 27 And then
ſhall he ſend his angels, and ſhall gather together his
elect from the four winds, from the uttermoſt part of
the earth, to the uttermoſt part of heaven 28 [g] Now
learn a parable of the fig tree When her branch is yet
tender, and putteth forth leaves, ye know that ſummer
is near 29 So ye in like manner, when ye ſhall ſee
theſe things come to paſs, know that it is nigh, *even* at
the doors 30 Verily I ſay unto you, [h] that this gene-
ration ſhall not paſs, till all theſe things be done 31

[a] 1 Theſſ v 3 Eph v 6 Col ii 8 2 Theſſ ii 3
[d] Jer xiv 14 & xxiii 21 John v 43
[e] Ver 22 Acts v 36, 37 Rev
[f] Zech xiv
[h] Matt x 17 Or Chriſt birth pains Matt xxiv 8
[k] Matt x 18 John xv 20 & xvi 2 Rev ii 10 Acts xvi
[l] Rom x 18 Col i 6
[m] Matt x 17 Micah vii 6 Matt x 21
[n] Dan xii 12 Matt Rev ii 10
[o] Matt xxiv 15 Luke xxi 20
[p] Dan ix 27 & xii 11
[q] Dan ix 23
[r] Prov xxii 3
[s] Luke xxiii 29
[t] Dan xii 1 Joel ii 2
[u] Isa i 9 Zech
[x] Luke xvii 23
[y] Deut xiii
[z] 2 Theſſ ii 9, 10
[a] John x 28, 29 Rom viii
[b] 2 Tim iii 1 2 Pet iii 17
[c] Matt xxiv 29 Luke xxi 25
[d] Iſa xiii 10 Ezek xxxii 7 Joel ii 10, 31 Rev vi 12
[e] Dan vii 13 Chap xiv 62 Rev i 7
[f] Matt xvi 27
[g] Matt xxiv 32 1 Cor xv
[h] 1 Theſſ iv 16
[h] Matt xxiv 34 Luke xxi 32
[i] Matt xvi 28

k Isa. li. 6 [k] Heaven and earth shall pass away [l] but my words
2 Pet. iii. 7, 10 shall not pass away 32 ¶ But of that day and *that*
l Isa. xl. 8 hour knoweth no man, no not the angels which are in
Mat. v. 18 heaven, neither the Son, [m] but the Father 33 [n] Take
m John xiv. 7 Acts i. 7 ye heed, watch and pray for ye know not when the
n Mat. xxv. 13 1 Thes. v. 6 time is 34 *For the Son of man is* as a man taking a
far journey, who left his house, and gave authority to
his servants, and to every man his work, and command-
ed the porter to watch 35 [o] Watch ye therefore; (for
o 2 Pet. iii. 10 Rev. xvi. 15 ye know not when the master of the house cometh, at
even, or at midnight, or at the cock-crowing, or in the
morning) 36 Lest coming suddenly, he find you
sleeping 37 And what I say unto you, I say unto
all, Watch

v 24—37 The things here predicted primarily refer to the destruction of the Jewish people, but they seem also to have respect to the final appearing to judgment of our great God and Saviour Jesus Christ As his hand visibly appeared in the ruin of Jerusalem, the temple, and Jewish nation, and also in his separating his disciples, when the calamity came near, who fled to Pella, and escaped the Roman sword, so will he fulfil this prophecy in the approaching dissolution of all things, when he shall personally appear, coming in the clouds with power and great glory, to execute judgment on all impenitent sinners, and to gather his elect into his eternal kingdom Concerning these great events he warns them,

1 That the time of their fulfilment is near, and they might judge of their approach by the preceding signs, just as surely as they would of the summer's drawing nigh by the budding of the fig-tree Some of that generation would live to see the utter ruin of Judea and Jerusalem his prophetic word must infallibly take place, and heaven and earth sooner pass away, than one tittle of his predictions fail Near also, even at the door, is the great day of judgment The period of time, which yet remains, we know is short, how short, who can tell?

2 The time when is uncertain None in heaven or earth precisely knows the hour, not even the Son, as man, or in virtue of his designation to the mediatorial office; it is a secret locked up in God's eternal mind, and neither revealed to men nor angels We are left in this awful uncertainty, that we may be always ready.

3 He admonishes them, in the view of what he had spoken, to watch and pray, which he enforces by the following parable His appearing would be like that of a master, who took a long journey, committed to his stewards the management of his affairs, and directed the work in which he would have his servants employed during his absence, charging the porter to take especial care that no thief broke in, and that all should be ready to receive him at his return, which he left uncertain, that they might be in constant expectation of him, and prepared to welcome him Thus when Jesus ascended up on high, he left a charge with all his servants, whether ministers or private christians, to employ themselves diligently in the work he hath appointed them, and to be prepared to give an account of their fidelity He is coming again to make a solemn enquiry, the time when is uncertain, every hour we stand in jeopardy, not knowing whether by day or by night the calls of death or judgment may place us before him Our care therefore must be, above all things, that we are not surprized by him, slothful, negligent, and unprepared to meet him, though he come never so suddenly What, therefore, our Lord inculcates upon his disciples, we are alike bound to hear, for unto us it is alike addressed, *I say unto all, Watch* *Note*, Our great concern upon earth is to be ready for death and judgment; each breath we draw may be our last let us seize then the moment as it flies, and whilst the hour lasts, give all diligence, that we may be found of him in peace

CHAP XIV

In this chapter we have, 1 The plot of the chief priests and scribes against Christ, ver 1, 2 *2 The anointing of Christ's head at a supper in Bethany,* ver 3—9 *3 The contract Judas made with the chief priests to betray him,* ver 10, 11 *4 Christ's eating the passover with his disciples, his instituting the Lord's supper, and his discourse with his disciples at and after supper,* ver. 12—31 *5 Christ's agony in the garden,* ver 32—42 *6 The betraying of him by Judas, and the apprehending of him by the chief priest's agents,* ver 43—52 *7 His arraignment before the high priest, his conviction, and the indignities done him at that bar,* ver 53—65 *8 Peter's denying him,* ver 66—72 *Most of which passages we had before,* Matt xxvi

a Mat. xxvi. 2 Luke xxii. 1 1 AFTER two days was *the feast of* the passover,
and of unleavened bread and the chief priests
John xi. 17 and the scribes [b] sought how they might take him by
Acts iv. 20—28 craft, and put him to death. 2. But they said, Not
on the feast-*day*, [c] lest there be an uproar of the people c John xi. 40.
3 ¶ And being in Bethany, in the house of Simon the
leper, as he sat at meat, [d] there came a woman, having d Mat. xxvi. 7 Luke vii. 37 John xii. 3
an alabaster-box of ointment of † spikenard, very pre-
cious, and she brake the box, and poured it on his head † Or pure Nard
4 And there were some that had indignation within
themselves, and said, Why was this waste of the oint-
ment made? 5 For it might have been sold for more
than three hundred [e] pence, and have been given to e Mat. xviii. 8
the poor And they murmured against her 6 And
Jesus said, Let her alone, why trouble ye her? she hath
wrought a good work on me. 7 For [f] ye have the f Deu. xv. 11 John xii. 8
poor with you always, and whensoever ye will, [g] ye may
do them good but me ye have not always. 8 She g John xii. 33 & xiv. 19
hath done what she could. she is come aforehand to
anoint my body to the burying 9 Verily I say unto
you, Wheresoever this gospel shall be preached through
out the whole world, *this* also that she hath done, shall
be spoken of for a memorial of her 10 ¶ [h] And h Mat. xxvi. 14 Luke xxii. 4
Judas Iscariot, one of the twelve, went unto the chief
priests, to betray him unto them. 11 And when they
heard *it*, they were glad, and promised to give him
[i] money And he sought how he might conveniently i Zech. xi. 12. 1 Tim. vi. 10
betray him

v 1—11 The scene of our Saviour's sufferings now approaching, we have here the steps preparatory thereunto

1 The anointing him as he sat in the house of Simon the leper, so called, probably, as having been cured by Jesus of that nauseous disease *Note*, When the sin is forgiven, and the backslider restored, the reproach will still frequently abide. Whilst Jesus was at supper, a woman, supposed to be Mary Magdalene, or Lazarus' sister, came behind him, and poured upon his head a box of precious spikenard Some of the disciples, with Judas at their head, with indignation beheld what they esteemed such unnecessary waste, the value of the ointment amounting to above nine pounds, which they suggested might have been much more profitably employed in charitable uses, but Christ, who knew the secret murmurs they were afraid to utter, reproved their rash censures, and commended the deed as highly praise-worthy, it being intended as a burial unction, which, according to her power, willing to honour her Lord whilst alive, she thus anticipated, as she would not have an opportunity to do it for him after his death Their care indeed for the poor was commendable, but they being ever present, abundant occasions would offer to relieve them But as he was ready to depart, it was the only opportunity of shewing him respect which would be ever afforded her therefore to her honour shall this be mentioned, wherever in future days the gospel shall be preached, and this remarkable instance of her faith and love shall for ever accompany the narrative of his death and resurrection *Note*, (1) They who love the Lord Jesus Christ, never think they can do enough to testify their regard for him (2) They who honour him, whatever censures others may cast on them, he will honour

2 The scheme laid for his betrayal and ruin Determined upon his death, the chief priests and scribes consulted only on the means of effecting it with the least noise, and at first bethought them, that on the feast-day it would be dangerous to arrest him, for fear of the people but whilst they were in council, a most unexpected incident fixed their resolutions Judas, one of the twelve apostles, came and offered to betray his master The bargain was instantly struck, the money engaged for, and immediately he set himself to find the properest opportunity to put him into the hands of these his implacable enemies *Note*, (1) Where the love of filthy lucre reigns, whatever profession a man may make, there wants nothing but temptation to draw forth the apostacy of his heart (2) The devil often favours his servants with most unexpected success, in order to embolden and harden them in wickedness, and to bind them faster in his chains

12 ¶ [k] And [l] the first day of unleavened bread, k Mat. xxvi. 17 Luke xxii. 4
when they † killed the passover, his disciples said unto
him, Where wilt thou that we go and prepare, that l Exod. xii. 6
thou mayest eat the passover? 13 And he sendeth † Or sacrificed
forth two of his disciples, and saith unto them, Go ye
into the city, and there shall meet you a man bearing
a pitcher of water follow him. 14 And wheresoever
he shall go in, say ye to the good-man of the house,
The Master saith, Where is the guest chamber, where
I shall eat the passover with my disciples? 15 And he
will shew you a large upper room furnished and pre-
pared there make ready for us 16 And his disciples
went forth, and came into the city, and found as he
had said unto them and they made ready the passover

17 And in the evening he cometh with the twelve
18 And as they ſat and did eat, Jeſus ſaid, Verily I ſay
unto you, [m] One of you which eateth with me, ſhall be-
tray me 19 And they began to be ſorrowful, and to ſay
unto him one by one, Is it I? and another *ſaid*, Is it I?
20 And he anſwered and ſaid unto them, *It is* one of
the twelve, that dippeth with me in the diſh 21 The
Son of man indeed goeth, [n] as it is written of him but
wo to that man by whom the Son of man is betrayed
good were it for that man if he had never been born
22 ¶ And as they did eat, [o] Jeſus took bread, and bleſſed,
and brake *it*, and gave to them, and ſaid, Take eat, this
is my body 23 And he took the cup, and when he had
given thanks, he gave *it* to them and [p] they all drank
of it 24 And he ſaid unto them, This is my blood
of [r] the New Teſtament, which is ſhed [s] for many 25
Verily I ſay unto you, I will drink no more of the
fruit of the vine, [t] until that day that I drink it new
in the kingdom of God 26 ¶ And when they had
ſung an ‡ hymn, they went out into the mount of
Olives 27 [u] And Jeſus ſaith unto them, All ye ſhall
be [x] offended becauſe of me this night for it is writ-
ten, [y] I will ſmite the ſhepherd, and the ſheep ſhall be
ſcattered 28 But after that I am riſen, [z] I will go be-
fore you into Galilee 29 But Peter ſaid unto him,
[a] Although all ſhall be offended, yet *will* not I 30
And Jeſus ſaith unto him, [b] Verily I ſay unto thee,
that this day, *even* in this night before the cock crow
twice, thou ſhalt deny me thrice 31 But he ſpake
the more vehemently, If I ſhould die with thee, I will
not deny thee in any wiſe Likewiſe alſo ſaid they all

m Pſ xl 9 John xiii 21 &c
n Pſ xxii Iſa liii &c Dan ix 26.
o Mat xxvi 26. Luke xxii 19. 1 Cor xi 23
p 1 Cor x 4
r Jer xxxi 31
s Mat. xx 28 Rom v 15
t Acts x 41
‡ Or pſalm Some think pſalms cxiii—cxviii
u Mat. xxvi 31 &c
x Mat xi 6
y Zech xiii 7 John xvi 32
z Chap xvi 7
a 2 Kings viii 13
b John xiii 38 1 Cor x 12.

v 12—31 We have here,

1 Chriſt's celebration of the paſſover with his diſciples By his orders, two of them had been ſent with particular directions where to prepare it, and having accordingly found the perſon with the pitcher of water, and followed him home, they were ſhewn by the maſter of the houſe a furniſhed room, where they prepared the ſupper, and in the evening Jeſus came with the reſt of the diſciples, and ſat down to eat the paſchal Lamb *Note*, (1) When we have our Lord's orders, we muſt go forth depending on his providence, even when we know not whither we go (2) The pureſt communions will not be without falſe brethren this ſide heaven; of twelve apoſtles, one was a traitor

2 At the table he ſtartled his diſciples with an information the moſt alarming, that one of them, who now appeared ſo friendly, would prove a traitor, and betray him into the hands of his enemies Exceedingly grieved at ſuch an aſſurance, each unwilling to ſuſpect another, and unconſcious of ſuch deſign, Judas excepted, began to ſay, *Lord, is it I?* I dread the thought of ſuch villainy, and wiſh not a moment to lie under the ſuſpicion of it In anſwer to their queſtion, Chriſt points out the traitor, by directing them to one of the twelve then dipping in the diſh with him, adding a moſt fearful commination againſt him, *v* 21 if any thing at laſt might touch that hardned traitor's conſcience *Note*, (1) A zealous ſoul is grieved but to be ſuſpected of unfaithfulneſs (2) We cannot be too jealous over ourſelves A ſincere diſciple wiſhes others to ſearch him, and prays the Lord each day to try the ground of his heart, and ſhew him if there be any hidden iniquity there, that it may be repented of and renounced (3) Not one jot or tittle of God's word can fail, and all his decrees infallibly have their accompliſhment, even wicked men, when moſt invenomed againſt him, are nevertheleſs made ſubſervient to his purpoſes, though this neither extenuates their guilt, nor will at all mitigate their puniſhment

3 At the cloſe of the paſchal ſupper, our Lord inſtituted that ordinance, which in his church ſhould ſuperſede, and ſupply the place of this ſolemn feaſt Having taken bread, he bleſſed it, brake, and gave to each of them, to be eaten in remembrance of his broken body, which ſhould procure for them a more glorious redemption than in the paſſover they commemorated, a redemption from ſin, and death, and hell Then taking the cup in like manner, after his ſolemn benediction, he bid them all drink of it, as they did, and this he explains as his *blood of the New Teſtament*; by the ſhedding of which, all the promiſes of the covenant of grace would be confirmed to them, and to as many as in faith received theſe inſtituted ſeals of that covenant And hereupon our Lord takes his farewell of them, till the day came when they ſhould ſit down with him in glory, and drink the new wine in the kingdom of God, partaking of the joys at his right hand for evermore Then cloſing the ſolemnity with an hymn, they departed for the mount of Olives

4 In the way to the retirement whither Jeſus went, he took occaſion to warn his diſciples of their approaching deſertion of him, which the ſcripture had foretold, and they were about to fulfil that very night But to encourage them to return to him again, he lets them know, though he ſhould be ſmitten, and they ſcattered from him, yet after his reſurrection, they ſhould again ſee him to their comfort in Galilee Peter, ſhocked at the thought, *confident in himſelf*, and *with warmth* reſenting the ſuſpicion, ſolemnly engages, though every one of his brethren, like Judas, ſhould deſert his maſter, he never would And, notwithſtanding the repeated warnings our Lord gives him, that he would not only forſake, but deny him before the morning returned, more reſolute and peremptory than before, Peter with vehemence inſiſts he will die with him, ſooner than deny him And all the reſt, unwilling to be outdone in aſſurances of fidelity, declared this alſo to be their determined reſolution *Note*, (1) We know not our own hearts, when we confidently boaſt what we will do The firſt temptation will prove our weakneſs (2) Many are diſcouraged from the Lord's table, for fear of falling afterwards, as if every ſubſequent ſin was mortal, but though no doubt we are called to uſe peculiar watchfulneſs, we muſt not think, if we fall, the door of grace is ſhut The diſciples, immediately after the ſacrament, fell, and foully too; and yet the Lord recalled and *recovered* them Let us not then deſpair

32 [c] And they came to a place which was named
Gethſemane and he ſaith to his diſciples, *Sit ye here*,
while I ſhall pray 33 And he taketh with him Peter,
and James, and John, and began to be ſore amazed,
and to be very heavy, 34 And ſaith unto them, [d] My
ſoul is exceeding ſorrowful unto death tarry ye here,
and watch 35 And he went forward a little, and fell
on the ground, and [e] prayed, that if it were poſſible
the hour might paſs from him 36 And he ſaid,
[f] Abba, Father, all things *are* poſſible unto thee, take
away [g] this cup from me neverthelеſs, [h] not what I will,
but what thou wilt. 37 And he cometh and findeth
them [i] ſleeping, and ſaith unto Peter, Simon, ſleepeſt
thou? couldeſt not thou watch one hour? 38 [k] Watch
ye, and pray, leſt ye enter into temptation the ſpirit
truly *is* ready, [l] but the fleſh *is* weak 39 And [m] again
he went away and prayed, and ſpake the ſame words
40 And when he returned, he found them aſleep again
(for [n] their eyes were heavy) neither wiſt they what to an-
ſwer him 41 And he *cometh the third time*, and ſaith
unto them, Sleep on now, and take your reſt it is
enough, the hour is come; behold, the Son of man is
betrayed into the hands of ſinners 42 Ariſe up, let us
go, lo, he that betrayeth me is at hand

c Mat xxvi 36 Luke xxii 39 John xviii 1
d Pſ xxii 14 & cxvi 3 John xii 27
e Heb v 7.
f Rom viii. 15 Gal iv 6
g Mat xx 22
h John vi. 38
i Mat xxv. 5 Ver 34.
k Chap xiii. 33 Eph vi. 18
l Pſ lxxviii. 39 Rom vii 22 Gal. v 17
m Luke xviii. 1 2 Cor xii 8
n Cant v 2.

v 32—42 We have before us the amazing ſcene of the Redeemer's agony in the garden Gethſemane Having left eight of his diſciples at a greater diſtance, he took three of them to be nearer ſpectators of his ſufferings

1 His anguiſh was unutterable Amazement and horror ſeized his ſoul, and a ſenſe of the divine wrath oppreſſed his conſcience with its intolerable load Sorrows, like the agonies of death, compaſſed him about, and pains, like thoſe the damned feel, gat hold upon him He acquaints his three diſciples with ſomething of what he endured, which words were too feeble to expreſs, and bids them tarry there, and watch with him, in this hour of temptation We may here, as in a glaſs, obſerve, (1) The dreadful evil of ſin, and every pang the Redeemer feels ſhould be a dagger to our hearts, begetting deepeſt ſelf-abhorrence and moſt unfeigned grief for thoſe abominations, which nothing but theſe ſufferings of the Son of God could expiate (2) The ſure foundation of our faith The Lord hath laid on him the iniquities of us all theſe agonizing pains are the ranſom he pays to ſatisfy the juſtice of an offended God, and having accepted one for all, there is no more condemnation to thoſe that are in Chriſt Jeſus (3) The inexpreſſibly tranſcendent love of our Lord and Saviour, willingly reſigning himſelf thus for our ſakes what returns, then, do we not owe him? (4) The comfort procured for us under our affliction and dejection Whatever we ſuffer, Jeſus hath drank deeper of the bitter cup, and having been thus tempted himſelf, can tenderly feel for us, and will ſuccour us under our ſorrows, and bring us happily to the end of them

2 His prayer was humble, fervent, importunate, ſubmiſſive As *man*, he could not but wiſh the bitter cup might remove, as *mediator*, he bowed ſubmiſſive to his Father's will, content, whatever muſt be endured, to finiſh the work which God had given him to do Thrice he renews the ſame requeſt, and thrice reſigns himſelf to ſuffer whatever might be for the glory of the divine Juſtice to inflict *Note*, (1) We are not forbid to mourn and pray for the removal of our burdens, even when moſt reſigned to ſuffer God's holy will (2) Though our troubles are not ſoon removed, we muſt not be weary in wait-

ing

ing upon God In his time they ſhall end, and we ſhall finally receive the anſwer of peace, if we faint not, either deliverance from our trials, or ſtrength to endure them

3 On coming to his diſciples, he finds them aſleep, and therefore rouſes them with a juſt and ſharp rebuke, eſpecially addreſſed to Simon, who had lately appeared ſo zealous, and promiſed ſuch diſtinguiſhed fidelity How ſhameful that they could not watch one hour with their agonizing maſter! or if not for his ſake, at leaſt for their own, when it was ſo needful for them to watch and pray, ſuch temptation being ready to overtake them, as nothing but almighty grace could enable them to bear but whilſt he thus upbraids and warns, the tender Saviour pities them, and kindly ſeeks to excuſe what he muſt condemn Their ſpirit was willing, he knew their hearts, but the fleſh was weak to withſtand the effects of wearineſs and the oppreſſions of grief and the infirmities incident to this feeble frame, diſabled them from doing what they deſired A ſecond time he goes to pour out his ſorrows before God, again he returns, and they are aſleep, and when awaked, unable to anſwer his juſt rebuke, after having received ſuch repeated admonition The third time he retires to redouble his cries, yet finds them on his return ſleeping ſtill Now therefore he bids them *ſleep on*, if they dared any longer, or rather, *will ye ſleep yet?* when danger was now at the door, he calls them, therefore, to go with him, to meet his betrayer *Note*, (1) Slothfulneſs in prayer is uſually the forerunner of ſad falls (2) Jeſus, by his word and providences, is repeatedly knocking at our ſtupid hearts, to awaken our attention, and rouſe us to watchfulneſs and prayer (3) Thoſe who have made the ſtrongeſt profeſſions are peculiarly criminal if they act unſuitably (4) It is well for us we have a compaſſionate high prieſt who can be touched with the feeling of our infirmities, and ſees that the ſpirit of his people is willing, even when through the frailty of our nature we cannot always ſtand upright (5) They who do not watch and pray when danger threatens, will be unprepared to meet it, and ſink under the temptation

o Mat. xxvi 47 Luke xxii 47 John xviii 3 p Acts i 16 q Pſ iii 1
43 ¶ o And immediately, while he yet ſpake, p cometh
Judas, one of the twelve, and with him q a great mul-
titude with ſwords and ſtaves, from the chief prieſts,
and the ſcribes, and the elders 44 And he that be-
trayed him, had given them a token, ſaying, Whom-
ſoever I ſhall kiſs, that ſame is he, take him, and lead
him away ſafely 45 And as ſoon as he was come, he
goeth ſtraightway to him, and ſaith, Maſter, maſter,
r 2 Sam xx 9 s Lam iv 20 Acts ii 23 t Rom xii 19
and r kiſſed him 46 ¶ And s they laid their hands on
him, and took him 47 And one of them that ſtood
by, t drew a ſword, and ſmote a ſervant of the high
prieſt, and cut off his ear 48 And Jeſus anſwered and
ſaid unto them, Are ye come out as againſt a thief,
with ſwords and *with* ſtaves, to take me? 49 I was
daily with you in the temple, teaching, and ye took me
v Pſ xxii 1– 18 Iſai 7 Dan ix 26 Acts xxvi 23 x Joh xix 13 Ver
not but v the ſcriptures muſt be fulfilled 50 And x
they all forſook him and fled 51 And there followed
him a certain young man, having a linen cloth caſt a-
bout his naked body, and the young men laid hold on
him 52 And he left the linen cloth, and fled from
them naked

v 43—52 His internal ſufferings in the garden being ended, his external ſufferings begin, ſo ſtill doth billow roll on billow, till all the ſtorms of wrath are gone over him

1 He is apprehended by a band of men ſent from the chief prieſts, ſcribes, and elders, under the conduct of Judas the traitor, who, as it was night, that they might not miſtake the perſon of Jeſus, gave them this ſignal, that they might know him, by his going up and kiſſing him And hereupon, with great pretended reſpect, approaching Chriſt, he kiſſed him, and they who were at his heels laid hands upon him *Note*, (1) Apoſtates ever prove the blackeſt inſtruments of hell, and no height of office, or profeſſion, is ſafe from temptation We need not ſtumble at the falls of the greateſt apparent chriſtians, when we ſee an apoſtle a traitor and a devil (2) The blackeſt ſchemes of villainy are often crowned with ſucceſs, and the wicked triumph awhile, but their time is ſhort

2 Peter, ever violent, no ſooner ſaw his maſter apprehended, than he attempted a reſcue, and drawing his ſword, ſtruck at one of the men who had ſeized Jeſus, and cut off his ear his intention was good, but his zeal intemperate *Note*, (1) Many have more zeal than prudence, and their good intentions are no excuſe for their raſhneſs (2) In times of perſecution, it is much eaſier to draw the ſword and fight, than patiently to bow down and meekly ſuffer

3 Chriſt expoſtulates with his enemies on this clandeſtine manner of apprehending him, as if he had been ſome infamous villain and murderer that needed to be ſeized, and overpowered with arms and numbers, when they knew he had every day appeared in the temple, where they might eaſily have taken him, but the ſcriptures muſt be fulfilled that ſpoke of his betrayal and ſufferings, and the flight of his diſciples for they no ſooner ſaw him ſubmit quietly to be bound, than they all forſook him and fled, glad every one to ſhift for himſelf, leaſt they alſo ſhould be apprehended *Note*, (1) The moſt innocent men are often proceeded againſt, as if they were the vileſt of mankind, and ſuch apprehenſions ſtudiouſly raiſed againſt them, to cloak the malice of their perſecutors (2) The fulfilment of the ſcriptures ſhould be a great comfort to us under all our ſufferings for Chriſt's ſake thus, we ſee, it muſt be (3) We need not think it ſtrange, if in times when we moſt need ſuch ſupport, our deareſt friends abandon us, through fear of being involved in our troubles In theſe ſeaſons we ſhould remember Jeſus in the garden

4 A young man near the garden, probably diſturbed by the noiſe, ſtarted up from his bed, and ran down with only a ſheet about him, or ſome linen garment, to enquire into the cauſe, and followed the crowd a little way Being obſerved by one of the ſoldiers, and perhaps ſuſpected for a diſciple, they attempted to lay hold of him, but with the loſs of his garment, he got looſe, and fled naked This incident ſeems to be related to ſhew the inveteracy of theſe enemies of Jeſus, none that looked like his diſciples might expect to meet any quarter with them

y Mat xxvi 57 Luke xxii 54 John xviii 13 z Pſ xxii 16
53 ¶ And y they led Jeſus away to the high prieſt
and z with him were aſſembled all the chief prieſts, and
the elders and the ſcribes. 54 And Peter followed him
afar off, even into the palace of the high prieſt and he
ſat with the ſervants, and warmed himſelf at the fire
55 And the chief prieſts, and all the counſel ſought for
witneſs againſt Jeſus to put him to death, and found
a Pſ xxvii 12 & xxxv 11
none 56 For a many bare falſe witneſs againſt him,
but their witneſs agreed not together 57 And there
arose certain, and bare falſe witneſs againſt him, ſaying,
b Ch xv 29 John ii 19
58 We heard him ſay, b I will deſtroy this temple that
is made with hands, and within three days I will build
another made without hands 59 But neither ſo did
their witneſs agree together 60 And the high prieſt
ſtood up in the midſt, and aſked Jeſus, ſaying, Anſwer-
eſt thou nothing? what is it which theſe witneſs againſt
c Pſ xxxviii 13 Iſa liii 7
thee? 61 But c he held his peace, and anſwered no-
thing Again the high prieſt d aſked him, and ſaid un-
to him, Art thou the Chriſt, the Son of the Bleſſed?
d Mat xxvi 63
62 And Jeſus ſaid, I am and e ye ſhall ſee the Son of
e Dan vii 13 f Mat xxiv 30
man ſitting on the right hand of power, and f coming
in the clouds of heaven 63 Then the high prieſt
rent his clothes, and ſaith, What need we any further
witneſſes? 64 Ye have heard the blaſphemy what
think ye? And they all condemned him g to be guilty
of death 65 And ſome began to h ſpit on him, and to
cover his face, and to buffet him, and to ſay unto him,
Propheſy and the ſervants i did ſtrike him with the
palms of their hands

v 53—65 Our bleſſed Lord, after being dragged through the ſtreets, as a criminal, is here carried before the high-prieſt and Sanhedrim, in order that ſome matter of accuſation might be found whereon to ground his condemnation and Peter, now a little recovered from his fright, and prompted by ſtrong curioſity to ſee the end, at a diſtance followed the band, and having got admiſſion into the palace, ſat and warmed himſelf with the ſervants at the fire, preſuming in ſuch company none would take him for a diſciple We are here informed,

1 What pains were taken to ſuborn falſe witneſſes, in order to have a pretence for putting Jeſus to death this being their bloody reſolution, and the proceſs a mere vail to cover the murder But though many, to pleaſe the prieſts, witneſſed againſt him, and ſome perverting the words which he had ſpoken of the temple of his body ſome years before, and applying them to the temple of Jeruſalem, would have repreſented him as an enemy to their worſhip and religion, yet all the charges they could muſter up amounted to nothing capital, whilſt the moſt glaring contradictions appeared in their evidence

2 Unable to condemn him upon the evidence of others, the high-prieſt ſeeks to extort from himſelf ſomething more material Finding him ſilent under all theſe frivolous and falſe accuſations, and not to be prevailed upon to reply ought to their charges, he roſe with vehemence, and ſolemnly adjured him to ſay directly, whether he really was, as he pretended, the Meſſiah, the Son of the bleſſed God? Then Jeſus, undiſmayed, with dignity becoming his office, aſſerted his divine miſſion and character, with an awful warning to them who now thus deſpiſed and ſet him at nought, that the time would come when they ſhould tremble at his preſence, and behold him executing his temporal judgments on their place and nation, and yet more fearfully meet him at the great day, when they muſt ſtand at his tribunal, and periſh eternally Pretending much aſtoniſhment

what he termed blasphemy, the high-priest rent his cloaths, exclaimed against the need of further evidence, and, branding him as a blasphemer, appealed to the rest for their opinion, who, following such a wicked example, unanimously condemned him to death. *Note*, (1) We may not be staggered if we see the most reverend, aged, wise, and noble, conspiring against the cause of Jesus, and persecuting his people. By such was Jesus himself condemned. (2) The silence of our Redeemer under every accusation should teach us patience when we are thus reviled, committing our cause to him that judgeth righteously. (3) It is easy to brand those as blasphemers who in the highest, desire to give glory to God. The best men have often been dressed up in the most shocking colours, and blackened with the most opprobrious names, in order to make the persecution of them appear necessary and laudable.

3. No sooner was judgment given against him, than they began to insult him with the most grievous indignities. They spit upon him, blindfolded him, buffeted him, struck him on the face, and in derision bid him exercise his prophetical office, by telling who smote him. Thus did not he hide his face from shame and spitting, that we might be enabled without shame to stand before the tribunal of God.

k Matt. xxvi. 69. Luke xxii. 55. John xviii. 16.
66 ¶ k And as Peter was beneath in the palace,
there cometh one of the maids of the high priest. 67
And when she saw Peter warming himself, she looked
upon him, and said, And thou also wast with Jesus of
l Matt. xxvi. 70. Nazareth. 68 l But he denied, saying, I know not,
neither understand I what thou sayest. And he went
out into the porch; and the cock crew. 69 And a
maid saw him again, and began to say to them that stood
by, This is *one* of them. 70 And he denied it again.
And a little after, they that stood by said again to Peter,
Surely thou art *one* of them: for thou art a Galilean,
m Matt. xxvi. 74. and thy speech agreeth *thereto*. 71 But m he began to
curse and to swear, *saying*, I know not this man of
whom ye speak. 72 And the second time the cock
n ver. 30. crew. And Peter called to mind n the word that Jesus
said unto him, Before the cock crow twice, thou shalt
† Or, he covered his head, he wept. Zech. xii. 10. Matt. xxvi. 75. 2 Cor. vii. 11.
deny me thrice. And † when he thought thereon,
he wept.

v. 66—72. Peter's fall had been foretold, and we here see the prediction fully verified.

1. He had rushed needlessly into temptation, and thrust himself into the midst of bad company, and then no marvel he fell. He was first ashamed of Christ, and that was but one step from denying him. *Note*, They who are not to be found among the disciples of Jesus because it is reproachful, and associate with the world in order to gain estimation, and to be thought well of, will pierce themselves through with many sorrows.

2. On the slightest trial Peter repeatedly denied and disowned his Master, and from words descended to oaths, seeking perfidy and lies with foulest perjury. Lord, what is man, when left to himself! A servant-maid confounded the chief of the apostles, when trusting for a moment to the strength of his own resolution. Peter's mouth hardly knew how to pronounce an oath, and would before have shuddered at the thought; but, when once he had first opened the door, profaneness and perjury easily entered. When once we turn aside from the path of truth never so little, none know to what dreadful lengths they may be hurried. Complicated crimes wounded the apostle's conscience, denial of his Master, falsehood before God, repeated lies, horrid profaneness, and wilful perjury. Yet even this is of use. Many a poor sinner might have despaired, if he had not seen such examples, and read in their pardon and recovery the possibility of his own.

3. When he was sunk into the lowest depth of sin, then was the time for the almighty, sovereign, saving grace of Jesus to appear. Once had the cock crowed, after his first denial of his Master, and that warning had passed unnoticed; for, till God soften the heart, all alarms of providence or the word are disregarded. The second time after his repeated crimes this herald of God reminds him of his Master's words, and his dire fulfilment of them. And now in full view his horrid guilt stared him in the face; every reflection shocked him, and, unable to bear the place, he retired to pour out in tears his bitter anguish. Some render the words, *covering his face* as a mourner, *he wept* bitterly, with penitential sorrow returning to a pardoning God. And it stands upon record, for the comfort of the chief of sinners, that he found mercy with him.

CHAP. XV.

Here we have, 1. Christ arraigned and accused before Pilate the Roman governor, ver. 1—5. *2. Cried out against by the common people at the instigation of the priests, ver.* 6—14. *3. Condemned to be crucified* [illegible] *ver.* 15. *4. Abused in a* [illegible]

mock-king by the Roman soldiers, ver. 16—19. *5. Led out to the place of execution with all possible ignominy and disgrace, ver.* 20—22. *6. Nailed to the cross between two thieves, ver.* 23—28. *7. Reviled and abused by all that passed by, ver.* 29—32. *8. Forsaken for a time by his Father, ver.* 33—36. *9. Dying and rending the vail, ver.* 37, 38. *10. Attested and witnessed to be the Christ by the centurion and others, ver.* 39, 40, 41. *11. Buried in the sepulchre of Joseph of Arimathea, ver.* 42—47.

1 AND a straightway in the morning the chief a Matt. xxvii. 1. Luke xxii. 66.
priests b held a consultation with the elders and b John xviii. 28.
scribes, and the whole council, and bound Jesus, and Acts iv. 26.
carried *him* away, and delivered *him* to Pilate. 2 And c Luke xxiii. 3.
Pilate asked him, Art thou the King of the Jews? And d 1 Tim. vi. 13.
he answering said unto him, d Thou sayest *it*. 3 And
the chief priests e accused him of many things: but e he e Matt. xxvii. 12.
answered nothing. 4 And Pilate asked him again,
saying, Answerest thou nothing? behold how many
things they witness against thee. 5 But Jesus yet answered
nothing, so that Pilate marvelled. 6 Now at
that feast he released unto them one prisoner, whomsoever
they desired. 7 And there was *one* named f Barabbas, f John xviii. 40.
which lay bound with them that had made insurrection
with him, who had committed murder in the insurrection.
8 And the multitude crying aloud, began to
desire *him to do* as he had ever done unto them. 9 But
Pilate answered them, saying, Will ye that I release
unto you the King of the Jews? 10 (For he knew g Acts viii. 9.
that the chief priests had delivered him g for envy.) h Acts iii. 14.
11 But h the chief priests moved the people, that he
should rather release Barabbas unto them. 12 And
Pilate answered, and said again unto them, What will
ye then that I shall do *unto him* whom ye call the
King of the Jews? 13 And they cried out again,
Crucify him. 14 Then Pilate said unto them, Why,
what evil hath he done? And they cried out the more
exceedingly, Crucify him.

v. 1—14. Unwearied in wickedness, we see those who had great part of the night sat up to seize and condemn the Lord Jesus, early in the morning again in consultation how to get their sentence confirmed by the Roman governor, and executed. Let it shame our slothfulness, that they should be carried farther by enmity against Christ, than we by zeal to serve him.

1. They bound and led him prisoner to Pilate's tribunal. Our mighty Sampson might indeed easily have snapped these cords asunder; but, faster bound with bands of love to our sinful souls, he quietly submitted to be led as a lamb to the slaughter.

2. Before Pilate our Lord witnessed the good confession. In answer to his interrogatories, he confessed, and denied not, that he was the Christ, the King of his spiritual Israel; but to the clamorous charges of the priests, his invenomed persecutors, he observed a profound silence; nor, when urged to answer by Pilate, deigned to make the least reply. He despised their malice; he was prepared to suffer; he desired not to be delivered; and he knew it in vain to remonstrate with those who wilfully and obstinately rejected the truth; and therefore, to Pilate's admiration, he still held his peace. *Note*, (1.) Christ is a king, and they who refuse to bow as willing subjects to his government, will find him able to punish the rebels that will not have him to reign over them. (2.) We need not marvel if false brethren are our bitterest accusers. Read the scriptures, and from the beginning it will be seen, that wicked, worldly, and sensual priests are ever the most invenomed enemies to the cause of truth. (3.) Silence is the best answer to false and scurrilous invective.

3. Pilate, convinced of the innocence of Jesus, greatly desired to deliver him from his enemies, as he plainly saw, that the envy of the priests was alone the cause of this malicious prosecution; and as it was an established custom at the passover, to gratify the people by the release of any prisoner they desired, he bethought him of an expedient which he imagined could scarce fail of success. There was a most infamous miscreant then in prison for murder and insurrection, and he doubted not, but if he proposed to the people these two, Jesus and Barabbas, they would infallibly prefer the former. The supposition was reasonable, but he was disappointed in the issue. *Note*, (1.) When people think to extricate themselves from their difficulties by indirect means, because if they act openly and honestly it may expose them to censure, they often but farther involve themselves. (2.) Whatever many pretend as the specious pleas for reviling the zealous ministers of truth, it is envy that instigates their enmity; they cannot bear the reproof of their lives and doctrine.

4. Swayed by the malignant insinuations of the priests and elders, who, forgetting their dignity, mingled with the crowd, the people rejected Jesus, and demanded Barabbas. Pilate, amazed, laboured still to get Jesus off, and proposed the question

tion to them, what he ſhould do with that poor man, who was called the King of the Jews, and more to be pitied than feared They cried out all together, *Crucify him, crucify him* In vain the governor attempted to expoſtulate on the injuſtice, the cruelty *of ſuch a puniſhment, where a man* had been proved guilty of no crime, they only grew more outrageous and clamorous, and tumultuouſly demanded an inſtant compliance with their requeſt *Note*, We muſt not judge of the juſtice of a caſe by the clamours of the populace the voice of truth is *often ſilenced amidſt the louder cries of prejudice*

i Mat xxvii 26 John xix 1 — 15 ¶ [i] And *ſo* Pilate willing to content the people,
releaſed Barabbas unto them, and delivered Jeſus, when
he had ſcourged *him*, to be crucified 16 And the ſol-
diers led him away into the hall, called Pretorium, and
they call together the whole band 17 And they
k Luke xxiii 11 — [k] cloathed *him* with purple, and platted a crown of
thorns, and put it about his *head*, 18 And began to
ſalute him, Hail, king of the Jews 19 And they ſmote
l Iſa l 6 Chap xiv 65 — him on the head with a reed, and did [l] ſpit upon him,
and bowing *their* knees, worſhipped him 20 And
when they had mocked him, they took off the purple
m Chap xii 8 Heb xiii 12 — from him, and put his own clothes on him, and [m] led
him out to crucify him 21 [n] And they compel one
n Mat xxvii 32 Luke xxiii 26 — Simon a Cyrenian, who paſſed by, coming out of the
country, the father of Alexander and Rufus, *to* bear
his croſs

v 15—21 The importunity and clamour of the people overcame the convictions of Pilate's conſcience To content them, *he releaſed Barabbas, pronounced ſentence of crucifixion on* Jeſus, and delivered him up for execution, having before ſcourged him, in hopes of moving their compaſſion But,

1 The ſoldiers, in order more bitterly to inſult him, dragged him to the hall called *Pretorium*, and gathering their whole company, *in deriſion of the pretenſions of Jeſus*, arrayed him as a king in a purple robe, placed a crown of thorns upon his head, and, ridiculing his mock-dignity, wiſhed all happineſs to the King of the Jews, ſtriking him on the head with the cane which they had put into his hand, to make the thorns on his head pierce the deeper, ſpitting upon him in contempt, whilſt they fell on their knees pretending to pay him homage Thus, becauſe ſinful man had affected to be like God, he who came to bear the puniſhment of our pride, muſt ſubmit to the baſeſt indignities to expiate our guilt With wonder and love then let us behold the man, aſtoniſhed at his humiliation, and bowing with no fictitious homage, but with deepeſt reverence before him, as our incarnate God and King

2 When they were tired of this inhuman ſport, they diſarrayed him of the purple robe, put on his own garment, and led him away to the place of execution, bearing his croſs But being unable to ſupport the load, leſt he ſhould die by the way, and diſappoint their cruelty, they took it off from him, and ſeizing one who paſſed by, perhaps known to be a diſciple, the father of Alexander and Rufus, men afterwards of note among the faithful, they compelled him to carry the croſs after Jeſus to Calvary *Note*, (1) Unexpected croſſes often come upon us, it is well to be habitually prepared for them (2) However ignominiouſly *we may be treated now for Chriſt's ſake*, it ſhall hereafter redound to our everlaſting honour

o Mat xxvii 33 Luke xxiii 33 John xix 17 — 22 [o] And they bring him unto the place Golgotha,
which is, being interpreted, the place of a ſcull 23
p Pſ lxix 21 — And [p] they gave him to drink wine mingled with myrrh
but he received *it* not 24 And when they had cruci-
q Pſ xxii 18 John xix 23 — fied him, [q] they parted his garments, caſting lots upon
them, what every man ſhould take 25 And it was
the third hour, and they crucified him 26 And the
ſuperſcription of his accuſation was written over, THE
KING OF THE JEWS 27 And with him they
crucified two thieves; the one on his right hand, and
the other on his left 28 And the ſcripture was ful-
r Iſa liii 12 — filled, which ſaith, [r] And he was numbred with the
tranſgreſſors 29 And they that paſſed by, railed on
s Pſ xxii 7 & cix 25 — him, wagging their heads, and ſaying, Ah, [t] thou that
t John ii 19 Chap xiv 58 — deſtroyeſt the temple, and buildeſt *it* in three days, 30
Save thyſelf, and come down from the croſs. 31 Like-
wiſe alſo the chief prieſts mocking, ſaid among them-
ſelves, with the ſcribes, He ſaved others, himſelf he can-
not ſave 32 Let Chriſt the King of Iſrael deſcend now
from the croſs, that we may ſee, and believe. And
u Luke xxiii 39 &c — [u] they that were crucified with him, reviled him

v 22—32 We are here led to the loweſt ſtep of the Saviour's humiliation, his obedience to death, even the death of the croſs

1 They crucified him about nine o'clock on mount Golgotha, a puniſhment and death the moſt painful, ignominious, and accurſed The hands and feet torn with the nails, excited the moſt excruciating pain, the whole body hanging on the wounds, the bones diſlocated, the blood ſtreaming down, and, lingering in agonies inexpreſſible, he felt all the horrors of death in its moſt tremendous form None but the vileſt miſcreants and *ſlaves were thus puniſhed*, and *God in his law had* branded the death upon a tree with his curſe, *Deut* xxi 23 He who ſtood in the room of ſinners, of the chief of ſinners, therefore ſubmitted to bear their ſins in his own body on the tree, to endure all the ſhame, the pain, the curſe, which they *had deſerved, and thus to take away ſin by the ſacrifice of* himſelf

2 On the tree he continued to endure every freſh inſult and cruelty which malice could deviſe [1] Inſtead of the intoxicating draught uſually given to criminals, he was offered ſour wine, mixed with bitter ingredients, which *he refuſed* to drink [2] Whilſt he hung in agonies, the four ſoldiers more immediately his executioners, ſported themſelves with dividing his clothes as their fee, and caſting lots for their ſeveral ſhares [3] The ſuperſcription over his croſs, though it faſtened no crime *upon him, was an inſult on his pretenſions* [4] Two thieves were crucified with him, one on each ſide, that he might not only appear numbered with the tranſgreſſors, but branded as the vileſt of the vile Thus undeſignedly they fulfilled the ſcriptures concerning him, *Iſa* liii 12 [5] Every paſſenger with bittereſt ſarcaſms caſt in his teeth what they regarded as his arrogant boaſts, *v* 29 wagging their heads in ſcorn, and bidding him prove the miſſion which he challenged by coming down *from the croſs* The *chief prieſts and ſcribes* alſo, who came to glut their vengeance with this ſpectacle, and to ſee the execution performed with every circumſtance of ignominy and cruelty, now triumphed over him, deriding his pretenſions as a Saviour to others, who was ſo little able to ſave himſelf, inſultingly *demanding now that he would ſhew himſelf* the *Meſſiah*, the King of Iſrael, and promiſing to believe on him, if he can give an inſtance of the power he aſſumed, by unfaſtening himſelf from the tree, and coming down before them all Nay, even the very thieves who hung by his ſide, vented their rage and reviling againſt him, *ſo hardened even in the jaws of death* Whilſt with horror and amaze at ſuch wickedneſs we read and tremble, let us fear that we do not repeat theſe crimes we ſo condemn, by our ſins crucifying the Son of God afreſh, and putting him to open ſhame

33 And [x] when the ſixth hour was come, there was — x Mat xxvii 45 Luke xxiii 44
darkneſs over the whole † land, until the ninth hour — † Gr earth.
34 And at the ninth hour Jeſus cried with a loud voice,
ſaying, Eloi, Eloi, lama ſabachthani? which is, being
interpreted, [y] My God, my God, why haſt thou forſaken — y Pſ xxii 1
me? 35 And ſome of them that ſtood by, when they
heard *it*, ſaid, Behold, he calleth Elias 36 And [z] one — z John xix 29
ran and filled a ſpunge full of [a] vinegar, and put *it* on — a Pſ lxix 21
a reed, and gave him to drink, ſaying, Let alone, let
us ſee whether Elias will come to take him down 37
And Jeſus cried with a loud voice, and [b] gave up the ghoſt — b Heb x
38 And [c] the veil of the temple was rent in twain, — c Ex xxvi 31
from the top to the bottom. 39 ¶ And when the cen-
turion which ſtood over-againſt him, ſaw that he ſo cried
out, and gave up the ghoſt, he ſaid, [d] Truly this man — d Pſ lxxxix 27 Mat iii 17
was the Son of God 40 There were alſo women
[e] looking on afar off among whom was Mary Magda- — e Pſ xxxviii 11
lene, and Mary the mother of James the leſs, and of
Joſes, and of Salome, 41 Who alſo when he was in
Galilee, [f] followed him, and miniſtred unto him, and — f Luke viii 2
many other women which came up with him unto Je-
ruſalem

v 33—41 Death at laſt brings the welcome releaſe from ſuch uncommon wretchedneſs, after Jeſus had hung on the tree about ſix hours, during which we are told,

1 The dreadful darkneſs that for the three laſt hours covered the earth, portending that fearful ſtate of blindneſs and hardneſs of heart to which the Jewiſh people were now abandoned *for their wickedneſs* The Sun of righteouſneſs was now ſetting, to riſe on them no more, and moſt juſtly do thoſe who hate the light, deſerve to be deprived of it, and to be left to the darkneſs of their fallen minds

2 The darkneſs of the ſun was but the emblem of the more dreadful darkneſs which involved the Redeemer's ſoul and extorted from him that exceeding bitter cry, *My God, my God, why haſt thou forſaken me?* Such a complaint from the mouth of the Son of God may well amaze every heart The arrows of wrath now drank up his ſpirit, the powers of darkneſs ſtruggled with their might, and all that *Jeſus could endure* was laid upon him Never had ſuch an hour paſſed ſince the ſun began

its revolutions, nor shall be again, till he is plucked from his sphere

3 Astonishingly hardened, notwithstanding all that had passed, some that stood by mocked him, as if he now wanted Elias to come, and running and filling a spunge with vinegar, they put it to his lips, the more to insult him, whilst others said, *Let alone*, let us see whether Elias will appear to save him or no Thus they regarded him as abandoned of God, and concluded, that none in earth or heaven desired to help him

4 Having finished the atonement, he dismissed his spirit, and left the lifeless corpse upon the tree *He cried with a loud voice*, not as one worn out with pains, but as a triumphant conqueror, and vanquished as he fell, by death destroying him that had the power of death, that is, the devil

5 At that instant the vail of the temple was rent in twain from the top to the bottom, intimating the abolition of the ritual service, the rending the Jewish state in pieces, and the access opened now through the cross of Jesus, and his body there offered, for every sinner into the holiest of all, God being reconciled through the blood of his cross, and willing to receive all that come unto him through this dying Redeemer

6 This amazing cry, and sudden departure of Jesus, deeply affected the Roman centurion, under whose command the soldiers were, and, convinced by what he saw and heard of his innocence, and the truth of that assertion for which he suffered, he could not but confess, that *this was verily the Son of God*. He was the first fruits of the Gentile confessors, and appointed to bear testimony to the Redeemer's glory in the hour of his deepest humiliation

7 Those pious women who had followed Jesus from Galilee, and supported him out of their substance, continued with him to the last The names of some of them are mentioned to their everlasting honour Mary Magdalen was one much had been forgiven her, and she thus proved how much she loved the Saviour in return and *Mary the mother of James the less*, so called probably from his low stature, *and Salome*, the mother of Zebedee's children and now all their hopes seemed to be extinguished by the death of their Lord Thus when we seem sunk into the lowest depths, then doth the glory of God more eminently appear in raising our desponding souls, and filling us with the triumphs of faith and joy

42 ¶ [g] And now when the even was come (because [g Matt. xxvii 57. Luke xxiii 50. John xix 38.]
it was the preparation, that is, the day before the sabbath) 43 Joseph of Arimathea, an honourable counsellor, [h] which also waited for the kingdom of God, [h Luke ii 25, 38.]
came, and went in boldly unto Pilate, and craved the
body of Jesus 44 And Pilate marvelled if he were
already dead and calling unto him the centurion, he
asked him whether he had been any while dead 45
And when he knew *it* of the centurion, he gave the
body to Joseph. 46 And he bought fine linen, and
took him down, and wrapped him in the linen, and
[i] laid him in a sepulchre which was hewn out of a rock, [i Is. liii 9. Matt. xxvii. 60.]
and rolled a stone unto the door of the sepulchre 47
And Mary Magdalene, and Mary the mother of Joses,
beheld where he was laid

v 42—47 Nothing now remained but to take down the bodies as the evening approached, longer than which they were forbidden to hang there, and also it being the preparation of the sabbath, the work needed to be hastened But who shall perform this last kind office to the corpse of Jesus. The Lord hath prepared an unexpected person for the service, Joseph of Arimathea, a person of distinction, a counsellor, probably one of the great sanhedrim, a secret disciple of Jesus, and who, notwithstanding his sufferings and death, expected that his glorious kingdom would come, and in faith waited for it

1 He went in *boldly* to Pilate, and begged the body of Jesus, when none of his apostles or followers had the courage to own him Pilate, who could hardly believe that Christ was yet dead, called the centurion, and, when he was assured of the fact, readily granted Joseph's request, and gave an order for delivering the body *Note*, (1) In Christ's cause we have need of courage They who dare appear on the side of the people that are every where spoken against, must not be ashamed (2) God hath his chosen among the great, the noble, and honourable counsellors; though not many, yet enough to leave the rest inexcusable in their infidelity

2 Joseph with great respect having taken down the mangled corpse of his Lord, and wrapped it in fine linen bought for the occasion, interred the body in his own new tomb, which was hewn out of a rock, and closed the door with a large stone, whilst the two Mary's, who had continued near the cross, now followed their Master to his grave, and marked the place, intending, after the sabbath to embalm the corpse *Note*, (1) They who love the Lord Jesus, serve him with their best, and count nothing too much to bestow for his honour (2) In the grave of Jesus the poor sinner beholds with joy all his iniquities buried, and never more shall they rise up to condemn or destroy him (3) Visits to the grave are very useful, they serve to quicken us to prepare for our great change.

CHAP XVI

Christ's love, 1 *Rises from the dead*, ver 1—8 2 *Appears to Mary Magdalene*, ver 9—11 3 *To two of his disciples*, *then to the eleven*, ver 12—14 4 *Invests them with their commission to preach the gospel*, ver 15—18 5 *He ascends into heaven*, ver 19, 20

1 [a] AND when the sabbath was past, Mary Mag- [a Matt. xxviii 1. Luke xxiv 1. John xx 1.]
dalene, and Mary *the mother* of James, and
Salome, [b] had brought sweet spices, that they might come [b Luke xxiii 56. John xix 39.]
and anoint him 2 And very early in the morning, the
first *day* of the week, they came unto the sepulchre at the
rising of the sun 3 And they said among themselves,
Who shall roll us away the stone from the door of the se-
pulchre? 4 (And when they looked, they saw that the
stone was rolled away) for it was very great 5 [c] And [c John xx 12.]
entring into the sepulchre, they saw a young man sitting
on the right side, clothed in a long white garment, and
[d] they were affrighted 6 And he saith unto them, Be [d Dan x 8. Luke i 12, 29. Chap xvi 5, 8.]
not affrighted ye seek Jesus of Nazareth, which was
crucified [e] he is risen, he is not here behold the place
where they laid him 7 But go your way, tell his dis-
ciples and Peter, that he goeth before you into Galilee
there shall ye see him, [f] as he said unto you 8 And [f Chap xiv 28.]
they went out quickly, and fled from the sepulchre, for
[g] they trembled, and were amazed neither said they [g Matt. xxviii 8.]
any thing to any man, for they were afraid

v 1—8 No sooner was the sabbath past, during which Christ had lain in the grave, than we find,

1 Early in the morning, on the first day of the week, the pious women, who the preceding evening had provided spices for embalming the body, little expecting his resurrection from the dead, set out from the city for the sepulchre, which they reached just at sun-rising, and by the way having expressed to each other their concern how to roll back the ponderous stone from the mouth of the cave, to their surprize they beheld it already done for them *Note*, (1) Though difficulties at a distance seem unsurmountable, when we go on steadily depending upon God, we shall often meet with unexpected assistances (2) It is mentioned to their distinguished honour, how assiduous and faithful the women who followed Jesus proved, when the men forsook him. The weaker vessel is often seen to be the stronger Christian

2 An angel appears to them As they entred into the sepulchre, to their great surprize and terror, they beheld one in the likeness of a young man, in long white robes sitting within But the angel soon quieted their fears, bids them not be terrified, he knew their business there was to seek the crucified Jesus, and, to their inexpressible joy, informs them, he is no longer numbered with the dead, but *risen* There was the place where he lay they are therefore enjoined without delay to carry the glad tidings to Peter and the rest of the apostles, and to tell them, according to his promise, that their glorified Master will meet them in Galilee, and make them happy with his presence and converse *Note*, (1) We are often apt to fear where no fear is, and to dread our mercies as miseries (2) They who seek a crucified Jesus, are sure to find comfort to their souls (3) Though we for our unfaithfulness might justly be left to mourn our folly, Christ is a compassionate Saviour, willing to pardon, and in haste to speak peace to the souls of his afflicted disciples. (4) Peter is particularly mentioned; had he not, perhaps he would have thought the message was good news for the rest, but not for him, as having rendered himself unworthy the name of a disciple but where sin hath abounded, there will the Lord make his grace much more to abound (5) They who know the joy of meeting Jesus, and of his spiritual presence in the ordinances of his worship, will not count the way long to go, where his word is dispensed, and his voice is still heard

3 The women ran eagerly to carry the message, trembling with a mixture of surprize and joy, and spoke to no man by the way, afraid the news was too good to be true, or that the Jews would be exasperated if they heard it, and say they had stolen the body *Note*, The great good news of a finished salvation, perfect and entire in Christ Jesus, appears to the trembling sinner almost beyond belief

9 ¶ Now when *Jesus* was risen early the first *day* of
the week, [h] he appeared first to Mary Magdalene, out of [h John xx 14.]
whom he had cast seven devils 10 *And* she went and
told them that had been with him, [i] as they mourned [i Mat. v 4.]
and

and wept 11 And they, when they had heard that he
was alive, and had been ſeen of her, [k] believed not 12
¶ After that he appeared in another form unto [l] two of
them, as they walked, and went into the country 13
And they went and told *it* unto the reſidue neither believed they them

k Luke xxiv 11
l Luke xxiv 13, &c

v 9—13 Chriſt here appears,

1 To Mary Magdalen, the morning he roſe, that remarkable ſinner, out of whom he had caſt ſeven devils Sometimes the greateſt ſinners prove the greateſt ſaints, and deareſt to the Saviour She immediately carried the joyful news to the eleven, who, inconſolable, with bitter anguiſh lamented their departed Lord, and their own unfaithfulneſs to him, and ſeemed ſunk in deſpair of ever ſeeing him again Nay, ſo ſlow of heart were they to believe, notwithſtanding the repeated predictions Chriſt had given them of his riſing from the dead, that they received her declarations as a mere fancy, and imagined her deceived by ſome ſpectre or apparition *Note*, (1) The moſt reviving comforts uſually are ſent when we are moſt dejected and deſponding (2) The very incredulity of the diſciples tends to the confirmation of our faith it ſhews, they were not themſelves willing to believe, but upon the moſt indubitable evidence

2 The ſame day at evening he appeared to two others of his diſciples, who were going towards Emmaus, a village about ſeven miles from Jeruſalem, but perhaps being in a different dreſs from what he uſually wore, and *their eyes being holden that they ſhould not know him*, Luke xxiv 16—31 they converſed with him for a while, and at laſt their eyes were opened, and they knew him whereupon they inſtantly returned to acquaint their brethren, and even then they would not be perſuaded, though the witneſſes were ſo unexceptionable

14 ¶ [m] Afterward he appeared unto the eleven as
they ſat † at meat, and upbraided them with their unbelief, and hardneſs of heart, becauſe they believed not
them which had ſeen him after he was riſen 15 And
he ſaid unto them, Go ye into all the world, and [n] preach
the goſpel to every creature 16 [o] He that believeth
and [p] is baptized, ſhall be ſaved, but [q] he that believeth
not, ſhall be damned 17 And theſe ſigns ſhall follow
them that believe, [r] In my name ſhall they caſt out devils, [s] they ſhall ſpeak with new tongues, 18 [t] They
ſhall take up ſerpents, and if they drink any deadly
thing, it ſhall not hurt them, [u] they ſhall lay hands on
the ſick, and they ſhall recover

m Luke xxiv 36 John xx 19 1 Cor xv 7
† Or together
n Rom x 18 Col i 23
o John iii 18, 36 Rom x 9
p Acts ii 38 1 Pet iii 21
q John xii 48
r Acts v 16 & xvi 18
s Acts ii 4 & x 46
t Luke x 19 Acts xxviii 5
u Acts xxviii 8 Jam v 14, 15

v 14—18 Since they are ſo loath to believe the report of others, Jeſus condeſcends to put the matter beyond diſpute, by appearing himſelf the ſame evening unto all the apoſtles, except Thomas, as they were ſitting at table together

1 He *upbraids them with their unbelief and hardneſs of heart*, that they were ſo backward to receive the teſtimony of thoſe who had ſeen him, notwithſtanding the many aſſurances of his riſing again, which he had given them before his death *Note*, (1) Unbelief is a moſt beſetting ſin, and highly diſpleaſing to the Lord Jeſus (2) Naturally we are indiſpoſed to believe farther than we can ſee, and yet, if even we did ſee, it would not truly produce faith in any ſoul that is not ſatisfied with the evidence of the goſpel

2 He ſolemnly inveſts them with authority to go and preach the goſpel among all nations, and to confirm their miſſion by the miracles he would enable them to work This tranſaction paſſed, it ſhould ſeem, not at the time of his firſt appearing to them, but afterwards, juſt before his aſcenſion

[1] He enlarges their commiſſion to go into all the world, and to preach that goſpel, which had been hitherto confined to the Jewiſh people, to every human creature, as far as their labours would reach, with power alſo to ſend out others, as fellow-labourers with them, to ſpread the ſavour of the truth in every place

[2] The ſummary of their preaching muſt be faith in the Son of God, in his life, death, and reſurrection, the neceſſity of the ſalvation obtained by his obedience and ſufferings for loſt ſinners, the fulneſs and all-ſufficiency of it to procure pardon, life, and glory for all who truſt in him, and the ſin and danger of thoſe who reject this method of divine wiſdom and love, and refuſe obedience to the faith of the goſpel, their damnation being as inevitable, as the ſalvation of thoſe who believe in Jeſus, and in conſequence thereof make open profeſſion of their faith and are by baptiſm received into the boſom of the church, is ſure and certain *Note*, Under the goſpel none periſh becauſe of the greatneſs of their ſins, but becauſe they ſin againſt the remedy, and ſeal themſelves up under wrath by their unbelief

[3] In confirmation of their doctrine they are impowered to work the moſt aſtoniſhing miracles *In the name of Jeſus*, depending on his power, and to advance his goſpel, they ſhall be enabled *to caſt out devils* from thoſe that were poſſeſſed, *to ſpeak with new tongues*, which they had never learnt, with the moſt entire fluency and readineſs, as if they had ſeverally been their native language *They ſhall take up ſerpents*, the moſt venomous, without the leaſt harm, See Acts xxviii 3—6 *If they drink any deadly thing, it ſhall not hurt them*, when thus openly or ſecretly their perſecutors might ſtrive to make away with them *They ſhall lay hands on the ſick, and they ſhall recover*, every diſeaſe giving way to their healing touch And theſe miraculous powers they not only poſſeſſed themſelves, but were enabled to impart to others, and were continued till Chriſtianity got firm footing in the world, ſince which theſe miracles, being no longer neceſſary, are ceaſed

19 ¶ So then [x] after the Lord had ſpoken unto them, x Luke xx…
[y] he was received up into heaven, and [z] ſat on the right y Acts i …
hand of God 20 And they went forth, and preached z Pſ. cx 1
every where, the Lord working with them, and [a] confirming the word with ſigns following Amen

a Acts … Heb ii 4

v 19, 20 When our Lord had thus commiſſioned and qualified them for the great work he had committed to their charge, we ſee him,

1 Aſcending to his throne of glory, and exalted to the right hand of Majeſty on high Having finiſhed the work of redemption in behalf of his people, all power is put into his hands, to beſtow eternal life on as many as the Father hath given him, and to reign in and over them as his faithful ſubjects, whilſt his enemies, as vanquiſhed, muſt bow before him, and whether they are devils or wicked men, will ſhortly receive from his lips their eternal doom

2 We ſee them going forth according to their Maſter's orders, preaching the goſpel in defiance of all oppoſition from earth and hell, the Lord ſupporting them againſt all their perſecutors, giving the moſt amazing ſucceſs to their labours, by wondrous miracles atteſting their miſſion to be divine, and by the power of the Holy Ghoſt making their word powerfully effectual to the converſion of the hearts of innumerable multitudes And this ſign will ever follow the goſpel to the end of time, wherever it is preached in ſpirit and in truth, it will be found the power of God unto ſalvation and as the Evangeliſt adds his *Amen* hereunto, ſo are we alſo bound to do, aſſured that thus it *will* be, and praying that thus it *may* be, that the word may daily run and be glorified, till the ends of the earth ſhall remember themſelves, and be turned to the Lord, and all fleſh ſhall ſee the ſalvation of our God Amen So come, Lord Jeſus!

5

THE

THE EVANGELICAL EXPOSITOR; OR, A PRACTICAL COMMENT Upon the GOSPEL according to St. LUKE.

THE penman of this Epistle is Luke, *of what country is uncertain · I incline to their opinion who suppose him a native Israelite He was, it seems, a physician,* Col iv 14 *and though* Religio Medici *is used as a proverb, we find an Evangelist of that profession He is mentioned with honour as the companion of the blessed Apostle* Paul *in his prison,* 2 Tim iv 11. *and is supposed to be that brother so esteemed in the churches,* 2 Cor viii 18 *The date of his gospel is not fixed, some regarding him as the first of the Evangelists, others say, he wrote during his travels with* Paul *in Achaia, about seventeen years after Christ's ascension, and many conclude it was written at Rome, during Paul's imprisonment, and just before the history of the* Acts of the Apostles, *and then it will be fixed about the twenty-seventh year after Christ, and the fourth of the reign of Nero but whenever or wherever he composed it, it is generally received as genuine, and written by divine inspiration, and, as such, stands among the records of our holy religion*

CHAP I

In this chapter we have, 1 *Luke's preface to his gospel,* ver 1—4 2 *The prophesy and history of the conception of John Baptist, who was Christ's forerunner,* ver 5—25 3 *The annunciation of the virgin Mary,* ver 26—38 4 *The interview between Mary the mother of Jesus, and Elisabeth the mother of John,* ver 39—56 5 *The birth and circumcision of John Baptist, six months before the birth of Christ,* ver 57—66 6 *Zachariah's song of praise, in thankfulness for the birth of John, and in prospect of the birth of Jesus,* ver 67—69 7 *A short account of John Baptist's infancy,* ver 80

1. FORASMUCH as many have taken in hand to set forth in order a declaration of those things which are most surely believed among us,
2 [a] Even as they delivered them unto us, [b] which from the beginning were eye-witnesses, and ministers of the word
3 [c] It seemed good to me also, having had perfect understanding of all things from the very first, to write unto thee in order, [d] most excellent Theophilus,
4 [e] That thou mightest know the certainty of those things wherein thou hast been instructed

[illegible marginal references]

Ver 1—4 Dedications are usually but the feather with which flattery tickles the pride of the great, but here is one, whose simplicity bespeaks the Christian spirit of the author, and recommend the book not to the patronage of his noble friend, as needing his countenance, but to the consideration of his pupil, in order to instruct his conscience, and direct his practice

The Evangelist opens with his reason for writing Because many had undertaken to publish narratives of the birth, life, doctrines, miracles, sufferings, death, and resurrection of Jesus, who, though probably well-meaning disciples, wrote under no infallible guidance of the Spirit, it appeared therefore to be the will of God, and highly proper, that he should compose a connected history, and particular account of all things from the beginning, to prevent the errors and mistakes which might arise from uninspired writings

1 He professes to confine himself to *the things most surely believed* among the faithful not matters of doubtful disputation, but facts established by the most indubitable evidence of those who *from the beginning were eye-witnesses, and ministers of the word*, heard the doctrines, and saw the miracles of Jesus, and were divinely commissioned by him to go forth and preach the gospel he had delivered to them

2 He was fully qualified for the work he undertook, *having had perfect understanding of all things from the very first*, and this not merely received by tradition from the best attested reports, but as the words (παρηκολουθηκοτι ανωθεν) may be rendered, *having attained to the exact understanding of all things from above*, which inspiration he had diligently sought, and sacredly followed

3 The end he proposed was, *that Theophilus*, whom he addressed with the respectable title of *most excellent*, being, it seems, a man of rank and fashion, *might know the certainty of those things wherein he had been instructed*, or *catechised* Probably Luke had been the means of his conversion, and had taught him by word of mouth the great principles of the Christian religion, and therefore, that his memory might be assisted, his knowledge increased, and his faith more firmly established in the truths of the gospel, he drew up the following history *Note*, (1) The gospel of Jesus Christ is not a cunningly devised fable, but contains fact supported by the most incontestible evidence, and truths the most sure and certain, whereon our faith may stand unshaken (2) Catechising was the antient method of communicating

meating to the youth, and newly-converted persons, the knowledge of the great doctrines of religion, and perhaps our present deplorable ignorance is owing to no one cause more than to the perfunctory discharge or total neglect of this most useful method of instruction (3) Christianity, though it forbids to give flattering titles, enjoins us to pay honour to whom honour is due, it teaches us politeness without falshood, simplicity without rudeness, respect without servility, and courtesy without cringing

5 THERE was [f] in the days of Herod the king of
Judea, a certain priest named Zacharias, [g] of
the course of Abia and his wife *was* of the daughters
of Aaron, and her name *was* Elisabeth 6 And [h] they
were both righteous before God, [i] walking in all the
commandments and ordinances of the Lord, blameless
7 And they had no child, because that Elisabeth was
barren, and they both were *now* well stricken in years 8
And it came to pass, that while he executed the priest's
office before God in the order of his course, 9 Ac-
cording to the custom of the priest's office, his [k] lot was
[l] to burn incense when he went into the temple of the
Lord 10 And [m] the whole multitude of the people
were praying without, at the time of incense 11 And
there appeared unto him an angel of the Lord, standing
on the right side of the altar of incense 12 And
when Zacharias saw *him*, he was troubled, and [o] fear
fell upon him 13 But the angel said unto him, [p] Fear
not, Zacharias, for thy prayer is heard, and thy wife
Elisabeth shall bear thee a son, and thou shalt call his
name John 14 And thou shalt have joy and gladness,
and [q] many shall rejoice at his birth 15 For he shall
be great in the sight of the Lord, and [r] shall drink nei-
ther wine nor strong drink, and he shall be filled with
the holy Ghost, [u] even from his mother's womb 16
And [x] many of the children of Israel shall he turn to
the Lord their God 17 And [y] he shall go before him
in the spirit and power of Elias, to turn the hearts of
the fathers to the children, and the disobedient † to the
wisdom of the just, [z] to make ready a people prepared
for the Lord 18 And Zacharias said unto the angel,
[a] Whereby shall I know this? for I am an old man,
and my wife well stricken in years 19 And the angel
answering said unto him, I am Gabriel, [c] that stand in
the presence of God and am sent to speak unto thee,
and to shew thee these glad tidings 20 And behold,
thou shalt be dumb, and not able to speak, until the
day that these things shall be performed, because thou
believest not my words, which shall be fulfilled in their
season 21 And the people waited for Zacharias, and
marvelled that he tarried so long in the temple 22
And when he came out, he could not speak unto them
and they perceived that he had seen a vision in the
temple for he beckoned unto them, and remained
speechless 23 And it came to pass, that as soon as the
days of his ministration were accomplished, he departed
to his own house 24 And after those days his wife
Elisabeth conceived, and hid herself five months, saying,
25 Thus hath the Lord dealt with me, in the days
wherein he looked on me, to take away my reproach
among men

v 5—25 The other Evangelists commenced their history from the conception and birth of Jesus, Luke begins farther back, with that of John the Baptist, his forerunner, which was attended with extraordinary circumstances well deserving our regard

1 We have an account of his parents They lived in the reign of Herod, an Idumean, who held his kingdom under the Roman emperor Both Zacharias and Elisabeth were of the sacerdotal family he was of the course of Abia, the eighth of those four and twenty into which the priests were divided, (1 *Chron* xxiv 7—10) To the honour of this aged pair it is recorded, that their piety was most exemplary, they approved themselves to God in a holy blameless conversation, living by faith in the expected Messiah, whom they regarded in the use of all the divine institutions, and were sincerely observant of all the ordinances of worship, and duties of morality But notwithstanding the distinguished excellence of their characters, it was their infelicity to be destitute of children, Elisabeth being barren, and both of them now so advanced in years, as in the common course of nature to deprive them of the hope of issue *Note*, (1) In the worst of times God preserves some faithful ones as eminent instances of his grace, and reprovers of the world which lieth in wickedness (2) Our mercies are often long deferred, to make them at last the more welcome

2 An angel appeared to Zacharias as he was discharging his ministry in the temple The services to be performed by the course in waiting were determined by lot his office was to burn incense in the sanctuary, and whilst this was performing, the holy worshippers without in silent aspirations lifted up their prayers to God, expecting acceptance through the intercession of Christ, which the smoke of the incense offered by the priest represented, *See Rev* viii 1—4 And whilst Zacharias was thus employed, *an angel of the Lord* appeared to him on *the right side of the altar of incense*, and, struck with the glorious sight and unusual appearance, Zacharias trembled, and feared greatly what such vision might portend *Note*, (1) Visits from another world may well fill even good men with terror, not only through the weakness of the human frame, but also from the consciousness of their guilt and sinfulness (2) Prayer is the service God's people never neglect, and herein their care is to lift up their hearts unto God, not so sollicitous about the choice of words, as that a fervent desire may speak the language of their souls (3) All our services and prayers must be offered through the mediation of Jesus, for then only can they be acceptable unto God

3 The angel delivers to him the message with which he was sent Having first kindly quieted his fears, he assures him of gracious acceptance with God, and an answer to his prayers Probably at that time he had particularly been crying for the coming of the promised Messiah, as he had formerly often asked for a son, and both are now granted him, the latter first, in order to introduce the former *Thy wife Elisabeth*, so long barren, and now aged, *shall bear thee a son, and thou shalt call his name John*, which signifies *gracious*, and was most admirably suited for him who should be so great in spiritual gifts and graces, and the harbinger of the Messiah and his kingdom *And thou shalt have joy and gladness*, not only in him, so welcome a child given after so long waiting, but in the view of the high character and office he is ordained to bear *and many shall rejoice at his birth*, congratulating his parents on such an unexpected blessing And it will afford yet farther cause of joy to multitudes, who afterwards shall be blessed with his ministry and labours, *for he shall be great in the sight of the Lord*, highly honoured of God, and blessed with singular endowments from him *and shall drink neither wine nor strong drink*, a Nazarite from his birth, for it becomes those designed for eminent services, to live a life of eminent self-denial, and dead to sensual delights *He shall be filled with the Holy Ghost, even from his mother's womb*, sanctified, set apart, and qualified fully for the ministry to which he was appointed *And many of the children of Israel shall he turn to the Lord their God*, the Messiah, their incarnate God, then ready to appear *and he shall go before him*, as his messenger and harbinger, the morning-star that ushers in the rising sun, *in the spirit and power of Elias*, endued with the zeal of that eminent reformer, and in austerity of manners nearly resembling him *to turn the hearts of the fathers to the children*, either the Jews to the Gentiles, removing their prejudices and enmity against them, or *with the children*, converting young and old by his preaching, *and the disobedient to the wisdom of the just*, convincing the most rebellious sinners, and leading them to Christ for justification, even to the wisdom that maketh wise unto salvation and thus *to make ready a people prepared for the Lord*, raising their expectations of him, removing their prejudices, and pointing him personally out to them as their Lord and Saviour, or *prepared by the Lord*, according to his eternal counsels ordained to life and glory, and now by John's ministry to be called to faith in the Son of God *Note*, (1) Though our requests are long delayed, they are not therefore denied, and the mercy at last comes enhanced in value, as the answer of many prayers (2) True greatness is not to be estimated by outward grandeur or wealth, God's favour, and the possession of the gifts and graces of his Spirit, these alone make a man great in his eyes who is the fountain of honour (3) The great end of a zealous minister of God's word is to convert the souls of men, and turn them to the Lord Jesus nor need they despair of the most disobedient sinners, almighty grace can bend the most stubborn heart

4 Zacharias, looking at human probabilities, staggered at the promise through unbelief, and wanted some further sign to remove his doubts He and his wife being now grown old, the age as well as barrenness of Elisabeth made him regard the event as incredible Very unlike a son of Abraham! *Rom* iv 19, 20

5 The angel gives him the sign he asked, and therewith the just punishment of his unbelief *I am Gabriel*; my very appearance to you should have been sufficient to beget confidence in my word, because *that I stand in the presence of God*, attentive to his orders, and employed in his service *and am sent* expressly *to thee* with this message, *and to shew thee these glad tidings*, which should have been received with thankfulness and joy but since thou afkest a sign, *behold, thou shalt be dumb*, and no more able to object to the truth of what I say, *and not able to speak, until*

the day that these things shall be performed, as a punishment upon thee, *because thou hast not believed my words, which*, notwithstanding all the obstacles unbelief suggests, *shall be fulfilled in their season*. Note, (1) Our unbelief is very dishonourable and displeasing to God. (2) God's promises will take effect, notwithstanding our unbelief, and though we suffer for our distrusts of him, he will not cast us off from him.

6 Zacharias returns to the people, who wondered at the length of his stay in the temple, and were waiting for the usual benediction before they retired. And their wonder increased, when coming forth he was unable to speak a word, and by his signs they perceived he had seen a vision in the temple, and for a time continued deaf and dumb, (*See ver* 62.) The Aaronical priesthood was now about to be silenced, and the dumb signs of typical institutions to be set aside by the clear voice of gospel grace.

7 The angelic message quickly received its accomplishment. Having staved out the days of his ministration in the temple, he returned home with his wife, who immediately conceived by him; and thereupon, as she was to bring forth a Nazarite, kept herself for five months close retired from all company, that she might contract no ceremonial uncleanness, spending the time in thankfulness, praise, and devotion, blessing God for the singular mercy, in removing the reproach of barrenness from her, under which she had so long laboured, and at last bestowing on her, in so extraordinary a way, that son who should be the harbinger of the Messiah. *Note*, In all our mercies God is ever to be acknowledged; and particularly we are assured, that children and the fruit of the womb are the heritage and gift that cometh from the Lord.

26 And in the sixth month the angel Gabriel was
sent from God, unto a city of Galilee, named Nazareth,
27 To a virgin [h] espoused to a man whose name was
Joseph, of the house of David; and the virgin's name
was Mary. 28 And the angel came in unto her, and
said, Hail, [i] thou that art † highly favoured, the Lord
is with thee: [k] blessed *art* thou among women. 29
And when she saw him, she was troubled at his saying,
and cast in her mind what manner of salutation this
should be. 30 And the angel said unto her, Fear not,
Mary: for thou hast found favour with God. 31 And
[l] behold, thou shalt conceive in thy womb, and bring
forth a son, and [m] shalt call his name Jesus. 32 He
shall be great, and [n] shall be called the Son of the Highest;
and [o] the Lord God [p] shall give unto him the throne
of his father David. 33 And [q] he shall reign over the
house of Jacob for ever, and [r] of his kingdom there
shall be no end. 34 Then said Mary unto the angel,
How shall this be, seeing I know not a man? 35
And the angel answered and said unto her, [s] The holy
Ghost shall come upon thee, and the power of the
Highest shall overshadow thee: therefore also that holy
thing which shall be born of thee, shall be called the
Son of God. 36 And behold, thy cousin Elisabeth,
she hath also conceived a son in her old age: and this
is the sixth month with her who was called barren.
37 For [t] with God nothing shall be impossible. 38
And Mary said, Behold the handmaid of the Lord; be it
unto me according to thy word. And the angel departed
from her.

[h] Mat i 18. [i] Dan ix 23. Ver 19. † Or, graciously accepted, or much graced. [k] Ver 42. Judg v 24. [l] Isa vii 14. Mat i 21. [m] Chap ii 21. [n] Mark v 7. [o] Isa ix 6, 7. & xvi 5. [p] Ps cxxxii 11. Rev iii 7. [q] Dan ii 44. & vii 14, 27. Mic iv 7. [r] Heb i 8. [s] Mat i 20. [t] Gen xviii 14. Job xlii 2. Jer xxxii 17. Zech viii 6. Chap xviii 27.

v. 26—38 Six months after the former miraculous conception of Elisabeth, the same angel Gabriel is sent on a more important message, to foretel the conception and birth of the Lord's Christ. We have here,

1 The person from whom the human nature of the Son of God was to be taken. Her name was Mary, of the royal race of David, but now reduced to very mean circumstances; a virgin unspotted, espoused to Joseph of the same royal line, dwelling in a remote corner of the land, and in a place despicable almost to a proverb, *See John* i 46.

2 The angel's address and salutation. *Hail, thou that art highly favoured, &c.* He wishes her all peace, prosperity, and joy; assures her of the favour of the Most High; that his gracious presence was with her; and that she of all others was singled out to be distinguished with peculiar honour, and to be called blessed in all generations, as the mother of the adored Messiah. The popish plea for the adoration of the virgin Mary, taken from hence, is absurd, and utterly unsupported; these words in no wise implying prayer or worship, but merely a friendly salutation.

3 Mary's surprise on the angel's appearance and address. She was greatly astonished at such an unexpected visit, and the respect paid to her, a woman so unknown and unnoticed; and much perplexed, reasoned with herself what this blessedness should mean, which was pronounced with such solemnity.

4 The angel, to remove the perplexity and confusion under which she appeared, proceeds with his message. *Fear not, Mary: for thou hast found favour with God*; and when this is the case, all disquieting fears are groundless. *And behold*, astonishing as the tidings are, yet true, *thou shalt conceive in thy womb*, tho' a virgin immaculate, (*Isa* vii 14.) *and bring forth a son, and shalt call his name Jesus*, the same as Joshua, or Saviour; of whom the former deliverers of Israel were types and figures. *He shall be great*, in dignity, person, offices, and works; *and shall be called the Son of the Highest*, shall really be so, partaking of the same divine nature. *And the Lord shall give unto him*, as the Messiah, *the throne of David his father*, from whom, as man, he descended, and whose kingdom was typical of that spiritual dominion which Jesus should erect in the hearts of his people, sitting as a king upon his holy hill of Sion, the church of his redeemed. *And he shall reign over the house of Jacob*, the true Israel of God, whether Jews or Gentiles brought to the obedience of the faith; and his throne shall be established *for ever, and of his kingdom there shall be no end*; enduring as the days of time, and subject to none of the vicissitudes and changes which attend earthly sovereignty; and, when time shall end, this kingdom shall be continued in a more glorious form, coeval with the ages of eternity.

5 The Virgin, not distrusting the truth, or questioning the possibility of what he said, humbly desires to be informed by what means this should be brought to pass, seeing she was conscious of her own virginity.

6 He vouchsafes to inform her as much as she need wish to know. *The Holy Ghost, the power of the Highest*, exerting his almighty influence, will by his immediate agency, as he moved upon the face of the water in the first creation, enable her to conceive: and therefore, because in this miraculous manner the body of the child Jesus should be formed, he shall be *a holy thing*, from his conception not partaking of the taint of human corruption, as all flesh do in the ordinary course of generation; and shall be called *the Son of God*, being as such now manifested in the human nature; and that which she conceived, henceforward and insolubly subsisting in personal union with the second person of the sacred trinity, should henceforth bear his name. And he adds, as an encouragement to strengthen her faith in his word, that *her cousin Elisabeth*, who was by one of her parents allied it seems to the house of David, as by the other descended from Aaron, was now with child, though so stricken in years, and in the sixth month of her pregnancy, who had before been barren. The same power therefore which had wrought this miracle, would work this greater one, of which he assured her; *for with God nothing is impossible*; however it exceeds human power of conception, what he promises he can and will surely perform.

7 Mary with deep humility and submission yields herself up to the Lord, as his handmaid, desiring him to do with her whatever he pleased; utterly unworthy so great an honour, yet, since such was his promise, begging it might be fulfilled, and faithfully depending upon the Lord's almighty power and grace. Hereupon the angel departed, having finished the work the Lord had given him to do. *Note*, (1) However wonderful and surpassing great God's promises are, it becomes us to credit his word, and rest our everlasting hopes thereon; then we glorify him. (2) Angelic visions here below were only transient; shortly these blessed spirits will be our companions to eternity.

39 And Mary arose in those days, and went [u] into
the hill-country with haste, into a city of Judah; 40 And
entred into the house of Zacharias, and saluted Elisabeth.
41 And it came to pass, that when Elisabeth
heard the salutation of Mary, the babe leaped in her
womb; and Elisabeth was filled with the Holy Ghost:
42 And she spake out with a loud voice, and said,
[x] Blessed *art* thou among women, and blessed *is* the
fruit of thy womb. 43 And whence *is* this to me,
that the mother of my Lord should come to me? 44
For lo, as soon as the voice of thy salutation sounded
in mine ears, the babe leaped in my womb for joy.
45 And [y] blessed *is* she that believed: || for there shall
be a performance of those things which were told her
from the Lord. 46 And Mary said, [z] My soul doth
magnify the Lord, 47 [a] And my spirit hath rejoiced
in God my Saviour. 48 For [a] he hath regarded || the
low estate of his handmaiden: for behold, from henceforth
[b] all generations shall call me blessed. 49 For he
that is mighty hath done to me great things; and [c] holy
is his name. 50 And [d] his mercy *is* on them that fear
him, from generation to generation. 51 [e] He hath
shewed strength with his arm; [f] he hath scattered the
proud in the imagination of their hearts. 52 [g] He
hath put down the mighty from *their* seats, and exalted
them of low degree. 53 [h] He hath filled the
hungry

[u] Josh xxi 10, 11. [x] Ver 28. [y] John xx 29. 1 Pet i 8. || Or, that there shall be, &c. [z] 1 Sam ii 1. Ps xxxiv 2. & xxxv 9. [a] Ps cxxxvi 23. & cxxxviii 6. || Or, lowliness. Isa lxvi 2. Mat v 3. [b] Chap xi 27. [c] Ps cxi 9. [d] Ex xx 6. Ps ciii 17. [e] Ps xcviii 1. & cxviii 15, 16. Isa li 9. & lii 10. [f] Ps xxxiii 10. 1 Pet v 5. [g] 1 Sam ii 6, &c. Job v 11. Ps cxiii 6. [h] 1 Sam ii 5. Ps xxxiv 10.

hungry with good things, and the rich he hath sent
i Ps xcviii 3 Jer xxxi 3, 20 Ver 72 empty away 54 He hath holpen his servant Israel, i in
remembrance of *his* mercy, 55 k As he spake to our
k Gen xvii 19 Ps cxxxii 11 fathers, to Abraham and to his seed for ever 56 And
Mary abode with her about three months, and returned
to her own house

v 39—56 Quickly after the angel's departure we are informed,

1 Of Mary's visit to her cousin Elisabeth in haste, to confer with her on these strange events, that they may confirm each other's faith, and rejoice in their singular mercies The journey was long from Galilee to the hill-country of Judea, probably to Hebron, a city of priests, but the converse of such a friend as Elisabeth would repay all her pains *Note*, Nothing is more encouraging, comforting, and quickening, than when the faithful communicate their mutual experiences

2 Their meeting was accompanied with circumstances very remarkable No sooner had Mary entered the house of Zacharias, and saluted Elisabeth, than the babe, as under a divine impulse, leaped in her womb, seeming to congratulate the blessed Virgin's arrival *and Elisabeth was filled with the Holy Ghost*, with the extraordinary afflatus of the divine Spirit, revealing to her mind the Messiah's conception, the message of the angel to Mary, her faith therein, and the sure performance of what was then promised and addressing her welcome and highly honoured guest, she spake aloud, with a transport of holy joy, as the Spirit gave her utterance, saying, *Blessed art thou among women*, distinguished above all others with peculiar marks of divine favour, and, far from envying, Elisabeth warmly congratulated her on the honour *and blessed is the fruit of thy womb*, that divine Messiah being there conceived, in whom all nations of the world should be blessed, and who is in himself, in the glory of the divine nature, God over all blessed for ever *And whence is this to me?* how great the condescension, *that the mother of my Lord should come to me?* that she should honour me with her company, from whom a body is preparing for the great Lord of all, to appear in the human nature *For lo!* with wonder hear what with wonder I relate, *as soon as the voice of thy salutation sounded in mine ears, the babe leaped in my womb for joy*, as if conscious of the nearness of his Lord, and welcoming her who should bring forth that Messiah, whose harbinger he is appointed to be *And blessed is she that believed*, not staggering at the promise, but acquiescing in the divine word, which shall infallibly be accomplished, *for there shall be a performance of those things which were told her from the Lord* *Note*, (1) True grace makes us thankful for our own mercies, and to rejoice without envy in others greater attainments (2) When the gospel's joyful sound reaches our ears, and the sweet name of Jesus is proclaimed, then should our hearts leap as this babe, and bless the God of our salvation (3) Believing souls must be blessed Christ is now formed in their hearts the hope of glory, and they shall assuredly see the eternal performance of all the great and precious promises which the faithful God hath given them

3 Mary, deeply affected with the words of Elisabeth, and moved with the same divine inspiration, echoes back her praises, and foresees and foretels the great salvation of the Messiah now in her womb

[1] She rejoices in God for the distinguished honour conferred upon her *My soul doth magnify the Lord*, exalting his great and glorious name, and admiring and adoring the wonders of his goodness, *and my spirit hath rejoiced in God my Saviour* and justly was it a greater cause of joy to her, that she knew herself interested in his salvation, than that after the flesh she should be honoured as his mother, for without the former, the latter could have profited her nothing *For he hath regarded the low estate of his handmaiden*, though in outward circumstances contemptible and mean, and as a poor sinner, vile and unworthy, he hath been pleased to honour me so highly *for behold, from henceforth all generations shall call me blessed*, as distinguished with this singular mark of his favour, as interested through faith in the salvation of Jesus, and as the happy instrument chosen to bring forth that Redeemer, who should be the great blessing of mankind *For he that is mighty hath done to me great things*, displaying his power beyond all conception, in the incarnation of his son, and his sovereign grace *to me*, appointed to bring him forth, *and holy is his name*, as all his works and ways declare, therefore from men and angels to him all praise is due, and may it be for ever ascribed to him by all the hosts of earth and heaven! *Note*, (1) When Christ is known *as our God and Saviour*, then shall we rejoice in him, and magnify his name (2) The lower we are in our own eyes, the more admiring thoughts shall we have of the distinguishing grace of our Lord

[2] She praises him for the wonders he doth for his people in the ways of his providence and grace *His mercy is on them that fear him, from generation to generation*; not to me only, but to all who with filial reverence and godly fear worship and serve him *His mercy* to such is rich and gracious; and now more eminently displayed than ever, in the incarnation of his Son, given to bring in an everlasting righteousness, and work out an everlasting salvation, in which whosoever trusts, from generation to generation, will find mercy for ever *He hath shewed strength with his arm*, chusing the weak things of the world to confound the mighty, raising up so glorious a Redeemer from a birth so obscure *he hath scattered the proud in the imagination of their hearts*, disappointing their schemes, and humbling them in the dust Both in the dispensations of his providence and grace, *he hath put down the mighty from their seats*, the proud oppressors of his people of old, as Pharoah, Sennacherib, &c and the spiritually proud, the lofty Pharisees, and all self-righteous sinners, these he hurls from their fancied dignity, destroys their vain confidences, and casts them down as contemptible and vile *and exalted them of low degree*, he hath done so, and continues so to do, raising up by his providence the oppressed as Joseph from the prison to sit among the princes, and by his grace reviving the hearts of poor and contrite sinners, exalting them to his favour, and delighting to honour them *He hath filled the hungry*, those that hunger after righteousness, and feel their utter need of Jesus, *with good things*, satisfying their souls out of his fulness, *and the rich*, who, admiring their own excellencies, see no want of a better righteousness, those *he hath sent empty away*, destitute of all true grace, without the least mark of his favour, and given up to their own delusions *He hath holpen his servant Israel*, in all past ages, by extraordinary interpositions on their behalf, and now more eminently, in raising them up a Saviour from their most dangerous spiritual enemies, *in remembrance of his mercy*, which from eternity dwelt in his mind towards them, and which at sundry times he revealed to them, *as he spake to our fathers, Abraham and his seed for ever*, to whom he had promised, that in his seed all nations of the world should be blessed, which promise God was now about to fulfil *Note*, (1) Pride will surely have a fall No height of station or self confidence can protect those whom God abhors (2) There is help laid on one mighty to save, and all the poor, the weak, and helpless of God's Israel, may come to him, and be holpen (3) All God's promises will, sooner or later, receive their accomplishment, and blessed are they who wait for him

4 Mary, after a visit of three months, returned to Nazareth, satisfied now of her own conception, and thereby assured of the truth of the angel's and Elisabeth's predictions

57 Now Elisabeth's full time came, that she should
be delivered, and she brought forth a son 58 And
her neighbours and her cousins heard how the Lord had
shewed great mercy upon her, and l they rejoiced with l Ver 14
her 59 And it came to pass, that m on the eighth day m Gen xvii 12
they came to circumcise the child, and they called him Lev xii 3
Zacharias, after the name of his father 60 And his
mother answered and said, Not *so*, but n he shall be call- n Ver 13
ed John, 61 And they said unto her, There is none
of thy kindred that is called by this name 62 And
they made signs to his father, how he would have him
called 63 And he asked for a writing table, and wrote,
saying, n His name is John And they marvelled all
64 And his mouth was opened immediately, and his
tongue *loosed*, and he spake, and praised God 65 And
fear came on all that dwelt round about them and all
these † sayings were noised abroad throughout all the † Or things
hill-country of Judea 66 And all they that had heard
them, o laid *them* up in their hearts, saying, What manner o Chap ii
of child shall this be? And the hand of the Lord was 19, 51
with him.

v 57—66 Elisabeth's full time being come, we have here,

1 The birth of her son, and the great joy attending it Tidings of so extraordinary an event were soon spread among her relations and neighbours, and they could not but magnify the Lord for so signal a mercy vouchsafed to her, who was both barren and aged, and they came to congratulate her on the occasion, and rejoice with her *Note*, A gracious heart takes pleasure in the comforts which others enjoy, and rejoices with those that rejoice

2 On the eighth day, when the child was to be circumcised, as it was usual at that time to give him a name after some of his ancestors, the friends and relations, who met on that occasion, would have called him Zacharias, after his father, but Elisabeth, informed by writing from her husband, or by revelation, objected, insisting the child should be called John They who were present expressed their surprize at this, and objected against what was so unusual, none of her kindred bearing that name the matter therefore was referred to the father for his decision, who being deaf and dumb, they made signs to him that he would fix the child's name, and he making sign for a writing-table, to the astonishment of the company, wrote, *His name is John* *Note*, (1) The first concern we owe our children is, early to dedicate them to God (2) Every John

ſhould remember the import of his name, and ſhew himſelf truly *gracious*

3 Zacharias immediately thereupon recovered his ſpeech, and, as the firſt and beſt uſe of his tongue, offered up his praiſes and thankſgivings to the God of his mercies

4 Theſe extraordinary events, which now were ſpread, and in every body's mouth, filled the people with aſtoniſhment and reverential fear, in awful expectation of what would be the iſſue, treaſuring up in their memories, and often pondering in their mind, the wonderful circumſtances attending the birth of this extraordinary child, and from his earlieſt infancy ſomething amazingly great and gracious was ſeen in him, which farther engaged their attention, it evidently appearing that *the hand of the Lord was with him*, and that he was taken under the care and guidance of his peculiar providence and grace *Note*, God has ways we know not of, to communicate his grace to the ſouls of infants, and make them partakers of the Holy Ghoſt, even before they are partakers of reaſon who then can ſay, why ſuch ſhould not be baptized?

67 And his father Zacharias was filled with the Ho-
ly Ghoſt, and propheſied, ſaying, 68 ᵖ Bleſſed be the
Lord God of Iſrael, for ᵍ he hath viſited and redeemed
his people, 69 And ʳ hath raiſed up an horn of ſalva-
tion for us, in the houſe of his ſervant David; 70 ˢ As
he ſpake by the mouth of his holy prophets, which have
been ſince the world began, 71 ᵗ That we ſhould be
ſaved from our enemies, and from the hand of all that
hate us 72 To perform the mercy *promiſed* to our
fathers, and ᵘ to remember his holy covenant 73
ˣ The oath which he ſware to our father Abraham, 74
That he would grant unto us, that we being delivered
out of the hands of our enemies, ʸ might ſerve him
without fear, 75 ᶻ In holineſs and righteouſneſs before
him all the days of our life 76 And thou child ſhalt
be called the prophet of the Higheſt for ᵃ thou ſhalt
go before the face of the Lord, to prepare his ways,
77 To give knowledge of ſalvation unto his people,
† by the remiſſion of their ſins, 78 Through the
‡ tender mercy of our God, whereby the § day-ſpring
from on high hath viſited us, 79 ᵇ To give light to
them that ſit in darkneſs, and in the ſhadow of death,
to guide our feet into the way of peace 80 And ᶜ the
child grew, and waxed ſtrong in ſpirit, and ᵈ was in
the deſarts till the day of his ſhewing unto Iſrael

ᵖ Pſ lxxii 18 ᵍ Ex iii 16 — iv 31 ʳ Pſ cxxxii 17 ˢ Jer xxiii 5 & xxx 10. Acts iii 21 ᵗ Pſ cvi 10. ᵘ Lev xxvi 42. ˣ Gen xii 3 & xvii 4 & xxii 16 Heb vi 13 17 ʸ Jer xxxii 40 Heb ix 14 ᶻ Theſ iv 7. 2 Tim i 9 Tit ii 12 1 Pet i 15 ᵃ Iſa xl 3 Mal iii 1 & iv 5 Ver 17 † Or for Chap iii 3 ‡ Or, Bowels of the mercy, &c. § Or, ſun-riſing or branch Num xxiv 17 Iſa xi 1 Zech iii 8 & vi 12 Mal iv ᵇ Iſa ix 2 & lx 1 Matt iv 16 Acts xxvi 18 ᶜ Chap ii 40 ᵈ Mat iii 1

v 67—80 Zacharias, filled with the Holy Ghoſt, among his other aſcriptions of praiſe to the Lord, when his tongue was looſed, uttered the following prophetic ſong, relative to the Meſſiah's incarnation and redemption, and the fulfilment of the everlaſting covenant of grace to his people

1 He bleſſes, adores, and praiſes the God of his Iſrael for the ſalvation to be obtained by the Meſſiah, *who hath viſited and redeemed his people*, hath often done it before, but now more ſignally than ever, by that eternal redemption which his incarnate Son was about to obtain for his elect *and hath raiſed up a horn of ſalvation for us in the houſe of his ſervant David*, one able to ſave to the uttermoſt, and before whom all his foes muſt fall, ſprung from the royal race of David, according to his faithful promiſes, *as he ſpake by the mouth of his holy prophets, which have been ſince the world began*, from the promiſe made to fallen man in Paradiſe had this Saviour been the conſtant ſubject of the prophetic word, as the ſeed of the woman, the deſcendant of Abraham, of the tribe of Judah, and the family of David, and lo, the event verifies all the predictions The expected Saviour is now incarnate, and ready to appear, *that we ſhould be ſaved from our enemies*, the worſt of enemies, ſin, Satan, death, and hell, *and from the hand of all that hate us*, from this preſent evil world, and all the wicked who inhabit it, not a temporal, but, what is infinitely better, a ſpiritual ſalvation from all the powers of darkneſs and corruption *to perform the mercy promiſed to our fathers*, that mercy of all mercies, the ſending the Meſſiah, *and to remember his holy covenant*, which from eternity was eſtabliſhed, and is now about to be fulfilled by the obedience and death of Jeſus in behalf of his people, whereby all our forfeited mercies might be reſtored, and our title to glory be recovered, according to *the oath which he ſware to our father Abraham*, the father of all the faithful, both Jews and Gentiles, *that he would grant unto us*, in virtue of our divine Redeemer's undertaking, *that we being delivered out of the hands of our enemies*, thoſe ſpiritual enemies by whom we were enſlaved, and muſt have for ever continued under the bondage of corruption, unleſs the Son had made us free but, bleſſed be his name! he hath brought us by his blood, his righteouſneſs and grace, into the glorious liberty of the ſons of God, that we *might ſerve him without fear*, no longer in the ſpirit of a ſlave, but under the influence of that free ſpirit of adoption, where love caſteth out ſervile fear, and enables us to walk willingly and cheerfully, *in holineſs and righteouſneſs before him*, in the univerſal diſcharge of the duties of piety towards God, and juſtice towards men, at leaſt, under a prevailing deſire to do ſo, with ceaſeleſs prayer for divine aſſiſtance, *all the days of our life*, faithful and perſevering until death in his bleſſed ſervice and they who have found this fulfilled to them, have reaſon indeed to praiſe God without ceaſing

2 He bleſſes God for the particular mercy ſhewn to himſelf in giving him ſuch a ſon, whoſe office and dignity he in ſpirit foreſees *And thou child ſhalt be called the prophet of the Higheſt*, of that divine Immanuel, who is God over all, bleſſed for ever *for thou ſhalt go before the face of the Lord*, as the harbinger of the King of Glory, *to prepare his ways*, by preaching repentance, and directing ſinners to him, as the only Saviour of loſt ſouls *to give knowledge of ſalvation unto his people*, of a ſpiritual and eternal ſalvation wrought out by Jeſus, which he declared to them a ſalvation not obtained by any perſonal righteouſneſs of their own, as a matter of deſert, but freely beſtowed on them *by the remiſſion of their ſins thro' the tender mercy of our God*, the original fountain from whence all the great ſalvation flows, *whereby the day-ſpring*, or riſing ſun of righteouſneſs, *from on high hath viſited us*, with his reviving and refreſhing beams of grace, *to give light to them that ſit in darkneſs and in the ſhadow of death*, to thoſe who before through a veil darkly in types and figures caught the glimmering day, to diffuſe his bright influences amidſt the heathen world, covered with thickeſt darkneſs of idolatry and ignorance; and to ſhine into the minds of blind, ſtupid, and hardened ſinners, diſpelling the miſts of error, and chaſing the clouds of ſin away, enlightening the conſcience, and ſoftening the heart, in order *to guide our feet into the way of peace*; to peace with God through the atoning blood, to peace within, through the application of it to our ſouls, to peace with men, through the ſpirit of univerſal love, to eternal peace, the conſummation of our felicity

3 The younger years of the Baptiſt ſtrongly corroborated this prediction concerning him *He grew, and waxed ſtrong in ſpirit*, his parts and capacity increaſed wonderfully with his ſtature, and his ſoul was filled with uncommon wiſdom, fortitude, and grace *and he was in the deſarts till the day of his ſhewing unto Iſrael*, living in ſolitude, retirement, and devotion, till the time appointed for his entering upon his prophetic office *Note*, They who moſt carefully improve their younger days in the ſchool of true wiſdom, will be beſt qualified to appear, and moſt likely to be ſucceſsful, when they are called forth to miniſter in public

CHAP II.

In this chapter we have, 1 *The birth of Chriſt at Bethlehem* 2. *The notifying of his birth to the ſhepherds in that neighbourhood by an angel, the ſong of praiſe which the angels ſung upon that occaſion, and the ſpreading of the report of it by the ſhepherds*, ver 8—20 3 *The circumciſion of Chriſt, and the naming of him*, ver 21 4 *The preſenting of him in the temple*, ver 22—24 5 *The teſtimonies of Simeon and Anna the propheteſs concerning him*, ver 25—39 6 *Chriſt's growth and pregnancy*, ver 40—52 7 *His obſerving the paſſover at twelve years old, and his diſcourſe with the doctors in the temple*, ver 41—51

1 AND it came to paſs in thoſe days, that there
went out a decree from Cæſar Auguſtus, that
all the world ſhould be † taxed 2 (And this taxing
was firſt ‡ made when Cyrenius was governor of Syria)
3 And all went to be taxed, every one into his own
city 4 And Joſeph alſo went up from Galilee, out
of the city of Nazareth, into Judea, unto the city of
David, which is called ᵃ Bethlehem (becauſe ᵇ he was of
the houſe and lineage of David) 5 To be taxed with
Mary his eſpouſed wife, being great with child 6
And ſo it was, that while they were there, the days
were accompliſhed that ſhe ſhould be delivered 7
And ᶜ ſhe brought forth her firſt born ſon, and wrapped
him in ſwaddling clothes, and laid him in a manger, be-
cauſe there was no room for them in the inn.

† Or enrolled ‡ Or executed ᵃ Mic v 2. Mat ii 5, 6. John vii 42 ᵇ Mat i ᶜ Mat i 25

v 1—7 The morning ſtar being riſen, the ſun of righteouſneſs cannot be far behind in the fulneſs of time God ſends forth his Son, born of a woman We have here,

1 The time of Chriſt's birth; in the reign of Auguſtus Cæſar When he had extended the Roman monarchy to the greater part of the known world, and was now in perfect peace throughout his vaſt empire, he ordered a general enrollment to be made through the provinces, that every man, according to his ability, might pay a ſuitable tax and this was done under the inſpection of Cyrenius, the governor of Syria, with which Judea was joined in one province, ſo that it evidently appeared the ſcepter was departed from Judah, by this badge of ſervitude,

107

servitude, *Gen* xlix 10 the fourth monarchy was now risen to its glory, *Dan* ii 44 and therefore in this time of peace was the proper and appointed period fixed by the antient prophecies for the appearing of the Prince of peace, the Messiah

2 The place where Jesus was born, at Bethlehem whither his parents were obliged to travel, on account of this enrollment, they being of the lineage of David, and therefore called to appear at the seat of their ancestors Augustus only meant his own glory and advantage in this matter, but God had designs to serve by him, he knew not it was thus evident that our Lord sprung from David, and the scripture was fulfilled which fixed his going forth from Bethlehem, *Micah* v 2 By such mysterious ways doth God work, accomplishing the purposes of his own will, and making those who least intend it, subservient to his own designs

3 The wretched circumstances in which Christ came into the world Though a first-born son, and of royal extraction, not to mention his divine honours, yet was he born in the stable of an inn, and his cradle a manger, his parents being so poor as to be unable to procure better accommodations Thus did the everlasting Father become an infant of days, He who bound up the deep in swaddling bands, was himself swathed as a babe, He whom the heaven, and the heaven of heavens cannot contain, was laid in a manger, He, who in uncreated glory on his eternal throne, was the object of adoration to all the angelic hosts, is thrust into a stable to dwell among the beasts of the earth So low did he humble himself when he became man for us men and for our salvation, and took the form of a servant, as a prelude to his submitting to the death of a slave

8 And there were in the same country shepherds
abiding in the field, keeping † watch over their flock
by night 9 And lo, the angel of the Lord came upon
them, and the glory of the Lord shone round about
them, and ᵉ they were sore afraid 10 And the angel
said unto them, ᶠ Fear not for behold, I bring you
good tidings of great joy, which shall be to all people
11 For ᵍ unto you is born this day, in the city of David, a Saviour, ʰ which is Christ the Lord 12 And
this *shall be* a sign unto you, Ye shall find the babe
wrapped in swaddling clothes, lying in a manger 13
And suddenly there was with the angel ⁱ a multitude of
the heavenly host praising God, and saying, 14 ᵏ Glory
to God in the highest, and on earth ˡ peace, good will
towards men 15 And it came to pass, as the angels
were gone away from them into heaven, ‡ the shepherds
said one to another, Let us now go even unto Bethlehem, and see this thing which is come to pass, which
the Lord hath made known unto us 16 And they
came with haste, and found Mary and Joseph, and the
babe lying in a manger 17 And when they had seen
it, they made known abroad the saying which was told
them concerning this child 18 And all they that
heard *it*, wondred at those things which were told them
by the shepherds 19 But Mary ᵐ kept all these things,
and pondered *them* in her heart 20 And the shepherds
returned, glorifying and praising God for all the things
that they had heard and seen, as it was told unto them

† Or night watches
ᵈ Chap ix 31
ᵉ Ibid i 12
ᶠ Id 13 30 Rev i 17
ᵍ Isa ix 6
ʰ Chap i 43
ⁱ Heb i 6
ᵏ Chap xix 38
ˡ Isa lvii 19 Mic iv 2 Rom v 1 Eph ii 17
‡ Gr The men the shepherds
ᵐ Chap i 66 Ver 51 Gen xxxvii 11

v 8—20 Amidst the deepest humiliations of Jesus, some bright displays of his uncreated glory still broke forth, that we might not stumble at the meanness of his appearing in the flesh, but be made to confess, truly this is the Son of God We have here,

1 The appearance of an angelic minister to notify the birth of the Prince of peace, not to the mighty monarchs of the earth that they should come and pay their homage before the King of kings, and Lord of lords, but to poor shepherds, who were by night watching their flock The things that are despised from the beginning hath God chosen They were employed in their honest calling, and then were favoured with this unexpected visit from above God will put the honour upon industry The angel *stood over them* in the air, and the earth shone with his brightness, a divine glory compassed him about, and fear seized their minds at the presence of this celestial messenger Visits from the unseen world to men conscious how ill they have deserved at God's hand, may well alarm us, and make even gracious souls afraid

2 The heavenly visitant soon quieted their troubled minds, saying, *Fear not*, no danger is near, no evil portended, but the very contrary, *for behold* (with wonder and delight attend my message) *I bring you good tidings of great joy*, the happiest news that ever reached the sinful sons of men, and *which shall be to all people*, not to the Jews only, but to the Gentiles also, alike interested in this message *For unto you is born this day, in the city of David, a Saviour, which is Christ the Lord*, the long expected Messiah, the Lord of life and glory, *the Saviour* to the uttermost, *to you*, and all those who come to God by him, and that without him must have been for ever undone *And this shall be a sign unto you*, whereby you may assuredly know him, and a strange sign indeed it was, *ye shall find the babe wrapped in swaddling clothes, lying in a manger*, the last place surely where they would ever have sought the Messiah, after such a glorious herald had proclaimed his birth and titles, but the most eminent distinction of God incarnate was his deep *humiliation* *Note*, (1) If there be a Saviour born, we must seek him for ourselves that we may obtain an interest in him (2) None perish in their sins, but they who will not come to him that they may have life, for he is able to save to the uttermost all who come to God by him, seeing he is Christ the Lord

3 Suddenly a multitude of the angelic host joined this celestial messenger, to celebrate the divine glory, and to congratulate the sons of men on this auspicious occasion The morning stars that sing together, and all those sons of God who shouted for joy to see the world's foundation laid, now join with greater transport to adore this more transcendent display of the divine benignity in the redemption of sinners by the incarnation of Jehovah (1) They ascribe to God *glory in the highest*, all his divine perfections are to the uttermost exalted, his infinite mercy that moved him to pity sinners, his surpassing wisdom that contrived, and his Almighty power and grace that accomplished the wondrous means of man's salvation, his inviolable justice, his matchless love, his unchangeable faithfulness to his promises, all shine with peculiar lustre in the redemption which is by Jesus Christ (2) They congratulate the sinful sons of Adam on the peace sent down from heaven to earth Peace with God, as reconciled through his Son, peace in the sinner's conscience now undisturbed with fears of guilt, peace between the discordant sons of men, and all these blessings in time and eternity purely flowing from God's *good will*, not for the sake of any thing in us, but according to his good pleasure, and to the praise of the glory of his grace If angels sing, shall men be silent? How ought we to echo back the sound, for us, and not for them is this salvation wrought, to us this mercy is extended, most bounden therefore are we for ever to bless and praise the God of all grace for this inestimable gift, the Son of his love

4 No sooner had these angelic ministers finished the heavenly song, and returned to their shining realms of bliss, than instantly the shepherds resolved to go and see this wondrous child, fully persuaded of the truth of what they had heard, and acknowledging the distinguishing mercy of God in having thus revealed it unto them Hasting therefore to Bethlehem, they found every circumstance as it had been told them, and *the babe lying in the manger* *Note*, When God sends us on his errands, we should make no delay all must be left to go where he calls

5 Fully confirmed in the persuasion that this was the promised Saviour, they failed not to spread the glad tidings, relating all they had seen and heard from the angel, or Mary, concerning this child And as they were plain and unexceptionable men, concurred in the same report, were eye and ear-witnesses of the facts they asserted, it exceedingly amazed all those to whom they told the story, they knew not how to question the truth, and yet that the Messiah should be born in a stable, that his parents should be persons so obscure, that poor shepherds only should be favoured with the notice of his birth, and not the chief priests and rulers of the nation, all these circumstances staggered them Thus the report was the wonder of a day, and soon died away, and was forgotten, *but Mary kept all these things, and pondered them in her heart*, comparing them with what had before passed, confirmed thereby in her faith and hope, and silently storing up every circumstance in her memory against some future occasion Mean time the shepherds returned to their former occupation, blessing and praising God for what they had heard and seen, so exactly correspondent with all that the angels had told them, and waiting, no doubt, in hope for the day when the child should come to manhood, and publicly appear as Israel's Saviour

21 And ⁿ when eight days were accomplished for
the circumcising of the child, his name was called
ᵒ JESUS, which was so named of the angel before he
was conceived in the womb 22 And when ᵖ the days
of her purification, according to the law of Moses, were
accomplished, they brought him to Jerusalem, to present
him to the Lord, 23 (As it is written in the law of
the Lord, ᑫ Every male that openeth the womb, shall be
called holy to the Lord) 24 And to offer a sacrifice
according to that which is said in the law of the Lord, ʳ
A pair of turtle-doves, or two young pigeons

ⁿ Gen xvii 12 Lev xii 3
ᵒ Mat i 21 Chap i 31
ᵖ Lev xii 2
ᑫ Exod xiii 2 Numb iii 13 viii 17
ʳ Lev xii 8

v 21—24 He who was made under the law *for us*, submitted not only to all the moral precepts, but to the ceremonial institutions

1 He was circumcised the eighth day, thus submitting himself thereby to the observance of the law, humbling himself to the painful rite, as born in the likeness of sinful flesh, owning himself

of the seed o Abraham, and wearing his badge of the children of God, as under the instituted seal of the covenant devoted to him At this time, as usual, his name was also given him, and he was called *Jesus*, having been so named of the angel before his conception, to signify his glorious character as *a Saviour* from sin Satan, death, and hell

2 He was, at the end of the time appointed for his mother's purification, or forty days, *their* purification, as some copies read, *Lev* xii 24 presented in the temple as holy to the Lord, *Exod* xiii 2 God having reserved to himself the first-born of Israel, in commemoration of his sparing them when he slew the Egyptians, and they were to be redeemed at the price of *five shekels*, about Twelve Shillings and Six-pence, *Numb* xviii 16 whilst his mother also brought an offering for herself, according to the prescription of the same law, a pair of turtle-doves, or young pigeons, which in case of poverty were accepted instead of a lamb and a dove, *Lev* xii 6—8 the one as a sin-offering of atonement, in testimony of her unworthiness of the mercy she had received, the other as a burnt-offering, expressive of her thankfulness

25 And behold there was a man in Jerusalem, whose name *was* Simeon, and the same man *was* just and devout, waiting for the consolation of Israel and the holy Ghost was upon him 26 And it was revealed unto him by the *holy Ghost*, that he should not see death before he had seen the Lord's Christ 27 And he came by the spirit into the temple and when the parents brought in the child Jesus, to do for him after the custom of the law, 28 Then took he him up in his arms, and blessed God, and said, 29 Lord, now lettest thou thy servant depart in peace, according to thy word, 30 For mine eyes have seen thy salvation 31 Which thou hast prepared before the face of all people 32 A light to lighten the Gentiles, and the glory of thy people Israel 33 And Joseph and his mother marvelled at those things which were spoken of him 34 And Simeon blessed them, and said unto Mary his mother, Behold, this *child* is set for the fall and rising again of many in Israel, and for a sign which shall be spoken against 35 (Yea, a sword shall pierce through thy own soul also) that the thoughts of many hearts may be revealed 36 And there was one Anna a prophetess, the daughter of Phanuel, of the tribe of Aser, she was of a great age, and had lived with an husband seven years from her virginity 37 And she *was* a widow of about fourscore and four years which departed not from the temple, but served *God* with fastings and prayers night and day 38 And she coming in that instant, gave thanks likewise unto the Lord, and spake of him to all them that looked for redemption in Jerusalem

v 25—38 Amidst all the meanness and poverty of Jesus, very glorious were the testimonies born to him from heaven and upon earth We have here,

1 The public declarations of Simeon, a man, it seems, of distinguished note in Jerusalem, who just then came, by divine direction, into the temple

[1] The account here given concerning him is greatly to his honour *He was just*, toward men, *and devout*, eminently religious toward God, *waiting* in faith and patience *for the consolation of Israel*, the promised Messiah, whose coming in the flesh was to be the great joy of all his people, Gentile as well as Jew, the time of whose appearing, fixed in the prophetic writings, was now at hand *and the Holy Ghost was upon him*, not only as a spirit of holiness, but as a spirit of prophecy *And it was revealed unto him by* the secret inspiration of *the Holy Ghost, that he should not see death before he had seen the Lord's Christ*, whom his eyes should behold before they were closed in the dust *And accordingly*, just at that instant, *he came by the spirit into the temple*, under some divine warning of what was doing there *and when the parents brought in the child Jesus, to do for him after the custom of the law*, to present him to the Lord, and pay the price of redemption, *then took he him up in his arms*, in a transport of joy, at having found him whom he had so long and so earnestly expected *and blessed God*, and broke forth into the following prophetic song of praise *Note*, (1) We must not be weary of waiting, though the Lord may for a while exercise our patience, all his promises are sure (2) Christ the consolation of his Israel, he makes all those happy who by faith embrace him (3) They who have Jesus in their arms, in their hearts, can look death in the face with confidence

[2] His discourse on this occasion was solemn and joyful He said, *Lord, now lettest thou thy servant depart in peace, according to thy word*, I crave life, welcome death! He is now content to be gone, since God hath thus graciously fulfilled his promise to him, and cheerfully resigns his soul in confidence of exchanging a perishing world for an eternity of glory *For mine eyes have seen thy salvation*, that Messiah, who is come to be the author of eternal salvation to his redeemed, *which thou hast prepared before the face of all people*, provided according to the eternal counsels, and now manifested in the flesh to accomplish the glorious work, *A light to lighten the Gentiles*, who have long sat in darkness, ignorance, and idolatry, but now shall be made partakers of the light of truth and the grace of the gospel, *and the glory of thy people Israel*, among whom his personal ministry was employed, who were spectators of his miracles, from whom he descended after the flesh, by whom, as his apostles and evangelists, he first propagated the knowledge of his salvation, and in him all the spiritual Israel are justified, and shall glory, *Isa* xlv 25 *Note*, (1) A believing sight of Christ, and of the great things he hath prepared for his people, will not only enable us to overcome the terrors of death, but to triumph in its approach (2) We may not leave our post till the Lord grants us our dismission, our time is in his hand, whilst he hath work for us to do, we must be content to be here, till he calls us to depart, and be with Christ, which is far better (3) Christ is the sun of righteousness, there is nothing but darkness and death in the spiritual world, till he arises with healing in his wings

[3] Simeon concludes with his benediction on the parents of Jesus, and a prediction for their notice They marvelled at these transcendently glorious testimonies which were born to their infant son, whilst Simeon congratulated them on their distinguished felicity, and prayed that the best of blessings might descend upon them *He blessed them, and said unto Mary his mother*, as more especially the parent of Jesus, and interested in what he was about to say, *behold*, with wonder and confidence of the truth which I declare, *this child is set for the fall and rising again of many in Israel*, he will be to many native Jews a stone of stumbling, and a rock of offence, *Isa* viii 14—18 whilst by his power and grace others shall be raised up to newness of life, even many who at first were offended at him, and he shall quicken all his spiritual Israel throughout the world, and bring them to a state of happiness and glory, *and for a sign which shall be spoken against*, his humiliation and sufferings will give handle to his persecutors to blaspheme and revile him, *yea*, and so bitter will the enmity be against him, that it will extend to all his relations and friends, *a sword shall pierce through thy own soul also*, such anguish and pain you will endure from the view of his insults and sufferings, and those you may be called to endure for the profession of your faith in him, *that the thoughts of many hearts may be revealed*, these times of persecution most effectually serving to discover the faithful disciples from the hypocrites and apostates *Note*, (1) The same gospel is to some the savour of death unto death, which to others is the savour of life unto life (2) They whom Jesus raises, must first be laid low in the dust of humiliation (3) All our comforts in this world have some bitterness annexed to them, we must look only for perfect happiness in a better

2 Anna the prophetess confirms, just at the same instant, what Simeon had spoken concerning the glory of the child Jesus

[1] Her person and character are described Her name was Anna, whom the Lord had endued with a spirit of prophecy She was the daughter of Phanuel, a person probably of some note, and of the tribe of Asher, a very aged woman, having lived seven years with a husband, and ever since continued *a widow of about eighty-four years*, a great age, if comprehending the whole of her life, but if reckoned as her years of widowhood, will carry her age at lowest to above a hundred years Yet though so old, she constantly attended the stated worship of the temple morning and evening, and on all solemn occasions, and was much in fasting and prayer, a singular instance of piety and devotion

[2] Her testimony concerning Jesus is recorded Just at the instant that Simeon was discoursing concerning him, she came in, and with thanksgiving and praise to the Lord, confirmed what he had spoken concerning this child And among all her religious acquaintance, who were expecting the Messiah's appearing, and looking for his redemption, she spake of the Son of Mary, the person raised up of God for this great design *Note*, (1) They who are constant at the temple, meet a refund to keep up communion with God, will find many a blessed and happy visit from him which they perhaps little expected (2) They who know Jesus themselves, are in duty bound to spread the knowledge far and wide, and to endeavour to bring others to an acquaintance with his salvation

39 And when they had performed all things according to the law of the Lord, they returned into Galilee, to their own city Nazareth 40 And the child grew, and waxed strong in spirit, filled with wisdom, and the grace of God was upon him 41 ¶ Now his parents went to Jerusalem every year at the feast of the passover 42 And when he was twelve years old,

they

they went up to Jerusalem after the custom of the feast,
43 And when they had fulfilled the days, as they re-
turned, the child Jesus tarried behind in Jerusalem,
and Joseph and his mother knew not *of it* 44 But
they supposing him to have been in the company, went
a days journey, and they sought him among *their* kins-
folk and among their acquaintance 45 And when
they found him not, they turned back again to Jerusa-
lem, seeking him 46 And it came to pass, that after
three days they found him in the temple, sitting in the
midst of the doctors, both hearing them, and asking
f Mat vii 28 Mark i 22 Chap iv 22, 32 John vii 15, 46 them questions 47 And f all that heard him were asto-
nished at his understanding and answers 48 And when
they saw him, they were amazed and his mother said
unto him, Son, why hast thou thus dealt with us? be-
hold thy father and I have sought thee sorrowing 49
And he said unto them, How is it that ye sought me?
g John ii 16 wist ye not that I must be g about my Father's business?
h Chap ix 45 & xviii 34 50 And h they understood not the saying which he spake
unto them 51 And he went down with them, and
came to Nazareth, and was subject unto them but his
i Gen xxxvii 11 Dan vii 28 Ver 19 mother i kept all these sayings in her heart 52 And
k 1 Sam ii 26 Ver 40. Jesus k increased in wisdom and † stature, and in favour
† Or age with God and men.

v 39—52 Our curiosity might have tempted us to wish for some more large and particular accounts of the infancy and childhood of Jesus, but as till his public appearance in the character of the Messiah we had no particular need of it, all that the Holy Ghost hath been pleased to record of the first twenty-nine years of his life, is contained in these few verses, where some beams of his glory, even from his earliest days, are seen to break forth, as presages of his future greatness

1 After he was presented in the temple, till twelve years of age, he for the most part lived with his parents at Nazareth, whither they were directed to go, after their return from Egypt, *Mat* ii There he grew up as other children do, and as his stature increased, and reason began to dawn, he displayed the most uncommon natural abilities, was endued with wisdom far beyond his years, and instead of that foolishness which is bound up in the heart of all other children, and immediately begins to discover itself with the first dawnings of sense, in him nothing was seen of folly or perverseness The grace of God eminently governed his spirit and conduct from his tenderest years, and the favour of God towards him appeared most evident and singular

2 At the age of twelve, he gave some amazing evidences of his extraordinary wisdom, and some intimations of the great work he had in view

[1] At this time he went up to Jerusalem with his parents to the passover, where all the males, from that age, were commanded to appear to celebrate this solemnity *Note*, It is highly incumbent on parents to acquaint their children betimes with their covenant relation to God, and to endeavour to engage them early, with their own free choice, to surrender themselves up to him as his willing servants

[2] When they had stayed during the seven days of the feast, and then set out on their return for Nazareth, the child Jesus tarried behind in Jerusalem, probably when they went up to worship, on the morning before they proceeded on their journey, he left them in the temple, and as the men and women travelled in different companies, each of his parents supposed he had been with the other, or with some of their kins-folk, great numbers of which travelled together, till at even, when they met, to their surprize they missed their Son, and after a fruitless search among all their kinsfolk and acquaintance, they turned back to Jerusalem in the morning to seek for him *Note*, (1) They who have lost the presence of Jesus, after having ever tasted the blessedness of his company, cannot but be solicitous to find him again, and will enquire earnestly, *Saw ye him whom my soul loveth?* (2) Our kinsfolk and acquaintance are too often unable to direct us to Jesus, we must go farther for our information

[3] At last they found him on the third day in the temple, in one of the chambers, probably where the Sanhedrim sat, or where the wise men instructed their catechumens, there Jesus was, among other young persons, hearing their discourses, answering their questions with the most amazing acuteness, and proposing others to them, which shewed uncommon wisdom and penetration, insomuch that they were all astonished at the sagacity of his replies, and the depth of his understanding, so exceedingly beyond his years, and such as made him appear worthy a place among the highest rabbi's, instead of a seat at their feet as a catechumen

[4] Having found him, they were amazed to see him thus admired and esteemed by the doctors, and his mother began tenderly to expostulate with him on his stay, which had given them such anxiety and grief but he gently rebuked her solicitude, who, after all that had passed, ought not to be surprized at finding him there Where should he be so properly as in the courts of his Father's house, and what so fit an employment for him, as to be thus *about his Father's business*? But they *understood* not his meaning his regal office, as the Messiah, the son of David, they believed, but his prophetical character, and the nature of his spiritual kingdom, they seem not yet to have known

3 He returned to Nazareth, submitting to his parents in every instance of filial duty, and his mother stored up his sayings in her mind, expecting, that though she now understood them not, hereafter they would be explained more fully Till he was near thirty years of age, he continued in this obscure abode, and under the government of his parents, probably working as a carpenter for their maintenance and his own and as he advanced to manhood, his attainments in wisdom and understanding were amazing, his faculties most enlarged, and his soul filled with all those gifts and graces which the human nature, by its union with the divine, was prepared to receive. Thus he grew highly in God's favour, and admired and esteemed by all who were acquainted with his singular excellencies *Note*, (1) Let children, when grown up, learn of Jesus subjection to their parents, that is a duty we must ever pay (2) Though the truths of God which we are taught may not at first be understood by us, yet the knowledge of them will prove highly useful, when afterwards God gives the spiritual understanding (3) Those children are indeed their parents glory and joy, whose wisdom and graces increase with their years, and exceed them

CHAP III

In this chapter we have, 1 *The beginning of John's baptism, and the scope and intention of it,* ver 1—6 *His exhortation to the multitude,* ver 7—9 *And the particular instructions he gave to those who desired to be told their duty,* ver 10—14 2 *The notice he gave them of the approach of the Messiah,* ver 15—18 *to which is added (though it happened after what follows) the mention of his imprisonment,* ver 19, 20 3 *Christ coming to be baptised of John, and his entrance thereon upon the execution of his prophetical office,* ver 21, 22 4 *His pedigree and genealogy recorded up to Adam,* ver 23—38

1 NOW in the fifteenth year of the reign of
Tiberius Cesar, Pontius Pilate being governor
of Judea, and Herod being tetrarch of Galilee, and his
brother Philip tetrarch of Iturea, and of the region of
Trachonitis, and Lysanias the tetrarch of Abilene, 2
a Annas and Caiaphas being the high priests, the word a John xi 49, 51 & xviii 13 Acts iv 6
of God came unto John the son of Zacharias in the
wilderness 3 b And he came into all the country about b Mat iii 1 &c Mark i 4 &c
Jordan, preaching the baptism of c repentance for the
remission of sins, 4 As it is written in the book of
the words of Esaias the prophet, saying, d The voice of c Ezek xviii 30
one crying in the wilderness, Prepare ye the way of the d Isa xl 3 John i 23
Lord, make his paths straight 5 Every valley shall
be filled, and every mountain and hill shall be brought
low, and the crooked shall be made straight, and the
rough ways shall be made smooth; 6 And e all flesh e Isa lii 10.
shall see the salvation of God 7 Then said he to the
multitude that came forth to be baptized of him, f O f Mat iii 7 & xii 34 & xxiii 33
generation of vipers, who hath warned you to flee from
g the wrath to come? 8 Bring forth therefore fruits g Rom v 9 1 Thes i 10
worthy of repentance, and begin not to say within
yourselves, h We have Abraham to *our* father for I h John viii 33, 39 Acts xiii 26
say unto you, that God is able of these stones to raise
up children unto Abraham 9 And now also the ax
is laid unto the root of the trees i every tree therefore i Mat vii 19 John xv 6
which bringeth not forth good fruit, is hewn down,
and cast into the fire 10 And the people asked him,
saying, k What shall we do then? 11 He answereth k Acts ii 37
and saith unto them, l He that hath two coats, let him l Chap xi 41 Jam ii 15, 16. 1 John iii 17
impart to him that hath none; and he that hath meat,
let him do likewise 12. Then came also m publicans
to be baptized, and said unto him, Master, what shall m Mat xxi 32
we do? 13 And he said unto them, Exact no more
than that which is appointed you 14 And the sol-
diers likewise demanded of him, saying, And what shall
we do? And he said unto them, † Do violence to no † Or put no man in fear
man, neither accuse *any* falsly, and be content with
your ‡ wages ‡ Or allowance

v 1—14 Great expectations had been raised concerning the son of Zacharias from his infancy, and now he appears to answer them

1 The

1 The time of his entring publicly on his ministry, is here observed It was in the reign of Tiberius, when Pontius Pilate was governor of Judea, Herod tetrarch of Galilee, his brother Philip of Iturea, and Lysanias of Abilene They were called tetrarchs, either as having each the fourth part of what was under the dominion of Herod the Great, or as standing in the fourth rank of governors, which are reckoned thus, the emperor, proconsuls, kings, tetrarchs They were all foreigners, a mark of the sad subjection of the Jewish people, now reduced entirely under the Roman yoke, the sceptre being finally departed from Judah and the very kingly office abolished in Judea *Annas and Caiaphas being the high-priests*, not that they both bore that office at the same time, but Annas had been, and Caiaphas was now in that station, or as some suppose, Annas was the *sagan*, or chief of the priests, who stood next to the high priest in rank and honour

2 The origin and tendency of his ministry is declared *The word of God came to him in the wilderness*, he was inwardly moved by the Holy Ghost to go forth, being endued with extraordinary gifts and graces, and possessed of the spirit of prophecy, and hereupon leaving the solitude where he had hitherto abode, he came into a more populous part of the country near to Jordan, preaching publickly the necessity of repentance, and admitting to his baptism those who made profession of it, as the sign and seal of the remission of their sins *Note*, All who by faith turn to Jesus, and repent them truly of their sins, are assured of their pardon

3 John herein eminently fulfilled the prophecy of Isaiah, *chap* xl 3—5 He was *the voice of one crying in the wilderness*, loud and vehement, *prepare ye the way of the Lord* into your hearts, by a deep and humbling sense of your sins *make his paths straight*, let every obstruction from pride and ignorance be removed, as the harbinger clears the way for the entry of the king *Every valley shall be filled*, the lowly and depressed with sin shall be raised up by pardoning grace and divine consolations, *and every mountain and hill shall be brought low*, the proud and self-righteous shall be humbled into the dust of humiliation, or sunk into the belly of hell, *and the crooked shall be made straight*, the perverse dispositions and conduct of sinners shall by divine grace be rectified, *and the rough ways shall be made smooth*, the most untractable spirits softened and subdued, or every difficulty in the way of men's receiving the Messiah shall be removed *And all flesh*, not of the Jews only, but of the Gentiles also, *shall see the salvation of God*, many of all nations, ranks, and ages shall embrace the gospel of Jesus, and partake of his eternal redemption

4 He addressed himself with very awakening language to the multitude who came to him He charges them as *a generation of vipers*, full of venom, hypocrisy, and Satanical subtilty, and asks, *who hath warned you to flee from the wrath to come?* from the national judgments ready to descend upon them, or the more terrible and eternal vengeance hanging over every guilty sinner's head He warns them therefore of the necessity of a speedy and real change of heart and life, evident in the fruits of all holy conversation and godliness without which, their boasted privilege as Abraham's descendants, would profit them nothing, but rather aggravate their guilt God wanted them not, he could, and would, from stones, from Gentiles, raise up a more illustrious and numerous race, the heirs of Abraham's faith, his spiritual children, who should supply their place, if they continued hypocritical and impenitent now therefore the call of mercy was sent to them, that they might prevent their impending doom, before the ax of divine vengeance was laid to their roots, and they, as barren trees, cut down and cast into the fire, utterly destroyed as a nation, and as the sinners of old, suffering also the vengeance of eternal fire *Note*, (1) The sinner hath no moment to lose, death and judgment are at his heels (2) No outward privilege can profit those, whose hearts remain unrenewed and unholy (3) True repentance will be seen by its fruits, the change will be internal, universal, evident, abiding (4) It is a fearful thing for an impenitent soul to fall into the hands of the living God

5 The Pharisees and Sadducees were probably disgusted at these hard sayings, and left him, but the people, the publicans and soldiers, were deeply affected, and earnestly sollicitous to know what those fruits of repentance were, which they were required to produce and a blessed symptom it is of real conversion, when we are thus diligent to enquire what is the mind of God, and really disposed through grace to follow it To these, therefore, John directs his instruction suited to their several circumstances and temptations.

[1] To the people in general he recommends a liberal distribution to the necessities of their brethren, supplying them according to their ability with food and raiment, and where the call was urgent, straitning themselves rather than suffer their neighbours to perish with cold, or be famished with hunger and a truly charitable soul is not only to his power, but sometimes above his power, willing

[2] To the publicans, the collectors of the public taxes, many of whom were Jews, he gave in charge that they should use no extortion, nor levy more than the government demanded their employment, though in general odious to the people, was not in itself unlawful, whilst they demeaned themselves in it with justice and integrity

[3] To the soldiers, who seem to have been also Hebrews, perhaps the guards of Philip, or Herod, he said, *do violence to no man*, extort nothing from the people by threatning, behave not insolent, nor outrageous in your quarters, when employed in war, use no unnecessary devastations, nor wanton cruelty; *neither accuse any falsly*, neither their comrades to their officers, or the people where they might be stationed, through malice, or for the sake of money, *and be content with your wages*, neither increasing them by plunder, nor seeking to advance them by mutiny, a caution well deserving the notice of all servants, who, if once they give way to discontent, will soon be tempted to use unlawful means to gratify their covetousness

15 And as the people were in † expectation, and all † Or suspense
men mused in their hearts of John, whether he were the
Christ, or not, 16 John answered, saying unto them
all, ⁿ I indeed baptize you with water, but one mightier ⁿ Acts i 5
than I cometh, the latchet of whose shoes I am not wor- & xi 16 & xix 4
thy to unloose ᵒ he shall baptize you with the Holy ᵒ Isa xliv 3
Ghost, and with fire 17 ᵖ Whose fan *is* in his hand, Joel ii 28
and he will throughly purge his floor, and will gather ᵖ Mal iii 3
the wheat into his garner, but ᑫ the chaff he will burn ᑫ Mal iv 1
with fire unquenchable 18 And many other things in
his exhortation preached he unto the people 19 ʳ But ʳ Mat xiv 3
Herod the tetrarch, being reproved by him for Herodias Mark vi 17
his brother Philip's wife, and for all the evils which
Herod had done, 20 Added yet this above all, that
he shut up John in prison

v 15—20 We have here,

1 The general expectations which the people were in of the Messiah The sceptre was departed from Judah, and the prophecies of Daniel concerning him now required his coming, which made many turn their eyes to John, who appeared with marks of such singular distinction, and spoke with such authority and zeal, that they began to suspect this might be the long-expected Messiah

2 John immediately undeceived them, disclaiming all pretensions to that honour, and directs them to expect shortly the *Great Prophet*, whose forerunner he was The meanest office under him he acknowledges himself unworthy to discharge, and his baptism was not worthy to be compared with the more powerful and efficacious influences of that Holy Ghost, that, under the ministry of Jesus, should be abundantly dispensed, and act, like fire, with resistless energy upon the souls of men By *his gospel* he would make a thorough separation between the faithful and the hypocrites, and by *his judgments* on the Jewish people sweep them away as the chaff before the fan, and, when he hath gathered in his chosen, the wheat, into his garner, the wicked, the self-righteous, and the apostate, will be cast into the everlasting burnings An awful declaration, which deserves the most awakened attention

These and many other things did John with great freedom and fidelity deliver, preaching the glad tidings of the gospel (ευηγγελιζετο) to the people, and urging upon their consciences the importance of the truths he declared Such ministers ought all, who are put in trust with the gospel, to be, warm, zealous, indefatigable, free, copious, evangelical Then may we expect to reap the fruit of our labours, in a harvest of immortal souls

3 After a short but glorious course of about a year and a half, a sudden stop is put to the Baptist's ministry by a most unjust imprisonment Unable to flatter, yet zealous to reprove the most exalted sinners, Herod the tetrarch escaped not his sharp rebukes for the complicated crime of taking his brother Philip's wife, and marrying her even during his life, and though she had children by him, thus joining incest to adultery, *and for all the other evils which Herod had done*, which were many and notorious Exasperated at the plain and faithful dealing, he added this to all his other wickedness, that he shut up John in prison, and after a while was prevailed upon to take away his life. *Note*, (1) When God's ministers are thus compelled to an involuntary silence, their sufferings speak as loud as their sermons (2) Mysterious are the ways of Providence The excellent of the earth become a prey to persecutors, who triumph at their fall Where, will some say, is the God of judgment? Wait a moment The mystery will soon be unfolded

21 Now when all the people were baptized, ˢ it came ˢ Mat iii 13 Mark i 9
to pass, that Jesus also being baptized, and praying, the
heaven was opened 22 And the Holy Ghost descended
in a bodily shape like a dove ᵗ upon him, and ᵘ a voice ᵗ Isa xi 2
came from heaven, which said, ˣ Thou art my beloved ᵘ John xii 28
Son, in thee I am well pleased 23 And Jesus himself ˣ Psal ii 7 Isa xlii 1 Chap ix 35 2 Pet i 17
‖ began to be about thirty years of age, being (as was ‖ Or being about thirty years old when he began his ministry Num iv 3, 35, 39

(supposed) [y] the son of Joseph, which was *the son* of Heli,
24 Which was *the son* of Matthat, which was *the son*
of Levi, which was *the son* of Melchi, which was *the son*
of Janna, which was *the son* of Joseph, 25 Which was
the son of Mattathias, which was *the son* of Amos, which
was *the son* of Naum, which was *the son* of Esli, which
was *the son* of Nagge, 26 Which was *the son* of Maath,
which was *the son* of Mattathias, which was *the son* of
Semei, which was *the son* of Joseph, which was *the son*
of Judah, 27 Which was *the son* of Joanna, which
was *the son* of † Rhesa, which was *the son* of Zorobabel,
which was *the son* of Salathiel, which was *the son* of Neri,
28 Which was *the son* of Melchi, which was *the son* of
Addi, which was *the son* of Cosam, which was *the son*
of Elmodam, which was *the son* of Er, 29 Which was
the son of Jose, which was *the son* of Eliezer, which was
the son of Jorim, which was *the son* of Matthat, which
was *the son* of Levi, 30 Which was *the son* of Simeon,
which was *the son* of Juda, which was *the son* of Joseph,
which was *the son* of Jonan, which was *the son* of Eliakim,
31 Which was *the son* of Melea, which was *the*
son of Menan, which was *the son* of Mattatha, which was
the son of [z] Nathan, [a] which was *the son* of David,
32 [b] Which was *the son* of Jesse, which was *the son* of
Obed, which was *the son* of Booz, which was *the son* of
Salmon, which was *the son* of Naasson, 33 Which was
the son of Aminadab, which was *the son* of Aram, which
was *the son* of Esrom, which was *the son* of Phares, which
was *the son* of Juda, 34 Which was *the son* of Jacob,
which was *the son* of Isaac, which was *the son* of Abraham,
[c] which was *the son* of Thara, which was *the son* of Nachor,
35 Which was *the son* of Saruch, which was *the*
son of Ragau, which was *the son* of Phalec, which was
the son of Heber, which was *the son* of Sala, 36 Which
was *the son* of § Cainan, which was the *son* of Arphaxad,
[d] which was *the son* of Sem, which was *the son* of Noe,
which was *the son* of Lamech, 37 Which was *the son*
of Mathusala, which was *the son* of Enoch, which was
the son of Jared, which was *the son* of Maleleel, which
was *the son* of Cainan, 38 Which was *the son* of Enos,
which was *the son* of Seth, which was *the son* of Adam,
which was *the son* of God

[y] Mat xiii 55 John vi 42.
† These 19, from Joseph to Rhesa, were Christ's natural fathers, those mentioned Mat i 13—16 were his kindred and fathers by right of government
[z] Zech xii 12
[a] 2 Sam v 14 1 Chron iii 5
[b] Ruth iv 18 1 Chron ii 10
[c] Gen xi 24, 26
§ St Luke follows the Septuagint, in which Cainan is mentioned, though he is not in the Hebrew Gen x 24 & xi 12
[d] Gen xi 10.

v 21—38 The Evangelist finishes the history of John's ministry, which continued near a year after Christ's baptism, before he enters upon the publick appearance of Jesus

1 After a multitude of others had been baptised, at last Jesus also comes to John, and is baptised of him in Jordan when, looking up in prayer to his Father, instantly the heavens were opened, and the Holy Ghost in a bodily shape descended upon him, both to qualify him for his mediatorial work, and to be a sign to John that he was the Messiah, which was farther confirmed by an audible voice from heaven, God the Father testifying his delight in this Son of his love, and his perfect satisfaction in his undertaking *Note*, (1) Christ prayed, to set us the example In this way the communion between earth and heaven is to be maintained (2) If God be well pleased in his Son, then may we confidently rest our souls on him as our Saviour, and never doubt of the fulness of the redemption he hath obtained for us

2 The age and pedigree of Jesus are recorded by the Evangelist He was about thirty years of age when he entered upon the mediatorial office Descended from David by his mother's side, whose genealogy is here given, as well as by Joseph's his reputed father Some difficulties occur, in computing the genealogies Joseph, said in Matthew to be the son of Jacob, is here said to be the son of Heli, which some avoid by reading the words (*as was supposed the son of Joseph*) in a parenthesis, intimating that in reality Jesus was the son of Heli, Mary's father Or Joseph, being her husband, might be called, in right of his wife, Heli's son

Some have observed also, that the words (ως ενομιζετο) *as it was supposed*, may be rendered *as it was found in the record* of the genealogy, which the Evangelist copied, and none at that time ever contradicted

The inserting the name of Cainan between Sala and Arphaxad is of more difficult solution, it not agreeing with the Hebrew copies, nor any ancient version except the Septuagint, and is thought not to have been there originally, but that some early transcriber of Luke's gospel inserting this name by mistake, it afterwards crept into that translation The matter indeed is of little moment, and doth not in the least affect our salvation

Some, to whose sentiment I accede, chuse to carry the name of Jesus through all his ancestors, instead of connecting each with his immediate predecessor As thus, *Jesus* the son of Heli, of Matthat, *&c* till we come to the top of the line, as the son of Adam in his human, the Son of God in his divine nature, uniting both in his own person, and yet not two, but one Christ

CHAP IV

We left Christ newly baptized, and owned by a voice from heaven, and the descent of the Holy Ghost upon him Now in this chapter we have, 1 A further preparation of him for his public ministry by his being tempted in the wilderness *2 His entrance upon his public work in Galilee,* ver 14, 15 *particularly, (1) At Nazareth, the city where he had been bred up,* ver 16—30 *which we had no account of before in Matthew (2) At Capernaum, where, having preached to admiration,* ver 31, 32 *he cast the devil out of a man that was possessed,* ver 33—37 *Cured Peter's mother-in-law of a fever,* ver 38, 39 *And many others that were sick and possessed,* ver 40, 41 *And then went and did the same in other cities of Galilee,* ver 42—44

1 AND Jesus, being full of the Holy Ghost, returned from Jordan, and [a] was led by the Spirit
into the wilderness, 2 Being [b] forty days [c] tempted of
the devil, and in those days he did eat nothing and
when they were ended, he afterward hungred 3 And
the devil said unto him, If thou be the Son of God,
command this stone that it be made bread 4 And
Jesus answered him, saying, It is written, that [f] man
shall not live by bread alone, but by every word of God
5 And the devil, taking him up into an high mountain,
shewed unto him all the kingdoms of the world in a
moment of time 6 And the devil said unto him, All
this power will I give thee, and the glory of them, for
[g] that is delivered unto me, and to whomsoever I will I
give it 7 If thou therefore wilt worship me, all shall
be thine 8 And Jesus answered and said unto him,
Get thee behind me, Satan for it is written, [h] Thou
shalt worship the Lord thy God, and him only shalt thou
serve 9 And he brought him to Jerusalem, and set
him on a pinnacle of the temple, and said unto him, If
thou be the Son of God, cast thyself down from hence
10 For it is written, [i] He shall give his angels charge
over thee, to keep thee 11 And in *their* hands they
shall bear thee up, lest at any time thou dash thy foot
against a stone 12 And Jesus, answering, said unto
him, It is said, [k] Thou shalt not tempt the Lord thy
God 13 And when the devil had ended all the temptation,
[l] he departed from him [m] for a season

[a] Mat iv 1 Mark i 12
[c] Ex xxxiv 28 1 Kings xix 8
[e] Ecclus ii 1
[f] Deut viii 3
[g] Rev xiii 7
[h] Deut vi 13 &c
[i] Ps xci 11
[k] Deut vi 16
[l] Jam iv 7
[m] John xiv 30

v 1—13 As the great enemy of souls had foiled the first man in the midst of a paradise of delights, the second man, the Lord from heaven, who came to destroy the works of the devil, that he might render his victory more illustrious, gives the tempter every advantage Though deep retired in a dreary desert, without human converse, without food, during forty days, to satisfy his hunger, he stood like a rock in the midst of the sea, defying the impotent attacks of the raging fiend of darkness *Being full of the Holy Ghost*, and just then anointed for his mediatorial office, and furnished with the fulness of divine grace, Satan, to his bitter shame and vexation, found him immoveable, and every attack he made but signalized his own defeat

1 He tempted him to distrust his Father's care, and insinuated his suspicion of the character he assumed as the Son of God seeking to shake the faith of the Redeemer, and challenging him to give a proof of it by working so needful a miracle for his own supply But Jesus refused to gratify him, and by the sword of the Spirit, the word of God, foiled his assault, testifying his confidence in his Father's provision for him, refusing to take the matter out of his hand, and persuaded that he could by other means than by bread alone preserve his life and satisfy his hunger Hereby teaching us, (1) Under every temptation to have recourse to the word and promises of God (2) Not to give place to the devil, by harbouring for a moment his suggestions (3) Never to desire to be our own carvers, or think by our own contrivance and wisdom, exclusive of God, to extricate ourselves from our difficulties, or gain our own end, but quietly to resign ourselves to him, submissive to his providences, and constantly depending upon his blessing and support (4) That we should not estimate God's favour by his outward dispensations, nor call in question our adoption of him, though never so severely exercised Many of God's dearest children have known the pinchings of hunger, to prove their faith and try their patience

2 He tempted him with the enticing offers of temporal grandeur This St Matthew places the last, and such it seems to have been; though Luke inverts the order Taking him up into a mountain, the devil in a moment caused all the kingdoms of the world in their greatest glory to pass in review before our Lord,

Lord, as if to dazzle and charm him with their united ſplendor then boldly challenging them as his own, as if delivered to him, either by the Moſt High, which was falſe, or by the willing ſubjection of theſe nations and their kings, who yielded themſelves up to the devil's power, and, as Lord of all, he pretends therefore a right to diſpoſe of them at his pleaſure on one condition he proffers to lay them all at the feet of Jeſus, and conſtitute him the univerſal ſovereign, *If thou wilt worſhip me, all ſhall be thine* With indignation and abhorrence at ſuch inſolence and impiety, he rejects the tempter's offer, and, ſtill drawing his weapons from the ſacred magazine of Scripture, condemns the daring attempt of this hateful ſpirit thus to invade the divine prerogative, and confounds him with producing that eternal and invariable rule of worſhip, *Thou ſhalt worſhip the Lord thy God, and him only ſhalt thou ſerve* *Note*, All adoration of ſaints, angels, and the Virgin, is in fact but the worſhip of Satan, and as much a *ſacrifice to devils*, (1 Cor x 20) as the religious ſervices of Paganiſm

3 Once more the devil returns to the charge, and, ſince Chriſt is unmoved with grandeur, and unſhaken with diſtruſt, he tries to fill him with unwarrantable preſumption, and, ſetting him on a pinnacle of the temple, bids him caſt himſelf down into the court of worſhippers below, and, if he was really the Son of God, to prove it by ſuch a ſign from heaven as the Jews ſought, which, he ſuggeſts, would not fail of engaging them to receive him as the Meſſiah, nor could there be danger in the experiment, ſince God had given him an expreſs promiſe of protection, and he was under angelic care, *Pſalm* xci 11, 12 Chriſt ſeemed to lay ſuch ſtreſs upon the Scripture, therefore Satan quotes it too to ſupport his cauſe The word of God, in the hands of wicked men, is thus often perverted and wreſted to ſerve the vileſt purpoſes But Jeſus detects Satan's fallacy God is to be truſted, not tempted, as it is written, *Deut* vi 16 In the way of duty he will hold us up if, without any warrant from him, we expoſe ourſelves to needleſs danger, we have not the leaſt ground to hope for preſervation

Utterly defeated now, the devil quits the field, covered with ſhame, in malice ſtill inveterate Waiting therefore for a more favourable ſeaſon, he departed, reſolving to ſeize the firſt occaſion of returning with ſharpened malignity, *ſee Luke* xxii 53

n Matt iv 12 John iv 43. 14 ¶ n And Jeſus returned in the power of the Spirit
into o Galilee and there went out a fame of him through
o Acts x 37. all the region round about 15 And he taught in their
ſynagogues, being glorified of all 16 ¶ And he came
p Matt ii 23. to Nazareth, p where he had been brought up and as
q Acts xvii. his cuſtom was q he went into the ſynagogue on the ſabbath day, and ſtood up for to read 17 And there was
delivered unto him the book of the prophet Eſaias and
when he had opened the book, he found the place where
r Iſa lxi 1. it was written, 18 r The Spirit of the Lord *is* upon
me, becauſe he hath anointed me to preach the goſpel to
the poor, he hath ſent me to heal the broken hearted,
to preach deliverance to the captives, and recovering of
ſight to the blind, to ſet at liberty them that are bruiſed,
19 To preach the acceptable year of the Lord 20 And
he cloſed the book, and he gave *it* again to the miniſter,
and ſat down and the eyes of all them that were in the
ſynagogue were faſtened on him 21 And he began to
ſay unto them, This day is this ſcripture fulfilled in your
ears 22 And all bare him witneſs, and wondered at
the gracious words which proceeded out of his mouth
And they ſaid, s Is not this *Joſeph's* ſon? 23 And he
ſaid unto them, Ye will ſurely ſay unto me this proverb,
Phyſician, heal thyſelf whatſoever we have heard done
in Capernaum, do alſo here in thy country 24 And
he ſaid, Verily I ſay unto you, u No prophet is accepted
in his own country 25 But I tell you of a truth,
Many widows were in Iſrael in the days of Elias, x when
the heaven was ſhut up three years and ſix months,
when great famine was throughout all the land 26
y 1 Kings xvii 9. But unto none of them was Elias ſent y ſave unto Sarepta,
a city of Sidon, unto a woman *that was* a widow. 27
And many lepers were in Iſrael in the time of Eliſeus
z 2 Kings v 14. the prophet and z none of them was cleanſed ſaving
Naaman the Syrian 28 And all they in the ſynagogue,
when they heard theſe things, were filled with wrath,
29 And roſe up and thruſt him out of the city, and led
‖ Or, edge. him unto the ‖ brow of the hill (whereon their city was
a John viii 59 & x 39. built) that they might caſt him down headlong 30
But a he, paſſing through the midſt of them, went his
way.

v 14—30 Having vanquiſhed his infernal foe in the wilderneſs, Jeſus enters upon his miniſterial office, and publickly appears, deſtroying, by his doctrine and miracles, the power of Satan over the bodies and ſouls of men

1 *In the power of the Spirit he returned to Galilee*, ſtrengthened with might in the inner man for the arduous work which he had undertaken, and immediately he ſet himſelf to diſcharge his high commiſſion, preaching in their ſynagogues the goſpel of the kingdom, and ſuch power accompanied his word, and ſuch miracles confirmed his doctrine, that the people in general admired and extolled him, and his fame quickly ſpread through all that country

2 After paſſing through other parts of Galilee he came to Nazareth, where he had been brought up and, *as his cuſtom was*, he went into the ſynagogue on *the ſabbath-day, and ſtood up to read* ſome ſection of Scripture, as was uſually done on that day and a moſt laudable cuſtom is this, in every worſhipping aſſembly, to read the word of God The volume, which was delivered to him for this purpoſe by the miniſter of the ſynagogue, contained the prophecy of Iſaiah, and, unrolling the parchment on which it was written, he found the place, *Iſa* lxi 1, 2 which ſpake ſo evidently of himſelf Whether it was the portion of Scripture for the day, or that he choſe it as the propereſt introduction to his diſcourſe, is uncertain, but, whichever was the caſe, it gave him the faireſt opportunity to deſcribe his own office and character, and left them inexcuſable who ſhould reject him, notwithſtanding the voice of the prophets read every ſabbath-day

(1) The text gave a full account of the Redeemer's undertaking 1 He was eminently qualified for his arduous work by that plenitude of gifts and graces conferred upon him by the Spirit of the Lord, and fully commiſſioned by this unction from the Holy One for the diſcharge of his mediatorial office 2 The great end of his miſſion is ſet forth (1) *To preach the goſpel to the poor*, to evangelize them, not only to ſpeak to their ears, but to make his work effectual, to convert their hearts And by *the poor* are meant not merely the indigent and common people, though of ſuch were Chriſt's diſciples chiefly taken, but *the poor in ſpirit*, who, convinced of their ſpiritual wants and wretchedneſs, would gladly embrace that free pardon, righteouſneſs, and ſalvation, which the goſpel revealed to them (2) *To heal the broken-hearted*, whoſe ſins pierced their ſouls with ſorrow, and whoſe troubled conſciences and corrupted hearts nothing but the balm of his blood and grace could relieve and cure (3) *To preach deliverance to the captives*, to ſinful ſouls enſlaved by Satan's power Their chains of guilt are broken through the atonement of Jeſus, and by his Spirit they are delivered from the bondage of corruption into the glorious liberty of the ſons of God (4) To preach *recovering of ſight to the blind*, to open the darkened underſtanding of fallen man, and to ſhine into his heart, communicating the knowledge of the ſalvation which is by grace (5) *To ſet at liberty them that are bruiſed*, to break off the galling yoke of the law from the necks of thoſe who, under a ſpirit of bondage, continued miſerable and unhappy, and, in its ſtead, to give them the ſpirit of adoption, and liberty from every ſlaviſh fear (6) *To preach the acceptable year of the Lord*, that joyful year of goſpel jubilee, when inſolvent ſinners ſhall obtain free remiſſion of all their ſins, deliverance from their miſeries, reſtoration to the divine favour, and their forfeited inheritance in the heavenly Canaan

(2) Having read this text, and delivered the roll again to the miniſter, he ſat down, as was the cuſtom of the Jewiſh doctors, and began to diſcourſe at large on all the various particulars, ſhewing how the words referred to the Meſſiah and his office, and were that very day fulfilled in himſelf

3 The audience hung with attention on his lips, their eyes eagerly faſtened on him, and admiration ſeized every hearer, ſuch eminent wiſdom, ſuch energy of diction, ſuch majeſty and grace, appeared in all his words and his addreſs, that they were aſtoniſhed above meaſure, eſpecially conſidering the meanneſs of his birth and education *Is not this Joſeph's ſon*, the carpenter? Which, though it increaſed their wonder at his diſcourſe, prejudiced them againſt his perſon, and would not ſuffer them to admit the application to himſelf of the high office of the Meſſiah *Note*, (1) To have our eyes directed to the miniſter ſerves often to fix the attention to his diſcourſe (2) Many admire the preaching, and are pleaſed with the orator, whoſe hearts are never truly converted by what they hear

4 He anticipates and anſwers the objection he ſaw riſing in the hearts of many againſt him *Ye will ſurely ſay to me this proverb, Phyſician, heal thyſelf* if thou art the wondrous Perſonage, as reported, ſhew it, by working the ſame miracles at home *which we have heard done in Capernaum* But, in anſwer hereunto, he aſſures them, that, if he did the ſame or greater wonders amongſt them, he knew their prejudices againſt him were ſuch, they would notwithſtanding reject him, *no prophet being accepted in his own country*, they would ſtill think meanly of him who had known his parentage and education, and been uſed for ſo long a time to regard him as vaſtly their inferior But he ſhews them, that though he with-held his favours from them it would be no proof againſt him, ſince he had the examples of former prophets to plead, and God was the ſovereign diſpoſer of his own gifts, and beſtows them not on thoſe whom men judge moſt fit, but on ſuch as he pleaſes Thus Elijah ſup-

ported

ported miraculouſly a widow of Sarepta, a Gentile city, during the famine which raged, whilſt many as neceſſitous remained in Iſrael without any ſuch relief, and Eliſha alſo, paſſing by the multitude of his own leprous countrymen, cleanſed only Naaman the Syrian, a Gentile, and hereditary enemy to Iſrael As great or greater objections would therefore lie againſt theſe prophets than they ſuggeſted againſt him

5 The people were highly exaſperated at the reproach which they apprehended was couched under theſe inſtances, as if they of Nazareth were as wicked as the Iſraelites in the days of Ahab, and that even Gentiles would be preferred before them in the *divine regard* Though ſo lately they admired his gracious words, this application cut them to the heart, and, riſing in a popular tumult, they caſt him out of the ſynagogue, hurried him through the city, and, dragging him to the brow of the hill on which their city was built, intended to hurl him headlong down, and daſh him in pieces *Note*, It is a mercy that even the madneſs of the people is under a divine reſtraint elſe how many of God's faithful miniſters had met an untimely death?

6 Jeſus diſappoints their malice His time to ſuffer was not yet come, and therefore, by his divine power, either holding their eyes, or rendering himſelf inviſible, or ſtriking them to the earth, as the guard who afterwards came to arreſt him, he paſſed ſafe through the midſt of them, leaving them to their impenitence and ruin *Note*, They who reject Jeſus and his goſpel are juſtly given up to a reprobate mind

b Mat iv 13 Mark i 21 — 31 [b] And came down to Capernaum, a city of Galilee,
and taught them on the ſabbath-days 32 And they
c Mat vii 29 Tit ii 15 — were aſtoniſhed at his doctrine for [c] his word was with
power 33 ¶ [d] And in the ſynagogue there was a man
d Mark i 23 &c — which had a ſpirit of an unclean devil, and cried out
e Mat viii 29 — with a loud voice, 34 Saying, Let us alone, [e] what
have we to do with thee, thou Jeſus of Nazareth? art
f Ver 41 — thou come to deſtroy us? [f] I know thee who thou art,
g Dan ix 20 Ch p i 35 — [g] the holy One of God 35 And Jeſus rebuked him,
ſaying, Hold thy peace, and come out of him And,
when the devil had thrown him in the midſt, he came
out of him, and hurt him not 36 And they were all
amazed, and ſpake among themſelves, ſaying, What a
word *is* this? for with authority and power he commandeth
the unclean ſpirits, and they come out 37 And
the fame of him went out into every place of the country
round about 38 ¶ And he aroſe out of the ſynagogue,
h Mat viii 14 Mark i 29 — and [h] entred into Simon's houſe And Simon's
wife's mother was taken with a great fever, and they
beſought him for her 39 And he ſtood over her, and
rebuked the fever, and it left her And immediately ſhe
i Mat viii 16 Mark i 32 — aroſe and miniſtred unto them 40 ¶ [i] Now when
k Ja iv 4 Mat viii 17 — the ſun was ſetting, all they that had any [k] ſick with
divers diſeaſes brought them unto him and he laid his
hands on every one of them, and healed them. 41 And
devils alſo came out of many, crying out, and ſaying,
l Ver 34 — [l] Thou art Chriſt the Son of God And he rebuking
m Acts xvi 17, 18 — them, [m] ſuffered them not ‖ to ſpeak for they knew
‖ Or to ſay that they knew him — that he was Chriſt 42 And [n] when it was day, he
n Mark i 35 — departed, and went into a deſert place and the people
ſought him, and came unto him, and ſtayed him, that
he ſhould not depart from them 43 And he ſaid unto
them, I muſt preach the kingdom of God to other cities
o Is lxi 1 — alſo [o] for therefore am I ſent 44 And he preached
in the ſynagogues of Galilee.

¶ 31—44 When Jeſus departed from Nazareth he returned to Capernaum, and, as uſual, on the ſabbath-day he taught the people in their ſynagogues, to the aſtoniſhment of all who heard him, ſuch divine authority and commanding energy accompanied his word In proof of the doctrine he advanced, we have here,

1 A notable miracle performed in the preſence of the congregation where he preached, *ſee Mark* i 23 A man with the ſpirit of an unclean devil was in the ſynagogue Filled with enmity againſt Chriſt and his goſpel, and terrified with juſt fears that Jeſus would diſpoſſeſs him, the devil, uſing the man's organs of ſpeech, cried out, *Let us alone*, &c These wicked ſpirits dread their doom, and fearfully look forward to their terrible judgment They knew the power of Jeſus of Nazareth, for they had proved it in the wilderneſs, and, fully ſatisfied concerning his miſſion, they confeſs him to be *the Holy One of God*, though with no kind intention, malice dictated here the language of truth, and they would fain fix upon him the ſuſpicion of a confederacy with them, by bearing ſuch an honourable teſtimony to him But Jeſus in a moment ſilenced this foul fiend, and with a word releaſed the miſerable man from his power With rage, compelled to depart, the devil vented his laſt efforts, throwing the man down with violent convulſions, as if he would have torn him in pieces, but his power was broken, he was unable to hurt him, and the cure was compleat Amazed, the whole congregation beheld and queſtioned with each other concerning a miracle ſo wondrous and incontestible Never had ſuch power and authority appeared before, that with a word the infernal ſpirits ſhould thus be diſpoſſeſſed, without the leaſt ability to make reſiſtance And immediately the fame of the cure ſpread far and wide *Note*, The power of Satan, as an unclean ſpirit, over the ſouls of men, is ſtill exceeding great, and nothing but the powerful word of goſpel-grace can caſt him out

2 No ſooner was he returned from the ſynagogue than Peter's wife's mother, who lay ill of a fever, experienced his healing grace At the requeſt of ſome of the company, who mentioned her diſorder, he aroſe, ſtood by her bed-ſide, rebuked the fever with a word, and inſtantly ſhe was ſo perfectly reſtored to health as to be able to wait on the gueſts who were in the houſe *Note*, (1) When they who are near and dear to us are ſick, we muſt beſeech Jeſus on their behalf, and the prayer of faith ſtill availeth much (2) They who are reſtored to ſpiritual health by the Saviour's grace, will be ready to diſcharge every kind office of love and ſervice to the leaſt of his people

3 A multitude of other cures were performed by him the ſame day at even All who had friends or relations diſeaſed applied to him, and, whatever was their malady, he with a touch healed them all even devils, unable to ſtand before his word, came out of thoſe that were poſſeſſed, confeſſing him to be the Meſſiah, but he ſilenced them, refuſing to receive any teſtimony from ſuch as they were *Note*, When they who we know bear enmity towards us ſpeak us moſt reſpectfully, their civilities are to be moſt ſuſpected of deſign

4 Early next morning he departed from Capernaum to a ſolitude for retirement Thither the people followed him, and intreated him to return to their city but he choſe to diffuſe the favour of his goſpel, and diſpenſe his miracles of mercy in the country around, for this was the deſign of his miſſion, to be a general bleſſing *Note*, (1) They who have much public work have eſpecial need of ſeaſonable retirement alſo To be *alone with God* is the beſt preparative for the pulpit (2) They who have found Chriſt's preſence ſo deſireable, naturally wiſh for its continuance And though he refuſed his bodily preſence to *them*, he hath engaged to his people, who ſeek him, that he will abide with them for ever

CHAP. V

In this chapter we have, 1 Chriſt's preaching to the people out of Peter's ſhip, ver 1—3 2 The miraculous draught of fiſh, ver 4—11 3 His cleanſing the leper, ver 12—15 4 A ſhort account of his private devotion and public miniſtry, ver 16, 17 5 His cure of the man ſick of the palſy, ver 18—26 6 His calling Levi the publican, and converſing with publicans on that occaſion, ver 27—32 7 His juſtifying his diſciples in not faſting ſo frequently as the diſciples of John and the Phariſees did, ver 33 ad finem

1 AND [a] it came to paſs, that as the people preſſed — a Mat iv 18 Mark i 16
upon him to hear the word of God, he ſtood
by the lake of Genneſareth, 2 And ſaw two ſhips
ſtanding by the lake but the fiſhermen were gone out
of them, and were waſhing *their* nets 3 And he entred
into one of the ſhips, which was Simon's, and
prayed him that he would thruſt out a little from the
land and he ſat down, and taught the people out of
the ſhip 4 Now, when he had left ſpeaking, he ſaid
unto Simon, [b] Launch out into the deep, and let down — b John xxi 6
your nets for a draught 5. And Simon anſwering ſaid
unto him, Maſter, we have toiled all the night, and
have taken nothing nevertheleſs at thy word I will let
down the net 6 And, when they had this done, they
incloſed a great multitude of fiſhes, and their net brake
7 And they beckned unto *their* partners which were in
the other ſhip, that they ſhould come and help them
And they came and filled both the ſhips, ſo that they
began to ſink 8 When Simon Peter ſaw *it*, he fell
down at Jeſus's knees, ſaying, [c] Depart from me, for I — c [illegible]
am a ſinful man, O Lord. 9 For he was aſtoniſhed,
and all that were with him, at the draught of the fiſhes
which they had taken 10 And ſo *was* alſo James and
John the ſons of Zebedee, which were partners with — d [illegible]
Simon And Jeſus ſaid unto Simon, Fear not, [d] from
henceforth thou ſhalt catch men 11 And, when they
had brought their ſhips to land, [e] they forſook all, and — e [illegible]
followed him

v 1—11 Vaſt was the concourſe that attended the preaching of Jeſus, and whilſt the Scribes and Phariſees, the wiſe doctors of the law, deſpiſed him, the common people were eager to hear him, and preſſed through the crowd to get nearer Hereupon,

1 Chriſt deſired the uſe of a fiſherman's boat, for the greater convenience of being heard, and to be leſs incommoded with the throng, and there he ſat down and taught the people who ſtood before him on the ſhore

2 When he had done preaching he deſired Simon, in whoſe boat he was, to lanch out farther into the lake and let down their nets Simon told him the ill ſucceſs they had met with, but, though they had wearied themſelves all night, and waſhed their nets, if he bid them they would chearfully make another trial *Note*, (1) The moſt diligent and laborious ſometimes meet with diſappointments, and are apt to be diſcouraged by the little fruit they ſee of their labours, but they muſt perſiſt in the way of duty, and leave the event to God (2) If our bread be eaſily earned, and our reſt ſweet unto us, we ſhould remember charitably thoſe who labour hard for little gain, and wake, at their toils, when we are ſleeping

3 Moſt amazing was the quantity of fiſhes they incloſed their net began to give way with the weight, and, unable to draw them up themſelves, they beckoned to their partners to come to their aſſiſtance, and loaded both their boats ſo deep, that they were in danger of ſinking Peter was now abundantly repaid for the loan of his boat, and in this diſplay of his Maſter's power in the ſea as well as on the land, might be confirmed in his faith of the doctrine which he delivered

4 Peter, deeply affected with what he ſaw, and perceiving the danger they were in, *fell down at Jeſus's knees*, and, under the deepeſt ſenſe of his own unworthineſs, cried out, *ſaying, Depart from me, for I am a ſinful man, O Lord* Conſcious of his guilt and ſinfulneſs, he trembled, leſt the Lord was come to puniſh inſtead of bleſſing him, and was afraid of his very mercies *for he was aſtoniſhed, and all that were with him, at the draught of fiſhes they had taken*, though brought up to this buſineſs from their youth, they had never ſeen any thing at all to be compared with this in their whole lives *Note*, (1) The beſt of men are *ſinful men*, and need continually to fall at Jeſus's feet in deepeſt ſelf-abaſement (2) Though we have grievouſly offended our Lord, we may not ſay, *Depart from me*, but, Stay with me, or, Return to me in mercy, for nothing but his preſence and grace can keep us from ſinking

5 Jeſus quiets their fears He is not come to them in anger, but in mercy and he hath ſtill greater kindneſs in ſtore for them than this cargo of fiſhes, therefore *he ſaid unto Simon, Fear not, from henceforth thou ſhalt catch men*, and be more ſucceſsful in caſting the goſpel-net, and drawing greater multitudes out of the depths of ſin and miſery to life and ſalvation Which was eminently fulfilled, *Acts* ii 41

6 No ſooner were they come to land than Simon and Andrew, and the ſons of Zebedee their partners, obeying his call, immediately left their boats, and all they had, quitting their employment at the time when it appeared moſt ſucceſsful, and commenced thenceforward conſtant attendants on the Lord Jeſus *Note*, They who know the bleſſedneſs of Chriſt's ſervice will count nothing too much to part with for his ſake

f Mat viii 2 Mark i 40 — 12 ¶ f And it came to paſs, when he was in a certain
g Lev xiii 44 Chron xxvi 23 — city, behold, a man g full of leproſy who, ſeeing Jeſus,
fell on *his* face, and beſought him, ſaying, Lord, if thou
wilt, thou canſt make me clean 13 And he put forth
his hand, and touched him, ſaying, I will, be thou clean
And immediately the leproſy departed from him 14
h Mark v 43 — And h he charged him to tell no man but go and ſhew
i Lev xiv 4 10 — thyſelf to the prieſt, and offer for thy cleanſing i accord-
ing as Moſes commanded, for a teſtimony unto them
k Mat iv 24 — 15 But ſo much the more k went there a fame abroad
of him and great multitudes came together to hear,
and to be healed by him of their infirmities 16 ¶ And
l Mat vi 46 — l he withdrew himſelf into the wilderneſs, and prayed

v 12—16 We have here,

1 The cleanſing of the leper This ſtory both the former evangeliſts have recorded It affords us,

(1) A ſtriking emblem of our true ſtate So corrupt is our nature, ſo ſpotted are our ſouls, ſo loathſome in the eyes of God, and by all human means ſo utterly incurable is the diſeaſe of ſin

(2) It directs us where our only hope lies, even in Jeſus, the great phyſician To him, with deep humiliation and confuſion of face, in the ſight of our own vileneſs, ſhould we make application, crying earneſtly for his healing grace, depending on his power to ſave to the uttermoſt, and caſting ourſelves wholly on his mercy

(3) Chriſt appears a gracious Saviour, ready to hear the prayer of the poor deſtitute, and able to ſave to the uttermoſt all who come to him both to pardon the ſinner's guilt, however aggravated, and to deliver him from the power of his corruptions, however inveterate

(4) Every cleanſed ſinner will obediently follow the commands of Jeſus, will offer up himſelf a living ſacrifice to God, and in the bleſſed, evident, and univerſal change wrought upon him, will leave thoſe without excuſe, who will not acknowledge the divine power and grace magnified in ſuch a converſion

2 Great multitudes reſorted to him from every quarter to hear him and to be healed The more he ſought to be hid, the more his fame ſpread The gratitude and tranſport of joy this poor man felt on his cure would not permit him to hold his tongue and conceal the glory of his great benefactor Modeſt worth, that wiſhes to be concealed, ſhines the brighter

3 He withdrew, after the labours of the day, from the crowd, and, retiring into a ſolitary place, ſpent ſome time alone in prayer To teach us this neceſſary duty, which nothing ſhould intrench upon or interrupt

17 And it came to paſs on a certain day, as he was
teaching, that m there were Phariſees and doctors of the — m Jer xvii 15
law ſitting by, which were come out of every town of
Galilee, and Judea, and Jeruſalem and the power of
the Lord was *preſent* to heal them 18 ¶ n And behold, — n Mat ix 2 Mark ii 3
men brought in a bed a man which was taken with the
palſy and they ſought means to bring him in, and to
lay *him* before him 19 And when they could not find
by what way they might bring him in, becauſe of the
multitude, they went upon the houſe-top, and let him
down through the tiling with *his* couch, into the midſt
before Jeſus 20 And when he ſaw their faith, he ſaid
unto him, Man, o thy ſins are forgiven thee 21 And — o Pſ ciii 3 If xxxviii 17 & xliv 22 John v 14
the ſcribes and Phariſees began to reaſon, ſaying, Who
is this which ſpeaketh blaſphemies? p Who can forgive
ſins but God alone? 22 But when q Jeſus perceived — p Job xiv 4 Iſa liii 5
their thoughts, he, anſwering, ſaid unto them, What rea- — q Pſ cxxxix 2 John ii 24 & vi 6
ſon ye in your hearts? 23 Whether is eaſier to ſay,
Thy ſins be forgiven thee, or to ſay, Riſe up and walk?
24 But that ye may know that r the Son of man hath — r John xvii 2 Acts v 31
power upon earth to forgive ſins, (he ſaith unto the ſick
of the palſy) I ſay unto thee, Ariſe, and take up thy
couch, and go into thine houſe 25 And immediately
he roſe up before them, and took up that whereon he
lay, and departed to his own houſe, glorifying God.
26 And they were all amazed, and they glorified God,
and were filled with fear, ſaying, We have ſeen ſtrange
things to day

v 17—26 Chriſt ceaſed not his indefatigable labours

1 He preached in a houſe on a week-day at Capernaum, for no day, no place, is unſuitable or unſeaſonable when an opportunity offers to ſpeak a word for God, and for the good of men's ſouls Among others of his audience, were a large number of Scribes and Phariſees, who, with no good intention, were come from the diſtant places, not to hear and learn, but to *ſit by*, to make remarks and cavil, *and the power of the Lord was preſent to heal them*, not the Phariſees, but many of the multitude who came to him with their ſeveral diſeaſes, thus at leaſt to leave without excuſe thoſe who reſiſted the evidence of ſuch inconteſtible miracles *Note*, (1) When perſons come to hear the word of God, not to profit themſelves, but to prejudice others againſt it, great is their guilt (2) Though we know the malice of thoſe who watch for our halting, we muſt not be diſcouraged from perſevering in the way of duty (3) The power of the Lord is preſent to heal wherever his goſpel is preached, but they who reject the counſel of God againſt their own ſouls, have only themſelves to blame for their deſtruction

2 Juſt at that time a paralytic man was brought to Jeſus, unable to gain acceſs by the door, becauſe of the multitude, his friends carried him up to the top of the houſe, and let him down through the roof into the room where Jeſus was Beholding their faith, he pronounces the pardon of his ſins, and notwithſtanding all the cavil of the Phariſees which he knew, Jeſus confirms the divine authority he aſſumed, by an immediate cure of the paralytic man, proving thereby, that he who could thus ſovereignly, by his own power, remove the effects of ſin, had an undoubted right to pardon it The cure was inſtantaneous and perfect, and to the amaze of all, who were ſtruck with ſacred reverence and awe when they ſaw him, who the moment before lay ſtretched ſo helpleſs, now riſe with full ſtrength and vigour, take up his own bed, and go away, glorifying God for the aſtoniſhing mercy, and the people in general acknowledged, that no ſuch ſtrange miracles were ever before ſeen or heard of *Note*, (1) All our diſeaſes are the fruit of ſin, and that ſhould ever humble us under them before God (2) Jeſus hath power to forgive ſin, and they who by faith come to him, ſhall know it by bleſſed experience (3) If our ſin be pardoned, the bitterneſs of ſickneſs and death is paſſed

and your soul rejoicing in God, as his Saviour, hath nothing to complain of (4) When we have received mercy at God's hand, we are bound to ascribe to him the glory due unto his name, and to speak to his praise.

a Matt ix 9 Mark ii 13 — 27 ¶ a And after these things he went forth, and saw
a publican named Levi, sitting at the receipt of custom
and he said unto him, Follow me 28 And he left all,
rose up, and followed him 29 And Levi made him a
great feast in his own house and there was a great
company of publicans, and of others that sat down with
them 30 But their scribes and Pharisees murmured
c Gen xliii 32 Luke xv 2 Acts x 28 — against his disciples, saying, c Why do ye eat and drink
with publicans and sinners? 31 And Jesus, answering,
said unto them, They that are whole need not a phy-
u Chap xviii 10—14 & xix 10 Rom v 6, 8 1 Tim i 15 — sician, but they that are sick 32 u I came not to call
the righteous, but sinners to repentance 33 ¶ And
they said unto him, x Why do the disciples of John
x Matt ix 14 Mark ii 18 — fast often, and make prayers, and likewise *the disciples*
of the Pharisees, but thine eat and drink? 34 And
y Chap xviii 12 z John iii 29 a Acts i 9 b Acts xiii 3 — he said unto them, Can ye make the children of the
bride-chamber fast, while y the bridegroom is with them?
35 But the days will come, a when the bridegroom shall
be taken away from them, and b then shall they fast in
c Matt ix 16 Mark ii 21 — those days 36 ¶ And he spake also a parable unto
them, c No man putteth a piece of a new garment upon
an old if otherwise, then both the new maketh a rent,
and the piece that was *taken* out of the new agreeth not
with the old 37 And no man putteth new wine into
old bottles, else the new wine will burst the bottles,
and be spilled, and the bottles shall perish 38 But
new wine must be put into new bottles, and both are
preserved 39 No man also, having drunk old *wine*,
straightway desireth new for he saith, The old is bet-
ter

v 27—39 The conversion of the sinner's heart to God is equally a matter of wonder, and as great an evidence of divine power, as cleansing the leper, or raising the dead We have here,

1 The calling of Matthew, or Levi the publican, and his ready obedience to the command of Jesus, instantly leaving all, he followed him The vilest sinners, and those who have the greatest obstacles lying in the way of their salvation, are, when Jesus speaks to the heart, effectually wrought upon Nothing is above his almighty grace

2 The gracious condescension of the Lord to those publicans, whom Matthew invited to his house Our Lord disdained not to sit down with them, and vindicates his conduct from the envious, malicious, and censorious suggestions of the Pharisees He associated not with them as approving their ways, or countenancing them in evil, but as a physician visits the diseased, the whole, at least they who fancy themselves so, need not his care The business of the Saviour in the world was not with the righteous, or those who were vainly puffed up with a conceit of their own excellence, as was the case of the Pharisees, he came to call poor sinners, as the publicans were, to repentance, and would kindly receive them, when sensible of their guilt and sinfulness they turned to him And he is still the same gracious Lord, no miserable sinner need despair, let him look unto Jesus and be saved, only those perish who know not their need of him, or proudly fancy they are righteous

3 He vindicates his disciples from the censures of the Pharisees respecting fasting It was not fit they should fast, whilst their Master was with them they were not yet prepared to endure this discipline Such austerities might tempt them to draw back, as new fermenting wine would burst old bottles, their exercises must be proportioned to their strength At present they could not bear it, but hereafter the time would come when losing their Master, and called out to labour in his cause, they would learn to fast, 2 Cor xi 27 Not that the Pharisees need boast of such a strictness upon their own bodily services though, like new fermenting wine that sparkles high, they made a fair shew in the flesh, their form of godliness was not to be compared with the life and power of religion, *the old wine*, which the disciples possessed, and which every spiritual person, who hath a true relish for the things of God, far prefers

CHAP VI

In this chapter we have, 1 A proof of the lawful use of works of necessity and mercy on the sabbath day, ver 1—11 2 Christ's retirement for secret prayer, ver 12 3 His calling his twelve apostles, ver 13—16 4 His curing the multitudes of all sorts of diseases who came to him, ver 17, —19 5 The sermon that he preached to his disciples and the multitude, instructing them in their duty both to God and man, ver 20—49

1 AND a it came to pass on the second sabbath after — a Matt xii 1 Mark ii 23
the first, that he went through the corn fields
and his disciples b plucked the ears of corn, and did eat, — b Deut xxiii 25
rubbing *them* in *their* hands 2 And certain of the
Pharisees said unto them, Why do ye that which is not
lawful to do on the sabbath-days? 3 And Jesus, an-
swering them, said, Have ye not read so much as this,
c what David did, when himself was an hungred, and — c 1 Sam xxi 6
they which were with him 4 How he went into the
house of God, and did take and eat the shew-bread, and
gave also to them that were with him, d which is not — d Exod xxix 33 Lev xxiv 9
lawful to eat, but for the priests alone? 5 And he said
unto them, That the Son of man is Lord also of the
sabbath 6 e And it came to pass also on another sab- — e Matt xii 9 Mark iii 1
bath, that he entered into the synagogue and taught
and there was a man whose right hand was withered
7 And the scribes and Pharisees watched him, f whether — f Chap xiv 3
he would heal on the sabbath day that they might
find an accusation against him 8 But he knew their — John ii 25
thoughts, and said to the man which had the withered
hand, Rise up, and stand forth in the midst And he
arose, and stood forth 9 Then said Jesus unto them,
I will ask you one thing, Is it lawful on the sabbath days
to do good, or to do evil? to save life, or to destroy *it*?
10 And, looking round about upon them all, he said
unto the man, g Stretch forth thy hand And he did so — g Exod xiv 26
and his hand was restored whole as the other 11 And
they were filled with madness, and h communed one with — h Chap xix 47
another what they might do to Jesus

v 1—11 These passages we had before in the other evangelists The time when the first of these events happened is said to be *the second sabbath after the first*, or rather *the first sabbath after the second day* of the Passover, from whence were reckoned the seven weeks to the feast of Pentecost

1 Our Lord vindicates his disciples from the censures of the Pharisees, and proves, by the example of David, the lawfulness of rubbing out the ears of corn, and eating them on the sabbath, when hunger called for food *Note*, (1) Works of necessity are always allowable (2) The greatest censurers of the innocent actions of others are often most indulgent to their own iniquities

2 He vindicates himself from the same malignant cavillers As he preached in the synagogue on another sabbath, there was a man present who had a withered hand Jesus bid him stand forth in the midst of the congregation, and, knowing the malicious purposes of his watchful enemies, who, from such a gracious work as he was about to do, intended to ground an accusation against him, as if he was a sabbath-breaker, he appeals to themselves whether they thought the fourth commandment could possibly forbid the doing good, or saving a man's life on the sabbath day Unable to reply, yet resolved to find fault, they were silent On which he with a word restored the withered hand And thereat his enemies were so enraged, that, with fury rising to madness, they consulted how they might destroy him *Note*, (1) They who would be cured of their spiritual infirmities must be found in the assembly of the faithful, where Christ usually dispenses his healing grace (2) Men's perverseness and wickedness must not deter nor discourage us from the work in which the Lord would have us employed (3) All passion is temporary madness during its fury neither reason nor conscience are regarded

12 And it came to pass in those days, that he went
out into a mountain to pray, and continued all night in
prayer to God 13 ¶ And when it was day, i he called — i Matt x 1
unto him his disciples k and of them l he chose twelve, — k Mark iii 13 l Chap ix 1
whom he also named apostles 14 Simon (whom he — m John i 42
also named Peter) and Andrew his brother, James and — Acts i 13
John, Philip and Bartholomew, 15 Matthew and Tho-
mas, James *the son* of Alphæus, and Simon called Zelo-
tes 16 And Judas n *the brother* of James, and Judas — n Jude 1
Iscariot, which also was the traitor 17 ¶ And he
came down with them, and stood in the plain, and the
company of his disciples, and a great multitude of people
out of all Judea and Jerusalem, and from the sea coast
of Tyre and Sidon, which came to hear him, and to be
healed of their diseases 18 And they that were vexed
with unclean spirits and they were healed 19 And — o Matt xiv 36
the whole multitude sought to touch him for there
went virtue out of him, and healed *them* all

5 — 20 — 20

v 12—19 We have here,

1 Our Lord's retirement *He went out to a mountain to pray, and continued all night in prayer to God*, (εν τη προσευχη του Θεου) which may signify either the object to whom his prayer was directed, or the fervency of his requests, or, as some suppose, the house of prayer or *proseucha*, to which he retired, such oratories, it seems, being common in that country The length of the time he spent there bespoke the importance of the occasion, he being about to chuse and ordain his twelve apostles *Note*, When matters of deep concern lie upon our souls, we are especially called to spread the case before God for his direction and blessing

2 The calling and appointment of the twelve apostles. These he ordained to be his chief ministers in that kingdom which he was come to establish, putting them in trust with his gospel, and empowering them to work miracles in confirmation of their mission The names of the apostles are the same as before, only he who was called Lebbeus, and surnamed Thaddeus, is here called Judas the brother of James, these names belonging to the same person, and Simon the Canaanite is here named *Simon Zelotes*, being probably, before his conversion, of the sect of the Zealots

3 Having finished this work, he came down with the twelve to the plain, where great multitudes attended from the most distant parts of the country, to hear his discourses and to partake of his wondrous cures Nor were they disappointed he graciously taught them and richly dispensed his favours, healing all the diseased, and casting out the unclean spirits from such as were possessed, yea, such virtue went out of him, that *the whole multitude* of miserable patients, who came to him, *sought but to touch him*, fully persuaded that this would be effectual to heal them, and found, according to their faith, that their cure was instantly effected

20 ¶ And he lifted up his eyes on his disciples, and
said, Blessed *be* ye poor for yours is the kingdom of
God 21 Blessed *are* ye that hunger now for ye
shall be filled Blessed *are* ye that weep now for ye
shall laugh 22 Blessed are ye when men shall hate
you, and when they shall separate you *from their com-
pany*, and shall reproach *you*, and cast out your name as
evil, for the Son of man's sake 23 Rejoice ye in
that day, and leap for joy for behold, your reward *is*
great in heaven for in the like manner did their fathers
unto the prophets 24 But wo unto you that are
rich for ye have received your consolation 25 Wo
unto you that are full for ye shall hunger Wo unto
you that laugh now for ye shall mourn and weep
26 Wo unto you when all *men* shall speak well of you
for so did their fathers to the false prophets

v 20—26 Some have supposed this is an abridgment of the same discourse preached *Matt* v—vii others that it was delivered at a different time and place, though the matter be similar And this seems most probable, as there it is said he went up into a mountain and sat, here, that he came down and stood in the plain

As the disciples of Jesus would, for their attachment to him, be called to endure many hardships and sufferings, he here, fixing his eyes upon them, addresses them for their encouragement

1 He pronounces those blessed whom the world in general counts to be of all men most miserable (1) *Blessed are ye poor*, destitute of all earthly substance, or who have left all to follow me, and whose spirits are humbled into the dust under the sense of your sinfulness and spiritual poverty *yours is the kingdom of God*, the present riches of grace in your treasury, and the eternal inheritance above reserved for you as your exceeding great reward (2) *Blessed are ye that hunger now*, either wanting necessary food for the sake of Christ and his gospel, or to denote after spiritual blessings as the hungry crave for meat, *for ye shall be filled* with food to satisfy the cravings of hunger, or better, with that supply of righteousness and grace which the soul desires (3) *Blessed are ye that weep now*, under affliction for Christ's sake, or mourning over sin in yourselves and others, *for ye shall laugh*, filled with eternal consolations in that kingdom where every tear shall be for ever wiped away from your eyes (4) *Blessed are ye when men shall hate you* for your attachment to Christ and his gospel, *and when they shall separate you* from their company, counting it infamous to associate with a person so obnoxious, as well as from their religious assemblies, *and shall reproach you*, branding you with every malicious slander, and treating you with insult and contempt as the vilest of mankind, *and cast out your name as evil*, never mentioning you but with indignity, obloquy, and violence, during you whenever they [illegible] *for the Son of man's sake*, because you espouse his interest, profess your faith in him, and live to his glory, which is indeed the cause of all their enmity at the bottom, whatever specious pretences they alledge their malevolence. Not-
withstanding their curses, ye are truly blessed *Rejoice ye in that day* therefore, *and leap for joy*, such reproach is your highest honour, and will prove your eternal advantage, *for behold, your reward is great in heaven* and this reward will abundantly overpay all your losses and sufferings *for in the like manner did their fathers unto the prophets* In every age, the faithful, from the beginning, have met the same treatment from the world of the ungodly It is your honour to be made like in such company, and to partake of the same cross they endured is the way to the crown they have won Let us weigh well these things, and we shall say, welcome reproach, welcome every opprobrious name, welcome enmity, reviling, insolence This is the way to glory

2 He pronounces fearful woes on those whom the world calls happy, so different are God's thoughts from man's thoughts (1) *Wo unto you that are rich*, who, possessed of affluence, idolize the creature, seek your happiness from worldly enjoyments, and trust in these vanities, *for ye have received your consolation* you have your all in hand and have nothing to hope for in eternity (2) *Wo unto you that are full*, living in all fleshly gratifications and faring sumptuously every day, *for ye shall hunger*, emptied of all your present abundance, and left to the rage of craving appetite, that can never be satisfied, and to raging thirst, where not a drop of water is granted to cool a flaming tongue (3) *Wo unto you that laugh now*, spending your days in mirth, pleasure, and sinful joy, *for ye shall mourn and weep*, where the sorrow will be unavailing as the torment which occasions it will be intolerable and eternal (4) *Wo unto you when all men shall speak well of you*, a sure sign that you do nothing to reprove them, either by your profession or Christian conversation, flattering them in their sin, and never offending them by your fidelity to their souls, then you will gain their approbation, *for so did their fathers to the false prophets*, whose smooth and deceitful prophecies obtained them the caresses of their countrymen, whilst the faithful prophets, who knew not to flatter, were abhorred and persecuted And all these things are eminently verified and verifying every day

27 ¶ But I say unto you which hear, Love your
enemies, do good to them which hate you 28 Bless
them that curse you, and pray for them which despite-
fully use you 29 And unto him that smiteth thee
on the *one* cheek, offer also the other and him that
taketh away thy cloke, forbid not *to take thy* coat also
30 Give to every man that asketh of thee, and of him
that taketh away thy goods, ask *them* not again 31
And as ye would that men should do to you, do ye
also to them likewise 32 For if ye love them which
love you, what thank have ye? for sinners also love those
that love them 33 And if ye do good to them which
do good to you, what thank have ye? for sinners also
do even the same 34 And if ye lend to them of
whom ye hope to receive, what thank have ye? for
sinners also lend *to sinners*, to receive as much again
35 But love ye your enemies, and do good, and lend,
hoping for nothing again and your reward shall be
great, and ye shall be the children of the Highest
for he is kind unto the unthankful, and *to* the evil
36 Be ye therefore merciful, as your Father also is
merciful

v 27—36 The same truths are here delivered in *Matth* v 38—48. Our Lord inculcates that universal charity which is the eminent characteristic of his religion Our love must extend even to our bitterest enemies, and make us ready to every good word and work for their service, returning to them blessing for curses, love with prayers, and return prayers for despiteful usage Christian charity must lead us to put up with affronts without resentment, and to suffer wrongs without revenging them, or seeking litigious redress, *v* 29 Charity must open our heart to feel the distresses of the indigent, and our hand liberally, according to our ability, to relieve them, often lending without the hope of repayment, and willing to cancel the debts of the insolvent, whom unforeseen providences have disabled from the power of discharging, *v* 30 Charity teaches us to put ourselves in the place of others, and act toward them in such a manner, as, in their circumstances, we could wish to be treated, *v* 31 And there are three reasons urged for this generous conduct

1 That this is the distinguishing badge of our profession To love, serve, and lend to those who make us a return in kind, is no more than the most selfish would do and the faith which worketh by love must carry us much farther than this

2 Our reward will be great in heaven, whatever ungrateful returns we may meet from men on earth

3 As we shall herein most distinguishedly resemble the Father of mercies, *who is kind to the unthankful and evil* He will
unknow-

away a soul rejoicing in God, as his Saviour, hath nothing to complain of (4) When we have received mercy at God's hand, we are bound to ascribe to him the glory due unto his name, and to speak to his praise

27 ¶ And after these things he went forth, and saw
a publican named Levi, sitting at the receipt of custom
and he said unto him, Follow me 28 And he left all,
rose up, and followed him 29 And Levi made him a
great feast in his own house and there was a great
company of publicans, and of others that sat down with
them 30 But their scribes and Pharisees murmured
against his disciples, saying, Why do ye eat and drink
with publicans and sinners? 31 And Jesus, answering,
said unto them, They that are whole need not a phy-
sician, but they that are sick 32 I came not to call
the righteous, but sinners to repentance 33 ¶ And
they said unto him, Why do the disciples of John
fast often, and make prayers, and likewise *the disciples*
of the Pharisees, but thine eat and drink? 34 And
he said unto them, Can ye make the children of the
bride chamber fast, while the bridegroom is with them?
35 But the days will come, when the bridegroom shall
be taken away from them, and then shall they fast in
those days 36 ¶ And he spake also a parable unto
them, No man putteth a piece of a new garment upon
an old if otherwise, then both the new maketh a rent,
and the piece that was *taken* out of the new agreeth not
with the old 37 And no man putteth new wine into
old bottles, else the new wine will burst the bottles,
and be spilled, and the bottles shall perish 38 But
new wine must be put into new bottles, and both are
preserved 39 No man also, having drunk old *wine*,
straightway desireth new for he saith, The old is bet-
ter

v 27—39 The conversion of the sinner's heart to God is equally a matter of wonder, and as great an evidence of divine power, as cleansing the leper, or raising the dead We have here,

1 The calling of Matthew, or Levi the publican, and his ready obedience to the command of Jesus, instantly leaving all, he followed him The vilest sinners, and those who have the greatest obstacles lying in the way of their salvation, are, when Jesus speaks to the heart, effectually wrought upon Nothing is above his almighty grace

2 The gracious condescension of the Lord to those publicans, whom Matthew invited to his house Our Lord disdained *not to sit down with them*, and vindicates his conduct from the envious, malicious, and censorious suggestions of the Pharisees He associated not with them as approving their ways, or countenancing them in evil, but as a physician visits the diseased, the whole, at least they who fancy themselves so, need not his care The business of the Saviour in the world was not with the righteous, or those who were vainly puffed up with a conceit of their own excellence, as was the case of the Pharisees, he came to call poor sinners, as the publicans were, to repentance, and would kindly receive them, when sensible of their guilt and sinfulness they turned to him And he is still the same gracious Lord, no miserable sinner need despair, let him look unto Jesus and be saved, only those perish who know not their need of him, or proudly fancy they are righteous

3 He vindicates his disciples from the censures of the Pharisees respecting fasting It was not fit they should fast, whilst their Master was with them they were not yet prepared to endure this discipline Such austerities might tempt them to draw back, as new fermenting wine would burst old bottles, their exercises must be proportioned to their strength At present they could not bear it, but hereafter the time would come when losing their Master, and called out to labour in his cause, they would learn to fast, 1 Cor ix 27 Not that the Pharisees need lay such a stress upon their own bodily services though, like new fermenting wine that sparkles high, they made a fair shew in the flesh, their form of godliness was not to be compared with the life and power of religion, *the old wine*, which the disciples possessed, and which every spiritual person, who hath a true relish for the things of God, prefers

CHAP VI

In this chapter we have, 1 A proof of the lawfulness of works of necessity and mercy on the sabbath-day, ver 1—11 2 Christ's retirement for secret prayer, ver 12 3 His calling his twelve apostles, ver 13—16 4 His curing the multitudes of their various diseases, who came then applauding to him, ver 17—19 5 The sermon that he preached to his disciples and the multitude, instructing them in their duty both to God and man, ver 20—49

1 AND it came to pass on the second sabbath after
the first, that he went through the corn fields
and his disciples plucked the ears of corn, and did eat,
rubbing *them* in *their* hands 2 And certain of the
Pharisees said unto them, Why do ye that which is not
lawful to do on the sabbath-days? 3 And Jesus, an-
swering them, said, Have ye not read so much as this,
what David did, when himself was an hungred, and
they which were with him 4 How he went into the
house of God, and did take and eat the shew-bread, and
gave also to them that were with him, which is not
lawful to eat, but for the priests alone? 5 And he said
unto them, That the Son of man is Lord also of the
sabbath 6 And it came to pass also on another sab-
bath, that he entred into the synagogue and taught
and there was a man whose right hand was withered
7 And the scribes and Pharisees watched him, whether
he would heal on the sabbath day that they might
find an accusation against him 8 But he knew their
thoughts, and said to the man which had the withered
hand, Rise up, and stand forth in the midst And he
arose, and stood forth 9 Then said Jesus unto them,
I will ask you one thing, Is it lawful on the sabbath-days
to do good, or to do evil? to save life, or to destroy *it*?
10 And, looking round about upon them all, he said
unto the man, Stretch forth thy hand And he did so
and his hand was restored whole as the other 11 And
they were filled with madness, and communed one with
another what they might do to Jesus

v 1—11 These passages we had before in the other evangelists The time when the first of these events happened is said to be *the second sabbath after the first*, or rather *the first sabbath after the second* day of the Passover, from whence were reckoned the seven weeks to the feast of Pentecost

1 Our Lord vindicates his disciples from the censures of the Pharisees, and proves, by the example of David, the lawfulness of rubbing out the ears of corn, and eating them on the sabbath, when hunger called for food *Note*, (1) Works of necessity are always allowable (2) The greatest censurers of the innocent actions of others are often most indulgent to their own iniquities

2 He vindicates himself from the same malignant cavillers As he preached in the synagogue on another sabbath, there was a man present who had a withered hand Jesus bid him stand *forth in the midst of the congregation*, and, knowing the malicious purposes of his watchful enemies, who, from such a gracious work as he was about to do, intended to ground an accusation against him as if he was a sabbath breaker, he appeals to themselves whether they thought the fourth commandment could possibly forbid the doing good, or saving a man's life on the sabbath-day Unable to reply, yet resolved to find fault, they were silent On which he with a word restored the withered hand And thereat his enemies were so enraged, that, with fury rising to madness, they consulted how they might destroy him *Note*, (1) They who would be cured of their spiritual infirmities must be found in the assembly of the faithful, where Christ usually dispenses his healing grace (2) Men's perverseness and wickedness must not deter nor discourage us from the work in which the Lord would have us employed (3) All passion is temporary madness during it we have neither reason nor conscience to regard

12 And it came to pass in those days, that he went
out into a mountain to pray, and continued all night in
prayer to God 13 ¶ And when it was day, he called
unto him his disciples and of them he chose twelve,
whom he also named apostles 14 Simon (whom he
also named Peter) and Andrew his brother, James and
John, Philip and Bartholomew, 15 Matthew and Tho-
mas, James *the son* of Alpheus, and Simon called Zelo-
tes 16 And Judas *the brother* of James, and Judas
Iscariot, which also was the traitor 17 ¶ And he
came down with them, and stood in the plain, and the
company of his disciples, and a great multitude of people
out of all Judea and Jerusalem, and from the sea coast
of Tyre and Sidon which came to hear him, and to be
healed of their diseases, 18 And they that were vexed
with unclean spirits and they were healed 19 And
the whole multitude sought to touch him for there
went virtue out of him, and healed them all

v. 12—19. We have here,

1. Our Lord's retirement. *He went out to a mountain to pray, and continued all night in prayer to God,* (εν τη προσευχη του Θεου) which may signify either the object to whom his prayer was directed, or the fervency of his requests; or, as some suppose, the house of prayer, or *proseucha*, to which he retired, such oratories, it seems, being common in that country. The length of the time he spent there bespoke the importance of the occasion, he being about to chuse and ordain his twelve apostles. *Note,* When matters of deep concern lie upon our souls, we are especially called to spread the case before God for his direction and blessing.

2. The calling and appointment of the twelve apostles. These the Lord intended to be his chief ministers in that kingdom which he was come to establish, putting them in trust with his gospel, and empowering them to work miracles in confirmation of their mission. The names of the apostles are the same as before, only he who was called Lebbeus, and surnamed Thaddeus, is here called Judas the brother of James, these names belonging to the same person; and Simon the Canaanite is here named *Simon Zelotes,* being probably, before his conversion, of the sect of the Zealots.

3. Having finished this work, he came down with the twelve to the plain, where great multitudes attended from the most distant parts of the country, to hear his discourses and to partake of his wondrous cures. Nor were they disappointed: he graciously taught them and richly dispensed his favours, healing all the diseased, and casting out the unclean spirits from such as were possessed; yea, such virtue went out of him, that *the whole multitude* of miserable patients, who came to him, *sought but to touch him,* fully persuaded that this would be effectual to heal them, and found, according to their faith, that their cure was instantly effected.

20 ¶ And he lifted up his eyes on his disciples, and
said, [a] Blessed *be* ye poor: for yours is the kingdom of
God. 21 [b] Blessed *are* ye that hunger now: [c] for ye
shall be filled. [d] Blessed *are* ye that weep now: for ye
shall laugh. 22 [e] Blessed are ye, when men shall hate
you, and when they [f] shall separate you *from their com-*
pany, and shall reproach *you,* and cast out your name as
evil, for the Son of man's sake. 23 [g] Rejoice ye in
that day, and leap for joy: for behold, your reward *is*
great in heaven: [h] for in the like manner did their fathers
unto the prophets. 24 But [i] wo unto you that [k] are
rich: for [l] ye have received your consolation. 25 [m] Wo
unto you that are full: for ye shall hunger. [n] Wo unto
you that laugh now: for ye shall mourn and weep.
26 [o] Wo unto you when all men shall speak well of you:
for so did their fathers [p] to the false prophets.

v. 20—26. Some have supposed this is an abridgment of the same discourse preached *Mat.* v—vii. others that it was delivered at a different time and place, though the matter be similar. And this seems most probable, as there it is said he went up into a mountain and sat, here, that he came down and stood in the plain.

As the disciples of Jesus would, for their attachment to him, be called to endure many hardships and sufferings, he here, fixing his eyes upon them, addresses them for their encouragement.

1. He pronounces those blessed whom the world in general counts to be of all men most miserable. (1.) *Blessed are ye poor,* destitute of [illegible] worldly substance, or who have left all to follow me, and whose spirits are humbled into the dust under the sense of your sinfulness and spiritual poverty: *yours is the kingdom of God,* the present riches of grace are your treasure, and the eternal inheritance above is reserved for you as your exceeding great reward. (2.) *Blessed are ye that hunger now,* either wanting necessary food for the sake of Christ and his gospel, or so earnest after spiritual blessings as the hungry crave for meat; *for ye shall be filled* with food to satisfy the cravings of hunger, or, better, with that supply of righteousness and grace which the soul desires. (3.) *Blessed are ye that weep now,* under afflictions for Christ's sake, or mourning over sin in yourselves and others, *for ye shall laugh,* filled with eternal consolations in that kingdom where every tear shall be for ever wiped away from your eyes. (4.) *Blessed are ye when men shall hate you* for your attachment to Christ and his gospel, *and when they shall separate you* from their communion, counting it infamous to associate with a person so obnoxious, as well as from their religious assemblies; *and shall reproach you,* branding you with every malicious slander, and treating you with insult and contempt as the vilest of mankind: *and cast out your name as evil,* never mentioning you but with malignity, obloquy, and virulence, shunning you wherever they go, and all this *for the Son of man's sake,* because you espouse his interests, profess your faith in him, and live to his glory; which is indeed the cause of all their enmity at the bottom, with whatever specious pretence they cloak their malevolence. Notwithstanding their curses, ye are truly blessed. *Rejoice ye in that day therefore, and leap for joy,* such reproach is your highest honour, and will prove your eternal advantage; *for behold your reward is great in heaven,* and this reward [illegible] will infinitely overpay all your losses and sufferings: *for in like manner did their fathers unto the prophets.* In every age, the faithful, from the beginning, have met the same treatment from the world of the ungodly. It is your honour to be made like to such company, and to partake of the same cross they endured as the way to the crown they have won. Let us weigh well these things, and we shall say, welcome reproach, welcome every opprobrious name, welcome enmity, reviling, insolence. This is the way to glory.

2. He pronounces fearful woes on those whom the world calls happy, so different are God's thoughts from man's thoughts. (1.) *Wo unto you that are rich,* who, possessed of affluence, idolize the creature, seek your happiness from worldly enjoyments, and trust in these vanities; *for ye have received your consolation,* you have your all in hand, and have nothing to hope for in eternity. (2.) *Wo unto you that are full,* living in all fleshly gratifications, and faring sumptuously every day; *for ye shall hunger,* emptied of all your present abundance, and left to the rage of craving appetite, that can never be satisfied, and to raging thirst, where not a drop of water is granted to cool a flaming tongue. (3.) *Wo unto you that laugh now,* spending your days in mirth, pleasure, and sensual joy, *for ye shall mourn and weep,* where the sorrow will be as unavailing as the torment which occasions it will be intolerable and eternal. (4.) *Wo unto you when all men shall speak well of you,* a sure sign that you do nothing to reprove them, either by your profession or Christian conversation, flattering them in their sin, and never offending them by your fidelity to their souls, then you will gain their approbation; *for so did their fathers to the false prophets,* whose smooth and deceitful prophecies obtained them the caresses of their countrymen, whilst the faithful prophets, who knew not to flatter, were abhorred and persecuted. And all these things are eminently verified and verifying every day.

27 ¶ But I say unto you which hear, [q] Love your
enemies, [r] do good to them which hate you, 28 [s] Bless
them that curse you, and [t] pray for them which despite-
fully use you. 29 And [u] unto him that smiteth thee
on the *one* cheek, offer also the other: and [x] him that
taketh away thy cloke, forbid not *to take thy* coat also.
30 [y] Give to every man that asketh of thee, and of him
that taketh away thy goods, ask *them* not again. 31
And [z] as ye would that men should do to you, do ye
also to them likewise. 32 For [a] if ye love them which
love you, what thank have ye? for sinners also love those
that love them. 33 And if ye do good to them which
do good to you, what thank have ye? for sinners also
do even the same. 34 And [b] if ye lend *to them* of
whom ye hope to receive, what thank have ye? for
sinners also lend to sinners, to receive as much again.
35 But [c] love ye your enemies, and do good, and lend,
hoping for nothing again: and your reward shall be
great, and [d] ye shall be the children of the Highest:
for he is kind unto the unthankful, and *to* the evil.
36 [e] Be ye therefore merciful, as your Father also is
merciful.

[q] Matt. v. 44. [r] Lev. xxiii. 4. Prov. xxv. 21. Rom. xii. 20. [s] Rom. xii. 14. 1 Pet. iii. 9. [t] Chap. xxiii. 34. Acts vii. 60. [u] Isa. l. 6. Lam. iii. 30. Matt. v. 39. [x] 1 Cor. vi. 7. [y] Deut. xv. 7. Prov. xxi. 26. [z] Matt. vii. 12. [a] Matt. v. 46. [b] Matt. v. 42. Deut. xv. 8. [c] Ver. 27. [d] Matt. v. 45. [e] Matt. v. 48.

v. 27—36. The same truths are here delivered as *Matth.* v. 38—48. Our Lord inculcates that universal charity which is the eminent characteristic of his religion. Our love must extend even to our bitterest enemies, and make us ready to every good word and work for their service, rendering to them blessing for curse. Love will make us return prayer for despiteful usage. Christian charity must lead us to put up with affronts without resentment, and to suffer wrongs without avenging them, or seeking injurious redress, *v.* 29. Charity must open our hearts to feel the distresses of the indigent, and our hands liberally, according to our ability, to relieve them, often lending without the hope of repayment, and willing to cancel the debts of the insolvent, whom unforeseen providences have disabled from the power of discharging, *v.* 30. Charity teaches us to put ourselves in the place of others, and act toward them in such a manner as, in their circumstances, we could with reason have expected from them, *v.* 31. And there are three reasons urged for this generous conversation.

1. That this is the distinguishing badge of our profession. To love, serve, and lend to those who make us a return in kind, is no more than the most self-interested worldling doth: and the faith which worketh by love must carry us much farther than this.

2. Our reward will be great in heaven, whatever ungrateful returns we may meet from men on earth.

3. As we shall herein most strikingly resemble the Father of mercies, *who is kind to the evil and unthankful.* He will acknow-

acknowledge us as his children, which is the moſt exalted honour and dignity

37 [x] Judge not, and ye ſhall not be judged condemn
not, and ye ſhall not be condemned forgive, and ye
ſhall be forgiven 38 [y] Give, and it ſhall be given
unto you, good meaſure, preſſed down, and ſhaken to-
gether, and running over, ſhall men give into your boſom
For [z] with the ſame meaſure that ye mete withal, it ſhall
be meaſured to you again 39 And he ſpake a para-
ble unto them, [a] Can the blind lead the blind? ſhall
they not both fall into the ditch? 40 [b] The diſciple is
not above his maſter but every one that is perfect ſhall
be as his maſter 41 And [c] why beholdeſt thou the
mote that is in thy brother's eye, but perceiveſt not the
beam that is in thine own eye? 42 Either how canſt
thou ſay to thy brother, Brother, let me pull out the
mote that is in thine eye, when thou thyſelf beholdeſt
not the beam that is in thine own eye? Thou hypo-
crite, [d] caſt out firſt the beam out of thine own eye, and
then ſhalt thou ſee clearly to pull out the mote that is
in thy brother's eye 43 For [e] a good tree bringeth not
forth corrupt fruit neither doth a corrupt tree bring
forth good fruit 44 For [f] every tree is known by his
own fruit for of thorns men do not gather figs, nor of
a bramble-buſh gather they † grapes 45 [g] A good
man out of the good treaſure of his heart, bringeth forth
that which is good and an evil man, out of the evil
treaſure of his heart, bringeth forth that which is evil
for of the abundance of the heart his mouth ſpeaketh
46 ¶ And [h] why call ye me Lord, Lord, and do not
the things which I ſay? 47 [i] Whoſoever cometh to me,
and heareth my ſayings, and doth them, I will ſhew you
to whom he is like 48 He is like a man which built
an houſe, and digged deep, and [k] laid the foundation on
a rock and when the flood aroſe, the ſtream beat ve-
hemently upon that houſe, and could not ſhake it for
it was founded upon a rock 49 But he that heareth
and doth not, is like a man that without a foundation
built an houſe upon the earth, againſt which the ſtream
did beat vehemently, and immediately it fell, and the
ruin of that houſe was great

[x] Mat vii 1 Rom ii 1 & xiv 4 10 Jam iv 11, 12 [y] Prov xix 17 [z] Mat vii 2 Mark iv 24 [a] Iſa ix 16 & xlii 19 Mat xv 14 [b] Mat x 24 John xiii 16 & xv 20 [c] Mat vii 3 [d] Prov xviii 1 [e] Mat vii 17 & xii 33 [f] Mat vii 16 † Gr A grape [g] Mat xii 35 [h] Mal i 6 Mat vii 21 Chap xiii 25 [i] Mat vii 24 [k] 1 Cor iii 11

v 37—49 Theſe wiſe ſayings we have conſidered before, *Mat* vii and in other places They give us the moſt noble directions whereon to form our judgment and conduct, happy they who obſerve them

1 In judging we muſt ever be candid, and lean to the moſt favourable ſide, interpreting the words and actions of others with thoſe allowances which we wiſh and need for our own and then we ſhall find the ſame candor from others which we exerciſe towards them

2 We muſt give and forgive, ready to relieve the neceſſitous, and to paſs by the offences of our brethren charitable and merciful, as we ourſelves expect mercy from God, and live penſioners on his bounty And this will engage others the more readily to forgive us, and even in this life we ſhall often reap the fruits of our liberality

3 As we deal with others, we may expect to be dealt with ourſelves Our rigour and ſeverity to others, will provoke men to treat us with the ſame, when we fall into their power, *Judg* i 7 whilſt our known benevolence will uſually engage a like return

4 Ignorant and blind guides, who know not the way of ſalvation themſelves, can never lead others aright, they who follow ſuch, will periſh with them It is hardly poſſible they ſhould teach others the bitterneſs and burden of ſin who have never felt either, nor acquaint them with the unſearchable riches of Chriſt, who have not experimentally found him precious to their own ſouls

5 Chriſt's followers may not expect kinder treatment from the world than their maſter met The higheſt perfection of the diſciple lies in conformity to his example, and when like his Lord, he is enabled to lead a life of ſelf-denial and deadneſs to the world, then he will be prepared to ſuffer whatever for his ſake he may be called to

6 They who ſet up for reformers of others, need firſt look well to their own ſouls to be quick-ſighted to others faults, and blind to our own, muſt make our rebukes abſurd, and they would be juſtly retorted When we are enabled to keep our own conſcience void of offence, then our reproofs will come commended by the weight of example, and be doubly weighty

7 Men's actions will be good, or evil, according to their inward principle A tree may be known by its fruit, ſo may a man by his conduct and converſation according to the good or evil treaſure in the heart, ſuch will be the produce *A good man*, by divine grace, truly renewed in the ſpirit of his mind, brings forth the genuine fruits of righteouſneſs and true holineſs *an evil man*, whoſe heart is unchanged, and under the power of native corruption, can do nothing truly pleaſing to God, his words and ways are all corrupt before God, either groſsly vicious, or he habitually forgets God, or if he pretends to ſerve him, pride and hypocriſy ſtamp his duties as an abomination

8 It is not pompous profeſſions, but real fidelity, which makes a man a true diſciple of Jeſus They who call him Lord, muſt give a proof of their ſincerity by their obedience it is not merely *hearing*, but *doing*, which he requires They who believe indeed to the ſaving of their ſouls, whoſe practice evidences their faith unfeigned, are like the wiſe builder, whoſe houſe, founded on a rock, defied the floods and ſtorm They ſtand faſt in the hour of temptation, and are not moved away from the hope of the goſpel, they perſevere in God's holy ways, and are kept by his power unto ſalvation But the careleſs hearer, on whoſe ſoul the word of Jeſus doth not take effect, builds his hopes of heaven on a ſandy foundation, and flatters himſelf to his ruin The hour of temptation here often proves him an apoſtate, or at leaſt in death the hope of the hypocrite periſheth Let us look well then to the ground on which we ſtand, that we may not too late perceive our irretrievable error

CHAP VII

In this chapter we have, 1 *Chriſt curing the centurion's ſervant,* ver 1—10 *and raiſing one to life that was dead, the widow's ſon at Naim,* ver 11—18 2 *Chriſt's anſwer to John's queſtion,* ver 19—23 *To which he adds an honourable teſtimony concerning John, and a juſt reproof to the men of that generation for the contempt they put upon him and his doctrine,* ver 24—35 3 *Chriſt comforting and pardoning a poor penitent, and juſtifying himſelf in the favour he ſhewed her, againſt the cavils of a proud Phariſee,* ver 36—50

1 NOW when he had ended all his ſayings in the
audience of the people, [a] he entred into Caper-
naum 2 And a certain centurion's ſervant, who was
dear unto him, was ſick, and ready to die 3 And
when he heard of Jeſus, he ſent unto him the elders of
the Jews, beſeeching him that he would come and heal
his ſervant 4 And when they came to Jeſus, they be-
ſought him inſtantly, ſaying, That he was worthy for
whom he ſhould do this 5 For he loveth our nation,
and he hath built us a ſynagogue 6 Then Jeſus went
with them And when he was now not far from the
houſe, the centurion ſent friends to him, ſaying, Lord,
trouble not thyſelf, for [b] I am not worthy that thou
ſhouldeſt enter under my roof 7 Wherefore neither
thought I myſelf worthy to come unto thee but [c] ſay
in a word, and my ſervant ſhall be healed 8 For I alſo
am a man ſet under authority, having under me ſoldiers,
and I ſay unto one, Go, and he goeth and to another,
Come, and he cometh and to my ſervant, Do this,
and he doeth it 9 When Jeſus heard theſe things, he
marvelled at him, and turned him about, and ſaid unto
the people that followed him, I ſay unto you, I have
not found ſo great faith, no, not in Iſrael 10 And
they that were ſent, returning to the houſe, found the
ſervant whole that had been ſick

[a] Mat viii 5 &c [b] Prov xxvii 2 Ver 4 [c] Pſ cvii 20

v 1—10 When Jeſus had finiſhed his diſcourſe in the audience of the people, an occaſion offers, to confirm by a miracle, the truths he had been declaring The ſame ſtory we had, *Mat* viii 5 different circumſtances are here inſerted, ſuch as the ſending of the elders of the Jews, and afterwards his friends, before the centurion came himſelf, as it ſeems probable he did at laſt, but his application by them was in fact the ſame, as if he had come in perſon at firſt

1 Hearing the fame of Jeſus, and having faith in him, he greatly deſired his help in behalf of a ſick ſervant, whoſe fidelity and diligence had endeared him to his maſter; and ſuppoſing that he, who was a Gentile, and a Roman officer, might not ſo eaſily obtain the favour, he engaged the elders of the Jews to be advocates for him, who readily undertook to ſerve him, as being under great obligations to him They earneſtly therefore beſought Jeſus for him, as one worthy his regard, having ever teſtified a great reſpect for the Jewiſh nation and religion, and at his own expence built them a ſynagogue for divine worſhip *Note,* (1) A ſervant truly faithful and induſtrious deſerves that eſteem he thus ſtudies to engage (2) It is good having an intereſt in their prayers whom the Lord Jeſus reſpects

2 As Chriſt was in the way to the centurion's houſe, he no ſooner heard of his condeſcenſion than in great humility he ſent other friends in his name, as unwilling to give the Lord

this trouble, and counting his house unworthy of such a guest, and himself undeserving of his honoured presence, which was indeed the reason he did not in person at first make the application. He professes his faith to be such in Christ's power, that all diseases would obey his orders, more readily even than the soldiers the word of their commanding officer; and that he need not be present to perform the cure; if he spoke, he believed it would instantly be done.

3. Christ expresses his admiration and approbation of such uncommon faith: even among all the Jewish people had never yet appeared so remarkable an instance of humble assured faith, as in this Gentile; therefore he puts honour upon him, and with pleasure grants his request. The disease immediately departed, and the persons who had been sent from the centurion's house, on their return found the servant perfectly restored to health. *Note*, True humility, and firm trust in his power and love, above all things commend us to the Saviour's regard.

11 ¶ And it came to pass the day after, that he
went into a city called Nain; and many of his disciples
went with him, and much people. 12 Now when he
came nigh to the gate of the city, behold, there was a
d Zech. xii. 10. dead man carried out, d the only son of his mother, and
she was a widow: and much people of the city was with
her. 13 And when the Lord saw her, he had com-
passion on her, and said unto her, Weep not. 14. And
† Or, coffin. he came and touched the † bier (and they that bare him
e Ez. xxxvii. 4. Eph. v. 14. stood still) and he said, Young man, I say unto thee, e
Arise. 15 And he that was dead sat up, and began
to speak: and he delivered him to his mother. 16.
And there came a fear on all: and they glorified God,
saying, That a great prophet is risen up among us; and,
f Ch. i. 68. That f God hath visited his people. 17 And this ru-
mour of him went forth throughout all Judea, and
throughout all the region round about. 18 And the
disciples of John shewed him of all these things.

v. 11—18. Another notable miracle wrought the day after the former, is here recorded.

1. The place where it was done was in the gate of the city, in the presence of all the multitude who followed Jesus, and of the company who attended the funeral, so that there was no want of evidences to attest the certainty of the fact.

2. The subject of the miracle was the dead corpse of a young man then carrying to his grave, the only son of an afflicted widow, and all the circumstances of the case rendered it peculiarly affecting. (1.) He was *a son, an only son*, probably the staff of her old age, and the support and comfort of her widowhood. (2.) He was a young man, cut down in the flower of his age, a warning to every one who looked upon his bier not to promise themselves continuance here, for childhood and youth are vanity. (3.) His mother was a *widow*, one terrible stroke of death had separated her from the partner of her bosom. This son alone remained to cheer her solitude, the staff of her age, and now he too is taken away; so numerous, so repeated, are our troubles in this vale of misery and tears: like Job's messengers of evil, scarce the sound of one is out of our ears, before another more grievous follows. May every pang we feel, but disengage us from the world, and teach us to seek more earnestly our rest above; then shall our severest losses prove our truest gain.

3. Compassion moved the Saviour's bosom. He ever tenderly felt for human woe, and unasked he brings relief. It was kind in those who attended this poor disconsolate widow, to condole with her, and endeavour to alleviate her sorrows. They could but weep with her, Jesus alone was able to say unto her, *weep not*; and by removing the cause, to wipe away the tears from her eyes. Approaching the bier whereon the corpse lay, the bearers halted, and with a word of power, in all the majesty of essential deity, *he said, Young man, I say unto thee, Arise*; instantly his spirit returned, *he that was dead sat up* on the bier where he was stretched out, all his senses were perfectly restored, *and he began to speak*; when with delight Jesus *delivered him back to his* transported *mother*. *Note*, (1.) The bowels of Jesus yearn over the miserable, and in all the afflictions of his people he is afflicted. Let the mourners remember, that Jesus compassionates their sorrows; and if he doth not appear to restore those dear pledges which are gone from our arms, he will bring us together at the resurrection day. (2.) Power accompanies the word of Jesus. Though dead sinners cannot of themselves hear or awake, the gospel call is not therefore in vain; but by the Redeemer's grace is made effectual to quicken the soul, and raise it from the death of sin unto the life of righteousness. (3.) Though Jesus might justly have claimed a right in him whom he had thus restored to life, he delivered him to his mother, intimating to us the great obligation lying on children to be dutiful to their parents, and a comfort and support to them in their old age.

4. Amazement and fear seized on the beholders. Astonished at this evidence of divine power, they *glorified God* for such an eminent instance of his goodness, and more especially that at last he had sent the *Great Prophet*, the expected Messiah, and in mercy visited his people; for these works of wonder proclaimed aloud that this was he who should come. Swift the fame of Jesus spread through Judea, and the country round; this amazing miracle bespoke his character; and among the rest John's disciples carried the report to their master, now bound in prison for his zeal and fidelity. *Note*, When dead souls are raised up to newness of life, we must give the glory to God of his great work: and these miracles, blessed be his name, are not yet ceased.

19 ¶ And John calling unto him two of his dis-
ciples, g sent *them* unto Jesus, saying, h Art thou he that g Mat. xi. 2.
should come, or look we for another? 20 When the h Gen. xlix. 10. Dan.
men were come unto him, they said, John Baptist hath ix. 24. John
sent us unto thee, saying, Art thou he that should come, vi. 14.
or look we for another? 21 And in that same hour
he cured many of *their* infirmities, and plagues, and of
evil spirits; and unto many that were blind he gave
sight. 22 Then Jesus answering, said unto them, Go
your way, and tell John what things ye have seen and
heard; how that i the blind see, the lame walk, the i Pf. cxlvi. 8. Isa.
lepers are cleansed, the deaf hear, the dead are raised, xxix. 18. &
k to the poor the gospel is preached. 23 And l blessed is xxxv. 5, 6.
he whosoever shall m not be offended in me. 24 ¶ And k Ch. iv. 18. l Jam. ii. 5.
n when the messengers of John were departed, he began 1 Cor. i.
to speak unto the people concerning John, What went 28. m Chap. ii.
ye out into the wilderness for to see? o A reed shaken 34. 1 Pet.
with the wind? 25 But what went ye out for to see? ii. 8. n Mat. xi. 7.
A man clothed in soft raiment? Behold, they which o Eph. iv.
are gorgeously apparelled, and live delicately, are in 14.
king's courts. 26 But what went ye out for to see? A
prophet? Yea, I say unto you, and much more than a
prophet. 27 This is he of whom it is written, p Behold, p Mal. iii. 1. Mark i. 2.
I send my messenger before thy face, which shall prepare
thy way before thee. 28 For I say unto you, q Among q Chap. i. 15.
those that are born of women, there is not a greater pro-
phet than John the Baptist: But he that is least in the
kingdom of God, is greater than he. 29 And all the
people that heard *him*, and the publicans justified God,
r being baptised with the baptism of John. 30 But the r Mat. iii. 5.
Pharisees and lawyers rejected s the counsel of God against s Acts xx.
themselves, being not baptized of him. 31 ¶ And 27.
the Lord said, t Whereunto then shall I liken the men t Mat. xi.
of this generation? and to what are they like? 32. 16.
They are like unto children sitting in the market-place,
and calling one to another, and saying, We have piped
unto you, and ye have not danced; we have mourned
unto you, and ye have not wept. 33 For u John the u Chap. i.
Baptist came neither eating bread, nor drinking wine; 15.
and ye say, He hath a devil. 34. x The Son of man is x Mat. xi.
come eating and drinking; and ye say, Behold, a glut- 11.
tonous man, and a wine bibber, a friend of publicans
and sinners. 35 But wisdom is justified of all her
children.

v. 19—35. This passage of history was before recorded. It contains,

1. The message sent by John from his prison, *v.* 19. not so much for his own satisfaction, as for the sake of his disciples, whose faith needed every confirmation, when combated by all the national prejudices so early imbibed. They found nothing of that grandeur and earthly greatness about Jesus, which they expected in the Messiah.

2. The answer of Jesus. His works, as well as words, sufficiently bespoke his real character. In the presence of the messengers from John, he performed a multitude of miraculous cures, and dispossessed many evil spirits: then bid them report to their master what they had heard and seen, *that the blind see, the lame walk, the lepers are cleansed, the dead are raised*, evidences incontestible of his mission as the Messiah, and figures of the more beneficial works which he came to perform on the souls of men; opening the eyes of the understanding, strengthening the impotent, curing the most inveterate habits of sin, and the desperate wickedness of the heart, and quickening the dead in trespasses and sin; for which end, *to the poor the gospel is preached*, wherein were fulfilled the prophecies which had gone before concerning him, *Isa.* lxi. 1. xxxv. 5, 6. *Psal.* lxxii. 13. and least, notwithstanding, they should be in danger of stumbling at the meanness of his appearance, and the enmity wherewith he was treated by the most respected characters of the Jewish people, the chief priests, scribes, and pharisees, he cautions

them against being offended at these things, since he alone was happy and blessed, who through all this cloud of prejudice received him as the Christ, and believed in his word

3 When the disciples of John were departed, Jesus began to give him just and high commendations He was a man of unshaken fortitude and unwavering fidelity, uniformly bearing testimony to Christ, and not plying like a reed under the contradiction of sinners, but boldly testifying against their iniquities dead to the delights of sense and glory of the world, he affected not soft raiment as a courtier, but as a mortified prophet lived what he preached greater in one sense than any of the former prophets, as the immediate forerunner of the Messiah, and as seeing him appear of whom they spake His success also was great, multitudes who heard him, and many of the vilest sinners, even publicans, affected by his discourses, glorified God, acknowledging their own sins, and the just punishment due to them, and in humble penitence sought for pardon, submitting to John's baptism, and professing thereby for the future to devote themselves to God's service But the proud and self-righteous Pharisees, puffed up with the vain conceit of their own excellence, fancied they were just persons who needed no repentance, therefore in general they rejected his preaching, and refused to submit to his baptism, thereby sealing themselves up under wrath, and the case is much the same to this day Those who are converted by the ministry of the word, are chiefly of the common people, and many whom the self-righteous despise as vile and abandoned, whilst the rulers pay little regard to the gospel-word, the wise men of this world disregard it as foolishness, and the persons of most admired goodness cannot bear to be set on a level with the chief of sinners, cannot stoop to receive the grace of Jesus freely, and thus perish in their pride

4 Christ upbraids the perverseness of the men of that generation No similitude could sufficiently describe their wilfulness and obstinacy, like froward and surly children, they neither would join their companions when in their play they imitated a feast or a funeral Thus the austerities of John, his life of self-denial, and doctrine of repentance disgusted them, and they reproached him as melancholy, or a demoniac The Son of man, on the other hand, more familiarly associated with others, refused not an invitation to a wedding, or a feast, and they reviled him as a glutton, a drunkard, and a loose companion *But wisdom is justified of all her children*, those who are truly made wise unto salvation, justify God in those methods he uses for their conversion, and approve and honour the Lord Jesus, who is the wisdom of God in all his works and ways *Note*, (1) They who resolve to cavil, will never want a handle (2) Different men and ministers have different tempers and manners, some are naturally more austere and reserved, others more free and open, some more powerfully urge the thunders of Sinai upon the sinner's conscience, others dwell upon the softer accents of gospel-grace And this diversity of dispositions in which men are led is beautiful, though malice will find the matter of objection against both (3) We must take care not to judge of others by ourselves, not branding on the one hand the reserved, as morose, nor, on the other, charging innocent freedom as licentiousness, but ever put the most candid constructions on men's tempers and manners.

36 ¶ And one of the Pharisees desired him that
y Mat xxvi 6 Mark xiv 3 John xi 2 he would eat with him And y he went into the Pha-
risee's house, and sat down to meat 37 And behold,
a woman in the city, which was a sinner, when she
knew that Jesus sat at meat in the Pharisee's house,
brought an alabaster box of ointment, 38 And stood
at his feet behind him weeping, and began to wash his
feet with tears, and did wipe *them* with the hairs of
her head, and kissed his feet, and anointed *them* with
the ointment 39 Now when the Pharisee which had
bidden him, saw *it*, he spake within himself, saying,
z Chap xv 2 z This man, if he were a prophet, would have known
who and what manner of woman *this is* that toucheth
him for she is a sinner 40 And Jesus answering,
said unto him, Simon, I have somewhat to say unto
thee And he saith, Master, say on 41 There was
a Mat vi 12 Ver 47 a certain creditor which had two a debtors the one
owed five hundred † pence, and the other fifty 42
b Mat xviii 28 And when b they had nothing to pay, he c frankly for-
c Ps xlix 8 gave them both Tell me therefore, which of them
d Rom iii 24 will love him most? 43 Simon answered and said, I
e Ver 47 suppose that e he to whom he forgave most. And he said
unto him, Thou hast rightly judged 44 And he turn-
ed to the woman, and said unto Simon, Seest thou this
woman? I entred into thine house, thou gavest me no
water for my feet but she hath washed my feet with
tears, and wiped *them* with the hairs of her head. 45
Thou gavest me no kiss but this woman, since the
time I came in, hath not ceased to kiss my feet 46
Mine head with oil thou didst not anoint but this wo-
man hath anointed my feet with ointment 47 Where-
fore I say unto thee, f Her sins, which are many, are for- f 1 Tim i 14
given, † for she loved much but to whom little is † Or therefore
forgiven, the same loveth little 48 And he said unto
her, Thy sins are forgiven 49 And they that sat
at meat with him, began to say within themselves,
g Who is this that forgiveth sins also? 50 And he g Mark ii 7
said to the woman, h Thy faith hath saved thee, go in h Mat ix 22 Mark v 34 Chap viii 48 xviii 42
peace

℣ 36—50 Our Lord behaved himself courteous to all, and though the Pharisees had shewn themselves his bitter enemies, he refused not the invitation of one of them, and readily went to eat at his house And we are told,

1 A singular circumstance which happen'd on that occasion A woman, whose character had been notoriously infamous, but by the preaching and grace of the Redeemer was become a real penitent, and true believer, came in, urged by her deep affection for her Lord, and standing behind him as he lay along (which was their custom at meals) with penitential tears she bedewed his feet, wiped them with her once braided, but now dishevelled hair, and kissing them in humble adoration, anointed them, as a token of her high respect, with precious ointment from an alabaster box *Note*, (1) They who truly draw near to Jesus, cannot but feel their hearts bleed, and their eyes overflow, in the remembrance of past ingratitude. (2) A soul that loves the Lord Jesus, counts nothing too good to employ in his service (3) When the eyes, full of adultery, become fountains of tears, and all the ornaments of pride, the lure of lust, are laid aside, these are blessed symptoms of a happy change

2 The Pharisee was highly offended at Christ for suffering such a woman to approach him, and thought within himself, if Jesus were the prophet he pretended to be, he must have known, and spurned from his feet a creature so infamous Thus whilst persons of a proud and self-righteous spirit are looking with contempt on a poor harlot, and saying, *Stand by thyself, come not near me, I am holier than thou*, they are not aware that this high conceit of themselves, and despising others, is in God's sight an abomination far greater, even than those outward evils which they condemn in others

3 Christ justifies the woman from Simon's censures The Pharisee questioned Christ's prophetical character, therefore the Lord, by answering his thoughts, will give him an evidence of it, and draw the poor woman's vindication from his own lips and this he doth by an apposite parable, having informed Simon he had something of importance to say to him, to which he professes himself all attention

(1) The parable respected two debtors, the one of whom owed ten times more than the other, but being both insolvent, the creditor freely forgave them Christ hereupon appeals to Simon for an answer, which of the two will love their gracious benefactor most? The reply was evident, he to whom most was forgiven *The debt is sin*, and sinners are deep in arrears to God, they have never paid him the obedience they owe, and are become liable to the arrests of judgment All are guilty, but some are more notorious offenders, and have sinned with greater aggravations than others, yet the least transgressor is an insolvent debtor, he can never make God a compensation for the least of his iniquities, and must perish eternally with the vilest, unless he is convinced of his sinfulness, and flies to the free grace of God in Jesus Christ In him there is plenteous redemption, the chief of sinners are sure of finding pardon tho' the ransom he hath paid, and none who come to him shall be in any wise cast out A sense of this abounding grace will not fail to engage the believing sinner's heart, and in proportion to the discovery he hath of his own guilt, should his gratitude be for the rich mercy vouchsafed to him The chief of sinners are bound to become the chief of saints, to love much, because the Lord hath forgiven them much

(2) Christ applies the parable to the case before him This woman was the debtor who owed the five hundred pence, and she had been forgiven, no marvel, therefore, her expressions of gratitude were singular, for which, so far from being condemned, she rather deserved to be commended All she had done flowed from this source, and herein she had exceeded Simon in her returns of love, as much as she had done in the offensiveness and notoriety of her transgression (1) Instead of the water, which he had neglected to bring, she had, with penitential tears, bedewed his feet, and wiped them with her hair (2) The kiss of peace and salutation Simon had not given to his sacred guest, but this poor sinner had not ceased to express her humble gratitude and love, by repeatedly kissing even his feet (3) The common civility of oil to anoint his head the Pharisee had with-held, but she had poured this costly ointment on his feet, the expression of her faith in him as the Messiah, and of that unfeigned regard which made her account the greatest cost well employed in his service therefore he seals afresh the

the pardon which he had beſtowed upon her, on account of which ſhe loved him ſo greatly Whilſt ſuch as Simon, who were leſs acquainted with their own guilt and ſinfulneſs, and did not ſee their great need of a pardon, would feel themſelves leſs obliged to the Saviour's grace, and teſtify, as Simon had done, leſs regard for him

(3) He particularly addreſſes himſelf to the poor woman, to ſilence her fears, and encourage her under the Phariſee's frowns He repeats his aſſurances, *Thy ſins are forgiven thee*, and though he knew the murmurs this raiſed, and the offence it gave among the phariſaical tribe who were at the table, as if his arrogating ſuch a power was impious, nay, blaſphemous, he, ſo far from receding, confirms her ſalvation, to which, through faith in him, ſhe was now aſſuredly entitled, and therefore he bids her *go in peace*, every fear of guilt removed, her conſcience at eaſe, regardleſs of the reproaches of the proud, and waiting confidently for the eternal reſt that remaineth for the people of God *Note*, (1) As nothing renders us ſo fearful as the conſciouſneſs of guilt, we need promiſe upon promiſe to encourage our truſt and hope (2) Faith alone can pacify the conſcience, and produce that genuine love and evangelical ſorrow, which worketh repentance unto ſalvation never to be repented of

CHAP VIII

Here is, 1 Chriſt's preaching, and ſubſiſtence by the charitable contributions of good people, ver 1—3 2 The parable of the ſower, ver 4—18 3 The preference which Chriſt gave to his obedient diſciples, before his neareſt relations according to the fleſh, ver 19—21 4 His ſtilling a ſtorm at ſea with a word's ſpeaking, ver 22—25 5 His caſting a legion of devils out of a man that was poſſeſſed by them, ver 26—40 6 His healing the woman that had the bloody iſſue, and raiſing Jairus's daughter to life, ver 41—56

1 AND it came to paſs afterward, that he went
throughout every city and village preaching,
and ſhewing the glad tidings of the kingdom of God
and the twelve *were* with him, 2 And [a] certain women [a Mat xxvii 55, 56]
which had been healed of evil ſpirits and infirmities,
Mary called Magdalene, [b] out of whom went ſeven [b Mark xvi 9]
devils, 3 And Joanna the wife of Chuza, Herod's
ſteward, and Suſanna, and many others, which miniſtred
unto him of their ſubſtance

v 1—3 With unwearied labours the divine Redeemer went about doing good

1 He viſited round all the cities and villages in Galilee, preached the glad tidings of the kingdom of God, and opened the nature, bleſſings, and privileges of that goſpel-church which he came to erect His twelve apoſtles attended him to be witneſſes of his miracles, and to learn from his lips the doctrines they were afterwards appointed to preach

2 His ſupport aroſe from the contributions of ſome pious women who followed him, who had experienced his healing grace both in their bodies and their ſouls Among many others, three are particularly mentioned, Mary Magdalene, out of whom Jeſus had caſt ſeven devils, Joanna, the wife, perhaps now the widow, of Chuza, Herod's ſteward, probably a perſon of conſiderable rank and fortune, and Suſanna These, with many others, furniſhed him with a ſubſiſtence, and he, in great humility, condeſcended to be thus ſupported, rather than by exerting his own miraculous power *Note*, (1) Chriſt lived upon alms, to teach us never to deſpiſe the poor, nor, if we are reduced, proudly to ſcorn being obliged to others for a maintenance (2) They who love the goſpel, cannot but delight to contribute liberally for the ſupport of it (3) If we have been truly healed by the grace of Jeſus, we ſhall commence thenceforward his inſeparable followers in all holy converſation and godlineſs

4 ¶ And when much people were gathered together, [c Mat xiii 2 Mark iv 1]
and were come to him out of every city, he ſpake by a
parable 5 A ſower went out to ſow his ſeed and as
he ſowed, ſome fell by the way-ſide, and it was trodden
down, and the fowls of the air devoured it 6 And
ſome fell upon a rock, and as ſoon as it was ſprung up,
it withered away, becauſe it lacked moiſture 7 And
ſome fell among thorns, and the thorns ſprang up with [d John xv 5]
it, and choked it 8 And other fell on good ground,
and ſprang up, and [e] bare fruit an hundred fold And
when he had ſaid theſe things, he cried, [f] He that hath [f Mat xi 15]
ears to hear, let him hear 9 And his diſciples aſked
him, ſaying, What might this parable be? 10 And [g 1 Cor ii 10]
he ſaid, [g] Unto you it is given to know the myſteries of
the kingdom of God but to others in parables, [h] that [h Iſa vi 9 John xii 40]
ſeeing they might not ſee, and hearing they might not
underſtand 11 [i] Now the parable is this The ſeed is [i Mat xiii 18 Mark iv 14]
the word of God 12 Thoſe by the way-ſide, are they
that hear then cometh the devil, and taketh away the
word out of their hearts, leſt they ſhould believe and be
ſaved 13 They on the rock, *are they*, which when
they hear, [k] receive the word with joy, and theſe have [k Iſa lviii 2 Ezek xxxiii 31 Mark vi 20 John v 35]
no root, [l] which for a while believe, and in time of temp- [l Hoſ vi 4]
tation fall away 14 And that which fell [m] among [m Jer iv 3]
thorns, are they, which when they have heard, go forth, [n Mat xix 23 1 Tim vi 9]
and [n] are choked with cares, and riches, and pleaſures
of *this* life, and bring no fruit to perfection 15 But
that on the good ground, are they which in an honeſt [o John xv 8]
and good heart, having heard the word, keep it, and [o]
bring forth fruit [p] with patience 16 ¶ No man [q] when [p Heb x 36]
he hath lighted a candle, covereth it with a veſſel, or [q Mat v 15 Mark iv 21]
putteth *it* under a bed but ſetteth it on a candleſtick, [Chap xi 33]
that they which enter in may ſee the light 17 For [r] [r Job xii 22 Mat x 26]
nothing is ſecret, that ſhall not be made manifeſt neither [Chap xii 2]
any thing hid, that ſhall not be known, and come a-
broad 18 Take heed therefore how ye hear [s] for [s Mat xiii 12 & xxv 29]
whoſoever hath, to him ſhall be given, and whoſoever [Chap xix 26]
hath not, from him ſhall be taken even that which he
ſeemeth to have 19 ¶ [t] Then came to him his mo- [t Mat xii 46 Mark iii 31]
ther and his brethren, and could not come at him for
the preſs 20 And it was told him *by certain*, which
ſaid, Thy mother and thy brethren ſtand without, de-
ſiring to ſee thee 21 And he anſwered and ſaid unto
them, [u] My mother and my brethren are theſe which [u John xv 14]
hear the word of God, and do it

v 4—21 Great multitudes being collected together from all the neighbouring cities and villages, he took occaſion to repreſent the nature of the goſpel-diſpenſation by the parable of the ſower, which we had, *Mat* xiii 3 the explication of which, he vouchſafes to give to his inquiſitive diſciples in private, it being their peculiar mercy, that what was left myſterious to others, ſhould be explained to them And a ſingular favour is this, if whilſt others are left in darkneſs, we are brought into the marvellous light of goſpel-truth

1 Concerning the parable, we may obſerve, (1) How vigilant *is our adverſary the devil, in every place where the word* of God is diſpenſed, to harden the heart againſt receiving it, leaſt *we ſhould believe and be ſaved*, and this he doth, by diſtracting the attention, by ſuggeſting ſome vain or worldly thoughts immediately after we have heard God's word preached, by inſtilling prejudices againſt the ſower, or doubts about the ſcripture itſelf, and thus preventing the admiſſion or abidance of the truth in the minds of the hearers the conſequence of which is, that men neglect and deſpiſe the great ſalvation of God (2) Among the multitudes who appear from time to time to be affected with the goſpel, and make ſome profeſſion, the greater number fall ſhort of the kingdom, diſcouraged by the frowns, or ſeduced by the ſmiles of this preſent evil world, they grow cold and careleſs, the love of pleaſure and eaſe, anxious cares, or inordinate love of riches, deſtroy and choak the word, and they either openly apoſtatize, or in their hearts, at leaſt, depart from the living God Hence, out of many who are called, few are choſen (3) There is a remnant, according to the election of grace, to whom the ſeed of the goſpel-word becomes the power of God unto ſalvation They ſeriouſly hear, ſedately weigh, and faithfully embrace the truth, as it is in Jeſus their heart, by divine grace, are made honeſt and ſincere, and patiently perſevering in well-doing, they hold the beginning of their confidence ſtedfaſt unto the end, not ſeduced by any enticements, nor deterred by any perſecutions, which for the word' ſake may ariſe Thus their fruit abides and abounds, and they ſtand ready for the harveſt of eternal glory

2 By another parable of a lighted candle, Chriſt teaches his diſciples, and others, what was expected from them, even to ſhine as lights in the world, holding forth the word of life This being the great deſign of all the private inſtructions he gave them, that they ſhould afterwards plainly and fully declare to the world, the great truths couched under theſe ſimilitudes As therefore they muſt give a ſolemn account for the particular advantages they enjoyed, they muſt take heed how they hear, when ſo much was hereby entruſted to them, and expected from them; which, if they improved, farther aſſiſtances of ſpiritual light, and greater gifts ſhould be given them but if they neglected to profit by theſe means of wiſdom and grace vouchſafed to them, the conſequence would be, that the gifts and knowledge which they ſeemed to have, would decay, and be taken from them, and darkneſs and error ſucceed

3 Chriſt acknowledges thoſe who truly hear the word of God, and do it, as his neareſt and deareſt relations His mother and his brethren deſired to ſee and ſpeak with him, but unable to approach him, becauſe of the crowd, ſome of thoſe who

who ſtood around him, informed him of their requeſt, but he was otherwiſe engaged in his Father's work, and took occaſion hence to encourage thoſe who were his diligent attendants, aſſuring them they ſhared his regards above the neareſt relatives after the fleſh

u Mat viii 23, Mark iv 35 — 22 ¶ [u] Now it came to paſs on a certain day, that
he went into a ſhip with his diſciples and he ſaid unto
them, Let us go over unto the other ſide of the lake
x Pſ x 1 Iſa xlv 15 y Iſa liv 11 — And they launched forth. 23 But as they ſailed, [x] he
fell aſleep and there came down [y] a ſtorm of wind on
the lake, and they were filled *with water*, and were in
jeopardy 24 And they came to him, and awoke him,
ſaying, Maſter, maſter, we periſh Then he aroſe, and
z Pſ cvi 13 — [z] rebuked the wind, and the raging of the water and
they ceaſed, and there was a calm 25 And he ſaid
unto them, Where is your faith? And they being afraid,
wondered, ſaying one to another, What manner of man
a Pſ lxv 7 & lxxxix 9 & cvii 25, 29 — is this? for [a] he commandeth even the winds and water,
and they obey him 26 ¶ And [b] they arrived at the
country of the Gadarenes, which is over againſt Galilee
b Mat viii 28 Mark v 1 — 27 And when he went forth to land, there met him
out of the city a certain man which had devils long
time, and ware no clothes, neither abode in *any* houſe,
but in the tombs 28 When he ſaw Jeſus, he cried
out, and fell down before him, and with a loud voice
ſaid, What have I to do with thee, Jeſus, thou Son of
c 2 Pet ii 4 Jude 6 — God moſt high? I beſeech thee [c] torment me not
29 (For he had commanded the unclean ſpirit to come
out of the man For oftentimes it had caught him
and he was kept bound with chains, and in fetters,
and he brake the bands, and was driven of the devil
into the wilderneſs) 30 And Jeſus aſked him, ſay-
ing, What is thy name? And he ſaid, Legion becauſe
many devils were entred into him 31 And they be-
ſought him that he would not command them to go
d Rev xx 3 — out into [d] the deep 32 And there was there an herd
of many ſwine feeding on the mountain and they be-
ſought him that he would ſuffer them to enter into
them And he ſuffered them 33 Then went the devils
out of the man, and entred into the ſwine, and the
herd ran violently down a ſteep place into the lake,
and were choked 34 When they that fed them ſaw
what was done, they fled, and went and told *it* in the
city and in the country 35 Then went they out to
ſee what was done, and came to Jeſus, and found the
man out of whom the devils were departed, ſitting at
the feet of Jeſus, clothed, and in his right mind and
they were afraid 36 They alſo which ſaw *it*, told
them by what means he that was poſſeſſed of the devils
was healed 37 ¶ Then the whole multitude of the
e Deut v 25 Chap v 8 Acts xvi 39 — country of the Gadarenes round about, [e] beſought him
to depart from them, for they were taken with great
fear and he went up into the ſhip, and returned back
f Mark v 18 — again 38 Now [f] the man out of whom the devils were
departed, beſought him that he might be with him
but Jeſus ſent him away, ſaying, 39 ¶ Return to
thine own houſe, and ſhew how great things God hath
done unto thee And he went his way, and publiſhed
throughout the whole city, how great things Jeſus had
done unto him

v 22—39 We had before an account of theſe two illuſtrious miracles, *Mat* viii We ſee,

1 Chriſt's wonders in the deep He, at whoſe word the ſtormy waves ariſe, can in a moment alſo reſtrain their rage, and ſilence their roaring Chriſt ſent his diſciples by ſea on purpoſe to give them this freſh evidence of his omnipotence They embarked at his word, and little expected danger, but oftentimes, when we are lulled into ſecurity, our peril is moſt imminent they had him with them however, and therefore need not fear but he was aſleep, for ſo regardleſs he ſometimes appears towards his people in their diſtreſs, and then danger ſtaggered their faith, and filled their heart with fears, as their boat was filled with water The ſtrongeſt believers are ſometimes ſhaken, prayer was now their recourſe, to Chriſt they fly, and awaken him with their cries He ſlept with this deſign, to quicken their deſires after him, to affect them with a deeper ſenſe of their want of him, and teſtify toward them more abundantly his power and his love When we feel ourſelves undone and periſhing, then is Chriſt truly precious to us, none ever periſhed who thus fled to him He roſe, and with a word ſtilled the raging ſea, and quieted their fears He delights to ſpeak peace to the troubled conſcience, and they who wait on him ſhall not be aſhamed of their confidence Their only ſhame will ariſe from their diſhonourable diſtruſts of him, for theſe he juſtly reproves them, *Where is your faith?* Faith they had in habit, but not in exerciſe, their jeopardy for a moment ſuppreſſed its vigorous actings, their ſudden deliverance amazed them, and filled with reverential fear at ſuch a diſplay of divine power, they could not but conclude he muſt be more than man, whom winds and waves obeyed

2 Chriſt's dominion over the powers of darkneſs, raging devils can no more reſiſt his power, than raging winds and waves, and this is an unſpeakable comfort to all God's people, that Satan is a vanquiſhed foe, and cannot harm, even a ſwine, without permiſſion A legion here poſſeſſed one man, how numberleſs then theſe malignant ſpirits, how unequal a match muſt we be for them, if left to ourſelves! No chains could hold this poor demoniac, in cold and nakedneſs, without clothes or covering, he was driven to the tombs ſo ungovernable are we when under the influence of Satanical tempers, a terror to others, a burden to ourſelves At the feet of Jeſus he fell, whilſt the foul ſpirit within cried out in terror, dreading to be diſpoſſeſſed, and ſent to the abyſs, the place of torment A laviſh fear of hell ſometimes drives men thus to their knees they dread the puniſhment but do not loath their ſins, they cry for releaſe from their pains, not for deliverance from their corruptions When the devil is compelled to quit his hold of the man, he fain would be doing miſchief, if but among the ſwine, and in correction to ſome, and as a warning to others, Chriſt permits this viſitation on their property But when they heard from the affrighted keepers the loſs they had ſuſtained, they deſired him to depart out of their coaſt, dreading the conſequences of his ſtay, and he departed The viſitations which ſhould humble, often ſerve but to harden the ſouls of ſinners inſtead of coming to Chriſt, they would get as far from him as poſſible The poor man, however, who was now reſtored to his right mind, and ſitting at Jeſus's feet, would fain have followed him, but he is ſent back to proclaim the mercy he hath experienced When by divine grace a *right mind* is reſtored to us, and the power of ſin and Satan is broken, we are called upon to acknowledge the mercy to the praiſe of Jeſus, and to tell what great things he hath done for our ſouls, inviting others to come and taſte how gracious the Lord is

40 And it came to paſs, that when Jeſus was re-
turned, the people *gladly* received him for they were
all waiting for him 41 ¶ [g] And behold, there came a — g Mat ix 18 Mark v 22
man named Jairus, and he was a ruler of the ſynagogue
and he fell down at Jeſus feet, and beſought him that
he would come into his houſe 42 For he had one only
daughter, about twelve years of age, and ſhe lay [h] a — h Mat ix 18
dying But as he went, the people thronged him
43 ¶ And a woman [i] having an iſſue of blood twelve — i Lev xv 25
years, which had ſpent all her living upon phyſicians,
neither could be healed of any, 44 Came behind him,
and touched the border of his garment and imme-
diately her iſſue of blood ſtanched 45 And [k] Jeſus — k Mark v 30
ſaid, Who touched me? When all denied, Peter, and
they that were with him, ſaid, Maſter, the multitude
throng thee, and preſs *thee*, and ſayeſt thou, Who
touched me? 46 And Jeſus ſaid, Some body hath
touched me for I perceive that virtue is gone out of
me 47 And when the woman ſaw that ſhe was not
hid, ſhe came trembling, and falling down before him,
ſhe declared unto him before all the people, for what
cauſe ſhe had touched him, and how ſhe was healed
immediately 48 And he ſaid unto her, Daughter, be
of good comfort [l] thy faith hath made thee whole, go — l Chap vii 50 & xvii 19 & xviii 42
in peace 49 ¶ While he yet ſpake, there cometh one
from the ruler of the ſynagogue's *houſe*, ſaying to him,
Thy daughter is dead, trouble not the Maſter 50 But
when Jeſus heard *it*, he anſwered him, ſaying, Fear
not [m] believe only, and ſhe ſhall be made whole 51 — m John xi 25
And when he came into the houſe, he ſuffered no man
to go in, ſave Peter, and James, and John, and the fa-
ther and the mother of the maiden 52 And all wept,
and bewailed her but he ſaid, Weep not, ſhe is not
dead, but [n] ſleepeth 53 And they laughed him to — n John xi 11
ſcorn, knowing that ſhe was dead 54 And [o] he put — o Acts ix 40
them all out, and took her by the hand, and called, ſay-
ing, Maid, ariſe 55 And her ſpirit came again, and
ſhe aroſe ſtraightway and he commanded to give her
meat 56 And her parents were aſtoniſhed [p] but he — p Mat viii 4 & ix 30 Chap v 14
charged them that they ſhould tell no man what was
done

v 40—56

v 40—56 Though the Gadarenes were glad to get rid of Jesus, the men of Galilee with open arms received him, eagerly waiting for his return. If in one place the gospel be despised and expelled, another door of utterance shall be opened, and some will be glad to welcome the ejected ministers of Christ.

No sooner was Jesus arrived, than we find an application made to him by a ruler, in behalf of his daughter at the point of death, and whilst he goes to perform one miracle, by the way he works another.

1 A poor diseased woman, who was ashamed to make a public application to him, persuaded that a touch of his garment would effect that which all her physicians had attempted in vain, came in secret among the crowd, and touching his garment, found, according to her faith, a perfect cure. But it was neither possible nor proper that it should be hid: for the glory of Jesus, and the comfort of her own soul, she is called upon to make an acknowledgment of the mercy. Persuaded, that he who felt virtue go out of him, and wrought the cure, could not be at a loss to find out the patient, no sooner did she hear his enquiries, than she fell trembling at his feet, acknowledged her boldness, and owned the blessing she had received. Far from being displeased, he who healed her body, now comforts her soul, and commending her faith, dismisses her in peace. *Note*, (1.) There is that fulness of grace in Christ, that whoever comes to him, shall be holpen. (2.) We cannot be hid from the eye of Jesus, and a gracious soul desires it not; he would tell him of all his wretchedness, and pour out his heart in simplicity before him. (3.) Christ delights to raise up the trembling sinner, and speaks comfort to his poor in spirit: such need not fear, the language of Jesus to them shall be the voice of peace and love.

2 The ruler's daughter had now closed her eyes in death, and therefore his friends imagined it useless to trouble Jesus farther. In lesser trials many thus pretend to trust him, who, in greater, are ready to despair; but he, who by a word can heal the diseased, can by the same power raise the dead; he encourages, therefore, the ruler's faith; not only whilst there is life there is hope, but even in death the case is not desperate, when he, who is the resurrection and the life, is the physician. With three of his disciples, and the parents of the child, he went into the room where she lay, sending forth those as unworthy to be spectators of his power, who, when he would dry up their tears with good words and comfortable, laughed at his saying that she only slept, because they knew she was dead; but knew not that to him it was as easy to call her from the arms of death, as to awaken her from sleep. The bed of death is the place of repose for those who fall asleep in Jesus; there they sweetly rest, till they are awakened in the resurrection morn to rise in that eternal day, when sleep and death will be no more. At his word the damsel arose; his hand of grace, his word of power, communicated life, and brought back the spirit which had fled: in perfect health her astonished parents behold her restored to their longing arms. He commanded them hereupon to give her some food, and charged them to conceal the miracle; he wanted not men to spread his fame, his works were sufficient heralds. By the effectual word of Jesus is the sinner, dead in trespasses, thus quickened to spiritual life; and when the union between the body and soul is dissolved, he takes care of both in their state of separation, and will bring the spirit again in the resurrection-day, and prepare for it a body glorified like his own.

CHAP. IX.

In this chapter we have, 1. The commission Christ gave his twelve apostles to preach the gospel, and confirm it by miracles, ver. 1—6. *2. Herod's terror at the growing greatness of our Lord Jesus,* ver. 7—9. *3. The apostles return to Christ, his retirement with them into a place of solitude, the great resort of people to them notwithstanding, and his feeding five thousand men with five loaves and two fishes,* ver. 10—17. *4. His discourse with his disciples concerning himself, and his own sufferings for them, and theirs for him,* ver. 18—27. *5. Christ's transfiguration,* ver. 28—36. *6. The cure of a lunatick child,* ver. 37—42. *7. The repeated notice Christ gave his disciples of his approaching sufferings,* ver. 43—45. *8. His check to the ambition of his disciples,* ver. 46—48. *and to their monopolizing of the power over devils to themselves,* ver. 49, 50. *9. The rebuke he gave them for their resentment of an affront given him by a village of the Samaritans,* ver. 51—56. *10. The answers he gave to several that were inclined to follow him, but not considerately, or not zealously and heartily so inclined,* ver. 57—62.

1 THEN he called his twelve disciples together, [a Mat. x. 1. Mark iii. 13]
and gave them power and authority over all
devils, and to cure diseases. 2 And he sent them to
preach the kingdom of God, and to heal the sick.
3 And he said unto them, [b] Take nothing for your jour- [b Chap. x. 4]
ney, neither staves, nor scrip, neither bread, neither
money; neither have two coats apiece. 4 And [c] what- [c Chap. x. 5, 6]
soever house ye enter into, there abide, and thence de-
part. 5 And whosoever will not receive you, when ye
go out of that city, [d] shake off the very dust from your [d Acts xiii. 51. & xviii. 6]
feet for a testimony against them. 6 And they departed,
and went through the towns, preaching the gospel, and
[e] healing every where. 7 ¶ [f] Now Herod the tetrarch [e Ver. 1 / f Mat. xiv. 1. Mark vi. 14]
heard of all that was done by him: and he was [g] perplex-
ed, because that it was said of some, that John was risen [g Ps. xiv. 5]
from the dead; 8 And of some, that [h] Elias had ap- [h Mat. xvi. 14]
peared; and of others, that one of the old prophets was
risen again. 9 And Herod said, John have I behead-
ed: but who is this of whom I hear such things? And
he desired to see him.

v 1—9 Our Lord having called his twelve apostles to closer attendance upon himself, that they might be qualified for the work in which he designed to employ them, now sends them forth in his name, and invests them with miraculous powers, as a proof of their divine mission.

1 He directs them *what* to say and do. The subject of their preaching must be the gospel of the kingdom, and by their beneficent acts of healing men's bodies, they would *not only* confirm, but recommend also their doctrine to men's souls.

2 He directs them *how* to go on this errand. They must make no preparation for the journey; but in their fisher's garments, without change of raiment, without money, or provision, they must go forth, trusting entirely on divine providence for the supply of all their wants; taking up their quarters with the *first family who should receive them,* and *abiding in the same house* during their stay, to avoid all appearance of fickleness or nicety. But if any refused them a welcome entertainment, leaving that city to its fate, they need only shake off the dust of their feet, and that should stand as an eternal testimony against them for rejecting the gospel, and ensure their destruction.

3 They immediately obeyed, and executed their commission; for every gracious soul delights to be employed for Christ, and runs at his command.

4 Herod the tetrarch was exceedingly perplexed and terrified at the reports, which on this occasion reached his ears. The country rang with the miracles performed by Jesus and his apostles, and people offered various conjectures concerning this great personage, who not only wrought such wonders himself, but was able to communicate this extraordinary power to others. Some said it was John revived; others that Elias was come, the expected forerunner of the Messiah; others, that one of the old prophets was risen again. Herod's guilty conscience smote him, justly fearing that the murdered Baptist was indeed risen, or some more mighty instrument of God to avenge his quarrel, and *he desired to see him.*

10 ¶ And the apostles when they were returned, told
him all that they had done. [i] And he took them, and [i Mat. xiv. 13. Mark vi. 31]
went aside privately into a desert place, belonging to the
city called Bethsaida. 11 And the people when they
knew *it*, followed him: and he received them, and
spake unto them of the kingdom of God, and healed
them that had need of healing. 12 [k] And when the day [k John vi. 5]
began to wear away, then came the twelve and said
unto him, Send the multitude away, that they may go
into the towns and country round about, and lodge, and
get victuals: for we are here in a desert place. 13 But
he said unto them, Give ye them to eat. And they
said, We have no more but five loaves and two fishes;
[l] except we should go and buy meat for all this people. [l Num. xi. 22. 2 Kings iv. 43]
14 For they were about five thousand men. And he
said to his disciples, Make them sit down by fifties in a
company. 15 And they did so, and made them all sit
down. 16 Then he took the five loaves, and the two
fishes, and looking up to heaven, [m] he blessed them, and [m Mat. xv. 36. & xxvi. 26. Rom. xiv. 6]
brake, and gave to the disciples [n] to set before the mul-
titude. 17 And they did eat, and were all filled: and [n Mat. xxiv. 45]
there was taken up of fragments that remained to them,
twelve baskets.

v 10—17 When they had finished their work, they returned to give their master an account. He is the chief shepherd to whom we are all responsible. The remembrance that we must appear before him shortly to answer for our ministry, should quicken our diligence. Christ took them for a while into a retirement: he is a good master, and delights not to weary out his servants; rest after labour is needful. But the people, eager to hear and be healed, broke in upon their retirement; and Jesus, unwearied in labour of love, preached to them, as usual, the gospel of the kingdom, and healed their diseases. He is so gracious, that none who come to him with their complaints, shall be in any wise cast out Yea, he not only feeds their souls with heavenly manna, but their bodies with miraculous food five thousand men, besides women and children, are made to feast on five loaves and two small fishes This miracle is recorded by all the evangelists, and affords us still food for our faith (1) In times of want and distress, our care must be cast on the Lord, he feedeth the hungry (2) If we have but little, yet let us not fear to divide our morsel with the poor, like the widow's cruse, it shall not be diminished hereby (3) When we look up to heaven for a blessing from God, though we by our sins have forfeited all title to our creature-comforts, in Christ Jesus they will be restored to us, and then when we eat and drink, it will be to the glory of God

o Mat xvi 13 Mark viii 27
18 ¶ o And it came to pass as he was alone praying,
his disciples were with him and he asked them, saying,
Whom say the people that I am? 19 They answering,
said, John the Baptist but some *say*, Elias and others
say, that one of the old prophets is risen again 20 He
said unto them, But whom say ye that I am? Peter an-
p John vi 69 & xi 27 Acts viii 37 1 John iv 15 q Mat xvi 20
swering, said, p The Christ of God 21 And q he straitly
charged them, and commanded *them* to tell no man that
thing, 22 Saying, r The Son of man must suffer many
r Ver 44 Chap xviii 31 & xxiv 7
things, and be rejected of the elders, and chief priests,
and scribes, and be slain, and be raised the third day
23 ¶ And he said to them all, If any man will come
s Mat x 38 Acts xiv 22 1 Thess iii 3 2 Tim iii 12
after me, let him deny himself, and s take up his cross
daily, and follow me 24 For t whosoever will save his
t Chap xvii 33 John xii 25
life, shall lose it but whosoever will lose his life for my
sake, the same shall save it 25 For what is a man ad-
vantaged, if he gain the whole world, and lose himself,
u Mat x 33 Chap xii 9 2 Tim ii 12
or be cast away? 26 For u whosoever shall be ashamed
of me and of my words, of him shall the Son of man be
x Mat xxv 31
ashamed, when x he shall come in his own glory, and
y Dan vii 10 Jude 14
in his Father's, and y of the holy angels 27 But I tell
z Mat xxiv 34
you of a truth, there be some standing here which shall
not taste of death, z till they see the kingdom of God

v 18—27 Christ having dismissed the multitude whom he had fed, retired with his disciples, to pray with them and for them, as the master of this little family, and to teach us in our houses to follow his example And when he had finished, we are told,

1 The *enquiries* he made concerning the general opinion formed of him The disciples informed him the people were divided in sentiment some said he was John, revived, others, Elias, others, one of the old prophets risen again On putting the question to them, what they thought of him, Peter, the spokesman for his brethren, declared their faith in him as the Christ of God He said the truth, but as it was not proper that this should be publickly and expressly urged, least tumults should ensue among the people who expected a temporal Messiah, he at present enjoined them silence on this head, till the great day of his resurrection should manifest the glory of his character

2 The *warning* he gave them of his own sufferings and death, and this he immediately adds after the confession they had made of him as the Messiah, in order to prepare them for what might stagger them if it came upon them unawares, and to correct the common prejudices concerning the Messiah's temporal kingdom, which they, as well as their countrymen, had imbibed

3 The *admonition* he gave them of the sufferings they must expect to endure for his sake Instead of the ambitious hopes they entertained, they must prepare by a course of habitual self-denial for the hardships and persecutions they would be called to endure in his service, and be ready to take up every cross which in the way of their duty was laid upon them, even, if need be, to martyrdom itself They might be tempted, indeed, by the terror of suffering, or the allurements of the world, to save their lives by base compliances, but this was the way assuredly in eternity to lose what they meant to preserve, whilst a bold and faithful profession, though it exposed them even to death, would be recompensed with a better life in the eternal world If they were unfaithful and apostatized, nothing could balance their loss, the gain of the whole world would be no compensation for the perdition of an immortal soul and if they were ashamed of, and disowned him, their Master, the consequence would inevitably be, that they must be disowned by him, *when in his own glory*, as mediator, and in his *Father's glory*, as having all power in heaven and earth delegated to him, and in the glory *of his holy angels*, the attendants of his triumph, and the spirits that minister before his throne, he shall appear to judge the world *Note*, The realizing view of a judgment day are powerfully effectual to engage the believer to take up every cross, to hesitate at no loss, shame or suffering, for Christ's sake He knows that these shall finally prove his eternal gain, his immortal honour

4 The *encouragement* he suggests for his disciples support

Some of them then present should live to see the kingdom of the Messiah erected, in defiance of all opposition, his gospel spread through the earth, and condign vengeance executed on the Jewish people their persecutors and his murderers It is a comfort to every suffering saint of God that the time is short, in a moment he shall be triumphant over every foe

28 ¶ a And it came to pass about an eight days a Mat xvii 1 Mark ix 2
after these sayings, he took Peter and John and James,
and went up into a mountain to pray 29 And as
he prayed, b the fashion of his countenance was altered, b 2 Pet i 16
and his raiment *was* c white and glistering 30 And c Dan vii 9
behold, there talked with him two men, which were
Moses and Elias 31 Who appeared in glory, and
spake of his decease which he should accomplish at Je-
rusalem 32 But Peter, and they that were with him,
d were heavy with sleep and when they were awake, d Dan viii 18 & x 9
they saw his glory, and the two men that stood with
him 33 And it came to pass, as they departed from
him, Peter said unto Jesus, Master, it is good for us to
be here, and let us make three tabernacles, one for
thee, and one for Moses, and one for Elias not know-
ing what he said 34 While he thus spake, there came
a cloud, and overshadowed them and they feared as
they entred into the cloud 35 And e there came a e 2 Pet i 17
voice out of the cloud, saying, f This is my beloved f Mat iii 17 Chap iii 22
Son, g hear him 36 And when the voice was past, g Acts iii 22
Jesus was found alone and h they kept *it* close, and h Mat xvii 9
told no man in those days any of those things which
they had seen

v 28—36 The story of the transfiguration was recorded in the other evangelists Some circumstances are here added

1 Christ went up into this mountain to pray, and then his glory broke forth, which should be an engagement and encouragement to us to maintain communion with God in prayer, since by such approach to him the glory of transforming grace is derived from him, and we become changed into his image

2 Moses and Elias *appeared in glory*, as all Christ's saints shall shortly do They spake of his departure (ἔξοδον) his Exodus, in allusion to the departure of Israel from Egypt, so happy an exit was Jesus shortly to make from this miserable world to the land of eternal rest and blessedness The prophets had foretold his sufferings, and they talk with him on this subject the time being at hand, and Jerusalem the place where he must be put to death The way to glory lies through the grave, in our happiest days on earth this should be ever in our view, and this will reconcile us to all the horrors of death, when we consider it as opening the door of eternal life

3 The disciples were heavy with sleep, probably it was night, and they had been wearied with the labours of the day but when they were awake, they beheld their master and his two attendants beaming with irradiation, and bright as the light *Note*, By our drowsy frame of spirit we are ready to lose many of those glorious visits from above, which the watchful and praying saints of God are favoured with, and it is a mercy that recovering grace suffers us not to sleep the sleep of death

4 Peter, charmed with the vision, is for taking up his abode there, and proposes erecting three tabernacles, *not knowing what he said* The saints of God who have once quitted this miserable abode, wish not again to take up their dwelling here, they have an infinitely nobler place, a house not made with hands eternal in the heavens

5 Fear seized them, as the bright cloud, the emblem of the divine presence, overspread them, and separated Moses and Elias from their view, but the voice of God silenced their fears, enjoining them with solemn attention to hear and obey *his well-beloved Son* If he be with us, and we are following his revealed word, we need not be dismayed with any cloud which may come over us, he will bring us safely through

6 The apostles kept the vision close, and *told no man in those days*, as Jesus had commanded them The relation would meet with readier credence after his resurrection, for which time it was reserved

37 ¶ i And it came to pass, that on the next day, i Mat xvii 14 Mark ix 14
when they were come down from the hill, much people
met him. 38 And behold, a man of the company
cried out, saying, Master, I beseech thee, look upon my
son, for he is mine only child. 39 And lo, a spirit
taketh him, and he suddenly crieth out, and it teareth
him that he foameth again, and bruising him, hardly de-
parteth from him 40 And I besought thy disciples to
cast him out, and they could not 41 And Jesus an-
swering said, O faithless and perverse generation, how

lon-

long shall I be with you, and suffer you? Bring thy son
[k] Mar. i. 26. Rev. xii. 12. hither. 42 And [k] as he was yet a coming, the devil
threw him down, and tare *him*. And Jesus rebuked the
unclean spirit, and healed the child, and delivered him
again to his father.

v. 37—42. It seems that Jesus and his three disciples continued all night on the mountain. The next day, descending to the multitude, he found his presence greatly needed. The people eagerly ran to him, and the father of a poor lunatic child earnestly besought that help from him, which his disciples had in vain attempted to give. The case was very affective: he was *an only child*, and so fearfully torn by the malicious spirit. What a mercy we are not left to his power! what an invaluable privilege that we have the almighty Jesus near, to whom we can apply, and who is able to save to the uttermost. Rebuking the unbelief of that perverse generation, particularly of the scribes and Pharisees, who began to insult over the disciples, he gives them a convincing proof that his arm is not shortened, nor his power abated. With a word the raging devil is dispossessed, and the child is delivered to his father perfectly cured.

43 ¶ And they were all amazed at the mighty power
of God. But while they wondered every one at all things
which Jesus did, he said unto his disciples, 44 Let
[l] Ver. 22. these sayings sink down into your ears: for [l] the Son of
man shall be delivered into the hands of men. 45 But
[m] Chap. xviii. 34. [m] they understood not this saying, and it was hid from
them, that they perceived it not: and they feared to ask
[n] Mat. xviii. 1. Mark ix. 34. Chap. xxii. 24. him of that saying. 46 ¶ [n] Then there arose a reasoning
among them, which of them should be greatest.
47 And Jesus, perceiving the thought of their heart,
took a child, and set him by him, 48 And said unto
[o] Mat. x. 42. Chap. x. 16. [p] John xiii. 20. them, [o] Whosoever shall receive this child in my name,
receiveth me: and [p] whosoever shall receive me, receiveth
him that sent me: for he that is least among you all,
[q] Mark ix. 38. the same shall be great. 49 ¶ [q] And John answered
and said, Master, we saw one casting out devils in thy
[r] Numb. xi. 28. name, and [r] we forbad him, because he followeth not
with us. 50 And Jesus said unto him, Forbid *him* not:
[s] Mat. xii. 30. for [s] he that is not against us, is for us.

v. 43—50. The works of the Lord are great, and worthy our admiration.

1. This miracle filled the people with amazement *at the mighty power of God*. His hand here so evidently appeared. Is any *soul* recovered from Satan's power, much more may we say, *This is the finger of God*.

2. Christ informs the disciples of his approaching sufferings. They were very backward to receive what was so contrary to their ideas of the Messiah's kingdom, and so destructive of the ambitious hopes they had entertained. Therefore he prefaces his discourse with a solemn warning to them deeply to consider and carefully to remember what he said; but they understood not his meaning, blinded by their prejudices, and afraid to ask him, lest they should be reproached with their dulness, or meet the same reproof as Peter had before received, if they presumed to raise objections. *Note*, The plainest truths, when we are under the power of prejudice, are mistaken or perverted.

3. All that they heard had no effect upon them to cure their aspiring views. They disputed among themselves, as they travelled, who should have the first post of honour in that temporal kingdom which they expected. Jesus knew the subject of their reasoning, and, by a most apposite emblem of a little child, teaches them the only spirit and temper which would make a soul truly great in the eyes of God. So meek, so lowly, so free from ambition, envy, and malice, should they be; delighting in, and receiving with warmest affection, all who shewed such a childlike temper: and every kindness shewn to such persons, he tells them, he would receive as done to himself; yea, God the Father would regard it with highest approbation, and reward them. *Note*, (1.) Jesus is the searcher of hearts, our thoughts are known to him, we need keep a strict guard over them. (2.) Nothing is more contrary to the spirit of a disciple of the lowly Jesus, than the affectation of earthly grandeur and the pride of life.

4. Christ checks the narrow party spirit which appeared in John and others of his disciples. He had forbad one whom he saw casting out devils in the name of Jesus, because he followed not with them, and for this probably expected his Master's approbation: but Christ saith, *Forbid him not, for he that is not against us, is for us*. Though he may not join us, if he concur in carrying on the same design, he is to be encouraged rather than silenced. *Note*, Though others follow not exactly our mode of worship, or refuse to join in our communion, let us not therefore stamp them as heretical or schismatic, and oppress or silence them. Do they labour to pull down Satan's kingdom, and spread the savour of the Redeemer's name? then, however Christ is preached, it becometh us therein to rejoice.

51 ¶ And it came to pass, when [t] the time was [t] Mar. xvi. 19. Acts i. 2.
come that he should be received up, he stedfastly set his
face to go to Jerusalem, 52 And sent messengers be-
fore his face: and they went, and entered into a village
of the Samaritans to make ready for him. 53 And
[u] they did not receive him, because his face was as [u] John iv. 9.
though he would go to Jerusalem. 54 And when his
disciples James and John saw this, they said, Lord,
wilt thou that we command fire to come down from hea-
ven, and consume them, [w] even as Elias did? 55 But [w] 2 Kings i. 10.
he turned, and rebuked them, and said, Ye know not
what manner of spirit ye are of. 56 For [x] the Son of [x] John iii. 17. & xii. 47.
man is not come to destroy mens lives, but to save *them*.
And they went to another village.

v. 51—56. Nothing is more contrary to the spirit of Christianity, which breathes universal love, than the fury of bigotry and the flames of persecution. We have here,

1. Our Lord stedfastly setting his face to Jerusalem, which was shortly to be the scene of his sufferings. The time fixed in the divine decree was come, when he should go up from Galilee, to return thither no more till after his resurrection: or this may refer to his ascension, when he should be received up into glory; and, knowing what followed, and all before him, with unshaken courage and confidence he went forth to meet them. *Note*, (1.) When sufferings for Christ's sake stand in the way of duty, like him we should stedfastly set our face to meet them, and neither fail nor be discouraged. (2.) It is a comfort to look forward to the day when all our present troubles shall have an end, and we shall be *received up* to the place whither Jesus is gone before.

2. As Samaria lay in his way, he sent some of his disciples forward to prepare some refreshment in one of the villages, that he might not be delayed in his journey. But, as there was the most deadly feud between the Jews and Samaritans about the proper place of worship, each preferring their own, when they perceived that Christ and his disciples were bent for Jerusalem, probably to celebrate the feast of tabernacles there, they were incensed against him for thus preferring the temple in mount Zion to theirs on mount Gerizim, and therefore refused to grant him or his followers any entertainment among them. *Note*, If we are treated with rudeness and incivility, our Master was thus used before us.

3. John and James, fired at this indignity put on their Master, would instantly, with their Lord's permission, have poured vengeance on the place, consuming them with fire from heaven, as Elias did, 2 *Kings* i. 9—12. They knew, if Christ gave them leave, one word would compleat the overthrow of the city, and make it as Sodom and Gomorrah. But he rebukes their fiery spirit, and said, *Ye know not what manner of spirit ye are of*. They seemed to be actuated by zeal for his glory, but really were under the influence of pride, passion, and revenge. How different from that spirit of peace, love, patience, and forbearance, which his gospel breathed! *for the Son of man is not come to destroy mens lives*, by making his enemies monuments of vengeance, *but to save them*, not only by miracles of healing to cure their bodies, but by all meekness and long-suffering, and every mild and endearing method of grace, to work upon their hearts, and melt them with these coals of love heaped upon them. *Note*, (1.) Even good men are sometimes carried away, and do not see the malignity and selfish passions which lurk under the guise of zeal for God. (2.) The examples of former saints are not to be pleaded as *precedents*, unless the cases be parallel, and we have the same warrant and authority under which they acted. (3.) The religion of Jesus is never to be propagated by fire and sword, but by soft persuasion, and every work and labour of love. Force may make men hypocrites: choice alone can make them Christians.

4. Christ hereupon patiently put up the affront, and quietly went with his disciples to another village, where they met a more hospitable reception. *Note*, To conquer our own spirit is a greater victory than to lay our bitterest enemy at our feet.

57 ¶ [y] And it came to pass, that as they went in the [y] Mat. viii. 19, &c.
way, a certain man said unto him, Lord, I will follow
thee whithersoever thou goest. 58 And Jesus said un-
to him, Foxes have holes, and birds of the air *have*
nests, but the son of man hath not where to lay *his* head.
59 And he said unto another, Follow me. But he said,
Lord, suffer me first to go and bury my father. 60 Je-
sus said unto him, Let the dead bury their dead: but
go thou and preach the kingdom of God. 61 And
another also said, Lord, I will follow thee; [z] but let me [z] 1 Kings xix. 20.
first go bid them farewel which are at home at my
house. 62 And Jesus said unto him, No man having
put his hand to the plough, and [b] looking back, is fit [b] Gen. xix. 26.
for the kingdom of God.

v. 57—62.

v 5,—62 They who would follow Christ must count the cost, and be ready, without hesitation, to part with all for his sake We have here,

1 The offer of one who, expecting the Messiah was about to set up his kingdom, professes his zeal to serve him, in hopes he shall be well reward d for i But Christ undeceives him He would meet with none of the honours he expected, and innumerable hardships of which he seemed not to be aware The Son of man, so far from providing for his followers, was more destitute than the foxes of the desert or the fowls of heaven, having neither house nor home So poor, for our sakes, he became, to teach us contentment in the lowest station of life, never to aspire at this world's greatness, patiently to submit to every want we may be called to endure, to expect tribulations and look for no rest below, till the day comes that we shall rest in the dust, and then enter into our kingdom

2 Another, called to follow Christ, wanted to make excuse, and solicits a delay, pretending piety towards an aged parent, and desiring to perform the last offices to him before he commenced Christ's constant follower But Christ denies his request a more urgent duty lay upon him there were enough dead sinners to bury the dead corpse, whilst he, as a living soul, was needed to preach the everlasting gospel *Note*, (1) Delays are dangerous many a soul hath been lost by plausible excuses for withdrawing from present duty, and putting off the concerns of eternity to a more convenient season (2) Religion teaches us to shew piety at home, and to requite our parents, but, if the dearest relation in life would divert us from the service of Jesus and his gospel, then we must leave father and mother to follow the Master's call, and shew our obedience to his commands

3 A third person makes a voluntary tender of his service to Christ, and only begs that he may first bid adieu to his friends, and settle his worldly affairs But Christ, who saw that his heart was entangled with worldly things, lets him know the impossibility of uniting the incompatible services of God and Mammon *No man, having laid his hand to the plough, and looking back, is fit for the kingdom of God* Whilst he hankers after the world, and parts from it with reluctance, he will not heartily discharge the gospel ministry *Note*, (1) Worldly things are the most dangerous snares to draw the heart from Christ even those that we may lawfully mind are apt to engage unlawful and inordinate affections after them (2) When we have once set our faces heavenward, let us never look back Remember Lot's wife

CHAP. X

In this chapter we have, 1 Christ's commission to the seventy disciples, ver 1—16 2 The reports which the seventy disciples made to their Master of the success of their negotiation, and his discourse thereupon, ver 17—24 3 Christ's discourse with a lawyer concerning the way to heaven, and the instructions Christ gave him by a parable to look upon every one as his neighbour, ver 25—37 4 Christ's entertainment at Martha's house, the reproof he gave to her for her care about the world, and his commendation of Mary for her care about her soul, ver 38—42

1 AFTER these things, the Lord appointed other
seventy also, and sent them two and two before
his face into every city and place whither he himself
a Mat ix 37 John iv 35 would come 2 Therefore said he unto them, [a] The
harvest truly *is* great, but the labourers *are* few [b] pray
b 2 Thes iii 1 ye therefore the Lord of the harvest, that he would send
forth labourers into his harvest 3. Go your ways
c Mat x 16 [c] behold, I send you forth as lambs among wolves 4
d Mat x 9 10 [d] Carry neither purse, nor scrip, nor shoes and [e] salute
e 2 Kings iv 29 no man by the way 5 And [f] into whatsoever house ye
f Mat x 11 enter, first say, Peace *be* to this house 6 And, if the
son of peace be there, your peace shall rest upon it if
not, it shall turn to you again. 7 And in the same
g 1 Cor x 27 house remain, [g] eating and drinking such things as they
h 1 Cor ix 4 &c give for [h] the labourer is worthy of his hire Go not
i Tim v 18 from house to house 8 And into whatsoever city ye
enter, and they receive you, eat such things as are set
before you 9 And heal the sick that are therein, and
i Mat iii 2 & iv 17 say unto them, [i] The kingdom of God is come nigh un-
to you 10 But into whatsoever city ye enter, and
they receive you not, go your ways out into the streets
k Chap ix 5 Acts xiii 51 & xviii 6 of the same, [k] and say, 11 Even the very dust of your
city, which cleaveth on us, we do wipe off against you
notwithstanding, be ye sure of this, that the kingdom of
God is come nigh unto you 12 But I say unto you,
l Mat x 15 & xi 22 24 that [l] it shall be more tolerable in that day for Sodom
than for that city 13 Wo unto thee, Chorazin, wo
unto thee, Bethsaida for if the mighty works had been
done in Tyre and Sidon, which have been done in you,
[m] they had a great while ago repented, [n] sitting in sack- m Ezek iii 6
cloth and ashes 14 But it shall be more tolerable for n Jonah iii 8
Tyre and Sidon at the judgment than for you 15
And thou, Capernaum, [o] which art exalted to heaven, o Isa xiv 13 Jer li 53
shalt be thrust down to hell 16 [p] He that heareth you, p Mat x 40 John xiii 20
heareth me and [q] he that despiseth you, despiseth me q Exod xvi 8 1 Thess iv 8
and he that despiseth me, despiseth him that sent me

v 1—16 The harvest was plenteous, but hitherto the labourers had been few We have here seventy disciples ordained to the ministry, invested with miraculous powers, and sent as harbingers to prepare the way of Christ in all the adjacent country whither he was preparing to go Their number corresponds with the elders of Israel on whom the Spirit of the Lord rested in the wilderness, and they were sent two and two for their mutual comfort and encouragement

1 They must address themselves in prayer to God for success upon their own labours, and that he would raise up and qualify many more to go forth and preach the gospel And this must be still the constant subject of our requests to God the more we look round on the world, and see immortal souls perishing for lack of knowledge, the more zealously should we labour, and the more fervently pray that the Lord would send forth labourers into his harvest

2 He tells them what they may expect to meet Though they were never so harmless and inoffensive, and their discourses breathed nothing but peace and love, they would have enemies to encounter, fierce and savage as wolves but he who sent them would afford them protection, and minister strength and courage to them in their work And, if God be with us, we need not fear who are against us

3 He orders them to make no provision for their journey, but trust on Providence for the supply of their wants and, as their work required dispatch, they must not lose any time in unnecessary discourse or civilities with any person whom they met Not that Christ enjoined rudeness and incivility, but there was now no time for compliments, when the service was urgent

4 Where-ever they entered into a house, and were hospitably received, there he orders them to say, *Peace be to this house*, praying that all blessings, spiritual, temporal, and eternal, might rest upon those who dwelt there *And if the son of peace be there*, any into whose hearts the Son of God hath put a desire to hear and receive the gospel of peace, then an answer of peace should be given to their prayers, *your peace shall rest upon it*, but *if not*, if there be no chosen vessel in the family, whose hearts are open to embrace the truth, *it shall return unto you again*, and your prayers for them shall be answered in blessings on your own souls *Note*, (1) They who preach the gospel of peace cannot but fervently desire, for all those among whom they minister, that God would speak peace by them to the consciences of their hearers (2) Some receive, but more reject, our preaching and prayers, yet even to those that perish our labours and prayers are not in vain, we are still a sweet savour of Christ, and, though they reject the salvation we bring, Christ will approve and reward our fidelity

5 In whatever house they were at first received, there they must abide, thankfully and chearfully making use of the provision set before them, and not doubting but their labours would procure them that welcome they deserved They must be content with the meanest fare, and never, affecting nicety, change their lodgings for better accommodations, lest they should incur the suspicion of fickleness, or flesh-pleasers *Note*, (1) Christ's ministers have a right to a maintenance (2) When the love of souls, not of filthy lucre, draws men to labour in the gospel, they will learn in whatsoever state they are, therewith to be content, and put up with the poorest accommodations

6 He directs them what must be the subject of their preaching They must say, *The kingdom of God is come nigh unto you*, the kingdom of the Messiah, with all its inestimable blessings and privileges, is now ready to appear; prepare to receive him, and he empowers them to heal the sick, in confirmation of their preaching, as well as in return for the kind civilities which they received *Note*, Nothing is ever lost by kindness shewn to Jesus and his servants

7 In case their ministry is rejected, and they are driven from their work, they are to leave that devoted city, publickly declaring the doom ready to light upon the place, and shaking off the dust of their feet for a testimony against them, assuring them of the nearness of the Messiah's kingdom, and the dreadful consequences which must unavoidably ensue from their obstinacy and impenitence And in a day of judgment it shall be more tolerable for Sodom than for that city, because they have rejected greater means of grace than were vouchsafed to that abandoned city *Note*, (1) None sink under such aggravated guilt as those who despise and reject the gospel (2) The day is near when these despisers will wonder and perish

8 On this occasion our Lord turns his discourse to those cities where such multitudes of his miracles had been wrought, and who

who notwithstanding continued impenitent Chorazin, Bethsaida, have their fearful doom read Had the most wicked cities of the Gentiles enjoyed their blessings and privileges, and calls to repentance, even Tyre and Sidon had long ago been brought into the dust of humiliation. Therefore the judgment of the heathen, in the day of vengeance, shall be more tolerable than theirs and Capernaum, exalted to heaven in privileges, shall sink as low in hell under the wrath of God, provoked by their hardened infidelity Let the lands and places that enjoy the gospel light hear and tremble at these denunciations

9. He encourages the seventy to go forth They are his ambassadors he will reckon the treatment they meet with as shewn to himself Those who heard and respected them he would regard, as if they shewed this attention and kindness to his own person, whilst they who despised their persons, and rejected their ministry, insulted him, and put contempt on God who sent him *Note*, Many ill-use, slight, and contemn Christ's ministers, and treat them as mean and despicable, but they will shortly feel, to their cost, that the King of glory will fearfully avenge the insults shewn to his ambassadors

17 ¶ And the seventy returned again with joy, say-
ing, Lord, even the devils are subject unto us through
thy name 18 And he said unto them, f I beheld Satan
as lightning fall from heaven 19 Behold, g I give
unto you power to tread on serpents and scorpions, and
over all the power of the enemy, and nothing shall by
any means hurt you 20 Notwithstanding in this re-
joice not, that the spirits are subject unto you but ra-
ther rejoice, because h your names are written in heaven
21 ¶ In that hour Jesus rejoiced in spirit, and said, I
thank thee, O Father, Lord of heaven and earth, that
u thou hast hid these things from the wise and prudent,
and x hast revealed them unto babes even so, Father,
for so it seemed good in thy sight 22 y All things are
delivered to me of my Father and no man knoweth
who the Son is, but the Father, and z who the Father
is, but the Son, and *he* to whom the Son will reveal *him*
23 ¶ And he turned him unto *his* disciples, and said
privately, a Blessed *are* the eyes which see the things that
ye see 24 For I tell you, that b many prophets and
kings have desired to see those things which ye see, and
have not seen *them*, and to hear those things which ye
hear, and have not heard *them*

f John xii 31 Rev xii 9
g Mark xvi 18 Acts xxviii 5
h Ex xxxii 32 Ps lxix 28 Dan xii 1 Phil iv 3 Heb xii 23 Rev xiii 8
u Isa xxix 14 & xliv 25 1 Cor i 19
x Mat xi 25 (?) 1 Cor ii 10
y Mat xxviii 18 John iii 35
z John i 18 & x 15
a Mat xiii 16
b 1 Pet i 10

v 17—24 Having finished their ministry, we have here,

1 The return of the disciples to their Master, transported to find that even the devils were subject unto them, and ascribing the glory to him, in whose name they were enabled to work such stupendous miracles *Note*, All our victories over Satan must be ascribed to the grace and power of the great Captain of our salvation, and in him we may and ought to rejoice greatly

2 He received them very graciously

(1) He informs them it was no news to him that the devils were subject unto them *I saw*, when I sent you forth to preach the gospel and work miracles, *Satan falling as lightning from heaven*, his power and kingdom began now to be shaken and totter, and this was the presage of his more irrecoverable ruin, when in the Gentile world the gospel should quickly spread, and, rooting up idolatry and spiritual darkness, turn the hearts of sinners from the power of Satan unto God

(2) He enlarges their powers, as the reward of their fidelity, and an encouragement to persevere They shall tread upon serpents and scorpions unhurt, and the old serpent, and his venomous associates, whether men or devils, should be bruised under their feet *And nothing shall by any means hurt you* Under almighty protection you may defy every danger *Note*, They have nothing to fear who have Christ for their master, and execute his commission

(3) He checks their joy on this singular distinction with which he endued them, and directs them to a nobler cause for it, *rather rejoice that your names are written in heaven*, else, though they had cast out devils, they might themselves finally perish, and become companions with them It is not gifts, but graces, that evidence our adoption of God, which should afford us most joy *Note*, (1) God knoweth those that are his, their names are registered in the records of eternity (2) The eternal predestination of God a matter of most comfortable meditation to those who, by faith embracing the promises, feel in their hearts the witnessing of God's Spirit, sealing them unto the day of redemption

(4) Christ expresses his delight and thankfulness for the blessings conferred on these his poor disciples and to this hour nothing rejoices the hearts of his people so greatly as beholding the progress of his gospel, the fall of Satan, and the conversion of men's souls He said, *I thank thee, O Father, Lord of heaven and earth*, the great Disposer of all things, *that thou hast hid these things from the wise and prudent, and hast revealed them unto babes*, leaving the proud scribes and doctors of the law under the darkness of pretended science, prejudiced against and strangers to the mysteries of grace, whilst poor illiterate men, of low capacities, and contemptible in the eyes of the worldly wise, are put in trust with the gospel, and enlightened with the Spirit of truth. *Even so, Father, for so it seemed good in thy sight* such was the pleasure of infinite wisdom, who sovereignly dispenses his gifts, the more to manifest his own glory *All things are delivered to me of my Father*, all power and authority, all wisdom and grace to communicate to his chosen In Jesus are all the treasures laid up, and out of his fulness we must receive *And no man knoweth who the Son is but the Father, and who the Father is but the Son, and he to whom the Son will reveal him* the perfections of the divine nature are only fully known by the divine Persons themselves, and we can only be acquainted with them, and their eternal purposes of infinite wisdom and grace, so far as the Son of God is pleased to reveal them to us

(5) Turning to his disciples privately he pronounces them truly blessed, favoured with the sight of the Lord's Christ, and enjoying the clearest discoveries of that kingdom of grace which the Messiah was now come to erect in the world Prophets and kings in former ages desired in vain to see and hear what they, more highly favoured, saw and heard *Note*, The distinguishing mercies we enjoy should excite our thankfulness, and quicken our diligence to improve them

25 ¶ And behold, a certain lawyer stood up, and
tempted him, saying, c Master, what shall I do to in-
herit eternal life? 26 He said unto him, What is writ-
ten in the law? how readest thou? 27 And he an-
swering, said, d Thou shalt love the Lord thy God with
all thy heart, and with all thy soul, and with all thy
strength, and with all thy mind, and e thy neighbour as
thyself 28. And he said unto him, Thou hast answered
right f this do, and thou shalt live 29 But he, g wil-
ling to justify himself, said unto Jesus, And who is my
neighbour? 30. And Jesus answering, said, A certain
man went down from Jerusalem to Jericho, and fell among
thieves, which stripped him of his raiment, and wounded
him, and departed, leaving *him* half dead 31 And by
chance there came down a certain priest that way, and
when he saw him, h he passed by on the other side
32 And likewise a Levite, when he was at the place,
came and looked *on him*, and passed by on the other side
33 But a certain i Samaritan, as he journeyed, came
where he was and when he saw him, he had compassion
on him, 34 And went to him, and bound up his wounds,
pouring in oil and wine, and set him on his own beast,
and brought him to an inn, and took care of him
35 And on the morrow, when he departed, he took out
two k pence, and gave *them* to the host, and said unto
him, Take care of him, and whatsoever thou spendest
more, when I come again, I will repay thee 36 Which
now of these three, thinkest thou, was neighbour unto
him that fell among the thieves? 37 And he said,
He that shewed mercy on him Then said Jesus unto
him, Go, and do thou likewise

c Mat xxii, 35 Mark xii 28
d Deut vi 5. & x 12 & xxx 6
e Lev xix 18 Rom. xiii 9 Gal. v 14 Jam ii 8
f Lev xviii 5 Ezek xx 11, 13, 21 Rom x 5
g Chap xvi 15
h Ps xxxviii 11
i John iv 9.
k Mat xviii 28

v 25—37 We have the same question proposed by one of the scribes as was put by the young ruler, *Mark* x 17 not so much with a view to be informed, as with the intention to entangle our Lord in his talk

1 In answer to his question Christ turns him over to the law, in which he fancied himself deeply conversant, and bid him say what he read there, as the way of obtaining the eternal life he sought and when the scribe replied the conditions there prescribed were the perfect love of God and our neighbour, Christ approves the answer, and assures him, *Do this, and thou shalt live* Such perfection of obedience will entitle those who can plead it to the reward But where, alas! is this to be found? The more we read the tenor of the covenant of works, the more, if our minds are enlightened, shall we be driven to despair of ourselves, conscious how far we have been from continuing in all the things written in the book of the law to do them But with this view had not the lawyer read Yet,

2 *He, willing to justify himself*, as if he had kept the whole law, desired to know who was to be reckoned his neighbour, conceiting, probably, his justice and charity had been so extensive to the whole house of Israel, that he might justly claim the reward of perfect obedience

3 Christ, by an apposite case in point, lets him see his ignorance of the divine law, and the defectiveness of his charity, correcting at the same time the corrupt notions of the Jewish teachers, who reckoned themselves not at all obliged to shew the least kindness to those who were out of the pale of their communion. The story here represented is very beautiful and affecting

1 A Jew, as he travelled from Jerusalem to Jericho, *fell among thieves*, with *which* the road was greatly infested, and these, not satisfied with having plundered and *stripped him of his raiment*, inhumanly *wounded him, and departed, leaving him* weltering in his blood, *half dead*, and ready to expire This case may fitly represent the state of mankind; way-laid by Satan the great enemy of souls, robbed of the garments of innocence, wounded and dying in their sins, without power or strength to help themselves

2 In this disastrous condition, in which the poor wounded traveller lay, *by chance*, so Providence ordered it, *there came down a certain priest that way*, whose office and character should have engaged him to exercise his humanity and compassion towards an object so pitiable, especially to one of his own nation and religion, but his unfeeling heart was steeled against his brother, and, turning to the other side of the road, he pursued his journey unconcerned A Levite quickly followed, as callous to every humane sensation he just came and looked on, and, not caring to be at the trouble or expence of providing for a dying man, he kept on his way, and left him to perish there Hard-hearted monsters! cries every tongue But, alas! such Levites and priests are found in every age, who not only with-hold their hand from relieving the wants of the miserable, but leave the more precious souls of men to perish, unconcerned what becomes of them Some suppose that these represent the law of Moses, from which no mercy is to be expected it makes no provision for man a sinner, nor speaks one word of comfort to the guilty, but leaves the soul under a curse which extends to eternal death

3 A *Samaritan*, one of that despised and detested nation, travelling that way, saw the miserable object, and compassion instantly melted his heart Without waiting to know of what country he was, he went to him, and pouring oil and wine into his wounds, he bound them carefully up, perhaps with the very linnen garments he wore, and, gently setting him on his own beast, he carried him to the nearest inn, and saw every accommodation provided for him which the place would afford And on the morrow, having waited that night to see the poor patient well provided for, he gave the host, on parting, two pence, about fifteen pence of our money, with a charge to take all possible care of the wounded man, and engaged to defray, on his return, whatever expence might be farther incurred A noble instance indeed of humanity and generosity We cannot be at a loss to whom this character of the good Samaritan eminently belongs Jesus is come down from heaven, he sees his people lying in their blood, helpless and desperate; his compassions are kindled towards them; he binds up the wounds of the guilty sinner's soul, his own blood is the healing balm he pours into them, he brings them into his church, were they are fed with the provision of his ordinances, he clothes them with his righteousness, revives them with the cordials of his love, and bears their charges through the inn of this world, supporting them with the riches of his grace, he commends them to the care of his ministers, and at his second coming will not fail to reward their care and diligence

4 Christ proposes to the lawyer the question, which of these was the neighbour to the wounded traveller? and the case was too clear to admit of hesitation, he could not but answer, *He that shewed mercy on him* *Then said Jesus unto him, Go, and do thou likewise* Think not you have kept the law, or even understood the extent of the command, before you feel the same compassionate spirit, the same readiness to relieve even a Samaritan, as he shewed towards this Jew An extent of charity to which he had been hitherto an utter stranger, and therefore his self-justification was but self-delusion

38 ¶ Now it came to pass, as they went, he entred
into a certain village and a certain woman, named
[l] Martha, received him into her house. 39 And she
had a sister called Mary, [m] which also [n] sat at Jesus's feet,
and heard his word 40 But Martha was cumbred about
much serving, and came to him, and said, Lord, dost
thou not care that my sister hath left me to serve alone?
bid her therefore that she help me. 41. And Jesus answered, and said unto her, Martha, Martha, thou art
careful, and troubled about many things 42 But [o] one
thing is needful And Mary hath chosen that good part,
which shall not be taken away from her

[l] John xi 1 & xii 2, 3. [m] 1 Cor vii 32 [n] Chap viii 35 Acts xxii 3 [o] Ps xxvii 4

v 38—42 We have here,

1 The hospitable entertainment given to our blessed Lord by a good woman who lived at Bethany, named Martha Though his character was obnoxious, and his retinue numerous and poor, yet she was not ashamed of owning her respect for him, and was happy to furnish him with the best her house afforded. A gracious heart makes an open hand We should grudge no expence when Christ's cause demands our support

2 Mary, the sister of Martha, sat at Jesus's feet, attentive to his divine instructions; and as, according to his usual custom, he began to discourse about the glad tidings of his salvation, she listened with eagerness to the gracious words which proceeded out of his mouth *Note*, (1) Ministers, not only in public, but from house to house, should delight to dispense the gospel-word They are profitable visits when a gracious discourse seasons the entertainment. (2) They who would be wise unto salvation must sit at Jesus's feet. We cannot hear his voice indeed, but in his blessed word he yet speaketh

3 Martha, desirous to shew her respect for her honoured guest, was very busy in providing the entertainment Her diligence was commendable, but *she was* too much taken up, *cumbered with much serving*, she wanted to make the feast splendid, and was so distracted with these worldly engagements, that she could not find leisure to attend the heavenly discourse of the Redeemer *Note*, (1) Family cares inordinately engaging the mind are a great snare to our souls (2) Christ's servants should not cumber themselves with much serving They who eat and drink to the glory of God will not affect dainties

4 Displeased that Mary came not to her assistance, Martha brings her complaint to Christ, *Lord, dost thou not care that my sister hath left me to serve alone?* She seems not only to blame Mary's backwardness to assist her, but to reflect upon Jesus, that he should suffer her to sit there, when she wanted her help in the family, and therefore suggests that it was but reasonable, that he should *bid her go* and assist in providing for the guests. *Note*, (1) They who have their own hearts much set upon the world are ready to find fault with those as negligent who shew not the same anxiety after it (2) Too many, like Martha, are apt to think, that the exercises of religion incroach upon the duties of our station, but, usually speaking, the fault is, as here, far on the other side.

5 Christ reproves her inordinate carefulness *Martha, Martha*, he speaks with earnestness and pity, *thou art careful, and troubled about many things*, giving herself unnecessary anxiety, when Christ required no such sumptuous entertainment. *But one thing is needful*, to know Christ and partake of his salvation. Compared with this, every thing besides is unimportant, therefore should this engage our first and chief concern and we are highly culpable when other things divert us from attending to the interests of our immortal souls *Note*, (1) Faithful rebukes are the truest marks of genuine love (2) They who are full of inordinate care are sure to involve themselves in many troubles (3) Christ's disciples have need deeply to remember this reproof and caution, for Martha's anxiety is a besetting evil

6 Instead of blaming Mary, as her sister expected, Christ commends her choice, and approves her conduct, *She hath chosen that good part, which shall not be taken from her* *Note*, (1) However serious godliness may provoke the censures of the lukewarm, Jesus will commend what they condemn (2) They who have chosen Christ as their portion, and his word as their rule, have wisely determined, and shall never repent of their choice (3) If we have by faith embraced the Saviour, and truly been made partakers of his grace, then we have an interest in that eternal blessedness, of which none of the powers of earth or hell can deprive us

CHAP XI

In this chapter, 1 *Christ teacheth his disciples to pray*, ver 1—13 2 *He fully answereth the blasphemous imputation of the Pharisees*, ver 14—26 3 *He shews the honour of obedient disciples to be greater than that of his own mother*, ver 27, 28 4 *He upbraids the men of that generation for their infidelity and obstinacy*, ver 29—36 5 *He severely reproves the Pharisees and lawyers for their hypocrisy, pride, and their oppressing the consciences of those that submitted to them, and their hating and persecuting those that witnessed against their wickedness*, ver 37—54

1 AND it came to pass, that as he was praying in
a certain place, when he ceased, one of his disciples said unto him, Lord, teach us to pray, as John
also taught his disciples 2 And he said unto them,
[a] When ye pray, say, Our Father [b] which art in heaven,
[c] Hallowed be thy Name. [d] Thy kingdom come [e] Thy
will be done, [f] as in heaven, so in earth 3. [g] Give us
day by day our daily bread 4. And forgive us our sins,
for we also forgive every one that is indebted to us
And [h] lead us not into temptation, but [i] deliver us from
evil 5 And he said unto them, Which of you shall
have a friend, and shall go unto him at midnight, and
say unto him, Friend, lend me three loaves, 6 For a
friend of mine in his journey is come to me, and I have
nothing to set before him 7 And he from within shall
answer and say, Trouble me not the door is now shut,
and my children are with me in bed, I cannot rise and
give thee. 8. I say unto you, Though he will not rise
and give him, because he is his friend: [k] yet because of
his importunity, he will rise and give him as many as he
need-

[a] Mat vi 9, &c [b] Ps xi 4 Isa lxvi 1. [c] John xii 28 [d] Mat iv 17 [e] Mat xxvi 42 Acts xxi 14 [f] 1 Cor x 31 [g] Job xxiii 12 Mat iv 4 John vi 33—58 [h] Mat xxvi 41 1 Cor x 13 Rev iii 10 [i] John xvii 15 2 Pet ii 9 [k] Chap xviii 1, &c.

needeth 9 And I ſay unto you, [l] Aſk, and it ſhall be
given you ſeek, and ye ſhall find knock, and it ſhall
be opened unto you 10 For [m] every one that aſketh,
receiveth and he that ſeeketh, findeth and to him
that knocketh, it ſhall be opened 11 If a ſon ſhall
aſk bread of any of you that is a father, will he give him
a ſtone? or if *he aſk* a fiſh, will he for a fiſh give him a
ſerpent? 12 Or if he ſhall aſk an egg, will he offer
him a ſcorpion? 13. [n] If ye then, being evil, know
how to give good gifts unto your children how much
more ſhall *your* heavenly Father give the holy Spirit to
them that aſk him?

l Pſ cxviii 5 Mat vii 7 & xxi 22 John xvi 23 24. Jam i 5 6 1 John v 14
m Prov viii. 17 Jer xxix 12.
n Mat. vii. 9

v 1—13 Prayer is the great inſtituted means of maintaining communion with God it is as the breath of every ſpiritually living ſoul There can be no ſurer proof of our being dead in treſpaſſes and ſins than the habitual neglect of it The prayerleſs live without God, and muſt die without hope Our Lord himſelf was much in prayer, to ſet us an example and his diſciples, deſirous to follow him, are repreſented here as preferring their requeſt to him, that he would inſtruct them both concerning the matter and manner of their prayers, and give them a form or directory, as John had done for his diſciples *Note,* Unleſs the Lord *teach us to pray*, and pour out upon us the ſpirit of prayer and ſupplications, we can offer no acceptable ſervice

1 Chriſt condeſcends to grant their requeſt, and gives them the following ſhort but moſt comprehenſive form of prayer

Our Father which art in heaven, thou great Creator and univerſal Lord, whoſe throne is in the heavens, and to whom ten thouſand times ten thouſand angels and archangels pay their ceaſeleſs adorations, to thee do we ſinful worms and duſt of the earth addreſs our prayer, regarding thee not only as our common Parent and Maker of all things, but in the more endeared relation of our reconciled God and Father in Jeſus Chriſt. *Hallowed be thy name* may I and every other creature exalt thy glory, and, according to the diſplays of thy glorious perfections made in thy works and word, may we ever admire, adore, honour, love, and ſerve thee *Thy kingdom come* erect the throne of thy grace in our hearts, O viſit us with thy ſalvation, give us the light of thy truth, and the effectual influences of thy Spirit, that we may become thy faithful ſubjects and ſervants Send forth thy goſpel into the world, accompany it with thy mighty power, and make it effectual to the converſion of ſinners ſouls, build us up together in thy faith, fear, and love, and prepare us daily, in the exerciſe of all holy converſation and godlineſs, for thy eternal preſence, then come and take us to thy throne above, where, day and night for ever, we may ſerve thee in thy temple, and go out no more *Thy will be done, as in heaven, ſo in earth*, may we emulate the lively, conſtant, univerſal obedience paid by thy celeſtial hoſts Let thy revealed word be our invariable rule, and may we, without partiality and without hypocriſy, deſire to know and with delight fulfil what thou doſt command and in every diſpenſation of thy providence may our ſpirits be reſigned, ſubmiſſive, ſatisfied, content to wait thy leiſure, and meekly caſting our care upon thee *Give us day by day our daily bread* on thee, O Lord, we depend for the needful proviſion for our bodies during the days of our pilgrimage, let us, as thy children, be ſupplied by thy bounty, enable us to live in a conſtant dependence upon thee, content with the portion thou art pleaſed to aſſign us, and confident thou wilt not leave us to want any manner of thing which is good for us and, whilſt our bodies are fed by thy providence, let our ſouls be nouriſhed with the better bread of life which cometh down from heaven *And forgive us our ſins*, many, great, and aggravated as they have been blot them out through the Redeemer's blood, ſpeak peace and pardon to our guilty ſouls, and glorify thyſelf in mercy And we are emboldened, Lord, to hope for an anſwer of peace, *for we alſo forgive every one that is indebted to us*, readily paſſing by their offences and treſpaſſes againſt us, as we hope to be forgiven ourſelves, and pleading thy promiſe, that, when we are enabled thus to do, we ſhall aſſuredly find mercy with thee our moſt highly and juſtly offended God Remember therefore the word wherein thou haſt cauſed us to put our truſt *And lead us not into temptation*, keep us from every ſnare laid for our ſouls, and ſuffer us not to fall under the trials we may be called to endure *but deliver us from evil*, from the evil one, the evil world, and that greateſt enemy our own evil hearts, deceitful above all things and deſperately wicked Save us with thine uttermoſt ſalvation, and bring us at laſt to that eternal kingdom where no temptation nor evil can ever enter

2 Chriſt directs them as to the *manner* of their prayers, to be fervent, perſevering, and importunate; the effects of which he inſtances in the caſe of a man, who, having a ſudden viſit from a friend on his journey, and nothing for him to eat, ſhould run to his neighbour's houſe at midnight, and deſire to borrow three loaves. At that unſeaſonable hour his neighbour would be apt to make many excuſes, and endeavour to put him off, rather than diſturb his family yet, if he is very importunate, that will uſually prevail; and, if but to be rid of his importunity, he will lend him what he aſks Now if one, who ſhews ſo much reluctance to yield, is overcome by entreaty, much more will our gracious God, who is ever more willing to hear than we to pray, and wont to give more than we deſire or deſerve, anſwer the ſupplications of his people, if they faint not Let them *aſk* in faith, nothing doubting, let them *ſeek* with diligence unwearied, let them *knock* aloud, with cries fervent and reiterated, and then they will ſurely find an anſwer of peace, their prayers ſhall be heard, their requeſts granted, and the door of mercy be opened

3 Our Lord ſuggeſts yet farther encouragement to prayer from the conſideration of our relation to God as our father If the bowels of earthly parents yearn over their children's wants, and none are found ſo inhuman as, inſtead of the bread and meat which they crave, to give them things noxious and poiſonous If men, by nature ſinful, feel ſuch tenderneſs towards their offſpring, how infinitely ſurpaſſing are the compaſſions of our Father in heaven, and, as his power is equal to his love, much more will he ſupply all the ſpiritual neceſſities of our ſouls, and give his Holy Spirit, which compriſes all bleſſedneſs, to them that aſk him

14 ¶ And [o] he was caſting out a devil, and it was
dumb And it came to paſs, when the devil was gone
out, the dumb ſpake and the people wondered 15
But ſome of them ſaid, [p] He caſteth out devils through
† Beelzebub the chief of the devils 16 And others,
tempting *him*, [q] ſought of him a ſign from heaven 17
But he, knowing their thoughts, ſaid unto them, Every
kingdom divided againſt itſelf is brought to deſolation
and a houſe *divided* againſt a houſe falleth 18 If Satan
alſo be divided againſt himſelf, how ſhall his kingdom
ſtand? becauſe ye ſay, that I caſt out devils through
Beelzebub. 19 And if I by Beelzebub caſt out devils,
by whom do your ſons caſt them out? therefore ſhall
they be your judges 20 But if I [r] with the finger of
God caſt out devils, no doubt [s] the kingdom of God is
come upon you 21 [t] When a ſtrong man armed keepeth
his palace, his goods are in peace 22. But [u] when
a ſtronger than he ſhall come upon him, and overcome
him, he taketh from him all his armour wherein he
truſted, and divideth his ſpoils 23 [x] He that is not
with me, is againſt me and he that gathereth not with
me, ſcattereth 24 [y] When the unclean ſpirit is gone
out of a man, [z] he walketh through dry places, ſeeking
reſt and finding none, he ſaith, I will return unto my
houſe whence I came out 25 And when he cometh,
he findeth *it* ſwept and garniſhed 26 Then goeth he,
and taketh to him ſeven other ſpirits more wicked than
himſelf, and they enter in, and dwell there and [a] the
laſt ſtate of that man is worſe than the firſt

o Mat ix 32 & xii 22
p Mark iii 22 John viii 48, 52
† Gr Beelzebub
Ver 18, 19.
q Mat xii 38 & xvi 1.
Ver 29
1 Cor i 22
r Ex viii 19
s Dan ii 44
Chap i 33
t Mat xii 29
u Iſa xlix 24 & liii 12. Col ii 15
x Mat xii. 30
y Mat xii 43
z Job i 7
1 Pet v 8.
a Heb vi 4, &c. & x 26
2 Pet ii 20.

v 14—26 The moſt amazing manifeſtations of Chriſt's power and glory, and his noble acts of beneficence towards men's bodies and ſouls, could not prevent the invenomed tongue of malice from caſting upon him the moſt malignant aſperſions We have here,

1 The wicked inference drawn by the Phariſees, on ſeeing a moſt aſtoniſhing inſtance of Chriſt's power in the diſpoſſeſſing a devil from a man that was dumb, who immediately recovered his ſpeech to the amazement of the ſpectators To counteract the effects of this miraculous cure among the people, ſome of them, who could not deny the fact, ſuggeſted that it was performed by a confederacy between *Jeſus* and the *prince of the devils* whilſt others challenged him to give a ſign from heaven of his divine miſſion, as if all beſides was unſatisfactory So perverſe and abſurd are uſually the objections of obſtinate infidelity

2 Chriſt knew their thoughts, and what ſuggeſtions they were labouring to inſtil into the minds of the people, and confutes them with the moſt unanſwerable arguments It was as abſurd to ſuppoſe ſo ſubtil an enemy as Satan would ever concur in eſtabliſhing that doctrine which radically overthrew his empire over the ſouls of men, as that any community or family ſhould propoſe their eſtabliſhment by diviſion between the members that compoſe it, which muſt evidently tend to their mutual deſtruction Beſides, they condemned themſelves herein, when they admitted that many of their own kindred and followers, by exorciſms were, in the name of God, enabled to caſt out devils, and never ſuppoſed any diabolical combination in their caſe This malignant oppoſition to him therefore tended moſt effectually to their own ruin and deſtruction, for, ſince *the finger of God* was evident in theſe miraculous works, and proved *the kingdom of God* was come, which the Meſſiah ſhould erect in the world, in rejecting the evidence of his miſſion they excluded themſelves from all the bleſſings and privileges of his kingdom And to ſhew farther the real deſtruction of Satan's power by his miracles and doctrine, he illuſtrates the matter by a ſimilitude, *v.* 21, 22 As a ſtrong man will not quit his palace, which he-

holds

holds with an armed force, unleſs he be vanquiſhed by a ſuperior foe, no more will Satan quit his hold of men's bodies and ſouls till compelled by the power of the almighty Saviour. When the prey therefore is taken from this mighty one, it is a ſure proof that his power is broken, and his intereſts ruined. Nor can there be any neutrality between Chriſt and Belial. They who halt between two opinions, who do not join Chriſt's cauſe, admit the evidence of his miſſion, and profeſs diſcipleſhip, muſt expect to be treated by him as enemies, and to be ſcattered in his wrath.

The Redeemer's victories over Satan are ſtill daily ſeen; yea, we are bound to experience them in our own ſouls, or it had been good for us we had never been born. For by nature we are children of wrath, born ſlaves of corruption, and under the power of this wicked one. Our deſperately wicked hearts are the palace where he ſits enthroned, and there his deſpotic orders are obeyed; by every prejudice, every allurement, every temptation, he ſtrengthens his intereſt againſt Chriſt and his truth, and flatters with viſions of peace the ſinner's ſoul, filling him with falſe confidence, keeping him in darkneſs with reſpect to his danger, lulling him aſleep in ſecurity, ſuffering him to entertain no doubt of the goodneſs of his heart and the ſafety of his ſtate, and turning him away from whatever tends to diſturb this deceitful repoſe. But, when Chriſt comes by his word and Spirit, the conflict begins, unuſual diſtreſs and terrors ſeize the ſoul, the enemy ſtruggles hard to keep his hold, but the ſtronger grace and power of the Saviour prevail, the ſtrong holds of Satan are laid low, the ſinner's proud imaginations humbled, his falſe confidences, his own righteouſneſs and ſelf-ſufficiency, levelled with the duſt, Chriſt comes and takes poſſeſſion of the heart, by his enlightening, ſanctifying grace diſpels the darkneſs of ignorance and error, and looſes the bonds of ſin and corruption, taking the prey from the mighty, and employing to his own glory the body, ſoul, ſpirit, and all the faculties of the redeemed ſinner.

3. Chriſt intimates to them their truly deplorable condition, under another ſimilitude. They were like a man, out of whom the evil ſpirit departed for a while, ſeeking a ſettlement elſewhere, but, finding none to his mind, he returned to his former houſe, and found it ready prepared for his reception; where, entering with ſeven worſe ſpirits, he took up his abode, and the caſe of that man was more deſperate than ever. Thus now that Satan's kingdom was ſhaken in Judea, he had retired for a while into the Gentile world; but when, after the reſurrection of Jeſus, and the preaching of his goſpel among the heathen, he could find no reſt there, his idols being demoliſhed and his votaries converted, then would he return again to the Jewiſh people, who had rejected their Meſſiah, and find them ready to welcome him into their hearts: with ſevenfold greater influence over them he ſhall take poſſeſſion of them for his own, and, by hurrying them on to fill up the meaſure of their iniquities, will haſten the deſtruction of their country, and effectually ruin both body and ſoul in hell.

This alſo repreſents the ſtate of every hypocrite and apoſtate. An outward reformation may be wrought, and Satan's power for a time ſuſpended; the houſe may be ſwept from groſſer immoralities, and garniſhed with the form of godlineſs, with common gifts of ſpeculative knowledge, or a fair ſhew of profeſſion, whilſt the heart remains unchanged, unhumbled, and unholy: for a while they endure; but, when the hour of temptation comes, Satan finds a ready acceſs, and enters with greater power than ever into the heart; the ſins which were before hid under the veil of hypocriſy break forth, apoſtaſy enſues: and theſe uſually prove the vileſt and moſt abandoned of all ſinners, and will receive the greater damnation.

27 ¶ And it came to paſs, as he ſpake theſe things,
a certain woman of the company lift up her voice, and
ſaid unto him, [b] Bleſſed is the womb that bare thee, and
the paps which thou haſt ſucked. 28 But he ſaid, Yea,
[c] rather bleſſed are they that hear the word of God, and
keep it.

[b] Chap. i. 48.
[c] Mat. vii. 21. Chap. viii. 21. Jam. i. 25.

v. 27, 28. Struck with the miracle ſhe had ſeen, and deeply affected with the convincing force of evidence which appeared in our Lord's diſcourſe, a gracious woman of the company could not reſtrain the glowing rapture of her heart, and burſt forth into expreſſions of wonder and admiration at what ſhe heard and ſaw, counting her inexpreſſibly bleſſed and happy who was the mother of ſuch a ſon. But Chriſt took occaſion to point her to an unſpeakably greater honour and happineſs, of which ſhe herſelf might become poſſeſſed: to hear the word of God and keep it, ſo to receive the love of the truth as to be ſaved thereby, was a far greater bleſſedneſs than, after the fleſh, to have been found among his neareſt relatives.

29 ¶ [d] And when the people were gathered thick
together, he began to ſay, This is an evil generation:
they ſeek a ſign, and there ſhall no ſign be given it,
but the ſign of Jonas the prophet. 30 For [f] as Jonas
was a ſign unto the Ninevites, ſo ſhall alſo the Son of man
be to this generation. 31 The queen of the ſouth ſhall
riſe up in the judgment with the men of this generation,
and condemn them: for [g] ſhe came from the utmoſt parts
of the earth, to hear the wiſdom of Solomon; and be-
hold, a greater than Solomon is here. 32 The men of
Nineveh [h] ſhall riſe up in the judgment with this genera-
tion, and ſhall condemn it: for [i] they repented at the
preaching of Jonas; and behold, a greater than Jonas is
here. 33 [k] No man, when he hath lighted a candle,
putteth it in a ſecret place, neither under a buſhel, but
on a candleſtick, that they which come in may ſee the
light. 34 [l] The light of the body is the eye: therefore
when thine eye is ſingle, thy whole body alſo is full of
light; but when *thine eye* is evil, thy body alſo is full of
darkneſs. 35 Take heed therefore, that the light which
is in thee be not darkneſs. 36 If thy whole body there-
fore *be* full of light, having no part dark, the whole
ſhall be full of light, as when † the bright ſhining of a
candle doth give thee light.

[d] Mat. xii. 38.
[e] 1 Cor. i. 22.
[f] Jon. i. 17. & ii. 10.
[g] 1 Kings x. 1.
[h] Jer. iii. 11. Ezek. xvi. 51. Rom. ii. 27.
[i] Jon. iii. 5.
[k] Mat. v. 15. Mark iv. 21. Chap. viii. 16.
[l] Mat. vi. 22.
† Gr. a candle by its bright ſhining.

v. 29—36. As they were ſo obſtinate in rejecting the ſigns he had given them, and ſtill demand one from heaven, as a ſubterfuge for their unbelief, Chriſt rejects their petition, and, before the people, who were gathered thick around him, ſhews them,

1. That no ſign ſhall be given them from heaven but only that of which Jonas was the type and figure, even the reſurrection of the Son of man from the dead; and their rejection of that would ſeal them up under final impenitence.

2. He warns them of the dreadfulneſs of their guilt, and the aggravated ruin which muſt be the conſequence of rejecting him and his goſpel. As he was far greater than Solomon or Jonah, the queen of Sheba who came ſo far to hear the wiſdom of the one, and the Ninevites who repented at the preaching of the other, would riſe up in a judgment-day to upbraid and condemn their perverſeneſs and unbelief.

3. They had yet the light of truth among them: they were therefore inexcuſable if they abode in darkneſs, and wilfully ſhut their eyes againſt conviction. They who embraced the goſpel, receiving it in the light and the love of it, would be eternally bleſſed and benefited thereby; thoſe who rejected it would be given up juſtly to the blindneſs of their heart, and left to fall into eternal darkneſs. *Note,* (1.) The goſpel is *the lighted candle,* ſet up on the candleſtick of the public miniſtry, to guide benighted ſouls into the paths of everlaſting peace. (2.) What the eye is to the body, that faith is to the ſoul, enabling us to ſee the great things which pertain unto our eternal life, and to embrace them; and, as the bleſſed effect thereof, we are enabled to walk in comfort and holineſs, growing in grace, till the bleſſed day comes when no cloud of ignorance, or ſpot of ſin, ſhall hide the full luſtre of the beatific viſion. (3.) Whilſt the heart remains under the power of native corruption, the underſtanding is darkened, the judgment corrupted by depraved affections, and all the glories of the goſpel day ſhine around ſuch in vain, as the ſun's brighteſt beams convey no light to the perſon whoſe organs of viſion are obſtructed by vicious humours. (4.) We have great need to beware how we trifle with the goſpel, leſt we provoke the Lord to withdraw the light of truth from us, and ſeal us up under judicial blindneſs and hardneſs of heart; and then, *how great is that darkneſs!*

37 ¶ And as he ſpake, a certain Phariſee beſought
him to dine with him: and he went in and ſat down to
meat. 38 And [m] when the Phariſee ſaw *it*, he marvel-
led that he had not firſt waſhed before dinner. 39 And
the Lord ſaid unto him, [n] Now do ye Phariſees make
clean the outſide of the cup and the platter; but [o] your
inward part is full of ravening and wickedneſs. 40 Ye
fools, did not he that made that which is without, make
that which is within alſo? 41 But rather [p] give alms
of ſuch things as you have; and behold, all things are
clean unto you. 42 But [q] wo unto you Phariſees: for
ye tithe mint and rue and all manner of herbs, and
[r] paſs over judgment and the love of God: theſe ought
ye to have done, and not to leave the other undone.
43 Wo unto you Phariſees: for [s] ye love the uppermoſt
ſeats in the ſynagogues, and greetings in the markets.
44 [t] Wo unto you ſcribes and Phariſees, hypocrites:
for [u] ye are as graves which appear not, and the men that
walk over *them* are not aware of *them*. 45 ¶ Then
anſwered one of the lawyers, and ſaid unto him, Maſter,
thus ſaying, thou reproacheſt us alſo. 46 And he ſaid,
[x] Wo unto you alſo, ye lawyers: for ye lade men with
burdens grievous to be born, and ye yourſelves touch not
the

[m] Mark vii. 3.
[n] Mat. xxiii. 25.
[o] Tit. i. 15.
[p] Iſa. lviii. 7. Dan. iv. 27. Chap. xii. 33.
[q] Mat. xxiii. 23.
[r] 1 Sam. xv. 22. Hoſ. vi. 6. Mic. vi. 8. Mat. ix. 13. & xii. 7.
[s] Mat. xxiii. 6. Mark xii. 38, 39. 3 John 9.
[t] Mat. xxiii. 27.
[u] Pſ. v. 9.
[x] Mat. xxiii. 4. Acts xv. 10. Gal. vi. 13.

the burdens with one of your fingers 47 [z] Wo un- [z Mat xxiii 29]
to you for ye build the ſepulchres of the prophets,
and your fathers killed them 48 Truly [a] ye bear [a Pſ lxiv 8]
witneſs that ye allow the deeds of your fathers for
[b] they indeed killed them, and ye build their ſepul-
chres 49 Therefore alſo ſaid the wiſdom of God, [b Acts vii 51 52]
'I will ſend them prophets and apoſtles, and [d] *ſome* of [c Mat xxiii]
them they ſhall ſlay and [e] perſecute 50 That the [d Acts viii]
blood of all the prophets, which was ſhed from the foun- [e Chap xxi]
dation of the world, may be required of this generation,
51 From [f] the blood of Abel unto [g] the blood of Za- [f Gen iv 8 g 2 Chron xxiv 21]
charias, which periſhed between the altar and the temple
verily I ſay unto you, it ſhall be required of this gene-
ration 52 [h] Wo unto you, lawyers for ye have [h Mat xxiii 13]
taken away the key of knowledge ye entred not in your-
ſelves, and them that were entring in, ye † hindred 53 [† Or forbad]
And as he ſaid theſe things unto them, the ſcribes and
Phariſees began to urge *him* vehemently, and to provoke
him to ſpeak of many things 54 Laying wait for
him, and ſeeking to catch ſomething out of his mouth,
that they might accuſe him

v 37—54 We have here,

1 The invitation which one of the Phariſees gave our Lord to dine with him, which he accepted, went to the houſe, and ſat down to meat

2 The Phariſee obſerved, and was much offended, that Chriſt did not waſh before he ſat down at the table, according to the tradition of the elders, which he and his brethren ſo ſcrupulouſly obſerved

3 Chriſt, who knew this proud Phariſee's thoughts, took occaſion freely to reprove their folly and hypocriſy, who had placed the ſubſtance of their religion in theſe uſeleſs and ſuperſtitious obſervances, whilſt they neglected the great and moſt important commands of God He denounces therefore his woes againſt them, [1] For their *hypocriſy*, in ſhewing ſuch ſollicitude to obſerve the various waſhings of their cups and platters, in conformity with the traditions of the elders, whilſt they took no pains to cleanſe their ſouls from the deep pollutions of ſin, from the inward extortion and covetouſneſs, which rendered them abominable in the ſight of God What egregious folly! If God required outward cleanneſs, muſt he not much more expect internal purity? The way to have a ſanctified uſe of their creature-comforts was by charitable diſtribution to the poor, (*Deut* xxvi 12—15) and when this proceeded out of a pure heart, and faith unfeigned, all things would then be clean unto them (*Tit* i 15) but without this, all the water in Jordan would never cleanſe them from their filthineſs [2] For their *injuſtice* and *irreligion* whilſt they pretended the moſt ſcrupulous regard to God's ſervice, tithing even the herbs in their garden, they lived in the groſs violation of the moſt weighty precepts of the moral law, paſſing over *judgment* partial as magiſtrates, extortioners in their dealings, and as void of the *love of God*, as of charity, to their neighbour duties, which being of the firſt importance, demanded their chief attention [3] For their *pride* They were fond of preeminence, expected the moſt honourable ſeat in places of worſhip, where humility was eſpecially required, and affected ſounding titles of homage to be paid them in public, as if they were beings of a ſuperior rank [4] For their *inward filthineſs* Notwithſtanding all the ſpecious appearances of devotion and piety which they wore, their hearts were a ſink of uncleanneſs, and as graves concealed, which men, ere they were aware, walked over, and were defiled by them, ſo did their principles, practice, and converſation, corrupt thoſe who followed their deſtructive ways

4 One of the lawyers, or ſcribes, whoſe office it was in general to expound the law to the people, conceived theſe reproofs on the Phariſees included reproaches on them alſo, and our Lord, without reſpect of perſons, does not ſpare them They were alike culpable, and the ſame woes and wrath hung over them [1] Becauſe they added to the divine precepts an inſupportable load of human traditions, and whilſt to themſelves they were abundantly indulgent, and made the path of ſelf-denial ſufficiently eaſy, they exacted with rigour a ſcrupulous conformity from others to their human impoſitions [2] Becauſe they pretended reverence for the memory of the prophets, and erected noble monuments over the graves of thoſe whom their fathers had murdered, but even the care of the prophets tombs perpetuated the memory of their anceſtors crimes, which they were ready to repeat, being actuated by the ſame malignant ſpirit, *therefore alſo ſaith the wiſdom of God*, Jeſus the divine *Logos*, in whom are hid all the treaſures of wiſdom and knowledge, *I will ſend them prophets and apoſtles, and ſome of them they ſhall ſlay and perſecute*, exceeding all the outrages of their forefathers, more bloody minded and inveterate againſt the miniſters of the goſpel filling up hereby the meaſure of their iniquities, and bringing upon themſelves the vengeance due for all the righteous blood ſhed from Abel to Zacharias, who for his fidelity was ſtoned in the very courts of the temple, (2 *Chron* xxiv 20—22) At the hands of this generation, ſaith he, ſhall it be required and the prediction was fearfully verified in the dreadful and utter deſtruction ſhortly after poured out upon the city, temple, and nation [3] Becauſe *they had taken away the key of knowledge*, arrogating to themſelves the right of expounding the ſcriptures, they miſled the people by corrupt gloſſes They perverted the texts which had the plaineſt reference to the Meſſiah, and the cleareſt accompliſhment in Jeſus, inſtilling wrong notions of his temporal kingdom, they prejudiced the people againſt Chriſt and his goſpel, and refuſing to enter themſelves into the number of his diſciples, they uſed all their art and influence to prevent others from joining them who were diſpoſed to acknowledge his miſſion and character

5 Cut with theſe ſharp rebukes, which unhumbled ſinners regard as affronts and reproaches, *they began to urge him vehemently*, with captious queſtions, *and to provoke him to ſpeak of many things*, trying to ruffle his temper, or draw from him ſome unguarded expreſſion, which to ground ſome accuſation againſt him, either to render him odious to the people, or obnoxious to the government, but his patience and prudence diſappointed their malice *Note*, Fidelity in reproving men's ſins will often procure us inveterate enemies, and we have need watch over the temper of our hearts, and the door of our lips, when in the moſt of thoſe who we know lie in wait for our halting

CHAP XII

Chriſt here, 1 Warns his diſciples to take heed of hypocriſy, and of cowardice in profeſſing Chriſt anity and preaching the goſpel, ver 1—12 2 He gives a caution againſt covetouſneſs, ver 13—21 3 He encourageth his diſciples to caſt all their care upon God, and engageth them to make religion their main buſineſs, ver 22—34 4 He ſtirs them up to watchfulneſs, ver 35—48 5 He bids them expect trouble and perſecution, ver 49—53 6 He warns the people to obſerve and improve the day of their opportunities, and to make their peace with God in time, ver 54—59

1 IN the mean time, [a] when there were gathered to- [a Mat xvi 6 Mark viii 15]
gether an innumerable multitude of people, inſo-
much that they trode upon one another, he began to ſay
unto his diſciples firſt of all, [b] Beware ye of the leaven of [b Mat xvi 12]
the Phariſees, which is hypocriſy 2 For [c] there is no- [c Mat x 26 Mark iv 22 Chap viii 17]
thing covered, that ſhall not be revealed, neither hid,
that ſhall not be known 3 Therefore whatſoever ye
have ſpoken in darkneſs, ſhall be heard in the light and
that which ye have ſpoken in the ear in cloſets, ſhall be
proclaimed upon the houſe-tops 4 [d] And I ſay unto [d Mat x 28 &c]
you, [e] my friends, [f] Be not afraid of them that kill the [e John xv 15]
body, and after that have no more that they can do 5 [f Iſa li 12]
But I will forewarn you whom you ſhall fear Fear him,
which after he hath killed, hath power to caſt into hell,
yea, I ſay unto you, Fear him 6 Are not five ſparrows
ſold for two † farthings, and not one of them is forgot- [† Mat x 29]
ten before God? 7 But even [g] the very hairs of your [g 1 Sam xiv 45 Chap xxi 18 Acts xxvii 34]
head are all numbred Fear not therefore ye are of
more value than many ſparrows 8 Alſo I ſay unto you,
[h] Whoſoever ſhall confeſs me before men, [i] him ſhall the [h Rom x 9]
Son of man alſo confeſs before the angels of God 9
But [k] he that denieth me before men, ſhall be denied be- [i Rev iii 5 k Chap ix 26 2 Tim ii 12]
fore the angels of God 10 And [l] whoſoever ſhall ſpeak
a word againſt the Son of man, it ſhall be forgiven him [l Mat xii 31 Mark iii 28]
[m] but unto him that blaſphemeth againſt the Holy Ghoſt,
it ſhall not be forgiven 11 And [n] when they bring [m 1 John v 16]
you unto the ſynagogues and *unto* magiſtrates and pow- [n Mat x 19 Mark xiii 11]
ers, [o] take ye no thought how or what thing ye ſhall an-
ſwer, or what ye ſhall ſay 12 For the holy Ghoſt ſhall [o Jer i 7 Chap xxi 14]
teach you in the ſame hour what ye ought to ſay

v 1—12 Our Lord inculcated the ſame truth on different occaſions We need line upon line, and precept upon precept. A vaſt auditory was now aſſembled, and, as he was ever ready to ſpeak when they deſired to hear, he took occaſion,

1 To caution his diſciples in public againſt that hypocriſy of the Phariſees which he had juſt before ſo ſharply rebuked in private He calls it *the leaven of the Phariſees* Their hearts, lips, and lives were wholly infected thereby ſwoln with pride and ſelf-importance, and ſoured with envy and malice, all their ſpecious pretences to religion were but an abomination Chriſt therefore warns his diſciples to ſhun this hateful evil themſelves, and not to be impoſed upon by the fair profeſſions of theſe deſigning men And he urges, as a powerful argument, the ſure detection of hypocriſy, either in this world, or in the day when the ſecrets of all hearts ſhall be revealed Then moſt retired communications, even the whiſpers in a cloſet, muſt all ſhortly be proclaimed before the aſſembled world How careful then need

need we be over every thought and word, considering that all-seeing and heart-searching God with whom we have to do

2 He charges them to be faithful to their trust, and never to suppress, through fear or shame, one tittle of their message, but what they have learnt of him in private, that must they boldly and publicly declare in the face of all opposition And to encourage them to approve their fidelity unshaken, he addresses them, [1] As his *friends*, whom he dearly loved, and would not fail to support under every trial [2] He lets them know, that the most inveterate malice of their foes can only reach the perishing body, they cannot touch the immortal soul Better therefore, infinitely better would it be for them, by a steady testimony to the truth, bravely to put their lives in their hands, and meet, if the Lord so permitted, the worst death their enemies could inflict, than by a cowardly silence, or suppression of the offensive doctrines of the gospel, to provoke a jealous God, whose wrath reaches not only to the body, but to the soul, sinking both into the flames of hell, and enduring to eternity The fear of him should swallow up every other fear [3] That guardian Providence, which watches over and orders the most minute events, would take peculiar care of them Not a sparrow is forgotten of God, or falls unnoticed, yea, the very hairs of their head are numbered, their most invenomed foes cannot touch one of them without divine permission, therefore they need not fear what man can do unto them [4] According to their fidelity or unfaithfulness, so would they be owned or disowned by him at the last great day They who, fearless of reproach or suffering, dared make confession of him in the world, shall be with honour acknowledged as his disciples, in the presence of angels at the resurrection of the just, whilst to decline bearing a testimony for him before men, to avoid loss or infamy, would infallibly provoke Jesus to renounce all relation to them, and expose them to everlasting shame and contempt in the dreadful day of judgment When we are tempted to be ashamed of Christ, or to deny our profession, let us seriously remember this warning, and be wise [5] Contempt of their testimony, and blasphemy against the Holy Ghost, would expose their persecutors to endless wrath All the revilings now cast out against the Son of man in his state of humiliation were pardonable, but after his ascension, and the descent of the Holy Ghost upon them, to ascribe the miracles they wrought in confirmation of the resurrection of Jesus, to diabolical agency, would be to resist the only means of conviction, and must exclude such blasphemers from the possibility of repentance or forgiveness [6] In all emergencies, where they were called to answer before the tribunals of their persecutors, whether Jews or Gentiles, Christ undertakes to furnish them with a tongue, and wisdom which none of their adversaries shall be able to gainsay or resist They need not take thought a moment what to speak in their own defence, the Holy Ghost should effectually furnish them with every thing proper for the occasion, and with such encouragements before them, they may boldly go forth, and fear not

13 ¶ And one of the company said unto him, Mas-
ter, speak to my brother, that he divide the inheritance
with me 14 And he said unto him, [p] Man, who made
me a judge, or a divider over you? 15 And he said
unto them, [q] Take heed and beware of covetousness for
a man's life consisteth not in the abundance of the things
which he possesseth 16 And he spake a parable unto
them, saying, The ground of a certain rich man brought
forth plentifully 17 And he thought within himself,
saying, What shall I do, because I have no room where
to bestow my fruits? 18 And he said, This will I do
I will pull down my barns, and build greater, and there
will I bestow all my fruits and my goods 19 And I
will say to my soul, [r] Soul, thou hast much goods laid
up for many years, take thine ease, eat, drink, *and* be
merry 20 But God said unto him, *Thou* fool, this night
[s] thy soul shall be required of thee [t] then whose shall
those things be which thou hast provided? 21 [u] So *is*
he that layeth up treasure for himself, and is not rich
towards God

p John xviii 36

q 1 Tim vi [illegible]

r Eccl xi 9 1 Cor xv 32 Jam v 5

s Job xx 22 & xxvii 8 Pf lii 7

t Pf xxxix 6 Jer xvii 11

u Matt vi 20 Ver 33 1 Tim vi 18

v 13—21 We have here,

1 The application made to Christ by one of the company, desiring him, as a person of authority, to interpose on his behalf with his brother, who either unjustly kept him out of his part of the inheritance, or being the elder, and having by law a double portion, this worldly-minded man would fain come in for an equal share

2 Christ refuses to interpose The exercise of temporal power and authority did not belong to that kingdom he came to establish, nay, had he interfered, they would have perhaps made it a ground of accusation, and quarrelled with him for daring to make himself a ruler and a judge (*See Exod* ii 14)

3 He takes occasion from the unreasonable application to warn his disciples against the great sin and danger of covetousness, which being a most insinuating evil, they had need carefully guard their hearts against it Men are apt to fancy, that this world's goods are most essential to happiness, but *a man's life consisteth not in the abundance of the things which he possesseth*, they conduce nothing to the spiritual satisfaction of the soul, they cannot prolong our lives a day, an hour, nay, instead of being comforts to us, they often prove a plague and snare here below besides all the hindrances they put in our way, to obstruct our entrance into the kingdom of heaven To give the greater force to this admonition, he illustrates it by a striking example

The ground of a certain rich man brought forth plentifully, (Χώρα, *a region*) His estate was vast, as the produce of it was abundant These common gifts of providence the evil and unthankful often enjoy in the largest measure, but we may not judge of God's love or of real felicity from hence The *rich* man is far from being usually the *happy* man We are told,

[1] What anxious cares his wealth occasioned *He thought within himself, saying, What shall I do, because I have no room where to bestow my fruits?* He appears as full of perplexity as if he knew not where to get another morsel to satisfy the cravings of hunger Such is the usual effect of increasing wealth, it brings an increase of cares and disquietude

[2] The result of his thoughts was this *I will pull down my barns, and build greater, and there will I bestow all my fruits and my goods*, a resolution, that spoke great folly, as well as ungodliness He calls these *his* fruits, which were really but lent him of the Lord To hoard up *all*, when so many empty barns of the poor, and hungry bellies might have charitably eased him of somewhat of his load of plenty, was vilely covetous To call these his *goods*, which must perish in the using, proved his utter ignorance of a better portion *Greater barns* would only bring greater expence and greater care, besides the plague of building, and his presumptuous *I will*, shewed he left God far above out of his sight So ready are they who trust in uncertain riches to forget the living God

[3] He flatters himself with the most pleasing prospects, when his schemes were completed, of sitting down and enjoying at ease the store he had collected *I will say to my soul, Soul, thou hast much goods laid up for many years, take thine ease, eat, drink, and be merry* How absurd the conclusion? Could his *soul* relish the gratifications of a beast, or feel any satisfaction from the indulgence of appetite? The wealth of the world, and the plenitudes of sense, are not a portion at all suited to its wants their God alone with a sense of his love and favour can supply He promised himself *many years* to enjoy his affluence when he knew not what a day might bring forth, he ensured the safety of his goods, when in the shortest space fire or tempest might lay his storehouses in ruins so precarious are all our earthly possessions But if he saw his barns rise, and brooded over his plenty, *ease* was what he could no more secure to his soul, than his toil All his fruits and his goods could no more dispel the pains of an aching head, than cure the [illegible] of an aching heart One stroke of sickness or disease must embitter all his abundance, and leave him pining in the midst of plenty one unhappy incident in his family might forbid him to taste the least satisfaction in all his affluence So poor, so precarious a portion is all sublunary good

[4] God suddenly confounds his schemes, and blasts his hopes He said unto him, *Thou fool, this night thy soul shall be required of thee then whose shall those things be which thou hast provided?* Death in a moment darkens all the gay prospect, and dashes the painted bubble which flattering hope had blown The day is near, when every carnal worldling, whom men applaud [illegible], and praised as *doing well to himself*, (*Ps* xlix 18) shall feel with terrible conviction his egregious folly, and hear *thou fool* pronounced upon him by the lips of eternal wisdom The affluence of the wicked must quickly change its owner, and nothing remain for them but a dreary grave, and a certain fearful looking-for of judgment Death, whenever it come to them, will be a terrible surprize, and dreadful night of horror will surround them, as, dragged reluctant from the body, their soul, their guilty soul, must go where riches profit not to bribe a verdict in their favour, nor can all their wealth procure one drop of water to cool their tongue in those eternal flames which never shall be quenched

[5] Our Lord applies the parable in general to every worldly-minded man, *that layeth up treasure for himself* sets his heart upon riches, expects his happiness from them, and all whose concerns are engrossed merely about himself, without regard to God's glory, or care for his neighbour *and is not rich towards God*, destitute of the treasures of grace, and without the least title to the eternal inheritance *so is he*, so blind are his schemes, so fruitless his cares, and so miserable will be his end Let us be warned therefore in time, and not foolishly prefer gold to godliness, the body to the soul, and time to eternity

22 ¶ And he said unto his disciples, Therefore I
say unto you, [x] Take no thought for your life, what ye
shall eat, neither for the body, what ye shall put on
23 The life is more than meat, and the body is *more*
than

x Matt vi 25 [illegible]

than raiment 24 Consider the ravens for they nei-
ther sow nor reap, which neither have storehouse nor
barn, and God feedeth them How much more are
ye better than the fowls? 25 And which of you with
taking thought can add to his stature one cubit? 26
If ye then be not able to do that thing which is least,
why take ye thought for the rest? 27 Consider the li-
lies how they grow they toil not, they spin not and
yet I say unto you, that Solomon in all his glory was
not arrayed like one of these 28 If then God so clothe
the grass, which is to-day in the field, and to-morrow is
cast into the oven how much more *will he clothe* you,
O ye of little faith? 29 And seek not ye what ye shall
eat, or what ye shall drink, neither be ye of doubtful
mind 30 For all these things do the nations of the
world seek after and your Father knoweth that ye
have need of these things 31 ¶ But rather [a] seek ye
the kingdom of God, and all these things shall be added
unto you 32 Fear not, † little flock, [*] for it is your
Father's good pleasure to give you the kingdom 33
[b] Sell that ye have, and give alms provide yourselves
bags which wax not old, a treasure in the heavens that
faileth not, where no thief approacheth, neither moth
corrupteth 34 [c] For where your treasure is, there will
your heart be also 35 [d] Let your loins be girded about,
and [e] *your* lights burning? 36 And ye yourselves like
unto men that wait for their Lord, when he will return
from the wedding, that when he cometh and knocketh,
they may open unto him immediately 37 [f] Blessed
are those servants, whom the Lord when he cometh shall
find watching verily I say unto you, that he shall gird
himself, and make them to sit down to meat, and will
come forth and serve them 38 And if he shall come
in the second watch, or come in the third watch, and
find *them* so, blessed are those servants 39 And this
know, that [g] if the good man of the house had known
what hour the thief would come, he would have watched,
and not have suffered his house to be broken through
40 [h] Be ye therefore ready also for the Son of man
cometh at an hour when ye think not

v 22—40 The following instructions we have considered before in the other Evangelists, but they are of such importance, as to deserve our hearing once, yea twice, that they may be graven on our hearts, for nothing is a more fatal snare to the soul, than inordinate desire after the wealth of this world

1 Christ enjoins his disciples to cast their care upon God, and never to disquiet or perplex themselves about a worldly provision, *anxious sollicitude* being as criminal as *sensual indulgence* We must *take no thought* about the necessaries of life, disquieting ourselves with the fears of hunger or nakedness, but in the way of duty chearfully trust him with our support, who gave us our being, *v* 23 Even the ravens are fed by his providence, and the lily is clothed with beauty, such as Solomon arrayed in all his glory could not vie with and shall he not much more feed and clothe us, who in excellence, as creatures, are so much better, and, as a peculiar people, are so much dearer to him? The cause of all our anxious cares and fears is our unbelief not that our sollicitude will mend our circumstances, it is as useless as it is needless We cannot add to our *stature* a cubit, or to our *age* a day, and if in the least things all our thought must be unavailing, why should we distress ourselves about the rest? Dependent therefore on the Divine Providence, we need not be distressed, perplexed, and fluctuating like meteors, about a subsistence, for this would shew we had no more confidence in God than heathens, and intimate the most criminal distrust of the power and care of him we call our *Father*, who knows all our wants, is able to supply them, and hath engaged that we shall want no manner of thing that is truly good for us We have indeed greater things in view than food and raiment, even *the kingdom of God*, the blessings of grace and glory these must engage our first concern and then we may safely trust the Lord with all our temporal affairs

2 He encourages them not to fear want, when they are the assured heirs of the eternal King *Fear not, little flock* Christ's children are like a *flock*, united in love under their kind shepherd's care *a little flock*, few, compared with the world which lieth in wickedness yet, though compassed with enemies, they need *not fear* their Redeemer is mighty as he is precious *It is your Father's good pleasure to give you the kingdom*; a kingdom of glory that fadeth not away, the gift of sovereign grace, bestowed not according to our desert, but the good pleasure of his own will, and if he hath provided a throne in the heavens, we may rest assured he will not leave us to want on earth Instead therefore of desiring to hoard unnecessary wealth, or being, under anxiety about food or raiment, our hearts and hands should be open, according to our abilities, to relieve the necessitous, and, when God's providence calls for it, ready to part with all we possess, sending it before us, as the surest and most abiding portion, which will enrich us in the eternal world, where it will be incorruptible and inexhaustible This will raise our affections to high and heavenly things, and there where our treasure is, our heart will be

3 He bids them prepare for the day when he, their Master, shall come to take them with him to the mansions provided for them, and to partake of the pleasures which are at his right hand for evermore Christ, our Master, is gone up to heaven, to prepare for himself his spouse, the church we are his servants, appointed to watch till his return, and to be ready to meet him, the oil of grace burning in our lamps, and our souls active in his service As many as he finds thus expecting him, and welcoming his arrival, he will reward with distinguished blessedness, and entertain them with all the unutterable delights of the eternal world, taking them with him to sit down in the kingdom of God As the time of Christ's coming is uncertain, like the wise housholder, we need be habitually on our guard, and awake with the first alarm, that we may not be unexpectedly surprised, as by a thief in the night, *for the Son of man cometh at an hour when ye think not*, and wo to those whom he finds sleeping in sin and carnal security

41 ¶ Then Peter said unto him, Lord, speakest thou
this parable unto us, or even to all? 42 And the
Lord said, [i] Who then is that faithful and wise steward,
whom *his* lord shall make ruler over his houshold, to
give *them their* portion of meat in due season? 43
Blessed *is* that servant, whom his lord when he cometh
shall find so doing 44 Of a truth I say unto you, that
[k] he will make him ruler over all that he hath 45
But and if that servant say in his heart, My lord delayeth
his coming, and shall begin to beat the men-servants,
and maidens, and to eat and drink, and to be drunken
46 The lord of that servant will come in a day when
he looketh not for him, and at an hour when he is not
aware, [l] and will cut him in sunder, and will appoint
him his portion with the unbelievers 47 And [m] that
servant which knew his Lord's will, and prepared not
himself, neither did according to his will, shall be beaten
with many *stripes* 48 But [n] he that knew not, and did
commit things worthy of stripes, shall be beaten with
few *stripes* For unto whomsoever much is given, of
him shall be much required and to whom men have
committed much, of him they will ask the more 49
¶ [o] I am come to send fire on the earth, and what will
I, if it be already kindled? 50 But [p] I have a bap-
tism to be baptized with, and how am I straitened till it
be accomplished! 51 Suppose ye that I am come to
give peace on earth? I tell you, Nay, [q] but rather di-
vision 52 For from henceforth there shall be five in
one house divided, three against two, and two against
three 53 [r] The father shall be divided against the son,
and the son against the father the mother against the
daughter, and the daughter against the mother the mo-
ther-in-law against her daughter-in-law, and the daugh-
ter-in-law against her mother-in-law

v 41—53 Peter, the warm-hearted disciple, the ready spokesman, desires to know if our Lord's discourse was directed to the apostles in particular, or to all the disciples in general? Hereupon,

1 Christ replies to his question What he had spoken had both a general view to all the disciples, and was particularly applicable to them who were advanced to the most honoured posts, as stewards of the Lord's houshold (1) Their *duty* was, as put in trust with the care of men's souls, to be wise and faithful dispensers of the gospel, and the instituted ordinances of grace, considering the several cases and states of those to whom they ministred, and seasonably and rightly dividing to each the word of truth, for their conviction, edification, or comfort (2) The *blessedness* of fidelity would be great whoever shall be found at Christ's appearing, thus zealously, diligently, perseveringly employed, shall be highly advanced by him in glory, and placed, like Joseph in Egypt, at the King's right hand (3) As great will be the *misery*, sin, and danger of those who shall be found unfaithful It is shocking to think there should be such a character as a minister of Christ in profession, quarrelsome, oppressive, abusive, prophane, drunken, yet such there have been, there will be, and the cause of these, and the like enormities, is intimated, such a one saith, *My Lord delayeth his coming*, and therefore in security grows negligent and treacherous to his trust, and insensible to the awful account he must shortly make But such insensibility retards not the ap-
proach

2

Job [illegible] 41 [illegible] Psalm [illegible] 9
[a] 1 Kings [illegible] Mat vi 33 [illegible] Pf xxxiv 9 [illegible] Mark x [illegible] 1 Tim [illegible]
† Or, Little [illegible] flock
[*] Chap xii [illegible]
[b] [illegible]
[c] Mat [illegible] 21
[d] Chap [illegible] Acts [illegible] 45 [illegible] 1 Tim [illegible]
[e] Mat vi [illegible]
[f] Heb [illegible] 1 Pet [illegible]
[g] Mat xxiv [illegible]
[h] Mat xxiv 40 [illegible]
[g] Mat xxiv 43, 1 Thes v 2 2 Pet iii 10 Rev iii 3 & xvi [illegible]
[h] Mat xxiv 44 & xxv 13, 1 Thes v 6
[i] Mat xxiv 45 & xxv 21 1 Cor iv 2
[k] Chap xxiv 29
[l] Mat xxiv 51
[m] Num xv 30 Deut xxv 2 Jam iv 17
[n] Lev v 17
[o] Mat x 34 Ver 51
[p] Mat xx 22
[q] Mic vii 6 John x 26 & x 19
[r] Mat x 35

proach of danger, the dreadful hour of reckoning draws near, the Judge will suddenly and unexpectedly appear, and pronounce their tremendous doom according to the light and advantages they have enjoyed, shall be the measure of their punishment The stripes shall be fewer, where through ignorance men have erred and offended, whilst the heaviest strokes of vengeance shall fall on those who have abused the greatest gifts, and in opposition to knowledge and conscience have been unfaithful to their trust and this is agreeable to the strictest rules of equity, that where a greater trust hath been committed, a proportionable improvement should be required, whilst unfaithfulness and negligence in such a case, become more aggravatedly criminal

2 Christ admonishes them of the fiery trials which he and they must go through His gospel, though breathing the spirit of peace and love, yet being so opposite to the pride and prejudices of men, would give occasion to the bitterest animosities and persecutions This fire was already kindled in the rancour shewn him by the Scribes and Pharisees, but will he desist from his glorious undertaking, or suppress the offensive truths? No, in no wise Since by no other means, than the sufferings he foresaw, the salvation of his people could be obtained, he willingly offers himself to the bloody baptism before him, eagerly longing for the time when it should be accomplished in the garden, and on the cross How astonishing his love towards us! He forewarns his disciples, that they must expect their cross also, for from that temporal kingdom of peace and prosperity with which they flattered themselves, war and tumult are before them The gospel they preached would be opposed with the fiercest rage of men and devils, and the greatest miseries and confusions the consequence Even among nearest relations it would occasion the most grievous divisions in families where but should be converted, and part remain in their sins, the bitterest animosities would arise in the bosoms of those who rejected the counsel of God And such will be their enmity against those who embrace the truth, that it will break through all ties of blood, duty, and friendship, making the father unnatural, the son undutiful, even in the hearts of those, whose softer sex should breathe greater mildness, the spirit of superstition and bigotry will quench all natural affection, so that even parents shall persecute their children, and children their parents, exasperated by the reproof of their holy lives, and inflamed with rage at the gentlest remonstrances, and the most endearing persuasions of those who labour for their conversion And thus it continues to this day, and must to the end of the world let us not think it strange

54 ¶ And he said also to the people, [a] When ye see
a cloud rise out of the west, straightway ye say, There
cometh a shower, and so it is 55 And when *ye see*
the south wind blow, ye say, There will be heat, and
it cometh to pass 56 Ye hypocrites, ye can discern
the face of the sky, and of the earth but how is it,
that ye do not discern this time? 57 Yea, and why
even of yourselves judge ye not what is right? 58 ¶ [c]
When thou goest with thine adversary to the magistrate,
[d] *as thou art* in the way, give diligence that thou mayest
be delivered from him, lest he hale thee to the judge,
and the judge deliver thee to the officer, and the officer
cast thee into prison 59 I tell thee, thou shalt not depart
thence, till thou hast paid the very last mite

a Mat xvi 2
b p xix 14
c Mat v 25
d Isa lv 6
e Job xxii 21
f Job v
g Mat xiii 2

v 54—59 The former discourse was addressed to the disciples, this to the multitude

1 Christ upbraids them for their stupidity and perverseness in not attending to, or rejecting the evidences of his mission They judged what weather there would be by the prognosticks which experience had taught them how inexcusable then were they not to discern *this time*, fixed for the Messiah's appearing, and how hypocritical and false their pretences to wisdom and knowledge of the prophets, when they disregarded or perverted the plainest declarations of the scriptures, concerning the birth, family, life, doctrine, and kingdom of the Messiah, and thus knew not the day of their visitation! Amazing that they should not even of themselves, discern what was right, when the evidence was so cogent, and that whilst they shewed observation and judgment in matters of less concern, in this of infinitely greater moment to their souls, they should act so strangely infatuated!

2 He admonishes them of the necessity of a speedy accommodation of their matter with an offended God, before it was too late A common prudence would dictate the necessity of seeking an amicable agreement with our adversary, rather than push matters to extremities where the cause must infallibly be carried against us, and a prison be the issue of the trial, much more should we, in the matters of our souls, shew greater concern to obtain reconciliation with God, who by our sins is become our adversary To attempt our own justification before him, were folly, and to escape from his sentence, is impossible Whilst

therefore, we are *in the way* of life, our wisdom is to cast ourselves at his feet, acknowledging our offences, and through faith in Jesus, our surety, to plead for mercy, least death should drag us to his dread tribunal in unpardoned guilt, and the ministers of vengeance seize us in consequence of the judgment pronounced, and cast us into the prison of hell, where even eternal torments can never satisfy offended justice, or cancel the infinite debt of sin

CHAP XIII

In this chapter we have, 1 The good improvement Christ made of the massacre of some Galileans, ver 1—5 2 The parable of the barren fig-tree, ver 6—9 3 Christ's healing a poor infirm woman on the sabbath day, ver 11—17 4 A repetition of the parables of the grain of mustard-seed, and the leaven, ver 18—22. 5 His answer to the question concerning the number of the saved, ver 23—30 6 The slight he put upon Herod's malice and menaces, and the doom of Jerusalem read, ver 31—35

1 THERE were present at that season, some that
told him of the Galileans, whose blood Pilate
had mingled with their sacrifices 2 And Jesus answering,
said unto them, Suppose ye that these Galileans
were sinners above all the Galileans, because they
suffered such things? 3 I tell you, Nay but except
ye repent, ye shall all likewise perish 4 Or those
eighteen, upon whom the tower of Siloam fell, and slew
them, think ye that these † sinners above all men
that dwell in Jerusalem? 5 I tell you, Nay but
except ye repent, ye shall all likewise perish

† Gr Debtors
Mat vi 12
& xviii 24
Ezek xviii 30

v 1—5 We have here,

1 A tragical story reported to our Lord by some who were present Probably these Galileans had been followers of Judas of Galilee, *Acts* v 37 of whom Pilate having got information, fell upon them when they came up to the temple to worship, and mingled their blood with their sacrifices Perhaps what our Lord had been speaking of the necessity of always watching, and the importance of securing peace with God, gave occasion to the remark or, as it seems from the sequel, they meant to insinuate, that these must needs be very wicked persons, who were given up to so dreadful a judgment

2 Jesus seeks to turn this event to their profit, and to ground thereon an exhortation to repentance He reproves the uncharitable censure they seemed to cast on these unhappy men, as if their crimes had brought them to this untimely death, whereas such afflictive visitations were no proof of guilt, the best of men have sometimes suffered most Nor may we judge of God's love or hatred to any man by the outward dispensations of his providence If they meant to reflect on them as Galileans, and thereby to throw some reproach on Christ and his disciples, who were their countrymen, Christ instances a recent calamity of as melancholy a nature which lately happened at Jerusalem, when eighteen persons were suddenly crushed to death by the fall of a tower in Siloam, so that these calamities were not singular, or confined to persons in one place more than another, nor were they to conclude, that these men perished because they were greater sinners than others in Galilee or Jerusalem But he solemnly warns them, that a heavier doom hung over their heads except they repented, when their blood too should be shed by the Roman sword in the midst of their sacred solemnities, and they be buried as the men in the tower of Siloam, under the ruin of their city, and perish temporally, and eternally and this is applicable to every sinner (1) His desert is to perish under the wrath of God (2) Nothing but repentance can prevent his ruin (3) The judgments of God on others are loud warnings to us (4) Consciousness of our own sinfulness and provocations, should make us very careful how we censure others (5) They who are severe in judging, may expect judgment without mercy

6 ¶ He spake also this parable [b] A certain man had
a fig-tree planted in his vineyard, and he came and
sought fruit thereon, and found none. 7 Then said
he unto the dresser of his vineyard, Behold, these three
years I come seeking fruit on this fig-tree, and find
none [c] cut it down, why cumbreth it the ground? 8
And he answering, said unto him, Lord, [d] let it alone
this year also, till I shall dig about it, and dung *it* 9
And if it bear fruit *well* and if not, *then* [e] after that,
thou shalt cut it down

b Isa v 2 Mat xxi 19
c Luke iii 9
d Dan iv 27
e Heb vi 8
f Rom xi 22

v 6—9 This parable is designed to enforce the foregoing admonition It seems primarily to be applicable to the Jewish people, blessed with peculiar advantages, but disappointing God's expectations, yet spared a little longer at the Redeemer's intercession, till having tried them another space, and used in vain the moſt powerful means for their converſion in the miſſion of his apoſtles, at laſt he devotes them to utter ruin for their unbelief and impenitence, cutting them down as a barren tree, and caſting them into the fire But whatever reference the parable hath to them, it is of more extenſive uſe, as containing a warning to all who enjoy the means of grace, and who, if they are not converted by them, will fall under heavier wrath and condemnation

1 Great were the advantages this fig-tree enjoyed It was planted *in a vineyard*, in the beſt ſoil, and under the owner's peculiar care and culture The church is the vineyard of God, every viſible member hath a place there, ſitting under the rain of goſpel doctrine, and bleſt with the miniſterial labours of Chriſt's faithful ſervants

2 The owner juſtly expected to find fruit on this tree, as the Lord doth from all who have a place in his church, of whom he requires the fruits of grace and holineſs, as well as the leaves of profeſſion

3 Great was his diſappointment *he found none*, and therefore complains to the vine-dreſſer how long he had waited, and how uſeleſs was this tree, which impoveriſhed the ground, and occupied the room of one that might be profitable With much more reaſon may the Lord complain of many profeſſors, who bring him no honour, and continue barren and unfruitful He comes from year to year, for three, for thirty, yea, ſometimes for threeſcore years together, ſo wonderful is his patience and forbearance, and finds them ſtill *cumberers of the ground*, whoſe ill example is more extenſively pernicious the longer they are permitted to ſtand

4 He dooms it to fall, *cut it down*, ſince the tree bore no fruit, it was only fit for the flames Such is the awful ſentence of God againſt the impenitent ſinner, *cut it down*, and death is ready to lift the ax, and caſt body and ſoul into the fire of hell How awful, how alarming the thought!

5 The vine-dreſſer begs another year, if it be ſpared, he will take freſh pains, it may yet bear, and then all will be well, but if not, he conſents to leave the tree to its juſt doom Chriſt is this vine-dreſſer, at his interceſſion are ſinners ſpared, and every miniſter under him fails not in like manner to be an advocate for thoſe among whom he labours But, (1) If through the interceſſion of Jeſus our lives are prolonged, and we have another year granted, we ſhould know and improve the day of our viſitation The time is ſhort, reprieves are not pardons, though we are ſpared never ſo long, if we continue in our ſins, we muſt periſh at the laſt (2) Whilſt the Lord ſpares the ſinner, miniſters muſt never be weary of labouring, and ſhould try every method, digging up the heart by the terrors of the law, and ſeeking to dung it with the quickening manure of the goſpel (3) It is never too late to amend, the moſt barren and unfruitful, who by grace at laſt are turned to God, will find mercy with him, the paſt tranſgreſſions ſhall be forgiven, the preſent ſervice accepted, and all ſhall be well, (4) God's patience, though it bear long, will not bear always, they who provoke and grieve his holy ſpirit by their obſtinate impenitence, will at laſt be left to the deſtruction they have choſen, and every day of his forbearance which they have abuſed, ſhall add a treaſure of wrath againſt the day of wrath

10 And he was teaching in one of the ſyna-
gogues on the ſabbath 11 ¶ And behold, there was a
woman which had a ſpirit of infirmity eighteen years,
and was bowed together, and could in no wiſe lift up
herſelf 12 And when Jeſus ſaw her, he called *her* to
him, and ſaid unto her, Woman, thou art looſed from
g Mark xvi 18 Acts ix, 1 thine infirmity 13 And [g] he laid *his* hands on her
and immediately ſhe was made ſtraight, and glorified
God 14. And the ruler of the ſynagogue anſwered
with indignation, becauſe that Jeſus had healed on the
h Exod xx 9 & xxiii 12 ſabbath-day, and ſaid unto the people, [h] There are ſix
days in which men ought to work in them therefore
i Chap vi 7 & xiv 3 come and be healed, and [i] not on the ſabbath-day 15
The Lord then anſwered him, and ſaid, Thou hypo-
k Chap. xiv 5 crite, [k] doth not each one of you on the ſabbath looſe
his ox or *his* aſs from the ſtall, and lead *him* away to
l Chap xix 9 watering 16 And ought not this woman, [l] being a
daughter of Abraham, whom Satan hath bound, lo theſe
eighteen years, be looſed from this bond on the ſabbath-
day? 17 And when he had ſaid theſe things, all his
adverſaries were aſhamed and all the people rejoiced
for all the glorious things that were done by him

v 10—17 Chriſt was an unwearied preacher, and, as uſual, was now in the ſynagogue on the ſabbath-day To confirm the doctrine he taught, we are told,

1 The notable miracle he wrought on an infirm woman who was preſent Her caſe was very pitiable under the power of Satan her body was ſo convulſed and contracted, that ſhe was bent double, and could not ſtand erect, and as the diſorder had been of ſo long ſtanding as eighteen years, all hope of a cure was deſperate Yet ſhe made a ſhift to crawl to the ſynagogue, and did not, as many might have done, make her weakneſs, or deformity, a plea for abſenting from God's worſhip There the compaſſionate eye of Jeſus remarked her unhappy ſituation, and, unſolicited, he called and cured her, looſing her from Satan's bonds, and enabling her inſtantly to ſtand upright, for which ſhe moſt heartily expreſſed her gratitude, glorifying and praiſing God for this extraordinary and unexpected mercy *Note*, (1) So weak and infirm are our ſouls by nature, unable to lift up their affections to high and heavenly things, and ever bowed down to earthly ſenſual objects (2) Chriſt ſeeks us, not we him, and is pleaſed to call to us in the goſpel-word, that coming to him we might be cured (3) The powerful hand of his grace effectually relieves the ſoul from the bondage of guilt and corruption, and when at any time we are afterwards bowed down with fear, and go heavily through manifold temptations, he giveth ſtrength to the weak (4) It will be the delight and duty of all who experience his healing, to glorify him in their lips and in their lives, walking upright before him

2 The envious and malicious ruler of the ſynagogue, inſtead of glorifying God for the miracle, hardened with bigotry and prejudice, ſharply reprimanded the people, as if the ſabbath was violated by their coming to be healed on that day *Note*, They who reſolve to find fault, and not to be convinced, will cavil againſt the moſt glaring evidence

3 Our Lord juſtifies his own conduct, and upbraids him with his hypocriſy The zeal he pretended for the ſabbath was a mere pretence, to hide that enmity which raged in his heart againſt Chriſt and his goſpel His own daily practice condemned and confuted his unreaſonable and uncharitable cenſures None of thoſe, who moſt rigidly obſerved the ſabbath, thought it any breach of the ſacred reſt, to looſe their beaſt from the ſtall, and lead him to water And if an ox or an aſs might have ſuch pains beſtowed on them on the ſabbath, with how much greater reaſon did mercy and charity plead, that a human creature, a daughter of Abraham too, bound by Satan's power, and ſo long and ſo grievouſly afflicted, ſhould be relieved, when without the leaſt labour it could be done by a ſingle word?

4 The argument was moſt concluſive, and confuſion covered his adverſaries, whilſt all the people, who were ſtruck with wonder at his miracles, and the force of his reaſoning, rejoiced at theſe glorious works of power and grace which they beheld. *Note*, Sooner or later all the foes of Chriſt and his people ſhall be confounded, and all his faithful triumph in his great ſalvation

18 ¶ [m] Then ſaid he, Unto what is the kingdom of m Mat xiii 31 Mark iv 30
God like? and whereunto ſhall I reſemble it? 19 It
is like a grain of muſtard-ſeed, which a man took and
caſt into his garden, and it grew, and [n] waxed a great n Pſ lxxx 8—11 Prov iv 18
tree and the fowls of the air lodged in the branches
of it 20 And again he ſaid, Whereunto ſhall I liken
the kingdom of God? 21 [o] It is like leaven, which a o Mat xiii. 33
woman took and [p] hid in three † meaſures of meal, [q] till p Pſ cxix 11
the whole was leavened 22 And [r] he went through † Mat xiii. 33
the cities and villages, teaching and journeying towards q 1 Cor v 7
Jeruſalem r Mat ix. 35 Mark vi 6

v 18—22 We have here,

1 Two parables which were before recorded, *Mat* xiii 31 repreſenting the gradual increaſe of Chriſt's church, and the ſecret, but effectual ſpreading of the goſpel-leaven Though the beginnings were ſmall, as the grain of muſtard-ſeed when ſown, yet, in proceſs of time, like a far-ſpreading tree, the kingdom of the Meſſiah would be erected throughout all the world, and Gentiles, as well as Jews, flock into it And like leaven, though no external force be employed, the doctrines of truth would inſenſibly, but powerfully work, till their influence was diffuſed through all the earth

2 Our Lord continued his courſe towards Jeruſalem, preaching and teaching in all the cities and villages as he journeyed. Wherever Providence directs our way, we ſhould be glad to improve every opportunity to ſpeak a word for the good of immortal ſouls

s 2 Tim viii. 1 † Or, Agonize Mat xi 12. t Mat vii. 13 u John vii 34 & viii 21 Rom ix 31 x Pſ xxxii 6 Iſa lv. 6 y Mat xxv 10 z Chap vi. 46 a Mat vii 23 & xxv 12

23 Then ſaid one unto him, Lord, are [s] there few
that be ſaved? And he ſaid unto them, 24 ¶ † Strive
to [t] enter in at the ſtrait gate for [u] many, I ſay unto
you, will ſeek to enter in, and ſhall not be able 25
[x] When once the maſter of the houſe is riſen up, and
[y] hath ſhut to the door, and ye begin to ſtand without,
and to knock at the door, ſaying, [z] Lord, Lord, open
unto us, and he ſhall anſwer, and ſay unto you, [a] I
know you not whence you are 26 Then ſhall ye be-
gin to ſay, We have eaten and drunk in thy preſence,

and thou hast taught in our streets 27 But he shall

say, I tell you, I know you not whence you are, [t] de-
part from me all ye workers of iniquity 28 [c] There
shall be weeping and gnashing of teeth, [d] when ye shall
see Abraham, and Isaac, and Jacob, and all the pro-
phets in the kingdom of God, and you *yourselves* thrust
out 29 And [e] they shall come from the east, and *from*
the west, and *from* the north, and *from* the south, and
shall sit down in the kingdom of God 30 And be-
hold, [f] there are last which shall be first, and there are
first which shall be last

t Ps vi 8 Mat xxv 41 — c Mat viii 12 xiii 42 & xx — d Mat viii 11 Mark xii — f Mat xix 30 & xx 16

v 23—30 We have here,

1 The question put to our Lord, *Are there few that shall be saved?* Perhaps the design of it was captious, to represent him as rigid and uncharitable, or it might be mere curiosity, many being more inquisitive who shall be saved, and who not, than about what they must do to secure their own salvation

2 Our Lord answers the question in a way which seemed most profitable for the enquirer, directing him at least to give diligence to ensure the salvation of his own soul

(1) His exhortation is, *Strive to enter in at the strait gate*, the way to heaven is difficult, ten thousand obstructions, both without and within, straiten the passage, great diligence and incessant prayer, therefore, are needful, that, strengthened by power from on high, we may be able to hold on, and to hold out, and so to run as to obtain the prize

(2) He enforces his exhortation by various motives, [1] *Many will seek to enter in, and shall not be able*, willing indeed to go to heaven, but unwilling to use the necessary means, resting in cold formality, or lazy endeavours, bound with the fetters of sloth, or blinded with pride and self-righteousness, and so mistaking the way, or coming short of the kingdom [2] If the present moment be neglected, it will shortly be too late The door of mercy through the gospel, which is now open, will shortly be shut, when Jesus the master of the house, in death or judgment, requires the sinner's soul, and then the most importunate cries will be unavailing it is now or never that prayer can profit us [3] Many who entertained the most confident hopes of heaven, will be found to have a lie in their right hand They will knock as if they had a right to admission, plead relation to Christ as their Lord, that they were constant attendants on his word, and communicants at his table, yet will Christ utterly disown them in that day, and drive them with indignation from his presence, as *workers of iniquity*, whatever pretences to religion they made, their hearts were not whole with him, their professions were hypocritical, and secret sins were harboured, delighted in, and gratified Doomed, therefore, to be thrust into the outer darkness, with every dreadful expression of horror and despair, with weeping, and gnashing of teeth, in vain shall they bewail their folly, and pining with envy, and vexation, shall behold the patriarchs, prophets, and saints of God in glory exalted, and enjoying those unutterable delights of the heavenly kingdom, from which themselves must be eternally excluded, the sight of which will aggravate every pang they feel How awful a scene! what diligence, what carefulness should it beget in us, that we come not into this place of torment! How jealous need we be over our hearts, that we rest not in outward privileges, and deceive not ourselves with vain hopes thousands have gone out of this world dreaming of heaven, and have awaked in hell

(3) Some shall be saved though *few*, comparatively speaking, in any one place or age, yet *many*, when collected into the great congregation and there, such as seemed the most unlikely, coming from Gentile lands, from the east, and from the west, and from the north, and from the south, and admitted into the church of the redeemed, whilst the Jewish people, who were *first* in privilege, shall be *last*, rejected for their impenitence, and the heathen, who were *last* in their call, shall be *first* in the kingdom *Note*, When we come to heaven, we shall meet many there whom we least expected, and miss many, of whom we entertained the most confident assurances

31 ¶ The same day there came certain of the Phari-
sees, saying unto him, Get thee out, and depart hence
for Herod will kill thee 32 And he said unto them,
Go ye and tell that fox, Behold, I cast out devils, and
I do cures to day and to morrow, and the third day [i] I
shall be perfected 33 Nevertheless, I must walk to-
day and to morrow, and the day following for it cannot
be that a prophet perish out of Jerusalem 34 [k] O Je-
rusalem, Jerusalem, [l] which killest the prophets, and
stonest them that are sent unto thee how often would
[k] I have gathered thy children together, as a hen *doth*
gather her brood [l] under *her* wings, and [m] ye would not?
35 Behold, [n] your house is left unto you desolate And
verily I say unto you, ye shall not see me, until the time
come when ye shall say, [o] Blessed *is* he that cometh in
the name of the Lord

i Heb ii 10 — h Mat xxiii 37 — 2 Chron xxxvi 15 Neh ix 26 — k 2 [illegible] — Ps xvii 8 — 1 Kings [illegible] — Mic [illegible] — o Ps cxviii 26

v 31—35 Christ's inveterate enemies are ceaseless in their malice, seeking to distress and destroy him

1 Certain Pharisees pretending regard for his safety, brought him information that his life was in danger from Herod either this was a contrivance of their own, who wanted to get rid of Christ, whose preaching and practice so reproved and cut them to the heart, or it may be, Herod employed them to drive Christ out of his dominions, being willing enough to have done him a mischief, but fearing the consequences of attempting to seize him, because of his interest in the people *Note*, It is no unusual artifice with wicked men to seek, by suggestions of danger, to deter the faithful from their duty

2 Christ defies Herod's menaces *Go tell that fox*, saith he, whose craft, treachery, and rapine were notorious, *Behold, I cast out devils, and do cures to day and to morrow*, not desisting from his work, nor intimidated with these threatnings, *and the third day I shall be perfected*, shortly my work will be finished, and by my sufferings and death I shall compleat the salvation of my people and till then, it is neither in the power of Herod, or any of the emissaries of hell, to stop me in my work, and take away my life *Nevertheless*, as my hour is not yet come, *I must walk to day and to morrow, and the day following*, continuing his ministry in Galilee, without fear of interruption *for* as my death, and the place of it, are fore-ordained of God, *it cannot be that a prophet perish out of Jerusalem*, where alone the great council sat, to whom it belonged to judge those who laid claim to the gift of prophecy, and to put those whom they counted impostors to death *Note*, (1) All the powers of earth or hell cannot hurt or destroy us, till the appointed time comes (2) The day of death will be the time when the faithful shall be perfected, a consummation devoutly to be wished for

3 On this occasion, at the mention of Jerusalem, Christ laments over her wickedness, and foretels the wrath ready to descend on that devoted city Not knowing the day of her visitation, she was abandoned to ruin, and too late would be convinced of his divine mission, and wish for a part in his salvation, when he should come shortly to execute his temporal judgments, or in the great day, to pour the vials of his eternal wrath on those who had rejected him

CHAP XIV

In this chapter we have, 1 *The cure which Christ wrought upon a man that had the dropsy, on the sabbath-day, and his justifying himself therein, against those who were offended at his doing it on that day*, ver 1—6 2 *A lesson of humility given to those who were ambitious of the highest rooms*, ver 7—11 3 *A lesson of charity to those who feasted the rich and did not feed the poor*, ver 12, 13, 14 4 *The success of the gospel foretold in the parable of the guests invited to a feast*, ver 15—24 5 *The great law of discipleship laid down, with a caution to all that will be Christ's disciples, to undertake it deliberately, and with consideration, and particularly to ministers, to retain their favour*, ver 25—35

1 AND it came to pass, as he went into the house
of one of the chief Pharisees to eat bread on
the sabbath day, that they watched him 2 And be-
hold, there was a certain man before him, which had
the dropsy 3 And Jesus answering, spake unto the
lawyers and Pharisees, saying, [a] Is it lawful to heal on
the sabbath day? 4 And they held their peace And
he took *him* and healed him, and let *him* go 5 And
answered them, saying, [b] Which of you shall have an
ass, or an ox fallen into a pit, and will not straightway
pull him out on the sabbath-day? 6 And they could
not answer him again to these things

a Chap xiii 14 — b Exod xxiii 5 Deut xxii 4 Chap xiii 15

v 1—6 Christ refused not the invitations of those he knew were his enemies, and though he was well aware of their malicious intentions, he behaved to them with all kindness and courtesy

1 He dined with a chief Pharisee on the sabbath-day, and there being present a pitiable object, who was swollen with a dropsy, they *watched* whether he would heal him, intending, if he did, to accuse him as a sabbath breaker

2 Christ, who knew their thoughts, interrogates them on the subject, Whether *it was lawful to heal on the sabbath-day?* But they observed a sullen silence, unwilling to preclude the accusation they meditated, by admitting it to be lawful, and yet not knowing how to maintain the unlawfulness of so good a deed

3 *He took* the man aside, *and healed him*, reducing in a moment his distended body, and sending him away perfectly cured

And

And in his own justification, and to their conviction and confusion, urges their own practice, to prove the lawfulness of such a work of charity. If they admitted that an ox or an ass fallen into a pit, should be lifted out on the sabbath-day, least it should perish there, how much more forcible was the argument for the cure of a diseased person, whose life was in danger? and how evident did it appear, that their zeal for the sabbath was mere hypocrisy, designed only to cover their malignity against him?

4 *They could not answer him again to these things*, their own conduct spoke their condemnation. *Note*, At Christ's bar every mouth shall be stopped.

7 ¶ And he put forth a parable to those which were
bidden, when he marked how they chose out the chief
rooms; saying unto them, 8 When thou art bidden
of any man to a wedding, sit not down in the highest
room; lest a more honourable man than thou be bidden
of him; 9 And he that bade thee and him, come and
say to thee, Give this man place; and thou begin with
shame to take the lowest room. 10 But [c] when thou
c Prov xxv 6 7 art bidden, go and sit down in the lowest room; that
when he that bade thee cometh, he may say unto thee,
Friend, go up higher: then shalt thou have worship in
the presence of them that sit at meat with thee. 11 For
[d] whosoever exalteth himself, shall be abased; and [e] he
d Job xxii 29 Psal xviii 7 Prov xxix 23, Chap xvi 15 & xviii 14 Jam iv 6. 1 Pet v 5 e Prov xv 33 that humbleth himself, shall be exalted. 12 ¶ Then
said he also to him that bade him, When thou makest a
dinner or a supper, call not thy friends, nor thy bre-
thren, neither thy kinsmen, nor *thy* rich neighbours; lest
they also bid thee again, and a recompense be made
thee. 13 But when thou makest a feast, [f] call the poor,
f Neh viii 12 Tobit iv. 7 the maimed, the lame, the blind: 14 And thou shalt
be blessed; for they cannot recompense thee: for thou
shalt be recompensed at the resurrection of the just.

v 7—14 Though our Lord was courteous, he was far above the flattery of compliment. When he saw occasion for rebuke, he would not, even in the company of persons most distinguished, refrain from faithful admonition.

1 He rebukes the guests for that affectation of preeminence which he observed among them, each coveting the most honourable seat at the table. Such pride would expose them to contempt, whilst humility was the way to honour: for they who assumingly thrust themselves into the seat of precedence which did not belong to them, might expect to be degraded, when a more honourable personage coming in, the master of the house would say, *Give this man place*; and this could not fail of covering with confusion the conceited intruder, who must go down lower, and expose himself to the contempt of the company. Much more to their honour would it be, humbly to take the lowest place, as ready to give the preference to others; for then the master, attentive to place his guests, according to their rank, would respectfully desire them to come up higher, and their modesty and humility would gain the regard and esteem of all that sit at table. And as this is the case among men, so is it also before God, *whosoever exalteth himself*, in a proud conceit of his own excellence above other men, *shall be abased*, treated with contempt and abhorrence by him who trieth the heart, and knows the true characters of men; *and he that humbleth himself*, under the deepest sense of his vileness and unworthiness, *shall be exalted* to the favour of God on earth, and to the enjoyment of his glory in heaven. *Note*, (1.) Pride is a sin alike odious in the sight of God and man. (2.) Modest diffidence gives a brighter lustre to real worth.

2 He rebukes the master of the house for his inviting the rich, and neglecting the poor. It bespeaks the pride, selfishness, and luxury of the heart, to make profuse entertainments, and invite only the wealthy, at whose tables we expect to be entertained in return. Such feasting is evil; it is an abuse of the creatures of God, and robbery of the poor: not that we are forbid welcoming our friends, or returning their visits: it is the profusion, which would render us incapable of relieving the indigent, the vain affectation of show, the ambition of keeping grand company, and the expectation of a recompence in kind, which our Lord condemns. He bids us, on the contrary, with charitable hospitality feed the poor, not sturdy beggars, for that is no charity, but an encouragement to idleness; *but the maimed, the lame, the blind*: these cannot indeed return the favour; but we shall be no losers, God will remember and reward these labours of love at *the resurrection of the just*.

15 ¶ And when one of them that sat at meat with
g Rev xix 9 him, heard these things, he said unto him, [g] Blessed *is*
h Mat xxii 2 he that shall eat bread in the kingdom of God. 16
i Prov ix 3 &c Then said he unto him, [h] A certain man made a great
supper, and bade many: 17 And [i] sent his servant at
supper-time to say to them that were bidden, Come, for
all things are now ready. 18 And they all with one
consent [k] began to make excuse. The first said unto k John v 40
him, [l] I have bought a piece of ground, and I must l 1 Tim vi 9 10
needs go and see it: I pray thee have me excused. 19
And another said, I have bought five yoke of oxen,
and I go to prove them: I pray thee have me excused.
20 And another said, I have married a wife, and there-
fore I cannot come. 21 So that servant came, and
shewed his lord these things. Then the master of the
house being angry, said to his servant, Go out quickly
into the streets and lanes of the city, and bring in hither
[m] the poor, and the maimed, and [n] the halt, and [o] the m Mat v 3. Jam ii 5
blind. 22 And the servant said, Lord, it is done as n Mic iv 6, 7 Zeph iii 19
thou hast commanded, and yet there is room. 23 And o John ix 39 Rev. iii 17 18
the Lord said unto the servant, Go out into [p] the high- p Prov i 20, &c
ways, and hedges, and [q] compel them to come in, that q Chap xxiv 29 Acts xvi 15 2 Cor v 20 2 Tim iv 2
my house may be filled. 24 For I say unto you, that r Mat xxi 43
[r] none of those men which were bidden, shall taste of
my supper.

v 15—24 Affected with the discourse of Christ, which breathed such humility and charity, one of the guests broke forth as in a transport, looking forward to the days of the Messiah, when they expected that all plenty, piety, and happiness would universally abound, and said, *Blessed is he that shall eat bread in the kingdom of God*. Christ immediately replied to this observation by a parable, drawn from the feast before them, and containing intimations which they would be very backward to receive; insinuating to them, that however great the Messiah's kingdom might be, the Jews in general would reject it, and the despised Gentiles chiefly partake of the privileges of the gospel.

1 *A certain man made a great supper, and bade many*. Christ is the master of the feast; all the riches of gospel-grace are provided by him for the entertainment of miserable sinners, and his invitation is free and gracious. He bids his servants say, whosoever will, let him *come, for all things are now ready*; the present moment is the accepted time, there must be no delay; and if we feel our want of pardon, peace, grace, and glory, we shall make none, but press eagerly to be fed with these heavenly provisions.

2 The guests gave the servants a cold reception, and pretended other engagements. The Jewish people in general rejected the gospel, and turned a deaf ear to the apostles and evangelists; and too many in every age resemble them, and find some frivolous excuse for their conduct. One had purchased a farm, and he must needs go and see it; another had bought five yoke of oxen, and he wanted to try them; and a third is just married, and therefore pleads, *I cannot come*. But the truth is, *I will not*; his wife would have found a welcome too, that need not have hindered him. *Note*, (1.) Any thing will serve for a hindrance to those who want an excuse; and the devil will take care that they shall not be at a loss, who have no inclination to duty. (2.) Hearts full of worldly cares, and set on amassing wealth, must needs be deaf to gospel-calls. (3.) The folly of the men of the world is great as their sin; for what trifles do they barter heaven! (4.) Inordinate affection to lawful comforts, even to our dearest relatives, may prove a dangerous stumbling-block in our way to glory.

3 The servants returned with grief to their master, and reported the repulse they had met with; and just indignation kindled in the master's bosom at the ingratitude and contempt shown to his gracious invitation. *Note*, (1.) Ministers carry their complaints to God against the souls among whom they have laboured in vain, and spent their strength for nought; and a fearful account will such despisers of the gospel shortly give. (2.) Abused mercy turns to fiercest wrath; rejection of the calls of grace must needs issue in ruin.

4 Though they who were invited refused to come, the feast shall not be lost. The master bids his servants *go into the streets and lanes of the city, and bring in the poor, the maimed, the halt, and the blind*; since the Scribes and Pharisees, with all the rich and noble among the Jews, rejected his salvation, the gospel was to be preached to the lowest of the people, many of whom were brought to the obedience of faith. And when the servants having executed their commission, reported that yet there was room, their Lord sends them *into the highways and hedges*, even to the Gentile world, to call the vilest sinners, and urge them to come in, assuring them of a hearty welcome. *Note*, (1.) The unbelief of the impenitent shall not prevent the promise of God from taking effect. Christ will have a church and people in the world, though the wise, mighty, and noble reject him. (2.) The gospel hath usually most success among those whom the proud, the wise, and self-righteous, despise, even the ignorant, the poor, the publicans and open sinners; nor must the servants think it any disparagement to themselves or their master, that of such is the kingdom of heaven. (3.) The compulsion which Christ's ministers must use is, the force of argument and

per

perſuaſion, not violence, or the civil power, which can only make men hypocrites (4) None are excluded from Chriſt who do not exclude themſelves, there is room, and we are welcome if we refuſe to come, our ruin lieth at our own door

5 He ſeals up the deſpiſers of the goſpel under wrath and reprobacy *I ſay unto you, that none of thoſe who were bidden, ſhall taſte of my ſupper* The unbelieving Jews, to whom the goſpel was firſt preached, and all who hear and reject the counſel of God againſt their own ſouls, are juſtly abandoned to the deluſions they have choſen, and left to periſh in their ſins

25 ¶ And there went great multitudes with him
and he turned, and ſaid unto them, 26 [s] If any man
come to me, [t] and hate not his father, and mother, and
wife, and children, and brethren, and ſiſters, [u] yea, and
his own life alſo, he cannot be my diſciple 27 And
[x] whoſoever doth not bear his croſs, and come after me,
cannot be my diſciple 28 For [y] which of you intend-
ing to build a tower, ſitteth not down firſt, and count-
eth the coſt, whether he have *ſufficient* to finiſh *it*?
29 Leſt haply after he hath laid the foundation, and
[z] is not able to finiſh *it*, all that behold *it*, begin to
mock him, 30 Saying, This man began to build, and
was not able to finiſh 31 Or [a] what king going to
make war againſt another king, ſitteth not down firſt,
and conſulteth whether he be able with ten thouſand
to meet him that cometh againſt him with twenty
thouſand? 32 Or elſe, while the other is yet a great
way off, he ſendeth an ambaſſage, and deſireth condi-
tions of peace 33 So likewiſe, whoſoever he be of
you, that forſaketh not all that he hath, he cannot be
my diſciple 34 ¶ [b] Salt *is* good [c] but if the ſalt have
loſt its favour, [d] wherewith ſhall it be ſeaſoned? 35 It
is neither fit for the land, nor yet for the dunghill,
but men caſt it out He that hath ears to hear, let
him hear

[s] Deut xiii 6 & xxxiii 9 Mat. x 37 [t] Rom ix. 13 [u] Rev xii. 11 [x] Chap ix 23 2 Tim iii 12 [y] Prov xxiv 27 [z] 2 John 8 [a] Prov xx 18 [b] Col iv 6 [c] Mat v 13 Mark ix 50 [d] Heb vi 4—6

v 25—34 Multitudes followed Chriſt, probably in hopes to ſhare in that temporal kingdom which they expected the Meſſiah would ſet up To undeceive them, he lets them know,

1 The terms of diſcipleſhip They will not find that eaſe, affluence, and honour, with which they flattered themſelves, but the very reverſe they muſt be ready to quit their neareſt and deareſt relations, when Chriſt's ſervice calls for them, muſt be content to leave all behind, and to be baniſhed from their beſt friends if parents commands come in competition with our duty to him, we muſt not heſitate whom we ſhall obey nay, our own lives muſt not be dear to us, when his glory requires us to lay them down The love of him muſt conſtrain us ſtronger than death, every croſs which he is pleaſed to lay upon us, cheerfully ſhould we take up, content to be nailed to it, if he ſo ordained And if without ſuch entire ſurrender of ourſelves to him, we cannot be his diſciples, much leſs may we think we belong to him, if we are afraid to diſoblige a friend or a relation for his ſake, if we cannot bear a name of infamy, or a badge of reproach Such as ſhrink from theſe leſſer trials, and are aſhamed to make profeſſion of him, will certainly never go with him to priſon, or to death

2 He exhorts his followers ſeriouſly and deliberately to weigh the difficulties and dangers, before they embark in his cauſe, leſt after having made a profeſſion, they ſhould expoſe themſelves to contempt, and bring heavier ruin upon their ſoul, by drawing back unto perdition, and this he illuſtrates by two compariſons, (1) By a man ſitting down to build a tower, who makes an eſtimate of the charge before he begins the fabric, leaſt otherwiſe, raſhly embarking in a work for which his abilities are not ſufficient, the unfiniſhed ruins ſhould expoſe him to contempt We have the tower of ſalvation to build on Jeſus, the ſure foundation, it will coſt us much labour, prayer, ſelf-denial, reproach, loſs, perhaps of life itſelf, ere it be finiſhed Before, therefore, we commence profeſſed diſciples, we ſhould well weigh the conſequences, whether we have really power from on high, divine faith, and a vital principle of grace, to carry us through Many have begun, and failed, and thereby expoſed themſelves to juſt contempt, for even the wicked world, to whom they return, will ridicule and deſpiſe thoſe who draw back from their holy profeſſion (2) By one King going to war againſt another Before he takes the field, he will weigh the danger, and conſider whether he is a match for his antagoniſt; and if he finds his ſtrength utterly unequal, it is wiſeſt, before matters are driven to extremities, to ſend ambaſſadors, and ſeek peace Such is our caſe each Chriſtian is a ſoldier, who muſt expect and prepare to endure *hardneſs* the powers of earth, corruption, and hell, under Satan, their king, are the *twenty thouſand* with whom we have to conflict Clothed, therefore, in the panoply of God, and ſupported with his might in the inner man, we ſhould go forth and the ſword once drawn we muſt never ſheath it till death But if deterred by difficulties, perſecutions, and ſufferings, we ſeek an ignominious peace with the world *which lieth in wickedneſs*, under the government of that wicked one, and inſtead of *forſaking all*, ſtagger in the hour of trial, the caſe is deſperate, we ſhall continue enſlaved by ſin, and cannot be Chriſt's diſciples

3 He warns them againſt apoſtacy, whether miniſters or people *Salt is good*, my goſpel, and they who diſpenſe it, are the ſalt of the earth, *but if the ſalt hath loſt its ſavour*, and thoſe who profeſs to ſpread the lively truths of God, adulterate the word, and grow degenerate in their temper and manners, *wherewith ſhall it be ſeaſoned*? The caſe appears deſperate, where ſuch rooted departure from the truth in practice and principle prevails; *it is neither fit for the land, nor yet for the dunghill*, ſuch perſons are not only uſeleſs, but noxious, and therefore *men caſt it out*, all good men abandon ſuch faithleſs profeſſors, and they ſhould be caſt out of the church, as they will infallibly be ſeparated eternally from the communion of the faithful in heaven *He that hath ears to hear let him hear*, and let him that thinketh he ſtandeth, take heed leſt he fall

CHAP XV.

Chriſt vindicates himſelf from the cavils of the Phariſees, offended at his converſing with publicans and ſinners ver 1, 2 *in three parables* 1 *Of the loſt ſheep*, ver 3—7. 2 *Of the loſt ſilver*, ver 8, 9, 10 3 *Of the prodigal ſon*, ver 11—32

1 THEN drew near unto him [a] all the publicans
and ſinners for to hear him 2 And the
Phariſees and ſcribes murmured, ſaying, [b] This man re-
ceiveth ſinners, and [c] eateth with them 3 ¶ And he
ſpake this parable unto them, ſaying, 4 [d] What man
of you having an hundred ſheep, if he [e] loſe one of
them, doth not leave the ninety and nine in the wilder-
neſs, and [f] go after that which is loſt, until he find it?
5 And when he hath found *it*, [g] he layeth *it* on his
ſhoulders, rejoicing 6 And when he cometh home,
he calleth together *his* friends and neighbours, ſaying
unto them, Rejoice with me, for [h] I have found my ſheep
which was loſt 7 I ſay unto you, that likewiſe joy
ſhall be in heaven over one ſinner that repenteth [i], more
than over ninety and nine juſt perſons, which need no
repentance 8 ¶ Either what woman having ten †
pieces of ſilver, if ſhe loſe one piece, doth not light a
candle, and ſweep the houſe, and ſeek diligently till ſhe
find *it*? 9 And when ſhe hath found *it*, ſhe calleth
her friends, and *her* neighbours together, ſaying, Rejoice
with me, for I have found the piece which I had loſt
10 Likewiſe I ſay unto you, There is joy in the pre-
ſence of the angels of God, over one ſinner that re-
penteth

[a] Mat ix 10 Chap v 29 [b] Mat xi 19 Chap xix 10 1 Tim i 15 [c] Acts xi 3 Gal ii 12. [d] Mat xviii 12 [e] Iſa liii 6. Jer l 6 [f] Ezek xxxiv 16. Chap xix 10 [g] Iſa xl 11 [h] 1 Pet. ii 10 25 [i] Chap v 32 † A Drachma was equal to a Roman Penny and worth ſeven pence Half penny

v 1—10 Offended, perhaps, with the hard ſayings of the former chapter, many of his attendants withdrew, and made way for another ſet of hearers

1 *The publicans and ſinners drew near to hear him* The *publicans* were uſually perſons of the moſt infamous character, and the *ſinners* were either public and notorious offenders, or it may be ſome of the heathen, or from the multitude of ſtrangers who dwelt there, the country was called *Galilee of the Gentiles*, theſe aſſembled around him, they needed ſuch a gracious Saviour

2 The proud Phariſees and Scribes hereupon expreſſed their diſpleaſure, offended, that one who profeſſed himſelf a prophet, ſhould deign to permit ſuch wretches to approach him, receive them with kindneſs, and ſit with them at the ſame table Their inſolent ſelf-conceit would have ſaid, *Come not near me*, but he, who came to be the ſinner's friend, did not diſdain their company, they were the loſt he came to ſave *Note*, The cenſure of the ſelf-righteous falls heavieſt uſually on the moſt excellent perſons, in their nobleſt exerciſes of charity

3 Chriſt vindicates himſelf from their reproaches, in two parables, and ſhews, that the higheſt glory would redound to God from the converſion of theſe ſinners, and joy fill the celeſtial hoſt, on that occaſion We have,

(1) The parable of the loſt ſheep, wherein we may obſerve, [1] The caſe of the miſerable ſinner, he is *loſt*, gone aſtray from God's fold, wandering endleſsly in mazes of ignorance and error; a ſtranger to all ſpiritual comfort and happineſs, running headlong to deſtruction, and ready to periſh everlaſtingly [2] The peculiar care of the Saviour towards his people in their loſt eſtate, like a ſhepherd who leaves his flock in the wilderneſs to ſeek one ſtraying ſheep, ſo doth the Lord purſue his wanderers he finds them when they do not ſeek him, takes them up in the arms of his grace, weak and impotent of themſelves to return, and brings them back to his fold with that effectual power and tender pity, which ſecures

them

them from all harm (3) There is greater joy in heaven over one such sinner recovered by sovereign grace, than *over ninety and nine just persons which need no repentance*, which seems to be spoken with a peculiar reference to the Pharisees who trusted that they were righteous, and needed no repentance These our Lord *left in the wilderness* of unregeneracy, to perish in their pride the conversion of one poor Gentile sinner, the recovery of the most notorious offender, was matter of greater rejoicing in heaven, and brought more glory to God, than that form of godliness in which they boasted

(2) The parable of the lost piece of money, which is nearly of the same import as the foregoing The *woman* represents the Lord, the possessor of all, the *silver*, the souls of men, infinitely more precious, the *nine pieces* design the Scribes and Pharisees, and all self-righteous persons, the *one lost piece*, the heathen, or any poor perishing sinner, sunk in the dregs of pollution, or lost in the dirt of worldly-mindedness and sensuality, *The candle* is the blessed gospel which shines in this dark place the world, where the sinner lies buried in corruption, *the sweeping the house* represents the diligence of the faithful ministers of Christ whose instrumentality he uses to seek after lost souls, and when he hath designs of grace towards a soul, he never ceases seeking him, till the means are made effectual to his conversion and salvation, and great is the joy arising from this happy event The angels of God rejoice in it, and the more desperate the case seemed, and the more unexpected the recovery, the more sensible is the pleasure To see the chief of sinners brought to repentance, raises their loudest songs of praise Those therefore, who made such objections to his receiving sinners, evidently shewed themselves destitute of a heavenly mind, and unlike the angels of God

11 ¶ And he said, A certain man had two sons
12 And the younger of them said to *his* father, [k] Father,
give me the portion of goods that falleth *to me* And
he divided unto them *his* living 13 And not many
days after, the younger son gathered all together, and
[l] took his journey into a far country, and there wasted
his substance with riotous living 14 And when he had
spent all, there arose a mighty [m] famine in that land,
and he began to be in want 15 And he went and
joined himself to a citizen of that country, and he sent
him into his fields to feed swine 16 And [n] he would
fain have filled his belly with the husks that the swine
did eat, and no man gave unto him 17 And when
he came to himself, he said, How many hired servants
of my father's have bread enough and to spare, and I
perish with hunger! 18 [o] I will arise and go to my
father, and will say unto him, Father, I have sinned against heaven, and before thee, 19 And am no more
worthy to be called thy son make me as one of thy
hired servants 20 And he arose, and came to his
father But when [q] he was yet a great way off, his
father saw him, and [r] had compassion, and ran and fell
on his neck, and kissed him 21 And the son said
unto him, Father, [s] I have sinned against heaven, and [t]
in thy sight, and [u] am no more worthy to be called thy
son 22 [x] But the father said to his servants, Bring
forth [y] the best robe, and put *it* on him, and put a
ring on his hand, and shoes on *his* feet 23 And
bring hither the fatted calf, and kill *it*, and let us eat
and be merry 24 For this my son [z] was dead, and is
alive again, he was lost, and is found And they began to be merry 25 Now his elder son was in the
field and as he came and drew nigh to the house, he
heard musick and dancing 26 And he called one of the
servants, and asked what these things meant 27 And
he said unto him, Thy brother is come, and thy father
hath killed the fatted calf, because he hath received
him safe and sound 28 And he was angry, and would
not go in therefore came his father out, and intreated
him 29 And he answering, said to *his* father, Lo,
these many years do I serve thee, neither transgressed I at
any time thy commandment, and yet thou never gavest
me a kid, that I might make merry with my friends
30 But as soon as this thy son was come, which hath
devoured thy living with harlots, thou hast killed for
him the fatted calf 31 And he said unto him, Son,
thou art ever with me, and all that I have is thine.
32 It was meet that we should make merry, and be
glad for this thy brother was dead, and is alive again,
and was lost, and is found

v 11—32 Yet farther, to shew how little cause the Scribes and Pharisees had to murmur at the favour shewn to publicans and sinners, he added a third beautiful parable, wherein miserable and wretched sinners may ever read the compassions of a pardoning God, and be engaged by the riches of his grace to return to the arms of his mercy

The certain man here spoken of, is God, the common Father of all the *two sons* are either the Jews, the elder brother, and the Gentiles, the younger, or rather, by the one are meant the Scribes and Pharisees, by the other the publicans and sinners, both, as descendants of Abraham, the children of God, in a covenant of peculiarity And to this latter sense, the occasion of the parable seems to direct us

The character of the miserable sinner is here drawn under the figure of the younger son We have,

1 His departure from home, and the miseries into which his extravagance brought him

(1) He was *impatient* of restraint, as young men usually are, wanted to get from *his father's eye*, conceited himself able to manage better for himself than his aged parent for him, and therefore forwardly demands, *Give me the portion of goods which falleth to me*, as if he had a right to challenge them as his due just such are we all by nature (1) Discontent under God's government, and affecting independency (2) Desirous to fly from him, and foolishly flattering ourselves that we can be hid (3) Puffed up with high imaginations of our own abilities and excellence (4) Looking upon God's gifts as our own property, for the use of which we are accountable to none (5) Coveting a present portion, and seeking all our happiness from the world, careless and unconcerned about our future state

(2) The father, though he might justly except to such a *forward demand*, divided *his substance*, and gave the younger son his share, evidently shewing, he was not that morose and harsh parent, which this headstrong youth probably represented him Thus God bestows liberally the bounties of his providence on the evil and unthankful, and leaves his own children for a while to the devices of their own hearts, that dire conviction may teach them their folly and their sin

(3) No sooner had he got his share, than in haste to be gone, he stayed but a few days to pack up his all, and took his journey into a far country, where he apprehended no rebuke from his watchful father, and there giving a loose to every appetite, he soon dissipated his fortune among women wine, and riotous living How exact the representation! (1) Such wanderers are we, as soon as we are born we go astray (2) In this alienation from God the sinner habitually continues, fulfilling the desires of the flesh and of the mind (3) We are enslaved by vile affections, and naturally devoted to those youthful lusts which war against the soul (4) Present gratification usually weighs with us more than any considerations about futurity (5) As extravagance and whoredom have the most direct tendency to rob us of our substance, much more will these, and the like sins, infallibly ruin our soul.

(4) Great were the miseries in which this prodigal now felt himself involved *When he had spent all*, which would not hold long in such bad company as he kept, *there arose a mighty famine in that land*, *and* as those on whom he had lavished his money, now dropped off from his acquaintance as the leaves in autumn, *he began to be in want*, without a morsel of bread to appease the cravings of hunger Reduced now to the utmost distress, without a farthing in his pocket, without a friend to assist him, necessity drives him to court the meanest drudgery to keep life and soul together, *he went and joined himself to a citizen of that country, and he sent him into his fields to feed swine*, yet even there he could not earn enough to satisfy his hunger, he envied the very swine their husks, and *would fain have filled his belly* with them, but could not, or was not permitted that favour, and *no man* had the least compassion for his case, or *gave unto him* the least morsel of sustenance such is the misery of the sinner (1) He is in *want* of all true comfort, and destitute of all grace, the favour of God, as the dew of heaven, is with-held, his hard heart produces nothing good, and he pines away in his iniquities (2) He is the vilest slave in nature, the devil is the citizen, in whose hard service he is employed he is like the swine, wallowing in the lusts of uncleanness, or groveling in worldly-mindedness (3) His soul is harrassed with raging desires, which none of his pursuits can gratify, for they who depart from God, to seek satisfaction in the creature, must feel the cravings of incessant hunger, and find nothing but husks before them The world, and all the things of it, can provide no solid food for an immortal soul

Some give a different interpretation of the word They suppose the *citizen of that country* to be a *Pharisaical legal preacher*, to whom the awakened sinner flies under his distress He sets him to work *in his fields*, directs him to moral duties, to the law, to the *conditions of the covenant*, *in order to obtain peace* with God, but the husks of self-righteousness are unsatisfactory, conscience is unappeased, guilt unatoned for, corruption unmortified, and he continues a companion of swine

2 Distress at last brought him to consider the wofulness of

his state, and what possibility there yet was of preventing his dying for want in that strange land. *When he came to himself*, for hitherto he had acted as a madman, or one possessed, he began to reflect on the plenty which reigned in his father's family, where there was not a hired servant, but had *bread enough and to spare*: *and I*, says he, *perish with hunger*. He resolves therefore to return, and cast himself on his father's mercy, acknowledging his sin against heaven and against him, owning it his just desert to be disowned as a son, and begging it, as the highest favour he dares ask, to be admitted among the hired servants. And what he resolved, he immediately executed; his urgent want admitted not of delay. Happy the soul in whom such a gracious purpose is stirred up! *Note*, (1.) Every impenitent sinner is *beside himself*; all his thoughts, words, and ways bespeak him mad; fancying himself wise, great, happy, when infatuated, poor, and miserable; and putting a value upon the straws of his cell, the gain and pleasures of this world, as if they were sterling gold, whilst he is insensible to all the eternal glories that are above. (2.) In our most desperate estate, whilst there is life there is hope; it is never too late to return to God; the vilest sinner may find mercy, the most abominable be converted and changed. (3.) Afflictions are often made the blessed means of driving our souls to God: softened by the rod of correction the heart is made tender, and disposed to listen to the words of wisdom, which were before despised and rejected. (4.) Though the conversion of the soul to God is alone effected by the power of divine grace, yet he works in such a way, as that it is our own choice, and the result of reason, consideration, and conviction. He opens our understandings to see our true state, and beholding the inevitable ruin which is before us, we are driven by mere necessity to Christ for pardon and salvation. (5.) None need perish who return unto God right humbly; there is with him grace abounding, *bread enough, and to spare*. (6.) In our returns to God, we must all adopt the prodigal's spirit and language: *we have sinned* more than we can express or conceive; we should reflect upon all the aggravations of our sin, how ungratefully we have behaved towards the Father of mercies, how impiously affronted the Most High, whose throne is in the heavens, that so we may truly loath ourselves for all our abominations. (7.) We are never truly humbled for sin, till we feel and own our unworthiness of the least mercy, and our just desert of being utterly abandoned and rejected of God; so that if the least favour be shewn us, we shall acknowledge it with deepest gratitude. (8.) Vile and wicked as we may have been, we must not forget that endearing name of *Father*, to encourage our hopes, to awaken genuine and godly sorrow, and to embolden our faith to approach him. (9.) When God is working with our hearts, all depends upon our immediate obedience to his calls and warnings. To-day, whilst it is called to-day, harden not your heart.

3. His reception was unspeakably beyond his expectations. *He came to his Father*, and was welcomed with open arms. Let offended parents learn such compassions towards their returning prodigals. *When he was yet a great way off*, as if the Father's longing eyes had been looking out for his coming, *he saw him*, and though in rags and nakedness, emaciated and changed, so that no other could scarce have known him, he discerned the long-lost child. Melted with compassion at his piteous case, yet overjoyed once more to behold him, *he ran* with eagerness, *fell on his neck*, embracing him with the warmest emotions of parental tenderness, *and kissed him*, the token of welcome, the seal of pardon. Such are the tender mercies of our God toward poor sinners; he sees, well pleased, the first rising desire in our hearts towards him; he pities our misery, though we have brought it upon ourselves, and have so highly dishonoured him; his arms of grace are open to receive us; he will not upbraid our folly, but is ready instantly to pardon our sin, and through Christ Jesus to forgive and forget all that is past, sealing our pardon, and speaking peace to our souls. The prodigal, deeply affected with his own vileness, and now more deeply struck with his ingratitude than ever, under the resentment of such amazing tenderness as his father shewed him, with grief and shame unfeigned, cries, *Father, I have sinned*, &c. The sense of God's pardoning love, instead of making the sinner proud, sinks him to the dust, and makes him abhor himself for having ever offended a God so gracious. The son would have proceeded, but the father's heart is so overjoyed, he prevents him with blessings and loving kindness, commanding the most splendid dress and the noblest entertainment to be provided for him. So far is the Lord from upbraiding poor returning penitents, that their iniquities, like a cloud, are blotted out, and glory and honour are put upon them.

[1.] The father commands his servants to bring forth *the best robe*, to put *a ring on his hand, and shoes on his feet*, that his nakedness may not only be covered, and his filthy garments taken away, but that he may be adorned as became a dear child of that noble family. And how much more glorious the provision which Jesus hath made for his returning prodigals! *A robe of righteousness*, perfect and everlasting, is provided for them, arrayed in which, they appear without spot even in the presence of God. Their filthy garments of sin are taken away, and beautiful in holiness impressed, as well as righteousness imputed, they all are seen to be the children of a King. *The ring*, the seal of reconciliation and union, the spirit of Jesus gives, sealing them unto the day of redemption; and shod with the preparation of the gospel of peace, they run the way of God's commandments with delight.

[2.] The noblest entertainment is ordered. *Bring hither the fatted calf, and kill it, and let us eat and be merry*. Hungry and faint, he had long been a stranger to such rich provision, and pining in want and wretchedness, was a stranger to joy: but now he shall be fed to the full, and partake of the general gladness which his return occasions. *Note*, (1.) In the gospel, the richest provision is made for the hungry; Christ with all his fulness is provided, and faith feeds upon him, to the strengthening and refreshing of the soul. (2.) They who are brought by grace to taste of the sweetness of God's love, will truly feel, that every thing compared with this, is but husks. (3.) There is joy among all the household of God when one poor sinner returns to join the happy family.

[3.] The cause of the father's joy is this, *My son was dead and is alive again; he was lost, and is found*; he was as bad as dead, yea, worse than dead, whilst living in riot and excess, lost to his family, undone himself; but his return is life from the dead. *Note*, (1.) Every impenitent sinner in the midst of life is in death, spiritually dead to God, and ready to suffer the wages of eternal death in hell. (2.) The soul lost in sin, is lost for ever, unless recovered by sovereign grace. (3.) Though God's dearest children may lie down in common with others, sunk under guilt, and enslaved by corruption, yet in God's purposes they are still his, and this blessed and happy change shall pass upon them. The dead shall live, the lost be found.

4. The family readily joined the master of the house, rejoicing with him on the present happy occasion. The elder son alone appeared discontented; he was in the field when his brother returned, and heard with surprize, as he drew near to the house, the music and dancing. Enquiring of one of the servants, he soon learns the occasion, and expresses his disgust and discontent against his father's behaviour, as if the kindness shewn to his brother was an injury done to himself, who, he conceives, had deserved so much better at his father's hand. This character properly belonged to the Pharisees, and is applicable to all who are influenced by the same spirit of pride and self-righteousness. They are *in the field* of this world, in a state of unregeneracy, the slaves of earth, minding worldly things, working for life, and expecting to receive the harvest of eternal glory as the fruit of their own labours. They *draw nigh to the house*, the church of God, in profession, but never enter it by a spiritual union with the head of the church, Christ Jesus. *They hear the music and dancing*, the sweet sound of the great and precious promises, which makes the hearts of the miserable and guilty dance for joy; and strangers to this divine consolation themselves, they are vexed that any others should partake of it, and *angry*, that those should be admitted to the enjoyment of all the riches of his grace who have behaved so profligately, and be put on a level with themselves, who have, as they conceit, deserved so well at God's hands. *They will not go in*, not submitting to the righteousness, not content to receive the salvation of God freely, as lost and undone, as much as the vilest of mankind. In vain the Lord, by the ministry of the word, remonstrates with them on their perverseness, and urges upon them the necessity of a better righteousness than their own, *intreating* them to accept of that provided by the Redeemer, and thus come in and partake of the feast. They vaunt their own meritorious services, and in their own conceit fancy *they never transgressed at any time the commandments*, and therefore have a claim to the divine favour. They cannot regard publicans as their *brethren*, and think the kindness of God to perishing sinners is injustice to them, and unbecoming him; that these, instead of being received into his arms, should smart under his rod, and at least only be received into a lower place, after having done long penance for their offences.

Some suppose that *the elder brother* represents a gracious man, who having himself escaped from the grosser pollutions that are in the world, is apt to entertain too high thoughts of himself, and too little compassion toward such as have more grossly offended. To avoid which, we should learn, (1.) To entertain the lowliest thoughts of ourselves, and especially to watch against spiritual pride. (2.) Never to complain of God as *unjust* to us, but to acknowledge ourselves *unworthy* of the least of all his mercies. (3.) Not to harbour unkindness against, and treat with severity, those who may have dishonoured their profession by their unfaithfulness, but to be happy to give them again the right hand of fellowship, whenever they return to God. (4.) To rejoice in the gifts and graces of those who have been most eminent sinners, and not to envy them their distinguished mercies, though they may now far outshine and eclipse ourselves.

5. The father silences and rebukes his unreasonable murmurs. *Son, thou art ever with me*; the Scribes and Pharisees, or the Jewish people, enjoyed peculiar privileges, the ordinances

of

of worſhip, and the ſpecial preſence of God in the midſt of them, *and all that I have is thine*, if by their unbelief they did not cut themſelves off, the mercy ſhewn to Gentiles, to the chief of ſinners, would prove no diminution of the favours they ſhould enjoy *It was meet that we ſhould make merry and be glad for this thy brother was dead and is alive again, and was loſt and is found*, the converſion of the Gentiles and other notorious ſinners, dead in treſpaſſes, and ready to periſh for ever, ſo far from being a ground of diſcontent, ſhould be to all matter of rejoicing *Note*, (1) They who are truly God's children, may be aſſured that *all things* are theirs, all ſpiritual bleſſings in time and in eternity (2) The abounding grace of God is never exhauſted by the myriads who partake of it the happineſs of others is no diminution of our own, but rather increaſes our delight (3) Whatever God doth is well done, every murmur muſt be ſilenced before him, and in all the diſpenſations of his providence and grace, he is ever to be acknowledged as righteous, juſt, and good

CHAP XVI

We have here, 1 The right uſe of worldly enjoyments repreſented in the parable of the unjuſt ſteward, ver 1—13 2 *A reproof of the Phariſees for their covetouſneſs*, ver 14—18 3 *The danger of ſetting our hearts on an earthly portion, illuſtrated in the parable of the rich man and Lazarus*, ver 19—31

1 AND he ſaid alſo unto his diſciples, There was
a certain rich man which had a ſteward, and
the ſame was accuſed unto him that he had waſted his
goods 2 And he called him, and ſaid unto him,
How is it that I hear this of thee? give an account of
thy ſtewardſhip. for thou mayeſt be no longer ſteward
3 Then the ſteward ſaid within himſelf, What ſhall I
do? for my lord taketh away from me the ſtewardſhip
I cannot dig, to beg I am aſhamed 4 I am reſolved
what to do, that when I am put out of the ſtewardſhip,
they may receive me into their houſes 5 So he called
every one of his lords debtors unto him, and he ſaid un-
to the firſt, How much oweſt thou unto my lord? 6
And he ſaid, An hundred † meaſures of oil And he
ſaid unto him, Take thy bill, and ſit down quickly, and
write fifty 7 Then ſaid he to another, And how much
oweſt thou? And he ſaid, An hundred ‡ meaſures of
wheat And he ſaid unto him, Take thy bill, and
write fourſcore 8 And the lord commended the un-
juſt ſteward, becauſe he had done wiſely for the chil-
dren of this world are in their generation wiſer than [a]
the children of light 9 And I ſay unto you, [b] Make
to yourſelves friends of the ‖ mammon of unrighteouſ-
neſs, that when ye fail, they may receive you into ever-
laſting habitations 10 [c] He that is faithful in that
which is leaſt, is faithful alſo in much and he that is
unjuſt in the leaſt, is unjuſt alſo in much 11 If there-
fore ye have not been faithful in the unrighteous mam-
mon, who will commit to your truſt the true *riches*?
12 And if ye have not been faithful in that which is
another man's, who ſhall give you that which is your
own? 13 ¶ No ſervant can ſerve two maſters for
either he will hate the one and love the other, or elſe
he will hold to the one, and deſpiſe the other Ye can-
not ſerve God and mammon 14 And the Phariſees
alſo, [e] who were covetous, heard all theſe things and
they derided him 15 And he ſaid unto them, Ye are
they which juſtify yourſelves before men, but [f] God
knoweth your hearts for [g] that which is highly eſteem-
ed amongſt men, is abomination in the ſight of God
16 [h] The law and the prophets *were* until John [i] ſince
that time the kingdom of God is preached, and [k] every
man preſſeth into it 17 And [l] it is eaſier for heaven
and earth to paſs, than one tittle of the law to fail
18 Whoſoever putteth away his wife, and marrieth
another, committeth adultery and whoſoever marrieth
her that is put away from *her* huſband, committeth
adultery

V 1—18 To direct us in the right improvement of worldly wealth, we have here,

1 The parable of the unjuſt ſteward God is our maſter and lord all who are intruſted with any of his gifts, are his ſtewards, and ſhould improve them to his glory This man was accuſed of waſting his maſter's goods, and how juſtly liable are we to the ſame charge? How often have we abuſed the ſubſtance we have enjoyed, and the abilities we have been bleſt with, to God's diſhonour? In conſequence of his ill management, he is called to an account, ordered to leave the ſervice and a terrible reckoning will there be for us, if, hurried away by death, we are called to God's bar, cut off in the midſt of our ſins, and baniſhed for ever from his preſence Too lazy to dig for his maintenance, too proud to beg, he reſolves, by deeper frauds, to ſecure for himſelf a maintenance, and calling privately his lord's debtors, whoſe accounts were in his hands, he agreed with them to draw a new ſtate of their debts, abating twenty meaſures of wheat to one, and fifty of oil to another, thus endeavouring to make them his friends, that, when he was diſmiſſed from his lord's ſervice, he might have their houſes to receive him *Note*, (1) One ſtep in ſin always tends to lead on to farther abominations (2) Pride and lazineſs often drive men to the moſt wicked methods to ſupply their wants, unable to bear the labours of honeſt induſtry for a ſubſiſtence, or to ſubmit to aſk relief (3) They who truſt too much to ſtewards, and ſeldom inſpect their own accounts, will uſually ſuffer for it

2 The Lord commended the unjuſt ſteward's conduct, not as truly laudable in itſelf, but as an inſtance of foreſight, care, and contrivance, worthy imitation in a better way, *for the children of this world*, ſuch as this man was, who place their happineſs in earth and a portion here below, *are in their generation wiſer*, act more prudently, and ſhew greater induſtry to ſecure worldly advantages, *than the children* do to obtain the infinitely more momentous acquiſitions of grace and glory Let us go to them, therefore, to learn, and be aſhamed to ſee ourſelves outdone in diligence by thoſe who purſue a periſhing world, when we have at ſtake the intereſt of an immortal ſoul and an awful eternity

3 Chriſt applies the parable to his diſciples *I ſay unto you, Make to yourſelves friends of the mammon of unrighteouſneſs*, employ your worldly goods in ſuch a way, as ſhall be to your own advantage in the day of judgment, *that when ye fail*, and at death this periſhing world is left behind with all its enjoyments, *they may receive you into everlaſting habitations*, they who have received the comfort of your bounty, God's poor ſaints, or Chriſt and God himſelf, who will reward ſuch works of faith, and labours of love, with everlaſting glory *Note*, (1) This world's wealth is called *the mammon of unrighteouſneſs*, or *of deceit*, becauſe uſually it is abuſed to the vileſt purpoſes, and gotten by unjuſt and deceitful means (2) The only way of turning thoſe riches to our advantage, which others abuſe to their ruin, is by employing them for the glory of God, and the good of our fellow-creatures, and then they will be bleſſings (3) At death all things fail us, nothing of our earthly affluence can go down with us to the grave, unleſs we have ſent our treaſures before us, they can then afford us no ſatisfaction (4) Our one great buſineſs here below is to ſecure for ourſelves the everlaſting habitations, and though no money can purchaſe a manſion in glory, yet will they, who have laid out their talents in God's bleſſed ſervice, find themſelves hereafter repaid with the richeſt intereſt

4 Our Lord enforces his exhortation by the following arguments, (1) That the miſimprovement of the gifts of God's providence muſt effectually exclude them from the treaſures of his grace, for as a ſervant who is faithful in a little matter, gains our confidence to be entruſted with more, ſo where he is unjuſt in trifles, no prudent maſter would care to employ him in matters of greater importance If therefore we are unfaithful in the abuſe of worldly things, it cannot be thought we ſhould make a better improvement of the nobler talents, the means of divine wiſdom and grace, and therefore theſe *true riches* he will juſtly with-hold from us, (2) and if we have behaved as diſhoneſt ſtewards in that which God hath entruſted us with, and which is not our own, but his, how can it be expected that we ſhould poſſeſs that *good part*, the riches of grace, which moſt properly may be called *our own*, becauſe once poſſeſſed, it ſhall never be taken *from us*? (3) It is impoſſible to ſerve two maſters, God and mammon, becauſe their demands being oppoſite and contradictory, ſo far as we love and ſerve the world, we muſt hate and diſobey God and on the other hand, if we love and ſerve him, we muſt be dead to the world, and ready to forego all its honours, intereſts, pleaſures, and eſteem, whenever they ſtand in competition with his glory God requires the heart, he cannot ſuffer a rival, nor will admit of an allowed partition to attempt reconciling the inconſiſtent ſervices of God and mammon, is but the devil's aſk to enſure our ruin

5 The Phariſees were highly offended with truths which touched them ſo nearly Their character was drawn in the unjuſt ſteward, and their covetous, worldly minded hearts, under all their moſt plauſible guiſe of religion, were the ſlaves of mammon they treated him therefore with the greateſt diſdain and contempt *Note*, (1) The inordinate love of the world is the bane of many a fair profeſſor (2) When the word of God preſſes the conſcience hard, the obſtinate ſinner often affects to deſpiſe, and turn off with a laugh, what he feels himſelf unable to anſwer (3) If we are treated with inſult and

deriſion

† The Batus contained nine gallons three quarts Ezek xlv 11 14
‡ The Homer contained fourteen buſhels and a pottle
a John xii 36 Eph v 8 1 Theſ v 5
b Dan iv 27 Matt vi 19 & xix 21 Chap xi 41 1 Tim vi 19
‖ Or riches
c Chap xix 17
d Matt vi 24
e Matt xxiii 14
f Pſ vii 9
g 1 Sam xvi 7
h Matt xi 12 13
i Ibid iii 2
k Chap vii 29
l Pſ cii 26 Iſa li 6 Matt v 18 1 Pet i 25
m Matt v 32 & xix 9 Mark x 11 1 Cor vii 10, 11

derision by those to whom we minister the gospel, Jesus our master endured the like treatment before us.

6. Christ sharply rebukes their hypocrisy and worldly-mindedness. He despised their reviling, yet warns them of their ruin, that they might yet repent of their sins before it was too late. *Ye are they which justify yourselves before men*, pretending the strictest piety and most scrupulous devotion, *but God knoweth your hearts*, that they are full of deadly poison, of pride, envy, covetousness, falsehood, and oppression: *for that which is highly esteemed among men*, these pompous shews of exterior sanctity, *is abomination in the sight of God*, who sees the odious principles which actuate your whole conduct, and abhors all your pretended services. *Note*, (1.) The most rigid services of formal religion, instead of justifying men before God, render them only the more abhorred. (2.) The opinion of the world is a very fallacious rule of judgment: usually the most admired characters in the eye of men, are in his regards an abomination; and they who are set up as patterns of piety, will be found in fact a sink of iniquity.

7. He turns to the poor publicans and sinners, whom the Pharisees despised, encouraging them to press into that kingdom which his grace had opened to them. The Old Testament dispensation was now at an end, since the preaching of John the Baptist; the prophecies concerning the Messiah were about to receive their accomplishment, and the free grace of the gospel to be universally published through the world, when the distinction of Jew and Gentile should cease. Every man therefore, without exclusion of any sinners, whatever crimes he may have committed, is welcome to the Saviour, and sure to find mercy. And these glad tidings engaged the hearts of many, whom the self-righteous Pharisees despised, to press into it amidst all opposition. *Note*, They must strive against the world who would enter into heaven.

8. He precludes an objection which his self-righteous enemies would be ready to start, that he meant to invalidate the authority of the divine law. No. The frame of heaven and earth shall sooner be dissolved than one tittle of the law can fail; all the prophecies, types, and figures, must receive their accomplishment, the precepts, in their true spiritual meaning, were now more than ever explained by Christ's preaching, and magnified by his own obedience to them; and, far from admitting a laxer system of moral duty, this holy law must abide the unchangeable rule of righteousness, and conformity to it would now be enforced by the strongest motives: as for instance in the article of marriage: divorce under the law of Moses was permitted to prevent greater evils, but under the gospel it is entirely prohibited, and marriage restored to its primitive institution, nothing being admitted as a plea for its dissolution but unfaithfulness to the marriage-bed. Whosoever therefore for any other cause putteth away his wife, and marries again, is in adultery; as is he also who shall marry her who is divorced. The gospel, wherever it is truly received, strikes at the root of corrupt affections, and engages us to walk not after the flesh, but after the spirit.

19 ¶ There was a certain rich man, m which was
m Ps. lxxiii. 5, &c. clothed in purple and fine linen, and fared sumptuously
every day. 20 And there was a certain beggar named
Lazarus, n which was laid at his gate full of sores, 21
And desiring to be fed with the crumbs which fell from
the rich man's table: moreover, the dogs came and
licked his sores. 22 And it came to pass that o the
o Job xxi. 25, 26. beggar died, and was carried by the angels into Abra-
ham's bosom: p the rich man also died, and was buried.
23 And in hell he lift up his eyes, being in torments,
p Chap. xiii. 28. and q seeth Abraham afar off, and Lazarus in his bosom.
24 And he cried and said, Father Abraham, have mercy
on me, and send Lazarus, that he may dip the tip of his
q Zech. xiv. 12. finger in water, and r cool my tongue; for s I am tor-
r Is. lxvi. 24. Mark ix. 44. mented in this flame. 25 But Abraham said, Son, re-
member that t thou in thy life time receivedst thy good
things, and likewise Lazarus evil things: but now he is
comforted, and thou art tormented. 26 And besides
all this, between us and you there is a great gulf fixed:
so that they which would pass from hence to you, can-
not; neither can they pass to us, that *would come* from
thence. 27 Then he said, I pray thee therefore, father,
that thou wouldest send him to my father's house: 28
For I have five brethren, that he may testify unto them,
lest they also come into this place of torment. 29
u Is. viii. 20. &c. Abraham saith unto him, u They have Moses and the
prophets, let them hear them. 30 And he said, Nay,
father Abraham: but if one went unto them from the
dead, they will repent. 31 And he said unto him, If
w John xii. 10, 11. they hear not Moses and the prophets, w neither will they
be persuaded, though one rose from the dead.

v. 19—31. This parable seems to be particularly designed to rebuke the pride of the Jews, who, enriched with outward privileges, treated the poor Gentiles with disdain, as unworthy a place among the dogs of their flock; and yet there was grace in store for the poor diseased sinners whom they despised, whilst, through their unbelief and impenitence, they themselves would be rejected and ruined. It is also more generally applicable to what we see sadly verified every day, that rich epicures wallow in luxury, whilst God's dear children pine under want and hunger, whose end will be as it is here represented; where the veil is taken off from the world to come, and we behold the glories of the one, and the unutterable miseries of the other.

1. The state of a rich wicked man is set before us. *There was a certain rich man*, whose fortune enabled him to gratify every appetite. He appeared in the most splendid robes, equalling the majesty of princes, *clothed in purple and fine linen*; and his table was spread with every delicacy, *he fared sumptuously every day*. It may be said, Where is the harm of this? he was born to his estate, and the expence was no more than he could afford. Admit the fact. The harm was not in the use, but the abuse, of the creatures of God. He lived a life of sensuality, and sat unconcerned about the miseries of others. And it is designed to teach us, (1.) That this world's riches are often given to those who know not God, and that his love and favour are never to be judged of by outward things. (2.) That wealth and affluence are dangerous to the soul, and, affording the means to gratify men's bestial appetites, often plunge them in perdition and destruction.

2. The state of a poor godly man. He is called *Lazarus*, and to the miseries of poverty were added the more afflicting portion of a nauseous disease: wanting a morsel of bread, overspread with ulcers, without even rags to cover them, unable to walk, he is carried to the rich man's gate, and laid on the cold ground, desiring to be fed, if but with the crumbs which fell from the table. We hear no complaints, no murmuring at his condition: he was reduced to want, and not ashamed to beg; but, for what appears, he begged in vain; either his requests were refused, or, which amounted to the same thing, neglected and disregarded: but the dogs, possessed of more humanity than their master, came and licked his sores. Behold here the condition of a dear saint of God, and learn of him, (1.) Not to estimate a man's spiritual state by his afflictions: for it is often seen, that those whom the Lord most loveth he is pleased most severely to exercise. (2.) Patient submission to God's providential chastisements is a gracious proof of our adoption. (3.) The cries of the poor, which have been rejected or unnoticed, will by and by be remembered to the confusion of those who thus unkindly treated them. (4.) They will have a grievous account to answer for, who have spent more on their dogs than they ever gave to the necessitous, and fed them well fed, when many of their fellow-creatures are famishing.

3. Death at last came with friendly hand to remove at once all the poor beggar's miseries. Emaciated with hunger and disease, worn down with pain and misery, he closed his eyes, and bid adieu to human wretchedness, seeking a refuge in the grave, where the wicked cease from troubling. We hear of no burial given him: probably some hole was dug to remove the nusance from the gate, and, buried with the burial of an ass, not a friend followed the bier, not a tear was dropped over the grave: but he rests in peace, and now his eternal triumph begins: attending angels, who minister to the heirs of salvation, and hover round their dying beds, received the departing spirit, and, on their wings mounting to the skies, shouted aloud, Lift up your heads ye gates, and be ye lift up ye everlasting doors, that an heir of glory may come in. Led to his seat on high, admitted to the richest entertainment of that blest world, he is placed next to Abraham, and receives that distinguished honour of leaning on the patriarch's bosom. What a glorious prospect does this present! amidst all our present evil, how should such a hope support and comfort us! Death must be the farthest limits of a believer's sufferings; beyond the grave, all is happiness eternal and bliss uninterrupted.

4. *The rich man also died, and was buried.* Probably his funeral was pompous, as his living was grand. A noble tomb received the corpse, and spices and perfumes made the clods of the valley sweet unto him, whilst perhaps charity wept on the monument, and the flattering marble proclaimed his munificence, liberality, and every virtue that ever yet adorned man. How vain this pageantry! to which the body is now insensible, and the soul, ah! whither is it fled? *In hell he lift up his eyes, being in torments*, the just punishment of his abused affluence: and now how changed are circumstances! He sees, with astonishment, *Abraham afar off*, and *Lazarus*, the poor despised Lazarus, *in his bosom*, admitted to this state of highest honour and dignity. *Note*, (1.) The misery of the wicked, and the happiness of the just, immediately commence at their death. (2.) Every sight in hell is aggravating; even the prospect of heaven before the damned can only torment them with the view of that glory into which they must never enter.

5. In this fearful situation we have the rich man's request. *He cried*, with earnestness and importunity, extorted by the pangs he

he felt How different from the songs of riot that before echoed through his palace! *Father Abraham, have mercy on me* perhaps in his cups he had ridiculed the old story of Abraham; or it may be he had depended upon his outward privileges as descended from him, but now found how vain were his expectations *Note*, Many, who have never prayed before, will pray loud enough in hell, but pray in vain His request seems small, *Send Lazarus, that he may dip the tip of his finger in water, and cool my tongue, for I am tormented in this flame* how is his proud crest fallen? he who did not give this poor beggar a crumb from his table now would fain crave a drop of water at his hands He little thought once he should be so reduced Observe, (1) His complaint, *I am tormented in this flame* Damned sinners have no hing but wrath before them, that preys like fire upon their souls, as much as their bodies are tortured by the everlasting burnings They who will not hear and fear, and do no more wickedly, in this day of mercy, will then feel, when every pang will be embittered with despair (2) The day is near, when they who despised the people of God would be glad to receive from them the least favours

6 Abraham's answer is most confounding and unbending for in hell no requests are granted, not even a drop of water to cool a flaming tongue They who neglect the day of grace have nothing before them but misery, without abatement, and without end *Son, remember that thou in thy life-time receivedst thy good things, and likewise Lazarus evil things, but now he is comforted, and thou art tormented* (1) He addresses him as a *son*, the remembrance of which relation aggravated the guilt of his degenerate conduct Our abused privileges will increase the measure of our guilt (2) He bids him *remember*, for conscience then will be awake, and self-tormenting reflections embitter every pang The sinner will remember every means of grace he hath trifled with, every call of God he hath slighted, every affliction which he hath misimproved, every blessing he hath abused (3) He reminds him of the *good things* which he had received, and misapplied, unthankful for them, placing his happiness in them, prostituting them to the basest purposes of serving his lusts and pleasures, and, as he reckoned these during life his chief good, he had his all in hand, and nothing to expect after death but wrath to the uttermost (4) He leads him to reflect on the *evil things* Lazarus had received, which patiently he had born, though denied at his gate a crumb which fell from the table (5) He bids him now observe how the tables are turned *he is comforted*, the miseries of a child of God, however sharp, are, comparatively speaking, light afflictions, which are but for a moment death will put an end to every sorrow, and instantly his everlasting bliss will commence *But thou art tormented* the triumphing of the wicked is but for a moment, they can carry nothing with them into the grave, and the joys and delights, in which they wallowed before, will only make the change more terrible, when they are driven into the everlasting burnings, where there is weeping and wailing and gnashing of teeth (6) He leaves him without hope of mercy, or prospect of the least relief for, *besides all this, between us and you there is a great gulf fixed*, impassable on either side, *so that they who would pass from hence to you cannot* if a glorified saint wished to afford the least relief to a damned sinner, it would be in vain not that he will ever feel such a desire, but will approve and applaud the justice of God in their eternal torment *Neither can they pass to us that would come from thence* when once the pit of hell hath closed its mouth upon the miserable soul, despair seals up the door of mercy, no gleam of hope ever reaches that dire abode the decree once gone forth is irreversible, as the tree falleth it must lie How awful! how awakening the thought! Sinner, hear and tremble The door of mercy yet is not shut against thee Oh flee quickly thither Cry mightily to God, if yet there may be hope, in a moment it will be too late to knock when the door is shut

7 Again he prefers another request, but meets with a second repulse Since he is doomed in despair to suffer himself, he cannot, without increasing horror, reflect on meeting his brethren in that place of torment, whom he probably had greatly been instrumental to ruin by his bad example and influence, and whose bitter upbraidings he wished to prevent for not love of their souls, but desire to prevent an increase of his own misery, seems to have dictated the request Earnestly therefore doth he entreat, that, if Lazarus may not come to him, he may go to them, and prevent *their* eternal ruin, if he may not alleviate *his* torment *Note*, (1) They who have been tempters to others, and companions in sin, will shortly become mutual tormentors (2) Even a tormented sinner in hell expresses a concern for the souls of his brethren, when thousands on earth never give themselves a thought about them

Abraham denies the request it is unnecessary and it is impossible *They have Moses and the prophets, let them hear them* They wanted not the means of conviction and conversion, if they did not obstinately harden their heart *Note*, The Scriptures are the ordinary means God employs to turn men's hearts They who neglect to attend to these sacred oracles are left to their own devices, and sealed up under wrath

8 Once more he redoubles his plea, yet meets with no more success In hell no prayers are answered, it is here alone that prayers can prosper He replied, *Nay, father Abraham*, tho' they may pay no regard to Moses and the prophets, too long, it may be, accustomed to treat all revelation with contempt, *yet, if one went unto them from the dead, they will repent* such a messenger must needs carry conviction along with him, and compel them to turn from the error of their ways So ready are foolish men to be requiring evidence which God is not pleased to give, and which, should he comply with their request, would still be utterly ineffectual for, as Abraham declares, *if they hear not Moses and the prophets, neither will they be persuaded though one rose from the dead* Indeed it is impossible they should One from the dead could not speak with more authority and certainty than the Scriptures We should have much more reason there to suspect a delusion, than in the oracles of truth And though we might perhaps be terrified with the apparition, our hearts could never be changed thereby, since that the power of God alone can effect We should by degrees recover from the fright, or be laughed out of our fears, and our corruptions would soon get the better of our convictions The word of God therefore is ordinarily the alone, and sufficient, means he is pleased to use it is presumption in us to prescribe, and folly to desire any other If we harden our hearts against the warnings therein contained, visits from the dead, yea being dragged through the belly of hell itself, and sent back again to earth, would be utterly ineffectual to convert our souls *To the law therefore and the testimony*, Isa viii 19, 20

CHAP XVII.

In this chapter, 1 *Christ teaches his disciples to take heed of giving offence, and to forgive the injuries done them*, ver 1—4 *To pray for the increase of their faith*, ver 5, 6 *And then teacheth them humility, whatever service they had done for God*, ver 7—10 2 *He cleanses ten lepers, one of whom only thanks him, and he a Samaritan*, ver 11—19 3 *He discourses with his disciples upon occasion of an enquiry of the Pharisees, when the kingdom of God should appear*, ver 20—37

1 THEN said he unto the disciples, [a] It is im- [a] Mat xviii
possible but that offences will come [b] but wo 6, 7 Mark
unto him through whom they come 2 It were better ix 42
for him that a milstone were hanged about his neck, 1 Cor xi 19
and he cast into the sea, than that he should offend one [b] Mat xxvi 24
of these little ones 3 ¶ Take heed to yourselves [c] If [c] Mat xviii 15, 21
thy brother trespass against thee, [d] rebuke him, and if he [d] Lev xix 17
repent, forgive him. 4 And if he trespass against thee Prov xvii 10
seven times in a day, and seven times in a day turn again Jam v 19.
to thee, saying, I repent, thou shalt forgive him 5
And the apostles said unto the Lord, Increase our faith
6 And the Lord said, [e] If ye had faith as a grain of [e] Mat xvii 20 & xxi 21 Mark xi 23
mustard-seed, ye might say unto this sycamine-tree, Be 1 Cor xiii 2.
thou plucked up by the root, and be thou planted in
the sea, and it should obey you 7 But which of you
having a servant plowing, or feeding cattle, will say un-
to him by and by, when he is come from the field, Go,
and sit down to meat? 8 And will not rather say unto
him, Make ready wherewith I may sup, and gird thy-
self, [f] and serve me till I have eaten and drunken, and [f] Chap xii 37
afterward thou shalt eat and drink? 9 Doth he thank
that servant because he did the things that were com-
manded him? I trow not 10 So likewise ye, when ye
shall have done all those things which are commanded
you, say, [g] We are unprofitable servants we have done [g] Job xxii 3 & xxxv 7 Mat xxv 30 Rom xi 35
that which was our duty to do.

℣ 1—10 This discourse is particularly addressed to the disciples, and contains,

1 A *warning* against giving offence It must need be, considering the corruption of our nature, the craft of Satan, and the temptations of the world, that offences come, but wo to *persecutors*, who discourage and oppose the work of God, wo to *seducers*, who corrupt the truth, and deceive the souls of men with pernicious heresies wo *to faithless professors*, whose carnal lives stumble the weak and harden the wicked better were it for them to die with the vilest of malefactors than live to increase their everlasting misery

2 A *command* to forgive all injuries *Take heed to yourselves*, as not to give offence, so also not to take it When others are provoking, hold in your own spirit, and in patience possess your soul let no angry thought, no passionate word nor wish, no violence break forth Mildly endeavour to convince an offending brother, and, the moment he expresses his repentance, let the arm of forgiveness and reconciliation be open to him, yea, if he, through weakness or forgetfulness, seven times in a day repeat the offence, and turn again, professing his sorrow, and pro-

promiſing greater watchfulneſs, we muſt ſtill forgive, and neither upbraid him, nor keep in mind his repeated provocations

3 Here is *inſtruction* given, how we can alone diſcharge this difficult duty *Lord*, ſay the apoſtles, *Increaſe our faith* This is the root from whence all other graces flow, as this ſtrengthens, they are in exerciſe The apoſtles themſelves were conſcious of the weakneſs of their faith, they knew his grace alone could ſupply their wants, therefore in prayer to him they make their application We muſt go to the ſame Saviour, and he will not ſend us empty away To their requeſt the Lord replied, *If ye had faith as a grain of muſtard-ſeed, ye might ſay unto this ſycamine-tree, Be thou plucked up by the root, and be thou planted in the ſea; and it ſhould obey you*, ſuch being the mighty efficacy of divine faith, and every duty, under its influence, becomes practicable

4 Chriſt enjoins upon them humility in all their ſervices Whatever works they were enabled to perform, whatever difficulties they might be called to encounter, they muſt regard themſelves as his *ſervants*, and fulfil the duties of their ſtation, nor think they had merited any thing by their labours, for, as a ſervant, when he returns from his work in the field, doth not expect to be attended, but is required firſt to wait on his maſter before he ſups himſelf, nor is thanked for ſo doing, becauſe it is his duty, in like manner muſt Chriſt's miniſters and ſervants, when they have done their beſt, acknowledge they are unprofitable ſervants, and, if they had indeed performed *all things* commanded them, they would have done no more than was *their duty to do*, and would have no merit to plead, *our goodneſs extendeth not to God*, we can never make him our debtor for duty, whilſt we muſt daily own ourſelves his debtors for pardoning and ſanctifying grace

11 ¶ And it came to paſs, as he went to Jeruſalem,
that he paſſed through the midſt of Samaria and Galilee
12 And as he entred into a certain village, there met
him ten men that were [h] lepers, [i] which ſtood afar off
13 And they lifted up *their* voices, and ſaid, [k] Jeſus,
Maſter, have mercy on us 14 And when he ſaw *them*,
he ſaid unto them, [l] Go ſhew yourſelves unto the prieſts
And it came to paſs, that, as they went, they were cleanſed
15 And one of them, when he ſaw that he was
healed, turned back, and with a loud voice glorified
God, 16 And fell down on *his* face at his feet, giving
him thanks and he was a Samaritan 17 And Jeſus
anſwering ſaid, Were there not ten cleanſed? but where
are the nine? 18 There are not found that returned to
give glory to God, ſave this ſtranger 19 And he ſaid
unto him, Ariſe, go thy way, [m] thy faith hath made
thee whole.

[h] Lev xiii 46 [i] 2 Chron xxvi 21 [k] Chap xviii 37 [l] Mat viii 4 Lev xiii 2 & xiv 2 Chap v 14 [m] Chap vii 50 & viii 48 & xviii 42

v 11—19 The leproſy was a diſorder not only incurable, and moſt nauſeous, but which rendered the unhappy patient ceremonially defiled, and excluded him from the comforts of human ſociety We have here the miraculous cure of ten men afflicted with that miſerable diſeaſe

1 They met Chriſt on his journey, hearing it may be of his coming that way, and aſſembled to move his compaſſion, and unite their ſupplications to him Keeping at a humble diſtance, they lifted up their voice and cried aloud for mercy to him, whom fame had proclaimed the Saviour of the miſerable *Note*, (1) A humble ſenſe of our own vileneſs ſhould deeply affect our ſouls in all our approaches to God (2) Joint ſufferers ſhould unite their prayer, and thus more powerfully beſiege the throne of grace

2 Chriſt ſent them to the prieſts for inſpection, whom the law had made the judges of leproſy And herein he intimated his deſign to cleanſe them, if they in faith obeyed his direction, and withal hereby his power and glory would be made evident to thoſe in the ſanctuary, who, pronouncing theſe perſons clean, might learn by what means the wondrous cure was wrought

3 *As they went they were healed* They did not heſitate about the journey, or ſay, To what purpoſe ſhould we go? but went in faith, and were accordingly healed for in the way of duty we may expect Chriſt's powerful hand of grace to work effectually for us where we are utterly unable to help ourſelves

4 One of the poor lepers no ſooner received his cure than he immediately returned, *with a loud voice glorifying God*, adoring the power and grace which he had ſo richly experienced, and fell at *the feet of Jeſus*, with warmeſt gratitude expreſſing his acknowledgments of the mercy which he had received *Note*, The leaſt we can render to God for his goodneſs towards us is praiſe, and therein we are bound to be ſpeedy and hearty, deeply ſenſible that we are leſs than the leaſt of all his mercies

5 Chriſt expreſſes his approbation of his conduct, and encourages his faith Nine out of the ten went on, but this man, though *a Samaritan*, a *ſtranger* to the commonwealth of Iſrael, evidenced deeper gratitude and more unfeigned religion than thoſe who profeſſed to know the true God Our Lord therefore diſmiſſes him with an aſſurance of his ſalvation His faith had not only obtained his cure in common with the reſt, but had ſaved his ſoul alſo *Note*, (1) Ingratitude is a common ſin How many more receive mercies from God than are thankful for them? (2) We often meet with the greateſt gratitude where we leaſt expected it, whilſt ſometimes they who make profeſſion of religion moſt grievouſly diſappoint us

20 ¶ And when he was demanded of the Phariſees,
when the kingdom of God ſhould come, he anſwered
them, and ſaid, The kingdom of God cometh not with
† obſervation 21 Neither ſhall they ſay, Lo here, or
lo there for behold, the kingdom of God is ‡ within
you. 22 And he ſaid unto the diſciples, The days
will come when ye ſhall deſire to ſee one of the days
of the Son of man, and ye ſhall not ſee *it* 23 And
[n] they ſhall ſay to you, See here, or ſee there: go not
after *them*, nor follow *them* 24 [o] For as the lightning
that lighteneth out of the one *part* under heaven, ſhineth
unto the other *part* under heaven ſo ſhall alſo the Son
of man be in his day 25 But firſt [p] muſt he ſuffer
many things, and be rejected of this generation. 26
And [q] as it was in the days of Noe, [r] ſo ſhall it be alſo
in the days of the Son of man 27 They did eat, they
drank, they married wives, they were given in marriage,
until the day that Noe entred into the ark and the flood
came and deſtroyed them all 28 Likewiſe alſo as it
was in the days of Lot, they did eat, they drank, they
bought, they ſold, they planted, they builded 29 But
the ſame day that Lot went out of Sodom, [s] it rained
fire and brimſtone from heaven, and deſtroyed them all
30 Even thus ſhall it be in the day [t] when the Son of
man is revealed 31 In that day, he [u] which ſhall be
upon the houſe top, and his ſtuff in the houſe, let him
not come down to take it away and he that is in the
field, let him likewiſe not return back 32 [x] Remember
Lot's wife. 33 [y] Whoſoever ſhall ſeek to ſave his
life, ſhall loſe it and whoſoever ſhall loſe his life, ſhall
preſerve it 34 [z] I tell you, in that night there ſhall
be two men in one bed, the one ſhall be taken, and the
other ſhall be left 35 Two women ſhall be grinding
together, the one ſhall be taken, and the other left
36 § Two men ſhall be in the field, the one ſhall be
taken, and the other left 37 And they anſwered and
ſaid unto him, Where, Lord? And he ſaid unto them,
[a] Whereſoever the body *is*, thither will the eagles be gathered together

† Or, outward ſhew ‡ Or among you [n] Mat xxiv 23 Mark xiii 21 Chap xxi 8 [o] Mat xxiv 27 [p] Chap ix 22 & xviii 31 & xxiv 7 26 [q] Gen vi 3—7 & vii 5, &c Mat xxiv 37 1 Pet iii 20 [r] 1 Theſ v 3 [s] Gen xix 24 [t] 2 Theſſ i 7 [u] Mat xxiv 17 Mark xiii 15 [x] Gen xix 26 [y] Chap ix 24 John xii 25 [z] Mat xxiv 40, 41 1 Theſ iv 17 § Some Greek copies want this verſe [a] Job xxxix 30 Mat xxiv 28

v 20—37 We have here our Lord's anſwer to the Phariſees queſtion, *when the kingdom of God ſhould come*, that glorious temporal kingdom of the Meſſiah which their prejudices taught them to expect

1 He informs them that it will come with none of that outward ſhew which they imagined, nor occaſion any ſuch obſervation, as when a prince makes his progreſs through the kingdom, every mouth is full of it, *Lo here* he comes, *or lo there* he reſides *for behold the kingdom of God is within you*, the heart is the ſeat of the Meſſiah's kingdom, there he ſets up his throne, bringing the ſoul, with all its faculties, into obedience to his bleſſed Self *Note*, (1) Chriſtianity knows no ſect or party, Chriſt is not confined here or there, but all, who believe in him and love him in ſincerity, are ſubjects of his happy government (2) We muſt look into our hearts, whether Chriſt be formed in us All true religion is internal and experimental, and without this the form and ſhew of godlineſs avail nothing

2 He directs his diſcourſe to his diſciples, with a view to warn them of the difficulties they muſt encounter Far from becoming great men in this world, eſteemed and honoured as they flattered themſelves, they would meet with ſuch ſeaſons of diſtreſs and perſecution, as would make them look back with deſire and regret upon one of theſe days, when they enjoyed Chriſt's perſonal preſence with them, and wiſh for it in vain

3 He foretells them of his ſpeedy and unexpected appearance to deſtroy the Jewiſh people, when, driven to extremities, they would be ready to hearken to every impoſtor who pretended Chriſt was here or there, ready to reſcue them from the power of the Romans, but, like lightning, he would appear and utterly conſume that devoted city and nation Or this may repreſent alſo the mighty efficacy of his goſpel, which, with irreſiſtible power and rapidity, ſhould ſpread to the ends of the earth, notwithſtanding all oppoſition

4 He informs them the Meſſiah *muſt ſuffer many things, and be rejected of that generation* but when, by death, he hath accompliſhed the ſalvation of his people, then all his enemies and theirs muſt fall before him

5 He

5 His coming to destroy Jerusalem would be sudden and terrible, as the flood which consumed the old world, and the fire that devoured the cities of Sodom, whilst the sensuality and carnal security of the Jewish people would be like that which prevailed in the days of Lot and Noah, whose warnings were despised and disbelieved, till the threatned ruin came, and, too late, brought the due conviction of their truth So would the unbelieving Jews reject the warnings of Christ and his apostles, and perish as these despisers of old *Note*, (1) The inordinate pursuit of this world's gratifications is apt to lull the soul into a fatal security (2) It is common for sinners to go fast asleep into eternal misery, and not to be apprehensive of their danger till they lift up their eyes in torments (3) A few, in the most evil days, are rescued, whom God will take care of amidst every danger (4) The coming of our Lord Jesus Christ will be matter of the same surprize to a careless world at the last day as his judgments of old have been

6 He admonishes his disciples, as soon as they saw the danger approach, and the Roman army advancing to Jerusalem, to flee without delay, nor to regard what they may have left behind in the city, nor stop to cast a look thitherwards, lest, as Lot's wife was made a monument of divine vengeance, a like destruction should overtake them, if, sollicitous about what they left, they should look back, or go back to save it In these days of persecution, when tempted to save their lives by base compliances, they must remember this would be the sure way to perish everlastingly, whilst readiness to meet death itself, in the way of duty, would most effectually secure their eternal life and glory *Note*, (1) We should often remember Lot's wife, and tremble at the thought of drawing back (2) If we would make a right estimation of our gain and loss, we must look forward to eternity, and take that in to the reckoning

7 God's distinguishing providence will in that day take care of his own people, who, though exposed to the same dangers as others, shall be then singularly preserved, and escape from the general desolation *Note*, God knoweth those that are his, and will always take care they shall be safe, either beneath the sun or above it

8 In answer to his disciples, who enquired, *Where, Lord?* what will become of those who are left, and where shall the judgment light, he informs them, *Where the body is, there will the eagles be gathered together* wherever the Jews are, the Romans, as eagles, will pursue them, seize them in their fastnesses, and utterly root them out of the land And this may be applied to Christ himself, to whom all his people eagerly flock, and feed on him, to the great strengthening and comfort of their souls.

CHAP XVIII

In this chapter we have, 1 The parable of the importunate widow, designed to teach us fervency in prayer, ver 1—8 2 The parable of the Pharisee and Publican, designed to teach us humility, and humiliation for sin in prayer, ver 9—14 3 Christ's favour to little children that were brought to him, ver 15, 16, 17 4 The rich man, who loved his wealth more than Christ, ver 18—30 5 Christ's foretelling of his own death and sufferings, ver 31—34 6 His restoring sight to a blind man, ver 35—43 And these four passages we had before in Matthew and Mark

1 AND he spake a parable unto them, *to this end*,
that [a] men ought always to pray, and not to
faint, 2 Saying, There was in a city a judge, which
feared not God, neither regarded man 3 And there
was a widow in that city, and she came unto him, saying, Avenge me of mine adversary 4 And he would
not for a while but afterward he said within himself,
Though I fear not God, nor regard man, 5 [b] Yet,
because this widow troubleth me, I will avenge her, lest
by her continual coming she weary me 6 And the
Lord said, Hear what the unjust judge saith 7 And
[c] shall not God avenge his own elect, which cry day and
night unto him, though he bear long with them? 8 I
tell you that [d] he will avenge them speedily Never-
theless, when the Son of man cometh, shall he find faith
on the earth?

[a] Chap xxi 36 Rom xii 12 Eph vi 18 Col iv 2 1 Thess v 17
[b] Chap xi 8.
[c] Rev vi 10 Ps lxx 18 Isa lx 1 Rev vi 10
[d] Heb x 37 2 Pet iii 9

v 1—8 The intention of the parable before us, as we are informed in the first verse, is to encourage us in persevering prayer, even though we may not always find the immediate answer of our requests. We have,

1 The parable of the importunate widow and unjust judge. He was a man of abandoned principles, destitute of religion and honesty, *neither fearing God nor regarding man* and miserable is that country where such magistrates are in office A poor oppressed widow appealed to him for relief cruelly taking advantage of her weakness, some crafty or covetous wretch had defrauded or injured her, and with ceaseless importunity, at the judge's gate, she cried for justice to be done her. Deaf for a while to her intreaties, he paid no regard to her cause, till, wearied out with her perpetual clamour, merely to get rid of it, he granted her suit, and redressed her wrongs

2 Christ applies the case, for the encouragement of his praying people If the unjust judge was thus prevailed upon by importunity, how much more *shall God avenge his own elect, who cry to him day and night, though he bear long with them? I tell you that he will avenge them speedily* *Note*, (1) God's people are his *elect*, they have not chosen him, but he hath chosen them (2) Dear as they are to him, they meet with many a sore trial, and much oppression in this world, and to him they carry all their complaints (3) We must not be weary, though our requests do not immediately succeed, but patiently persevere in calling upon God day and night (4) God *bears long* with his enemies, to see if they will yet repent and turn to him, and he defers *long* the prayers of his people, to exercise their graces, but he will *speedily* avenge them, punishing their enemies, and rescuing them from their sufferings

3 He foretells his disciples how little faith would be found among the Jewish people when he came to judge them and at his second coming the remnant of the faithful would be alike small a fearful consideration! Let him that thinketh he standeth take heed lest he fall, and redouble his prayers that he may never faint nor fail under any trials

9 ¶ And he spake this parable unto certain [e] which
trusted in themselves † that they were righteous, and de-
spised others 10 Two men went up into the temple
to pray, the one a Pharisee, and the other a publican
11 The Pharisee stood and prayed thus with himself,
[f] God, I thank thee, that I am not as other men *are*,
extortioners, unjust, adulterers, or even as this publican
12 I fast twice in the week, I give tithes of all that I
possess 13 And the publican, standing afar off, [g] would
not lift up so much as his eyes unto heaven, but [h] smote
upon his breast, saying, God be merciful to me [i] a sin-
ner 14 I tell you, this man went down to his house
justified *rather* than the other for [k] every one that exalt-
eth himself, shall be abased, and he that humbleth him-
self, shall be exalted

[e] Chap xvi 15 † Or be cause
[f] Isa lxv 5 Chap xviii 1 Rev iii 17
[g] Ps xl 12
[h] Jer xxxi 19
[i] Job xl 4. Rom vii 24.
[k] Job xxii 29 Chap xiv 11 Jam iv 6. 1 Pet v 5 6.

v 9—14 The purport of this parable is intimated in the opening of it, *He spake this parable unto certain who trusted in themselves that they were righteous, and despised others* They were puffed up with a vain conceit of their excellence above other men, they presumed their own doings and duties would ensure their acceptance with God, and, high in self opinion, looked down with contempt on the herd of vulgar sinners as far beneath them though in God's sight they were infinitely more vile and abominable than those whom they despised We have,

1 The account of two men of very different characters, who went up to the temple to pray The one *a Pharisee*, proud, self-righteous, who, confident of his own goodness, expected the admiration of men, and counted even God his debtor The other *a publican*, a poor broken hearted, self-condemned sinner, who, feeling his misery fled to God for mercy *Note*, (1) Prayer is every man's duty They must be inexcusable who live in the neglect of it (2) The temple was the type of Jesus Christ, through whom alone our prayers can come up before God with any prospect of acceptance

2 The Pharisee's address to God bespoke the abominable arrogance of his heart *He stood and prayed thus with himself*, in some conspicuous place where others might admire his devotion and piety, *God, I thank thee that I am not as other men are, extortioners, unjust, adulterers, or even as this publican* He pretends to thank God, but in fact all he said was merely a compliment on himself Much evil he had avoided, much good he had done, not only abstaining from grosser vices, from extortion, adultery, injustice, but also he was often in fastings, and scrupulous in paying tythes of all that he possessed, and with much self-complacence congratulates himself that he was so much superior to other men, and boasts to God how far he exceeded in goodness that vile publican, whom he passed in the outer court of the temple Thus spoke this swelling worm what he called his prayers breathed nothing but the language of pride, uncharitableness, and censure Yet, detested as this character appears, how many who hope for heaven come short of it, and live indulging those vices from which even this Pharisee was free?

3 The publican's prayer was just the very reverse In humility, self abhorrence, and earnest desire after mercy, he bows into the dust before God *He stood afar off*, keeping a humble distance from the Pharisee, whom he counted so much his superior, or in the outer court of the Gentiles, as unworthy a place among true Israelites, *and would not lift up so much as his eyes unto heaven*, with down-cast looks, which bespoke the deep dejection of his soul, as if he was unworthy to turn even his eyes towards God's holy habitation; *but smote upon his breast*, where that vile heart lodged in which so much evil had dwelt,

and

and against which he would express a holy indignation Then raising, as it were, a deep sigh from his inmost soul, in one short ejaculation he breathed forth the desires of his sinful soul, *God be merciful to me a sinner!* He *owns his guilt*, by nature, by practice, ill-deserving, hell-deserving, he disclaims all hope and dependence upon himself, and trusts alone upon the promised *mercy* of God through the blood of atonement, assured he must otherwise eternally perish and therefore he casts his soul down before the throne of God's grace, earnestly begging that mercy which he so greatly needed A pattern which every poor sinner must imitate, and in this way alone may the miserable hope to find mercy We are all in this publican's state, and, if ever we would be saved, we must learn his spirit and adopt his prayer

4 Very different was the acceptance which these men's prayers met at a throne of grace However to outward view the specious Pharisee might be generally among men preferred to this despised publican, God seeth not as man seeth *this* poor, self-abased, and penitent sinner *went down to his house justified*, his sins pardoned, his person accepted, his prayer granted, and peace spoken to his soul, *and not the other*, the proud self-justifier was left to his native guilt and sin, abhorred of God, his very prayers an abomination, and all his boasts were but delusion, and must prove his destruction And the reason of this is added, which contains also an axiom which will be for ever proved true, *every one that exalteth himself*, in the vain imagination of his own self-sufficiency and righteousness before God, looking down with disdain upon others, as so much his inferiors in goodness, he *shall be abased*, his pride will be mortified, his sins will take hold of him, and the wrath of God in hell for ever abide upon him whilst *he that humbleth himself*, taking shame for his sinfulness and baseness before God, confessing his guilt, and acknowledging his unworthiness of the least mercy, *shall be exalted* to the favour of God in this world, and to his eternal glory in a better

l Mat xix 13 Mark x 13
m Psal cxxxi 2 1 Cor xiv 20 1 Pet ii 2
n Mark x 15

15 And [l] they brought unto him also infants, that
he would touch them but, when *his* disciples saw *it*,
they rebuked them 16 But Jesus called them unto
him, and said, Suffer little children to come unto me,
and forbid them not for [m] of such is the kingdom of
God 17 [n] Verily I say unto you, Whosoever shall not
receive the kingdom of God as a little child, shall in no
wise enter therein

v 15—17 This passage of story hath before been twice recorded, and a third time it is profitable to consider it

1 As an encouragement to parents early to bring their babes to Jesus, in prayer committing them to his benediction, by baptism offering them to become visible members of his church, and engaging to bring them up in the nurture and admonition of the Lord

2 We must not be disheartened in our applications, if we find those discountenance us from whom we hoped for encouragement, the Master himself will treat us more kindly

3 The longest day we live we need still to set before us a little child for our pattern In the school of teachableness, humility, and simplicity, the best and wisest have yet many lessons to learn

o Mat xix 16 Mark x 17
p Ex xx 13 Deut v 17 Rom xiii 9
q Mark vii 10 Eph vi 2 Col iii 20
r Phil iii 6
s Chap xii 33 & xvi 9 Acts iv 34 1 Tim vi 19
t Prov xi 28 1 Cor i 26 1 Tim vi 17
u Gen xviii 14 Jer xxxii 17 Zech viii 6 Chap i 37
x Deut xxxiii 9 Mat iv 20
y Job xlii 12

18 And [o] a certain ruler asked him, saying, Good
Master, what shall I do to inherit eternal life? 19 And
Jesus said unto him, Why callest thou me good? none
is good save one, *that is* God 20 Thou knowest the
commandments, [p] Do not commit adultery, Do not kill,
Do not steal, Do not bear false witness, [q] Honour thy
father and thy mother 21 And he said, [r] All these
have I kept from my youth up 22 Now when Jesus
heard these things, he said unto him, Yet lackest thou
one thing Sell all that thou hast, and distribute unto
the poor, and thou shalt have treasure in heaven and
come, follow me 23 And when he heard this, he
was very sorrowful for he was very rich 24 And
when Jesus saw that he was very sorrowful, he said,
[t] How hardly shall they that have riches enter into the
kingdom of God! 25 For it is easier for a camel to
go through a needle's eye, than for a rich man to enter
into the kingdom of God 26 And they that heard *it*
said, Who then can be saved? 27 And he said, The
things which are impossible with men, [u] are possible
with God 28 Then Peter said, Lo, [x] we have left all,
and followed thee 29 And he said unto them, Verily
I say unto you, there is no man that hath left house, or
parents, or brethren, or wife, or children, for the kingdom
of God's sake, 30 [y] Who shall not receive manifold
more in this present time, and in the world to come
life everlasting

v 18—30 We have here,

1 Our Lord's discourse with the young ruler, who enquired after the way to eternal life The enquiry was important, and what the greatest of men need seriously to consider, for they are dying worms as well as others Could man keep the commandments, this would be still the road to glory, but since the fall, that door of paradise is barred, and none can any longer hope to enter heaven by personal obedience, since all have sinned and come short of the glory of God To flatter ourselves we have kept the commandments would prove our ignorance of the spirituality of God's law, and of the corruption of our own hearts Thus deceived was this young ruler, and the delusion was evident the moment he was called upon to part with all for Christ, when, unable to bear that hard saying, he departed sorrowful *Note*, Worldly things are usually dire hindrances in the way to glory for the sake of some one darling lust, how many make shipwreck of their souls

2 Our Lord took occasion from hence to warn his disciples, whose hearts were too full of the hopes of temporal grandeur, how difficult, and next to impossible, it was for a rich man to enter the kingdom of God And, when they expressed their astonishment thereat, he refers them to that almighty grace which can effect that for us which we could never do for ourselves *Note*, Instead of grasping at abundance, we should tremble at the perilousness of our situation, if God in his providence gives us much we have so many more hindrances in our way to heaven, unless he gives us also proportionable grace to improve our talents to his glory

3 In answer to Peter's question, what they should have who left all to follow him, Christ replies, they should be abundant gainers thereby, receiving *manifold more in this present time*, if not in kind, yet in comfort, in the present graces and gifts of God's Spirit, and in the enjoyment of his love and favour, *and in the world to come life everlasting*, which will infinitely overpay all our present losses

z Chap ix 22 & xvii 25 & xxiv 6
a Ps xxii Is liii
b Chap xxiii
c Is l 6

31 ¶ [z] Then he took unto him the twelve, and said
unto them, Behold, we go up to Jerusalem, and [a] all
things that are written by the prophets concerning the
Son of man shall be accomplished 32 For [b] he shall
be delivered unto the Gentiles, and shall be mocked, and
spitefully entreated, and [c] spitted on, 33 And they
shall scourge *him*, and put him to death and the third
day he shall rise again. 34 And they understood none
of these things and this saying was hid from them,
neither knew they the things which were spoken.

v 31—34 We have here,

1 The warning Christ gave his disciples of the sufferings he must endure, to arm them against that dire event He was about to suffer every indignity, and at last death itself Nor ought this to surprize them, since the Scriptures had foretold that thus it must be, and not one jot or tittle of the divine word can fail But as they declared his sufferings, they had insured his resurrection also, and therefore his disciples need not despond, having this glorious event in their view

2 So strong were the unhappy prejudices the apostles had imbibed, that they understood none of these things The prophecies which spoke of the Messiah's sufferings and reproaches were hid from them, they could not reconcile the glorious things spoken of his kingdom to such a scene of indignities and humiliation and, having their eyes dazzled with the temporal grandeur of the Messiah's kingdom, they overlooked all beside But then, now, and ever, ought we to remember, that the way to glory, both for the head and the members, lies through much tribulation, and *no cross, no crown*

d Mat xx 29 Mark x 46
e Chap vii Joh ix
f Ver 15
g Mat xx
h Is xxxv
i Chap vii
k Chap i

35 ¶ [d] And it came to pass, that as he was come
nigh unto Jericho, a certain [e] blind man sat by the way-
side begging 36 And hearing the multitude pass by,
he asked what it meant 37 And they told him, that
Jesus of Nazareth passeth by 38 And he cried, saying,
Jesus, thou son of David, have mercy on me 39 And
they which went before rebuked him, that he should
hold his peace but [f] he cried so much the more, Thou
son of David, have mercy on me 40 And Jesus stood
and commanded him to be brought unto him and,
when he was come near, he asked him, 41 Saying,
[g] What wilt thou that I shall do unto thee? And he
said, Lord, [h] that I may receive my sight 42 And
Jesus said unto him, Receive thy sight [i] thy faith hath
saved thee 43 And immediately [k] he received his sight,
and followed him, glorifying God and all the people,
when they saw *it*, gave praise unto God

v 35—43 It was prophesied of the Messiah, that he should open the eyes of the blind here we see him fulfilling the prophetic word And he who gave light to the darkened body

shine

shines still with brighter beams as the sun of righteousness into the benighted soul, and communicates also the faculty of spiritual vision to those whose souls the God of this world had blinded

1 The patient here was blind and poor, and such beggars have a claim upon our charity

2 He sat by the way-side, where he hoped for relief, and there he found more than his most sanguine wishes expected for, whilst we are waiting upon God in his ways, he is pleased often to give us more than we can ask or think He heard of the multitude that Jesus passed by, and now resolved to seize the happy moment to prefer his request, nor would be silenced by any rebukes of those who were near him, crying with loud and ceaseless importunity, *Jesus, thou son of David, have mercy on me* *Note*, Wherever God thus pours out a spirit of prayer and supplication, it is a sure earnest that he intends to grant our petitions

3 Christ, in his wonted compassion, calls the poor man, bids him prefer his petition, and grants his request, giving him sight according to his desire The tender-hearted Saviour feels for human wretchedness, and will not send the poor and humble supplicant away without an answer of peace If we have faith to trust him, he hath power and willingness to heal all our infirmities, and to supply all our wants

4 The poor beggar, now restored to sight, with delight followed Jesus in the way, glorifying God for the mercy he had experienced, and all the people joined his praises *Note*, (1) If we have received spiritual sight, then shall we follow Jesus without delay in all his holy ways (2) The mercies of others demand our thankfulness, as well as our own, for we are members one of another

CHAP XIX

In this chapter we have, 1 The conversion of Zaccheus the publican at Jericho, ver 1—10 2 *The parable of the pounds which the king intrusted with his servants, and of his rebellious citizens*, ver 11—27 3 *Christ's riding in triumph into Jerusalem, and his lamentation in prospect of the ruin of that city*, ver 28—44. 4 *His teaching in the temple, and casting the buyers and sellers out of it*, ver 45—48

1. AND *Jesus* entred, and passed through Jericho
2 And behold, *there was* a man named Zac-
cheus, which was the chief among the publicans, and
he was rich 3 And he sought to see Jesus, who he
was, and could not for the press, because he was little
of stature 4 And he ran before, and climbed up into
a sycamore-tree to see him, for he was to pass that way
5 And when Jesus came to the place, he looked up
and saw him, and said unto him, Zaccheus, make haste,
and come down, for to day I must abide at thy house
6. And he made haste, and came down, and received
him joyfully 7 And when they saw *it*, they all mur-
a Isa, lx 11 mured, saying, that [a] he was gone to be guest with a
man that is a sinner 8 And Zaccheus stood, and said
unto the Lord, Behold, Lord, the half of my goods I
give to the poor and if I have taken any thing from
b Exod xxii 1 any man by false accusation, [b] I restore *him* four-fold.
Chap iii 14 9 And Jesus said unto him, This day is salvation come
c Rom iv 11, 12, 16 to this house, forasmuch as [c] he also is [d] the son of Abra-
Gal iii 7 ham 10 For [e] the Son of man is come to seek and save
d Chap xiii 16 that which was lost

e Mat x 6, & xviii 11 Chap xv 24 *v* 1—10 Whilst the conversion of every sinner's heart be speaks the great power of God, the change wrought on some appears still more worthy to be remembered and admired, as in the case of Zaccheus

1 He was a publican, yea *chief among the publicans*, and rich, two great obstructions, in human view, to the salvation of his soul but Christ has his elect among the great and wealthy, as well as among the poor, and nothing is too hard for his almighty grace The chief of sinners he can make the chief of saints.

2 He took great pains to get a sight of Christ, and to satisfy a curiosity which the great fame of him had raised being short, and unable to overlook the crowd of people that usually attended Jesus in his travels, he ran before, and climbed up into a sycamore tree, that he might see him as he passed by *Note*, (1) They who would gain a sight of Jesus must break through every obstacle in their way (2) Curiosity, though often blameable, in many cases is praise-worthy To see and hear those of whom there are strange reports is the best way to judge for ourselves

3 There the eye of Jesus discovered him, and, as he had led him to that tree by the hand of his providence, he now surprizes him with the calls of his grace, and, by name addressing him, desires him to come down quickly, intending to be that day his guest With joy the publican obeyed, little expecting such a favour, and received him with heartiest welcome *Note*, (1) Many who have come merely through curiosity to hear and see some minister, whose fame hath been spread abroad, have been graciously surprised with the call of God, and from that hour converted unto him (2) There is a wondrous providential disposition of our affairs, which, when we are turned to God, we can reflect upon with amazement, and see his hand leading us when we had not one thought of his designs (3) When Christ calls we should gladly run, his word can open for him a welcome into our house and our hearts, and make us with delight reply, *Come in, dear Lord, to me* (4) *Come down* is the gospel call, we must sink low in our own eyes, to rise high in God's favour

4 Many, who were present, were exceedingly offended, that one, who professed himself a prophet of such distinguished sanctity, should go to eat with a person who was so notorious a sinner His profession made him odious as a publican, his riches might be regarded as the fruit of extortion, and his character might be known as infamous but it did not follow, because he had been bad, that he was so, as their censure implied, nor was Jesus to be blamed for visiting those, who, the more desperate their case seemed, so much the more needed his healing grace

5 Whatever Zaccheus had been, he now gives the most undoubted proofs of genuine and unfeigned repentance The grace of Jesus had powerfully wrought upon his heart, and the effects of it appeared visible in his words and actions However grasping he had been of wealth, and intent on gain, now at a stroke half his goods he gives to the poor, and, if any man had ought to lay against him of fraud or extortion, he was ready to make the utmost restitution which the law demanded *Note*, (1) One of the best symptoms of real conversion to God is deadness to the world (2) There can be no true repentance without restitution, at least without the desire to make it to the utmost of our power (3) They who would shew the spirit of true charity, should not leave it merely to their wills to bequeath their wealth to pious uses, but employ it during their lives

6 Christ testified his approbation of Zaccheus's conduct, and comforted him with the assurance of that salvation which was now come to him and to his house, forasmuch as he also was a son of Abraham He now shewed himself a genuine descendant of this father of the faithful his salvation was therefore secured, his sins pardoned, his person accepted, and eternal glory his portion, whilst all his family also shared his mercy. And what Christ had done in this case was in direct conformity with the great design of his coming into the world, *to seek and save that which was lost* *Note*, (1) Every sinner is a lost soul, lost in error and sin, unable to recover himself, and ready to perish eternally and a great point is gained, when we begin to be deeply convinced of this alarming truth (2) Christ is the Saviour of the desperate none are so far gone as to be past his recovery (3) He must first seek us, or we shall never seek to him for salvation

11 And as they heard these things, he added, and
spake a parable, because he was nigh to Jerusalem, and
because they thought that the kingdom of God should
immediately appear 12 He said therefore, [f] A certain f Mat xxv 14
noble-man [g] went into a far country, to receive for him g Acts i 11
self a kingdom, and to return 13 And he called his
ten servants, and delivered them ten † pounds, and said † A mina was worth 3l 2s 6d
unto them, [h] Occupy till I come 14 But his citizens
hated him, and sent a message after him, saying, We h 1 Cor xii 7.
will not have this man to reign over us 15 And it
came to pass, that when he was returned, having re-
ceived the kingdom, then he commanded these servants
to be called unto him, to whom he had given the ‡ mo ‡ Or silver Ver 23
ney, [i] that he might know how much every man had i Rom xiv 12
gained by trading 16 Then came the first, saying,
Lord, [k] thy pound hath gained ten pounds 17 And k Jam ii 18
he said unto him, Well, thou good servant because
thou hast been faithful in a very little, [l] have thou au l Gen xxxix 4 Mat xxiv 47 & xxv 21
thority over ten cities 18 And the second came, say-
ing, Lord, thy pound hath gained five pounds 19
And he said likewise to him, Be thou also over five cities
20. And another came, saying, Lord, behold, *here is*
thy pound which I have kept laid up in a napkin 21
For I feared thee, [m] because thou art an austere man m Mat xxv 24
thou takest up that thou layedst not down, and reapest
that thou didst not sow 22 And he saith unto him,
[n] Out of thine own mouth will I judge thee, thou wicked n 2 Sam i 16 Job xv 6 Mat xii 37
servant. Thou knewest that I was an austere man,
taking up that I laid not down, and reaping that I did
not sow 23 Wherefore then gavest not thou my mo-
ney into the bank, that at my coming I might have re

quired mine own with uſury? 24 And he ſaid unto
them that ſtood by, Take from him the pound, and give
it to him that hath ten pounds 25 (And they ſaid un-
to him, Lord, he hath ten pounds) 26 For I ſay unto
o Mat xiii 12 & xxv 29 Chap viii 18 you, that ° unto every one which hath ſhall be given
and from him that hath not, even that he hath ſhall be
taken away from him 27 But thoſe mine enemies,
which would not that I ſhould reign over them, bring
hither, and ſlay *them* before me

v 11—27 What Chriſt had ſaid to Zaccheus gave occaſion to ſome, who heard him, to conclude, that the temporal kingdom of the Meſſiah was about to be ſet up in the world, and that, on his arrival at Jeruſalem, he would declare himſelf openly To rectify ſuch a miſtake therefore he ſpake the following parable, intimating to them therein, that the generality of the Jewiſh people would not ſubmit to the kingdom of his grace, and that the kingdom of his glory was more diſtant than they imagined

1 *A certain nobleman*, a perſon of high birth, *went into a far country, to receive for himſelf a kingdom*, to be inveſted with ſovereign authority, as the governors of Judah were by the Roman emperors, *and to return*, with full power and authority, to reward or puniſh his ſubjects Thus the Lord Jeſus aſcended into heaven, to receive the mediatorial kingdom, and ſat down at the right hand of the Majeſty on high, being quickly to return from thence in the miſſion of his Spirit, to ſpread his goſpel through the earth, in the deſtruction of the Jewiſh people and nation, and finally at the day of judgment And as ſurely as he once came into the world, ſo ſurely will he return again, and will not tarry

2 He committed to his ſervants a certain ſum of money, that during his abſence they might *trade* (πραγματεύσασθε) and improve their capital, in order that at his return he might receive the fruits of their induſtry The miniſters of Chriſt in particular, and all his people in general, are thoſe ſervants, each hath his portion of gifts, natural or providential, which he is required to employ for his Maſter's honour and intereſt All we have is derived from him, and ſhould be devoted to him Till he comes, we are called upon to uſe all diligence Every ſoul won by us will prove our own unſpeakable gain, and whatever be the ſucceſs of our labours, whether more or leſs, if we approve ourſelves faithful to him till death, we are ſure not to loſe our reward

3 Two of the ſervants, on their maſter's return, with ſatisfaction appeared before him, and rendered him a faithful account of the truſt committed to them The one had gained more, the other leſs, but both had been diligent, received his commendation, and were preferred according to the advantages they had made Whence we are taught, (1) That we muſt one day be called upon to give a ſolemn account to our great Lord and Maſter of all the means and mercies, gifts and grace, which we have enjoyed, and our profiting thereby (2) They who are found faithful will receive the approbation of the Chief Shepherd, and be rewarded by him (3) Whatever ſucceſs we have, we muſt, to the glory of our Lord, own, that it is *thy pound* hath gained it, for not to our endeavours, but to his grace, are we indebted for the effect of our miniſtry (4) If we have the Saviour's commendation of our diligence, we need not care who may find fault with us (5) They who are moſt zealous in their labours for Chriſt will receive the greater reward, exalted, as one ſtar differeth from another ſtar in glory

4 The third, ſunk in ſloth and careleſsneſs, began to ſeek excuſes, and, having produced the pound committed to his charge, pretended his fear of his maſter's auſterity, as if he would caſt on him the blame of his own idleneſs But out of his own mouth was this wicked ſervant condemned, ſince that apprehenſion he pleaded of his maſter's auſterity ſhould at leaſt have led him to place the money at the banker's, where, with lawful intereſt, he might have received his own Juſtly therefore he commanded the pound to be taken from him, and given to him who had gained the ten pounds for his having ſo much is ſo far from being an objection, as ſome preſent intimated, *v* 25 that it was a reaſon why he ſhould have more, having made ſo good a uſe of the former truſt, whilſt he, who made no uſe, or ſo bad a one, of the pound delivered to him, juſtly deſerved to have it taken from him *Note*, (1) Not only the abuſe of our gifts, but our negligence to improve and employ them for Chriſt's honour and the good of men's ſouls, will be eſteemed highly criminal (2) The pleas of ſlothful profeſſors, in the judgment day, ſhall turn to their everlaſting confuſion and condemnation (3) Idle ſervants are wicked ſervants Miniſters who are not active in Chriſt's ſervice effectually ſerve the intereſt of Satan (4) Hard thoughts of God are at the bottom of every unhumbled ſinner's heart (5) Diligence to improve the gifts and graces, which the Lord hath beſtowed on us, is the ſure way to have both abundantly increaſed under his bleſſing, whilſt ſloth makes all our attainments to wither and decay

5 He foretells the ruin of the Jewiſh people in general. They were the *citizens* who ſent after him in his abſence, refuſing to ſubmit to his government they paid no regard to his apoſtles and miniſters when he was aſcended into heaven and, having filled up the meaſure of their iniquities by rejecting his goſpel, he ſeized the rebels with his arm of judgment, and the Roman ſword miſerably maſſacred innumerable multitudes of this devoted people, and ruined their country And ſuch will be the caſe with all impenitent ſinners They ſay, in the pride and rebellion of their hearts, *We will not have this man to reign over us*, rejecting the government of his laws and the warnings of his ſervants but their terrible deſtruction approaches the King, their Judge, clothed with vengeance, is ready to be revealed from heaven, when wrath to the uttermoſt will come upon them, and they who refuſed to bow to the ſceptre of his grace ſhall be broken with the rod of his judgments They who will not be *ruled* muſt be eternally *ruined*

28 ¶ And when he had thus ſpoken, he went before,
ascending up to Jeruſalem 29 p And it came to paſs, p Mat xxi 1 Mark xi 1
when he was come nigh to Bethphage and Bethany, at
the mount called *the mount* of Olives, he ſent two of his
diſciples, 30 Saying, Go ye into the village over againſt
you, in the which at your entering ye ſhall find a colt tied,
whereon yet never man ſat looſe him, and bring *him*
hither 31 And if any man aſk you, Why do ye looſe
him? thus ſhall ye ſay unto him, Becauſe the Lord hath
need of him 32 And they that were ſent, went their
way, and found even as he had ſaid unto them 33
And as they were looſing the colt, the owners thereof
ſaid unto them, Why looſe ye the colt? 34 And they
ſaid, The Lord hath need of him 35 And they brought
him to Jeſus and q they caſt their garments upon the q 2 Kings ix 13
colt, and r they ſet Jeſus thereon 36 And as he went, r Zech ix 9
they ſpread their clothes in the way 37 And when he
was come nigh, even now at the deſcent of the mount
of Olives, the whole multitude of the diſciples began to
rejoice, and praiſe God with a loud voice, for all the
mighty works that they had ſeen, 38 Saying, s Bleſſed s Pſ cxviii 26
be the King that cometh in the name of the Lord
t peace in heaven, and glory in the higheſt 39 And t Chap ii 14 Eph ii 14
ſome of the Phariſees from among the multitude ſaid
unto him, Maſter, rebuke thy diſciples 40 And he
anſwered and ſaid unto them, I tell you, that if theſe
ſhould hold their peace, u the ſtones would immediately u Hab ii 11
cry out

v 28—40 Eager to accompliſh the ſalvation of his people, the bleſſed Jeſus haſtens to the ſcene of his ſufferings, not intimidated by all the dreadful events he foreſaw Was he ſo willing to die for us, and ſhall we be cowards in his ſervice? We have here what we met with twice before

1 The triumphant entry of Jeſus into Jeruſalem, amidſt the acclamations of the multitude He was mounted, not as a conqueror on a triumphal car, but, as Zion's lowly King, on an aſs's colt, and that not his own He ſent to borrow it for this occaſion, and, having the dominion over all creatures, and in his hands the hearts of all men, the owners readily ſent him at the Saviour's bidding Mounted thereon, the garments of his poor diſciples were the trappings, and ſerved as carpets ſpread to adorn his entry whilſt, filled with wonder and praiſe at all the miracles they had ſeen, the multitude cried, *Bleſſed be the King*, Meſſiah, may all happineſs and proſperity attend him *that cometh in the name of the Lord*, inveſted with divine authority and power *peace in heaven*, let the God of heaven bleſs his undertaking, and crown it with ſucceſs, appearing now a reconciled God to us, *and glory in the higheſt*, let the greateſt honour, praiſe, and adoration redound to him for this ſalvation, and be aſcribed to him by men on earth and angels in heaven

2 Chriſt vindicates his diſciples from the envious cavil of the Phariſees, who could not bear to hear ſuch acclamations, and would inſinuate that it was the higheſt pride to permit ſuch incenſe to be offered to him But, though he came in great humility, the preſent occaſion demanded theſe praiſes, and, if the multitude had been ſilent, he aſſured theſe cavillers the very ſtones would cry out, reproaching their ſtupidity, and aſcribing to God the glory due unto his name

41 ¶ And when he was come near, he beheld the
city, and wept over it, 42 Saying, If thou hadſt
known, even thou, at leaſt in this thy day, the things
which belong unto thy peace! but now they are hid from
thine eyes 43 For the days ſhall come upon thee, that
thine enemies ſhall caſt a trench about thee, and compaſs
thee round, and keep thee in on every ſide, 44 And x
x ſhall lay thee even with the ground, and thy children x Matt xxiv 2
within

y Chap. xxi within thee, and y they ſhall not leave in thee one ſtone
upon another z becauſe thou kneweſt not the time of
z Dan ix 24 thy viſitation 45 a And he went into the temple, and
a Matt xxi 12 began to caſt out them that ſold therein, and them that
bought, 46 Saying unto them, It is written, b My
b Iſa lvi 7 houſe is the houſe of prayer but c ye have made it a
c Jer vii 11 den of thieves 47 And he taught daily in the temple
But d the chief prieſts and the ſcribes, and the chief of
d Mark xi 18 John vii 19 the people thought to deſtroy him, 48 And could not
find what they might do for all the people † were very
† Or, Hang upon him attentive to hear him

v 41—48 We have here,

1 The tears of Jeſus ſhed over the devoted city Jeruſalem Being now in full view of that rejected place, and foreſeeing the impending miſeries ready to overwhelm the inhabitants, *he wept over it*, as man, feeling the tendereſt compaſſion towards them, *ſaying, If thou hadſt known*, or, *O that thou hadſt known! even thou*, a wicked and bloody city as thou haſt been, *at leaſt in this thy day*, when the moſt abundant means of grace have been vouchſafed to thee, *the things* which belong *unto thy peace*, temporal and eternal, *but now they are hid from thine eyes*, thou art abandoned to judicial blindneſs, and utter reprobacy, the conſequence of which will ſhortly be utter ruin, when thine enemies ſhall beſiege and enter into thee, maſſacre the inhabitants, and leave not one ſtone upon another, *becauſe thou kneweſt not the time of thy viſitation*, rejecting the light of my goſpel, the warnings of my miniſters, and the overtures of mercy, which were vouchſafed to thee *Note*, (1) A Chriſtian's heart, like his Maſter's, feels the tendereſt compaſſion towards periſhing ſinners, and grieves to behold their approaching miſeries (2) There is a time of viſitation, when the Lord is pleaſed to ſet before us the things which belong to our pardon, peace, and ſalvation, and to urge them upon us by his providence, his word, his Spirit not to know, or abuſe this day of grace, is to be undone (3) However long we have treſpaſſed on God's patience, or however greatly we have provoked him, if at laſt we are prevailed upon to return to him, it is never too late to find favour with him Let none therefore deſpair, who deſire *now* to return without delay to the Lord (4) Juſtly are they given up to judicial blindneſs and hardneſs of heart, who reject the counſel of God againſt their own ſouls (5) All the threatnings of Jeſus will be as ſurely fulfilled, as we have ſeen this againſt Jeruſalem accompliſhed in the total overthrow of that city and people Let every ſinful city, every ſinful ſoul, take warning by her fall

2 Being come to Jeruſalem, he goes immediately to the temple, cleanſes it from the profanations there practiſed, caſting out the *buyers and ſellers*, who had made that *houſe of prayer a den of thieves*, teſtifying his zeal for his Father's honour, and when he had thus purged this holy place from ſuch groſs abuſes, he preached there to the people the doctrines of his rich grace *Note*, The preaching of the goſpel is the great glory of every temple devoted to the Saviour's honour

3 The chief prieſts, ſcribes, and rulers, were highly exaſperated at his diſcourſes and conduct, which ſo deeply reflected on their corruptions, and therefore ſought how to murder him immediately, but they could not juſt then contrive any ſcheme for the execution of their bloody purpoſes, the people in general being very attentive to his diſcourſes, (ἐξεκρέματο) they *hung upon* his lips, eagerly catching every word which dropped, for he ſpoke with ſuch power, energy, and conviction, as from their own ſcribes they had never heard before

CHAP XX

In this chapter we have, 1 Chriſt's anſwer to the chief prieſts queſtion concerning his authority, ver 1—8 2 *The parable of the vineyard let out to the unjuſt and rebellious huſbandmen*, ver 9—19 3 *Chriſt's anſwer to the queſtion propoſed to him concerning the lawfulneſs of paying tribute to Ceſar*, ver 20—26 4 *His vindication of the reſurrection of the dead and the future ſtate, from the fooliſh cavils of the Sadducees*, ver 27—38 5 *His puzzling the ſcribes with a queſtion concerning the Meſſiah's being the ſon of David*, ver 39—44 6 *The caution he gave his diſciples to take heed of the ſcribes*, ver 45—47

a Matt xxi 23 Mark xi 27 1 AND a it came to paſs, that on one of thoſe days,
as he taught the people in the temple, and
preached the goſpel, the chief prieſts and the ſcribes
came upon him, with the elders, 2 And ſpake unto
b Acts iv 7 him, ſaying, Tell us, b by what authority doſt thou theſe
things? or who is he that gave thee this authority? 3
And he anſwered and ſaid unto them, I will alſo aſk you
c John i 25 one thing, and anſwer me 4 c The baptiſm of John,
was it from heaven, or of men? 5 And they reaſoned
with themſelves, ſaying, If we ſhall ſay, From heaven,
he will ſay, Why then believed ye him not? 6 But
and if we ſay, Of men, all the people will ſtone us for
d they be perſuaded that John was a prophet 7 And d Matt xiv 5
they anſwered, that e they could not tell whence *it was* e Job v 13
8 And Jeſus ſaid unto them, Neither tell I you by what
authority I do theſe things

v 1—8 Whilſt Jeſus was engaged in the bleſſed work of preaching to the people the glad tidings of ſalvation, the chief prieſts, ſcribes, and elders came upon him, to interrupt him in theſe labours of love *Note*, We may not wonder, if in the ſervice of the goſpel we meet with many interruptions from the great enemy of ſouls, and his emiſſaries

They demanded his authority for what he ſaid and did, inſinuating, that as it belonged to them to judge of the pretenſions of thoſe who aſſumed the prophetical character, unleſs he produced his commiſſion, they muſt proceed againſt him as a deceiver He anſwers their queſtion by another, reſpecting the baptiſm of John, which not caring to anſwer for fear of the people, and unwilling to own the divine miſſion of the Baptiſt, they pretended ignorance, and gave him a juſt reaſon to refuſe them a farther account of himſelf, ſeeing they had already rejected the plaineſt evidence *Note*, It is but loſt labour to endeavour to perſuade thoſe, who are before reſolved not to be convinced

9 f Then began he to ſpeak to the people this para- f Matt xxi 33 Mark xii 1
ble g A certain man planted a vineyard, and let it forth
to huſbandmen, and went into a far country for a long g Iſa v 1 Jer ii 21
time 10 And at the ſeaſon, h he ſent a ſervant to the
huſbandmen, that they ſhould give him of the fruit of h 2 Chron xxxvi 15
the vineyard but the huſbandmen i beat him, and ſent i 2 Chron xxxvi 16
him away empty 11 And again he ſent another ſer- Neh ix 26
vant, and they beat him alſo, and entreated *him* ſhame- Matt xxiii 34
fully, and ſent *him* away empty 12 And again he ſent Acts vii 52
the third, and i they wounded him alſo, and caſt *him* 1 Theſſ ii 15 Heb
out 13 Then ſaid the lord of the vineyard, What ſhall xi 36
I do? I will ſend my beloved ſon it may be they will
reverence *him* when they ſee him 14 But when the
huſbandmen ſaw him, they reaſoned among themſelves,
ſaying, k This is the heir l come, let us kill him, that k Heb i 2
the inheritance may be ours 15 So m they caſt him l Chap xxi 2
out of the vineyard, and killed *him* What therefore m Heb xiii 12
ſhall the lord of the vineyard do unto them? 16 He
ſhall come and deſtroy theſe huſbandmen, and n ſhall n Acts xiii 46 & xviii 6
give the vineyard to others And when they heard *it*,
they ſaid, God forbid 17 And he beheld them, and
ſaid, What is this then that is written, o The ſtone which o Pſ cxviii 22 Iſa
the builders rejected, the ſame is become the head of the xxviii 16
corner? 18 Whoſoever ſhall fall upon that ſtone ſhall Acts iv 11
be broken but p on whomſoever it ſhall fall, it will 1 Pet ii 7
grind him to powder 19 ¶ And the chief prieſts and p Dan ii 34, 35 Matt
the ſcribes the ſame hour ſought to lay hands on him, xxi 44
and q they feared the people for they perceived that he q Ver 6.
had ſpoken this parable againſt them

v 9—19 This parable is deſigned for a warning to the prieſts and rulers, of the ruin coming upon them and their nation, for their perſecutions of the meſſengers of God, and their rejection of the Meſſiah

1 The vineyard was the Jewiſh people, which had been taken under God's peculiar care, and having inſtituted a magiſtracy and miniſtry among them, he expected ſuitable returns of love and duty from them, but inſtead of that, they treated with the greateſt cruelty thoſe divinely-appointed meſſengers, whom he ſent to remind them of his juſt expectations, and now were about to murder the ſon, who was come on the ſame errand, the conſequence of which would be the ruin of the nation, and the eternal deſtruction of theſe miſcreants *Note*, (1) The beſt of men have often met with the cruelleſt uſage from thoſe, whoſe good alone was the object of their labours (2) The end of obſtinate tranſgreſſors is to be rooted out at the laſt

2 Struck with the denunciation of vengeance, they could not but deprecate the wrath threatened, and expreſs their abhorrence of ſuch a crime as the murder of the Meſſiah, but Chriſt with deepeſt concern beheld them, aſſured of their determined obſtinacy, and approaching ruin Though their efforts would all be fruitleſs, that ſtone which these Jewiſh builders rejected, would, notwithſtanding, become the head of the corner This Jeſus, whom they deſpiſed, would be exalted to the right hand of Majeſty on high, and inveſted with all power and authority in heaven and in earth, and his enemies, who were offended at him, and on whom his vengeance would light, muſt terribly periſh

3 The chief prieſts plainly perceived the drift of the parable, and rage boiled in their boſoms They would gladly have ſeized and murdered him on the ſpot, but were deterred through

fear of the people, and forced reluctantly to defer their bloody purpose to a more convenient opportunity So little effect have the fairest warnings upon those who harden their hearts against conviction

r Mat xxii 15 Mark xii 13 — 20 And they watched him, and r sent forth spies,
which should feign themselves just men, that they might
take hold of his words, that so they might deliver him
unto the power and authority of the governor 21 And
s Ps xii 2 — they asked him, saying, s Master, we know that thou
sayest and teachest rightly, neither acceptest thou the
† Or of a truth thou teachest the way of God — person *of any*, but † teachest the way of God truly. 22
Is it lawful for us to give tribute unto Cesar, or no ?
23 But he perceived their craftiness, and said unto them,
‡ Mark xii 15 — Why tempt ye me ? 24 Shew me ‡ a penny · whose
image and superscription hath it ? They answered and
t Rom xiii 7 — said, Cesar's 25 And he said unto them, t Render
therefore unto Cesar the things which be Cesar's, and
unto God the things which be God's 26 And they
could not take hold of his words before the people and
they marvelled at his answer, and held their peace

v 20—26 Resolved if possible to destroy him, and not having the power in their own hands, they determined to try if they could not ensnare him, and render him obnoxious to the Roman government, as a seditious person, for which purpose we have here,

1 The insidious question proposed to him by certain of the Pharisees and Herodians, who, under the guise of conscientious regard to their duty, pretended a great concern to know whether it was lawful to give tribute to Cesar, or not, and thereby acknowledge themselves the subjects of a foreign power They suggest their fullest confidence in the rectitude of his decisions, their opinion of his integrity unawed by the fear of men, and their satisfiedness in that divine commission under which he acted; and thus they endeavoured to flatter him into an unguarded freedom, which either must embroil him with the civil powers, or render him odious to the people *Note*, (1) The garb of piety hath often served to cover the vilest designs We need be on our guard against some who feign themselves just men, and not credulously trust to every specious professor To be wise as serpents is our duty, as well as to be harmless as doves (2) It hath been the common artifice of persecutors to endeavour to represent the faithful as enemies to the state, and thus to gain the civil powers to oppress them

2 His answer confounds and silences his enemies *He perceived their craftiness*, for from him nothing is hid, nothing is secret, and out of their own mouth draws a decision of the question, to which they cannot object As they own their money bore Cesar's image and superscription, he had certainly a right to his own, though this interfered not with God's demands, to whose worship and service their hearts and lives must be devoted Unable to object, in sullen silence they held their peace, marvelling at his wisdom, yet obstinate in their infidelity

u Mat xxii 23 Mark xii 18 — 27 ¶ u Then came to him certain of the Sadducees
w Acts xxiii 8 — (w which deny that there is any resurrection) and they
asked him, 28 Saying, Master, y Moses wrote unto us,
y Deut xxv 5 — If any man's brother die, having a wife, and he die
without children, that his brother should take his wife,
z Job iii 8 — and raise up seed unto his brother 29 z There were
therefore seven brethren and the first took a wife, and
died without children 30 And the second took her to
wife, and he died childless 31 And the third took
her; and in like manner the seven also And they left
no children, and died 32 Last of all the woman died
also 33 Therefore in the resurrection, whose wife of
them is she ? for seven had her to wife 34. And Jesus
answering said unto them, The children of this world
marry, and are given in marriage 35 But they which
shall be accounted worthy to obtain that world, and the
resurrection from the dead, *neither marry*, nor are given
a 1 Cor xv — in marriage. 36 a Neither can they die any more, for
b 1 John iii — b they are equal unto the angels, and are the children of
c Rom viii 23 — God, c being the children of the resurrection. 37 Now
that the dead are raised, even Moses shewed at the bush,
d Ex iii 6 Acts vii 32 Heb xi 16 — when d he calleth the Lord the God of Abraham, and
the God of Isaac, and the God of Jacob 38 For he is
e Rom xiv — not a God of the dead, but of the living for e all live
unto him

v 27—38 The confutation of the Sadducean objection to the resurrection of the dead was considered before, *Mat* xxii 23 *Mark* xii 18 But our Lord here enlarges somewhat concerning that awful state which after death succeeds *The children of this world marry, and are given in marriage* necessary it is that the world should thus be supplied with inhabitants, and the ravages of death be repaired by the rising generation *but they which shall be accounted worthy to obtain that world, and the resurrection from the dead*, have higher joys than even the marriage state can afford, and need not to increase, where death is swallowed up in victory They are said to *be accounted worthy*, not that in and of ourselves we have any merit, our worthiness consists in being found in Christ, justified by his blood, complete in his righteousness, and sanctified by his spirit In that unseen world to which the blessed go, [1] *They neither marry, nor are given in marriage*, their holiness and happiness is compleat without it the delights of sense are swallowed up in the infinitely surpassing ecstacies of the soul [2] *Neither can they die any more* that world needs not to be replenished with new inhabitants, where life eternal reigns, and death never enters [3] *They are equal to the angels*, partaking in their service, enjoying the same bliss, glorious and immortal as these seraphic spirits [4] They *are the children of God, being the children of the resurrection*, as adopted sons, they have now the title to the eternal glory, and at the resurrection day will be put in possession of the purchased inheritance

39 ¶ Then certain of the scribes answering, said,
Master, thou hast well said 40 And after that they
durst not ask him any question at all 41 And he said
unto them, f How say they that Christ is David's son ? — f Mat xxii 42 Mark xii 35
42 And David himself saith in the book of Psalms,
g The LORD said unto my Lord, Sit thou on my right — g Ps cx 1 Acts ii 34
hand, 43 Till I make thine enemies thy footstool — Heb i 13
44 David therefore calleth him Lord, h how is he then — h Rev xxii 16
his son ? 45 ¶ Then in the audience of all the people,
he said unto his disciples, 46 i Beware of the scribes,
k which desire to walk in long robes, and l love greet- — i Mark xii 38 &c
ings in the markets, and the highest seats in the syna- — k Mat xxiii 5
gogues, and the chief rooms at feasts, 47 m Which — l Chap. xi 43
devour widows houses, and for a shew make long prayers — m Mat xxiii 14 2 Tim iii 6 Tit. i 11
the same shall receive greater damnation

v 39—47 The scribes, the established expositors of the law, expressed their high approbation of his answer to their Sadducean opponents, and, struck with the surpassing wisdom which appeared in all his discourses, declined attempting any further to encounter him, conscious of his superiority But though they had done with him, Christ hath not done with them

1 *He proposes to them a question*, which seemed of easy solution, but which quite disconcerted them for an answer Ignorant of the mystery of the person of the Messiah, in whom the divine and human natures should be united, they could not account how David's Son should be David's Lord To us this mystery is unfolded we behold God and man in one Christ

2 He condemns the hypocrisy and covetousness of the scribes, and cautions his disciples against them They made a vast parade of profession, and with flowing robes in solemn stateliness as they passed, expected homage, as due to their superiority, delighted in hearing the incense offered to their vanity, proudly affected precedency, and whilst by their long prayers they insinuated themselves into the confidence of widows, they basely and wickedly abused the trust reposed in them, and devoured their substance *These shall receive greater damnation* wickedness committed under such a veil of piety, brings the most aggravated guilt on the conscience, and must be attended with the most terrible vengeance of God

CHAP XXI

In this chapter we have, 1 Christ's approbation of a poor widow that cast two mites into the treasury ver 1—4 2 *A prediction of the destruction of Jerusalem, and of the second coming of Jesus Christ to judge the world, under the type and figure of that*, ver 5—33 3 *A practical application of this by way of caution and counsel*, ver 34—36 4 *An account of Christ's preaching, and the people's attendance on it*, ver 37, 38

1 AND he looked up, and a saw the rich men cast- — a Mark xii 41
ing their gifts into b the treasury 2 And he — b 2 Kings xii 9
saw also a certain poor widow casting in thither two
mites 3 And he said, Of a truth I say unto you,
c that this poor widow hath cast in more than they all — c 2 Cor viii 12
4. For all these have of their abundance cast in unto the
offerings of God but she of her penury hath cast in all
the living that she had

v 1—4 The commendation of this poor widow's offering we heard, *Mark* xii 41 We may observe, (1) That it is the duty of all, according to their ability, to contribute to the service of the sanctuary, the maintenance of a gospel ministry,

the

the education of youth, and the relief of the necessitous (2) The least mite which is given to the offerings of God from a heart zealous for his glory, and breathing fervent charity, shall be remembered, and infinitely recompensed in the great day

5. ¶ And [d] as some spake of the temple, how it was
adorned with goodly stones and gifts, he said, 6 *As
for* these things which ye behold, the days will come, in
the which [e] there shall not be left one stone upon ano-
ther, that shall not be thrown down 7 And they asked
him, saying, Master, but when shall these things be?
and what sign *will there be* when these things shall come
to pass? 8 And he said, [f] Take heed that ye be not
deceived for [g] many shall come in my name, saying,
I am *Christ*, and the time draweth near go ye not
therefore after them 9 But when ye shall hear of wars
and commotions, be not terrified for these things must
first come to pass, but the end *is* not by and by 10
Then said he unto them, [h] Nation shall rise against na-
tion, and kingdom against kingdom, 11 And great
earthquakes shall be in divers places, and [i] famines, and
pestilences, and fearful sights, and great signs shall there
be from heaven 12 But before all these, they shall
lay their hands on you, and [k] persecute *you*, [l] delivering
you up to the synagogues, and [m] into prisons, [n] being
brought before kings and rulers [o] for my name's sake
13 And [p] it shall turn to you for a testimony. 14
Settle *it* therefore in your hearts, not to meditate before
what ye shall answer 15 For [q] I will give you a mouth
and wisdom, [r] which all your adversaries shall not be
able to gainsay nor resist 16 And [s] ye shall be be-
trayed both by parents and brethren, and kinsfolks and
friends, and [t] *some* of you shall they cause to be put to
death 17 And ye shall be hated of all *men* for my
name's sake 18 But [u] there shall not an hair of
your head perish 19 In your patience possess ye your
souls

d Mat xxiv 1 Mark xiii 1
e 1 Kings ix Jer xxvi 18 Mic iii 12 Chap xix 44
f Jer xxix 8 Eph v 6 Col ii 8 2 Thes ii 3 1 John iv 1
g Jer xiv 14 & xxiii 21 Acts v 36 37
h Hag ii 22 Zech xiv 13
i Acts xi 28
k John xv 20
l Mat x 17
m Acts v 18 & xii 4
n Acts xvi 24 Rev ii 10
o Acts iv 7 & xxv 23
p 1 Pet iv 14 Phil i 28
q Ex iv 12 Jer i 9
r Chap xii 12 Acts ii 4
s Isa lix 17 Acts vi 10 Mic vii 6 Mat x 21
t Acts vii 59 & xii 2
u Mat x 30

v 5—19 The disciples, vastly pleased with the magnificence of the temple, and the gifts with which it was enriched, could not but grieve at the thoughts that it should be utterly destroyed, and fain would move the Saviour's compassion to reverse the sentence he had pronounced, but he confirms the doom of that devoted place, and in answer to their request informs them of the signs preceding the threatned desolation

1 False Christs would arise, making great profession of delivering the Jews from the Roman yoke, and affirming the time fixed in the antient prophecies was near, when the temporal kingdom of the Messiah should be set up But they are to beware of such deceivers, and neither follow nor be led by them His kingdom they had been often advised was not of this world, nor must they look for any other Messiah but himself

2 Terrible commotions and awakening judgments would precede the day of his coming to destroy the Jewish nation Bloody wars and tumults would ravage the country, earthquakes rock the ground, famines and pestilence desolate the land, and fearful sights in the heavens terrify the beholders, and portend the approaching dire calamities But they must not be *terrified* at the signs, nor apprehensive of the consequence, for they shall be under the peculiar care of the divine Providence, though greater evils are still behind

3 They must expect fiery persecutions, and will find their nearest and dearest relations, filled with enmity against the gospel, their bitterest enemies They will be scourged in the synagogues by their own countrymen, cast into prison, brought before heathen magistrates and kings, hated of all men, and called to resist unto blood, sealing the truth they professed with martyrdom But to support and encourage them herein, Christ assures them, [1] That their sufferings and persecutions shall tend to make the gospel-word more diffused, and be a testimony against those who maliciously and cruelly persecuted them [2] He promises them extraordinary aids in times of extraordinary trials They need not be sollicitous about the answer they should make, when cited before the tribunals of magistrates and kings, nor must they depend upon their own prudence for their defence, but expect divine assistance *I will give you a mouth and wisdom, which all your adversaries shall not be able to gainsay or resist* The Holy Ghost should furnish them with *matter* and *words*, fill their mouths with such arguments, and give such energy to their discourse, as should quite confound and silence their persecutors, if it did not convince them And all God's faithful ministers and people, when suffering for the truth's sake, and called in defence of the gospel to answer before the rulers, may still depend on the same superior help, (*See Acts* iv, v, vi) [3] Out of all their severest trials God will save them harmless *Not an hair of your head shall perish* either literally he would strangely deliver them from the most imminent perils, as he saved them out of Jerusalem when the Romans came to besiege the city, or figuratively it expresses his singular care of them, so that though they should be delivered to prison, or to death, his eye should be upon them for good, and give them at least a happy issue out of all their afflictions, bringing them through these tribulations to eternal life and glory, so that they should be infinitely gainers by all their sufferings [4] He exhorts them patiently to bear up under every temptation, and not be ruffled or discomposed, but with holy serenity and calm resignation to cast their care upon God, and quietly wait for his salvation *Note*, (1) In trying times the hardest conflict is within, to preserve the tranquility of our own souls by humble confidence in God (2) A little patience will bring us to the end of every human woe

20 And [x] when ye shall see Jerusalem compassed
with armies, then know that [y] the desolation thereof is
nigh. 21 Then let them which are in Judea, [z] flee to
the mountains, and let them which are in the midst of
it, depart out, and let not them that are in the coun-
tries enter thereinto 22 For these be the days of ven-
geance, that all things [a] which are written may be ful-
filled 23 But [b] wo unto them that are with child, and
to them that give suck in those days for there shall
be great distress in the land, and wrath upon this people
24 And they shall fall by the edge of the sword, and
shall be led away captive into all nations and Jerusalem
shall be troden down of the Gentiles, [d] until the times of
the Gentiles be fulfilled 25 ¶ And [e] there shall be
signs in the sun, and in the moon, and in the stars, and
upon the earth distress of nations, with perplexity, the
sea and the waves roaring, 26 Men's hearts failing
them for fear, and for looking after those things which
are coming on the earth for the powers of heaven shall
be shaken 27 And [f] then shall they see the Son of
man coming in a cloud with power and [g] great glory
28 And when these things begin to come to pass, then
look up, and lift up your heads, for [h] your redemption
draweth nigh

x Mat xxiv 15 Mark xiii 14
y Chap xix 43
z Dan xxii 3
a Dan ix 26 27 Zech xi 1
b Chap xxiii 29
c Dan viii
d Dan ix 27 & xii 7 Rom xi 25
e Isa xiii 10 Ezek xxxii 7 Joel ii 10 31 & iii 15 2 Pet iii 10 Rev vi 12
f Dan vii 13 Mat xxvi 64 Rev i 7
g Mat xvi 27
h Rom viii 19, 23

v 20—28 Having exhorted them to bear up in these dangerous days that should precede the final destruction of Jerusalem, he passes on to describe her utter overthrow

1 After a variety of fearful signs, at last the destroying army of the Romans shall approach, the signal for the faithful to leave the devoted place, and fly for their lives, as history informs us every Christian did, so that not one perished in Jerusalem The days of vengeance then shall come upon the Jewish nation for all their wickedness, and especially for that blood of the Messiah, the curse of which they imprecated upon their heads, and now shall terribly seize them Great indeed would be the distress of those who fled, especially of such as were with child, or who gave suck, because this must retard their speed, and add to their other afflictions, yet greater far would be the misery of those who remained, on whom the full vials of wrath would be poured out, the sword making the most fearful ravages among them, and the few who remained alive after the siege being led captives, and dispersed into all nations, whilst their once glorious city, razed from the foundations, should long lie in ruins, and never be restored to its former grandeur, but continue under the power of the Gentiles, *until the times of the Gentiles be fulfilled*, when the fulness of them in the last days being come in, we have hope that Israel shall again be gathered, and Jerusalem, as some suppose, be again restored, and inhabited by the Jewish converts This desolation of Judea would be terrible, as if the very elements were dissolving around them their whole civil and ecclesiastical polity would be utterly destroyed, and, half dead with terror and dismay, the wretched inhabitants would sink under the load of complicated evil Then to their confusion they will too late perceive, that he whom they crucified was the true Messiah, when, according to his predictions, they shall behold him coming thus terribly to take vengeance on them, and to set up his gospel kingdom, in defiance of all opposition Such fearful signs shall also precede the final dissolution of all things, when the Judge of quick and dead shall at last be revealed from heaven, taking vengeance on all that know not God, and obey not his gospel

2 Christ encourages his disciples, when these calamities begin, to lift up their heads in joyful hope, knowing that their *redemption draweth nigh* The destruction of the Jewish people, who were the most inveterate persecutors of the first Christians, would be to them a great deliverance, and afford matter for their thankfulness to God, who had avenged them of these bitter enemies And thus in the day of final judgment shall the destruction of the ungodly be the triumph of the saints

29 [i] And he spake to them a parable, Behold the fig-
tree, and all the trees; 30 When they now shoot forth,

i Mat xxiv 32 Mark xiii 28

ye see and know of your own selves that summer is now
nigh at hand 31 So likewise ye, when ye see these
things come to pass, know ye that the kingdom of God
k Mat xvi 28 is nigh at hand 32 Verily I say unto you, k This ge-
neration shall not pass away, till all be fulfilled 33
l Isa li 6 2 Pet iii 7, 10 l Heaven and earth shall pass away m but my word shall
m Isa xl 8 Mat v 18 not pass away 34 ¶ And n take heed to yourselves,
n Rom xiii 13 1 Thes v 6 1 Pet iv 7 lest at any time your hearts be overcharged with surfeit-
ing and drunkenness and cares of this life, and so that
day come upon you unawares 35 For o as a snare
o 1 Thes v 2 2 Pet iii 10 Rev iii 3 & xvi 15 shall it come on all them that dwell on the face of the
p Eph vi 18 whole earth 36 p Watch ye therefore, and q pray al-
q Chap xviii 1 1 Thes v 17 ways, that ye may be accounted worthy to escape all
r Eph vi 13 these things that shall come to pass, and r to stand before
s John viii 1 2 the Son of man 37 And s in the day-time he was
t Chap xxii 39 teaching in the temple, and t at night he went out, and
abode in the mount that is called *the mount* of Olives
38 And all the people came early in the morning to
him in the temple for to hear him

v 29—38 These signs of the times which Christ had set before them, if duly remarked, would as clearly point out to them the approach of the threatned judgments, as the summer is known to be at hand, when the buds and flowers of spring appear The time for the fulfilment of this prophecy was near, and the accomplishment of it sure therefore,

1 He cautions them to beware of sensuality and security, lest the day of his coming should surprize them unprepared to meet him *Note*, (1) We are in jeopardy every hour the day of death and judgment is uncertain, we need be every moment on our guard They who are immersed in the cares and pleasures of the world, will be terribly surprized by it, and wo to those on whom it shall come as a snare, and seize them in their sins (2) If we would meet our Judge with comfort, and be found of him in peace, we must keep a strict rein on inordinate appetite, and learn to die daily to the world, and sit loose to all its cares and enticements They who are dead to the world whilst they are in it, will be the readiest to go out of it at the most sudden summons (3) Surfeiting and drunkenness must necessarily unqualify us to meet our God A glutton! a drunkard! what a fearful reckoning must he make in the day of judgment! (4) The cares of this world as effectually stupify the conscience, as the fumes of liquor do the body, and though men are apt to think a sober worldling a decent character, compared with a notorious drunkard, yet is their state equally dangerous, and perhaps the former the most difficult to be wrought upon The drunkard sleeps, and is sober, but the worldly-minded rises up as he lay down, *overcharged* with the same load of worldly anxiety and carking sollicitude

2 He exhorts them *to watch and pray always, that they may be accounted worthy to escape all these things that shall come to pass, and to stand before the Son of man*, with comfort and confidence of his favour and regard Not that our watchfulness and prayers confer any merit, we must be counted *worthy and accepted in the beloved*, but these are the means God hath appointed, in the use of which he hath promised his grace and blessing to us and whilst we are awake, and expect our Lord's arrival, and look up to him for strength continually, he will bring us safe through every temptation, and give us to partake at last in his final salvation

3 During these few days between his triumph and his sufferings, he continued indefatigable in his labours, preaching daily in the temple, and when the evening came, he retired to the Mount of Olives for prayer and meditation, returning in the morning to his delightful work in the temple, where an attentive auditory waited eager to hear his divine discourses

CHAP XXII

In this chapter we have, 1 The plot to take Jesus, and Judas's coming into it, ver 1—6 2 *Christ's eating the passover with his disciples,* ver 7—18 3 *The instituting of the Lord's supper,* ver 19, 20. 4 *Christ's discourse with his disciples after supper, upon several heads,* ver 21—38 5 *His agony in the garden,* ver 39—46 6 *The apprehending of him, by the assistance of Judas,* ver 47—53 7 *Peter's denying him,* ver 54—62 8 *The indignities done to Christ by those that had him in custody, and his trial and condemnation in the ecclesiastical court,* ver 63—71

a Mat xxvi Mark xiv 1 a NOW b the feast of unleavened bread drew
nigh, which is called the pass-over 2 And
c Ps ii 2 John xi 47 Acts iv 27 the chief priests and scribes c sought how they might
kill him, for they feared the people 3 ¶ Then d en-
d John xiii 2, 27 Acts i tred Satan into Judas surnamed Iscariot, being of the
number of the twelve. 4 And he went his way, and
communed with the chief priests and captains, how he
might betray him unto them 5 And they were glad,
e Zec xi 12 and covenanted to e give him money 6 And he pro-
† Or, without tumult mised, and sought opportunity to betray him unto them
† in the absence of the multitude

v 1—6 The awful hour now approaches, when the great Redeemer must offer himself a sacrifice for the sins of his people We have,

1 The chief priests and scribes consulting how to perpetrate the bloody deed they had resolved The fear of the people restrained them from open violence, and now they plotted how to take him off secretly

2 Judas, the traitor, opportunely appeared to further their scheme Satan, whose slave he had ever continued, even tho' advanced to the dignity of an Apostle, now urged him on to the precipice of ruin, and going to the chief priests, in council assembled, who gladly embraced the offer he made, they soon struck up the bargain, and for thirty pieces of silver he engaged to betray his Master, and accordingly he watched for a secret opportunity, when, in the absence of the people, they might seize him without fear of a tumult *Note*, (1) All the malice of open enemies do not strike at the cause of Christ so deeply as the perfidy of false disciples (2) The devil watches the weak side of professors, and whether it be gold, or wine, or women, &c he prepares the bait, and apostates readily catch at it

7 ¶ f Then came g the day of unleavened bread, f Mat xxvi 17 Mark xiv 12
when the passover must be killed 8 And he sent Pe- g Ex xii 6
ter and John, saying, Go and prepare us the passover,
that we may eat 9 And they said unto him, Where
wilt thou that we prepare? 10 And he said unto them,
Behold, when ye are entred into the city, there shall a
man meet you, bearing a pitcher of water, follow him
into the house where he entreth in 11 And ye shall
say unto the good man of the house, The Master saith
unto thee, Where is the guest chamber, where I shall
eat the passover with my disciples? 12 And he shall
shew you a large upper room furnished there make
ready 13 And they went and found as he had said
unto them and they made ready the passover 14
And when the hour was come, he sat down, and the
twelve apostles with him 15 And he said unto them,
With desire I have desired to eat this passover with you
before I suffer 16 For I say unto you, I will not any
more eat thereof, h until it be fulfilled in the kingdom h Chap xiv 15
of God 17 And he took ‡ the cup, and gave thanks, ‡ The first cup being to the passover
and said, Take this, and divide *it* among yourselves
18 For I say unto you, I will not drink of the fruit of
the vine, until the kingdom of God shall come 19
¶ And i he took bread, and k gave thanks, and brake i 1 Cor xi 23
it, and gave unto them, saying, This is my body which k Rom xiv 6
is given for you this do in remembrance of me 20 1 Tim iv 5
Likewise also the cup after supper, saying, This cup *is*
the new testament in my blood, which is shed for you

v 7—20 The day of the preparation of the passover being come, we have,

1 The solemnization of it according to the law His disciples, Peter and John, had been sent to make ready, and directed whither to go, and having followed the orders of their Master, and prepared the paschal lamb, at even he came and sat down with the twelve, Judas being still of the number, his treachery not having yet openly appeared Being seated, with warm affection he addressed them, saying, *With desire I have desired to eat this passover with you before I suffer* He was happy to have this last meeting with them, he longed for the hour when the great work he had undertaken should be accomplished, and that was now at hand He welcomed those approaching sufferings which procured their salvation, and was now about to put a period to all the ceremonial institution Therefore he adds, *I will not any more eat thereof, until it be fulfilled in the kingdom of God* for when, as the Lamb of God, *he* should be offered, who was the true passover, this typical ordinance must cease of course In the gospel kingdom, the supper he was now about to institute, would supersede it, and in the great day of his appearing and glory, most eminently they should rejoice together in the final accomplishment of their glorious liberty; when departed from this world, the house of their prison, they should enter with him into the heavenly Canaan of eternal rest Presenting therefore the passover-cup to the disciples, in which it was usual for the company to pledge the master, he takes a solemn farewel of *the fruit of the vine, until the kingdom of God come*, either when, after his exaltation, his gospel should be spread through the earth, and his presence be manifested in the midst of his church, where his disciples assembled to partake of

his

his ſupper or when the heavenly kingdom ſhould come, where his redeemed people ſhall be for ever ſatisfied with the pleaſures that are at his right hand.

2 The inſtitution of *the Lord's ſupper*, which ſhould be continually celebrated in his church, in memory of a greater redemption than that from Egypt, even the deliverance which he hath obtained for us by the ſacrifice of himſelf, from Satan, ſin, death, and hell The bread is broken in token of his body being broken on the croſs it is given us as ſpiritual food for our immortal ſouls, that by faith feeding upon the great doctrines of his atonement and righteouſneſs, we may be comforted and ſtrengthened with might in the inner man And the wine repreſents to us that blood he ſhed for the remiſſion of our ſins, and ſeals to us all the promiſes of the everlaſting covenant, of which we are aſſured partakers, when faith realizes the ſigns, and makes Chriſt's fleſh meat indeed, and his blood drink indeed, for then we have *everlaſting life* in him

21 ¶ But behold, [l] the hand of him that betrayeth
me, *is* with me on the table, 22 And truly the Son
of man goeth [m] as it was determined but wo unto that
man by whom he is betrayed 23 And they began to
inquire among themſelves, which of them it was that
ſhould do this thing. 24 ¶ And there was alſo a ſtrife
among them, which of them ſhould be accounted the
greateſt 25 And he ſaid unto them, [n] The kings of
the Gentiles exerciſe lordſhip over them , and they that
exerciſe authority upon them, are called benefactors
26 [o] But ye *ſhall* not *be* ſo but he that is greateſt
among you, let him be as the younger , and he that is
chief, [p] as he that doth ſerve 27 For whether *is*
greater, he that ſitteth at meat, or he that ſerveth ? *is*
not he that ſitteth at meat ? but [q] I am among you as
he that ſerveth 28 Ye are they which have continued
with me in [r] my temptations 29 And [s] I appoint unto you a kingdom, as my Father hath appointed unto
me 30 [t] That ye may eat and drink at my table in
my kingdom, and [u] ſit on thrones, judging the twelve
tribes of Iſrael 31 ¶ And the Lord ſaid, Simon, Simon, behold, [x] Satan hath deſired *to have* you, that he
may ſift *you* as wheat 32 But [y] I have prayed for
thee, that thy faith fail not , and [z] when thou art converted, ſtrengthen thy brethren 33 And he ſaid unto
him, Lord, I am ready to go with thee both into priſon,
and to death 34 [a] And he ſaid, I tell thee, Peter,
the cock ſhall not crow this day, before that thou ſhalt
thrice deny that thou knoweſt me 35 [b] And he ſaid
unto them, When I ſent you without purſe, and ſcrip,
and ſhoes, lacked ye any thing ? And they ſaid, Nothing 36 Then ſaid he unto them, But now he that
hath a purſe, let him take *it*, and likewiſe *his* ſcrip
and he that hath no ſword, let him ſell his garment, and
buy one 37 For I ſay unto you, that this that is
written, muſt yet be accompliſhed in me, [c] And he was
reckoned among the tranſgreſſors for the things concerning me have an end 38 And they ſaid, Lord, behold, here *are* two ſwords. And he ſaid unto them, It
is enough

l Pſ. xl. 9. Mat. xxvi. 21. Mark xiv. 18. John xiii. 21. m Acts ii. 23. & iv. 28. n Mat. xx. 25. Mark x. 42. o 1 Pet. v. 3. p 1 Cor. ix. 19. q Mat. xx. 28. John xiii. 13, 14. Phil. ii. 7. r Heb. iv. 15. s Mat. xxiv. 47. Chap. xii. 32. t Chap. xiv. 15. Rev. xix. 9. u Pſ. xlix. 14. Mat. xix. 28. Rev. iii. 21. x 1 Pet. v. 8. y John xvii. 9, 11, 15. z Pſ. li. 13. John xxi. 15—17. a Mat. xxvi. 34. Mark xiv. 30. John xiii. 38. b Chap. ix. 3. & x. 4. c Iſa. liii. 12. Mark xv. 28.

v 21—38 Chriſt having finiſhed the ſupper, addreſſes himſelf to his diſciples

1 He admoniſhes them, that, though ſtrange the relation, yet one of them ſhould betray him That he ſhould thus go, was ordained by the determinate counſel and foreknowledge of God , yet dreadful would be the guilt of that wretch who ſhould perpetrate the horrid deed Aſtoniſhed at the information, the diſciples with anxious ſollicitude began to enquire which of them he pointed at, ſhocked with the thought of being guilty of ſuch enormous wickedneſs *Note*, (1) There are in every age traitors, who eat of Chriſt's bread, and yet betray him (2) Though God foreſees and permits the wickedneſs of ſinners, yet will not this at all exculpate them from their guilt (3) Holy jealouſy over ourſelves, leſt we ſhould be faithleſs , is the ſureſt way to preſerve our fidelity inviolable

2 He rebukes the ſinful affectation of precedency, for which his apoſtles, whoſe heads were ſtill full of his temporal kingdom, had been diſputing among themſelves . He corrects their vain imaginations, and aſſures them, that the kingdom he was about to erect, was in no wiſe like the kingdoms of the Gentiles, where the princes and rulers exerciſed deſpotic ſway over their ſubjects, affected the title of benefactors, and were flattered with it by their ſubjects but they who bore his commiſſion muſt not imitate ſuch example , nor think of lordſhip over their brethren The way in which his miniſters can only hope to riſe in eminence, is by condeſcending to every work and labour of love , to ſerve the meaneſt and leaſt of his diſciples , in honour preferring others to themſelves, and being ever little and low in their own eyes His own example was a powerful argument to enforce humility upon them Though he was their Maſter, and they his ſervants, he ſubmitted even to waſh their feet, that they might learn of him Hitherto they had continued with him during all his trials and humiliations they have only to perſevere in the ſame way, expecting nothing on earth but ſufferings, and looking for higher honours than the fading ones of this world , either in *the kingdom of grace*, in which they ſhould fill the moſt important ſtation , be made eminent inſtruments of God for good to men's ſouls, and partake of the rich proviſion of goſpel ordinances , or, *in the kingdom of glory*, where they ſhould reign with their exalted Lord, filled with eternal conſolations, and ſit down on thrones prepared for them at his right hand, aſſeſſors with him in the judgment, as he himſelf was now about to take the mediatorial throne appointed to him by his Father, and ſhould reign over his redeemed people in glory everlaſting *Note*, (1) In Chriſt's kingdom humility is the only way to honour , and our ambition muſt be, not to be admired as *great*, but to lay ourſelves out in doing *good* (2) They who faithfully adhere to the Saviour in the midſt of manifold temptations, ſhall find, that as their tribulations abound for Chriſt, their conſolations even in this world ſhall abound alſo, and that they ſhall, in the world to come, obtain a throne of glory that fadeth not away (3) Thoſe who receive the kingdom of grace or glory, are purely indebted for it to the gift of Jeſus (4) The ſaints of God are now uſually deſpiſed and trampled upon , but ſhortly their revilers and perſecutors ſhall ſee them exalted to a throne, and aſſeſſors with the great Judge, before whoſe bar they muſt ſtand trembling, and be covered with everlaſting ſhame and contempt

3 He warns Peter of his approaching fall, but aſſures him withal of his grace to recover him, that he ſhould not finally be caſt away *Simon, Simon, Satan hath deſired to have you*, even all of you, as he deſired God's permiſſion to tempt Job, without which he dared not touch a hair of his head and his purpoſe is, *to ſift you as wheat* , hoping either to prove them chaff, and deſtroy them by apoſtacy or at leaſt to diſtreſs , terrify, and ſcatter them in the hour of temptation *but I have prayed for thee*, in particular, againſt whom the fierceſt attack will be made, *that thy faith fail not*, totally and finally, though it will be grievouſly ſhaken *And when thou art converted*, recovered from this grievous fall and temptation, *ſtrengthen thy brethren* , taught by experience, admoniſh others of the rock of ſelf-confidence on which thou haſt ſtruck, and to beware of temptation But if they are overcome, encourage them again to return, and not to deſpair, ſince there is mercy for the baſeſt backſliders, and no repenting ſinner is rejected *Note*, (1) Satan is unable without leave to hurt the leaſt of God's ſaints (2) A perſon may be overcome by temptation, and yet their faith not utterly fail (3) Where true faith is in the heart, the ſoul cannot finally periſh (4) All our perſeverance and ſtability is not to be aſcribed to any reſolution of our own, but to the ceaſeleſs interceſſion of our divine advocate (5) When we have fallen, we may not lie down in deſpair, but riſe, and return with ſhame and humble confeſſion to a pardoning God, that we may find mercy (6) They who have been moſt tempted and exerciſed themſelves, are the beſt counſellors for others under the like trials, and will have moſt compaſſion for them, and be able by their own experience to comfort and encourage them in their diſtreſs

4 He ſilences Peter's boaſts with expreſs aſſurance of his being about to deny him thrice Peter reſolutely declared, neither priſon nor death ſhould ever make him be falſe to his Maſter, or quit him for a moment but Chriſt aſſures him, that night he would have a dire conviction of the weakneſs of his reſolutions, and the ſtrength of the tempter's power over him, even ſo far as to make him deny that he ever knew his Maſter *Note*, We could not ſuſpect there was ſo much evil in our hearts, if in a day of temptation we had not proved it to our grief , but Chriſt knows it all, and provides the grace for our recovery, even before we have fallen

5 He appeals to his diſciples for his paſt care over them ; and they own, that in all their journey , when they travelled without money or proviſions, they lacked nothing *Note*, (1) The more we reflect on the divine Providence in the days that are paſt, the more we ſhall be compelled to acknowledge, that hitherto God hath helped us (2) Paſt experience of the Lord's goodneſs ſhould engage our preſent confidence in his mercy (3) Chriſt's diſciples muſt be ſatisfied with a little, and their Maſter will take care they ſhall not be deſtitute

6 He bids them now prepare for and expect more perilous times , and days of greater diſtreſs. He was about to ſuffer among tranſgreſſors , in the greateſt torment and ignominy, according to the ancient prophecies concerning him, all which now were ready to be accompliſhed and they, for the teſtimony of his goſpel, would be expoſed to want and ſuffering They muſt now take all they have, and employ it in providing hoſe neceſſaries for themſelves which they will want , and really, that at the expence of their garments, ſuch as a ſword, is more

needful

needful for their own defence against the perils of robbers, which they may be called to encounter in their travels Or, figuratively, they may rather refer to the persecutions and violence of their enemies, against which it would require all their fortitude and courage to bear up The disciples, supposing that he meant literally, that they should repel force by force, replied, *Lord, here are two swords*, as if they wished to know whether they should procure more, but *he said unto them, It is enough*, these were sufficient to answer the instructive design for which he mentioned them It was not by those weapons of war that his kingdom was to be spread, or their safety secured, but by the sword of the Spirit, which is the word of God, and by the armour of righteousness on the right hand and the left

39 ¶ [d] And he came out, and [e] went, as he was
wont, to the mount of Olives, and his disciples also
followed him 40. And when he was at the place, he
said unto them, [f] Pray, that ye enter not into temptation
41 And [g] he was withdrawn from them about a stone's
cast, and kneeled down, and prayed, 42 Saying, Father,
if thou be willing, remove [h] this cup from me nevertheless,
[i] not my will, but thine be done 43 And
[k] there appeared an angel unto him from heaven,
strengthening him 44 And being in an agony, [l] he
prayed more earnestly and his sweat was as it were
great drops of blood falling down to the ground 45
And when he rose up from prayer, and was come to his
disciples, he found them sleeping for sorrow, 46 And
said unto them, Why sleep ye? rise and [m] pray, lest ye
enter into temptation.

[d] Mat xxvi 36 Mark xiv 32 John xviii 1 [e] Chap xxi 37 [f] Chap. xi 4 Ver 46 [g] Mat xxvi 39 [h] Mat xx 22 [i] John v 30 & vi 38 [k] Mat iv 11 Heb i 14 [l] Heb v 7 [m] Ver 40

v 39—46 We have here Christ's agony in the garden, the account of which the other Evangelists had given us in nearly the same words *See Mat* xxvi 36 *Mark* xiv 32 Three circumstances are here particularly taken notice of

1 That *an angel appeared from heaven, strengthening him* in his agony, probably suggesting to him, as man, some powerful inducements to encourage and support him under his unutterable distress, that the conflict would be short, the issue glorious, the victory sure, and the eternal salvation of his people be the great reward So low did the Son of God humble himself, as to need their services, who were the work of his own hands and they who ministred to *him*, will not fail to perform the like kind offices to the heirs of salvation If the Lord lays upon us heavy burdens, he will send us help in the needful time of trouble

2 That *being in an agony, he prayed more earnestly* All the storms and billows of divine wrath were now going over him, and the great enemy of souls with all his fury hurled his fiery darts against him With strong crying and tears he redoubled therefore his supplications, and was heard *Note*, Prayer is at all times seasonable, but when we are under distress of body or soul, we are peculiarly called to cry mightily to him, whose strength is made perfect in weakness, and every *wrestling* Jacob will be a *prevailing* Israel

3 *His sweat was as it were great drops of blood falling down to the ground* The intenseness of his agony threw the humours of his body into so violent a fermentation, that though it was night, and he lay on the cold ground, the blood commixed with his sweat through the pores, and the reeking drops trickling down, dyed the earth on which he lay What a bloody baptism was he baptized with! My soul, behold, admire, and adore! It was love for thee that brought thy Saviour thus low these drops of bloody sweat are the expiation of thy iniquities

47 ¶ [n] And while he yet spake, behold, a multitude,
and he that was called Judas, one of the twelve, [o] went
before them, and drew near unto Jesus, [p] to kiss him
48 But Jesus said unto him, Judas, betrayest thou the
Son of man with a kiss? 49 When they which were
about him, saw what would follow, they said unto him,
Lord, shall we smite with [q] the sword? 50 ¶ And one
of them [r] smote the servant of the high priest, and cut
off his right ear 51 And Jesus answered and said,
Suffer ye thus far And he touched his ear, and healed
him 52 Then Jesus said unto the chief priests, and
captains of the temple, and the elders which were come
to him, Be ye come out as against a thief, with swords
and staves? 53 When [s] I was daily with you in the
temple, ye stretched forth no hands against me But
[t] this is your hour, and the power of darkness

[n] Mat xxvi 47 Mark xiv 43 John xviii 3 [o] Acts i 16 [p] 2 Sam xx 9 [q] 2 Cor x 4 [r] Rom xii 19 [s] Chap iv 21 [t] John xii 27

v. 47—53 The traitor with an armed band now appears, and we have,

1 Christ betrayed The signal given by Judas was a kiss Adding hypocrisy to his treachery he approached him, and Jesus, who well knew his design, with one kind word of expostulation on his baseness, readily surrendered himself into the hands of his enemies *Note*, The Lord is privy to the secret thoughts of apostates in heart, and sees the traitor under all the specious profession he makes

2 The disciples, who instantly would have stood on their defence, and rescued him, asked his leave to unsheath their swords, but Peter, too impatient to wait for an answer, drew, and aiming a blow at one of those who were active in seizing on his Master, a servant of the high priest's, the sword glanced down the side of his head, and took off his right ear But Christ rebuked Peter for his rashness, and desires his enemies not to resent the blow which Peter had struck, the damage of which he immediately repairs, and on the spot gave them an evidence of his power and grace, by healing the servant, and restoring his lost ear, which, if their hearts had not been hardened as the nether millstone, could not fail to have convinced them both of the wickedness and ingratitude of their conduct May we learn of our Lord thus ever to render good for evil

3 He expostulates with the chief priests, and the captains of the temple, and elders, some of whom, even at that unseasonable hour, forgetting their dignity, and instigated by their malice, now mingled with the soldiers, and came to make sure of their prey Christ reasons with them on the uselessness of such a military force, when he never would have attempted resistance, nor ever meant to abscond, since he appeared daily in public in the temple *But*, says he, *this is your hour, and the power of darkness* Till that hour came, all the powers of earth and hell could not prevail against him, now it was come, they would find no difficulty in performing what was the predetermined counsel of God

54 Then [u] took they him, and [x] led *him*, and brought
him into the high priest's house And Peter followed
afar off 55 And when they had kindled a fire in the
midst of the hall, and were set down together, [y] Peter
[z] sat down among them 56 But a certain maid beheld
him as he sat by the fire, and earnestly looked upon
him, and said, This man was also with him 57 And
[a] he denied him, saying, Woman, I know him not 58
And after a little while another saw him, and said, Thou
art also of them And Peter said, Man, I am not 59
And about the space of one hour after, another confidently
affirmed, saying, Of a truth this *fellow* also was
with him, for he is a Galilean 60 And Peter said,
Man, I know not what thou sayest And immediately,
while he yet spake, the cock crew 61 And the Lord
turned, and looked upon Peter, and Peter remembered
the word of the Lord, how he had said unto him, [b] Before
the cock crow, thou shalt deny me thrice 62
And Peter [c] went out, and [d] wept bitterly

[u] Mat xxvi 57 [x] Mat xxvi 57 Mark xiv 53 John xviii 12 [y] Mat xxvi 69 Mark xiv 66 John xviii 16 [z] Psal xlix 16 [a] Ver 33 [b] Ver 34 [c] Mark xiv 6 [d] Zech xii 10 Cor vii 11

v 54—62 We have here,

1 Peter's sad fall Willing to see what would be the end of his Master's trials, he stole into the palace, and hoped to pass unperceived among the croud, but his look, his behaviour, his speech, discovered him, and excited repeated charges from the by-standers, which he solemnly disowned, declaring he did not know the man Jesus whom they spoke of and confirming the horrid lie with the most profane oaths and perjury One wilful lie has often led men on to the most dreadful lengths None know where they shall stop, when for a moment they deviate from the path of truth

2 His gracious recovery The cock crew to warn him of his guilt, and rung in Peter's ear a peal of loudest thunder, and one look of Jesus broke his heart with anguish *He turned, and looked upon Peter*, and that glance spoke more than words could utter It shewed him, that, though now on his trial, Christ was apprized of all that passed it conveyed the deepest conviction, the tenderest expostulation, the kindest compassion and the most effectual calls of grace to his heart Peter's guilt now rose in blackest colours to his view, his baseness, his ingratitude, every aggravating circumstance returned to his memory, and, overwhelmed with grief, anguish, horror, and shame, *he went out, and wept bitterly*

63 ¶ [e] And the men that held Jesus [f] mocked him,
and smote *him* 64 And when they had blindfolded
him, they [g] struck him on the face, and asked him, saying,
Prophesy, who is it that smote thee? 65 And
many other things blasphemously spake they against him
66 ¶ And as soon as it was day, [h] the elders of the
people, and the chief priests, and the scribes came together,
and led him into their council, 67 Saying, Art
thou the Christ? tell us And he said unto them, If I
tell you, you will not believe 68 And if I also ask
you, you will not answer me, nor let *me* go 69 [i] Hereafter
shall the Son of man sit on the right hand of the
power of God 70 Then said they all, Art thou then
the

[e] Mat xxvi 67 Mark xiv 65 [f] [illegible] [g] Job xvi 10 [h] Psal ii 2 Acts iv 26 [i] Dan vii 13 Chap [illegible] Heb i 3 [illegible]

k Mark xiv 62 the Son of God? And he said unto them, [k] Ye say
that I am 71 And they said, What need we any fur-
ther witness? for we ourselves have heard of his own
mouth

v 63—71 Behold with horror and indignation,

1 The insults put on this innocent sufferer by the objects who gathered themselves against him The servants who kept Jesus in custody till the council met, mocked him, buffeted him, and blindfolding him, in derision of his prophetical character, struck him on the face, and bid him tell who smote him with other blasphemies, which he silently and patiently endured.

2 The injustice and cruel oppression which his judges, the chief priests and Scribes, shewed at his trial Early they arose, at break of day, eager to hasten his condemnation, and having brought him before them, demanded a direct answer, whether he were the Messiah, or no Christ knew that their wicked design was to employ his own words as the ground of his condemnation, and therefore expostulates with them on their unfair and unreasonable proceedings *If I tell you, ye will not believe* they were resolved at all events, in hardened obstinacy, to reject his pretentions, *and if I ask you* what you can object to the evidences of my divine mission which I have given, *you will not answer me* unable to refute them, yet determined not to be convinced by them, though reduced to silence *nor will you let me go*, though unable to prove a single charge against me Therefore he refers them for conviction to his coming with vengeance on the throne of judgment, when they should know, to their cost, whether he really was possessed of that character which he assumed With indignation they tumultuously asked whether he dared arrogate the title of *the Son of God?* He boldly replied in the affirmative, so they said, and so indeed he was With one voice they instantly condemned him as a blasphemer, counting any further witness unnecessary, when his own confession proved, as they concluded, the blasphemy of his pretensions So were they given up to a reprobate mind, and blind to the clearest evidence of truth, wilfully rushed on their eternal ruin, filling up the measure of their iniquities

CHAP XXIII

This chapter carries on and concludes the history of Christ's sufferings and death We have here, 1 His arraignment before Pilate the Roman governor, ver 1—5 2 His examination before Herod, ver 6—12 3 Pilate's struggle with the people, to release Jesus, 'et last he condemns him to be crucified, ver 13—25 4 An account of what passed as they led him to be crucified, ver 26—34 5 An account of what passed at the place of execution, ver 32—38 6 The conversion of one of the thieves, as Christ was hanging on the cross, ver 39—43 7 The death of Christ, and the prodigies that attended it, ver 44—49 8 His burial, ver 50—56

a Mat xxvii 2. Mark xv 1 John xviii 28
b Ch p xvii
c 1 Kings xviii 17. Acts xvii 7
d Ch xx 25
e John xix 12
f Mat xxvii 11
g 1 Tim vi 13

1 [a] AND the whole multitude of them arose, and
[b] led him unto Pilate 2 And they began to
accuse him, saying, We found [c] this *fellow* perverting
the nation, and [d] forbidding to give tribute to Cæsar,
saying, [e] that he himself is Christ a king 3 And
Pilate asked him, saying, [f] Art thou the king of the
Jews? And he answered him and said, [g] Thou sayest
it 4 Then said Pilate to the chief priests, and *to* the
people, I find no fault in this man 5 And they were
the more fierce, saying, He stirreth up the people,
teaching throughout all Jewry, beginning from Galilee
to this place 6 When Pilate heard of Galilee, he ask-
ed whether the man were a Galilean 7 And as soon
h Chap iii 1 as he knew that he belonged unto [h] Herod's jurisdic-
tion, he sent him to Herod, who himself was also at Je-
rusalem at that time. 8 ¶ And when Herod saw Jesus
i Chap ix 9 he was exceeding glad for [i] he was desirous to see him
k Mat xiv 1 of a long season, because [k] he had heard many things of
him, and he hoped to have seen some miracle done by
him 9 Then he questioned with him in many words,
but he answered him nothing 10 And the chief priests
and scribes stood and vehemently accused him 11
l Is liii 3 And Herod with his men of war [l] set him at nought,
and mocked *him*, and arrayed him in a gorgeous robe,
and sent him again to Pilate 12 ¶ And the same day
m Acts iv 27 [m] Pilate and Herod were made friends together, for
n Chap xxii before they were at enmity between themselves

v 1—12 Though they had condemned our Lord as worthy to die as a blasphemer, yet not having the power of life and death in their hands, and the pretended crime not being of such a nature as the Roman government might deem capital, in order to execute their bloody purposes the chief priests are obliged to have recourse to some other charge Therefore,

1 They accuse him to Pilate, as a fomenter of sedition, setting up himself for king, and forbidding to give tribute to Cæsar, though he had so expressly enjoined it, when they meant to ensnare him, and so far from affecting royalty, had opposed the mistaken zeal of his followers, who would have set him up for their king, *John* vi 15 But the purest innocence is no defence against the blackest calumny Nay, in the present case, they knew themselves in their hearts to be the rebels, they abhorred the Roman government, and so far from thinking it a crime to oppose it, would gladly have embraced the first favourable occasion to revolt And by the just judgment of God, that *pretended crime*, on account of which they demanded the condemnation of Jesus, was shortly after *the real crime*, for which themselves, and the whole Jewish nation, were destroyed by the Romans *Note*, The poisoned chalice will return to him who mingled it

2 Christ plainly and directly answers Pilate's interrogatories, and confesses himself indeed *King of the Jews*, but not in opposition to Cæsar, with whose government he never interfered His kingdom was of a quite different nature, not *of this world*, but purely spiritual over the hearts of men

3 Pilate, convinced of the innocence of Jesus, declares he can find no fault in him, whatever religious doctrines he taught, they came not under his cognizance, and therefore he would have released him but the chief priests, exasperated even to fury at the thought of his being discharged, insisted upon it they could prove him guilty of many seditious discourses, and attempts to raise insurrections through Galilee, the chief scene of his preaching, and in all Judea

4 Pilate, on the mention of Galilee, having found he was of that country, would very gladly have rid himself of this disagreeable affair, and Herod the tetrarch of Galilee, being then at Jerusalem, to whose jurisdiction he belonged, he referred them to him and thus was the scripture fulfilled, *Psal* ii 2 *Acts* iv 26, 27

5 Herod was highly pleased at the sight of Jesus The fame of his mighty works had long excited a desire to see him, and he hoped his curiosity would be gratified by seeing some miracle now performed by him But he was mistaken as Christ knew the spirit with which he put the several questions to him relative to his miracles, he deigned not to make the least reply The poorest beggar that came with his diseased body, would have met the kindest words and speediest relief, but he will not prostitute his power to gratify the curiosity of the proudest potentate

6 Whilst Jesus held his peace, his accusers, with open mouths, belched out their malice, endeavouring to exasperate Herod against him, and to awaken his jealousy with charges of his seditious conduct in Galilee but Herod thought him an object rather to be despised than feared, and after treating him as a weak silly wretch, and suffering his soldiers to make sport of him, in derision of the pretences which Jesus was said to form, he decked him in a robe of mock-majesty, and sent him back to Pilate, desirous he should determine concerning him as he thought fit *Note*, If we are set at nought, insulted, despised, and treated as fools or madmen, let it not be grievous to us, we are but like our Lord

7 Pilate and Herod were on this occasion reconciled They had been at enmity between themselves, on what account is not said, perhaps on account of the slaughter of the Galileans, Herod's subjects, mentioned *Luke* xiii 1 but the mutual civility which passed on this occasion, healed the breach, and made them friends again He who came to remove the enmity which subsisted between God and man, is here the peace-maker even between his persecutors

o Mat xxvii 23. Mark xv 14. John xix 4
p Acts iii 14
q Mat xxvii 26

13 ¶ And [o] Pilate, when he had called together the
chief priests and the rulers and the people, 14 Said
unto them, Ye have brought this man unto me, as
one that perverteth the people and behold, I having
examined *him* before you, have found no fault in this
man touching those things whereof ye accuse him, 15
No, nor yet Herod for I sent you to him, and lo no-
thing worthy of death is done unto him 16 I will
therefore chastise him, and release *him* 17 For of ne-
cessity he must release one unto them at the feast 18
And they cried out all at once, saying, [p] Away with this
man, and release unto us Barabbas 19 (Who for a
certain sedition made in the city, and for murder was
cast into prison) 20 Pilate therefore willing to release
Jesus, spake again to them 21 But they cried, say-
ing, Crucify *him*, crucify him 22 And he said unto
them the third time, Why, what evil hath he done?
I have found no cause of death in him I will therefore
chastise him, and let *him* go 23 And they were instant
with loud voices, requiring that he might be crucified
and

and the voices of them, and of the chief priests prevail-
ed 24 And Pilate gave sentence that it should be as
they required 25 And q he released unto them him
that for sedition and murder was cast into prison, whom
they had desired, but he delivered Jesus to their will

q Prov xvii 15 Isa v 23 & lix 14.

v 13—25 Jesus being brought again from Herod to Pilate,
1 He called the chief priests and rulers, and the people, and convinced of the innocence of the prisoner, he declares, after the strictest examination, he can find no shadow of a crime nor had Herod testified the least mark of his displeasure against Jesus as a criminal, or as one deserving capital punishment He offers, therefore, to *chastise* him, as if he were a criminal, to gratify them, and cover their prosecution from the suspicion of malice and since he must release one to them at the feast, he proposes Christ as the person, who, though his life was spared, would be thus stigmatized as a malefactor Thus doth this corrupt judge desire to trim between his conscience and the people, unwilling to imbrue his hands in innocent blood, yet sollicitous to show his utmost complaisance to them

2 The proposal was abortive The people instigated by their priests and rulers, rejected the offer, *demanding the release* of Barabbas, whose notorious crimes of murder and insurrection called for the severest punishment, and cried out for the immediate execution of Jesus In vain Pilate, again and again, remonstrated against the injustice and cruelty of such a demand, but they only grew more outrageous at his opposition, and not satisfied with the chastisement he offered to inflict upon Jesus, demanded his crucifixion with such clamour, noise, and violence, as quite terrified Pilate into a compliance He feared men more than God, and dared not disoblige a lawless multitude, though at the expence of innocent blood

3 Pilate, though reluctantly, at last pronounces the sentence of execution upon the innocent Saviour, and having released that infamous criminal Barabbas, as preferred before him, *delivers Jesus to their will*, and the enmity which they had shewn against him plainly foretold, that their tender mercies would be cruelty

26 r And as they led him away, they laid hold of one
Simon a Cyrenian, coming out of the country, and on
him they laid the cross, that he might bear it after
Jesus 27 ¶ And there followed him a great company
of people, and of women, which also bewailed and la-
mented him 28 But Jesus turning unto them, said,
Daughters of Jerusalem, weep not for me, but weep for
yourselves, and for your children 29 For behold, the
days are coming, in the which they shall say, Blessed *are*
the barren, and the wombs that never bare, and the
paps which never gave suck 30 s Then shall they be-
gin to say to the mountains, Fall on us, and to the hills,
Cover us 31 t For if they do these things in a green
tree, what shall be done in the dry?

r Mat xxvii 32. Mark xv 21

s Isa ii 19 Hos x 8 Rev vi 16 & ix 6

t Jer xxv 29 Ezek xx 47 1 Pet iv 17

v 26—31 Behold the Lamb of God led to the slaughter, amidst the tears of Jerusalem's daughters

1 His executioners seized on Simon, a Cyrenian, compelling him to bear the cross under which Christ was ready to expire, and not out of pity, but least by death he should elude their malice, they released him for a moment, that they might shortly bind him faster to it with iron

2 A multitude followed him, and among them many women bewailing his unhappy fate, and touched with tenderest sympathy at his innocent sufferings *Note*, A sight of the cross-bearing Saviour may well excite our deepest grief For he bore our sins, and carried our sorrow

3 He addresses the mourners, and kindly bids them direct their tears into another channel, *weep not for me, but weep for yourselves, and for your children*, deep as his agonies were, he freely submitted to them, his sufferings were voluntary, and the issue of them would be glorious, but the judgment coming upon their people and nation, would be imbittered with the wrath of God, and end in their utter destruction Then barrenness would be accounted a blessing for better were it to be destitute of children, than to see them devoured by famine and the sword A refuge then, under falling rocks and mountains, would be welcome, rather than to meet the fearful executioners of God's vengeance, *for if they have done this thing in the green tree, what shall be done in the dry?* If these wicked men have inflicted such sufferings on me, who am innocent, what shall be done to them who, by their sins, are as fuel prepared for the devouring flames And if the Romans, whom they have instigated, are permitted to exercise such cruelty on me who have never given them provocation, what vengeance will they wreak on the Jewish people, when to the utmost exasperated, and consuming them as fire doth the dry wood? *Note*, (1) Though barrenness is often counted a misery, the days may come when not to have children may be reckoned among our mercies (2) They who will not fly to the arms of Jesus for mercy, will cry in vain to rocks and mountains to shelter them from the frowns of his wrath (3) Every view of the sufferings of Jesus should fill us with horror at the dreadful evil and danger of sin, if when it was *imputed* to him only, the wrath of God fell so heavy upon him, with what an intolerable load must the impenitent soul be overwhelmed, when all the wrath of God due for his *own* sins shall light down on his devoted head If Christ's sufferings were so great, what must the torment of the damned be?

32 And u there were also two other malefactors led
with him to be put to death 33 And x when they were
come to the place which is called ‖ Calvary, there they
crucified him, and the malefactors, one on the right
hand, and the other on the left 34 ¶ Then said Jesus,
Father, y forgive them, for z they know not what they
do And a they parted his raiment, and cast lots 35
And b the people stood beholding and the rulers also
with them derided *him*, saying, He saved others, let
him save himself, if he be Christ the chosen of God
36 And the soldiers also mocked him, coming to him,
and c offering him vinegar, 37 And saying, If thou be
the king of the Jews, save thyself 38 And a super-
scription also was written over him in letters of Greek
and Latin, and Hebrew, THIS IS THE KING OF
THE JEWS 39 ¶ And one of the malefactors
which were hanged, railed on him, saying, If thou be
Christ, save thyself and us 40 But the other answer-
ing, rebuked him, saying, Dost not thou fear God,
seeing thou art in the same condemnation? 41 And
we indeed justly, for we receive the due reward of our
deeds but this man hath done nothing amiss 42
And he said unto Jesus, Lord, remember me when thou
comest into thy kingdom 43 And Jesus said unto
him, Verily I say unto thee, To day shalt thou be with
me in paradise

v 32—43 We have here,

1 The crucifixion of the Son of God between two malefactors, who, to increase the ignominy of his sufferings, were led with him to Calvary, the place of execution, and crucified on each side of him There, amidst the taunts and insults of his enemies, he was hung up, in torments to expire and over his head his pretended crime was written in Hebrew, Greek, and Latin, *This is the King of the Jews* Whilst they are mocking, let us bow down with adoration, and wonder at that love which fastened him to the accursed tree If, as they challenged him to do, he refused to *save himself*, it was because he could not then have *saved us*, it was needful that he should die upon the cross, that we might not eternally perish under the wrath of God

2 His prayer for his murderers *Father, forgive them, for they know not what they do*, they were blinded by prejudice and ignorance, and as the dying Sufferer forgave them, he became, as mediator, their advocate with his Father, that he might obtain their pardon, and prevailed Some of those who nailed him to the tree, experienced the glorious efficacy of that atoning blood with which their hands were stained *Note*, (1) There are no crimes so great but the blood of Jesus can cleanse us from them, even murder itself is not unpardonable (2) The persecutors of God's people know not what they do, and this should be an argument with us, after our Lord's example, to bear with, forgive, pity, and pray for them

3 The conversion of the thief upon the cross, wherein we behold a most glorious evidence of the mighty efficacy of the Saviour's grace, even in the lowest step of his humiliation, and a striking display of the great design of his sufferings, to save that which was lost We are told by the other evangelists, that both the malefactors reviled him, as I am inclined to believe at first they did, though afterwards one of them, by the effectual sovereign grace of God, became a signal monument of mercy, as is here related One indeed continued hardened to the last, railing on him, and challenging him if he was the Christ, to save himself and them Thus afflictive providences, without the grace of God, serve only to harden and exasperate, instead of humbling the impenitent The other, snatched as a brand from the burning, is here held up an illustrious monument of the salvation of Jesus, even to the uttermost; an object which stains the pride of human glory, and renders all self-wrought human righteousness contemptible, when such a wretch enters the eternal kingdom, from which the most devout, decent, and orderly Pharisee must be for ever excluded The fear which some have expressed lest this example should embolden sinners, and the many insinuations they have suggested to evince the good character of the thief, as if he had never heard of Christ before, that it was the first crime, &c appear unnecessary, not to say unchristian, and whatever specious shew of piety they bear, are calculated merely to tarnish the transcend-

u Isa liii 12 Mat xxvii 38 Mark xv 27 John xix 18

x Mat xxvii 33 Mark xv 22 John xix 17

‖ Or, the place of a skull

y Mat v 44 Acts vii 60 1 Cor iv 12

z Acts iii 17

a Mat xxvii 35 Mark xv 24 John xix 23

b Psal xxii 17 Zech xii 10

c Mat xxvii 34 48

ent lustre of the unsearchable riches of Christ, and to derogate from the sovereignty and freedom of the grace of God It is enough that the Saviour was pleased to exercise a signal act of favour towards one desperate sinner, as an encouragement to the most miserable still to trust in his mercy

(1) The behaviour of this malefactor evidenced the blessed influence which a sense of redeeming love instantly wrought on his heart No sooner was he struck with the conviction, that the suffering man who hung by his side was the true Messiah, and God's eternal Son, than instantly his tone is changed to every expression of real penitence (1) He sharply rebukes his companion, *Dost thou not fear God?* When ready to appear at his tremendous bar, how unsuitable is such reviling in thy lips, *seeing thou art in the same condemnation*, suffering the same kind of punishment, and therefore humanity dictated mutual compassion (2) He reminds him of the justness of their punishment, and takes shame to himself for his crimes *We indeed suffer justly, for we receive the just reward of our deeds*, and that should have covered them both with confusion, and sealed up their lips in silence Thus every real penitent justifies God in his judgments, and owns all he suffers to be no more than his sins deserve (3) He bears testimony to the innocence of Jesus, *this man hath done nothing amiss*, he was fully convinced his sufferings were for sins not his own, and his confession seems to intimate he was well acquainted with the Saviour's character, and what he had seen of Christ's behaviour on the cross, his meekness, patience, and charity towards his murderers, were striking evidences of his innocence (4) He addresses himself to the dying Redeemer, as a dying sinner commending himself to his mercy, *Lord, remember me when thou comest into thy kingdom* His faith staggered not at the ignominious circumstances in which he beheld the Son of God, he pays him the divine honours due to him as *the Lord* of life and glory, he professes unshaken dependance on his all sufficiency to save, even at the latest gasp, the vilest of sinners Humbly he presents his request, one kind remembrance only he asks, unworthy the least regard, but if the Lord will think of him in that glorious kingdom, to which he is now assured he is about to be advanced, that will be enough to ensure his salvation Lord, give me like faith in thy power and love! Thus dying, may I be able to commend my spirit into thy hands! Content to stand on a level with this wretched malefactor, and founding all my hopes on thy rich and sovereign grace alone!

(2) Christ is pleased most graciously to answer his requests, and to give him even more than he asks *Verily I say unto thee*, and my word is truth, my promises sure, *this day shalt thou be with me in paradise*, thy soul, as soon as it departs from the body, shall join the assembly of the blessed in that state of happiness and glory, which God hath prepared for his redeemed people *Note*, (1) The prayer of faith is sure of an answer of peace, the chief of sinners, when they return to God, shall be placed among his saints in glory everlasting (2) There is a state of blessedness immediately prepared for the souls of the faithful, where they are in joy and felicity before the resurrection day, when in body and soul their happiness will be complete (3) Where Christ is, there is heaven, to be with him, is to be eternally blessed

d Mat xxvii 45 Mark xv 33 e Amos viii 9 f Ex xxvi 31 2 Chron iii 14 Heb x 19 g Ps xxxi 5 1 Pet ii 23 h Acts vii 59 i Mat xxvii 54 Mark xv 39 k John xix 25 Ps xxxviii 11

44 d And it was about the sixth hour, and there was
a darkness over all the earth until the ninth hour 45
And e the sun was darkened, and f the vail of the temple
was rent in the midst 46 ¶ And when Jesus had
cried with a loud voice, he said, Father, g into thy
hands I commend my spirit and having said thus, h he
gave up the ghost 47 Now when the centurion saw
what was done, he glorified God, saying, i Certainly this
was a righteous man 48 And all the people that came
together to that sight, beholding the things which were
done, smote their breasts, and returned 49 And all his
acquaintance, and the women that followed him from
Galilee, k stood afar off beholding these things.

v 44—49 We are told,

1 The prodigies which happened whilst Jesus hung on the tree The sun was eclipsed from twelve o'clock at noon till three, and the vail of the temple rent, signifying the state of judicial blindness, to which the Jewish people were abandoned, the abolition of all the typical institution, the one great sacrifice being now offered which they represented, and the free access which all, whether Jew or Gentile, now have to a throne of grace, *through the new and living way consecrated through the vail, that is to say, his flesh*, Heb x 19, 20

2 The last dying words of Jesus, which he uttered aloud, not as one exhausted, but as having still his full strength, *Father, into thy hands I commend my spirit and having thus said, he gave up the ghost* He borrows the Psalmist's words, for scripture language is ever most expressive in our addresses to God He testifies the fullest confidence in the favour of God his *Father*, as the great high-priest and sacrifice, he, by the eternal Spirit, offers himself for the sins of his people and now, by his death, pays down the ransom in full to divine justice, he commits his human body and soul, that now were to be separated, to his Father's care, and waits in hope until the third day, when they should be reunited, and he should rise again And thus must the dying saints of God by faith, cheerfully commend their departing souls to their Father's keeping, until the happy resurrection morn, when, fashioned like to Christ's glorious body, our sleeping ashes shall be re-animated, and we shall be taken to dwell with him in his eternal kingdom

3 The centurion's confession Deeply affected with what he saw and heard, he could not refrain from expressing his fullest conviction of the innocence of Jesus, and, to the glory of God, acknowledges the righteousness of his eternal Son

4 The spectators, many of them at least, perhaps some also who had cried, *Crucify him* now full of anguish and remorse, returned smiting on their breasts The prodigies they beheld startled their consciences, and terrified them with the apprehension of what would be the consequence of this atrocious deed, at which even the heavens above, and the earth under their feet, testified their indignation

5 A multitude of his disciples, and of the women who followed Jesus from Galilee, stood at a distance, overwhelmed with grief at what they saw, and under the deepest dejection, as if the cross of Jesus was the death of all their hopes when, in fact, by these sufferings alone his victories were to be obtained, and his kingdom established

50 ¶ l And behold, *there was* a man named Joseph, l Mat xxvii 57 Mark xv 42 John xix 38
a counsellor, *and he was* a good man, and a just 51
(The same had not consented to the counsel and deed
of them) *he was* of Arimathea, a city of the Jews
(m who also himself waited for the kingdom of God) m Chap ii 25 38
52 This man went unto Pilate, and begged the body
of Jesus 53 And he took it down, and wrapped it in
linen, and n laid it in a sepulchre that was hewn in stone, n Isa liii 9 Mat xxvii 60
wherein never man before was laid 54 And that day
was the preparation, and the sabbath drew on 55 And
the women also o which came with him from Galilee, o Chap viii 2
followed after, and beheld the sepulchre, and how his
body was laid 56 And they returned, and prepared
spices and ointments, and rested the sabbath-day, p ac- p Ex xx 10
cording to the commandment

v 50—56 The corpse of Jesus was now in danger of being cast with those of the malefactors into a common grave, but when none of his other disciples had courage to appear, or ability to give him an honourable interment, God is pleased to raise up one to discharge this last kind office

1 His name and character are here given us He was called Joseph, a man of signal piety and probity, *a counsellor*, probably one of the great Sanhedrim, *who consented not to the counsel and deed of them*, either he entered his protest against their proceedings, or seeing opposition in vain, withdrew *He was of Arimathea, a city of the Jews, who also himself waited for the kingdom of God*, expecting, according to the prophecies, that it would shortly appear

2 He went unto Pilate, and having obtained permission to take down the body from the cross, he wrapped it in linen, and laid it in his own new tomb, where never man before lay, in haste to finish the funeral, because the sabbath drew on The women, the constant attendants of Jesus, followed the corpse to the grave, and returning, prepared spices and ointment, that they might come and embalm him, as soon as the sabbath was past, during which, they observed the rest enjoined on that holy day *Note*, The Lord's day now, as the sabbath of old, is sacred, all our affairs must be so ordered, as not to break in upon the hours expressly set apart for the immediate service of God

CHAP XXIV

We have here glorious testimonies born to the resurrection of Jesus, 1 By two angels, to the women, who reported it to the apostles, ver 1—12 2 By Christ himself, to two of the disciples, as they went to Emmaus, ver 13—35 3 He appears to the eleven disciples themselves, the same day at evening, ver 36—48 4 He ascends into heaven, to the joy and praise of his disciples, whom he left behind, ver 49—53

1 a NOW upon the first day of the week, very early a Mat xxviii 1 Mark xvi 1 John xx 1 Chap xxiii 56
in the morning, they came unto the sepulchre,
bringing the spices which they had prepared, and cer-
tain *others* with them 2 And they found the stone
rolled away from the sepulchre 3 And they entred
in, and found not the body of the Lord Jesus 4 And
it came to pass, as they were much perplexed there-
about,

c Gen xviii 2 John xx 13 Acts i 10. about, behold, c two men ſtood by them in ſhining
garments 5 And as they were afraid, and bowed
down *their* faces to the earth, they ſaid unto them,
† Or The living one Heb vii 8. Why ſeek ye † the living among the dead? 6 He is
not here, but is riſen remember d how he ſpake unto
d Chap ix 22 & xviii 33 you when he was yet in Galilee 7 Saying, The Son
of man muſt be delivered into the hands of ſinful men,
and be crucified, and the third day riſe again 8 And
e John ii 22 e they remembered his words, 9 And returned from
the ſepulchre, and told all theſe things unto the eleven,
and to all the reſt 10 It was Mary Magdalene, and
f Chap viii 3 f Joanna, and Mary *the mother* of James, and other *wo-
men that were* with them, which told theſe things unto
the apoſtles. 11 And their words ſeemed to them as
g Ver 25 idle tales, and g they believed them not 12 Then a-
h John xx 3 6 roſe Peter, and h ran unto the ſepulchre, and ſtooping
down, he beheld the linen clothes laid by themſelves,
and departed, wondring in himſelf at that which was
come to paſs

v 1—12 The ſabbath being ended, the good women who had prepared the ſpices to embalm the body, were early up, to viſit the ſepulchre, and, to their ſurprize, found the ſtone rolled away from the door and, to increaſe their perplexity, on entring the ſepulchre, they found not the body Whereupon we are told,

1 The glorious viſion which appeared to them of two angels, whoſe preſence at firſt greatly terrified them, and with deep reſpect they bowed their faces to the ground, but theſe heavenly meſſengers ſoon relieved them from their diſtreſs, with words of kindeſt conſolation, *Why ſeek ye the living among the dead? He is not here, but is riſen*, Jeſus, your maſter, is no longer the priſoner of the grave, he lives, for ever lives, the conqueror of all his foes, *remember how he ſpake unto you when he was yet in Galilee*, it need not ſurprize them when he had ſo repeatedly foretold the ſufferings and death he muſt undergo from the hands of wicked men, and his reſurrection which would follow and on being reminded of this, they remembered the prediction which the angel mentioned *Note*, We are ſtrangely forgetful of the great things which Jeſus hath ſpoken, and need to have our memories often refreſhed, that we may not let them ſlip

2 The haſte the women made to apprize the apoſtles, and the reſt of the diſciples, of what they had ſeen and heard But, though the fact was aſſerted by the women, ſo ſlow of heart were they to believe, that they treated the report *as idle tales, and believed them not*, they imputed it to the power of imagination, and were ſo ſunk in deſpair, and ſo totally unapprehenſive of Chriſt's reſurrection, that they ſeem not to have the leaſt expectation of it, nor the leaſt remembrance of the aſſurances concerning his riſing again, which he had ſo repeatedly given them

3 Peter, rouſed by the report, reſolved however to ſee for himſelf, and ran immediately to the ſepulchre, and ſtooping down, ſaw the grave cloaths regularly folded up, and laid ſeparate, but the body gone, whereupon *he departed, wondring in himſelf at that which was come to paſs* Not having the leaſt expectation of his maſter's reſurrection, he could not account for theſe ſtrange circumſtances Had he remembered the words of Jeſus, his wonder muſt have ceaſed

i Mark xvi 12. 13 ¶ i And behold, two of them went that ſame day
to a village called Emmaus, which was from Jeruſalem
about threeſcore furlongs 14 And they talked toge-
ther of all theſe things which had happened 15 And
it came to paſs, that while they communed *together*, and
k Matt xviii 20 Ver 36. reaſoned, k Jeſus himſelf drew near, and went with
them 16 But their eyes were holden, that they ſhould
not know him 17 And he ſaid unto them, What
manner of communications are theſe that ye have one
to another, as ye walk, and are ſad? 18 And the
one of them, whoſe name was Cleopas, anſwering,
ſaid unto him, Art thou only a ſtranger in Jeruſalem,
and haſt not known the things which are come to paſs
there in theſe days? 19 And he ſaid unto them,
What things? And they ſaid unto him, Concerning
l Matt xxi 11 Chap vii 16 John iv 19 m Acts vii 22 n Chap i 68 Acts i 6 Ver 1 Jeſus of Nazareth, l which was a prophet m mighty in
deed and word before God and all the people 20 And
how the chief prieſts and our rulers delivered him to
be condemned to death, and have crucified him 21
But we truſted that it had been he n which ſhould have
redeemed Iſrael and beſide all this, to day is the third
day ſince theſe things were done 22 Yea, and certain
women alſo of our company made us aſtoniſhed, o which
were early at the ſepulchre 23 And when they found
not his body, they came, ſaying, that they had alſo ſeen
a viſion of angels, which ſaid that he was alive 24
p Ver 12 And p certain of them which were with us, went to the
ſepulchre, and found *it* even ſo as the women had ſaid,
but him they ſaw not 25 Then he ſaid unto them,
O fools, and ſlow of heart to believe all that the pro-
q Or, ought he not to have ſuffered &c. Ver 46 phets have ſpoken! 26 q Ought not Chriſt to have
ſuffered theſe things, and to enter into his glory? 27
r Gen iii 15 & xxii 18 s Deut xviii 15 And beginning at r Moſes, and s all the prophets, he
expounded unto them in all the ſcriptures the things
concerning himſelf 28 And they drew nigh unto the
village whither they went and he made as though he
would have gone further 29 But t they conſtrained
him, ſaying, Abide with us, for it is towards evening,
and the day is far ſpent And he went in to tarry with
them 30 And it came to paſs as he ſat at meat with
them, he took bread, and bleſſed *it*, and brake, and
gave to them 31 And their eyes were opened, and
they knew him, and he vaniſhed out of their ſight
32 And they ſaid one to another, Did not our heart
burn within us, while he talked with us by the way,
and while he opened to us the ſcriptures? 33 And
they roſe up the ſame hour, and returned to Jeruſalem
and found the eleven gathered together, and them that
u 1 Cor 15 5 were with them, 34 Saying, The Lord is riſen indeed,
and u hath appeared to Simon 35 And they told what
things *were done* in the way, and how he was known of
them in breaking of bread.

v 13—35 This paſſage juſt mentioned by Mark, is here more at large related We have,

1 The diſcourſe of two of the diſciples as they walked to a village called Emmaus, about ſeven or eight miles from Jeruſalem Their buſineſs we are not told, perhaps deſpair had ſeized upon their hearts of ever again ſeeing their crucified maſter, and they were now returning homewards And as they went, the melancholy events which had paſſed, were the *ſubject of their converſation*, together with the report which the women had ſpread of the reſurrection of their Lord, on the probability of which they might be reaſoning *Note*, Godly converſation makes the moſt pleaſing journey

2 An unknown ſtranger, to appearance, joins them on the road, as they were in deep diſcourſe, and walking with them, kindly enquires what cauſed their melancholy looks and earneſt converſation They little thought who now was of their company, either their ſight was miraculouſly affected, or their downcaſt eyes were never lifted up to look upon the perſon who had overtaken them *Note*, (1) Where two of Chriſt's diſciples meet to talk about the things which appertain to his kingdom and glory, he will be in the midſt of them, inſtructing and comforting them (2) The children of God are often, without reaſon, ſad, and fear their caſe is deſperate, when their ſalvation is moſt ſecure, but *their eyes are holden* through their weakneſs of their faith they cannot take the comfort which is offered to them (3) When we are ſad and dejected, ſolitude increaſes the evil, whilſt the converſe of a gracious friend ſerves to alleviate our ſorrows and where we are fellow-mourners, by comparing our caſes, we ſhould ſeek to be mutual comforters

3 In anſwer to his queſtion, Cleopas replied, *Art thou only a ſtranger in Jeruſalem, and haſt not known the things which are come to paſs there in theſe days?* The city had rung of the horrid execution of Jeſus, and Cleopas preſumes that no man who came from thence, could poſſibly be unacquainted with the tranſaction which had paſſed on that occaſion

4 When Chriſt ſtill pretended ignorance of the thing to which Cleopas alluded, in order to draw on farther diſcourſe in anſwer to his queſtion, Cleopas ſuccinctly relates the paſt and preſent ſtate of the affair He begins with an account of his dear Lord and Maſter *Jeſus of Nazareth, who was a prophet*, a teacher come from God, who confirmed his divine miſſion by the heavenly doctrine he taught and the miracles he wrought, was evidently approved of the Moſt High, who endued him with ſuch mighty powers, and bore witneſs to him from heaven, and was for a while greatly careſſed and admired by the people, who in crowds attended his miniſtry Him, at the inſtigation of the chief prieſts and rulers, the Roman governor had crucified, though confeſſedly innocent, the remembrance of which proceedings ſeems deeply afflicted them eſpecially as they acknowledge themſelves his diſciples, and own their fond ſanguine hope, that this *had been he, who ſhould have redeemed Iſrael*, the promiſed Meſſiah, the great prophet, whom Moſes had bid them expect But, alas! their hopes were now almoſt buried in their Maſter's grave it was true indeed, he talked about riſing on the third day, which was now drawing to a period, and certain ſtrange reports had been ſpread by ſome women of their company, who had been that morning at the ſepulchre to look after the body,

and

and astonished them with an account of having seen a vision of angels, who said he was alive, but they gave little credit to the report. Some of their men, however, hereupon ran to the tomb, and found the body gone, as the women had said, but saw nothing of the angels or their Master, which rendered the matter very suspicious, and made them suppose the women mistaken, since if he was really arisen, they could not but conclude he would rather have notified it to his apostles than to them, so that on the whole they were deeply dejected, and once entertained the least prospect of ever seeing him again.

5. The unknown traveller hereupon took up the discourse. He begins with a just rebuke of their folly and unbelief. *O fools, and slow of heart to believe all that the prophets have spoken.* Had ye reflected upon, and embraced the prophetic writings, you might as soon have entertained suspicions about the rising of the sun, as the resurrection of Jesus: for *ought not Christ to suffer these things*, according to the eternal counsels of God, the express declarations of his prophets, and for the honour of the divine justice, and *to enter into his glory*, the reward of his sufferings and death? So far, therefore, from harbouring doubts because of these, that he could not be the Messiah, nor would ever rise again, what he endured was absolutely a proof of the reality of the character he assumed, and should have encouraged their fullest confidence, that as they had beheld his humiliation on the cross, they should also see his exaltation to the mediatorial throne. Then beginning from the books of Moses, he proceeded through the prophets, expounding to them the types and prophecies which related to himself, and spoke of his sufferings, and the glory which should follow. *Note*, The Old Testament, as well as the New, is full of Christ. We never understand Moses and the prophets aright, unless we see him as the great object which they continually hold forth to us.

6. At last Christ discovers himself unto them. Drawing nigh to Emmaus, he made as if he would have parted company, and passed on further, but they were too much charmed with his discourse to let him go, and therefore as the evening was advanced, they pressed him to stay; and at their importunate request he went in with them. And sitting down at table, with authority, as the master of the house, took bread, according to his usual manner, and craving the divine benediction, brake, and gave to them. Immediately their eyes were opened, they looked up, and discovered the well-known features of their crucified Master, when instantly he became invisible and withdrew, leaving them to reflect on what they had seen and heard. *Note*, (1.) They who wish for Christ's company must solicit the favour; he loves the importunity of prayer. (2.) If we have tasted the satisfaction of communion with Jesus, like the spouse we shall hold him fast in the arms of faith and love, and determine never to let him go. (3.) Our meals must be sanctified by prayer and thanksgiving, and then they will serve to minister food to our souls as well as our bodies. (4.) In the ways of his ordinances, the Lord opens the eyes of our faith, and enables us to behold his glory; he hath often since that made himself known to his people *in the breaking of bread* at his table. (5.) The visits of Jesus upon earth are transient; in heaven alone we can expect the uninterrupted beatific vision.

7. The disciples could not help hereupon reflecting on the lively impression the discourse of Jesus had made upon them in the way. On comparing, they found that both their hearts had glowed with holy ardour as he spoke, such irradiation darted into their minds, whilst he opened to them the scripture, such life and energy accompanied his discourse, that they cannot but marvel at their own stupidity not to have discovered him before, since none could have taught them with such demonstration of the Spirit and power, but he who spake *like as never man spake* before. *Note*, Nothing can warm the sinner's frozen heart like the preaching of a crucified Jesus, and his delightful name should be the continual subject of our discourse.

8. They immediately resolved to return, and carry the glad tidings to their brethren at Jerusalem. Not a moment was to be lost; they knew by what themselves had felt how melancholy and distressed their fellow disciples were, and how they could bring them news that would warm their heart, as it had fired their own. Accordingly, though it was evening, they hasted back, and found opportunely the apostles assembled with the rest of the faithful, who, before they had power to speak, eagerly prevented them, saying, *the Lord is risen indeed, and hath appeared unto Simon*; so that it is not a woman's report merely, but a certain fact. The two disciples then corroborated the evidence with what had passed in the way, and the discovery which Jesus made of himself to them *in breaking of bread*, when they sat down together to take some refreshment. *Note*, (1.) The gracious experiences which the Saviour gives us of his love, we should delight to communicate for the comfort and encouragement of our brethren. (2.) Nothing serves more to confirm the faith, and enliven the hope of real christians, than comparing their observations, and the dealings of God with their souls. As iron sharpeneth iron, so doth such gracious communication mutually quicken and warm their hearts.

36 ¶ [x] And as they thus spake, Jesus himself stood
in the midst of them, and saith unto them, Peace *be*
unto you. 37 But they were terrified and affrighted,
and supposed that they had seen a spirit. 38 And he
said unto them, Why are ye troubled? and why do
thoughts arise in your hearts? 39 Behold my hands
and my feet, that it is I myself: [y] handle me, and see;
for a spirit hath not flesh and bones, as ye see me have.
40 And when he had thus spoken, he shewed them *his*
hands and *his* feet. 41 And while they yet believed
not [z] for joy, and wondered, he said unto them, [a] Have
ye here any meat? 42 And they gave him a piece of
a broiled fish, and of an honey-comb. 43 And he took
it, and did eat before them. 44 And he said unto
them, [b] These *are* the words which I spake unto you,
while I was yet with you, that all things must be fulfilled
which were written in the law of Moses, and *in* the prophets,
and *in* the psalms concerning me. 45 Then [c]
opened he their understanding, that they might understand
the scriptures, 46 And said unto them, Thus it
is written, and thus it behoved Christ to suffer, and to
rise from the dead the third day: 47 And [e] that repentance
and [f] remission of sins should be preached in his
name [g] among all nations, [h] beginning at Jerusalem.
48 And [i] ye are witnesses of these things. 49 ¶ And
behold, [k] I send the promise of my Father upon you:
but tarry ye in the city of Jerusalem, until ye be endued
with power from on high.

[x] Mark xvi. 14. John xx. 19. 1 Cor. xv. [y] John xx. 27. [z] John xxi. [illegible] [a] Gen. xlv. 26. John xxi. 10. [b] Chap. ix. 22. & xvii. 31. Ver. 6. [c] Acts xvi. 14. [illegible] Acts xvii. 3. [e] Acts v. 31. & xiii. 38. [f] John iii. [g] Isa. xlix. 6. [h] Acts i. 4. [i] John xv. 27. Acts i. 8. [k] Isa. xliv. 3. John xiv. 26. & xv. 26. & xvi. 7. Acts ii. 4. [l] Acts i. 4.

Ver. 36—49. This is the fifth appearance of Jesus the same day he arose. First he was seen by Mary, *John* xx. 14. Then by the women, *Matt.* xxviii. 9. By Peter alone, 1 *Cor.* xv. 5. By the two disciples, and now by all who were assembled together.

1. He suddenly appeared in the midst of them, whilst they were talking over this glorious event, the resurrection of their Lord, and with most encouraging words of consolation, wishes them all peace and happiness. He mentions not one upbraiding word of their perfidy in forsaking him, of Peter's profaneness and perjury in denying him; they had turned again, and he had sealed their pardon; the past, therefore, is not only forgiven, but forgotten, and he is come to assure them of his unchangeable love.

2. They were terrified and affrighted at his presence, and supposed at first it was an apparition, or a spirit, that had assumed the form of Jesus. So surprized were they, that they forgat the proofs of his resurrection for a moment, on which they had been just discoursing.

3. He soon convinced them of the groundlessness of their fears, and their folly to be startled at his appearance, which should have been their greatest joy. *Why are ye troubled, and why do thoughts arise in your hearts?* *Note*, We often cause ourselves needless disquiet, brooding over melancholy apprehensions, when perhaps the very distress we feel is a symptom for good, as the deep conviction of sin shew the Spirit of God is at work with our hearts, and will shortly fill us with peace and joy in believing. To remove, therefore, their doubts,

(1.) He bids them examine him, and gain the fullest evidence to their senses. There were his hands and his feet, where still the scars of the nails remained, those glorious scars in his victorious conflict over all the powers of darkness, their enemies; and his *handle me, and see*; satisfy yourselves fully in the certainty of my resurrection, and the identity of my body; *for a spirit hath not flesh and bones, as ye see me have*, but is incorporeal, though it may appear under the resemblance of a human form. Accordingly he shewed them his hands, his feet, his side, that they might have the fullest conviction of his being the same Jesus, for bearing testimony to whose resurrection, they would afterwards be exposed to the most furious persecutions, and therefore it was needful that their own assurance of the fact should be put beyond a doubt.

(2.) He eats and drinks with them, to prove most fully to them, that he had really a living body like their own. The astonishment they were in, and the inexpressible joy they felt, quite overcame them; they were ready to believe, that what they saw and heard, was too great and too good news to be true, and could not yet credit the testimony of their own senses. To give them time to recover from this ecstasy, and confirm their faith, he sat down with them, and did eat in their presence some broiled fish, and a piece of an honey-comb, which they gave him, so that they might be assured hereby he was no spectre.

(3.) He not only gave this conviction to their sense, but poured a flood of divine light upon their souls. He refers them to his former discourses with them, concerning the things written in the law, the prophets, and psalms, relative to his sufferings and glory; and by the powerful operation of his Spirit he wonderfully brought all he had spoken to their memory, and opened the intent and meaning of the ſcriptures to their hearts with ſuch evidence, clearneſs, and certainty, that they perceived the full accompliſhment of all in him *Note*, (1) Our underſtandings are darkened, till Chriſt ſhines upon us as the ſun of righteouſneſs, and alſo by his ſpirit communicates the faculty of viſion (2) The moſt enlightened mind hath daily need to cry, *open thou mine eyes* (3) The way in which Chriſt teaches is in and by the ſcriptures, we muſt look for no wiſdom unto ſalvation out of the written word Though, (4) The plaineſt truths of God's revealed will are never be ſpiritually diſcerned, till the Holy Ghoſt guides us into the ſenſe and meaning of them

(4) He gives them inſtructions for the work in which they were now about to be employed (1) They were to be witneſſes of his death and reſurrection, proving from the ſcriptures the predictions concerning both, which were now accompliſhed in him, in conſequence whereof, *repentance and remiſſion muſt be preached by them in his name among all nations, beginning at Jeruſalem* He being exalted at the right hand of God, in conſequence of his ſufferings, to beſtow thoſe ineſtimable bleſſings on as many as believed in his name, not of the Jews only, but of the Gentiles alſo and nothing could ſo powerfully influence and engage the hearts of ſinners to return to God, as this free and full ſalvation preached to them in his name They muſt begin at Jeruſalem, which had been the chief ſcene of his life and ſufferings, the oracles of God, to which they appealed, were in the hands of the Jews, there the facts were tranſacted, to the truth of which they might moſt confidently appeal, and there his murderers dwelt, who moſt eſpecially needed to be called to repentance, and to many of whom he would ſignalize the riches of his grace, in pardoning and ſaving them The goſpel is grace abounding to the chief of ſinners (2) He bids them wait a while at Jeruſalem, and in a few days he would pour out upon them the Spirit from on high, which he had promiſed them, to qualify them for their arduous undertaking, and ſtrengthen them in the diſcharge of it His kingdom was to be eſtabliſhed, not by human endeavours, but by divine energy, therefore the inſtruments were poor weak illiterate fiſhermen, and this the more magnified the effectual working of that mighty power which appeared in them They were endued with ſuch wiſdom as none of their adverſaries could reſiſt, with ſuch courage, that no danger could diſmay them, with ſuch miraculous powers, as evidently ſpoke the finger of God, and were bleſſed with ſuch amazing ſucceſs, that in ſpite of all oppoſition, they were enabled to lay the foundations of that church, againſt which the gates of hell can never prevail

50 ¶ And he led them out [m] as far as to Bethany — m Acts i 12
and he lift up his hands, and bleſſed them 51 And — n Mark xvi
it came to paſs, while he bleſſed them, [n] he was parted — 19 Acts i 9
from them, and carried up into heaven 52 [o] And they — o Matt
worſhipped him, and returned to Jeruſalem with great — xxviii 9
joy 53 And [p] were continually in the temple, praiſing — p Acts ii 46
and bleſſing God Amen — & v 42

v 50—53 We have here the account of the aſcenſion of Jeſus into heaven, after he had forty days converſed with his diſciples after his reſurrection

1 He gives them his parting benediction He *led them out as far as to Bethany*, from whence he had made his triumphant entry into Jeruſalem, ſome few days before his death And lifting up his hands, as the great high prieſt, *Lev* ix 22 he pronounced a bleſſing upon them

2 He was parted from them juſt as he had finiſhed his benediction, as Elijah from Eliſha, *and carried up into heaven*, either by the miniſtry of angels, or his own divine power, making his triumphant entry into the glorious courts above, and ſitting down on the mediatorial throne prepared for him as the reward of his ſufferings *Note*, Though deareſt friends muſt now part, we follow Jeſus to that kingdom where we ſhall part no more

3 The diſciples bowed down in adoration before him, as the very God, who though in his human nature removed out of ſight, yet filled heaven and earth with his preſence *Note*, The incarnate Jeſus juſtly claims the worſhip and ſervice of all his faithful followers

4 *They returned to Jeruſalem with great joy* Their ſorrows now were baniſhed, bright hope and burning love poſſeſſed every boſom, and they waited confidently expecting the fulfilment of the promiſe their Lord had given them, *and were continually in the temple*, at the ſtated hours of worſhip, perhaps, as ſome ſuggeſt, they took up their abode in one of the rooms which adjoined to it, through the favour of ſome Levite, who might be a diſciple, *Acts* i 14 *praiſing and bleſſing God*, joining the temple ſongs, and offering their joyful acknowledgments for all the wondrous mercies they had received, and for the promiſes of greater yet in ſtore for them *Amen* May we in our bleſſing and praiſes ſeek to emulate theſe happy diſciples, till we come to join the ſongs of eternity, and in the better temple, among the bleſſed, ſhall day and night for ever celebrate redeeming love

THE

THE

EVANGELICAL EXPOSITOR;

OR, A

PRACTICAL COMMENT

Upon the GOSPEL according to

St. JOHN.

JOHN, the writer of this Gospel, was the favoured disciple whom Jesus peculiarly loved, and who leaned on his bosom He wrote the last of all the apostles, and some suppose, even after he had lived to see the destruction of Jerusalem, though the year and place when and where this gospel was written are not certainly fixed He relates much of what the other evangelists had omitted, especially some of the most spiritual discourses of Jesus, and explicitly asserts and proves his divine power and Godhead He is said to have lived to a great age, and to be the only one of the twelve apostles who died a natural death, the rest having all sealed their testimony with their blood

CHAP I

The scope and design of this chapter is to confirm our faith in Christ as the eternal Son of God, and the true Messiah and Saviour of the world, that we may be brought to receive him, and rely upon him as our prophet, priest, and king, and to give up ourselves to be ruled, and taught, and saved by him In order to this, we have here, 1 An account given of him by the inspired penman himself, ver 1—5 And again, ver 10—14 And again, ver 16, 17, 18 2 The testimony of John Baptist concerning him, ver 6—9 And again, ver 15 But most fully and particularly, ver 19—37 3 His own manifestation of himself to Andrew and Peter, ver 38—42 to Philip and Nathanael, ver 43—51

a Prov viii 22 &c Col i 17 1 John i 1 Rev xix 13 b Prov viii 30 Chap xvii 5 1 John i 2 c Chap x 30 Phil ii 6 [illegible] d Gen i 1 e Ps xxxiii 6 Ver 10 Col i 16 Heb i 2 Rev iv 11 f Chap v 26 1 John v 11 g Chap viii 12 & ix 5 [illegible] h Chap iii 19

1 [a] IN the beginning was the Word, and [b] the Word
was with God, and [c] the Word was God 2 [d]
The same was in the beginning with God 3
[e] All things were made by him, and without
him was not any thing made that was made 4 [f] In him
was life, and [g] the life was the light of men 5 And
the light shineth in darkness, and the darkness com-
prehended it not

Ver 1—5 St John opens his gospel with an account of that divine personage, concerning whom he was about to write He is called the Word, or Logos, the essential word of God, to whom he ascribes all the attributes peculiar to the One Jehovah We have,

1 His eternal self existence *In the beginning was the Word,* not only before his incarnation, but ere creation rose, or time began to measure its periods, from everlasting, he existed, the great I AM

His co-existence with the Father *The Word was with God, and the Word was God,* not as one God with another, but as one divine person co-existing with another in the same godhead, and partaking with the Father in the same divine nature and essential perfections *The same was in the beginning with God,* before any creature had yet been spoken into being

3 His agency, in the formation of the world, and all things therein *All things were made by him,* not as a subordinate instrument, but as the self-sufficient author of them, *and without him was not any thing made that was made,* from the highest to the lowest all are the creatures of his hand, and such power proves him to be very God, *Isa* xliv 24

4 He is the original of life and light to all the creatures he hath made *In him was life,* self-existent and independent, and he is the eternal fount from whence all beings, sensitive or rational, receive their life, and are maintained by supplies out of his fulness, *and the life was the light of men,* from him was communicated to us all that reason and understanding of which we are possessed, and from him alone comes all divine light and life since the fall, by which we can be restored to the knowledge and enjoyment of God

5 *The light shineth in darkness* By the fall all divine light is utterly banished from the minds of men, and they are by nature sunk in the blackness of spiritual darkness The glimmering of *tradition,* and the brighter light of *revelation,* shining in the shadows and types of the law, or the prophecies and promises of the Old Testament, were utterly ineffectual to lead men to eternal life and salvation, without divine illumination *the darkness comprehended it not* the plainest and most obvious truths the natural man can no more comprehend, than the blind can discern the object before them He, therefore, who first gave eyes to our bodies, must, by the same divine power, give light to our darkened minds, or we must for ever remain under spiritual darkness and ignorance

6 ¶ [i] There was a man sent from God, whose name
was John 7 The same came for a witness, to bear
witness of the light, that all men through him might
believe 8 He was not that light, but *was sent* to
bear witness of that light 9 [k] *That* was the true light,
which lighteth every man that cometh into the world
10 He

i Mal iii 1 Mat xi 10 Ver 33 k [illegible] Ver 4

10 He was in the world, and [l] the world was made
by him, and the world knew him not 11 [m] He came
unto his own, and [n] his own received him not 12 But
[o] as many as received him, to them gave he power to
become the sons of God, *even* to them that believe on
his name 13 [p] Which were born, not of blood, nor
of the will of the flesh, nor of the will of man, but
of God 14 And [q] the Word [r] was made [s] flesh, and
dwelt among us (and [t] we beheld his glory, the glory
as of the only begotten of the Father) [u] full of grace
and truth

l Ver 3 Ep iii 9 Heb i 2 & xi 3
m Mat xv 24 Acts iii 26 Rom xv 8
n Luke xix 14
o Isa lvi 5 Rom viii 15 Gal iii 26 2 Pet i 4 1 John iii 1
p Chap iii 5 Jam i 18 1 Pet i 23
q Mat i 16 1 Tim iii 16
r Rom i 3 Gal iv 4 Heb ii 14
s Isa xl 5
t Mat xvii 2 2 Pet i 17
u Col i 19 & ii 9

v 6—14 The clearest revelation of gospel light began with the Baptist's ministry To him therefore the Evangelist refers, as leading the most glorious testimony to the *uncreated Word*

1 He relates the mission and preaching of John *There was a man sent from God, whose name was John* his miraculous birth, his extraordinary gifts, and remarkable sanctity, were plain indications of his mission from above *The same came for a witness, to bear witness of the light*, to point out to their notice the Sun of righteousness, that was now about to arise, but to whom, through the hardness of their hearts, they were indisposed to pay due attention and regard, and to testify that this was the Messiah of God *that all men through him might believe*, not every individual, but men of all sorts, who were, without distinction, invited by him to look to Jesus and to be saved *He was not that light*, though his energetical discourses, and mighty influence, raised in the minds of many an apprehension that he was the promised Christ, he assumed no such title, *but* his honour was to be the morning star, the harbinger of day, to usher in the rising Sun *he was sent to bear witness of that light*, and prepare the way of the Lord Whilst we rejoice in the light of ministers, we must remember they are only witnesses to the Light, and as they preach not themselves, but Christ Jesus the Lord, to him must our eyes be alone directed

2 Before he proceeds farther with John's testimony, the Evangelist enlarges on the glorious character and office of him, to whom the Baptist bore record *That was the true light*, in opposition to the false lights of Gentile philosophy, and in contradistinction to the glimmering taper of ceremonial types and figures he was eminently *the true light*, the fountain from which all wisdom and knowledge flow, *which lighteth every man that cometh into the world*, either as the author of natural reason to all men, or as sending the light of his gospel to all nations, or rather as the giver of spiritual light to the soul of every sinner who is brought out of the kingdom of darkness, and translated into that new world the kingdom of God's dear Son *He was in the world, and the world was made by him* from the beginning his power and providence were displayed, but such was the blindness and stupidity of mankind, that *the world knew him not*, nor in the expanded volume of nature, opened to their view, discerned his eternal Godhead Nay, *he came unto his own*, appearing incarnate in the fulness of time and manifesting himself by his doctrine and miracles to the Jewish people, who were *his own* in a covenant of peculiarity, and his kinsmen according to the flesh, *and his own received him not*, they were in general hardened and obstinate, and rejected their God and Saviour *But* a remnant according to the election of grace received, and *to as many as received him* in his real character, as the promised Messiah, the Prophet, Priest, and King of his people, *to them gave he power to become the sons of God, even to them that believe on his name* By faith embracing him as their God and Saviour, and placing their whole dependance on his atonement and righteousness, they were advanced to the high dignity and privilege of being accounted the sons and daughters of the Lord Almighty, entitled to the inheritance of glory as joint heirs with Christ, and endued with all those heavenly graces and filial dispositions which proved their adoption of God And all who truly believe in and receive the same Jesus into their heart, trusting on him alone as the atoning Saviour, and are devoted to him as their Lord and Master, shall be made partakers of the same invaluable blessings and honours We, who were by nature *children of wrath*, are now become *the children of God by faith in Jesus Christ* And this is not merely a *relative* change, but a *real* one where God confers the dignity of a child, he gives the spirit of adoption Those therefore are his sons, *which were born not of blood*, not by *natural descent*, for nothing but corruption runs in the blood of all the fallen sons of Adam, nor by *circumcision*, which was only the outward sign of an inward and spiritual grace, without which that bloody rite availed nothing to the soul, *nor of the will of the flesh*, our regeneration springs not from any power or ability in ourselves, for we are not sufficient of ourselves to think any thing as of ourselves, *nor doth it come of the will of man*, the wisest reasoners, the most powerful orators, spend their rhetorick in vain, moral suasion is ineffectual, unless enforced by divine operation, and therefore the Evangelist adds, *but of God*, the conversion of the soul is the work of sovereign and almighty grace alone and we can only be quickened from the death of trespasses and sins to spiritual life by the same divine power and energy which first breathed into the lifeless clay a living soul *And*, in order to this great design of man's salvation, *the Word was made flesh*, became incarnate, *not by the conversion of the Godhead into flesh, but by taking the manhood into God* he took our nature, that, in *the likeness of sinful flesh*, he might make reconciliation, *and dwelt among us*, in all the fulness of the Godhead taking up his abode in the body, which was prepared for him, as the Shechinah dwelt in the temple (*And we beheld his glory*, the brightness of which darted through the veil that for a time obscured its lustre, and appeared in all the miracles he wrought, in the transcendent wisdom, goodness, grace, power, and majesty he displayed on various occasions, and particularly blazed forth at his transfiguration, his resurrection, and ascension all which divine manifestations of himself, the more they considered, the more were they filled with reverence and godly fear, and could not but regard *the glory* of Jesus *as the* glory *of the only begotten of the Father*) such as it became this divine Personage to appear in, who was *the brightness of his Father's glory, and the express image of his person*, and who was *full of grace and truth*, *full of grace*, of all spiritual blessings to bestow on his people, *and of truth*, fulfilling in his own person, as *the substance*, all those typical institutions which were *the shadows of good things to come*, together with the prophecies which chiefly centred in him, and accomplishing all the engagements he had undertaken in the behalf of his people With what entire satisfaction then may we rest our souls on this adored Redeemer, so admirably qualified for the office of Mediator, possessed of all the excellence which the human nature is capable of receiving, and infinitely exalted in the uncreated glory of the divine The more we consider his humiliation in becoming incarnate, the more deeply should we be affected with the sense of his grace and love, and, whilst we view the man Christ Jesus as *the very God of very God*, the more confidently should we trust upon his compleat salvation

15 ¶ [x] John bare witness of him, and cried, saying,
This is he of whom I spake, [y] He that cometh after
me, is preferred before me, for [z] he was before me
16 And of [a] his fulness have all we received, and grace
for grace 17 For [b] the law was given by Moses, but
grace and truth came by Jesus Christ 18 [c] No man
hath seen God at any time, the only begotten Son,
which is in the bosom of the Father, he hath declared
him

x Chap i 32
y Ver 27 30 Chap iii 31
z Chap viii 58 Col i 17
a Chap iii 34 Col i 19 & ii 9, 10
b Exod xx 1 &c
c Exod xxxiii 20 Luke x 22 1 Tim vi 16 1 John iv 12

v 15—18 We have here,

1 The Baptist's farther testimony to Christ *John bare witness of him, and cried, saying, This is he of whom I spake, He that cometh after me is preferred before me* He was the herald sent to prepare the way of the King Messiah, to proclaim aloud the coming of the incarnate God, and at his baptism to point him out to the notice of the world, as infinitely his superior in dignity, though after him, in point of time, entering upon his ministry and mission And this preeminence he justly ascribes to him, both in the view of his eternal existence as a divine Person, and also of his constitution to the office of Mediator before the worlds were, *for he was before me* *Note*, (1) The greatest of ministers and the chief of saints are always most careful to ascribe nothing to themselves, but ever to exalt the name of their adored Lord and Master as alone worthy of all honour and glory (2) The younger in office is often seen to be the greater in grace

2 The Evangelist takes up the word, and expatiates on the unsearchable riches of Christ in connection with what he had said, *v* 14 *Out of his fulness*, the plenitude of gifts and graces resident in this Son of God's eternal love, *have we all received* not only they, as apostles, were indebted to their incarnate Lord for all the wondrous abilities with which they were qualified for the discharge of the trust committed to them, but also all Christians, of every degree, in every age, draw from the ever-flowing, overflowing, fountain of a Saviour's grace the supply of all their spiritual wants, *and grace for grace*, which singular expression is differently interpreted, either as representing the fulness as well as freedom of the gospel blessings, as *grace upon grace*, heaped up unto glory, or as the supply suited to our necessities, and effectual to strengthen us for all the work and duty to which the Saviour calls us, or such grace as exactly corresponds to that which is in him, transforming us into the same image, as the wax bears the impression of the seal, or as descriptive of the more abundant measure of grace dispensed under the gospel than under the law, to which sense the following verse seems to direct us *For the law came by Moses* he as the minister of God, declared his will to the Jewish people, and it was a matter of grace and favour that God by him revealed himself and his law unto them *but* one unspeakably greater than Moses is here, the author of a new dispensation, which in glory far excelleth, 2 Cor iii 10 for *grace and truth came by Jesus Christ* He is the sum and fulfilment of all the types and prophecies, and in him they receive their accomplishment the gospel, which he declared, contained the brightest

discoveries of the divine grace and goodness, and the most re- viving promises, confirmed by the veracity of the unchangeable God, and as he reveals the only way of obtaining the divine favour, and how we may walk so as to please God, he ministers also the ability for that which he enjoins, and his gospel is *a law of the Spirit of life*, communicating spiritual life and power to the soul. The greatest prophets who went before him are not to be compared with him, and his word must needs, in the clearness and fulness of it, excel all the other revelations of his will which God hath been pleased to vouchsafe to the sons of men, for *no man hath seen God at any time*, neither men nor angels are capable of that intimate knowledge of the divine coun- sels, nor were ever admitted into his secrets: *the only begotten Son, which is in the bosom of the Father*, and by his participation of the Godhead most perfectly understands all the designs of grace which were in the eternal mind, in nature one with the Father, and infinitely dear to him, *he hath declared him*, being most transcendently qualified to make such discoveries of God and his eternal counsels, particularly of his wisdom and grace in the redemption of lost sinners, as none of the prophets, nor John himself, could be supposed to do, they being but servants over the house of God, he the Son in his own house, and therefore hath more gloriously and distinctly than ever, brought life and immortality to light by his gospel. They who went before us saw but through a glass darkly, we with a cleardness of vision, like that of face to face. May the light of gospel *truth*, so clearly revealed to us in and by the Son, be accompanied with the effectual power of gospel *grace* to our hearts!

19 ¶ And [a] this is the record of John, when the
Jews sent priests and Levites from Jerusalem to ask him,
Who art thou? 20 And [c] he confessed, and denied
not, but confessed, I am not the Christ. 21 And they
asked him, What then? Art thou [f] Elias? And he
saith, I am not. Art thou [h] that prophet? And he
answered, No. 22 Then said they unto him, Who art
thou? that we may give an answer to them that sent us.
What sayest thou of thyself? 23 [h] He said, I *am* the
voice of one crying in the wilderness, Make straight
the way of the Lord, [i] as said the prophet Esaias.
24 And they which were sent, were of the Pharisees.
25 And they asked him, and said unto him, Why bap-
tizest thou then, if thou be not that Christ, nor Elias,
neither that prophet? 26 John answered them, say-
ing, [k] I baptize with water: but there standeth one
among you, whom ye know not; 27 [l] He it is who
coming after me, is preferred before me, whose shoes
latchet I am not worthy to unloose. 28 These things
were done in Bethabara beyond Jordan, where John was
baptizing.

[a] Chap. v. [c] Luke iii 16 [?] Acts xiii 25 [f] Mal iv 5 Matt xvii 10 [h] Deut xviii 15, 18 [h] Isa xl 3 Luke iii 4 [i] Isa xl 3 [k] Matt iii 11 Acts i 5 [l] Ver 15, 30 Acts xix 4

v. 19—28 The testimony of John is here reassumed, which he delivered to those who were sent from Jerusalem to examine into his credentials.

1 The sanhedrim, whose business it was to take cognizance of all religious matters, sent priests and Levites to enquire who he was, and what character he assumed; the time being at hand when the Messiah, according to the prophets, was now about to appear. And many took John to be the Christ, or at least an extraordinary person raised up for some great purposes, they wanted to learn from his own lips what he professed himself to be.

2 John's answer to their question were direct and faithful. As to his being the Messiah, he freely and earnestly dis- claims every such pretension: *he confessed, and denied not, but confessed, I am not the Christ*. Note, We must never arrogate to ourselves honours which do not belong to us, but should reject every temptation to pride with abhorrence. In reply to their question, *whether he were Elias?* he said, *No*. The Jews looked for the person of Elias, John only came in the spirit and power of that zealous reformer, and therefore was not the Elijah they expected. He declares himself to be neither Jere- miah nor *that prophet* of which Moses spake, nor any of the an- cient prophets risen again, one of whom they supposed would precede the coming of Elias. Hereupon they urge him to give them a positive answer who he was, if he was neither of those whom they had mentioned, that they might carry back some- thing determinate to those who sent them. To this he gives a direct answer in the words of Scripture, Isa xl 3. *I am the voice of one crying in the wilderness, Make straight the way of the Lord, as said the prophet Esaias*. He is the harbinger of the Messiah: his office was to cry aloud and spare not, rebuking them and reproving the errors of the people, and thus calling upon them to prepare to meet their God incarnate. And this is the great work of every true minister of Christ: with zeal, which fires his discourses, he labours to call sinners to the Saviour, and, eager in his exhortations, desires to lead them to repentance unto life. ——Since he disclaimed the character of the Messiah, and those prophets which they had mentioned, they expostulated with him on his assuming authority to baptise, for it seems those Pharisees, who were most bigotted in this commission, tenacious of their traditions, and proud in the con- ceit of their own goodness, fancied they needed no repentance, and unable to brook the freedom and severity of the Baptist's rebukes, would gladly have taken occasion to suppress and silence him. In answer to their question he replies, *I baptize with water*, as the outward sign of an inward and spiritual grace, which I pretend not to confer, *but there standeth one among you*, or there lately *stood one among you*, even Jesus, who had been baptized by him, *whom ye know not*, he not having yet publickly appeared in his glorious character as the Messiah, *He it is who, coming after me, is preferred before me*, is infinitely my superior, *whose shoes latchet I am not worthy to unloose*: so transcendently glorious and exalted is his dignity, that to be employed in the meanest office about his person is an honour far beyond all that I can pre- tend to deserve. This conversation passed at Bethabara beyond Jordan, where John was baptising; but they made no enquiries after him, concerning whom John informed them.

29 ¶ The next day John seeth Jesus coming unto him,
and saith, Behold [m] the Lamb of God, which † taketh
away the sin of the world. 30 [n] This is he of whom
I said, After me cometh a man which is preferred be-
fore me: for he was before me. 31 And I knew him
not: but that he should be made manifest to Israel, there-
fore am I come [o] baptizing with water. 32 And John
bare record, saying, [p] I saw the Spirit descending from
heaven like a dove, and it abode upon him. 33 And I
knew him not: but he that sent me to baptize with
water, the same said unto me, Upon whom thou shalt
see the Spirit descending and remaining on him, [q] the
same is he which baptizeth with the Holy Ghost. 34
And I saw, and bare record that this is the Son of God.
35 ¶ Again the next day after, John stood, and two
of his disciples: 36 And looking upon Jesus as he
walked, he saith, [r] Behold the Lamb of God.

[m] Exod xii 3 Isa liii 7 Ver 36 Acts viii 32 1 Pet i 19 † Or, beareth [n] Ver 15, 27 [o] Matt iii 6 [p] Matt iii 16 Luke iii 22 [q] Matt iii 11 Acts i 5 [r] Ver 29

v. 29—36 Jesus had now finished his glorious conflict with the great enemy of souls, and was returned from the wilderness victorious to the banks of Jordan. There John saw him, and bore repeated testimony to him as the Christ of God.

1 He points out Jesus to the notice of his disciples, as he walked near the river's side, saying, *Behold the Lamb of God, which taketh away the sin of the world*. He is the *Lamb* without spot and blemish, which the daily sacrifice and paschal lamb prefigured; he is the Lamb *of God*, appointed by him as the great oblation which should once be offered, with whose sacri- fice he would be well pleased, *taking away the sin of the world*, of all his people, not of the Jews only, but of the Gentiles also; and by the one oblation he hath once offered hath fully, completely, and everlastingly made the atonement, so that all, in every age or place, under whatever degree of guilt or power of corruption they lie, who come to him, are sure to find a complete salvation wrought out for them: and therefore we are directed to *behold* him, to look to him with an eye of faith, that we may be made partakers of the eternal redemption that is in him.

2 He declares this is the person to whom he had before born witness: *This is he of whom I said, After me cometh a man which is preferred before me, for he was before me*; a man, yet more than man, even God-man. *And I knew him not*, there was no personal acquaintance between them before, nor were they in league together to serve any sinister end or purpose: *but that he should be made manifest to Israel, therefore am I come baptizing with water*: this was the great end of John's ministry, to point out to Israel the anointed Saviour.

3 He mentions the sign which the Lord had given him to discover this distinguished Personage whose forerunner he was, but of whom till then he had no personal knowledge. The sign given was the visible descent of the Spirit as a dove, and on whomsoever of those, who came to him to be baptised, he should see it light, he might be fully assured that this was *he which baptizeth with the Holy Ghost*. This he saw at Jordan, when Jesus came to be baptized of him, and heard the voice from heaven mentioned Matth iii 17. On their information he there- fore *bare record* then, and ever after continued to repeat the same testimony, *that this is the Son of God* incarnate, the true Messiah promised from the beginning.

4 The next day again looking earnestly on Jesus as he walked, he pointed him out to two of his disciples, saying, *Behold the Lamb of God*, desirous to engage their attention to the heavenly Saviour, and to lead them to value, regard, and embrace him, as the one great atoning sacrifice for the sins of men, which all those offered under the law prefigured and re- presented. Note, (1) The doctrine of Christ sacrifice for our sins is the glorious subject on which ministers must continually insist. (2) They who have beheld the excellency of Jesus

cannot

cannot but delight to recommend him to the regard and notice of others

37 And the two disciples heard him speak, and they
followed Jesus 38 Then Jesus turned, and saw them
following, and saith unto them, What seek ye? They
said unto him, Rabbi, (which is to say, being inter-
† Or, abidest. preted, Master) where † dwellest thou? 39 He saith
unto them, Come and see They came and saw where
he dwelt, and abode with him that day for it was
‡ i.e. Two hours before night. about the ‡ tenth hour 40 One of the two which
heard John *speak*, and followed him, was * Andrew,
* Matt. iv. 18. Simon Peter's brother 41 He first findeth his own
brother Simon, and saith unto him, We have found
§ Or, the Anointed. the Messias, which is, being interpreted, § the Christ
42 And he brought him to Jesus And when Jesus
beheld him, he said, Thou art Simon the son of Jona
‖ Matt. xvi. 18. ‖ Or, Peter. thou shalt be called Cephas, which is by interpretation,
‖ a stone

v. 37—42 The first disciples of Jesus here begin to commence their acquaintance with him

1 The two, who were with John when he pointed out Jesus to their notice, immediately followed him, desiring to be indulged in a greater intimacy with him And the gracious Lord, who observes and is delighted with the first steps a soul takes in approaching him, kindly accosted them, and enquired what they sought With respectful address and humble enquiry they replied, *Rabbi, where dwellest thou?* Rabbi was the title given to the most famed of their wise men, and most deserving of it must be he in whom dwelt all the treasures of wisdom and knowledge They desire to be admitted to a longer conversation with him than they could enjoy as they walked, and would gladly, if they might be permitted, wait upon him to receive his divine instructions *Note*, Abiding communion with Jesus is the thing a soul, who is at all acquainted with him, importunately desires Christ courteously invites them to his lodgings, *Come and see* he was ready to give them an immediate welcome, for his arms are ever open to receive those who desire to come to him With thankfulness and joy they immediately embraced the offer Where the soul is at stake, every delay is dangerous *They came and saw where he dwelt, and abode with him that day for it was about the tenth hour* so that they spent that day in delightful conversation with him The name of one of these disciples was Andrew, Simon Peter's brother, the other probably the author of this gospel, who here, as in other places, modestly suppresses his own name, when the mention of it would be to his honour A noble instance of his unfeigned humility

2 A third disciple is added Andrew, eager to communicate the glad tidings to his brother Simon, findeth him, and with exultation relates the important discovery they had made, *We have found the Messias, (which is, being interpreted in the Greek language, the Christ)* the anointed of the Lord, so often spoken of in the Scriptures, *and he brought him to Jesus*, who took particular notice of him, and calling him by his name, which, though a stranger to him probably before, he well knew, he gives him a new name, *Cephas*, which signifies *a stone*, adopting him into his family, and intimating the steadiness of his heart in the work of the gospel, and his being appointed one of those pillars on which, with his brethren the apostles, the church should stand firm, grounded on Jesus the chief corner-stone and sure foundation *Note*, (1) They who have tasted the riches of a Saviour's grace themselves cannot but be active to draw others unto him There is in Christ enough and to spare (2) They who are nearly related to us in blood claim a peculiar interest in our regard and prayers, and the best token of our love to them will be shewn in leading them to Jesus (3) The faithful in Christ Jesus stand firm, a rock, unmoved with the storms of tribulation which for his sake they may be called to endure

[illegible margin notes]
43 ¶ The day following Jesus would go forth into
Galilee, and findeth Philip, and saith unto him, Follow
me 44 Now * Philip was of Bethsaida, the city of
Andrew and Peter 45 Philip findeth * Nathanael, and
saith unto him, We have found him of whom * Moses
in the law, and the prophets did write, Jesus * of Na-
zareth, the son of Joseph 46 And Nathanael said un-
to him, * Can there any good thing come out of Naza-
reth? Philip saith unto him, Come and see 47 Jesus
saw Nathanael coming to him, and saith of him, Be-
hold * an Israelite indeed, * in whom is no guile 48
Nathanael saith unto him, Whence knowest thou me?
Jesus answered and said unto him, Before that Philip
called thee, when thou wast under the fig-tree, I saw
thee 49 Nathanael answered and saith unto him,
Rabbi, thou art * the Son of God, thou art * the King
of Israel 50 Jesus answered and said unto him, Be-
cause I said unto thee, I saw thee under the fig tree,
believest thou? thou shalt see greater things than these
51 And he saith unto him, Verily, verily I say unto
you, * Hereafter you shall see heaven open, and the
angels of God ascending and descending upon the Son
of man [illegible margin notes]

v. 43—51 Our Lord having begun to make choice of his disciples, adds two more to the number, in Galilee, whither he went the day following

1 Christ himself calls Philip He *found* him, not by accident, but design, as the great Shepherd, seeking after his lost sheep, and gathering them unto himself, not one of whom shall perish he knoweth their wanderings, and will bring them to his fold *He saith unto him, Follow me*, and Christ's word instantly wrought effectually upon him *He was of Bethsaida*, a town on the lake of Gennesareth, and a place very abandoned, *Matth* xi 21 yet there Andrew and Peter also dwelt, for in the worst of places God hath some chosen vessels, to be to the praise of the glory of his grace

2 Philip immediately went in quest of some friends to whom he might carry the glad tidings, and finding Nathanael, he with joy communicates the news, *We have found him of whom Moses in the law, and the prophets did write, Jesus of Nazareth, the son of Joseph* Probably our Lord had opened these scriptures concerning himself to Philip's fullest satisfaction But Nathanael, on the mention of Nazareth, starts an objection, *Can any good thing come out of Nazareth?* a place mean and despicable to a proverb Philip, unable to solve the difficulty, yet not shaken in his own faith, saith, *Come and see*, persuaded that Jesus himself could easily silence that and every other objection which might be raised against him *Note*, (1) They, who have found Christ, cannot but exult in this happy acquisition (2) Tho' we may not be capable of answering every objection which may be started, we are not therefore to conclude our religion is a delusion, but examine further, and then we shall find enough to satisfy us that we have not believed cunningly devised fables (3) When we are in doubt we must come to Jesus, and by prayer and attention to his word may be confident he will lead us into all truth

3 Nathanael yielded to Philip's invitation, and quickly was convinced of the unreasonableness of the prejudices which he had entertained (1) Christ highly commends his character as he saw him coming near, saying to those who were in company with him at that time, *Behold an Israelite indeed, in whom is no guile*, a genuine son of simple-hearted Jacob *Note*, It is a great thing to be *an Israelite indeed*, in spirit and temper such as our profession demands, without allowed guile either towards God or man, but with regard to both keeping a conscience void of offence (2) Nathanael expresses his surprize how Jesus should know him, whom he had never seen before, but the confirmation of it, which Christ gave, yet more amazed him, and silenced all his doubts, as it proved his omniscience *Before that Philip called thee, when thou wast under the fig-tree, I saw thee* Probably Nathanael had retired thither for some religious exercises, where no eye could see him, and there had offered up his fervent supplication to God for the Messiah's coming, or might be employed in meditation, perhaps on that dream of Jacob, *Gen* xxviii 12 to which our Lord refers, *v.* 51 and such an instance of his knowing both the place of his retirement, and the very sentiments of his soul, could not but give Nathanael the strongest evidence of his being indeed the Messiah, as Philip had affirmed *Note*, The eye of Jesus is upon us in our most retired moments, and he is acquainted with every sentiment of our souls And this cannot but afford much comfort to a gracious soul and speak confusion to every hypocrite (3) Nathanael, fully convinced, bows down before him, and makes solemn profession of his faith in him as the Messiah, *Rabbi, thou art the Son of God, thou art the King of Israel* His prejudices instantly vanished, and, assured of the divine mission and character of Jesus, he gladly yields himself up a loyal subject to Israel's King, trusting on him for salvation from all enemies

4 Christ, with approbation of his faith, and admiration of his noble confession, assures Nathanael he shall shortly see greater and more glorious evidence of his divine wisdom and power, to confirm his confidence *Verily, verily I say unto you*, who am the faithful and true witness, *Hereafter you shall see heaven opened*, or *from henceforth*, when, entering upon his publick ministry, he should begin to manifest his glory in the miracles he wrought and the doctrines he taught, *and ye shall see the angels of God ascending and descending upon the Son of man*, either literally, in their ministrations to him at his resurrection and ascension, or rather figuratively, such a friendly intercourse between heaven and earth would now appear to be restored, and such wonders wrought by Jesus in confirmation of his mission, that it would be proved with evidence strong, and strong as if they saw the heaven themselves opened, and the angels employed in carrying on a correspondence between God the Father and

the Son became man for us men and for our salvation. Note, Through the Son of man the kingdom of heaven is opened to all believers, the angels of God minister to the heirs of salvation, and we may now enter boldly into the holiest of all, ascending by him, who is unto us, as the ladder of Jacob, the way to God and glory.

CHAP II.

In this chapter we have, 1. The story of the first miracle which Jesus wrought, turning water into wine, at Cana of Galilee, ver. 1—11 and his appearing at Capernaum, ver. 12. 2. The story of the first passover he kept at Jerusalem after he began his public ministry. His driving the buyers and sellers out of the temple, ver. 13—17 and the sign he gave to them who questioned his authority for it, ver. 18—22. The account of some that believed him thereupon for some time, ver. 23, 24, 25 until he saw them [illegible] to put no confidence in them.

1 AND the third day there was a marriage in Cana
of Galilee, and the mother of Jesus was there.
2 And both Jesus was called, and his disciples, to the
marriage. 3 And when they wanted wine, the mother
of Jesus saith unto him, They have no wine. 4 Jesus
saith unto her, ᵃ Woman, what have I to do with thee?
ᵇ mine hour is not yet come. 5 His mother saith unto
the servants, Whatsoever he saith unto you, do it. 6
And there were set there six water-pots of stone, ᶜ after
the manner of the purifying of the Jews, containing two
or three firkins apiece. 7 Jesus saith unto them, Fill
the water-pots with water. And they filled them up to
the brim. 8 And he saith unto them, Draw out now,
and bear unto the governor of the feast. And they bare
it. 9 When the ruler of the feast had tasted the water
that was made wine, and knew not whence it was, (but
the servants which drew the water knew) the governor
of the feast called the bridegroom, 10 And saith unto
him, Every man at the beginning doth set forth good
wine, and when men have well drunk, then that which
is worse: *but* thou hast kept the good wine until now.
11 This beginning of miracles did Jesus in Cana of
Galilee, and ᵈ manifested forth his glory, and his disci-
ples believed on him.

ᵃ Chap. xix. [illegible] ᵇ [illegible] ᶜ [illegible] ᵈ Chap. i. 14.

¶ 1—11 The first miracle of Jesus was wrought at a marriage-feast in Cana of Galilee. It was probably a marriage of some near relation of his mother Mary's, who seemed not to be there merely as a guest, but as one of the family. Christ was invited, and refused not the invitation given him on this occasion; but went with his disciples to grace the bridal feast with his presence and company, and put an honour upon the institution. *Note*, (1.) Our marriages can only then be expected to prove happy, when Jesus with his benediction crowns the nuptial [illegible] (2.) Religion teaches none to be unsocial or uncivil, but commands us to rejoice with those that rejoice. We are told,

1. The concern expressed by the mother of Jesus to her Son on account of the deficiency of the wine at this entertainment. The number of the guests, perhaps more than were expected, exceeded the small quantity which these persons who were probably in mean circumstances had provided, and they might not be able to afford more. It seems she expected that he would soon begin to display his glorious power, and intimated that the present necessity afforded an opportunity for his miraculous [illegible]. *Note*, (1.) In the height of our earthly joys, [illegible] we shall be wanting. We must look only for perfect bliss in that kingdom where they neither marry nor are given in marriage. (2.) A [illegible] heart interests itself in the distresses of its friends, and, when he can do no more to relieve them, fails not to commend their case to the kind Saviour's notice.

2. He gave her a reprimand for interfering in matters which did not belong to her. Though he was her son after the flesh, yet in the exercise of his miraculous power, he acted as Son of God, and owed her no obedience, and to intermeddle in the direction of his conduct, respecting the affairs of his kingdom, was a very blameable presumption. What a direct condemnation of the horrid idolatry of that church, which prays to the mother to command her Son? Besides he tells, *My hour is not yet come*, either it was not yet time to work this miracle, till all the wine was spent, or rather the time for the publick manifestation of his glory, by his open performing miracles, was not yet come, and whatever he might do in private, he was not to be directed by her, or any other, when or how to act.

3. Then, like an obedient friend, submitted to his pleasure, she entertained apprehension that he would grant her request, and [illegible] the matter into his consideration, and therefore privately bid the servants obey whatever orders he should give them. *Note*, (1.) We must not be discouraged in our faith, if our prayers are not immediately answered. (2.) Christ's commands are implicitly to be obeyed, without reasoning or hesitation.

4. Christ performs the needful miracle, and with circumstances that eminently displayed his glory. Six water-pots of stone were placed there, containing about *two or three firkins* each, which some suppose to be a quantity about nine gallons; it being customary with the Jews to use [illegible] washings, some of which were enjoined by the law of God, and more by the tradition of the elders, and therefore, where such a number of guests were present, much water was necessary. These water-pots Christ bids the servants fill *with water* to the brim, that there might be no suspicion of fraud in the miracle. They obeyed, and instantly the transformation was wrought. He orders them to take up a [illegible] and carry this liquor *to the governor of the feast*, the person who was either the master of the ceremonies, or [illegible] on that occasion, or was the *architriclinus*, the priest or Levite, who blessed the cup before it was sent round to the guests. No sooner had he tasted the wine which had been water than he was struck with the delicious flavour, and, unacquainted whence it came, he observed with surprize to the bridegroom his unusual method of procedure. Others usually produced their best wine first, and afterwards, when men have well drunk, that which is worse, (or [illegible]) of a weaker body, but he had kept *the good wine* to the last, as the grace-cup, to conclude the entertainment. *Note*, (1.) God's creatures, and wine among the rest, are given us richly to enjoy. It is no sin to be pleased with the delicious flavour of the grape, when we remember with thankfulness who gave it that quality, only we must be sure that we do not by intemperance abuse our mercies, and turn our blessings into a curse by excess or drunkenness. (2.) It suits need a [illegible] to rest in the irregularities of those who [illegible] perhaps, to their shame, would have no government over themselves. (3.) Whatever consolations believers here enjoy, the greatest are reserved for them at last, when, at the marriage-supper of the Lamb, they shall drink the new wine in the kingdom of God.

5. At the conclusion of this miracle the Evangelist observes, that this was the first Jesus performed after his entrance on his ministry. Wherein *he manifested forth his glory* in such displays of his power and grace, who spake by his authoritative word, [illegible] exerted his own greatness, and proved his own eternal Godhead and glory, *and his disciples believed on him*, confirmed in their assurance of the truth of that high character which he assumed. *Note*, The more we become acquainted with Christ in his word, the more shall we be convinced that this is he who should come, and shall be engaged to rest our souls on him for life and salvation.

12 ¶ After this, he went down to Capernaum, he,
and his mother, and ᵉ his brethren, and his disciples, and
they continued there not many days. 13 ¶ And the
ᶠ Jews passover was at hand, and Jesus went up to Jeru-
salem, 14 And ᵍ found in the temple those that sold
oxen, and sheep, and doves, and the changers of money,
sitting. 15 And when he had made a scourge of small
cords, he drove them all out of the temple, and the
sheep, and the oxen, and poured out the changers
money, and overthrew the tables, 16 And said unto
them that sold doves, Take these things hence, make
not my Father's house an house of merchandise. 17
And his disciples remembered that it was written, ʰ The
zeal of thine house hath eaten me up. 18 ¶ Then an-
swered the Jews, and said unto him, ⁱ What sign shew-
est thou unto us, seeing that thou dost these things?
19 Jesus answered and said unto them, ᵏ Destroy this
temple, and in three days I will raise it up. 20 Then
said the Jews, Forty and six years was this temple in
building, and wilt thou rear it up in three days? 21
But he spake of ˡ the temple of his body. 22 When
therefore he was risen from the dead, ᵐ his disciples re-
membered that he had said this unto them; and they
believed the scripture, and the word which Jesus had
said.

ᵉ Mat. xii. 46. ᶠ Exod. xii. 14. ᵍ Mat. xxi. 12. Mar. xi. 15. Luke xix. 45. ʰ Psal. lxix. 9. ⁱ Mat. xii. 38. Chap. vi. 30. ᵏ Mat. xxvi. 61. & xxvii. 40. ˡ Heb. viii. 2. ᵐ Luke xxiv. 8.

¶ 12—22 Capernaum was the place where Christ usually resided, *Matth.* iv. 13. Thither he came with his mother, brethren, and disciples, who, struck with what they had seen, attended him to observe the further manifestations of his divine power and glory which he should make. He abode at this time at Capernaum but not many days, the Passover being at hand, which called him up to Jerusalem. Where we find him,

1. Purging the temple of those intruders who had defiled the holy place. Under pretence of accommodating those who came up to worship, with sacrifices and change of money, a market was kept in the temple by the connivance of the priests, who probably made some considerable advantage by permitting such

such a profanation But Christ, beholding with indignation such corruptions in the house of God, immediately began to vindicate the honour of that sacred inclosure, and, having made a scourge of cords, he drove out the traders with their beasts, overturned the tables of the money-changers, and bad those who sold doves to take them away, remonstrating with them on the wickedness of their conduct, *Make not my Father's house an house of merchandise*, and, standing in so near a relation to the God of the temple, he could not endure to see him thus dishonoured *Note,* (1) The love of filthy lucre is generally at the root of the corruptions which creep into the church of God (2) If God is our father, we cannot but be grieved to see him dishonoured, and shall zealously appear in his cause (3) They who are bold and faithful for God will often see that one can chase a thousand, and that, if we dare stand up in his name, the consciences of sinners will cover them with confusion

2 The disciples *remembered that it was written, The zeal of thine house hath eaten me up* And this confirmed still the more their faith, as they observed all the Scripture prophecies accomplished in him

3 Being questioned by the Jews concerning the authority on which he acted, and required to give a sign in proof of the mission to which he pretended, *He answered and said unto them, Destroy this temple, and in three days I will raise it up* Since they refused to be convinced by other miracles, he refers them to the last sign which should be wrought, even his resurrection from the dead by his own divine power, after they had destroyed the temple of his body as he had now cleansed his house from their profanations, so would he raise his own body, which they should slay, and never suffer it to see corruption They understood him as if he meant the material temple where he then was, which had now been forty-six years building and beautifying since Herod took down that erected by Zerubbabel, and raised the present fabric on the same spot, which, though the body of it was finished in eight years, might probably till that time have continued to be more highly ornamented though some suppose the words are to be interpreted of the time which Zerubbabel's temple was in building However, they looked upon it as a most absurd pretension, for a mere man, as they presumed him to be, to assert he could do that in three days, which had employed thousands of workmen so many years Thus they ridiculed his assertion, though it appears they understood something of his meaning *Note,* (1) It is just with God to give those up to their vain imaginations, who have no love of the truth, but have pleasure in unrighteousness (2) The grossest mistakes have been entertained by understanding literally what the Scriptures have spoken figuratively, as in the doctrine of *transubstantiation*, drawn from the words of Christ, *This is my body* (3) The body of Jesus was the true temple, in which the fulness of the Godhead dwelt, and of him the temple at Jerusalem was but the type and figure (4) As the temple was the medium of worship, and they who prayed turned their faces thitherwards, so is it through Christ Jesus alone that we can have access to and acceptance with God

4 His disciples, though they, no more than the Jews, understood his meaning at that time, yet afterwards, when the events verified the prediction, and the Spirit poured out from on high opened their minds to understand the Scriptures, reflected on this prophecy, and, seeing the accomplishment of it in his resurrection, were the more deeply confirmed in their faith of the *scripture, and the word which Jesus had said* *Note,* The truths of Scripture which we learn in younger years, though not understood at that time, yet are of singular use when, in any future time, it pleases God to shine into our heart, and open the eyes of our minds

23 ¶ Now when he was at Jerusalem at the passover, in the feast *day*, many believed in his name, when they saw the miracles which he did. 24 But Jesus did not commit himself unto them, because he knew all men, 25 And needed not that any should testify of man for he knew what was in man

v 23—25 During the seven days of the feast Christ preached openly the doctrines of his kingdom, and wrought mighty miracles in confirmation of the truth he taught The effect of which, we are told, was,

1 *That many believed in his name*, at least for the time they were so struck with his miracles as to give their assent to his doctrine, and own him as the Messiah But,

2 *Jesus did not commit himself unto them*, did not trust himself with them, or repose any confidence upon them, *because he knew all men*, the fickleness of some, who would play the hypocrite in order to betray him, and the weakness of others, who in a time of danger might through timidity be tempted to desert him, or through mistake and indiscretion raise some disturbance, through their vain imaginations that his kingdom was *temporal*, and his throne to be established by arms *And*, being thus all-wise, *he needed not that any should testify of man for he knew what was in man*, how deceitful above all things and desperately wicked his heart was, and therefore how little to be trusted

Note, (1) We should be cautious in whom we confide, and try before we trust (2) Christ knows the secrets of all hearts, he sees the devices of his *fiercest enemies*, and the falsehood of *pretended friends*, and he will bring every thing to judgment, and every secret thing, whether it be good or whether it be evil

CHAP III

In this chapter we have, 1 Christ's discourse with Nicodemus, ver 1—21 2 John Baptist's discourse with his disciples concerning Christ, ver 22—36

1 THERE was a man of the Pharisees, named
Nicodemus, a ruler of the Jews 2 The
same came to Jesus by night, and said unto him, Rabbi,
we know that thou art a teacher come from God for
no man can do these miracles that thou doest, except
God be with him 3 Jesus answered and said unto
him, Verily, verily I say unto thee, Except a man be
born again, he cannot see the kingdom of God 4
Nicodemus saith unto him, How can a man be born
when he is old? can he enter the second time into his
mother's womb, and be born? 5 Jesus answered, Ve-
rily, verily I say unto thee, Except a man be born of
water and *of* the Spirit, he cannot enter into the king-
dom of God 6 That which is born of the flesh, is
flesh, and that which is born of the Spirit, is spirit
7 Marvel not that I said unto thee, Ye must be born
again 8 The wind bloweth where it listeth, and
thou hearest the sound thereof, but canst not tell whence
it cometh, and whither it goeth so is every one that
is born of the Spirit 9 Nicodemus answered and said
unto him, How can these things be? 10 Jesus an-
swered and said unto him, Art thou a master of Israel,
and knowest not these things? 11 Verily, verily I say
unto thee, We speak that we know, and testify that we
have seen, and ye receive not our witness 12 If I
have told you earthly things, and ye believe not, how
shall ye believe, if I tell you of heavenly things 13
And no man hath ascended up to heaven, but he that
came down from heaven, *even* the Son of man which is
in heaven 14 ¶ And as Moses lifted up the serpent
in the wilderness, even so must the Son of man be
lifted up 15 That whosoever believeth in him should
not perish, but have eternal life 16 ¶ For God so
loved the world, that he gave his only begotten Son,
that whosoever believeth in him, should not perish, but
have everlasting life 17. For God sent not his Son
into the world to condemn the world, but that the
world through him might be saved 18 ¶ He that
believeth on him, is not condemned but he that be-
lieveth not, is condemned already, because he hath not
believed in the name of the only begotten Son of God
19 And this is the condemnation, that light is come
into the world, and men loved darkness rather than light,
because their deeds were evil 20 For every one that
doth evil, hateth the light, neither cometh to the light,
lest his deeds should be reproved 21 But he that
doth truth, cometh to the light, that his deeds may be
made manifest, that they are wrought in God

v 1—21 Though not many mighty are called, we have here a singular instance of one made a monument of divine grace

1 *There was a man* of great note and eminence, *of the Pharisees*, the sect which ever expressed the bitterest enmity against our Lord, *named Nicodemus, a ruler of the Jews*, a member of the sanhedrim, *the same came to Jesus by night*, solicitous to have some particular discourse with him concerning the things he had heard him preach, and he chose this time, as some suppose, out of shame and cowardice, as not daring to appear publickly with him for fear of the Jews, or because this was the season when Christ would be most at leisure, being engaged all the day in publick, and when he might more freely and at large talk over with him the important point concerning which he desired to be resolved With great respect he addressed him, *and said unto him, Rabbi, we know that thou art a teacher come from God for no man can do these miracles that thou doest, except God be with him* These were such credentials of his divine mission, and wrought with such notorious evidence, that the more they were examined, the more forcibly they proved the author of them sent from God *Note,* (1) The grace of Jesus can reach those

those whose condition in life is most dangerous, and their prejudices the strongest against his gospel (2) When the profession of the true religion is reproachful and unfashionable, some, who dare not openly avow their sentiments, in secret approve the truths which others despise, and will slip in among the faithful, if they cannot be seen, as Nicodemus by night (3) Christ is come to be a teacher of babes, to lead a dark world to the light of life, and guide the erring feet of sinners into the paths of everlasting peace May we be humble scholars then, and learn of him!

2 In consequence of the application of Nicodemus, Christ addresses him in the following instructive discourse

(1) On the nature and necessity of regeneration *Verily, verily I say unto thee, Except a man be born again, or from above, he cannot see the kingdom of God* Nicodemus, as the rest of his countrymen, tinctured with the common prejudices concerning the Messiah's kingdom, supposed the seed of Abraham would be all admitted to an honourable place in it But Christ strikes at that radical mistake, assuring him, that no man's external privileges, religious profession, or moral attainments, availed any thing, if his heart and life were not effectually wrought upon by the regenerating influences of the Spirit of God For, as we are born by nature corrupt and polluted with sin, and spiritually dead in trespasses we must receive another, a new divine nature, the work of God, as much as the life which he first gave to the clay, in order that man might be a living soul And, unless this supernatural change passes upon us, we can neither understand the nature of the Messiah's kingdom, nor receive any of the blessings and benefits which it was designed to convey to us

Nicodemus, mistaking Christ's meaning, and understanding the words in a literal sense, expresses his surprize at the assertion, not comprehending how it was possible for a man, old as he was, to pass the second time through his mother's womb In answer to his objection Christ enforces and explains his declarations, *Verily verily I say unto thee*, a truth that is of most infallible certainty, *Except a man be born of water and the Spirit, he cannot enter into the kingdom of God* Christ's word, however strange and unintelligible to the natural man, cannot change There can be no entrance into glory, without that new birth which gives a meetness for it The soul, by the powerful agency of the Spirit of God, must be cleansed from its natural pollution, as water purifies the body from any filth it hath contracted, and by the ordinance of baptism, as the initiatory rite, regenerate souls are to be admitted into the visible communion of the faithful And the necessity of such a spiritual change is evident, because *that which is born of the flesh is flesh* could a man a thousand times pass through the womb, he would come forth still the same corrupted creature, unfit for the kingdom of God, man's nature being utterly sinful in his present fallen state, and all his appetites, delights, and pursuits, being after the flesh, and the things which gratify his bestial part so that the soul is utterly enslaved, and the whole man flesh and not spirit Whilst, on the contrary, *that which is born of the Spirit is spirit* when the Holy Ghost works effectually on the heart, it is refined from the dregs of sensuality, the soul is restored to spiritual understanding, and the whole man, now brought under the influence of a new, divine, implanted principle of grace, becomes spiritual, in his affections, pursuits and designs, delivered from the bondage of base lust and vile corruption into the glorious liberty of the sons of God, and restored to a capacity of enjoying him *Marvel not* therefore, adds the Lord, *that I said unto thee, Ye must be born again*, nor, though we are ignorant of the manner in which this divine change is wrought, is that any objection to the thing for, in the world around us, we see effects, the immediate cause of which we are ignorant of As for instance, *The wind bloweth where it listeth*, without controul from any creature, *and thou hearest the sound thereof, but canst not tell whence it cometh, nor whither it goeth* the effects produced by it are sensibly felt, but why it blows at one time stronger than at another, why from one point rather than another, where it begins and where it ends, these are secrets known only to him who bringeth the wind out of his treasures *So is every one that is born of the Spirit* with such sovereignty doth the uncreated Spirit work, affecting the conscience of some, and not of others, with power irresistible bearing down every obstruction, quickening, comforting, sanctifying the sinner's soul, and giving him blessed experience of his effectual power and influence, though he work mysteriously, and leaves the manner of his operations still a secret to us

(2) When yet Nicodemus appeared ignorant, and questioned how these things could be, for to the natural man the things of the Spirit of God are foolishness, Christ proceeds to reprove his dulness, and to enlarge on the certainty and sublimity of those glorious truths which he advanced *Art thou a master in Israel*, a famed teacher, and professor of divinity, *and knowest not these things?* *Note*, It is a shame for those who undertake to instruct others to be ignorant themselves, and, whilst they affect to pass for men of deep learning and erudition, to be unacquainted with the most important truths that pertain unto salvation *Verily, verily I say unto thee, We speak that we do know* the truths Christ taught were of infallible certainty, he spoke as commissioned by his Father, and under the influences of the Spirit, in correspondence with what all the prophets and John had before declared *and testify that we have seen*, not speaking on hearsay, but on the most undoubted evidence, and with the clearest assurance *and ye receive not our witness* Such was the blindness, such the prejudice, that had spread over the Jews in general, and the Pharisees and rulers in particular, that they refused to receive and embrace the doctrines of salvation taught by the Son of God, though so infallibly true, so plainly delivered, and attested by such miracles so that they were without excuse As all infidels are, who refuse to submit to the evidence of revelation *If therefore I have told you earthly things*, illustrating, with the familiar instances of water and the wind, the necessity of a spiritual change in the hearts of sinners here below, *and ye believe not*, comprehend not the meaning, nor give credit to the truths advanced, *how shall ye believe, if I tell you of heavenly things?* of the more sublime doctrines of the gospel, the amazing union of the divine and human nature, the design of the incarnation of the Son of God, his sufferings, death, exaltation, the nature of his spiritual kingdom, and of the beatific vision how much more must these be mysterious, when delivered in language suitable to the vast subject, if the plainer truths appear so difficult to be understood? For instance, *No man hath ascended up to heaven, but he that came down from heaven* the prophets of God indeed had spoken under a divine inspiration, and what they said came from heaven, but none of them ever spoke of their own knowledge, as having been with God in glory, acquainted with all the secrets of his will, this was the distinguished privilege of the Son of man, the Messiah, who from eternity was in the bosom of the Father and was now come down from heaven, as a teacher eminently sent from God, and who, though upon earth, was even then *the Son of man which is in heaven*, though in his human nature he stood and talked with Nicodemus, his divine nature filled heaven and earth, was every where present, and, in virtue of that communication of properties which subsists between the two natures, the Son of man, though on earth, was, as God, in heaven, as *the Lord of life and glory* is said to be *crucified* 1 Cor ii 8 and God, who is incorporeal, is said to purchase the church with *his own blood*, Acts xx 28 that which was done by him in one nature being ascribed to him in the other *Note*, (1) There are mysteries above our comprehension, which are to be received on the evidence of God's word Where reason fails, faith must be exercised (2) In all the humiliation of the Son of man, we must never forget that he is unchangeably the same, *God over all, blessed for ever*

(3) As the great prophet he proceeds to describe the end of his incarnation, and the eternal blessedness of those who truly believe in him He came to seek and save that which was lost, to heal our mortal wounds, and to recover our perishing souls

[1] *He came to heal our mortal wounds*, as the antitype of the brazen serpent which Moses in the wilderness lifted up, that those who were stung by the fiery serpents might look and live *And as Moses lifted up the serpent in the wilderness, even so must the Son of man be lifted up, that whosoever believeth in him should not perish, but have everlasting life* (1) We are mortally stung by the old fiery serpent Satan, and the deadly poison of sin is diffused throughout our nature, the wound incurable, the torment intolerable and eternal, unless more than human help and healing be vouchsafed to us (2) Christ is the only hope of the desperate, the brazen serpent lifted up, for the healing of the nations, on the pole of the everlasting gospel, once crucified on a tree, but now exalted to the throne, bright-shining with beams of grace on every miserable soul that turns the eye of faith towards him (3) It is looking to him alone which performs the wondrous cure The soul that looks to any other physician, or refuses this simple method of cure, *Look to me and be ye saved*, Isa xlv 22 perishes without remedy, whilst faith infallibly brings health and healing for, (4) However obnoxious we are by sin to the wrath of God, however deep our guilt, or aggravated our iniquities, he is a Saviour to the uttermost whosoever look to him shall live, though, like the dying thief, reduced to the last gasp, yea only the chief of sinners shall be rescued from the eternal ruin he justly apprehended and fears, but shall have *eternal life*, entitled to all the bliss and blessedness of glory, through the complete and finished salvation which is in Jesus Christ, and can never afterwards perish

[2] He came to save our lost souls by the sacrifice of himself *For God so loved the world, that he gave his only begotten Son, that whosoever believeth in him should not perish, but have everlasting life* (1) Christ is the universal Saviour, not of the Jews only, but of the Gentiles also, and, as his free invitation is preached to all, whosoever will is invited to come to him They who reject him tell sin against their own mercies (2) He is *the only begotten of God*, which bespeaks his infinite dignity and all-sufficiency to save those for whose sake he came into the world (3) The love of God in thinking upon us in our ruined state, and sending his Son to be the propitiation for our sins is the astonishment of angels, and should be matter of our unceasing wonder, praise, and adoration (4) Whosoever by faith receive the Lord Jesus, as the Son of God and the Redeemer of lost souls, placing their whole dependance on his blood and righteous-

righteousness, are sure to obtain the remission of all their sins, and, in the world to come life everlasting *For God sent not his Son into the world to condemn the world*, as the Jews supposed their Messiah would destroy the Gentile nations, and exalt them, *but that the world through him might be saved* Even the vilest and most guilty, who believe in him, whether Jews or Gentiles, may now through him obtain salvation, whilst, out of him, ruin and despair must seize the whole fallen race *He that believeth on him is not condemned there is no condemnation to them that are in Christ Jesus*, nor will any charge lie against those whom God justifieth, and for whom the Saviour of sinners shed his blood *But*, (5) Destruction inevitable and eternal must be the portion of those who neglect or despise so great a salvation, *he that believeth not* the gospel-word preached unto them, whether Jew or Gentile, *is condemned already*, lies at present under the curse which is the wages of sin, and is as surely a lost soul, as when the sentence shall be executed in the great day, *because he hath not believed in the name of the only begotten Son of God* Unbelief is the great damning sin there can be no cure for those who reject the only remedy, and when God hath been so rich in grace, as to give his only begotten Son, the baseness of the ingratitude in rejecting him cannot but bring aggravated guilt and perdition on the sinner's soul *And this is the greatest* and most fatal cause of their *condemnation, that light is come into the world*, the light of the glorious gospel of Christ, in which he shines as the sun of righteousness arisen to guide our feet into the ways of peace *and men*, notwithstanding, *loved darkness rather than light* The Jews hold fast their corrupt traditions, the Gentiles, their idolatrous superstitions, and both shun the light of truth, which makes manifest and condemns their works of darkness, *because their deeds are evil*, therefore are they sealed up under wrath, and such wilful ignorance, and obstinate rejection of the truth, must needs fill up the measure of their iniquities (6) This then will be the test between the wilfully impenitent and the sincere enquirer after truth *For every one that doth evil*, makes it his practice and his delight, and is wedded to his sins, *hateth the light*, his carnal mind is at enmity with Christ and his gospel, *neither cometh to the light*, but shuns the means of grace, the ministrations of the faithful, and the company and converse of such whose words and works would be a rebuke to his darkness, *lest his deeds should be reproved*, lest his darling corruptions should be held up to him in their own hideous form, his danger faithfully set before him, and his conscience wounded with remorse *But he that doth the truth*, in simplicity following the mind of God, as far as it is revealed to him, open to conviction, and willing to be searched, *cometh to the light* of God's word, desirous to know, and disposed to follow it, however contrary to his own natural inclination or worldly interests, *that his deeds may be made manifest*, his heart examined, his principles brought to the test, his mind enlightened, and his conduct regulated, so that it may appear he is now under the influence of a regenerate spirit, designing in all his works the divine glory, and evidencing *that they are wrought in God*, by his gracious influence, according to his holy will, and in a state of union and communion with him Blessed and happy are the people who are in such a case!

b Chap iv 2 · c Mat iii 6 Mark i 4 Luke iii 3 · d Mat xiv 3 · e Chap i 7, 15 27 34 · f 1 Cor iv 7 Heb v 4 Jam i 17 · † Or, take unto him self · g Chap i 20, 27 · h Mal iii 1 Mark i 2 Luke i 17 · i 2 Cor xi 2 · k Cant v 1 · l Chap i 15, 27 · m Chap viii 23 1 Cor xv 47 · n Eph i 21 1 Pet iii 22 · o Ver 11 Chap vii 16 & viii 26 & xii 49 · p Rom iii 4 1 John v 10 · q Chap i 16 · r Chap v 20 · s Dan vii 14 Mat xi 27 & xxviii 18 Chap xvii 2 Heb ii 8 · t Hab ii 4 Ver 15, 16 Rom i 17 1 John v 10

22 ¶ After these things came Jesus and his disciples
into the land of Judea, and there he tarried with them,
and [b] baptized 23. ¶ And [c] John also was baptizing
in Enon, near to Salim, because there was much water
there and they came, and were baptized 24 For
[d] John was not yet cast into prison 25 ¶ Then there
arose a question between *some* of John's disciples and
the Jews, about purifying 26 And they came unto
John, and said unto him, Rabbi, he that was with
thee beyond Jordan, [e] to whom thou bearest witness,
behold, the same baptizeth, and all men come to him
27 John answered and said, [f] A man can † receive no-
thing, except it be given him from heaven 28 Ye
yourselves bear me witness, that I said, [g] I am not the
Christ, but that [h] I am sent before him 29 He that
hath the bride, is [i] the bridegroom but [k] the friend of
the bridegroom, which standeth and heareth him, re-
joiceth greatly because of the bridegroom's voice this
my joy therefore is fulfilled 30 He must increase, but
I *must* decrease 31 He that cometh from above, [l] is
above all [m] he that is of the earth, is earthly, and speak-
eth of the earth he that cometh from heaven, [n] is above
all 32 And [o] what he hath seen and heard, that he
testifieth, and no man receiveth his testimony 33 He
that hath received his testimony, [p] hath set to his seal,
that God is true 34 For he whom God hath sent,
speaketh the words of God for God giveth not the Spi-
rit by measure *unto him* 35 [q] The Father loveth the
Son, and [r] hath given all things into his hand 36
[s] He that believeth on the Son, hath everlasting life; and
he that believeth not the Son, shall not see life, but the
wrath of God abideth on him

v 22—36 When our Lord had finished his discourse with Nicodemus, we are told,

1 Whither he went, and what he did He left Jerusalem, and travelled into the country of Judea, where he continued some time, preaching the gospel of the kingdom, and by the ordinance of baptism, which his apostles administred, admitted those who professed their faith in him into the number of his avowed disciples

2 John continued his ministry in another part of the country with success He did not join with Jesus, lest their enemies should pretend there was a combination between them, nor did he desist from his labours, though he knew his superior was now gone forth to minister, but continued to preach and baptize all who came to him, having fixed himself at a place where were many streams of water, that rendered it convenient to administer baptism to the multitudes which resorted to him, for as yet *he was not cast into prison*, as he shortly afterwards was, and a period put to his farther usefulness *Note*, The work of the ministry is wide, there is room for the exercise of all our several talents, nor must any be discouraged by their own comparative inferiority they are suited for their place, and may hope to see their labours successful

3 A contest arose between some of John's disciples and the Jews, concerning *purifying* It would seem as if the disciples of John exalted their master's baptism above the ceremonial ablutions of Moses, or the purifications enjoined by the traditions of the elders, whilst many of the Jews probably contended for their own more antient and authorised customs, and looked upon John's baptism as an innovation, suggesting that there would be no end to such novelties, as another person, one Jesus, was as much or more followed than their master, and his disciples would cry up his baptism as better than John's

4 Puzzled with this difficulty, John's disciples carry the case to their master, and, jealous for his honour and their own, who were connected with him, report with concern what they had lately heard, *and said unto him, Rabbi, he that was with thee beyond Jordan*, and, among others, received baptism, *to whom thou bearest witness*, pointing him out with peculiar distinction; *behold, the same baptizeth*, setting up himself as a rival to thee, *and all men come to him* They look upon it as a piece of presumption in Jesus to assume the Baptist's office, and ungrateful to make use of the testimony which John had born, in prejudice to him nor could they without envy behold their master eclipsed by him whom they regarded as lately but his disciple, and as one of themselves So ready are good men to be under the temptation of a party-spirit, and to feel unbecoming jealousies, and risings of envy against superior excellence, which seems to eclipse their own

5 John's answer shewed what spirit he was of Far from envying Jesus as his rival, he rejoices in his success, and confirming the testimony he had before born to him, chearfully turns over to him all his interest in Israel

John answered and said, A man can receive nothing, except it be given him from heaven God gives to every man severally as he wills, gifts, endowments, and success If he is pleased to bestow more on one than another, there is no room for complaint whatever our measure is, it is a matter of favour to us, and we have reason to be thankful, nor ought to envy the superior honours or usefulness of others and this consideration should in every case silence every murmur of discontent or envy The words also may have another reference, and intimate, that it was evident the plainest truths were insufficient, unless they were favoured with divine illumination, else could not his disciples, after what he had so repeatedly spoken of Christ, have stumbled at the rising fame of Jesus, and the application of the multitudes to him And this is a universal truth, that unless a man be taught of God, he never can understand and heartily embrace the truths of God, which must be spiritually discerned

He appeals to what he had uniformly advanced from the beginning *Ye yourselves bear me witness, that I said, I am not the Christ, but that I am sent before him* All the honour he had ever assumed was that of being his harbinger, and going before the face of the Lord to prepare his way and therefore he was now arrived, his forerunner, far from being grieved, must rejoice in it *He that hath the bride, is the bridegroom*, Christ hath alone the right over his church, and to him must the gathering of the people be He is come from heaven to espouse it to himself, the heavenly bridegroom, and having loved his people from eternity, draws their hearts to him in faith and love There can be no reason therefore for murmurs or jealousy, *but*, far otherwise, *the friend of the bridegroom*, as he was, *which standeth and heareth him*, waiting upon him as his attendant, helping forward his interests, and desiring to advance his honour, *rejoiceth greatly because of the bridegroom's voice*, when he comes to take his bride, and issues his orders and instructions to those who wait in his train *This my joy therefore is fulfilled*, to hear that Christ appears publicly, inviting his bride, his redeemed people, to come to him, and that multitudes flock to him, embracing the offers of his grace. And thus doth every faithful miniſter ſtand before the great bridegroom of ſouls, to receive his commands, and deliver the meſſages of love to his church, delighted to behold the happy effects produced by them, when his people become a willing people in the day of his power, and rejoicing greatly in every ſoul converted to Jeſus, and brought by faith and love to cleave to him alone.

Far from envying the riſing glory of his Lord, John beholds with pleaſure the fulfilment of the divine decree. *He muſt increaſe, but I muſt decreaſe*, his fame muſt ſpread, his glory be manifeſted, his diſciples multiply, and to him doth John gladly turn over all his intereſt, content to fade before his ſuperior brightneſs, as the morning ſtar diſappears before the riſing ſun, and well-pleaſed to ſee that kingdom of the Meſſiah eſtabliſhed and increaſing, that muſt ſpread from pole to pole, and endure to the end of time. And to behold this, cannot but give the moſt ſingular delight to every faithful miniſter.

The glory of his perſon, and the ſurpaſſing excellence of his office, cannot but give him this ſuperiority. *He that cometh from above, is above all*: his nature and original being divine, he muſt needs have the indiſputed precedency, and ſupreme authority, over all other meſſengers ſent from God, who ſpeak only in his name, and by his commiſſion. *He that is of the earth*, and ſuch are the greateſt ſaints and prophets, *is earthly, and ſpeaketh of the earth*: as he is ſprung from the duſt, and muſt return to the duſt, he is naturally attached to earthly things, his conceptions low and groveling, and, when even under divine inſpiration, unable adequately to expreſs the ſublime myſteries of infinite wiſdom, whilſt *he that cometh from heaven, is above all*. Contraſted with the teachings of Jeſus, in whom from eternity dwelt all the treaſures of wiſdom, as being one of the ſacred ſelf-exiſtent Godhead, the wiſdom of the wiſeſt is weakneſs, and their ſpeech not to be compared with his preaching. *And* the reaſon is evident, becauſe *what he hath ſeen and heard, that he teſtifieth*, from the moſt intimate knowledge of the divine nature and counſels, both as God incarnate, and in the human nature poſſeſſing the Spirit without meaſure. But ſuch was the blindneſs and obſtinacy of thoſe to whom he ſpoke, that, though he was greatly attended, *and* John's *diſciples apprehended* all who followed him believed in him, he lets them know the caſe was far otherwiſe: *no man receiveth his teſtimony*, none, comparatively ſpeaking, ſo few of the multitudes who came to him would be found his real diſciples. Many are called by the goſpel, but few truly converted by it, bleſſed and happy however are thoſe who receive it in the light and love of it, for *he that hath received his teſtimony, hath ſet to his ſeal, that God is true*. He ſubſcribes to the faithfulneſs and veracity of God, in having fulfilled all the propheſies concerning the Meſſiah, and embraces, with full confidence of their completion, the gracious promiſes of his goſpel, as being all Yea and Amen in Chriſt Jeſus. And herein God is glorified, when we truſt our everlaſting hopes upon the word he hath delivered to us by his Son, *for he whom God hath ſent, ſpeaketh the words of God*, all his language ſpoke the divinity reſident in him, and no word of human infirmity ever dropped from his lips, *for God giveth not the Spirit by meaſure unto him*. All the other prophets, who were ſent of God, poſſeſſed but a meaſure of the Spirit, and only ſpoke under his immediate inſpiration on ſome particular occaſions, being, at other times left to ſpeak *their own words*, but he in whom dwelt the fulneſs of the Godhead bodily, ever ſpoke the *words of God*. *The Father loveth the Son* with a peculiar and tranſcendent regard, as being poſſeſſed of the ſame nature and perfections. He delights in his Son's undertaking, as Mediator, *and hath given all things into his hand*, inveſting him in his human nature with all power and authority in heaven and in earth. All the great affairs of the kingdom of providence, grace, and glory, are committed to his management, that his enemies may feel his vengeance, that his faithful ones may experience his bleſſing, protection, and care, and all at laſt appear before him as their eternal Judge. *He that believeth*, therefore, *on the Son*, receives him as God manifeſt in the fleſh, and reſts his hopes on the rich grace revealed in the goſpel alone, *hath everlaſting life*, he ſhall not only hereafter be put in poſſeſſion of it, but hath actually already in himſelf the beginnings and foretaſtes of it, and poſſeſſes that title to it, confirmed by the immutable oath and promiſe of God, which never can be loſt: *and*, on the contrary, *he that believeth not the Son*, rejecting his divine authority and miſſion, incredulous of his word, and diſobedient to his will, *ſhall not ſee life*: whilſt he remains under the power of unbelief, he is dead in treſpaſſes and ſins, and nothing *but* miſery inconceivable and eternal awaits him, becauſe *the wrath of God*, which is for ever wrath to come, *abideth on him*. How terrible is the end of all who believe not God, and obey not the goſpel of his dear Son!

CHAP. IV.

In this chapter we have Chriſt, 1. *Departing out of Judea*, ver. 1—3. 2. *Paſſing through Samaria,* (1.) *His coming into Samaria*, ver. 4—6. (2.) *His diſcourſe with the Samaritan woman at a well*, ver. 7—26. (3.) *The notice which the woman gave of him to the city*, ver. 27—30. (4.) *Chriſt's talk with his diſciples in the mean time*, ver. 31—38. (5.) *The good effect of this among the Samaritans*, ver. 39—42. 3. *We find him reſiding for ſome time in Galilee*, ver. 43—46. *and his curing of a nobleman's ſon there that was at death's door*, ver. 46—54.

1 WHEN therefore the Lord knew how the Pha-
riſees had heard that Jeſus made and [a] bap- [a] Chap. iii. 22.
tized more diſciples than John, 2 (Though Jeſus him-
ſelf baptized not, but *his* diſciples) 3 [b] He left Judea, [b] Chap. vii. 1—3.
and departed again into Galilee.

v. 1—3. Judea being now become a dangerous abode, thro' the malice of the Phariſees, Our Lord retires into Galilee, that he might be farther removed from Jeruſalem, where his bitter enemies chiefly reſided. He had continued about eight months (*See ver.* 35.) in Judea, and as his preaching had been very ſucceſsful, and great multitudes followed him, who were admitted by baptiſm into the number of his profeſſing diſciples, he knew the wicked deſigns which his Phariſaical enemies had formed, on the information they received concerning his growing fame and intereſt among the people, as if he far exceeded John in his popularity and the number of converts, and therefore was to be apprehended as a more dangerous rival than the Baptiſt. Though in ſome particulars the information given to the Phariſees ſeems to be falſe, for as it is not probable, that they who were baptized by the diſciples of Jeſus were more than thoſe whom John had baptized, ſo it is certain, that Jeſus baptized not, but his diſciples, maintaining the dignity of his character, as ſent to baptize with the Holy Ghoſt, and far ſuperior to John, or any others. Or it may be alſo to remove all emulation among his diſciples, which might ariſe, if he baptized ſome, and his ſervants others, or to ſhew, that the validity of the ordinance depended not on the worthineſs of the miniſtry, but on his bleſſing and inſtitution. *Note*, (1.) The enemies of the goſpel are ever envious and exaſperated at its *ſucceſs*. (2.) When danger threatens, it is prudent to avoid the ſtorm by flight, where duty does not require us to ſtand and ſuffer.

4 And he muſt needs go through Samaria. 5 Then
cometh he to a city of Samaria, which is called Sy-
char, near to the parcel of ground [c] that Jacob gave [c] Gen. xxxiii. 19. & xlviii. 22. Joſh. xxiv. 32.
to his ſon Joſeph. 6 Now Jacob's well was there.
Jeſus therefore being wearied with *his* journey, ſat thus
on the well: and it was about the ſixth hour. 7 There
cometh a woman of Samaria to draw water: Jeſus ſaith
unto her, Give me to drink. 8. For his diſciples were
gone away unto the city to buy meat. 9. Then ſaith
the woman of Samaria unto him, How is it that thou
being a Jew, aſkeſt drink of me, which am a woman of
Samaria? for [d] the Jews have no dealings with the Sa- [d] 2 Kings xvii. 24. Luke ix. 52, 53. Acts x. 28.
maritans. 10 Jeſus anſwered and ſaid unto her, If
thou kneweſt the gift of God, and who it is that ſaith
to thee, Give me to drink; thou wouldeſt have aſked of
him, and he would have given thee [e] living water. 11 [e] Jer. ii. 13. Zech. xiv. 8.
The woman ſaith unto him, Sir, thou haſt nothing to
draw with, and the well is deep: from whence then haſt
thou that living water? 12 Art thou greater than
our father Jacob, which gave us the well, and drank
thereof himſelf, and his children, and his cattle? 13
Jeſus anſwered and ſaid unto her, Whoſoever drinketh
of this water ſhall thirſt again: 14 But [f] whoſoever [f] Chap. vi. 35, 58.
drinketh of the water that I ſhall give him, ſhall never
thirſt; but the water that I ſhall give him, [g] ſhall be in [g] Chap. vii. 38.
him a well of water ſpringing up into everlaſting life.
15 The woman ſaith unto him, [h] Sir, give me this wa- [h] Chap. vi. 34.
ter, that I thirſt not, neither come hither to draw. 16
Jeſus ſaith unto her, Go, call thy huſband, and come
hither. 17 The woman anſwered and ſaid, I have no
huſband. Jeſus ſaid unto her, Thou haſt well ſaid, I
have no huſband: 18 For thou haſt had five huſbands,
and he whom thou now haſt is not thy huſband: in
that ſaidſt thou truly. 19 The woman ſaith unto him, [i] Luke vii. 16. & xxiv. 19. Chap. vi. 14.
Sir, [i] I perceive that thou art a prophet. 20 Our fa-
thers worſhipped in this mountain; and ye ſay, that
[k] in Jeruſalem is the place where men ought to wor- [k] Deut. xii. 5, 11. 1 Kings ix. 3. 2 Chr. vii. 12.
ſhip. 21 Jeſus ſaith unto her, Woman, believe me,
the hour cometh, [l] when ye ſhall neither in this moun- [l] Mal. i. 11.
tain, nor yet at Jeruſalem worſhip the Father. 22 Ye
worſhip [m] ye know not what: we know what we wor- [m] 2 Kings xvii. 29.
ſhip: for [n] ſalvation is of the Jews. 23 But the hour [n] Iſa. ii. 3. Rom. ix. 4.
cometh, and now is, when the true worſhippers ſhall
worſhip

o Phil iii 3 worship the Father o in spirit and p in truth: for the
p Heb x 22 Father seeketh such to worship him. 24 q God is a
q 2 Cor iii 17 Spirit, and they that worship him, must worship *him* in
spirit and in truth. 25 The woman saith unto him, I
know that Messias cometh which is called Christ: when
r Ver 29, 39 he is come, r he will tell us all things. 26 Jesus saith
s Chap ix 37 unto her, s I that speak unto thee, am *he*.

v 4—26 As Samaria lay between Judea and Galilee, he must necessarily pass through it in his way thither, unless he took a large compass about. That country was inhabited by the posterity of the colonies which the king of Assyria had planted there after the captivity; and being mingled with many apostate Jews, became a mongrel race, who, though retaining many heathen idolatries and superstitions, professed themselves worshippers of Israel's God, and received the books of Moses; were circumcised, and erected a temple on mount Gerizim, in opposition to that at Jerusalem, pretending that this was the spot where God ought to be worshipped. Hence arose the bitterest animosity between the Samaritans and the Jews, who regarded them as the most abominable of mankind. In this journey we are told,

1 The place where our Lord stayed to rest himself a while, being wearied with his journey. It was by a well-side belonging to a city of Samaria, called Sychar, (or Shechem, as is supposed) which city bordered on a piece of land which Jacob, having purchased of the sons of Hamor, had given to his son Joseph, (*See Gen* xlviii 22 *Josh* xxiv 32) The well was called *Jacob's*, either because he dug it, or used it for himself and family. Our Lord here appears truly man, subject to our sinless infirmities, weariness, thirst, and hunger; for it became him in all things to become like unto his brethren, sin only excepted. *It was about the sixth hour*, or mid-day, according to the Jewish computation of time; or six in the evening, if we follow the Roman method of reckoning.

2 The discourse which passed between Jesus and a woman of Samaria. She happened just at this time to come to draw water; so divine Providence ordered it, leading her to Christ in a way she knew not, (*See Gen* xix 2 xxiv 11 *Exod* ii. 15) The disciples being gone into the city to buy meat, he was alone, and is pleased graciously to improve that moment's leisure for the benefit of this poor stranger's soul, she being one of those lost sheep he came to seek and save.

He addressed her first, begging a little water to drink; for though he was rich, for our sakes he became thus poor, and condescends to ask a cup of cold water. Yet he had a further end in view, even to engage her in conversation, and thereby to effect the purposes of his grace toward her. Occasional discourse with strangers hath been often found to have a blessed and abiding influence, and should encourage us, when travelling, to open our mouths, and speak a word for God, and for immortal souls.

The woman expressed her surprize, that he who appeared to be a Jew, should deign to receive any act of kindness at the hands of a Samaritan; or that he should expect the least favour would be granted from one to the other, where the enmity between the two nations was so bitter and irreconcileable, as to cut off all manner of friendly intercourse between them. Religious quarrels are thus usually seen to be the most implacable; but where the spirit of bigotry and uncharitableness dwells, whichever side is right in the point disputed, the spirit of both is wrong, and utterly opposite to pure religion and undefiled.

Waving the subject of the controversy between the Jews and Samaritans, Christ designed to lead her to the knowledge of himself, and therefore replied, *If thou knewest the gift of God*, what an unexampled instance of his love he hath given in sending his own Son into the world, *and who it is that saith to thee, Give me to drink*, even that divine person now become incarnate, *thou wouldst* have laid aside all these national prejudices, and *have asked of him, and he would have given thee living water*, those gifts of grace, and comforts of his spirit, which to the sinner's soul are more desirable than the coolest and most refreshing stream to the parched throat and weary traveller. *Note*, (1) Christ is the fountain of gardens, and well of living water, open for every poor sinner, and freely given, that whosoever will, may come unto him, and drink of the riches of his grace. (2) Many wickedly disregard the invaluable blessings of the gospel, because they perceive not their excellence, nor their own want of them. (3) They who would obtain the blessings of grace from Jesus, and his holy Spirit, must seek them in importunate prayer; and he who is faithful and true, hath promised that none such shall ask in vain.

The woman mistaking Christ's meaning, and taking his discourse literally with some sort of disdain answered, *Sir, thou hast nothing to draw with, and the well is deep; from whence then hast thou that living water?* and therefore concludes his boasts were absurd, and his offers a mere jest. They who are wholly taken up with the objects of sense, have no understanding of spiritual things; they are foolishness to them: the hidden springs of grace in Christ being unseen, are disbelieved. Besides, she regards it as a great piece of presumption in him, to prefer any other waters before those of a well so highly distinguished. *Art thou greater than our father Jacob*, from whom we Samaritans, as well as you Jews, claim our descent, *which gave us this well, and drank thereof himself, and his children, and his cattle?* Vain boasts these! when they had so poor a title to claim kindred with the patriarch, and were no better than usurpers of that country, which they pretended came to them by gift from Jacob to Joseph, and so in a right line of descent to them. The bitterest enemies of the church thus often usurp, and would monopolize its privileges.

Though she had spoken foolishly and perversely, Christ kindly bore with her, and continued his discourse, saying, *Whosoever drinketh of this water shall thirst again*; this was but common water, and could only slake the present thirst, which must soon return: *but whosoever drinketh of the water that I shall give him, shall never thirst*. All the comforts of the world are insufficient to give any abiding satisfaction; Christ alone can bestow the substantial portion on the soul. They who pant after the earth, and its enjoyments, drink and thirst again; *but the water that I shall give him, shall be in him a well of water springing up into everlasting life*. Such is Christ, when formed in the believer's heart. [1] He delivers the soul from the dominion of all the former unsuitable appetites and inclinations after sensual objects. [2] He furnishes us with continual supplies of grace and consolation from himself, the everflowing, overflowing fountain of mercies; so that in our heavenly journey we can never faint nor be weary, drinking of these living streams, as of the water from the rock, which followed Israel's camp through the desert. [3] Wherever his grace is thus implanted in the soul, it bears the affections heavenward, and never fails till it is consummated in glory everlasting.

The woman, either seriously desiring what could it be possessed, would save her so much trouble, or ridiculing pretensions she had no apprehension he could make good, replied, *Sir, give me this water, that I thirst not, neither come hither to draw*.

To impress deeper seriousness upon her soul, or to convince her of the dignity of his character, of which she was not at all apprized, Jesus turned the discourse to another topic, which he knew must nearly and deeply affect her, and bringing her sin home to her conscience, would engage her to embrace him as her Saviour. Therefore he saith unto her, *Go, call thy husband, and come hither*. Conscious of the guilty state in which she at present lived, she wanted to conceal her shame, and said, *I have no husband*, conceiving it impossible for him to detect the lie. But, to her amazement, she finds him intimately acquainted with all the most secret transactions of her life, which he lays before her. *Thou hast well said, I have no husband*; so far is true; *for thou hast had five husbands*, from whom, probably for her adulterous conduct, she had been successively divorced; *and he whom thou now hast, is not thy husband: in that saidst thou truly*, the person with whom she now cohabited, not being married to her, or her former husbands being yet living. He doth not reproach her either with her evasion or lewdness, but rather leaves it to her conscience to make the application. Gentle reproofs, by insinuation, are often more effectual than more immediate and rough rebuke.

Struck with what she heard, and convicted in her own conscience, she would willingly have turned off the discourse from so painful a subject; and persuaded, by what he had told her, of his more than human knowledge, she proposes to him the grand point in debate between the Jews and Samaritans. *Sir, I perceive that thou art a prophet. Our fathers worshipped in this mountain*; there Abraham built an altar (*Gen* xii 6, 7) and the tribe of Joseph stood, when the blessings and curses were pronounced by the tribes on mount Ebal and Gerizim; and therefore on this mountain Gerizim, the Samaritans insisted sacrifices and offerings should alone be offered to God, in the temple which they built there: *and ye*, that are Jews, *say, that in Jerusalem is the place where men ought to worship*, in the temple on Mount Zion, where alone the oblations on God's altar are accepted; and therefore she wished, that he, who appeared so able, would resolve her in this important point. That God should be worshipped, there was no doubt: they who live in the neglect of his worship, are worse than Jews or Samaritans. The question was, Where was the place of divine appointment? and herein she did well to improve the present opportunity in converse about divine things, when she had with her so able an adviser.

Jesus kindly leads her even further than her enquiry reached. *He saith unto her, Woman, believe me*, and, since you esteem me a prophet, weigh well what I am now about to declare, *the hour cometh*, when a final period shall be put to all ceremonial distinctions, and the peculiar honours of places set apart for the worship of the Divine Being, *when ye shall neither in this mountain, nor yet at Jerusalem, worship the Father*, that is to say, exclusively; since under the gospel dispensation every place was alike acceptable to God, where holy hands were lifted up without wrath or doubting; and shortly both the temple at Gerizim and on mount Zion would be made desolate, and no sacrifice be any longer offered there. Indeed at present the Samaritans

were

were wholly wrong. *Ye worship ye know not what*, ignorant of the true God (2 Kings xvii 26), regarding him as a local deity, and debasing the worship which they pretended to pay him, with idolatrous superstitions. *We know what we worship*; for God is known in Israel, and he as one of that nation after the flesh, reckoned himself among the true worshippers, who paid their adoration according to the divine prescription, and were instructed in the revelation which he had been graciously pleased to make of himself in his sacred oracles. *For salvation is of the Jews*: the promises of salvation were peculiarly made to them, the means of grace confined for the most part to them, and he who came to be the salvation of the ends of the earth, sprang from them. *But*, though in this respect the Samaritans were utterly wrong, and not to be compared with Abraham's true descendants, yet these distinctions of nations and places were now about to cease, *the hour cometh, and now is, when the true worshippers shall worship the Father in spirit and in truth*. The place of worship is now become indifferent, the spirit and temper of the worshipper alone makes the acceptable service. All carnal ordinances are abolished, and a spiritual worship is introduced, wherein the heart, under the powerful influences of the Holy Ghost, must be lifted up in faith and love to God, and *in truth*, with simplicity and godly sincerity, according to the divine institution, and through Christ alone, who is the way, *the truth*, and the life; *for the Father seeketh such to worship him*; he will graciously accept their services, and can be pleased with no other, and such worshippers by his grace he fashions and finds, though few, compared with the formal, lifeless, hypocritical, or ignorant worshippers, who are utter strangers to such spirituality. *For God is a Spirit*, of infinite perfections, incorporeal, invisible, eternal, omniscient, requiring not the adoration of the lip or the knee, but of the heart, *and they that worship him, must worship him in spirit and in truth*: without which, the place, the form, the manner of our religious worship, avails nothing, and are in his view of no account. And what Christ saith to her is an eternal truth, and merits our most serious notice and regard, that so we may not mock God, and deceive ourselves, when we approach him in the ordinances of his worship.

The woman, though unable to object to the truths he advanced, yet professes to suspend her judgment till he should come, who would set all things right. *She saith unto him, I know that Messias cometh, (which is called*, in the Greek, *Christ*, or the anointed), this expectation being generally entertained by the Samaritans, as well as Jews. *When he is come*, whom we expect as ready to appear, *he will tell us all things*, will put an end to our controversies, clear up our doubts, and give us a distinct knowledge of all the will of God. Hereupon Jesus, in answer to her expectation of the Messiah's coming, plainly declares to her his character: *I that speak unto thee, am he*. So much nearer to us is the dear Saviour often than we are aware. Speak, Lord, to my heart, and make me to know that thou art with me, in me!

27 ¶ And upon this came his disciples, and mar-
velled that he talked with the woman: yet no man said,
What seekest thou? or, Why talkest thou with her?
28 The woman then left her water-pot, and went her
way into the city, and saith to the men, 29 Come,
see a man which told me all things that ever I did: is
not this the Christ? 30 Then they went out of the
city, and came unto him. 31 ¶ In the mean while his
disciples prayed him, saying, Master, eat. 32 But he
said unto them, I have meat to eat that ye know not of.
33 Therefore said the disciples one to another, Hath
any man brought him *ought* to eat? 34 Jesus saith
unto them, My meat is to do the will of him that sent
me, and to finish his work. 35 Say not ye, There
are yet four months, and *then* cometh harvest? behold,
I say unto you, Lift up your eyes, and look on the
fields; for they are white already to harvest. 36
And he that reapeth receiveth wages, and gathereth
fruit unto life eternal: that both he that soweth, and he
that reapeth, may rejoice together. 37 And herein is
that saying true, One soweth, and another reapeth. 38
I sent you to reap that whereon ye bestowed no labour:
other men laboured, and ye are entred into their labours.
39 ¶ And many of the Samaritans of that city believed
on him, for the saying of the woman, which testified,
He told me all that ever I did. 40 So when the Sa-
maritans were come unto him, they besought him, that
he would tarry with them: and he abode there two
days. 41 And many more believed because of his
own word; 42 And said unto the woman, Now we
believe, not because of thy saying: for we have heard
him ourselves, and know that this is indeed the Christ,
the Saviour of the world.

℣ 27—42 Just as the Lord had so far advanced in his discourse, and manifested his glorious character to this poor Samaritan, we are told,

1 The interruption given to the conversation by the arrival of the disciples, who had been sent to procure provisions, and, influenced by the common Jewish prejudices, they marvelled to see him thus engaged with a Samaritan woman. Yet, submitting to his will and wisdom, and with deepest reverence silent before him, none dared presume to ask him, what he sought of the woman, or what he said to her. *Note*, We may not question the Lord concerning any of the dispensations of his providence or grace, but rest assured that he doth all things well.

2 Deeply convinced, by what Jesus had spoken, of his being indeed the Messiah, with eagerness and joy the woman ran back to the city, leaving her water-pot behind her, careless about that, when greater concerns engaged her soul, *and saith to the men*, the inhabitants of the place, *Come*; opportunity is precious, and not a moment to be lost: *come, see a man which told me all things that ever I did: is not this the Christ?* He told me such secret passages of my life, which none but God could know, and hath impressed such a sense of them on my conscience, as fully convinces me he is the promised Messiah; haste therefore to him, and judge for yourselves, that you may be convinced also. *Note*, (1) They who run on Christ's errands, gladly disencumber themselves of every thing which would retard their speed, and sit loose to all they leave behind them. (2) When we have ourselves tasted that the Lord is gracious, we cannot but delight to invite others to come and see how good he is, and to partake with us in his tender mercies. (3) We never know Christ truly, till experimentally feeling the convictions of his word and Spirit, and brought to a deep and humbling discovery of our sins, we feel the necessity of that salvation which he brings.

3 Multitudes on this strange report, bad as the woman's character had been, resolved to go and see for themselves, no doubt invisibly drawn also by the Saviour's grace to come to him, who had such signal mercies in store for them.

4 Christ in the mean time improved the interval in profitable discourse with his disciples. So set was his mind on the blessed work before him, that, though hungry, he forgat for a while to eat his bread. The disciples pressed him, as weary, and fasting too long, to eat of the provision they had brought; *but he said unto them, I have meat to eat that ye know not of*. The gracious work begun on the heart of this poor Samaritan woman, and the prospect of multitudes flocking towards him, were more delightful and refreshing to his soul, than the richest entertainment to his body. The disciples, who understood him literally, with surprize *said one to another, Hath any man brought him ought to eat?* So dull were they of understanding. But their Master soon corrected their mistake, saying unto them, *My meat is to do the will of him that sent me, and to finish his work*; this is my greatest satisfaction, to be engaged in the blessed work of seeking and saving that which was lost, for which great end I came into the world, and from which I shall never desist till it is completed; and what was his delight should be theirs, as the husbandman labours with satisfaction in the view of the approaching harvest. *Say not ye, There are yet four months, and then cometh harvest?* Doth that joyous season please you in the prospect? *Behold*, an infinitely better is in view, *I say unto you, Lift up your eyes, and look on the fields*, (where probably multitudes of the Samaritans now appeared in view), *for they are white already to harvest*, immortal souls are ready to be gathered into the gospel church, and therefore this is no time to eat and drink, but to rise and labour. *And*, for an inducement hereunto, he suggests the glorious recompense of reward, which would be the wages of their fidelity: *He that reapeth, receiveth wages, and gathereth fruit unto eternal life*; the wages of present comfort here, supplying strength and success in his labours, and in the world to come life everlasting; and this not only for himself, but for many of those among whom he ministers; for he shall not only save his own soul, but those that hear him, 1 Tim. iv. 16. the blessed effect of which will be, *that both he that soweth, and he that reapeth, may rejoice together*. The minister who began, and they who carry on the good work, will alike partake of the comfort of it. *And herein is that proverbial saying true, One soweth, and another reapeth*. The apostles reaped what the prophets sowed; and, after their Master's resurrection, gathered a plenteous harvest of souls, among whom he had sown the seed of eternal life. *I sent you to reap that whereon ye bestowed no labour: other men laboured, and ye are entred into their labours*: the writings of the prophets, and the preaching of John, greatly facilitated their ministry, and contributed to its success; and going forth with such advantages, they had peculiar encouragement, and double cause for their diligence. *Note*, (1) Gospel ministers, as harvest men, must labour diligently and cheerfully in the service of God, and of immortal souls. (2) When the people appear eager and attentive to hear, it is a most power-

ful

ful excitement to the miniſter, to preach with livelineſs and zeal (3) Nothing will turn to ſo glorious an account in the day of God, as immortal ſouls gained to his kingdom through our miniſtry (4) The preachers of the goſpel have different talents, ſome more adapted to break up the fallow ground, and ſow the ſeed, others, to nouriſh up, and rear to maturity, the trees of righteouſneſs each are uſeful in their place, and will rejoice together at the laſt in the fruit of their joint labours.

5 Great was the effect of the woman's teſtimony concerning Chriſt *Many of the Samaritans of that city believed on him for the ſaying of the woman, which teſtified, He told me all that ever I did* She was indeed a weak inſtrument, but God can work by the moſt unlikely means Perſuaded of his prophetical character, and receiving him as the Meſſiah, they humbly beſought him to favour them with his company for a while, that they might enjoy his holy inſtructions Nor did he diſdain their requeſt, but abode with them two days, teaching them concerning the things that made for their everlaſting peace And ſo powerful was his miniſtry among them, that *many more believed becauſe of his word* not only thoſe who believed in him on the woman's report, were confirmed in the faith, but thoſe who had paid leſs regard to her, now felt the divine conviction of the Saviour's diſcourſes, *and ſaid unto the woman, Now we believe, not becauſe of thy ſaying*, merely, but on the moſt unſhaken authority of the word of Jeſus himſelf, *for we have heard him ourſelves, and know*, by the powerful energy of his word upon our conſciences, *that this is indeed the Chriſt, the* ſo long promiſed and expected *Saviour of the world*, not of the Jews only, but of the Samaritans alſo, and of all the nations of the earth, to whom his goſpel ſhould come, and who ſhould receive this word of ſalvation *Note*, (1) The greateſt fruit is often reaped where it was leaſt expected The Samaritans readily embraced that Saviour whom the Jews rejected (2) Chriſt is indeed the Saviour of the world, but we muſt believe in him before we ourſelves can be experimentally acquainted with his ſalvation

43 ¶ Now after two days he departed thence, and went into Galilee 44 For [a] Jeſus himſelf teſtified, that a prophet hath no honour in his own country 45 Then when he was come into Galilee, the Galileans received him, having ſeen all the things that he did at Jeruſalem at [b] the feaſt for they alſo went unto the feaſt 46 So Jeſus came again into Cana of Galilee, [c] where he made the water wine And there was a certain † nobleman, whoſe ſon was ſick at Capernaum 47 When he heard that Jeſus was come out of Judea into Galilee, he went unto him, and [d] beſought him that he would come down and heal his ſon for he was at the point of death 48 Then ſaid Jeſus unto him, [e] Except ye ſee ſigns and wonders, ye will not believe 49 The nobleman ſaith unto him, Sir, come down ere my child die 50 Jeſus ſaith unto him, Go thy way, thy ſon liveth And the man believed the word that Jeſus had ſpoken unto him, and he went his way 51 And as he was now going down, his ſervants met him, and told *him*, ſaying, Thy ſon liveth 52 Then enquired he of them the hour when he began to amend and they ſaid unto him, Yeſterday at the ſeventh hour the fever left him 53 So the father knew that *it was* at the ſame hour in the which Jeſus ſaid unto him, Thy ſon liveth, and himſelf believed, and his whole houſe 54 This *is* again the ſecond miracle *that* Jeſus did, when he was come out of Judea into Galilee

[a] Mat xiii 57 Mark vi 4 Luke iv 24

[b] Ex xxiii 15

[c] Chap ii 9

† Or courtier, or ruler

[d] Hoſ v 15

[e] Chap. iv 28 1 Cor i 22

v 43—54 Jeſus made but a ſhort viſit to Sychar, he had other work to do, and therefore *after two days he departed thence* Yet perhaps two more ſucceſſful days paſſed not during his miniſtry, a gracious earneſt of the ſucceſs which his goſpel ſhould meet in the heathen world, when, inſtead of being confined almoſt wholly, as at preſent, to the loſt ſheep of the houſe of Iſrael, it ſhould be preached to every creature

1 Chriſt purſued his journey to Galilee, but went not to Nazareth, well knowing, as he had before obſerved and experienced, *that a prophet hath no honour in his own country* Thoſe with whom we have been brought up from infancy, uſually paying little reſpect to the perſon of their teacher, with whom they have been familiar, as their junior, their ſchoolfellow, or their companion

2 The Galileans gladly received him, having ſeen his miracles at the feaſt of the paſſover, to celebrate which, diſtant as they were, they went up with the other Jews to Jeruſalem *Note*, They who love God's ordinances, will not grudge to go far to enjoy them, and will have never reaſon to regret their pains

3 He viſited, among other places, Cana where his firſt miracle was wrought of turning the water into wine, and there another notable miracle is wrought by him, which is not recorded by any of the other Evangeliſts

[1] The perſon who made application to him was a nobleman, probably one of Herod's courtiers, perhaps Chuza, (*Luke* viii 3) or Manaen, (*Acts* xiii 1) and the patient was his own ſon *Note*, (1) Greatneſs is no protection from diſeaſe, nor from any of the common calamities incident to humanity (2) Afflictions often drive thoſe to Chriſt, who otherwiſe, probably had never applied to him, and then indeed they are bleſſings in diſguiſe

[2] His addreſs was earneſt, and beſpoke his confidence in the power of Jeſus He came himſelf from Capernaum to Cana, about fifteen miles, to beg his help The caſe was deſperate, and paſt all other aid but his, for his child was *at the point of death*, and therefore he intreats him to haſten down without delay He thought the preſence of Jeſus was needful to the cure, herein diſhonourably limiting the holy One of Iſrael *Note*, Our ſins have reduced us all to the point of eternal death unleſs Jeſus ſave, we muſt inevitably periſh

[3] Chriſt rebukes his confined notions of his almighty power, and the backwardneſs of the Jews in general to believe The Samaritans believed as ſoon as he had preached among them, but they required repeated ſigns and wonders, not ſatisfied with thoſe which they had already ſeen him work at Jeruſalem, during the feaſt

[4] The nobleman renews his importunate requeſt Every moment of delay was, in his apprehenſion, imminently dangerous, for though he had faith in Chriſt, that he could cure his ſon, if he was preſent with him, yet he ſeems to have no apprehenſion that he could heal at a diſtance, or, if the child was dead, reſtore him to life again

[5] Chriſt relieves him of his pain, ſaying, *Go thy way, thy ſon liveth* Nothing more was needful to the cure his word wrought as effectually at diſtance, as if he had gone in perſon He ſpeaks, and it is done Oh that we had but faith to truſt him at all times!

[6] The power which wrought the cure of the ſon, as effectually influenced the heart of the father, ſo that in full aſſurance of faith he departed, perfectly ſatisfied, that the word which Jeſus had ſpoken was ſure, and that he ſhould find his ſon alive and well He appeared thus a true ſon of Abraham, and none like him ever truſted the Lord, and was confounded

[7] His ſervants met him, as he returned, with the joyful news of his ſon's recovery, and on enquiring when the happy change took place, they told him, *at the ſeventh hour the fever left him*, not gradually, but in a moment he recovered, and the father immediately remembered that was preciſely the hour when Jeſus had ſpoken to him

[8] The effect of this miracle was the converſion of himſelf and his family *Himſelf believed, and his whole houſe* He had begun to believe before, now his faith was more confirmed in Jeſus as the Meſſiah, and he became a profeſſed diſciple, whilſt his houſhold, who were eye-witneſſes of the miracle, followed his example *Note*, (1) One word of Jeſus ſpoken to the heart, works effectually to our ſalvation (2) When the maſter of the family ſets the gracious example, it is often greatly influential to all his houſe

Laſtly, The evangeliſt remarks this, as the ſecond miracle Jeſus had wrought in Cana of Galilee By two and three witneſſes thus he eſtabliſhed the authority of his miſſion, and probably the quality of the patient made the cure to be the more obſerved When perſons of ſuperior rank are ſingled out by the grace of the Redeemer, the change wrought on them engages more particular attention

CHAP V

Here been in the chapter a miracle and a ſermon 1 The miracle was the cure of an impotent man, that had been diſeaſed thirty-eight years, ver 1—16 2 The ſermon was Chriſt's vindication of himſelf before the Sanhedrim, when he was proſecuted as a criminal for healing the man on the ſabbath-day, in which, (1) He aſſerts his authority as Meſſiah, and Mediator between God and man, ver 17—29 (2) He proves it by the teſtimony of his Father, of John Baptiſt, of his miracles, and of the ſcriptures of the Old Teſtament, and condemns the Jews for their unbelief, ver 30—47

1 AFTER this [a] there was a feaſt of the Jews, and Jeſus went up to Jeruſalem 2 Now there is at Jeruſalem [b] by the ſheep | *market* a pool, which is called in the Hebrew tongue, ‖ Betheſda, having five porches 3 In theſe lay a great multitude of impotent folk, of blind, halt, withered, waiting for the moving of the water 4 For an angel went down at a certain ſeaſon into the pool, and troubled the water whoſoever then firſt after the troubling of the water ſtepped in, was made whole of whatſoever diſeaſe he had 5 And a certain man was there, which had an infirmity thirty and eight years 6 When Jeſus ſaw him lie, and knew that

[a] Lev xxiii 2 Deut xvi 1

[b] Neh iii 1

| Or gate

‖ That is, The houſe of mercy

that he had been now a long time *in that case*, he saith
unto him, Wilt thou be made whole? 7 The impo-
tent man answered him, Sir, I have no man, when the
water is troubled, to put me into the pool but while
I am coming, another steppeth down before me 8
Jesus saith unto him, ᵉ Rise, take up thy bed, and walk
9 And immediately the man was made whole, and took
up his bed, and walked and ᵈ on the same day was the
sabbath 10 ¶ The Jews therefore said unto him that
was cured, It is the sabbath-day, ᵉ it is not lawful for
thee to carry *thy* bed 11 He answered them, He that
made me whole, the same said unto me, Take up thy
bed and walk 12 Then asked they him, What man
is that which said unto thee, Take up thy bed and
walk? 13 And he that was healed wist not who it
was for Jesus had conveyed himself away, a multitude
being in *that* place 14 Afterward Jesus findeth him
in the temple, and said unto him, Behold, thou art
made whole ᶠ sin no more, lest a worse thing come unto
thee 15 The man departed, and told the Jews that
it was Jesus which had made him whole 16 And
therefore did the Jews persecute Jesus, and sought to
slay him, because he had done these things on the sab-
bath-day

ᵛ 1—16 The feast here spoken of was probably the pas-
over, the second, which our Lord kept at Jerusalem, after his
public entrance on the ministry, and there he works the fol-
lowing notable miracle.

1 The place where the miracle was wrought, is very re-
markable It was a pool of water near *the sheep-gate*, Neh iii
1 called *Bethesda*, or the House of Mercy, surrounded with
cloysters, or covered walks, where the impotent lay sheltered,
who came with their several complaints, blind, halt, withered,
waiting for the moving of the water in hopes of a cure For
the pool was impregnated with a strange virtue at certain sea-
sons, owing to the descent of an angel who troubled the waters,
and the first person who immediately stepped in, was cured of
whatever disease he had

When this healing power began to be communicated to the
waters, or when it ceased, the Jewish historians are entirely
silent, it served however to shew, God had not left his people
without witness, and represented that fountain which should be
opened in the Saviour's side, in which whosoever washed should
be made clean This fountain hath not at seasons merely, but
at all times, the power of healing, and therefore whosoever con-
tinues under his spiritual maladies, has only his own negligence
to blame, that he will not come to Christ that he may be
cured

2 The person on whom the cure was wrought had been
thirty-eight years under his infirmity, probably paralytic, and
unable to move, and therefore, when Jesus passing by, com-
passionately observed his pitiable case, and graciously addressed him,
Wilt thou be made whole? He relates his unhappy condition, and
his continual disappointment, whilst some other stepped in before
he could find a friend to assist him to reach the troubled waters,
so that he began now to despair of ever obtaining his cure
Note, (1) What thankfulness do we owe to our preserving
God, if we enjoy perfect health and strength, whilst others tot-
ter with weakness and disease, and wearisome days and nights
are appointed to them (2) The compassionate eye of Jesus
is on the afflicted, and though he suffers them to be long exer-
cised, he will pity them in due season, and deliver them
(3) They who would receive a cure from him of their spiritual
maladies, ought at least to be waiting at the pool of ordinances,
where Jesus usually manifests his power and grace

3 Christ with a word heals his disease, bidding him
rise, take up his bed, and walk, and such power accom-
panied his command, that the impotent man instantly felt his
strength return [illegible] perfectly cured, and taking up his bed,
walked away in the sight, and to the amazement of the be-
holders and *the same day was the sabbath* *Note*, (1) When
Christ speaks to the impotent soul, he gives ability for that
which he commands (2) They who are healed by his grace,
will instantly be obedient to his will

4 As according to the tradition of the elders, it was ac-
counted unlawful to carry a bed on the sabbath-day, the Jews
jealous, therefore, for the honour of that sacred day of rest, re-
buked him for being guilty of such a profanation The man
thought he had sufficient authority, when he who healed him
gave him his orders, and pleads the command of the person who
had wrought the cure upon him They suspected who had done
the miracle, and wanted the man to accuse his kind benefactor,
against whom they wished to proceed as a sabbath-breaker.
What man is that which said unto thee, Take up thy bed and walk?
With such contempt and indignation do they speak of Christ,
as if he was a mere man, and a wicked man too, notoriously
guilty of a breach of God's law The man, who knew [illegible]

Jesus, could give them no information, for he had disappeared
immediately, mixing among the croud, probably to avoid the
admiration of some, and the malignity of others, who he knew
would be offended at him for this glorious act of mercy, be-
cause it was the sabbath day *Note*, (1) The sabbath was made
for man, not man for the sabbath, therefore works of mercy
and charity are always commendable (2) They who are
eminent for well doing, may expect to pass through evil report
as well as good report

5 Soon after the poor man going up to the temple, probably
to return thanks for his late mercies, met Jesus there, who
gave him a solemn caution with regard to his future con-
duct *Sin no more, lest a worse thing come unto thee* Should he
provoke the wrath of God by his sins, it would yet be worse
than his past long affliction The man in the simplicity of his
heart went and *told the Jews that it was Jesus which had made him
whole* probably he hoped this notable miracle might en-
gage them to acknowledge him as the Messiah, but so far were
they from being led to admire his character, that filled with
envy and enmity, they sought to slay Jesus, and for a pretext,
pleaded that this work of mercy was a profanation of the sab-
bath *Note*, (1) They who have received signal mercies from
God, are peculiarly bound to be found in the temple, offering
up their thanksgivings (2) In the Lord's house we may ex-
pect to be favoured with his presence (3) Sin is at the root
of all our sufferings, in time and eternity (4) They who are
by grace delivered from the power and punishment of sin, should
be doubly watchful not to return again unto folly (5) Many
cover, with pretended zeal for religion, their enmity against
the most faithful servants of Christ

17 ¶ But Jesus answered them, ᵍ My Father worketh
hitherto, and I work 18 Therefore the Jews ʰ sought
the more to kill him, because he not only had broken
the sabbath, but said also, that God was his Father,
ⁱ making himself equal with God 19 Then answered
Jesus, and said unto them, Verily, verily I say unto
you, ᵏ The Son can do nothing of himself, but what he
seeth the Father do for what things soever he doth,
these also doth the Son likewise 20 For ˡ the Father
loveth the Son, and ᵐ sheweth him all things that him-
self doth and he will shew him greater works than
these, that ye may marvel 21 For as the Father
raiseth up the dead, and quickeneth *them* even so ⁿ the
Son quickeneth whom he will 22 For the Father
judgeth no man, ᵒ but hath committed all judgment un-
to the Son 23 That all men should honour the Son,
even as they honour the Father ᵖ He that honoureth
not the Son, honoureth not the Father which hath sent
him. 24 Verily, verily I say unto you, ᑫ He that hear-
eth my word, and believeth on him that sent me, hath
everlasting life, and ʳ shall not come into condemnation,
ˢ but is passed from death unto life 25 Verily, verily
I say unto you, The hour is coming, and now is, when
ᵗ the dead shall hear the voice of the Son of God and
they that hear shall live 26 For as the Father hath
life in himself, so hath he given to the Son to have life
in himself 27 And ᵘ hath given him authority to exe-
cute judgment also, ˣ because he is the Son of man 28
Marvel not at this for the hour is coming, in the which
all that are in the graves shall hear his voice, 29 And
ʸ shall come forth, ᶻ they that have done good unto the
resurrection of life, and they that have done evil, unto
the resurrection of damnation 30 ᵃ I can of mine own
self do nothing as I hear I judge and ᵇ my judgment
is just, because I seek not mine own will, but the will
of the Father which hath sent me

ᵛ 17—30 We have here our Lord's vindication of himself
from the charge laid against him as a sabbath breaker

1 He argues from his Father's work to his own *My Fa-
ther worketh hitherto*, by his continual operation, every day he
administers the affairs of the kingdom of providence, *and I work*
as one with him, in nature and operation, and therefore my
work of power and grace can be no more the subject of blame,
than his Most absurd, therefore, was the charge laid against
him as a sabbath breaker, who was Lord of the sabbath, and
one with the eternal Father, the Maker and Preserver of all
things

2 This defence exasperated them but the more Such a
claim to God as *his own father* (πατέρα ἴδιον) in that peculiar
sense, as implied a coequality with him in power, authority,
and operation, they regarded as the highest blasphemy, and
more deserving of death than even the breach of the sabbath

3 Far from blaming his enemies perverting his word, he
vindicates what he had said, asserting and proving in the most
exalted

exalted sense the eternal union and co-equality between the Father and the Son, and his title to the dignity of the undivided godhead, *Verily, verily, I say unto you*, what I speak is certain, and my words truth itself, *The Son can do nothing of himself, but what he seeth the Father do*, such is the unity of their nature, that they are alike intimately acquainted with each others counsels and designs, having one eternal mind. The Son, therefore, never acts separate from the Father, but with his consent and co-operation. *for what things soever he doth, these also doth the Son likewise*, whatever the Father doth in the continual agency of his providence, the Son, as one with him, is a co-worker, and acts with the same divine power and authority as the Father himself. *For the Father loveth the Son*, an infinite mutual complacence subsists between the divine persons, *and sheweth him all things that himself doth*, communicating with him all his counsels and designs, and doing nothing in the kingdom of grace or providence, but in conjunction with him. *and he will shew him greater things than these*, performing by him and with him, greater miracles of power and goodness than this wrought on the impotent man, *that ye may marvel*, either led to admire my works, and believe in my divine mission, or to wonder and perish in obstinate infidelity.

In confirmation of what he had said, he instances his own divine power in two most remarkable particulars, each of which are interwoven in his discourse, and nearly connected.

[1.] He hath power equally with the Father to quicken the dead. He is *the prince of life*, and by his own sovereign will and pleasure raises up whom he will. Self-existent as the Father, he hath life in himself, *v.* 26. or *as the Father hath life in himself*, intending in his eternal mind to bestow it on his chosen people, *so hath he given the Son to have life in himself*, in the œconomy of man's redemption this life eternal is lodged in the hands of the Son, resides in him, and is to be derived from him, and he bestows it sovereignly according to the good pleasure of his will. By him,

(1.) The souls of sinners are raised from the death of trespasses in which they lay, by the effectual word of gospel-grace they are called from the grave of corruption, and awake to newness of life. *and the hour is coming, yea, now is*, when this great work shall be performed, *now* by his own ministry, hereafter more abundantly by his apostles preaching. *Note*, (1.) Our souls, by the fall, are become utterly incapable of all spiritual good, insensible to our real state of misery, and altogether dead before God, as much as the corpse which is laid in the coffin is insensible to what passes around it, and utterly disqualified for every action of life. (2.) Our hearts must experience a spiritual resurrection to newness of life here, or we can never hope for eternal life hereafter. (3.) The voice of Jesus in his word made effectual by his spirit, is the powerful agent which accomplishes this glorious work.

(2.) By him the dead bodies of men shall be raised up at the last day. Nor need any *marvel*, that he who first created man upon earth, should be able to repair the ruined tabernacle, and restore it from dust. *all*, from the first man whom God formed, to the last whom death shall seize, *shall hear the voice of the Son of God*, and instantly at his word *shall come forth*, leaving the prison of the grave, restored to life that never more shall end. Though according to their several characters, very different will their doom be; *they that have done good*, whose hearts were renewed by divine grace, and whose works and ways evidenced faith unfeigned, and love without dissimulation, they, and only they, will rise *unto the resurrection of life*, to that state of immortal bliss and glory, which shall be the reward of their fidelity; *and they that have done evil*, have continued under the power and dominion of their native corruption, have lived without experiencing a divine change upon their hearts, and died under the guilt of unrepented sin, they shall rise *unto the resurrection of damnation*, condemned to those eternal torments which are the wages of sin without measure and without end, lying down in hell under the wrath of God, which is for ever wrath to come. How awful! how alarming the admonition! oh that we might feel the weighty import of it, and prepare to meet our God!

[2.] He hath the power of finally determining the everlasting state of men and angels. Not only is God the Son the judge of all, in common with the Father, administering all the affairs of the kingdom of providence and grace, and without him *the Father judgeth no man*; but as mediator also, he hath a peculiar authority delegated to him, to execute judgment as the Son of man, to pronounce sentence from his throne at the last day, to take vengeance on all who have been rebellious against his government, and despised or rejected his salvation; and to fix, by an irrevocable decree, the eternal blessedness of his redeemed people; and the rule of his judgment at that day will be his own word, *Verily, verily, I say unto you, He that heareth my word, and believeth on him that sent me, hath everlasting life, and shall not come into condemnation, but is passed from death unto life*; where we may observe, (1.) The sinner's title to glory, *faith in the Redeemer*. (2.) The effect of it, deliverance from all condemnation in time and eternity; for who can lay ought to the charge of those whom God justifieth? (3.) They who have passed from spiritual death to spiritual life, have therein the earnest and foretaste of eternal life. (4.) *The judgment* of Jesus is *just*, ver. 30. for all he doth is according to the eternal counsels of wisdom between the Father and the Son, *v.* 29. in correspondence with the will of the Father, and according to the commission he hath received from him. Such, then, being his infinite dignity, the Son, who is in glory equal, in majesty coeternal, must be *honoured*, worshipped, and adored, even *as the Father*; and so far from its being blasphemous, and derogatory from the Father's glory, that he should thus claim equality with him, in nature, perfections, and uncreated excellence, so inseparably connected are they, and their honour and interest so entirely the same, that the Father regards every instance of disrespect shewn to his Son, as dishonour done to himself, both as he is one with him in the same undivided Godhead, and also as he is the Son of man sent from him, commissioned by him, and, as his ambassador, representing himself.

31 ⁿ If I bear witness of myself, my witness † is not
true. 32 ¶ ᵉ There is another that beareth witness of
me, and I know that the witness which he witnesseth
of me, is true. 33 Ye sent unto John, and ᶠ he bare
witness unto the truth. 34 But I receive not testi-
mony from man: but these things I say, that ye might
be saved. 35 He was a burning and a shining light:
and ᵍ ye were willing ʰ for a season to rejoice in his light.
36 ¶ But ⁱ I have greater witness than *that* of John:
for ᵏ the works which the Father hath given me to finish,
the same works that I do, bear witness of me, that the
Father hath sent me. 37 And ˡ the Father himself
which hath sent me, hath born witness of me. Ye
have neither heard his voice at any time, ᵐ nor seen his
shape. 38 And ye have not his word abiding in you:
for whom he hath sent, him ye believe not. 39 ⁿ Search
the scriptures, for in them ye think ye have eternal
life, and ᵒ they are they which testify of me. 40 And
ᵖ ye will not come to me, that ye might have life.
41 ᑫ I receive not honour from men. 42 But I know
you, that ye have not the love of God in you. 43 I
am come in my Father's name, and ye receive me not:
if another shall come in his own name, him ye will
receive. 44 ʳ How can ye believe, which receive ho-
nour one of another, and seek not ˢ the honour that *cometh*
from God only? 45 Do not think that I will accuse
you to the Father: there is *one* that accuseth you, *even*
Moses, in whom ye trust. 46 For had ye believed
Moses, ye would have believed me: for ᵗ he wrote of
me. 47 But if ye believe not his writings, how shall
ye believe my words?

v. 31—47. In confirmation of the glorious character he assumed, and his mission from the Father, he proceeds to produce other evidence than his own, admitting, that if what he asserted was utterly unsupported, they might reject his testimony of himself as untrue.

1. John the Baptist bore witness of him, and to his evidence Christ appeals, fully assured it was true: and they themselves, who applied to him as a prophet, were bound to embrace his testimony, which in the most solemn manner he delivered to those deputies of the Sanhedrim who were sent to enquire who he was, and under what authority he acted. He plainly asserted Christ's divine character, (ch. i. 19—30.) and his evidence they could not but allow to be most respectable. For though he was not *that light*, the Messiah, *he was a burning and a shining light*; his exemplary conduct and zealous preaching bespoke the simplicity of his soul, *and ye were willing for a season to rejoice in his light*. They gloried in him at first, and raised their expectations high; but when he would neither himself assume the character of the Messiah, nor declare himself that Messiah whom they expected, they could not bear the sharpness of his rebukes, and the plainness of his testimony to that Messiah whom they rejected, and therefore they soon fell off and neglected him. not that Christ indeed needed human testimony; he had far greater. But for their conviction he mentions this, as it might be the means of rescuing them from ruin. *Note*, (1.) Every minister of Jesus, like John, should burn with zeal for his glory, and shine in all holy conversation, that he may ad[illegible] and give weight to the doctrine he preaches. (2.) Many at first seem to rejoice in the light of the gospel, who soon grow cold and careless, and neglect so great a salvation. (3.) They who trifle with their mercies, are justly deprived of them.

2. He appeals to a greater witness than that of John, even to his own works, which bore witness of him. His whole life and ministry bespoke his [illegible] character, and especially his miracles, wrought by his own divine power, evidenced his mis-

sion

sion from God And greater works than he had yet done remained for him to finish, to leave them at least without excuse, if they obstinately persisted in their infidelity

3 God the Father himself had expressly born witness to him by a voice from heaven at his baptism, *Mat* iii 16, 17 which was solemnly repeated, *Mat* xvii 5 a high distinguished attestation, such as had never before on any occasion been vouchsafed *Ye have neither heard his voice at any time, nor seen his shape*, all the voices that were heard, and the appearances that were seen, under the Old Testament, were either those of the Son in a human form, or of the angels employed by him in this ministry, then first when the Father in person spoke from heaven at the baptism of his Son, was his voice audibly heard, and a visible manifestation made of his glory *And ye have not his word abiding in you*, neither this immediate testimony from heaven, nor his former word by his prophets had ever made any abiding impression, *for whom he hath sent, him ye believe not*, after all this evidence they, notwithstanding, rejected the testimony of God, and refused to believe in his Messiah *Note*, (1) When God sends, he will bear witness to his own servants, and attest with his spirit the commission he hath given them (2) Many have the word of God in their hands, and sounding in their ears, and yet have it not abiding in their hearts

He refers them to their own scriptures for the proof of his divine character and mission *Search the scriptures, or ye do search them* The scriptures were by many of them much studied, and they boasted of their wisdom in these sacred oracles, but they were really great strangers to the meaning of them, they had need therefore look farther and deeper than ever yet they had done, and he ventures to rest his cause upon an appeal to these authentic records, which they themselves so highly and justly valued *for in them ye think ye have eternal life*, they placed the chief stress of their religion upon the knowledge of the law, and flattered themselves, by constantly reading these sacred writings, and getting them by rote, they were sure of heaven Now *these*, saith he, *are they that testify of me*, all the types, promises, prophecies, center in him, and refer to him, and *yet ye will not come to me, that ye may have life*, such were their prejudices and wilful blindness, that though the scriptures were so express in pointing him out to their notice, they would not come to apply to him, that they might obtain the pardon life and salvation which he alone could give Not that he affected to exalt himself, to gather a party, or obtain temporal dominion *I receive not honour from men*, he neither courted nor needed human applause, his only aim was to advance his Father's glory *But I know you, that ye have not the love of God in you*, he tried their hearts, and notwithstanding all their high pretences of zeal for God's honour, the love of the world predominated in their affections, and they had really no heartfelt and sincere regard to God or godliness, and rejected him because he did not correspond with their earthly expectations Hence, though *I am come in my Father's name*, with evidences of a divine mission so strong and striking, *ye receive me not*, because the salvation he brought was spiritual from sin, and death, and hell and he so sharply rebuked their vices, and undeceived them in their vain expectation of a temporal Messiah, who should come with outward pomp and grandeur, therefore they rejected him but *if another shall come in his own name, him ye will receive*, eager to embrace every impostor who pretended to deliver them from the Roman yoke, and aggrandize their nation, though vouching no authority but his own vain boastings And being under the influence of such a carnal mind, *how can ye believe, which receive honour one of another, and seek not the honour which cometh from God only*? Their spirit and temper, and proud affectation of pre-eminence, were the reverse of the kingdom which Christ came to erect, where humility and self-denial stood in the first and most distinguished place, and must for ever exclude them from the spiritual, substantial, and eternal honour which God alone bestows on the children of his grace, and the heirs of his glory Learn hence, (1) The necessity of deep and serious examination of the scriptures, comparing spiritual things with spiritual, and diligently seeking for Christ in them, who is the sum and substance of them, for without the practical knowledge of him, all other attainments in the letter, language, and phrases of the scripture, are really no better than splendid ignorance (2) In the scriptures eternal life is to be obtained, because they reveal to us that Redeemer, who is the author of it, to all who obey him The Old Testament, as well as the new, is full of him, the moral law drives us for refuge to him, the type of the ceremonial law all prefigure him, the prophecies all center in him He is indeed all, and in all (3) All who come by faith to Christ, embracing the salvation which is in him, will assuredly find pardon, grace, and glory, the reason why any sinner perish is this, that blinded by ignorance, or perverted by pride and self-righteousness, they *will* not come to Christ, that they might have life Their eternal ruin, therefore, lies at their own door (4) Christ searcheth the heart and trieth the reins, he knoweth what is in man, and under the mask of warmest profession of religion can discover the enmity which reigns within, against himself and his gospel (5) Where inordinate love of this world prevails, and ambition, covetousness, and desire of human applause, possess the soul, it is impossible the love of God should dwell there No man can serve two masters (6) When men chuse those false prophets, who flatter them in their iniquities, and run without being sent, and pleased with their smooth prophecies turn a deaf ear to the warning voice of truth, justly doth God give up such to the delusions they have chosen (7) True honour comes from God alone, his estimation of us, not that of all the world beside, stamps our character with excellence or infamy His approbation, therefore, a gracious soul desires in the first place (8) Whilst our hearts chiefly affect earthly honours, it is impossible we should believe in, embrace, and submit to him, whose kingdom is not of this world, and whose first demand from us is to take up our cross and follow him, as men wondered at

Lastly, Christ turns them over to Moses, in whose writings they so much gloried, for a proof of his mission, and as their accuser, if they persisted in their infidelity *Do not think that I will accuse you to the Father*, as if I came to spy out your faults, with a view to your condemnation, No *there is one that accuseth you, even Moses, in whom ye trust* That law on which they trusted for salvation must needs condemn them as transgressors, and Moses in person at the last day must, to their confusion, testify against their impenitence and unbelief *For had ye believed Moses, ye would have believed me for he wrote of me*, as the great Prophet who should rise, as the great End of the Law, moral and ceremonial, to whom both pointed, *but if ye believe not his writings*, for whom you pretend such high veneration, and are not convinced by them of my divine mission, *how shall ye believe my words*? against whom you entertain such inveterate prejudices, and whom you treat with such insolent contempt? *Note*, (1) Many make their boast of those privileges which will at last prove their more aggravated condemnation, because they have abused them (2) They who refuse to fly by faith for refuge to the gospel of Christ, must inevitably perish under the accusations of the law of Moses

CHAP VI

In this chapter we have, 1 *The miracle of the loaves*, ver 1—14 2 *Christ's walking upon the water*, ver 15—21 3 *The people's flocking after him to Capernaum*, ver 22—25 4 *His conference with them, occasioned by the miracle of the loaves, in which he reproves them for seeking carnal food, and directs them to spiritual food*, ver 26—27 *shewing them how they must labour for spiritual food*, ver 28, 29 *and what that spiritual food is*, ver 30—59 5 *Their discontent at what he said, and the reproof he gave them for it*, ver 60—65 6 *The apostasy of many from him, and his discourse with his disciples that adhered to him upon that occasion*, ver 66—71

1 AFTER these things Jesus went over the sea
of Galilee, which is *the sea* of Tiberias 2 And
a great multitude followed him, because they saw his
miracles which he did on them that were diseased 3
And [a] Jesus went up into a mountain, and there he sat
with his disciples. 4 And [b] the passover, a feast of the
Jews, was nigh 5 ¶ When Jesus then lift up *his* eyes,
and saw a great company come unto him, he saith unto
Philip, Whence shall we buy bread that these may eat?
6 (And this he said to prove him for he himself
knew what he would do) 7 Philip answered him, [d]
Two hundred penny worth of bread is not sufficient
for them, that every one of them may take a little 8
One of his disciples, Andrew, Simon Peter's brother,
saith unto him, 9 There is a lad here, which hath five
barley-loaves, and two small fishes [e] but what are they
among so many? 10 And Jesus said, Make the men
sit down Now there was much grass in the place So
the men sat down, in number about five thousand
11 And Jesus took the loaves, and when [f] he had given
thanks, [g] he distributed to the disciples, and [g] the disciples
to them that were set down, and likewise of the
fishes, as much as they would 12 When they were
filled, he said to his disciples, Gather up the fragments
that remain, that nothing be lost 13 Therefore they
gathered *them* together, and filled twelve baskets with
the fragments of the five barley-loaves, which remained
over and above unto them that had eaten 14 Then
those men, when they had seen the miracle that Jesus
did, said, This is of a truth [h] that prophet that should
come into the world

a Luke ix 10 b Lev xxiii 5 7 Deut xvi 1 c Mat xiv 14 Mark vi 35 Luke ix 12 d Num xi 22 [?] Mat xviii 28 e 2 Kings iv 43 f Mat xv 36 & xxvi 26 Rom xiv 6 g Mat xxiv 45 h Deut xviii 15, 18 & vi 40

Ver 1—14 The miracle here recorded is the only one, which all the four evangelists have mentioned We have

The

1 The time and place, when and where it was wrought Chriſt had croſſed the Lake Genneſaret, called the ſea of Tiberias, from a city Herod had built on the borders of it, in honour of the Emperor Tiberius Multitudes followed him, not ſo much, it ſeems, affected by his doctrine, as drawn by his miracles However the Lord was ready to receive them, and going up into a mountain, for the convenience of being heard, ſat there with his diſciples, and taught the liſtening crowd *and the paſſover*, the third ſince his entrance on the miniſtry, now approached

2 The miracle itſelf Beholding with compaſſion the multitudes who were aſſembled on this occaſion, our Lord addreſſed himſelf to Philip, and aſked him, in order to try his faith, being himſelf reſolved what to do, Where they could get bread to feed that multitude? Philip, dull of apprehenſion, looked only to human aid, and ſuggeſts, that two hundred pennyworth of bread (about ſix pounds five ſhillings, which probably was all their common ſtock) would not be ſufficient to give each a morſel Andrew hearing the diſcourſe, ſuggeſts, there was a lad in the company that had five barley loaves and two ſmall fiſhes, but these indeed would be as nothing among ſuch a multitude But where human means fail, the divine power is not ſtraitned Commanding his diſciples, therefore, to ſeat the multitude in order, *where the graſs was their carpet*, and the earth their table, with his divine benediction he conſecrated the ſcanty proviſion, and breaking the bread and fiſhes, gave them to his diſciples, who diſtributed them to the multitude, and marvellous to behold! under their hands the meat continued to grow as it deſcended down the ranks, and not only afforded enough for a plentiful meal to all that vaſt multitude, but ſuch a quantity of fragments as filled twelve baſkets full *Note*, (1) When the Lord is pleaſed at times to leave us in perplexity, he hath deſigns of his own to anſwer, and knows what he intends to do (2) Chriſt's diſciples muſt not diſdain coarſe and ſcanty fare, but be content, when his providence ſo ordains, to put up with barley cakes, and be thankful for them, and then this poor proviſion, with the benediction of Jeſus, ſhall yield a richer entertainment than all the delicacies of the luxurious (3) They who call a fiſh-meal faſting, ſeem to caſt reproach on the rich feaſt with which Jeſus entertained his followers (4) Bread muſt never be waſted, even the fragments of barley cakes are carefully gathered up If we are full, others are faſting, who will be glad of our leavings, good œconomy is the means to enable us for more extenſive charity

3 Great was the effect, for the time at leaſt, produced by this miracle on the minds of the people They concluded this muſt be *that* great *prophet* ſpoken of by Moſes, *Deut* xviii 15 who ſhould come into the world

15 ¶ When Jeſus therefore perceived that they would
come and take him by force, to make him a king, he
departed again into a mountain himſelf alone 16 And
i Mat xiv 23 Mark vi 17 [i] when even was *now* come, his diſciples went down unto
the ſea, 17 And entred into a ſhip, and went over
the ſea towards Capernaum and it was now dark, and
k Pſ cvii 23, &c Jeſus was not come to them. 18 And [k] the ſea aroſe,
by reaſon of a great wind that blew 19 So when they
had rowed about five and twenty or thirty furlongs, they
l Job ix 8 ſee Jeſus [l] walking on the ſea, and drawing nigh unto
the ſhip and they were afraid 20 But he ſaith unto
m Cant iii 1 them, It is I, be not afraid 21 Then [m] they willingly
received him into the ſhip and immediately the ſhip
was at the land whither they went

v 15—21 We have here,

1 The retirement of the Lord Jeſus They, whom he had in ſo aſtoniſhing a manner fed, were immediately for proclaiming him King of the Jews, and erecting his ſtandard, expecting, according to their miſtaken prejudices, that he would ſet up a temporal dominion, reſcue them from the Roman yoke, and place them at the head of the nations But far different was the kingdom he came to eſtabliſh, therefore, fearing leaſt their irregular zeal ſhould hurry them into ſome ſeditious behaviour, and that againſt his will they might attempt to force the royalty upon him, he left them, and went up again into the mountain alone *Note*, (1) Chriſt's kingdom is not of this world, his true diſciples will never ſeek their portion here below (2) His miniſters muſt avoid every thing that may give the ſhadow of offence to the ſecular powers, never intermeddling with civil affairs, but teaching all dutiful ſubmiſſion to the powers that are

2 Whilſt the maſter was in the mountain, the diſciples were toſſing on the tempeſtuous waves By the command of their Lord they had gone on ſhipboard, in order to croſs the lake, but now the ſtorm aroſe, the night was dark, the wind contrary, and their maſter not come to them, which heightened their diſtreſs *Note*, (1) After the ſweeteſt ſeaſons of refreſhment, ſometimes the darkeſt days of temptation ſucceed (2) It is one of the heavieſt afflictions to the ſoul under trials, when the preſence of Jeſus is withdrawn, and we are left under darkneſs and deſertion (3) They who embark in Chriſt's cauſe, muſt prepare for a ſtorm The way to glory lies through much tribulation.

3 In their extremity help approaches In the way of duty we need never deſpair, Chriſt will deliver us in the needful time of trouble He came to them miraculouſly walking on the waters, but they, affrighted, thought it had been an apparition, till his well-known voice quieted their fears when he was ſo nigh, no evil could hurt them *Note*, (1) We often terrify ourſelves with unneceſſary apprehenſions of danger, and when our minds are dejected, are ready to fear that the very means that are working for our good, portend an increaſe of our miſery (2) Jeſus alone, by his all-powerful word, can ſpeak peace to the ſinner's troubled mind

4 With joy they welcomed their maſter's arrival, and in a moment the ſhip, by a miracle, was at the place of their deſtination *Note*, (1) Chriſt is doubly precious to the ſoul, when mourning after him, and walking in darkneſs, he returns, and lifts up the light of his countenance, and diſſipates every cloud of ſorrow (2) The church, and every faithful ſoul embarked on this tempeſtuous world, experience many a ſtorm, but *their everlaſting ſafety is ſecured, they ſhall never finally be caſt away* (3) It will be a pleaſing ſurprize to many a trembling believer, when he ſhall find himſelf at death ſafely landed on the ſhores of eternal reſt

22 ¶ The day following, when the people which
ſtood on the other ſide of the ſea, ſaw that there was
none other boat there, ſave that one whereinto his diſ-
ciples were entred, and that Jeſus went not with his
diſciples into the boat, but *that* his diſciples were gone
away alone 23. (Howbeit there came other boats from
Tiberias, nigh unto the place [n] where they did eat n Ver. 11
bread, after that the Lord had given thanks) 24 When
the people therefore ſaw that Jeſus was not there, neither
his diſciples, they alſo took ſhipping, and came to Ca-
pernaum, ſeeking for Jeſus 25 And when they had
found him on the other ſide of the ſea, they ſaid unto
him, Rabbi, when cameſt thou hither? 26 Jeſus
anſwered them, and ſaid, Verily, verily I ſay unto you,
Ye ſeek me, not becauſe ye ſaw the miracles, but be-
cauſe ye did eat of the loaves, and were filled 27 La-
bour not for the meat which periſheth, but for [o] that o Ver 54, 63 Chap xiv 14
meat which endureth unto everlaſting life, which the
Son of man ſhall give unto you for [p] him hath God p Mat iii 17 & xvii 5 ...
the Father ſealed

v 22—27 All night the multitude ſeem to have waited for the return of Jeſus from the mountain in the morning, for as they ſaw the diſciples embark, and leave their maſter behind them, and there was no other boat in which he could follow them, they concluded he muſt ſtill be on that ſide the water, but not finding him there as they expected, we are told,

1 How carefully they followed him Some boats arriving in the morning from Tiberias, near that place where they had been miraculouſly fed through the benediction of Jeſus, they croſſed the lake to Capernaum, hoping to find him there, where he uſually made his abode *Note*, (1) They who love Chriſt truly, will ſtick at no pains in following him (2) When we are found in God's way, his providence is often ſeen moſt graciouſly to ſecond our good deſigns and deſires

2 They found him on the other ſide of the ſea, and could not but expreſs their aſtoniſhment how he could come thither, having no conveniences for croſſing the lake *Note*, Many eagerly run after Chriſt and his goſpel, pretending great zeal for hearing, who never truly come to him by faith, nor receive the ingrafted word to the ſaving of their ſouls

3 Chriſt, who knew the ſpirit and temper with which they followed him, replies to their queſtion in ſuch a manner, as he ſaw their ſtate required

[1] He rebukes them for the corrupt principle on which they acted They followed him, not becauſe they were convinced by his doctrine and miracles, and believed in him to the ſaving of their ſouls, but merely becauſe they had been fed at his coſt, and expected yet greater temporal advantages from him when he ſhould ſet up his kingdom *Note*, Many follow Chriſt for the loaves, who have no love for his goſpel

[2] He exhorts them to ſeek a better portion *Labour not for the meat which periſheth, but for that meat which endureth unto everlaſting life, which the Son of man ſhall give unto you* The world and all the things of it periſh in the uſing, and we are dying daily, and cannot long poſſeſs any thing here below It were therefore the moſt egregious folly to lay out all our labour on ſo tranſitory a portion, and moſt criminal to make our profeſſion of religion ſubſervient to the baſe purpoſes of earthly advantage Chriſt propoſes to us a nobler good, even that

ſpiri-

ſpiritual food of his grace, by which our immortal ſouls may be fed, and we may grow up to the participation of that eternal life, which the ſon of man hath to beſtow on every truly faithful ſoul *for him hath God the Father ſealed*, fully commiſſioned and authoriſed him to give this eternal life to his redeemed people, and to feed them with that living bread, of which, if a man eat, he ſhall never die *Note*, (1) All our bleſſings, in time and eternity, come from the free gift of our Redeemer (2) None who come to Jeſus, ſeeking the living bread, will be denied, for *he feedeth the hungry*

28 Then ſaid they unto him, What ſhall we do, that
we might work the works of God? 29 Jeſus anſwer-
ed and ſaid unto them, This is the work of God, [q] that
ye believe on him whom he hath ſent 30 They ſaid
therefore unto him, [r] What ſign ſheweſt thou then, that
we may ſee, and believe thee? what doſt thou work?
31 [s] Our fathers did eat manna in the deſert, as it is
written, [t] He gave them bread from heaven to eat 32
Then Jeſus ſaid unto them, Verily, verily I ſay unto
you, Moſes gave you not that bread from heaven, but
my Father giveth you [u] the true bread from heaven
33 For the bread of God is he which cometh down
from heaven, and giveth life unto the world 34 Then
ſaid they unto him, [x] Lord, evermore give us this bread
35 And Jeſus ſaid unto them, I am the bread of life [y]
he that cometh to me, ſhall never hunger, and he that
believeth on me, ſhall never thirſt 36 But I ſaid unto
you, that ye alſo have ſeen me, and believe not 37
All that the Father giveth me, ſhall come to me, and
[z] him that cometh to me, I will in no wiſe caſt out
38 For I came down from heaven, [a] not to do mine
own will, [b] but the will of him that ſent me 39
And this is the Father's will which hath ſent me, [c] that
of all which he hath given me, I ſhould loſe nothing,
but ſhould raiſe it up again at the laſt day 40 And
this is the will of him that ſent me, that [d] every one
which ſeeth the Son, and believeth on him, may have
everlaſting life and I will raiſe him up at the laſt day
41 The Jews then murmured at him, becauſe he ſaid,
I am the bread which came down from heaven 42
And they ſaid, [e] Is not this Jeſus the ſon of Joſeph,
whoſe father and mother we know? how is it then
that he ſaith, I came down from heaven? 43 Jeſus
therefore anſwered and ſaid unto them, Murmur not a-
mong yourſelves 44 [f] No man can come to me,
except the Father which hath ſent me, draw him and I
will raiſe him up at the laſt day 45 [g] It is written in
the prophets, And they ſhall be all taught of God
Every man therefore that hath heard, and hath learned
of the Father, cometh unto me 46 Not that any man
hath ſeen the Father, [i] ſave he which is of God, he hath
ſeen the Father 47 Verily, verily I ſay unto you,
[i] He that believeth on me hath everlaſting life 48 [k] I
am that bread of life 49 [l] Your fathers did eat manna
in the wilderneſs, and are dead 50 [n] This is the bread
which cometh down from heaven, that a man may eat
thereof, and not die 51 I am the living bread, [n] which
came down from heaven if any man eat of this bread,
he ſhall live for ever and the bread that I will give, is
my fleſh, [o] which I will give for the life of the world
52 The Jews therefore [p] ſtrove amongſt themſelves,
ſaying, [q] How can this man give us *his* fleſh to eat? 53
Then Jeſus ſaid unto them, Verily, verily I ſay unto
you, Except ye [r] eat the fleſh of the Son of man, and
drink his blood, ye have no life in you 54 [s] Whoſo
eateth my fleſh, and drinketh my blood, hath eternal
life, and I will raiſe him up at the laſt day 55 For
my fleſh is meat indeed, and my blood is drink indeed
56 He that eateth my fleſh, and drinketh my blood, [t]
dwelleth in me and I in him 57 As the living Father
hath ſent me, and I live by the Father ſo he that eat-
eth me, even he ſhall live by me 58 [u] This is that
bread which came down from heaven not as your fa-
thers did eat manna, and are dead he that eateth of this
bread ſhall live for ever 59 Theſe things ſaid he in
the ſynagogue, as he taught in Capernaum

v 28—59 In conſequence of what he had ſpoken, the perſons who heard him entered into conference with him, how they might attain that everlaſting life he mentioned

1 *They ſaid unto him, What ſhall we do, that we might work the works of God?* He had commanded them to labour for the enduring meat, and they wanted to know what they muſt do, whether any thing more was neceſſary than obedience to the law of Moſes for they founded all their expectations on their own doings and duties, and thought of no other way to righteouſneſs and life eternal than by the works of the law

2 Chriſt replied, *This is the work of God, that ye believe on him whom he hath ſent* It is not by doing, but by believing, that righteouſneſs and ſalvation are attainable, faith in Jeſus, in his divine character as the Meſſiah, and in the all-ſufficiency of his blood and righteouſneſs, to juſtify the ungodly is the principal thing, without which it is impoſſible to pleaſe God And this faith is his own work in the ſoul, which we can no more give ourſelves, than we can create a world

3 They anſwered again, *What ſign ſheweſt thou then, that we may ſee, and believe thee, what doſt thou work?* They overlooked the miracles he had already performed, and demanded greater For ſince he ſeemed to aſſume higher authority than that of Moſes, they thought he ſhould produce greater evidences of a divine commiſſion it is true he had by miracle yeſterday fed five thouſand, but they ſuggeſt Moſes did much more *Our Fathers did eat manna in the deſert, as it is written, He gave them bread from heaven to eat* The number there was much greater, the miracle daily continued, and the fare far more delicious than barley loaves

4 Chriſt rectifies their miſtake They aſcribed to Moſes what was not his, but God's gift *Verily, verily I ſay unto you, Moſes gave you not that bread from heaven*, it doth not appear he had the leaſt concern in procuring it, neither did it come from heaven, as they imagined, but merely from the clouds, and ſerved only to ſupport a mortal life *but my Father*, who gave you the manna, *giveth you the true bread from heaven*, of which that was the type and figure *For the bread of God is he* (or that) *which cometh down from heaven, and giveth life unto the world*, a proviſion as much ſuperior to the manna in the wilderneſs, as the throne of God is beyond the clouds, and life eternal exceeds the preſent moment of mortality

5 Ignorantly miſtaking his meaning, as if he ſpoke of material bread, *they ſaid unto him, Lord, evermore give us this bread* They eagerly deſire that heavenly proviſion, whoſe properties were ſo excellent, and ſo far ſurpaſſed the manna which their fathers did eat in the wilderneſs They indeed underſtood not what they aſked, but if we have taſted of the heavenly manna, have fed upon the word of Jeſus, and feaſted on the ſweet and precious promiſes which are in him, we ſhall not ceaſe with deep ſenſibility to cry, *Lord, evermore give us this bread!*

6 Chriſt plainly informs them of his meaning *I am the bread of life*, he ſpake not of bread literally, or of a merely temporal happineſs, but of himſelf, a divine perſon become incarnate to give ſpiritual life to immortal ſouls He is the *bread of life*, our bodies could better live without daily food, than our ſpirit without the conſtant ſupplies of his grace He is both the quickening principle of our ſpiritual life, and the conſtant ſupport of it Therefore, ſaith Chriſt, *he that cometh to me ſhall never hunger, and he that believeth in me, ſhall never thirſt*, whoſoever by faith applies to Jeſus, ſhall never want the richeſt proviſion to ſatisfy the moſt enlarged deſires of his ſoul *But I ſaid unto you, that ye alſo have ſeen me, and believe not*, they had ſeen his miracles, yet through their earthly-mindedneſs and attachment to worldly intereſts, they received him not as a ſpiritual Redeemer, nor truſted upon him for eternal life Some, indeed, there were who would embrace his goſpel, and be ſaved by it *All that the Father giveth me*, according to the everlaſting covenant of grace, as a peculiar people, *ſhall come unto me*, drawn by Almighty cords of grace irreſiſtible, and enabled to exerciſe faith in me *and him that cometh to me*, under whatever load of guilt or corruption he groans, *I will in no wiſe caſt out* The Saviour's arms of mercy are open to receive the miſerable and the deſperate no ſinner who flies to him need fear a repulſe, however great or aggravated his iniquities may be, pardon, peace, grace, and glory, are aſſured to him by the promiſe of the God who cannot lie *For I came down from heaven, not to do mine own will, but the will of him that ſent me*, not on an errand of uncertainty, or to carry on any deſign ſeparately from his Father, but as his ambaſſador, qualified and commiſſioned to execute that glorious work of man's redemption, to which he was appointed, and ready to do and ſuffer whatever the determinate counſel of God hath ordained *And this is the Father's will which hath ſent me, that of all which he hath given me, I ſhould loſe none, but ſhould raiſe it up again at the laſt day* From whence we learn, (1) That according to the covenant of redemption, a certain number of ſinners are given to Jeſus Chriſt, in whom he ſhall ſee the travel of his ſoul and herein he acts as the eternal King, ſovereignly exerciſing mercy to ſome, when he might, in juſtice, have condemned all to ſuffer the wages of ſin (2) Chriſt will infallibly take care of thoſe whoſe intereſts are lodged in his hands, his grace ſhall find them out, his power preſerve them, and neither the wiles of Satan, nor the temptations of the world, nor the perverſeneſs of the fallen heart, ſhall be able to defeat his purpoſe of love toward them not one ſhall be loſt, of thoſe whoſe ſins he

bore

Lord (3) As the Saviour undertakes to deliver his people from ſin and all its conſequences, death, which is the wages of ſin, ſhall not have dominion over them, as by his grace their ſouls are reſcued from the power of corruption, their bodies ſhall alſo be redeemed from the grave, and raiſed up in glory at the great day of his appearing (4) All thoſe have a part in this ſalvation who hear, *and by* faith, embrace the goſpel which Chriſt declares For *this is the will of him that ſent me, that every one that ſeeth the Son, and believeth on him, may have everlaſting life and I will raiſe him up at the laſt day*, the goſpel propoſes a free ſalvation, through Jeſus, to every miſerable ſinner, and who ever receives the record of God concerning his Son, ſees his own deep need of the Saviour and the all-ſufficiency of Jeſus, becomes a partaker of that preſent life of grace, which is the earneſt of the eternal life of glory They who periſh owe it to their infidelity, they reject the counſel of God againſt their own ſouls, and will not come to Chriſt that they may have life, either through ignorance, inſenſible to their own miſery and want of a Saviour, or through pride, going about to eſtabliſh their own righteouſneſs inſtead of ſubmitting to the righteouſneſs of God

7 Perceiving now that Chriſt plainly pointed at himſelf, as the living bread endued with ſuch wondrous properties, the Jews murmured and cavilled at him, as if he aſſumed to himſelf extravagant honours, in pretending to come down from heaven, and being the bread of life, and they objected his known deſcent from Joſeph and Mary *Is not this Jeſus the ſon of Joſeph, whoſe father and mother we know? How is it then that he ſaith, I came down from heaven?* when his earthly original is ſo evident

8 Chriſt confutes their cavils, and anſwers their murmurings *He ſaid unto them, Murmur not among yourſelves*, he knew their thoughts, and the prejudices they entertained againſt him, ariſing from that native corruption of their hearts, which nothing but Almighty grace could ſubdue *For no man can come to me, except the Father which hath ſent me, draw him*, ſuch is the preſent ſtate of fallen man, that he is under an utter impotence to turn unto God, unleſs drawn by the ſpirit of God, and enabled to believe in his dear Son And to as many as are thus drawn to him, Chriſt ſaith, *I will raiſe him up at the laſt day*, and the way in which the ſinner is thus wrought upon, is according as *it is written in the prophets*, Iſa liv 13 Jer xxxi 34 *They ſhall be all taught of God*, by his revealed word, and the illumination of his ſpirit *Every one therefore that hath heard and learned of the Father*, ſpeaking in his word, and by his ſpirit to the ſoul, *cometh unto me*, truſting on Jeſus alone for pardon, righteouſneſs, and ſalvation, and without ſuch divine teaching and ſpiritual illumination, the natural man cannot receive the truths of revelation, nor believe in the Son of God *Not that any man hath ſeen the Father*, viſibly or perſonally inſtructing him, *ſave he which is of God*, his incarnate Son, *he hath ſeen the Father*, is privy to all his councils and deſigns, by him all divine diſcoveries are made, and through his agency the effectual power is communicated to our ſouls, to hear and receive the goſpel-word *Verily, verily I ſay unto you*, as a moſt undoubted truth, *He that believeth on me, hath everlaſting life*, the true believer is already poſſeſſed of it by right and title, through Jeſus, his glorious covenant-head and repreſentative, embraces it in faith and hope, hath the earneſt and foretaſtes of it in preſent grace, and muſt neceſſarily be brought to the actual enjoyment of eternal glory hereafter *I am that bread of life*, it is from Chriſt our ſpiritual life is derived, through him it is ſupported, and by him it ſhall be perfected *Your fathers did eat manna in the wilderneſs, and are dead*, miraculous as their proviſion was, it only maintained for a while a temporal life, and did not prevent the ravages of death, or render them immortal But *this is the bread which cometh down from heaven, that a man may eat thereof, and not die*, for whoever by faith truly feeds upon Chriſt, ſhall never die eternally *I am the living bread which came down from heaven*, to be the author of ſpiritual and eternal life *if any man eat of this bread*, hungering after the pardon, righteouſneſs, and ſalvation which Jeſus brings, *he ſhall live for ever*, though not immortal upon earth, yet ſure of an eternity of glory in heaven *and the bread that I will give, is my fleſh, which I will give for the life of the world* His human body, offered up as the great ſacrifice for ſinners, would be the grand procuring cauſe of all thoſe ineſtimable bleſſings he had mentioned, of which not only the Jews, but the Gentile world would be made partaker

9 The groſs and carnal ideas of the Jews ſtill prevented them from comprehending his meaning And *they ſtrove among themſelves, ſaying, How can this man give us his fleſh to eat?* Concluding his aſſertion abſurd and improbable, becauſe they underſtood him, as if ſpeaking of his human fleſh, which ſhould be eaten like bread An opinion as monſtrous, as that which the Romiſh church hath ſince aſſerted concerning the fleſh of Jeſus, as corporally eaten in the eucharist

Laſtly, Chriſt confirms and explains what he had ſaid concerning his fleſh It was of abſolute neceſſity, that in a ſpiritual ſenſe, that ſhould be done which was figuratively repreſented by eating his fleſh, and drinking his blood, even that they ſhould be vitally united to him by faith, and become one with him, as the food which is eaten incorporates with our bodies For *verily, verily I ſay unto you, Except ye eat the fleſh of the Son of man, and drink his blood, ye have no life in you*, without this union of our ſouls to him, we can neither have ſpiritual life here, nor eternal life hereafter But *whoſo eateth my fleſh, and drinketh my blood*, not merely partaking of the elements which repreſent theſe, depending on which, many deceive themſelves, and think, if they can but receive the ſacrament before they die, they ſhall infallibly be ſaved, when neither living nor dying will thoſe outward ſigns at all profit thoſe who are ſtrangers to the inward and ſpiritual grace, I ſay, it is not partaking of the outward elements, but the ſpiritual feeding upon Chriſt and his ſaving benefits by faith which is here meant, and whoever doth that, *hath eternal life*, is now entitled to it, and will ſhortly be put in poſſeſſion of it, *and I will raiſe him up at the laſt day For my fleſh is meat indeed, and my blood is drink indeed*, affording the moſt delightful nouriſhment and feaſt for the ſoul, infinitely exceeding any corporal refreſhment *He that eateth my fleſh, and drinketh my blood*, with ſpiritual appetite and diſcernment, *dwelleth in me, and I in him* He is incorporated with Chriſt, as a member of his body myſtical, is entitled to the remiſſion of ſins and acceptance with God, which, by the blood-ſhedding of Jeſus, is obtained for all who believe in him, and hath Chriſt as the quickning ſpirit formed in his heart, the principle of ſpiritual life, which ſhall reach its utmoſt perfection in eternal glory, the union between him and us once formed, being ever after indiſſoluble *For as the living Father*, who is the fountain of life to every creature, *hath ſent me, and I*, as man and mediator, commiſſioned by him, *live by the Father*, ſupported and enabled to finiſh the work he hath given me to do, *ſo he that eateth me*, united to me by faith, *ſhall live by me*, receiving out of my fulneſs, as the branches are fed by the living root, and their life is eternal as my own Becauſe I live, ye ſhall live alſo *This then is* the concluſion of the whole, I am *that bread which came down from heaven*, concerning which I ſpoke before, and the properties of which are ſo tranſcendently excellent *not as your fathers did eat manna*, far different is this bread, *that* was from the clouds, *this* from the higheſt heavens, that was but the type, this the antitype and ſubſtance, that only ſupported a momentary life, they who fed thereupon, were ſubject to all the diſeaſes and decays incident to mortality, *and are dead*, but *he that eateth of this bread ſhall live for ever*

This diſcourſe Jeſus held in the ſynagogue at Capernaum, publicly and openly, that all who deſired it might hear and receive his heavenly doctrines *Note*, Truth ſeeks no covert The goſpel of Jeſus muſt be declared openly, and will bear the ſevereſt enquiry His word is truth

60 Many therefore of his diſciples, when they had
heard *this*, ſaid, This is an hard ſaying, who can hear
it? 61 When Jeſus knew in himſelf, that his diſciples
murmured at it, he ſaid unto them, Doth this offend
you? 62 [x] *What* and if ye ſhall ſee the Son of man [x] Chap iii
aſcend up where he was before? 63 [y] It is the ſpirit 13 Acts i
that quickneth, the fleſh profiteth nothing the words 9 Eph iv
that I ſpeak unto you, *they* are ſpirit, and *they* are life 8 [y] 2 Cor iii 6
64 But there are ſome of you that believe not For
[z] Jeſus knew from the beginning, who they were that [z] Chap ii
believed not, and who ſhould betray him 65 And he 24 25 & xiii 11
ſaid, Therefore [a] ſaid I unto you, that no man can come [a] Ver 44
unto me, except it were given unto him of my Father 45
66 ¶ From that *time* many of his diſciples went back,
and walked no more with him 67 Then ſaid Jeſus
unto the twelve, Will ye alſo go away? 68 Then Simon
Peter anſwered him, Lord, to whom ſhall we go?
thou haſt [b] the words of eternal life 69 And [c] we [b] Acts v
believe, and are ſure that thou art that Chriſt the Son [c] Mat xvi 16 Chap i
of the living God 70 Jeſus anſwered them, [d] Have 49 & xi
not I choſen you twelve, and [e] one of you is a devil? [d] Luke vi 13
71 He ſpake of Judas Iſcariot, *the ſon* of Simon for [e] Chap xiii
he it was that ſhould betray him, being one of the 27
twelve

v 60—71 We have here an account of the different effects produced by this diſcourſe on the mind of the hearers

1 Many who had followed him till then as his nominal diſciples were highly ſhocked at what they heard, taking it in a groſs and carnal ſenſe, and not entering into the ſpirit of his words, or they were offended at the divine original and operation which he claimed as coequal with God the Father, or, becauſe it was myſterious, they diſbelieved his doctrine as abſurd as the infidels and ſcoffers of our day, who, becauſe the myſteries of grace appear not agreeable to their fallen reaſon, ſuppoſe it a mark of ſuperior underſtanding to reject them

2 Chriſt was appriſed of their murmurings, for he ſees the hard thoughts which ſinners entertain of him, as well as hears their hard ſpeeches He ſearcheth the heart, and therefore replies,

plies, *Doth this offend you?* If the coming down of the Son of man from heaven appears so incredible, *What and if ye shall see the Son of man ascend up where he was before?* This would perhaps yet more astonish them, considering the meanness of his present appearance, and might seem still more improbable to happen. As to what he had observed about eating his flesh, this must be understood not corporeally, but spiritually. *It is the spirit that quickeneth, the flesh profiteth nothing*: the bare participation of the outward ordinances avails nothing to procure eternal life. The sinner's soul must first be quickened by the power of the Spirit of Jesus, and brought to the discernment of spiritual things, otherwise the most nourishing words of his gospel convey no more to the inward man, than meat doth to the dead corpse. *The words that I speak unto you, saith he, they are spirit, and they are life*; to be understood not in a literal but spiritual sense, and, accompanied by the power of the Holy Ghost, become the means of quickening the dead sinner's soul, and maintaining the life which Christ bestows, till it is perfected in eternity. *But there are some of you that believe not*; professing to be disciples, but in truth not at all experimentally acquainted with the doctrines of the gospel: *for Jesus knew from the beginning who they were that believed not, and who should betray him. And he said, Therefore said I unto you, that no man can come unto me, except it were given unto him of my Father*, being powerfully drawn by his effectual grace. *Note*, (1.) Christ knoweth the heart, and sees the infidelity which reigns within, though covered with the most plausible cloak of profession. (2.) Apostates prove they were always hypocrites. (3.) Unless the Lord draw us by his grace, we have neither inclination nor ability to follow him.

3. Many, who had murmured before, now utterly withdrew, and returned to their former occupations, to their own sinful ways, and pharisaical teachers, and never made any farther profession, nor attended any more on his ministry. We are not to wonder if we see apostates, nay *many*, of whom we had formed the most sanguine hopes, go back: it was so from the beginning.

4. Christ hereupon addressed his twelve chosen ones, that he might draw from them a profession of their faith in him. *Will ye also go away?* Not that he doubted their sincerity, but it bespeaks his affection towards them, and his confidence in them, that, whatever others did, they would never follow so bad examples, but in general, at least, cleave to him with unshaken fidelity.

5. Peter's zealous heart cannot bear the suspicion which the question seemed to intimate, and therefore, in the name of his brethren, he nobly replies, *Lord, to whom shall we go?* Out of thee we can hope for neither pardon, peace, grace nor glory. Turn where we will, misery and destruction meet us. *Thou*, and thou alone, *hast the words of eternal life*, and *we believe* all that thou hast lately spoken, *and are sure that thou art that Christ, the Son of the living God*. *Note*, (1.) Peter's reply must be the answer of every faithful soul, when tempted to quit his profession. *To whom shall we go* for life and peace? To our sins? they will destroy us. To our own works and endeavours? they cannot justify or save us. To the world? it will deceive our expectations. Christ, and Christ alone, is the only foundation of hope and fountain of happiness to a fallen sinner: out of him, nothing but wrath and ruin remain for us. (2.) The more steadily and fiercely we trust in the Son of God, the more we honour him: And that faith which gives him glory, will bring us the most reviving consolations.

6. *Jesus answered them*, to check too great self-confidence, and prepare them for the issue, *Have not I chosen you twelve* to the distinguished honour of apostleship, *and one of you is a devil?* possessed by that wicked spirit, in his heart a traitor and a murderer. *He spake of Judas Iscariot, the son of Simon, for he it was that should betray him*, as Christ full well knew; though he was one of the twelve, which aggravated his guilt. *Note*, (1.) A man, like Judas, may have been the means of casting out devils from others, and yet be a devil himself. Among the most flaming professors there will be found hypocrites and apostates. Let him that thinketh he standeth take heed lest he fall. (2.) The purest societies on earth cannot answer for all their members: it is in heaven alone that the wheat will be free from the chaff.

CHAP. VII.

In this chapter we have, 1. Christ's declining for some time to appear publicly in Judea, ver. 1. 2. His design to go up to Jerusalem at the feast of tabernacles, and his discourse with his kindred in Galilee concerning his going up to this feast, ver. 3—13. 3. *His preaching publicly in the temple at that feast. (1.) In the midst of the feast*, ver. 14, 15. *we have his discourse with the Jews, [1.] Concerning his doctrine*, ver. 16—18. *[2.] Concerning the crime of sabbath-breaking laid to his charge*, ver. 19—24. *[3.] Concerning himself, both whence he came, and whither he was going*, ver. 25—36. *(2.) On the last day of the feast, [1.] His gracious invitation to poor souls to come to him*, ver. 37—39. *[2.] The reception that it met with. 1. Many of the people disputed about it*, ver. 40—44. *2. The chief priests would have brought him into trouble for it, but were first balked by their officers*, ver. 45—49. *and then silenced by one of their own court*, ver. 50—53.

1 AFTER these things, Jesus walked in Galilee:
for he would not walk in Jewry, because [a] the
Jews sought to kill him. 2 Now [b] the Jews feast of
tabernacles was at hand. 3 [c] His brethren therefore
said unto him, Depart hence, and go into Judea, that
thy disciples also may see the works that thou dost. 4
For *there is* no man *that* doth any thing in secret, and he
himself seeketh to be known openly. If thou do these
things, shew thyself to the world. 5 For [d] neither did
his brethren believe in him. 6 Then Jesus said unto
them, [e] My time is not yet come: but your time is al-
way ready. 7 [f] The world cannot hate you; but me
it hateth, [g] because I testify of it that the works thereof
are evil. 8 Go ye up unto this feast: I go not up yet
unto this feast; for [h] my time is not yet full come. 9
When he had said these words unto them, he abode *still*
in Galilee. 10 ¶ But when his brethren were gone up,
then went he also up unto the feast, not openly, but as it
were in secret. 11 Then [i] the Jews sought him at the
feast, and said, Where is he? 12 And [k] there was
much murmuring among the people concerning him:
for [l] some said, He is a good man: others said, Nay;
but he deceiveth the people. 13 Howbeit, no man
spake openly of him, [m] for fear of the Jews.

[a] Chap. v. 16, 18. [b] Lev. xxiii. 34. [c] Mat. xii. 46. Mark iii. 31. Acts i. 14. [d] Mark iii. 21. [e] Chap. ii. 4. & viii. 20. Ver. 8, 30. [f] Chap. xv. 19. [g] Chap. iii. 19. [h] Chap. viii. 20. [i] Chap. xi. 56. [k] Chap. ix. 16. & x. 19. [l] Mat. xxi. 46. Luke vii. 16. Chap. vi. 14. Ver. 40. [m] Chap. ix. 22. & xii. 42. & xix. 38.

V. 1—13. As the inveterate malignity of the chief priests and Pharisees led them to determine the death of Jesus, by popular fury or by form of law; to avoid their devices, he continued in Galilee. They who had refused the light of truth, have it justly withdrawn from them; and where our enemies rage, and our safety is in danger, it is prudent to depart, and carry that gospel of God to others, which sinners against their own souls reject and persecute. We have here,

1. The conversation which passed in Galilee between Jesus and some of his relations. The feast of tabernacles being at hand, when a great concourse of people would be assembled in Jerusalem:

(1.) They urge him to make his public appearance there, and not stay in that obscure part of the country, but go up to the metropolis and *shew himself*, and his wondrous works, if really they would bear the test of examination: since this could not fail of getting him disciples among the great men at Jerusalem, and of confirming those he had already made, who would be assembled there on this solemnity. And they suggest this would be the way most effectually to advance his own reputation and honour, which they sinfully imagined he, like the men of the world, designed. *For neither did his brethren believe in him.* As he did not answer their expectations in erecting a temporal kingdom, they began to suspect he was not *the Messiah*, which they at first hoped; and therefore wanted him to declare himself, and produce his credentials, or go up to Jerusalem, where his pretensions, if false, might be detected. *Note*, (1.) Many appear at public ordinances *to shew themselves*, not to give the glory to God, but to secure reputation to themselves. (2.) They who want a temporal kingdom evidently prove that they are faithless followers of Christ.

(2.) Christ mildly replies to their perverse suggestions, *My time is not yet come* for going up to the feast, *but your time is always ready*, you may appear there at any time without any danger; they seek not your lives, as they do mine. *The world cannot hate you*, because your spirit, temper, and conduct, are but too conformed thereunto, *but me it hateth, because I testify of it, that the works thereof are evil*, which cannot but exasperate those who determine not to part with their beloved sin. *Go ye therefore up unto the feast* without delay: *I go not up yet unto the feast, for my time is not yet full come*. *Note*, (1.) Christ hath fixed the time for all his purposes, and we may be assured that is the best time, and therefore are bound cheerfully and confidently to wait his leisure. (2.) Sinners hate the light of truth, and cannot but be exasperated with those reproofs, to which they obstinately refuse to submit. (3.) Whatever pretence men make for their enmity against the gospel and the preachers of it, the true cause is this, they cannot endure the testimony born against their evil deeds. (4.) They who go to ordinances with an hypocritical spirit may never expect the comfort of Christ's presence in them.

2. The journey of Jesus to Jerusalem. He staid a while longer in Galilee, till his brethren were gone up to the feast, and then, when his time was come, he went himself, *not openly, but as it were in secret*, that he might give no offence to the ruling powers, who, if he came with a multitude, might interpret it into a seditious design. *Note*, Though the cause of Christ cannot be carried on without *notice*, it will be prudent to

do it with as little *noiſe* as poſſible We need not provoke needleſs oppoſition it will come faſt enough upon us, if we are faithful

3 The expectation which was raiſed of him *The Jews ſought him at the feaſt, and ſaid, Where is he?* Some wiſhed to ſee him out of curioſity, ſome out of malice, hoping to deſtroy him, and ſome out of better motives, expecting to receive ſome gracious inſtruction from him *And there was much murmuring among the people concerning him*, their ſentiments being greatly divided *ſome ſaid he is a good man*, convinced by his miracles, ſtruck with his exemplary life, and influenced by his holy doctrine, *others*, hardened in infidelity, though they had not one ſingle charge of evil to produce againſt him, *ſaid, Nay, but he deceiveth the people*, as if there was ſome latent impoſture under theſe ſpecious appearances *Howbeit, no man ſpake openly of him, for fear of the Jews* Whatever good opinion any formed of him, they were very cautious how they ſpoke their ſentiments, it being highly dangerous to appear among his approvers, when thoſe who were in power were known to be the avowed enemies and bitter perſecutors of him and his diſciples *Note*, (1) Chriſt's miniſters, like himſelf, muſt expect to paſs *through evil report and good report, as deceivers, and yet true* (2) They who are obſtinate in rejecting the truth, will find ſomething to quarrel with in the moſt ſpotleſs characters, and ſuppoſe thoſe who act with greateſt ſimplicity to God's glory, are carrying on ſome deſign of their own

14 ¶ Now about the midſt of the feaſt, Jeſus went
up into the temple, and taught 15 And the Jews
n Mark vi 3 marvelled, ſaying, n How knoweth this man letters,
having never learned? 16 Jeſus anſwered them, and
o Chap viii 28 & xii 49 & xiv 10 24 ſaid, o My doctrine is not mine, but his that ſent me
17 p If any man † will do his will, he ſhall know of
p Ecclus xxi 11 the doctrine, whether it be of God, or *whether* I ſpeak
of myſelf 18 q He that ſpeaketh of himſelf, ſeeketh
† Or is willing to do his own glory but he that ſeeketh his glory that ſent
q Chap v 41 him, the ſame is true, and no unrighteouſneſs is in him
19 r Did not Moſes give you the law, and *yet* none of
r Ex xxiv 3 Acts vii 35, &c you keepeth the law? s Why go ye about to kill me?
s Chap v 16, 18 & xi 53 20 The people anſwered and ſaid, t Thou haſt a devil
who goeth about to kill thee? 21 Jeſus anſwered and
t Chap viii 48, 52 & x 20 ſaid unto them, I have done one work, and ye all marvel
22 u Moſes therefore gave unto you circumciſion,
u Lev xii 3 (not becauſe it is of Moſes, x but of the fathers) and ye
x Gen xvii 10 on the ſabbath-day circumciſe a man 23 If a man on
the ſabbath-day receive circumciſion, that the law of
Moſes ſhould not be broken, are ye angry at me, be-
y Chap v 8 9 cauſe y I have made a man every whit whole on the ſab-
z Deut i 16 17 Prov xxiv 23 bath-day? 24 z Judge not according to the appearance,
but judge righteous judgment 25 Then ſaid
a Ver 19 ſome of them of Jeruſalem, Is not this he a whom they
ſeek to kill? 26 But lo, he ſpeaketh boldly, and they
ſay nothing unto him do the rulers know indeed that
b Mat xiii 55 Mark vi 3 Luke iv this is the very Chriſt? 27 Howbeit b we know this
man whence he is but when Chriſt cometh, no man
knoweth whence he is 28 Then cried Jeſus in the tem-
c Chap viii 14 ple as he taught, ſaying, c Ye both know me, and ye
d Chap v 43 & viii 42 know whence I am and d I am not come of myſelf, but
e Chap v 32 & viii 26 Rom iii 4 he that ſent me e is true, f whom ye know not 29 But
f Chap i 18 & viii 55 g I know him, for I am from him, and he hath ſent me
g Mat xi 27 Chap x 15 30 Then h they ſought to take him but i no man laid
h Mark xi 18 Luke xix 47 & xx 19 hands on him, becauſe his hour was not yet come. 31
i Ver 19 Chap viii 37 And k many of the people believed on him, and ſaid,
When Chriſt cometh, will he do more miracles than
k Chap viii 30 theſe which this *man* hath done? 32 ¶ The Phariſees
heard that the people murmured ſuch things concerning
him and the Phariſees, and the chief prieſts ſent officers
to take him 33 Then ſaid Jeſus unto them, l Yet a
l Chap xvi 16 little while am I with you, and *then* I go unto him that
ſent me 34 m Ye ſhall ſeek me, and ſhall not find *me*
m Hoſ v 6 Chap viii 21 & xiii 33 and where I am, *thither* ye cannot come 35 Then
ſaid the Jews among themſelves, Whither will he go
that we ſhall not find him? will he go unto n the diſ-
n Iſa xi 12 Jam i 1 1 Pet i 1 perſed among the ‖ Gentiles, and teach the Gentiles?
‖ Or, Greeks 36 What *manner of* ſaying is this that he ſaid, Ye ſhall
ſeek me, and ſhall not find *me* and where I am, *thither*
ye cannot come.

v 14—36 When Chriſt was come up to Jeruſalem, *about the midſt of the feaſt*, we find him, where indeed we might expect to meet him, in the temple, teaching the people He would ſhew, he was neither aſhamed of the doctrine he preached, nor afraid of the enemies who threatened him We are told,

1 The admiration which the hearers expreſſed at his preaching, ſaying, *How knoweth this man letters, having never learned?* Though he had been brought up in none of their ſchools, he appeared ſo wiſe in the Scriptures, opened them with ſuch evidence, and reaſoned upon them with ſuch force of argument, as could not but aſtoniſh them, and probably led ſome to conclude, that ſuch extraordinary gifts were not attained without diabolical aſſiſtance

2 The reply of Jeſus *My doctrine is not mine, but his that ſent me* As Mediator, he received his miſſion, and ability to diſcharge his office, from his Father, and needed no human aſſiſtance, nor advanced ought of his own invention What he taught was divine in its original, and deſigned ultimately to advance the glory of God, from whom it came *If any man will do his will, he ſhall know of the doctrine, whether it be of God, or whether I ſpeak of myſelf* he that, laying aſide his prejudice, as an humble enquirer, comes, deſiring to be taught, ſhall find ſuch evidence in the goſpel, as to demonſtrate the divine authority of its author, and ſhall experience ſuch powerful and bleſſed effects produced thereby, as ſhall moſt indubitably prove it to be the word (not of man, but) of God *He that ſpeaketh of himſelf, ſeeketh his own glory* an impoſtor would ſeek to advance his own reputation and intereſts, as the falſe teachers did *but he that ſeeketh his glory that ſent him*, as Chriſt did, and all his faithful miniſters will do, *the ſame is true*, he evidences hereby the ſimplicity of his heart, *and no unrighteouſneſs is in him*, no fraud nor falſehood in his preaching or deſigns They pretended indeed great zeal for the law of Moſes, and founded their ſuggeſtions of his being an impoſtor on the ſuppoſition that he violated the ſabbath, and taught men to diſregard the Moſaical inſtitutions, when, in fact, they themſelves were living in the groſſeſt violation of the plaineſt precepts of it *Did not Moſes give you the law? and yet none of you keepeth the law Why go ye about to kill me?* purpoſing to murder him, becauſe of the miracle he had wrought on the impotent man on the ſabbath-day *Note*, (1) They who ſpeak *of themſelves*, without a divine call, and *for themſelves*, with a view to their own honour and advantage, evidently ſhew the falſehood of their religious pretenſions. theſe God hath never ſent (2) Many pretend a great zeal for the intereſts of morality, and a jealouſy leſt the grace of the goſpel ſhould entrench upon them, who live themſelves in the open violation of the divine law

3 The people, who were really ignorant of the deſigns of the enemies of Jeſus, or at leaſt affected to be ſo, expreſs their ſurpriſe at the accuſation he brought againſt them *They anſwered and ſaid, Thou haſt a devil*, thou talkeſt as one poſſeſſed *Who goeth about to kill thee?* They would inſinuate that his fears were groundleſs, the charge unjuſt, and himſelf a liar Let us not wonder if we ſuffer the moſt vile aſperſions, are counted madmen, liars, devils The Son of God was thus reproached before us

4 Overlooking their perverſeneſs and abuſe, our Lord proceeds to vindicate that action which they had ſo much condemned, and for which they went about to kill him *I have done one work*, in healing the impotent man, *and ye all marvel*, becauſe it was done on the ſabbath-day, as if this was inconſiſtent with the character he profeſſed as a teacher ſent from God And yet they themſelves commonly practiſed what might much more juſtly be regarded as a breach of the ſabbath, than his healing a cripple by a word ſpeaking *Moſes therefore gave unto you circumciſion*, as an ordinance to be obſerved among you, (*not becauſe it is of Moſes*, inſtituted by him, *but of the fathers*, being commanded of God to Abraham long before the days of Moſes) *and ye on the ſabbath circumciſe a man If a man on the ſabbath-day receive circumciſion, that the law of Moſes ſhould not be broken*, which enjoins it to be performed on the eighth day, whenever that happened, *are ye angry with me, becauſe I made a man every whit whole on the ſabbath-day?* where they allowed themſelves to circumciſe and dreſs a wound on that day, how could they, with any ſhew of reaſon, cenſure him, who, without the leaſt trouble, merely by a word, had cured an object ſo miſerable? Partial judges were they indeed, and juſtly therefore doth he rebuke them, *Judge not according to appearance*, with reſpect of perſons, condemning that in him which they allowed in their own countrymen, or becauſe of the meanneſs of his outward circumſtances, paying a higher reſpect to the deciſions of their own more ſpecious and pompous rabbi's than to his *but judge righteous judgment*, weighing the real merits of the caſe, without prejudice, and then they would be convinced, that their own practice would be a full vindication of his conduct *Note*, (1) Unreaſonable and wicked men are they indeed, who cenſure and condemn others for what they allow, nay approve, in themſelves (2) Such is the force of prejudice, that it often blinds the eyes againſt the moſt glaring conviction (3) All is not gold which glitters we muſt look farther than appearances, if we would learn the true characters of men (4) Chriſt's words and works demand nothing but an impartial examination to prove their excellence

5 Some of the inhabitants of Jeruſalem, to whom the deſigns of the chief prieſts and rulers were no ſecret, were exceedingly aſtoniſhed at the boldneſs of Chriſt's diſcourſe, and wondered they

they did not immediately attempt to ſeize him, ſuggeſting as if their with-holding their hands from him gave ſuſpicion that they had changed their ſentiments concerning him, and began themſelves to think him the Meſſiah As for themſelves, they could entertain no ſuch imagination, becauſe they knew *whence he was but, when Chriſt cometh, no man knoweth whence he is*, the Scripture having ſpoken of him as like Melchizedek, whoſe deſcent is unknown, as one whoſe goings forth have been from everlaſting, and whoſe generation none can declare Their reaſoning however was fallacious for, though theſe ſcriptures were true with regard to his divine nature and deſignation to his mediatorial office, of whom he ſhould ſpring, and where he ſhould be born, as his human nature, had been expreſsly determined *Note*, (1) God hath reſtraints upon the hands and hearts of wicked men, and marvellouſly withholds them from the evil which they deſign and have an opportunity to perform (2) They who miſtake the Scriptures err moſt dangerouſly, as they ſupport themſelves in their own imagination with the conceit of divine authority

6 Chriſt replies to theſe cavils It was true they knew his earthly deſcent their grand miſtake lay in not looking higher, to his original from above, and his miſſion from God *I am not come of myſelf*, aſſuming this honour, *but he that ſent me is true* to all his promiſes made of and to the Meſſiah, *whom ye know not*, for, though they believed in one eternal Jehovah, they did not truly know the *Scripture God*, as ſubſiſting in Father, Son, and Holy Ghoſt, *but I know him*, his perfections and purpoſes, *for I am from him*, by eſſential emanation, as the beams from the ſun, *and he hath ſent me*, in the character of Mediator, to accompliſh the ſalvation of his people

7 Very different were the effects produced upon the hearers Some were highly incenſed by his declarations, and would have inſtantly ſeized him, but they were under a divine reſtraint, the determinate hour fixed in the divine counſels not being yet come Others, eſpecially of the common people, ſtruck with what they heard and ſaw, could not withhold from expreſſing their perſuaſion that this muſt be the Chriſt for it could not be conceived, wherever he came, that he ſhould do greater miracles than Jeſus wrought *Note*, (1) Though the enmity of wicked men be never ſo great againſt us, it is a comfortable conſideration that they can do nothing without a divine permiſſion, and all their power or policy muſt prove abortive to oppreſs the faithful miniſters of Chriſt, who bear teſtimony to his truth, till the hour appointed in God's eternal counſels comes (2) They who receive the goſpel of Jeſus are uſually ſuch as man deſpiſeth, as being of the poor and unlearned multitude What therefore the world accounts their reproach, that they are chiefly followed by ſuch, the miniſters of the goſpel ſhould eſteem their honour

8 The Phariſees and rulers, jealous leſt his credit and influence with the people ſhould increaſe, could not hear theſe murmurs without indignation, and therefore immediately diſpatched officers to arreſt him, and to bring him before the ſanhedrim *Note*, Wicked inſtruments will not be wanting, where power is in the hands of perſecutors

9 Chriſt, who knew what was plotting againſt him, addreſſed the officers and people, ſaying, *Yet a little while I am with you*, and till that time was expired all their malicious attempts were impotent, *and then I go unto him that ſent me*, to my Father, from whom I came *Ye ſhall ſeek me*, when your calamity comes you will wiſh for the Meſſiah, *and ſhall not find me*, nor obtain the leaſt relief or reſpite, looking for help from heaven in vain *and where I am, thither ye cannot come*, baniſhed for ever from that glory where *I am* Though Chriſt's human nature was on earth, in his divine nature he was ſtill enthroned in the light, which no man can approach unto *Note*, (1) It is too late to cry for mercy when it is the time of judgment They who reject the Saviour upon earth, and die faithleſs and impenitent, muſt never hope to be with him where he is, in heaven (2) A little while will deliver the faithful out of all their troubles Let us therefore patiently endure The time is ſhort

Laſtly, Miſtaking his meaning, they bewildered themſelves in idle and vain reaſonings whither he would go, that they ſhould not find him, whether among the diſperſed Jews, or among the Gentiles, as if he could find no diſciples among thoſe, who were judges of his pretenſions, or as defying him to go where they could not follow him

37 [a] In the laſt day, that great *day* of the feaſt,
Jeſus ſtood and cried, ſaying, [b] If any man thirſt, let
him come unto me, and drink 38 He that believeth
on me, as the ſcripture hath ſaid, [c] out of his belly ſhall
flow rivers of living water 39 (But [d] this ſpake he of
the Spirit, [e] which they that believe on him ſhould receive
for the holy Ghoſt was not yet *given*, becauſe
that Jeſus was not yet glorified) 40 ¶ Many of the
people therefore, when they heard this ſaying, ſaid, Of a
truth this is [f] the prophet 41 Others ſaid, [g] This is
the Chriſt But ſome ſaid, [x] Shall Chriſt come out of
Galilee? 42 Hath not the ſcripture ſaid, That Chriſt
cometh [y] of the ſeed of David, and [z] out of the town of
Bethlehem, where David was? 43 So [a] there was a
diviſion among the people becauſe of him 44 And
[b] ſome of them would have taken him, but no man laid
hands on him

[a] Lev xxiii 36 [b] Iſa lv 1 Chap vi 35 Rev xxii 17 [c] Deut xviii 15 [d] Prov xviii 4 Iſa xliv 3 Chap iv 14 [e] Joel ii 28 Acts ii 17 Chap vi 2 Acts ii 33 Acts xix 2 [f] Ch xvi 7 [g] Chap iv 42 [x] Ver 52 Chap i 46

[y] Pſ cxxxii 11 [z] Mic v 2 [a] Ver 12 Chap ix 16 & x 19 [b] Ver 30

v 37—44 The officers returned without executing their commiſſion, and Jeſus went on in the public exerciſe of his miniſtry We have,

1 His diſcourſe in the laſt day of the feaſt, when a vaſt concourſe attended at the temple, and they uſed with great ſolemnity to draw water from the pool of Siloam, and pour it out with great rejoicings On which he took occaſion to ſpeak of himſelf as the living water *He cried, If any man thirſt, let him come unto me, and drink* Earneſt to invite poor ſinners to partake of his rich grace, he lifted up his voice aloud, and urged them to come to him and be happy The invitation is general, to *any man that thirſts* and none can truly come to Chriſt but they who feel their want of him, and therefore hunger and thirſt after him and his righteouſneſs, to ſuch Chriſt is a fountain of living waters, refreſhing and ſatisfying the longing deſires of the ſoul *He that believeth on me*, as the only Saviour, and repoſes his entire confidence on my all-ſufficiency to ſupply his every want, *as the ſcripture hath ſaid, out of his belly ſhall flow rivers of living water*, ſuch an abundance of ſpiritual gifts, graces, and conſolations, ſhall be beſtowed upon him, that, like a perpetual and copious fountain, they ſhall flow forth in ſtreams of righteouſneſs, and diffuſive bleſſings on every ſide, *Iſa* xli 18 xliii 20 xliv 3 lviii 2 *Joel* ii 28

2 The Evangeliſt explains the meaning of Chriſt's words *This ſpake he of the Spirit, which they that believe on him ſhould receive*, in a more abundant and glorious manner than had been ever vouchſafed before *for the holy Ghoſt was not yet given*, in that moſt plentiful effuſion of his divine influences which was promiſed, *Joel* ii 28 *becauſe that Jeſus was not yet glorified* and it was needful he ſhould firſt paſs through his ſtate of humiliation, and enter into his glory, when, on the day of Pentecoſt, the moſt aſtoniſhing out-pouring of the Spirit ſhould atteſt the Saviour's exaltation, and not only the miraculous powers communicated by him ſhould evidence the divine authority under which the apoſtles acted, but the ſtrongeſt demonſtration of his effectual power ſhould accompany their preaching, and under the goſpel diſpenſation the ſouls of thoſe who were converted ſhould be filled with the largeſt meaſures of light, holineſs, and joy

3 The people were divided greatly in their ſentiments concerning Chriſt Many, ſtruck with his divine teaching, could not help expreſſing their perſuaſion of his miſſion from God, as that *prophet* promiſed, *Deut* xviii 15 which they underſtood as the forerunner of the Meſſiah Others went farther, thinking him not the harbinger, but the King Meſſiah himſelf But others, prejudiced by their national pride and falſe notions of the Meſſiah, objected that he came out of Galilee, whereas Chriſt was to deſcend from the lineage of David, and to come from Bethlehem, the reſidence of David's anceſtors, as he did, though they knew it not Thus, whilſt the ſentiments of the people were divided, the officers and his enemies, though they would fain have arreſted him, were reſtrained by a divine power, and offered him no violence *Note*, (1) The goſpel of Chriſt often creates great diviſions, for, though it breathes nothing but peace, they who refuſe to receive the truth cannot but oppoſe it (2) Many flatter themſelves they have right on their ſide, for want of examining into facts and evidences, when their concluſions would often be found utterly unſupported

45 Then came the officers to the chief prieſts and
Phariſees, and they ſaid unto them, Why have ye not
brought him? 46 The officers anſwered, [c] Never man
ſpake like this man 47 Then anſwered them the Phariſees,
Are ye alſo deceived? 48 [d] Have any of the
rulers, or of the Phariſees believed on him? 49 But
this people who knoweth not the law are curſed 50
Nicodemus ſaith unto them, ([e] he that came † to Jeſus
by night, being one of them) 51 [f] Doth our law judge
any man before it hear him, and know what he doth?
52 They anſwered and ſaid unto him, Art thou alſo
of Galilee? Search and look for out of Galilee ariſeth
no prophet 53 And every man went unto his own
houſe

[c] Mat vii 29 [d] Chap xii 42 Acts vi 7 1 Cor i 26 & ii 8 [e] Chap iii 2 † Gr To him [f] Deut i 17 & xix 15 [g] Iſa ix 1 2 Mat iv 15 Chap i 46

v 45—53 Whilſt the chief prieſts and Phariſees, as in duty bound, ſhould have been in the temple, leading the devotions of the people, we find them maliciouſly conſulting how to deſtroy the Lord of that ſacred place, for which they profeſſed ſo high a veneration

1 The officers returned without the priſoner, and are ſharply queſtioned why they have not executed their orders They honeſtly acknowledge they could not, they were ſo over-awed with the majeſty of Jeſus, with the power and evidence of his diſcourſe,

discourse, that their hearts failed them *Never man spake like this man*. *Note*, There is a power accompanying the preaching of the gospel, which hath often disarmed the rage of bitterest enemies, and made those bow down before the word of truth who came to disturb the preacher

2 The Pharisees, with indignation, upbraided them with their weakness *Are ye also deceived?* Can men of your sense and rank be imposed upon by such a delusion? *Have any of the rulers, or of the Pharisees, believed on him?* Men of the greatest abilities, fashion, and reputation, the wisest and most devout *but this people who know not the law*, the vulgar herd, *are cursed*, abandoned of God to every impostor, and through their ignorance of the law, unable to judge of his pretensions *Note*, (1) Few of the rulers and Pharisees, the great men, and pious devotees, who value themselves on their own goodness, are found among the disciples of Jesus in any age (2) Many are prejudiced against the gospel, because they see the profession of it is unfashionable, and not the way to this world's preferment (3) It is common with this world's wise men to treat the poor disciples of Jesus as an ignorant, contemptible, deluded set of creatures, yet to the babes hath God revealed, what they, who boast of their superior wisdom, never knew (4) The curse causeless will not fall, but upon the head of him that utters it

3 Nicodemus, who had visited Jesus by night, *chap* iii 2 and was secretly a disciple, could not hear those infamous and unjust reflections, unmoved, and therefore assuming courage, he remonstrated against their unreasonable and illegal manner of proceeding They condemned unheard, contrary to all rules of justice and equity, whereas, at least, they should have given Christ an impartial hearing, and examined thoroughly into facts, before they decided on the merits of the case Nothing could be more sensible and just than the maxim, but it doth not appear that any seconded or supported the motion *Note*, (1) Christ hath some that dare own his cause, even among the great and noble (2) It is highly wicked and unjust to condemn any man till he hath had a fair hearing, and liberty to speak in his own defence

4 Instead of refuting the force of his argument, they fell to reviling, *Art thou also of Galilee?* A disciple of this despicable Galilean? *Search, and look, for out of Galilee ariseth no prophet* They concluded Jesus had been born in Galilee, because he had made it his chief abode, and as false was their assertion concerning the scriptures, for Jonah was of Galilee, and probably Nahum and Elijah also *Note*, (1) It is a sure sign of a bad cause, when men have recourse to abuse in the stead of argument (2) Many confidently appeal to the scriptures, as if it was the same thing to assert and prove, but we must examine for ourselves, and not take the scripture upon trust

5 Hereupon the council separated, and each retired to his own home, unable to answer Nicodemus, and ashamed to proceed further, where the injustice was so glaring *Note*, One faithful man, who dares make a stand for Christ, will often silence and confound a whole company of gainsayers

CHAP VIII

In this chapter we have, 1 Christ's evading the snare which the Jews laid for him, in bringing to him a woman taken in adultery, ver 1—11 2 *Divers discourses or conferences of his with the Jews that cavilled at him, and sought occasion against him, and made every thing he said a matter of a controversy* (1) *Concerning his being* the light of the world, *ver* 12—20 (2) *Concerning the ruin of the unbelieving Jews*, ver 21—30 (3) *Concerning liberty and bondage*, ver 31—37 (4) *Concerning his Father and their Father*, ver 38—47 (5) *Here is his discourse in answer to their blasphemous reproaches*, ver 48—50 (6) *Concerning the immortality of believers*, ver 51—59 *And in all this he endured the contradiction of sinners against himself*

1 JESUS went unto the mount of olives 2 And
early in the morning he came again into the temple,
and all the people came unto him, and he sat down and
taught them 3 And the scribes and Pharisees brought
unto him a woman taken in adultery, and when they
had set her in the midst, 4 They say unto him, Master,
this woman was taken in adultery, in the very act.
5 Now [a] Moses in the law commanded us, that such
should be stoned but what sayest thou? 6 This they
said, tempting him, that they might have to accuse him
But Jesus stooped down, and with *his* finger wrote on
the ground as though he heard them not 7 So when
they continued asking him, he lifted up himself, and said
unto them, [b] He that is without sin among you, let him
first cast a stone at her 8 And again he stooped down,
and wrote on the ground 9 And they which heard *it*,
being convicted by their own conscience, went out one
by one, beginning at the eldest, *even* unto the last and
Jesus was left alone, and the woman standing in the
midst 10 When Jesus had lifted up himself, and saw
none but the woman, he said unto her, Woman, where
are those thine accusers? hath no man condemned thee?
11 She said, no man, Lord. And Jesus said unto her,
[c] Neither do I condemn thee go, and sin no more

a Lev xx 10. Deut xxii 22

b Deut xvii 7 Rom ii 1

c ...

v 1—11 According to his usual custom, our Lord in the evening went unto the mount of olives, perhaps to the house of his friend Lazarus, or to retire for communion with God, or to avoid the danger of some popular tumult, which his implacable enemies might attempt to raise against him in the night In the morning early he returned to the temple, and sat down, as one having authority, to preach the gospel to the multitude which crowded around him *Note*, Early rising to wait upon God will be a gracious presage of a happy day

Whilst Christ was engaged in this blessed employment, we are told the interruption he met with from his invenomed enemies

1 They proposed a case to him, the decision of which they flattered themselves would bring him into disgrace with the people, or embroil him with the government They bring a woman *taken in adultery*, *in the very act*, for, though such deeds of darkness usually are concealed with deepest cunning, God is sometimes pleased strangely to bring to light such deadly works, and to expose those to the infamy of the world, who were emboldened to transgress in the foolish confidence that *no eye shall see me* The proof was evident, the law express, but, as he assumed authority to make alterations therein, they desire to know what was his judgment on the case, hoping to get some matter of accusation against him On the one hand, if he should command the law to be put in force, they would accuse him to the Roman government as pronouncing sentence of death, and assuming judicial authority, and to the people, as acting inconsistent with himself, who invited publicans and sinners to come to him, and willingly conversed and eat and drank with them On the other, if he should acquit her, or refuse to confirm the sentence the law had pronounced, they would brand him as an enemy to the divine institutions, a violater of the law, and a patron of the most scandalous enormities

2 Christ, who knew their wickedness, seemed to pay no regard to the case they proposed, stooping down and writing on the ground, as though he heard them not But, as they now thought he was in a dilemma from which he could not disentangle himself, they urged him vehemently to answer their question When raising himself, with majesty and wisdom which confounded his enemies, he bids *him that was without sin cast the first stone at her* Since the hands of the witnesses should be first upon the criminals, *Deut* xvii 7 it became them, who appeared so zealous in punishing the sins of others, to see that they were themselves free from the like or more infamous crimes, else it would be strangely absurd in them to execute the sentence, however just Thus he testified his approbation of the law, without encouraging their prosecution, and effectually saved his own reputation, without any express condemnation of the poor criminal *Note*, (1) When we have to deal with crafty foes, a cautious answer is but needful prudence (2) Before we condemn others, we should first take care that we are not chargeable with the same or greater evils than we censure in them

3 Whilst he stooped again to the ground, to give them a moment's time to pause, reflect, and retire, they, convicted by their consciences, slunk away, fearing lest their own sins should be brought to light to their confusion The eldest led the way, and the younger followed so that, all these indignant accusers being fled, the woman was left alone with Jesus, and those who before had been attending his ministry *Note*, (1) Many are more afraid of being *shamed* for their sins than of being *damned* (2) They, who, under convictions, fly from Christ, to get rid of them, instead of coming to him with humble confession to obtain pardon, wilfully destroy themselves

4 The trembling criminal still stood at his bar, when, lifting up himself, the merciful Judge questions her, *Where are those thine accusers? hath none condemned thee?* none offered to cast a stone at thee? *She saith, No man, Lord And Jesus said, Neither do I condemn thee go, and sin no more* As he came not upon earth to be a temporal judge, he left the sword of magistracy to the powers that ruled, and dismissed her, with a solemn warning, to beware of returning again unto wickedness, lest a more dreadful punishment than the civil magistrate could inflict should be her portion in the last great day *Note*, (1) Jesus is now a merciful Saviour he will shortly be an inexorable Judge Wise and happy are they who improve the moment of opportunity, and seek to him for mercy whilst mercy may be found (2) The greatest crimes, even adultery, may be forgiven to those who come by faith to a dying Redeemer, and wash their polluted souls in the fountain of his blood (3) Those whom Jesus pardons he saves not *in* their sin, but *from* them they go to lead a new life, whose sentence of death he reverses There is an inseparable union between justifying and sanctifying grace

12 ¶ Then spake Jesus again unto them, saying, [d] I
am the light of the world he that followeth me shall
not walk in darkness, but shall have the light of life
13 The Pharisees therefore said unto him, [e] Thou bear-
est record of thyself, thy record is not true 14 Jesus
answered and said unto them, Though I bear record of
myself, *yet* my record is true for I know whence I came,
and whither I go, but [f] ye cannot tell whence I come,
and whither I go 15 [g] Ye judge after the flesh, [h] I
judge no man 16 And yet if I judge, my judgment
is true for [i] I am not alone, but I and the Father that
sent me 17 It is also written in your law, that [k] the
testimony of two men is true 18 I am one that bear
witness of myself, and [l] the Father that sent me, beareth
witness of me 19 Then said they unto him, Where
is thy Father? Jesus answered, [m] Ye neither know me,
nor my Father [n] if ye had known me, ye should have
known my Father also 20 These words spake Jesus
in the treasury as he taught in the temple and [o] no man
laid hands on him, [p] for his hour was not yet come

d Isa xlix 6 Chap i 4 5, 9 & ix 5 & xii 35, 36
e Chap v 31
f Chap vii 28 & ix 29
g Chap vii 24
h Chap iii 17 & xii 47
i Ver 29
k Deut xvii 6 & xix 15 Heb x 28
l Chap v 37
m Chap xvi 3
n Chap xiv 9
o Chap vii 30
p Chap vii 8

v 12—20 Though the Pharisaical accusers of the adulteress had been confounded, some of their brethren remained to cavil at the gracious words which proceeded out of the Saviour's lips

1 Christ, re-assuming his discourse to the people, took occasion to speak of himself under the glorious character of the Sun of righteousness, *saying, I am the Light of the world* What the sun is to the world, that Christ must be to the soul Without him, universal spiritual darkness spreads over us its dreadful, baleful influence But *he that followeth me*, receives my gospel, and treads in my steps, *shall not walk in darkness*, the eyes of his mind shall be enlightened to know the truth, and his soul enabled for and directed in the practice of it, so that the darkness of error and sin shall not deceive and mislead him, *but he shall have the light of life*, the saving light of gospel grace here, and the eternal life of glory hereafter Blessed and happy are they who walk in this light of the Lord

3 He vindicates himself from the objection which the Pharisees made, who said, *Thou bearest record of thyself, thy record is not true* as if, in his own cause, these assertions were the mere boasts of self-commendation overlooking the testimony which John bore to his character, and the evidence which all the miracles Christ did brought along with them *He answered and said unto them, Though I bear record of myself, yet my record is true* If, in ordinary cases, a man's own testimony concerning himself may be well called in question, yet, in the case of messengers sent from God, the matter is otherwise The message he brought was itself a proof of his mission, considering the circumstances in which he appeared *For I know whence I came, and whither I go* He knew his own divine mission, and that, as he came from the Father, he must shortly return to him again, of which he had given them striking evidence in the miracles he had wrought *But ye cannot tell whence I come, nor whither I go*, wilfully blind to the truths he brought, and rejecting the credentials which he produced *Ye judge after the flesh*, and from the meanness of his outward appearance concluded, it was impossible that this should be he who should deliver Israel and they who thus judge after the flesh in spiritual matters are sure to be in the wrong *I judge no man*, not at all intermeddling in acts of judicial power, nor assuming any authority, nor was it his office at present to condemn any, but to seek and save that which was lost *And yet, if I judge, my judgment is true*, as being the searcher of all hearts, and beholding all things naked and open before him *for I am not alone, but I and the Father that sent me*, such an inseparable union subsisting between us, so that my judgment is according to his, and all I speak is in express conformity with his will, who gave me my mission *It is also written in your law, that the testimony of two men*, credible witnesses, *is true*, and sufficient for the proof of any matter of the greatest consequence *I am one that bear witness of myself*, as the Messiah, which my doctrine and works declare me to be, *and the Father that sent me beareth witness of me*, not only in all the prophecies of old, but in repeated voices heard from heaven Here therefore are two witnesses of divine authority to prove the truth

4 The Pharisees, with contempt of his pretensions, replied, *Where is thy father?* what, Joseph the carpenter? is he the witness? *Jesus answered, Ye neither know me, nor my Father*, are not acquainted with my divine original *if ye had known me*, as the Son of God, *ye should have known my Father also*, as we are one in nature, counsel, and operation the knowledge of me include the knowledge of my Father, as I am the brightness of his glory, and the express image of his person Thus freely and fully doth Jesus assert his eternal power, Godhead, and unity with the Father *These words spake Jesus in the treasury, as he taught in the temple and no man laid hand on him, for his hour was not yet come* And, till God's decreed and appointed moment comes, the malice of persecutors and the rage of devils are alike impotent and vain

21 Then said Jesus again unto them, I go my way,
and [q] ye shall seek me, and shall die in your sins whi-
ther I go, ye cannot come 22 Then said the Jews,
Will he kill himself? because he saith, Whither I go,
ye cannot come 23 And he said unto them, [r] Ye are
from beneath, I am from above ye are of this world,
I am not of this world 24 I said therefore unto you,
that ye shall die in your sins [s] for if ye believe not that
I am *he*, ye shall die in your sins 25 Then said they
unto him, Who art thou? And Jesus saith unto them,
Even *the same* that I said unto you from the beginning
26 I have many things to say, and to judge of you
but [t] he that sent me is true, and [u] I speak to the world
those things which I have heard of him 27 They
understood not that he spake to them of the Father
28 Then said Jesus unto them, When ye [x] have lift up
the Son of man, [y] then shall ye know that I am *he*, and
that I do nothing of myself, but as my Father hath
taught me, I speak these things 29 And [z] he that
sent me, is with me [b] the Father hath not left me alone
for [c] I do always those things that please him 30 As
he spake these words, [d] many believed on him

q Chap vii 34 & xiii 33
r Chap iii 31
s Ver [illegible]
t Chap vii 28
u Chap iii 32 & xv 15
x Chap iii 14 & xii 32
y Rom i 4
z Chap xiv 10, 30
a Chap xiv 10
b Ver 16 Chap xvi 32
c Chap iv 34 & v 30
d Chap vii 31

v 21—30 Words of terror to awaken their consciences, as well as words of grace to engage their hearts, did the Redeemer employ, if any thing might at last effectually work upon them

1 He warns them of their approaching ruin, and the cause of it *Then said Jesus again unto them, I go my way*, to the Father, *and ye shall seek me*, when your calamities overtake you, and shall long for the Messiah to save you from them, *and shall die in your sins*, or *your sin*, under the guilt of all your other iniquities, and especially that capital one of unbelief, and rejection of me and my gospel *whither I go, ye cannot come*, the gates of eternal life and glory will be for ever barred against you, and no entrance permitted you into those regions of blessedness, which I shall shortly be *Note*, (1) Unbelief is the damning evil It is the sin against our remedy, and necessarily leads men to destruction (2) They who refuse to embrace the Saviour in faith and love, and to follow him in holy obedience here, must never expect admission into his eternal kingdom of glory hereafter

2 The Jews, instead of trembling before the warnings of Jesus, treated them with derision, saying, *Will he kill himself?* to get rid of his enemies, and be out of their reach

3 In reply to their malicious suggestion, he answers, *Ye are from beneath*, earthly and sensual in your spirit and temper, and therefore cannot understand and follow me, *I am from above*, celestial in my original, and my conversation in heaven *ye are of this world*, affecting and pursuing its honours, interests, pleasures, and esteem, *I am not of this world*, dead to it in my affections, and looking forward to that blessed world to which I go *I said therefore unto you, that ye shall die in your sins*, as you must infallibly do, if you continue in your present state of impenitence, worldly-mindedness, and unbelief *for if ye believe not that I am he*, the eternal, unchangeable Jehovah, or the Messiah, the Light of the world, the Saviour of the miserable, *ye shall die in your sins*, no pardon or redemption being possible for those who reject the grace of the gospel Jesus alone can deliver the soul from the guilt, power, and punishment of sin, and out of him there is no help or hope of salvation

4 With a repetition of the like taunt as before, they replied, *Who art thou?* that talkest such great things, and threatenest so highly? *Jesus saith unto them, Even the same that I said unto you from the beginning*, the great object of faith since the first promise was given, and the same Messiah which from the beginning of my ministry I have proved myself to be. *I have many things to say and to judge of you*, to upbraid your infidelity, and prove the inexcusableness of your impenitence, these are reserved for an after-reckoning *but he that sent me is true*, both in fulfilling his promises and his threatenings, *and I speak to the world those things which I have heard of him*, both the purposes of his grace to his people, and the inevitable ruin which will attend those who reject his Christ, and which the issue will infallibly prove to be a true testimony *They understood not that he spake to them of the Father*, their hearts were hardened in sin, and their minds blinded by prejudice *Note*, The plainest truths of God, the most solemn warnings of danger, are not apprehended nor understood The God of this world hath blinded the minds of sinners, and they continue stupid and insensible

5 Christ refers them to a future day for a full conviction of what at present they will not believe *When ye have lift up the Son of man* upon a cross, as the brasen serpent, in consequence of which sufferings, his exaltation to glory would follow, *then shall ye know that I am he*, the true Messiah, as the wonders which happened during his hanging upon the cross bespoke him

to be, as was proved by his resurrection and ascension to glory, as many of them to their eternal comfort perceived, when by his Spirit their souls were converted, and turned to him whom they had pierced, and as the rest would terribly feel, when shortly he should take vengeance on their nation, cut them off by the Roman sword, and doom them to eternal misery. Then shall ye be convinced, saith he, *that I do nothing of myself*, without divine authority, *but as the Father hath taught me, I speak these things*, in exact correspondence with the instructions that, as man and mediator, I have received from him, *and he that sent me, is with me*, Christ being in nature and essence one with the Father, and having his presence, power, and Spirit, to enable him for, and encourage him in, the great work of redemption. *The Father hath not left me alone*, without the clearest demonstrations of his favour and regard, *for I do always those things that please him*, and therefore he cannot but take the highest complacency in me and my undertaking, which is in such exact conformity to his will, and ultimately tends so highly to advance his glory. *Note*, (1.) All must know, by happy or dreadful experience, that Jesus is the Christ; they who are not convinced of it by his word and Spirit, will prove it in the judgments he will inflict upon them. (2.) However much we may be deserted of the world, God will never leave nor forsake his faithful servants, and we can want neither company nor comfort, if his blessed presence be with us.

6. Great was the effect produced by these words. *As he spake these, many believed on him*, as come with a divine commission from God, and the true Messiah; at least, so far were they convinced, as to make a profession of their faith, though by the sequel it seems, that many of them were far from being sound converts. *Note*, Many for a time make a fair profession, whose hearts are not right with God, and who abide not steadfastly in his covenant.

31 Then said Jesus to those Jews which believed on
him, [e] If ye continue in my word, *then* are ye my disci-
ples indeed; 32 And ye shall know the truth, and
[f] the truth shall make you free. 33 ¶ They answered
him, [g] We be Abraham's seed, and were never in bon-
dage to any man: how sayest thou, Ye shall be made
free? 34 Jesus answered them, Verily, verily I say
unto you, [h] Whosoever committeth sin, is the servant of
sin. 35 And [i] the servant abideth not in the house for
ever: *but* the Son abideth ever. 36 [k] If the Son there-
fore shall make you free, ye shall be free indeed. 37
I know that ye are Abraham's seed; but [l] ye seek to kill
me, because my word hath no place in you.

e Heb. iii. 14. f Ver. 30. Rom. vi. 14, 18. & viii. 2. Jam. i. 25. g Mat. iii. 9. Ver. 39. h Rom. vi. 16, 20. 2 Pe. ii. 19. i Gen. xxi. 10. Gal. iv. 30. k Rom. viii. 2. Gal. v. 1. l Chap. vii. 19, 25, 32.

v. 31—37. We have here,

1. Christ's address to those Jews who professed to believe in him. *If ye continue in my word*, faithfully adhere to the gospel and the profession of it, unmoved with any opposition, and cordially prove your obedience to it in all holy conversation and godliness, *then are ye my disciples indeed*; I will own and accept you as such: *and ye shall know the truth*, obtain deeper and clearer discoveries of it, *and the truth shall make you free*, free from guilt, through the knowledge of the Redeemer's blood and righteousness, free from the dominion of sin and Satan, through the powerful operations of the Spirit, free from ignorance and error, through divine teaching, free from the bondage of the law and corruption, and brought into the glorious liberty of the Son of God. *Note*, (1.) The proof of true discipleship is seen in our *abiding* faith in, and adherence to, Jesus and his gospel. Many profess to believe for a while, who, in time of temptation, fall away. (2.) Our measure of attainments in knowledge and grace is very imperfect here, we have need to be looking up continually for daily supplies of divine light and love, and Christ's faithful followers shall find both abundantly dispensed to them from on high. (3.) That is true liberty, when our souls are brought to God's happy service, and delivered from the servitude of sin and Satan.

2. The Jews who heard him, felt their pride hurt by the insinuation of their subjection, which Christ intimated, and with indignation replied, *We are Abraham's seed, and were never in bondage to any man: how sayest thou, Ye shall be made free?* They boast of their descent from that patriarch, as their great honour, and with the strangest effrontery profess to have enjoyed uninterrupted liberty as their birthright and privilege, when it was so notorious, that under a multitude of enemies they had suffered the most afflictive servitude and captivity, and were now a conquered province of the Roman Empire.

3. Waving the discussion of the point relative to their civil liberty, concerning which he spake not, he lets them know there is a more dreadful servitude than that of the body, even of the immortal soul, under the yoke of sin and Satan. *Whosoever committeth sin, is the servant of sin*, he that makes a practice of sin, and lives habitually under the power of it, is the worst of slaves, whatever his civil liberties may be, how ever noble his descent, or high his church privilege. *And the servant abideth not in the house always*, but as the son of the bondwoman was cast out of Abraham's family, so would all the impenitent and unbelieving among the Jews be cut off from the church of God, as every unfaithful professor will be, who continues to live in his sins, however high an opinion he may have entertained of himself, or however respectfully others may have thought of him: *but the Son abideth ever*, he who is Abraham's promised seed emphatically, the true Isaac, his is the inheritance, and all who claim under him, as the sons of God by faith, have a sure title to a place among the houshold of God. *If the Son therefore shall make you free*, the Son of God, the Lord of the house, where Moses himself was but a servant, *ye shall be free indeed*, not with that *imaginary* freedom, of which the Jews boasted, but (ὄντως) that *real* liberty which only Jesus can give to the fallen, corrupt, and guilty soul. He makes his people free, (1.) From the arrests *of the law*, by an obedience unto death he hath satisfied all its demands, and found a ransom for us. (2.) From *corruption*, his Spirit both delivers us from the blindness of error, and from the power of sin. (3.) As free-born sons, we are adopted into God's family, enjoy all the privileges, to which perfect obedience in our own persons could have entitled us, and have an assured title to the eternal kingdom.

4. He applies the case to them. *I know that ye are Abraham's seed*, but, very unlike that patriarch in your spirit and temper, *ye seek to kill me*, and the reason is, *because my word hath no place in you*, your hearts are steeled against it, you cannot bear the humbling truths I deliver, and your pride, prejudices, and self-righteousness, effectually prevent their influence, and where this is the case with any soul, there the gospel is as water spilt on the ground, utterly unprofitable.

38 [m] I speak that which I have seen with my Father:
and ye do that which ye have seen with your father.
39 They answered and said unto him, [n] Abraham is
our father. Jesus saith unto them, [o] If ye were Abra-
ham's children, ye would do the works of Abraham.
40 But now [p] ye seek to kill me, a man that hath told
you the truth, which I have heard of God: this did not
Abraham. 41 Ye do the deeds of your father. Then
said they to him, We be not born of fornication; [q] we
have one Father, *even* God. 42 Jesus said unto them,
[r] If God were your Father, ye would love me: for I
proceeded forth, and came from God; [s] neither came I
of myself, but he sent me. 43 [t] Why do ye not un-
derstand my speech? *even* because ye cannot hear my
word. 44 [u] Ye are of *your* father the devil, and the
lusts of your father ye will do: he was a murderer from
the beginning, and [x] abode not in the truth, because
there is no truth in him. When he speaketh a lie, he
speaketh of his own: for he is a liar, and the father of
it. 45 And because I tell *you* the truth, ye believe me
not. 46 Which of you convinceth me of sin? And
if I say the truth, why do ye not believe me? 47 [y] He
that is of God, heareth God's words: ye therefore hear
them not, because ye are not of God.

m Chap. v. 19, 30. & xiv. 10. n Mat. iii. 9. Ver. 33. o Rom. ii. 28. & ix. 7. Gal. iii. 7, 29. p Chap. vii. 19. Ver. 37. q Isa. lxiii. 16. Mal. i. 6. r 1 John v. 1. s Chap. v. 43. & vii. 28, 29. t Chap. vii. 17. u Mat. xiii. 38. 1 John iii. 8. x Jude 6. y 1 John iv. 6.

v. 38—47. Christ proceeds in his discourse.

1. He points out the cause of the contrariety of sentiments which subsisted between them. *I speak that which I have seen with my Father*, as perfectly knowing his mind and will, and from eternity acquainted with all his councils and designs; *and ye do that which ye have seen with your father*, your works shew whose children you are, whose example you imitate, and under what father's tuition you have been brought up.

2. Fired with resentment, as if he reflected upon their progeny, they boasted their descent from Abraham, the friend of God, of whom they could surely learn nothing that was evil. Jesus answered them, *If ye were Abraham's children, ye would do the works of Abraham*; but, very opposite to his faith and obedience is your conduct, *ye seek to kill me, a man that hath told you the truth, which I have heard from God*, a truth so needful to be known, that I am the very promised Messiah, the eternal Son of the Father: *this did not Abraham*, his submission to the first notice of God's will was eminent, and such a murderous spirit, as to contrive the death of any man, much less of a messenger sent from heaven, never dwelt in his bosom; therefore it is sufficiently evident, that your relation to him can never be proved by your temper; *for ye do the deeds of your father*, and who that is, let your conduct tell. *Note*, It is often prudent, in conveying unpleasing truths, to state the premises, and let the persons themselves draw the conclusion.

3. With indignation they replied, perceiving he spoke not in a literal but figurative sense, *We be not born of fornication*: are not idolaters, nor their descendants, have never gone a whoring from God: *we have one Father*, whom we worship and adore, *even* Jehovah, the only living and true *God*. But all, they who flatter themselves they have the true religion, because they make profession of it, whilst their practice is utterly contradictory to sound godliness, deceive their own souls.

4. Christ

4 Christ shews them their fatal mistake. God could not be their Father, whilst their ways were so perverse before him. *If God were your Father, you would love me*, and embrace the truth I deliver to you, *for I proceeded forth, and came from God*, as my Father, and one in nature with him: *neither came I of myself, but he sent me*, to accomplish the great designs of his grace, as the redeemer of his elect children. *Why do ye not understand my speech?* The reason is, *because ye cannot hear my words*, your hearts are averse to the truth, and prejudiced against me, and how then can God be your Father? *Ye are of your father the devil*, he is the spirit which worketh in you, *and the lusts of your father ye will do*, obstinately bent on following the dictates of pride, malice, and envy, the grand characteristics of this foul fiend. *He was a murderer from the beginning*, seducing man in paradise from his allegiance to God, he thereby exposed the whole human race to death spiritual, temporal, and eternal; and ever since, from the days of righteous Abel, at his instigation have those horrid deeds of bloodshed and murder been committed, under which the earth groans. *And he abode not in the truth*, he lost the purity and rectitude of his own nature, and then by a daring lie tempted man to disbelieve the divine commination respecting the forbidden fruit, *because there is no truth in him*, his kingdom is supported by falshood and delusion; all the errors and heresies that rend the church, and all the vain hopes that lull sinners to ruin, derive from him their origin. *When he speaketh a lie, he speaketh of his own, for he is a liar, and the father of it*: all his temptations from the beginning have been, and are, a tissue of falshoods, his own devising, the genuine offspring of his apostate spirit: and as he is in himself faithless in his nature, so is he the father of all lies and liars; they are his children, they bear his strong and striking lineaments, and evidence clearly from whom they are descended; they obey his commands, and follow his example. *And because I tell you the truth*, the truth of my gospel, mission, and divine character, *ye believe me not*: such is your miserable infatuation and delusion, that ye are more disposed to believe the devil's lie, than God's truth, so enslaved are you by this wicked spirit. *Which of you convinceth me of sin?* either of immorality in conduct, or unsoundness in doctrine? *And if I say the truth, why do ye not believe me?* when every circumstance conspires to prove my mission divine, how inexcusable is your obstinacy? *He that is of God*, as you pretend to be, *heareth God's word*, desirous to know, and willing to obey it: *ye therefore hear them not*, and pay no regard to what I declare to you, *because ye are not of God*, are not his children, nor influenced by his spirit, but under the power and dominion of the god of this world, the spirit that worketh in the children of disobedience. *Note*, (1) They who have God for their Father, will shew it by an unfeigned love to the Lord Jesus Christ, by a solemn attention to his word, and faithful obedience to his will. (2) They who do the devil's works, are infallibly the devil's children. By their fruit ye shall know them. Pride, envy, malice, enmity against those that are good, lying, rage, &c. these are the features of Satan, and mark his genuine offspring. (3) Christ's ministers and people, like their Master, must give diligence to keep a conscience void of offence, that their most envenomed enemies may have no evil thing *justly* to say of them. (4) They who slight and disregard the Redeemer's gospel, and those who preach it, despise not men, but God, and therein prove the unsubdued enmity and apostacy of their hearts.

48 Then answered the Jews, and said unto him, Say
we not well, that thou art a Samaritan, and [z] hast a de-
vil? 49 Jesus answered, I have not a devil; but I
honour my Father, and ye do dishonour me. 50 And
[a] I seek not mine own glory: there is one that seeketh
and judgeth. 51 Verily, verily I say unto you, [b] If a
man keep my saying, he shall never see death. 52.
Then said the Jews unto him, Now we know that thou
hast a devil. [c] Abraham is dead, and [d] the prophets;
and thou sayest, If a man keep my saying, he shall never
taste of death. 53 Art thou greater than our father
Abraham, which is dead? and the prophets are dead:
whom makest thou thyself? 54 Jesus answered, [e] If I
honour myself, my honour is nothing: [f] it is my Father
that honoureth me; [g] of whom ye say that he is your
God: 55 Yet [h] ye have not known him; but I know
him: and if I should say, I know him not, I should be
a liar like unto you: but I know him, and keep his
saying. 56 Your father Abraham rejoiced to see my
day: and he saw it, and was glad. 57. Then said the
Jews unto him, Thou art not yet fifty years old, and
hast thou seen Abraham? 58 Jesus said unto them,
Verily, verily I say unto you, Before Abraham was, I
am. 59 Then took they up stones to cast at him: but
Jesus hid himself, and went out of the temple, going
through the midst of them, and so passed by.

z Chap. vii. 20. & x. 20.
a Chap. v. 41. & vii. 18.
b Chap. v. 24. & xi. 26.
c Heb. xi. 13.
d Zech. i. 5.
e Chap. v. 31.
f Chap. xvi. 14. & xvii. 1, 5.
g Ver. 41.
h Chap. vii. 28, 29.

v. 48—59. The Jews, cut to the heart at this sharp rebuke, were exceedingly exasperated.

1 They began to abuse him with the most virulent language. *Say we not well, that thou art a Samaritan, and hast a devil?* They would represent him as an enemy to their religion and nation, as one in league with Satan, to whose influence they ascribed the miracles Christ performed; or as a lunatic and madman, possessed by this spirit, thus to call the children of Abraham the children of the devil. *Note*, It is no uncommon thing to hear the best of men branded with the most opprobrious names, abused as satanical, or treated with contempt as madmen; but wisdom is justified of all her children.

2 Christ meekly replies to so unjust and malicious an accusation, *I have not a devil*, neither act in concert with him, nor am possessed by him: *but I honour my Father*, far from derogating from his honour, as you would infer from my pretensions, the great end I propose in all my words and works is to advance it, *and I seek not my own glory*, in contradistinction to him; *there is one that seeketh and judgeth*, that will secure me an interest in the hearts of his people, will vindicate my injured character, and avenge the contempt and indignity you cast upon me. But, however slightly and meanly you may think of me, *verily, verily I say unto you*, is the most assured truth, *If a man keep my saying*, really believes, embraces, and obeys my gospel, *he shall never see death*, the second, the eternal death, the wages of sin. *Note*, (1) The most unprovoked abuse must be returned with mildness; the wrath of man worketh not the righteousness of God. (2) When we are conscious our design is the advancement of the divine glory, we need not be concerned about any malignant interpretations put on our conduct. (3) They are disciples indeed, who hear the word of God and *keep* it, embracing the promises as the most invaluable treasure, and obedient to the commands, as the approved rule of duty. (4) They who thus walk, have nothing to fear from death; the sting of it is taken away, the power of spiritual death is destroyed, and the grave is now become the gate of eternal life and glory.

3 More confirmed in their prejudices, instead of embracing the glorious privilege to which Christ invited them, they said, *Now we know that thou hast a devil*, and art stark mad to talk at so strange a rate. *Abraham is dead, and the prophets, and thou sayest, If a man keep my saying, he shall never taste of death. Art thou greater than our father Abraham, which is dead?* though so eminently the friend of God, *and the prophets are dead*, who were so highly favoured of him, *whom makest thou thyself?* what insufferable arrogance, to pretend a power of bestowing that immortality upon thy followers, which God himself never vouchsafed to his most eminent saints and servants?

4 Christ answers their cavil, and vindicates what he had asserted. *If I honour myself*, and assumed a character which I could not support with the most powerful evidence, *my honour is nothing*, and you might treat it as an empty boast: *but it is my Father that honoureth me*, bearing witness to my divine mission and authority, and expressing his full approbation of me as his Son, *of whom ye say that he is your God*, glorying, as descendants from the patriarchs, in your covenant relation to him. *Yet ye have not known him*, his nature and perfections, his mind and will; *but I know him*, most intimately acquainted with his person and counsels: *and if I should say, I know him not*, and should retract ought that I have advanced concerning the perfect knowledge I have of him from eternity, *I should be a liar like unto you: but I know him, and keep his saying*, always doing the things which please him, and acting in exact conformity with his mind and will. *Your father Abraham rejoiced*, or was very desirous, *to see my day*, and longed for my coming in the human nature to redeem the Israel of God; *and he saw it* by faith, tho' distant, yet surely approaching. He beheld in Isaac born, in the promise made to his seed, in Melchisedech, in the sacrifice of his son, and the ram provided in his stead, and in the visible appearance of the Lord himself, Gen. xviii. 2. in all these he beheld the incarnate Saviour, *and was glad*, exulted in the glorious hope of my appearing in the fulness of time. *Note*, (1) The affectation of honour, and courting men's admiration, is the sure evidence of not deserving it. (2) What was Christ's labour must be ours, to advance not our own, but God's glory. (3) Many profess to know God, who in works deny him, and against whom their very privileges and opportunities of knowing him will rise up to their greater condemnation. (4) The surest evidence of a right knowledge of God is our practical improvement of his sayings, and submitting to his blessed word and will. (5) The appearing of Christ is the desire and delight of the faithful, as it is the terror of the wicked; and he will come, and will not tarry. The Lord is at hand. (6) They who by faith now look to Jesus, and wait for him, shall soon see him face to face, and rejoice with joy unspeakable and full of glory.

5 With sovereign contempt do the Jews treat this declaration, perverting his word, as if he had asserted, that Abraham saw him in the flesh. *Thou art not yet fifty years old, and hast thou seen Abraham?* or he thee, when he hath been dead above two thousand years before? How ridiculous the pretension!

They

They judged of Chriſt's age probably by his look: inceſſant labours perhaps had marred his viſage, and brought on, before their time, the wrinkles of age.

6. He plainly aſſerts to them his eternal ſelf-exiſtence, as an anſwer to their objection: *Verily, verily I ſay unto you*, as the moſt certain and undoubted truth, *Before Abraham was* born, or had a being, *I am*, the ſame unchangeable Jehovah, who by this name made myſelf known to Moſes in the buſh, *Exod.* iii. 14. and therefore muſt be infinitely ſuperior and prior to Abraham.

7. Enraged beyond all bounds of forbearance at ſuch an aſſertion, which they regarded as the moſt impudent blaſphemy, the Jews *took up ſtones to caſt at him*, intending to murder him on the ſpot: *but Jeſus hid himſelf*, by his divine power probably withholding their eyes from perceiving him, *and went out of the temple, going through the midſt of them, and ſo paſſed by*, eſcaping their fury, becauſe his hour was not yet come. *Note*, (1.) It is prudent to hide ourſelves when we ſee the approaching danger. (2.) They who drive Chriſt from them, are juſtly abandoned by him to judicial blindneſs and hardneſs of heart.

CHAP. IX.

In this chapter we have, 1. *The miraculous cure of a man that was born blind*, ver. 1—7. 2. *The diſcourſes which were occaſioned by it*: (1.) *A diſcourſe of the neighbours among themſelves, and with the man*, ver. 8—12. (2.) *Between the Phariſees and the man*, ver. 13—34. (3.) *Between Chriſt and the poor man*, ver. 35—38. (4.) *Between Chriſt and the Phariſees*, ver. 39. ad finem.

1 AND as *Jeſus* paſſed by, he ſaw a man which
was blind from *his* birth. 2 And his diſciples
aſked him, ſaying, Maſter, who did ſin, this man, or his
parents, that he was born blind? 3 Jeſus anſwered,
Neither hath this man ſinned, nor his parents: [a] but
that the works of God ſhould be made manifeſt in him.
4 [b] I muſt work the works of him that ſent me, while
it is day: [c] the night cometh when no man can work.
5 As long as I am in the world, [d] I am the light of the
world. 6 When he had thus ſpoken, [e] he ſpat on the
ground, and made clay of the ſpittle, and [f] he anointed
the eyes of the blind man with the clay, 7 And ſaid
unto him, Go waſh in the pool of Siloam (which is by
interpretation, Sent.) He went his way therefore, and
waſhed, and came ſeeing.

[a] Chap. xi. 4.
[b] Chap. v. 19. & xvii. 4.
[c] Chap. xi. 9. & xii. 35.
[d] Chap. i. 5, 9. & viii. 12. & xii. 35, 46.
[e] Mark vii. 33. & viii. 23.
[f] Rev. iii. 18.

v. 1—7. The connection between this chapter and the foregoing ſeems to ſpeak as if the events here recorded immediately followed the preceding, though others ſuppoſe they happened at the diſtance of three months, thoſe being done at the feaſt of tabernacles, theſe at the feaſt of dedication, *Chap.* x. 22. We have here the cure of a poor blind man.

1. Jeſus obſerved him as he paſſed by, and knew his pitiable caſe, that he was *blind from his birth*. Such are we by nature, born in ſin, and conceived in wickedneſs, blind to every ſpiritual object, and utterly unable to find the way to eternal life and peace, till Jeſus paſſeth by, regards us with the eyes of his compaſſion, and is found by them who ſought him not.

2. The diſciples hereupon propoſed a curious queſtion to their Maſter: *Who did ſin, this man, or his parents, that he was born blind?* They ſeem to have entertained ſomething of the Pythagorean opinion concerning the pre-exiſtence and tranſmigration of ſouls from one body to another, and that the puniſhment of ſome ſignal offence in a former body might be puniſhed with the preſent affliction, or that the ſin of the parents might have entailed this judgment on their offſpring.

3. Chriſt anſwers their queſtion, by way of rectifying their miſtakes, and checking ſuch cenſorious concluſions. *Neither hath this man ſinned, nor his parents*, not that they had never committed actual ſin, nor been born in original corruption, but that it was not becauſe of any particular crime which either had committed, that this blindneſs was inflicted, *but that the works of God ſhould be made manifeſt in him*, and the Meſſiah be exalted in working a miraculous cure upon him. *Note*, (1.) We are not to judge of men's ſins by their ſufferings, it being often the lot of God's deareſt children to be moſt ſeverely afflicted. (2.) God has purpoſes of his own glory to anſwer in thoſe afflictive providences, the reaſon of which we cannot always diſcern, and this is at leaſt a ſufficient reaſon to reconcile us to them.

4. He gives the reaſon of his readineſs to help this poor man: *I muſt work the works of him that ſent me, while it is yet day*. He was ſent upon earth to do good to the bodies as well as ſouls of men, and therefore whilſt his perſonal miniſtry laſted, this was his proper employment. *The night cometh when no man can work*, when death ſhould put a period to his mortal days, his work of healing would then be done. *As long as I am in the world, I am the light of the world*, both corporally giving eyes to the blind, and enabling them to ſee the day, but more peculiarly in a ſpiritual ſenſe, as the Sun of Righteouſneſs ariſen with healing in his wings, the only true light that can guide the benighted ſouls of men into the paths of eternal life. *Note*, (1.) Life is our day of uſefulneſs, the moment in which we can ſerve and glorify God, we have need therefore to be diligent to redeem the time, and lay ourſelves out in his bleſſed ſervice. The night of death is near, when no work can be done for Chriſt and for ſouls, how precious then is every paſſing hour! (2.) What the ſun is to the natural world, that is Chriſt to the ſpiritual world: without him all is darkneſs, we know nothing of God, or ourſelves, our true happineſs, our proper work, or the great end of our being, and he muſt not only ſhine upon us as the light, but ſhine *into* our hearts, giving us alſo the faculty of viſion.

5. He gives ſight to the blind man, and this in a way different from the miracles he uſually performed, which were done with a word. *He ſpat on the ground, and made clay of the ſpittle, and he anointed the eyes of the blind man with the clay, and ſaid unto him, Go waſh in the pool of Siloam (which is by interpretation, Sent,)* and was the figure of the kingdom of the Meſſiah, (*Iſa.* viii. 6.) The blind man immediately obeyed his orders, and inſtantly felt his eyes opened, and his ſight perfectly reſtored. *Note*, (1.) The word of the goſpel is as this clay, unable of itſelf to communicate ſpiritual light to the ſoul, but, when applied by the powerful hand of Jeſus, becomes effectual to open the eyes of the mind. (2.) Obedient faith never fails of bringing relief. They who at Chriſt's command perſeveringly wait upon him in the way of his ordinances, will find their darkneſs enlightened, their doubts removed, their weakneſs ſtrengthened, their ſouls comforted.

8 ¶ The neighbours therefore, and they which be-
fore had ſeen him, that he was blind, ſaid, Is not this
he that ſat and begged? 9 Some ſaid, This is he:
others *ſaid*, He is like him: *but* he ſaid, I am *he*. 10.
Therefore ſaid they unto him, How were thine eyes
opened? 11 He anſwered and ſaid, A man that is
called Jeſus, made clay, and anointed mine eyes, and
ſaid unto me, Go to the pool of Siloam, and waſh:
and I went and waſhed, and I received ſight. 12 Then
ſaid they unto him, Where is he? He ſaid, I know
not.

v. 8—12. We have here,

1. The amazement of the neighbours, who could ſcarce perſuade themſelves that he was the ſame man whom they had ſeen ſtretched along, a poor blind beggar, by the way-ſide during ſo many years. Some affirmed it was the ſame man, others doubted, though they owned the reſemblance, till the man himſelf ended the diſpute, by affirming he was the very perſon. *Note*, They who have experienced the power of the healing grace of Jeſus upon their ſouls, ſhould be ready to own it, to the glory of his great name.

2. In anſwer to their queſtion, how he came to recover his ſight, after being blind from his birth, he informed them, that a man called Jeſus, had made clay, anointed his eyes, ſent him to the pool of Siloam to waſh, and that inſtantly thereupon he received his ſight. *Note*, If the opening of the eyes of a dark body awakened ſuch concern to enquire how it was done, much more ought the opening the eyes of the darkened minds of ſinners to be matter of aſtoniſhment, and awaken our notice and enquiries.

3. They hereupon put another queſtion to him, either out of deſire to know this wonderful perſon, or more probably with a malicious deſign to ſeize one whom the Phariſees had proſcribed. *Where is he? He ſaid, I know not*, Chriſt having departed when he had performed the cure. Thus in the work of grace upon the ſoul we ſee and feel the bleſſed change, though the hand which produces it is unſeen.

13 ¶ They brought to the Phariſees him that afore-
time was blind. 14 And it was the ſabbath-day when
Jeſus made the clay, and opened his eyes. 15 Then
again the Phariſees alſo aſked him how he had received
his ſight. He ſaid unto them, [g] He put clay upon
mine eyes, and I waſhed, and do ſee. 16 Therefore
ſaid ſome of the Phariſees, This man is not of God, be-
cauſe he keepeth not the ſabbath-day. Others ſaid, [h]
How can a man that is a ſinner do ſuch miracles? And
[i] there was a diviſion among them. 17 They ſay unto
the blind man again, What ſayeſt thou of him, that he
hath opened thine eyes? He ſaid, [k] He is a prophet.
18 But the Jews did not believe concerning him, that
he had been blind, and received his ſight, until they had
called the parents of him that had received his ſight.
19. And they aſked them, ſaying, Is this your ſon, who

[g] Ver. 6.
[h] Ver. 33. Chap. iii. 2.
[i] Chap. vii. 43. & x. 19.
[k] Chap. iv. 19. & vi. 14.

ye say was born blind? how then doth he now see?
20 His parents answered them and said, We know that
this is our son, and that he was born blind 21 But
by what means he now seeth, we know not or who
hath opened his eyes, we know not he is of age, ask
him, he shall speak for himself 22 These words spake
his parents, because they feared the Jews for the Jews
had agreed already, that if any man did confess that he
was Christ, ° he should be put out of the synagogue
23 Therefore said his parents, He is of age, ask him
24 Then again called they the man that was blind, and
said unto him, Give God the praise we know that this
man is a sinner 25 He answered and said, Whether
he be a sinner *or no*, I know not one thing I know,
that whereas I was blind, now I see 26 Then said they
to him again, What did he to thee? how opened he
thine eyes? 27 He answered them, I have told you
already, and ye did not hear wherefore would ye hear
it again? will ye also be his disciples? 28 Then they
reviled him, and said, Thou art his disciple, but we are
Moses' disciples 29 We know that God spake unto
Moses as for this fellow, ᵖ we know not from whence
he is 30 The man answered and said unto them,
Why, herein is a marvellous thing, that ye know not
from whence he is, and *yet* he hath opened mine eyes
31 Now we know that ᵍ God heareth not sinners but
if any man be a worshipper of God, and doth his will,
him he heareth 32 Since the world began was it not
heard that any man opened the eyes of one that was
born blind 33 ʳ If this man were not of God, he could
do nothing 34 They answered and said unto him,
ˢ Thou wast altogether born in sins, and dost thou teach
us? And they † cast him out

o Chap vii & xii & xix Acts — Chap xvi — r Ver 16 — Zech vii 11 — p Chap ix 14 — q Job xxvii 9 & xxxv 12 Psal xviii 41 & lxvi 18 Prov i 28 & xxviii 29 Isa i 15 Jer xi 11 & xiv 12 Ezek viii 18 Mic iii 4 Zech vii 13 — r Ver 16 — s Ver 2 — † Or excommunicated him

v 13—34 Far from being induced by this wondrous miracle to admire the person who wrought it, we find them incensed, and ready to prosecute Jesus as a criminal

1 Information is lodged against him before the rulers and the Pharisees, and the man who had been lately blind, is brought before the Sanhedrim, because *it was the sabbath day when Jesus made the clay, and opened his eyes*, which they regarded as a vile profanation of the day

2 The Pharisees interrogate the man concerning the matter, very loth to be persuaded of the fact, and determined to find fault where wonder and praise should have filled their hearts and tongues The man simply gives a narrative of his case and cure, which divided the sentiments of the council Some said, admitting the fact, *this man is not of God*, whatever miracles he may pretend to work, *because he keepeth not the sabbath-day*, for they regarded the making clay of the spittle as a violation of the strict rest enjoined by the tradition of the elders Others were loth to admit the fact, and would fain overthrow its evidence, fearing, lest if it was allowed to be true, the people would justly conclude that no wicked man could work such miracles, and thereby the authority of Jesus would be established or rather, *How can a man that is a sinner do such miracles?* are the words of some, such as Joseph and Nicodemus, who justly objected, that such miracles of grace were a strong evidence of a divine mission, and of God's approbation of the person who wrought them, and this occasioned some debate in the council Some of them hereupon demanded of the man what he thought of Jesus, and whether he had really opened his eyes The man from just experience owns, he could not but conclude he must be a prophet *Note*, (1) A poor blind beggar often judges more wisely concerning Christ and his character, than those who boast themselves masters in Israel (2) Some, even of the great, are called, and their conduct and testimony leaves the rest at least more inexcusable

3 They cite the father and mother of the man to appear at their bar, hoping to find some way to invalidate the credit of the miracle, but they only the more confirmed it, so easily can God take the wise in their own craftiness They question the parents of the man, *Whether this was their son? whether he was born blind?* and *how* he now came to see? To the two first questions they gave a clear and explicit answer He was their son, and had been born blind How he now saw was a question, which they cared not, for certain reasons, to enter into, and therefore rather referred the matter to their son, who was of age, and therefore able to answer for himself For the truth was, they were timorous and apprehensive of the consequences of making that open confession, which gratitude and truth demanded, because they were afraid they should be excommunicated, according to the Jewish law which the Sanhedrim had passed, that if any should own Jesus as the Messiah, he should be put out of the synagogue, and therefore they were willing to *trim*, and leave the question for their son to resolve *Note*, (1) The church's censures, when wicked men are in authority, have often been laid on her best friends (2) The true religion of Jesus will ever be a suffering cause, even where the public profession of it is made experimental godliness being only possessed by a few (3) When the profession of Christ exposes us to persecution, many are ready to conceal their religion in order to escape the cross

4 The council finding they got nothing to their satisfaction from the parents, again called the man himself, and unable to deny that a notable miracle was wrought, endeavour to rob the Lord Jesus of the honour due to him for it, saying, *Give God the praise*, who hath done the work, but *we know that this man is a sinner*, and therefore though God may please to use wicked instruments for the accomplishment of his purposes yet the praise is only due to himself So confidently do they speak, who, when challenged to bring a single proof of sin against Jesus, could not have the confidence to lodge one accusation *Note*, Many endeavour thus to supply the want of argument, with confident assertions of virulent abuse

5 The man replied, *Whether he be a sinner or no, I know not*, I will not determine, though I have all the reason in the world to believe the contrary but *one thing I know*, by happy experience, *that whereas I was blind, now I see*, and cannot be persuaded out of my senses *Note*, Many captious questions may be put to a gracious soul, in order to shake the ground of his confidence, but though he may not be able to give a distinct account how that spiritual change is wrought, which he experiences, yet he can say, I know it is wrought my understanding is enlightened, my heart is changed

6 Again they demand an answer to their questions, in hopes that through inadvertence or fear he might falter in his evidence, or vary from what he had advanced but his reply more exasperated them *He answered them, I have told you already*, distinctly and clearly, *and ye did not hear*, so as to regard or credit what I said *wherefore would ye hear it again?* to what purpose do you desire it? *will ye also be his disciples?* which he suggests either ironically, as knowing their aversion to Jesus, or seriously, as very willing to repeat what he had said a thousand times over, if they had the least disposition to hear and believe him, and come to Jesus as their Lord and Master

7 With rage and resentment at the mention of this, they bitterly revile him *Thou art his disciple*, a poor deluded wretch, *but we are Moses' disciples*, the followers of that great lawgiver of Israel, and who ought to be regarded as the guides in religious matters, and not to be taught by such a fellow as thee. *We know that God spake by Moses*, face to face on the Mount, and delivered the law under a divine commission but *as for this fellow, we know not from whence he is* in truth they desired not to know, and would not examine the evidence he had produced of his divine original and authority, for then they might have seen that there was a perfect agreement between Jesus and Moses, and that instead of the worthless fellow whom they scornfully rejected, this was the great Prophet, of whom Moses spake *Note*, (1) Many boast of these external privileges which only serve to aggravate their guilt (2) The servants of Jesus, like their master, have often been treated with insolence and contempt, as upstart fellows whom nobody knows (3) Many are branded as forsaking the good old religion, who are in fact the very espousers of it, by those who, resting upon the form of godliness, are utter strangers to the power of it

8 Once more the man replies, *Why, herein is a marvellous thing, that ye know not from whence he is*, when he hath given such an incontestible evidence of his divine mission by this amazing miracle, *and he hath opened mine eyes Now we know*, we, who are common people, and much more persons of your learning and sagacity, *that God heareth not sinners*, nor grants their prayers, much less would he enable them to perform miracles to support an imposture *but if any man be a worshipper of God, and doth his will, him he heareth*, and in the present case, the miracle Jesus hath wrought is an express testimony of God's approbation of him *Since the world began was it not heard that any man opened the eyes of one that was born blind*, such a thing, not the greatest of the prophets, not even Moses himself had ever performed *If*, therefore, *this man was not of God*, sent by him, and owned of him, *he could do nothing*, since it cannot be imagined God would enable a bad man to work such extraordinary miracles to carry on a bad cause, and promote a delusion A conclusion most reasonable and unanswerable, and drawn from premises the most evident and allowed *Note*, (1) An impenitent sinner, who persists in his iniquities, can never expect God will hear or answer his prayers (2) They who in spirit worship God, and in simplicity obey him, may be assured he will hear and grant all their petitions (3) A poor unlettered man, when taught of God, is able to confound the wisest doctors who are, with all their learning, strangers to divine teaching

9 Unable to answer his reasoning, they make up in violence and abuse what they want in argument *Thou wast altogether born in sin, and dost thou teach us?* Thou, a vile fellow, stigmatized from thy birth, as carrying a body inhabited by a vile soul, a poor ignorant wretch, a companion of beggars from thy birth, dost thou pretend to direct us, the guides and

rulers of the church, famed for wisdom and sanctity, and invested with chief authority What insolence, what arrogance is thine! *And they cast him out*, excommunicated him immediately, and cut him off from the congregation of Israel But the curse causeless shall not fall, the anathemas of church rulers, who abuse their authority, shall only light upon their own head *Note*, Proud worldly-wise men despise the poor, and think their own self-sufficiency above all need of others help and teaching whereas none who know themselves, will ever think themselves too wise to learn, or too good to mend

35 Jesus heard that they had cast him out, and
when he had found him, he said unto him, Dost thou
believe on [t] the Son of God? 36 He answered and
said, Who is he, Lord, that I might believe on him?
37 And Jesus said unto him, Thou hast both seen him,
and [u] it is he that talketh with thee 38 And he said,
Lord, I believe And he worshipped him

[t] Ps ii 7
[u] Mat iii 17 & xiv 33 & xxvi 63

v 35—38 The unjust act of these oppressive church rulers was soon noised abroad, and came to the ears of Jesus Hereupon we are told,

1 That Christ *found him*, he went in search of him, probably to encourage and comfort him under the persecution he suffered for the truth, *and said unto him, Dost thou believe on the Son of God*, the promised Messiah? *Note*, (1) Though wicked men may bust their power in casting out the faithful servants of Jesus, he will visit his outcasts with his love, and own them under their sufferings for his sake (2) True faith in the Son of God is the great attainment, to know and trust in him, is everlasting life

2 The poor man replied with earnestness, *Who is he, Lord, that I might believe on him?* I do expect him, and should be happy to find him, and wish for nothing more than to be directed to him, that I might by faith embrace him

3 Christ gives him a clear declaration of his own office and character *Thou hast both seen him, and it is he that talketh with thee*, whose power thou hast experienced, and is so much nearer to thee than thou art aware of, as he often is to his dear people, when they are afflicted and mourning his absence

4 That moment, by the power of Jesus, he was enabled to exercise divine faith in his heart, and he makes an open profession of it, *Lord, I believe, and he worshipped him*, giving him that divine honour which was due to him, as the eternal Son of God For they who truly know and believe in him, pay the same worship and honour to the Son, even as to the Father

39 ¶ And Jesus said, [x] For judgment I am come
into this world [y] that they which see not might see,
and that they which see, [z] might be made blind 40
And *some* of the Pharisees which were with him, heard
these words, and said unto him, [a] Are we blind also?
41 Jesus said unto them, [b] If ye were blind, ye should
have no sin but now ye say, We see, therefore your
sin remaineth.

[x] Chap v 22, 27 Chap iii 17 & xii 47
[y] Mat xiii 13
[z] Mat xi 25, 2 Cor iii 14
[a] Rom ii 19
[b] Chap xv 22—24

v. 39—41 Whilst Jesus so kindly encouraged and comforted the poor sufferer, he pronounces just judgment on his malicious persecutors

1 He gives a general account of the design of his mission *Jesus said, For judgment am I come into this world*, to fulfil the decree of God, revealing his truth for the illumination of some, and inflicting judicial blindness on others who rejected it *that they which see not, might see*, both corporally and spiritually, not only opening, by miracle, the eyes of men's bodies, but by his grace shining into the benighted souls of men *and that they which see*, conceit themselves wise and knowing in the things of God, *might be made blind*, given up for their pride and self-sufficiency to the blindness, hardness, and impenitence of their own hearts

2 The Pharisees supposing they were meant, with indignation replied, *Are we blind also?* Dare you insolently suggest, that we, the guides of the people, and the light of the land, are in darkness ourselves? *Note*, Nothing more offends the proud and self-righteous, than to call in question their knowledge or goodness and their passion on such occasions is a fresh proof of the truth of the charge laid against them

3 Christ answered, *If ye were blind*, really destitute of the means of knowledge, as the Gentile world, or, deeply sensible of your own native blindness, desired to be led unto me the light of life, *ye should have no sin*, none comparatively speaking, or you would have submitted to a better wisdom and righteousness than your own, whereby ye might have been justified from all things, and your sins be pardoned *but now ye say, We see*, conceited of your knowledge, and puffed up with pride, and *therefore your sin remaineth*, aggravated by the pretensions you make and the abuse of the means of grace you have enjoyed *Note*, None are so far from divine wisdom, as those who are wise in their own conceits, none so far from real goodness, as

they who value themselves on their own excellence Publicans and harlots shall enter the kingdom of heaven before such as these

CHAP X

In this chapter, we have, 1 Christ's parabolical discourse concerning himself, as the door of the sheep, and the shepherd of the sheep, ver 1—18 2 The various sentiments of people upon it, ver 19—21 3 The dispute Christ had with the Jews in the temple at the feast of dedication, ver 22—39 4 His departure into the country thereupon, ver 40—42

1 VERILY I say unto you, [a] He that entreth not
by the door into the sheepfold, but climbeth
up some other way, the same is a thief and a robber
2 But he that entreth in by the door, is the shepherd
of the sheep 3 To him the porter openeth and the
sheep hear his voice and he calleth his own sheep by
name, and leadeth them out 4 And when he putteth
forth his own sheep, he goeth before them, and the
sheep follow him for they know his voice 5 And
a stranger will they not follow, but will flee from him,
for they know not the voice of strangers 6 This parable
spake Jesus unto them but they understood not
what things they were which he spake unto them 7
Then said Jesus unto them again, Verily, verily I say
unto you, [b] I am the door of [c] the sheep 8 All that
ever came before me, [d] are thieves and robbers but the
sheep did not hear them 9 I am the door [e] by me if
any man enter in, he shall be saved, and [f] shall go in
and out, and [g] find pasture 10 [h] The thief cometh not,
but for to steal, and to kill, and to destroy I am come
[i] that they might have life, and that they might have *it*
more abundantly 11 [k] I am the good shepherd [l] the
good shepherd giveth his life for the sheep 12 But he
that is an hireling, and not the shepherd, whose own the
sheep are not, seeth the wolf coming, and [m] leaveth the
sheep, and fleeth and the wolf catcheth them, and
scattereth the sheep 13 The hireling fleeth, because he is
an hireling, and careth not for the sheep 14 I am the
good shepherd, [n] and know my *sheep*, and [o] am known of
mine 15 [p] As the Father knoweth me, even so know
I the Father and I lay down my life for the sheep
16 And [q] other sheep I have, which are not of this fold
them also I must bring, and they shall hear my voice,
and [r] there shall be one fold, *and* one shepherd. 17
Therefore doth my Father love me, [s] because I lay down
my life, that I might take it again 18 No man taketh
it from me, but I lay it down of myself I have power
to lay it down, and [t] I have power to take it again
[u] This commandment have I received of my Father

[a] Heb. x 4
[b] Chap xiv 6 Eph ii 18
[c] Ezek xxxiv 31
[d] Jer xxiii 1 & 6
[e] Chap xiv 6
[f] Zech x 12
[g] Ps xxiii 2 Ezek xxxiv 14
[h] 1 Pet ii 25
[i] Ezek xxxiv 15
[k] Isa xl 11 Ezek xxxiv 12 & xxxvii 24 Heb xiii 20 1 Pet v 4
[l] Acts xx 28
[m] Zech xi 16 17
[n] Chap xvii 18 2 Tim ii 19
[o] 2 Tim i 12
[p] Mat xi 27
[q] Isa lvi 8
[r] Ezek xxxvii 22 Eph ii 14 1 Pet ii 25
[s] Isa liii 8 12 Heb ii 9
[t] Chap ii 19
[u] Acts ii 24

v 1—18 As the Pharisees and priests arrogated to themselves the dominion over the church, and boasted of their authority, wisdom, and sanctity, as the only true pastors, traducing Jesus as an impostor, because he acted without their ordination Christ here, in a parable, warns the people against these faithless pastors

1 He proposes a parable to them, borrowed from a shepherd and his flock *Verily, verily I say unto you*, with deepest solemnity, and most infallible certainty, *He that entreth not by the door into the sheepfold, but climbeth up some other way, the same is a thief and a robber*, such a clandestine entry shews the ill design on which he comes *The sheepfold is the church of God*, where the faithful are united together in love, and share in the provision of gospel-ordinances provided for them, *the door is Christ* himself, by whom the faithful enter, and who by his spirit calls and qualifies his ministers for their work *The thieves* are those who intrude into the ministry without a divine call, influenced by the hopes of the honours and profits of the service, instead of being *inwardly moved by the Holy Ghost*, and animated by love to Jesus, and zeal for immortal souls *But he that entreth in by the door, is the shepherd of the sheep*, whom Jesus calls and qualifies for his office, and who, with fidelity and diligence attends, feeds, and watches over those gracious souls, whom the Saviour commits to his care *To him the porter openeth, and the sheep hear his voice* the spirit of God makes his ministry successful, and opens the hearts of sinners to receive the gospel he preaches *and he calleth his own sheep by name*, the Lord knoweth those that are his, and by his effectual power upon their hearts, calls them to himself by the instrumentality of his under-shepherds, who also are personally and particularly acquainted with their own peculiar flocks *and leadeth them out* into green pastures of ordinances, and beside the waters of comfort *And when he putteth*

putteth forth his own sheep, he goeth before them as their shepherd, to protect them from danger, *and the sheep follow him*, close at his footsteps, imitating his example, *for they know his voice*, they have a discernment of gospel-truth, and approve of, and submit to his teachings. *But a stranger will they not follow, for they know not the voice of strangers*, they discover the false principles or bad practices of those who set up for pretended guides, and will not put their souls under their tuition, or be influenced by their examples.

2. The Jews understood not the meaning of his discourse, and therefore Christ more explicitly opens to them his meaning.

(1.) He is *the door*, the only way of access to God and glory is through him, and none can enter into the ministry but by his call, and under his commission. All that went before, with pretensions to the character of the Messiah, and those who, without an eye to him, exercised their ministry, or who endeavoured, as the Scribes and Pharisees of that age did, to prejudice the people against the true Messiah's character, all these were thieves and robbers, intruders into the office to which God never called them, and robbing him of his glory: but from their delusive teachings the Lord preserved his own people, so that they were not deceived by them, nor paid regard to the teachings of these false shepherds. But of himself Christ saith, *I am the door* of access to, and acceptance with God; *by me*, through faith in my name, *if any man enter in, he shall be saved* from sin, from the condemning guilt and enslaving power of it, from the law, and the curse which it pronounces; from Satan, and all the powers of evil, from deceivers, and all their wiles; yea, he shall be saved with an everlasting salvation, *and shall go in and out, and shall find pasture*, during his journey through life, he shall have free access to the ordinances, possess a glorious liberty in his spirit, be safe under the shepherd's constant care, and be fed with the sweetest refreshments which the grace of the gospel ministers. Blessed and happy are they, who thus walk under the constant guard and guidance of the divine Redeemer.

(2.) He is *the shepherd*, the great, the good, the true shepherd.

[1.] The gracious design which he is come upon, is quite different from that of the false teachers. They, by their pernicious heresies, steal away the heart of the unwary, prejudice them against the truth, and whilst they promise them life and salvation, really murder their souls, and seek by persecutions to destroy or disperse the flock of Christ, which they cannot deceive: whilst he is come, that his people and the sheep of his pasture may have life, the life of grace here, and of glory hereafter: yea, that they might have it *more abundantly*, fuller assurance of it than they ever had before, or in a more abundant measure, and with greater glory and advantage than even Adam in innocence possessed.

[2.] The way in which he obtains these privileges for his people, is by his death for them. *I am the good shepherd*, eminently so, and as the greatest instance of it, *the good shepherd giveth his life for the sheep*, as I am ready to do, dying in their stead to redeem them from sin, death, and hell. And herein Christ's love towards them is in the most convincing manner evidenced. *But he that is an hireling, and not the shepherd*, who serves for lucre merely, not for the love of souls, *whose own the sheep are not*, regarding them with none of that affectionate concern which the owner feels; such a one *seeth the wolf coming, and leaveth the sheep*, whenever danger approaches, he deserts his post, *and the wolf catcheth them, and scattereth the sheep*, perverting and seducing them. *The hireling fleeth, because he is an hireling, and careth not for the sheep*: behold the true character of the false and faithless shepherd. (1.) He is one who serves for hire, and makes the ministry his trade. (2.) He feels no concern about the souls of men, and if he gets the revenues of the church, concerns himself not if the devil runs away with his flock. (3.) He never exposes himself to any danger nor labours in the ministry, only careful about his own safety, and consulting his own ease. The very reverse is the character of a good minister: like his master, his bosom glows with desire after the salvation of men's souls; he is ready to spend and be spent in the service of the ministry; he labours willingly, not for hire but from principle, and no dangers can deter him from his duty, or drive him to desert his post.

[3.] As the good shepherd, he is acquainted intimately with his flock and their concerns, and takes care of them. *I am the good shepherd, and know my sheep, and am known of mine*; Christ knows particularly those that are his, he regards them with tenderest affection, takes cognizance of all their wants, and kindly relieves and supplies them: and he is known by his people as the great object of their faith and hope, the author of their joy and happiness. *As the Father knoweth me, even so know I the Father*; such intimate knowledge of each other as subsists between the father and the son, subsists also between Christ and his people: *and I lay down my life for the sheep*, to testify his love, and to accomplish the eternal designs of grace towards them. *And other sheep I have, which are not of this fold*, out of the pale of the Jewish church, *them also I must bring*, according to the eternal decrees of the covenant of grace, from their guilt, misery, and ruin, into a state of favour and acceptance with God; *and they shall hear my voice*, effectually wrought upon by the mighty and irresistible influences of the divine Spirit, *and there shall be one fold, and one shepherd*, when all true believers, both Jews and Gentiles, shall be united in one glorious church, under their common head Christ Jesus, and share the same blessings and privileges. *Therefore doth my Father love me, because I lay down my life*, highly well pleased in my undertaking, whereby such glory would accrue to him, and salvation certain and eternal be obtained for the redeemed: for I lay it down *that I might take it again*, rising for their justification, and thus effectually triumphing over all their foes. *No man taketh it from me*, neither force nor fraud avail any thing, till my own time comes, *but I lay it down of myself*, voluntarily, with my own consent. *I have power to lay it down*, a right and authority to lay it down, as a satisfaction to divine justice, *and I have power to take it again*, having made the atonement, by my own almighty power I will quicken my dead body, and raise it to eternal life and glory. *This commandment have I received of my Father*, according to the eternal counsels between them, he had engaged thus to die for his people, and herein he delighted to do the will of God.

19 ¶ [x] There was a division therefore again among
the Jews for these sayings. 20 And many of them said,
[y] He hath a devil, and is mad; why hear ye him? 21
Others said, These are not the words of him that hath a
devil. [z] Can a devil [a] open the eyes of the blind?

[x] Chap. vii. 43. & ix. 16. [y] Chap. vii. 20. & viii. 48, 52. [z] Exod. iv. 11. Psal. xciv. 9. & cxlvi. 8. [a] Chap. ix. 6, 7.

v. 19—21. The discourse of Jesus gave occasion for warm debates among the Jews, whose sentiments were greatly divided concerning him.

1. Many, who were his enemies, cried out, *He hath a devil, and is mad; why hear ye him?* Can you be so weak and deluded, as to attend to such absurd and blasphemous nonsense? Thus doth the world often scoff at the serious discourses of Christ's faithful ministers, and ridicule and revile those who pay attention to their preaching: but we should neither be threatened nor laughed out of our religion.

2. Others entertained very different sentiments, and said very sensibly, *These are not the words of him that hath a devil*; the nature of his doctrine, and his manner of speaking, savour nothing of insanity, nor can possibly tend to advance, but to destroy Satan's kingdom. Besides, *Can a devil open the eyes of the blind?* Can a madman, or much less a bad man, under diabolical influence, perform such a miracle? The supposition is absurd and incredible. It evidently appeared that this was the finger of God.

22 ¶ And it was at Jerusalem [b] the feast of the dedi-
cation, and it was winter. 23 And Jesus walked in the
temple in [c] Solomon's porch. 24 Then came the Jews
round about him, and said unto him, How long dost
thou † make us to doubt? If thou be the Christ, tell us
plainly. 25 Jesus answered them, I told you, and ye
believed not: [d] the works that I do in my Father's name,
they bear witness of me. 26 [e] But ye believe not, be-
cause ye are not my sheep, as I said unto you. 27 [f] My
sheep hear my voice, and I know them, and they follow
me: 28 And [g] I give unto them eternal life; and [h] they
shall never perish, neither shall any pluck them out of
my hand. 29 [i] My Father which gave *them* me, is
greater than all; and none is able to pluck them out of
my Father's hand. 30 [k] I and *my* Father are one. 31
Then [l] the Jews took up stones again to stone him. 32
Jesus answered them, Many good works have I shewed
you from my Father; for which of those works do ye
stone me? 33 The Jews answered him, saying, For a
good work we stone thee not; but for blasphemy; and be-
cause that thou, being a man, [m] makest thyself God. 34
Jesus answered them, [n] Is it not written in your law, I
said, Ye are gods? 35 If [o] he called them gods, [p] un-
to whom the word of God came, and the scripture cannot
be broken; 36 Say ye of him, [q] whom the Father hath
sanctified, and sent into the world, Thou blasphemest;
[r] because I said, I am [s] the Son of God? 37 [t] If I do
not the works of my Father, believe me not. 38 But if
I do, though ye believe not me, [u] believe the works: that
ye may know and believe that [x] the Father *is* in me, and
I in him.

[b] 1 Mac. iv. 59. [c] Acts iii. 11. & v. 12. † Gr. Take away our souls. [d] Ver. 38. Chap. v. 36. [e] Ibid. viii. 47. 1 John iv. 6. [f] Ver. 4, 14. [g] Ver. 10. 15. Chap. xvii. 2. Rom. vi. 23. [h] Chap. xvii. 12. & xviii. 9. [i] Chap. xiv. 28. [k] Ibid. xvii. 11, 22. [l] Chap. viii. 59. [m] Ibid. v. 18. [n] Psal. lxxxii. 6. [o] Rom. xiii. 1. [p] Chap. vi. 27. [q] Ibid. v. 17, 18. [r] Luke i. 35. [s] Chap. xv. 24. [t] Chap. v. 36. & xiv. 11. [x] Chap. xiv. 11. & xvii. 21.

v. 22—38. We have here another discourse between Jesus and the Jews. We have,

1. The time and place. It was at the feast of dedication, observed in remembrance of the renovation of the temple-service, when Judas Maccabæus dedicated the new altar, and cleansed the temple which Antiochus had profaned, which was in the winter,

winter, in the month of December And therefore Chriſt walked under cover, in a place called Solomon's porch, a magnificent building, which ſtanding on the ſame ground where Solomon's porch formerly ſtood, continued to bear that name

2 Hither the Jews came to him, and ſurrounding him, in order to pick a quarrel with him, they urged him to tell them plainly and boldly, and keep them no longer in ſuſpence by his figurative and dark expreſſions, whether he were the Chriſt or not

3 Chriſt knew their malicious deſigns, and therefore *anſwered them, I told you* in terms ſufficiently plain, if you choſe to underſtand them, *and ye believed not*, and were determined not to believe it was vain, therefore, to add farther aſſertions, and he choſe to refer them to the miracles which abundantly proved his miſſion *the works that I do in my Father's name, they bear witneſs of me But ye believe not*, obſtinate in your infidelity, *becauſe ye are not of my ſheep, as I ſaid unto you*, their tempers and diſpoſitions plainly ſhewed they were not, and Chriſt knew they were not of thoſe whom the Father had given him, whoſe character and conduct he deſcribes *My ſheep hear my voice*, with attention, diſcernment, and ſpiritual delight, *and I know them*, take cognizance of them, and diſtinguiſh them with my peculiar favour and regard, *and they follow me* in the ways of truth and righteouſneſs, obedient to my word, and imitating my example *And I give unto them eternal life*, they have a preſent ſure title thereto, experience the beginnings of it here, and ſhall be put into the full poſſeſſion of it after death, *and they ſhall never periſh*, no wiles of Satan, no craft of men, no power of corruption, ſhall be able finally and fatally to prevail againſt them, and ſeparate them from the love and protection of me their ſhepherd *neither ſhall any pluck them out of my hand*, whatever efforts the devil, the world, and the fleſh may make to deſtroy them *My Father, which gave them me, is greater than all* their foes, *and none is able to pluck them out of my Father's hand*, they muſt be ſafe when omnipotence is their guard *I and my Father are one*, in nature, eſſence, and perfections, and our power, wiſdom, and truth, are engaged for the preſervation of the redeemed flock *Note*, (1) Eternal life is wholly the gift of God through Jeſus Chriſt (2) They whom Chriſt will ſave, can never periſh O that we had faith to truſt him!

4 The Jews, fired with rage, could no longer refrain, *but took up ſtones to ſtone him* as a blaſphemer

5 Jeſus mildly expoſtulated with them on their baſeneſs, ſaying, *Many good works have I ſhewed you from my Father*, works of ſuch benevolence and wonder, as evidenced his miſſion divine *for which of thoſe works do ye ſtone me?* how horrid is your ingratitude! how baſe your returns! *Note*, (1) Nothing aggravates our ſins againſt God, ſo much as our vile ingratitude (2) If we meet with the moſt ungrateful returns from thoſe on whom we had conferred the greateſt obligations, we may not think it ſtrange Jeſus was ſo treated before us

6 The Jews attempt to vindicate their conduct, ſaying, *For a good work we ſtone thee not, but for blaſphemy, and becauſe that thou, being a man, makeſt thyſelf God*, for in this light they interpreted his claim of unity with the Father, and his aſſuming the incommunicable attributes of the Deity *Note*, Pretended zeal for God's honour hath been the pretext which perſecutors have often uſed to cover the moſt violent outrages againſt his moſt faithful ſervants

7 Chriſt proves he had the fulleſt right to thoſe divine honours which he claimed *Is it not written in your law, I ſaid ye are gods?* Pſ lxxxii 6 *If he called them gods*, who as magiſtrates were types of the King Meſſiah, and *unto whom the word of God came*, entruſted by him with the government of the Jewiſh church and nation, *and the ſcripture cannot be broken*, but muſt receive its accompliſhment in that Meſſiah, who really poſſeſſes divine honour and authority, and is intitled to that high name which they bore as his repreſentatives, *ſay ye then of him whom the Father hath ſanctified*, and ſet apart before the worlds were, *and* in the fulneſs of time *ſent into the world, Thou blaſphemeſt, becauſe I ſaid, I am the Son of God?* But beſides the ſcripture teſtimony, I appeal to my miracles *If I do not the works of my Father*, as great as might be expected from him, and by my own power as God, if theſe do not ſpeak my divine character, and that I am entitled to the honour I claim as Son of God, *believe me not*, I am content to be rejected by you *but if I do* works ſo great, and in ſuch a manner, as declare my divine power and godhead, *though ye believe not me*, on my own word and aſſertions, *believe the works*, thoſe unexceptionable evidence, *that ye may know and believe that the Father is in me, and I in him*, we being one in nature and eſſence, having the moſt intimate union and communion in the ſame undivided Godhead

y Chap viii 59 & ... 39 ʸ Therefore they ſought again to take him but he
eſcaped out of their hand, 40 And went away again
beyond Jordan, into the place ᶻ where John at firſt bap-
tized, and there he abode 41 And many reſorted
unto him, and ſaid, John did no miracle ᵃ but all things
that John ſpake of this man were true 42 And many
believed on him there

v 39—42 Far from appeaſing their fury, Chriſt, by maintaining his right to the eſſential glories of divinity, exaſperated them to the higheſt pitch Whereupon,

1 *They ſought again to take him*, concluding they had now full evidence againſt him to convict him as a blaſphemer, and get him legally condemned by the Sanhedrim, and put to death

2 As the time for Chriſt's ſuffering was not yet come, *he eſcaped out of their hand*, either holding their arms by an inviſible power from ſeizing him, or their eyes from ſeeing him

3 He retired *beyond Jordan, into the place where John at firſt baptized, and there he abode*, preaching the goſpel of the kingdom, and gathering probably ſome fruit from the ſeed, which John had ſown here about two or three years before

4 Multitudes *reſorted to him* there, drawn by his preaching and miracles, *and ſaid, John did no miracle but all things that John ſpake of this man were true* He appears with that tranſcendent greatneſs and glory, in which John ſpake of him *And many believed on him there*, as the true Meſſiah *Note*, (1) Tho' perſecutors drive the miniſters of Chriſt from one place, God will take care to ſend them where he hath ſtill greater work for them to do (2) Jeſus will be peculiarly welcome with his goſpel to thoſe, whoſe hearts, by the ſharp convictions of the law, as by the auſtere Baptiſt's miniſtry, are broken with a humbling ſenſe of ſin

CHAP XI

Here is, 1 The tidings ſent to our Lord Jeſus of the ſickneſs of Lazarus, and his entertainment of thoſe tidings, ver 1—16 2 *The viſit he made to Lazarus's relations when he had heard of his death, and their entertainment of the viſit*, ver 17—32 3 *The miracle wrought in the raiſing of Lazarus from the dead*, ver 33—44 4 *The effect wrought by this miracle upon others*, ver 45—57

1 NOW a certain man was ſick, *named* Lazarus of
Bethany, the town of ᵃ Mary and her ſiſter
Martha 2 (It was *that* Mary ᵇ which anointed the ᵃ Luke x 38
Lord with ointment, and wiped his feet with her hair, ᵇ Mat xxvi 7 Mark
whoſe brother Lazarus was ſick) 3 Therefore his ſiſters xiv 3
ſent unto him, ſaying, Lord, behold, he whom thou Chap. xii 3
loveſt is ſick 4 When Jeſus heard *that*, he ſaid, This
ſickneſs is not unto death, ᶜ but for the glory of God, ᶜ Chap ix
that the Son of God might be glorified thereby 5 Now 3 Ver 40
Jeſus loved Martha, and her ſiſter, and Lazarus 6
When he had heard therefore that he was ſick, ᵈ he a- ᵈ Chap x
bode two days ſtill in the ſame place where he was 7 40
Then after that, ſaith he to *his* diſciples, Let us go into
Judea again 8 *His* diſciples ſay unto him, Maſter, ᵉ the ᵉ Ibid 31
Jews of late ſought to ſtone thee, and goeſt thou thither
again? 9 Jeſus anſwered, Are there not twelve hours
in the day? ᶠ If any man walk in the day, he ſtumbleth ᶠ Ibid ix 4
not, becauſe he ſeeth the light of this world 10 But
ᵍ if a man walk in the night, he ſtumbleth, becauſe there ᵍ Ibid xii
is no light in him. 11 Theſe things ſaid he and after 35
that, he ſaith unto them, Our friend Lazarus ʰ ſleepeth, ʰ Mat ix
but I go that I may awake him out of ſleep 12 Then 24
ſaid his diſciples, Lord, if he ſleep, he ſhall do well
13 Howbeit Jeſus ſpake of his death but they thought
that he had ſpoken of taking reſt in ſleep. 14 Then
ſaid Jeſus unto them plainly, Lazarus is dead 15 And
I am glad for your ſakes, that I was not there (to the
intent ye may believe) nevertheleſs, let us go unto him
16 Then ſaid Thomas, which is called Didymus, unto
his fellow-diſciples, Let us alſo go, that we may die
with him

v 1—16 The miracle contained in this chapter is recorded by this evangeliſt alone We have,

1 The perſons particularly intereſted *Lazarus*, a particular friend of Chriſt's, who was now ſick at Bethany, a little village near Jeruſalem, where he had lived with Mary and her ſiſter Martha, at whoſe houſe Jeſus ſeems to have chiefly reſided when he went up to Jeruſalem on the great feſtivals Mary whoſe brother was ill, was a woman of ſingular piety, which particularly appeared in the reſpect ſhe paid our Lord ſome time after this, *chap* xii 3 when at a public entertainment ſhe anointed his feet with a box of precious ointment, and wiped them with her hair *Note*, Chriſt keeps a faithful account, and will not fail to make honourable mention of all the work of faith and labours of love done for his ſake by his faithful people

2 The ſiſters, anxious for their brother, who was ſo dear to them,

them, dispatched a messenger to acquaint their Lord and master of his imminent danger, knowing it would be enough to mention the case to him, since *he who was sick* was a person *he loved* so tenderly. *Note,* (1.) When we ourselves, or our dear relatives, are sick, we must spread the case before the compassionate Saviour, and commit it with humble submission to his care. (2.) They are happy souls indeed, who are distinguished as the disciples whom Jesus eminently loves. (3.) The dearest children of God share in the common afflictions incident to humanity; yea, often are most severely exercised.

3. Christ foretold the issue of the sickness, that it should not be *unto death*; at least that death should not keep him as his prisoner, but that the *glory of God* should be most eminently displayed in his recovery, for which end this sickness was sent. *Note,* (1.) It is a great consolation to every child of God, that in all his sufferings, God hath purposes of his own glory to answer. (2.) Though we are sick, even unto death, we know if Jesus loves us, that the perishing of the outward man can do us no real harm, but will open for our disembodied souls a passage to eternal life and blessedness.

4. He defers his visit to Lazarus two days, though his love to him and the family was well known, and very singular; and this he did to prove their faith and patience, and give them a more signal manifestation of his power and grace. *Note,* Christ's very delays, however irksome and trying to us, are designed in the issue for our greater comfort and his greater glory.

5. When the two days were expired, Christ calls upon his disciples to attend him to Bethany, designing to carry relief to the afflicted family there. But they expostulate with him on the danger to which he must expose himself by such a journey, when so lately the Jews had attempted to murder him, and still harboured the same malicious intentions: but perhaps this concern for his safety was not without some regard to their own also, who were so nearly connected with him; for very apt are we to mix selfish considerations where we seem to mean only our divine master's honour and interests. In reply to their suggestion, he answers, *Are there not twelve hours in the day,* according to general estimation, allotted for labour? *if any man walk in the day he stumbleth not, because he seeth the light of the world,* that sun which gilds his path, and makes his way plain before his face. Thus whilst the time of life appointed by the Father lasts, I fear no danger, and go forward in my work; *but if a man walk in the night he stumbleth, because there is no light in him.* So when my day of work expires, then, and not till then, shall I be suffered to fall into the hands of my foes. *Note,* (1.) The consideration how soon the night of death approaches, should quicken our diligence, whilst yet the day of life continues, to redeem the time, and finish the work Christ hath given us to do. (2.) They who walk under the guidance of the word and spirit of Jesus, go on their way unmoved, whilst they who follow any other guide are sure to stumble upon the dark mountains of error, and fall into the pit of destruction.

6. He informs them of the death of their common friend Lazarus, and his design to raise him up again to life, which he represents under the figure of sleep. *Our friend Lazarus sleepeth, but I go, that I may awake him out of sleep.* The disciples understanding him literally, thought this a favourable symptom, and that he would do well without their master's going into the jaws of danger. But as he spake of his death under this figure, and not of common rest, as they apprehended, he rectified their mistake by plainly telling them, *Lazarus is dead;* and adds, *I am glad, for your sakes, that I was not there* before he died, *to the intent ye may believe,* when by his resurrection from the grave, after so long a time, your faith may receive the greater confirmation. *Nevertheless,* though he is dead, *let us go unto him.* *Note,* (1.) Sleep is death's lesser mysteries; and every day that we wake from our beds, we experience a kind of resurrection. (2.) The great restorative to weak and wearied nature is soft repose; but no sleep is so sweet to the body, as the sleep of death to the gracious soul, from which he awakes in eternal day.

7. Thomas, called Didymus, or the twin, on hearing what Jesus had said, and his resolution to go into Judea, said to his fellow-disciples, *let us also go, that we may die with him;* either with Lazarus, whom he loved so much as not to wish to survive him, or rather with their master, who, by going, seemed to expose his life to inevitable danger: and he, zealous to attend him, offers himself, and encourages his brethren to cleave to him wherever he went, though death itself should be the consequence. *Note,* (1.) The loss of those on whom our fond affections were placed, often embitters life, and makes death appear desirable. (2.) To go to join the spirits of just men made perfect, is indeed a consummation devoutly to be wished for. (3.) A faithful disciple will be intimidated by no danger from following his master, and encouraging each other to stand fast in the day of trial.

17 Then when Jesus came, he found that he had lain
in the grave four days already. 18 (Now Bethany was
nigh unto Jerusalem, about † fifteen furlongs off.) 19
And many of the Jews came to Martha and Mary, to
comfort them concerning their brother. 20 Then Mar-
tha, as soon as she heard that Jesus was coming, went
and met him: but Mary sat *still* in the house. 21 Then
said Martha unto Jesus, Lord, if thou hadst been here,
my brother had not died. 22 But I know, that even
now, ¹ whatsoever thou wilt ask of God, God will give ¹ Chap. ix. 31.
it thee. 23 Jesus saith unto her, Thy brother shall rise
again. 24 Martha saith unto him, ᵏ I know that he ᵏ Luke xiv. 14. Chap. v. 29.
shall rise again in the resurrection at the last day. 25
Jesus said unto her, ˡ I am the resurrection, and the life: ˡ Chap. v. 21. & vi. 39, 40, 44.
ᵐ he that believeth in me, though he were dead, yet ᵐ Chap. iii. 36. 1 John v. 10, &c.
shall he live: 26 And whosoever liveth and believeth
in me, ⁿ shall never die. Believest thou this? 27 She ⁿ Rev. xx. 6.
saith unto him, Yea, Lord: I believe that ᵒ thou art the ᵒ Mat. xvi. 16. Chap. iv. 42. & vi. 69.
Christ, the Son of God, which should come into the
world. 28 And when she had so said, she went her
way, and called Mary her sister secretly, saying, The
Master is come, and calleth for thee. 29 As soon as
she heard *that,* she arose quickly, and came unto him.
30 Now Jesus was not yet come into the town, but
was in that place where Martha met him. 31 The Jews
then which were with her in the house, and ᵖ comforted ᵖ Ver. 19.
her, when they saw Mary that she rose up hastily, and
went out, followed her, saying, She goeth unto the
grave, to weep there. 32 Then when Mary was come
where Jesus was, and saw him, she fell down at his feet,
saying unto him, Lord, ᑫ if thou hadst been here, my ᑫ Ver. 21.
brother had not died.

† Or, About two miles.

v. 17—32. Jesus having declared his purpose, began his journey with his disciples, and arrived at Bethany, which was distant from Jerusalem about two miles.

1. He found a melancholy scene. The house, where with joy he had lately been entertained, is drowned in tears; such woeful changes do we often see after the shortest absence from our friends. Lazarus had lain in the grave four days already, and many of the Jews from Jerusalem, which was near, had come to console the afflicted sisters. *Note,* (1.) It is kind to weep with those that weep, and by partaking, to relieve the sorrows of the miserable. (2.) When we lose our dearest relatives, if they fall asleep in Jesus, we have abundant reason to be comforted *concerning our brother;* his lot is to be envied; our tears should rather flow for ourselves left yet behind, to conflict with the powers of evil. (3.) The house of most distinguished piety is not barred against affliction; but though we sorrow as men, we can rejoice as believers. There is hope in the end.

2. Martha no sooner heard of the Master's approach, than she went to meet him; whilst Mary, who had not yet heard of his arrival, sat still in the house. We are here told what passed at this first interview.

[1.] Martha, with deep respect addressing the Saviour, said, *Lord, if thou hadst been here, my brother had not died;* so confident was she of his power and compassions, though her weakness appeared in supposing his bodily presence necessary to the cure. *But I know that even now,* desperate as the case is, *whatsoever thou wilt ask of God, God will give it thee;* she mentioned no particular, but meekly referred the case to his grace and wisdom. *Note,* In our deepest sorrows, our only relief is to draw near to Jesus, to tell him our sorrows, and cast our care upon him.

[2.] Christ answers her with good words, and comfortable words. *Thy brother shall rise again.* He expressed it so as to leave it doubtful, whether he meant a present or future resurrection: in either view it administred matter for her faith and hope and consolation. *Note,* It is a most reviving consideration when death robs us of our brethren in Jesus, that the separation is but short; we shall meet them again at the resurrection of the just.

[3.] Martha professes her faith in what her Lord had spoken. *I know that he shall rise again in the resurrection at the last day;* that there should be a resurrection she was persuaded, and that Lazarus would rise among the just; but though this was some consolation, her loss hung heavy upon her.

[4.] *Jesus said unto her, I am the resurrection and the life;* not only by his prayer could he obtain life from God for whom he would, but he had the power of life in himself, and at his own pleasure could raise the dead, and call the things that are not, as though they were. *He that believeth in me, though he were dead, yet shall he live;* his body, as well as soul, shall live in the eternal world; *and whosoever liveth and believeth in me,* quickened to spiritual life, and walking now by faith, *shall never die;* shall never lose the life of grace he possesses, which is the beginning of the life of glory; and though this body may return to the dust, from whence it came, yet shall it be raised again, and be made immortal as his never-dying soul. *Believest thou this?* A solemn question which we should often put to ourselves. The resurrection of the body is to sense improbable, impossible; but faith overlooks every difficulty. He who raised us from the dust at first, can again re-assemble the scattered atoms, and bring

bring bone to his bone *Note*, (1) Chriſt is the author of *natural life*, in him we live, and move, and have our being, of *ſpiritual life*, by his power and his ſpirit are we quickened from the death of ſin *of eternal life*, as he hath procured the title for us, and by him we ſhall be raiſed up at the laſt day (2) They who have this faith in them, are truly bleſſed and happy, they live in comfort, and die in hope

[5] Martha ſaid unto him, *Yea, Lord, I believe that thou art the Chriſt, the Son of God, which ſhould come into the world*, the true Meſſiah ſo long promiſed, ſo greatly expected, and that thou haſt all power to do whatſoever thou pleaſeſt, and that nothing is impoſſible with thee *Note*, They who know the Saviour's all-ſufficiency, may comfortably and confidently reſt all their hopes upon him

3 Mary comes to meet the Lord Martha, in haſte to communicate the glad news, and to make her ſiſter partaker of the bleſſings of his converſe, goes and ſecretly whiſpers to her that Jeſus the Maſter was come, and wiſhed to ſee her Eager to meet him, ſhe haſtily aroſe, and came to him without the town where he had halted, as nearer the grave where his buſineſs lay The Jews, who came to condole with her, obſerving her ſudden departure, concluded ſhe was gone to the grave to weep, and followed her But Mary had now found her Lord, and at his feet poured out with tears her ſorrowful complaint, *Lord, if thou hadſt been here, my brother had not died* *Note*, (1) Gracious ſouls delight to be inſtrumental in bringing others to Jeſus, to partake of his conſolations (2) Chriſt is a better comforter than ten thouſand friends at his feet under all our ſorrows let us be found, and he will calm our troubled breaſts (3) It is kind to viſit the houſe of mourning, and ſeek to divert from inordinate ſorrow the afflicted, who often ſtudy how to ſharpen and aggravate their own griefs (4) We are often apt to torment and grieve ourſelves unneceſſarily with apprehenſions that ſomething was neglected or overlooked, that might have been done for our departed friends, instead of ſubmitting to the divine decree with ſilent reſignation

33 When Jeſus therefore ſaw her weeping, and the
Jews alſo weeping which came with her, he groaned in
the ſpirit, and was troubled, 34 And ſaid, Where have
ye laid him? They ſay unto him, Lord, come and ſee
r Luke xix 41 Rom xii 15 35 r Jeſus wept 36 Then ſaid the Jews, Behold how
he loved him! 37 And ſome of them ſaid, Could not
s Chap ix 6 this man, s which opened the eyes of the blind, have
cauſed that even this man ſhould not have died? 38
Jeſus therefore again groaning in himſelf, cometh to the
grave It was a cave, and a ſtone lay upon it 39
Jeſus ſaid, Take ye away the ſtone Martha, the ſiſter
of him that was dead, ſaith unto him, Lord, by this time
he ſtinketh for he hath been *dead* four days 40 Jeſus
ſaith unto her, Said I not unto thee, that if thou wouldſt
t Ver 4 believe, t thou ſhouldſt ſee the glory of God? 41 Then
they took away the ſtone *from the place* where the dead
was laid And Jeſus lifted up *his* eyes, and ſaid, Father,
I thank thee that thou haſt heard me 42 And I knew
u Chap xii 30 that thou heareſt me always: but u becauſe of the people
which ſtand by, I ſaid *it*, that they may believe that
thou haſt ſent me 43 And when he had thus ſpoken,
he cried with a loud voice, Lazarus, come forth 44
And he that was dead came forth, bound hand and foot
x Chap xx 7 with grave clothes and x his face was bound about
with a napkin. Jeſus ſaith unto them, Looſe him, and
let him go

v 33—44 We have here,

1 The compaſſion of Jeſus He felt for the anguiſh which appeared in the tears ſo plentifully ſhed, *he groaned in the ſpirit, and was troubled*, either ſympathizing with Mary and her friends in their grief, or, as the words ſeem in their ſignification to intimate, with indignation at the unbelief and hardneſs of heart which he ſaw in many of the Jews there preſent and knowing his own deſign of grace, he aſked, *Where have ye laid him?* Not that he could be unacquainted with any event, but that it might appear there was no contrivance between him and the relations of the deceaſed, *They ſay unto him, Lord, come and ſee*, and being come to the place, he, whoſe tender heart felt deeply for human miſery, and as man poſſeſſed the tendereſt feelings of our nature, gave vent to his grief *Jeſus wept* *Note*, (1) Jeſus was very man as well as very God, and ſubject to all our ſinleſs paſſions and infirmities (2) Tears of tender ſympathy become the diſciples of Jeſus, who are commanded to weep with thoſe that weep

2 The reflections made by thoſe preſent on the tears of Jeſus Some ſaid, and the obſervation was moſt natural, *Behold how he loved him!* Others with more malignant inſinuations, ſuggeſt, *Could not this man, which opened the eyes of the blind, have cauſed that even this man ſhould not have died?* Intimating, that had he really poſſeſſed the power he pretended, he would have kept his friend from death, but as he could not do this, it was to be ſuſpected that what had paſſed for ſo extraordinary a miracle before, was really a mere ſham *Note*, (1) If we conſider what Jeſus hath done, how he hath ſhed not only tears, but drops of blood for us, with much more reaſon may we ſay, *Behold how he loved us!* (2) They who determine to cavil, will always find a pretence

3 Jeſus groaning in ſpirit at the malice and wickedneſs of ſuch a ſuggeſtion, *cometh to the grave*, which, according to their uſual method of burying the dead, was a cave, with a ſtone laid on its mouth This he bids them remove, that all might be convinced of the reality of Lazarus's death, by the putrefaction of the corpſe Martha, concluding from the time he had lain in the grave, that the body muſt be very offenſive, and thinking it too late to hope for his revival, would have diverted Jeſus from his purpoſe, but *he ſaid unto her, Said I not unto thee, that if thou wouldſt believe, thou ſhouldſt ſee the glory of God* diſplayed in a more eminent manner than hath yet appeared? And herein probably he refers to ſomething which he had ſaid in the former converſation with her, which is not recorded by the evangeliſt *Note*, (1) Nothing ſerves more deeply to mortify our pride on any bodily excellencies, than the reflection how awful will be the change, when we have lain but a few days in the grave (2) If we have true faith, we ſhall ſurely ſee the great ſalvation of God, whatever difficulties may ſeem to be in our way

4 The grave being opened, and the corpſe diſcovered, *Jeſus lift up his eyes to heaven, and ſaid, Father, I thank thee that thou haſt heard me*, not as imploring aſſiſtance for the performing the miracle of Lazarus's reſurrection, which by his own power he would accompliſh, but as thanking him for the preſent opportunity afforded him, for the diſplay of his divine power and authority *And I knew that thou heareſt me alway*, becauſe my will and thine are one, *but becauſe of the people which ſtand by, I ſaid it, that they might believe that thou haſt ſent me*, and be aſſured of my being the true Meſſiah by this ſtupendous miracle, which will add ſtill greater evidence to my miſſion *Note*, (1) In our approaches to God, we ſhould draw near to him as the Father of mercies, with full confidence in his faithfulneſs, power, and love (2) Thankſgivings for paſt mercies are an encouragement to the preſent exerciſe of our faith (3) Chriſt is an all-prevailing advocate, his prayers for us are always heard, therefore we may boldly draw near to a throne of grace

5 By a word the miracle is wrought With the voice of Majeſty, as the Lord of life, he ſpeaks aloud, *Lazarus, come forth*, and inſtantly, obedient to his command, death ſurrenders his priſoner, by omnipotent power the corpſe is raiſed, Lazarus comes forth alive, enveloped with all the ſwathings and the napkin round his face, as he was laid in the grave Jeſus bids them *looſe him, and let him go*, being perfectly reſtored to health and ſtrength, he was able as ever to walk to his own houſe *Note*, (1) Such is the mighty call of Jeſus to the ſoul dead in treſpaſſes and ſins, and power accompanies his goſpel, by which the dead are quickened to newneſs of life (2) The change in the reſurrection day will be thus inſtantaneous, in a moment, in the twinkling of an eye, 1 Cor xv 52

45 Then many of the Jews which came to Mary, and
y had ſeen the things which Jeſus did, believed on him y Chap ii 23 xii 11
46 But ſome of them went their ways to the Phariſees,
and told them what things Jeſus had done. 47 ¶ Then
z gathered the chief prieſts and the Phariſees a council, z Pſ ii 2 Mat xxvi 3 Mark xiv 1
and ſaid, a What do we? for this man doth many mi- a Chap xii 19 Acts iv 16
racles 48 If we let him thus alone, all men will believe
on him, and the Romans ſhall come and take away both
our place and nation 49 And one of them named b b Luke iii 2 Acts iv 6
Caiaphas, being the high prieſt that ſame year, ſaid unto
them, Ye know nothing at all, 50 Nor conſider that
c it is expedient for us, that one man ſhould die for the c Chap xviii 14
people, and that the whole nation periſh not 51 And
this he ſpake not of himſelf but being high prieſt that
year, he propheſied that Jeſus ſhould die for that nation
52 And d not for that nation only, e but that alſo he d Iſa xlix 6 1 John ii 2 e Eph i 10
ſhould gather together in one, the children of God that
were ſcattered abroad 53 Then from that day forth
they took counſel together for to put him to death 54
Jeſus therefore walked no more openly among the Jews,
but went thence into a country near to the wilderneſs,
into a city called f Ephraim, and there continued with f 2 Chr xiii 19
his diſciples 55 ¶ And the Jews paſſover was nigh at
hand and many went out of the country up to Jeruſa-
lem before the paſſover, to purify themſelves 56
g Then ſought they for Jeſus, and ſpake among them- g Chap vii 11
ſelves, as they ſtood in the temple, What think ye, that
he will not come to the feaſt? 57 Now both the chief
prieſts

priests and the Pharisees had given a commandment, that if any man knew where he were, he should shew *it*, that they might take him

v. 45—57 This miracle produced very different effects upon the spectators

1 Many of the Jews there present, who had come to console the sorrowful sisters, struck with the evidence of the divine power of Jesus, believed in him as the Messiah Thus their kindness to the afflicted was repaid with the best of spiritual blessings upon their own souls

2 Others, obstinate in infidelity, and exasperated, instead of being convinced, by what they had seen, went with malicious wickedness to the Pharisees, who were members of the Sanhedrim and informed them what was done, that they might take measures to suppress the increasing fame of Jesus

3 A council is instantly summoned, in order to deliberate on some more vigorous methods to stop this man Being assembled, they said, *What do we?* How dilatory are our proceedings? How long shall we see ourselves run down, and our interests in the people usurped? *for this man doth many miracles*, which could not be denied, and *if we let him thus alone* to root himself in the people's affections, *all men will believe on him* as the Messiah, and set him up as king the consequence of which will be, that *the Romans will come to crush* such a rebellion, *and take away both our place and nation* This they dreadfully apprehended, and by the very methods they took to prevent it, filled up the measure of their iniquities, and brought that very destruction which they feared upon their own heads *Note*, (1) The enemies of Christ have often pretended zeal for the public good, as a pretence to persecute the public's best friends (2) They who, under the influence of carnal policy, by wicked methods think to extricate themselves from their difficulties, only pull down the more surely that ruin which they seek to shun

4 Caiaphas, the high-priest that year (this dignity and office under the Roman government having become venal, and the persons being often changed) a man of a Sadducean spirit, *Acts* v 17 unconcerned about a judgment to come, with daring effrontery and haughtiness, said, *Ye know nothing at all*, to sit thus debating and deliberating, *nor consider that it is expedient for us, that one man should die for the people, and that the whole nation perish not* when matters are come to such a crisis there can be no ground to hesitate about proceeding, nor need we enter into the enquiry whether he be a prophet or no, the case is desperate, and requires a desperate remedy better is it, tho' he were innocent, to destroy him, than endanger, by a foolish lenity, the safety of the nation *Note*, (1) When secular interest, court favour, bribery, and corruption, exalt men to the highest offices in the church, no marvel if the chief rulers are arch-persecutors (2) Reason and justice stand in little stead, where power is in the hand of oppressors

5 The evangelist informs us, that Caiaphas *spake not this of himself but being high priest that year*, whose words would be looked upon as oracular, God so ordered it that he should express his sentiments in such a way, as that though he designed the most malignant and murderous counsel, he declared the most important and glorious truth, *he prophesied that Jesus should die for that nation*, as the Messiah, to redeem his people *and not for that nation only*, to save the elect remnant, *Rom* xi 5 of the Jewish people, *but that also he should gather in one the children of God that were scattered abroad*, even those of the Gentiles also, wherever dispersed, as well as Jews, who were predestinated to the adoption of children by Christ Jesus, *Eph* i 5 and designed to become one fold under one shepherd

6 Caiaphas's discourse determined the council, and from that day forward, with resolute purpose, they took counsel to put Jesus to death, and thought only on the properest means to execute their design

7 Christ, who knew this combination against him, and the determination of his implacable enemies, withdrew, and *walked no more openly among the Jews*, retiring to a city called Ephraim, in the least frequented part of the country, where he spent his time in conversation with his disciples The hour of his departure approaching, this season was most usefully employed in teaching them the things which pertained to the kingdom of God

8 The last passover which our Lord was to celebrate on earth, now drew nigh, and multitudes, according to custom, resorted to Jerusalem to purify themselves from any ceremonial uncleanness which they had contracted, before the feast began, that they might be legally prepared to partake of it Many enquiries were then made concerning Jesus, by those who met together in the temple, it being a question much agitated among them, whether he would venture to come up to the feast or not? For the chief priests had issued strict orders, that if any man knew where he was, he should shew it, that they might arrest him, and put him to death And this made some doubt, whether such an open declaration of their intention might not intimidate him, whilst others would have been glad to have had an opportunity of delivering him up to his implacable enemies *Note*, When rulers are wicked, they never want instruments to execute their iniquitous purposes

CHAP XII

In this chapter we are told, 1 *How Mary anointed the feet of Jesus at Bethany*, ver 1—8 2 *The consultation of the chief priests to kill him and Lazarus, whom the people flocked to see*, ver 9—11 3 *He enters Jerusalem in triumph*, ver 12—19 4 *The Greeks desire to see him*, ver 20—22 5 *He foretels his death*, ver 23—33 6 *He solemnly warns the Jews*, ver 34—36 7 *They in general persist in their infidelity, though some of the rulers believe, but durst not own him*, ver 37—43 8 *He asserts his divine mission*, ver 44—50

1 THEN Jesus, six days before the passover, came
to Bethany, where Lazarus was which had been
dead, whom he raised from the dead 2 [a] There they a Mat xxvi 6 Mark xiv 3
made him a supper, and Martha served but Lazarus
was one of them that sat at the table with him 3 Then
took [b] Mary a pound of ointment of † spikenard very b Luke x 39 Chap xi 2 † Or pure nard
costly, and anointed the feet of Jesus, and wiped his
feet with her hair and the house was filled with the
odour of the ointment 4 Then saith one of his disciples,
Judas Iscariot, Simon's *son*, which should betray
him, 5 Why was not this ointment sold for three
hundred ‡ pence, and given to the poor? 6 This he ‡ Mat xviii 28
said, not that he cared for the poor, but because he was
a thief, and [c] had the bag, and bare what was put therein. c Chap xiii 29
7 Then said Jesus, Let her alone against the day
of my burying hath she kept this 8 For [d] the poor d Deut xv 11
always ye have with you, but me ye have not always
9 Much people of the Jews therefore knew that he was
there and they came, not for Jesus sake only, but that
they might see Lazarus also, [e] whom he had raised from e Chap xi 44
the dead 10 ¶ But the chief priests consulted, that
they might put Lazarus also to death, 11 Because
that [f] by reason of him many of the Jews went away, f Chap xi 45 & xi 45
and believed on Jesus

v 1—11 We have here,

1 The visit of Jesus to Bethany He came there six days before the passover, and took up his lodgings with Lazarus, a person now uncommonly distinguished, as having been dead, and miraculously restored to life by his power He knew the danger to which he exposed himself, but his hour approached, and therefore he offered himself a willing sacrifice, as the true paschal Lamb, who should be sacrificed for us

2 Lazarus and his sisters gave him a most welcome reception, and in honour of their guest made a great supper and Martha, to do honour to her heavenly visitant, waited herself upon him, whilst Lazarus sat at the table with him, a living monument of his power and grace

3 During the entertainment, Mary, to testify her deep respect for her divine Lord and Master, came with a pound of very costly spikenard, and anointed his feet, wiping them with her hair, and the odour of the ointment filled the house expressing hereby her faith, love, and deep humility, receiving him as the anointed Messiah, and paying her dutiful homage to him *Note*, No fragrance of the sweetest perfume can adequately represent that sweet savour of Christ, and of the graces of his Spirit, which fill the believer's soul with joy unspeakable and full of glory

4 Judas, in heart a traitor, but yet in profession ranked among the apostles, pretending charity for the poor, testified indignation at this act of respect shewn to his Master, as if it had been an unnecessary piece of waste not indeed that this divine grace of charity ever glowed in his false bosom, but *because he was a thief*, and being intrusted with the common purse, he had purloined part of the money which was put in it, and applied it to his own use, and hoped if this ointment had been sold, and the money brought into their joint stock, some part of it might be easily secreted *Note*, (1) Hypocrites, when they make the most zealous profession, really dislike that serious godliness they discover in others, and their worldly mindedness in trifles shews how ready they will be to apostatize, the moment a greater temptation is before them (2) Satan transforms himself often into an angel of light, and gilds with specious names and pretences the vilest purposes Thus *worldly wisdom* is called *rational prudence*, and *covetousness* wears the mask of *zeal against others extravagance* (3) The love of money is usually most fatal to the soul They who are fond of the bag, will not long be faithful to their Lord

5 Christ vindicates what Mary did from the ill construction which Judas had put upon it *Jesus said, Let her alone*, neither

neither blame nor trouble her, *against the day of my burial hath she kept this*, so Divine Providence ordered it, that, though she knew not his approaching death, she thus should embalm him when alive, because she would have no opportunity to perform that kind office when he was dead Besides, he adds, *the poor always ye have with you*, such objects would never be wanting whereon to exercise their charity *but me ye have not always*, and therefore, during the short moment of his stay with them, they could not be too sedulous to shew him every token of respect and honour *Note*, Opportunities to serve Christ are precious, and must be embraced without delay

6 Multitudes of people from Jerusalem flocked to Bethany, in order to gratify their curiosity with a sight of Jesus, concerning whom they had heard so much, and also to see Lazarus, who had been raised from the dead, the fame of which miracle had been greatly spread

7 The chief-priests, far from being affected with such an instance of Christ's power, not only persisted in their bloody purpose to murder him, but also consulted to put Lazarus to death, being filled with rage and envy, that many of the Jews, struck with the evidence of this miracle, had deserted their party, and joined themselves to Jesus, professing their faith in him as the Messiah *Note*, (1) They who are most eminently distinguished with God's favour, are the objects against whom wicked men level their most malignant enmity (2) The stronger the evidence is, the more exasperated do they grow who obstinately resolve not to be convinced

f Mat xxi 8 Mark xi 8 Luke xix 35
h 1 Mac xiii 51 2 Mac x 7
i Ps cxviii 25, 26
k Zech ix 9
l Chap vii 39
m Chap xiv 26
n Chap xi 47

12 ¶ [f] On the next day, much people that were come
to the feast, when they heard that Jesus was coming to
Jerusalem, 13 [h] Took branches of palm-trees, and
went forth to meet him, and cried, [i] Hosanna, blessed
is the King of Israel that cometh in the name of the Lord
14 And Jesus when he had found a young ass, sat there-
on, [k] as it is written, 15 Fear not, daughter of Sion
behold thy King cometh, sitting on an ass's colt 16
These things understood not his disciples at the first
But when [l] Jesus was glorified, [m] then remembred they
that these things were written of him, and *that* they had
done these things unto him 17 The people therefore
that was with him, when he called Lazarus out of his
grave, and raised him from the dead, bare record 18
For this cause the people also met him, for that they heard
that he had done this miracle 19 The Pharisees there-
fore said among themselves, [n] Perceive ye how ye prevail
nothing? behold, the world is gone after him

v 12—19 The triumphal entry of our Lord into Jerusalem is recorded by all the evangelists

1 A vast crowd, with loudest acclamation, and every expression of joy, attended him *A great multitude, who were come to the feast, when they heard that Jesus was coming to Jerusalem*, from Bethany, *went forth to meet him*, and welcome his arrival, with palm-branches in their hands, the emblem of that victory which Jesus was shortly to obtain over sin and Satan, the issue of which conflict was already sure, and with loud hosannas they cried, *Blessed is the King of Israel, that cometh in the name of the Lord* They acknowledge Jesus as the King Messiah, so long expected to sit on David's throne, they wish him all prosperity, success, and happiness, and hail the glad day of his appearing *Note*, With greater joy doth the sinner welcome the Saviour to the throne of his heart, and wishes him to set up his throne there for ever and ever

2 He made his entry, not with the pomp of earthly majesty, but, as better suited his state of humiliation, on an ass's colt, that thus also he might fulfil the Scripture, which had said, *Fear not, daughter of Sion behold thy King cometh*, to save thee from all thy spiritual foes, *sitting on an ass's colt*, that humble supplicants may be emboldened to approach him, and present their petitions *These things understood not his disciples at the first but when Jesus was glorified*, and from his throne on high had sent his Spirit into their hearts, to open their understandings, that they might understand the Scripture, *then remembred they that these things were written of him, and that*, though at the time they had no thought about the fulfilment of the Scripture, *they had done these things unto him*, which had been foretold *Note*, (1) Christ is Zion's King, and he must reign till he hath put all his enemies under his feet (2) The Scriptures are often fulfilled by those who at the time have not the least intention so to do (3) Many times the Scriptures are read without the least knowledge of their true meaning, but, when God opens the understanding, the Bible then becomes a book perfectly new, and treasures of wisdom are discovered in it which were utterly unknown before

3 The reason of so great a multitude coming to usher Jesus into Jerusalem at this time was, that many of those who beheld the miracle of Lazarus's resurrection declared what they had seen and such an astonishing work, attested by so many and credible eye-witnesses, could not but procure general admiration

4 The Pharisees beheld, with the utmost rage and vexation, the increasing respect paid to Jesus, and said one to another, *Perceive ye how ye prevail nothing?* instead of crushing him, all our attempts are baffled, and his rising fame threatens utterly to supplant us in the esteem of the people *behold, the world is gone after him*, the generality of our followers have forsaken us, and commenced his disciples It is high time to put some stop to these proceedings, or the grievance will be past redress *Note*, (1) They who oppose Christ, in vain lift up their impotent arm against his church and kingdom no powers of earth or hell shall be able finally to prevail (2) Obstinate sinners grow more resolute and determined in sin, by the very checks which God gives them, and madly rush *on the thick bosses of his buckler*

o Acts xvii 4
p Acts viii 27
q Chap i 44
r Chap xiii 32, & xvii 1
s 1 Cor xv 36
t Mat x 39 & xvi 25
u Chap xiv 3 & xvii 24 1 Thes iv 17

20 ¶ And there were [o] certain Greeks among them,
[p] that came up to worship at the feast 21 The same
came therefore to Philip, [q] which was of Bethsaida of
Galilee, and desired him, saying, Sir, we would see Jesus
22 Philip cometh and telleth Andrew and again, An-
drew and Philip told Jesus 23 ¶ And Jesus answered
them, saying, [r] The hour is come, that the Son of man
should be glorified 24 Verily, verily I say unto you,
[s] Except a corn of wheat fall into the ground and die,
it abideth alone but if it die, it bringeth forth much
fruit 25 [t] He that loveth his life shall lose it and he
that hateth his life in this world, shall keep it unto life
eternal 26 If any man serve me, let him follow me,
and [u] where I am, there shall also my servant be if any
man serve me, him will *my* Father honour

v 20—26 Christ's fame had been spread far and wide We have here,

1 The enquiry of some Greeks after him They seem to have been devout men, proselytes from among the Gentiles, who came up to Jerusalem to worship, and, having heard so much of Jesus, were greatly desirous to see and converse with him for which purpose they applied to Philip, with whom probably they might formerly have had some acquaintance *Note*, (1) They who have a real desire after Christ will seek him, and beg advice and assistance from those who are his ministring servants It is good to know those that know the Saviour (2) The awakened sinner desires to see Jesus, his fulness of grace and all-sufficiency to save, to obtain an interest in his regard, and be admitted to communion with him

2 Philip first consulted his brother Andrew, whether it was proper to mention the request of Gentiles to their Master, and, being agreed on the point, they informed Jesus of the matter *Note*, In doubtful cases it is wisdom to consult a faithful friend

3 Christ took occasion, from this application to him, to discourse on the glorious issue of his undertaking, when Jews and Gentiles by the power of his Spirit should be converted unto him *The hour is come that the Son of man should be glorified*, when, being lifted up on the cross, and exalted to the throne of his glory, he should draw all men unto him, and be honoured in the salvation of sinners from every nation, without distinction *Verily, verily I say unto you, Except a corn of wheat fall into the ground and die, it abideth alone but if it die, it bringeth forth much fruit* So, he intimates, must he die, and be laid in the earth, that, having thereby made the atonement, and brought in an everlasting righteousness, he might in his resurrection become the root and author of spiritual life to innumerable multitudes of his redeemed people, who should be raised by him from the death of sin unto the life of righteousness, and bring forth abundant fruits of grace, the glory of which would be ascribed to him alone And as those, whom he died to save, would for his sake, when called and converted unto him, be exposed to the greatest sufferings, he suggests the most powerful arguments to engage their fidelity *He that loveth his life*, and, for fear of losing a temporal being, or the advantages of this world, deserts the cause of Jesus, *shall lose it*, and perish everlastingly *and he that hateth his life in this world*, sitting loose to its honours, ease, and interests, when they stand in competition with Christ, and sends, if need be, to seal his testimony with his blood, he *shall keep it unto life eternal*, and be made for ever happy with God in glory So that, *if any man serve me, let him follow me*, my example, the teachings of my word and Spirit, and the directions of my providence, *and* then, whatever difficulties, dangers, or sufferings he may be exposed to, *where I am, there shall also my servant be*, inheriting the same glory to which I shall be advanced *if any man serve me*, in simplicity and godly sincerity, *him will my Father honour*, setting him at his own right hand, and causing him to sit down on my throne, as I am sat down with the Father on his throne *Note*, (1) They who would faithfully follow Christ must prepare for sufferings (2) When we by faith look to and realize the glories of the world above, we cannot but sit loose to every thing here below (3) If Christ be our master, and our affections are placed upon him, where he is we shall shortly be (4) However dishonoured we may be by a world which lieth in wicked-

ness,

neſs, we ſhall find the moſt abundant recompenſe in the honour which cometh from God only.

27 [x] Now is my ſoul troubled, and what ſhall I ſay?
[y] Father, ſave me from this hour: but [z] for this cauſe
came I unto this hour. 28 Father, glorify thy name.
[a] Then came there a voice from heaven, *ſaying*, I have
both glorified *it*, and will glorify *it* again. 29 The
people therefore that ſtood by, and heard *it*, ſaid that
it thundered: others ſaid, An angel ſpake to him. 30
Jeſus anſwered and ſaid, [a] This voice came not becauſe
of me, but for your ſakes. 31 Now is the judgment
of this world: [b] now ſhall the prince of this world be
caſt out. 32 And I, if [c] I be lifted up from the earth,
will [d] draw all men unto me. 33 (This he ſaid, ſigni-
fying what death he ſhould die.) 34 The people an-
ſwered him, We have heard out of the law, that [e] Chriſt
abideth for ever: and how ſayeſt thou, The Son of man
muſt be lifted up? who is this Son of man? 35 Then
Jeſus ſaid unto them, Yet a little while [f] is the light
with you: [g] walk while ye have the light, leſt darkneſs
come upon you: for [h] he that walketh in darkneſs,
knoweth not whither he goeth. 36 While ye have the
light, believe in the light, that ye may be [i] the children of
light. Theſe things ſpake Jeſus and departed, [k] and did
hide himſelf from them.

v. 27—36. We have here,

1. The addreſs of Jeſus to his heavenly Father. *Now is my ſoul troubled*, with the proſpect of his approaching ſufferings, from which the humanity ſhrunk back; *and what ſhall I ſay*, in this diſtreſs? *Father, ſave me from this hour?* ſhall I deſire to be excuſed the pains and death which I foreſee? No: *but for this cauſe came I unto this hour*, according to the eternal counſels being appointed in the ſtead of ſinners to bear their ſins and carry their ſorrows, and therefore he deſired not to be ſaved from the ſufferings to which he had conſented, but to be ſupported under them. *Father, glorify thy name*, and by my death diſplay, in the moſt eminent manner, the glory of thy juſtice, faithfulneſs, mercy, and every divine perfection. *Note*, (1.) The remembrance of the diſtreſs of the Redeemer's ſoul ſhould be a relief to us when our ſpirits are troubled. He gave *his* ſoul an offering for ſin, that he might take away the bitterneſs of it from *ours*. (2.) Though *now* for a little moment we feel diſtreſs, the time is near, when every trouble ſhall end in everlaſting joy. (3.) When we are under difficulties we muſt fly to God, humbly reſign ourſelves to his will, and beg for ſtrength to glorify him in the fire.

2. The Father anſwers him by a voice from heaven. *Then came there a voice from heaven, ſaying, I have both glorified it*, in the incarnation, obedience, miracles, and doctrine of Jeſus, *and will glorify it again*, by his death, reſurrection, and aſcenſion.

3. The people who ſtood by heard with aſtoniſhment the voice; ſome more confuſedly, who ſaid *it thundered*; others more diſtinctly, who ſaid that *an angel ſpake to him*; either ignorantly or wilfully miſtaking the glorious teſtimony.

4. Chriſt declares to them the meaning of what they heard. *This voice came not becauſe of me*, for my ſatiſfaction merely, *but for your ſakes*, that you my diſciples might be encouraged by this teſtimony born to my divine miſſion. *Now is the judgment of this world*, the hour is near when the Jewiſh nation ſhall receive their doom, and a bleſſed change be wrought in the heathen world, when God ſhall ſeparate the precious from the vile, and gather his choſen people to himſelf, the power of ſin and Satan being broken: *for now ſhall the prince of this world be caſt out*, the devil's uſurped dominion over the ſouls of men ſhall be deſtroyed, his oracles in the heathen world be ſilenced, and at laſt his kingdom ſhall be finally rooted up: and this by a method which to human view may appear the moſt unlikely. *And I, if I be*, or *when I am, lifted up from the earth*, on the croſs, as a ſacrifice for ſin, *will draw all men unto me*, Gentiles as well as Jews, who ſhould be made partakers of all the ineſtimable bleſſings of his blood-ſhedding, and drawn to him by the irreſiſtible cords of his dying love. (*This he ſaid, ſignifying what death he ſhould die*, even by crucifixion.) *Note*, (1.) Satan is now a vanquiſhed foe, ſince Chriſt hath died, the head of the old ſerpent is bruiſed. (2.) Chriſt is the glorious center of unity, the banner under which his redeemed with delight are gathered, and, cleaving to him in faith and love, are made more than conquerors by him over all their enemies. (3.) The croſs of Chriſt is the powerfully attractive object, and therein all the glories of redeeming love are moſt eminently diſplayed, which effectually conquer the ſinner's ſoul.

5. The people, hearing him ſpeak of himſelf as about to be lifted up and die, object this as a contradiction of the character which he aſſumed as the Meſſiah, becauſe the Scripture ſpoke of his continuing a king and prieſt *for ever*, Pſal. cx. 4. lxxxix. 29. but they overlooked what the ſame ſcriptures had ſaid concerning his ſufferings, and would not attend to the repeated notices which Chriſt had given of his riſing again, and thus entring into his glory, which made his ſufferings not at all inconſiſtent with his everlaſting dominion: therefore they inſultingly aſk, *Who is this Son of man?* As if he himſelf could not poſſibly be the perſon of whom Daniel propheſied, ſince he acknowledged he muſt be lifted up and die. *Note*, They cannot but err, who take one part or text of Scripture, without conſidering its connection and relation with the reſt. Thus many pervert the very life-giving truths of God, and make them a ſavour of death.

6. As Chriſt ſaw the ill ſpirit and temper that raiſed theſe cavils, he declines a direct anſwer to their queſtion, and rather chuſes to reply by warning them of their danger, if they neglected the preſent opportunity vouchſafed unto them. *Then ſaid Jeſus unto them, Yet a little while is the light with you*, either meaning himſelf, the Sun of righteouſneſs, now about to ſet in blood, or the goſpel, which ſhould for a ſeaſon be continued among them: *walk while ye have the light*, make uſe of your day of grace; *leſt darkneſs come upon you*, as it certainly will if you neglect the preſent ſalvation; you will then be given up to judicial blindneſs, the light of the goſpel will be removed, and you will be left, as a man benighted, to ſtumble and fall into eternal miſery: *for he that walketh in darkneſs knoweth not whither he goeth*, not appriſed of the precipice which is before him, and the ruin which approaches. *While therefore ye have the light* of my preſence and goſpel, *believe in the light*, receive me as the Meſſiah, and walk under the influence of my word, *that ye may be the children of light*, the children of grace on earth, of glory in heaven, admitted *to the inheritance among the ſaints in light*. *Note*, (1.) Nothing is more conducive to awaken the conſcience, than the remembrance of the *momentarineſs of our time*, and the infinite importance of that eternity which depends upon our improvement of it. The day of life is ſhort, the day of grace may be much ſhorter. To-day therefore, whilſt it is called to-day, harden not your hearts. (2.) They who are favoured with the light of the goſpel, are under peculiar obligations to know and improve the day of their viſitation. (3.) Chriſt is the light of a benighted world, and out of him there is nothing but blackneſs of darkneſs. They who know him not, nor the rich ſalvation which his blood and righteouſneſs have obtained for us, are walking in the darkneſs of error and ſin, and haſtening into that eternal darkneſs where there is weeping and wailing, and gnaſhing of teeth. (4.) They only are children of the light who walk in the light as Chriſt alſo walked, habitually looking to him for direction, and deſiring to follow his example.

Laſtly, Chriſt, having finiſhed this diſcourſe, withdrew, *and did hide himſelf from them*. He knew their wicked deſigns to apprehend him, and therefore, as his hour was not yet come, he concealed himſelf, probably at Bethany, abandoning them alſo hereby to their impenitence and unbelief. Wo to the ſinner from whom Jeſus finally departs, and leaves him to his own heart. His ruin is inevitable.

37 But though he had done ſo many miracles before
them, yet they believed not on him: 38 That the
ſaying of Eſaias the prophet might be fulfilled, which
he ſpake, [l] Lord, who hath believed our report? and — l Iſa. liii. 1. Rom. x. 16.
to whom hath the arm of the Lord been revealed? 39
Therefore they could not believe, becauſe that Eſaias
ſaid again, 40 [m] He hath blinded their eyes, and hard- — m Iſa. vi. 10.
ned their heart, that they ſhould not ſee with *their* eyes,
nor underſtand with *their* heart, and be converted, and
I ſhould heal them. 41 [n] Theſe things ſaid Eſaias, — n Iſa. vi. 1.
when he ſaw his glory, and ſpake of him. 42 ¶ Ne-
vertheleſs, [o] among the chief rulers alſo many believed — o Chap. vii. 48.
on him, but [p] becauſe of the Phariſees they did not — p Chap. vii. 13. & ix. 22.
confeſs *him*, leſt they ſhould be put out of the ſynagogue. — q Chap. v. 44.
43 For [q] they loved the praiſe of men more than the
praiſe of God.

v. 37—43. The miracles and preaching of the Lord Jeſus were, we find, ineffectual to the converſion of the Jewiſh people.

1. *Though he had done ſo many miracles before them, yet they believed not on him*. In general their hearts were obſtinately hardned, and they could not bear to think of acknowledging one who appeared ſo mean and poor as their Meſſiah, concerning whom they had formed ſuch high expectations.

2. Herein the prophecy of Iſaiah was eminently fulfilled. *Lord, who hath believed our report?* the declaration made by Jeſus and his miniſters; *and to whom hath the arm of the Lord been revealed?* how few have been effectually wrought upon by the power of the Spirit, and brought to the obedience of faith? *Therefore they could not believe*; they were under, not a fatal neceſſity, but a moral impotency; God had determined to leave them to the hardneſs and impenitency of their hearts, and had predicted their infidelity and deſtruction; which prophecy, the-

fore now received its accomplishment, *because that Esaias said again*, Isa vi 9, 10 *He hath blinded their eyes, and hardened their hearts*, giving them up to follow their own devices, and punishing them with the curse of impenitence; *that they should not see with their eyes, nor hear with their ears, nor understand with their heart, and be converted, and I should heal them* they would not, and therefore they *shall* not He abandons them to their wickedness, and they awfully fulfil the prophetic word *Note*, (1) God's spiritual judgments are a great deep We know he is righteous, and will be found just when he judgeth (2) They cannot believe to whom the arm of the Lord is not revealed for our minds are darkness, till God shines into us, to give us the light of the knowledge of his glory in the face of Jesus Christ (3) The Scripture must be fulfilled, and they cannot but perish whom God abandons to their own heart's lusts

3 The Evangelist shews that the prophecy he had quoted looked farther than the times of Isaiah, even to the days of the Messiah, when the prophet *saw his glory, and spake of it* The place referred to is *Isa* vi 1—10 and contains one of the most glorious visions of the eternal Jehovah in the whole book of Scripture, and the strongest and clearest proof of the proper and essential divinity of Jesus our Lord

4 Though in general Christ was rejected by the Jewish people, *Nevertheless, among the chief rulers also many believed on him*, convinced in their consciences that he was the Messiah, *but, because of the Pharisees, they did not confess him, lest they should be put out of the synagogue*, the sanhedrim, his inveterate enemies, having thus determined, and, unwilling to take up this reproach of Christ, they were ashamed to own what they felt, *for they loved the praise of men more than the praise of God* *Note*, (1) Many approve in their hearts the truths and practices, which the fear of men and the reproach of the world deter them from professing and following (2) They who are ashamed of Christ, and his gospel, may justly expect to be disowned by him in the great day of his appearing

44 Jesus cried, and said, [r] He that believeth on me, believeth not on me, but on him that sent me 45 And [s] he that seeth me, seeth him that sent me 46 [t] I am come a light into the world, that whosoever believeth on me, should not abide in darkness 47 And if any man hear my words, and believe not, [u] I judge him not for [x] I came not to judge the world, but to save the world 48 [y] He that rejecteth me, and receiveth not my words, hath one that judgeth him [z] the word that I have spoken, the same shall judge him in the last day 49 For [a] I have not spoken of myself, but the Father which sent me, he gave me a commandment, [b] what I should say, and what I should speak 50 And I know that his commandment is life everlasting whatsoever I speak therefore, even as the Father said unto me, so I speak

r Mark ix 37. 1 Pet i 21. s Chap xiv 9. t Ver 36. Chap iii 19 & viii 12. & ix 5, 39. u Chap v 45 & viii 15, 26. x Chap iii 17. y Deut xviii 19. Luke x 16. z Mark xvi 16. a Chap viii 38 & xiv 10. b Deut. xviii 18.

v 44—50 Jesus takes his last farewel of them, and leaves his finishing testimony, with earnestness addressing to them his discourse, if so be that at last, in this their day, they might know the things which made for their everlasting peace, before they should be for ever hid from their eyes

1 He shews the excellence of faith *Jesus cried and said, He that believeth on me* as the Messiah, the true and only Saviour of lost souls, *believeth not on me* only, or ultimately, *but on him that sent me* *And he that seeth me*, by faith in my true character as God, as well as man, and in my office as commissioned from my Father, *seeth him that sent me*, from whom as Mediator I derive my authority, and whose glory and perfections are manifested in and by me *for I am come a light into the world*, from heaven, where I shine eternally bright in uncreated glory, *that whosoever believeth on me* as the Author of eternal salvation, and bringing life and immortality to light by the gospel, expecting to receive from me direction and guidance in the way to glory, *should not abide in darkness*, in the ways of error and sin, or go down into eternal darkness *Note*, They who walk by faith in Jesus have the light of life before them, and can never finally or fatally err

2 He warns them of the great peril of unbelief *If any man hear my words, and believe not*, wilfully rejecting the incontestible evidence of my divine mission, *I judge him not*, do not yet pass sentence upon him, but give him a longer respite *for I came not to judge the world*, to take vengeance upon sinners, *but to save the world*, to bring to all in general, Gentiles as well as Jews, the glad tidings of a free and full salvation *He that rejecteth me, and receiveth not my words*, making light of the gospel, and despising its offers, *hath one that judgeth him* *the word that I have spoken, the same shall judge him in the last day*, and rise up to witness against his obstinate infidelity and hardened impenitence *Note*, (1) The great end of Christ's coming into the world was the salvation of lost souls They who reject him sin against their own mercies (2) In a judgment-day, nothing will rise up to aggravate more fearfully the guilt of those that perish, than all the means of grace which they have abused, and the word of the gospel preached to them, which they have slighted.

3 He declares the authority on which he acted *For I have not spoken of myself*, as a private person, on my own authority, *but the Father, which sent me, he gave me a commandment, what I should say, and what I should speak*, under whose commission I act, and from whom I have received my instructions, *and I know that his commandment is life everlasting*, the doctrines, which from him I declare unto you, are the only means of leading sinners to eternal blessedness *whatsoever I speak therefore, even as the Father said unto me, so I speak*, and acting under his authority, and declaring his will, it would be at their peril if they rejected the truths which from God he delivered unto them *Note*, (1) They who would obtain everlasting life must attend to the word of Jesus There, and only there, is it to be found (2) They who reject the gospel do it at their peril Their ruin is inevitable

CHAP XIII

Having finished his public discourses, our Saviour improves the time in private with his disciples In this chapter, 1 He washes his disciples feet, ver 1—17 2 He foretels who should betray him, ver 1—30 3 He instructs them in the great doctrine of his own death, and the great duty of brotherly love, ver 31—35 4 He foretels Peter's denying of him, ver 36—38

1 NOW [a] before the feast of the passover, when Jesus knew that [b] his hour was come, that he should depart out of this world unto the Father, having loved his own which were in the world, [c] he loved them unto the end 2 And supper being ended, [d] (the devil having now put into the heart of Judas Iscariot, Simon's *son*, to betray him) 3 Jesus knowing that [e] the Father had given all things into his hands, and that [f] he was come from God, and went to God, 4 He riseth from supper, and laid aside his garments, and took a towel and girded himself 5 After that, he poureth water into a bason, and began to wash the disciples feet, and to wipe *them* with the towel wherewith he was girded 6 Then cometh he to Simon Peter and † Peter saith unto him, Lord, [g] dost thou wash my feet? 7 Jesus answered and said unto him, What I do, thou knowest not now, but thou shalt know hereafter 8 Peter saith unto him, Thou shalt never wash my feet Jesus answered him, [h] If I wash thee not, thou hast no part with me. 9 Simon Peter saith unto him, Lord, not my feet only, but *also* my hands and *my* head 10 Jesus saith to him, He that is washed, needeth not, save to wash *his* feet, but is clean every whit and [i] ye are clean, but not all. 11 For [k] he knew who should betray him, therefore, said he, Ye are not all clean 12 So after he had washed their feet, and had taken his garments, and was set down again, he said unto them, Know ye what I have done to you? 13 [l] Ye call me, Master, and Lord and ye say well, for *so* I am 14 [m] If I then *your* Lord and Master have washed your feet, [n] ye also ought to wash one anothers feet 15 For [o] I have given you an example, that ye should do as I have done to you 16 Verily, verily I say unto you, [p] The servant is not greater than his Lord, neither he that is sent, greater than he that sent him 17 [q] If ye know these things, happy are ye if ye do them

a Mat xxvi 2. b Chap xii 23, & xvii 1. c [illegible] d Luke xxii 3. e Mat xi 27 & xxviii 18. Chap iii 35. Heb ii 8. f Chap viii 42. † Gr He. g Mat iii 14. h Chap iii 5. 1 Cor vi 11. Eph v 26. Tit iii 5. Heb x 22. i Chap xv 3. k Chap vi 64. l Mat xxiii 8. 10. 1 Cor viii 6. & xii 3. Phil ii 11. m Luke xxii 27. n Gal vi 1. o Mat xi 29. 1 Pet ii 21. 1 John ii 6. p [illegible] Luke vi 40. Chap xv 20. q Jam i 25.

v 1—17 This transaction is supposed by some to have passed two days before the passover, during the supper at Simon's house in Bethany, though others imagine it was done at the paschal supper itself

1 Christ in deepest humility condescends to wash his disciples feet, to testify his love towards them, and set them an example *When he knew that his hour was come, that he should depart out of this world to the Father*, by his death, resurrection, and ascension, *having loved his own which were in the world*, with an everlasting love, *he loved them unto the end*, unchangeable in his regards, and purposing to bring them to a state of everlasting happiness with himself *And*, as an instance of his love, *supper being ended*, or it being supper time, (*the devil having now put into the heart of Judas Iscariot, Simon's son, to betray him*) *Jesus, knowing that the Father had given all things into his hands*, all power in heaven and in earth, *and that he was come from God, and went to God*, notwithstanding the transcendent glory which he possessed in consequence thereof, yet, to make his humiliation more illustrious, and his love appear more astonishing, *he riseth from supper, and laid aside his upper garments, and, as a servant, took a towel and girded himself*, tucked it round his waist [illegible] *poureth water into a bason, and began to wash the disciples feet, and to wipe them with the towel wherewith he was girded* [illegible] *Note*, (1) Christ hath a peculiar people in the world whom he [illegible]

guishes from all others with special marks of his love and regard, for whose sake he came into the world, and whom he will love to eternity, perfecting their salvation, and bringing them to be with him to enjoy him for ever and ever (2) The devil's wiles are fatally prevalent even an apostle becomes his prey Who need not then tremble for himself (3) Whilst the amazing humility of Jesus raises our highest admiration, we should learn to imitate his bright example, and count nothing beneath us which may tend to God's glory, or the good of immortal souls

2 We have the conversation which past between Christ and Peter on this occasion After having washed the feet of others, he came to Peter, who, amazed at such condescension, could not bear to see his Master in so servile an office, and saith, *Lord, dost thou*, the God of glory, the divine Messiah, *wash my feet*, a vile sinner as I am? *Jesus answered and said, What I do, thou knowest not now, but thou shalt know hereafter*, be made acquainted with my purpose and design in this matter *Peter saith unto him, Thou shalt never wash my feet* he was shocked at the thought of his Master's degrading himself so low, and thought he never would consent that he should perform so mean a service to so worthless a creature as he felt himself to be *Jesus answered him, If I wash thee not*, if thou art not spiritually washed from thy sins by my blood, and cleansed by my Spirit, which is signified by this washing of water, *thou hast no part with me*, no communion with me, no interest in me *Simon Peter saith unto him, Lord, not my feet only, but also my hands and my head*, convinced of his error, and desiring nothing so much as his favour, and communion with him, and sensible how polluted he was throughout, he longs to be thoroughly purged from corruption, and to be washed all over *Jesus saith to him, He that is washed*, justified and sanctified, *needeth not, save to wash his feet* by daily application to the same fountain of my blood, to cleanse him from the remaining corruption which cleaves to him, and the guilt daily contracted in this polluted world, and will not be hereby cast out of my favour, *but is clean every whit*, regarded as compleat in me, and habitually freed from the dominion of sin *and ye are clean* in this sense, *but not all*, not every individual of you *For he knew who should betray him, therefore he said, ye are not all clean*, Judas the traitor being of their number *Note*, (1) The condescensions of Jesus cannot but be the astonishment of the enlightened soul (2) Though God's dispensations appear dark and intricate, it becomes us never to object we know not now, but we shall know hereafter, the reasons of his procedure (3) None have a part in Christ who are not cleansed by his heavenly washing We cannot partake of his glory, if we are not first made partakers of his grace, washed in his blood and cleansed by his Spirit (4) It is good not to be peremptory in our resolves, as we may see cause to change our minds (5) They who have tasted the grace of God in truth, desire the perfect sanctification of their hearts and lives (6) We need not only once come to Jesus for pardon and grace, but every day to renew the exercise of faith and repentance (7) Christ tries the hearts of his professing people, and knows who are hypocrites, and who are disciples indeed.

3 Christ explains to them the meaning of what he had done *Ye call me Master, and Lord and ye say well, for so I am If I then, your Lord and Master, have washed your feet, ye ought also to wash one another's feet*, condescending to every office of kindness towards the meanest disciple And, to reconcile them to duties so self-denying, he adds, *Verily, verily I say unto you, The servant is not greater than his Lord, neither he that is sent, greater than he that sent him* With such an example therefore before them, they need not think the lowest offices of charity a disparagement to them *If ye know these things*, and understand my meaning, *happy are ye if ye do them*, are in your spirit and practice conform to my precepts and pattern *Note*, (1) Jesus is our Lord and Master his teaching we must observe, his command obey (2) A faithful disciple of Jesus studies how to serve his brethren, and is ready to condescend to the lowest in every work of faith and labour of love (3) Christ hath set us an example that we should follow his steps, what he enjoins on us he hath practised first himself (4) Knowledge is good, but practice is the life of religion They are doubly criminal who know better and do worse

18 ¶ I speak not of you all; I know whom I have
chosen but that the scripture may be fulfilled, He
that eateth bread with me, hath lifted up his heel against
me 19 Now I tell you before it come, that when
it is come to pass, ye may believe that I am *he* 20
Verily, verily I say unto you, He that receiveth whom-
soever I send, receiveth me and he that receiveth me,
receiveth him that sent me 21 When Jesus had thus
said, he was troubled in spirit, and testified, and said,
Verily, verily I say unto you, that one of you shall be-
tray me 22 Then the disciples looked one on another,
doubting of whom he spake 23 Now there was lean-
ing on Jesus bosom, one of his disciples whom Jesus
loved 24 Simon Peter therefore beckoned to him,
that he should ask who it should be of whom he spake
25 He then lying on Jesus breast, saith unto him, Lord,
who is it? 26 Jesus answered, He it is to whom I
shall give a sop, when I have dipped it And when he
had dipped the sop, he gave it to Judas Iscariot, *the son*
of Simon 27 And after the sop, Satan entred into
him Then said Jesus unto him, That thou doest, do
quickly 28 Now no man at the table knew for what
intent he spake this unto him 29 For some *of them*
thought, because Judas had the bag, that Jesus had
said unto him, Buy *those things* that we have need of
against the feast or that he should give some thing to
the poor 30 He then having received the sop, went
immediately out and it was night

v 18—30 Christ knew who should betray him, and here he begins to point out the traitor to his disciples

1 In general he lets them know there was a false disciple among them, on whom none of the things he had spoken would have had any effect *I speak not of you all* as clean and faithful, *I know whom I have chosen* to salvation, as well as apostleship *but that the scripture may be fulfilled*, which saith, *He that eateth bread with me hath lifted up his heel against me*, therefore have I called one to be an apostle whom I know to be a traitor, notwithstanding all the kindness I have shewn him *Now I tell you before it come, that when it is come to pass, ye may believe that I am he*, and may be the more confirmed in your faith of my divine omniscience and mediatorial character, when you see this prediction awfully verified And to encourage you to be faithful, whatever falsehood you may see in others, or whatever humbling services you may be called to, *Verily, verily I say unto you, He that receiveth whomsoever I send, receiveth me*, and testifies his respect for me, in the honour paid to my ambassador, *and he that receiveth me* as the Messiah sent of God, *receiveth him that sent me* *When Jesus had thus said, he was troubled in spirit*, deeply affected with the traitor's guilt, and the ruin hanging over his head, *and testified, and said, Verily, verily I say unto you, that one of you shall betray me* *Note*, (1) The Lord knows those that are his, and whom he hath chosen to grace and glory, and they shall never perish (2) Many eat at Christ's table who most ungratefully lift up their heel against him, and with aggravated guilt prove faithless and betray him (3) Every true minister of Jesus is his ambassador, and represents his Prince's person For his sake therefore is he to be honoured

2 He points out Judas in particular as the person designed. Shocked at what they heard, doubtful which of them was meant, and anxious to know, each of them looked at the other, to observe whether either would betray any symptoms of guilt; and, as John the beloved disciple lay on the couch next below Jesus, as it were in his bosom, Simon Peter, eager to be resolved, privately gave him a hint that he should softly ask their Master who was meant When, taking an opportunity, he whispered, *Lord, who is it? Jesus answered*, so low as not to be heard by the rest, *He it is to whom I shall give a sop, when I have dipped it* in the sauce *and when he had dipped the sop, he gave it to Judas Iscariot, the son of Simon*, intimating to John that he was the person *Note*, (1) It is a bitter grief to true disciples to hear of the scandals brought upon Jesus by false professors of religion (2) Those are happy whom Jesus favours with his especial regard, and lays in the bosom of his love

3 Judas immediately sets himself to accomplish his hellish purpose *After the sop, Satan entred into him*, possessed his body and soul, and drove him to the precipice of destruction *Then said Jesus, What thou doest, do quickly*, either challenging him to do his worst, or abandoning him to Satan's device Now at the table having heard what he had said to John, they suspected Christ had given Judas orders to provide something against the feast, or to distribute some relief to the poor, he being the purse-bearer Urged on by the power of the wicked one, *he went out presently*, fixed in his base and wicked purpose, *and it was night*, the fittest time for such deeds of darkness and, however unseasonable the hour, so eager was he bent upon his treachery, that nothing could delay him *Note*, (1) When Christ abandons the sinner to Satan's power, he rather hardens him (2) They who withdraw from the society of the faithful, begin to shew the apostacy of their hearts

31 ¶ Therefore when he was gone out, Jesus said,
Now is the Son of man glorified, and God is glorified
in him 32 If God be glorified in him, God shall
also glorify him in himself, and shall straightway glo-
rify him 33 Little children, yet a little while I am
with you Ye shall seek me and as I said unto the
Jews, Whither I go, ye cannot come so now I say un-
to you 34 A new commandment I give unto you,
That ye love one another, as I have loved you, that
ye also love one another 35 By this shall all men
know

know that ye are my disciples, if ye have love one to another

v. 31—35. When Judas was gone out, Jesus addressed himself to his faithful apostles

1. He informs them, that the hour of his glorification was now really arrived. *Jesus said, Now is the Son of man glorified*, he is ready by his sufferings to obtain the glorious victory over all his own and his people's foes, sin, Satan, death, and hell; *and God is glorified in him*, all his divine perfections being most eminently displayed in the obedience to death of the Redeemer. *If God be glorified in him*, his justice, truth, wisdom, mercy exalted to the highest by his cross, *God shall also glorify him in himself*, or *with himself*, bringing him to the mediatorial throne in heaven, *and shall straightway glorify him*, in the amazing signs and wonders which should accompany the death of Jesus, and especially by his speedy resurrection.

2. He intimates to them, that the time of his stay with them would be very short. *Little children*, so tenderly and affectionately doth the Lord Jesus regard his dear people, *yet a little while I am with you. Ye shall seek me*, longing for my bodily presence with you; *and as I said unto the Jews, Whither I go, ye cannot come; so now I say to you*, you must be content for a while under the irksome separation, till the hour of your glory shall also arrive, (v. 36.) and ye shall then come to be with me where I am.

3. He charges them to cultivate mutual love. *A new commandment I give unto you*, not indeed now first enjoined, since it was the old commandment which had been from the beginning, but through the degeneracy of the times it had ceased to be practised, but was now more clearly explained, and enforced by new motives, a command the most excellent, and the fundamental law of that kingdom which he came to establish, *that ye love one another, as I have loved you*, ready to every act of kindness, and to part with every thing, if need be, even life itself, for the good of your brethren: and this was to be the characteristic mark of their discipleship, *for by this shall all men know that ye are my disciples, if ye have love one to another*, they shall take knowledge of you, that you have been with me, and learnt of me. *Note*, The distinguishing badge of true Christianity is this spirit of fervent charity. Love is the image of Jesus: he that dwelleth in love, dwelleth in him. This will make us meek and lowly towards our brethren, ready to pass by their provocations, to forgive their offences, to pity their infirmities, to bear with their differences in opinion or practice, to delight in their prosperity, to promote their good, spiritual and temporal, and ever to maintain towards them the kindest sentiments, and be constant in warmest applications to the throne of grace on their behalf. Then shall the wondring world say of us as of old, *See how these Christians love one another*. A spirit of selfishness, narrowness, bitterness, dispute, animosity, is a reproach to the profession of Christianity, and proves, that those who are actuated by it, deceive their own selves, when they call themselves the followers of Jesus.

36 ¶ Simon Peter said unto him, Lord, whither goest
thou? Jesus answered him, Whither I go, thou canst
not follow me now; but [l] thou shalt follow me after-
wards. 37 Peter said unto him, Lord, why cannot I
follow thee now? [k] I will lay down my life for thy sake.
38 Jesus answered him, Wilt thou lay down thy life for
my sake? Verily, verily I say unto thee, The cock shall
not crow, till thou hast denied me thrice.

[l] Chap. xxi. 18. 2 Pet. i. 14. [k] Mat. xxvi. 33. Mark xiv. 31. Luke xxii. 33.

v. 36—38. We have here a conference between Christ and Peter on what he had said, v. 33.

1. Peter, dissatisfied perhaps with what Christ had spoken, was solicitous to know whither he was going, and therefore eagerly enquires. Probably he thought he was about to quit Judea, and, according to their prejudiced opinions of the Messiah, to erect his kingdom in some other part of the world.

2. *Jesus answered him, Whither I go, thou canst not follow me now*. Christ had work yet for Peter to do upon earth, before he should gain the glorious crown of martyrdom. *But thou shalt follow me afterwards*, partaking both of my sufferings and glory. *Note*, Our eternal inheritance is secured for us: and tho' here we wait and suffer a while, the happy hour will arrive, when we shall come to be with Jesus where he is.

3. Peter, with too much self-confidence, unwilling his Master should doubt his courage, or determined purpose to cleave to him wherever he went, replied, *Lord, why cannot I follow thee now?* what dangers or difficulties can deter me? *I will lay down my life for thy sake*, and will die sooner than desert thee.

4. Christ warns him of the weakness of his resolution, and how unable he would find himself for the least part of what he promised. *Wilt thou lay down thy life for my sake?* how little dost thou know thy own weakness! *Verily, verily I say unto thee*, I affirm it as the most certain truth, *The cock shall not crow, till thou hast denied me thrice*, before another sun shall rise, and the time of cock-crowing is over, thou shalt not only deny me as thy Master, but disown the very knowledge of my person. *Note*, We know not our weakness till the temptation comes, and every boast of self-confidence is a certain prelude to a fall.

CHAP. XIV.

This chapter is a continuation of Christ's discourse with his disciples after supper. When he had convicted and discarded Judas, he set himself to comfort the rest, who were full of sorrow upon what he had said of leaving them, and a great many good words and comfortable words he here speaks to them. The general scope of this chapter is in the first verse, it is designed to keep trouble from their hearts: now in order to that, they must believe. And let them consider, 1. Heaven as their everlasting rest, ver. 2, 3. 2. Christ himself as their way, ver. 4—11. 3. The great power they shall be clothed with by the prevalency of their prayers, ver. 12—14. 4. The coming of another comforter, ver. 15—17. 5. The fellowship and communion that should be between him and them after his departure, ver. 18—24. 6. The instructions which the Holy Ghost should give them, ver. 25, 26. 7. The peace Christ bequeathed to them, ver. 27. 8. Christ's own chearfulness in his departure, ver. 28—31. And this which he said to them, is designed for the comfort of all his faithful followers.

1. [a] LET not your heart be troubled: ye believe in
God, believe also in me. 2 In my Father's
house are many mansions: if *it were* not *so*, I would
have told you. [b] I go to prepare a place for you. 3
And [c] if I go and prepare a place for you, [d] I will come
again, and receive you unto myself; that [e] where I am,
there ye may be also.

[a] Ver. 27. Chap. xvi. 22. [b] Chap. xiii. 33, 36. [c] Ver. 18. [d] Acts i. 11. [e] Chap. xii. 26. & xvii. 24.

v. 1—3. To comfort them against the approaching trials, which would be apt to shake the foundation of all their hopes,

1. He exhorts them to maintain unshaken confidence in him amidst all their difficulties. *Let not your heart be troubled*: the thought that one disciple should betray him, another deny him, that he should suffer, die, and leave them, these things deeply affected them, and he, who knows the souls of his people in adversity, endeavours to provide for their comfort. *Ye believe in God*, according to the revelation he hath made of himself in his word, *believe also in me*, as the true Messiah, as the almighty Saviour, able to support you in all your exigencies, and to comfort you under every affliction. Or it may be read, *Believe in God*, live in the constant exercise of faith in the power and grace of my Father: and *believe also in me*, have the same confidence in me, who am one with him in the same undivided Godhead.

2. He assures them his absence would be to their great advantage. *In my father's house*, in heaven, the place where the eternal Father makes the brightest manifestations of his glory, there are *many mansions*, abiding dwelling-places, where there is perfect peace and joy, and love and happiness. *If it were not so, I would have told you*, and not encouraged you to follow me at the loss of all things, if I had not an eternal recompense to bestow upon you. *I go to prepare a place for you*, as your forerunner, to take possession of the purchased inheritance, to be ready there to receive and welcome you, having prepared you for the mansions prepared for you. *And if I go and prepare a place for you*, as surely as I leave you now, *I will come again*, and that quickly, *and receive you unto myself, that where I am, there ye may be also*, admitted to my presence, partaking of my glory, and made for ever blessed and happy in the enjoyment of my love and favour. *Note*, (1.) The believing prospect of the glory which shall be revealed, should comfort us under all our present trials and afflictions. (2.) In heaven there are mansions for the many sons whom Jesus shall bring home to his Father's house: *none shall thrust his mate, for there is room enough for all*. (3.) None who trust on Jesus, whatever they may quit or lose for his sake, shall ever have cause to lament their choice: in heaven they will be abundantly repaid. (4.) They who look for a better country, that is, an heavenly, shall by blessed experience shortly prove the faithfulness of him who hath promised to bring them thither, who also will do it. (5.) As surely as Christ is gone into heaven, so surely will he come to bring his people home to himself, either calling them away by death, or finally appearing at the great judgment-day, when all his elect shall be gathered together unto him, and be taken to reign with him in glory everlasting; and well may we comfort one another with these words.

4 And whither I go ye know, and the way ye know.
5 Thomas saith unto him, Lord, we know not whither
thou goest; and how can we know the way? 6 Jesus
saith unto him, [f] I am the way, and [g] the truth, and [h] the
life: [i] no man cometh unto the Father but by me. 7
If

[f] Isa. xxxv. 8. [h] Heb. ix. 8. [g] Chap. i. 17. & viii. 32. [f] Chap. i. 4. & v. [i] Chap. x. 9.

[h] If ye had known me, ye ſhould have known my Fa-
ther alſo and from henceforth ye know him, and have
ſeen him 8 Philip ſaith unto him, Lord, ſhew us the
Father, and it ſufficeth us 9 Jeſus ſaith unto him,
Have I been ſo long time with you, and yet haſt thou
not known me, Philip? [i] he that hath ſeen me, hath
ſeen the Father, and how ſayeſt thou *then*, Shew us the
Father? 10 Believeſt thou not that [m] I am in the Fa-
ther, and the Father in me? the words that I ſpeak un-
to you, [n] I ſpeak not of myſelf but the Father that
dwelleth in me, he doth the works 11. Believe me
that I *am* in the Father, and the Father in me or elſe
believe me for the very works ſake

[h] Chap. viii. 19.
[i] Chap. xii. 45. Col. i. 15. Heb. i. 3.
[m] Ver. 20. Chap. x. 38. & xvii. 21, 23.
[n] Chap. v. 19. & viii. 28. & xii. 49.

v. 4—11 Having ſet before them the happineſs provided for them, Chriſt further encourages them, ſaying, *Whither I go ye know*, I have repeatedly told you, *and the way ye know*, which I have taught you by my word and my example

1 Thomas replied to this, *We know not whither thou goeſt, and how can we know the way?* Though in general they had ſome knowledge of the way to heaven, whither Chriſt was going, yet miſtaking his diſcourſe, and having his head filled with the conceits of Chriſt's temporal kingdom, Thomas, like the reſt, ſuppoſes he was going ſomewhere to erect his throne upon earth, but where was a ſecret to him, and he wiſhed to know, as Peter had done, that, though with leſs ſelf-confidence, he might follow his Maſter

2 Jeſus anſwers, *I am the way*, through his blood alone there is acceſs unto God, and by his grace can we only be enabled to walk in the path which leads to eternal glory *the truth*, whom all the ritual ſervices prefigured, in whom they were fulfilled, whoſe promiſes are faithful, and who hath never failed thoſe that truſt him, *and the life*, who hath life in himſelf, and is the author of ſpiritual and eternal life to his people *no man cometh to the Father, but by me*, in our preſent fallen ſtate we can neither draw near to a throne of grace with acceptance, but by Jeſus Chriſt as our advocate and ſurety, nor can we ever hope to appear before the throne of glory, but as complete in him, and making mention of his righteouſneſs only *If ye had known me*, in my true character as God, as well as man, *ye ſhould have known my Father alſo*, foraſmuch as we are in nature and eſſence one *and from henceforth*, as by this intimation you may perceive my meaning, *ye know him, and have ſeen him*, in me *Note*, (1) The knowledge of the Godhead of the Redeemer is eſſential to ſalvation (2) Chriſt can diſcover in his diſciples more knowledge of his bleſſed ſelf than they think themſelves poſſeſſed of, and are therefore complaining of their ignorance

3 Philip, not yet entring fully into his Maſter's meaning, *ſaith unto him, Lord, ſhew us the Father*, ſome viſible and corporeal repreſentation of him, *and it ſufficeth us*, this will fully ſatisfy us, and ſilence all our further enquiries

4 Jeſus gently rebukes the dulneſs of his comprehenſion, and *ſaith unto him, Have I been ſo long time with you, and yet haſt thou not known me, Philip?* my divine original, as well as miſſion *He that hath ſeen me, hath ſeen the Father*, the divine perfections which I have diſplayed, prove my eſſential Godhead, as partaker of the ſame nature, attributes, and glory with him *and how ſayeſt thou, Shew us the Father? believeſt thou that I am in the Father, and the Father in me?* though in perſon diſtinct, yet in eſſence one, inſeparably united in the ſame eternal Godhead *The words I ſpeak to you*, deep and myſterious as ſome of the doctrines are which I declare, *I ſpeak not of myſelf*, by any authority purely my own, or as apart from the Father, *but the Father that dwelleth in me, he doth the works*, which confirm my divine miſſion, and ſet God's ſeal to the truths which I deliver *Believe me that I am in the Father, and the Father in me*, upon the credit of the teſtimony which I bear, *or elſe*, if you think that inſufficient, *believe me for the very works ſake*, which are ſuch convincing proofs of the truths which I preach, and done in ſuch a godlike manner, by my word, in my own name, and by my own power, as ſhews my Godhead and glory *Note*, (1) They who have been long in Chriſt's ſchool, ſhould make their profiting appear They are juſtly culpable who, bleſſed with the richeſt means, do not grow in grace and in the knowledge of our Lord and Saviour Jeſus Chriſt (2) In Chriſt Jeſus we behold a brighter diſplay of God's glory and preſence than ever before appeared, ſeeing in him dwelt all the fulneſs of the Godhead bodily

12 Verily, verily I ſay unto you, [o] He that believeth
on me, the works that I do, ſhall he do alſo, and greater
works than theſe ſhall he do, becauſe I go unto my Fa-
ther 13 And [p] whatſoever ye ſhall aſk in my name,
that will I do, that the Father may be glorified in the
Son 14 If ye ſhall aſk any thing in my name, I will
do *it*

[o] Mat. xxi. 21. Mark xvi. 17.
[p] Mat. vii. 7. & xxi. 22. Mark xi. 24. Chap. xv. 7, 16. & xvi. 23. 1 John iii. 22. & v. 14.

v. 12—14 The loſs of their Maſter's preſence and company dejected his poor diſciples To comfort them, he promiſes,

1 To endue them with the moſt aſtoniſhing miraculous powers *Verily, verily I ſay unto you, He that believeth on me*, as you do, *the works that I do, ſhall he do alſo*, the ſame miracles ye have ſeen me perform *yea, and greater works than theſe ſhall he do*, more numerous, and more wonderful, (*See Acts* v. 15 xix. 12) And particularly this may refer to *the gift of tongues*, and the vaſtly ſuperior ſucceſs which ſhould attend the preaching of the apoſtles, and the much more numerous converts they ſhould make, than their Maſter had done, and this, *becauſe I go to the Father*, when having received all power in heaven and earth, he would in the moſt abundant manner pour out the Spirit upon them from on high, to enable them for the great work whereunto he had ordained them

2 To grant them all their petitions *Whatſoever ye ſhall aſk in my name*, pleading my promiſe, and depending on my advocacy, *that I will do*, by my own divine power, giving you an anſwer to every prayer according to the various neceſſities of your ſouls, *that the Father may be glorified in the Son*, and his glory ſhould be the end of all our petitions, and in gratifying them Chriſt deſigns to advance his Father's honour, and manifeſt his power, grace, and faithfulneſs *If ye ſhall aſk any thing in my name, I will do it*, granting you every needful ſupply of grace and ſtrength for your ſupport and ſucceſs in the work of the goſpel

15 [q] If ye love me, keep my commandments 16.
And I will pray the Father, and [r] he ſhall give you an-
other comforter, that he may abide with you for ever,
17 *Even* [s] the Spirit of truth, whom the world cannot
receive, becauſe it ſeeth him not, neither knoweth him,
but ye know him, for he dwelleth with you, and ſhall
be in you

[q] Ver. 21, 23. Chap. xv. 10, 14. 1 John v. 3.
[r] Chap. xv. 26. & xvi. 7. Rom. viii. 26, 27.
[s] Chap. xvi. 13. 1 John iv. 6.

v. 15—17 Our Lord proceeds to encourage and comfort them in the view of the ſervice before them, and in the proſpect of his departure from them

1 They muſt give a proof of their love of him by their obſervance of his commandments *If ye love me, keep my commandments* He ſpeaks not as doubting the truth of their regard, but as quickening them to give increaſing proofs of the ſincerity of their love, by a conſcientious reſpect to all his precepts

2 He promiſes to ſend them another comforter, who ſhould abundantly ſupply the loſs of his bodily preſence *I will pray the Father*, and effectually be your advocate, *and he ſhall give you another comforter*, and counſellor, to ſupport, direct, and quicken you, whoſe loſs they ſhould no more fear, for Chriſt will take care *that he may abide with you for ever*, carrying you through all your trials, and death itſelf, to an eternal inheritance in glory, *even the Spirit of truth*, the Spirit of the true God, whoſe inſpiration dictates the ſacred oracles, and who leads the minds of benighted ſinners into the knowledge of all truth, *whom the world cannot receive*, the men of the world, who harden their hearts in pride and impenitence, *becauſe it ſeeth him not, neither knoweth him*, are ſtrangers to his operations, are led by ſight, not by faith, and therefore count his teaching to be fooliſhneſs and enthuſiaſm *But ye know him*, as having already illuminated your hearts, and ſanctified in a meaſure your ſouls *for he dwelleth with you, and ſhall be in you*, as his living temples, guiding, governing, ſtrengthening, comforting, and bleſſing you continually *Note*, (1) In the one Godhead there are three perſons, Father, Son, and Holy Spirit, each poſſeſſed of the ſame divine perfections (2) All Chriſt's true diſciples to the end of time may expect divine teaching and conſolation amidſt all their trials, and, whilſt they are looking to him, ſhall be ſtrengthened, quickened, and comforted in his bleſſed work and ways (3) Every faithful ſoul is the temple of the Holy Ghoſt, and by experience feels the indwelling power of his effectual grace.

18 [t] I will not leave you † comfortleſs, [u] I will come
to you 19 Yet a little while, and the world ſeeth me
no more but [x] ye ſee me [y] becauſe I live, ye ſhall
live alſo 20 At that day ye ſhall know that [z] I am
in my Father, and you in me, and I in you 21 [a] He
that hath my commandments, and keepeth them, he it
is that loveth me and he that loveth me, ſhall be loved
of my Father, and I will love him, and will manifeſt
myſelf to him. 22 Judas ſaith unto him, not Iſcariot,
Lord, how is it that thou wilt manifeſt thyſelf unto us,
and not unto the world? 23 Jeſus anſwered and ſaid
unto him, [b] If a man love me, he will keep my words
and my Father will love him, [c] and we will come unto
him,

[t] Mat. xxviii. 20.
† Or, orphans.
[u] Ver. 3, 28.
[x] Chap. xvi. 16.
[y] 1 Cor. xv. 13, 20. 1 Theſ. iv. 14.
[z] Ver. 10. Chap. x. 38. & xvii. 21, 23.
[a] Ver. 15, 23. 1 John ii. 5. & v. 3.
[b] Ver. 15.
[c] 1 John ii. 24. Rev. iii. 20.

him, and make our abode with him. 24 He that
d Ver. 10. Chap. v. 38. & xii. 48. loveth me not, keepeth not my ſayings: and [d] the word
which you hear, is not mine, but the Father's which
ſent me.

v. 18—24. Chriſt purſues the ſame reviving ſubject. He was indeed going from them for a while, but his abſence would not be long.

1. *I will not leave you comfortleſs*, as orphans: *I will come to you*, either at his reſurrection, or by the miſſion of his Spirit, or by his final appearing to judgment. *Yet a little while, and the world ſeeth me no more*; they who rejected him, would no more be favoured with a ſight of him after his reſurrection: *but ye ſee me*, I will appear to you; ye ſhall ſee me now by faith, and ſhortly ſhall eternally enjoy the full viſion of me in glory. *Becauſe I live, ye ſhall live alſo*; I, as the fountain-head of ſpiritual life, will communicate the living influences to you my members, and, vitally united to me, you ſhall live in holy conformity to me here, and in the eternal enjoyment of me hereafter. If we are diſciples indeed, our life is bound up with that of the Son of God himſelf, nor can death deſtroy our union with him: he that liveth and believeth in him ſhall never die eternally. *At that day*, of Chriſt's reſurrection as a triumphant conqueror over all his foes, or when by the effuſion of the Holy Ghoſt their minds ſhould be more deeply illuminated, and moſt eſpecially when they ſhould come to meet him in the kingdom of his glory, *ye ſhall know that I am in my Father*, one in eſſential union, *and you in me, and I in you*, as living members of my body myſtical, joined to me in one ſpirit. And in conſequence of this, *he that hath my commandments, and keepeth them*, is enabled truly to underſtand, and in ſimplicity to obey them; *he it is that loveth me*, he gives hereby an undoubted proof of his unfeigned affection to me: *and he that loveth me, ſhall be loved of my Father*, is the object of his favour, delight, and complacence: *and I will love him*, with unchangeable regard, *and will manifeſt myſelf to him*, making the richeſt diſcoveries of grace and glory to his ſoul. *Note*, (1.) Every faithful ſoul is a partaker of a divine nature, and lives in a ſtate of inſeparable union with the Son of God. (2.) Chriſt gives increaſing diſcoveries of his truth and love to the ſouls of his people, till they are brought to ſee him face to face. (3.) The proof of our love to Jeſus muſt appear in our fidelity and obedience. *If we ſay we abide in him, and walk in darkneſs, we lie.* (4.) Though our love to him is not the cauſe of his love to us, but the effect; yet, as we are enabled to make it appear more clearly, we ſhall find brighter manifeſtations made to our ſouls of our intereſt in him, ſhall experience ſweeter foretaſtes of the eternal bliſs which is promiſed, and ſhall receive increaſing ſupplies of the Spirit, to perfect in us what is yet lacking, and prepare us for our eternal abode with him.

2. One of Chriſt's diſciples, either not apprehending fully his meaning, deſired him to explain it; or overwhelmed with admiration, could not but wonder at the endearing condeſcenſions of Jeſus *to them* in particular. *Judas ſaith unto him, not Iſcariot*, but Jude the brother of James, another of the twelve apoſtles, *How is it that thou wilt manifeſt thyſelf unto us, and not unto the world?* *Note*, They who are the objects of God's diſtinguiſhing favour, cannot but admire the grace of which they are partakers, and with wonder cry, *Why me, Lord?*

3. Chriſt graciouſly confirms and explains what he had ſpoken. *Jeſus anſwered and ſaid unto him, If a man love me, he will keep my words, and my Father will love him*, and make the moſt delightful diſcoveries to him of his grace and favour; *and we will come unto him, and make our abode with him*, taking up our dwelling in the temple of his heart, manifeſting our gracious preſence to him, and maintaining, through the Spirit, in the word and ordinances, the moſt bleſſed and abiding communion with him. On the other hand, *He that loveth me not, keepeth not my ſayings*, diſobeys my commands, and neglects my inſtitutions, and thereby proving his averſion to me, ſhuts the door of his heart againſt me, and wilfully rejects my goſpel, with all its ineſtimable bleſſings. *And the word which you hear is not mine, but the Father's, who ſent me*; therefore they who diſreliſh and reject it, muſt be neceſſarily excluded from his favour as well as mine.

25 Theſe things have I ſpoken unto you, being *yet*
e Ver. 16. preſent with you. 26 But the Comforter, *which is*
the Holy Ghoſt, whom the Father will ſend in my name,
f Chap. xvi. 26. & xvi. 13. 1 John ii. 20, 27. Phil. iv. 7. Col. iii. 15. [f] he ſhall teach you all things, and bring all things to
your remembrance, whatſoever I have ſaid unto you.
27 [g] Peace I leave with you, my peace I give unto you:
not as the world giveth, give I unto you. [h] Let not
h Ver. 1. your heart be troubled, neither let it be afraid. 28 Ye
i Ver. 3. have heard how [i] I ſaid unto you, I go away, and come
again unto you. If ye loved me, ye would rejoice, be-
k Chap. x. 29. & xiv. 9. Phil. ii. 6. l Chap. xiii. 19. & xvi. 4. cauſe I ſaid, I go unto the Father: for [k] my Father is
greater than I. 29 And [l] now I have told you before
it come to paſs, that when it is come to paſs, ye might
believe. 30 Hereafter I will not talk much with you:
m Chap. xii. 31. & xvi. 11. for [m] the prince of this world cometh, and hath nothing
in me. 31 But that the world may know that I love
n Chap. x. 18. the Father; and [n] as the Father gave me command-
ment, even ſo I do. Ariſe, let us go hence.

v. 25—31. For the further encouragement of his diſciples he proceeds,

1. To aſſure them of the teachings and conſolations of the Holy Ghoſt. *Theſe things have I ſpoken, being yet preſent with you*; the time being ſhort, I have endeavoured to lay them clearly before you: *but the Comforter, which is the Holy Ghoſt*, the third perſon in the ſacred Trinity, *whom the Father will ſend in my name*, at my interceſſion, to ſupply my abſence, and to advance my kingdom and glory; *he ſhall teach you all things*, opening your underſtandings to clearer diſcoveries of the truth, enlarging your capacities, and ſtrengthening your memories; for he ſhall *bring all things things to your remembrance whatſoever I have ſaid unto you*; he would not only revive the memory of all the works and diſcourſes of Chriſt, which they had forgotten, but give them a diſtinct knowledge of what, at the time Chriſt ſpoke, they did not underſtand.

2. He engages to give them peace in the midſt of all their troubles. *Peace I leave with you, my peace I give unto you*, as my laſt bequeſt; *peace* with God, as reconciled to you; *peace* in your own conſciences, from the confidence of his love; *peace* with each other, united in bonds of firmeſt union; *my peace*, which none but I your Maſter could procure or beſtow, the purchaſe of my blood, the fruit of my interceſſion; *I give it*, freely, fully, *to you*, and all who follow you as my diſciples. *Not as the world giveth, give I it to you*; not as a piece of compliment, but as a real bleſſing; not as worldly gifts, uncertain and precarious, but as a gift infinitely more valuable than all that earth can beſtow, and infinitely more abiding. It is what the world can neither give, and, bleſſed be God, can never take away from us. *Let not your heart be troubled, neither let it be afraid*, under the apprehenſion of any ſufferings or trials when I am abſent from you: my peace, which paſſeth all underſtanding, ſhall keep your hearts and minds.

3. He aſſures them his departure would be for his own glory and their good, and therefore they ought rather to rejoice than be ſorry for it. *Ye have heard how I ſaid unto you, I go away, and come again unto you*, to take you to the manſions prepared for you. *If ye loved me, ye would rejoice, becauſe I ſaid, I go unto the Father*, to receive the mediatorial throne; *for my Father is greater than I*, not in his divine nature, but as in the œconomy of man's ſalvation, the Son of God humbled himſelf to take the human nature, and ſubmitted to the form of a ſervant: *though equal to the Father, as touching his Godhead, yet inferior to the Father, as touching his manhood*; therefore in his exaltation, as the man Chriſt Jeſus, it became them to be joyful. *And now I have told you before it come to paſs, that when it is come to paſs*, in my death, reſurrection, aſcenſion, and the effuſion of the Holy Ghoſt, *ye may believe*, that I am the true Meſſiah, and will aſſuredly fulfil all the promiſes which I have made to you.

4. He tells them, that the great enemy of ſouls would now be finally vanquiſhed. *Hereafter I will not talk much with you*, the time of my departure is at hand: *for the prince of this world*, he who hath uſurped the dominion over the hearts of fallen men, and once pretended to offer me the kingdoms of the world, (*Luke* iv. 5—7.) he *cometh*, with all his fury and rage, to make his laſt, his deſperate attack; *and hath nothing in me*; all his attempts will be baffled, and his malice recoil upon his own head with greater aggravation of his guilt, and to his utter confuſion and deſtruction; he will find no guilt in me to accuſe my conſcience, no legal power over me in conſequence of ſin, (*See Heb.* ii. 14.) no corruption to work upon, or afford an opening for his temptations: and as Chriſt once conquered for his people in his own perſon, ſo will he conquer in them, and bruiſe Satan ſhortly under their feet.

5. He informs them, that his departure from them was according to the Father's commandment, and a matter of his moſt willing obedience. *But, that the world may know, that I love the Father*, though Satan hath no power over me, I am ready to lay down my life, according to my Father's will: *and as the Father hath given me commandment, even ſo I do*, readily offering myſelf to ſuffer according to his eternal counſels: *Ariſe, let us go hence*, and meet the approaching danger. *Note*, When duty calls, and God ſo ordains, inſtead of flying from ſufferings, we muſt cheerfully offer ourſelves up, willing to glorify God, if he ſo pleaſes, even in the fires.

CHAP. XV.

In this chapter, 1. Chriſt ſpeaks of himſelf under the figure of a vine, ver. 1—7. *2. Commands them to abound in fruits of love*, ver. 8—17. *3. Comforts them againſt the world's hatred*, ver. 18—27.

a Mat. xxi. 33. 1 Pet. ii. 5.
1 I Am the true vine, and [a] my Father is the huſ-
bandman. 2 [b] Every branch in me that beareth
not

not fruit, he taketh away and every *branch* [c] that bear-
eth fruit, he purgeth it, that it may bring forth more
fruit 3 [d] Now ye are clean through the word which I
have ſpoken unto you 4 [e] Abide in me, and I in you
As the branch cannot bear fruit of itſelf, except it abide
in the vine no more can ye, except ye abide in me
5 I am the vine, ye *are* the branches He that abideth
in me, and I in him, the ſame bringeth forth much
[f] fruit for without me ye can do nothing 6 If a man
abide not in me, [g] he is caſt forth as a branch, and is
withered, and men gather them, and caſt *them* into the
fire, and they are burned 7 If ye abide in me, and
my words abide in you, [h] ye ſhall aſk what you will, and
it ſhall be done unto you 8 [i] Herein is my Father
glorified, that ye bear much fruit, ſo ſhall ye be my
diſciples

c Gal v 22– Eph v 9
d Chap xiii 10 & xvii 17 Eph v 26 1 Pet i 22
e Col i 23
f Hoſ xiv 8 Phil i 11
g Mat iii 10 & vii 19
h Ver 16 Chap xiv 13, 1 John iii 22
i Mat v 16 Phil i 11

v 1—8 We have here a continuation of Chriſt's farewel diſcourſe to his diſconſolate diſciples

1 He repreſents himſelf to them under the figure of a vine *I am the true vine*, as a vine, mean and weak in his outward appearance, yet ſpreading on every ſide, ſending his ſalvation to the ends of the earth, and bringing forth the moſt reviving fruits, pleaſing to God, and chearing to man *the true vine*, the life-giving ſource of ſpiritual influences, conveyed from him to all the branches of his body myſtical, and thoſe who are ingrafted upon him, will never find him to fail or deceive them *and my Father is the huſbandman*, who planted it in the earth, and with watchfulneſs and care every moment preſerves and waters it, ſupporting Chriſt in the exerciſe of his mediatorial office, with complacence delighting in him, and guarding him and every member of his church, who are grafted upon him, from every evil

2 His profeſſing people are the branches, on whom the great huſbandman employs his care *Every branch in me that beareth not fruit, he taketh away* Some profeſſing members of Chriſt are only nominally diſciples, not vitally united to Jeſus by faith and love, and bearing no true fruits of grace and holineſs, theſe the Lord taketh away In time of perſecution they fall off, or they turn aſide into ſuch errors in principle, or immoralities in conduct, as diſcover their hypocriſy, or, if they are ſpared to the laſt, by death they are cut off, and then the hypocrite's hope periſheth *And every branch in me that beareth fruit*, truly engrafted into Chriſt, partaking of the quickening influences of his Spirit, and bringing forth the fruits of righteouſneſs, which are by Jeſus Chriſt to the praiſe and glory of God, *he purgeth it, that it may bring forth more fruit* by his word, his Spirit, his afflictive providences, he continues to cut off the luxuriant and noxious ſhoots of pride, luſt, and worldlineſs, which would ſtill ſpring from the remainders of in-dwelling corruption, even in the hearts of the faithful, and to encourage, cultivate, and increaſe the gracious diſpoſitions he hath implanted, that they may ſhoot more vigorouſly, and bring forth more abundantly in all good converſation and godlineſs

3 As he had now purged out Judas from among them, he exhorts them to approve their fidelity *Now ye are clean through the word which I have ſpoken unto you*, your hearts being purified by faith, in which way the word becomes effectual to all Chriſt's diſciples in every age, purging out the droſs of in-dwelling evil, and ſanctifying the ſoul *Abide in me*, as the root and ſtock from whence all ſpiritual ſupplies of grace are drawn, placing all your dependance on my blood and righteouſneſs, my Spirit and power, *and I will then abide in you*, as the living principle of all goodneſs *As the branch cannot bear fruit of itſelf, except it abide in the vine*, and maintain a conſtant communication with the root, *no more can ye, except ye abide in me* The beſt of men have no ſtock of grace within themſelves, but muſt maintain habitual communion with Jeſus, if they would continue to bring forth fruit unto God *I am the vine, ye are the branches he that abideth in me*, in the conſtant exerciſe of faith, *and I in him*, by the powerful operation of my Spirit, *the ſame bringeth forth much fruit for without me*, ſeparate from me, and for a moment deſtitute of my quickening influence, *ye can do nothing* truly good and acceptable to God, but muſt wither, droop, and die, as branches deprived of communication with the living root Without Chriſt we can do nothing towards our juſtification, ſanctification, or glorification, he muſt be to us *all* and *in all*

4 He warns them of the fatal conſequences of departure from him *If any man abide not in me*, baſely deſert my cauſe, and make ſhipwreck of faith and a good conſcience, or, whilſt he hath a name to live, be really found dead in treſpaſſes and ſins, *he is caſt forth as a branch*, excommunicated from the company of the faithful here below, if his iniquities are brought to light, or, at fartheſt, cut off at death from the ſociety of the bleſſed, *and is withered*, his piety withers, his zeal grows cold, his devotion dies, his reputation decays, his hopes periſh; *and men gather them and caſt them into the fire, and they are burned*, and thus ſhall the angels of God at the laſt gather out of Chriſt's kingdom all that offend and do iniquity, when hypocrites will have their portion with the unbelievers and impenitent, and be caſt together into the everlaſting burnings Let us read and tremble

5 He aſſures them the prayers of all his faithful people ſhou'd be heard and anſwered *If ye abide in me*, ſteadily cleaving to me under all diſcouragements, *and my words abide in you*, and habitually influence your conduct, *ye ſhall aſk what ye will, and it ſhall be done unto you*, whatever is for his glory and our good ſhall be granted And *herein is my Father glorified*, by your abiding in me, and aſking and receiving out of my fulneſs, *that ye bear much fruit* of grace, which will redound to his praiſe, *ſo ſhall ye be my diſciples*, evidently proved to be ſuch by your good converſation and approved fidelity, and ſhall be acknowledged by me in the day of my appearing and glory

9 As the Father hath loved me, ſo have I loved you
continue ye in my love 10 [k] If ye keep my command-
ments, ye ſhall abide in my love even as I have kept
my Father's commandments, and abide in his love
11 These things have I ſpoken unto you that my joy
might remain in you, and [l] *that* your joy might be full
12 [m] This is my commandment, That ye love one an-
other, as I have loved you 13 [n] Greater love hath no
man than this, that a man lay down his life for his friends
14 [o] Ye are my friends, if ye do whatſoever I command
you 15 Henceforth I call you not ſervants, for the
ſervant knoweth not what his lord doth but I have
called you friends, for [p] all things that I have heard of
my Father, I have made known unto you 16 [q] Ye
have not choſen me, but I have choſen you, and [r] or-
dained you, that you ſhould go and bring forth fruit,
and *that* your fruit ſhould remain that [s] whatſoever ye
ſhall aſk of the Father in my name, he may give it
you 17 Theſe things I command you, that ye love
one another

k Chap xiv 15, 21, 23
l Chap xvi 24 & xvii 13 1 John i 4
m Chap xiii 34 1 Theſ iv 9 1 Pet iv 8 1 John iii 11 & iv 21
n Rom v 7 1 John iii 16
o Chap xiv 15 23 Mat xii 50
p Eph i 9
q 1 John iv 10 19
r Mat xxviii 19 1 Tim ii 7
s Mat xxi 22 Ver 7 Chap xiv 13
t Ver 12

v 9—17 We have here,

1 The love of Chriſt towards his people *As the Father hath loved me, ſo have I loved you*, and this love of his appeared moſt eminent and ſingular

(1) In his laying down his life for them *Greater love hath no man than this, that a man lay down his life for his friends* but greater even than this hath been the love of Jeſus, when we were enemies Chriſt died for us

(2) In his kindneſs towards them, admitting them into his favour and friendſhip *Ye are my friends, if ye do whatſoever I command you*, and herein ſhew yourſelves faithful to me *Henceforth I call you not ſervants*, though to be employed by ſuch a Maſter, and that he condeſcends to accept of our ſervices, is abundant honour, *for the ſervant knoweth not what his lord doth*, nor is admitted to any ſuch intimacy and familiarity as you have been indulged with *but I have called you* by the honourable name of *friends*, and have treated you with the moſt cordial affection and confidence, *for all things that I have heard of my Father, I have made known unto you* All things that as Mediator he came to preach and teach, reſpecting the ſalvation of ſinners, and the counſels of grace, he had kept back nothing from them, and his Spirit would ſhortly give them a clearer knowledge of what he had revealed to them

(3) In his ordaining them to the high dignity of apoſtleſhip, as well as to eternal life and glory *Ye have not choſen me*, and by your choice laid any obligations on me to return the kindneſs, *but I have choſen you*, of my ſovereign will and pleaſure, and to manifeſt the riches of my grace and love, *and ordained you*, both to your office as apoſtles, and to ſalvation, as elect veſſels, *that ye ſhould go and bring forth fruit*, in the purity of your converſations, and the abundant ſucceſs of your miniſtry, *and that your fruit ſhould remain*, when your fidelity ſhall receive an eternal recompenſe, and the bleſſed effects of your labours, preaching, and writings, remain to the lateſt ages

(4) In his granting them all their petitions *That whatſoever ye ſhall aſk of the Father in my name, he may give it you*, and the aſſurance of being heard is the great inducement and encouragement to us to pray How can we but be happy to draw near to God, when we are thus conſtantly aſſured of receiving an anſwer of peace?

2 He exhorts them, from the conſideration of his love to them, to make the due and grateful return to him, by loving and ſerving him, and one another *Continue ye in my love*, ſtedfaſtly cleave to me, and believe my regard to you will be invariable and unchangeable *If ye keep my commandments, ye ſhall abide in my love*; if you approve your fidelity, you ſhall have the unutterable ſatisfaction of my approbation, and have increaſing ſupplies of grace miniſtred to you, yet farther to eſtabliſh, ſtrengthen, and ſettle you *Even as I have kept my Father's commandments*, with unabating ardor and conſtancy *and abide in his love*, am now, and ſhall for ever be, the object of his higheſt delight and complacence, as you ſhall be of mine And next to your love of me, *this is my commandment, that ye*

love one another, as I have loved you And again, *v* 17 this being among the best proofs of real love to Jeſus, and the great commandment which he eſpecially enjoins, as the diſtinguiſhing badge of true diſcipleſhip *Note,* (1) The love of Chriſt known and believed, can alone engage our hearts to a return of love (2) The purpoſe of univerſal obedience to Chriſt's commands, is the ſure evidence of love without diſſimulation (3) No duty is more frequently and earneſtly urged upon us, than chriſtian charity, becauſe nothing is more ornamental to our profeſſion, nor do we in any thing more reſemble him, whoſe nature and name is love

a 1 John iii 13
b John xv 5
c Chap xvii 14
x Mat x 24 Luke vi 40 Chap xiii 16
y Ezek iii
z Mat x 22 & xxiv 9 Chap xvi 3
a Chap ix 41
b Jam iv 17
† Or excuſe
c 1 John ii 23
d Chap iii 2 & ix 32
e Pſ xxxv 19 & lxix 4

18 [a] If the world hate you, ye know that it hated me
before *it hated you* 19 [b] If ye were of the world, the
world would love his own but [c] becauſe ye are not of
the world, but I have choſen you out of the world, there-
fore the world hateth you 20 Remember the word
that I ſaid unto you, [x] The ſervant is not greater than
the lord If they have perſecuted me, they will alſo per-
ſecute you [y] if they have kept my ſaying, they will keep
yours alſo 21 But [z] all theſe things will they do unto
you for my name's ſake, becauſe they know not him that
ſent me 22 [a] If I had not come and ſpoken unto them,
they had not had ſin [b] but now they have no † cloke
for their ſin 23 [c] He that hateth me, hateth my Fa-
ther alſo 24 If I had not done among them the works
[d] which none other man did, they had not had ſin but
now they have both ſeen, and hated both me and my
Father 25 But *this cometh to paſs,* that the word might
be fulfilled that is written in their law, [e] They hated me
without a cauſe

v 18—25 They who will be faithful to the Saviour, muſt expect the enmity of a ſinful world, where wicked men, many and mighty, will unite in hatred, oppoſition, and perſecution againſt them

1 The followers of Jeſus may expect to be hated, perſecuted, deſpiſed Since the original enmity put between the ſeed of the ſerpent, and the ſeed of the woman, never was there one truly godly man, but more or leſs experienced the like treatment

2 So dealt they with our great Lord and Maſter, whoſe example ſhould reconcile us to ſuffer with him *If the world hate you, marvel not, ye know that it hated me before it hated you* never was character ſo ſpotleſs as his, never one ſuffered ſo much from the enmity of the world

3 The reaſon for the world's hatred of us is evident *If ye were of the world,* conformed to it in your tempers, manners, and practice, *the world would love his own,* would careſs and eſteem you, *but becauſe ye are not of the world, but I have choſen you out of the world, therefore the world hateth you,* becauſe by my diſtinguiſhing grace I have taken you for my own, and ordained you to eternal life and glory, your heavenly minds and converſation cannot but witneſs againſt, and reprove their vain and wicked ways, and therefore their anger riſes *Note,* The men of the world have not only a hatred of real chriſtians in general, but an eſpecial enmity againſt goſpel miniſters, whoſe preaching and rebukes exaſperate thoſe who reject the counſel of God againſt their own ſouls

4 He reminds them, that this was no more than he had all along taught them to expect *Remember the word that I ſaid unto you, The ſervant is not greater than the lord,* nor may expect more reſpectful treatment *If they have perſecuted me,* with all manner of rancour, reviling, and injuries, *they will alſo perſecute you,* my ambaſſadors, who bear the ſame meſſage, and go forth into the ſame world that lieth in wickedneſs *If they have kept my ſayings, they will keep yours alſo,* the goſpel you preach will be deſpiſed and rejected, and your words be miſrepreſented, cavilled at, and ridiculed, as mine in general have been *But all theſe things will they do unto you for my name's ſake,* becauſe you have an intereſt in my love, vindicate my honour, and preach my goſpel, whatever other pretences they may feign as the ground of their oppoſition, *becauſe they know not him that ſent me,* their minds are blinded by pride and prejudice, ignorant of the true God and his Meſſiah *Note,* (1) All who will live godly in Chriſt Jeſus, may expect perſecution of one kind or other (2) The faithful miniſters of the goſpel may not be ſurprized, if their preaching is treated with contempt or ridicule, their Lord was ſo inſulted (3) Perſecutors often pretend other cauſes to cover their enmity againſt God's people, but whatever be their pretext, the true reaſon is his image in them which they cannot bear, and his goſpel which they abhor

5 Chriſt ſuggeſts the inexcuſable guilt of thoſe who rejected him and his goſpel *If I had not come and ſpoken unto them, they had not had ſin,* comparatively ſpeaking, *but now they have no cloke for their ſin,* their infidelity is wilful, their impenitence obſtinate *He that hateth me, hateth my Father alſo,* the hatred ſhewn to his perſon, miniſter, and goſpel, ultimately center in God himſelf *If I had not done among them the works which none other man did,* ſuch ſtupendous miracles, as inconteſtibly proved my divine miſſion, *they had not had ſin,* they might have had ſome cloak for their unbelief, *but now they have both ſeen, and hated both me and my Father,* rejecting the teſtimony he thus hath born to me, and fixed in a rooted averſion to me and him *But this cometh to paſs, that the word might be fulfilled that is written,* Pſal lxix 4 *in their law, They hated me without a cauſe* *Note,* (1) They are left moſt inexcuſable, and their guilt moſt aggravated, who perſiſt in unbelief, and go to hell with bibles in their hands (2) They who hate the goſpel, and Chriſt, the author of it, whatever they may pretend, truly hate God Enemies to the chriſtian religion, are enemies to all religion, and Deiſt is really but another ſofter name for Atheiſt (3) Enmity againſt Chriſt and his goſpel is moſt abſurd and unreaſonable, it is quarrelling with our own mercies, and being, in fact, the worſt enemies to ourſelves

f Luke xxiv 49 Chap xiv 17, 26 & xvi
g Acts ii
h Acts i 8 & iv 20 & v 32 &
k Luke i 2 1 John i 1

26 But [f] when the Comforter is come, whom I will
ſend unto you from the Father, *even* the Spirit of truth,
which proceedeth from the Father, he ſhall teſtify of
me 27 And [g] ye alſo ſhall bear witneſs, becauſe [h] ye
have been with me from the beginning

v 26, 27 Though the enemies of Jeſus and his people are many and mighty, he hath provided ſuch ſupports for them, as ſhall enable them to triumph over all oppoſition

1 His Spirit ſhall be their comfort and ſtrength *But when the Comforter is come, whom I will ſend unto you from the Father, even the Spirit of truth, which proceedeth from the Father, he ſhall teſtify of me* On the day of Pentecoſt, the moſt abundant influences of the Holy Ghoſt were to be poured forth upon them, he being the third perſon in the ſacred Trinity, proceeding from the Father and the Son, whoſe peculiar office in the œconomy of man's ſalvation is to teſtify of Chriſt, as the Spirit of truth ſpeaking in the apoſtles, and bearing witneſs to the divine glory and grace of the Redeemer, and making the preaching of the goſpel effectual to the conſciences of men He is *the advocate,* convincing men of ſin, righteouſneſs, and judgment, *the Comforter,* filling the ſouls of Chriſt's faithful people with joy unſpeakable and full of glory

2 They ſhall themſelves hereby be enabled to bear a noble teſtimony for Chriſt *Ye alſo ſhall bear witneſs,* preaching my goſpel in the face of all oppoſers, and confirming it by the miraculous powers with which you ſhall be inveſted and your evidence cannot be juſtly excepted againſt, *becauſe ye have been with me from the beginning,* and ſpeak the things of which you have yourſelves the moſt undoubted aſſurance *Note,* Miniſters can then powerfully preach Chriſt, when they have themſelves experimentally known him, have been with him in faith and love, and for a ſeaſon have walked in a ſtate of communion with him

CHAP XVI

We have here the concluſion of Chriſt's diſcourſe 1 *He warns them of their approaching trials* 2 *He promiſes,* (1) *That he would ſend them the Comforter,* ver 7—15 (2) *That he would viſit them again at his reſurrection,* ver 16—22 (3) *That he would ſecure to them an anſwer of peace to all their prayers,* ver 23—27 (4) *That he was now but returning to his Father,* ver 28—32 (5) *That whatever troubles they might meet with in this world by virtue of his victory over it, they ſhould be ſure of peace in him,* ver 33

a Mat xi 6
b Chap ix 22 34 xii 42
c Mat xxiv 9
d Chap xv 21 & 1 Cor ii 8
e Chap xiii 19 & xiv 29
f Mat ix 15
g Chap vii 33 & xiv 28 ver 10 16
h Chap xiv 1 27
i Chap xiv 16 26 & xv 26
k Acts ii 1
l Or convince
m Acts ii 37
n Rom i 24
o Luke xxiv 17
p 1 John v 20
q Acts ii 32 Rev xxii 16
r Chap xii 31
s Mark iv 33 1 Cor iii 1

1 THESE things have I ſpoken unto you, that [a] ye
ſhould not be offended 2 [b] They ſhall put you
out of the ſynagogues yea, the time cometh, that who-
ſoever killeth you, will think that he doth God ſervice
3 And [c] theſe things will they do unto you, becauſe
they have not known the Father, nor me 4 But [d] theſe
things have I told you, that when the time ſhall come,
ye may remember that I told you of them And [e] theſe
things I ſaid not unto you at the beginning, becauſe I was
with you 5 But [f] now I go my way to him that ſent
me, and none of you aſketh me, Whither goeſt thou?
6 But becauſe I have ſaid theſe things unto you, [g] ſor-
row hath filled your heart 7 Nevertheleſs, I tell you
the truth, It is expedient for you that I go away, for if
I go not away, [h] the Comforter will not come unto you,
but [i] if I depart, I will ſend him unto you 8 And
when he is come, he will [l] reprove the world of ſin,
and of righteouſneſs, and of judgment 9 [m] Of ſin, be-
cauſe they believe not on me, 10 Of righteouſneſs,
becauſe I go to my Father, and ye ſee me no more,
11 [n] Of judgment, becauſe [o] the prince of this world is
judged 12 I have yet many things to ſay unto you,
but

but ye cannot bear them now 13 Howbeit, when he
p the Spirit of truth is come, q he will guide you into all
truth for he shall not speak of himself, but whatsoever
he shall hear, *that* shall he speak and r he will shew you
things to come 14 He shall glorify me for he shall
receive of mine, and shall shew it unto you 15 s All
things that the Father hath, are mine therefore said I,
that he shall take of mine, and shall shew it unto you

p Chap. xv. 26. q Ver. 6. r John ii. s Chap. xvii. 10.

v 1—15 To be forewarned is to be forearmed Christ lets his disciples know what they had to expect

1 He tells them what they must expect, and warns them to prepare for it *These things have I spoken unto you, that ye should not be offended*, that you might not be discouraged by sufferings, faint under the cross, and desert the path of duty *They shall put you out of the synagogues*, excommunicate you from their society, and thrust you from divine worship *yea the time cometh*, when, so infatuated and bloody will their persecution be, *that whosoever killeth you, will think that he doth God service* Note, (1) The best friends of the church of Christ have often been branded by those who pretend to be church-rulers as her worst enemies (2) Blind bigotry raises the bitterest persecution, the blood of martyrs hath never flowed more liberally than by their hands, who murdered them as excommunicate heretics in the name of the Lord

2 He suggests the real cause of this treatment *These things will they do unto you, because they have not known the Father, nor me*, though they may pretend the highest attainments of wisdom and piety, and persecute you as a sect of poor illiterate deluded enthusiasts, yet they are sunk in spiritual ignorance, which though no excuse for their wickedness, is an argument for you to bear patiently with them, and to pity and pray for them

3 He lets them know that he gave them these warnings for the confirmation of their faith in him, and to encourage them to bear up when the day of temptation came upon them *These things have I told you, that when the time shall come, ye may remember that I told you of them*, and have a fresh proof of my omniscience and faithfulness to you *And these things I said not unto you at the beginning, because I was with you*, to bear the chief burden myself, and to comfort and support you Note, Christ graciously proportions our trials to our strength, and will never suffer us to be tempted above what he will enable us to bear

4 He assures them, though he was going, and they were dejected, it would be abundantly for their good *But now I go my way to him that sent me, and none of you asketh me, Whither goest thou?* Though they had asked him with a temporal view, they had no apprehension that he was going to heaven, to prepare an abode for them in glory, and therefore did not pursue their enquiries *But because I have said these things unto you*, of my departure, and your approaching troubles, *sorrow hath filled your heart*, when you ought rather to rejoice *Nevertheless, I tell you the truth*, greatly as you dread my going from you, *it is expedient for you that I go away*, and a kind father will give his children not what they foolishly wish, but what he knows will be best for them, *for if I go not away, the Comforter will not come unto you*, such being the decree of the most high *but if I depart*, according to the eternal counsels, finishing my work, and entering into my glory, *I will send him unto you*, as the fruit of my death, and the effect of my intercession, and this would more than supply the loss of his bodily presence Note, We are often melancholy, when we ought to rejoice, much readier to pore over our corruptions, and terrify ourselves with the fear of our enemies, than to exult in the promises, and look up with confidence to Christ Jesus, and this is as dishonourable to him, as uncomfortable to ourselves

5 He describes the blessed work of the Spirit which he promised to send *When he is come, he shall convince the world of sin, of righteousness, and of judgment*

[1] *Of sin*, awakening the conscience of many, both Jews and Gentiles, to a discovery of their native corruption, actual transgression, exceeding sinfulness, and liableness to the wrath of an offended God, especially of the great sin of unbelief, this being the damning iniquity, and the cause of sinners destruction, *because they believe not in me* for pardon, grace, life and salvation, and under this view of themselves, he lays them in the dust of deepest abasement

[2] *Of righteousness*, of the perfect personal righteousness of Jesus, whom the Jews had so blasphemed, and of the completeness of that everlasting righteousness which, as the mediator, he wrought out for miserable sinners, and to which the Spirit directed the self-despairing soul to look, as the grand foundation of hope towards God, *because I go to my Father, and ye see me no more*, his exaltation to the right hand of God being the fullest token of his Father's approbation of him, and that he was well pleased for his righteousness sake, and therefore he was no more to appear in his present state of humiliation, because he had, to his Father's entire satisfaction, finished the work he had given him to do

[3] *Of judgment*, that all power is given to Christ, in heaven and in earth, to sanctify and renew the hearts of his people, and execute judgment upon all their enemies and his, the finally impenitent and obstinate sinners, *because the prince of this world*, the devil, *is judged*, his power is broken his kingdom destroyed, and whilst the triumphs of a Redeemer's grace are now continually spreading through the earth in multitudes rescued from the hands of this enemy, he and all his adherents shall shortly be brought to receive their final sentence at the bar of this eternal judge, and wicked devils and wicked men together be cast into the lake which burneth with fire and brimstone, which is the second death

6 The Spirit shall wonderfully enlarge their understandings, and give them a clear insight into many glorious truths, that as yet they did not fully apprehend *I have many things to say unto you*, respecting the abolition of the Mosaical œconomy the calling the Gentiles, the rejection of the Jews, &c *but ye cannot bear them now*, through the deep rooted prejudices which still held possession of their hearts, bigotted to the ritual institutions, and expecting a temporal kingdom *Howbeit, when he the Spirit of truth is come*, then they should be enabled to receive those discoveries which they now could not bear, *for he shall guide you into all truth*, opening their understandings to understand the scriptures, as an unerring guide leading them into the most explicit views of the gospel-truths, and enabling them to speak and act under his direction with infallible wisdom *for he shall not speak of himself*, as a private person or serving any interest merely his own, *but*, in exact correspondence with Christ and the Father, *whatsoever he shall hear, that shall he speak*, according to the eternal counsels of peace between them both, with which he is fully acquainted, searching *the deep things of God, and he will shew you things to come*, as a spirit of prophecy, enabling them to look into futurity, and make known to the church the things which in succeeding ages should come to pass, even to the end of time

7 In all this work of the divine Spirit, his intention eminently is to glorify the Redeemer *He shall glorify me*, all the gifts and graces he bestows, and the miracles he enabled the apostles to perform, were designed to exalt Jesus as the great Redeemer of men, and bear witness to his divine mission, *for he shall receive of mine, and shall shew it unto you* Christ hath obtained all blessings for us, the office of the Spirit is to apply them to our hearts, and put us in possession of that pardon, righteousness, adoption, comfort, grace, and glory, which he hath purchased by his obedience unto death in behalf of his people *All things that the Father hath, are mine*, not only as we are one in nature, perfections, and unity of interests, but as all the blessings he designs for his chosen people, are lodged in my hands as mediator, *therefore said I, he shall take of mine, and shall shew it unto you* Spirit of truth and grace, apply these inestimable blessings to my soul!

16 t A little while and ye shall not see me and again,
a little while, and ye shall see me, because I go to the
Father 17 Then said *some* of his disciples among them-
selves, What is this that he saith unto us, A little while
and ye shall not see me and again, a little while and ye
shall see me and, Because I go to the Father? 18 They
said therefore, What is this that he saith, A little while?
we cannot tell what he saith 19 Now Jesus knew that
they were desirous to ask him, and said unto them, Do ye
enquire among yourselves of that I said, A little while
and ye shall not see me and again, a little while and ye
shall see me? 20 Verily, verily I say unto you, that
u ye shall weep and lament, but the world shall rejoice
and ye shall be sorrowful, but your sorrow shall be turn-
ed into joy 21 x A woman when she is in travail, hath
sorrow, because her hour is come but as soon as she is
delivered of the child, she remembreth no more the an-
guish, for joy that a man is born into the world 22
And ye now therefore have sorrow but I will see you
again, and y your heart shall rejoice, and your joy no man
taketh from you

t Chap. vii. 33. & xiii. 33. & xiv. 19. u Luke xxiv. 17. Ver. 22. x Isa. xxvi. 17. y Luke xxiv. 41. 52. Chap. xx. 20.

v 16—22 To comfort his sorrowful disciples, the gracious Saviour suggests fresh grounds of encouragement to them

1 He promises them to visit them again shortly *A little while and ye shall not see me*, he should be laid in the grave, *and again, a little while and ye shall see me*, after my resurrection, *because I go to the Father*, to enter upon his glory, to appear in the presence of God as his people's advocate, to take possession of the purchased inheritance for them, and at last to bring them to be with him where he is

2 Some of the disciples, blinded with their national prejudices, and stupid with sorrow, were at a loss to comprehend his meaning, and repeating his words, enquired of one another what they understood by them, and all confessed they knew not what he meant by *a little while*

3 Christ, who knew the secrets of their hearts, and what was the subject of their whispers, prevented their enquiry by explain-

explaining the meaning of *the little while* he spoke of *Verily, verily I say unto you, that ye shall lament and weep* at his sufferings and death with all the circumstances of ignominy wherewith it would be attended, *but the world shall rejoice*, the wicked world the scribes and rulers would triumph, as if they had obtained a compleat victory over him, *and ye shall be sorrowful*, sunk in deep dejection, their hopes swallowed up in despair, *but your sorrow shall be turned into joy*, when seeing him arisen from the dead they would triumph, fully assured of his being the Messiah and with joy still more unspeakable and full of glory would they be filled, when, after beholding his ascension into heaven, the Holy Ghost should from on high be shed abroad in their hearts Then all their pangs, like those of a woman in travail, when her son is born, would be swallowed up and forgotten in the comfort which should succeed, v 21 *Ye now therefore have sorrow*, because I am leaving you, *but I will see you again*, certainly and shortly, *and your heart shall rejoice, and your joy no man taketh from you*, it will never again be interrupted by any more distress and fears, but continue permanent as the source from whence it flows *Note*, (1) Though we may sometimes be in heaviness, through manifold temptations, it is our comfort that we know our sorrow will be momentary, but our joys, which shall succeed, eternal (2) The triumphing of the wicked is but for a moment, and must end in eternal disappointment and misery (3) Though children are certain cares, uncertain comforts, we naturally rejoice at their birth, but when we see what a world of sin they are come into, and what snares are before them, we need tremble for them and pray, least it should be *better for them they had never been born* (4) In heaven all our sorrows will be forgotten, and every tear wiped away from our eyes Then shall we lament no more the absence of Jesus, but without interruption behold the beatific vision (5) Christ hath spiritual joys to bestow on his people, of which a malicious persecuting world can never rob them

23 And in that day ye shall ask me nothing Verily,
verily I say unto you, z Whatsoever ye shall ask the Father
in my name, he will give *it* you 24 Hitherto have ye
asked nothing in my name ask, and ye shall receive,
a that your joy may be full 25 These things have I
spoken unto you in †† proverbs · the time cometh when
I shall no more speak unto you in †† proverbs, but I
shall shew you plainly of the Father. 26. b At that day
ye shall ask in my name and I say not unto you, that
I will pray the Father for you: 27 For c the Father
himself loveth you, because ye have loved me, and d
have believed that I came out from God 28 e I came
forth from the Father, and am come into the world
again, f I leave the world, and go to the Father 29
His disciples said unto him, Lo, now speakest thou
plainly, and speakest no proverb. 30 Now are we sure
that g thou knowest all things, and needest not that any
man should ask thee by this h we believe that thou
camest forth from God 31 Jesus answered them, Do
ye now believe? 32 i Behold, the hour cometh, yea,
is now come, that ye shall be scattered k every man to
his own, and shall leave me alone and l yet I am not
alone, because the Father is with me 33 These things
I have spoken unto you, that m in me ye might have
peace In the world ye shall have tribulation but be
of good cheer, n I have overcome the world

z Mat vii 7 & xxi 22. Chap xiv 13 & xv 16 Jam i 5. a Chap xv 11. †† Or parables Ver 19. b Ver 23. c Chap xiv 21, 23. d Ibid iii 13 & xvii 8. e Chap xiii 3. f Chap vii 33 & xiv 28 Ver 5, 16. g Chap xxi 17. h Ibid xvii 8. i Mat xxvi 31 Mark xiv 27. k Chap xx 10. l Chap viii 29 & xiv 10. m Isa ix 6 Chap xiv 27 Rom v 1 Eph ii 14 Col i 20. n 1 John v 4 & iv 4.

V 23—33 An answer to all their enquiries and prayer is promised them *in that day*, when under the Spirit's mighty influences, they should in all things be taught and directed

1 *In that day ye shall ask me nothing*, shall not need to make any further enquiries about *these things*, concerning which you are now at a loss, and which *I have spoken unto you in proverbs*, under similitudes, in parables, and short sentences, and though sufficiently plain, you, through your present prejudices and sorrow, have not understood *The time cometh when I shall no more speak unto you in proverbs, but I shall shew you plainly of the Father*, make such clear discoveries to your minds by my Spirit, of the whole system of gospel-truths, of the divine perfections and personality of the Father, of his gracious designs towards his people, of the nature and end of all my sufferings, and of the glory thence accruing to God, as will be perfectly satisfactory *Note*, All the great and glorious truths of God's word are dark and unintelligible, till he is pleased by his Spirit to shine into our hearts, to give the light of the knowledge of his glory, and make us acquainted with the great mysteries of godliness

2 All their prayer shall be answered *Verily, verily I say unto you, Whatsoever ye shall ask the Father in my name*, as your exalted Saviour and great high-priest, entered for you into heaven itself, and ever living to make intercession for you, *he will give it you* *Hitherto have ye asked nothing in my name*, nothing to plead as they were now invited to do, or rather had not in their addresses to the Father made use of his mediation, or pleaded his blood and righteousness as the ground of their hope *ask, and ye shall receive, that your joy may be full*, all that you can wish or desire shall be granted, till the abundant joys of present grace and divine consolations shall reach their perfection in eternal glory *At that day*, when the Spirit shall be poured out upon you, *ye shall ask in my name*, with entire dependance on my atonement, and all-prevailing advocacy, *and I say not unto you, I will pray the Father for you*, not that he would ever cease to intercede for them, but that the Father would be ready of himself to grant all their petitions *for the Father himself loveth you*, is your friend and Father, and reconciled God, *because ye have loved me*, this blessed effect produced on their hearts might assure them of the Father's love, which was the cause of it, *and have believed that I came out from God*, as the true Messiah, executing the divine commission received from him *Note*, (1) What an encouragement have we to pray, when the promise is so full? All the blessings which, in humble dependance on our Jesus, we can ask, believing, we are sure to receive (2) Nothing so directly tends to increase our spiritual comforts, as the abiding prayer of faith (3) God delights in those whom Jesus hath redeemed, and as he hath loved them with an everlasting love, he will never cease heaping upon them the constant gracious tokens of his regard, when they approach him as their reconciled God and Father in Jesus Christ (4) True faith always works by fervent love, they who know Jesus as their Saviour, cannot but feel their hearts drawn out towards him with enlarged affection, and shortly they shall be made perfect in love

3 He sums up plainly for their comfort all he had been saying to them *I came forth from the Father*, where from everlasting I am, and voluntarily submitted to my present state of humiliation *again*, having finished the work which was given me to do, and obtained the eternal redemption of my people, *I leave the world, and go to my Father*, to that eternal glory which I had with him before the worlds were This therefore should be matter of their joy, not sorrow

4 The disciples now enlightened to understand his discourse, with delight express their satisfaction in what he had said, and their entire faith in him as the true Messiah *Lo, now speakest thou plainly, and speakest no proverb*, the meaning is no longer dark or doubtful *Now are we sure that thou knowest all things, and needest not that any man should ask thee*, we perceive thou art acquainted with our inmost thoughts, and canst answer us, even before we have proposed our questions *by this we believe that thou camest forth from God* *Note*, Truths, though plain, affect us not, till Christ speaks to the soul, and then we wonder how we could have overlooked before what now we see so clearly

5 Jesus, who saw that their faith was less established than they apprehended, warns them how soon it would be shaken *Do ye now believe? Behold*, as a farther proof of my omniscience, *the hour cometh, yea, now is*, the moment is at hand *that* I shall be betrayed into the hands of sinners, *and ye shall be scattered every man to his own*, flying for safety to any friend's house that will conceal you, *and shall leave me alone*, in the power of my enemies *and yet I am not alone, because the Father is with me*, not only as one in nature, and in the inseparable union of the godhead, but his gracious presence would be with him, as Mediator, supporting him under all his sufferings *Note*, (1) In trying times, many are apt to desert the profession they have made, unwilling to suffer for Christ and his cause (2) They who think that they do believe, must not be self-confident he that thinketh he standeth, must take heed least he fall (3) God never forsakes his afflicted people, when all the world, yea, their nearest and dearest friends desert them, a sense of his love, the light of his countenance, and his supporting presence, will make them an abundant recompence for the loss of all besides

6 For their comfort, he assures them, the issue of all their trials and his would be peace *These things have I spoken unto you, that in me ye might have peace*, whatever happen unto them, what he had spoken would afford them a sufficient ground for their support and comfort *In him*, by faith in his passion, and all-sufficient sacrifice and righteousness, they would find such a peace as the world never knew, beholding their sins pardoned, and God reconciled to them, enjoying delightful communion with him, and amidst all their trials, their souls kept serene and calm in the confidence of his power and grace to carry them through, and in the prospect of the glory which should be revealed in them *In the world ye shall have tribulation*, you must expect and prepare for it, *but be of good cheer*, be confident of my power and grace, and courageously stand in the evil day, *I have overcome the world*, I have vanquished the god of this world with all his wicked instruments, and have triumphed over every difficulty which stood in the way of your salvation, and you may comfortably be assured, through my grace and love, you also shall be made more than conquerors *Note*, (1) Every real christian must expect his cross, and prepare for tribulation, it is inseparable from his profession (2) No outward or inward troubles should deject or dishearten us, our Redeemer is mighty, yea, almighty to save (3) Peace in our con-

conſciences is our privilege and portion if we do indeed belong to Chriſt, and uſually as our tribulations for Chriſt abound, our conſolations which are by him, abound alſo (4) The world, and the things of it, are great enemies to our ſouls, and the means which the devil employs to enſnare and deſtroy us, but Chriſt hath overcome for us, and he will, by his grace, overcome in us, till all our foes ſhall be made our footſtool

CHAP XVII

This chapter is a prayer, the departing prayer of the Lord Jeſus Chriſt Obſerve, 1 The circumſtances of the prayer, ver 1 2 The prayer itſelf (1) He prays for himſelf, ver 1—5 (2) He prays for thoſe that are his And here, [1] The general pleas with which he introduceth his petitions for them, ver 6—10 [2] The particular petitions he puts up for them, 1 That they might be kept, ver 11—16 2 That they might be ſanctified, ver 17—19 3 That they might be united, ver 11 and ver 20—23 4 That they might be glorified, ver 24—26

1 THESE words ſpake Jeſus, and lift up his eyes
to heaven and ſaid, Father, [a] the hour is come,
[b] glorify thy Son, that thy Son alſo might glorify thee
2 As thou haſt given him power over all fleſh, that he
ſhould give eternal life to as many [c] as thou haſt given
him 3 And [d] this is life eternal, that they may know
thee the only true God, and Jeſus Chriſt whom thou
haſt ſent 4 [e] I have glorified thee on the earth [f] I
have finiſhed the work [g] which thou gaveſt me to do
5 And now, O Father, glorify thou with me with thine
own ſelf, with the glory [h] which I had with thee before
the world was

[a] Chap xii 23 & xiii 1 [b] Chap xiii 31 [c] Mat xi 27 & xxviii 18 Chap iii 35 [d] Chap v 32 [e] Chap xiii 31 [f] Chap xix 30 Heb x 8 [g] Chap iv 34 [h] Iſa liii 12 Phil ii 6 Chap i 1, 2 & x 30 & xiv 9

v 1—5 Our Lord having finiſhed his farewel diſcourſe, cloſes it with a prayer, for thoſe whom we preach to, we ſhould pray for He here recommends his redeemed to the care and keeping of the Father of mercies, and the bleſſed effects of it we continue to reap to this hour, and ſo ſhall all his church to the end of time

1 He addreſſes his prayer to the *Father*, whom, as mediator and head of his church, he regarded as his ſuperior, and in whoſe love he herein expreſſes his confidence He approaches him as a ſon with reverence and godly fear, *lifting up his eyes to heaven*, the place where he peculiarly manifeſts his tranſcendent glory *Note*, (1) The object of prayer is God only, and when we approach him, it muſt be as to our reconciled God and Father in Jeſus Chriſt (2) Chriſt lifted up his eyes to heaven to ſanctify this geſture to us, and to juſtify it againſt the ridicule of ſcoffers (3) None can poſſibly belong to Chriſt who do not ſhew, in a courſe of habitual and conſtant prayer, their dependance upon the Father of Mercies

2 He prays for himſelf, that he may be glorified, and enabled, in the completion of the work he had undertaken, moſt eminently to exalt his Father's glory *Father, the hour is come*, fixed in the eternal counſels for his death, and though it approached with horrors unſpeakable, he welcomed its arrival, becauſe he ſaw that the ſalvation of his people would be the happy fruit thereof *glorify thy Son*, as man and Mediator, he looked for ſupport under his ſufferings, that ſome beams of glory might gild that gloomy ſcene, that triumphant over death and hell, he might riſe on the third day, aſcend into heaven, and ſit on the throne prepared for him, where angels, principalities, and powers ſhould be made ſubject unto him and from thence he ſhould ſend down his ſpirit effectually, to eſtabliſh his kingdom in the earth and his judgments upon the Jewiſh people, deſtroying their city and nation, *that thy Son alſo might glorify thee*, by ſuffering in the ſtead of ſinners, and thereby bringing the higheſt glory to all the divine perfections, as alſo by the diſcharge of his mediatorial office when exalted to the throne of glory, by the miſſion of his ſpirit, and the miniſtry of his ſervants, his goſpel ſhould be ſpread abroad, and God's name magnified among the heathen *Note*, God's glory ſhould always be the great end we propoſe, in all our prayers and ſervices

3 He pleads the covenant ſubſiſting between them, and the power with which, in conſequence thereof, he was inveſted, as the argument to enforce his requeſt *As thou haſt given him power over all fleſh, that he ſhould give eternal life to as many as thou haſt given him*, all the concerns of fallen man were put into the Redeemer's hand, and in that peculiar remnant, who were to be the travel of his ſoul, was God peculiarly to be glorified *Note*, (1) Man in his fallen ſtate is become fleſh and not ſpirit, brutiſh in his appetites, paſſions, and purſuits (2) Chriſt hath all human affairs under his mediatorial government, and as ſuch is not only a King of ſaints, but a King of kings, and Lord of lords He orders all the temporal affairs of men as ſhall be moſt ſubſervient to the ſalvation of his elect, and will at laſt be the judge of quick and dead (3) Eternal life is the gift of Jeſus Chriſt, he hath purchaſed for his people the title to it, and hath, in virtue of his obedience unto death, a right to beſtow this ineſtimable privilege on the many ſons whom he will bring unto glory May I be of that bleſſed number!

4 He explains wherein this eternal life conſiſts, *and* what is the way to it *This is life eternal*, the earneſt, foretaſte, and aſſurance of it, *to know thee the only true God, and Jeſus Chriſt whom thou haſt ſent*, not a ſpeculative knowledge merely, but ſuch as engages fiducial confidence in God, as the only worthy object of our truſt and worſhip, in oppoſition to all idols, and ſuch a full perſuaſion of the divine miſſion of Jeſus, as leads us to him as the only Mediator between God and Man, and ſatisfies the ſoul in the clear views of his fulneſs and all-ſufficiency to ſave to the uttermoſt all who come to God by him

5 He pleads what he had done to glorify God upon earth, as the reaſon and ground of his prayer and confidence, that the Father would glorify him with himſelf in heaven *I have glorified thee upon earth*, in my doctrines, miracles, and life, *I have finiſhed the work which thou gaveſt me to do*, of perfect ſinleſs obedience to death, even the death of the croſs, for the redemption of ſinners He was now on the very point of concluding his undertaking, and being fully purpoſed to go through with it, he ſpeaks of it as already accompliſhed *And now O Father, glorify thou me with the glory which I had with thee before the world was* Having finiſhed his mediatorial work, he became intitled to the promiſed reward, and confidently expects to be exalted to the mediatorial throne, and to return to heaven again, there to make diſplay of his own eternal and uncreated glory, which, during his humiliation, he ſuffered to be obſcured by the vail of fleſh *Note*, (1) The Redeemer's work is a *finiſhed work*, he hath left nothing for us to do, pardon, comfort, grace, glory, are effectually purchaſed, and his free gift to the miſerable and deſperate (2) They who by grace, through faith, are intereſted in this eternal redemption, having the ſame mind which was in Chriſt Jeſus, deſire to live only to glorify God upon earth

6 I have manifeſted thy name unto the men [i] which
thou gaveſt me out of the world thine they were, and
thou gaveſt them me, and they have kept thy word
7 Now they have known that all things whatſoever
thou haſt given me, are of thee 8 For I have given
unto them the words [m] which thou gaveſt me, and they
have received them, and [n] have known ſurely that I
came out from thee, and they have believed that thou
didſt ſend me 9 I pray for them I pray not for the
world, but for them which thou haſt given me, for they
are thine 10 And all mine are thine, and [o] thine are
mine, and I am glorified in them.

[i] Chap. vi 37 & x 29 Ver 9, 11, 24 [m] Chap viii 28 & xii 49 & xiv 10 [n] Chap xvi 27, 30 [o] Chap xvi 15

v 6—10 Having offered up his prayer for himſelf, he proceeds to enlarge on the behalf of his apoſtles in particular, and the diſciples in general, who had heard and believed his word *I have manifeſted thy name unto the men which thou gaveſt me out of the world*, have particularly revealed to them thy glorious perfections, and the eternal deſigns of grace diſplayed in my goſpel, foraſmuch as they were given to me in a diſtinguiſhing way from the reſt of mankind *thine they were*, not only by creation as men, but by election, as choſen veſſels, *and thou gaveſt them me*, as the fruit of my travail, to be a peculiar people to me, favoured with my love, and under my eſpecial care, *and they have kept thy word*, embracing faithfully the doctrines which I have delivered unto them, publickly profeſſing, and zealouſly propagating the *goſpel of the kingdom* *Now*, of late their minds have been more clearly enlightened, and *they have known that all things whatſoever thou haſt given me, are of thee*, that what I have taught them hath the ſeal of heaven upon it, and that I have acted in all things in perfect conformity as Mediator to the commiſſion I have received *For I have given unto them the words which thou gaveſt me*, all the doctrines of goſpel grace relative to men's everlaſting peace, how pardon, peace, righteouſneſs, and ſalvation may be attained by me, *and they have received them*, in the light and love of them, *and have known ſurely that I came out from thee, and they have believed that thou didſt ſend me*, as the promiſed and true Meſſiah, inveſted with divine authority to ſeek and ſave loſt ſouls, and to accompliſh the redemption of his people *I pray for them*, that they may be preſerved and kept, and the begun work perfected in them; *I pray not for the world* in general, *but for them which thou haſt given me*, that remnant, according to the election of grace, for whoſe ſake particularly I became incarnate, *for they are thine* by eternal deſignation, and now by their own voluntary choice and ſurrender *And all mine are thine, and thine are mine*, our intereſts are inſeparably the ſame, as we are one in nature, eſſence, and operation, and the redeemed are alike indebted to both for all the bleſſings of the covenant of grace, *and I am glorified in them*, in their complete redemption; and by their faith, love, worſhip, and obedience here below, as I ſhall be the object of their eternal praiſes in glory everlaſting From whence we learn, (1) That the redemption, which is by Christ Jesus, extends not universally to every particular of mankind, but is confined to those whom the Father hath given him out of the world. (2) Those for whom Christ doth not pray are called *the world*: all their joys, desires, pursuits, and aims, center in worldly things. They live after the fashion of the world, and will be condemned with the world. (3) Christ's undertaking was not uncertain respecting its success: he knew that those whom the Father had given him would come to him, and they can never perish whose interests are lodged in his hands. (4) Keeping Christ's word, holding fast his doctrine, and adorning it by a good conversation, is the substantial evidence of our belonging to him. (5) The study and delight of every redeemed soul is to exalt the name of Jesus, and to ascribe entirely to him the glory of that rich, full, and free salvation, of which he hath made them partakers.

11 And now I am no more in the world, but these
are in the world, and I come to thee. Holy Father,
keep through thine own name those whom thou hast
given me, that they may be one, as we *are*. 12
While I was with them in the world, I kept them in
thy name: those that thou gavest me I have kept, and
none of them is lost, but the son of perdition; that
the scripture might be fulfilled. 13 And now come
I to thee, and these things I speak in the world, that
they might have my joy fulfilled in themselves. 14 I
have given them thy word, and the world hath hated
them, because they are not of the world, even as I am
not of the world. 15 I pray not that thou shouldest
take them out of the world, but that thou shouldest
keep them from the evil. 16 They are not of the
world, even as I am not of the world.

1 Pet. i. 5. Jude 1. Ver. 21, &c. Chap. x. 30. Chap. vi. 39. & x. 28. Heb. ii. 13. Chap. xviii. 9. 1 John ii. 19. Chap. vi. 70. & xiii. 18. Ps. cix. 8. Chap. xv. 11. Ver. 8. Chap. xv. 18, 19. Ver. 16. Matt. vi. 13. Gal. i. 4. 2 Thess. iii. 4. 1 John v. 18, 19.

v. 11—16. Our Lord proceeds in his prayer for his dear disciples, whom he was going to leave, and therefore, as man and mediator, commends them to his Father's care and keeping. *And now I am no more in the world*, ready to depart, and return to my radiant throne in glory, *but these are in the world*, left to conflict a while with temptations, corruptions, afflictions, persecutions, *and I* am going from them, so that they will be deprived of the comfort of my bodily presence, when *I come to thee. Holy Father*, essentially holy in thyself, and the Author and Source of all holiness to thy creatures, *keep, through thine own name, those whom thou hast given me*, by thy almighty power, and for thy own glory, preserve them from sinking under their trials, strengthen them against their spiritual foes, Satan, the world, and sin, keep them by thy grace, till thou shalt bring them to thy glory, *that they may be one as we are*, united in affection and labours, and having the same interests and designs. *While I was with them in the world, I kept them in thy name* from apostacy, according to the commission with which I was invested, and by the influences of thy grace: *those that thou gavest me* to be my apostles, *I have kept* in the faith and hope of the gospel, unmoved, *and none of them is lost*, and left to perish, *but the son of perdition*, that traitor Judas, who was from the beginning a child of the devil, *that the scripture might be fulfilled*, Psalm xli. 9. cix. 8. *And now come I to thee*, having finished my work, and returning to my glorious rest: *and these things I speak in the world*, and offer these requests on their behalf, *that they might have my joy fulfilled in themselves*, happy in the present experience of my love, in the quickening, guiding, and comforting influences of my Spirit, and in the hope inspired by the great and precious promises that are in me, so that their joys on earth may increase, and be growing up to perfection in heaven. *I have given them thy word*, have put them in trust with thy gospel, and furnished them with gifts to publish it through the world, *and*, because they have embraced the truth, and boldly confessed it, *the world hath hated them*, unable to bear the reproofs of their preaching and practice, *because they are not of the world*, in their principles, tempers, and conduct, opposite to the carnal mind and conversation of natural and sensual men, who mind earthly things, *as I am not of the world*, and my example and doctrine have they faithfully observed. *I pray not that thou shouldest take them out of the world*, deliver them at once from all the power of their enemies, and put an immediate period to all their trials and troubles, *but that thou shouldest keep them from the evil*, supporting them under all their sufferings, preserving them from falling into sin, and bruising *the wicked one*, Satan, under their feet, thus enabling them to triumph over all opposition. *They are not of the world, even as I am not of the world*, therefore they will be persecuted, as I have been; and, as thou hast supported me, let them experience the like protection, and share thy care and love. *Note*, (1) The prospect of going to be with God in glory cannot but make it pleasing to quit a world of wretchedness: the hour of our dissolution will be the beginning of our endless felicity. (2) It is a pleasing, comforting consideration, that our stability depends not upon ourselves, but is secured by the divine grace and faithfulness: they must needs be safe kept whom God keeps. (3) The world is the Christian's grand enemy; and the victory that overcometh it is *our faith*, and this is the gift of God. (4) Christ's people have work to do for him in the world; and, however desireable it is to be with him, they must not be in haste to go before his time, but patiently take up their cross, fight the good fight, and hope unto the end. (5) No man's profession, privileges, gifts, or apparent attainments, where *the heart is not right with God*, will stand him in any stead when the hour of trial comes; he will be proved, like Judas, *a son of perdition*. (6) The Lord will have his disciples walk joyfully, not mournfully, before him; and he hath for this end left us the exceeding great and precious promises, and ever lives to make intercession for us. (7) The faithful servants of Jesus, who keep his word, and refuse to be conformed to the ways and manners of this wicked world, may expect to be hated by those, against whom their words and works cannot but testify that their deeds are evil.

17 Sanctify them through thy truth: thy word
is truth. 18 As thou hast sent me into the world,
even so have I also sent them into the world. 19 And
for their sakes I sanctify myself, that they also might
be † sanctified through the truth.

Chap. xv. 3. Acts xx. 32. Eph. v. 26. 1 Tim. iv. 5. 2 Sam. vii. 28. Ps. cxix. 151. Chap. xiii. 1. Chap. xx. 21. 1 Cor. i. 2. Heb. ii. 11. & x. 10. † Or, truly sanctified.

v. 17—19. Our Lord had before prayed for his disciples preservation, here he prays for their sanctification.

Sanctify them through thy truth, consecrate them for their sacred office, and let them be under the powerful influences of thy word and Spirit, that in their own souls they may experience increasing purity, and be enabled for the propagation of the truth of the gospel through the world: *thy word is truth*, infallibly certain in itself, and the great means of purifying the heart. *As thou hast sent me into the world, even so send I them*, with the same gospel, and on the same errand, to advance thy glory, and promote the salvation of immortal souls. *And for their sakes I sanctify myself*, am now ready to offer up myself a sacrifice, and to enter on my mediatorial office in glory, as their great High-priest, to be their eternal Advocate, *that they also*, in virtue of my intercession for them, and by the mission of the Holy Ghost into their hearts, *might be sanctified through thy truth*, enabled for the practice of all true godliness, and, possessed of the knowledge of the glorious gospel, may be strengthened and made successful in propagating the glad tidings to the ends of the earth. *Note*, (1) All Christ's people are made partakers of true holiness: he saves none whom he does not sanctify. (2) What was his prayer for us, must be ours daily for ourselves, that God would carry on the blessed work of his grace upon our hearts, and perfect that which he hath begun. (3) The word of God is the great means of our sanctification, and by it, thro' the quickening influences of the Holy Ghost, are we enabled to grow up into him in all things who is our head, even Christ. (4) The ministers of Jesus are his peculiar concern, and they who are truly his, prove it by the practical influence his word hath on their own hearts, and the zeal with which they preach the truth to others. (5) They who go into the ministry under a divine mission and call, may confidently expect the divine assistance and blessing. (6) All that Christ did and suffered was for our benefit and advantage, and as the merit is transferred to us, if we are by faith united to him, we may confidently expect the reward, in present grace and future glory.

20 Neither pray I for these alone, but for them also
which shall believe on me through their word; 21 That
they all may be one; as thou, Father, *art* in me, and
I in thee, that they also may be one in us: that the world
may believe that thou hast sent me. 22 And the glory
which thou gavest me, I have given them; that they
may be one, even as we are one: 23 I in them, and
thou in me, that they may be made perfect in one;
and that the world may know that thou hast sent me,
and hast loved them, as thou hast loved me.

Ver. 11, 22, 23. Chap. x. 38. & xiv. 11. Chap. xiv. 20. Col. iii. 14.

v. 20—23. Christ's prayer terminates not merely in requests for his disciples of that day, but includes all his redeemed to the latest ages.

Neither pray I for these alone, my first ministers and apostles, *but for them also which shall believe on me through their word*, in all succeeding generations, *that they all may be one* in faith and love, by the preaching of the gospel collected together, and united in one body under the same living head, *as thou, Father, art in me, and I in thee, that they also may be one in us*, animated by the same spirit, one in judgment, disposition, designs, desires, and admitted into the nearest fellowship with the Father and his Son Jesus Christ, *that the world may believe that thou hast sent me*, beholding the powerful effects of my grace upon them. *And the glory which thou gavest me, I have given them*, either the gospel, with all its inestimable blessings, or the grace and glory which he, as the great covenant-head of his people, hath obtained in order to bestow upon them, *that they may be one, even as we are one*, in strictest and most inseparable union with us, and with each

each other through the same Spirit *I in them*, as the head of vital influence to them, *and thou in me*, by thy Spirit given without measure unto me, *that they may be made perfect in one*, attaining to the highest perfection of which their nature is capable in eternal glory, *and that the world may know that thou hast sent me*, convinced by the present power of thy grace, displayed in their concord, unity, and mutual love, or beyond doubt assured of my divine character, when they shall be glorified together with me *And it shall then appear that thou hast loved them, as thou hast loved me*, when they are made kings and priests, and shall reign with us for ever and ever *Note*, (1) The ministry of the word is the great instrument Christ is pleased to make use of, in order to beget faith in the souls of his redeemed people, and to as many as he will call, and for whom he prays, it will be certainly effectual (2) All true Christians are one in Christ Jesus he is their living head they are by faith and love united to him, and joined in one spirit to each other, and what is now begun in grace shall be shortly complicated in glory (3) They who are one with Christ, sprinkled with his blood, cloathed with his righteousness, and joined to him in one spirit, are complete in him, and as such cannot but be the objects of the same love as God the Father shewed to him the Mediator (4) They who despise, insult, and ridicule the followers of Jesus, will shortly be convinced, to their confusion, how highly they are, and shall be to eternity, the objects of his love

24 ᵐ Father, I will that they also whom thou hast
given me, be with me where I am, that they may behold
my glory which thou hast given me for thou lovedst me
before the foundation of the world 25 O righteous
Father, ⁿ the world hath not known thee, but ° I have
known thee, and ᵖ these have not known that thou hast
sent me 26 And I have declared unto them thy name,
and will declare *it* ᑫ that the love wherewith thou hast
loved me, may be in them, and I in them

ᵐ Chap xii 26 & xiv 3, 1 Thes iv 17 ⁿ Chap xv 21 & xvi 3 ° Chap vii 29 & viii 55 & x 15 ᵖ Ver 8 Chap xvi ᑫ Chap xv 9

v 24—26 Our Lord here concludes his prayer for his dear people, with the most comfortable assurance of their everlasting blessedness being secured to them

Father, I will that they also, whom thou hast given me, all my redeemed, *be with me where I am* It is my demand, and I claim it as my right, *that they* be brought to my eternal kingdom, and *may behold my glory which thou hast given me*, transformed into the same image, adoring and rejoicing, *for thou lovedst me before the foundation of the world*, and therefore wilt grant all my requests *O righteous Father*, whose decrees are just, and whose promises are all faithful and true, *the world hath not known thee*, thy perfections, counsels, or designs, *but I have known thee* most intimately and perfectly, *and these* my present apostles and disciples *have known that thou hast sent me*, the promised Messiah *And I have declared unto them thy name*, thy nature, attributes, and designs of grace according to the everlasting covenant, *and will declare it*, by farther discoveries to them of thy mind and will, after my resurrection, and by the mission of the Spirit, *that the love wherewith thou hast loved me may be in them*, and they, knowing it, may, by experience of the same love, be made unutterably blessed and happy, *and I in them*, taking up my residence in their hearts, and thus preparing them for and bringing them to the fruition of the eternal felicity provided for them before the foundation of the world *Note*, (1) Christ's intercession is not uncertain in its effect, but what he asks must be granted, since he claims only what he is intitled to *Father, I will* (2) All Christ's people must be with him where he is, and in his presence is the fulness of joy (3) The world lieth in ignorance and wickedness happy are they who are enlightened by Jesus, and called out of the world (4) God loves his people with an everlasting love, and a sense of this shed abroad in the heart is heaven begun (5) Where Christ now dwelleth in the hearts of his people by faith and love, they have an earnest of the eternal glory which shall be revealed in them when they come to dwell with him in heaven

CHAP XVIII

This chapter relates, 1 *How Christ was arrested in the garden, and surrendered himself a prisoner*, ver 1—12 2 *How he was abused in the high priest's court, and how Peter in the mean time denied him*, ver 13—27 3 *How he was prosecuted before Pilate*, ver 28—40

1 WHEN Jesus had spoken these words, ᵃ he
went forth with his disciples over ᵇ the brook
Cedron, where was a garden, into the which he entred,
and his disciples 2 And Judas also which betrayed
him, knew the place for ᶜ Jesus oft-times resorted thi-
ther with his disciples 3 ᵈ Judas then having received
a band *of men*, and officers from the chief-priests and
Pharisees, cometh thither with lanterns, and torches,
and weapons 4 Jesus therefore knowing all things that
should come upon him, went forth, and said unto them,
Whom seek ye? 5 They answered him, Jesus of Na-
zareth Jesus saith unto them, † I am *he* And Judas
also which betrayed him, stood with them 6 As soon
then as he had said unto them, I am *he*, they went
backward and fell to the ground 7 Then asked he
them again, Whom seek ye? and they said, Jesus of
Nazareth 8 Jesus answered, I have told ye that I am
he If therefore ye seek me, let these go their way
9 That the saying might be fulfilled which he spake,
ᶠ Of them which thou gavest me, have I lost none
10 ᵍ Then Simon Peter having a sword, drew it, and
ʰ smote the high-priest's servant, and cut off his right ear
The servant's name was Malchus 11 Then said Jesus
unto Peter, Put up thy sword into the sheath ⁱ the cup
which my Father hath given me, shall I not drink it?
12 Then the band, and the captain, and officers of the
Jews ᵏ took Jesus, and bound him 13 And led him
away to ˡ Annas first (for he was father-in-law to Caia-
phas, which was the high-priest that same year) 14
Now ᵐ Caiaphas was he which gave counsel to the Jews,
that it was expedient that one man should die for the
people

ᵃ Mat xxvi 36 Mark xiv 32 Luke xxii 39 ᵇ 2 Sam xv 23 ᶜ Luke xxi 37 & xxii 39 ᵈ Mat xxvi 47 Mark xiv 43 Luke xxii 47 Acts i 16 † Or I am *he* ᵉ Ps xxvii 2 ᶠ Chap xvii 12 ᵍ Mat xxvi 51 Mark xiv 47 Luke xxii 50 ʰ Zech xiii 7 ⁱ Mat xx 22 & xxvi 39, 42 ᵏ Lam iv 20 Acts ii 23 ˡ Luke iii 2 ᵐ Chap xi 50

v 1—14. His hour being come, the Son of man surrenders himself into the hands of his enemies, having first given them a demonstration both of his power and his grace

1 Having finished his discourse, he retired over the brook Cedron to the garden whither he was wont to resort with his disciples, a place the traitor Judas well knew, and which he judged the most convenient to betray him A garden was the scene of the first man's rebellion and apostacy, and in a garden the atoning sufferings of the second man, the Lord from heaven, began

2 Judas, having laid the plot with the chief-priests and Pharisees, now got a band of soldiers, together with the servants and officers of these inveterate enemies of Jesus, with whom also some of their masters went themselves, to make sure of their prey, and, as it was night, they took lanterns and torches, as well as weapons, that they might search him out, and, if any resistance was made, overpower his few disciples Jews and Gentiles concur in bringing him to the accursed tree, who was ordained to reconcile both to God by the blood of his cross

3 Jesus, far from declining to meet them, or seeking to escape the danger, goes forth to meet them He knew what was coming upon him he had undertaken to suffer, and therefore, having asked their business, and being informed by them that they sought Jesus of Nazareth, not ashamed of that reproachful name, he saith, *I am he*, readily offering himself to them, Judas the traitor being at their head *Note*, (1) When duty calls, no danger must deter us from appearing boldly and openly for Christ (2) We must not be ashamed of any reproachful name which for the sake of Jesus we are called to bear His reproach is our real honour (3) It is a dreadful change to see the man, who was once numbered among the disciples, herding with enemies and persecutors

4 Wonderfully powerful was the word of Jesus No sooner had he uttered it, than, struck by an unseen hand, *they went backward and fell to the ground* He that laid them thus low could in an instant have laid them lower in the belly of hell, but this was the day of his patience, and therefore, though he would give them an evidence of his power, he will yet give them space to repent

5 Once more he asks them whom they sought, if they dared persist in their atrocious designs, and they, with hardened obstinacy, answered, Jesus of Nazareth He mildly replied, *I have told you I am he*, ready to yield up himself, but desirous to secure his disciples from danger, *if therefore ye seek me, let these go their way*, do them no harm and this he said with reference to a late declaration he had made, *of them whom thou gavest me I have lost none*, and by his present protection of them gave them an earnest of the fulfilment of all the other promises which he had made to them *Note*, (1) Hearts hardened in sin will be restrained by no warnings, nor checked by any providences, but rush madly on to ruin (2) Christ knows how to suit our trials to our strength, and will not suffer his disciples to be tempted above what he knows they are able to bear (3) He who gave himself to be a ransom, hath by his bonds obtained our discharge The justice of God hath no more demands, nor need we fear the penalty of a broken law He hath purchased, by the offering of his own body, eternal redemption for us (4) None can be finally lost whom Christ hath undertaken to save

6 Peter, fired at what he saw, immediately drew his sword, and, in the heat of inconsiderate rashness, smote a domestick of the high-priest, whose name was Malchus, and cut off his ear. But Jesus, displeased at this unseasonable zeal, bids him

sheath the sword, and urges as a reason, *the cup which my Father hath given me, shall I not drink it?* His resolution was fixed, his sufferings necessary, and, whatever power he was possessed of to rescue himself from his enemies, he freely resigned himself into their hands, to do with him according to the determinate counsel and foreknowledge of God. *Note,* (1.) They who are most hasty in their zeal are not always most steady in their service. Of this, Peter's desertion and conduct afford a sufficient proof. (2.) Christ's cause is not to be maintained by the sword. The weapons of our warfare are not carnal, but spiritual, and by our meekness we should seek to disarm the madness of our foes.

7. The soldiers, with the officers of the Jews, therefore now seized and bound the voluntary prisoner, and, as a criminal, shamefully dragged him through the streets to the palace of Annas, the father-in-law of Caiaphas the high-priest that year; such sad and frequent changes were now made in that high office. This Caiaphas it was, who in a former debate had shewed his inveterate enmity against Christ, and determined, right or wrong, that it was better to put him to death than provoke the Romans to destroy the nation, as he apprehended would be the consequence, if Jesus were suffered to set up himself as the Messiah. *Note,* (1.) The bonds of Christ are significant. He was bound with cords, that we might be loosed from the chains of our sins, and that henceforth his constraining love might effectually bind our hearts to him in cords of gratitude, which never should be broken. (2.) If we are in bonds for Christ, it will reconcile us to suffer joyfully, when we reflect that he was first bound for us. (3.) If one man, Christ Jesus, had not died for the sins of his people, they must have perished everlastingly.

n Mat. xxvi. 58. Mark xiv. 54. Luke xxii. 54.
o Mat. xxvi. 69.

15 ¶ And [n] Simon Peter followed Jesus, and *so did*
another disciple: That disciple was known unto the high
priest, and went in with Jesus into the palace of the
high priest. 16 [o] But Peter stood at the door without.
Then went out that other disciple which was known
unto the high priest, and spake unto her that kept the
door, and brought in Peter. 17 Then saith the damsel
that kept the door unto Peter, Art not thou also *one* of
this man's disciples? He saith, I am not. 18 And
the servants and officers stood there, who had made a
fire of coals, (for it was cold) and they warmed them-
selves: and Peter [p] stood with them, and warmed him-
self. 19 ¶ The high priest then asked Jesus of his dis-
ciples, and of his doctrine. 20 Jesus answered him,
[q] I spake openly to the world; I ever taught in the syna-
gogue, and in the temple, whither the Jews always resort;
and in secret have I said nothing. 21 Why askest thou
me? ask them which heard me, what I have said unto
them: behold, they know what I said. 22 And when
he had thus spoken, one of the officers which stood by,
[r] struck Jesus [‖] with the palm of his hand, saying, An-
swerest thou the high priest so? 23 Jesus answered
him, If I have spoken evil, bear witness of the evil: but
if well, why smitest thou me? 24 [s] (Now Annas had
sent him bound unto Caiaphas the high priest.) 25 And
Simon Peter stood and warmed himself. [t] They said
therefore unto him, Art not thou also one of his disci-
ples? He denied, and said, I am not. 26 One of the
servants of the high priest (being his kinsman whose ear
Peter cut off) saith, Did not I see thee in the garden
with him? 27 Peter then denied again, and immedi-
ately [u] the cock crew.

p Ps. i. 1.
q Chap. vii. 26.
r Jer. xx. 2. Is. l. 6.
‖ Or, with a rod.
s Mat. xxvi. 57.
t Mat. xxvi. 69, 71. Mark xiv. 69. Luke xxii. 58.
u Chap. xiii. 38.

v. 15—27. Annas, highly approving the deed, and confirming them in their purpose, soon dispatched the innocent prisoner to Caiaphas, to be condemned. Perhaps his age prevented him from attending in the council; but he wished them to proceed, and would give his sanction to their prosecution. We have an account of what passed in the high priest's palace.

1. Peter denies his Master the first time.

(1.) He followed at a distance to the door of the palace, his courage having somewhat revived, and his curiosity being strong to see what would be the issue of the matter. Thus unnecessarily he ran into temptation, and no good can then be expected from him. We have no promise of protection, when we wilfully thrust ourselves into danger.

(2.) A disciple, who was known to the high priest, seeing Peter at the gate, let him in. Some have supposed this was John, who in some other parts of the gospel thus modestly suppresses his own name; but it rather seems improbable that a poor fisherman of Galilee should have such an acquaintance with Caiaphas; and with more it is the probability the person spoken of was one of those chief rulers who believed on Jesus, but dared not confess him for fear of the Jews. But what was intended as a kindness, really proved a snare, so oft do we hurt by the misguided affection of our friend.

(3.) The first and feeblest attack quite disconcerted the self-confident disciple. A servant girl, that kept the door, observing probably his dejected looks, and recollecting his countenance among the followers of Jesus, charged him as *his master's disciple*, which he instantly denied; and, as if to avoid every suspicion of belonging to Christ, he joined the servants and officers, who, it being cold, and at night, had kindled a fire in the hall, and warmed themselves. *Note,* (1.) We know not how weak we are till we are tried. (2.) They who mix with vain and worldly company, to avoid the imputation of being over-righteous, will usually, if there be any sensibility remaining in their consciences, pierce themselves through with many sorrows.

2. Whilst Peter, instead of appearing in behalf of his Master, was basely denying him, the high-priest began to interrogate Jesus concerning his disciples and his doctrine, hoping to find some charge of sedition or blasphemy whereon to ground an accusation against him.

3. Christ appeals to all who had heard him preach, for an answer to his interrogatories. If he had done or taught any thing criminal, there could be no want of witness, when many then present had often heard him, and knew the doctrines which he taught. He ever spake freely, boldly, and openly, preaching in the synagogues, the places of chief resort; and he advanced nothing in private different from what he avowed publicly, nor wished to conceal his sentiments from the world, but to make all men know the truth. *Note,* Truth neither needs nor seeks the covert; and God's ministers must boldly, openly, and uniformly declare their message to the world, whether men will hear, or whether they will forbear.

4. Just and mild as Christ's answer was to a question so malicious and captious, an insolent officer, who stood by, struck the innocent prisoner with his hand or his staff, and haughtily suggests as if his answer to the high-priest was unbecoming. He knew, however infamous such behaviour was, his master would countenance it, and that his insolence would recommend him. When rulers are wicked, their servants will readily imitate their ill examples, and the insults of such abjects are peculiarly bitter. But to this, for our sakes, the Son of God submitted, and thus fulfilled the Scripture, *Isa.* l. 6. *Mic.* v. 1.

5. Christ, with astonishing patience, instead of striking him dead, meekly replied, *If I have spoken evil*, now, or at any other time, *bear witness of the evil* before the court; *but if well*, and I have spoken nothing justly blameable, *why smitest thou me?* *Note,* (1.) When we are suffering, however unjustly, we must in our patience possess our souls, and neither entertain undue resentment nor seek to revenge. (2.) Mild remonstrances, not railing accusations, become the children of God.

6. A second time Peter is beset, and falls. As he stood at the fire, some who stood by challenged him again as a follower of Jesus; and now, sunk under temptation, he repeats the shameful lie, *I am not*. *Note,* (1.) They who are fallen under one temptation feel themselves less able to resist the next. (2.) Many who make confident profession, when the cause of Christ flourishes, soon disown and renounce it, when called to suffer shame for his sake.

7. One of the by-standers, a relation of him whose ear Peter had cut off, hearing him so stoutly deny all connection with Jesus, on observing him attentively recollected his face, and urged the question stronger upon him, *Did not I see thee in the garden with him?* So close an attack more sadly disconcerted the unhappy disciple, and urged him the more solemnly to repeat his denial: *and immediately the cock crew*. *Note,* (1.) Every sin hardens the heart, and naturally paves the way for a greater. (2.) The slightest incidents of Providence, which others disregard, God can make to us a most alarming call.

28 ¶ [x] Then led they Jesus from Caiaphas unto
[‖] the hall of judgment: and [y] it was early; and they
themselves went not into the judgment hall, [z] lest they
should be defiled; but that they might eat the passover.
29 Pilate then went out unto them, and said, What
accusation bring you against this man? 30 They an-
swered and said unto him, If he were not a malefactor,
we would not have delivered him up unto thee. 31
Then said Pilate unto them, Take ye him, and judge
him according to your law. The Jews therefore said
unto him, [a] It is not lawful for us to put any man to
death: 32 That [b] the saying of Jesus might be ful-
filled, which he spake, signifying what death he should
die. 33 [c] Then Pilate entered into the judgment-hall
again, and called Jesus, and said unto him, Art thou
the King of the Jews? 34 Jesus answered him, Sayest
thou this thing of thyself, or did others tell it thee of me?
35 Pilate answered, Am I a Jew? Thine own nation,
and the chief priests have delivered thee unto me: What
hast thou done? 36 [d] Jesus answered, [e] My kingdom

x Mat. xxvii. 2. Mark xv. 1. Luke xxiii. 1.
‖ Or, Pilate's house.
y Mat. xxvii. 1.
z Acts x. 28.
a Gen. xlix. 10.
b Mat. xx. 19. Chap. xii. 32.
c Mat. xxvii. 11.
d 1 Tim. vi. 13.
e Luke xii. 14.

is not of this world if my kingdom were of this world,
then would my servants fight, that I should not be deli-
vered to the Jews but now is my kingdom not from
hence 37 Pilate therefore said unto him, Art thou
a king then? Jesus answered, Thou sayest that I am
a king To this end was I born, and for this cause
came I into the world, that I should bear witness unto the
truth Every one that is of the truth, heareth my
voice 38 Pilate saith unto him, What is truth? And
when he had said this, he went out again unto the Jews,
and saith unto them, I find in him no fault at all
39 But ye have a custom, that I should release unto you
one at the passover will ye therefore that I release unto
you the king of the Jews? 40 Then cried they all
again, saying, Not this man, but Barabbas Now
Barabbas was a robber

v 28—40 His envenomed enemies, determined on his ruin, dragged the innocent Jesus very early in the morning, after suffering during the night the greatest insults and indignities, to Pilate the Roman governor, in order to get him legally condemned and crucified, desirous that he should suffer in the most ignominious way And we are told,

1 The hypocritical scrupulosity of these pretended priests They would not enter the judgment-hall, lest they should be defiled by the touch and company of heathens, and thereby, being rendered ceremonially unclean according to their traditions, should be debarred from partaking of the passover-feast, and the sacrifices which were offered the day after the passover Thus strictly devout would they appear, with innocent blood upon their heads Well was it said of them, *Ye strain at a gnat and swallow a camel*

2 Pilate, at whose bar Jesus was placed as a criminal, came forth to them in great complaisance, desiring to know their accusation against the prisoner In answer to so reasonable a question, they haughtily reply, *If he were not a malefactor*, a person notoriously infamous, *we would not have delivered him up unto thee*, as if from persons of their eminent sanctity a general charge was a sufficient proof of the prisoner's crimes Pilate, justly offended at so insolent a reply, and so unreasonable a procedure, bid them take him and judge him according to their law, desirous to rid himself of so disagreeable a cause They replied, *It is not lawful for us to put any man to death*, either they had been deprived of the power of capital punishments, or they dared not exert it through the frequency of the people's crimes but there was a further view, which they undesignedly answered hereby, even the fulfilling of the prophecy of Jesus, who had signified *by what death he should die*, Matth xx 19 and crucifixion being not a Jewish but a Roman punishment, it was necessary he should be delivered to the Romans, and executed by them *Note*, (1) Many of the best of men, like Jesus, have been branded as the vilest of malefactors, without one real crime proved against them (2) God can over-rule the wickedness of the most envenomed persecutors to his own glory, and make them, when they mean only to gratify their own malice, the means of fulfilling the prophecies of his word

3 Pilate, having heard the tremendous accusations lodged against Jesus by his accusers, ordered the prisoner to be brought, and examined him as touching the things laid to his charge, the chief of which was setting up in opposition to Cæsar, and therefore he demands if it were true, that he assumed the character of *King of the Jews*? Jesus answered, *Sayest thou this thing of thyself*, under any real suspicion of the truth of the fact? *or did others tell it thee of me*, by whose falsehood and malice thou art influenced? Pilate, in a kind of derision at the expectation the Jewish people formed of their Messiah, answered, *Am I a Jew?* no I concern myself about none of these matters *Thine own nation and the chief priests have delivered thee unto me* as a traitor and seditious person, setting up for a king in opposition to Cæsar *What hast thou done?* It is to be supposed persons of so respectable a character would not, without cause, lodge such an accusation *Note*, Many think there must be something wrong, when they who are esteemed the most learned and pious condemn and persecute but we must not take our opinion from the judgment of men, but from the word of God Otherwise, like Pilate, we shall be in danger of condemning the innocent

4 Christ informs Pilate of the nature of that kingdom which he came to erect *Jesus answered, My kingdom is not of this world*, promising no earthly honour nor emolument, nor interfering with any secular system, but is purely spiritual, consisting in a dominion over the souls of men *If my kingdom were of this world, then would my servants fight, that I should not be delivered to the Jews*, but there never had been the least attempt to rescue him, nor any sedition or tumult excited by him, which must have been the case had he affected temporal authority *but now is my kingdom not from hence*, it takes not its rise from earth, is not supported by the arm of flesh, nor governed by worldly maxims and human policy

5 Pilate, beholding his mean, wretched, and low estate, could not help exclaiming at the pretensions which Jesus seemed here to advance *Art thou a king then?* Yes, saith Jesus, *Thou sayest that I am a king*, and so it is, for *to this end was I born, and for this cause came I into the world, that I should bear witness unto the truth* of the gospel word in general, and to this truth in particular, that I am that King Messiah who should come into the world *Every one that is of the truth*, effectually wrought upon by the Spirit of truth, *heareth my voice*, receives my word, acknowledges my mission, and bows to the sceptre of grace I stretch forth to the miserable and the desperate *Pilate saith unto him, What is truth?* either he spoke it contemptuously, deriding his pretensions, who set himself up as the voice of truth itself, or if he put the question curiously, seriously, or judicially, he seems not to have waited for an answer, or Jesus vouchsafed not to return one *Note*, (1) Is Christ born a King? then should we yield our hearts willing subjects to his blessed government (2) They only know that truth which makes wise unto salvation, who hear and spiritually understand the voice of Jesus speaking in his gospel

6 Pilate, in his conscience now satisfied of the innocence of Jesus, led him forth, and declared before them all, that *he found no fault in him* Willing therefore to obtain his discharge, he proposed it to them, as it was an established custom at that feast to release some prisoner unto them, whether it should not be this miserable object, whom, in derision of his pretensions, he calls *the king of the Jews* But they, instigated by their malicious priests, rejected the proposition, and demanded Barabbas, a noted murderer and robber, preferring him before the Lord of life and glory *Note*, (1) He who suffered for sins not his own, even by his judge was acknowledged to be innocent (2) They who, under the dictates of worldly wisdom seek to please men, and maintain a good conscience with it, will find the impracticability of the attempt (3) The cry is ever against the cause of truth, but, though it be oppressed for a while, it shall finally prevail

CHAP XIX.

In this chapter we have, 1 *The remainder of Christ's trial before Pilate, which was tumultuous and confused*, ver 1—15 2 *Sentence given, and execution done upon it*, ver 16—18 3 *The title over his head*, ver 19—22 4 *The parting of his garment*, ver 23, 24 5 *The care he took of his mother*, ver 25—27 6 *The giving him vinegar to drink*, ver 28, 29 7 *His dying word*, ver 30 8 *The piercing of his side*, ver 31—37 9 *The burial of his body*, ver 38—42 *O that in meditating on these things, we may experimentally know the power of Christ's death, and the fellowship of his sufferings!*

1 THEN Pilate therefore took Jesus, and scourg- a Mat xxvii 26 Mark xv 15
ed *him* 2 And the soldiers platted a crown
of thorns, and put it on his head, and they put on him b Is l 6
a purple robe, 3 And said, Hail, king of the Jews
and they smote him with their hands 4 Pilate there-
fore went forth again, and saith unto them, Behold, I
bring him forth to you, that ye may know that I find c Chap xviii 38 Ver 6
no fault with him 5 Then came Jesus forth, wearing
the crown of thorns, and the purple robe And *Pilate*
saith unto them, Behold the man 6 When the chief
priests therefore and officers saw him, they cried out, d Ver 15 Acts iii 13
saying, Crucify *him*, crucify *him* Pilate saith unto them,
Take ye him, and crucify *him* for I find no fault in
him 7 The Jews answered him, We have a law, and e Lev xxiv 16.
by our law he ought to die, because he made himself f Mat xxvi 65 Chap v 18 & x 38
the Son of God 8 ¶ When Pilate therefore heard that
saying, he was the more afraid; 9 And went again
into the judgment hall, and saith unto Jesus, Whence
art thou? But Jesus gave him no answer 10 Then
saith Pilate unto him, Speakest thou not unto me?
Knowest thou not, that I have power to crucify thee,
and have power to release thee? 11 Jesus answered,
Thou couldst have no power at all against me, except it
were given thee from above therefore he that delivered
me unto thee hath the greater sin 12 And from
thenceforth Pilate sought to release him but the Jews
cried out, saying, If thou let this man go, thou art not h Luke xxiii 2
Cæsar's friend whosoever maketh himself a king, speak- i Acts xvii 7
eth against Cæsar 13 ¶ When Pilate therefore heard
that saying, he brought Jesus forth, and sat down in the
judgment-seat, in a place that is called the Pavement,
but in the Hebrew, Gabbatha 14 And it was the k Mat xxvii 62.
preparation of the passover, and about the sixth hour
and he saith unto the Jews, Behold your king 15
But they cried out, Away with *him*, away with *him*,

crucify

l Ver 6 m Gen xlix 10 n Mat xxvii 26 Mark xv 15 Luke xxiii 24 o Luke xxiii 33 Heb xiii 12 13

[l] crucify him Pilate saith unto them, Shall I crucify
your king? The chief priests answered, [m] We have no
king but Cesar 16 [n] Then delivered he him therefore
unto them to be crucified And they took Jesus and
led him away 17 And he bearing his cross, [o] went
forth into a place called *the place* of a skull, which is
called in the Hebrew, Golgotha 18 Where they cru-
cified him, and two other with him, on either side one,
and Jesus in the midst

v 1—18 Having failed in his first attempt to release the innocent prisoner, he bethought him of another, to move the people's compassion

1 He delivered him up to the officers to be publicly scourged, hoping probably, that after this ignominy and punishment their fury might be appeased The soldiers to whose custody Jesus had been committed, added the most cruel mockery to his sufferings, and, in derision of the dignity to which he pretended, *platted a crown of thorns, and put it on his head*, arrayed him in robes of mock-majesty, and bowing the knee, saluted him king of the Jews, whilst with their hands they smote him, and offered him the vilest indignities *Note*, (1) By these stripes he fulfilled the prophetic word, and procured the healing of our guilty souls (2) Many make a jest of things sacred now, who will shortly prove them to their cost serious realities (3) He who endured such pain and shame for us, hath left us his example of patient suffering how dare we at any time complain, when we see what he endured?

2 Thus arrayed, Pilate once more ordered him to be led forth, hoping this would satisfy his persecutors, and that they might be prevailed upon to let him go, when he adds withal his solemn testimony, that he found *no fault in him*, and that he therefore regarded him as an object rather to be pitied than feared, and pointing to him as he stood, wearing the crown of thorns and purple robe, his face black with buffetting, and fine red with blood, he said, *Behold the man!* and let such an object of misery plead with you for mercy *Note*, (1) That man, once treated with such insult and contempt, should be for ever in our eyes the object of our admiration, love, and praise, for as he humbled himself thus low, the more we see of his abasement, the more the riches of his grace should rise in our esteem (2) If we are hooted at, and made a gazing-stock by wicked men, we are only called to a fellowship in Christ's sufferings, and should therein rejoice

3 Far from being softened and melted by the misery of the innocent sufferer, the chief priests and their officers, more exasperated through the fear of losing their prey, instigated the people, and in a most tumultuous manner headed the mob, and led the cry, *Crucify him, crucify him* Pilate, shocked at their cruelty and injustice, or ironically reproaching them, who pretended to so much sanctity, with so wicked a deed, replies, *Take ye him, and crucify him*, if ye are so madly set upon it, I chuse to have nothing to do with so base an action, for *I find no fault in him* Fearing that Jesus should yet escape them, they produce a new accusation of a capital nature Before they charged him as a traitor against the government, now as a blasphemer against God, pretending, that according to their law he ought to die, *because he made himself the Son of God*, and pretended to the incommunicable honours of the Godhead

4 Pilate, more terrified at that saying, lest he should bring the divine vengeance more fearfully on his head, determined to examine farther into the matter, and therefore taking Jesus into the judgment-hall, demanded whence he came, whether of human or divine extraction But Jesus, knowing it was useless to reply, gave him no answer Pilate resenting his silence as a contempt of his authority, with haughtiness adds, *Speakest thou not unto me?* art thou mute, though a prisoner at my bar? *knowest thou not that I have power to crucify thee, and have power to release thee?* He boasts of his authority as absolute, as able to save or to destroy so apt are proud worms in office to magnify themselves, and to affect a display of their power

5 Christ nobly checks his arrogance, and exposes the vanity of his boasts *Thou couldest have no power at all against me, except it were given thee from above*, as a magistrate, it was from heaven he received his authority, and should rule with justice, and in this particular case, had he not been delivered by the determinate counsel of God, not all the Roman powers combined could have prevailed in the minutest particular against him *Therefore he that delivered me unto thee*, Judas the traitor, or Caiaphas the high-priest, *hath the greater sin* *Note*, There is a difference in sin, some transgress with much more aggravated guilt than others, as they act against greater light, and offend with more deliberate malice

6 Pilate, now more deeply stung in his conscience, sought earnestly to obtain the release of Jesus, but in vain Had he acted as an upright magistrate, and according to the convictions of his conscience, he would have braved all popular resentment; but his corruptions overcame his convictions, and the fear of offending the people, and perhaps endangering himself, at last prevailed The Jews perceiving how he was disposed, in order to compel him to consent, clamoured loud, and urged, that if he *let this man go*, he could not be *Cesar's friend*, since whoever made himself *a king*, spoke against Cesar, and was a rebel against his government, tho' the fact was so notoriously false, Christ having never assumed the least temporal authority, he commanded, on the contrary, the tribute to be paid to Cesar, and when the people would have made him a king by force, he left them, and disappointed their designs But this they craftily urge, as what must most powerfully influence Pilate, who might now be liable to an accusation before the emperor for betraying his trust, if he should let one go, whom they accused as a traitor Thus they who in heart abhorred the Roman government now would appear the most zealous subjects of Cesar Wicked men to effect their purposes can transform themselves into every shape

7 Pilate, terrified into compliance with their request by this suggestion, and well apprized of the cruel and suspicious temper of Tiberius the Roman emperor, sat down on the judgment-seat, in a place called *Gabbatha*, or *the pavement*, in order to pronounce sentence upon the prisoner *And it was the preparation day of the passover* sabbath, a solemn season, when very different subjects should have engaged their time and thoughts, *and about the sixth hour* Once more to try if any thing would work upon them, Pilate bids them *behold* their *king*, and think a moment if such a miserable object could afford any real cause to fear his pretensions, even if he had affected royalty But they, impatient for his execution, shouted, *Away with him, crucify him*, they will hear nothing in his favour, and are determined in their bloody purpose Pilate remonstrates with them hereupon, *Shall I crucify your king?* either meaning to excite their compassions, or ridiculing their hopes of the Messiah They who at other times ever testified their abhorrence of the Roman yoke, now eagerly embrace it, and with deep professions of loyalty cry, *We have no king but Cesar* Pilate then seeing it in vain to contend, pronounced sentence, and delivered up the innocent prisoner to them to be crucified Thus was he arraigned and condemned for us, for a pretended crime, that the condemnation due to us for our real rebellions against God might be removed

8 The sentence is immediately put in execution by his blood-thirsty persecutors, with every circumstance of ignominy They drag him to the place where malefactors were executed without the city, bearing his own cross, and there nail him to the accursed tree, between two infamous criminals, who were executed with him, to make him appear the vilest of the vile, thus fulfilling the scriptures, which foretold he should be *numbered with the transgressors*, *Isa* liii 12 We cannot too frequently in our meditations come and see this great sight Calvary offers the noblest subject to our view, God incarnate dying for our iniquities with what anguish for our guilt, which brought the Saviour to the cross, with what love to him, who so freely consented to bear our sins in his own body on the tree, should we then look up to a crucified Jesus!

19 ¶ [p] And Pilate wrote a title, and put it on the
cross And the writing was, JESUS OF NAZARETH
THE KING OF THE JEWS 20 This title then
read many of the Jews For the place where Jesus was
crucified was nigh to the city And it was written in
Hebrew, *and* Greek, *and* Latin 21 Then said the
chief priests of the Jews to Pilate, Write not, The king
of the Jews, but that he said, I am king of the Jews
22 Pilate answered, What I have written, I have writ-
ten 23 ¶ Then [q] the soldiers, when they had cruci-
fied Jesus, took his garments (and made four parts, to
every soldier a part) and also *his* coat Now the coat
was without seam, woven from the top throughout
24 They said therefore among themselves, Let us not
rent it, but cast lots for it, whose it shall be that the
scripture might be fulfilled, which saith, [r] They parted
my raiment among them, and for my vesture they did
cast lots These things therefore the soldiers did 25
[s] Now there stood by the cross of Jesus, his mother, and
his mother's sister, Mary *the wife* of [t] Cleophas, and
Mary Magdalene 26 When Jesus therefore saw his
mother and the disciple standing by, [u] whom he loved,
he saith unto his mother, [w] Woman, behold thy son
27 Then saith he to the disciple, Behold thy mother
And from that hour that disciple took her unto his own
home 28 ¶ After this, Jesus knowing that all things
were now accomplished, [x] that the scripture might be
fulfilled, saith, I thirst 29 Now there was set a vessel
full of vinegar and they filled a spunge with vinegar,
and put it upon hyssop, and put it to his mouth 30
When Jesus therefore had received the vinegar, he said,

p Mat xxvii 37 Mark xv 26 Luke xxiii 38
q Mat xxvii 35 Mark xv 24 Luke xxiii 34
r Ps xxii 18
s Mat xxvii 55 Mark xv 40 Luke xxiii 49
t Or Cleopas
u Chap xiii 23 xxi 20 24
w Chap ii 4
x Ps lxix 21

It

y Chap. xvi. 4 ʸ It is finiſhed: and he bowed his head, and gave up the ghoſt.

v. 19—30. The circumſtances of Chriſt's death are here ſomewhat more fully related than by the other Evangeliſts.

1. On a tablet at the top of his croſs Pilate wrote a ſuperſcription in Hebrew, Greek, and Latin, containing the accuſation laid againſt him, *Jeſus of Nazareth the King of the Jews.* Multitudes of the Jews then, who came from the city to the place of execution, read the ſuperſcription; and the chief prieſts, offended at the title given him, regarded it as a brand of infamy upon their nation, and therefore wiſhed him to alter the writing into another form, and not to call him abſolutely *King of the Jews*, but *that he ſaid, I am King of the Jews*, deſiring to fix upon his memory this infamy of an impoſtor. But Pilate, indignant at the injuſtice they had driven him to commit, with diſpleaſure rejects their requeſt, ſaying, *What I have written, I have written*, and will not alter it. *Note*, (1.) The innocence of Jeſus this very ſuperſcription proved. No crime was charged upon him, but his aſſerting his real character as the King Meſſiah. (2.) God holds the hands and lips of wicked men, and can, when he pleaſes, make them write and ſpeak in ſuch a way, as ſhall bear teſtimony to his truth.

2. The ſoldiers who crucified him, as he hung on the tree, ſat down to part his garments among them; and, unwilling to rend his ſeamleſs coat, determined rather to caſt lots which of them ſhould have it, fulfilling literally the ſcripture, which had ſaid, *They parted my raiment among them, and for my veſture they did caſt lots*, (Pſ. xxii. 18.) *Theſe things therefore the ſoldiers did*, being under the ſecret influence of his power, whom they knew not.

3. In the midſt of his agonies Jeſus ſhewed the tendereſt concern for his afflicted mother, who ſtood by his croſs, with the diſciple whom he loved; and kindly addreſſing her, he recommends her to the care of his beloved John, deſiring her to regard him henceforward as a ſon, and directing him to pay her the duty and affection due to a mother; *and from that hour that diſciple took her to his own home*, glad to obey the commands of his dying Maſter, and well pleaſed to have an opportunity of teſtifying his unfeigned love towards him. *Note*, (1.) Chriſt on the croſs hath taught all children an eminent inſtance of filial duty towards their parents, whoſe wants to the utmoſt they are bound to provide for. (2.) When one friend fails, the Lord can raiſe us up another; if we truſt him, we ſhall not be deſtitute. (3.) They who love the adored Jeſus, will be happy to embrace every opportunity of teſtifying their regard for him.

4. Chriſt knowing *that all things were now accompliſhed*, and his work of redemption nearly complete, *that the ſcripture might be fulfilled*, (Pſ. xxii. 15. lxix. 21.) *ſaith, I thirſt*; and a veſſel of vinegar being near, which was probably mixed with water, as drink for the Roman ſoldiers, they dipped a ſpunge in the liquor, and on a ſtalk of hyſſop lifted it to his lips. Jeſus felt that wrath of God, and thirſted, which had he not endured, we muſt for ever have lain down in everlaſting burnings, without one drop of water to cool our tongues.

5. Jeſus having received the vinegar, ſaith, *It is finiſhed*; the victory is obtained over death and hell; the work of redemption compleated; the full atonement made; all the types and prophecies fulfilled; the law magnified by a perfect obedience unto death; the juſtice of God ſatisfied; the ſalvation of ſinners ſecured; and therefore now his ſufferings end. *He bowed his head, and gave up the ghoſt*, freely reſigning his ſoul into his Father's hands, and ſurrendering that life, which otherwiſe none could have taken from him, *a ranſom for many*.

31 The Jews therefore, because it was the prepara-
z Deut. xxi. 23. tion, that ᶻ the bodies ſhould not remain upon the croſs
on the ſabbath day (for that ſabbath-day was an high
day) beſought Pilate that their legs might be broken,
and *that* they might be taken away. 32 Then came
the ſoldiers, and brake the legs of the firſt, and of the
other which was crucified with him. 33 But when they
came to Jeſus, and ſaw that he was dead already, they
brake not his legs: 34 But one of the ſoldiers with a
a 1 John v. 6, 8. ſpear pierced his ſide, and forthwith ᵃ came thereout
blood and water. 35 And he that ſaw it bare record,
and his record is true: and he knoweth that he ſaith
true, that ye might believe. 36 For theſe things were
b Ex. xii. 46. Numb. ix. 12. Pſ. xxxiv. 20. done, that the ſcripture ſhould be fulfilled, ᵇ A bone of
him ſhall not be broken. 37 And again another
c Zech. xii. 10. ſcripture ſaith, ᶜ They ſhall look on him whom they
pierced.

v. 31—37. This laſt indignity ſhown to our Lord's body is only recorded by this Evangeliſt.

1. The Jews, ſuperſtitiouſly obſervant of the ſabbath, and hypocritically pretending reverence for that ſacred inſtitution, whilſt their hands were red with the blood of him who was Lord of the ſabbath, that the bodies might not hang on the trees till evening, when the ſabbath began, which was a high day, and kept with great ſolemnity, they deſired Pilate that *their legs might be broken, and that they might be taken away*, to kill them outright, if they were not dead before, and to bury them immediately. *Note*, Hypocrites often appear very ſcrupulous about the ceremonials of religion, whilſt they are living in open violation of its moſt eſſential precepts.

2. Pilate granted their requeſt, and the two malefactors, not being yet dead, had the dreadful operation performed on them: but when the ſoldiers came to Jeſus, perceiving him already dead, they brake not his legs; but one of the ſoldiers, to put the matter paſt diſpute, *thruſt his ſpear into his ſide, and forthwith came thereout blood and water*; either the pericardium being pierced, and thus the water it contained ruſhed out with the blood, or this ſeparate diſcharge was miraculous, and typical of the great bleſſings of juſtification and ſanctification obtained by Chriſt's blood ſhedding for us. And John, who was ſtanding by, adds his atteſtation, as an eye-witneſs to this fact, as moſt indubitably true, that we *might believe* the certainty of Chriſt's death, and receive the ineſtimable bleſſings which this blood and water ſignified. *Note*, (1.) We are polluted with guilt, and defiled with corruption; but this is the fountain opened for ſin and for uncleanneſs. Jeſus came *by blood* to make the atonement, *by water* to purge our conſciences from dead works to ſerve the living God: whoſoever therefore cometh to him, ſhall find the mighty efficacy of his blood to pardon the moſt guilty, and of his grace to purify the moſt polluted ſoul. (2.) We have not followed cunningly deviſed fables in the goſpel of our ſalvation, but believe on the evidence of facts, ſupported by the moſt unſhaken authority, and atteſted by the moſt competent witneſſes.

3. In this tranſaction particular notice is taken of the fulfilment of two ſcriptures. [1.] *A bone of him ſhall not be broken*, (Exod. xii. 46.) which, though ſpoken of the paſchal lamb, yet eſpecially regarded him, who in the fulneſs of time, as our *paſſover*, ſhould be ſacrificed for us, (1 Cor. v. 7.) Another ſcripture had ſaid, (Zech. xii. 10.) *They ſhall look on him whom they pierced*. Thus were the prophecies accompliſhed by thoſe, who thought of nothing leſs in what they did, than the confirmation of our faith in Jeſus as the true Meſſiah.

38 ¶ ᵈ And after this, Joſeph of Arimathea (being a d Mat. xxvii. 57. Mark xv. 42. Luke xxiii. 50.
diſciple of Jeſus, but ſecretly ᵉ for fear of the Jews) be- e Chap. ix. 22. & xii. 42.
ſought Pilate that he might take away the body of Jeſus:
and Pilate gave him leave. He came therefore and took
the body of Jeſus. 39 And there came alſo ᶠ Nicode- f Chap. iii. 1, 2. & vii. 50.
mus (which at firſt came to Jeſus by night) and brought
a mixture of myrrh and aloes, about an hundred pound
weight. 40 Then took they the body of Jeſus, and
ᵍ wound it in linen clothes, with the ſpices, as the man- g Acts v. 6.
ner of the Jews is to bury. 41 Now in the place
where he was crucified, there was a garden; and in the
garden a new ſepulchre, wherein was never man yet
laid. 42 ʰ There laid they Jeſus therefore, becauſe of h Iſa. liii. 9. Mat. xxvii. 60.
the Jews preparation-*day*; for the ſepulchre was nigh at
hand.

v. 38—42. Though now Jeſus ſeemed deſerted of all, and his corpſe ready to be laid with malefactors in a common grave, God raiſes up one who is appointed to give it a more honourable interment.

1. Joſeph of Arimathea, who through fear of the Jews had concealed his ſentiments, and, though ſecretly a diſciple of Jeſus, dared not to profeſs it, now boldly appears, and begs of the governor the body of Jeſus, which was granted. *Note*, (1.) The higher men are in the world, the greater temptation they are under to ſhun the reproach of the croſs; and, though perſuaded of the truth of the goſpel, not to make bold and open profeſſion of it. (2.) When the more courageous diſciples are foiled, God can ſay to the fearful heart, Be ſtrong, and embolden them to appear boldly in the cauſe of God and truth.

2. Nicodemus, who at the firſt appearing of Jeſus came to him by night, now joined Joſeph in this pious work, and provided a large quantity of myrrh and aloes, in order to embalm the body of Jeſus, as was often done to men of eminent reputation and dignity. No expence to ſerve him will be grudged by thoſe who truly love the Lord Jeſus Chriſt.

3. They took down the body, and wrapped it in linen clothes, with the ſpices, as was the manner of the Jews to bury their great men: and as Joſeph had a garden near the place where Jeſus was crucified, in which he had prepared for himſelf a new tomb, hewn out of a rock, where never man had lain before, there laid they the body of Jeſus, it being very convenient, as they were ſtraitened for time, the preparation day being far advanced, and the ſabbath approaching. Thus was our great ſurety laid under the arreſt of death, and conſigned to the ſilent grave, that he might make the clods of the valley ſweet to us, prepare our bed of duſt perfumed with his own glorious body

body, and comfort us in the reviving hope of following him through the grave, the gate of death, unto a joyful immortality

CHAP XX.

The proofs of Christ's resurrection which we have in this chapter, are, 1 Such as occurred immediately at the sepulchre (1) The sepulchre found empty, and the grave-clothes in good order, ver 1—10 (2) Two angels appearing to Mary Magdalene at the sepulchre, ver 11—13 (3) Christ himself appearing to her, ver 14—18 2 Such as occurred afterwards at the meetings of the apostles (1) At one, the same day at evening that Christ rose, when Thomas was absent, ver 19—25 At another, that day seven-night, when Thomas was with him, ver 26—31

a Mat xxviii 1 Mark xvi 1 Luke xxiv 1 1 [a] THE first *day* of the week cometh Mary Mag-
dalene, early when it was yet dark, unto the
sepulchre, and seeth the stone taken away from the sepul-
chre 2 Then she runneth, and cometh to Simon Peter,
b Chap xiii 23 & xxi 7, 20 24 and to [b] the other disciple whom Jesus loved, and saith
unto them, They have taken away the Lord out of the
sepulchre, and we know not where they have laid him
c Luke xxiv 12 3 [c] Peter therefore went forth, and that other disciple,
and came to the sepulchre 4 So they ran both to-
gether And the other disciple did out-run Peter, and
came first to the sepulchre 5 And he stooping down,
d Chap. xix 40 *and looking in*, saw [d] the linen clothes lying, yet went he
not in 6 Then cometh Simon Peter following him,
and went into the sepulchre, and seeth the linen clothes
e Chap xi 44 lie 7 And [e] the napkin that was about his head,
not lying with the linen clothes, but wrapped together
in a place by itself 8 Then went in also that other
disciple which came first to the sepulchre, and he saw,
f Ps xvi 10 Acts ii 25, 31 & xiii 35 and believed 9 For as yet they knew not [f] the
scripture, that he must rise again from the dead 10
Then the disciples went away again unto their own
home.

v 1—10 The reconciling the accounts of the several Evangelists, with regard to the circumstances attending the resurrection, hath exercised the ingenuity of many learned expositors The fact itself is proved by a great cloud of witnesses

1 Mary Magdalene very early, while it was yet dark, sat out for the sepulchre, where she arrived about sun-rising, and to her surprize found the stone removed from the door Hereupon looking in, and missing the body of Jesus, she, with the other women, ran to Peter and John, and with great concern informed them of the removal of the body of Jesus, they knew not whither *Note*, (1) They who truly love Christ, will delight to meet him early (2) It is a bitter grief to a gracious soul to feel the absence of Jesus, and not to know where he may be found (3) We often make that matter of our mourning, which should afford us real cause for joy (4) The communication of our sorrows is often the nearest way to recover our lost comforts

2 Peter and John immediately went forth, desirous to inform themselves how matters stood, and running together, John out-ran Peter, and came first to the sepulchre, where stooping down, and looking in, he saw the linen clothes lying, yet went not in Peter, more courageous, no sooner reached the place, than he went in to gain the fullest satisfaction possible, and observed the grave-clothes, not carelessly thrown down, but each part separately folded up, and laid by itself, a certain proof, that whoever removed the body, did it deliberately, and not in haste Hereupon John also now ventured in after Peter, *and he saw, and believed*, either that the body was removed, or that Christ was really risen from the dead, for hitherto none of the disciples had entertained any right notions of the Messiah, nor, after all the scripture prophecies, and their Master's predictions, seem at all to have expected his resurrection from the dead

3 Hereupon the disciples return to their companions, to communicate to them the state of the matter as it appeared to them, and to wait the event

g Mark xvi 5 11 ¶ [g] But Mary stood without at the sepulchre,
weeping and as she wept, she stooped down, *and looked*
into the sepulchre, 12 And seeth two angels in white,
sitting the one at the head, and the other at the feet,
where the body of Jesus had lain 13 And they say
h Ver 15. unto her, [h] Woman, why weepest thou? She saith unto
i Mat xxviii 9 Mark xvi 9 them, Because they have taken away my Lord, and I
k Luke xxiv 16, 31 Chap xxi 4 know not where they have laid him 14 [i] And when
she had thus said, she turned herself back, and saw
Jesus standing, and [k] knew not that it was Jesus 15
Jesus saith unto her, Woman, why weepest thou? whom
seekest thou? she supposing him to be the gardener,
saith unto him, Sir, if thou have borne him hence, tell
me where thou hast laid him, and I will take him away
16 Jesus saith unto her, Mary She turned herself,
and saith unto him, Rabboni, which is to say, Master
17 Jesus saith unto her, Touch me not for I am not
yet ascended to my Father but go to [l] my brethren, l Ps xxii 22 Mat xxviii 10 Heb ii 11
and say unto them, [m] I ascend unto my Father and m Chap xvi 28
your Father, and *to* [n] my God and your God 18 Ma- n Eph i 17
ry Magdelene came and told the disciples, that she
had seen the Lord, and that he had spoken these things
unto her.

v 11—18. Christ's first appearance was to Mary Magdalene Much had been forgiven her, and she loved much Her past conduct was all forgotten, and her unfeigned present attachment to Jesus made her now justly dear to him, and she is favoured with this distinguished token of his regard

1 She stood without at the sepulchre weeping, being returned the second time to seek farther after her dear Lord and they who wait constantly upon him, though he withdraw for a while, yet shall they find him at the last, and what they sow in tears, they shall reap in joy

2 As she wept, she stooped down, and looked into the sepulchre, and saw two angels in human forms, (the same, as some suppose, which appeared to her before, *Luke* xxiv 3—6) They were clothed in white, the emblem of their spotless purity, and sat one at the head, and the other at the feet, where the body of Jesus had lain, to pay him honour, and to be the messengers of his resurrection

3 They kindly addressed her, *Woman, why weepest thou?* She, whose heart overflowed with sorrow, as her eyes with tears, replied, *Because they have taken away my Lord, and I know not where they have laid him* and this she thought a sufficient reason for her grief, but our vexations, like hers, are often imaginary, and of our own making had we but faith, the clouds would immediately disappear

4 Christ manifests himself to her, for they who can rest in nothing short of Christ and his love, shall not be disappointed As she turned herself, *she saw Jesus standing, and*, because either her eyes were holden, or they were so filled with tears, she *knew not that it was Jesus* So much nearer is he to his mourning saints, than they oftentimes are aware He kindly addressed her in the words of his angelic ministers, *Woman, why weepest thou?* and she not attending to him closely, and supposing him probably the gardener, begged to be informed if he had borne the body away, or could give her any intelligence concerning it, that she might give it an honourable interment elsewhere, if it might not lie there *Jesus saith unto her, Mary* his altered tone of voice, and calling her by her name, assured her instantly who spoke, and turning to him, she casts herself at his feet with reverence and rapturous joy, crying, *Rabboni*, my Master! how welcome, unutterably welcome to her longing heart! *Note*, When Christ returns after a season of darkness and weeping, then, as the sun shining after rain, the beams of his love are more delightful than ever to the soul

5 He sends her with the kindest message to his disciples *Touch me not*, stay not to express your affectionate regard, the moment is precious, *for I am not yet ascended to my Father*, you will therefore have other opportunities of seeing and conversing with me *But go to my brethren* without delay, in such affectionate terms doth he address those who had so lately shamefully fled and left him, *and say unto them, I ascend unto my Father and your Father, and to my God and your God* Christ owns them in the endeared relation of brethren, assures them he was now entering into his glory, as the covenant head of his redeemed people, returning to his Father by eternal generation, and theirs by adoption and grace, to his God, whom, as the man Christ Jesus, the head of his redeemed people, he loved, obeyed, and worshipped; and their God, in a covenant of everlasting love, to *bless them with all spiritual blessings in heavenly things in Christ* Blessed and happy are they who can say, The God and Father of our Lord Jesus Christ is *my* Father and *my* God

6 Mary hastens to carry the glad news to the disconsolate disciples, and with a transport of joy declares she has seen him, and reports the kind message which he had delivered to her They who have seen Christ by faith, and tasted of his consolations, cannot but delight to tell of him, and to spread the knowledge of his grace

19 ¶ [o] Then the same day at evening, being the first o Mark xvi 14 Luke xxiv 36
day of the week, when the doors were shut, where the
disciples were assembled for fear of the Jews, came Jesus 1 Cor xv 5
and stood in the midst, and saith unto them, Peace *be*
unto you 20 And when he had so said, [p] he shewed p Ver 27
unto them *his* hands and his side Then [q] were the dis- q John xvi 22 Chap
ciples glad when they saw the Lord 21 Then said

John:

r Matt. xxviii. 18. Chap. xvii. 18. Heb. iii. 1. 2 Tim. ii. 2.
s Matt. xvi. 19. & xviii. 18. 1 Cor. v. 4, 5.
t Chap. xi. 16.

Jesus to them again, Peace *be* unto you: r as *my* Father
hath sent me, even so send I you. 22 And when he
had said this, he breathed on *them*, and saith unto them,
Receive ye the holy Ghost. 23 s Whosesoever sins ye
remit, they are remitted unto them; *and* whosesoever
sins ye retain, they are retained. 24. ¶ But Thomas,
one of the twelve, t called Didymus, was not with them
when Jesus came. 25 The other disciples therefore said
unto him, We have seen the Lord. But he said unto
them, Except I shall see in his hands the print of the
nails, and put my finger into the print of the nails, and
thrust my hand into his side, I will not believe.

v. 19—25. The reports of Mary and the women produced little conviction in the minds of the disciples; such fools, and slow of heart were they to believe; Jesus therefore appears to them himself, to put the matter out of doubt.

1. The apostles were all assembled, Thomas excepted, on the evening of the day in which Christ rose from the dead, which was the first day of the week. For fear of the Jews they had shut and barred the doors, when on a sudden, probably whilst they were considering over the strange reports which they had heard, and examining into their credibility, or praying for farther light and direction, Jesus appears in the midst of them, and with the kindest salutation addresses them, *Peace be unto you.* He upbraids them not with any thing that had passed; it was forgiven and forgotten; and now he is come to put them in possession of that peace which before his death he had so solemnly bequeathed to them. *Note*, (1.) Where the disciples of Jesus assemble in his name, there will he be in the midst of them. (2.) The peace which our Redeemer bestows, lifts us superior to all our fears.

2. To give them undoubted assurance of the identity of his person, and the certainty of his resurrection, he shewed them his hands and his side, which still bore the glorious scars gotten in that conflict he had endured for their sakes, when all their foes were vanquished; and, fully satisfied that it was indeed their adored Master himself, joy and gladness were diffused thro' every heart, and sat on every countenance. *Note*, Those love-prints in the Saviour's flesh should still be gazed upon by us with faith, delight, and wonder. Whilst they are pleading before the throne, who shall lay ought to our charge?

3. He solemnly invests them anew with their commission from him. *Then said Jesus unto them again, Peace be unto you:* he would remove every remaining fear, and recover them from their astonishment, that they might hear and receive the commission he delivered to them. *As my Father hath sent me, even so send I you*; giving you full authority to go and preach my gospel, engaging to qualify you for the work, and to give you to see the most abundant success of your labours. *And when he had said this, he breathed on them, and saith unto them, Receive ye the Holy Ghost*; by this emblem signifying to them, that the Spirit which proceeded from him, as the breath from the body, should rest upon them, as a quickening Spirit, like that which God breathed at first into the lifeless clay, (*Gen.* ii. 7.) and should enable them with the abundance of his gifts and graces to discharge that high office to which they were ordained. And as one branch of their divinely-delegated authority, he saith, *Whosesoever sins ye remit*, according to the gospel which they preached, and as possessed of that discernment of spirits, whereby they were enabled to distinguish the truly faithful, *they are remitted unto them*, the absolution which they pronounce on earth, he engages to ratify in heaven: *and whosesoever sins ye retain*, because of their impenitence and unbelief, *they are retained*; and if they die in their sins, the wrath of God, according to their denunciations, must for ever abide upon them. *Note*, (1.) Though men may give an outward mission, it is the office of the Holy Ghost to call and qualify every true minister of Christ; and, without his inspiration, they who run unsent, will be accounted as thieves and robbers. (2.) Though ministers have no power of their own to pardon sins, or bind them upon the soul, yet, where they speak according to Christ's word, he will confirm their sentence.

4. Thomas, called Didymus, one of the twelve apostles who were first ordained, though now reduced to eleven by the apostacy of Judas, happened not to be present when Jesus shewed himself to the rest. By what he was detained, is not said; perhaps the fear which made them lock the doors, kept him away: and if so, for his cowardice and neglect he is justly punished with the loss of that blessed sight which his brethren enjoyed. But whether he was before in fault or not, his incredulity was justly blameable, when his brethren in a transport of joy assured him they had *seen the Lord*. Resolute in unbelief, he declares nothing shall convince him, but the evidence of his own senses. *Except I shall see in his hands the print of the nails, and put my finger into the print of the nails, and thrust my hand into his side, I will not believe*; a very criminal incredulity, yet was it so over-ruled by divine providence, as to add additional evidence to the certainty of Jesus's resurrection. So far were his own apostles from easily satisfying themselves about the fact, that nothing but the most infallible evidence could have convinced them: and indeed when they looked forward to what they must expect to meet with on account of their testimony, they needed the fullest conviction of the truth in their own souls, to bear them out in their sufferings.

x Ver. 19.
y Ver. 25.
z 1 John i. 1.
a 2 Cor. v. 7. 1 Pet. i. 8.
b Chap. xxi. 25.
b Luke i. 4.
c Chap. iii. 15, 16. & v. 24. 1 Pet. i. 9.

26 ¶ And after eight days again his disciples were
within, and Thomas with them: *then* came Jesus, the
doors being shut, and stood in the midst, and said, x Peace
be unto you. 27 Then saith he to Thomas, y Reach
hither thy finger, and behold my hands; and reach hither
thy hand, and thrust it into my side: and be not
faithless, but believing. 28 And Thomas answered
and said unto him, My Lord and my God. 29 Jesus
saith unto him, Thomas, because thou hast seen me, thou
hast believed: z blessed *are* they that have not seen, and
yet have believed. 30 ¶ And a many other signs truly
did Jesus in the presence of his disciples, which are not
written in this book: 31 b But these are written, that
ye might believe that Jesus is the Christ the Son of
God; and c that believing ye might have life through his
name.

v. 26—31. Our Lord by his resurrection consecrated the first day of the week; then his disciples assembled, and he appeared to them. A week after he repeated his visit, to put a farther honour on the day, which was henceforward to be observed as the Christian sabbath.

1. Christ appears to them, where they were met together, and Thomas with them, having shut the doors for fear of the Jews. Seven days Thomas was left to his unbelieving doubts, and in a miserable state of suspence, whilst the other disciples rejoiced in their risen Redeemer. But now having punished him for his former neglect and absence, and being joined again in communion with his fellow-apostles, he is favoured with the sight of Jesus, who graciously condescends to give him all that satisfaction which he perversely required. *He stood in the midst, and said, Peace be unto you*, according to his former gracious salutation: then particularly addressing himself to Thomas, to rebuke his infidelity, and satisfy his doubts, he bids him, since nothing else would convince him, put his finger upon the scars in his hands, and examine with his hand the wound in his side, and feel and see the certainty of that resurrection he would not credit, *and be not faithless, or incredulous, but believing. Note*, Unbelief is the injurious bar which robs us of our comfort, and God of his glory; most justly therefore does it deserve rebuke from Christ, and call for deep humiliation from us.

2. Thomas, quite overcome with the evidence and confounded and ashamed at his own incredulity, cries out, *My Lord and my God*, in the fullest assurance of faith, and with the deepest reverence and adoration of his glorious Master. He acknowledges his divinity, and worships him as the object of highest honour, as very God. *Note*, (1.) True faith regards Jesus not only as God and Lord, but as *my* God, and *my* Lord, in whose favour and love we have an assured interest. (2.) We are then disciples indeed, when Jesus is exalted in our hearts, and in our lips and life we confess him our Lord and Master.

3. For a reproof to Thomas, and an encouragement to those who should come after, Jesus replies, *Thomas, because thou hast seen me, thou hast believed*, refusing every proof but the evidence of his own senses; and, though convinced at last, yet was he culpable in rejecting the testimony which his brethren had born, in which way the rest of the world must be converted to the faith. And therefore Christ adds, *Blessed are they that have not seen, and yet have believed*, as the Old Testament saints had done, and as must be the case with those who afterwards should believe the gospel on the testimony of the inspired witnesses: their faith is more noble, spiritual, and honourable to God, and will procure the most transcendent blessings upon their own souls.

4. The Evangelist observes, that many other signs were given of the resurrection of Jesus, during the forty days he was seen of them, than those recorded in the sacred writings; but the evidence contained in the book of God is fully satisfactory to those who humbly desire information, and who search the scriptures to be made wise unto salvation through them: they will be convinced from these sacred records, *that Jesus is the Christ*, the promised Messiah, *the Son of God*, possessed of the same divine nature and perfections, and declared to be so *by his resurrection from the dead* (*Rom.* i. 4.); and they who believe on him may be assured *of life through his name*, the life of grace with all its comforts here, and the life of glory with all its unutterable blessedness hereafter, both being effectually obtained by the death and resurrection of Jesus, who hath *opened the kingdom of heaven to all believers.*

CHAP. XXI

We have here another appearance of Christ We are told, 1 How he discovered himself to them as they were fishing, filled their net, and then very familiarly came and dined with them upon what they had caught, ver 1—14 2 *What discourse he had with Peter after dinner (1) Concerning himself,* ver 15—20 (2) *Concerning John,* ver 21—23 (3) *The solemn conclusion of this gospel,* ver 24, 25

1 AFTER these things Jesus shewed himself again
to the disciples at the sea of Tiberias, and on
this wise shewed he *himself* 2 There were together Si-
a Chap i 45 mon Peter, and Thomas called Didymus, and a Natha-
b Mat iv 21 nael of Cana in Galilee, and b the *sons* of Zebedee, and
two other of his disciples 3 Simon Peter saith unto
them, I go a fishing They say unto him, We also go
with thee They went forth, and entred into a ship im-
mediately, and that night they caught nothing 4 But
when the morning was now come, Jesus stood on the
c Luke xxiv 16 Chap xx 14 shore but c the disciples knew not that it was Jesus 5
Then d Jesus saith unto them, Children, have ye any
d Luke xxiv 41 meat? They answered him, No 6 And he said unto
e Luke v 4, &c them, e Cast the net on the right side of the ship, and ye
shall find They cast therefore, and now they were not
able to draw it for the multitude of fishes 7 Therefore
f Chap xiii 23 & xx 2 Ver 20 that disciple f whom Jesus loved, saith unto Peter, It is
the Lord Now when Simon Peter heard that it was
the Lord, he girt *his* fisher's coat *unto him*, (for he was
naked) and did cast himself into the sea 8 And the
other disciples came in a little ship (for they were not far
from land, but as it were two hundred cubits) dragging
the net with fishes 9 As soon then as they were come
to land, they saw a fire of coals there, and fish laid there-
on, and bread 10 Jesus saith unto them, Bring of the
fish, which ye have now caught 11 Simon Peter went
up, and drew the net to land full of great fishes, an hun-
dred and fifty and three and for all there were so ma-
ny, yet was not the net broken 12 Jesus saith unto
g Acts x 41 them, g Come *and* dine And none of the disciples durst
ask him, Who art thou? knowing that it was the Lord.
13 Jesus then cometh and taketh bread, and giveth
h Chap xx 19, 26 them, and fish likewise 14 This is now h the third
time that Jesus shewed himself to his disciples, after that
he was risen from the dead

℣ 1—14 The disciples being appointed to meet their Lord in Galilee, returned thither, and, till the time came, employed themselves in their former occupation Christ's servants must never be idlers

1 Christ appears to them at the sea of Tiberias, where Simon Peter, Thomas, Nathanael, the sons of Zebedee, and two other disciples were fishing They were unsuccessful all night, and toiled in vain in the morning Jesus stood on the shore, and, at the distance they were, the disciples knew him not *Note,* (1) God's ministers sometimes labour long, and see little fruit, but they must not be weary, nor faint in their minds patient perseverance shall at last be crowned with success (2) They who are diligent in their honest calling, are in Christ's way, and may expect his blessing

2 Christ addresses them in his familiar manner, *Children, have ye any meat? They answered, No He said unto them, Cast the net on the right side of the ship* Rather than return empty, they resolved to make the trial, and to their astonishment found the net so full, *that they were not able to draw it up into the boat for the multitude of fishes* *Note,* (1) Christ takes cognizance of his disciples wants; he will see that they have meat to eat (2) Our success depends not on our own labours, but on Christ's blessing (3) They who go under a divine call, shall find at last, that their labour is not in vain in the Lord

3 *John hereupon suggests* this must needs be the Lord Peter instantly caught the hint, and, fired with zeal and love, girt up his coat, and plunged into the sea, impatient to be at his dear Master's feet, whilst the other disciples, who were but a little way from shore, about an hundred yards, hasted to land, dragging the net with them Simon joined them, and assisted them in their labour, and to their astonishment counted one hundred and fifty-three large fishes, and yet the net remained unbroken, which still increased the miracle *Note,* (1) Different disciples excel in different gifts and graces some are more quick to discern, others more intrepid to execute, some move slowly, but steadily, others blaze with zeal, though not equally uniform, and each especially serviceable in their places (2) God's people will all be brought safe to the shores of everlasting rest through every tribulation, and when they are counted over, not one will be lacking of those which gospel grace effectually drew to Jesus

4 Their Master, who had given them this *miraculous* draught of fishes, had provided also for their refreshment on shore They found *a fire, and fish laid thereon, and bread,* to which he bids them add some of those they had caught, and then kindly and familiarly, as formerly, invites them to come and refresh themselves, whilst they in sacred awe at his presence and miracles, kept at a respectful distance, *nor durst ask him, Who art thou?* which would have implied unbelief, when indeed they were fully satisfied that it was the Lord *Note,* (1) They who act under the command of Jesus, and go forth in his name, shall not want a provision *Verily they shall be fed* (2) In the ordinances a rich repast is provided for the faithful, and the Master in them will break the bread of life to our souls (3) The gospel word is, *Come,* Christ's arms are open to his people, they will be welcome to all the rich provision of his grace

5 Christ, as the master of the feast, distributes the bread and fish to them, and did eat and drink with them, to shew himself truly alive, and to confirm them in the certainty of his resurrection, (*Acts* x 41) And still he is the same gracious Lord they who hunger and thirst after righteousness, shall be filled, and all the cravings of their souls relieved by the abundance of his grace

6 The Evangelist remarks, that this was the third public appearance of Jesus to any considerable number of his disciples together, whose faith would hereby be more confirmed Or this was the third day that he appeared to them the first day of his resurrection he appeared five several times, once the week after, and now again for the third time, and every repeated visit brought new tokens of his love

15 ¶ So when they had dined, Jesus saith to Simon
Peter, Simon *son* of Jonas, lovest thou me more than
these? He saith unto him, Yea, Lord, thou knowest
that I love thee He saith unto him, Feed my lambs
16 He saith to him again the second time, Simon *son* of
Jonas, lovest thou me? He saith unto him, Yea, Lord,
thou knowest that I love thee He saith unto him
i Feed my sheep 17 He saith unto him the third time, i Acts xx 28 1 Pet v 2
Simon *son* of Jonas, lovest thou me? Peter was grieved,
because he said unto him k *the third time,* Lovest thou k Chap xiii 38
me? And he said unto him, Lord, l thou knowest all l Chap ii 25 & xvi 30
things, thou knowest that I love thee Jesus saith unto
him, Feed my sheep 18 Verily, verily I say unto
thee, When thou wast young, thou girdest thyself, and
walkedst whither thou wouldest but when thou shalt
be old, thou shalt stretch forth thy hands, and another
shall gird thee, and m carry *thee* whither thou wouldest m Acts xxi 11
not 19 This spake he, signifying n by what death he n 2 Pet i 14
should glorify God And when he had spoken this, he
saith unto him, Follow me

℣ 15—19 When dinner was ended, Christ addressed himself to Peter He knew Peter's conscious heart upbraided him bitterly for his past conduct, and now, to silence his fears, whilst he tacitly reproves his unfaithfulness, confirms him in his office, as fully restored to his favour and love

We have,

1 The question thrice put to him, *Lovest thou me?* and the first time Christ adds, *more than these?* more than he loved his dearest relatives who were present, or more than the ship, and nets, and fish, and all earthly comforts and gain, or rather, more than these love me, because he had once so boldly and forwardly intimated his superior attachment to him, that *though all men should be offended, yet will not I,* and then it implied a tacit rebuke for this vain-glorious boast But now that he was restored to favour again, this new obligation conferred upon him required an especial return of love *Note,* (1) Nothing begets genuine repentance, but a sense of Christ's love engaging ours (2) When we do amiss, we must not be displeased to have our sincerity questioned (3) True love to Christ will make us count every thing trivial in comparison with him (4) It is a commendable ambition to desire to love Christ more than others, whilst we feel how peculiar our obligations to him are

2 Three times Peter makes the same reply *Thou knowest that I love thee* he will not pretend any more to a superiority over his brethren, though conscious of the sincerity of his love The third time, grieved at the repeated question, which seemed to intimate a suspicion of his sincerity, and reminded him of his threefold denial, he adds, *Thou knowest all things, Lord, thou knowest that I love thee,* and for this he can appeal to him, as the searcher of hearts *Note,* (1) They who are sincere in their attachment to Christ, can appeal for their simplicity to the searcher of their hearts (2) Every remembrance of past unfaithfulness should grieve us, though it be forgiven of our Lord, and forgotten

3 Thrice Jeſus bids him prove the ſincerity of his love by his diligence and labour in the miniſtry *Feed my lambs, feed my ſheep* Since his iniquity is pardoned, his commiſſion is renewed and with more abundant diligence he is called upon to diſcharge his awful truſt He muſt feed *the lambs*, the young diſciples, and thoſe who are moſt weak and feeble, conſidering their weakneſs and having compaſſion on their infirmities, as remembering his own He muſt feed *the ſheep*, the ſtrong of the flock, willing to expoſe himſelf to any dangers for their ſake, and faithfully miniſtring to them the rich food of the goſpel word, for their nouriſhment and growth in grace

4 Chriſt foretels the ſufferings which awaited him in the diſcharge of his miniſtry He muſt ſeal the truth he preached by enduring martyrdom *Verily, verily I ſay unto thee, When thou waſt young, thou girdeſt thyſelf*, full of vigour, *and walkedſt whither thou wouldeſt, but when thou ſhalt be old*, after a long life of labour *thou ſhalt ſtretch forth thy hands, and another ſhall gird thee, and carry thee whither thou wouldeſt not*, even to priſon *and this he ſpake, ſignifying by what death he ſhould die*, and the concurring teſtimony of antiquity reports, that he was crucified at Rome *Note*, (1) Nature ſtarts from death, is reluctant to go, but grace can enable us to meet it in its moſt tremendous forms (2) Every ſaint of God deſires to die, as he lived, to God's glory, patiently reſigned to his will, commending with his dying breath the good ways of the Lord, and rejoicing in hope of the glory ready to be revealed in him

5 He gives Peter a ſignificant ſign of what he required of him Riſing from table, he ſaith unto him, *Follow me*, copy my example, follow my inſtructions, and if he was called to the croſs, he muſt remember, it would be no more than his Maſter for his ſake had endured before Whatever we ſuffer, we ſhould never forget how much more our Maſter endured, and that this is the way to come to be with him in his glory We muſt bear the croſs before we wear the crown

20 Then Peter turning about, ſeeth the diſciple
o Chap xiii 23, & xx 2 ver — o whom Jeſus loved, following, which alſo leaned on his
breaſt at ſupper, and ſaid, Lord, which is he that be-
trayeth thee? 21 Peter ſeeing him, ſaith to Jeſus,
Lord, and what *ſhall* this man *do*? 22 Jeſus ſaith unto
p Mat xvi 28 — him, If I will that p he tarry till I come, what *is that* to
q Ver 19 — thee? q Follow thou me 23 Then went this ſaying
abroad among the brethren, that that diſciple ſhould not
die yet Jeſus ſaid not unto him, He ſhall not die but,
If I will that he tarry till I come, what *is that* to thee?
24 This is the diſciple which teſtifieth of theſe things,
r Chap xix 35. 3 John 12 — and wrote theſe things and we know that his teſti-
mony is true 25 s And there are alſo many other
s Chap xx 30. — things which Jeſus did, the which if they ſhould be
written every one, I ſuppoſe that even the world itſelf
could not contain the books that ſhould be written
Amen

V 20—25 Peter riſing up to follow his Maſter, on looking back, beheld John the beloved diſciple juſt behind him Hereupon,

1 He begs Jeſus to ſay, what ſhould be John's lot and labour Either he was curious to know, or tenderly concerned, leſt the ſame ſufferings waited his dear fellow labourer True Chriſtian charity will make us feel for our brethren as for ourſelves

2 Chriſt checks his curioſity, whilſt he anſwers his queſtion *If I will that he tarry till I come*, in ſome peculiarly glorious diſplay of my power, ſuch as the deſtruction of the Jewiſh nation would be, *what is that to thee? follow thou me* *Note*, (1) It is the will of Jeſus, that we ſhould follow ſteadily the path of duty, without curiouſly deſiring to pry into futurity, content to leave all our concerns in his hands (2) Our Lord directs all things according to the counſels of his own will, and that ſhould at all times ſatisfy us, and make us humbly ſay, *The will of the Lord be done*

3 From a miſtake of Chriſt's meaning a report ſpread among the brethren, as if that diſciple *ſhould not die*, whereas Chriſt ſaid no ſuch thing, but, *If I will that he tarry till I come*, meaning that he ſhould live to ſee the deſtruction of the Jewiſh ſtate and polity, and afterwards die not a violent but a natural death From whence we may obſerve, the uncertainty of all *human traditions*, and the great danger of ſubmitting implicitly to human expoſitions of ſcripture, however ſupported by numbers, authority, or antiquity We have the book of God before us, we have the Spirit of God promiſed to teach us, let us therefore, after all that others ſay, read, hear, and judge for ourſelves

4 The Evangeliſt now drawing to a concluſion, ſolemnly atteſts the truth of all he had recorded, being an eye and ear-witneſs of what he writes, and as he was himſelf abſolutely certain of what he ſaid, ſo were all his brethren, and the truths contained in this goſpel are attended with ſuch evidence as muſt convince every impartial enquirer They who reject the ſcripture teſtimony, wilfully ſhut their eyes againſt the light, and, whatever they may pretend, have no cloak for their obſtinate infidelity

5 He cloſes with a declaration, that innumerable other miracles were performed by Jeſus beſides thoſe here recorded, which, if they were all related with the circumſtances ſeverally attending them, not all the ſcribes in the world could have written them, nor the moſt retentive memory contain them Nor would the unbelieving world, who reject the preſent evidence, have received the truth, though innumerable volumes of Chriſt's miracles had been written for their conviction Hereto the Evangeliſt ſets his *Amen!* What he wrote was infallibly certain let us add our *Amen* to his, perfectly ſatisfied in his teſtimony, by faith embracing the glorious truths he records, and fervently praying for the accompliſhment of all the ineſtimable bleſſings which are promiſed Amen! Amen!

THE

EVANGELICAL EXPOSITOR;

OR, A

PRACTICAL COMMENT

UPON THE

ACTS of the APOSTLES.

THE Author of this volume is usually supposed to be Luke the beloved physician, who wrote the third of the four gospels, which bears his name, and who was very probably one of the seventy disciples, whose commission, Luke x 1, &c *was little inferior to that of the twelve apostles This Luke was very much a companion of Paul's in his services and sufferings* · Only Luke is with me, 2 *Tim* iv 11. *We may know by his stile in the latter part of this book when and where he was with him, for then he writes we did so and so, as* chap. xvi. 10 xx 6 *and from thenceforward to the end of the book He was with Paul in his dangerous voyage to Rome, when he was carried thither a prisoner, was with him when from his prison there he wrote his epistles to the Colossians and Philemon, in both which he is named. And it should seem that St Luke wrote this history when he was with St Paul at Rome during his imprisonment there, and was assistant to him, for the history concludes with St Paul's preaching there in his* own hired house *It is called,* The Acts of the Apostles, of the holy Apostles, *so the Greek copies generally read it, and so they are called,* Rev xviii 20 Rejoice over her, ye holy apostles *One copy inscribes it,* The Acts of the Apostles by Luke the Evangelist. 1. *It is the history of the apostles, yet here is in it the history of Stephen, Barnabas, and some other apostolical men, who, though not of the twelve, yet were endued with the same Spirit, and employed in the same work And of those that were apostles, it is the history of Peter and Paul only that is here recorded, and Paul was not of the twelve. But this sufficeth as a specimen of what the rest did in other places, pursuant to their commission, for they were none of them idle And as we are to think what is related in the gospels concerning Christ sufficient, because infinite wisdom thought so, the same we are to think here concerning what is related of the apostles and their labours, for what more is told us from tradition of the labours and sufferings of the apostles, and the churches they planted, is altogether doubtful and uncertain, and what I think we cannot build upon with any satisfaction at all, this is* gold, silver, *and* precious stones, *built upon the* foundation, *that is* wood, hay, and stubble 2 *It is called their acts, or* doings, *giving an account of their preaching, sufferings, miracles, success, the planting of the Christian churches by their means, and the vast progress of the gospel through their indefatigable labours The history ends with the first imprisonment of Paul at Rome, about thirty years after our Lord's ascension*

CHAP I

The inspired historian begins his narrative of the Acts of the Apostles, 1 With a review of the gospel history from the resurrection to the ascension of our Lord, ver 1—11 2 *With a general idea of the embryo of the Christian church, and its state from Christ's ascension to the pouring out of the Spirit,* ver 12—14 3 *With a particular account of the filling up of the vacancy that was made in the sacred college by the death of Judas, by the electing of Matthias in his room,* ver 15—26

a Luke i 3 1 THE former treatise have I made, O [a] Theo-
b Mark xvi 19 Luke xxiv 51 1 Tim iii 16 philus, of all that Jesus began both to do
and teach, 2 Until the day in which he
was taken up, after that he through the
holy Ghost [c] had given commandments unto the apostles, c Mat xxviii 19 Mark xvi 15
whom he had chosen 3 [d] To whom also he shewed John xx 21 Chap x 41
himself alive after his passion, by many infallible proofs, 1 John xx 19 26
being seen of them forty days, and speaking of the things & xxi 1
pertaining to the kingdom of God 4 [e] And being 1 Cor xv 5 e Luke xxiv
assembled together with them, commanded them that 49 17
they should not depart from Jerusalem, but wait for the f John xiv 16, 26, 27
promise of the Father, [f] which, *saith he*, you have heard & xv 26
of me 5 For [g] John truly baptized with water, [h] but & xvi 7
ye shall be baptized with the holy Ghost, not many days g Mat iii 11 Chap xi 16 & xix 4
hence h Joel ii 28 Chap ii 4 & xi 15

v 1—5 St Luke, the supposed penman of this book, dedicates it, as he had done his gospel, to Theophilus his noble catechumen

2 He

1 He reminds him of the former treatise which he had written for his edification and instruction, containing an account *of all that Jesus began both to do and teach*, laying the foundation of that Christian church on which they were to build, *until the day in which he was taken up*, continuing to instruct them in the nature of his kingdom, *after that he, through the Holy Ghost*, which the Father gave without measure unto him, *had given commandments unto the apostles whom he had chosen*, commissioning them to preach his gospel, and, according to the plenitude of his power, enabling them for this arduous work *Note*, They who *teach*, must *do* a minister's practice must be correspondent with his precepts

2 He mentions some of those many infallible signs which Jesus gave of his resurrection He shewed himself to his disciples alive, convinced them fully of the identity of his person, was seen of them several times, in different places, during the forty days that he continued on earth, eat, drank, and conversed freely with them, instructing them in *the things pertaining to the kingdom of God*, informing them of the nature of his kingdom, the powers they should be endued with, the success of their ministry, and the glory which was prepared for them

3 Christ ordered them, at one of their solemn meetings, not to depart from Jerusalem, whither they had probably come from Galilee, after they had seen him on the mountain where he appointed them to meet him, *but wait for the promise of the Father, which, saith he, you have heard of me*, fully and confidently expecting that Spirit whom the ancient prophecies had foretold should be abundantly poured out in the days of the Messiah, and of whom he had so often spoken to them before his departure, as the Comforter that he would send unto them from the Father, to enable them for the glorious work which was before them *For John truly baptized with water*, and that was all he pretended to do, *but ye*, according to his declarations, *shall be baptized with the Holy Ghost not many days hence*, receiving such abundant measures of light, grace, wisdom, courage, and utterance, as effectually to carry them through every temptation, and make them successful in spreading the gospel, in defiance of all opposition *Note*, We must patiently wait, and then we shall assuredly see the salvation of God

6 When they therefore were come together, they asked of him, saying, ^i^ Lord, wilt thou at this time restore again the kingdom to Israel? 7 And he said unto them, ^k^ It is not for you to know ^l^ the times or the seasons, which the Father hath put in his own power 8 But ^m^ ye shall receive † power, ^n^ after that the Holy Ghost is come upon you and ^o^ ye shall be witnesses unto me, both in Jerusalem, and in all Judea, and in Samaria, and unto the uttermost part of the earth 9 And ^p^ when he had spoken these things, while they beheld, ^q^ he was taken up, and a cloud received him out of their sight 10 And while they looked stedfastly toward heaven, as he went up, behold, two men stood by them ^r^ in white apparel, 11 Which also said, ^s^ Ye men of Galilee, why stand ye gazing up into heaven? this same Jesus, which is taken up from you into heaven, ^t^ shall so come in like manner as ye have seen him go into heaven

i Mat xxiv 3
k Mat xxiv 36 Mark xiii 32 1 Thes v 1
l Chap ii 1 4
† Or the power of the Holy Ghost coming upon you
m Luke xxiv 49
n Luke xxiv 48 John xv 27 Ver 22 Chap ii 32
o Luke xxiv 51
p Ver 2
q Mat xxviii 3 Chap x 30
r Chap ii 7 & xiii 31
s Dan vii 13 Mat xxiv 30 1 Thes i 10 2 Thes i 10 Rev i 7

v 6—11 The apostles had not yet quite dropped their apprehensions of the Messiah's temporal kingdom, and the resurrection of Jesus probably flattered them with new hopes

1 They put the question therefore to him, whether *at this time* he would *restore again the kingdom to Israel*, raising the Jewish people to the highest pitch of grandeur, and bringing all the kingdoms of the earth in subjection to them So hard is it to eradicate early prejudices And even good men are apt to look for a church triumphant instead of a church militant upon earth but, when the Spirit is poured out more abundantly, we shall learn to expect nothing here but reproach and the cross, and wait for another world to sit down in the kingdom

2 Christ checks their vain curiosity And, as the Spirit, which should be given them, would shortly rectify their mistakes, he tells them it was not for them *to know the times and seasons* when those great expected revolutions should be brought about, *which the Father hath put in his own power*, and which are secrets concealed in the divine mind *Note*, (1) Secret things belong unto God Curiosity to be wise above what is written, is foolish as well as fruitless (2) The uncertainty in which it hath pleased God to leave us, concerning future events, is graciously ordered, to the intent we might be always prepared for that which God hath prepared for us

3 He assures them, that, poor, illiterate, and despised instruments as they appeared, they should be endued with the most astonishing spiritual power, through the mighty influence of the Holy Ghost, which should *come upon them*, when, filled with zeal, courage, and wisdom, which none of their adversaries could gainsay or resist, they should be witnesses unto him, asserting his character as the divine Messiah, bearing testimony to his resurrection, publishing the glad tidings of salvation through his name, and confirming the truth of their words by the exertion of the most amazing miracles beginning at Jerusalem, then going to the Samaritans, among whom before they had been with-held from preaching, and then to spreading the glorious gospel to the ends of the earth, not only among the dispersed Jews, but among the Gentiles also *Note*, Gospel ministers must preach Jesus Christ, bearing witness to his grace and glory, and publishing to all, the free and full redemption which is obtained for lost sinners through his blood and righteousness

4 *When he had spoken these things, while they beheld*, earnestly regarding him, and duly attentive to the gracious words which proceeded out of his mouth, *he was taken up, and* with eager looks they followed him, till *a cloud received him out of their sight*, and, amidst congratulating angels, he ascended to the throne of his glory May I follow thee, Lord, with eyes of faith now, and, when it shall please thee, ascend to behold thee face to face

5 An angelic vision appears to them, as they stood gazing towards heaven after their dear Lord, *as he went up*, willing to catch the last possible glimpse of him, and keeping still their eyes fixed on the place where he became invisible to them Two celestial spirits in human forms, arrayed in white apparel, the emblem of their purity and splendor, stood by them, and kindly addressed them, saying, *Ye men of Galilee, why stand ye gazing up into heaven?* as if ye expected your Lord and Master to return quickly unto you *this same Jesus*, who was delivered for your offences, and died on a tree, *is now taken up from you into heaven*, exalted to the mediatorial throne, as having finished the redemption of his people, and is gone to prepare a place for them, *shall so come in like manner*, at the last day of his return in glory, in the clouds of heaven, attended by his angelic host, *as ye have seen him go into heaven* On that event, be ready to meet him in that great day! Oh that the expectation of it might be deep upon our minds continually!

12 ^u^ Then returned they unto Jerusalem from the mount called Olivet, which is from Jerusalem a sabbath-day's journey 13 And when they were come in, they went up ^x^ into an upper room, where abode both ^y^ Peter, and James, and John, and Andrew, Philip, and Thomas, Bartholomew, and Matthew, James *the son* of Alpheus, and ^z^ Simon Zelotes, and ^a^ Judas *the brother* of James 14 ^b^ These all continued with one accord in prayer and supplication with the women, and Mary the mother of Jesus, and with ^c^ his brethren

u Luke xxiv 52
x Chap ix 37 39 & xx 8
y Mat x 2 3
z Luke vi 15
a Jude 1
b Chap ii 1 42, 46
c Mat xiii 55

v 12—14 We have here,

1 The place from whence our Lord ascended, *the mount Olivet*, about a mile from Jerusalem There his sufferings began, in the garden, and thence he entered into his glory as a triumphant conqueror, (*Zech* xiv 4) in full view of that devoted city, for which judgment was now prepared

2 The return of the disciples They came back to the city according to their Master's orders, *and when they were come in*, either into a private house, or, as some suppose, into the temple itself, *see Luke* xxiv 53 *they went into an upper room*, for greater secrecy If this was in the temple, they might be accommodated by some priest or Levite, who was a hidden disciple, with a room there, or, if it was in the city, though they constantly attended the temple service, they met in private there, and spent their time, *with one accord*, in prayer and supplications for the coming of that Comforter who was promised The eleven apostles are particularly mentioned, all of whom kept close together, with the women, who had approved their fidelity, love, and zeal, in a very distinguished manner, and *Mary the mother of Jesus*, concerning whom we hear no more mention ever after, and *his brethren*, those of Christ's kinsmen who now believed on him, *see Matth* xiii 55 with many other *Note*, (1) It is good for the disciples of Jesus to unite together the world is closely leagued against them They need therefore maintain the closest fellowship with each other (2) Prayer is the blessed and constant employment of God's people, and especially in all seasons of particular trial, when their faith and patience are called into exercise, they have need to redouble their supplications (3) Nothing can be denied to the united prayers of the faithful, who with one accord surround a throne of grace in the name of Jesus

15 ¶ And in those days Peter stood up in the midst of the disciples, and said, (the number of ^d^ the names together were about an hundred and twenty) 16 Men and brethren, this scripture must needs have been fulfilled, ^e^ which the holy Ghost by the mouth of David spake before concerning Judas, ^f^ which was guide to them that took Jesus 17 For ^g^ he was numbered with us, and had obtained part of ^h^ this ministry 18 ^i^ Now this man purchased a field with the reward of iniquity, and falling headlong, he burst asunder in the midst, and all

d Rev iii 4
e Psal xli 9
f John xviii 3
g Luke vi 16
h Chap xii 25 & xxi 19
i Mat xxvii 5

all his bowels gushed out 19 And it was known unto
all the dwellers at Jerusalem, insomuch as that field is
called in their proper tongue, Aceldama, that is to say,
The field of blood 20 For it is written in the book
of Psalms, [k] Let his habitation be desolate, and let no
man dwell therein and [l] his [†] bishoprick let another
take. 21 Wherefore of these men which have accom-
panied with us all the time that the Lord Jesus went in
and out among us, 22 Beginning from the baptism
of John, unto that same day that [n] he was taken up from
us, must one be ordained to be a witness with us of his
resurrection 23 And they appointed two, Joseph cal-
led [p] Barsabas, who was surnamed Justus, and Matthias
24 And they prayed, and said, Thou, Lord, [q] which
knowest the hearts of all men, shew whether of these
two thou hast chosen, 25 That he may take part of
this ministry and apostleship, from which Judas by trans-
gression fell, that he might go to his own place 26
And [r] they gave forth their lots, and the lot fell upon
Matthias, and he was numbred with the eleven apostles

k Psal lxix 25. l Psal cix 8. † Or, office, or charge. n Ver 9. q 1 Sam xvi 7. Jer xi 20. Chap xv 8. Rev ii 23. r 1 Chron xxiv 5.

v 15—26 At one of those solemn meetings, where about an hundred and twenty of the disciples were assembled, Peter, the zealous servant of his Lord, *stood up* in the midst of them, not affecting to *sit*, as their master or superior, but proposing a matter to them as his equals We have,

1 His speech He addresses them as his friends, companions, and brethren in Christ, and having an important proposal to make to them, he reminds them of the fulfilment of the scripture, in the wickedness and miserable end of Judas the traitor, whose treachery the Holy Ghost having foreseen and foretold, it could not but come to pass, and none ought to be offended thereat As an aggravation of his guilt, Peter observes,

(1) The high dignity to which he was advanced *He was numbred with us, and had obtained part of this ministry*, and this but the more aggravated his sin and ruin *Note*, Many are numbred *with us* who are not *of us*, but *a name to live*, whilst persons are really *dead in trespasses and sins*, will avail nothing

(2) His sin was treachery He was *guide to them that took Jesus*, a ringleader in iniquity, as apostates usually prove

(3) His end was notorious His money, the wages of unrighteousness, served only to buy a field to bury strangers, and driven by the devil and a despairing conscience, he went and hanged himself when the rope, or the place on which he hung, giving way, he fell, and his belly bursting asunder, his bowels gushed out, a fearful exit! of which great notice was deservedly taken, the fact being publickly known in Jerusalem, and noised abroad, insomuch that the people called the field purchased by this money, Aceldama, or *The field of blood*, with respect to the innocent blood, of which it was the price, perpetuating thereby the infamy, not only of the traitor who sold his master, but of the rulers who tempted him to this atrocious deed

(4) He cites the Book of Psalms, in which the prophecy relating to Judas was found *Let his habitation be desolate, and let no man dwell therein*, Psal lxix 25 *and his bishoprick let another take*, Psal cix 8

(5) He proposes to them, according to this prophetic word, that the sacred college should be filled up, by the addition of one to their number, out of those who had approved themselves from the beginning faithful, and had been among the first who followed Jesus, and privy to all the transactions concerning him, from the time he was baptized of John in Jordan, till his ascension to glory, that he might with them be *a witness of his resurrection*, of that grand article of truth, as well as of all the other glorious things relative to Christ's divine mission and character *Note*, (1) None should be admitted into the ministry but such as for a season have proved their fidelity to Christ, in a course of holy walking with him (2) They who have known Christ, and the power of his resurrection in their souls, cannot but make him the subject of all their discourse.

2 The church approving the proposal, nominated two, Joseph and Matthias, and not knowing which to prefer, they applied to God, the searcher of hearts, by prayer for direction, that he would be pleased to shew them, which of these he had chosen *to take part of that ministry and apostleship, from which Judas by transgression fell, that he might go to his own place*, the dire abode prepared for fallen angels and rebellious sinners *Note*, (1) In our concernments, we should never fail to look up to God for direction (2) Apostates from Christ necessarily plunge themselves into perdition and destruction

3 Having commended the matter to God's determination, they solemnly cast lots, when the Lord, at whose disposal the lot is, *Prov* xvi 33 appointed Matthias, who was thenceforward numbered with the eleven apostles.

CHAP II

Here is, 1 The descent of the Spirit upon the apostles, and those that were with them, on the day of Pentecost, ver 1—4 *2 The various speculations which this occasioned among the people that were now met in Jerusalem from all parts*, ver 5—13 *3 The sermon which Peter preached to them hereupon*, ver 14—36 *4 The good effect of this sermon in the conversion of many to the faith of Christ, and their addition to the church*, ver 37—41 *5 The eminent piety and charity of these primitive Christians, and the manifest tokens of God's presence with them*, ver 42—47

1 AND when [a] the day of Pentecost was fully come,
[b] they were all with one accord in one place 2
And suddenly there came a sound from heaven, as of a
rushing mighty wind, and [c] it filled all the house where
they were sitting 3 And there appeared unto them
cloven tongues, [d] like as of fire, and it sat upon each of
them 4 And [e] they were all filled with the Holy Ghost,
and began to [f] speak with other tongues, as the Spirit
gave them utterance

a Lev xxiii 15. Deut xvi 9. b Chap i 14. c Chap iv 31.

v 1—4 The great promise here receives its accomplishment in the mission of the Holy Ghost upon the disciples We have,

1 The time *When the day of Pentecost*, the fiftieth from the passover, *was fully come*, in the morning, *they were all with one accord in one place*, it being the first day of the week, which they observed in memory of their Lord's resurrection, and consecrated also now by the pouring out of the Spirit upon them No longer strifes or discord divided them, united in fervent charity, they waited the fulfilment of their master's promise *Note*, (1) They who wait upon God in the assembly of his saints, shall find him by his Spirit still present in the midst of them (2) God will delight to dwell with those whose hearts, by fervent charity, are united in his service

2 The manner in which the Holy Ghost descended *Suddenly there came a sound from heaven, as of a rushing mighty wind*, an emblem of the freedom of the Spirit's operations, and of his irresistible energy on the minds of men, *and it filled all the house where they were sitting And there appeared unto them cloven tongues, like as of fire*, signifying the illuminating, warming, and purifying influences of the Spirit upon their souls, and the amazing gift of tongues bestowed upon them with that freedom of utterance, whereby they were enabled to preach the gospel among all nations, and *it*, or *he*, *sat upon each of them*, the Holy Ghost, in all the fulness of his miraculous operations, now taking up his constant residence in them, to qualify them for the arduous service to which they were ordained *And they were all filled with the Holy Ghost*, not only the apostles, but all the disciples, and probably the women, as well as the men, v 17, 18 experiencing such divine joys and consolation as they had never experienced before, *and began to speak with other tongues*, in all the variety of languages, *as the Spirit gave them utterance*, suggesting both the matter and words, and enabling them with the greatest copiousness and most forcible energy to declare the wonderful works of God, v 11 in the gospel of his dear Son

5 And there were dwelling at Jerusalem Jews, de-
vout men, out of every nation under heaven 6 Now
when this was noised abroad, the multitude came to-
gether, and were [†] confounded, because that every man
heard them speak in his own language 7 And they
were all amazed and marvelled, saying one to another,
Behold, are not all these which speak, [g] Galileans? 8
And how hear we every man in our own tongue, where-
in we were born? 9 Parthians, and Medes, and Ela-
mites, and the dwellers in Mesopotamia, and in Judea,
and Cappadocia, in Pontus, and Asia, 10 Phrygia,
and Pamphylia, in Egypt, and in the parts of Libya
about Cyrene, and strangers of Rome, Jews and pro-
selytes, 11 Cretes and Arabians, we do hear them
speak in our tongues the wonderful works of God 12
And they were all amazed, and were in doubt, saying
one to another, What meaneth this? 13 Others mock-
ing, said, These men are [h] full of new wine

† Or, troubled in mind. g Chap i 11. h Matt xi 19.

v 5—13 Such an extraordinary occurrence was soon spread abroad, and brought a vast concourse together We have,

1 The persons *Devout men, who dwelt at Jerusalem, out of every nation under heaven*, both Jews and Proselytes, who were now assembled at the feast of Pentecost, or as some suppose, had taken up their residence there, in expectation of the speedy appearing of the Messiah

2 The

2 The amazement which filled them at hearing these men, that were poor illiterate Galileans, speak with such fluency and propriety, all the various languages and dialects of their respective countries, *Parthians, Medes, &c.* They could not, therefore, but with wonder and surprize, observe to each other, how astonishing was this miracle, and question what could be the meaning of it, and whether it ushered in the long-expected kingdom of the Messiah? for they heard them speak in their several native tongues *the great things of God*, respecting the redemption which was in Jesus Christ, and the glorious privileges obtained by his death, resurrection, and ascension for all believers.

3 Some *mocking, said, These men are full of new wine*, a cavil most wicked, absurd, and blasphemous. Probably these were inhabitants of Jerusalem, the scribes and Pharisees, who not understanding the languages which the inspired disciples spoke, thought it nonsense, and would fain have branded them as drunkards, that they might prejudice the people against them, by this most malicious falshood. *Note*, There are still too many to whom the great things of God appear unintelligible, and because they are themselves destitute of spiritual understanding, they brand the preachers of them as enthusiasts, *speaking evil of the things they know not*.

14 ¶ But Peter standing up with the eleven, lift up
his voice, and said unto them, Ye men of Judea, and all
ye that dwell at Jerusalem, be this known unto you, and
hearken to my words. 15 For these are not drunken,
as ye suppose, seeing it is but the third hour of the day.
16 But this is that which was spoken by the prophet
Joel. 17 And it shall come to pass in the last days,
(saith God) I will pour out of my Spirit upon all flesh:
and your sons and your daughters shall prophesy, and
your young men shall see visions, and your old men
shall dream dreams. 18 And on my servants, and on
my handmaidens I will pour out in those days of my
Spirit, and they shall prophesy. 19 And I will shew
wonders in heaven above, and signs in the earth beneath,
blood, and fire, and vapour of smoke. 20 The sun
shall be turned into darkness, and the moon into blood,
before that great and notable day of the Lord come.
21 And it shall come to pass, that whosoever shall call
on the name of the Lord, shall be saved. 22 Ye men
of Israel, hear these words, Jesus of Nazareth, a man
approved of God among you, by miracles and wonders
and signs, which God did by him in the midst of you,
as ye yourselves also know. 23 Him, being delivered
by the determinate counsel and foreknowledge of God,
ye have taken, and by wicked hands have crucified and
slain. 24 Whom God hath raised up, having loosed
the pains of death: because it was not possible that he
should be holden of it. 25 For David speaketh con-
cerning him, I foresaw the Lord always before my face,
for he is on my right hand, that I should not be moved.
26 Therefore did my heart rejoice, and my tongue was
glad: moreover also, my flesh shall rest in hope. 27
Because thou wilt not leave my soul in hell, neither wilt
thou suffer thine holy One to see corruption. 28 Thou
hast made known to me the ways of life, thou shalt make
me full of joy with thy countenance. 29 Men *and*
brethren, let me freely speak unto you of the patriarch
David, that he is both dead and buried, and his sepul-
chre is with us unto this day. 30 Therefore being a
prophet, and knowing that God had sworn with an
oath to him, that of the fruit of his loins, according
to the flesh, he would raise up Christ to sit on his
throne: 31 He seeing this before, spake of the resur-
rection of Christ, that his soul was not left in hell,
neither his flesh did see corruption. 32 This Jesus
hath God raised up, whereof we all are witnesses. 33
Therefore being by the right hand of God exalted,
and having received of the Father the promise of the
Holy Ghost, he hath shed forth this, which ye now
see and hear. 34 For David is not ascended into the
heavens: but he saith himself, The Lord said unto my
Lord, Sit thou on my right hand, 35 Until I make thy
foes thy footstool. 36 Therefore let all the house of
Israel know assuredly, that God hath made that same
Jesus whom ye have crucified, both Lord and Christ.

v. 14—36. In answer to the malicious cavil of these enemies to the truth, Peter, the zealous apostle, and now inspired by peculiar influences from on high, rose and boldly addressed to these mockers this awakening discourse.

1 *He stood up with the eleven*, to shew the falshood of the charge, and vindicate themselves from so malicious an accusation; and aloud directing his discourse to the Jews, who were present, begs attention to the words of truth and soberness, which he was about to utter. *Note*, We must not return a sharp answer to a reviling accusation, but *with meekness answer those who oppose themselves* against us.

2 He denies the calumny, and shews it to be as absurd as malicious. *These men are not drunken, as ye suppose*, and would insinuate, *seeing it is but the third hour of the day*, but nine o'clock in the morning, and till then, on the sabbaths and festivals, the Jews usually did neither eat nor drink, nor was it at all probable, that so many as they were, they should have been guilty of such a debauch, or dare appear intoxicated in the house of God.

3 He explains to them the affair which they counted so strange, which some admired and others ridiculed. This was the accomplishment of the prophecy of Joel, *chap.* ii. 28—32. which he cites at large; for though himself inspired, the Spirit was not given to supersede the scriptures, but to enable us to understand them. God had promised *in the last days*, the days of the Messiah, which ushered in the last dispensation of grace, *I will pour out of my Spirit*, in a more extraordinary measure than ever before, *upon all flesh*, on some of all ranks and conditions, or upon the Gentiles as well as Jews; *and your sons and your daughters shall prophesy*, foretelling future events, *chap.* xxi. 9, 10. *and your young men shall see visions, and your old men shall dream dreams*, God, in these ways, revealing to them his mind and will: *and on my servants, and my handmaidens*, on persons of all conditions, women as well as men, without distinction of rank or sex, *I will pour out in those days of my Spirit*, as from an inexhaustible fountain, *and they shall prophesy*: *and I will shew wonders in heaven above*, dreadful prodigies in the air, which were the prelude to the approaching ruin of the Jewish nation, for their obstinate infidelity and rejection of the Messiah; *and signs in the earth beneath*, dire presages of impending woes; *blood, and fire, and pillars of smoke*, the blood of the people shed by the invading foe, whose devastations should spread through the country, and the smoak of their cities consumed in flames, which should obscure the sky. *The sun shall be turned into darkness, and the moon into blood*, suffering unusual eclipses, or looking red, through the dusky clouds of smoke; or this may signify the approaching total dissolution of their government, *before the great and terrible day of the Lord come*, when he shall execute such condign vengeance on his murderers, as no nation, since the burning of Sodom, ever suffered, and when he shall be glorified in his judgments. *And it shall come to pass, that whosoever*, discerning the signs of these times, *shall call on the name of the Lord*, the almighty Jehovah, Jesus, spoken of in this prophecy, placing their dependance on him alone for salvation, and in fervent prayer making their application to him for help, they *shall be saved* by his power and grace from all the evils they fear, in time or eternity, and be made partakers of his eternal glory. Lord, pour out a spirit of prayer and supplication upon me, that I may be of this blessed number!

4 He improves this occasion, in order to preach to them Jesus, whose gift and purchase this Spirit was, which now was shed abroad so abundantly upon them, intreating their attention to the important truths he was about to deliver.

[1.] He reminds them of his well-known life and character. *Jesus of Nazareth*, a name they gave him by way of reproach, but *a man approved of God among you*, evidently signalized with his peculiar favour, *by miracles, and wonders, and signs*, which he was enabled to work in proof of his divine mission, *which God did by him in the midst of you, as ye yourselves also know*, bearing his attestation to the character he assumed, and they themselves had been eye-witnesses of these wonderful works.

[2.] They had, notwithstanding, rejected his credentials, and hung him on a tree. *Him*, this glorious Messiah, *delivered by the determinate counsel and foreknowledge of God*, ordained a sacrifice to divine justice, *ye have taken* and seized as a criminal, *and by wicked hands have crucified and slain*, engaging the Gentile governor to bring him to this ignominious death, and his innocent blood is now upon your heads.

[3.] *God had raised him*, notwithstanding all their enmity, rage, and malice, *having loosed the pains of death*, judicially discharging him from the grave, and from all the sorrows of death, which, as the substitute of his people, he contented to endure, *because it was not possible he should be holden of them*. The dignity of his person, the perfection of his sacrifice, and the prophecies concerning him, rendered it impossible that he should remain longer the prisoner of death; whom by dying he had destroyed, and as a triumphant conqueror, rose to lead his captivity captive.

[4.] He shews that this was foretold by the Royal Psalmist, who, personating Jesus, the true Messiah, thus *speaketh concerning him, I foresaw the Lord always before my face*, he walked under the constant sense of his Father's presence, and with an eye to his glory, *for he is on my right hand*, to support and carry me through my arduous undertaking, *that I should not be moved* with any of the sufferings of life, or the terrors

terrors of death *Therefore did my heart rejoice* in his power, faithfulness, and love, *and my tongue was glad*, praising him for the experience of his almighty grace, and the assured salvation of his people, which he had promised him as the travail of his soul *my flesh also shall rest in hope*, entirely satisfied of a glorious issue, and entring the grave in the fullest assurance of a speedy resurrection, *because*, or *that thou wilt not leave my soul in hell*, to abide, like other departed spirits, in the invisible world, nor his body in the dust, *neither wilt thou suffer thy holy One to see corruption*, and putrify in the tomb, being *the holy One* of God, and having by a perfect obedience to death, even the death of the cross, compleated the redemption of his people, he had a right to a speedy discharge from that lowest step of his humiliation *Thou hast made known to me the ways of life*, which he through the gates of death, and Christ, the first-fruits of those that slept, is gone before, having raised himself to an endless life, and leading his people after him to a glorious immortality *thou shalt make me full of joy with thy countenance*, in that state of bliss and blessedness to which, as Mediator, he should be exalted and what is here primarily spoken concerning the great head of the church, is true of every member of his body mystical (1) They live for God, designing his glory as their end, and resting upon his promises, his power, and grace, as their abiding support, comfort, and joy (2) They *die in hope*, committing their souls into the hands of a faithful Creator, and rejoicing in the prospect of eternal life and glory which the gospel sets before them, and of which faith assures them

[5] He comments on the text he had quoted Great and respectable as *the patriarch David* was, the head of the royal race of Judah, yet he saw corruption, and they, as reasonable men, and his countrymen, if they dispassionately considered these words, must needs be convinced that the Psalmist spake not this of himself, he dying, and being buried as other men, and his tomb being extant to this day, but *being a prophet, and knowing that God had sworn with an oath to him*, Ps cxxxii 11 *that of the fruit of his loins, according to the flesh, he would raise up Christ to sit upon his throne*, as Israel's king, in the most exalted sense, reigning in the hearts of his redeemed people *he seeing this before*, by the spirit of prophecy, *spake of the resurrection of Christ*, whom he personates when he saith, *that his soul was not left in hell, neither did his flesh see corruption* *This Jesus*, who lately lay in the grave, the Son of David after the flesh, the person of whom he, as a prophet, speaks, *God hath raised up, whereof we all are witnesses*, having been his constant followers before his death, and having often seen, conversed, and eat and drank with him since his resurrection, till the day that we beheld him ascend up to heaven

[6] The gifts of the Spirit were the fruit of his exaltation *Therefore being by the right hand of God exalted* to the mediatorial throne, and possessed of the most transcendent dignity and glory, *and having received of the Father the promise of the Holy Ghost*, the purchase of his obedience to death in the behalf of his people, *he hath shed forth this, which ye now see and hear*, the flames of fire, and gift of tongues, which appeared to them so strange And his ascension also David had foretold, *Psal* cx 1 *For David is not ascended into the heavens*, as the person, in whose name he speaks, evidently was, *but* the Lord Jesus is gone thither, *as he saith himself*, *The Lord*, Jehovah, *said unto my Lord*, the Messiah, *Sit thou on my right hand*, in the highest dignity, and possessed of universal dominion and authority, *until I make thy foes thy footstool*, until sin, Satan, death, and every enemy of the Redeemer and his people, shall be finally and for ever destroyed

[7] He warmly applies the matter to their consciences *Therefore let all the house of Israel know assuredly*, as a truth most infallible and certain, *that God hath made that same Jesus whom ye have crucified, both Lord and Christ*, and there could not be a greater aggravation of their wickedness than this, that whom the Lord had glorified, they had crucified, nor a more tremendous consideration than that he was now exalted to a throne of glory to execute vengeance on all his murderers, who obstinately persisted in their impenitence

g Zech xii 10 37 ¶ Now when they heard *this*, [g] they were pricked in their heart, and said unto Peter, and to the rest of the
h Luke iii 10 Chap ix 6 & xvi 30 apostles, Men *and* brethren, [h] what shall we do? 38.
Then Peter said unto them, [i] Repent, and be baptized
i Luke xxiv 47 Chap iii 19 every one of you in the name of Jesus Christ for the remission of sins, and ye shall receive the gift of the Holy
k Chap iii 25 & xiii 46 Ghost 39 For the promise is [k] unto you, and [l] to your
l Joel ii 28 children, and [m] to all that are afar off, even as many as
m Chap xxviii 28 Eph ii 13 the Lord our God shall call 40. And with many other
words did he testify and exhort, saying, Save yourselves
from this untoward generation 41 ¶ Then they that
gladly received his word, were baptized and the same
day there were added *unto them* about three thousand
souls.

v 37—41 The power of the Spirit upon the apostles themselves appeared gloriously evident in the boldness wherewith he inspired them, as well as in the miraculous gifts with which he endued them here we have also a proof of his energetic influence on the consciences of the hearers, accompanying his own word in the mouths of his servants

1 Many of the hearers, struck with conscious guilt at what they heard, *were pricked in their heart* with sharp and deep convictions of their sin and danger, and in great distress of conscience, *said unto Peter and the rest of the apostles*, whom just before they had mocked at, *Men and brethren, what shall we do*, to avert the dire vengeance we have provoked, and to obtain pardon for a deed so atrocious? *Note*, (1) When the Spirit of God opens the sinner's conscience to discern his hell-deserving guilt, his hard heart then is broken with the most fearful apprehensions of his danger (2) Ministers are the physicians to whom convinced sinners should apply, and they have balm to cure the mortal wound which sin hath made in their souls (3) They who truly feel their lost estate, cannot but desire, above all things, to know if yet there may be hope

2 *Peter*, in the name of his brethren, *said unto them*, your case, however dangerous, is not desperate, *Repent*, under a sense of redeeming love be deeply humbled for your guilt and ingratitude, and with deep self-abhorrence, and a thorough change of temper and conduct, turn unto the Lord, *and be baptized every one of you in the name of Jesus Christ*, professing your faith in him as the true Messiah, and sincerely yielding up yourselves to him as his willing subjects, *for the remission of sins*, purchased by him, and freely bestowed on the chief of sinners, *and* herewith also *ye shall receive the gift of the Holy Ghost*, of his comforting and sanctifying influences, as also (it is probable) of his miraculous powers *For the promise*, v 38 of pardon and the Holy Ghost, or the great promise made to Abraham and his seed, *is to you and to your children*, his descendants, *and to all that are afar off*, dispersed Jews or Gentiles, yet more distant from the covenant of promise, *even as many as the Lord our God shall call* to the knowledge of his Son, and to faith in him, who shall be blessed with faithful Abraham *Note*, (1) No sinner need despair, the gospel holds forth, through the blood of Jesus, a free pardon to the most guilty of the sons of Adam, and he that believes shall be saved (2) Where the Lord gives remission of sins, he sends his Holy Ghost effectually to produce that repentance which he enjoins (3) None can come to God but those whom he calls not merely by the outward voice of his word, but by the internal power of his Spirit

3 The apostle enlarged on this subject *And with many other words did he testify and exhort, saying, Save yourselves from this untoward generation*, come out from among them, and be ye separate, renounce the false tenets and corrupt practices of the Scribes and Pharisees, that ye may escape the plagues ready to descend upon this sinful people, abandoned to their infidelity and destruction *Note*, They who would be saved among Christ's people, must be separated from the ways of this wicked world, and from the familiar society of careless sinners, shunning their assemblies, as a man dreads the house infected by the plague

4 Great was the effect produced by this discourse, through the Spirit's mighty energy No less than three thousand souls immediately embraced, and *gladly received*, the word of gospel-grace, and believing in a crucified Redeemer now risen from the dead, made open profession of their faith, and were baptized in his name *Note*, (1) The salvation which is by Jesus Christ, is glad news to the sinner who is pricked to the heart with a sense of his guilt and danger (2) They who are truly turned to the Lord, will boldly make profession of his name, and join themselves to the society of the faithful, whatever danger or reproach they may be exposed to thereby

42 And [n] they continued stedfastly in the apostles n Chap i 14 Ver 46
doctrine and fellowship, and [o] in breaking of bread, and o Chap xx 7
[p] in prayers 43 And fear came upon every soul and p Rom xii 12 Col iv 2
[q] many wonders and signs were done by the apostles q Mark xvi 17 Chap v 12
44 And all that believed were together, and [r] had all r Chap iv 32
things common, 45 And [s] sold their possessions and s Ibid 34
goods, and [t] parted them to all men, as every man had t Isa lviii 7
need 46. And [u] they continuing daily with one accord u Chap i 14
[x] in the temple, and [y] breaking bread from house to x Luke xxiv 53 Chap v 42
house, did eat their meat with gladness and singleness of y Ver 42
heart, 47 Praising God, [z] and having favour with all z Luke ii 52 Chap iv 33 Rom xiv 18
the people And [a] the Lord added to the church daily a Chap v 14
such as should be saved

v 42—47 We have here the practice of the primitive church

1 They were united in holy ordinances *They continued stedfastly in the apostles' doctrine*, professing their faith in Christ and his gospel, and attending on the apostles ministry *and fellowship*, maintaining the closest communion with them, *and in breaking of bread*, celebrating the Lord's Supper, *and in prayers* social and public, *continuing daily with one accord in the temple* at the stated hours of service, *and praising God* for all the inestimable blessings bestowed, through Jesus Christ, upon them N,

They who have tasted of the blessing of communion with God, will delight to maintain it in the diligent use of all holy ordinances

2 A solemn awe restrained their enemies from molesting them *Fear came upon every soul and many wonders and signs were done by the apostles*, so that it evidently appeared that God was with them *Note*, God can put his bridle in the jaws of persecutors, and say, Touch not my prophets, and do my anointed no harm

3 A spirit of most noble and disinterested charity appeared among them *All that believed were together*, they were of one heart and mind, and assembled in several companies, as many as conveniently could meet in one place, *and had all things common*, each casting his all into the common stock, *and* as the necessity of the times was urgent, and they knew the sure and near approach of Jerusalem's overthrow, they *sold their possessions and goods, and parted them to all men, as every man*, of their society, *had need*, and as they assembled daily with one accord in the temple, so did they *break bread from house to house*, provided out of the common stock, eating their meat together *with gladness and singleness of heart*, fervent in love to each other, thankful to God, and conscious of their own undissembled simplicity and sincerity before him *Note*, Who should rejoice, if the children of God do not?

4 They were highly esteemed, and their numbers daily increased They had *favour with the people*, their undissembled piety commanded respect, and the miraculous powers with which they were invested, excited reverence *And the Lord* so eminently blessed their ministrations, that there were *added unto the church daily such as should be saved* *Note*, (1) Those whom the Lord will save, he will take care so effectually to call, as that they *shall* come to him (2) It is the Lord's work to add converts to his church in dependance on his power and promise, we labour with comfort and confidence

CHAP III

In this chapter we have a miracle and a sermon 1 *The miracle is the healing of a man that was lame from his birth, with a word speaking*, ver 1—8 *And the impression which this made upon the people*, ver 9—11 2 *The scope of the sermon which was preached thereupon, was to bring people to Christ, to repent of their sin in crucifying him*, ver 12—19 *And to believe in him now he was glorified*, ver 20—26

1 NOW Peter and John went up together [a] into the temple, at the hour of prayer, [b] *being* the ninth hour 2 And [c] a certain man lame from his mother's womb was carried, whom they laid daily at the gate of the temple which is called Beautiful, [d] to ask alms of them that entred into the temple 3 Who seeing Peter and John about to go into the temple, asked an alms 4 And Peter fastning his eyes upon him, with John, said, Look on us 5 And he gave heed unto them, expecting to receive something of them 6 Then Peter said, Silver and gold have I none, but such as I have give I thee [e] In the name of Jesus Christ of Nazareth, rise up and walk 7 And he took him by the right hand, and lifted *him* up, and immediately his feet and ancle bones received strength 8 And he leaping up, stood, and walked, and entred with them into the temple, [f] walking, and leaping, and praising God 9 And all the people saw him walking and praising God 10 And they knew that it was he which sat for alms at the Beautiful gate of the temple and they were filled with wonder and amazement at that which had happened unto him 11 And as the lame man which was healed held Peter and John, all the people ran together unto them in the porch [g] that is called Solomon's, greatly wondering

a Chap. ii. [illegible]
c Chap. xiv. 8
e Chap. iv. [illegible]

Ver 1—11 Among the many miracles performed by the apostles, one notable one is here recorded

1 The apostles by whom it was done were Peter and John, they were going up to the temple together at the stated hour of prayer, probably the same day in which Peter had preached in the morning, being *the ninth hour*, or three o clock in the afternoon *Note*, They who love the temple service, will be glad to be there twice a day

2 The poor object, on whom the miracle was performed, was a beggar, a cripple from his mother's womb, who lay *at the beautiful gate of the temple*, which was made of Corinthian brass, more precious than gold and asked *alms of them that entered into the temple*, seeing Peter and John, therefore, about to enter, he asked of them *an alms* *Note*, (1) Those who are poor and incapable of working, are the true objects of charity (2) They who are drawn to the temple by the love of God, will have their hearts enlarged in tenderest compassion towards the wants of the necessitous

3 Peter and John looking earnestly at him, bid him attend to them, as about to shew him a singular favour, and the poor man expecting an alms, looked attentively at them When Peter, the forward speaker, addressed him, saying, *Silver and gold have I none, but such as I have*, and what silver and gold never could procure, *give I thee In the name of Jesus Christ of Nazareth, rise up and walk*, by his authority I speak, and his power shall enable thee for what I command Then *taking him by the right hand, he lift him up, and immediately* the astonishing cure was wrought, *his feet and ancle bones received strength* *Note*, (1) The riches of grace are infinitely more valuable than the treasures of both the Indies (2) According to our abilities, we must be ready to communicate of the gifts of God with which he hath entrusted us, whether temporal or spiritual (3) In this impotent man, every sinner may read his own case and cure 1 By nature, from our birth, thus spiritually paralytic are we, and utterly unable to walk one step in God's ways 2 The temple is the place where the poor impotent sinner should be found, for there the Lord usually dispenses the alms of his grace 3 The ministers of Christ say not in vain *arise and walk*, to those who have no power of themselves to help themselves, for he, in whose name they speak, doth by his Spirit accompanying their word, enable the helpless soul for that which they enjoin 4 Christ first lays hold of us by the hand of his grace, and then we lay hold of him by the hand of faith, and feel an unusual power communicated to our paralytic souls

4 The lame man, transported with joy at the strange alteration he instantly felt, *leaped up* with astonishing agility, and *stood* firm on his feet, and *walked* about before all present, in token of his perfect cure, and entred with his benefactors into the temple, *walking, and leaping, and praising God* *Note*, (1) If our souls have received a spiritual cure, then will our hearts and lips be filled with praise and thanksgiving to the God of all grace, and we shall be happy in employing the strength he hath given us in walking in his holy ways (2) They who have found a blessing from the ministry of Christ's servants, will not fail to accompany them into the temple, that they may reap farther benefit from their company and discourse

5 The people who beheld him were struck with wonder and surprize, at seeing him thus walking and praising God, knowing that it was the same cripple who had lain at the gate of the temple, and whilst, as in an ecstasy, he hung about Peter and John, expressing his unutterable gratitude for this mercy received by their means, the people gathered round them in the part of the temple called Solomon's porch, *greatly wondering* at this amazing miracle, and at those who wrought it *Note*, They who have been made the instruments of good to our souls, cannot but be dear to us, and embraced with peculiar affection

12 ¶ And when Peter saw *it*, he answered unto the people, Ye men of Israel, why marvel ye at this? or why look ye so earnestly on us, [i] as though by our own power or holiness we had made this man to walk? 13 [k] The God of Abraham, and of Isaac, and of Jacob, the God of our fathers [l] hath glorified his Son Jesus, whom ye delivered up, and [m] denied him in the presence of Pilate, when he was determined to let *him* go 14 But ye denied [n] the holy One, and [o] the just, and desired a murderer to be granted unto you, 15 And killed the prince of life, [p] whom God hath raised from the dead, [q] whereof we are witnesses 16 And his name through faith in his name hath made this man strong, whom ye see and know yea, the faith which is by him hath given this perfect soundness in the presence of you all 17 And now, brethren, I wot that [r] through ignorance ye did *it*, as *did* also your rulers 18 But those things which God before had shewed by the mouth of all his prophets, that Christ should suffer, he hath so fulfilled 19 ¶ [s] Repent ye therefore and be converted, that your sins may be blotted out, when the times of refreshing shall come from the presence of the Lord 20 And he shall send Jesus Christ, [t] which was before preached unto you 21 Whom the heaven must receive, until the times of restitution of all things, which God hath spoken by the mouth of all his holy prophets [u] since the world began 22 For Moses truly said unto the fathers, A prophet shall the Lord your God raise up unto you of your brethren, like unto me him shall ye hear in all things whatsoever he shall say unto you 23 And it shall come to pass, *that* every soul which will not hear that prophet, shall be destroyed from among the people 24 Yea, and all the prophets from Samuel, and those that follow after, as many as have spoken, have likewise

y Gen xii 3 & xviii 18 & xxii 18 & xxvi 4 Gal iii 8 z Luke xxiv 47 Chap xiii 46 a Ver 19

foretold of these days 25 Ye are the children of the
prophets, and of the covenant which God made with
our fathers, saying unto Abraham, y And in thy seed
shall all the kindreds of the earth be blessed 26 z Un-
to you first, God having raised up his Son Jesus, sent
him to bless you, a in turning away every one of you
from his iniquities

v 12—26 Peter beholding the concourse of people assembled on this occasion, improves so happy an opportunity to preach the gospel to those who seemed so affected with the miracle before them A word in season, how good is it!

1 He humbly disclaims all the honour of the miracle, which was due to his Master alone *Ye men of Israel, why marvel ye at this?* when so much greater cures have been before performed among you by the Lord Jesus, *or why look ye so earnestly on us, as though by our own power or holiness we had made this man walk?* *Note*, (1) The most successful ministers must be the most humble, the more they are admired of others, the lower they must lie down at the feet of Jesus, ascribing to him alone the praise (2) We are too apt to idolize the men and ministers, who have been made signal instruments of good to us, but we should look further, even to him who alone *giveth the increase*

2 He preaches to them that Jesus, whom they crucified, by whose power alone this miracle was wrought *The God of Abraham, and of Isaac, and of Jacob*, that covenant-keeping God, *the God of our fathers, hath glorified his Son Jesus*, owning him in this high character, not only by all the miracles which he had wrought, but by his resurrection from the dead, and ascension to heaven, *whom ye delivered up* as a malefactor, into the hands of the Roman governor, *and denied him in the presence of Pilate*, as your King Messiah, requiring his crucifixion, *when he*, convinced of his innocency, *was determined to let him go* *But ye*, instigated by the priests and rulers, with savage barbarity *denied the holy One, and the Just*, whom none could ever convince of sin, or impeach his spotless purity and as the most provoking aggravation of your guilt, *desired a murderer to be granted unto you*, in preference to him, *and killed the Prince of Life*, the author and fountain of natural, spiritual, and eternal life; *whom God hath raised from the dead*, defeating all the malice of his enemies, rolling away the reproach of the cross, and exalting him to a state of the most transcendent glory, *whereof we are witnesses*, have seen and conversed with him after his resurrection, and are endued with these miraculous powers by him, to make our testimony more regarded *And his name, through faith in his name, hath made this man strong whom ye see and know*, acting under his authority, and trusting on his power, hath this incontestible miracle been performed *yea, the faith which is by him*, exercised upon him as the object, and wrought in us by him as the author, *hath given him this perfect soundness in the presence of you all*, for this thing was not done in a corner, but publickly in the temple, and the perfection of the cure was evident to every beholder

3 Yet dreadful as their guilt was, he means not to drive them to despair *And now, brethren*, exceeding sinful as your conduct hath been, *I wot that through ignorance ye did it, as did also your rulers*, I persuade myself that many, I would hope the most, who were engaged in that black deed, were blindly hurried on by their passions and prejudices, and knew not what they did, else would they not have crucified the Lord of glory, 1 Cor ii 8 *But those things which God before had shewed by the mouth of all his prophets, that Christ should suffer, he hath so fulfilled*, and though this be no extenuation of your wickedness, yet since the very end of his dying was, in order to obtain remission of sins for the most miserable and desperate, there is still hope, even for those, whose hands are red with his blood *Note*, (1) Charity bids us hope the best, even of the vilest, and not to impute to them worse motives to their actions than really influence them (2) The wickedness of men God can over-rule, and bring good out of their evil

4 He exhorts to immediate penitent return to him whom they had crucified *Repent ye, therefore*, of this atrocious deed, *and* since there is yet hope toward God, *be converted* turn to this Jesus, as the true Messiah laying aside your pride and prejudices, yield up your hearts to his guidance and government, and fly to the atoning blood of his cross, which was shed for this very purpose, *that your sins*, however great, numberless, and aggravated, *may be blotted out*, and your guilt cancelled, *when the times of refreshing shall come from the presence of the Lord*, those joyful seasons of consolation which now you will experience, when turning unto him you shall be filled with joy and peace in believing, and shall also find favour with him, and be acknowledged by him, when he shall come to be glorified in his saints, and to be admired of all that believe, in his presence then shall you possess bliss unutterable, and under his shadow enjoy an eternal rest from all the burdens of sin, sorrow, *and* temptation *For he shall send Jesus*, this *Jesus* whom he hath made both Lord and *Christ*, and appointed the Judge of quick and dead, even him *which before was preached unto you*, in all the sacred oracles, and by his own blessed ministry, *whom the heaven must receive*, whither we have seen him ascend, and where he now sits enthroned in glory, *until the times of restitution of all things*, when the mystery of godliness shall be finished, all his elect people be gathered in to him, and his kingdom shall finally come at the great day of his appearing to judge the world *Note*, (1) The great inducement to evangelical repentance, is the promise of pardon and forgiveness (2) They who truly turn to Jesus, shall find refreshing and rest to their souls, and reconciliation with a pardoning God (3) Though Christ be now exalted to his throne, we expect his coming a second time oh that we may be prepared to meet him! then shall it be a *time of refreshing*, when seeing him face to face, we shall be changed into the same image, be like and with him for ever

5 He supports what he had said by an appeal and reference to the scriptures, in which they believed For these were the things *which God hath spoken by the mouth of all his holy prophets since the world began*, concerning the kingdom of his Messiah For instance, *Moses*, that great law-giver, in whom you glory, he bore a noble testimony to Jesus, *and truly said unto the fathers* in the wilderness, *A prophet shall the Lord your God raise up unto you of your brethren*, sprung from the stock of Abraham, *like unto me*, who shall with far greater dignity be a mediator between God and you, shall deliver you from worse than Egyptian bondage, and from the most intimate knowledge of God, shall reveal to you his mind and will *him shall ye hear in all things whatsoever he shall say unto you*, embracing his doctrines, obedient to his precepts, and observant of his institutions with implicit faith, unbounded love, and unreserved submission, yielding up your souls to his guidance and government *And it shall come to pass, that every soul which will not hear that prophet*, and believe and obey him, *shall be destroyed from among the people*, cut off by some notorious stroke of divine vengeance *Yea, and all the prophets from Samuel*, in whom the spirit of prophecy revived, *and those that follow after*, in a long succession, *as many as have spoken, have likewise foretold of these days*, speaking of the Messiah, his sufferings, glory, and kingdom, from its beginning on earth, till its consummation in heaven

6 He draws a most encouraging motive from their relation to the prophets, to receive their word, and believe in the Messiah, of whom they testified *Ye are the children of the prophets*, their disciples and descendants from the patriarchs, *and heirs of the covenant which God made with our fathers, saying unto Abraham, In thy seed shall all the kindreds of the earth be blessed*, which seed was Christ, whose salvation shall extend to all nations, therefore, being the immediate offspring of the great father of the faithful, *Unto you first, God having raised up his Son Jesus*, sending him in the human nature, and raising him from the dead, hath *sent him to bless you*, by his own ministry and labours, and now by investing us with power and authority to preach his gospel, *in* which the most powerful motives are urged, in order to your conversion, and which his Spirit makes effectual to the *turning every one of you*, that believe in him, *from his iniquities*, and bringing you to pardon, salvation, and life eternal *Note*, (1) Jesus is come to be the blessing of the world Without him, the curse and wrath of God must have for ever abode upon us (2) Iniquity is the cause of all our misery, when Christ comes to the sinner, he not only pardons his guilt, but converts his soul, and thus effectually recovers him to the life of grace, in order to bring him to the life of glory

CHAP. IV

In this chapter the persecution against the apostles begins 1 *Peter and John are taken up upon a warrant from the priests, and committed to jail*, ver 1—4 2 *They are examined by a committee of the great Sanhedrim*, ver 5—7 3 *They bravely avow what they have done, and preach Christ to their persecutors*, ver 8—12 4 *Their persecutors, being unable to answer them, enjoin them silence, threaten them if they go on to preach the gospel, and so dismiss them*, ver 13—22 5 *They apply themselves to God by prayer, for the further operations of that grace which they had already experienced*, ver 23—30 6 *God owns them, both outwardly and inwardly, by manifest tokens of his presence with them*, ver 31—33 7 *The believers had their hearts knit together in holy love, and enlarged their charity to the poor, and the church flourished more than ever, to the glory of Christ*, ver 33, 34—37

1 AND as they spake unto the people, the priests
and the captain of the temple, and the Saddu-
cees a came upon them, 2 Being grieved that they b Chap v
taught the people, and b preached through Jesus the re- [illegible]
surrection from the dead 3 And they laid hands on [illegible]
them, and put them in hold unto the next day for it
was now eventide 4 Howbeit, many of them c which [illegible]
heard the word, believed, and the number of the men [illegible]
was about five thousand.

v. 1—4 The success of the gospel could not but provoke Satan's enmity, and the inveterate enemies of the name of Christ cannot be expected long to be at rest.

1. The apostles continued to teach the people, and, as their grand subject, *preached through Jesus the resurrection from the dead.* They both testified the certainty of his resurrection, and affirmed, that he was raised up for this purpose, to be the author of spiritual and eternal life to his people, who should be raised up by him at the last day to a glorious immortality.

2. Multitudes of their hearers believed; and, notwithstanding the enmity to which they saw their preachers exposed, five thousand converts more were added to the church; so mightily grew the word of God, and prevailed. *Note,* Where the gospel meets with the greatest opposition, it is usually attended with the most remarkable success.

3. The priests, the captain of the temple, who presided over the watches, and the Sadducees, grieved and vexed to the heart, that the doctrine of Jesus, which they had taken such pains to suppress, should now spread with greater rapidity than ever; and that he whom they had ignominiously crucified, should be exalted as the resurrection and life, as the author of all blessedness in time and eternity; rushed upon the apostles suddenly, seized them as criminals, and committed them to the custody for the night, it being eventide, that they might be brought before the sanhedrim the next day. *Note,* They who preach Christ, must prepare to suffer for him.

5 ¶ And it came to pass on the morrow, that their
rulers, and elders, and scribes, 6 And [d] Annas the high
priest, and Caiaphas, and John, and Alexander, and as
many as were of the kindred of the high priest, were gathered
together at Jerusalem. 7 And when they had
set them in the midst, they asked, [e] By what power, or
by what name have ye done this? 8 Then Peter [f] filled
with the Holy Ghost, said unto them, Ye rulers of the
people, and elders of Israel, 9 If we this day be examined
of [g] the good deed done to the impotent man,
by what means he is made whole; 10 Be it known
unto you all, and to all the people of Israel, that by the
name of Jesus Christ of Nazareth, whom ye crucified, [h]
whom God raised from the dead, even by him doth this
man stand here before you whole. 11 [i] This is the
stone which was set at nought of you builders, which
is become the head of the corner. 12 [k] Neither is there
salvation in any other: for there is none other name under
heaven given among men whereby we must be saved.
13 ¶ Now when they saw the boldness of Peter and
John, and perceived that they were unlearned and ignorant
men, [l] they marvelled; and they took knowledge
of them, that they had been with Jesus. 14 And beholding
the man which was healed standing with them,
[m] they could say nothing against it.

[d] Luke iii. 2. John xi. 49. [e] Exod. ii. 14. Matt. xxi. 23. Chap. vii. 27. [f] Luke xii. 11, 12. [g] Chap. iii. 6, 16. [h] Chap. ii. 24. [i] Psal. cxviii. 22. Isa. xxviii. 16. Matt. xxi. 42. [k] Matt. i. 21. 1 Tim. ii. 5, 6. [l] Chap. iii. 7. [m] Ver. 10.

v. 5—14 No sooner was the morning returned than we have,

1. The court assembled to try the innocent prisoners; but little justice can be expected, when their judges are known to be their avowed and inveterate enemies. The rulers, elders, and scribes, the high priest Annas, who now enjoyed that dignity, with Caiaphas, who had sat in the chair the year preceding, with John and Alexander, persons of distinguished note, and others of the high priest's kindred, were all leagued against two poor fishermen, to try if their power could not intimidate, or their learning confute, or their authority silence them.

2. The prisoners are arraigned. *They set them in the midst,* to answer before their judges the interrogatories which they chose to put to them, and haughtily demanded, *by what power,* human, divine, or diabolical, *or by what name,* by virtue of whose authority, or by the invocation of what name, *have ye done this?*

3. Peter, *filled with the Holy Ghost,* endued with singular boldness, and directed by his immediate influence, according to Christ's promise, (Mark xiii. 11.) *said unto them,* respectfully addressing them as magistrates and men of rank, *Ye rulers of the people, and elders of Israel, if we be examined as criminals this day, of the good deed done to the impotent man,* and you demand information, *by what means* such an act of mercy and power was performed, and *he is made whole,* we with pleasure appear to give you the fullest satisfaction. Therefore, *be it known unto you all, and to all the people of Israel,* whom it highly concerns, *that by the name,* the precious, powerful, all-prevailing name *of Jesus of Nazareth, whom ye* have treated with the highest contempt, and most ignominiously *crucified,* but *whom God raised from the dead,* in disappointment the impotent malice of his murderers, *even by him,* by this once despised, but now glorified Jesus, and by no power of our own, by no magic charms, but by faith in him alone, *doth this man stand here before you whole. This is the stone* [illegible] *which was set at nought of you,* who by station and office should be *builders* of

God's spiritual temple, but *which is now exalted of God, and become the head of the corner,* by which the church of God is supported, and firmly knit together. *Neither is there salvation in any other;* there is no spiritual or eternal salvation out of him, by the deeds of the law, or by any human power or righteousness whatsoever; *for there is none other name under heaven given among men, whereby we must be saved,* God having appointed him to be the only redeemer from sin, death, and hell; and all who believe not in him, must therefore perish everlastingly. *Note,* (1.) Salvation is every sinner's great concern. (2.) In and of ourselves we have nothing but misery, sin, and wrath, and have no power of ourselves to help ourselves. (3.) Christ alone can save a sinful soul by the merit of his blood and righteousness. (4.) God freely offers him in the gospel to the miserable, and invites all men to believe on him to the saving of their souls. (5.) They must inevitably and eternally perish, who neglect so great a salvation.

4. Such an answer quite confounded the court. *When they saw the boldness of Peter and John,* their undaunted courage, their readiness of speech, and powerful elocution; *and perceived that they were unlearned and ignorant men,* and been brought up at none of the public seminaries, at the feet of none of their rabbins, nor had ever the least advantages of education; *they marvelled* at the intrepidity, wisdom, and eloquence that appeared in them; *and they took knowledge of them that they had been with Jesus,* in whose company they recollected they had seen them formerly; *and beholding the man which was healed standing with them,* who probably came ready to bear testimony for them, and to do honour to his benefactors, to whatever danger it might expose him, *they could say nothing against it;* the miracle was too notorious to be contradicted. *Note,* (1.) In Christ's cause, even before the greatest, we may well boldly stand forth; he will bear us through. (2.) They who have been with Jesus, will carry the marks of it visibly about them, like Moses on the mount, their faces will shine, and their holy and heavenly conversations proclaim their Master's glory.

15 But when they had commanded them to go aside
out of the council, they conferred among themselves,
16 Saying, [n] What shall we do to these men? for that
indeed a notable miracle hath been done by them *is* manifest
to all them that dwell in Jerusalem; and [o] we cannot
deny *it.* 17 But that it spread no further among
the people, let us straitly threaten them, that they speak
henceforth to no man in this name. 18 And they
called them, and [p] commanded them not to speak at all,
nor teach in the name of Jesus. 19 But Peter and
John answered and said unto them, [q] Whether it be
right in the sight of God, to hearken unto you more
than unto God, judge ye. 20 For we cannot but
speak the things [r] which we have seen and heard. 21
So when they had further threatned them, they let them
go, finding nothing how they might punish them, [s] because
of the people: for all *men* glorified God for that
which was done. 22 For the man was above forty
years old, on whom this miracle of healing was shewed.

[n] John xi. 47. [o] Ver. 14. [p] Chap. v. 40. [q] Chap. v. 29. [r] Ibid. xxii. 15. 2 Pet. i. 16. 1 John i. 3. [s] Matt. xxi. 26. Luke xx. 6, 19. & xxii. 2. Chap. v. 26.

v. 15—22 How to punish those against whom they had no charge to lay they knew not, yet fain would they brand them, if possible, with some mark of infamy.

1. In order to consult upon the case the more freely, *they commanded* the apostles to be led out of the council-chamber, whilst *they conferred among themselves, saying, what shall we do to these men?* our difficulties are greater than ever, *for that indeed a notable miracle hath been done by them is manifest to all them that dwell in Jerusalem, and we cannot deny it,* so that to attempt it would but expose our own character: *but, that it spread no further among the people,* neither the fame of the miracle, nor the doctrine of Christ in confirmation of which it was wrought, *let us straitly threaten them,* on pain of our highest displeasure, and at the peril of suffering the punishment due to their contumacy, *that they speak henceforth to no man in this name.* Thus they hope, by their terrors, the ministers, to suppress the doctrine of the gospel. *And they called them, and commanded them not to speak at all, nor teach in the name of Jesus,* breathing forth their impotent malice. *Note,* (1.) The enemies of the gospel often join in close cabal how to suppress the growing progress of the truth; but he who sitteth on the heavens laughs them to scorn. (2.) Many a faithful minister of Jesus, for the truths which he hath maintained, hath met the frowns and threatenings of proud priests and prelates, who would fain intimidate and silence them, that they should speak no more in the name of Jesus; but they despise their menaces, they are prepared to suffer, but will not be silent.

2. The prisoners gave in their answer; they needed no premeditation to reply, and said unto them, *Whether it be right in the sight of God to hearken unto you more than unto God, judge ye.* Can it be possible we should be silent, when lying under his express injunctions, or how can we thus acquit ourselves to our con-

conſciences, or mankind, for whoſe ſake we preach this ſalvation of Jeſus? Your commands therefore being incompatible with the ſuperior obedience we owe to God, cannot poſſibly be obſerved, *for we cannot but ſpeak the things which we have ſeen and heard*, a neceſſity is laid upon us, and woe unto us if we preach not the goſpel *Note*, (1) Where the injunctions of men are contrary to the word of God, we muſt not heſitate a moment which we ſhall obey (2) They who have experimentally known the ſalvation which is in Jeſus, and taſted its ſweetneſs, cannot but delight to ſpread the ſavour of his name, and to make all men, as far as their influence reaches, know the grace which is in him

3 Unable to fix the leaſt accuſation againſt the apoſtles, they were compelled reluctantly to let them go, repeating their former threatnings, to try if that would intimidate them, and *finding nothing how they might puniſh them*, as they earneſtly wiſhed to do, *becauſe of the people*, who would have riſen up againſt them for ſuch a flagrant act of injuſtice, *for all men glorified God for that which was done*, the multitude in general were convinced that this was the finger of God, and could not but adore him, who had enabled theſe men to perform this act of power and mercy, *for the man was above forty years of age, on whom this miracle of healing was ſhewed*, and had been ſo long known by the people, that the cure was rendered thereby the more ſingular and aſtoniſhing *Note*, (1) God can put his reſtraints upon perſecutors, and prevent them, by various conſiderations, from doing all the miſchief to which they are inclined (2) They who in old age are cured by the goſpel word, are more eminent monuments of divine mercy

[f Chap. x. 2] 23 ¶ And being let go, [f] they went to their own company, and reported all that the chief prieſts and elders had ſaid unto them 24 And when they heard that, they lift up their voice to God with one accord, and ſaid, Lord, thou *art* God which haſt made heaven and earth, and the ſea, and all that in them is 25 Who by the mouth of thy ſervant David haſt ſaid, [u Pſal. ii. 1] [u] Why did the heathen rage, and the people imagine vain things? 26 The kings of the earth ſtood up, and the rulers were gathered together againſt the Lord, and againſt his Chriſt 27 For of a truth againſt thy holy child Jeſus, [x] whom thou haſt anointed, [y] both Herod and Pontius Pilate, with the Gentiles and the people of Iſrael, were gathered together, 28 For [z] to do whatſoever thy hand and thy counſel determined before to be done 29 And now, Lord, behold their threatnings and grant unto thy ſervants, [a] that with all boldneſs they may ſpeak thy word, 30 By ſtretching forth thine hand to heal and [b] that ſigns and wonders may be done by the name of thy holy child Jeſus 31 ¶ And when they had prayed, [c] the place was ſhaken where they were aſſembled together, and they were all filled with the holy Ghoſt, and they ſpake the word of God with boldneſs

[x Iſa. lxi. 1. Luke iv. 18. y Matt. xxvi. 3. Luke xxiii. 1. 8. z Matt. xxvi. 24. Chap. ii. 23. a Eph. vi. 19. b Chap. iii. 6. 16. Ver. 10. c Chap. ii. 2. 4. & xvi. 26.]

v 23—31 No ſooner were the two apoſtles diſmiſſed than,

1 They returned *to their own company*, not aſhamed or afraid to join them, notwithſtanding all the threatnings of the prieſts, *and reported all that the chief prieſts and elders had ſaid unto them*, and moſt probably their reply *Note*, We muſt never deſert the ſociety of our brethren The world hath its end, if it can confine our religion to our cloſets, and prevent our open profeſſion of it, by joining thoſe who appear on the Lord's ſide

2 *When they heard that, they lift up their voice to God*, in prayer and praiſe, *with one accord*, under the influence of the Holy Ghoſt, ſpeaking as if animated by one ſoul, *and ſaid, Lord, thou art God*, infinite in power, *which haſt made heaven and earth, and the ſea, and all that in them is*, the great Creator and Governor, in whoſe hand are the hearts of all men, and all events directed by thy providence are under thy controul, *who by the mouth of thy ſervant David haſt ſaid, Why did the heathen rage, and the people imagine vain things?* endeavouring to ſuppreſs the glorious goſpel of Jeſus *The kings of the earth ſtood up, and the rulers were gathered together againſt the Lord, and againſt his Chriſt* And now this prophecy is eminently fulfilled, *for of a truth againſt thy holy child Jeſus, whom thou haſt anointed* as the true Meſſiah promiſed ſo long before, *both Herod and Pontius Pilate, with the Gentiles, and the people of Iſrael, were gathered together*, conſpiring to deſtroy the adorable Redeemer, but, in the execution of their barbarous and malicious deſigns, thou didſt over-rule their wickedneſs *for to do whatſoever thy hand and thy counſel determined before to be done*, executing thy eternal decrees, and bringing to thyſelf the greateſt glory, to the Redeemer the greateſt honour, and to loſt ſouls a free and full ſalvation *And now, Lord, behold their threatnings*, reſtrain and diſappoint their rage and malice, *and grant unto thy ſervants, that with all boldneſs they may ſpeak thy word*, openly and zealouſly preaching thy goſpel, in nothing diſmayed by their adverſaries, and own them in their teſtimony, *by ſtretching forth thine hand to heal and that ſigns and wonders may be done by the name of thy holy child Jeſus*, by the authority derived from this thy incarnate Son, and to the glory of his great name *Note*, (1) In all our dangers we ſhould make application to him who is able to help us (2) All the wickedneſs and wrath of man ſhall turn to God's praiſe, and the remainder of that wrath he will reſtrain (3) The ſin of perſecutors is not the leſs malignant, becauſe God over-rules it to ſubſerve purpoſes of his own glory (4) God takes cogniſance of all the malice of his people's foes, and hears their threatnings, therefore we need not fear them (5) They who are to preach the goſpel to a gainſaying world need to be often ſecretly looking up to God for boldneſs, that, through fear or ſhame, they may not be unfaithful to men's ſouls (6) Tokens of God's preſence and bleſſing with us, are the comfortable encouragement to us to perſevere even through much tribulation

3 Their prayer receives an immediate anſwer from God *When they had prayed, the place was ſhaken where they were aſſembled together*, as a ſenſible token of the divine preſence in the midſt of them, *and they were all filled with the Holy Ghoſt*, feeling a growing ardor in their ſouls, experiencing freſh meaſures of ſtrength, courage, and conſolation communicated to them, *and they ſpake the word of God with boldneſs* *Note*, When God is for us, we need neither fear nor care who are againſt us

[d 1 Pet. iii. 8. e Chap. ii. 44. f Chap. i. 8. 22. g Chap. ii. 47. h Ver. 37. Chap. v. 2. i Ver. 35.]

32 And the multitude of them that believed, [d] were of one heart, and of one ſoul [e] neither ſaid any *of them*, that ought of the things which he poſſeſſed was his own, but they had all things common 33 And with great power [f] gave the apoſtles witneſs of the reſurrection of the Lord Jeſus and [g] great grace was upon them all 34 Neither was there any among them that lacked, for as many as were poſſeſſors of lands or houſes, ſold them, and brought the prices of the things that were ſold, 35 And [h] laid *them* down at the apoſtles feet and diſtribution was made unto every man according as he had need 36 And Joſes, who by the apoſtles was ſurnamed Barnabas (which is, being interpreted, The ſon of conſolation) a Levite, *and* of the country of Cyprus, 37 Having land, ſold *it*, and brought the money, and [i] laid *it* at the apoſtles feet

v 32—37 How beautiful is the ſcene here preſented to us! how unlike the ſchiſms and diviſions which have ſince unhappily rent the church of Chriſt

1 *The multitude of them that believed*, vaſt as the acceſſions lately made had been, *were of one heart*, knit together in love, united in ſentiment, *and* ſeemed as it were actuated by *one ſoul*

2 *With great power gave the apoſtles witneſs of the reſurrection of the Lord Jeſus*, proving the fact by inconteſtible evidence, and enforcing the truths connected therewith, confirming their teſtimony with ſigns and wonders, and preaching, with the moſt intrepid boldneſs and zeal, the glorious goſpel committed to them, *and great grace was upon them all*, the moſt evident tokens of the divine favour reſted upon them, and the effects of it were an entire contempt of the world, and moſt fervent charity towards all men

3 *They had all things common*, and none ſaid *that ought of the things which he poſſeſſed was his own*, but freely gave up all for the general ſervice, hence there was not *any among them that lacked*, the pooreſt being equally ſupported out of the common ſtock, whilſt the richer members of the church, *as many as were poſſeſſors of lands or houſes ſold them, and*, of their own accord, freely *brought the prices of the things that were ſold, and laid them down at the apoſtles feet*, as truſtees for the good of the community, *and diſtribution was made unto every man*, by theſe faithful ſtewards, *according as he had need* *And Joſes, who was by the apoſtles ſurnamed Barnabas (which is, being interpreted, a ſon of conſolation)* probably from the admirable faculty he poſſeſſed of ſpeaking peace to wounded conſciences, *a Levite, and of the country of Cyprus, having land*, either in Judea or in his own country, *ſold it, and brought the* purchaſe *money*, which ſeems to have been very conſiderable, *and laid it at the apoſtles feet* a noble inſtance of enlarged and diſintereſted charity, deſerving a particular memorial *Note*, (1) What we have in the world is not *our own*, but God's, and, whenever he is pleaſed to call for it, ſhould be employed in his ſervice (2) If we are not called now to the ſame exerciſe of charity as in theſe days of the church's infancy, yet the rich muſt remember they are ſtill but God's almoners, and ſhould approve themſelves faithful ſtewards of the gifts entruſted to them (3) Objects of real *need* have a title to our relief according to our ability, eſpecially thoſe that are of the houſehold of faith (4) Our bright example provokes the zeal of others, and none that ſhew themſelves faithful to Jeſus and his cauſe ſhall be forgotten by him

CHAP

CHAP. V.

In this chapter we have, 1 *The sin and punishment of Ananias and Sapphira,* ver 1—11 2 *The flourishing state of the church, in the power that went along with the preaching of the gospel,* ver 12—16 3 *The imprisonment of the apostles, and their miraculous discharge out of prison, with fresh orders to go on to preach the gospel, which they did, to the great vexation of their persecutors,* ver 17—26 4 *Their arraignment before the great Sanhedrim, and their justification of themselves in what they did,* ver 27—33 5 *Gamaliel's counsel concerning them, that they should not persecute them, but let them alone, and see what would come of it, and their concurrence for the present with this advice, in the dismission of the apostles with no more but a scourging,* ver 34—40 6 *The apostles chearful progress in their work, notwithstanding the prohibition laid upon them, and the indignity done them,* ver 41, 42

1 BUT a certain man named Ananias, with Sap-
phira his wife, sold a possession, 2 And kept
back *part* of the price, his wife also being privy *to it*,
[a Chap iv 37] and brought a certain part, and [a] laid *it* at the apostles
feet 3 But Peter said, Ananias, why hath Satan filled
thine heart to lie to the holy Ghost, and to keep back
part of the price of the land? 4 Whilst it remained,
was it not thine own? and after it was sold, was it not
in thine own power? why hast thou conceived this thing
in thine heart? thou hast not lied unto men, but unto
God 5 And Ananias hearing these words, fell down
and gave up the ghost and [b] great fear came on all them
[b Chap. ii 43 Ver 11] that heard these things 6 And the young men arose,
[c] wound him up, and carried *him* out, and buried *him*
[c John xix 40] 7 And it was about the space of three hours after, when
his wife, not knowing what was done, came in 8 And
Peter answered unto her, Tell me whether ye sold the
land for so much And she said, Yea, for so much.
9 Then Peter said unto her, How is it that ye have
agreed together, [d] to tempt the Spirit of the Lord?
[d Ver 3] behold, the feet of them which have buried thy husband
are at the door, and shall carry thee out 10 Then fell
she down straightway at his feet, and yielded up the
ghost and the young men came in and found her dead,
and carrying *her* forth, buried *her* by her husband 11
[e Ver 5] And [e] great fear came upon all the church, and upon as
many as heard these things

v 1—11 The purest societies on this side heaven have some hypocrites, as we see here

1 Ananias, with Sapphira his wife, willing to appear among the foremost of the distinguished disciples of Jesus, sold a possession, and publickly brought a part of the money, which they would insinuate was the whole, and laid it at the apostles feet, whilst their covetous heart secretly reserved a part, and still halted between God and Mammon, though they desired to make a fair shew in the flesh, and thought to impose upon the apostles *Note*, Hypocrites may go far in appearance, and even, through a sping of zeal, forgo for a while some temporal advantage, or endure loss, but their heart is not right with God, and therefore there is still a reserve made, which serves to make them more eminently miserable, parting with many of the comforts of this world, and yet having no sure portion in a better

2 *Peter*, who knew by divine revelation the falsehood of the pretended disciple, said unto him, *Why hath Satan filled thy heart* with such covetousness and falsehood, *to lie to the Holy Ghost*, either to think thus to impose upon the apostles, who were endued with the discernment of spirits by the Holy Ghost, or by pretending to act under his impulse and influence, when in fact he was under the spirit of the devil, *and to keep back part of the price*, though intimating that the land was parted with for pious purposes, and devoted to the service of the church *While it remained, was it not thine own? and after it was sold, was it not thine own?* both the sale and surrender of the price being a voluntary act, and none were compelled to do either, but were left to their own pious zeal *Why hast thou conceived this thing in thine heart?* and harboured the suggestion of Satan to contrive so base a deed, *thou hast not lied unto men, but unto God*, to that eternal Spirit which resided in the apostles, who searcheth the hearts of all men, and from whom nothing is hid, nothing is secret *Note*, (1) Nothing betrays persons more frequently into the sin of lying than the affectation of appearing high in other esteem (2) They who conceive *falsehood in their hearts* are filled with Satan, a lying spirit in his strongest resemblance (3) The Holy Ghost is God omniscient Let those whom pride, worldly-mindedness, or any mean motive, drives into the ministry, take heed how they presume to declare they are inward is moved by him, lest, like Ananias and Sapphira, they be detected, if not here, yet hereafter to their everlasting confusion

3 Behold a fearful example of divine vengeance! No sooner had Peter spoken than Ananias *fell down and gave up the ghost*, struck by an invisible hand, as the just punishment of his wickedness, and to make one example to deter others from such impious hypocrisy *And great fear came on all them that heard these things* it impressed an awe upon the minds of those who had joined themselves to the church, and served to keep off from the society of the apostles those who would have been spots in their assembly

4 The young men present removed the corpse, wrapped it in grave-clothes, and buried it

5 Sapphira, the wife of Ananias, who was privy to his falsehood, ignorant of what had passed, about three hours after joined the assembly, and, being required of Peter to answer if they had sold the land for so much, without hesitation she affirmed the lie, foolishly presuming none could disprove it Her doom therefore is pronounced, being the partner of her husband's sin, she shares his punishment *Peter said unto her, How is it that ye have agreed to tempt the Spirit of the Lord?* how astonishing is your stupidity, as well as monstrous your wickedness, to attempt imposing upon the omniscient God? *behold the feet of them which have buried thy husband are at the door, and shall carry thee out* Instantly, death-struck, she fell at his feet, and they carried her out and buried her with her husband, whilst all the church were filled with reverence and godly fear at that jealous God, who thus appeared the avenger of falsehood and hypocrisy, and all others, that heard these judgments, were afraid of provoking or tempting the apostles, whose very word seemed cloathed with death *Note*, (1) It is truly grievous when near relations serve to encourage each other in iniquity (2) God, though patient under numberless provocations, is pleased to make some sinners monuments of his vengeance, that men may hear and fear, and do no more wickedly

12 ¶ And [f] by the hands of the apostles were many [f Chap ii 43 Rom xv 19 Heb ii 4]
signs and wonders wrought among the people, (and they
were all with one accord [g] in Solomon's porch 13 And [g Chap iii 11]
[h] of the rest durst no man join himself to them but [i] the [h John ix 22 & xii 42 & xix 38]
people magnified them 14 And [k] believers were the
more added to the Lord, multitudes both of men and
women) 15 Insomuch that they brought forth the sick [i Chap iv. 21]
into the streets, and laid *them* on beds and couches, [l] that
at the least the shadow of Peter passing by, might over- [k Chap. ii 41 47]
shadow some of them 16 There came also a multi- [l Mat ix 21 & xiv 36 Chap xix 12]
tude *out* of the cities round about unto Jerusalem, bring-
ing [m] sick folks, and them which were vexed with un-
clean spirits and they were healed every one [m Mark xvi 17, 18]

v 12—16 We are here told,

1 Of the many and great miracles performed by the apostles, in proof of their divine mission, and so much were the people in general convinced of the mighty powers they possessed, that they brought forth the sick in beds and couches and laid them in the streets, *that at least the shadow of Peter passing by might overshadow some of them*, persuaded that this would be effectual to work a cure and from the country vast multitudes of patients, sick and vexed with unclean spirits, were brought to them, *and they were healed every one* none being rejected who made application to them

2 Of the vast veneration in which the apostles were held *They were all with one accord in Solomon's porch*, appearing and teaching publickly in the temple with the greatest unanimity among themselves *and of the rest durst no man join himself unto them*, either none of the disciples presumed to set themselves on a level with the apostles, or rather none durst make a hypocritical profession of Christianity, who were not conscious of the simplicity of their heart, being terrified with the doom of Ananias and Sapphira *but the people magnified them*, held them in the highest veneration, and spoke of them with the highest esteem, beholding the wonders which they wrought, and the presence and power of God evident in the midst of them

3 Of the vast accession of converts made to the church *Believers were the more added to the Lord*, and made open profession of their faith in Christ, *multitudes both of men and women*, so mightily grew the word of God and increased

17 ¶ Then the high priest rose up, and all they that
were with him, (which is the sect of the Sadducees) and
were filled with [n] indignation, 18 And laid their hands [n Or envy]
on the apostles, and put them in the common prison
19 But [o] the angel of the Lord by night opened the [o Chap. xii 7 & xvi 26]
prison doors, and brought them forth, and said, 20
Go, stand and speak in the temple to the people, all [p John vi 68]
the words of this life 21 And when they heard *that*
they entered into the temple early in the morning, and
taught. But [q] the high priest came, and they that were [q Chap iv 6]
with

with him, and called the council together, and all the senate of the children of Israel, and sent to the prison to have them brought 22 But when the officers came, and found them not in the prison, they returned, and told, 23 Saying, The prison truly found we shut with all safety, and the keepers standing without before the doors but when we had opened, we found no man within 24 Now when the high priest, and [q] the captain of the temple, and the chief priests heard these things, they doubted of them whereunto this would grow 25 Then came one and told them, saying, Behold, the men whom ye put in prison, [r] are standing in the temple, and teaching the people

[q] Luke xxii 4 Chap iv 1 [r] Ver. 20, 21

v. 17—25 It cannot be supposed that the inveterate enemies of the gospel would long be quiet, or Satan rest when his kingdom was falling to ruins before the gospel word

1 The apostles are seized and imprisoned The hand of the high-priest was first in this transgression, supported by the Sadducean sect, who could not endure the testimony born to the resurrection of Jesus, which radically struck at all their tenets exasperated to fury, they could contain no longer, and with lawless violence laid hands on them, and, to put the greater disgrace upon them, dragged them to the common prison among the vilest malefactors *Note,* (1) The success of the gospel is a vexation to wicked men, and, when they have power in their hands, the disciples of Jesus shall feel their oppression (2) It is Satan's artifice, by endeavouring to make the ministers of Christ despicable, to prejudice the people against them

2 The Lord miraculously delivers his servants, by the hand of an angel, from their confinement The commitment was illegal, therefore the great Judge of all sends his messenger to discharge them honourably and, by his power opening the prison doors, he *said, Go, stand and speak in the temple, to the people, all the words of this life*, not the least intimidated by all the malice of their inveterate foes, but in their very ears, in the temple, the most publick place, must they declare the life-giving truths of the gospel word, and the offensive doctrines of a risen Redeemer *Note,* (1) God can make the most lonesome prison a paradise of delights, when he manifests his presence there (2) They who are put in trust with the gospel must not, in the most publick manner, shun to declare the whole counsel of God, however offensive it may prove, and whatever may be the consequence to themselves

3 Without delay they obey the heavenly command, and early, as soon as the temple doors were open, they went thither, and boldly taught as before, fearless of any consequences *Note,* When duty calls, no danger must deter us

4 An extraordinary council was assembled by the high-priest and his abettors, consisting not only of the sanhedrim, *but of all the senate of the children of Israel* And now, ready to proceed to trial, the prisoners are commanded to be brought forth, when, big with expectations of their appearing in chains before them, they are astonished with the report of their officers, that the prison was safe as they left it, and the guards upon duty, but none of the prisoners, whom they had committed thither, were to be found Such an account threw them into the greatest perplexity, they knew not what course to take, and began to be under terrible apprehensions *whereunto this would grow* when, to their greater confusion, tidings are brought them, that the men whom they sought, and had the evening before committed to prison, were preaching openly in the temple, in defiance of all their menaces *Note,* (1) They who fight against God must needs involve themselves in many troubles (2) The Lord can deliver his people out of all their trials, in spite of the malice of their most invenomed persecutors

26 Then went the captain with the officers, and brought them without violence (for [s] they feared the people, lest they should have been stoned) 27 And when they had brought them, they set *them* before the council and the high-priest asked them, 28 Saying, [t] Did not we straitly command you, that you should not teach in this name? and behold ye have filled Jerusalem with your doctrine, and intend to bring [u] this man's blood upon us 29 ¶ Then Peter and the *other* apostles answered and said, [x] We ought to obey God rather than man 30 [y] The God of our fathers raised up Jesus, whom ye slew and [z] hanged on a tree 31 [a] Him hath God exalted with his right hand *to be* [b] a Prince and a Saviour, [c] for to give repentance to Israel, and [d] forgiveness of sins 32 And [e] we are his witnesses of these things, and [f] *so is* also the holy Ghost, [g] whom God hath given to them that obey him. 33 ¶ [h] When they heard *that*, they were cut *to the heart*, and took counsel to slay them 34 Then stood there up one in the council, a Pharisee, named [i] Gamaliel, a doctor of law, had in reputation among all the people, and commanded to put the apostles forth a little space, 35 And said unto them, Ye men of Israel, take heed to yourselves, what ye intend to do as touching these men 36 For before these days rose up Theudas boasting himself to be somebody, to whom a number of men, about four hundred, joined themselves who was slain, and all, as many as obeyed him, were scattered and brought to nought 37 After this man rose up Judas of Galilee, in the days of the taxing, and drew away much people after him he also perished, and all, even as many as obeyed him, were dispersed 38 And now I say unto you, Refrain from these men, and let them alone for [k] if this counsel, or this work be of men, it will come to nought 39 But [l] if it be of God, ye cannot overthrow it, lest haply ye be found even [m] to fight against God 40 And to him they agreed and when they had called the apostles and [n] beaten *them*, [o] they commanded that they should not speak in the name of Jesus, and let them go 41 ¶ And they departed from the presence of the council, [p] rejoicing that they were counted worthy to suffer shame for his name 42 And daily [q] in the temple, and in every house, they ceased not to teach and preach Jesus Christ

[s] Matt xxi 26 Chap iv 21 [t] Chap iv 18 [u] Chap ii 23, 36 [x] Chap iv 19 [y] Chap iii 13 [z] Chap x 39 1 Pet ii 24 [a] Chap ii 33 Heb ii 10 [b] Luke xxiv 47 [c] Chap iii 15 [d] Chap iii 26 [e] Chap xiii 38 [f] John xv 26 [g] Chap ii 4 [h] Chap ii 37 [i] Chap xxii 3 [k] Matt xv 13 [l] 1 Cor i 25 [m] Chap ix 5 [n] Matt x 17 [o] Chap iv 18 [p] Matt v 12 1 Pet iv 13 [q] Chap ii 46

v. 26—42 We have here,

1 The peaceable submission of the apostles to the officers, who came to seize them a second time in the temple They dared not use violence, for fear lest the people should have rose upon them, who held in just veneration the character of the apostles The captain therefore, with his attendants, spoke them fair, and they, not unwilling nor afraid to appear before the council, consented to go with them

2 The insolent reprimand given them by the high-priest, for daring to disobey the charge given them *Did not we straitly command you, that you should not teach in this name?* and ye have treated our orders with contempt, *and behold, ye have filled Jerusalem with your doctrine*, most detestable and pernicious as it is, *and intend to bring this man's blood upon us*, both to expose us to the people, and lay the guilt of it at our doors, as if we had murdered an innocent man, and one whom you cry up so highly But had not the apostles told them before, they must obey God rather than man? and had they not themselves invoked the blood of Jesus upon them, when Pilate would have let him go? Why then should they be angry?

3 The apostles boldly replied, *We ought to obey God rather than man*, and, far from softening any of the truths they declared, or the accusations they brought against them as the murderers of the Son of God, to their faces they dare declare it, and charge this atrocious deed on their consciences *The God of our fathers raised up Jesus*, testifying his highest approbation of him, *whom ye slew and hanged on a tree*, with the most impious cruelty and injustice, *him hath God exalted with his right hand* to a throne of glory in the heavens, *to be a Prince and a Saviour* to his redeemed people, *to give repentance to his Israel, and remission of sins*, freely and fully pardoning the transgressions of all who by true faith turn unto him, and working that conversion and faith in their hearts by the power of his grace *And we are his witnesses of these things*, appointed by him, and speaking with the greatest assurance the truths we most certainly know, *and so is the Holy Ghost, whom God hath given to those that obey him*, who in all his miraculous gifts, as well as by the mighty energy of his gospel on our own hearts and the hearts of others, attests the truths which we declare *Note,* (1) Christ, as a Saviour, offers the free and full remission of their sins, be they never so many, great, or aggravated, to those who fly to him as their refuge (2) The promises of pardon are the great motives and causes of evangelical repentance (3) All who embrace Jesus as their Saviour, submit to him as their Prince, they who would reign *with* him, must be ruled *by* him (4) Beside all the great and glorious external evidences of Christianity, every obedient believer hath the internal witness of the Spirit in his heart, which is to him instead of a thousand arguments, and, without this divine conviction of the truth, though we may silence and confound gainsayers, we never can convert them

4 *When they heard this*, far from submitting to the Saviour, and seeking the remission of sin which he is exalted to give, *they were cut to the heart*, malice, indignation, and rage, burned in their bosom, *and* instantly they *took counsel to slay them*, resolving to rid themselves at once of their troublers, and murder them together *Note,* The bosom of the wicked, when triumphant in iniquity, is a present hell, whilst, even in their sufferings for righteousness sake, the faithful feel their heaven begun

5 To check the fury of these zealots, Gamaliel, a man of more moderate counsels, arose He was *a Pharisee, a doctor of the law* by profession, and his high reputation among the people

gave him weight and influence in the aſſembly and he is ſaid to have been now the preſident of the ſanhedrim *He commanded to put the apoſtles forth a little ſpace*, that he might ſpeak more freely Whereupon, addreſſing his brethren, (1) He adviſes them not to act too raſhly *Ye men of Iſrael, take heed to yourſelves what ye intend to do as touching theſe men*, leſt by ſome haſty reſolution ye bring guilt upon your ſouls, and provoke God's diſpleaſure (2) He inſtances the ruin of ſome late impoſtors, who ſoon came to nothing, which would now be the caſe with theſe men, if the matter was a mere human contrivance Theudas and Judas, two late pretenders, had ariſen and collected a number of followers, but both were quickly deſtroyed, their followers diſperſed, and their attempts abortive and they might reaſonably expect the ſame would be the iſſue of the preſent diſturbance, if the thing was a mere artifice of deceivers, without embroiling themſelves, and taking the matter out of God's hand *Therefore*, (3) His advice is for the preſent to *refrain from theſe men, and let them alone*, and wait a while to ſee what courſe matters will take, *for if this counſel or this work be of men*, a mere invention of the crafty, or the folly of deluded enthuſiaſts, *it will come to nought*, the deceit will be ſoon detected, and their attempts end in their own confuſion, without our interfering, *but if it be of God*, though you oppoſe it with never ſo much violence, *ye cannot overthrow it*, and reſiſtance would be as vain as impious Therefore wait quietly the event, *leſt haply ye be found even to fight againſt God*, the madneſs of which is evident, and the conſequence cannot but be your own confuſion and ruin *Note*, (1) Perſecution for conſcience ſake is as abſurd as it is wicked (2) They who oppoſe Chriſt's miniſters and goſpel fight againſt God, and the iſſue of that conflict muſt needs be fatal to his enemies

6 Gamaliel's counſel ſo far prevailed as to reſcue the apoſtles from immediate death, but their enemies could not ſo entirely abſtain from them as to diſcharge them unhurt, their rage muſt be vented on their backs, though reſtrained from their blood they *called in the apoſtles*, and, having ignominiouſly and ſeverely ſcourged them as malefactors, diſmiſſed them, with the moſt expreſs injunctions of never more ſpeaking in the name of Jeſus, at the peril of all the pains and penalties which would attend their diſobedience

7 With admirable conſtancy the apoſtles bore their ſufferings, and boldly perſiſted in their glorious work *They departed from the preſence of the council*, without a word of reproach or reviling, patiently ſubmitting to theſe indignities, and, ſo far from being aſhamed or intimidated, *rejoicing that they were counted worthy to ſuffer ſhame for his name* This reproach was their higheſt honour, theſe ſtripes their glory, *and*, ſo far from deſiſting and being ſilent, as they were commanded, *daily in the temple*, in defiance of their perſecutors, *and in every houſe*, where they reſorted, *they ceaſed not to teach and preach Jeſus Chriſt* He was the great theme of all their diſcourſe, and the complete redemption which was in him they explained and enforced, inviting all to come and ſhare their mercy, and believe to the ſaving of their ſouls *Note*, (1) When for the ſake of Jeſus and his truth we are called to ſuffer, we ſhould take pleaſure in reproaches, and rejoice at the inſults we meet with they ſhall iſſue to our more abundant glory (2) A crucified Jeſus muſt be the conſtant ſubject of our miniſtrations, and publickly when called into the pulpit, and privately, when viſiting from houſe to houſe, *him* ſhould we ceaſeleſs teach and preach

CHAP VI

In this chapter we have, 1 *The diſcontent about the diſtribution of the public charity*, ver 1 2 *The ordination of ſeven deacons to eaſe the apoſtles of the burden*, ver 2—6 3 *The increaſe of the church*, ver 7 4 *A particular account of Stephen, one of the ſeven* (1) *His great activity for Chriſt*, ver 8 (2) *The oppoſition he met with*, ver 9, 10 (3) *The convening of him before the great ſanhedrim, and the crimes laid to his charge*, ver 11—14 (4) *God's owning him upon his trial*, ver 15

a Chap ii. 41, 47 & v 14
b Chap ix 29 & xi 20.
c Chap iv 35
d Ex xviii 17
e Deut i 13 Chap i 21 & xvi 2 1 Tim iii 7
f Chap ii 42
g Chap. xi 24
h Chap viii 5 26 & xxi 8
i Rev. ii 6, 15

1 AND in thoſe days, when [a] the number of the
diſciples was multiplied, there aroſe a murmur
ing of [b] the Grecians againſt the Hebrews, becauſe their
widows were neglected in [c] the daily miniſtration 2
Then the twelve called the multitude of the diſciples un
to them, and ſaid, [d] It is not reaſon that we ſhould leave
the word of God, and ſerve tables 3 Wherefore, bre-
thren, [e] look ye out among you ſeven men of honeſt
report, full of the holy Ghoſt and wiſdom, whom we
may appoint over this buſineſs 4 But [f] we will give
ourſelves continually to prayer, and to the miniſtry of the
word. 5 ¶ And the ſaying pleaſed the whole multi
tude and they choſe Stephen, [g] a man full of faith and
of the holy Ghoſt, and [h] Philip, and Prochorus, and
Nicanor, and Timon, and Parmenas, and [i] Nicolas a
proſelyte of Antioch. 6 Whom they ſet before the apo
ſtles and when [k] they had prayed, [l] they laid *their* hands
on them 7 And [m] the word of God increaſed, and
[n] the number of the diſciples multiplied in Jeruſalem
greatly, and a great company of [o] the prieſts were obe-
dient to the faith

k Chap i 24
l Chap viii 17 & xiii 3 1 Tim iv 14 & v 22 2 Tim i 6
m Chap xii 24 & xix 20 Col i 6
n Ver 1
o John xii 42

v 1—7 The admirable peace and harmony of the church here ſuffers ſome ſlight interruption, and yet good ariſes out of the evil We have,

1 The cauſe, whether real or imaginary, of the diſcontent which appeared among ſome of the members of the church *In thoſe days, when the number of diſciples was multiplied*, for the ſufferings of the apoſtles, ſo far from checking the progreſs of the goſpel, proved its furtherance, *there aroſe a murmuring of the Grecians*, or Helleniſt Jews, who were chiefly foreigners, and were ſo called from the Greek language, which they ſpoke, and uſed in their ſynagogues, *againſt the Hebrews*, who were inhabitants of Judea, and made uſe of the Hebrew language in reading the Old Teſtament, and they complained, *becauſe their widows were neglected in the daily miniſtration*, as if there was a partiality ſhewn to the poor, who were Hebrews, and *theirs* either paſſed over, or ſcantily ſupplied The complaint might poſſibly be real, in the multiplicity of affairs which lay on the apoſtles hands, they might be unable to look minutely into the wants of the ſeveral widows, or other poor, who had made application to them for relief, or perhaps, as the public ſtock was chiefly raiſed by the Hebrews, they might count that the widows and other poor of that denomination were entitled to the preference, but probably mere ſuſpicion dictated the complaint, and, as they lay under ſome kind of diſadvantages as foreigners, they were jealous, leſt they ſhould be ſlighted, for thoſe who are poor are too apt to be querulous, to eye with jealouſy what is beſtowed on others, and to clamour, as if any kindneſs done to them was an injuſtice to themſelves *Note*, (1) Money matters are too often the cauſes of much diſſatisfaction even among thoſe who profeſs to be dead to the world (2) In the beſt ordered church ſome imperfections will be found, and the moſt careful paſtors may hear of ſome real or pretended cauſe of complaint

2 The apoſtles propoſe an excellent expedient to remove all cauſe of murmuring, and this not only for the ſatisfaction of others, but for their own relief, their neceſſary employment, in preaching the word of God, being too much interrupted by minding theſe ſecular concerns They aſſembled *the multitude of the diſciples*, it being a matter of common concern, *and ſaid, It is not reaſon that we ſhould leave the word of God, and ſerve tables*, theſe avocations of providing for the poor diverting them too much from the great buſineſs of preaching the goſpel *Wherefore, brethren, look ye out among you men of honeſt report, full of the Holy Ghoſt and wiſdom, whom we may appoint over this buſineſs*, men of eſtabliſhed reputation and integrity, endued with a diſtinguiſhed meaſure of the gifts and graces of the Spirit, to enable them for the faithful diſcharge of their office, and whoſe wiſdom and prudence are eminent, that they may manage the church's ſtock to greateſt advantage Theſe were to be choſen by the people themſelves, who could not afterwards reaſonably find fault with the perſons of their own appointment, and the apoſtles would *ordain them* to their office, that they might be inveſted with due authority, and that thoſe who were concerned might know to whom they muſt apply in theſe matters *but we will give ourſelves continually to prayer, and to the miniſtry of the word*, as our more immediate and proper employment *Note*, (1) They who are appointed to any holy office, even the loweſt in the church, may here behold the requiſites thereto They muſt be perſons of *blameleſs character*, *men of parts and abilities* for the diſcharge of their truſt *with wiſdom*, and above all experimentally *acquainted with the grace of God* in their ſouls, and partakers of the Holy Ghoſt To ordain perſons immoral, ignorant, deſtitute of experimental religion, and to count them fit for the miniſtry who are fit for nothing elſe, how ſhocking! how contrary to the apoſtolic practice! and what a ſcandal muſt ſuch be to the office they bear! (2) Diveſted as much as poſſible of worldly cares, Chriſt's ambaſſadors ſhould be occupied wholly in his work and the ſervice of immortal ſouls, preaching his goſpel in ſeaſon and out of ſeaſon, and watering with their prayers the labours of the pulpit, that God may give the increaſe

3 The propoſal met with general approbation, and, after ſerious deliberation, they, with joint concurrence and perfect unanimity, made choice of ſeven perſons, whoſe names are recorded, and ſeem to be of the Helleniſt Jews, which would moſt effectually ſerve to ſilence all future murmurings among them Stephen ſtands firſt in the catalogue, with a moſt honourable teſtimony borne to him, he was *full of faith and of the Holy Ghoſt*, a man eminent for parts and grace Philip, who follows him, we find afterwards ſucceſsfully employed in preaching the goſpel, *chap* viii Of the reſt we have no particular account, unleſs Nicolas, as ſome have ſuggeſted, was the founder of that ſect which St John mentions with abhorrence, *Rev* ii 6—15 Theſe ſeven being preſented to the apoſtles, *they prayed* with them and for them, that they might be qualified for their work,

and approve themselves faithful, and then, by the imposition of hands, solemnly separated them for this service, to which they were chosen

4 The church continued to increase greatly, the intestine murmurs being silenced, the apostles being more disincumbered, and all zealously attending to their several charges Thus the gospel-word spread its blessed influence around, the *disciples multiplied in Jerusalem*, where, during our Lord's ministry, few seem to have believed in him, and what is still more astonishing, and to be reckoned among the chief wonders of grace, *a great company of the priests were obedient to the faith*, who had been the most inveterate enemies of Christ and his gospel, but now embraced the profession of Christianity, and proved by their holy conversation the unfeigned faith which was in them *Note*, True faith in Jesus as a Saviour ever produces sincere obedience to him as our Master

p Ver 5 Chap vii 5 8 And Stephen [p] full of faith and power did great
wonders and miracles among the people 9 ¶ Then
there arose certain of the synagogue, which is called *the*
synagogue of the Libertines and Cyrenians, and Alexan-
drians, and of them of Cilicia, and of Asia, disputing
q Luke xxi 15 Ex iv 12 Isa liv 17 with Stephen 10 And [q] they were not able to resist
the wisdom and the spirit by which he spake 11 Then
they suborned men which said, We have heard him speak
blasphemous words against Moses, and *against* God 12
And they stirred up the people, and the elders, and the
scribes, and came upon *him*, and caught him, and
brought *him* to the council, 13 And set up false wit-
nesses, which said, This man ceaseth not to speak blas-
phemous words against this holy place and the law 14
For we have heard him say, that this Jesus of Nazareth
r 2 Chron vii 21 Dan ix 26 Mat xxiv 2 & xxvi 61 † Or rite shall [r] destroy this place, and shall change the † customs
which Moses delivered us 15 And all that sat in the
council, looking stedfastly on him, saw his face as it had
been the face of an angel

ỽ 8—15 Stephen, the first of the seven deacons, not only discharged the office to which he was appointed, but also appeared a zealous preacher of the gospel

1 *He was full of faith and power*, endued with an eminent measure of courage and zeal for Christ, and, in confirmation of the truths he preached, *did great wonders and miracles among the people*

2 He appeared a bold disputant against those who opposed the cause of truth *There arose certain of the synagogue, which is called the synagogue of the Libertines*, such Jews as were honoured with the freedom of the city of Rome, *and Cyrenians, and Alexandrians, and of them of Cilicia, and of Asia, disputing with Stephen* These Hellenist Jews and proselytes being generally the greatest zealots for Judaism, and perhaps being eminently skilled in Grecian literature, thought they could soon confute and confound this zealous advocate for Christianity, and challenged him to a public disputation Probably Paul of Tarsus, a city of Cilicia, was among the foremost of them Stephen declined not the opportunity of vindicating the glorious truths of the gospel, and this he did with such clearness of argument, force of reasoning, energy of diction, and piercing application, *that they were not able to resist the wisdom and the spirit by which he spake*, confounded, silenced, and unable to make any reply which carried the shadow of argument

3 Enraged at being thus baffled, and instigated by malice and revenge, *they suborned witnesses, which said, We have heard him speak blasphemous words against Moses, and against God*, endeavouring by perjury and murder to silence him for ever, whose arguments they felt themselves so utterly unable to answer *And*, working upon their prejudices and passions, *they stirred up the people, and the elders, and the scribes, and* in a popular tumult they *came upon him, and caught him*, as a criminal, *and brought him to the council*, as a blasphemer, *and set up false witnesses*, which they had hired and instructed what to swear against Stephen, who *said*, *This man ceaseth not to speak blasphemous words against this holy place*, the temple, *and against the law* *For we have heard him say*, what fully amounts to the charge we produce against him, *that this Jesus*, the contemptible Nazarene who was crucified, *shall destroy this place*, this sacred house, *and shall change the customs which Moses delivered us*, abolishing all the ceremonial institutions of our celebrated law-giver, and introducing others of his own appointment in their stead

Such was the charge; which, if real, was far from amounting to blasphemy, and these things actually came to pass, though probably even in this they falsified, as the apostles themselves seem not to have been yet apprized, that the ceremonial law should be utterly abolished, but whatever he might have said, we may suppose they put upon it the most malicious construction it would bear *Note*, It is no new thing for the faithful to be branded as blasphemers; and it is only wonderful, that when the enemies of the gospel make no conscience of an oath, they do not by more frequent perjuries attempt to blacken or destroy those whom they so much abhor

4 God owned his suffering servant by a signal mark of his favour visible even to his persecutors *All that sat in the council, looking stedfastly on him*, to observe if he betrayed any tokens of fear or guilt, *saw his face as it had been the face of an angel*, such deliberate courage, such undisturbed serenity, such majesty and mildness sat on his countenance; perhaps a divine splendor beamed from it, like that of Moses when he came from the mount, and seemed to make him appear more than human

CHAP VII

In this chapter we have the martyrdom of Stephen, the first of the noble army of martyrs Here is his defence of himself before the council 1 He shews, by going over the history of the Old Testament, that God never intended to confine his favours to that place or that ceremonial law, and that they had no reason to expect he should, for the people of the Jews had always been a provoking people, and had forfeited the privileges of their peculiarity Nay, that that holy place and that law were but figures of good things to come, and it was no disparagement at all to them to say, that they must give place to better things, ver 1—50 *And then, 2 He applies this to them that prosecuted him, and sat in judgment upon him, sharply reproving them for their wickedness, by which they had brought upon themselves the ruin of their place and nation, and they could not bear to hear of it*, ver 51—53 *3 The putting of him to death by stoning of him, and his patient, chearful, pious submission to it*, ver 54—60

1 THEN said the high priest, Are these things so?
2 And he said, [a] Men, brethren, and fathers,
hearken, The God of glory appeared unto our father
Abraham when he was in Mesopotamia, before he dwelt
in Charran, 3 And said unto him, [b] Get thee out of
thy country, and from thy kindred, and come into the
land which I shall shew thee 4 Then [c] came he out
of the land of the Chaldeans, and dwelt in Charran and
from thence, when his father was dead, he removed him
into this land wherein ye now dwell 5 And he gave
him none inheritance in it, no not *so much as* to set his
foot on [d] yet he promised that he would give it to him
for a possession, and to his seed after him, when *as yet*
he had no child 6 And God spake on this wise, [e] that
his seed should sojourn in a strange land, and that they
should bring them into bondage, and entreat *them* evil
[f] four hundred years 7 And the nation to whom they
shall be in bondage, will I judge, said God and after
that shall they come forth, and [g] serve me in this place
8 And [h] he gave him the covenant of circumcision
and so [i] *Abraham* begat Isaac, and circumcised him the
eighth day, and [k] Isaac *begat* Jacob, and [l] Jacob *begat*
the twelve patriarchs 9 And [m] the patriarchs moved
with envy sold Joseph into Egypt but [n] God was with
him, 10 And [o] delivered him out of all his afflictions,
and [p] gave him favour and wisdom in the sight of Pha-
raoh king of Egypt, and he made him governor over
Egypt and all his house 11 [q] Now there came a dearth
over all the land of Egypt and Canaan, and great af-
fliction, and our fathers found no sustenance 12 [r] But
when Jacob heard that there was corn in Egypt, he sent
out our fathers first 13 And [s] at the second *time* Jo-
seph was made known to his brethren, and Joseph's
kindred was made known unto Pharaoh 14 Then
sent Joseph, and called his father Jacob to him, and [t] all
his kindred, threescore and fifteen souls 15 So [u] Ja-
cob went down into Egypt, [x] and died, he and our fa-
thers, 16 And [y] were carried over into Sychem, and
laid in [z] the sepulchre that Abraham bought for a sum
of money of the sons of Emmor, *the father* of Sychem

ỽ 1—16 This noble confessor is now before his judges assembled in full council, with the high priest at their head, all his known, avowed, and inveterate enemies, yet, in answer to the high priest's demand, *Are these things so?* he boldly undertakes his defence The scriptures are the armoury from whence he draws the weapons of his warfare, and we find him a compleat master of his subject Being a Hellenist Jew, he quotes the septuagint, as the version commonly in use in their synagogues, though containing some variations from the original Hebrew He begins,

1 With a respectful and affectionate address, intreating their unprejudiced attention, *Men, brethren, and fathers, hearken*

2 He lays before them a concise view of the patriarchal history, in order that they might remember, that God had a church and

and people in the world before the law was given, and ſtill would have one when all the ceremonial inſtitutions were aboliſhed

1 He opens with the call of Abraham, to whom *the God of glory appeared*, in ſome viſible diſplay of his preſence, *when he was in Meſopotamia, before he dwelt in Charran*, in an idolatrous land, *and ſaid unto him, Get thee out of thy country, and from thy kindred, and come into the land which I ſhall ſhew thee* Accordingly he immediately left his country, and removed to Charran, and after his father's death, receiving a ſecond call, he came into the land of Canaan, and abode there where they now dwelt

From hence it appeared, that Abraham was in God's favour before he was circumciſed, and that God's Shechinah had viſited Ur of the Chaldees, before it appeared in Canaan, and therefore they might ſee, that neither the diſpenſation of the law, nor the land of Iſrael, were needful for the acceptable worſhip of God *Note*, (1) Though we may not ſee clearly whether God is leading us, yet when we have his call we may confidently go forward (2) They who are travelling to the heavenly Canaan, chearfully turn their backs on earth with all its allurements

2 Though God had promiſed Abraham the land of Canaan for a poſſeſſion, and to his ſeed after him, *when as yet he had no child*, yet he gave him not a foot of land for a preſent inheritance, nor for four hundred years after, reckoning from the birth of Iſaac did any of his poſterity enjoy the promiſed inheritance, but lived unſettled, and afflicted, under the tyranny of ſtrangers, till at the expiration of the time appointed, God engaged to *judge* their Egyptian oppreſſors, and to bring them at laſt to ſerve him in this place And this Stephen ſuggeſts, in order to lower their pride on their original, and from the length of time which elapſed between the promiſe and the fulfilment of it, as well as from the hardſhips their fathers endured in the intermediate ſpace, to ſhew them, that the principal object to which the Lord intended to lead them, was the heavenly Canaan, of which this was but the figure, and therefore it could be no blaſphemy to ſay, that Jeſus would deſtroy this country, when he promiſed to bring them to the heavenly Canaan, and the Jeruſalem which is above *Note*, (1) Though God's promiſes may be long in their fulfilment, they are ſure (2) The children of God's love may be, and uſually are, called to endure the ſevereſt afflictions here (3) He will finally avenge them on their oppreſſors

3 Having called Abraham to be his ſervant, God gave him the covenant of circumciſion, as a ſeal of the righteouſneſs of that faith which he had being yet uncircumciſed, and this rite he tranſmitted to his poſterity, circumciſing his ſon Iſaac on the eighth day, according to the divine command And Iſaac begat Jacob and the twelve patriarchs, in whom the family of Abraham began to enlarge yet even then did the ſame ſpirit of envy break forth againſt Joſeph, as they who boaſted themſelves deſcendants from these patriarchs afterwards ſhewed to Jeſus, of whom Joſeph was an eminent type, both in his ſufferings and exaltation *The patriarchs, moved with envy, ſold him into Egypt but God was with him, and delivered him out of all his afflictions*, and endued him with ſuch wiſdom as recommended him to Pharaoh's favour, who conſtituted him *governor over Egypt and all his houſe*. And thus had God exalted his ſon Jeſus, whom they had brought to the loweſt ſtate of ignominy and abaſement, to a throne of glory A dearth which Joſeph had foretold, ſhortly after drove the brethren of Joſeph from Canaan to Egypt, where, through his care, proviſion had been laid up againſt the years of famine There at the ſecond interview, to the aſtoniſhment of his brethren, Joſeph made himſelf known to them, and Pharaoh being acquainted with his kindred, at his ſeeking Joſeph invited his father and all his family into Egypt, conſiſting of ſeventy-five perſons There Jacob with the patriarchs died, and in the faith of the fulfilment of God's promiſe to Abraham, the patriarchs' bones were carried out of Egypt, and *laid in the ſepulchre which* Jacob the grandſon of *Abraham bought for a ſum of money, of the ſons of Emmor the father of Sychem* Thus they might obſerve, that the land on which they ſet ſo high a value was afflicted with famine, that the patriarchs, of whom they boaſted, all died in a ſtrange country, yet were accepted of God, and died in faith, expecting that heavenly country to which Jeſus was appointed to bring all the Iſrael of God

17 But when the time of the promiſe drew nigh,
which God had ſworn to Abraham, [a] the people grew [a Ex i — ; Ps cv 24.]
and multiplied in Egypt, 18 Till another king aroſe,
which knew not Joſeph 19 The ſame dealt ſubtilly
with our kindred, and evil entreated our fathers, ſo [b] that [b Ex i 22]
they caſt out their young children, to the end they might
not not live 20 In which time Moſes was born, and [c Ex ii 2. d Heb xi 23]
[d] was exceeding fair, and nouriſhed up in his father's
houſe three months 21 And when he was caſt out,
[e] Pharaoh's daughter took him up, and nouriſhed him [e Ex ii 10]
for her own ſon 22 And Moſes was learned in all the
wiſdom of the Egyptians, and [f] was mighty in words [f Luke xxiv 19]
and in deeds 23 And when he was full forty years
old, it came into his heart to viſit his brethren the chil-
dren of Iſrael 24 [g] And ſeeing one of *them* ſuffer [g Ex ii 11]
wrong, he defended *him*, and avenged him that was op-
preſſed, and ſmote the Egyptian 25 For he ſuppoſed
his brethren would have underſtood how that God by
his hand would deliver them but they underſtood not
26 [h] And the next day he ſhewed himſelf unto them as [h Ex ii 13.]
they ſtrove, and would have ſet them at one again, ſay-
ing, Sirs, ye are brethren, why do ye wrong one to an-
other? 27 But he that did his neighbour wrong, thruſt
him away, ſaying, [i] Who made thee a ruler and a judge [i Chap iv —]
over us? 28 Wilt thou kill me as thou killedſt the
Egyptian yeſterday? 29 [k] Then fled Moſes at this ſay- [k Ex ii 15.]
ing, and was a ſtranger in the land of Madian, where
he begat two ſons

v 17—29 Stephen proceeds with the hiſtory of the Jewiſh people

1 *When the time of the promiſe drew near*, they multiplied exceedingly Then a new king aroſe, *which knew not Joſeph*, nor remembered what a ſaviour he had been to the land, but, jealous of the increaſe of the Iſraelites, with helliſh craft he ſought to extirpate them by a bloody edict to kill all the male children which ſhould be born, whilſt by the moſt ſervile and inceſſant toils and labour he ſought to harraſs to death their fathers And thus were they acting againſt the diſciples of Jeſus and his infant church, but their ſubtilty and malice would be equally abortive, the followers of Jeſus but increaſed and multiplied the more

2 *In this ſtate of diſtreſs Moſes was born, deſigned of God* for their great deliverer, for when God's people are at the laſt extremity, he is ready glorioully to appear on their behalf The child was *exceeding fair*, ſomething peculiarly beautiful appeared on his infant countenance After being concealed three months, he was at laſt expoſed, and ſo providence ordered it, that Pharaoh's daughter, coming down to the ſpot to bathe, found the babe, and was ſo ſtruck with his beauty and tears, that ſhe took and brought him up as her own ſon, giving him the moſt accompliſhed education, ſo that he was *learned in all the wiſdom of the Egyptians, and was mighty in words and deeds*, remarkably judicious in his counſels, and eminent for his courage

Stephen ſhewed hereby, that, far from diſhonouring Moſes, he regarded him with greateſt admiration, and ſpoke of him with the higheſt encomiums He was alſo an eminent figure of Chriſt, expoſed to like danger in his infancy, and raiſed up of God to be a greater Saviour to his people

3 Being arrived at the prime of life, and at the height of grandeur and affluence, moved by divine impulſe, he reſolved to leave the court of Pharaoh, and viſit his afflicted brethren And ſeeing one of them moſt unjuſtly abuſed and beaten, he interpoſed in his behalf, and ſlew the Egyptian, as a ſpecimen of that authority with which he was inveſted, as their appointed deliverer, ſuppoſing by this action they would underſtand what God intended to do for them by his means, *but they underſtood not The next day he ſhewed himſelf* again *unto them as they ſtrove*, and as a peace-maker would fain have reconciled the two Hebrews which quarrelled with each other, ſuggeſting their near relation, and how unbecoming it was in them to abuſe and fight with one another But he who was the aggreſſor, impatient of the rebuke, (as thoſe uſually are, who are in the wrong) inſultingly rejects his interpoſition, ſaying, *Who made thee a ruler and a judge over us?* as if he aſſumed an authority to which he had no title, and upbraids him with what he had done the day before, *Wilt thou kill me as thou killedſt the Egyptian yeſterday?* Perceiving hereby the danger in which he was, and the ingratitude and baſeneſs of his brethren, *Moſes fled*, leſt the fact being publiſhed, he ſhould be arreſted as a murderer, and taking up his abode in the land of Midian, he ſpent another forty years there, where he begat two ſons

Now Stephen inſinuates it was no new thing with them to reject and ill-uſe their divinely-appointed deliverers As their fathers perverſely ſhut their eyes againſt the pretenſions of Moſes, ſo had they refuſed Jeſus the prince of glory, who came to deliver them from a worſe than Egyptian bondage, even from the tyranny of ſin and Satan, and from the power of death and hell

30 [l] And when forty years were expired, there ap- [l Ex iii 2]
peared to him in the wilderneſs of mount Sina, an angel
of the Lord in a flame of fire in a buſh 31 When
Moſes ſaw *it*, he wondered at the ſight and as he drew
near to behold *it*, the voice of the Lord came unto him,
32 *Saying*, [m] I *am* the God of thy fathers, the God of [m Mat xxii 32 Heb xi 16.]
Abraham, and the God of Iſaac, and the God of Jacob
Then Moſes trembled, and durſt not behold 33 [n] Then [n Joſh v 15]
ſaid the Lord to him, Put off thy ſhoes from thy feet

for the place where thou standest is holy ground 34
I have seen, I have seen the affliction of my people which
is in Egypt, and I have heard their groaning, and am
come down to deliver them And now come, I will send
thee into Egypt 35 This Moses whom they refused,
saying, ᵖ Who made thee a ruler and a judge? the same
did God send *to be* a ruler, and a deliverer, ᵍ by the hands
of the angel ʳ which appeared to him in the bush 36
He brought them out, after that he had ˢ shewed wonders
and signs in the land of Egypt, and in the Red sea, and
ᵗ in the wilderness forty years 37 ¶ This is that Mo-
ses which said unto the children of Israel, ᵘ A prophet
shall the Lord your God raise up unto you of your bre-
thren, like unto me, ˣ him shall ye hear. 38 ʸ This is
he that was in the church in the wilderness, with ᶻ the
angel which spake to him in the mount Sina, and *with*
our fathers who received the lively ᵃ oracles to give
unto us 39 To whom our fathers would not obey,
but thrust *him* from them, and in their hearts turned
back again into Egypt, 40 ᵇ Saying unto Aaron, Make
us gods to go before us for *as for* this Moses, which
brought us out of the land of Egypt, we wot not what
is become of him. 41 And ᶜ they made a calf in those
days, and offered sacrifice unto the idol, and rejoiced in
the works of their own hands 42 Then God turned,
and ᵈ gave them up to ᵉ worship the host of heaven, as
it is written in the book of the prophets, ᶠ O ye house
of Israel, have ye offered to me slain beasts, and sacri-
fices, by the space of forty years in the wilderness? 43
Yea, ye took up the tabernacle of Moloch, and the star
of your god Remphan, figures which ye made, to wor-
ship them and I will carry you away beyond Babylon.

Ver 7
p Ex ii 14
q Num xx 16
r Ex iii 2
s Ex vii — xiv
t Ex xvi 1
u Deut xviii 15 18 Chap iii 22
x Mat xvii 5
y Ex xix 3, 17
z Isa lxiii 9 Gal iii 19
a Ver 53 Rom iii 2
b Ex xxxii 1
c Deut ix 16 Neh ix 18 Ps cvi 19
d Ps lxxxi 12 Rom i 24 2 Thes ii 11
e Jer vii 18 & xix 13 & xliv 17 Ezek viii 16
f Am v 25

v 30—43 Stephen proceeds in his account of Moses, and, far from speaking ought that could be construed into blasphemy against him, none could ever make more honourable mention of this great law-giver

1 At the expiration of forty years, the great angel of the covenant, who in the fulness of time was to come into the world as God incarnate, in the person of the man Christ Jesus, appeared to him in a bush, which seemed all on fire, yet remained unconsumed Struck with astonishment at this strange sight, when Moses approached to take a nearer view, the voice of God was heard from the midst of the bush, saying, *I am the God of thy fathers, the God of Abraham, and the God of Isaac, and the God of Jacob*, remembring his covenant, and now about to fulfil his promises to their seed, after so long a time The doctrine of a resurrection then, at which the Sadducees were so offended, hath Moses for its voucher and God had not limited his presence to the temple, but had here displayed his glory in a wilderness, and that very covenant of promise made unto the fathers, which God spake of to Moses, Stephen preached, shewing its most evident and glorious accomplishment in the spiritual salvation of Jesus, so far was he from contradicting, and much more from blaspheming Moses, as they alledged

2 Struck with sacred reverence, his eyes fixed on the earth, Moses durst not behold Then God bids him put his shoes from his feet, as standing now on holy ground, and gives him his commission *I have seen, I have seen the affliction of my people which is in Egypt, and I have heard their groaning, and am come down to deliver them.* Though God suffer his people to be in distress, he hears their cry, and in his good time will help them *This Moses whom they refused, saying, Who made thee a ruler and a judge? the same did God send to be a ruler, and a deliverer, by the hands of the angel which appeared to him in the bush*, and thus had God exalted Jesus, whom they had in like manner rejected, to be a Prince and Saviour

3 Moses faithfully executed his commission, and *brought them out* from the house of bondage, *after he had shewed signs and wonders in the land of Egypt, and in the Red sea, and in the wilderness forty years* So highly does he speak of Israel's deliverer, nor was it any derogation from him, that a greater than he should arise, accomplishing a more glorious redemption for them, since of such a one doth Moses himself prophesy

4 *This is that Moses*, the very person for whose honour they were so jealous was he *which said unto the children of Israel, A prophet shall the Lord your God raise up unto you of your brethren, like unto me*, a new law-giver, who should introduce another dispensation, or *as me*, as he hath raised up me, so shall there arise another, invested with divine authority and power *him shall ye hear*, submitting to his word, and obedient to his voice in all things Far therefore from dishonouring Moses, Stephen shews the accomplishment of his prophecy, and that they ought to testify their real veneration for his memory, by obeying his injunctions, and submitting to that new and spiritual dispensation which Jesus the great prophet came to introduce

5 Notwithstanding all the services which Moses did them, and all the honour God had conferred upon him, their fathers had treated him with the highest contempt and ingratitude *This is he that was in the church in the wilderness*, as their captain and leader, *with the angel*, that uncreated angel of the covenant, the great Jehovah Jesus, *which spake to him in the mount Sina, and with our fathers*, face to face, as a man talketh to his friend, *who received the lively oracles to give unto us*, *oracles*, as being of infallible certainty, and *lively*, sharp, and piercing the conscience, or leading those who truly understood them to eternal life Yet greatly as Moses was honoured of God herein, *our fathers would not obey him, but thrust him from them, and in their hearts turned back again into Egypt*, murmuring and mutinying against him, and, at the very time when, as their mediator, he was in the mount with God, sinking into the grossest idolatry, *saying unto Aaron, Make us gods to go before us for as for this Moses, which brought us out of the land of Egypt, we wot not what is become of him* So disrespectfully did they speak of their great deliverer *And* accordingly *they made a calf in those days*, in imitation of the Egyptian god Apis, *and offered sacrifice unto the idol, and rejoiced in the work of their own hands* Instead therefore of charging Stephen with blasphemy, they would do well to remember what their own ancestors had done

6 For these abominations God was justly provoked *Then he turned*, withdrew from them his grace and favour, *and gave them up to worship the host of heaven*, leaving them in righteous judgment to their own inventions In consequence of which they neglected God, and all the newly-instituted ordinances, and relapsed, after they came into Canaan, into the grossest idolatry, for which he quotes a prophet's word, whose authority they would not dispute, (*Amos* v 25—27) *Have ye offered unto me slain beasts, and sacrifices, by the space of forty years in the wilderness?* No they neglected his worship, and what they offered was to devils, and not to God, (*Deut* xxxii 17) so that they themselves disused for forty years those very customs which Moses had delivered to them And, worse still, *ye took up the tabernacle of Moloch*, the image of this idol inclosed in a shrine, *and the star of your god Remphan, figures which ye made to worship them*, in express contradiction to the commands of God *and* for this he threatens them with condign punishment, *I will carry you away beyond Babylon*, (*See 2 Kings* xvii 5—8)

Now if God dealt thus severely with them for despising Moses's law, of how much sorer punishment, than even their ancestors received, would they be counted worthy, for rejecting the dispensation of grace which Jesus, so far greater than Moses, came from God to reveal to them?

44 Our fathers had the tabernacle of witness in the
wilderness, as he had appointed, † speaking unto Moses,
ᵍ that he should make it according to the fashion that he
had seen 45 ʰ Which also our fathers ‡ that came af-
ter, brought in with § Jesus into the possession of the
Gentiles, ⁱ whom God drave out before the face of our
fathers, unto the days of David 46 ᵏ Who found fa-
vour before God, and ˡ desired to find a tabernacle for
the God of Jacob 47 ᵐ But Solomon built him an
house 48 Howbeit ⁿ the most High dwelleth not in
temples made with hands, as saith the prophet, 49
ᵒ Heaven *is* my throne, and earth *is* my footstool what
house will ye build me? saith the Lord or what *is* the
place of my rest? 50 Hath not my hand made all
these things?

† Gr. Who spake
g Ex xxv 40 Heb viii 5
h Josh iii 14
‡ Or having received
§ i e Joshua, So Heb iv 8
i Deut iv 38 & vii 1 Ps lxxviii 55
k 1 Sam xvi 1 Chap xiii 22
l Ps cxxxii 4
m 1 Kings vi 1 1 Chron xvii 12
n 1 Kings viii 27 Chap xvii 24
o Isa lxvi 1 Mat v 34 & xxiii 22

v 44—50 The accusation lodged against Stephen was for speaking against the temple, as if that was blasphemous, whereas he shews, that their fathers worshipped God acceptably for ages before any temple was built

1 It was not till they came into *the wilderness*, that *the tabernacle of witness* was reared, according to the model which God shewed to Moses in the mount God accepted his faithful worshippers before there was any tabernacle, and they might again serve him as acceptably, if *the holy place*, the temple, were destroyed and the very care shewn in the making of this tent according to the divine model, intimated, that it was a shadow of good things to come, being typical of the incarnation of the Son of God, and of his spiritual and gracious presence in his church

2 This tabernacle Joshua brought into the possession of the Gentiles, whom God drave out before him, and if it was set up in that polluted land of Canaan, why might not God now erect his spiritual tabernacle among the nations of the heathen?

3 Till David's time God was pleased to dwell in this mean and moveable tent, above four hundred years, and when David was desirous to build a temple for the Lord, he forbad him, reserving that honour for Solomon, who *built him an house* It appeared therefore evident, that God was not solicitous to have a temple for his abode, as if that was necessary for their acceptable worship, and also, that if Solomon might change the tabernacle for a temple, God might no doubt, if he pleased, de-

stroy

ſtroy that, and make his abode in his ſpiritual temple, the church of the redeemed

4 Though God ordered the erection of the tabernacle, and the building of the temple, it could not be conceived, that his immenſity could be circumſcribed by theſe narrow bounds, when, as the prophet, (*Iſa* lxvi 1, 2) had obſerved, *Heaven is his throne, and earth his footſtool* No houſe made with hands can then be comparable to that glorious temple the univerſe, which himſelf hath reared nor can he need a place to repoſe himſelf, when all things and creatures whatever are the work of his hands Therefore it was no diſparagement to the temple, to affirm, that Jeſus ſhould deſtroy this temple, and ſet up another, into which all nations ſhould flow together, and their worſhip be acceptable to him

51 ¶ Ye stiff necked and uncircumciſed in heart
and ears, ye do always reſiſt the holy Ghoſt as your
fathers *did*, ſo *do* ye 52 Which of the prophets have
not your fathers perſecuted? and they have ſlain them
which ſhewed before of the coming of the juſt One,
of whom ye have been now the betrayers and murder
ers 53 Who have received the law by the diſpoſi
tion of angels, and have not kept *it*

v 51—53 Probably Stephen was proceeding to ſhew, that the temple and its ſervice muſt come to an end, but perceiving the rage that fired the boſoms of his enemies ſparkling in their eyes, and expecting ſoon to be interrupted, he cloſes with a word of piercing application

1 He charges them with their obſtinacy and ſtubbornneſs, like unto their fathers *Ye ſtiff-necked, and uncircumciſed in heart and ears*, in profeſſion God's ſervants, but hardened in pride and prejudice againſt the cleareſt intimations of his will, *ye do always reſiſt the Holy Ghoſt*, rejecting the evidence of his miracles, wilfully blind to the cleareſt prophecies, and fighting againſt the convictions of your own conſciences *As your fathers did, ſo do ye*, refuſing to hearken unto us the inſpired ſervants of Jeſus, as they turned a deaf ear to the warnings of the prophets and juſt is it in God to devote thoſe to ruin, who will not hearken to his admonitions, but obſtinately harden their hearts

2 They were perſecutors and murderers, like their fathers *Which of the prophets have not your fathers perſecuted?* more or leſs reviling or oppoſing them *and they have ſlain them which ſhewed before the coming of the juſt One*, the divine Meſſiah, Jeſus, the holy One of God, ſent to bring in an everlaſting righteouſneſs, by his perfect obedience in the ſinner's ſtead, *of whom ye*, treading cloſely in your anceſtors ſteps, and exceeding them in wickedneſs, *have been the betrayers and murderers*

3 They had rejected God's word, as their fathers before them, *who have received the law*, delivered in the moſt auguſt manner, *by the diſpoſition of angels*, whoſe miniſtry God employed on mount Sinai, when in ſhining ranks they graced that ſolemnity, as attendants on the King of Glory, *and have not kept it*, have, like them, broken its moſt eſſential precepts, and added to all their guilt the rejection of the goſpel alſo, notwithſtanding all the glorious evidence wherewith it hath been attended, and how then can ye hope to eſcape the vengeance of an offended God?

54 ¶ When they heard theſe things, they were cut
to the heart, and they gnaſhed on him with *their* teeth
55 But he being full of the holy Ghoſt, looked up
ſtedfaſtly into heaven and ſaw the glory of God, and
Jeſus ſtanding on the right hand of God 56 And
ſaid, Behold, I ſee the heavens opened, and the Son
of man ſtanding on the right hand of God 57 Then
they cried out with a loud voice, and ſtopped their ears,
and ran upon him with one accord, 58 And caſt
him out of the city, and ſtoned *him* and the witneſſes
laid down their clothes at a young man's feet, whoſe
name was Saul 59 And they ſtoned Stephen, call-
ing upon *God*, and ſaying, Lord Jeſus receive my ſpi-
rit 60 And he kneeled down and cried with a loud
voice, Lord, lay not this ſin to their charge And
when he had ſaid this, he fell aſleep

v 54—60 We have here the glorious and triumphant death of the firſt chriſtian martyr

1 *When they heard theſe things, they were cut to the heart*, ſo filled were they with envy, indignation, and malice, as if ſawn aſunder *and they gnaſhed upon him with their teeth*, as if they would have devoured him alive *Note*, Wicked men carry their hell about with them, in thoſe diabolical tempers and raging paſſions, which make them their own tormentors

2 Stephen, unterrified with their malice, and *being full of the Holy Ghoſt*, receiving an abundant increaſe of grace and conſolation ſuited to his preſent condition, *looked up ſtedfaſtly into heaven*, appealing to God, confidently expecting divine ſupport, and eagerly longing after that crown of glory that now ſhone bright in his view, and enabled him to look down with contempt upon the malice of his enemies, *and*, by a miraculous manifeſtation, *ſaw the glory of God*, ſome viſible emblem of the eternal Majeſty, ſuch as the Shechinah, *and Jeſus ſtanding at the right hand of God*, in his human nature as mediator, exalted to the higheſt honour and dignity, appearing as the advocate of his ſuffering ſaint, to ſtrengthen him boldly to reſiſt unto blood, to crown him with martyrdom, and ſhortly to avenge him of his bloody perſecutors Tranſported with this beatific viſion, he *ſaid*, with wonder and delight, *Behold, I ſee the heavens opened, and the Son of man ſtanding at the right hand of God* *Note*, (1) In times of ſuffering, our eyes ſhould be lifted up to heaven, ſo from thence cometh our help (2) As our tribulations for Chriſt abound, he is pleaſed, by the moſt gracious manifeſtation of himſelf, to cauſe our conſolations to abound alſo (3) A ſight of Jeſus, at the right hand of God, will carry us triumphantly through death, armed with all its terrors, and enable us to defy the ſtroke

3 Concluding now that they had full cauſe for his condemnation, *They cried with a loud voice*, to drown his ſpeech, to expreſs their deteſtation of what they heard, and ſharpen each others fury, *and ſtopped their ears*, as if ſhocked at his blaſphemy, *and ran upon him with one accord*, the whole multitude of the people riſing in tumultuous rage, *and caſt him out of the city*, as a wretch not fit to live, and who defiled that holy place where he ſtood, *and ſtoned him*, as a blaſphemer, *Lev* xxiv 16 *and the witneſſes*, whoſe hands were firſt upon him, *Deut* xvii 6, 7 *laid down their clothes at a young man's feet, whoſe name was Saul*, a fiery zealot, who with pleaſure ſaw the bloody execution of this holy martyr *Note*, (1) The cauſe of Chriſt is often run down with clamour, and rage ſupplies the place of reaſon (2) Many of the deareſt ſaints upon earth have been counted as the off-ſcouring of all things, and thought unworthy of the air they breathed

4 *They ſtoned Stephen, calling upon God*, tho' caſt out from earth, as unworthy to live, he had a ſure intereſt in heaven, *ſaying, Lord Jeſus receive my ſpirit*, *and*, now ready to expire, *he kneeled down and cried with a loud voice*, expreſſive of the vehemence of his deſire, *Lord, lay not this ſin to their charge*, copying cloſely his divine Maſter's example, *and when he had ſaid this he fell aſleep*, as theſe words dropped from his lips, the mortal blow reached him, and in the arms of everlaſting love he ſweetly reſted from ſuffering and ſorrow for ever *Note*, (1) In a dying hour, we cannot be better employed than in commending our ſouls into the arms of Jeſus (2) If our immortal part be ſafe, it little matters what becomes of the fleſhly tabernacle (3) Jeſus is very God, the object of his people's adoration, and as by faith in him we can only live comfortably, ſo by an eye to him, as the reſurrection and the life, can we die happily (4) Our bittereſt perſecutors muſt ſhare our prayers, and the more wicked they are, the more they need them (5) When we come to die, it will be eſſential to our own comfort, that we are truly in charity with all men (6) Death to a believer is but a ſleep, repoſing a while in that bed of duſt where our Lord hath lain, his voice ſhall waken us up in the reſurrection morn, and we ſhall ariſe to ſhare with him the triumphs of that eternal day, *when our ſun ſhall no more go down, nor our moon withdraw itſelf, but the Lord ſhall be our everlaſting light, and our God our glory*

CHAP VIII

We have here, 1 The perſecution of the church, ver 1—3 2 *Its enlargements by Philip's preaching at Samaria*, ver 4—13 3 *Peter and John confirm the diſciples there, and rebuke Simon Magus*, ver 14—25 4 *Philip, by divine direction, preaches to, converts, and baptizes the Ethiopian eunuch*, ver 26—38 5 *He returns*, ver 39, 40

1 AND Saul was conſenting unto his death And
at that time there was a great perſecution againſt
the church which was at Jeruſalem, and they were all
ſcattered abroad throughout the regions of Judea and
Samaria, except the apoſtles 2 And devout men car-
ried Stephen *to his burial*, and made great lamentation
over him 3 As for Saul, he made havock of the
church, entering into every houſe, and haling men and
women, committed *them* to priſon.

a Chap vii 58 & xxii 20 b Chap xi 19 c Gen xxiii 2 & l 10 2 Sam iii 31 d Chap ix 1 & xxii 4 & xxvi 10, 11 1 Cor xv 9 Gal i 13 1 Tim i 13

v 1—3 We are here told,

1 The pleaſure and ſatisfaction Saul took in ſeeing the firſt martyr bleed He not only conſented to the deed, but, as the word ſignifies, feaſted his eyes with the ſhocking ſpectacle, in hopes ſuch ſharp methods would ſoon put a ſtop to the progreſs of that goſpel which he abhorred

2 The chief prieſts and rulers determined to purſue their blow, and whilſt the fury of the people laſted, ſeverely perſecuted the church at Jeruſalem, ſo that the preachers, who were the great objects of enmity, were forced to withdraw, and diſperſe

themselves through Judea and Samaria, except the apostles, who still continued at Jerusalem, and were preserved safe from the rage of their blood-thirsty enemies

3 Stephen's friends, *devout men*, eminent for their piety, dared, notwithstanding the danger to which they were exposed, to gather up his broken remains, and *carried him to his burial*, and though they could not but rejoice in his triumphant death, they bewailed their own and the church's loss, deprived of so able an advocate for the cause of Christ *Note*, (1) The departure of the eminent servants of Jesus demands a tear; though it be their gain, it is our loss, and we should weep for ourselves (2) The corpse is honourable in which a heavenly spirit hath dwelt, and should be decently laid in the dust, in sure and certain confidence of a glorious resurrection, when it shall awake in brighter array

4 *Saul*, the invenomed foe to the Christian name, a fiery zealot, the fittest tool the priests could have chosen for their service, *made havock of the church*, persecuting them even unto death, as he owns, (*Acts* xxii 4) *entring into every house, and*, sparing neither age nor sex, *haling men and women, committed them to prison* To such low and dirty work doth enmity against the gospel lead a man of note, a gentleman, a scholar, as if every mark of contempt and cruelty to a Christian was meritorious and commendable

e Mat x.23 Chap xi 19 f Chap vi 5 4. Therefore [e] they that were scattered abroad, went
every where preaching the word 5 Then [f] Philip went
down to the city of Samaria, and preached Christ unto
them 6 And the people with one accord gave heed
unto those things which Philip spake, hearing and seeing
g Mark xvi 17 the miracles which he did 7 For [g] unclean spirits,
crying with a loud voice, came out of many that were
possessed *with them* and many taken with palsies, and
that were lame, were healed 8 And there was great
joy in that city 9. But there was a certain man called
h Chap xiii 8 Simon, which before-time in the same city [h] used sorcery, and bewitched the people of Samaria, giving out
that himself was some great one. 10 To whom they
all gave heed from the least to the greatest, saying, This
man is the great power of God 11 And to him they
had regard, because that of long time he had bewitched
them with sorceries 12 But when they believed Phi-
i Chap i 3 lip, preaching the things [i] concerning the kingdom of
k Mat xxviii 19 God, and the name of Jesus Christ, [k] they were baptized both men and women 13 Then Simon himself
believed also, and when he was baptized, he continued
† Or Signs and great miracles with Philip, and wondered, beholding the † miracles and
signs which were done

v 4—13 The attempt to extinguish and suppress the rising flame of Christianity, served but the more to spread the sacred fire *They that were scattered abroad, went every where preaching the word*, not hiding themselves in corners, or seeking concealment by their silence, but publishing throughout the country the glad tidings of salvation by Jesus Christ Philip, the second of the deacons, and now the first since Stephen had finished his glorious course, was among the chief of these dispersed Evangelists.

1 He went *down to the city of Samaria*, to the metropolis of the country, which was either Samaria, or, as some think, Sychar, or Shechem, where Jesus had been formerly, (*John* iv 5) *and preached Christ unto them* As an herald he publickly proclaimed his name, as exalted to the throne of glory, and invited all to come and share the blessings of his happy government and this must be our constant theme, Christ crucified, glorified

2 Great was the success that attended his labours *The people with one accord*, in general, *gave heed unto those things which Philip spake*, shewing the most serious attention to his discourses, *hearing and seeing the miracles which he did*, in proof of his divine mission, and of the gospel of Jesus which he declared unto them Miracles of the most stupendous nature, such as dispossessing unclean spirits, who with the utmost rage exclaimed at the power they could not withstand, curing the paralytic, and restoring the use of their limbs to the lame, when all human help was desperate *And there was great joy in that city*, the people transported beheld these amazing works of divine power and grace, and rejoiced in the glad news of pardon and salvation preached to them through the Redeemer *Note*, (1) So far as the gospel effectually reaches the heart, Satan's power is broken, and his kingdom of uncleanness within is destroyed (2) The grace of God cures the moral impotence of our fallen nature, and enables the lame man to leap like an hart, and the paralytic soul to walk and run the way of God's commandments (3) The great things which make for our everlasting peace, deserve our most serious attention, and the more we attend unto them, the more shall we consult our own happiness (4) True religion will make none melancholy, but wherever the gospel is known and believed, there the soul will taste the sweetest and most substantial joy

3 What made the success of the gospel in this place still more extraordinary, was the delusion under which the people had lain, through the feats of a certain sorcerer named Simon, who had *bewitched the people of Samaria*, astonishing them with his magic arts and diabolical illusions, *giving out that himself was some great one*, the great God himself, or, as others suppose, the expected Messiah; and such was the influence which his pretended miracles had on the minds of the people, that *they all gave heed* unto him, *from the least to the greatest*, high and low, young and old, *saying, This man is the great power of God*, as if he was endued with almighty power, equal to the great God himself, so strangely had he for a considerable time *bewitched them with his sorceries*

4 Before the gospel word the kingdom of Satan fell *When they believed Philip, preaching the things concerning the kingdom of God*, the blessings and privileges, the doctrines and ordinances of it, *and the name of Jesus Christ*, as the great Saviour of lost sinners, the head of his church, the author of all mercies here, and glorious hopes hereafter, they gladly embraced his salvation, abandoned the impostor Simon, and by baptism made open profession of their faith in Jesus, *both men and women*. *Note*, (1) They who are most bewitched by Satan's sorceries, and the power of sin, are not beyond the recovering influence of the Redeemer's grace (2) When we truly believe in Jesus, we shall openly and boldly profess him before men

5 Even Simon the magician himself was so astonished at the real miracles and signs which Philip wrought, that he *believed also*, so far at least, as to make outward profession of Christ as the true Messiah, and to desire and be admitted to baptism in his name *Note*, (1) They who have been most atrociously wicked, when they make profession of repentance and conversion to God, are to be received cordially into the church, notwithstanding all that is past (2) Though many hypocrites may and do join themselves with God's people, yet we must leave men's hearts to the searcher of hearts, and judge of others with all candour and charity, till they give evident proofs of their unfaithfulness

14 Now when the apostles which were at Jerusalem,
heard that Samaria had received the word of God, they
sent unto them Peter and John 15 Who when they
were come down, prayed for them [l] that they might re- l Chap ii 38
ceive the holy Ghost 16 (For [m] as yet he was fallen m Chap xix 2
upon none of them only [n] they were baptized in [o] the n Mat xxviii 19
name of the Lord Jesus) 17 Then [p] laid they *their* o Chap x 48 & xix 5
hands on them, and they received the holy Ghost. 18 p Chap vi 6 & xix 6 Heb vi 2
And when Simon saw that through laying on of the
apostles hands the holy Ghost was given, he offered them
money, 19 Saying, Give me also this power, that on
whomsoever I lay hands, he may receive the holy Ghost.
20 But Peter said unto him, Thy money perish with
thee, because [q] thou hast thought that the gift of God q Mat x 8 2 Kings v 16
may be purchased with money 21 Thou hast neither
part nor lot in this matter for thy heart is not right in
the sight of God 22 Repent therefore of this thy
wickedness, and pray God, [r] if perhaps the thought of r Dan iv 27 2 Tim ii 25
thine heart may be forgiven thee 23 For I perceive
that thou art in [s] the gall of bitterness, and *in* the bond s Heb xii 15
of iniquity 24 Then answered Simon, and said, [t] Pray t Num xxi 7 1 Kings xiii 6
ye to the Lord for me, that none of these things which
ye have spoken come upon me 25 And they, when
they had testified and preached the word of the Lord,
returned to Jerusalem, and preached the gospel in many villages of the Samaritans

v 14—25 The glad tidings soon reached Jerusalem of the happy progress of the gospel at Samaria, and the apostles, for the furtherance of the blessed work, dispatched two of their body, Peter and John, immediately, to confirm the disciples, and communicate unto them those extraordinary gifts which the apostles alone could confer We have,

1 The success of their journey *They prayed for them, that they might receive the Holy Ghost*, in his miraculous gifts, and be set on a level with the Jewish converts, *for as yet he had fallen upon none of them*, though they had experienced his illuminating, sanctifying, and comforting influence upon their souls, in consequence of which they *had been baptized in the name of the Lord Jesus*, yet they had not, by any visible appearance of the Holy Ghost, received the gift of tongues, or prophecy, or the power to work miracles But when the apostles had prayed, and were assured of an answer to their requests, *then laid they their hands on them, and they received the Holy Ghost*, in some visible manner, at least many of them, on whom the apostles laid their hands, and probably ordained them to the ministry of the word, for which they were thus more eminently qualified *Note*, Though we may not expect [illegible: miraculous powers], yet the same

Holy

Holy Ghoſt, in all his gracious influences, is ſtill given in anſwer to the prayer of faith

2 Simon's hypocriſy on this occaſion appeared *When he ſaw that through the laying on of the apoſtles hands the Holy Ghoſt was given*, he was vaſtly ambitious of poſſeſſing the ſame apoſtolic power, and thought he could well reimburſe himſelf any expence, could he but obtain it, therefore, ſuppoſing their views mercenary as his own, *he offered them money, ſaying, Give me this power alſo, that on whomſoever I lay hands, he may receive the Holy Ghoſt*, thus diſcovering both his ambition and avarice, and ſhewing the rottenneſs of his heart, notwithſtanding his pretended converſion

3 Peter, with abhorrence, rejects the propoſal, and denounces his doom *Thy money periſh with thee*, thou and it muſt periſh together, if in this temper of mind thou abideſt as for us, we deteſt thy mercenary offer, *becauſe thou haſt thought that the gift of God may be purchaſed with money*, an imagination as abſurdly fooliſh, as impiouſly wicked *Thou haſt neither part nor lot in this matter*, art neither a partaker of the gifts or graces of the Spirit, and as yet an alien from the kingdom of grace, and deſtitute of the hope of glory *for thy heart is not right in the ſight of God*, but under the ſpecious profeſſion of Chriſtianity, lurks the fouleſt hypocriſy *Repent therefore of this thy wickedneſs*, ſo great and aggravated, if yet repentance may be given, *and pray God, if perhaps the thought of thine heart may be forgiven thee*, and there be a poſſibility of pardon *For I perceive* by this propoſal, *that thou art in the gall of bitterneſs*, in a ſtate of unregeneracy, under the dominion of the moſt abhorred corruptions, *and in the bond of iniquity*, enſlaved by Satan and ſin, and as a criminal carrying to execution, expoſed to the ſevereſt vengeance of an offended God *Note*, (1) The fatal bait of money, how many ſouls hath it plunged into perdition and deſtruction? (2) Where the heart is not right with God, though a *form* of godlineſs may conceal the hypocriſy from men, there is one that ſeeth and judgeth (3) Sin is the odious thing which renders the ſoul abominable to God, and when it breaks forth in an apoſtate, juſtly expoſes his character to the deteſtation of all good men (4) They who are now held in bonds of iniquity, may aſſuredly expect to be bound over to everlaſting ſhame and puniſhment (5) The vileſt of ſinners muſt not be abandoned, but ſtill invited to repentance and prayer, whilſt there is life, there is hope

4 Simon, terrified at this dire commination and reproof, intreats their prayers for him, not ſo much that his heart might be renewed, as that the threatned vengeance might be averted and that is a ſure ſign of an unhumbled ſpirit, when it is more affected with the dread of ſuffering, than with the evil of ſin

5 The apoſtles, *when they had teſtified and preached the word of the Lord*, confirming and eſtabliſhing the faith of the diſciples at Samaria, *returned to Jeruſalem*, to give an account to their brethren, of their proceedings and ſucceſs, *and*, in their way, *they preached the goſpel in many villages of the Samaritans*, improving every ſtage of their journey, and taking every opportunity of publiſhing the great ſalvation of their maſter Jeſus Let us imitate ſuch worthy examples, preaching the word *in ſeaſon*, and as ſome may think, *out of ſeaſon*

26 And the angel of the Lord ſpake unto Philip, ſaying, Ariſe and go toward the ſouth, unto the way that
goeth down from Jeruſalem unto Gaza, which is deſert
u Pſ lxviii 31. Zeph iii 10. 27 And he aroſe and went: and behold, [u] a man of
Ethiopia, an eunuch of great authority under Candace
queen of the Ethiopians, who had the charge of all her
x John xii 20. treaſure, and [x] had come to Jeruſalem for to worſhip,
28 Was returning, and ſitting in his chariot, read Eſaias
the prophet 29 Then the Spirit ſaid unto Philip, Go
near, and join thyſelf to this chariot 30 And Philip
ran thither to him, and heard him read the prophet
Eſaias, and ſaid, Underſtandeſt thou what thou readeſt?
31 And he ſaid, How can I, except ſome man ſhould
guide me? and he deſired Philip that he would come
up and ſit with him 32 The place of the ſcripture
y Iſa liii 7 which he read, was this, [y] He was led as a ſheep to the
ſlaughter, and like a lamb dumb before his ſhearer, ſo
opened he not his mouth 33 In his humiliation his
judgment was taken away and who ſhall declare his
generation? for his life is taken from the earth 34
And the eunuch anſwered Philip, and ſaid, I pray thee,
of whom ſpeaketh the prophet this? of himſelf, or of
ſome other man? 35 Then Philip opened his mouth,
z Chap x 43. and began at the ſame ſcripture, and preached unto him
a Mat xvi 16. John vi 69. & xi 27. Chap ix 20. 1 John iv 15. & v 5 Jeſus 36 And as they went on *their* way, they came
unto a certain water and the eunuch ſaid, See, *here is*
water, [z] what doth hinder me to be baptized? 37 And
Philip ſaid, If thou believeſt with all thine heart, thou
mayeſt And he anſwered and ſaid, I believe that [a] Jeſus
Chriſt is the Son of God 38 And he commanded the
chariot to ſtand ſtill and they went down both into the
water, both Philip and the eunuch, and he baptized
him 39 And when they were come up out of the
water, [b] the Spirit of the Lord caught away Philip, that b 1 Kings xviii 12. 2 Kings ii 16 Ezek iii 12, 14.
the eunuch ſaw him no more and he went on his
way rejoicing 40 But Philip was found at Azotus
and paſſing through, he preached in all the cities till he
came to Ceſarea

v 26—40 We have here the converſion of the Ethiopian eunuch, by whom it is generally ſuppoſed Chriſtianity was firſt planted in that country, and the ſcripture fulfilled, *Pſal* lxviii 30

1 Philip, who continued ſtill at Samaria, is directed by an angel to depart thence, and *go towards the ſouth, unto the way that goeth from Jeruſalem to Gaza, which is deſert* And immediately, obedient to the heavenly call, *he aroſe and went* *Note*, Though we ſee not at firſt the reaſons on which God's providential diſpoſition of us is founded, yet when we bow to his command, we ſhall ſee cauſe to acknowledge his wiſdom and goodneſs

2 He there met a man of ſingular diſtinction, *an Ethiopian*, an inhabitant of Africa, *an eunuch*, either really ſuch, they being formerly often preferred to the firſt offices of ſtate, or this may ſignify his ſtation at the court, as the word is uſed of Potiphar, *Gen* xxxix 1 being a man *of great authority under Candace queen of the Ethiopians, who had the charge of all her treaſure*, a poſt of diſtinguiſhed eminence, *and had come to Jeruſalem for to worſhip*, either being a Jew, or a proſelyte to their religion *Note*, God hath taken ſome of all nations, and all ranks, to be to the praiſe of the glory of his grace

3 Philip receives an intimation from the Holy Spirit, *to go near, and join himſelf to this chariot*, where he found him reading aloud the prophet Eſaias, perhaps the portions which he had heard expounded at Jeruſalem, where though he muſt have heard of Chriſt and his apoſtles, yet he ſeems to have paid no regard to them, and was returning attached as much as ever to the Jewiſh religion *Note*, (1) The Lord, by ſtrange providences, often brings about great events; even when we travel on the road, we know not what good may be done, though among ſtrangers, if we have but the heart to ſpeak a word for Chriſt (2) The ſcriptures ſhould be much in our hands; they are the beſt companion on our journeys, and will ſupply matter for the choiceſt meditation (3) It is no evil for men of ſtation and affluence to ride in their chariots, if that, as well as every other gift, be ſanctified by the word of God, and by prayer

4 Philip hearing him read the prophet Eſaias, puts a queſtion to him of great moment, and which we ſhould often put to ourſelves, when peruſing the ſacred oracles, *Underſtandeſt thou what thou readeſt?* His reply was ſingularly humble far from taking the queſtion ill, though from a ſtranger on foot, and meanly dreſſed, he anſwers with the moſt modeſt acknowledgment of his own poor attainments, *How can I, except ſome man ſhould guide me? and*, willing to be inſtructed, and glad to embrace every opportunity of increaſing his knowledge of theſe bleſſed propheciecs, *he deſired Philip*, who appeared to be intelligent in theſe matters, *to come up* into the chariot, *and ſit with him*, well judging that the honour he did the evangeliſt, would be abundantly repaid by the inſtructions he ſhould receive *Note*, (1) To ſhew a teachable ſpirit, is the ſureſt way to become wiſe unto ſalvation (2) The ſcriptures, eſpecially the prophecies, are many of them hard to be underſtood, and we ſhould therefore call in the aſſiſtance of good men, and good books, to aſſiſt our enquiries, and above all, look up to the Spirit of wiſdom for an enlightened underſtanding

5 This illuſtrious Ethiopian having ſeated him in the chariot, enquires of Philip the meaning of the paſſage he had been reading, *Iſa* liii 7, 8 where, according to the ſeptuagint verſion, it was written, *He was led as a ſheep to the ſlaughter, and like a lamb dumb before his ſhearer, ſo opened he not his mouth In his humiliation his judgment was taken away, and who ſhall declare his generation? for his life is taken from the earth*, the Ethiopian therefore begs Philip to inform him, of whom the prophet in this paſſage ſpeaks, *of himſelf, or of ſome other man?* Hereupon *Philip opened his mouth, and*, glad of ſo fair an opening, *began at the ſame ſcripture, and preached unto him Jeſus*, the great ſubject of the prophecy He was *the ſheep led to the ſlaughter*, willingly offering himſelf a ſacrifice for the ſins of his people, ſilent *before his ſhearers as a lamb*, neither upbraiding nor threatning, but meek and patient under all the indignities ſhewn him, he humbled himſelf to the loweſt ſtate, to the life of a ſervant, and the death of a ſlave *In his humiliation his judgment was taken away*, he was treated in the moſt unjuſt and cruel manner, hurried from one judgment ſeat to another, and though confeſſedly innocent, executed as the vileſt of malefactors *and who ſhall declare his generation?* the wickedneſs and impiety of the men of that age in which he ſuffered theſe things, *for his life is taken from the earth*, and by wicked hands he was crucified and ſlain, cut off as a criminal un-

unworthy to live Yet God raised him from the dead, exalted him to his right hand, in token of his fullest approbation, and having accepted his sacrifice for the sins of his people, hath given power to his ministers to preach remission of sins to all nations, and by the ordinance of baptism, to admit those who professed faith in him to baptism, as the initiatory ordinance into his church

6 Convinced of the truth by Philip's discourse, he embraced the gospel of Jesus which the evangelist preached, and *as they went on their way*, Philip opening the truth at large, and the eunuch attentively listening, *they came unto a certain water*, when, desirous to make open profession of his faith by baptism, if Philip had no objection, he humbly proposes it, that he might be baptized *Philip said, If thou believest with all thine heart*, the great truths on which I have been discoursing, trusting on Jesus alone for pardon, righteousness, and salvation, and willing to yield thyself to his government and service, *thou mayest He answered, I believe that Jesus Christ is the Son of God*, the divine, all-sufficient, and promised Saviour, the true Messiah, God incarnate Satisfied with this confession of his faith, Philip consents to his proposal, and the eunuch ordering his chariot to stop, *they went down into the water, both Philip and the eunuch, and he baptized him* *Note*, (1) Nothing affects the consciences of men like the preaching of a crucified Jesus (2) Faith is not a mere speculative assent to gospel truths, but the embracing with the heart a salvation suited to the case of a lost sinner (3) No man can truly say that Jesus is the Christ, but by the Spirit of God, and the real knowledge of this truth secures eternal life

7 Philip and the eunuch are parted as miraculously as they were brought together *When they were come up out of the water, the Spirit of the Lord caught away Philip, that the eunuch saw him no more*, and this miracle served to bear testimony to his doctrine, *and he went on his way rejoicing* in Christ Jesus, with whose salvation he was now become acquainted, and happy in the hope of carrying the glad tidings to his countrymen *But Philip was found at Azotus*, or Ashdod, upwards of thirty miles from Gaza, *and passing through, he preached* as he travelled, *in all the cities, till he came to Cesarea*, where afterwards, it seems, he chiefly took up his abode, *Acts* xx 8

CHAP IX

In this chapter we have, 1 The famous story of St Paul's conversion (1) His awakening call as he went to Damascus, ver 1—9 *(2) How he was baptized by Ananias*, ver 10—19 *(3) How he immediately preached the faith of Christ*, ver 20—22 *(4) How he was persecuted, and narrowly escaped with his life*, ver 23—25 *(5) How he was admitted among the brethren at Jerusalem, how he preached and was persecuted there*, ver 26—30 *(6) The rest and quietness which the churches enjoyed for some time after this*, ver 31 *2 The cure wrought by Peter on Æneas, who had long been laid up of a palsy*, ver 32—35 *3. The raising of Tabitha from death to life at the prayer of Peter*, ver 36—44

a Chap. viii 3. Gal. i 13. 1 Tim. i 13. — 1. AND [a] Saul yet breathing out threatnings and
slaughter against the disciples of the Lord, went
unto the high-priest, 2 And desired of him letters to
b Chap. xix 9, 23. — Damascus to the synagogues, that if he found any of [b]
this way, whether they were men or women, he might
c Chap. xxii 6 & xxvi 12. 1 Cor. xv 8. — bring them bound unto Jerusalem 3 And [c] as he
journeyed, he came near Damascus and suddenly there
shined round about him a light from heaven 4 And
he fell to the earth, and heard a voice saying unto him,
d Matt. xxv 40, &c. — Saul, Saul, [d] why persecutest thou me? 5 And he said,
Who art thou, Lord? And the Lord said, I am Jesus
e Chap. v 39. — whom thou persecutest [e] *It is* hard for thee to kick a-
gainst the pricks 6 And he trembling and astonished
f Luke iii 10. Chap. ii 37. & xvi 30. — said, Lord, [f] what wilt thou have me to do? And the
Lord *said* unto him, Arise, and go into the city, and it
g Dan. x 7. Chap. xxii 9. & xxvi 13. — shall be told thee what thou must do 7 And [g] the men
which journeyed with him stood speechless, hearing a
voice, but seeing no man 8 And Saul arose from the
earth, and when his eyes were opened, he saw no man
but they led him by the hand, and brought *him* into
Damascus 9 And he was three days without sight, and
neither did eat nor drink

(ver 1—9) Saul the bloody persecutor of the church, again appears, but hence forward to support a very different character His Hebrew name, *Saul*, signifies *desired*, his Roman name, *Paul, little* He was by birth a Cilician, of the city of Tarsus, sprung from the tribe of Benjamin, a Hebrew of Hebrews, skilled deeply in Grecian literature, as well as Jewish theology, brought up under the greatest masters of the time, a very zealot for the law, a man of rank, though a tent-maker (it being a custom with the Jews to instruct all those, who were bred scholars, in some handicraft trade) and a Roman, born a freeman of that city His conversion, which holds so distinguished a place in the records of Christianity, happened about a year after our Lord's ascension We are here told, in conformity with the former account given of him,

1 With what rage he persecuted the disciples of Jesus *He yet breathed out threatnings and slaughter*, not satiated with the blood of martyrs which he had shed, his fury grasped at the utter extirpation of the Christian name, determined to intimidate them from their profession, and drive them to blaspheme, or murder the obstinately faithful For this end, not content with the mischief he had done at Jerusalem, he pursued them to other cities, and *desired*, and obtained, *letters from the high-priest*, and *the whole estate of the elders*, Acts xxii 5 empowering him to act in their name at Damascus, and if in the synagogue there he found any *of this way*, favourers of this new religion, Christianity, *whether they were men or women, he might bring them bound unto Jerusalem*, to be tried and punished by their spiritual court, the Sanhedrim Thus was Saul employed when the Lord stopped him in his mad career Let us admire the wonders of grace, and never despair of the chief of sinners

2 God marvellously arrests him in the midst of his mad career He was now arrived near the place of his destination, and already, in imagination, triumphed in the havock he should make but how far are God's ways above our ways, and his thoughts above our thoughts! When sinners are driving to the heighth of wickedness, he is sometimes pleased to magnify his power and grace, in bending their iron necks to his yoke *As he journeyed, he came near Damascus and suddenly there shined round about him a light from heaven*, brighter than the meridian sun, the dazzling lustre of which quite overpowered him, and the presence of Jesus in his glory filled him with such amazement *and* confusion, that *he fell to the earth*, unable to stand on his feet, or being more probably on horseback, he was struck down, as with a blast of lightning *Note*, Those whom God designs for eminent usefulness, he sometimes exercises with the deepest terrors and distress, and lays them in the lowest pit of humiliation

3 Christ having seized him as his prisoner, addresses him out of the glorious light which shone around him *He heard a voice saying, Saul, Saul*, Christ speaks with vehemence, as to one who stood on the precipice of ruin, insensible of his danger, and with fervent compassion, as desirous to snatch him from instant ruin, *why persecutest thou me?* with daring impiety lifting thy rebel arm against the Almighty, with black ingratitude thus returning the love of him who died to redeem thee, with cruel enmity persecuting those who never injured thee, and in them, my people, striking at me their Lord and Master *Note*, (1) When Christ comes with his Spirit, convincing the soul of sin, he brings the matter home to the conscience, and the sinner hears him say, Thou art the man (2) The Lord resents the insults shown to his people, as injuries done to himself

4 The affrighted criminal, now cited to answer at the bar of this justly offended Redeemer, with terror replies, *Who art thou, Lord* desirous to be acquainted with him, whose heavenly voice he heard *And the Lord said, I am Jesus, whom thou persecutest*, that name thou hast so often blasphemed, and against whom thou art now acting with such invenomed malice and enmity, *it is hard for thee to kick against the pricks*, as blind and self-destructive must these attempts against my church and people prove, as with the naked foot to kick against a sharp iron goad *Trembling and astonished*, Saul enquires, *Lord, what wilt thou have me to do?* A flood of light now broke in upon his soul, his sins, in all their aggravations, rose up to his view, the dreadful consequences he had justly to apprehend from the wrath of an offended Saviour, stared him in the face, and made him willing now to do and suffer any thing, if he may escape the vengeance which he hath provoked he earnestly begs information, if yet there may be hope of mercy, pardon, and salvation And the Lord said unto him, *Arise, and go into the city, and it shall be told thee what thou must do*, he leaves him for a while to ruminate in darkness on the past, yet with some gracious hope of hearing farther from him, for he might well conclude, that had Christ intended to destroy him, he would not thus have spared and spoken to him *Note*, (1) They who rebel against the convictions of their conscience, the warnings of God's word, and the calls of God's ministers, will pierce themselves through with many sorrows (2) When God's Spirit sets a man's sins in array before him, and opens his eyes to see the flaming gulph on the brink of which he stands, no marvel if horror and a terrible dread seize upon him, and like Belshazzar, his knees smite against each other (3) Our terrors of conscience must not drive us from Christ, but to him, enquiring into his will, and what hope of salvation remains for us Let not the greatest sinner add despair to all his crimes (4) Though the Lord may not give present ease, or relief, to the troubled conscience, yet we must wait his leisure, and be found at his feet, where never miserable soul yet perished

5 Saul's fellow-travellers, the guards, sent to assist him in executing the high priests and sanhedrim's commission, *stood speechless*, when risen from the ground to which they had been struck down, *hearing a voice*, some tremendous sound, like thunder, or words, the meaning of which they did not understand and though they heard Paul speak *seeing no man*, to whom he addressed himself

6 *Saul* himself *arose from the earth* at Christ's bidding, and now opening his eyelids, his sightless eyeballs no longer met the light of day, he is taken off from the view of outward objects, that he may turn his thoughts more intensely to what appears within Thus blind, his companions *led him by the hand, and brought him to Damascus*, a spectacle of wretchedness, where he purposed, a few moments before, in pomp to make his entry so soon can God change the sinner's mirth into mourning, and humble his pride in the dust. *Three days and nights* he continued dark in his body, and probably under deeper distress and darkness in his soul, *and he neither did eat nor drink* his troubled mind destroyed all relish for food, and in fasting and prayer he spent these three melancholy days, the most dreadful hours that he ever knew.

10 ¶ And there was a certain disciple at Damascus,
ʰ named Ananias, and to him said the Lord in a vision,
Ananias. And he said, Behold, I *am here*, Lord 11
And the Lord *said* unto him, Arise, and go into the
street which is called Straight, and inquire in the house
of Judas, for *one* called Saul ᵏ of Tarsus for behold, he
prayeth, 12 And hath seen in a vision a man named
Ananias, coming in, and putting *his* hand on him, that
he might receive his sight 13 Then Ananias answered,
Lord, I have heard by many of this man, ˡ how
much evil he hath done to thy saints at Jerusalem 14
And here he hath authority from the chief priests, to
bind all ˡ that call on thy name 15 But the Lord said
unto him, Go thy way for ᵐ he is a chosen vessel unto
me, ⁿ to bear my name before the ᵒ Gentiles, and ᵖ kings,
and the children of Israel 16 For ᑫ I will shew him
how great things he must suffer for my name's sake
17 And ʳ Ananias went his way, and entred into the
house, and ˢ putting his hands on him, said, Brother
Saul, the Lord (*even* Jesus that appeared unto thee in
the way as thou camest) hath sent me, that thou mightest
receive thy sight, and ᵗ be filled with the Holy Ghost.
18 And immediately there fell from his eyes as it had
been scales, and he received sight forthwith, and arose,
and was baptized 19 And when he had received
meat, he was strengthened Then was Saul certain days
with the disciples which were at Damascus 20 And
straightway he preached Christ in the synagogues, that ᵘ
he is the Son of God 21 But all that heard *him* were
amazed, and said, ˣ Is not this he that destroyed them
which called on this name in Jerusalem, and came hither
for that intent, that he might bring them bound unto
the chief priests? 22 But Saul increased the more in
strength, and confounded the Jews which dwelt at Damascus,
proving that this is very Christ

v 10—22 The Lord now returns to visit the distressed, afflicted Saul, for he will not leave those to despair whom he calls down with convictions

1 The Lord in a vision speaks to a disciple at Damascus named Ananias, who, with ready attention and obedience, attends his order. He bids him *arise, and go into the street which is called Straight, and enquire in the house of Judas, for one Saul of Tarsus*, a person of distinguished name, for *behold*, an astonishing change is passed upon him, humbled in the dust *he prayeth, and hath*, in answer to his prayer, *seen in a vision a man named Ananias, coming in, and putting his hand on him, that he might receive his sight*; he being therefore the person pointed out for this service, must go without delay *Note*, (1) God sees the distresses of the afflicted, he will hear their cry, and will help them (2) The moment a soul is truly turned to God, the evidence of spiritual life will immediately appear, *behold, he prayeth* Those who are prayerless, are evidently yet dead in trespasses and sin (3) When Christ calls us to his service, we should with delight and readiness answer, Here am I

2 Ananias at first objects to go but is quickly satisfied The well-known character of Saul made him apprehensive of danger, should he put himself within the reach of such a bigotted persecutor, who had not only done so much evil at Jerusalem, but had come to Damascus, armed with the chief priests commission, to bind all that called on the name of Jesus and carry them as criminals to Jerusalem But Christ silences his objections, *the Lord said unto him, Go thy way*, there is no danger, *for he is a chosen vessel unto me*, appointed to distinguished honour and eminent usefulness, *to bear my name before the Gentiles, and kings, and the children of Israel*, preaching that faith he once destroyed *For I will shew him how great things he must suffer for my name's sake*, and will enable him to endure the most severe persecutions, and at last, in testimony of the truth of his mission, to seal it with his blood *Note*, (1) All God's people are elect vessels, though some are chosen to more distinguished honour and usefulness than others (2) They who embark in Christ's cause, especially as ministers of his gospel, must prepare for the cross, and learn to endure hardness, as good soldiers

3 Ananias hereupon immediately obeys, and entering the house where Saul lodged, and *putting his hands on him, said, Brother Saul*, now adopted into the family of God, a child of grace, an heir of glory with us, and henceforward separated into the ministry of the gospel, *the Lord (even Jesus that appeared to thee in the way as thou camest*, and struck thee with blindness) *hath sent me, that thou mightest receive thy bodily sight*, the emblem of the happier illumination of thy soul, with the light of truth, *and* that thou mightest *be filled with the Holy Ghost*, with his miraculous gifts, as well as the most abundant measure of his grace, in order to qualify thee for the great and glorious service to which thou art appointed *Note*, (1) When God is pleased to work a change on the vilest, we must, with open arms, receive them as our brethren (2) Where the Lord wounds, he will heal

4 No sooner had Ananias spoken, than the cure was wrought The scales fell from his eyes, *he received sight forthwith, and arose, and was baptized*, openly making profession of that faith which he now most heartily embraced No longer the blind Pharisee, but the enlightened Christian, delivered from the horrible darkness of terrifying guilt, and rejoicing in the sun of righteousness arisen upon him with healing in his wings

5 Behold the fierce persecutor instantly commencing a faithful preacher Having refreshed himself with proper food after so long fasting, he was strengthened in body, as well as soul, *then* he joined the faithful disciples of Jesus at Damascus, and instead of the threatnings he lately breathed against them, he was united with them in the closest bonds of Christian communion, appeared openly among them, and immediately *preached Christ in the synagogues, that he is the Son of God*, the true Messiah, to the astonishment of all who heard him, for knowing his past conduct, and the intention of his journey thither, they could not but stand amazed at this wondrous change But far from being ashamed of the apostacy with which some reproached him, or dubious about the merits of that cause, which his former Jewish friends so decried, and still with bitterness opposed, *Saul increased the more in strength*, supernaturally taught and strengthened, and daily growing more bold and zealous in defence of that faith which he had embraced, pleading the cause of Jesus against every gainsayer, and *confounded the Jews which dwelt at Damascus, proving that this is very Christ*, by such irrefragable arguments, as left them nothing to reply *Note*, (1) Christ is the glorious subject, on which his faithful ministers delight to dwell (2) It justly excites astonishment, and serves for a fresh confirmation of the truth of the gospel, when bitter opposers, by the power of divine grace, appear advocates for the cause which they once decried

23 ¶ And after that many days were fulfilled, the
Jews took counsel to kill him 24 But ʸ their laying
await was known of Saul and they watched the gates
day and night to kill him 25 Then the disciples took
him by night, and ᶻ let *him* down by the wall in a
basket 26 And ᵃ when Saul was come to Jerusalem,
he assayed to join himself to the disciples but they were
all afraid of him, and believed not that he was a disciple
27 But ᵇ Barnabas took him, and brought *him* to the
apostles, and declared unto them how he had seen the
Lord in the way, and that he had spoken to him, and
how he had preached boldly at Damascus in the name of
Jesus 28 And ᶜ he was with them coming in and going
out at Jerusalem 29 And ᵈ he spake boldly in the
name of the Lord Jesus, and disputed against the Grecians,
ᵉ but they went about to slay him 30 *Which*
when the brethren knew, they brought him down to
Cesarea, and sent him forth to Tarsus 31 Then ᶠ had
the churches rest throughout all Judea, and Galilee,
and Samaria, and were edified, and walking in the fear
of the Lord, and in the comfort of the Holy Ghost,
were multiplied

v 23—31 The transactions here recorded, happened three years after the foregoing, during which, the apostle went into Arabia, preaching to the Jews who were settled in that country, and then returned again to Damascus, Gal i 17, 18 where we find,

1 The narrow escape he had out of the jaws of his inveterate persecutors Enraged at his apostacy from them, they ...

regarded it, and unable to bear the powerful energy of his discourses, inculcating the glorious truths of the gospel, they resolved to dispatch him, and having gained the governor to their side, they watched the gates day and night in order to murder him but impotent is the malice of the wicked against those whom the Lord will protect, their scheme was discovered either by some friend, or by revelation, and the brethren, in order to elude the vigilance of these bloody-minded persecutors, let the apostle *down by the wall in a basket by night*, and so he escaped *Note*, If we are for the Lord's sake brought into the greatest straits and temptations, he is still able to make a way for us to escape

2 He proceeded to Jerusalem, and there he met new difficulties *See Gal* i 18

(1) From the brethren themselves He immediately *assayed to join himself to the disciples*, his former noble friends he had now forsaken, and wished to be admitted among the poor and persecuted disciples of Jesus *but they were at first afraid of him*, not having heard ought about him probably during the three years he was in Arabia, *and believed not that he was a disciple* knowing his past enmity, they suspected his present conversion might be feigned Caution is needful, we should be well acquainted with those whom we admit into our communion, least they be wolves in sheep's cloathing *believe not every spirit* But Barnabas, who had received full information concerning Paul's case, soon satisfied the minds of the disciples, and bringing Paul to the apostles James and Peter, who alone were then at Jerusalem, he told them all the circumstances of his extraordinary conversion, and his approved fidelity and zealous labours ever since, particularly at Damascus Hereupon they gladly gave him the right hand of fellowship, and he appeared publickly among the disciples, going in and out with them, joining in their worshipping assemblies, *and spake boldly in the name of Jesus* They who have so good a cause, may well courageously appear in defence of it, Christ's service will bear us out

(2) From the Jews The Hellenists, who were most bigotted to Judaism, encountered him, and he *disputed* with them with such evidence, power, and demonstration, that unable to stand before the force of his arguments, they determined to silence him by the sword Therefore, after a short abode of fifteen days at Jerusalem, having received a revelation from God, directing him in his labours, *Acts* xxii 17, 18 and the brethren being sollicitous for his safety, he was brought by them as far as Cesarea, and from thence was sent to Tarsus, his native city, where he continued preaching the gospel, till Barnabas joined him, *chap* xi 25 *Note*, (1) It is a sure sign of a bad cause, where recourse is had to violence instead of argument (2) Whatever plots the wicked contrive against the ministers of truth, the Lord will take care of them, till they have finished their testimony

3 *Then had the churches rest throughout all Judea, and Galilee, and Samaria*, Paul being removed, the flames of persecution which were again kindling, abated and a little respite was a great mercy to them, after they had been so harrassed by their foes, nor did they fail to improve it, they *were edified* in knowledge and faith, enjoying more quietly the means of grace, and assembling more undisturbed, *and walking in the fear of God*, a filial, reverent fear, which made them circumspect and holy in all manner of conversation, *and in the comfort of the Holy Ghost*, enjoying much of his light, love, and consolations, *were multiplied*, increasing in numbers, and growing in grace *Note*, They who walk most nearly and humbly with God, will enjoy most of the comforts of his Spirit

32 ¶ And it came to pass, as Peter passed through-
out all *quarters*, he came down also to the saints which
dwelt at Lydda 33 And there he found a certain man
named Eneas, which had kept his bed eight years, and
was sick of the palsy 34 And Peter said unto him,
Eneas, Jesus Christ maketh thee whole arise and make
thy bed And he arose immediately 35 And all that
f 1 Chron v 16. dwelt at Lydda, and f Saron, saw him, and turned to
the Lord

v 32—35 The historian for a while leaves Paul to his labours, and returns to relate the ministry of Peter

1 He travelled about to visit the churches which had been planted, to confirm the disciples, and ordain ministers among them, and among other places, *he came down to the saints which dwelt at Lydda* *Note*, They who are called to be Christians, are by their very profession saints, separated from the world, and devoted to God

2 Peter there performed a notable miracle, which is here recorded A man, whose name was Eneas, had been bed ridden eight years, through the palsy, and all possibility of a cure by human means, was despaired of, but when the apostle saw him, he said, *Eneas, Jesus Christ maketh thee whole arise, and make thy bed* and instantly the cure was wrought, and the man was restored to perfect health and strength *Note*, (1) By nature we are absolutely impotent to all good, and no man can afford us the least relief (2) Christ is the great physician, he can cure those whose state is the most deplorable and desperate (3) When he speaks to the soul, power accompanies his word, and we are enabled to rise from the bed of spiritual weakness and impotence, by the mighty power of his grace

3 Great was the effect produced by this miracle The people of Lydda and Saron in general, convinced of the divine power evident in the cure, *turned to the Lord*, and made profession of Christianity, and then was the scripture eminently fulfilled, which said, *They should see the glory of the Lord, and become a fold of flocks*, Isa xxxv 2 lxv 10

36 ¶ Now there was at Joppa a certain disciple
named Tabitha, which by interpretation is called † Dor-
† i e A doe kind of deer cas this woman was g full of good works and alms-
g 1 Tim ii 8 deeds which she did 37 And it came to pass in those
days, that she was sick, and died whom when they had
h Chap i 13 washed, they laid *her* in h an upper chamber 38 And
forasmuch as Lydda was nigh to Joppa, and the disciples
had heard that Peter was there, they sent unto him two
men, desiring *him* that he would not delay to come to
them 39 Then Peter arose, and went with them
When he was come, they brought him into the upper
chamber and all the widows stood by him weeping,
and shewing the coats and garments which Dorcas made
while she was with them 40 But Peter put them all
forth, and i kneeled down and prayed, and turning *him* i Chap vii 60.
to the body, said, Tabitha, arise And she opened her
eyes and when she saw Peter, she sat up 41 And he
gave her his hand, and lift her up and when he had
called the saints and widows, presented her alive 42
And it was known throughout all Joppa, and many be-
lieved in the Lord 43 And it came to pass, that he
tarried many days in Joppa with one k Simon a tanner k Chap x 6

v 36—43 Another, and a still greater miracle is here wrought, in confirmation of the divine authority, under which Peter acted We have,

1 The sickness and death of an excellent woman, whose name was *Tabitha*, in Greek, *Dorcas*, or a Doe, she was an inhabitress of Joppa, and adorned the profession of Christianity which she made, being full *of good works*, the genuine proofs of the truth of the faith she possessed, *and of alms-deeds which she did*, not only bestowing her substance liberally to the necessitous, but labouring with her hands, that she might be more extensive in her beneficence, for real Christians will shew the fruits of grace, their works will speak their praise In the midst of her useful life, it pleased God to cut her off, she fell sick and died From the ravages of mortality the best have no exemption, and according to their custom, they had now washed the body, and laid it out for interment

2 The disciples at Joppa who heard of Peter's being so near as Lydda, and of the miracle he had there wrought, sent two of their number to him, informing him of the present afflictive Providence, and intreating him to come to them, to comfort them under their grief, and probably with some expectations, that he might yet restore to life their departed sister

3 Peter, without delay, complied with their request, and when he came, found the body laid out in the upper chamber, and the widows lamenting their loss of such a bountiful friend, shewing the coats and garments which perhaps they then wore, the tokens of her charity, diligence, and pity to the poor, whilst she was with them *Note*, (1) The fatherless and widows are peculiar objects of compassion, to them the hand of charity should be liberally stretched forth (2) Though they who are truly charitable will ever be silent, and desire no commendation or return, yet those who reap the blessings of their bounty, ought not to be so [illegible] gratitude, at least, to the tribute which they owe

4 Peter, who following his master's example, *Matt* ix 25 declined all appearance of vain-glory, put forth the company, and after kneeling down and praying, he turned to the body, and said, *Tabitha, arise*, in the full confidence of the power which accompanied his word, and immediately opening her eyes, which had been closed in death, when *she saw Peter, she sat up*, and Peter giving her his hand, assisted her to rise from the bier where she lay, and calling the widows, *presented her alive*, to their great astonishment and joy

5 The fame of the miracle quickly spread through Joppa, and was in every body's mouth, and many, struck with the evidence of God's approbation of the doctrine which Peter preached, *believed in the Lord*, and made public profession of his gospel Encouraged by such a prospect of success, the apostle made some considerable abode in that place, lodging in the house of *one Simon a tanner*, satisfied with any accommodations, and only intent upon preaching the gospel of his adored Lord and Master

CHAP

CHAP X

¶ Gentiles here begin to be admitted into the church 1 *Cornelius is directed by a viſion to ſend for Peter, and ſends for him accordingly,* ver 1—8 2 *Peter is directed by a viſion to go to Cornelius, though he was a Gentile,* ver 9—23 3 *The happy interview between Peter and Cornelius at Ceſarea,* ver 24—33 4 *The ſermon Peter preached in the houſe of Cornelius to him and to his friends,* ver 34—43 5 *The baptizing of Cornelius and his friends with the Holy Ghoſt firſt, and then with water,* ver 44—48

1 THere was a certain man in Ceſarea, called Cornelius, a centurion of the band called the Italian
band, 2 [a] A devout *man*, and one that feared God with [a Chap xxii 12]
all his houſe, which gave much alms to the people, and
prayed to God alway 3 He ſaw in a viſion evidently,
about the ninth hour of the day, an angel of God coming
in to him, and ſaying unto him, Cornelius 4 And
when he looked on him, he was afraid, and ſaid, What
is it, Lord? And he ſaid unto him, Thy prayers and
thine alms are come up for a memorial before God 5
And now ſend men to Joppa, and call for *one* [b] Simon, [b Ver 32]
whoſe ſurname is Peter 6 He lodgeth with one [c] Simon a tanner, whoſe houſe is by the ſea-ſide [d] he ſhall [c Chap ix 43] [d Ibid]
tell thee what thou oughteſt to do 7 And when the
angel, which ſpake unto Cornelius, was departed, he
called two of his houſhold ſervants, and a devout ſoldier
of them that waited on him continually 8 And when
he had declared all *theſe* things unto them, [e] he ſent them [e Ver Chap xi]
to Joppa

¶ 1—8 The goſpel had for about ſeven years been preached to Jews only, and the apoſtles as yet ſeem not to be fully apprized of the extent of their commiſſion But now a door of faith is opened to the Gentiles, and Peter is firſt ſent expreſsly to preach the goſpel to them We have an account,

1 Of Cornelius, the firſt fruits of the Gentiles unto Chriſt He was a centurion, captain over a hundred ſoldiers, belonging to the regiment or band called *the Italian*, in garriſon at Ceſarea, and though arms were his profeſſion, and from a Gentile nothing good could well be expected, yet he was ſingularly *devout*, having abandoned the idolatry in which he was bred, and become a proſelyte of righteouſneſs, worſhipping and fearing *God with all his houſe*, who were influenced by his pious example, a man of diſtinguiſhed liberality, who *gave much alms to the people*, Jews or Gentiles, who appeared truly neceſſitous, *and prayed to God always*, obſerving the Jewiſh ſtated hours of prayer *Note*, (1) It is no diſparagement to a ſoldier to be found upon his knees he who truly fears God, will be moſt ready to fight and die for his country (2) Where the maſter of a family fears God, we may be aſſured his houſe will be a houſe of prayer (3) Charity is the inſeparable attendant on a gracious character, whilſt a niggard's hand and heart prove the total abſence of vital godlineſs

2 An angel appears to Cornelius as he was at prayer, about three o'clock in the afternoon, at the time of the evening oblation Affrighted with this celeſtial viſitant, the centurion with deepeſt reverence deſires to know the purport of his coming, fearing leſt he brought ſome meſſage of evil But the angel ſoon quieted his fears, and ſaid unto him, *Thy prayers and thine alms are come up for a memorial before God*, are graciouſly accepted as the genuine fruit of thy faith and love, according to the meaſure of light thou haſt received *And now ſend men to Joppa, and call for one Simon, whoſe ſurname is Peter, he lodgeth with one Simon a tanner, whoſe houſe is by the ſea ſide, he ſhall tell thee what thou oughteſt to do* Cornelius ſeems already to have been a proſelyte, and to have been living in the faith of the promiſed Meſſiah, according to the prophecies, but as yet he had not heard him preached, or actually become incarnate, and this was moſt needful for him to know, according to the preſent diſpenſation of grace, in order to his ſalvation And to put an honour on the goſpel miniſtry, the angel gives him no further information, but refers him to the diſtinct, appointed miniſter of the word

3 No ſooner was the angel departed, than immediately Cornelius called two of *his houſhold ſervants, and a devout ſoldier that waited on him continually*, who being truly religious like his maſter, was always kept near his perſon To theſe he related his extraordinary viſion, and ordered them early in the morning to proceed to Joppa, and telling Peter the occaſion, to deſire he would return with them to Ceſarea *Note*, They who are truly godly themſelves, delight to have thoſe near them as ſervants, who are partakers of the ſame grace

9 ¶ On the morrow as they went on their journey, [f Chap xi 5]
and drew nigh unto the city, [f] Peter went up upon the
houſe top to pray, about the ſixth hour 10 And he
became very hungry, and would have eaten but while
they made ready, he fell into a trance, 11 And [g] ſaw [g Chap vii 56 Rev iv 1]
heaven opened, and a certain veſſel deſcending unto him,
as it had been a great ſheet, knit at the four corners, and
let down to the earth 12 Wherein were all manner of
four-footed beaſts of the earth, and wild beaſts, and
creeping things, and fowls of the air 13 And there
came a voice to him, Riſe, Peter, kill, and eat 14
But Peter ſaid, Not ſo, Lord, for I have never eaten [h] [h Lev xi 4, &c Deut xiv 3, &c]
any thing that is common or unclean 15 And the
voice *ſpake* unto him again the ſecond time, [i] What God [i Ver 28 Mat xv 11 Chap xi 9 Rom xiv 14 1 Tim iv 4 Tit i 15]
hath cleanſed, *that* call not thou common 16 This
was done thrice and the veſſel was received up again
into heaven 17 Now while Peter doubted in himſelf
what this viſion which he had ſeen ſhould mean, behold, the men which were ſent from Cornelius, had
made enquiry for Simon's houſe, and ſtood before the
gate, 18 And called, and aſked whether Simon which
was ſurnamed Peter, were lodged there. 19 ¶ While
Peter thought on the viſion, the Spirit ſaid unto him,
Behold three men ſeek thee 20 [k] Ariſe therefore, and [k Chap xv 7]
get thee down, and go with them, doubting nothing
for I have ſent them

¶ 9—20 The ſervants of Cornelius departing early in queſt of Peter, the Lord prepares him to give them a welcome reception He, like his countrymen, was ſtill prejudiced againſt the Gentiles, and thought all familiar communication with them was unlawful, the Lord therefore in a marvellous way is pleaſed to over rule their prepoſſeſſion.

1 A viſion appears to him when he went up to the top of the houſe to pray, where he might be moſt retired, juſt before the ſervants of Cornelius arrived It was noon, and whilſt he was thus devoutly engaged, *he became very hungry, and would have eaten, but while they made ready* ſome refreſhment for him, *he fell into a trance*, a ſupernatural ecſtacy came upon him, *and*, to ſhew him the myſtery of the calling of the Gentiles into the church, whom he had been uſed to regard as perſons unclean, *he ſaw heaven opened*, in token of ſome farther revelation of God's will now about to be made to him, *and a certain veſſel deſcending unto him, as it had been a great ſheet knit at the four corners, and let down to the earth, wherein*, ſuitably to his preſent hungry ſituation, *there were all manner of four-footed beaſts of the earth, and wild beaſts, and creeping things, and fowls of the air, and there came a voice to him*, ſaying, *Riſe, Peter, kill and eat*, without diſtinction of clean or unclean Peter, though hungry, objected to the propoſal, *Not ſo, Lord* he could not think of tranſgreſſing the ceremonial law, *for*, ſaith he, *I have never eaten any thing that is common or unclean* The voice *a ſecond time* addreſſed him, ſaying, *What God hath cleanſed, that call not thou common* He who firſt commanded a diſtinction of meats, had a right to abrogate it again if he pleaſed, and as he had taken the Jews for his peculiar people, he might alſo bring the Gentiles to ſhare the bleſſings of the ſame gracious covenant and as this was now his purpoſe, Peter might ſafely eat whatever was ſet before him, and go and converſe with, and preach to the Gentiles, without fear of pollution *This was done thrice*, to ſhew the certainty of the viſion, and engage his attention to it, *and the veſſel was received up again into heaven*

2 The viſion ſoon receives an explication Peter was now ſeriouſly conſidering, but at a loſs to know what this viſion meant, and juſt then the men whom Cornelius had ſent were at the door enquiring for him The Spirit therefore gives him an intimation what meſſenger waited for him below, and tho' they were Gentiles, bid him go with them, *doubting nothing* of the unlawfulneſs of being in their company, for they were divinely ſent by his order. *Note*, Whilſt we are in ſimplicity deſiring in our difficulties to know God's will, he will by ſome gracious intimation direct us aright

21 Then Peter went down to the men which were
ſent unto him from Cornelius, and ſaid, Behold, I am
he whom ye ſeek what *is* the cauſe wherefore ye are
come? 22 And they ſaid, Cornelius the centurion, [l] a [l Ver 1 Chap xxii 12]
juſt man, and one that feareth God, and of good report
among all the nation of the Jews, was warned from God
by an holy angel, to ſend for thee into his houſe, and to
hear words of thee 23 Then called he them in, and
lodged *them* And on the morrow Peter went away with
them, and certain brethren from Joppa accompanied
him 24 And the morrow after they entered into Ceſarea And Cornelius waited for them, and had called together his kinſmen and near friends 25 And as Peter
was coming in, Cornelius met him, and fell down at his
feet, and worſhipped *him* 26 But Peter took him up,
ſaying,

saying, Stand up, [m] I myself also am a man 27 And
as he talked with him, he went in, and found [n] many
that were come together 28 And he said unto them,
Ye know how that [o] it is an unlawful thing for a man
that is a Jew, to keep company, or come unto one of
another nation but [p] God hath shewed me, that I should
not call any man common or unclean 29 Therefore
came I *unto you* without gainsaying, as soon as I was sent
for. I ask therefore for what intent ye have sent for me
30 And Cornelius said, Four days ago I was fasting
until this hour, and at the ninth hour I prayed in my
house, and behold, [q] a man stood before me [r] in bright
clothing, 31 And said, Cornelius, thy prayer is heard,
and thine alms are had in remembrance in the sight of
God 32 Send therefore to Joppa, and call hither
Simon whose surname is Peter, he is lodged in the house
of *one* Simon a tanner, by the sea-side, who when he
cometh, shall speak unto thee. 33 Immediately therefore
I sent to thee, and thou hast well done that thou art
come Now therefore are we all here present before God,
to hear all things that are commanded thee of God.

v 21—33 Peter, having received full satisfaction, went down without delay to the messengers

1 Having told them he was the person whom they sought, he desired to be informed of the cause of their coming and *they said, Cornelius the centurion, a just man,* eminent for his probity and integrity among men, *and one that feareth God,* though a Gentile, a worshipper of the God of Israel, *and of good report among all the nation of the Jews,* who respect his amiable and exemplary character, *was warned of God by an holy angel to send for thee into his house, and to hear words of thee* concerning the things that make for his everlasting peace

2 Peter courteously hereupon received and lodged the messengers that night, *and on the morrow went away with them for Cesarea,* accompanied by certain brethren from Joppa, who might desire to be present at this interview, or more probably went at Peter's request, that they might be witnesses for him, if at any time he should be blamed by his Jewish brethren for visiting a Gentile family *Note,* (1) It becomes ministers and all Christians to be hospitable (2) When there is danger that our conduct may be censured, or our conversation misrepresented, it is prudent to have witnesses for what passes, to whom we can appeal

3 The second day, in the afternoon, Peter and the messengers entered Cesarea, where Cornelius with eager expectation waited his arrival, having called *his kinsmen and near friends* to share with him the blessing of Peter's discourse *Note,* The greatest kindness we can shew our friends is to invite them to partake with us our spiritual mercies, and to join in our religious exercises

4 Cornelius received the Apostle with deepest reverence and respect, and paid him honour which Peter thought excessive, he fell at his feet, as he entered the house, and *worshipped* him, prostrate before him, as if he had been the mightiest potentate But the apostle, too humble and modest to accept such profound admiration, *took him up,* and would not suffer him to stay in that posture, *saying, Stand up I myself am also a man,* a poor sinful worm, though honoured with this office of apostleship And thereupon familiarly conversing with him, he entered into the house, where a number of persons was assembled, desirous to hear Peter's words, and affording him a larger field of usefulness than he might have expected *Note,* It is a great encouragement to speak where we meet a large and attentive audience

5 Peter enquires the cause wherefore Cornelius sent for him, saying to him and the company, *Ye know that it is unlawful,* and looked upon as an abominable thing, *for one that is a Jew,* as I am, *to keep company or come unto one of another nation* in any way of familiar intercourse *But,* though I long thought so, *God hath* of late *shewed me that I should not call any man common or unclean,* on account of his being of a different nation Obedient *therefore* to the admonition of God, *came I unto you, without gainsaying, as soon as I was sent for* perfectly persuaded of his will in this matter *I ask therefore for what intent ye have sent for me?* that I may be able suitably to improve the present opportunity, to God's glory, and for your good

6 Cornelius relates the late occurrences, which occasioned the present meeting *Four days ago I was fasting until this hour, and at the ninth hour I prayed in my house,* when the evening sacrifice was offering, the usual hour of prayer, *and behold,* in answer to my requests for divine direction and guidance, *a man stood before me in bright clothing,* an angel in human form, *and,* addressing me, *said, Cornelius, thy prayer is heard, and thine alms are had in remembrance in the sight of God Send therefore to Joppa, and call hither Simon, whose surname is Peter, he is lodged in the house of one Simon, a tanner, by the sea side, who, when he cometh, shall speak unto thee,* and give thee the direction thou art seeking *Immediately therefore* without delay, *I sent to thee, and thou hast well done that thou art come* We are all [illegible] and [illegible] come to us, and doubt not but it will be greatly pleasing to God

Now therefore are we all here present before God, met in his fear, hoping for his mercy, and expecting his special presence and blessing, seriously disposed *to hear,* and desirous to embrace and obey *all things that are commanded thee of God,* whom we with all reverence receive as a messenger expressly sent from him to lead us in the way of salvation *Note,* (1) The gospel then comes with effect, when those who sit under it shew solemn attention and seriousness, receiving it not as the word of man, but as the word of God (2) They who are sincere with God desire to hear and know *all* his will, not merely what he promises, but what he commands, however displeasing it may be to flesh and blood

34 ¶ Then Peter opened *his* mouth, and said, [s] Of
a truth I perceive that God is no respecter of persons
35 But [t] in every nation, [u] he that feareth him, and
worketh righteousness, is accepted with him 36 The
word which God sent unto the children of Israel, [x] preach-
ing peace by Jesus Christ ([y] he is Lord of all) 37 That
word (*I say*) you know, which was published throughout
all Judea, and [z] began from Galilee, after the baptism
which John preached 38 How [a] God anointed Jesus
of Nazareth with the holy Ghost, and with power, who
went about doing good, and healing all that were op-
pressed of the devil for [b] God was with him 39 And
[c] we are witnesses of all things which he did, both in the
land of the Jews, and in Jerusalem whom they slew
and hanged on a tree 40 [d] Him God raised up the
third day, and shewed him openly, 41 [e] Not to all
the people, but unto witnesses, chosen before of God,
even to us, [f] who did eat and drink with him after he rose
from the dead 42 And [g] he commanded us to preach
unto the people, and to testify that [h] it is he which was
ordained of God *to be* the judge [i] of quick and dead
43 [k] To him give all the prophets witness, that through
his name [l] whosoever believeth in him, shall receive re-
mission of sins

v 34—43 Peter, on comparing his own vision with that which Cornelius related, was now fully persuaded of God's gracious designs towards the Gentiles, and therefore with great warmth of affection, delight, and earnestness, addressed this attentive auditory

1 He expresses his full persuasion, notwithstanding all his former prejudices, that the Lord had now abolished all national distinctions, and designed his gospel should indiscriminately be preached to Jews and Gentiles *Of a truth I perceive that God is no respecter of persons,* on account of any external circumstances of birth, rank, or country, *but in every nation, he that feareth him, and worketh righteousness, is accepted with him* Not that we are to conceive that any unenlightened Gentile was capable of fearing God or working righteousness by any power in himself, or that these are the ground of acceptance before God no they are only the fruits of faith, and are descriptive not of the conditions of acceptance with God, but of the person who is in a state of favour with him The meaning of the Apostle seems to be, That Gentiles, as well as Jews, though uncircumcised, were capable of partaking of God's favour through the gospel, and their works were accepted through faith Of this number Cornelius was one, who had known so much of the gospel doctrine as a proselyte, as to build his hopes thereon, and act [illegible] thereunto and God in mercy therefore was now leading him into fuller discoveries of the truth, as it is in Jesus

2 He refers them to the report that had been every where spread of the life, miracles, doctrines, death and resurrection of Jesus *The word which God sent unto the children of Israel, preaching peace by Jesus Christ,* the glad tidings of reconciliation with an offended God through him, (*He is Lord of all,* the self-existent Deity, God over all, and as Mediator incarnate invested with all power in heaven and earth) *that word, I say, you know, which was published throughout Judea, after the baptism which John preached,* by John himself and his disciples, the fame of which could not but have reached them, *How God anointed Jesus of Nazareth with the Holy Ghost and with power,* authorizing and enabling him to perform the most astonishing miracles in proof of his divine mission, *who went about doing good* to the bodies and souls of men, by his heavenly doctrine instructing them, *and* by his miracles of grace *healing all that were oppressed of the devil,* under whatever disease or torment, or corporal possession, they laboured *for God was with him,* mightily supporting him, and testifying his high approbation of him *And we are witnesses of all things which he did both in the land of the Jews and in Jerusalem* having been his constant followers and disciples, *whom they slew and hanged on a tree,* a death the most painful and ignominious, in hatred of his pretensions as the promised Messiah, because he corresponded not with their carnal notions of [illegible] and [illegible] *him God raised up the third day,* to the

confusion, and in testimony of his perfect satisfaction in this divine Redeemer's undertaking, *and shewed him openly*, after his resurrection, *not to all the people*, who had so obstinately rejected the clearest evidence of truth, *but unto witnesses chosen before of God even to us, who did eat and drink with him after he rose from the dead*, and, from the fullest conviction of our senses, were assured of his resurrection, and were appointed by him to bear our testimony thereto *And he commanded us to preach unto the people, and to testify that it is he which was ordained of God to be the Judge of quick and dead*, before whom all must appear, and give an account of the things done in the body *To him give all the prophets witness*, from the beginning speaking of him as the great subject of their discourses, and pointing to him under various types and figures, *that through his name*, through his sacrifice and obedience unto death, *whosoever believeth in him shall receive remission of sins*, justified freely and fully from all his transgressions, whether he be Jew or Gentile, and thus prepared to stand before his judgment-seat with confidence of acceptance *Note*, (1) The remission of sins is the first and great gospel promise, and the door of admission to all the rest (2) If we believe that Jesus shall indeed shortly be our Judge, we cannot but be anxiously sollicitous to secure an interest in his favour

n Chap xv 8 & xv 15 44 ¶ While Peter yet spake these words, n the holy
Ghost fell on all them which heard the word 45 And
they of the circumcision which believed, were astonished,
as many as came with Peter, because that on the Gentiles
also was poured out the gift of the holy Ghost 46 For
they heard them speak with tongues, and magnify God
Then answered Peter, 47 Can any man forbid water,
that these should not be baptized, which have received
Chap xv the holy Ghost " as well as we? 48 And ° he com-
manded them to be baptized p in the name of the Lord
° Chap i 5 1 Cor i 14 17 p Chap viii 16 Then prayed they him to tarry certain days

v 44—48 While these words were yet dropping from the Apostle's lips, God himself appears, bearing witness to the gospel which Peter preached

1 *The Holy Ghost*, in his miraculous gifts as well as gracious influences, *fell on all them which heard the word*, as on the disciples at the day of Pentecost, *and they of the circumcision, which believed, were astonished, as many as came with Peter, because that on the Gentiles also was poured out the gift of the Holy Ghost*, though they were neither circumcised nor baptized, *for they heard them speak with tongues, and magnify God*, like the other ministers of the gospel, they were equally qualified for that service, in which probably the Lord designed to employ the first fruits of the Gentiles, and in the various languages which they spoke adored God for the blessings of that redemption in Christ Jesus, of which they now were made partakers *Note*, They who have received the Holy Ghost cannot but desire to magnify God, both in the exercise of his gifts and graces seeking the divine glory

2 Peter, no longer dubious, hesitates not to admit them into the church by the instituted rite of baptism It would be highly absurd for the most rigid Jewish Christian to object against admitting those to the sign and seal of the covenant, who had received the gifts and graces of the covenant *Can any man forbid water, that these should not be baptised, which have received the Holy Ghost as well as we?* The point was too clear to admit of a scruple, and therefore *he commanded them to be baptised in the name of the Lord* Hence it appears evidently, that water-baptism is an ordinance to be used by those who are most clearly baptised with the Holy Ghost

3 They entreated Peter to tarry *certain days* with them, that they might enjoy the edification and comfort of his farther ministrations *Note*, (1) They who have received a blessing under the discourse of a gospel minister, covet to hear more (2) The most advanced in gifts and graces are never to think themselves above the ministry of the word

CHAP XI.

In this chapter we have, 1 Peter's necessary vindication of what he did in receiving Cornelius and his friends into the church, from the censure he lay under for it among the brethren, and their acquiescence in it, ver 1—18 2 The good success of the gospel at Antioch, and the parts adjacent, ver 19—21 3 The carrying on of the good work that was begun at Antioch, by the ministry of Barnabas first, and afterwards of Paul in conjunction with him, and the lasting name of Christian first given to the disciples there, ver 22—26 4 A prediction of an approaching famine, and the contribution that was made among the Gentile converts for the relief of the poor saints in Judea upon that occasion, ver 27—30

1 AND the apostles and brethren that were in Ju-
dea, heard that the Gentiles had also received
a Chap x 45 the word of God 2 And when Peter was come up to
Jerusalem, a they that were of the circumcision contend-

ed with him, 3 Saying, b Thou wentest in to men un- b Chap x 28
circumcised, c and didst eat with them 4 But Peter c Gal ii 12
rehearsed *the matter* from the beginning, and expounded
it d by order unto them, saying, 5 e I was in the city d Luke i 3
of Joppa praying, and in a trance I saw a vision, A e Chap. x 9 &c
certain vessel descend, as it had been a great sheet, let
down from heaven by four corners, and it came even to
me 6 Upon the which when I had fastned mine eyes,
I considered, and saw four-footed beasts of the earth,
and wild beasts, and creeping things, and fowls of the
air 7 And I heard a voice saying unto me, Arise,
Peter, slay and eat 8 But I said, Not so Lord for
nothing common or unclean hath at any time entred in-
to my mouth 9 But the voice answered me again
from heaven, What God hath cleansed, *that* call not
thou common 10 And this was done three times and
all were drawn up again into heaven 11 And behold,
immediately there were three men already come unto the
house where I was, sent from Cesarea unto me 12
And f the Spirit bade me go with them, nothing doubt- f Chap x 19 & xv 7
ing. Moreover, these six brethren accompanied me,
and we entred into the man's house 13 And he
shewed us how he had seen an angel in his house, which
stood and said unto him, Send men to Joppa, and call
for Simon, whose surname is Peter 14 Who shall tell
thee words, whereby thou and all thy house shall be saved
15 And as I began to speak, the holy Ghost fell on
them, g as on us at the beginning 16 Then remem- g Chap ii 4
bred I the word of the Lord, how that he said, John h Chap i 5 & xix 4
indeed baptized with water, but i ye shall be baptized
with the holy Ghost 17 Forasmuch then as k God i Isa xliv 3 Joel ii 28
gave them the like gift as *he did* unto us, who believed k Chap xv 8
on the Lord Jesus Christ, l what was I, that I could l Chap x 47.
withstand God? 18 When they heard these things they
held their peace, and glorified God, saying, Then hath
God also to the Gentiles granted repentance unto life

v 1—18 The conversion of the Gentiles, and the admission of those into the Christian church who were uncircumcised, was a thing so new and extraordinary, that it soon reached Jerusalem And we are told,

1 What offence it gave to some of the Christians there, who were as yet wedded to the Jewish ritual *They that were of the circumcision contended with Peter*, so far were they from entertaining any thought of his supremacy or infallibility, which his pretended successors have since claimed, that they called him to account for what he had done, as if it was matter of blame, *saying, Thou wentest in to men uncircumcised, and didst eat with them*, supposing it a prostitution of their privileges, and high disgrace to the apostolic character *Note*, (1) Even good men are sometimes strangely enslaved by prejudices and bigotry (2) Rash censures sometimes drop from gracious men, and we must mildly bear with them, and answer in the spirit of meekness Even godlike charity will be sometimes called latitudinarian by narrow minds, that never tasted the warm sensations of generous, catholic love

2 Peter relates the whole transaction from the beginning, and then refers the matter to their judgment He might have despised their censures, but it is a debt we sometimes owe ourselves, to set what is misrepresented in its true colours, and remove, as far as we can, the prejudices of our brethren

(1) He informs them of the vision which he himself had seen in all its particulars, wherein God intimated to him that all the Mosaical distinctions between meats and persons were now at an end

(2) He relates the vision which Cornelius was favoured with, and the express command given him to send for Peter from Joppa, as the person by whose word he and his house *should be saved*, through faith in that Saviour whom the Apostle should preach unto him, and out of whom there is no salvation

(3) He declares the express command he had from the Spirit to go with the messenger Cornelius sent, and his prudent precaution to take several of the brethren with him, that his journey might be the less subject to any misrepresentation, when he had them as witnesses for his conduct

(4) He pleads, what above all other arguments vindicated his procedure, the attestation which the Holy Ghost bore to his word almost as soon as he began to speak to them of the gospel salvation, giving them the same miraculous gifts as he bestowed on themselves at the beginning And this brought to his mind *the word of the Lord*, just before his ascension, *Acts* i 5 *how that he said, John indeed baptised with water, but ye shall be baptised with the Holy Ghost* Seeing therefore this promise thus eminently fulfilled, and that God made no distinction between Gentile and Jewish converts, who, though not of the seed of Abraham, *believed on the Lord Jesus Christ*, and expected salvation by him

in him alone, *what was I that I could withstand God?* or refuse to admit to baptism those whom he had so eminently called into the participation of the glorious privileges of the gospel

3 An account so satisfactory silenced every cavil No objections could possibly be made to Peter, but contrariwise, *they glorified God* for this unexpected event, *saying*, with wonder and delight, *Then hath God also to the Gentiles granted repentance unto life* *Note*, (1) Repentance is God's gift it is not in the power of our own will, nor to be produced by judgments or mercies, but comes purely from his Spirit working effectually upon the conscience, without which we must for ever continue under our native blindness and hardness of heart (2) Where repentance is evangelical, and the gift of God, there it is the sure symptom of present spiritual life, and the earnest of that which is eternal

[n] Chap viii 1 19 ¶ Now they which were scattered abroad, upon
the persecution that arose about Stephen, travelled as far
as Phenice, and Cyprus, and Antioch, preaching the
word to none but unto the Jews only 20 And some
of them were men of Cyprus and Cyrene, which when
they were come to Antioch, spake unto the Grecians,
[n] Chap ii 47 preaching the Lord Jesus 21 And [n] the hand of the
[o] Ver 24 Lord was with them and [o] a great number believed,
and turned unto the Lord 22 ¶ Then tidings of these
things came unto the ears of the church which was in
Jerusalem and they sent forth Barnabas, that he should
go as far as Antioch 23 Who when he came, and had
[p] Chap xiii 43 & xiv 22 seen the grace of God, was glad, and [p] exhorted them
all, that with purpose of heart they would cleave unto
[q] Chap vi 5 the Lord 24 For he was a good man, and [q] full of
the holy Ghost, and of faith and much people was add-
ed unto the Lord 25 Then departed Barnabas to
[r] Chap ix 30 [r] Tarsus, for to seek Saul 26 And when he had
found him, he brought him unto Antioch And it came
to pass, that a whole year they assembled themselves
† Or, in the church † with the church, and taught much people, and the
disciples were called Christians first in Antioch

v 19—26 We have here an account of the planting the gospel at Antioch the metropolis of Syria, and one of the most famous cities in the Roman empire

1 The preachers of the gospel, who, on the persecution which arose after Stephen's death, were dispersed abroad, carried the glad tidings of the gospel as far as Phenice, a province of Syria and Cyprus, a large island of the Mediterranean sea, and Antioch But, as they knew not yet the extent of their commission, as reaching to all nations and every creature, they confined themselves wholly to the Jews who were dispersed in these countries *And some of them were men of Cyprus and Cyrene*, a city in Africa, *which, when they were come to Antioch, spake unto the Grecians*, either unto the Hellenist Jews, or, as some suppose, on hearing of the conversion of Cornelius and his friends, and that the preaching the gospel to the Gentiles had been approved by the apostles, they enlarged their field of usefulness, *preaching* to the Grecian Gentiles *the Lord Jesus*, whose character, offices, grace, and glory, were the constant subject of their ministrations *And the hand of the Lord was with them*, not only enabling them to perform astonishing miracles, but blessing their labours with signal success, *and a great number believed, and turned unto the Lord*, effectually brought to Jesus as their only Redeemer and Saviour, on whose righteousness and grace they placed their entire dependance *Note*, (1) The labours of God's ministers are only then effectual, when *the hand of the Lord is with them* without him, Paul must plant and Apollos water in vain (2) True faith will ever shew itself in real conversion of heart, from the ways of sin and the world, to the love and service of the blessed God

2 The church at Jerusalem, whither the apostles still frequently resorted, no sooner heard these glad tidings, than they sent forth *Barnabas*, a Hellenist, a native of Cyprus, and a man of singular abilities, *that he should go as far as Antioch*, passing through the places where the gospel had got footing, to strengthen and establish the new convert. Barnabas readily accepted the mission, and proceeded to Antioch, and when he *had seen the grace of God*, visibly manifested in the conversion and conversation of those whom the Lord by his gospel had called in that city, *he was glad, and exhorted them all, that with purpose of heart they would cleave unto the Lord*, encouraging them to maintain their profession amidst all opposition, and suggesting the most powerful arguments to establish their fidelity. *For he was a good man*, of a noble, generous, disinterested spirit, sweet and affable in his discourse, *and full of the Holy Ghost*, possessed of very eminent gifts and graces, *and of faith* in a most abundant measure *and much people was added unto the Lord* by his ministry and labour *Note*, (1) They who are truly partakers of the grace of God in their own souls, behold with singular delight the powerful effects of the same grace upon the hearts of others

(2) They who turn to the Lord must cleave to him in a persevering course of fidelity but if any man draw back, aggravated perdition must be the consequence (3) When we are ourselves deeply and fully persuaded of the truth, we shall be enabled to speak more forcibly and powerfully to others

3 The field being large, and the prospect promising, Barnabas sought an able fellow-helper, and knowing that Paul was yet at Tarsus, about an hundred miles off, he went to seek him, and invite him to Antioch, where his labours were greatly wanted Having found him at Tarsus, he invited him to return with him Antioch, to which Paul readily consented, and for a year *they assembled themselves with the church*, leading the religious assemblies of the faithful, *and taught much people*, vast multitudes attending their ministrations *Note*, (1) They who have the glory of their Lord simply at heart, can take pleasure in the greater gifts and abilities of others, and are happy to procure their assistance, though they may be more admired and useful preachers than themselves (2) The work of the ministry is doubly pleasing, when we see the fruits of our labour in the growing edification of the faithful, and the conversion of sinners to God

4 *The disciples were called Christians first at Antioch*, not probably by their enemies as a term of reproach, but, as the word (χρηματίσαι) seems to imply, by some divine intimation, and solemn act of their own Thus they would abolish the distinction of Jew and Gentile, and in their very name, as *Christians*, make profession of their full and entire dependance on Christ as their Lord and Saviour Are we Christians then? let our lives prove the reality of the profession we make

27 ¶ And in these days came [s] prophets from Jeru- [s] Chap. xiii 1 & xv 32
salem unto Antioch 28 And there stood up one of them
named [t] Agabus, and signified by the Spirit, that there [t] Chap xxi 10
should be great dearth throughout all the world which
came to pass in the days of Claudius Cesar 29 Then
the disciples, every man according to his ability, [u] deter- [u] Cor. Gal.
mined to send relief unto the brethren which dwelt in
Judea 30 [x] Which also they did, and sent it to the [x] Chap xii 25
elders by the hands of Barnabas and Saul

v 27—30. Among the eminent gifts bestowed on the primitive Christians, some were endued with the spirit of prophecy We are here told,

1 Of a visit from certain prophets of Jerusalem, who, hearing the great success of the gospel at Antioch, came thither to help forward the glorious work, and to comfort and establish the hearts of the disciples

2 One of them, named Agabus, had it revealed to him by the Spirit, *that there should be a great dearth throughout all the world*, and, standing up in the midst of the assembled church, signified to them this afflictive event, which accordingly came to pass about two years afterwards, in the reign of Claudius Cesar

3 *Then the disciples, every man according to his ability, determined to send relief unto the brethren which dwelt in Judea*, who, by the persecutions they had suffered, were greatly reduced, and those who had riches, had at the first parted with all for the service of the gospel, and probably it was suggested that the famine would be most severely felt in those parts No sooner was the matter resolved than the contribution was made, *and they sent it to the elders by the hands of Barnabas and Saul*, to be distributed according to the necessities of the faithful, than which nothing could serve more to conciliate their minds to the Gentile converts, and to remove their deep rooted prejudices *Note*, (1) Every Christian, according to his ability, is bound to contribute to the assistance of his brethren (2) God will take care of his poor, and by some means or other provide that in the time of dearth they shall be supplied He that feedeth the ravens, will not leave his children to famish

CHAP XII

In this chapter we have the story, 1 Of the martyrdom of James the apostle, and the imprisonment of Peter, by Herod Agrippa, who now reigned as king in Judea, ver 1—4 2 *The miraculous deliverance of Peter out of prison*, ver 5—19 3 *The cutting off of Herod in the height of his pride by the stroke of an angel, the minister of God's justice*, ver 20—23 4 *Barnabas and Saul return to Antioch*, ver 24, 25

1 NOW about that time, Herod the king stretched
forth *his* hands to vex certain of the church
2 And [a] he killed James [b] the brother of John with the [illegible]
sword 3 And because he saw it pleased the Jews, he
proceeded further to take Peter also (Then were [c] the
days of unleavened bread) 4 And [d] when he had ap-
prehended him, he put him in prison, and delivered him
to

to four quaternions of soldiers, to keep him, intending after Easter to bring him forth to the people

v 1—4 Herod, the grandson of Herod the great, and father of Agrippa, before whom Paul pleaded his cause, *chap* xxvi 1—28 had now, through the favour of Claudius the Roman emperor, received the government of Judea as well as Galilee Being a bitter enemy to Christianity, he interrupted the rest which the church had for a while enjoyed, and lighted up afresh the fire of persecution

1 He began to harrass and distress the saints at Jerusalem, either countenancing those who insulted and abused them, or imprisoning and persecuting them on account of their profession The faithful may expect short respite from tribulation in this world, and must be always prepared to suffer.

2 *He killed James, the brother of John, with the sword* Thus did he drink of the cup with his Lord, as was foretold, *Matth* xx 23 and first of the apostles sealed his testimony with his blood He was probably executed in prison, like the Baptist, by a private order from the king, and led the way to his brethren, who were hereby taught to prepare for the like fate, and be faithful unto death

3 *Because he saw it pleased the Jews, he proceeded further to take Peter also,* glad to ingratiate himself with the people, at the same time that he gratified his own enmity against the disciples of Jesus and Peter, as an especially active, zealous preacher, was peculiarly obnoxious *Then were the days of unleavened bread,* the feast of the passover approaching *When* therefore *he had apprehended him, he put him in prison, and delivered him to four quaternions of soldiers,* sixteen in number, who guarded him by four at a time, and relieved each other, *to keep him,* that he might not escape, *intending after Easter,* or the Passover, *to bring him forth to the people,* to gratify them with the pleasing spectacle of his ignominious execution *Note,* (1) They who study to please men will be led into many a guilty deed (2) Success in wickedness often emboldens sinners to proceed to greater lengths

[† Or earnest prayer was made] 5 Peter therefore was kept in prison, but † prayer
was made without ceasing of the church unto God for
him 6 And when Herod would have brought him
forth, the same night Peter was sleeping between two
soldiers, bound with two chains, and the keepers before
the door kept the prison 7 And behold, [e] the angel [e Chap v 19]
of the Lord came upon him, and a light shined in the
prison and he smote Peter on the side, and raised him
up, saying, Arise up quickly And his chains fell off
from *his* hands 8 And the angel said unto him, Gird
thyself, and bind on thy sandals and so he did And
he saith unto him, Cast thy garment about thee, and
follow me 9 And he went out, and followed him,
and [f] wist not that it was true which was done by the [f Ps cxxvi 1]
angel but thought he saw a vision 10 When they
were past the first and the second ward, they came unto
the iron gate that leadeth unto the city, [g] which opened [g Chap xvi 26]
to them of his own accord and they went out, and
passed on through one street, and forthwith the angel
departed from him 11 And when Peter was come to
himself, he said, Now I know of a surety, that [h] the [h Dan vi 22]
Lord hath sent his angel, and hath delivered me out
of the hand of Herod, and *from* all the expectation of
the people of the Jews 12 And when he had considered
the thing, [i] he came to the house of Mary the mother of [i Chap iv 23]
[k] John, whose surname was Mark, where many were [k Chap. xv 37]
gathered together, [l] praying 13 And as Peter knock- [l Ver 5]
ed at the door of the gate, a damsel came to ‡ hearken, [‡ Or ask who was there]
named Rhoda 14 And when she knew Peter's voice,
she opened not the gate for gladness, but ran in, and
told how Peter stood before the gate 15 And they
said unto her, Thou art mad But she constantly af-
firmed that it was even so Then said they, It is [m] his [m Mat xviii 10]
angel 16 But Peter continued knocking and when
they had opened *the door,* and saw him, they were asto-
nished 17 But he [n] beckoning unto them with the [n Chap xiii 16 & xix 33, & xxi 40]
hand to hold their peace, declared unto them how the
Lord had brought him out of the prison And he said,
Go shew these things unto James, and to the brethren
And he departed, and went into another place 18
Now as soon as it was day, there was no small stir among
the soldiers, what was become of Peter 19 And when
Herod had sought for him, and found him not, he exa
mined the keepers, and commanded that *they* should be
put to death And he went down from Judea to Cesarea,
and *there* abode

v 5—19 To human view Peter's case seemed desperate, and a few days would complete the triumph of his persecutors But God had otherwise ordained, and then the craft of the wisest and the power of the mightiest are alike vain

1 During Peter's imprisonment, *prayer was made without ceasing of the church unto God for him,* they were fervent and frequent at a throne of grace, perhaps one company after another continued their incessant supplications, deeply concerned for fear of losing him after all their other breaches, and trusting that, though no human prospect of his deliverance appeared, the Lord would, in his own time and way, rescue his suffering servant from the hands of his blood-thirsty persecutors *Note,* When the faithful ministers of Jesus are suffering for their testimony, the church is called to pray earnestly for them, that, if the Lord so pleases, they may be delivered from unreasonable and wicked men, and spared for further usefulness

2 The time appointed for Peter's execution now drew near, the next was the fatal day appointed to bring him forth to the people Peter mean-time was kept with greatest care, chained to two soldiers within the prison, whilst without the guards kept the door, to prevent any rescue or escape, and never could greater precaution be taken Yet, though his danger was so imminent, his case so desperate, unterrified, composed, in peace he sweetly slept, whilst probably the eyes of his malicious foes were held waking, and their disturbed minds could take no rest on beds of ivory A good cause, a good conscience, and the desire to glorify God, whether by life or death, raised him superior to every fear, and, though expecting no deliverance, he took his wonted repose *Note,* (1) God suffers us sometimes to be reduced to extremities, that his power and grace in rescuing us from our trials may appear with more distinguished lustre (2) When wicked men seem to have ensured the success of their enterprises, God is often pleased to blast their designs, and to cover them with confusion

3 God sends his angel to deliver the faithful prisoner, and he, whom gates nor guards could exclude, suddenly entering the prison in a blaze of light, with a gentle touch awakened Peter from his slumbers, then, bidding him arise, his chains marvellously *fell off from his hands,* and, being now at liberty, the angel *said unto him, Gird thyself, and bind on thy sandals, and so he did And he saith unto him, Cast thy garment about thee, and follow me* Peter obeyed, and as yet apprehended not the reality of the facts, but supposed the scene was merely visionary Passing now the first and second bodies of guards without molestation, who were cast into a profound sleep, or terrified with the angelic minister's appearance, they came unto the iron gate, *which opened of its own accord,* and, being now in the city, the angel accompanied Peter through one street, and then departed, his presence being no longer needful, and Peter could then provide for his own safety *Note,* (1) We have in Peter's deliverance a lively image of our redemption We lie by nature fast bound in the chains of sin, and sleep securely, not apprehensive of danger, though ruin is before us Then God sends his gospel as this angel, and by his Spirit shines in our heart awakens us from our security and insensibility Quickened by grace, the chains of corruption fall off, and we are now enabled to rise and walk, clothed with the garment of righteousness, and our feet shod with the preparation of the gospel of peace Under divine light and guidance we are enabled to pass through numberless difficulties, and through hosts of enemies hold on our way, till the iron gate of death opens in view, and, opening wide, admits us into the new Jerusalem (2) No difficulties are insurmountable, if God be for us (3) When we have the ordinary means before us, we are not to expect miracles

4 Peter, being left alone, soon recovered from his surprise, and, reflecting on what was past, was fully assured the scene was not visionary, but real, *that the Lord had sent his angel, and delivered him out of the hand of Herod, and from all the expectation of the people of the Jews,* who waited impatiently for his execution Deliberating then whither in prudence he should direct his steps, *he came to the house of Mary the mother of John, whose surname was Mark, where many were gathered together, praying,* and importunate no doubt they were when the danger was now so near when, lo! a most astonishing answer is given to their prayers, behold, *Peter knocked at the door,* a visitant little expected by them A damsel, named Rhoda, ran immediately into the porch, to listen whether it were a friend or foe, before she opened the gate, when, hearing Peter's well-known voice, so transported was she, that, instead of opening the door, she ran to her mistress, where they were all assembled for prayer, and told them, to their astonishment, that *Peter stood before the gate* Unable to credit so strange a story, they said, *thou art mad,* it is impossible But she *constantly affirmed* the certainty of the fact, *that it was even so Then said they, It is his angel,* a messenger come from him, or one of the celestial spirits, who imitates his voice, and brings some tidings concerning him Mean-time Peter repeated his knocks at the gate, and, going down, they opened the door, when with amazement they beheld him, and, eager to know the circumstances of this extraordinary event, they together began to ask him concerning

it whereupon he beckoned with his hand, commanding ſilence, whilſt he declared to them his miraculous deliverance And, as no time was to be loſt to ſecure himſelf, having charged them to inform James and the brethren of his eſcape, for their comfort and encouragement, *he departed, and went into another place*, where he might be ſecured from the danger *Note*, (1) They who perſevere in prayer will at laſt meet an anſwer of peace (2) Sudden and great joy for the time often deſtroys reflection, and makes us forget what we ſay or do (3) Though, when called of God, neither death nor danger muſt deter us from the way of duty, yet, when the Lord opens a door for our eſcape, we may lawfully provide for our own ſafety

5 The next morning the guards were in the utmoſt conſternation at finding their priſoner gone, and juſtly dreaded the rage of the king, as if they had been chargeable with neglect or connivance In vain ſtrict ſearch is made by Herod every where, and, unable to find Peter, he wreaks his vengeance on the keepers, who could not give the leaſt ſatisfactory account of the matter, and therefore were ordered to be put to death for their ſuppoſed negligence or corruption Then retiring from Judea to Ceſarea, in order, it is ſaid, to celebrate games in honour of Auguſtus Cæſar, for ſome time *he abode there* *Note*, God can, when he pleaſes, hide his people from the malice of their moſt invenomed foes

20 ¶ And Herod was highly diſpleaſed with them of
Tyre and Sidon but they came with one accord to him,
and having made Blaſtus the king's chamberlain their
friend, deſired peace, becauſe [o] their country was nou-
riſhed by the king's *country* 21 And upon a ſet day,
Herod arrayed in royal apparel, ſat upon his throne, and
made an oration unto them 22 And the people gave
a ſhout, *ſaying*, *It is* the voice of a god, and not of a
man 23 And immediately the angel of the Lord ſmote
him, becauſe he gave not God the glory and he was
eaten of worms, and gave up the ghoſt 24 ¶ But
[p] the word of God grew and multiplied 25 And
Barnabas and Saul returned from Jeruſalem, when they
had fulfilled *their* † miniſtry, and [q] took with them John
whoſe ſurname was Mark

[o] 1 Kings v 9 11 Ezek xxvii 17
[p] Iſa lv 11 Chap vi 7 & xix 20 Col i 6
† Or charge Chap xi 29 30
[q] Chap xiii 5, 13

v 20—25 Proud perſecutors juſtly meet an avenging God

1 Herod's pride now reached the ſummit of wickedneſs On ſome provocation given him by the maritime cities of Tyre and Sidon, Herod was highly offended, and, juſtly fearing the wrath of this haughty monarch, they inſtantly diſpatched embaſſadors to him to make their ſubmiſſion, and deprecate his diſpleaſure, for, as they chiefly drew their proviſion from his territories, if he prohibited his ſubjects from ſupplying them, it would have expoſed them to a famine Therefore having, by preſents probably, gained Blaſtus the king's chamberlain for their friend, who had a conſiderable influence with his maſter, *they deſired peace*, and a day was fixed to give them public audience Herod, arrayed in royal robes, glittering, ſays Joſephus, with ſilver, and reflecting the ſun beams ſo ſtrongly as dazzled the eyes of the ſpectators, and ſeated on his gorgeous throne, *made an oration to the people*, probably expatiating on the provocations of the Tyrians, and diſplaying his own clemency in pardoning them on their ſubmiſſion The people, delighted with his ſplendid appearance, pleaſed with his diſcourſe, and willing to flatter his pride, ſhouted their blaſphemous admiration, as if they heard a preſent deity, ſaying, *It is the voice of a god, and not of a man*, whilſt he, well-pleaſed, received the impious adulation

2 Inſtantly God ſmote him, and hurled him from his towering height of pride into the abyſs of deſpicable wretchedneſs An angel, the executioner of wrath, ſtruck the fatal blow, *becauſe he gave not God the glory*, and dared accept ſuch adoration A foul, filthy, and tormenting diſeaſe ſeized his vitals, in agonies he lingered five days, worms bred in his putrid carcaſe, and, devoured alive, he miſerably periſhed, a ſpectacle of horror to every beholder So eaſily can God abaſe thoſe who walk in pride, and make the meaneſt worm that crawls an inſtrument of his vengeance

3 In ſpite of all perſecution and oppoſition, *the word of God grew and multiplied*, ſpreading with rapidity and vaſt ſucceſs And Barnabas and Saul, having finiſhed their buſineſs at Jeruſalem, returned again to Antioch, taking with them John, whoſe ſurname was Mark, Barnabas's nephew *Note*, When miniſters are called abroad, and have finiſhed their work, they muſt haſten home again, where their ſtated labour awaits them

CHAP XIII

Here is, 1 The ſolemn ordination of Barnabas and Saul, by divine direction, to the great work of ſpreading the goſpel among the Gentiles, ver 1—3 2 Their preaching the goſpel in Cyprus, and the oppoſition they met with there from Elymas the ſorcerer, ver 4—13 3 The heads of a ſermon which Paul preached at Antioch in Piſidia, ver 14—41 4 The preaching of the goſpel to the Gentiles at their requeſt, and upon the Jews refuſal of it, ver 42—49 5 The trouble which the infidel Jews gave to the apoſtles, which obliged them to remove to another place, ver 50—52

1 NOW there were [a] in the church that was at
Antioch, certain prophets and teachers, as Bar-
nabas, and Simeon that was called Niger, and [b] Lucius
of Cyrene, and Manaen, which had been brought up
with Herod the tetrarch, and Saul 2 As they mini-
ſtred to the Lord, and faſted, the holy Ghoſt ſaid,
[c] Separate me Barnabas and Saul, for the work [d] where-
unto I have called them 3 And [e] when they had faſted
and prayed, and laid their hands on them, they ſent *them*
away

[a] Chap xi 26
[b] Rom xvi 21
[c] Chap ix 15 & xxii 21 Rom i 1 Gal i 15
[d] Matt ix 38 Rom x 15 Heb v 4
[e] Chap vi 6

v 1—3 Though the goſpel had now begun to make its entrance into the Gentile world, none had yet been particularly ordained and appointed to that ſervice, till Paul and Barnabas, by the immediate order of the Holy Ghoſt, were called thereunto

1 The church at Antioch flouriſhed greatly There were *certain prophets*, who ranked next to the apoſtles in the church, *and teachers*, eminent for their gifts and graces, *as Barnabas, and Simeon*, who, probably from his dark complexion, *was called Niger, and Lucius of Cyrene*, an African by birth, and *Manaen, who had been brought up with Herod* Antipas, *the tetrarch* of Galilee, his friend and companion, but now had quitted the honours of a court for the reproach of the goſpel, *and Saul*, ſo famous in the records of Chriſtianity *Theſe miniſtred to the Lord, and faſted*, diligently employed in the ſervice of immortal ſouls, and at ſeaſons, in more ſolemn acts of prayer and faſting, waited upon God for his bleſſing and direction

2 Whilſt they were, on a certain day, thus engaged, *the Holy Ghoſt*, by his immediate ſuggeſtion, and by his own divine authority, *ſaid, Separate me Paul and Barnabas for the work whereunto I have called them*, to preach among the Gentiles the unſearchable riches of Chriſt, and to be chiefly employed in their ſervice Learn hence, (1) The perſonality of the Holy Ghoſt, and his co-equal glory with the Father and Son (2) The true call to the miniſtry muſt come from above

3 Purſuant to this order, Paul and Barnabas were ſolemnly ſet apart, with faſting and prayer and impoſition of hands, for the peculiar ſervice to which the Holy Ghoſt had appointed them and, wiſhing them all ſucceſs in their arduous undertaking, the brethren *ſent them away* And henceforward we find them the two great apoſtles of the Gentiles ſpread the glorious goſpel to diſtant lands, whither the glad tidings had never reached before

4 ¶ So they being ſent forth by the holy Ghoſt, de-
parted unto Seleucia, and from thence they ſailed to [f] Cy-
prus 5 And when they were at Salamis, they preached
the word of God in the ſynagogues of the Jews and they
had alſo [g] John to *their* miniſter 6 And when they had
gone through the iſle unto Paphos, they found a certain
ſorcerer, a falſe prophet, a Jew, whoſe name *was* Barjeſus
7 Which was with the deputy of the country, Sergius
Paulus, a prudent man, who called for Barnabas and Saul,
and deſired to hear the word of God 8 But [h] Elymas
the ſorcerer (for ſo is his name by interpretation) with
ſtood them, ſeeking to turn away the deputy from the
faith 9 Then Saul (who alſo *is called* Paul) filled with
the holy Ghoſt, ſet his eyes on him, 10 And ſaid, O
full of all ſubtilty and all miſchief, [i] thou child of the
devil, thou enemy of all righteouſneſs, wilt thou not
ceaſe to pervert the right ways of the Lord? 11 And
now behold, the hand of the Lord *is* upon thee, and
thou ſhalt be blind, not ſeeing the ſun for a ſeaſon
And immediately there fell on him a miſt and a dark
neſs, and he went about ſeeking ſome to lead him by the
hand 12 Then the deputy, when he ſaw what was
done, believed, being aſtoniſhed at the doctrine of the
Lord 13 Now when Paul and his company looſed
from Paphos, they came to Perga in Pamphylia and
[k] John departing from them, returned to Jeruſalem

[f] Chap iv 36
[g] Chap xii 25
[h] Exod vii 11 2 Tim iii 8
[i] Matt xiii 38 John viii 44 1 John iii 8
[k] Chap xv 38

v 4—13 Being in this ſolemn manner ſent forth, Paul and Barnabas immediately applied themſelves to their work

1 They directed their courſe to Cyprus, the native land of Barnabas, going to Seleucia, and thence ſailed for Salamis, the chief town of the eaſtern part of the iſland And firſt, as was their cuſtom, *they preached the word in the ſynagogue of the Jews*, giving them the preference and, if they rejected the goſpel, leaving them thereby inexcuſable *and they had John to their miniſter*

minister, to assist them in their work, provide necessaries for them, and execute any service which might be appointed him

2 They travelled through the greatest part of the island, preaching the gospel, till they came to Paphos, the chief city, on the western coast, famous for the temple of Venus There they met with one *Barjesus*, which signifies the son of Joshua, a Jew by birth, addicted to magic, who set up for a prophet, and had insinuated himself into the favour of Sergius Paulus, the Roman governor of the island, *a prudent*, considerate, thinking *man*, who, hearing of the fame of Barnabas and Saul, desired to learn from themselves that new doctrine which they taught as a revelation from God But Elymas, the sorcerer, knowing that, if the deputy received the gospel, his influence with him would be at an end, set himself to oppose these ministers of Christ, and to turn away the deputy from the faith *Note*, (1) It is prudence to prove all things, and hold fast that which is good (2) Where-ever the gospel comes, Satan will find some tool to employ, in order to cast stumbling-blocks in the way of those who desire to hear

3 *Saul*, who henceforward is always called by his Roman name Paul, as more agreeable to the Gentiles among whom for the future he chiefly conversed, *filled with the Holy Ghost*, fired with zeal for the gospel, and under a divine afflatus, *set his eyes on him*, with indignation and abhorrence of his wickedness, *and said*, *O full of all subtilty*, expert in every art of deceit, taught by the great deceiver, *and*, like him, set on *all mischief*, *thou enemy of all righteousness*, the implacable foe to truth and godliness, and that gospel which is designed to promote them, *wilt thou not cease to pervert the right ways of the Lord?* to misrepresent them, and by every artful and malicious suggestion to prejudice men against the Lord Jesus, and those ways of his grace, which alone can lead to eternal life and glory? *And now behold*, as an evident token of God's displeasure, *the hand of the Lord is upon thee*, in righteous judgment; *and thou shalt be blind, not seeing the sun for a season* the emblem and punishment of the wilful blindness of thy heart *Note*, (1) Subtilty and delight in mischief united, form the strongest image of the devil (2) They who are enemies to the gospel, must be enemies to all righteousness, since this alone can effectually produce true holiness in the heart (3) The Lord's ways are all right, and lead direct to happiness and heaven they who pervert or misrepresent them, as unreasonable, unpleasant, or unprofitable, shall bear their burden

4 His doom is no sooner pronounced than executed *Immediately there fell on him a mist and darkness*, *and*, his sight being entirely lost, *he went about* groping his way, *and seeking some to lead him by the hand* Struck with the evidence of the miracle, perceiving the sorcerer confounded by the arguments, and unable to stand before the power with which Paul appeared to be invested, *the deputy believed* in Jesus, *being astonished at the doctrine of the Lord*, which came with such convincing power and energy to his heart, and contained such amazing discoveries of God and his great salvation, with which he had been before utterly unacquainted

5 Having shortly after set sail from Paphos, Paul and his companions directed their course to Perga, a city of Pamphylia, situate in lesser Asia There John, their minister, quitted them, and returned to Jerusalem A worldly or timid spirit prevailed against him he wanted to see his mother, or he was weary of the fatigues of the Gentile mission, or some temporal affair drew off his attention from the ministry of the word which Paul much resented, and laid a ground of future contention between him and Barnabas

14 ¶ But when they departed from Perga, they came
to Antioch in Pisidia, and [l] went into the synagogue on
the sabbath day, and sat down 15 And [m] after the
reading of the law and the prophets, the rulers of the
synagogue sent unto them, saying, Ye men *and* brethren,
if ye have [n] any word of exhortation for the people, say
on 16 Then Paul stood up, and [o] beckoning with *his*
hand, said, Men of Israel, and [p] ye that fear God, give
audience 17 The God of this people of Israel chose
our fathers, and exalted the people, when [q] they dwelt
as strangers in the land of Egypt, and [r] with an high
arm brought he them out of it 18 And [s] about the
time of forty years † suffered he their manners in the
wilderness 19 And when [t] he had destroyed seven nations
in the land of Canaan, [u] he divided their land to
them by lot 20 And after that [x] he gave *unto them*
judges about the space of four hundred and fifty years,
until Samuel the prophet 21 And afterward [y] they
desired a king [z] and God gave unto them Saul the son
of Cis, a man of the tribe of Benjamin, by the space
of forty years 22 And when he had removed him,
[a] he raised up unto them David to be their king, to
whom also he gave testimony, and said, [b] I have found
David the *son* of Jesse, [c] a man after mine own heart,
which shall fulfil all my will 23 [d] Of this man's seed
hath God, [e] according to *his* promise, raised unto Israel
a Saviour Jesus 24 [f] When John had first preached
before his coming, the baptism of repentance to all the
people of Israel 25 And as John fulfilled his course,
he said, [g] Whom think ye that I am? I am not *he*
But behold, there cometh one after me, whose shoes of
his feet I am not worthy to loose 26 Men *and* brethren,
children of the stock of Abraham, and whosoever
among you feareth God, [h] to you is the word of this
salvation sent 27 For they that dwell at Jerusalem,
and their rulers, [i] because they knew him not, nor yet
the voices of the prophets which are read every sabbath-day,
they have fulfilled *them* in condemning *him* 28
And [k] though they found no cause of death *in him*, yet
desired they [l] Pilate that he should be slain 29 And
when they had fulfilled all that was written of him,
[n] they took *him* down from the tree, and laid *him* in a
sepulchre 30 But [o] God raised him from the dead
31 And [p] he was seen many days of them which came
up with him [q] from Galilee to Jerusalem, [r] who are his
witnesses unto the people 32 And we declare unto you
glad tidings, how that [s] the promise which was made
unto the fathers, 33 God hath fulfilled the same unto
us their children, in that he hath raised up Jesus again,
as it is also written in the second psalm, [t] Thou art my
son, this day have I begotten thee 34 And as concerning
that he raised him up from the dead, *now* no
more to return to corruption, he said on this wise, [u] I will
give you the ‡ sure mercies of David 35 Wherefore
he saith also in another *psalm*, [x] Thou shalt not suffer
thine holy One to see corruption 36 For David, after
he had § served his own generation by the will of God,
[y] fell on sleep, and was laid unto his fathers, and saw
corruption 37 But he whom God raised again, saw
no corruption 38 ¶ Be it known unto you therefore,
men *and* brethren, that through this man is preached
unto you the forgiveness of sins 39 And [a] by him all
that believe are justified from all things, from which ye
could not be justified by the law of Moses 40 Beware
therefore, lest that come upon you [b] which is spoken of
in the prophets, 41 Behold, ye despisers, and wonder,
and perish for I work a work in your days, a work
which ye shall in no wise believe, though a man declare
it unto you

[l] Chap xvi 13 & xvii 2 & xviii 4 [m] Luke iv 16 Ver 27 [n] Heb xiii 22 [o] Chap xii 17 [p] Ver 42, 43 [q] Ex i 1 [r] Ex vi 6 & xiii 14, 16 [s] Exod xvi 35 Pf xcv 10 † Or bore them like a nurse Deut i 31 [t] Deut vii 1 [u] Josh xiv 1, 2 Ps lxxviii 55 [x] Judg ii 16 [y] 1 Sam viii 5 [z] 1 Sam x 1 [a] 1 Sam xvi 13 [b] Pf lxxxix 20 [c] 1 Sam xiii 14 [d] Isa xi 1 Mat i 1 [e] 2 Sam vii 12 [f] Mat iii 1 [g] Mat iii 11 John i 20 [h] Mat x 6 Chap iii 26 Ver 46 [i] Chap iii 17 1 Cor ii 8 [k] Chap iii 13 [l] Mat xxvii 22 John xix 6 [m] Chap iii 13 [n] Mat xxvii 59 [o] Chap ii 24 [p] Mat xxviii 16 Chap i 3 1 Cor xv 5, 6 [q] Chap i 11 [r] Chap i 8 [s] Gen iii 15 & xxii 18 Deut xviii 15 Isa liii 10 Jer ... [t] Heb i 5 & v 5 ‡ Gr holy or just things [x] Isa lv 3 [y] Pf xvi 10 Chap ii 27, 31 § Or served the will of God in his generation [y] 1 Kin ii 10 Chap ii 29 [z] Dan ix 24 Luke xxiv 47 [a] Chap ii 38 & v 31 & x 43 Rom iii 25 Heb ix 15 [a] Rom iii 28 & viii 3 Heb vii 19 [b] Isa xxviii 14 Hab i 5

v 14—41 How long they stayed, and what success the apostles had at Perga, is not recorded, but more is preserved of their labour at Antioch, the capital of Pisidia, which was their next remove

1 On the sabbath day, according to their custom, they went into the synagogue, and sat down, waiting a proper opportunity to deliver the message which they brought

2 After the reading the law and prophets as usual, *the rulers of the synagogue*, probably being acquainted with their public characters, and willing to hear what they had to say, *sent unto them, saying, Ye men and brethren, if ye have any word of exhortation*, or consolation, *to the people, say on* *Note*, (1) In public worship the reading the Scriptures should always have a place (2) The preaching the word, and expounding it with application to the hearts of the hearers, is one most essential end and use of our assembling on the Lord's day

3 Paul declined not the invitation, but gracefully rising, and waving his hand that silence might be kept, he very affectionately and seriously addresses his brethren, intreating a patient and attentive audience

1 He opens with reminding them of the peculiar favour which God had shewn to their fathers God had chosen the Jewish people in a covenant of peculiarity, and, according to the promise made unto their fathers, had wonderfully multiplied and exalted them in Egypt, where they sojourned, and at last, when they were oppressed by Pharaoh, had brought them thence with a high hand, *v* 17 In the wilderness, amidst all their provocations, his patience bore with them, his bounty had fed them forty years, *v* 18 After destroying the accursed nations of Canaan, he gave them the country by lot, for their inheritance, *v* 19 and, for about the space of four hundred and fifty years from their deliverance from Egypt, continued, in their emergencies, to raise them up divinely appointed officers, called judges, to save them from the hands of their enemies, until the time of Samuel the prophet, *v* 20 Afterward, indulging them in their desire, he appointed Saul the son of Cis, a Benjamite, their king, whose reign, with Samuel's government, filled the space of forty years, *v* 21 And when he was rejected, then was David anointed to sit on Israel's throne and

raised from his low estate to that high dignity, a man, to whom God bore the most honourable testimony, as one *after mine own heart*, approved and known to be faithful, *which shall fulfil all my pleasure*, and answer all my purposes and designs

Herein the apostle seems to desire to conciliate the Jews to him, and engage their regard to his discourse, when it appears, that, far from having any prejudice against the Jewish nation, as was suggested, or despising their peculiar honours, he dwells upon them with pleasure, in order to introduce the discourse of the Messiah, the Son of David, which was the great object he had in view

2 As God had made to David a promise, that of his seed the Messiah should spring, the glorious hope of Israel, that promise he had now fulfilled in Jesus, the Saviour of his people from sin, misery, death, and hell, to introduce whose appearing, John had preached *the baptism of repentance to all the people of Israel*, inviting them to turn to that Messiah, whose forerunner he was, that by faith in him they might obtain remission of sins, (*Mark* i 4 *Luke* iii 3) disclaiming that title himself, when the people were in doubt whether he were the Christ or not, but directing them to one presently to appear after him, so far transcending him in dignity, that he should count it an honour of which he was unworthy, to perform the meanest offices to him This being then the main point in view, to bring them acquainted with him, to whom John bore record, he pathetically urges them to consider the matter *Men and brethren*, possessed of rational and immortal souls, *children of the stock of Abraham*, and of the promise made unto our fathers, *and whosoever among you feareth God*, whether Jews or proselytes, *to you is the word of this salvation sent*, and you are first called to partake of the inestimable blessings of the redemption which this Jesus hath obtained *Note*, (1) It is among the most invaluable mercies, to have the word of salvation sent to us (2) No condemnation will be so great and aggravated as theirs who reject the gospel-word

3 He plainly tells them of the great guilt and wickedness of the Jewish rulers, in rejecting, persecuting, and murdering the Lord's Christ *They knew him not*, so fatally blinded were their minds by the prejudices which they had entertained, and the expectations they had formed of a temporal Messiah, *nor yet the voices of the prophets, which are read every sabbath-day*, in which the sufferings and death of the Messiah were at large foretold but God so over-ruled their wickedness, that undesignedly *they have fulfill'd these scriptures in condemning him and though*, even by the confession of his judge, his innocence was acknowledged, and *they found no cause of death in him*, yet, so malicious and enraged were they against him *they desired Pilate that he should be slain And when they had fulfilled all that was written of him*, concerning his sufferings and death, even in the most minute particulars, *they took him down from the tree, and laid him in a sepulchre*, brought to the dust of death, the lowest step of his humiliation *Note*, (1) Ignorance of the scriptures is often found, where the sound of them in the ears is heard every sabbath-day (2) It will not excuse the sins of persecutors, that they did it ignorantly in unbelief, when they rejected the means of better information

4 He insists at large on his glorious resurrection, as the grand foundation on which all the sure hope of salvation through Jesus was built His enemies thought they had effectually defeated all his pretensions when they laid him in the grave, *but God raised him from the dead*, to their confusion, and as a token of the fullest approbation of his character and undertaking, a fact attested by a great cloud of witnesses, who had been most intimately acquainted with him before his death, and, during forty days, had many conferences with him, and eat and drink with him after his resurrection, the truth of which some of them had already sealed with their blood, and others in the face of death and danger still continued to declare And to this resurrection of Jesus we now present our testimony, proclaiming it as the most joyful tidings, that *the promise made unto the fathers*, of that Messiah in whom all nations of the world should be blessed, *he hath now fulfilled unto us their children, in that he hath raised up Jesus again*, whereby it appears that he was the glorious personage of whom David spoke, *as it is written also in the second Psalm, Thou art my Son, this day have I begotten thee*, from eternity the [illegible], and as God bore testimony to the dignity and divine character of his Son, his baptism and transfiguration, so most eminently was Jesus *declared to be the Son of God with power by the resurrection from the dead*, (*Rom* i 4) And that God raised him from the dead, no more to see corruption, is evident from [illegible] where he said, *I will give you the sure mercies of David* Having then appointed his Son, according to the tenor of the everlasting covenant, *the leader and commander of the people*, and by an oath confirmed his promise, it became necessary, that he who by his sufferings and death was to ratify the covenant, and obtain these mercies for his people, should rise again to [illegible] them, and ever live to maintain them in the possession of their invaluable privileges In farther proof of which, *he saith also in another Psalm, Thou shalt not suffer thine Holy One to see corruption*, (*Psal* xvi 10) which words can only be applicable to the Messiah, for as to David himself, it is evident, *after he had served his generation by the will of God*, discharging his high office with great fidelity for his people's good, *he fell asleep* in the arms of death, resting from all his labours, *and was laid unto his fathers, and saw corruption*, his corpse, like others, returning unto dust *but he whom God raised*, even Jesus, the Messiah, of whom David spake in this Psalm, exactly fulfilled it, *and* rising on the third day, *saw no corruption*, nor ever shall, God having exalted him to his own right hand in glory everlasting, to bestow these covenant mercies on all his redeemed people, until time shall be no more *Note*, (1) Like David we must learn not to live for ourselves, but for God's glory, and the good of mankind (2) To a faithful soul death is but a sleep, when he rests from his labours, and is in joy and felicity (3) The more we examine the scriptures, the more confirmed shall we be, that Jesus is the Christ, in whom we shall see all the prophecies so eminently and exactly fulfilled

5 He applies what he said to their hearts, as a matter in which they were most nearly concerned *Be it known unto you therefore, men and brethren, that through this man is preached unto you the forgiveness of sins*, by his sufferings it is obtained, in his name it is declared, and by his authority bestowed *and by him*, through the merit of his obedience unto death, *all that believe are justified from all things*, discharged from the condemnation of the law, and the guilt of all their transgressions, be they never so many, great, or aggravated, *from which ye could not be justified by the law of Moses*, legal or ceremonial, none being able to fulfil the moral law in perfection, and the ceremonial prescribed no sacrifice for wilful transgression and therefore all who looked for justification by the deeds of the law, were necessarily left under wrath and condemnation *Note*, (1) The great gospel promise and privilege is forgiveness of sins In Christ Jesus there is a free and full pardon promised to the miserable and the desperate (2) It is impossible for a fallen sinner to be just before God by any obedience of his own, or by any other means and method than that of his own appointment, even faith in the blood and righteousness of him who justifieth the ungodly (3) All who truly believe in Jesus, are compleat in him, all he did, all he suffered, is reckoned to our account, and God is therefore righteous and just in forgiving our sins, since he hath accepted one for all, *the just for the unjust*

Lastly, He solemnly warns them of the danger of rejecting this salvation *Beware therefore, lest*, through your obstinate infidelity, *that* fearful and alarming threatening *should come upon you, which is spoken of in one of the prophets*, (*Hab* i 5) concerning the men of that generation in which he lived, *Behold, ye despisers*, and *wonder* at your own stupidity, and my vengeance ready to light upon you, *and perish*, be covered with shame, and hide yourselves in terrors at the approaching judgments, *for I work a work, which you shall in no wise believe, though a man declare it unto you*, such as the destruction of their temple and nation by the Romans, a judgment more terrible than ever before fell upon them by the hand of the Chaldeans Or perhaps it may refer to the glorious work of redemption and mercy which should be extended to the Gentiles, whilst the Jews would be rejected for their wilful unbelief and impenitence, neither of which would they believe, though told them by persons of the most undoubted credit and authority

42 And when the Jews were gone out of the synagogue, the Gentiles besought that these words might be
preached to them † the next sabbath 43 Now when † Or in the week between
the congregation was broken up, many of the Jews, and
religious proselytes followed Paul and Barnabas, who
speaking to them, persuaded them to [c] continue in the c Chap xi 23 & xiv 22 Heb iii 6, 14
grace of God 44 ¶ And the next sabbath day came
almost the whole city together to hear the word of God
45 But when the Jews saw the multitudes, they were
filled with envy, and [d] spake against those things which d Chap xviii 6 1 Pet iv 4
were spoken by Paul, contradicting and blaspheming
46 Then Paul and Barnabas waxed bold, and said, [e] It e Matt x 6 Chap iii 26 Rom i 16
was necessary that the word of God should first have
been spoken to you but [f] seeing ye put it from you, f Ex xxxii [illegible]
and judge yourselves unworthy of everlasting life, lo,
[g] we turn to the Gentiles 47 For so hath the Lord g Matt xxi 43 Rom x 19
commanded us, *saying*, [h] I have set thee to be a light of h Chap xviii 6 & xxviii 28 i Isa xlii 6, & xlix 6 Luke ii 32 k Chap ii 47
the Gentiles, that thou shouldest be for salvation unto
the ends of the earth 48 And when the Gentiles heard
this, they were glad, and glorified the word of the Lord
and [k] as many as were ordained to eternal life, believed
49 And the word of the Lord was published throughout
all the region 50 But the Jews stirred up the devout
and honourable women, and the chief men of the
city, and [l] raised persecution against Paul and Barna- l 2 Tim iii 11
bas, and expelled them out of their coasts 51 But
[m] they shook off the dust of their feet against them, and m Matt x 14 Chap xviii 6
came unto Iconium 52 And the disciples were filled
with joy, and with the holy Ghost

v 42—52

v 42—52 Nothing could be more kindly spoken than this discourse of the apostle, and more respectful to the Jewish people But we are told,

1 The ill reception many of the Jews gave to his sermon They went *out of the synagogue*, in open contempt of the apostle, and of the doctrine of Christ which he preached, intimating thereby an avowed resolution never to hear him again, or regard ought that he could say And justly are they abandoned to their infidelity, who obstinately reject the counsel of the Lord against their own souls, and will not even give the gospel a candid hearing

2 The Gentiles hereupon, the proselytes of righteousness, who attended the Jewish worship, *besought*, that if the Jews refused to receive the gracious message, *these words might be preached to them the next sabbath* They longed for that salvation which the others slighted

3 Though the generality of the Jews turned their backs on the apostles and their preaching, many were affected by what they heard, both of the native Jews, and religious proselytes, and they *followed Paul and Barnabas*, that they might in private have some farther conference with them on a matter so important and glad to see them thus impressed, they conversed freely with them on the subject, to carry on the good work begun on their hearts, warmly exhorting and persuading them by every powerful argument, *to continue in the grace of God*, faithfully embracing and boldly professing the gospel doctrines, depending on the Spirit's influence, and waiting in the use of all appointed means upon the Lord *Note*, (1) They who truly receive the word of Christ, will follow his ministers, and long for farther instruction in righteousness (2) Continuance in the grace of God, must prove we are truly partakers of it

4 The next sabbath the auditory was immense Probably, in the week days, the apostles had improved every opportunity to spread the truths of God, and as the Gentiles were graciously received by them, they flocked together on the sabbath, and not only the religious proselytes, but many of those who were before idolatrous, invited by curiosity, or from better motives, assembled *to hear the word of God*

5 *When the Jews*, who were enemies to the gospel, *saw the multitudes*, and among them many of the idolatrous Gentiles whom they abhorred, *they were filled with envy*, that to them the word of God should be spoken, and that these new preachers should grow so popular, *and spake against those things which were spoken by Paul, contradicting and blaspheming*, with the utmost rage and passion they disputed against the doctrines of the gospel, abused and vilified the preacher, and blasphemed the holy name of Jesus, who was the great subject of the apostle's discourse *Note*, It is no new thing to hear the glorious truths of Christ and his salvation, treated with virulence and blasphemy by men of corrupt minds

6 *Then Paul and Barnabas waxed bold*, far from being intimidated by such opposition, they appeared inspired with greater zeal, and shewed more undaunted courage in delivering their message, *and said, It was necessary that the word of God should first have been spoken unto you*, in respect to the privileges of your birth, and the command of our master, who sent us forth to publish his gospel, beginning at Jerusalem, and sending the first calls to the lost sheep of the house of Israel *but seeing ye put it from you*, and wilfully reject and vilify the great salvation of the Messiah, *and judge yourselves unworthy of eternal life*, which can only be obtained by that faith in him and his gospel, which you despise, and are unworthy to hear any more, *lo, we turn to the Gentiles*, leaving you of this place to your obstinate impenitence and infidelity, and henceforth proclaiming the salvation which is in Jesus Christ to the heathen, and herein we act by divine warrant, and in exact correspondence with the scriptures *For so hath the Lord commanded us, saying, I have set thee to be a light of the Gentiles, that thou shouldest be for salvation unto the ends of the earth*, Isa xlix 6 *Note*, (1) The more obstinately sinners oppose the word of God, the more bold and zealous should his ministers be, in maintaining the truth of his gospel (2) They who reject God's ministers, and their message, pronounce sentence on themselves, *as unworthy of eternal life* (3) Christ is the sun of righteousness risen on the benighted world, in him we see the way to present and eternal salvation opened, and all, to the end of the earth, are invited to look to him, and be saved

7 *When the Gentiles heard this*, that the salvation which the apostles preached extended to them, according to God's express word and warrant, *they were glad, and glorified the word of the Lord*, praising him for sending the light of his truth among them, *and as many as were ordained to eternal life*, who not only, like the stony ground hearers, expressed a transitory joy in what they heard, but were in God's eternal and all-wise decrees appointed unto glory, to stand amidst the shining ranks of the church triumphant, *they believed* to the saving of their soul *And the word of the Lord*, which was with such gracious effect preached in the capital, *was published throughout all the region*, both by the apostolic labours, and the Gentile converts, who longed to engage their brethren to share with them in the common salvation. *Note*, (1) The gospel is glad news to the sinner that sees and feels the need of the pardon and grace therein promised (2) They who have tasted the preciousness of God's word, cannot but glorify him for his unspeakable gift (3) Eternal life is the gift of God and in their hearts, who are ordained to partake of it, doth he work the work of faith with power (4) If we have ourselves received the knowledge of Jesus, and his rich grace, we shall delight to spread abroad the savour of his name

8 The unbelieving Jews, filled with malice and enmity against the apostles, *stirred up the devout and honourable women*, who were proselytes, and most zealous for Judaism *and the chief men of the city*, probably by their means, representing the apostles as dangerous men, *and raised persecution against Paul and Barnabas, and expelled them out of their coasts* *Note*, (1) Wherever the gospel is preached with success there the ministers of it may expect the devil's rage (2) None persecute so bitterly as those who are devout and make profession of religion (3) The best of men have been expelled with ignominy from places where their successful labours provoked the enmity of those, who should have protected and honoured them, but such reproach is their highest honour, such suffering their truest preferment

Lastly, Being thus violently driven out of the city, *they shook off the dust of their feet against them*, in detestation of their wickedness, and as a testimony against their persecutors in the judgment-day, according to their master's order, Luke ix 5 *and they came to Iconium*, the chief city of Lycaonia, a neighbouring province *And the disciples*, whom they left behind, though deprived of their faithful teachers, and beholding these persecutions, far from being disheartened, *were filled with joy, and with the Holy Ghost*, blest with the most abundant consolations in their souls, mightily enriched with the gifts and graces of the Spirit, and making a bold and noble profession of their faith, amidst all opposition *Note*, (1) Where the place against which the rejected ministers of Jesus shake off the dust of their feet, Sodom's vengeance shall be light compared with the doom of that city (2) As our tribulations for Christ abound, he can, and usually doth, cause our consolations to abound also

CHAP XIV

We have in this chapter a farther account of the progress of the gospel, by the ministry of Paul and Barnabas, among the Gentiles Here is, 1 Their successful preaching at Iconium, and their being driven thence by the violence of their persecutors, ver 1—7 2 Their healing of a lame man at Lystra, and the difficulty they found to restrain the people from worshipping them as gods, ver 8—18 3 The outrage of the people against Paul, at the instigation of the Jews, the effect of which was, that they stoned him, as they thought, to death, but he was wonderfully restored again, ver 19, 20 4 The visit which Paul and Barnabas made to the churches which they had planted, to confirm and put them into order, ver 21—23 5 Their return to Antioch, from whence they were sent forth, the good they did by the way, and the report they made to the church of Antioch of their expedition, ver 24—28

1 AND it came to pass in Iconium, that they went
both together into the synagogue of the Jews,
and so spake, that a great multitude both of the Jews
and also of the Greeks believed 2 But the unbelieving
Jews stirred up the Gentiles, and made their minds evil
affected against the brethren 3 Long time therefore
abode they speaking boldly in the Lord, [a] which gave
testimony unto the word of his grace, and granted [b] signs
and wonders to be done by their hands 4 But the
multitude of the city was divided and part held with
the Jews, and part with the apostles 5 And when
there was an assault made both of the Gentiles, and also
of the Jews, with their rulers, [c] to use *them* despitefully,
and to stone them, 6 They were ware of *it*, and [d] fled
unto Lystra and Derbe, cities of Lycaonia, and unto the
region that lieth round about 7 And there they
preached the gospel

[a] Mark xvi 20 Heb ii 4

[b] Chap xix 11

[c] 2 Tim iii 11

[d] Matt x 23 Chap viii 1

ver 1—7 Though the apostles were so ignominiously treated by the Jews at Antioch, yet did they not desist from their accustomed manner of visiting their synagogues but at Iconium, and making them the offer of the gospel

1 *They went both together into the synagogue* as mutual fellow-helpers, and that out of the mouth of two witnesses every word might be established, *and so spake, that a great multitude both of Jews and also of the Greeks believed* So powerful was their preaching, and so mightily did the Spirit of God bless their ministrations, to the conviction and conversion of many hearers.

2 The success, as usual, exasperated the unbelieving Jews, who stirred up the Gentiles *and made their minds evil affected against the brethren*, by representing them and their conduct as what was dangerous

carrying on some bad design. Persecutors would thus always cover malignity under specious pretences.

3. Though the apostles saw the prejudices and rancour entertained against them and their new converts, they were not disheartened, but *abode long time speaking boldly in the Lord*, in his glorious cause, and supported by his power and Spirit, *which gave testimony unto the word of his grace, and granted signs and wonders to be done by their hands*, in attestation to the truth of the gospel which they preached. *Note*, (1.) The gospel is *the word of Christ's grace*, containing the richest discoveries of free, boundless, and undeserved mercy to the sinful sons of men. (2.) They who go forth in the strength of the Lord, will not be dismayed at the frowns of their enemies.

4. Notwithstanding the malice of the Jews, a strong party was formed for the apostles, and the city was divided, and for a time the persecution was restrained. At last, the Jewish party prevailing, an assault was made both of the Gentiles and Jews, supported by the magistrates, in order to seize the apostles, and *use them despitefully*, treating them with every kind of ignominy, *and then to stone them*, as blasphemers and miscreants unworthy to live. *Note*, (1.) If the gospel makes a division in a place or city that was before at peace, it is not to be imputed to any tendency which the gracious message hath to create such disturbance, but to the enmity of the natural heart against God, which cannot bear to see the power of gospel grace in the conversations of others. And far better is it to bear reproach and persecution, as the troublers of the false peace of sinners, than to suffer them to swim securely down the stream into the gulph of perdition. (2.) If the enemies of the truth are so unanimous in opposition, shall the friends of the gospel be less united in the glorious cause?

5. The apostles got intelligence of this conspiracy, and to escape *from the hands of these blood-thirsty men, fled to Lystra and Derbe, cities of Lycaonia, and unto the region that lieth round about, and there they preached the gospel*, not desisting from their labours, though compelled to fly for their lives. Thus the enmity of their persecutors contributed but the more to spread that gospel which they opposed.

e Chap. iii. 2. 8 ¶ And [e] there sat a certain man at Lystra, impotent in his feet, being a cripple from his mother's womb, who never had walked: 9 The same heard Paul speak:
f Mat. ix. 28. who stedfastly beholding him, and perceiving that [f] he had faith to be healed, 10 Said with a loud voice,
g Isa. xxxv. 6. Stand upright on thy feet. [g] And he leaped and walked.
11 And when the people saw what Paul had done, they lifted up their voices, saying in the speech of Lycaonia,
h Chap. xxviii. 6. [h] The gods are come down to us in the likeness of men.
12 And they called Barnabas, Jupiter; and Paul, Mercurius, because he was the chief speaker. 13 Then the priest of Jupiter, which was before their city, brought
i Dan. ii. 46. oxen and garlands unto the gates, and [i] would have done sacrifice with the people. 14 *Which* when the apostles
k Mat. xxvi. 65. Barnabas and Paul heard *of*, [k] they rent their clothes, and ran in among the people, crying out, 15 And saying,
l Chap. x. 25, 26. Rev. xix. 10. & xxii. 9. Sirs, [l] why do ye these things? [m] We also are men of like passions with you, and preach unto you, that ye
m Jam. v. 17. should turn from [n] these vanities unto the living God,
n 1 Sam. xii. 21. [o] which made heaven and earth, and the sea, and all
o Gen. i. 1. Psal. cxlvi. 6. Rev. xiv. 7. things that are therein: 16 [p] Who in times past suffered all nations to walk in their own ways. 17 [q] Nevertheless he left not himself without witness, in that he
p Psal. lxxxi. 12. Chap. xvii. 30. did good, and gave us rain from heaven, and fruitful seasons, filling our hearts with food and gladness. 18
1 Pet. iv. 3. And with these sayings scarce restrained they the people,
q Chap. xvii. 27. Rom. i. 20. that they had not done sacrifice unto them.

v. 8—18. During their stay at Lystra we are told,

1. Of a notable cure performed by Paul on a man lame from his birth. In the assembly where Paul was preaching, he sat attentive to his discourse, when the apostle *stedfastly beholding him, and perceiving*, by the spirit of discernment, *that he had faith to be healed*, and was persuaded of the power with which the apostles were endued to cure his lameness, incurable as it was by any human means, he *said with a loud voice*, that all present might hear and take notice of the miracle, *Stand upright on thy feet*, *and* instantly *he leaped and walked*, restored to perfect strength. *Note*, (1.) They who love the word of God, though they are lame, and cannot walk, will be carried to hear it. (2.) The pains which some take to attend God's worship, through lameness and infirmity, will rise up to condemn their sloth and negligence, who, though so much better able to go, indulge themselves at home. (3.) When Jesus speaks to the impotent soul in his word then, tho' helpless to all good before, our hearts exult with holy joy, and rise to run the way of his commandments.

2. Astonished at what they had seen, the idolatrous Gentiles who were present, concluded, according to the notions of their

pagan theology, that the gods were come down to them in the likeness of men, and in an ecstacy of joy at this supposed honour done them, in their own language expressed aloud the sentiments of their hearts; and, agreeable to the absurd ideas which they had received of their gods, *they called Barnabas Jupiter*, being probably the elder man, and his stature more majestic; *and Paul Mercurius, because he was the chief speaker*, Mercury being the god of eloquence, and reputed the messenger who went on the errands of Jove and the superior deities. *Then the priest of Jupiter which was before their city*, reputed their patron God, or whose temple stood in the suburbs, *brought oxen and garlands unto the gates*, the place of concourse, where Paul and Barnabas were speaking to the people, or to the door of the house where they lodged, *and would have done sacrifice with the people*, crowning them with their garlands, and offering their sacrifices before them.

3. With horror and indignation, when the apostles perceived their design, *they rent their clothes, and ran in among the people, crying out, and saying, Sirs, why do ye these things?* Far from suffering the people to continue in so dangerous a mistake, though it brought them such honour, they desired to renounce all such vain glory, and with earnestness remonstrated against a design so impious and idolatrous. Far from assuming divinity, *we also are men of like passions with you*, subject to all the infirmities of humanity, and corrupt and sinful worms of the earth, as the rest of mankind, *and preach unto you*, as ministers and ambassadors of Christ, which is the highest honour we claim, *that ye should turn from these vanities*, these absurd, useless, unprofitable deities, which are mere nothings, creatures of the fancy which never existed, and whose worship is the height of folly, as well as impiety; and that ye should be brought *unto* the worship and service of *the living God*, who alone is worthy to be feared and adored, as the fountain of life, and the great Creator of all, *which made heaven and earth, and the sea, and things that are therein*, visible or invisible; *who in times past*, in his mysterious ways of providence, which are all righteous and just, *suffered all nations to walk in their own ways*, with much long-suffering bearing with their provocations. *Nevertheless, he left not himself without witness*, but gave them sufficient evidences of his wisdom and goodness, of his eternal power and Godhead, (*Rom.* i. 20.) *in that he did good, and gave us rain from heaven, and fruitful seasons, filling our hearts with food and gladness*, which gifts of his beneficence should have led up our hearts unto him, and left us without excuse in our ignorance of him, neglect, and unthankfulness: to persist therefore in these abominations of idolatry, now the gospel light was come unto them, would be peculiarly criminal. *Note*, (1.) All our temporal mercies should lead up our hearts to God, and looking above all second causes, the great Author of all should be constantly seen in all the bounties of his providence, in every drop of dew that waters the earth, and every blade that breaks the clod. (2.) The goodness of God to us should engage our hearts towards him, and if we have lived in ignorance before, we are called to improve what better light he now graciously communicates. (3.) Our gratitude is due to God, not only for the food he bestows, but for the gladness of heart which he gives to make use of his blessings.

4. *With these sayings scarce restrained they the people, that they had not done sacrifice unto them*; all their expostulations and entreaties with difficulty prevailed upon them to desist, so foolishly obstinate were they in their mistaken persuasion.

19 ¶ And there came thither certain Jews from Antioch and Iconium, who persuaded the people, and
[r] having stoned Paul, drew *him* out of the city, [s] sup- r 2 Cor. xi. 25. 2 Tim. iii. 11.
posing he had been dead. 20 Howbeit, as the disciples s 2 Cor. xii. 2.
stood round about him, he rose up, and came into the
city: and the next day he departed with Barnabas to
Derbe. 21 And when they had preached the gospel to
that city, and had † taught many, they returned again † Gr. Made disciples of many. St Mat. xxviii. 19.
to Lystra, and *to* Iconium, and Antioch, 22 Con-
firming the souls of the disciples, *and* [t] exhorting them t Chap. xi. 23. & xiii. 43.
to continue in the faith, and that [u] we must through u Mat. x. 38. & xvi. 24. Rom. viii. 17. 2 Tim. iii. 12.
much tribulation enter into the kingdom of God. 23
And when [x] they had ‡ ordained them elders in every x Tit. i. 5.
church, and had prayed with fasting, they commended ‡ Gr. chose them by the lifting up of hands.
them to the Lord, on whom they believed. 24 And
after they had passed through Pisidia, they came to Pam-
phylia. 25 And when they had preached the word in
Perga, they went down into Attalia: 26 And thence
sailed to Antioch, [y] from whence they had been recom- y Chap. xiii. 1, 3.
mended to the grace of God, for the work which they
fulfilled. 27 And when they were come, and had ga-
thered the church together, [z] they rehearsed all that God z Chap. xv. 4, 12. & xxi. 19.
had done with them, and how he had [a] opened the door a 1 Cor. xvi. 9. 2 Cor. ii. 12.
of faith unto the Gentiles. 28 And there they abode
long time with the disciples.

v 19—28 How fickle is the mind of vain men! how soon are they, who have no foundation, carried about with every wind They who are deified to day, are thus often detested to-morrow It becomes us, if we would have abiding honour, to seek that which cometh from God only

1 The apostles are brought into the most imminent dangers, and Paul stoned and left for dead The Jews, their implacable enemies, followed them from Iconium and Antioch on purpose to counteract their labours, and with diabolical malice to prevent, to their utmost, the progress of the gospel And soon they found means to *persuade* the wavering multitude that these men were deceivers, turbulent and seditious, and exasperated them so highly that seizing Paul, against whom they bore the bitterest grudge as the chief preacher, *they stoned him* in a popular tumult, *and drew him out of the city, supposing he had been dead* Howbeit, *as the disciples stood round about him*, lamenting over him, praying he might be restored to life, or with an intent to bury him, *he rose up*, quickened by miraculous power, *and*, notwithstanding the late wounds and bruises he had received, *he came into the city*, strengthened in his body, and not daunted in his mind by all that he had endured *Note*, (1) True disciples will not forsake their persecuted ministers, but own them in the face of every reproach and danger (2) God's faithful servants, though brought to the gates of the grave, shall not die till their work is done

2 The *next day, Paul departed with Barnabas for Derbe*, and when, as usual, they had preached the gospel, and *taught*, their ministry being blessed to the conversion of *many*, they returned back again to the cities of Lystra, Iconium, and Antioch, *confirming the souls of the disciples*, settling them on Christ the great foundation, that no troubles felt or feared, no cares or temptations, might move them away from the hope of the gospel, *and exhorting them to continue in the faith* of Jesus, in the belief of his office, glory, and gospel, and in the bold and open profession of his name, *and saying, that we must through much tribulation enter into the kingdom of God*, for which therefore they must prepare, and count as if some strange thing happened unto them, since all that will live godly in Christ Jesus, must share this common lot *Note*, (1) They who have received the gospel-word, have still need of further confirmation, that they may be built up on their most holy faith, and ministers must labour to establish the professors, as well as to awaken the careless (2) Nothing but faith can enable us to overcome the frowns, the allurements, and discouragements of this present evil world, they who would stand in the evil day, must continue to hold fast on Christ (3) The way to heaven lies through much tribulation, but let us look to the end, and keep the far more exceeding and eternal weight of glory in view, and then we shall count all the sufferings of the present time as light affliction that are but for a moment

3 They *ordained elders*, or presbyters, *in every church*, to lead their devotions, to minister the sacrament, preach the word, and watch over the flock of God committed to their charge, men of gravity and piety, selected from the other disciples, and judged best qualified for the arduous work of the ministry, and having *prayed with fasting*, for the supplies of grace and the divine benediction upon them, *they commended them to the Lord, on whom they believed*, both the elders and their congregations, begging that the Lord, who had begun the good work, would perfect the same, nourishing them up in the words of sound doctrine, and preserving them unto his everlasting kingdom *Note*, (1) The work of the ministry cannot be undertaken with too great solemnity, and they who feel the weight of it, will not fail importunately to seek, by prayer, for more than human power, to carry them through (2) We may comfortably and confidently commit to the divine keeping, those who have faithfully obeyed the call of divine grace, for none shall pluck them out of the Saviour's hand (3) The best parting of friends is in prayer to the Lord, mutually commending ourselves to his care and love

4 The apostles continued their journey to Antioch in Syria, passing through Pisidia, till they came to Pamphylia, where they preached the word at *Perga*, a city of that province, and *Attalia* another town on the sea-coast, and from thence they failed to Antioch, *from whence they had been recommended to the grace of God, for the work which they fulfilled*, and now were returned from their successful expedition, bringing back a full answer to the prayer that had been put up at their departure *And when they were come, and had gathered the church together, they rehearsed all that God had done with them*, ascribing nothing to themselves, but giving him the glory to whom alone the praise of all was due, *and how he had opened a door of faith unto the Gentiles*, great multitudes of whom had been converted unto the faith of Jesus *And there*, at Antioch, *they abode long time with the disciples*, comforting, establishing, strengthening them *Note*, (1) Whatever good is done by our preaching, we must remember, that all the efficacy proceeds not from us, but from the grace of God (2) The way into the kingdom of grace and glory lies through the door of faith, which God alone can open

CHAP XV

Unhappy divisions here first appear in the Christian church, but they are soon allayed Here is, 1 A controversy raised at Antioch by the judaizing teachers about circumcising the Gentile converts, and causing them to observe the ceremonial law ver 1, 2 2 *A consultation had with the church at Jerusalem about this matter, and the sending of delegates thither for that purpose*, ver 2—5 3 *An account of what passed in the synod that was convened upon this occasion*, ver 6 *What Peter said*, ver 7—11 *What Paul and Barnabas discoursed of*, ver 12 *And lastly, what James proposed for the settling of this matter*, ver 13—21 4 *The result of this debate, and the circular letter that was written to the Gentile converts, directing them how to govern themselves with respect to the Jews*, ver 23—29 5 *The delivering of this determination to the church at Antioch, and the satisfaction it gave them*, ver 30—35 6 *A second expedition designed by Paul and Barnabas to preach to the Gentiles, in which they quarrelled about their assistant, and parted upon it, one steering one course, and the other another*, ver 30—41

1 AND certain men which came down from Judea,
taught the brethren, *and said*, [a] Except ye be [a] John vii
circumcised [b] after the manner of Moses, ye cannot be 22 Gal v 2 Phil iii
saved 2 When therefore Paul and Barnabas had no 2 Col ii 8 11 16
small dissention and disputation with them, they deter- [b] Gen xvii
mined that [c] Paul and Barnabas, and certain other of 10 Lev xii
them, should go up to Jerusalem unto the apostles and 3 [c] Gal ii 1
elders about this question 3 And [d] being brought on [d] Rom xv
their way by the church, they passed through Phenice 24 1 Cor xvi 6 11
and Samaria, [e] declaring the conversion of the Gentiles [e] Chap xiv 27
and they caused great joy unto all the brethren 4
And when they were come to Jerusalem, they were re-
ceived of the church, and *of* the apostles and elders, and
[f] they declared all things that God had done with them [f] Ver 12
5 But † there rose up certain of the sect of the Pharisees † Or there rose up said they, certain
which believed, saying, [g] That it was needful to cir-
cumcise them, and to command *them* to keep the law of
Moses. [g] Ver 1.

v 1—5 The peace of that happy society at Antioch, which was the envy of the devil, begins to be interrupted by some, who sowed the seeds of controversy, the bane of the Christian church

1 *Certain men came down from Judea*, not sent by the apostles, but instigated by their own pride and prejudices, *and taught the Gentile brethren, saying, Except ye be circumcised after the manner of Moses, ye cannot be saved*, as if their faith in Christ and adherence to the gospel was insufficient, unless they also submitted to this distinguishing ordinance, and the other rites of the ceremonial law The Jewish Christians, at least, themselves were *zealous for the law*, (*Acts* xxi 20) and were permitted to observe the Jewish ritual as a thing in its nature indifferent, and from which the destruction of the temple, and the dissolution of the Jewish polity, would soon emancipate them but not satisfied with being themselves indulged in this practice, they wanted to enslave the consciences of the Gentile converts under the same yoke, and that on peril of their damnation if they rejected it *Note*, Men are strangely disposed to make their own opinion and practice the standard for others, and to enforce their fancies and inventions as of essential consequence, liberally denouncing their anathemas, and consigning to the pit of destruction all who will not conform to their mode of thinking and worship, and submit their consciences to their yoke but when we are making God's word our rule, and, according to our best light, following his will, we need little regard their rash denunciations

2 Paul and Barnabas boldly withstood these judaizing teachers, and disputed against them as the corrupters of genuine Christianity, and when a growing dissention seemed to threaten this flourishing church, *they determined that Paul and Barnabas, and certain other of them, should go up to Jerusalem unto the apostles and elders about this question*, that the matter being discussed in a full assembly of all the chief ministers of the church, the pretensions of these corruptors might be confounded, and the liberty of the Gentiles confirmed

3 The two great Apostles of the Gentiles hereupon departed, being respectfully attended part of the way by some chief brethren of the church, and as they passed through Phenice and Samaria, *they caused great joy unto all the brethren, declaring the conversion of the Gentiles*, for to faithful souls nothing is matter of more pure unfeigned delight, than to hear that others are made partakers of the same grace which we have tasted

4 *The church at Jerusalem*, and *the Apostles* Cephas, James, and John, and *the elders*, or presbyters, received these distinguished messengers with high respect, and expected their full

approbation of their conduct, when they heard what they had done, and their success among the Gentiles but *certain of the sect of the Pharisees, which believed* in Jesus as the Messiah, and made profession of faith in him, still retained many of their former tenets, and were bigotted to the ceremonial law, they *rose up* therefore, insisting, that it was needful for them not only to believe in Jesus, but also to be circumcised, and keep the law, in order to obtain acceptance with God, thus most highly derogating from the free grace of God, and the great doctrine of justification by faith alone

6 ¶ And the apostles and elders came together for to
consider of this matter 7 And when there had been
much disputing, Peter rose up and said unto them,
[h] Men *and* brethren, ye know how that a good while ago,
God made choice among us, that the Gentiles by my
mouth should hear the word of the gospel, and believe
8 And God [i] which knoweth the hearts, bare them witness,
[k] giving them the holy Ghost, even as *he did* unto
us 9 And [l] put no difference between us and them,
[m] purifying their hearts by faith 10 Now therefore
why tempt ye God, to [n] put a yoke upon the neck of
the disciples, which neither our fathers nor we were able
to bear? 11 But [o] we believe that through the grace
of the Lord Jesus Christ we shall be saved even as they.
12 ¶ Then all the multitude kept silence, and gave audience
to Barnabas and Paul, [p] declaring what miracles
and wonders God had wrought among the Gentiles by
them 13 ¶ And after they had held their peace,
[q] James answered, saying, Men *and* brethren, hearken
unto me 14 Simeon hath declared how God at the
first did visit the Gentiles, to take out of them a people
for his name 15 And to this agree the words of the
prophets as it is written, 16 [r] After this I will return,
and will build again the tabernacle of David, which
is fallen down and I will build again the ruins thereof,
and I will set it up 17 That the residue of men might
seek after the Lord, and all the Gentiles upon whom my
name is called, saith the Lord, who doth all these things
18 Known unto God are all his works from the beginning
of the world 19 Wherefore [s] my sentence is,
that we trouble not them, which from among the Gentiles
are turned to God 20 But that we write unto
them, that they abstain [t] from pollutions of idols, and
[u] *from* fornication, and *from* things strangled, and [x] *from*
blood 21 For Moses of old time hath in every city
them that preach him, [y] being read in the synagogues
every sabbath day

[h] Chap x 20 & xi 12
[i] 1 Chron xxviii 9 Jer xi 20 & xvii 10 Chap i 24
[k] Chap x 44
[l] Chap x 28
[m] Chap x 43 1 Cor i 2 1 Pet i 22
[n] Mat xxiii 4 Gal v 1
[o] Gal ii 16 Eph ii 8 Tit ii 11 & iii 4
[p] Chap xiv 27
[q] Chap xii 17
[r] Am ix 11, 12
[s] Ver 28
[t] Ex xxxiv 15 1 Cor viii 1 & x 20
[u] 1 Thes iv 3
[x] Gen ix 4 Lev iii 17 & vii 26 & xvii 14
[y] Chap xiii 15, 27

v 6—21 The first general council that had yet sat to decide on the unhappy disputes which were beginning to arise in the church, is here with great seriousness assembled, to hear, consider, and determine After much disputing on the subject, we have,

1 Peter's speech on the occasion He had heard what had been said on both sides of the argument, and therefore, as one of the most respectable personages in that assembly, rises to deliver his opinion

He reminds them how God had sent him several years before to preach the gospel to Cornelius and the Gentiles who were with him, and had thereby led them by faith to Jesus Christ for life and salvation The same gifts had been bestowed on them, as on the Jewish converts, and God had himself herein testified his acceptance and approbation of them, making no difference between them, *purifying their hearts by faith*, as justified and sanctified by the blood, the righteousness, and grace of Jesus, without the least need of circumcision and the ceremonial observances Since therefore God had so evidently decided the matter, it was the highest presumption, and no better than tempting God, arraigning his wisdom and authority, to pretend a right to counteract what he had done, and repeal what he had determined and it was a great injury to the Gentile brethren, to put that yoke of ceremonial institutions upon their neck, that had been so burthensome to themselves and their fathers, and which was now absolutely useless, since the salvation by Jesus Christ was alike free to Jew and Gentile, and both were to be saved by grace through faith, without the least respect to circumcision, or any legal institutions *We* therefore, says Peter, expect to be *saved even as they*, and they as freely as we *Note*, (1) The salvation of the gospel is a common salvation, free from all terms and conditions whatsoever, bestowed by grace, and accepted by faith alone (2) They who have the real faith of the gospel, will certainly evidence its purifying efficacy upon their hearts (3) All who hold the head Christ, and walk in holiness as Christ also walked, however in some sentiments they may differ from us, are cordially to be embraced by us as brethren

2 Paul and Barnabas, instead of ten thousand arguments, related simply *the miracles and wonders which God had wrought among the Gentiles by them, whilst all the multitude kept* a profound *silence*, listening attentively to so wonderful and pleasing a narrative, wherein it evidently appeared, both by the *miracles* which God enabled them to work, and by the *success* he gave them in the conversion of the Gentiles, that he approved their labours, and bore testimony to the acceptance of these Gentile converts What need could there be, that they should be burdened with the works of the law, who *had received the Holy Ghost by the hearing of faith?* (*See Gal* iii 2)

3 On their closing their discourse, James, the last speaker in this council, sums up the debate, and delivers his opinion

[1] After a respectful address to them, as men of reason and consideration, and brethren in the Lord, he reminds them of what Peter had said, by whose preaching first God *did visit the Gentiles* with the knowledge of his gospel, and the gifts of his grace, *to take out of them a people for his name*, to be to the praise of his glory

[2] He observes, that God herein exactly fulfilled his own word in the mouth of his prophets, which had so long ago foretold this great event, *as it is written*, (*Amos* ix 11) *After this I will return*, and recover the scattered remnant of Israel, *and will build again the tabernacle of David, which is fallen down*, in and by the divine Messiah, who, when the house of David was reduced to the lowest state of want and contempt, should arise to set up that spiritual and everlasting kingdom, of which David's house and kingdom were the figures *and I will build again the ruins thereof, and I will set it up*, great and glorious, *that the residue of men*, even the nations who had before been left of God to walk in their own ways, *might seek after the Lord*, submitting to the Messiah's sceptre, and becoming obedient to the gospel word, *and all the Gentiles*, whether proselytes or idolaters, converted to the faith of Christ, *upon whom my name is called*, as elect vessels, separated for his glory, *saith the Lord who doth all these things*, whose word is faithful, whose power alone could effect this wondrous conversion in the heathen world, and who in so doing testified his acceptance of the Gentile converts

[3] He resolves the matter into God's eternal purpose *Known unto God are all his works from the beginning of the world*, what he decreed from eternity he had foretold, and now fulfilled, and they might be fully assured, all his counsels were holy, just, and good, and therefore to be acquiesced in by them without a moment's hesitation

[4] He delivers his opinion concerning what he judges proper to be done on the present occasion *My sentence is, that we trouble not them, which from among the Gentiles are turned to God*, by the imposition of the unnecessary yoke of legal observances on their consciences, *but that*, to avoid all offence to the believing brethren among the Jews, and to remove whatever would prevent their communion with the Gentile converts, *we write unto them, that they abstain from the pollution of idols*, from eating or drinking any thing offered to idols, *and from fornication*, and all impure embraces, *and from things strangled, and from blood*, for as fornication, though so common and allowed among the Gentiles, must be abstained from as a moral evil, other things, though indifferent in themselves, were then needful to be observed, in order to promote mutual love and communion between the Jewish and Gentile brethren For as the writings of Moses, in which these things are forbidden, had been of old read every sabbath-day, and the Jewish converts still retained a high veneration for the law, they owed them this indulgence to their long-received usage in these indifferent matters *Note*, Great allowances are to be made to the prejudices of education, and therefore in indifferent matters we should show to each other a spirit of mutual charity and forbearance, desiring to please every man his neighbour for his good to edification

22 Then pleased it the apostles and elders, with the
whole church, to send chosen men of their own company
to Antioch, with Paul and Barnabas, *namely*, Judas surnamed
Barsabas and Silas, chief men among the brethren
23 And wrote letters by them after this manner,
The apostles, and elders, and brethren send greeting
unto the brethren which are of the Gentiles in Antioch,
and Syria, and Cilicia 24 Forasmuch as we have
heard, that [a] certain which went out from us have
troubled you with words, subverting your souls, saying,
Ye must be circumcised, and keep the law, to whom we
gave no *such* commandment 25 It seemed good unto
us, being assembled with one accord, to send chosen
men unto you, with our beloved Barnabas and Paul,
26 [b] Men that have hazarded their lives for the name of
our Lord Jesus Christ 27 We have sent therefore Judas
and Silas, who shall also tell you the same things by
mouth 28 For it seemed good to the holy Ghost, and

Chap ... 23
[a] Ver 1
[b] Chap ... 27

and to us, to lay upon you no greater burden than theſe
necessary things; 29 [e] That ye abſtain from meats [e Ver 20 Chap xxi]
offered to idols, and from blood, and from things ſtran
gled, and from fornication: from which if ye keep
yourſelves, ye ſhall do well. Fare ye well. 30 So
when they were diſmiſſed, they came to Antioch: and
when they had gathered the multitude together, they de-
livered the epiſtle. 31 *Which* when they had read, they
rejoiced for the † conſolation. 32 And Judas and Silas [† Or, exhortation]
being prophets alſo themſelves, [f] exhorted the brethren [f Chap xiv]
with many words, and confirmed *them*. 33 And after
they had tarried *there* a ſpace, they were let [e] go in peace [e 1 Cor xvi 11 Heb xi 31]
from the brethren unto the apoſtles. 34 Notwithſtand-
ing it pleaſed Silas to abide there ſtill. 35 Paul alſo
and Barnabas continued in Antioch, teaching and preach-
ing the word of the Lord, with many others alſo.

v 22—35. The matter being now brought to a concluſion, and the aſſembly concurring in their approbation of the opinion which James had delivered, we have,

1. The choice of two perſons from the brethren at Jeruſalem, eminent for their gifts and graces, Barſabas and Silas, to accompany Paul and Barnabas to Antioch, with letters containing the decree of the council, both as a teſtimony of reſpect towards their Gentile fellow-Chriſtians, and as helpers to eſtabliſh the work begun among them.

2. The letters themſelves contained,

[1.] A moſt reſpectful addreſs. *The apoſtles, and elders, and brethren ſend greeting unto the brethren which are of the Gentiles in Antioch, and Syria, and Cilicia*: they aſſume no authoritative ſtile, nor ſounding titles; but ſtretch out the hand of fellowſhip, giving them the reſult of their conſultations.

[2.] They recite the cauſe on which their council was held, marking with juſt diſapprobation the diſturbers of the church's peace. *We have heard, that certain which went out from us have troubled you with words, ſubverting your ſouls, ſaying, Ye muſt be circumciſed, and keep the law; to whom we gave no ſuch commandment*: they pretended that they acted under the apoſtolic commiſſion and authority, but this is here utterly diſclaimed. *Note*, (1.) Nothing ſo fatally *ſubverts* the ſoul, as the inſiſting upon any thing, as neceſſary to our acceptance and juſtification before God, beſides faith only. (2.) Many pretend a miſſion from God and his church, whoſe pretenſions, when examined, are found utterly falſe and deluſive.

[3.] They make honourable mention of the bearers of their epiſtle, whom they with one accord agreed to ſend. *It ſeemed good unto us, being aſſembled with one accord, to ſend choſen men unto you, with our beloved Barnabas and Paul*, for whom they expreſſed their higheſt regard, and teſtified the moſt entire approbation of their conduct, *men that have hazarded their lives for the name of our Lord Jeſus Chriſt*; a noble evidence of their approved fidelity. *We have ſent therefore Judas and Silas, who*, leſt any cavil ſhould be raiſed about the meaning or intention of the contents of our letters, *ſhall alſo tell you the ſame things by mouth*.

[4.] They plainly determine concerning the diſputed point. *It ſeemed good to the Holy Ghoſt*, according to his word in the prophets, and the intimations of his will in the converſions already wrought among the Gentiles by his power; *and to us*, aſſembled in his name, and under his influence, *to lay upon you no greater burden than theſe neceſſary things: That ye abſtain from meats offered to idols, and from blood, and from things ſtrangled, and from fornication*. The avoiding fornication is *neceſſary* for Chriſtians at all times; the other things were merely temporal prohibitions, enjoined for a particular purpoſe, in order to prevent offence, and to remove all cauſe of diſunion between them and their Jewiſh brethren; but theſe were *not* things of moral and perpetual obligation, but were to ceaſe when, the Jewiſh polity being deſtroyed, all the ceremonial inſtitutions would be at an end.

[5.] They bid them a kind *farewel*, wiſhing them all proſperity in body and ſoul, and recommending them to ſubmit to their deciſion; not with proud anathemas if they diſobeyed, but with the more apoſtolic language of kind entreaty and affectionate perſuaſion. *If ye keep yourſelves* from theſe things, *ye ſhall do well*; it will be to the glory of God, the peace of the church, and the furtherance of the goſpel.

3. The bearers no ſooner arrived, than they aſſembled the multitude, and delivered the epiſtle, who read with pleaſure the determination of the controverſy ſo much to the ſatiſfaction of the Gentile brethren: *and Judas and Silas being prophets alſo themſelves*, endued with eminent gifts of wiſdom and knowledge, *exhorted the brethren with many words*, to perſevere in the faith and obedience of the goſpel, *and confirmed them* in the doctrines of truth which they had embraced. Where the goſpel is truly and powerfully preached, the occaſional aſſiſtance of new miniſters is ſtill advantageous, and ſerves to help forward the work of God.

4. After ſome conſiderable ſtay, the meſſengers from the apoſtles were *let go in peace*, with the thanks of the church for all their kind and uſeful labours, and had the ſatiſfaction to ſee peace perfectly re-eſtabliſhed, which could not but be glad news to the brethren at Jeruſalem. Silas however choſe ſtill to continue at Antioch, where Paul and Barnabas, and many others, with great ſucceſs, taught and preached *the word of the Lord*. *Note*, Where God opens a great door of uſefulneſs, there a double obligation lies upon his miniſters to improve the opportunity, and to labour more abundantly in the bleſſed work.

36 ¶ And ſome days after Paul ſaid unto Barnabas,
Let us go again and viſit our brethren, in every city
[f] where we have preached the word of the Lord, *and ſee* [f Chap xiii 4 13 & xiv 1, 21]
how they do. 37 And Barnabas determined to take
with them [g] John, whoſe ſurname was Mark. 38 But [g Chap xii 12 25 & xiii 5 Col iv 10]
Paul thought not good to take him with them, [h] who
departed from them from Pamphylia, and went not with [h Chap xiii 13]
them to the work. 39 And the contention was ſo
ſharp between them, that they departed aſunder one from
the other: and ſo Barnabas took Mark, and ſailed un-
to Cyprus; 40 And Paul choſe Silas, and departed,
[i] being recommended by the brethren unto the grace of [i Chap xiv 26]
God. 41 And he went through Syria and Cilicia, con-
firming the churches.

v 36—41. The beſt of men are but men at the beſt, and liable to the ſame paſſions as others. The ſacred hiſtorians generouſly record their own faults, that we ſhould not think of them more highly than we ought to think.

1. The zealous Paul propoſes to his faithful aſſociate Barnabas a ſecond expedition among the Gentiles, and particularly with a view to viſit their brethren in all the places where they had preached the word, to ſee how they ſtood, to communicate a ſecond bleſſing to them, and to exhort, encourage, rebuke, and quicken them according to their ſeveral needs. *Note*, Thoſe lie eſpecially near a miniſter's heart, to whom, under God, he hath been a ſpiritual father: and if providence removes him for a while from them, he cannot but be anxiouſly concerned for their welfare, and long for their eſtabliſhment.

2. A diſagreement unhappily aroſe between Paul and Barnabas on this occaſion. Barnabas readily conſented to the propoſal, but determined to take his nephew John Mark, partial probably to him on account of his relation. Paul warmly oppoſed it, and would by no means conſent, thinking him unworthy of that honour, *who departed from them from Pamphylia, and went not with them to the work*, intimidated by the danger, or weary of the fatigue, or diverted by ſome worldly motive from the ſervice of the goſpel. They who have proved themſelves unfaithful, ſhould be tried, ere they are again truſted.

3. The iſſue of the contention was ſo ſharp that they parted. Both were obſtinate, both heated with the diſpute; and, whichever was in the right in the ſubject of the contention, both were, it ſhould ſeem, wrong in the haſty unyielding ſpirit with which it was managed. *Note*, (1.) Tho' we may ſee good men upon a time unhappily betrayed into a temporary fit of paſſion, we muſt beware not to make their evil a plea in our own excuſe. (2.) Truly wiſe and good men may differ in ſome opinions, ſentiments, and views, and contend too warmly for their own. Let us not be offended thereat; it is the infirmity of this mortal ſtate, where darkneſs and imperfection will ſtill be found. It is reſerved for the felicity of the heavenly ſtate, to be entirely of one heart and one mind.

4. Though they diſputed about a circumſtance of little importance perhaps, (and ſuch hath often bred the ſharpeſt contentions) yet both heartily perſiſted in their former gracious purpoſe; and even their ſeparation was over-ruled for the furtherance of the goſpel. *Barnabas took Mark, and ſailed unto Cyprus; and Paul choſe Silas, and departed, being recommended by the brethren unto the grace of God*; which ſeems to intimate, that they thought Paul in the right in refuſing Mark, and favoured him with a particular mark of their approbation. *And he went through Syria and Cilicia, confirming the churches*, and eſtabliſhing them in the faith and practice of the goſpel.

Whatever juſt cauſe of diſpleaſure Paul might now have againſt Mark, we find with pleaſure, that afterwards he ſhewed him the moſt cordial regard, and profeſſed the higheſt opinion of him, (2 *Tim* iv 11 *Col* iv 10.) We ſhould learn therefore to judge with much temper and candour, even of thoſe who may have taken a wrong ſtep, leſt their future conduct ſhould make us grieve for the ſeverity with which we treated them: and though they have juſtly deſerved ſharp rebuke, when they again approve their fidelity, and teſtify their repentance, we ſhould forget all that is paſt, give them the right hand of fellowſhip, and truſt and honour them as before.

CHAP.

CHAP XVI

This hiſtory henceforward chiefly records the travels, labours, and ſufferings of Paul Here is, 1 The beginning of his acquaintance with Timothy, and taking him to be his aſſiſtant, ver 1—3 2 The viſit he made to the churches for their eſtabliſhment, ver 4, 5 3 His call to Macedonia, and his coming to Philippi, with his entertainment there, ver 6—13 4 The converſion of Lydia, ver 14, 15 5 The caſting of an evil ſpirit out of a damſel, ver 16—18 6 The accuſing and abuſing Paul and Silas for it, their impriſonment, and the indignities done them, ver 19—24 7 The miraculous converſion of the jailer to the faith of Chriſt, ver 25—34 8 The honourable diſcharge of Paul and Silas by the magiſtrates, ver 35—40

a Chap xv 6 b Rom xvi 21 Phil ii 19 1 Theſ iii 2 c 2 Tim i 5 d Chap vi 3 e 1 Cor ix 20 Gal ii 3 1 THEN came he to a Derbe and Lyſtra and be-
hold, a certain diſciple was there b named Ti-
motheus, c the ſon of a certain woman, which was a
Jeweſs, and believed, but his father *was* a Greek 2
Which was d well reported of by the brethren that were
at Lyſtra and Iconium 3 Him would Paul have to
go forth with him, and e took and circumciſed him,
becauſe of the Jews which were in thoſe quarters for
they knew all that his father was a Greek 4 And as
f Chap xv 29 g Id 41 they went through the cities, they delivered them the
decrees for to keep, f that were ordained by the apoſtles
and elders which were at Jeruſalem 5 And g ſo were
the churches eſtabliſhed in the faith, and increaſed in
number daily

v 1—5 We have here an account of Paul's travels, and his acquaintance with Timothy, who under his tuition afterwards grew ſo eminent

1 Paul's firſt viſit was to Derbe and Lyſtra, where the Lord had provided for him an aſſiſtant and companion in his travels, *a certain diſciple*, a young man named Timothy, whoſe mother was a Jeweſs, his father a Gentile His exemplary conduct and excellent parts had gained him a great character among the brethren at Lyſtra and Iconium, Paul therefore was deſirous to engage him to go with him, and the zealous youth readily conſenting, *he took and circumciſed him*, not as neceſſary to ſalvation, or as an obligation on him to obſerve the ceremonial law, that having been ſettled by the apoſtolic decree, but as a matter in itſelf indifferent, and becauſe he knew the prejudices the Jews who believed not would entertain againſt him, becauſe they knew his father was a Greek, and that unleſs he were circumciſed, they never would admit him to preach in any of their ſynagogues, or converſe with him, which might greatly obſtruct the uſefulneſs of his miniſtry In condeſcenſion therefore to the prejudices of his countrymen he took this ſtep, and to the Jews became as a Jew, that he might gain the Jews, a proof of his warm affection towards his kinſmen after the fleſh, though perſecuted by them as their inveterate enemy

2 *As they went through the cities, they delivered them the decrees for to keep, that were ordained by the apoſtles and elders which were at Jeruſalem* Though he had for a particular reaſon circumciſed Timothy, he meant not to lay any ſtumbling-block in the way of the Gentile converts thereby, but aſſerted their entire liberty from all the legal inſtitutions, according to the copies of the apoſtolic decree which he delivered to them *And ſo were the churches eſtabliſhed in the faith*, in the great doctrines of juſtification by faith alone, and of acceptance with God through Jeſus Chriſt, without any reſpect to circumciſion or the Moſaical ordinances, *and increaſed in number daily*, the Lord, by the miniſtration of Paul and his young aſſiſtant, adding to the church ſuch as ſhould be ſaved And this is the ſupreme joy of the faithful miniſters of Chriſt, and a freſh bond to quicken their zeal and diligence, when Chriſt is pleaſed to make them ſee this travail of their ſoul

6 Now when they had gone throughout Phrygia, and
the region of Galatia, and were forbidden of the holy
Ghoſt to preach the word in Aſia, 7 After they were
come to Myſia, they aſſayed to go into Bithynia but
the Spirit ſuffered them not 8 And they paſſing by
h 2 Cor ii 12 Myſia, h came down to Troas 9 And a viſion ap-
i Chap x 30 peared to Paul in the night There ſtood i a man of
Macedonia, and prayed him, ſaying, Come over into
Macedonia, and help us 10 And after he had ſeen
k 2 Cor ii 13 the viſion, immediately we endeavoured to go k into Ma-
cedonia, aſſuredly gathering, that the Lord had called us
for to preach the goſpel unto them 11 Therefore
looſing from Troas, we came with a ſtrait courſe to Sa-
mothracia, and the next *day* to Neapolis 12 And
from thence to Philippi, which is the chief city of that
part of Macedonia, *and* a colony and we were in that
city abiding certain days 13 And on the ſabbath we
went out of the city by a river-ſide, where prayer was
wont to be made, and we ſat down, and ſpake unto the
women which reſorted *thither* 14 ¶ And a certain
woman named Lydia, a ſeller of purple, of the city of
Thyatira, which worſhipped God, heard *us* l whoſe l Luke xxiv 45
heart the Lord opened, that ſhe attended unto the
things which were ſpoken of Paul 15 And when
ſhe was baptized, and her houſhold, ſhe beſought *us*,
ſaying, If ye have judged me to be faithful to the Lord,
come into my houſe and abide *there* And m ſhe con- m Gen xix 3 & xxxiii 11 Judg xix 21 Luke xxiv 29 Heb xiii 2
ſtrained us.

v 6—15 We have here,

1 Paul's travels continued through Phrygia and Galatia He had purpoſed to go on through the proconſular Aſia, but by a ſecret impulſe of the Holy Ghoſt, he was forbid, other work being provided for him His next remove was to Myſia, a people deſpicable to a proverb, but the grace of Jeſus knows no reſpect of perſons From thence they had deſigned to go into Bithynia, another province of leſſer Aſia, *but the Spirit ſuffered them not*, under whoſe guidance they directed all their motions Therefore paſſing by Myſia, without making any ſtay, they came to Troas, near the place where the ancient city of Troy had ſtood, and here, it is ſuppoſed, Luke, the writer of this hiſtory, joined Paul and his company, as henceforward he uſually ſays, *we*, as one of thoſe who travelled with the apoſtle

2 At Troas, the Lord in a viſion directed Paul which way to bend his courſe An angel, in the garb of a Macedonian, ſtood by him, and intreated him to come over into Macedonia and help them, by his prayers and preaching Hereupon, aſſuredly concluding this was a divine call to preach the goſpel unto them, he and his fellow-travellers immediately prepared for their voyage, and came to Samothracia, a little iſland lying in the Archipelago, or Ægean Sea, and the next day they arrived at Neapolis, a port on the confines of Macedonia, and continuing their courſe, they reached Philippi, the chief city of that part of Macedonia, and a Roman colony, governed by the Roman laws and magiſtrates *Note*, (1) When we ſee an evident call of God to a place, we may go to our work with confidence, aſſuredly gathering that God hath there a people to praiſe him (2) They who are ſent on God's work, muſt run at his bidding, and make no delay (3) Chief cities uſually afford the greateſt field of uſefulneſs, and the goſpel ſent thither becomes a more general bleſſing

3 The firſt days of their arrival ſeemed to promiſe but little ſucceſs they abode there *certain days*, perhaps unnoticed, and unable to find a door of utterance There ſeems to have been no ſynagogue of the Jews in this place, but ſome devout women, whether Jews or proſelytes, reſorted to an oratory without the city, near the river ſide, where they uſed to meet for prayer on the ſabbath-day thither the apoſtle and his fellow-travellers went, and joined their devotions, taking an opportunity to preach to them the goſpel, and lead them to the knowledge of the great ſalvation which is in Jeſus Chriſt

4 A bleſſing attended their labours *A certain woman named Lydia, a ſeller of purple*, either of ſilk or cloth, or the purple dye, a native *of Thyatira*, a city of Aſia, but who was now ſettled at Philippi, and *worſhipped God*, as a proſelyte of the gate, *heard us* with great ſeriouſneſs, *whoſe heart the Lord opened* by the powerful efficacy of his grace, *that ſhe attended unto the things which were ſpoken of Paul*, and received the truth, in the light and love of it And as ſhe made immediate profeſſion of her faith, ſhe was *baptized, and her houſhold*, whereupon ſhe beſought Paul and his friends, ſaying, *If ye have judged me to be faithful to the Lord*, ſeeing ye have received me into your number, ſhew me the confidence you place in me, and *come into my houſe and abide there*, ſo deſirous was ſhe of teſtifying her gratitude to thoſe from whom ſhe had received ſo great ſpiritual bleſſings, and ſollicitous to enjoy as much as poſſible of their converſation, that ſhe might grow more eſtabliſhed in the truth, *and ſhe conſtrained us*, unwilling to be burdenſome, they were at firſt backward to accept her invitation, but at laſt, overcome with her importunity, they conſented *Note*, (1) One ſoul turned to God is a great acquiſition, and well worthy to be recorded (2) Providence ſometimes brings us far from our native home, with views we little thought of, and ſo orders the place of our abode as to be greatly ſubſervient to the ſalvation of our ſouls (3) Faith cometh by hearing, and hearing by the word of God, they who ſit under a preached goſpel are in the Lord's way (4) The heart, by nature, is cloſe ſhut againſt the light of truth by ignorance, blindneſs, prejudice, and error it is God's almighty power and grace alone which can open a way for the entrance of his goſpel, and make it effectual to the converſion of the ſoul (5) They who have received a bleſſing from God's miniſters, and owe to them, under God, their ſouls, think they can never ſufficiently ſhew their gratitude to them for their labour of love (6) We cannot but deſire the approbation of thoſe who are eminently good, and wiſh ſo to act, as that they may judge us *faithful to the Lord*

16 ¶ And

16 ¶ And it came to pass, as we went to prayer, a certain damsel, ⁿ possessed with a spirit of † divination, met us, which brought her masters ° much gain by soothsaying 17 The same followed Paul and us, and cried, saying, These men are the servants of the most high God, which shew unto us the way of salvation 18 And this did she many days But Paul ᵖ being grieved, turned and said to the spirit, I command thee in the name of Jesus Christ to come out of her And ᵍ he came out the same hour 19 ¶ And ʳ when her masters saw that the hope of their gains was gone, ˢ they caught Paul and Silas, and drew *them* into the ‡ market-place, unto the rulers, 20 And brought them to the magistrates, saying, These men being Jews, ᵗ do exceedingly trouble our city, 21 And teach customs which are not lawful for us to receive, neither to observe, being Romans 22 And the multitude rose up together against them and the magistrates rent off their clothes, and ᵘ commanded to beat *them* 23 And when they had laid many stripes upon them, they cast *them* into prison, charging the jailer to keep them safely 24 Who having received such a charge, thrust them into the inner prison, and ˣ made their feet fast in the stocks

ⁿ 1 Sam xxviii 7 † Gr Python ° Chap xix 24. ᵖ Mark i 25, 34 ᵍ Mark xvi 17 ʳ Chap xix 25, 26 ˢ 2 Cor vi 5 ᵗ 1 Kings xviii 17 Chap xvii 6 ᵘ 2 Cor xi 25 1 Thes ii 2 ˣ Jer xx 2

not stagger at any reproach which, for his sake, they may be called to bear

25 ¶ And at midnight Paul and Silas prayed, and sang praises unto God and the prisoners heard them 26 ʸ And suddenly there was a great earthquake, so that the foundations of the prison were shaken and immediately ᶻ all the doors were opened, and every one's bands were loosed 27 And the keeper of the prison awaking out of his sleep, and seeing the prison doors open, he drew out his sword, and would have killed himself, supposing that the prisoners had been fled 28 But Paul cried with a loud voice, saying, Do thyself no harm, for we are all here 29 Then he called for a light, and sprang in, and came trembling, and fell down before Paul and Silas 30 And brought them out, and said, ᵃ Sirs, what must I do to be saved? 31 And they said, ᵇ Believe on the Lord Jesus Christ, and thou shalt be saved, and thy house 32 And they spake unto him the word of the Lord, and to all that were in his house 33 And he took them the same hour of the night, and washed *their* stripes, and was baptized, he and all his, straightway 34 And when he had brought them into his house, ᶜ he set meat before them, and rejoiced, believing in God with all his house

ʸ Chap iv 31 ᶻ Chap v 19 ᵃ Luke iii 10 Chap ii 37 & ix 6 ᵇ John iii 16, 36 & vi 47 1 John v 10 ᶜ Luke v 29 & xix 6

v 16—24 A singular occurrence soon made the preachers of the gospel more taken notice of

1 There was a damsel possessed *with a spirit of divination*, for in these times of ignorance and idolatry, the devil used many such deluding instruments, who pretended to foretel future events, and to return oracular answers to those who foolishly put their trust in such jugglers and as they paid for consulting them, this maid being reputed of extraordinary skill, brought *her masters much gain by her soothsaying* And when Paul and his companions went out of the city to their oratory, this damsel for several days followed them, crying, *These men are the servants of the most high God, which shew unto us the way of salvation*, and this was either a testimony extorted by the divine power to leave the men of Philippi more inexcusable, for rejecting what themselves deemed to be oracular, or as others suggest, the devil designed to prejudice the cause of Christ, as if these preachers were promoting the same interests, and influenced by the same spirit as this soothsayer *Note*, (1) It is the honour of ministers, that they are servants of the most high God (2) There is no way of salvation, but that which the gospel points out to us, without it we must for ever lie down in ignorance, guilt, and misery

2 Grieved at her continual clamours, and justly apprehensive, lest there should seem to be a confederacy between them and her, or sorry that Satan, by her means, should deceive and delude the people of Philippi, *Paul turned and said to the spirit, I command thee in the name of Jesus Christ, to come out of her*, and instantly Satan's power was broken, *and he came out the same hour*

3 Her masters, highly exasperated to find all their gains gone, and her soothsaying at an end, caught Paul and Silas, the two most active persons, and dragging them violently along to the forum, where the magistrates sat to administer justice, preferred a heavy complaint against them, covering their private revenge with the pretence of zeal for the public welfare, saying, *These men being Jews*, the refuse of the earth, and the pests of society, *do exceedingly trouble our city*, fomenting riots and disturbances, and interrupting the peace of the people, *and teach customs which are not lawful for us to receive, neither to observe, being Romans*, their doctrines and practices being utterly opposite to, and subversive of the worship of our gods, the manners of our country, and the laws of the empire *Note*, (1) The love of money is the root of all evil (2) Revenge and malice often wear the cloak of religious zeal, to conceal their malignity (3) They who are the preachers of the gospel of peace, have often thus been branded as the disturbers of society, and as the firebrands of discord

4 The giddy multitude, inflamed by a charge so invidious, rose up in a popular tumult ready to tear them in pieces, and the magistrates, without form of trial, twinming with the stream, rent off their clothes, and commanded the lictors, their officers, *to scourge them* with rods severely, as the most infamous malefactors, 2 *Thess* ii 2 and not content with this cruel treatment, after the many and deep stripes they had laid on them, they committed them to the town prison, strictly charging the jailer *to keep them safely*, that they might not escape, whilst they consulted what farther to do with them And he, an instrument fit as his masters could desire, failed not to execute the charge with abundant severity, thrusting them into *the inner prison*, the place allotted to the vilest criminals, and to prevent all possibility of escape, as well as to add to the miseries of these innocent sufferers, *he made their feet fast in the stocks* *Note*, Christ's servants must prepare for sufferings, and

v 25—34 The misery, pain, and wretched condition in which these two innocent prisoners might be supposed to lie, would lead us to expect many a doleful groan, but, wonderful to tell! we find them happier in their filthy prison, than their persecutors on beds of down

1 *At midnight Paul and Silas prayed*, committing themselves cheerfully to God, and looking up to him for strength to bear whatever more might be laid upon them, remembering, no doubt, their persecutors, and begging God to forgive them, not forgetting their inhuman jailor, *and they* not only prayed, but *sang praises unto God*, rejoicing in their bonds, that they were counted worthy to suffer for their master's name, and were filled with such divine consolations as made them forget all the horrors of a prison, and brought down to that dreary mansion a taste of heavenly felicity, *and the prisoners heard them*, so loud, so hearty were their praises, not ashamed of their master's name and service *Note*, (1) Prayer is an ease to the heart in every affliction, and joint sufferers should unite their supplications (2) Our trials should never untune our hearts for praise, in the midst of all, we have much, very much, for which we should be thankful (3) Psalm-singing is a blessed gospel ordinance, and we should never be ashamed of being heard in our families, though foolish and wicked men may ridicule the service

2 God miraculously gives a token of his presence with them, and of his acceptance of their prayers and praises *Suddenly there was a great earthquake*, a testimony of God's displeasure against their persecutors, and of his appearance on the behalf of his suffering ministers, *so that the foundations of the prison were shaken, and immediately all the doors were opened, and every one's bands were loosed*, an intimation to the prisoners, that the gospel which these faithful preachers declared, was designed to deliver their souls from the more grievous bondage of guilt and corruption

3 The jailor himself becomes a convert

(1) Awaked by the terrible shock, and starting from his bed, he saw with astonishment the prison doors wide open, and supposing all the prisoners fled, for whose escape his own life must pay, in the first transports of despair he drew his sword, to put an end to his life, in order to prevent a more dreaded public execution

(2) Paul, who probably by divine revelation knew the fatal resolution the jailor was about to take, with a loud voice stays his uplifted arm, saying, *Do thyself no harm, for we are all here* Paul and Silas thought not of escaping, and the rest were held by an invisible power, fast as the chains which bound them *Note*, The gospel word is, *Do thyself no harm*, all God's warnings, rebukes, and calls, are purely to rescue us from the ruin into which we were running, and to save us from sin, the cause of all our miseries

(3) The jailor, whose conscience the convictions of sin and now shook more terribly, than the earthquake the prison's foundations, *called for a light, and sprang in hastily, and came trembling*, under the most fearful sense of his dreadful guilt, *and fell down before Paul and Silas*, with deepest respect and veneration, *and brought them out* of the horrid dungeon where they were, *and said, Sirs, What must I do to be saved?* He now felt all the wickedness of his past conduct, particularly his cruel behaviour to these messengers of God, and confounded at his provocations, eagerly begs their forgiveness and direction, how he may obtain pardon at the hands of God *Note*, (1) God's

7 I Spirit

Spirit works in different ways on different persons, some, like Lydia, are gently led to Christ, others pass first through the most dreadful terrors, sometimes brought to the gates of despair, and even tempted to self-murder, and yet even this works together for their good, in order to make Christ more precious to their souls. (2.) They who have despised and ill used God's ministers before, when seized by conviction of sin, will entertain very different apprehensions of them, and address them with very different language. (3.) To a soul convinced of sin, all other considerations are swallowed up in that one great concern, *What must I do to be saved?*

(4.) Paul and Silas have an immediate answer ready for his question. *Believe on the Lord Jesus Christ, and thou shalt be saved, and thy house*, the salvation which they preached, being free for him, though an idolatrous Gentile and bitter persecutor, and his family also would be admitted to share his blessing. *And they spake unto him the word of the Lord, and to all that were in the house*, who were assembled on this joyful occasion. *Note*, (1.) The gospel proposes free salvation in Jesus Christ to the chief of sinners. (2.) Nothing but faith in a Redeemer can bring true peace to a guilty conscience, or obtain the salvation which a sinner needs. (3.) Masters of families, who know the Lord themselves, cannot but be desirous that all under their roof may share their blessings, and be brought with them to the knowledge of the truth.

(5.) Filled now with gratitude and love, the jailor, deeply affected with the blessed truths which he heard, *took them, and washed their stripes*, to supple and ease the wounds which their severe scourging had made on their backs, *and was baptized, he and all his, straightway*, desirous to come under the bonds of the covenant with his family, and to make public profession of Christianity. Which done, he brought Paul and Silas into his house, and *set meat before them*, to refresh them, after the fatigues and fasting which they had endured, *and rejoiced, believing in God with all his house*, who rejoiced with him in the salvation which they had now embraced, or *over all his house*, going from one room to another in a transport of joy. *Note*, (1.) Believing in Christ, is called *believing in God*, for he is very God, and on his being so, our everlasting hopes depend. (2.) Joy is the happy fruit of faith, they who see a reconciled God blotting out all their transgressions, cannot but rejoice in his salvation.

35 And when it was day, the magistrates sent the ser-
jeants, saying, Let those men go. 36 And the keeper
of the prison told this saying to Paul, The magistrates
have sent to let you go: now therefore depart, and go
in peace. 37 But Paul said unto them, They have
d Chap. xxi. 25 beaten us openly uncondemned, [d] being Romans, and
have cast us into prison; and now do they thrust us out
privily? nay, verily, but let them come themselves, and
fetch us out. 38 And the serjeants told these words
unto the magistrates: and they feared when they heard
that they were Romans. 39 And they came and be-
e Mat. viii. 34 sought them, and brought *them* out, and [e] desired *them*
to depart out of the city. 40 And they went out of
f Ver. 14 the prison, and [f] entered into *the house of* Lydia: and
when they had seen the brethren, they comforted them,
and departed.

v. 35—40. We have here,

1. The message of the magistrates to these prisoners. In the morning, when their passion was cooler, they probably reflected upon the illegality of their proceedings, and if they felt the earthquake, this might still more alarm their fears. Therefore they sent their serjeants to the jailor, with orders to dismiss the prisoners, willing to hush up the matter, without farther animadversion.

2. The jailor, glad to convey this message to his guests now, rather than his prisoners, informed them they were at liberty to depart, and advises them to haste away, lest perhaps the present mind of these magistrates should change, and he wishes that all blessing and happiness may attend them.

3. Paul appears in no haste to go. His own innocence required vindication, and for the sake of the disciples, he meant to assert his civil rights and privileges, and therefore bid the serjeants carry back this message to their masters, *They have beaten us openly*, cruelly and ignominiously, tho' *uncondemned*, without even a form of trial, *being Romans*, whose privileges, as citizens, are not thus insolently to be trampled upon, *and have cast us into prison*, as if we were the vilest slaves and criminals, *and now do they thrust us out privily?* as if we wanted a clandestine escape, and had broke from prison? *nay, verily*, we will accept of our liberty on no such terms, *but let them come themselves, and fetch us out*, acknowledging our innocence publickly, removing the reproach they have cast upon our characters, and taking shame to themselves for their illegal and tyrannical procedure, that they may act more gently for the future. Our civil rights are thus often a barrier against the fury of persecutors; the fear of the law often restrains those, who are with-held from injuring us by no fear of the Lord.

4. The magistrates, justly apprehensive of the consequence, if Paul should cite them before the tribunal of their superiors for their illegal proceedings, *came* very submissively, *and besought them* not to take advantage of the law against them, but to forgive the injuries they had received, *and brought them out* of the prison, publickly acknowledging hereby their innocence, *and desired them to depart out of their city*, that there might be no farther disturbance. Thus hath the violence of persecutors often involved them in proceedings which they were unable to vindicate, and which have at last brought shame and confusion upon their own heads.

5. Being thus honourably discharged, *they went out of the prison and entered into the house of Lydia*, their former hostess, *and when they had seen the brethren, they comforted them*, with an account of God's wondrous appearance for them, and the success of the gospel, even in their prison, encouraging them therefore to stand fast in the confidence of support under all their trials, *and* hereupon they *departed*, to spread the gospel through the other provinces of Greece, leaving behind them a very flourishing church, which, from these small beginnings, rose to singular eminence.

CHAP. XVII.

Here is a further account of the travels of Paul, and his services and sufferings for Christ. We have him, 1. Preaching and persecuted at Thessalonica, another city of Macedonia, ver. 1—9. 2. Preaching at Berea, where he met with an encouraging audience, but was driven thence also by persecution, ver. 10—15. 3. Disputing at Athens, the famous university of Greece, ver. 16—21. and the account he gave of natural religion, for the conviction of those that were addicted to polytheism and idolatry, and to lead them to the Christian religion, ver. 22—31. together with the success of this sermon, ver. 32, 33, 34.

1 NOW when they had passed through Amphipolis,
and Apollonia, they came to Thessalonica, where
was a synagogue of the Jews. 2 And Paul, as his
manner was, [a] went in unto them, and three sabbath a Luke iv. 16
days reasoned with them out of the scriptures, 3 Open-
ing and alledging, [b] that Christ must needs have suffer- b Luke xxiv. 26, 46.
ed, and risen again from the dead; and [c] that this Jesus, c Chap. ix. 22.
† whom I preach unto you is Christ. 4 And [d] some
of them believed, and consorted with Paul and Silas; † Or, whom, said he, I preach.
and of [e] the devout Greeks a great multitude, and of the d Chap. xxviii. 24.
chief women not a few. 5 ¶ But the Jews which be- e Ver. 17.
lieved not, moved with envy, took unto them certain
lewd fellows of the baser sort, and gathered a company,
and set all the city on an uproar, and assaulted the house
of Jason, and sought to bring them out to the people.
6 And when they found them not, they drew Jason,
and certain brethren, unto the rulers of the city, crying,
These that [f] have turned the world upside down, are f 1 Kings xviii. 17. Chap. xvi. 20.
come hither also; 7 Whom Jason hath received: and
these all do contrary to the decrees of Cesar, [g] saying,
that there is another king, *one* Jesus. 8 And they g Luke xxiii. 2. John xix. 12.
troubled the people, and the rulers of the city, when
they heard these things. 9 And when they had taken
security of Jason, and of the other, they let them go.

v. 1—9. As the stile of the chapter and the following changes from *we* to *they*, it hath been conjectured that Luke staid at Philippi till Paul returned thither, *chap.* xx. 5, 6. His further travels are here recorded.

1. He, with his companions, Silas and Timothy, passed through Amphipolis and Apollonia, whether he preached in either of these places, we are not told, his route was directed probably under a divine impulse to Thessalonica, the metropolis of Macedonia. Not discouraged by his ill usage at Philippi, he was bold in his God, to speak the gospel unto them also, 1 *Thess.* ii. 2. and as his manner was, having found there a synagogue of Jews, he went in unto them, to make them the first tender of the gospel word. Three sabbath-days successively *he reasoned with them out of the scriptures*, and as they admitted the sacred authority of Moses and the prophets, he appealed to their writings, in proof of the doctrines which he advanced, *opening* their scope and intention, *and* particularly by the texts which related to the Messiah, *alledging* from them, *that Christ*, far from being that temporal king and earthly conqueror, which they expected, *must needs have suffered*, in order to obtain spiritual and eternal redemption for his people, *and* must have *risen again from the dead*, in proof of his having compleated the work which he had undertaken, evidently proving from the scripture, that these things must be accomplished in the Messiah, *and that this Jesus whom I preach unto you, is Christ*, in whom all the prophecies

concerning the Messiah were fulfilled, and in no other; and that the one this must be he that should come, nor must they look for another.

2. His preaching was powerful and convincing, and the spirit of truth set it home to the consciences of many of his hearers. *Some of them*, who were Jews, *believed, and* made immediate profession of the truth which they had embraced; they *consorted with Paul and Silas*, as casting in their lot with them, and ready to share their weal and woe, *and of the devout Greeks a great multitude, and of the chief women not a few*. Thus the foundations were laid of a most flourishing church, multitudes of Gentiles, as well as proselytes, being converted by the great apostles' labours, 1 Thess. 1. 9.

3. Now where could they find rest from the malice of their inveterate enemies. *The Jews which believed not, moved with envy* at the success of Paul's preaching, and the respect paid to him by the Gentiles, as well as by many of their own synagogue, *took unto them certain lewd fellows of the baser sort, and gathered a company*, a profligate mob, the scum of the earth, and by these *they set all the city in an uproar*, raising a riot against the preachers of the gospel, *and assaulted the house of Jason* where Paul and his companions lodged, *and sought to bring them out to the people*, that they might expose them to the exasperated populace. *And when they found them not*, they having prudently withdrawn for their security, *they drew Jason, and certain brethren*, who were at his house, *unto the rulers of the city, crying, These that have turned the world upside down, are come hither also*, spreading their pestilential errors, to the destruction of all peace and good neighbourhood, and sowing the seeds of discord and sedition, to the ruin of the state, *whom Jason hath received* into his house, countenanced and abetted. *And these all do contrary to the decrees of Cæsar*, and evidently shew their disaffection and disloyalty to his government, *saying, that there is another king, one Jesus*, who is the universal Lord of all, to whom every knee must bow, in opposition to Cæsar our only lord and emperor. *And they troubled the people and rulers of the city when they heard these things*, lest some rebellion was really meditating, or lest the jealous emperor Claudius should entertain suspicions of their negligence, however innocent they knew the apostles to be, and however they suspected the wickedness of the accusation. *Note*, (1.) They who are the enemies and disturbers of the people of God, are usually the vilest of mankind, abandoned profligates, lost to all sense of justice and virtue. (2.) If men offend, the magistrates are to judge; but to make the rabble judges and executioners, is to place madness on the seat of justice. (3.) It hath been a common accusation, that the gospel turns the world upside down, and creates all disturbances; but they who bring the charge, will not see that they themselves are the troublers, and that their own passions and perverseness occasion the very evils of which they complain. (4.) The kingdom of Jesus is far from interfering with the civil government, nay, it is one essential part of it to be subordinate to the powers that be; so malicious is the accusation of those, who would insinuate its dangerous tendency to the peace of kingdoms.

4. The magistrates, on enquiry, finding no ground for the accusation, discharged Jason and his friends, on security taken for their appearance, if required. And thus ended this threatening affair, through the moderation of the rulers, without any farther ill consequence.

Chap. ix. 10 ¶ And [b] the brethren immediately sent away Paul and Silas by night unto Berea: who coming thither, went into the synagogue of the Jews. 11 These were more noble than those in Thessalonica, in that they received the word with all readiness of mind, and searched the scriptures daily, whether those things were so. 12 Therefore many of them believed; also of honourable women which were Greeks, and of men not a few. 13 But when the Jews of Thessalonica had knowledge that the word of God was preached of Paul at Berea, they came thither also, and stirred up the people. 14 And [c] then immediately the brethren sent away Paul, to go as it were to the sea: but Silas and Timotheus abode there still. 15 And they that conducted Paul, brought him unto Athens: and [d] receiving a commandment unto Silas and Timotheus, for to come to him with all speed, they departed.

ver. 10—15. Though forced to avoid the present storm, Paul and his companions were obliged to fly from Thessalonica, the Lord had work for them to do elsewhere.

1. *The brethren sent them away by night unto Berea*, to conceal them from the fury of their persecutors; and no sooner were they arrived, than they took the first opportunity of going into the synagogue of the Jews, to preach the gospel to them, nothing entreated, as they had so lately been by them at Philippi and Thessalonica. True charity is never weary of well doing, nor tired out with repeated provocations.

2. These Jews of Berea *were more noble than those of Thessa-*

lonica, freer from prejudices, more candid enquirers after truth, of more enlarged sentiments, and ready to give a fair hearing to those who differed from them in opinion; and therefore *they received the word with all readiness of mind*, embracing it most cheerfully, as soon as they were convinced of the truth; and not taking the matter upon trust, but they *searched the scriptures daily, whether those things were so*, comparing diligently Paul's preaching with the scriptures to which he appealed, and examining carefully the passages which he explained, that they might comprehend their genuine meaning. *Note*, (1.) The doctrines of the gospel fear no scrutiny: we wish for nothing more, than that our hearers would seriously examine whether these things are so. (2.) Searching the scriptures should be our daily business and delight, and their minds will be filled with noble and exalted sentiments and principles, who follow in simplicity these sacred oracles.

3. Great was the effect of Paul's preaching, on minds so disposed to examine candidly into what they heard. *Many of the Jews believed; also of honourable women which were Greeks, and of men not a few.*

4. The restless malice of the Jews will not suffer the apostle to rest in peace in any place. Hearing of the success of the word of God at Berea, *they came thither also, and stirred up the people*, using every calumny to incense them against them.

5. The brethren at Berea knowing that against Paul the malice of the Jews was principally levelled, sent him away, *as it were unto the sea*, to prevent farther search: *but Silas and Timotheus abode still* at Berea, to confirm the disciples, and carry on the work of God.

6. Paul, with those who accompanied him, took the road to Athens, the most renowned university of Greece; and when the brethren returned, he sent orders to Silas and Timotheus to follow him speedily.

16 ¶ Now while Paul waited for them at Athens, [m] his spirit was stirred in him, when he saw the city wholly given to idolatry. 17 Therefore disputed he in the synagogue with the Jews, and with [n] the devout persons, and in the market daily with them that met with him. 18 Then certain philosophers of the Epicureans, and of the Stoics, encountered him. And some said, What will this babbler say? other some, He seemeth to be a setter forth of strange gods: because he preached unto them Jesus, and the resurrection. 19 And they took him, and brought him unto [†] Areopagus, saying, May we know what this new doctrine whereof thou speakest is? 20 For thou bringest certain strange things to our ears: we would know therefore what these things mean. 21 (For all the Athenians and strangers which were there, spent their time in nothing else, but either to tell or to hear some new thing.)

[m] 2 Pet. ii. 8.

[n] Ver. 4.

[†] Or Mars-hill. Ver. 22. It was the highest court in Athens.

ver. 16—21. While Paul waited at Athens for the arrival of his fellow-labourers, we are told,

1. With what grief and indignation he beheld the idolatry of the inhabitants, and what zeal burned in his bosom, on seeing these abominations. Unable, therefore, to contain any longer, he entered the synagogue, beginning, as usual, with the Jews and devout proselytes, disputing boldly with them, and answering all their objections against that Messiah whom he preached unto them: and not resting there, he daily talked with those he met in the places of public concourse, remonstrating against their absurd idolatry, and seeking to turn them from their stocks and stones which they worshipped, to the service of the living God. *Note*, When we have Christ's cause at heart, we shall be ready to speak a word for him in all companies, and have his interests constantly uppermost.

2. The philosophers, with which this seat of Greek literature abounded, could not silently pass by, unnoticed, this zealous disputant; and therefore some of the Stoics and Epicureans, their two most famed sects, though in opinion utterly opposite, united their forces against him. Some of them with infinite contempt said, *What will this babbler say?* prating at this strange rate: others, with indignation at his attempt to introduce what they thought new deities, said, *He seemeth to be a setter forth of strange gods*, or foreign demons, *because he preached unto them Jesus, and the resurrection* (ἀνάστασιν) which they took to be a goddess, according to their dark and blind apprehension.

3. In order to hear at large what he had to say for himself, they invited him to Areopagus, hill dedicated to Mars, where the supreme court of the judges sat, who determined all matters, civil or religious; and a number of philosophers being assembled, they said, *May we know what this new doctrine, whereof thou speakest, is? For thou bringest certain strange things unto our ears: we would know therefore what these things mean.* Among all the volumes that crowded their libraries, the writings of Moses and the prophets, probably, were unknown to them: and since their professed research was after truth, they desired, if, like the

mysteries

myſteries of their gods, no ſecreſy was enjoined, that they might hear a full and plain diſcuſſion of the doctrine which he maintained and inculcated. And in this matter, curioſity ſeems to have prompted them more than any real deſire of being informed. It being the character of the Athenians in general, that they, and the ſtrangers who reſorted thither, *ſpent their time in nothing elſe, but either to tell or to hear ſome new thing*. *Note*, It is a miſerable waſte of precious time, thus to ſpend it in gaping after news and novelty; and inſtead of real wiſdom, can only produce ſuperficial talkativeneſs.

22 ¶ Then ſtood Paul in the midſt of Mars hill, and ſaid, Ye men of Athens, I perceive that in all things ye are too ſuperſtitious. 23 For as I paſſed by, and beheld † your devotions, I found an altar with this inſcription, TO THE UNKNOWN GOD. Whom therefore ye ignorantly worſhip, him declare I unto you. 24 [o] God that made the world, and all things therein, ſeeing that he is Lord of heaven and earth, [p] dwelleth not in temples made with hands. 25 Neither is worſhipped with men's hands, [q] as though he needed any thing, ſeeing [r] he giveth to all life, and breath, and all things; 26 And hath made of one blood, all nations of men, for to dwell on all the face of the earth, and hath determined the times before appointed, and [s] the bounds of their habitation; 27 [t] That they ſhould ſeek the Lord, if haply they might feel after him, and find him, [u] though he be not far from every one of us: 28 For [x] in him we live, and move, and have our being; [y] as certain alſo of your own poets have ſaid, For we are alſo his offspring. 29 Forasmuch then as we are the offspring of God, [z] we ought not to think that the God-head is like unto gold, or ſilver, or ſtone graven by art and man's device. 30 And [a] the times of this ignorance God winked at; but now [b] commandeth all men every where to repent: 31 Becauſe he hath appointed a day in the which [c] he will judge the world in righteouſneſs, by *that* man whom he hath ordained, whereof he hath given aſſurance unto all men, in that [d] he hath raiſed him from the dead.

† Or the gods that you worſhip. a 2 Theſ. ii. 4. o Chap. xiv. 15. p Chap. vii. 48. q Pſ. l. 8. r Gen. ii. 7. Job xii. 10. & xxxiii. 4. Iſa. xlii. 5. s Deut. xxxii. 8. t Rom. i. 20. u Chap. xiv. 17. x Col. i. 17. Heb. i. 3. y Tit. i. 12. z Iſa. xl. 18. a Chap. xiv. 16. Epheſ. iii. 5. 1 Pet. i. 14. b Luke xxiv. 47. c John v. 22. Chap. x. 42. Rom. ii. 16. 2 Tim. iv. 1. d Chap. ii. 24.

v. 22—31. Never was diſcourſe more admirably ſuited to the auditory, than this. Having now to do, not with Jews who admitted revelation, but with idolatrous philoſophers, who, amidſt their innumerable deities, were without God in the world, the apoſtle ſets himſelf to lead them to the knowledge of Him, whom they ignorantly worſhipped.

1. In the midſt of a numerous audience of ſenators, philoſophers, and others, who deſired to hear what he had to ſay, he begins with a general remark, which he had made during his abode among them, *Ye men of Athens, I perceive that in all things ye are too ſuperſtitious* (δεισιδαιμονεστέρους), *more addicted to the worſhip of gods* than other people; which he mentions, not perhaps with a view immediately to upbraid them with it, as their crime, but to engage their attention to his diſcourſe, as perſons of more than ordinary profeſſed devotion.

2. He informs them, that he had particularly obſerved on one of their altars, this inſcription, *TO THE UNKNOWN GOD*, which, though a confeſſion of their ignorance, intimated a deſire to know and worſhip him; and ſome have thought that this altar was dedicated to the God of Iſrael, whoſe name *Jehovah*, the Jews never pronounced.

3. He tells them that this God whom they ignorantly worſhipped, him declared he unto them. Not as a ſetter forth of *ſtrange* gods, to add to their number other deities, nor of *new* gods; but to bring them to the knowledge of him, who was the only living and true God, and to direct them how he was acceptably to be ſerved, whom they, with blind devotion, adored, though unknown. So prudently and perſuaſively does he introduce and urge the glorious truths he had to deliver, even from the idolatry which he condemned.

4. He deſcribes the God he preached as the great Creator, Governor, and Lord of all, the author of life and being to every creature, and who filleth heaven and earth with his preſence. *He made the world, and all things therein*, which ſprung not from a fortuitous concourſe of atoms, nor ſubſiſted from eternity, as the different ſects of philoſophers taught, but were the work of the Almighty, and ſpoken into being at his word; who, *ſeeing that he is Lord of heaven and earth*, the author and owner of all, *dwelleth not in temples made with hands*, nor can his immenſity be circumſcribed by theſe narrow bounds; *neither is worſhipped, or ſerved with mens hands, as though he needed any thing*, ſacrifices, ſtatues, temples, or offerings, to increaſe his felicity, who is in himſelf infinitely bleſſed and glorious, and incapable of receiving any addition to his ſelf-ſufficient happineſs; *ſeeing* all that the creature poſſeſſes come from him, *for he giveth to all, life, and breath, and all things*, their being, with all the ſupports and comforts of it, they receive from him, but can add nothing to him: *and hath made of one blood, all nations of men, for to dwell on all the face of the earth*, who are originally deſcended from the ſame pair, which ſhould ſtain the pride of pedigree, and teach us to love as brethren: *and hath determined the times before appointed, and the bounds of their habitations*, having fixed in his eternal purpoſe the various events, and the periods of time in which each ſhould happen, appointing to nations and individuals their place and abode on this habitable globe. And in all the diſpenſations of his providence, the end he propoſes is, *that they ſhould ſeek the Lord* engaged by all the kindneſs and bounties of his providential hand, *if haply*, amidſt the darkneſs, blindneſs, and ignorance of their fallen mind, *they might feel after him, and find him*, groping as the blind, through the creatures, and riſing from the conſideration of the viſible objects around them, to the knowledge of his eternal power and godhead: *though he be not far from every one of us*, filling heaven and earth with his preſence, and exerting in every place his perpetual agency; *for in him we live, and move, and have our being*, brought into being by his power, ſupported by his providence, and preſerved by his care; *as certain alſo of your own poets have ſaid*, particularly Aratus, *For we are his offspring*. *Note*, (1.) He who gives us our being, has a full right to diſpoſe of us according to the good pleaſure of his will: to murmur at our lot, is to rebel againſt his providence. (2.) Our times are in God's hand, the number of our days is with him, he hath appointed us our bounds, which we cannot paſs. (3.) Though God hath revealed enough of his glory to leave the world without excuſe, yet ſuch is the blindneſs of fallen man, that the wiſeſt of men knew not God, nor ever would have known him, but for *the fooliſhneſs of preaching*, even that preaching, which the wiſdom of this world ſtill brands as folly. (4.) We can never enough be thankful for that bleſſed book of God that teaches more ſubſtantial wiſdom in one page, yea, in one line, than is contained in all the volumes of poets and philoſophers.

4. As the conſequence of the doctrine which he advanced, he infers the abſurdity of idolatry, and exhorts them to turn unto the living God. *Foraſmuch then as we are the offspring of God*, created by him, and in his image, *we ought not* to put ſo groſs an affront upon him, as *to think that the godhead is like unto gold or ſilver, or ſtone graven by art and man's device*, however rich the materials, or exquiſite the workmanſhip. *And the times of this ignorance God winked at*, with wondrous patience and long-ſuffering bearing with their abominations, and leaving the Gentiles as neglected, without the light of revelation; *but now*, in the riches of his grace, overlooking all that is paſt, he is pleaſed to make a revelation of himſelf, and his deſigns to the world in general, *and commandeth all men every where to repent*, engaging them thereunto by the moſt engaging promiſes of pardon and acceptance through a Redeemer, and warning them by all the awful judgments which will deſcend on the heads of thoſe who perſiſt in their impenitence and idolatry, *becauſe he hath appointed a day in the which he will judge the world in righteouſneſs, by that man whom he hath ordained, whereof he hath given aſſurance unto all men, in that he hath raiſed him from the dead*. The day is fixed in the eternal counſels, the judgment will be impartial and ſtrict, from the fulleſt knowledge of the characters of men, the perſon is appointed to whom all judgment is committed, his reſurrection from the dead gives the fulleſt aſſurance to all who will enquire into the evidence of the fact, with its connections, of God's approbation of him, and his appointment to this high office: and as there can be no exception to his ſentence, there lies no appeal from his bar. An awful ſcene, which we cannot too often place before us, and under which our daily conduct ſhould be influenced, that we may be found of him in peace at that day.

32 ¶ And when they heard of the reſurrection of the dead, ſome mocked: and others ſaid, [e] We will hear thee again of this matter. 33 So Paul departed from among them. 34 Howbeit, certain men clave unto him, and believed: among the which *was* Dionyſius the Areopagite, and a woman named Damaris, and others with them.

e Chap. xxiv. 25.

v. 32—34. We have here an account of the effects of Paul's preaching to this philoſophic audience.

1. Some ridiculed his ſtrange notions, and on the mention of *the reſurrection of the dead*, ſo contrary to the maxims of their philoſophy, they mocked at the abſurdity of ſuch an aſſertion; whilſt others, deferring to determine upon the matter for the preſent, promiſed to give it a ſecond hearing at their leiſure. *Note*, (1.) We are not to think the worſe of the ſacred truths of God, becauſe profane philoſophers or wits ridicule, and make a jeſt of them. (2.) They who put off the concerns of their ſoul, which demand preſent attention, to ſome future day, uſually find ſomething elſe continues to engage them, till it is too late.

2. The apoſtle's words were not however wholly ineffectual. Though the majority perſiſted in their ſcientific arrogance and philoſophic pride, yet when Paul departed, and the aſſembly broke up, *certain men clave unto him*, immediately commencing a connection

nection with him, *and believed* that good which he preached unto them, *among the which was Dionysius the Areopagite*, a member of the supreme court of judicature before whom Paul appeared, *and a woman of note* and distinction, *named Damaris, and others with them*, who by the power of divine grace were effectually *turned from idols to the* living and true *God*

CHAP XVIII

In this chapter we have, 1 Paul's coming to Corinth, his private converse with Aquila and Priscilla, and his public reasonings with the Jews, from whom, when they rejected him, he turned to the Gentiles, ver 1—6 2 The great success of his ministry there, and the encouraging vision given him to continue his labours there, ver 7—11 3 The molestation which after some time he met with there from the Jews, but Gallio the Roman governor refused to intermeddle in the cause, ver 12—17 4 The progress Paul made through many countries, after he had continued long at Corinth, for the edifying and watering of the churches which he had founded and planted, in which course he made a short visit to Jerusalem, ver 18—23 5 An account of Apollos's improvement in knowledge, and of his usefulness in the church, ver 24—28

1 AFTER these things, Paul departed from Athens, and came to Corinth 2 And found a certain Jew named [a] Aquila, born in Pontus, lately come from Italy, with his wife Priscilla (because that Claudius had commanded all Jews to depart from Rome) and came unto them 3 And because he was of the same craft, he abode with them, and [b] wrought (for by their occupation they were tent-makers) 4 And he reasoned in the synagogue every sabbath, and persuaded the Jews, and the Greeks 5 And [c] when Silas and Timotheus were come from Macedonia, Paul [d] was pressed in spirit, and testified to the Jews that Jesus was Christ 6 And [e] when they opposed themselves, and blasphemed, [f] he shook *his* raiment, and said unto them, [g] Your blood *be* upon your own heads, [h] I *am* clean [i] from henceforth I will go unto the Gentiles

[a] Rom xvi 3. 1 Cor xvi 19. [b] Ch xx 34. 1 Cor iv 12. 1 Thess ii 9. 2 Thess iii 8. [c] Chap xvii 14. [d] Job xxxii 18. [e] Chap xiii 45. 1 Pet iv 4. [f] Neh v 13. Matt x 14. Chap xiii 51. [g] 2 Sam i 16. Ezek xviii 13. & xxxiii 4. [h] Ezek iii 18, 19. & xxxiii 9. [i] Chap xiii 46. & xxviii 28. & xxviii

v 1—6 At Athens Paul seems to have made no long stay Probably the pride of philosophy permitted little success to the gospel which he preached He therefore next visited Corinth, a city famous through all Greece for trade and opulence

1 The apostle, unwilling to be burdensome for a maintenance, highly as he was intitled to the most liberal provision, worked for bread at his trade of tent-making, all the Jewish students being brought up to some handicraft business Aquila, a converted Jew, with his wife Priscilla, who were of this occupation, being banished from Rome, with all the other Jews, by the jealous emperor Claudius, and settled at Corinth To them, whom he found excellent people, and deeply versed in the things of God, he applied for work, and disdained not to labour for a subsistence A noble instance of that disinterested zeal which burned in his bosom, and made him willing to undergo any hardship, to prevent the least prejudice which might arise, however unreasonably, against the gospel that he preached! *Note*, Those who are seeking a favour would do well to settle with those from whom they are likely to reap good to their soul

2 While he laboured six days for a maintenance, every sabbath, with indefatigable diligence and zeal, he visited the synagogue, where *he reasoned* with the Jews and Grecian proselytes, proving from the Scriptures the doctrines which he preached with unanswerable arguments, and silencing all their objections, *and persuaded* them to embrace the salvation which was in Christ Jesus and, with respect to many, not without success And being still more animated by the coming of Silas and Timothy, who brought him the glad tidings of the establishment and increase of the churches which he had planted, he urged with greater warmth and earnestness the grand truth, that Jesus is the Christ, the promised Messiah, and that there was no salvation out of him, grieved to behold the obstinate infidelity of the Jews, and mightily constrained with love towards them, and desire after their conversion *Note*, A true zeal for Jesus, and love for immortal souls, will give warmth, energy, and spirit to our discourses

3 When he found all his labour for them rejected with scorn, and returned with reviling, that they opposed with determined obstinacy what they could not answer, and blasphemed that divine Redeemer whom he preached unto them, with just indignation *he shook his raiment, and*, abandoning them to their wilful impenitence, *said unto them, Your blood be upon your own heads, I am clean*, having given you solemn warning, and laboured to rescue you from that guilt and ruin which you are terribly and surely bringing upon your souls *from henceforth*, since all my words are ineffectual, and rejected by you, *I will go unto the Gentiles*, not doubting but they will give the gospel word a more welcome reception *Note*, (1) They who wilfully oppose the gospel, exasperated, instead of convinced, go on often to add blasphemy to impenitence (2) It is a comfort to a faithful minister at last to be conscious that he is free from the blood of all men (3) Woe unto those against whom the very ministers of grace shall rise up in judgment to accuse and condemn them

7 ¶ And he departed thence, and entred into a certain man's house, named Justus, one that worshipped God, whose house joined hard to the synagogue 8 [k] And Crispus the chief ruler of the synagogue believed on the Lord with all his house and many of the Corinthians, hearing, believed, and were baptized 9 Then [l] spake the Lord to Paul in the night by a vision, Be not afraid, but [m] speak, and hold not thy peace 10 For [n] I am with thee, and [o] no man shall set on thee to hurt thee for I have much people in this city 11 And he [p] continued there a year and six months, teaching the word of God among them

[k] 1 Cor i 14. [l] Chap xxiii 11. [m] Matt x 19. [n] Jer i 18. & Matt xxviii 20. [o] Isa liv 17. [p] Gr sat

v 7—11 Having solemnly warned the Jews of the danger and ruin which would be the consequence of their impenitence, he departed

1 From the synagogue he went to the house adjoining, which belonged to one named Justus, a proselyte, whither those who desired to hear him might come And though the greater body of the Jews rejected his preaching, yet he saw rich fruits of his labours; Crispus, the ruler of the synagogue, being converted to the faith, with all his house and a great number of the Corinthians, hearing the gospel, *believed and were baptized* *Note*, (1) Though some reject the gospel, it is a great comfort to a minister's soul to see others not only hear it with attention, but embrace it with affection (2) Not many noble and rulers are called, yet here and there one, to leave the rest at least inexcusable

2 Amidst all Paul's discouragements the Lord is with him to support and comfort him, and by a vision in the night intimates him boldly to persevere, saying, *Be not afraid* of the opposition and malice of the Jews, *but speak, and hold not thy peace*, with all diligence, fidelity, and zeal, declaring the gospel, deterred by no menaces or opposition of the most malignant persecutors, *for I am with thee*, to support, protect, and prosper thee in all thy labours, *and no man shall set on thee to hurt thee*, restrained by a secret over-ruling hand from injuring your person, or silencing your ministry, *for I have much people in this city*, whom I have ordained unto eternal life, and who shall be called and converted by thy ministry *Note*, (1) If God be with us and for us, we need not be intimidated by the many or the mighty who may rise up against us (2) They who are labouring for Christ, though they be not visited with night visions, shall find internal divine supports ministered to them amidst all their tribulation (3) Where God hath a people, he will send to them his gospel, and all that the Father hath given his Son *shall* come unto him

3 Encouraged by this declaration, the apostle continued at Corinth a year and six months, with unwearied diligence and fervent zeal preaching the gospel, and seeing numbers daily added to the church of such as should be saved, God opening to him a great door and effectual, though there were many adversaries, 1 Cor xvi 9

12 ¶ And when Gallio was the deputy of Achaia, the Jews made insurrection with one accord against Paul, and brought him to the judgment seat, 13 Saying, This fellow persuadeth men to worship God contrary to the law 14 And when Paul was now about to open his mouth, Gallio said unto the Jews, [q] If it were a matter of wrong or wicked lewdness, O ye Jews, reason would that I should bear with you 15 But if it be a question of words and names, and of your law, look ye *to it*, for I will be no judge of such matters 16 And he drave them from the judgment seat 17 Then all the Greeks took [r] Sosthenes, the chief ruler of the synagogue, and beat him before the judgment seat And Gallio [s] cared for none of those things

[q] Chap xxiii 29. & xxv 11, 19. [r] 1 Cor i 1. [s] Amos vi 6.

v 12—17 Though God had promised to save the apostle from hurt, he doth not engage to exempt him from the malicious efforts of his enemies

1 The Jews, as they had elsewhere done, raised an insurrection, and in a popular tumult dragged Paul before Gallio the proconsul, who was the brother of Seneca the philosopher, and is said to have been of the most sweet and gentle disposition, and universally beloved Their accusation against the apostle was, that *this fellow*, so contemptuously do they speak of him, *persuadeth men to worship God contrary to the law*, and because they were allowed the exercise of their religion by the edicts of the Roman emperors,

empire, they pretend it was highly criminal for any Jew to worship God any other way than they did.

2 Paul was just going to make his defence, and shew the falshood as well as indignity of the accusation. But Gallio, understanding it was a merely religious matter, refused to interfere, and dismissed the cause, saying, *if it were a matter of wrong, or wicked lewdness*, where any injury had been done, or theft or immorality committed, *O ye Jews, reason were that I should bear with you*, and do you justice, indecently clamorous as you are: *but if it be a question of names and of your law*, whether Jesus, whom Paul preaches, be your Messiah, and what obligation there lies on him, or those whom he teaches, to worship God after the law of Moses, *look ye to it*, and end such disputes among yourselves, *for I will be no judge of such matters*, it is no concern to me how any man worships God, whilst he approves himself a good subject, and disturbs not the peace of the state. *And he drave them from the judgment-seat*, expressing his displeasure at their troublesome and impertinent clamours. *Note*, Magistrates are bound to right the injured; but, where the accusation is evidently frivolous or malicious, such causes should be discountenanced and dismissed.

3 Exasperated at their disappointment, the unbelieving Greeks took hold of Sosthenes, the chief ruler of the synagogue, Paul's friend, 1 Cor. i. 1. and fellow-labourer, and, to vent their resentment, *they beat him before the judgment-seat*, in the face of the governor. *And Gallio cared for none of these things*, rather chusing to wink at the affront and riot, than embroil himself with an enraged populace.

Some suppose that Sosthenes was not yet a convert, but headed the accusation against the apostle, and that, as the Jews were in general hated, the profane Greeks, seeing the governor favourable to Paul, were encouraged to put this insult upon them in the person of their chief ruler. Whichever was the case, the behaviour of Gallio was justly to be blamed; for, whether Sosthenes was a good or bad man at that time, such illegal proceedings deserved animadversion: but he seems to have been too indifferent about the matter, and merely to consult his own ease.

18 ¶ And Paul *after this* tarried *there* yet a good
while, and then took his leave of the brethren, and sailed
thence into Syria, and with him Priscilla and Aquila; ᵃ Numb vi 18. Chap xxi 24.
ᵃ having shorn *his* head in Cenchrea: for he had a vow.
19 And he came to Ephesus, and left them there: but
he himself entred into the synagogue, and reasoned with
the Jews. 20 When they desired *him* to tarry longer
time with them, he consented not; 21 But bade them
farewel, saying, ᵗ I must by all means keep this feast that ᵗ Chap xix 21.
cometh in Jerusalem: but I will return again unto you,
ᵘ if God will. And he sailed from Ephesus. 22 And ᵘ 1 Cor iv 19. Heb vi 3. Jam iv 15.
when he had landed at Cesarea, and gone up and saluted
the church, he went down to Antioch. 23 And after
he had spent some time *there*, he departed, and went
over all the country of Galatia and Phrygia in order, ʸ Gal i 2. Chap xiv 22. & xv 3.
ʸ strengthening all the disciples.

v. 18—23. After a long abode at Corinth, and seeing abundant success of his labours, we have here,

1 The apostle's departure. Having taken a solemn farewell of the brethren, he set sail for Syria, Priscilla and Aquila accompanying him, *having shorn his head at Cenchrea, for he had a vow*, willing, as far as was lawful, to comply with the Jews, that he might prepare them the more readily to hear him. And now the time of his vow of Nazaritism, under which he had bound himself, being expired, his head was shaved according to the law, *Numb* vi. 1—21. *Note*, In all indifferent matters we should become all things to all men, in order, if it please God, that we may by any means gain some to the knowledge of Christ.

2 His arrival at Ephesus, the chief city of the proconsular Asia. There, as his custom was, he entred into the synagogue of the Jews, and *reasoned* with them concerning the great truths of Christianity. But his stay was very short, as he hastened to Jerusalem: and therefore, leaving Aquila and Priscilla there, though they, and probably the other Jews, desired him to make some longer abode with them, they could not prevail with him, he having urgent business, which called him to Jerusalem, where he intended to keep the approaching feast, probably the passover. But with God's permission he engaged to return to them again, and make some longer stay among them, to dispense that gospel which they seemed desirous to hear. *Note*, As all our motions are under the Divine Providence, and our times are in his hands, a gracious soul determines nothing absolutely, but adds to all his purposes, *if it please the Lord*.

3 Sailing from Ephesus, he arrived at Cesarea, where landing, he went up to Jerusalem, and saluted the church, enquiring of their welfare, gladdening them with the tidings he brought, and maintaining communion with his brethren the apostles, who might still make that the chief place of their resort. And such friendly visits of Christ's ministers are a great comfort and mutual encouragement to each other.

4 From Jerusalem he departed for Antioch, the most famed Gentile church, from whence he had been at first sent forth, and whither now the second time he returned with still more joyful accounts of the progress of the gospel. After some time spent there, he proceeded on a third visitation, going over *all the country of Galatia and Phrygia in order, strengthening all the disciples*, confirming them in the faith, encouraging them to persevere, and suggesting the strongest motives and arguments to engage them to take up the cross, and patiently in well-doing to approve their fidelity to their blessed Lord and Master.

24 ¶ And ᶻ a certain Jew named Apollos, born at ᶻ 1 Cor. i. 12.
Alexandria, an eloquent man, *and* mighty in the scrip-
tures, came to Ephesus. 25 This man was instructed
in the way of the Lord; and ᵃ being fervent in the spirit, ᵃ Rom xii 11.
he spake and taught diligently the things of the Lord,
ᵇ knowing only the baptism of John. 26 And he began ᵇ Chap xix 3.
to speak boldly in the synagogue: Whom when Aquila
and Priscilla had heard, they took him unto them, and
expounded unto him the way of God more perfectly.
27 And when he was disposed to pass into Achaia, the
brethren wrote, exhorting the disciples to receive him:
who, when he was come, ᶜ helped them much which had ᶜ 1 Cor. iii. 6.
believed through grace. 28 For he mightily convinced
the Jews, *and that* publicly, ᵈ shewing by the scriptures ᵈ Ver. 5.
that Jesus was Christ.

v. 24—28. Whilst the apostle was on his travels, under a promise of returning to Ephesus, the Lord was raising up in that place an eminently useful minister in the person of Apollos.

1 The account given of him is, that he was a Jew by birth, a native of Alexandria in Egypt, a man of singular abilities, possessed of a fund of solid learning, and endued with a most persuasive faculty of elocution, deeply read in the Scriptures, and every way highly qualified for the work of the ministry. *This man was instructed in the way of the Lord*, and, as far as John's ministry went, embraced the principles of the doctrine of Christ; *and*, so far as his knowledge reached, *being fervent in spirit*, and impressed with a warm zeal for God's glory, and the good of men's souls, *he spake and taught diligently the things of the Lord*, with much study and pains, according to his best light, *knowing only the baptism of John*, who spake of the approaching Messiah, and exhorted all men to prepare for his reception. *And he began to speak boldly in the synagogue*, with great freedom of speech and intrepidity of mind, fearless of the faces of men. A noble pattern for our imitation! And happy is it for that people to whom the Lord is pleased to send such a helper, whose heart, enriched with grace, zealously longs for their salvation, and whose gifts of wisdom and elocution enable him in the most engaging and powerful manner to urge the truths he preaches upon the conscience.

2 Aquila and Priscilla with pleasure heard him, and, observing his simplicity and zeal, they invited him to their lodging, and, being far more experienced and enlightened Christians, *they expounded unto him the way of God more perfectly*, which it seems he never had an opportunity of being informed of before, having probably lived at Alexandria till now, and he immediately embraced the gospel, as soon as he heard it. Herein we may observe, (1.) The gracious conduct of Aquila and Priscilla. Though far more experienced in the truths of God, they attended the ministry of Apollos, encouraged him in his work, and helped him greatly by their private conversation with him. Older Christians should thus be ready to assist young ministers with their advice, and countenance them in their labours. (2.) The great teachableness of Apollos. Though a man so ingenious, learned, and eloquent, he disdained not to sit as a scholar at the feet of a poor tent-maker and his wife, and to learn of them the good ways of God. Thus should young ministers covet the acquaintance of more aged and wiser Christians: and much, very much, may be learned from conversation with poor old men and women, despicable as they may appear in the eyes of scientific pride. (3.) Whatever our attainments are, we should never think ourselves too wise to learn. They who know most will covet to know more, and have their ears open to those who can expound to them the way of God more perfectly.

3 When, after some stay at Ephesus, Apollos was *disposed to pass into Achaia*, to preach the gospel there, particularly at Corinth, Aquila and Priscilla recommended him by letter to the brethren as an able and faithful servant of the Lord Jesus; and, when he came thither, *he helped them much which had believed through grace*, establishing their faith, comforting their hearts, and building them up on that foundation which Paul had laid; *for he mightily convinced the Jews, and that publickly*, in their synagogues and before all the people, *shewing by the scriptures*, with the most convincing argument and close application, *that Jesus was Christ*, the true expected Messiah, by faith in whom alone salvation

salvation could be obtained *Note*, (1) Faith is the gift of God, it is by his grace alone that we are enabled to receive the salvation which is in his Son (2) Though we have true faith, yet we need help and quickning, that we may be more confirmed and established in the truth (3) They who are put in trust with the gospel should be able to defend the great truths which they preach, and from the Scriptures, with all zeal and meekness, to convince gainsayers and confirm the faithful

CHAP XIX

We have here Paul's return to Ephesus according to his promise, and his imparting the Holy Ghost to some who had known only John's baptism, preaching the gospel to the Jews three months, and being persecuted by them, he turns to the Gentiles, preaching the gospel to them in the school of one Tyrannus during two years, and confirming his preaching by miracles, ver 1—12 2 *What was the fruit of his labour*, ver 13—20 3 *What projects he had of further usefulness*, ver 21, 22 *and what would at length be met with at Ephesus from the silversmiths, which forced him thence to pursue the measures he had laid, how a mob was raised by Demetrius to cry up Diana*, ver 23—34 *and how it was suppressed and dispersed by the town clerk*, ver 35—41

1 AND it came to pass, that while Apollos was at Corinth, Paul having passed through the upper coasts, came to Ephesus and finding certain disciples, 2 He said unto them, Have ye received the holy Ghost since ye believed? And they said unto him, We have not so much as heard whether there be any holy Ghost 3 And he said unto them, Unto what then were ye baptized? And they said, Unto John's baptism. 4 Then said Paul, John verily baptized with the baptism of repentance, saying unto the people, That they should believe on him which should come after him, that is, on Christ Jesus 5 When they heard *this*, they were baptized in the name of the Lord Jesus 6 And when Paul had laid *his* hands upon them, the holy Ghost came on them, and they spake with tongues, and prophesied 7 And all the men were about twelve

v 1—7 Whilst Apollos was at Corinth, labouring in the vineyard which Paul had planted, he was travelling through Phrygia and Galatia towards Ephesus, where he arrived

1 He found there certain disciples, who had been baptized either by John or some of his followers, with reference to the Messiah as ready to appear, and who, till now, seem to have been out of the way of receiving further information concerning him Paul therefore enquired of them, as they made profession of their faith, *Have ye received the Holy Ghost, since ye believed* in his miraculous gifts? They own they had not, nor even heard that any such were bestowed by him, *We have not so much as heard whether there be any Holy Ghost* They knew there would be an abundant effusion of his mighty influences, according to the promise, in the days of the Messiah But as yet they had received no intelligence that any such extraordinary gifts had been bestowed The Apostle, with some surprize, then asked them, *Unto what then were ye baptized?* on what account, in whose name, or to the profession of what doctrine? *They said, Unto John's baptism*, in the faith of the Messiah, who was quickly to be revealed *Note*, (1) Though we may not look for the miraculous powers, we may, we must, be partakers of the mighty influences of the Spirit in our hearts If we make profession of our faith, we should therefore seriously enquire into its reality, and whether the Holy Ghost witnesses to his own work in our souls (2) They who are baptized, and have received the outward and visible sign, should often examine themselves, whether they possess the inward and spiritual grace, else the washing of water will be a merely unprofitable ceremony

2 Paul hereupon set himself to explain the true intent of John's baptism *John verily baptized with the baptism of repentance*, exhorting and encouraging men to turn to God, from the view of the riches of his grace, shortly about to be displayed in the kingdom of the Messiah, *saying unto the people, that they should believe on him which should come after him, that is, on Jesus Christ*, the only Saviour from guilt and misery And *when the people*, who attended John's ministry, *heard this, they were baptized in the name of the Lord Jesus*, devoted to the Messiah's service, who was then just appearing, and professing their faith in him The Messiah was now come and accomplished the work of redemption, was exalted to the right hand of God, and had already poured out his Spirit in a miraculous manner upon his disciples.

3 When the Apostle had thus informed them of the grand intention of John's baptism, and they gladly embraced the word, *he laid his hands upon them*, and *the Holy Ghost came on them*, endowing them with miraculous gifts, *and they spake with tongues*, *and prophesied*, as the disciples did at the first effusion of the Spirit They were twelve in number, and probably destined for the ministry of the word at Ephesus, to which they were hereby eminently qualified

8 And he went into the synagogue, and spake boldly for the space of three months, disputing and persuading the things concerning the kingdom of God 9 But when divers were hardened, and believed not, but spake evil of that way before the multitude, he departed from them, and separated the disciples, disputing daily in the school of one Tyrannus 10 And this continued by the space of two years, so that all they which dwelt in Asia, heard the word of the Lord Jesus, both Jews and Greeks 11 And God wrought special miracles by the hands of Paul 12 So that from his body were brought unto the sick handkerchiefs or aprons, and the diseases departed from them, and the evil spirits went out of them.

v 8—12 Paul having thus opened his commission, and produced such authentic evidences of his mission, we find him,

1 According to his custom in the synagogue, where, during three months, he continued speaking boldly in the name of the Lord Jesus, preaching his gospel, *and disputing and persuading the things concerning the kingdom of God*, reasoning with them on the subject, rectifying their mistaken notions, answering their objections, earnestly and affectionately urging them to accept the proffered grace of the Redeemer, and commence subjects of that happy kingdom which the adored Messiah was come to erect here below, that they might be admitted hereafter to partake of his glory in a better world

2 When, after so long a season, the generality seemed but more rivetted in their pride and prejudices, and hardened in their sins, not only obstinately rejecting the gospel themselves, but seeking to prejudice others against it, *speaking evil of that way before the multitude, he then departed from them*, abandoning them to their determined infidelity, *and separated the disciples* from such incorrigible blasphemers, collecting them into a Christian society, and laying the foundation of the Ephesian church, afterwards so renowned, *disputing daily in the school of one Tyrannus*, whither all, both Gentiles and Jews, might resort to him, and hear the gospel which he preached defended by the most convincing arguments Two years he continued there his daily labours, *so that all they that dwelt in Asia*, who resorted on various accounts to this famed city, first or last *heard the word of the Lord Jesus, both Jews and Greeks*, either from Paul himself, or from those who spread the report of his preaching on their return into the country, as perhaps some of his assistants made excursions into parts adjacent, and helped to spread abroad the glad tidings

3 In confirmation of the doctrine which Paul preached, and to give greater weight to his discourses, *God wrought special miracles* by his hand, such as were not only out of the common course of nature, but which none of the other apostles had wrought, so that even *handkerchiefs or aprons*, either such as he wore, or which were sent to him, *were brought from his body unto the sick*, and with such miraculous efficacy were they as it were impregnated by his touch, that the diseases were instantly cured, and the devil dispossessed An emblem of the greater cures which the gospel he preached was designed to work, even to deliver the souls of sinners from their more fatal spiritual maladies, and to rescue them from the bondage of sin and Satan

13 ¶ Then certain of the vagabond Jews, exorcists, took upon them to call over them which had evil spirits the name of the Lord Jesus, saying, We adjure you by Jesus whom Paul preacheth 14 And there were seven sons of *one* Sceva a Jew, *and* chief of the priests, which did so 15 And the evil spirit answered and said, Jesus I know, and Paul I know, but who are ye? 16 And the man in whom the evil spirit was, leapt on them, and overcame them, and prevailed against them, so that they fled out of that house naked and wounded 17 And this was known to all the Jews and Greeks also dwelling at Ephesus, and fear fell on them all, and the name of the Lord Jesus was magnified 18 And many that believed came, and confessed, and shewed their deeds 19 Many also of them which used curious arts, brought their books together, and burned them before all men and they counted the price of them, and found it fifty thousand pieces of silver 20 So mightily grew the word of God, and prevailed

v 13—20 We have here

1 The presumptuous attempt of certain vagabond Jews, exorcists, who pretended by charms to cure diseases and tell fortunes

[illegible] 5 Observing

Observing the admiration in which the apostle was held through the astonishing miracles he performed, hence undertook to do the same, and to cast out devils as well as he, supposing that the name of Jesus, invoked and pronounced by way of charm, would enable them to perform the same cures. *And there were seven sons of one Sceva a Jew, and chief of the priests*, who was probably the head of one of the twenty-four courses, *which did this*, leading this strolling life, and pretending to perform these feats of conjuration. Accordingly, having a patient brought to them, possessed of a devil, they began their exorcisms over him, saying, *We adjure you by Jesus, whom Paul preacheth*, solemnly commanding you, by that name which Paul proclaims, to depart immediately.

2. Insufficient was the effect of their adjuration from their expectations. Instead of obeying their commands, the evil spirit, using the man's organs of speech, insultingly replied, in contempt of their words, *Jesus I know, and Paul I know*, too well he knew the divine power of the one, and the authority with which the other was invested; *but who are ye?* a vagabond crew, without power or authority; *and the man, in whom the evil spirit was, leapt on them* with fury and rage, *and overcame them, and*, in spite of all their efforts, *prevailed against them, so that they fled out of that house naked and wounded*, their cloaths torn from their backs, and heartily beaten, bruised, and bloody, the just derision of the spectators. *And*, as this was transacted publickly, *it was known to all the Jews and Greeks dwelling at Ephesus, and fear fell on them all*, dreading the power of these infernal spirits, nor daring any more to mock God by such incantations, lest he should let loose these furies upon them, *and the name of the Lord Jesus was magnified*, it evidently appearing that he alone could dispossess these fiends of darkness, and therefore he was regarded with highest honour, and his name mentioned with reverence.

3. Seeing these exorcists thus shamefully defeated, many who had before time used the like magic arts and charms, but now by the grace of God were brought to faith in the Lord Jesus, *came and confessed their deeds*, with shame and confusion of face before God and man, *and brought their books together*, out of which they had learnt their spells and methods of divination, fortune-telling, casting of nativities, interpreting dreams, discovering lost goods, laying spirits, and the like diabolical arts, *and burned them before all men*, in detestation of such wickedness, and to prevent their falling into the hands of others. *And they counted the price of them, and found it fifty thousand pieces of silver*, so scarce and curious were these manuscripts. *So mightily grew the word of God and prevailed!* Note, (1.) They who are brought to the faith of the gospel, will be instantly led to sacrifice their dearest and most beloved iniquities, with holy indignation at the *remembrance of them*. (2.) They who know the evil of sin, will be careful to remove every temptation thereunto out of their own and others way. (3.) True converts desire to take shame before all men, and to give to the Lord Jesus the glory due unto his name in the most substantial proofs of their real conversion to him.

u Rom. xv 25 Gal. i 2 x Ch. xx 22 y Ch. xviii 21 Rom. xv 23-28 z Chap. xiii 5 a Rom. xvi 23 2 Tim. iv 20 b 2 Cor. i 8 c Ch. ix 2 d Chap. xvi 16, 19

21 ¶ [u] After these things were ended, Paul [x] pur-
posed in the spirit, when he had passed through Mace-
donia and Achaia, to go to Jerusalem, saying, After I
have been there, [y] I must also see Rome. 22 So he
sent into Macedonia two of them that ministred unto
him, [z] Timotheus and [a] Erastus, *but* he himself stayed in
Asia for a season. 23 And [b] the same time there arose
no small stir about [c] that way. 24 For a certain *man*
named Demetrius, a silversmith, which made silver shrines
for Diana, brought [d] no small gain unto the craftsmen.
25 Whom he called together with the workmen of like
occupation, and said, Sirs, ye know that by this craft
we have our wealth. 26 Moreover, ye see and hear
that not alone at Ephesus, but almost throughout all
Asia, this Paul hath persuaded and turned away much
people, saying, That they be no gods which are made
with hands. 27 So that not only this our craft is in
danger to be set at nought, but also that the temple of
the great goddess Diana should be despised, and her
magnificence should be destroyed, whom all Asia and the
world worshippeth. 28 And when they heard *these say-
ings*, they were full of wrath, and cried out, saying,
Great *is* Diana of the Ephesians. 29 And the whole
city was filled with confusion: and having caught [e] Gaius
and [f] Aristarchus, men of Macedonia, Paul's companions
in travel, they rushed with one accord into the theatre.
30 And when Paul would have entred in unto the peo-
ple, the disciples suffered him not. 31 And certain of
the chief of Asia, which were his friends, sent unto him,
desiring *him* that he would not adventure himself into the
theatre. 32 Some therefore cried one thing, and some

e Ps. xcv 3 1 Cor. x 3 f 1 Cor. i 14 g Ch. xx 4 xxvii 2 Col. iv 10

another: for the assembly was confused, and the more
part knew not wherefore they were come together. 33
And they drew Alexander out of the multitude, the Jews
putting him forward. And Alexander [h] beckned with — h Chap. xii 17 & xxi 40
the hand, and would have made his defence unto the
people. 34 But when they knew that he was a Jew,
all with one voice about the space of two hours cried out,
Great *is* Diana of the Ephesians. 35 And when the
town-clerk had appeased the people, he said, *Ye* men
of Ephesus, what man is there that knoweth not how
that the city of the Ephesians is a † worshipper of the — † Or the keeper of the temple
great goddess Diana, and of the *image* which fell down
from Jupiter? 36 Seeing then that these things can-
not be spoken against, ye ought to be quiet, and to do
nothing rashly. 37 For ye have brought hither these
men, which are neither robbers of churches, nor yet
blasphemers of your goddess. 38 Wherefore if Deme-
trius and the craftsmen which are with him, have a mat-
ter against any man, ‡ the law is open, and there are — ‡ Or the court days are kept
deputies, let them implead one another. 39 But if ye
inquire any thing concerning other matters, it shall be
determined in a lawful assembly. 40 For we are in
danger to be called in question for this days uproar,
there being no cause whereby we may give an account
of this concourse. 41 And when he had thus spoken,
he dismissed the assembly.

v. 21—41. Just as Paul thought of departing from Ephesus, an unexpected storm arose.

1. After a stay of about three years at Ephesus from his first coming thither, he resolved to visit the churches he had planted in Macedonia and Achaia, purposing from thence to go to Jerusalem, and, under the influence of the Holy Ghost, determined afterwards to see Rome also, the seat of empire, and there preach the glorious gospel of Christ. He sent therefore Timotheus and Erastus before him, to give them notice of his intentions, and prepare their collection for the poor saints at Jerusalem, whilst he himself stayed a while in Asia, carrying on the blessed work which was there begun.

2. During his stay, *there arose no small stir about that way*, the way of Christ, which Paul preached, the occasion and consequences of which are here related.

(1.) The ringleader, who stirred up the tumult was one *Demetrius, a silversmith*, whose most gainful branch of business lay in making silver models of the temple of Diana, with her image in miniature within, which the superstitious worshippers used to carry home with them, for the gratifying the curiosity of their neighbours, or for the purposes of devotion. This man, calling his fellow craftsmen together, harangued them on the danger in which their trade stood, from whence all their wealth arose, and this through the preaching of Paul, who, instead of paying the least regard to their shrines, or the great Diana and her temple, persuaded and turned away the people, almost throughout all Asia, from the worship of their goddess, *saying, That they be no gods which are made with hands*, despising the images and deities to whom their ancestors had ever paid such veneration: and, in consequence thereof, not only their craft was in danger, and that was a point which he knew lay near their hearts, but he pretends a higher motive for his present application to them, even his zeal for the great goddess Diana, the object of their own and of universal devotion, who was now likely to grow into contempt, and her magnificent temple to be abandoned, if this new religion should be suffered to gain ground; and therefore it was high time for them to bestir themselves, and oppose the growing evil. *Note*, (1.) Pomp and numbers are still on the side of idol-worship in the papal church, falsely called Christian. (2.) They who make gain of their religion, and follow it as their craft, evidently shew to whom they pay their adoration, not to God, but Mammon.

(2.) This harangue had its desired effect. The craftsmen, enflamed to fury with the apprehension that both their gain and their goddess were in danger, with wild uproar filled the streets, shouting, *Great is Diana of the Ephesians*. The mob readily joined them, and the whole city immediately became a scene of tumult and confusion.

3. Gaius and Aristarchus, *men of Macedonia, Paul's companions*, falling in their way, they seized them, and hurried them to the theatre, where the public games were celebrated, and criminals thrown to wild beasts, and compelled to fight them, *see* 1 Cor. xv. 32. intending probably there to dispatch these fellow-labourers of the apostle. Paul, nobly prodigal of his life in defence of the gospel and of his suffering friends, would fain *have entred in to the people*, and attempted to reason with them on their wickedness: *but the disciples*, justly apprehensive of the imminent danger to which he would be exposed, earnestly dissuaded him, and insisted upon his not going; which were also further enforced by a message from *certain of the chief of Asia*, who presided over the public games, and had the direction

of

of the theatre, *which were his friends*, and consulted his safety, and therefore desired *that he would not adventure himself into the theatre*, where all their influence and authority might be unable to restrain an enraged populace from some fatal acts of violence. *Note*, The lives of great and good men are precious: though they are prodigal of them, and willing to spend and be spent in the service of Christ, their friends should be more careful of them than they are of themselves.

4. The mob, now prodigiously increased, roared out, *some one thing, some another; for the assembly was confused, and the more part knew not wherefore they were come together*: and some of them *drew Alexander out of the multitude*, to call him to an account, *the Jews putting him forward*, either helping to expose him to the rage of the people, being equally enemies to the Christian name; or, if he was one of their body, encouraging him to declaim against Paul, and excuse them, who were alike hated on account of their known aversion to idolatry. *And Alexander beckoned with his hand*, desiring silence, *and would have made his defence unto the people*, either for himself and the Christians, if he was of their number, or rather, being a Jew, he intended to throw the odium upon the apostle, and exculpate his countrymen. But no sooner was it known that he was a Jew, the professed enemy of idol-worship, than they stopped their ears, and would not hear a word; but *all with one accord, about the space of three hours*, continued crying out and shouting, *Great is Diana of the Ephesians!* as if their noise had not proved the truth of her deity. Thus often is the cause of God and truth run down by those who madly refuse to hear the voice of reason.

5. The *town clerk*, or rather the chief magistrate, who presided over the public games, with difficulty at last silenced the uproar, and remonstrated against the tumult, saying, *Ye men of Ephesus, what man is there that knoweth not how that the city of the Ephesians is a worshipper of the great goddess Diana*, devoted to her service, and by their charter engaged to take care of her temple and worship, *and of the image which fell down from Jupiter*, which therefore is not of the gods made with men's hands, against whom Paul declaims. *Seeing then that these things cannot be spoken against*, being universally received among us as certain, *ye ought to be quiet, and to do nothing rashly* against the persons whom ye have seized. *For ye have brought hither these men* as criminals, *which are neither* proved to be *robbers of temples, nor yet blasphemers of your goddess*, treating her with no opprobrious language, nor guilty of any sacrilege. *Wherefore if Demetrius and the craftsmen which are with him*, who have fomented this riot, *have a matter against any man, the law is open, and there are deputies*, where justice will readily be done them, *let them implead one another*, and submit to the decision of the proper judges. *But if ye enquire any thing concerning other matters*, of more general concern, relative to the state or religion, *it shall be determined in a lawful assembly*, convoked for that purpose. *For*, so far from deciding at present upon the merits of the cause, *we are in danger of being called in question for this day's uproar*, if complaint be carried to the emperor against us, *there being no just cause whereby we may give an account of this concourse*, if we should be summoned before our superiors.

And when he had thus spoken, to soothe and quiet the inflamed multitude, *he dismissed the assembly*, enjoining them peaceably to retire to their own homes. *Note*, (1.) God hath a variety of ways to rescue his people out of their troubles, and can raise them up friends from quarters where they least expected them. (2.) It is a constant and universal rule to do nothing rashly, for whatever is done in a passion we shall infallibly wish undone. (3.) The terror of the law is usually a greater restraint than the fear of God. Happy were it for us if we remembered, whenever inordinate passion begins to swell in our bosom, that we are liable to be called in question for the uproar, and should therefore check the rising storm.

CHAP. XX.

In this chapter we have, 1. *Paul's travels through Macedonia, Greece, and Asia, and his coming at length to Troas*, ver. 1—6. 2. *A particular account of his spending one Lord's day at Troas, and his raising Eutychus to life there*, ver. 7—12. 3. *His progress, or circuit, for the visiting of the churches he had planted, in his way towards Jerusalem, where he designed to be by the next feast of pentecost*, ver. 13—16. 4. *The farewel sermon he preached to the presbyters of Ephesus, now he was leaving that country*, ver. 17—35. 5. *The very sorrowful parting between him and them*, ver. 36, 37, 38.

1 AND [a] after the uproar was ceased, Paul called unto him the disciples, and [b] embraced *them*, ... [a] Chap. xix. 41. [b] Acts xxi. ...
and departed for to go into Macedonia. 2 And when
he had gone over those parts, and had given them much
exhortation, he came into Greece, 3 And *there* abode ... [c] Chap. xx. ...
three months. And when [d] the Jews laid wait for him, as ... [d] Chap. ix. 24.
he was about to sail into Syria, he purposed to return
through Macedonia. 4 And there accompanied him
into Asia, Sopater of Berea; and of the Thessalonians,
[e] Aristarchus and Secundus; and Gaius of Derbe, and [e] Chap. xix. 29.
Timotheus; and of Asia, [f] Tychicus and [g] Trophimus. [f] Eph. vi. 21. Col. iv. 7.
5 These going before, tarried for us at Troas. 6 And [g] Chap. xxi. 29.
we sailed away from Philippi, after the days of unleavened bread, and came unto them [h] to Troas in five days, [h] Chap. xvi. 8.
where we abode seven days.

1—6. Soon after the uproar, which Demetrius had raised, was ceased, Paul determined to proceed on his journey, as he had before purposed.

1. After an affectionate parting with the brethren, Paul departed for Macedonia to visit the churches he had planted; and, having gone over those parts, and given them *much exhortation* to persevere, amidst all opposition, in the profession of the faith which they had embraced, he came into Greece, into Achaia, where he abode *three months*, employed in the same profitable manner, confirming and strengthening the faithful; and from thence was purposing to sail for Syria, in order to go directly to Jerusalem; but, by intelligence or inspiration, having learnt that the Jews intended to waylay, murder, and rob him of the collection which the churches had made for their poor brethren in Judea, he changed his route, and returned through Macedonia.

2. The companions of his travels into Asia were *Sopater of Berea*, Rom. xvi. 21. *of the Thessalonians, Aristarchus and Secundus, and Gaius of Derbe, and Timotheus, and of Asia, Tychicus and Trophimus*; and now Luke the historian, who had probably been left in those parts before, to carry on the work so prosperously begun, seems to have joined the apostle's train. The rest, *going before, tarried for* Paul and Luke, and those who accompanied them *at Troas*, whither they followed immediately after the passover, sailing from Philippi, and in five days joined their companions at Troas, where they stayed seven days.

7 And upon [i] the first *day* of the week, when the dis- [i] 1 Cor. xvi. 2. Rev. i. 10.
ciples came together [k] to break bread, Paul preached unto [k] Chap. ii. 42, 46.
them, ready to depart on the morrow; and continued his 1 Cor. x. 16.
speech until midnight. 8 And there were many lights in & xi. 20, &c.
the upper [l] chamber, where they were gathered together. [l] Chap. i. 13.
9 And there sat in a window a certain young man named
Eutychus, being fallen into a deep sleep: and as Paul was
long preaching, he sunk down with sleep, and fell down
from the third loft, and was taken up dead. 10 And
Paul went down, and [m] fell on him, and embracing *him*, [m] 1 Kings xvii. 21.
said, [n] Trouble not yourselves; for his life is in him. 2 Kings iv. 34.
11 When he therefore was come up again, and had [n] Mat. ix.
broken bread, and eaten, and talked a long while, even 24.
till break of day, so he departed. 12 And they brought
the young man alive, and were not a little comforted.

v. 7—12. Seven days the apostle abode at Troas, desirous to spend one Lord's day with the disciples before he went on his journey. And a blessed day, no doubt, it was to the church in that place.

1. According to their established custom, *upon the first day of the week*, which had succeeded to the Jewish sabbath, and in memory of the Lord's resurrection, and the descent of the Holy Ghost, was consecrated henceforward to God's more immediate service in all acts of religious worship, and for the publick administration of the ordinances, *the disciples came together to break bread*, commemorating, as they constantly did every week, the sacrifice and sufferings of their Lord. *Paul preached unto them, ready to depart on the morrow*; and, having much to say, and being probably not likely ever again to have another opportunity of speaking to them, his warm heart led him on, so that *he continued his speech until midnight*, unwearied in exhortation, and addressing himself to those who counted the longest of his discourses short. *And there were many lights in the upper chamber, where they were gathered together*; they were content to put up with this mean inconvenient place of meeting; and, as no deeds of darkness were found among them, they took care the place should be well illumined, to confute the invidious insinuations of their enemies. *Note*, According to the practice of the apostles and the primitive church, the first day of the week is appointed for the assemblies of the faithful disciples of Jesus to join in all acts of religious worship, hear his word, partake of his ordinances, and maintain communion with each other. They who neglect the assembling of themselves together, as the manner of some is, evidently shew that they have renounced Christianity, and have no part nor lot among the faithful in Christ Jesus.

2. A melancholy accident happened to a youth in the company, whose name was Eutychus. He sat in a window that was open; and, the apostle lengthening his sermon so much more than usual, sleep overtook the young man, and falling backward through the window, which was three stories high, he was killed on the spot. A warning to those who sleep under

sermon, where they have none of those things to plead which might be urged in his excuse.

3. Paul raises him again to life. It served for a momentary interruption to the assembly, but [illegible] contributed to the further[illegible] of their faith and joy. The apostle immediately *went down, and fell on him, and embracing him*, as Elijah stretched himself on the dead corpse of the widow of Sarepta's son, 1 Kings xvii. 21. *said, Trouble not yourselves, for his life is in him*, restored by divine power. Then he returned to the room where they had assembled, and, after the administration of the Lord's supper, spent the remainder of the night, till break of day, in sweet communion and conversation, when, in the most affectionate manner, he took his leave. But, before they parted, *they brought the young man alive* into the assembly, *and were not a little comforted*, as some reproach might have been cast upon them, had he thus died, but now it tended to the credit of the gospel. *Note*, (1.) They who know the sweetness and profit of Christian conferences, [illegible] to improve every moment of the company of those faithful ministers whose discourse so greatly tends to quicken and comfort them. (2.) Providences that appear at first view very afflictive, God can and often doth over-rule to the increase of our joy.

13 ¶ And we went before to ship, and sailed unto Assos, there intending to take in Paul: for so had he appointed, minding himself to go afoot. 14 And when he met with us at Assos, we took him in, and came to Mitylene. 15 And we sailed thence, and came the next *day* over against Chios; and the next *day* we arrived at Samos, and tarried at Trogyllium; and the next *day* we came to Miletus. 16 For Paul had determined to sail by Ephesus, because he would not spend the time in Asia: for he hasted, if it were possible for him, [p] to be at Jerusalem the day of Pentecost.

v. 13—16. Paul now without delay hastened to Jerusalem. His companions went by ship before to Assos, where they were to take in Paul, who for some important reasons, which we are not told, resolved to go thither on foot. Here embarking, they all sailed for Mitylene, the chief city of the isle of Lesbos, from whence, without stopping, they proceeded the next day as far as the isle of Chios, and the next, arriving at Samos, they made a short stay at Trogyllium, a harbour in the promontory of Mycale in Asia, and the next day arrived at Miletus, sailing by Ephesus, *because he would not spend the time in Asia: for he hasted, if it were possible for him, to be at Jerusalem the day of Pentecost*, and he apprehended the importunity of his Ephesian friends might have delayed him. *Note*, When the glory of God, and the business of our station, call for our attendance, pleasant and delightful as it is to enjoy the company of our dear friends, we must forego this satisfaction.

17 ¶ And from Miletus he sent to Ephesus, and called the elders of the church. 18 And when they were come to him, he said unto them, Ye know, [q] from the first day that I came into Asia, after what manner I have been with you at all seasons, 19 Serving the Lord with all humility of mind, and with many tears, and temptations, which befel me by the lying in wait of the Jews: 20 *And* how I kept back nothing that was profitable *unto you*, but have shewed you, and have taught you publickly, and from house to house, 21 Testifying both to the Jews, and also to the Greeks, [r] repentance toward God, and faith toward our Lord Jesus Christ. 22 And now behold, [s] I go bound in the spirit unto Jerusalem, not knowing the things that shall befal me there: 23 Save that [u] the holy Ghost witnesseth in every city, saying, that bonds and [x] afflictions abide me. 24 But [y] none of these things move me, [z] neither count I my life dear unto myself, [a] so that I might finish my course with joy, and [b] the ministry, which I have received of the Lord Jesus, to testify the gospel of the grace of God. 25 And now behold, I know that ye all among whom I have gone preaching the kingdom of God, [c] shall see my face no more. 26 Wherefore I take you to record this day, that I am [d] pure from the blood of all *men*. 27 For [e] I have not shunned to declare unto you all [f] the counsel of God. 28 ¶ Take heed therefore unto yourselves, and to all the flock, over the which [g] the holy Ghost hath made you overseers, to [h] feed the church of God, [i] which he hath purchased [k] with his own blood. 29 For I know this, that after my departing [l] shall grievous wolves enter in among you, not sparing the flock. 30 Also of your own selves shall men arise, [m] speaking perverse things, to draw away disciples after them. 31 Therefore watch, and remember that [n] by the space of three years, I ceased not to warn every one night and day with tears. 32 And now, brethren, I commend you to God, and [o] to the word of his grace, which is able [p] to build you up, and to give you [q] an inheritance among all them which are sanctified. 33 [u] I have coveted no man's silver, or gold, or apparel. 34 Yea, you yourselves know, that [x] these hands have ministred unto my necessities, and to them that were with me. 35 I have shewed you all things, how [y] that so labouring ye ought to support the weak, and to remember the words of the Lord Jesus, how he said, It is more blessed to give than to receive.

v. 17—35. Though Paul would not call at Ephesus, he greatly desired to see the [*] elders of the church, and therefore sent for them to Miletus, who gladly attended him, where he addressed to them this most affecting and solemn discourse, that can scarce now be read by any gracious heart without a tear.

1. He opens with an appeal to them concerning his life and doctrine during the time he had sojourned among them.

(1.) As to his life, *Ye know, from the first day that I came into Asia, after what manner I have been with you at all seasons*, how exemplary, holy, and unblameable his conversation had been, how uniform his conduct, how steady amidst all his trials, *serving the Lord with all humility of mind*. His Master's service was his one business, and, amidst all the honour which the Lord had put upon him, he sought no glory nor applause, but, with the lowliest thoughts of himself, and deepest condescension towards others, was ready to stoop to any service, even to the meanest, whereby the Saviour might be glorified, and the bodies or souls of men be benefited, *and with many tears*, in his prayers for them, and affectionate discourses to them, deeply concerned for those who obstinately rejected the counsel of God against their own souls, tenderly sympathizing with the afflictions of the faithful, and lamenting over backsliders and apostates, *and with many temptations which befel me by the lying in wait of the Jews*, ever contriving his destruction; in all which his approved fidelity had been abundantly manifested, and his example remained for their imitation.

(2.) As to his doctrine. *Ye know how I kept back from you nothing that was profitable unto you*, not shunning with all simplicity and sincerity to declare the whole counsel of God, unawed by fears, undismayed by difficulties, uninfluenced by any worldly motives, *and have shewed and taught you publickly* in the congregation, *and* privately *from house to house*, continually labouring to diffuse the sweet savour of Christ, and to communicate edification, encouragement, and consolation, wherever he went, *testifying both to the Jews, and also to the Greeks*, with the most earnest affection and concern, *repentance towards God*, the necessity and nature of it, as implying a deep and humbling sense of sin, its evil, malignity, and danger, a genuine self-abhorrence in the view of its guilt and ingratitude, with an unfeigned and unreserved renunciation of it, and a real conversion of heart to the love and service of a pardoning God, *and faith toward our Lord Jesus Christ*, directing sinners to him as the great object of all their hopes, describing the fulness, freedom, and all-sufficiency of his salvation, and urging them to trust in his blood, righteousness, and grace, for pardon, peace, adoption, glory. *Note*, (1.) What was Paul's doctrine must be ours, if ever we would approve ourselves to God, and profit men's souls, under the influence of the Spirit desiring to lead them to a deep conviction of their ruin, and a humbling sense of their sin, and then to point out the glorious remedy provided in a crucified Jesus. (2.) They who have the care of immortal souls lying upon them can never be enough diligent. Their private conversation must breathe the same spirit as their discourse in the pulpit, and every company where they are found should be the wiser and better for them. (3.) No fear of man should ever lead us to suppress a tittle of those glorious gospel truths which are so offensive to human pride, at least it should be our labour to deliver our own souls, whether men will hear or whether they will forbear.

* It has been urged by those who plead for a parity among the ministers of the gospel, that these elders are called *episcopoi*, bishops, [illegible] 28. But, since John addresses himself to a person in the singular number, as the angel of the church, Rev. ii. 1. and it appears from Ignatius that Onesimus was in his time bishop of that church, not long after the death of the apostle John, who is generally supposed to have spent his latter days there, and in the persecution [illegible] I cannot but think it carries with it [illegible] argument that though during the time they were under immediate apostolical inspection [illegible] were men [illegible] of the same rank and order, yet by the [illegible] appointed [illegible] officers over them [illegible] they [illegible] were [illegible] invested with the superintendency of the ministers in [illegible] and adjacent country, and who [illegible] admitted to their successors [illegible] delegated to them for the well government of the church. [illegible] that the [illegible] however [illegible] between [illegible] primitive episcopacy [illegible] the order [illegible] station.

2 He lets them know what a scene of sufferings were before him He left them not to avoid the cross, but was about to encounter greater persecutions than ever *And now, behold, I go bound in the Spirit unto Jerusalem*, by the mighty constraining of the Holy Ghost led thither, and fully determined in my own soul to follow his guidance and direction, *not knowing the things that shall befal me there*, the particular sufferings to which he should be exposed God had not revealed to him *Save that the Holy Ghost witnesseth in every city, saying, that bonds and afflictions abide me*, either in general he had this notice given him, or in every city he passed through the divinely inspired prophets foretold the sufferings which awaited him *But none of these things move me*, to terrify him from his duty, or shake his constant mind, *neither count I my life dear unto myself*, dear as it was, he paid no regard to it, when the cause of Christ called him to brave death and danger, content to suffer whatever the Lord pleased to permit *so that I might finish my course with joy*, accomplishing his blessed Master's work, and reaching the prize of his high calling, *and the ministry which I have received of the Lord Jesus, to testify the gospel of the grace of God*, freely and openly publishing the unsearchable riches of Christ, and proving by the fullest evidence the truth he declared, displaying in the most ravishing manner the sovereign, unmerited, boundless love and [illegible] grace of God, manifested in the gospel of his dear Son [illegible] sinners *Note*, (1.) If our hearts are truly fixed on God, and on the consideration of heaven, we shall look down upon the [illegible] and deaths as unable to hurt us, and hold ourselves put our lives in our hands, when Christ calls to them (2.) Life is our race, and death the goal, our one concern is to finish our course with joy, and that by persevering fidelity approving ourselves to God, we may receive the crown of life and glory which the Lord, the righteous Judge, shall give to all his faithful servants (3.) Our ministry is received of the Lord, and to him must we shortly render up the solemn account (4.) The grand subject of all our discourses, if we would fulfil that ministry we have received of the Lord, must be *the gospel of the grace of God*, in opposition to all the pride of duties and human self-sufficiency, labouring to make lost sinners know the necessity of a free justification through the blood and righteousness of a Redeemer, and, from a view of their utter impotence and corruption, to lead them to those supplies of grace and strength which can only be derived from him

3 He informs them that he is now taking his last leave of them, and appeals to God for his freedom from the blood of all men *And now, behold, I know, that ye all, among whom I have gone preaching the kingdom of God*, the doctrines, privileges, and duties thereof, *shall see my face no more*, nor ever again enjoy my personal ministry among you *Wherefore I take you to record this day, that I am pure from the blood of all men, for I have not shunned to declare unto you all the counsel of God* He appeals therefore to them in the presence of God for his fidelity the whole truth of the gospel, so far as God had revealed it to him, he had declared, and now, if any soul among them perished, their blood was on their own head, he was free *Note*, (1.) It is a singular satisfaction when we can make such an appeal to God, and those to whom we have ministred, for our simplicity and faithfulness in the discharge of our sacred trust (2.) The whole counsel of God, without reserve, must be declared, the truths of God need no concealment and they shew their ignorance of the spirit of the gospel, who with timidity mention its glorious privileges, pretending fear lest the sovereign, free, and boundless grace of God should be perverted to licentiousness We must declare it, let men abuse it at their peril

4 He gives them a solemn parting charge *Take heed to yourselves*, that your own conversation may be exemplary, and your souls influenced by that gospel you preach to others, *and to the flock* committed to your charge, for whom you must give an awful account shortly before the great Shepherd and Bishop of souls, *over the which the Holy Ghost hath made you overseers*, appointing you to your office, and furnishing you with gifts for the discharge of it, *to feed the church of God* with knowledge and understanding, and with wisdom and meekness to preside over them, *which he hath purchased with his own blood*; the inestimable value of their souls therefore is evident, when he who is very God became incarnate, and submitted to the death of the cross, to make atonement for their sins and to purchase them for his own Did Jesus bleed to redeem his people, and can we be his servants, and not desire to spend and be spent in the service of [illegible] the [illegible] negligent minister, beyond all others, trampl[illegible] [illegible] the blood of the Son of God

[illegible] *He warns them of the dangers which they would be called to [illegible]*, [illegible] to be [illegible] faithful *For I know* [illegible] by revelation *that after my departure shall grievous wolves enter in among you*, both persecutors without, and false teachers [illegible] to corrupt the truth, and ruin the souls of the people, *not sparing the flock*, [illegible] to holiness, [illegible] *Also of your own selves shall men arise*, [illegible] [illegible] part up [illegible] ambition, and of whom you [illegible] *speaking perverse things*, departing from the simplicity of the gospel, broaching pernicious heresies, [illegible] dangerous innovation, *to draw away disciples after*

them [illegible] [illegible] 2 Tim 3: 15 [illegible] [illegible] the [illegible] would be necessary, and [illegible] [illegible] and should [illegible] [illegible] disciples [illegible] [illegible] they [illegible] [illegible] gospel, *and [illegible]* [illegible] you needed [illegible] [illegible] *I [illegible]* [illegible] [illegible] concerned for them, carefully observing the first motions of declension, [illegible] appearances of declension from the purity of the truth, or the simplicity of the gospel, [illegible] [illegible] or [illegible] [illegible] [illegible] protection, [illegible] [illegible] recover the fallen, [illegible] [illegible] [illegible] [illegible] [illegible] with the gospel, may be enabled to shew such zeal, fidelity, and affectionate concern over the souls of our people

6 He solemnly commends them to the divine care and keeping *And now, brethren*, having admonished you of the dangers you must encounter and knowing [illegible] more than [illegible] [illegible] [illegible] [illegible] your fidelity to Christ, *I commend you to God* to his power to protect, his wisdom to guide, his [illegible] to comfort you, *and to the word of his grace*, to his written and revealed word, for your conduct and direction, or to the [illegible] Christ Jesus, out of whose [illegible] [illegible] [illegible] [illegible] preserved and kept through [illegible] all the [illegible] [illegible] opposition of persecutors [illegible] *able to build you up*, in faith, hope, and [illegible] *and to give you an inheritance among all them which are sanctified*, preparing you for that kingdom which he hath prepared for you, and bringing you at last to inherit [illegible] [illegible] in light and glory [illegible] (1.) [illegible] not in our own [illegible] [illegible] [illegible] [illegible] [illegible] we are saved (2.) [illegible] hope [illegible] God's saints in heaven, who are not partakers of their grace upon earth, and sanctified by the Holy Ghost (3.) [illegible] [illegible] means of producing, through the power of his might, true sanctification (4.) The kingdom of glory is the *inheritance* of God's people, being chosen in Christ Jesus before the foundation of the world, called by his word, and justified by faith, their title is indefeasible, and the possession secured, they can never perish, but shall have everlasting life

7 He particularly reminds them of the disinterestedness which he had shewn to this world, and his labours, that he might not be beholden to any man for a provision, while he freely preached the gospel *I have coveted no man's silver or gold, or apparel*, content with what he could obtain from his own industry, and burdensome to none of them for maintenance *Yea, you yourselves know, that these hands have ministred unto my necessities*, entitled as he was to a liberal provision, he chose, for the sake of the gospel, to waive his right, and to work hard at his trade, by which he was enabled to earn a subsistence not only for himself, but also *to help them that were with me*, who [illegible] to provide for themselves [illegible] [illegible] particular [illegible] teacher, that he might [illegible] every [illegible] [illegible] they would [illegible] [illegible] by my example, *I have shewed you all things, how that so labouring*, as I have done, *ye ought to support the weak*, [illegible] and [illegible] their wants, and removing every [illegible] of prejudice which the deceivers might seek to instil into the minds of the weak brethren, as if they laboured for [illegible] *and to remember the words of the Lord Jesus, how he said, It is more blessed to give than to receive*, it is more [illegible] [illegible] to relieve the wants of others, and lay out ourselves for them, and without recompence, than to be beholden to them for maintenance

36 ¶ And when he had thus spoken, he kneeled down, and prayed with them all 37 And they all wept sore, and fell on Paul's neck, and kissed him, 38 Sorrowing most of all for the words which he spake, that they should see his face no more And they accompanied him unto the ship

[illegible] 36—38 Having finished this most affectionate discourse,

1 *He kneeled down and prayed with them all*, commending them solemnly to the Lord [illegible] [illegible] they might be enabled faithfully to discharge the solemn trust committed to them, and observe the good counsel he had delivered *Note*, (1.) Ministers must water the word sown with their prayers, that God may give the increase (2.) Friends will do well to part in prayer, that [illegible] [illegible] meet here again in peace, and, if not, that they may together finally unite [illegible] [illegible] [illegible] the throne of God and of the Lamb

2 They parted with floods of tears and the most affectionate embraces [illegible]

his prayer, and his departure from them, *and fell on Paul's neck and kissed him*, taking their last farewel of their dear pastor, with hearts full of love, and swelling with grief, *sorrowing most of all for the words which he spake, that they should see his face no more* To part was bitter, to part for a long while, would have been yet more irksome, but to part, without the hope of ever meeting again among the living, this added peculiar anguish to the separation, and antedated the funeral sorrows it was a kind of living burial *And they accompanied him unto the ship*, willing to enjoy his company to the last moment, and to testify their deep respect and fervent love towards him *Note*, Tho' our friends may be separated from us, so that we can see their face no more, it is our consolation, if we are united in one Jesus, that we shall assuredly meet in a better world, never to part again

CHAP XXI

In this chapter we have, 1 A journal of Paul's voyage from Ephesus to Cesarea, ver 1—7 *2 The struggles he had with his friends at Cesarea, who mightily opposed his going up to Jerusalem, but could not prevail*, ver 8—14 *3 Paul's journey from Cesarea to Jerusalem, and the kind entertainment which the Christians there gave him*, ver 15—17 *4 In condescension to the prejudices of the Jews, and by the advice of the brethren he purifies himself in the temple according to the law*, ver 18—26 *5 The turning of this very thing against him by the Jews, and the apprehending of him in the temple as a criminal thereupon*, ver 27—30 *6 The fair escape he had of being pulled to pieces by the rabble, and the taking of him into fair and legal custody by the chief captain, who permitted him to speak for himself to the people*, ver 31—40.

† Or, Torn or pulled away with violence 1 AND it came to pass, that after we were † gotten
from them, and had lanched, we came with a
straight course unto Coos, and the *day* following unto
Rhodes, and from thence unto Patara 2 And finding a
ship sailing over unto Phenicia, we went aboard, and set
forth 3 Now when we had discovered Cyprus, we
left it on the left hand, and sailed into Syria, and landed
at Tyre for there the ship was to unlade her burden
a Isa. xxiii. 18 4 And a finding disciples, we tarried there seven days
b Chap. xx. 23. Ver. 12 b who said to Paul through the Spirit, that he should not
go up to Jerusalem 5 And when we had accomplished
those days, we departed, and went our way, and they
all brought us on our way, with wives and children, till
c Chap. xx. 36 *we were* out of the city and c we kneeled down on the
shore, and prayed 6 And when we had taken our
leave one of another, we took ship, and they returned
home again 7 And when we had finished *our* course
from Tyre, we came to Ptolemais, and saluted the brethren, and abode with them one day

v 1—7 With deepest reluctance he had, as it were by violence, torn himself from the embraces of his dear Ephesian brethren, and now, since God had so ordained, he pursues his voyage

1 He proceeds to Tyre They came in a straight course to Coos, the next day to Rhodes, famed for its Colossus, and thence to Patara, whither the ship in which they sailed was bound, or was from thence to take a different course from that which they pursued, therefore providentially finding another ship ready to sail for Phenicia, they embarked, and leaving Cyprus on the left, arrived on the coasts of Syria, and landed at Tyre, where the ship was *to unlade her burden*

2 Seven days Paul and his companions halted at this famed mart, spending one Lord's day with the disciples which they found there, and improving his short stay for their edification and comfort *Note*, When we travel, we should enquire after the disciples, their profession will make them singular, and they may be easily found

3 There he received from some of the inspired prophets of the church, a warning of the dangers which were before him, and that if he meant to escape them, he must not go to Jerusalem, but his resolution was fixed, and his call evident, and therefore he departed at the expiration of the seven days

4 They took a solemn farewel of him, when he thus determined to proceed, and *brought us on our way, with wives and children, till we were out of the city*, willing to shew the apostle and his companion the greatest honour and respect, and desirous that they and theirs might to the last moment improve the blessing of his presence and company *and we kneeled down on the shore, and prayed* for the blessing of God on their voyage, and upon those who were left behind Then affectionately taking their leave of each other, the apostle and his friend proceeded on their course, and the Tyrian brethren returned

5 From Tyre they sailed to Ptolemais, where Paul went on shore, desirous to salute the brethren, though he could stay but one day with them, yet one day of his company must have been a singular blessing and comfort to them The visits of such men, though short, are highly to be prized

8 And the next *day* we that were of Paul's company
departed, and came unto Cesarea, and we entred into
the house of Philip d the evangelist, (e which was *one* of
the seven) and abode with him 9 And the same man
had four daughters, virgins, f which did prophesy 10
And as we tarried *there* many days, there came down
from Judea a certain prophet, named g Agabus 11
And when he was come unto us, he took Paul's girdle,
and bound his own hands and feet, and said, Thus saith
the holy Ghost, h So shall the Jews at Jerusalem bind
the man that owneth this girdle, and shall deliver *him*
into the hands of the Gentiles 12 And when we heard
these things, both we and they of that place, i besought
him not to go up to Jerusalem 13 Then Paul answered, What mean ye to weep, and to break mine heart?
for I am ready not to be bound only, k but also to die at
Jerusalem for the name of the Lord Jesus 14 And
when he would not be persuaded, we ceased, saying, l The
will of the Lord be done

v 8—14 From Ptolemais they journeyed to Cesarea, where they designed to make some considerable stay

1 At Cesarea Philip the evangelist hospitably received them He was one of the seven deacons, and, after his successful labours among the Samaritans, and with the Ethiopian eunuch, was now settled in this great city *He had four daughters, virgins, which did prophesy*, endued with the miraculous gift of foretelling future events, (*Joel* ii 28)

2 There Paul receives a full prediction of the sufferings which were before him *As we tarried there many days, there came down from Judea a certain prophet, named Agabus*, who had foretold the famine, (*chap* xi 28) and now probably on purpose came with this prophetic intelligence Taking up Paul's girdle, he bound his own hands, and then his feet therewith, to affect the spectators the more by this significant action, which he explained, as what should shortly happen to the owner of that girdle, whom the Jews should thus bind, and deliver as a criminal to the Romans

3 Paul's companions, as well as the brethren at Cesarea, hearing these melancholy tidings, united in dissuading him from going to Jerusalem, and with tears entreated him to consult the safety of that life, which, however *ready* he might be to part with, would be to them a loss irreparable

4 Paul nobly replied to their intreaties, *What mean ye to weep, and to break mine heart?* Their tears affected him more than all his own expected sufferings, they were a temptation to shake his courage, and it troubled him, both that they should shew such timorousness, and dissuade him from what was his duty and that he should be obliged to deny them any request, since he could not comply with them without grieving the Spirit under whose influence he now acted, and therefore he dares defy the fury of all his persecutors, *for I am ready not to be bound only, but also to die at Jerusalem for the name of the Lord Jesus*, prepared, if God so pleased, to shed his blood in confirmation of the truth which he preached, and to glorify his Master, as a martyr in his cause *Note*, (1) The foolish fondness of our friends is often a more dangerous trial than the avowed opposition of our enemies (2) Faithful souls are unmoved with the fear of sufferings Death is welcome, if Jesus be but glorified thereby

5 Perceiving his unshaken resolution, his friends desisted, submitting to *the will of God*, and acquiescing in his determination, which they perceived proceeded not from any inflexibility of temper, but from the *conviction* that he acted agreeably to the call of God's Spirit *Note*, Submission to God's will is not only our duty, but should be our delight, when we know that all he does is righteous, and that it will ultimately tend to our good, as well as his own glory

15 And after those days we took up our carriages,
and went up to Jerusalem 16 There went with us also
certain of the disciples of Cesarea, and brought with
them one Mnason of Cyprus, an old disciple, with whom
we should lodge 17. And when we were come to Jerusalem, the brethren received us gladly 18 And the
day following, Paul went in with us unto m James, and
all the elders were present 19 And when he had saluted them, he n declared particularly what things God
had wrought among the Gentiles by his ministry 20
And when they heard *it*, they glorified the Lord, and
said unto him, Thou seest, brother, how many thousands
of Jews there are which believe, and they are all o zealous of the law 21 And they are informed of thee,

that thou teachest all the Jews which are among the Gentiles, to forsake Moses, saying, that they ought not to circumcise *their* children, neither to walk after the customs. 22 What is it therefore? the multitude must needs come together: for they will hear that thou art come. 23 Do therefore this that we say to thee: we have four men which have a vow on them; 24 Them take, and purify thyself with them, and be at charges with them, that they may p shave *their* heads: and all may know that those things whereof they were informed concerning thee, are nothing; but *that* thou thyself also walkest orderly, and keepest the law. 25 As touching the Gentiles which believe, q we have written and concluded, that they observe no such things, save only that they keep themselves from *things* offered to idols, and from blood, and from *things* strangled, and from fornication. 26 Then Paul took the men, and the next day purifying himself with them, r entred into the temple, s to signify the accomplishment of the days of purification, until that an offering should be offered for every one of them.

p Numb. vi. 2, 13, 18. Chap. xviii. 18.
q Chap. xv. 20, 29.
r Chap. xxiv. 18.
s Numb. vi. 13.

v. 15—26. We have here,

1. The journey of Paul and his companions to Jerusalem. His resolution was taken, and they, as they cannot dissuade him from his purpose, are ready cheerfully to share the danger: they therefore packed up their baggage, which they perhaps carried on their backs, and marched forward, accompanied by other brethren of Cæsarea, and brought with them one Mnason of Cyprus, *an old disciple*, venerable for his age, and his long standing in the profession of Christianity, *with whom we should lodge*, he having a house at Jerusalem, and during the festival lodgings were difficult to be obtained.

2. The brethren at Jerusalem gave him at his arrival a most hearty welcome. *And the day following Paul went in with us unto James*, the only apostle who seems to have been at that time resident at Jerusalem, *and all the elders were present*; when, after friendly salutations passed, Paul gave them a particular and distinct account of all the churches which had been planted by his ministry, and the great success which God had given to his labours; which gave them the most singular satisfaction, and excited their warmest praises, *they glorified the Lord*, who had done such great things by him. *Note*, God must have the glory of all our success; for whatever our labours are, it is he who giveth the increase.

3. James, in the name of the rest, hereupon offers his brother Paul his advice, desiring him, in condescension to the prejudices of the Jewish brethren, to shew his compliance with the ceremonial law. For though it was by no means to be imposed on the Gentile converts, nor was any justification before God in whole or in part to be expected from it; yet being still attached to these rites, to which from their infancy they had been taught to pay such reverence, as being of divine appointment, the Jewish converts in general were zealous for their observance; and as it was not sinful to comply with them herein, they judged it would be prudent in him to conform to them for the maintenance of mutual love and peace. The number of the disciples from the Jews was now increased to *many thousands*, or rather *myriads*, ten thousands; and many had imbibed prejudices against Paul, through the false reports of the Judaizing teachers, as if, not content with teaching the Gentiles that *they* were free from the ceremonial law, he had also dissuaded the Jews from conforming thereto, leading them to apostatize from the institution of Moses, and to discontinue the usage of circumcision. What therefore was to be done in the present case? the multitude must soon know of his coming, and there was danger of their assembling together to complain of him, as prejudiced against him. To promote therefore Paul's usefulness, which might be impeded thereby, and to reconcile them to him, who had deserved so highly of the church of God, they propose to him an expedient which would silence the cavillers, and remove the prejudices of his Jewish brethren, who, when they saw him conform to the law, would be convinced of the falshood of the report which had been propagated concerning him. They advise him therefore to join himself with four other converted Jews, who were under a vow of Nazaritism, and to go through the usual rite with them, providing the sacrifices offered on this occasion, (*Numb.* vi. 1—8.) which would most effectually silence gainsayers: not that this should be any infringement of the Gentile liberty, that being already determined by a solemn decree.

4. Paul, willing to the weak to become as weak, readily yielded to their proposal: and taking with him the men who were under a vow of Nazaritism, entered peaceably into the temple, *to signify the accomplishment of the days of purification* to the priests, which they would observe with the usual rite, *until that an offering should be offered for every one of them*, as the law directed, *Numb.* vi. 13—20.

Some have censured Paul's compliance, as countenancing the Jews in prejudices which ought to have been opposed; but it should seem that the thing was justifiable, and agreeable to the avowed maxim on which he always proceeded, (1 *Cor.* ix. 20.) for which end he had also circumcised Timothy; willing to please all men for their good to edification: charitably condescending to the infirmities of the weak, desirous, so far as he could with a good conscience, to comply with them in all indifferent matters, if by any means he might save some.

27 And when the seven days were almost ended, t the Jews which were of Asia, when they saw him in the temple, stirred up all the people, and u laid hands on him, 28 Crying out, Men of Israel, help: This is the man that teacheth all men every where against the people, and the law, and this place: and further, x brought Greeks also into the temple, and hath polluted this holy place. 29 (For they had seen before with him in the city, y Trophimus an Ephesian, whom they supposed that Paul had brought into the temple.) 30 And z all the city was moved, and the people ran together: and they took Paul, and drew him out of the temple: and forthwith the doors were shut. 31 And as they went about to kill him, tidings came unto the chief captain of the band, that all Jerusalem was in an uproar. 32 Who immediately took soldiers, and centurions, and ran down unto them: and when they saw the chief captain and the soldiers, they left beating of Paul. 33 Then the chief captain came near, and took him, and commanded *him* a to be bound with two chains; and demanded who he was, and what he had done. 34 And some cried one thing, and some another, among the multitude: and when he could not know the certainty for the tumult, he commanded him to be carried into the castle. 35 And when he came upon the stairs, so it was that he was born of the soldiers, for the violence of the people. 36 For the multitude of the people followed after, crying, b Away with him. 37 And as Paul was to be led into the castle, he said unto the chief captain, May I speak unto thee? Who said, Canst thou speak Greek? 38 Art not thou that Egyptian which before these days madest an uproar, and leddest out into the wilderness four thousand men that were murderers? 39 But Paul said, c I am a man which am a Jew of Tarsus, *a city* in Cilicia, a citizen of no mean city: and I beseech thee, suffer me to speak unto the people. 40 And when he had given him licence, Paul stood on the stairs, and d beckoned with the hand unto the people: and when there was made a great silence, he spake unto them in the Hebrew tongue, saying,

t Chap. xxiv. 18.
u Chap. xxvi. 21.
x Chap. xxiv. 6.
y Chap. xx. 4.
z Chap. xxvi. 21.
a Chap. xx. 23. Ver. 11.
b Luke xxiii. 18. John xix. 15. Chap. xxii. 22.
c Chap. ix. 11. & xxii. 3.
d Chap. xii. 17. & xix. 33.

v. 27—40. Henceforward we shall find the faithful Paul in bonds, and see him no more at liberty to the end of this history.

1. A tumult is raised against Paul. When he had nearly accomplished the seven days attendance on the temple, and was about to offer his sacrifice, the Jews of Asia, who had come up to celebrate the pentecost, observed him in the temple; and, fired with rage, as if his presence there was a profanation of the holy place, they incense the people against him, and raising a mob, as if he was the vilest criminal alive, they cried out for every Israelite to help in seizing and punishing most exemplarily such a miscreant, whom they accuse of apostacy from their religion, and as the rich seducer, *teaching every where*, with a view to prejudice men against the Jewish church and nation, against the sacred law of Moses, and that hallowed temple in which they so highly gloried. And not content herewith, they charge him with the most atrocious profanation of that holy place, by introducing uncircumcised Gentiles into the court of the Israelites; a calumny malicious and false in the highest degree, and grounded on their seeing Trophimus, an Ephesian, in Paul's company in the city. *Note*, (1.) The cause of Christ hath been often run down by noise and clamour; and the ministers of truth have been still branded with invidious names, and then suggestions have been cast out against them, as if they were guilty of all things. (2.) Innocence is no protection against calumny: some strained innuendo, or misrepresentation, easily turns the most innocent word or action into something highly criminal.

2. The city was soon in an uproar [illegible] by their suggestions, the people ran together, and [illegible] Paul, dragged him out of the temple, *and forthwith the doors were shut*, to prevent Paul's flying to the horns of the altar, or the Gentiles from following him, so that this holy place might not be defiled.

filed with his blood, for the intention of the people was evidently to murder him, and they began now violently to beat him, and must quickly have dispatched him

3 Paul is through the divine providence rescued from instant death The chief captain of the Roman forces, which kept garrison in the castle of Antonia, hearing of the uproar, ran down with a detachment to quell the tumult, and seeing him appear with an armed force, the people immediately desisted from beating Paul The captain hereupon having seized and bound him, that it might appear he intended not to rescue him, but to proceed against him in a legal way, demanded *who he was, and what he had done* *Note*, (1) Popular tumults are highly dangerous, and to be suppressed at their first rising (2) God can raise up instruments to rescue his suffering servants from a quarter they least expected, and often makes even *the earth to help the woman*, Rev xii 16

4 The noise was so great, and the clamours so various, that it was impossible for the chief captain to get a satisfactory answer, whilst *some cried one thing, some another, among the multitude* Therefore he commanded the prisoner to be carried into the castle, where he might examine into the affair, and as the soldiers guarded Paul thither, the crowd pressed so hard upon them, crying, *Away with him*, hang him, crucify him, that they were forced to take him in their arms, to prevent his being pulled to pieces, or smothered in the throng

5 The apostle respectfully begs leave to speak a word with the chief captain, who expresses his surprize to hear him talk the Greek language, and intimates his suspicion of him, that he had been that Egyptian impostor, who, a few years before, had raised a sedition at the head of four thousand murderers, who soon increased to a considerable army, but they were defeated, and the ringleader, with a few of his accomplices only, escaped Paul soon undeceived him, informing him, that he was by birth and religion a Jew, a citizen of Tarsus in Cilicia, a city of distinguished renown, and wished he might be permitted to speak unto the people, to clear himself from the malicious accusations of his persecutors *Note*, Many are run down thro misrepresentation, and oppressed by those who, if they knew the truth, would never have joined in the cry against them

6 Lysias, the chief captain, readily granted his request, when Paul standing on the stairs, beckoned with his hand, intimating his desire to speak to them, and a great silence being made thereupon, he addressed to them, in the Hebrew tongue, in that dialect which was in common use, the noble defence recorded in the following chapter

CHAP XXII

We have here, 1 Paul's address to the people, and their attention to it, ver 1, 2 2 The account he gives of himself (1) What a [illegible] he had been in the beginning of his time, ver 3—5 (2) How he was miraculously converted, and brought over to the faith of Christ, ver 6—11 (3) How he was confirmed and baptized by the ministry of Ananias, ver 12—16 (4) How he was afterwards called, by an immediate warrant from heaven, to be the apostle of the Gentiles, ver 17—21 3 The interruption given him upon this by the rabble, ver 22, 23 4 Paul's second rescue out of their hands, and the further course which the chief captain took to find out the true reason of this mighty clamour against Paul, ver 24, 25 5 Paul's pleading his privilege as a Roman citizen, by which he was exempted from scourging, ver 25—29 6 The chief captain's removing the cause into the high priest's court, and Paul's appearing there, ver. 30

1 MEN, [a] brethren, and fathers, hear ye my de-
fence *which I make* now unto you. 2 (And
when they heard that he spake in the Hebrew tongue
to them, they kept the more silence and he saith) 3
[b] I am verily a man which am a Jew, born in Tarsus, *a
city* in Cilicia, yet brought up in this city, [c] at the feet
of [d] Gamaliel, *and* taught according to the perfect man-
ner of the law of the fathers, and [e] was zealous towards
God, [f] as ye all are this day 4 And [g] I persecuted
[h] this way unto the death, binding and delivering into
prisons both men and women 5 As also the high
priest doth bear me witness, and [i] all the estate of the
elders [k] from whom also I received letters unto the
brethren, and went to Damascus, to bring them which
were there bound unto Jerusalem, for to be punished
6 And it came to pass, that [l] as I made my journey, and
was come nigh unto Damascus, about noon, suddenly
there shone from heaven a great light round about me
7 And I fell unto the ground, and heard a voice saying
unto me, Saul, Saul, why persecutest thou me? 8
And I answered, Who art thou, Lord? And he said un-
to me, I am Jesus of Nazareth whom thou persecutest

a Chap vii 2
b Chap xxi 39 2 Cor xi 22
c Deut xxxiii 3 2 Kings iv 38 Luke x 39
d Chap v 34
e Chap xxi 20 Gal i 14
f Rom x 2
g Chap viii 3
h Chap ix 2
i Luke xxii 66
k Chap ix 2
l Ch ix 3 & xxvi 12, &c

9 And [m] they that were with me saw indeed the light,
and were afraid, but they † heard not the voice of him
that spake to me 10 And I said, What shall I do,
Lord? And the Lord said unto me, Arise, and go into
Damascus, and there it shall be told thee of all things
which are appointed for thee to do 11 And when I
could not see for the glory of that light, being led by
the hand of them that were with me, I came into Da-
mascus 12 And [n] one Ananias, a devout man accord-
ing to the law, [o] having a good report of all the Jews
which dwelt *there*, 13 Came unto me, and stood, and
said unto me, Brother Saul, receive thy sight And the
same hour I looked up upon him 14 And he said,
The God of our fathers [p] hath chosen thee, that thou
shouldest know his will, and [q] see [r] that just One, and
shouldest hear the voice of his mouth 15 For thou
shalt be his witness unto all men, of [s] what thou hast
seen and heard. 16 And now why tarriest thou? arise,
and be baptized, and [t] wash away thy sins, [u] calling on
the name of the Lord 17 And [x] it came to pass, that
when I was come again to Jerusalem, even while I prayed
in the temple, I was in a trance, 18 And saw him,
saying unto me, [y] Make haste, and get thee quickly out
of Jerusalem for they will not receive thy testimony
concerning me 19 And I said, Lord, they know [z] that
I imprisoned and [a] beat in every synagogue them that
believed on thee 20 And [b] when the blood of thy
martyr Stephen was shed, I also was standing by, and
[c] consenting unto his death, and kept the raiment of them
that slew him 21 And he said unto me, Depart for
[d] I will send thee far hence unto the Gentiles

m Chap ix 7 Dan x 7
n Chap ix 10
o Chap x 22 1 Tim iii 7
p Chap xxvi 16
q 1 Cor ix 1 & xv 8
r Chap iii 14 & vii 52
t Chap ii 38
x Chap ix 26
y Chap ix 29
z Ver 4
a Matt x 17
b Chap vii 58 & viii 1
c Luke xi 48
d Chap xiii 2

v 1—21 No sooner had he obtained permission to speak, and all in silence listened, than with noble composure of mind, and in the most respectful manner, he addressed himself unto the people, saying, *Men, brethren, and fathers, hear ye my defence which I make now unto you* He makes no mention of their violence, but merely aims to apologize for himself, and undeceive them, respecting the false charges laid against him, and it is the greatest injustice to condemn any man, till he hath been heard impartially in his own defence

As he spoke aloud to them in the Hebrew dialect, which they understood, they kept the more silence, and he proceeded as follows

1 He gives them an account of his parentage and education He was one of their own body, a native Jew, a Hebrew of Hebrews, not a poor obscure fellow, nor illiterate, as some might have scandalized him, but a freeman of Tarsus in Cilicia, and educated under the most famous of their Rabbi's, at the feet of the learned Gamaliel and as he was thus early initiated in the most critical and accurate knowledge of the Mosaical law, with all the traditional comments of the elders thereupon, so was he most zealous for these institutions, and for the observance of these traditions, from a conscientious regard to God's glory, as they themselves now appeared to be

2 He informs them of the bitter enmity which he had himself formerly expressed against that religion of Jesus which he now preached He had been a bloody persecutor of the disciples of Jesus, furious to extirpate the Christian name from the earth, seizing, without respect of rank, age, or sex, the professors of Christianity, and dragging them to prisons, endeavoured by every ignominy and cruelty to compel them to blaspheme and recant And for this he appeals to the high priest and sanhedrim, by whom he had been employed, and under the sanction of whose commission he had been sent to Damascus, to seize and carry prisoners to Jerusalem all who should be there found professing the Christian religion, that they might be proceeded against, and punished as apostates None could have been further from Christianity than himself the bitterest of those who now persecuted him, came short of the enmity which he had shewn against it

3 He relates the history of his conversion It proceeded from no affectation of novelty, no discontent at being disappointed of preferment, from no worldly motive, nor the sophistry of others, but was the immediate miraculous work of God For as he was ready to enter Damascus, with all his prejudices, and breathing out threatenings and slaughter, suddenly at noon a light from heaven, brighter than the meridian sun, shone around him, and falling in terror to the earth, he heard the voice of Jesus, saying, *Saul, Saul, why persecutest thou me* And when, trembling and astonished, he answered, *Who art thou, Lord* it was replied, *I am Jesus of Nazareth, whom thou persecutest* Convinced now of his own dreadful guilt, and anxious to escape the fearful consequences thereof, he begs to be informed what he must do, when the Lord bid him go to Damascus, and there he should receive information of every thing that was *appointed for him to do* And being now raised from

from the earth, and blinded with the heavenly light, his companions led him by the hand to Damascus, for the truth of which facts they could witness, this being no fancy or delusion, for though they heard not distinctly the words that were spoken, they saw the light, were terrified, and fell to the earth together with him, and heard the sound of a voice, though not the articulate discourse.

4. He declares the further instructions and cure which he received from Ananias, whose character he describes, to recommend him to their regard. He was *a devout man according to the law*, and, though a Christian, still zealously observed the ritual service, *having a good report of all the Jews that dwelt there*, for his exemplary life and conversation, and attachment to the temple worship. He came, and said, *Brother Saul, receive thy sight*, which was no sooner spoken than done: *the same hour I looked up upon him*. Then Ananias delivered his message, and said, *The God of our fathers hath chosen thee*, in his eternal counsels, *that thou shouldst know his will*, as revealed in the gospel, *and see that just One*, who so wrongfully suffered, *and shouldst hear the voice of his mouth*, and in some future time receive a fuller commission and farther instructions from him. *For thou shalt be his witness unto all men*, to the Jews and Gentiles, *of what thou hast seen and heard*. *And now why tarriest thou?* without delay *arise, and be baptized*, receiving this instituted sign of admission into his church, and to all the privileges of it, *and wash away thy sins*, now pardoned through his atoning blood, *calling on the name of the Lord*, the only Saviour, that all the blessings of his everlasting covenant may be conferred upon thee, according to his promises. *Note*, (1.) The great gospel privilege is remission of sins. (2.) All who are brought truly to the Lord, from that hour cease not to call upon him, living in constant dependence on his grace.

5. He informs them of the divine warrant by which he was commissioned to go and preach to the Gentiles. It was given him at Jerusalem, while he was in the temple praying, where he fell into a trance, and saw this divine Redeemer, who said unto him, *Get thee quickly out of Jerusalem, for they will not receive thy testimony*, being obstinately prejudiced against it. *And I said*, unwilling to leave my dear countrymen, for whose souls I so earnestly longed, and to whom I fancied my ministry might be more particularly convincing, *Lord, they know that I imprisoned and beat in every synagogue them that believed on thee. And when the blood of thy martyr Stephen was shed, I also was standing by, and consenting unto his death, and kept the raiment of them that slew him*. And this he urges as a reason why the people would now more readily regard his testimony, when he preached that faith he once destroyed, since it must need be a supernatural power which could produce so wonderful a conversion. But the Lord, who knew the hearts of all men, and that his ministry would be rejected by the Jews, repeated his commands, *Depart*, and appointed him other work, *for I will send thee far hence unto the Gentiles*.

From all which they might see clearly how far he was from being that enemy to the Jewish nation and worship which he was represented to be, how earnestly he would have continued labouring amongst them, how reluctantly he quitted Jerusalem, and by what most express divine authority he acted in his labours among the Gentiles.

v. 22—30. Hitherto with patience the Jews gave audience to the apostle's discourse, but the very mention of the Gentiles fired their indignation, and they would hear no more.

1. They cried out with the most raging fury, *Away with such a fellow from the earth, for it is not fit that he should live*. The very thought, that the idolatrous Gentiles should be preferred to them, exasperated them beyond bounds, and they imagined no punishment was equal to the desert of such a miscreant, who could dare plead a divine commission to preach to the abhorred heathen. Therefore *they cried out* against him with the utmost detestation, *and cast off their clothes*, resolved to stone him on the spot as an apostate and blasphemer, *and threw dust into the air*, as if they wanted to bury him alive. Thus have the greatest and best of men the world was ever blest with, been treated as the off-scouring of all things, and unworthy of the air they breathed.

2. The chief captain Lysias, seeing such madness and fury expressed by the people, *commanded Paul to be brought into the castle*, partly to shelter him from the popular rage, partly from the apprehension, that he must needs have been guilty of some enormous wickedness, which could occasion such general abhorrence, and therefore most unjustly *commanded*, without further enquiry, *that he should be examined by scourging*, to extort a confession from himself of the supposed crime, which made the people so violent against him.

3. When the soldiers, who were about to execute the chief captain's commands, were binding him with thongs to the pillar, in order to be scourged, Paul mildly addressed himself to the centurion who stood by, and said, *Is it lawful for you to scourge a man that is a Roman, and uncondemned?* The centurion, startled at this intimation, and knowing the dangerous consequence of such a procedure, stayed the soldiers, and went immediately to acquaint the chief captain, suggesting to him the necessity of proceeding with caution, since the person whom they had in custody was one of much greater distinction than they apprehended, a Roman citizen.

4. The chief captain Lysias, knowing the jealousy of the Roman citizens, and the severity of the law against those who should dare to bind or scourge any of them, especially without a fair and public trial, came directly, and desired to be informed in this point, saying, *Art thou a Roman citizen?* Paul said, *Yea*. The chief captain, surprized at this, answered, *With a great sum obtained I this freedom*, and you seem a poor Jew, unable to purchase so high a dignity. *And Paul*, who held his privilege from a more honourable source, *said, But I was free born*.

5. Instantly orders were given for his being loosed; they who were about to scourge him departed, and the chief captain himself was under terrible apprehensions, lest, if Paul should complain of this outrage, it might be attended with very ill consequence to him, that he had rashly proceeded so far as to bind him, being a Roman. Our civil privileges are an invaluable blessing, and the fear of man often restrains those who know no fear of God.

6. The next day the governor, desirous of coming at the certainty of the thing laid to Paul's charge, *commanded the chief priests and all their council to appear*, and having loosed him *from his bands*, that he might not seem to prejudge his cause, and treat him as a criminal without proof, *he brought Paul down, and set him before them*, that they might bring their accusations, and he be at liberty to answer in his own defence.

22. And they gave him audience unto this word, and
e Chap. xxi. 36. f Chap. xxv. 24. *then* lifted up their voices, and said, [e] Away with such a fellow from the earth: for [f] it is not fit that he should live. 23 And as they cried out, and cast off *their* clothes, and threw dust into the air, 24 The chief captain commanded him to be brought into the castle, and bade that he should be examined by scourging; that he might know wherefore they cried so against him.
25 And as they bound him with thongs, Paul said unto
g Chap. xvi. 37. the centurion that stood by, [g] Is it lawful for you to scourge a man that is a Roman, and uncondemned?
26 When the centurion heard *that*, he went and told the chief captain, saying, Take heed what thou doest: for this man is a Roman. 27 Then the chief captain came, and said unto him, Tell me, art thou a Roman? He said, Yea. 28 And the chief captain answered, With a great sum obtained I this freedom. And Paul said, But I was *free* born. 29 Then straightway they
† Or, tortured him. Ver. 24. Heb. xi. 3. departed from him which should have † examined him: and the chief captain also was afraid, after he knew that he was a Roman, and because he had bound him. 30 On the morrow, because he would have known the certainty wherefore he was accused of the Jews, he loosed him from *his* bands, and commanded the chief priests and all their council to appear, and brought Paul down, and set him before them.

CHAP. XXIII.

We have here, 1. Paul's protestation of his own integrity, and of a civil respect to the high priest, however he had upon a sudden spoken warmly to him, and justly, ver. 1—5. *2. Paul's prudent contrivance to get himself clear of them, by setting the Pharisees and Sadducees at variance one with another,* ver. 6—9. *3. The governor's seasonable interposal to rescue him out of their hands likewise,* ver. 10. *4. Christ's more comfortable appearing to him, to animate him against those difficulties that lay before him, and to tell him what he must expect,* ver. 11. *5. A bloody conspiracy of some desperate Jews to kill Paul,* ver. 12—15. *6. A discovery of this conspiracy to Paul, and by him to the chief captain,* ver. 16—22. *7. The chief captain's care of Paul's safety, who sent him away immediately under a strong guard from Jerusalem to Cæsarea, which was now the residence of Felix the Roman governor, and there he safely arrived,* ver. 23—35.

1. AND Paul earnestly beholding the council, said, Men *and* brethren, [a] I have lived in all good conscience before God until this day. 2 And the high priest Ananias commanded them that stood by him [b] to smite him on the mouth. 3 Then said Paul unto him, God shall smite thee, *thou* whited wall: for sittest thou to judge me after the law, and [c] commandest me to be smitten contrary to the law? 4 And they that stood by said, Revilest thou God's high priest? 5 Then said Paul,

a Chap. xxiv. 16. 2 Cor. i. 12. 2 Tim. i. 3. Heb. xiii. 18. b 1 Kings xxii. 24. Jer. xx. 2. John xviii. 22. c Lev. xix. 35. Deut. xxv. 1, 2.

Paul, I wist not, brethren, that he was the high priest
For it is written, [d] Thou shalt not speak evil of the ru
ler of thy people

℣ 1—5 Paul with undaunted courage appears before this august assembly, nor fears their faces, though well persuaded of their inveterate enmity against him

1 He makes a solemn profession of his own integrity *Men and brethren, I have lived in all good conscience before God until this day*, even in his unregenerate state he had, according to his best light and knowledge, acted with conscientious zeal for God's glory, and his outward conversation had been ever unimpeached And as to his conversion to Christianity he had embraced the gospel upon the strongest evidence, so had he ever since with all fidelity approved himself to God, and they who have this testimony of a good conscience, need never be ashamed

2 Ananias the high priest, highly offended at such a protestation of his innocence, commanded one of the officers who stood by Paul to strike him on the mouth, and not suffer him to proceed with such confidence and effrontery of address

3 Justly indignant at such an insult, and not actuated by private revenge, but by prophetic impulse, he denounces the doom of this proud high priest *God shall smite thee, thou whited wall*, with some stroke of his vengeance for thy pride and hypocrisy *for sittest thou to judge me after the law, and commandest me to be smitten contrary to the law?* how unjust and iniquitous is such a procedure! *Note*, Proud persecutors are but whited walls, and shall soon feel how unable they are to stand before the storm of divine judgments

4 Some who were present were highly offended at the apostle's freedom, as an unbecoming insult on the high priest's character and office, saying, *Revilest thou God's high priest?*

5 Paul immediately apologized for what he had said, unwilling to prejudice his Jewish brethren against him, however great the provocation which had been given him *I wist not, brethren, that he was the high priest*, either he did not advert to his dignity at that time, or he did not consider him as the high priest, another being lawfully entitled to that office, and Ananias but an intruder *for* he meant not to speak disrespectfully of that high office, since *it is written, Thou shalt not speak evil of the ruler of thy people*, and he always desired to have his conduct governed by God's revealed word, and to honour the magistrate, however wicked the man might be

6. But when Paul perceived that the one part were
Sadducees, and the other Pharisees, he cried out in the
council, Men *and* brethren, [e] I am a Pharisee, the son of
a Pharisee [f] of the hope and resurrection of the dead, I
am called in question 7 And when he had so said,
there arose a dissension between the Pharisees and
Sadducees and the multitude was divided 8 For
[g] the Sadducees say that there is no resurrection, neither
angel nor spirit but the Pharisees confess both 9
And there arose a great cry and the scribes *that were* of
the Pharisees part arose, and strove, saying, [h] We find no
evil in this man but [i] if a spirit or an angel hath spok-
en to him, [k] let us not fight against God 10 And
when there arose a great dissension, the chief captain
fearing lest Paul should have been pulled in pieces of
them, commanded the soldiers to go down, and to take
him by force from among them, and to bring him into
the castle 11 And the night following, the Lord
stood by him, and said, Be of good cheer, Paul for as
thou hast testified of me in Jerusalem, so must thou bear
witness also at Rome

℣ 6—11 Since the apostle had to do with men on whom he might now easily perceive he could not hope to prevail by pleading the cause which they were determined to persecute, he here,

1 Prudently disconcerted all their measures by a plea which they little apprehended He observed the council was divided into two sects, of Pharisees and Sadducees, and if he can wisely gain one party of them to his side, he may more easily extricate himself from his difficulties Accordingly he cried aloud, *Men and brethren, I am a Pharisee, the son of a Pharisee*, have always been brought up in the faith of their distinguishing tenets, and among the chief articles thereof we reckon the resurrection of the dead, for which hope *I am called in question*, the grand foundation of all that doctrine of the gospel which I preach being built on the resurrection of the Redeemer

2 This immediately, as he expected, raised a division in the court the Pharisees espousing this great truth, the Sadducees opposing it *for* the Sadducees denied the resurrection of the body, the immortality of the soul, and any future state of rewards and punishments, whilst the Pharisees, though wedded to their traditions, stiffly maintained these great doctrines of truth Hence arose a schism between them, and the fury

against Paul was now turned into a sharp contention between themselves, so that a great cry arose, and in mere opposition to the Sadducees, the Pharisees took the apostle's part, and contended for him as orthodox in his principles, and innocent in his behaviour *But if an angel or spirit hath spoken to him*, as it is possible may be the case, *let us not fight against God*, since all opposition to such a heavenly message would be in fact rebellion against God himself, according to the advice which Gamaliel had formerly given, (*chap* v 38, 39)

3 A violent tumult hereupon rose, the Sadducees were enraged at the opposition they met with, and in the quarrel between his friends and foes, Paul was in danger of being torn limb from limb, so that the chief captain was again compelled to interpose, and with his soldiers to carry him off, and secure him in the castle, lest he should be pulled in pieces by them Thus the Lord again providentially rescued him from the jaws of death

4 The night following *the Lord stood by him*, in a vision, to comfort and encourage him with unshaken fortitude to stand fast *and said, Be of good cheer, Paul*, be confident of the supports of my power and love, and let no dangers dismay thee *for as thou hast testified of me in Jerusalem, so must thou bear witness also at Rome* So he had designed formerly, (*chap* xix 21) and now the Lord will make even the malice of his persecutors the means of carrying him thither *Note*, If the Lord speak comfort to our souls, and stand by us, then our prison shall be a palace, and our sufferings our joy

12. And when it was day, certain of the Jews band-
ed together, and [m] bound themselves † under a curse, say-
ing, that they would neither eat nor drink till they had
killed Paul 13 And they were more than forty which
had made this conspiracy 14 And they came to the
chief priests and elders, and said, We have bound our-
selves under a great curse, that we will eat nothing until
we have slain Paul 15 Now therefore ye with the
council signify to the chief captain, that he bring him
down unto you to morrow, as though you would enquire
something more perfectly concerning him and we, or
ever he come near, are ready to kill him 16 And
when Paul's sister's son heard of their lying in wait, he
went and entred into the castle, and told Paul 17
Then Paul called one of the centurions unto him, and
said, Bring this young man unto the chief captain for
he hath a certain thing to tell him 18 So he took
him, and brought him to the chief captain, and said,
Paul the prisoner called me unto him, and prayed me
to bring this young man unto thee, who hath something
to say unto thee 19 Then the chief captain took him
by the hand, and went *with him* aside privately, and ask-
ed *him*, What is it that thou hast to tell me? 20 And
he said, The Jews have agreed to desire thee, [o] that thou
wouldest bring down Paul to morrow into the council,
as though they would enquire somewhat of him more
perfectly 21 But do not thou yield unto them for
there lie in wait for him of them more than forty men,
which [p] have bound themselves with an oath, that they
will neither eat nor drink till they have killed him and
now are they ready, looking for a promise from thee.
22 So the chief captain *then* let the young man depart
and charged *him, See thou* tell no man that thou hast
shewed these things to me 23 And he called unto him
two centurions, saying, Make ready two hundred sol-
diers to go to Cesarea, and horsemen threescore and ten,
and spearmen two hundred, at the third hour of the
night 24 And provide *them* beasts, that they may set
Paul on, and bring *him* safe unto Felix the governor
25 And he wrote a letter after this manner 26 Clau-
dius Lysias, unto the most excellent governor Felix,
sendeth greeting 27 This man was taken of the
Jews, and should have been killed of them then came
I with an army, and rescued him, having understood
that he was a Roman 28 And [r] when I would have
known the cause wherefore they accused him, I brought
him forth into their council 29 Whom I perceived
to [s] be accused of questions of their law, but to have
nothing laid to his charge worthy of death or of bonds
30 And when it was told me, *how* that the Jews laid
wait for the man, I sent straightway to thee, and [t] gave
commandment to his accusers also, to say before thee
what *they had* against him Farewel 31 Then the
soldiers, as it was commanded them, took Paul and
brought *him* by night to Antipatris 32 On the mor

row they left the horsemen to go with him, and returned to the castle 33 Who when they came to Cesarea, and delivered the epistle to the governor, presented Paul also before him 34 And when the governor had read *the letter*, he asked of what province he was And when he understood that he was of Cilicia, 35 I will hear thee, said he, when thine accusers are also come And he commanded him to be kept in Herod's judgment-hall

v 12—35 We have here a desperate plot laid against the innocent apostle, but by the divine providence discovered and defeated

1 The plot was deeply laid, and ready to be executed Since they could gain their ends no other way, the next day some of his most invenomed foes determined to assassinate him The number of the conspirators amounted to more than forty, who by a dreadful oath bound their souls to be faithful to each other, and neither to *eat or drink till they had killed Paul* And this their horrid design they communicated to the chief priests and elders for their approbation, who they knew would stick at nothing to destroy a man whom they so abhorred They proposed therefore, that they should desire the chief captain to bring Paul once more to the council-board to be examined, and they undertook to dispatch him by the way as he came nor did the chief priest, it seems, or elders, hesitate at the proposal

2 God brought this bloody conspiracy to light A nephew of Paul's, his sister's son, got some intelligence of their design, and instantly ran to the castle, to acquaint the apostle of his danger, who begged the favour of one of the centurions to introduce the young man to the chief captain, having some very interesting intelligence to communicate The centurion very obligingly went, and informed Lysias of Paul's request, and he without delay gave the young man a private audience Taking him kindly by the hand, he led him aside, and bid him speak freely what he had to say whereupon he informed him of the whole conspiracy, which was ready to be put in execution, and that they were now coming to ask his consent to their request, with regard to the bringing down of Paul before them, under pretence of a more exact enquiry into the charges laid against him the young man therefore humbly begs, that he will not *yield to them* in this matter The chief captain, with a solemn injunction of secresy, hereupon dismissed him, engaging to take effectual care of Paul *Note*, (1) The Lord often wonderfully brings to light the hidden things of darkness, and lays open by strange methods the deep designs of bloody conspirators (2) It is a high commendation to men of rank who are in office, to be easy of access, and not proudly to disregard their poor suitors (3) Secresy is often most essential to the success of our affairs

3 Lysias immediately took the most effectual method to prevent this horrid assassination, and fearing lest, if he kept Paul in the castle, their madness might hurry them to some dreadful outrage, or to attempt by one method or other to compass his death, he called two centurions, and bid them get two hundred soldiers, and as many spearmen, with seventy horsemen, ready to march to Cesarea by nine o'clock that evening, and to *provide beasts*, one or more, for Paul's use, or perhaps for some of his companions who might chuse to attend him, and deliver him up safe to Felix the governor, treating the prisoner with all possible respect, and desirous thus to rescue him from the hands of the conspirators

4 With the prisoner he sent the following letter *Claudius Lysias unto the most excellent Felix, sendeth greeting*, wishing him all prosperity *This man*, whom I have sent, *was taken of the Jews*, in a tumultuous manner, *and would have been killed by them*, had I not interposed *Then*, hearing of the riot which was made, *I came with an army* to quell the disturbance, *and rescued him, having understood that he was a Roman* citizen *And when I would have known the cause wherefore they accused him*, willing to give the matter an impartial hearing, *I brought him forth into their council*, to know what they had to say against him, *whom I perceived to be accused of questions of their law, but to have nothing* really criminal *laid to his charge worthy of death or of bonds And when it was told me, how that the Jews laid wait for the man* to assassinate him, to prevent so base a deed, *I sent straightway to thee*, referring the whole matter to your Excellency's cognizance, *and gave commandment to his accusers also, to say before thee what they had against him*, as a more competent judge, and fitter to decide on this matter *Farewel*

5 The soldiers under the command of the centurions at night departed, and before morning had brought Paul safe to Antipatris, when, being out of danger, the soldiers and spearmen returned, and left the seventy horse to conduct him to Cesarea, who on their arrival delivered the letter to the governor, and presented the prisoner before him When Felix had perused the contents, he asked Paul of what province he was, and having understood that he belonged to Cilicia, *I will hear thee, said he, when thine accusers are also come And he commanded him to be kept in Herod's judgment hall*, assigning him an apartment in the palace, and, though under confinement, permitting his friends to visit him without restraint

CHAP XXIV

We left Paul a prisoner at Cesarea in this chapter we have his arraignment and trial before Felix the governor Here is, 1 The appearing of the prosecutors against him, and the bringing of the prisoner to the bar, ver 1, 2 *2 The opening of the indictment against him by Tertullus*, ver 2—8 *3 The corroborating of the charge by the testimony of the witnesses, or rather the prosecutors themselves*, ver 9 *4 The prisoner's defence made by himself, with all due deference to the governor*, ver 10 *he denies the charge, and challengeth them to prove it*, ver 11—13 *owns the truth, and makes an unexceptionable profession of his faith, which he declares was that he suffered him for*, ver 14—16 *and gives a particular account of what had passed from their first seizing of him, challenging them to instance in any ill that they had found in him*, ver 17—21 *5 The adjourning of the cause, and the continuing of the prisoner in custody*, ver 22, 23 *6 The private conversation that was between the prisoner and the judge, by which the prisoner hoped to do good to the judge, and the judge thought to get money by the prisoner, but both in vain*, ver 24—26 *7 The lengthening out of Paul's imprisonment for two years, till another governor came*, ver 27

1 AND after five days, [a] Ananias the high priest descended with the elders, and *with* a certain orator *named* Tertullus, who informed the governor against Paul 2 And when he was called forth, Tertullus began to accuse *him*, saying, Seeing that by thee we enjoy great quietness, and that very worthy deeds are done unto this nation by thy providence, 3 We accept *it* always, and in all places, most noble Felix, with all thankfulness 4 Notwithstanding, that I be not further tedious unto thee, I pray thee, that thou wouldest hear us of thy clemency a few words 5 For we have found this man [b] a [†] pestilent fellow, and a mover of sedition among all the Jews throughout the world, and a ringleader of the sect of the Nazarenes 6 [c] Who also hath gone about to profane the temple whom we took, and would have judged according to our law 7 But the chief captain Lysias came upon us, and with great violence took *him* away out of our hands, 8 [d] Commanding his accusers to come unto thee by examining of whom, thyself mayest take knowledge of all these things whereof we accuse him 9 And the Jews also assented, saying, that these things were so

a Chap xxiii

b Kings xviii 17, Chap xvi 20 & xvii 6

† Gr a pest

c Chap xxi 28

d Chap xxiii 30 & xxv 16

v 1—9 Lysias no doubt informed the chief priests and elders what he had done, and referred them to Felix, if they chose further to prosecute Paul Whereupon,

1 Without loss of time, *after five days*, reckoning from the time they first apprehended him, they came down to Cesarea, with Ananias the high priest at their head, and appearing in a body before Felix, to give the greater weight to their cause, they desired to be heard against Paul, and had engaged an artful and plausible counsellor, one Tertullus, to plead for them *Note*, Inveterate malice against the gospel will sometimes make the most reverend characters stoop to the meanest actions

2 Paul being brought forth, Tertullus, with many oratorial flourishes, and a most flattering address to the judge, opens his speech against the prisoner at the bar

[1] He compliments the governor on his administration Though universally known to be one of the most oppressive, covetous, and cruel, that had ever ruled over Judea, yet, to court his favour, and win him to their party, he, as one that pleaded not for truth but for hire, daubs thick his adulations *Seeing that by thee we enjoy great quietness, and that very worthy deeds are done unto this nation by thy providence*, penetration, and prudent care, *we accept it always, and in all places, most noble Felix, with all thankfulness*, professing the deepest sense of our obligations for such singular favours, and emboldened thereby to hope more confidently for the justice we demand against the prisoner *But that I be not further tedious unto thee, I pray thee, that thou wouldest hear us of thy clemency a few words*, the case being so clear, that it can take up very little of your Excellency's time, to be convinced of the prisoner's guilt

It was well known how the Jewish nation in general, and the elders in particular, hated Felix and his government, but now, when they have a point to carry, they liberally offer at his feet their flattering applause

[2] He comes to the point, and boldly alledges many pernicious crimes, with which he charges the innocent prisoner *We found this man a pestilent fellow*, propagating his pernicious tenets like a plague, the very pest of society, *and a mover of sedition among all the Jews throughout the world*, exciting tumults

wherever he goes against the Roman government, *and a ringleader of the sect of the Nazarenes*, a promoter of that detestable heresy, for which, and his notoriously seditious principles, the first author of it, one Jesus of Nazareth, was crucified some years ago. *Who also hath gone about to profane the temple*, with daring impiety introducing those who were by the law forbid admission there.

All these charges are a tissue of falshoods. All the pestilence Paul carried with him was the gospel of salvation, doing good to men's bodies and souls wherever he came. Far from sedition, he taught the most conscientious obedience to the ruling powers. The tumults complained of, were made not by him, but by his accusers themselves. He set himself up for no head of a sect, nor attempted to draw any man to his standard, but to his divine Master: and so far from profaning the temple, none could behave with greater piety, seriousness, and conformity to the law, than he had done. *Note*, (1.) The purest innocence is no protection from the vilest aspersions. They who make no conscience of lies, with solemn assurances, and repeated falshoods, will strive hard but they will blacken the fairest character. (2.) The charge against the gospel and its ministers hath often been, that they raise disturbances and riots, when in fact the very persons who lay this accusation against them, are the very persons who raise the tumults; like Nero, who set Rome on fire, and then persecuted the Christians for that atrocious deed: but there is one who seeth and judgeth.

[3.] He insinuates the equity with which they were proceeding against the prisoner, by a fair trial according to the law, when Lysias, the chief captain, interrupting the course of justice, by violence seized the prisoner, and carried him off, obliging them to all this trouble and expence, by bringing the cause hither: but he hopes now at least justice will be done, and that the governor fully satisfied of Paul's guilt, will pronounce sentence against him.

Nothing could be more false and invidious than this assertion; but Lysias was not here to disprove it, and he hoped the weight of evidence which he brought with him would prevail.

3. The high priests and elders added their solemn attestation to the truth of Tertullus's harangue: nor is it a marvel, that they, who wanted to murder Paul by assassination, should now attempt to carry their point by the blackest perjury.

10 Then Paul, after that the governor had beckoned unto him to speak, answered, Forasmuch as I know that thou hast been of many years a judge unto this nation, I do the more cheerfully answer for myself: 11 Because that thou mayest understand, that there are yet but twelve days since I went up to Jerusalem for to worship.
12 And [e] they neither found me in the temple disputing with any man, neither raising up the people, neither in the synagogues, nor in the city: 13 Neither can they prove the things whereof they now accuse me. 14 But this I confess unto thee, that after [f] the way which they call heresy, so worship I [g] the God of my fathers, believing all things which are written in [h] the law and the prophets: 15 And have hope towards God, which they themselves also allow, that [i] there shall be a resurrection of the dead, both of the just and unjust. 16 And herein do I exercise myself [k] to have always a conscience void of offence toward God and *toward* men. 17 Now after many years, [l] I came to bring alms to my nation, and offerings. 18 Whereupon [m] certain Jews from Asia found me purified in the temple, neither with multitude, nor with tumult. 19 [n] Who ought to have been here before thee, and object, if they had ought against me. 20 Or else let these same *here* say, if they have found any evil doing in me, while I stood before the council, 21 Except it be for this one voice, that I cried standing among them, [o] Touching the resurrection of the dead, I am called in question by you this day.

e Chap. xxv. 8. & xxviii. 17.
f Chap. ix. 2.
g 2 Tim. i. 3.
h Ch. xxvi. 22. & xxviii. 23.
i Dan. xii. 2. John v. 28, 29. Chap. xxiii. 6.
k 2 Cor. i. 12. & iv. 2. Heb. xiii. 18.
l Chap. xi. 29, 30. Rom. xv. 25. Gal. ii. 10.
m Chap. xxi. 26.
n Chap. xxiii. 30. & xxv. 16.
o Chap. xxiii. 6.

10—21. How different is the spirit which breathes in the defence of Paul, from that which actuated the plausible orator, Tertullus. He is not exasperated with the falshood which were advanced, or in a heat to reply, but waited the governor's permission to speak, which when Felix had signified, he rose with [illegible], to pour confusion on the charges of his adversaries.

1. With deep respect for his judge, which was consistent with Christian [illegible] and the truth which became him, he opens his discourse, *Forasmuch as I know that thou hast been of many years a judge unto this nation, I do the more cheerfully answer for myself* [illegible]. Felix well knew the spirit and temper of the Jews by his long acquaintance with them, and could not wonder at the malice of their [illegible] had all the things been true,

which they alledged, the governor had, no doubt, heard of Paul before.

2. He flatly denies the charges of *sedition*, of which he was accused. It was but twelve days since he came to Jerusalem, not to *profane the temple*, but, with high respect of that sacred place, *to worship* there, where they neither found him disputing with any man, either about religion or government, nor fomenting the least disturbance in the synagogues or the city; but demeaning himself with all peaceableness, and he defies his accusers to prove one of the charges which they so peremptorily alledged. *Note*, It is in every villain's power to propagate falshood, and to bring the heaviest charges against the noblest characters; but every sedate hearer and upright judge will not rest in his assertions, but requires proof of the facts.

3. He owns and glories in the acknowledgment, that after the way which they stigmatized as heresy, so worshipped he the God of his fathers, *believing all things which are written in the law and the prophets*, the divine authority of the precepts, and the accomplishment of the promises, and his hope towards God, and preaching, were in exact correspondence with the fundamental doctrine of the orthodox faith which they themselves held, that there should *be a resurrection of the dead, both of the just and of the unjust*, who must answer before the eternal judge, that divine Messiah, Jesus of Nazareth, whom the Jews had crucified. *And herein do I exercise myself*, persuaded of this solemn day's approach, and expecting to stand before the great Judge of all, endeavouring *to keep a conscience void of offence toward God and toward men*. *Note*, (1.) The scriptures are the only rule of faith and practice, to them we must cleave. (2.) As there will be a resurrection of the just and of the unjust, it is a matter of awful consideration to enquire, which character is ours. (3.) Hope towards God, is an anchor which will keep the soul stedfast in every storm. (4.) A good conscience is our best friend. Perfection is not attainable in this world; but that in simplicity and godly sincerity we desire to have our conversation, this is our rejoicing.

4. As to his *profaning the temple*, this was of a piece with the other falshoods advanced; the very contrary was evident. He had, after a considerable absence from Jerusalem, returned with charitable contributions for the poor saints who dwelt there, and having a religious vow, had brought his own offerings to the temple, where certain Jews of Asia saw him, purifying himself according to the law, *not with multitude nor with tumult*, only four persons who had vows, like himself, were with him, demeaning themselves with all possible quietness and regularity: and as to the supposed offence of having brought Greeks into the temple, which was suggested as the occasion of the riot which was raised, he challenges them to produce these men of Asia who raised this report, and ought to be here, if they had any thing to object. Or since they were absent, he appeals to his accusers themselves, if on examination before the council, any one misdemeanour was so much as proved against him, except they reckoned his declaration concerning the resurrection of the dead to be such, wherein he had been supported and countenanced by the most respectable part of that assembly.

A defence so clear, so ingenuous, so convincing, as carried its own evidence along with it, and demonstrated his innocence of every crime they had alledged against him.

22 And when Felix heard these things, having more perfect knowledge of *that* way, he deferred them, and said, When Lysias the chief captain shall come down, I will know the uttermost of your matter. 23 And he commanded a centurion to keep Paul, and to let *him* have liberty, and [p] that he should forbid none of his acquaintance to minister, or come unto him. 24 And after certain days, when Felix came with his wife, Drusilla, which was a Jewess, he sent for Paul, and heard him concerning the faith in Christ. 25 And as he reasoned of [q] righteousness, temperance, and judgment to come, Felix trembled, and answered, Go thy way for this time; [r] when I have a convenient season, I will call for thee. 26 He hoped also that money should have been given him of Paul, that he might loose him: wherefore he sent for him the oftener, and communed with him. 27 But after two years, Porcius Festus came into Felix' room: and Felix, willing to shew the Jews [s] a pleasure, left Paul bound.

p Chap. xxvii. 3. & xxviii. 16.
q Tit. ii. 11, 12.
r Chap. xiii. 7.
s Chap. xxv. 9.

v. 22—27. Felix patiently heard the parties, but deferred passing judgment upon the cause.

1. He put off the determination till the arrival of Lysias, on whom they seemed to reflect, when he could more thoroughly examine into the circumstances; and probably, though unwilling to disoblige the chief men of the nation, he was little apprehensive of any danger of sedition from the professors of christianity, *having more perfect knowledge of that way*. As Cornelius, a centurion, long ago had been converted to the Christian faith at Cæsarea, and many others, Felix was no doubt well acquainted with

them

their principles, and an eye-witness of their peaceable conduct, and therefore did not readily believe these atrocious accusations against Paul.

2 He committed the apostle to the custody of a centurion, who should let him enjoy all liberty to walk about as a prisoner at large, permitting any of his friends to visit, converse with him, and supply him with whatever he wanted. Thus the malignant priests were disappointed, and Paul, though justice was delayed, had reason to be thankful for his escape from their malice.

3 The curiosity of Felix, and of his wife Drusilla, who, though a Jewess, had married him a heathen, and had forsaken her former husband Azizus, king of Emessa, prompted them to hear from this celebrated preacher, an account of the Christian religion, and of that faith in Christ which he inculcated. *Note*, Many are willing to know the speculative principles of religion, whose hearts have no relish for the practice of it.

4 Paul readily appeared to give an account of his doctrine before them, not as mere speculative opinions, but as practical principles; and knowing the characters of the persons before whom he spoke, he failed not to reason powerfully on the nature and necessity of righteousness and temperance, the guilt and danger of the opposite vices, of injustice, oppression, excess, and impurity, and on the awful account which all must shortly give before the Judge of quick and dead, when, without respect of persons, *the everlasting state of men must be determined*. So faithfully should Christ's ministers bring home to men's consciences the word of truth, whether they will hear, or whether they will forbear.

5 Felix, with conscious guilt, trembled as he sat, and affrighted, heard these alarming words: but more in haste to get rid of his convictions than his sins, he dismissed the apostle with an intimation, that when his affairs were less urgent, he would hear him again on the subject. *Note*, (1.) The word of God will sometimes make the stoutest hearted sinner tremble. (2.) Many are terrified with the apprehensions of their sins, and afraid to think of death and judgment, who, notwithstanding, live and die the slaves of corruption. (3.) In the concerns of our souls nothing is more fatal than delay. If God's word hath spread an alarm in the conscience, Satan seldom asks more than to defer the matter to a more convenient season, till we are older, or have less worldly engagements: and if he can thus far prevail, the cause is gained, and we, like Felix, are undone.

6 Though many future conferences passed between them, Felix never brought religion on the carpet. His covetous heart thought to make a good advantage of his prisoner, and knowing how high Paul was in the esteem of his friends, he hoped they would have proposed a considerable ransom to obtain his discharge: but though they would have done so, probably Paul resolved never to be indebted for his liberty to any such indirect method; and therefore, after two years, Felix being recalled from his government, to answer for his male-administration, and justly apprehensive that the elders of Judea would swell the number of his accusers, he endeavoured to gain their favour, by leaving Paul bound in the hands of Porcius Festus, his successor.

CHAP. XXV.

We have here, 1. *Paul accused before Festus*, ver. 1—7. 2. *His appeal unto Cesar*, ver. 8—12. 3. *Festus relating the case to king Agrippa, he desires to hear him, and Paul is accordingly brought forth*, ver. 13—27.

1 NOW when Festus was come into the province,
after three days he ascended from Cesarea to
Jerusalem. 2 Then [a] the high priest, and the chief of
the Jews informed him against Paul, and besought him,
3 And desired favour against him, that he would send
for him to Jerusalem, [b] laying wait in the way to kill
him. 4 But Festus answered, that Paul should be kept
at Cesarea, and that he himself would depart shortly
thither. 5 Let them therefore, said he, which among
you are able, go down with *me*, and accuse this man, if
there be any wickedness in him. 6 And when he had
tarried among them † more than ten days, he went down
unto Cesarea, and the next day sitting on the judgment
seat, commanded Paul to be brought. 7 And when
he was come, the Jews which came down from Jerusalem,
stood round about, and laid many and grievous
complaints against Paul, which they could not prove,
8 While he answered for himself, Neither against the
law of the Jews, neither against the temple, nor yet against
Cesar, have I offended any thing at all. 9 But
Festus, [d] willing to do the Jews a pleasure, answered
Paul, and said, Wilt thou go up to Jerusalem, and there
be judged of these things before me? 10 Then said
Paul, I stand at Cesar's judgment-seat, where I ought to
be judged: to the Jews have I done no wrong, as thou
very well knowest. 11 For [e] if I be an offender, or
have committed any thing worthy of death, I refuse not
to die: but if there be none of these things whereof these
accuse me, no man may deliver me unto them. [f] I appeal
unto Cesar. 12 Then Festus when he had conferred
with the council, answered, Hast thou appealed
unto Cesar? unto Cesar shalt thou go.

[a] Chap. xxiv. 1.
[b] Chap. xxiii. 15.
† Or, as some copies read, no more than eight or ten days.
[c] Chap. xxiv. 5. & xxviii. 17.
[d] Chap. xxiv. 27.
[e] Chap. xxiii. 29.
[f] Chap. xxvi. 32.

§ 1—12. No sooner was Festus entered upon his government, than Paul's implacable enemies beset him.

1 After three days stay at Cesarea, Festus proceeded to Jerusalem, where he no sooner arrived, than the high priest and elders, coming in a body to pay their compliments to the governor, failed not to seize the opportunity to prepossess his mind, informing him against Paul, and setting the affair in the most invidious light, they besought him to give judgment against the prisoner, and for that purpose, begged the favour of him, that he might be sent for to Jerusalem, resuming the old scheme to assassinate him by the way. How restless are the struggles of malice! and what wickedness is not the wretched heart of man capable of, when enslaved by envy and revenge?

2 Festus excused himself from granting their request, chusing rather to decide the matter at Cesarea, either he thought their desire unreasonable, or perhaps suspected some design; and therefore informing them that he should shortly depart thither, he assured them, if they would prepare their evidence, and those who were best able to manage the prosecution would go down with him, and could prove him guilty of any crime or misdemeanour, he would grant them impartial justice.

3 After ten days stay at *Jerusalem* Festus went down to Cesarea with those who were to carry on the prosecution against Paul, and without delay, the very next day the prisoner is brought to the bar, and his enemies surrounding the judge, as if to intimidate him into compliance, or by their number to give weight to the cause, laid many and grievous accusations against the apostle, as if he was the vilest of the vile: but when the evidences which should support these allegations were required, it evidently appeared they could not prove one of their charges. While, in his defence, Paul confidently denied every accusation, having neither offended against the law, the temple, or the civil government, and defied them to produce a single instance wherein he had acted unbecoming his profession, as a Jew, or his allegiance to Cesar. *Note*, Nothing is easier than to advance high charges against Christ's people, but laying and proving are usually found to be different things.

4 Festus could not but perceive the malice of the accusation, and the innocence of the prisoner: but willing on his first coming to Cesarea, to ingratiate himself with the Jews, by granting them the favour which they desired, of having Paul tried at Jerusalem, he asked him whether he would go up thither, and have the cause decided by him in presence of the Sanhedrim? Too well Paul knew the designs of his persecutors, to consent to a proposal so dangerous; therefore he wisely pleads his privilege as a Roman, and appeals unto Cesar. *I stand*, saith he, *at Cesar's judgment seat, where I ought to be judged*, and am ready to appear: *to the Jews have I done no wrong, as thou very well knowest. For if I be an offender, or have committed any thing worthy of death*, according to the laws of the empire, *I refuse not to die*, content to suffer the desert of my offences: *but if there be none of these things whereof they accuse me*, and the charge be evidently false and malicious, *no man may deliver me unto them*, and put me in their power. I claim my right, as a freeman of Rome, to be only judged there, and *appeal unto Cesar*. *Note*, (1.) The wisdom of the serpent is needful with the harmlessness of the dove, when we have to do with unreasonable and wicked men. (2.) It is a debt we owe ourselves to claim the protection of the law, against those who maliciously attempt to wound our fame, or injure our person.

5 Festus acquiesces in his appeal. *He conferred with the council*, who assisted him in the management of affairs, and as they admitted the right of the prisoner to claim this privilege, he answered, *Hast thou appealed unto Cesar, unto Cesar shalt thou go*, not unwilling, perhaps, thus to rid his hand so fairly of a cause which might have involved him in much trouble.

13 And after certain days, king Agrippa and Bernice
came unto Cesarea to salute Festus. 14 And when
they had been there many days, Festus declared Paul's
cause unto the king, saying, [g] There is a certain man
left in bonds by Felix: 15 [h] About whom, when I
was at Jerusalem, the chief priests and the elders of the
Jews informed *me*, desiring *to have* judgment against him.
16 To whom I answered, It is not the manner of the
Romans to deliver any man to die, before that he which
is accused have the accusers face to face, and have licence

[g] Chap. xxiv. 27.
[h] Ver. 2, 3.

to

to answer for himself concerning the crime laid against
him 17 Therefore when they were come hither, with-
out any delay on the morrow I sat on the judgment-seat,
and I commanded the man to be brought forth 18
Against whom when the accusers stood up, they brought
none accusation of such things as I supposed 19 But
i Chap xviii 15 & xxiii 29 had i certain questions against him of their own supersti-
tion, and of one Jesus which was dead, whom Paul af-
k Rev i 18 firmed k to be alive 20 And because I doubted of such
manner of questions, I asked *him* whether he would go
to Jerusalem, and there be judged of these matters 21
‡ Or cognisance But when Paul had appealed to be reserved unto the ‡
hearing of Augustus, I commanded him to be kept till
I might send him to Cesar 22 Then Agrippa said
unto Festus, I would also hear the man myself To-
morrow, said he, thou shalt hear him 23 And on the
l Eccles i 2 1 Cor vii 31 morrow, when Agrippa was come, and Bernice, l with
great pomp, and was entred into the place of hearing,
with the chief captains, and principal men of the city,
at Festus commandment Paul was brought forth 24
And Festus said, King Agrippa, and all men which are
here present with us, ye see this man, about whom all
the multitude of the Jews have dealt with me, both at
m Chap xxii 22 Jerusalem, and also here, crying that m he ought not to
n Chap xxiii 9 & xxvi 31 live any longer 25 But when I found that n he had
committed nothing worthy of death, and that he himself
hath appealed to Augustus, I have determined to send
him 26 Of whom I have no certain thing to write
‡ Or The lord Job xxxii 21 unto ‡ my lord Wherefore I have brought him forth
o Chap xxvi 3 before you, and o especially before thee, O king Agrippa,
that after examination had I might have something to
write 27 For it seemeth to me unreasonable to send
a prisoner, and not withal to signify the crimes *laid* a-
gainst him

v 13—27 As Christ had told his disciples that they should be brought before governors and kings, so doth he order it in his providence, that their persecutors are made the instruments of leading those great men to hear the gospel, who perhaps otherwise never would have heard it We have here,

1 The visit of Agrippa to Festus, to congratulate him on his coming to his government He was the son of that Herod who slew the apostle James Claudius, the Roman emperor, had given him the title of king, and the tetrarchy which belonged to his uncle Philip Bernice, who accompanied him, was his sister, but was accused of too great familiarity with her brother such were the great folks of those times, when viewing then the present corruptions of the age, *say not the former days were better*, the world was always the same

2 As Agrippa and Bernice were both brought up in the Jewish religion, after they had been at Cesarea some time, in conversation one day Paul's case happened to be the subject, which Festus related to the king, either to entertain him with the story, or to have his advice how to act, as better acquainted with the Jewish rites and customs, than he, a stranger, could be supposed to be He had found Paul in bonds, when Felix resigned the government to him, and had no sooner come to Jerusalem, to take possession of his province, than the chief priests and elders clamoured for judgment against him, but he excused himself from a hasty decision of the matter, alledging the constant custom of the Romans to adjudge no man to death, nor to consign him to destruction, through any favour or partiality, but first to have the person accused, and his accuser, face to face, that he might have liberty to exculpate himself from any crime laid to his charge And to dispatch the matter without delay, the next day after his arrival, the prisoner was brought to the bar, when, to his surprize, he found no one accusation of a criminal nature could be proved, such as came under his cognizance as a magistrate, but that the charge turned upon certain questions of a religious nature, respecting the tenets he held, contrary to their law, and *about one Jesus, who was dead, whom Paul affirmed to be al... again* counting himself an incompetent judge of such superstitious controversies, as he regarded them, he proposed to Paul to have the matter discussed before the Sanhedrim at Jerusalem, but the prisoner objecting to them, had pleaded his privilege, and appealed unto Cesar, he was therefore still in custody, till an opportunity offered to send him to Rome *Note*, (1) Every man has a natural right to be heard before he is condemned To determine a cause where only one side of the question is told, is the sure way to err, and may be the means of irreparable injury to the purest innocence (2) They who know not Jesus, speak slightly of him, but to those who feel their guilt, and need of a Saviour, whether he be alive again or no, is a matter of infinite importance, on which their everlasting hopes depend

3 Agrippa, curious to know what Paul had to say for himself, intimated a desire to hear him, Festus gladly consented to it, and appointed the next day On the morrow Agrippa and Bernice in vast pomp, arrayed in gorgeous apparel, attended by their royal retinue, entered the judgment-hall, where all the chief captains and principal men of the city attended, drawn by curiosity, or to pay their respects to the noble personages who were present when being seated, the prisoner, at the commandment of Festus, is brought forth, more adorned with his prison garments and glorious bonds, than they in all their vain splendor and empty magnificence

4 Festus with respect hereupon addressed himself to King Agrippa, and the principal men who were present, and opened the occasion of their meeting with an account of the prisoner before them, concerning whom he had been sollicited with great importunity by all the Jews, both at Jerusalem and Cesarea, to pass sentence of death upon him, as a miscreant unworthy to live But when on a fair trial nothing criminal could be proved against him, and Paul had appealed to Augustus for the final decision of his cause, he was resolved to send him and as it looked absurd and unreasonable to send a prisoner, without signifying what crimes he stood accused of, he had therefore brought Paul forth before that honourable assembly, especially before King Agrippa, who was most acquainted with the Jewish laws and customs, that after a full discussion of the case, he might have something determinate to write to his imperial master, concerning the prisoner who had appealed to his judgment.

CHAP XXVI

In this chapter we have, 1 The account Paul gives of himself in answer to the calumnies of the Jews And in that, (1) His humble address to king Agrippa, and the compliment he passed upon him, ver 1—3 (2) *His account of his original and education, and his profession as a Pharisee, and his adherence still to that which was then the main article of his creed, in distinction from the Sadducees, the* resurrection of the dead, *however his nation's he had since departed from it,* ver 4—8 (3) *Of his zeal against the Christian religion, and the professors of it in the beginning of his time,* ver 9—11 (4) *Of his miraculous conversion to the faith of Christ,* ver 12—16 (5) *Of the commission he received from heaven to preach the gospel to the Gentiles,* ver 17, 18 (6) *Of his proceedings pursuant to that commission, which had given this mighty offence to the Jews,* ver 19—21 (7) *Of the doctrine which he had made it his business to preach to the Gentiles, which was so far from destroying the law and the prophets, that it shewed the fulfilling of both,* ver 22, 23 2 *The remarks that were made upon his apology* (1) *Festus thought he never heard a man talk so madly, and slighted him as crazed,* ver 24 *And in answer to him he denies the charge, and appeals to king Agrippa,* ver 25, 26 (2) *King Agrippa being more closely and particularly dealt with, thinks he never heard a man talk more rationally and convincingly, and owns himself almost his convert,* ver 28 *And Paul heartily wishes him so,* ver 29 (3) *They all agree that he was an innocent man, and that he ought to be set at liberty, and it was pity he was provoked to put a bar in his own door by appealing to Cesar,* ver 30, 31

1 THEN Agrippa said unto Paul, Thou art per-
mitted to speak for thyself Then Paul stretched
forth the hand, and answered for himself, 2 I think my-
self happy, king Agrippa, because I shall answer for my-
self this day before thee, touching all the things whereof
I am accused of the Jews 3 Especially because I know
thee a to be expert in all customs and questions which a Deut xv
are among the Jews wherefore I beseech thee to hear 18
me patiently 4 My manner of life from my youth,
which was at the first among mine own nation at Jerusa-
lem, know all the Jews, 5 Which knew me from the b Chap xx
beginning, (if they would testify) that b after the most 3 & xxiii 6
straitest sect of our religion, I lived a Pharisee 6 And Phil iii 5
now I stand, and am judged for the hope of c the promise c Chap iii 25 & xxv
made of God unto our fathers 7 Unto which *promise* 4 & chap
our twelve tribes instantly serving *God* d day and night, Luke i
e hope to come for which hope's sake, king Agrippa, I 27 d J
am accused of the Jews 8 Why should it be thought Dan xii
a thing incredible with you, that God should raise the d Luke ii
dead? 9 I verily thought with myself that I ought to 3 1 Tim
do many things contrary to the name of Jesus of Naza- e Luke xi
reth. 10 f Which thing I also did in Jerusalem and Chap xx
many of the saints did I shut up in prison, g having re- f Chap viii
ceived authority from the chief priests, and when they 3
were put to death I gave my voice against *them* 11 And r Chap
h I punished them oft in every synagogue, and compelled 14
them to blaspheme, and being exceedingly mad against h Chap
them, i I persecuted *them* even unto strange cities

v. 1—11. As Agrippa was the principal perſonage in that aſſembly to whom Feſtus had particularly addreſſed himſelf, he ſignified to Paul, who waited the order of his ſuperiors, that he was permitted to ſpeak for himſelf. Glad of the opportunity to vindicate the glorious cauſe of God and truth, whilſt he apologized for himſelf, with dignity ſtretching out his hand, the great apoſtle, with conſcious uprightneſs and unaffected ſimplicity, began,

1. With the ſatiſfaction he felt on the occaſion now given him of anſwering before ſo able and candid a judge. *I think myſelf happy, king Agrippa, becauſe I ſhall anſwer for myſelf this day before thee,* concerning the charges laid againſt me by my countrymen, *eſpecially becauſe I know thee to be expert in all queſtions and cuſtoms which are among the Jews. Wherefore I beſeech thee to hear me patiently,* whilſt I deſire, without art or diſguiſe, to relate the principles which have influenced my conduct from the firſt day until now.

2. He freely appeals to the Jews themſelves, who knew *his manner of life from his youth up,* that he had been educated at Jeruſalem, under the moſt celebrated of their doctors, had early embraced the principles of Phariſaiſm, and, according to their moſt rigid interpretations, had conformed to all the rites, Moſaical or traditionary, and obſerved, with moſt conſcientious regard, the commandments of the law, blameleſs in all his converſation. So that it was neither ignorance, prejudice, looſe principles, or immoral conduct, which could be urged as a reaſon for the change wrought upon him.

3. He declares freely the cauſe of his preſent bonds. It was for hoping *the hope of the promiſe made of God unto the fathers,* of a reſurrection to eternal life and glory through the divine Meſſiah, who had appeared in the perſon of Jeſus of Nazareth, and by his riſing from the dead had fully proved his own glorious character, and ſecured the reſurrection of all his redeemed people. *Unto which promiſe* not only he, but all the truly religious of the twelve tribes, hoped to come, with fervency and conſtancy, day and night, in their prayers, labouring to arrive at the poſſeſſion of the bleſſings promiſed through this Meſſiah. And for this hope's ſake was he accuſed, for preaching this Meſſiah, the ſalvation which was in him, and a reſurrection to everlaſting bleſſedneſs through faith in his name. So that, inſtead of being an apoſtate from the fundamental articles of the Jewiſh faith, according to the malicious accuſations of his perſecutors, he maintained them with all his might and diligence. Nor did he urge any thing abſurd or unreaſonable, when he aſſerted the reſurrection of Jeſus, as the firſt fruits of his people: for *why ſhould it be thought a thing incredible that God ſhould raiſe the dead?* is any thing beyond God's power? and ought we not implicitly to credit his promiſe? *Note,* (1.) All our hopes toward God are founded on his promiſes. (2.) They who would come to the poſſeſſion of the eternal bleſſedneſs, are called upon to ſerve God day and night in ceaſeleſs and importunate prayer.

4. He owns the inveterate prejudices againſt Chriſtianity under which he formerly lay. *I verily thought with myſelf that I ought to do many things contrary to the name of Jeſus of Nazareth,* ſuppoſing it a duty I owed to God and my brethren, to ſuppreſs, by every means, the doctrine and pretenſions of one who appeared ſo deſpicable: *which thing alſo I did in Jeruſalem,* being moſt zealous againſt his diſciples, *and many of the ſaints did I ſhut up in priſon, having received authority from the high-prieſts; and, when they were put to death, I gave my voice againſt them,* juſtifying the moſt bloody meaſures, and teſtifying my fulleſt approbation of theſe horrid executions: *and I puniſhed them oft in every ſynagogue,* with reſtleſs eagerneſs purſuing them, *and compelled them,* through the dread of ſcourgings, infamy, or death, *to blaſpheme* that holy Name whereby they were called, *and, being exceedingly mad againſt them,* to find many of them obſtinate in their faith, and to ſee the number of the diſciples increaſe in ſpite of all the load of oppreſſion, *I perſecuted them even unto ſtrange cities,* longing, if poſſible, to extirpate the very Chriſtian name. If he was now therefore a preacher and a ſufferer for that faith which once he ſo furiouſly perſecuted, it could ariſe only from the deepeſt conviction, and his converſion was itſelf a proof of the truth of Chriſtianity. *Note,* (1.) It is poſſible for thoſe who ſeem moſt confident they are in the right, and are moſt violent in ſupport of their opinions, to be moſt dangerouſly deceived. I doubt not that many to this hour perſecute the truth, and think they do God ſervice. (2.) Nothing will lie heavier on the awakened conſcience than the remembrance of former injuries done to the ſouls of men, the effect of which perhaps are now irreparable.

12 Whereupon [k] as I went to Damaſcus, with au-
thority and commiſſion from the chief prieſts, 13 At
mid-day, O king, I ſaw in the way a light from heaven,
above the brightneſs of the ſun, ſhining round about me,
and them which journeyed with me. 14 And when we
were all fallen to the earth, I heard a voice ſpeaking un-
to me, and ſaying in the Hebrew tongue, Saul, Saul,
why perſecuteſt thou me? *It is* hard for thee to kick
againſt the pricks. 15 And I ſaid, Who art thou,
Lord? And he ſaid, I am Jeſus whom thou perſecuteſt.
16 But riſe, and ſtand upon thy feet: for I have ap-
peared unto thee for this purpoſe, [l] to make thee a mi-
niſter and a witneſs both [m] of theſe things which thou
haſt ſeen, and [n] of thoſe things in the which I will ap-
pear unto thee; 17 Delivering thee from the people,
and *from* the Gentiles, [o] unto whom now I ſend thee,
18 [p] To open their eyes, and to turn *them* from dark-
neſs to light, and *from* the power of Satan unto God,
[q] that they may receive forgiveneſs of ſins, and [r] inhe-
ritance among them which are [s] ſanctified by faith that
is in me. 19 Whereupon, O king Agrippa, [t] I was not
diſobedient unto the heavenly viſion: 20 But [u] ſhewed
firſt unto them of Damaſcus, and at Jeruſalem, and
throughout all the coaſts of Judea, and *then* [x] to the
Gentiles, that they ſhould repent and turn to God, and
do [y] works meet for repentance. 21 For theſe cauſes
[z] the Jews caught me in the temple, and went about to
kill *me*. 22 Having therefore obtained help of God,
I continue unto this day, witneſſing both to ſmall and
great, ſaying none other things than thoſe [a] which the
prophets and Moſes did ſay ſhould come: 23 That
[b] Chriſt ſhould ſuffer, *and* [c] that he ſhould be the firſt
that ſhould riſe from the dead, and [e] ſhould ſhew light
unto the people, and to the Gentiles.

[l] 1 Tim. i. 12. [m] Chap. xxi. [n] 2 Cor. x. [o] Chap. ix. 15. [q] Luke xxiv. 47. [z] Chap. xxi. [a] Chap. ix. [y] Chap. xxi. [x] Matt. iii. 8. [b] Luke xxiv. 27. [c] 1 Cor. xv. 20. Col. i. 18. Rev. i. 5. [e] Iſa. xlii. 6. Luke ii. 32.

v. 12—23. The apoſtle, having related his former life and converſation, proceeds to account for the amazing change which had been wrought in him.

1. He declares the manner of his converſion. As he approached Damaſcus to execute the high-prieſts commiſſion, at mid-day a light, brighter than the ſun, darted from heaven upon him and his companions; and, when in conſternation they were fallen together to the earth, a voice of majeſty addreſſed him, *Saul, Saul, why perſecuteſt thou me? It is hard for thee to kick againſt the pricks:* theſe mad attempts to wound me in my members muſt be attended with ruin to thy own ſoul. Terrified with this interrogation, when he replied, *Who art thou, Lord?* the voice anſwered, *I am Jeſus, whom thou perſecuteſt.* That deſpiſed Nazarene, whom he branded as an impoſtor, now demonſtrated to him his divine power and glory with ſuch evidence as in a moment bore down all his prejudices, and ſtruck him to the heart with horror, ſhame, and remorſe.

2. He who had laid him in the duſt, with infinite condeſcenſion raiſed him up, and inveſted him with that commiſſion under which he now acted. He ſaid, *Riſe, and ſtand upon thy feet; for I have appeared unto thee,* not to deſtroy thee, as thou haſt deſerved, but *for this purpoſe, to make thee a miniſter and a witneſs both of theſe things which thou haſt ſeen, and of thoſe things in the which I will appear unto thee,* giving thee farther diſcoveries of my mind and will, and directions for thy conduct; and amidſt all the dangers to which hereafter for my name's ſake thou muſt be expoſed, *delivering thee from the Jewiſh people, and from the Gentiles, unto whom now I ſend thee,* with an apoſtolic commiſſion to publiſh the glad tidings of ſalvation, *to open their eyes,* through a divine illumination attending thy preaching, *to turn them from the darkneſs* of ſuperſtition, idolatry, ignorance, and error, *to* the ſaving *light* and knowledge of the grace which is in Jeſus Chriſt, *and from the power of Satan,* who now reigns in their hearts, *unto God,* effectually converting their ſouls from the dominion of ſin to the love and ſervice of the holy, ever bleſſed God, *that they may receive forgiveneſs of ſins,* through me, the great Redeemer of loſt ſouls, *and inheritance among them that are ſanctified by faith that is in me,* prepared for and intitled to the eternal manſions of bleſſedneſs, through that divine faith which worketh by love, and purifies the ſouls of all my redeemed people. *Note,* (1.) The whole world lieth in darkneſs and wickedneſs, until the light of the goſpel-word and the power of goſpel-grace be ſhed abroad in the heart. (2.) The great end of the Chriſtian miniſtry is in order to the converſion of men's ſouls to God. They are not ſent of him, who are never made uſe of by him to this bleſſed end, and neither know nor expect ſuch fruit of their labours. (3.) Forgiveneſs of ſins is the great foundation on which alone repentance towards God can be effectually preached. We muſt believe that he is a pardoning God, before we can have any hope of returning to his favour. (4.) There can be no true juſtification but what flows from faith which worketh by love. (5.) Our title to glory is not of debt, but of grace. Jeſus hath purchaſed it for us, and freely beſtows it upon his people, who are the children which his Father hath given him. (6.) Though our title to the eternal inheritance is the finiſhed work of Jeſus, it becomes us to experience a meetneſs for it by the power of his Spirit in our hearts. We muſt be ſanctified before we can be glorified.

3. Borne down by ſuch irreſiſtible evidence, he could not heſitate a moment. *Whereupon, O king Agrippa, I was not diſobedient unto the heavenly viſion,* but, inſtantly becoming a con-

vert to the truth, *I shewed first to them of Damascus, and then at Jerusalem, and throughout all the coast of Judea, and then to the Gentiles,* according to the orders given me, *that they should repent and turn to God,* deeply convinced of their guilt and danger, filled with self-abhorrence, and in simplicity desiring to renounce their sins, whilst they drew near to a throne of grace through a crucified Jesus; *and do works meet for repentance,* to evidence the genuine conversion of their hearts to God. *Note,* Unless our fruits prove the truth of the grace which is in us, we deceive ourselves, if we think that we are real converts.

4. His indefatigable labours and zeal in preaching these benevolent and infinitely momentous doctrines were the only causes of provocation given to his unbelieving brethren, who, obstinate against his testimony, and exasperated at his preaching, seized him in the temple, and in a tumultuous manner, if he had not been rescued, would have pulled him in pieces on the spot. Let the impartial judge if he had deserved such treatment.

5. Not intimidated by his past dangers, and *having,* according to the divine promise, ver. 17. *obtained help from God,* he stedfastly persevered, supported and encouraged by the Spirit's inward assistances, and the gracious interpositions of the Lord's providence in his behalf, *witnessing both to small and great,* without respect of persons, or fear of man, that great salvation which is brought to light by the gospel, and most clearly revealed through the death and resurrection of Jesus; *saying none other things than those which the prophets and Moses did say, that Christ should suffer,* and not be a temporal conqueror, but devoted to death for the sins of his people, Isa. liii. 8. *and that he should be the first that should rise from the dead,* to die no more, and as the *first-fruits of them that slept,* who, by virtue of their relation to him, should be quickened by his power at the last day; *and should shew light unto the people, and to the Gentiles,* diffusing the knowledge of his great salvation not only among his ancient favourites the Jews, but extending his grace to the ends of the earth, and sending out the light of his gospel, as the light of his sun, to his people of all nations, tongues, and languages, who are freely called to partake of all the blessings and privileges of his kingdom.

24 And as he thus spake for himself, Festus said
[f 2 Kings ix. 11. John x. 20. 1 Cor. iv. 10.] with a loud voice, Paul, [f] thou art beside thyself; much
learning doth make thee mad. 25 But he said, I am
not mad, most noble Festus; but speak forth the words
of truth and soberness. 26 For the king knoweth of
these things, before whom also I speak freely: for I am
persuaded that none of these things are hidden from him;
for this thing was not done in a corner. 27 King
Agrippa, believest thou the prophets? I know that thou
believest. 28 Then Agrippa said unto Paul, Almost
thou persuadest me to be a Christian. 29 And Paul
[g 1 Cor. vii. 7.] said, [g] I would to God, that not only thou, but also all
that hear me this day, were both almost, and altogether
such as I am, except these bonds. 30 And when he
had thus spoken, the king rose up, and the governor,
and Bernice, and they that sat with them: 31 And
when they were gone aside, they talked between them-
[h Chap. xxiii. 9. & xxv. 25.] selves, saying, [h] This man doth nothing worthy of death,
or of bonds. 32 Then said Agrippa unto Festus, This
[i Chap. xxv. 11.] man might have been set at liberty, [i] if he had not ap-
pealed unto Cesar.

Ver. 24—32. Whilst Paul, warmed by the glorious subject on which he had entered, was proceeding to display the great truths of his Redeemer's person, offices, and character, he is here,

1. Interrupted by Festus. Unable to hear with patience what he, a heathen, counted so absurd as the resurrection of a dead man, and so strange as the miraculous conversion, he said aloud, *Paul, thou art beside thyself; much learning doth make thee mad.* He looked upon him with an air of disdain, as rather to be pitied as a lunatic, than condemned as a criminal. Perhaps the warmth which Paul expressed, as he advanced in his speech, made him think his imagination was over-heated with the intenseness of his application. *Note,* It is no unusual thing for those who never knew the light of truth, and the zeal of warm affection for a Redeemer, to stamp those who appear fervent in his cause as enthusiasts or madmen.

2. Paul's reply was a sufficient proof of the falseness of this invidious imputation. *I am not mad, most noble Festus; but speak forth the words of truth and soberness,* matters of infinite importance, and supported by the most substantial evidence. He does not resent the suggestion of the governor, but by the meekness of his reply proves the unruffled serenity of his own mind; and, referring himself to Agrippa, he adds, *For the king knoweth of these things, before whom I speak freely,* being conversant in the writings of Moses and the prophets, where the sufferings and resurrection of the Messiah are foretold; and hath heard how they have been fulfilled in Jesus of Nazareth: *for I am persuaded that none of these things are hidden from him;* he must have been long ago told of the death and resurrection of Jesus Christ, and of my singular conversion; *for this thing was not done in a corner,* but publickly known, and attested by unexceptionable witnesses, many of whom have, and many more are ready to seal their testimony with their blood.

3. Turning then from Festus to Agrippa, in the most affecting and pathetic manner he applied himself to the conscience of his royal auditor. *King Agrippa, believest thou the prophets? I know that thou believest.* He cannot entertain a suspicion to the contrary, and with confidence expresses his assurance of his faith in the inspired writings; paying him the greatest compliment, whilst he presses on him the most important truths.

4. Agrippa is nearly staggered with this close application; and, struck with the polite yet serious address of the apostle, replies, *Almost thou persuadest me to be a Christian.* So much reason and evidence appeared in Paul's discourse, that, were it not for a regard to his dignity and temporal interests, he could become a convert to Christianity. *Note,* Many, unable to stand before the evidence of truth, are *almost persuaded,* but the world holds them in fetters, and they dare not pursue their own convictions.

5. With inimitable address, where the piety of the Christian was blended with the politeness of the Roman, Paul replied, *I would to God that not only thou, but also all that hear me this day, were both almost and altogether such as I am, except these bonds.* He wished him and them all the happiness which himself enjoyed in Christ, and exempt from all the ignominy and sufferings to which for the sake of Jesus he was exposed.

6. The king hereupon arose, unable perhaps any longer to stand against the powerful evidence of truth, and afraid of some more moving strokes on his conscience: the governor and Bernice followed him, with the rest of the principal persons. And as they retired together, and talked of Paul's case and his defence, they perfectly agreed that *this man,* however great the clamour was against him, had done *nothing worthy of death or of bonds,* so clear was the innocence of the apostle. *Then said Agrippa unto Festus, This man might have been set at liberty, if he had not appealed unto Cesar.*

CHAP. XXVII.

This whole chapter is taken up with an account of Paul's voyage towards Rome, when he was sent thither a prisoner by Festus the governor, upon his appeal to Cesar. 1. *The beginning of the voyage was calm and prosperous,* ver. 1—8. 2. *Paul gave them notice of a storm coming, but could not prevail with them to lie by,* ver. 9—11. 3. *As they pursued their voyage, they met with a great deal of tempestuous weather, which reduced them to such extremity, that they counted upon nothing but being cast away,* ver. 12—20. 4. *Paul assured them, that though they would not be advised by him to prevent their coming into this danger, yet by the good providence of God they should be brought safely through it, and none of them should be lost,* ver. 21—26. 5. *They are shipwrecked in the isle of Malta, and by Paul's counsel all got safe to land,* ver. 27—44.

1 AND when [a] it was determined that we should sail [a Chap. xxv. 12.]
into Italy, they delivered Paul and certain other
prisoners unto one named Julius, a centurion of Augus-
tus's band. 2 And entering into a ship of Adramyt-
tium, we launched, meaning to sail by the coasts of Asia;
one [b] Aristarchus, a Macedonian, of Thessalonica, being [b Chap. xix. 29.]
with us. 3 And the next *day* we touched at Sidon.
And Julius [c] courteously entreated Paul, and gave *him* [c Chap. xxiv. 23.]
liberty to go unto his friends to refresh himself. 4 And
when we had launched from thence, we sailed unto Cy-
prus, because the winds were contrary. 5 And when
we had sailed over the sea of Cilicia and Pamphylia, we
came to Myra, *a city* of Lycia. 6 And there the centu-
rion found a ship of Alexandria sailing into Italy; and
he put us therein. 7 And when we had sailed slowly
many days, and scarce were come over against Cnidus,
the wind not suffering us, we sailed under Crete, over
against Salmone; 8 And hardly passing it, came unto
a place which is called The fair havens, nigh whereunto
was the city *of* Lasea. 9 Now when much time was
spent, and when sailing was now dangerous, because the [d Lev. xvi.]
fast was now already past, Paul admonished *them*, 10
And said unto them, Sirs, I perceive that this voyage
will be with hurt and much damage, not only of the
lading and ship, but also of our lives. 11 Neverthe-
less the centurion believed the master and the owner of
the ship, more than those things which were spoken by
Paul. 12 And because the haven was not commodious
to winter in, the more part advised to depart thence also,
if by any means they might attain to Phenice, *and there*
to winter; *which is* an haven of Crete, and lieth toward
the south west, and north-west.

v 1—12 How long Paul continued at Cesarea is not said, probably on the first opportunity he was shipped for Rome We have here,

1 His embarkation Paul and some other prisoners were put on board a ship of Adramyttium, under the care of one Julius, a centurion of the legion which bore the name of Augustus Luke the evangelist, and Aristarchus a Macedonian, accompanied the apostle, whose presence and society could not but be a singular blessing to him in this tedious voyage

2 His progress The next day after they sailed they touched at Sidon, where Julius reposed such confidence in his prisoner, that, on his parole, he permitted him to visit his friends, that he might have the comfort of refreshing himself with their company and conversation, and be supplied with proper provisions for the voyage Loosing from thence they beat up under the island of Cyprus, the wind being against them, and, coasting the Cilician and Pamphylian shore, they arrived at Myra a city of Lycia There the centurion finding a ship of Alexandria sailing to Italy with a loading of wheat, he contracted for a passage, and carried the prisoners and the companions of the apostle aboard, and putting to sea, through contrary winds, they made but little way, in many days scarce reaching Cnidus, a promontory in Caria, and, instead of leaving Crete on the left, they were forced to beat up on the other side, over against the eastern cape called Salmone, and, with great difficulty weathering the point, cast anchor in a bay called The fair havens, near the city of Lasea *Note*, (1) In our voyage through this tempestuous world we may expect to meet many an unfavourable gale (2) Though the wind of afflictions and temptations blow hard against us, and we can scarcely bear up against it, if we steadily hold on our course, we shall at last reach the fair havens where we would be

3 His advice As the autumn was far advanced, and the fast on the great day of atonement was now passed, the season of the year began to grow tempestuous, and sailing to be dangerous Paul therefore admonished them not to proceed farther till the spring, foretelling by a prophetic impulse, that if they did they would repent their rashness, and not only sustain great damage in the loss of their ship, but also greatly endanger their lives But, the master and owner of the ship being of a different opinion, the centurion, who chose rather to be guided by their judgment in this matter, disregarded Paul's admonition, and *The fair havens* being an inconvenient port to winter in, the majority of the ship's company advised to sail for Phenice, a haven in Crete, at no great distance, that was made by two points of land that ran south-east and north-west, and was more sheltered from the winds, and more commodious for a winter station

13 And when the south wind blew softly, supposing
that they had obtained *their* purpose, loosing *thence* they
sailed close by Crete 14 But not long after there
† arose against it a tempestuous wind, called Euroclydon † Or beat
15 And when the ship was caught, and could not bear
up into the wind, we let *her* drive 16 And running
under a certain island which is called Clauda, we had
much work to come by the boat 17 Which when
they had taken up, they used helps, undergirding the
ship, and fearing lest they should fall into the quick-
sands, strake sail, and so were driven 18 And we be-
ing exceedingly tossed with a tempest, the next *day* they
lightened the ship, 19 And the third *day* [e] we cast out e Jonah i 5
with our own hands the tackling of the ship 20 And
when neither sun nor stars in many days appeared, and
no small tempest lay on *us*, all hope that we should be
saved was then taken away

v 13—20 In consequence of the advice of the majority, we have here,

1 The ship pursuing her voyage with a prosperous gale The south wind blowing gently encouraged them to put to sea, and now, concluding they could not fail to reach their desired port, they coasted along the island of Crete but the gale of prosperity is often but a short-lived delusion For,

2 The wind suddenly shifted to an opposite quarter, and a hurricane, called Euroclydon, arose, and blew so vehemently, that the ship was ready to be swallowed up in the waves, so that, unable to bear up against the storm, or keep their course, they let her drive at random, and, running under an island called Clauda, with great difficulty they hoisted the boat on board, then undergirding the ship with ropes, to prevent her going to pieces, and fearing lest they should be driven on the quicksands of the African shore, they reefed their sails, and drove before the wind under the bare pole Thus they continued to be tossed about violently, whilst lowering clouds obscured the skies, and neither sun nor stars for many days appeared, so that they knew not where they were *Note*, (1) We should never be too elated the transition from the height of prosperity to the depth of adversity is often very sudden (2) Many of God's dearest children have known such melancholy seasons, when Christ, their polar star, hath been obscured, and spiritual darkness hath compassed them round on every side

3 All attempts which human prudence dictated they now made use of The next day after the storm began, in order to lighten the ship, they cast out the merchandize into the sea, and, when still the danger increased, passengers as well as seamen were called upon deck, and the third day they threw overboard the utensils and unnecessary tackling of the ship, when their lives were each moment in jeopardy, they cared not for any loss besides but when, after all their efforts, for many days the storm raged with unabating severity, despair sat in general upon the countenance of the seamen, and they expected nothing but to be swallowed up of the merciless waves *Note*, (1) If men are so prodigal of their goods to save their bodies, when in danger, how much readier should we be to part with them, rather than seek to preserve them at the peril of our souls? (2) Long-continued trials are apt to lead us to despair It requires strong faith to walk in darkness and see no light, and yet to stay ourselves upon God

21 But after long abstinence, Paul stood forth in the
midst of them, and said, Sirs, ye should have hearkned
unto me, and not have loosed from Crete, and to have
gained this harm and loss 22 And now I exhort you
to be of good cheer for there shall be no loss of *any man's*
life among you, but of the ship 23 For there stood
by me this night the angel of God, whose I am, and
[f] whom I serve, 24 Saying, Fear not, Paul, [g] thou f Rom i 9 2 Tim i 3
must be brought before Cesar and lo, [h] God hath given g Chap xxiii 11
thee all them that sail with thee 25 Wherefore, Sirs, h Gen xxxix 5
be of good cheer for [i] I believe God, that it shall be
even as it was told me 26 Howbeit [k] we must be cast i Luke i 45 John iv 50
upon a certain island 27 But when the fourteenth night Rom iv 20
was come, as we were driven up and down in Adria 2 Tim i 12
about midnight, the shipmen deemed that they drew near k Chap xxviii 1
to some country 28 And sounded, and found it twenty
fathoms and when they had gone a little further, they
sounded again, and found it fifteen fathoms 29 Then
fearing lest they should have fallen upon rocks, they cast
four anchors out of the stern, and wished for the day
30 And as the shipmen were about to flee out of the
ship, when they had let down the boat into the sea, un-
der colour as though they would have cast anchors out
of the foreship, 31 Paul said to the centurion, and to
the soldiers, Except these abide in the ship, ye cannot be
saved 32 Then the soldiers cut off the ropes of the
boat, and let her fall off 33 And while the day was
coming on, Paul besought them all to take meat, say-
ing, [l] This day is the fourteenth day that ye have tarried, l Or ye have continued without meat expecting the 14th day
and continued fasted, having taken nothing 34 Where-
fore I pray you to take *some* meat, for this is for your
health for [l] there shall not an hair fall from the head 1 1 Kings i 52 Matt x
of any of you 35 And when he had thus spoken, he
took bread, and [m] gave thanks to God in presence of them m 1 Sam ix 13 John vi 11 1 Tim iv 3, 4
all, and when he had broken *it*, he began to eat. 36
Then were they all of good cheer, and they also took
some meat 37 And we were in all in the ship, two
hundred and threescore and sixteen souls 38 And when
they had eaten enough, they lightened the ship, and cast
out the wheat into the sea 39 And when it was day
they knew not the land but they discovered a certain
creek with a shore, into the which they were minded,
if it were possible, to thrust in the ship 40 And when
they had taken up the anchors, they committed *themselves*
unto the sea, and loosed the rudder bands, and hoised up
the mainsail to the wind, and made toward shore 41
And falling into a place where two seas met, [n] they ran n 2 Cor xi 25
the ship aground, and the forepart stuck fast, and re-
mained unmoveable, but the hinder part was broken
with the violence of the waves 42 And the soldiers
counsel was to kill the prisoners, lest any of them should
swim out and escape 43 But the centurion, willing
to save Paul, kept them from *their* purpose, and com-
manded that they which could swim, should cast *them-
selves* first into the sea, and get to land 44 And the
rest, some on boards, and some on *broken pieces* of the
ship And so it came to pass that they escaped all safe
to land

v 21—44 Man's extremity is God's opportunity when we are at our wits end, he can still open a door for us to escape

1 Paul

1. Paul chears their hearts with the aſſurance, that though they gave themſelves over for loſt, and abandoned themſelves to deſpair, not a man of the company ſhould periſh.

(1.) He gently reminds them of his advice which they had diſregarded. They ſhould have followed his prophetic warning, and then they would have prevented the danger, loſs, and injury, which they had now ſuſtained. *Note*, Moſt of the miſeries in which we involve ourſelves, are owing to our own obſtinacy, and diſregard of the admonitions of our wiſer friends.

(2.) He confidently aſſures them of the ſafety of their perſons, though their ſhip muſt be wrecked, and therefore exhorts them to be of good cheer. Notwithſtanding their contempt of his advice, he deſired to revive their deſponding hearts, and to quicken them to beſtir themſelves in the confidence of being preſerved through the divine mercy. *Note*, Though others involve themſelves in trouble by neglecting our counſel, we muſt nevertheleſs be ready to lend them our aſſiſtance, to comfort them under their trials, or to extricate them from their difficulties.

(3.) He produces divine authority for what he ſaid, that they might reſt ſatisfied with the truth of his aſſertion, however improbable it might appear. *There ſtood by me this night*, in viſion, *the angel of God*, a celeſtial meſſenger ſent from that glorious Lord, *whoſe I am*, his peculiar property by redemption, as well as creation, and by his ſpecial appointment conſtituted an apoſtle, *and whom I ſerve*, making it the buſineſs and happineſs of my life to promote his glory in the goſpel of his dear Son, and yielding up my body, ſoul, and ſpirit, with unreſerved devotedneſs, to his bleſſed work and ſervice. And this heavenly miniſter addreſſed me, *ſaying, Fear not, Paul*, thou art ſafe in the midſt of danger, *for thou muſt be brought before Ceſar: and lo! God hath given thee all them that ſail with thee*, who for thy ſake ſhall be preſerved. Such a public bleſſing is one good man; and they who are hated and perſecuted of the world, as not worthy to live, are indeed the very perſons for whoſe ſake it is preſerved.

(4.) He comforts them, and encourages them to truſt in God. *Wherefore, ſirs, be of good cheer: for I believe God that it ſhall be even as it was told me*, and doubt not but the event will confirm his gracious promiſe.

(5.) He tells them, they muſt, however, expect to be ſhipwrecked on a certain iſland, which, among other things, when it came to paſs, would evidence the divine inſpiration by which the apoſtle ſpoke.

2. After many days of terror and diſmay, on the fourteenth night, as they were toſſed to and fro by the tempeſt in the Adriatic ſea, the ſeamen about midnight apprehended they were near land, and ſounding, at firſt found twenty fathoms of water, and a little further, fifteen: leſt therefore they ſhould be driven aſhore in the dark, or ſtrike upon ſome rock, they caſt anchor, and longed impatiently for day-light, that they might ſee in what ſituation they were. *Note*, In the dark and ſtormy night of temptation, deſertion, or affliction, the anchor of hope, which enters into that within the vail, muſt hold the ſoul ſure and ſtedfaſt, until the ſun of righteouſneſs ariſe, and lift up the light of his countenance upon us.

3. The ſailors, diſregarding Paul's aſſurances of ſafety, thought to ſecure themſelves, whatever became of the reſt; and therefore hoiſting out the boat, under pretence of caſting anchor out of the foreſhip, they intended to make for the ſhore, and leave the ſhip and the paſſengers to ſhift for themſelves. Paul, probably by divine intimation, perceived their deſign, and immediately acquainted the centurion and ſoldiers, aſſuring them, that though God had promiſed to preſerve them, it was to be effected in the uſe of the neceſſary means; and that if the ſeamen, who ſhould work the ſhip, were ſuffered to eſcape, they muſt not expect to be ſaved. In the way of duty we may only hope for the fulfilment of the promiſes. The ſoldiers therefore, apprized of the danger, immediately cut the ropes, and let the boat drive.

4. While they waited for the morning light, Paul, the comforter and encourager of his dejected ſhip-mates, *beſought them to take meat*, and refreſh themſelves after their toils, *ſaying, This day is the fourteenth day that ye have tarried*, in ſuſpenſe between life and death, *and continued faſting*, without any inclination to food, *having taken nothing*, at leaſt no regular nor hearty meal. *Wherefore I pray you to take ſome meat, for this is for your health*, and will conduce to your ſafety: *for there ſhall not an hair fall from the head of any of you*. And when he had thus heartened them with his chearful counſel and countenance, *he took bread, and gave thanks to God in the preſence of them all*, for their paſt preſervation, the promiſe of aſſured ſafety, and the proviſion that was now before them: *and when he had broken it, he began to eat*, ſetting them an example. Revived by this repeated aſſurance and exhortation, and ſeeing him ſo ſatisfied, they all took refreſhment, their number conſiſting of two hundred and threeſcore perſons: and being ſtrengthened by a hearty meal, they lightened the ſhip, caſting the wheat, of which part of her cargo conſiſted, into the ſea, that ſhe might draw the leſs water, as they intended to run her aſhore.

5. When welcome day-light appeared, they deſcried the land not very diſtant, though what country it was they knew not: but obſerving a creek which ran up within the ſhore, they reſolved, if poſſible, to ſteer the ſhip thither; and weighing the anchors, or ſlipping the cables, they hoiſted the mainſail, and looſed the rudder, which had been faſtened, and made for ſhore: but ſtriking on a ſhoal where two currents met, the prow ſtuck faſt, and the waves daſhing on the ſtern, ſhe ſoon went to pieces.

6. In this extremity the inhuman ſoldiers propoſed the bloody expedient of murdering all the priſoners, leſt any of them ſhould eſcape, and they become anſwerable for them: a ſhocking propoſal! But the centurion, who now ſaw more reaſon than ever to value Paul, for his ſake would not permit ſo cruel a project to be executed: and therefore commanded every one to conſult in the beſt manner poſſible for their own ſafety; whereupon ſome by ſwimming, and others on parts of the wreck, got ſafe to ſhore, and not one perſon of the whole company was drowned, according to Paul's prediction. *Note*, (1.) Many a faithful ſoul reaches the ſhores of eternal reſt in a ſtorm; and however great his fears, or imminent his danger, he will find his ſafety ſecured. (2.) After long beating on life's tempeſtuous ocean, though we leave earth and all its things behind us, we ſhall not regret their loſs, when we feel ourſelves entred into the land of reſt which remaineth for the people of God.

CHAP. XXVIII.

We have here, 1. Paul's miraculous eſcape, after his ſhipwreck, from a viper which faſtened on his hand, ver. 1—6. 2. The great good he did in the iſland of Malta, and the reſpect ſhewed him there, ver. 7—10. 3. The completion of his voyage, and his journey to Rome, ver. 11—16. *4. The conference he held with the Jews on his arrival, ſome of whom believed, and others were hardened,* ver. 17—29. *5. The liberty he had, though a priſoner, to preach in his own hired houſe during two years,* ver. 30, 31.

1 AND when they were eſcaped, then they knew
that [a] the iſland was called Melita. 2 And the
barbarous people ſhewed us no little kindneſs: for they a Chap. xxvii.
kindled a fire, and received us every one, becauſe of the
preſent rain, and becauſe of the cold. 3 And when
Paul had gathered a bundle of ſticks, and laid them on
the fire, there came a viper out of the heat, and faſtned
on his hand. 4 And when the barbarians ſaw the venomous
beaſt hang on his hand, they ſaid among themſelves,
No doubt this man is a murderer, whom though
he hath eſcaped the ſea, yet vengeance ſuffereth not to
live. 5 And he ſhook off the beaſt into the fire, and
[b] felt no harm. 6 Howbeit, they looked when he
ſhould have ſwoln, or fallen down dead ſuddenly: but b Mark xvi. 18. Luke x. 19.
after they had looked a great while, and ſaw no harm
come to him, they changed their minds, and [c] ſaid that
he was a god. 7 In the ſame quarters were poſſeſſions c Chap. xiv. 11.
of the chief man of the iſland, whoſe name was Publius,
who received us and lodged us three days courteouſly.
8 And it came to paſs that the father of Publius lay
ſick of a fever, and of a bloody flux, to whom Paul
entred in, and [d] prayed, and laid his hands on him, and
healed him. 9 So when this was done, others alſo d James v. 14.
which had diſeaſes in the iſland came, and were healed:
10 Who alſo [e] honoured us with many honours, and
when we departed they laded *us* with ſuch things as were e 1 Tim. v. 17.
neceſſary.

2. 1—10. The iſle of Melita, or Malta, ſince ſo famed for the noble ſtand its knights made againſt all the power of the Ottoman empire, was the place where they found themſelves on ſhore.

1. They received great courteſy from the people of the iſland, who are called *barbarous*, not as being ſavage in their manners, the very contrary of which appeared, but as unpoliſhed iſlanders, and unacquainted with Grecian literature. They were ſo far from being engaged in plundering the wreck, that their attention was taken up about the poor people who had eſcaped, wet and cold as they were: they therefore kindled a fire to dry them, and took them under ſhelter from the rain, which fell heavily, and from the cold. *Note*, (1.) Shipwrecked mariners are entitled to the greateſt humanity. It is a pitch of ſavage brutality beyond what heathens ſhewed, to plunder the little remains of their misfortune; yet, ſhocking to tell, even in a Chriſtian land, are wretches found ſo deſtitute of every feeling of humanity, as to be more intent on the wreck, than ſollicitous about the lives of the people; yea, to ſtrip and rob them even when caſt on ſhore, inſtead of helping and aſſiſting them. Sure-

ly they will receive judgment without mercy, who have thus shewed no mercy (2) Fuel is as needful a charity for the poor as food or raiment When we hear the wintry winds blow, and feel the cold even in our warm rooms, we should remember those who shiver over the scarce smoaking embers, and through whose miserable cottages the wind and rain find a free passage

2 Paul, ever active and ready to serve his fellow-creatures in the lowest offices of kindness, had gathered a bundle of sticks, and laid them on the fire, when a viper, which had been unobserved in the faggot, perceiving the heat, leaped out and fastened on his hand, which when these unlettered islanders beheld, they concluded this must be some notorious murderer, who, though he had escaped shipwreck, the divine vengeance thus signally overtook, and would not suffer to live, and they expected each moment to see him swell and drop down dead *Note*, (1) Though this is not usual, the place of retribution, yet God is sometimes pleased to make even here some signal monuments of his vengeance (2) We must not interpret every sudden stroke of God, or remarkable affliction, as a divine judgment the best of men have been often most severely exercised

3 The apostle, with perfect composure of mind, and trust on Christ's promise, (*Mark* xvi 18) shook off the venomous animal into the fire, and remaining to their astonishment unhurt, they, after a while, changed their opinion of him, and fancied he must be more than human, even one of their immortal gods, who could thus defy the viper's venom So changeable are the sentiments of the populace, he that is run down as a murderer to-day, is sometimes cried up as a god to-morrow

4 The possessions of the chief man of the island, whose name was Publius, lay near the place where the ship had been cast away, and he most hospitably entertained them three days, till they could be otherwise provided for and in return for his civility, God so ordered it in his providence, that he should not lose his reward Publius's father now lay dangerously ill of a fever and the bloody flux, Paul therefore went in, and praying over him, *laid his hands on him*, and in the name of his divine Master *healed him* instantaneously The fame of which miracle soon spread, and others who were diseased made their applications to the apostle, and freely received the cure of all their several maladies *Note*, (1) They who have large possessions should exercise proportionable hospitality, and be generous stewards of these temporal gifts of God (2) Kindness shewn to God's ministers, their Master somehow or other will take care to repay

5 This grateful people, during their stay, failed not to pay them the highest veneration and respect Most probably the apostle not only healed their bodily diseases, but with his companions preached to them the gospel of Jesus for the healing of their souls, and therefore the Maltese at their departure liberally furnished them with all necessaries for the voyage Having shared their spiritual things, they gladly in return communicated of their worldly things

11 And after three months we departed in a ship of
Alexandria, which had wintered in the isle, whose sign
was Castor and Pollux 12 And landing at Syracuse,
we tarried *there* three days 13 And from thence we
fet a compass, and came to Rhegium and after one day
the south wind blew, and we came the next day to Pu-
teoli 14 Where we found brethren, and were desired
to tarry with them seven days and so we went toward
Rome 15 And from thence, when the brethren heard
of us, they came to meet us as far as Appii forum, and
the three taverns whom when Paul saw, he thanked
God, and took courage 16 And when we came to
Rome, the centurion delivered the prisoners to the cap-
tain of the guard but [f] Paul was suffered to dwell by
himself, with a soldier that kept him

[f] Chap xxiv 23 & xxvii 3

v. 11—16 After three months stay on the island, when the spring returned, they once more pursued their voyage, and met with no more disaster

1 They embarked in another ship of Alexandria, which had wintered at Malta, and bore the image of Castor and Pollux, under whose protection the wretched idolaters expected safety

2 After a prosperous voyage they landed at Syracuse in the isle of Sicily, where they stayed three days From thence they fetched a compass round, and arrived at Rhegium, the first port they made in Italy, The next day, taking advantage of the south wind, they proceeded to Puteoli, near Naples, from whence they were to travel by land to Rome At Puteoli Paul and his companions, to their great comfort, found some Christian brethren, who requested him to stay a week with them, that they might spend one Lord's-day together, which the centurion kindly permitted him to do, and from thence they set forward for the great metropolis of the world, the place of their destination

3 The Christians who were at Rome no sooner heard of his coming from Puteoli, than they set forward to meet him on the road, to shew respect to one who had so eminently distinguished himself in the cause, and was particularly endeared to them by the affectionate epistle which they had received from him Some of them went as far as the town called *Appii-forum*, above fifty miles, and others as far as *the three taverns*, (*tres tabernæ*), a place upwards of thirty miles from Rome, to receive him, not ashamed of his bonds Their presence much refreshed his heart, when he saw them, *he thanked God* for the grace which appeared in these faithful brethren, *and took courage*, his drooping spirits revived, and now he can boldly face the bloody Nero, before whom he must appear Nothing so encourages the hearts of ministers amidst the greatest opposition of enemies, as the company and countenance of some faithful friends, who dare own and stand by them in defiance of reproach or danger

4 On their arrival at Rome, the centurion delivered up his charge of prisoners to the captain of the guard The rest probably were committed to close custody, but Paul, either thro' the letter of Festus, or the request of Julius, was left a prisoner at large, being permitted to dwell in lodgings, with a soldier chained to him as his guard

17 And it came to pass, that after three days, Paul
called the chief of the Jews together. And when they
were come together, he said unto them, Men *and* bre-
thren, though [g] I have committed nothing against the [g] Chap xxv 8
people or customs of our fathers, yet [h] was I delivered [h] Chap xxi. 33
prisoner from Jerusalem into the hands of the Romans
18 Who [i] when they had examined me, would have let [i] Chap xxiv. 10 & xxv 8 & xxvi 31
me go, because there was no cause of death in me 19
But when the Jews spake against *it*, [k] I was constrained [k] Chap xxv. 11
to appeal unto Cesar, not that I had ought to accuse my
nation of 20 For this cause therefore have I called
for you, to see *you*, and to speak with *you* because that
[l] for the hope of Israel I am bound with [m] this chain [l] Chap xxvi 6, 7
21 And they said unto him, We neither received letters [m] Ibid 29 Eph iii 20 & vi 20 2 Tim i 16
out of Judea concerning thee, neither any of the brethren
that came, shewed or spake any harm of thee 22 But
we desire to hear of thee what thou thinkest for as
concerning this sect, we know that [n] every where it is [n] Luke ii 34 Chap xxiv 5 14.
spoken against

v 17—22 Though by the edict of Claudius all the Jews had been banished from Rome, at the accession of Nero they returned, and many were now settled there, opulent and men of distinction To them, after three days rest from his journey, Paul addressed himself, and, since he could not wait on them, begged the favour of their company at his lodgings, and when they were assembled there, being desirous to stand right in their opinion,

1 He relates his case to them, as to men of humanity, his brethren after the flesh, and worshippers of the true God, from whom he might expect friendship and affection Though he appeared in bonds, it was not for any crime he had committed, nor for any violation of the sacred rites and institutions delivered by Moses to their fathers, that he had been sent a prisoner to Rome The Roman governors, both Felix and Festus, before whom he had been examined, were sensible of his innocence, and would have discharged him, but some violent persons of his own countrymen, filled with prejudices against him, objected to his release, and urged the governor Festus to bring him back to Jerusalem, so that he was obliged to appeal unto Cesar, merely for his own preservation, not that he meant any accusation of his countrymen before the emperor, but only to defend himself, and obtain his liberty He therefore called them together to assure them, that the chain he wore was purely for preaching *the hope* of every true Israelite, even the coming of the divine Messiah, who had, according to the prophecies, appeared, and accomplished the salvation of his people, and for declaring the resurrection to eternal life, as the privilege of all who believed in him *Note*, Christ is the only hope of the Israel of God A sinner who knows his real state, sees nothing out of Jesus but black despair and wrath to the uttermost, but in him there appears grace abounding to the miserable and the desperate, *reigning through righteousness unto eternal life*

2 In reply the Jews said unto him, *We neither received letters out of Judea concerning thee, neither any of the brethren that came shewed or spake any harm of thee*, so that they own they had no crime to charge him with Probably his accusers dared not appear before the emperor, conscious of the danger to which they might expose themselves *But we desire to hear of thee what thou thinkest*, and would impartially examine into the new opinions you broach, and are willing to know how you can prove, that Jesus of Nazareth is that hope of Israel, of whom the prophets have spoken *for* this seems to us highly im ro-

unprobable, and *as concerning this sect*, which he hath founded, *we know that every where it is spoken against*, as maintaining heretical opinions, and disturbing the peace of mankind *Note*, (1) Christianity is no sect, built on narrow opinions, aiming at secular advantages, or tending to sow division in the world No just the very contrary it embraces all mankind who acknowledge Jesus as the Saviour, directs us to seek our happiness and true interests in another world, and breathes nothing but peace and love (2) We may not wonder if the true gospel of the grace of God be still every where spoken against it must be so, whilst the generality rest in the form, and deny the power of godliness

23 And when they had appointed him a day, there
came many to him into his lodging to whom he ex-
pounded and testified the kingdom of God, persuading
a Luke xxiv 27 John i 45 — them concerning Jesus, a both out of the law of Moses,
and *out of* the prophets, from morning till evening 24
p Chap xvii. 4 — And p some believed the things which were spoken, and
some believed not 25 And when they agreed not a-
mong themselves, they departed, after that Paul had
spoken one word, Well spake the holy Ghost by Esaias
q Isa vi 9 Matt xiii 14 Mark iv 12 Luke viii 10 John xii 40 Rom xi 8 — the prophet unto our fathers, 26 Saying, q Go unto
this people, and say, Hearing ye shall hear, and shall
not understand, and seeing ye shall see, and not per-
ceive 27 For the heart of this people is waxed gross,
and their ears are dull of hearing, and their eyes have
they closed, lest they should see with *their* eyes, and
hear with *their* ears, and understand with *their* heart,
and should be converted, and I should heal them 28
Be it known therefore unto you, that the salvation of
r Chap xiii 46 & xviii 6 — God is sent r unto the Gentiles, and *that* they will hear
it 29 And when he had said these words, the Jews de-
parted, and had great reasoning among themselves

v 23—29 Though naturally prejudiced, as Jews, against the doctrines of Jesus, they consented to appoint a day, and met at the apostle's lodgings in great numbers, to hear what he had to say on the subject Hereupon,

1 Paul *expounded* to them the nature, doctrines, and privileges of that kingdom of God which he preached; explained to them all the prophecies and types of the Old Testament, shewing how they centred in Jesus of Nazareth, and received their full accomplishment in his life, death, and resurrection, *testifying*, from his own and others experience, the power of this divine Saviour's grace upon the heart, and *persuading* them with the warmest affection and zeal, to submit to this Redeemer, and embrace that divine Messiah, to whom both the law and the prophets bore witness, that they might partake of that spiritual salvation which he had obtained for his people As the matter was of such vast importance, he reasoned with them from morning until evening, answering probably all their objections, and proving at large, by the most convincing arguments, that Jesus is the Christ

2 His discourse, as usual, produced different effects on his hearers. *Some believed* the truths he preached, and others remained hardened in their prejudices, and *believed not*, which occasioned a disagreement in their sentiments, the infidel party being incensed against the gospel word Thus is the same gospel to some a savour of life unto life, to others, of death unto death

3 Before they parted, the apostle addressed to them one awakening word *Well spake the Holy Ghost by Esaias the prophet*, even that glorious Jehovah who inspired the sacred penmen, *saying, Go unto this people, and say, Hearing ye shall hear, and shall not understand, and seeing ye shall see, and not perceive*, amidst the clearest preaching of the gospel-word, and the fullest discoveries of gospel-grace, they were abandoned of God for their obstinacy to judicial blindness and obduracy *For the heart of this people is waxed gross*, stupid, senseless, and obstinate, thro' pride, prejudice, and passion *and their ears are dull of hearing*, inattentive to the preaching of the truth *and their eyes have they closed*, wilfully blind against the evidence of miracles performed, of prophecies fulfilled, and the divine attestation given to the character of Jesus as the Messiah, *lest they should see with their eyes, and hear with their ears, and understand with their heart, and should be converted, and I should heal them* *Be it known therefore unto you, that*, since ye thus with determined obstinacy reject the counsel of God against your own souls, and exactly fulfil this prophecy, in your present rejection of Christ and his gospel, *the salvation of God*, which you neglect and despise, *is sent unto the Gentiles, and they will hear it*, and partake of the invaluable blessings and privileges of the Messiah's kingdom *Note*, They who refuse to hearken to God's word, and wilfully harden their hearts against his warnings, are justly given up to a reprobate mind, and left to the ruin which they have chosen

4 The assembly hereupon broke up, and warm debates ensued on the subjects concerning which he had spoken, some vindicating what they had heard, as righteous, just, and good, others exasperated against the preacher and his doctrine, and unable to think of the Gentiles being admitted into the Messiah's kingdom, without the utmost indignation

30 And Paul dwelt two whole years in his own hired
house, and received all that came in unto him, 31.
Preaching the kingdom of God, and teaching those
things which concern the Lord Jesus Christ, s with all — s Chap ... 31
confidence, no man forbidding him.

v 30, 31 The apostle had been already near three years a prisoner, and still longer is ordained to wear the honourable bonds of Christ It was at Rome however a consolation to him, that he was so much his own master, as to be able to dwell in his own hired house, and to have all company whom he chose admitted these years therefore that he abode at Rome, we are told, were profitably spent

1 *He received all that came to him*, his doors were ever open, and whosoever would, might hear him and, no doubt, multitudes, drawn by the desire of instruction, the comfort of his company, or curiosity to know what so remarkable a person had to say, attended him *Note*, (1) Every minister's house should be readily accessible to all who seek instruction for their souls (2) Our houses, by godly conversation and discourse, by prayer and praise, should be consecrated to God's service, and where two or three are met in his name, he will be in the midst of them

2 The subject of his preaching to those who came to hear, was concerning the kingdom of God, and the things which related to the Lord Jesus Christ, the Alpha and Omega of all his discourses His person, offices, character, his incarnation, sufferings, and glory, with all the great and inestimable blessings and privileges derived from thence, were the delightful theme on which he insisted Happy were it, if all who call themselves Christ's ministers followed so bright an example How dry and unaffecting is that discourse, where Jesus is not exalted as all and in all!

3 He preached *with all confidence*, with the greatest liberty and freedom in his own spirit, most fully assured of the doctrines which he taught, using all plainness of speech, and with the most undaunted courage, *no man forbidding him*, neither the Roman emperor restrained him, nor could the Jews hinder him so that, though a prisoner, God made him eminently useful in his bonds, and there were saints converted by his ministry even in Cæsar's houshold, *Phil* iv 22 Here also he wrote those epistles to the Ephesians, Colossians, Philemon, and the Philippians, wherein, though dead, he yet speaketh, and we in them enjoy the most blessed fruits of his prison labours

The historian leaves him in this confinement After two years he regained his liberty Concerning his future labour we have nothing certain the received tradition is, that after visiting Spain, Crete, Judea, and the churches of Asia, he came to Rome the second time, where he suffered martyrdom, and went to receive the crown of glory which fadeth not away

THE

THE

EVANGELICAL EXPOSITOR;

OR, A

PRACTICAL COMMENT

UPON THE

Epistle of St. Paul to the ROMANS.

WE are now entring upon the most peculiarly profitable parts of the book of God All scripture is given by inspiration of God, but among the bright volumes it contains, Paul's Epistles shine with distinguished lustre, in which the grand truths of Christianity appear in all their glory, illustrated, defended, the objections against them answered, and the doctrines of grace explicitly taught, and urged with the warmth of a heart which felt its need of them

Though others of the epistles in order of time precede this to the Romans, it stands first in the collection, as being the largest, and containing the most comprehensive view of the peculiar doctrines and duties of our holy religion It was written, as is generally supposed, about the year 57, *from Corinth, just before the apostle departed for Troas in his way to Jerusalem,* See Acts xx 2, 3, &c

The chief design of this epistle is to shew the only way of a sinner's acceptance with God, whether he be Jew or Gentile, even through faith in the blood and righteousness of Jesus, to exalt the glory of God's grace in this method of salvation, and to vindicate it from the objections of the Judaizing Christians, who by placing some dependance on the works of the law, moral and ceremonial, debased the purity of the gospel In the first fifteen verses the apostle introduces and asserts the doctrine of a free salvation by Jesus Christ, the necessity of which he proves in the remaining part of that chapter and the following, where it appears, that the Gentiles could not be justified by the law of nature, nor the Jews by the law of Moses, that both being guilty before God, must be justified freely by faith in Jesus Christ, or perish, and that Abraham, the father of the faithful, thus found acceptance with God, (chap IV 1, 2, 3, 4) *He pursues the argument in the 5th chapter as far as the fall of man, the cause of all the sin and misery which are in the world, and forms a striking contrast between the first covenant-head of mankind, who fell, and the second man the Lord from heaven, who came to rescue his people from the miseries in which they were involved And here the glory of the Redeemer's grace shines the more illustrious, when considered in the view of the desperateness and universality of the guilt and ruin in which we are involved From the riches of the grace which is in Jesus Christ, he proceeds to infer the necessity of dying unto sin, and living unto God, declares, amidst all the struggles of in-dwelling corruption, the happy deliverance from the dominion of sin which believers enjoy, describes their transcendently great and glorious privileges in Christ, including deliverance from condemnation, the spirit of adoption, victory over all tribulation, even death itself, the redemption of the body in the resurrection-day and the perfection of bliss and blessedness in the eternal enjoyment of the love of God,* (chap VI, VII, VIII) *He thence traces up these inestimable mercies to their source, as flowing from the eternal, sovereign, and absolutely free purpose and grace of God, wherein he shews, that the rejection of the Jews, and the calling of the Gentiles, were according to the everlasting counsels of his own will, revealed in the prophetic word, and every way consistent with his wisdom, righteousness, and grace He answers the objections of those who cavilled at the divine sovereignty displayed in this awful pleasing dispensation,* (chap. IX, X, XI) *On these doctrines he grounds his exhortations to the practice of a variety of personal relative duties, which by the faithful in Christ Jesus are bound to adorn the doctrine of God their Saviour in all things,* (chap XII, XIII, XIV, XV, to ver 14) *and the whole closes with affectionate salutations, the promise of a speedy visit, if the Lord permitted, his benediction, and doxology*

Many expositors have grievously debased the great and glorious doctrines herein contained, respecting the free grace and justification of the gospel, and would fain insinuate, that the works concerning which the apostle speaks, are not the moral, but ceremonial *works of the law, that the election spoken of is* national, *respecting Jews*

3 and

and Gentiles, and not to be interpreted of individuals; and the privileges to which some are chosen in preference to others, are merely external, and have no reference to their eternal state: the contrary of which many faithful and able advocates have fully evinced, among the least of whom I shall count it an honour to be numbered, and wish to plead with them the cause of sovereign grace. Not that any one can be reasoned into the reception of these humbling truths: man's fallen spirit, his pride, and prejudices, must revolt against them, till enlightened from above, brought under a divine conviction of sin, *and led to a discovery of the desperate wickedness, the absolute impotence, and the inconceivable deceitfulness of his naturally corrupted heart, he bows into the dust, is content to be saved as desperate, and to acknowledge himself indebted for his whole salvation to God's free choice and everlasting love. All the truths of God here described must till then appear absurd, unreasonable, derogatory, according to the notions he hath formed, to all the divine perfections, perhaps impious, nay even blasphemous. But when the Spirit of God discovers to us our real state of enormous guilt, the exceeding sinfulness of sin, and writes despair on every effort and attempt to help ourselves, then, like a mathematical proposition, which before appeared inexplicable, because the principles on which alone it could be solved were unknown, we trace, admiring and adoring, the various steps of gospel grace from everlasting to everlasting: divine evidence accompanies the process, and in the full blaze of truth we discover in this most astonishing scheme of salvation the offspring of eternal love, planned by infinite wisdom, and executed by almighty power, we discover glory given to God in the highest, the honour of the incarnate Saviour exalted to the uttermost, the sinner reduced to the lowest state of humiliation, yet most effectually engaged to love and serve the God of all grace. Thus as many as it pleaseth the Lord our God to call out of darkness into his marvellous light, they see and believe the love which God hath towards them, whilst all the labour of critics, philosophers, and merely letter-learned divines, leaves them just where it found them, groping for the wall as blind.*

CHAP. I.

In this chapter we may observe, 1. The preface or introduction to the whole epistle, to ver. 15. 2. A description of the deplorable condition of the Gentile world, which begins the proof of the doctrine of justification by faith, here laid down at ver. 17.

a 1 Cor. ix. 1. 2 Cor. xii. 11. b Acts ix. 15. & xiii. 2. Gal. i. 15, 16. c Gen. iii. 15. & xxii. 18. & xlix. 10. Deut. xviii. 15. Isa. vii. 14. & ix. 6. & xl. 10. & liii. 4, &c. Jer. xxiii. 5, 6. Dan. ix. 24. Acts x. 43. Gal. iii. 8. 1 Pet. i. 10, 11. d Mat. iii. 17. 2 Pet. i. 17. e Mat. i. 1. Luke i. 32. f Mat. xii. 40. Acts xiii. 33. g John i. 16. Chap. v. h Chap. iii. 29. Eph. iii. 8. i Mat. xxviii. 19. Eph. iii. 8. 1 Tim. ii. 7. k Chap. xvi. 26. l 1 Thes. iv. 7. 1 Cor. i. 2. m Chap. xvi. 20, 24. 1 Cor. i. 3. 2 Cor. i. 2. 1 Thes. i. 1.

1 PAUL, a servant of Jesus Christ, called *to be* [a] an apostle, [b] separated unto the gospel of God, 2. ([c] which he had promised afore by his prophets in the holy scriptures) 3 Concerning [d] his Son Jesus Christ our Lord, which was made of [e] the seed of David according to the flesh, 4 And declared *to be* the Son of God with power, according to the Spirit of holiness, [f] by the resurrection from the dead: 5 [g] By whom [h] we have received grace and [i] apostleship [k] for obedience to the faith among all nations for his name: 6. Among whom are ye also the called of Jesus Christ. 7 To all that be in Rome, beloved of God, [l] called *to be* saints: [m] Grace to you, and peace from God our Father, and the Lord Jesus Christ.

v. 1—7. The epistle opens,

1. With an account of the author. *Paul a servant of Jesus Christ*, once an inveterate persecutor, but now *called to be an apostle*, and glorying in this honourable name, *separated unto the gospel of God*, to that delightful and happy work of preaching the glad tidings of salvation through a dying Redeemer, signally distinguished by the Spirit's call, qualified by the effectual working of his mighty power, and solemnly dedicated and devoted to the service.

2. The apostle no sooner mentions the gospel of God, than his heart fires at the views of its glory and excellence. The wondrous scheme had been planned in the divine mind from eternity, had been the burden of the prophetic word from the beginning, where various hints of it had been given, and promises made of a more clear revelation of the divine mind and will, which might be expected in the fulness of time. The grand subject of this gospel is *Jesus Christ*, the Messiah, the anointed Saviour, and *our Lord*, the object of our faith and worship, and the King to whom we owe all duty and allegiance, who in his *human nature was made of the seed of David according to the flesh*, as had been foretold, (*Psal.* cxxxii. 11.) and as to his divine nature, he *was declared to be the Son of God with power, according to the Spirit of holiness, by the resurrection from the dead*. As the eternal Son of God, he possessed the same divine nature and perfections with the Father, they being one in the *Spirit of holiness*, in the essence of the undivided Godhead, a demonstration of which appeared, when by the exertion of his own power, through the operation of the holy Spirit, he raised his body from the grave, so that he appears to be God and man in one Christ.

3. From this risen Saviour he professes to have received, together with his brethren, *grace and apostleship*, both the high honour of this office, and ability to discharge it to the glory of God, *for obedience to the faith among all nations for his name*, that being the great end of their ministry, to bring all men, both Jews and Gentiles, to the faith of the gospel, and that holy obedience which flows from it, by which the name of Jesus should be to eternity exalted. *Note*, As obedience to God's law is the great fruit of faith, so is faith itself a most eminent part of obedience, when considered as an act of submission to the righteousness of God.

4. He with pleasure mentions the happy lot they had among those who were become obedient to the faith, *among whom are ye also the called of Christ Jesus*, by his word and spirit effectually brought to the participation of all the privileges of the gospel, *beloved of God* from eternity, and in his good time *called to be saints*, separated from a world that lieth in wickedness, for his peculiar people. *Note*, Every one truly called of Jesus is the happy object of the divine regard, and obliged to answer in their spirit and conversation the honourable title they bear, as the *saints* of God.

5. To these the apostle addresses his epistle. *To all that be in Rome*, professors of the faith, and in the judgment of charity partakers of the grace of God in truth, may *grace*, pardoning, comforting, quickening, sanctifying, be multiplied *to you; and peace*, the blessed effect thereof, *from God our Father, and the Lord Jesus Christ*.

8 First, [n] I thank my God through Jesus Christ for you all, that [o] your faith is spoken of throughout the whole world. 9 For [p] God is my witness, [q] whom I serve with my spirit in the gospel of his Son, that [r] without ceasing I make mention of you always in my prayers, 10. Making request, (if by any means now at length I might have a prosperous journey [s] by the will of God) to come unto you. 11 For I long to see you, that [t] I may impart unto you some spiritual gift, to the end you may be established, 12 That is, that [u] I may be comforted together with you, by the mutual faith both of you and me. 13. Now I would not have you ignorant, brethren, that [x] oftentimes I purposed to come unto you (but was let hitherto) that [y] I might have some fruit among you also, even as among other Gentiles. 14 [z] I am debtor both to the Greeks, and to the barbarians, both to the wise, and to the unwise. 15. So, as much as in me is, I am ready to preach the gospel to you that are at Rome also.

n Eph. i. 16. o Chap. xvi. 19. 1 Thes. i. 8. 2 John 4. p Chap. ix. 1. 2 Cor. i. 23. & xi. 31. q John iv. 23. Phil. iii. 3. r 1 Thes. iii. 10. 2 Tim. i. 3. s Jam. iv. 15. Chap. xv. 29. t Ibid. 3 John 3. u Acts xvi. 21. 1 Tit. x Phil. iv. 17. 1 Cor. iv. 16—23. 2 Cor. xi. 28, 29.

v. 8—15. After the warmest wishes for all spiritual blessings upon them, and his authoritative benediction, in the fullest confidence that the grace and peace he prayed for, would be bestowed upon them,

1. He thanks God on their behalf, whom he calls *my God*, happy in an assured interest in his favour and love *through Jesus Christ*, by whom alone every mercy descended on him or them. And the matter of his thanksgiving was, their *faith spoken of throughout the world*, they had approved themselves eminently faithful, and were the glory and joy of the churches, who triumphed in their eminent attainments. *Note*, (1.) When faith can say, *my God*, then the heart will be filled with thanksgiving and praise. (2.) A Christian's heart glows with gratitude, when he beholds the power of divine grace shining in the conversation of his brethren. (3.) Though we may not affect a name in the world, yet it is highly desirable to be spoken of by good men, and that our faith and conduct should receive their approbation.

2. He appeals to God for his incessant prayers on their behalf. *God is my witness, whom I serve with my spirit in the gospel of his Son*,

Son, most willingly, affectionately, and faithfully preaching the glad tidings of salvation through the divine Redeemer; *that without ceasing I make mention of you always in my prayers*, begging the best of blessings may descend upon you; and particularly *making request*, (*if by any means now at length I might have a prosperous journey by the will of God*) *to come unto you*, and enjoy the comfort of personal conversation with you. *Note*, (1.) Those whom we truly love, we shall remember without ceasing at the throne of grace. (2.) God's service must engage our souls: nothing is acceptable to him, but what is done heartily with an eye to his glory. (3.) In all our journeys the Lord should be regarded: though we devise our way, he must direct our steps.

3. The ends he proposed to himself in this visit, were, [1.] Their benefit. *For I long to see you, that I may impart unto you some spiritual gift, to the end ye may be established*, confirmed, if it please God, by his labours and ministry in the faith; guarded against seducers, and their ministers furnished with greater gifts for the edifying of the church. [2.] Their mutual consolation. *That is, that I may be comforted together with you, by the mutual faith both of you and me*; when by communicating their mutual experience, they might discover the effectual workings of the same divine faith, and rejoice together in the glorious hope set before them. *Note*, (1.) The highest advanced in faith and grace have need of farther establishment. We have not yet attained, nor are already perfect. (2.) Mutual communications of the dealings of God with our souls, greatly tend both to our comfort and establishment in the faith.

4. He informs them that he had long meditated a visit to them, though hitherto he had been providentially hindered by the difficulties he had to encounter, and the engagements which lay upon him; being earnestly desirous to *have some fruits among them, even as among other Gentiles*; that he might see his ministry attended with the same blessed effects, as in so many other places. And in these his labours he looked upon himself as *a debtor both to the Greeks and to the barbarians*; his call of God to the office of apostleship, and the qualifications he was endued with, obliged him to be faithful to his trust: and as the deepest adepts in Grecian literature were, respecting the way of salvation, as far removed from the truth as the most unpolished barbarian, he endeavoured to suit his discourses to both, that the wise men of this world might become wise unto salvation through gospel word, and the weaker and more unlearned be fed with the sincere milk of heavenly truth. *Note*, (1.) All our abilities and gifts of nature, providence, or grace, are lent us of the Lord, and to be accounted for to him, as being his debtors for them. (2.) We must suit our discourses to our auditory; and though the matter be the same, the manner should be varied, to give every man his portion in due season.

5. He professes the alacrity and cheerfulness wherewith he looks towards Rome, amidst all the dangers he might expect to encounter there, ready to preach the gospel in the most public manner, and fearless of any consequences from the opposition of the many or the mighty. The ministers of grace should thus be bold as lions in the cause of truth, nor fear the faces of men.

16 For [a] I am not ashamed of the gospel of Christ:
for [b] it is the power of God unto salvation, to every one
that believeth; to the Jew first, and [c] also to the Greek.
17 For therein is [d] the righteousness of God revealed
[e] from faith to faith: [f] as it is written, The just shall
live by faith. 18 For [g] the wrath of God is revealed
from heaven against all ungodliness, and unrighteousness
of men, who hold the truth in unrighteousness.

a Mark viii. 38. Acts … 2 Tim. i. 8. b 1 Cor. i. 18. c Acts xiii. 46. d Chap. iii. 21. f Hab. ii. 4. Gal. iii. 11. Heb. x. 38. g 2 Cor. vi. 7.

v. 16—18. The apostle having experienced the power of the gospel on his own soul, so far was he from being ashamed of the reproach of the cross, which to the Jews was a stumbling-block, and to the Greeks foolishness, that he gloried in the honour of being sent to publish to small and great the glad tidings of salvation through a crucified Jesus; and he gives his reason for so doing.

1. Because the gospel which he preached was *the power of God unto salvation, to every one that believeth, to the Jew first, and also to the Greek*; this being the great means God is pleased to make use of, and through the Spirit's effectual working comes with demonstration to the sinner's heart: and it was sent to the Jews first, and then more generally to the Gentile world, that as many of both as were ordained unto eternal life, might believe the divine report, and by faith embrace and lay hold of the hope of eternal life revealed in the gospel; *for therein is the righteousness of God revealed*, that transcendently glorious righteousness, which God the Son incarnate hath wrought out for us, and God the Father, according to the tenor of the everlasting covenant of grace, hath appointed as the condition of our salvation, hath declared his acceptance of, by the resurrection of Jesus, and imputes to our account, and which is set forth in the gospel, as the great object of our faith, the meritorious cause of our justification, and our title to eternal glory: *from faith to faith*, being wholly of faith, exclusive of all works and duties of our own, (*See chap. vi. 12. 2 Cor. iii. 18.*) or from the doctrine of faith in the word, to the grace of faith in the heart; or rather from one degree of faith to another, as we gain clearer discoveries of the fulness, suitableness, and transcendent glory of that finished salvation which is revealed to us in the gospel. *As it is written*, in the Old Testament, which exactly corresponds in doctrine with the New, *The just*, or justified man, *shall live by faith*; thereby he is brought into, and continues in, a state of spiritual life; so that death, the wages of sin, can have no more dominion over him; and being regarded in God's sight as righteous and just, he possesses a title sure and unalienable to that eternal life which is brought to light in the gospel, as the reward of the Redeemer's obedience unto death, even the death of the cross.

2. Because without this method of gospel grace every human creature must lie down under eternal wrath and despair: *for the wrath of God is revealed from heaven against all ungodliness, and unrighteousness of men, who hold the truth in unrighteousness*. God's word denounces vengeance on every transgressor; his judgments past have often terribly spoken his displeasure against him; and the whole world are found guilty before him, since all have sinned in opposition to their better knowledge, whether Jews, who enjoyed the light of revelation, or Gentiles, whom God left not without witness, giving them sufficient traditionary notices of his being, perfections, and attributes, which the visible objects around them served to explain, so as to leave them without excuse in their idolatry and disobedience. *Note*, (1.) Every sinner at God's bar will find self-condemned; he will be made to own he knew better, and did worse. (2.) Fearful is the wrath revealed against all ungodliness and unrighteousness of men: if it once seize on the sinner, it will burn, and never can be quenched. (3.) How highly should we value, and how eagerly embrace that glorious gospel, which alone can afford us shelter from those terrible blasts of the divine vengeance!

19 Because [h] that which may be known of God, is
manifest in them; for God hath shewed it unto them.
20 For [i] the invisible things of him from the creation
of the world are clearly seen, being understood by the
things that are made, *even* his eternal power and God-
head; so that they are without excuse. 21 Because
that when they knew God, they glorified him not as
God, neither were thankful; but [k] became vain in their
imaginations, and their foolish heart was darkened. 22
[l] Professing themselves to be wise, they became fools,
23 And [m] changed the glory of the incorruptible God,
into an image made like to corruptible man, and to
birds, and four footed beasts, and creeping things. 24
Wherefore [n] God also gave them up to uncleanness,
through the lusts of their own hearts, to dishonour their
own bodies between themselves: 25 [o] Who changed
the truth of God into a lie, and worshipped and served
the creature more than the Creator, [p] who is blessed for
ever. Amen. 26 For this cause God gave them up
unto vile affections: [q] for even their women did change
the natural use into that which is against nature: 27
And likewise also the men, leaving the natural use of the
woman, burned in their lust one toward another; men
with men working that which is unseemly, and receiving
in themselves that recompence of their error which was
meet. 28 And [r] even as they did not like ‖ to retain
God in *their* knowledge, God gave them over to a re-
probate mind, to do those things which are not conve-
nient; 29 Being filled with all unrighteousness, forni-
cation, wickedness, covetousness, maliciousness; full of
envy, murder, debate, deceit, malignity; whisperers, 30
Backbiters, haters of God, despiteful, proud, boasters,
inventers of evil things, disobedient to parents, 31
Without understanding, covenant-breakers, without na-
tural affection, implacable, unmerciful: 32 Who know-
ing the judgment of God, (that they which commit such
things are worthy of death) not only do the same, but
[s] have pleasure in them that do them.

i Acts … k 2 Kings xvii. 15. Eph. iv. 17, 18. l Jer. x. 14. … m 2 Kings xvii. 29. … n Psal. lxxxi. 12. … 1 Pet. iv. 3. … 2 Cor. xi. … Eph. v. 12. Jude 7. r Wisd. xiv. … ‖ Or, to acknowledge. s Hos. vii. 3. …

v. 19—32. The deplorable state of guilt in which the Gentile world lay is here pathetically described, and the judgment of God against them therefore evidently appears to be most righteous.

1. They had, though not the light of revelation, yet such notices of God's being and attributes, as left them inexcusable. *Because that which may be known of God, is manifest in them*, or among them; not, I apprehend, by any light of nature, which comes with every man into the world, as some suppose; for the fallen soul is darkness itself; but *God hath shewed it unto them*, by the traditionary notices delivered down from the beginning, and by the works of creation and providence, which confirm and

and evidence the truth of the being and glory of the eternal Jehovah, whose *invisible things*, his divine perfections, his eternal power and Godhead, his self-existence, incorporeal nature, infinite wisdom and goodness, *are clearly seen, being understood by the things that are made*: the intellectual faculties contemplating the visible objects, and man himself (ποιημα) the most remarkable creature upon earth, might *from the creation of the world* receive the fullest confirmation of what God had shewed unto men concerning himself.

2 They notwithstanding fell into the grossest and most inexcusable idolatry. *When they knew God*, had some notions of his being and attributes, and might have obtained clearer discoveries had they attended to the means of instruction which he afforded them, *they glorified him not as God*, neither in their hearts, their worship, or their conduct, regarding and treating him suitably to his nature and perfections, *neither were thankful*, insensible to the blessings of his providence, and imputing to second causes all the mercies which they received from the first. Hence *they became vain in their own imaginations*, indulging their fancies, and, proudly reasoning about matters which were too high for them, the philosophers set up their various systems, and in their contests and disputations for their own opinions erred alike from the truth, *and their foolish heart was darkened*, their boasted wisdom became folly, the corruption of their nature blinded their understanding, and, in the midst of the highest pretensions to science, they sunk into the most fatal depths of ignorance and error, *professing themselves to be wise*, puffed up with the conceit of their vast attainments, *they became fools*, perfect ideots in the most obvious matters respecting the divine Being and worship, *and*, instead of a Spirit immortal, invisible, eternal, they *changed the glory of the incorruptible God into an image made like unto corruptible man, and to birds, and four-footed beasts, and creeping things*, so shockingly debasing his dignity, so horridly infatuated in their wild imaginations, *changing the truth of God into a lie*, ascribing to idols the honour due to Jehovah, making such false representations of him, as if he were corporeal, and worshipping and serving *the creature more than the Creator*, (παρα) *above, besides*, or *contrary* to him. Though they acknowledged a supreme Numen, their worship was chiefly directed to their inferior deities, and all the services which they paid to their idols were the greatest dishonour to God, and reflected most highly upon his being and perfections, *who is blessed for ever. Amen!* He is infinitely and necessarily blessed and glorious in himself, the only author of blessedness to all his creatures, and the alone worthy object of their worship and adoration, to whom may it be for ever rendered and ascribed!

3 In just judgment upon them for such abominable idolatry, and direct opposition to the notices he had given them concerning himself, *He gave them up*, abandoned them to their own hearts lusts, which, when his restraining grace was withdrawn, hurried them headlong into the foulest and most unnatural acts of uncleanness, the very mention of which should make us shudder with horror, and to be ignorant of the very ideas of such horrid deeds is most desireable. To commit such uncleanness with greediness was at once the filling up the measure of their iniquities, and the heavy and deserved punishment inflicted for their idolatry, *the recompence of their error which was meet*. *And as they did not like to retain God in their knowledge*, but quenched the gift he had bestowed, and acted in opposition to the knowledge he had vouchsafed to them, *God gave them up to a reprobate mind*, rejected them with abhorrence, and left them to the blindness, hardness, and malignity of their fallen hearts, *to do those things which are not convenient*, detestable to God, dishonourable to themselves, and the consequences of which must be eternally ruinous; *being filled with all unrighteousness*. And the dreadful catalogue of sins here given, *v.* 29—31 was not merely applicable to the more ignorant and unrefined part of the Gentile world, but was notoriously true of their wisest philosophers and their most refined moralists, *who knowing the judgment of God*, and having sufficient light in their consciences to discover, *that they which commit such things are worthy of death*, as transgressors against the majesty on high, yet so enslaved were they by their vile affections, that they *not only do the same* themselves, *but have pleasure in them that do them*, encourage, countenance, and take delight in others who commit the same abominations. From all which it is most evident, that men of such a character as these can never, by any work of righteousness which they can pretend to, be justified before God, but must be saved by abounding grace, or perish. *Note*, (1) Nothing is a sorer punishment than for the sinner to be given up to his own hearts lusts. (2) When God withdraws his restraint, there are no abominations into which we shall not rush headlong, as the horse rusheth into the battle. (3) When we see the dire iniquities here recorded, and behold them in the practice and temper of others, we should reflect, for our own humiliation, that our hearts are the same, our nature alike corrupt, and that, if we are restrained from the like wickedness, we owe it not to ourselves. (4) Sin against light and knowledge is most exceeding sinful, but the summit of iniquity is to take a diabolical pleasure in the wickedness of others, and to love sin for its own sake.

CHAP II

The Gentiles have been found guilty. The Jews are here shewn to be in the same condemnation. 1 He proves in general that Jews and Gentiles stand upon the same level before the justice of God, to ver 17. 2 He shews more particularly what sins the Jews were guilty of, notwithstanding their profession and vain presumptions, ver 17 to the end.

1 [a] THerefore thou art inexcuseable, O man, who-
soever thou art that judgest: for wherein thou
judgest another, thou condemnest thyself; for thou that
judgest dost the same things. 2 But we are sure that
the judgment of God is according to truth, against them
which commit such things. 3 And [b] thinkest thou this,
O man, that judgest them which do such things, and
dost the same, that thou shalt escape the judgment of
God? 4 Or despisest thou [c] the riches of his goodness,
and forbearance, and long-suffering, not knowing that
[d] the goodness of God leadeth thee to repentance? 5
But [e] after thy hardness and impenitent heart, [f] trea-
surest up unto thyself wrath against the day of wrath,
and revelation of the righteous judgment of God, 6
[g] Who will render to every man according to his deeds:
7 To them, who by patient continuance in well doing,
seek for glory, and honour, and immortality, eternal life:
8 But [h] unto them that are contentious, and do not obey
the truth, but obey unrighteousness, indignation and
wrath, 9 Tribulation and anguish upon every soul of
man that doth evil, [i] of the Jew first, and also of the
Gentile; 10 But [k] glory, honour, and peace to every
man that worketh good, to the Jew first, and also to the
Gentile: 11 For [l] there is no respect of persons with
God. 12 For [m] as many as have sinned without law,
shall also perish without law: and as many as have sin-
ned in the law, shall be judged by the law; 13 (For
[n] not the hearers of the law are just before God, but the
doers of the law shall be justified. 14 For when the
Gentiles which have not the law, do by nature the things
contained in the law, these, having not the law, are a
law unto themselves: 15 Which shew the work of the
law written in their hearts, their conscience also bearing
witness, and † *their* thoughts the mean while accusing,
or else excusing one another) 16 In the day when [o] God
shall judge the secrets of men [p] by Jesus Christ, [q] accord-
ing to my gospel.

v. 1—16 Nothing could be urged against the profane Gentiles which the Jews would not with satisfaction admit. But, whilst they judged them, they in fact condemned themselves, being chargeable with the same abominations, and that with more aggravated guilt because of their superior advantages. To them therefore the apostle addresses himself, and proves them most inexcusable in their censures, and liable to the same wrath of a justly offended God.

1 They were guilty of the same sins which the Gentiles committed, yet flattered themselves that they should escape the judgment of God. But it was folly in them to promise themselves impunity, when the God of truth and judgment had fully declared his determined purpose to punish such workers of iniquity; and all who knew the unchangeableness of his word, were sure that vengeance must overtake the transgressors, whether they were Jews or Gentiles. *Note*, (1) It is vile hypocrisy to condemn that in others which we allow and practise ourselves. (2) God's judgment will be according to truth, and none shall be able to object to the righteousness of his sentence, any more than they can escape from the execution of it.

2 They abused God's patience, and made the most ungrateful returns for his goodness. Presuming on the mercies they had enjoyed, the most wonderful forbearance they had experienced, and all his multiplied favours had the most direct tendency to melt down their obdurate hearts into an ingenuous frame and contrition, and to engage them to return to God; but they considered not their deep obligations, were insensible to all the wonders of his grace, and *after their hardness, and impenitent hearts, treasured up unto themselves wrath against the day of wrath, and revelation of the righteous judgment of God*, to be executed in punishment of their iniquities, as if they were heaping up the most valuable treasure. *Note*, (1) There is a day of wrath, of terrible wrath, approaching, when inexorable judgment will seize the impenitent soul. (2) In all God's decisions his righteousness will appear, and even the damned be forced to own their sentence just. (3) They are past remedy, whom the goodness of God leads not to repentance. (4) A hard and impenitent heart

a Sam. xii. ... Luke vi. 37 ... Jam. ii. 11
b Jam. i
c Eph. i. 7 & ii. 4
d Isa. xxx. 18 ... e ... 20 ...
f Amos iii. 10 Jam. v. 3
g Job xxxiv. 11 ... Mat. xvi. 27 ... 2 Cor. v. 10 ... Rev. xxii. 12
h ... The. i. 8
i Luke xii. 47
k 1 Pet. i. 7
l Deut. x. 17 Acts x. 34
m Luke xii. 48
n Mat. vii. 21 John xiii. 17 Jam. i. 22 &c.
† Or, between themselves accusing, or excusing their consciences
o Eccles. xii. 14 1 Cor. iv. 5
p John v. 22 Acts x. 42 & xvii. 31
q 2 Tim. ii. 8

heart is the greatest plague on this side of hell. (5) The time of God's patience is expiring, and abused patience will bring down the heaviest vengeance.

3. God, in his procedure at the day of judgment, will act with the greatest impartiality, rendering *to every man according to his works*. (1) *To them who by patient continuance in well-doing*, who in the persevering exercise of faith in a Redeemer, are in the use of the appointed means working out their salvation, *seek for the glory, honour, and immortality* which is brought to light in the gospel, to them God will give *eternal life*; *glory, honour, and peace*, are the assured portion secured *to every man that*, under the influence of faith and love, *worketh good*, actuated by gospel principles, and proposing as his end the divine glory. And herein there is no difference between Jew or Gentile, nor is God a respecter of one more than the other; the faithful of both denominations shall share the same blessedness; as being interested in the same divine righteousness, they shall be entitled to the same reward. (2) On the other hand, *unto them that are contentious, and do not obey the truth*, contradicting and opposing the method of divine grace revealed in the gospel, *but obey unrighteousness*, walking in unbelief, iniquity, and impenitence, *indignation and wrath, tribulation and anguish*, even all the terrors of vengeance which a righteous Judge will inflict, must be poured out *upon every man that doth evil, of the Jew first*, to whom all his outward privileges will be no protection, *and also of the Gentile*, who shall no more escape than the Jew, if he neglects the great salvation of the gospel; and each will bear their punishment according to the advantages which they have enjoyed, and the means and mercies which they have abused.

4. In judging the world, God will regard the different measures of light against which men have sinned, and will punish them according to the several aggravations of their guilt.

The Gentiles, who *have sinned without law*, must perish *without law*. They have not had indeed the same clear revelation as was made to the Jews at Sinai, but they have a law written on their hearts, some more obscure traces of God's will have been delivered down to them, and their consciences, though defiled, have some general notions of good and evil, right and wrong, truth and falsehood; by which means these heathens, though *not having the law, are a law unto themselves*; and, when they correspond in their practice with these dictates of natural conscience, their thoughts and judgment acquit and approve them, or, if they deviate therefrom, they are accused, reproached, and condemned in their own hearts. The Gentiles therefore, though not so criminal as the Jews who resist clearer manifestations of the divine will, yet cannot plead ignorance; they sin against their partial convictions, are without excuse, and God is just in executing his judgments against them.

The Jews, and *as many as have sinned in the law*, against the holy commandments which were delivered unto them, *shall be judged by the law*; and, as their sin is more aggravated, their condemnation will be more grievous. And though they valued themselves highly on their external privileges as the disciples of Moses, and thought themselves the favourites of heaven, because they were acquainted with God's law, and heard it constantly read and explained to them, they were most fatally deceived; since *not the hearers of the law are just before God, but the doers of the law shall be justified*: and, if they cannot produce a righteousness perfect and complete, so far from profiting them, the law, in which they boast themselves, denounces all its curses on their guilty heads.

In the day therefore *when God shall judge the secrets of men by Jesus Christ*, to whom all judgment is committed, *according to the gospel*, which Paul calls *my gospel*, not as if he was the author of it, but as being put in trust with it, then shall impartial justice be executed on transgressors, and according to the measure of their guilt shall be their condemnation. *Note*, (1) An awful day of judgment approaches: it highly imports every soul to enquire how they shall come and appear before God. (2) Whatever is now concealed with most cautious care shall soon be brought to light: we believe that he shall be our Judge, from whom nothing is hid, nothing is secret.

17 Behold, thou art called a Jew, and [r] restest in the
law, and [s] makest thy boast of God, 18 And [t] know-
est *his* will, and [u] approvest the things that are more ex-
cellent, being instructed out of the law; 19 And [x] art
confident that thou thyself art a guide of the blind, a
light of them *which are* in darkness, 20 An instructer
of the foolish, a teacher of babes, [y] which hast the form
of knowledge and of the truth in the law. 21 Thou
therefore which teachest another, teachest thou not thy-
self? thou that preachest a man should not steal, dost
thou steal? 22 Thou that sayest a man should not
commit adultery, [a] dost thou commit adultery? thou
that abhorrest idols, [b] dost thou commit sacrilege? 23
Thou that makest thy boast of the law, through break-
ing the law dishonourest thou God? 24 [c] For the name
of God is blasphemed among the Gentiles, through you,
as it is written. 25 For circumcision verily profiteth,
if thou keep the law: but [e] if thou be a breaker of the
law, thy circumcision is made uncircumcision. 26
Therefore, [f] if the uncircumcision keep the righteousness
of the law, shall not his uncircumcision be counted for
circumcision? 27 And [g] shall not uncircumcision which
is by nature, if it fulfil the law, judge thee, who by the
letter and circumcision dost transgress the law? 28 For
[h] he is not a Jew, which is one outwardly, neither *is that*
circumcision, which is outward in the flesh: 29 But he
is a Jew, [i] which is one inwardly; and [k] circumcision *is*
that of the heart, [l] in the spirit, *and* not in the letter;
[m] whose praise *is* not of men, but of God.

r Jer. vii. 4. Zeph. iii. 11. s Isa. xlviii. 2. Mic. iii. 11. John viii. 41. t Ps. cxlvii. 19. u Phil. i. 10. x Isa. xlii. 19. Mat. xxiii. 24. y Chap. vi. 17. 1 Tim. i. 16. Mat. xxiii. 3. a Jer. iii. 8. b Mal. iii. 8. c 2 Sam. xii. 14. Ezek. xxxvi. 20—.

e Lev. xxvi. 41. Chap. iii. 20. e Acts vii. 51. Gal. vi. 3. f Mat. viii. 10. g Mat. xii. 41. h John viii. 39. Chap. ix. 6. i 1 Pet. iii. 4. k Deut. xxx. 6. Jer. iv. 4. Col. ii. 11. l Chap. vii. 6. Phil. iii. 3. m 1 Cor. iv. 5. 2 Thes. ii. 4.

Ver. 17—29. The great rock on which the Jews split was their vain dependance on the law of Moses, when in fact that very law on which they trusted denounced indignation and wrath upon them as transgressors of it.

1. The apostle mentions various particulars in which they proudly gloried. *Behold thou art called a Jew*; they valued themselves highly on their descent from Abraham, *and restest in the law*, secure of heaven because they had Moses for their teacher, though they obeyed not his injunctions; *and makest thy boast in God*, as if peculiarly interested in him, and, exclusive of all other nations, possessing his favour and regard; *and knowest his will, and approvest the things that are more excellent, being instructed out of the law*, puffed up with the conceit of their superior knowledge of God's mind above any other people, accurate to discern truth from falsehood, professing their high estimation of the divine law, and from earliest youth (κατηχούμενος) catechised and instructed out of it; *and art confident that thou thyself art a guide of the blind, a light of them which are in darkness, an instructor of the foolish, a teacher of babes*, such high and lofty titles they assumed, when regarding their Gentile neighbours, on whom they looked down with sovereign contempt, and thought the wisest heathens were but as infants to them, and needed to come to their school to learn the elements of divine knowledge, when, in fact, all they possessed was but *a form of knowledge and of the truth in the law*; for in reality they neither understood its nature, extent, or spirituality, nor practised its precepts. *Note*, (1) External privileges rested upon, instead of improved, tend but more fatally to deceive and destroy us. (2) Unsanctified knowledge is a dangerous possession, puffing up the soul in pride, and leading it to perdition. (3) A form of sound words in our lips may impose upon men, but without the power of divine grace in the heart, all the rest is no better than sounding brass and tinkling cymbal.

2. He charges them with various crimes, the more aggravated because of the privileges in which they boasted, and the knowledge which they professed. Whilst they taught others, they never preached to their own hearts, their lives gave the lie to their instruction. They declaimed against theft, yet practised it themselves, *Matth.* xxiii. 14. and lived in the adultery they so sharply condemned in others; they testified their abhorrence of idols, yet sacrilegiously robbed God of his honour, not only withholding their tythes and offerings from his altar, but more abundantly by making void his law through their traditions; and, whilst scrupulous in trifles, neglecting the weightier matters. Thus they stood most inexcusably guilty, and by such flagrant breaches of his law, even whilst they boasted of it as their great privilege, and trusted on it as their security, they put the highest dishonour upon God, and brought the greatest reproach on their profession, giving occasion to the very Gentiles to blaspheme and speak evil of their religion, the professors of which were so infamously vile; and acting over the same part *as it is written* their fathers had done before them, *Ezek.* xxxvi. 20—23. *Note*, (1) Example influences more than precept. Indeed how can it be expected that the people should believe those, who shew by their practice that they do not believe themselves? (2) They who prove false to their professions, give the deepest stab to the cause of God and truth.

3. The apostle considers the Jewish plea of circumcision, and proves the vanity of it. It profited them, if they kept the law perfectly, to which they bound themselves thereby; but, in case of transgression, it stood them in no stead, nor were they at all more acceptable to God than an uncircumcised Gentile. And if, for argument's sake, it be supposed that a heathen should observe all the precepts of the law, would he not be an object of God's regard, as much as if he had been circumcised? and would not such a moral heathen, though uncircumcised, condemn thee a Jew, and circumcised, if he observed that law which you, though professing to hold, and by circumcision obliging yourself to keep, notwithstanding transgress? Undoubtedly he would. *Note*, The comparative exemplariness of those who enjoy less means, and make less profession of religion, will justly condemn those, who with greater advantages, and more pretension to piety, dishonour by their unfaithfulness, the holy name whereby they are called.

4 He describes the true circumcision It is not mere outward profession which seals a man a true Israelite, neither is that circumcision, which is outward in the flesh, available to any saving purpose but he is the true son of Abraham, who in faith and spirit resembles this eminent friend of God, and the true circumcision, which God regards, *is that of the heart*, purified by faith, *in the spirit, and not in the letter*, where not only a profession is made, but a real inward change is wrought by the power of the Holy Ghost, *whose praise is not of men, but of God*, it is what men cannot discern, and as they who possess it desire not human but divine approbation, their great care and concern is that they may be accepted of God *Note*, It is the heart which God regards Let us remember then, that we have to do with him, on whom the most plausible professions cannot impose

CHAP III.

Having proved the guilt both of Gentiles and Jews, the apostle in this chapter, 1 Answers some objections that might be made against what he had said about the Jews, ver 1—9 2 He asserts the guilt and corruption of mankind in common, both Jews and Gentiles, ver 9—19 3, He argues from thence, that justification must needs be by faith, and not by the law, ver 19 to the end

1 WHAT advantage then hath the Jew? or what
profit is there of circumcision? 2 Much
every way ᵃ chiefly, because that unto them were com-
mitted the oracles of God 3 For what if ᵇ some did
not believe? ᶜ shall their unbelief make the faith of God
without effect? 4 God forbid yea, ᵈ let God be true
but ᵉ every man a liar as it is written, ᶠ That thou
mightest be justified in thy sayings, and mightest over-
come when thou art judged 5 But if ᵍ our unrighte-
ousness commend the righteousness of God, what shall
we say? Is God unrighteous who taketh vengeance?
(I speak as a man) 6 God forbid for then ʰ how shall
God judge the world? 7 For if the truth of God hath
more abounded through my lie unto his glory, why yet
am I also judged as a sinner? 8 And not *rather*, (as
we be slanderously reported, and as some affirm that we
say) ⁱ Let us do evil that good may come? whose dam-
nation is just 9 What then? are we better *than they*?
No, in no wise for we have before † proved both Jews
and Gentiles, that ᵏ they are all under sin, 10 ˡ As it
is written, There is none righteous, no not one 11
There is none that understandeth, there is none that seek-
eth after God 12 They are all gone out of the way,
they are altogether become unprofitable, there is none
that doth good, no not one 13 ᵐ Their throat is an
open sepulchre, with their tongues they have used de-
ceit, ⁿ the poison of asps is under their lips 14 ᵒ Whose
mouth is full of cursing and bitterness 15 ᵖ Their feet
are swift to shed blood 16 Destruction and misery *are*
in their ways 17 And the way of peace have they
not known 18 ᑫ There is no fear of God before their
eyes

a Deut iv 8 Ps cxlvii 19 Chap ix 4 b Heb iv 2 c Numb xxiii 19 Chap ix 6 2 Tim ii 13 d John iii 33 e Ps lxxxvi 11 & cxvi 11 f Ps li 4 g Chap v 8 h Gen xviii 25 Job viii 3 i Chap vi 1 15 † Gr charged k Gal iii 22 l Ps xiv 1—3 & liii 1—3 m Ps v 9 n Ps cxl 3 o Ps x 7 p Prov i 16 Isai lix 7, 8 q Ps xxxvi 1

ver 1—18 The apostle proceeds to answer the objections raised against the doctrine he had advanced, and to confirm the truth which he had asserted

1 He answers the objections raised against his positions

(1) If the Jews are thus in the same condemnation as the Gentiles, what advantage have they, notwithstanding the peculiar favours shewn them of God, and the divinely instituted rites, particularly circumcision, which he appointed them? The apostle answers, *Much every way chiefly because that unto them were committed the oracles of God* In the law and the prophets they had the most blessed means vouchsafed them to come to the knowledge of the truth, and especially of that Messiah who was the sum and substance of the oracles of God and it was also their honour to be intrusted with the keeping of these sacred records Their advantages therefore above the Gentiles were very great and singular *Note*, Among our most invaluable blessings we should always reckon our Bibles, for in them we have eternal life revealed to us

(2) If it be objected to this, that, though the Jews had the oracles of God, *some did not believe*, admit it But what then? *Shall their unbelief make the faith of God without effect?* Shall the faithful God, because of the infidelity of some, fail of fulfilling his promise to Abraham and his spiritual seed, who trust upon him according to his word? *God forbid!* His word must be accomplished, and his promises are sure *Yea, let God be true*, let it be for ever acknowledged that he is so, *but let every man*, who dare dispute his veracity and truth, know that he must be found *a liar* Men are inconstant, deceitful, and vain, no confidence is to be placed in them, but God never can nor will deceive us *as it is written, That thou mightest be justified in thy sayings, and mightest overcome when thou art judged*, as David acknowledged, *Ps* li 4 for, notwithstanding his foul falls and great unfaithfulness, God would not alter the word which was gone out of his mouth concerning that Messiah who should spring from his loins And he will for ever stand clear of all imputations which foolish men may cast upon him, and be found faithful and true, though we presumptuously dare arraign his righteousness, or censure his conduct

(3) But some perverse Jew may say, whose character I will personate, speaking *as such a man*, *If our unrighteousness commend the righteousness of God*, and he gains glory by our wickedness and unbelief, both glorifying his justice in our punishment, and his grace in calling the Gentile sinners in our stead, and justifying them by the righteousness of his son, *what shall we say? Is not God unrighteous* (*ὁ ἐπιφέρων τὴν ὀργήν*) *who taketh vengeance* for that unbelief and unrighteousness, which serves at the last more eminently to display the lustre of his divine perfections, his truth, holiness, and grace? With abhorrence the apostle rejects the insinuation *God forbid! for then how shall God judge the world?* If he were not infinitely righteous in his nature, he would be unfit for this high office and if he, by his over-ruling providence, brings good out of evil, and magnifies his grace more eminently where sin hath most abounded, sin hath not therefore the less evil or malignity, nor hath the sinner ought to plead, since he designs nothing less than the divine glory

(4) But the same carnal Jew, whom I have personated before, may further urge, *If the truth of God hath more abounded through my lie unto his glory*, and my unbelief, which gives the lie to his promises, and my wickedness, which gives the lie to my profession, serves to magnify his veracity, *why yet am I also judged as a sinner?* and punished for transgressions that serve rather to magnify God than to dishonour him? *and may we not rather* abandon ourselves to evil, in order that *good may come?* and God's grace and truth receive greater glory in justifying those who believe on his Son? And such malicious and blasphemous reports are spread by our Jewish enemies, who confidently affirm that this is the doctrine which we as apostles preach, and as Christians believe But we abhor the suggestion, and declare to such slanderers of us and the truth, and to all who dare thus abuse the holy doctrines of grace, that their *damnation is just*, and inevitable *Note*, (1) The best of ministers and of men have had the foulest aspersions cast on them, and been charged with holding the most abhorred blasphemies (2) The injured characters of his ambassadors God will avenge (3) They who abuse the doctrines of grace, as arguments for licentiousness, will perish with most aggravated guilt

2 The apostle returns, after confuting the Jewish objections, to the main point in debate, whether Jews, as well as Gentiles, were not all under sin *Are we better than they? No, in no wise for we have before proved* at large in the two former chapters, *that both Jews and Gentiles are all under sin*, condemned by the guilt, enslaved by the power, and liable to the eternal wrath which is the wages of sin, so that all need a better righteousness than their own to justify them before God And to enforce this truth, the apostle quotes the Scriptures, which the Jews admitted, as containing the fullest proof of his assertion God declares, *Ps* xiv 1 *that there is none righteous*, according to the perfect demands of his holy law, *no not one* so corrupted is our nature, *that there is none that understandeth*, the human mind is darkened, and cannot discover or receive the things that be of the Spirit of God, *there is none that seeketh after God*, no one good disposition remaining in the natural heart, nor desire after communion with God, but evil, and only evil, and that continually Hence of all men the Psalmist asserts, that *they are all gone out of the way*, following the bent of their native corruption, *they are altogether become unprofitable*, bringing forth no fruit to God's glory, *there is none that doth good, no not one* And the foul streams which flow from this polluted fountain are described in other places of the Scripture *their throat is an open sepulchre*, voracious and insatiable in the pursuits of their lusts and covetousness, *with their tongues they have used deceit*, flattering, false, faithless, *the poison of asps is under their lips*, secretly, artfully, incurably, does their tongue drop the malignant venom, to blast the fame or destroy the life of their neighbour, *whose mouth is full of cursing and bitterness*, blaspheming God himself, and shooting out their bitter words of rancour and reviling against the people and the good ways of the Lord, *their feet are swift to shed blood*, every member of their body is a ready instrument of iniquity, *destruction and misery are in their ways*, and wherever they go they mark their path with mischief, spreading their wickedness as a plague, pestilential to others, and at last bringing perdition on themselves, *and the way of peace have they not known*, strangers to whatever would conduce to their own peace and happiness both here and hereafter, disturbing, as far as they can, by their malignity and perverseness, the peace of mankind *there is no fear of God before their eyes*, destitute of every gracious principle and this, as it is the root of all their wickedness, so it is the summit of all their ungodliness, they leave God far above out of their sight And such being the divine description of every man by nature, declared by him

who

who searcheth the heart, and knoweth what is in man, the universal guilt and desperate wickedness of the whole human race, both Jews and Gentiles, cannot but be most evident Whilst we read the dreadful charge, may we be led to a humbling acknowledgment of the truth, and from the deepest heart-felt conviction be laid in the dust, submitting wholly to the righteousness of God!

19 Now we know that what things soever the law
saith, it saith to them who are under the law that
every mouth may be stopped, and all the world may
become guilty before God 20 Therefore by the deeds
of the law there shall no flesh be justified in his
sight for by the law is the knowledge of sin 21
But now the righteousness of God without the law
is manifested, being witnessed by the law and the
prophets, 22 Even the righteousness of God, which is
by faith of Jesus Christ unto all, and upon all them
that believe, for there is no difference 23 For all
have sinned, and come short of the glory of God; 24
Being justified freely by his grace, through the redemp-
tion that is in Jesus Christ 25 Whom God hath
set forth to be a propitiation through faith in his
blood, to declare his righteousness for the remission of
sins that are past, through the forbearance of God, 26
To declare, *I say*, at this time his righteousness, that he
might be just, and the justifier of him which believeth
in Jesus 27 Where is boasting then? It is excluded
By what law? of works? Nay but by the law of
faith 28 Therefore we conclude, that a man is justi-
fied by faith without the deeds of the law 29 *Is he* the
God of the Jews only? *Is he* not also of the Gen-
tiles? Yes, of the Gentiles also 30 Seeing *it is* one
God which shall justify the circumcision by faith, and
uncircumcision through faith 31 Do we then make
void the law through faith? God forbid yea, we esta-
blish the law.

v 19—31 The apostle proceeds to apply the truths which he had advanced and proved

1 *All the World* is become guilty before God, and no flesh can be justified in God's sight by the deeds of the law, because *all have sinned and come short of the glory of God*, have come short of righteousness, and therefore of heaven, *v* 23 According to the several dispensations under which they have lived, the law speaketh both to Jews and Gentiles, and condemns them as transgressors, The Gentiles have offended against those precepts of the moral law, which God, though more obscurely, hath shewed them And the Jews, against the clearer revelation, which in the Scriptures they have enjoyed, so that *every mouth must be stopped*, and guilt evident and confessed appear upon every living soul *For by the law is the knowledge of sin*, so far from being able to justify any man, it is the glass that can only shew him his deformity, the strait rule to mark his sad deviations from it *Note*, (1) Man in his nature is become *flesh*, fallen and corrupted, and therefore it is impossible that, in his present ruined state, he should be just before God (2) The law is designed to discover sin to the conscience, not to justify any, but to convince all men of the necessity of a better righteousness than their own to appear in before God (3) All flesh must plead guilty at God's bar, and no man can possibly be saved, till he hath seen, felt, and owned that he hath deserved most justly to be damned

2 To those who, from the conviction which the law brings to their consciences, are driven to despair of acceptance with God, on account of any doings and duties of their own, the gospel reveals the method of divine grace, appointed and provided for the sinner's justification before God *But now*, since all hope is fled of obtaining favour with God on the footing of our own obedience, *the righteousness of God*, that divine righteousness which God incarnate wrought out, and which God the Father accepts on our behalf, *without the law*, which the moral law never discovered, but required personal, not imputed righteousness, and which is complete, exclusive of all respect to any obedience of ours to the law, *is manifested* in the person of Jesus Christ, and by the preaching of the gospel, *being witnessed by* all the types and figures of the ceremonial *law*, *and by the prophets*, *Isai* xlv 24, 25 *Jer* xxiii 6 *Dan* ix 24 So that even during the time that the Mosaical dispensation lasted, the Jews were taught to look for a better righteousness than that which they could obtain by the deeds of the law, *even the righteousness of God*, of our divine substitute and surety, who for us men and our salvation became obedient unto death even the death of the cross, and which is now received *by faith in* this adored redeemer *Jesus Christ*, and judicially made over, and reckoned to the account of every soul who, renouncing every other hope, lays hold on this set before him, and it is *unto all and upon all them that believe*, whether Jew or Gentile, *for there is no difference*, they alike need it, as having all sinned and come short of God's glory, and he freely bestows it on them without any regard to the degrees of their guilt, or the different measures of their faith, the weakest believer, though the chief of sinners, being freely, fully, and everlastingly justified before God thro' this divine righteousness Nor is there the least moving cause in any of us to engage God to have respect to us, We lie in one promiscuous mass of corruption till *justified freely by his Grace*, by his sovereign and undeserved mercy, *through the redemption which is in Jesus Christ*, who by his obedience unto death paid down the invaluable price of our redemption, which doth not at all affect the riches of the grace respecting us, though bought with his blood, it is sovereignly and freely imputed to our account, and we owe it to God's boundless mercy, that he provided, qualified, and accepted our glorious surety, and freely gave him up for us all *Whom God hath set forth*, predestinating him in his eternal counsels, and in the fulness of time sending him in the human nature, *to be a propitiation*, to be the one great propitiatory sacrifice, that *through faith in his blood*, the chief of sinners might boldly approach a throne of grace And hereby, (1) The best of blessings is secured to us, even *the remission of sins that are past, through the forbearance of God* The sacrifices under the law were insufficient to take away sin, the faithful therefore under the Old Testament had recourse to this atoning blood which in the fulness of time should be shed, and in the view thereof God bore with them, pardoned and accepted them And we are ultimately indebted to this blood, that speaks before the throne, and to the forbearance of God with us, in consequence thereof, that we have not through our repeated provocations been cut off long since, as we have deserved, and cast into hell for our sins (2) Hereby the greatest honour redounds to God, for in this his method of dealing with sinners, he shews and demonstrates *his own righteousness*, both the glory of his justice in the punishment of sin, and the transcendent excellence and perfection of the Redeemer's righteousness, by means of which, consistent with the divine glory, an honourable provision was made for the pardon of sin, and neither God's truth, justice, or holiness impeached by the grace extended to the sinner so that *at this time*, under the gospel dispensation, he *declares his righteousness*, *that he might be just*, *and* withal, *the justifier of him which believeth in Jesus* Never was God's displeasure against sin more awfully displayed than when he laid upon his son the iniquities of us all. Having exacted from him the debt of suffering, it is now become an act of justice that we should be discharged, our surety's obedience being accepted in our stead, we have by right a title to the divine favour (3) Hereby all boasting is excluded from the sons of men, none can say he is accepted before God on account of any works of righteousness done by him, or foreseen in him, all are excluded *By what Law? Of works? Nay, but by the law of faith*, by that gracious evangelical dispensation, wherein the blood and righteousness of God our Redeemer are proposed as the only meritorious cause of the sinner's acceptance.

The conclusion then from the above premises is evident, that a man is and can be justified before God in no other way than *by faith only*, *without the deeds of the law*, the only justifying righteousness being that of the Saviour which faith apprehends, and exclusive of all other considerations, whether of our duties or our sin, entitles the believer to the favour of God

3 This privilege of free justification, through a Redeemer's righteousness, is common to the Gentile as well as Jew Is God then in this new dispensation of his grace in the gospel of his dear son, *the God of the Jews only? or peculiarly? Is he not of the Gentiles also? Yes, of the Gentiles also* It is a common salvation, and both are alike freely invited to partake of it *Seeing it is one God which shall justify the circumcision by faith, and the uncircumcision through faith*, both Jews and Gentiles standing exactly on the same footing, without respect of persons, or any difference in the way of their acceptance.

4 He concludes with obviating an objection, which some might raise, as if he hereby *made void the* moral *law*, the eternal rule of righteousness, as useless and insignificant, but he rejects with detestation the suggestion, *God forbid! Yea*, so far from making it void, we *establish the law* It remains the same as ever to convince of sin, to be not a covenant of life, but a rule of obedience, and that faith which shews it magnified in the highest, by the perfect righteousness of our Redeemer, as it works by love, is the most powerful principle to engage our hearts to delight in the law of God after the inner man, and to run the way of his commandments walking in the glorious liberty of the children of God, a liberty, not to transgress, but to obey

CHAP IV

Nothing could serve so effectually to prove the argument he advanced, as to prove that Abraham in whom the Jews so highly gloried, was justified by faith only The apostle therefore, in this chapter, 1 enters into the evidence of this fact, ver 1—8 2 *He observes when and why Abraham was so justified*, ver 9—17 3 *He describes*

describes and commends that faith of his, ver 17—22 4 *He applies all this to us*, ver 23—25

a [illegible] 1 WHAT shall we say then, a that Abraham our
Phil. iii 4 father, as pertaining to the flesh, hath found?
b Chap iii 27 Eph ii 9 2 For b if Abraham were justified by works, he hath
whereof to glory, but not before God 3 For what
c Gen xv 6 Gal iii 6 Jam ii 23 saith the scripture? c Abraham believed God, and it
was counted unto him for righteousness 4 Now
d Matt xx 7 d to him that worketh, is the reward reckoned not of grace
Chap xi 6 but of debt 5 But e to him that worketh not, but
e Josh xxiv 2 Chap v 6 believeth on him that justifieth the ungodly, his
faith is counted for righteousness. 6 Even as David
also describeth the blessedness of the man unto whom
f Ps xxxii 1, 2 God imputeth righteousness without works 7 f *Saying*,
Blessed are they whose iniquities are forgiven, and whose
sins are covered 8 Blessed *is* the man to whom the
Lord will not impute sin

v 1—8 Abraham was the renowned ancestor, on their descent from whom the Jews so highly prided themselves If therefore it can be made appear, that he who was so eminent for his obedience was justified not by works but by faith, then surely none of his descendants, who came so short of his excellent character, may expect to be justified in any other way

What shall we say then, that Abraham our father, as pertaining to the flesh, hath found? Did he obtain justification by the efforts of his natural wisdom and strength, or by circumcision, or his other outward privileges and performances? No, in nowise For,

1 If he were justified by works, he might have had room for boasting, but whatever excellence there was in his character before men, he had nothing whereof *to glory before God* for in the Lord alone can we be justified or permitted to glory Therefore, when speaking of Abraham, the Scripture expressly observes, *Gen* xv 6 *Abraham believed God, and it was counted to him for righteousness*, that which he believed respecting the promised seed, who should suffer and obey in his stead, was reckoned to his account, as the ground of his justification and righteousness before God, and not any doings or duties of his own so that he had no room for glorying, except in the Lord his righteousness

2 If Abraham were justified by works, his reward would have been of debt, not of grace, for perfect obedience would have entitled any man to eternal life but God called Abraham when he was (ασεβη) an ungodly idolatrous heathen, and justified him through faith in the promised Messiah *And to him that worketh not*, who is utterly unable to perform that perfect righteousness which God requires, *but believeth on him that justifieth the ungodly*, conscious that this is his character, and perceiving the absolute necessity of a better righteousness than his own, even that which God hath provided in his Son, *his faith*, not the act, but the object of it, the righteousness of Jesus Christ, is counted and *imputed to him* for his justifying *righteousness* and title to God's favour If Abraham then must be justified as an ungodly sinner, as one *that worketh not*, it would be strange presumption in his descendants, or any others, to expect justification in any other way

3 He argues the necessity of free justification from the declarations of the psalmist, who describes him as the truly blessed man, not who hath no sins to answer for, but who hath them not imputed to him, being justified from them all by the free grace of God, *without* any *works* of his own, of whatever kind, to recommend him to the divine regard Indeed how else could he regard us, since all have sinned, are chargeable with iniquity, and liable to wrath? But God forgives, covers, doth not impute our sins to us, but to our surety, and reckons his righteousness to our account, and this is the ground of all true blessedness in time or eternity From hence flow forgiveness of sin, admission to God's favour, and a title to the eternal inheritance and blessed indeed and happy are they, who through a Redeemer are thus justified from all things, and shall never more enter into condemnation !

9 *Cometh* this blessedness then upon the circumcision *only*, or upon the uncircumcision also? For we
say that faith was reckoned to Abraham for righteous-
ness. 10 How was it then reckoned, when he was
in circumcision, or in uncircumcision? not in circum-
g Gen xvii 11 cision, but in uncircumcision 11 And g he received the
sign of circumcision, a seal of the righteousness of the
h Luke xix 9 Ver 17, 18 Gal iii 7 faith, which *he had yet* being uncircumcised h that he
might be the father of all them that believe, though
they be not circumcised, that righteousness might be
imputed unto them also 12 And the father of circum-
cision to them who are not of the circumcision only, but
also walk in the steps of that faith of our father Abraham,
which *he had* being *yet* uncircumcised

v 9—12 The blessedness above described is, no doubt, most desirable, the question is, to whom it belongs? Is it peculiar to the circumcised Jews, or common to the uncircumcised Gentiles? The former would fain monopolize it as the sole privilege of those, who were within the pale of circumcision, but the gospel declares the uncircumcised Gentiles alike capable of receiving it

It was faith, the object of it, even the divine righteousness of a Redeemer, not circumcision, which was Abraham's justifying righteousness, as hath before been shewn This was imputed to him, and in consequence thereof he was a justified man, fourteen years before he was circumcised It is evident therefore that when he afterwards submitted to this instituted ordinance of God, and received *the sign of circumcision*, it was not in order to his being justified, since that he had been long before, but as *a seal of the righteousness of the faith which he had, being yet uncircumcised*, a visible token that God had taken him and his seed into the bond of the covenant, and an assurance to him of all the blessings which were to be procured by that Redeemer in whom he had believed Thus, in this eminent instance of him, who bore the distinguished title of father of the faithful, and from whom the Messiah should spring in whom all nations were to be blessed, the Gentiles, though uncircumcised, might behold the way of justification freely opened to them, and stand in the nearest relation to Abraham, whose faith they followed, as his spiritual children, and though they were not his natural descendants, might share in all his most distinguished blessings, through that *righteousness* which should be *imputed unto them also*, in like manner as it was to him, during his uncircumcised state

And herein also God shewed to the Jews, that it was not their being the natural descendants of Abraham, and partakers of circumcision with him, which entitled them to pardon, but that the distinguishing privileges of that covenant of grace into which Abraham was admitted, belonged only to those *who walked in the steps of that faith of our father Abraham which he had, being yet uncircumcised*, and without which, circumcision, and all their other duties and performances, would never procure for them *justification to life*

13 For i the promise that he should be the heir of the i Gen. xii 3 & xv 6 & xvii 10 Gal iii 16
world, *was* not to Abraham, or to his seed through the
law, but through the righteousness of faith 14 For
if they which are of the law be heirs, faith is made void,
and the promise made of none effect. 15 Because k the law k Chap [illegible]
worketh wrath for where no law is, *there is* no trans-
gression 16 Therefore *it is* of faith, that *it might be* [illegible] Gal iii
by grace, to the end m the promise might be sure to all 1 John iv 10
the seed, not to that only which is of the law, but to that [illegible] Chap
also which is of the faith of Abraham, who is the father [illegible]
of us all, 17 (As it is written, n I have made thee m Chap. iii 3 & xv 6
a father of many nations) before him whom he be- n Gen xvii 5
lieved, *even* o God who quickneth the dead, and o Heb xi 12
calleth those things which be not as though they were o Chap [illegible] 11
18 p Who against hope believed in hope, that he might p Gen xv 5, 6
become the father of many nations according to that
which was spoken, So shall thy seed be 19 And
being not weak in faith, q he considered not his own q Gen xvii 17 & xviii 11 Heb xi 11, 12
body now dead, when he was about an hundred years
old, neither yet the deadness of Sarah's womb 20 He
staggered not at the promise of God through unbelief,
but was strong in faith, giving glory to God 21 And
being fully persuaded, that what he had promised, he r Heb [illegible]
was able also to perform 22 And therefore it was im-
puted to him for righteousness

v 13—22 As circumcision was not a justifying righteousness to Abraham, nor to any of his seed, neither was the law, in which the Jewish people trusted *For the promise, that he should be heir of the world*, inheriting all true blessedness both here and hereafter, *was not to Abraham or to his seed through the law* of Moses, which was not yet given, nor in virtue of any personal obedience of his or theirs, *but through the righteousness of faith For if they which are of the law be heirs*, and the title to the blessings promised arose from the fulfilling the law, whether that of Moses or any other, *then faith is made void*, there is no place for the exercise of it, *and the promise is of no effect*, since the inheritance would depend on our obedience, and if that were not perfect, the promise would be useless, which must necessarily be the case in our present corrupted state, *because the law worketh wrath*, and can only deliver over every man to the righteous judgment of God, as transgressor Had there indeed been no law given, had no notice of God's will, traditionary or revealed, been afforded, there would have been no conscience of sin, *for where no law is there is no transgression*, but now that there is a law, the offender is obnoxious to the curse, which is the sanction annexed to the transgression of it *Therefore*, since none by their obedience to any law, moral or ceremonial, could possibly be entitled to the promised blessing, God so ordained,

tha

that it should be *of faith, that it might be of grace*, that the promise, and all the blessings contained in it, of pardon, adoption, and eternal life, might appear to be given of God's mere goodness and sovereign pleasure, without the least desert on our part, faith stretching out its empty hand to receive the inestimable treasure, and that faith too the gift of God, that it might be wholly of grace, *to the end that the promise might be sure*, and notwithstanding our unworthiness, secured to us in our divine substitute and covenant head Christ Jesus, independent of any obedience of our own for such is our frailty and corruption, that if it depended upon our own obedience as the condition of it, not a moment could we be sure of it, but now it is infallibly ascertained *to all the seed*, to the spiritual seed of Abraham, even all true believers, *not to that only which is of the law*, who live under the Mosaical dispensation, *but to that also which is of the faith of Abraham*, though Gentiles by birth and profession, yet through faith become, in God's account, the children of this eminent patriarch, *who is the father of us all*, whether believing Jews or Gentiles, *as it is written, I have made thee a father of many nations* in a spiritual sense, *before him whom he believed, even God*, was he thus reputed as the father of nations, even before him *who quickneth the dead*, Abraham and his wife, whose bodies were now as good as dead, or the Gentiles dead in trespasses and sins, or the bodies of the deceased in the last day *and* who in virtue of his almighty power, *calleth the things which be not as though they were*, since whatever he wills, at his word starts into being Persuaded of this, notwithstanding all the difficulties which his faith had to encounter, *Abraham against hope*, if reason were consulted, *believed in hope*, and against all arguments which sense or experience urged, he rested satisfied in the fulfilment of the promise, *that he should become the father of many nations, according to that which was spoken*, Gen xv 5 when, pointing him to the stars, God assured him, *so shall thy seed be*, so numberless, so illustrious Having this divine promise, he staggered not a moment through any improbabilities which unbelief might suggest, from the consideration of his own great age, which, with regard to his having children, rendered his body as if already dead, nor at *the deadness of Sarah's womb*, long since past child bearing, *but was strong in faith, giving glory to God*, with the fullest assurance expecting the fulfilment of what God *had promised, and was able also to perform* And *therefore it was imputed to him for righteousness*, and what he saw about to be done by the promised seed, Christ Jesus, was now reckoned to his account, and he stood thereby justified before God *Note*, (1) Where God hath promised, whatever objections carnal reason and unbelief may make, it is our wisdom to turn a deaf ear to every suggestion, and confidently wait the accomplishment of his word, and this gives God the highest glory (2) Though unbelief will war against the soul, yet in every child of Abraham faith will get the victory

23 [a] Now it was not written for his sake alone, that
it was imputed to him, 24 But for us also, to whom it
shall be imputed, if we believe on him [t] who raised up
Jesus our Lord from the dead, 25 [u] Who was deli-
vered for our offences, and [x] was raised again for our
justification

v 23—25 Great was the faith of the patriarch, great the honour put upon him thereby But this record borne to him of his acceptance before God was not written *for his sake alone*, historically to inform us of that which rendered him so eminent, *but for us also*, as a pattern, comfort, and encouragement to us, and an assurance that the same divine righteousness shall be imputed to us, for our justification, if we, as true sons of the father of the faithful, believe as he did, *on him that raised up Jesus Christ our Lord from the dead, who*, as our substitute and surety, *was delivered for our offences*, to bear our sins in his own body on the tree, and, by his obedience unto death, to bring in an everlasting righteousness, *and*, having so done, *was raised again for our justification*, who, in virtue of his finished work, are now by faith in him entitled to pardon, acceptance, and eternal life *Note*, There is but one justifying righteousness before God, even that of Jesus Christ In that Abraham stood accepted, and all his seed must look for no other

CHAP V

The apostle having made out his point, and fully proved justification by faith, doth in this chapter proceed in the explication, illustration, and application of that truth (1) He shews the fruits of justification, ver 1—11 (2) He shews the fountain and foundation of justification in the death and righteousness of Jesus Christ, which he discourseth of at large in the rest of the chapter

1 THerefore [a] being justified by faith, [b] we have
peace with God through our Lord Jesus Christ
2 [c] By whom also we have access by faith into this
grace wherein we stand, [d] and rejoice in hope of the
glory of God 3 And not only so, but [e] we glory in
tribulations also, [f] knowing that tribulation worketh
patience 4 [g] And patience, experience and experi-
ence, hope 5 [h] And hope maketh not ashamed, be-
cause [i] the love of God is shed abroad in our hearts by
the Holy Ghost which is given unto us

v 1—5 The sinner's justification before God through faith being set forth, the blessed effects of it are here described Not that faith is the meritorious cause of our justification, as any act of our own, or any work of grace wrought in us, *but we are justified by faith*, as the means whereby we receive the righteousness of Jesus as our own, and thereby appear complete in him And being now justified,

1 *We have peace with God* The dreadful breach which sin had made is repaired, the enmity between God and us is removed, and being restored to a state of favour and reconciliation with him, we have that peace of God in our souls which passeth all understanding, and which none can know or taste till they have, through Jesus Christ our Lord, received the atonement, and seen the arms of everlasting love stretched out to receive their sinful souls

2 *We have*, by him, *access into this grace wherein we stand*, have freedom and liberty to approach a throne of grace, as abiding in a state of constant acceptance before God, and are assured that all our requests shall, through our great high priest, be always heard and answered

3 We *rejoice in the hope of the glory of God*, that glory which shall be revealed in us, at the day of the appearing of our great God and Saviour Jesus Christ, which being secured to us by the promises of the unchangeable God, and our title clear through the divine righteousness of the Redeemer, we can even now antedate by faith our blessedness, and rejoice in the purchased possession prepared for us in heaven

4 Even our severest trials now have in them matter of abundant joy *And* we can *not only* rejoice in the prospect before us, *but we glory in tribulations also*, in all our afflictions, persecutions, sufferings, and reproaches for Christ, *knowing that*, however grievous to flesh and blood these things at present may be, in the issue they shall prove blessings in disguise, whilst *tribulation worketh patience*, and gives us an opportunity to exercise submission to God's holy will, and, without repining, cheerfully to resign ourselves into his hands, neither angry at the instruments of our troubles, nor resenting their indignities *And patience* brings *experience* of God's power, grace and faithfulness, supporting us under our trials, and extricating us out of them; and of our own frailty and fidelity, whilst we feel how weak we are in ourselves, yet that we can do all things through Christ strengthening us *And experience* begets *hope*, every support he ministers, every deliverance which he gives, confirms and encourages our hope in God, *and hope maketh not ashamed*, will never disappoint nor deceive us, *because the love of God is shed abroad in our hearts, by the Holy Ghost which is given unto us*, and our hope rests not on any goodness, or strength in ourselves, but on the sovereign, free, and boundless love, which, in the most copious streams, is poured forth by the Holy Ghost into our hearts, in the richest manifestations, and produces these blessed and happy effects

6 For when [k] we were yet without strength, in due
time [l] Christ died for the ungodly 7 For scarcely for
a righteous man will one die yet [m] peradventure for a
good man some would even dare to die 8 But [n] God
commendeth his love towards us, in that while we were
yet sinners Christ died for us 9 Much more then be-
ing now justified by his blood, we shall be saved [o] from
wrath through him 10 For if when we were enemies,
[p] we were reconciled to God by the death of his Son
much more being reconciled, [q] we shall be saved by his
life 11 And not only so, but we also joy in God,
through our Lord Jesus Christ, by whom we have [r] now
received the atonement

v 6—11 The apostle having mentioned that delightful theme, the love of God which is in Christ Jesus our Lord, cannot but expatiate thereon It is amazing love, if we consider the persons to whom it is shewn, the manner in which it is expressed, and the blessings thence derived (1) The *persons* were ungodly wretches, apostates from God, desperately wicked, sunk in the lowest abyss of misery, *sinners* in nature, in practice, and exposed to all the terrible wrath of an offended God, *without strength* to afford ourselves the least relief, or to take a single step, in order to escape the just and inevitable destruction which was before us, yea, *enemies*, determinately set on evil, and rebels, open and avowed against God's crown and dignity (2) In this state of deadly guilt and hopeless misery, *in due time*, according to the divine appointment, *Christ died for the ungodly*, an instance of such transcendant grace and love, as never had appeared on earth before Were we to search the world through-

out,

out, scarce could we find a man who, for the most righteous, excellent, and amiable person, would lay down his own life or risk it for him *though peradventure for a good man*, whose public usefulness was eminent, or to whom he owed the deepest obligations, one might be found so generous and grateful, as even to dare to die in his stead And with what astonishment would such an heroic action be heard, and preserved in the records of fame, for the admiration of all succeeding ages! But lo! with infinitely transcending glory doth God commend the surpassing excellence of *his love towards us, in that while we were yet sinners Christ died for us*, took our nature, stood in our place, endured the curse which we had deserved, and by the ransom of his own blood redeemed us from our state of guilt, misery, and despair Hear it, ye angels, with admiration and astonishment! Hear it, ye sinful sons of men, with wonder and love, and henceforth let heaven echo and earth resound with the praises of redeeming love! (3) Inestimable are the blessings derived to us through this love of God in Jesus Christ

1 We *are now justified through his blood*, and *reconciled* to God *by his death* All the enmity between us is done away, his favour is restored, and we are accepted in the beloved

2 Much more then may be depended upon it, as a most assured truth, that if we are now justified before God, *we shall be saved from wrath through him*, shall never enter again into condemnation, but shall hold fast the most assured hope of eternal life *For if when enemies, we were reconciled to God by the death of his Son, much more being* now in a state of *reconciliation*, and having an everlasting advocate in our ascended Jesus, to whom all power is given in heaven and in earth, *shall we be saved by his life* Because he lives, we shall live also, and reign with him in glory everlasting

3 Such a prospect ministers the most enlivened delight to the soul *Not only* are we reconciled, and raised superior to all tribulations, but having *through Jesus Christ now received the atonement*, and being actually made partakers of the justification, acceptance, and title to glory, which, by his obedience to death, he purchased for us, we *joy in God through our Lord Jesus Christ*, as our God for ever and ever, our portion and exceeding great reward, in whose present and eternal favour we have a sure and indefeasible interest. Blessed and happy the people that are in such a case!

r Gen iii 6 Chap vi 23 1 Cor xv 21 † Or in whom t Chap iv 15 1 John iii 4 u 1 Cor xv 22, 45

12 Wherefore, r as by one man sin entered into the
world, and death by sin and so death passed upon all
men, † for that all have sinned 13 For until the law
sin was in the world, but t sin is not imputed when
there is no law 14 Nevertheless, death reigned from
Adam to Moses, even over them that had not sinned
after the similitude of Adam's transgression, u who is the
figure of him that was to come 15 But not as the
offence, so also *is* the free gift For if through the offence
of one, many be dead, much more the grace of God,
and the gift by grace, *which is* by one man, Jesus
Christ, hath abounded x unto many 16 And not as
it was by one that sinned, *so is* the gift for the judgment
was by one to condemnation, but the free gift *is*
of many offences unto justification. 17 For if by one
man's offence, death reigned by one, much more they
which receive abundance of grace, and of the gift of
righteousness, y shall reign in life by one, Jesus Christ.
18 Therefore as by ‡ the offence of one, *judgment came*
upon all men to condemnation, even so ‖ by the
righteousness of one, *the free gift came* upon all men unto
justification of life 19 For as by one man's disobedience
many were made sinners so by the obedience of
one shall many be made righteous, 20 Moreover the
law entered, that the offence might abound but where sin
abounded, a grace did much more abound 21 That
as sin hath reigned unto death, even so might grace reign
through righteousness unto eternal life, by Jesus Christ
our Lord

x Mat xx 28 & xxvi 28 John i 16. y Rev v 10 & xx 4 & xxii 5 ‡ Or one offence ‖ Or one righteousness z Chap iii 20 & iv 15 & vii 8 Gal iii 19, 23 a Luke vii 47 1 Tim i 14

v. 12—21 In these verses the apostle draws a parallel between the two covenant-heads, Adam and Christ, between the guilt and misery derived from the one, and the blessedness obtained by the other for his people where it appears how men came into the wretched state of sin in which at present they appear, and how rich was that love of God which drew them out of it

By one man sin entered into the world, one sin opened the flood-gates of ungodliness, and deluged the world, overwhelming it with miseries innumerable, *and death by sin*, in every tremendous form, seized on the human nature, *and so death*, the wages of sin, death temporal, spiritual, and eternal, *passed upon all men, for that*, or *in whom* (ἐφ' ᾧ) *all have sinned* Adam was the common parent and covenant-head of mankind, and at that time possessed the whole human nature, so that all his posterity, being in his loins, (*Heb* vii 9, 10) fell with him his offence became theirs, is imputed to them, and renders them obnoxious to the same punishment with himself So that it appears hereby that Jews as well as Gentiles are in the same state of condemnation *For until the law*, before the revelation of God's will on mount Sinai was made, *sin was in the world*, with death and all its attendant miseries, *but* this supposes some law in force, before that which was given by Moses, for *sin is not imputed where there is no law*, nor would any punishment have been inflicted where there was no offence committed But though the law of Moses was not in being, *nevertheless death reigned from Adam to Moses*, not only over actual transgressors, grown up to the knowledge of good and evil, but *even over them that had not sinned after the similitude of Adam's transgression*, multitudes of infants suffering in the deluge and desolations of Sodom and Gomorrah, and daily their dying groans and agonies testify that sin is in them, because the wages of it is exacted from them, and evidently prove that they are involved in the guilt of that one man's disobedience by which sin and death entered into the world, and *who is the figure of him that was to come*, the type of our second covenant-head and representative, Jesus Christ, who in the fulness of time should become incarnate, that as sin and death are communicated to us by the one, so should righteousness and life be obtained for us by the other *But*, though the parallel between them is striking, yet in comparing them the latter far excelleth *for not as the offence, so also is the free gift*, the benefit accruing from the divine righteousness, doth not barely answer the dire effects of the first man's sin, it doth much more *For if through the offence of one, many be dead*, the dreadful sentence being passed upon them, *much more the grace of God, and the gift by grace, which is by one man, Jesus Christ*, who hath wrought out that righteousness, by which the most unsearchable riches of divine grace are procured for his people, *hath abounded unto mercy*, securing to them not merely such a life as Adam had in innocence, but one far surpassing in glory, and eternal in its endurance *And not as it was by one that sinned, so is the gift*, the dissimilitude is considerable with regard to the *efficacious influence* of the transactions of the two great covenant-heads *for the judgment*, the guilt and sentence in consequence thereof, *was by one* sin, of one man, *to the condemnation* of all his posterity whom he represented, *but the free gift* of God through the Redeemer's obedience to death, reaches not to the pardon of one sin, but *of many offences unto justification* all the sins of his elect, actual as well as original, being laid on their substitute, and they through faith in him are freely and fully delivered from all condemnation, and accepted as righteous before God *For if by one man's offence, or by one offence, death reigned by one*, and set up the pillars of his throne, bringing the whole human race under his mortal power, *much more they which receive abundance of grace*, even all that fulness which is laid up for them in Jesus Christ, *and of the gift of righteousness*, that everlastingly glorious, and infinitely meritorious righteousness of their Lord, *shall reign in life by one, Christ Jesus*, triumphant over sin, its guilt and power, quickened to spiritual life here, and looking for that life of glory hereafter, when they shall reign with Jesus in heaven, and see sin and death and hell for ever put under their feet *Therefore as by the offence of one*, or *by one offence*, *judgment came*, (or, sin entered, as it may be supplied) *upon all men to condemnation*, and they were exposed to death eternal thereby, *even so by the righteousness of one*, the second man, the Lord from heaven, the free gift came *upon all men to justification of life*, their Redeemer having provided the complete righteousness which contains their title to life and glory, and which God accepts and graciously makes over to all the heirs of promise, so that in both cases God appears as a righteous judge, placing the acts of the representatives to those, whose persons and characters they bore, and who were, in the eye of the law, one with them *For as by one man's disobedience, many were made sinners*, ([illegible]) and in virtue of the imputation of his sin, regarded in the eye of the law as guilty, and condemned as one, in crime and punishment, with their covenant-head, *so by the obedience of one shall many be made righteous*, his righteousness being imputed to them, and they thereby being, in the eye even of the holy law, regarded as righteous, and declared to be so, complete in him *Moreover*, let it be observed, that long after sin and death were in the world, *the law entered*, which was given on mount Sinai, not that the Jews might be justified thereby, but *that the offence might abound*, and sin be more clearly discovered to the conscience, and appear exceeding sinful *but where sin abounded, grace did much more abound*, God taking occasion, even from the creature's violence, to magnify the more transcendently the riches of his own free mercy, in pardoning, justifying, and saving lost souls, and raising them to higher glory than that which they had lost by the first man's disobedience *So that as sin hath reigned unto death*, and, usurping the throne, spread its dire dominion over the fallen sons of men, *even so might* victorious *grace* erect her throne on the ruins of these vanquished foes, and *reign through* that *righteousness* which is brought in, *by Jesus Christ our Lord*, over all his redeemed people *unto eternal life*, releasing them from the power of sin and death, bringing them into a ſtate of favour with God, which is better than life itſelf, quickening them to ſpiritual life here, and ſecuring to them eternal life hereafter Thou God of all grace, ſet up this bleſſed kingdom in my heart, and reign for ever there!

CHAP VI

The apoſtle having at large aſſerted, opened, and proved the great doctrine of juſtification by faith, leſt any ſhould turn this grace of God into licentiouſneſs, he doth with a like zeal, copiouſneſs of expreſſion, and cogency of argument, preſs the abſolute neceſſity of ſanctification, as the inſeparable fruit and companion of juſtification The water and the blood came ſtreaming together out of the pierced ſide of the dying Jeſus and what God hath thus joined together, let not us dare to put aſunder

1 WHAT ſhall we ſay then? ᵃ ſhall we continue
in ſin that grace may abound? 2 ᵇ God for-
bid ᶜ how ſhall we that are dead to ſin live any longer
therein? 3 Know ye not that ᵈ ſo many of us as were
baptized into Jeſus Chriſt, were baptized into his death?
4 Therefore ᵉ we are buried with him by baptiſm into
death that ᶠ like as Chriſt was raiſed up from the dead
by the glory of the Father, ᵍ even ſo we alſo ſhould walk
in newneſs of life 5 For if we have been planted to-
gether in the likeneſs of his death we ſhall be alſo *in
the likeneſs* of *his* reſurrection 6 Knowing this, that
ʰ our old man is crucified with him, that the body of ſin
might be deſtroyed, that henceforth we ſhould not ſerve
ſin 7 For ⁱ he that is dead is freed from ſin 8
Now ᵏ if we be dead with Chriſt, we believe that we
ſhall alſo live with him 9 Knowing that ˡ Chriſt being
raiſed from the dead, dieth no more, death hath no more
dominion over him 10 For in that he died, ᵐ he died
unto ſin once but in that he liveth, ⁿ he liveth unto
God 11 Likewiſe reckon ye alſo yourſelves ᵒ to be
dead indeed unto ſin, but alive unto God through Jeſus
Chriſt our Lord 12 ᵖ Let not ſin therefore reign in
your mortal body, that ye ſhould obey it in the luſts
thereof 13 ᵠ Neither yield ye your members as † in-
ſtruments of unrighteouſneſs unto ſin but ʳ yield your-
ſelves unto God, as thoſe that are alive from the dead,
and your members as ‡ inſtruments of righteouſneſs un-
to God 14 For ˢ ſin ſhall not have dominion over
you for ye are not under the law, but under grace
15 What then? ᵗ ſhall we ſin becauſe we are not under
the law, but under grace? God forbid 16 Know ye
not, that ᵘ to whom ye yield yourſelves ſervants to obey,
his ſervants ye are to whom ye obey, whether of ſin
unto death, or of obedience unto righteouſneſs? 17
But God be thanked, that ye were the ſervants of ſin,
but ˣ ye have obeyed from the heart that form of doc-
trine § which was delivered you 18 ʸ Being then
made free from ſin, ye became the ſervants of righte-
ouſneſs 19 I ſpeak after the manner of men becauſe
of the infirmity of your fleſh for as ye have yielded
your members ſervants to uncleanneſs and to iniquity,
unto iniquity, even ſo now yield your members ſervants
to righteouſneſs, unto holineſs 20 For ᶻ when ye were
the ſervants of ſin, ye were free from righteouſneſs 21
ᵃ What fruit had ye then in thoſe things, whereof ye
are now aſhamed? for the end of thoſe things *is* death
22 But now being made free from ſin, and become
ſervants to God, ye have your fruit unto holineſs, and
ᵇ the end everlaſting life 23 For ᶜ the wages of ſin *is*
death but ᵈ the gift of God *is* eternal life, through Je-
ſus Chriſt our Lord

ᵃ Chap iii. 8 ᵇ Mat iv. 10 ᶜ Col iii 3 1 Pet. ii 24 ᵈ Gal iii. 27 ᵉ Col. ii 12 ᶠ Chap viii 11 Phil iii 10, 11 ᵍ Eph iv 22 Col iii 10 ʰ Gal ii 20 & v 24 Col iii 5, 9 ⁱ 1 Pet iv 1 ᵏ 2 Tim ii 11 ˡ Rev i 18 ᵐ Heb ix. 28 ⁿ Luke xx 38 ᵒ Gal ii 19 ᵖ Pſ cxix 133 ᵠ 1 Pet. iv 2 † Or Weapons ʳ Chap xii 1 Col iii 5 ˢ Chap v 20. Heb viii 10 ᵗ 1 Cor ix 21 Gal. ii 18 ᵘ Mat vi 24 John viii 34 2 Pet ii 19 ˣ 2 Tim i 13 § Whereto ye were delivered ʸ John viii 32 1 Cor vii 22 Gal v 1 ᶻ Mat vii 18 ᵃ Chap vii 5 ᵇ Chap v 1 ᶜ Gen ii 17 Chap ii 8 ᵈ v 12 Jam i 15 ᵈ 1 Pet i 3

v 1—23 The riches of the grace which he had diſplayed in the former chapter, the apoſtle clearly foreſaw would furniſh objections againſt his doctrine, which he therefore ſtates and obviates *What ſhall we ſay then?* Is this a licentious doctrine? and *ſhall we continue in ſin, that grace may abound? God forbid* the apoſtle rejects the thought with abhorrence, as the vileſt abuſe of this moſt bleſſed truth *How ſhall we that are dead to ſin, live any longer therein?* under its power and dominion How inconſiſtent would it be with our character, how contrary to the obligations of gratitude and duty lying upon us, and how deſtructive of our peace and hope! Our very baptiſm repreſents our profeſſion, and intimates to us the converſation becoming the name we bear *Know ye not, that ſo many of us as were baptized into Jeſus Chriſt*, into the faith of his name, and obedience to his authority, *were baptized into his death?* that we ſhould reſemble him, dying to ſin, as he died for it, and correſponding with his great deſign in ſuffering, which was to redeem us from all iniquity. *Therefore we are buried with him by baptiſm into death*, partaking of the benefits of his death, and, as a corpſe laid in the grave, which ceaſes from the actions of life, ſo ſhould we ſhew an abiding deadneſs to ſin, *that like as Chriſt was raiſed up from the dead by the glory of the Father*, by his almighty power, *even ſo we alſo ſhould walk in newneſs of life*, quickened by virtue derived from him, our head of vital influence, as well as repreſentative, and having received a new nature, new principles, and new hearts from him, we are bound to his praiſe to ſhew forth in all holy converſation and godlineſs, the real and univerſal happy change which is paſſed upon us to the praiſe of the glory of his grace *For if we have been planted together in the likeneſs of his death*, engrafted into him, and one with him as the members of his body myſtical, ſharing in the bleſſed effects of his death and experiencing its efficacy in ſeparating our ſouls from ſin, as death ſeparated his body and ſoul, *we ſhall be alſo planted in the likeneſs of his reſurrection*, quickened by his divine power, and enabled to walk before God in holineſs here, till we ſhall come in perfect holineſs to dwell with him for ever in glory *Knowing this, that our old man*, that fallen nature derived from Adam, and coeval with our very being, *is crucified with him*, ſo that its condemning guilt is aboliſhed, and its tyrannizing power is broken And though it be a painful lingring death, and the remainders of in-dwelling ſin will ſtruggle to the laſt, yet we know Chriſt died, *that the body of ſin might be deſtroyed, that henceforth we ſhould not ſerve ſin*, ſhould no longer be the ſlaves of corruption as before, and that ſhortly its very being in us might be at an end *For he that is dead is freed from ſin* as a man that is dead can have no further claims laid againſt him, ſo if we are crucified with Chriſt, we are freed from the legal power and dominion of our former maſter, ſhall never periſh under guilt, nor return to the bondage of corruption yea, though we may be overtaken by temptation, we ſhall not finally or fatally be enſlaved by ſin *Now if we be* thus *dead with Chriſt*, through union with his crucified body, and virtue thence derived, *we believe that we ſhall alſo live with him*, quickened to a life of grace here, and ſhortly to be raiſed to a life of eternal bleſſedneſs and glory, to reign with him in heaven *Knowing that Chriſt*, our covenant-head and repreſentative, *being raiſed from the dead, dieth no more, death hath no more dominion over him*, he hath for ever ſatisfied all the demands of juſtice *for in that he died, he died for ſin once*, and by one oblation once offered hath obtained eternal redemption for us *but in that he liveth, he liveth unto God*, a life heavenly, immortal, which death can never more affect, being exalted to the right hand of Majeſty on high, as our covenant-head of righteouſneſs, and the eternal ſource of vital influence to all the members of his body myſtical, and becauſe he liveth, we muſt live alſo, our life being eternal as his own

From theſe glorious views which the apoſtle ſets before us of our union and communion with Chriſt in his death and reſurrection, the apoſtle proceeds to urge upon the faithful two things (1) That they *ſhould reckon themſelves dead indeed unto ſin*, not only diſcharged from its condemning guilt, but delivered from its power and dominion, ſo as henceforward willingly to have no more fellowſhip with the unfruitful works of darkneſs, ceaſing from them as a dead man doth from the actions of life (2) That they ſhould reckon themſelves *alive unto God through Jeſus Chriſt our Lord*, quickened by his grace, as the divine principle, to newneſs of life, and engaged and inclined to live to his glory as their great end

This being then the great privilege, dignity, and duty of believers, we are moſt powerfully urged to walk agreeably thereunto *Let not ſin therefore reign in your mortal body, that ye ſhould obey the luſts thereof* Whilſt we carry a mortal body about us, we muſt expect to feel the warrings of in-dwelling ſin till death comes, the conflict will not end, we need therefore to watch and pray, which are the great appointed means of grace, that the tyrant which is dethroned, may not again uſurp dominion over us, and particularly are called upon to deny the craving of bodily appetite, by which the ſtrongeſt temptations to ſin enter, that, however beſet, we may not yield a willing obedience to the former luſts, in which we walked in the days of our ignorance But, though overtaken, nay overcome, we may not, muſt not, cannot lie down contented ſlaves, but ſhall riſe thro' the power of divine grace, and caſt the hateful yoke away, under which we groan being burdened *Neither yield ye your members*, neither thoſe of your bodies, nor the faculties of your ſoul, *as inſtruments of unrighteouſneſs unto ſin*, to war in that hateful cauſe, under ſo foul a captain *but yield yourſelves unto God, as thoſe that are alive from the dead, and your members as inſtruments of righteouſneſs unto God*, living henceforward for his glory, and employing body, ſoul, and ſpirit in his bleſſed ſervice, and to advance his kingdom and intereſt in the world, fighting under his banner, and faithful unto death *For ſin ſhall not have dominion over you*, though it may ſurprize and prevail againſt you for a while, it ſhall not gain your approbation, lord it over you abidingly or unreſiſted, nor obtain an allowed ſovereignty But though the conflict be sometimes sharp and afflictive, the victory is sure at the last, *for ye are not under the law*, as a covenant of works, which can give no hope of pardon for guilt, nor afford any assistance against the power of sin, *but under grace*, under that gracious covenant established with the second Adam, wherein the pardon of all sins is granted, where unchangeable promises secure our stability, and never-failing springs of divine support and assistance shall make us at last more than conquerors and what can afford such an encouraging argument to strive against sin, as the assurance that we shall overcome?

But some man might object to this, that if this be the case, and we are no more under the law, we may live as we list The apostle prevents and refutes the objection *What then? shall we sin because we are not under the law, but under grace? God forbid* this would be to act in opposition to the whole design of the gospel salvation, and inconsistently with all our professions as children of grace For *know ye not, that* it is a truth obvious and incontestable, *to whom ye yield yourselves servants to obey, his servants ye are to whom ye obey, whether of sin unto death, or of obedience unto righteousness?* No man can serve two masters utterly contradictory in their commands The servants of sin, who willingly surrender themselves to this tyrant's will, must infallibly reap eternal death as the wages of their work, whilst the servants of God are servants *of obedience unto righteousness*, his interests being thus served and advanced, and their end is eternal life according therefore to the service in which we are employed, we shew what master we serve, and to whom we belong *But God be thanked, that though ye were*, in times past, *the servants of sin*, ye do not continue so, *but ye have obeyed from the heart that form of doctrine which was delivered unto you*, both in heart and conduct now cast into the mould of the glorious gospel, (τυπον εις ον παρεδοθητε) and bearing all its amiable lineaments, in the most blessed and happy conformity to him who is the great Author of it, Jesus Christ

Being then made free from sin, by the power of the eternal Spirit through the gospel effectually operating to destroy the dominion, tyranny, and love of sin, *ye became the servants of righteousness*, discharged from the hateful servitude of iniquity, and entered into the service of a better master, which is perfect freedom, the willing subjects of the holy Jesus, your rightful Lord and Sovereign *I speak after the manner of men*, representing this matter under the familiar images of masters and servants, *because of the infirmity of your flesh*, the understanding being still dark thro the remainders of corruption, and most easily receives spiritual ideas, when communicated under the vail of sensible objects *For as*, in time past, *ye yielded your members*, both body and soul, *servants to uncleanness, and to iniquity, unto iniquity*, willing slaves to every vile affection, going from evil to worse, and fulfilling all the corrupt desires of the flesh and of the mind, *even so now yield your members servants of righteousness, unto holiness*, let every member of your body and faculty of your soul be as freely, delightfully, constantly, and universally employed in the service of the blessed Jesus your Master, and in the practice of righteousness and true holiness, as by nature they were before engaged in the service of sin

And surely the strongest obligations now lie upon you thus to walk in holiness *for when ye were the servants of sin*, wholly devoted to its service, *ye were free from righteousness*, not from the obligations to it, which are immutable and eternal, but ye cast off all restraint, were utterly averse to the rule of righteousness, and boasted of liberty, when the most wretched slaves of corruption And a moment's reflection will now convince you of the misery of that state in which you lay, for *what fruit had ye then in those things, whereof ye are now ashamed?* did not the curse of sin follow you close as your shadow? did not the sting of it at times torment and make you miserable in the midst of your enjoyments? did not the very pursuits in which you were engaged, involve you in trouble, disappointment, vexation? and were you not always unsatisfied, and felt an aching void, which nothing you possessed could fill? and with what shame, horror, and remorse, do you now reflect upon your past conduct? *for*, careless and thoughtless as you then were, you now know, *that the end of those things is death* eternal, which must have been your miserable lot, if divine grace had not interposed, and plucked you as brands from the burning *But now being made free from sin, and become servants to God*, since this blessed exchange of masters, *ye have your fruit unto holiness*, walking in that good conversation and godliness which brings glory to God, and is most comfortable to your own souls, *and the* blessed *end* and issue of which will be *everlasting life* *For the wages of sin*, the accursed master whom ye formerly served, *is death*, including all miseries, both here and hereafter, of soul and body, and that to eternity *but the gift of God is eternal life*, which he bestows not out of respect of any service or desert of ours, but as a matter of mere grace and favour, *through Jesus Christ our Lord*, in whom this eternal life is secured to us, and for whose righteousness sake it is bestowed upon us, purchased by the Saviour, but absolutely free to the sinner

Let us examine ourselves then, whether we are in the faith, and with deepest self-application consider what the apostle hath here advanced Our everlasting hopes depend on our experience of these things We most fatally deceive ourselves, if we talk of grace, and promise ourselves heaven, and live and die the servants of corruption

CHAP VII

We may observe in this chapter, 1 Our freedom from the law further urged as an argument to press upon us sanctification, ver 1—6 2 The excellency and usefulness of the law asserted and proved from the apostle's own experience notwithstanding, ver 7—14 3 A description of the conflict between grace and corruption in the heart, ver 14, 15, to the end

1 KNOW ye not, brethren, (for I speak to them
that know the law) how that [a] the law hath do-
minion over a man as long as he liveth? 2 For [b] the [a] Chap 19
woman which hath an husband, is bound by the law to [b] Prov vi 32 1 Cor
her husband so long as he liveth but if the husband vii 10, 39
be dead, she is loosed from the law of *her* husband 3
So then [c] if while *her* husband liveth, she be married to [c] Num v
another man, she shall be called an adulteress but [d] if 20, 21 Judg
her husband be dead, she is free from that law, so that xiv 20 Mat v
she is no adulteress, though she be married to another [d] Ruth i
man 4 Wherefore, my brethren, [e] ye also are become 13 1 Tim v 14
dead to the law [f] by the body of Christ, that [g] ye should [e] Chap vi 2 Gal ii
be married to another, *even* to him who is raised from 19
the dead, that we should bring forth fruit unto God, [f] Col ii 14, [g] 2 Cor xi
5 For when we were in the flesh, [h] the motions of sins 2
which were by the law, did work in our members [i] to [h] Chap vi
bring forth fruit unto death 6 But now we are deli- 19 Gal v 19
vered from the law, that being dead wherein we were [i] Chap vi
held, [k] that we should serve in newness of spirit, and 21 Jam i 15
not *in* the oldness of the letter [k] Luke i 74, John iv 23, Chap ii 29, 2 Cor iii 6

v 1—6 The apostle had asserted, that we are not under the law, and in what sense he here explains He was addressing himself to them who knew the law, and would admit it as the most obvious truth, that the law can no longer be binding, than the person lives under it As for instance *The woman which hath an husband, is bound by the law to her husband so long as he liveth but if her husband be dead*, the bond of wedlock is dissolved, and *she is loosed from the law of her husband So then if while her husband liveth, she be married to another man, she shall be called an adulteress*, but the case is quite different *if her husband be dead*, for then *she is free from the law, so that she is no adulteress, though she be married to another man*

Now such was our case

1 Our first marriage was to the law, we were under it as a covenant of works, and the fruits of that marriage were dreadful *For when we*, Jews as well as Gentiles, *were in the flesh*, in our natural, corrupt, and unregenerate state, *the motions of sin*, the passions and vile affections of our fallen hearts, *which were by the law* considered as a covenant of works, which demanded a perfection we could not pay, and denounced a curse we could not endure, our corruptions, I say, were but the more irritated by the strictness of the prohibition, and the severity of the sanction, and *did work in our members* with such mighty and irresistible energy, as *to bring forth fruit unto death*, producing all those actual transgressions which spring from the original root of bitterness in our nature, and, unless we were delivered from the guilt and dominion of them, must issue in eternal death and as long as any soul is under the law as a covenant, this must be his miserable case But,

2 We are married to another, even to Christ Jesus Our first husband *the law being dead, wherein we were held, we are delivered* from its obligations as a covenant, and from the curse it denounced on the transgressors We are no more in these respects under it, than a wife is subject to her departed husband *We are become dead to the law*, and the law unto us, *by the body of Christ*, for he hath satisfied all its demands and we are thus discharged from all connection with, and obligation to, our former husband, *that we might be married to another, even to him who is raised from the dead*, the risen and exalted Saviour, to whom we now pledge our fidelity, and by ties of love, that never can be dissolved, are drawn to a willing subjection to his pleasing yoke, *that we should bring forth fruit unto God*, the fruits of grace and holiness produced through the quickening influences of his Spirit, which, till this union with Christ commences, never can be brought forth, and tending to advance the divine glory, acceptable also to God through Jesus Christ and *that we should serve in newness of spirit, and not in the oldness of the letter* though made free from the law as a covenant of life, yet under the law to Christ, receiving from him the new heart, walking before him under the influence of new principles, and enabled to shew forth a very different conversation in righteousness and true holiness, from what we ever did or could practise, when under the power of the old man, and spending the

the law as a covenant of life, which only provoked, instead of reſtraining, the corruption of our hearts

7 What ſhall we ſay then? Is the law ſin? God for-
bid Nay, [l] I had not known ſin, but by the law: for
I had not known † luſt, except the law had ſaid, [m] Thou
ſhalt not covet 8 But [n] ſin taking occaſion by the com-
mandment, wrought in me all manner of concupiſcence
For [o] without the law ſin *was* dead 9 For I was alive
without the law once, [p] but when the commandment
came, [q] ſin revived, and I died 10 And the com-
mandment [r] which was *ordained* to life, [s] I found to be
unto death 11 For ſin taking occaſion by the com-
mandment, deceived me, and by it ſlew me 12 Where-
fore [t] the law *is* holy, and the commandment holy, and
juſt, and good

l Chap iii 20. † O concupiſcence. m Ex xx 17. n Chap v 20. 1 Cor xv 56. o Mark x 20. p Chap x 5. Gal iii 10. q Pſ xxxvii 4—8. r Lev xviii 5. s 2 Cor iii 7. t Pſ xix 8 & ſ. cxix 96.

v 7—12 An objection might be raiſed from what the apoſtle had ſaid, as if he had moſt diſhonourably reflected on the law *What ſhall we ſay then? is the law ſin?* with indignation he replies, *God forbid* the law is good, the evil is all in ourſelves

1 The law is in itſelf moſt *holy, juſt, and good*, it contains a tranſcript of God's purity, inculcates the moſt perfect obedience, demands nothing but what eſſentially flows from the very relation of Creator and creature, and in its nature is like its Author, excellent.

2 The advantages of the law are great, as it convinces the conſcience, and humbles the ſoul under a ſenſe of ſin *I had not known ſin, but by the law*, ſo far is the law from leading to ſin, or approving it, that it diſcovers and condemns the moſt ſecret workings of evil *For I had not known luſt*, the ſinfulneſs of the firſt motions of corrupt deſire, *except the law had ſaid, Thou ſhalt not covet* the law therefore is not ſinful *but*, as the bright mirror, diſcovers that deformity which would otherwiſe have been overlooked The evil is all in ourſelves, where *ſin taking occaſion by the commandment*, raged even the more violently becauſe of the prohibition, and *wrought in me all manner of concupiſcence For without the law*, whilſt in my Phariſaical ſtate I knew not its ſpirituality and extenſive demands, *ſin was dead*, did not terrify my conſcience, and to my apprehenſion was entirely ſubdued, ſo that I counted myſelf, as touching the righteouſneſs which is by the law, blameleſs *For I was alive without the law once*, in thoſe days of my vanity, when Phariſaical pride ſwelled my boſom, I counted my title to life clear on the footing of my own obedience, being a perfect ſtranger to the ſpiritual nature and extent of the law *but when the commandment came*, laid open to my conſcience by the Spirit in its purity and ſpirituality, conviction flaſhed on my mind, *ſin revived*, and brought unnumbered charges againſt me, which I had overlooked, and I felt its living power in my heart, when I thought it had been utterly deſtroyed, *and*, in conſequence thereof, *I died*, I ſaw myſelf a condemned criminal, moſt juſtly obnoxious to the divine diſpleaſure, and in the eye of the law under the fearful ſentence of eternal death *And the commandment which*, if perfectly obeyed, *was ordained to* be a covenant of *life* to man in innocence, *I found to be unto death*, and through the corruption of my nature rendering me incapable of keeping it, I perceived the only thing it could do for me was, to conſign me over to the wrath of God as a tranſgreſſor *For ſin*, that native principle of corruption in my heart, *taking occaſion by the commandment* to rebel againſt the law, as if it was unreaſonably ſevere, *deceived me* with hopes of pleaſure and impunity, *and by it ſlew me*, like an aſſaſſin, that having miſled the traveller, plunges his dagger into his heart *Wherefore* all theſe dire conſequences are to be aſcribed wholly to our deſperate corruption, whilſt *the law is holy*, and no blame to be laid againſt it, *and the commandment is holy, juſt, and good*

13 Was then that which is good made death unto
me? God forbid. But ſin, that it might appear ſin,
working death in me by that which is good, that ſin
by the commandment might become exceeding ſinful
14 For we know that [u] the law is ſpiritual but [x] I
am carnal, [y] ſold under ſin 15 For that which I do,
I allow not [z] for that I would, that do I not, but what
I hate, that do I 16 If then I do that which I would
not, I conſent unto the law, that *it is* good 17 Now
then it is no more I that do it, but ſin that dwelleth in
me 18 For I know that [a] in me (that is in my fleſh)
dwelleth no good thing for to will is preſent with me,
but *how* to perform that which is good I find not 19
For the good that I would, I do not but the evil
which I would not, that I do 20 Now if I do that I
would not, it is no more I that do it, but ſin that dwell-
eth in me 21 I find then a law, that when I would
do good, evil is preſent with me 22 For [b] I delight
in the law of God, after the inward man 23 [c] But I
ſee another law in my members, warring againſt the law
of my mind, and [d] bringing me into captivity to the
law of ſin, which is in my members 24 [e] O wretched
man that I am! who ſhall deliver me from the body of
this death? 25 [f] I thank God through Jeſus Chriſt
our Lord So then with the mind I myſelf ſerve the
law of God, but with the fleſh the law of ſin

u Heb iv 12. x 1 Cor iii 1. y 1 Kings xxi 20. z Gal v 17. a Gen vi 5 & viii 21. Iſa i 6 & lxiv 6. b Pſ i 2. 2 Cor iv 16. Col iii 10. c Gal v 17. Jam iv 1. d Prov xxiv 16. Jam iii 2. e Job xl 4. Pſ xxxviii 3, 5. f 1 Cor xv 57.

v 13—25 A new objection is ſtarted from the title he gives to the law as *good* *Was then that which is good made death unto me?* might one ſuggeſt, can that which is ſo good in its nature be in its effects ſo deadly? and is the law of God the cauſe of all human miſeries? *God forbid* It is not the law, *but* the crime committed againſt it, which cauſes the death of the malefactor Thus *ſin*, the concupiſcence of my corrupted nature, *that it might appear ſin*, and be diſcovered to my conſcience in its true malignity, *working death in me by that which is good*, and taking occaſion to rebel from the very purity and perfection of the holy law of God, brought the ſentence of death upon me, *that ſin by the commandment*, ſo clearly forbidden, yet riſing in wilful oppoſition thereto, *might appear exceeding ſinful* and that this corruption of my nature, the ſource of all my actual tranſgreſſions, might be ſeen in the blackeſt colours that words can expreſs, or thought conceive, (καθ' ὑπερβολὴν ἁμαρτωλός)

Such was the apoſtle's ſtate before converſion, and afterwards he ſtill proved the ſevereſt conflicts with indwelling ſin, and ſaw how unable he was to ſtand before the demands of a holy law *For we know*, I Paul, and all who are enlightened to a knowledge of the truth, *that the law is ſpiritual*, reaching to the thoughts and intents of the heart, and requiring perfection of nature, as well as outward obedience, *but I am carnal*, feel myſelf a poor fallen creature, *ſold under ſin*, by the firſt man's tranſgreſſion delivered into the ſerpent's hands, and born the ſlave of corruption, the dire effects of which I daily feel, and groan under them *For that which I do, I allow not*, when in thought, word, or deed, my wretched heart yields to the tempter's wiles, my judgment diſapproves the evil I commit, and, far from a deliberate choice, my ſoul riſes againſt it, and I loathe both the ſin and myſelf *For what I would*, and in my better part approve and deſire, *that do I not*, I deſire always with the moſt intenſe application, that my ſoul ſhould be fixed on God, and engaged in his bleſſed work and ſervice yet how ſhort do I come of that ſpirituality of temper and conduct which I wiſh to exerciſe? *But what I hate, that do I*, inſenſibly, through infirmity, ſurprize, or temptation, betrayed into things that habitually I abhor *If then I do that which I would not*, and am overcome by the power of in-dwelling ſin, whilſt I feel a ſettled averſion to this hateful ſervice, *I conſent unto the law*, (σύμφημι) give my full approbation to it, *that it is good*, moſt excellent in itſelf, moſt becoming God to enjoin, and me to obey, and even if its fearful penalty were levied upon me, I muſt own the ſentence righteous, juſt, and good *Now then it is no more I*, as a new man, *that do it, but ſin*, the old native corruption, *that dwelleth in me*, like the Canaanites, and is a burdenſome to me, as they were to God's Iſrael *For I know*, by ſad experience, *that in me (that is in my fleſh)*, in my carnal ſelf, there *dwelleth no good thing*, but evil, and only evil, and that continually *for to will is preſent with me*, and under the influence of the divine nature, of which I am made a partaker, my judgment approves the things that are excellent, and my choice determines me to walk and pleaſe God, *but how to perform that which is good I find not*, the ſtorms of temptation, and the current of corruption carry me out of the courſe I mean to ſteer, ſo that I cannot keep in the ſtraight way of holineſs, nor proceed with that ſteadineſs and ſpeed I hoped and purpoſed *For the good that I would*, even to be found complete in all the will of God, *I do not*, cannot attain unto, *but the evil which I would not*, but condemn, diſapprove, and diſallow, *that I do*, feeling myſelf weak as an infant, and unable to make reſiſtance *Now if I do that I would not*, as I ſaid before, *it is no more I that do it*, ſin is in my eyes an abominable thing, and my renewed part feels an averſion to it, and a hearty approbation of the holy law of God, *but* all the evil proceeds from *ſin*, that corrupted principle, *which* ſtill *dwelleth in me* *I find then a law*, of my fallen nature acting in me with ſuch mighty influence, *that when I would do good, evil is preſent with me*, ſome diſcouragements ſuggeſted to deter me, ſome ſnare to allure me, or ſome evil deſire riſes up, quenches the gracious purpoſe I had formed, and turns me aſide from the path of righteouſneſs *For I* can ſay with the greateſt truth, *I delight in the law of God, after the inward man* my inmoſt ſoul, renewed by grace, doth not only approve the law in all its ſpirituality as good, but feels a complacency therein, and knows no happineſs equal to that perfect conformity thereto, which it deſires, and to which it hopes one day to arrive *But*, what is the bittereſt burden I groan under, *I ſee another law in my members*, the mighty workings of remaining corruption, *warring againſt the law of my mind*, my better part, which divine grace hath renewed, and though habitually the power of the new nature predominates, yet the war is often ſharp, *and* ſometimes corruption prevails, *bringing me into captivity to the law of ſin, which is in my members*, whilſt for a time overpowered, reluctantly I am drawn aſide, not a willing ſlave, but an unhappy captive *O wretched man that I am!* thus tied and bound with the chain of my ſins, *who ſhall deliver me from the body of this death?* from this fallen nature, which, like a body conſiſting of various members, works ſo powerfully, and muſt, for any thing I can do to help myſelf, bring me under the ſentence of eternal death But though I feel my helpleſſneſs, and lie down under ſelf-deſpair, *I thank God through Jeſus Chriſt our Lord.* By his grace I am already delivered from condemnation, by his Spirit I ſhall be ſaved from the power of evil, and his unchangeable promiſes aſſure me of a compleat victory ſhortly, when all the remainders of ſin ſhall be finally and utterly deſtroyed *So then* the ſum of the matter is ſhortly this *with my mind*, in my ſettled judgment and choice, *I myſelf*, (αυτος εγω) my real ſelf, with my renewed heart in the inner man, I *ſerve the law of God*, with full conſent, and willing ſubjection, *but with my fleſh the law of ſin*, feeling its workings in me, though diſallowed and condemned, and ſometimes, though reluctantly, brought under its hateful power

Many have aſſerted, that Paul in this whole deſcription perſonates an unregenerate man, and ſeem to think it highly derogatory to his high character to ſuppoſe, that ſo great a Chriſtian, the chief of the apoſtles, ſhould feel ſuch a war of corruption as is here deſcribed but if any man conſiders the expreſſions of *his hating* and *not allowing the evil he did*, *his conſenting to the law as good*, *delighting in it after the inward man*, (with which compare 2 *Cor* iv 16 *Eph* iii 16) *ſerving it with his mind*, &c and contraſts herewith the ſtate of unregeneracy deſcribed in the former chapter, *v* 12, 13, 16, 19 he will ſee that the apoſtle ſpoke indeed of *himſelf*, and not another perſon And will not the experience of the deareſt children of God correſpond herewith, whoſe minds are truly enlightened to know the ſpirituality of the law, and the corruption of their nature? Thoſe who are ignorant of the one, and feel not the other, may fancy themſelves indeed to have attained, and be already perfect but to that the apoſtle pretended not, *Phil*, iii 12 and thoſe who like him experimentally know their fallen ſtate, and impotence to obey the perfect law of God, will ſtill adopt his complaint, and feel the neceſſity of living conſtantly on the riches of that grace which is revealed in the goſpel

CHAP VIII

The apoſtle having fully explained the doctrine of juſtification, *and preſſed the neceſſity of* ſanctification, *in this chapter applies himſelf to the* conſolation *of the Lord's people Miniſters are helpers of the joy of the ſaints* Comfort ye, comfort ye my people, *ſo runs our commiſſion,* Iſa xl 1 *It is the will of God, that his people ſhould be a comforted people And we have here ſuch a draught of the goſpel-charter, ſuch a diſplay of the unſpeakable privileges of true believers, as may furniſh us with abundant matter for joy and peace in believing, that by all theſe immutable things, in which it is impoſſible for God to lye, we might have ſtrong conſolation And many of the people of God have accordingly found this chapter a well-ſpring of comfort to their ſouls, living and dying, and have ſucked and been ſatisfied from theſe breaſts of conſolation, and with joy drawn water out of theſe wells of ſalvation There are three things in this chapter,* 1 *The particular inſtances of a Chriſtian's privileges,* ver 1—29 2 *The ground thereof laid in predeſtination,* ver 29, 30 3 *The apoſtle's triumph herein, in the name of all the ſaints,* ver 31, *to the end*

a John xv 4 Heb v 18 | 1 [a] *THERE is* therefore now no condemnation to
b Chap vii 6 Gal v 16, 25 | them which are in Chriſt Jeſus, [b] who walk
c John vi 63 & viii 32 36 2 Cor iii 6 Gal ii 19 | not after the fleſh, but after the Spirit 2 For [c] the law
d Heb vii 18, 19 & ix 9 | of the Spirit of life in Chriſt Jeſus, hath made me free
e John iii 17 Acts xiii 39 2 Cor v 21 Gal iii 13 | from the law of ſin and death 3 For [d] what the law
f John iii 6 | could not do, in that it was weak through the fleſh, [e] God
g Gal v 25 | ſending his own Son in the likeneſs of ſinful fleſh, and
h Chap vi 21 Gal vi 8 | for ſin, condemned ſin in the fleſh 4 That the righte-
i Jam iv 4 | ouſneſs of the law might be fulfilled in us, who walk
k 1 Cor ii 14 | not after the fleſh, but after the Spirit 5 For [f] they
that are after the fleſh, do mind the things of the fleſh
but [g] they that are after the Spirit, the things of the Spi-
rit 6 For [h] to be carnally minded, *is* death, but to
be ſpiritually minded, *is* life and peace 7 Becauſe
[i] the carnal mind *is* enmity againſt God [k] for it is not
ſubject to the law of God, neither indeed can be 8. So
then they that are in the fleſh cannot pleaſe God

v 1—8 This chapter opens with a moſt reviving view of the ſafety of every believer in their great covenant-head Chriſt Jeſus, notwithſtanding all the accuſations of guilt, and the ſtruggle of remaining corruption *There is therefore now no condemnation to them which are in Chriſt Jeſus*, being united to him by faith as their ſurety, the ſentence of the law is reverſed though they deſerve wrath as much as others, though Satan lays many grievous charges againſt them, and God himſelf is pleaſed to viſit ſometimes their iniquities with a rod, and their ſin with ſcourges, yet the bitterneſs of death is paſt Since they have fled for refuge to the blood and righteouſneſs of a Redeemer, they are ſafe for eternity And they are to be known by their daily converſation, as thoſe *who walk not after the fleſh*, under the habitual dominion of their fallen nature and corrupt affections, *but after the Spirit*, directed by God's word as their rule, and under the teachings, guidance, and influence of the Holy Ghoſt, who hath implanted a new and divine nature in them *For the law of the Spirit of life in Chriſt Jeſus*, either that goſpel which, where truly embraced, operates moſt powerfully in conſtraining the conſcience by love unto obedience, through the quickening influence of the divine Spirit, or that moral law which, through the eternal Spirit, in its utmoſt perfection both in heart and practice, Jeſus, as our ſubſtitute, obeyed, and having thereby brought in an everlaſting righteouſneſs, *hath made me free from the law of ſin and death*, delivering me from the condemning ſentence of that law which diſcovered ſin to my conſcience, and denounced wrath as the wages due to it, and from the enſlaving power of corruption, through the grace purchaſed by the Redeemer's obedience unto death *For what the law could not do, in that it was weak through the fleſh*, becauſe of the corruption of our nature it was impoſſible that, as a covenant of works, any fallen creature could obtain life and ſalvation by the law, and it neither provided nor admitted any atonement or expiation for guilt, *God ſending his own Son in the likeneſs of ſinful fleſh, and for ſin, condemned ſin in the fleſh*, reſcuing us in his infinite grace from the ruin which a broken law, never to be repaired, threatned, and this in a way ſo tranſcendently glorious, even by the incarnation of his coequal Son, who took the human nature, with all its ſinleſs infirmities, and ſtood in the ſinner's ſtead, and laying upon him the iniquities of us all, God teſtified, in the ſufferings of his own Son *for* the *ſin* we had committed, the abhorrence he had of ſin, and exacted the puniſhment due to it from the incarnate Saviour, *that the righteouſneſs of the law might be fulfilled in us*, who, in virtue of our union with Jeſus, as our covenant-head and repreſentative, are now perſonally, legally, and perfectly juſtified, even by that law which before condemned us, becauſe being *compleat in him*, we are now poſſeſſed of a righteouſneſs adequate to all the demands of the law, yea in the higheſt magnifying the law, and making it honourable And all *who* are thus vitally united to Chriſt as their head, *walk not after the fleſh, but after the Spirit*, for they are not only brought into a new ſtate, but are made partakers of a new and divine nature, which now influences and actuates them in all their converſation *For they that are after the fleſh*, under the dominion of their native corruption, *do mind the things of the fleſh*, reliſh, delight in, and purſue the things that are pleaſing only to the carnal mind and ſenſual appetite *but they that are after the Spirit*, partakers of his effectual grace, through union with Jeſus the living head of vital influence to his people, they (φρονουσι) underſtand, are attached to, delight in, and follow *the things of the Spirit*, both the doctrines he reveals, the bleſſings he beſtows, and the ſervices which he enjoins, and for which he enables them *For to be carnally minded*, to live under the reigning dominion of the fallen ſpirit, governed by lawleſs paſſions and ſenſual appetites, *is death*, is a preſent ſtate of ſpiritual death, and muſt end in death eternal *but to be ſpiritually minded*, renewed by the Holy Ghoſt, under the habitual influence of his grace, and ſupremely and abidingly attached to, and engaged in, the purſuit of ſpiritual objects, this *is life and peace*, it is the proof of the divine life begun in the ſoul, peace of conſcience is the preſent happy fruit which it produces, and it will iſſue in eternal peace and bleſſedneſs *Becauſe the carnal mind is enmity againſt God*, and ſtands in direct oppoſition to his perfections and authority, abhorring the government of his providence, and hating the reſtraints and injunctions of his law *for it is not ſubject to the law of God, neither indeed can be*. There is an abſolute impoſſibility of ſuch a nature's being brought into conformity to the holy will of God, and till a new heart and right ſpirit be given from above, the enmity muſt for ever remain inveterate and unſubdued *So then they that are in the fleſh cannot pleaſe God*, whilſt they continue in this ſtate, every thing they do is defiled, and the very duties they perform, however right in themſelves, are abominable in his ſight So deſperate is our condition by nature, till the almighty grace of God works the bleſſed change, enabling us to walk and pleaſe God.

9 But ye are not in the fleſh, but in the Spirit, if ſo
be that [l] the Spirit of God dwell in you Now [m] if any | l 1 Cor [illegible] vi 19
man have not the Spirit of Chriſt, he is none of his | m Gal iv 6
10 And if [n] Chriſt *be* in you, the body *is* dead becauſe | n Eph iii 17
of ſin, but the Spirit *is* life, becauſe of righteouſneſs | o Acts ii 24
11 But if the Spirit of [o] him that raiſed up Jeſus from | 1 Cor vi 14
the dead dwell in you, he that raiſed up Chriſt from | Col ii 12
the dead [p] ſhall alſo quicken your mortal bodies by his | p 1 Cor xv
Spirit that dwelleth in you 12 Therefore, brethren, | 2 Cor iv 14
[q] we are debtors not to the fleſh, to live after the fleſh | q 1 Cor vi 20
13 For [r] if ye live after the fleſh, ye ſhall die but if | r Gal vi 8 Col iii 5

ye

ye through the Spirit do mortify the deeds of the body,
ye shall live 14 For [s] as many as are led by the Spirit
of God, they are the sons of God 15 For [t] ye have
not received the spirit of bondage again [u] to fear, but
ye have received [x] the Spirit of adoption, whereby we
cry, Abba, Father 16 [y] The Spirit itself beareth wit-
ness with our spirit, that we are the children of God

s John i 12 Gal v 18. t 1 Cor ii 12. u 2 Tim i 7 Heb ii 15. x Isa lvi 5 Gal iv 6. y 2 Cor i 22 & v 5 Eph i 13, & iv 30 1 John iii 24.

v 9—16 With comfort the apostle addresses the believers at Rome, confident of their interest in the blessed Spirit of all grace *But ye are not in the flesh*, under the dominion and influence of the carnal mind, *but in the Spirit*, being regenerate and born again, *if so be*, or *seeing that*, *the Spirit of God dwelleth in you*, as in his peculiar temple, taking up his abode in your hearts, manifesting there his presence and love, and shewing his powerful and perpetual agency But *now, if any man have not the Spirit of Christ*, who is the very God from whom, as from the Father, that one Spirit proceeds, and be not renewed by his grace, and under his guidance and influence, *he is none of his* whatever his professions may be, he doth not belong to Christ as a member of his body mystical, he is not a child of his family, nor a subject of his kingdom, and must be eternally disowned by him and separated from him, if he dies in this unregenerate state *And*, on the other hand, *if Christ be in you*, by his Spirit dwelling in your hearts, *the body indeed is dead because of sin*, and must lie down in the dust, *but the spirit*, the immortal part, *is life, because of righteousness*, raised from spiritual death in virtue of the Redeemer's righteousness here, and entitled to eternal life hereafter, and by the divine principle implanted in you made meet for the inheritance among the saints in light *but if the Spirit of him that raised up Jesus from the dead*, being one in essence and co-operation with the Father and the Son, (comp 1 Cor vi 14 *John* v 28, 29) and concurring in the work of raising the body of Jesus, *dwell in you* as his temple, *he that raised up Christ from the dead*, as the pledge of our resurrection, and the first fruits of them that slept, *shall quicken your mortal bodies by his Spirit that dwelleth in you*, your bodies shall, by the same indwelling almighty power which raised him, be ransomed from the grave, and become immortal and glorious, fashioned like to your exalted Head *Therefore, brethren, we are debtors, not to the flesh, to live after the flesh*, we have neither obligation nor inducement to follow the cravings of corrupt nature, but, on the contrary, are under every bond of love and duty to live for God, in the daily and habitual mortification of every vile affection *for if ye live after the flesh*, the slaves of corruption, *ye shall die eternally*, *but if ye through the Spirit do mortify the deeds of the body*, denying your corrupt affections and sensual appetites, and through the power of the Spirit growing conformed to your crucified Lord, *ye shall live* with him in glory everlasting *For as many as are led by the Spirit of God*, under his conduct, enlightened, directed, and supported by him, *they are the sons of God*, made his children by adoption and grace, and bearing in their renewed minds his image and likeness *For ye have not received the Spirit of bondage again to fear*, are not under that slavery to your lusts and passions, which was attended with a fearful looking for of judgment, nor under that legal dispensation which brought the conscience into distress and darkness, exacting an obedience that could not be paid, nor under those horrors which, on the first discoveries of your danger in a state of unregeneracy, seized on your souls *but ye have received the Spirit of adoption*, being admitted by God's sovereign grace into that high relation of children, he hath sent the Spirit of his Son into our hearts, producing every childlike disposition of filial love, confidence, and delight in him, *whereby we* are emboldened to approach him with faith and joy, and to *cry, Abba, Father*, before him *The Spirit itself*, in such approaches to God, when in simplicity we offer our hearts unto him, *beareth witness with our spirits*, shining upon his own work in our souls, and testifying our consciences *that we are the children of God*, and may take the comfort of that blessed and honourable relation

17 And if children, then heirs, heirs of God, and
joint-heirs with Christ if so be that we suffer with *him*,
that we may be also glorified together 18 For I rec-
kon, that the sufferings of this present time, *are* not
worthy *to be compared* with the glory which shall be
revealed in us 19 For the earnest expectation of the
creature waiteth for the manifestation of the sons of
God 20 For [d] the creature was made subject to vanity,
not willingly, but by reason of him who hath subjected
the same in hope 21 Because the creature itself also
shall be delivered from the bondage of corruption, into
the glorious liberty of the children of God 22 For
we know that the whole creation groaneth and travail-
eth in pain together until now 23 And not only *they*,
but ourselves also, which have the first fruits of the
Spirit, even we ourselves groan within ourselves, wait-
ing for the adoption, *to wit*, the redemption of our body
24 For we are saved by hope But [k] hope that is seen
is not hope for what a man seeth why doth he yet hope
for? 25 But if we hope for that we see not, *then* do
we with patience wait for it

k 2 Cor v 7 Heb xi 1

v 17—25 The inheritance of glory is the necessary consequence of our adoption of God To this transcendently excellent privilege the apostle therefore passeth *and* concludes, that *if children* by adoption and grace, *then are we heirs*, and entitled to the eternal inheritance, *heirs of God*, made so by his Spirit, and receiving from him all the blessedness which he hath to bestow, and hath promised in his Son, *and joint-heirs with Christ*, who is the first-born of many brethren, and hath secured to them, as for himself, the title to eternal life *if so be that we suffer with him*, as we must expect to do in his service, this being the inseparable attendant of it, that all who will live godly in Christ Jesus must suffer persecution, but the issue will be highly to our advantage, *that we may be also glorified together* at the great day of his appearing, when he shall bestow the promised crown, and before men and angels acknowledge us as his brethren And such a prospect makes all our trials light and easy *For I reckon* (λογίζομαι), on summing up the account of our loss and gain, *that the sufferings of this present time*, however acute or continued, *are not worthy to be compared with the glory which shall be revealed in us*, but, when placed against the glory of eternity, they appear trivial and momentary, and sink unnoticed as the drop into the boundless ocean *For the earnest expectation of the creature waiteth for the manifestation of the sons of God*, which some understand of the Gentile world, and the elect of God among them who through the power of Satan had been made subject to vanity and idolatry, but now, being themselves rescued from the bondage of corruption, they earnestly expected, as a woman in travail, the happy time, when, by the more abundant outpouring of the Spirit, a more general conversion should be wrought in the earth, and far greater multitudes of lost souls be released from the dominion of the wicked one, and brought into the glorious liberty of the sons of God Others suppose that the creature, even the whole creation (πᾶσα κτίσις) in general, animate or inanimate, is here by a noble prosopopeia introduced, as waiting with eager impatience for that blessed alteration which the gospel will make, when the creatures of God shall be no more abused as they have been, but shall be recovered from their present disordered state, and employed by the sons of God, according to their original design, to exalt their Maker's glory *For the creature was made subject to vanity*, the very ground being cursed for man's sin, and all the creatures perverted, through the corruption which is in the human nature, from their original design and use, *not willingly*, by any choice or tendency of their own, or any sin in them, *but by reason of him who hath subjected the same*, and by that sin to which Adam was instigated through the malice of the devil, were involved in the miseries of his fall Not that they should always remain under the dreadful abuses which they suffer, but they rest *in hope that the creature itself also shall be delivered from the bondage of corruption*, under which they lie at present, *into the glorious liberty of the sons of God*, restored by them to answer the great end for which they were created, and expecting the general restitution of all things, when the *new heavens and new earth* shall arise, *wherein dwelleth righteousness* *For we know that the whole creation groaneth and travaileth in pain together until now*, under the grievous burden of abuses which the creatures suffer, and longing for deliverance *And not only they, but ourselves also which have the first fruits of the Spirit*, in his present sealing, sanctifying, and comforting operations, the earnests of the eternal felicity provided for us in a better world, *even we ourselves*, notwithstanding the riches of the grace of which we have been made partakers, yet, *groan within ourselves*, under the remainder of indwelling sin, and the afflictions which still lie heavy upon us till death, *waiting for the adoption*, when Christ will publickly own the relation he bears to us before men and angels at the great day, to wit, *the redemption of our body*, when, triumphant over the grave, we shall reach the summit of heavenly felicity our souls perfected in holiness, our bodies fashioned like to Christ's glorious body, and the whole man shall together be blest with the fruition of God himself as his everlasting portion *For we are saved by hope* though we are not yet in possession of the purchased glory, we hold our title in sure and certain hope *but hope that is seen is not hope*, when the object is possessed hope ceases *for what a man seeth why doth he yet hope for?* *But if we hope for that we see not*, expecting shortly perfect deliverance from all our corruptions and afflictions, *then do we with patience wait for it*, persuaded that the Lord, in his own good time, will fulfil his promises, and bring us at last, through all our trials, to the inheritance incorruptible undefiled, which fadeth not away reserved for us in the heavens And blessed and happy are all they who thus wait for him

26 Likewise the Spirit also helpeth our infirmities
for [l] we know not what we should pray for as we ought
but [m] the Spirit itself maketh intercession for us with

l Matt xx 22 Jam iv 3. m Zech xii 10.

groan-n 1 Chron xxviii 9 Ps vii 9 Jer xi 20 o 1 John v 14 p Gen l 20 Prov vi 1 Chap v 3 4 q Chap ix 11 2 Tim i 9

groanings which cannot be uttered 27 And he [n] that
searcheth the hearts, knoweth what *is* the mind of the
Spirit, because he maketh intercession for the saints,
[o] according to *the will of* God 28 And we know that
[p] all things work together for good to them that love
God, [q] to them who are called according to *his* pur-
pose.

v. 26—28 We have not only a glorious hope before us, but have *likewise* the most reviving supports by the way, for *the Spirit* of our God, quickening, comforting, strengthening us, *helpeth our infirmities*, that we may not sink under our burdens, or be discouraged by our trials, or err through our remaining darkness (συναντιλαμβανεται) having implanted the graces of hope and patience, he still supports us in the exercise of them, and particularly in our approaches to God in prayer, *for we know not what to pray for as we ought*, ignorant, and knowing not what is best for us, weak, and unable to express our wants aright, our affections so cold, our attention so distracted, and sometimes our lips sealed up, that we cannot speak before God *but the Spirit itself*, by his gracious suggestions, *maketh intercession for us*, pouring out a spirit of prayer and supplication upon our hearts, giving us such a sense of our wants, and exciting desires after God so intense and affecting as words cannot express, which can only be breathed forth *with groanings which cannot be uttered* *And he that searcheth the hearts*, the all-seeing God, *knoweth what is the mind of the Spirit*, though our tongue may not form an articulate sound in prayer, God regards and will answer these gracious workings of his Spirit in our hearts, *because he maketh intercession for the saints according to the will of God*, inclining us always to ask according to the mind and will of God, and engaging us humbly to resign ourselves, for an answer to our prayers, in time, manner, and measure, to his good pleasure *And we know*, by the assured promises of his word, by the experience of all his saints, and by our own, when thus unreservedly casting our care upon him, *that all things work together for good to them that love God*, and however dark, and for the time grievous to flesh and blood, the dispensations of Providence may appear, we are now assured, and we shall hereafter prove, that the circumstances which seemed most afflictive we could not have done without, and that they especially conduced to promote our spiritual and eternal welfare, and this is one of the inestimable privileges peculiar *to them who are called according to his eternal purpose*, and by the gospel, through the power of the Spirit, effectually turned to God

r Ex xxxiii 12 Jer i 5 Chap xi 2 2 Tim ii 19 s Eph i 5 11 t 2 Thes ii 13 1 Pet i 2 u Col i 18 x Isa xliii 1 & li y 1 Cor i 24 Heb ix 15 1 Pet iii 9 z Chap v 1 & ix 24 a John xvii

29 For [r] whom he did foreknow, [s] he also did pre-
destinate [t] *to be* conformed to the image of his Son, [u] that
he might be the first-born among many brethren 30
Moreover, whom he did predestinate, [x] them he also
called and whom he called, [y] them he also justified
and whom he justified, [z] them he also glorified

v. 29, 30 The apostle, having mentioned several of the inestimable privileges which belong to the faithful in Christ Jesus, here traces them up to their origin in God's predestination, and to their issue in our eternal glory *For whom he did foreknow*, as the objects of his eternal love, chosen of his sovereign will and pleasure to be to the praise of the glory of his grace, *he also did predestinate to be conformed to the image of his Son*, in holiness of heart and life, in sufferings here, and in eternal glory hereafter, *that he might be the first-born among many brethren*, their Prince and Pattern, having in all things the pre-eminence, the first begotten from the dead, and the forerunner in our name and nature entered for us into possession of the heavenly inheritance *Moreover, whom he did predestinate* to holiness and sufferings as the way, and heaven as the end, *them he also called* by his grace, through the gospel word, to know, embrace, and profess the truth of Jesus, *and whom he called, them he also justified*, discharging them from all guilt and condemnation, and accepting them as righteous through their Covenant Head and Substitute, *and whom he justified, them he also glorified*, advancing them to his own right hand, and making them to sit down with him on his eternal throne And this, being sure to be accomplished in all God's redeemed people, is spoken of as already done, because not one can perish of the many sons whom the Lord Christ is appointed to bring unto glory *Note*, (1) God doth not choose us for any good in us, or done by us, or which he foresaw we should do afterwards, but merely of his sovereign will and pleasure (2) God's predestination is so far from leading us to live as we list, as some suppose, that it is the most powerful argument to walk in holiness as Christ also walked, whereunto we are appointed (3) It were the height of folly to flatter ourselves we shall live with Christ hereafter, if we are not like him now (4) The Redeemer's undertaking was not uncertain; he knew that none whom he purchased should ever perish (5) God by his word, his providence, his Spirit calls all those whom he hath chosen, and so effectually, that they cannot but hear and obey him (6) They who obedient to the gospel call, have fled for refuge to lay hold upon the hope set before them, are justified from all things, and shall never again enter into condemnation, so as finally to perish (7) All the redeemed must be glorified Our salvation stands not upon our frail and sinful selves, but upon the well-ordered covenant, and the perfection of our divine Substitute we are complete in him, and are already sat down in heavenly places with and in Christ Jesus

31 What shall we then say to these things? [a] If God
be for us, who *can be* against us? 32 [b] He that spared
not his own Son, but [c] delivered him up for us all,
[d] how shall he not with him also freely give us all things?
33 [e] Who shall lay any thing to the charge of God's
elect? *It is* God that justifieth 34 [f] Who *is* he that
condemneth? [g] *It is* Christ that died, yea rather that is
risen again, who is even at the right hand of God, [h] who
also maketh intercession for us 35 [i] Who shall sepa-
rate us from the love of Christ? *shall* tribulation? or dis-
tress? or persecution? or famine? or nakedness? or pe-
ril? or sword? 36 (As it is written, [k] For thy sake
we are killed all the day long, we are accounted as sheep
for the slaughter) 37 [l] Nay in all these things we are
more than conquerors through him that loved us 38
For I am persuaded, that neither death, nor life, nor
angels, [m] nor principalities, nor powers, nor things pre-
sent, nor things to come, 39 Nor height, nor depth,
nor any other creature, shall be able to separate us from
the love of God which is in Christ Jesus our Lord

a 2 Kn vi 16 Ps cxviii 6 b Gen xxii 12 Zech xiii 7 c Isa liii John i 29 Chap iv 25 d Ps lxxxiv 11 Mat vi 33 1 Tim iv 8 e Isa l 8 Rev xii 10 f Job xxxiv 29 g Chap. iv 25 h Chap v 1 Heb vii 25 1 John ii 1 i John x k Ps xliv 22 2 Cor iv 11 l 2 Cor ii 14 Rev xii 11 m Eph vi 12

v. 31—39 Having enumerated the distinguishing blessings of the faithful, the apostle triumphantly exults in the assurance of God's unchangeable regard

1 In the view of what God hath done he defies all accusers *What shall we then say to these things?* shall we start back from sufferings when the issue is so glorious? what can we wish or desire more transcendently glorious than these great and precious promises *If God be for us*, with infinite wisdom to guide, almighty power to protect, and boundless love to comfort us, *who can be against us?* what have we to fear from men or devils? they cannot frustrate his purposes of grace, nor disappoint his designs *He that spared not his own Son, but delivered him up for us all*, of his own good pleasure freely gave him to become incarnate, laid upon him our iniquities, and exacted from him all that punishment which his people had deserved, *how shall he not with him also freely give us all things?* what can he now withhold, when, compared with the gift of his Son, every thing besides must appear but little? since he hath given *him*, we may surely conclude he will much more add all the rest, and freely enrich us with all spiritual and eternal blessings in Christ Jesus *Who shall lay any thing to the charge of God's elect?* be their transgressions never so many, great, and aggravated, *it is God that justifieth* them, and, since he hath accepted them in their Surety, they can appear with boldness at his tribunal, and plead that perfect atonement and righteousness which even justice itself must approve *Who is he that condemneth?* let the law accuse, let conscience plead guilty, yet, since he who hath redeemed us from the curse of the law is our Advocate, there is no condemnation, for *it is Christ that died*, he hath paid the ransom, *yea rather that is risen again*, God hath testified his full approbation thereof of his undertaking, and that his justice is completely satisfied, so that we may safely trust upon his finished salvation, *who is even at the right hand of God*, exalted to the highest dignity and glory, as a Prince and Saviour, to give repentance and remission of sins, *who also maketh intercession for us*, our friend in every time of need, and, in the all-prevailing merit of his atonement, pleading effectually our cause, and securing our eternal salvation *Note*, The views of a dying, risen, ascended, glorified Redeemer, should silence all our fears and doubts, and engage us comfortably and confidently to trust him under all our trials for time and for eternity

2 He professes his confidence that, with such a Saviour at the right hand of God, no sufferings shall ever separate our souls from Christ and his love *Who shall separate us from the love of Christ?* what shall be able to quench the flame of his affection towards us, or extinguish the sacred flame which he hath kindled in our bosom? *shall tribulation, or distress, or persecution or famine, or nakedness, or peril, or sword*, shall all the various ills that flesh is heir to, from sickness, pain, poverty, a malignant world, a corrupted nature, a tempting devil, shall these separate us from the Redeemer's arms? No That we must suffer, he hath foretold us, *as it is written, For thy sake we are killed all the day long, we are accounted as sheep for the slaughter*, butchered without remorse by our cruel persecutors, and for the sake of Jesus in jeopardy every hour But do these things move us? Nay, so far from it, that *in all these things we are more than conquerors*, rising superior to every foe, *through him that loved us*, whose inward supports, and consolations over balance all our sufferings, and whose power and grace, continually exerted on our behalf, carry us triumphantly through our conflicts Fr

I am perſuaded, that neither death, with all its terrors, *nor life*, with all its allurements, *nor angels, nor principalities, nor powers*, neither the fiends of darkneſs, nor the perſecuting rulers of the earth, *nor things preſent*, the afflictions and temptations now felt, *nor things to come*, the greater evils which we fear, *nor height* of proſperity, *nor depth* of adverſity, *nor any other creature, ſhall be able to ſeparate us from the love of God which is in Chriſt Jeſus our Lord* Till the Son be ſeparated from the Father's boſom, we never can be ſeparated from his love, for we are one with him in union indiſſoluble When any gracious ſoul is tempted to doubt their final perſeverance, and ready to ſink under preſent trials, let them read this bleſſed chapter, and in the unchangeable love of God in Chriſt ſweetly repoſe He is faithful, therefore we ſhall never periſh

CHAP IX

The apoſtle, 1 Expreſſes his deep concern for his countrymen who rejected the goſpel, ver 1—5 2 *He proves that the promiſes made to the fathers are nevertheleſs made good, ver* 6—13 3 *He anſwers the objections raiſed againſt God's ſovereignty and predeſtination, both with regard to his dealings with Jews and Gentiles, ver* 14—29 4 *If the Gentiles obtained righteouſneſs and ſalvation, and the Jews did not, it was becauſe they ſought it in a wrong way, ver* 30—33

a Chap i 9 2 Cor i 23 ... b Chap x 1 Jer ... c Ex xxxii ... d Deut vii 6 e Ex iv ... Jer xxx 9 f 1 Sam iv ... g Je xxxi ... h ... i ... Chap ... k ... l ... m ... Eph ... Phil ii 9

1 ^a I Say the truth in Chriſt, I lie not, my conſcience
also bearing me witneſs in the holy Ghoſt, 2
That ^b I have great heavineſs and continual ſorrow in
my heart 3 For ^c I could wiſh that myſelf were ac-
curſed from Chriſt for my brethren, my kinſmen accord-
ing to the fleſh 4 ^d Who are Iſraelites, to whom *per-*
taineth ^e the adoption, and ^f the glory, and ^g the cove
nants, and ^h the giving of the law, and the ſervice *of*
God, and the ^i promiſes, 5 ^k Whoſe *are* the fathers,
and ^l of whom as concerning the fleſh Chriſt *came*, ^m who
is over all, God bleſſed for ever Amen

v 1—5 The Jewiſh bigots looked upon Paul as a ſignal apoſtate, and perſecuted him with peculiar virulence and enmity He wiſhed therefore to ſoften their exaſperated ſpirits, whilſt he makes profeſſion of his own tender concern for their welfare and ſalvation And there is a peculiar propriety in his introduction, when we conſider the offenſive truths he was about to advance

1 He makes a ſolemn proteſtation of the very fervent regard he bore towards them *I ſay the truth in Chriſt*, ſolemnly appealing to him who is the ſearcher of hearts, and knoweth that *I lie not, my conſcience alſo bearing me witneſs in the Holy Ghoſt* to the ſimplicity and ſincerity of what I am going to ſay, *that*, far from entertaining the leaſt prejudice or ill-will againſt my countrymen, *I have great heavineſs and continual ſorrow in my heart*, feeling the acuteſt pangs of grief, when I think of their fearful condition, and what muſt be the inevitable conſequences of their unbelief *For I could wiſh that myſelf were accurſed from Chriſt* (ἀνάθεμα), content to be cut off from all my privileges as an apoſtle, and to be ſeparated from the ſociety of the faithful with ſhame and diſgrace, yea to undergo the moſt ignominious and tormenting death, *for my brethren, my kinſmen according to the fleſh*

2 He mentions the diſtinguiſhed privileges with which they had been favoured of God, which could not but make their rejection peculiarly grievous to him *Who are Iſraelites*, bearing the name of their eminent progenitor Jacob *to whom pertaineth the adoption*, taken into that covenant of peculiarity in which God regarded the whole nation as his children, *Exod* iv 22 *and the glory*, the ark, the ſhechinah, the mercy-ſeat, the tokens and emblems of the Divine Preſence in the midſt of them, *and the covenants*, the covenant of circumciſion made with Abraham, and renewed with Iſaac and Jacob, and that of Sinai with the whole body of Iſrael, *and the giving of the law*, containing God's ordinances, *moral, judicial, and ceremonial, and the ſervice of God*, in what manner his worſhip ſhould be performed, *and the promiſes*, of temporal proſperity, which would be the reward of their obedience, and of the Meſſiah and his great ſalvation, *whoſe are the fathers*, the deſcendants of the famed patriarchs, *and of whom, as concerning the fleſh, Chriſt came*, the promiſed ſeed of Abraham in his human nature, but *who* in his divine, *is over all, God bleſſed for ever Amen!* Note, (1) The divinity of our incarnate Saviour is a chief article of our creed Thereon depend the perfection of his work on our behalf (2) A God, the Lord Jeſus is the great object of worſhip, and our prayers and praiſes muſt be addreſſed immediately to him

n Heb ... Acts ... o Chap ... p John viii ... q ...

6 ^n Not as though the word of God hath taken none
effect For they *are* not all Iſrael, which are of Iſrael
7 ^p Neither becauſe they are the ſeed of Abraham, *are*
they all children but ^q in Iſaac ſhall thy ſeed be called ^q Gen xxi 12
8 That is, They which are the children of the fleſh,
theſe *are* not the children of God but ^r the children of ^r Gal iv 28
the promiſe are counted for the ſeed 9 For this *is* the
word of promiſe, ^s At this time will I come, and Sara ^s Gen xviii 10
ſhall have a ſon 10 And not only *this*, but when
^t Rebecca alſo had conceived by one, *even* by our father ^t Gen xxv 21
Iſaac, 11 (For *the children* being not yet born, neither
having done any good or evil, that the purpoſe of
God according to election might ſtand, ^u not of works, ^u 2 Tim i 9
but of him that calleth) 12 It was ſaid unto her,
^x The elder ſhall ſerve the younger 13 As it is writ- ^x Gen xxv 23
ten, ^y Jacob have I loved, but Eſau have I hated ^y Mal i 2

v 6—13 Grief for his unhappy countrymen filled the apoſtle's heart But, though the generality of them periſhed, the promiſe made to Abraham would not be fruſtrated He would *not* therefore have them ſuppoſe *as though the word of God had taken none effect*, and failed of its accompliſhment, becauſe they believed not *It is not poſſible* (as the words may be rendered) *that the word of God ſhould fail For they are not all Iſrael*, true Iſraelites, and ſavingly intereſted in the ſpiritual bleſſings of the covenant, *which are of Iſrael*, the offspring of Jacob, *neither becauſe they are the ſeed of Abraham, are they all children* of God, and ſure of acceptance with him and of ſalvation, as they flattered themſelves External privileges never intitled any ſoul to life and glory And they might very eaſily obſerve that,

1 In the difference made between the two ſons of Abraham, not in Iſhmael, *but in Iſaac* (ſays God, *Gen* xxi 12) *ſhall thy ſeed be called*, from him the Meſſiah was to ſpring, in his line only was the favoured poſterity of Abraham to be reckoned, and like him were the ſpiritual ſeed to be, the children of the free woman, *Gal* iv 22 and partakers of eternal bleſſedneſs *That is, They which are the children of the fleſh*, the natural deſcendants of Abraham, *they are not all the children of God but*, as was evident from the firſt in the caſe of Iſhmael and Iſaac, *the children of the promiſe are counted for the ſeed*, even thoſe who, as Iſaac, are born not of the will of the fleſh, nor of man, but of God, and through faith embrace the great promiſe of ſalvation through Jeſus Chriſt *For this is the word of promiſe, At this time will I come, and Sarah ſhall have a ſon* When Sarah had been long ſince paſt child-bearing, this ſon, the type and figure of the ſpiritual ſeed, was raiſed up through the ſupernatural agency of God according to his promiſe

2 The ſame diſtinction is alſo obſervable between the ſons of Iſaac, though ſprung from the ſame mother, and this too before they were born, and could have done any perſonal acts to cauſe the difference which God was pleaſed to put between them *And not only was this* the caſe with the ſons of Abraham, *but when Rebecca alſo had conceived by one, even by our father Iſaac*, though twins in the ſame womb, God preferred one to the other (*For the children being not yet born, neither having done any good or evil*, there could be nothing in them to influence God's choice, both being alike born in ſin yet were they ſovereignly diſtinguiſhed from each other, *that the purpoſe of God according to election might ſtand* firm and immutable, *not of works*, either done or foreſeen, *but of him that calleth* effectually, according to the good pleaſure of his will) When therefore the children were yet in the womb, *it was ſaid unto her, The elder ſhall ſerve the younger*, Jacob inheriting the birthright and bleſſing, whilſt Eſau was rejected, and in after age the poſterity of the elder became tributary to Iſrael, 2 *Sam* viii 14 *As it is written, Jacob have I loved, but Eſau have I hated* Which ſome refer to the election and rejection of their poſterity, others of their perſon, God ſovereignly chuſing Jacob to be an heir of grace, and leaving Eſau under the corruption and wrath of a fallen nature *Note*, Though none are damned but for their ſin, yet all who are ſaved owe it to God's free and ſovereign grace alone

14 What ſhall we ſay then? ^z *Is there* unrighteouſ- ^z Deut xxxii 4 2 Chron xix 7 Ps xcii 15
neſs with God? God forbid. 15 For he ſaith to Moſes,
^a I will have mercy on whom I will have mercy, and I ^a Ex xxxiii 19
will have compaſſion on whom I will have compaſſion
16 So then ^b *it is* not of him that willeth, nor of him ^b Isa lxv 1
that runneth, but of God that ſheweth mercy 17 For
the ſcripture ſaith unto Pharaoh, ^c Even for this ſame ^c Ex ix 16 Prov xvi 4
purpoſe have I raiſed thee up, that I might ſhew my
power in thee, and that my name might be declared
throughout all the earth 18 Therefore hath he mercy ^d Luke x 21
on whom he will *have mercy*, and whom he will he ^e Job ix 4
hardeneth 19 Thou wilt ſay then unto me, Why doth
he yet find fault? For who hath reſiſted his will? 20 ^f Ps xlvi 9
^g Nay but, O man, who art thou that repliest againſt
God? ^f Shall the thing formed ſay to him that formed *it*,
Why haſt thou made me thus? 21 ^k Hath not the ^k Jer xviii 6
potter power over the clay, of the ſame lump to make
one

one vessel unto honour, and another unto dishonour?
22 *What* if God, willing to shew *his* wrath, and to
make his power known, endured with much long-suffer-
ing [h] the vessels of wrath [i] fitted to destruction: 23.
And that he might make known [k] the riches of his glory
on the vessels of mercy, which he had afore prepared
unto glory? 24 Even us whom he hath called, [l] not
of the Jews only, but also of the Gentiles?

h 1 Thes. v. 9. i 1 Pet. ii. 8. Jude 4. k Eph. i. 7. Col. i. 27. 2 Tim. i. 9. & ii. 21. l Eph. ii. 14. &c.

v. 14—24. The apostle proceeds to vindicate the ways of God to men, and to answer the objections which every fallen spirit naturally raises against the sovereignty of God. *What shall we say then?* If he thus of his mere pleasure chuses one, and leaves another, *Is there* not *unrighteousness with God?* Is not this procedure unjust and partial? *God forbid.* His grace is his own. The favour shewn to some is no injustice to others from whom he is pleased to withhold it.

1. He sovereignly extends mercy to some. *For he saith to Moses, I will have mercy on whom I will have mercy, and I will have compassion on whom I will have compassion.* And such an exercise of his power and grace, in rescuing some of the apostate race of mankind who deserve nothing from him, can be no injustice to the rest. His prerogative it is to do what he will with his own, and whatever he doth must be right. *So then it is not of him that willeth, nor of him that runneth, but of God that sheweth mercy*; the sinner's salvation comes not from any works or will, or ability of his own, recommending him to the divine favour in preference to another, but is an act of sovereign mercy, according to God's eternal purpose.

2. He sovereignly passes by others, and leaves them to the miseries of their fallen nature, as in the case of Pharaoh. *For the scripture saith unto Pharaoh, Even for this same purpose have I raised thee up* to the throne of Egypt, *that I might shew my power in thee*, making this impious king's stubbornness and rebellion the means of more gloriously displaying his own might, and shewing, that those who walk in pride he is able to abase, *and that my name might be declared throughout all the earth*, in the manifestation of my patience and righteous vengeance towards my enemies, and of my love and faithfulness to my chosen.

3. *Therefore*, it is evident, *he hath mercy on whom he will have mercy*, according to the good pleasure of his own will, *and whom he will he hardeneth*, leaving them, like Pharaoh, to the stupidity and pride of their fallen hearts, and, when they have resisted all his warnings and corrections, he delivers them up to judicial blindness and impenitence. And herein he is righteous: as he owes no man any thing, those who are left to themselves have no right to complain, since they are alone the authors of their own miseries, whilst those who are rescued from the ruins of their fallen nature ascribe their recovery to his sovereign and boundless grace.

4. The apostle foresees an objection which would immediately be started against the sovereignty of God, in bestowing his peculiar and distinguishing grace on some, and withholding it from others. *Why doth he yet find fault?* and threaten to punish the disobedience he will not prevent? *for who hath resisted his will?* if he give men up to follow their own hearts, and they cannot but do evil, how can that be construed resistance against him which he abandons them to commit? *Note*, When we hear the same objections now raised against us as were of old against the apostle, it is a strong presumption that our doctrine is the same, and we will answer as he doth.

5. *Nay but, O man, who art thou that repliest against God?* what arrogance for a despicable worm to dispute with his Creator? for a fallen sinner to question a holy God on his procedures? and for folly itself to arraign infinite wisdom at its bar? *Shall the thing formed say to him that formed it, Why hast thou made me thus?* in the dispensations of thy providence and grace leaving me to perish, whilst others equally guilty are saved? *Hath not the potter power over the clay, of the same lump to make one vessel unto honour, and another unto dishonour?* and hath not God the same authority, out of the same mass of the human nature, to form vessels of wrath and mercy, exalting some to undeserved blessedness, and leaving others to most deserved contempt? *What if God, willing to shew his wrath, and to make his power known*, in punishing the wicked, *endured with much long-suffering the vessels of wrath fitted to destruction*: Is this unrighteous? No. The objects of his vengeance most justly suffer. They are corrupted creatures, children of wrath by nature, have rejected his warnings, abused his patience, and filled up the measure of their iniquities: *and* if God hath taken this course, *that he might more eminently make known the riches of his glory on the vessels of mercy, which he had afore prepared unto glory*, can any man object to the riches of his grace, manifested to those whom in his eternal purpose he appointed, and in the fulness of time prepared, for the inheritance among the saints in light? Surely he hath full right to exercise such favour, in preference to others, as he hath done *even to us whom he hath called, not of the Jews only, but also of the Gentiles*. If they are the objects of his love, and the people of his choice, it matters not of what nation they are, he regards them as Abraham's seed, and heirs according to the promise. *Note*, (1.) How hard is it to submit to God's sovereignty, and to be satisfied to be passive

as the clay in the hands of the potter? (2.) None go to hell but those whose sins have fitted them for destruction: none go to heaven but those whom God hath afore prepared unto glory. For which place then are we on the wheel?

25 As he saith also in Osee, [m] I will call them my
people, which were not my people; and her, beloved,
which was not beloved. 26 And [n] it shall come to pass,
that in the place where it was said unto them, Ye *are* not
my people; there shall they be called the children of the
living God. 27 Esaias also crieth concerning Israel,
[o] Though the number of the children of Israel be as the
sand of the sea, [p] a remnant shall be saved: 28. For he
will finish the work, and cut *it* short in righteousness:
because a short work will the Lord make upon the earth.
29 And as Esaias said before, [q] Except the Lord of
sabaoth had left us a seed, we had been [r] as Sodoma,
and been made like unto Gomorrha.

m Hos. ii. 23. 1 Pet. ii. 10. n Hos. i. 10. o Isa. x. 22. p Ch. xi. 5. q Isa. i. 9. Lam. iii. 22. r Gen. xix. 24. Isa. xiii. 19. &c.

v. 25—29. As it was a truth so hard to be digested, and so contrary to the apprehensions of the Jews concerning the promises made unto their fathers, the apostle from the Old Testament proves, that the calling of the Gentiles to all the privileges of children of Abraham had been long since foretold.

1. In Hosea it was said, *I will call them my people, which were not my people, and her beloved, which was not beloved*, bringing the Gentiles, who before were aliens, and disregarded of God, into a covenant relation as his chosen, and treating them as the objects of his peculiar love. *And again* in another place, *It shall come to pass, that in the place where it was said unto them, Ye are not my people, there shall they be called the children of the living God*, admitted to all the privileges of adoption and grace.

2. In Isaiah the rejection of the far greater number of the Jews is declared, into whose room the Gentiles were to succeed. Thus *Esaias also crieth concerning Israel, Though the number of the children of Israel be as the sand of the sea, a remnant* only, according to the election of grace, *shall be saved*, *for*, the prophet in another place adds, *He will finish the work*, and close his accounts, *and cut it short in righteousness*, consuming with just vengeance the apostates: *because a short work will the Lord make upon the earth*, those who are left as monuments of grace will be comparatively but few, whilst the generality of the Jewish nation will quickly be consumed from the face of the earth. *And again, as Esaias had said before* to the same purpose, he adds, *Except the Lord of sabaoth had left us a seed*, at whose disposal are all the hosts of heaven and earth, *we had been as Sodoma, and been made like unto Gomorrha*, utterly cut off as these devoted cities. *Note*, Considering the sinfulness of man, the wonder is not that so few but that any should be saved. When justice might well have destroyed all, it is a matter of astonishing grace that mercy hath been extended to so many.

30 What shall we say then? That the Gentiles [s] which
followed not after righteousness, [t] have attained to righ-
teousness, even the righteousness which is of faith. 31
But Israel, [u] which followed after the law of righteousness,
[x] hath not attained to the law of righteousness. 32
Wherefore? Because *they sought it* not by faith, but as
it were by the works of the law: for [y] they stumbled at
that stumbling stone; 33 As it is written, [z] Behold,
I lay in Sion a stumbling-stone, and rock of offence:
and [a] whosoever believeth on him, shall not be ashamed.

s Ch. iv. 11. t Chap. iii. 21. u Chap. x. 2, 3. x Chap. xi. 7. y Luke ii. 34. 1 Cor. i. 23. z Isa. viii. 14. & xxviii. 16. Matt. xxi. 42. a Chap. x. 11.

v. 30—33. Having proved the rejection of the Jews and the calling of the Gentiles, he suggests the reason. *What shall we say then* further in vindication of God's free grace in saving some, and leaving the rest to perish? It is evident, *that the Gentiles, which followed not after righteousness*, neither knew their malady nor sought their remedy, have notwithstanding *attained to righteousness, even the righteousness which is of faith*, being accepted of God as righteous through faith in Christ Jesus: *but Israel, which followed after the law of righteousness*, and sought justification before God by their own obedience, *hath not attained to righteousness*, not being capable of performing that perfect righteousness which the law demands, and therefore being left under the curse as transgressors. *Wherefore* have they not attained? *Because they sought it not by faith* in the righteousness of another, *but as it were by the works of the law*, placing their dependance upon their own doings and duties, either in part or in the whole, for their acceptance with God: *for they stumbled at that stumbling stone*, the crucified Galilean, whose lowly appearance offended them, and they could not think of embracing him as their Messiah. *As it is written* in Isaiah, *Behold, I lay in Sion a stumbling stone, and rock of offence*, that Messiah who should be the *tried stone* and *sure foundation* to those who believed, and would to those who rejected him be as the rock which dashes those to pieces who fall thereon: *and whosoever believeth on him shall not be ashamed*, though the generality perish in their impenitence and unbelief, yet those few who dare trust him

him for pardon, life, and ſalvation, ſhall never be diſappointed of their hopes, but find him a Saviour to the uttermoſt. *Note*, Nothing is ſo fatal to the ſoul as dependance upon our own righteouſneſs, either in whole or in part, for acceptance with God, whilſt thoſe who, ſelf-deſpairing, fly to the righteouſneſs of faith revealed in the goſpel, are ſure to be juſtified from all things, and ſaved with an everlaſting ſalvation.

CHAP. X.

The apoſtle again (1) repeats his hearty wiſh for the ſalvation of his brethren. (2) Shews the difference between the righteouſneſs of faith and the righteouſneſs of the law, by which they ought to be juſtified, ver. 5—11. (3) *Declares that Jews and Gentiles are on a level, with reſpect to juſtification before God, ver.* 12—18. (4) *He proves this from their own ſcriptures, ver.* 19—21.

a Chap. ix. 1.
1 [a] BRETHREN, my heart's deſire and prayer
to God for Iſrael is, that they might be ſaved.
b Acts xx.
2 For I bear them record, [b] that they have a zeal of
c & xxii.
God, but not according to knowledge. 3 For they
Gal. i.
being ignorant of [c] God's righteouſneſs, and [d] going
& iv. 17.
c Chap. i. 17.
about to eſtabliſh their own righteouſneſs, have not ſub-
d Luke xviii.
11. Chap.
mitted themſelves unto the righteouſneſs of God. 4 For
ix. 31. Phil.
iii. 9.
[e] Chriſt is the end of the law for righteouſneſs to every
e Matt. v. 17.
Acts xiii. 39.
Chap. viii. 3.
Gal. iii. 24.
one that believeth.

v. 1—4. The apoſtle here,

1. Expreſſes his fervent deſire for the ſalvation of his countrymen. *Brethren, my heart's deſire and prayer to God for Iſrael is, that they might be ſaved.* Notwithſtanding what he was, in the the diſcharge of his office, compelled to ſay concerning the general rejection of the Jews, he was yet affectionately deſirous of their ſalvation, and ceaſeleſs in ſupplications at a throne of grace that they might yet be convinced and converted, and thereby plucked as brands from the burning. *Note*, (1.) Thoſe we preach to, we muſt fervently pray for, that God may give them repentance to the acknowledgment of the truth. (2.) They who know the value of immortal ſouls, will feel their eternal intereſts warm upon their hearts.

2. He ſpeaks moſt reſpectfully of them, *For I bear them record, that they have a zeal for God*, a fixed averſion to idolatry, a ſtrong attachment to his law and divinely inſtituted ordinances, and in their perſecutions of Chriſtianity really think they do God ſervice; *but* they are miſguided, and do *not* act *according to knowledge*; they underſtand not the nature and deſign of the law, and have imbibed the ſtrongeſt prejudices againſt the true Meſſiah and the way of ſalvation, which he hath brought to light by the goſpel. *For they being ignorant of God's righteouſneſs*, ignorant of the perfection of obedience which he requires, as the only title to life by the law; ignorant of the ſtrictneſs of his juſtice, which can overlook no flaw, and will accept nothing but what is abſolutely complete; and ignorant of that righteouſneſs, which he hath provided in the incarnate Redeemer whom they rejected, *and going about to eſtabliſh their own righteouſneſs*, reſting their acceptance before God on the footing of their own moral and ceremonial ſervices, *have not ſubmitted to the righteouſneſs of God*, even that divine righteouſneſs which he hath provided and accepted in his dear Son, and which, embraced by faith, is, and can be, the only ground of the ſinner's juſtification before God. *For Chriſt is the end of the law for righteouſneſs to every one that believeth.* He alone perfectly fulfilled the *moral* law, and in his life and death fully ſatisfied the demands of divine juſtice. He hath aboliſhed the *ceremonial* law, being himſelf the ſubſtance of which that was the ſhadow; and the righteouſneſs complete and perfect which he hath wrought out, is the only one, which, being embraced by faith, can juſtify the ſinner before God; to which all, both Jew and Gentile, muſt flee or periſh. *Note*, Nothing is more fatally dangerous to the ſoul, than ignorance of the ſpirituality of God's law, and of our own inability to anſwer its demands. The more zealouſly we ſtrive to commend ourſelves to God, on the footing of our own duties, the more fearfully do we ſeal up our ſouls under wrath.

5 For Moſes deſcribeth the righteouſneſs which *is* of
f Lev. xviii. 5. Gal. iii. 12.
the law, That [f] the man which doth thoſe things, ſhall
live by them. 6 But the righteouſneſs which is of faith,
g Deut. xxx. 12.
ſpeaketh on this wiſe, [g] Say not in thine heart, Who ſhall
aſcend into heaven? (that is, to bring Chriſt down *from
above*:) 7 Or, Who ſhall deſcend into the deep? (that
is, to bring up Chriſt again from the dead.) 8 But what
h Deut. xxx. 14.
ſaith it? [h] The word is nigh thee, *even* in thy mouth,
and in thy heart: that is, the word of faith which we
i Matt. x. 32.
preach, 9 That [i] if thou ſhalt confeſs with thy mouth
k Acts viii. 37.
the Lord Jeſus, and [k] ſhalt believe in thine heart that
God hath raiſed him from the dead, thou ſhalt be ſaved.
10 For with the heart man believeth unto righteouſneſs,
and [l] with the mouth confeſſion is made unto ſalvation. l Phil. ii. 11.
11 For the Scripture ſaith, [m] Whoſoever believeth on m Iſa. xxviii. 16. & xlix. 23. Jer. xvii. 7. Chap. ix. 33.
him ſhall not be aſhamed.

v. 5—11. There are two methods of righteouſneſs.

1. By the law; and that righteouſneſs is thus deſcribed by Moſes, *The man that doth thoſe things*, all that is written in the book of the law perfectly, univerſally, and through, without failure, flaw, or infirmity, *ſhall live by them*, and be entitled to life eternal. But no fallen creature ever did, or ever can do this; therefore juſtification and ſalvation are not this way attainable.

2. By the Redeemer's ſubſtitution and obedience in our ſtead. The law, in our preſent condition, only preaches deſpair; *but the righteouſneſs which is of faith*, which God hath provided and accepted, and faith embraces, *ſpeaketh on this wiſe*, to the conſcience burdened with ſin and guilt, *Say not in thine heart*, as if deſpairing of juſtification before God, *Who ſhall aſcend into heaven, that is, to bring Chriſt down from above* to make atonement for ſin: it is needleſs, ſeeing by one oblation, once offered, he hath perfected for ever his redeemed: *or who ſhall deſcend into the deep? that is, to bring up Chriſt again from the dead.* This is already done, and God, by the reſurrection of Jeſus, hath teſtified the full ſatisfaction which hath been made to his law and juſtice, ſo that the bar to our acceptance before God is now removed. Inſtead therefore of the impoſſibilities, which guilty fear and unbelief would ſuggeſt, the goſpel opens a door of hope to the miſerable and the deſperate. *But what ſaith it?* Why, all that we can wiſh and deſire, to ſilence our terrors and revive our drooping hearts. *The word is nigh thee, even in thy mouth, and in thy heart*, brought near in the goſpel revelation, acknowledged, and made effectual by the ſpirit to the heart; *that is the word of faith which we preach*, holding up Chriſt as the glorious object, whom faith embraces for righteouſneſs and ſalvation: the tenor of our declarations, as authorized of God to ſpeak, is this, *that if thou ſhalt confeſs with thy mouth the Lord Jeſus*, as the true Meſſiah, *and ſhalt believe in thine heart that God hath raiſed him from the dead, thou ſhalt be ſaved.* No works of the law, nor other title whatever, is needful to eternal life but this; and all who, renouncing themſelves, repoſe their whole confidence upon Jeſus, as delivered for their offences, and raiſed for their juſtification, are built on that foundation which never can be moved. *For with the heart man believeth unto righteouſneſs*; faith is not a mere notion entertained in the head, but the cordial ſubmiſſion of the heart to the Redeemer's righteouſneſs, as a matter in which it is deeply intereſted; *and with the mouth confeſſion is made* of our faith before God and men *unto ſalvation*, there being an inſeparable connection between true faith and eternal bleſſedneſs; *for the ſcripture ſaith, whoſoever believeth on him ſhall not be aſhamed*, whatever his condition hath been, he will never be aſhamed of Chriſt, and however great his guilt, no condemnation ſhall lie againſt him, either in time or eternity, but he ſhall have boldneſs in the day of judgment. Lord, in this faith may I be found, living and dying! making mention of thy righteouſneſs only!

12 For [n] there is no difference between the Jew and n Acts x. 34. & xv. 9. Chap. iii. 22, 29.
the Greek: for the ſame Lord over all, [o] is rich unto o Eph. i. 7. & ii. 4.
all that call upon him. 13 For [p] whoſoever ſhall call p Joel ii. 32. Acts ii. 21.
upon the name of the Lord, ſhall be ſaved. 14 [q] How
then ſhall they call on him in whom they have not be-
lieved? and [r] how ſhall they believe in him of whom q Heb. xi. 6.
they have not heard? and [s] how ſhall they hear without r John xv. 22.
a preacher? 15 And [t] how ſhall they preach, except
they be ſent? as it is written, [u] How beautiful are the s Tit. i. 3.
feet of them that preach the goſpel of peace, and bring t Matt. ix. 38.
glad tidings of good things! 16 But [x] they have not u Iſa. lii. 7. Nah. i. 15.
all obeyed the goſpel. For Eſaias ſaith, [y] Lord, who x Heb. iv.
hath believed our report? 17 So then faith *cometh* by y Iſa. liii. 1. John xii. 38.
hearing, and hearing by the word of God. 18 But I
ſay, Have they not heard? Yes verily, [z] their ſound z Pſ. xix. 4. Matt. xxiv.
went into all the earth, and their words unto the ends of 14. & xxviii. 19. Col. i.
the world. 19 But I ſay, Did not Iſrael know? Firſt 6, 23.
Moſes ſaith, [a] I will provoke you to jealouſy by *them* a Deut. xxxii. 21.
that are no people, *and* by a fooliſh nation I will anger
you. 20 But Eſaias is very bold, and ſaith, [b] I was b Iſa. lxv. 1. Chap. ix. 30.
found of them that ſought me not; I was made manifeſt
unto them that aſked not after me. 21 But to Iſrael
he ſaith, [c] All day long I have ſtretched forth my hands c Prov. i. 24. Iſa. lxv. 2.
unto a diſobedient and gainſaying people.

v. 12—21. Under the goſpel diſpenſation mankind are on a level, without reſpect to any people or nation. *For there is no difference between the Jew and the Greek*; both have ſinned, and come ſhort of the glory of God; both muſt be ſaved freely by grace, through the redemption which is in Jeſus Chriſt, or periſh everlaſtingly: *for the ſame* Redeemer, who is *Lord over all, is rich* in grace, and boundleſs in mercy *unto all that call upon him*, as periſhing and helpleſs without him. *For*, ſo it was foretold,

Joel ii 32 *whoſoever*, without exception, *ſhall call upon the name of the Lord* Jeſus, depending upon his atonement and righteouſneſs alone, *ſhall be ſaved* from guilt and ſin, and wrath and hell, and advanced to eternal glory But if the Gentiles are included in the diſpenſation of the goſpel, then

1 It was needful that the goſpel ſhould be preached to them, and Paul's brethren had no juſt ground for their enmity againſt him, becauſe he was appointed the apoſtle of the Gentiles For *How then ſhall they call on him in whom they have not believed?* Faith is eſſential to the very being of prayer, and without it the ſervice of the lip and the knee is vain and unprofitable, *and how ſhall they believe in him of whom they have not heard?* They muſt hear of Jeſus in his ſaving offices, before they can poſſibly truſt in him *and how ſhall they hear without a preacher*, to make known to them the revelation of God's will? *and how ſhall they preach except they be ſent* with a divine commiſſion? *Note*, Before any preſume to preach, let it be clear that they have a miſſion from God To run unſent is inſolent preſumption

2 The goſpel contains the beſt news which ever reached mortal ears, and ſhould be matter of joy wherever it is carried, *as it is written*, Iſaiah lii 7 *How beautiful are the feet of them that preach the goſpel of peace, and bring glad tidings of good things!* which prophecy terminated not in the joyful meſſages of Iſrael's deliverance from Babylon, but looked forward to the great redemption of Jeſus, and that goſpel which his miniſters ſhould publiſh, *a goſpel of peace*, where God was in Chriſt, reconciling ſinners to himſelf, and proclaiming the glad news of pardon and ſalvation to guilty and periſhing ſouls, and they who feel the comfort of the meſſage, cannot but, for its ſake, delight in and honour the meſſengers

3 Though the goſpel in itſelf contained ſuch a welcome meſſage, yet in general, both among Jews and Gentiles, it hath been rejected *But they have not all obeyed the goſpel*, and yielded themſelves up to the Saviour No, contrariwiſe the generality of thoſe, to whom it is preached, harden their hearts *For Eſaias ſaith*, foreſeeing the little ſucceſs which the miniſters of Chriſt ſhould meet with, *Who hath believed our report?* How few are found faithful among the many called? Yet the goſpel report is the ſavour of life unto life in them who are ſaved *So then faith cometh by hearing, and hearing by the word of God*, this being the ordinary means, and made effectual by the ſpirit's power, *that arm of the Lord* which reveals Chriſt to the heart

4 *But I ſay, have they not heard*, both Jews and Gentiles, the goſpel word? *Yes verily, their ſound went into all the earth, and their words unto the ends of the world* And this extenſive ſpread of the goſpel, by thoſe preachers whom he ſent forth, however the multitude rejected the counſel of God, was a token of his good will to the Gentiles, and of his deſign to gather out of them a people to be to the praiſe of the glory of his grace

5 *But I ſay, did not Iſrael know* that God deſigned to ſhew mercy to the Gentiles? Had they attended to their own prophets, they would have ſeen how groundleſs their imaginations were that the bleſſings of the Meſſiah's kingdom ſhould be confined to them, and the Gentiles excluded For *firſt Moſes ſaith*, for whom they profeſs peculiar veneration, *I will provoke you to jealouſy by them that are no people, and by a fooliſh nation will I anger you* The Gentiles were long excluded from God's regard, and, amidſt all their wiſdom, were entirely ignorant of ſpiritual things to have them now brought into favour, and made wiſe unto ſalvation, ſhould have provoked a holy emulation in the Jewiſh nation, but it wrought a contrary effect, exciting the greateſt bitterneſs and enmity againſt the converted Gentiles (2) He produces another ſcripture, ſtrongly proving the divine determination, with regard to the calling of the Gentiles and the rejection of the Jews Moſes had intimated it, *but Eſaias is very bold*, and, with great plainneſs and freedom, foretells to his countrymen this mortifying event, *and ſaith, I was found of them that ſought me not, I was made manifeſt unto them that aſked not after me*, preventing the Gentiles with the bleſſings of his goodneſs, and the calls of his grace, when they were without one thought of God, worſhipping their idols, and had not ſo much as a deſire in their hearts after him *But to Iſrael he ſaith*, now to be rejected for their impenitence and obſtinacy, *all day long I have ſtretched forth my hands unto a diſobedient and gainſaying people*, his patience therefore being wearied out, eſpecially by their oppoſition to the goſpel, he abandons them to ruin *Note*, (1) If God had not firſt ſought us, we ſhould never have enquired after him (2) When the Lord hath waited long to be gracious, and uſed the moſt powerful means to work upon the ſinner's heart, if he ſtill rejects the counſel of God againſt his own ſoul, juſtly doth God decree, my ſpirit ſhall not always ſtrive, and leaves him to the deſtruction which he hath choſen

CHAP XI

The apoſtle having reconciled that great truth of the rejection of the Jews with the promiſes made to the fathers, is in this chapter farther labouring to mollify the harſhneſs of it, and to reconcile it to the divine goodneſs in general It might be ſaid, Hath God then caſt away his people? *The apoſtle therefore ſets himſelf in this chapter to give an anſwer to this objection, and that two ways 1 He ſhews at large what the mercy is, that is mixed with this wrath*, ver 1—32 *2 He infers from thence the infinite wiſdom and ſovereignty of God, with the adoration of which he concludes this chapter and ſubject*, ver 33—36

1 I SAY then, [a] Hath God caſt away his people? God
forbid For [b] I alſo am an Iſraelite, of the ſeed of
Abraham, *of* the tribe of Benjamin 2 God hath not
caſt away his people [c] which he foreknew Wot ye not
what the ſcripture ſaith of Elias? how he maketh in-
terceſſion to God againſt Iſrael, ſaying, 3 [d] Lord, they
have killed thy prophets, and digged down thine altars,
and I am left alone, and they ſeek my life 4 But
what ſaith the anſwer of God unto him? [e] I have reſerved
to myſelf ſeven thouſand men, who have not bowed
the knee to *the image of* Baal 5 Even ſo then at this
preſent time alſo [f] there is a remnant according to the
election of grace 6 And [g] if by grace, then *is it* no
more of works otherwiſe grace is no more grace But
if *it be* of works, then is it no more grace otherwiſe
work is no more work 7 What then? [h] Iſrael hath not
obtained that which he ſeeketh for, but the election
hath obtained it, and [i] the reſt were blinded 8 Ac
cording as it is written, [k] God hath given them the ſpirit
of ſlumber, [l] eyes that they ſhould not ſee, and ears that
they ſhould not hear, unto this day 9 And David
ſaith, [m] Let their table be made a ſnare, and a trap, and
a ſtumbling-block, and a recompence unto them 10
Let their eyes be darkened, that they may not ſee, and
bow down their back alway. 11 I ſay then, Have
they ſtumbled that they ſhould fall? God forbid but
rather [n] through their fall ſalvation *is come* unto the
Gentiles, [o] for to provoke them to jealouſy 12 Now
if the fall of them *be* the riches of the world, and the di-
miniſhing of them the riches of the Gentiles how much
more their fulneſs? 13 For I ſpeak to you Gentiles,
in as much as [p] I am the apoſtle of the Gentiles, I
magnify mine office 14. [q] If by any means I may
provoke to emulation *them which are* my fleſh, and might
ſave ſome of them 15 For if the caſting away of
them *be* the reconciling of the world what *ſhall* the
receiving *of them be*, but life from the dead? 16 For
[r] if the firſt fruit *be* holy, the lump *is* alſo *holy* and if the
root *be* holy, ſo *are* the branches 17 And if [s] ſome
of the branches be broken off, and [t] thou being a wild
olive-tree, wert graffed in amongſt them, and with them
partakeſt of the root and fatneſs of the olive-tree,
18 [u] Boaſt not againſt the branches but, if thou boaſt,
thou beareſt not the root, but the root thee 19 Thou
wilt ſay then, The branches were broken off, that I
might be graffed in 20 Well, becauſe of unbelief
they were broken off, and thou ſtandeſt by faith Be
not high-minded, but [x] fear 21 For if God ſpared not
the natural branches, *take heed* leſt he alſo ſpare not
thee 22 Behold therefore the goodneſs and ſeverity
of God, on them which fell, ſeverity, but towards
thee, goodneſs, [y] if thou continue in *his* goodneſs
otherwiſe [z] thou alſo ſhalt be cut off 23 And they
alſo, if they bide not ſtill in unbelief, ſhall be graffed
in for God is able to [a] graff them in again 24 For
if thou wert cut out of the olive tree which is wild by
nature, and wert graffed contrary to nature into a good
olive-tree how much more ſhall theſe which be the
natural *branches*, be graffed into their own olive-tree?
25 For I would not, brethren, that ye ſhould be igno
rant of this myſtery, ([b] leſt ye ſhould be wiſe in your
own conceits) that [c] blindneſs in part is happened to
Iſrael, [d] until the fulneſs of the Gentiles be come in
26 And ſo all Iſrael ſhall be ſaved as it is written,
[e] There ſhall come out of Sion the deliverer, and ſhall
turn away ungodlineſs from Jacob 27 For [f] this *is*
my covenant unto them, when I ſhall take away their
ſins 28 As concerning the goſpel, *they are* enemies for
your ſake but as touching the election, [g] *they are* be-
loved for the fathers ſakes 29 For the gifts and cal-
ling of God *are* without repentance. 30 For [h] as ye
in times paſt have not believed God, yet have now
obtained mercy through their unbelief 31 Even ſo
have

have these also now not † believed, that through your mercy they also may obtain mercy 32 For ‡ God hath concluded them all in unbelief, that he might have mercy upon all

† Or, obeyed ‡ Or, shut them all up together Gal iii.

v 1—32 Nothing could be more grating to the Jews than this subject of their rejection, and some one might say, *Hath God cast away his people*, universally, and finally? *God forbid*

1 Though some are cast off, yet not all

2 If the nation of Jews in general be at present abandoned, the Gentiles are called into the Messiah's kingdom

3 The time will come when the Jews shall be brought back, and admitted into the church of the redeemed

1 Though some are cast off, yet not all of this Paul was himself an instance *For I also am an Israelite, of the seed of Abraham, of the tribe of Benjamin*, and though none shewed greater bitterness against the gospel, yet have I obtained mercy, and multitudes besides, of the Jewish people, share the same blessing, for *God hath not cast away his people which he foreknew*, having a chosen generation, whom he from eternity decreed to bring up to glory, though the generality should perish in their unbelief, and these were more than might be at first imagined, as was the case in the days of Elias, when, on account of their general defection to idolatry, and persecution of God's prophets, that zealous reformer complained to God as if he was left alone, and his life daily in jeopardy, and, from the melancholy appearances, could not but conclude that the people were ripe for ruin But God informs him that, bad as things were, he had still reserved seven thousand faithful worshippers, who had not bowed to Baal, *even so then at this present time also there is a remnant according to the election of grace* *Note*, (1) There are many more faithful souls than we, looking round on the general apostacy, are ready to suppose (2) In every age the children of God have been but few, like these seven thousand, compared with the myriads of Israel (3) If any soul be kept from swimming down the stream of general corruption, it is of God's mere grace, or we had been exactly like our neighbours (4) When religion is out of countenance, it is a great thing to dare to be singular, and not bow the knee to Baal (5) If there had not been an *election of grace*, the whole human race had been as the angels which left their first estate, and had perished with them —*And if* this election of some, in preference to others, be *by grace*, of God's mere sovereign and undeserved favour, *then is it no more of works*, either done by them, or foreseen in them, as the motive for his choice of them, for, *otherwise, grace is no more grace* The very idea of grace would be destroyed, if any thing in the objects recommended them, in preference to others, to the divine regard *But if*, on the other hand, *it be of works*, in any sense whatever, *then it is no more grace, otherwise work is no more work*, these standing in direct opposition to each other Salvation must therefore be wholly of the one or the other, but it cannot be of works, for we have none which can bear the severity of God's justice it must therefore be of grace, or not at all *What then* is the case? Why the fact is evident, *Israel hath not attained that which he seeketh for*, the reason of which is given, *chap* ix 31, 32 *but the election hath obtained it*, through faith in Jesus, professing that righteousness which entitles them to life eternal, *and the rest were blinded*, left to their impenitence and unbelief, and perishing by the sentence of that law, for their obedience to which they expected justification before God *Note*, (1) Our election of God is the groundwork of all our hopes and happiness in time and eternity (2) They who trust in whole or in part on their works for salvation, make Christ to have died in vain, and the grace of God of no effect (3) They who trust on their own righteousness, are ever most hardened against the gospel method of salvation

In proof of what he had alledged, terrible as it might appear to some, he appeals to the scriptures, *according as it is written, God hath given them the spirit of slumber, eyes that they should not see, and ears that they should not hear unto this day* They are sunk into stupidity, and insensibility, and in just judgment for their rejection of all the means, mercies, and corrections vouchsafed to them, especially for their wilful unbelief of the gospel, God hath abandoned them to a reprobate mind, and unto this day it continues *And*, to the same effect, *David saith*, when speaking of the enemies of the Messiah, *Let their table be made a snare, and a trap, and a stumbling block, and a recompence unto them* Their altar, and all the ritual service on which they depended, would prove the means of their ruin, or those bounties of Providence, which they abused to pride and luxury, should intoxicate them, and, like drunken men, for the punishment of their infidelity, they should stumble into perdition *Let their eyes be darkened, that they may not see*, since they hate the light, they shall be left in blindness, *and bow down their back alway*, under perpetual bondage and servitude, enslaved by the powers of earth, and more enslaved by worldly-mindedness, by sin and Satan *Note*, (1) Of all judgments, spiritual ones are most to be dreaded, and yet are usually least perceived (2) They who mind earthly things, ... but will in darkness

2 Though the Jews were cast off for a while, the Gentiles were called into the church

I say then, have they stumbled that they should fall, utterly and irrecoverably? *God forbid but rather* so hath God ordered it in his providence, *that through their fall salvation is come unto the Gentiles* (see *Acts* xiii 46, 47) *for to provoke them to jealousy*, that, ashamed to be outdone by the Gentiles, they may be stirred up to a noble emulation *Now if the fall of them be the riches of the world, and the diminishing of them the riches of the Gentiles*, God in his infinite wisdom and mysterious designs making the apostacy and obstinacy of the Jews the occasion of spreading his gospel the sooner among the Gentiles, whom he is pleased to enrich with the abundance of his grace, *how much more* will the Gentiles be confirmed in the faith, and the multitude of converts increase when they shall see *their fulness*, the restoration of the dispersed Jews to their forfeited privileges, when at the last they shall be turned to the Lord? *For I speak to you Gentiles*, for your comfort and caution, *in as much as I am the apostle of the Gentiles*, particularly appointed of God to preach the gospel to you, *I magnify mine office*, I glory in my employment, and bless God for having honoured me so far as to appoint me thereunto And this I say, *If by any means I may provoke to emulation them which are my flesh*, to outstrip the Gentiles, ashamed to be exceeded by them in faith and holiness, *and might thus save some of them*, by leading them to Christ for pardon, grace, and eternal life, *for*, as I said, *if the casting away of them be the reconciling of the world*, the gospel, through their infidelity, being sent unto the Gentiles, *what shall the receiving of them be, but life from the dead*? How surprizing and delightful will that great event be, when the Jews in general shall be converted to Christ, and restored to the church as men raised from the dead, and their conversion inspire the Gentiles with fresh life and vigour! *For if the first fruits be holy* and some few converts of the Jewish people now appear the pledges and earnests of what God will do for the nation hereafter, *the lump is also holy*, and they shall at last be wholly consecrated as a nation to God *and if the root be holy*, Abraham and the patriarchs, from whom the Jews descended, considered as their fœderal head, to whom and his seed the promises were made, *so are the branches*, they have a relative holiness in virtue of their descent, and though at present their unbelief cuts them off from all the privileges of the covenant, yet for the fathers sake, in future ages God's love to them, as a nation, shall appear, and they shall again be received into the bosom of his church *And if some of the branches be broken off*, for their unbelief, *and thou*, a Gentile, *being a wild olive-tree*, by birth an alien from the commonwealth of Israel, and a stranger to the covenants of promise, *wert graffed in amongst them, and with them partakest of the root and fatness of the olive-tree*, admitted in common with Abraham's natural descendants, who believe, to share in all the blessings and privileges of the covenant of grace, *boast not against the branches*, looking down with scorn on the Jews, who for their infidelity are broken off, *but if thou boast*, and grow proud of thy advancement, remember, *thou bearest not the root, but the root thee*, and all the mercies thou enjoyest are from the Jews; from them, according to the flesh, Christ descended, the first preachers of the gospel were of their nation, and all church privileges are derived from Abraham, the great father of the faithful therefore this people, though now fallen, must not be trampled upon *Thou wilt say then*, perhaps, *The branches were broken off, that I might be graffed in*, I was preferred to them, and have reason to esteem myself above them *Well, because of unbelief they were broken off*, it was not on account of any goodness in you, but because of their own infidelity, *and thou standest by faith*, not holding your privileges on account of any desert, but through God's free grace in Christ Jesus and therefore all boasting is excluded *Be not then high minded but fear*, lest you also fall, through the same example of unbelief *For if God spared not the natural branches, take heed lest he also spare not thee*, if the Gentiles imitated their pride and unbelief, they might much more apprehend he would deal with them in the same manner, and deprive them of all the privileges to which he had admitted them *Behold therefore*, and admire *the goodness and severity of God on them which fell*, he hath executed just *severity*, cutting them off from his church, and depriving them of all the privileges of his people, *but towards thee*, unworthy as thou art, he hath shewn the most transcendent *goodness*, admitting thee, a despised idolatrous Gentile, into his kingdom, and will continue to bless thee, *if thou continue in his goodness*, and do not abuse the merciful dispensation, under which you at present stand, by pride and infidelity *otherwise thou also shalt be cut off*, and no nominal profession of Christianity, if the heart prove apostate, will secure any man from the wrath of God

3 There is still hope in the end, that all Israel, notwithstanding their present rejection, shall at last be converted and saved *And they also, if they abide not still in unbelief, shall be graffed in* and when they receive the gospel, and believe in Jesus, as the Messiah, shall be readmitted into the church of the redeemed, *for God is able to graff them in again*, as the children of believing Abraham Nor is this at all inconceivable or improbable, *for if thou wert cut out of the olive tree, which is wild by nature*, sprung from the Gentile stock, which was out of the covenant, *and wert graffed contrary to nature into a good olive tree*, which is like graffing a wild scion on a good tree, *how much more shall these*, which

which be the natural branches, and descendants of Abraham, *be grafted into their own olive tree?* and be received into the gospel-church, which was once wholly confined to their people and nation. *For I would not, brethren, that ye should be ignorant of this mystery, (lest ye should be wise in your own conceits,* puffed up with an opinion of your own excellence, and fancying that the favour of God is henceforth to be confined to you alone), *that blindness in part is happened to Israel,* and they are left to their unbelief for a while, *until the fulness of the Gentiles be come in,* when in the latter days the nations of the earth shall, in a more general manner than ever, become obedient to the faith. *And so all Israel shall be saved,* in general they shall be brought into the gospel-church, and converted to the Lord: *as it is written, There shall come out of Sion the deliverer, and shall turn away ungodliness from Jacob,* the adored Messiah in the last days shall go forth in the power of his gospel, and by the efficacy of his word and Spirit shall turn these disobedient unto the wisdom of the just, so that all their iniquities shall be pardoned, and the enmity of their hearts be subdued by his almighty grace. *For this is my covenant unto them,* and he will fulfil his promises, as will be seen in the latter day, *when I shall take away their sins,* freely pardoning, for his name's sake, all that is past, and receiving them into the arms of his everlasting love.

Upon the whole then the state of the case stands thus: *As concerning the gospel, they are at present enemies to it,* and permitted so to be *for your sake,* that the gospel might be the sooner and farther diffused thro' the Gentile world, (*Acts* xiii 46, 47.) *But as touching the election* of them as a nation to be his peculiar people, *they are beloved for the fathers' sakes,* and though for the present abandoned, yet there is still mercy in store for them. *For the gifts and calling of God are without repentance,* God is in one mind, and cannot change, and having made his promises to Israel, as a chosen nation, they shall assuredly be called again into his church, and the elect among them be made partakers of eternal salvation. *For as ye in times past have not believed God,* but lived without him in the world, serving stocks and stones, *yet have now obtained mercy,* through God's boundless grace admitted into the fellowship and privileges of the gospel, *through their unbelief,* who put that gospel from them: *even so have these also now not believed,* but have been left to infidelity, *that through your mercy they also may obtain mercy,* provoked to emulation by you, and led by it to embrace the same Redeemer, through whom the Gentiles have found acceptance with God. And this conversion of the Jews is at least as likely, and will be as sure, as the conversion of the idolatrous Gentiles. *For God hath concluded them all in unbelief,* both Jews and Gentiles have been left by turns under the power of infidelity, *that he might glorify the riches of his grace* towards both, *and have mercy upon all,* upon the body of Jews and Gentiles in general, making them at last one fold under one shepherd.

Some suppose this conversion of the Jews is already past, and that, after the destruction of their city and temple, multitudes were convinced, and converted to Jesus as the Messiah: but I am much more inclined to think, that this prophecy is yet to receive its accomplishment. And it is a very remarkable circumstance, that the Jewish people, in all their dispersions, are still as distinct from the nations among whom they dwell, as ever, and, no doubt, are thus by divine providence preserved for this great event.

33 O the depth of the riches both of the wisdom and
knowledge of God! [k] how unsearchable *are* his judgments,
and [l] his ways past finding out! 34 For [m] who hath
known the mind of the Lord, or [n] who hath been his
counsellor? 35 Or who hath first given to him, and
it shall be recompensed unto him again? 36 For [o] of
him, and through him, and to him, *are* all things: to
whom *be* glory for ever. Amen.

k Job v 9 Ps xxxvi 6. l Job xi 7. m Job xv 8 Jer xxiii 18 Wisd ix 13 1 Cor ii 16. n Isa xl 13 Job xxxv 7 Chap xi 11. o 1 Cor viii 6 Col i 16.

v 33—36. Having evidently reconciled the *rejection* of the Jews with the justice and goodness of God, and shewn that there was mercy yet in store for them, in the view of this astonishing dispensation the apostle breaks out, *O the depth of the riches both of the wisdom and knowledge of God! how unsearchable are his judgments, and his ways past finding out!* Rather the apostle dare no pry into the divine counsels, but stands admiring on the ocean's brink, and cries, O the depth of the riches of that grace, which both Jews and Gentiles experience, unworthy as they are of the least of it! What wisdom and knowledge appear in the contrivance of this admirable scheme, planned in the divine mind, to make even the rejection of the Jews subservient to the calling of the Gentiles, and their conversion, the means at last of restoring the Jews to the divine favour. These counsels are too deep for us to fathom, the reasons of his determinations are hid in his own eternal mind, and the methods which in his providence he takes to effect his own purposes, are beyond our ken, we are lost in the labyrinth of which he who is infinite in wisdom only holds the clue. *For who hath known the mind of the Lord?* what creature ever pried into the deep things of God, or could discover his eternal counsels? *Or who hath been his counsellor?* nor man nor angel were consulted in planning his designs of grace, where all was fixed by his infinite wisdom, according to his sovereign pleasure. *Or who hath first given to him, and it shall be recompensed unto him again?* Who can claim any thing by right from him? He is debtor neither to Jew nor Gentile, and how then dare any arraign his procedure, or say unto him, What dost thou? *For of him, and through him, and to him are all things,* all things in nature and providence own him their former and upholder, their efficient cause, and ultimate end; and in the dispensation of his grace especially, the whole of the sinner's salvation from first to last is derived from him, arising from his sovereign pleasure, the effect of his infinite wisdom and love, accomplished by his power, and designed for the advancement of his glory; *to whom therefore* it is most fit, that the redeemed upon earth, and the exalted spirits in heaven, should ascribe *glory for ever!* and all who have tasted of his grace, will add their joyful *Amen!* Note, Though we have the deepest insight into the mysteries of grace, the wisest must own, that they know but a part of God's ways. There are many things which our short line cannot fathom, and we can only resolve into the divine sovereignty: our business there is not to dispute, but believe; not to demand God's reasons, but to acquiesce in his determinations; not to cavil, but to admire and adore!

CHAP. XII.

The apostle having at large cleared and confirmed the principal fundamental doctrines of Christianity, comes in the next place to press the principal duties. We mistake our religion, if we look upon it only as a system of notions, and a guide to speculation. No, it is a practical religion, that tends to the right ordering of the conversation. It is designed not only to inform our judgment, but to convert our souls, and amend our lives. The riches of grace revealed in the gospel are designed to engage our hearts to God, and to make us holy and happy. This chapter contains an exhortation to believers, engaging them, 1. To dedicate themselves wholly to God, ver. 1, 2. *2. To walk humbly before him,* ver. 3—5. *3. To use faithfully their gifts to God's glory, and their brethren's edification,* ver. 6—8. *4. To discharge the various duties which adorn their character,* ver. 9—21.

1 [a] I BESEECH you therefore, brethren, by the
mercies of God, that [b] ye present [c] your bodies
[d] a living sacrifice, holy, acceptable unto God, [e] *which is*
your reasonable service. 2 And [f] be not conformed to
this world: but [g] be ye transformed by the renewing of
your mind, [h] that ye may prove what *is* that good and
acceptable and perfect will of God. 3 For I say,
[i] through the grace given unto me, to every man that is
among you, [k] not to think *of himself* more highly than he
ought to think; but to think soberly, according [l] as God
hath dealt to every man the measure of faith. 4 For as
we have many members in one body, and all members
have not the same office: 5 So [m] we being many are
one body in Christ, and every one members one of another.
6 [n] Having then gifts, differing according to
the grace that is given to us, whether prophecy, *let us prophesy*
[o] according to the proportion of faith; 7 Or ministry,
[p] *let us wait* on *our* ministring; or he that teacheth,
on teaching; 8 Or he that exhorteth, on exhortation:
[q] he that giveth, *let him do it* with simplicity;
[r] he that ruleth, with diligence; he that sheweth mercy,
with cheerfulness. 9 [s] *Let* love *be* without dissimulation.
[t] Abhor that which is evil; cleave to that which is good.
10 [u] *Be* kindly affectioned one to another with brotherly
love; [x] in honour preferring one another; 11 [y] Not
slothful in business; [z] fervent in spirit; serving the Lord;
12 [a] Rejoicing in hope; [b] patient in tribulation; [c] continuing
instant in prayer; 13 Distributing to the necessity
of saints; [e] given to hospitality. 14 [f] Bless
them which persecute you: bless, and curse not. 15
[g] Rejoice with them that do rejoice, and weep with them
that weep. 16 [h] *Be* of the same mind one towards another.
[i] Mind not high things, but condescend to men
of low estate. [k] Be not wise in your own conceits. 17
[l] Recompense to no man evil for evil. [m] Provide things
honest in the sight of all men. 18 If it be possible, as
much as lieth in you, [n] live peaceably with all men.
19 Dearly beloved, [o] avenge not yourselves, but rather
give place unto wrath: for it is written, Vengeance *is*
mine; I will repay, saith the Lord. 20 Therefore if
thine enemy hunger, feed him; if he thirst, give him
drink: for in so doing thou shalt heap coals of fire on

a 2 Cor x 1. b 1 Pet ii 5. Chap vi 13. Luke i 74, 75. 1 Cor vi 20. Heb x 20. 1 Pet ii 5. 1 Cor vi 20. 1 Pet iv 2. 1 John ii 15. Eph iv 23. Acts xv. 1 Cor iii. Prov xxvi 12. 1 Cor iv. Eph. 1 Tim vi 17. 1 Pet iv 10. 1 John. Acts. 1 Pet i 22. Phil ii. Prov xii. 1 Pet iv. Chap xvi. James ii. 1 Thess. Matt v. 1 Cor x. Heb xiii. Jer. 1 Cor. Matt v 39. 1 Cor vi. Heb. Lev xix 18.

5

q Prov xxiv 21. his head 21 q Be not overcome of evil, but overcome evil with good

v 1—21 The doctrines of grace are so far from leading to licentiousness, that nothing but these can effectually engage the heart to walk in holiness as Christ also walked

1 The apostle exhorts them to yield themselves wholly to God *I beseech you therefore, brethren, by the mercies of God*, by the consideration of that sovereign, boundless, undeserved grace, which you have tasted, *that*, constrained by a sense of such distinguishing and astonishing love, *ye*, as spiritual priests, *present your bodies*, not the carcase of a dead animal, but a nobler oblation than any which were offered under the law, even *a living sacrifice*, your whole selves to be employed for God's glory, *holy*, without allowed guile, in spirit, temper, and conduct, conformed to his will, and *acceptable to God* thro Jesus Christ, in whom your persons and services are regarded as a sacrifice of a sweet smell, all *which is your reasonable service*, to be performed with all the powers of your rational souls, and most fit and right, considering the infinite obligations lying upon you *And* in order hereunto, *be not conformed to this world*, to its temper, maxims, fashions, manners, *but be ye transformed by the renewing of your mind*, after the image of God in righteousness and true holiness, *that ye may prove what is that good, and acceptable, and perfect will of God*, discerning what is the mind of God in his word, commending to others the excellence and importance of the revelation he hath made, and cast into the very mould of the gospel, the best proof of your approbation of it *Note*, (1) No argument is so powerful to engage the ingenuous heart, as a sense of the mercies of God (2) The most acceptable sacrifice to God is the surrender of our whole selves to him at the feet of the cross of Jesus, the altar which sanctifies the gift (3) They who yield themselves to God, must prove their simplicity in all holy conversation and godliness (4) Religion is indeed a reasonable service, the more we consider what we owe to God, the more shall we be bound to acknowledge, that he deserves to be served with every faculty of our soul, and every member of our body (5) They who partake of the true grace of God, and experience its transforming efficacy upon their tempers and conduct, they die unto the world, and live only for God

2 He enforces upon them humility and lowliness of mind, that great ornament of the Christian character *For I say, through the grace given unto me*, in virtue of the office with which I am invested, *to every man that is among you*, whatever his rank or attainments may be, *not to think of himself more highly than he ought to think*, affecting a superiority over others, or pretending to be wise above what is written, and to intrude into things that are too high for him, *but to think soberly* and lowly of his gifts, graces, and attainments, *according as God hath dealt to every man the measure of faith*, and acknowledging, that whatever measure of faith he possesses, or however distinguished his endowments by nature or grace may be, yet he hath nothing which he *hath not received*, and therefore all boasting is excluded And as our talents are merely lent us for our own soul's good, and the edification of others, it will become us to see that our profiting appears *For as we have many members in one body, and all members have not the same office*, but each discharges his separate function, and all are alike needful in their place, and contribute to the good of the whole, *so we being many are one body in Christ, and every one members one of another*, united under our adored head, each occupying his respective place according to the measure of the gift of Christ, and therefore, instead of being puffed up in pride, and despising one another, we should give diligence to discharge the several services allotted to every member, acknowledging the mutual obligation which one hath to the other, and contributing heartily to the prosperity of the whole *Having then gifts, differing according to the grace that is given unto us*, as the Lord hath sovereignly been pleased to dispense to every man, let it be our care to improve them, according to our respective offices and station, for the glory of God, and the good of our fellow-member. *Whether prophecy, let us prophesy according to the proportion of faith* They who are put in trust with the gospel, must preach it with all fidelity and diligence, according to the measure of light, faith, and experience which they have received or, *according to the analogy of faith*, in exact consistence with the grand principle laid down in the word of God, in scripture-language, and with attention to the context *Or ministry, let us wait on our ministring*, in the inferior departments of the church, where attention, care, and constancy are required *Or he that teacheth, on teaching*, opening, explaining, and defending the doctrine of the scripture *Or he that exhorteth, on exhortation*, with warmth applying the word to the conscience, warning the unruly, supporting the feeble-minded, reproving the guilty, comforting the dejected, and, according to the different state of the people's souls, suiting his discourse for their edification and consolation *He that giveth*, and is entrusted with the distribution of the public stock appropriated to charitable uses, *let him do it with simplicity*, without fraud, favour, or affection, according to the real want of the church's poor *He that ruleth*, and hath the management of affairs, must do it *with diligence*, careful that proper discipline be observed *He that sheweth mercy*, *with chearfulness*, ready to every work and labour of love not dragged reluctantly to visit the sick or afflicted, or grudging the time, trouble, or expence, not treating the poor with illness, or sternness, but with that affability, tenderness, and compassion, which bespeak the pleasure that he takes in relieving the [illegible] *Note*, (1) Pride is a busy sin, we can never be enough on our guard against it The very gifts and graces of God, (such is our corruption) we are ready to abuse, and plume ourselves upon them (2) If God hath put us in trust with any office, our business is to approve our fidelity to him, employing the talents which he hath lent us, not puffed up with any distinction which he may have made between us and others, but remembring the solemn account we must shortly make before him, when he calleth us to give an account of our stewardship (3) Ministers have different gifts, all excellent in their place One is blessed with a clearer judgment, another with a warmer heart, and all for the edification of the body of Christ

3 The apostle proceeds to urge Christians in general to walk before God and man in such a way, as may most eminently adorn the doctrine they profess, and glorify their divine Master

Let love be without dissimulation Let your love to God in Christ be supreme, and your love to your brethren unfeigned and hearty, the living principle of every good word and work, and without which all our doings are nothing worth

Abhor that which is evil Turn away with abhorrence from all manner of iniquity, harbouring no allowed sin in yourself, and testifying your hatred of it wherever it appears, though in those who are nearest and dearest to you And on the contrary, *cleave to that which is good*, to God, his people, his word, his worship, will, and ways, never deterred by any danger, or seduced by any allurements, from the path of duty

Be kindly affectioned one to another, tenderly desiring to promote each other's happiness, delighting in each other's prosperity, bearing each other's burdens, and ready to every word and work which fervent charity dictates *with brotherly love*; *in honour preferring one another*, casting the veil of oblivion over the faults of others, and humbly acknowledging your own, thinking and speaking honourably of the gifts, graces, and attainments of your brethren, and entertaining lowly thoughts of yourselves

Not slothful in business In the business of your station be vigorous and active and whatever thy hand findeth to do, do it with thy might, but especially in all the work of God be lively, *fervent in spirit*, animated with burning love and holy zeal for his glory, *serving the Lord* in prayer, and praise, and all his ordinances, in persevering obedience to his will, [illegible] providences, approving your fidelity, until [illegible] Jesus

Rejoicing in hope, believing the faithfulness of God [illegible] mises, and going forward with chearfulness [illegible] work and ways, knowing that your labour [illegible] in the Lord

Patient in tribulation, resigned to the divine providence [illegible] under every provocation, with holy courage sustaining the [illegible] test shocks of opposition and persecution, and, under the [illegible] affliction, quietly waiting to see the salvation of God

Continuing instant in prayer, fervently and frequently approaching a throne of grace, seeking help and strength for all the work and service to which you are called, deeply conscious of your own insufficiency, without continual supplies of power from on high, to do any thing aright before God

Distributing to the necessity of saints, chearfully, liberally, according to their wants, and your abilities *Given to hospitality*, welcoming to your house and table those who for the sake of Christ are destitute, and giving them that warm and cordial reception which true charity dictates

Bless them which persecute you bless, and curse not speaking of them and to them respectfully, commending what is praiseworthy in them, never returning a thing for railing, never harbouring a thought of resentment against your most malignant revilers, forgiving them, and praying to God that he would forgive them also, and turn their heart

Rejoice with them that do rejoice, sharing their joys, and, instead of envying, sincerely partaking of their prosperity *and weep with them that weep*, feeling the tenderest sympathy with them in their sufferings, and by prayer, advice, and every assistance, desirous to alleviate or remove the sorrows of the miserable

Be of the same mind one towards another, united as much as may be in sentiment, and where any lesser difference in judgment subsists, still preserving the same warm affection toward each other, wishing all good to your brethren, and seeking to promote each other's happiness

Mind not high things, affect not pre-eminence, aspire not after the honours and dignities of the world, nor court the company of the great *but condescend to men of low estate*, treating your inferiors with kindness, and to whatever eminence or affluence you may arise, be courteous, affable, and free to the lowest, ready to stoop to every proper office of love for the service and comfort of the meanest saint of God Or, *condescend to mean things*, as the word may be rendered, let your mind be humbled to your condition, and chearfully acquiesce in every dispensation of providence, however strait and necessitous your circumstances may be

Be not wise in your own conceits Beware of entertaining a high imagination of your own abilities, gifts, or graces, treating the advice and admonitions of others with scorn, as if you were above all teaching, and satisfied in your own self-sufficiency

Recompense to no man evil for evil, neither in looks, words, or works

Provide things honest in the sight of all men, not only taking care of your families and worldly concerns, but so ordering the general course of your conduct and conversation, that the unprejudiced part of mankind, at least, may bear you an honourable testimony, and that none may be able to reproach you with any thing mean, or unbecoming your Christian character

If it be possible, as much as lieth in you, live peaceably with all men, studiously avoiding whatever may bring on disputes or uneasiness, and, as far as is consistent with truth, charity, and the glory of God, cultivating a spirit of love and peace, that at least, if through the perverseness of others it be not possible to avoid contentions, you may have the satisfaction of your own conscience in the reflection, that, *as much as lieth in you*, it hath been your endeavour to please all men for their good to edification

Dearly beloved, avenge not yourselves, but rather give place unto wrath forgive the injuries you receive, take no private revenge, suppress the angry passions which naturally rise within you, give the soft answer which turneth away wrath, not, by opposing, irritate, but however unreasonable others may appear, yield, or go away till the storm hath subsided and if, after all, you meet with implacable resentment, refer the matter to God, *for it is written, Vengeance is mine, I will repay, saith the Lord* This is his prerogative, and not to be invaded by us As magistracy is his ordinance, in some cases for the good of society we are bound to have recourse thereto, in others, where ourselves are only concerned, we must wait the great decisive day, when every man shall receive according as his work is *Therefore if thine enemy hunger, feed him, if he thirst, give him drink for in so doing thou shalt heap coals of fire on his head*, either by such instances of kindness you will melt him down, (as the refiners do their metals) into repentance, and gain his heart to love you, or, if he continues obstinate in hatred, it will exceedingly aggravate his condemnation, to add base ingratitude to his unprovoked enmity

Finally, *Be not overcome of evil*, let no ill usage, however aggravated, repeated, or persisted in, discompose your spirit, weary out your patience, or quench your charity, so as that you should give way to anger, be enslaved by corruption, and afford the enemy an occasion to triumph over your infirmity *But overcome evil with good*, which is the most glorious conquest, the proof of the noblest spirit, and the assured evidence that you are born of him who causeth his sun to rise upon the evil and the good, and sendeth his rain upon the just and upon the unjust Lord Jesus, give me such a heart, and stamp this thy image on my soul!

CHAP XIII

There are three good lessons taught us in this chapter 1 *A lesson of subjection to lawful authority*, ver 1—6 2 *A lesson of justice and love to our brethren*, ver 7—10 3 *A lesson of sobriety and godliness in ourselves*, ver 11 *to the end*

a Tit. iii. 1. 1 Pet. ii. 13. 1 LET every soul be subject unto the higher pow-
b Prov. viii. 15. Dan. ii. 21 & iv. 32. ers For b there is no power but of God the
c 1 Sam. xxiv. 6. xxvi. 9. powers that be are ordained of God 2 c Whosoever
therefore resisteth the power, resisteth the ordinance of
God and they that resist shall receive to themselves
d 1 Pet. ii. 14 & iii. 13. damnation 3 d For rulers are not a terror to good
works, but to the evil Wilt thou then not be afraid of
the power? do that which is good, and thou shalt have
praise of the same 4 For he is the minister of God
to thee for good But if thou do that which is evil, be
e Jer. xxv. 9. afraid, for he beareth not the sword in vain for e he is
the minister of God, a revenger to *execute* wrath upon
f Eccl. viii. 2. him that doth evil 5 Wherefore f *ye* must needs be
g 1 Pet. ii. 19. subject, not only for wrath, g but also for conscience sake
6 For, for this cause pay you tribute also for they are
God's ministers, attending continually upon this very
h Matt. xxii. 21. thing 7 h Render therefore to all their dues tribute
i Luke xx. 25. to whom tribute *is due*, custom to whom custom, i fear
to whom fear, honour to whom honour

v 1—7 From the duties they owed to each other, as members of civil society, the apostle proceeds to enforce submission in all lawful things to the authority of the civil government under which they lived The Christian doctrine makes no alteration in the natural and civil rights of mankind Dominion is not founded in grace, therefore *let every soul be subject unto the higher powers*, respectful and obedient to all lawful magistrates, from the highest to the lowest, and willingly observant of the laws with the execution of which they are entrusted *For there is no power but of God*, he is the source of all authority, dignity, and honour, by him kings reign *The powers that be are ordained of God*, whatever be the mode of government, whether the ruling power be lodged in the hands of one person or many, submission is our duty, and though the men who are invested with the authority be never so vile and wicked, their lawful commands are nevertheless to be obeyed, and the magistrate is to be honoured, however despicable the man may appear *Whosoever therefore resisteth the power*, and refuses obedience to the lawful orders of the established government, *resisteth the ordinance of God, and they that resist shall receive to themselves damnation*, (κρίμα), the punishment due to their offence, according to the laws, from the sword of the magistrate, and judgment also from God, for the transgression against his ordinance *For rulers are not a terror to good works* they who behave quiet and submissive have nothing to fear, for such subjects the magistrates are bound to protect and cherish, *but* they are appointed *to restrain the evil* actions of men, which tend to disturb the peace of society, to dishonour God, or injure their neighbour *Wilt thou then not be afraid of the power? do that which is good*, peaceable and obedient to the laws, *and thou shalt have praise of the same*, in every well-ordered government such subjects will be protected and encouraged *For he is the minister of God*, appointed to preserve the peace of the state, to redress injuries, administer justice, suppress vice, prophaneness, and immorality, to punish offenders, and promote the general welfare and therefore if thou art found obedient, the office of magistracy will be *to thee for good* *But if thou do that which is evil*, and violate the established laws, *be afraid, for he beareth not the sword in vain*, being obliged by his very office impartially to inflict the penalty due to every offence, *for he is the minister of God*, who puts the sword of judgment into his hands, as *a revenger to execute wrath upon him that doth evil*, not out of any private personal resentment, but coolly as God's vicegerent, without partiality or favour, according to the dictates of justice *Wherefore ye must needs be subject, not only for wrath*, merely through fear of punishment and penalties, *but also for conscience sake*, from a principle of duty towards God, whose ordinance is binding, and obedience for his sake is due to human laws, though no pains or penalties were annexed *For, for this cause pay you tribute also*, the taxes and duties necessary for the support of the government, whose protection you enjoy *for they are God's ministers, attending continually upon this very thing*, and therefore every fraud committed against the public is even more criminal, than if it merely affected an individual *Render therefore to all their dues*, according to the laws human or divine *tribute to whom tribute is due, custom to whom custom*, all subsidies, taxes, &c imposed by lawful authority *fear to whom fear* and reverence should be paid, *honour to whom honour* is due, according to the superior rank and relation in which by the providence of God they are placed

8 Owe no man any thing, but to love one another
for k he that loveth another, hath fulfilled the law 9 k Gal. v. 13. 1 Tim. i. 5.
For this, l Thou shalt not commit adultery, Thou shalt Jam. ii. 8.
not kill, Thou shalt not steal, Thou shalt not bear false l Ex. xx. 13 &c.
witness, Thou shalt not covet, and if *there be* any other Deut. v. 17 &c.
commandment, it is briefly comprehended in this saying,
namely, m Thou shalt love thy neighbour as thyself m Lev. xix. 18.
10 Love worketh no ill to his neighbour therefore n Matt. xxii. 40. Ver. 8.
n love *is* the fulfilling of the law.

v 8—10 From the payment of dues to magistrates the apostle passes on to enforce the discharge of every debt, to whomsoever due

Owe no man any thing, never run in debt where you have no immediate prospect of paying, nor continue in debt when you have ability to discharge it, and in every relation of life be ready to fulfil the duty which you owe One debt there is, however, and *but* one, where, though ever paying, you neither wish nor desire that it should be less, and that is, *to love one another* as men, and especially as Christians, seeking to promote each other's present and eternal welfare, and this is the great and reigning principle in all your conduct *for he that loveth another*, and, from a sense of the love of God in Christ, experiences this God-like charity, *hath fulfilled the law*, if his love were perfect, he would be complete in all the will of God, which is not indeed the lot of man in this life, it is reserved for the felicity of a better Yet so far as love is in vigorous exercise, so far will his spiritual obedience advance towards perfection *For this, thou shalt not commit adultery, thou shalt not kill, thou shalt not steal, thou shalt not bear false witness, thou shalt not covet, and if there be any other commandment, it is briefly comprehended in this saying, namely, Thou shalt love thy neighbour as thyself*, and act conscientiously toward them, as, were our circumstances reversed, we might reasonably expect they should behave towards us, so then,

We

were there no human restraints or punishments, love would itself effectually prevent every violation of our neighbour's person, goods, or fame we cannot hurt the body, which we love, we cannot defraud those we love, we cannot speak evil of those we love, we cannot defile those we love, though lawless lust (which is real hatred) often covers its horrid features with the false vizor of this sacred name *Love worketh no ill to his neighbour*, neither in act, or intention, *therefore love is the fulfilling of the law*

11 And that, knowing the time, that now *it is* high
time to ° awake out of sleep for now *is* our salvation
nearer than when we believed. 12 The night is far
spent, ᵖ the day is at hand ᑫ let us therefore cast off the
works of darkness, and ʳ let us put on the armour of
light 13 ˢ Let us walk honestly as in the day, ᵗ not
in rioting and drunkenness, ᵘ not in chambering and
wantonness, ˣ not in strife and envying 14 But ʸ put
ye on the Lord Jesus Christ, and ᶻ make not provision
for the flesh, to *fulfil* the lusts *thereof*

v 11—14 The apostle enforces what he had been recommending to their practice by a very awful consideration *And this* duty of love I press upon you, *knowing the time*, the day of gospel grace and light having broke upon us, so *that now it is high time to awake out of sleep*, and shake off all spiritual sloth, and carnal security *for now is our salvation nearer than when we believed*, and as our journey's end draws nearer, we should mend our pace, nor loiter, when the mansions of eternal rest are, as it were, in view *The night is far spent*, the night of trials and afflictions, of remaining ignorance and corruption, is drawing to an end, *the day* of our complete redemption from darkness, trouble, sin and suffering, *is at hand*, when in eternal glory our sun shall rise to set no more *let us therefore cast off the works of darkness*, as persons rising from their beds remove the cloaths, so must we reject and put far away all those sinful tempers and practices, which are opposite to the light of truth, are usually done in secret, and for which the blackness of darkness is the reserved punishment, *and let us put on the armour of light*, all those bright and shining graces of the spirit, which adorn our holy profession, and enable us to stand against the assaults of sin, the world, and Satan, till triumphantly we shall appear in all the lustre of eternal glory Therefore *let us walk honestly as in the day*, shewing a conversation such as becometh Godliness in the eyes of men, guided by the light of truth, and the spirit of purity; and able to bear the strictest scrutiny of our observers, *not in rioting and drunkenness*, indulging to excess in meat and drink our sensual appetites, *not in chambering and wantonness*, for which sensuality supplies the fuel, but restraining every lascivious thought, immodest word, indecent action, as well as abstaining from the grosser pollutions which are in the world through lust, *not in strife and envying*, contentious, quarrelsome, and grieved, instead of rejoicing in the prosperity of our neighbours *But put ye on the Lord Jesus Christ*, that you may be complete in him, put on his righteousness, as your glorious dress, put on his image, that, being like him, you may come to be with him, put on his holy profession, owning your entire dependance upon him, as your prophet, priest, and king, that all who see you may take knowledge of you that you indeed belong to him, *and make not provision for the flesh, to fulfil the lusts thereof*, let your soul, and your eternal interests, be your great concern, without anxiety about a worldly provision, and, especially, mortify your sensual appetites in whatever would tend to inflame the native corruption of your hearts, and to as many as walk after this rule, peace be on them and mercy, and on the Israel of God

CHAP XIV

The apostle, in order to cultivate mutual love and peace between the Jewish and Gentile converts, (1) Cautions the one against judging, and the other against despising their brethren in indifferent things, ver 1—13 (2) *He exhorts the Gentiles rather to forego the use of their Christian liberty, than offend their Jewish brethren in these things*, ver 14—23

1 ᵃ HIM that is weak in the faith receive you, *but*
not to doubtful disputations 2 For ᵇ one
believeth that he may eat all things another, who is
weak, eateth herbs 3 ᶜ Let not him that eateth, de-
spise him that eateth not, and let not him which eateth
not, judge him that eateth for God hath received him
4 ᵈ Who art thou that judgest another man's servant?
to his own master he standeth or falleth Yea, he shall
be holden up for God is able to make him stand 5.
ᵉ One man esteemeth one day above another another
esteemeth every day *alike* ᶠ Let every man be fully
persuaded in his own mind 6 ᵍ He that regardeth the
day, regardeth *it* unto the Lord, and he that regardeth
not the day, to the Lord he doth not regard *it* He
that eateth, eateth to the Lord, for ʰ he giveth God
thanks, and he that eateth not, to the Lord he eateth not,
and giveth God thanks 7 For ⁱ none of us liveth to
himself, and no man dieth to himself 8 For ᵏ whether
we live, we live unto the Lord, and whether we die, we
die unto the Lord whether we live therefore or die,
we are the Lord's 9 For ˡ to this end Christ both
died, and rose, and revived, that he might be Lord both
of the dead and living 10 But why dost thou judge
thy brother? or why dost thou set at nought thy brother?
for ᵐ we shall all stand before the judgment seat of Christ
11 For it is written, ⁿ *As* I live, saith the Lord every
knee shall bow to me, and every tongue shall confess to
God 12 So then ° every one of us shall give account
of himself to God 13 Let us not therefore judge
one another any more but judge this rather, that ᵖ no
man put a stumbling-block, or an occasion to fall in *his*
brother's way

v 1—13 As many of the Jewish converts still retained a high veneration for the Mosaical institution, and were scrupulous in observing a distinction of *meats* and *days*, from which the Gentile Christians justly apprehended themselves entirely at liberty, the apostle therefore recommends a kind condescension to the educational prejudices of their Jewish brethren, and that there should be no coolness or distance between them on account of these indifferent matters *Him that is weak in the faith receive you*, heartily embracing and welcoming them, *but not to doubtful disputations*, not perplexing them with useless disputes about things of a trivial nature

1 Respecting *meats* *One believeth that he may eat all things*, and, satisfied about the abolition of the ceremonial law, counts nothing any longer common or unclean, eating, without scruple, whatever kind of wholesome food is set before him *Another who is weak*, through the prejudice of education, or want of light, fearful of using any meat but what is permitted by the law of Moses, and killed according to the manner there prescribed, (*Lev* xvii 10—14) when he is invited to eat with Gentiles, least he should incur ceremonial defilement, abstains from their victuals, *and eateth only herbs* *Let not him that eateth, despise him that eateth not*, as weak and superstitious, priding himself on his superior knowledge, and clearer views of his Christian liberty *and*, on the other hand, *let not him that eateth not, judge him that eateth*, and being prejudiced and narrow in his own conceptions, dare uncharitably to censure his brother as a loose liver, and irreligious professor, because he hath no such scruples about indifferent matters, *for God hath received him* into his favour, and therefore, whom he accepts, none should condemn *Who art thou that judgest another man's servant? to his own master he standeth or falleth* It is the highest arrogance to usurp God's throne, and sit in judgment on our brother, who is responsible to God alone, and uses only that liberty which he is in conscience satisfied God allows *Yea*, and whatever risk censures the weak and superstitious may cast upon him, *he shall be holden up*, the Lord will strengthen and preserve him through faith unto salvation, *for God is able to make him stand*, perfecting him in fidelity unto the end, and appearing with boldness in the day of judgment *Note*, (1) Nothing is more contrary to the spirit of charity than rash and hasty censures (2) We must leave every man to the great judge, nor should pretend to decide upon their everlasting state, without the clearest warrant of God's word

2 Respecting *days* *One man esteemeth one day above another*, as the Jewish converts did, who paid a particular regard to the passover, pentecost, new moon, and other feast and fast days, as more sacred than other *another esteemeth every day alike*, counting all these Jewish distinctions abolished *Let every man be fully persuaded in his own mind*, and, being satisfied in his own conscience, be content that others should judge for themselves, allowing them the same liberty we claim ourselves, charitably concluding, that *he that regardeth the day, regardeth it unto the Lord*, intending therein to glorify the Lord Jesus, who on mount Sinai at first enjoined the ceremonial law *and he that regardeth not the day, to the Lord he doth not regard it*, from the same principle, and with a view to the Redeemer's glory, by whose authority they suppose the Mosaical institutions are laid aside *He that eateth*, as the converted Gentile, every kind of meat without scruple, *eateth to the Lord, for he giveth God thanks*, and is persuaded that all the creatures of God are good, when sanctified by the word of God, and by prayer *and he that eateth not*, supposing that the prohibition of a variety of meats enjoined by Moses is still in force, *to the Lord he eateth not*, persuaded in conscience he ought to abstain, *and giveth God thanks* for the food which he hath allowed him under the law In these points, therefore, we should bear with each other, nor, for such trifles, dispute and break the band of Christian love

3 Our

3 Our grand end and aim in these things, and all others, should be the glory of God *For none of us liveth to himself*, we are not our own, and must not live as self-seekers, or self-pleasers, we are bought with a price, that we should glorify God in our bodies and in our spirits, which are his *and no man dieth to himself*, wishing to get rid of his troubles, or to gain a name, or selfishly desiring his crown before the time when God shall appoint him an end to his warfare, *for whether we*, who are truly the servants of Jesus, *live, we live unto the Lord*, desirous to be, and do, and suffer according to his holy will and pleasure, *or whether we die* a natural, lingring, sudden, or violent death, *we die unto the Lord*, resigned to his will, committing all our concerns into his hands, and with our departing breath desiring to exalt his great and glorious name, and to commend the goodness of our God, *whether we live therefore or die, we are the Lord's*, belong to him as his devoted servants, as his inseparable property depending on him, and singly aiming at his glory And thus, whether we are weaker or stronger believers, we have all one purpose, one end, one home *For to this end Christ both died, and rose and revived*, having made the great atonement for the sins of his people, and being raised in token of God's approbation of his undertaking, and seated on the mediatorial throne, *that he might be Lord both of the dead and living*, is head over all things to his church, invested with universal dominion and authority, to rule the living, to revive the dead, and when in the day of his appearing and glory, the dead shall rise, the living be changed, he will be the object of their everlasting praises Since then we are Christ's, and he alone hath dominion over us, it becomes us never to usurp authority over the consciences of our brethren, or to pass censures on the dead or the living We have one master only, whose approbation we need be sollicitous to secure.

4 We must each, shortly, answer for ourselves before God, and therefore to his judgment all should be referred *But why dost thou judge thy brother*, as lax and latitudinarian, because you are rigid and scrupulous? *or why*, on the other hand, *dost thou set at nought thy brother*, as an ignorant, weak, and despicable bigot, because he thinks that evil, which you know to be innocent? This is to take the matter out of God's hands, and to erect an unhallowed tribunal, *for we shall all stand before the judgment seat of Christ*, and by his sentence, and no other, must stand or fall for ever *For it is written, As I live, saith the Lord, every knee shall bow to me, and every tongue shall confess to God*, owning me the eternal Jehovah, acknowledging my eternal glory and Godhead, and bowing before the sceptre of my judgment, as accountable to me alone, and expecting from my lips the decision of their eternal state for happiness or misery *so then every one of us shall give an account of himself to God*, to Christ, to whom all judgment is committed, and who is essentially very God *Let us not therefore judge one another any more* with any rash and precipitate censures, *but judge this rather, that no man put a stumbling-block, or an occasion to fall in his brother's way*, and whatever knowledge he may have of Christian liberty, yet to be careful so to use it, as not willingly to grieve or ensnare his brother, by tempting him to sin, by giving a handle for censure, or emboldening him to do what his conscience may not be satisfied is right *Note*, Our great concern is to prepare for a judgment day, and the best means to be ready for it is to keep it often in our view, and to bring ourselves thither in self-examination, before the Lord shall cite us to his bar

14 I know, and am persuaded by the Lord Jesus, that
p there is nothing unclean of itself but q to him that
esteemeth any thing to be unclean, to him *it is* unclean
15 But if thy brother be grieved with *thy* meat, now
walkest thou not charitably r Destroy not him with thy
meat, for whom Christ died. 16 Let not then your
good be evil spoken of 17 For s the kingdom of God
is not meat and drink, t but righteousness, and peace,
and joy in the holy Ghost 18 For he that in these
things serveth Christ, *is* acceptable to God, and approved
of men. 19 Let us therefore follow after the things
which u make for peace, and things x wherewith one may
edify another 20 For meat destroy not the work of
God y All things indeed *are* pure, but *it is* evil for
that man who eateth with offence 21 z *It is* good neither to eat flesh, nor to drink wine, nor *any thing* whereby
thy brother stumbleth, or is offended, or is made weak
22 Hast thou faith? have it to thyself before God
a Happy *is* he that condemneth not himself in that thing
which he alloweth. 23 And he that doubteth, is damned
if he eat, because *he eateth* not of faith for b whatsoever
is not of faith, is sin

p Acts x 15 1 Tim iv 4 Tit i 15
q Ver 23
r 1 Cor viii 11
s 1 Cor viii 8 Heb. xiii 9
t Chap xv 13 Gal v 22
u Ps xxxiv 14
x Chap xv 2 1 Cor xiv 12
y Matt xv 11 Ver 14
z 1 Cor viii 13
a 1 John iii 21
b Tit i 15

v 13—23 The apostle had just intimated, that they should desire mutual edification, and not abuse their Christian liberty to others detriment.

1 As to his own sense of these ceremonial things, he saith, *I know, and am persuaded by the Lord Jesus, that there is nothing unclean of itself*, the ceremonial law concerning meats being wholly abrogated, and these communicate no moral defilement to the conscience, *but to him that esteemeth any thing to be unclean, to him it is unclean*, as he would act against his conscience if he should eat, and though his conscience be erroneous, he would do evil

But, 2 Whatever conviction any man may have of the lawfulness of all kinds of food, yet, *if thy brother be grieved with thy meat*, through his educational prejudices and you unkindly persist in the use of your liberty, and eat before him what he esteems forbidden, *now walkest thou not charitably, destroy not him with thy meat, for whom Christ died*, destroy not the peace of his mind, by giving him unnecessary offence, or, at least, be not the means of stumbling such as, in the judgment of charity, we may reckon among the redeemed Those who are really the purchase of Christ's blood, can indeed never perish, but what hath in its nature but the most distant tendency to endanger them, must carefully be avoided

3 Another reason why you should abridge yourself of something of your Christian liberty, is this *Let not then your good be evil spoken of*, do not provoke those who are misinformed to speak evil of you, for that which is itself lawful, nor do any thing which may lessen you in men's esteem, and prevent your usefulness, nor give occasion to the enemy, by needless contentions, to speak evil of Christianity itself

4 As the greatest points of Christianity stand distinct from all these trivial matters, no stress should be laid upon them *For the kingdom of God is not meat and drink*, consists not in using or abstaining from the ceremonial institutions which the law prescribed concerning these things, *but it is righteousness, and peace, and joy in the Holy Ghost* These are the grand essential matters *Righteousness*, imputed and implanted, *peace* with God through Jesus Christ, and the sense of his love kindling ours, and engaging us to live peaceably with all men, *and joy in the Holy Ghost*, which this divine spirit communicates to our souls, making us happy in God and his holy ways *For he that in these things serveth Christ*, faithful to his cause, and in simplicity designing his honour, whatever his practice or sentiments may be in unessential matters, *is acceptable to God*, his person and services are accepted in the beloved, *and he is approved of man*, as a sincere convert, at least by all those of sound judgment and solid experience

He therefore exhorts, 5 *Let us therefore follow after the things which make for peace*, laying aside all uncharitable contentions, *and things whereby one may edify another*, not seeking our own pleasure merely but others good *For* so trivial a consideration as this or that kind of *meat*, *destroy not the work of God*, nor disturb the peace, and love, and harmony, which should subsist between fellow-Christians, and which it is the great design of God in his gospel to produce in the hearts of the faithful *All things indeed are pure*, I will admit, to those who have knowledge, *but it is evil for that man who eateth with offence*, and the liberty of using any meat, which in itself was lawful, becomes criminal, when we chuse rather to offend a weak brother, than forego the gratification of our appetite for his sake In such a case *it is good neither to eat flesh, nor to drink wine, nor any thing whereby thy brother stumbleth, or is offended, or is made weak* It would be right and prudent to abstain from any of these creatures, however good in themselves, and lawful to be used, rather than be a hindrance to the weak, grieve or discourage the less enlightened, or tempt our brother rashly to censure us, or with a doubting conscience to follow our example *Hast thou faith*, and art satisfied concerning the abrogation of the ceremonial institution, *have it to thyself before God*, and use thy liberty to God's glory on proper occasions *Happy is he that condemneth not himself in that thing which he alloweth*, and never exposes himself to the just reproaches of his conscience, by warping his better judgment to gratify his covetousness, his pleasure, or his pride *And* where this is the case, *he that doubteth* about the propriety of what he is going to do, supposes there may be a difference between meats lawful and unlawful, and therefore hesitates whether he shall eat or not, *is damned if he eat*, his conscience will condemn him, *because he* is not sure that he hath God's warrant for what he doth, and *eateth not of faith*, *for whatsoever is not of faith, is sin* God's word must be our rule, we must ever from thence receive our direction, and where our minds are not fully satisfied concerning his will, nothing must tempt us to take one step further We are safe, though mistaken, when we thus jealously abridge ourselves of our liberty, but where we presumptuously act, tho' doubts remain, we shew an evident disregard to God's authority, and violate the sacred dictates of conscience

CHAP XV

The apostle, in pursuance of his discourse (1) Directs the strong in faith to bear with the weak, ver 1—6 (2) That all should receive one another as brethren, ver 7—12. (3) Draws to a conclusion of his epistle, ver 13—33

1 ᵃ WE then that are ſtrong ought to bear the in-
firmities of the weak, and not to pleaſe our-
ſelves 2 ᵇ Let every one of us pleaſe *his* neighbour for
his good ᶜ to edification 3 For even Chriſt pleaſed not
himſelf, but as it is written, ᵈ The reproaches of them
that reproached thee, fell on me 4 For ᵉ whatſoever
things were written aforetime, were written for our learn-
ing, ᶠ that we through patience and comfort of the ſcrip-
tures might have hope 5 Now ᵍ the God of patience
and conſolation grant you to ʰ be like-minded one to-
wards another, according to Chriſt Jeſus 6 That ye
may with one mind *and* one mouth glorify God, even the
Father of our Lord Jeſus Chriſt

ᵃ Chap xiv 1 1 Cor ix. 22 Gal vi. 1 ᵇ 1 Cor ix 19. & x 24, 33 Phil ii 4 ᶜ Chap xiv. 19 ᵈ Pſ lxix 9 ſ Chap iv 23, 1 Cor ix 10 & x 11 2 Tim iii 16 ᵍ Chap xii. 16 ʰ 1 Cor i 10 Phil ii 2

v 1—6 The apoſtle infers from what he had advanced in the foregoing chapter,

1 That, *We then that are ſtrong ought to bear the infirmities of the weak, and not to pleaſe ourſelves*, having compaſſion towards them, making every kind allowance for their prejudices and ſcruples, not provoked by their raſh cenſures, and deſirous to prevent them by foregoing our own pleaſure for their profit *Let every one of us* therefore *pleaſe his neighbour for his good to edification*, not complying with him in any thing that is ſinful, but in all indifferent matters ready to yield to him, in order to inſinuate into his confidence, for the advantage of his ſoul

2 He enforces his exhortation by the ſtrongeſt motive of Chriſt's example *For even Chriſt pleaſed not himſelf*, when he was under no obligations to us, he freely ſubmitted to all hardſhips and ſufferings for our ſakes, *as it is written, The reproaches of them that reproached thee, fell on me*, he willingly bore the contradiction of ſinners againſt himſelf, and all the reproaches which tranſgreſſors by their offences had caſt on the bleſſed God, he bore in his own body on the tree, when he made atonement for them And in this ſcripture, as well as others, we are not to ſuppoſe David ſpeaks of himſelf, but of Chriſt, and with a view to the edification of his people *For whatſoever things were written aforetime, were written for our learning, that we through patience and comfort of the ſcriptures might have hope*, animated by the examples there ſet forth, to ſhew the ſame meekneſs, patience, and forbearance, revived by the views of the great and precious promiſes, and comforted in the aſſured hope of eternal life therein revealed to us *Note*, (1) Chriſt's pattern ſhould be ever in our view "Would the Lord Jeſus "in our ſituation have thus thought, ſpoke, and acted," ſhould be our enquiry? (2) They are the truly wiſe who are learned in the ſcriptures, and know the way to everlaſting life (3) The ſcriptures afford us the moſt powerful arguments for patience under all our trials and provocations, and furniſh us with the moſt ſubſtantial comforts under all our diſcouragements, both in the precious promiſes of preſent divine ſupport, and in the proſpect of the glory which ſhall be revealed

3 He ſeconds his exhortations with his prayers We can only ſpeak to the ear, God muſt make it effectual to the heart *Now the God of patience and conſolation*, who is ſo long-ſuffering towards us, and ready to comfort the afflicted, and is the ſource and author of all patience, to us, and the giver of all conſolation, *grant you to be like minded one towards another*, united in ſentiment and affection, *according to Chriſt Jeſus*; copying his example, and obedient to his holy will, *that ye may with one mind and one mouth*, as if animated by one ſoul, in your religious aſſemblies, and in ſocial converſe, *glorify God, even the Father of our Lord Jeſus Chriſt*, in ſpirit and converſation deſirous to exalt his great and glorious name, and ſhew forth his praiſes *Note*, (1) Chriſtians ſhould be united in one mind, and join in the ſame worſhip, all ſchiſmatical diviſions are God's abhorrence (2) Our prayers muſt follow our preaching, that God may give the bleſſing

7 Wherefore ⁱ receive ye one another, ᵏ as Chriſt alſo
received us, to the glory of God 8 Now I ſay, that
ˡ Jeſus Chriſt was a miniſter of the circumciſion for the
truth of God, ᵐ to confirm the promiſes *made* unto the
fathers 9. And ⁿ that the Gentiles might glorify God
for *his* mercy, as it is written, ᵒ For this cauſe I will
confeſs to thee among the Gentiles, and ſing unto thy
name 10 And again he ſaith, ᵖ Rejoice, ye Gentiles,
with his people 11 And again, ᑫ Praiſe the Lord, all
ye Gentiles, and laud him, all ye people 12. And
again Eſaias ſaith, ʳ There ſhall be a root of Jeſſe, and
he that ſhall riſe to reign over the Gentiles, in him ſhall
the Gentiles truſt 13 Now the God of hope fill you
with ˢ all joy and peace in believing, that ye may abound
in hope through the power of the holy Ghoſt

ⁱ Chap xiv 1 ᵏ John vi 37 ˡ Mat xv 24 Acts iii 25 ᵐ 2 Cor i 20 ⁿ John x 16 ᵒ 2 Sam xxii 50 Pſ xviii 49 ᵖ Deut xxxii 43 ᑫ Pſ cxvii 1 ʳ Iſa xi 1, 10 ˢ Chap xiv 17 1 Pet i 8

v 7—13 The apoſtle returns to enforce his former exhortation *Wherefore receive ye one another*, with brotherly affection, in friendly intercourſe, and holy communion, *as Chriſt alſo received us*, whether Jews or Gentiles, notwithſtanding all our infirmities, *to the glory of God*, as this was the end he had in view, the ſame muſt we propoſe to ourſelves

1 Chriſt had received the Jewiſh converts *Now I ſay, that Jeſus Chriſt was a miniſter of the circumciſion*, ſubmitted himſelf to that bloody rite, and perſonally miniſtred to the loſt ſheep of the houſe of Iſrael, *for the truth of God*, to diſplay his faithfulneſs to his covenant, and *to confirm the promiſes made unto the fathers*, that of their ſeed Chriſt ſhould come Now as this put a peculiar honour upon the Jews, their Gentile brethren ſhould not deſpiſe them, becauſe of any weak attachment to the ceremonial inſtitutions

2 Chriſt had alſo received the Gentiles to the participation of the ſame privileges, *and* therefore this ſhould engage the brotherly regards of their Jewiſh brethren, ſince the ſalvation that Jeſus obtained was to extend to them, *that the Gentiles might glorify God for his mercy*, who now at laſt looked with compaſſion upon them, and had called them into his church *as it is written, For this cauſe I will confeſs to thee among the Gentiles, and ſing unto thy name* Becauſe thou haſt given me the heathen for my inheritance, I will declare thy word among them, and call upon them to offer their thankſgivings for the ineſtimable bleſſings of which in the goſpel they are made partakers *And again*, in another prophecy, *he ſaith, Rejoice, ye Gentiles, with his people*, incorporated with them, ſharing their privileges, and therefore happy in the experience of the ſame goſpel grace *And again*, it is ſaid, *Praiſe the Lord, all ye Gentiles, and laud him, all ye people*, joining your voices together in the great congregation, the partition-wall being taken down *And again, Eſaias ſaith, There ſhall be a root of Jeſſe*, the divine Meſſiah, *and he that ſhall riſe to reign over the Gentiles*, exalted to the mediatorial throne, and extending his conqueſts over the ſouls of ſinners to the ends of the earth, *in him ſhall the Gentiles truſt*, placing their dependance upon him as their only Lord and Saviour All which prophecies clearly ſhew, that the time ſhould come, when the Gentiles ſhould be fellow-heirs, and of the ſame body, and therefore the Jewiſh converts ſhould with hearty affection embrace their Gentile brethren, as all one in Chriſt Jeſus

3 The apoſtle adds his affectionate prayer for them both *Now the God of hope*, who in Chriſt Jeſus is the ground and author of our hope of all the ſpiritual and eternal bleſſings, *fill you with all joy and peace in believing*, enabling you to lay hold of the promiſes of the everlaſting covenant, and giving you the abundance of divine conſolations, and of that peace which paſſeth all underſtanding, *that ye may abound in hope through the power of the Holy Ghoſt*, in the fulleſt aſſurance of poſſeſſing the eternal bleſſedneſs above, the earneſts and foretaſtes of which the Spirit gives, in the light, ſtrength, and comfort which he now communicates *Note*, (1) When faith is in exerciſe, then our ſouls will be happy even here below (2) The Chriſtian's hope never makes aſhamed, becauſe it never can diſappoint him (3) They who would abound in hope, peace, and joy, ſhould be much in prayer to him who is the giver of every good gift, and whoſe face none ſeek in vain

14 And I myſelf alſo am perſuaded of you, my bre-
thren, that ᵗ ye alſo are full of goodneſs, filled with all
knowledge, able alſo to admoniſh one another 15
Nevertheleſs, brethren, I have written the more boldly
unto you, in ſome ſort, ᵘ as putting you in mind, ˣ be-
cauſe of the grace that is given to me of God, 16
ʸ That I ſhould be the miniſter of Jeſus Chriſt to the
Gentiles, miniſtring the goſpel of God, that the offer-
ing up of the Gentiles might be acceptable, being ſanc-
tified by the holy Ghoſt

ᵗ 2 Pet i. 12 1 John ii 21 ᵘ 2 Pet i 12 ˣ Chap i 5 & xii 3 ʸ Act ix 15 Gal i 16 1 Tim ii 7 2 Tim i 11 Iſa lxvi 20 Phil ii 17

v 14—16 St Paul here,

1 Expreſſes the high eſtimation in which he held them *And I myſelf alſo am perſuaded of you, my brethren*, from the gracious teſtimony born to you by thoſe who are acquainted with your ſtate, *that ye alſo are full of goodneſs*, enriched with every precious fruit of the Spirit, with tender benevolence and ſympathy willing to bear and forbear, and united in love and peace, notwithſtanding any leſſer differences of opinion *filled with all knowledge*, in the great eſſential points of the goſpel revelation, *able alſo to admoniſh one another*, and to communicate your gifts for mutual edification

2 He elegantly apologizes for the freedom he had taken in reproving, adviſing, and exhorting them, who were themſelves ſo eminent in gifts and graces *Nevertheleſs, brethren, I have written the more boldly unto you, in ſome ſort, as putting you in mind*, rather as your monitor to refreſh your memory, than ſetting up myſelf for your inſtructor, as if you were ignorant The liberty he uſed with them was what his office obliged him to *becauſe of the grace that is given to me of God*, honoured by him with apoſtleſhip, *that I ſhould be the miniſter of Jeſus Chriſt to the Gentiles, miniſtring the goſpel of God*, diſcharging the office of a Chriſtian prieſt with unwearied diligence, fidelity, and zeal, *that the offering up of the Gentiles*, their ſpiritual ſacrifices of prayer and praiſe, *might be acceptable* through Jeſus Chriſt, *being ſanctified by the Holy Ghoſt*, and thereby infinitely more excel-

lent,

lent than any of the oblations that were ever made at the temple

17 I have therefore whereof I may glory through
a Heb v 1 Jesus Christ, in a those things which pertain to God
b 2 Cor x 15 18 For b I will not dare to speak any of those things,
c Chap i 5 & xvi 26 which Christ hath not wrought by me, c to make the
d Acts xix 11 12 2 Cor xii 12 Gentiles obedient, by word and deed, 19 d Through
mighty signs and wonders, by the power of the Spirit of
God, so that from Jerusalem, and round about Illyri-
cum, I have fully preached the gospel of Christ 20
Yea, so have I strived to preach the gospel, not where
e 2 Cor x 15 16 Christ was named, e lest I should build upon another
f Isa lii 15 man's foundation 21 But as it is written, f To whom
he was not spoken of, they shall see and they that have
not heard, shall understand

v 17—21 Having mentioned his office, as the apostle of the Gentiles, he glories therein *I have therefore whereof I may glory through Jesus Christ*, by whose grace I have been so supported, and who hath given such eminent success to my labours, *in those things which pertain to God*, wherein his glory is so greatly concerned, and in the conversion of the Gentiles so highly exalted Or the words may be rendered, *I have therefore a rejoicing in Christ concerning the things of God*, that is, the Gentiles, who are offered up to him as living sacrifices, in which he felt the most unfeigned satisfaction *For I will not dare to speak of any of those things which Christ hath not wrought by me*, far be all arrogant boasts from me, nor would I ascribe the least honour to myself, but only to him whose efficacious grace, under my preaching, hath wrought powerfully, *to make the Gentiles obedient by word and deed*, shewing forth by an open confession, and a becoming conversation, the reality of their conversion to God, *through mighty signs and wonders*, which were wrought in confirmation of my divine mission, *by the power of the Spirit of God*, whose mighty influence gives energy and demonstration to the word preached, *so that from Jerusalem and round about unto Illyricum, I have fully preached the gospel of Christ*, diffusing with indefatigable labours the light of truth through Syria, Lesser Asia, and Greece, and keeping back nothing of the whole counsel of God concerning the free and perfect salvation of sinners through the great Redeemer *Yea, so have I strived to preach the gospel, not where Christ was named*, but with a holy ambition I went rather to the places where he was wholly unknown, *lest I should build upon another man's foundation*, and be thought to be a terror to those who went before, and to have borrowed my knowledge from them, and so should have wanted a signal proof of my doctrine and office, as immediately received from Christ himself *But as it is written*, (Isa lii 15) so hath it been fulfilled by my ministry, *To whom he was not spoken of, they shall see and they that have not heard, shall understand* the Gentiles, who lay in darkness, utterly ignorant of the Messiah and his kingdom, shall see the light of life, and be made wise unto salvation *Note*, Whatever success attends our labours, God must have all the glory, who alone giveth the increase.

g Chap i 13 22 For which cause also I have been much hindred
from coming to you 23 But now having no more
h Acts xix 21 Chap i 11 place in these parts, and h having a great desire these
many years to come unto you, 24 Whensoever I take
my journey into Spain, I will come to you for I trust
to see you in my journey, and to be brought on my way
thitherward by you, if first I be somewhat filled with
your *company* 25 But now I go unto Jerusalem to mi-
i 2 Cor viii 1, &c & ix 2 nister unto the saints 26 For i it hath pleased them of
Macedonia and Achaia, to make a certain contribution
for the poor saints which are at Jerusalem 27 It hath
k 1 Cor ix 11 Gal vi 6 pleased them *verily*, and their debtors they are For k if
the Gentiles have been made partakers of their spiritual
things, their duty is also to minister unto them in carnal
things 28 When therefore I have performed this, and
l Phil iv 17 l have sealed to them this fruit, I will come by you into
m Chap i 11 Spain 29 And m I am sure that when I come unto
you, I shall come in the fulness of the blessing of the
gospel of Christ

v 22—29 St Paul had travelled far, but he intended still to extend his labours to a wider circle, and visit Rome also, and the regions beyond it

1 He had long proposed to visit them, but his many avocations had hitherto prevented him *For which cause also I have been much hindred from coming to you, but now having no more place in these parts*, the gospel being fully preached, and Christian churches planted throughout the country between Jerusalem and Italy *and having a great desire these many years to come unto you*, that I might impart to you some spiritual gifts, and be comforted by you, *whensoever I take my journey into Spain*, where I I purpose, God willing, to erect the gospel-standard, *I will come to you*, and take you in my way, *for I trust to see you in my journey, and*, according to the kind reception I have met in other churches, *to be brought on my way thitherward by you*, some of you going with me, and giving me such directions and necessaries as may conduce to the success of the expedition, *if first I be somewhat, or in part, filled with your company*, enjoying the satisfaction of their conversation, rejoicing in their steadfastness, and tasting a little of the sweetness of that communion of saints which he hoped in perfection to enjoy with them in heaven. *Note*, (1) When duty detains us from those whose company we most delight in, we are ever chearfully to forego our own pleasure, for the sake of our master's service (2) All our purposes should be formed in subordination to Divine Providence (3) Christian fellowship is one of the greatest joys on earth, and a little foretaste of what we expect, when we shall join the spirits of the just made perfect

2 He at present was obliged to return to Jerusalem with the collections of the several churches for their poor brethren in Judea, who by persecution and the famine were in great distress *But now I go unto Jerusalem to minister unto the saints*, to distribute among them the generous contributions of their Gentile brethren, *For it hath pleased them of Macedonia and Achaia, to make a certain contribution for the poor saints which are at Jerusalem It hath pleased them verily*, thus freely and liberally to contribute of their substance, and afford a noble example of Christian benevolence *and their debtors they are*, gratitude as well as charity required this at their hands *For if the Gentiles have been made partakers of their spiritual things*, and have been called to share in those privileges that were long peculiar to the church of Israel, *their duty is also*, in return, *to minister unto them in carnal things*, (λειτουργησαι), honouring God by a conscientious and liberal supply of their wants

3 When he had finished this work, he expresses his confidence that he shall come to them *When therefore I have performed* my present journey and service, *and have sealed to them this fruit*, careful that it be rendered up to them undiminished, *I will come by you into Spain And I am sure that when I come unto you, I shall come in the fulness of the blessing of the gospel of Christ*, as a merchant vessel richly fraught, bringing with me the inestimable treasures of the gospel-word, for your most abundant edification and comfort *Note*, It is a happy meeting between a minister and his people, when he thus comes to them in the fulness of the blessing of the gospel of Christ

30 Now I beseech you, brethren, for the Lord Jesus
Christ's sake, and n for the love of the Spirit, that ye n Phil ii 1
strive together with me in *your* prayers to God for me o 2 Cor i 11 Col iv 12
31 p That I may be delivered from them that do not
believe in Judea, and that my service which *I have* for p Acts xx 23 & xxi 27 2 Thess iii 2
Jerusalem, may be accepted of the saints 32 q That I
may come unto you with joy r by the will of God, and q Chap i 10
may with you be refreshed 33 Now s the God of r 1 Cor iv 19 James iv 15
peace *be* with you all Amen s Chap xvi 20 2 Thess iii 16

v 30—33 Having declared to them his purpose, he intreats their prayers, that he may be able to accomplish it

Now I beseech you, brethren, for the Lord Jesus Christ's sake, by every powerful argument which can be drawn from the grace which is in him, whose I am, and whom I serve, *and for the love of the Spirit*, who visited your souls with his blessed influence, and is a proof of your being possessed of this divine principle, *that ye strive together with me in your prayers to God for me*, fervently and importunately joining me in my earnest cries to God, *that I may be delivered from them that do not believe in Judea*, those most envenomed foes, his own infidel and wicked countrymen, *and that my service which I have for Jerusalem, may be accepted of the saints*, that all their prejudices against him and the Gentile converts might be removed, and this benevolence thankfully and chearfully received, to the cementing a nearer union between them And also, *that I may come unto you with joy by the will of God*, having found success in this ministry, if the Lord so pleased, *and may with you be refreshed*, in the enjoyment of your company, and the communication of our mutual happy experience *Now*, in return for the favour I ask, may *the God of peace be with you all*, uniting your hearts in love to his blessed self, and to one another, and filling you with all peace and prosperity in your souls *Amen* I pray that this may, and trust that it will, be your happy case *Note*, (1) We are bound to desire each other's prayers, and should count these among the greatest obligations which can be conferred upon us (2) Our applications to a throne of grace must be fervent and agonizing, as becomes those who know the inestimable value of the prize for which they wrestle

CHAP

CHAP XVI

Paul is now concluding this long and excellent epistle, and he doth it with a great deal of affection 1 *He recommends one friend to the Roman Christians, and particularly salutes several among them,* ver 1—16 2 *He gives a caution to take heed of those who caused divisions,* ver 17—20 3 *Salutations are added from some who were with Paul,* ver 21—24 4 *He concludes with a solemn celebration of the glory of God,* ver 25—27

1 I Commend unto you Phebe our sister, which is a
servant of the church which is at Cenchrea 2
a Phil ii 29 That a ye receive her in the Lord, as becometh saints,
and that ye assist her in whatsoever business she hath need
of you for she hath been a succourer of many, and of
b Acts xviii 2 myself also 3 Greet b Priscilla and Aquila my helpers
in Christ Jesus 4 (Who have for my life laid down
their own necks unto whom not only I give thanks,
but also all the churches of the Gentiles) 5 Likewise
c Mat xviii 20 1 Cor xvi 19 Col iv 15 Philem 2 greet c the church that is in their house Salute my well-
d 1 Cor xvi 15 beloved Epenetus, d who is the first-fruits of Achaia un-
to Christ 6 Greet Mary, who bestowed much labour
on us 7 Salute Andronicus and Junia my kinsmen
and my fellow-prisoners, who are of note among the apo-
e Gal i 22 stles, e who also were in Christ before me 8 Greet
Amplias my beloved in the Lord 9 Salute Urbane
our helper in Christ, and Stachys my beloved 10 Sa-
lute Apelles approved in Christ Salute them which are
of Aristobulus *houshold* 11 Salute Herodion my kins-
man Greet them that be of the *houshold* of Narcissus,
which are in the Lord 12 Salute Tryphena and Try-
phosa, who labour in the Lord Salute the beloved
Persis, which laboured much in the Lord 13 Salute
f 2 John 1 Rufus chosen in the Lord, and his mother and f mine
14 Salute Asyncritus, Phlegon, Hermas, Patrobas,
Hermes, and the brethren which are with them 15
Salute Philologus, and Julia, Nereus, and his sister, and
Olympas, and all the saints which are with them 16
g 1 Cor xvi 20 2 Cor xiii 12 1 Thess v 26 1 Pet v 14 g Salute one another with an holy kiss The churches
of Christ salute you

v 1—16 The apostle now takes his leave of them

1 With commending to them the bearer *I commend unto you Phebe our sister* in the Lord, *which is a servant*, or a deaconess, *of the church which is at Cenchrea*, in the neighbourhood of Corinth She was one of those who devoted her time and substance to the service of the cause of Christ probably her house served for the assemblies of the church, and she entertained those who came to preach the gospel among them Therefore he desires, *That ye receive her in the Lord*, with all holy affection, in the Redeemer's name and for his sake, *as becometh saints*, such as ye profess yourselves to be, *and that ye assist her in whatsoever business she hath need of you*, shewing her every mark of kindness and respect *for she hath been a succourer of many*, and hath most hospitably received and entertained them; *and of myself also*, with gratitude therefore I desire to acknowledge her kindness and generosity *Note*, The least return we can make for favours is to testify our gratitude to our kind benefactors

2 He sends his affectionate salutations to many at Rome

(1) To Priscilla and Aquila, of whom he speaks with deepest regard as his *helpers in Christ Jesus*, who had been particularly assistant to him in his labours at Corinth, and had for his *life laid down their own necks*, and when he was in danger rescued him at the hazard of their lives, *Acts* xviii 12—17 For which noble instance of generous love, saith he, *not only I give thanks, but also all the churches of the Gentiles*, who owe the continuance of my ministry to their zeal and interposition *Likewise greet the church that is in their house*, either their family, who were all professors of the faith, or the saints who usually assembled there for publick worship

(2) To Epenetus, whom he entitles his *well-beloved* So tenderly affectionate was the apostle's heart towards his spiritual children, and especially to Epenetus, as being the first-fruits of his ministry in Achaia unto Christ, and the earnest of that plenteous harvest which followed

(3) To *Mary*, whom he distinguishes as having *bestowed much labour on us*, peculiarly assiduous in every kind office of love towards me and my fellow-labourer

(4) To Andronicus and Junia, who some suppose to be husband and wife, but others more probably to be brothers They were Jews, near kinsmen to the apostle, had been endeared to him by confinement in the same prison for Christ, were persons eminent for their gifts, graces, sufferings, and services, and, he adds to their honour, *who were in Christ before me*, called among the earliest converts, and preaching the faith whilst he destroyed it

(5) To divers others, the most of whom he mentions with some note of distinction *Greet Amplias, my beloved in the Lord*, who bears his image, and is most amiable in the relation wherein he stands to the same divine Master *Salute Urbane, our helper in Christ*, and fellow-labourer in the glorious gospel, *and Stachys my beloved* *Salute Apelles, approved in Christ*, whose constancy and fidelity have appeared in many trials *Salute them which are of Aristobulus' houshold* *Salute Herodion my kinsman* both in the flesh and in the spirit *Greet them that be of the houshold of Narcissus, which are in the Lord*, vitally united by faith unto him *Salute Tryphena and Tryphosa*, those excellent women, *who labour in the Lord*, in their place and station indefatigable to serve the interests of the gospel *Salute the beloved Persis, which laboured much in the Lord*, remarkably diligent in her sphere to advance the cause of God *Salute Rufus, chosen in the Lord*, eminent for gifts and graces, and an elect vessel of distinguished honour, *and his mother and mine*, whose kindness to me lays me under such obligations of filial love as if I were by birth her son *Salute Asyncritus, Phlegon, Hermas, Patrobas, Hermes, and the brethren which are with them*, and belong to their families, from the highest to the lowest *Salute Philologus and Julia, Nereus, and his sister, and Olympas, and all the saints which are with them*, of their respective housholds *Salute one another with an holy kiss*, loving one another out of a pure heart fervently *The churches of Christ salute you*, joining me in the most affectionate remembrances, prayers, and good wishes

17 Now I beseech you, brethren, h mark them which h Acts xv 24 Col ii 8
cause divisions and offences, contrary to the doctrine
which ye have learned, and i avoid them 18 For they i 1 Cor v 11 2 Thess iii 6
that are such, serve not our Lord Jesus Christ, but k their 1 Tim vi 3—5
own belly, and l by good words and fair speeches de- 2 John 10
ceive the hearts of the simple 19 For m your obedience k Phil iii 19
is come abroad unto all men I am glad therefore on l Ezek xiii 18 1 Tim vi 5
your behalf but yet n I would have you wise unto that 2 Pet ii 3 Jude 16
which is good, and simple concerning evil 20 And m Chap i 8
o the God of peace p shall bruise Satan under your feet n Mat x 16 1 Cor xiv 20
shortly q The grace of our Lord Jesus Christ be with o Chap xv 33
you Amen p Gen iii 15
q Ver 24

v 17—20 Having testified his own warm affection towards them, and sought to unite them in mutual love, he adds,

1 A solemn caution *Now I beseech you, brethren, mark them which cause divisions and offences*, so opposite to the spirit of vital Christianity, and so *contrary to the doctrine which ye have learned* *Mark*, with holy jealousy, those deceivers, who, under plausible pretences of greater purity of worship, rend the peace of the church, *and avoid them*, join not with them in communion, and shun, as the greatest evil, whatever would introduce or perpetuate needless divisions

2 He discovers to them the true character of these pretenders, as the strongest argument to avoid them *For they that are such, serve not our Lord Jesus Christ*, whatever plausible pretences and professions they make, they have not really his glory and interest at heart, *but their own belly*, designing some mean, selfish, sinister, worldly advantage, *and by good words and fair speeches deceive the hearts of the simple*, who credulously follow them in their destructive ways Of you I am persuaded better things, *for your obedience is come abroad unto all men*, and, to your honour, mention is made through all the churches of your professed and exemplary subjection to the gospel of Christ *I am glad therefore on your behalf*, that you are so well established, and have not been beguiled by these false teachers *But yet*, knowing the weakness and folly of our fallen nature, and the subtilty of deceivers, I warn you to watch against the first effort, *for I would have you wise unto that which is good, and simple concerning evil*, cautious to discern truth from error, and joining the wisdom of the serpent to the harmlessness of the dove

3 He expresses his confidence in the Lord's preservation of them from all their enemies and seducers Now *the God of peace*, reconciled to you in a covenant of everlasting love, to whose blessing and protection I have recommended you, *shall bruise Satan under your feet shortly*, and all his instruments, though never so crafty *The grace of our Lord Jesus Christ be with you*, to strengthen, stablish, settle you, and make you more than conquerors *Amen!* *Note*, (1) None do the devil's work more effectually than those who foment needless divisions among the people of God (2) Satan is a vanquished foe, and whomsoever it is possible for him to deceive, he cannot, we know, deceive the elect (3) The confidence of victory secured for us in Christ is the greatest encouragement boldly to conflict with our spiritual enemies (4) The time is short, if faith and patience hold out a moment longer, we shall be placed for ever out of the reach of sin and Satan, and reign triumphant with him who shall make our foes become our footstool (5) The grace of our Lord Jesus Christ must do all for us, and therefore to his glory must all our victories be ascribed

Acts xvi 1
21 Timotheus my work-fellow, and Lucius, and
Jaſon, and Soſipater, my kinſmen ſalute you 22 I
Tertius, who wrote *this* epiſtle, ſalute you in the Lord
23 Gaius mine hoſt, and of the whole church, ſaluteth
you Eraſtus the chamberlain of the city ſaluteth you,
Ver. 20. 1 Cor xvi 23 Phil iv 23 1 Theſ v 28 Rev xxii. 21
and Quartus a brother 24 The grace of our Lord
Jeſus Chriſt *be* with you all Amen

v 21—24 As the apoſtle had before ſaluted many of the ſaints by name, he adds,

1 The affectionate remembrances of ſome of thoſe who were at preſent his companions *Timotheus my work-fellow*, as a ſon with a father, ſerving with me in the goſpel, *and Lucius, and Jaſon, and Soſipater, my kinſmen, ſalute you I Tertius, who wrote this epiſtle*, as the apoſtle's amanuenſis, *ſalute you in the Lord Gaius mine hoſt, and of the whole church*, whoſe hoſpitable doors are ever open to the faithful, *ſaluteth you Eraſtus the chamberlain of the city ſaluteth you*, ſuch had been his high office, and perhaps he ſtill continued in his poſt, though converted to the faith, one of the *not many noble* who were called, *and Quartus a brother* in Chriſt Jeſus, for all who have him for their Saviour, have one Father, even God

2 He repeats his fervent prayers for their ſpiritual proſperity *The grace of our Lord Jeſus Chriſt be with you all* May you experience his pardoning, comforting, ſtrengthening, ſanctifying grace below, and come to his compleat and eternal glory above *Amen!* I pray it may be ſo I truſt it ſhall be

Eph iii 20, Jud 24
25 Now to him that is of power to ſtabliſh you according to my goſpel, and the preaching of Jeſus Chriſt,
Chap ii 16
(according to the revelation of the myſtery which was
1 Cor ii 7 Eph iii 3, 9 Col i 26
kept ſecret ſince the world began, 26 But now is
2 Tim i 10 Tit i 3
made manifeſt, and by the ſcriptures of the prophets
according to the commandment of the everlaſting God,
Acts vi 7 Chap i 5
made known to all nations for the obedience of faith)
27. To God only wiſe, *be* glory through Jeſus Chriſt 1 Tim i 17 Jude 25
for ever Amen

v 25—27 Once and again, when he ſeemed to cloſe his epiſtle, ſome new matter aroſe to his mind, here he ſolemnly takes his leave of them

1 He commends them to God and the word of his grace *Now* I commend you *to him that is of power to eſtabliſh you*, and keep you from falling, *according to my goſpel*, which, by divine authority commiſſioned, I here declare unto you, *and* according to *the preaching of Jeſus Chriſt*, agreeably to what he himſelf taught, and I ſpeak in his name, pointing him out as the great ſum and ſubſtance of the goſpel, the hope and help of his people, *according to the revelation of the myſtery which was kept ſecret ſince the world began*, wholly hid from the Gentiles, and but obſcurely intimated to the Jews in types and dark prophecies, *but now is made manifeſt* by the miniſtry of the divinely illuminated ſervants of Jeſus, *and by the ſcriptures of the prophets*, which, having received their accompliſhment, are unveiled, and clearly underſtood, *according to the commandment of the everlaſting God*, who hath given his miniſters an expreſs commiſſion to declare the unchangeable purpoſes of his grace, that they might be *made known to all nations*, Gentiles as well as Jews, *for* this glorious end, that they might be brought to *the obedience of faith*, receiving the teſtimony of his word, and from the divine principle of faith, which worketh by love, engaged to walk before him in righteouſneſs and true holineſs

2 He concludes with a doxology *To God only wiſe*, eſſentially wiſe in himſelf, and ſeen eſpecially to be ſo in the amazing contrivance of the goſpel method of ſalvation, *be glory* and honour aſcribed, *through Jeſus Chriſt* the only Mediator, *for ever Amen* May his ſaints on earth perpetuate with their lateſt breath his praiſes! and in heaven he ſhall for ever be to all his hoſts the glorious object of their unceaſing adorations Amen and Amen!

THE

EVANGELICAL EXPOSITOR;

OR, A

PRACTICAL COMMENT

Upon the FIRST EPISTLE of

St. Paul to the CORINTHIANS.

CORINTH was a famed city of that part of Greece called Achaia, situated on the neck of land which joined the Peloponnesus, now called Morea, to Greece. Its very situation made it a most convenient mart, and, in consequence of the vast trade carried on there, it became exceeding rich and populous, so that the place was noted for pride and luxury, and lewd to a proverb. Here was the gospel standard erected by the blessed Paul, and abundant fruit of his labours appeared during his two years stay: but, on his absence, factions arose, false teachers sought to raise a party against the apostle, disputes followed, disorders in discipline, doctrine, and morals, were introduced, and these grievous abuses, which had come to the apostle's ears, are severely reprehended. After a short introduction at the beginning of the epistle, he first blames them for their discord and factions, enters into the original and source of them, shews them how much pride and vanity, and the affectation of science, learning, and eloquence, flattered by false teachers, had contributed to the scandalous schism, and prescribes humility and submission to divine instruction, to the teaching of God by his Spirit, both by external revelation and internal illumination, as a remedy for the evils that abounded amongst them. He shews them the vanity of their pretended science and eloquence on many accounts. This he doth through the first four chapters. In the fifth he treats of the case of the incestuous person, and orders him to be put out from amongst them. Nor is what the ancients say improbable, that this incestuous person was a man in great esteem, and head of one party at least amongst them. The apostle seems to tax them with being puffed up on his account, chap. v. 2. *In the sixth chapter he blames them for their law suits carried on before heathen judges, when their disputes about property should have been amicably determined amongst themselves, and in the close of the chapter warns them against the sin of fornication, and urges his caution with variety of arguments. In the seventh chapter he gives advice upon a case of conscience, which some of that church had proposed to him in an epistle, about marriage, and shews it to be appointed of God as a remedy against fornication, that the ties of it were not dissolved though an husband or wife continued an heathen when the other became a Christian, and, in short, that Christianity made no change in men's civil states and relations. He gives also some directions here about virgins, in answer, as is probable, to the Corinthians enquiries. In the eighth he directs them about meats offered to idols, and cautions them against abusing their Christian liberty. From whence he also takes occasion in the ninth chapter to expatiate a little on his own conduct upon this head of liberty. For though he might have insisted on a maintenance from the churches where he ministred, he waved this demand, that he* might make the gospel of Christ without charge; *and did in other things comply with and suit himself to the tempers and circumstances of those among whom he laboured, for their good. In the tenth chapter he dissuades them, from the example of the Jews, against having communion with idolaters, by eating of their sacrifices, inasmuch as they could not be at once partakers of the Lord's table and the table of devils, though they were not bound to enquire concerning meat sold in the shambles, or set before them at a feast made by unbelievers, whether it were a part of the idol sacrifices or no, but were at liberty to eat without asking questions. In the eleventh chapter he gives direction about their habit in publick worship, blames them for their gross irregularities and scandalous disorders in receiving the Lord's supper, and solemnly warns them against the abuse of so sacred an institution. In the twelfth chapter he enters on the consideration of spiritual gifts, which were poured forth in great abundance on this church, upon which they were not a little elated. He tells them in this chapter, that all came from the same original, and were all directed to the same end. They issued from one Spirit, and were intended for the good of the church, and must be abused when they were not made to minister to this purpose. Towards the close he informs them, that they were indeed valuable gifts, but he could recommend to them ſomewhat far more excellent Upon which he breaks out, in the thirteenth chapter, into the commendation and characters of charity And then in the fourteenth directs them how to keep up decency and order in the churches in the uſe of their ſpiritual gifts, in which they ſeem to have been exceeding irregular, through pride of their gifts, and a vanity of ſhewing them The fifteenth chapter is taken up in confirming and explaining the great doctrine of the reſurrection The laſt chapter conſiſts of ſome particular advices and ſalutations, and thus the epiſtle cloſes*

CHAP I

In this chapter we have, 1 The preface or introduction to the whole epiſtle, ver 1—10 2 One principal occaſion of writing it hinted, viz their diviſions and the original of them, ver 10—13 3 An account of Paul's miniſtry among them, which was principally preaching the goſpel, ver 13—17 4 The manner wherein he preached the goſpel, and the different ſucceſs of it, with an account how admirably it was fitted to bring glory to God, and beat down the pride and vanity of man, ver 17 ad finem

1. PAUL called *to be* an apoſtle of Jeſus Chriſt,
[a] through the will of God, and [b] Soſthenes
our brother, 2 Unto the church of God
which is at Corinth, to them [c] that are ſancti-
fied in Chriſt Jeſu, [d] called *to be* ſaints, with all that in
every place [e] call upon the name of Jeſus Chriſt our
Lord, [f] both theirs and ours 3 [g] Grace *be* unto you,
and peace from God our Father, and *from* the Lord
Jeſus Chriſt. 4 [h] I thank my God always on your
behalf, for the grace of God which is given you by Jeſus
Chriſt, 5 That in every thing [i] ye are enriched by
him, [k] in all utterance, and *in* all knowledge 6 Even
as [l] the teſtimony of Chriſt was confirmed in you 7 So
that ye come behind in no gift, [m] waiting for the † com-
ing of our Lord Jeſus Chriſt 8 [n] Who ſhall alſo con-
firm you unto the end, [o] *that ye may be* blameleſs in the
day of our Lord Jeſus Chriſt 9 [p] God *is* faithful, by
whom ye were called unto [q] the fellowſhip of his Son
Jeſus Chriſt our Lord

a Col i 1 b Acts xviii 17 c John xvii 19 Acts xv 9 d Rom i 7 1 Theſ iv 7 e Acts ix 14 21 2 Tim ii 22 f Rom iii 22, 29 Chap viii 6 g Rom i 7 Eph i 2 1 Pet i 2 h Rom i 8 i Chap v 8 k Chap xii 8 2 Cor viii 7 l 2 Theſ i 10 Rev i 2 m Phil iii 20 Tit ii 13 2 Pet iii 12 † Gr Revelation n 1 Theſ iii 13 o Col i 22 1 Theſ v 23 p Chap x 13 1 Theſ v 24 2 Theſ iii 3 Heb x 23 q John xvii 21 Eph iii 9 1 John i 3

v 1—9 The apoſtle opens his epiſtle,

1 With an aſſertion of his apoſtolic character, which ſome among them affected to traduce and vilify, as if he had aſſumed an honour to which he was in no wiſe entitled He affirms therefore the divine authority upon which he acted, not ſelf-conſtituted, but called of Jeſus Chriſt to the high honour and important charge of apoſtleſhip. And Soſthenes, a fellow-miniſter, joins him in affectionate ſalutations *Note*, There are times when to vindicate our real character, and magnify our office, is not pride, but a debt we owe to the church of God

2 He addreſſes himſelf to the church of God at Corinth, as *to them that are ſanctified in Chriſt Jeſus*, ſet apart by God's eternal deſignation in Chriſt their head, ſeparated by his grace from the world which lieth in wickedneſs, incorporated in his name, and making open profeſſion of their faith in him by baptiſm, *called to be ſaints*, juſtly ſo denominated, and proving by their conduct the propriety of the name they bore, *with all that in every place call upon the name of Jeſus Chriſt our Lord, both theirs and ours*, in whom we have a joint intereſt, and are all one in him *Note*, (1) All who profeſs the name of Jeſus are called to prove their relation to him by the holineſs of their walk (2) Since Chriſt is propoſed to us as the object of our worſhip, he muſt needs be very God (3) The life of a Chriſtian is an habitual courſe of calling upon God To live without prayer is the ſureſt mark of a Chriſtleſs ſoul

3 He gives them his apoſtolical benediction *Grace be unto you, and peace from God our Father, and from the Lord Jeſus Chriſt* *Grace*, the ſource of every bleſſing, and *peace* with a reconciled God through Jeſus Chriſt *Note*, (1) Every mercy a ſinner enjoys in time, or hopes for in eternity, flows purely from the ſovereign, free, and boundleſs grace of God in Jeſus Chriſt (2) All ſolid peace of conſcience can only ariſe from a ſenſe of God's favour, and reconciliation through the Redeemer

4 He thanks God, on their account, for the graces and gifts which were beſtowed upon them *I thank my God* (and bleſſed and happy are they who can call him ſo) *always on your behalf*, (ſo conſtantly did he feel a tender concern for them upon his heart) *for the grace of God which is given you by Jeſus Chriſt*, as the great Head of his people, to whom they are united, and from whom, as the fountain of vital influence, they draw continual ſupplies of ſtrength and conſolation And as he charitably hoped the generality of them were partakers of the grace of God in truth, he had alſo another cauſe for thankfulneſs, *because in every thing ye are enriched by him, in all utterance and in all knowledge*, endued with clear views of that rich ſalvation which is in a crucified Jeſus, and capable of expreſſing themſelves on the ſubject with ſingular fluency of ſpeech and energy of diction, *as the teſtimony of Chriſt was confirmed in you*, the Holy Ghoſt giving the fulleſt demonſtration to their conſciences of the truth of that goſpel which was preached unto them, *ſo that ye come behind in no gift*, in nothing inferior to any church which had been planted, in theſe diſtinguiſhed gifts of the Spirit, *waiting for the coming of our Lord Jeſus Chriſt*, according to the declarations of his word, which they had heard and embraced, preparing to meet him, and, with patient but joyful expectation, looking for the day of his appearing *Note*, They who are Chriſtians indeed cannot but rejoice in the proſpect, that, when Chriſt who is our hope ſhall appear, then ſhall we alſo appear with him in glory

5 The apoſtle profeſſes his confidence in them, that they will never be moved from the hope of the goſpel *Who ſhall alſo confirm you unto the end*, in faith and holineſs, enabling you to perſevere unſhaken amidſt all your trials, *that ye may be blameleſs in the day of our Lord Jeſus Chriſt*, being found complete in him, and then transformed wholly into his image And this his expectation Paul builds on the ſureſt foundation, even becauſe *God is faithful* to all his promiſes, and never can or will fail his people, *by whom ye were called unto the fellowſhip of his Son Jeſus Chriſt our Lord*, and the ſame almighty grace which brought you into this bleſſed eſtate is engaged to cement the union, till it ſhall be perfected in glory *Note*, (1) They who are Chriſt's are ſure finally to overcome none can pluck them out of his hand (2) The faithfulneſs of God ſhould be matter of our frequent meditation, ſince nothing enlivens the heart with hope, and quickens it to walk in holineſs, as the aſſured confidence that nothing ſhall ever be able to ſeparate us from the love of God which is in Chriſt Jeſus our Lord

10 Now I beſeech you, brethren, by the name of
our Lord Jeſus Chriſt, that ye all ſpeak the ſame thing,
and *that* there be no † diviſions among you, but *that*
ye be perfectly joined together in the ſame mind, and
in the ſame judgment 11 For it hath been declared
unto me of you, my brethren, by them, *which are of the*
houſe of Chloe, that [s] there are contentions among you
12 Now this I ſay, [t] that every one of you ſaith, I am
of Paul, and I of [u] Apollos, and I of [x] Cephas, and I
of Chriſt 13 [y] Is Chriſt divided? was Paul crucified
for you? or were ye baptized in the name of Paul?
14 I thank God that I baptized none of you, but [z] Criſ-
pus and [a] Gaius 15 Leſt any ſhould ſay, that I had
baptized in mine own name 16 And I baptized alſo
the houſhold of [b] Stephanas beſides, I know not whe-
ther I baptized any other

† Or ſchiſms. Chap xi 18 r Rom xii 16 & xv 5 2 Cor xiii 11 Phil iii 16 s Prov xiii 10 t Chap iii 4 u Acts xviii 24 x John i 42 y Gal i 7 Eph iv 5 z Acts xviii 8 a Rom xvi 23 b Chap xvi 15, 17

v 10—16 One chief end of writing this epiſtle appears to be the healing thoſe diviſions of which Paul had been informed He therefore,

1 Exhorts them to union among themſelves, in ſentiment and affection to have their hearts knit together, avoiding, as the moſt dangerous rock, thoſe diſputes and diviſions, which muſt be the bane of Chriſtian charity, and could not but end in the ruin of the church And he urges this by the moſt powerful motive, even *by the name of our Lord Jeſus Chriſt*, not only as one authoriſed to enjoin this upon them, but ſuggeſting that the very mention of the endearing name of Jeſus ſhould ſilence every jar, and fill their ſouls with love to him and one another *Note*, Internal diviſions among the members of Chriſt have more wounded his cauſe than all the external attacks of earth or hell

2 He informs them whence he received his information of thoſe evils which he ſo juſtly condemns, and ſolemnly remonſtrates againſt their making ſo ill a uſe of his name, as well as of his brethren, to range themſelves in different parties, whilſt ſome ſaid, *I am of Paul, and I of Apollos, and I am of Cephas*, or Peter, depreciating the one and exalting the other, as if it mattered ought by whoſe inſtrumentality they were converted to the faith whilſt others, as if above all means and inſtruments, boaſted, *I am of Chriſt*, and ſo immediately under the teachings of his Spirit as to need no other inſtructor But how abſurd were theſe pretenſions, and how dangerous theſe diſcords! *Is Chriſt divided?* so as to act ſeparately from the means of his own appointment? or can there be the leaſt ſort of diviſion between him and thoſe who act by his authority? and with whom he hath promiſed to be to the end of the world? or can his church, which is his body, and one with him, be disjointed, and his members ſubſiſt ſeparately from each other? ſurely no

And as for those ministers, under whose names you range yourselves, let me ask, applying it to myself, *Was Paul crucified for you?* Did I, or my brethren, ever pretend that we were your saviours? *or were ye baptized in the name of Paul*, by my authority, as my disciples, professing your faith in me, or obedience to my service? God forbid Neither I, nor my fellow labourers, ever taught you to hope for any other atonement but in a crucified Jesus, nor baptized you in any other name but his *I thank God*, since this matter hath been so abused by many of you, *that I baptised none of you but Crispus and Gaius, lest any should say, that I had baptised in my own name*, and sought to set myself at the head of a party *I baptised also the household of Stephanas besides, I know not whether I baptised any other* *Note*, A faithful minister of Christ rejects with abhorrence all attempts to set him at the head of a party, sollicitous only that his master should be glorified, and jealous above all things never to rob him of his peculiar honours

17 For Christ sent me not to baptize, but to preach
the gospel [c] not with wisdom of words, lest the cross of
Christ should be made of none effect 18 For [d] the
preaching of the cross is to them that perish, [d] foolish
ness but unto us which are saved, [e] it is the power of
God 19 For it is written, [f] I will destroy the wisdom
of the wise, and will bring to nothing the understanding
of the prudent 20 [g] Where is the wise? where is
the scribe? where is the disputer of this world? [h] hath
not God made foolish the wisdom of this world? 21
[i] For after that, in the wisdom of God, the world by
wisdom knew not God, it pleased God by the foolishness
of preaching to save them that believe 22 For [k] the
Jews require a sign, and the Greeks seek after wisdom
23 But we preach Christ crucified, [l] unto the Jews a
stumbling-block, and [m] unto the Greeks foolishness,
24 But unto them which are called, both Jews and
Greeks, Christ [n] the power of God, and [o] the wisdom of
God 25 Because the foolishness of God is wiser than
men, and the weakness of God is stronger than men
26 For ye see your calling, brethren, how that [p] not
many wise men after the flesh, [q] not many mighty, not
many noble, *are called* 27 But God hath chosen the
foolish things of the world, [s] to confound the wise, and
God hath chosen the weak things of the world, to confound the things which are mighty, 28 And [t] base
things of the world, and things which are despised, hath
God chosen, *yea*, [u] and things which are not, to bring
to nought the things that are 29 [x] That no flesh
should glory in his presence 30 But of him are ye
in Christ Jesus, who of God is made unto us [y] wisdom,
and [z] righteousness, and [a] sanctification, [b] and redemption
31 That according as it is written, [c] He that glorieth,
let him glory in the Lord

c Chap ii 1, 4 1 Pet i 16 d Acts xvii 18 Chap ii 14 e Rom i 16 f Job v 12 Isai xxix 14 g Isai xxxiii 18 h Job xii 17 Isai xliv 25 i Rom i 28 See Matt xi 25 k Matt xii 38 John iv 48 l Isai viii 14 1 Pet ii 8 m Chap ii 14 n Rom i 16 o Col ii 3 p Matt xi 25 John vii 48 q Rev vi 15 r Ps viii 2 2 Cor x 5 s Jam ii 5 u Rom iv 17 x Rom iii 27 Eph ii 9 y Col ii 3 z Jer xxiii 6 Rom iv 25 2 Cor v 21 a John xvii 19 b Eph i 7 1 Thess iv 14 c Jer ix 23, 24 2 Cor x 17

v 17—31 Having vindicated himself from every insinuation that he designed to form a party by baptising disciples, he disclaims next every attempt to aggrandize himself in the manner in which he preached the gospel unto them *For*, saith he, *Christ*, from whom immediately I received my commission, *sent me not to baptise* as my principal business, *but to preach the gospel*, according to the revelation made known unto me, and he informs them,

1 Of the manner in which he preached, *not with wisdom of words*, with affected flourishes of oratory, or to gratify philosophic pride, *least the cross of Christ should be made of none effect*, the simple truth of a crucified Jesus should be obscured, its efficacy defeated, its honour tarnished, and the success be ascribed not to the divine simplicity and native force of the truth, but to the art and eloquence of those who preached the gospel *Note*, Though eloquence, without ostentation, is both lawful and laudable, yet, as Luther says, he is the best preacher that can speak the most familiarly, and suits his discourse best to the capacity and understanding of the hearer, more sollicitous to be understood than to be admired

2 Of the effect of his preaching *For the preaching of the cross*, and the great salvation obtained by the blood-shedding of the Redeemer on the ignominious tree, *is to them that perish, foolishness* They who are puffed up in pride on their own sufficiency, or ignorant of their guilt and sinfulness, and their need of the redemption which is in Christ, reject the gospel as nonsense and absurdity, and perish in their impenitence and unbelief (1) The doctrine of the cross was to the Jews *a stumbling-block*, *v* 23 They could not bear to receive him for their Messiah, who made so mean an appearance in his life, and died as a malefactor on a tree Rejecting all the amazing miracles which he wrought, they required a sign from heaven, *Mat* xii 38 expecting he should appear in all worldly pomp and grandeur, as their temporal, instead of a spiritual, Redeemer (2) To the Greeks this doctrine *was foolishness* *They sought after wisdom*, *v* 22 they received nothing but what was demonstrable on what they termed the principles of reason, and since their philosophic minds could perceive no connection between a man who was crucified, and the redemption of sinners, nor esteemed it possible, on their principles, that he who could not, as they conceived, save himself from the cross, should be able to save others from death and hell they stamped the declaration with folly, and rejected it as absurd But, (3) Unto us who are called, and *saved* by grace, however proud Greeks or self-righteous Jews may think of it, *Christ*, and the doctrine of salvation through his cross, appears to be *the power of God, and the wisdom of God* *The power of God is seen* to be most gloriously displayed in the Mediator's undertaking and sufferings, in his miracles, resurrection, ascension, and especially in the mighty efficacy with which his gospel is attended, through the influences of his Spirit, effectually quickening the dead in trespasses and sins, turning them from darkness to light, and from the power of Satan unto God *The wisdom of God* is astonishingly displayed in the stupendous scheme of man's redemption, wherein the sinner, consistent with the glory of every divine perfection, can be received *into the bosom of mercy*, and pardon, righteousness, and glory, be bestowed on him, without dishonour to God's government or law, and this through the substitution of the second Adam, the Lord from heaven, in our stead

3 He shews the triumph of this doctrine of a crucified Jesus over all the inventions of the wisest sages, their schemes and systems could never relieve a guilty conscience, or lay a solid foundation for the sinner's hope The Lord therefore, according to his word, *Isai* xxix 14 stamps all human wisdom as folly *Where is the wise* philosopher? *Where is the learned scribe*, deep read in traditions? *Where is the disputer of this world*, whether Jew or Gentile? Can the one or the other give the least satisfactory account, how a guilty sinner can be reconciled to an offended God? *Hath not God made foolish the wisdom of this world?* and left philosophers and Rabbins to grope for the wall as blind? *For after that*, or *since*, *in the wisdom of God*, it was so ordered, *that the world by wisdom knew not God*, but their most learned sages were permitted to become vain in their imaginations, see *Rom* i 21, 22 ignorant of God, his worship, and ways, *it pleased God* in his infinite grace and love, to make a more transcendent display of his own glory, *by the foolishness of preaching*, (for so would a wise world call the doctrine of the cross) *to save them that believe*, making it effectual to their eternal peace and joy This contrivance of divine wisdom, to save lost souls by the incarnation of Jesus, is deemed the greatest folly, but *the foolishness of God is wiser than men* infinitely excelling all their boasted researches, and ingenious systems, *and the weakness of God is stronger than men*, however inadequate the gospel method in their eyes may appear, and however weak the instruments are, which are chiefly employed in the work, yet it was clear to demonstration, that what all the precepts of philosophy, and the power of oratory, never produced, the doctrine of the cross effected, destroying the kingdom of sin and Satan in the hearts of men, and causing such an evident change in their tempers and conduct, as spoke the finger of God *Note*, Wherever the gospel is truly preached, however weak the instrument may be, God will bear testimony to his own word, that the excellency of the power may appear to be of God and not of us

4 He appeals to them for the truth of what he had advanced, as verified by experience *For ye see your calling, brethren*, and cannot but observe who are the partakers of the gospel salvation, *how that not many wise men after the flesh, not many mighty, not many noble are called*, some few singular instances of these may be observed, whom the sovereign grace of God hath effectually wrought upon but, in general, the proud philosopher, the self righteous scribes, and the men of high birth and affluence, refuse to submit to the humbling and self-denying doctrines of the cross and, leaving them to their folly and ruin, *God hath chosen the foolish things of the world to confound the wise*, that an illiterate Christian should shame the proud philosopher, and shew the surpassing influence of the doctrine of Jesus, above all his learned precepts *And God hath chosen the weak things of the world*, men in the meanest outward circumstances, *to confound the things which are mighty*, to stamp vanity on human grandeur, and to shew that his kingdom stands without any earthly support, nay, in defiance of all worldly power and influence, *and base things of the world, and things which are despised*, even the poor Gentiles, whom the self-righteous Jews would have disdained to put among the dogs of their flock, these *hath God chosen, yea, and things which are not*, who never had a name or place in the church of God before, *to bring to nothing* (καταργήσῃ) *to abolish, the things that are*, putting a period to the covenant of peculiarity, under which the Jewish people formerly stood, and thought themselves, exclusive of all others, the only favourites of heaven but now all difference ceases, *that no flesh should glory in his presence*, on account of any imagined superiority in wisdom, wealth, nobility, or any external privileges, but *that, as it is written, he that glorieth should glory in the Lord*, ascribing the whole of their salvation to his sovereign, rich, and boundless grace, as revealed in the gospel of Jesus to the miserable and the desperate

5 He reminds them of the inestimable blessings, to which, in virtue of their interest in Christ, they were intitled. They had in themselves nothing to glory in, nothing but weakness and wickedness; *but of him are ye in Christ Jesus*, chosen from eternity, called in the fulness of time into the fellowship of the gospel, and incorporated into the mystical body of Christ, *who of God is made unto us*, according to the constitution of the covenant of grace, *wisdom and righteousness, and sanctification and redemption*. (1) *Wisdom*, we are naturally foolish, deceived, and ignorant; but all the treasures of wisdom reside in our exalted head; and, as the prophet of his church, it is his office to lead us into all truth, for which end he hath given us his word, and promises his Spirit, that we may be taught of God, and thereby be made wise unto salvation. (2) *Righteousness*, by his obedience unto death he hath brought in an everlasting righteousness for our use, in which we can appear complete before God, and, sinful and corrupt as we are in ourselves, we are ever accepted in this beloved, and God justifies us, though ungodly, because found in him, who is the Lord our righteousness. (3) *Sanctification*, he is the head of vital influence, and, as a quickening spirit, works effectually in the hearts of his people, mortifying their corrupt and vile affections, and daily renewing them in the inner man, that their spirits and temper may be brought to a nearer conformity with his own. (4) *Redemption*, his work is perfect, he hath obtained eternal redemption for his people, they can therefore never perish. The trials of time cannot separate us from his love; we shall now be saved from the dominion of sin, at death, the very being of it shall be destroyed in us, and though our bodies return to the dust from whence they came, at the great resurrection-day we shall awake in the perfection of beauty, no more to see corruption, our bodies glorious and immortal as his own. Thus Christ is to us all in all, and to him alone must all the glory be ascribed.

CHAP. II.

The apostle proceeds with his argument in this chapter, and, (1) Reminds the Corinthians of the plain manner wherein he delivered the gospel to them, ver. 1—5. But yet, (2) Shews them that he hath communicated to them a treasure of the truest and highest wisdom, such as exceeded all the attainments of learned men, such as could never have entered into the heart of man, if it had not been revealed, nor can be received and improved to salvation, but by the light and influence of that Spirit who revealed it, ver. 6 ad finem.

1 AND I, brethren, when I came to you, came not with excellency of speech, or of wisdom, declaring unto you the testimony of God. 2 For I determined not to know any thing among you, save Jesus Christ, and him crucified. 3 And I was with you in weakness, and in fear, and in much trembling. 4 And my speech, and my preaching *was* not with enticing words of man's wisdom, but in demonstration of the Spirit, and of power: 5 That your faith should not stand in the wisdom of men, but in the power of God.

v. 1—5. The apostle here before declared with what unadorned simplicity he had preached to them the doctrines of the gospel; they needed no varnish, and he trusted to their native weight and evidence to recommend them. *And I, brethren, when I came to you, came not with excellency of speech, or of wisdom, declaring unto you the testimony of God*, he used no rhetorical arts, nor affected curious speculations, but plainly declared the message which he had received of the Lord, the truth of which was attested by prophecies and miracles, and sealed to their hearts by the demonstration of the Spirit. *For I determined not to know any thing among you, save Jesus Christ, and him crucified*, avoiding all shew of Jewish or Grecian literature, and simply confining myself to that one distinguished point, in which all the lines of our salvation meet as in one centre, from which all the privileges of the gospel flow as from their source, and under the influence of which we can alone be engaged and inclined to all the service to which the Saviour calls us, constrained by his dying love. *And I was with you in weakness, and in fear, and in much trembling*, deeply sensible of his own insufficiency for the arduous work, in his outward circumstances and appearance, poor and despicable, exposed to innumerable difficulties from the enmity of the world without, and the envy of some within, who wanted to make a party against him, and above all, deeply exercised in his own soul, lest his message should be despised and rejected by them to their eternal ruin. *And my speech, and my preaching, was not with enticing words of man's wisdom*, these he studiously avoided, *but* he taught with much more effectual evidence, *in demonstration of the Spirit and of power*, not only by the miracles which he wrought in confirmation of his mission, but by the energy with which the Holy Ghost accompanied his preaching, to their consciences: *that your faith should not stand in the wisdom of men*, as supported by human evidence, or wrought by moral persuasion or argument, *but in the power of God*, arising from a divine conviction of the truth, resting on divine testimony, and produced by the operation of God. *Note*, (1) Nothing is more contrary to the spirit of the gospel than the affectation of being admired as orators, instead of being useful preachers. (2) Christ, in his person and offices, should be the great subject of all our discourses, nothing so effectually reaches the conscience as the doctrine of the cross. (3) Faithful ministers have peculiar trials, both from without and within, trembling sometimes for themselves, conscious of their own infirmities; trembling for the people, least that which should be to them a savour of life unto life, should, by their unbelief and prejudices, become a savour of death unto death. (4) The faith of God's elect is not the effect of human persuasion, but of divine operation.

6 Howbeit we speak wisdom among them that are perfect: yet not the wisdom of this world, nor of the princes of this world, that come to nought: 7 But we speak the wisdom of God in a mystery, *even* the hidden *wisdom*, which God ordained before the world unto our glory: 8 Which none of the princes of this world knew: for had they known *it*, they would not have crucified the Lord of glory. 9 But as it is written, Eye hath not seen, nor ear heard, neither have entered into the heart of man, the things which God hath prepared for them that love him. 10 But God hath revealed *them* unto us by his Spirit: for the Spirit searcheth all things, yea, the deep things of God. 11 For what *man* knoweth the things of a man, save the spirit of man which is in him? even so the things of God knoweth no man, but the Spirit of God. 12 Now we have received, not the spirit of the world, but the Spirit which is of God; that we might know the things that are freely given to us of God. 13 Which things also we speak, not in the words which man's wisdom teacheth, but which the holy Ghost teacheth; comparing spiritual things with spiritual. 14 But the natural man receiveth not the things of the Spirit of God: for they are foolishness unto him; neither can he know *them*, because they are spiritually discerned. 15 But he that is spiritual, judgeth all things, yet he himself is judged of no man. 16 For who hath known the mind of the Lord, that he may instruct him? But we have the mind of Christ.

v. 6—16. The apostle had disclaimed all affectation of human wisdom. *Howbeit*, says he, *we speak wisdom among them that are perfect*, (τελειοις) and grown up to greater maturity in knowledge, understanding, and grace, demonstrating the infinite wisdom, and suitableness of the divine contrivance, in the grand scheme of man's salvation, through faith in a crucified Jesus. *Yet not the wisdom of this world*, such as the heathen philosophers have invented or will approve, *nor of the princes of this world*, such as the proud Rabbies, and great men of the earth comprehend, or can conceive, who, with all their boasts of science, *come to nought*, and perish in their pride. *But we speak the wisdom of God in a mystery, even the hidden wisdom which God ordained before the world unto our glory*. The divine contrivance of the salvation of lost sinners had been unknown to the Gentile world, and but dimly revealed to the Jews in mysterious types and figures; but now the fulness of time was come, fore-ordained in the eternal councils, when the mystery of grace should be unfolded, and the elect of God effectually brought to his kingdom and glory. And this design of the divine wisdom *none of the princes of this world knew*, neither the Roman governor, nor the high priest and elders of the Jews, *for had they known it, they would not have crucified him*, who in essential deity is one with the Father, and justly claims the title of *the Lord of Glory*. *But as it is written, Eye hath not seen, nor ear heard, neither have entered into the heart of man, the things which God hath prepared for them that love him*. Low as their apprehensions were of the crucified Redeemer, yet hath he brought in a salvation for lost souls, unutterably glorious, by a contrivance far above human conception, and hath prepared for those who, sensible of his amazing grace, feel the constraining of divine love in their hearts, such inestimable blessings as pass man's understanding. *But these* glorious things, which are hidden from others, *God hath revealed unto us by his Spirit*, by a divine illumination in the preaching of the gospel, *for the Spirit*, who is the great agent in the conversion of the sinner's soul, illuminating his darkness, and quickening him from his state of death, *searcheth all things, yea, the deep things of God*, and who alone being perfectly acquainted with his counsels, is fully able to reveal them to us. *For what man knoweth the things of a man, save the spirit of man which is in him?* None but our own spirit can discover what passes in our secret thoughts; *even so the things of God knoweth no man, but the Spirit of God* The wisest and weakest are equally at a loss respecting God's eternal councils and designs, and none but that eternal Spirit, who is essentially God, and one with the Father and the Son, (as a man's soul is one with him, and conscious of all that passes in his breast) can know or reveal these unto us *Now we have received, not the spirit of the world,* that we should be guided by its wisdom, or follow its maxims, *but the Spirit which is of God,* whose office it is, in the œconomy of man's salvation, to enlighten the darkened mind, *that we might know the things that are freely given to us of God,* even all those inestimable blessings and privileges, of which, by grace through faith, we are made partakers *Which things also we speak,* declaring, from happy experience, the truths which the Spirit hath revealed to us, *not in the words which man's wisdom teacheth,* affecting to set them off with figures of oratory, *but which the Holy Ghost teacheth,* to add to which would be but to gild the brilliant, which shines infinitely brighter in its native lustre *comparing spiritual things with spiritual,* the types with the antitype, the prophecies with their fulfilment, the Old Testament with the New, which serve to cast mutual light and glory on each other, and supply us with expressions, which most forcibly and clearly convey the Spirit's meaning to the heart *But the natural man,* who continues under the darkness of his fallen mind, whatever attainments in human wisdom and literature he may have made, *receiveth not the things of the Spirit of God for they are foolishness unto him,* because he cannot reconcile them to his corrupted reason and defiled mind, *neither can he know them,* he is as much under a moral incapacity of ever attaining to the true understanding of spiritual things, as the blind man is under a natural incapacity of discovering the brightest objects, till the faculty of vision is given him, *because they are spiritually discerned,* and therefore cannot be comprehended without divine illumination *But he that is spiritual,* and effectually taught of God, *judgeth all things,* discovering the excellence, all-sufficiency, and suitableness of God's method of salvation, and distinguishing truth from error *Yet he himself is judged of no man,* no natural man, however wise or learned, discerns the principles upon which he acts, or can comprehend the truths which the spiritual man experimentally knows, or can confute him by any reasonings, when he sees that he hath the word of God for his guide, and the Spirit of God promised to lead him into all truth *For who hath known the mind of the Lord?* what philosopher ever soared so high as to penetrate into the secrets of God's eternal mind, *that he may instruct him* who is spiritual, in these supernatural truths? Darkness and folly are evident in all the schemes and notions of the wisest sages, *but we have the mind of Christ,* are divinely led into the knowledge of his designs of grace, and therefore can never be moved away from the hope of the gospel, by any pretenders to science, or by the disputations of philosophers, with whatever founding names or titles they may be dignified Learn hence, (1) That the wisest sage and the most illiterate peasant are on a level, respecting the knowledge which maketh wise unto salvation (2) If all the wisdom which ever existed in the whole fallen race was centered in one person, he would be as incapable of communicating one tittle of divine truth to us, as the glow-worm of enlightening the universe (3) It is the distinguished character of the redeemed, that they are all taught of God, not only by external revelation, but by the Spirit's internal illumination (4) The love of God, now shed abroad in our hearts, is the earnest of that inheritance which he hath prepared for us (5) We are not to wonder that those, who are mostly versed in human literature, are usually most averse to the truth of God The reason is evident, *ver* 14 (6) A spiritual understanding of the Scriptures is a better qualification for the ministry than all Roman or Grecian literature.

CHAP III

In this chapter the apostle (1) Blames the Corinthians for their carnality and divisions, ver 1—4 *(2) He instructs them how what was amiss among them might be rectified, by reminding, (1) That their ministers were no more than ministers,* ver 5 *(2) That they were united, and carried on the same design,* ver 5—10 *(3) That they built on one and the same foundation,* ver 11—16 *(3) He exhorts them to give due honour to their bodies, by keeping them pure,* ver 16, 17 *And to humility and self-diffidence,* ver 18—21 *(4) And dehorts them from glorying in particular ministers, because of the equal interest they had in all,* ver 21, to the end

1 AND I, brethren, could not speak unto you as
unto spiritual, but as unto carnal, *even* as unto
babes in Christ 2 I have fed you with milk, and
not with meat for hitherto ye were not able *to bear it,*
neither yet now are ye able 3 For ye are yet carnal
for whereas *there is* among you envying and strife,
and divisions, are ye not carnal, and walk as men?
4 For while one saith, I am of Paul, and another, I

am of Apollos, are ye not carnal? 5 Who then is
Paul, and who *is* Apollos, but ministers by whom ye
believed, even as the Lord gave to every man? 6 I
have planted, Apollos watered but God gave the
increase 7 So then, neither is he that planteth any
thing, neither he that watereth but God that giveth
the increase

v 1—7 The apostle proceeds here,

1 To rebuke the carnality, and contentions which reigned among the members of the Corinthian church *I brethren,* (for as such I regard you, notwithstanding the many imperfections I perceive among you) *could not speak unto you as unto spiritual, but as unto carnal, even as unto babes in Christ,* for greatly, as many were enriched in gifts, (see *chap* 1 5) yet in grace your attainments were very low, and your affections groveling still on earth and therefore as babes *I have fed you with milk,* with the simplest and plainest truths of the gospel, *and not with meat,* the more sublime points of revelation and the deep things of God, *for hitherto ye were not able to bear it, neither yet are ye able,* you would not have been edified by them, but have abused them, and made them minister to your pride and disputatious humour *For ye are yet carnal,* and shew too much of an unrenewed spirit, *for whereas,* or since *there is among you envying and strife, and divisions, are ye not carnal, and walk as men?* Whilst under the power of such evil tempers, wherein do you differ from the world that lieth in wickedness? *For while one saith, I am of Paul, and another, I am of Apollos, are ye not carnal?* Doth not such a spirit of party prove the deep, unmortified remainders of carnality in your hearts? Assuredly *Note,* (1) Ministers must be faithful to the souls of the people, and never flatter (2) There may be great attainments in knowledge, and yet little grace in the heart, and this wisdom puffeth up (3) Among real Christians, there are great differences to be observed, some are weak as babes, others, strong as men grown to maturity Our wisdom, as ministers, is therefore to give to every man his portion in due season (4) Nothing is more contrary to the spirit of Christianity than angry disputes, and schismatical divisions.

2 The apostle ascribes to the rich grace of God all the success which the gospel had met with among them It became effectual, not through human instruments, but by divine energy *Who then is Paul, and who is Apollos, but ministers by whom ye believed, even as the Lord gave to every man?* The men were mere instruments, it was the Lord alone who made their ministry effectual *I have planted,* by first preaching the gospel to you, *Apollos watered,* succeeding me in labouring among you *but God gave the increase,* without whose special operation and mighty influence, however great the natural abilities of either may have been, I must have planted and Apollos watered in vain *So then, neither is he that planteth any thing, neither he that watereth, but God that giveth the increase,* to whom the whole glory must be ascribed, exclusive of all the instruments he may have been pleased to employ And therefore they are not to be set up either as the authors of the gospel, or the cause of its efficacy *Note,* (1) If any man believe the gospel word, this must be the gift of God, for we can neither give ourselves faith, nor can the most powerful preachers communicate it to us (2) Ministers should ever be careful to ascribe to God the glory of all the success they meet with, we are nothing, he is all in all

8 Now he that planteth, and he that watereth are
one and every man shall receive his own reward, according
to his own labour 9 For we are labourers
together with God ye are God's husbandry, *ye*
are God's building 10 According to the grace of
God which is given unto me, as a wise master builder,
I have laid the foundation, and another buildeth thereon
But let every man take heed how he buildeth
thereupon 11 For other foundation can no man lay,
than that is laid, which is Jesus Christ 12 Now if
any man build upon this foundation, gold, silver, precious
stones, wood, hay, stubble 13 Every man's
work shall be made manifest For the day shall declare
it, because it shall be revealed by fire, and the fire
shall try every man's work, of what sort it is 14 If
any man's work abide which he hath built thereupon, he
shall receive a reward 15 If any man's work shall be
burnt, he shall suffer loss but he himself shall be saved,
yet so, as by fire

v 8—15 All faithful ministers are engaged in the same blessed cause, and have but one end in view, to glorify Christ and save immortal souls, and they shall not lose their reward *Now he that planteth,* by first preaching the gospel word, *and he that watereth* the seed sown by coming after him, *are one* in affection and intention and therefore those who are converted

under

under their preaching should be united also, nor think of setting up one against another *and every one shall receive his own reward, according to his own labour*, when the great Master comes, he will give to every man according as his work is; to secure his approbation must therefore be our great design, and not the empty honour which cometh from man only, which some of you affect *For we are labourers together with God*, united in the same service, and honoured abundantly by the very work committed to us whilst *ye are God's husbandry*, your hearts the field wherein he sows the seed of eternal life, *ye are God's building*, the spiritual temple which he erects, and where he is well pleased to take up his abode, for ye are the habitation of God through the Spirit Of this building we may observe,

1 The foundation is Jesus Christ *According to the grace of God which is given unto me*, who hath appointed me to the office, and qualified me for the service, *as a wise master-builder I have laid the foundation* of your faith and hope in crucified Jesus, *and another buildeth thereon*, succeeding ministers have carried on the blessed work begun in your hearts *but*, it is a needful and important caution, *let every man take heed how he buildeth thereupon For other foundation can no man lay than that is laid, which is Jesus Christ*, the rock of ages, the only hope of the miserable and desperate, and out of whom there is no salvation

2 The superstructure must correspond with the foundation *Now if any man build upon this foundation, gold, silver, precious stones*, inculcating the holy doctrines of the gospel, and exhorting men to a heavenly conversation which may adorn them, such labourer's work will bear the severest scrutiny, and shine gloriously before the eyes of men, but if they build *wood, hay, stubble*, urging their own conceits and fancies, and zealous about things insignificant and unessential, whilst the weightier matters are neglected, *every man's work shall be made manifest, for the day* of judgment *shall* shortly *declare it, because it shall be revealed by fire, and*, as the refiner tries the metal in the furnace, *the fire shall try every man's work, of what sort it is*, the exact scrutiny of that day shall prove whether every man's opinion and practices corresponded with the scripture standard or not, and the consequence of the trial will be awful (1) *If any man's work abide which he hath built thereupon*, and it appears before the great Judge that he hath followed his plan, and corresponded with his designs, in building up men's souls in the doctrines of grace and holiness, *he shall receive a reward*, eminent and distinguished, according to his labours and fidelity (2) *If any man's work shall be burnt*, and his opinions and practices be found unscriptural and erroneous, however highly he may have valued himself upon his abilities, *he shall suffer loss*, and see his fine-spun conceits all destroyed *but*, if he hath himself been founded upon Christ, and, though weak or mistaken, yet was not allowedly wicked or licentious, *he himself shall be saved* from the wrath to come, *yet so as by fire*, with such difficulty as a man escapes naked from his house when in flames *Note*, (1) Before the great trying-day comes, we should be often examining ourselves by that word of God whereby we must at last be justified or condemned (2) We may not be liberal of rash censures concerning the eternal states of men, but, whilst we condemn their opinions, must leave their hearts to the great Judge

16 [a] Know ye not that ye are the temple of God,
and *that* the Spirit of God dwelleth in you? 17 If any
man defile the temple of God, him shall God destroy
for the temple of God is holy, which *temple* ye are 18
[b] Let no man deceive himself If any man among you
seemeth to be wise in this world, let him become a fool,
that he may be wise 19 For the wisdom of this world
is foolishness with God for it is written, [c] He taketh
the wise in their own craftiness 20 And again, [d] The
Lord knoweth the thoughts of the wise, that they are
vain 21 [e] Therefore let no man glory in men for all
things are yours 22 Whether Paul, or Apollos, or
Cephas, or the world, or life, or death, or things present,
or things to come, [f] all are yours 23 And [g] ye
are Christ's, and Christ *is* God's

[a] Chap vi 19 2 Cor vi 16 Eph ii 21, 22 Heb iii 6 1 Pet ii 5
[b] Prov [illegible] 7 [illegible] 21 Chap [illegible]
[c] Job v 13 [illegible]
[d] Ps xciv 11
[e] Ver 7
[f] Rom viii 28 2 Cor iv 5 15
[g] Chap xi 3 2 Cor x 7 Eph i 10 [illegible]

v 16—23 The apostle here,

1 Presses the argument of holiness upon them from the consideration suggested *Know ye not that ye are the temple of God*, designed in a more peculiar manner for his abode than that house which Solomon built, *and that the Spirit of God dwelleth in you*, in his gracious presence and mighty operation *If any man defile the temple of God*, and seek, by broaching his corrupt opinions, to subvert the foundation, or by evil practice to seduce and draw men away from the truth of the gospel, *him shall God destroy*, with more terrible judgment than was threatened against the defilers of the material temple *for the temple of God is holy*, set apart for himself, *which temple ye are*, and therefore are bound to be holy in all manner of conversation

2 He warns them against the danger of vain conceit on their gifts and attainments *Let no man deceive himself* with high imaginations of his own superior excellence and in consequence propagate as truth his own erroneous opinions *If any man among you seemeth to be wise in this world*, and values himself upon his attainments in philosophy and human literature, *let him become a fool, that he may be wise*, renouncing all so far as it would beget perverse reasonings against the humbling truths of revelation, and content simply to embrace the doctrine of the cross, which the wise world counts foolishness, for thus only can any man become wise unto salvation *for the wisdom of this world is foolishness with God*, all their systems of theology, and their learned disquisitions on religion, are mere folly, compared with his glorious scheme of salvation through a dying Redeemer *for it is written, He taketh the wise in their own craftiness*, their fine-spun reasonings are the nets wherein they entangle and ruin themselves *and again, The Lord knoweth the thoughts of the wise, that they are but vain*, all their projects and designs, however deep concealed, are open to his eye, and, compared with his thoughts, weakness, folly, and vanity, are stamped upon them *Note*, (1) No man can become truly wise till, sensible of his spiritual ignorance, like a little child he comes to God's word to learn the first elements of truth (2) How amazingly foolish will all the wisdom of this world shortly appear, when those who trusted on the powers of their fallen reason to lead them to happiness, will find it to have been, like the deceitful meteor, a light only to delude them into eternal darkness

3 He warns them against exalting men, even the best and wisest, or following any minister implicitly, when their faith ought to stand not in the wisdom of men, but in the power of God *Therefore let no man glory in men*, as being this or that man's disciples, despising others and undervaluing their ministry *for all things are yours*, appointed and ordained for your blessing and advantage, *whether Paul, or Apollos, or Cephas*, the gifts are bestowed on them for the edification of the body of Christ, *or the world*, the administration of it is in the hands of Jesus, and he will give his people such a portion of it as shall be most for their good, *or life*, he will preserve you so long, and in such circumstances, as shall be most for his glory and your eternal happiness, *or death*, he will disarm it of its sting, and, in whatever manner it may come upon you, will cause it to prove your greatest gain, *or things present*, you shall be cared for through all your pilgrimage by his gracious providence, *or things to come*, an eternity of glory is before you, *all are yours*, secured to you in the everlasting covenant, and working together for your present and eternal benefit, *and ye are Christ's*, the objects of his love, the purchase of his blood, the members of his body, *and Christ is God's*, the appointed Mediator, the great Covenant-Head, who hath all things in his hands, and ever lives to perfect the salvation of his people, and to bring them to reign with him in heaven, to the eternal praise of the glory of God's grace

CHAP IV

In this chapter the apostle, 1 *Directs them how to account of him and his fellow ministers, and therein, tacitly at last, reproves them for their unworthy carriage towards him*, ver 1—6 2 *He cautions them against pride and self-elation, and hints at the many temptations they had to conceive too highly of themselves, and despise him, and other apostles, because of the great disparity in their circumstances and condition*, ver 7—14 3 *He challenges their regard to him as their father in Christ*, ver 15—17 4 *He tells them of his having sent Timothy to them, and of his own purpose to come to them shortly, however some among them had pleased themselves, and grown vain upon the quite contrary expectation*, ver 18, ad finem

1 LET a man so account of us, [a] as of the ministers
of Christ, and [b] stewards of the mysteries of God
2 Moreover [c] it is required in stewards, that a man be
found faithful 3 But with me it is a very small thing
that I should be judged of you, or of man's ‖ judgment
yea, I judge not mine own self 4 For I know nothing
by myself, [d] yet am I not hereby justified but he that
judgeth me is the Lord 5 [e] Therefore judge nothing
before the time, [f] until the Lord come, who both will
bring to light the hidden things of darkness, and will
make manifest the counsels of the hearts and then shall
every man have praise of God 6 And these things,
brethren, I have in a figure transferred to myself, and
to Apollos for your sakes that ye might learn in us
[i] not to think *of men* above that which is written, that
no one of you be puffed up for one against another

[a] Matt xxiv [illegible] Chap [illegible]
[b] [illegible] Cor [illegible] Luke [illegible]
‖ Gr day
[c] [illegible]
[d] [illegible]
[e] Matt vii 1 Rom ii 1 [illegible]
[f] [illegible]
[i] [illegible] Chap [illegible]

v 1—6 The apostle here,

1 States the true character of gospel ministers, and the esteem in which they should be held *Let a man so account of us, as of the ministers of Christ* (servants) [illegible], whatever is of the vessel, where Christ is the pilot, and labour with all their might to bring it to the haven of eternal rest, *and stewards of the mysteries of God*, dispensing to the household of faith the precious truths in the [illegible] word [illegible] growth in [illegible]

grace *Moreover it is required in stewards that a man be found faithful*, true to the trust committed to them, and zealous for their Master's interest and honour

2 Whatever they might think of him, he could appeal to God for his own simplicity and godly sincerity *But*, though some among you in the spirit of party are crying up one minister and censuring another, *with me it is a very small thing that I should be judged of you, or of man's judgment*, though I am desirous, for the honour of Christ and the success of my ministry, to vindicate my integrity before men, yet their censures are comparatively insignificant the approbation of the Lord, in the great day, is my important concern *Yea*, conscious of the corruption of my own heart, *I judge not mine own self, for though I know nothing by myself*, nor am at all conscious of allowed guile or unfaithfulness, *yet am I not hereby justified*, I would not on my consideration rest my justification before God on the footing of my own sincere obedience, he knows the deceitfulness of my heart better than I can, and may condemn me for what I have overlooked *but*, living upon his grace, and enabled to appeal to him for my simplicity, I wait the great decisive day, knowing that *he that judgeth me is the Lord*, to whose blood and righteousness I have fled for acceptance, and by whose grace I am what I am *Note*, (1) It is a comfort to us that men, even the best of men, are not our judges (2) Though we must in a becoming care about our character before men, our great concern must be to approve ourselves to God, and where we are conscious that this is our desire and labour, then we may sit loose to every malevolent censure (3) The fidelity of a steward, and the diligent labours of a servant, characterise the real minister of the gospel

3 He warns them against hasty judgment *Therefore judge nothing before the time*, suspend every rash censure *until the Lord come, who both will bring to light the hidden things of darkness, and will make manifest the counsels of the hearts*, when every man's principles, as well as practices, will be laid naked and open *and then shall every man*, who shall be found faithful, *have praise of God*, and be acknowledged and commended by the great Judge of all *Note*, (1) The prospect of a judgment day should make us careful how we dare judge others They shall then have judgment without mercy, who shewed no mercy (2) However sin be now concealed, and false principles put on the most specious appearances, the cheat cannot be long undiscovered the day is near when the secrets of all hearts shall be made known (3) They who can now approve themselves to their Lord, however reviled or maligned, shall shortly be owned by the eternal Judge

4 To avoid every offence, he tells them, *These things, brethren, I have in a figure transferred to myself and to Apollos for your sakes*, chusing to make use of his own name, and that of Apollos, rather than to apply the matter to any of those who headed parties among them, which might but exasperate And I do this *that ye might learn in us*, who, though chief in labours among you, disclaim all authority over your consciences, *not to think of men above that which is written*, setting them up as the Lords of your faith, and implicitly following their opinions, *and that no one of you be puffed up for one against another*, exalting the character of one minister upon the ruins of another, but giving God the glory of the various gifts he hath bestowed on different men, and thankful for the benefit of their ministry

7 For who maketh thee to differ *from another*? and
[f] what hast thou that thou didst not receive? now if thou
didst receive *it*, why dost thou glory as if thou hadst not
received *it*? 8 Now ye are full, [k] now ye are rich, ye
have reigned as kings without us and I would to God
ye did reign, that we also might reign with you 9 For
I think that God hath set forth us the apostles last, [l] as
it were appointed to death For [m] we are made a spectacle
unto the world, and to angels, and to men 10
We *are* [n] fools for Christ's sake, but ye *are* wise in Christ,
[o] we *are* weak, but ye *are* strong ye *are* honourable,
but we *are* despised 11 Even unto this present hour,
[p] we both hunger and thirst, and are naked, and [q] are
buffeted, and have no certain dwelling place, 12 And
labour, [r] working with our own hands [s] being reviled,
we bless being persecuted, we suffer it 13 Being
defamed, we intreat [t] we are made as the filth of the
world, *and are* the offscouring of all things unto this
day

[f] John iii 27 James i 17 1 Pet iv 10
[k] Rev iii 17
[l] Ps xliv 22 Chap xv 30 2 Cor iv 11 & vi 9
[m] Heb x 33
[n] 2 Kings ix 11 Acts xvii 18 & xxvi 24 Chap iii 18
[o] Chap ii 3 2 Cor xiii 9
[p] 2 Cor xi 27 Phil iv 12
[q] Acts xxiii 2
[r] 2 Cor vi 4 &c
[s] Acts xx 34 1 Thess ii 9
[t] Lam iii 45

v 7—13 As they were puffed up with a high conceit of themselves, and their unreasonable partiality for one minister above another, arose from an opinion of their own superior taste and judgment, the apostle rebukes this unchristian spirit

1 He reminds them that all they possessed was of God's mere grace *For who hath made thee to differ from another*, admitting your attainments may be singular? *and what hast thou that thou didst not receive* from above, as a matter of sovereign favour *Now if thou didst receive it, why dost thou glory as if thou hadst not received it?* and that it was not owing to his grace, but to your own desert, diligence, or ability? a claim how insolent, ungrateful, and impious? *Note*, There is nothing we can properly call our own but sin all good cometh from above, and God must have the glory of his own work it is the worst of sacrilege to plume ourselves on the gifts or graces which he bestows

2 He ironically reproves their vain imaginations of their own excellence *Now ye are full, now ye are rich*, abounding in worldly wealth, high in spiritual gifts, and flattering yourselves with the apprehension of your exalted attainments in grace, *ye have reigned as kings without us*, priding yourselves as if you had attained the summit of prosperity, without any obligations to us, or any assistance of ours who first preached the gospel unto you *and I would to God ye did reign*, far from envying you, I should be happy in your advancement, and wish for nothing more earnestly than that you really were as great and excellent as the glass of self-deceit represents you to be, *that we also might reign with you*, rejoicing in your attainments, and partaking of your glory as the instruments who contributed so greatly to your conversion and edification, whom you would then honour and respect, instead of adding to our troubles by your unbecoming conduct and ingratitude *For I think that God hath set forth us the apostles*, who were last called to the ministry of the word, *as it were appointed unto death*, ordained to suffer peculiar afflictions, and every day exposed to danger and death *for we are*, as publick criminals, exposed to beasts in the theatres, and devoted to destruction, *made a spectacle unto the world, and to angels, and to men*, exposed to every ignominy, reproach, and suffering from the world which lieth in wickedness, whilst angels and good men admire our constancy and pity our sufferings, and devils and wicked men insult, revile, and persecute us But whilst *we are* counted *fools for Christ's sake*, thus to expose ourselves for the sake of our crucified Master, and for our preaching the doctrines of the cross, which the world counts foolishness, *ye are wise in Christ*, and, varnishing over the offensive truths of the gospel, value yourselves on your wisdom and prudence in escaping that cross under which we groan *we are weak*, oppressed with sorrows and sufferings till our strength is ready to fail, *but ye are strong*, and know none of our tribulations to harass you *ye are honourable*, and maintain a respectable character in the world, and with lukewarm professors of Christianity, *but we are despised* for our fidelity, which draws upon us the reproaches and persecutions under which we appear so contemptible Whilst you enjoy ease and affluence, *even unto this present hour, we both hunger and thirst, and are naked, and are buffeted, and have no certain dwelling-place*, like our Master, without a settled abode to lay our head, *and labour, working with our own hands*, for that maintenance which you should supply, but which, for the gospel's sake, we rather choose to earn with the sweat of our brow than demand *being reviled, we bless, being persecuted, we suffer it* patiently, *being defamed, we intreat*, return no opprobrious language, but mildly remonstrate, and humbly beg a hearing *we are made as the filth of the world, and are the off-scouring of all things unto this day*, treated as the vilest malefactors, and as wretches chosen from the dregs of the people, who, being regarded by the heathen as the authors of all their publick calamities, are offered in sacrifice to appease the wrath of their supposed offended deities *Note*, (1) Many dangerously mistake, who judge of themselves by their gifts It is not great knowledge, but great grace, which constitutes the eminent Christian (2) They who will be faithful in the ministry should count the cost, and go forth with a readiness to suffer, if need be, the loss of all things (3) Nothing can serve to shew the character of the blessed Paul in a more distinguished light than the account he here gives of himself May we learn to copy his disinterested zeal, and bear our sufferings with the like meekness and unshaken fidelity!

14 I write not these things to shame you, but [u] as
my beloved sons I warn *you* 15 For though you have
ten thousand instructors in Christ, yet *have ye* not many
fathers for [x] in Christ Jesus I have begotten you thro'
the gospel 16 Wherefore I beseech you, [y] be ye followers
of me 17 For this cause have I sent unto you
Timotheus, [z] who is my beloved son, and faithful in
the Lord, who shall bring you [a] into remembrance of
my ways which be in Christ, as I teach every where in
every church 18 Now some are puffed up as though
I would not come to you 19 But I will come to you
shortly, [b] if the Lord will, and will know, not the speech
of them which are puffed up, but the power 20 For
the kingdom of God *is* not in word, but in power
21 What will ye? [c] shall I come unto you with a rod,
or in love, and *in* the spirit of meekness?

[u] 1 Thess ii 11
[x] Chap ix 12 Gal iv 19 Philem 10 James i 18
[y] Chap xi 1 Phil iii 17 1 Thess i 6 2 Thess iii 9
[z] Acts xix 22 Chap xvi 10 Phil ii 19 1 Thess iii 2 1 Tim i 2 2 Tim i 2
[a] Chap xi 2
[b] Acts xviii 21 Rom xv 32 Heb vi 3 James iv 15
[c] 2 Cor x 2 & xiii 10

v 14—21 The apostle with singular address,

1 Insinuates the kind intentions he had in the discourse *I write not these things to shame or upbraid you, but as a father*, tenderly

tenderly concerned for *my beloved sons*, *I warn you* to be aware of a conduct that is so unbecoming you, which must in the issue prove so much to your dishonour, and which it is highly incumbent on you to observe, lament, and amend *For though ye have ten thousand instructors in Christ*, who help to build you up in the faith, *yet have ye not many fathers*, to whose ministry ye were indebted for being called to the knowledge of the truth *for in Christ Jesus I have begotten you through the gospel*, he using my instrumentality, and sending me first among you to preach his great salvation, and the most of you, through his effectual grace, by my ministry, have been called to the knowledge of the truth, and faith in him, and therefore I have a peculiar title to your esteem and regard *Wherefore I beseech you, be ye followers of me* as dear children, not led away by those who would pervert you from the simplicity of the gospel, and steal your affections from me that you might idolize them Remember my example, and, as far as I appeared to imitate my divine Master, copy after the pattern *Note*, (1) Those rebukes will be most effectual, where kindness gives weight to the admonition (2) The way to reclaim any man from the error of his ways is not by publickly exposing him to shame, but by secret and gentle remonstrances (3) They who have been our spiritual fathers have a title to our peculiar affection (4) Every minister by his example should adorn the doctrine he preaches, that he may with some humble confidence be able to say, "Be ye followers of me"

2 He tells them what were his kind intentions in sending the bearer of this epistle *For this cause have I sent unto you Timotheus*, to second this letter by his exhortations and ministry, *who is my beloved son*, begotten in the gospel, and dear to me as a child, *and faithful in the Lord*, proved to be so by long experience, *who shall bring you into remembrance of my ways which be in Christ, as I teach every where in every church*, preaching the same doctrine, and walking in the same steps *Note*, (1) The great doctrines of the gospel can admit of no change like their Author, they are the same yesterday, to-day, and for ever (2) All faithful ministers of Christ bring the same message, walk after the same rule, and mind the same things Novelty is the proof of error

3 He assures them of his intention to visit them himself, notwithstanding the insinuations of some of their false teachers *Now some are puffed up as though I would not come to you*, as if I was ashamed or afraid personally to meet them, and perhaps may make the sending of Timothy an argument to support their suggestions *but I will come to you shortly*, it is my firm determination so to do, *if the Lord will*, in whose hands are all our ways, *and will know not the speech of them which are puffed up, but the power*, examining into their credentials, and not to be deluded with the glare of their eloquence or learning, but enquiring what power accompanies their ministrations, and what efficacy their discourses have on the hearts of the hearers *For the kingdom of God is not in word*, the church of the Redeemer is neither erected nor supported by human wisdom, nor doth mere profession constitute the Christian character, *but* it stands *in the power of God*, not by man's eloquence, but through the preaching of the cross, made effectual through the Spirit's energy, is this kingdom set up and maintained in the hearts of the redeemed

4 He concludes with an authoritative question *What will ye?* how would you chuse I should visit you? *shall I come unto you with a rod*, according to my apostolic power, severely to chastise those offenders and disturbers of your peace? this would be my grief as well as yours, *or shall I come to you*, as I desire to do, *in love, and in the spirit of meekness?* rejoicing to find a thorough reformation of whatever hath been amiss, forgetting what is past, and affectionately embracing you as my dear children *Note*, (1) Obstinate offenders call for the rod, and though it be painful, parents, masters, ministers, must not spare (2) Love and meekness are the ornament of the Christian character, and in these the preachers of the gospel should excel.

CHAP. V.

In this chapter the apostle, 1 Blames them for their indulgence in the case of the incestuous person, and orders him to be excommunicated and delivered to Satan, ver 1—7 *2 He exhorts them to Christian purity, by purging out the old leaven*, ver 7, 8 *And*, *3 Directs them to shun even the common conversation of Christians who were guilty of any notorious and flagitious wickedness*, ver 9 ad finem

1 IT is reported commonly *that there is* fornication
among you, and such fornication as is not so much
as [a]named among the Gentiles, [b]that one should have
his father's wife 2 And ye are puffed up, and have
not rather mourned, that he that hath done this deed
[c]might be taken away from among you 3 For I verily
[d]as absent in body, but present in spirit, have judged
already, as though I were present, *concerning* him that
hath so done this deed, 4 In the name of our Lord
Jesus Christ, when ye are gathered together, and my
spirit, [e]with the power of our Lord Jesus Christ, 5
[f]To deliver such an one unto Satan for the destruction
of the flesh, that the spirit may be saved in the day
of the Lord Jesus 6 [g]Your glorying *is* not good
Know ye not that [h]a little leaven leaveneth the whole
lump? 7 Purge out therefore the old leaven, that ye
may be a new lump, as ye are unleavened For even
[i]Christ our passover is sacrificed for us 8 Therefore
[k]let us keep the feast, [l]not with old leaven, neither
with the leaven of malice and wickedness, but with the
unleavened *bread* of sincerity and truth

a Eph v 3 b Lev xviii 8 Deut xxii 30 & xxvii 20 c Lev xx 11 d Col ii 5

e Matt xviii 18 John xx 23 2 Cor ii 10 f 1 Tim i 20 g Jam iv 16 h Chap xv 33 Gal v 9 i Exod xii 3 &c Isa liii 7 John i 29 1 Pet i 19 k Exod xii 15 l Deut xvi 3

v 1—8 The apostle, after reproving their party disputes, passes on to other gross offences which subsisted among them

1 A most gross and scandalous crime had been committed by one of the members of the church, that he should have his father's wife, either after his father's death, or, as seems more likely, during his father's life a species of fornication abominable even in the eyes of civilized heathens, and bringing the greatest reproach on their profession as Christians

2 What had been one man's sin in the commission had become the sin of the whole by their connivance *Ye are puffed up* Perhaps this was some factious leader, whom his party screened from censure, and gloried still in his gifts, or the opposite party triumphed maliciously in his fall, or their outward prosperity made them negligent of inward purity among the members of the church, and therefore, without mourning over such a scandalous offender, and casting him out of the church, as they ought to have done, he still continued to assemble with them, and they countenanced him in his wickedness *Note*, (1) In the most flourishing churches corruptions will creep in (2) Party divisions fill the heart with malice, and cause men to ascribe to the whole the faults of individuals (3) A Christian's heart mourns over the offences of his brethren, and cannot but sensibly feel the wounds given thereby to the Redeemer's cause

3 The apostle pronounces sentence upon this incestuous Corinthian, and enjoins them to put it in force against him by an immediate excommunication *I verily, as absent in body, but present in spirit*, having my heart ever solicitous for your welfare, and knowing by revelation the true state of this case, *have judged already, as though I were present, concerning him who hath so done this deed*, that he be without delay cast out from among you *In the name of our Lord Jesus Christ, when ye are gathered together* to consult on this affair, *and my spirit* is among you *with the power of our Lord Jesus Christ*, who hath left his authority to his church for the maintenance of holy discipline among the professing members of it, I have determined that you are in duty bound *to deliver such an one unto Satan for the destruction of the flesh*, expelling him from the society of the faithful, and delivering him back into the world that lieth under the dominion of the wicked one And perhaps some signal mark of wrath was suffered to be inflicted upon his body, that, thus exposed to shame and suffering, he might yet perhaps be brought to repentance, and *that the spirit may be saved in the day of the Lord Jesus* *Note*, It is as necessary for the backslider as it is for the glory of God, that he should smart for his unfaithfulness such chastisement is for his salvation, not destruction

4 He exhorts them to purge out the leaven of wickedness from among them *Your glorying is not good*, it is peculiarly unseasonable and strange, when such offences are committed among you with impunity *Know ye not that a little leaven leaveneth the whole lump?* and that in like manner corrupt principles and practices, connived at in the least measure, may soon spread, and communicate universal infection to the church *Purge out therefore the old leaven*, search out and remove the scandalous person from among you, as carefully as the Jews examine their houses before the passover, *that ye may be* in reality *a new lump, as ye are* in profession *unleavened*, in simplicity and truth devoted to the Lord Jesus as his peculiar people, and departing from all iniquity as the evidence that you belong to him *Note*, (1) The beginnings of evil are to be watched against and checked, lest, like the spreading mortification, the whole body become infected (2) They who are Christ's are new creatures If we say we abide in him, and walk in darkness, we lie, and do not the truth

5 He urges his exhortation by the strongest argument *For even Christ our passover*, who was typified by the paschal lamb, *is sacrificed for us*, that he might cleanse us from all iniquity, this being the great end of his death *Therefore let us keep the feast* which he hath instituted instead of the paschal supper, *not with old leaven*, admitting profane and scandalous offenders to the table of the Lord, *neither with the leaven of malice and wickedness*, not harbouring allowed sin, or living under the power of corruption, defiled in body, or soured with pride and party-disputes *but with the unleavened bread of sincerity and truth*, with real attachment of heart to the Saviour, and unfeigned love

to

to the brethren *Note*, (1) The sacrifice of Christ, which we commemorate, should be a rich feast to our souls, since thereby every blessing in time and eternity is secured to us (2) They who approach the Lord's table should examine themselves, whether their old leaven be purged out, and their hearts in simplicity brought to the spirit and temper of the gospel

9 I wrote unto you in an epistle, [m] not to company
with fornicators 10 Yet not altogether with the for-
nicators [n] of this world, or with the covetous, or ex-
tortioners, or with idolaters, [o] for then must ye needs
go out of the world 11 But now I have written unto
you, not to keep company, [p] if any man that is called
a brother be a fornicator, or covetous, or an idolater,
or a railer, or a drunkard, or an extortioner, with such
an one, no not to eat 12 For what have I to do to
judge [q] them also that are without? do not ye judge [r] them
that are within? 13 But them that are without, God
judgeth Therefore [s] put away from among yourselves
that wicked person

v 9—13 Some conceive that the apostle here refers to a former epistle which he had written to the Corinthians, others to one he was writing when he heard from them, and began a new letter in answer to them, though perhaps what he speaks may have only respect to what he had said before in this same epistle *I wrote unto you in an epistle, not to company with fornicators*, to be separate from all familiar intercourse with those who bring such reproach on the Christian name *Yet* my intention is *not* that you should be altogether secluded from the world, and refuse all civil intercourse *with the fornicators of this world, or with the covetous, or extortioners, or with idolaters, for then must ye needs go out of the world*, so few would be left with whom to have any commerce or society in such an evil world as this is *But now I have written unto you, not to keep company, if any man that is called a brother be a fornicator, or covetous, or an idolater, or a railer, or a drunkard, or an extortioner, with such an one, no not to eat*, not only he should be excluded from eating bread with you at the Lord's table, but even all intercourse and connection with him should be cut off, and he should be shunned and avoided by you more than even the heathen themselves, that, being put to shame, he may yet be brought to repentance, and restored to the bosom of the church *For what have I to do to judge them also that are without?* as they make no profession of Christianity, they lie under no censures, and in civil affairs, as duty calls, may lawfully be conversed with *but do not ye judge them that are within?* The professing members of the church come under your jurisdiction, and are, when under censure, to be treated with this peculiar distance *But them that are without*, who are open offenders, and live carelessly after the fashion of the world, *God judgeth*, to whose judgment they must be left *Therefore*, since your power extends over your own community, *put away from yourselves that wicked person*

CHAP VI

In this chapter the apostle, 1 Reproves them for going to law with one another about small matters, and bringing the cause before heathen judges, ver 1—8 *2 He takes occasion hence to warn them against many gross sins to which they had been formerly addicted,* ver 9—12 *3 And having cautioned them against the abuse of their liberty, he vehemently dehorts them from fornication by various arguments,* ver 12 ad finem

1 DARE any of you, having a matter against an-
other, go to law before the unjust, and not
before the saints? 2 Do ye not know that [a] the saints
shall judge the world? and if the world shall be judged
by you, are ye unworthy to judge the smallest matters?
3 Know ye not that [b] we shall judge angels? how much
more things that pertain to this life? 4 If then ye have
judgments of things pertaining to this life, set them to
judge who are least esteemed in the church 5 I speak
to your shame Is it so, that there is not a wise man
amongst you? no not one that shall be able to judge
between his brethren? 6 But brother goeth to law with
brother, and that before the unbelievers 7 Now there-
fore there is utterly a fault among you, because ye go
to law with one another [c] why do ye not rather take
wrong? why do ye not rather suffer yourselves to be
defrauded? 8 Nay, you do wrong and defraud, and
that *your* brethren

v 1—8 The apostle proceeds to censure another grievous fault among them A litigious spirit prevailed, and, to the shame of their holy profession, brother went to law against brother, *and that before the unbelievers*, the heathen magistrates

1 He rebukes them for thus going to law among themselves, and that too, as appears, *v* 2, 7 on matters of small importance, which, without great detriment to themselves or families, they might have quietly passed by, and borne the loss rather than seek a litigious redress and, worst of all, they chose rather to carry their causes before the heathen tribunals, than refer them to the decision of their own members, the saints of God, foolishly exposing themselves thereby to the partiality which might be expected from unjust judges, and giving the enemy occasion to triumph in their quarrels

2 He suggests, as an aggravation of their fault, the honour and dignity to which the saints of God must shortly be exalted as assessors with the eternal Judge on his throne, whilst fallen angels and a guilty world stand at his bar, and receive from his lips their eternal doom And if so, how strange must it be that they should not now be able to judge of the smallest matters, and determine concerning the trivial affairs of this life, which even those who are least esteemed in the church would be much fitter to decide than the heathen magistrates before whom they carried their disputes

3 With a warm expostulation on their folly and perverseness he points out to them a remedy for the evil *I speak to your shame* In what an unbecoming and unchristian manner do you act *Is it so, that there is not a wise man amongst you? no not one that shall be able to judge between his brethren?* Where they boasted of such high attainments in wisdom, it would be very strange if they could not find a better umpire of their disputes among the whole body of their church, than to have recourse to Gentile tribunals There was therefore, no doubt, a fault in this matter, and far better was it for them to suffer some wrong and loss, than to seek redress in such a way But, instead of this meekness, patience, and forgiveness, *you do wrong and defraud, and that your brethren*, to the great dishonour of your Christian profession *Note*, All differences among Christians should be amicably determined by their brethren at least, in lesser matters, it were better to quit our right than have recourse to the wrangling bar

9 Know ye not that the unrighteous shall not inherit
the kingdom of God? Be not deceived [d] neither forni-
cators, nor idolaters, nor adulterers, nor effeminate, nor
abusers of themselves with mankind, 10 Nor thieves,
nor covetous, nor drunkards, nor revilers, nor extortion-
ers, shall inherit the kingdom of God 11 And [e] such
were some of you [f] but ye are washed, but ye are sanc-
tified, but ye are justified in the name of the Lord Jesus,
and by the Spirit of our God

v 9—11 The apostle, having warned them against some particular offences, passes on to enumerate a black catalogue, of which they had formerly been guilty, and under the power of which whosoever continued to walk, he never could inherit the kingdom of God

1 The sins mentioned are fornication, idolatry, adultery, effeminacy and lasciviousness, sodomy, theft, avarice, drunkenness, reviling, extortion, crimes which if indulged must necessarily exclude the soul from any part in the kingdom of grace, and for ever banish it from the presence of God in glory

2 He warns them against all self-delusion in this matter There was a heathen then right-hand, if they flattered themselves with any vain imaginations that they had yet hope towards God, whilst walking in such abominations, which then, now, and for ever, if not forgiven and forsaken, must inevitably destroy both body and soul in hell

3 He reminds them of the blessed change which had passed upon them, that they might not again return unto folly *Such were some of you but*, glory be to God sovereign, rich, and boundless grace, *ye are washed, but ye are sanctified, but ye are justified in the name of the Lord Jesus, and by the Spirit of our God* ye are washed in the fountain opened for sin and uncleanness, by the atoning blood and righteousness of the adored Redeemer your iniquities are pardoned, great and aggravated as they were, and your persons presented spotless before the throne of God, and you are not only accounted righteous, but made pure in heart by the mighty operation of the Divine Spirit, and in body, soul, and spirit, renewed, that you might be made meet for the inheritance among the saints in light *Note*, (1) The greatest crimes exclude none from salvation who fly to the atoning blood of Jesus In him there is grace abounding for the chief of sinners (2) All who are justified by grace are sanctified by the Spirit We deceive ourselves, if we think we have an interest in the one, if we do not experience the effectual operation of the other (3) Nothing is so strong an argument to a redeemed soul to fly from sin, as the remembrance of the mercy he hath tasted, and of the ransom which hath been paid

12 [g] All things are lawful unto me, but all things
are not expedient all things are lawful for me, but I
will not be brought under the power of any 13 [h] Meats
for the belly, and the belly for meats but God shall
destroy both it and them Now the body is not for

forni-

fornication, [i] but for the Lord, and the Lord for the
body 14 And [k] God hath both raiſed up the Lord,
and [l] will alſo raiſe up us by his own power 15 Know
ye not, that [m] your bodies are the members of Chriſt?
ſhall I then take the members of Chriſt, and make them
the members of an harlot? God forbid 16 What,
know ye not that he which is joined to an harlot, is one
body? for [n] two (ſaith he) ſhall be one fleſh 17 But
he that is joined unto the Lord, [o] is one ſpirit 18 Flee
fornication Every ſin that a man doth, is without the
body but he that committeth fornication [p] ſinneth
againſt his own body 19 What, know ye not that
[q] your body is the temple of the holy Ghoſt *which is* in
you, which ye have of God, and [r] ye are not your own?
20 For [s] ye are bought with a price therefore glo-
rify God in your body, and in your ſpirit, which are
God's

[i] Ver 19 20 2 Cor xi 2 [k] Acts ii 24 [l] Rom vi 5, 8 & viii 11 2 Cor iv 14 [m] Rom xii 5 Chap xii 27 Eph v 30. [n] Gen ii 24 Mat xix 5 Eph v 31 [o] John xvii 21, 23 Eph iv 4 & v 30 32 [p] Rom i 24 1 Thes iv 4 [q] Chap. iii 16 2 Cor vi 16 Eph ii 21 [r] Rom xiv 7 [s] Acts xx 28 Chap vii 23 Heb ix 12 1 Pet i 18

v 12—20 As ſome of them at Corinth appeared to have too light thoughts of the ſin of fornication, which the apoſtle ranked under the damning ſins, and ſeem to have ſet it on a footing only with the meats forbidden to the Gentile converts, (*Acts* xv 29) the apoſtle ſtrongly ſets himſelf to ſhew their dangerous error With regard to meats forbidden by the Levitical law, or offered to idols, *All things are lawful unto me*, which Chriſt hath not forbidden, and are not in their own nature ſinful, *but all things are not expedient*, even in indifferent matters, for the ſake of others, it is right to forego our Chriſtian liberty *All things are lawful for me, but I will not be brought under the power of any*, ſo as to have my affections enſlaved by them, or to have my conſcience ſubjected to any human arbitrary authority *Meats for the belly, and the belly for meats*, all wholeſome food is deſigned for our uſe, *but* these are things of trivial conſequence, ſince *God ſhall* ſhortly *deſtroy both it and them* In the eternal world the ranſomed will not need these bodily refreſhments, for they ſhall hunger no more, nor thirſt any more but reſpecting fornication, the matter is very different, though the belly is not at all defiled by meats, the body is by fornication

He urges this matter by various arguments

1 *Now the body is not for fornication*, it was not made to be proſtituted to impurity, *but for the Lord*, to be employed for his glory, *and the Lord for the body*, who, as the bridegroom of his church and people, requires their bodies as well as ſouls to be under his holy government *And*,

2 *God hath both raiſed up the Lord Jeſus* from the dead, that his quickened body might be the pledge and earneſt of our reſurrection, *and will alſo raiſe up us by his own power* our bodies therefore that ſhall be faſhioned like to his glorious body, ought not now to be polluted by fornication and uncleanneſs

3 *Know ye not, that your bodies are the members of Chriſt?* through faith we are united to Chriſt as our living head, and compoſe a part of his body myſtical *ſhall I then take the members of Chriſt, and make them the members of an harlot?* how horrid the very ſuggeſtion! and every Chriſtian heart, with deteſtation of the thought, cannot but cry, *God forbid!* *What, know ye not that he which is joined to an harlot, is one body?* ſuch an unhallowed connection is moſt contrary to the union of the heart with Jeſus *for two, ſaith he, ſhall be one fleſh* A fornicator becomes united to an harlot, and not to Chriſt, *but he that is joined to the Lord*, in real vital union of heart and perſon, *is one ſpirit*, actuated and influenced by the ſame divine Spirit, which in all its fulneſs dwells in our exalted head Therefore *flee fornication*, as the higheſt indignity we can offer to the Lord, of whoſe body we are members *Note*, In temptations to lewdneſs flight is often the only preſervative

4 *Every other ſin that a man doth, is without the body*, and terminates upon an object without himſelf, not immediately defiling the body, though it brings guilt upon his ſoul, *but he that committeth fornication ſinneth againſt his own body*, not only offending againſt God and his neighbour, but immediately contaminating his own fleſh by ſuch an abomination

5 *What* ſhall I farther urge? *Know ye not that your body is the temple of the Holy Ghoſt which is in you, which ye have of God?* and, ſince he hath been pleaſed to take up his abode in your hearts, *ye are not your own*, but bound to yield yourſelves to his will and guidance, and to do nothing which ſhould provoke the divine inhabitant to quit his temple with abhorrence

6 *For*, to finiſh with one argument more, *ye are bought with a price*, even the amazing price of a Redeemer's blood, from the curſe of the law, and the bondage of corruption, that you might be reſtored to the ſervice and enjoyment of the bleſſed God *Therefore*, ſince this was one great end of your redemption, *glorify God in your body, and in your ſpirit, which are God's*, nor dare to alienate your affection from him, or to diſhonour your bodies by fornication, which ſhould be employed in his bleſſed work, and wholly and unreſervedly devoted to his glory

CHAP VII

In this chapter the apoſtle anſwers ſome caſes propoſed to him by the Corinthians about marriage He, 1 Shews them that marriage was appointed as a remedy againſt fornication, and therefore perſons had better marry than burn, ver 1—10 2 *He gives direction to thoſe who were married to continue together, though they might have an unbelieving relation, unleſs the unbeliever would part, in which caſe a Chriſtian would not be in bondage*, ver 10—17 3 *He ſhews them, that becoming Chriſtians does not change their external ſtate, and therefore adviſes every one to continue, in the general, in that ſtate in which he was called*, ver 17—25 4 *He adviſes them, by reaſon of the preſent diſtreſs, to keep themſelves unmarried hints the ſhortneſs of time, and how they ſhould improve it, ſo as to grow dead and indifferent to the comforts of the world, and ſhews them how worldly cares hinder their devotions, and diſtract them in the ſervice of God*, ver 25—35 5 *He directs them in the diſpoſal of their virgins*, ver 36—39 6 *And cloſes the chapter with advice to widows, how to diſpoſe of themſelves in that ſtate*, ver 39, 40

1 NOW concerning the things whereof ye wrote
unto me [a] *It is* good for a man not to touch
a woman 2 Nevertheleſs, *to avoid* fornication, let
every man have his own wife, and let every woman have
her own huſband 3 [b] Let the huſband render unto the
wife due benevolence and likewiſe alſo the wife unto
the huſband 4 The wife hath not power of her own
body, but the huſband and likewiſe alſo the huſband
hath not power of his own body, but the wife 5 [c] De-
fraud you not one the other, except *it be* with conſent
for a time, that ye may give yourſelves to faſting and
prayer, and come together again, [d] that Satan tempt
you not for your incontinency 6 But I ſpeak this by
permiſſion, *and* [e] not of commandment 7 For I would
that all men were even as I myſelf but [f] every man
hath his proper gift of God, one after this manner, and
another after that 8 I ſay therefore to the unmarried
and widows, [g] It is good for them if they abide even as
I 9 But [h] if they cannot contain, let them marry for
it is better to marry than to burn

[a] Ver 6 [b] Ex xxi 10 1 Pet iii 7 [c] Ex xix 15 1 Sam xxi 4 Joel ii 16 [d] 1 Theſ iii 5 [e] Ver 12 2 Cor viii 8 & xi 17 [f] Mat xix 11 [g] Ver 26 [h] 1 Tim v 14

v 1—9 In anſwer to ſome caſes of conſcience, which the Corinthians had ſent to the apoſtle for his ſolution, he here replies

1 In the perſecuted ſtate of the church, and conſidering the incumbrances which a married ſtate neceſſarily produced, he ſuggeſts, that it would be well for thoſe who had the gift of continence to keep themſelves ſingle, and in order to avoid exciting any deſire for women, that they ſhould obſerve a cautious diſtance, and never touch them

2 Yet he was far from enjoining celibacy as a duty *To avoid fornication*, where the gift of continence was not poſſeſſed, and circumſtances made it more eligible, it was adviſeable that every man and woman ſhould enter into the honourable eſtate of marriage, with all conjugal fidelity and love cleaving alone to thoſe with whom they are thus united

3 For thoſe who are married, he lays down this rule That neither of them afterward have a right to withhold their bodies from each other, but mutually owe the duty of the marriage-bed And though on ſome extraordinary occaſions they may forego thoſe lawful delights which they take in each other, it muſt be *by conſent*, when peculiar ſeaſons of humiliation call for prayer and faſting, and only for *a time*, nor defrauding each other of that which is now a mutual duty, but coming together as before, *that Satan tempt you not for your incontinency*, and, whilſt you wrongly abſtain from what is lawful, he ſhould lead you to what is criminal, and enſnare your affections with other objects

4 The apoſtle declares, *I ſpeak this by permiſſion*, as my advice, *and not of commandment*, as what is abſolutely neceſſary for every individual, not as if it were every man's duty to marry, who was thereto inclined, there were caſes and circumſtances when perſons could beſt judge for themſelves *For I would that all men were even as I myſelf*, and could as contentedly continue in a ſtate of celibacy, *but every man hath his proper gift of God, one after this manner, and another after that*, according to their different diſpoſitions and conſtitution *I ſay therefore to the unmarried and widows, It is good for them if*, in theſe perilous times, *they abide even as I*, and can with ſafety and ſatisfaction continue ſingle *But if they cannot contain*, and they find their animal appetites too ſtrong to be kept under, *let them marry* this then becomes a duty, and it would be ſinful to neglect the ordinance of God *for it is better to marry than to burn*, and be harraſſed with tormenting deſire

10 And unto the married I command, *yet* not I, but
the Lord, Let not the wife depart from *her* husband
11 But and if she depart, let her remain unmarried, or
be reconciled to *her* husband and let not the husband
put away *his* wife 12 But to the rest speak I, not
the Lord, If any brother hath a wife that believeth not,
and she be pleased to dwell with him let him not put
her away 13 And the woman which hath a husband
that believeth not, and if he be pleased to dwell with
her, let her not leave him 14 For the unbelieving
husband is sanctified by the wife, and the unbelieving
wife is sanctified by the husband, else were your chil-
dren unclean, but now are they holy 15 But if the
unbelieving depart, let him depart A brother or a
sister is not under bondage in such *cases* but God
hath called us † to peace 16 For what knowest thou,
O wife, whether thou shalt save *thy* husband? or how
knowest thou, O man, whether thou shalt save *thy* wife?
17 But as God hath distributed to every man, as the
Lord hath called every one, so let him walk and so
ordain I in all churches

v 10—17 As many who had been called in a conjugal state had partners of their bed, who still continued in heathenism, and divorces were common among the Jews, the apostle, by immediate authority from his Lord, declares what was their duty in such circumstances

1 The wife may on no considerations (adultery excepted) depart from her husband *But if she depart* voluntarily, or be dismissed through any quarrel, *let her remain unmarried, or be reconciled to her husband*, whose regard it is her duty by all lawful means to endeavour to regain *And let not the husband put away his wife*, on any consideration but the defilement of the marriage bed *Note*, Those who are married should desire and delight to make that state a comfort to each other every breach involves both in misery

2 With regard to those who have partners that continue in unbelief, whilst they themselves are called to the knowledge of the truth, the following directions I give by the Spirit, the Lord having left no express command concerning the matter

(1) If any unbelieving wife or husband chuse to cohabit with their partner, who is converted to the faith of Christ, the believing wife or husband must not separate themselves from the unbeliever on account of religion And he suggests his reasons for what he enjoined [1] The state is sanctified by the faith of either of the parties *The unbelieving husband is sanctified by*, or in, *the wife, and the unbelieving wife is sanctified by*, or in, *the husband*, they being one by virtue of the marriage union, and all their lawful marriage enjoyments sanctified to the faithful person, *else were your children unclean*, and not entitled to the blessings and privileges that belong to the visible church, *but now are they holy*, capable of being received into the congregation of the faithful, and admitted to the seal of the covenant, as much as if they descended from parents who were both believers in profession [2] *God hath called us to peace*, and therefore, so far as we can maintain it with our unbelieving relatives, we are bound to do it, and not make our different sentiments in religious matters the ground of contention and angry dispute and tho we wish they were even as we, yet should we not quarrel with them because they refuse to be of the same mind with us, but bear with the perverseness and displeasure which they may testify against us on account of our profession [3] Whilst thus walking in love, peace, and charity, *what knowest thou, O wife, whether thou shalt save thy husband? or how knowest thou, O man, whether thou shalt save thy wife?* and be made the instrument of her conversion *But*, whether this be the case or not, *as God hath distributed to every man, as the Lord hath called every one*, in whatever state or relation, *so let him walk*, as may most adorn his holy profession, *and so ordain I in all churches*, laying this down as a general rule, to be accommodated to particular case

But, (2) The case however is quite different, *if the unbelieving depart*, and, offended at their partner for embracing the gospel, for that cause refuse any longer to cohabit with them, and, all kind means being tried, insist on a separation, *a brother or a sister is not under bondage in such cases*, not obliged to detain them when they desire to depart Nay, some suppose, that such a malicious and obstinate desertion, where all proposals of reconciliation and return are rejected, amount to the dissolution of the marriage covenant, with regard to the injured party, like death itself but I should think otherwise, unless the desertion accompanied with adultery in the unbeliever, and even then, though in God's sight the marriage bond is broken, the civil contract can be dissolved only by proper authority

18 Is any man called being circumcised? let him
not become uncircumcised Is any called in uncircum-
cision? let him not become circumcised 19 Circum-
cision is nothing, and uncircumcision is nothing but
the keeping of the commandments of God 20 Let
every man abide in the same calling wherein he was
called 21 Art thou called *being* a servant? care not
for it, but if thou mayest be made free, use *it* rather
22 For he that is called in the Lord, *being* a servant,
is the Lord's freeman likewise also he that is called
being free, is Christ's servant 23 Ye are bought
with a price, be not ye the servants of men 24 Bre-
thren, let every man wherein he is called, therein abide
with God

v 18—24 The apostle passes on to other cases

1 Respecting circumcision *Is any man called being circumcised*, Jew or proselyte, *let him not become uncircumcised*, or regret that he submitted to this rite *Is any one called in uncircumcision? let him not become circumcised*, all these marks of peculiarity being abolished under the gospel Jew and Gentile have now but one way to glory *Circumcision is nothing, and uncircumcision is nothing*, of no avail at all to salvation, *but* the grand point is, *the keeping the commandments of God*, from the divine principle of faith which worketh by love

2 With regard to men's station in life, *Let every man abide in the same calling wherein he was called*, desiring no alteration in his circumstances, but satisfied with the dispensations of God's providence *Art thou called being a servant? care not for it*, as if because a servant or slave, therefore the less acceptable to God With him there is no respect of persons *But if thou mayest be made free, use it rather*, if the Lord open a door for your liberty, thankfully accept it, mean time resigned to his will *For he that is called in the Lord, being a servant, is the Lord's freeman*, brought from the bondage of corruption to the most desirable freedom, even into the glorious liberty of the sons of God *Likewise also he that is called being free, is Christ's servant* whatever our civil privileges may be, when we have taken the Lord for our Master, we are, as much as the meanest slave, bound to yield ourselves to him, obedient in all things *Ye are bought with a price*, both one and the other with the same price, even the blood of Jesus *be not ye* therefore *the servants of men*, but whenever their commands interfere with the will of your great Master, hesitate not a moment whom you shall obey Upon the whole, *brethren*, this is my injunction, *Let every man wherein he is called*, whatever his station in life may be, *therein abide with God*, resigned to his will, aiming at his glory, maintaining communion with him, and looking up for grace to serve him acceptably *Note*, (1) As our worldly circumstances are ordered by divine appointment, to repine is to rebel against God (2) No attainments in religion give us a right to any superiority in worldly things Dominion is not founded in grace

25 Now concerning virgins, I have no command-
ment of the Lord yet I give my judgment as one that
hath obtained mercy of the Lord to be faithful 26
I suppose therefore that this is good for the present di-
stress, *I say*, that *it is* good for a man so to be 27 Art
thou bound unto a wife? seek not to be loosed Art
thou loosed from a wife? seek not a wife 28 But and
if thou marry, thou hast not sinned, and if a virgin
marry, she hath not sinned nevertheless, such shall have
trouble in the flesh, but I spare you 29 But this I
say, brethren the time is short It remaineth that both
they that have wives be as though they had none, 30
And they that weep, as though they wept not, and they
that rejoice, as though they rejoiced not, and they that
buy, as though they possessed not, 31 And they that
use this world, as not abusing it for the fashion of this
world passeth away 32 But I would have you without
carefulness He that is unmarried, careth for the things
that belong to the Lord, how he may please the Lord
33 But he that is married, careth for the things that
are of the world, how he may please *his* wife 34
There is difference also between a wife and a virgin
The unmarried woman careth for the things of the Lord,
that she may be holy, both in body and in spirit but she
that is married, careth for the things of the world, how
she may please *her* husband 35 And this I speak for
your own profit, not that I may cast a snare upon you,
but for that which is comely, and that you may attend
upon the Lord without distraction.

v 25—35 In answer to their question with regard to unmarried persons, though our Lord had given no particular directions, yet the apostle, under divine inspiration, delivers his judgment

1 Considering the troublesome times, and the present distress they were under, he advises those who with chastity could, to

contin-

continue single. If they were already married, they must be content in that state, nor seek to loose that indissoluble bond, but if unmarried, they would do well not hastily to change their condition.

2 If any person found it more adviseable or necessary for them to marry, they would commit no sin in so doing, marriage being honourable in all, only they would encumber themselves more in the world, and in those days of persecution expose themselves to more dangerous trials. But he urges not the point, lest he should bring them into a snare, when he only meant to suggest the cautions which prudence dictated.

3 Whatever was their state, married or unmarried, he had one important charge to give them. *This I say, brethren, the time is short*, eternity is advancing swiftly, and the days which here are allotted us draw to their end. Since therefore our great concern in this world is to prepare for a better, *it remaineth that both they that have wives be as though they had none*, not setting their affections on a dying world, or retarded from the pursuit of heavenly things by any engagements or attachments here below; *and they that weep, as though they wept not*, restraining all inordinate grief for the loss of dearest relatives, or for any other afflictions, since all present sufferings must so quickly have an end; *and they that rejoice, as tho' they rejoiced not*, considering the transitory nature of all their worldly comforts, and therefore sitting loose to them; *and they that buy, as though they possessed not*, not trusting in uncertain riches, nor placing their happiness in these possessions, but looking for a more enduring substance; *and they that use this world, as not abusing it*, to flatter their pride, or gratify their luxury; *for the fashion of this world passeth away*, all things below are fleeting as the shadow, and will shortly vanish as the dream when one awaketh. *Note*, (1) A deep sense of the vanity of time, and the importance of eternity, is needful to regulate both our joys and sorrows, and to keep our affections disengaged from the objects of sense which would otherwise enslave us. (2) We are dying worms in a dying world: the longest life is but *a short time*, every moment we are in jeopardy; and what is all the world to a dying man?

4. He suggests the general reason on which he grounded the foregoing advice. *I would have you without carefulness*, not to lay a snare upon you by enforcing celibacy, but that those who have the gift, *may attend on the Lord without distraction*. The advantage of the unmarried state is this, that being less incumbred with worldly cares, the single brother or sister are more at leisure for the service of the Redeemer, and can more entirely devote their time and talents, and employ both body and spirit in his blessed work: whilst the married person must necessarily be more engaged in the care of a family, and the needful provision for them, and have the partner of their bosom to please in all lawful things, sollicitous to promote their temporal and eternal happiness. *Note*, (1) That is always best for a Christian, which is best for his soul. (2) Our first desire should be to please the Lord, and, whether married or single, to be holy both in body and spirit.

36 But if any man think that he behaveth himself
uncomely toward his virgin, if she pass the flower of
her age, and need so require, let him do what he will, he
sinneth not: let them marry. 37 Nevertheless, he that
standeth stedfast in his heart, having no necessity, but
hath power over his own will, and hath so decreed in
his heart that he will keep his virgin, doth well. 38
So then, he that giveth *her* in marriage [i] doth well; but
he that giveth *her* not in marriage doth better. 39
[j] The wife is bound by the law as long as her husband
liveth; but if her husband be dead, she is at liberty to
be married to whom she will, [k] only in the Lord. 40
But she is happier if she so abide, [l] after my judgment:
and [m] I think also that I have the Spirit of God.

i Heb. xiii. 4. j Rom. vii. 2. k 2 Cor. vi. 14. l Ver. 25. m 1 Thess. iv. 8.

v. 36—40. The apostle proceeds with farther directions concerning marriage.

1 Concerning virgins. *If any man think that he behaveth himself uncomely towards his virgin*, by restraining his daughter or ward, who is disposed thereto, from marrying, *if she pass the flower of her age*, and is come to years of maturity, *and need so require*, on deliberating the matter, it seems most eligible she should change her condition, *let him do what he will, he sinneth not* in disposing of her, *let him marry her* to a proper partner. *Nevertheless, he that standeth stedfast in his heart*, resolved to keep his ward or daughter single, *having no necessity, but hath power over his own will, and hath so decreed in his heart*, with her consent, that *he will keep his virgin* as she is, *doth well*, and shews in such trying times a prudent care of her. *So then, he that giveth her in marriage*, when it becomes needful, *doth well*, acts a lawful and commendable part; *but he that giveth her not in marriage, doth better*, provides more for her comfort, and keeps her more at her liberty to serve the Lord.

Some suppose (*τὴν παρθένον ἑαυτοῦ*) signifies not his virgin, but the state of virginity, and give the sense, that if any man continued single beyond the usual time when it was thought reputable to marry, and afterwards should think that he had put an undue restraint upon himself, and see cause to change his condition, it would be lawful for him, even if advanced in years, to take a wife: for though it might be most commendable if he could keep his first purpose, yet, if he finds the state of wedlock needful, he is at liberty and may marry.

2 Concerning widows. The wife is bound by the law to her husband for life, unless by obstinate desertion and adultery the marriage-bond is cancelled. *But if her husband be dead, she is at liberty to be married to whom she will, only in the Lord*, careful not to be unequally yoked with an unbeliever, and giving her hand to no man, who hath not, as far as she can judge, given his heart to Christ. *But*, in most cases, *she is happier if she so abide, in my judgment*, and live unmarried; *and*, in what I here advise, *I think also*, whatever false teachers may suggest, *that I have the Spirit of God*, and now speak under his immediate inspiration.

CHAP. VIII.

The apostle in this chapter answers another case proposed to him by some of the Corinthians, about eating those things that had been sacrificed to idols. 1. He hints at the occasion of this case, and gives a caution against too high esteem of their knowledge, ver. 1—3. 2. He asserts the vanity of idols, and the unity of the Godhead, and the sole mediation of Christ between God and man, ver. 4—7. 3. He tells them, that upon supposition that it were lawful in itself to eat of things offered to idols, for that they themselves are nothing, yet regard must be had to the weakness of Christian brethren, and nothing done that would lay a stumbling block before them, and occasion their sin and destruction, ver. 7, ad finem.

1 NOW [a] as touching things offered unto idols,
We know that [b] we all have knowledge.
[c] Knowledge puffeth up, but charity edifieth. 2 And
if any man think that he knoweth any thing, [d] he know-
eth nothing yet as he ought to know. 3. But if any
man love God, [e] the same is known of him. 4 As con-
cerning therefore the eating of those things that are of-
fered in sacrifice unto idols, we know that [f] an idol *is*
nothing in the world, and that [g] *there is* none other God
but one. 5 For though there be [h] that are called gods,
whether in heaven or in earth, (as there be gods many,
and lords many) 6 But [i] to us *there is but* one God, the
Father, [k] of whom *are* all things, and we in him; and
[l] one Lord Jesus Christ, [m] by whom *are* all things, and
we by him.

a Acts xv. 20. b Rom. xiv. 14. c Rom. xiv. 3. Ch. iv. 18. Gal. vi. 3. d Gal. vi. 3. e Exod. xxxiii. 12. Nah. i. 7. Gal. iv. 9. 2 Tim. ii. 19. f Isa. xli. 24. & xliv. 8. Jer. x. 11. g Deut. iv. 39. Mark xii. 29. Eph. iv. 6. h John x. 34, 35. i Mal. ii. 10. k Acts xvii. 28. Rom. xi. 36. l John xiii. 13. Phil. ii. 11. m John i. 3. Col. i. 16. Heb. i. 2.

v. 1—6. The apostle proceeds to consider the case of eating the flesh of animals which had been offered in sacrifice to idols. Sometimes the idolaters feasted their friends thereon in the idol-temples, sometimes in their own houses, and what they did not make use of, was sold in the shambles.

1 He warns them against leaning upon their own understanding, and proudly abusing their Christian liberty. *Now as touching things offered unto such, we know that we all* in general *have knowledge*, and are persuaded of the vanity of idols, as well as you. Nevertheless, *knowledge*, without grace, *puffeth up, but charity edifieth*, and will engage us not merely to consider what is lawful, but what is expedient, making us condescending to those whose attainments are less, and who do not see things as clearly as we may. *And if any man think that he knoweth any thing*, self-opinionated, and above attending to the sentiments or weakness of his brethren, *he knoweth nothing yet as he ought to know. But if any man love God*, and from that blessed principle is engaged to make a practical improvement of his knowledge for God's glory, and his neighbour's edification, *the same is known of him*, and will receive his approbation. *Note*, (1) That is the truly valuable knowledge which enables us to be most useful. (2) Self-conceit is a sure proof of ignorance. (3) There may be much knowledge in the head, where there is little charity in the heart.

2 He admits, that an idol is nothing, a mere imaginary being, and that, abstractedly considered, the eating meat offered in sacrifice to them is no evil, since *there is no other God but one*, whose creatures are all good in themselves. *For though there be that are called gods, whether in heaven or in earth, (as there be gods many, and lords many)*, multitudes of celestial and terrestrial deities being worshipped by the deluded heathen; *but to us there is but one God*, in opposition to the pagan polytheism, one in essence and operation, who is represented in the gospel revelation as *the Father, of whom are all things*, the Creator, Governor, and Preserver of all, *and we in him*, living, moving, and having our being; *and one Lord Jesus Christ*, not another God, and, like the heathen deities, of an inferior nature, but a partaker of the same undivided Godhead and glory, *by whom are all things, and we by him*, one in operation with the Father, the Creator of all, and the

Mediator, in his perſonal character appointed to govern the peculiar kingdom delegated to him, to be our advocate for all bleſſings, and the diſpenſer of them to his redeemed people

7. Howbeit *there is* not in every man that knowledge
for ſome with conſcience of the idol unto this hour, eat
it as a thing offered unto an idol, and their conſcience
being weak, is defiled. 8 But meat commendeth us
not to God for neither if we eat, are we the better,
neither if we eat not, are we the worſe 9 But take
heed leſt by any means this liberty of yours become a
ſtumbling-block to them that are weak 10 For
if any man ſee thee which haſt knowledge ſit at
meat in the idol's temple, ſhall not the conſcience of
him which is weak be emboldened to eat thoſe things
which are offered to idols 11 And through thy
knowledge ſhall the weak brother periſh, for whom
Chriſt died? 12 But when ye ſin ſo againſt the brethren,
and wound their weak conſcience, ye ſin againſt
Chriſt 13 Wherefore if meat make my brother to
offend, I will eat no fleſh while the world ſtandeth, leſt
I make my brother to offend

v. 7—13 Admitting the vanity of idols, the apoſtle ſhews, that for the ſake of a weak brother they ought, notwithſtanding, to abridge themſelves of that liberty they might otherwiſe take, and not offend them by eating what was offered in ſacrifice to thoſe abominable deities For,

1 Some of the new converts, not having entirely loſt their veneration for thoſe idols which they uſed to worſhip, nor as yet wholly perſuaded of their vanity, ſtill when they eat their ſacrifices, pay them ſome ſort of honour and regard, and *their conſcience being thus weak*, through their remaining ignorance, *is defiled with the guilt of idolatry*

2 We ſhould be cautious therefore for others' ſake, though we ourſelves have knowledge, leſt we ſhould become a ſtumbling-block to *them that are weak*, conſidering that meat of one kind or another, uſed or abſtained from, is no recommendation to God's favour *for neither if we eat* the food, without any reſpect to the idol, *are we the better*, *neither if we eat not*, prudently abſtaining for others' ſake, *are we the worſe* But though the eating of the idol ſacrifices be never ſo innocent in itſelf, yet it may prove a great hurt to the conſciences of the weak, who ſeeing you eating in an idol-temple, may be emboldened by your example, though not ſatisfied of the lawfulneſs of the action, to do the like, and thus what you, who know the vanity of idols, might otherwiſe do innocently, may be the means of leading a weaker brother to wound his conſcience with guilt, *for whom Chriſt died*, and who, having made profeſſion of his faith, is, in the judgment of charity, to be reckoned among his redeemed people *But when ye ſin ſo againſt the brethren, and wound their weak conſcience, ye ſin againſt Chriſt*, whoſe compaſſions towards the lambs of his flock are great, and he will reſent every ſlight put upon them, and every offence given to them *Wherefore if meat* offered to idols *make my brother to offend, I will eat no fleſh while the world ſtandeth*, of any ſuch ſacrifice, however innocent the thing may be in itſelf, *leſt I make my brother to offend* *Note*, It is not enough that we avoid what is ſinful ourſelves, Chriſtian charity will teach us even to abridge ourſelves of liberty in lawful things for others' good

CHAP IX

In this chapter the apoſtle ſeems to anſwer ſome cavils againſt himſelf 1 He aſſerts his apoſtolical miſſion and authority, and gives in his ſucceſs amongſt them, as a teſtimony to it, ver 1—3 *2 He claims a right to ſubſiſt by his miniſtry, and defends it by ſeveral arguments from natural reaſon and the Moſaical law, and aſſerts it alſo to be a conſtitution of Chriſt*, ver 3—15 *3. He ſhews that he had willingly waved this privilege and power for their benefit*, ver 15—20 *4 He inſtances in ſeveral other things, in which he had denied himſelf for the ſake of other men's ſpiritual intereſt and ſalvation*, ver 20—24 *And, 5 Concludes this argument by ſhewing what animated him to this courſe, even the proſpect of an incorruptible crown*, ver 24, ad finem

1 AM I not an apoſtle? am I not free? have I
not ſeen Jeſus Chriſt our Lord? are not you
my work in the Lord? 2 If I be not an apoſtle unto
others, yet doubtleſs I am to you for the ſeal of mine
apoſtleſhip are ye in the Lord 3 Mine anſwer to them
that do examine me, is this, 4 Have we not power
to eat and to drink? 5 Have we not power to lead
about a ſiſter a wife as well as other apoſtles, and *as* the
brethren of the Lord, and Cephas? 6 Or I only and
Barnabas, have not we power to forbear working? 7
Who goeth a warfare any time at his own charges?
Who planteth a vineyard, and eateth not of the fruit
thereof? or who feedeth a flock, and eateth not of the
milk of the flock? 8 Say I theſe things as a man?
or ſaith not the law the ſame alſo? 9 For it is written
in the law of Moſes, Thou ſhalt not muzzle the mouth
of the ox that treadeth out the corn Doth God take
care for oxen? 10 Or ſaith he it altogether for our
ſakes? for our ſakes, no doubt, this is written that
he that ploweth ſhould plow in hope, and that he
that threſheth in hope ſhould be partaker of his hope
11 If we have ſown unto you ſpiritual things, *is it* a
great thing if we ſhall reap your carnal things? 12
If others be partakers of *this* power over you, *are* not
we rather? Nevertheleſs, we have not uſed this power,
but ſuffer all things, leſt we ſhould hinder the goſpel
of Chriſt 13 Do ye not know that they which miniſter
about holy things, live *of the things* of the temple?
and they which wait at the altar are partakers with
the altar? 14 Even ſo hath the Lord ordained,
that they which preach the goſpel, ſhould live of the
goſpel

v. 1—14 It ſeems probable that the falſe teachers had raiſed ſome objection againſt Paul's authority as an apoſtle, becauſe he had not aſſerted that right to a maintenance which was due to his office, and waving his privilege had refuſed to be burdenſome to them

1 He vindicates his authority If he had not inſiſted on a maintenance, it was for their ſakes he had waved this right *Am not I an apoſtle*, becauſe I have acted thus diſintereſted? *am not I free* to claim a ſubſiſtance, if I chooſe it? *have I not ſeen Jeſus Chriſt our Lord?* and received my commiſſion immediately from him? *Are not you my work in the Lord?* the converts of my miniſtry, and the fruit of my labour in the goſpel *If I be not an apoſtle to others, yet doubtleſs I am to you*, who owe to me chiefly, as the inſtrument, all you know and are *for the ſeal of my apoſtleſhip are ye in the Lord*, the Lord atteſting the truth of my miſſion, by the ſucceſs with which he bleſſed my miniſtry to your ſouls *Note*, (1) The beſt of men and miniſters may expect to meet with malignant revilers (2) They who have been bleſt under our miniſtry have in themſelves the ſtrongeſt proof that we are ſent of God

2 He aſſerts his right to all the privileges of an apoſtle In anſwer to thoſe who preſumed to ſit in judgment on his character, he replies, *Have we not power to eat and to drink?* have not Barnabas and I a claim upon you for a maintenance, tho' we have not exerted it? *Have we not power to lead about a ſiſter a wife*, and to expect a proviſion for our families as we are travelling from place to place, *as well as other apoſtles, and as the brethren of the Lord, and Cephas? Or I only and Barnabas*, who were particularly ſent to the Gentiles, *have not we power to forbear working?* and muſt earn with our hands that maintenance which the other apoſtles are entitled to for their work's ſake? How abſurd and unreaſonable is ſuch a ſuppoſition! *Who goeth a warfare any time at his own charges?* the ſoldier hath his ſtipend and proviſions *Who planteth a vineyard, and eateth not of the fruit thereof?* the vine-dreſſer is fed with the produce of his toil *or who feedeth a flock, and eateth not of the milk of the flock?* If theſe are juſtly entitled to eat the labour of their hands, much more have the miniſters of the goſpel, who ſuſtain all theſe characters, a right to a competent proviſion *Say I theſe things as a man?* merely on the footing of equity, *or ſaith not the law the ſame alſo?* let even my Judaizing oppoſers and miſtaken judges *For it is written in the law of Moſes, Thou ſhalt not muzzle the mouth of the ox that treadeth out the corn*, but whilſt he works, he ſhall be permitted to eat *Doth God take care for oxen?* was this precept given merely with a reference to them, *or ſaith he it altogether for our ſakes*, who labour in the goſpel? *for our ſakes, no doubt, this is written, that he that ploweth*, breaking up the fallow ground of the ſinner's heart, *ſhould plow in hope* of a reaſonable return, *and that he that threſheth in hope*, ſeparating the chaff of corruption from the good ſeed of grace in the heart, *ſhould be partaker of his hope* And as the ploughman and threſher eat the fruit of their toils, ſo much more ſhould the labouring miniſter in God's ſpiritual huſbandry have a juſt recompence of reward. *If we have ſown unto you ſpiritual things, is it a great thing*, or unreaſonable for us to expect, or for you to give, *that we ſhould reap your carnal things*, and have a maintenance, when the value between the ſpiritual bleſſings we communicate, and the pittance we ſhould receive, is ſo diſproportionate? *If others be partakers of this power over you*, and are ſupported at your expence, to whom ye never were or can be ſo indebted as unto us, *are not we rather* entitled to a proviſion, if we choſe to claim it? *Nevertheleſs, we have not uſed this power*, nor inſiſted on what we had a right to demand, *but ſuffer all things*, chuſing to undergo any want and hardſhips, *leſt we ſhould hinder the goſpel of Chriſt*, and raiſe a prejudice in your minds, that our views were merce-

nary But *do ye not know, that they which minister about holy things, live of the things of the temple? and they which wait at the altar are partakers with the altar*, and receive their maintenance from their ſhare in the ſacrifices and oblations? *Even ſo hath the Lord ordained, that they which preach the goſpel, ſhould live of the goſpel* So that it appears, (1) In the very reaſon of the thing, (2) From the law of Moſes, (3) From Chriſt's expreſs inſtitution, (*Luke* x 7) that the miniſters of Chriſt have a right to be ſupported becomingly by thoſe among whom they labour

x V. 12. 1 Theſ. ii 9. 2 Theſ. iii 8. y 2 Cor. xi 10, &c. z Amos iii 8. Rom. i 14. a Chap. iii 8. b Chap. iv 1. Col. i 25.

15 x But I have uſed none of theſe things Neither
have I written theſe things that it ſhould be ſo done
unto me. for y it were better for me to die than that
any man ſhould make my glorying void 16 For
though I preach the goſpel, I have nothing to glory
of for z neceſſity is laid upon me, yea, wo is unto
me, if I preach not the goſpel 17 For if I do this
thing willingly, a I have a reward but if againſt my
will, b a diſpenſation *of the goſpel* is committed unto
me 18 What is my reward then? verily, that
when I preach the goſpel, I may make the goſpel of
Chriſt without charge, that I abuſe not my power in
the goſpel.

v 15—18 The apoſtle mentions his own diſintereſted conduct, for nothing is more oppoſite to the character of a Chriſtian miniſter, than the very ſhadow of mercenary views *I have uſed none of theſe things*, nor ever claimed my right among you, *neither have I written theſe things that it ſhould be ſo done unto me*, on any future occaſion *for it were better for me to die, than that any man ſhould make my glorying void* I had rather wear out my body with labour to miniſter to my own wants, than not preach the goſpel to you freely, and thereby cut off occaſion from thoſe, who, if I received any recompenſe, would thence take a handle to prejudice you againſt me *For though I preach the goſpel, I have nothing to glory of for neceſſity is laid upon me*, and I cannot but obey the Maſter's orders *yea, wo is unto me if I preach not the goſpel*, I muſt be expoſed to the bittereſt accuſations of unfaithfulneſs, and juſtly ſink under the heavieſt vengeance *For if I do this thing willingly, I have a reward*, the conſciouſneſs of diſintereſted zeal is a ſatisfaction to my own ſoul, and the Lord will remember and reward my labours of love *but if againſt my will I labour, a diſpenſation of the goſpel is committed unto me*, and I am bound to be faithful. *What is my reward then? verily that when I preach the goſpel, I may make the goſpel of Chriſt without charge*, ſhewing the diſintereſted fidelity with which I act, and approving myſelf to God, and to my own conſcience, *that I abuſe not my power in the goſpel*, nor exact even what I have authority to demand, demonſtrating to the people, that I ſeek not theirs, but them *Note*, For the ſake of Chriſt it is prudent often to forego our rights and privileges, and to wave the claims to that reward, to which our office and labours may entitle us

c Chap. x 33. Gal. v 13. d 1 Pet. iii 1. e Acts xvi 3. & xviii 18. & xxi 26. f Gal. ii 3. g Chap. vii 22. h Rom. xv 1. 2 Cor. xi 29. i Chap. x 33. k Rom. xi 14. Chap. vii 16.

19 For though I be free from all men, c yet have I
made myſelf ſervant unto all, that d I might gain the
more 20 And e unto the Jews I became as a Jew,
that I might gain the Jews, to them that are under the
law, as under the law, that I might gain them that are
under the law, 21 f To them that are without law, as
without law, (g being not without law to God, but under
the law to Chriſt) that I might gain them that are
without law 22 h To the weak became I as weak,
that I might gain the weak i I am made all things to
all men, k that I might by all means ſave ſome 23
And this I do for the goſpel's ſake, that I might be partaker
thereof with *you*

v 19—23 In other inſtances of Chriſtian liberty, as well as the foregoing, the apoſtle ſets us a noble example of ſelf-denial *For though I be free from all men*, and under no obligations to be ſubſervient to their will or humour, *yet have I made myſelf ſervant unto all*, willing in all indifferent matters to conform to them, and deny myſelf, *that* thus engaging their affections and attention, *I might gain the more*, and win them over to embrace the doctrines and ways of the goſpel *And* for this purpoſe, *unto the Jews I became as a Jew, that I might gain the Jews*; not refuſing to obſerve thoſe ceremonials in their worſhip, to which, though indifferent in themſelves, they were ſtill attached *To them that are under the law, as under the law, that I might gain them that are under the law*, ſubmitting to many of its ordinances, to engage the affection of my Jewiſh brethren, who ſtill maintain their veneration for the divinely-inſtituted ſervice of the ſanctuary *To them that are without law, as without law*, not urging on them circumciſion, or any of the ceremonial inſtitution, as at all neceſſary to ſalvation, but inſiſting on the neceſſity of faith in Chriſt alone, (*being not without law to God*, as if the moral law was abrogated, as well as the ceremonial, *but under the law to Chriſt*, walking in faith and holineſs, according to the obligations which the goſpel lays upon me,) *that I might gain them that are without law*, and lay no needleſs obſtacles in the way of the Gentiles, but preaching the ſimple goſpel, might engage their hearts to Jeſus and his bleſſed ſervice *To the weak became I as weak*, condeſcending to their infirmities, and abſtaining even from things innocent and lawful, where their conſcience was ſcrupulous, *that I might gain the weak*, and lead them on to farther attainments of knowledge and grace In ſhort, *I am made all things to all men*, ſtudying to pleaſe every man for his good to edification, *that I might by all means ſave ſome*, and, through the bleſſing of the Redeemer, be made the inſtrument of their converſion *And this I do for the goſpel's ſake*, if poſſible to remove all prejudice and objections, *that I might be partaker thereof with you*, and come to ſhare with you in all its ſaving bleſſings and benefits *Note*, It is highly our duty to avoid every unneceſſary occaſion of offence, and in all indifferent things to forego our own will and pleaſure for the profit of our neighbour

l Gal. ii 2. Phil. ii 16. 2 Tim. iv 7. Heb. xii 1. m Eph. vi 12. 1 Tim. vi 12. 2 Tim. ii 5. & iv 7. n 2 Tim. iv 8. Jam. i 12. 1 Pet. v 4. Rev. ii 10. & iii 11. o Rom. viii 13. Col. iii 5. p Rom. vi 19.

24 Know ye not that they which run in a race, run
all, but one receiveth the prize? l ſo run that ye may
obtain 25 And every man that m ſtriveth for the maſtery,
is temperate in all things Now, they *do it* to obtain
a corruptible crown, but we n an incorruptible 26
I therefore ſo run, not as uncertainly, ſo fight I, not as
one that beateth the air 27 But o I keep under my
body, and p bring it into ſubjection leſt that by any
means when I have preached to others, I myſelf ſhould
be a caſt-away

v 24—27 To quicken them to imitate his own example, and give all diligence to make their calling and election ſure, he propoſes to them the caſe of thoſe who in the Iſthmian games contended for victory *Know ye not that they which run in a race, run all, but one receiveth the prize?* the prize itſelf was in value trivial, though ſuch pains were uſed to obtain it, and only one could there poſſeſs the honour Here the prize is no leſs than eternal life, and *all* who run are ſure to win *ſo run* then with faith, patience, and perſeverance, *that ye may obtain* the ineſtimable reward *And* again, *every man that ſtriveth for the maſtery*, and would overcome, as wreſtlers or boxers in the games, *is temperate in all things*, that by obſerving the moſt exact regimen, and bringing their bodies into the beſt order, they may be the better prepared for the conflict *Now they do it to obtain a corruptible crown*, of withering leaves or flowers, *but we* have *an incorruptible* crown of glory in view, compared with which theirs is poor and trivial; and therefore how much more are we bound to deny our appetites, with how much greater earneſtneſs ought we to contend for victory, where we are ſure, if we fight manfully, to conquer, and the reward will be ſo unutterably and eternally glorious *I therefore*, in this view, *ſo run* with unwearied diligence my Chriſtian courſe, *not as uncertainly*, obſerving the path of duty preſcribed, not dubious concerning the iſſue, but ſure through Chriſt to win the prize *So fight I* againſt the world, the fleſh, and the devil, *not as one that beateth the air*, not merely exerciſing my arms as the boxers, that they might be ready for the combat, *but I keep under my body*, (ὑπωπιαζω) mortify its corrupt appetites, as the boxers, who beat their antagoniſts black and blue, *and bring it into ſubjection*, (δουλαγωγω) as the wreſtlers, when their adverſary was thrown under them, *leſt that by any means when I have preached to others* the neceſſity of ſuch mortification, diligence, and ſelf-denial, *I myſelf*, through negligence or unfaithfulneſs, *ſhould* be overcome by my corrupted nature and ſpiritual foes, and *be a caſt-away* at laſt (αδοκιμος), rejected by the great Judge, and counted unfit for the promiſed reward And the holy jealouſy which I feel for myſelf, I inculcate upon you, that in the uſe of all appointed means you may ſecure the glorious prize, and be approved of the Lord in the great day of his appearing *Note*, (1) In our Chriſtian race and warfare, what diligence, conſtancy, and courage do we not need? bleſſed be God there is help laid on one mighty to ſave, and looking to him we are ſure to gain the prize (2) Our bodies are our great ſnare, and the mortification of ſenſual appetite is abſolutely neceſſary in order to the ſalvation of the immortal ſoul (3) Holy jealouſy over ourſelves is the great preſervative againſt apoſtacy (4) Tho' God's elect can never be finally caſt away, and the apoſtle ſtrove not *as uncertainly*, yet we muſt remember God hath ordained the means as well as the end, and that we but deceive ourſelves, if we promiſe ourſelves ſafety, when we grow negligent, and work not out our ſalvation with fear and trembling (5) Many have appeared with zeal in the cauſe of Chriſt, and have been the means of ſaving others, who have periſhed themſelves Let him that thinketh he ſtandeth, take heed leſt he fall

CHAP X

In this chapter the apostle prosecutes the argument at the close of the last, and (1) Warns the Corinthians against security by the example of the Jews, whose history is left upon record for the admonition of Christians, ver 1—15 *(2) He resumes his former argument,* chap viii *about eating things* offered to idols, *and shews that it is utterly inconsistent with true Christianity,* ver 15—23 *(3) He lets them yet know, that though they must not eat of things sacrificed to idols as such, and out of any regard to the idol, yet they might buy such flesh in the markets, and eat it at the table of heathen acquaintance, without asking any questions for that the heathen's abuse of them did not render the creatures of God unfit to be the food of his servants Yet liberty of this kind must be used with a due regard to weak consciences, and no offence given by it to Jew or Gentile, or the church of God,* ver 23, ad finem

1 MOreover, brethren, I would not that ye should
be ignorant, how that all our fathers were
under [a] the cloud, and all passed [b] through the sea,
2 And were all baptized unto Moses in the cloud, and
in the sea, 3. And did all eat the same [c] spiritual
meat, 4 And did all drink the same [d] spiritual drink
(For they drank of that spiritual Rock that [e] followed
them: and that Rock was Christ) 5 But with many
of them God was not well pleased for [f] they were over-
thrown in the wilderness 6 Now these things were our
examples, to the intent we should not lust after evil
things, as [g] they also lusted 7 [h] Neither be ye idola-
ters, as *were* some of them, as it is written, [i] The
people sat down to eat and drink, and rose up to play
8 [k] Neither let us commit fornication, as some of them
committed, and [l] fell in one day three and twenty thou-
sand 9 Neither let us tempt Christ, as [m] some of them
also tempted, and [n] were destroyed of serpents 10
Neither murmur ye, as [o] some of them also murmured,
and [p] were destroyed of the destroyer 11 Now all
these things happened unto them for ensamples and
[q] they are written for our admonition, [r] upon whom the
ends of the world are come 12 Wherefore [s] let him
that thinketh he standeth, take heed lest he fall 13
There hath no temptation taken you, but such as is com-
mon to man but [t] God *is* faithful, [u] who will not suffer
you to be tempted above that ye are able, but will with
the temptation also [x] make a way to escape, that ye may
be able to bear *it*

a Ex. xiii. 21 Num x 18, & Neh ix 19, &c Ps lxxviii 14, &c b Ex xiv 22 Heb xi 29 c Ex xvi 15 & John vi 49 50 d Ex xvii 6 Num xx. 11 Psal cv 41 e Deut ix 21 f Num. xxvi 64, 65 Heb iii 17 g Num xi 4, 33, 34 h 1 John v 21 i Ex xxxii 6 k Chap vi 18 l Num xxv 1, 9 m Ex xvii 2, 7 Num xxi 5 n Num xxi 6 o Ex xvi 2 & xvii 2 Num xiv 2 p Num xiv 37 q Rom xv 4 r Phil iv 5 s Rom xi 20 t 1 Thess v 24 u Psal cxxv 3 x Jer xxix 11

v 1—13 The apostle returns to the subject of eating the sacrifices offered to idols

1 He reminds the Corinthians of the distinguished privileges, and fatal overthrows of the Israelites in the wilderness *Moreover, brethren, I would not that ye should be ignorant, how that all our fathers were under the cloud, and all passed through the sea,* led by divine protection, covered from the heat by day, and cheered by the light of fire by night, preserved amidst the watery walls, and safely traversing the ocean's bed, *and were all baptised unto Moses in the cloud, and in the sea,* sprinkled with some drops from the cloud, or the spray of the dashing waves, and were all brought under the Mosaical law, as we by baptism are visibly admitted into the church of Christ, and devoted to his service *And did all eat of the same spiritual meat,* the manna which fell around their tents, the figure of Christ, the true bread which came down from heaven, on whom his redeemed sacramentally feed to the end of time, *and did all drink of the same spiritual drink, for they drank of that spiritual rock which followed them, and that rock was Christ* Through all the desert the living streams gushed forth to slake their thirst, and that divine Redeemer, whom the rock prefigured, the fountain of living waters, and streams from Lebanon, he, by his gracious presence, was in the midst of them as he is still in the hearts of all his people a well of water springing up into everlasting life *But,* though all enjoyed these distinguishing privileges, *with many of them God was not well pleased, for they were overthrown in the wilderness,* and, for their disobedience and rebellions, were not suffered to enter into the land of promise, the type of the heavenly Canaan, but their carcases fell in the desart *Note,* It is not outward privileges enjoyed, but inward grace possessed, which alone can bring us to the eternal inheritance, and the rest which remaineth for the people of God

2 From their examples, the apostle warns the Corinthians not to be secure, notwithstanding their distinguished privileges, lest, imitating their sin, they should be exposed to like punishment (1) He cautions them against the indulgence of their appetite Dissatisfied with the manna, the Israelites lusted after flesh to eat Against such luxury they must beware, and particularly avoid the idol-feasts or sacrifices, which could not but have the most fatal consequences *Note,* To please the palate, how many have plunged both body and soul into hell! (2) He warns them against idolatry, such as the Israelites committed, when, having offered their sacrifices to the calf, they sat down to feast upon them, and according to the heathen custom, rose up to dance around him to do him honour, but they severely smarted for their folly, *Exod* xxxii 10, 28 (3) He admonishes them against fornication, such as the Jews committed with the daughters of Moab, and to which they were led at their idol feasts, the dire consequence of which was, that in one day three and twenty thousand were cut off by the immediate judgment of God With such an instance of divine vengeance before them, they had need tremble for themselves in a city so abandoned to lewdness as Corinth was, knowing that none of their privileges could protect them, if they sinned, but that whoremongers, and adulterers, God will judge (4) He warns them against all dishonourable distrust of the power and grace of Christ to carry them through their difficulties, remembering the vengeance inflicted upon those of old, who tempted and provoked God by their unbelief, *Numb* xx 14 and were destroyed by the fiery serpents *Note,* When unbelief prevails, then the old serpent, the devil, resumes his dominion over the soul (5) He cautions them against all discontent under their sufferings or trials, and to beware of those who would instigate them to murmur against him, and the other ministers of Christ, for what they delivered from him Thus murmured the Israelites against Moses and Aaron, and at the difficulties they apprehended, and were destroyed by the angel's hand These things were all recorded for the admonition of the church, and what befel God's professing people of old, should be a warning to us at present, who live under the last dispensation which God will ever grant, that, having their fearful punishment, we might avoid the like provocations *Wherefore, let him that thinketh he standeth,* secure and immoveable, *take heed, lest,* puffed up with high imaginations of his own sufficiency, *he fall,* as the Israelites did of old *Note,* (1) Others falls should be our warnings (2) Distrust of ourselves, and dependance upon the power and grace of the Redeemer, are our great stability

3 He encourages the faithful among them, under all their trials, to trust and not be afraid *There hath no temptation taken you, but such as is common to man,* such as you might expect from the world around, or such as is incident to the human nature, or, at least, none so grievous but you may well bear up under it *But* however severe your temptations may be, *God is faithful* to his promises, *who will not suffer you to be tempted above what ye are able, but will with the temptation also make a way to escape, that ye may be able to bear it,* supporting you whilst it lasts, and in his good time giving you deliverance from it, so that you shall neither be drawn into sin, nor faint under your sufferings *Note* (1) We must not think our trials, however severe, singular, and murmur, others have felt the same before us (2) God's faithfulness should be the anchor of our hope (3) Our Redeemer is mighty, we may safely trust him (4) God knows best what afflictions we need, and how long we should be exercised with them To him let us always refer ourselves, casting our care upon him

14 Wherefore, my dearly beloved, [y] flee from idolatry
15 I speak as to wise men [z] judge ye what I say 16
The cup of blessing which we bless, [a] is it not the com-
munion of the blood of Christ? The bread which we
break, [b] is it not the communion of the body of Christ?
17 For [c] we being many are one bread, and one body
for we are all partakers of that [d] one bread 18. [e] Be-
hold Israel after the flesh are not they which eat of the
sacrifices partakers of the altar? 19 What say I then?
[f] that the idol is any thing, or that which is offered in
sacrifice to idols is any thing? 20. But *I say,* that the
things which the Gentiles sacrifice, [g] they sacrifice to
devils, and not to God and I would not that ye should
have fellowship with devils 21 [h] Ye cannot drink the
cup of the Lord, and the cup of devils ye cannot be
partakers of the Lord's table, and of the table of devils
22 [i] Do we provoke the Lord to jealousy? [k] are we
stronger than he?

y 1 John v 21 z 1 Thess v 21 a Matt xxvi 27 b Chap xi 24 c Rom xii 5 Chap xii 27 d John vi 35 e Lev iii 3 & vii 15 f Chap viii 4 g Lev xvii 7 Deut xxxii 17 Psal cvi 37 Rev ix 20 h 2 Cor vi 15, 16 i Deut xxxii 21 k Job ix 19 Ezek xxii 14

v 14—22 From the foregoing premises the apostle returns to urge the necessity of shunning idolatry, in its most distant approaches, knowing the dreadful consequences of it on the one hand, and the divine assistance promised on the other He therefore, as *dearly beloved,* with warm affection, warns them to *flee from idolatry,* and as to *wise men,* whether really possessed of spiritual wisdom, or vainly puffed up with their fancied high attainments, he appeals to them for the reasonableness of what he advanced

1 He instances in the case of the Lord's supper *The cup of blessing which we bless, is it not the communion of the blood of Christ?* Do we not therein profess to hold communion with Christ in all his

his faving bleffings? Do we not therein acknowledge our obligations to him as bought with a price, to glorify him in our bodies and our fpirits, which are his? *The bread, or loaf, which we break, is it not the communion of the body of Chrift?* Doth it not reprefent to us his broken body? Doth not our feeding upon it fignify our communion with him, who is the living bread? And do we not hereby profefs our folemn devotednefs to him, and union with each other? *For we being many are one bread*, as the different corns of wheat are moulded into one loaf, *and* intimately united *in one body*, of which Chrift is the living head, *for we are all partakers of that one bread*, feafting together upon the facrifice of Chrift, herein fhadowed forth; partakers of all the benefits obtained by his one oblation once offered, and thereby united to him in love, and to one another

2 The cafe is the fame with regard to the Jewifh facrifices *Behold Ifrael after the flefh*, in their obfervance of the ritual fervices, *are not they which eat of the facrifices partakers of the altar?* When they feaft upon the remainder of the peace offerings, they profefs communion with, and fubjection to that God, on whofe altar they offered their facrifice

3 He applies what he had faid to the point in hand *What fay I then, that the idol is any thing, or that which is facrificed to idols is any thing?* No, I have declared the contrary, *chap* viii The idol is nothing, and the meat is in its nature not altered *But I fay, that the things which the Gentiles facrifice, they facrifice to devils, and not to God* The demons whom they worfhip are wicked and fallen fpirits, with whom, in thefe facrifices, they maintain communion and to whom they pay divine honours *And I would not that ye fhould have fellowfhip with devils*, as by parity of reafon, confidering the foregoing cafes, you muft, if you feaft with the idolaters on their facrifices *Ye cannot drink the cup of the Lord*, the fymbol of his blood, *and the cup of devils*, the libations confecrated to the dæmons, *ye cannot be partakers of the Lord's table, and of the table of devils*, there is an utter inconfiftency in fuch a conduct, Chrift and Belial can have no communion To feaft, therefore, in idol temples, is to renounce Chriftianity, its fentiments, and privileges *Do we provoke the Lord Jefus to jealoufy*, by fuch idolatry, in direct oppofition to his holy law *Exod* xx 3—5 *Are we ftronger than he?* and do we defy the wrath of the Almighty? Surely deftruction muft be the confequence *Note*, When we have to do with a jealous God, how careful fhould we be that no idol in our hearts, as well as no outward object of idolatry, rob him of his peculiar honour!

23 [l] All things are lawful for me, but all things are
not † expedient all things are lawful for me, but all
things edify not 24 [m] Let no man feek his own but
every man another's wealth 25 [n] Whatfoever is fold in
the fhambles, *that* eat, afking no queftion for confcience
fake 26 For [o] the earth *is* the Lord's, and the fulnefs
thereof 27 If any of them that believe not bid you *to
a feaft*, and ye be difpofed to go, [p] whatfoever is fet before
you eat, afking no queftion for confcience fake
28 But if any man fay unto you, This is offered in facrifice
unto idols, eat not, [q] for his fake that fhewed it,
and for confcience fake [r] For the earth *is* the Lord's,
and the fulnefs thereof 29 Confcience, I fay, not thine
own, but of the others for [s] why is my liberty judged of
another man's confcience? 30 For, if I by grace be a
partaker, [t] why am I evil fpoken of for that which I give
thanks? 31 [u] Whether therefore ye eat or drink, or
whatfoever ye do, do all to the glory of God 32 [x] Give
none offence, neither to the Jews nor to the Gentiles, nor
to the church of God 33 Even as [y] I pleafe all men in
all things, not feeking mine own profit, but the *profit* of
many, that they may be faved

[l] Chap vi 12 † Or profitable [m] Rom xv 1, 2 Chap xiii 5 Phil ii 4 [n] 1 Tim iv 4 [o] Deut x 14 Pf xxiv 1 & l 12 Ver 28 [p] Luke x 7 [q] Chap viii 10 12 [r] Ver 26 [s] Rom xiv 16 [t] 1 Tim iv 3 4 [u] Col iii 17 1 Pet iv 11 [x] Rom xiv 13 Chap viii 13 [y] Chap ix 22 [z] Rom xv 2 Chap ix 19 2 Cor xii 19

v 23—33 The apoftle here,

1 In general warns them againft every abufe of their Chriftian liberty *All things are lawful for me*, and thefe meats offered to idols are not thereby defiled, *but all things are not expedient* There are circumftances in which it would be duty to abftain from what is, in its own nature, innocent and indifferent *all things are lawful for me, but all things edify not*, and therefore, if eating thefe facrifices give offence to a weak brother, it would be then duty to abftain, however clear I might be in the lawfulnefs of the thing And this is a rule applicable to many other cafes, therefore, generally, *let* it be your practice that *no man feek his own* will, humour, or benefit, *but every man another's wealth*, ready to deny himfelf, in order to promote their advantage and edification

2 He fhews in what particular inftances the meat offered to idols might be fafely eaten (1) If it was expofed in the public market to be fold, then they need not make any enquiries *for confcience fake* whence it came, but buy and ufe it for common food *For the earth is the Lord's, and the fulnefs thereof*, and all the creatures are good, when ufed to his glory (2) If any heathen acquaintance bid you to a feaft, and you have any inducement or obligation to go, whatever the table affords may be eaten without fcruple, but if any perfon at the table fuggefts, *this is offered in facrifice unto idols, eat not, for his fake that fhewed it, and for confcience fake*, bearing your teftimony thereby againft all fuch impious honours offered to dæmons, and keeping your confcience void of offence *For the earth is the Lord's, and the fulnefs thereof*, and he hath provided fufficiency of other food, without difhonouring him by the leaft thing which might feem to countenance idolatrous worfhip Abftain for *confcience* fake, *I fay, not thine own, but of the others*, who informed you, and might be grieved or ftumbled by your example, though your own might receive no damage

3 He anfwers an objection which might be raifed *For why is my liberty judged of another man's confcience?* His confcience is not to be the rule of my conduct *For if I by grace be a partaker, why am I evil fpoken of for that, for which I give thanks?*— In anfwer, he replies, that the following rules muft be applied to all particular circumftances Some underftand the apoftle, not as fpeaking in the perfon of an objector, but as declaring what he did in fuch a cafe, and intimating how imprudent it would be to give others occafion to pafs a wrong judgment upon him, for however lawful it might be for him to eat the meat which had been offered to idols, yet he was, for the fake of his influence and ufefulnefs, to take care, that *his good* might *not be evil fpoken of*, Rom xiv 16 and therefore he would abftain Two general rules he prefcribes,

1 *Whether therefore ye eat or drink, or whatfoever ye do, do all to the glory of God*, making that the ultimate end of all your actions

2 *Give none offence, neither to the Jews, nor to the Gentiles, nor to the church of God* Do nothing which fhould grieve or ftumble them, particularly, avoid the meat offered to idols, which the Jews abominated, and might prove a fnare to the weaker Gentile converts And what he recommended to them, he practifed himfelf *Even as I pleafe all men in all things*, that I lawfully can, *not feeking my own profit*, humour, or inclination, *but the profit of many, that they may be faved*, follicitous, by every means, to win fouls to the adored Redeemer, and to lead them in the ways of everlafting life

CHAP XI

In this chapter the apoftle blames, and endeavours to rectify, fome great indecencies and manifeft diforders in the church of Corinth. As (1) *The mifconduct of their women in the public affembly*, ver. 1—17 (2) *He blames them for their difcord, riot, and neglect and contempt of the poor at the Lord's-fupper*, ver 17—23 (3) *To rectify thefe fcandalous diforders, he fets before them the nature and intentions of this holy inftitution, directs them how they fhould attend on it, and warns them of the danger of a conduct fo indecent as theirs, and of all unworthy receiving*, ver 23, to the end

1 [a] BE ye followers of me, even as I alfo *am* of
Chrift 2 Now I praife you, brethren, that
[b] you remember me in all things, and [c] keep the ordinances,
as I delivered *them* to you 3 But I would have
you know, that [d] the head of every man is Chrift, and [e]
the head of the woman, *is* the man, and [f] the head of
Chrift, *is* God 4 Every man praying or prophefying,
having *his* head covered, difhonoureth his head
5 But every woman that prayeth, or [g] prophefieth with
her head uncovered, difhonoureth her head for that
is even all one as if fhe were fhaven 6 For if the
woman be not covered, let her alfo be fhorn but if
it be [h] a fhame for a woman to be fhorn or fhaven, let
her be covered. 7 For a man indeed ought not to
cover *his* head, forafmuch as [i] he is the image and
glory of God but the woman is the glory of the
man 8 For the man is not of the woman but [k] the
woman of the man 9. Neither was the man created
for the woman [l] but the woman for the man 10 For
this caufe ought the woman [m] to have power on *her*
head, [n] becaufe of the angels 11 Neverthelefs, neither
is the man without the woman, neither the woman
without the man in the Lord 12 For as the woman
is of the man, even fo *is* the man alfo by the woman
but [o] all things of God 13 Judge in yourfelves is
it comely that a woman pray unto God uncovered?
14 Doth not even nature itfelf teach you, that if a
man have long hair, it is a fhame unto him? 15 But
if a woman have long hair, it is a glory to her for
her hair is given her for a covering 16 But [p] if any
man feem to be contentious, we have no fuch cuftom,
[q] neither the churches of God.

[a] Chap iv 16 Eph. v 1 Col iii 17 1 Thef i 6 2 Thef iii 9 [b] Chap iv 17 [c] 2 Thef ii 15 & iii 6 [d] Rom xii 5 Eph v 23 Phil ii 10 11 [e] Gen iii 16 1 Pet iii 1, 6 [f] John xiv 28 Chap iii 23 & xv 28 [g] Acts xxi 9 [h] Num v 18 Deu xxii 5 [i] Gen ... Jam iii 9 [k] Gen ii [l] Gen ii 18 [m] Gen xxiv 65 [n] Ecclef v 6 [o] Rom xi 36 [p] 1 Tim vi 4 [q] Chap xiv 33

v 1—16

v. 1—16 The apostle had promised to them, in the conclusion of the former chapter, his own example, and he here exhorts them, *Be ye followers of me, as I also am of Christ* He copied after his divine master, and therefore could speak freely, when his own practice was so eminently a comment on his discourses

1 To introduce, with greater effect, the reproofs which he was constrained to give, he commends them for what was praise-worthy among them *Now I praise you, brethren, that you remember me in all things, and keep the ordinances, as I delivered them to you*, at least, the main body of the church loved, honoured, and respected him, and were obedient to his instructions

2 He lays a foundation for the rebuke which he was obliged to give, by reminding them of the superiority of the man over the woman *I would have you know, that the head of every man is Christ*, he is the Creator and Governor of all, and, in a peculiar manner, the head of his church *and the head of the woman is the man*, who both by creation and nature the superiority, and therefore the woman should be in subjection *And the head of Christ is God*, considered as Mediator, and, in his human nature, he is inferior to the Father, though, in his Godhead, co-equal and co-eternal

3 The thing he blames is, that their men prayed and prophesied covered, the women, uncovered Veiling the head, in the Eastern countries, was regarded as a token of modesty and subjection in the woman, and having the head uncovered, betokened the superiority of the man when therefore any man prayed or prophesied, leading the devotions of the congregation, with a covering on his head, he dishonoured Christ his head, who had given him the superiority, on the contrary, if any woman, under an extraordinary inspiration, prays or prophesies in public, with her head uncovered, she dishonours the man who is her head, by such an affectation of appearing like him and, instead of modest subjection, pretends to an equality with him, and she might, with equal decency, cut her hair short, and wear it in the form peculiar to men, and thus appear unveiled But if such a sight would appear shocking and highly immodest, in a religious assembly, then *let her be covered* *The man ought not to cover his head*, it would be to debase his dignity, *forasmuch as he is the image and glory of God*, invested with the supreme dominion, *but the woman is the glory of the man*, who hath the honour of being placed in the rank of creation above her, and hath a becoming dominion over her *For the man is not of the woman*, created from her substance, *but the woman is of the man*, from his rib *Neither was the man created for the woman*, seeing he was in being before her, *but the woman for the man*, to be his help-mate, and herein was implied a reasonable subjection to him *For this cause ought the woman to have power over her head*, and to be veiled, in token of her subjection, *because of the angels*, or messengers of Christ, who should preside in the church, and it would be highly arrogant to affect equality with them *Nevertheless, neither is the man without the woman, neither the woman without the man in the Lord*, both sexes partaking alike of that common salvation which is in Jesus Christ, so that though subjection be due, the woman is not to be tyrannized over as a slave, but to be cherished with warmest affection and becoming respect *For as the woman is of the man*, taken from his side, *even so is the man also by the woman*, springing from her, *but all things of God*, who hath placed each in their respective stations, which, therefore, for conscience sake, they should discharge *Judge in yourselves, is it comely that a woman pray unto God uncovered*, affecting to be like the men, and inverting the established order of God? *Doth not nature itself teach you*, that a distinction should be observed in the dress of the different sexes? And as such is the custom of the country where you live, to cut the hair short, it is regarded as a token of great effeminacy to appear otherwise *So that if a man have long hair, it is a shame unto him But if a woman have long hair, it is a glory to her*, comely, and becoming her sex, *for her hair is given her for a covering*, and should be managed so as to avoid all confusion of dress between the sexes *But if any man seem to be contentious*, and disposed to vindicate such a preposterous practice, *we have no such custom, neither the churches of God*, where every appearance of a contentious spirit is condemned, and all such indecent affectation discountenanced

17 Now in this that I declare *unto you* I praise *you*
not, that you come together, not for the better, but for
the worse 18 For first of all, when ye come together
in the church, I hear that [f] there be [|] divisions among
you, and I partly believe it 19 For [g] there must be
also heresies among you, [h] that they which are approved
may be made manifest among you 20 When ye come
together therefore into one place, *this is* not to eat the
Lord's supper 21 For in eating every one taketh be-
fore *other*, his own supper and one is hungry, and
[i] another is drunken 22 What, have ye not houses to
eat and to drink in? or [k] despise ye the church of God,
and [l] shame them that have not? What shall I say to
you? shall I praise you in this? I praise *you* not

[f] Chap i 10, 11 & iii 3 [|] Or schisms [g] Mat xviii 7 [h] ... xi 19 ... [i] Jude 12 [l] ... xx ... [k] Jam ii 6

v 17—22 Shocking abuses early crept into the Corinthian church, some of which the apostle mentions, and sharply rebukes the offenders Though he would praise them (ver 2) in general, there were some among them who were a dishonour to their holy profession, who met with them, *not for the better*, to receive edification, *but for the worse*, growing more corrupt, even in the very use of holy ordinances

1 *When ye come together in the church, I hear that there be divisions among you*, one being for Paul, and another for Apollos, and the church thus torn with factions, *and I partly believe it For there must be also heresies among you*, such is the corruption of man's nature, and the craft of the wicked one, that tares will be sown amongst the wheat, and for wise purposes God permits it should be so, *that they which are approved may be made manifest among you*, their faith tried, and their sincerity evidenced *Note*, (1) Nothing is more fatal to the church of Christ, than uncharitable divisions and discords between the members (2) God can over-rule, even the wickedness of apostates, to the furtherance of his people in faith and holiness

2 Some of them committed the most scandalous irregularities at the Lord's table *When ye come therefore into one place, this is not to eat the Lord's supper*, the method in which you proceed being utterly subversive of the very intention of that holy ordinance, *for in eating, every one taketh, before other, his own supper*, as if it was a mere common meal, and what is still worse, *one is hungry*, the poor man goes away without any refreshment, the bread and wine being devoured by those who come first, *and another is drunken*, the rich indulging themselves to the full, if not to excess *What a scandalous abuse! Have ye not houses to eat and to drink in?* when you want to nourish your bodies? *or despise ye the church of God*, and put contempt on the poor members of it, *and shame them that have not*, have no houses of their own, nor abilities to provide the elements for themselves? *What shall I say to you? shall I praise you in this*, thus to form parties even in the church, and devour the provision of which the poor should partake No, assuredly, *I praise you not*, I blame you exceedingly

23 For [a] I have received of the Lord, that which also [a] Chap xv 3.
I delivered unto you, That the Lord Jesus, [*] the *same* [*] Mat xxvi 26
night in which he was betrayed, took bread 24 And
when he had given thanks, he brake *it*, and said, Take,
eat, this is my body, which is broken for you this
do in remembrance of me 25 After the same manner
also *he took* the cup, when he had supped, saying, This
cup is the New Testament in my blood this do ye, as
oft as ye drink *it*, in remembrance of me 26 For as
often as ye eat this bread, and drink this cup, ye do
shew the Lord's death [b] till he come 27 Wherefore [b] John xiv. 3 Acts i 11 1 Thes iv 16 Jude 14 15
whosoever shall eat this bread and drink *this* cup of
the Lord [c] unworthily, shall be guilty of the body and [c] John vi 63 & xiii 27 Chap x 21
blood of the Lord 28 But [d] let a man examine him- [d] 2 Cor xiii. 5 Gal vi 4
self, and so [e] let him eat of *that* bread, and drink of *that* [e] Num ix 13
cup 29 For he that eateth and drinketh unworthily, [†] Or judgment
eateth and drinketh [†] damnation to himself, not discern- Rom xiii. 2.
ing the Lord's body 30 For this cause many *are* weak Ver 34
and sickly among you, and many sleep 31 For [f] if [f] Ps xxxii 5. Jer vi 8
we would judge ourselves, we should not be judged [g] Ps xciv 12 Heb. xii 5, 10.
32 But when we are judged, [g] we are chastened of the [h] Ver 22
Lord, that we should not be condemned with the world [i] Chap vii 17 Tit i 5
33 Wherefore, my brethren, when ye come together to [k] Chap iv. 19
eat, tarry one for another 34 And if any man hunger,
[h] let him eat at home, that ye come not together unto
condemnation. And the rest [i] will I set in order [k] when
I come

v 23—34 To rectify the gross abuses which he reprehended, the apostle set before them,

1 The true nature of the sacred institution, as he received it from the Lord, and had faithfully delivered it unto them *The Lord Jesus*, the king of his church, *the same night in which he was betrayed took bread and when he had given thanks, he brake it, and said, Take, eat, this bread is* the symbol and representation *of my body, which is broken for you*, and offered upon the cross in your stead, *this do in remembrance of me* continue, in this ordinance, a constant memorial of my dying love, and of the benefits you receive thereby, *After the same manner also he took the cup, when he had supped, saying, This cup is the New Testament*, or covenant *in my blood*, which is now ratified by the blood-shedding of the Mediator, and all the inestimable privileges contained in it secured to every believer *This do ye, as oft as ye drink it, in remembrance of me*, frequently meeting to celebrate this sacred feast, remembering therein my matchless grace, manifest in those precious and plenteous drops of blood shed for your redemption, *for as often as ye eat this bread, and drink this cup ye do shew the Lord's death till he come*, declaring your dependence thereon, as the ground of all your hope towards God, and openly professing your faith in a crucified Redeemer, to all his

people

people are called upon to do, until the day comes when they shall appear with him in glory

2 He warns them of the danger of an irreverent use of this holy ordinance, *Wherefore, whosoever eateth and drinketh this cup of the Lord unworthily*, in such a scandalous, factious, and sensual manner, *shall be guilty of the body and blood of the Lord*, incurring the heavy guilt of treating with contempt the blood of the covenant *But let a man examine himself*, with regard to the truth of his faith, love, and conversion to God, and his knowledge of the design of this sacred institution, *and so let him eat of that bread and drink of that cup*, to his soul's edification and comfort *For he who eateth and drinketh unworthily*, in the shocking manner before described, *eateth and drinketh damnation to himself*, provoking some temporal judgment of God upon him, *not discerning the Lord's body*, nor making a difference between the sacred symbol thereof, and common food *For this cause many are weak and sickly among you, and many sleep*, God visiting in sickness, disease, and death, your provocations *For if we would judge ourselves*, and seriously examine into our conduct, that with real penitence we might return unto God, *we should not be judged* with such heavy providential afflictions *But when we are thus judged, we are chastened of the Lord* in mercy, *that we should not be condemned with the world*, left to go on securely, and perish in our sins *Note*, (1) None should be discouraged from the Lord's table, who, on examining themselves, can say, that in simplicity they desire to approve themselves to him (2) God never casts away his people, though often for their good he visits their offences with a rod, and their sin with scourges

3 He directs them now to celebrate this sacred ordinance *Wherefore, my brethren, when ye come together to eat, tarry one for another* till all are assembled, and you can eat together, sitting down, as children of one family, at the table of the Lord *And if any man hunger, let him eat at home*, this being not designed as an ordinary meal, *that ye come not together to condemnation*, provoking God by your irreverence, dissensions, or excess *And the rest*, if there be any thing further amiss, respecting the proper discipline to be observed, *will I set in order when I come*

CHAP XII.

In this chapter the apostle, (1) Considers the case of spiritual gifts, which were very plentifully poured out on the Corinthian church He considers their original, that they are from God, their variety and use, that they were all intended for one and the same general end, the advancement of Christianity, and the church's edification, ver 1—11 *(2) He illustrates this by an allusion to an human body, in which all the members have a mutual relation and subserviency, and each its proper place and use,* ver 12—27 *(3) He tells us, that the church is the body of Christ, and the members are variously gifted, for the benefit of the whole body and each particular member,* ver 27—30 *And then, (4) Closes with an exhortation to seek somewhat more beneficial than these gifts,* ver 31

1. NOW [a] concerning spiritual *gifts*, brethren, I would not have you ignorant 2 Ye know that [b] ye were Gentiles, carried away unto these dumb idols, even as ye were led 3 Wherefore I give you to understand, that [c] no man speaking by the Spirit of God, calleth Jesus accursed and *that* [d] no man can say that Jesus is the Lord, but by the holy Ghost 4 Now there are diversities of gifts, [e] but the same Spirit 5 And there are differences of administrations, but the same Lord 6 And there are diversities of operations, but it is the same God [g] which worketh all in all 7 But the manifestation of the Spirit is given to every man to profit withal 8 For to one is given by the Spirit [h] the word of wisdom, to another [i] the word of knowledge by the same Spirit, 9 To another [k] faith by the same Spirit, to another [l] the gifts of healing by the same Spirit; 10 To another [m] the working of miracles, to another [n] prophecy, to another [o] discerning of spirits, to another [p] *divers* kinds of tongues, to another [q] the interpretation of tongues 11 But all these worketh that one and the self-same Spirit, [r] dividing to every man severally [s] as he will

a Chap xiv 1 b Chap vi 11 Eph ii 11, 12 1 Pet iv 3 c Mark ix 39 d Mat xvi 17 2 Cor iii 5 1 John iv 2, 3 e Rom xii 4, 6, 8 Eph iv 11 1 Pet iv 10 f Eph iv 4 g Eph i 23 h Chap ii 6 i Chap xiii 2 k Mat xvii 21 Chap xiii 2 Heb xi 3 l Mark xvi 18 Jam v 14 m Acts xiv 10 & xx 12 n Acts xi 28 o Acts v 3 or Chap xiv 29 p Acts ii 4 q Chap xiv 28 r Chap vii 7 Eph iv 7 s John iii 8 Heb ii 4

v 1—11. The church of Corinth was greatly enriched in spiritual gifts, and these had been sadly abused, and made an occasion of much pride and contention The apostle therefore here leads them to consider the author, nature, design, and use of the extraordinary powers which were given them

1 He reminds them, for their humiliation, of their former state, *Ye know that ye were Gentiles, carried away unto these dumb idols, even as ye were led*, hurried on blindfold to worship the senseless stocks and stones *Wherefore I give you to understand*, now that God hath brought you out of darkness into his marvellous light, *that no man speaking by the Spirit of God calleth Jesus accursed*, it being a sure proof that both the Jewish exorcists, and the heathen diviners who pretend to such inspiration, yet blaspheme him from whom the Spirit proceeds, are liars, and of their father the devil, *and*, on the other hand, *no man can say that Jesus is the Christ, but by the Spirit of God*, to discover his all-sufficiency for the work of redemption, and his suitableness to every necessity of our souls, we need a divine illumination and though we may confess him to be the Christ with our lips, yet we can never experimentally know him to be our anointed Saviour, till it please God to reveal his Son in us And all the miracles which are wrought in confirmation of this truth, are by the power of the holy Ghost, who intends thereby to glorify Christ Let a man pretend to what he will, if he doth not know and love the Lord Jesus, he must be destitute of the Spirit, but if he doth, then, however low his gifts may be, he hath an assured interest in the Saviour

2 He directs them in the proper *use* of the spiritual gifts which they enjoyed *Now there are diversities of gifts, but the same Spirit*, who bestows them in all their variety on private Christians, or ministers, *and there are differences of administrations*, of offices and services, some superior to the others, *but the same Lord* appoints to each his employment, and they act under his authority *And there are diversities of operations*, and miraculous powers, *but it is the same Lord which worketh all in all*, by whose mighty energy alone they are performed *But the manifestation of the Spirit is given to every man to profit withal*, whatever gifts or powers he is endowed with, that manifest the presence and energy of the holy Ghost, they are designed to promote the edification of the body of Christ, and to advance his glory *For to one is given by the Spirit the word of wisdom*, a clear understanding of the great doctrines of the gospel, and ability to express them with judgment and eloquence, *to another the word of knowledge by the same Spirit*, an insight into the types and prophecies of the Old Testament, and a readiness to explain and apply them *To another faith by the same Spirit*, so that in the midst of the most threatning dangers, he is enabled, confidently and quietly, to repose on God *To another the gifts of healing by the same Spirit*, all manner of bodily diseases, by a word or a touch instantaneously *To another the working of miracles*, in mercy, or judgment, Acts viii 40 Acts v 5, 10 *To another prophecy*, or the power of foretelling future events, *to another the discerning of spirits*, under what influence, divine or diabolical, men act, what is their real design and qualifications, and who are fit to be publickly employed in the church, *to another divers kinds of tongues*, so as to understand and speak fluently languages he had never learnt, *to another the interpretation of tongues*, the ability of rendering with exactness and propriety a foreign tongue, which the congregation may not understand, into their own native language *But all these worketh that one and the selfsame Spirit, dividing to every man severally*, and sovereignly, *as he will* *Note*, (1) The Holy Ghost is a divine person, he acts with sovereignty in the distribution of his own gifts, and in energy and operation is one with the Father and the Son (2) All our gifts are bestowed for service, not to advance our own honour and interest, but the glory of God, and the salvation of men's souls

12 For [t] as the body is one, and hath many members, and all the members of that one body, being many, are one body [u] so also *is* Christ 13 For [x] by one Spirit are we all baptized into one body, [y] whether *we be* Jews or Gentiles, whether *we be* bond or free, and [z] have been all made to drink into one Spirit 14 For the body is not one member, but many 15 If the foot shall say, Because I am not the hand, I am not of the body, is it therefore not of the body? 16 And if the ear shall say, Because I am not the eye, I am not of the body, is it therefore not of the body? 17 If the whole body *were* an eye, where *were* the hearing? if the whole *were* hearing, where *were* the smelling? 18 But now hath [a] God set the members, every one of them in the body, [b] as it hath pleased him 19 And if they were all one member, where *were* the body? 20 But now *are they* many members, yet but one body. 21 And the eye cannot say unto the hand, I have no need of thee nor again, the head to the feet, I have no need of you 22 Nay, much more those members of the body which seem to be more feeble, are necessary 23 And those *members* of the body, which we think to be less honourable, upon these we bestow more abundant honour, and our uncomely *parts* have more abundant comeliness 24 For our comely *parts* have no need but God hath tempered the body together, having given more abundant honour to that *part* which lacked. 25 That there should be no [c] schism in the body,

t Rom xii 4 Eph iv 4 16 u Ver 27 x Rom vi 3 y Gal iii 28 Eph ii 13 16 Col iii 11 z John vii 37, 39 a Ver 28 b Rom xii 3 c Or division

body, but *that* the members should have the same care
one for another 26 And whether one member suffer,
all the members suffer with it or one member be ho
noured, all the members rejoice with it.

v 12—26 The apostle represents the union subsisting between the faithful who partake of the several gifts of the Spirit, under the similitude of a human body consisting of many members it is but *one*, though composed of various parts, which have each their particular function for the good of the whole *So also is* the mystical body of *Christ*, tho' consisting of different persons, with different gifts, and appointed to different stations, yet all who are vitally united to him compose but one spiritual body, into which all, whether Jews or Gentiles, who have been baptised with water and the Holy Ghost, are by faith incorporated, and are nourished by that one Divine Spirit that resides in all his fulness in Christ, and is from him diffused through the several members, who thereby maintain communion with their exalted Head Now in the natural body, (1) Each member constitutes a part of the whole, and the meanest are needful *the foot* and *the ear*, though less useful perhaps than the *hand* and *eye*, are yet equally parts of the body The meanest Christian is dear to the Saviour, and regarded by him as truly a member of his body as the noblest (2) There is a beauty in the variety of the different members if the body were all eye or all ear, it would be defective and monstrous Thus the diversity of offices and gifts in the church display a beautiful symmetry (3) As in the body natural God gives, as he pleases, to every member its proper office, so, in the body mystical, the Lord appoints to each his station, and furnishes him with gifts, which he is bound to receive with thankfulness, to use with diligence, and neither to murmur against the giver, nor envy the superiority of others (4) Every member of the body contributes to the good of the whole The eye wants the hand, the head the feet, nay the feeblest members are necessary Thus do those who are in the most exalted stations in the church need the inferior members, and must not despise them as insignificant or useless (5) In the body we shew peculiar regard to our uncomely parts, covering them with proper cloathing, which our comely parts do not need, and thus hath God ordered it, that we should give more abundant honour to the part which lacketh In like manner ought the more eminent in gifts and abilities in the church to hide the infirmities of their weaker brethren, not to reproach or despise them, but treat them with kindness and regard, and desire to make them appear in the most respectable manner (6) In the body the suffering of one member gives pain to the whole, and all the members share in the honour conferred on any particular part such a mutual sympathy prevents all schism in the body, and obliges the members to *have the same care one for another* The like fellow-feeling should every Christian have for his brother we should tenderly sympathize with the afflicted in body or soul, and their temporal or spiritual prosperity, far from being the occasion of our envy, should be matter of our sincerest joy All coldness and distance is as unnatural as a schism between the members, and should be shunned as the most dangerous evil

27 Now are [c] ye the body of Christ, and members in
particular 28 And [d] God hath set some in the church,
[e] first apostles, secondarily prophets, [f] thirdly teachers,
after that miracles, then gifts of healing, [g] helps, [h] go-
vernments, diversities of tongues 29 [i] *Are* all apo-
stles? *are* all prophets? *are* all teachers? *are* all workers
of miracles? 30 Have all the gifts of healing? do all
speak with tongues? do all interpret? 31 But [k] covet
earnestly the best gifts [l] And yet shew I unto you a
more excellent way

v 27—31 The apostle particularly applies the case in hand *Now are ye the* mystical *body of Christ, and members in particular*, each being a part of the whole *And God*, in infinite wisdom and with admirable propriety, *hath set some in the church*, appointing one to a higher, another to a lower station In the *first* rank stand the *apostles*, who received their commission immediately from Christ himself *secondarily prophets*, who are endued with the gift of foretelling future events *thirdly teachers*, who labour in the word and doctrine, and are the ordinary ministers of the gospel *after that miracles*, which some are endued with the power of working *then gifts of healing* the sick *helps*, such as are assistants to the superior ministers *governments*, those who preside over the affairs of the church others are endued with *diversities of tongues*, the ability to speak or interpret them *Are all apostles? are all prophets? are all teachers? are all workers of miracles? have all the gifts of healing? do all speak with tongues? do all interpret?* No Each hath his appointed station and peculiar gifts, wherein the highest are not to be envied, nor the lowest to be despised *But covet earnestly the best gifts* It may be regarded as his advice or it may be read as an affirmation, *Ye do covet the best gifts*, and blameably desire to excel in these extraordinary endowments, or are in emulation, *Do ye covet earnestly the best gifts? and envy each other's superior attainments? Yet shew I unto you a more excellent way* a spirit of love, which prompts to every good word and work for the glory of God and the profit of men's souls, is far better and more desireable than the most shining gifts *Note*, (1) Gifts, when valued because of the esteem which they procure us, more than for their use to the souls of men, prove the most fatal snare to the soul (2) One spark of godlike charity is infinitely preferable to all the glare of the most eminent titles or abilities

CHAP XIII.

In this chapter the apostle, 1 *Recommends it by shewing the necessity and importance of it,* ver 1—4 2 *By giving a description of the properties and fruits,* ver 4—8 3 *By shewing how much it excels the best of gifts and other graces, by its continuance, when they shall be no longer in being or of any use,* ver 8 to the end

1. THOUGH I speak with the tongues of men
and of angels, and have not charity, I am be-
come *as* sounding brass, or a tinkling cymbal 2 And
though I have *the gift of* [a] prophecy, and understand all
mysteries, and [b] all knowledge, and though I have [c] all
faith, so that I could remove mountains, and have not
charity, I am nothing 3 And [d] though I bestow all
my goods to feed the poor, and [e] though I give my
body to be burned, and have not charity, it profiteth me
nothing

v 1—3 The more excellent way, which the apostle had been recommending, he here describes, and that is charity or love, which is the greatest of graces, shall endure for ever, when gifts are vanished away, and without it they are nothing worth

1 *Though I speak with the tongues of men*, in all the various languages of the globe, *or even of angels, and have not charity*, or love, *I am become as sounding brass, or a tinkling cymbal*, so inharmonious, and a mere empty noise Little reason therefore had the Corinthians to value themselves upon the gifts of tongues, which only afforded occasion for pride and contention *And*,

2 *Though I have the gift of prophecy*, can foretel future events, *and understand all mysteries*, through divine illumination discovering the meaning of the most abstruse prophecies and figures, *and have all knowledge*, such as never mortal man attained before, *and have not charity*, or *love*, it signifies nothing to my salvation. Such light would only be sufficient to lead me into eternal darkness

3 *And though I had all faith*, to work the most stupendous miracles, *so that I could remove mountains, and have no love, I am nothing* in God's account, and utterly destitute of the spirit of vital Christianity

4 *And though I bestow all my goods to feed the poor*, it would be utterly unprofitable to myself, if divine love was not the principle from which my almsgiving proceeded *Note*, Many give largely to the poor, who never did a *truly charitable act* in their lives

5 *And though I give my body to be burned*, for my profession of the gospel, *and have not charity*, or *love* to the Redeemer, and to men for his sake, *it profiteth me nothing* The affectation of leaving a great name, or the conceit of the meritoriousness of such a sacrifice, may even lead a man to a stake He may burn for Christ, and yet be disowned by him, if this genuine mark of discipleship be lacking

4 [f] Charity suffereth long, *and* is kind, charity [g] en-
vieth not, charity [h] vaunteth not itself, [i] is not puffed
up, 5 Doth not behave itself unseemly, [j] seeketh not
her own, [k] is not easily provoked, thinketh no evil, 6
[l] Rejoiceth not in iniquity, [m] but rejoiceth in the truth
7 [n] Beareth all things, [o] believeth all things, hopeth all
things, [p] endureth all things

v 4—7 We have here the true properties of that most excellent of graces, *charity*, or love

1 It *suffereth long*, patiently enduring provocation, unruffled with affronts, passing by offences, and suppressing every motion of resentment that would rise within the soul

2 It *is kind*, courteous, affable, benevolent, and opens the lips, the hand, and heart, to every good word and work

3 *Charity envieth not* the superior gifts, graces, attainments, honours, or affluence, which others enjoy, but takes pleasure in them, as if they were his own

4 *Charity vaunteth not itself*, is not ostentatious of any excellencies or superior advantages, doth not treat inferiors with contempt and insolence, nor rashly or perversely utter any thing to a brother's disadvantage

5 *It is not puffed up*, doth not fill the head with vain conceit of its own importance, nor suffer him to think more highly of himself than he ought to think

6 It

6 It *doth not behave itself unseemly*, admits of no conduct unsuitable to the age, station, or circumstances, of the person, suffers nothing mean, indecent, or dishonourable, to enter the mind, or be carried into act

7 It *seeketh not her own*, is influenced by no mercenary motives, nor pursues any private ends, inordinately craving honour, gain, or applause, but is generous, noble, and disinterested, sacrificing her own advantage for the good of others

8 It *is not easily provoked*, but, under the most exasperating insults, can preserve a holy serenity, and even be angry, and sin not, displeased at the sin, yet pitying the sinner, always restraining just resentment within bounds, and ready to be reconciled

9 It *thinketh no evil*, never seeking to pry into others conduct to discover faults, but ever ready to put the best construction on their words and actions, entertains no undue suspicions, and is willing to forget as well as forgive every injury

10 It *rejoiceth not in iniquity*, nor looks, but with grief and sorrow, on the sins, perverseness, and infirmities of others *But*,

11 *Rejoiceth in the truth*, glad of the success of the gospel, pleased with beholding its influence, where-ever it appears, and ever delighting to bear testimony to the truth, and speaking from the heart

12 It *beareth all things*, covers men's faults with the mantle of love, pities their weakness, and suffers without the thought of retaliating their perverseness

13 It *believeth all things*, willing to entertain the most favourable opinion of all, averse to every ungrounded suspicion, and candidly disposed to receive the excuse and explanation where aught may have been mistaken

14 It *hopeth all things*, where matters appear dark, and cannot but raise doubts, still charity will not despair but that they can yet be cleared up satisfactorily, or, where the evil is evident, that the fault will be repented of and amended

15 It *endureth all things*, with unshaken fortitude bearing up under every affliction, temptation, and persecution, and for the sake of Christ and his people ready to undergo any sufferings

Such is this transcendent grace of charity In the glass of which we should often look, compare our features with this perfect pattern, and daily seek that we may grow more like him whose nature and name is Love

8 Charity never faileth but whether *there be* pro-
phecies, they shall fail, whether *there be* tongues, they
shall cease, whether *there be* knowledge, it shall vanish
away 9 For we know in part, and we prophesy in
part 10 But when that which is perfect is come, then
that which is in part shall be done away 11 When I
was a child, I spake as a child, I understood as a child,
I † thought as a child but when I became a man, I put
away childish things 12 For [a] now we see through a
glass ‡ darkly, but then face to face now I know in
part, but [r] then shall I know even as also I am known
13 And now abideth faith, hope, charity, these three,
but the greatest of these *is* charity

† Or reasoned
[q] 2 Cor iii 18 & v 7
‡ Gr In a riddle
[r] Mat xviii 10 1 John iii 2

v 8—13 The apostle proceeds in his commendation of charity, not only as superior to all gifts, but as the chief of all graces

1 *Charity never faileth*, *but* will continue in the heart where it hath been once planted, enduring as the days of eternity All gifts must quickly have an end, *whether they be prophecies*, the gift of foretelling future events, or interpreting the Scriptures, *they shall fail*, and be of no further use in the eternal world, *whether there be tongues, they shall cease*, when they have answered their present use of spreading the gospel through the world, and in heaven we shall have but one language, *whether there be knowledge*, the extraordinary insight into divine truth, *it shall vanish away*, in glory this knowledge will be no longer needed

2 All gifts are suited only to a state of imperfection, when we arrive to maturity in glory we shall be above them *For we know in part, and prophesy in part*, our greatest attainments are at present defective, *but when that which is perfect is come, then that which is in part shall be done away*, and our nature being exalted to the highest pitch of which it is capable, all imperfection will be swallowed up in perfection of knowledge and holiness, absolute and everlasting Our present and future state differ as much as manhood does from infancy *When I was a child, I spake as a child, I understood as a child, I thought as a child*, and such the infirmities were all then highest present attainments, no better than the poor conceptions and lispings of babes *but when I became a man, I put away childish things*, and in the heavenly state so low thoughts shall we entertain of all our present most esteemed acquisitions, despise what in the days of childish folly we valued, and see, with a distinctness of spiritual vision, as much above our present state, as the thoughts of manhood are superior to the fancies of infancy *for now we see through a glass darkly*, the mirrour reflecting the object indistinctly, and, like a riddle, the truth is involved with obscurity, *but then face to face*, clearly and fully, by intuition, without any darkening medium *Now know I in part*, and with all my singular gifts know but in part, *but then shall I know even as also I am known*, comprehending heavenly objects with the most distinct knowledge, and in the same way that God, who is a spirit, and his angels, know me

3 Charity is the most excellent of graces, as well as above all gifts *And now abideth faith, hope, charity, these three* cardinal graces, inseparable from the Christian character, and which till death must be in constant exercise, *but the greatest of these is charity*, the others being as means to this as the end And when faith is swallowed up in sight, and hope in the fruition of the eternal blessedness, love, the bright image of the Deity, shall glow towards the eternal Three, and the celestial hosts, in every bosom of the redeemed, and continue to burn, with unextinguished ardor, throughout the countless ages of eternity

CHAP XIV

In this chapter the apostle, 1 *Begins with advising them of all spiritual gifts to prefer prophesying*, ver 1—6 2 *He goes on to shew them how unprofitable the speaking foreign languages was, and useless to the church, whereas gifts should be used for the good of the church*, ver 6—15 3 *He advises that worship should be celebrated so as the most ignorant might understand and join in prayer and praise, and presses the advice by his own example*, ver 15—21. 4 *He informs them, that tongues were a sign for unbelievers rather than those that believe, and represents the advantage of prophecy above speaking with tongues, from the different suggestions they would give to the mind of an unbeliever coming into their assemblies*, ver 21—26 5 *Blames them for the disorder and confusion they had brought into the assembly by their vanity and ostentation of their gifts, and directs them in using their gifts both of tongues and prophecy*, ver 26—34 6 *Forbids women speaking in the church, and closes the subject by requiring them to perform every thing in the public worship with order and decency*, ver 34 to the end

1 FOLLOW after charity, and [a] desire spiritual
gifts, but [b] rather that ye may prophesy 2 For
[c] he that speaketh in an *unknown* tongue, speaketh not
unto men, but unto God for no man understandeth
him, howbeit in the spirit he speaketh mysteries 3 But
[d] he that prophesieth, speaketh unto men to edification,
and exhortation, and comfort 4 He that speaketh in
an *unknown* tongue, edifieth himself but he that pro-
phesieth, edifieth the church 5 [e] I would that ye all
spake with tongues, but rather that ye prophesied. for
greater *is* he that prophesieth than he that speaketh with
tongues, except he interpret, that the church may receive
edifying

[a] Chap xii 31
[b] Numb xi 25
[c] Acts ii 4 & x 46
[d] Act x . & xix 14
[e] Numb xi 29

v 1—5 Having recommended charity in the first place, he proceeds to shew what spiritual gifts were most desireable

1 *Follow after charity* (διωκετε), pursue it with the greatest eagerness, *and desire spiritual gifts* for the glory of God and the good of the church, *but rather*, or chiefly, *that ye may prophesy*, so as by divine illumination to be enabled most profitably to open and apply the Scriptures to the consciences of men for their comfort and edification

2 He assigns this reason for his exhortation, *He that speaketh in an unknown tongue speaketh not to men*, who cannot understand him, *but unto God*, *for no man understandeth him*, *howbeit in the spirit he speaketh mysteries*, and advances the most glorious and important truths *but he that prophesieth*, explaining and opening the Scriptures to the understanding and capacity of the hearers, *speaketh unto men to edification*, *and exhortation*, *and comfort*, and his ministry and gifts are made useful to their souls *He that speaketh in an unknown tongue, edifieth himself*, *but he that prophesieth, edifieth the church*, and communicates an extensive benefit to others as well as to his own heart *I would that ye all spake with tongues*, and were furnished with this great gift, *but rather that ye prophesied* *for greater is he that prophesieth than he that speaketh with tongues*, he is a more useful and therefore a more excellent man, and to be more highly esteemed by the hearers, *except he interpret, that the church may receive edifying* Note, Our discourses should be adapted to the capacity of our hearers high flights of eloquence, or affectation of learning, are absurd where the audience is illiterate Our ambition must be to stoop, and we should ever be more sollicitous to be understood than to be admired

6 Now brethren, if I come unto you speaking with
tongues, what shall I profit you, except I shall speak to
you [f] either by revelation, or by knowledge, or by pro-
phesying, or by doctrine? 7 And even things without
life giving sound, whether pipe or harp, except they give
a distinction in the † sounds, how shall it be known

[f] Ver
† Or tunes

what is piped or harped? 8 For if the trumpet give an
uncertain ſound, who ſhall prepare himſelf to the battle?
‡ Or ſignifi- 9. So likewiſe you, except ye utter by the tongue ‡ words
cant words eaſy to be underſtood, how ſhall it be known what is
ſpoken? for ye ſhall ſpeak into the air 10 There are,
it may be, ſo many kinds of voices in the world, and
none of them *is* without ſignification 11. Therefore if
I know not the meaning of the voice, I ſhall be unto
him that ſpeaketh, a barbarian, and he that ſpeaketh
ſhall be a barbarian unto me. 12 Even ſo ye, foraſmuch
g Chap xii as g ye are zealous of ſpiritual *gifts*, ſeek that ye may ex
31 ver 1 cel to the edifying of the church 13 Wherefore let him
that ſpeaketh in an *unknown* tongue, pray that he may
interpret 14 For if I pray in an *unknown* tongue, my
ſpirit prayeth, but my underſtanding is unfruitful

v 6—14 The apoſtle goes on to ſhew the abſurdity of making an oſtentatious ſhew of gifts, and ſpeaks in his own perſon to inſinuate the reproof which they deſerved for their vanity in this reſpect *Now brethren, if I come unto you ſpeaking with tongues, what ſhall I profit you, except I ſhall ſpeak to you*, interpreting what is made known unto me in an intelligible manner, *either by revelation*, if it be a new truth, *or by knowledge, or by propheſying, or by doctrine?* opening the Scriptures, and enforcing them on the conſcience He illuſtrates this,

1 By a *pipe or harp* Unleſs theſe inſtruments give a diſtinction of ſounds to direct the dancer's motion, or to excite the different paſſions which muſic raiſes, they will be uſeleſs and inharmonious and juſt ſo muſt ſpeaking in an unknown tongue be abſurd to one who is a ſtranger to the language

2 By a *trumpet*, which *if it give an uncertain ſound, who ſhall prepare himſelf to the battle?* And as the ſoldier in ſuch a caſe muſt be utterly at a loſs, ſo muſt the congregation be where the diſcourſe is in an unknown tongue, or above their capacities, and ſuch preaching is to them no better than the whiſtling of the wind

3 A perſon ſpeaking in ſuch an unknown tongue appears as a barbarian to the hearers Various as the languages are in the world, each ſerves to convey the ideas of the mind to thoſe who are acquainted with it, but to no others therefore, if I know not the meaning of the language, it will appear mere gibberiſh, the ſpeaker will appear a barbarian to me, and I to him

Now this being evidently the caſe, the apoſtle exhorts them, ſince they ſo eagerly coveted ſpiritual gifts, to deſire thoſe that were of the moſt uſeful tendency, and if they ſpoke with tongues, to pray that they might be able to interpret them for the edifying of the church *For if I pray in an unknown tongue, my ſpirit prayeth*, and my own ſoul may be engaged in devotion, *but my underſtanding is unfruitful*, and my prayers of no uſe to the hearer

15 What is it then? I will pray with the ſpirit, and
h Eph v 19 I will pray with the underſtanding alſo I will ſing with
Col iii 16 the ſpirit, and I will ſing h with the underſtanding alſo
Pſ xlvii 7 16 Elſe when thou ſhalt bleſs with the ſpirit, how ſhall
he that occupieth the room of the unlearned, ſay Amen
at thy giving of thanks, ſeeing he underſtandeth not
what thou ſayeſt? 17 For thou verily giveſt thanks
well, but the other is not edified 18 I thank my God,
k Rom xv k I ſpeak with tongues more than you all 19 Yet in
19. the church I had rather ſpeak five words with my under-
ſtanding, that *by my voice* I might teach others alſo, than
ten thouſand words in an *unknown* tongue 20 Bre-
l Pſ cxix 99 thren, l be not children in underſtanding howbeit, m in
Rom xvi malice be ye children, but in underſtanding be † men

19. Eph iv 14. Heb v 12
m Pſ cxxxi 2 Mat xviii 3
† Gr Perfect, or full grown
Chap ii 6

v 15—20 The apoſtle ſums up what he had been ſaying

What is it then that is proper to be done? *I will pray with the ſpirit*, under a divine afflatus, and with any of the tongues which he hath given on proper occaſions, *and I will*, in the congregation, *pray with my underſtanding alſo*, in ſuch manner as that others may be edified *I will ſing with the ſpirit*, when under a divine inſpiration, in whatever language he is pleaſed to enable me to utter his praiſes, *and I will*, in public, *ſing with my underſtanding alſo*, that the church may join in my aſcriptions of praiſe to God *Elſe, when thou ſhalt bleſs with the ſpirit*, though under his immediate inſpiration, if it be in an unknown tongue, *how ſhall he that occupieth the room of the unlearned ſay Amen at thy giving of thanks, ſeeing he underſtandeth not what thou ſayeſt*, and therefore cannot join in the ſervice? *For thou verily giveſt thanks well, but the other*, who knoweth not the meaning of the words, *is not edified* *I thank my God* (and happy is it when we can call him *mine*), *I ſpeak with tongues more than you all*, he did not depreciate this gift therefore becauſe he poſſeſſed it not, but becauſe they made ſo evil a uſe of it *yet in the church I had rather ſpeak five words with my underſtanding, that by my voice I might teach others alſo, than ten thouſand words in an unknown tongue*, from which none of the hearers could receive the leaſt benefit Therefore *brethren, be not children in underſtanding*, and fooliſhly boaſt yourſelves on the ſhowy gift of tongues *howbeit in malice be ye children*, free from the malignant paſſions of envy, malice, and pride, *but in underſtanding be men*, and prove yourſelves to be Chriſtians grown to riper years, by knowing how to value things according to their intrinſic worth, and to prefer godlike charity to the moſt aſtoniſhing gifts *Note*, (1) That church muſt be erroneous, where ignorance is regarded as the mother of devotion, and the prayers are offered in an unknown tongue (2) The leaſt good done to the meaneſt ſoul is an unſpeakably greater acquiſition than the higheſt applauſe gained to ourſelves (3) A malicious, envious ſpirit is directly contrary to true Chriſtianity Among the firſt leſſons of that ſchool, we muſt learn to become as little children

21 In the law it is written, n With *men of* other n Iſ. xxviii
tongues and other lips, will I ſpeak unto this people 11, 12
and yet for all that will they not hear me, ſaith the Lord
22 Wherefore tongues are for a ſign, not to them that
believe, but to them that believe not but propheſying
ſerveth not for them that believe not, but for them which
believe 23 If therefore the whole church be come to-
gether into one place, and all ſpeak with tongues, and
there come in thoſe that are unlearned, or unbelievers,
o will they not ſay that ye are mad? 24 But if all pro- o Acts ii. 13
pheſy, and there come in one that believeth not, or *one*
unlearned, he is convinced of all, he is judged of all
25 And thus are the ſecrets of his heart made manifeſt,
and ſo falling down on *his* face he will worſhip God, and
report that p God is in you of a truth p Iſ. xlv 14. Zech viii 23

v 21—25 The apoſtle further enforces what he had advanced by obſerving,

1 That it had been threatened to the Jews, as the puniſhment of their infidelity, that *with men of other tongues, and other lips, will I ſpeak unto this people, and yet for all that will they not hear me, ſaith the Lord* which was *primarily* fulfilled when they were ſent into captivity to Babylon, where they heard the ſtrange language of their conquerors, and *ſecondarily* when, on the day of Pentecoſt, they heard the apoſtles ſpeak with tongues, yet rejected the evidence which the Holy Ghoſt bore thereby to the doctrine which they preached, deaf to the warnings of Providence and the calls of grace The Corinthians ſhould not therefore be ſo inordinately fond of what God had before uſed in a way of judgment upon Iſrael *Wherefore*,

2 *Tongues are for a ſign, not to them that believe, but for them that believe not*, to carry the goſpel into the lands of infidelity, and bear a teſtimony to the truth of it, which thoſe who believe do not ſo much need, *but propheſying ſerveth not for them that believe not* merely, *but is alſo for them that believe*, that they may be built up on the true foundation So that to ſpeak with tongues in a Chriſtian aſſembly was uſeleſs and abſurd, becauſe none could be profited thereby

3 The credit of their profeſſion ſhould reſtrain them from an oſtentation of their gift of tongues. *If therefore the whole church be come together into one place, and all ſpeak with tongues*, it will appear a ſecond Babel *and if there come in thoſe that are unlearned*, either private Chriſtians or other common people, *and unbelievers, will they not ſay that ye are mad*, and, inſtead of being converted, ridicule you as a parcel of frantic enthuſiaſts? *But if all propheſy*, in their turn preaching, praying, or praiſing, in an intelligible manner, *and there come in one that believeth not*, out of curioſity or by accident, *or one unlearned*, or ignorant *he is convinced of all, he is judged of all*, his conſcience is pricked under the word, his ſin is brought to his remembrance, and the juſt wrath of God due thereunto is ſet before him *and thus are the ſecrets of his heart made manifeſt*, as if the preacher had known his very ſoul, and deſcribed his caſe particularly, *and ſo, falling down on his face, he will worſhip God*, convinced, by what he hears, that this is his work, *and report that God is in you of a truth*, ſince none could ſo diſcover the inmoſt ſoul, and ſpeak with ſuch power and energy, unleſs God's Spirit inſtructed them and accompanied their miniſtrations *Note*, The word of truth, when rightly diſpenſed, is a diſcerner of the thoughts and intent of the heart and many, who have heard it, have felt by experience, that God's miniſters often deſcribe their caſe particularly as if they knew the ſecrets of their ſoul, and they wonder who hath told them

26 How is it then, brethren? when ye come toge- q Ver 6
ther, every one of you hath a pſalm, q hath a doctrine, Chap xii 8
hath a tongue, hath a revelation, hath an interpretation
r Let all things be done to edifying 27 If any man r Chap xii
ſpeak in an *unknown* tongue, *let it be* by two, or at the 12 Eph iv 12
moſt *by* three, and that by courſe, and let one interpret
28 But if there be no interpreter, let him keep ſilence
in the church, and let him ſpeak to himſelf and to God

29 Let the prophets speak two or three, and ᵗ let the
other judge 30 If *any thing* be revealed to another,
that sitteth by, let the first hold his peace 31 For ye
may all prophesy one by one, that all may learn, and
all may be comforted 32 And the spirits of the pro-
phets are subject to the prophets 33 For God is not
the author of † confusion, ᵘ but of peace, as in all churches
of the saints

ᵗ Chap. xii 15 & xiv 30 † Or tumult ᵘ Chap. xi 16 & xii 5

v 26—33 The apostle reproves their ill behaviour, and gives them rules for their conduct

1 He blames their irregularities in the church *How is it then, brethren,* that you behave so unseemly in the house of God? for, *when ye come together, every one of you hath a psalm, hath a doctrine, hath a tongue, hath a revelation, hath an interpretation*, and, whilst every one is forward to exercise his own gift, the whole is a scene of disorder and confusion *Let all things be done to edifying*, and no such unseasonable and unprofitable exercise of these divinely communicated gifts be permitted

2 He orders how they should proceed in the congregation (1) *If any man speak in an unknown tongue, let it be by two, or at the most by three*, no more than these should at one meeting speak, *and that by course*, in their proper turn, *and let one interpret*, that the audience may receive instruction *but, if there be no interpreter, let him* that speaks in an unknown tongue *keep silence in the church*, and not interrupt what is to the use of edifying, *and let him speak to himself and to God* in private prayer (2) *Let the prophets speak two or three*, at one assembly, and after each other, *and let the other judge* whether those who profess to be prophets really are so, and examine what they say by the word of truth (3) *If any thing* of peculiar importance *be revealed to another* prophet *who sitteth by, let the first* who was speaking hasten to conclude his discourse, and *hold his peace for ye may all prophesy one by one*, at proper opportunities, *that all may learn, and all may be comforted*, this being the great end for which the gift of prophecy is bestowed *And the spirits of the prophets are subject to the prophets*, these who are truly inspired are not like those under diabolical possession, but have the due government of themselves, and will not be hurried into any indecency or impropriety, as to the matter, time, or manner, of their speaking

3 He enforces his discourse with this argument, *For God is not the author of confusion, but of peace*, such disorderly proceedings as these here remarked cannot arise from him, but *as in all* the other *churches of the saints*, so among you, it is his pleasure, and for his glory, that due order should be observed

34 ʷ Let your women keep silence in the churches
for it is not permitted unto them to speak, but ˣ *they
are commanded* to be under obedience, ʸ as also saith the
law 35 And if they will learn any thing, let them
ask their husbands at home for it is a shame for women
to speak in the church

ʷ 1 Tim ii 11 12 ˣ Chap xi 3 Eph v 22 Col iii 18 1 Pet iii 1 ʸ Gen iii 16

v 34—35 We have here silence imposed on women in the church *For it is not permitted unto them to speak* as public teachers, *but they are commanded to be under obedience, as also saith the law*, and to shew it by such a modest silence *And if they will learn any thing*, and desire that what they have heard may be farther explained, *let them ask their husbands at home for it is a shame for women to speak in the church*, and renounce that due subordination which God hath enjoined *Note*, (1) If it be the woman's duty to learn in subjection, it is the husband's duty equally to maintain his superiority by shewing himself able to inform her (2) Modesty is a woman's greatest ornament, and in them all boldness is peculiarly shocking

36 What? came the word of God out from you?
or came it unto you only? 37 ᶻ If any man think
himself to be a prophet, or spiritual, let him acknow-
ledge that the things that I write unto you are the
commandments of the Lord 38 But if any man be
ignorant, let him be ignorant 39 Wherefore, bre-
thren, ᵃ covet to prophesy, and forbid not to speak with
tongues. 40 ᵇ Let all things be done decently, and in
order

ᶻ 2 Cor x 7 1 John iv 6 ᵃ Chap xii 31 Ver 1 ᵇ Chap xi 34

v 36—40 The apostle closes his discourse with warmth on this head *What* mean you by your irregular behaviour? *Came the word of God out from you? or came it unto you only?* Are you the mother church? ought you to set up yourselves as oracles and are you to pay no respect to the usages of other churches, as if your own was infallible? how intolerably assuming is such behaviour? *If any man think himself a prophet, and spiritual, let him* prove the truth of the inspiration which he challenges, by subscribing to these truths, and *acknowledge that the things that I write unto you are the commandments of the Lord*, since no man, truly under the influence of the Spirit, can possibly contradict what that Spirit, speaking in his apostles, dictates *but if any man be ignorant*, and obstinately refuses to submit to these commands, *let him be ignorant*, treated with deserved contempt, and left to follow the wilful blindness and perverseness of his own heart *Wherefore brethren*, on the whole, *covet to prophesy*, as the most excellent gift, *and forbid not to speak with tongues*, which are useful when managed according to the manner above prescribed And for a general rule in all things pertaining to the publick worship, *let all things be done decently, and in order*, and let every indecency and irregularity be banished from the house of God *Note*, (1) They who continue wilfully ignorant of, or obstinately reject the commandments of the Lord, evidently shew by whose spirit they are led (2) When a man hates the light, he is justly abandoned to the darkness he hath chosen (3) In the public worship of God all the service should be rational, composed, orderly, edifying

CHAP XV.

In this chapter the apostle treats of the resurrection of the dead. 1 *He establishes the certainty of our Saviour's resurrection*, ver. 1—11 2 *He from this truth sets himself to refute those who said there is no resurrection of the dead*, ver 12—20 3 *From our Saviour's resurrection he establishes the resurrection of the dead, and confirms the Corinthians in the belief of it by some other considerations*, ver 21—35 4 *He answers an objection against this truth, and takes an occasion thence to shew what a vast change will be made in the bodies of believers at the resurrection*, ver 36—51. 5 *He informs us what a change will be made in them that shall be living at the sound of the last trumpet, and the complete conquest the just shall then obtain over death and the grave*, ver 52—57 *And*, 6 *Sums up the argument with a very serious exhortation to Christians to be resolved and diligent in their Lord's service, because they know they shall be so gloriously rewarded by him*, ver 58

1 MOREOVER, brethren, I declare unto you
the gospel ᵃ which I preached unto you, which
also you have received, and ᵇ wherein ye stand, 2 ᶜ By
which also ye are saved, if ye † keep in memory what
I preached unto you, ᵈ unless ye have believed in vain
3 For I delivered unto you first of all, ᵉ that which I
also received, how that Christ died for our sins ᶠ accord-
ing to the scriptures 4 And that he was buried, and
ᵍ that he rose again the third day according to the scrip-
tures. 5 And that ʰ he was seen of Cephas, then ⁱ of
the twelve. 6 After that, ᵏ he was seen of above five
hundred brethren at once of whom the greater part re-
main unto this present, but some are fallen asleep. 7
After that, he was seen of James, then of all the apo-
stles 8 And ˡ last of all he was seen of me also, as of
one born out of due time 9 For ᵐ I am the least of the
apostles, that am not meet to be called an apostle, be-
cause ⁿ I persecuted the church of God. 10 But ᵒ by
the grace of God I am what I am and ᵖ his grace which
was bestowed upon me was not in vain, but ᑫ I laboured
more abundantly than they all ʳ yet not I, but the grace
of God which was with me 11 Therefore whether *it
were* I or they, so we preach, and so ye believed.

ᵃ Acts xvii. 4 ᵇ Rom v 2 2 Cor i 24 ᶜ Rom i. 16. Chap. i. 21 † Or hold fast Heb. x 23 ᵈ Gal iii 4. ᵉ Chap. xi. 23 ᶠ Isa. liii 5. & Dan ix 26 1 Pet ii 24 ᵍ Ps xvi 10 Isa liii. 10 Hos vi 2 Mat xii. 40 Acts xiii 33. & xxvi 22 23, 1 Pet i 11 ʰ Luke xxiv 34 ⁱ John xx 24 ᵏ Mat xxvi 32 ˡ Acts ix 4 ᵐ Eph iii 8 ⁿ Acts viii. 3 ix 1 1 Tim i 13 ᵒ Eph ii 8 ᵖ 2 Cor xi 23 ᑫ Acts xx 19 20 Rom xv 19. 2 Cor xi 23, ʳ Mat x 20. 2 Cor iii 5 Phil ii 13. 1 Tim i 12

v 1—11 The resurrection of the dead being a chief article of the Christian faith, the apostle here asserts and establishes the doctrine, in opposition to some false teachers who had attempted to undermine and overturn this glorious truth, 2 *Tim* ii 17, 18

1 He reminds them of that gospel which he had formerly preached unto them, which they had received from his lips, and in the faith of which they had hitherto persevered *By which also*, he adds, *ye are saved* with an everlasting salvation, *if ye keep in memory*, or *hold fast, what I preached unto you*, as ye certainly will, *unless ye have believed in vain*, taking up with mere notions, and resting in outward profession, without having ever really the root of the matter in you *For I delivered unto you first of all*, or among the most capital points of the Christian faith, and as the foundation on which all our hopes in time and eternity are built, *that which I also received* by immediate revelation, *how that Christ died for our sins according to the scriptures*, which had foretold his substitution and sufferings in the sinner's stead, *and that he was buried*, having truly tasted of death, he was laid in the grave, *and that he rose again the third day according to the scriptures*, being delivered for our offences, he was raised again for our justification, and in his resurrection we have an earnest of our own, sin, which was the cause of death, being by him done away *And* of the fact of his being risen we have the most authentic evidence, as I have told you, *that he was seen of Cephas, then of the twelve*, which name they bore, though their original number, by the apostacy of Judas and the absence of Thomas, was not complete *After that he was seen of above five hundred brethren at once; of whom the greater part remain unto this present, but some are fallen asleep* in Jesus *After that he was seen of James*, the brother or near kinsman of the

Lord;

Lord, *then of all the apoſtles*, all of whom were ready to ſeal their teſtimony with their blood, men, who could not be deceived themſelves, nor could be under the leaſt temptation of deceiving others, when they expected nothing but ſuffering and death in every tremendous ſhape for their fidelity *And laſt of all he was ſeen of me alſo*, that I might be an eye-witneſs of his reſurrection, when called in ſo miraculous a way to the office and honour of an apoſtle Hereupon,

2 He makes a beautiful digreſſion, with the deepeſt humility acknowledging his own unworthineſs, and Chriſt's rich grace in calling and qualifying him for the work of apoſtleſhip He was ſeen of me, *as of one born out of due time*, deſpicable as an abortive fœtus, and brought forth with violent pangs *for I am the leaſt of the apoſtles*, utterly unworthy of the high honour, and laſt called to it, *that am not meet to be called an apoſtle*, but deſerved to have an eternal brand of infamy ſtamped upon me, *becauſe I perſecuted the church of God But by the grace of God*, his amazingly rich and boundleſs grace, a happy alteration is wrought in me, and *I am what I am*, have obtained mercy, and been called not only to the faith of the goſpel, but to the dignity of an apoſtle, *and his grace which was beſtowed upon me was not in vain, but* wrought moſt effectually, ſo that under the influence of it *I laboured more abundantly than they all*, undergoing greater hardſhips, expoſed to greater dangers, and with the moſt unwearied diligence ſpreading the goſpel through the world *Yet not I* tho' conſtrained to vindicate my character, I impute nothing to myſelf, *but to the grace of God which was with me*, enabling me for his work, and crowning it with ſucceſs *Therefore, whether it were I or they, ſo we preach, and ſo ye believed* all of us bore the ſame teſtimony to a crucified and riſen Redeemer, and you profeſſed to make him your whole dependance for pardon, grace, life, and ſalvation *Note*, (1) A gracious ſoul remembers with deep humility thoſe ſad days when he lived in rebellion againſt God (2) Whatever we are or do, to the grace of God alone we are indebted for it, and he muſt have the glory (3) All true miniſters of Jeſus bring one meſſage, determined to know nothing but Chriſt, and him crucified, glorified, for he is all, and in all

12 Now if Chriſt be preached that he roſe from the
dead, [s] how ſay ſome among you that there is no reſur-
rection of the dead? 13 But if there be no reſurrection
of the dead, [t] then is Chriſt not riſen 14 And if Chriſt
be not riſen, then *is* our preaching vain, and your faith
is alſo vain 15 Yea, and we are found falſe witneſſes
of God, becauſe [u] we have teſtified of God, that he
raiſed up Chriſt whom he raiſed not up, if ſo be that
the dead riſe not 16 For if the dead riſe not, then is
not Chriſt raiſed: 17 And if Chriſt be not raiſed,
your faith *is* vain, [x] ye are yet in your ſins 18 Then
they alſo which are fallen aſleep in Chriſt are periſhed
19 If in this life only we have hope in Chriſt, [y] we are
of all men moſt miſerable

s Acts xvii 32 2 Tim ii 18
t John xiv 19. 2 Cor iv 14 1 Theſ iv 14.
u Acts ii 24, 32 & xiii 30.
x Acts v 31 Rom iv 25
y 2 Tim iii 12.

v 12—19 Having proved the certainty of Chriſt's reſurrection, he proceeds to ſhew the certainty of ours, refuting the opinion of thoſe heretical teachers, who ſuggeſted that it was impoſſible, or that Chriſt did not riſe in a *public capacity*, as the head and firſt fruits of his redeemed people *Now if Chriſt be preached that he roſe from the dead, how ſay ſome among you that there is no reſurrection of the dead?* which, if it were true, then the following abſurdities muſt be admitted

1 *If there be no reſurrection of the dead, then is Chriſt not riſen*, notwithſtanding all the prophecies, and the undoubted teſtimony of ſo many unexceptionable witneſſes

2 *If Chriſt be not riſen, then is our preaching vain*, uſeleſs, and unprofitable, the reſurrection of Jeſus being the grand truth on which the whole goſpel depends, *and your faith is alſo vain*, the doctrine on which it is built would have no ſolid foundation, and the hopes you derive from thence muſt diſappoint and deceive you *Yea, and*, on this ſuppoſition, *we are found falſe witneſſes of God*, and muſt have made uſe of his ſacred name to ſupport a moſt impious falſhood, *becauſe we have teſtified of God*, profeſſing to act by his authority, and under his commiſſion, *that he raiſed up Chriſt* to a glorious and immortal life, in token of his acceptance of his undertaking, as the reward of his ſufferings, and as the head of his redeemed people, who ſhould follow him into his kingdom *whom he raiſed not up, if ſo be that the dead riſe not for it is evident, if the dead riſe not, then is not Chriſt*, who was once numbered among the dead, *raiſed and if Chriſt be not raiſed, your faith is vain*, and all the hopes ariſing from him are deluſive *ye are yet in your ſins*, under the guilt and condemnation of them for as there is no atonement for ſin, but that which he offered, and on his reſurrection the acceptance of his ſacrifice depended, if he had continued in the grave, and ſeen corruption, we muſt have ſunk into deſpair, and concluded his oblation unſatiſfactory, nor could we have expected, that he who remained himſelf the priſoner of death, ſhould ever be able to deliver us from the power of it

3 *Then they alſo which are fallen aſleep in Chriſt are periſhed*, this being the neceſſary conſequence of the above horrid ſuppoſition, for if Chriſt be not riſen, then hope in him is vain, and then, though they died martyrs for his cauſe, they have departed with a lie in their right hand, and are loſt for ever, than which thought nothing can be more ſhocking or diſcouraging to ſurviving Chriſtians

4 *If* this were the caſe, that *in this life only we have hope in Chriſt*, and after death have nothing to look for, *we*, who are Chriſtians by profeſſion, and eſpecially the miniſters of Chriſt, who ſtand moſt expoſed to perſecution and all kinds of ſuffering for his ſake, *are of all men moſt miſerable*, foregoing all the comforts and advantages of this life, and wading through a ſea of difficulties and trials and how abſurd would this be, if after death we had no reſpect to the recompenſe of reward, and expected not a joyful reſurrection! and who would ever ſeek to be crucified unto the world, and the world unto him, if he looked no farther than the grave, and hoped for nothing in eternity?

20 But [z] now is Chriſt riſen from the dead, *and* [a] be-
come the firſt-fruits of them that ſlept 21 For ſince
[b] by man *came* death, [c] by man *came* alſo the reſurrection
of the dead 22 For as in Adam all die, even ſo in
Chriſt ſhall all be made alive 23 But [d] every man in
his own order Chriſt the firſt-fruits, afterward they
that are Chriſt's, at his coming 24 Then *cometh* the
end, when he ſhall have delivered up the kingdom to
God, even the Father, when [e] he ſhall have put down
all rule and all authority and power 25 For he muſt
reign [f] till he hath put all enemies under his feet 26
[g] The laſt enemy *that* ſhall be deſtroyed *is* death 27
For [h] he hath put all things under his feet But when
he ſaith all things are put under *him*, *it is* manifeſt that
he is excepted which did put all things under him 28
And when [i] all things ſhall be ſubdued unto him, then
[k] ſhall the Son alſo himſelf be ſubject unto him that put
all things under him, that God may be all in all 29
Elſe what ſhall they do which are baptized for the dead,
if the dead riſe not at all? why are they then baptized
for the dead? 30 And [l] why ſtand we in jeopardy
every hour? 31 I proteſt by [m] your rejoicing which
I have in Chriſt Jeſus our Lord, [n] I die daily 32 If
after the manner of men [o] I have fought with beaſts at
Epheſus, what advantageth it me, if the dead riſe not?
[p] let us eat and drink, for to morrow we die 33 Be
not deceived [q] Evil communications corrupt good
manners 34 [r] Awake to righteouſneſs, and ſin not,
for ſome have not the knowledge of God: [s] I ſpeak
this to your ſhame.

z Ver 4
a Acts xxvi 23 Col i 18 Rev i 5
b Gen iii [illegible] Rom v [illegible]
c John xi 25
d 1 Theſ iv 16
e Dan vii 14 1 Tim vi 15
f Pſ cx 1 Eph i 22 Heb x 13
g 2 Tim i 10 Heb ii 14 Rev xx 14
h Pſ viii 6 Mat xxviii 18 Heb ii 8
i Phil iii 21
k Chap iii 23 & xi 3
l Gal v 11
m 1 Theſ ii 19
n Rom viii 36 Chap iv 9 2 Cor i 8 & iv 10.
o Acts xix 28
p Iſa xxii 13 & lvi 12 Wiſd ii 6
q Pſ xviii 26 Prov xiii 20 Gal v 9
r Rom xiii 11 Eph v 14
s Chap vi 5

v 20—34 The certainty of Chriſt's reſurrection being proved, and the glaring abſurdities demonſtrated which muſt follow from a contrary ſuppoſition, the apoſtle paſſes on to the bleſſed effects of Chriſt's reſurrection, as enſuring ours, which he proves,

1 Becauſe *Chriſt is riſen from the dead, and become the firſt fruits of them that ſlept*, and ſhall ſleep in him He is *the firſt-begotten from the dead*, and *the firſt-born of many brethren*, whom he ſhall bring unto glory, and his reſurrection is the pledge and earneſt that all his redeemed ſhall live with him for ever God in raiſing him up hath given them aſſurance, that they ſhall be bleſſed and gathered in with him in their ſeaſon *For ſince*, or becauſe, *by one man came death*, which followed on the firſt ſin, *by man came alſo the reſurrection of the dead*, by the ſecond man, the Lord from heaven *For as in Adam*, our common parent, and covenant-head, *all die*, involved in his guilt, and expoſed to death, ſpiritual, temporal, and eternal, *ſo in Chriſt*, the other covenant head of his redeemed, *ſhall all* thoſe, whoſe ſins he bore in his own body on the tree, *be made alive*, by virtue of their union with him, raiſed to a life of grace here, and to a life of glory hereafter *But every man in his own order*, (τάγματι), Chriſt and his members ſhall each in their time, rank, and order, riſe in glory *Chriſt the firſt fruits*, who conſecrate the harveſt, and is the pledge of our reſurrection; *afterwards they that are Chriſt's, at his coming*, his peculiar people, whoſe eternal redemption he hath compleated

2 The apoſtle proves we muſt riſe, becauſe death is among thoſe enemies, which the exalted Mediator ſhall deſtroy *Then cometh the end* of the world, and of all the ſorrows of the faithful, *when*, having gathered in all his redeemed, and not one of them being wanting, *he ſhall have delivered up the kingdom to God, even the Father*, that mediatorial kingdom, the peculiar adminiſtration of which hath been entruſted to him as the Son of man *when he ſhall have put down all rule, and all authority and power*, aboliſhing every form of civil and eccleſiaſtical government, and ſubduing every enemy, human or diabolical, that tyrannized over his people, *for he muſt reign*, as Mediator, *till he hath put all enemies under his feet. The laſt enemy that ſhall be deſtroyed, is death*,

death, when the dead bodies of his people ſhall be raiſed to immortal life, no more to ſee corruption *For he*, even God the Father, *hath put all things under his feet*, and appointed him to be head over all things to his church *But when he ſaith all things are put under him, it is manifeſt that* this refers only to all *created beings*, and that *he is excepted which did put all things under him*, for God himſelf can be ſubject to none *And when all things ſhall be ſubdued unto him*, and the ends of his mediatorial kingdom anſwered in the compleat ſalvation of his people, both in body and ſoul, *then ſhall the Son alſo himſelf be ſubject unto him that put all things under him*, he will then reſign the peculiar adminiſtration committed to him, ſurrendering himſelf as the head of his church, and the members of his body myſtical, into his Father's hands, to receive thoſe eternal rewards which are due to him in virtue of his finiſhed work, *that God may be all in all* and henceforth the delegated power and authority of Jeſus, as Mediator, ſhall ceaſe, and the one glorious God, the Father, Son, and the Holy Ghoſt, ſhall be the immediate fountain of dominion and bleſſedneſs to the church triumphant for ever

3 He argues the certainty of the reſurrection from the very baptiſm of Chriſtians *Elſe what ſhall they do which are baptized*? if there be no reſurrection, how abſurd and ſtrange would it be to take up the Chriſtian profeſſion, when, if they had nothing in proſpect after death, and here ſtood expoſed to every miſery, and the danger of daily martyrdom, they would ſeem merely baptized *for the dead*, and to be of all men moſt miſerable, *if the dead riſe not at all Why are they then baptized for the dead*? who with ſuch a proſpect would ever be prevailed on to embrace Chriſtianity? *And why ſtand we in jeopardy every hour*, and ready to ſeal our teſtimony with our blood, if we had not the glorious hope of a better reſurrection? *I proteſt by your rejoicing which I have in Chriſt Jeſus*, by all the comforts of Chriſtianity, and as ſurely as that Spirit lives who is the author of them, *I die daily*, living continually in the neareſt views and expectations of martyrdom *If after the manner of men I have fought with beaſts at Epheſus*, encountering men brutiſh and ſavage in their tempers, and have expoſed myſelf to conflicts as dangerous as thoſe which the condemned criminals ſuſtain, when obliged to encounter wild beaſts in the public theatres, *what advantageth it me*, what benefit could I reap from ſuch perilous adventures, or what could ever induce me thus to hazard my life, *if the dead riſe not*? Surely if this was the caſe, that nothing was to be hoped for after the grave, it would be our wiſdom rather to adopt the principles of Epicurus, than of Chriſtianity, and to ſay, *Let us eat and drink, for to-morrow we die*, and rather enjoy preſent pleaſure, than ſuffer needleſs pain, if there were no hereafter, and death put an end to us for ever *Note*, (1) Nothing but the proſpects of eternity can poſſibly engage any to the practice of Chriſtianity 'Till we have realizing views by faith of the things not ſeen, it is impoſſible we ſhould truly take up the croſs (2) One great ſupport in ſuffering, is a reſpect to the recompenſe of the reward

4 The apoſtle cloſes with a ſolemn caution *Be not deceived* by thoſe falſe teachers who endeavour to ſap the foundation of your hopes *Evil communications corrupt good manners*, the bad principles of thoſe ſeducers could not but produce immoral practice, and to be connected and intimate with ſuch men was dangerouſly infectious *Note*, Bad company ſhould be ſhunned as the plague *Awake* then *to righteouſneſs*, be on your guard, and ſee that ye walk as becomes your holy profeſſion *for* I perceive by theſe dangerous doctrines which are broached among you, that *ſome of you have not the knowledge of God*, and of his mind and will, as revealed in his goſpel *I ſpeak this to your ſhame*, that men of ſuch bad principles and corrupt converſation ſhould be among you, permitted as teachers, or ſuffered to communicate with the church as members *Note*, We are blameable not only for the evils we commit ourſelves, but for thoſe which we connive at in others

t Ezek. xxxvii. 3 35 But ſome man will ſay, t How are the dead raiſed
up? and with what body do they come? 36 Thou
u John xii. 24 fool, u that which thou ſoweſt is not quickened except
it die 37 And that which thou ſoweſt, thou ſoweſt
not that body that ſhall be, but bare grain, it may
chance of wheat, or of ſome other *grain* 38 But God
giveth it a body as it hath pleaſed him, and to every
ſeed his own body 39 All fleſh *is* not the ſame fleſh
but *there is* one *kind of* fleſh of men, another fleſh of
beaſts, another of fiſhes, *and* another of birds 40 *There
are* alſo celeſtial bodies, and bodies terreſtrial but the
glory of the celeſtial *is* one, and the *glory* of the terreſtrial
is another 41 There is one glory of the ſun, and another
glory of the moon, and another glory of the ſtars,
x Dan. xii. 3. Matt. xiii. 43 y Phil. iii. 21 for *one* ſtar differeth from *another* ſtar in glory 42 x So
alſo *is* the reſurrection of the dead y It is ſown in corruption,
it is raiſed in incorruption 43 It is ſown in
diſhonour, it is raiſed in glory it is ſown in weakneſs,
it is raiſed in power 44 It is ſown a natural body, it
is raiſed a ſpiritual body There is a natural body, and
there is a ſpiritual body 45 And ſo it is written,
z The firſt man Adam was made a living ſoul, the laſt z Gen. ii. 7
Adam *was made* a a quickening ſpirit 46 Howbeit, a John v. 21
that *was* not firſt which is ſpiritual, but that which is natural,
and afterward that which is ſpiritual 47 The Phil. iii. 21
firſt man *is* b of the earth, c earthy the ſecond man *is* b Gen. ii. 19
the Lord d from heaven 48. e As *is* the earthy, ſuch c John iii. 31
are they alſo that are earthy and as *is* the heavenly, d John iii. 31
ſuch *are* they alſo that are heavenly 49 And as f we e Phil. iii. 6
have born the image of the earthy, g we ſhall alſo bear f Gen. v. 3
the image of the heavenly g 2 Cor. iii. 18 1 John iii. 2

v 35—49 Two plauſible objections againſt the reſurrection are here ſuggeſted (1) *How are the dead raiſed up*? what power is ſufficient for ſuch a work, to recover the ſcattered atoms? and, (2) *With what body do they come*? with the ſame identical particles, or in ſome other ſhape and form In anſwer to the objector, the apoſtle replies, *Thou fool* Probably the perſons who oppoſed the doctrine of the reſurrection pretended to high attainments in ſcience, and to reaſon as philoſophers, but they proved their ignorance, rather than their wiſdom, and erred, not knowing the ſcriptures, nor the power of God

1 *That which thou ſoweſt is not quickened except it die* The ſame power therefore that every year raiſes from under the clod, where the ſeed was ſown and corrupted, a plenteous harveſt, can raiſe from the grave the body which hath returned to its duſt again, and it would be as abſurd to object againſt the *poſſibility* of the one as the other

2 As to the *manner* of the reſurrection, *and with what body* we ſhall come from the grave, to continue the ſimilitude, I anſwer, *That which thou ſoweſt, thou ſoweſt not that body that ſhall be, but bare grain*, without any of that rich cloathing which afterward it produces, the blade, the ear, and then the full corn in the ear, *it may chance of wheat, or of ſome other grain*, that dies and revives again *but God giveth it a body as it hath pleaſed him, and to every ſeed his own body*, ſo ordering it in infinite wiſdom, that every ſeed produces its own ſpecies In quality indeed the reſurrection-body will differ from the preſent, though in identity of perſon the ſame Nor is this ſtrange, when we ſee out of the ſame materials, that bodies of very different qualities are formed *All fleſh is not the ſame fleſh but there is one kind of fleſh of men, another fleſh of beaſts, another of fiſhes, and another of birds*, the ſubſtance is originally the ſame, though by divine power wonderfully diverſified in quality *There are alſo celeſtial bodies, and bodies terreſtrial*, *but* though all formed of the firſt created matter, they greatly differ in excellence, *the glory of the celeſtial is one, and the glory of the terreſtrial is another* Such difference will there be between the preſent and the reſurrection-body, as between a clod and a ſtar *There is one glory of the ſun, and another glory of the moon, and another glory of the ſtars, for one ſtar differeth from another ſtar in glory*, is of greater magnitude, and ſhines with greater ſplendor, *ſo alſo is the reſurrection of the dead* we are raiſed by the ſame divine power as the corn vegetates, and that almighty hand which modifies the ſame matter in the different bodies around us, can make the like glorious difference between our preſent and our reſurrection body, though the manner *how* may be to us inconceivable *It is ſown in corruption*, from the day of its generation till it is putrefied in the duſt, *it is raiſed in incorruption*, incapable of putrefaction or diſſolution *It is ſown in diſhonour*, in life full of defilement, covered with ſhame, in death loathſome and moſt contemptible, *it is raiſed in glory*, like unto Chriſt's glorious body, ſhining as the ſtars for ever and ever *It is ſown in weakneſs*, is at preſent liable to a thouſand infirmities, pain, wearineſs, ſickneſs, accidents, and death, and in the grave muſt be a prey for worms *it is raiſed in power*, vigorous and active, fit to join the immortal ſoul, and without wearineſs to ſerve God in his temple day and night without ceaſing for ever *It is ſown a natural body*, that needs the conſtant ſupport of meat, and drink, and ſleep, like the beaſts that periſh *it is raiſed a ſpiritual body*, requiring none of theſe animal refreſhments, and will be like the angels *There is a natural body*, ſuch as we now poſſeſs, *and there is a ſpiritual body*, ſuited to the celeſtial world which is the inheritance of the ſaints *And ſo it is written, The firſt man Adam*, from whom we derive our preſent body, *was made a living ſoul*, was endued with animal life, and required all thoſe ſupports which we do *the laſt Adam*, the Lord Jeſus, our ſecond covenant-head and repreſentative, *was made a quickening ſpirit*, poſſeſſing life in himſelf, and the fountain of it to his people, having ſince his reſurrection a ſpiritual body, and by virtue of his power, and our union with him, he ſhall faſhion our bodies like his own *Howbeit, that was not firſt which is ſpiritual, but that which is natural, and afterward that which is ſpiritual* Adam's animal body was firſt, Chriſt's ſpiritual body afterward, and ſuch is the order alſo eſtabliſhed for us, firſt to bear the natural, then to receive the ſpiritual body *The firſt man was of the earth*, formed from the clay, and by his ſin he became *earthy*, returning to the duſt from whence he came *The ſecond man*, our better repreſentative,

1 t,

tive, *is the Lord from heaven*, coming from thence to take our nature upon him, is now returned thither with this nature glorified, and we expect him to come from thence to make us like himself *As is the earthy, such are they also that are earthy*, as Adam's body was, so must ours be, who sprung from him, mortal and corruptible, *and as is the heavenly, such are they also that are heavenly*, as many as are born from above, and made partakers of a divine nature, shall be conformed in their bodies to their Lord, and shall shortly be glorified together *And as we have born the image of the earthy*, by nature the children of corruption, sprung from a fallen parent, and like him must return to dust, *we shall also bear the image of the heavenly*, as many as are by faith united to Jesus, and renewed in the spirit of their mind, shall bear shortly his bright image in their bodies as well as soul for ever

50 Now this I say, brethren, that [h] flesh and blood
cannot inherit the kingdom of God, neither doth cor-
ruption inherit incorruption 51 Behold, I shew you a
mystery, [i] We shall not all sleep, but we shall all be
changed, 52 In a moment, in the twinkling of an
eye, at the last trump (for [k] the trumpet shall sound) and
the dead shall be raised incorruptible, and we shall be
changed 53 For this corruptible must put on incor-
ruption, and this mortal *must* put on immortality 54
So when this corruptible shall have put on incorruption,
and [l] this mortal shall have put on immortality, then
shall be brought to pass the saying that is written,
[m] Death is swallowed up in victory 55 [n] O death,
where *is* thy sting? O † grave, where *is* thy victory?
56 The sting of death is sin, and [o] the strength of sin *is*
the law. 57 But thanks *be* to God, [p] which giveth us
the victory through our Lord Jesus Christ 58 [q] There-
fore, my beloved brethren, [r] be ye stedfast, unmoveable,
always abounding in the work of the Lord, forasmuch
[s] as ye know that your labour is not in vain in the Lord

h John iii … Ch … 1 Cor … 1 Thes iv 15—17
k Mat xxiv 31 John … 1 Thes iv 16
l Cor v 4
m Isa xxv 8 Heb … x 14
n Hos xiii 14
† Or Hades
o Rom … 13, & vii 5
p Rom … 1 John v 4
q 1 Pet iii …
r 2 Cor … 2
s Eph vi 10.

v 50—58 The apostle here,

1 Gives the reason of the change which he had described *Now this I say, brethren, that flesh and blood*, such as our bodies are at present, *cannot inherit the kingdom of God*, they are unable to bear the eternal weight of glory, and incapable of tasting the delights, or being employed in the services of that blest world to which we go *Neither doth corruption inherit incorruption* The body must be refined from its corruptible dross, before it can enter upon or enjoy the incorruptible inheritance

2 He informs them of a secret unknown to them *Behold, I shew you a mystery, we shall not all sleep* in the dust, *but we shall all be changed*, on as many of his people as shall be found alive at Christ's last appearing, a change will pass equivalent to death and resurrection, *in a moment, in the twinkling of an eye, at the last trump*, when the voice of Jesus shall awake the dead *For the trumpet shall sound, and the dead shall be raised incorruptible, and we shall be changed*, our bodies undergoing a happy alteration in their qualities, though preserving their identity, *for this corruptible* body, which we carry about, *must put on incorruption, and this mortal must put on immortality*, that we may be capable of enjoying that celestial happiness for which we are designed

3 When this awful season comes, then shall death be for ever abolished. *So when this corruptible shall have put on incorruption, and this mortal shall have put on immortality, then shall be brought to pass the saying that is written*, Isa xxv 8 *Death is swallowed up in victory* And that king of terrors shall be so utterly destroyed, that he shall never more be able to lift his arm against one of the redeemed, and, in the prospect of this glorious day, the faithful soul can even now antedate his eternal triumphs, and exulting, cry, *O death, where is thy sting?* I defy it *O grave, where is thy victory?* I rise immortal, and tread thee beneath my feet for ever

4 The ground of the believer's triumph is here declared *The sting of death is sin*, this arms the monster with all his terrors, *and the strength of sin is the law*, binding over the transgressor to a future judgment, and not merely denouncing bodily death as the wages of sin, but passing sentence of eternal death, and consigning body and soul to hell *But thanks be to God which giveth us the victory through Jesus Christ our Lord* In his adored name we lift up our banners, in his righteousness we make our boast, since he hath died in our stead, he hath led our captivity captive, though we see corruption in the grave, death cannot hold dominion over us, we shall rise glorious and immortal, and, through our dear Redeemer's power and grace, come and reign with him in glory everlasting *Note*, (1) Death is no longer dreadful when the sting of sin through the atoning blood is taken out of the conscience We shall find in the grave the golden gates of life and immortality, which open into the paradise of God (2) That which will be the subject of our everlasting praises, should now be the matter of our songs, and since the victory is actually obtained, we should antedate the triumphs of eternity, and to our Redeemer's honour adore him in the full assurance of the conquest which he hath completed

5 He closes the whole with a warm exhortation arising from the foregoing discourse *Therefore, my beloved brethren, be ye stedfast*, firm and unwavering in the faith and hope of the gospel, especially in the great doctrines of the atoning death, and resurrection of Jesus, with the blessed effects thence flowing of our immortal life and glory, *unmoveable* by any of the artifices of Satan, the craft of seducers, or the corruptions of your own hearts, founded on the rock which storms assail in vain, *always abounding in the work of the Lord*, zealously and abidingly engaged in his service, chearful and willing to undergo any sufferings, in spite of every opposition, increasing with the increase of God, *knowing*, as the most assured truth, *that your labour shall not be in vain in the Lord*, but that he, to whom you are by faith united as your living head of vital influence, will strengthen, uphold, and own you in life, in death, and after death, raise up your bodies to immortal life, and bestow the never-fading crown of righteousness and glory upon you, the reward, not indeed of debt, but of grace *Note*, (1) Our practice will bear pace always with the strength of our faith, the more sure and realizing our views of eternal things are, the more vigorously shall we press towards the mark for the prize of the high calling in Christ Jesus (2) It is the strongest encouragement to labour for the Lord, because we are sure to succeed in his service (3) Whatever we do or suffer for Christ, we shall never regret it in a resurrection day, and shall only then be ashamed that we have loved him no more, and served him no better

CHAP XVI

In this chapter the apostle (1) *Gives direction about some charitable collection to be made*, ver 1—5 (2) *He talks of making them a visit*, ver 6—10 (3) *He recommends Timothy to them, and tells them Apollos intended to come to them*, ver 11—13 (4) *He presses them to watchfulness, constancy charity, and to pay a due regard to all who helped him, and his fellow-labourers in their work*, ver 14—19 (5) *After salutations from others, and his own, he closes the epistle with a solemn admonition to them, and his good wishes for them*, ver 20, to the end

1 NOW concerning the [a] the collection for the saints,
[b] as I have given orders to the churches of Ga-
latia, even so do ye 2 Upon † the first *day* of the
week, let every one of you lay by him in store, as *God*
hath prospered him, that there be no gatherings when I
come 3 And when I come, whomsoever you shall ap-
prove by *your* letters, [c] them will I send to bring your
‡ liberality unto Jerusalem 4 And if it be meet that
I go also, they shall go with me

a Acts xi 29 Rom xv 25 & xv 26
b Gal i 2
† Or one of the sabbaths Luke xxiv 1 Acts xx 7 Rev 10
c 2 Cor viii 16
‡ Or free gift

v 1—4 The church at Jerusalem having undergone peculiar oppression and sufferings, and many of the saints being reduced to great poverty, the Gentile brethren, at the apostle's instigation, generously contributed for their relief

Now as concerning the collection for the saints in Judea, *as I have given order to the churches of Galatia, even so do ye* Since in wealth the Corinthians exceeded the Galatians, and in spiritual gifts were so eminent, it would be a shame if they came behind in benevolence and charity *Upon the first day of the week*, the day held sacred among Christians, and hallowed by their solemn assemblies, *let every one of you lay by him in store*, contributing to the collection for the poor, *as God hath prospered him*, each according to their ability, the rich more abundantly, and they who have little, chearfully giving a portion out of that little, *that there be no gatherings when I come* And, being thus in readiness *when I come, whomsoever you shall approve by your letters*, and recommend as faithful men, *them will I send to bring your liberality unto Jerusalem*, concurring in your recommendation *And if it be meet*, and judged necessary for this benevolent design, *that I go also, they shall go with me* *Note*, (1) Every Christian is bound, according to his ability, to minister to the necessities of his brethren (2) All our success comes from God's gracious providence, and is gratefully to be acknowledged (3) The more we receive from God, the more are we called, as good stewards, to improve it for his glory, and the advantage of our brethren

5 Now I will come unto you, [d] when I shall pass
through Macedonia (for I do pass through Macedonia)
6 And it may be that I will abide, yea and winter with
you, that ye may bring me on my journey whithersoever
I go 7 For I will not see you now by the way, but
I trust to tarry a while with you, [f] if the Lord permit
8 But I will tarry at Ephesus until Pentecost 9 For
a great door and effectual is opened unto me, and [h] *there
are* many adversaries

d Acts xix 21 2 Cor i 16.
e Acts xv 3 & xx 38 … vii 5
f Acts xviii 21 Jam iv 15
g Acts xiv 27 2 Cor ii 12 Col iv 3 Rev iii 8
h Acts … 9, 23

v 5—9 The apostle, in his own mind, had planned a visit to Corinth, of which he informs them, though Providence prevented, at this time, the execution of his design

Now I will come unto you, such is my present intention, if the Lord please, *when I shall pass through Macedonia, for I do purpose soon to pass through Macedonia And it may be that I will abide* a considerable time among you, *yea and winter with you, that ye may bring me on my journey whithersoever I go*, returning to your

former

former affection, and testifying your wonted respect for me, notwithstanding those prejudices which the false teachers have laboured to instil *For I will not see you now in the way* (ἐν παρόδῳ) to make a transient visit, which would not answer the end I propose of settling your affairs, establishing you in the truth, and enjoying your company, *but I trust to tarry a while with you, if the Lord permit*, at whose disposal I am, and by whose providence I desire ever to be directed *But I will tarry at Ephesus* (from whence he seems to have written this epistle) *until Pentecost*, either till that feast was past, or till its approach, when he intended to be at Jerusalem, a great concourse of Jews from all parts assembling there at that season And the reason for his long stay at Ephesus he gives, *for a great door and effectual is opened unto me*, a signal blessing hath attended my labours, and great multitudes are by the Spirit converted to the faith of Christ, *and*, as might be expected, *there are many adversaries*, both Jews and Gentiles, who, instigated by Satan, oppose with all their might and craft the progress of the gospel, against whom he chose personally to stand up, and boldly to vindicate the glorious cause *Note*, (1) Wherever Christ is preached successfully, there the malice and cunning of earth and hell will be exerted, to stop the rising interest of truth and godliness (2) Success in our labours is a great argument and encouragement boldly to persevere (3) Faithful ministers, instead of being daunted by outward opposition, have their zeal but the more kindled What weakens their hands and discourages their hearts, is the unfaithfulness of professors, and the unfruitfulness of their hearers

10 Now if Timotheus come, see that he may be with
you without fear for [i] he worketh the work of the
Lord, as I also *do* 11 Let [k] no man therefore despise
him but conduct him forth in peace, that he may come
unto me for I look for him with the brethren 12 As
touching *our* brother Apollos, I greatly desired him to
come unto you with the brethren but his will was not
at all to come at this time, but he will come when he
shall have convenient time

i Chap. iv. 17. Phil. ii. 20. 1 Thess. iii. 2. k 1 Tim. iv. 12. l Acts xviii. 24. & xix. 1.

v. 10—12 The apostle here,

1 Recommends Timothy to them, who was *now* on his journey to Corinth *If Timotheus come, see that he may be with you without fear* of any insult from any of the factious leaders, regard him with affection, treat him with respect, and hear him with attention *for he worketh the work of the Lord, as I also do*, zealous for the cause of the same divine master, and tried and found faithful *Let no man therefore despise him* because of his youth, slight his reproofs, or think lightly of his ministry, *but conduct him forth in peace*, give him a proof of your affection and esteem, by providing him with necessaries for his journey, and bringing him on his way, *that he may come unto me for I look for him with the brethren*, either I and the brethren here expect him, or I desire his return with the brethren who may accompany him hither *Note*, Young ministers should be encouraged, not despised, and their ministrations, though without the sanction of grey hairs, yet, seconded with the weight of zeal and piety, deserve the most serious attention

2 He informs them that Apollos declined a visit to them at present, though he had earnestly pressed him thereto *As touching our brother Apollos, I greatly desired him to come unto you with the brethren, but his will was not at all to come at this time, but he will come when he shall have convenient time* Though a party at Corinth had affected to set up Apollos in preference to Paul, the apostle entertained no jealousy of his brother-labourer, assured that he never would encourage but discountenance such a spirit of division The faithful ministers of Christ will not harbour mean distrust of each other, no, not though those who love to sow discord among brethren, endeavour to instil base suspicions On the other hand, Apollos, probably out of respect to his honoured brother Paul, declined at that time the visit, lest, in the present ill disposition of the Corinthians, it might be abused by those who wanted to make him the head of a party Though when the present feuds were subsided, he meant to go thither, and labour among them Such a spirit of love should ministers cultivate, jealous for each other's reputation as their own, and frowning on every flatterer that would attempt to raise their credit at the expence of their brother

13 [m] Watch ye, [n] stand fast in the faith, quit you
like men, [o] be strong 14 [p] Let all your things be
done with charity 15 I beseech you, brethren, (ye
know the house of Stephanas, that [q] it is the first fruits
of Achaia, and *that* they have addicted themselves to [r]
the ministry of the saints) 16 That [s] ye submit your-
selves unto such, and to every one that helpeth with *us*
and laboureth 17 I am glad of the coming of Stepha-
nas and Fortunatus, and Achaicus for [t] that which was
lacking on your part they have supplied 18 For they
have refreshed my spirit and yours therefore [u] acknow-
ledge ye them that are such

m Mat. xxiv. 42. 1 Pet. v. 8. n 1 Cor. i. 24. Phil. i. 27. & iv. 1. Col. iv. 12. 1 Thess. iii. 8. o Jude 3. p Eph. vi. 10. q Chap. xiii. 4. 7. r Rom. xvi. 5. s 2 Cor. ix. 1. t Phil. ii. 29. u 1 Tim. v. 17. Heb. xiii. 17. Chap. xi. 9. Phil. ii. 30. w 1 Thess. v. 12.

v. 13—18 The apostle proceeds,

1 To some general exhortations *Watch ye* against every enemy of your souls, especially those who would seduce you from the doctrines of truth, *stand fast in the faith*, grounded and settled in the hope of the gospel, so as never to be moved from your holy profession, *quit you like men*, with wisdom, zeal, and fidelity, in the midst of the opposition of enemies, and the snares of deceivers, *be strong* in the grace which is in Jesus Christ, exercising yourselves unto godliness, and fighting manfully under the Lord's banners, against every enemy within and without And whilst you thus shew yourselves courageous for the truth, *let all your things be done in charity*, and let the spirit of meekness temper all your zeal *Note*, (1) A Christian is compassed with enemies, he need be ever on his guard (2) When we are firmly established in the principles of the gospel, no danger or sufferings will deter us from the path of duty, (3) Charity is the great ornament of our profession, to bear with the perverseness of mistaken friends, and meekly to sustain the attacks of avowed enemies, is to be like our master

2 He commends to their particular regard the house of Stephanas *I beseech you, brethren, (ye know the house of Stephanas, that it is the first fruits of Achaia*, converted by my ministry, and whom I baptised myself, *and that they have addicted themselves to the ministry of the saints*, laying themselves out in the Lord's immediate service, and zealously employed in assisting his people to their utmost, both in their temporal and spiritual concerns) I beseech you, brethren, *that ye submit yourselves to such*, directed by them, imitating their examples, and not led away by upstart teachers, and that ye in like manner reverence, regard, and attend *to*, *every one that helpeth with us and laboureth* to promote the interests of the same divine master, and the edification of your souls

3 He testifies his satisfaction in the good account he had lately heard concerning them *I am glad of the coming of Stephanas and Fortunatus, and Achaicus, for that which was lacking on your part, they have supplied*, giving the apostle a more clear state of the matter than was conveyed in the letter they brought, and explaining things much to his satisfaction, which reports had greatly exaggerated *Note*, It is a great joy to every minister and Christian's heart to hear unfavourable reports of their brethren contradicted by those who are best acquainted with their circumstances

4 He enjoins them to respect those faithful men at their return *For they have refreshed my spirit* by their conversation, and the accounts they have given, and this cannot but afford like satisfaction to *yours therefore acknowledge ye them that are such*, and shew them that respect and regard, which their kind, candid, and charitable construction of your conduct merits at your hands *Note*, Good offices done us demand a grateful return

19 The churches of Asia salute you Aquila and
Priscilla salute you much in the Lord, with [x] the church
that is in their house 20 All the brethren greet you
[y] Greet ye one another with an holy kiss 21 [z] The
salutation of *me* Paul with mine own hand. 22 [a] If any
man love not the Lord Jesus Christ, let him be anathema,
maran atha 23 [b] The grace of our Lord Jesus Christ
be with you. 24 My love *be* with you all in Christ
Jesus. Amen

x Rom. xvi. 5. 15. 16. y Rom. xvi. 16. z Col. iv. 18. 2 Thess. iii. 17. a Gal. i. 8. 9. John. viii. b Rom. xvi. 24.

v. 19—24 St Paul closes his epistle,

1 With affectionate salutations *All the churches of Asia salute you*, cordially wishing you every blessing of the everlasting gospel *Aquila and Priscilla salute you much in the Lord, with the church that is in their house*, even all the members of that amiable family which compose a little church among themselves, and such a family is happy indeed *All the brethren salute you* with warm affection *Greet ye one another with an holy kiss The salutation of me Paul with mine own hand* And thus he signs what his amanuensis wrote from his lips, as genuine and authentic

2 He subjoins a solemn warning *If any man love not the Lord Jesus Christ*, be his eminence of station never so great, his gifts never so extraordinary, his profession never so glowing, if his heart be unsound, his principles erroneous, and his practice dishonourable to the gospel, fomenting divisions, puffed up with pride, and at bottom an apostate, *let him be anathema, maran atha*, excommunicated from the body of the faithful, and consigned over to that fearful judgment, which the righteous Lord, in the day of his appearing and glory, will inflict on such impenitent offenders *Note*, (1) It is not enough to be Christian in word and tongue, do we love the Lord Jesus Christ in sincerity? that is the question (2) None sink under heavier vengeance than those who have been false and faithless to their holy profession

3 He concludes with his usual benediction and prayer *The grace of our Lord Jesus Christ be with you*, and therein is comprehended every blessing in time and in eternity *My love be with you all in Christ Jesus* Sharply as I have been constrained to rebuke you, in him I love you affectionately, and every thing I have said flows from the most unfeigned desire to promote your present and eternal happiness *Amen!* May this be the happy issue Believe my kind intentions and regard, join with me in my prayers, and then the issue shall be peace

THE

EVANGELICAL EXPOSITOR;

OR, A

PRACTICAL COMMENT

Upon the SECOND EPISTLE of

St. Paul to the CORINTHIANS.

IN his former epistle the apostle had signified his intention of coming to Corinth as he passed through Macedonia, *chap.* xvi 6 *but being providentially hindered for some time, he writeth this second epistle to them about a year after the former, and there seem to be these two great urgent occasions.* 1 *The case of the incestuous person that lay under censure, required that with all speed he should be restored and received again into communion. This therefore he giveth directions about,* chap ii *and afterwards,* chap vii *he declareth the satisfaction he had upon the intelligence he received of their good behaviour in that affair.* 2 *There was a contribution now making for the poor saints at Jerusalem, which he exhorteth the Corinthians to join in,* chap viii *and* ix

There are divers other things very observable in this epistle, e. g. (1) *The account the apostle giveth of his labours and success in preaching the gospel in several places,* chap. ii (2) *The comparison he maketh between the Old and New Testament dispensation,* chap iii (3) *The manifold sufferings that he and his fellow-labourers met with, and the motives and encouragements for their diligence and patience,* chap iv, v. (4) *The caution he gives the Corinthians against mingling themselves with unbelievers,* chap vi (5) *The way and manner in which he justifieth himself and his apostleship from the opprobrious insinuations and accusations of false teachers that endeavoured to ruin his reputation at Corinth,* chap x, xi, xii *and throughout the whole epistle*

CHAP I

After the introduction, ver 1, 2 *the apostle begins with the narrative of his troubles and God's goodness which he had met with in Asia, by way of thanksgiving to God,* ver 3—6 *and for the edification of the Corinthians,* ver 7—11 *Then he attests his and his fellow labourers integrity,* ver 12, 13, 14 *and afterwards vindicateth himself from the imputation of levity and inconstancy,* ver 15—24

1 [a] PAUL an apostle of Jesus Christ by the will
of God, and Timothy *our* brother, unto the
church of God which is at Corinth, with
all the saints which are in all Achaia. 2
[b] Grace *be* to you, and peace from God our Father, and
from the Lord Jesus Christ. 3 [c] Blessed *be* God, even
the Father of our Lord Jesus Christ, [d] the Father of
mercies, and the God of all comfort; 4 [e] Who com-
forteth us in all our tribulation, that we may be able to
comfort them which are in any trouble, by the comfort
wherewith we ourselves are comforted of God. 5. For
as [f] the sufferings of Christ abound in us, [g] so our con-
solation also aboundeth by Christ. 6. And whether we
be afflicted, [h] *it is* for your consolation and salvation, which
is effectual in the enduring of the same sufferings which
we also suffer: or whether we be comforted, *it is* for
your consolation and salvation.

v 1—6 The apostle opens the epistle,

1 With his usual address and salutation. *Paul an apostle of Jesus Christ, by the will of God* eminently called to this high office, *and Timothy our brother*, who joins me in heartiest affection towards you, *unto the church of God which is at Corinth, with all the saints which are in all Achaia*, who in profession and practice appear to be separated from the world as the Lord's people. *Grace be to you and peace*, with all their happy fruits, *from God the Father*, the author of all our blessings, *and from the Lord Jesus Christ*, the meritorious cause of them.

2 He blesseth God for the signal mercies he had experienced. *Blessed be God, even the Father of our Lord Jesus Christ*, and who in and through him, as the divine Mediator, is now become to us *the Father of mercies, and the God of all comfort*, multiplying his pardons, showering down his benefits, and giving us spiritual, temporal, and eternal consolation through this Son of his love, *who comforteth us in all our tribulation*, by his word and Spirit bringing home the great and precious promises with power to our soul, and shedding abroad his love in our hearts, *that*, from experience of the riches of his goodness, *we may be able to comfort them that are in trouble*, whether in soul or body, *by the comfort wherewith we ourselves are comforted of God*, tenderly sympathizing with them, and suggesting the encouraging word of scripture, which, in distress, we have found reviving to our own souls. *For as the sufferings of Christ abound in us*, to whom

whom we are thus conformed, and who is still afflicted in all the affliction of his members, *so our consolation also aboundeth by Christ*, who fails not to minister supports and comforts proportionable to our sufferings *And whether we be afflicted, it is for your consolation and salvation*, it is designed for your advantage, that by our examples of patience, fortitude, and perseverance, you may be encouraged to bear up under every trial, and boldly stand fast, till your salvation is completed, *which is effectual*, and greatly promoted by such exercises of faith and patience, *in the enduring of the same sufferings which we also suffer* *or whether we be comforted*, by divine supports under our afflictions, or by seasonable deliverances from them, *it is also ordered for your consolation and salvation* *Note*, (1) All our mercies from God call for perpetual grateful acknowledgments (2) They who have been exercised with trials in their own souls and bodies, will be the most able comforters to others under the like troubles We speak best, when we speak from experience (3) Though our afflictions may be at present grievous, the time will come when we shall see peculiar reason to bless God for them, and know that they have been especially conducive to our eternal salvation (4) All our comforts flow from God in Christ, as reconciled to us in a covenant of everlasting love

i Rom v 3, 4 & viii 17 — 7 And our hope of you *is* stedfast, knowing that i as
you are partakers of the sufferings, so *shall ye be* also of
k Acts xix 23, 1 Cor xv 32 — the consolation 8 For we would not, brethren, have
you ignorant of our trouble k which came to us in Asia,
that we were pressed out of measure, above strength,
insomuch that we despaired even of life 9 But we
l Jer xvii 5, 7 — had the sentence of death in ourselves, l that we should
not trust in ourselves, but in God which raiseth the dead
10 Who delivered us from so great a death, and doth
deliver in whom we trust that he will yet deliver *us*
m Rom xv 30, Phil i 19, Philem 22 — 11 You also m helping together by prayer for us, that
n Chap iv 15 — n for the gift *bestowed* upon us by the means of many
persons, thanks may be given by many on our behalf

v 7—11 St Paul,

1 Expresses his confidence in them, *And our hope of you is stedfast*, that ye will never be discouraged by any tribulations which you see us endure, or are called to bear yourselves, *knowing, that as you are partakers of the sufferings* with us, *so shall ye be also of the consolation*, rejoicing with us here in the experience of God's love, and shortly to arrive where sorrow shall be for ever banished, and our joys will be perfected

2 He informs them what a fight of afflictions they had undergone *For we would not, brethren, have you ignorant of our trouble which came to us in Asia*, (see Acts xix xvi xix) *that we were pressed out of measure, above strength*, loaded with burdens more than our natural strength could sustain, *so that we despaired even of life*, not knowing which way to escape, and our case to all appearance desperate *But we had the sentence of death in ourselves*, and concluded we must be destroyed, the Lord in his providence suffering us to be brought to these extremities, *that we should not trust in ourselves*, feeling by experience our own utter insufficiency to help ourselves, *but in God which raiseth the dead*, whose wisdom, power, and grace alone could extricate us from our troubles, and save us from the jaws of death *Note*, The Lord suffers his people often to be reduced as it were to the last gasp, that he may convince them more deeply of their own helplessness, and magnify his grace and power more signally in their deliverance

3 He gratefully acknowledges the divine interposition *Who delivered us from so great a death*, when to human view it appeared inevitable, *and doth deliver*, in jeopardy as we stand every hour *in whom we trust that he will yet deliver us*, content to cast our care upon him, in the fullest confidence of his protection and support *You also helping together by prayer for us*, and joining in affectionate supplications on our behalf, that we may be still preserved in the midst of danger, *that for the gift* of so signal a deliverance as we have experienced, *bestowed upon us by the means of many persons*, in answer to the prayers of those faithful souls who, centered at a throne of grace, besought the Lord for us, *thanks may be given by many on our behalf*, and God glorified and praised for the mercy he hath extended towards us *Note*, (1) Past experience of God's interposition should engage us still to hope in his mercy (2) None ever trusted God and were confounded (3) We owe much to the prayers of those who interest themselves for us in their approaches to God (4) The blessings received in answer to prayer call loud for a due return of praise

12 For our rejoicing is this, the testimony of our
o Chap ii 17 & iv 2 — conscience, that o in simplicity and godly sincerity, p not
p 1 Cor ii 4, 13 — with fleshly wisdom, but by the grace of God, we have
had our conversation in the world, and more abundantly
to you wards. 13 For we write none other things unto you, than what you read or acknowledge, and I trust
you shall acknowledge even to the end 14 As also
you have acknowledged us in part, that q we are your — q Chap v 12
rejoicing, even as r ye also *are* ours in the day of the — r Phil ii 16
Lord Jesus — 1 Thess ii 19, 20

v 12—14 The apostle here,

1 Vindicates himself in general from the insinuations of his traducers *For our rejoicing is this, the testimony of our conscience, that in simplicity and godly sincerity*, maintaining a single eye to God's glory, *not with fleshly wisdom*, purposing any mean ends, or selfish designs of our own, *but by the grace of God*, having this for our governing principle, taught by his word, and guided by his Spirit, *we have had our conversation in the world, and more abundantly to you wards*, who cannot but be conscious how holily and unblameably we behaved ourselves among you, and if I have now disappointed you of my intended visit, it was no double-mindedness, but the providence of God, which prevented me *Note*, A good conscience affords always matter of real joy

2 He appeals to themselves for the truth of what he said *For we write none other things unto you than what you read or acknowledge, and I trust you shall acknowledge even to the end*, our future conversation shall, we trust, be as exemplary as the past *As also you have acknowledged us in part, that we are your rejoicing, even as ye also are ours in the day of the Lord Jesus*, when we hope to appear with you before him as the seals of our ministry, our joy and crown

15 And in this confidence I was minded to come un-
to you before, that you might have s a second benefit — s Rom i 11
16 And to pass by you into Macedonia, and to come
again out of Macedonia unto you, and of you to be
brought on my way toward Judea 17 When I there-
fore was thus minded did I use lightness? or the things
that I purpose, do I purpose according to the flesh, that
with me there should be yea, yea, and nay, nay? 18
But *as* God *is* true, our † word toward you was not yea — † Or, preaching
and nay 19 For the Son of God, Jesus Christ, who
was preached among you by us, *even* by me, and Silva-
nus, and Timotheus, was not yea and nay, but in him
was yea. 20 For all the promises of God in him *are*
yea, and in him amen, unto the glory of God by us
21 Now he which stablisheth us with you in Christ, and
t hath anointed us, *is* God 22 u Who hath also sealed — t 1 John ii 20, 27
us, and x given the earnest of the Spirit in our hearts — u Eph i 13, & iv 30, 2 Tim ii 19, Rev ii 17
23 Moreover, y I call God for a record upon my soul, — x Chap v 5, Eph i 14
that z to spare you I came not as yet unto Corinth 24 — y Rom i 9, Gal i 20
a Not for that we have dominion over your faith, but — z 1 Cor iv 21, Chap xii 20 & xiii 2, 10
are helpers of your joy for b by faith ye stand — a 1 Cor iii 5, 1 Pet v 3, b Rom xi 20

v 15—24 In answer to the insinuations of his enemies, who accused him of levity and inconstancy,

1 He avers the sincerity of his intentions at the time he gave them his promise *In the confidence* of their affection and esteem, he was fully purposed to visit them, in hopes of affording them further spiritual assistance, and not merely to call on them in his way to Macedonia, but to return from thence, and make some considerable stay among them, and then to have been helped forward on his journey by them to Jerusalem *When I therefore was thus minded, did I use lightness*, promising rashly, and altering my mind without sufficient reason? *or the things that I purpose, do I purpose according to the flesh?* was I influenced by any secular views? or did I want to flatter you, and tell you what I never intended to perform? *that with me there should be yea, yea, and nay, nay*, talking backwards and forwards to serve a turn? No Paul, as every faithful man doth, spoke the truth from his heart

2 He vindicates his doctrine, which the seducers wanted to represent as equally erroneous as his promise was deceitful, and this he doth with a solemn appeal to God *But, as God is true, our word toward you was not yea and nay*, our doctrine was not various and changeable, but uniformly the same, *for the Son of God, Jesus Christ, who was preached among you by us, even by me and Silvanus and Timotheus, was not yea and nay, but in him was yea*, the same crucified Jesus was the subject of our ministry, and we taught with perfect harmony all the glorious truths of gospel grace *for all the promises of God in him are yea, and in him amen*, infallibly certain, and invariably the same, not conditional, and depending upon any thing in our miserable selves, but everlastingly sure, flowing from the sovereign favour and love of God, purchased by the obedience to death, and ratified by the blood shedding, of the Redeemer, *unto the glory of God by us*, who by our ministrations is thus exalted in the highest

3 He mentions some of the inestimable blessings which God in Christ Jesus had bestowed (1) *Now he which stablisheth us with you in Christ is God*, we are built up in him, and, being together united to him as our living Head, nothing shall ever be able to separate us from him (2) He *hath anointed us* with the gifts and graces of his Spirit (3) He *hath also sealed us* unto the day of redemption, securing us for his own in a cove-
nant

mint of grace, and ſtamping his bleſſed image on our ſouls. (4.) He *hath given us the earneſt of the Spirit in our hearts*, ſhedding abroad his love, as the pledge of that eternal felicity whereunto we are appointed.

4. He gives a weighty reaſon for not coming at preſent to Corinth, and ſolemnly calls God to witneſs thereto, that it was out of mere tenderneſs towards them, *to ſpare* them, that he might not be obliged to inflict on the offenders condign puniſhment. But, to prevent miſtakes, he adds, *Not for that we have dominion over your faith*, we aſſume no tyrannical power, nor pretend to be lords over your conſcience, *but are helpers of your joy*, deſiring to promote your ſpiritual and eternal conſolation: *for by faith ye ſtand*, grounded not on fallible human teſtimony, but on the word of God, and therefore ſhall never be moved away from the hope of the goſpel. *Note*, They who have true faith ſhall never finally or fatally fall.

CHAP. II.

In this chapter the apoſtle proceedeth in the account of the reaſons why he did not come to Corinth, ver. 1—4. *Then he writeth concerning the inceſtuous perſon, that lay under cenſure, and giveth directions for the reſtoring him, together with the reaſons for then ſo doing*, ver. 5—11. *And afterwards informeth them of his labours and ſucceſs in preaching the goſpel in ſeveral places*, ver. 12—17.

1 BUT I determined this with myſelf, that I would
not come again to you in heavineſs. 2 For if I
make you ſorry, who is he then that maketh me glad,
but the ſame which is made ſorry by me? 3 And I
wrote this ſame unto you, leſt when I came [a] I ſhould
have ſorrow from them of whom I ought to rejoice,
[b] having confidence in you all, that my joy is *the joy* of
you all. 4 For out of much affliction and anguiſh of
heart, I wrote unto you with many tears; not that you
ſhould be grieved, but that ye might know the love
which I have more abundantly unto you.

a Chap. xii. [illegible]
b Chap. vii. [illegible]

v. 1—4. The apoſtle ſuggeſts another reaſon why he would not come now to Corinth, leſt he ſhould be compelled to exercise ſuch ſeverity on offenders as would be bitter to them and painful to himſelf; and in ſuch circumſtances it muſt be a melancholy meeting, when he muſt make thoſe ſorrowful who ſhould have made him glad; and, whilſt this was the caſe, his tender ſympathy with them muſt occaſion heavineſs to his own ſpirit. He wiſhed therefore rather that all offences might be firſt removed, for which end he had written the former letter, and that he might not be obliged to ſorrow over thoſe as impenitent, in whom he hoped to rejoice as faithful: and he would fain hope, from his confidence in their affection and regard, that *his joy* was *theirs*, and that they would be ready to remove every cauſe of uneaſineſs, and delight to make him happy. With much anguiſh of heart, and many tears, he had dictated this epiſtle, not to grieve them, but to profit them, and that his own love towards them, and jealouſy over them, might be more abundantly manifeſted. *Note*, (1.) Faithful rebuke is the trueſt mark of love. (2.) Correction is an unpleaſing though neceſſary taſk. (3.) The deſign of every reproof ſhould not be to grieve but to recover.

5 But [c] if any have cauſed grief, [d] he hath not grieved
me, but in part: that I may not overcharge you all.
6 Sufficient to ſuch a man *is* this puniſhment, [e] which
was inflicted of many. 7 So that contrariwiſe, [f] *ye ought*
rather to forgive *him*, and comfort *him*, leſt perhaps ſuch
a one ſhould be ſwallowed up with overmuch ſorrow.
8 Wherefore I beſeech you that ye would confirm *your*
love towards him. 9 For to this end alſo did I write,
that I might know the proof of you, [g] whether ye be
obedient in all things. 10 To whom ye forgive any
thing, I *forgive* alſo: for if I forgave any thing, to whom
I forgave *it*, for your ſakes *forgave I it*, in the perſon of
Chriſt; 11 [h] Leſt Satan ſhould get an advantage of us:
for we are not ignorant of [i] his devices.

c 1 Cor. v. 1. Gal. iv. [illegible]
d Chap. [illegible] 1 Cor. v. [illegible]
e 1 Cor. v. [illegible] Gal. [illegible]
f Chap. vii. 15. & x. 6.
h Luke xxii. 31. 1 Cor. vii. 5. Chap. xi. 3. 1 Pet. v. 8. Eph. vi. 11, 16. 2 Tim. ii. [illegible] Rev. ii. [illegible]

v. 5—11. The apoſtle here directs them how to behave toward the inceſtuous perſon, who had been, according to his orders, excommunicated.

1. He had been grieved *in part* that he was compelled to puniſh; but, ſince the man had teſtified his repentance, the cauſe of his ſorrow was removed: and though he had found fault with many who were puffed up, and had not mourned on this occaſion, he would not overcharge them with farther reproof, ſince they had, as a body, cleared themſelves by their obedience to his letter.

2. The puniſhment which had been inflicted on the offender was ſufficient; and, ſince he was humbled and reſtored, the ſentence of excommunication ſhould be removed. He exhorts them therefore, (1.) *to forgive* him. (2.) to *comfort* him under the deep wounds of ſhame and remorſe which he muſt have felt, leſt Satan ſhould take advantage of his diſtreſs to overwhelm him with deſpair. (3.) To *confirm* their love towards him, and receive him into their church, and into their boſom, with all the cordiality of warm affection. *Note*, We ought to be peculiarly tender of broken ſpirits, not aggravating their offences, but ſympathizing with their anguiſh.

3. This was the end the apoſtle propoſed, both in his former and preſent epiſtle, that he might have a proof of their obedience. And, to engage them to a ready compliance with his preſent exhortation, he mentions his own willingneſs to concur with them in forgiving this penitent; and, according to the divine authority delegated to him, in the name of Jeſus Chriſt he pronounced his abſolution; and this he did for their ſakes, as a freſh mark of his love to them, and to promote their welfare, leſt Satan ſhould take advantage, from any ſeverity ſhewn to this offender, to diſcourage the hearts of backſliders from returning, through deſpair of pardon, or raiſe prejudices againſt the members of the church as of an unforgiving and uncharitable ſpirit. *For we are not*, ſays he, *ignorant of his devices*, how by every method he ſtrives to obſtruct the ſucceſs of the goſpel, and diſturb the peace of the church.

12 Furthermore, [k] when I came to Troas to *preach*
Chriſt's goſpel, and [l] a door was opened unto me of the
Lord, 13 I had no reſt in my ſpirit, becauſe I found
not [m] Titus my brother: but taking my leave of them,
I went from thence into Macedonia. 14 Now thanks
be unto God, [n] which always cauſeth us to triumph in
Chriſt, and maketh manifeſt [o] the ſavour of his know-
ledge by us in every place. 15 For [p] we are unto God
a ſweet ſavour of Chriſt, in them that are ſaved, and in
them that periſh: 16 [q] To the one *we are* the ſavour
of death unto death; and to the other the ſavour of life
unto life. And [r] who *is* ſufficient for theſe things? 17
For we are not as many, which [s] corrupt the word of
God: but as of ſincerity, but as of God, in the ſight
of God ſpeak we in Chriſt.

k Acts xvi. 8. & xx. 6.
l 1 Cor. xvi. 9.
m Chap. vii. 6.
n [illegible]
o Cant. i. 3.
p 1 Cor. i. 18.
q Luke ii. 34. John ix. 39. Acts xiii. 46. 1 Pet. ii. 7, 8.
r Chap. iii. 5, 6.
s Or, adulterate. Isa. i. 22. Chap. iv. 2. 2 Pet. ii. 3.

v. 12—17. The apoſtle,

1. Acquaints them with another thing which retarded his journey to Corinth. *Furthermore, when I came to Troas, to preach Chriſt's goſpel*, that conſtant delightful theme on which I dwell, *and a door was opened unto me of the Lord*, he, who hath the hearts of all men in his hand, having given me a pleaſing proſpect of ſucceſs; yet ſo anxious was I to hear of you, that *I had no reſt in my ſpirit, becauſe I found not Titus my brother*, whom I expected to arrive there from you: *but, taking my leave of them, I went from thence into Macedonia*, where I met him, and heard with delight the account which he brought from you.

2. Having hinted his ſucceſsful labours at Troas, he breaks forth into thankſgiving to God. *Now thanks be unto God, which always cauſeth us to triumph*, in the midſt of all our tribulations raiſing us ſuperior to our foes, and filling us with exultation and joy *in Chriſt* the rock of our confidence, *and maketh manifeſt the ſavour of his knowledge by us in every place*, diffuſing his goſpel as fragrance, and cauſing our labours to be acceptable to himſelf, and profitable to thoſe among whom he ſends us to miniſter. *For we are unto God a ſweet ſavour of Chriſt*, his precious name in our lips, and his grace in our hearts, render us pleaſing to God, *in them that are ſaved*, in whom God's rich mercy is magnified, being called by him to the faith and privileges of the goſpel; *and alſo in them that periſh*, in whom his juſtice is diſplayed in puniſhing their obſtinate infidelity; and, though they are not gathered, yet are we alike glorious in the eyes of the Lord, who regards not our ſucceſs, but our fidelity. *To the one we are the ſavour of death unto death*, a deſpiſed and abuſed goſpel aggravating their guilt, and increaſing their condemnation; *and to the other the ſavour of life unto life*, like a ſweet perfume, that recovers the fainting ſpirit, ſo doth the goſpel, through the power of the Holy Ghoſt, quicken the ſouls of many from the death of ſin unto a life of righteouſneſs, and continue to refreſh and revive them amidſt all their trials and ſufferings here, till they come to eternal life and glory hereafter. *And*, in the view of theſe eternally important events, and the awful and dangerous charge lying upon us, who need not to tremble for himſelf, and to cry out, *Who is ſufficient for theſe things?* The greateſt, the beſt of men, will be moſt conſcious of their own weakneſs, and be looking up for more than human power to enable them for the diſcharge of this arduous employment. *Note*, (1.) They who are truly found in Chriſt will always have cauſe to triumph in him over all their foes. (2.) The goſpel word never returns void. Where it is not a ſavour of life, it will be a ſavour of death. (3.) The more we are ſenſible of our own inſufficiency, the more ſhall we look up to him who giveth ſtrength to the work.

3. He vindicates himſelf, and glances at their falſe teachers. *For we are not as many, which corrupt*, and adulterate *the word of*

God, to make advantage thereby; but as of sincerity, without guile or deceit, but as of God, speaking under his witness, guidance, and authority, in the sight of God speak we in Christ, approving ourselves to the great Searcher of hearts, with a single eye to the Redeemer's glory, and making him the grand subject of all our ministrations.

CHAP. III.

The apostle makes an apology for not seeming to commend himself, and is careful not to assume too much to himself, but to ascribe all praise unto God, ver. 1—5. He then draws a comparison between the Old Testament and the New, and sets forth the excellency of the latter above the former, ver. 6—11. From thence he infers what is the duty of gospel ministers, and the advantage of those who live under the gospel, above those that lived under the law, ver. 12, to the end.

a 1 Cor. iv. 1.
DO we begin again to commend ourselves? or
need we, as some *others*, epistles of commen-
dation to you, or *letters* of commendation from you?
2 b Ye are our epistle written in our hearts, known and
read of all men: 3 *Forasmuch as ye are* manifestly
declared to be the epistle of Christ, ministred by us,
written not with ink, but with the Spirit of the living
God; c not in tables of stone, but d in fleshly tables of
the heart. 4 And such trust have we through Christ to
God-ward: 5 Not that we are sufficient of ourselves
to think any thing as of ourselves; e but our sufficiency
is of God.

a 2 Cor. iv. 2. & v. 12. & x. 8. & xii. 11. Chap. ii. 17. b 1 Cor. ix. 2. c Ex. xxiv. 12. & xxxiv. 1. d Ps. xl. 8. Jer. xxxi. 33. Ezek. xi. 19. & xxxvi. 26. Heb. viii. 10. e John xv. 5. Chap. ii. 16. f 1 Cor. xv. 10. Phil. ii. 13.

Ver. 1—5. To silence his traducers the apostle was compelled to protect his sincerity, and here,

1. He apologizes for seeming thus to commend himself. *Do we begin again to commend ourselves? or need we, as some others,* the false apostles, *epistles of commendation to you* from other churches, *or letters of commendation from you,* in order to gain credit and influence? no; we need them not: our conduct speaks for us. And ye yourselves *are our epistle*, our best letters testimonial, *written in our hearts*, in the deep affection we bear you; *known and read of all men*, whereas your conversion bore an honourable testimony to the instrument of it, *known and read of all men*, who observe the work of God's grace evident in you through our labours, *forasmuch as ye are manifestly declared to be the epistle of Christ, ministred by us,* written *not with ink, but with the Spirit of the living God*, the author of all the gifts and graces which you possess, *not on tables of stone*, as the law of Moses, *but in the fleshly tables of the heart*, softened and renewed by grace, where the impression of the gospel would be deep and lasting. *And such trust have we through Christ to God-ward*, that our ministry hath been made thus effectual to you, to God's glory, your benefit, and our own commendation.

2. He prevents any suggestion as if he had arrogated ought to himself. *Not that we are sufficient of ourselves to think any thing as of ourselves*, who cannot from ourselves spiritually produce one good thought, and much less by the mere power of our reasoning effect your conversion; no, *but our sufficiency is of God*, who alone furnishes us with ability, and crowns our labours with success. To him alone should the praise of all be for ever ascribed. Note; The best of men have always the lowliest thoughts of themselves.

f Chap. v. 18.
6 f Who also hath made us able ministers of h the
New Testament; i not of the letter, but of the Spirit:
for k the letter killeth, but l the Spirit giveth life. 7
But if m the ministration of death, n written *and* engraven
in stones, was glorious, o so that the children of Israel
could not stedfastly behold the face of Moses, for the
glory of his countenance; which *glory* was to be done away;
8 How shall not p the ministration of the Spirit be ra-
ther glorious? 9 For if the ministration of condemna-
tion *be* glory, much more doth the ministration of q righ-
teousness exceed in glory. 10 For even that which was
made glorious, had no glory in this respect, by reason
of the glory that excelleth. 11 For if that which is
done away *was* glorious, much more that which remain-
eth *is* glorious.

f Chap. v. 18. h Jer. xxxi. 31. Matt. xxvi. 28. i Rom. ii. 29. & vii. 6. k Rom. iii. 20. & iv. 15. & vii. 9, &c. Gal. iii. 10. l John vi. 63. m Rom. vii. 10. n Deut. x. 1, &c. o Ex. xxxiv. 29, 30. p Gal. iii. 5. q Rom. i. 17. & iii. 21.

Ver. 6—11. The apostle runs a parallel between the Mosaical and gospel dispensation, shewing the superior excellency of the latter, and the honour of those who were the ministers of it.

Who also hath made us able ministers of the New Testament, furnishing us with abilities and giving us success, *not of the letter,* not ministers of *the law*, which the Judaizing teachers so insisted, *but of the spirit*, of the gospel, which the Holy Ghost accompanies with his divine energy: *for the letter*, the law, *killeth*, commanding a perfection men cannot perform, and denouncing a curse on the least transgression, *but the spirit*, the gospel, attended with the quickening power of the Holy Ghost, *giveth life*, bringing sinners into a state of favour with God, raising them to spiritual life here, as the pledge and beginning of eternal life hereafter.

But if the law, which was *the ministration of death, written and engraven in stones, was glorious*, which it certainly was, delivered with such solemn pomp on Sinai, *so that the children of Israel could not stedfastly behold the face of Moses, for the glory of his countenance*, so bright it shone, *which glory was to be done away* in a while, *how shall not the ministration of the Spirit*, the gospel, *be rather glorious*, which is attended with such mighty energy, and quickening influence? and how much do its ministers also exceed in glory? *for if the ministration of condemnation*, which could only denounce wrath on the disobedient, *be glory, much more doth the ministration of righteousness*, even of the righteousness of God by faith, *exceed in glory.* And they who minister this glorious gospel must as much excel the ministers of the law, as righteousness and eternal life are preferable to condemnation and wrath. *For even that which was made glorious, had no glory in this respect, by reason of the glory that excelleth*, as stars disappear before the rising sun. *For if that which is done away*, as is now the case with the Mosaical dispensation, *was glorious*, and introduced with such majesty and splendour, *much more that which remaineth*, the gospel dispensation, *is glorious*; its privileges and blessings are infinitely greater, and will endure to eternity.

12 Seeing then that we have such hope, r we use
great † plainness of speech: 13 And not as Moses,
s *which* put a veil over his face, that the children of Israel
could not stedfastly look to t the end of that which is
abolished: 14 But u their minds were blinded: for un-
til this day remaineth the same veil untaken away, in
the reading of the Old Testament; which *veil* is done
away in Christ. 15 But even unto this day, when
Moses is read, the veil is upon their heart. 16 Never-
theless, x when it shall turn to the Lord, y the veil shall
be taken away. 17 Now the Lord is that Spirit: and
z where the Spirit of the Lord *is*, there *is* liberty. 18
But we all with open face beholding a as in a glass b the
glory of the Lord, c are changed into the same image,
from glory to glory, *even* as by the Spirit of the Lord.

r Eph. vi. 19. † Or, boldness. s Ex. xxxiv. 33, &c. t Rom. x. 4. Gal. iii. 24. u Isa. vi. 10. x Rom. xi. 23, 26. y Isa. xxv. 7. z John viii. 36. a 1 Cor. xiii. 12. b Chap. iv. 4, 6. 1 Tim. i. 11. c Rom. viii. 29. 1 Cor. xv. 49.

Ver. 12—18. These words are the inference from the foregoing comparison.

Seeing then that we have such hope in the superior excellence of the gospel above the law, and trust on the divine power to make it effectual, *we use great plainness of speech*, freely delivering our message, and seeking no embellishments. *Not as Moses, which put a veil over his face*, to hide the splendour of his countenance, intimating thereby, *that the children of Israel could not stedfastly look to the end of that which is abolished*, they stuck at the letter and the shadows, and perceived not that it was intended to lead them to Christ, that they might be justified by faith; *but their minds were blinded*, stupified (ἐπωρώθη) for not only then, but *until this day remaineth the same veil untaken away in the reading of the Old Testament*, besides the natural veil of darkness on their minds, there is an obscurity in the very institution itself as wrapped up in types and figures, and though they read the Scriptures, they understood not their true meaning and design, *which veil is done away in Christ*, in whom all the types and prophecies received their accomplishment, and who is the end of the law for righteousness to every one that believeth, as they know who behold him shining with the light of his gospel. *But even unto this day, when Moses is read*, the carnal Jew is so hardened through pride, prejudice, and sensuality, that *the veil is still upon their heart*, and they continue ignorant of him to whom the law and the prophets bear witness. *Nevertheless, when it shall turn to the Lord*, either the heart of any individual among them, or the people in general in the last days, *the veil shall be taken away*, and they shall acknowledge and receive the true Messiah. *Now the Lord Jesus Christ is that quickening Spirit*, who alone can effect this mighty work: *and where the Spirit of the Lord is*, and the gospel is truly embraced, *there is liberty*, freedom from darkness, guilt, and bondage, and access with boldness to a reconciled God. *But we all with open face*, who, through the illumination of his Spirit, have received the gospel in the light and love of it, *beholding*, there, *as in a glass*, or mirrour, which distinctly reflects the rays, *the glory of the Lord, are changed into the same image* of the adored Jesus, *from glory to glory*, from the bright traces which he hath begun in time till his likeness in us is perfected in eternity: and all this is effected, *even as by the Spirit of the Lord*, or, *by the Lord the Spirit*, the great and glorious Agent in this new creation, who is very God, and in the ministration of his gospel effectually forms the redeemed to the measure of the stature of the fulness of Christ. Lord, thou Spirit of all grace, thus transform my soul into the Saviour's perfect image!

CHAP.

CHAP. IV.

In this chapter we have an account, 1. Of the constancy of the apostle and his fellow-labourers in their work. Their conduct, that it is described, ver. 1, 2. Their success is considered, ver. 3, 4. An objection is obviated, ver. 3, 4; and their sincerity proved, ver. 5, 6, 7. 2. Of their courage and patience under their sufferings. Which see what their sufferings were, together with their effects, ver. 8—12. And what it was that kept them from sinking and fainting under them, ver. 13 to the end.

1 THerefore seeing we have this ministry, as we have received mercy, we faint not. 2 But have renounced the hidden things of dishonesty, not walking in craftiness, nor handling the word of God deceitfully, but by manifestation of the truth commending ourselves to every man's conscience in the sight of God. 3 But if our gospel be hid, it is hid to them that are lost. 4 In whom the god of this world hath blinded the minds of them which believe not, lest the light of the glorious gospel of Christ, who is the image of God, should shine unto them. 5 For we preach not ourselves, but Christ Jesus the Lord, and ourselves your servants for Jesus sake. 6 For God, who commanded the light to shine out of darkness, hath shined in our hearts to give the light of the knowledge of the glory of God in the face of Jesus Christ. 7 But we have this treasure in earthen vessels, that the excellency of the power may be of God, and not of us.

v. 1—7 The apostle, having shewn the excellence of the gospel above the law, passes on to give an account of the diligence and sincerity with which he and his companions discharged their ministry.

1. They laboured with perseverance and fidelity. *Therefore seeing we have this ministry*, from the Lord, *as we have received mercy*, and support under all our infirmities, *we faint not*, under our greatest trials cheerfully holding on unwearied in our glorious course, *but have renounced the hidden things of dishonesty*, abhorring every thing scandalous or reproachful, using no cover or concealment, *not walking in craftiness*, to beguile unstable souls by any mean arts, *nor handling the word of God deceitfully*, corrupting the pure truth by any base alloy of our own, or attempting to accommodate it to the taste of our hearers, *but by manifestation of the truth, commending ourselves to every man's conscience in the sight of God*, in all plainness of speech applying the gospel to men's hearts, under a deep sense of the solemn account we must shortly give of our ministry. *Note*, (1.) The business of ministers is not to adapt their words to men's humours, but to strike at their hearts. (2.) They who lay their hands to the gospel plough must never faint, or look back, whatever trials they may meet in the discharge of their office.

2. He obviates an objection, How, if he spoke so plainly, the truth was yet received by so few. *But if our gospel*, after all the pains we take, *be hid, it is hid to them that are lost*, who wilfully persist in their impenitence and unbelief, and reject the counsel of God against their own souls, *in whom the god of this world*, the devil, *hath blinded the minds of them which believe not*, increasing and confirming, by his malignant influence, the native blindness and darkness of their hearts, by his allurements or discouragements keeping them under his dominion, *lest the light of the glorious gospel of Christ, who is the image of God*, the brightness of his glory and the express image of his person, *should shine unto them*, enlighten their darkness, and convert their souls. *Note*, (1.) They must be lost from whom the gospel is hid, since it is the only means of salvation. (2.) The devil hath the general sway in the world, and is, though men perceive it not, the real object of their worship. (3.) The way in which Satan's kingdom is maintained in the world is by ignorance, and the prejudices he raises against the glorious gospel of Christ.

3. He declares their sincerity. *For we preach not ourselves*, not our own inventions, nor seek to promote our own honour or interest, *but Christ Jesus the Lord*, making him the grand subject of all our discourses, his person, offices, grace, righteousness; *and ourselves your servants for Jesus sake*, whose glory we seek to advance in the salvation of your souls. *For God, who commanded the light to shine out of darkness*, by his almighty word in the beginning, *hath*, by the like divine energy, *shined in our hearts*, dispelling the thick clouds of spiritual darkness, *to give the light of the knowledge of the glory of God in the face of Jesus Christ*, as it appears in the glorious gospel of which he is the sum and substance, and wherein all the divine perfections are exalted to the highest. *But we have this treasure of the gospel in earthen vessels*, committed to frail, poor, and perishing worms, such as we are, *that the excellency of the power may be of God, and not of us*. When such weak instruments are enabled to bear up under all persecutions, and are made so amazingly successful in their labours, it must with the strongest demonstration be evident, that the work is more than human, even of divine operation. *Note*, (1.) None can illuminate the dark mind of a fallen soul but he that at first said, *Let there be light, and there was light*. (2.) The meaner the instruments are, the more is the power and grace of God magnified, who worketh by them, and makes their ministry effectual to the salvation of lost sinners.

8 *We are* troubled on every side, yet not distressed; *we are* perplexed, but not in despair; 9 Persecuted, but not forsaken; cast down, but not destroyed; 10 Always bearing about in the body the dying of the Lord Jesus, that the life also of Jesus might be made manifest in our body. 11 For we which live, are alway delivered unto death for Jesus sake, that the life also of Jesus might be made manifest in our mortal flesh. 12 So then death worketh in us, but life in you. 13 We having the same spirit of faith, according as it is written, I believed, and therefore have I spoken; we also believe, and therefore speak; 14 Knowing that he which raised up the Lord Jesus, shall raise up us also by Jesus, and shall present *us* with you. 15 For all things *are* for your sakes, that the abundant grace might, through the thanksgiving of many, redound to the glory of God. 16 For which cause we faint not; but though our outward man perish, yet the inward man is renewed day by day. 17 For our light affliction, which is but for a moment, worketh for us a far more exceeding *and* eternal weight of glory; 18 While we look not at the things which are seen, but at the things which are not seen: for the things which *are* seen, *are* temporal; but the things which are not seen, *are* eternal.

v. 8—18 Many were the dangers to which, for the gospel's sake, the ministers of Christ were exposed, yet none of these things moved them.

1. Their trials were great. *We are troubled on every side*, with manifold afflictions in every place, *yet not distressed* with anxiety, or discomposed as if we had no way to escape; *we are perplexed*, and in doubt what step to take, *but not in despair* of the Lord's help and interposition, *persecuted* by wicked men with unrelenting malice, *but not forsaken* of God, so as to be given up for a prey to their teeth, *cast down* through the infirmity of our flesh, and the prevalence of fear and unbelief, *but not destroyed* as the wicked, but rising again by grace, and triumphant over all the power of evil: *always bearing about in the body the dying of the Lord Jesus*, carrying the marks of his sufferings, to shew we belong to our crucified Master, who sympathizes with us and counts our griefs his own, *that the life also of Jesus might be made manifest in our body*, He, as the living principle within, sustaining us under all our conflicts. *For we which live*, spiritually by his grace, and, amidst our continual persecutions, are still preserved, *are always delivered unto death for Jesus sake*, each day in jeopardy, and ready to be cut off for the testimony which we bear, *that the life also of Jesus might be made manifest in our mortal flesh*, it being evidently seen, by the protection he vouchsafes to us, that he is alive, and at the right hand of God; and that his Spirit hath quickened us to newness of life, whilst with unshaken courage, patience, and perseverance, in the midst of our sufferings, we desire to finish our course after his example. *So then death worketh in us*, and we, who are Christ's ministers, are exposed to the most fearful dangers, *but life in you*, who enjoy all comfort and peace, and even our sufferings are the confirmation of the gospel which we preach, and the means of deriving your spiritual and eternal life.

2. If their trials were great, their supports were great.

(1.) They stood by faith. *We having the same spirit of faith* with the saints of old, which animated the divine psalmist, and is wrought by the Holy Ghost in us and you, *according as it is written, I believed, and therefore have I spoken; we also believe, and therefore speak*, fully persuaded of the heavenly divine truths which we preach, and confident that the Lord will support us in our testimony to his gospel, and fulfil all his promises to us both in time and eternity. *Note*, They who have true faith will never faint. (2.) They were upheld by the hope of a joyful resurrection. *Knowing* with fullest assurance, *that he which raised up the Lord Jesus, shall raise up us also by Jesus*, in virtue of our union with him, *and shall present us with you*, a faultless band, before the throne of his glory, and the expectation of this raises us above the fears of death. (3.) The consolation that God would be glorified, and men's souls profited, supported and quickened them. *For all things are for your sakes*, all our labours and sufferings ultimately tend to promote your present and eternal happiness, *that the abundant grace*, held forth in our ministration, *might, through the thanksgiving of many, redound to the*

glory

glory of God, who, embracing the gospel, and made partakers of its inestimable blessings cannot but with ceaseless praises adore and magnify that gracious God, who hath called them to his kingdom and glory *For which cause we faint not*, but for your sakes, and God's glory, patiently and cheerfully persevere (4) Their own souls were profited by their afflictions, which was another reason why they should bear up under them *But though our outward man perish* through our hardships, labours, and sufferings, *yet the inward man is renewed day by day*, with fresh supplies of grace, strength, and consolation, growing more meet for the eternal world to which we are going, and we may well be content with every outward cross that tends to bring us thus nearer to our crown (5) The near and assured prospect of glory was their great support and comfort *For our light affliction, which is but for a moment*, so faith teaches us to judge, our afflictions are *light*, compared with the weight of glory which we expect, and *momentary*, however long continued through life, if viewed against the eternity which succeeds, and what is more, *worketh for us a far more exceeding and eternal weight of glory* The words are amazingly emphatical, ... and such as no translation can fully render. Steadily therefore we persevere, *while we look not at the things which are seen, but at the things which are not seen*, the glorious objects above, which faith realizes to the soul, *for the things which are seen are temporal*, transitory, and momentary, *but the things which are not seen are eternal*, glorious beyond conception, and to be enjoyed without measure and without end

CHAP. V.

The apostle proceeds to shew the reasons why they did not faint under their afflictions, viz their expectation, desire, and assurance of happiness after death, ver. 1—5 and makes an inference for the comfort of believers in their present state, ver 6, 7, 8 and urges it to a diligent attention to their duty, ver 9, 10, 11 Then he mentions an apology for seeming to commend himself, and giveth a good reason for his zeal and diligence, ver 12—15 And mentions two things that are necessary in order to our being in Christ, viz regeneration and reconciliation ver 16, ad finem

a Job iv. 19. 2 Pet i 13, 14. 1 FOR we know, that if a our earthly house of *this* tabernacle were dissolved, we have a building of God, an house not made with hands, eternal in the heavens 2 For in this b we groan earnestly, desiring to be clothed upon with our house which is from heaven
b Rom viii 23.
c Rev iii 18. & xvi 15. 3 If so be that c being clothed we shall not be found naked 4 For we that are in *this* tabernacle do groan, being burdened not for that we would be unclothed, but d clothed upon, that mortality might be swallowed up of life 5 Now e he that hath wrought us for the selfsame thing, *is* God, f who also hath given unto us the earnest of the Spirit 6 Therefore *we are* always confident, knowing that, whilst we are at home in the body, we are absent from the Lord 7 (For h we walk by faith, not by sight) 8 We are confident, *I say*, and i willing rather to be absent from the body, and to be present with the Lord 9 Wherefore k we labour, that whether present or absent we may be accepted of him 10 For l we must all appear before the judgment seat of Christ, m that every one may receive the things *done* in his body, according to that he hath done, whether *it be* good or bad 11 Knowing therefore n the terror of the Lord, we persuade men, but we are made manifest unto God, and I trust also are made manifest in your consciences

d 1 Cor xv 53, 54.
e Isa xxix 23. Eph ii 10.
f Rom viii 16, 23. Chap i 22. Eph i 14. & iv 30.
g Heb xi 13.
h Rom viii 24. 1 Cor xiii 12. Chap iv 18. Heb xi 1.
i Phil i 23.
k Or, endeavour.
l Matt xxv 31, 32. Rom xiv 10.
m Gal vi 7. Rom ii 6.
n Heb x 31. Jude 23.

v 1—11 No marvel, with such a scene full in his view, the apostle fainted not. He enlarges here on the delightful theme, which cannot but minister to nothing of the like courage and consolation to every gracious soul. We have,

1 The apostle's expectation: and a like, which every faithful servant of Jesus can, in a measure, adopt as his own *For we know*, by the evidence of God's word, the testimony of our conscience, and the witness of the Spirit, *that if our house of this tabernacle*, the frail body in which we are pilgrims at present sojourn for a day, *be dissolved*, and returned to the dust from whence it came, *we have a building of God*, infinitely more magnificent, *a house not made with hands, eternal in the heavens*, a celestial palace prepared for our everlasting residence, and suited to the excellence of the glorified soul *For in this tabernacle of clay we groan earnestly*, loaded with many affliction, and burdened with many corruption *desiring to be clothed with our house, which is from heaven*, and to arrive at the celestial city, where sin nor sorrow shall ever enter more *If so be that, or since, being thus arrayed with robes of light and purity we shall not be found naked*, exposed my horrors to the storms of this wretched world, but be invested in joy and felicity. *For we that are in this tabernacle do groan, being burdened*, longing for our perfect state of holiness and happiness, when we shall be for ever released from the burdens of outward afflictions, and indwelling sin *not for that we would be unclothed*, and wish to part with our bodies, *but clothed upon, that mortality might be swallowed up of life*, transformed, as those who shall be changed in a moment, as their bodies shall be, who are alive at the coming of the Lord *Note*, (1) Our present abode is a wretched tabernacle that must quickly be taken down, but we an eternal mansion ready to receive the immortal soul? (2) To a soul that hath ever tasted of the bitterness of sin, and groaned under the trials and temptations of this mortal state, the exchange of worlds is a consummation devoutly to be wished for

2 The apostle mentions the ground of his expectation and hope *Now he that hath wrought us for the selfsame thing is God*, whose mighty energy hath spiritualized our souls, and lifted them up to seek those high and heavenly things, *who also hath given unto us the earnest of the Spirit*, in his graces, consolations, and abiding residence in our hearts, which seal to us the purchased possession *Therefore we are always confident*, in the assurance of the fulfilment of the divine promises, and of support under all our trials till they shall happily end, *knowing that whilst we are at home in the body, we are absent from the Lord*, and, like pilgrims, distant from our true home and rest *For we walk by faith, not by sight*, looking above all present objects to the eternal world, and having our hearts influenced, and our conduct regulated accordingly, *we are confident, I say*, in the experience of God's present love, and the assurance of his eternal favour, *and willing rather to be absent from the body and to be present with the Lord*, well pleased, if God so ordained, to bid an eternal adieu to all our infirmities and afflictions, and enter immediately into the beatific vision of our Lord *Wherefore we labour, that whether present or absent, we may be accepted of him* This is our holy ambition, so to be found in him, sprinkled with his blood, clothed with his righteousness, and walking under the influence of his grace, that now, and in the day of his appearing and glory, both our persons and services may meet with his approbation *Note*, (1) None enter the heavenly world, but those who have the earnest of the Spirit in their hearts, and are made meet for the inheritance among the saints in light (2) Faith in God's promises inspires confidence of their fulfilment, we know we have not followed cunningly-devised fables (3) They who have seen the glories of a better world, and are assured of their portion there, cannot but with pleasure look forward to the happy change (4) The more sure our hope of heaven is, the more enlivened will be our diligence in the way that leads thither

3 He reminds them of the awful day which approached, as a spur to himself, and a warning to them *For we must all appear before the judgment-seat of Christ*, where without disguise every man's real character will appear, *that every one may receive the things done in his body, according to that he hath done, whether it be good or bad*, admitted graciously to the reward of eternal blessedness, or sinking under righteous vengeance into the abyss of endless misery *Knowing therefore the terror of the Lord*, and the fearful end of the hypocrite and ungodly, *we persuade men*, by every alarming and alluring motive, to fly from the wrath to come, and embrace the gospel which we proclaim *But*, whether they will hear or forbear, *we are made manifest to God*, who knows our simplicity in all our ministrations, *and I trust also are made manifest in your consciences*, for our labours and sufferings bear witness to the unfeigned concern we have shewn for your souls *Note*, (1) The sense of an approaching judgment should awaken a holy solicitude to be ready for it (2) The terror of the Lord his minister must use to rouse the lethargic sinner, and urge him to fly from his impending ruin

12 For o we commend not ourselves again unto you, but give you occasion p to glory on our behalf, that you may have somewhat to *answer* them which glory in appearance, and not in heart 13 For whether we be q besides ourselves, *it is* to God or whether we be sober, *it is* for your cause 14 For r the love of Christ constraineth us, because we thus judge, that s if one died for all, then were all dead 15 And *that* he died for all, t that they which live, should not henceforth live unto themselves, but unto him which died for them, and rose again

o Chap iii 1.
p Chap i 14.
q Chap xi 1, 16, 17.
r Chap xii 11.
s Rom v 15.
t Rom xiv 7, 8. 1 Cor vi 19. Gal ii 20. 1 Thess v 10. 1 Pet iv 2.

v 12—15. The apostle,

1 Prevents an insinuation which might have been suggested by his enemies, as if he meant to commend himself *For we commend not ourselves again unto you*, nor speak thus with a view of ingratiating ourselves into your good opinion, *but to give you occasion to glory on our behalf, that you may have somewhat to answer them which glory in appearance, and not in heart*, furnishing you with arguments to silence the vain boasting of those judaizing teachers, who would malign and traduce us *For whether we be beside ourselves*, and in our zeal for the gospel talk as men distracted, as they would insinuate, *it is to God*, and for his glory,

that we thus ſpeak, *or if we be ſober*, and, as the wiſer part among you juſtly think, ſay nothing but the words of truth and ſoberneſs, *it is* for your cauſe, whoſe ſalvation we ſeek to promote.

2 He declares the noble principle which influenced his preaching and practice *For the love of Chriſt conſtraineth us, becauſe we thus judge*, and have determined, on matureſt deliberation, *that if one died for all*, for ſinners of all degrees, whether Jews or Gentiles, without diſtinction, *then were all dead*, alike in need of his redemption, by nature the children of wrath, and under the curſe of a broken law, or all thoſe for whom he died became myſtically dead in him, delivered from the curſe and condemnation of the law, by his ſuffering the penalty in their ſtead, *and that he died for all, that they which live*, redeemed by his blood, and quickened by his Spirit, *ſhould not henceforth live unto themſelves*, for their own eaſe, intereſts, or honour, *but unto him which died for them, and roſe again*, devoting themſelves to his bleſſed ſervice, who purchaſed them at ſo dear a rate *Note*, (1) A ſenſe of Chriſt's love upon the heart is the only genuine principle of true obedience (2) We then truly live, when the Redeemer's glory is made the grand aim of all our converſation

16 Wherefore [y] henceforth know we no man after
the fleſh yea, though [z] we have known Chriſt after the
fleſh, yet now henceforth know we *him* no more 17
Therefore if any man [a] *be* in Chriſt, [b] *he is* a new crea-
ture [c] old things are paſt away, behold, all things are
become new 18 And all things *are* of God, [d] who
hath reconciled us to himſelf by Jeſus Chriſt, and hath
given to us the miniſtry of reconciliation, 19 To wit,
that [e] God was in Chriſt, reconciling the world unto
himſelf, not imputing their treſpaſſes unto them, and
hath committed unto us the word of reconciliation 20
Now then [f] we are ambaſſadors for Chriſt, as though God
did beſeech *you* by us we pray *you* in Chriſt's ſtead, Be
ye reconciled to God 21 For [g] he hath made him *to be*
ſin for us, [h] who knew no ſin, that we might be made
[i] the righteouſneſs of God in him

y Mat xi 50 (?) ... iii 11 z John xvi 6, 7 & xx 17 a Rom viii 9 10 b Gal vi 15 c Rom vi 11 Eph ii ... &c & iv 2, &c Rev xxi 5 d Rom v 10 Eph ii 16 Col i 20 1 John iv 10 e Rom iii 25 f Mal ii 7 Eph vi 20 g Iſa liii 6 ... Gal iii 13 1 Pet ii 24 h John viii 46 1 Pet ii 22 i Rom i 17, & x 4 Phil iii 9

v 16—21 From the foregoing premiſes,

1 The apoſtle determines, without reſpect of perſons, to preach the goſpel alike to Jews and Gentiles, who are both redeemed by the ſame Lord *Wherefore henceforth know we no man after the fleſh*, paying no regard to any external privileges of deſcent from Abraham or circumciſion *yea, though we have known Chriſt after the fleſh*, and formerly thought, during his abode on earth, that he was come to erect a temporal kingdom, and exalt the Jewiſh nation to the pinnacle of human glory, *yet now henceforth know we him no more*, theſe fooliſh prejudices are removed, we have got an acquaintance with the ſpiritual nature of his ſalvation, and know that the great deſign for which he became incarnate was to advance the divine glory in the recovery of loſt ſouls, whether Jews or Gentiles, without diſtinction, even of as many as ſhould believe in his name

2 He urges, as the main point of Chriſtianity, a real change of heart *Therefore if any man be in Chriſt*, vitally united to him, *he is a new creature*, though the ſame perſon, yet morally ſo renewed in the ſpirit of his mind, and in underſtanding, will, and affections ſo ſpiritualized, that he is quite different from his former ſelf *old things are paſt away*, his naturally corrupt principles and practices are laid aſide, and *behold*, with wonder, the amazing alteration! *all things are become new*, he hath new light in his mind, a new bias given to his will and affections, his whole courſe of life is altered, his principles, proſpects, ways, thoughts, purſuits, company, are as directly oppoſite to what they were before, as if he were really another man Reader, haſt thou experienced this change?

3 The new creation is God's work, and wrought by means of his goſpel *And all things are of God, who* planned and executed the wondrous ſcheme of our ſalvation, and *hath reconciled us to himſelf by Jeſus Chriſt*, through his atoning blood and juſtifying righteouſneſs, *and hath given to us the miniſtry of reconciliation, to wit, that God was in Chriſt* according to his eternal council, *reconciling the world*, Gentiles as well as Jews, *unto himſelf*, by that amazing expedient of the ſubſtitution of his own Son in the ſinner's ſtead, *not imputing their treſpaſſes unto them*, but laying upon him the iniquities of us all, *and hath committed unto us the word of reconciliation*, that we ſhould publiſh this goſpel of peace to every creature *Now then we are ambaſſadors for Chriſt*, ſent, in his name, to heal the dangerous breach between the holy God and the ſinful ſoul, *as though God did beſeech you by us*, under whoſe commiſſion we act with authority and ſpeak in his name *we pray you*, by every endearing argument, as you value your immortal ſouls, and urge you *in Chriſt's ſtead*, whoſe perſon we repreſent, and whoſe goſpel we miniſter, *be ye reconciled to God*, ſubmit to his righteouſneſs, accept his proffered pardon and grace bow humbly at his feet without reſerve yield up yourſelves to him, that the reconciliation may be mutual, and the friendſhip eternal *For he hath*

made him to be ſin, a ſin-offering, *for us, who knew no ſin* of his own, but willingly took our iniquities upon himſelf, and ſuffered for them, making a full atonement and ſatisfaction to the juſtice of God, *that we might be made the righteouſneſs of God in him*, by virtue of our union with him, intereſted in his everlaſting righteouſneſs, accepted and regarded of God for ever as complete and perfect, and entitled thereby to eternal life and glory My ſoul, with wonder and delight hear and embrace theſe glad tidings, be thy ſins all laid at Jeſus's feet, and in his righteouſneſs arrayed thou mayeſt boldly appear in the preſence of God!

CHAP VI

In this chapter the apoſtle, (1) giveth an account of his general errand to all that he preached unto, with the ſeveral arguments and methods he uſed, ver 1—10 (2) He addreſſes himſelf particularly to the Corinthians, giving them good cautions with much affection and ſtrong arguments, ver 11—18

1 WE then, † *as* [a] workers together *with him*, [b] be-
ſeech *you* alſo, that ye [c] receive not the grace
of God in vain 2 (For he ſaith, [d] I have heard thee
in a time accepted, and in the day of ſalvation have I
ſuccoured thee behold, [e] now *is* the accepted time,
behold, now *is* the day of ſalvation) 3 [f] Giving no
offence in any thing, that the miniſtry be not blamed
4 But in all things [g] approving ourſelves as the mi-
niſters of God, [h] in much patience, in afflictions, in ne-
ceſſities, in diſtreſſes, 5 [i] In ſtripes, in impriſonments,
in tumults, in labours, in watchings, in faſtings, 6
By pureneſs, by knowledge, by long ſuffering, by kind-
neſs, by the holy Ghoſt, by love unfeigned 7 By the
word of truth, [k] by the power of God, [l] by the armour
of righteouſneſs on the right hand and on the left,
8 By honour and diſhonour, [m] by evil report and good
report, as deceivers, and *yet* true, 9 As unknown,
and yet well known, [n] as dying, and behold, we live,
[o] as chaſtened, and not killed, 10 As [p] ſorrowful, yet
alway rejoicing, [q] as poor, yet making many rich, as
having nothing, [r] and *yet* poſſeſſing all things

† Or as fellow labourers a 1 Cor iii 9 b Chap v 20 c Heb xii 15 d Iſa xlix 8 e Iſa lxi 2 Rom xiii 11 Heb iii 7, 13 f Rom xiv 13 1 Cor viii 13 & x 32 g Chap iv 2 & v 11 h 2 Tim iii 10 &c i Chap xi 23 &c k 1 Cor ii 4 l Chap x 4 Eph vi 11, 13 2 Tim iv 7 m Mat xxvii 63 John vii 12 n Chap iv 10, 11 o Pſ cxviii 18 p Mat v 12 Acts v 41 & xvi 25 Heb x 34 q Prov xiii 7 r Phil iv 18.

v 1—10 We have here an account,

1 Of the general exhortation which, as ambaſſadors for Chriſt, Paul and his fellow-labourers addreſſed to all their hearers *We then as workers together with him*, as the inſtruments he employs in calling loſt ſinners to a ſtate of reconciliation with God, *beſeech you alſo*, among others to whom we are ſent, *that ye receive not the grace of God in vain*, nor ſlight his goſpel, remaining empty profeſſors, inſtead of actual poſſeſſing the power and life of godlineſs *For he ſaith*, addreſſing his Son, the Meſſiah, *Iſa* xlix 4—6 *I have heard thee in a time accepted, and in the day of ſalvation have I ſuccoured thee* anſwering his prayers, as moſt acceptable before him, and ſupplying him with the needful ſtrength to finiſh his arduous undertaking for the complete redemption of his people *behold, now is the accepted time*, when the ſinners of every nation are invited to partake of the bleſſings he hath purchaſed, and are ſure of acceptance with God through his dear Son, *behold, now is the day of ſalvation* ſeize therefore the preſent moment, and fly for refuge to Jeſus the hope ſet before you, and then you will be ſaved with an everlaſting ſalvation *Note*, (1) To-day God invites, to-day we ſhould hear and obey, no moment is to be trifled with, every breath we draw is precarious, to-morrow may not belong to time, but to eternity What an awakening conſideration! how are we called to improve the preſent *NOW*! (2) Miniſters muſt with importunity and earneſtneſs urge upon dying men the neceſſity of attending inſtantly to the things of their everlaſting peace, before they be hid from their eyes

2 Of their carefulneſs to avoid every occaſion of offence *Giving no offence in any thing, that the miniſtry be not blamed* behaving ſo diſcreetly, both among Jews and Gentiles, as to give neither any ground of prejudice againſt that goſpel which we preach, *but in all things approving ourſelves as the miniſters of God*, becoming the character we bear *in much patience*, meekly reſigned, and ſteadily perſevering, *in afflictions*, of various kinds, which we ſuffer for our work's ſake, *in neceſſities*, wanting even food and raiment, *in diſtreſſes*, from which we ſee no way to extricate ourſelves, *in ſtripes*, beaten both in the ſynagogues and before the heathen tribunals, *in impriſonments*, caſt into dungeons; *in tumults*, from outrageous mobs; *in labours*, unceaſing, *in watchings*, *in faſtings*, having our reſt broken, and our proviſion ſcanty, and ſometimes voluntarily denying ourſelves food and ſleep on a religious account And in theſe ſufferings we are ſupported *by pureneſs*, acting with the greateſt ſimplicity of intention, and integrity of conduct, *by knowledge*, fully acquainted with the truths which we deliver, *by long-ſuffering*, bearing with the perverſeneſs and provocation of

Vol II

12/

8 ...

oppoſers

opposers, *by kindness*, in temper and manners gentle and courteous, *by the Holy Ghost*, of whose gifts, graces, and consolations we abundantly partake, *by love unfeigned* to God and man, *by the word of truth*, which unadulterated we deliver, *by the power of God*, whose everlasting arms are under us, and who, in the miracles he enables us to work, bears testimony to our doctrine, *by the armour of righteousness on the right hand and on the left*, furnished out of the armoury of God with every thing necessary for our spiritual warfare; *by honour and dishonour*, not elated with the high esteem of some, nor discouraged by the insolent contempt of others, *by evil report and good report*, mentioned with great commendation by our friends, and branded with the most infamous slanders by our enemies, *as deceivers*, so treated by many, *and yet true*, proved and found faithful to Christ, and the souls of men, *as unknown*, represented as men of no figure and despicable, *yet well known*, those who are best acquainted with us, are sensible of our real characters, of our importance and usefulness, *as dying*, and every hour in jeopardy, *and behold we live*, amidst all our dangers, *as chastened* from the Lord, and by the hands of men, *and not killed*, immortal till God's time comes, *as sorrowful*, under manifold temptations, *yet always rejoicing* in a sense of the divine love and favour, *as poor* in this world, *yet making many rich*, in spiritual and eternal treasures, *as having nothing*, that here we can call our own, dependent on Providence for daily bread, *and yet possessing all things*, having a present fulness in the contentment we enjoy, blessed with all the internal riches of grace, and holding firm a sure title to the eternal riches of glory

11 O ye Corinthians, our mouth is open unto you,
ᵃ our heart is enlarged 12 Ye are not straitned in us,
but ᵇ ye are straitned in your own bowels 13 Now
for a recompence in the same, (ᶜ I speak as unto *my*
children) be ye also enlarged 14 ˣ Be ye not unequally
yoked together with unbelievers for ʸ what fellowship
hath righteousness with unrighteousness? and what com-
munion hath light with darkness? 15 And ᶻ what con-
cord hath Christ with Belial? or ᵃ what part hath he that
believeth, with an infidel? 16 And what agreement
hath the temple of God with idols? for ᵇ ye are the tem-
ple of the living God, as God hath said, I ᶜ will dwell
in them, and walk in *them*, and I will be their God, and
they shall be my people 17 Wherefore ᵈ come out
from among them, and be ye separate, saith the Lord,
and touch not the unclean thing, and I will receive you,
18 ᵉ And I will be a Father unto you, and ye shall be
my sons and daughters, saith the Lord Almighty

a Chap vii 3. b Chap xii 15. c 1 Cor iv 14. x Deut vii 3. 1 Cor vii 9. y 1 Kings xviii 21. Prov xxix 27. 1 Cor x 21. Eph v 11. z 1 Sam v. 2, 3. a Acts viii 21. b 1 Cor iii 16 & vi 19. Eph ii 21. c Lev xxvi 12. Ezek xxxvii 28. d Isa lii 11. Jer li. 6. Rev xviii 4. e Jer xxxi 9, 33. Rev xxi

ℓ 11—18 The apostle's heart glowed with warm affection, and he cannot but unbosom himself *O ye Corinthians, our mouth is opened unto you, our heart is enlarged*, we speak with the greatest freedom, and long for your salvation *Ye are not straitned in us*, we love you ardently, we would keep back nothing from you that could promote your spiritual and eternal interests, *but ye are straitned in your own bowels*, and fail to make the suitable returns of gratitude, nor are open to receive the blessings we communicate *Now for a recompence in the same, (I speak as unto my children*, from whom I may justly expect the strongest filial regard) *be ye also enlarged*, in mutual love towards us your faithful ministers, and in your cordial reception of that blessed gospel, with all its precious doctrines and inestimable privileges which we declare unto you As a father then I admonish you, for the credit of your profession, and for the good of your own souls, *Be not unequally yoked together with unbelievers*, intermarrying with the unconverted heathen, or otherwise entering into near and close connection with them, particularly not joining in any of their religious services *for what fellowship hath righteousness with unrighteousness?* What holy friendship can subsist between a renewed and an unsanctified soul? *And what communion*, in society and converse, *hath* the enlightened Christian with the unenlightened sinner any more than *light with darkness? And what concord hath Christ with Belial?* What harmony can subsist between the members of Christ and the children of the wicked one? *Or what part* or lot *hath he that believeth with an infidel? and what agreement hath the temple of God with idols?* How can the worshipper of the true Jehovah, and who are themselves his living temple, join with heathens in their idolatrous worship? How absurd is it and incongruous? *for ye are the temple of the living God*, where his divine Spirit is pleased to take up his abode, *as God hath said, I will dwell in them, and walk in them*, in a nobler sense than he ever was in his temple of old, blessing them with his presence and abiding communion; *and I will be their God*, in an everlasting covenant, in which all my perfections are engaged to make them happy, *and they shall be my people*, cheerfully engaged to yield themselves up to my service, and, by my power and grace, made such as I would have them be *Wherefore come out from among them, and be ye separate* from all unnecessary intercourse and familiarity with the unconverted heathen, *saith the Lord, and touch not the unclean thing*, keep at

the greatest possible distance from idolatry, and every abomination, *and I will receive you* as my peculiar people, *and will be a Father unto you*, shewing you the most endeared affection, *and ye shall be my sons and daughters, saith the Lord Almighty*, admitted to that high dignity and most inestimable privilege *Note*, (1) A child of God must separate himself from the ways and manners of a world that lieth in wickedness (2) God cannot bear a rival in our hearts, no idols must be harboured there (3) The covenant of grace saith, *I will*, and *you shall*, for it is entirely God's work, that we are conformed to his will

CHAP VII

This chapter begins with an exhortation to progressive holiness, and a due regard to the ministers of the gospel, ver 1—4 Then the apostle returns from a long digression, to speak further of the affair concerning the incestuous person, and tells them what comfort he received in his distress about that matter upon his meeting with Titus, ver 5, 6, 7 and how he rejoiced in their repentance, with the evidences thereof, ver 8—11 And lastly, he concludeth with endeavouring to comfort the Corinthians, upon whom his admonitions had had so good an effect, ver 12—16

1 ᵃ HAVING therefore these promises, dearly be-
loved, let us cleanse ourselves from all filthi-
ness of the flesh and spirit, ᵇ perfecting holiness in the fear
of God. 2 Receive us we have wronged no man,
we have corrupted no man, ᶜ we have defrauded no man
3 I speak not this to condemn *you*. for ᵈ I have said
before, that you are in our hearts to die and live with
you 4. ᵉ Great *is* my boldness of speech toward you,
ᶠ great *is* my glorying of you ᵍ I am filled with comfort,
ʰ I am exceeding joyful in all our tribulation 5 For
ⁱ when we were come into Macedonia, our flesh had no
rest, but we were troubled on every side, without *were*
fightings, within *were* fears. 6 Nevertheless God, ᵏ that
comforteth those that are cast down, ˡ comforted us by
the coming of Titus 7 And not by his coming only,
but by the consolation wherewith he was comforted in
you, when he told us your earnest desire, your mourning,
ᵐ your fervent mind toward me, so that I rejoiced the
more. 8 For though I made you sorry with a letter, I
do not repent, ⁿ though I did repent for I perceive that
the same epistle made you sorry, though *it were* but for a
season 9 Now I rejoice, not that ye were made sorry,
but that ye sorrowed to repentance for ye were made
sorry † after a godly manner, that ye might receive da-
mage by us in nothing 10 For ᵒ godly sorrow work-
eth repentance to salvation not to be repented of but ᵖ the
sorrow of the world worketh death 11 For behold,
this self-same thing that ye sorrowed after a godly sort,
what carefulness it wrought in you, yea, *what* clearing of
yourselves, yea, *what* indignation, yea, *what* fear, yea,
what vehement desire, yea, *what* zeal, yea, *what* re-
venge! In all things ye have approved yourselves to be
clear in this matter

a Chap vi. 16 John iii 3. b 1 Cor ix. c Acts xx 33. Chap xii. 1 Thes 5. d Chap vi. 11. e Chap iii. 12. f Chap ix. g Phil ii. Col i. 24. h Matt v. Acts v. Rom v 3. i Acts xvi 19. k Chap i. l Chap ii 13. m Prov xxviii. n Chap ii 4. † Gr according to God. o 2 Sam xii 13. Matt xxvi 75. Luke xviii 13. p Matt xxvii 4, 5 Heb xii

ℓ 1—11 Having mentioned the amazingly rich and gracious promises of God, he makes here,

1 An inference from them *Having therefore these promises, dearly beloved, let us cleanse ourselves from all filthiness of the flesh and spirit*, avoiding every kind of intemperance or uncleanness, which would pollute our bodies, and mortifying the inward abominations of pride, malice, falshood, &c which defile the soul, *perfecting holiness in the fear of God*, growing in grace, and going on till ultimately our course shall be completed in finished perfection

2 He returns from the digression he had made, to vindicate himself and his fellow-labourers from the slanders of the false teacher *Receive us* with cordial regard *we have wronged no man, we have corrupted no man, we have defrauded no man*, our principles have been according to God's word, and our practice upright and unblameable *I speak not this to condemn you*, reflecting on you as a body, as having traduced us *for I have said before, that you are in our hearts to die and live with you*, such confidence have we in you, and such warm affection toward you *Great is my boldness of speech towards you*, in reproving the disorders among you, *great is my glorying of you*, as my genuine, obedient children, and ornaments of your profession *I am filled with comfort in you, I am exceeding joyful in all our tribulation*, to hear the [illegible] account from you *For when we were come into Macedonia, in need of Titus, our flesh had no rest, but we were troubled on every side*, not only with the opposition of our enemies but with the [illegible] of our minds on your account, *without were fightings* from [illegible], *within were fears* for you, lest you should be removed from [illegible] in Christ

[illegible]

Nevertheless, God that comforteth those that are cast down, comforted us by the coming of Titus, whose arrival revived our drooping hearts: *and not by his coming only, but by the consolation wherewith he was comforted in you*, by the affectionate and respectful reception he met with at Corinth, *when he told us your earnest desire* to obey our injunctions, *your mourning* for the offences which had been committed, *your fervent mind towards me*, vindicating with zeal my character against the false teachers, and longing for my coming, *so that I rejoiced the more*, and his report exceedingly heightened the pleasure of his arrival. *For though I made you sorry with a letter*, wherein I was constrained to use sharp rebukes, *I do not repent, though I did repent*, and grieved exceedingly, even at the time, that I should be necessitated to use such severity: *for I perceive the same epistle made you sorry, though it were but for a season*, and engaged you immediately to correct what was amiss. *Now I rejoice, not that ye were made sorry*, in that I could have no satisfaction, and sympathized tenderly with you, *but that ye sorrowed to repentance: for ye were made sorry after a godly manner*, mourning over your unfaithfulness, and returning in deep humility to God, *that ye might receive damage by us in nothing*, but contrariwise be abundantly profited. *For godly sorrow worketh repentance unto salvation, not to be repented of*, and what hath such a gracious effect cannot but in the issue prove matter of the most solid satisfaction: *but the sorrow of the world*, which men of earthly minds feel, on account of the losses and crosses here below, *worketh death*, driving them to despair, impairing their health, and sometimes even causing them to lay violent hands on themselves. *For behold, this self-same thing that ye sorrowed after a godly sort*, what a blessed influence it had upon you! *what carefulness it wrought in you* to remove the cause of offence, *yea, what clearing of yourselves* from any connivance of iniquity, *yea, what indignation* against what was evil in yourselves, or in the notorious delinquent, *yea, what fear* of God, and jealousy for yourselves, *yea, what vehement desire* to make a thorough reformation of all disorders, *yea, what zeal* for God's glory, and the honour of your holy profession, *yea, what revenge*, punishing with due severity the criminal! *In all things you have approved yourselves to be clear in this matter*, by your ready amendment. *Note*, (1.) Godly sorrow is the most profitable physic for the soul. (2.) Whatever bitterness we may have tasted, we shall never at last repent of that which worketh repentance unto salvation.

12 Wherefore, though I wrote unto you, *I did it* not
for his cause [q] that had done the wrong, nor for his — q 1 Cor. v. 1.
cause that suffered wrong, [r] but that our care for you — r Chap. ii. 9.
in the sight of God might appear unto you. 13 Therefore we were comforted in your comfort: yea, and exceedingly the more joyed we for the joy of Titus, because his spirit was refreshed by you all. 14 For if
I have boasted any thing to him of you, I am not
ashamed; [s] but as we spake all things to you in truth, — s Chap. ii. 17. & iv. 2. & vi. 7.
even so our boasting which *I made* before Titus is found
a truth. 15 And his [†] inward affection is more abun- — † Gr. bowels.
dant toward you, whilst he remembreth the obedience of
you all, how with fear and trembling you received him.
16 I rejoice therefore that [t] I have confidence in you in — t Phil. i. 22. 2 Thes. iii. 4. Philem. 8.
all things.

v. 12—16. Since his admonition had so good an effect, the apostle cannot but rejoice. *Wherefore, though I wrote unto you*, with some sharpness, *I did it not for his cause that had done the wrong*, not merely that the incestuous person should be punished, *nor for his sake that suffered wrong*, out of any partial favour to his injured father, *but that our care for you in the sight of God might appear unto you*, and the church be preserved from scandal. *Therefore we were comforted in your comfort*, the peace and purity of your society being restored: *yea, and exceedingly the more joyed we for the joy of Titus, because his spirit was refreshed by you all*, by the kind, obedient, respectful, and affectionate behaviour which you shewed toward him. *For if I have boasted any thing to him of you, I am not ashamed* of the character I gave you; *but as we spake all things to you in truth*, in simplicity and godly sincerity, *even so our boasting which I made before Titus is found a truth*, and the commendation I gave you hath been proved to be but just. *And his inward affection is more abundant toward you, whilst he remembreth the obedience of you all* to my apostolic injunctions, *how with fear and trembling you received him*, with deepest reverence and holy jealousy, lest you should not duly profit by his advice. *I rejoice therefore that I have confidence in you in all things*, that you will continue to obey my admonition, and to refresh my spirit by your dutiful and becoming conduct on every occasion. *Note*, It is a singular comfort to a minister, that he hath confidence in the fidelity of his people.

CHAP. VIII.

In this chapter he acquainteth the Corinthians with, and commendeth, the good example of the Macedonians in their works of charity, and that Titus was sent to Corinth to collect their bounty, ver. 1—6. He then proceedeth to urge this duty with several cogent arguments, ver. 7—15. and commendeth the persons that were employed in this affair, ver. 16—24.

1 MOREOVER, brethren, we [†] do you to wit of — † Gr. make known to you.
the grace of God bestowed on the churches of
Macedonia. 2 How that [a] in a great trial of affliction, — a 1 Thes. i. 6.
the abundance of their joy, and [b] their deep poverty — b Mark xii.
abounded unto the riches of their [‡] liberality. 3 For to — ‡ Gr. simplicity.
their power (I bear record) yea, and beyond their power,
they were willing of themselves; 4 Praying us with
much intreaty, that we would receive the gift, and *take*
upon us [c] the fellowship of the ministring to the saints. 5 — c Acts xi. 29. Rom. xv. 25. 1 Cor. xvi. 4. Chap. ix. 1.
And *this they did*, not as we hoped, but first gave their
own selves to the Lord, and unto us by the will of God.
6 Insomuch that [d] we desired Titus, that as he had be- — d Chap. xii. 18.
gun, so he would also finish in you the same grace also.

v. 1—6. As the brethren in Judea had undergone peculiar sufferings, and were reduced to great poverty, the Gentile churches, at the instigation of the apostles, had made a collection for their relief. The churches of Macedonia had begun it, and the churches of Achaia ought not to be backward in so good a work.

1. The apostle acquaints them with the generous conduct of the Macedonian brethren. *Moreover, brethren, we do you to wit of the grace of God bestowed on the churches of Macedonia*, inclining them to exercise their generous benevolence. *How that in a great trial of affliction*, amidst sore persecutions, *the abundance of their joy* in the Holy Ghost, *and their deep poverty abounded unto the riches of their liberality*, and set off, with greater lustre, their distinguished charity. *For to their power (I bear record) yea, and beyond their power, they were willing of themselves*, needing no instigation, *but praying us, with much intreaty, that we would receive the gift* of their kindness, *and take upon us the fellowship of the ministring to the saints*, distributing their bounty to the Christians in Judea. *And this they did, not as we hoped*, only, *but* with a noble generosity, far exceeding our most sanguine expectations, they *first gave their own selves to the Lord*, solemnly surrendering themselves, and all their possessions, to his glory, *and unto us by the will of God*, resolving to be directed by us as his ministring servants, according to his revealed word. *Note*, (1.) The grace of God opens the heart with love, and the hand with liberality. A lively Christian will rather go beyond his power, than be backward in acts of piety and charity. (2.) They who have truly given themselves to the Lord, will hold back nothing from him, which may serve to promote his glory and the interests of his kingdom.

2. He commended it to Titus, who had been so acceptable to them before, to go and finish what he had begun, exciting them to the exercise of the *same grace* of liberality, which had so eminently appeared in the Macedonian churches. *Note*, The success of our designs, in a great measure, depends upon the choice of proper instruments.

7 Therefore as [e] ye abound in every thing, in faith, — e 1 Cor. i. 5.
in utterance, and knowledge, and in all diligence, and
in your love to us, *see* that ye abound in this grace
also. 8 [f] I speak not by commandment, but by occasion — f 1 Cor. vii. 6.
of the forwardness of others, and to prove the sincerity
of your love. 9 For ye know the grace of our Lord
Jesus Christ, that [g] though he was rich, yet for your — g Luke ix. 58. Phil. ii. 7.
sakes he became poor, that ye through his poverty
might be rich. 10 And herein [h] I give *my* advice: for — h 1 Cor. vii. 25.
[i] this is expedient for you, who have begun before, not — i Prov. xix. 17. Matt. x. 42. 1 Tim. vi. 18, 19.
only to do, but also to be [‡] forward a year ago. 11 — ‡ Gr. willing.
Now therefore perform the doing of it; that as *there was*
a readiness to will, so *there may be* a performance also
out of that which you have. 12 For [k] if there be first — k Chap. ix. 7. Mark xii. 43.
a willing mind, *it is* accepted according to that a man
hath, *and* not according to that he hath not. 13 For
[l] *I mean* not that other men be eased, and you burdened: — l Acts iv. 34.
14 But by an equality, *that* now at this time your
abundance *may be a supply* for their want, that their
abundance also may be *a supply* for your want; that there
may be equality: 15 As it is written, [m] He that *had* — m Exod. xvi. 18.
gathered much had nothing over; and he that *had gathered* little, had no lack.

v. 7—15. The apostle proceeds to excite the Corinthians to give liberally to the necessities of their brethren, by the most persuasive arguments.

1. The eminence in other gifts and graces should make them ambitious to excel in this. *Therefore, as, or but as, you abound in every thing, great and glorious, in faith, in utterance*, and eloquence, in clear *knowledge* of the mysteries of the gospel, *and in all*

all diligence, to advance the Redeemer's cause and interest, *and in your love to us, see that ye abound in this grace also*, of Christian liberality And this *I speak not by commandment*, as particularly ordered of God, or by my apostolic authority, *but* rather recommend it to you, *by occasion of the forwardness of others*, that you may not come behind them in any spiritual attainments, *and to prove the sincerity of your love* to Jesus and to his poor members for his sake *Note*, (1) We should be ashamed to be outdone in liberality by those who have less ability than ourselves (2) Where our love to Jesus is sincere, it will appear by a readiness to every good word and work

2 He urges the example of the great Redeemer *For ye know the grace of our Lord Jesus Christ*, the greatness of his love to poor and perishing souls, *that though he was rich* in uncreated glory, the Maker and Governor of all things, *yet for your sakes he became poor*, so poor, as to want a house of his own to cover him when alive, and, when dead, was indebted to the charity of a friend for a grave And to this he submitted, *that you through his poverty might be rich*, filled with all the treasures of his grace here, and his glory hereafter therefore standing so indebted to him, how could they with-hold a pittance of their perishing goods from his necessitous saints and their brethren?

3 Their promising beginnings called for a suitable conclusion *And herein I give my advice for this is expedient for you*, and becoming the high rank in which you stand, *who have begun before, not only to do* something by way of such a collection, *but also to be forward a year ago*, testifying the greatest readiness to concur in this generous service *Now therefore perform the doing of it, that as there was a readiness to will, so there may be a performance also out of that which ye have*, that your practice may correspond with your professions, and your contributions be according to your abilities *for if there be first a willing mind*, and real charity in the heart, the gift *is accepted according to that a man hath, and not according to that he hath not*, for it is not the sum contributed, so much as the spirit from whence it proceeds, that God regards

4 Since the divine providence had favoured them with abundance of worldly goods, they were peculiarly obliged to liberal distribution to the poor *For I mean not that other men be eased, and you burdened*, either that you should impoverish yourselves, to enrich the poor in Judea, or that other churches should be excused, and you alone be called upon to bear the whole charge of their necessary relief no, *but by an equality*, proportioning your gifts to your abilities, *that now at this time your abundance may be a supply for their want, that*, if by the strange vicissitudes of divine providence you should be hereafter reduced, and they prosperous, *their abundance may be a supply for your want, that there may be equality*, in the mutual beneficence exercised towards each other *As it is written*, concerning the manna, *He that had gathered much had nothing over, and he that had gathered little had no lack*, each had their omer, what remained to those who had gathered more being given to supply the wants of the aged and infirm, who had gathered less In like manner should we who abound, reckon our superfluities as the debt we owe to the indigent

16 But thanks *be* to God, which put the same earnest
care into the heart of Titus for you 17 For indeed
he accepted the exhortation, but being more forward, of
his own accord he went unto you 18 And we have
sent with him [n] the brother, whose praise *is* in the gospel [n Chap xii 18]
throughout all the churches 19 (And not *that* only,
but who was also chosen of the churches to travel with
us with this † grace which is administred by us to the glory [† Or gift]
of the same Lord, and *declaration of* your ready mind)
20 Avoiding this, that no man should blame us in this
abundance, which is administred by us, 21 [p] Providing [p Rom xii 17 Phil iv 8 1 Pet ii 12]
for honest things, not only in the sight of the Lord,
but also in the sight of men 22 And we have sent
with them our brother, whom we have oftentimes proved
diligent in many things, but now much more diligent,
upon the great confidence which ‡ *I have* in you [‡ Or, He hath]
23 Whether *any do enquire* of Titus, *he is* my partner,
and fellow helper concerning you or our brethren *be
enquired of, they are* [q] the messengers of the churches, *and* [q Phil ii 25]
the glory of Christ 24 Wherefore shew ye to them,
and before the churches, the proof of your love, and [r] of [r Chap vii 14 & ix 2]
our boasting on your behalf

v 16—24 The apostle here,

1 Thanks God, who put the same earnest care into the heart of Titus, to engage them *in this blessed work*, so that he needed no entreaty to undertake the journey, but full of zeal, as the apostle himself, for the honour of the Corinthian brethren, and for the relief of the poor, he was a volunteer in the service, and under a divine direction readily undertook to go *Note*, Readiness to a good work shews the temper right

2 He commends to them a brother, who accompanied Titus *and we have sent with him the brother, whose praise is in the gospel throughout all the churches*, for his fidelity and zeal in the ministry, *and not that only, but who was also chosen of the churches to travel with us with this grace*, or free gift, *which is administred by us*, and to be distributed to the necessitous in Judea, *to the glory of the same Lord*, who is hereby honoured as our common Master, *and* to the *declaration of your ready* and liberal *mind*, which is hereby manifested

3 He intimates the care he took to remove all suspicion of dishonesty or partiality, by thus having others joined with him in this charge *Avoiding this, that no man should blame us in this abundance, which is administred by us*, as if we misapplied or embezzled the least mite *providing things honest, not only in the sight of the Lord, but also in the sight of men*, whom we would convince of our unblemished integrity *Note*, In this censorious world we cannot be too careful to avoid every occasion of scandal, and ministers for the gospel's sake should be peculiarly cautious, and especially in money matters

4 He commends to them another brother, who also accompanied Titus, but who it was is uncertain He speaks of him with distinguished respect, as one *whom we have oftentimes proved diligent in many things, but now much more diligent, upon the great confidence which I have in you*, that ye will receive him with respect, and attend to his exhortations

5 In answer to any cavils of the false teachers he adds, *Whether any do enquire of Titus, he is my partner, and fellow-helper concerning you* in the work of the ministry *or our brethren be enquired of, they are the messengers of the churches*, deputed by them to this service, *and the glory of Christ*, ornaments to the gospel which they preached *Wherefore shew ye to them, and before the churches, the proof of your love* to Christ, to me, and your afflicted brethren, *and of our boasting on your behalf*, that you may be found to answer the high opinion we have entertained of you, and the encomiums we have bestowed upon you

CHAP IX

In this chapter the apostle seemeth to excuse his earnestness in pressing the Corinthians to the duty of charity, ver 1—5 *And proceedeth to give directions about the acceptable way and manner of performing it, viz bountifully, deliberately, and freely, and giveth good encouragement for so doing*, ver 6, *to the end*

1 FOR as touching [a] the ministring to the saints, it [a Acts xi 29 Rom xv 26 1 Cor xvi 1]
is superfluous for me to write to you 2 For I
know the forwardness of your mind, [b] for which I boast [b Chap viii 24]
of you to them of Macedonia, that Achaia was ready
a year ago; and your zeal hath provoked very many [c Chap viii 10]
3 Yet have I sent the brethren, lest our boasting of you
should be in vain in this behalf, that, as I said, ye may
be ready 4 Lest haply if they of Macedonia come
with me, and find you unprepared, we (that we say not,
you) should be ashamed in this same confident boasting
5 Therefore I thought it necessary to exhort the brethren,
that they would go before unto you, and make
up beforehand your † bounty, ‡ whereof ye had notice [† Or blessing]
before, that the same might be ready as *a matter of* bounty, [‡ Or which hath been spoken of before Land Ver]
and not as *of* covetousness

v 1—5 The apostle, with admirable address, whilst he seems to waive many arguments he might have urged, yet by his confidence expressed in their readiness to comply with his request, lays the strongest obligations on them to shew their generosity He knew *their forwardness*, he boasted of *their zeal*, and it had excited a holy ambition in the Macedonians to follow them For their own sake therefore, as well as his, he wished them to be ready, and had sent Titus and the brethren for this purpose, that if any of the Macedonians came with them, he, not to say they themselves, would be put to shame in the confident boasting he had made of them, should they be found unprepared, and their collections not compleated He sent therefore, that having timely notice, all might be ready in the way most honourable for them, and most agreeable to the commendations he had given them, not an extorted alms, but a noble, generous, willing contribution, the grateful acknowledgment due to God for all the singular mercies they had received *Note*, Alms given with reluctance, or squeezed out by mere importunity, only prove the covetousness, not the charity of the giver

6 But this *I say*, [d] He which soweth sparingly shall [d Prov xi 24 & xix 17 Gal vi 7]
reap also sparingly and he which soweth bountifully [e Deut xv 7]
shall reap also bountifully 7 Every man according as [f Ex xxv 2 & xxxv 5 1 Cor xvi 2 Rom xii 8 Chap viii 12]
he purposeth in his heart, *so let him give*, [e] not grudgingly,
or of necessity for [f] God loveth a chearful giver
8 And [g] God *is* able to make all grace abound towards [g Phil iv 19]
you, that [h] ye always having all sufficiency in all things, [h Pro xi 25]
may abound to every good work 9 (As it is written,

[i] He hath dispersed abroad, he hath given to the poor
his righteousness remaineth for ever 10 Now he that
[k] ministreth seed to the sower, both minister bread for
your food, and multiply your seed sown, and increase the
fruits of your righteousness) 11 Being enriched in eve
ry thing to all † bountifulness, [l] which causeth through
us thanksgiving to God 12 For the administration
of this service not only supplieth the want of the saints,
but is abundant also by many thanksgivings unto God,
13 (Whiles by the experiment of this ministration,
[m] they glorify God for your professed subjection unto
the gospel of Christ, and [n] for your liberal distribution
unto them, and unto all men) 14 And by their prayer
for you, which long after you, [o] for the exceeding grace
of God in you 15 Thanks *be* unto God for his un-
speakable gift.

v 6—15 The apostle proceeds to direct them,

1 Concerning the right manner of giving It must be done, (1) *Bountifully*, according to our abilities (2) *With deliberation*, not inconsiderately, but after weighing well what we can afford, consistent with the provision we owe to our own house (3) *Not grudgingly, or of necessity*, as if it was extorted by importunity, or that we were ashamed not to do as others, or as if our heart grieved to part with what our hand bestowed such a spirit would mar the deed

2 He suggests the strongest reasons to excite their liberality (1) It would be highly for their own advantage *He which soweth sparingly shall reap also sparingly and he which soweth bountifully shall reap also bountifully* (2) *God loveth a chearful giver*, and his love is the greatest of blessings (3) He is able abundantly to recompense you, both in spiritual graces, and worldly goods, so that you shall still have an abundant sufficiency thro' his good providence, and be enabled to abound in every good work, finding yourselves never the poorer for what is spent in his blessed service (4) They would hereby secure lasting honour, since the scripture testifies of him who liberally dispenses to the poor, that *his righteousness*, or alms, *remaineth for ever*, and shall bring forth the most blessed fruits in everlasting life, when the great Judge in the day of his appearing shall remember and reward him (5) Much glory will hereby accrue to God, as well as much good be done to the poor saints, who experiencing the riches of your bounty, will be excited to offer their thanksgivings to God for this proof of your fraternal love, and of your real *subjection to the gospel of Christ*, manifested in such liberality shewn to them, and unto all men as occasion requireth *Note*, Where true Christianity is enthroned in the heart, it will ever appear in godlike charity (5) This will also engage the prayers of those who partake of your bounty, and an interest in the supplications of the saints at a throne of grace, will abundantly repay us for every kindness done to them *Note*, When we can make no other acknowledgment, we must pray for our kind Benefactors, that God, the poor man's friend, may reward them

3 The apostle offers up his own earnest prayers for them *Now he that ministreth seed to the sower*, so that there is corn enough for the year's provision, and a sufficiency again to sow the ground, *both minister bread for your food*, and give you always a supply, *and multiply your seed sown*, restoring a hundred fold into your bosoms, *and increase the fruits of your righteousness*, enabling you to abound in liberality more and more, and I have confidence he will, *being enriched in every thing*, with all the blessings of grace and providence, which can enable and dispose you *to* exercise *all bountifulness, which causeth through us thanksgiving to God*, who bless his name both for the abundance he hath bestowed upon you, and for the heart he hath given you to employ it to his glory

4 He concludes the effort with this doxology, *Thanks be unto God for his unspeakable gift*, for all he hath done for you, in you, and by you; above all, for Jesus Christ, that most transcendently invaluable gift, which comprehends all others, and for which all language is insufficient to express our gratitude

CHAP X

In this chapter the apostle, in a mild and humble manner, asserteth his authority, ver 1—6 He then proceeds to reason the case with the Corinthians, and refuseth to justify himself, or to act by such rules as the false teachers did, but according to the better rules he had fixed for himself, ver 7, to the end

1 NOW [a] I Paul myself beseech you, by the meek
ness and gentleness of Christ, [b] who in presence
am base among you, but being absent am bold toward
you 2 But I beseech you, that I may not be bold
when I am present, with that confidence wherewith I
think to be bold against some which think of us as if
we walked according to the flesh 3 For though we
walk in the flesh, we do not war after the flesh 4
(For [d] the weapons of [e] our warfare *are* not carnal, but
† mighty through God [f] to the pulling down of strong
holds) 5 [g] Casting down ‡ imaginations, and every
high thing that exalteth itself against the knowledge of
God, and bringing into captivity every thought to the
obedience of Christ 6 And [i] having in a readiness to
revenge all disobedience, when [l] your obedience is ful-
filled

v 1—6 No where had the apostle met with more malignant insinuations, than from the false teachers at Corinth, he is obliged therefore, in justice to himself, to refute their slanders

1 Though he had it in his power to punish, he rather chose mildly to intreat, imitating the meekness and gentleness of his blessed Master The false teachers reviled him as a poor despicable animal, and mean in his abilities, as diminutive in his stature, who fawned and cringed when present, but when absent wrote in such a magisterial stile, terrifying them into compliance with his will, by vain boasts of his apostolic rod But he wished not to be compelled to exercise the power wherewith he was invested, and to their faces boldly to rebuke, and severely chastise, those who dared insinuate as if he *walked after the flesh*, with views of secular advantage, and influenced by carnal policy *Note*, (1) However great provocations we may meet with, the example of the meek and gentle Lamb of God should ever be in our eye (2) If men will not be reformed, they must be ruined (3) The best of men and ministers may expect malignant traducers

2 He asserts the integrity of his preaching and conduct *For though we walk in the flesh*, surrounded with the common infirmities of humanity, *we do not war after the flesh*, under the maxims of fleshly wisdom, or for any selfish ends *For the weapons of our warfare are not carnal*, we war not against the powers of evil with an arm of flesh, or pretend to convince by mere human persuasion, *but* that gospel we preach becomes effectual through divine operation, and is *mighty through God*, the Spirit's energy, *to the pulling down of the strong holds* of sin and Satan in the world, and in the hearts of men, *casting down imaginations*, confuting the corrupt reasonings of self-righteous Pharisees and proud philosophers, *and every high thing that exalteth itself against the knowledge of God*, confounding the pride and self-sufficiency of the unhumbled heart, *and bringing into captivity every thought to the obedience of Christ* engaging the sinner to bow to his gentle yoke, submitting his reason to revelation, his will to the commands of Jesus, and in every sentiment of his soul yielding a willing subjection to the authority of the great Redeemer *Note*, (1) Men are not to be persuaded by the sword but by the gospel (2) Satan's power is strong in the human heart, nothing but the power of Jesus can dethrone him (3) Nothing is more opposite to *the knowledge of God*, than a high conceit of our own wisdom and righteousness

3 He threatens the offender, *having in a readiness to revenge all disobedience*, and inflict condign punishment on those false teachers, and maligners of the true apostles, *when your obedience is fulfilled*, and mild methods have recovered the penitent members from those who continue refractory

7 [k] Do ye look on things after the outward appear-
ance? [l] If any man trust to himself, that he is Christ's,
let him of himself think this again, that as he *is* Christ's
even [m] so *are* we Christ's 8 For though I should boast
somewhat more of our authority, ([n] which the Lord hath
given us for edification, and not for your destruction)
[o] I should not be ashamed 9 That I may not seem
[p] as if I would terrify you by letters 10 For *his* let-
ters, (say they) *are* weighty and powerful, but *his* bodily
presence *is* weak, and [q] *his* speech contemptible 11
Let such an one think this, [r] that such as we are in word
by letters, when we are absent, such *will we be* also in
deed when we are present 12 For [s] we dare not make
ourselves of the number, or compare ourselves with some
that commend themselves but they measuring them
selves by themselves, and comparing themselves amongst
themselves, are not wise 13 But we will not boast of
things without *our* measure, but according to the mea-
sure of the rule which God hath distributed to us, a mea-
sure to reach even unto you 14 For we stretch not
ourselves beyond *our measure*, as though we reached not
unto you, for [t] we are come as far as to you also in
preaching the gospel of Christ 15 Not boasting of
things without *our* measure, *that is*, [u] of other men's la-
bours, but having hope when your faith is increased,
that we shall be | enlarged by you according to our rule
abundantly, 16 To preach the gospel in the *regions*

beyond you, *and* not to boast in another man's line of
things made ready to our hand 17 But [x] he that glo-
rieth, let him glory in the Lord 18 For [y] not he that
commendeth himself is approved, [z] but whom the Lord
commendeth

x Isa lxv 16 Jer ix 24 1 Cor i 31 y Prov xxvii 2 z Rom ii 29. 1 Cor iv 5

v 7—18 The apostle reasons the case with the Corinthians *Do ye look on things after the outward appearance?* and form your judgment merely on external show? *If any man trust to himself, that he is Christ's,* that he belongs to him as a member of his body mystical, or is commissioned by him as a minister, *let him of himself think this again, that as he is Christ's, even so are we Christ's,* whatever evidence he may produce of the one or the other, I can at least equal him *For though I should boast somewhat more of our authority,* than I have done, or than the vainest of my traducers dare to do concerning the powers with which they are invested, (which authority *the Lord hath given us for edification* of his church, *and not for your destruction,* to drive offenders to despair by severity), *I should not be ashamed,* but dare speak with truth and confidence But I forbear, *that I may not seem,* as these men suggest, *as if I would terrify you by letters For his letters, say they, are weighty and powerful,* wrote in an authoritative strain, and big with menaces *but his bodily presence is weak, and his speech contemptible,* he appears with no dignity of presence and aspect, and his parts and elocution are as despicable as his stature In answer to such a contemptuous insult, I reply,

1 *Let such an one think this,* and be assured, *that such as we are in word by letters, when we are absent, such will we be also in deed when we are present,* and execute every threatening we denounce against the obstinately impenitent

2 We never act with falsehood and ostentation, like these seducers, *For we dare not make ourselves of the number, or compare ourselves with some that commend themselves,* puffed up with vain conceit, and blinded with self-admiration *but whilst they* fondly value themselves on their imaginary greatness, *measuring themselves by themselves,* and supposing themselves the standard of excellence, *and comparing themselves amongst themselves,* by the poor and insignificant endowments of others equally vain, they *are not wise,* foolishly fancying they are something, when in fact they are nothing *Note,* All self-applause is hateful We should look to others superior excellencies to be humble, and not proudly vaunt ourselves over those beneath us

3 The apostle lays down the proper rule of conduct *But we will not boast of things without our measure, but according to the measure of the rule which God hath distributed to us, a measure to reach even unto you* Like those who run in the Isthmian games, we have kept the line marked out for our race, and in a regular course have preached the gospel as far as Corinth *For we stretch not ourselves beyond our measure,* as these false apostles do, *as though we reached not unto you,* and had in coming to Corinth entered into another man's province, *for we are come as far as to you also in preaching the gospel of Christ,* through countries where his name had not been heard before *not boasting of things without our measure, that is, of other men's labours,* and taking, to myself the credit of their success, *but having hope, when your faith is increased,* your church fully regulated, and your divisions healed, *that we shall be enlarged by you according to our rule abundantly, to preach the gospel in the regions beyond you,* where darkness still reigns uncontrouled, *and not to boast in another man's line of things made ready to our hand,* assuming to myself the honour of their labours *But he that glorieth, let him glory in the Lord,* ascribing to the grace of God alone the whole of whatever gifts he enjoys, or success he may be blessed with and taking no praise to himself *For not he that commendeth himself is approved, but whom the Lord commendeth,* and his approbation is the only true and substantial honour

CHAP XI

In this chapter the apostle apologizeth for his being about to commend himself, and giveth the reasons for what he did, ver 1—4 After which he maintaineth, in his own necessary vindication, his equality with the other apostles, and with the false apostles in this particular, of preaching the gospel to the Corinthians freely without wages, ver 5—15 Then he maketh another preface to what he was about further to say in his own justification, ver 16—21 And lastly he giveth a large account of his qualifications, labours, and sufferings, in which he exceeded the false apostles, ver 22, to the end

a Chap v 13 Ver 16 b Chap xii 17 18 c Hos ii 19 20 d Lev xxi 13 e Gen iii 4 John viii 44 f Gal i 6 8 g Acts xx 28 Heb xii 17

1 WOULD to God you could bear with me a
little in my folly, and indeed bear with me
2 For I am jealous over you with godly jealousy for
I have espoused you to one husband, that I may pre-
sent you as a chaste virgin to Christ 3 But I fear lest
by any means, as the serpent beguiled Eve through his
subtilty, so your minds should be corrupted from the
simplicity that is in Christ 4 For if he that cometh
preacheth another Jesus whom we have not preached, or
if ye receive another Spirit, which ye have not received,
or [h] another gospel, which ye have not accepted, ye might
well bear with *him*

h Gal i 8

v 1—4 The apostle begins,

1 With an apology for what he was about to say *Would to God you could bear with me a little in my folly, and indeed bear with me,* compelled reluctantly to speak in my own commendation

2 He gives the reasons for what he was about to say It was,

(1.) Out of jealousy for them *For I am jealous over you with godly jealousy for I have espoused you to one husband, that I may present you as a chaste virgin to Christ,* true to your solemn engagements, and faithful in all your conduct to this heavenly bridegroom of souls *But I fear,* knowing the wiles of the false teachers, *lest by any means, as the serpent beguiled Eve through his subtilty, so your minds should be corrupted from the simplicity that is in Christ,* perverted from the principles, or seduced from the practice of the gospel

(2.) Out of justice to himself *For if he that cometh preacheth another Jesus whom we have not preached, or if ye receive another Spirit, which ye have not received, or another gospel, which ye have not accepted, ye might well bear with him* but since there is but *one* Jesus, *one* Spirit, *one* gospel, it was shrewdly to be suspected, that the person who pretended to preach another Jesus, boasted of a better Spirit, and a more excellent gospel than that by which they had at first been converted to the faith, was a deceiver, and, instead of being connived at or caressed, should be rejected with abhorrence

5 For I suppose [i] I was not a whit behind the very
chiefest apostles. 6 But though [k] *I be* rude in speech,
yet [l] not in knowledge, but [m] we have been thorough-
ly made manifest among you in all things 7 Have I
committed an offence [n] in abasing myself that you might
be exalted, because I have preached to you the gospel of
God freely? 8 I robbed other churches, taking wages
of them to do you service 9 And when I was present
with you and wanted, [o] I was chargeable to no man
for that which was lacking to me the brethren which
came from Macedonia supplied and in all things I have
kept myself from being burdensome unto you, and *so*
will I keep *myself* 10 [p] As the truth of Christ is in
me, [q] no man shall stop me of this boasting in the re-
gions of Achaia 11. Wherefore? [r] because I love you
not? God knoweth 12 But what I do, that I will do,
[s] that I may cut off occasion from them which desire
occasion, that wherein they glory, they may be found
even as we 13 For [t] such *are* false apostles, [u] deceitful
workers, transforming themselves [x] into the apostles of
Christ 14 And no marvel, for Satan himself is trans-
formed into an angel of light 15 Therefore *it is* no
great thing if his ministers also be transformed as the
ministers of righteousness, [y] whose end shall be accord-
ing to their works

i 1 Cor xv 10 Chap xii 11 k 1 Cor i 17 & ii 1 13 l Eph iii 4 m Chap iv 2 & v 11 & xii 2 n 1 Cor ix 6, 12 Chap xii 13 o Chap xii 13 1 Thes ii 9 2 Thes iii 8 p Rom ix 1 q 1 Cor ix 15 r Chap xii 15 s 1 Cor ix 12 t Gal i 7 Phil i 15 1 John iv 1 u Gal i x Rev ii 2 y Phil iii 19

v 5—15 Constrained by the insinuations which had been cast out against him, the blessed Paul,

1 Asserts his equality with the very chief of the apostles Though *rude in speech,* my stile simple, my elocution not so graceful as some others, yet my knowledge of the gospel-mysteries is inferior to none *But we have been thoroughly made manifest among you in all things,* your consciences have born witness to the efficacy of our preaching, and our conversation among you, as you know, hath been most unblameable

2 He asserts his disinterested conduct, and vindicates himself from the cavils of his adversaries, who suggested, as though he acted below the apostolic character, in not receiving his maintenance from the church at Corinth *Have I committed an offence in abasing myself,* to work for my subsistence, *that you might be exalted* to the participation of the gospel privileges, *because I preached the gospel to you freely,* that no prejudices might obstruct your receiving our word, which such disinterested zeal could not but recommend? *I robbed other churches, taking wages of them to do you service,* not really plundering them, but living upon their voluntary contributions, when the Corinthians, so much richer, should have rather afforded him a maintenance However, he neither had been, nor would be, a burden to them his former want the Macedonians supplied, and he was firmly resolved, that none in all Achaia, in any future time, should have reason to reproach him on this behalf, or stop his glorying of having preached to them the gospel freely

Wherefore do I this? out of pride or distrust, as the false teachers would insinuate, and *because I love you not?* No, *God knoweth* these were not my motives But I have and will this act, *that I may cut off occasion from them which desire occasion,* and would be ready to catch at any handle to fleece you, if I received any

thing

taking from you Therefore I would wish, *that wherein they glory, they may be found even as we*, and as free from every mercenary view *for in truth such are false apostles*, assuming a character to which they have not the least title, *deceitful workers*, corrupting the word of God, *transforming themselves into the apostles of Christ*, appearing under the most specious professions *And no marvel, for Satan himself is transformed into an angel of light*, as he appeared when he came to seduce Eve from her integrity *Therefore it is no great thing if his ministers also be transformed as the ministers of righteousness, whose end shall be according to their works*, and the issue be their everlasting destruction

16 I say again, Let no man think me a fool, if
otherwise, yet as a fool receive me, that I may boast my-
self a little 17 That which I speak, I speak *it* not
after the Lord, but as it were foolishly in this confi-
dence of boasting 18 Seeing that many glory after
the flesh, I will glory also 19 For ye suffer fools glad-
ly, seeing ye *yourselves* are wise 20 For ye suffer if a
man bring you into bondage, if a man devour *you*, if a
man take *of you*, if a man exalt himself, if a man smite
you on the face 21 I speak as concerning reproach,
as though we had been weak howbeit, whereinsoever
any is bold (I speak foolishly) I am bold also 22 Are
they Hebrews? so *am* I are they Israelites? so *am* I
are they the seed of Abraham? so *am* I 23 Are they
ministers of Christ? (I speak as a fool) I *am* more in
labours more abundant, in stripes above measure, in
prisons more frequent, in deaths oft 24 Of the Jews
five times received I forty *stripes* save one 25 Thrice
was I beaten with rods, once was I stoned, thrice I suf-
fered shipwreck, a night and a day I have been in the
deep 26 *In* journeyings often, *in* perils of waters, *in*
perils of robbers, *in* perils by *mine own* countrymen, *in*
perils by the heathen, *in* perils in the city, *in* perils in
the wilderness, *in* perils in the sea, *in* perils among false
brethren, 27 In weariness and painfulness, in watch-
ings often, in hunger and thirst, in fastings often, in
cold and nakedness 28 Besides those things that are
without, that which cometh upon me daily, the care of
all the churches 29 Who is weak, and I am not
weak? who is offended, and I burn not? 30 If I must
needs glory, I will glory of the things which concern
mine infirmities 31 The God and Father of our
Lord Jesus Christ, which is blessed for evermore, know-
eth that I lye not. 32 In Damascus the governor un-
der Aretas the king kept the city of the Damascenes
with a garrison, desirous to apprehend me 33 And
through a window in a basket was I let down by the wall,
and escaped his hands

v 16—33 The apostle with reluctance enters upon the subject of his own vindication *I say again, Let no man think me a fool, if otherwise, yet as a fool receive me, that I may boast myself a little*, such boasts in general being indeed the indications of a vain mind *That which I speak, I speak it not after the Lord, but as it were foolishly in this confidence of boasting* but since I am compelled by the unhappy circumstances in which I stand, and *seeing that many glory after the flesh*, in their external privileges, *I will glory also* *For ye suffer fools gladly*, the arrogant boasters among you, *seeing ye yourselves are wise* Probably the words are spoken ironically Wise men indeed ye are, to be dupes to such ostentatious deceivers *For ye suffer if a man bring you into bondage*, tyrannizing over your consciences, *if a man devour you* under the specious pretence of religion, *if a man take of you* presents and salaries for preaching, *if a man exalt himself*, and treat you with lordly contempt, *if a man smite you on the face*, submissive to every insult *I speak as concerning reproach*, with which these deceivers have treated you, *as though we had been weak*, and had no right to exert such authority as they pretend to claim *howbeit, whereinsoever any is bold (I speak foolishly) I am bold also*, and can produce as long a catalogue of privileges as the chief of these arrogant men

1 As to *external Jewish privileges* of descent, *Are they Hebrews? so am I*, by both my parents, (Phil iii 5) *are they Israelites?* the sons of Jacob, *so am I are they the seed of Abraham? so am I*, a true descendant of this eminent patriarch

2 As to *gospel privileges*, *Are they ministers of Christ?* commissioned by him, *(I speak as a fool)*, admitting their plea, tho' false, to be true, *I am more*, having a more extraordinary commission, more eminent endowments, and suffering for the cause more than any of them *In labours more abundant, in stripes above measure*, unmercifully beaten *in prisons more frequent, in deaths oft*, exposed to the most imminent dangers, a short enumeration of which will prove what I assert *Of the Jews five times received I forty stripes save one. Thrice was I beaten with rods*, by the Roman lictors, *once was I stoned*, and left for dead, *thrice I suffered shipwreck, a night and a day I have been in the deep*, tossed on the foaming waves, and every moment ready to be swallowed up by them *In journeyings often, in perils of waters*, in fording rivers, or by land-floods, *in perils of robbers, in perils by mine own countrymen*, who lay in wait for me, *in perils by the heathen, in perils in the city*, from dangerous insurrections, *in perils in the wilderness*, during my travels, *in perils in the sea, in perils among false brethren*, the most dangerous of all enemies *In weariness and painfulness*, under the most fatiguing labours, *in watchings oft*, my rest being broken, *in hunger and thirst*, for want of needful refreshments, *in fastings often*, voluntary, or necessitated by mere want, *in cold and nakedness*, exposed to the inclemency of the weather, and without sufficient clothing to keep me warm *Besides those things* which affect my *body*, a heavier load of cares lies upon my mind, *that which cometh upon me daily, the care of all the churches*, to advance their purity and peace, rectify their disorders, and guard them against seducers *Who is weak, and I am not weak?* sympathizing with him in his infirmity of body or mind? *who is offended, and I burn not* with jealousy for the offence, and zeal to restore him? *If I must needs glory, I will glory of the things which concern mine infirmities*, and rather mention my sufferings and hardships, than my privileges *The God and Father of our Lord Jesus Christ, which is blessed for evermore, knoweth that I lye not* *In Damascus the governor under Aretas the king kept the city of the Damascenes with a garrison, desirous to apprehend me And through a window in a basket was I let down by the wall, and escaped his hands*, snatched as it were from inevitable death Such a glorious course marked indeed the great apostle such sufferings for righteousness sake are the highest honour

CHAP XII

In this chapter the apostle, first, maketh mention of the favour God had shewn him, and the honour done him, and the methods God took to keep him humble, and the use he made of this dispensation, ver 1—10 Then he addresseth himself to the Corinthians, blaming them for what was faulty among them, and giving a large account of his behaviour, and kind intentions towards them, ver 11, to the end

1 IT is not expedient for me doubtless to glory I
will come to visions and revelations of the Lord
2 I knew a man in Christ above fourteen years ago
(whether in the body, I cannot tell, or whether out of
the body, I cannot tell God knoweth) such an one
caught up to the third heaven 3 And I knew such a
man (whether in the body, or out of the body, I cannot
tell God knoweth) 4 How that he was caught up into
paradise, and heard unspeakable words, which it is not law-
ful for a man to utter 5 Of such an one will I glory
yet of myself I will not glory, but in mine infirmities
6 For though I would desire to glory, I shall not be
a fool, for I will say the truth but *now* I forbear, lest
any man should think of me above that which he seeth
me *to be*, or *that* he heareth of me 7 And lest I
should be exalted above measure through the abundance
of the revelations, there was given to me a thorn in
the flesh, the messenger of Satan to buffet me, lest I
should be exalted above measure 8 For this thing I
besought the Lord thrice, that it might depart from
me 9 And he said unto me, My grace is sufficient
for thee for my strength is made perfect in weakness
Most gladly therefore will I rather glory in my infirmi-
ties, that the power of Christ may rest upon me 10
Therefore I take pleasure in infirmities, in reproaches,
in necessities, in persecutions, in distresses for Christ's
sake for when I am weak, then am I strong

v 1—10 Once more he will speak Though (ordinarily he confesseth) *it is not expedient for me doubtless to glory*, *but* others boast of extraordinary manifestations, *I will come to visions and revelations of the Lord*, one remarkable instance of which I will only mention

I knew, or I know, *a man in Christ*, a faithful soul, *above fourteen years ago, (whether in the body I cannot tell, or whether out of the body*, whether in his spirit only, or in his whole man, *I cannot tell God knoweth) such an one caught up to the third heaven*, where angels dwell, and the most illustrious display of the divine glory is made *And I knew such a man, (whether in the body, or out of the body, I cannot tell God knoweth) how that he was caught up into paradise*, the region of the blessed, *and heard unspeakable words*, which contained such sublimity of ideas, and were delivered in such language, *as it is not lawful*, or possible, *for a man to utter*, in his present mortal state of weakness. *Of such an one will I glory yet of myself I will not glory, but in mine infirmities*, and in such things as carry evident marks of my own weakness

Let

For though I would desire to glory, I shall not be a fool, for I will say the truth, and appeal to the heart-searching God for what I say: *but now I forbear, lest any man should think of me above that he seeth me to be, or that he heareth of me*, supposing me to be more than human, who am a mere worm. *And lest I should be exalted above measure through the abundance of the revelations, there was given to me a thorn in the flesh, the messenger of Satan, to buffet me, lest I should be exalted above measure*: what this was, whether some bodily affliction, or outward reproach, or more probably the workings of evil corruptions, whatever it was, it was very grievous, yet sent for the most blessed purpose, and served to keep him humble. *For this thing I besought the Lord thrice* importunately, *that it might depart from me. And he said unto me*, by an audible voice, or some divine impression on my spirit, *My grace is sufficient for thee: for my strength is made perfect in weakness*, and I will carry thee victorious through all opposing foes without, and corruptions within. *Most gladly therefore will I rather glory in my infirmities, that the power of Christ may rest upon me*, and be the more transcendently exalted in rescuing me out of all my trials, and carrying me safe through every temptation. *Therefore I take pleasure in infirmities, in reproaches, in necessities, in persecutions, in distresses for Christ's sake*, not only resigned, but happy, rejoicing in the sufferings I endure: *for when I am weak, then am I strong*, and rise victorious over every foe, through the power of omnipotent grace. *Note*, (1) To be humble in the midst of high attainments is doubly excellent. (2) No thorn more grievous to a gracious soul, than the workings and buffetings of in-dwelling sin. (3) Prayer is the great relief under every distress. (4) Though God doth not always answer us according to our petitions, yet if he gives us strength to stand in our difficulties, we are bound to acknowledge that our prayers are answered. (5) There is sufficiency of grace in the Redeemer to carry us safe through every trial, and to make us at last more than conquerors. (6) The more we see and feel our own weakness, the more firm we stand in the power of God.

11 [l] I am become a fool in glorying, ye have com-
pelled me: for I ought to have been commended of
you: for [m] in nothing am I behind the very chiefest
apostles, [n] though I be nothing. 12 [o] Truly the signs
of an apostle were wrought among you in all patience,
in signs and wonders and mighty deeds. 13 For [p] what
is it wherein ye were inferior to other churches, except *it
be* that I myself was not burdensome to you? forgive
me this wrong. 14 [q] Behold, the third time I am
ready to come to you, and I will not be burdensome
to you; for [r] I seek not yours, but you: for the children
ought not to lay up for the parents, but the parents for
the children. 15 And [s] I will very gladly spend and
be spent [t] for you, though [u] the more abundantly I
love you, the less I be loved. 16 But be it so, [x] I did
not burden you: nevertheless being crafty, I caught you
with guile. 17 Did I make a gain of you by any of
them whom I sent unto you? 18 [y] I desired Titus,
and [z] with *him* I sent a brother: did Titus make a gain
of you? walked we not in the same spirit? *walked we*
not in the same steps? 19 [a] Again, think you that we
excuse ourselves unto you? we speak before God in
Christ: but *we do* all things, dearly beloved, for your
edifying. 20 For I fear, lest when I come I shall not
find you such as I would, and *that* I shall be found un-
to you such as ye would not: lest *there be* debates, en-
vyings, wraths, strifes, backbitings, whisperings, swell-
ings, tumults: 21 *And* lest when I come again, my
God will humble me among you, and *that* I shall bewail
many which have sinned already, and have not repented
of the uncleanness, and fornication, and lasciviousness,
which they have committed.

m 11—21. The apostle returns again,

1. To apologize for what might seem an act of vanity. *I am become a fool in glorying; ye have compelled me: for I ought to have been commended of you*, who have received such peculiar benefit by my means: *for in nothing am I behind the very chiefest apostle*, in my [illegible] and labours, *though I be nothing*, considered in myself, [illegible] and success is of God. *Truly the signs of an apostle were wrought among you in all patience*, amidst innumerable provocations and sufferings, *in signs*, miracles, *and wonders*, [illegible] *and mighty deeds*, which speak the arm of omnipotence. *For what is it wherein ye were inferior to other churches* in gifts and privileges, *except it be that I myself was not burdensome to you? forgive me this wrong*, that which never was a wrong [illegible], and [illegible], though polite, rebukes, [illegible] spoken ironically [illegible] for refusing their reward from them, which might be construed as a mark of dif-

dain. *Note*, (1) Where we have received spiritual benefit, it is a debt we owe to our ministers to vindicate their injured characters. (2) The greatest of men and ministers, when viewing themselves in their true colours, cannot but own, I am nothing.

2. He declares his purpose to shew the same disinterested conduct. *Behold, the third time I am ready to come to you*, having the second time been disappointed, *and I will not be burdensome to you*, but will preach the gospel to you freely: *for I seek not yours, but you*, your spiritual benefit, not your worldly substance. *For* I consider myself as your father in Christ, and shall treat you with paternal care, not desiring nor accepting ought at your hands; *for*, in general, *the children ought not to lay up for the parents, but the parents for the children. And* all I have shall be willingly laid out for you, for *I will very gladly spend and be spent for you*, to promote the good of your souls, ready, if need be, to lay down my own life, *though* I should meet with the most ungrateful returns, and *the more abundantly I love you, the less I be loved*, and even those who seduce you be preferred before me. *Note*, (1) A true minister of Christ never serves for hire, but for love, delighting to feed, not to fleece the flock. (2) True zeal for Christ and his cause will make his servants nobly prodigal of life, unto their power, and sometimes above their power exerting themselves in his service. (3) The most ungrateful returns must not stay us from doing good even to the evil and unthankful.

3. He obviates an insinuation which the seducers suggested, that though he took no wages himself, those whom he sent were well paid. *Be it so*, they will argue, *I did not burden you: nevertheless being crafty, I caught you with guile*; so invidiously would they misrepresent my conduct. But in answer, I appeal to yourselves, *Did I make a gain of you by any of them whom I sent unto you? I desired Titus, and with him I sent a brother: did Titus make a gain of you? walked we not in the same spirit? walked we not in the same steps?* shewing the same disinterested generosity, and following my example in preaching the gospel freely, without any expence to you? *Again*,

4. *Think you that we excuse ourselves unto you?* and want by specious pretences, for sinister ends, to insinuate into your regard, or to get off from visiting you as I promised? *We speak before God in Christ*, appealing to him for our sincerity; *but we do all things, dearly beloved, for your edifying*, having this great end ever in view.

5. He declares his jealous fears for them. *For I fear, lest when I come I shall not find you such as I would*, obedient and orderly, *and that I shall be found unto you such as ye would not*, obliged, though with reluctance, to exert my apostolic authority; *lest there be debates, envyings, wraths, strifes, backbitings, whisperings, swellings, tumults*, and all other evil fruits of a proud, contentious, uncharitable spirit. *And lest when I come again, my God will humble me among you, and that I shall bewail many which have sinned already, and have not repented of the uncleanness, and fornication, and lasciviousness which they have committed. Note*, (1) The falls of professors are a real grief to their faithful ministers, and every gracious soul cannot but mourn over them. (2) They who persist in their iniquities must be faithfully rebuked, and, if they do not amend, their obstinate impenitence will inevitably issue in final perdition.

CHAP. XIII.

In this chapter the apostle threateneth to be severe against obstinate sinners, and assigneth the reason thereof, ver. 1—6. Then he maketh a suitable prayer to God on the behalf of the Corinthians, with the reasons inducing him thereto, ver. 7—10. And concludeth his epistle with a valediction and a benediction, ver. 11—14.

1 [a] THIS *is* the third time I am coming to you.
[b] In the mouth of two or three witnesses shall
every word be established. 2 [c] I told you before, and
foretel you as if I were present the second time; and be-
ing absent, now I write to them [d] which heretofore have
sinned, and to all other, that if I come again I will not
spare: 3 Since ye seek a proof of Christ [e] speaking in
me, which to you-ward is not weak, but [f] is mighty in
you. 4 For [g] though he was crucified through weak-
ness, yet [h] he liveth by the power of God. For we also
are weak in him, but [i] we shall live with him by the
power of God toward you. 5 [k] Examine yourselves,
whether ye be in the faith; prove your own selves. Know
ye not your own selves, *how* that Jesus Christ is in you,
except ye be reprobates? 6 But I trust that ye shall
know that we are not reprobates.

n 1—6. Having once and again warned them by his epistles to amend their disorders, with Sosthenes and Timothy, who

joined

joined in his admonitions, he is now the third time ready to appear in person Therefore,

1 He assures them, that if any continued yet refractory and disorderly, notwithstanding these repeated rebukes, he *would not spare*, but inflict condign punishment on such obstinate offenders *Note*, No patience, human or divine, will always bear there is an approaching end, when wrath to the uttermost will overtake the ungodly

2 Since they demanded a proof of his apostleship, they should receive it *Since ye seek a proof of Christ speaking in me*, as if I threatened what I had no power or authority to execute, when you have had such demonstration before of that gospel which I preach, and of that authority with which I am invested, *which to you ward is not weak, but is mighty in you*, who have experienced the efficacy of my preaching, and begun to smart under the chastening rod, (1 *Cor* xi 30) *For though he was crucified through weakness, yet he liveth by the power of God*, and hath all power now committed into his hands *for we also are weak in him*, and, because of our present sufferings, treated by many of you as despicable, and possessed of no authority from him *but we shall live with him by the power of God towards you*, and as surely as he lives, shall we prove ourselves cloathed with his power to punish offenders And this would soon be experienced by them, if they did not instantly amend their ways

3 He urges them to judge themselves, that they might not be judged of the Lord, or his ministers *Examine yourselves, whether ye be in the faith*, bring your hearts to the touchstone of God's revealed will *prove your own selves*, by this divine rule *know ye not your own selves, how that Jesus Christ is in you*, formed in your hearts by his Spirit, *except ye be reprobates*, and when brought to the test, like false metal, rejected as refuse, and found hypocrites *But I trust that ye shall know that we are not reprobates*, but approved and allowed of our divine Master, and acknowledged by him as faithful in all things

7 Now I pray to God that ye do no evil, not that
we should appear approved, but that ye should do that l Chap vi 9
which is honest [l] though we be as reprobates 8 For
[m] we can do nothing against the truth, but for the truth m 1 Tim i 9
9 For we are glad when [n] we are weak, and ye are n Chap xi 30 & xii 5, 9
strong and this also we wish, [o] *even* your perfection o 1 Thess iii 10
10 Therefore [p] I write these things being absent, lest
being present I should use sharpness, [q] according to the p 1 Cor iv 21 Chap. ii 3 & x 2 & xii 20
power which the Lord hath given me to edification, and
not to destruction. q Chap x 8

v 7—10 The apostle adds his fervent prayer for them *Now I pray to God that ye do no evil*, nor incur censure from us, or wrath from God *not that we should appear approved*, and by the punishment we inflict, give a demonstration of our apostolic power, *but that ye should do that which is honest*, and praiseworthy, *though we be as reprobates*, and, having no need to exert our power, should be thought of as insignificant persons, who really had it not *For we can do nothing against the truth*, nor dare lift up the rod against such as walk according to the gospel, *but* our power is to be exercised *for the truth*, to defend it against heretical teachers, and to recover backsliders by needful correction *For we are glad when we are weak, and ye are strong*, and when your exemplary practice renders censure unnecessary, and we appear as if we had no authority to inflict it *And this also we wish, even your perfection*, or *restoration*, that every offence were removed, the church knit together in perfect harmony and union, and every member of it growing up to the measure of the stature of the fulness of Christ *Therefore I write these things being absent, lest being present I should use sharpness, according to the power which the Lord hath given me to edification, and not to destruction*, desirous rather that all evils among you should be amended, and our reproofs effectual for your reformation, than that we should be constrained to give a proof of our power in executing deserved punishment on the impenitent

11 Finally, brethren, farewel Be perfect, be of good
comfort, [r] be of one mind, live in peace, and [s] the God r Rom xii 16 Phil ii 2 1 Pet iii 8
of love and peace shall be with you 12 [t] Greet one s Rom xv 33
another with an holy kiss 13 All the saints salute t Rom xvi 16
you 14 [u] The grace of the Lord Jesus Christ, and the u Rom xvi 24
love of God, and the communion of the holy Ghost, *be* x Phil ii 1
with you all Amen

v 11—14 The apostle here,

1 Takes his leave of them with affectionate exhortations. *Finally, my brethren, farewel Be perfect*, united to each other, walking in the purity of the gospel, and reforming every disorder *be of good comfort, be of one mind*; let every dispute be silenced, and the spirit of party subside *Live in peace* and love, *and the God of love and peace shall be with you*, and dwell in the midst of you with his especial presence and blessing *Greet one another with an holy kiss All the saints salute you*, wishing you all prosperity in your souls and bodies, in time and in eternity *Note*, (1) Union in affection and sentiment is the sure mark of the prosperity of the church (2) The God of love and peace commands us to be like himself, and that is to be happy

2 He concludes with his apostolical benediction *The grace of our Lord Jesus Christ, and the love of God, and the communion of the Holy Ghost be with you all*, may the grace of a dying Redeemer, which includes all spiritual and eternal blessings, be your portion ! may a sense of the Father's love, the spring and source of your redemption, be warm upon your hearts ! and may the richest communications from the Holy Ghost revive, quicken, strengthen, comfort, stablish you ever more and more, till by the mighty operation of this triune God your salvation shall be completed in glory everlasting, and your happy service be his never-ending praise ! Such is my prayer for you cease not to join my supplications for these inestimable benefits, and let every soul among you with faith and fervency say, *Amen* !

THE

EVANGELICAL EXPOSITOR;

OR, A

PRACTICAL COMMENT

Upon the EPISTLE of

St. PAUL to the GALATIANS.

THIS epistle of Paul, written, as is supposed, about the year 59, is directed not to the church or churches of a single city, as some others are, but of a country or province, for so Galatia was. It is very probable, that these Galatians were first converted to the Christian faith by his ministry, but if he was not the instrument of planting, yet at least he had been employed in watering these churches, as is evident from this epistle itself, and also from Acts xviii 23 *where we find him going over all the country of Galatia and Phrygia in order, strengthening all the disciples.*

While he was with them, they had expressed the greatest esteem and affection both for his person and ministry, but he had not been long absent from them before some judaizing teachers got in among them, by whose arts and insinuations they were soon drawn into a meaner opinion both of the one and of the other

That which these false teachers chiefly aimed at, was to draw them off from the truth as it is in Jesus, particularly in the great doctrine of justification, which they grossly perverted, by asserting the necessity of joining the observation of the law of Moses with faith in Christ in order to it, and the better to accomplish this their design, they did all they could to lessen the character and reputation of the apostle, and to raise up their own on the ruins of his, representing him as one who, if he was to be owned as an apostle, yet was much inferior to others, and particularly who deserved not such a regard as Peter, James, and John, whose followers, it is likely, they pretended to be and in both these attempts they had but too great success

This was the occasion of his writing this epistle, wherein he expresses his great concern, that they had suffered themselves to be so soon turned aside from the faith of the gospel, vindicates his own character and authority as an apostle against the aspersions of his enemies, shewing that his mission and doctrine were both divine, and that he was not, upon any account, behind the very chiefest of the apostles, 2 Cor xi 5. *He then sets himself to assert and maintain the great gospel-doctrine of justification by faith without the works of the law, and to obviate some difficulties that might be apt to arise in their minds concerning it · and having established this important doctrine, he exhorts them to stand fast in the liberty wherewith Christ had made them free, cautions them against the abuse of this liberty, gives them several very needful counsels and directions, and then concludes the epistle with giving them the true character of those false teachers by whom they had been ensnared, and, on the contrary, remind them of his own temper and behaviour In all which, his great scope and design was, to recover those that had been perverted, to settle those that might be wavering, and to confirm such among them as had kept their integrity*

CHAP I

In this chapter, after the preface or introduction, ver 1—6 *the apostle severely reproves these churches for their defection from the faith,* ver 6—10 *And then proves his own apostleship, which his enemies had brought them to question* 1 *From his end and design in preaching the gospel,* ver 10 2 *From his having received it by immediate revelation,* ver 11, 12 *For the proof of which he acquaints them,* (1) *What his former conversation was,* ver 13, 14 (2) *How he was converted, and called to the apostleship,* ver 15, 16 (3) *How he behaved himself afterwards,* ver 16, to the end

1 PAUL, an apostle ([a] not of men, neither by
man, [b] but by Jesus Christ, and God the Fa-
ther, [c] who raised him from the dead) 2
And all the brethren which are with me, unto
the churches of Galatia · 3 [d] Grace *be* to you, and peace
from God the Father, and *from* our Lord Jesus Christ,
4 [e] Who gave himself for our sins, that he might deliver
us from [f] this present evil world, according to the will of
God and our Father 5 To whom *be* glory for ever
and ever Amen.

[a] Ver 11, 12
[b] Tit i 3
[c] Acts ii 24 & iv 10
[d] Rom i 7 1 Cor i 3 2 Cor i 2 1 Thes i 1 2 Thes i 2
[e] Chap ii 20 Eph v 2 Tit ii 14
[f] 1 John v 19

v 1—5

v 1—5 Among the heaviest burdens which lay on the great apostle Paul was the care of all the churches, where many errors soon crept in, and judaizing teachers sought to corrupt the simplicity of the gospel, and therewith to decry him who was the zealous defender of its glorious privileges No where had these seducers practised with more success than among the Galatians, for whose recovery to the purity of the faith, the apostle writes this epistle

1 He begins with his apostolical address *Paul an apostle, not of men, neither by man*, not assuming a character to which he had no title, nor acting under any ordination merely human, *but* immediately called to this high office, and commissioned *by Jesus Christ* himself, who personally appeared to him, *and God the Father, who raised him from the dead*, declaring thereby his perfect satisfaction in the atonement and righteousness of his Son and therefore Paul's commission bore this eminent distinction, that, whilst the chief apostles were only ordained by Jesus in the days of his humiliation, the great apostle of the Gentiles received his call and office from the glorified Redeemer, exalted on his mediatorial throne

2 All the brethren which were with him joined the apostle in his address to the churches of Galatia, concurring with him in sentiment, and declaring thereby their approbation of the doctrines which he maintained, and of the just reproofs he was about to give No titles of respect or regard are added their general defection probably withheld him from making any honourable mention of them, as was usual in his other epistles Only,

3 He wishes that the best of blessings may attend them *Grace be with you*, in all its happy effects of pardon, comfort, strength, purity, perseverance, *and peace*, the consequence thereof both proceeding as a free and sovereign act of favour *from God the Father, and from our Lord Jesus Christ*, the meritorious cause of all our mercies, *who gave himself for our sins*, in infinite compassion to our wretched state, humbling himself to take our nature upon him, and as our substitute and representative to bear our sins in his own body on the tree, *that he might* obtain eternal redemption for us, and *deliver us from this present evil world*, from the guilt and condemnation under which it lies, and from the power of iniquity by which it is enslaved; and this hath our adored Redeemer done for us *according to the will of God and, or even, our Father*, who is reconciled to us by the blood of his cross, and regards us as dear children *To whom be glory for ever and ever, Amen!* Both to the Father and his coequal Son, for such a contrivance of infinite love and grace, in order to the redemption of lost souls, be all praise and honour ascribed by men and angels, in time and to eternity *Note*, (1) The oblation of Jesus once for all, is the only substantial foundation of the sinner's hope towards God (2) This world in which we dwell is full of evil we must in spirit and temper be delivered from it, or we shall be condemned with it

6 I marvel that ye are so soon removed from him
that called you into the grace of Christ unto another
g2 Cor xi 4 gospel: 7 ᵍ Which is not another, but ʰ there be some
h Acts xv that trouble you, and ⁱ would pervert the gospel of
1, 24 Chap v 10, Christ 8 But ᵏ though we, or an angel from heaven,
12 preach any other gospel unto you, than that which we
i 2 Cor ii have preached unto you, let him be accursed 9 As
17 k 1 Cor xvi we said before, so say I now again, if any *man* preach
22 any other gospel unto you, ˡ than that ye have received,
l Deut iv 2 & xii 32 Prov xxx 6 Rev xxii 18 let him be accursed

v 6—9 Abrupt the apostle hastens to his point, and expresses,

1 His astonishment at their defection from the faith *I marvel that ye are so soon removed from him that called you into the grace of Christ*, from the blessed God himself, and from us his ministers, *unto another gospel*, different from that which we preached to you, wherein the glorious grace of a Redeemer was exalted; *which* new doctrine *is not indeed another* gospel, bringing no glad tidings to the sinful soul of free pardon and salvation by Jesus Christ, but is clogged with conditions which it is impracticable for a fallen creature to perform *but*, the truth is, *there be some that trouble you, and would pervert the gospel of Christ*, destroying the riches of the grace, and adulterating the truth with the base alloy of error *Note*, (1) They who in whole or in part would introduce works as the gospel condition of justification before God, are the most dangerous perverters of the souls of men (2) There is but one way to regain the lost favour of God, and that is through grace by faith, and they who propose any other must perish with a lie in their right hand

2 He expresses his detestation of any other pretended gospel, besides that which he had preached to them *But though we, or an angel from heaven*, if we could suppose it possible, *preach any other gospel unto you than that which we have preached unto you, let him be accursed*, and lie down under the most dreadful anathemas of divine vengeance *As we said before*, with the deepest solemnity I repeat it, *If any man preach any other gospel unto you than that ye have received* from us, *let him be accursed.*

10 For ᵐ do I now ⁿ persuade men, or God? or ᵒ do m 1 Thes ii 4
I seek to please men? for if I yet pleased men, I should n 1 Sam
not be the servant of Christ 11 ᵖ But I certify you, xxiv 7 Mat xxviii
brethren, that the gospel which was preached of me is 13
not after man 12 For ᑫ I neither received it of man, o Jam iv 4
neither was I taught *it*, but ʳ by the revelation of Jesus p 1 Cor xv 1
Christ. 13 For ye have heard of my conversation in q 1 Cor xv 3 Ver 1
time past, in the Jews religion, *how* that beyond mea- r Eph iii 3
sure I persecuted the church of God, and ˢ wasted it s Acts ix 1 & xxii 4
14 And profited in the Jews religion, above many my t Acts viii 3
equals in mine own nation, ᵘ being more exceedingly u Acts xxii 3
zealous of the traditions ˣ of my fathers 15 But when x Jer i 5
it pleased God, ʸ who separated me from my mother's y Isa xlix 1
womb, and ᶻ called *me* by his grace, 16 ᵃ To reveal Jer i 5
his Son in me, ᵇ that I might preach him among the hea- z Acts xiii 2 Rom i 1
then, immediately I conferred not with flesh and blood a Mat xvi
17 Neither went I up to Jerusalem, to them which 17 2 Cor iv 6
were apostles before me, but I went into Arabia, and b Acts ix
returned again unto Damascus 18 Then after three 15 & xxii 21 Rom
years ᶜ I went up to Jerusalem to see Peter, and abode xi 13 Eph iii 8
with him fifteen days 19 But ᵈ other of the apostles c Acts ix 26
saw I none, save ᵉ James the Lord's brother 20 Now d 1 Cor ix 5
the things which I write unto you, ᶠ behold, before God, e Mark vi 3
I lye not 21 ᵍ Afterwards I came into the regions of f Rom ix 1
Syria and Cilicia, 22 And was unknown by face unto g Acts ix 30
ʰ the churches of Judea, which ⁱ were in Christ 23 h 1 Thes ii 14
But they had heard only, That he which persecuted us i Rom xvi 7
in times past, now preacheth the faith which once he
destroyed 24 And they glorified God in me

v 10—24 To vindicate himself from the aspersions of the judaizing teachers, who affected to set up Peter and the other apostles as far his superiors, he enters into a detail of his divine mission and ministry

1 He declares the scope of his preaching *Do I now persuade men, or God*, endeavouring to engage them to obey human inventions, or to submit to the gospel of the blessed God? *or do I seek to please men*, and ingratiate myself with you, as the Jewish zealots? No *For* I am well persuaded, that *if I yet pleased men*, and made that my study to accommodate the gospel to their prejudices, *I should not be the servant of Christ*, and with fidelity and simplicity discharge the trust committed to me *Note*, (1) To please God, not men, must be our great design (2) It is impossible that our fidelity in preaching the gospel should not offend those who, in pride and self-sufficiency, cannot bear the humbling truth of the necessity of submission to the righteousness of God therein revealed

2 He demonstrates to them the divinity of his mission The gospel he preached was not *after man*, a human invention, or received at second hand from men's information, but immediately by *revelation* from the exalted Jesus, now entered into his glory They knew his past conversation what a bigot he had been for Judaism, how greatly he had excelled many of his fellow-students in rabbinical knowledge, exactly skilled in all their laws and traditions to propagate these he had exerted all his zeal, and, with rage approaching madness, had persecuted the professors of the Christian name with the savage fury of the most barbarous foe No prejudices of education therefore could have led him to embrace Christianity, but, on the contrary, such a rivetted enmity against it, could be only overcome by some very extraordinary method of conviction *But when it pleased God*, who hath in his hands the hearts of all men, *who* of his rich and sovereign grace *separated me from my mother's womb*, having predestinated me for his own, to serve him in the gospel, *and called me by his grace*, in such a distinguishing manner, when I was going with the most implacable enmity to persecute the disciples at Damascus, when, I say, God graciously was pleased then *to reveal his Son in me*, making my inmost soul, by divine irradiation, acquainted with the fulness of the redemption which is in him, *that I might preach him among the heathen*, as peculiarly ordained to be their apostle, *immediately I conferred not with flesh and blood*, consulting no longer my own worldly ease, interest, or honour, or asking advice about what God had so clearly determined *neither went I up to Jerusalem, to them which were apostles before me*, as if I needed instruction, or a confirmation in my office, *but*, divinely taught and ordained, *I* immediately entered on my work, and *went into Arabia*, where the gospel had not been preached before, *and returned again unto Damascus Then, after three years, I went up to Jerusalem to see Peter*, not to learn of him, but to communicate the success of my labours, and enjoy the comforts of Christian fellowship with him and the rest of the brethren there; *and abode with him only fifteen days But other of the apostles saw I none, save James the Lord's brother*, or near kinsman, so that I received not my knowledge or commission from them *Now the things which I write unto you, behold, before God I lie not*, but with the deepest solemnity appeal to him for the truths I advance *Afterwards I came into the regions of*

Syria

Syria and Cilicia, preaching the gospel, *and was,* during many years, *unknown by face unto the churches which were in Christ,* and professed faith in his name, so that from them I could not have received any knowledge of the truth *But they had heard only, That he which persecuted us in times past, now preacheth the faith which he once destroyed And they glorified God in me,* ascribing to him praise for my wondrous conversion *Note,* (1) Christ must be revealed by his Spirit in us, as well as by his word to us, if we would know him to the saving of our souls (2) When occasion requires it, we honour God by a solemn appeal to him

CHAP II

The apostle in this chapter continues the relation of his past life and conduct, and with the same view, 1 Informs them of another journey which he took to Jerusalem many years after the former, and how he behaved himself at that time, ver 1—11 And, 2 Gives them an account of another interview he had with the apostle Peter at Antioch, and how he was obliged to behave himself towards him there And from the subject matter of that conversation he proceeds to discourse on the great doctrine of justification by faith in Christ without the works of the law, which it was the main design of this epistle to establish, and which he enlarges more upon in the two following chapters

1 THEN fourteen years after [a] I went up again
to Jerusalem with Barnabas, and took Titus
with me also 2 And I went up by revelation, and
[b] communicated unto them that gospel which I preach
among the Gentiles, but † privately to them which were
of reputation, lest by any means [c] I should run, or had
run in vain 3 But neither Titus, who was with me,
being a Greek, was compelled to be circumcised 4
And that because of [d] false brethren unawares brought in,
who came in privily to spy out [e] our liberty which we
have in Christ Jesus, [f] that they might bring us into
bondage 5 To whom we gave place by subjection, no
not for an hour, that [g] the truth of the gospel might
continue with you 6 But of those, [h] who seemed to be
somewhat, (whatsoever they were, it maketh no matter
to me [i] God accepteth no man's person) for they who
seemed *to be somewhat,* in conference [k] added nothing to
me 7 But contrariwise, when they saw that the
gospel of the uncircumcision was committed unto me,
as *the gospel* of the circumcision was unto Peter, 8 (For
he that wrought effectually in Peter to the apostleship
of the circumcision, [m] the same was [n] mighty in me to-
wards the Gentiles) 9 And when James, Cephas, and
John, who seemed to be [o] pillars, perceived [p] the grace
that was given unto me, they gave to me and Barnabas
the right hands of fellowship, that we *should go* unto
the heathen, and they unto the circumcision 10 Only
they would that we should remember the poor, [q] the same
which I also was forward to do

a Acts xv 2. b Acts xv 12. † Or, severally. c Phil ii 16. 1 Thess iii 5. d 2 Cor xi 26. e Chap iii 25. f Chap iv 9. v 1, 13. g Ver 14. h Chap vi 3. i Deut x 17. Acts x 34. Rom ii 11. 1 Pet i 17. k 2 Cor xi 11. l Acts xiii 2. Rom xi 13. 1 Tim ii 7. 2 Tim i 11. m Acts ix 15. xxii 21. Chap i 16. n Chap iii 5. o Matt xvi 18. Eph ii 20. Rev xxi 14. p Rom i 5. xii 3. & xv 15. Eph iii 8. q Acts xi 30. xxiv 17. Rom xv 25. 1 Cor xvi 1. 2 Cor viii & ix.

v 1—10 The apostle, in vindication of his divine mission and authority, as in nothing inferior to the other apostles, relates what passed at Jerusalem, when, fourteen years after his conversion, he went up thither, with Barnabas and Titus, by a special revelation from God, on occasion of the dissensions which the Jewish teachers had raised in the church of Antioch about the necessity of circumcising the Gentiles, and engaging them to keep the law of Moses

1 He communicated, and explained in conversation, to those who were of greatest note and *reputation,* the gospel which he preached among the Gentiles, in all its freedom and latitude, *but privately,* because of the known prejudices which many of the Jewish Christians entertained concerning the necessity of still observing the law And this method he took, *lest by any means he should run or had run in vain;* and, through the clamours of the hot zealots for Judaism, his *past* labours should have been in some measure rendered abortive, or his future usefulness be obstructed

2 Though he acted with all prudence, he made no sinful compliance to their prejudices, maintaining the purity of the gospel, and firm to his principles that the Gentiles were in no manner obliged to the observation of the Mosaical law therefore, though Titus was a Greek, he was not compelled to be circumcised, nor did the apostles insist upon it And Paul took Titus a Gentile Christian and minister of the gospel, on purpose that in him he might bear a public testimony against those false brethren who had craftily insinuated themselves into the church at Antioch, and with prying eye observed the apostle's conduct at Jerusalem, whether he would there maintain the liberty of the Christian gentiles from the Mosaical institutions For they would have been happy if they could have had such a plea as the circumcision of Titus, to urge the same upon the Gentile converts But *not for an hour* would the apostle and his collegue Barnabas give way to such a dangerous imposition, *that the truth* and freedom *of the gospel* might be maintained inviolable, and the Gentiles enjoy that entire liberty from every yoke of bondage, which in Christ Jesus was preached unto them *Note,* False brethren are our most dangerous foes Against them we need peculiar watchfulness

3 Though he conferred with the apostles of chief eminence, and who were so preferred to him by the judaizing teachers, whatever had been the case *formerly* (ποτε), and whatever privileges they had enjoyed above him, that affected not the matter at present God, who *accepteth no man's person,* can, when he pleases, reveal his gospel to the bitterest enemy of the truth, and raise the vilest persecutor to the honour of apostleship. However great the names of Peter, James, and John were, *they added nothing* to him, nor contributed the least to his improvement in knowledge, so thoroughly had he been taught of God the mysteries of gospel truth

4 The issue of the conference was the perfect satisfaction expressed by the apostles at Jerusalem in what they heard, it appearing most undeniably, that the same Lord, who had wrought by Peter's ministry among the Jews, who was more particularly sent to them, had wrought as effectually by Paul among the Gentiles, to whom they therefore concluded the apostleship of the Gentiles was committed Therefore these pillars of the church, James, Cephas, and John, convinced of the grace and apostleship conferred upon him, with cordial affection gave to him and Barnabas the right hands of fellowship, and concurred in their sentiments, that it fully appeared the will of God, that Paul and his fellow-labourer should go to the Gentiles more immediately, whilst their own ministry was more generally confined to the Jews only they recommended it to them that they should remember the poor saints in Judea, and obtain some relief for them from the Gentile churches A service in which Paul warmly engaged. So that it was evident, from the result of this conversation, that there was a perfect harmony in doctrine between Paul and the apostles at Jerusalem, and that they fully recognized his divine authority and mission.

11 But [r] when Peter was come to Antioch, I with-
stood him to the face, because he was to be blamed.
12 For before that certain came from James, [s] he did eat
with the Gentiles but when they were come, he with-
drew, and separated himself, fearing them which were
of the circumcision. 13 And the other Jews dissembled
likewise with him, insomuch that Barnabas also was
carried away with their dissimulation 14 But when I
saw that they walked not uprightly according to [t] the
truth of the gospel, I said unto Peter [u] before *them* all,
[x] If thou, being a Jew, livest after the manner of Gen-
tiles, and not as do the Jews, why compellest thou the
Gentiles to live as do the Jews? 15 We *who are* [y] Jews
by nature, and not [z] sinners of the Gentiles, 16 [a] Know-
ing that a man is not justified by the works of the law,
but [b] by the faith of Jesus Christ, even we have believed
in Jesus Christ, that we might be justified by the faith
of Christ, and not by the works of the law for [c] by
the works of the law shall no flesh be justified 17 But
if, while we seek to be justified by Christ, we ourselves
also are found [d] sinners, *is* therefore Christ the minister
of sin? God forbid 18 For if I build again the things
which I destroyed, I make myself a transgressor 19
For I [e] through the law [f] am dead to the law, that I
might [g] live unto God. 20 I am [h] crucified with Christ.
nevertheless I live, yet not I, but Christ liveth in me
and the life which I now live in the flesh, [i] I live by the
faith of the Son of God, [k] who loved me, and gave him-
self for me 21 I do not frustrate the grace of God
for [l] if righteousness *come* by the law, then Christ is dead
in vain

r Acts xv 35. s Acts x 28. & xi 3. t Ver 5. u 1 Tim v 20. x Acts x 28. y Acts xv 10, 11. z Matt ix 11. Eph ii 3, 12. a Acts xiii 38. b Rom iii 22, 28 & viii 3. Heb vii 18, 19. c Psal cxliii 2. Rom iii 20. Chap iii 11. d 1 John iii 8, 9. e Rom viii 2. f Rom vii 4. g Rom vi 11. 2 Cor v 15. 1 Thess v 10. Heb ix 14. 1 Pet iv 2. h Rom vi 6. Chap v 24. i 2 Cor v 15. 1 Pet iv 2. k Chap i 4. Eph v 2. Tit ii 14. l Heb vii 11. Rom xi 6. Chap v 4.

v 11—21 Nothing could serve more effectually to establish the character of the great apostle of the Gentiles than the occurrence here recorded, wherein, so far from being Peter's inferior, as the judaizing teachers suggested, he appears his faithful and zealous reprover

1 Peter's fault was, that, at his coming to Antioch, he freely communed with the Gentile Christians, and eat and drank with them, though uncircumcised, but, on the arrival of some Jewish brethren sent from James, he temporized, and, for fear of offending the prejudiced Judaizer, to the great discouragement of the Gentile brethren, he suspended his former [illegible] intercourse with them, and, influenced by him, the Jewish Christians at Antioch dissembled likewise, and withdrew from free converse, as before, with their Gentile brethren, and,

over-

overcome by such bad examples, even Barnabas himself was carried away with their dissimulation, and, contrary to all his former conduct and teaching, joined in this separation for which Peter most justly was to be blamed *Note*, (1) The fear of men, and undue desire of their esteem, hath sometimes warped the most steady Christians from the simplicity of the gospel (2) Bad examples are ever dangerous, especially the examples of those who are high in men's esteem, and whose influence is most extensive

2 The rebuke Paul gave him was such as his dissimulation deserved And as the offence given was public, publickly and to his face he with noble fidelity withstood him, and, seeing him so sadly decline from the path of truth, and the liberty of the gospel, he addressed himself to Peter, and said unto him before them all, *If thou, being a Jew, livest after the manner of Gentiles, and not as do the Jews*, satisfied that the ceremonial law is no longer binding, *why compellest thou the Gentiles to live as do the Jews*, and by the example thou hast lately shewn wouldst enslave their consciences to the Mosaical institutions, as if necessary to their acceptance with God? What a glaring contradiction appears between such a conduct and your late avowed principles and practice!

3 He suggests the strongest arguments for the unreasonableness of such a conduct, since all distinction of Jew and Gentile now was ceased, both needing the same Redeemer, and expecting to be justified by the same rich grace of the gospel *We who are Jews by nature*, God's chosen people, and trained up in the law, *and not sinners of the Gentiles*, who in general are looked upon by the Jews as persons abandoned and reprobate, *knowing that a man is not*, cannot be *justified by the works of the law*, which none can perfectly fulfil, *but by the faith of Jesus Christ*, *even we have believed in Jesus Christ* for pardon and acceptance with God, *that we might be justified by the faith of Christ*, through that divine righteousness which he wrought out for us, *and not by the works of the law* and if this was the case with us, much more must the Gentiles have recourse to the same free grace, *for by the works of the law*, moral or ceremonial, *shall no flesh be justified*, none being able to produce a righteousness adequate to its demands *But if, while we seek to be justified by Christ, we ourselves are found sinners*, as must be the case of those who are under the law, Rom iii 9 *is therefore Christ the minister of sin*, who, notwithstanding all he hath done for us and in us, would in such a case leave us under the condemning guilt and prevailing power of sin? *God forbid*, with abhorrence is the thought to be rejected Yet would this be the consequence of seeking to the law for acceptance with God, *for if I build again the things which I destroyed*, and, after preaching the grace of the gospel, have recourse to the law for justification before God, *I make myself a transgressor*, contradict my own doctrine, and acknowledge myself still under guilt and condemnation, which my faith in Christ hath not removed So inconsistent was this behaviour therefore in Peter and his associates

4 Though some might object to the doctrine of free justification without the deeds of the law, the apostle declares his own and every believer's judgment and practice *For I through the law am dead to the law*, unable to obey it as a covenant of life, and renouncing all my expectations from it, *that I might live unto God*, abiding in a constant state of favour with him through the Redeemer's righteousness, and quickned by his grace to newness of life *I am crucified with Christ*, as my law-fulfiller, in him the law is satisfied, and hath no more demands upon me than it hath upon the dead *nevertheless I live* in a state of reconciliation with God, bringing forth the fruits of righteousness, *yet not I*, by any inherent power or principle in myself, *but Christ liveth in me*, by virtue of union with him I possess that righteousness which gives me a title to life, and receive from him, as my head of vital influence, his quickening Spirit *and the life which I now live in the flesh, I live* not after the flesh, but *by the faith of the Son of God*, placing my whole dependance upon him, and drawing continual supplies of grace and strength out of his fulness, *who loved me, and gave himself for me*, to make a complete atonement, and to bring in an everlasting righteousness, for me and all who embrace his great salvation *I do not frustrate the grace of God*, and slight, as of no value, the transcendent favour of God's dear Son, and the righteousness unto life which is in him, as they do who go to the works of the law for acceptance with God *for if righteousness come by the law*, and were to be obtained by our personal obedience, *then Christ is dead in vain*, for in that case righteousness and salvation might have been obtained without him *Note*, (1) We must die to the law, and renounce all hope of being justified thereby, before we can fly to Jesus, and live unto God (2) By faith alone is the life of our souls maintained, whilst from the fulness of our Redeemer we derive the constant supplies of grace and strength (3) All who either in whole or part place their dependance on their own doings and duties for acceptance with God, they make Christ to have died in vain

CHAP III

The apostle, in this chapter, 1 Reproves the Galatians for their folly in suffering themselves to be drawn away from the faith of the gospel 2 He proves the doctrine which he had reproved them for departing from, viz That of justification by faith without the works of the law (1) From the example of Abraham's justification (2) From the nature and tenor of the law (3) From the express testimony of the Old Testament And (4) From the stability of the covenant of God with Abraham And lest any should hereupon say, Wherefore then serveth the law? He answers, [1] It was added because of transgression [2] It was given to convince the world of the necessity of a Saviour [3] It was designed as a schoolmaster to bring us to Christ And then he concludes the chapter, by acquainting us with the privilege of Christians under the gospel-state

1 O Foolish Galatians, [a] who hath bewitched you, [a] Chap v 7.
that you should not obey the truth, before whose
eyes Jesus Christ hath been evidently set forth, crucified
among you? 2 This only would I learn of you, Re-
ceived ye [b] the Spirit by the works of the law, or [c] by [b] Acts ii 38 & viii 15 & xv 8
the hearing of faith? 3 Are ye so foolish? having [c] Eph i 13 Heb vi 4
begun in the Spirit, are ye now made perfect by the flesh? [e] Rom x 17
4 [d] Have ye suffered so † many things in vain? if it be [d] 2 John 8.
yet in vain 5 He therefore [e] that ministreth to you † Or great
the Spirit, and worketh miracles among you, doth he it [e] 2 Cor iii 8
by the works of the law, or by the hearing of faith?

v 1—5 With warm expostulation, and sharp rebuke, the apostle upbraids the stupidity and folly of these Galatians, who had departed so grievously from the simplicity of the gospel *O foolish Galatians, who hath bewitched you*, what emissary of Satan by his craft hath perverted your souls, *that you should not obey the truth*, but depart from the grand principles of the gospel, renouncing the doctrine of free justification through the Redeemer's blood and righteousness? Several things served to aggravate their folly

1 The clear display of the truth which had been made to them *Before whose eyes Jesus Christ hath been evidently set forth*, and his death and sufferings, with all the effects and design of them, represented in such a lively manner, as if he had been *crucified among you*

2 What they had received under the ministration of the gospel *This only would I learn of you, Received ye the Spirit*, his gifts and grace, *by the works of the law*, by the ministration of it or obedience to it, *or by the hearing of faith*, the preaching of justification through the free grace of a Redeemer? They must own it was through the latter and therefore most inexcuseable was their folly to quit that gospel, the blessed and most happy effects of which they had experienced

3 *Having begun in the Spirit, are ye now made perfect by the flesh?* and, forsaking your dependence on the grace of the gospel, do you expect to reach perfection by your obedience to the law? *Are ye so foolish* to have recourse to the ministration of death, in order to obtain righteousness unto life?

4 *Have ye suffered so many things in vain*, for the cause of Christ and the profession of the gospel? How absurd were it to expose yourselves thus, *if it be yet in vain*, and after all you should apostatize, and lose the blessings of your profession and sufferings? You must then of all men be most foolish and most miserable

5 *He therefore that ministreth to you the Spirit, and worketh miracles among you, doth he it by the works of the law*, as the way of justification, *or by the hearing of faith*, in the ministry of the gospel? If these miracles, as was evident, were wrought in confirmation of the doctrines of grace, how preposterously absurd were they to quit the truth confirmed by such divine and incontestible evidence!

6 Even as [f] Abraham believed God, and it was ac- [f] Gen xv 6 Rom iv 3 Jam ii 23
counted to him for righteousness 7 Know ye there- [g] Rom iv 11 12, 16
fore, that [g] they which are of faith, the same are the [h] Rom ix 7 Ver 22
children of Abraham 8. And [h] the scripture, foresee- [i] Gen xii 3. & xviii 18 & xxii 18 Acts iii 25
ing that God would justify the heathen through faith, [k] Deut xxvii 26 Jer xi 3
preached before the gospel unto Abraham, *saying*, [i] In [l] Chap ii 16
thee shall all nations be blessed 9 So then they which [m] Hab ii 4 Rom i 17 Heb x 38.
be of faith, are blessed with faithful Abraham 10 For [n] Rom iv 4, 5 & x 5, 6 & xi. 6
as many as are of the works of the law, are under the [o] Lev xviii 5 Neh ix 29 Ezek xx 11
curse for it is written, [k] Cursed *is* every one that con- [p] Rom viii 3 2 Cor v. 21 Chap iv 5
tinueth not in all things which are written in the book [q] Deut xxi 23
of the law to do them 11 But that [l] no man is justi- [r] Acts i 25
fied by the law in the sight of God, *it is* evident for, [s] Isa xxxii 15 & xliv 3 Jer xxxi 33 & xxxii 40 Ezek xi 19 & xxxvi 26 Joel ii 28 Zech xii 10.
[m] The just shall live by faith 12 And [n] the law is not
of faith but, [o] The man that doth them, shall live in
them 13 [p] Christ hath redeemed us from the curse of
the law, being made a curse for us for it is written,
[q] Cursed *is* every one that hangeth on a tree 14
[r] That the blessing of Abraham might come on the Gen-
tiles through Jesus Christ; that we might receive [s] the
promise of the Spirit through faith 15. Brethren, I

[t] Heb ix 17 ſpeak after the manner of men, [t] though it be but a
man's covenant, yet if it be confirmed, no man diſan-
[u] Gen xvii 7 Ver 8 nulleth nor addeth thereto 16 Now [u] to Abraham
and his ſeed were the promiſes made He ſaith not,
And to ſeeds, as of many, but as of one, and to thy
ſeed, which is Chriſt 17 And this I ſay, *that* the co-
venant that was confirmed before of God in Chriſt, the
[x] Exod xii 40 41 law [x] which was four hundred and thirty years after can
not diſannul, that it ſhould make the promiſe of none
[y] Rom viii 17 effect 18 For [y] if the inheritance *be* of the law, [z] *it is*
[z] Rom iv 14 no more of promiſe but God gave *it* to Abraham by
promiſe

v 6—18 The apoſtle, having ſharply rebuked the folly of the Galatians in departing from the truth, proceeds to confirm the great doctrine of juſtification by faith alone, from which they had been ſeduced And he proves it,

1 By the example of Abraham He *believed God, and it was accounted to him for righteouſneſs* the Lord Meſſiah, on whom his faith reſted, became his juſtifying righteouſneſs before God *Know ye therefore, that they which are of faith*, and place their whole dependance for acceptance with God on *the ſame* object, they *are the* ſpiritual *children of Abraham And the ſcripture, foreſeeing that God would juſtify the heathen through faith, preached before the goſpel unto Abraham*, when neither circumciſion was yet inſtituted, nor the law given, *ſaying, In thee*, that is, in thy ſeed, the Meſſiah, *ſhall all nations be bleſſed*, accepted of God in him, and admitted to the participation of all the privileges of God's peculiar people *So then* it is evident from hence, that *they which be of faith are bleſſed with faithful Abraham*, without the leaſt reſpect to the works of the law

2 It is impoſſible for any man to be juſtified before God any other way than by faith *For as many as are of the works of the law*, and ſeek juſtification and ſalvation on the footing of perſonal righteouſneſs, *are*, and muſt be, *under the curſe* denounced on every tranſgreſſor *for it is written, Curſed is every one that continueth not in all things which are written in the book of the law to do them*, the leaſt failure in thought, word, or deed, but once, even in the longeſt life, effectually cuts off the ſinner from all hope by the law, and leaves him under the wrath of an offended God Therefore *Chriſt*, viewing our deſperate guilt and hopeleſs miſery, *hath redeemed us from the curſe of the law*, by the price of his own blood, *being made a curſe for us*, by divine conſtitution appointed to be our ſurety, treated by inexorable juſtice as a tranſgreſſor, and bearing, in his own body on the croſs, the puniſhment due to our iniquities *for it is written, Curſed is every one that hangeth on a tree* And to this moſt painful, ſhameful, and accurſed death he ſubmitted, *that the bleſſing of Abraham might come on the Gentiles through Jeſus Chriſt*, and righteouſneſs be imputed to them alſo for juſtification, *that we*, whether Jews or Gentiles, being taken into a ſtate of acceptance with God, *might receive the promiſe of the Spirit*, in all his plenitude of gifts, graces, and conſolations, *through faith* in the Redeemer, and not on account of any works of our own, or legal ſervices *Note*, (1) Every man, being unable to keep the law in perfection, is conſequently a tranſgreſſor, and ſealed up under wrath (2) Deſpair is written on every effort of the fallen ſinner to eſcape from the condemnation under which he lies (3) The goſpel brings relief to the deſperate, by revealing to us a divine Subſtitute, all-ſufficient to bear our ſins, and to reſtore us to the enjoyment of God's forfeited favour (4) By faith alone we embrace, and actually poſſeſs, all the bleſſings obtained for us in and by the great Redeemer

3 The ſcriptures of the Old Teſtament are expreſs to the point *But that no man is juſtified by the works of the law in the ſight of God, it is evident for the juſt ſhall live by faith*, or the *juſt by faith ſhall live*; he only who by faith is counted righteous before God, can live here in a ſtate of favour with him, and hereafter be admitted to the enjoyment of him *And the law is not of faith but* the way it preſcribes for juſtification is directly oppoſite, even by perfect perſonal obedience, *The man that doth them*, and keeps in ſpirit and practice, univerſally and abidingly, all the commands enjoined, *ſhall live in them*, but every defect, flaw, or failure, brings down death as the wages of ſin So that the ſaints of old were juſtified in the ſame way as we are, and the goſpel was preached to them even as unto us

4 The ſtability of the covenant made with Abraham could not be vacated by the law *Brethren, I ſpeak after the manner of men*, and uſe a familiar inſtance to elucidate the point in hand *though it be but a man's covenant, yet, if it be confirmed*, and duly ſigned and ſealed, *no man diſannulleth or addeth thereunto*, except the parties intereſted by mutual conſent *Now to Abraham and his ſeed were the promiſes made*, of juſtification, adoption, grace, and glory *He ſaith not to ſeeds, as of many*, as if the promiſe referred to all his *natural* as well as *ſpiritual* children, *but as of one*, in the ſingular number, *and to thy ſeed, which is Chriſt*, who was *perſonally* meant, and in whom all the ſpiritual ſeed are myſtically included *And this I ſay*, is evident, *that the covenant which was confirmed before*, to Abraham, *of God in Chriſt*, or *with reſpect to Chriſt*, who was the Mediator, Surety, and ſubſtance of the covenant in his own perſon, *the law, which was four hundred and thirty years after, cannot diſannul, that it ſhould make the promiſe of none effect*, and introduce another way of juſtification before God, different from, yea contrary to, that which God had before eſtabliſhed with Abraham *For if the inheritance be of the law*, and the title to eternal life be obtained by perſonal obedience, *it is no more of promiſe but God gave it*, graciouſly and abſolutely, *to Abraham by promiſe*, which no ſubſequent diſpenſation could ſet aſide, for God is not a man that he ſhould lie, nor the ſon of man that he ſhould repent, and therefore the promiſe of juſtification, adoption, and the eternal inheritance, is in Chriſt ſecured to all the ſpiritual ſeed of faithful Abraham

19 Wherefore then *ſerveth* the law? [a] it was added [a] John xv 22 Rom iv 15 & v 20 1 Tim i 9
becauſe of tranſgreſſions, till the ſeed ſhould come, [b] to [b] Ver 16
whom the promiſe was made, *and it was* ordained [c] by [c] Acts vii 53
angels in the hand [d] of a mediator 20 Now a media- [d] Deut v 5 John i 17 Acts vii 38 1 Tim ii 5
tor is not *a mediator* of one, but God is one 21 *Is* the
law then againſt the promiſes of God? God forbid for
if there had been a law given which could have given
life, verily righteouſneſs ſhould have been by the law
22 But [e] the ſcripture hath concluded [f] all under ſin, [e] Ver 8 [f] Pſ xiv 3 Rom iii 9, 19 23, & xi 32
that the promiſe by faith of Jeſus Chriſt might be given
to them that believe 23 But before faith came, we
were kept under the law, ſhut up unto the faith which
ſhould afterwards be revealed 24 Wherefore [g] the law [g] Rom x 4
was our ſchoolmaſter *to bring us* unto Chriſt, [h] that we [h] Acts xiii 39
might be juſtified by faith 25 But after that faith is
come, we are no longer under a ſchoolmaſter 26 For
[i] ye are all the children of God by faith in Chriſt Jeſus [i] John i 12 Rom viii 14, Chap iv
27 For [k] as many of you as have been baptized into [k] Rom vi 3
Chriſt, [l] have put on Chriſt 28 [m] There is neither Jew [l] Rom xiii 14
nor Greek, there is neither bond nor free, there is nei- [m] Rom x 12 1 Cor xii 13 Col iii 11
ther male nor female for ye are all [n] one in Chriſt Jeſus [n] Eph ii 14 15
29 And [o] if ye *be* Chriſt's, then are ye Abraham's ſeed, [o] Gen xxi 12 Rom ix 7 Heb xi 18
and [p] heirs according to the promiſe [p] Eph iii 6

v 19—29 In anſwer to the objections which he knew the Jewiſh zealots would raiſe, as if he derogated from the honour of the law, and rendered it uſeleſs, he ſtates and anſwers them

1. They might ſay, *Wherefore then ſerveth the law*, if no creature can be juſtified or ſaved by it? I reply, *It was added becauſe of tranſgreſſions*, in ſubſervience to the deſign of the covenant of grace, in order to reſtrain by its penalty, and to convince, diſcover, and condemn the tranſgreſſors, ſhewing them the neceſſity of a better righteouſneſs than their own, *till the ſeed ſhould come, to whom the promiſe was made*, and who ſhould be the end of the law for righteouſneſs to every believer, *and it was ordained by angels*, delivered by their miniſtry, *in the hand of a mediator*, even Moſes, who was typical of the great Mediator, Jeſus Chriſt *Now a mediator is not a mediator of one*, but ſtands between the two parties, *but God is one*, unchangeable in his purpoſes and promiſes, and as the Gentiles were not repreſented at all at mount Sinai, nor regarded as one of the parties in that covenant, which was a tranſaction merely between God and Abraham's natural ſeed, this cannot exclude them from the benefit of the antecedent promiſe which God made to Abraham and his ſpiritual ſeed

2 Some may argue from hence, *Is the law then againſt the promiſes of God*, made to Abraham and his ſeed? are they at variance with each other? *God forbid* there is the moſt perfect harmony between them *For if there had been a law given which could have given life, verily righteouſneſs ſhould have been by the law* and could man have kept in his own perſon the righteouſneſs of the law, his title to life would have been clear, and the promiſed Subſtitute had been unneceſſary *but the ſcripture hath concluded all under ſin*, hath ſhut up every man, as in a dungeon, under the guilt and condemnation of ſin, all having come ſhort of the glory of God, *that the promiſe by faith of Jeſus Chriſt might be given to them that believe*, and that pardon and ſalvation might come to us as the free gift of God in him *But before faith came*, before Chriſt, the great object of faith, appeared incarnate, and his goſpel was more clearly manifeſted, *we*, who were under the Moſaic diſpenſation, *were kept under the law*, as in a caſtle, ſeparate from other nations, and, as captives under a yoke of bondage, *ſhut up* in cloſe cuſtody *unto the faith which ſhould afterwards be revealed*, and till Chriſt, opening to us a door of hope, ſhould bring us from this ſtate of ſervitude into the glorious liberty of the ſons of God *Wherefore the law was our ſchoolmaſter*, and ſerved moſt directly *to bring us unto Chriſt, that we might be juſtified by faith* the *moral* precepts and ſanction convinced us of our deſperate caſe, as unable to anſwer the demands of the law, and obnoxious to the curſe, the *ceremonial* inſtitutions led us to look for the divine Subſtitute, in all the ſacrifices which were enjoined for the expiation of ſin, and both taught the neceſſity of juſtification by faith through a better righteouſneſs than our own *But after that faith is come*, and Chriſt,

the

the sinner's substitute, hath appeared, and is held forth to us in the gospel, *we are no longer under a schoolmaster*, being delivered from our former state of minority and legal bondage *For now ye* who believe *are all the children of God by faith in Jesus Christ*, arrived to maturity of age, and entitled to all the blessings of adoption, which Jesus hath obtained for the many sons whom he shall bring unto glory *For as many of you*, whether Jews or Gentiles, *as have been baptised into Christ*, by faith really united to him, and by baptism making open profession of him, *have put on Christ*, and, cloathed in his divine righteousness, have a title to all spiritual and eternal blessings *There is now neither Jew nor Greek, there is neither bond nor free, there is neither male nor female*, all distinction of nation, sex, condition, is ceased *for ye*, who believe, *are all one in Christ Jesus*, united to him in one body, and alike freely partakers of all the privileges contained in the eternal covenant of redemption *And if ye be Christ's*, living members of his body mystical, *then are ye Abraham's seed* in a spiritual sense, *and heirs according to the promise*, entitled to claim, under Christ, your great covenant-head, all the blessings which he hath purchased for his redeemed So that circumcision, and the Mosaical institutions, are in no wise necessary, either for present pardon or eternal salvation

CHAP IV

The apostle in this chapter, in correspondence with his great design, shews us, (1) The great excellence of the gospel-state above the legal, ver 1—8 (2) The happy change that was made in them at their conversion, ver 8—12 (3) The affection they had had for him and his ministry, ver 12—17 (4) The character of the false teachers by whom they had been perverted, ver 17, 18 (5) The very tender affection he had for them, ver 19, 20 (6) The history of Isaac and Ishmael, by a comparison taken from which he illustrates the difference between such as rested in Christ and such as trusted in the law

1 NOW I say, *that* the heir as long as he is a
child, differeth nothing from a servant, though
he be Lord of all, 2 But is under tutors and gover-
nors, until the time appointed of the father 3 Even
so we, when we were children, [a] were in bondage un-
der the elements of the world 4 But [b] when the ful-
ness of the time was come, God sent forth his Son,
[c] made [d] of a woman, [e] made under the law, 5 [f] To
redeem them that were under the law, [g] that we might
receive the adoption of sons 6. And because ye are
sons, [h] God hath sent forth the Spirit of his Son into
your hearts, crying, Abba, Father 7. Wherefore thou
art no more a servant, but a son, [i] and if a son, then an
heir of God through Christ

[a] Chap iii 23 Col ii 20. [b] Dan ix 24 Mark i 15 Eph i 10. [c] John i 14 Rom i 3 Phil ii 7. [d] Gen iii 15 Isa vii 14 Mic v 3 Mat i 23. [e] Mat xx 28 Heb ix 12. [g] John i 12 Chap iii 26 Eph i 5 1 John iii 1. [h] Rom viii 15. [i] Rom viii 16, 17.

v 1—7 The apostle had hinted before, that the state of those who were under the law, was a kind of minority He here enlarges on that subject, shewing the vast superiority of the gospel above the legal dispensation

1 Before Christ came, they were in a state of non-age *Now I say that the heir, as long as he is a child, differeth nothing from a servant, though he be Lord of all*, and entitled to the inheritance, *but is under tutors and governors, until the time appointed of the father*, when he should be declared of age, and enter upon the management of his own affairs *Even so we*, and all the people of God under the Old Testament, *when we were children*, in the infantile state of the church, *were in bondage under the elements of the world*, subject to the law, with all the carnal ordinances, which were, as the first letters of the alphabet, designed to lead us on to higher attainments, and kept us, during this time of non-age, in a state of fear, as children who dread correction, if they perform not their appointed tasks *But*,

2 Under the gospel dispensation our condition is much happier *When the fulness of the time was come*, appointed in the eternal decree, *God sent forth his Son*, his only begotten, one in the same divine nature and essence, *born of a woman*, that he might be manifested in the flesh, *made under the law*, appointed both to endure the penalty due to our transgressions, and by his obedience to the precept in our stead, *to bring* in an everlasting righteousness for us, that he might *redeem them that were under the law*, under its bondage and curse, *that we*, who believe in him, *might receive the adoption of sons*, admitted to that high privilege, with all its happy consequences *And because ye are sons, God hath sent forth the Spirit of his Son into your hearts*, through the glorified Redeemer, who hath all fulness of the Spirit to bestow on his people, and forms their hearts, by his divine operations, to the temper becoming the high dignity and relation with which they are honoured; so that, through the effectual working of the Holy Ghost, we are enabled, with filial dependance, filial love, and sacred joy, to approach a throne of grace, *crying, Abba, Father* *Wherefore*, wherever this Spirit is given, *thou art no more a servant, but a son*, admitted to that honourable place in God's family, *and if a son, then an heir of God through Christ*, and entitled to everlasting blessedness So that to return to the law for acceptance with God, is absurd and needless *Note*, (1) God manifest in the flesh is the foundation of every hope to the sinner (2) If any man have not the Spirit of Christ, he is none of his, the grace of adoption always accompanies the privilege of adoption (3) 'Tis happy for the soul, that is enabled with humble boldness to approach in holy God, *crying, Abba, Father*, and claiming this kindred with him, which he will not disown (4) Our present adoption is the earnest of our eternal redemption

8 Howbeit, [k] then when ye knew not God, [l] ye did
service unto them which by nature are no gods 9 But
now after that ye have known God, or rather [n] are
known of God, [n] how turn ye again to [o] the weak and
beggarly elements, whereunto ye desire again to be in
bondage? 10 [p] Ye observe days, and months, and
times, and years 11 I am afraid of you, [q] lest I have
bestowed upon you labour in vain

[k] Eph ii 12. [l] Rom i 25, 1 Cor xii 2, 1 Thes i 9. [m] 1 Cor viii 3 2 Tim ii 19. [n] Col ii 20. [o] Heb vii 18. [p] Rom xiv 5 Col ii 16. [q] Chap ii 2 1 Thes iii 5.

v 8—11 To shew them the glaring folly of their having recourse to the law for justification, he reminds them,

1 Of their former state of Gentilism *Howbeit, then when ye knew not God*, grossly ignorant of his being, perfections, and attributes, and, in fact, without God in the world, *ye did service unto them which by nature are no gods*, worshipping senseless idols, and ascribing divinity to stocks and stones In this state of horrid ignorance and guilt did the gospel find them, and called them out of darkness into marvellous light

2 How absurd then was their defection from the truth which they had received! *But now after that ye have known God*, thro' the gospel of his dear Son, *or rather are known of God*, approved and accepted of him in the Redeemer, *now turn ye again to the weak and beggarly elements, whereunto ye desire again to be in bondage?* What infatuation hath seized you, to leave the gospel dispensation of light, love, and liberty, for the bondage, darkness, and fear of the Mosaical institutions, *weak* and insufficient to cleanse the soul from guilt, or to obtain acceptance with God, and *beggarly*, when compared to the superior riches of gospel grace *Ye observe days, and months, and times, and years*, placing dependance on the ceremonial ordinances of the Jewish ritual, as essential to your justification before God And where this is the case, *I am afraid of you, lest I have bestowed upon you labour in vain*, and departing thus from the fundamentals of the gospel, notwithstanding all our preaching, you should finally perish *Note*, (1) Many who make, for a while, fair professions, prove, in the end, foul apostates (2) Nothing more effectually destroys the soul, than a departure from that fundamental point of the gospel, *justification by faith alone* (3) It is a deep concern to the true ministers of Christ, when they, in whom they hoped to see the fruit of their labours, disappoint their expectations

12 Brethren, I beseech you, be as I *am*, for I *am* as
ye *are* [r] ye have not injured me at all 13 Ye know
how [s] through infirmity of the flesh, I preached the gos
pel unto you at the first. 14. And my temptation which
was in the flesh ye despised not, nor rejected, but re-
ceived me [t] as an angel of God, [u] *even* as Christ Jesus
15 [‡] Where is then the blessedness you spake of? for
I bear you record, that if *it had been* possible, ye would
have plucked out your own eyes, and have given them
to me 16 Am I therefore become your enemy, be-
cause [x] I tell you the truth?

[r] 2 Cor ii 5. [s] 1 Cor ii 3 2 Cor xi 30. [t] Mal ii 7. [u] Mat x 40 John xiii 20 1 Thes ii 13. [‡] Or, what was then. [x] Chap ii 14.

v 12—16 The apostle here,

1 With affectionate address desires to win upon them *Brethren, I beseech you, be as I am*, united with me in affection as I am to you, and imitate my example, leaving these Jewish rites as matters of indifference, and cleaving to Christ and his righteousness only for justification before God, *for I am as ye are*, one with you in fervent charity, and we are equally entitled to the privileges of the gospel *ye have not injured me at all*; the injury you do is to Christ, and your own souls, and what I say proceeds not from my private resentment, but purely from a zeal for his glory and your good, and if any disrespect may have been cast on me, I entirely overlook it *Note*, The rebuke, that is tempered with love, will always be most effectual

2 He reminds them of the former affection and esteem which they had shewed him *Ye know, how through infirmity of the flesh, I preached the gospel unto you at the first And my temptation in the flesh*, (whether his sufferings, weakness of body, or ungraceful appearance, they knew what he meant, though we do not for certain, but whatever it was, he could say) *ye despised not, nor rejected*; did not therefore slight my ministry, nor treat my person with contempt, *but received me as an angel of God*, with all veneration and regard, as a messenger sent from heaven, yea, *even as Christ Jesus*, had he himself appeared in the flesh among you, religious adoration excepted, ye could not have paid him greater respect *Where is then the blessedness you spake of?* that ardent wish for my happiness, and the delight you expressed in the

the gospel which I preached unto you? *for I bear you record, that if it had been possible, ye would have plucked out your own eyes, and have given them unto me*, counting nothing too great to testify the sense of your gratitude towards me. *Note*, Many in their first love, are all on fire for Christ, and never think they can enough testify their regard to the ministers of their conversion, who by and by grow cold or perverted from the truth, and treat with contempt those whom they once respected as almost angelical.

3. He expostulates with them on the strange alteration which now appeared. *Am I therefore become your enemy, because I tell you the truth*, and kindly warn you of the deadly consequences of your defection from the purity of the gospel? *Note*, (1) Truth, honestly spoken, often creates us enemies. (2) Ministers may expect that their fidelity will offend. (3) Whether men will hear or forbear, we must speak, nor fear any consequences.

17 They [y] zealously affect you, *but* not well, yea, they would exclude † you, that you might affect them.
18 But *it is* good to be zealously affected always in a good thing, and not only when I am present with you.

[y] Rom. x. 2. † Or, us.

v. 17—18. St. Paul knew the spirit and temper with which the judaizing teachers acted, and he,

1. Warns the Galatians of it. *They zealously affect you*, and pretend great zeal for you, *but not well*; their professions are dissembled, and their design is crafty, *yea, they would exclude you* from me and your true friends, who preach the pure gospel to you, *that you might affect them*, and yield your consciences up to their direction. *Note*, All is not gold which glitters; we should try, before we trust; hypocrisy, for selfish ends, can put on the purest guise of truth.

2. He points out to them the rule they should follow. *But it is good*, and the proof of an excellent spirit, *to be zealously affected always in a good thing*, or to a good man, *and not only when I am present with you*, whilst an unsteady, wavering conduct, shews that the heart is not well grounded in the truth, and discovers a dishonourable levity and inconstancy.

19 [z] My little children, of whom I travail in birth
again, until Christ be formed in you, 20 I desire to be
present with you now, and to change my voice, for I
† stand in doubt of you. 21 Tell me, ye that desire
to be under the law, do ye not hear the law? 22 For
it is written, that Abraham had two sons, [a] the one by
a bond-maid, [b] the other by a free-woman. 23 But he
who was of the bond-woman, [c] was born after the flesh;
but he of the free-woman *was* by promise. 24 Which
things are an allegory; for these are the two † covenants,
the one from the mount Sinai, [d] which gendereth to bon-
dage, which is Agar. 25 For this Agar is mount Sinai
in Arabia, and answereth to Jerusalem which now is, and
is in bondage with her children. 26 But [e] Jerusalem
which is above is free, which is the mother of us all.
27 For it is written, [f] Rejoice, thou barren, that bearest
not; break forth and cry, thou that travailest not: for
the desolate hath many more children than she which hath
an husband. 28 Now we, brethren, as Isaac was, [g] are
the children of promise. 29 But as then [h] he that was
born after the flesh persecuted him *that was born* after the
Spirit, [i] even so *it is* now. 30 Nevertheless, what saith
the scripture? [k] Cast out the bond-woman and her son:
for [l] the son of the bond-woman shall not be heir with the
son of the free-woman. 31 So then, brethren, we are
not children of the bond-woman, [m] but of the free.

[z] 1 Cor. iv. 15. Philem. 10. Jam. i. 18. † Or, am perplexed in, or for you. [a] Gen. xvi. 15. [b] Gen. xxi. 2. Heb. xi. 11. [c] Rom. ix. 7. † Or, testaments. [d] Chap. v. 1. [e] Isa. ii. 2. Heb. xii. 22. Rev. iii. 12. & xxi. 2, 10. [f] Isa. liv. 1. [g] Rom. ix. 8. Chap. iii. 29. [h] Gen. xxi. 9. [i] Chap. v. 11. & vi. 12. [k] Gen. xxi. 10, 12. [l] John viii. 35. [m] John viii. 36. Chap. iii. 29. & v. 1, 13.

v. 19—31. To engage their hearts, and prevail on them to return from their sad defection from the truth,

1. He expresses his tender affection towards them. *My little children*, dear to me as such, amidst all the weakness you discover, *of whom I travail in birth again*, with such agonies of spirit, longing for your present recovery, as when I first desired to turn you from your soul idolatry, *until Christ be formed in you*, your souls effectually brought under the influence of his gospel, and his image stamped upon your hearts, *I desire to be present with you*, that I might more fully enter upon the subject, confound the gainsayers, and defend the fundamental article of Christianity from which you have swerved, *and*, if it so pleased the Lord to make my preaching effectual to your conversion, *to change my voice* from rebuke to consolation, *for* I own it present, *I stand in doubt of you*, whether you have ever truly believed to the saving of your souls, and may not yet be cast away. *Note*, (1) Ministers travail in birth for immortal souls, and feel an affection for those whom they have begotten in the gospel, like the tender mother's sensibility towards her infant offspring. (2) Christ can never be formed in the heart, where self-righteousness and self dependance still prevail. (3) It is no charity to think

well, when we see evidently what is evil, though we wish to change our voice, and to behold a happy reformation.

2. He expostulates with the Judaizers, who sought justification by the deeds of the law. *Tell me, ye that desire to be under the law, do ye not hear the law?* If you attentively considered the history of Abraham, you would see the folly of your attempt. *For it is written, that Abraham had two sons, the one by a bond-maid*, Hagar an Egyptian, *the other by a free woman*, Sarah. *And he who was of the bond maid*, Ishmael, *was born after the flesh*, in the ordinary course of nature: *but he of the free-woman*, Isaac, *was by promise*, given of God, when both his parents were naturally incapable of issue. *Which things are an allegory, or allegorized*, and have a spiritual meaning, beyond the mere letter of the words; *for these*, Hagar and Sarah, *are the* figures of the *two covenants, the one from the mount Sinai, which gendreth to bondage*, begetting a slavish spirit, and leaving the soul under condemnation, *which is Agar*, and represented by her. *For this Agar is mount Sinai in Arabia*, and her being cast out with her son, is a lively figure of the rejection of those who are under the law, which was delivered on that mountain, *and* this bondwoman *answereth to Jerusalem which now is, and is in bondage with her children*, abandoned for their infidelity, and excluded from all the blessings of the covenant. *But Jerusalem which is above*, the church of the redeemed, who by faith in Christ look for glory and immortality, *is free* from all the condemnation of sin and the law, of *which* Sarah *is* the type, and may be considered as *the mother of us all*, whether Jews or Gentiles, who, like her son Isaac, are entitled to all the promised blessings. *For it is written*, with particular reference to Sarah and Hagar, *Rejoice, thou barren, that bearest not; break forth and cry, thou that travailest not*; thou Gentile land, which, like Sarah, hast long been without ever bringing forth one child for God, now exult in thy vast progeny, *for the desolate hath many more children than she which hath an husband*, more converts springing from among the heathen, where all hope of such a seed was despaired of, than are to be found among those who, under the Sinai covenant, were, during so many hundreds of years, espoused to the Lord as their husband. *Now we, brethren*, who through grace are joined to Christ by faith, *as Isaac was, are the children of the promise*, and heirs of the eternal inheritance. *But as then he that was born after the flesh* (Ishmael) *persecuted*, with mockery and reproaches, *him that was born after the Spirit*, to wit, Isaac, the child of the promise, *even so it is now*, the carnal Jews, who contend for justification by the works of the law, deride and persecute us, who maintain that justification is by faith alone. *Nevertheless, what saith the Scripture? Cast out the bond-woman and her son: for the son of the bond woman shall not be heir with the son of the free woman*; and so surely will they be excluded from the heavenly inheritance, who seek it by the deeds of the law. *So then we, brethren*, who expect justification by faith only, *are not children of the bond woman, but of the free*, and shall inherit that eternal life, from which they who are of the law, and depend upon their own doings for their acceptance with God, must be for ever excluded. *Note*, (1) To understand the Scriptures, we must look further than the letter. (2) Reproach and ridicule are, in God's account, persecution; and this, at least all who live godly in Christ Jesus, must endure.

CHAP. V.

In this chapter the apostle (1) applies his foregoing discourse exhorting them to stand fast in the liberty of the gospel, ver. 1—12. *(2) He cautions them against abusing their liberty*, ver. 13—15. *(3) Exhorts them to walk after the Spirit, and not after the flesh, enumerating the works of each*, ver. 16—25.

1 STAND fast therefore in [a] the liberty wherewith
Christ hath made us free, and be not entangled
again [b] with the yoke of bondage. 2 Behold, I Paul
say unto you, that [c] if ye be circumcised, Christ shall pro-
fit you nothing. 3 For I testify again to every man
that is circumcised, that he is a debtor to do the whole
law. 4 [d] Christ is become of no effect unto you, who-
soever of you are justified by the law; [e] ye are fallen from
grace. 5 For we through the Spirit wait for [f] the hope
of righteousness by faith. 6 For [g] in Jesus Christ neither
circumcision availeth any thing, nor uncircumcision; but
[h] faith which worketh by love. 7 Ye did [i] run well;
[k] who did hinder you, that ye should not obey the truth?
8 This persuasion *cometh* not of him [l] that calleth you.
9 [m] A little leaven leaveneth the whole lump. 10 [n] I
have confidence in you through the Lord, that you will
be none otherwise minded: but [o] he that troubleth you
[p] shall bear *his* judgment, whosoever he be. 11 [q] And
I, brethren, if I yet preach circumcision, [r] why do I yet
suffer persecution? then [s] is the offence of the cross
ceased. 12 [t] I would they were even cut off [u] which
trouble you.

[a] John viii. 32. Rom. vi. 18. 1 Pet. ii. 16. [b] Acts xv. 10. Chap. ii. 4. [c] Acts xv. 1. [d] Rom. ix. 31, 32. Chap. ii. 21. [e] Heb. xii. 15. [f] Rom. viii. 24, 25. 2 Tim. iv. 8. [g] 1 Cor. vii. 19. Chap. iii. 28. & vi. 15. [h] 1 Thess. i. 3. Jam. ii. 18, 20, 22. [i] 1 Cor. ix. 24. [k] Chap. iii. 1. [l] Chap. i. 6. [m] 1 Cor. v. 6. & xv. 33. [n] 2 Cor. ii. 3. & viii. 22. [o] Chap. i. 7. [p] 2 Cor. x. 6. [q] 1 Cor. xv. 30. [r] Chap. iv. 29. & vi. 17. [s] 1 Cor. i. 23. [t] Josh. vii. 25. 1 Cor. v. 13. Chap. i. 8, 9. [u] Acts xv. 1, 2, 24.

v. 1—12.

v 1—12 Having established the doctrine which he undertook to prove, of free justification by faith alone, without the works of the law, he passes on to exhort them steadily to hold fast the truth. *Stand fast therefore in the liberty wherewith Christ hath made us free* from the curse of the law, and its obligation as a covenant of works, seeing for us he hath endured the one and fulfilled the other, *and be not entangled again with the yoke of bondage*, and by submitting to circumcision, return to the Mosaical law as obligatory, and necessary to salvation *Note*, (1) Every believer is Christ's freed-man, and hath nothing to fear from the law as denouncing a curse, and owes it no obedience as a covenant (2) The liberty of the gospel is not a liberty to sin, but to serve God, with freedom of spirit and willing obedience. The apostle enforces his exhortation with several arguments

1 *Behold, I Paul say unto you, that if ye be circumcised, Christ shall profit you nothing* If you depend on these things as essential to your justification before God, all Christ hath done and suffered will be of no avail to you, *v* 4 *ye are fallen from grace*, and excluded from all the blessings of the gospel, whose doctrines you once professed to hold *Note*, The moment we pretend to join any thing of our own, any doings, duties, deserts, or deserts, to Christ's finished work of atonement and righteousness, this is so high a contempt upon him, as must necessarily cut us off from all the blessings of that complete salvation which he hath wrought out, and of which he expects to have the entire glory

2 Every man, who was circumcised, was obliged to perfect obedience to the law, under the penalty of the curse it denounces *For I testify again* (so earnest am I that this important matter be clearly understood) *to every man that is circumcised, that he is a debtor to keep the whole law*, and having laid himself under such an obligation, must perish under the least failure, whilst he expects eternal life on the footing of his own obedience

3 *For even we*, who are Jews, whose consciences have been enlightened to see the spiritual demands of the law, despairing of acceptance with God that way, do *through the Spirit*, under his divine illumination and influence, *wait for the hope of righteousness by faith*, expecting earnestly and patiently that eternal life which God hath promised, not by the works of the law, but through faith in the righteousness of our great Redeemer, as our only sufficient title, and availing plea, and if the Jews were thus necessitated to renounce all dependence on their circumcision, and the legal institutions under which they had been brought up, what folly would it be for Gentiles, who had never been subject to the law, to have recourse thereto? *Note*, Our hope towards God is founded on a better righteousness than our own, even on that of our divine Substitute and Surety

4. The gospel hath cancelled all distinction of Jew and Gentile *For in Christ Jesus*, and under that gracious dispensation which he hath introduced, *neither circumcision availeth any thing, nor uncircumcision*, as a recommendation to God's favour, *but it is faith which worketh by love*, that alone is available to salvation, faith, which lays our whole dependance on Christ alone, and, from a confidence in his love, engages our souls in love to him, and in universal benevolence to mankind *Note*, (1) Christ is to the believer all and in all (2) Faith justifies, not as a grace in us, but as it receives and embraces the divine righteousness provided in the gospel, and leads us to renounce every other hope (3) Wherever faith is unfeigned, the genuine fruits of love will spring from it, and hereby it shall be proved and evidenced

5 It was the more grievous for them to depart from the faith, whose beginnings had been so exceedingly promising *Ye did run well, who did hinder you* from proceeding in the happy ways of the gospel, and hath diverted you from your course, *that you should not obey the truth*, which once you embraced? *This persuasion cometh not of him that calleth you* these judaizing sentiments I never taught you, and God, by his Spirit in the gospel, laid down a quite different method for your acceptance before him *Note*, (1) Many run well for a season, who afterwards falter in their heavenly course (2) It should be matter of serious enquiry to us, what hath turned us aside or retarded us in our Christian race? (3) They who receive the truth in the light of it, must shew their love of it also by the unfeigned obedience of their hearts thereunto

6 The insinuation of such dangerous tenets was likely to produce the most fatal effect *A little leaven leaveneth the whole lump* Where once a departure from the principles of truth begins, like the plague it spreads through the whole body, and one corrupt member in the church may communicate the most fatal and pernicious heresies to the whole

7 The apostle, notwithstanding the fears he could not but entertain, yet charitably expresses his confidence in many of them, that they would resist these innovations *I have confidence in you through the Lord, that you will be none otherwise minded*, and cleave unshaken to the principles of the gospel *but he that troubleth you*, (ὁ ταράσσων) the arch heretic, and author of these pernicious opinions, *shall bear his burden*, and be laid under the just censure of the church, *whosoever he be*, however great and distinguished, at least the righteous judgment of God shall surely overtake him at the last

8 He exculpates himself from every insinuation, which these seducers suggested as if he himself was of their sentiments *And I brethren, if I yet preach circumcision* as necessary to salvation, which they would make you believe, *why do I yet suffer persecution* from the Jewish zealots, my most inveterate foes? *then is the offence of the cross ceased* if this were the case, there would be no reason for them to be any longer exasperated with me. His sufferings therefore proved the zeal wherewith he opposed a notion so subversive of the fundamentals of Christianity

9 He, with just indignation, expresses his earnest wish, that these troublers of the church's peace had their desert *I would they were even cut off that trouble you*, excommunicated from the society of the faithful, or silenced by the righteous vengeance of God *Note*, The troublers of the church's peace, who broach their destructive opinions, sow dissensions, and promote schisms in the undivided body of Christ, shall be severely dealt with in the day of recompence

13 For, brethren, ye have been called unto liberty,
only [x] use not liberty for an occasion to the flesh, but by x 1 Cor viii 9
[y] love serve one another 14 For [z] all the law is ful- 1 Pet ii 16 2 Pet ii 19
filled in one word, *even* in this, [a] Thou shalt love thy y 1 Cor ix 19 Chap vi 2
neighbour as thyself 15 But if ye bite and devour one z Matt vii 12 James ii 8
another, take heed that ye be not consumed one of an- a Lev xix 18 Matt xxii 39 Rom xiii 9
other.

v 13—15 As the apostle had before exhorted them to hold fast their liberty, he here teaches them wherein that liberty consisted *For, brethren, ye have been called unto liberty, only use not liberty for an occasion to the flesh*, as if you were discharged from every moral obligation, and might gratify the corrupt desires of the flesh and of the mind, *but* the gospel of grace teaches us a different lesson, and engages us, by the most powerful principle, even *by love to serve one another*, in every instance of brotherly affection seeking to promote each other's spiritual, temporal, and eternal interests *For all the law is fulfilled in one word*, all the precepts of the second table are summed up in one, *even in this, Thou shalt love thy neighbour as thyself* *But if ye bite and devour one another*, disputing, reviling, and with fierce contentions, like savage beasts exasperated against each other, *take heed that ye be not consumed one of another*, and, forsaken of God, be given up to the evil of your own hearts, which must end in your ruin *Note*, Nothing tends to the destruction of Christianity so immediately as dissensions among those who bear the Christian name

16 *This* I say then, [b] Walk in the Spirit, and ye shall b Rom vi 12 & viii 1, 4 & xiii 14
not fulfil the lust of the flesh 17 [c] For the flesh lusteth 1 Pet ii 11
against the Spirit, and the Spirit against the flesh and c Rom vii 23 &c
these are contrary the one to the other, so that ye cannot d Rom vi 14 & viii 2
do the things that ye would 18 [d] But if ye be led by the e 1 Cor iii 3 Eph v 3 Col iii 5 Jam iii 14
Spirit, ye are not under the law 19 Now [e] the works of the
flesh are manifest, which are *these*, Adultery, fornication,
uncleanness, lasciviousness, 20 Idolatry, witchcraft,
hatred, variance, emulations, wrath, strife, seditions,
heresies, 21 Envyings, murders, drunkenness, revel
lings, and such like of the which I tell you before, as
I have also told you in time past, that [f] they which do f 1 Cor vi 9 Eph v 5 Col iii 6
such things shall not inherit the kingdom of God 22 Rev xxii 15
But [g] the fruit of the Spirit is love, joy, peace, long suff g John xv 2 Eph v 9
ing, [h] gentleness, [i] goodness, faith, 23 Meekness, tem h Col iii 12
perance [k] against such there is no law 24 And they i Rom xv 14
that are Christ's have crucified the flesh with the affec k 1 Tim i 9
tions and lusts 25 [m] If we live in the Spirit, let us also l Rom vi 6 Chap ii 20
walk in the Spirit 26 [n] Let us not be desirous of vain m Rom viii 4, 5
glory, provoking one another, envying one another n Phil ii 3

v 16—26 The advice which St Paul upon the whole gives is this,

1 In general, *This I say then, Walk in the Spirit* under his blessed influence, dictates, and guidance, according to the gospel word, *and ye shall not fulfil the lust of the flesh*, be given up to the native corruptions of your heart, and to finish and perfect it, (ἐπιτελεῖν) as to become absolute slaves to it, and to perish under its reigning dominion In this imperfect state indeed you will not be free from the workings of in-dwelling evil, *for* there are two contending principles in every believer's heart, corruption and grace, *the flesh lusteth against the Spirit*, craving indulgence and gratification, *and the Spirit against the flesh*, opposing and mortifying its corrupt desires, *and these are contrary the one to the other*, in their nature, acting, and tendencies, *so that ye cannot do, or ye do not, the things that ye would*, the workings of the old man are checked and restrained by the power of divine grace, and though the propensity to evil remain in the regenerate, he is enabled by the nobler and divine nature, which he hath received, to oppose its carnal will and affection, though the conflict is often sharp, and sometimes corruption may prevail *But if ye be led by the Spirit*, habitually under his influence, *ye are not under the law*, its condemnation is no longer to be apprehended,

nor are ye subject to it as a covenant of works, but brought into the glorious liberty of the sons of God

2 He particularly enumerates those works of the flesh which must be avoided, and those gracious fruits of the spirit which should be produced by them *Now*,

1 *The works of the flesh*, of the corrupt nature which is in fallen man, *are manifest, which are these, adultery, fornication, uncleanness, lasciviousness*, with every act of bodily pollution, or mental impurity Also, *idolatry, witchcraft, hatred, variance, emulations, wrath, strife, seditions, heresies, envyings*, which more immediately are the iniquities of the carnal mind Add to these the deadly crimes of *murder, drunkenness, revellings, and such like* debaucheries and abominations, *of the which I tell you before* the day of vengeance comes, *as I have also told you in time past, that they which do such things*, unless they repent, *shall not inherit the kingdom of God* Reader, mark these awful words, so express, so full, so distinct Examine thyself, are either of these things found allowed, indulged in thy heart or conduct? Then assuredly the wrath of God abideth on thee *But*,

2 *The fruit of the Spirit*, which he produces in the souls of the redeemed, *is love* to God and men, *joy* in the Lord through Jesus Christ, *in his people* who live to his glory, *in his ordinances*, now become our delight, *peace* of conscience, and with all mankind, *long-suffering*, under all afflictive providences, or the provocations of the perverse, *gentleness* of temper and manners towards every creature, *goodness*, that makes us ready to every word and work for the benefit of others, *faith* and truth in all our promises, engagements, and dealings, *meekness*, that is not easily provoked, and is instantly pacified, *temperance* in all our desires, and in the use of every earthly enjoyment *against such* dispositions and those who are possessed of them, *there is no law*, nor any condemnation to be apprehended

3 *They that are Christ's*, in reality living members of his body mystical, will give demonstrative proof of the truth of their profession by their spiritual practice, for they *have crucified the flesh with their affections and lusts* Their old man is nailed to their Redeemer's cross, and though not utterly dead, yet is dying daily, till, with the death of the body, the body of sin shall be utterly abolished, and buried with the corpse never to rise up again And whilst we are here in a state of warfare, *if we live in the Spirit*, actuated and influenced by his mighty energy, *let us also walk in the Spirit*, and act according to our profession as believers, and the obligations we are under to die daily unto sin, and to live unto righteousness *Let us not be desirous of vain-glory*, puffed up with a high conceit of our attainments or performances, and affecting human approbation, *provoking one another* by a proud superciliousness, or *envying one another* for their superior gifts, tempers the most opposite and contradictory to the profession of Christianity *Note*, (1) All, who are truly Christ's, evidence it by their conduct, the same mind in a measure is in them, and they follow his steps, if we say we have fellowship with him, and walk in darkness, we lie (2) Only from pride cometh contention, envy, and every evil work, this must therefore be mortified, or we cannot be saved

CHAP VI

This chapter chiefly consists of two parts In the former the apostle gives us several plain and practical directions, which more especially tend to instruct Christians in their duty to one another, and to promote the communion of saints in love, from ver 1 to ver 10 In the latter he resumes the main design of the epistle, which was to fortify the Galatians against the arts of their judaizing teachers, and confirm them in the truth and liberty of the gospel To which purpose he, 1 Gives them the true character of these teachers, and shews them from what motives, and with what views they acted, from ver 10 to ver 1[illegible] *And, 2 On the other hand he acquaints them with his own temper and behaviour, from both which they might easily see how little reason they had to slight him, and to fall in with them And then he concludes the epistle with a solemn benediction*

1 BRETHREN, [a] if a man be overtaken in a fault,
ye [b] which are spiritual, [c] restore such an one [d]
in the the spirit of meekness; considering [e] thyself, lest thou
also be tempted 2 [f] Bear ye one another's burdens, and
so fulfil [g] the law of Christ 3 For [h] if a man think
himself to be something, when he is nothing, he deceiveth
himself 4 But [i] let every man prove his own
work, and then shall he have rejoicing in himself alone,
and [l] not in another 5 For [k] every man shall bear his
own burden 6 [l] Let him that is taught in the word,
communicate unto him that teacheth in all good things
7 Be [m] not deceived, God is not mocked for [n] whatsoever
a man soweth, that shall he also reap 8 For [o] he
that soweth to the flesh shall of the flesh reap corruption
but [p] he that soweth to the Spirit shall of the Spirit reap
life everlasting 9 And [q] let us not be weary in well
doing for in due season [r] we shall reap, if we faint not
10 [s] As we have therefore opportunity, [t] let us do good
unto all *men*, [u] especially unto them who are [x] of the
houshold of faith

v 1—10 As he had so warmly recommended to them that love, which would engage them to serve one another, he passes on to the exercise of it in several instances

1 *Brethren, if a man be overtaken in a fault*, through surprize, temptation, and human frailty, *ye which are spiritual*, and strong in the grace which is in Jesus Christ, *restore such an one in the spirit of meekness*, with all the tenderness that an able surgeon handles a dislocated joint, in order to reduce it, using, not rough reproaches, but tender expostulations, *considering thyself*, as no man is secure, *lest thou also be tempted*, and suffered to fall, to punish the undue severity you may have used towards others, and justly to smart under the same scourge *Note*, (1) A sense of our own weakness will make us compassionate towards an offending brother (2) Peculiar tenderness is needful, when the soul is already vexed and grieved by sin, least we drive those to despair, whom we should lead to repentance (3) Angry reproofs, however great the provocation may be, never can do good

2 *Bear ye one another's burdens*, sympathizing with the afflicted, patient with the infirmities of the weak, and desirous to alleviate every grief, under which your brethren groan, by your prayers, your counsel, or your substance, *and so fulfil the law of Christ*, that law of love, which he hath taught both by precept and example

3 In humility, every man should watch over, and examine himself *For if a man think himself to be something* extraordinary, and self-sufficient to withstand every temptation, *when in fact he is nothing*, and hath no strength of his own, *he deceiveth his own self*, as he will find, by dire experience, when he comes to be tried *But let every man prove his own work*, examining into his principles and practice according to the gospel rule, *and then*, if he finds a happy correspondence between them, *shall he have rejoicing in himself, and not in another*, he will exult in the blessed testimony of the spirit and his own conscience, ascribing to the grace of God what hath been wrought in him, and will seek no glory from human applause, nor desire to rake up other's faults as a foil to set off his own excellencies, satisfied in God in Christ Jesus accepts and approves his services *For every man shall bear his own burden*, and stand or fall, not according to the opinion he hath entertained of himself, or that others form of him, but according to the decision of the eternal judge *Note*, (1) A high opinion of ourselves ever argues great ignorance of our own hearts (2) The testimony of a good conscience is matter of solid satisfaction (3) Though we know nothing declaredly evil in ourselves, we must remember he that judgeth us is the Lord, who sees many evils, which we through blindness overlook, and therefore it becomes us ever to be humble before him

4 *Let him that is taught in the word, communicate unto him that teacheth in all good things*, contributing liberally and chearfully to the support of a gospel ministry, for the labourer is worthy of his hire *Be not deceived* by your deluding teachers, who would engross your regard, nor by the covetousness of your own hearts, that would divert you from this or any other instance of liberality, *God is not to be mocked* by vain pretences, *for whatsoever a man soweth, that shall he also reap*, according to his work will be his wages *For he that soweth to the flesh*, making provision for it to fulfil the lusts thereof, or inordinately anxious to hoard up worldly wealth, to the defrauding of God's altar or the poor, *such a man shall of the flesh reap corruption*, his perishing acquisitions will soon be fled, and endless misery succeed *but he that soweth to the Spirit*, in every instance of bounty and benevolence, under the Spirit's guidance, laying out himself, his time, his talents, for the glory of Christ, and the good of his people, *shall of the Spirit reap everlasting life*, and in eternity receive the blessed recompence of his deeds *And let us not be weary of well-doing*, though we may not see all the happy effects we expected, *for in due season we shall reap, if we faint not* Nothing can be lost which is employed in God's service, though like the seed under the clod it may seem to be buried for a while, it will surely spring up and afford a plenteous increase, often in this world, and always in a better

5 This is the day for labour, therefore we should diligently improve it And *as we have opportunity, let us*, according to our abilities, *do good unto all men*, with liberal hearts, and open hands, not restraining our charity to any party or nation, though *especially* extending it *unto them who are of the houshold of faith*, for whom we are bound particularly to interest ourselves, by peculiar ties of love and duty, as children of the same family, and heirs of the same inheritance

11 Ye see how large a letter I have written unto you
with mine own hand 12 As many as desire to make a
fair shew in the flesh, [y] they constrain you to be circumcised,
[z] only lest they [a] should suffer persecution for the

croſs of Chriſt 13 For neither they themſelves who
are circumciſed keep the law, but deſire to have you
circumciſed, that they may glory in your fleſh 14 But
[b] God forbid that I ſhould glory, ſave in the croſs of our
Lord Jeſus Chriſt, by whom the world [c] is crucified
unto me, and I unto the world 15 For [d] in Chriſt
Jeſus neither circumciſion availeth any thing, nor un-
circumciſion, but [e] a new creature 16 And [f] as many
as walk [g] according to this rule, peace *be* on them, and
mercy, and upon [h] the Iſrael of God 17 From hence-
forth let no man trouble me, for [i] I bear in my body
the marks of the Lord Jeſus 18 Brethren, [k] the grace
of our Lord Jeſus Chriſt *be* with your ſpirit Amen

[b] Phil iii 8 [c] Rom vi 6 Chap ii 20 [d] 1 Cor vii 19 Chap v 6 Col iii 11 [e] 2 Cor v 17 [f] Ps cxxv 5 [g] Phil iii 16 [h] Rom ii 28, 29 iv 12 Chap iii 9, 29 Phil iii 3 [i] 2 Cor iv 10 Col i 24 [k] 2 Tim iv 22 Philem 25

2 11—18 Though in his other epiſtles he uſually employed an amanuenſis, out of his great affection to them he wrote this long letter on ſo important a ſubject with his own hand And now, being about to conclude, he,

1 Marks out to them the true character of their ſeducing teachers, that they may beware of them *As many as deſire to make a fair ſhew in the fleſh*, and by their pompous profeſſions, and zeal for the ceremonials of religion, would inſinuate into your confidence, *they conſtrain you to be circumciſed*, and urge this upon you as neceſſary to ſalvation, when, in fact, their deſign is not your good, but their own eaſe and honour, for they do it *only leſt they ſhould ſuffer perſecution for the croſs of Chriſt* from the furious zealots for Judaiſm, who cannot bear the doctrine of free juſtification through faith in Chriſt alone, without circumciſion, or the works of the law *for*, eager as they are for your ſubmitting to this rite, *neither they themſelves, who are circumciſed, keep the law* in its moral purity and perfection, rigidly as they are attached to the ceremonials of it, *but they deſire to have you circumciſed, that they may glory in your fleſh*, and make a merit of it with their countrymen that you are their proſelytes to circumciſion *Note*, (1) They who are aſhamed of the croſs, are aſſuredly the enemies of Chriſt (2) Many make their boaſt of the form of religion, who are the greateſt ſtrangers to the power of it

2 He declares to them his own temper and conduct What the falſe teachers were aſhamed of, he gloried in *God forbid that I ſhould glory* in external privileges, attainments, gifts, duties, or any thing elſe, *ſave in the croſs of our Lord Jeſus Chriſt*, and in that atoning ſacrifice which he there offered, as my whole dependance for pardon and acceptance with God, *by whom alſo the world is crucified unto me, and I unto the world*, through faith in him I am mortified to all its allurements, honours, and intereſts, and content to be treated with that contempt and virulent enmity which for the truth ſake I ſuffer from a world that lieth in wickedneſs *Note*, (1) The croſs is the glorious object ever in the Chriſtian's eye, for to the ſacrifice there offered he is indebted for all his hopes in time and eternity (2) Faith in a crucified Jeſus is the victory that overcometh the world, and nothing elſe can enable us to do it

3 He lays down the eſſential point of true Chriſtianity *For in Chriſt Jeſus*, with regard to the ſalvation which is in him, *neither circumciſion availeth any thing, nor uncircumciſion*, the one is no advantage, the other no obſtruction, *but* that which muſt prove our intereſt in Chriſt, and that we are partakers of the grace of God in truth, is our becoming *a new creature*, having our principles, tempers and conduct, caſt into the mold of the goſpel, through the mighty energy of faith which worketh by love

4 He offers up his prayers for thoſe who hold faſt the truth *As many as walk according to this rule*, laid down in this epiſtle, with regard to juſtification by faith, and the new creature, without reſpect to circumciſion or uncircumciſion, *peace be upon them, and mercy, and upon the Iſrael of God*, may they enjoy peace with God and in their own conſciences, and every divine mercy which is purchaſed by the crucified Jeſus for his redeemed people, who, whether Jews or Gentiles, are God's ſpiritual Iſrael

5 He with authority enjoins them to give him no farther trouble on this point, but to ſubmit to his apoſtolic warnings and reproofs *From henceforth let no man trouble me* with farther diſputes and contentions, or with injurious reproaches, as tho' I had ever countenanced the doctrine of theſe judaizing teachers, the contrary of which is moſt evident I have ever oppoſed them, and ſeverely ſuffered for it, *for I bear in my body the marks of the Lord Jeſus*, the ſcars of the wounds and ſtripes endured for his ſake, the ſigns of my conformity to him, and of my adherence to the offenſive doctrines of his croſs, and particularly of juſtification by faith alone *Note*, It is a proof we believe the doctrines we preach, when we dare boldly ſuffer for them, and can produce the glorious ſcars received in the ſervice of the Captain of our ſalvation

6 He concludes with his uſual benediction *Brethren, the grace of our Lord Jeſus Chriſt be with your ſpirit, Amen!* The treatment he had received from them did not quench his love towards them Earneſt to promote their ſalvation, he prays that they may experience the ineſtimably precious love of a dying Redeemer, and partake of all the invaluable privileges which he freely beſtows on his choſen, even pardon, peace, comfort, holineſs, and eternal life

THE

THE

EVANGELICAL EXPOSITOR;

OR, A

PRACTICAL COMMENT

Upon the EPISTLE of

St. PAUL to the EPHESIANS.

THIS Epistle bears date out of a prison: and some have observed that what this apostle wrote when he was a prisoner had the greatest relish and savour in it of the things of God When his tribulations did abound, his consolations and experiences did much more abound From whence we may observe, that the afflictive exercises of God's people, and particularly of his ministers, do oftentimes tend to the advantage of others as well as to their own

The apostle's design is to settle and establish the Ephesians in the truth; and further to acquaint them with the mystery of the gospel in order to it In the former part he represents the great privilege of the Ephesians, who, being in time past idolatrous heathens, were now converted to Christianity, and received into covenant with God, which he illustrates from a view of their deplorable state before their conversion, chap i ii iii. *In the latter part (which we have in the fourth, fifth, and sixth chapters) he instructs them in the principal duties of religion, both personal and relative, and exhorts and quickens them to the faithful discharge of them Zanchius observes, that we have here an epitome of the whole Christian doctrine, and of almost all the chief heads of divinity*

Ephesus was the chief city of the proconsular Asia, and particularly famous for the magnificent temple of Diana Idolatry there reigned triumphant, till the standard of Christ was erected, the pillars of Satan's kingdom shaken, and multitudes brought by the preaching of Paul to the obedience of the faith

CHAP I

In this chapter we have 1 The introduction to the whole epistle, which is much the same as in others, ver 1, 2 *2 The apostle's thanksgivings and praises to God for his inestimable blessings bestowed on the believing Ephesians,* ver 3—14 *3 His earnest prayers to God in their behalf,* ver 15–23

1 PAUL an apostle of Jesus Christ, [a] by the
will of God, [b] to the saints which are at
Ephesus, and [c] to the faithful in Christ Jesus
2 [d] Grace *be* to you and peace from God
our Father, and *from* the Lord Jesus Christ

Ver 1, 2 The epistle opens with the apostle's usual address *Paul an apostle of Jesus Christ,* appointed to that high office and honour *by the will of God* immediately revealed from heaven, *to the saints which are at Ephesus,* by profession and practice separated from this present evil world, and sanctified by the Holy Ghost, *and to the faithful in Christ Jesus,* who by faith are united to him, and approve their fidelity before him *Grace be to you and peace,* in all their comprehensive import, *from God our Father,* the fountain of blessedness, *and from the Lord Jesus Christ,* the purchaser and bestower of every good and perfect gift Note, (1) All true Christians are *saints* upon earth (2) They who have obtained grace to be faithful have need still to look to the same fountain from whence they derive continual supplies, that their stability may be secured, and their peace be enlarged

3 [e] Blessed *be* the God and Father of our Lord Jesus
Christ, who hath blessed us with [f] all spiritual blessings
in heavenly † *places* in Christ 4 According as [g] he
hath chosen us in him before the foundation of the
world, [h] that we should be holy, and without blame
before him in love 5 [i] Having predestinated us [k] unto the adoption of children by Jesus Christ to himself,
[l] according to the good pleasure of his will, 6 To the
praise of the glory of his grace, [m] wherein he hath made
us accepted in [n] the Beloved 7 [o] In whom we have
redemption through his blood, the forgiveness of sins,
according to [p] the riches of his grace, 8 Wherein he
hath abounded towards us [q] in all wisdom and prudence,
9 [r] Having made known unto us the mystery of his
will according to his good pleasure, [s] which he hath
purposed in himself 10 That in the dispensation of
[t] the fulness of times [u] he might gather together in one
[x] all things in Christ, both which are in heaven, and
which are on earth, *even* in him 11 In whom also
we [y] have obtained an inheritance, being predestinated
according to the purpose of him who worketh all things

after

a 2 Cor i 1 b Rom i 7 2 Cor i 1 c 1 Cor iv 17 Col i 2 d Rom i 7 Col i 3

e 2 Cor i 3 1 Pet i 3 f Rom viii 32 † Or things 2 Thess ii 13 2 Tim i 9 h Luke i 75 Chap v 27 Col i 22 1 Thess iv 7 1 Pet i 2 i Rom viii 29 30 k Rom viii 15 Gal iv 5 1 John iii 1 l Mat xi 26 p Rom ii 4 n Mat iii 17 o Acts xx 28 Col i 14 Heb ix 12 1 Pet i 18 19 p Rom ii 4 Chap ii 7 r Rom xvi 25 Col i 26 s Chap iii 11 2 Tim i 9 t Gal iv 4 u 1 Cor xv 24 x Chap ii 15 Col i 20 y Acts xx 32 Acts xxvi 18 Col i 12

z Phil i 11 after the counsel of his own will 12 z That we should
a Jam i 18 be to the praise of his glory, a who first trusted in Christ
13 In whom ye also *trusted* after that ye heard the
word of truth, the gospel of your salvation in whom
b Rom viii 16 2 Cor i 22 Chap iv 30 also after that ye believed, b ye were sealed with that
holy Spirit of promise, 14 c Which is the earnest of
c 2 Cor v 5 d Luke xxi 28 Rom viii 23 Chap iv 30. our inheritance, d until the redemption of the purchased
possession, unto the praise of his glory

v 3—14 Deeply impressed with a sense of the inestimable blessings of which in Christ Jesus they had been made partakers, the grateful apostle breaks forth in praises and thanksgivings to the God of all grace

1 In general *Blessed be the God and Father of our Lord Jesus Christ*, the adored Redeemer, in whom he is now become our reconciled and covenant God, *who hath blessed us with all spiritual blessings in heavenly things* or *places in Christ*, blessings descending from above, and leading up our souls to high and heavenly things, till we reach the mansions of eternal blessedness And for all these rich gifts which we now enjoy, and all the greater glory which we hope for, be everlasting praise, honour, and thanksgiving ascribed to the ever-blessed fountain of mercies *Note*, (1) We cannot *bless* God as he *blesseth* us his blessings are real gifts conferred, ours are only the grateful acknowledgements we owe for them (2) In Christ Jesus *all* spiritual blessings are freely given to us, and though we are not in possession of them *all*, our title to them is sure

2 In particular,

(1) He praises God for the spiritual blessing of *election* *According as he hath chosen us in him before the foundation of the world*, in his own eternal mind having sovereignly fixed upon us as the objects of his love, not for any thing foreseen in us but as regarded in Christ, our covenant-head and representative, who is most eminently his *elect*, and in and with whom he hath predestinated us to life and salvation, and, as the way thereto, hath ordained, *that we should be holy, and without blame before him in love*, sanctified by his Spirit, in sincerity and truth enabled to approve ourselves before him, as acting under the influence of that divine principle of love which he hath shed abroad in our heart *having predestinated us unto the adoption of children by Jesus Christ unto himself*, from everlasting, in his eternal purpose, singling us out from the rest of mankind, and, through union with his own Son, admitting us to the high dignity of children, bestowing on us the Spirit of adoption, and designing us for the eternal inheritance, that we might be thus a people for his praise, *according to the good pleasure of his will*, not for any worthiness foreseen in us, or any previous obligation lying upon him so to do, but merely out of his own divine sovereignty, that we might be *to the praise of the glory of his grace*, which is thus magnified in the highest, and all the glory of a complete and finished salvation, from the beginning to the end, to be ascribed to him alone by every redeemed soul

(2) He blesses God for the reconciliation and acceptance obtained through Christ Jesus *Wherein he hath made us accepted in the Beloved*, in his boundless grace he hath taken us for his own, and, regarding us as we stand united with his dear Son, embraces us with the arms of his everlasting love, accepting both our persons and services for his sake, in whom, being found, we are esteemed complete and perfect, lacking nothing

(3) He praises God for the great and inestimable blessings of redemption and remission of sins through the adored Saviour *In whom we have redemption*, an entire deliverance from all evil, and a restoration to all blessedness, in virtue of the inestimable price which he hath paid, *through his most precious blood*, shed on purpose to satisfy divine justice, and obtain our deliverance from the curse of a broken law, in virtue whereof we have *the forgiveness of sins*, and are saved from all their deadly consequences in time and eternity, *according to the riches of his grace*, though it was due to our Substitute, the pardon is absolutely free to us, and that such a Redeemer should be ever provided was itself a matter of the most transcendent grace and favour, *wherein he hath abounded towards us in all wisdom and prudence*, manifesting the most astonishing depths of *wisdom* in the contrivance, and *prudence* in the execution of this wondrous scheme of salvation

(4) He blesses God for the knowledge he had communicated to them of his will *Having made known unto us the mystery of his will*, which was hid from former ages, or but darkly made known, but now is revealed to us, both by an external revelation of it clearly in his word, and by the internal illumination of his Spirit, *according to his good pleasure, which he hath purposed in himself*, flowing from his own sovereign determination, without the least inducement whatever thereunto moving him in those who were the objects of his choice, *that in the dispensation of the fulness of times* under the gospel, the last dispensation of grace which will be vouchsafed to the sinful sons of men, *he might gather together in one all things in Christ*, reducing things again to order from the confusion which sin had introduced, recovering his elect, whether Jews or Gentiles, from the miseries of their fallen state, and, under Christ as their living head, uniting them in one body, *both which are in heaven and which are on earth*, angels as well as saints being formed into one glorious company, *even in him*, who is their centre of union, whom they acknowledge as their common Lord, and alike owe to him their stability and eternal blessedness

(5) He blesses God for the glorious inheritance obtained for them in Christ *In whom also we have obtained an inheritance*, holding a title to eternal life on his complete obedience to death, and virtually possessed of it through him who, as our forerunner, is for us entered into heaven itself, *being predestinated* to this glorious portion, *according to the purpose of him who worketh all things* with irresistible efficacy (ἐνεργοῦντος) *after the counsel of his own will, that we*, to whom the word was first preached, *should be to the praise of his glory, who first trusted in Christ*, and embraced his gospel *In whom ye Gentiles also trusted*, and obtained a like inheritance with us, *after that ye heard the word of truth, the gospel of your salvation*, and became thereby obedient to the faith, and partakers in common of all our blessings

(6) He blessed God for the seal and assurance which they had received of their interest in the everlasting promises *In whom also, after that ye believed, ye were sealed with that holy Spirit of promise*, which, shining on his own work, conveyed the fullest evidence to your consciences of your particular interest in the salvation of the gospel, *which is the earnest of our inheritance*, a pledge and foretaste of the glory which shall be revealed, *until the redemption of the purchased possession*, when we, whom he purchased with his own blood, shall be brought to the perfection of holiness and happiness above, and the work be completed in the resurrection of a glorified body at the last day, *unto the praise of his glory*, when to eternity his great name shall be exalted by all the redeemed that shall surround his throne with never ending praises

15 Wherefore I also, e after I heard of your faith e Col i 4 Philem 5.
in the Lord Jesus, and love unto all the saints, 16
f Cease not to give thanks for you, making mention of f Rom i 9. Phil i 3, 4 1 Thes i 2 2 Thes i 3
you in my prayers, 17 That g the God of our Lord g John xx 17
Jesus Christ, the Father of glory, h may give unto you
the Spirit of wisdom and revelation, in the knowledge
of him 18 i The eyes of your understanding being h Col i 9 i Acts xxvi 18
enlightened, that ye may know what is the hope of his
calling, and what the riches of the glory of his inheritance in the saints, 19 And what *is* the exceeding greatness of his power to us-ward who believe, k according k Chap iii 7 Col ii 12
to the working of his mighty power; 20 Which he
wrought in Christ when l he raised him from the dead, l Acts ii 24
and m set him at his own right hand in the heavenly *places*, m Ps cx 1 Heb i 3 & x 12 1 Pet iii 22
21 n Far above all o principality, and power, and might,
and dominion, and every name that is named, not only
in this world, but also in that which is to come 22 n Phil ii 9. Col ii 10
And p hath put all things under his feet, and gave him o Rom viii 38 Col i 16
q *to be* the head over all things to the church, 23
r Which is his body, the fulness of him s that filleth all p Ps viii 6 1 Cor xv 27 Heb ii 8
in all

q Chap iv 15, 16 r Rom xii 5 1 Cor xii 27 Chap v 23 30 Col i 18 s 1 Cor xii 6 Chap iv 10 Col iii 11

v 15—23 The apostle accompanies his grateful thanksgiving with his affectionate prayers *Wherefore I also, after I heard of your faith in the Lord Jesus, and love unto all the saints*, shewn by the most genuine proofs, *cease not to give thanks for you* at every approach to the throne of grace, *making mention of you in my prayers, that the God of our Lord Jesus Christ*, and our covenant God in him, *the Father of glory, may give unto you the spirit of wisdom and revelation in the knowledge of him*, making a more clear and experimental discovery to you of the glorious truths of his word, and manifesting with greater energy his love to your souls, that you may know, chuse, and delight in him as your God, *the eyes of your understanding*, which by nature were darkened, *being now enlightened, that ye may know*, (1) *What is the hope of his calling*, assured with the utmost certainty of the solid foundation on which it is built, and seeing the unutterably glorious privileges which it comprehends *And*, (2) *What the riches of the glory of his inheritance in the saints*, at present in all the inestimably precious gifts and graces which he bestows, and hereafter in the complete and everlasting blessedness which he hath provided for them (3) *And what the exceeding greatness of his mighty power to us-ward who believe*; how surpassing marvellous, that we, who were dead in sins, should ever be quickened to the life of faith and grace, preserved midst all the enemies, spiritual and temporal, without and within, which fight against us, and our bodies at last raised from the dust in glory, *according to the working of his mighty power*, an act of omnipotence no less than that *which he wrought in Christ, when he raised him from the dead*, leading captivity captive, *and set him at his own right hand in the heavenly places*, triumphant over all his foes, and exalted to the throne of Majesty on high, *far above all principality, and power, and might, and dominion, and every name that is named, not only in this world, but also in that which is to come*, whether angels of light, or demons of darkness, or earthly potentates and princes, by whatever name or title distinguished, all are made subject unto him, *and hath put all things under his feet*, as the exalted Mediator, *and gave him to be head over all things to the church*, to govern, protect, and preserve it from all foes, and so to order every event, as that in its issue it shall conduce to the spiritual and eternal benefit of the whole and every individual believer, whilst he, as their living head of vital influence, actuates, quickens, and strengthens every member of his church, *which is his body* mystical, and in that sense they are *the fulness of him*, for if the least member were wanting, the body would be incomplete, though in himself Christ is infinitely perfect, and needeth us not, whilst we receive our all out of him *that filleth all in all*, supplying every want of his people, and bestowing on them the abundance of his grace, that they may grow up into him in all things, and be conformed to him their head. *Note*, (1) Prayer is the constant duty we owe to each other (2) The prospect of the glorious inheritance before us should quicken our desires after it (3) Every believer is as much an instance of omnipotent power, as if a dead body were raised from the dust (4) Christ hath all power committed to him for the good of his people, and they may be confident of his care and support in every time of need, nor shall any be able to pluck the meanest of his people out of his hands

CHAP II

This chapter contains an account, 1 Of the miserable condition of these Ephesians by nature, ver 1—3 and again, ver 11, 12 2 Of the glorious change that was wrought in them by converting grace, ver 4—10 and again, ver 13 3 Of the great and glorious privileges that converted Jews and Gentiles both receive from Christ, ver 14—22

1. AND ᵃ you *hath he quickned* who were dead in
trespasses and sins, 2 ᵇ Wherein in time past
ye walked according to the course of this world, accord-
ing to ᶜ the prince of the power of the air, the spirit that
now worketh in ᵈ the children of disobedience 3 ᵉ A-
mong whom also we all had our conversation in times
past, in the lusts of our flesh, fulfilling the desires of the
flesh and of the mind, and ᶠ were by nature the children
of wrath, even as others

ᵃ Col ii 13 ᵇ 1 Cor vi 11 Chap iv 22 Col iii 7 ᶜ John xvi 11 Chap vi 12 ᵈ Chap v 6 Col iii 6 ᵉ Tit iii 3 1 Pet iv 3 ᶠ Psal li 5 Rom v 12, 14.

v 1—3 Behold the miserable state of every man by nature

1 We are dead in trespasses and sins spiritually dead, as criminals under the curse and condemnation of a broken law, and the life of God extinguished in our souls, and in this state of desperate misery we must for ever continue, till redeemed by the blood, and quickened by the Spirit of the Lord Jesus

2 Though dead to God, we have been but too much alive to the practice of sin, *in which in time past we walked according to the course of this world*, our spirit apostate, our ways perverse, conformed to the maxims, and copying the manners of a world that lieth in wickedness, the consequence of which could not but be our condemnation with the world

3 We were at that time the bond-slaves of the god of this world, acting *according to* the instigation of *the prince of the power of the air*, the devil, who with his legions is permitted to exercise sometimes his power and agency in the aerial regions, and is *the spirit that now worketh in the children of disobedience*, by himself, and those foul fiends his fellows, tempting, seducing, governing, hardening the unbelieving and disobedient *among whom also we all*, Jews as well as Gentiles, even apostles as well as others, *had our conversation in time past*, enslaved by sin, and led captive by the devil at his will, a state how fearful!

4 We then lived *in the lusts of our flesh*, indulging every corrupt appetite, and *fulfilling the desires of the flesh and of the mind*, as the beasts which perish, devoted to the gratification of brutal passions, and in our soul filled with pride, envy, malice, hatred, revenge, and the whole train of spiritual wickednesses, disposed to every abomination, and only wanting temptation and opportunity to commit every iniquity in which body or soul can be engaged

5 As the source of all our evil, *we are by nature children of wrath*, obnoxious to the displeasure of that God who is of purer eyes than to behold iniquity, born with every evil propensity, and herein there is no difference even between the elect of God and others, all lying in the same corrupted mass, till separated by sovereign grace The more we are acquainted with this our natural state of desperate corruption, remediless guilt, and hopeless misery, the more we shall value the unsearchable riches of Christ, and be filled with admiration, love, and praise, in the view of an incarnate Redeemer

4 But God, ᵍ who is rich in mercy, for his great love
wherewith he loved us, 5 ʰ Even when we were dead
in sins, ⁱ hath quickned us together with Christ, (ᵏ by
grace ye are saved) 6. And hath raised *us* up together,
and ˡ made *us* sit together in heavenly *places* in Christ
Jesus 7 That in the ages to come he might shew
ᵐ the exceeding riches of his grace, in *his* kindness to-
wards us through Christ Jesus 8 For ⁿ by grace are ye
saved, ᵒ through faith, and that not of yourselves ᵖ *it is*
the gift of God 9 ᵍ Not of works, lest any man should
boast 10 For ʳ we are his workmanship, created in
Christ Jesus unto good works, which God hath before
ordained that we should walk in them 11 Wherefore
ˢ remember that ye *being* in time passed Gentiles in the
flesh, who are called Uncircumcision by that which is
called the Circumcision in the flesh ᵗ made by hands,
12 ᵘ That at that time ye were without Christ, ˣ being
aliens from the commonwealth of Israel, and strangers
from ʸ the covenants of promise, having no hope, and
ᶻ without God in the world 13 But now in Christ
Jesus, ye ᵃ who sometimes were far off, are made nigh
by the blood of Christ

ᵍ Rom x 12 ... ˡ Col iii 1 ᵐ Chap i 7 ⁿ Ver 5 ᵒ Rom iv 16 ᵖ Matt xvi 17 Rom x 14, 15, 17 ᵍ Rom iii 20, 27, 28 & iv 2 & ix 11 & xi 6 ʳ Col i 10 Tit ii 14 ˢ Col i 21 ᵗ Col ii 11 ᵘ Col i 21 ˣ Ezek xiii 9 ʸ Rom ix 4 ᶻ Gal iv 8 ᵃ Acts ii 39

v 4—13 With exultation and wonder should we contemplate the astonishing mystery of redeeming love Here in its brightest glories we see it displayed, and God in that delightful attribute of mercy appears exalted in the highest

1 The fontal cause of our redemption is God's eternal love and grace, who is *rich in mercy*, the source inexhaustible of all our blessings, not for any thing done by us, or foreseen in us, but purely to magnify *his own great love wherewith he loved us*, before the worlds were, having fixed upon us sovereignly as the objects of his choice, and predestinated us to grace in time, and glory in eternity

2 What serves as a foil to set off in the most distinguished lustre this mercy of our God, is the state in which we lay, *even when we were dead in trespasses and sins*, and, instead of any thing to engage his love, had in us every thing to excite his loathing even then, when we were foul, odious, and in a condition desperate as that of fallen angels, did the God of all grace regard us, and plucked us as brands from the burning Praise the Lord, O my soul, and forget not all his benefits

3 The inestimable blessings conferred upon such wretched sinners are, [1] *Life* in Christ our living head *He hath quickned us together with Christ* forasmuch as in his resurrection we see the sentence of death passed on our nature repealed, and the life which he possesses is for the use of his body mystical, who, as considered in him, are alive before God, and by virtue of union with him will in due time be raised to spiritual life, and conformed to the image of their living Lord *By grace ye are saved*, and thus, through the transcendently rich and sovereign love of God, restored to his favour here, and receive a sure title to his glory hereafter [2] *He hath also raised us up together, and made us sit together in heavenly places in Christ Jesus* for since he, as our forerunner and representative, is for us entred into the heavenly glory, we, as *virtually* included in him, may be said to be there also, and are thereby assured we shall in due time *actually* possess the same inheritance, and reign with him for ever May our affections then be ever placed above with our exalted head!

4 The end God proposes in this great salvation *That in the ages to come he might shew the exceeding riches of his grace, in his kindness towards us, through Jesus Christ*, encouraging to the latest days of time poor and perishing sinners to come and trust in this boundless mercy revealed in the gospel, and that in the better world, when all the glory of his grace in brightest colours shall appear, he might be the object of ceaseless praise and adoration to men and angels through all the countless ages of eternity

5 The means appointed to convey all these blessings to us is faith *For by grace ye are saved*, freely, fully, everlastingly, *through faith*, which is the way wherein we receive all the great and precious promises, *and that not of yourselves*, faith being not the produce of our own free-will, nor the effect of others reasonings, *but it is the gift of God*, and, like all other blessings, flows from his boundless love, and is the work of his Spirit in our hearts, and both the salvation itself, and the faith which embraces it, are bestowed without the least respect to any works of ours, that the glory of the divine grace might not suffer the least diminution *Not of works, lest any man should boast*, for could one fallen creature produce the least thought or action, which would give him a superiority over others, and recommend him to the divine favour, as a more worthy object than they, the salvation would be no more of grace, and the sinner might justly glory

6 Though our salvation be purely of grace, God hath taken care to engage our hearts to himself by the strongest ties, whilst all the work and all the glory appear to be his own *For we are his workmanship, created in Christ Jesus*, all that is excellent in us comes from his mere gift, our souls, by divine operation renewed, now produce the genuine fruits of righteousness, he works all that is good in us, and, though he exclude our glorying, secures our obedience *unto good works, which God hath before ordained that we should walk in them*, such being his eternal

purpose,

purpose, and he hath prepared (προητοίμασε) disposed us to, and enabled us for the practice of them. *Note*, The doctrines of grace, far from loosening, as some vainly imagine, the obligations to morality, can only effectually engage and enable the soul for the practice of righteousness and true holiness.

7 He reminds the Ephesians of what they should ever keep warm upon their memories, to awaken their gratitude, and bind their hearts to God. *Wherefore remember that ye being in time past Gentiles in the flesh, who are called uncircumcision by that which is called the circumcision in the flesh made with hands*, treated by the native Jews with contempt and disdain, and indeed excluded from all the peculiar privileges which they enjoyed: *that at that time ye were without Christ*, having neither knowledge of him, nor union with him; *being aliens from the commonwealth of Israel*, out of the pale of God's church, *and strangers from the covenants of promise*, which were peculiarly confirmed to Abraham's natural seed; *having no hope*, as left no well-grounded one, of God's favour and life eternal, *and without God in the world*, atheists, both *speculative* and *practical*, even whilst you worshipped gods many, being without the least knowledge of the one true Jehovah. *But now in Christ Jesus*, since by faith ye have been united to him, and heard and embraced his gospel, *ye who sometimes were far off* from all good, and all hope, *are made nigh by the blood of Christ*, received into a state of favour and reconciliation with God, and entitled to the eternal blessedness which he hath purchased. *Note*, Sinners in their natural state are far removed from God, and must, but for the redemption which is in Jesus Christ, remain so for ever.

14 For [b] he is our peace, [c] who hath made both one,
and hath broken down the middle wall of partition be-
tween us; 15 [d] Having abolished [e] in his flesh the en-
mity, *even* the law of commandments *contained* in ordi-
nances; for to make in himself of twain one new man,
so making peace; 16 And that he might reconcile
both unto God [g] in one body by the cross, [h] having slain
the enmity thereby. 17 And came and [i] preached
peace to you [k] which were afar off, and to them [l] that
were nigh. 18 For [m] through him we both have an
access by one Spirit unto the Father. 19 Now there-
fore ye are no more strangers and foreigners, but [n] fel-
low citizens with the saints, and of [o] the houshold of God;
20 And [p] are built [q] upon the foundation of the apostles
and prophets, Jesus Christ himself being [r] the chief corner-
stone; 21 [s] In whom all the building fitly framed together,
groweth unto [t] an holy temple in the Lord: 22 [u] In
whom you also are builded together for an habitation of
God through the Spirit.

b Isaiah ix. 6. John xvi. 33. Acts x. 36. Col. i. 20. c John x. 16. Gal. iii. 28. d Col. ii. 14. e Col. i. 22. f 2 Cor. v. 17. Gal. vi. 15. g Col. i. 22. h Rom. vi. 6. & viii. 3. Col. ii. 14. i Isa. lvii. 19. Zech. ix. 10. Acts x. 36. k Acts ii. 39. l Psal. cxlviii. 14. m John x. 9. Chap. iii. 12. Heb. iv. 16. & x. 19, 20. n Phil. iii. 20. Heb. xii. 22, 23. o Gal. vi. 10. p 1 Cor. iii. 9. & 1 Pet. ii. 4, 5. q Matt. xvi. 18. Rev. xxi. 14. r Psal. cxviii. 22. Isa. xxviii. 16. s Chap. iv. 16. t 1 Cor. iii. 16, 17. & vi. 19. 2 Cor. vi. 16. u 1 Pet. ii. 5.

v. 14—22. All the blessings in time and eternity, which sinners can ever hope for, flow down to them through the channel of a crucified Jesus. *For he is our peace*, having reconciled us to God by his own blood, *who hath made both one*, uniting Jews and Gentiles together in one body under himself our common head, *and hath broken down the middle wall of partition between us*, which till now excluded the nations from the blessings peculiar to Israel; *having abolished in his flesh the enmity*, that which had been the cause of much enmity between Jews and Gentiles, *even the ceremonial law*, called *the law of commandments contained in ordinances*, which, as they pointed all to Christ, were now fulfilled by him, and abrogated, he designing *for to make of twain*, of Jews and Gentiles, *one new man*, cementing them together in one church, and forming his own blessed image alike in their hearts, *so making peace* between them, as members of one body, united by faith and love in him; *and that he might reconcile both unto God*, who by nature and practice were alike estranged from him, and must have perished together, but for the same atoning blood which he shed, *in one body by the cross, having slain the enmity thereby*, sin, the cause of enmity between God and the sinner, being removed, and the ceremonial law, the great cause of variance between Jews and Gentiles, being abolished; *and came and preached peace*, by his divinely-constituted ministers, *to you*, Gentiles, *which were afar off*, inviting you, who were at the greatest distance from his church, to come and find pardon and peace with God; *and* the like message he *sent to them that were nigh*, to the Jewish people, who needed the same precious salvation, and could only through a Redeemer be saved from the curse of a broken law. *For through him we both have an access by one Spirit unto the Father*; the same spirit of adoption being shed abroad in both our hearts, the same advocate standing to plead for us, the same gracious God appearing as the Father of mercies, and ready alike to hear and answer our petitions. *Now therefore ye Gentiles are no more strangers and foreigners*, as before, *but fellow citizens with the saints*, partaking of the same privilege, *and of the houshold of God*, entitled to the same inheritance; *and are built upon the foundation of the apostles and prophets*, who both concurred in the same testimony, leading the souls of sinners to *Jesus Christ himself, who being the chief corner stone*, on whom alone they could safely build for eternity; *in whom all the building fitly framed together*, of Jews and Gentiles, *groweth unto an holy temple in the Lord*, daily accessions of converts being made to it, a temple infinitely more glorious than that of Solomon's, a living temple, where the Lord peculiarly dwells, as in his own house; *in whom you also are builded together*, and compose part of the glorious fabric, that ye might be *for an habitation of God through the Spirit*, who takes up his blest abode among you, and in your hearts, until ye shall come to the perfect enjoyment of him for ever in heaven. *Note*, (1.) There is but one safe foundation on which a sinful soul can build, and that is Jesus Christ. (2.) They who are truly grounded on him, shall never fail, but be growing, by the mighty agency of his in-dwelling Spirit, more holy and happy, till they arrive at the perfection of blessedness in glory everlasting.

CHAP. III.

This chapter consists of two parts: 1. Of the account which St. Paul gives the Ephesians concerning himself, as he was appointed by God to be the apostle of the Gentiles, ver. 1—13. 2. Of his devout and affectionate prayer to God for the Ephesians, ver. 14—21. We may observe it to have been very much the practice of this apostle to intermix, with his instructions and counsels, intercessions and prayers to God for those to whom he wrote, as knowing that all his instructions and teachings would be useless and vain, except God did render them effectual. This is an example that all the ministers of Christ should copy after; praying earnestly that the efficacious operations of the divine Spirit may attend their ministrations, and crown them with success.

1 FOR this cause I Paul [a] the prisoner of Jesus Christ
[b] for you Gentiles, 2 If ye have heard of the
dispensation of the grace of God, [c] which is given me
to you-ward: 3 [d] How that [e] by revelation [f] he made
known unto me the mystery, ([h] as I wrote afore in few
words, 4 Whereby when ye read ye may understand
my knowledge [i] in the mystery of Christ) 5 [k] Which
in other ages was not made known unto the sons of men,
[l] as it is now revealed unto his holy apostles and pro-
phets by the Spirit; 6 That the Gentiles [m] should be
fellow-heirs, and [n] of the same body, and [o] partakers of
his promise in Christ by the gospel: 7 Whereof I
was made a minister [p] according to the gift of the grace
of God given unto me by [q] the effectual working of
his power. 8 Unto me, [r] who am less than the least
of all saints, is this grace given, [s] that I should preach
among the Gentiles [t] the unsearchable riches of Christ;
9 And to make all men see what *is* the fellowship of
[u] the mystery, [x] which from the beginning of the world
hath been hid in God, [y] who created all things by Jesus
Christ: 10 [z] To the intent that now unto [a] the princi-
palities and powers in heavenly *places*, might be known
by the church [b] the manifold wisdom of God, 11 [c] Ac-
cording to the eternal purpose which he purposed in
Christ Jesus our Lord: 12 In whom we have boldness
and [d] access [e] with confidence by the faith of him. 13
Wherefore I desire that [f] ye faint not at my tribulations
[g] for you, which is your glory.

a Chap. iv. 1. 2 Cor. iv. 3. & Col. i. 24. b 2 Tim. ii. 10. c 1 Cor. iv. 1. Chap. ii. d Acts ix. 15. & xxii. 21. Gal. i. 16. e Acts xxii. 17, 21. f Gal. i. 12. g Rom. xvi. 25. Col. i. 26. h Chap. i. 9, 10. i 1 Cor. iv. 1. Chap. vi. 19. k Acts x. 28. l Chap. ii. 20. m Gal. iii. 28, 29. Chap. ii. 14. n Chap. ii. 15, 16. o Gal. iii. 14. p Rom. xv. 16. Chap. i. 19. q Chap. i. 19. r 1 Cor. xv. 9. 1 Tim. i. 15. s Gal. i. 16. & ii. 8. 1 Tim. ii. 7. 2 Tim. i. 11. t Chap. i. 7. & ii. 7. u Chap. i. 9. Ver. 3. x Rom. xvi. 25. Col. i. 26. y Psal. xxxiii. 6. John i. 3. Col. i. 16. Heb. i. 2. z 1 Pet. i. 12. a Rom. viii. 38. Chap. i. 21. b 1 Tim. iii. 16. c Chap. i. 9. d John xiv. 6. Rom. v. 2. Chap. ii. 18. e Heb. iv. 16. f Ver. 1. g Ver. 1.

v. 1—13. The apostle gives his beloved Ephesians an account of his sufferings for the truth which here he had asserted. *For this cause*, because I declare the privileges to which the Gentiles, in common with the Jews, are admitted through the gospel, *I Paul am the prisoner of Jesus Christ for you Gentiles*, and those are honourable bonds which in his service are laid upon us; *if*, or *since*, *ye have heard of the dispensation of the grace of God, which is given me to you-ward*, as especially commissioned and sent to preach the gospel to the Gentiles; and *how that by revelation he made known unto me the mystery* of his gospel, as a common salvation for men of all nations, (*as I wrote afore*, in this epistle, *in a few words, whereby when ye read ye may understand my knowledge in the mystery of Christ*, and how fully and clearly he hath acquainted me with his gracious design), *which in other ages was not made known unto the sons of men*, the Gentile world being left in utter ignorance, and those to whom the light of truth was revealed in types and prophecies, seeing but through a glass darkly, compared with the present clear dispensation of the gospel, *as it is now revealed unto his holy apostles and prophets by the Spirit*, since the ascension of Jesus into the heavens, *that the Gentiles should be fellow-heirs* with his Israel, *and of the same body*, incorporated in one church, *and partakers of his promise in Christ by the gospel*, sharing in all the present and eternal blessedness of his redeemed people, equally with the Jews. *Whereof I was made a minister*, by a divine call and ordination, not of men, nor by man, but immediately from Jesus Christ himself, *according to the gift of the grace of God given unto me*, appointing me to this office,

office, and qualifying me for the diſcharge of it, *by the effectual working of his power*, enabling me for my work, and crowning it with ſucceſs *Unto me, who am leſs than the leaſt of all ſaints*, ſo exceeding lowly doth the great apoſtle ſpeak of himſelf, and wants words ſufficiently abaſing to expreſs the ſenſe he entertained of his own unworthineſs of ſo high an honour, even to me, ſuch as I am, *is this grace given, that I ſhould preach among the Gentiles the unſearchable riches of Chriſt*, thoſe treaſures of grace and glory which reſide in him for his people's uſe, that can never be fathomed, never be exhauſted, a ſtore that mocks computation, and in which we know neither where to begin or where to end the wonderful account *And to make all men ſee*, as far as my miniſtry ſhould reach, *what is the fellowſhip of the myſtery*, and how bleſſed is that communion of ſaints into which by the goſpel they are admitted, even Gentiles as well as Jews, *which from the beginning of the world had been hid in God*, a ſecret lodged in his own eternal mind, *who created all things by Jeſus Chriſt*, without whoſe co-efficient agency was not any thing made that was made And the revelation of this myſtery, which was ſo long concealed, is made known, *to the intent that now unto the principalities and powers in heavenly places, might be known by the church the manifold wiſdom of God*, that freſh matter might thus be afforded to the angelic hoſt for their contemplation, wonder, and praiſe And all this great ſalvation is compleated, *according to the eternal purpoſe which he purpoſed in Chriſt Jeſus our Lord*, who was ordained to be the great agent in redemption, as he had been in creation *In whom we have boldneſs and acceſs with confidence by the faith of him*, faith, of which he is both the great author and object, whereby we can now approach the throne of grace with humble confidence, regarding God as our Father and friend, and admitted into the moſt endeared fellowſhip with him *Wherefore*, conſidering theſe ineſtimable bleſſings and privileges, *I deſire that ye faint not at my tribulations for you*, or be diſheartened or deſponding at theſe ſufferings, *which are your glory*, and ſhould miniſter to you continual matter of rejoicing in the honour thus conferred on me, and in the confirmation given thereby to the goſpel which you have received *Note*, (1) None can make goſpel miniſters but God only they who run unſent, muſt return unbleſt (2) The grace of God ſhould be the grand ſubject of our miniſtrations, for to preach this are we ſent (3) If we know the power of the goſpel, we ſhall not be aſhamed of that croſs, which for the ſake of it we ſhall be called to bear (4) The greateſt Chriſtians have the moſt lowly thoughts of themſelves their eyes being moſt enlightened, they diſcover more of their own imperfections and corruptions than others do (5) None can truly preach the *unſearchable riches of Chriſt* to others, who have not firſt experienced ſomething of them in their own ſouls (6) They who by faith in a Redeemer behold a reconciled God, will delight to approach him, and to maintain conſtant communion with him

14 For this cauſe I bow my knees unto the Father
of our Lord Jeſus Chriſt, 15 [h] Of whom the whole
family in heaven and earth is named, 16 That he
would grant you [i] according to the riches of his glory,
[k] to be ſtrengthened with might by his Spirit in [l] the inner
man, 17 That Chriſt may dwell in your hearts
by faith, that ye [m] being rooted and grounded in love,
18 [n] May be able to comprehend with all ſaints, what *is*
the breadth, and length, and depth, and height, 19
And to know the love of Chriſt, [o] which paſſeth knowledge,
that ye might be filled [p] with all the fulneſs of
God 20 Now [q] unto him that is able to do exceeding
abundantly above all that we aſk or think, according to
the power that worketh in us, 21 [r] Unto him *be* glory
in the church by Chriſt Jeſus throughout all ages, world
without end Amen.

h Chap i 10
i Rom ix 23 Chap i 7 Phil iv 19 Col i 27
k Chap vi 10
l Rom vii 22 2 Cor iv 16
m Col ii 7
n Chap i 18
o Phil iv 7
p John i 16 Chap i 23
q 1 Cor xvi 25 Jude 24
r Rom xi 36 & xvi 27 Heb xiii 21

v 14—21 The apoſtle informed us what was the ſubject of his preaching, and he failed not to water the ſeed ſown with his fervent and importunate prayers *To this cauſe*, that you may not faint, and that the goſpel may be made effectual to you, *I bow my knees unto the Father of our Lord Jeſus Chriſt*, and our Father in him, *of whom the whole family in heaven and earth is named*, both angels and men, ſaints on earth, and ſaints in heaven, who through their adored Saviour have obtained a more excellent title, as *children of God*, than that in which the carnal Jews boaſted, as *children of Abraham* Now the apoſtle prays for them,

1 *That he would grant you according to the riches of his glory*, out of the abundance of his grace, and for his great name's ſake, *to be ſtrengthened with might by his Spirit in the inner man*, to oppoſe all your ſpiritual foes, to reſiſt every temptation, to bear up under all perſecution, to diſcharge every duty and ſervice for God's glory and the good of immortal ſouls, and ſteadily and perſeveringly to hold on your heavenly courſe, till your warfare ſhall end, and your victory be complete *Note*, (1) Spiritual bleſſings are the beſt of bleſſings, and moſt earneſtly to be ſought (2) All our ſtrength cometh from above, and we may be confident, that the bleſſed Spirit who hath begun the good work, will perfect it even unto the end

2 *That Chriſt may dwell in your hearts by faith*, making your ſouls the place of his abode, bleſſing you with a ſenſe of his nearneſs and ſpecial preſence, and enabling you by faith to draw out of his fulneſs, *that ye being rooted and grounded in love*, fully perſuaded of God's love in Chriſt towards you, experiencing the richeſt manifeſtations of it in your hearts, and cleaving to him with fixed attachment, as the tree that hath ſtruck its roots deep into the earth, *may be able to comprehend with all ſaints*, to whom in bonds of fervent charity ye are united, *what is the breadth, and length, and depth, and height, and to know the love of Chriſt which paſſeth knowledge* Its fulneſs none, not even angels, can comprehend, but larger and more extenſive views of this love than we have yet attained to, we cannot but deſire, to behold its vaſt extent, as reaching to all nations and ſinners of every degree, its duration from everlaſting to everlaſting, the depths of wretchedneſs in which we lay, and of ſufferings to which for our ſakes the Son of God incarnate ſubmitted, and the tranſcendent heights of glory to which he himſelf is now exalted, and to which he hath engaged to bring us, that we may reign with him for ever and ever

3 *That ye may be filled with all the fulneſs of God*, completely made partakers of a divine nature, and to the utmoſt capacity of your ſouls may be enriched with all that light, grace, peace, joy, and holineſs, which God, as your covenant God, hath promiſed to his deareſt children in this world, and may you come to the eternal enjoyment of him in a better, to dwell in God, and God in you

4 He concludes with a doxology *Now unto him that is able to do exceeding abundantly above all that we aſk or think, according to the power that worketh in us*, who counts nothing too great or too good to beſtow on the children of his grace, and hath already given us the moſt encouraging experience of his power and grace, *unto him be glory in the church by Chriſt Jeſus throughout all ages, world without end*, eternal bleſſings, praiſe, and adoration be rendered unto him for this aſtoniſhing redemption, and let every member of the church, in heaven or in earth, with holy rapture and joy cry, *Amen!*

CHAP IV

Having laid down the glorious goſpel privileges, the apoſtle proceeds to enforce the obligations thence reſulting, for the doctrines of grace are the only powerful principles of true obedience In this chapter we have divers exhortations to important duties 1 One that is more general, ver 1 2 An exhortation to mutual love, unity, and concord, with the proper means and motives to promote them, ver 2—16 3 An exhortation to Chriſtian purity and holineſs of life, and that both more general, ver 17—24 and in ſeveral particular inſtances, ver 25, to the end

1 I Therefore [a] the priſoner † of the Lord, beſeech
you that ye [b] walk worthy of the vocation wherewith
ye are called 2 [c] With all lowlineſs and meekneſs,
with long-ſuffering, forbearing one another in love,
3 Endeavouring to keep the unity of the Spirit in [d] the
bond of peace 4 [e] *There is* one body, and [f] one Spirit,
even as ye are called in one hope of your calling, 5
[g] One Lord, [h] one faith, [i] one baptiſm, 6 [k] One God
and Father of all, who *is* above all, and [l] through all,
and in you all 7 But [m] unto every one of us is given
grace according to the meaſure of the gift of Chriſt 8
Wherefore he ſaith, [n] When he aſcended up on high, [o] he
led captivity captive, and gave gifts unto men 9 (Now
that he aſcended, what is it but that [p] he alſo deſcended
firſt into the lower parts of the earth? 10 He that
deſcended, is the ſame alſo [q] that aſcended up far above
all heavens, that [r] he might ‖ fill all things) 11 And
[s] he gave ſome, apoſtles, and ſome, prophets and ſome,
[t] evangeliſts, and ſome, [u] paſtors and [x] teachers, 12
For the perfecting of the ſaints, for the work of the miniſtry,
for the edifying of [y] the body of Chriſt 13
Till we all come in the unity of the faith, and [z] of the
knowledge of the Son of God, unto a perfect man, [a] unto
the meaſure of the ſtature of the fulneſs of Chriſt 14
That we henceforth be no more [b] children, [c] toſſed to
and fro, and carried about with every [d] wind of doctrine,
by the ſleight of men, *and* cunning craftineſs, whereby they
lie in wait to deceive 15 But [e] † ſpeaking the truth
in love, [f] may grow up into him in all things, [g] which is
the head, *even* Chriſt 16 From whom the whole body
fitly joined together, and compacted by that which every
joint ſupplieth, according to the effectual working in the
meaſure of every part, maketh increaſe of the body, unto
the edifying of itſelf in love.

a Chap iii 1
† Gr in
b Phil i 27 Col i 10 1 Theſſ ii 12
c Col iii 12, 13
d Col iii 14
e Rom xii 5 1 Cor xii 12, 13 Chap ii 16
f 1 Cor xii 4
g 1 Cor viii 6 & xii 5
h Gal i 7
i Gal iii 27 28
k Mal ii 10 1 Cor xii 6
l Rom xi 36
m Rom xii 6 1 Cor xii 11
n Pſ lxviii 18
o Col ii 15
p John iii 13
q Acts i 11 Heb iv 14 & vii 26 & ix 24
r Acts ii 33
‖ Or fulfil
s 1 Cor xii 28
t Acts xxi 8 2 Tim iv 5
u Acts xx 28
x Rom xii 7
y 1 Cor xii 27 Chap i 23 Col i 24
z Col ii 2
a Col i 28
b Iſa xxviii 9 1 Cor xiv 20
c Heb xiii 9
d Iſa xi ?
e Zech viii 16
† 2 Cor iv 2
† Or being ſincere in love 1 John iii 18
f Chap ii 21
g Chap i 22 Col i 18
h Col ii 19

v 1—16

v 1—16 The apostle addresses to them,

1 A general exhortation to walk worthy of their high vocation *I therefore, the prisoner of the Lord*, suffering now for my fidelity to his gospel, *beseech you*, by every endearing argument, *that ye walk worthy of the vocation wherewith ye are called*, adorning by your conversation the doctrine of God our Saviour in all things

2 He particularly exhorts them, (1) To behave *with all lowliness and meekness*, in humble thoughts of themselves, and the mildest deportment towards others, *with long-suffering* passing by offences, and overlooking the infirmities of their brethren, *forbearing one another in love*, influenced by this divine principle, and patient towards all men *Note*, True love, humility, unfeigned, and approved meekness, are the most striking lineaments of the Christian's character (2) In this manner *endeavouring to keep the unity of the Spirit in the bond of peace*, sweetly cemented together in holy fellowship, and the whole church being in perfect peace, no jarring discord should disturb the happy union.

3 He suggests the strongest motives to the practice which he recommends *There is one body*, of which we are all members, *and one Spirit*, which actuates the whole, and therefore we cannot, if this be the case, but have the tenderest concern for and closest union with each other, *even as ye are called in one hope of your calling*, looking for the same inheritance in glory, and expecting to spend a blessed eternity in your Father's house above There is *one Lord*, the Saviour of his people, and to whom they all owe duty and allegiance, *one faith*, the same gospel, and to be apprehended in the same way, *one baptism*, the sacramental rite of admission into the kingdom of grace, wherein we are solemnly dedicated to Father, Son, and Holy Ghost, *one God and Father of all*, who stands in this endeared relation to all that are the children of grace by faith in Jesus Christ, *who is above all*, exalted above all blessing and praise, *and through all*, dispensing his mighty influences through the whole mystical body, *and in you all*, making your hearts his temple and therefore, being connected by ties so many and so engaging, we should be most closely united together in love, and appear as actuated by one soul

4 The different gifts and graces bestowed on the members of the same body, far from producing any variance, should cement them the nearer, as they are given for the benefit of the whole *But unto every one of us is given grace, according to the measure of the gift of Christ*, each member hath his several office and endowment, and, according as the Lord sees fit, he dispenses sovereignly to every man the grace suited to his place and station *Wherefore he saith, When he ascended up on high, he led captivity captive*, triumphant over all his foes, having spoiled principalities and powers, and led Satan, sin, death, and hell, as vanquished enemies, bound to his chariot-wheels, *and gave gifts unto men*, the richest and most amazing gifts of his Spirit *Now that he ascended* in this glorious manner, *what is it* that is herein intimated to us, *but that he also descended first* from heaven *into the lower parts of the earth*, humbling himself to take the human nature into personal union with himself, and then to lie down in the grave, making atonement for our sins *He that descended is the same* divine Person, the Son of God, *who ascended above all heavens* to the state of most transcendent dignity, enthroned in majesty on high, *that he might fill all things*, and abundantly dispense to every member of his church the gifts and graces needful for them *And he gave some apostles*, to fill the highest station in his church, *and some prophets*, by inspiration to foretell future events, and to expound the prophetic word, *and some evangelists*, who were generally employed in preaching the word, *and some pastors and teachers*, to take care of particular churches, and minister unto them in holy things all which appointments to their several offices are designed *for the perfecting of the saints* (καταρτισμον) to join them in firm union together, and carry on the work of grace begun in them to its perfection in glory, *till we all come in the unity of the faith, and of the knowledge of the Son of God*, by means of the same blessed gospel, and by happy experience of the power and grace of the same adored Jesus, *unto a perfect man*, growing up to higher spiritual attainments, *unto the measure of the stature of the fulness of Christ*, when we shall bear his image complete, and when all the elect members shall be collected into his eternal kingdom, and form that glorious body of which he is the Head *That we henceforth be no more children*, weak in faith and knowledge, and every grace, and consequently liable to be *tossed to and fro, and carried about with every wind of doctrine, by the slight of men, and cunning craftiness whereby they lie in wait to deceive*, and by fair pretences seduce the simple and unwary into their pernicious heresies and destructive ways, *but, speaking the truth in love, may grow up into him in all things, which is the head, even Christ*, which growth in grace the blessed gospel, through the power of Jesus, tends effectually to promote, *from whom the whole body, fitly joined together* as members to the living Head, *and compacted by that which every joint supplieth according to the effectual working in the measure of every part*, by that divine energy that is communicated from the life-giving Spirit of the Lord, *maketh increase of the body, unto the edifying of itself in love*, till it come to perfect blessedness in the eternal world *Note*, Truth from the heart should ever be spoken among Christians, and with that love that may gain it a more welcome reception

17 This I say therefore, and testify in the Lord,
that [i] ye henceforth walk not as other Gentiles walk [k] in — i 1 Pet iv 3 k Rom i
the vanity of their mind, 18 [l] Having the understand- — 21
ing darkened, [m] being alienated from the life of God — l Chap v 8 m Chap ii
through the ignorance that is in them, because of [n] the — 12 1 Thes
blindness of their heart 19 [o] Who being past feeling, — iv 5 n Rom i
[p] have given themselves over unto lasciviousness, to work — 21 o 1 Tim iv
all uncleanness with greediness 20 But ye have not — 2
so learned Christ, 21 If so be that ye have heard him, — p Rom i
and have been taught by him, as the truth is in Jesus — 24 26
22 That ye [q] put off [r] concerning the former conversa- — q Col iii 8
tion, [s] the old man, which is corrupt according to the — & iii 8 r Heb xii 1
deceitful lusts 23 And [t] be renewed in the spirit of — s Chap ii 2 1 Pet
your mind, 24 And that ye [u] put on the new man, — iv 3
which after God [x] is created in righteousness and true — t Rom vi 6 u Rom xii
holiness 25 Wherefore putting away lying, [y] speak — x Rom xii
every man truth with his neighbour for [z] we are mem- — 2 Cor v
bers one of another 26 [a] Be ye angry, and sin not — 17 Chap
let not the sun go down upon your wrath 27 [b] Nei- — ii 10 Col iii 10
ther give place to the devil 28 Let him that stole steal — y Zech viii
no more but rather [c] let him labour, working with his — 16
hands the thing which is good, that he may have [d] to — z Rom xii
give to him that needeth 29 [e] Let no corrupt com- — 5 a Ps iv 4 & xxxvii 8
munication proceed out of your mouth, but [f] that which — b Jam iv 7 1 Pet v 9
is good to the use of edifying, [g] that it may minister — c Acts xx
grace unto the hearers 30 And [h] grieve not the holy — 35 1 Thes iv 11
Spirit of God, [i] whereby ye are sealed unto the day of — d Luke iii
[k] redemption 31 [l] Let all bitterness, and wrath, and — 11
anger, and clamour, and evil-speaking be put away from — e Chap v
you, [m] with all malice 32 And [n] be ye kind one to — 3 4 Mat xii 36
another, tender hearted, [o] forgiving one another, even — f Col iv 6
as God for Christ's sake hath forgiven you — g Col iii 16

h Isa lxiii 10. 1 Thes v. 19 i 2 Cor i 22 Chap i 13 k Luke xxi 28 Rom viii 23 l Col iii 8 m Tit iii 3 n 2 Cor ii 7 o Col iii 12 13 Mat vi 14 Mark xi 25

v 17—32 Having recommended to them close union, he proceeds to inculcate purity of heart and life

1 He warns them against the practices of the unconverted heathen *This I say therefore and testify in the Lord*, entreating and solemnly in his name enjoining it upon you as members of his undefiled body, *that ye henceforth walk not as other Gentiles walk*, in their sinful, idolatrous, sensual courses, *in the vanity of their mind*, acting after the dictates of their vain and corrupted heart, *having the understanding darkened* in all spiritual matters, *alienated from the life of God*, estranged from him who is the fountain of life, and averse to all his holy ways, *through the ignorance that is in them, because of the blindness of their hearts*, rejecting every means of instruction, wilfully perverse and obstinate against the notices of his will, and resisting the convictions of their own consciences, not liking to retain God in all their knowledge, *Rom* i 28 *who being past feeling*, their hearts impenetrably hardened in sin, *have given themselves over unto lasciviousness, to work all uncleanness with greediness*, abandoning themselves to every vile affection without restraint, and pursuing their guilty pleasures with insatiable desire

2 Far otherwise was the lesson the gospel had taught them *But ye have not so learned Christ*, since ye have known his grace, you have been directed to a different spirit and conduct, *if so be*, or *since that, ye have heard him* speaking in his word to your hearts, *and have been taught by him* through the illumination and powerful energy of his Spirit *as the truth is in Jesus*, even that pure unadulterated gospel which Jesus taught by his own ministry, and exemplified in his temper and conversation, whose bright example his living member delight to imitate *that ye put off, concerning the former conversation, the old man*, restraining and mortifying that body of sin which is born with you, and ever wars within you, *which is corrupt according to the deceitful lusts*, lusts which promise much gratification in the indulgence, but fatally deceive the soul into endless perdition *and be renewed in the spirit of your mind* yet more and more in knowledge, grace, and holiness, *and that ye put on the new man*, made partaker of a divine nature, and in spirit, temper, and conduct, quite changed from your former selves as if you had been really different persons, *which after God is created in righteousness and true holiness*, after his own image, and by his own power *Wherefore*, as those who are influenced by another Spirit, beware of those sins to which ye were formerly addicted, particularly,

(1) *Putting away lying, speak every man truth with his neighbour*, without deceit or prevarication, paying the strictest regard to your word in all things and in all circumstances and preferring the conduct rule of the strictest evil to the suppression of the least little good *for we are members one of another*, and therefore bound to use all simplicity and fidelity in our conversation with each other *Note*, An habitual liar is infallibly a child of wrath All Christ's members are bound to speak the truth from their heart

(2) *Be ye angry, and sin not*, for all anger is not in its own nature evil but as we are so prone, even where there is just cause, to exceed in our resentments, we must check the rising displeasure, and repress its workings therefore, whatever cause is given for it, *let not the sun go down upon your wrath*, but hasten to calm any tumult which may have arisen, that it fix not in hatred, or rankle into malice or revenge *neither give place to the devil*, who ever seeks to irritate the irascible nature which is in us, and to blow our passions into a flame *Note*, There is scarce a more besetting sin than anger, nor any against which we need be more habitually on our guard

(3) *Let him that stole steal no more*, utterly abhorring all such iniquitous practices, *but rather let him labour, working with his hand the thing which is good, that he may have to give to him that needeth*, and not only be saved from the temptation to dishonesty, whereunto idleness is the most direct road, but also be enabled by his honest industry to afford a pittance from his gains for the relief of the necessitous

(4) *Let no corrupt communication proceed out of your mouth*, nothing lewd, profane, opprobrious, light, which in its most distant tendency can lead to evil, *but that which is good to the use of edifying, that it may minister grace unto the hearers*, and serve to promote their spiritual and eternal benefit *Note*, Out of the abundance of the heart the mouth speaketh and a Christian spirit will appear in a readiness to introduce and maintain such conversation as is profitable and edifying

(5) *And grieve not the holy Spirit of God*, by these or any such like evils, lest you provoke him to withdraw his blessed influences from you, *whereby ye are sealed unto the day of redemption*, that glorious day when you shall be delivered from the burdens of the flesh, or when you shall rise again in glory to appear for ever in the presence of God Lord, take not thy holy Spirit from us!

(6) *Let all bitterness*, all rancour of spirit and acrimony in discourse, *and wrath, and clamour, and evil-speaking*, the fruits of a mind inflamed with passion and rage, *be put away from you, with all malice And be ye kind one to another*, gentle, courteous, affectionate, *tender-hearted*, sympathizing and full of pity towards the afflicted and the tempted, *forgiving one another* every provocation and injury, however great or aggravated, *even as God for Christ's sake hath forgiven you*, freely, fully, and for ever *Note*, (1) A sense how much we are ourselves indebted to the pardoning love of God, will engage us to exercise the like forgiveness to our brethren (2) A tongue that is set on fire of hell, and full of bitterness, &c hath never yet been brought under the restraints of a Redeemer's grace

CHAP. V.

We had several important exhortations in the close of the foregoing chapter, and they are continued in this particularly, 1 *We have here an exhortation to mutual love and charity,* ver 1, 2 2 *Against all manner of uncleanness,* ver 3—20 3 *The apostle directs to the conscientious discharge of relative duties,* from ver 21 *throughout this, and in the beginning of the next chapter*

1 [a] BE ye therefore followers of God, as dear child-
ren, 2 And [b] walk in love, as Christ also
hath loved us, and hath given himself for us [c] an offer-
ing and a sacrifice to God for a sweet smelling savour
3 But [d] fornication, and all uncleanness, or covetous-
ness, [e] let it not be once named amongst you, as be-
cometh saints 4 [f] Neither filthiness, nor foolish talk-
ing, nor jesting, [g] which are not convenient [h] but ra-
ther giving of thanks 5 For this ye know, that [k] no
whoremonger, nor unclean person, nor covetous man
[l] who is an idolater, [m] hath any inheritance in the king-
dom of Christ and of God 6 [n] Let no man deceive
you with vain words for [o] because of these things com-
eth the wrath of God upon the children of disobedience
7 Be not ye therefore partakers with them 8 For [p] ye
were sometimes [q] darkness, but now *are ye* [r] light in the
Lord walk as [s] children of light, 9 (For [t] the fruit
of the Spirit *is* in all goodness and righteousness and
truth) 10 [u] Proving what is acceptable unto the Lord
11 And [x] have no fellowship with [y] the unfruitful works
of darkness, [z] but rather reprove *them* 12 For [a] it is
a shame even to speak of those things which are done of
them in secret 13 But [b] all things that are reproved,
are made manifest by the light for whatsoever doth
make manifest is light 14 Wherefore he saith, [c] Awake
thou that sleepest, and [d] arise from the dead, and Christ
shall give thee light 15 See then that ye [e] walk cir-
cumspectly, not as fools, but as wise, 16 Redeeming
the time, [f] because the days are evil 17 Wherefore
be ye not unwise, [g] but understanding what the will of
the Lord *is* 18 And [h] be not drunk with wine, where-
in is excess, but be filled with the Spirit 19 Speak-
ing to yourselves [i] in psalms and hymns and spiritual
songs, singing and making melody in your heart to the
Lord, 20 [k] Giving thanks always for all things unto
God and the Father [l] in the name of our Lord Jesus
Christ,

a Mat v 4, 5 Chap iv 32 b John xiii 34 & xv 12 1 Thes iv 9 1 John iii 23 & iv 21 c Gal ii 20 Heb ix 14 d Heb xiii 3 & ix 26 & x 10 e Col iii 5 1 Thes iv 3, &c f 1 Cor v 1 Mat xii 35 Chap iv 29 Col iii 8 h Rom i 28 i Col i 12 k 1 Cor vi 9 Gal v 19 Rev xxi 8 l Col iii 5 1 Tim vi 17 m Gal v 21 n Jer xxix 8 Mat xxiv 4 Col ii 4, 8 o Col iii 6 p Chap ii 2 q Mat iv 16 r John viii 12 & xii 36 s Luke xvi 8 t Gal v 22 u Rom xii 2 Phil i 10 x 1 Cor v 9 y Rom vi 21 z Lev xix 17 a Rom i 24 b John iii 20 c Isa lx 1 Rom xiii 11 d John v 25 e Col iv 5 f Eccl xi 2 g Rom xii 2

h Prov xx 1 & xxiii 29 Isa v 11 Luke xxi 34 i 1 Cor xiv 26 Col iii 16 Jam v 13 k Ps xxxiv 1 Isa lxiii 7 Col iii 17 1 Thes v 18 l Heb xiii 15 1 Pet ii 5 & iv 11

v 1—20 Love is the divine principle through which alone the practice of all holiness can be made easy and natural to us This therefore,

1 The apostle inculcates *Be ye followers of God as dear children*, acting according to this high relation, and in your spirit and temper resembling your heavenly Father, *and walk in love*, which is his brightest attribute, and renders you most like the blessed Redeemer, *as Christ also hath loved us*, with a love so surpassing great, so free, so unchangeable, *and hath given himself for us an offering and a sacrifice to God for a sweet-smelling savour*, to make atonement for our sins, and to reconcile us to God by his own blood, his sacrifice being infinitely meritorious and acceptable *Note*, (1) Love is the characteristic mark of a child of God, and a disciple of Jesus, (2) The sacrifice of the Lamb of God is fully efficacious God is well pleased in the oblation of his Son, and all who draw near through him are sure of acceptance

2 He warns them against all manner of uncleanness *But fornication, and all uncleanness, or covetousness*, the lawless desires of fleshly concupiscence, *let it not be once named amongst you, as becometh saints*, but avoided with the utmost detestation, and never once so much as mentioned, *neither filthiness*, in gesture, habit, or discourse, *nor foolish talking*, in secret innuendos, or vain, light, and unprofitable conversation, *nor jesting*, with wantonness, about things sacred, or to the hurt of others, *which are not convenient*, *but* utterly unbecoming a Christian's profession, who should *rather* be employed in *giving thanks*, and use his tongue as an instrument to set forth God's glory

3 He enforces his exhortation by the most weighty arguments

(1) These sins must necessarily exclude us from heaven, and lay us under the eternal wrath of God *For this ye know*, according to the unchangeable word of God, *that no whoremonger, nor unclean person, nor covetous man*, whose heart is the stye of lewd desires, or *who* is inordinately eager after gain, and consequently *is an idolater*, loving and serving the creature more than the Creator, *hath any inheritance in the kingdom of Christ and of God*, but must be for ever excluded from the divine favour. *Let no man deceive you with vain words*, as if these sins were not so dangerous, and with some soft names of *human infirmity*, or *venial transgressions*, endeavour to satisfy your consciences, and embolden you to hope for impunity *for* know assuredly, *because of these things cometh the wrath of God upon the children of disobedience* and unbelief, who, despising God's warnings, perish eternally under the deluge of his fiery wrath *Be not ye therefore partakers with them*, by communion with them, or connivance at them, lest you become involved in their punishment *Note*, It is a fearful thing to fall into the hands of the living God. We should often consider it, that we might tremble, and avoid the very distant approaches of evil, that hath consequences so dreadfully dangerous

(2) What God hath done for us should engage us to be faithful to him *For ye were sometimes darkness*, and in this wretched state were blindly led on by vile affections to every abomination, ignorant of God and your own danger, and rushing headlong to ruin, *but now are ye light in the Lord*, since he hath shined into your hearts, and given you the knowledge of his will, and wrought effectually by his gospel to turn you to his blessed Self in the practice of true holiness, therefore *walk as children of the light*, agreeable to the obligations lying upon you, and the measure of knowledge and grace which you have received *For the fruit of the Spirit*, which the Lord hath given you to illumine your darkness, and quicken your souls from the death of sin, *is in all goodness and righteousness and truth*, it appear in every act of tenderness and beneficence towards the needy, in all purity of heart towards God, and uprightness in our dealing with men, and engage us to a holy simplicity and unimpeached fidelity in all our words and works, in which things, as children of light, you will therefore habitually walk, *proving what is acceptable unto the Lord*, desiring out of his word to learn his mind and will, and to approve yourselves to him in all holy conversation and godliness *And*, for this end, *have no fellowship with the unfruitful works of darkness*, neither by countenance or connivance at them in others, any more than by practising them yourselves, they are *works of darkness*, the deeds of a fallen and corrupted heart and that seek usually the covert of the night, *unfruitful* of every thing but misery, wrath, and wretchedness Instead therefore of joining in them, *rather*, wherever they appear in any brother, bear an open testimony against them, and with zeal, tempered with love, boldly *reprove them* *Note*, (1) The fallen mind is darkness itself they who are under its influence tread the paths of death and hell, and know not whither they are going (2) Why

God

God hath given us the light of his truth, every wilful ſin is infinitely aggravated (4) They who are truly ſenſible of the evil and danger of ſin, will not ſee it upon their brother, without a kind and faithful rebuke

3 The very ſhocking and ſhameful nature of theſe ſins ſhould deter us from them *For it is a ſhame even to ſpeak of thoſe things, which are done of them in ſecret*, the very mention of them muſt offend a modeſt ear, and how much more muſt the practice of them provoke a holy God? *But all things that are reproved*, as ſuch evils muſt be, *are made manifeſt by the light* of God's word, which hath ſhined into your hearts, and are thereby diſcovered in their native deformity, and hateful colours, *for whatſoever doth make manifeſt is light*, as the ſun illumines the world that otherwiſe would be covered in darkneſs, ſo doth Chriſt in his goſpel, ariſing as the ſun of righteouſneſs, ſhine into the hearts of his people, giving them light and diſcernment in ſpiritual things, which were before utterly hid from their eyes, and enabling them to ſee the evil and danger of thoſe tempers and practices, which before they never apprehended *Wherefore he ſaith*, when calling the ſouls of ſinners out of darkneſs into his marvellous light, *Awake, thou that ſleepeſt* in ſecurity, ignorance, and inſenſibility, *and ariſe from the dead*, from thy ſtate of death in treſpaſſes and ſins, *and Chriſt ſhall give thee light*, the light of life and truth, to conduct thee in the paths of holineſs to the regions of glory, and wherever this light is ſpoken into the ſoul, then it will be evident by an abhorrence of evil, and ſuch a converſation as will bear the ſtricteſt ſcrutiny

4 On what he had ſaid, he grounds this farther exhortation *See then that ye walk circumſpectly*, narrowly examining every ſtep you take, *not as fools, but as wiſe*, as thoſe who have been taught the truth as it is in Jeſus, *redeeming the time*, making the beſt improvement of the preſent moment, and deſirous to retrieve, in a meaſure, the time and opportunity which hath been loſt, *becauſe the days are evil*, and require greater watchfulneſs when iniquity ſo abounds, when temptations ſo many and great beſet you, and you know not how ſoon you may be cut off *Wherefore, be ye not unwiſe*, as in the former days of folly and unregeneracy, *but underſtanding what the will of the Lord is*, that ye may know how to walk and pleaſe him, and be found faithful to the light which he is pleaſed to give you *Note*, (1) If we conſider how much of our time we have abuſed and ſquandered, it will become us with peculiar diligence to improve the pittance which remains (2) Evil days require eſpecial circumſpection (3) The worſt and moſt fatal folly is the ignorance of God's word and neglect of our ſouls

How we muſt redeem our time, and walk according to the divine preſcription, the apoſtle, in ſeveral particulars, proceeds to ſhew,

1 *Be not drunk with wine, wherein is exceſs*, as the heathen at their Bacchanalian feaſts, and the dreadful conſequences of drunkenneſs are numberleſs, for when the mind is once intoxicated, a wide door is opened to every act of extravagance, folly, riot, debauchery, uncleanneſs, and there remains no reſtraint from the greateſt abominations

2 *But*, on the contrary, *be filled with the Spirit*, ſeek to drink deeper into the ſacred fountain of his divine light, grace, ſtrength, and conſolation, which will inſpire the moſt exquiſite and ſacred pleaſure and delight, not roaring round the board of riot, and joining the mad ſongs of the drunken, but *ſpeaking to yourſelves*, and each other, *in pſalms, and hymns, and ſpiritual ſongs*, uniting your voices in the Redeemer's praiſe, *ſinging and making melody in your hearts to the Lord*, with inward exultation in God as your Saviour, and every outward expreſſion that tends to exalt his great and glorious name, *giving thanks always for all things*, your hearts in every diſpenſation acknowledging a gracious God, and your tongue employed in thankſgiving *unto God and the Father, in the name of our Lord Jeſus Chriſt*, through whom all our ſervices are accepted, and by whom all the diſpenſations of providence and grace are made to work together for our good *Note*, (1) Pſalmody is a goſpel ordinance, and they who are happy in God will delight in his praiſes (2) Whatever our condition or circumſtances in life, there is always room for thankſgiving Afflictions, as well as mercies, demand a grateful acknowledgment, they are good for us, and we ſhall, in the iſſue, find the bleſſed effects of them

21 [m] Submitting yourſelves one to another in the fear
of God 22 [n] Wives, ſubmit yourſelves unto your own
huſbands, as unto the Lord 23 For [p] the huſband
is the head of the wife, [q] even as Chriſt is the head of
the church and he is the Saviour of the [r] body 24
Therefore as the church is ſubject unto Chriſt, ſo *let*
the wives *be* to their own huſbands in every thing
25 [s] Huſbands, love your wives, even as [t] Chriſt alſo
loved the church, and gave himſelf for it 26 That
he might ſanctify and cleanſe it [u] with the waſhing of
water [x] by the word, 27 That he might preſent it to
himſelf a glorious church, [y] not having ſpot or wrinkle,
or any ſuch thing, but that it ſhould be holy and
[z] without blemiſh 28 So ought men to love their wives,
as their own bodies he that loveth his wife, loveth
himſelf. 29 For no man ever yet hated his own fleſh,
but nouriſheth and cheriſheth it, even as the Lord the
church 30 For [a] we are members of his body, of his
fleſh, and of his bones 31 [b] For this cauſe ſhall a man
leave his father and mother, and ſhall be joined unto his
wife, and [c] they two ſhall be one fleſh 32 This is a
great myſtery but I ſpeak concerning Chriſt and the
church 33 Nevertheleſs let every one of you in particular ſo [d] love his wife even as himſelf, and the wife *ſee*
that ſhe reverence *her* huſband

m 1 Pet v 5 n Gen iii 16 1 Cor xiv 34 Col iii 18 Tit ii 5 1 Pet iii 1 o Chap vi 5 p 1 Cor xi 3 q Chap i 22 & iv 15 Col i 18 r Chap i 23 s Col iii 19 1 Pet iii 7 t Gal ii 20 Ver 2 u John iii 5 Tit iii 5 Heb x 22 1 John v 6 x John xv 3 & xvii 17 y Cant iv 7 Col i 22

z Chap i 4 a 1 Cor vi 15 & xii 27 b Gen ii 24 Mat xix 5 Mark x 7 c 1 Cor vi 16 d Col iii 19 1 Pet iii 7

v 21—33 The apoſtle proceeds to exhort them to the diſcharge of thoſe relative duties, which are the great ornament of Chriſtianity,

In general a ſpirit of gentleneſs and mutual forbearing muſt reign in you, *ſubmitting yourſelves one to another*, in all natural and civil relations, in public and private, making conſcience of diſcharging the duties of your ſeveral ſtations, and *in the fear of God*, willingly in ſubjection to thoſe whom he hath placed as your ſuperiors

1 Your duty as *wives* is to *ſubmit yourſelves unto your own huſbands*, in all reverence, honour, and dutiful obedience, conſulting their will, and content to be in ſubjection, *as unto the Lord*, regarding him as the author of your ſubordination, and ſubmitting, as the church doth to him *For the huſband is the head of the wife*, by divine appointment, *as Chriſt is the head of the church, and he is the Saviour of the body*, having bought her even at the expence of his own blood, and with the moſt endearing tenderneſs and affection providing whatever is needful for her ſupport and comfort *Therefore as the church is* bound, by every tie of love and duty, to be *ſubject unto Chriſt, ſo let the wives be to their own huſbands in every thing*, not contradictory to their duty towards God *Note*, The direction is clear and obvious, but the difficulty is for a fallen ſpirit to acquieſce Let thoſe therefore who enter into the marriage ſtate ſeriouſly conſider their obligations, before they lay themſelves under the ſolemn vow of *obedience in all things*

2 The duty of *huſbands* is this, *Love your wives* with ſingleneſs of affection, which ſpeaks in every word and look of tenderneſs, with gentleneſs deſiring to rule, not tyrannize, and, by every endearing art of perſuaſion, winning obedience, rather than haughtily and imperiouſly demanding ſubjection, remembering and imitating the love of Chriſt to his church, *who gave himſelf for it*, even to the death of the croſs, *that he might ſanctify and cleanſe it with the waſhing of water by the word*, in his atoning blood opening a fountain for ſin and uncleanneſs, to which, by faith, his people might come according to his word, and be effectually delivered from all their guilt, and defilement of body and ſoul, *that*, being thus cleanſed, *he might preſent it to himſelf*, as a chaſte virgin, adorned for her heavenly bridegroom, *a glorious church*, beautiful in his blood, and bright in the robe of his righteouſneſs, *not having ſpot or wrinkle, or any ſuch thing, but* appearing in perfect comelineſs and purity, *that*, as the ſacrifices under the law, *it ſhould be holy and without blemiſh* *So ought men to love their wives* according to this love of Chriſt, even *as their own bodies*, they being now a real part of themſelves *he that loveth his wife loveth himſelf* *For no man ever yet hated his own fleſh, but nouriſheth and cheriſheth it*, our own fleſh is not nearer to us than our wives, and the ſame affectionate care is due to them, *even as the Lord* hath ſhewed to *the church for we are members of his body* myſtical, *of his fleſh, and of his bones*, like the woman formed from the firſt man's ſide *For this cauſe*, ſeeing the union is ſo cloſe, *ſhall a man leave his father and mother, and ſhall be joined unto his wife*, in peculiar ſingleneſs of affection, *and they two ſhall be one fleſh*, as if they literally became one body *This is a great myſtery*, theſe words being figurative of a more happy and excellent marriage than that of the firſt man and woman, and I mean, in their application, to lead you, not merely to conſider the original law of marriage, *but I ſpeak concerning Chriſt and the church*, to whom they emphatically belong *Nevertheleſs let every one of you in particular ſo love his wife even as himſelf*, as the member of his own body, *and let the wife ſee that ſhe reverence her huſband* with all conjugal love, and jealous fear of offending

CHAP VI.

In this chapter, (1) The apoſtle proceeds in the exhortation to relative duties, which he began in the former Particularly he inſiſts on the duties of children and parents, and of ſervants and maſters, ver 1—9 (2) He exhorts and directs Chriſtians how to behave themſelves in the ſpiritual warfare with the enemies of their ſouls; and to the exerciſe of ſeveral Chriſtian graces, which he propoſes to them as ſo many pieces of ſpiritual armour, to preſerve and defend them in the conflict, ver 10—18 (3) He then cloſes the concluſion of the epiſtle, in which he takes his leave of them, commending himſelf to the prayers of the believing Epheſians, and praying for them, ver 19—24.

1 CHILDREN,

1 ᵃ CHILDREN, obey your parents in the Lord
for this is right 2 ᵇ Honour thy father and
mother, (which is the first commandment with promise)
3 That it may be well with thee, and thou mayest live
long on the earth 4 And ᶜ ye fathers, provoke not
your children to wrath but ᵈ bring them up in the nur-
ture and admonition of the Lord 5 ᵉ Servants, be obe-
dient to them that are *your* masters according to the flesh,
with fear and trembling, in singleness of your heart, as
unto Christ 6 ᶠ Not with eye-service, as men-pleasers,
but as the servants of Christ, doing the will of God from
the heart, 7 With good will doing service, ᵍ as to the
Lord, and not to men 8 ʰ Knowing that whatsoever
good thing any man doth, the same shall he receive of
the Lord, ⁱ whether *he be* bond or free 9 And ye
masters, do the same things unto them, † forbearing
threatning knowing that your master also is in heaven,
ᵏ neither is there respect of persons with him

ᵃ Prov xxiii 22 Col iii 20 ᵇ Ex xx 12 Deut v 16 & xxvii 16 Mat xv 4 ᶜ Col iii 21 ᵈ Deut vi 7 Ps lxxviii 4 Prov xix 18 & xxii 6 & xxix 17 ᵉ Col iii 22 1 Tim vi 1 Tit ii 9 1 Pet ii 18 ᶠ Col iii 22 ᵍ Ver 5 Col iii 23 ʰ Rom ii 6 2 Cor v 10 Col iii 24 ⁱ Col iii 11 ᵏ Lev xxv 43 Col iv 1 † Or mode rating ˡ Deut x 17 Rom ii 11 Col iii 25

v 1—9 The apostle proceeds with those relative duties which he had begun to enforce in the former chapter, beginning still with the inferior relation, for dutiful obedience will lay the strongest obligations on the superior to shew all condescension and love in return We have,

1 The duty of children to their parents *Children, obey your parents*, hear their counsels, and submit to their commands, this being the debt you owe them, both as the authors under God of your being, and for all the care they have shewn you, and this *in the Lord*, as fit and agreeable to his word, and for his glory *Honour thy father and mother*, saith the law, reverence them, speak respectfully to and of them, and if needful provide for them, (*which is the first commandment with* a particular *promise* annexed to it) *that it may be well with thee, and thou mayest live long on the earth*

2 The duty of parents *And ye fathers, provoke not your children to wrath*, by unreasonable tasks, severities, or restraints, *but* with all lenity, tenderness, and affection endeavour by love and kind persuasion to win upon them, and *bring them up in the nurture and admonition of the Lord*, instructing them in the knowledge of the Scriptures, setting before them a gracious example, directing them to the means of grace, and watching over them with holy jealousy

3 The duty of servants *Servants, be obedient to them that are your masters according to the flesh*, in all their lawful commands, *with* becoming *fear* of their displeasure, *and trembling* least at any time you should justly offend them, *in singleness of your heart, as unto Christ*, without flattery, deceit, or guile, with a regard to the Redeemer's glory *not with eye service, as men pleasers*, diligent only so long as they look over you, merely to curry favour with them, *but as the servants of Christ*, under his constant and all-seeing inspection, and therefore *doing the will of God from the heart*, and discharging the duties of the station in which he hath placed you with all fidelity and truth *With good will doing service*, with cheerfulness and alacrity, from a principle of love to your masters, and a real zeal for their honour and interest, and this *as to the Lord, and not to men*, desiring, not so much human, as the divine approbation, and acting from a sense of duty to the great Lord of all *Knowing that whatsoever good thing any man doth*, however mean his station, and inconsiderable in itself the service may be, *the same shall he receive of the Lord*, who will suitably reward his fidelity, *whether he be bond or free*

4 The duty of masters *And ye masters, do the same things unto them*, shew the same tenderness conscientiously to discharge your relation to them, *forbearing threatning*, not tyrannizing over them, and terrifying them with harshness and menaces, but chusing to rule by love rather than fear, *knowing that your master also is in heaven*, to whom you must give an account, *neither is there respect of persons with him*; all stand at his bar on a level, and must receive from his lips their eternal sentence for happiness or misery,

10 Finally, my brethren, be ᵐ strong in the Lord, and
ⁿ in the power of his might 11 ᵒ Put on the whole
armour of God, that ye may be able to stand against the
wiles of the devil 12 For we wrestle not against flesh
and blood, but against principalities, against powers,
against ᵖ the rulers of the darkness of this world, against
‡ spiritual wickedness in high *places* 13 ᑫ Wherefore
take unto you the whole armour of God, that ye may be
able to withstand in ʳ the evil day, and having done all to
stand 14 Stand therefore, ˢ having your loins girt
about with truth, ᵗ and having on the breast plate of
righteousness, 15 And ᵘ your feet shod with the pre-
paration of the gospel of peace, 16 Above all, taking
ˣ the shield of faith, wherewith ye shall be able to quench
all the fiery darts of the wicked 17 And ʸ take the
helmet of salvation, and ᶻ the sword of the Spirit, which

ᵐ Col i 11 ⁿ Chap i 19 & iii 16 ᵒ Rom xiii 12 2 Cor vi 7 1 Thes v 8 ᵖ Luke xxii 53 John xii 31 Acts xxvi 18 Col i 13 ‡ Or wicked spirits ᑫ 2 Cor x 4 ʳ Chap v 16 ˢ Isa xi 5 Luke xii 35 1 Pet i 13 ᵗ Isa lix 17 2 Cor vi 7 1 Thes v 8 ᵘ Isa lii 7 Rom x 15 ˣ 1 John v 4 ʸ Isa lix 17 1 Thes v 8 ᶻ Heb iv 12 Rev i 16

is the word of God 18 ᵃ Praying always with all
prayer and supplication in the Spirit, and ᵇ watching
thereunto with all perseverance, and supplication for all
saints, 19 ᶜ And for me, that utterance may be given
unto me, that I may open my mouth ᵈ boldly, to make
known the mystery of the gospel 20 For which ᵉ I am
an ambassador ᶠ in ‡ bonds that therein I may speak
boldly, as I ought to speak

ᵃ Luke xviii 1 Rom xii 12 Col iv 2 1 Thes v 17 ᵇ Mat xxvi 41 & xxv 13 ᶜ Acts iv 29 Col iv 3 2 Thes iii 1 ᵈ 2 Cor iii 12 ᵉ 2 Cor v 20 ᶠ Acts xxviii 20 Chap iii 1 & iv 1 Phil i 7 ‡ Or a chain

v 10—20 Every Christian is enlisted, under the banners of Jesus, to fight the Lord's battles, and to maintain unceasing war against sin, the world, and the devil The apostle therefore warmly exhorts them to quit themselves as men under the glorious captain of their salvation *Finally, my brethren, be strong in the Lord, and in the power of his might*, supported by those almighty influences of grace, which he supplies, in whom alone standeth our help, and from whom cometh our salvation *Put on the whole armour of God*, as a soldier covered from head to foot, with armour proof against every weapon, *that ye may be able to stand against the wiles of the devil*, and neither be seduced by his ensnaring temptations, nor terrified by his suggestions from the path of duty

1 The enemies we have to conflict with are described *For we wrestle not against flesh and blood*, not only against the corruptions implanted in our own nature, or the wicked men of this world, who oppose and persecute, *but against principalities, against powers, against the rulers of the darkness of this world, against spiritual wickedness in high places*, even against those legions of malignant spirits, who, under their hateful leader, have erected a kingdom of darkness, and enslaved the souls of men, and ever hover round us, watching for an opportunity to distress, harass, trouble, and, if they could, to destroy those who have escaped from their hateful bondage

2 Having such foes, we need be well armed against their assaults *Wherefore take unto you the whole armour of God*, so absolutely necessary for this dangerous conflict, *that ye may be able to withstand in the evil day*, when this hour of temptation and danger comes, *and having done all, to stand* faithfully, acquitting yourselves as good soldiers of Jesus Christ, through every trial, however sharp or prolonged, and more than conquerors at last, through him that loved you, when in a resurrection day you shall tread sin, satan, death and hell, for ever under your feet *Stand therefore*, the enemy advances, be ready to receive him, looking up to your almighty support, and invulnerable in the divine panoply. The Christian's complete armour, both offensive and defensive, is here in military terms described, the back alone is left unguarded, for we must conquer or die Flight is sure to be fatal to the coward soul

1 Truth must be our military girdle *Having your loins girt about with truth*, firm in the doctrines of the gospel, and sincere in the profession of it, in simplicity approving yourselves before the heart-searching God

2 Righteousness is our breast-plate *Having on the breast-plate of righteousness*, imputed and implanted, to guard the vital parts from the stroke of the invenomed foe

3 Our sandals must be the gospel of peace *Having your feet shod with the preparation of the gospel of peace*, that whatever rough ways we may walk in, and whatever difficulties we meet, we may stand fast in the gospel of Jesus, prepared for every conflict, stablished on the sure foundation, enjoying peace with God in our own souls, and following it with all men

4 Faith is our shield *Above all*, as the most necessary piece of armour, and that which covers the whole body, *taking the shield of faith*, having lively and realizing views of the divine promises of pardon, grace, righteousness, and glory, confidently resting upon them, *wherewith ye shall be able to quench all the fiery darts of the wicked*, when with fury he hurls his invenomed temptations at the soul, to despair, blasphemy, lewdness, rage, even to self-murder, seeking to bring horror, guilt, anguish, and distress upon the conscience, though he may not be able to destroy, but divine faith repels them all, quenches them, and they fall harmless at our feet

5 Salvation is our helmet *And take the helmet of salvation*, that sure hope of life eternal, grounded upon the faithfulness of the unchangeable God, that guards from dejection, and raises us superior to every fear

6 The mighty sword is the word of God *And take the sword of the Spirit, which is the word of God*, before which the legions of darkness cannot stand, when wielded by the faithful soldier, slaying every temptation, and opening a way through hosts of difficulties

7 Prayer must be added *Praying always with all prayer and supplication in the Spirit*, looking upwards constantly for divine support, in every emergence casting your care upon God, in ejaculations, and, at stated solemn seasons, commending yourselves into the Lord's hand, *and watching thereunto with all perseverance*, never weary or giving over, though the conflict be hard and long, and no immediate answer received, *and*, as for yourselves, so also continue earnest in *supplication for all saints*, engaged in the same warfare, contending with the same enemies,

and

and needing the ſame divine ſupport *And*, among others, *for me alſo*, under my trials, *that utterance may be given unto me, that I may open my mouth boldly*, fearleſs of any conſequences, *to make known the myſtery of the goſpel*, and publiſh the glad tidings with all zeal, openneſs, and freedom of ſpeech, without concealing any of the glorious truths, however offenſive they may be to men's pride or love of ſin *for which* fidelity *I am an ambaſſador* of Chriſt *in bonds*, ſuffering cheerfully, and ſtill deſiring, even in a priſon, to negociate the great affair of reconciliation between God and ſinners and I entreat your prayers, *that therein*, under whatever difficulties I ſtruggle, *I may ſpeak boldly, as I ought to ſpeak*, undaunted in my ſpirit, and without moleſtation *Note*, (1) Prayer is the Chriſtian's conſtant recourſe, and ſure ſupport in every exigence (2) Whilſt we continue perſevering in our ſupplications, we ſhall aſſuredly go on conquering and to conquer (3) We ſhould mutually remember each other at a throne of grace, all ſaints need our prayers, and ſhould have an intereſt in them

g Col iv 7. h 2 Tim iv 12. i Col iv 8.

21, But [g] that ye alſo may know my affairs, *and* how
I do, [h] Tychicus, a beloved brother and faithful miniſter
in the Lord, ſhall make known to you all things 22
[i] Whom I have ſent unto you for the ſame purpoſe, that ye
might know our affairs, and that he might comfort your
hearts 23 Peace *be* to the brethren, and love with faith
from God the Father, and the Lord Jeſus Chriſt 24
Grace *be* with all them that love our Lord Jeſus Chriſt
[k] † in ſincerity Amen

k Tit ii 7. † Or with uncorruptedneſs

v 21—24 Having deſired an intereſt in their prayers, he concludes his epiſtle,

1 With recommending Tychicus to them, the bearer of this epiſtle *But that ye alſo may know my affairs, and how I do* in my preſent confinement, *Tychicus, a beloved brother and faithful miniſter in the Lord, ſhall make known to you all things* concerning my ſituation, labours, treatment and ſucceſs, even in bonds *whom I have ſent unto you for the ſame purpoſe, that ye might know our affairs, and that he might comfort your hearts*, amidſt all the trials you meet, and encourage you, from my example, patiently and chearfully to perſevere in the good ways of the Lord

2 He cloſes with his uſual benediction and prayer *Peace be to the brethren*, may you enjoy a ſweet ſenſe of God's favour, be bleſt with all proſperity, temporal and ſpiritual, and live in the moſt uninterrupted harmony among yourſelves, *and* may *love* to God and to each other abound, *with faith*, in the moſt lively and vigorous exerciſe, all which ſpiritual bleſſings flow *from God the Father*, as their ſource in the œconomy of redemption, *and from the Lord Jeſus Chriſt*, as the purchaſer and diſpenſer of them to his choſen people *Grace be with all them that love our Lord Jeſus Chriſt in ſincerity*, (εν αφθαρσια) with unfeigned affection, or *in incorruption*, without adulterating the doctrines of truth, or admitting any earthly thing to rival him in their hearts, or *with immortality*, may his grace and your love be perfected in glory everlaſting Thus in faith he prays, and adds his joyful *Amen!* in confidence that the Lord will hear and anſwer his requeſts

THE

EVANGELICAL EXPOSITOR;

OR, A

PRACTICAL COMMENT

Upon the EPISTLE of

St. PAUL to the PHILIPPIANS.

PHILIPPI was a chief city of the western part of Macedonia, πρώτη τῆς μερίδος τῆς Μακεδονίας πόλις, Acts xvi 12 *It took its name from Philip, the famous king of Macedon, who repaired and beautified it, and was afterwards made a Roman colony. Near this place were the* Campi Philippici, *remarkable for the famous battles between Julius Cesar, and Pompey the Great, and that between Augustus and Antony on one side, and Cesar and Brutus on the other. But it is most remarkable among Christians for this epistle, which was written when Paul was* prisoner *at Rome,* A D 62

St Paul seems to have had a very particular kindness for the church at Philippi, which he himself had been instrumental in planting, and though he had the care of all the churches, *he had, upon that account, a particular* fatherly *tender care of this. He looked upon them as his* children, *and having* begotten them by the gospel, *he was desirous by the same gospel to* nourish *and nurse them up.*

From small beginnings they had arisen to a flourishing church, and in their liberality to the apostle were distinguished, of which he makes grateful and honourable mention, expressing his warm affection towards them, informing them of his success even in prison, encouraging them to bear up under all opposition, exhorting them to mutual love, warning them against deceivers, and stirring them up to all holy conversation and godliness.

CHAP I.

He begins with the inscription and benediction, ver 1, 2. He gives thanks for the saints at Philippi, ver 3—7. His great affection and concern for their spiritual welfare, ver 7—9. His prayer for them, ver 9—11. His care to prevent their offence at his sufferings, ver 12—20. His readiness to glorify Christ by life or death, ver 21—26. He concludes with a double exhortation to stedfastness and constancy, ver 27—30.

1 PAUL and Timotheus the servants of Jesus
Christ, to all the saints [a] in Christ Jesus which
are at Philippi, with the bishops and deacons.
2 [b] Grace *be* unto you, and peace from God
our Father, and *from* the Lord Jesus Christ.

a 1 Cor i 2

b Rom i 7. 1 Cor i 3. 2 Cor i 2. 1 Pet i 2.

ver 1—2 The apostolical inscription and benediction open the epistle. *Paul and Timotheus*, who join him in all cordial salutations, *the servants of Jesus Christ* in the gospel, *to all the saints in Christ Jesus which are at Philippi*, chosen in him, and in the fulness of time brought into real union with him in faith and holiness, *with the bishops*, the superior officers in the church, *and deacons*, their assistants. *Grace be unto you, and peace from God our Father, and from the Lord Jesus Christ.* Note, (1.) There can be no true peace but what flows from divine grace and favour. (2.) Every covenant mercy we receive at God's hands, comes to us as the fruit of our adored Redeemer's undertaking.

3 [c] I thank my God upon every remembrance of
you, 4 (Always in every prayer of mine for you all
making request with joy) 5 For [d] your fellowship in
the gospel from the first day until now; 6 Being con-
fident of this very thing, that he which hath begun [e] a
good work in you, will [f] perform *it* until the day of
Jesus Christ: 7 Even as it is meet for me to think
this of you all, because [g] I have you in my heart, inas-
much as both in my bonds, and in the defence and con-
firmation of the gospel, [h] ye all are partakers of my grace.
8 For [k] God is my record, [l] how greatly I long after
you all in the bowels of Jesus Christ. 9 And this I
pray, that [m] your love may abound yet more and more
[n] in knowledge, and *in* all judgment; 10 That ye may
approve things that are excellent; [p] that ye may be sin-
cere, and [q] without offence [r] till the day of Christ; 11
Being filled with the fruits of righteousness, [s] which are
by Jesus Christ, [t] unto the glory and praise of God.

c Rom i 8. 1 Cor i 4. Eph i 15, 16. Col i 3. 1 Thes i 2. d 2 Cor viii 1. 2 Cor. Ephes. iii 1. John i. e John vi 29. 1 Thes i 3. f Or, finish. Heb xii. g Ver 10. 2 Cor vii 3. h Eph iii 1 & iv 1. Col iv 3. 2 Tim i 8. i Chap iv 14. k Rom i 9. Gal i 20. l Chap ii 26. & iv 1. 1 Thes iii 12. m Eph i 17. n Philem 6. p Rom ii 18. & xii 2. q 1 Thes iii 13. Acts xxiv 16. 1 Cor x 32. r Ver 6. s John xv 4, 5. Eph ii 10. t John xv 8. Eph i 12.

ver 3—11 The apostle, after his gracious introduction, begins

1. With thanksgiving to God on their behalf. *I thank my God upon every remembrance of you*, and of the rich grace he hath bestowed upon you, (*always, in every prayer of mine for you all, making request with joy*, delighting in and over you) *for your fellowship in the gospel*, thankful for all the inestimable privileges [illegible]

to which you have been admitted, for the love and union maintained among you, and for your liberality in contributing to the furtherance of the gospel, *from the first day until now*, with steadfastness and perseverance, in the midst of all opposition, continuing to approve your fidelity. *Note*, (1.) It is a great joy to a minister's soul, when his people walk steadily in the fellowship of the gospel. (2.) Our grateful thanksgivings are ever due, whilst we are mentioning the divine mercies.

2. He expresses his confidence concerning them. *Being confident of this very thing, that he which hath begun a good work in you*, by his sovereign grace converting your souls, according to his unchangeable promises and love, *will perform* and finish *it until the day of Jesus Christ*, when your salvation shall be perfected for ever. *Note*, (1.) Whatever good is found in us, it comes from God, who worketh in us to will and to do of his good pleasure. (2.) He who is the author must also be the finisher of the work of grace, that in eternity he may have all the praise. (3.) Where God begins, we may be confident he will bring to a happy end. His work is perfect, and his gifts and callings without repentance.

3. He gives the reason for that confidence in them which he entertained. *Even as it is meet for me to think this of you all*, bound in the judgment of charity to esteem the whole church and every member true to their profession. And I the more readily entertain such a persuasion of you, *because I have you in my heart*, embraced with my warmest affections, and sharing my constant remembrances, *inasmuch as both in my bonds, and in the defence and confirmation of the gospel, ye are all partakers of my grace*, enduring the like tribulations as I suffer, and by your sympathy with me, and your readiness to assist me both in my bonds, and amidst all the opposition which I meet in defence of the gospel, ye manifestly appear to have received out of the same Redeemer's fulness. *Note*, We are bound to think well of those, who not only make a creditable profession, but dare to suffer for the truth themselves, or nobly own, even in bonds, those who do.

4. He appeals to God for the warm attachment of his heart unto them. *For God is my record, how greatly I long after you all in the bowels of Jesus Christ*, with the truest spiritual affection, like that which Jesus himself feels for precious souls.

5. He tells them what were his prayers for them. *And this I pray*, (1.) *That your love may abound yet more and more* towards God and one another. (2.) That ye may advance *in knowledge and in all judgment*, grounded and settled in the true principles of the gospel, and that thus your love may be increased day by day. (3.) *That ye may approve the things that are excellent*, bringing every thing to the test of God's word, that their different excellence may be ascertained, and examining by this unerring rule the doctrines of seducers, that the purity of the gospel may be maintained in opposition to their errors. (4.) *That ye may be sincere and without offence*, or allowed guile before God and man, true to your principles and upright in your conduct, *till the day of Christ*, persevering in your fidelity, and walking as those who constantly eye and are fearing God and a judgment-day. (5.) *If* thus found faithful, you will be *filled with the fruits of righteousness*, with every divine temper and gracious work which the Spirit of God produces in the redeemed, and *which are by Jesus Christ*, accepted through him as well as derived from him, *unto the praise and glory of God*. His own glory is the great end which he proposes in all his works, and which we therefore should ever regard as the great end of our being.

12 But I would ye should understand, brethren, that
the things *which happened* unto me have fallen out rather
unto the furtherance of the gospel. 13 So that my
bonds † in Christ are manifest ‡ in all the palace, and
‡ in all other *places*; 14 And many of the brethren in
the Lord waxing confident by my bonds, are much more
bold to speak the word without fear. 15 Some indeed
preach Christ even of envy ˣ and strife, and some also
of good will. 16 The one preach Christ of contention,
not sincerely, supposing to add affliction to my bonds:
17 But the other of love, knowing that I am set for the
defence of the gospel. 18 What then? notwithstand-
ing every way, whether in pretence, or in truth, Christ
is preached; and I therein do rejoice, yea, and will re-
joice. 19 For I know that this shall turn to my salva-
tion ʸ through your prayer, and the supply of ᶻ the Spi-
rit of Jesus Christ, 20 According to my earnest ex-
pectation, and my hope, that ᵃ in nothing I shall be
ashamed, but *that* with all boldness, as always, *so* now
also ᵇ Christ shall be magnified in my body, whether *it be*
by life or by death.

† Or, for Christ. ‡ Or, to all others. x Chap. ii. 3. y 2 Cor. i. 11. z Rom. viii. 9. a Rom. v. 5. b Acts xx. 24.

V. 12—20. Nothing could tend more gloriously to remove the ignominy of Paul's chain, or to comfort the hearts of his spiritual children, who might be much dejected at his reproaches and sufferings, than the account which he here gives.

1. Even in his bonds the gospel was not bound, *but* his sufferings tended to confirm and propagate the knowledge of the truth. *I would ye should understand, brethren, that the things which happened unto me*, dark and afflictive as the dispensation might appear to you, *have fallen out rather unto the furtherance of the gospel*; for God can easily bring the greatest good out of what appeared the greatest evil. Thus the blood of the martyrs hath ever been the seed of the church. *So that my bonds in Christ are manifest in all the palace*, where my sufferings for the gospel, and patient fortitude under them, are known to all the great men of Nero's court, *and in all other places*, and are made the happy occasion of raising enquiries about the gospel in those who might not otherwise have heard it, and of bringing some under the joyful sound even out of Cæsar's houshold. *And many of the brethren in the Lord, waxing confident by my bonds*, and fully satisfied of the goodness of the cause, and of the hand of the Lord visible in the support he gives me, *are much more bold* than ever *to speak the word without fear*, and to proclaim the salvation which is only to be found in a crucified Jesus. *Some indeed preach Christ even of envy, and strife*, taking this opportunity of my imprisonment to pursue the base end of setting up themselves, even under the covert of zeal for the gospel, envying my reputation, and hoping to supplant me in the affection of the churches; *and some also of good-will*, with hearty affection to the cause, and true regard for me. *The one preach Christ of contention*, out of mere pride and rivalship, *not sincerely*, from a right principle of love unfeigned, but from envy, *supposing to add affliction to my bonds*, by insinuating themselves, to my prejudice, with the members of the churches, or hoping to incense the government more against me by the noise they make, and the divisions they seek to raise. *But the other preach Christ of love*, truly attached to the Saviour, and longing to promote the salvation of immortal souls, *knowing that I am set for the defence of the gospel*, and suffered to bear these bonds on purpose to have an opportunity, before the highest in this world, publickly to vindicate and defend the cause of Christ. *Note*, (1.) Strange as it may appear, that any should preach Christ out of envy, so subtle is the tempter, and so corrupt the heart of man, that even the gospel may be turned into the gall of asps, and made the pedestal on which the proud self would erect its reputation. (2.) Faithful souls are whetted by opposition, and made more bold by bonds and reproaches.

2. He expresses the joy he felt in his own soul, amidst all he suffered from open enemies and false friends. *What then? tho'* some act on principles so base, *notwithstanding every way, whether in pretence or in truth, Christ is preached, and I therein do rejoice, yea, and will rejoice*: if his name is spread abroad, and his gospel propagated, that is matter of real joy, and the ministry may be blest, though the preacher perishes. *For I know that this shall turn to my salvation*, however different the designs of these men may be, and serve to procure my liberty the sooner, as well as to advance my soul's present and eternal benefit, *through your prayers* daily offered up for me, *and the supply of the Spirit of Jesus Christ*, which can enable me to improve under every dispensation, and cause it to work for good. *According to my earnest expectation and hope* that I shall be supported and delivered, and *that in nothing I shall be ashamed* of that glorious cause for which I suffer, *but that with all boldness*, and unshaken fortitude of mind, *as always* hitherto I have been enabled to act, *so now also Christ shall be magnified in my body, whether it be by life or by death*, by longer patient suffering, if such be his will, by a faithful discharge of my trust, should I regain my liberty, or by sealing the testimony with my blood, if his glory so require. *Note*, (1.) We are much indebted to our brethren's prayers. (2.) The supply of the Spirit of Christ can make up all other wants, and cause every providence to prove a blessing. (3.) If we are not a shame *to* the gospel, we need never be ashamed *of it*, though devoted, for the sake thereof, to the most ignominious death.

21 For † to me to live is Christ, and to die *is* gain.
22 But if I live in the flesh, this *is* the fruit of my la-
bour: yet what I shall choose I wot not. 23 For ᶜ I am
in a strait betwixt two, having a desire to depart, and
to be with Christ; which is far better: 24 Neverthe-
less, to abide in the flesh *is* more needful for you. 25
And ᵉ having this confidence, I know that I shall abide
and continue with you all for your furtherance and joy
of faith; 26 That ᶠ your rejoicing may be more abun-
dant in Jesus Christ for me, by my coming to you
again.

† Or, to me living and dying Christ is gain. c 2 Cor. v. 8. d 2 Tim. iv. 6. e Chap. ii. 24. f 2 Cor. i. 14. & v. 12.

V. 21—26. The apostle was happy to die, yet for their sakes content to live.

For to me to live is Christ, and to die is gain; living or dying, he is to me all and in all; for his glory I only desire to live, and in whatever way I die in his cause and service, I know it shall prove my everlasting gain. *But if I live in the flesh, this is the fruit of my labour*, to preach and suffer for the truth alike, in order to advance my great Master's cause; *yet what I shall choose I wot not*, whether life or death: *for I am in a strait be-*

twixt

twixt two, having a desire to depart and to be with Christ, longing for the heavenly blessedness in store, and to see him face to face, where sin, sorrow, and sighing, shall be for ever away, *which is far better* than any possible situation which I can be in here below. *Nevertheless, to abide in the flesh is more needful for you*, and for your benefit I can gladly forego for a while my own happiness, and conflict still amidst the opposing powers of earth and hell. *And having this confidence*, that my abode below will be for your edification, *I know* by divine intimation, *that I shall abide and continue with you all, for your furtherance and joy of faith*, to confirm and stablish you yet more and more, *that your rejoicing may be more abundant in Christ Jesus for me, by my coming to you again*, restored to liberty, and enabled to resume my useful labours among you. *Note*, (1.) If we can say with truth, *to live is Christ*, that his glory is our single aim, we may confidently add, *to die is gain*; how great, heaven can only tell. (2.) But for one thing can earth be truly desireable to the faithful, and that is the service which can be rendered to immortal souls, and the glory accruing thence to the Redeemer: for this therefore he lives.

f Eph. iv. 1. Col. i. 10. 1 Thess. ii. 12. & iv. 1. Eph. i. iv. 1. h Jude 3. i 2 Thess. k Rom. viii. 17. 2 Tim. ii. 11. l Acts v. 41. m Eph. ii. 8. n Col. ii. 1. o Acts xvi. 19, &c.

27 Only ^f let your conversation be as it becometh
the gospel of Christ: that whether I come and see you,
or else be absent, I may hear of your affairs, ^g that ye
stand fast in one spirit, with one mind, ^h striving together
for the faith of the gospel; 28 And in nothing terrified
by your adversaries: ^i which is to them an evident
token of perdition, ^k but to you of salvation, and that
of God. 29 For unto you ^l it is given in the behalf of
Christ, not only ^m to believe on him, but also to suffer
for his sake; 30 ^n Having the same conflict ^o which ye
saw in me, and now hear *to be* in me.

v. 27—30. The apostle closes with two exhortations.

1. *Only let your conversation be as becometh the gospel of Christ*, (πολιτευεσθε). Behave as citizens of the heavenly Jerusalem, walk worthy of your high vocation, adorning the doctrine of God our Saviour in all things, and proving the solidity of your hope by the spirituality of your conduct, *that whether I come and see you, or else be absent, I may hear of your affairs* with joy, *that ye stand fast in one spirit, with one mind, striving together for the faith of the gospel*, united in truth and love, resisting, with the most vigorous efforts, every persecuting or seducing foe, holding fast the unadulterated principles of grace, and building up each other in your most holy faith. *Note*, (1.) The faith of the gospel will ever meet with opposition. (2.) Unanimity among Christians is the great means of their establishment, while dissention and schism render them an easy prey.

2. *In nothing terrified by your adversaries*, however many or mighty, whether from earth or hell, but defy them in the mighty ... cleaving unshaken to the blessed gospel, *which is to them an evident token of perdition, but to you of salvation, and that of God*; such patient and faithful suffering for the truth proves your interest in it, while all the opposition of your foes must end in their eternal ruin. *For unto you it is given*, as your distinguished honour, *in the behalf of Christ, not only to believe on him* to the saving of your souls, which is an eminent gift of God, *but also to suffer for his sake, having the same conflict which ye saw in me* when I was with you, and steadily sustained the shock, *and now hear to be in me*. *Note*, (1.) Faith is the gift of God. (2.) Sufferings and reproaches on the behalf of Christ are real honours. (3.) It is an encouragement to us patiently to endure the cross, when we see others cheerfully bearing it before us, and glorying in tribulation.

CHAP. II.

The apostle proceeds to further exhortations to several duties, to be like minded, and lowly-minded, which he presses from the example of Christ, ver. 1—11. *And to diligence and seriousness in the Christian course*, ver. 12, 13. *And to adorn their Christian profession by several suitable graces*, ver. 14—18. *And concludes with particular notice and commendation of two good ministers, Timothy and Epaphroditus, whom he designed to send to them*, ver. 19—30.

a 2 Cor. xiii. 14. b Rom. xii. 16. & xv. 5. 1 Cor. i. 10. 2 Cor. xiii. 11. 1 Pet. iii. 8. c Gal. v. 26. Chap. i. 15. Jam. iv. 16. d Rom. xii. 10. 1 Pet. v. 5. e 1 Cor. x. 24. & xiii. 5. f Matt. xi. 29. John xiii. 15. 1 Pet. ii. 21. 1 John ii. 6. g John i. 1. 2 Cor. iv. 4. Col. i. 15. Heb. i. 3. h John v. 18. & x. 33.

1 IF *there be* therefore any consolation in Christ, if
any comfort of love, if any ^a fellowship of the Spirit,
if any bowels and mercies, 2 Fulfil ye my joy,
^b that ye be like-minded, having the same love, *being*
of one accord, of one mind. 3 *Let* ^c nothing *be done*
through strife or vain-glory; but in lowliness of mind
^d let each esteem other better than themselves. 4 ^e Look
not every man on his own things, but every man also
on the things of others. 5 ^f Let this mind be in you,
which was also in Christ Jesus: 6 Who ^g being in the
form of God, thought it not robbery ^h to be equal with
God: 7 ^i But made himself of no reputation, and took
upon him the form of ^k a servant, and ^l was made in
the likeness of men: 8 And being found in fashion as
a man, he humbled himself, and ^m became obedient unto
death, even the death of the cross. 9 ^n Wherefore God
also hath highly exalted him, and ^o given him a name
which is above every name: 10 That ^p at the name of
Jesus every knee should bow, of *things* in heaven, and
things in earth, and *things* under the earth; 11 And
^q that every tongue should confess, that Jesus Christ *is*
Lord, to the glory of God the Father.

i Ps. xxii. 6. Isa. liii. 3. Dan. ix. 26. Mark ix. 12. k Isa. xlii. 1. & xlix. 6. & lii. 13. Ezek. xxxiv. 23. Zech. iii. 8. l John i. 14. Rom. i. 3. Gal. iv. 4. Heb. ii. 14, 17. m Matt. xxvi. 39, 42. John x. 18. Heb. v. 8. n John xvii. 5. Heb. ii. 9. o Eph. i. 21. Heb. i. 4. p Isa. xlv. 23. Rom. xiv. 11. Rev. v. 13. q John xiii. 13.

v. 1—11. By every endearing argument the apostle exhorts his Philippian brethren,

1. To love, unity, and humility. *If there be any consolation in Christ*, (παρακλησις), if my *exhortation* hath any weight, and you experience any joy in the Redeemer; *if there be any comfort of love*, from the sense of the love of God shed abroad in your hearts; *if there be any fellowship of the Spirit*, in mutual union and complacence in each other, or through the Holy Ghost, with God the Father, and with his Son Jesus Christ; *if there be any bowels and mercies*, in the gracious Saviour towards you, or if you have ever felt the like tender compassions one towards another; if it be most desirable to abound in all these things, and you have already known their value and excellence, *fulfil ye my joy*, and continue to give me this highest satisfaction in you, *that ye be like minded*, animated as by one soul, *having the same love* one towards another, as the members of the same body, *being of one accord*, unanimous in desire and design to promote the Redeemer's glory, and the salvation of men's souls, and *of one mind*, holding the same principles and sentiments, according to the purity of the gospel. *Let nothing be done through strife or vain-glory*, affect no pre-eminence, dispute not for applause, nor speak or act under a contentious spirit, *but in lowliness of mind*, the great ornament of the Christian character, *let each esteem other better than themselves*, entertaining lowly thoughts of their own attainments, conscious of their manifold infirmities, and entertaining the best opinion of their brethren. *Look not every man at his own things*, to admire himself, or pursue his own selfish ends, his ease, honour, or worldly advantage, *but every man also on the things of others*, not as busy-bodies, to pry into them censoriously, but desiring to promote their real good, and from the view of their excellencies to be humble in your own eyes.

2. He enforces his exhortation with the most powerful argument, the example of the blessed Jesus. *Let this mind be in you, which was also in Christ Jesus*, even that lowliness which in him was so eminently exemplified, *who being in the form of God*, possessing every essential perfection of the divine nature, the brightness of the Father's glory, and the express image of his person, *thought it not robbery to be equal with God*, and justly to claim a parity with the Father in uncreated glory. *But*, in infinite condescension and pity towards us, he *made himself of no reputation*, laying aside the splendor of his divine majesty, *and took upon himself the form of a servant*, assuming the human nature in the lowest condition, *and was made in the likeness of men*, having the same reasonable soul, and human flesh, the corruption of our nature only excepted. *And being found in fashion as a man*, in all things made like unto his brethren, *he humbled himself* before God and man, through a life of affliction, *and*, at last, *became obedient to death*, for us men and for our salvation, *even the death of the cross*, that most painful, ignominious, and accursed death, submitting thereunto, that he might bear our sins in his own body on the tree. *Wherefore*, having finished the work which the Father had given him to do, to his fullest satisfaction, *God also hath highly exalted him* in his human nature to the mediatorial throne, as the reward of his sufferings, *and given him a name which is above every name*, all power, authority, and dominion being given to him over every creature, *that at the name of Jesus every knee should bow*, and divine honours be paid to the incarnate Son, *of things in heaven, and things in earth, and things under the earth*, by angels and men, and every intelligent creature; yea, even devils must be compelled to own his glory; *and that every tongue should confess that Jesus Christ is Lord*, the universal Sovereign, *to the glory of God the Father*, who, as man, hath thus exalted him to the throne of majesty on high, for the purposes of his own glory. *Note*, (1.) The example of our Lord should be ever before us, and that, if any thing can, will suppress the workings of pride. (2.) The love of a crucified Jesus should warm our hearts, and knit them in closest union to each other.

12 Wherefore my beloved, as ye have always obey-
ed, not as in my presence only, but now much more in
my absence, work out your own salvation with fear and
trembling. 13 For ^r it is God which worketh in you
both to will and to do of *his* good pleasure. 14 Do all
things ^s without murmurings, ^t and disputings: 15
That ye may be blameless and harmless, ^u the sons of
God, without rebuke, in the midst of ^x a crooked and

r Eph. iii. 20. 2 Cor. iii. 5. Heb. xiii. 21. s 1 Cor. x. 10. t Rom. xiv. 1. u Matt. v. 45. x Deut. xxxii. 5.

perverse nation among whom ye shine as lights in the
world 16 Holding forth the word of life, that I
may rejoice in the day of Christ, that I have not run in
vain, neither laboured in vain 17 Yea, and if I be
offered upon the sacrifice and service of your faith,
I joy, and rejoice with you all 18 For the same cause
also do ye joy, and rejoice with me

v 12—18 The apostle proceeds in his exhortations

1 To Christian diligence *Wherefore my beloved, as ye have always obeyed, not in my presence only, but now much more in my absence*, and therefore I entertain the fullest confidence of your perseverance in the same good ways of our God, *work out your own salvation with fear and trembling*, giving all diligence to make your calling and election sure in the use of every appointed means, jealous over your deceitful hearts, and watchful against every thing that might offend the Father of mercies, whose love you have tasted, and by whose grace your stability can only be secured, *for it is God which worketh in you both to will and to do of his good pleasure*, and you may firmly depend upon him, that, amidst all opposition, he will perfect in you the work which he hath begun *Note*, (1) God, who ordains the end, appoints the means, these are inseparable it were the height of folly and presumption to hope for salvation in the neglect of them (2) After all our diligence, our dependance must not be placed on ourselves but on him who worketh in us to will and to do, not according to our desert, nor merely at our desire, but of his own good pleasure (3) It is the strongest motive to exert ourselves, that we know our labour shall not be in vain in the Lord, for if he will work in us, for us, and with us, then shall we assuredly succeed

2 To an exemplary conversation, such as may confound their enemies, and comfort him their faithful servant under all his sufferings *Do all things without murmurings and disputings*, content under every providential dispensation, and studiously avoiding every occasion of contention among yourselves, *that ye may be blameless and harmless, the sons of God, without rebuke*, and behave so irreproachably, that your most malignant accusers may have no evil thing justly to say of you for ye dwell *in the midst of a crooked and perverse nation*, the keen eyes of your enemies are open, and they wait for your halting, gladly would they catch at any thing which might countenance them in their iniquities *among whom ye shine as lights in the world*, your bright examples, like suns in your several spheres, darting unwelcome light upon the workers of wickedness, and shining to the glory of God *Holding forth the word of life*, even the blessed gospel, both in your lips and in your conduct, *holding it fast* in all fidelity, *holding it up* with all zeal and boldness, if under God it may be blest to illuminate the darkness of those around you, and bring them to the Light of life, or at least to leave them inexcusable in their impenitence And this will be a singular satisfaction to me, when I find *that I have not run in vain, nor laboured in vain*, but behold in you such blessed effects of my ministry, and that all my conflicts shall at last be crowned with success *Yea, and if I be offered upon the sacrifice and service of your faith*, and should now be called as a victim to bleed in confirmation of the gospel which I preach, far from being intimidated with the prospect, *I joy and rejoice with you all*, congratulating you, and happy in myself that I am counted worthy of the crown of martyrdom, and enabled to leave so powerful a testimony behind me for the strengthening of your faith *For the same cause also do ye joy and rejoice with me*, and, far from being grieved or disheartened, should exult that I am enabled to be thus faithful unto death *Note*, (1) Every Christian is a city set on a hill, he needs peculiar circumspection, as flaws in his conduct will be exaggerated into faults of the first magnitude (2) We must hold up to the world, in our profession and example, the word of life, not ostentatiously proclaiming our own goodness, but, for God's glory and the profit of men's souls, shewing our light before men (3) Nothing can more revive a minister's heart, and make him so cheerfully content to suffer for the cause even to death, as seeing his labours successful and his ministry blest

19 But I trust in the Lord Jesus to send Timotheus
shortly unto you, that I also may be of good comfort
when I know your state 20 For I have no man like-
minded, who will naturally care for your state 21 For
all seek their own, not the things which are Jesus
Christ's 22 But ye know the proof of him, that as
a son with the father, he hath served with me in the gos-
pel 23 Him therefore I hope to send presently, so
soon as I shall see how it will go with me 24 But I
trust in the Lord, that I also myself shall come shortly
25 Yet I supposed it necessary to send to you Epa-
phroditus, my brother and companion in labour, and
fellow-soldier, but your messenger, and he that mi-
nistred to my wants 26 For he longed after you all,
and was full of heaviness, because that ye had heard that he
had been sick 27 For indeed he was sick nigh unto
death but God had mercy on him, and not on him
only, but on me also, lest I should have sorrow upon sor-
row 28 I sent him therefore the more carefully, that
when ye see him again, ye may rejoice, and that I may
be the less sorrowful 29 Receive him therefore in
the Lord with all gladness, and hold such in reputa-
tion 30 Because for the work of Christ he was nigh
unto death, not regarding his life to supply your lack
of service towards me

v 19—30 Since he was now unable to visit them himself, he promises to send them two of his dearest friends to supply his absence, and speaks of them in the highest terms of regard and commendation

1 He mentions Timothy Though he had spoken of his readiness to die, he informs them for their comfort, that he apprehended no immediate danger *But I trust*, says he, *in the Lord Jesus* that I shall be delivered, and, needful as his company is now to me, that I shall be able *to send Timothy shortly unto you, that I also may be of good comfort when I know your state*, and hear of your prosperity, *For I have no man likeminded*, so perfectly united in sentiment with me, and so in affection knit to you *who will therefore naturally care for your state* and with genuine regard desire to advance your soul's good *For all* here, too generally at least, *seek their own*, desirous of ease and carnal advantages, *not* with a single eye, as Timothy doth, pursuing *the things which are Jesus Christ's*, for his glory, and the edification of his people *But ye know the proof of him*, by past experience, with what zeal and fidelity he laboured among you, and *that as a son with the father, he hath served with me in the gospel*, willing to run all hazards, to share my fatigues and sufferings, and in all duty and affection obeying me as a child *Him therefore I hope to send presently, so soon as I shall see how it will go with me*, after I have appeared, as I shortly expect to do, at Cæsar's tribunal *but I trust in the Lord, that I also myself shall come shortly*, when I have regained my liberty *Note*, (1) They who enter the ministry with selfish views, seeking *their own things*, not those of Jesus Christ, shall bear their burden, when the great shepherd and bishop of souls appears (2) A faithful pastor feels the same tender concern for the children he hath begotten in the gospel, as if they were the offspring of his own body

2 He commends to them Epaphroditus, who brought this epistle to them *But I supposed it necessary*, being unable to come myself, or to spare Timothy just at this critical juncture, *to send to you Epaphroditus, my brother and companion in labour, and fellow-soldier*, who willingly served and suffered in the same blessed cause, *but your messenger, and he that ministered to my wants*, delivering your kind benefactions, and giving me every assistance which lay in his power *For he longed after you all*, and earnestly wished to be labouring again among you, *and was full of heaviness because that ye had heard that he had been sick*, knowing how deeply the sad news would affect you *For indeed he was sick nigh unto death*, his disease, to human view, mortal and desperate *but God had mercy on him*, and brought him back from the gates of the grave *and not on him only, but on me also, lest I should have sorrow upon sorrow*, anguish for his loss being added to my other burdens *I sent him therefore the more carefully*, and with greater haste, *that when ye see him again ye may rejoice* in his recovery and return to you, *and that I may be the less sorrowful* at his departure, when I know what delight and advantage his company will be to you *Receive him therefore in the Lord with all gladness*, with cordial regard, and as the ambassador of the Redeemer, *and hold such in reputation*, highly respecting them for their fidelity and zeal, *because for the work of Christ he was nigh unto death*, having contracted his illness from the fatigues he underwent, *not regarding his life*, but readily hazarding his health, *to supply your lack of service towards me*, which the distance rendered you incapable of affording me *Note*, (1) Though we must not carelessly neglect our health, yet, when the cause of Christ demand it, a faithful minister will shew a noble contempt of life, and be ready to expose himself to disease or death (2) They who know the value of a faithful minister, will count it a happiness to enjoy that he is longer spared to labour, and will rejoice in him before God

CHAP III

1 He cautions them against judaizing seducers, ver 1—3 2 Proposes his own example, and enumerates the privileges of his Jewish state which he rejected, ver 4—8 3 He describes the nature of his own choice, ver 9—14 4 He closes with an exhortation to beware of wicked men, and to follow his example, ver 15—21

1 FINALLY, my brethren, rejoice in the Lord
To write the same things to you, to me indeed
is not grievous, but for you it is safe 2 Beware of
dogs,

dogs, beware of [c] evil-workers, [d] beware of the conci-
sion. 3 For we are [e] the circumcision [f] which worship
God in the spirit, and rejoice in Christ Jesus, and have
no confidence in the flesh

a 2 Cor. iv 13. d Gal. v 2. e Deut. x 16. Jer. iv 4. Rom. ii 29. & iv 11, 12. Col. ii 11. f John iv 23, 24.

v 1—3 Into every church almost had the judaizing teachers crept, and caused much trouble to the great apostle The Philippians had been set at by them, and needed a caution against their seductions.

1 He exhorts them to rejoice in the Lord *Finally, my brethren*, after what I have said for your comfort, *rejoice in the Lord*, as your Redeemer and Saviour, assured of your interest in all the inestimable blessings of his gospel

2 He warns them against the false teachers *To write the same things to you*, which I have often spoken, and Epaphroditus has now in charge to deliver, *to me indeed is not grievous, but for you it is safe* to be reminded of your danger, and kept on your guard *Beware of dogs*, those cringing zealots, who fawn to ingratiate themselves with you, but design to introduce divisions among you, to bite and devour you, greedy, impudent, and worthless *Beware of evil workers*, whose practices declare the badness of their principles *Beware*, again I say, *of the concision*, no name being contemptible enough for them, who urging this abolished rite, would rend the peace of the church, would introduce confusion, and cut off the Gentiles from the privileges of the gospel

3 He describes true christianity *For we are the circumcision*, really in covenant with God, and entitled to all the spiritual blessings and privileges, *which worship God in spirit*, not with the outward pomp of ceremonial rites, but with the heart, according to the gospel institutions, *and rejoice*, or *glory*, *in Christ Jesus*, as our only hope towards God, placing our whole dependance upon him, happy in the perfection of the salvation which he hath wrought out for us, *and have no confidence in the flesh*, nor expect acceptance with God on account of any privileges of descent from Abraham, or any righteousness which we fallen creatures can perform *Note*, (1) All true Christians live in the constant worship of God, private and public, and that not formally, but in spirit and in truth (2) We must despair of ourselves, and renounce all dependance upon our own doings and duties, before we can exercise faith in Jesus, and know the joys of his salvation

4 Though [g] I might also have confidence in the flesh
If any other man thinketh that he hath whereof he
might trust in the flesh, I more 5 [h] Circumcised the
eight day, [i] of the stock of Israel, [k] *of* the tribe of Ben-
jamin, an Hebrew of the Hebrews, as touching the
law, a [l] Pharisee; 6 [m] Concerning zeal, [n] persecuting the
church, [o] touching the righteousness which is in the law,
blameless. 7 But [p] what things were gain to me, those
I counted loss for Christ 8 Yea doubtless, and I
count all things but loss, [q] for the excellency of the
knowledge of Christ Jesus my Lord for whom I have
suffered the loss of all things, and do count them but
dung that I may win Christ, 9 And be found in him,
not having mine own righteousness, [r] which is of the law,
but [s] that which is through the faith of Christ, the
righteousness which is of God by faith 10 That I
may know him, and the power of his resurrection, and
the [t] fellowship of his sufferings, being made conformable
unto his death, 11 If by any means [u] I might attain
unto the resurrection of the dead 12 Not as though
I had already [x] attained, either were already [y] perfect
but I follow after, if that I may apprehend that for which
also I am apprehended of Christ Jesus 13 Brethren, I
count not myself to have apprehended but *this* one
thing *I do*, [z] forgetting those things which are behind,
and [a] reaching forth unto those things which are before,
14 I press toward the mark, for the prize of [b] the high
calling of God in Christ Jesus

g 2 Cor. xi 18. h Gen. xvii 12. i 2 Cor. xi 22. k Rom. xi 1. l Acts xxiii 6. & xxvi 5. m Acts xxii 3. Gal. i 13, 14. n Acts viii 3. & ix 1. o Rom. x 5. p Mat. xiii 44. q Isa. liii 11. Jer. ix 24. John xvii 3. Col. ii 2. r Rom. x 5. s Rom. i 17. & iii 21, 22. & ix 30. t Rom. vi 3, 4, 5. [illegible] 2 Cor. iv 10. [illegible] 1 Tim. [illegible] 1 Pet. iv 13. u Luke xx 35. Acts xxvi 7. x 1 Tim. vi 12. y Heb. xii 23. z Ps. xlv 10. Luke ix 62. a 1 Cor. ix 24, 26. Heb. vi 1. b Heb. iii 1.

v 1—14 None had more outward privileges than Paul, none more heartily renounced them, and fled to a better hope His own example he proposes therefore for their imitation

1 If any man might have confidence in outward privileges, he had as many, or more, than any of the judaizing teachers a native Israelite, a descendant from Benjamin the son of the beloved Rachel, the tribe that clave to the house of David and the temple, when the rest revolted; on father and mother's side a Hebrew of pure extraction, circumcised according to the law, brought up after the strictest sect a Pharisee, in the observance both of the rites of the law, and the traditions of the elders, a zealot for Judaism, even so far as to be a bitter persecutor of Christianity, and in his outward conduct and conversation unblameable and unexceptionable

2 All these he renounced for Christ *But what things* I then thought *were gain to me*, and raised me in excellence above other men, *those I counted loss for Christ*, renouncing them utterly, assured if I trusted upon them for acceptance I must be undone, and therefore resting on Christ, on his blood and righteousness alone *Yea doubtless, and I count all things but loss*, I remain in the same sentiments, disclaiming all dependance upon my present as well as past doings and duties, *for the excellency of the knowledge of Christ Jesus my Lord*, compared with this, all besides is refuse, since I have known him as my Saviour, I want nothing more, *for whom I have suffered the loss of all things*, which this world holds dear, *and do count them but dung*, contemptible offals, fit to be cast only on the dunghill, *that I may win Christ*, and become partaker of the great salvation which he hath wrought out for his redeemed, *and be found in him*, as my city of refuge, my divine substitute and surety, my availing plea at the bar of God, *not having mine own righteousness, which is of the law*, nor daring in this to appear before the Judge, conscious how little it would bear the scrutiny, *but that which is through the faith of Christ, the righteousness which is of God by faith*, that divine, compleat, and spotless righteousness, which my Lord hath wrought out for me, which God imputes to me as my title to justification and life eternal, and which faith embraces as all my salvation *Note*, (1) Whatever we depend upon for justification, except on Christ alone, will assuredly prove to be our eternal loss (2) There is but one righteousness wherein a sinner can appear before God, and there never was, nor can be, another, besides that which Jesus of Nazareth completed when he died upon the cross

3 The apostle desired to know Christ, not only as his justifying righteousness, but as the Author of all spiritual life and eternal blessedness *That I may know him, and* experience *the power of his resurrection*, as the glorious head of vital influence to all his redeemed people, *and the fellowship of his sufferings*, daily experiencing the crucifixion of the old man, and willingly taking up my cross, however painful, *being made conformable unto his death*, dying unto sin, as Christ died for it, or ready to lay down my life for the gospel, whenever I may be called thereto *if by any means I might attain unto the resurrection of the dead*, raised to immortal life and glory in body as well as soul, and reaching the happy port of eternal rest, whither I steer my course *Not as though I had already attained, either were already perfect* in holiness, as I desire to be, *but I follow after*, eager to be at the goal, *if that I may apprehend that, for which also I am apprehended of Christ Jesus*, holding fast by that blessed Jesus, who first laid hold on me in my way to Damascus, and trusting on his power and grace to bring me to the eternal life which he hath promised, and whereunto he hath appointed me *Brethren, I count not myself to have apprehended*, or to be arrived at the summit of perfection, *but this one thing I do, forgetting those things which are behind*, resting in no present attainments, *and reaching forth unto those things which are before*, after higher measures of grace, *I press toward the mark, for the prize of the high calling of God in Christ Jesus*, with heaven in my eye I vigorously pursue my course, bending forwards eagerly as I run, and stretching out my arms to seize the crown of righteousness, which Jesus bestows, and is to be won only through the grace and strength which he supplies *Note*, (1) To know the power of Christ's resurrection, is to experience his quickening efficacy upon our souls, and to be raised from the death of sin to the life of righteousness, as his dead body was raised from the grave to the life of glory (2) The greatest saints are most sensible how short they come of perfection They who think they have grace enough, evidently shew they have none at all (3) Christ must apprehend us first, before we can apprehend him his power must keep us, or we shall never reach the salvation to which he hath called us (4) Heaven is the prize in view, happy the soul which reaches that goal

15 Let us therefore, as many as be [c] perfect, be thus
minded and if in any thing ye be otherwise minded,
God shall reveal even this unto you 16 Nevertheless,
whereto we have already attained, [d] let us walk [e] by the
same rule, [f] let us mind the same thing

c Rom. xv [illegible] Heb. v 14. d Rom. xii [illegible] e Gal. vi [illegible] f Chap. ii 2.

v 15, 16 The apostle exhorts them to be united in love, and like-minded with him *Let us therefore, as many as be perfect*, and far advanced in the Christian state, *be thus minded and if in any thing ye be otherwise minded*, and differ from me in sentiments, *God shall reveal even this unto you*, and clear up to your satisfaction whatever may yet be dark or doubtful *Nevertheless whereto we have already attained, let us walk by the same rule* of God's word, *let us mind the same thing*, wherein we are all agreed *Note*, Lesser differences of opinion should make no disunion of heart we must wait together on God, that he may instruct us in all his holy will

17 Brethren, [g] be followers together of me, and mark
them which walk so, as [h] ye have us for an ensample
18 (For [i] many walk, of whom I have told you often,
and now tell you even weeping, *that they are* the ene-

[illegible]

mies of the cross of Christ 19 Whose end *is* destruction, whose God *is their* belly and *whose* glory *is* in their shame, who mind earthly things) 20 For our conversation is in heaven, from whence also we look for the Saviour the Lord Jesus Christ 21 Who shall change our vile body, that it may be fashioned like unto his glorious body, according to the working whereby he is able even to subdue all things unto himself

V 17—21 With warnings and exhortations he closes the chapter

1 He warns them against the false teachers, whose character he describes *For many walk, of whom I have told you often, and now tell you even weeping*, concerned deeply for them, and jealous for you, *that they are the enemies of the cross of Christ*, both in their principles and their practice, their lives being as contrary to the spirit of purity, as their dependance on circumcision and the Mosaic rites is derogatory to the grace of the gospel, unwilling to profess, or suffer for, a crucified Jesus *whose end is destruction*, their errors and immoralities bringing upon them eternal ruin *whose God is their belly*, serving and indulging their sensual appetites, as their chief happiness *and whose glory is their shame*, boasting themselves in their evil ways, and proud of their privileges, which only serve to cover them with confusion, whilst they behave so unsuitably thereunto *who mind earthly things*, and have their groveling minds ever fixed on the interests, pleasures and honours of this miserable world *Note*, (1) They who make their belly their God, glory in their sins, and live after the fashion of the world, will infallibly find the end of their ways to be the destruction of both body and soul (2) It is a bitter grief to the faithful, when they behold any that bear the Christian name a dishonour to their holy profession.

2 He exhorts them to copy the good examples which he and others shewed them *Brethren, be ye followers together of me*, as I am of Christ, *and mark them which walk so, as ye have us for an ensample*, and adorn the gospel they profess *For our conversation is in heaven*, our traffic and concerns all lie there, and we regard ourselves as strangers upon earth, and denizens of the celestial city *from whence also we look for the Saviour, the Lord Jesus Christ*, to come at the last day, and bring us home to his blessed self, *who shall change our vile body*, that now bears the most humbling marks of weakness and infirmity, and will shortly be loathsome in the dust, *that it may be fashioned like unto his glorious body, according to the working whereby he is able even to subdue all things unto himself*, when death, the last of his enemies, shall be swallowed up in victory, and we shall rise, and shine, and reign with our exalted head in glory everlasting

CHAP IV

Exhortations to several Christian duties, as stedfastness, unanimity, joy, &c ver 1—9 The apostle's grateful acknowledgments of the Philippians kindness to him, with expressions of his own content, and desire of their good, ver 10—20 He concludes the epistle with praises, salutations, and blessings, ver 21—23.

1 THerefore, my brethren, dearly beloved and longed for, my joy and crown, so stand fast in the Lord, *my* dearly beloved 2 I beseech Euodias, and beseech Syntyche, that they be of the same mind in the Lord 3 And I intreat thee also, true yoke-fellow, help those women which laboured with me in the gospel, with Clement also, and *with* other my fellow-labourers, whose names *are* in the book of life 4 Rejoice in the Lord alway *and* again I say, Rejoice 5 Let your moderation be known unto all men The Lord *is* at hand 6 Be careful for nothing but in every thing by prayer and supplication with thanksgiving, let your requests be made known unto God 7 And the peace of God which passeth all understanding, shall keep your hearts and minds through Christ Jesus. 8 Finally, brethren, whatsoever things are true, whatsoever things *are* honest, whatsoever things *are* just, whatsoever things *are* pure, whatsoever things *are* lovely, whatsoever things *are* of good report, if *there be* any virtue, and if *there be* any praise, think on these things 9 Those things which ye have both learned and received, and heard and seen in me, do, and the God of peace shall be with you

V 1—9 The apostle,

1 With the most endearing appellations exhorts them to stand fast in the truth *Therefore, my brethren, dearly beloved and longed for*, to whom my whole soul is drawn out in warmest affection, and whose salvation I so earnestly desire, longing to see you, *my joy*, in every remembrance of your fidelity, *and crown*, whom now I esteem my chief honour, and who will be my most distinguished glory in the day of Christ, *so stand fast in the Lord, my dearly beloved*, cleaving to that divine Redeemer in whom you have believed, unshaken by danger, unterrified by opposition, and looking up for that almighty grace, which can make you more than conquerors *Note*, (1) None can tell the fervent longings of a faithful minister's heart after the salvation of his people's souls, but those that feel them (2) They who have already approved themselves faithful, are especially bound to persevere in the same blessed course

2 He intreats, that some individuals who were at variance, either with the church, or each other, might be happily reconciled *I beseech Euodias, and I beseech Syntyche, that they be of the same mind in the Lord*, and lay aside their disputes, united in love and peace *And I intreat thee also, true yoke-fellow*, who with me already hast heartily laboured in the cause of Christ, *help those women*, and endeavour to reconcile them to the church, and to each other, *which* have been so useful in former days, and *laboured with me in the gospel*, helping and assisting me, *with Clement also, and with other my fellow-labourers, whose names are in the book of life*, of the Lamb slain from the foundation of the world, registered among the elect of God, and heirs of salvation, and happy are they whose names shall be found written there

3 He exhorts them to holy joy *Rejoice in the Lord alway*, in all circumstances, and under every trial, maintain a holy delight in God, which will sweeten every affliction *and again I say, Rejoice* in him as your Saviour, your refuge, help, and hope, in every time of need

4 *Let your moderation be known unto all men*, (το επιεικες) shew a spirit of meekness and patience, that never is wearied out with provocations, and in affection be weaned from every inordinate attachment to this present world *The Lord is at hand*, and will soon confound your Jewish adversaries in the destruction of their city and temple, and shortly will put an end to all your trials in the great day of his appearing and glory

5 *Be careful for nothing*, without perplexity or tormenting sollicitude about the concerns of this world, and the difficulties in your way *but in every thing*, at all times, and in all circumstances, *by prayer and supplication with thanksgiving, let your requests be made known unto God*, casting all your care upon him, praising him for all the past mercies you have experienced, and trusting him for whatever may be yet to come *And the peace of God which passeth all understanding, shall keep your hearts and minds through Christ Jesus*, in answer to your prayers God will give you his blessed peace, preserving you sedate and calm amidst every storm, fortifying your minds against every foe, and keeping you in a happy serenity, neither discomposed, nor fainting under any of your troubles, till he brings you to the eternal rest which remaineth for his people in glory *Note*, (1) Though prudent forecast is not forbidden, all anxious fears, that imply distrust of God, and bring torment to the heart, are exceeding sinful (2) Prayer is the antidote to every ill, and whilst we have a throne of grace open, where we can pour all our complaints into the bosom of a compassionate God, however perplexed, we need never be in despair, but should quietly wait to see the salvation of God

6 *Finally, brethren, whatsoever things are true*, agreeable to the word of God, and the dictates of sincerity and truth; *whatsoever things are honest*, venerable and becoming in dress, language, and deportment, *whatsoever things are just*, and equitable in your dealings and transactions, *whatsoever things are pure*, in thought, word, and action, *whatsoever things are lovely*, and render you amiable in the sight of God and man, *whatsoever things are of good report*, among the truly religious, *if there be any virtue*, any thing truly noble, brave, and generous, *if there be any* thing that deserves *praise* and commendation, *think on these things*, and strenuously desire to be found in the exercise of them *Those things which ye have both learned and received, and heard and seen in me, do*, copy after my precepts and practice, *and then the God of peace shall be with you*, and bless you with his presence, and more abundant measures of his grace and love

10 But I rejoiced in the Lord greatly, that now at the last your care of me hath flourished again, wherein ye were also careful, but ye lacked opportunity. 11 Not that I speak in respect of want for I have learned in whatsoever state I am, therewith to be content 12 I know both *how* to be abased, and I know *how* to abound every where, and in all things I am instructed, both to be full and to be hungry, both to abound and to suffer need 13 I can do all things through Christ which strengtheneth me 14 Notwithstanding, ye have well done, that ye did communicate with my affliction 15 Now, ye Philippians, know also, that in the beginning of the gospel, when I departed from Macedonia, no church communicated with me, as concerning giving and receiving, but ye only 16 For even in Thessalonica ye sent once and again unto my necessity 17 Not because

[a] Rom. xv. 28. [illegible] [x] Chap. ii. 25. [y] Heb. xiii. 16. [z] 2 Cor. ix. 12. [a] [illegible] [b] [illegible] Eph. [illegible]

because I desire a gift: but I desire [a] fruit that may
abound to your account. 18 But I have all, and
abound: I am full, having received [x] of Epaphroditus
the things *which were sent* from you, [y] an odour of a
sweet smell, [z] a sacrifice acceptable, well-pleasing to God.
19 But my God [a] shall supply all your need, [b] according
to his riches in glory, by Christ Jesus.

v. 10—19. The Philippians had generously contributed to the apostle's support, and he gratefully mentions it to their honour.

1. He expresses his joy in the present fresh proof they had given of love to him, and regard for the cause of Christ. *But I rejoiced in the Lord greatly, that now at the last your care of me hath flourished again*, and you have added to your former instances of generosity; *wherein ye were also careful*, and would ere this have sent to my relief, *but ye lacked opportunity*.—Though it was a debt they justly owed him, he mentions it as a favour for which he esteemed himself much obliged.

2. He obviates an ill use which might be made of what he said. *Not that I speak in respect of want*, as though I was distrustful of a provision, or uneasy at my worldly circumstances; *for I have learned in whatsoever state I am, therewith to be content*, satisfied in all the will of God. *I know both how to be abased, and how to abound*: in the lowest circumstances composed, in the greatest affluence not elated. *Every where, and in all things I am instructed*, by my divine Master, to accommodate my mind to my situation; *both to be full, and to be hungry; both to abound, and to suffer need*; to know the want of bread without repining, and to have abundance without abusing it to excess. *I can do all things through Christ which strengtheneth me*, and enables me for all the services and sufferings to which in his providence he is pleased to call me. *Notwithstanding, ye have well done, that ye did communicate with my affliction*, in the seasonable relief you kindly sent. *Note*, (1.) Want is a great temptation to murmur, as abundance is to excess; but divine grace will enable us to accommodate our hearts to every circumstance. (2.) Though our strength is very weakness, the omnipotence of Jesus is engaged for us, and then nothing is impracticable.

3. He makes honourable mention of what they had formerly done. *Now ye Philippians, know also, that in the beginning of the gospel, when I departed from Macedonia*, or was *ready to depart*, to other parts, *no church communicated with me, as concerning giving and receiving, but ye only*; *for even in Thessalonica*, a city so much more wealthy than your own, where I was constrained to work hard for my bread, *ye sent once and again unto my necessity*, when my circumstances were very strait, and my wants pressing. *Not that* I mention these things *because I desire a gift*, and want to worm myself into your favour: no such mercenary views influence my conduct; *but I desire fruit that may abound to your account* in the great day of recompence, when these labours of love shall be remembred and rewarded.

4. He acknowledges the receipt of what Epaphroditus brought, and how sufficient it was for his needs; assuring them, that God would accept it as the most grateful sacrifice at their hands. *But I have all* I want, *and abound: I am full, having received of Epaphroditus the things which were sent from you, an odour of a sweet smell, a sacrifice acceptable, well-pleasing to God*, better than the fumes of incense, or the smoak of burnt-offerings. *But*, tho' I cannot repay you in kind, *my God*, who is all-sufficient, *shall supply all your need*, giving you the earthly good things you want, and especially bestowing all spiritual blessings upon you, *according to his riches in glory, by Christ Jesus*, which inestimable treasures he hath laid up for you, and will, through Christ Jesus, minister unto you both in time and eternity. *Note*, None were ever losers by what they lent to the Lord, and employed in the service of his blessed cause.

20 Now unto God our Father *be* glory for ever and
ever. Amen. 21 Salute every saint in Christ Jesus.
[c] The brethren which are with me greet you. 22 All
the saints salute you, [d] chiefly they that are of Cæsar's
houshold. 23 [e] The grace of our Lord Jesus Christ *be*
with you all. Amen.

[c] Gal. [illegible] [d] Chap. i. [illegible] [e] Rom. xvi. 24.

v. 20—23. We have here,

1. An ascription of praise to God. *Now unto God our Father be glory for ever and ever. Amen.* He is our Father to love us, our God abundantly to provide for us. We have long experienced his love and grace; with confidence let us trust him, and ascribe to him the praise we owe for all his past kindness and everlasting promises. *Note*, If God be our Father, we can want no manner of thing that is good.

2. Salutations to the brethren. *Salute every saint in Christ Jesus*, let every member of the church be assured of my most cordial regard, and kindest wishes. *The brethren which are with me greet you* with best remembrances. *All the saints salute you*, and join in Christian respects towards you; *chiefly they that are of Cæsar's houshold*, the domestics of his family, now converted to the faith, and one in affection with you. *Note*, It is a comfort to a real Christian to consider, that multitudes, whom he never saw or knew, bear him upon their hearts, and remember him in their prayers.

3. His closing benediction. *The grace of our Lord Jesus Christ*, in all its incomprehensible extent, and inconceivable fulness, *be with you all*; may the whole church, and every member, share it in the richest abundance. *Amen!*

2

THE

THE

EVANGELICAL EXPOSITOR;

OR, A

PRACTICAL COMMENT

Upon the EPISTLE of

St. PAUL to the COLOSSIANS.

COLOSSE was a considerable city of Phrygia, and probably not far from Laodicea and Hierapolis; we find these three mentioned together, chap iv 13 *It is now buried in ruins, and the memory of it chiefly preserved in this epistle The design of the epistle is to warn them of their danger from the Jewish zealots, who pressed the necessity of observing the ceremonial law, and to fortify them against the mixture of the Gentile philosophy with their Christian principles. He professes a great satisfaction in their stedfastness and constancy, and encourages them to* perseverance *It was written about the same time with the epistle to the Ephesians and Philippians,* Anno Domini 62 *and in the same place, while he was now prisoner at Rome. He was not idle in his confinement, and the word of God* was not bound

Who planted this church is not said, perhaps Epaphras, (chap i 6, 7) *Paul himself appears not yet to have seen them, but what he had heard of them engaged him, as the apostle of the Gentiles, to contribute to their edification*

CHAP. I.

The inscription as usual, ver 1, 2 *His thanksgiving to God for what he had heard concerning them, their faith, love, and hope,* ver 3—8 *He prays for their knowledge, fruitfulness, and strength,* ver 9—11 *Gives them an admirable summary of the Christian doctrine concerning the operation of the Spirit, the person of the Redeemer, the work of redemption, and the preaching of it in the gospel,* ver 12—28

1 PAUL an apostle of Jesus Christ, by the will
of God, and Timotheus *our* brother, 2
To [a] the saints and [b] faithful brethren in
Christ, which are at Colosse [c] Grace *be* unto
you, and peace from God our Father, and the Lord
Jesus Christ

v 1, 2 With his usual introduction the apostle opens his epistle *Paul an apostle of Jesus Christ, by the will of God,* appointed to that eminent honour and office by an immediate commission from heaven, *and Timotheus our brother,* who joins with me in this epistle, *to the saints and faithful brethren in Christ, which are at Colosse,* who are the living members of his body mystical, and in practice correspond with their holy profession, *Grace be unto you, and peace from God our Father, and the Lord Jesus Christ,* may every blessing of pardon, adoption, comfort, strength, perseverance, glory, be your happy portion!

3 [d] We give thanks to God, and the Father of our
Lord Jesus Christ, praying always for you 4 Since
[e] we heard of your faith in Christ Jesus, and of the love
which ye have to all the saints, 5 For the hope [f] which
is laid up for you in heaven, whereof ye heard before in
the word of the truth of the gospel 6 Which is come
unto you, [g] as *it is* in all the world, and [h] bringeth forth
fruit, as *it doth* also in you, since the day ye heard *of it,*
and knew the grace of God in truth 7 As ye also
learned of [i] Epaphras our dear fellow-servant, [k] who is
for you a faithful minister of Christ, 8 Who also declared unto us your [l] love in the Spirit. 9 [m] For this
cause we also, since the day we heard *it,* do not cease to
pray for you, and to desire [n] that ye might be filled
with [o] the knowledge of his will, in all wisdom and spiritual understanding 10 [p] That ye might walk worthy of the Lord [q] unto all pleasing, [r] being fruitful in
every good work, and increasing in the knowledge of
God, 11 [s] Strengthened with all might, according to
his glorious power, [t] unto all patience and long-suffering
[u] with joyfulness,

v 3—11 Though unknown to them in person, yet in heart and affection warmly attached to them, the blessed Paul,

1 Thanks God for the pleasing account which he had heard of them. *We give thanks to God, and the Father of our Lord Jesus Christ,* our reconciled and covenant God in him, *praying always for you,* that you may abide and abound in every thing that is excellent, and blessing God for what he hath already done on your behalf, *since we heard of your faith in Christ Jesus,* and how cordially you embraced his glorious gospel, and rested firm on him alone for acceptance and salvation *and of the love which ye have to all the saints,* the genuine fruit of your faith, and the proof of your unfeigned love to him, whose image they bear, *for the hope which is laid up for you in heaven,* even the eternal blessedness

[a] Rom i 7 Eph i 1 [b] 1 Cor iv 17 Eph vi [c] Gal i 3 1 Cor i 3

[d] 1 Eph i 16 Phil i 3 & iv 1 Thes i 2 [e] Eph i 15 Ibid 5 1 Cor i 1

[g] Mat xxiv 14 Rom x 18 Ver 23 [h] Mark iv 8 John xv 16 [i] Chap iv 12 Phil 23 [k] 2 Cor ii 23 1 Tim iv 6 [l] Rom xv 30 [m] Eph i 15 [n] 1 Cor i 5 [o] Rom xii 2 Eph v 17 [p] Eph iv 1 Phil i 27 [q] 1 Thes ii 12 [r] 1 Thes iv [s] John xv 16 Eph i 11 [t] Eph iii 16 & vi 10 [u] Rom v 3 Acts v 41 Heb x 34

blessedness which God hath prepared and promised, *whereof ye heard before in the word of the truth of the gospel which is come unto you*, through the Divine Providence it hath been preached among you, *as it is in all the world*, throughout the Roman empire, *and bringeth forth fruit*, made effectual by the Divine Power to the conversion of men's souls, *as it doth also in you* producing the most blessed effects, *since the day ye heard of it, and knew the grace of God in truth*, experimentally made acquainted therewith, receiving the gospel both in the light and in the love of it *As ye also learned of Epaphras, our dear fellow servant, who is for you a faithful minister of Christ*, for to his labours you are singularly indebted, *who also declared to us your love in the Spirit*, testifying his warm affection toward you, in the report he made of your unfeigned love to Christ and his people, the evidence of the effectual work of God's Spirit in your souls *Note*, (1) The mercies of which others, who are near and dear to us partake, call for our thankfulness, as well as those which we receive from God ourselves (2) It is a mercy, through Divine Providence, to hear *the word of the truth of the gospel* preached, but the grand matter is to receive it into our hearts, *and to know the grace of God in truth* (3) Wherever Divine Grace operates effectually, it will be seen in the blessed fruits which are produced thereby (4) A *faithful minister* is an invaluable blessing to any people, and highly are they bound to love and honour them

2 To his thanksgivings he adds his hearty prayers *For this cause we also, since the day we heard it, do not cease to pray for you*, (1) That ye may be made wise unto salvation, *and to desire that ye might be filled with the knowledge of his will*, your minds more clearly discerning the riches of his grace your privileges, and the practice of holiness which thence results, advancing *in all wisdom and spiritual understanding* and (2) Disposed to follow in simplicity the light which God bestows, *that ye might walk worthy of the Lord unto all pleasing*, adorning your holy profession by a suitable conversation, and desiring to approve yourselves to the great Master, *being fruitful*, as trees of righteousness, *in every good work* that is for the glory of God, and the benefit of your brethren, *and thus increasing in the knowledge of God* *Note*, As knowledge is essential to all acceptable service, so the more faithfully we improve the grace given unto us, the more fully shall we be let into the secrets of wisdom *For if any man doth his will, he shall know of the doctrine whether it be of God*, John vii 17. (3) We pray that ye may be *strengthened with all might* in the inner man, for the discharge of every duty, and to resist every enemy of your souls, *according to his glorious power*, which can support you abundantly *unto all patience and longsuffering with joyfulness*, bearing up with chearfulness under all persecutions or afflictions which may befal you, neither weary nor desponding, but with holy triumph exulting in the grace you have experienced, and the promises of continual help in every time of need *Note*, (1) All our strength must come from above, and is to be obtained in the way of prayer (2) Every believer, conflicting with sin and Satan, is a living monument of God's glorious power, and, like the burning bush, though compassed with temptations, is not consumed (3) However multiplied, prolonged, or afflictive our trials may be, we are called to exercise *all patience*, and neither to murmur nor faint under them, and hard as the work is, God can enable us for that which he doth command, yea, not only to be resigned, but to rejoice in the midst of tribulations

12 ˣ Giving thanks unto the Father, which hath made
us meet to be partakers of ʸ the inheritance of the saints
in light 13 Who hath delivered us ᶻ from the power
of darkness, and hath translated *us* into the kingdom of
his dear Son 14. ᵃ In whom we have redemption
ᵇ through his blood, *even* ᶜ the forgiveness of sins 15
Who is ᵈ the image of the invisible God, ᵉ the first-born
of every creature 16 For ᶠ by him were all things
created that are in heaven, and that are in earth, visible
and invisible, whether *they be* thrones, or ᵍ dominions, or
principalities, or powers all things were created ʰ by
him, and for him 17 And he is before all things, and
ⁱ by him all things consist 18 And ᵏ he is the head of
the body, the church who is the beginning, ˡ the first-
born from the dead, that in all things he might have the
preeminence. 19. For it pleased *the Father* that ᵐ in him
should all fulness dwell; 20 And (ⁿ having made peace
through the blood of his cross) ᵒ by him to reconcile ᵖ all
things unto himself, by him, *I say*, whether *they be* things
in earth, or things in heaven 21 And you ᵠ that were
sometimes alienated, and enemies in *your* mind ʳ by wicked
works, yet now hath he reconciled, 22 ˢ In the body
of his flesh through death, to present you ᵗ holy and un-
blameable, and unreproveable in his sight 23 ᵘ If ye
continue in the faith ˣ grounded and settled, and be not
moved away from the hope of the gospel, which ye have
heard, *and* ʸ which was preached ᶻ to every creature which
is under heaven, ᵃ whereof I Paul am made a minister
24 Who now rejoice in my sufferings ᶜ for you, and
fill up ᵈ that which is behind of the afflictions of Christ
in my flesh, for ᵉ his body's sake, which is the church
25 Whereof I am made a minister according to ᶠ the dis-
pensation of God, which is given to me for you, † to
fulfil the word of God, 26 *Even* ᵍ the mystery which
hath been hid from ages, and from generations, ʰ but
now is made manifest to his saints 27. ⁱ To whom
God would make known what is ᵏ the riches of the glory
of this mystery among the Gentiles, which is Christ in
you, ˡ the hope of glory 28 Whom we preach, ᵐ warn-
ing every man, and ⁿ teaching every man in all wisdom,
ᵒ that we may present every man perfect in Christ Jesus
29 Whereunto ᵖ I also labour, ᵠ striving according to his
working, which worketh in me mightily

v 12—29 The apostle returns again to thanksgiving,

1 In the view of the inestimable blessings to which they had been admitted *Giving thanks unto the Father, which hath made us meet to be partakers of the inheritance of the saints in light*, by his Spirit renewing our hearts, raising up our affections to high and heavenly things, and preparing us for that glory which he hath prepared for us *Note*, (1) Our inheritance is secured to us in Christ, and comes to us by grace, not by desert, he adopts us as children, and then we become heirs of consequence (2) All, who have this title, are educated as becomes the sons of God, and though the inheritance is sure to them in a covenant of promise, they are made meet for the enjoyment of it and it would be folly and delusion to expect our lot among the saints in light, if we have not our conversation among them here below

2 He gives thanks to God, *who hath delivered us from the power of darkness*, plucking us as brands from the burning, rescuing us from the slavery of sin and Satan, *and hath translated us into the kingdom of his dear Son*, admitting us to the inestimable privileges and blessings of that kingdom of light and grace which Jesus came to erect, that we might be brought under his happy government *Note*, (1) We are by nature slaves of sin and Satan, walking in darkness, and liable each moment to rush into eternal darkness (2) It is an act of sovereign and amazing grace, when God is pleased to pluck the sinner from this miserable state (3) They who are brought into the kingdom of the Son of God's love, will share that love with him, and be made eternally happy thereby

3 He blesses God for the salvation obtained through Christ, *in whom we have redemption through his blood*, including not only deliverance from wrath, but the purchased possession in glory, and, as the present earnest thereof, *the forgiveness of sins*, freely, fully, for ever so that we stand without fault before the throne of God

2 He describes the glorious personage to whom we are indebted for pardon, grace, glory, and every blessing, *who is the image of the invisible God*, one with the Father in essence and perfections, and, as incarnate, appears his visible representative, *the first born of every creature*, begotten before the worlds were, or *the first-begotten* (πρωτότοκος) *of every creature* *For by him were all things created that are in heaven, and that are in earth, visible and invisible*, from the lowest rank of beings to the highest archangel, *whether they be thrones, or dominions, or principalities, or powers*, by whatever names or titles distinguished, whether in heaven or in earth *all things were created by him, and for him*, by his power, and for his glory *And he is before all things*, in eternal pre-existence, *and by him all things consist*, preserved and upheld by his providence and care, as they were spoken into being at his word *And he is the head of the body*, in his peculiar character as mediator, not only as having the dominion over all things, but also as communicating vital influence to the several members, of which *the church* universal is composed *who is the beginning*, the principle of spiritual and eternal life to his people, *the first born from the dead*, who rose by his own power, and is the pledge, cause, and first-fruits of our resurrection, *that in all things he might have the pre-eminence*, exalted far above all creatures, the object of adoration to men and angels, and possessing the first place in their affection and regard *For it pleased the Father*, in consequence of the complete redemption which he hath obtained, *that in him should all fulness dwell* for the use of his church, all fulness of merit, righteousness, grace, gifts, according to their wants, to be freely dispensed to every member of his body mystical *And (having made peace through the blood of his cross*, receiving full satisfaction to his justice, by the oblation of the body of Jesus once for all, and now, consistent with his own glory, being able to extend mercy to the guilty sinner) it pleased the Father *to reconcile all things unto himself*, restoring them from their state of enmity to his forfeited regard, in a way as honourable to him, as happy and safe for them, *by him, I say, whether they be things on earth, or things in heaven*, the members of the church militant here below, or those already entered into rest above How glorious is the cross of Christ beheld in this delightful view! How justly worthy to be the ... and object ever

in our view, since to it we are indebted for all we possess here, and all we hope for hereafter!

3 He mentions with delight the particular interest which they, to whom he wrote, possessed in all the blessings of this glorious redemption *And you, that were sometimes utterly alienated from God, and enemies in your mind by wicked works*, by nature, by practice, rebels against the divine government, *yet now hath he reconciled, in the body of his flesh through death*, receiving you into the arms of his mercy, when drawing near to him by faith, through that new and living way which he hath consecrated through the vail of his crucified body, *to present you holy and unblamable, and unreproveable in his sight*, because accepted in the beloved, and being found in him, complete in the righteousness which he hath provided, the piercing eye of justice can discern no spot, nor wrinkle in you and this will infallibly be your happy case, both now and for ever, *if ye continue in the faith*, and really possess what you profess, or, *since ye continue in the faith*, and have given the strongest proofs of your union with the Lord, *grounded and settled* on him the true foundation, *and be not moved away from the hope of the gospel*, even that substantial hope, which springs from the perfect atonement, complete righteousness, and all sufficient grace secured to you in the great Redeemer, *which blessed gospel ye have*, through peculiar mercy, *heard, and which was preached to every creature which is under heaven*, is a common salvation, alike free for Gentiles as for Jews, and extending to sinners of every kind and condition *Note*, The gospel is grace abounding, none perish because of the greatness of their guilt, but because they reject the only remedy through pride and unbelief, and will not come to Christ, that they might have life

4 Having mentioned the gospel which was preached unto them, among others who were honoured with the dispensation of it, he humbly inserts his own name, *whereof I Paul am made a minister*, by special commission on behalf of the Gentiles *Who now rejoice in my sufferings* for the glorious truths which I have preached unto them, *and fill up that which is behind of the afflictions of Christ in my flesh, for his body's sake, which is the church*, not that the sufferings of Christ were incomplete, and needed any addition to them in order to obtain the redemption of his people, and make satisfaction to Divine Justice, but as the members of his body are all to go through tribulation to glory, I, who was the instrument of their sufferings formerly, now in turn receive my measure of afflictions, and with holy joy triumph under them, when I have cause to hope his church and people shall be profited thereby *whereof I am made a minister*, by a call immediately from heaven, *according to the dispensation of God*, in setting the œconomy of his peculiar family, *which is given to me for you Gentiles, to fulfil the word of God*; which was commanded me, or in correspondence with the prophecies which had foretold your call and conversion, *even the mystery which had been hid from ages, and from generations*, that the Gentiles should be fellow heirs, *but now is made manifest to his saints*, his prophets and apostles, and by them to all the faithful *to whom God would make known what is the riches of the glory of this mystery among the Gentiles*, who should be admitted to the participation of all the invaluable privileges of the gospel, the author, purchaser, and dispenser of *which is Christ in you*, formed in your hearts by faith, *the hope of glory whom we preach* as the only Saviour of the miserable and desperate, *warning every man* of the mortal danger of sin, and his inevitable ruin out of Christ, *and teaching every man in all wisdom* concerning the only method of safety, even faith in a crucified Saviour, *that we may present every man perfect in Christ Jesus*, complete in him as their head, and grown up to the perfection of knowledge, grace, and holiness, in the day of his appearing and glory *whereunto I also labour, striving* with every nerve, in the midst of opposing enemies, *according to his working which worketh in me mightily*, who enables me for the conflict, and crown my labours with success.

CHAP II

The apostle's concern for the Colossians, ver 1—4 *Repeated again*, ver 5 *He cautions them against false teachers among the Jews*, ver 6—8 *And against the Gentile philosophy*, ver 9—13 *Represents the privileges of Christians*, ver 14—16 *And concludes with a caution against the judaizing teachers, and those who would introduce the worship of angels*, ver 17—22

1 FOR I would that ye knew what great ᵃ conflict I — ᵃ Chap i 29
have for you, and *for* them at Laodicea, and *for* — Phil i 30
as many as have not seen my face in the flesh 2 ᵇ That — 1 Thes ii 2
their hearts might be comforted, ᶜ being knit together — ᵇ Chap i 6
in love, and unto all riches of the full assurance of un- — ᶜ Chap iii 14
derstanding, ᵈ to the acknowledgment of the mystery of — ᵈ Phil iii 8
God, and of the Father, and of Christ 3 In whom — 1 Cor i 24 Chap
are hid all the treasures of wisdom and knowledge — i 9

v 1—3 Though the apostle had no personal knowledge of the Colossians, the report he had heard engaged his warmest affections towards them *For I would that ye knew what great conflict I have for you*, how sollicitous I am for your welfare, and wrestle earnestly with God in prayer on your behalf, *and for them at Laodicea, and for as many as have not seen my face in the flesh* And this especially I ask of the Lord, *that their hearts might be comforted* under every trial, with those consolations which he bestows on his chosen, *being knit together in love* to Christ, and one another, *and unto all riches of the full assurance of understanding*, seeking to attain the most distinct and comprehensive knowledge of the gospel, with all its invaluable privileges, *to the acknowledgment of the mystery of God, and of the Father, and of Christ*, testifying the fullest approbation of that glorious scheme of salvation, which, though unknown before, is now revealed to the Gentiles, wherein God appears as their reconciled God and Father in Christ, the covenant-head of his redeemed *In whom are hid all the treasures of wisdom and knowledge*, for the use of his people, that he might so order all the dispensations of his providence and grace, as most effectually to conduct them into amidst all their difficulties to his eternal kingdom *Note*, (1) It is God's will that his people should be comforted, and for this his ministers should labour (2) Nothing tends more to cause our consolations to abound than the union of our hearts to Jesus, and to our brethren, in love unfeigned (3) Whatever remaining ignorance be in us, or darkness surround our steps, he who hath all the treasures of wisdom is our guide, and he will lead us by the right way

4 And this I say, ᶠ lest any man should beguile you — ᶠ Eph v 6
ᵍ with enticing words 5 For ʰ though I be absent in — Ver 18
the flesh, yet am I with you in the spirit, joying and — ᵍ Rom xvi 18
beholding ⁱ your order, and the stedfastness of your faith — ʰ 1 Cor v 3
in Christ 6 ᵏ As ye have therefore received Christ Je- — 1 Thes ii 17
sus the Lord, *so* walk ye in him 7 ˡ Rooted and built — ⁱ 1 Cor xiv 40
up in him, and stablished in the faith, as ye have been — ᵏ 1 Thes iv 1
taught, abounding therein with thanksgiving 8 ᵐ Be- — Jude iii
ware lest any man spoil you through philosophy and vain — ˡ Eph ii 21
deceit, after ⁿ the tradition of men, after ᵒ the rudiments — 22 & iii 17
of the world, and not after Christ 9 For ᵖ in him — ᵐ Jer xxix 8
dwelleth all the fulness of the Godhead bodily 10 And — Rom xvi 17
ᵠ ye are complete in him, ʳ which is the head of all — Heb xiii 9
principality and power 11 In whom also ye are ˢ cir — ⁿ Mat xv 2
cumcised with the circumcision made without hands, in — Gal i 14
ᵗ putting off the body of the sins of the flesh, by the — Ver 2
circumcision of Christ 12 ᵘ Buried with him in bap- — ᵒ Gal iv 3, 9 Ver 20
tism, wherein also you are risen with *him* through ˣ the — ᵖ Chap i 19
faith † of the operation of God, ʸ who hath raised him — ᵠ John i 16
from the dead 13 And ᶻ you being dead in your sins, — ʳ Eph i 21
and the uncircumcision of your flesh, hath he quickened — 1 Pet iii 22
together with him, having forgiven you all trespasses — ˢ Deut xxx 6 Jer iv 4
14 ᵃ Blotting out the hand-writing of ordinances that — Rom ii 29 Phil iii 3
was against us, which was contrary to us, and ᵇ took it — ᵗ Rom vi 6
out of the way, nailing it to his cross 15 And ᶜ ha- — Eph iv 22 Chap iii 8, 9
ving spoiled ᵈ principalities and powers, he made a shew — ᵘ Rom vi 4
of them openly, triumphing over them in it — ˣ Eph i 19 & iii 7

† Or in, or upon — Mark xi 22 — ʸ Acts ii 24 — ᶻ Eph ii 1, 5, 11 — ᵃ Eph ii 15, 16 — ᵇ Heb vii 18 & x 9 — ᶜ Gen iii 15 Ps lxviii 18 Isa liii 12 Mat xii 29 Luke x 18 John xii 31 & xvi 11 — ᵈ Eph iv 8 — Eph vi 12

v 4—15 The apostle felt the tenderest concern for them, and he testifies it by his jealousy over them

1 He warns them against the seducing, judaizing teachers *And this I say*, concerning my affection for you, and the all-sufficient wisdom of Jesus to direct you, *lest*, as Satan beguiled Eve through his subtilty, *any man should beguile you with enticing words*, perverting you from the simplicity of the gospel, under pretence of leading you to higher attainments *For though I be absent in the flesh, yet am I with you in the Spirit*; not only united to them in affection, but probably having some extraordinary discernment of their state from the Lord, *joying and beholding your order* and strict discipline, *and the stedfastness of your faith in Christ*, notwithstanding all the shocks of persecution, or the wiles of deceivers *As ye have therefore received Christ Jesus the Lord*, and made profession of your entire dependance upon him as your Prophet, Priest, and King, *so walk ye in him*, depending on the teachings of his word and Spirit, trusting on his atonement and righteousness, and desirous to obey his holy will in all things *rooted* as the tree, which no winds can blow down, *and built up in him, and stablished in the faith*, fixed immoveably on the rock of ages, and by faith growing up into him in all things who is the head, even Christ, *as ye have been taught* in the gospel preached to you, *abounding therein with thanksgiving*, enriched with all the fulness of divine grace, and excelling in praise to the great author of all your hope and happiness *Beware*, therefore, since ye have received the truth as it is in Jesus, *lest any man spoil you* of the inestimable treasure *through philosophy and vain deceit*, according to the corrupt systems of heathenism, misleading you from the purity of the gospel, *after the tradition of men*, whether of judaizing teachers or Gentile sages, *after the rudiments of the world*, those first elements, (*See on*) contained in the Mosaic œconomy, and suited only to the infant state of the church, *and which are not after Christ*, but tend to seduce the

heart from him, to direct the soul to rest on something else for salvation, besides his finished work, *in whom dwelleth all the fulness of the Godhead bodily*, all the divine perfections being, in their utmost fulness, perpetually resident in the person of the incarnate Jesus *Note*, (1) The discourse set off, with the most enticing words, must be brought to the test of God's revealed will, and if it correspond not therewith, whatever appearances of wisdom there may be, it is to be rejected with abhorrence (2) They who cleave to Christ, shall be preserved from delusion (3) He who is God as well as man in one Christ, must needs be able to save to the uttermost, and be the worthy object of our entire faith and dependance

2 He mentions the complete salvation, of which, in Christ, they had been made partakers *And ye are complete in him*, in virtue of your union with him, who is made of God unto you wisdom and righteousness, and sanctification and redemption, and *who is*, in his mediatorial character, *the head of all principality and power*, all in heaven, earth, and hell, from the highest creature to the lowest, being made subject unto him *In whom also ye are circumcised with the circumcision*, not that which is outward in the flesh, and now of no avail, but that *made without hands*, even the circumcision of the heart, evident *in the putting off the body of the sins of the flesh*, and mortifying the old man, which is corrupt, with the affections and lusts, *by the circumcision of Christ*, which he is the author of, and by his Spirit effects in the hearts of his people *Buried with him by baptism*, the ordinance which he hath instituted, superseding circumcision, and signifying to us our death unto sin, and new birth unto righteousness, *wherein also ye are risen with him*, quickened to newness of life, *through the faith of the operation of God, who hath raised him from the dead* The same divine power being needful to produce faith in the heart of the sinner, as to communicate life to the dead body of Jesus *And you being dead in your sins*, under the sentence of God's wrath, and separated from his favour, which is the true life of the soul, *and in the uncircumcision of your flesh*, serving divers lusts and pleasures, under the dominion of a corrupted nature, *hath he quickened together with him*, to a life of grace here, as the earnest and beginning of a life of glory in eternity, *having forgiven you all trespasses*, in virtue of the redemption of Jesus *Blotting out the hand-writing of ordinances that was against us, which was contrary to us*, by his blood cancelling the debt, and obliterating the bond, discharging us from the condemnation of the *moral* law, and abolishing the *ceremonial*, which separated Jews and Gentiles, and was the cause of enmity between them, *and took it out of the way, nailing it to his cross*, and rending it in pieces, *and having spoiled principalities and powers*, the apostate spirits of darkness, *he made a shew of them openly*, as their conqueror, on the tree, *triumphing over them in it*, and redeeming all his people thereby from their hateful dominion

How invaluable are the Christian's privileges! How precious should he be to us, who is the blessed author of them! (1) We are quickened by him from the death of sin (2) We have the free and full remission of all our iniquities (3) The curse of the law is satisfied, and there is no condemnation to those who are in Christ Jesus (4) Our spiritual enemies are vanquished, we need fear nothing from them, our Jesus is triumphant, and he will shortly make us, with himself, more than conquerors

16 Let no man therefore judge you ᵉ in meat or in
drink, or in respect ᶠ of an holy day, or of the new-
moon, or of the sabbath-*days* 17 ᵍ Which are a sha-
dow of things to come, but the body *is* of Christ 18
ʰ Let no man beguile you of your reward, in a voluntary
humility, and worshipping of angels, intruding into those
things ⁱ which he hath not seen, vainly puffed up by his
fleshly mind, 19 And not holding ᵏ the head, from
which all the body by joints and bands having nourish-
ment ministred, and knit together, increaseth with the
increase of God. 20 Wherefore if ye be ˡ dead with
Christ from ᵐ the rudiments of the world, ⁿ why, as
though living in the world, are ye subject to ordinances,
21 (ᵒ Touch not, taste not, handle not 22 ᵖ Which
all are to perish with the using) ᵠ after the command-
ments and doctrines of men? 23 Which things have
indeed a shew of wisdom in ʳ will worship and humility,
and neglecting of the body, not in any honour to the
satisfying of the flesh

ᵉ Rom xiv 2, 10, 17 ᶠ Gal iv 10 ᵍ Heb viii 5, & ix 9 & x 1 ʰ Ver 4 ⁱ Thes ii 3 Ezek xiii 3 1 Tim. 1 7 ᵏ Eph iv 15, 16 ˡ Rom vi 3, 5 vii 4, 6 Gal ii 19 ᵐ Ver 8 ⁿ Gal iv 3 ᵒ Rom xiv 1 ᵖ 1 Cor vi 13 ᵠ Isa xxix 13 Mat xv 9 Tit i 14 ʳ Ver 18

v 16—23 The apostle, from the foregoing consideration of the complete redemption which in Christ Jesus they had obtained, warns them against the judaizing zealot.

Let no man therefore judge or condemn you in meat or in drink, or in respect of an holy day, or of the new moon, or of the sabbath days, insisting on the necessity of observing their Jewish ceremonies, in order to salvation *which are a shadow of things to come, but the body is of Christ*, since he who is the substance of them hath appeared, they are now abolished, and no longer obligatory *Let no man beguile you of your reward*, or cheat you of the prize of your high calling in Christ Jesus, *in a voluntary humility*, leading you to a kind of abasement which the gospel never prescribed, *and worshipping of angels*, to the great dishonour of the one Mediator between God and man, *intruding into those things which he hath not seen, vainly puffed up by his fleshly mind*, falsely pretending to what he is ignorant of, and following the delusions of a heart eaten up with pride *and not holding the head*, Christ Jesus, *from whom alone the whole body* of his church, *by joints and bands having nourishment ministered, and knit together*, spiritually, as the members of the natural body are united to their common head, *increaseth with the increase of God*, in light, and love, and comfort, and holiness *Wherefore if*, or seeing, *ye be dead with Christ*, as your baptism intimated, *from the rudiments of the world*, and discharged from all obligation to the Mosaic œconomy, *why, as though living in the world*, and still under the legal dispensation, *are ye subject to ordinances*, and obey the dogmatical decisions of judaizing teachers, who cry, *Touch not, taste not, handle not*, as if the Levitical law was still in force, and the distinction of meats and drinks to be scrupulously observed by Christians, *which* meats *all perish with the using*, passing through the body, and cannot defile the soul, and are now no longer enjoined of divine authority, but merely *after the commandments and doctrines of men*, by these Jewish zealots? *Which things have indeed a shew of wisdom*, and pass under the specious pretence of paying to God service, even of supererogation, *in will-worship, and voluntary humility*, when his word hath never enjoined, *and neglecting of the body*, by affected austerities, *not in any honour*, these things are *not of any value* in the sight of God, but are *to the satisfying of the flesh*, serving only to foster man's pride, and to flatter him in a vain conceit of his own superior goodness *Note*, They who affect to be wise above what is written, will only in the issue expose their own absurd pride and egregious folly

CHAP III

The apostle exhorts us to set our hearts upon heaven, and take them off from this world, ver 1—4 *He exhorts to the mortification of sin, in the various instances of it*, ver 5—12 *and earnestly presses to mutual love and compassion*, ver 12—17 *And concludes with exhortations to relative duties, of wives and husbands, parents and children, masters and servants*, ver 18—25

1 IF ye then ᵃ be risen with Christ, seek those things
which are above, where ᵇ Christ sitteth on the right
hand of God 2 Set your affection ᶜ on things above,
not on things on the earth 3 For ᵈ ye are dead, and
your life is hid with Christ in God 4 When Christ
who is our life shall appear, ᵉ then shall ye also appear
ᶠ with him ᵍ in glory

ᵃ Rom vi 5 Eph ii 6 Chap ii 12 ᵇ Ps cx 1 Rom viii 34 Eph i 20 ᶜ John … ᵈ Rom vi 2 Gal ii 20 Chap ii 20 ᵉ John xi 25 ᶠ 1 Cor xv 51 ᶠ 1 Thes iv 17 ᵍ 1 Cor xv 43 Phil iii 21 1 John iii 2

v 1—4 The apostle having, in the former chapter, laid down the great fundamental doctrines of Christianity, and the invaluable privileges of true believers, proceeds here to exhort the Colossians to those tempers and practices which became their holy profession

1 He exhorts them to heavenly-mindedness *If ye then be risen with Christ*, in virtue of his resurrection, and of your union with him, *seek those things which are above*, even the eternal blessedness provided for you in heaven, *where Christ sitteth on the right hand of God*, gone before to prepare a place for you, and ever living to make intercession for you Therefore *set your affections on things above*, with faith, hope, and love, aspire after them, realizing them to your mind by frequent meditation and fervent prayer, seeking those influences of grace which may conduct you to the glory which shall be revealed, *and not on things on the earth*, whether Jewish ordinances, or earthly advantages and allurements, keep these under your feet, be weaned from them, and daily dying to them *Note*, A worldly mind, and a heavenly hope, are utterly inconsistent, no man can serve two masters

2 He supports his exhortation by the most powerful arguments *For ye are dead*, by your profession in baptism, and your obligations to a crucified Jesus, *and your life is hid with Christ*, both *your spiritual life*, with all its joys, is hid from the natural man, and by secret communications from your exalted head is still maintained till it shall be perfected above, *and your eternal life* is secured in him according to the secret purposes of God from the beginning, therefore, having such glorious expectations, look up, and live continually under the influence of them And then, *when Christ, who is our life*, the author, supporter, and finisher of it, *shall appear* in the great day of his second coming, *then shall ye also appear with him in glory*, and how much then doth it behove us to have our affections placed there, where we hope to spend an eternity with Christ in blessedness inconceivable!

5 ʰ Mortify therefore ⁱ your members which are up-
on the earth, ᵏ fornication, uncleanness, inordinate af-
fection, ˡ evil concupiscence, and covetousness, ᵐ which is
idolatry 6 ⁿ For which things sake the wrath of God

ʰ Rom viii 13 Gal v 24 ⁱ Rom vi 13 ᵏ Eph v 3 1 Thes iv 5 ⁿ Eph v 6 …

cometh

cometh on [b] the children of diſobedience 7 [p] In the
which ye alſo walked ſometime when ye lived in them
8 But [q] now you alſo put off all theſe, anger, wrath,
malice, blaſphemy, [r] filthy communication out of your
mouth 9 [s] Lye not one to another, [t] ſeeing that ye
have put off the old man with his deeds, 10 And
have put on the new man, [u] which is renewed in know-
ledge, [x] after the image of him [y] that created him 11
Where [z] there is neither Greek nor Jew, circumciſion nor
uncircumciſion, barbarian, Scythian, bond nor free but
Chriſt is all, and in all

o Eph ii 2. p Rom vi … 1 Cor vi 11. Tit iii 3. 1 Pet iv 3. q Eph iv 22. Jam i 21. 1 Pet ii 1. r Eph iv 29. & v 4. s Lev xix 11. Eph iv 25. Rev xxii 15. t Eph iv 22, 24. u Rom xii 2. x Gen i 26. Eph iv 24. y Eph ii 10. z Rom x 12. 1 Cor xii 13. Gal iii 28. & v 6. & vi 15.

v 5—11 If we would ſet our affections on things in heaven, our ſenſual and carnal affections muſt be mortified, and hereunto the apoſtle earneſtly exhorts them *Mortify therefore your members which are upon earth,* the remaining corruptions that ſtill war againſt you, ſuch as *fornication, uncleanneſs, inordinate affection, evil concupiſcence,* with every thought, word, or action, that hath the remoteſt tendency to excite impure deſire, *and covetouſneſs,* with every worldly luſt, *which is idolatry,* as it engages the heart to the creature, drawing it off from the love and ſervice of the Creator *for which things ſake the wrath of God cometh on the children of diſobedience,* and the conſequences of theſe ſins will infallibly be eternal death *In the which ye alſo,* as other Gentiles, *walked ſometime when ye lived in them* But now, ſince the light and grace of the bleſſed goſpel hath reached you, *ye alſo put off all theſe, anger, wrath, malice, blaſphemy,* ſpeaking reproachfully of God or things ſacred, or whatever would blaſt the reputation of others; and let no *filthy communication,* or immodeſt expreſſion, proceed *out of your mouth* *Lye not one to another,* but ever, in all your converſation, ſpeak the truth from your heart, and be faithful to every promiſe and engagement, *ſeeing that ye have put off the old man with his deeds,* the native corruption which came with you into the world, and works to bring forth fruit unto death, till ſubdued by the power of divine grace, *and ye have put on the new man, which is renewed in knowledge after the image of him that created him,* the heart, by the powerful operations of the Spirit, being renewed after the likeneſs of Jeſus the Creator, in light and holineſs, and his image defaced by the fall being now reſtored by efficacious grace *Where,* in this new creation, *there is neither Greek nor Jew, circumciſion nor uncircumciſion, barbarian, Scythian, bond nor free,* all diſtinction of nations, names, conditions, and external privileges is now aboliſhed *but Chriſt is all in all,* in him, all who believe, are *complete,* he is all to them in *wiſdom,* they need no other teacher, *all in righteouſneſs,* they want no commendation to God's favour but being found in him, all in *ſanctification,* their whole ſufficiency being derived from him, as the fountain of grace, all in *redemption,* as he hath by one oblation perfected for ever his people, and obtained, purely on account of what he hath done for them, all bleſſings in time and eternity *Note,* (1) We muſt mortify ſin, or ſin will eternally deſtroy us (2) Nothing is more dangerous than fleſhly luſts, which war againſt the ſoul, unleſs it be the corroding canker of covetouſneſs, which, though it may leſs ſhock the conſcience, is as fatally ruinous to the ſoul (3) The longer we have lived in ſin, the more urgently are we called to awake to newneſs of life, the time paſt may ſurely ſuffice to have wrought the will of the fleſh (4) Anger, malice, ſlander, and lies, are the ſtrongeſt lineaments of him who was a liar and murderer from the beginning (5) If we belong to Chriſt, we muſt prove it by the conformity of our temper and conduct to his, he that abideth in him, ought himſelf to walk as Chriſt alſo walked (6) If Chriſt be to us *all in all,* then are we bound to aſcribe to him the glory of all our ſalvation

12 [a] Put on therefore ([b] as the elect of God, holy and
beloved) [c] bowels of mercies, kindneſs, humbleneſs of
mind, meekneſs, long ſuffering, 13 Forbearing one
another, and [f] forgiving one another, if any man have a
quarrel againſt any [g] even as Chriſt forgave you, ſo
alſo do ye 14 [h] And above all theſe things [g] *put on* cha-
rity, which is [i] the bond of perfectneſs 15 [k] And let the
peace of God rule in your hearts, to the which alſo ye
are called [h] in one body, and be ye thankful. 16. Let
the word of Chriſt dwell in you richly in all wiſdom;
teaching and admoniſhing one another [l] in pſalms, and
hymns, and ſpiritual ſongs, ſinging [m] with grace in your
hearts to the Lord 17 And [n] whatſoever ye do in word
or deed, *do* all in the name of the Lord Jeſus, [o] giving
thanks to God and the Father by him

a Eph iv 24. … Theſ … e Eph iv 2. … Eph iv 3. … John xiii … Rom … Eph … Chap … John iv 21. Eph iv 3. … Chap … 1 Cor xiv 6. … Eph v 6. … Rom i 8. Eph v 20. 1 Theſ v 18. Heb …

v 12—17 The apoſtle proceeds to enforce the practice of all godlineſs upon them, as thoſe who were choſen in Chriſt Jeſus, *as the elect of God,* ordained to be *holy, and being beloved* by him, ſhould approve themſelves before him

1 *Put on therefore bowels of mercies,* ſuch as were in Jeſus Chriſt, towards the miſerable and afflicted, *kindneſs* in every word and deed, *humbleneſs of mind,* lowly in your own thoughts of yourſelves, and condeſcending to others, *meekneſs,* quietly ſubmitting to the diſpenſations of Providence, and enduring patiently every reproach and indignity, *long ſuffering* under repeated and aggravated provocations, *forbearing one another* under your ſeveral infirmities, *and forgiving one another* every offence or injury, *if any man have a quarrel againſt any even as Chriſt forgave you, ſo alſo do ye,* whoſe amazing grace to us ſhould powerfully engage our hearts to paſs by each other's tranſgreſſions, and not only to forgive, but to blot out of our remembrance every paſt offence *And*

2 *Above all theſe things,* as that which is moſt ſingularly neceſſary, or *over all theſe things,* as what ſets them off in their brighteſt luſtre, *put on charity,* that divine principle of all that is excellent, *which is the bond of perfectneſs,* uniting the whole body of the church together, and moſt effectual to preſerve them until they arrive at the perfection of holineſs and happineſs

3 *And let the peace of God rule in your hearts,* being at peace with him, carefully cultivate peace with each other, and let a ſenſe of his reconciliation to you ſway your hearts to mutual love and forbearance, *to the which alſo ye are called in one body,* as together united to Chriſt your common head, *and be ye thankful* for this invaluable bleſſing

4 *Let the word of Chriſt,* his bleſſed goſpel, *dwell in you richly* abiding in your hearts, the ſubject of your conſtant meditations, and delightful converſe, eſteem it as your moſt invaluable treaſure, and ſtore up the knowledge of it in your hearts, *in all wiſdom,* ready for uſe on every proper occaſion

5 As united in love, be *teaching and admoniſhing one another in pſalms, and hymns, and ſpiritual ſongs, ſinging with grace in your hearts to the Lord,* building up each other thus in your moſt holy faith, and helping forward your mutual joy in God, and his bleſſed ſervice *Note,* It is not the muſic of the voice, but the ſinging with grace in the heart which is the acceptable praiſe

6 *And whatſoever ye do in word or deed, do all in the name of the Lord Jeſus,* under the influence of his grace, with a regard to his will, and a ſingle eye to his glory, expecting the acceptance of every ſervice for his ſake alone, *giving thanks to God and the Father by him,* in whom our praiſes and prayers come up before the throne as ſacrifices of a ſweet ſmell *Note,* A Chriſtian can never want matter of praiſe, whenever he turns his thoughts towards the Lord Jeſus

18 [p] Wives, ſubmit yourſelves unto your own huſ-
bands, as it is fit in the Lord, 19 [q] Huſbands, love
your wives, and be not [r] bitter againſt them 20 [s] Chil-
dren, obey *your* parents in all things for this is well-
pleaſing unto the Lord 21. [t] Fathers, provoke not your
children *to anger,* leſt they be diſcouraged 22 [u] Ser-
vants, obey in all things *your* maſters [x] according to the
fleſh, not with eye-ſervice, as men-pleaſers, but in ſingle-
neſs of heart, fearing God 23 And [y] whatſoever ye
do, do it heartily, as to the Lord, and not unto men;
24 [z] Knowing that of the Lord ye ſhall receive the re-
ward of the inheritance for [a] ye ſerve the Lord Chriſt.
25 But he that doth wrong, ſhall receive for the wrong
which he hath done and [b] there is no reſpect of perſons

p Eph v 22. Tit ii 5. 1 Pet iii 1, 5. q Eph v 25, 28. 1 Pet iii 7. r Eph iv 31. s Eph vi 1. t Eph vi 4. u Eph vi 5, &c. 1 Tim vi 1. Tit ii 9. 1 Pet ii 18. x Philem 16. y Eph vi 6, 7. z Eph vi 8. a 1 Cor vii 22. b Acts x 34. Rom ii 11. Eph vi 9. 1 Pet i 17.

v 18—25 The apoſtle paſſes on to inculcate the diſcharge of the great relative duties, and he begins, as before, (*Eph* v 22) with the inferior relation, as ſubjection is peculiarly hard for creatures, who are naturally under the power of a ſpirit of pride and independence We have,

1 The duty of *wives* *Submit yourſelves unto your own huſbands,* be under their government, *as it is fit in the Lord,* according to the law of creation, and the divine conſtitution, obedient in all things which are not immediately inconſiſtent with your duty to the Lord Jeſus

2 The duty of *huſbands* *Love your wives* with all tenderneſs and ſingleneſs of affection, delighting in their company, and ſtudying to make them happy in their relation to you, *and be not bitter againſt them,* croſs, haſty, arbitrary, ſevere, with frowns or wrath, or ill uſage, making their yoke heavy

3 The duty of *children* *Obey your parents in all things* that are lawful, neither murmuring nor diſputing againſt their commands, or diſpoſals, *for this is well-pleaſing unto the Lord,* and a happy proof of your relation to the Father of Mercies

4 The duty of parents *Fathers, provoke not your children to anger,* by needleſs ſeverities, arbitrary reſtraints, harſh commands, and unreaſonable impoſitions, *leſt they be diſcouraged,* their ſpirits broken with ſuch treatment, and, through deſpair of pleaſing, they ſhould deſiſt even from the attempt.

5 The duty of *ſervants* *Obey in all things your maſters according to the fleſh,* whether Gentile or Chriſtian, diligent to obſerve all their juſt commands, *not with eye ſervice, as men-pleaſers,* merely whilſt they are looking on you, *but in ſingleneſs of heart, fearing God,* and equally faithful in the diſcharge of your duty when no eye ſeeth you but his, to whom it is your ſpecial care to approve yourſelves *and whatſoever ye do, do it heartily,* working with willingneſs and aſſiduity, *as to the Lord,* for his glory, *and not unto men,* merely with a view to their applauſe, *knowing that of the Lord ye ſhall receive the reward of the inheritance,* when the great Maſter ſhall appear to recompenſe the fidelity of his ſervants, in whatever condition or rank they have been placed

by him *for ye ſerve the Lord Chriſt*, and whatſoever ſervice ye do to them with a view to his honour, he will regard it as immediately rendered to himſelf, and reward it accordingly *But he that doth wrong* to his maſter, by fraud, connivance, ſloth, or negligence, *ſhall receive for the wrong which he hath done* the puniſhment due to his injuſtice *and there is no reſpect of perſons* with God, the meaneſt, at his bar, being accountable as well as the greateſt, and ſhall receive ſentence according to their deeds

CHAP IV.

He continues his account of the duty of maſters, from the cloſe of the former chapter, ver 1, 2 Exhorts to the duty of prayer, ver 3, 4 And to a prudent and decent carriage towards thoſe with whom we converſe, ver 5, 6 Cloſes the epiſtle with the mention of ſeveral of his friends, of whom he gives an honourable teſtimony, ver 7—18

a Eph vi 9 1 ^a MASTERS, give unto *your* ſervants that which is juſt and equal, knowing that ye alſo have a Maſter in heaven

v 1 This verſe ſhould moſt properly have cloſed the foregoing chapter, as it contains the duty of *maſters* *Give unto your ſervants that which is juſt and equal*, not treating them tyrannically, nor laying on them unreaſonable burdens, but uſing them kindly, giving them proper proviſion, paying them their wages punctually, according to agreement, and as much as they really deſerve, *knowing that ye alſo have a Maſter in heaven*, to whom you are reſponſible, and who regardeth the perſons of the rich no more than the poor

b Luke xviii 1 Rom xii 12 Eph vi 18 1 Theſ v 17 c Eph vi 19 2 Theſ iii 1 d 1 Cor xvi 9 2 Cor ii 12 e Mat xiii 11 1 Cor iv 1 Eph vi 19 Chap i 26 & ii 2 f Eph iii 1, Phila 7 13 g Eph v 15 1 Theſ iv 12 h Eph v 16. Eccleſ x 12 Chap iii 16 k Mark ix 50 l 1 Pet iii 15

2 ^b Continue in prayer, and watch in the ſame with
thankſgiving, 3 Withal, ^c praying alſo for us, that
God would ^d open unto us a door of utterance, to ſpeak
^e the myſtery of Chriſt, for which ^f I am alſo in bonds
4 That I may make it manifeſt, as I ought to ſpeak
5 ^g Walk in wiſdom toward them that are without,
^h redeeming the time 6 Let your ſpeech *be* alway
^i with grace, ^k ſeaſoned with ſalt, ^l that ye may know
how ye ought to anſwer every man

v 2—6 The apoſtle, having laid down the particular duties of each ſtation, proceeds to thoſe that more generally belong to all the members of Chriſt's church He exhorts them,

1 To unceaſing prayer *Continue in prayer* duly, at ſtated ſeaſons, and habitually in your mind diſpoſed to look up to God, *and watch in the ſame with thankſgiving*, engaged in the ſervice with warm affections, and intenſeneſs of mind, bleſſing and praiſing God for his goodneſs continually, *withal, praying alſo for us, that God would open unto us a door of utterance*, and give us both opportunity and ability *to ſpeak the myſtery of Chriſt*, his rich, free, and boundleſs grace, revealed to Gentiles as well as Jews, *for maintaining which I am alſo now in bonds* *that I may make it manifeſt, as I ought to ſpeak*, plainly and without reſerve, maintaining the equality of the Gentiles reſpecting all the privileges of the goſpel, and keeping back nothing of all the counſel of God, as becomes a faithful ambaſſador of Chriſt *Note*, Miniſters need their peoples prayers, and ſhould be conſtantly remembered by them in the view of their arduous work

2 To a becoming carriage towards thoſe who are as yet out of the pale of the church *Walk in wiſdom towards them who are without*, with all prudence and circumſpection, giving them no juſt occaſion of offence, guarding againſt all fellowſhip with them in what is evil, whilſt ready to every good word and work to do them ſervice, *redeeming the time*, deſiring to improve every opportunity of converſe with them for their benefit, and careful to avoid whatever might unneceſſarily provoke their malice and perſecution, and be the means to cut you off from life and uſefulneſs

3 *Let your ſpeech be alway with grace, ſeaſoned with ſalt*, edifying, diſcreet, and ſavoury, the proof of true grace in your own hearts, and the means of communicating it to others, *that ye may know how ye ought to anſwer every man*, whether the ſerious enquiries of thoſe who deſire inſtruction, the doubts of the ſcrupulous, or the cavils of adverſaries

m Eph vi 21 2

7 ^m All my ſtate ſhall Tychicus declare unto you,
who is a beloved brother, and a faithful miniſter, and
fellow ſervant in the Lord 8 Whom I have ſent unto
you for the ſame purpoſe, that he might know your
eſtate, and comfort your hearts 9 With ^n Oneſimus a
faithful and beloved brother, who is one of you They
ſhall make known unto you all things which *are done*
here 10 ^o Ariſtarchus my fellow priſoner ſaluteth you,
and ^p Marcus ſiſter's ſon to Barnabas (touching whom ye
received commandments if he come unto you, receive
him) 11 And Jeſus, which is called Juſtus, who are of
the circumciſion Theſe only *are my* fellow-workers
unto the kingdom of God, which have been a comfort
unto me 12 ^q Epaphras, who is one of you, a ſervant
of Chriſt, ſaluteth you, ^r always labouring fervently for
you in prayers, that ye may ſtand ^s perfect and complete
in all the will of God 13 For I bear him record,
that he hath a great zeal for you, and them that are
in Laodicea, and them in Hierapolis. 14 ^s Luke the
beloved phyſician, and ^t Demas greet you 15 Salute
the brethren which are in Laodicea and Nymphas,
and ^u the church which is in his houſe 16 And when
^x this epiſtle is read amongſt you, cauſe that it be read
alſo in the church of the Laodiceans, and that ye like-
wiſe read the epiſtle from Laodicea 17 And ſay to
^y Archippus, ^z Take heed to the miniſtry which thou haſt
received in the Lord, ^a that thou fulfil it 18 ^b The ſa-
lutation by the hand of me Paul ^c Remember my
bonds Grace *be* with you Amen

n Philem 10 o Acts xix 29 & xxvii 2 Philem 24 p Acts xv 37 2 Tim iv 11 q Chap i 7 Philem 23

s 2 Tim iv 11 t 2 Tim iv 10 u Rom xvi 5 1 Cor xvi 19 x 1 Theſ v 27 y Philem 2 z 1 Tim iv 16 a Rom xv 19 Chap i 25 b 1 Cor xvi 21 2 Theſ iii 17 c Heb xiii 3

v 7—18 The apoſtle cloſes his epiſtle with the commendation, and reſpectful mention of ſeveral of his brethren, who joined in ſalutations with him

1. Tychicus *All my ſtate ſhall Tychicus declare unto you*, the bearer of this epiſtle, *who* will give you a faithful account of my affairs, ſufferings, ſucceſs, and *is a beloved brother* in the goſpel, *and a faithful miniſter*, proved by long experience, *and fellow-ſervant* with me *in the Lord*, to promote the intereſts of his cauſe and kingdom *whom I have ſent unto you for the ſame purpoſe, that he might know your eſtate*, and bring me word how you fare and proſper, *and comfort your hearts*, under all your trials and ſufferings for the ſake of Chriſt and his goſpel

2 Oneſimus *With Oneſimus*, Tychicus's companion, *a faithful and beloved brother, who is one of you*, and now far different from the man who formerly fled his maſter's ſervice (See the epiſtle to Philemon) *They ſhall make known unto you all things which are done here*, for your comfort and encouragement, who cannot but rejoice to hear what ſupports I receive, and what a bleſſing is on my bonds

3 *Ariſtarchus my fellow-priſoner ſaluteth you, and Marcus ſiſter's ſon to Barnabas (touching whom ye received commandments, if he come unto you, receive him)* It appears hereby that though Mark was once under the apoſtle's diſpleaſure, he was now reſtored to his good graces, and having acknowledged his fault, had been heartily forgiven, and cordially received again *And Jeſus, which is called Juſtus, who are of the circumciſion, theſe* only of the Jewiſh brethren, *are my fellow-workers unto the kingdom of God, which have been a comfort unto me* under my ſufferings

4 *Epaphras, who is one of you, a ſervant of Jeſus Chriſt* in the goſpel, *ſaluteth you, always labouring fervently for you in prayers*, as in an agony wreſtling with God for a bleſſing upon your ſouls, *that ye may ſtand perfect and complete in all the will of God*, enlightened with the cleareſt diſcoveries of divine truth, and ſtedfaſt in the practice of all holineſs *For I bear him record, that he hath a great zeal for you, and them that are in Laodicea, and them in Hierapolis* Probably this faithful ſervant of Jeſus had been chiefly inſtrumental in planting theſe churches, and therefore bore them a very particular affection *Note*, (1) Thoſe whom we have begotten in the goſpel, we ſhall not fail earneſtly to commend to God's keeping and care, zeal for them will make our prayers importunate (2) Though we come however ſhort of the mark at which we aim, perfection complete and entire is that which the Chriſtian ſeeks as the ſummit of his felicity

5 *Luke the beloved phyſician*, by profeſſion a phyſician for the body, but now diſpenſes in the goſpel healing for the ſoul, *and Demas greet you*, wiſhing you the richeſt mercies of our God

6 *Salute the brethren which are in Laodicea, and Nymphas, and the church which is in his houſe* Probably there the faithful aſſembled for their ſtated worſhip, or his family, remarkable for their regularity, exemplarineſs, and daily worſhip of God, appeared a little church within themſelves *And when this epiſtle is read amongſt you, cauſe that it be read alſo in the churches of the Laodiceans, and that ye likewiſe read the epiſtle from Laodicea*, either that which was written from thence by the apoſtle, as ſome ſuggeſt, to Timothy, or rather an epiſtle from the church of the Laodiceans to the Coloſſians, which might contain matter of great edification *Note*, Religious letters are often ſingularly uſeful

7 *And ſay to Archippus*, their biſhop probably, who had need be peculiarly watchful over the flock, when ſeducers ſo abounded, *Take heed to the miniſtry which thou haſt received in the Lord, to fulfil it* with all zeal and fidelity, maintaining the doctrines of grace againſt all oppoſers, and adorning them in his converſation, building up the ſouls committed to his care in the true faith of the goſpel, labouring earneſtly for the edification of the ſaints, and for the converſion of ſinners *Note*, They who are put in truſt with the miniſtry, have a peculiarly important charge committed to them, and, if they grow cold and careleſs, their people may and ought, with becoming reſpect, to admoniſh them of their negligence

8 He concludes with his benediction and ſubſcription *The ſalutation by the hand of me Paul*, the mark of his genuine epiſtles *Remember my bonds*, which I now ſuffer for the ſake of the Gentiles, and ſhould eſpecially engage your prayers for me, and your affection towards me *Grace be with you*, may the ſovereign and rich favour of God, with all its bleſſed conſequences, be your preſent and everlaſting portion *Amen!*

THE

EVANGELICAL EXPOSITOR;

OR, A

PRACTICAL COMMENT

Upon the FIRST EPISTLE of

St. Paul to the THESSALONIANS.

Thessalonica was formerly the metropolis of Macedonia, it is now called Salonichi, and is the best peopled, and one of the best towns for commerce in the Levant. The apostle Paul, being diverted from his design of going into the provinces of Asia, properly so called, and directed after an extraordinary manner to preach the gospel in Macedonia, Acts xvi 9, 10 *in obedience to the call of God went from Tarsus to Samothracia, and from thence to Neapolis, and from thence to Philippi, where he had good success in his ministry; but met with hard usage, being cast into prison with Silas his companion in travel and labour, from whence being wonderfully delivered, they comforted the brethren there and departed. Passing through Amphipolis and Apollonia, they came to Thessalonica, where the apostle planted a church that consisted of some believing Jews, and many converted Gentiles,* Acts xvii 1—4. *But a tumult being raised in the city by the unbelieving Jews, and the lewd and baser sort of the inhabitants, Paul and Silas, for their safety, were sent away by night unto Berea, and afterwards Paul was conducted to Athens, leaving Silas and Timotheus behind him, but sent directions that they should come to him with all speed.*

When they were come, Timotheus was sent to Thessalonica to enquire after their welfare, and to establish them in the faith, 1 Thes iii 2, *who returned to Paul while he tarried at Athens, and was sent again, together with Silas, to visit the churches in Macedonia. So that Paul, being left at Athens alone,* 1 Thes iii 2 *departed from thence to Corinth, where he continued a year and a half, in which time Silas and Timotheus returned to him from Macedonia,* Acts xviii 5. *and then he wrote this epistle to the church of Christ at Thessalonica, which, though it is placed after the other epistles of this apostle, is supposed to be* first *in time of all Paul's epistles, and to be written about* A D 51.

The main scope whereof is to express the thankfulness of this apostle for the good success his preaching had among them, and to establish them in the faith, and persuade them to a holy conversation.

CHAP I

After the introduction, ver 1 *the apostle begins with a thanksgiving to God for the saving benefits bestowed on them,* ver 2—5 *And then mentions the sure evidences of the good success of the gospel among them, which was notorious and famous in several other places,* ver 6—10

a 2 Cor i 19 2 Thes i 1 1 Pet v 12
b Eph i 2 Phil i 1 Col i 2

1 PAUL, and a Silvanus, and Timotheus, unto the church of the Thessalonians, *which is* in God the Father, and *in* the Lord Jesus Christ b Grace *be* unto you, and peace from God our Father, and the Lord Jesus Christ

Ver 1 The apostle begins with his usual address, joining two of his brethren with himself *Paul, and Silvanus, and Timotheus, unto the church of the Thessalonians, which is in God the Father, and the Lord Jesus Christ,* called to the worship of the true God, chosen in Christ Jesus, and united to him by faith as living members of his body *grace be unto you, and peace from God our Father, and the Lord Jesus Christ,* may all the blessings of the everlasting covenant of redemption be your portion, partaking of the boundless grace of God, and enjoying that sweetest peace of conscience which results from a sense of his unchangeable love!

c Rom i 8 Eph i 16 Col i 3 Philem 4
d Chap ii 13
e John vi 29 Gal v 6 Jam ii [illegible]
f Rom xvi [illegible]
g Col [illegible] 2 Thes ii 13
i 1 Cor ii 4 [illegible]
k Col ii 2 [illegible]
l Chap ii [illegible]

2 c We give thanks to God always for you all, making mention of you in our prayers; 3 d Remembering without ceasing e your work of faith, f and labour of love, and patience of hope in our Lord Jesus Christ, in the sight of God, and our Father 4 Knowing, brethren beloved, g your election of God 5 For our gospel came not unto you in word only, h but also in power, and i in the holy Ghost, and k in much assurance, as l ye know what manner of men we were among you for your sake.

Ver 2—5 With thanksgiving and prayer the apostle on their behalf approached a throne of grace *We give thanks to God always for you all, making mention of you in our prayers*

3 Re

1 *Remembring, without ceasing,* (1) *your work of faith*, which is proved to be unfeigned by the blessed effects it produceth on your hearts and lives *And,* (2) Your *labour of love*, love to Jesus and one another engaging you to every good word and work, and making you willing to submit to any hardships, for his glory and the advantage of your brethren *And also,* (3) Your *patience of hope in our Lord Jesus Christ*, even that lively hope which faith in him inspires, and which strengthens you with patient perseverance to endure under every cross, *in the sight of God and our Father*, to whom we can appeal for our constant and thankful remembrance of you, and trust that in all fidelity you approve yourselves to him *knowing, brethren beloved, your election of God*, the objects of his eternal regard, and of his mere sovereign pleasure chosen to grace here and glory hereafter *Note,* (1) All our blessings flow from God's election We have not chosen him, but he hath chosen us (2) Those whom God chuses for his own he sanctifies, and prepares for the inheritance which he hath prepared for them

2 He thanks God for the success of his preaching among them *For our gospel came not unto you in word only* to your ears, *but also in power, and in the Holy Ghost*, who bore his attestation to the truth by miracles, accompanied it with divine evidence to the conscience, *and* caused it to enter into your hearts *with much assurance* of your personal interest in the promised blessings, *as ye know what manner of men we were among you for your sake*, with what patience and perseverance, in the midst of much persecution, we delivered our message, zealous for your souls, and how God was pleased graciously to own our labours *Note,* (1) Nothing fills a faithful minister's heart with deeper gratitude, than the beholding the success of his labours (2) Wherever the gospel is made effectual to the heart by the Holy Ghost, it comes with such evidence as bears down all objections, and powerfully bends the soul to the obedience of the faith

6 And [m] ye became followers of us, and of the Lord,
having received the word in much affliction, [n] with joy
in the holy Ghost 7 So that ye were ensamples to all
that believe in Macedonia and Achaia 8 For from
you [o] sounded out the word of the Lord, not only in
Macedonia and Achaia, but also [p] in every place your
faith to God-ward is spread abroad, so that we need
not to speak any thing 9 For they themselves shew
of us, [q] what manner of entring in we had unto you,
and [r] how ye turned to God from idols, to serve the
living and true God, 10. And [s] to wait for his Son
from heaven, [t] whom he raised from the dead, *even* Jesus,
which delivered us [u] from the wrath to come.

m 1 Cor xi 1 Phil iii 17 2 Thess iii 9 — n Acts v 41 Heb x 34 — o Rom x 18 — p Rom i 8 — q Chap ii 1 — r 1 Cor xii 2 — s 1 Cor i 7 Phil iii 20 Tit ii 13 2 Pet iii 12 — t Acts ii 24 — u Mat iii 7 Rom v 9 Chap v 9

v 6—10 The apostle describes the happy effects which the gospel produced among them

1 *Ye became followers of us* in faith, patience, and sufferings, *and of the Lord Jesus*, the perfect pattern which we desire to imitate, *having received the word in much affliction* far from being stumbled at the persecution which was raised against us, or being discouraged, ye were filled *with joy in the Holy Ghost* and, as your tribulations abounded, your consolation by Jesus Christ abounded also

2 Ye were eminently distinguished by your conduct on that occasion, *so that ye were ensamples* of courage, constancy, and zeal, *to all that believe in Macedonia and Achaia, for from you sounded out the word of the Lord*, the fame of your faith and the remarkable success of the gospel among you went forth, *not only in Macedonia and Achaia, but also in every place your faith God-ward is spread abroad*, and much spoken of, *so that we need not to speak any thing* in your commendation *for they themselves*, among whom this good report of you is spread, *shew of us, what manner of entring in we had unto you*, and need not our information, having been already made acquainted with all the circumstances, *and how ye turned to God from idols, to serve the living and true God*, who alone hath life in himself, and is the author thereof to all his creatures, and besides whom there is no God, *and to wait for his Son from heaven*, in faith and hope, *whom he raised from the dead* for our justification, *even Jesus*, the complete Saviour of his people, *which delivered us from the wrath to come*, and but for him we must all have perished eternally *Note,* (1) Good examples are mightily influential (2) Wherever the true grace of God comes, it will turn the heart from all its sinful pursuits, and from idols, to cleave to him in faith and love alone (3) We owe it to the Son of God that we are rescued from everlasting burning. Had he not interposed on our behalf, our estate had been desperate as that of the devils themselves (4) They who are partakers of the gospel salvation, constantly keep in mind the second coming of the Lord, waiting with desire his appearing, and making it their labour and prayer to be ready to meet him in clouds

CHAP II

In this chapter the apostle puts the Thessalonians in mind of the manner of his preaching among them, ver 1—6 Then of the manner of his conversation among them, ver 7—12 Afterwards of the success of his ministry, with the effects both on himself and themselves, ver 13—16 And then apologizeth for his absence, ver 17—20

1 FOR [a] yourselves, brethren, know our entrance
in unto you, that it was not in vain 2 But
even after that we had suffered before, and were shame-
fully entreated, as ye know, at [b] Philippi, [c] we were
bold in our God [d] to speak unto you the gospel of God
[e] with much contention 3 For [f] our exhortation *was*
not of deceit, nor of uncleanness, nor in guile 4 But
as [g] we were allowed of God [h] to be put in trust with
the gospel, even so we speak, [i] not as pleasing men,
but God, which trieth our hearts 5 For [k] neither at
any time used we flattering words, as ye know, nor a
cloak of covetousness, [l] God *is* witness 6 [m] Nor of
men sought we glory, neither of you, nor yet of others,
when [n] we might have † been [o] burdensome, [p] as the
apostles of Christ 7 But [q] we were gentle among you,
even as a nurse cherisheth her children 8 So being
affectionately desirous of you, we were willing [r] to have
imparted unto you, not the gospel of God only, but
also [s] our own souls, because ye were dear unto us
9 For ye remember, brethren, our labour and travel
for [t] labouring night and day, [u] because we would not
be chargeable unto any of you, we preached unto you
the gospel of God 10 Ye *are* witnesses, and God *also*,
[x] how holily, and justly, and unblameably we behaved
ourselves among you that believe 11 As you know,
how we exhorted and comforted, and charged every one
of you (as a father *doth* his children) 12 [y] That ye
would walk worthy of God, [z] who hath called you unto
his kingdom and glory

a Chap i 5, 9 — b Acts xvi 22 — c Chap i 5 — d Acts xvii 2 — e Phil i 30 Col ii 1 — f 2 Cor ii 17 & vii 2 — g 1 Tim i 11, 12 — h Gal ii 7 Tit i 3 — i Gal i 10 — k Acts xx 33 2 Cor ii 17 & vii 2 & xii 17 — l Rom i 9 — m John v 41, 44 & xii 43 — n 2 Cor x 2, 10 11 — † Or used authority — o 1 Cor ix 4, 6 — p 1 Cor ix — q 2 Tim ii 24 — r Rom i 11 — s 2 Cor xii 15 — t Acts xx 34 1 Cor iv 12 2 Cor xi 9 2 Thess iii 8 — u 2 Cor xii 13, 14 — x 2 Cor vii 2 2 Thess iii 7 — y Gen xvii 1 Eph iv 1 Phil i 27 Col i 10 Chap iv 1 — z 1 Cor i 9 Gal i 6 2 Pet v 10

v 1—12 The apostle reminds the Thessalonians,

1. Of his manner of preaching among them *For yourselves, brethren, know our entrance in unto you, that it was not in vain*, with great swelling words of vanity, or empty ineffectual harangues, but with the power of the gospel, and the mighty word of truth *But even after we had suffered before, and were shamefully entreated, as ye know, at Philippi*, undismayed at the persecutions that we had endured, *we were bold in our God to speak unto you the gospel of God with much contention*, as in an agony, labouring after your conversion amidst all the opposition which we had to encounter *For our exhortation was not of deceit*, we broached no false doctrine, nor had any intention to deceive, *nor of uncleanness*, but tending to discourage all manner of impurity; *nor of guile*, for we spoke the truth from the heart *but as we were allowed of God to be put in trust with the gospel*, and had this honour conferred upon us to be appointed his ambassadors, *even so we speak*, under a sense of the weighty charge committed to us, *not as pleasing men, but God, which trieth our hearts*, to whom we study to approve ourselves in simplicity and godly sincerity *for neither at any time used we flattering words*, in order to insinuate and ingratiate ourselves into your confidence, or to encourage you with the least imagination of impunity in your sins, *as ye know*, *nor* did we put on *a cloke* of religion to conceal our designs *of covetousness*, in order to make an advantage of you, *God is witness* to the uprightness of our hearts respecting you *Nor of men sought we glory, neither of you, nor yet of others*, desiring human applause or esteem, *when we might have been burdensome*, and demanded our maintenance of you, *as the apostles of Christ*

2 Of his conduct and conversation among them *But we were gentle among you, even as a nurse cherisheth her children*, with the greatest tenderness *So being affectionately desirous of you*, of your happiness and salvation, *we were willing to have imparted unto you, not the gospel of God only, but also our own souls*, ready to spend and be spent in the service of your faith, *because ye were dear unto us For ye remember, brethren, our labour and travail for labouring night and day*, with our own hands, to earn our maintenance, *because we would not be chargeable unto any of you, we preached unto you the gospel of God* freely *Ye are witnesses, and God also, how holily, and justly, and unblameably we behaved ourselves among you that believe*, conscientiously discharging every duty of religion towards God, and righteousness toward men *as you know how we exhorted and comforted, and charged every one of you, as a father doth his children*, with the affection and authority of the kindest parent, *that ye would walk worthy of God, who hath called you unto his kingdom and glory*, to the blessings of his grace in time, and of his glory in eternity *Note,* (1) They can speak boldly, who can appeal to their own conduct for the example of what they teach (2) The more love and tenderness accompanies our exhortations, the more effectual are they likely to prove (3) They who are called to God's kingdom

dom are bound to walk worthy of the high vocation, and to adorn the doctrine of Christ which they profess in all things.

13 For this cause also thank we God [a] without ceasing, because when ye received the word of God which ye heard of us, ye received *it* [b] not *as* the word of men, but (as it is in truth) the word of God, which effectually worketh also in you that believe. 14 For [c] ye, brethren, became followers of [d] the churches of God, which in Judea are in Christ Jesus: for [e] ye also have suffered like things of your own countrymen, [f] even as they *have* of the Jews: 15 [g] Who both killed the Lord Jesus, [h] and their own prophets, [i] and have [j] persecuted us; and they please not God, and are contrary to all men: 16 [k] Forbidding us to speak to the Gentiles that they might be saved, [l] to fill up their sins alway: for [m] the wrath is come upon them to the uttermost.

a Chap. i. 3. — b Mat. x. 40. Gal. iv. 14. 2 Pet. iii. 2. — c Chap. i. 6. — d Gal. i. 22. — e Acts xvii. 5. 13. — f Heb. x. 34. — g Acts vii. [illegible] — h Mat. xxiii. 34. 37. Luke xiii. 33. — i Acts viii. 4. & xi. 19. [illegible] — k Acts xiii. 50. & xiv. 5. 19. & xvii. 5. 13. & xviii. 12. & xix. 9. — l Gen. xv. 16. Mat. xxiii. 32. — m Mat. xxiv. 21.

v. 13—16. The apostle proceeds,

1. To thank God for their ready reception of the gospel word. *For this cause also thank we God without ceasing, because when ye received the word of God which ye heard of us, ye received it not as the word of man*, which may be fallacious, or at best of uncertain authority, *but as it is in truth, the word of God*, and is such deserving the deepest reverence, attention, and obedience, *which effectually worketh also in you that believe*, producing the most blessed consequences, and carrying with it the evidence of its divine original. *Note*, (1.) Though the treasure of God's word is committed to earthen vessels, its excellence is not therefore the less: and we must remember not who dispenses it, but whose word it is, that with reverence and godly fear we may hear and obey. (2.) Wherever the gospel is received into the heart, it works effectually to the salvation of the soul, changing the whole man into its blessed mold.

2. They were honoured with the cross, and bore it most exemplarily. *For ye, brethren, became followers of the churches of God, which in Judea are in Christ Jesus, for ye also have suffered like things of your own countrymen, even as they have of the Jews*, and sustained the shock of persecution with the same unshaken fortitude and unwearied patience.

3. He mentions with horror the dreadful guilt and rooted enmity of the Jewish zealots, his and their chief opponents, *who both killed the Lord Jesus*, with most atrocious wickedness imbruing their hands in his sacred blood, *and* murdered *their own prophets, and have* with the utmost virulence *persecuted us* his apostles; *and they please not God*, though they flatter themselves they are his only favourites, they act in direct opposition to his will, *and are contrary to all men*, abhorring both Gentiles and Christians, and filled with implacable malice against those who use any means for the conversion of the heathen to Christ, *forbidding us to speak to the Gentiles* the gospel of God's grace, *that they might be saved, to fill up* the measure of *their sins alway*, and to hasten the full vials of God's vengeance upon their devoted heads: *for the wrath is come upon them*, and hath begun to seize them in their rejection of God, and will be poured out *to the uttermost*, or *to the end*, in the entire destruction of their city, nation, and temple, and in the eternal perdition of the impenitent. *Note*, When the sinner's iniquities are at the full, then wrath cometh to the uttermost.

17 But we, brethren, being taken from you for a short time, [n] in presence, not in heart, endeavoured the more abundantly [o] to see your face with great desire. 18 Wherefore we would have come unto you (even I Paul) once and again; [p] but Satan hindered us. 19 For [q] what *is* our hope, or joy, or crown of rejoicing? [r] *Are* not even ye in the presence of our Lord Jesus Christ [s] at his coming? 20 For ye are our glory and joy.

n 1 Cor. v. 3. — o Chap. iii. 10. — p Rom. i. 13. & xv. 22. — q 2 Cor. i. 14. Phil. iv. 1. — r Rev. xxii. 12.

v. 17—20. The apostle,

1. Excuses his absence, which was not voluntary, but thro' unavoidable hindrance. *But we, brethren, being taken from you for a short time, in presence, not in heart*, and compelled reluctantly to leave you as helpless orphans, *endeavoured the more abundantly to see your face with great desire*, longing to converse with you, and build up your souls on the true foundation. *Wherefore we would have come unto you, (even I Paul), once and again*, and made efforts for that purpose; *but Satan hindered us*, sowing such dissension and raising such difficulties as made our abode in these parts, where we now are, absolutely necessary. *Note*, We have a busy enemy, who is ever seeking to lay obstacles in our way. We need therefore to watch against his devices, and to resist his wiles.

2. He assures them of his high affection and regard for them. *For what is our hope* in our labours, *or joy, or crown of rejoicing*, which revives, animates, and comforts our souls under all our work and sufferings? *Are not even ye in the presence of our Lord Jesus Christ at his coming?* Yes verily. *For ye are our glory and joy*, whilst, looking forward to the great day of Christ's appearing, we confidently hope to present you before him as the happy fruits of our labour, to your eternal blessedness and to our own immortal honour.

CHAP. III.

In this chapter the apostle giveth further evidence of his love to the Thessalonians, reminding them of his sending Timotheus to them, and the mention of his aim therein, and his reasons for so doing, ver. 1—5. By acquainting them of his great satisfaction at the return of Timothy, with good tidings concerning them, ver. 6—10. And concludeth with fervent prayer for them, ver. 11 to the end.

1 WHerefore [a] when we could no longer forbear, [b] we thought it good to be left at Athens alone; 2 And sent [c] Timotheus our brother and minister of God, and [d] our fellowlabourer in the gospel of Christ, to establish you, and to comfort you concerning your faith: 3 [e] That no man should be moved by these afflictions: for yourselves know that [f] we are appointed thereunto. 4 For verily when we were with you, we told you before [g] that we should suffer tribulation; even as it came to pass, and ye know. 5 For this cause, [h] when I could no longer forbear, I sent to know your faith, [i] lest by some means the tempter have tempted you, and [k] our labour be in vain.

a Ver. 5. — b Acts xvii. 15. — c Rom. xvi. 21. 1 Cor. xvi. 10. — d 1 Cor. iii. 9. — e Eph. iii. 13. — f Acts xiv. 22. 1 Cor. iv. 9. 2 Tim. iii. 12. 1 Pet. ii. 21. — g Acts xx. 24. — h Ver. 1. — i 1 Cor. vii. 5. 2 Cor. xi. 3. — k Gal. ii. 2. & iv. 11. Phil. ii. 16.

v. 1—5. The solicitude which the apostle felt towards them engaged him to send Timothy and be left alone at Athens, however useful or comfortable such a friend at that time might be to him. *Wherefore, when we could no longer forbear*, so anxious was I to hear of your affairs, *we thought it good to be left at Athens alone, and sent Timotheus our brother and minister of God, and our fellow-labourer in the gospel of Christ*, and this in order *to establish you* in the truth, to build you up in the glorious doctrines of the gospel of Jesus, *and to comfort you concerning your faith*, exhorting you to abide unshaken in your profession, and suggesting the most encouraging motives thereto, *that no man should be moved by these afflictions; for yourselves know that we are appointed thereunto*, according to God's eternal counsels, for wise and holy purposes of his own glory. *For verily, when we were with you*, we concealed nothing from you, but *told you* plainly *before* the persecutions came, *that we should suffer tribulation; even as it came to pass, and ye know. For this cause, when I could no longer forbear*, reflecting upon your very critical and trying circumstances, *I sent to know your faith, lest by some means the tempter should have tempted you* to turn back from the profession of Christ, *and our labour be in vain*, notwithstanding all the promising appearances which emboldened my confident hope in your fidelity. *Note*, (1.) We must count the cost, before we enlist under Christ's banner. All that will live godly in him shall suffer persecution. (2.) The devil usually seeks to discourage new converts by the violent opposition which he raises against them. (3.) Faithful ministers labour to confirm the faith and comfort the hearts of those who are suffering for righteousness sake. In this way only can we hope to enter into the kingdom of God.

6. [l] But now when Timotheus came from you unto us, and brought us good tidings of your faith and charity, and that ye have good remembrance of us always, desiring greatly to see us, [m] as we also *to see* you: 7 Therefore, brethren, we were comforted over you in all our affliction and distress by your faith: 8 For now we live, if ye stand fast in the Lord. 9 For what thanks can we render to God again for you, for all the joy wherewith we joy for your sakes before our God; 10 [n] Night and day [o] praying exceedingly [p] that we might see your face, and [q] might perfect that which is lacking in your faith? 11 Now God himself and our Father, and our Lord Jesus Christ direct our way unto you. 12 And the Lord [r] make you to increase and abound in love [s] one towards another, and towards all men, even as we *do* towards you: 13 To the end he may [t] stablish your hearts unblameable in holiness before God even our Father, at the coming of our Lord Jesus Christ [u] with all his saints.

l Acts xviii. 5. — m Phil. i. 8. — n Acts xxvi. 7. 2 Tim. i. 3. — o Rom. i. 10. 11. — p Chap. ii. 17. — q 2 Cor. xiii. 9. — r Chap. iv. 10. — s Chap. v. 15. 2 Pet. i. 7. — t 1 Cor. i. 8. Phil. i. 10. Chap. v. 23. 2 Thess. ii. 17. — u Jude 14.

v. 6—13. The apostle,

1. Expresses the vast satisfaction which he felt at Timothy's report. *But now, when Timotheus came from you unto us, and brought us good tidings of your* unshaken *faith* in Christ, *and* fervent *charity* towards each other; *and that ye have good remembrance of us always, desiring* earnestly *to see us, as we also to see you: therefore, brethren, we were comforted*, and all my anxious fears gave place to holy joy on account of you, *in all our affliction and distress*, which we were then suffering, when Timotheus arrived, but

but which were now made light and easy, *by* the knowledge of *your faith* in Jesus, and fidelity to his cause *for now we live*, and are happy in the midst of all our persecutions and dangers, *if*, or *seeing*, *ye stand fast in the Lord*, and are not moved away from the hope of the gospel *Note*, Nothing is such an encouragement to suffer for Christ and his gospel, as seeing the happy effects of our labours upon those among whom we minister

2. The glad news filled him with thankfulness to God, and opened his heart and lips in prayer *For what thanks can we render to God again for you*, or how sufficiently express our gratitude, *for all the joy wherewith we joy for your sakes before our God, night and day praying exceedingly*, with unusual fervor and vehemence, *that*, if the Lord so pleased, *we might see your face again, and might perfect that which is lacking in your faith?* helping you to farther and clearer discoveries of the gospel, and leading you to fuller and more assured confidence in the Lord *Note*, (1) The strongest believers need still to have their faith increased (2) The ministry of the word is the great means which God usually blesses for that happy purpose

3. He tells them what was the constant subject of his prayers for them *Now God himself and our Father*, who as *God* hath all power to supply every want of his people, and, as our *reconciled* God and *Father*, is in the fulness of his love and grace disposed most tenderly towards us, *and our Lord Jesus Christ*, who is equally with the Father the object of our prayers, and through whose mediation we receive an answer of peace, *direct our way unto you*, and in his providence enable us to accomplish the purposes we have formed *And the Lord make you to increase and abound in love one towards another, and towards all men, even as we do towards you*, advancing to higher attainments in this godlike temper, *to the end that he may stablish your hearts* in faith and love, *unblameable in holiness before God even our Father*, approving yourselves to him in all simplicity and godly sincerity, and acknowledged by him as his chosen *at the coming of our Lord Jesus Christ* to judgment, *with all his saints*, who in that day shall stand before his throne and share his triumphs *Note*, (1) Though we may purpose our goings, the Lord alone directeth our steps (2) An increase in love is the best symptom of the flourishing state of the Christian's soul (3) All God's people desire to be found unblameable in holiness before him, and so to walk as to please him well in all things (4) It is God alone by his grace who can make us such as he would have us to be therefore to him must we, without ceasing, direct our prayer (5) The Lord Jesus shall quickly come in glory with all his saints Happy the soul that shall then have boldness in his presence

CHAP IV

In this chapter the apostle gives earnest exhortations to abound in holiness, with a caution against uncleanness, enforced with several arguments, ver 1—8 *He then mentions the great duties of brotherly love, and quietness, with industry, in our callings*, ver 9—12 *and concludeth with comforting them that mourned for their relatives and friends that died in the Lord*, ver 13—18

1 FUrthermore then we beseech you, brethren, and
exhort *you* by the Lord Jesus, [a] that as ye have
received of us [b] how you ought to walk, [c] and to please
God, so ye would abound more and more 2 For ye
know what commandments we gave you by the Lord
Jesus 3 For this is [d] the will of God, *even* your sanc-
tification, that [e] ye should abstain from fornication 4
[f] That every one of you should know how to possess his
vessel in sanctification and honour, 5 Not in the lust
of concupiscence, [g] even as the Gentiles [h] which know
not God 6 [i] That no *man* go beyond, and [j] defraud
his brother in *any* matter, because that the Lord *is* the
avenger of all such, as we also have forewarned you and
testified 7. For God hath not called us unto unclean-
ness, but [k] unto holiness 8 [l] He therefore that de-
spiseth, despiseth not man, but God, [m] who hath also
given unto us his holy Spirit

a Col ii 6. b Chap ii 12. c Col i 10. d Eph v 17. e 1 Cor vi 15. f 1 Cor vi 18. g Rom i 24. h 1 Cor xv 34. Eph iv 17. i 1 Cor vi 8. j 1 Thes i 8. Or, oppress. k Lev xi 44. 2 Cor ... l Luke x 16. m Rom viii 9. 1 John iii ...

v 1—8 We have here,

1 An exhortation to all holy obedience *Furthermore then we beseech you, brethren, and exhort you by the Lord Jesus*, in his name and by his authority, *that as ye have received of us how you ought to walk, and to please God, so ye would abound more and more*, with greater watchfulness, diligence, and zeal, according to God's holy word *For ye know what commandments we gave you by the Lord Jesus*, so clearly that none can plead ignorance, and urged upon your conscience with those most powerful arguments which should engage your obedience thereunto *Note*, (1) The more clearly the path of duty is marked out to us, the more readily are we bound to walk in it (2) The best come very short of perfection, and have need to be exhorted to greater diligence and exemplariness in their walk and conversation

2 A caution against all impurity, as most opposite to the Christian character *For this is the will of God, even your sanctification*, that you should be in heart and conduct obedient to all his commands, particularly, *that ye should abstain from fornication*, that common sin among the Gentiles, and to which in the days of your unregeneracy you may have been addicted, *that every one of you should know how to possess his vessel*, his body, *in sanctification and honour*, with such purity and chastity as never to be guilty of an action unworthy those who are the temples of the Holy Ghost, and that would defile and disgrace you in the sight of God and every real Christian, *not in the lust of concupiscence*, indulging the vile affections of the natural heart, *even as the Gentiles do, which know not God*, *that no man go beyond and defraud his brother in any matter*, not only abstaining from every act of injustice, but especially by robbing them of that which is dearer to them than any earthly goods, the affections or the person of their wife, or drawing them into any horrid and unnatural acts of lewdness *because that the Lord is the avenger of all such, as we also have forewarned you and testified*, and will execute condign punishment on such workers of iniquity *For God hath not called us unto uncleanness, but unto holiness*, in his gospel enjoining all purity of heart and conversation on his people *He therefore that despiseth* our admonitions, *despiseth not man, but God, who hath also given unto us his holy Spirit*, by whose inspiration I now speak, and whose office it is to sanctify our bodies, souls, and spirits, and prepare us for the glory which is promised *Note*, Whoremongers and adulterers God will judge, and into his kingdom shall nothing enter which defileth or maketh unclean

9 But as touching brotherly love, [n] ye need not that
I write unto you for [o] ye yourselves are [p] taught of God
to love one another 10 And indeed ye do it towards
all the brethren which are in all Macedonia but we be-
seech you, brethren, [q] that ye increase more and more
11 And that ye study [r] to be quiet, and [s] to do your
own business, and [t] to work with your own hands (as
we commanded you) 12 [u] That ye may walk honestly
toward them that are without, and *that* ye may have lack
of nothing

n Chap v 1. o John xiii 34. & xiv ... Heb ... p 1 John ii 20, 27. q John xiii ... r Eph iv 28. 1 Pet ... s Chap. iii 12. t 1 Pet iv 15. u 2 Thes iii 12. ... Eph iv 28. 1 Thes ... Rom xiii 13. Col iv 5.

v 9—12 The apostle here inculcates,

1 The great duty of brotherly love *But as touching brotherly love, ye need not that I write unto you, for ye yourselves are taught of God to love one another*, and are already exemplary for your fervent and enlarged charity *and indeed ye do it*, not only towards the members of your own church, but *towards all the brethren which are in all Macedonia But*, as there is still room for much higher advancement, *we beseech you, brethren, that ye increase more and more Note*, (1) We are never so high in grace, but we have summits of holiness yet to climb, and shall continue to have, till we reach the heavenly Zion, and come to join the spirits of the just there made perfect (2) All good comes from God unless we are taught of him, no human lessons can lead us into the spirit of Christianity

2 Of quietness and industry in our callings *And that ye study to be quiet*, make it your holy ambition to live in peace with all men, not officiously intruding into other peoples affairs, *and to do your own business*, minding the concerns of your own family and calling, *and to work with your own hands*, as many as by your station must earn your bread by daily labour, *as we commanded you*, idleness and Christianity being utterly inconsistent *that ye may walk honestly toward them that are without*, paying every man his due, *and that ye may have lack of nothing*, but be furnished with all that yourselves and family may need, and not be burdensome to any

13 But I would not have you to be ignorant, bre-
thren, concerning them which are asleep, that ye sorrow
not, [x] even as others which have no hope 14 For [y] if
we believe that Jesus died, and rose again, even so
[z] them also which sleep in Jesus will God bring with him
15 For this we say unto you [a] by the word of the Lord,
[b] that we which are alive, and remain unto the coming
of the Lord, shall not prevent them which are asleep
16 For [c] the Lord himself shall descend from heaven
with a shout, with the voice of the archangel, and with
[d] the trump of God and [e] the dead in Christ shall rise
first 17 [f] Then we which are alive and remain, [g] shall
be caught up together with them in the clouds, to meet
the Lord in the air and so [h] shall we ever be with the
Lord. 18 [i] Wherefore || comfort one another with these
words

x Deut xiv 1. 2 Sam xii 20. y 1 Cor xv 13. z 1 Cor xv 23. Chap iii 13. a 1 Kings xiii 17. & xx ... b 1 Cor xv 51. c 2 Thes i 7. d 1 Cor xv 52. e 1 Cor xv 23. f 1 Cor xv 51. g Rev xi 12. h John xii 26. & xiv 3. & xvii 24. i Chap v 11. || Or, exhort.

v 13—18 The apostle here suggests the most encouraging arguments to support the Thessalonians under the loss of their near and dear relatives *But I would not have you to be ignorant, brethren, concerning them which are asleep*, and departed in the faith of Christ, *that ye sorrow not as others which have no hope*, as the heathen, who make such howling and lamentation for the dead, since we have a hope full of immortality *For if we believe that Jesus died, and rose again, even so them also which sleep in Jesus will God bring with him*, raising their bodies from the dust at the last day, as his was raised from the tomb *For this we say unto you by the word of the Lord, that we which are alive, and remain unto the coming of the Lord*, even those members of his church who shall be numbered among the living in the great day of his appearing and glory, *shall not prevent them which are asleep*, so as to anticipate their resurrection *for the Lord himself shall descend from heaven with a shout* of triumph and exultation, *with the voice of the archangel* that shall attend his orders, *and with the trump of God*, like that tremendous sound which once issued from Sinai's top, *and the dead in Christ*, those who departed in his faith and fear, shall rise first, in virtue of their union with their exalted Head *then we which are alive and remain*, as many as shall then be found among the living, *shall be caught up together with them in the clouds, to meet the Lord in the air, and so shall we ever be with the Lord*, enjoying that eternal blessedness in his immediate presence which is the summit of our felicity *Wherefore comfort one another with these words*, under all your present trials and discouragements, and in the prospect of your own approaching dissolution *Note*, (1) They who die in the faith of Christ return to his bosom, and their dust sleeps sweetly under his care, waiting a resurrection day (2) The faithful shall shortly meet together in bliss around the Redeemer's throne, and spend a happy eternity in his unceasing praises (3) This reviving hope is the comfort and support of the Christian, living and dying

CHAP V

The apostle having spoken in the end of the foregoing chapter concerning the resurrection, and the second coming of Christ, he proceeds to speak concerning the uselessness of enquiring after the particular time of Christ's coming, which would be sudden and terrible to the wicked, but comfortable to the saints, ver 1—5 He then exhorts them to the duties of watchfulness, sobriety, and the exercise of faith, hope, and love, ver 6—10 In the next words he exhorts them to several duties they owed to others, or to one another, ver 11—15 And afterwards to several other Christian duties of great importance, ver 16—22 And then concludes this epistle, ver 23—28

1 BUT of [a] the times and the seasons, brethren,
[b] ye have no need that I write unto you 2 For
yourselves know perfectly that [c] the day of the Lord so
cometh as a thief in the night 3 For when they shall
say, Peace and safety, [d] then sudden destruction cometh
upon them, [e] as travail upon a woman with child, and
they shall not escape 4 But ye, brethren, are not in
darkness, that that day should overtake you as a thief
5 [f] Ye are all the children of light, and the children of the
day we are not of the night, nor of darkness

[a] Mat xxiv 3, 36 Acts i 7 [b] Chap iv 9 [c] Mat xxiv 43, 44. 2 Pet iii 10 Rev iii 3 & xvi 15 [d] Luke xvii 27 & xxi 35 2 Thes i 9 [e] Isa xiii 8 [f] Eph v 8

v 1—5 Having mentioned the second advent of the Lord Jesus, he bids them prepare for it

1 Respecting the precise time of his coming, it is left in an awful uncertainty, that we might be always ready *But of the times and the seasons, brethren, ye have no need that I write unto you for yourselves know perfectly, that the day of the Lord so cometh as a thief in the night*, so suddenly and unexpectedly *Note*, It is a needless curiosity to desire precisely to know the hour of Christ's coming, but a most needful piece of wisdom to be always ready for his appearing

2 His coming will be the terror and surprize of an ungodly world *For when they*, who are secure in their sins, *shall say, Peace and safety*, promising themselves long years of sinful pleasures and indulgencies, *then sudden destruction cometh upon them, as travail upon a woman with child, and they shall not escape* *Note*, When the day of the Lord comes, it will spread a terrible alarm through a world that lieth in wickedness, and then the ungodly and the sinner will in vain cry to rocks and mountains to cover their guilty head

3 This will be a day of light and triumph to the people of God *But ye, brethren, are not in darkness*, sleeping in sinful and carnal security, but brought into the marvellous light of the gospel, and therefore need not fear *that that day should overtake you as a thief*, and find you unprepared *Ye are all the children of light, and the children of the day*, walking under the bright beams of the Sun of righteousness toward the kingdom of eternal glory *we are not of the night, nor of darkness*, in heathen ignorance, and under the blindness of the natural mind, but tread the shining path of truth, looking for and hastening unto the coming of the Son of man *Note*, It is an unspeakable blessing to be delivered from the darkness of the fallen heart, and, walking in the light of life, to have ever in our view the bright crown of righteousness which fadeth not away Then we can say, Come Lord Jesus, come quickly

6 [g] Therefore let us not sleep as *do* others, but [h] let
us watch and be sober 7 For [i] they that sleep, sleep
in the night, and they that be drunken, [k] are drunken
in the night 8 But let us, who are of the day, be
sober, [l] putting on the breast plate of faith and love, and
for an helmet, the hope of salvation 9 For [m] God
hath not appointed us to wrath, but [n] to obtain salva-
tion by our Lord Jesus Christ, 10 [o] Who died for us,
that, whether we wake or sleep, we should live together
with him 11 [p] Wherefore comfort yourselves toge-
ther, and edify one another, even as also ye do

[g] Mat xxv 5 [h] Mat xxv 42 & xxv 13 Rom xiii 11 1 Pet v 8 [i] Luke xxi 34, 36 Rom xiii 13 1 Cor xv 34 [k] Acts ii 15 [l] Isa lix 17 Eph vi 14 [m] Rom ix 22 Chap i 10 1 Pet ii 8 Jude 4 [n] 2 Thes ii 14 [o] Rom xiv 8, 9 2 Cor v 15 [p] Chap iv 18

v 6—11 On the foregoing considerations the apostle grounds his exhortations to the practice of several necessary duties

1 *Therefore let us not sleep as do others*, in carelessness about these eternal concerns, trifling away the precious moment of opportunity, *but let us watch and pray*, awake to the great affairs of our immortal souls, and ever listening when the sound, *Behold he cometh, Go ye out to meet him*, shall reach our ears Blessed is that servant whom his Lord, when he cometh, shall find watching *And*,

2 *Be sober*, temperate in the use of all God's creatures, neither overcharged with surfeiting or drunkenness nor with the cares or pleasures of this life *For they that sleep, sleep in the night, and they that be drunken, are drunken in the night*, and seek the darkness to hide their guilty head, stupifying their consciences till the dreadful hour shall startle them into sensibility *But let us who are of the day*, and walk in the light of truth, *be sober* (νηφωμεν) and vigilant, not intoxicated with any earthly pursuits or enjoyments, but seeking in the first place the kingdom of God and his righteousness

3 We must be armed, as well as on our guard, *putting on the breast-plate of faith and love, and for an helmet the hope of salvation*, these being the cardinal graces, by which the soul, like a warrior compleatly clad in armour, is able to resist every attack of the enemy, unhurt amidst all the fiery darts which sin and Satan can hurl against us *Note*, (1) We have mighty foes to grapple with, and need be well armed against them (2) Where faith is grounded on Christ, love in lively exercise, and hope with piercing eye looking up to eternal things, then none of our enemies can hurt us, nor will any of the snares of this world be able to prevail to draw our affections off from God and the things which are above

4 He encourages them, from past experience, with confidence still to trust on the Lord *For God hath not appointed us to wrath, but*, as is evident from his grace which we have already received, hath predestinated us *to obtain salvation by our Lord Jesus Christ, who died for us*, and thereby secured our eternal redemption, *that, whether we wake or sleep*, are numbered among the living or among the dead, at the day of his appearing, *we should then live together with him* in glory everlasting *Wherefore comfort yourselves together, or exhort and edify one another, even as also ye do*, nothing affording such animating ground of hope, and serving to quicken the soul in all holy walking before God, as these blessed prospects and expectations *Note*, (1) Our salvation in Jesus Christ is firmly secured, and the more we are enabled to exercise confidence in him, the more steadily shall we be upheld under all opposition (2) Christians should delight in exhorting, comforting, and edifying one another, and nothing can afford them more abundant matter than the expected coming of their Lord

12 And we beseech you, brethren, [q] to know them
which labour among you, and are over you in the Lord,
and admonish you, 13 And to esteem them very
highly in love for their work's sake *And* be at peace
among yourselves 14 Now we exhort you, brethren,
[r] warn them that are unruly, [s] comfort the feeble-
minded, [t] support the weak, be patient toward all men
15 [u] See that none render evil for evil unto any man
but ever [x] follow that which is good, both among your-
selves, and to all men

[q] 1 Cor xvi 18 Phil ii 29 1 Tim v 17 Heb xiii 7, 17 [r] 2 Thes iii 11 [s] Heb xii 12 [t] Rom xiv 1 Gal vi 1, 2 [u] Prov xvii 13 & xx 22 & xxiv 29 Mat v 39, 44 Rom xii 17 1 Cor vi 7 1 Pet iii 9 [x] Gal vi 10 Chap iii 12

v 12—15 The apostle passes on to other needful exhortations

1 He enjoins them to respect and honour their ministers *And we beseech you, brethren, to know them which labour among you, and are over you in the Lord*, presiding in your worshipping assemblies, *and admonish* and instruct *you* in the good ways of the Lord, *and to esteem them very highly in love for their work's sake* *Note*, (1) The duty of ministers is to *labour* with zeal and diligence for the good of their people's souls, to be *over them*, watching for their good as the shepherd tends his flock, with a constant eye to the great Shepherd who hath committed this trust to them, and to *admonish* them publickly and privately, without partiality, instructing them in all God's holy will (2) The duty of people to their ministers is to *love* them, to *esteem them highly* for their work's sake, to *know* and acknowledge them, with thankfulness for their labours, and serious attention to their advice

2 He

2 He exhorts them to the diſcharge of thoſe duties, which, as Chriſtians, they owed each other

(1) *Be at peace among yourſelves*, cultivating that mutual harmony and love with each other, and your miniſters, which, as a church, will moſt eſpecially tend to your eſtabliſhment

(2) *Now we exhort you, brethren, warn them that are unruly*, reprove them for their diſorderly walk, and threaten them with the church's cenſures if they amend not their ways, *comfort the feeble-minded*, whoſe hearts are ready to ſink under their trials, and are dejected with temptation or affliction, encourage them to bear up, and ſuggeſt every reviving motive to cheer their drooping ſpirits, *ſupport the weak*, whoſe attainments are low in grace and knowledge, and are therefore more eaſily offended, we ſhould therefore bear with their infirmities, and endeavour to ſtrengthen their faith, *be patient toward all men*, put up with every affront or provocation, forbearing and forgiving one another in love, and ſtill waiting and hoping for their amendment

3 *See that none render evil for evil unto any man*, in look, in word, or deed, *but ever follow that which is good, both among yourſelves, and to all men*, do good to their bodies and ſouls, and be ready to every work and labour of love

16. [i] Rejoice evermore 17 [k] Pray without ceaſing
18 [a] In every thing give thanks for this is the will of
God in Chriſt Jeſus concerning you 19 [b] Quench not
the Spirit. 20 [c] Deſpiſe not propheſyings 21 [d] Prove
all things [e] hold faſt that which is good 22 [f] Abſtain
from all appearance of evil

i Rom xii 12. Phil iv 4
k Luke xviii 1 & xxi 36. Rom xii 12. Eph vi 18
a Eph v 20. Col iii 17
b Eph iv 30. 2 Tim i 6
c 1 Cor xiv 1, 39
d 1 Cor ii 15. 1 John iv 1
e 2 Theſ ii 15
f Phil iv 8

v 16—22 We have here divers ſhort and weighty exhortations

1 *Rejoice evermore* in God as your Portion, in Chriſt as your Redeemer, in the Spirit as your Comforter, in one another, in all holy ordinances, and under every tribulation

2 *Pray without ceaſing*, be daily and often employed in this bleſſed work, in private in your families, or among the faithful *Note*, To live without prayer, is the ſure proof of an unregenerate heart

3 *In every thing give thanks*, under every diſpenſation of Providence, not only for mercies received, but alſo under every affliction, maintaining ſtill a chearful ſpirit *for this is the will of God in Chriſt Jeſus concerning you*, and the conſtant, grateful returns we owe for the rich redemption which we have obtained in his dear Son

4 *Quench not the Spirit*, by indulging any evil temper in your heart, or allowed ſin in your conduct, reſiſting his gracious motions, or neglecting thoſe means of grace wherein his divine influences are communicated to you

5 *Deſpiſe not propheſyings*, or *propheſies*, which ſtill contain much uſeful matter, and ſhould be conſtantly read and regarded, and attend upon the miniſtrations of the word

6 *Prove all things*, and try, by the goſpel teſt, every doctrine which is advanced, that you may not be a prey to deceivers *hold faſt that which is good*, unmoved by ſeducers among yourſelves, or the perſecutions of your enemies from without

7 *Abſtain from all appearance of evil*, dreading ſin in its moſt diſtant approaches, and avoiding whatever may have a tendency to lead you into evil, under however innocent a guiſe it may preſent itſelf unto you

23 And [g] the very God of peace [h] ſanctify you wholly
and *I pray God* your whole ſpirit and ſoul and body be
preſerved blameleſs unto the coming of our Lord Jeſus
Chriſt 24 [i] Faithful *is* he that calleth you, who alſo
will do *it* 25 Brethren, [k] pray for us. 26 [l] Greet all
the brethren with an holy kiſs 27 I † charge you by
the Lord, [m] that this epiſtle be read unto all the holy bre-
thren 28 [n] The grace of our Lord Jeſus Chriſt *be*
with you Amen

g Rom xv 33. Phil iv 9.
h Chap iii 13
i 1 Cor i 9 & x 13. 2 Theſ iii 3
k Col iv 3. 2 Theſ iii 1.
l Rom xvi 16. 1 Cor xvi 20.
† Or adjure
m Col iv 16. 2 Theſ iii 14
n Rom xvi 20, 24. 1 Cor xvi 23. 2 Cor xiii 14

v 23—28. The apoſtle concludes,

1 With his prayers for them *And the very God of peace ſanctify you wholly*, may he, who is the author and giver of peace to your conſciences, and who unites you together in this happy bond, may he cleanſe you from all iniquity, and perfect you in holineſs *and I pray God that your whole ſpirit, and ſoul and body*, in every member and every faculty, *be preſerved blameleſs unto the coming of our Lord Jeſus Chriſt* *Note*, (1) Prayer is the great means of ſanctification (2) He who hath called us to his kingdom and glory, muſt preſerve and keep us for himſelf, for of ourſelves we have no ſtrength

2 He expreſſes his confidence in God's promiſes and protection *Faithful is he that calleth you, who alſo will do it*, he never hath, never can fail thoſe that truſt him, and from his faithfulneſs we derive our fidelity

3 He entreats an intereſt in their prayers *Brethren, pray for us* The greateſt miniſters need the prayers of all their people, and the more they are mindful of them at a throne of grace, the more good will they receive from their miniſtrations

4 He adds his ſalutation *Greet all the brethren with an holy kiſs* Let every member of the church be aſſured of my moſt cordial and affectionate regards

5 He adjures them ſolemnly to read this epiſtle to the whole church *I charge you by the Lord*, in his name, *that this epiſtle be read unto all the holy brethren* *Note*, (1) All Chriſtians are bound to read the Scriptures diligently, nor can there be a ſtronger mark of antichriſt, than the keeping theſe ſacred records ſealed up in an unknown tongue (2) That public worſhip is very defective, where the Scriptures are not read in the congregation

6 He cloſes with his uſual benediction *The grace of our Lord Jeſus Chriſt be with you* May the ſovereign, boundleſs, and everlaſting favour of the adored Jeſus, be your portion now and for ever *Amen!*

THE EVANGELICAL EXPOSITOR; OR, A PRACTICAL COMMENT Upon the SECOND EPISTLE of St. PAUL to the THESSALONIANS.

THIS Second Epistle was written soon after the former, and seems to be designed to prevent their running into a mistake, which might arise from some passages in the former Epistle, concerning the Second coming of Christ, as if it were near at hand. The apostle in this Epistle is careful to prevent any wrong use some among them might make of those expressions of his, that were agreeable to the dialect of the prophets of the Old Testament, and informeth them that there were many intermediate counsels yet to be fulfilled before that day of the Lord shall come, though, because it is sure, he had spoken of it as near. There are other things he writeth about for their consolation under sufferings, and exhortation and direction in duty.

CHAP. I.

After the introduction, ver. 1, 2. the apostle begins this epistle with an account of his high esteem for these Thessalonians, ver. 3, 4. He then comforteth them under their afflictions and persecutions, ver. 5—10. And tells them what his prayers were to God for them, ver. 11, 12.

1 PAUL, and Silvanus, and Timotheus, unto
the church of the Thessalonians, in God our
Father, and the Lord Jesus Christ. 2
Grace unto you, and peace from God our
Father, and the Lord Jesus Christ. 3 We are bound
to thank God always for you, brethren, as it is meet,
because that your faith groweth exceedingly, and the
charity of every one of you all towards each other
aboundeth; 4 So that we ourselves glory in you in
the churches of God, for your patience and faith in all
your persecutions, and tribulations that ye endure: 5
Which is a manifest token of the righteous judgment of
God, that ye may be counted worthy of the kingdom of
God, for which ye also suffer: 6 Seeing *it is* a righte-
ous thing with God to recompense tribulation to them
that trouble you; 7 And to you who are troubled,
rest with us, when the Lord Jesus shall be revealed
from heaven with his mighty angels, 8 In flaming
fire, taking vengeance on them that know not God, and
that obey not the gospel of our Lord Jesus Christ: 9
Who shall be punished with everlasting destruction from
the presence of the Lord, and from the glory of his
power; 10 When he shall come to be glorified in his
saints, and to be admired in all them that believe
(because our testimony among you was believed) in that
day.

v. 1—2. The apostle joins the same persons in the inscription of this epistle with himself as in the former: *Paul, and Silvanus, and Timotheus, unto the church of the Thessalonians, in God our Father, and the Lord Jesus Christ: grace unto you, and peace from God our Father, and the Lord Jesus Christ.*

3. He expresses his thankfulness to God on their behalf: *We are bound to thank God always for you, brethren, as it is meet,* to [illegible] gratefully to acknowledge his blessings and mercies, especially those spiritual blessings, which he hath so richly bestowed upon you, *because that your faith groweth exceedingly,* in fuller discoveries of the gospel, and more unshaken confidence in the promises, as is evident in all the noble fruits of grace and holiness which flourish among you, *and the charity of every one of you all towards each other aboundeth,* the true proof of your faith unfeigned. *Note,* (1.) Faith, as well as every other grace, is at present imperfect, and they who are most advanced, have need to pray, *increase our faith.* (2.) Where true faith [illegible], every other grace must follow, for it worketh by love.

4. Their eminence in grace gave him occasion to boast of them to other churches: *So that we ourselves glory in you in the churches of God,* for your other gifts and graces, but especially *for your patience and faith in all your persecutions, and tribulations that ye endure* with holy intrepidity, unshaken perseverance, and calm submission bearing up under every trial. *Note,* The commendation of good men should be a powerful encouragement to us diligently to improve our fidelity in the cause of Christ.

5. Their sufferings could soon end in eternal glory, and the authors of them in fuller condemnation [illegible], *which is a manifest token of the righteous judgment of God,* who will soon make his impartial justice to appear, and even now it is your honour, as wisely ordered by him, that such tribulations should befall you, *that ye may be counted worthy of the kingdom of God, for which ye also suffer,* conformed thus to your head, and in his time to reign with him. *Seeing it is a righteous thing with God to recompense tribulation to them that trouble you,* who shall shortly feel the arm of an avenging judge; *but to you who are troubled, rest with us,* even the present rest in God, into which they who believe do now enter, and soon that eternal rest will come, which remaineth for

the people of God, *when the Lord Jesus shall be revealed from heaven with his mighty angels*, in all the pomp of tremendous majesty, *in flaming fire, taking vengeance on them that know not God, and that obey not the gospel of our Lord Jesus Christ*, whether idolatrous Gentiles, or unbelieving Jews, or impenitent sinners of every kind, *who shall be punished with everlasting destruction, from the presence of the Lord, and from the glory of his power*, driven into eternal banishment from his blissful abode, and suffering in body and soul the vengeance of eternal fire: *when*, in that happy day for his redeemed, *he shall come to be glorified in his saints*, whose perfect salvation shall then be accomplished, *and to be admired of all that believe*, being henceforward the subject of their everlasting adoration, love, and praise, *because our testimony among you was believed*, and you will reap the blessed fruits of your faith *in that great day*. *Note*, (1) There is a day at hand, when the persecutors and the persecuted will have impartial justice done them at the bar of God. (2) The prospect of that tribunal should comfort us under all the unjust reproaches, revilings, and tribulations which we now endure. (3) The appearing of the Lord will be terrible to the ungodly and the sinner, whose neglect of God and his gospel will then be avenged, when wrath to the uttermost shall overtake them, and, driven with confusion from the presence of an angry Judge, the jaws of hell shall yawn to receive them, and, deep ingulphed in everlasting burnings, they shall sink, and never rise up again. (4) Christ will be the eternal object of his people's admiration, and whilst with wonder they trace from first to last the amazing dispensation of his grace, their hearts will glow with rapture, and their tongues be filled with never-ending praise.

t 1 Thess. i. 2.

u 1 Pet. i. 7. & iv. 14.

11 Wherefore also t we pray always for you, that
our God would count you worthy of *this* calling, and
fulfil all the good pleasure of *his* goodness, and the work
of faith with power: 12 u That the name of our
Lord Jesus Christ may be glorified in you, and ye in
him, according to the grace of our God, and the Lord
Jesus Christ.

v. 11, 12. In the prospect of this day the apostle redoubled his supplications for them. *Wherefore also we pray always for you*,

1. *That our God*, in whose favour and love we have the most assured interest, *would count you worthy of this calling*, enabling you to walk as becomes your vocation, and bring you to the possession of the glory he hath promised, *and fulfil all the good pleasure of his goodness*, accomplishing the purposes of his sovereign grace towards you, carrying on and completing in you the salvation which he hath begun, *and the work of faith with power*, strengthening this radical grace, that all the rest may flourish with greater vigour. *Note*, (1) All our worthiness comes from God's good pleasure, who hath chosen, called, and led us hitherto, and to his sovereign grace we must be alike indebted for all that is yet to come, that we are enabled in faith to persevere, and shall reach at last the heavenly hill. (2) If our faith be wrought of God with power, then shall we never fail.

2. He prays, *That the name of our Lord Jesus Christ may be glorified in you*, by your exemplary conduct and conversation, *and ye in him*, as now united to him by faith, and soon to rise and reign with him eternally, *according to the grace of our God, and the Lord Jesus Christ*, which hath bestowed it on you for this great end, that his own glorious name might be for ever exalted, and all the praise of the sinner's salvation be ascribed to him alone.

CHAP. II.

The apostle is very careful to check the spreading of an error which some among them had fallen into, concerning the coming of Christ as being very near, ver. 1—3. *Then he proceedeth to confute this error he cautioned them against, by telling them of two great events that were antecedent to the coming of Christ, viz. a general apostasy, and the revelation of Antichrist, concerning whom the apostle tells them many remarkable things about his name, his character, his rise, his fall, his reign, and the sin and ruin of his subjects*, ver. 3—12. *He then comforts them against the terror of this apostasy, and exhorts them to stedfastness*, ver. 13—15. *And concludeth with a prayer for them*, ver. 16, 17.

a Mat. xxiv. 31. 1 Thess. iv. 16, 17. b Mat. xxiv. 4. Eph. v. 6. c 1 John iv. 1. d Jer. xxix. 8. Mat. xxiv. 4. 24. e 1 Tim. iv. 1. f Dan. vii. 25. 1 John ii. 18. Rev. xiii. 11. g John xvii. 12. h Isa. xiv. 13. Ezek. xxviii. 2, 6.

1 NOW we beseech you, brethren, a by the coming
of our Lord Jesus Christ, and *by* our gathering
together unto him, 2 b That ye be not soon shaken in
mind, or be troubled, neither by spirit, nor by word,
nor by letter, as from us, as that the day of Christ is at
hand. 3 c Let no man deceive you by any means: 4
For *that day shall not come*, d except there come a falling
away first, and e that man of sin be revealed, f the son of
perdition; 4 Who opposeth and g exalteth himself above
h all that is called God, or that is worshipped; so that
he as God sitteth in the temple of God, shewing himself
that he is God. 5 Remember ye not, that when I was
yet with you, I told you these things? 6 And now ye
know what withholdeth, that he might be revealed in his
time. 7 For k the mystery of iniquity doth already
work: only he who now letteth, *will let*, until he be
taken out of the way. 8 And then shall that wicked
be revealed, l whom the Lord shall consume m with the
spirit of his mouth, and shall destroy n with the bright-
ness of his coming: 9 *Even him* whose coming is o af-
ter the working of Satan, with all power, p and signs, and
lying wonders, 10 And with all deceiveableness of un-
righteousness in q them that perish; because they received
not the love of the truth, that they might be saved. 11
And r for this cause God shall send them strong delusion,
s that they should believe a lye: 12 That they all
might be damned who believed not the truth, but t had
pleasure in unrighteousness.

i 1 Cor. viii. 5. k 1 John ii. 18. & iv. 3. l Dan. vii. 10, 11. m Isa. xi. 4. Hos. vi. 5. Rev. ii. 16. & xix. 15. & xx. 1. n Chap. i. 8. 9. Heb. x. 27. o Eph. ii. 2. Rev. xiii. 13. p Deut. xiii. 1. Mat. xxiv. 24. Rev. xiii. 13. q 2 Cor. ii. 15. & iv. 3. r Rom. i. 24, &c. s 2 Chron. xviii. 22. Ezek. xiv. 9. t 1 Tim. iv. 1. u Rom. i. 32.

v. 1—12. An error of a dangerous tendency had, it seems, crept in to the church of the Thessalonians, that the coming of Christ to judge the world should be in their days. Whether this arose from their mistake of what the apostle had mentioned in his former epistle, or was broached by some who vouched his authority to support what they advanced, he sets himself to confute the assertion, and to rectify their judgment in this matter.

1. He solemnly warns them not to be troubled with needless fears and apprehensions. *Now we beseech you, brethren, by the coming of our Lord Jesus Christ, and by our gathering together unto him*, by all the hopes you entertain of meeting him with joy in that day, I adjure you, *that ye be not soon shaken in mind*, from the gospel which ye have embraced, and tossed to and fro with every wind of doctrine, *nor be troubled* by any assertions which may be advanced, or misconstructions which may arise, *neither by spirit*, by those who pretend to speak under divine inspiration, *nor by word*, however confidently any may advance this notion, *nor by letter, as from us*, either counterfeiting our hand, or perverting our meaning, *as that the day of Christ is at hand*. *Let no man deceive you by any means*: the consequence of such a persuasion would be very dangerous, and when you found yourselves disappointed of your vainly raised expectations, it might shake your faith in the truth of the whole gospel revelation. *Note*, (1) One way in which the arch deceiver strikes at the faith of God's elect, is by endeavouring, through his emissaries pretending to revelation, or a knowledge of the prophetic word, to raise groundless hopes in their minds, and from the disappointment of them to suggest, that the whole may be a delusion. (2) Tho' we cannot fix the time of Christ's coming, yet nothing is more certain, than that he that cometh shall come, and shall not tarry: may we without fear or dismay be ready to meet him. (3) However dispersed God's people now may be in different regions, and living in different ages, they shall one day be gathered together around the throne of Jesus, and so shall be ever with the Lord.

2. He confutes the error which was broached, by shewing, that many events, which would require much time to fulfil them, must precede the second coming of Christ.

(1) There must be first a general apostacy. *For that day shall not come, except there come a falling away first*, from the doctrine of the gospel, and the practice of godliness, which shall usher in the reign of Antichrist.

(2) The rise of the antichristian power is described, *v.* 3—10. To whom what is here spoken belongs, hath been matter of much dispute. I cannot but own, with the best protestant commentators, my full conviction, that the popish hierarchy is the subject of this prophecy, wherein we have,

[1] *The names* of this person, or rather state, here spoken of. *The man of sin, the son of perdition, that wicked one*, which do not point out any individual, but a succession of men, carrying on the same destructive designs, whose wicked practices and horrid delusions will be the cause of perdition to multitudes, who will perish with them.

[2] When *that man of sin is revealed, the son of perdition*, he may be known by these characters. *Who opposeth and exalteth himself above all that is called God, or that is worshipped*, assuming all power in heaven and in earth, undertaking to enact laws contrary to God's word and will, and setting up himself above kings and emperors, yea, and above the angels too, who are called Gods in scripture. *So that he as God*, arrogating divine perfections, *sitteth in the temple of God*, the church, where he hath erected his unhallowed throne, *shewing himself that he is God*, assuming the blasphemous titles of, *our God the pope, God upon earth*, &c. usurping divine authority over the bodies and consciences of men, pretending to pardon sin by his own power, and speaking great swelling words of blasphemy. *Remember ye not*, saith the apostle, *that when I was yet with you, I told you these things*.

[3] He

[3] His *rise* is pointed out *And now ye know*, if you reflect upon what I told you formerly, *what withholdeth*, that the man of sin doth not immediately appear, even the power of the heathen Roman emperors During their rule, the bishops of Rome were prevented from rising above their fellows, but this empire would in process of time moulder away, *that he may be revealed in his time*, when God, according to his own decrees, should permit the antichristian power to rear its head *For the mystery of iniquity doth already work*, and the seeds of pride, dissention, and worldly ambition, have begun to be sown *but he that letteth*, the Roman emperors, *will let, until he be taken out of the way*, their power declining, and the seat of empire being removed from Rome, *and then shall that wicked be revealed*, and the mystery of iniquity, and the tyranny of the popish power, arrive at their height

[4] His ruin is as certain as his rise *Whom the Lord shall consume with the spirit of his mouth, and shall destroy with the brightness of his coming*, raising up a noble army of preachers, who by the word of truth, accompanied with the Spirit's power, shall cut in sunder the fetters wherewith superstition hath enslaved the minds of men, and as the kingdom of Antichrist shall be overturned hereby, so shall he and all his followers at last perish in the lake of fire

[5] The way in which this wicked one shall maintain his usurped dominion is described *Whose coming is after the working of Satan, with all power, and signs, and lying wonders*, with all satanical influence and wiles, pretending to work miracles in support of his cause, *and* by a system of frauds deluding the nations of the earth, *with all deceivableness of unrighteousness in them that perish*, deceiving the souls of men to their eternal ruin, *because they received not the love of the truth, that they might be saved*, but turned aside to error, and chose their own delusions *And for this cause*, in just judgment upon them, *God shall send them strong delusion*, abandoning them to their own hearts, and giving them up to judicial blindness, *that they should believe a lye*, all those absurd legends, forgeries, and falshoods, with which the church of Rome abounds *that they all might be damned who believed not the truth* rejecting Christ and his gospel, *but had pleasure in unrighteousness*, delighting in their errors, superstitions, and bloody persecutions, to fill up the measure of their iniquities *Note*, It is just in God to abandon obstinate sinners to their own delusions, and leave them to the damnation which themselves have chosen

13. But [p] we are bound to give thanks alway to God
for you, brethren, beloved of the Lord, because God
hath [x] from the beginning [y] chosen you to salvation,
[z] through sanctification of the Spirit, and belief of the
truth 14 Whereunto he called you by our gospel, [a] to
the obtaining of the glory of our Lord Jesus Christ
15 Therefore, brethren, [b] stand fast, and hold [c] the tra-
ditions which ye have been taught, whether by word or
our epistle 16 [d] Now our Lord Jesus Christ himself,
and God even our Father, which hath loved us, and hath
given *us* everlasting consolation, [e] and good hope through
grace, 17 Comfort your hearts, [f] and stablish you in
every good word and work

[p] Chap ii 3
[x] Eph i 4 2 Tim i 9
[y] 1 Thes i 4
[z] Luke i 75 1 Pet i 2 John xvii 2.
[b] 1 Cor xv Phil iv
[c] 1 Cor xi 2 Chap iii 6
[d] Chap i -
[e] 1 Pet i
[f] 2 Cor i 21 1 Thes iii 13

v 13—17 The apostle,

1 Expresses his thankfulness to God for his electing love *But we are bound to give thanks alway to God for you, brethren beloved of the Lord, because* it is evident from your whole conduct and conversation that *God hath from the beginning chosen you to salvation*, having predestinated you, before the world were, to an eternity of blessedness, as elect vessels, separated by his sovereign grace from the corrupted mass of mankind, and, as the means of accomplishing the purposes of his eternal counsels, hath, *through sanctification of the Spirit, and belief of the truth*, begun to prepare you for the inheritance to which he hath appointed you; *whereunto he also called you by our gospel*, the happy instrument of your conversion, *to the obtaining of the glory of our Lord Jesus Christ*, which he hath procured for his people, and freely bestows upon them, according to the riches of grace *Note*, (1) God hath a people whom he hath chosen from the beginning unto salvation, and men, nor devils, nor sin, shall be able to frustrate the designs of his grace towards them (2) Wherever the Lord chuses a soul for glory, he inseparably annexes the means to the end, calling them by his gospel to faith and holiness, and working both in their hearts It would be the most absurd presumption to fancy we are the elect, if we cannot feel and demonstrate the work of the Spirit of faith and sanctification in our hearts and lives

2 He exhorts them to be faithful *Therefore, brethren*, in the assured prospect of success, *stand fast*, God's election of you should be the quickening and encouraging motive to make your own calling, and election sure, *and hold the traditions which ye have been taught*, the doctrines which we your faithful ministers have delivered to you, as received from Christ, *whether by word*, in our public preaching or private discourse, *or by our epistle*, lately sent to you *Note*, God's word is our only rule of duty, thereunto we must cleave

3 He closes with a fervent prayer for them *Now our Lord Jesus Christ himself, and God even our Father*, who alike are the objects of our worship, and are one in the glory of the same undivided Godhead, *who hath loved us, and hath given us everlasting consolation*, the foretastes of those joys that shall hereafter be uninterrupted and eternal, *and good hope through grace*, built on the substantial foundation of his unchangeable word, *comfort your hearts* with a clearer knowledge of your invaluable privileges, and a brighter manifestation of his love to your souls, amidst all your trials and sufferings, *and stablish you in every good word and work*, that you may approve yourselves faithful, and unto death persevere immoveably in the doctrine and practice of the blessed gospel *Note*, (1) God's everlasting love is the fountain of all our blessedness (2) Though our consolations may now be at times interrupted by the manifold temptations to which we are exposed, in eternity they will flow with an unceasing stream like a river (3) Good hope is still a sure anchor of the soul, when great joy may be withdrawn, and all is *through grace*, not for our desert, but according to the multitude of God's mercies (4) It is the Lord's work to comfort and stablish our hearts and whilst we are waiting upon him, we shall assuredly renew our strength

CHAP III

In the close of the foregoing chapter the apostle had prayed earnestly for the Thessalonians, and now he desireth their prayers, encouraging them to trust in God, to which he subjoins another petition for them, ver 1—5 He then proceedeth to give them commands and directions for the correcting some things he was informed were amiss among them, ver 6—15 And concludeth with benedictions and prayers, ver 16—18

1 FINALLY, brethren, [a] pray for us, that the
word of the Lord may † have *free* course, and be
glorified *even as it is* with you, 2 And [b] that we may
be delivered from unreasonable and wicked men for
[c] all *men* have not faith 3 But [d] the Lord is faithful,
who shall stablish you, and [e] keep *you* from evil 4
And [f] we have confidence in the Lord touching you,
that ye both do, and will do the things which we com-
mand you 5. And [g] the Lord direct your hearts into
the love of God, and into ‡ the patient waiting for
Christ

[a] Eph vi 19 Col iv 3
† Gr run
[b] Rom xv 31
[c] Rom x 16
[d] 1 Cor i 9 1 Thes v 24
[e] John xvii 15
[f] 2 Cor vii 16 Gal v 10
[g] 1 Chron xxix 18
‡ Or the patience of Christ

v 1—5 The apostle here draws to a conclusion, and,

1 Intreats their prayers *Finally, brethren, pray for us, that the word of the Lord may have free course*, and spread with increasing success, *and be glorified even as it is with you*, in the mighty effects produced by our ministration of it, *and that we may be delivered from unreasonable and wicked men*, hardened in pride and prejudice against the truth, who use every violent effort to oppose its progress, and silence the ministers of the gospel *for all men have not faith*, but even among professors of Christianity we often meet with the greatest opposers, and are in most danger from these false brethren *Note*, (1) The success of his labours lies nearest the heart of every gospel minister (2) All who have tasted of the grace of God in truth, are bound in ceaseless prayer to beg that the same word which they have received, may, in defiance of all opposition, run and be glorified, to the conviction of sinners, the confusion of gainsayers, and the edification of the faithful (3) Unreasonable and wicked men abound in every age, and they who, though professors of Christianity, are themselves destitute of divine faith, cannot but now, as then, testify the same enmity against the zealous preachers of the gospel

2 He expresses his confidence in them *But the Lord is faithful, who shall stablish you, and keep you from evil*, whatever wiles seducers may employ, or however severely you may be exposed to the enmity of persecutors, the Lord will never fail you and his grace shall make you more than conquerors *And we have confidence in the Lord touching you, that ye both do, and will do the things which we command you*, in his name, and by his authority *Note*, (1) Our great encouragement is God's fidelity to his promises he will not fail us, and therefore we cannot fail him (2) If the Lord did not keep us, we should not for a moment be able to keep ourselves, but when we have him at our right hand, neither the evil of sin shall prevail against us, nor the evil of suffering discourage us

3 He adds a short prayer for them, containing two important requests *And the Lord direct your hearts into the love of God*, turning your affections from every crooked path, and directly leading you to his blessed self, and to that happiness which is to be enjoyed in a sense of his present and everlasting love to your souls, *and into the patient waiting for Christ*, enabling you with chearfulness and submission to take up the cross, and to look for the

the coming of your Lord, when there shall be an end put to all your sufferings for ever.

6 Now we command you, brethren, in the name of
our Lord Jesus Christ, that ye withdraw yourselves
from every brother that walketh disorderly, and not
after the tradition which he received of us. 7 For
yourselves know how ye ought to follow us: for we
behaved not ourselves disorderly among you; 8 Neither
did we eat any man's bread for nought; but wrought
with labour and travail night and day, that we might
not be chargeable to any of you: 9 Not because we
have not power, but to make ourselves an ensample unto
you to follow us. 10 For even when we were with
you, this we commanded you, that if any would not
work, neither should he eat. 11 For we hear that
there are some which walk among you disorderly,
working not at all, but are busy-bodies. 12 Now
them that are such we command and exhort by our
Lord Jesus Christ, that with quietness they work, and
eat their own bread. 13 But ye, brethren, be not
weary in well doing. 14 And if any man obey not
our word by this epistle, note that man, and have
no company with him, that he may be ashamed. 15
Yet count him not as an enemy, but admonish him
as a brother.

v. 6—15. Though the apostle had so highly commended them, and expressed his confidence in them in general, yet there were some among them who needed sharp rebuke; and indeed in this imperfect state of things, no absolutely perfect and pure society of men is to be expected.

1. He warns them to avoid the company of such as walked disorderly among them, whose ill characters he here describes. *Now we command you, brethren, in the name of our Lord Jesus Christ*, and by the apostolic power committed to us, *that ye withdraw yourselves from every brother* that pretends to be a Christian, but *walketh disorderly, and not after the tradition which he received of us*, being a disgrace and a dishonour to his profession. *For yourselves know how ye ought to follow us*, and remember the practice we recommended to you, and the example which we set before you; *for we behaved not ourselves disorderly among you, neither did we eat any man's bread for nought*, without paying for it; *but wrought with labour and travail night and day*, to earn our own maintenance, *that we might not be chargeable to any of you*, and might preach the gospel freely, without putting you to the least expence. *Not because we have not power* to demand our subsistence, as due to our ministerial labour; *but* we rather chose to waive our right, *to make ourselves an example unto you to follow us*, encouraging industry, and discountenancing idleness. *For even when we were with you, this we commanded you, that if any would not work, neither should he eat*, nor receive any relief from the church, whose charity should be applied, not to the maintenance of the slothful, but to the support of the sick, infirm, and those who through age or accident are disabled from providing for themselves. *For we hear that there are some which walk among you disorderly, working not at all*, but depending on others for relief, and *are busy-bodies*, tattling from house to house, prying into the secrets of families, blowing up the coals of dissension, and the very pests of society. *Note*, (1.) When we can appeal to our people for the exemplariness of our own conversation, and for the conformity of our practice to our preaching, we may command and exhort them to their duty with confidence. (2.) Sloth and indolence are most opposite to the spirit of Christianity; and though men may plead they do no harm, yet if they neglect the duty of their calling and stations, God will reckon with them as with disorderly walkers. (3.) Idleness opens a door to every evil; and they who chuse not to do their own work, the devil will find them employ.

2. He addresses himself with authority to these disorderly walkers. *Now them that are such, we command and exhort by our Lord Jesus Christ*, by every endearing argument which his love can suggest, or the dread of his displeasure urges, *that with quietness they work, and eat their own bread*, peaceably minding their own affairs with diligence, and providing for themselves and families a becoming maintenance from the produce of their honest industry.

3. He directs the faithful and industrious how they should behave. *But ye brethren, be not weary in well-doing*, but with diligence discharge the labours of your calling; and if you have more than your own necessities require, there are many deserving objects who crave your charity. *And if any man among you obey not our word by this epistle*, and change not his ways, *note that man, and have no company with him*; permit him not to be your intimate, nor admit him to the table of the Lord; *that*, by your just censure of his conduct, *he may be ashamed*, and brought to repentance and amendment. *Yet count him not as an enemy* at once, and deal roughly, *but admonish him as a brother*, that, if it please the Lord, he may yet be reclaimed, and not be finally ruined. *Note*, (1.) We must not only walk orderly ourselves, but shew our disapprobation of those who behave dishonourable to their profession. (2.) Before more heavy censures are pronounced, every kind admonition must be attempted. Love will often shame those into ingenuous acknowledgments, that severity would but have exasperated and hardened.

16 Now the Lord of peace himself give you peace b Rom. xv.
always by all means. The Lord *be* with you all. 33. Phil. iv.
17 The salutation of Paul with mine own hand, 1 Thess. v.
which is the token in every epistle: so I write. 18 1 Cor. xvi.
The grace of our Lord Jesus Christ *be* with you all. 18.
Amen. Rom. xvi.
24.

v. 16—18. The apostle concludes with,

1. His prayer for them. *Now the Lord of peace himself*, who purchased it by his blood, and by his Spirit seals it to the hearts of his people, *give you peace always, by all means*, meeting you in the use of every instituted ordinance, filling you with a comfortable sense of his reconciliation to you, and giving you an happy union and harmony among each other. *The Lord be with you all*, may his presence and blessing be ever in the midst of you, and where he manifests himself, there heaven is already begun in the soul.

2. His subscription. *The salutation of Paul with mine own hand, which is the token in every epistle*, of its genuineness, to prevent the forgeries of seducers: *so I write*, in the close of every letter, when my amanuensis hath finished.

3. The benediction. *The grace of our Lord Jesus Christ be with you all*, may you share all the present and eternal blessedness included in his sovereign grace and love. *Amen!*

THE

THE

EVANGELICAL EXPOSITOR;

OR, A

PRACTICAL COMMENT

Upon the FIRST EPISTLE of

St. PAUL to TIMOTHY.

Hitherto Paul's Epistles were directed to churches, now follow some to particular persons, two to Timothy, one to Titus, and another to Philemon, all three ministers Timothy and Titus were Evangelists, an inferior order to the apostles, as appears by that, Eph iv 11 Some prophets, some apostles, some evangelists *Their commission and work was much the same with that of the apostles, to plant churches, and water the churches that were planted Timothy was first converted by Paul, and therefore he calls him his* own son in the faith, *we read of his conversion,* Acts xvi. 23

The scope of these two Epistles is, to direct Timothy how to discharge his office as an evangelist at Ephesus, where he now was, and where Paul ordered him for some time to reside, to perfect the good work which he had begun there.

CHAP I.

After the inscription in ver 1, 2 *we have,* 1 *The charge given to Timothy,* ver 3, 4 2 *The true end of the law,* ver 5—12 *where he shews it is entirely agreeable to the gospel* 3 *He mentions his own call to be an apostle, for which he expresses his thankfulness,* ver 12—16 5 *His doxology,* ver 17 6 *A renewal of the charge to Timothy,* ver 18 *And of Hymenaeus and Alexander,* ver 19, 20

a 1 Tim ix 15 & xxiii 21 b Chap 3 & iv 10 Tit i 3 c Col i 27 d Acts xvi 1 1 Cor iv 17 1 Thes iii 2 e 2 Tim i 2 Tit i 4 f Gal i 3 2 Tim i 2 1 Pet i 2 g Acts xx 1, 3 Phil ii 24 h Gal xv i Chap vi 3 k Chap iv 7 Tit i 14 & iii 9 l Chap vi 4

1 PAUL an apostle of Jesus Christ [a] by the commandment of [b] God our Saviour, and Lord Jesus Christ, [c] *which is* our hope, 2
Unto [d] Timothy, [e] *my* own son in the faith,
[f] grace, mercy, *and* peace from God our Father, and Jesus Christ our Lord 3 As I besought thee to abide still at Ephesus - when I went into Macedonia, that thou mightest charge some [h] that they teach no other doctrine,
4 [i] Neither give heed to fables, and endless genealogies, [k] which minister questions, rather than godly edifying, which is in faith *so do*

v 1—4 We have here,

1 The apostolical inscription *Paul an apostle of Jesus Christ,* the true Messiah, *by the express commandment of God* appointed to this office, who is *our Saviour,* having in his eternal mind designed the glorious plan of our redemption, *and of our Lord Jesus Christ,* one with the Father in glory and authority; *and who is* emphatically our hope, all our expectations in time and eternity resting upon his finished salvation, *unto Timothy my own son in the faith,* begotten by me in the gospel, is this epistle sent

2 His salutation *Grace, mercy, and peace,* be with you, *from God our Father,* in whose love we have a common interest, *and Jesus Christ our Lord,* who bought us with his blood, called us to the obedience of the faith, and, as his more immediate servants, put us in trust with his gospel

3 He reminds him of the design he had in leaving him at Ephesus, and exhorts him to be faithful to his charge *As I besought thee to abide still at Ephesus when I went into Macedonia, that thou mightest charge some, that they teach no other doctrine,* even those judaizing teachers, who would corrupt the simplicity of the gospel be faithful to thy trust, and warn the people to beware of these seducers, *neither to give heed to fables,* their absurd traditions, *and endless genealogies,* affecting to trace up their descent from Abraham and the patriarchs, and valuing themselves highly on such an ancestor, *which minister questions,* and endless disputes, *rather than godly edifying, which is in faith*
Note, (1) Unedifying disputes about unessential matters have the most pernicious tendency to destroy vital religion (2) There can be no true godliness, but what springs from faith as its principle (3) Ministers must watch over the flock, and guard them from the inroads of error, as well as impiety. (4) Broachers of new doctrine, contrary to the fundamental articles of faith, should receive from the bishops of the church deserved rebuke

5 Now [l] the end of the commandment is charity out of a pure heart, and *of* a good conscience, and *of* faith unfeigned 6 From which some having swerved, [m] have turned aside [n] unto vain jangling 7 Desiring to be teachers of the law, understanding neither what they say, nor whereof they affirm. 8 But we know that [o] the law *is* good, if a man use it lawfully; 9 Knowing this, that [p] the law is not made for a righteous man, but for the lawless and disobedient, for the ungodly and for sinners, for unholy and prophane, for murderers of fathers and murderers of mothers, for manslayers, 10
For whoremongers, for them that defile themselves with

l Rom xiii 8, 10. Gal v 14 m 2 Tim ii 22 n Chap v 15 & vi 20 2 Tim ii 18 o Chap vi 4, 20 2 Tim iv 4 p Rom vii 12 q Gal ii 19 & v 23

mankind, for men-stealers, for lyars, for perjured per-
sons, and if there be any other thing that is contrary
ʳ to sound doctrine, 11 According to the glorious gos-
pel of ˢ the blessed God, ᵗ which was committed to my
trust

ʳ Chap vi 3 2 Tim iv 3 Tit i 9 & ii 1 ˢ Chap vi 15 ᵗ Gal ii 7 1 Thes ii 4 Chap ii 7 Tit i 3

v 5—11 Having repeated the charge before given to Timothy, concerning the deluding teachers, he here,

1 Directs him what end he should aim at, the preservation of the church's peace *Now the end of the commandment*, (either of the moral law, or of the charge which the apostle had given him) *is* to promote *charity*, or love towards God and man, flowing *out of a pure heart*, sanctified by the blessed Spirit, *and of a good conscience*, purged from dead works by the blood of sprinkling, *and of faith unfeigned*, the radical grace, from whence love and every other divine temper springs *from all which some having swerved*, and wandring wide of the mark, *have turned aside unto vain jangling*, trifling questions, and idle disputes, *desiring to be teachers of the law*, setting up for great wisdom, as interpreters of it, and zealous to urge its observation upon the Gentiles as necessary to salvation, *understanding neither what they say, nor whereof they affirm*, real strangers to its spiritual nature, use, and design *Note*, (1) Love in the heart is the great preservative from all disputes and dissentions (2) It is a sad consideration, when ignorant men intrude into the ministry, strangers to the oracles of God, and unacquainted with any of the truths themselves in which they pretend to instruct others

2 The right use of the law is here declared *But*, however abused it may be, *we know that the law is good, if a man use it lawfully*, and apply it to the purposes for which God gave it, to convince the conscience of sin, to be a schoolmaster to lead us to Christ, and, though ceasing to be a covenant of works, yet continuing to be a rule of duty, according to which God will proceed in his judgment at the last day *Knowing this, that the law is not made for a righteous man*, nor doth the damning sentence of it lie against any faithful soul, that is righteous in Christ Jesus, *but for the lawless and disobedient, for the ungodly and for sinners, for unholy and prophane*, who with daring impenitence and wilful obstinacy transgress it, *for murderers of fathers and murderers of mothers, for manslayers, for whoremongers, for them that defile themselves with mankind, for men-stealers, for lyars, for perjured persons, and if there be any other thing that is contrary to sound doctrine*, all which, and every other crime, the law condemns, and the judgment denounced by the law is *according to the glorious gospel of the blessed God, which was committed to my trust*, there being the most perfect agreement in this respect between the law and gospel, which condemns all ungodliness, and teaches us to live righteously, soberly, and godly in this present evil world *Note*, The gospel is an awful glorious trust, and whilst we bless God for the honour he puts upon us in committing it to our charge, we need tremble for ourselves, lest we should be found unfaithful

ᵘ 2 Tim iv 17 ˣ 1 Cor vii 25 ʸ 2 Cor iii 6 ᶻ Acts viii 3, & ix 1 & xxii 4 1 Cor xv 9 Gal i 13 ᵃ John ix 39, 41 Acts iii 17 1 Cor ii 8 ᵇ Rom v 20 1 Cor xv 10 ᶜ 2 Tim i 13 ᵈ Luke vii 47 ᵉ Mat ix 13 Mark ii 17 Luke v 32 & xix 10 Rom v 8 1 John iii 5 ᶠ 1 Cor xv 9 ᵍ 2 Cor iv 1 ʰ Acts xiii 39 ⁱ 1 Chr xxix ... Psal x 16 ... ᵏ John i 18 ... ˡ Rom xvi 27 Jude 25 ᵐ 1 Chron xxix 11

12 And I thank Christ Jesus our Lord, ᵘ who hath
enabled me, for that ˣ he counted me faithful, ʸ putting
me into the ministry, 13 ᶻ Who was before a blas-
phemer, and a persecutor, and injurious But I obtained
mercy, because ᵃ I did *it* ignorantly in unbelief 14
And ᵇ the grace of our Lord was exceeding abundant,
ᶜ with faith, ᵈ and love which is in Christ Jesus 15
This *is* a faithful saying, and worthy of all acceptation,
that ᵉ Christ Jesus came into the world to save sinners,
ᶠ of whom I am chief 16 Howbeit, for this cause ᵍ I
obtained mercy, that in me first Jesus Christ might shew
forth all long-suffering, ʰ for a pattern to them which
should hereafter believe on him to life everlasting 17
Now unto ⁱ the King eternal, immortal, ᵏ invisible, ˡ the
only wise God, ᵐ *be* honour and glory for ever and
ever Amen

v 12—17 The apostle with deep gratitude acknowledges the distinguishing favour shown him of God, not only in calling him to the knowledge of his grace, but in putting him in trust with the gospel, and qualifying him for the discharge of it *I thank Christ Jesus our Lord, who hath enabled me, for that he counted me faithful, putting me into the ministry* *Note*, (1) None are Christ's ministers, but those whom he puts into their office (2) Whom he calls, he will qualify for the discharge of their ministry (3) Want of ministerial abilities is a sure proof that men run unsent

1 The apostle humbly owns the dreadful state out of which by divine grace he was called, *who was before a blasphemer* of Christ and his gospel, *and a persecutor* of his people, *and injurious*, branding the Christian name with every malignant aspersion *Note*, (1) The depth of our guilt serve to magnify but the more the riches of divine grace in our pardon and salvation (2) True converts are ever ready to take shame to themselves, and to confess their former abomination with deep regret

2 God had mercy on him *But I obtained mercy, because I did it ignorantly in unbelief*, which he mentions not as an extenuation of his guilt, but to shew the state of rooted prejudice, and hardened unbelief, in which the Lord found him *and the grace of our Lord was exceeding abundant*, beyond all conception wonderful, that it should be extended to such a wretch as me, *with faith, and love, which is in Christ Jesus*, and which in the richest measure the Lord was pleased to bestow upon my soul So that from the happiest experience I can now declare, that *this is a faithful saying, and worthy of all acceptation, that Christ Jesus came into the world to save sinners, of whom I am chief* none therefore, after the mercy which I have received, need despair *Howbeit*, notwithstanding my enormous guilt, *for this cause I obtained mercy, that in me first*, or the chief of sinners, *Jesus Christ might shew forth all long-suffering, for a pattern to them which should hereafter believe on him to life everlasting*, encouraging the vilest to hope and return to him, as being still willing and able to save to the uttermost *Note*, (1) Unbelief is at the bottom of every evil (2) The chief of sinners may be saved as freely as the least those only perish, who will not come to Christ that they may have life (3) They who are discouraged under a sense of the greatness of their sins, should remember those who have already found mercy, and from the deepest crimes have risen to the greatest heights of grace, witness David, Manasseh, Peter, and this apostle (4) All who by faith lay hold on Jesus Christ, have everlasting life, and shall never more enter into condemnation

3 He ascribes praise to God for all the rich grace which he had experienced *Now unto the King eternal, immortal, invisible, the only wise God* to Jesus, who in the highest possesses every divine attribute and perfection, *be honour and glory for ever Amen* *Note*, They who are sensible of their infinite obligations to Christ, will be ceaseless in their grateful acknowledgements to the Author of all their mercies

18 ⁿ This charge I commit unto thee, son Timothy, ⁿ Chap vi 13, Tim
ᵒ according to the prophecies which went before on thee, ᵒ Chap iv 14
that thou by them mightest ᵖ war a good warfare, 19 ᵖ Ch. p. vi 12 2 Tim ii 3
ᵠ Holding faith, and a good conscience, which some ᵠ Chap iii 9
having put away, concerning faith ʳ have made ship- ʳ Chap vi 9
wreck 20 Of whom is ˢ Hymeneus and ᵗ Alexander, ˢ 2 Tim ii 17
whom I have ᵘ delivered unto Satan, that they may learn ᵗ 2 Tim iv 14
not to blaspheme ᵘ 1 Cor v 5

v 18—20 The apostle repeats his charge to Timothy, mentioned *v* 3—5 *This charge I commit unto thee, son Timothy, according to the prophecies which went before on thee*, and marked thee out as appointed of God for signal service, *that*, remembring these things, *thou* mightest be quickened to correspond therewith, and *by them mightest war a good warfare*, as a faithful soldier of Christ, manfully fighting under his banner against sin and error *holding faith*, firmly attached to the purity of the gospel doctrines, *and* maintaining *a good conscience*, void of offence towards God and man, *which some having put away*, rejected and thrust from them, *concerning faith have made shipwreck*, and apostatized from the fair profession which once they made, *of whom is Hymeneus and Alexander*, those notorious heretics, *whom I have delivered unto Satan*, by my apostolic power assigning them over to that tormentor, to inflict upon them severe chastisement, *that they may learn not to blaspheme*, and that by their sufferings they may be brought to a conviction of their sins, or, at least, so terrified, as not to dare any longer to persist in their horrid blasphemies *Note*, (1) We are now engaged in a dangerous warfare, and the ministers of Christ especially will meet with the strongest opposition We have need therefore to hold fast by him who is our strength, that we may stand in the evil day (2) None usually turn out so dreadfully, and become such horrid blasphemers, as those who apostatize from the profession of religion which once they made

CHAP II

In this chapter St Paul treats, 1 Of prayer, with many reasons for it, ver 1—9 2 Of women's apparel, ver 9, 10 3 Of their subjection, with the reasons of it, ver 11—14 4 A promise given for their encouragement in child-bearing, ver 15.

ᵃ Jer xxix 7 ᵇ Chap i 1 Tit i 3 ᶜ Ezek xviii 23 Tit ii 11 2 Pet iii 9 ᵈ John x 30 Rom iii 29 ... ᵉ Gal iii 20 Heb ix 15 ᶠ Mat xx 28 ... ᵍ Gal iv 4 ... ʰ Acts ix 15 2 Tim i 11

1 I Exhort therefore that first of all, supplications,
prayers, intercessions, *and* giving of thanks be made
for all men 2 ᵃ For kings, and for all that are in
authority, that we may lead a quiet and peaceable life
in all godliness and honesty 3 For this *is* good and
acceptable in the sight of ᵇ God our Saviour 4 ᶜ Who
will have all men to be saved, and to come unto the
knowledge of the truth 5 For ᵈ *there is* one God, and
ᵉ one mediator between God and men, the man Christ
Jesus 6 ᶠ Who gave himself a ransom for all, to be
testified ᵍ in due time 7 ʰ Whereunto I am ordained a
preacher,

preacher, and an apostle, (ⁱ I speak the truth in Christ, *and* lye not) ᵏ a teacher of the Gentiles in faith and verity
8 I will therefore that men pray ˡ every where, ᵐ lifting up holy hands, ⁿ without wrath ᵒ and doubting

i Rom ix 1. k Acts xxii 21. Rom xi 13, xv 16. Eph iii 8. l Mal i 11. John iv 21. m Isa i 15. n Matt v 24. o James i 6.

v 1—8 The apostle exhorts,

1 That *supplications, prayers, intercessions, and giving of thanks be made* in the church for all ranks and conditions of men; particularly *for kings*, and *for all that are in authority*, the inferior magistrates, *that we may lead a quiet and peaceable life*, protected from all violence and injuries, and *in all godliness and honesty*, approving our unfeigned piety to God, and our unimpeached integrity towards men

2 He suggests the strongest reasons to support his exhortations *For this is good and acceptable in the sight of God our Saviour, who* enjoins universal charity, and *will have all men to be saved*, some of all nations, ranks, and conditions, Gentiles as well as Jews, high and low, rich and poor, *and*, in order thereunto, hath sent out his gospel *to* call them, that they may *come to the knowledge of the truth*, by the faith of which alone salvation can be obtained *For there is one God, and one mediator between God and men, the man Christ Jesus*, who, though very God, hath taken our nature into personal union with himself, and in his glorified body stands as the alone mediator before the throne, to make the persons, prayers, and services of his people accepted *Who gave himself a ransom for all*, paying down the price of our redemption in the drops of his own most precious blood, and thereby making a full satisfaction to divine justice for sinners of every condition and degree, as was foretold by the prophets, and *to be testified in due time* to all nations *Whereunto I am ordained a preacher, and an apostle*, by a divine commission, (*I speak the truth in Christ, and lye not*, as the heart-searching God doth bear me witness), *a teacher of the Gentiles*, to whom especially I am sent, *in faith and verity*, to bring them to the true faith of Christ, and this office I labour to discharge with all simplicity and faithfulness *Note*, (1) It is God's will that we should pray for others as well as for ourselves (2) Our encouragement to draw near to a throne of grace is this, that we have one Mediator there, who ever liveth to make intercession for us (3) Since Jesus hath paid, and God hath accepted the ransom, all that plead it have a right to the eternal redemption thereby obtained (4) None can be saved but by coming to the knowledge of the truth where Christ is not preached, there can be no hope, for there is salvation in no other (5) It is an inestimable blessing to enjoy the light of the gospel, and to sit under their ministry who preach it in faith and verity

3 He directs them how to pray *I will therefore that men*, who bear the Christian name, *pray every where*, not confined to any particular place, since God is alike present in all, in the closet, in the family, as well as in the great congregation only when we draw near to him, if we would obtain acceptance, we must be found *lifting up holy hands*, not polluted with allowed sin, but washed in atoning blood, *without wrath and doubting*, since harboured malice, unbelieving distrust of God, and a contentious spirit, must necessarily destroy all the efficacy of prayer

9 In like manner also, that ᵖ women adorn themselves in modest apparel, with shamefacedness and sobriety not with ‖ broidered hair, or gold, or pearls, or costly aray,
10 ᑫ But (which becometh women professing godliness) with good works
11 Let the woman learn in silence ʳ with all subjection.
12 But ˢ I suffer not a woman to teach, ᵗ nor to usurp authority over the man, but to be in silence
13 For ᵘ Adam was first formed, then Eve
14 And ˣ Adam was not deceived, but the woman being deceived was in the transgression
15 Notwithstanding she shall be saved in child-bearing, if they continue in faith and charity, and holiness with sobriety

p 1 Pet iii 3. ‖ Or plaited. q 1 Pet iii 4. r Gen iii 16. s 1 Cor xiv 34. t Eph v 22. u Gen i 27, ii 18, 22. 1 Cor xi 8, 9. x Gen iii 6. 2 Cor xi 3.

v 9—15 The apostle here directs how women professing godliness should behave

1 With modesty *In like manner also, that women adorn themselves in modest apparel, with shamefacedness and sobriety not with broidered hair, or gold, or pearls, or costly aray, but (which becometh women professing godliness) with good works* What a contrast to this description are our manners! yet, the truly gracious woman will still think modesty her brightest ornament, and when fashion imposes aught that is fantastical, extravagant, or immodest, will dare to disobey

2 *Let the woman learn in silence with all subjection*, not presuming to be speakers in the house of God, *but* hearers, *for I suffer not a woman to teach* in public, *nor to usurp authority over the man*, by that or any other instance of affected superiority, *but to be in silence For Adam was first formed, then Eve*, from his side, (*Gen* ii 22) to denote her inferiority *And Adam was not deceived* by the serpent, *but the woman being deceived was in the transgression*, and he, seduced by her, or out of fond affection determined to die with her, wilfully followed her example *Notwithstanding she shall be saved in child-bearing*, amidst all the anguish which flows from the sentence pronounced on her (*Gen* iii 16) and through that child which is born of woman, the adored Immanuel, she shall obtain everlasting salvation, *if they continue in faith and charity, and holiness with sobriety*, and prove themselves living members of Christ, in whom there is no difference between male or female, but both are alike called to partake of his grace and glory

CHAP III.

In this chapter our apostle treats of church officers And, 1 He gives us the qualifications of a person to be admitted to the office of a bishop, ver 1—8 2 Of the qualifications of deacons, ver 8—10 And of their wives, ver 11 And again of the deacons, ver 12, 13 3 Of the reasons of his writing to Timothy whereupon he speaks of the church and the foundation truth professed therein, ver 14, to the end

1 THIS is a true saying, If a man desire ᵃ the office of a bishop, he desireth ᵇ a good work
2 ᶜ A bishop then must be blameless, the husband of one wife, vigilant, sober, of good behaviour, given to hospitality, ᵈ apt to teach,
3 ᵉ Not given to wine, ᶠ no striker, ᵍ not greedy of filthy lucre, but patient, ʰ not a brawler, not covetous,
4 One that ruleth well his own house, ⁱ having his children in subjection with all gravity,
5 (For if a man know not how to rule his own house, how shall he take care of the church of God?)
6 Not a ‡ novice, lest being lifted up with pride, he fall into ᵏ the condemnation of the devil
7 Moreover, he must have a good report of them ˡ which are without, lest he fall into reproach, and the snare of the devil

a Acts xx 28. b Eph iv 12. c Tit i 6, &c. d 2 Tim ii 24. e Tit i 7. f 2 Tim ii 24. g 1 Pet v 2. h 2 Tim ii 24. i Tit i 6. ‡ Or, one newly come to the faith. k Isa xiv 12. l Acts xxii 12. m 1 Cor v 12. 1 Thes iv 12.

v 1—7 Timothy being left to preside over and regulate the affairs of the Ephesian church, the apostle gives him directions concerning those who should be ordained to ministerial offices among them

This is a true saying, If a man, inwardly moved by the Holy Ghost, *desireth the office of a bishop*, or overseer of the church of Christ, *he desireth a good work* the post is most honourable and important, yet withal most laborious, and requires singular qualifications for the right discharge thereof *A bishop then must*, (1) *Be blameless*, his morals irreproachable, and his character able to bear the nicest scrutiny (2) If he be not single, let him be *the husband of one wife*, that hath never given a divorce, in order to marry again, nor lives in poligamy (3) He must be *vigilant* over the souls committed to his care, and habitually resident among them (4) *Sober*, moderate in the use of every creature-comfort, and temperate in all things (5) *Of good behaviour*, courteous, engaging, prudent, edifying (6) *Given to hospitality*, ready to relieve strangers, and assist the necessitous (7) *Apt to teach*, furnished with Christian knowledge and experience, and possessing the faculty of communicating his sentiments with ease and propriety for the improvement of others (8) *Not given to wine*, not merely no drunkard, but never sitting long at the cup, or loving the glass (9) *No striker*, not passionate or quarrelsome (10) *Not greedy of filthy lucre*, and suspected of attachment to earthly gains and advantage, *but*, (11) *Patient*, a pattern of meekness and long-suffering (12) *Not a brawler*, clamorous, contentious, and talkative *nor*, (13) *Covetous*, seeking the fleece more than to feed the flock, and serving for hire, rather than for the love of men's souls (14) *One that ruleth well his own house*, with due discipline and authority, *having his children in subjection with all gravity for if a man know not how to rule his own house*, and so to behave there as to preserve order and decorum, *how shall he take care of the church of God*, where so much more difficulty may be expected, and so much more prudence is necessary? (15) *Not a novice*, and but lately acquainted with, and converted to, the faith of Christ, *lest being lifted up with pride*, thrusting himself arrogantly into an office for which he is not qualified, and ambitious of human honour, or popular applause, *he fall into the condemnation of the devil*, and sink the deeper from the height whereunto he affected to soar (16) *Moreover, he must have a good report of them which are without*, his conduct unsullied with any thing which would be an obstruction to his ministry, *lest he fall into reproach*, and grow contemptible, *and into the snare of the devil*

Ere any man appears a candidate for the ministry, let him solemnly consider these things It is not ease, or honour, or gain, or a genteel employment, that should lead us into the service these are motives dishonourable, unhallowed, impious Zeal for God, disinterested love of souls, must warm our bosoms, and unreserved devotedness of ourselves to Christ must mark each step And *Who is sufficient for these things*, may we well say? The best qualified will be most conscious how short they come, and

and be looking constantly up to him who hath promised, *Lo, I am with you alway, even to the end of the world*, Mat xxviii 20.

8 Likewise *must* [r] the deacons *be* grave, not double-tongued, [s] not given to much wine, not greedy of filthy lucre, 9 [t] Holding the mystery of the faith in a pure conscience 10 And let these also first be proved, then let them use the office of a deacon, being *found* blameless. 11 [q] Even so *must their* wives *be* grave, not slanderers, sober, faithful in all things 12 Let the deacons be the husbands of one wife, ruling their children and their own houses well 13 For [r] they that have used the office of a deacon well, purchase to themselves a good degree, and great boldness in the faith which is in Christ Jesus.

r Acts vi 3 · s Lev x 9 Ezek xliv 21 · t Chap i 19 · q Tit ii 3, &c · r Mat xxv 21

v 8—13 We have,

1 The character of the deacons, whose office it was chiefly to take care of the outward matters of the church, assist the ministers, provide for the poor, and manage the public stock

(1) They must be *grave*, men of venerable deportment (2) *Not double-tongued*, warping the truth to please in different companies, and speaking with design or dissimulation (3) *Not given to much wine*, but persons of exemplary temperance (4) *Not greedy of filthy lucre*, lest they be tempted to embezzle the church's stock (5) *Holding the mystery of the faith in a pure conscience*, cleaving steadily to the simplicity of the gospel doctrines, and adorning them by a becoming conversation (6) *And let these also first be proved, then let them use the office of a deacon, being found blameless*, having undergone a proper examination, and being approved, let them be invested with their office (6) *Let the deacons be the husbands of one wife*, avoiding all divorce and polygamy, *ruling their children and their own houses well*, setting them a good example, and maintaining due order and regularity *For they that have used the office of a deacon well*, with fidelity and diligence, true to the trust committed unto them, *purchase to themselves a good degree* of honour and respect in the church, *and great boldness in the faith which is in Christ Jesus*, God blessing such fidelity with an increase of grace, and greater openness and freedom in the profession of the gospel before men

2 The character of the deacons wives *Even so must their wives be grave*, in manners, dress, speech, and deportment *not slanderers*, speaking evil of persons behind their backs, and sowing discord in the church *sober*, and free from excess *faithful in all things*, that they may be a credit to their husbands, and adorn their station

14 These things write I unto thee, hoping [t] to come unto thee shortly 15 But if I tarry long, that thou mayest know how thou oughtest to behave thyself [r] in the house of God, which is the church of the living God, the pillar and ground of the truth 16 And without controversy great is the mystery of godliness [u] God was manifest in the flesh, [x] justified in the Spirit, [y] seen of angels, [z] preached unto the Gentiles, [a] believed on in the world, [b] received up into glory

t Chap iv 13 · r 2 Tim ii 20 · u John i 14 · 1 John i 2 · x Rom i 4 · 1 Pet iii 18 · y Mat xxviii 2 · John xx 12 · 1 Pet i 12 · z Eph iii 5, 6 · Col i 23 · a Col i 6 · b Luke xxiv 51 Acts i 9

v 14—16 Though he hoped to be with him at Ephesus shortly, yet, lest the Lord should call him elsewhere, he had sent the above directions *These things write I unto thee, hoping to come unto thee shortly but if I tarry long*, and arrive not so soon as I purpose, I have sent this epistle, *that thou mayest know how thou oughtest to behave thyself in the house of God, which is the church of the living God, the pillar and ground of the truth*, which last words some refer to the church, where the truth is held forth as an inscription written on a pillar, and maintained with all stedfastness others to Timothy himself, who was a firm pillar in that church but, best of all, they may be referred to Christ himself, the living God abiding in his own temple, and its true foundation and support *And without controversy great is the mystery of godliness*, especially in the following particulars *God was manifest in the flesh*, and took our nature upon him *justified in the Spirit*, when by his resurrection he was declared free from every charge, and God's justice fully satisfied *seen of angels*, when triumphant he ascended to the throne of majesty on high amidst their acclamations, *preached to the Gentiles*, as a Saviour to the uttermost, and freely inviting them to partake of all the blessings of his gospel *believed on in the world*, both by Jews and Gentiles, notwithstanding the ignominy of his cross *received up into glory*, to possess the reward of his sufferings or gloriously received, his gospel in the most astonishing manner spreading through the earth, and bringing vast multitudes of converts to the obedience of the faith *Note*, (1) The all sufficiency of the atonement of Jesus depends upon the divine glory of his person He who suffered on a cross was very God as well as very man (2) This is among the mysteries of godliness, where reason must bow down, and faith adore

CHAP. IV

St Paul here foretels, 1 *A dreadful apostasy*, ver 1—3 2 *He treats of Christian liberty*, ver 4, 5 3 *He gives Timothy divers directions with respect to himself, his doctrine, and the people under his care*, ver 6, to the end

1 NOW the Spirit [a] speaketh expresly that [b] in the latter times some shall depart from the faith, giving heed [c] to seducing spirits, and [d] doctrines of devils, 2 [e] Speaking lyes in hypocrisy, [f] having their consciences seared with a hot iron, 3 Forbidding to marry, *and commanding* to abstain from meats, which God hath created [g] to be received [h] with thanksgiving of them which believe and know the truth 4 For [i] every creature of God *is* good, and nothing to be refused, if it be received with thanksgiving 5 For it is sanctified by the word of God and prayer

a 2 Thes ii 3 · 2 Tim iii 1 · 2 Pet iii 3 · 1 John ii 18 · Jude 18 · b 1 Pet i 20 · c Rev xvi 14 · d Dan xi 37 38 · Rev ix 20 · e Rom xvi 18 · f Eph iv 19 · g Gen i 29, &c ix 3 · h Rom xiv 6 · 1 Cor x 30 · i Rom xiv 14 · 1 Cor x 25 · Tit i 15

v 1—5 We have here the prophecy of that dire apostacy from the faith, which was of old foretold, and which we have seen so strikingly and dreadfully verified in the corruptions of the church of Rome *Now the Spirit speaketh expresly*, in the prophetic writings, and by us who write under his immediate inspiration, *that in the latter times* of the present dispensation, *some shall depart from the faith*, and the marks of this apostacy he describes

1 The departure will arise from *giving heed to seducing spirits, and doctrines of devils*, or dæmons, reviving the errors of paganism in the worship of angels, dead saints, yea their very relicks, and making these a kind of mediators between God and them

2 *Speaking lyes in hypocrisy*, pretending to great zeal for the church and religion, yet propagating the most damnable heresies, such as justification by works, the freewill of man to good, *&c.* and by false legends, and forged miracles, deceiving the souls of the ignorant *having their consciences seared with a hot iron*, and sticking at no abominations which may contribute to advance their wicked ends, even consecrating regicide, dispensing with the most solemn oaths, and counting every species of barbarity lawful, yea laudable, to be perpetrated on those who oppose their destructive ways witness the blood of martyrs, that by popish cruelty hath dyed so plentifully this land

3 *Forbidding to marry*, speaking dishonourably of the ordinance itself, encouraging celibacy, and forbidding marriage to their clergy, monks, and nuns, in direct contradiction to God's word

4 Commanding *to abstain from meats*, under the hypocritical shew of self-denial, forbidding flesh in Lent, and enjoining fish instead of other animal food, *which God hath created to be received*, and eaten at all times, without distinction of days and seasons, if it be used *with* moderation and *thanksgiving of them which believe and know the truth For every creature of God is good, and nothing*, proper for food, *to be refused, if it be received with thanksgiving, for it is sanctified* for our use *by the word of God*, which declares there is nothing now common or unclean, *and by prayer* imploring his blessing, that we may use every creature-comfort to his glory *Note*, Our common meals should be ever sanctified with devotion, and God's blessing be implored before we presume to use his gifts

6 If thou put the brethren in remembrance of these things, thou shalt be a good minister of Jesus Christ, [k] nourished up in the words of faith, and of good doctrine, whereunto thou hast attained 7 But [l] refuse profane and old wives fables, and [m] exercise thyself *rather* unto godliness 8 For [n] bodily exercise profiteth † little but [o] godliness is profitable unto all things, [p] having promise of the life that now is, and of that which is to come 9 [q] This *is* a faithful saying, and worthy of all acceptation 10 For therefore we both labour, and suffer reproach, because we trust in the living God, [r] who is the Saviour of all men, especially of those that believe 11 These things command and teach 12 [s] Let no man despise thy youth, but [t] be thou an example of the believers, in word, in conversation, in charity, in spirit, in faith, in purity 13 Till I come, give attendance to reading, to exhortation, to doctrine 14 [u] Neglect not the gift that is in thee, which was given thee [x] by prophecy, [y] with the laying on of the hands of the presbytery 15 Meditate upon these things, give thyself wholly to them, that thy profiting may appear ‡ to all 16 [z] Take heed unto thyself, and unto thy doctrine, continue in them for in doing this thou shalt both save thyself and [a] them that hear thee

k 2 Tim iii 14, 15 · l Chap i 4 & vi 20 · 2 Tim ii 14 & iii 6 · m Heb v 14 · n Col ii 23 · † Or, a little, or in a few things · o Deut xxviii 12, xxx 9 · Ps lxxxiv 11 · Prov iii 16 · p Mat vi 33 · Mark x 30 · q Chap i 15 · r Ps xxxvi 6 & cvii 13 &c · s 1 Cor xvi 11 · Tit ii 15 · t Tit ii 7 · 1 Pet v 3 · u 2 Tim i 6 · x Chap i 18 · y Acts vi 6 · Chap v 22 · 2 Tim i 6 · ‡ Or, in all things · z Acts xx 28 · a Ezek xxxiii 9 · Rom xi 14 · 1 Cor ix 22 · Jam v 20

v 6—16 We have here,

1 The apostle's encouraging exhortation *If thou put the brethren in remembrance of these things, thou shalt be a good minister of Jesus Christ, nourished up in the words of faith and of good doctrine, whereunto thou hast attained* Such fidelity to his trust would bring down the blessing of the Lord upon his soul, and prove his own abundant advantage *Note*, Nothing is a greater means of edification to a minister's own soul, than his labours for the good of his brethren

2 He quickens him to diligence in his Christian calling *But refuse profane and old wives fables*, the absurd genealogies and traditions of the judaizing teachers, *and exercise thyself rather unto godliness*, strain every nerve to set forth the doctrines and duties of the gospel, and in thy own temper and conduct shew thyself eminently exemplary *For bodily exercise*, the most rigid observance of the externals of religion, *profiteth little, but godliness*, vital experimental religion, manifested in heart and life, *is profitable unto all things, having promise of the life that now is*, in the sanctified and happy use of worldly comforts, *and of that which is to come*, where God hath prepared for those that love him such good things as pass man's understanding *This is a faithful saying, and worthy of all acceptation*, as a truth which will be proved infallibly certain by every real Christian, and none will ever have reason to repent a life of godliness *Therefore we both labour and suffer reproach*, undismayed and unshaken, *because we trust in the living God*, who is able and ready to fulfil his promises, *who is the Saviour of all men*, bestowing innumerable providential blessings upon them, and rescuing them from many miseries but *especially of those that believe*, by his distinguishing grace and love bestowing upon them not only multiplied mercies in this world, but having purchased and secured for them an eternal salvation in heaven *Note*, (1) Though this world is not our home, nor our portion, yet, even here below, the truly godly are the most happy people (2) Christ hath a peculiar people, to whom he is in a special manner a Saviour, rescuing them from all spiritual evils, and bringing them to eternal blessedness

3 He directs him particularly how to demean himself *These things command and teach* with all authority *Let no man despise thy youth*, nor give them any occasion to do so, *but* behave so as to engage and command reverence and respect *and be thou an example of the believers, in word*, in all grave and edifying discourse, free from youthful levity, *in conversation*, strictly religious, and sincerely upright, *in charity*, fervent towards God, and the souls of men, *in spirit*, zealous for the cause of Jesus, and abounding in all the fruits of righteousness, *in faith*, unwavering, in profession bold, *in purity* of heart and conduct, without blemish or suspicion *Till I come, give attendance to reading* the scriptures in private, and in the congregation, *to exhortation*, bringing the word of God home to the consciences of the hearers, with warm application, for the conviction of some, and the consolation and edification of others, *to doctrine*, clearly stating the great points of the Christian faith, and vindicating them from all opposers *Neglect not the gift that is in thee*, but make the best improvement of the abilities with which God hath furnished you, and of the extraordinary gift *which was given thee by prophecy*, as some inspired men had foretold, *with the laying on of the hands of the presbytery*, when you were ordained to the work of the ministry *Meditate upon these things, give thyself wholly to them*, with such evident devotedness of heart, such delight in the service, and such exemplariness of conduct, *that thy profiting may appear to all Take heed unto thyself*, as a minister and a Christian, *and unto thy doctrine*, that it may exactly correspond with the gospel word, *for in doing this thou shalt both save thyself and them that hear thee* *Note*, (1) They who shew themselves examples to the flock, and evidently prove that they believe and practise themselves what they preach to others, tho young, will necessarily command respect and reverence, whilst grey hairs, dishonoured by an unbecoming conduct, will be justly despised (2) They who are to teach others, should be much in prayer and reading the scriptures, that they may lay in a fund of useful knowledge, and be full of matter for their public ministrations An idle minister must needs be an unprofitable preacher (3) They who have the charge of immortal souls should be wholly engrossed with this great concern, and give themselves up to their awful employment (4) It is our great encouragement to fidelity in the ministry, that not only our own soul shall be saved, but that we shall be made happily instrumental to the eternal salvation of others, who will be our joy and crown in the day of our Lord Jesus Christ

CHAP V

How the apostle directs Timothy 1 How to reprove, ver 1, 2 2 Of widows, both elder and younger, ver 3—16 3 Of elders, ver 17—19 4 Of public reproofs, ver 20, 5 Of caution in ordination, ver 21, 22 6 Of his health, ver 23 and of men's sins very different in their effects, ver 24, 25

a Lev xix 32 1 REBUKE not an elder, but intreat *him* as a father, *and* the younger men, as brethren, 2 The elder women, as mothers, the younger, as sisters, with all purity

v 1, 2 The apostle proceeds to give him farther directions concerning the needful, though less pleasing, work of rebuke Ministers are reprovers by office, and must be faithful to this trust

Rebuke not an elder, in years or office, if ought be found in him which demands censure, with a magisterial air, or unbecoming severity, *but*, with respect to his venerable years, *intreat him as a father* to remove the cause of offence *and the younger men as brethren*, with all freedom, yet with all in love and meekness *the elder women, as mothers*, with due respect, *the younger, as sisters, with all purity*, avoiding every thought, word, look, or gesture, that hath the most distant tendency to evil

3 Honour widows that are widows indeed 4 But b Ver 5 16
if any widow have children or nephews, let them learn
first to shew piety at home, and c to requite their pa- c Gen xlv 10 11 Matt xv 4 Eph vi 2
rents for that is good and acceptable before God 5
Now d she that is a widow indeed, and desolate, trusteth d 1 Cor vii 34
in God, and e continueth in supplications and prayers e Luke ii 37
f night and day 6 But she g that liveth in pleasure, f Acts xxvi 7
is dead while she liveth 7 And these things give in g Jam v 5 Or delicately, or wantonly
charge, that they may be blameless 8 But h if any h Isa lviii 7
provide not for his own, and especially for those of his i 2 Tim iii 5
own house, i he hath denied the faith, and is worse than k Tit i 16
an infidel 9 Let not a widow be taken into the num- l Luk ii 36 Chap iii 2
ber under threescore years old, l having been the wife m Heb xiii 2
of one man, 10 Well reported of for good works, if n 1 Pet iv 9
she have brought up children, if she have m lodged n Gen xviii 4 & xix 2 Luke vii 38, 44
strangers, if she have n washed the saints feet, if she have
relieved the afflicted, if she have diligently followed
every good work 11 But the younger widows refuse
for when they have begun to wax wanton against Christ,
they will marry, 12 Having damnation, because they
have cast off their first faith 13 And withal they learn
to be idle, o wandering about from house to house, and o Tit ii 5
not only idle, but tatlers also and busy-bodies, speaking
things which they ought not 14 I will therefore p that p 1 Cor vii 9
the younger women marry, bear children, guide the
house, give none occasion to the adversary to speak q Tit ii 8
reproachfully 15 For some are already turned aside
after Satan 16 If any man or woman that believeth
have widows, let them relieve them, and let not the
church be charged, that it may relieve them r that are r Ver 3, 5
widows indeed.

v 3—16 The apostle particularly directs Timothy how to behave in the case of widows who applied to be assisted out of the church's stock, and to be employed in pious offices under the direction of the deacons

1 *Honour widows that are widows indeed*, really in distress, in need of assistance, and deserving to be placed on the church's list, such as he describes, v 5 *Now she that is a widow indeed, and desolate*, without any friends to support her, *trusteth in God*, who is the friend of the friendless, and they who cast their care upon him shall not be destitute *and such a one continueth in supplications and prayers night and day*, depending upon the Lord's providential help, and shewing her undissembled piety *but she that liveth in pleasure*, gayly, idly, and voluptuously, *is dead while she liveth*, dead to God and godliness, and in no wise to be received of the church, or supported from the common stock *And these things give in charge, that they may be blameless*, and that no just offence may call for rebuke or censure *Note*, A life of carnal pleasures is a state of real death the soul then lies entombed in flesh, and such a person is really a living sepulchre

2 If any widows have near relations capable of providing for them, the church ought not to be burdened with their maintenance *If any widow have children or nephews*, or grandchildren, *let them learn first to shew piety at home, and to requite their parents*, by taking all care of them when labouring under age and infirmities, *for that is good and acceptable before God*, their bounden duty, and agreeable to his holy will *But if any*, who makes profession of the Christian name, refuse this assistance, which in such a case he is bound to afford, *and provide not for his own, and specially for those of his own house*, his aged parent, next to his wife and children, claiming a title to a maintenance, in part of that family which depend on him for a provision, *he hath denied the faith*, by such a conduct, *and is worse than an infidel* even the very heathen will rise up to condemn a conduct so base and unnatural *Therefore if any man or woman that believeth have widows*, mothers or grandmothers, *let them relieve them, and let not the church be charged, that it may* have sufficiency to *relieve them that are widows indeed*

3 He points out the age and qualifications of those who should be entred on the poor's list, or be taken into office and employed by the church under the deacons *Let not a widow be taken into the number under threescore years old, having been the wife of one man*, and never married to another after any divorce, *well reported of for good works* in her former better days, *if she have brought up children* in the nurture and admonition of the Lord, *if she have lodged strangers*, when brought by providence in her way, *if she have washed the saints feet*, condescending to the lowest offices of charity, *if she have relieved the afflicted*, with her help, her counsel, and her substance, *if she have diligently followed every good work*

4 *But the younger widows refuse for when they have begun to wax wanton against Christ*, as they may be in danger of doing, *they will* then *marry* improperly, perhaps wickedly, into some heathen family, *having* thus *damnation*, *because they have cast off their first faith*, and apostatized from the profession which they once made *and withal they learn to be idle*, *wandring about from house to house* in useless and impertinent visiting, *and not only idle, but tatlers also, and busy bodies*, officious and talkative *speaking things which they ought not*, to the hurt of their neighbour's reputation, and to the disturbance of society

17 Let the elders that rule well be counted worthy
of [r] double honour, especially they who labour in the
word and doctrine 18 For the scripture saith, [t] Thou
shalt not muzzle the ox that treadeth out the corn and,
[u] The labourer *is* worthy of his reward 19 Against
an elder receive not an accusation, but [x] before two or
three witnesses 20 [y] Them that sin rebuke before all,
[z] that others also may fear 21 [a] I charge *thee* before
God and the Lord Jesus Christ, and the elect angels,
that thou observe these things without preferring one
before another, doing nothing by partiality 22 [b] Lay
hands suddenly on no man, [c] neither be partaker of other
men's sins keep thyself pure 23 Drink no longer
water, but use a little wine [d] for thy stomach's sake, and
thine often infirmities 24 [e] Some men's sins are open
beforehand, going before to judgment, and some *men*
they follow after 25 Likewise also the good works *of*
some are manifest beforehand, and they that are other-
wise cannot be hid

r Rom xv 27 1 Cor ix 14 Gal vi 6 Phil ii 29 1 Thess v 12, 13 s Acts xxviii 10 t Deut xxv 4 1 Cor ix 9 u Lev xix 13 Deut xxiv 14 Mat x 10 Luke x 7 x Deut xix 15 y Gal ii 11, 14 z Deut xiii 11 a Chap vi 13 2 Tim ii 14 & iv 1 b Acts vi 6 & xiii 3 c 2 John 11 d Psal civ 15 e Gal v 19

v 17—25 The apostle here directs Timothy,

1. Concerning the proper maintenance of a gospel ministry *Let the elders that rule well be counted worthy of double honour*, highly esteemed and liberally provided for, *especially they who labour in the word and doctrine*, whose eminent zeal and diligence requires suitable acknowledgment *for the scripture saith, Thou shalt not muzzle the ox that treadeth out the corn*, but as he works he shall be freely allowed to eat *and* our Lord hath said, *The labourer is worthy of his reward* Note, The work of the ministry is laborious, and well do they who discharge it with zeal and diligence deserve an honourable provision

2 Concerning the accusation of an elder *Against an elder receive not an accusation, but before two or three witnesses* of character and credibility, and listen to no base surmises or slanderous suggestions *Them that sin before all*, being open, notorious, and scandalous offenders, *rebuke before all*, publickly and with sharpness, *that others also may fear*, respecting no man's rank or greatness *I charge thee before God, and the Lord Jesus Christ*, the eternal Judge, *and the elect angels*, who are the spirits that minister to the heirs of salvation, *that thou observe these things, without preferring one before another*, not prejudging the cause through favour or affection, *doing nothing by partiality*, nor suffering any consideration to prejudice or biass your minds for or against any man, but deciding according to truth

3 Concerning the ordination of ministers *Lay hands suddenly on no man* to put him into the ministry, till he hath been thoroughly tried, and found faithful and able, *neither be partakers of other men's sins*, by conniving at the intrusion of unfit persons into the sacred office *keep thyself pure* from the blood of all men, discountenancing all unbecoming behaviour, and in thy own conversation a pattern of purity and chastity

4 Concerning his own health *Drink no longer water, but use a little wine for thy stomach's sake, and thine often infirmities*, indefatigable labour, and strict abstemiousness, preyed upon a tender constitution probably, and required in moderation something more supporting than water, to which he had confined himself Note, The creatures of God are designed for our use and comfort, only let them be used with moderation, not to pamper the flesh, but so as to enable us the better to fulfil the duties of our station

5 With regard to censure and ordination, of which he had before spoken, he farther observes, *Some men's sins are open beforehand, going before to judgment*, and being notorious, such are to be rejected from the ministry, and laid under the church's censure, *and some men they follow after*, and though they studiously conceal their sin, yet, on deeper and closer examination, they will after a while come out, and therefore they should not hastily be admitted into sacred orders, without due probation *Likewise also the good works of some are manifest beforehand*, their whole character strikingly exemplary, and their ministerial gifts eminent, so that they may be admitted without hesitation *and they that are otherwise cannot be hid*, more caution is needful with those whose qualifications are dubious, and it requires some time to make it clear whether they should be received for, if they are really corrupt in principle or practice, they will soon betray themselves Note, (1) Before any be admitted into sacred orders, their character and qualifications should be well examined An ignorant and scandalous ministry is the greatest reproach to any church (2) However secretly men may hide their sins, yet usually in time their true character appears, and at least at a judgment-day no vail can hide the workers of iniquity

CHAP. VI

1 *He treats of the duty of servants*, ver 1, 2, 3 2 *Of teachers*, ver 3, 4, 5 3 *Of godliness and covetousness*, ver 6—11 4 *What Timothy was to flee, and what to follow*, ver 11—13 5 *A solemn charge*, ver 13—17, *And*, 6 *A charge for the rich*, ver 17, 18, 19 *And lastly*, *A charge to Timothy*, ver 20, 21

1 [a] LET as many servants as are under the yoke,
count their own masters worthy of all honour,
[b] that the name of God, and *his* doctrine be not blas-
phemed 2 And they that have believing masters, let
them not despise *them*, because they are brethren but
rather do *them* service, because they are faithful and be-
loved, partakers of the benefit [c] These things teach
and exhort 3 If any man [d] teach otherwise, and con-
sent not [e] to wholsome words, *even* the words of our
Lord Jesus Christ, and to [f] the doctrine which is ac-
cording to godliness, 4 He is proud, [g] knowing no-
thing, but † doting about [h] questions and strifes of words,
[i] whereof cometh envy, strife, railings, evil surmisings,
5 [k] Perverse disputings of [l] men of corrupt minds, and
destitute of the truth, [m] supposing that gain is godliness
from such withdraw thyself

a Eph vi 5 Col iii 22 1 Pet ii 18 b Ezek xxxvi 20 Tit ii 5 c Chap iv 11 d Chap i 3 e Chap i 10 2 Tim i 13 Tit i 9 f Tit i 1 g 1 Cor viii 2 † Gr sick h Chap i 4 & v 7 i 2 Tim ii 23 Tit iii 9 k 1 Cor xi 16 Chap i 6 l 2 Tim iii 8 m Tit i 11 2 Pet ii 3 Rom xvi 17 2 Tim iii 5

v 1—5 The apostle lays down,

1 The duty of Christian servants *Let as many servants as are under the yoke count their own masters worthy of all honour*, respect, and dutiful obedience, *that the name of God and his doctrine be not blasphemed*, and that unbelievers may never have occasion to reproach them, as if their religion had made them proud, lazy, or disobedient *And they that have believing masters, let them not despise them, because they are brethren*, as if Christianity destroyed the distinctions of providence, and brought all men on a level, no, *but rather do them service*, with peculiar submission, delight, diligence, and honesty, *because they are faithful and beloved, partakers of the benefit*, sharing all the blessings of the gospel salvation Note, (1) The gospel was never designed to destroy the distinctions God hath been pleased to make among men, but to direct every man how to adorn that station in which it hath pleased God to call him (2) The kindness and condescension of Christian masters must never teach servants to presume, but to treat them with greater respect, more affectionate regard, and unimpeached fidelity

2 He warns Timothy to teach steadily these truths, and to beware of deceivers *These things teach and exhort If any man teach otherwise*, as the judaizing teachers, who suggest as if it were unlawful for Christian slaves to obey their unbelieving masters, *and consent not to wholsome words, even the words of our Lord Jesus Christ, and to the doctrine which is according to godliness*, inculcating all dutiful discharge of our relations towards men, as well as piety towards God, *he is proud*, vainly puffed up with arrogant conceit of his own wisdom, though in fact *knowing nothing* as he ought to know, *but doting about questions and strifes of words*, engaged in vain and idle dispute about matters utterly insignificant, *whereof cometh envy, strife, railings, evil surmisings, perverse disputings of men of corrupt minds, and* who by such a spirit and temper evidently shew, that they are *destitute of the truth, supposing that gain is godliness*, serving merely their own worldly interests, and not the cause of Christ and immortal souls *from such withdraw thyself*, have no communion with them, nor suffer them to assemble among the faithful Note, (1) The doctrines of the gospel are doctrines according to godliness, and whatever would corrupt vital and practical religion cannot be the words of our Lord Jesus Christ (2) Proud disputers must needs be far from any true knowledge of that gospel whose whole injunctions are peace and love (3) They who make godliness in profession the ladder to earthly gain, will shortly find how fearful is their lot, when death shall hurl them into the abyss of wretchedness

I

6 But

6 But [o] godliness with contentment is great gain
7 For [p] we brought nothing into *this* world, *and it is*
certain we can carry nothing out 8 And [q] having food
and raiment, let us be therewith content 9 But [r] they
that will be rich, fall into temptation and [s] a snare, and
into many foolish and hurtful lusts, which drown men in
destruction and perdition 10 For the love of money
is the root of all evil [t] which while some coveted after,
they have erred from the faith, and pierced themselves
through with many sorrows 11 But thou, O [u] man
of God, flee these things, and follow after righteousness,
godliness, faith, love, patience, meekness 12 [x] Fight
the good fight of faith, [y] lay hold on eternal life, where-
unto thou art also called, [z] and hast professed a good
profession before many witnesses

[o] Prov xv 16 Isa. xxxiii 6 [p] Job i 21 Psal xlix 17 Eccles v 15 [q] Gen. xxviii 20 Prov xxx 8 Phil iv 11 Heb. xiii 5 [r] Prov xv 27 & xx 21 & xxviii 20 Mat xiii 22 Jam. v 1 [s] Chap iii 7 [t] 2 Tim iv 10 [u] 2 Tim iii 17 [x] 1 Cor ix 25 26 Chap i 18 2 Tim iv 7 [y] Phil iii 12, 14. Ver 19 [z] Heb xiii 23

v 6—12 From the mention of the abuses of some corrupters of godliness, the apostle,

1 Cautions Timothy against covetousness, and to possess a contented mind *But godliness with contentment is great gain*, making the mind happy in every state of life, and under every dispensation of providence, and this is the truest and most substantial gain even here below, where all our creature comforts are so precarious, insufficient, and perishing *For we brought nothing into this world, and it is certain we can carry nothing out*, but must return naked to the tomb, as we came from the womb *And* therefore *having food and raiment*, covering for our bodies, and refreshment such as nature craves, *let us be therewith content*, nor grasp after more, thankful for the mercies of the day, and trusting the Lord for the provision of to-morrow *But they that will be rich*, and, instead of being satisfied with their present allotted portion, are determined by every method to add to their store, and have their heart set upon wealth as their grand object, they *fall into temptation and a snare, and* become an easy prey to the devil, plunging themselves, in the unhallowed pursuit after riches, *into many foolish and hurtful lusts*, into deceit, fraud, lying, rapine, injustice, &c *which drown men in destruction and perdition*, and both body and soul perish for ever *For the love of money is the root of all evil*, and the source of every vile and scandalous action *which while some have coveted after*, we have seen the dreadful issue, *they have erred from the faith, and pierced themselves through with many sorrows*, besides all their crosses and vexations, laying up much bitterness for themselves, if they should hereafter be brought to repentance, and if not, treasuring up wrath against the day of wrath *But thou, O man of God, flee these things*, be warned by others sad examples, and shun with abhorrence all such covetous principles and practices *Note*, (1) There is no true contentment in this world but that which springs from real godliness (2) We consult our truest interests when our souls are our first concern (3) It is a mortifying reflection to every worldling, how short-lived must be his enjoyments, and that he can carry nothing with him to the grave but a shroud and a coffin (4) Nature is satisfied with little, grace with less, but covetousness with nothing (5) They who *will* be rich are in the high road to ruin, Satan desires no fairer mark (6) The love of money hath destroyed more than any one other vice whatever (7) They who, to gain the world, lose their own souls, will prove shortly their folly to be great as their sin

2 He enjoins him what was his proper pursuit *Follow after righteousness* in your transactions with men, *godliness*, and holiness of heart and life, *faith*, in increasing measure of the divine grace, and approved fidelity in all your conversation, *love* to God and men, *patience* under every provocation, and *meekness*, bearing with and gently instructing those that oppose themselves yet, shewing withal a becoming zeal for the truth, *fight the good fight of faith* against all opposing foes, from earth or hell, or inbred corruption, *lay hold on eternal life*, earnestly pressing towards the goal for the glorious prize, *whereunto thou art also called* by divine grace, as a Christian and an evangelist, *and hast professed a good profession before many witnesses* at thy ordination, and in the presence of those among whom thou hast preached and suffered for the gospel's sake *Note*, (1) We are engaged in an arduous warfare, and have need and must fight every step to heaven against a host of spiritual foes which oppose our progress (2) Eternal life, the glorious crown before us, should animate us for every conflict (3) The good profession we have once made should engage us with increasing diligence to approve our fidelity before God and man

13 [a] I give thee charge in the sight of God, [b] who
quickeneth all things, and *before* Christ Jesus, [c] who
before Pontius Pilate witnessed a good confession, 14
That thou keep *this* commandment without spot, un-
rebukeable, [d] until the appearing of our Lord Jesus
Christ 15. Which in his times he shall shew, [e] who
is the blessed and only Potentate, [f] the King of kings,
and Lord of lords, 16 [g] Who only hath immortality,
dwelling in the light which no man can approach unto,
[h] whom no man hath seen, nor can see [i] to whom *be*
honour and power everlasting Amen 17 Charge
them that are rich in this world, that they be not high-
minded, [k] nor trust in uncertain riches, but in [l] the liv-
ing God, [m] who giveth us richly all things to enjoy
18 That they do good, that they be [n] rich [o] in good
works, [p] ready to distribute, [q] willing to communicate,
19 [r] Laying up in store for themselves a good founda-
tion against the time to come, that they may [s] lay hold
on eternal life 20 O Timothy, [t] keep that which is
committed to thy trust, [u] avoiding profane *and* vain bab-
blings, and oppositions of science falsly so called 21
Which some professing, [x] have erred concerning the faith
Grace *be* with thee Amen

[a] Chap. v 21 [b] Deut xxxii 39 1 Sam ii 6 John v 21 [c] Mat xxvii 11 John xviii 37 [d] Phil i 6, 10 1 Thess iii 13 & v. 23 [e] Chap i 11 17 [f] Rev xvii 14 & xix 16 [g] Chap i 17 [h] Ex xxxiii 20 John i 18 1 John iv 12 [i] Jude 25 Rev i 6 & vii 12 [k] Job xxxi 24 Psal lxii 10 Mark x 24 [l] 1 Thess i 9 [m] Acts xiv 17 [n] Luke xii 21 Jam ii 5 [o] Tit iii 8 [p] Deut xv 7 Rom xii 13 [q] Heb xiii 16 [r] Mat vi 20 Luke xii 33 & xvi 9 [s] Ver 12 [t] 2 Tim i 14 Rev iii 3 [u] Chap i 4, 6 & iv 7 2 Tim ii 16 23, [x] Chap i 6, 19 2 Tim ii 18

v 13—21 The apostle concludes,

1 With repeating his solemn charge, and enforcing it with the most cogent arguments *I charge thee in the sight of God, who quickeneth all things*, the author of life to all his creatures, and the giver of spiritual life to his chosen, *and before Christ Jesus*, whose minister thou art, and *who* himself *before Pontius Pilate witnessed a good confession*, boldly asserting his own glorious character and office, *that thou keep this commandment without spot, unrebukeable*, faithful to the solemn trust reposed in thee, *until the appearing of our Lord Jesus Christ* at the great day *which in his times*, fixed in the eternal counsels, *he shall shew*, exactly accomplishing the promise of his coming, which he hath given to his people, according to the glorious names and characters which he bears, *who is the blessed and only Potentate*, to whom all in heaven and earth are subject, who hath the supreme and universal dominion and, as he is infinitely blessed in himself, he makes also his people happy under his government *the King of kings, and Lord of lords*, who all from him derive their power and authority, and to him are accountable, *who only hath immortality* in and of himself, and is the author of it to his creatures, whether angels or men, *dwelling* in uncreated glory, *in the light which no man*, in his present mortal state, *can approach unto, whom no man hath seen or can see*, in the full blaze of his divine perfections and attributes *to whom be honour and power everlasting* ascribed by all the hosts of earth and heaven *Amen!*

2 He gives him a particular charge to be delivered to the more opulent members of the church *Charge them that are rich in this world, that they be not high-minded*, puffed up on their worldly wealth and attainments, *nor trust in uncertain riches* as their dependence and rock, since these are transitory possessions, *but in the living God*, the only substantial and abiding good, *who giveth us richly all things to enjoy*, loading us with his benefits, and allowing us all sanctified use of his creatures wherefore they who are thus favoured must see *that they do good* with their wealth, not abusing it in luxury and extravagance, but *that they be rich in good works*, employing their treasures for the benefit of mankind, *ready to give*, even unasked, to the indigent and necessitous, *willing to communicate* of their substance, without grudging or niggardliness, *laying up in store for themselves a good foundation against the time to come*, disposing of their treasures in such a way as *that they may* have treasure in heaven, and *lay hold on eternal life* *Note*, (1) Wealth is a talent intrusted with us for the benefit of our brethren we are stewards, and must give an account of our profiting to the great Master (2) Riches are a great temptation to pride, therefore such as have affluence should be often admonished in their high estate to keep a humble mind (3) They are truly rich who are rich unto God, and improve their abundance to his glory

3 He warns him, as before, to take heed of deceivers *O Timothy, keep that which is committed to thy trust*, the unadulterated gospel word; *avoiding prophane and vain babblings, and oppositions of science falsly so called*, the noisy talk and proud boastings of judaizing teachers, pretending to high attainments in science, when in fact utter strangers to true wisdom, *which some professing, have erred concerning the faith*, and apostatized from the truth *Note*, That science which draws men from the simplicity of the gospel, however proud men may value themselves thereon, will be proved at last to be the most egregious folly

4 He gives him his parting benediction *Grace be with thee*, and that shall preserve thee from all error, and strengthen thee for the faithful discharge of the ministry *Amen!*

THE

THE EVANGELICAL EXPOSITOR; OR, A PRACTICAL COMMENT Upon the SECOND EPISTLE of St. PAUL to TIMOTHY.

THIS second epistle Paul wrote to Timothy from Rome, when he was a prisoner there, and in danger of his life. By these words, I am now ready to be offered, and the time of my departure is at hand, *chap.* iv. *ver.* vi. *it appears that his removal out of this world, in his own apprehension, was not far off, especially considering the rage and malice of his persecutors; and that he had been brought before the emperor Nero, which he calls* his first answer when no man stood with him, but all men forsook him. *chap.* iv. *ver.* 16. *And interpreters agree that this was the last epistle he wrote.*

Where Timothy now was, is not certain. The scope of this epistle somewhat differs from that of the former, not so much relating to his office as an evangelist, as to his personal conduct and behaviour.

CHAP. I.

After the introduction, ver. 1, 2. *we have,* 1. *Paul's sincere love to Timothy,* ver. 3—5. 2. *Divers exhortations given to him,* ver. 6—15. 3. *He speaks of Phygellus and Hermogenes, with others, and closes with Onesiphorus,* ver. 15, to the end.

1 PAUL, an apostle of Jesus Christ by the will
of God, according to the promise of life,
which is in Christ Jesus; 2 To Timothy,
a *my* dearly beloved son: b Grace, mercy, *and*
peace from God the Father, and Christ Jesus our Lord.
3 c I thank God, d whom I serve from *my* forefathers
with a pure conscience, that e without ceasing I have remembrance
of thee in my prayers night and day; 4
Greatly desiring to see thee, being mindful of thy tears,
that I may be filled with joy; 5 When I call to remembrance
f the unfeigned faith that is in thee, which
dwelt first in thy grandmother Lois, and g thy mother
Eunice; and I am persuaded that in thee also.

a 1 Cor. iv. 17. 1 Tim. i. 2. b Gal. i. 3. 1 Thess. i. 1. c Rom. i. 8. Eph. i. 16. d Acts xxiii. 1. & xxiv. 14. Rom. i. 9. e 1 Thess. i. 2. & iii. 10. f 1 Tim. i. 5. g Acts xvi. 1.

v. 1—5. St. Paul opens this epistle,

1. With his apostolic salutation to Timothy. *Paul an apostle of Jesus Christ by the will of God,* acting under a divine commission, *according to the promise of life, which is in Christ Jesus,* who hath to his people brought life and immortality to light by his gospel, *To Timothy, my dearly beloved son,* begotten by me in the gospel, and sharing my warmest paternal affection. *Grace, mercy, and peace,* with all the unutterable blessings therein contained, be with thee, *from God the Father, and Christ Jesus our Lord.* *Note,* (1.) True ministers of Christ feel the tenderest regard for their spiritual children, and cease not incessantly to pray that the best of blessings may descend upon them. (2.) All our mercies come to us as the free gift of God in Jesus Christ, whether the present pardon, peace, and grace which we receive here, or the promise of immortal life and glory which we expect hereafter.

2. He thanks God for him. *I thank God, whom I serve from my forefathers,* as a true child of Abraham, and descendant of the patriarchs, *with a pure conscience,* purged now from dead works by a Redeemer's blood, *that without ceasing I have remembrance of thee in my prayers night and day,* which I statedly offer at a throne of grace morning and evening; *greatly desiring to see thee, being mindful of thy tears,* and the distress which appeared at our last parting, *that I may be filled with joy,* if the Lord so pleases, by our happy meeting again; and it the more engages my heart to thee, *when I call to remembrance the unfeigned faith that is in thee,* and which hath been proved on so many occasions, *which dwelt first in thy grandmother Lois, and thy mother Eunice, and I am persuaded that in thee also,* who treadest in the same steps. *Note,* (1.) It is a singular blessing to have religious parents; for though grace come not by education, yet God often blesses effectually their labours, who study to bring up their children in the nurture and admonition of the Lord. (2.) Where unfeigned faith dwells, there every good fruit and gracious disposition will naturally be produced.

6. Wherefore I put thee in remembrance, h that thou
stir up the gift of God which is in thee, by the putting
on of my hands. 7 For i God hath not given us the
spirit of fear; k but of power, and of love, and of a sound
mind. 8 l Be not thou therefore ashamed of m the testimony
of our Lord, nor of me n his prisoner: but be
thou partaker of the afflictions of the gospel, according
to the power of God; 9 o Who hath saved us, and
called *us* with an holy calling, p not according to our
works, but q according to his own purpose and grace,
which was given us in Christ Jesus r before the world
began, 10 But s is now made manifest by the appearing
of our Saviour Jesus Christ, t who hath abolished
death,

death, and hath brought life and immortality to light
through the gospel 11. [y] Whereunto I am appointed
a preacher and an apostle, and a teacher of the Gentiles
12 [z] For the which cause I also suffer these things,
nevertheless I am not ashamed for [a] I know whom I
have believed, and I am persuaded that he is able [b] to
keep that which I have committed unto him [c] against
that day 13 [d] Hold fast [e] the form of sound words,
which thou hast heard of me, [f] in faith and love which
is in Christ Jesus 14 [g] That good thing which was
committed unto thee, keep by the holy Ghost [h] which
dwelleth in us

[y] Acts ix 15 1 Tim ii 7 [z] Eph iii 1 Chap ii to 1 Pet. iv 19. [b] 1 Tim. vi 20. [c] Chap iv. 8 [d] Chap iii 14 Tit i 9 [e] 1 John ii 24 [f] Rom vi 17 [g] 1 Tim i 14 [g] 1 Tim vi 20 [h] Rom viii 11

v 6—14 The apostle here,

1 Stirs up his dear son to the vigorous exercise of his ministry *Wherefore I put thee in remembrance, that thou stir up the gift of God which is in thee*, blowing the embers of divine love and zeal into a flame, and making the most profitable use of those distinguished spiritual gifts which God hath bestowed upon thee, *by the putting on of my hands* *For God hath not given us the spirit of fear*, that we should be discouraged by opposition, *but of power*, to bear up against every enemy undismayed, *and of love* to Christ and men's souls, which all the waters of persecution cannot quench, *and of a sound mind*, settled in the doctrines of truth, steady in attachment to them, and willing cheerfully to suffer for them May such a spirit be in every minister!

2 He exhorts him boldly to take up his cross *Be not thou therefore ashamed of the testimony of our Lord, nor of me his prisoner*, for they are honourable bonds, which are borne for the sake of Jesus and his cause *but be thou partaker of the afflictions of the gospel*, sympathizing with those that suffer, and willing to endure any persecutions on account of it, according to the power of God, which is engaged for the support of all those who are faithful *Note*, (1) All Christians, and ministers especially, must prepare for the cross, and expect it (2) They who dare commit their all to God, and look up to him for help, shall experience his almighty assistance in every time of need

3 He suggests the strongest motives to engage his fidelity to God and his gospel *Who hath saved us* with an everlasting salvation in the son of his love Christ Jesus, *and* hath *called us with an holy calling* by the word of his gospel, that we might be separate from a world that lieth in wickedness, and sanctified for his honour and glory, *not according to our works*, for the sake of any goodness foreseen in us, or works done by us, for all that we were, and could do, was an abomination in his sight, *but* our salvation was *according to his own* sovereign *purpose and grace, which was*, in God's eternal design and predestination, *given us in Christ*, the head and representative of his elect, *before the world began*, or any creature had their being, *but is now made manifest by the appearing of our Saviour Jesus Christ, who*, coming in the human nature, hath made the richest discoveries of God's grace to perishing sinners, and, by dying upon the cross as their substitute, *hath abolished death*, delivering them from the wages of sin, the curse of the law, and all the fearful consequences thereof in time and eternity, *and hath brought life and immortality to light by the gospel*, giving a brighter and clearer revelation of the eternal blessedness prepared for body and soul in a better world, and of the way which only leads thereto, than had ever before been made to the sons of men *Note*, (1) All who are effectually called of God, experience the power of his Spirit upon their hearts as a Spirit of holiness (2) Those who are saved by grace in time, were saved in the divine purpose from eternity, and their stability and perseverance secured in Christ Jesus before the world began (3) Every redeemed soul may regard death as a vanquished foe, since the sting of sin is taken out, we have nothing to fear, but every thing to hope, whilst in the grave we see the golden gates of life and immortality unfolded, and the bright beams of everlasting glory illuminating the dark valley of the shadow of death

4 He proposes to him his own example *Whereunto I am appointed a preacher, and an apostle, and a teacher of the Gentiles*, and count it my highest honour, *for the which cause I also suffer these things*, being now the prisoner of Jesus Christ for my fidelity in maintaining the privileges of the Gentiles, *nevertheless I am not ashamed*, neither of the gospel, nor of the chain he wore for the sake of it, *for I know whom I have believed*, the glories of his person, and the riches of his grace; *and I am persuaded that he is able*, as his promises assure me he is willing, *to keep that which I have committed to him*, even the precious deposit of my immortal soul, *against that day*, that great day of his appearing and glory *Note*, (1) Though we suffer for the gospel, we need not be ashamed, the cause will gloriously support us (2) What we have committed to Christ is safe for eternity; he never hath failed those that trust him blessed and happy the soul that can say, *I know whom I have believed*

5 He exhorts him to fidelity *Hold fast the form of sound words*, the sacred, unadulterated oracles of God, and the pure doctrines of the gospel, *which thou hast heard of me, in faith and love which is in Christ Jesus*, copy the pattern of my preaching, especially in these fundamental articles, and as thy faith in and love to the Redeemer hath appeared, with all fidelity and warm affection to the souls of men urge upon them the same blessed truths *That good thing which was committed unto thee, keep by the Holy Ghost which dwelleth in us*, be faithful to the solemn trust committed to thee; and by the power of the Holy Ghost, who abides in the hearts of all his people, with persevering diligence maintain the purity of the gospel *Note*, (1) Jesus is the glorious object of our faith and love, and to him should our hearts for ever cleave (2) The Lord must keep us, or we cannot keep ourselves, and the in-dwelling energy of the Holy Ghost alone can enable us to the discharge of every sacred trust which he hath committed to us

15 This thou knowest, that [i] all they which are in
Asia be turned away from me, of whom are Phygellus
and Hermogenes 16 The Lord give mercy unto [k] the
house of Onesiphorus, for he oft refreshed me, and was
not ashamed of [l] my chain 17 But when he was in
Rome, he sought me out very diligently, and found
me 18 The Lord grant unto him that he may find
mercy of the Lord in that day And in how many things
he ministred unto me at Ephesus thou knowest very well

[i] Chap iv 10, 15 [k] Chap iv. 19 [l] Acts xxviii 20

v 15—18 To engage his dear son Timothy's fidelity, he mentions the apostacy of some as a warning, and the steadfastness of Onesiphorus as an encouragement to him,

1 The apostacy of some *This thou knowest, that all they which are in Asia are turned away from me*, either the generality of the Asiatic churches and ministers, or rather such of the Asiatics as were at Rome, who were ashamed of his chain, and disowned him in his prison, *of whom are Phygellus and Hermogenes* *Note*, It is one of the bitterest pangs of suffering, to feel ourselves then deserted by those from whom we might reasonably, from their professions, have expected the greatest comfort and support

2 The steadfastness of Onesiphorus *The Lord give mercy unto the house of Onesiphorus*, probably he was an Ephesian, and absent from his family with the apostle, whom he attended and served with great fidelity and zeal, and therefore the grateful Paul in return repays him with his prayers, begging that the choicest blessings of God might descend upon him and his, *for he oft refreshed me* with seasonable visits, and supplies of necessaries, *and was not ashamed of my chain*, when cowardice and fear of reproach basely deterred others from coming near me *But when he was in Rome, he sought me out very diligently, and found me* *The Lord grant unto him that he may find mercy of the Lord in that day*, when Jesus shall come to reward every kindness shewn to his servants, especially to those who are suffering for righteousness sake *And in how many things he ministred unto me at Ephesus, thou knowest very well* *Note*, (1) When we can make no other return to our kind friends, at least in our prayers we are bound to recommend them to the Saviour's mercy, and beg him to reward them (2) *That day!* How should it be ever in our view, that great decisive day, when our eternity of happiness or misery must be determined! (3) We have nothing to cry for at God's hands but mercy, living or dying, the best have no merit to plead, but must expect eternal life as the *gift* of God through Jesus Christ our Lord

CHAP. II

In this chapter, 1 He encourages him in his work, shewing him from whence he must fetch help, ver 1 2 He must take care of a succession in the ministry, ver 2 3 He exhorts him to constancy and perseverance in this work, &c ver 3—15 4 He must shun profane and vain bablings, ver 16, 17, 18 for they will be pernicious and mischievous 5 He speaketh of the foundation of God which standeth sure, ver 19—21 6 What he is to avoid, youthful lusts, and foolish and unlearned questions, and what to do, ver 22 to the end

1 THOU therefore, [a] my son, [b] be strong in the
grace that is in Jesus Christ 2 And the
things that thou hast heard of me among many witnesses,
[d] the same commit thou to faithful men, who shall be
[e] able to teach others also 3 [f] Thou therefore endure
hardness, [g] as a good soldier of Jesus Christ 4 [h] No
man that warreth entangleth himself with the affairs of
this life, that he may please him who hath chosen him to
be a soldier 5 And [h] if a man also strive for masteries,
yet is he not crowned except he strive lawfully 6 [i] The
husbandman that laboureth, must be first partaker of the
fruits 7 Consider what I say, and the Lord give thee
understanding in all things

[a] 1 Tim i 2. [b] Eph vi 10 [c] Chap i 13 &c [d] Tit i 5 [e] 1 Tim iii 2. [f] Chap i 8. & iv 5 [g] 1 Tim i 18 [h] 1 Cor ix. 25 [i] 1 Cor ix. 10.

v 1—7 The apostle, in this chapter, continues his exhortations. *Thou therefore, my son, be strong in the grace that is in Jesus Christ*, sensible of thy own weakness, and dependent upon him who

alone

alone can enable thee for the arduous work *And the things that thou hast heard of me among many witnesses*, publickly declared, and proved by numerous testimonies of the law and prophets, *the same commit thou to faithful men*, whose sincerity and abilities have been tried and approved, *who shall be able to teach others also*, and preserve the glorious truths of gospel grace unadulterated *Thou therefore endure hardness*, all these persecutions and afflictions, to which, in the gospel warfare, thou must be exposed, acquitting thyself *as a good soldier of Jesus Christ*, fighting manfully under his banners with such courage, patience and perseverance, as may effectually secure the crown *No man that warreth entangleth himself with the affairs of this life*, his military service is incompatible with the pursuit of any other trade or profession, he must be at his General's call, and ever ready to obey his orders, *that he may please him who hath chosen him to be a soldier*, so must every minister of Christ be disengaged from worldly concerns, that he may be wholly employed in the service of the great Captain of our salvation, and make it his whole study and care to please him, and advance the interests of his kingdom *And if a man also strive for masteries* in the Olympic games, *yet is he not crowned* with that fading crown the reward of victory, *except he strive lawfully*, according to the rules prescribed, and much more should they, who have before them a crown of glory incorruptible, exert every effort according to the orders of their divine Master, to win the eternal prize *The husbandman that laboureth must be first partaker of the fruits*, or the husbandman must labour first before he partakes of the fruits, so must the faithful minister labour for the good of immortal souls, and patiently wait for the success of his ministry, and the expected reward in the day of Christ *Consider what I say, and the Lord give thee understanding in all things*, enabling thee to make deep application of these things to thy own soul, and, as a valiant soldier, a brave combatant, and laborious husbandman, to acquit thyself in thy ministerial office *Note*, Let all who look to the ministry, consider these things, and count the cost before they presume to appear a candidate for the service

8 Remember that Jesus Christ [k] of the seed of David
[l] was raised from the dead, [m] according to my gospel
9 [n] Wherein I suffer trouble as an evil doer, *even* unto
bonds, but the word of God is not bound 10 Therefore [o] I endure all things for the elect's sake, that they
may also obtain the salvation which is in Christ Jesus,
with eternal glory 11 *It is* a faithful saying for [q] if
we be dead *with him*, we shall also live *with him* 12
[r] If we suffer, we shall also reign *with him* [s] if we deny
him, he also will deny us 13 [t] If we believe not, *yet*
he abideth faithful, [u] he cannot deny himself

v 8—13 To encourage him boldly to suffer, the apostle suggests,

1 The grand foundation of their hope, as built upon the resurrection of Jesus *Remember that Jesus Christ*, the promised Messiah, *of the seed of David*, in his human nature, *was raised from the dead*, shewing thereby the complete redemption which he had obtained for his people, *according to my gospel* which I preached unto you

2 He set before him his own example *Wherein*, that is, for preaching which gospel, *I suffer trouble as an evil doer, even unto bonds but the word of God is not bound* even in my prison the gospel still runs and is glorified in the conversion of many souls, and others boldly labour and at large, though I am confined *Therefore* dependent upon the power of God, *I suffer all these things for the elect's sake*, willing to endure, if I am called thereunto, even death itself *that they may also obtain* (confirmed in the faith by my unshaken steadfastness in suffering for it) *the salvation which is in Jesus Christ, with eternal glory*, of which he is that to all, he is the author, finisher, and bestower, on all his chosen, and they are wholly indebted for it to his sovereign grace and love *Note*, (1) A noble example is a powerful encouragement to follow on (2) Though persecutors may confine the ministers, the word of God will still work effectually on as many as the Lord will call (3) All the elect shall infallibly obtain eternal salvation, for Christ hath secured it for them, and will bring them to be with himself where he is, that they may behold his glory

3 The reward of faithful suffering should engage him boldly to take up the cross *It is a faithful saying for if we be dead with him*, as vitally united to him in his death, or if called to die for his cause as he died for us, *we shall also live with him*, planted also in the likeness of his resurrection, and raised up to immortal life and glory *if we suffer* for him, *we shall reign with him*, sit down on his throne but *if we* prove faithless, and *deny him* in the hour of temptation, *he also will deny* and disown *us* in the great day of his appearing *if we believe not, yet he abideth faithful* his promises and threatenings will surely be accomplished, whether men believe them or no *he is immutable*, *he cannot deny himself*, or falsify his word *Note*, (1) It is our privilege to consider, when we see that the issue will be so glorious, (2) The hope of life with Jesus should raise us superior to all the fear of death, though in its most tremendous form (3) They who, for any

worldly interest or advantage, or to avoid shame, reproach, or suffering, disown the Lord Jesus, his gospel and suffering servants, will bear in eternity their burden, and be driven from his presence with everlasting contempt

14 Of these things put *them* in remembrance, [x] charg
ing *them* before the Lord, [y] that they strive not about
words to no profit, *but* to the subverting of the hearers
15 Study to shew thyself approved unto God, a work-
man that needeth not to be ashamed, rightly dividing
the word of truth 16 But [z] shun profane and vain
bablings, for they will increase unto more ungodliness
17 And their word will eat as doth a † canker of
whom is [a] Hymeneus and Philetus, 18 Who [b] con-
cerning the truth have erred, saying [c] that the resur-
rection is past already, and overthrow the faith of some.

v 14—18 The apostle proceeds to give further exhortations to Timothy

1 To seek the edification of those under his charge *Of these things put them in remembrance, charge them*, with all solemnity and authority, *before the Lord*, as in his presence, *that they strive not about words to no profit, but to the subverting of the hearers*, drawing them from the purity of the gospel, instead of promoting godly edifying *Note*, Any trivial matter will afford occasion of strife to a contentious spirit

2 He enjoins him to shew himself an able minister of Jesus Christ *Study to shew thyself approved unto God, a workman that needeth not to be ashamed*, diligent, faithful, laborious, skilful, *rightly dividing the word of truth*, and giving to each his portion in due season, according to the various cases and conditions of the people's souls *But shun profane and vain bablings*, the dreams of the judaizing teachers, *for they will increase unto more ungodliness*, and lead to the most pernicious errors in principles and practice *And their word will eat as doth a canker*, corroding the hearts of the hearers, and threatning their eternal death *of whom is Hymeneus and Philetus*, the chief heretical seducers, *who concerning the truth have erred, saying, that the resurrection is past already*; probably they asserted, that the resurrection was only mystical and spiritual, not of the body but of the soul, *and have overthrown the faith of some* *Note*, (1) Error is spreading as a gangrene, and, tho' it may appear little at first, threatens the most fatal consequences (2) They who love to hear themselves talk, will be sure to prove the truth of that scripture, that in the multitude of words there wanteth not folly (3) A true minister will labour to speak ever to the purpose, not curious about a fine harangue, but careful to apply the word of truth to the consciences of his hearers

19 Nevertheless [d] the foundation of God standeth
sure, having this seal, [e] The Lord knoweth them that are
his And, Let every one that nameth the name of
Christ depart from iniquity 20 But in a great house
there are not only vessels of gold and of silver, but also of
wood, and of earth; and [f] some to honour, and some to
dishonour 21 [g] If a man therefore purge himself from
these, he shall be a vessel unto honour, sanctified and
meet for the master's use, *and* [h] prepared unto every good
work

v 19—21 Among all the errors of deceivers, this is *nevertheless* our comfort

1 That *the foundation of God standeth sure*, the faith of God's elect can never be destroyed, however many false professors prove apostates, and God's design of grace towards them cannot be frustrated by any devices of the most subtle deceivers, for their stability is secured, *having this seal, The Lord knoweth them that are his*, and embraces them with the arms of everlasting love, from which neither men nor devils can pluck them *and*, in consequence of his sealing his people unto the day of redemption, this is his expectation from them, and will be their practice, *Let every one that nameth the name of Christ depart from iniquity*, and by the fruits of sanctification prove the certainty of their election

2 *But in a great house there are not only vessels of gold and of silver, but also of wood, and of earth, and some to honour, and some to dishonour*, so it need not be thought strange, that in the visible church, whilst some professors adorn the gospel, others appear a scandal to the name they bear, a dishonour to the Redeemer, and will, at the last, be rejected by him *If a man therefore purge himself from these* errors and practices of the seducing teachers, *he shall be a vessel unto honour, sanctified and meet for the master's use, and prepared unto every good work*, employed by him on earth with approbation, and then having finished the work which he hath given them to do below, shall be removed to shine in his better temple of eternal glory above Lord, may my lot be with these!

22 Flee also youthful lusts [i] but follow righteous-
ness, faith, charity, peace, with them [k] that call on the
Lord

[k] 1 Chron. xvii. 11. Rom. i. 3 [l] 1 Cor. xv. 4. [m] Rom. ii. 16 [n] Eph. iii. 1. Phil. i. 7. Col. iv. 3. [o] Eph. iii. 13. Col. i. 24. [q] Rom. vi. 5, 8. 2 Cor. iv. 10 [r] Rom. viii. 17. 1 Pet. iv. 13 [s] Mat. x. 33. Mark viii. 38. [t] Rom. iii. 3. & ix. 6 [u] Num. xxiii. 19

[x] 1 Tim. v. 21. & vi. 13. Chap. iv. 1 [y] 1 Tim. vi. 4 [z] 1 Tim. i. 4. & iv. 7. & vi. 20. Tit. i. 14. ... 9 † Or gangrene [a] 1 Tim. i. 20. [b] 1 Tim. vi. 21 [c] 1 Cor. xv. 12

[d] Mat. xxiv. 24. 1 John ii. 19 [e] Nah. i. 7. John x. 14, 27. Num. xvi. 5 [f] Rom. ix. 21 [g] Isa. lii. 11 [h] Chap. iii. 17

[i] 1 Tim. vi. 11 [k] Acts ix. 14. 1 Cor. i. 2

Lord [l] out of a pure heart. 23 But [m] foolish and un-
learned questions avoid, knowing that they do gender
strifes 24 And [n] the servant of the Lord must not
strive, but be gentle unto all *men*, [o] apt to teach, † pa-
tient, 25 [p] In meekness instructing those that oppose
themselves, [q] if God peradventure will give them repent-
ance [r] to the acknowledging of the truth, 26 And that
they may ‡ recover themselves out of [s] the snare of the
devil, who are taken § captive by him at his will

v 22—26 Some personal directions are here given the young evangelist

1 *Flee youthful lusts*, not merely those of the flesh, but the more dangerous ones of pride, love of pre-eminence, and popular applause, those fatal rocks against which so many make shipwreck, and need be shunned with peculiar care *But*,

2 *Follow righteousness* towards God and man, *faith, charity, peace, with* all the other train of heavenly tempers which abide in *them who call on the Lord out of a pure heart* *Note*, They who are Christians indeed, are constant at the throne of grace, and, in purity of heart and life, prove their professions sincere

3 *But foolish and unlearned questions avoid, knowing that they do gender strifes*, and open a field of endless and unprofitable controversy *And the servant of the Lord must not strive*, the follower of the Lamb of God should copy the pattern of his meekness, not quarrelsome, *but be gentle unto all men, apt to teach* in the most inoffensive way, *patient* under the provocations of the most untractable, and the prejudices of the weak *In meekness instructing those that oppose themselves* against the gospel doctrines, mildly arguing, and gently remonstrating, desirous to win them by love, and overcome them with kindness, *if God peradventure will give them repentance to the acknowledging of the truth*, as it is in Jesus, *and that they may recover themselves out of the snare of the devil, who are taken captive by him at his will*, as birds in the snare of the fowler, where they must lie and perish, unless Divine Grace breaks the snare, and delivers the miserable soul *Note*, (1) Nothing is more necessary for a minister than unwearied patience, and meekness (2) We must labour for the souls of men, but God only can give them repentance (3) The gospel word is the great instrument which the Lord employs for the conversion of the heart (4) They are the vilest of slaves who are led at the devil's beck to the service of divers lusts and pleasures, and happy is it for the soul that is delivered from this dreadful servitude by the power of Divine Grace, and brought into the glorious liberty of the sons of God

CHAP III

He foretels Timothy what the last days would be, with the reasons thereof ver 1—9 2 *Prescribes various remedies against them*, ver 10 to the end, *particularly his own example, and the knowledge of the holy scriptures, which are able to make us wise unto salvation, and will be the best antidote against the corruptions of the times we live in*

1 THIS know also, that [a] in the last days perilous
times shall come 2 For men shall be lovers
of their own selves, [b] covetous, [c] boasters, proud, blas-
phemers, disobedient to parents, unthankful, unholy,
3 Without natural affection, [d] truce-breakers, ‡ false
accusers, incontinent, fierce, despisers of those that are
good, 4 Traitors, heady, high-minded, lovers of plea-
sures more than lovers of God, 5 [e] Having a form of
godliness, but denying the power thereof [f] from such
also turn away

v 1—5 The apostle apprizes Timothy of the dangerous days which approached, that he might not be surprized when the offences came *This know also, that in the last days perilous times shall come*, when sad corruptions, creeping into the church, shall make it difficult to preserve a pure conscience *For men shall be lovers of their own selves*, wholly devoted to the pursuits of their worldly honour and interest, *covetous*, insatiate after filthy lucre, *proud*, and vain-glorious boasters, *blasphemers* of God and man, *disobedient to parents*, *unthankful* to their benefactors, *unholy* in heart and conversation, *without natural affection*, which appears even in brutes, *truce breakers*, perfidious to the most solemn engagements, *false accusers*, like devils incarnate, blackening, with every opprobrious calumny, their opponents, *incontinent*, indulging every bestial appetite, *fierce* and furious in their tempers, *despisers of those that are good*, and treating men, far their betters, with contempt, *traitors*, false to their trusts, betraying their nearest friends *heady*, driving furiously in their wicked courses, impatient of controul, *high minded*, puffed up with a vain conceit of their own superiority, *lovers of pleasures more than lovers of God*, and what is the aggravation of all these other abominations, making great pretensions to piety, *having a form of godliness*, and affecting rigid attachment to the externals of worship, *but denying the power of it*, real energetic vital religion *from such turn away*, and shun them as the plague

These corruptions began in the Gnosticks, which in the apostle's days appeared, and the perilous times advanced to their heighth, when the Roman pontiffs, after a train of diabolical practices, raised their blasphemous hierarchy, and consecrated their abominations. And to the papal apostacy are all these characters strikingly applicable

6 For [g] of this sort are they which creep into houses,
and lead captive silly women laden with sins, led away
with divers lusts, 7 Ever learning, and never able to
come to the knowledge of the truth 8 [h] Now as
Jannes and Jambres withstood Moses, so do these also
resist the truth [i] men of corrupt minds, [k] reprobate con-
cerning the faith 9. But they shall proceed no further;
for their folly shall be manifest unto all *men*, [l] as theirs also
was

v 6—9 The apostle proceeds,

1 To point out the artful and pernicious practices of the seducers *For of this sort are they which creep into houses* with every wheedling art, *and lead captive silly women laden with sins, led away with divers lusts*, imposing upon them with flattering speeches, and gaining them to their party, *ever learning* of these vain teachers, *and never able to come to the knowledge of the truth*, but bewildered in the endless mazes of error *Now as Jannes and Jambres withstood Moses*, setting up their pretended miracles in opposition to his divine commission, *so do these also resist the truth* of the gospel *men of* the like *corrupt minds* as these Egyptian sorcerers, *reprobate concerning the faith*, rejected and abhorred of God

2 He foretels that all their efforts should be impotent *But they shall proceed no further* than the magicians did, nor be able to deceive the elect, *for* an effectual check shall be given to them, and *their folly shall be manifest unto all men, as theirs also was*, and all their lying miracles shall be detected *Note*, Error may, for a time, prevail, but truth shall finally be triumphant

10. But thou ‖ hast fully known my doctrine, manner
of life, purpose, faith, long-suffering, charity, patience,
11 Persecutions, afflictions which came unto me [m] at
Antioch, [n] at Iconium, [o] at Lystra what persecutions I
endured but [p] out of them all the Lord delivered me
12 Yea, and [q] all that will live godly in Christ Jesus
shall suffer persecution 13 [r] But evil men and se-
ducers shall wax worse and worse, deceiving and being
deceived

v 10—13 Nothing could better serve to guard Timothy against these seducers than the striking contrast between their conduct and that of the blessed Paul

1 He reminds him of what he had seen *But thou hast fully known my doctrine*, the uniform tenor of my preaching, my exemplary *manner of life*, steady *purpose* to advance God's glory and the good of men's souls, unshaken *faith*, fervent *charity*, unwearied *patience*, amidst the many and grievous *persecutions, afflictions which came unto me at Antioch, at Iconium, at Lystra what persecutions I endured but out of them all the Lord delivered me* With such an example Timothy should be animated to fidelity, and might surely expect the same supports and deliverances

2 He informs him that suffering must be every Christian's lot *Yea, and all that will live godly in Christ Jesus shall suffer persecution*, of one kind or other, from mockery to martyrdom There is indeed a godliness in form that the world speaks well of, but to be *godly in Christ Jesus*, in spirit and temper conformed to him, will ever render us abhorred of a world that lieth in wickedness

3 He predicts the fatal end of these deceivers *But evil men and seducers shall wax worse and worse*, hurried on from one excess of wickedness to another, *deceiving and being deceived*, till, having filled up the measure of their iniquities, they perish with the arch-deceiver in everlasting burnings.

14 But [s] continue thou in the things which thou hast
learned and hast been assured of, knowing of whom thou
hast learned *them* 15 And that from a child thou hast
known the holy scriptures, [t] which are able to make thee
wise unto salvation, through faith which is in Christ Jesus
16 [u] All scripture *is* given by inspiration of God, [x] and
is profitable for doctrine, for reproof, for correction, for
instruction in righteousness 17 [y] That the man of God
may be perfect, [z] thoroughly furnished unto all good
works

v 14—17 As he would be exposed to great temptations, the apostle exhorts him to cleave to the scriptures, as the only infallible guide to truth.

But

But continue thou in the things which thou hast learned, and hast been assured of, the pure and unadulterated doctrines of the gospel, which, on the most satisfying evidence thou hast believed, *knowing of whom thou hast learned them,* even from me, divinely commissioned from the great Redeemer *and that from a child thou hast known the holy scriptures,* early initiated in these sacred records, *which are able to make thee wise unto salvation, through faith which is in Christ Jesus,* who is the sum and substance of the whole, and to whom both the law and the prophets bear witness *All scripture is given by inspiration of God,* both the Old and New Testament have the same divine original, *and is profitable for doctrine,* none demanding our credence and submission, but what can be clearly proved from thence, *for reproof* of errors, heresies, and all manner of evil, *for correction* of whatever is found amiss in the church, *for instruction in righteousness,* how righteousness before God can be obtained, through faith in a Redeemer, and how we can be enabled so to walk as to please God *that the man of God,* the true believer, *may be perfect, thoroughly* instructed in all the mind of God, and *furnished unto all good works,* whether as a Christian for those of his station, or as a minister for the arduous service in which he is engaged *Note,* (1) Parents should betimes endeavour to lead their children to the Bible (2) All the volumes of human learning can never teach us so much true wisdom as one page, one line of the book of God, after all these labours we must have been left to perish in ignorance, but in the oracles of truth, life and immortality are brought to light, and the poorest and most unlettered saint of God is wiser, in the things which make for his everlasting peace, than the deepest metaphysician, or the most profound philosopher (3) All scripture is of divine authority, therefore on God's testimony to be received with faith Our wisdom, where ought mysterious is revealed, is not to reason, but to believe (4) The book of God is the Christian's great magazine, he can be in no state and condition, but he will there find direction, instruction, reproof or comfort, exactly suited to his circumstances

CHAP. IV.

In this chapter St Paul, 1 Doth with great solemnity and earnestness press Timothy to the diligent and conscientious discharge of his work and office, as an evangelist, and the charge given to him, all gospel ministers are to take to themselves, ver 1—6 2 Why must Timothy now be instant in season, &c in a particular manner? Because the church was likely to be deprived of the apostle's labours, for his departure was at hand, ver 6, 7, 8 3 Divers particular matters, with an hint and caution about Alexander the coppersmith, ver 9—16 4 He informeth him of what befel him at his first answer, though men forsook him, the Lord stood by him, and that encouraged him to hope for future deliverance, ver 16—19 And then he concludes with salutations and a benediction, ver 19, to the end

1 [a] I Charge *thee* therefore before God and the Lord
Jesus Christ, [b] who shall judge the quick and the
dead at his appearing, and his kingdom 2 Preach the
word, be instant in season, out of season, reprove, [c] re-
buke, exhort with all long-suffering and doctrine 3
For [d] the time will come when they will not endure
[e] sound doctrine, [f] but after their own lusts shall they
heap to themselves teachers, having itching ears 4 And
they shall turn away *their* ears from the truth, and [g] shall
be turned unto fables 5 But watch thou in all things,
[h] endure afflictions, [i] do the work of an evangelist, † make
full proof of thy ministry 6 For I am now ready to
[k] be offered, and the time of my departure is at hand
7 I have fought [l] the good fight, I have finished [m] my
course, I have kept the faith 8. Henceforth there is
laid up for me [n] a crown of righteousness, which the
Lord the righteous judge shall give me [o] at that day
and not to me only, but unto all them that love his ap-
pearing

[a] 1 Tim v 21 Chap ii 14 [b] Acts x 42 [c] 1 Tim v 20 Tit ii 15 [d] Chap iii 1 [e] 1 Tim i 10 [f] Chap iii 6 [g] 1 Tim i 4 & iv 7 [h] Chap i 8 & ii 3 [i] Acts xxi 8 Eph iv 11 † Or fulfil Col i 25 & iv 17 [k] Phil ii 17 [l] 1 Tim vi 12 [m] 1 Cor ix 24 Phil iii 14 Heb xii 1 [n] Jam i 12 1 Pet v 4 Rev ii 10 [o] Chap i 12

v 1—8 The apostle, being now ready to conclude his epistle, gives Timothy,

1 His solemn charge *I charge thee before* the great heart-searching *God, and the Lord Jesus Christ, who shall judge the quick and the dead at his appearing and his kingdom,* in the last great day, when he shall come in his glory, and give to every man according to his work *preach the word,* proclaiming, as an herald aloud, the blessed gospel, *be instant in season,* and, as some may think, *out of season,* earnest to inculcate the truth upon men's consciences, both on the Lord's day, and every other opportunity, not only in time of peace, but amidst all opposition and persecution, *reprove, rebuke* gainsayers, backsliders, sinners; *exhort* and encourage the faithful, *with all long suffering,* unwearied in the service, nor discouraged at any difficulties in the way, *and with that doctrine,* which is according to the scripture, and profitable for the souls of men *Note,* (1) Ministers must not only *preach,* but be *instant,* frozen discourses, languidly delivered, will never fire the hearer's soul (2) They who have the work of Christ at heart, will be perhaps often thought very unseasonable in the frequency of their public ministrations, or the freedom of their private rebukes, but they have here a divine warrant

2 He warns him how difficult it will prove to be faithful amidst the abounding errors *For the time will come,* and the mystery of iniquity already begins to operate, *when they will not endure sound doctrine,* the pure gospel of Jesus Christ, *but after their own* depraved *lusts* and passions, *shall they heap to themselves teachers, having itching ears,* desiring to have their fancies entertained, and their corruptions flattered, instead of the free, honest, and faithful rebuke which the gospel ministers deliver *And they shall turn away their ears from the truth,* averse from it, and refusing to obey it, *and shall be turned unto fables,* listning to the seducing teachers, who with idle tales amuse, and with falshood lull their consciences asleep *Note,* They who like to be flattered in their sins, rather than to hear faithful reproof, are justly given up to their own delusions, and the blind are suffered to follow the blind, till both fall into the pit of hell

3 He admonishes Timothy to guard against these deceivers, and to caution the people that they be not imposed upon *But watch thou in all things* over thy own heart, and over the church committed to thy care, guarding against the first appearances of evil and error, *endure afflictions* with fortitude and patience, *do the work of an evangelist* with all fidelity and zeal, *make full proof of thy ministry,* that gainsayers may be silenced, and believers comforted and edified

4 He informs Timothy of his approaching dissolution and glorious hope, for his encouragement to follow his steps. *For I am now ready to be offered up,* and to pour out my blood as a libation in the service of the gospel *and the time of my departure is at hand,* when my disembodied soul shall go to the bosom of my Lord *I have fought a good fight,* and through grace can look back with satisfaction on my warfare, *I have finished my course,* and am near the glorious prize, *I have kept the faith,* maintaining the purity of the doctrines of Christ, and adorning them by unimpeached fidelity in my own conversation *Henceforth there is laid up for me a crown of righteousness, which the Lord, the righteous judge,* the rewarder of those whom he hath chosen and called, and strengthened for the conflict, *shall give me at that day* of his appearing and glory *and not to me only, but unto all them also that love his appearing,* and live under the influence, and in the prospect and earnest expectation of it *Note,* (1) The fidelity of others should be a quickning motive to excite our diligence, and their dying testimony to the blessedness of Christ's ways, should comfort and encourage us to persevere in them (2) When we have the sure hope of the crown of righteousness, the day of our departure will be the brightest which ever dawned upon us (3) They who are faithful unto death, may with delight look back, and, whilst they ascribe all to their Master's grace, they cannot but rejoice in the evidence, which the review affords of their approved sincerity before him (4) Whatever difficulties are in our way, we have a good cause to bear us out, and should comfortably and courageously persevere, whatever we lose for Christ here, we shall, at least in eternity, be unspeakable gainers by him (5) There is an awful day at hand, and a righteous judge expected Blessed and happy are they who truly love the day of his appearing, and can say with confidence, and real desire, Come, Lord Jesus, come quickly

9 Do thy diligence to come shortly unto me 10
For [p] Demas hath [q] forsaken me, having loved this pre-
sent world, and is departed unto Thessalonica Crescens
to Galatia, Titus unto Dalmatia 11 Only [r] Luke is
with me 14 Take [s] Mark and bring him with thee
for he is profitable to me for the ministry 12 And
[t] Tychicus have I sent to Ephesus 13 The cloke that
I left at Troas with Carpus, when thou comest, bring
with thee, and the books, *but* especially the parchments
14 [u] Alexander the coppersmith did me much evil [x] the
Lord reward him according to his works 15 Of whom
be thou ware also, for he hath greatly withstood our
words

[p] Col iv 14 Philem 24 [q] Chap i 15 Ver 16 [r] Col iv 14 [s] Acts xv 37 Col iv 10 [t] Acts xx 4 Eph vi 21 Col iv 7 Tit iii 12 [u] 1 Tim i 20 [x] Ps xxviii 4 Rev xviii 6

v 9—15 Several directions are here given to Timothy

1 *Do thy diligence to come shortly unto me,* as I especially need thy company at this time *For Demas hath forsaken me, having loved this present world,* and now, in this trying season, hath shamefully deserted me, pursuing his own base and worldly interest, *and is departed unto Thessalonica,* to be out of the danger to which here he might, as my companion, have been exposed *Crescens is gone,* on affairs of the church, *to Galatia, and Titus to Dalmatia,* so that I am almost left alone *Only Luke is with me,* my true and faithful fellow labourer, *and Tychicus have I sent to Ephesus* *Note,* The love of this present world hath fatally warped many from their fidelity to Christ

2 *Take Mark and bring him with thee for he is profitable to me for the ministry* Whatever just cause of umbrage the apostle

might

might have had formerly against him, he was now returned to his duty, and therewith to Paul's favour and regard *Note,* Those who have never so much offended us, we should cordially again receive, whenever they humbly desire to return to the right way

3 *The cloke,* or, as others render it, *the desk, that I left at Troas, with Carpus* my host, *when thou comest, bring with thee, and the books, but especially the parchments* What these writings contained, of which the apostle was so careful, is uncertain some have thought it was the roll of his freedom, others, the copies of his epistles, which had been sent to the several churches

4 He admonishes him to beware of a bitter enemy to Christianity *Alexander the coppersmith did me much evil,* (*Acts* xix 33) and still bears an implacable enmity to me *The Lord reward him according to his works,* to whose righteous judgment I leave him *Of whom be thou ware also, for he hath greatly withstood our words,* and endeavoured to prejudice both Jews and Gentiles against that gospel which we preach *Note,* Though no private revenge must dictate a thought or wish of resentment, yet obstinate and incorrigible enemies to truth and godliness are to be delivered up to an avenging God

16 At my first answer no man stood with me, but [y] all
y Chap i 15 *men* forsook me *I pray God* that it may not be laid to
z Mat x 19 their charge 17 Notwithstanding the Lord stood
with me, and strengthned me, that by me the preach-
ing might be fully known, and *that* all the Gentiles might
a Ps xxii 21 hear and I was delivered [a] out of the mouth of the lion
18 And the Lord shall deliver me from every evil work,
b Rom xvi 27 1 Tim and will preserve *me* unto his heavenly kingdom [b] to
vi 16 whom *be* glory for ever and ever Amen 19 Salute
c Acts xviii 2 [c] Prisca and Aquila, and [d] the houshold of Onesiphorus
d 2 Tim i 16 20 [e] Erastus abode at Corinth but [f] Trophimus have
e Acts xix 22 I left at Miletum sick 21 [g] Do thy diligence to come
before winter Eubulus greeteth thee, and Pudens,
f Acts xx 4 & xxi 29 and Linus, and Claudia, and all the brethren 22
g Chap i 4 [h] The Lord Jesus Christ *be* with thy spirit Grace *be* h Gal vi 18 Philem 25
with you Amen

v 16—22 The apostle here,

1 Informs Timothy of his present circumstances *At my first answer,* when I was called to defend myself before the emperor, *no man stood with me, but all,* who could be of any service by their countenance or presence, *forsook me,* through fear and cowardice *I pray God that it may not be laid to their charge,* but that he would pardon this unfaithfulness, and bring them to repentance *Notwithstanding,* though deserted by men, *the Lord stood with me and strengthened me* with boldness, freedom, and fidelity to plead the cause of his gospel, *that by me the preaching might be fully known, and that all the Gentiles might hear,* who were present at my trial, or to whom the substance of it should be related *and I was delivered out of the mouth of the lion,* from the cruel Nero, and the jaws of death, which seemed to yawn for me *And* I am fully confident, from long experience, that *the Lord shall deliver me from every evil work,* that I shall never speak nor act unbecoming the character I bear, intimidated by any fear of sufferings, *and will preserve me unto his heavenly kingdom,* giving me the inheritance in glory which he hath provided and promised *to whom be glory for ever and ever Amen!* *Note,* (1) In trying times we are not to be surprized if many desert us who promised very fair (2) If the Lord stand by us, we want no other support (3) It is our comfort, whatever befals us, that we have an heavenly kingdom secured, and then come life, come death all must be well

2 He sends his own and others salutations, and hastens Timothy to come to him *Salute Prisca and Aquila, and the houshold of Onesiphorus Erastus,* the chamberlain, *abode at Corinth but Trophimus have I left at Miletum sick,* not having any suggestion from the Lord, or power, miraculously to restore him *Do thy diligence to come before winter Eubulus greeteth thee, and Pudens, and Linus, and Claudia, and all the brethren* in these parts

3 He concludes with his hearty benediction and prayer for him *The Lord Jesus Christ be with thy spirit* to quicken, teach, guide, preserve thee *Grace be with you,* and all that love our Lord Jesus Christ in sincerity *Amen*

THE

EVANGELICAL EXPOSITOR;

OR, A

PRACTICAL COMMENT

Upon the EPISTLE of

St. PAUL to TITUS.

THIS Epistle of Paul to Titus is much of the same nature with those to Timothy, both were converts of Paul, and his companions in labours and sufferings, both in the office of evangelists, whose work was to water the churches planted by the apostles, and to set in order the things that were wanting in them. We read much of this Titus, his titles and character, and active usefulness in many places. He was a Greek, Gal ii 3. *St Paul called him* his son, *Tit* i 4. his brother, 2 *Cor.* ii. 13 his partner and fellow-helper, 2 *Cor* viii. 23 one that walked in the same Spirit, and in the same steps with himself *He went up with the apostle to the church at Jerusalem,* Gal ii 1 *was much conversant at Corinth, for which church he had* an earnest care, 2 *Cor* viii. 16. *Paul's second epistle to them, and probably his first also, was sent by his hand,* 2 Cor viii. 16, 17, 18, 23 *and* chap ix, 2, 3, 4 *and* chap xii. 18 *He was with the apostle at Rome, and thence went into Dalmatia,* 2 Tim iv 10 *after which no more occurs of him in the scriptures In Crete, a large island at the mouth of the Ægean sea, the gospel had got some footing, and here were Paul and Titus in one of their travels cultivating this plantation, but* the apostle of the Gentiles, *having on him* the care of all the churches, *could not himself tarry long at this place, therefore left Titus some time there to carry on the work which had been begun; wherein, probably meeting with more difficulty than ordinary, Paul wrote this epistle to him He was to see all the cities furnished with good pastors, to reject and keep out the unmeet and unworthy, to teach sound doctrine, and instruct all sorts in their duties, to set forth the free grace of God in man's salvation by Christ, and withal to shew the necessity of maintaining good works by those who have believed in God, and hope for eternal life from him*

CHAP I

In this chapter we have, (1) The preface or introduction to the epistle, ver 1—4 *(2) The end of Titus's being left at Crete,* ver 5 *And, (3) How the same should be pursued in reference both to good and bad ministers, from* ver 6, to the end

a 1 Tim iii 16 & vi 3. b Num xxiii 19. c Rom xvi 25. 2 Tim i 9. 1 Pet i 20. d Rom xvi 26. 2 Tim i 10. e 1 Thess ii 4. 1 Tim i 11. f 1 Tim i 1 & ii 3. g 2 Cor ii 13 & viii 6, 23. h 1 Tim i 2. i 2 Pet i 1. k Eph i 2. Col i 2.

1 PAUL, a servant of God, and an apostle of
Jesus Christ, according to the faith of God's
elect, and the acknowledging of the truth,
a which is after godliness 2 In hope of
eternal life, which God b that cannot lye, promised c be-
fore the world began; 3 d But hath in due times ma-
nifested his word through preaching, e which is commit-
ted unto me, f according to the commandment of God
our Saviour 4 g To Titus, h mine own son after i the
common faith k Grace, mercy, *and* peace from God the
Father, and the Lord Jesus Christ our Saviour

v 1—4 The apostle opens with his usual address

1 He sets forth his own divine commission and apostleship This epistle comes from *Paul,* who counts it his highest honour to be called *a servant of God* in the gospel of his dear Son, *and an apostle of Jesus Christ,* sent to bear the glad tidings of his salvation to Gentile lands, *according to the faith of God's elect,* the doctrine which is to be embraced by all whom the Lord hath chosen, *and* is pleased effectually to call to *the acknowledging of the truth, which is after godliness,* and which, having heartily embraced myself, I now with delight publish to others *in hope of eternal life, which* all, who live godly in Christ Jesus, are sure to attain unto, because *God, who cannot lye,* hath *promised* it unto them, in Christ their head, *before the world began, but hath in due times manifested his word through preaching, which is committed unto me, according to the commandment of God our Saviour* and I have with all fidelity laboured to discharge the important trust *Note,* (1) The highest dignity is to be the servant of the living God (2) There is an elect of God, to whom the gospel will be infallibly effectual (3) All, who are chosen in Christ Jesus before the world began, are in the fulness of time brought to contest the faith, acknowledge the truth, and in all godliness to shew its influence upon their heart (4) Eternal life is sure to all the faithful in the promise of an unchangeable God can make it he must be false to his word before they can fail of their inheritance in glory (5) They, who are ministers of God, must be indefatigable in preaching Dumb dogs that cannot, or will not bark, are not of the Great Shepherd's appointment

2 He-

2 He wiſhes Titus the beſt of bleſſings *To Titus, mine own ſon after the common faith*, my ſpiritual child, begotten in the goſpel, be *grace, mercy, and peace from God the Father, and the Lord Jeſus Chriſt our Saviour* Note, (1) All believers have one common faith, and are united to the ſame Jeſus (2) If Chriſt be indeed *our Saviour*, then God's ſovereign and everlaſting *love* and *mercy*, in all their boundleſs import of pardon and ſalvation to the uttermoſt, and *peace* of conſcience preſent and eternal, will be our bleſſed portion

5 For this cauſe left I thee in Crete, that thou
ſhouldſt [l] ſet in order the things that are wanting, and
[m] ordain elders in every city, as I had appointed thee
6 [n] If any be blameleſs, [o] the huſband of one wife,
[p] having faithful children, not accuſed of riot, or unruly
7 For a biſhop muſt be [q] blameleſs, [r] as the ſteward of
God, not ſelf-willed, not ſoon angry, [s] not given to
wine, [t] no ſtriker, [u] not given to filthy lucre, 8 [x] But
a lover of hoſpitality, a lover of † good men, ſober, juſt,
holy, temperate, 9 [y] Holding faſt [z] the faithful word,
‡ as he hath been taught, that he may be able by [a] ſound
doctrine, both to exhort and to convince the gainſayers
10 For [b] there are many unruly and vain talkers and
deceivers, eſpecially they of the circumciſion 11 Whoſe
mouths muſt be ſtopped, [c] who ſubvert whole houſes,
teaching things which they ought not, [d] for filthy lucre's
ſake

l 1 Cor xi 34. m Acts xiv 23. n 1 Tim iii 2, &c o 1 Tim iii 2 p 1 Tim iii 4 12 q 2 Cor vi 3 r 1 Cor iv 1 s Lev x 9 Ezek xliv 21 t 1 Tim iii 3 u 1 Tim iii 8 1 Pet v 2 x 1 Tim iii 2 † Or good things. y 2 Theſſ ii 15 z 1 Tim i 15 a 1 Tim i 10 & vi 3 ‡ Or in teaching. b Chap i 10 1 Tim i 6 c Mat xxiii 14 2 Tim iii 6 d 1 Tim vi 5

v 5—11 St Paul,

1 Reminds him of the end for which he was left in Crete *For this cauſe left I thee in Crete, that thou ſhouldſt ſet in order the things that are wanting*, directing them concerning the proper diſcipline, worſhip, and conduct, to be obſerved by this lately converted church, *and ordain elders in every city, as I have appointed thee*, ſuch as ſhall be found duly qualified for the miniſterial work

2 He deſcribes the character of thoſe whom he ſhould ordain *If any be blameleſs*, having a good report of thoſe who know him beſt, *the huſband of one wife*, no polygamiſt, *having faithful children*, brought up in the nurture and admonition of the Lord, *not accuſed of riot, or unruly*, diſſolute and refractory, but kept under due reſtraint, neither a diſgrace to themſelves or their parents *For a biſhop muſt be blameleſs, as the ſteward of God*, appointed to that high charge in his holy family, and therefore of a character irreproachable, *not ſelf-willed*, of a raſh and obſtinate temper, *not ſoon angry*, and firing at every provocation, *not given to wine*, addicted to drunkenneſs, or fond of the glaſs, *no ſtriker*, violent in his paſſions, *not given to filthy lucre*, a mercenary wretch, who ſerves for hire, *but* out of zeal for Chriſt and the ſouls of men He muſt be *alſo a lover of hoſpitality*, entertaining poor ſtrangers, and Chriſtians driven from their homes by the fury of perſecution, *a lover of good men*, without prejudice or exception, *ſober*, grave and prudent in his carriage and deportment, *juſt* and upright in his converſation, *holy* in all his conduct, *temperate* in his deſires and appetites, *holding faſt the faithful word*, maintaining the purity of the goſpel, and diſpenſing it with all fidelity, *as he hath been taught by us, that he may be able, by ſound doctrine, both to exhort* and comfort the true members of Chriſt's church, *and to convince gainſayers* of their errors For ſuch ſpiritual wiſdom is neceſſary, becauſe *there are many unruly and vain talkers and deceivers*, in Crete as well as other churches, who, though profeſſing Chriſtianity, walk diſorderly, and with their heretical tenets draw away diſciples after them, *eſpecially they of the circumciſion*, who are the great corrupters of the faith, urging circumciſion and the obſervance of the moſaical inſtitution as neceſſary to ſalvation, *whoſe mouths muſt be ſtopped*, not by force, but by ſound truth and ſcriptural arguments to detect their fallacies and ſilence their cavils, *who ſubvert whole houſes*, inſinuating themſelves into the families of profeſſors, *teaching things which they ought not, for filthy lucre's ſake*, adapting their teaching to the palates of their hearers, in order to inſinuate into their confidence, and enrich themſelves at their expence

12 [e] One of themſelves, *even* a prophet of their own,
ſaid, The Cretians *are* alway liars, evil beaſts, ſlow bel-
lies 13 This witneſs is true wherefore [f] rebuke them
ſharply, that they may be ſound in the faith, 14 [g] Not
giving heed to Jewiſh fables, and [h] commandments of
men that turn from the truth 15 [i] Unto the pure all
things *are* pure but [k] unto them that are defiled and
unbelieving, *is* nothing pure but even their mind and
conſcience is defiled 16 They profeſs that they know
God, [l] but in works they deny *him*, being abominable,
and diſobedient, [m] and unto every good work reprobate

e Acts xvii 28 f Chap ii 15 g 1 Tim i 4 & iv 7 h Mat xv 9 Col ii 22 i Luke xi 41 Rom xiv 14, 20 1 Cor x 23 25 1 Tim iv 3 k Rom xiv 23 l 2 Tim iii 5 m Rom i 28 2 Tim iii 8

v 12—16 The national character of the Cretians was very bad, therefore they would need ſharp rebuke

1 The apoſtle quotes one of their own writers *One of themſelves, even a prophet*, or poet, *of their own*, Epimenides, *ſaid, the Cretians are always liars*, peculiarly addicted to this ſin, *evil beaſts*, ravenous, gluttonous, and inſatiate in their appetites, *ſlow bellies*, luxurious and indolent and *this witneſs is true*, it is their juſt character *Wherefore*,

2 *Rebuke them ſharply*, ſuch ſcandalous deeds required ſevere and cutting remonſtrances, *that*, their ſin and danger being ſet before them, *they may be ſound in the faith*, warned by theſe rebukes of others to be more watchful, or recovered from ſuch grievous backſliding, *not giving heed to Jewiſh fables, and commandments of men*, the ridiculous legends and vain traditions of thoſe judaizing teachers, *that turn from the truth*, apoſtates themſelves, and labouring to pervert the faith of others, and to adulterate the bleſſed goſpel of grace, by enforcing upon the conſcience the abrogated rites of the moſaical law *Unto the pure all things are pure*, and no ceremonial uncleanneſs contracted by the touch or taſte of things forbidden by the levitical inſtitutions *but unto them that are defiled* by the reigning impurity of their hearts and lives, *and unbelieving*, deſtitute of faith in Jeſus, there *is nothing pure*, all they do and ſay is abominable in the ſight of God, *but even their mind and conſcience is defiled*, and, when the fountain is thus polluted, every ſtream which flows from it muſt needs be foul *They profeſs* indeed *to know God*, and make great boaſts of their wiſdom, *but in works they deny him*, and act as infidels, *being abominable* in their ſpirit *and* conduct, *diſobedient* to all God's holy laws, as well as enemies to his goſpel, *and*, in ſhort, *to every good work reprobate*, unfit and unable too, as well as diſinclined to, the practice of them *Note*, (1) Stubborn ſinners call for ſevere rebuke Lenity, where the knife is required, is real cruelty to the patient (2) The beſt preſervative againſt the wiles of deceivers is being found in the faith They who are ſure grounded on Chriſt will not eaſily be ſhaken (3) They who are deſtitute of right principles muſt neceſſarily err in all their conduct every thing they do, even what is in itſelf right, as to the matter and deed itſelf, becomes ſin to them, becauſe it proceeds from wrong principles, and is directed to wrong ends (4) It is not ſounding profeſſions, but holy lives, which characterize real Chriſtians. *Non magna loquimur, ſed vivimus*

CHAP II

The apoſtle here directs Titus about the faithful diſcharge of his own office, generally, ver 1 *and particularly, as to ſeveral ſorts of perſons*, ver 2—10 *and gives the grounds of theſe and of other following directions*, ver 11—14 *with a ſummary direction in the cloſe*, ver 15

1 BUT ſpeak thou the things which become
[a] ſound doctrine 2 That the aged men be
† ſober, grave, temperate, ſound in faith, in charity,
in patience 3 [b] The aged women likewiſe, that they
be in behaviour as becometh holineſs, not ‡ falſe accu-
ſers, not given to much wine, teachers of good things,
4 That they may teach the young women to be ſober,
to love their huſbands, [c] to love their children, 5 To
be diſcreet, chaſte, keepers at home, good, [d] obedient
to their own huſbands, [e] that the word of God be not
blaſphemed 6 Young men likewiſe exhort to be § ſober-
minded

a 1 Tim i 10 & vi 3 2 Tim i 13. Chap i 9 † Or vigilant b 1 Tim iii 9 &c 1 Pet iii 3 ‡ Or devils c 1 Tim iii 3 d 1 Tim v 14 Cen iii 16 1 Cor xiv 34. Eph v 22 Col iii 18 1 Pet iii 1 e Rom ii 24. 1 Tim vi 1 § Or diſcreet

v 1—6 The apoſtle proceeds to direct Titus in the faithful diſcharge of his office *But*, in contradiction to theſe deceivers, *ſpeak thou the things which become ſound doctrine*, the wholeſome truths of God's life giving word, dividing it aright to every man, according to their age, ſtation, and circumſtances

1 *That the aged men*, as their years as well as profeſſion eſpecially demand from them, *be ſober*, or *vigilant*, circumſpect in their conduct, *grave*, in habit, manners, converſation, that they may engage the reverence of their younger brethren, *temperate* and prudent, having their paſſions and appetites in ſubjection, *ſound in the faith*, in doctrine and practice, *in charity* enlarged, *in patience* exemplary, bearing the provocations of others with meekneſs, and not fretful under their own infirmities Such old diſciples are noble ornaments to their Chriſtian profeſſion.

2 *The aged women likewiſe, that they be in behaviour as becometh holineſs*, in dreſs, converſation, and deportment, *not falſe accuſers*, not ſlandering and defaming any, nor ſowing diſcord among brethren, *not given to much wine*, drunkenneſs, or the love of liquor, being in women doubly odious and hateful, *teachers of good things*, by their example and diſcourſe inculcating on their daughters every thing which may adorn the Chriſtian name

3 What the aged muſt teach, the younger women ſhould learn of them, *to be ſober*, avoiding every appearance of wantonneſs, exceſs, or levity, *to love their huſbands*, cleaving to them in warm affection, *to love their children*, training them up from infancy in the nurture and admonition of the Lord, *to be diſcreet* in the management of their families *chaſte*, ſhewing the moſt unfeigned modeſty and purity of manners, *keepers at home*, not gadding

gadding about to the neglect of their domestic affairs, but ever best pleased to be in their own house, *good*, kind and gentle to their servants, and, like Dorcas, full of almsdeeds and good works, *obedient to their own husbands*, delighting to serve and please them in all things, *that the word of God be not blasphemed* by a contrary behaviour, which would give the adversaries of Christianity occasion to speak reproachfully *Note*, Nothing makes Christianity appear so amiable as the conscientious discharge of the relative duties which it enjoins

4 *Young men likewise exhort to be sober-minded*, serious, solid, tractable, having a due sense of their own inexperience, and willing to be ruled and advised by their elder and wiser friends

7 [f] In all things shewing thyself a pattern of good
works in doctrine *shewing* uncorruptness, gravity, sin-
cerity, 8 [g] Sound speech that cannot be condemned,
[h] that he that is of the contrary part [i] may be ashamed,
having no evil thing to say of you

f 1 Tim iv 12 g 1 Tim vi 3 h 1 Tim v 14 1 Pet ii 12, 15 & iii 16 i 2 Thes iii 14

v 7, 8 We have a particular direction for Titus himself, who as a young man should be the example of what he taught to his brethren *In all things shewing thyself a pattern of good works*, practising what he preached *in doctrine shewing uncorruptness*, declaring the pure unadulterated truth, and maintaining a single eye to God's glory and the benefit of immortal souls, *gravity*, with all seriousness delivering his message, and with all *sincerity*, using *sound speech that cannot be condemned*, inculcating scripture truths in scripture language, and with such plainness and simplicity as *that he that is of the contrary part*, and would be glad to carp at and censure any ambiguous expression, *may be ashamed* of his malicious design, *having no evil thing to say of you*, finding no just charge of error in doctrine, or immorality in practice, to allege against you *Note*, (1) They who preach to others must by their practice prove that they believe themselves, else how can it be thought that others should credit them (2) Many watch for the halting of Christ's ministers, and the knowledge of this should make them more watchful over all that they speak or do, that confusion may cover their malignant enemies

9 *Exhort* [k] servants to be obedient unto their own
masters, *and* to please *them* well in all things, not answer-
ing again, 10 Not purloining, but shewing all good
fidelity; [l] that they may adorn the doctrine of God our
Saviour in all things

k Eph vi 5 Col iii 22 1 Tim vi 1, 2 1 Pet ii 18 l Matt v 16

v 9, 10 The duty of servants is here prescribed. *Exhort servants to be obedient unto their own masters*, with inward respect, as well as all outward dutiful submission, *and to please them well in all things* lawful to be done, *not answering again*, disputing their orders, murmuring at their commands, or daring to make an impertinent or saucy reply, *not purloining* the least thing from them, *but*, to a crumb of bread, strictly honest, nor conniving at the least waste or robbery committed by others, *shewing all good fidelity*, true to every trust reposed in them, speaking with the greatest veracity, and punctual in the observance of their orders, *that they may adorn the doctrine of God our Saviour in all things*, and even in the eyes of their unbelieving masters, if under such, recommend the religion which they profess *Note*, Such a servant as is here described is a great acquisition Would to God that those who make profession of godliness oftener read this apostolic directory!

11 For [m] the grace of God that bringeth salvation
[n] hath appeared to all men, 12 Teaching us, that
denying ungodliness [o] and worldly lusts, [p] we should live
soberly, righteously, and godly in this present world,
13 [q] Looking for that blessed hope, and the glorious
appearing of the great God, † and our Saviour Jesus
Christ 14 [r] Who gave himself for us, that he might
redeem us from all iniquity, and [s] purify unto himself [t] a
peculiar people, [u] zealous of good works 15 These
things speak and exhort, and [x] rebuke with all authority
[y] Let no man despise thee

m Chap. ii 4 n Luke iii 6 John i 9 o 1 Pet iv 2 1 John ii 16 p Eph i 4 Col i 22 q 1 Cor i 7 Phil iii 20 2 Pet iii 12 † Or, even r Gal i 4 & ii 20 1 Tim ii 6 s Heb ix 14 t Exod xix 5 Deut vii 6 u Eph ii 10 Chap iii 8 x Chap i 13 y 1 Cor xvi 11 1 Tim iv 12

v 11—15 The strongest motives are here suggested to enforce the practice before recommended

1 This is one great end of our redemption *For the grace of God*, displayed in the gospel word, *that bringeth salvation*, declaring the sovereign and free mercy of God in Christ to miserable sinners, *hath appeared* in the most illustrious manner *to all men*, to men of all ranks, degrees, and nations, *teaching us that, denying ungodliness* of every kind, *and worldly lusts*, whether of the flesh, of the eye, or the pride of life, (1 John ii 16) *we should live soberly*, in the government and subdual of every inordinate appetite and passion, *righteously*, with unimpeached integrity and uprightness in our dealings towards men, *and godly*, in all acts of publick and private devotion, in the use of every holy ordinance, and with a constant regard to the divine glory, *in this present world*, full as it is of evil and temptation *Note*, (1) Our salvation is purely a matter of grace, flowing from God's boundless and sovereign love, without respect to our deserts or desires (2) The gospel is a revelation of mercy to all ranks and degrees, and God appears eminently glorious therein, in justifying the chief of sinners who believe in Jesus (3) Whenever we are truly partakers of grace, the blessed influence thereof will appear on our hearts and lives, effectually engaging us to renounce every known sin, and powerfully quickening us for the discharge of every duty towards God, our neighbour, or ourselves. The doctrines of grace are the only principles which can produce righteousness and true holiness

2 We expect the appearing of the great Judge, and therefore are peculiarly called upon to prepare to meet him *Looking for that blessed hope*, the great object of it, the Lord from heaven, *and the glorious appearing of the great God, and*, or *even, our Saviour Jesus Christ*, who shall shortly sit upon the throne of his glory, when all nations shall be gathered before him, to receive from his lips their irreversible sentence, and in whose favour we have an assured interest, *who gave himself for us* an offering and a sacrifice to God, *that he might redeem us from all iniquity*, both from the guilt and power of it; *and might purify to himself a peculiar people*, the objects of his sovereign choice, taken from the corrupted mass of mankind to be to the praise of his glory and *zealous of good works*, influenced by the divine principle of faith which worketh by love, aiming at the advancement of their Redeemer's honour, and yielding themselves up to be guided by his word and will. *Note*, (1) Every believer hath a blessed hope before him, under the influence of which he lives comfortably, and supported by which he dies happily (2) They who would meet the great God their Saviour in peace, must be found among his redeemed, and experience a present deliverance from the reigning power of iniquity (3) Christ's people are indeed *peculiar* in their manners, temper, and conduct, distinguished from the world in which they dwell by the purity of their lives, and their zeal for good works

3 The apostle enjoins Titus to urge these things upon the consciences of his hearers *These things speak* with all freedom, *and exhort* them diligently to observe, *and rebuke with all authority* those who dare oppose the truth, and would maintain their erroneous principles and practices *Let no man despise thee* Behave in such a manner as may command respect, and if any notwithstanding presume to treat thee or thy ministry with contempt, it shall be at their peril.

CHAP III

Of duties which concern Christians more in common, and the reasons of them, ver 1—8 What Titus in teaching should avoid, and how he should deal with an heretic, with some other directions, ver 9—14 And salutations in the close, ver 15

1. PUT them in mind to [a] be subject to principali-
ties and powers, to obey magistrates, [b] to be ready
to every good work, 2 To speak evil of no man, [c] to
be no brawlers, *but* gentle, shewing all meekness unto all
men 3 For [d] we ourselves also were sometimes foolish,
disobedient, deceived, serving divers lusts and pleasures,
living in malice and envy, hateful, *and* hating one an-
other 4 But after that [e] the kindness and love of God
our Saviour toward man appeared, 5 [f] Not by works
of righteousness which we have done, [g] but according to
his mercy he saved us by [h] the washing of regeneration,
and renewing of the holy Ghost, 6 [i] Which he shed
on us † abundantly through Jesus Christ our Saviour
7 [k] That being justified by his grace, [l] we should be
made heirs according to the hope of eternal life

a Rom xiii 1 1 Pet ii 13 b Chap ii 14 Ve 8 c 2 Tim ii 24, 25 d 1 Cor vi 11 Eph ii 1 Col i 21 & iii 7 1 Pet iv 3 e Chap ii 11 f Rom iii 20 Gal ii 16 Eph ii 9 2 Tim i 9 g Acts xv 11 Eph v 26 1 John iii 5 h Ezek xxxvi 25 Acts ii 33 & x 45 Rom v 5 1 Cor xii ly i Rom iii 24 Chap ii 11 l Rom viii 23, 24

v 1—7 The apostle proceeds,

1 To direct Titus respecting the obedience which he must inculcate as due to the civil magistrate *Put them in mind to be subject to principalities and powers*, under whatever government they live, *to obey magistrates* with loyalty and willing submission, *to be ready to every good work*, rendering to all degrees of men the duty owing to them *to speak evil of* or *blaspheme no man*, reviling the magistrates, or raising any slanderous report *to be no brawlers*, disturbing the peace of society, turbulent and quarrelsome, *but gentle* in temper and manners, *shewing all meekness to all men*, however perverse or provoking their conduct may be towards us

2 He suggests the most cogent reasons to enforce his exhortation

(1) The consideration of their former sinful state and the more deeply we are sensible of our own vileness, the more we shall feel ourselves obliged to bear with others *For we ourselves also were sometimes foolish*, in our apostate nature, ignorant of divine truth, and under the darkness of our fallen minds, *disobedient* in spirit and practice, refusing to hear and obey the dictates of God's word, *deceived*, and wandering out of the way,

 under-

under the influence of a corrupted heart, and the wiles of Satan, *serving divers lusts and pleasures*, perfect slaves to our sensual appetites, the basest of all servitude *living in malice and envy*, possessed and governed by their diabolical passions, regarding others, who were more prosperous in the world, with a malignant eye, and pleased with any miseries which befel them *Hateful* to God, and all who bear his image, because of these abominations, *and hating one another*, with implacable resentment What a fearful description! yet in this glass may every enlightened sinner discover his own features, and own the humbling resemblance, for as face answereth face, so do the heart of man to man

[2] The kindness and love of God to them in their miserable estate should engage them to shew the like pity and compassion towards others *But after that*, vile as we were, *the kindness and love of God our Saviour*, notwithstanding, *towards man appeared*, most illustriously displayed in his glorious gospel, *not by works of righteousness which we have done*, for all our works were the very reverse, and merited only wrath to the uttermost, *but according to his mercy*, in the most astonishing manner extended to the miserable and the desperate, *he hath saved us*, freely, sovereignly, and for ever, *by the washing of regeneration, and renewing of the Holy Ghost*, who is the glorious agent of the divine change wrought in regeneration, cleansing our souls from the power of corruption, quickening us to a life of grace and holiness, maintaining and carrying it on day by day, till it is perfected in glory, *which* Holy Ghost *he shed on us abundantly*, both in his gifts and graces, *through Jesus Christ our Saviour*, the purchaser of every blessing for his redeemed people, and the dispenser of this Spirit unto them, *that being justified by his grace*, and through faith of the operation of God brought into a state of pardon and reconciliation, *we should be made heirs* of glory, *according to the hope of eternal life*, which he hath given us in that adored Redeemer, who hath obtained a compleat salvation for us, not only from all the miseries of sin, but unto all the blessedness of eternity *Note*, (1) The salvation of the sinner is entirely of grace, from the beginning to the end pardon, holiness, and hope of life eternal, are all the gift of God through Jesus Christ our Saviour (2) Though we are justified freely, not for any righteousness of our own, but of God's mere favour, yet do we from that moment become different men, and new creatures, by the Spirit of our God renewed in our minds, and preparing for the glory which is prepared for us

m 1 Tim i 15
n Eph ii 10 Chap ii 14 Ver 14
o 1 Tim i 4 & iv 7
2 Tim ii 23
p 2 Tim ii 14
q 2 Cor xiii 2
r Matt xviii 17 Rom xvi 17 2 Thess iii 6, 14 2 John 10

8 m *This is* a faithful saying, and these things I will
that thou affirm constantly, that they which have be-
lieved in God, n might be careful to maintain good
works these things are good and profitable unto men
9 But o avoid foolish questions, and genealogies, and
contentions, and strivings about the law, p for they are
unprofitable and vain 10 A man that is an heretic,
q after the first and second admonition, r reject 11
Knowing that he that is such is subverted, and sinneth,
being condemned of himself

v 8—11 The apostle here,

1 Inculcates the doctrine which Titus must preach *This is a faithful saying*, all that I have above declared of the duties incumbent on believers, the misery from which they have been redeemed, and the amazing grace of which they have been made partakers, is to be stedfastly believed and embraced *and these things I will that thou constantly affirm*, often insisting upon them in the course of thy ministry, to the end, *that they which have believed in God*, to the saving of their souls, *might be careful to maintain good works*, to excel, and lead the way to others (προΐστασθαι) with all diligence and zeal improving every opportunity which offers to be useful *These things are good and profitable unto men*, these doctrines here enforced have the most immediate tendency to advance the benefit of mankind, and promote their present and eternal good *Note*, The doctrine of justification by grace is so far from destroying the obligation to good works, that it is the only real and effectual principle which can make us careful to maintain them

2 He cautions him what to shun *But avoid foolish questions, and genealogies, and contentions, and strivings about the law*, which the judaizing teachers affect, to the great prejudice of Christianity, *for they are unprofitable and vain*, tending to no one useful purpose, but sowing discord in the church, and corrupting the simplicity of the gospel

3 *A man that is an heretic*, who openly professes and maintains doctrines subversive of the fundamental articles of faith, *after the first and second admonition, reject*, if he continues obstinate in his errors, remove him from your communion, and acknowledge him no longer as a brother *Knowing that he that is such is subverted*, apostate from Christ, the only foundation, *and sinneth* wilfully, *being condemned of himself*, openly broaching his sentiments, departing from the confession of faith which he formerly made, and avowedly separating himself from the church of God *Note*, They who refuse to be reclaimed from their errors by repeated admonition, must be cut off from the body of the visible church by excommunication

12 When I shall send Artemas unto thee, or s Ty- s Acts xx 4. 2 Tim iv 12
chicus, be diligent to come unto me to Nicopolis for
I have determined there to winter 13 Bring Zenas
the lawyer and t Apollos on their journey diligently, that t Acts xviii 24
nothing be wanting unto them 14 And let ours also
learn to u maintain good works for necessary uses, that u Ver 8 † Or profess honest trades
they x be not unfruitful 15 All that are with me sa-
lute thee Greet them that love us in the faith Grace x 1 Thess ii 9 2 Thess iii 8 Phil i 11 & iv 17 2 Pet i 8
be with you all Amen

v 12—15 We have here,

1 Some particular directions given to Titus (1) *When I shall send Artemas unto thee*, to supply thy absence, *or Tychicus, be diligent to come unto me to Nicopolis for I have determined there to winter* (2) *Bring Zenas the lawyer and Apollos on their journey diligently, that nothing be wanting unto them*, but that they be supplied with every necessary for their travels, when they remove to preach the gospel in some other place (3) *And let ours also learn to maintain good works for necessary uses, that they be not unfruitful*, but adorn the profession which they make, diligent in their several employments, and liberal according to their ability in the maintenance of their ministers, or in assisting any of their brethren who may need their support

2 He concludes with salutations and his apostolic benediction *All that are with me salute thee* affectionately *Greet them that love us in the faith*, and are one in sentiment and heart with us *Grace be with you all*, in its most abundant fruits and richest manifestations, *Amen!* so prays your faithful friend, confident that God will hear and answer his petition for you

THE EVANGELICAL EXPOSITOR;

OR, A

PRACTICAL COMMENT

Upon the EPISTLE of

St. PAUL to PHILEMON.

THIS epistle to Philemon is placed the last of those with the name of Paul to them, perhaps because the shortest, and of an argument peculiar and different from all the others, yet such as the Spirit of God, which indited it, saw would, in its kind, be very instructive and useful in the churches The occasion of it was this Philemon, one of note, and probably a minister in the church of Coloss, a city of Phrygia, had a servant named Onesimus, who having purloined his goods, ran away from him, and in his rambles came to Rome, where Paul was then a prisoner for the gospel, and providentially coming under his preaching there, was by the blessing of God converted by him, after which he ministred a while to the apostle in bonds, and might have been further useful to him, but understanding him to be another man's servant, he would not, without his consent, detain him, but sends him back with this letter commendatory, wherein he earnestly sues for his pardon and kind reception

CHAP I

In this epistle we have the preface, ver 1—7 The substance and body of it, ver 8—21 And then the conclusion, ver 22, to the end

1 PAUL [a] a prisoner of Jesus Christ, and Timothy *our* brother, unto Philemon our dearly beloved and fellow labourer, 2 And to *our* beloved Apphia, and [b] Archippus [c] our fellow-soldier, and to [d] the church in thy house 3
[e] Grace to you and peace from God our Father, and the
Lord Jesus Christ 4 [f] I thank my God, making mention of thee always in my prayers, 5 [g] Hearing of thy
love and faith, which thou hast toward the Lord Jesus,
and toward all saints, 6 That the communication of
thy faith may become effectual by [h] the acknowledging
of every good thing which is in you in Christ Jesus
7 For we have great joy and consolation in thy love,
because the bowels of the saints [i] are refreshed by thee,
brother

[a] Eph iii 1 & iv 1 2 Tim i 8 Ver 9
[b] Col iv 17
[c] Phil ii 25
[d] Rom xvi 5 1 Cor xvi 19
[e] Gal i 3 Eph i 2
[f] Eph i 16 Phil i 3 1 Thess i 2 2 Thess i 3
[g] Eph i 15 Col i 4
[h] Phil i 9
[i] 2 Tim i 16

v 1—7 We have here the preface to this short but beautiful epistle, and may observe,

1 The persons from whom it comes *from Paul, a prisoner of Jesus Christ*, now suffering for the gospel cause, *and Timothy our brother* and where two such eminent servants of the Saviour concurred in a request, what could be denied them?

2 The persons to whom it is directed *unto Philemon our dearly beloved brother in Christ, and fellow-labourer in the gospel, and to our beloved Apphia, and Archippus our fellow soldier*, in the glorious warfare under Christ the Captain of our salvation, *and to the church in thy house*, his whole family being converts to the faith, or the faithful at Colosse assembled there for worship, and by thus saluting them he seems desirous to interest them on his behalf, and to solicit their concurrence in the request he was about to make

3 The salutation *Grace to you*, in all its comprehensive import, *and peace*, flowing from a sense of pardon, acceptance, and the assured inheritance of glory, and both proceeding *from God the Father*, from his eternal, sovereign, boundless love, *and from the Lord Jesus Christ*, by whom all spiritual blessings have been purchased, and through whom alone they are bestowed upon us

4 His thankfulness and prayer *I thank my God*, in a covenant of everlasting love, *making mention of thee always in my prayers*, whenever I approach a throne of grace, *hearing of thy love and faith, which thou hast toward the Lord Jesus, and toward all saints*, for which I offer my unceasing praises, and add my fervent prayers, *that the communication of thy faith may become effectual*, to engage thee to every farther instance of generosity and benevolence, *by the acknowledging of every good thing which is in you in, or towards, Christ Jesus*, to whom much glory will redound, and many thanks be offered by those who feel the benefit of those gracious dispositions which the Saviour hath implanted, and which manifest themselves in every work and labour of love towards his people for his sake *for we have great joy and consolation in hearing of thy* distinguished *love, because the bowels of the saints are refreshed by thee, brother*, who gratefully acknowledge thy extensive charity, and this emboldens me to hope, that in the present instance my petition will be successful

8 Wherefore, [k] though I might be much bold in
Christ, to enjoin thee that which is convenient, 9
Yet for love's sake I rather beseech *thee*, being such an
one as Paul the aged, and now also [l] a prisoner of Jesus
Christ

[k] 1 Thess ii 6
[l] Ver 1

m Col ii 9 Christ 10 I beseech thee for my son m Onesimus,
n 1 Cor iv 15 Gal iv 19 n whom I have begotten in my bonds 11 Which in
time past was to thee unprofitable, but now profitable to
thee and to me 12 Whom I have sent again thou
therefore receive him, that is mine own bowels 13
o 1 Cor xvi 17 Phil ii 30 Whom I would have retained with me, o that in thy
stead he might have ministred unto me in the bonds of
the gospel 14 But without thy mind would I do no-
p 2 Cor ix 7 thing, p that thy benefit should not be as it were of ne-
cessity, but willingly

v 8—14 The apostle comes to the main business of the epistle, to intreat for poor Onesimus and he insinuates a multitude of the most powerful arguments, which should engage Philemon to grant his request, and be reconciled to his fugitive servant

1 He might have used his apostolic authority, but he prefers the intreaty of love *Wherefore, though I might be much bold in Christ, to enjoin thee that which is convenient*, and it would have been your duty in the present case implicitly to obey, *yet for love's sake I rather beseech thee*, waving all superiority, and pleading by that love which Jesus hath shown to you, and I feel towards you, *being such an one as Paul the aged*, grown old in the service of our common Lord, *and now also a prisoner of Jesus Christ*, therefore I cannot but be assured, whatever would be a comfort to me in these declining years, and serve to make my chain lighter, Philemon, for his Master's sake and mine, will not fail to grant —Inimitable is the manner in which the apostle introduces the point which he had in view Having raised every tender sentiment of love and friendship in his bosom, he,

2 Beautifully introduces in the most endearing light the subject of his request *I beseech thee for my son*, one that now stands in that near relation to me,—and startle not at the name,—strange as it may appear,—the person is no other than *Onesimus, whom I have begotten in my bonds* So mysterious are the ways of providence, that, though a fugitive from thee, divine grace has led him to my prison, there to become a partaker of the blessings of the gospel

3 He suggests the happy change now wrought upon him, *which in time past was to thee unprofitable*, with penitent shame he hath acknowledged his former ill behaviour, over which I would cast a veil of oblivion, *but now* can speak of him as a different man, whose spirit and actions I am confident will correspond with his name, and he will be found *profitable to thee*, if received again into thy service, *and*, as I have proved by some experience, would have been most useful *to me* *Note*, (1) When we speak of the faults of penitents, it should be with tenderness, not severity (2) Wherever divine grace comes, it makes a blessed alteration (3) A Christian servant is a truly profitable member in every family

4 His own love to this signal convert should engage Philemon's to him *Whom I have sent again* back to thy service, *thou therefore receive him, that is mine own bowels*, most tenderly beloved, and for whom I plead with all the affection that I should feel for my own child

5 He had deprived himself of the very useful service which Onesimus would have afforded him, that he might restore him to his rightful master, referring it to Philemon whether he would send him back again to Rome, or not *Whom I would have retained with me, that in thy stead he might have ministred unto me in the bonds of the gospel*, and done me those kind offices which I know thou wouldest have been happy to have afforded me thyself *But without thy mind would I do nothing*, nor detain him longer here, *that*, if it shall please thee to do me the favour of sending him hither again to minister unto me, *thy benefit should not* appear *to be as it were of necessity, but willingly*, as a voluntary act of generosity and friendship

15 For perhaps he therefore departed for a season,
that thou shouldst receive him for ever, 16 Not now
q 1 Tim vi 2 as a servant, but above a servant, q a brother beloved,
especially to me, but how much more unto thee, both in
the flesh and in the Lord? 17 If thou count me there-
r 2 Cor viii 23 fore r a partner, receive him as myself 18 If he hath
wronged thee, or oweth *thee* ought, put that on mine
account 19 I Paul have written *it* with mine own
hand, I will repay it albeit I do not say to thee how
thou owest unto me even thine own self besides 20
Yea, brother, let me have joy of thee in the Lord re-
s 2 Cor vii 16 fresh my bowels in the Lord 21 Having confidence
in thy obedience I wrote unto thee, knowing that thou
wilt also do more than I say

4

v 15—21 The apostle proceeds to suggest other arguments, to engage Philemon kindly to receive this fugitive

1 The mercy God had shewed him *For perhaps he therefore departed for a season*, so tenderly does the apostle mention his fault in flying his master's service, since it was now so wonderfully by God's good providence over-ruled for good, *that thou shouldst receive him for ever*, as a servant for life, to dwell together for eternity yet *not now as a* common *servant*, or slave, *but above a servant*, even as *a brother* in the gospel, *beloved* and dear, *especially to me*, who have been the happy instrument of his conversion, *but how much more to thee, both in the flesh*, as a member of thy family, become most faithful and industrious, *and in the Lord*, as equally a partaker in all the blessings of the Redeemer's grace and love *Note*, (1) God sometimes amazingly over-rules our most perverse ways, to bring out of them the greatest good Onesimus, under all the blessings of Philemon's ministry, and sharing all the ordinances of his holy family, continued abandoned, turns thief and runagate, and flies to Rome, there the Lord finds him, and makes him a monument of mercy (2) Though Christianity maintains in the strictest manner all due subordination of station, yet really Christian servants will have especial respect and regard shown them by their masters, who, as members of the same body, esteem them as their beloved brethren

2 The communion which subsisted between them, as fellow-heirs of the same kingdom *If thou count me therefore a partner*, a partaker of the same grace, and an inheritor of the same glory with thee, *receive him as myself*, with hearty affection and sincere reconciliation

3 He becomes Onesimus's surety for any wrong Philemon had sustained *If*, as I have reason to apprehend, *he hath wronged thee, or oweth thee ought, put that on mine account I Paul have written it with mine own hand, I will repay it*, and engage hereby to make you full satisfaction if demanded *Albeit I do not say to thee how* deeply thou art indebted to me, as the instrument under God, and that *thou owest unto me*, what is infinitely more valuable than all the wealth of the world, even *thine own soul also*

4 This instance of his condescension to his request would give the apostle singular satisfaction, as a fresh proof of Philemon's fidelity *Yea, brother, let me have joy of thee in the Lord* on thy own account, as well as for the sake of Onesimus, I ask it, that I may have rejoicing over thee, as a living member of Jesus *Refresh my bowels in the Lord*, and give me this consolation in my bonds, for that Redeemer's sake in whose name I urge my request *Note*, (1) Christians are brethren, and, as such, should delight to serve each other (2) It is highly the people's duty to endeavour to comfort their ministers, and to do every thing which may give them joy, and encourage them under their labours and sufferings for the gospel's sake

5 He concludes with expressing his confidence in Philemon, which laid the strongest obligations upon him not to disappoint his expectations *Having confidence in thy obedience* to our Lord's command to forgive every injury, *I wrote unto thee, knowing that thou wilt also do more than I say*, and shew greater kindness to poor Onesimus than I have requested, exceeding even my desire

22 But withal prepare me also a lodging for t I trust t Phil i 25 & ii 24
that u through your prayers I shall be given unto you u 2 Cor i 11
23 There salute thee x Epaphras, my fellow-prisoner in x Col i 7 & iv 12
Christ Jesus, 24 y Marcus, z Aristarchus, a Demas, y Acts xii 12 Col iv 10 z Acts xix 29
Lucas, my fellow-labourers 25 The grace of our Lord a Col iv 14 2 Tim iv 10
Jesus Christ *be* b with your spirit. Amen b 2 Tim iv 22

v 22—25 Having finished his main business, he closes,

1 With the intimation of a visit shortly *But withal prepare me also a lodging for I trust that through your prayers I shall* be delivered from my present confinement, and *be given unto you*, as a fresh act of favour from God, who for your further edification will enable me once more to minister his blessed gospel among you *Note*, (1) Prayer is the effectual means to procure all mercies for ourselves, and for each other (2) To have God's ministers spared to labour yet longer among us, is a signal favour

2 He sends the salutations of many who desired to be kindly remembered to him *There salute thee Epaphras, my fellow-prisoner in Christ Jesus*, sharing my honourable bonds for the same glorious cause, *Marcus, Aristarchus, Demas, Lucas, my fellow-labourers*

3 He concludes with his usual benediction *The grace of our Lord Jesus Christ*, in all its happy fruits, and eternally permanent effects, *be with your spirit*, with thee, and with all that are near and dear to thee, to bless, preserve, and keep you for his everlasting kingdom. *Amen*

THE

THE

EVANGELICAL EXPOSITOR;

OR, A

PRACTICAL COMMENT

Upon the EPISTLE to the

HEBREWS.

THIS epistle, though without a name, is generally ascribed to the apostle Paul: In the primitive times it was ascribed to him, and the stile and scope of it very well agrees with his spirit, whose main end and endeavour was to exalt Christ. And some think that the apostle Peter refers to this epistle, and proves Paul to be the penman of it, by telling the Hebrews, to whom he wrote, of Paul's having written to them, 2 Peter iii. 15. *And we read of no other epistle that he ever wrote to them but this. And though it has been objected, that since Paul put his name to all his other epistles, he would not have omitted it here, yet others have well answered, that he being the* apostle of the Gentiles, *who were odious to the Jews, might think fit to conceal his name, lest their prejudices against him might hinder them from reading and weighing it as they ought to do. As to the* scope *and* design *of this epistle, it is very evident it was clearly to inform the minds, and strongly to confirm the judgment of the Hebrews in the transcendent excellency of the* gospel *above the* law, *and so to take them off from the ceremonies of the law, to which they were so wedded, of which they were so fond, that they even doted on them. And those of them that were Christians retained too much of the* old leaven, *and wanted to be purged from it; he wanted therefore to persuade and press the believing Hebrews to a constant adherence to the Christian faith, and perseverance in it, notwithstanding all the sufferings they might meet with in so doing. In order to this, he speaks much of the excellency of the* author *of the gospel, the* glorious Jesus, *whose honour he advances, and whom he justly prefers before all others, shewing him to be all in all, and this in lofty strains of holy rhetoric. It must be acknowledged there are many things in this epistle hard to be understood, but the sweetness we shall find therein, will make us abundant amends for all the pains we take to understand it. And indeed if we compare all the epistles of the New Testament, we shall not find any of them more replenished with divine, heavenly matter than this to the Hebrews.*

CHAP. I.

In this chapter we have a twofold comparison stated. (1.) Between the evangelical and legal dispensation, and the excellency of the gospel above that of the law is asserted and proved, ver. 1, 2, 3. (2.) *Between the* glory of Christ, *and that of the* highest Creatures, *the angels, where the preeminence is justly given to the Lord Jesus Christ, and clearly demonstrated to belong unto him, from ver. 4, to the end of the chapter.*

1 GOD, who † at sundry times, [a] and in divers manners, spake in time past unto the
fathers by the prophets, 2 Hath [b] in
these last days [c] spoken unto us by *his* Son,
[d] whom he hath appointed heir of all things, [e] by whom
also he made the worlds. 3 [f] Who being the brightness of *his* glory, and the express image of his person, and
[g] upholding all things by the word of his power, when
[h] he had by himself purged our sins, [i] sat down on the
right hand of the Majesty on high. 4 Being made so
much better than the angels, as [k] he hath by inheritance
obtained a more excellent name than they. 5 For unto
which of the angels said he at any time, [l] Thou art my
Son, this day have I begotten thee? And again, [m] I will
be to him a Father, and he shall be to me a Son? 6
And † again, when he bringeth in [n] the First-begotten
into the world, he saith, And [o] let all the angels of God
worship him. 7 And of the angels he saith, [p] Who
maketh his angels spirits, and his ministers a flame of
fire. 8 But unto the Son *he saith,* [q] Thy throne, O God,
is for ever and ever; a sceptre of righteousness *is* the
sceptre of thy kingdom. 9 Thou hast loved righteousness, and hated iniquity; therefore [r] God, *even* thy God,
hath anointed thee with the oil of gladness above thy
fellows. 10 And, Thou, Lord, in the beginning hast
laid the foundation of the earth; and the heavens are the
works of thine hands. 11 [s] They shall perish, but thou
remainest; and they all shall wax old as doth a garment.
12 And as a vesture shalt thou fold them up, and they

shall

† Or, by several parts. [a] Num. xii. 6, 8. [b] Gal. iv. 4. Eph. i. 10. [c] John xv. 15. [d] Psal. ii. 8. Mat. xxi. 38. John iii. 35. [e] Eph. i. 22. [f] John i. 3. Eph. iii. 9. Col. i. 16. [f] Wisd. vii. 26. 2 Cor. iv. 4. Col. i. 15. [g] Col. i. 17. [h] Chap. ix. 12, 26. 1 Pet. ii. [illegible] [i] Eph. i. 20. Chap. x. 12. 1 Pet. iii. 22.

[k] Eph. i. 21. Phil. ii. 9, 10. [l] Psal. ii. 7. Acts xiii. 33. Chap. v. 5. [m] 2 Sam. vii. 14. 1 Chron. xxii. 10. [n] Psal. lxxxix. 27. † Or, when he bringeth again. [o] Rom. viii. 29. Col. i. 18. Deut. xxxii. 43. [illegible] xcvii. 7. [p] Psal. civ. 4. [q] Psal. xlv. 6, 7. [r] Acts x. 38. [illegible] [s] Isa. xxxiv. 4. & li. 6. 2 Pet. iii. 7, 10.

shall be changed but thou art the same, and thy years
shall not fail 13 But to which of the angels said he at
any time, ^u Sit on my right hand, until I make thine
enemies thy footstool? 14 ^x Are they not all ministring
spirits, sent forth to minister for them who shall be heirs
of salvation?

^u Ps cx 1 Mat xxii 44 Acts ii 34 1 Cor xv 25 Chap x 12
^x Ex xxiii 20 Ps xxxiv 7 & xci 11 Dan vi 22 Mat xviii 10 Acts v 19 & xii 7

v 1—14 The excellence of the gospel dispensation above the Mosaical opens this beautiful epistle The apostle shews,

1 The different way in which God communicated his will to the church of old, and to his people at present *God, who at sundry times*, by degrees, with increasing clearness, *and in divers manners*, by types, visions, dreams, audible voices, and immediate inspiration, *spake in time past unto the fathers by the prophets, hath in these last days*, at the close of the Jewish œconomy, and in that dispensation of grace which is the last which will be ever vouchsafed to the sons of men, and under this title of the *last days* hath been foretold by the inspired penmen, God hath, I say, now *spoken unto us by his Son*, the most glorious messenger who was ever yet employed in communicating the revelation of his will to man, in nature one with the Father, in majesty coeternal

2 He enlarges on the surpassing excellence of this Son of God, who had appeared in the human nature (1) It is He *whom he hath appointed heir of all things* as Mediator, exalting him to the sovereign and universal dominion over the works of his hands, and especially giving him to be head over all things to his church, in and through whom every member of it can only be entitled to the eternal inheritance (2) *By whom also he made the worlds*, exerting his co-agency and co-operation with the Father, not as an instrument, but as the great Creator (3) *Who being the brightness of his glory*, Light of Light, and very God of very God, possessing the essential attributes of Deity, *and the express image of his person*, bearing his exact resemblance in every divine perfection, appears his visible representative And, (4) As he is the Creator, so he continues *upholding all things by the word of his power*, supporting and governing them by his providence (5) *When he had by himself purged our sins, Himself*, the great High-priest and Sacrifice, expiating the transgressions of his people, which the blood of bulls and goats, shed by the levitical priests, could never take away, and by one oblation of himself, once offered, obtaining eternal redemption for us (6) When he had thus made the all-atoning sacrifice on the cross, *he sat down at the right hand of the Majesty on high*, in virtue of his own blood entering into the holy place not made with hands, and, as a priest upon his throne, *(Zech vi 13)* he is exalted to the highest dignity and glory in the human nature (7) He hath the pre-eminence, not only above the greatest prophets, but over the highest of the heavenly hosts, *being made so much better than the angels*, in his character as Mediator, as well as in the transcendent excellence of his divine nature, he infinitely surpasses the most glorious of all created beings, *as he hath by inheritance obtained a more excellent name than they*, even the name of *Son of God*, in a sense peculiar to himself, and which appears evident from the transcendent exaltation which in virtue of his sufferings he hath now by right obtained

3 In support of his argument, to prove the infinite pre-eminence of the incarnate Son above the highest of the angelic hosts, he brings the strongest proofs from those scriptures which the Jews admitted as of divine authority *For unto which of the angels said he at any time, Thou art my Son*, the same in essential Deity, *this day have I begotten thee*, even from eternity, which to God is one permanent unsuccessive day, or this refers to his resurrection from the dead, whereby his eternal Sonship was manifested, *(Rom i 4)* *And again, I will be to him a Father, and he shall be to me a Son*, treated with peculiar and distinguishing love, and raised to the eternal throne of glory *And again, when he bringeth in the First begotten*, the appointed Heir of all things, *into the world*, at his miraculous conception, *he saith, And let all the angels of God worship him*, and pay him that divine honour which is due to their Creator alone, and is the unalienable right of Deity *And of the angels he saith, Who maketh his angels spirits, and his ministers a flame of fire*, their highest honour and dignity is to be servants of the great Jehovah, and as flames of fire, with such activity and powerful agency, to execute his will and pleasure *But unto the Son*, as their eternal King, *he saith, Thy throne, O God*, who art the essential Jehovah, *is for ever and ever*, from everlasting unchangeably the same, and to eternity must endure, *a sceptre of righteousness is the sceptre of thy kingdom*, Thou hast the most indisputed title to reign, thy bosom is the seat of justice, and thy administration is marked with unsullied truth, holiness, and equity *Thou hast loved righteousness*, fulfilling it in thy own person and approving it in thy people, *and hated iniquity*, about to punish it with everlasting perdition, *therefore God, even thy God*, thy covenant God as the incarnate Mediator, *hath anointed thee* to the office of prophet, priest, and king, *with the oil of gladness*, with the most immeasurable fulness of spiritual gifts and graces, *above thy fellows*, whether angels or saints, kings, priests, or prophets *And thou, Lord, in the beginning*, before any creature yet had a being, by thy omnipotent creative power, *hast laid the foundation of the earth, and the heavens are the works of thine hands*, all the creatures, spiritual or corporeal, animate or inanimate, from the highest to the lowest, own thee their great Creator *They shall perish*, this visible creation of heaven and earth shall decay, *but thou remainest*, unchangeable, immortal, *and they all shall wax old as doth a garment*, the creatures of this lower world are mouldering daily, and nature's dissolution is at hand, *and as a vesture shalt thou fold them up, and they shall be changed, but thou art the same*, immutably, eternally, *and thy years shall not fail*, the same yesterday, to-day, and for ever *But to which of the angels said he at any time*, as he did to his incarnate Son, *Sit thou on my right hand*, enthroned in supreme majesty, *until I make thine enemies thy footstool*, and rule thee triumphant over every foe, when sin, Satan, death, and hell, shall be for ever put under thy feet? Such language belongs not to the highest of the angelic host for *are they not all ministring spirits*, servants to the great Mediator, and *sent forth*, under his command, *to minister for them*, in every kind office, *who shall be heirs of salvation*, appointed to the eternal inheritance in virtue of their relation to their exalted Head? From the whole we may observe, 1 The transcendent glory of the Lord Jesus (1) In his divine nature (2) In his mediatorial capacity The great Creator—the self-existent Jehovah—the eternal, immutable God—the object of adoration to the highest beings, angels as well as men—and reigning and to reign for ever and ever 2 The honour and office of the angelic hosts, to adore their King, to obey his mandates with delight and vigour, and to serve those highly distinguished sons of men who are appointed to be heirs of salvation 3 The dignity of God's children, standing in this high and holy relation to him as adopted by his grace and designed for the enjoyment of his glory, attended by ministers of flame, and shortly to be conducted by them to their eternal home 4 Vast and amazing as this visible creation now appears, the day approaches when, like the baseless fabric of a vision, all shall be dissolved, and by almighty power shall arise a new heaven and earth, to be the blest abode of the redeemed 5 Jesus must reign on his mediatorial throne till all his enemies are finally subdued, and his triumphant people shall come to reign with him in glory everlasting

CHAP II

In this chapter the apostle, 1 Makes some application of the doctrine laid down in the foregoing, concerning the excellency of the person of Christ, both by way of exhortation and argument, ver 1, 2, 3, 4 2 Enlarges farther upon the preeminence of Christ above the angels, ver 5, 6, 7 3 He proceeds to remove the scandal of the cross, ver 10—16 4 To assert the incarnation of Christ, taking upon him not the nature of angels, but the seed of Abraham, and assigns the reason of his so doing, ver 16 to the end

1 THerefore ^a we ought to give the more earnest
heed to the things which we have heard, lest at
any time we should | let *them* slip 2 For if the word
^b spoken by angels was stedfast, and ^c every transgression
and disobedience received a just recompence of reward,
3 ^d How shall we escape if we neglect so great salvation,
^e which at the first began to be spoken by the Lord,
and ^f was confirmed unto us by them that heard *him*,
4 ^g God also bearing them witness, both with signs and
wonders, and with divers miracles, and ^h gifts of the
Holy Ghost, according to his own will?

^a Chap iii 6
| Gr Run out as leaking vessels
^b Deut xxxiii 2 Acts vii 53 Gal iii 19
^c Deut xxvii 26 Chap x 28
^d Chap x 29 & xii 25
^e Mat iv 17 Mark i 14
^f Luke i 2
^g Mark xvi 20 Acts ii 22 & xiv 3 Rom xv 19
^h 1 Cor xii 4, 7, 11

v 1—4 The apostle, as he proceeds, applies the doctrine which he had advanced

Therefore we ought to give the more earnest heed to the things which we have heard, considering the infinite dignity and glory of the Speaker; eagerly attentive to his words, storing them up in our memory, and fixing them as principles of action in our hearts, *lest at any time we should let them slip*, and our treacherous memories, like leaking vessels, should suffer them to run out, or they should glide by us (παραρρυῶμεν) as a stream, unnoticed and neglected *For if the word spoken by angels*, the law given to Moses on mount Sinai, *was stedfast* and valid, stamped with divine authority, and guarded with the most awful sanctions, *and every transgression and disobedience received a just recompense of reward*, as the righteous punishment inflicted by divine justice, *how shall we escape*, what aggravated guilt and ruin must be on us who have heard *the gospel*, *if we neglect so great salvation*; great inexpressibly, if we consider the depths of the miseries into which we were fallen, the wonderful means used to extricate us, or the infinite mercies, blessings, and benefits, accruing to us thereby, a salvation, *which* comes recommended in the strongest manner, *as at the first it began to be spoken by the Lord* of life and glory incarnate, *and was confirmed unto us by them that heard him*, the apostles and others, who, commissioned by him, proclaimed the glad tidings of his gospel through the world *God also bearing them witness* to the divinity of that doctrine which they preached, *both with signs and wonders, and with divers verse miracles* of the most stupendous kind, *and gifts of the Holy Ghost*, the most astonishing and various, given *according to his own will*, for the confirmation of their testimony an attestation far more excellent than was given to the law of Moses *Note*, (1) When matters of such eternal importance are at stake, as the salvation of an immortal soul, we can never be sufficiently careful and attentive (2) Whatever punishments God inflicts on sinners, they are no more than the just reward of their deeds (3) Neglect of the gospel is among the most atrocious crimes, and will be visited with the severest judgments

5 For unto the angels hath he not put in subjection
ˡ Chap vi 5 ² Pe iii 13 ᵏ Pf viii 4, &c — ˡ the world to come, whereof we speak 6 But one
in a certain place testified, saying, ᵏ What is man that
thou art mindful of him? or the son of man, that thou
† Or a little while inferior to — visitest him? 7 Thou madest him † a little lower than
ˡ 1 Cor xv 27 Eph i 22 Chap i 13 — the angels, thou crownedst him with glory and honour,
and didst set him over the works of thy hands 8 ˡ Thou
hast put all things in subjection under his feet For in
that he put all in subjection under him, he left nothing
ᵐ 1 Cor xv 25 — *that is* not put under him But now ᵐ we see not yet
ⁿ Phil ii 7 — all things put under him 9 But we see Jesus, ⁿ who
° Acts ii 33 — was made a little lower than the angels, for the suffer-
ᵖ Rom v 8 2 Cor v 15 — ing of death, ° crowned with glory and honour, ᵖ that
he by the grace of God should taste death for every
man

v 5—9 The apostle returns to the comparison between the Mediator and the angelic hosts, shewing his surpassing excellence

For unto the angels hath he not put in subjection the world to come, whereof we speak, that is, the gospel dispensation, and the church under the new testament, not employing them as he did under the mosaical œconomy *But one in a certain place testified*, when contemplating the glories of creation, *What is man*, how despicable a worm, *that thou art mindful of him*, and shouldst send thy co-eternal Son to take man's nature upon him? *or* what is *the son of man*, a poor frail mortal, *that thou visitest him*, and in the person of the incarnate Saviour shouldst raise the human nature to such distinguished and transcendent glory *Thou madest him a little lower than the angels*, or *for a little while* (βραχύ τι) during his state of humiliation and sufferings unto death, *thou crownedst him with glory and honour*, raising him triumphant from the grave, *and*, exalting him to the throne of Majesty on high, *didst set him over the works of thy hands*, bestowing on him absolute and universal dominion over every creature *thou hast put all things in subjection under his feet*, not only all the enemies of himself and people, sin, Satan, death and hell, but all principalities and powers, and every name that is named, not only in this world, but in that also which is to come *For in that he put all in subjection under him, he left nothing that is not put under him*, angels, as well as others, being included within his absolute and universal empire *But now we see not yet all things put under him*, either *man in general*, or any individual of the human species, so that these words appertain not to any of Adam's natural descendants, or *under Jesus Christ himself* at present, who hath not yet utterly subdued all his enemies, the time of his final conquest not being arrived *But we see this blessed Jesus, who was made a little lower than the angels*, during a while, *for the sufferings of death*, that he might in the human nature die for the sins of his people, wherein he appeared inferior to their immortal spirits, we see him now *crowned with glory and honour*, on a throne, at the right hand of God, reigning till every foe shall become his footstool, *that he by the grace of God*, of his mere sovereign love and mercy, *should taste death for every man*, not for every individual of the human species, but for Jew and Gentile, for sinner of every rank and degree, even for all those many sons whom God before the world ordained unto glory *Note*, (1) The fontal cause of our salvation is the sovereign grace of God, the meritorious cause is the death of our incarnate Redeemer (2) In Christ man's nature is exalted above the angels, and we, by virtue of union with him, have obtained even a more excellent name than they

ᑫ Rom xi 36 — 10 For it became him ᑫ for whom *are* all things,
and by whom *are* all things, in bringing many sons un-
ʳ Acts iii 15 & v 31 ˢ Luke xiii 32 Chap v 9 — to glory, to make ʳ the captain of their salvation ˢ per-
ᵗ Chap x 10, 14 — fect through sufferings 11 For both he that sanctifieth,
ᵘ Acts xvii 26 — and ᵗ they who are sanctified, ᵘ *are* all of one for which
ˣ Mat xxviii 10 John xx 17 — cause he is not ashamed to call them ˣ brethren, 12
ʸ Ps xxii 22 — Saying, ʸ I will declare thy name unto my brethren, in
the midst of the church will I sing praise unto thee
ᶻ Ps xviii 2 — 13 And again, ᶻ I will put my trust in him And
ᵃ Isa viii 18 — again, ᵃ Behold, I and the children which God hath
given me

v 10—13 The cross was the offensive doctrine at which the Hebrews stumbled The apostle therefore shews the excellence of this method of salvation how glorious to God, how effectual for us

For it became him, for whom are all things, and by whom are all things, it was most suitable and becoming, and served most eminently to display the glory of all his divine perfections, *in bringing many sons unto glory*, even the multitude of the redeemed whom he had chosen in Christ Jesus, *to make the Captain* (ἀρχηγὸν) Leader and Author, *of their salvation perfect through sufferings*, completely fitted and consecrated thereby, for the execution of his mediatorial office, having made full satisfaction to the divine justice for the sins of his people *For both he that sanctifieth*, the Redeemer himself, who saves from the guilt and power of sin, *and they who are sanctified* by his blood and Spirit, *are all of one* blood, receiving the human nature from one common parent, and, as included in the same covenant of redemption, have one Father, even God *for which cause he is not ashamed to call them brethren*, but condescends to own the endearing relation, *saying*, (Psalm xxii 22) *I will declare thy name unto my brethren*, opening to them all the glories of divine grace displayed in the gospel, *in the midst of the church will I sing praise unto thee*, celebrating the wonders of thy love to thy peculiar people, (*Matth* xxvi 30) *And again*, (Ps xviii 2) *I will put my trust in him*, confident of his support under all my sufferings, and that they shall be effectual to the salvation of my people *And again Behold, I and the children which God hath given me*, as the travail of my soul, for whom I am ready to undergo every affliction, that I may at last be able to present them before the presence of his glory with exceeding great joy *Note*, (1) God hath many sons whom he hath decreed to bring unto glory, and though they be few in any one age or place, yet, when collected, they will be an innumerable multitude (2) We must be his children by adoption and grace, before we can receive the heavenly inheritance (3) In the method God hath taken to save sinners, by the incarnation of his Son, he hath acted eminently as became him, that, in the most amazing exercise of grace, he might withal make the most signal display of his justice and inexorable hatred of sin (4) The way to glory is through sufferings the Head and the members must walk in the same steps, and, since he hath gone before, he hath consecrated the cross, and to bear it is our honour, and will prove in the issue our unspeakable advantage (5) Christ is our elder brother, with what endearing affection ought we then to regard him, considering what he is to us, and what he hath done for us!

14 Forasmuch then as the children are partakers of
flesh and blood, ᵇ he also himself likewise took part of — ᵇ John i 14 Phil ii 7
the same ᶜ that through death he might destroy him — ᶜ 1 Cor xv 54, 55
that had the power of death, that is, the devil, 15
And ᵈ deliver them who through fear of death were all — ᵈ Luke i 74 2 Tim i 10
their life time subject to bondage 16 For verily † he
took not on him *the nature of* angels, but he took on him — † Gr He taketh not hold of angels, but of the seed
the seed of Abraham 17 Wherefore in all things it
behoved him to be ᵉ made like unto his brethren, that — ᵉ Phil ii 7
he might be ᶠ a merciful and faithful high priest, in — ᶠ Chap iv 15
things *pertaining* to God, to make reconciliation for the
sins of the people 18 For in that he himself hath
suffered, being tempted, he is able to succour them that
are tempted

v 14—18 By Christ's incarnation was the redemption of his people to be accomplished

Forasmuch then as the children, whom the Lord had given him, *are partakers of flesh and blood*, and as in the human nature sin had been committed, in this nature it must be expiated, therefore *he also himself likewise took part of the same*, made exactly in the likeness of sinful flesh, and one with them, *that through death*, giving himself to suffer in their stead, and bearing their sins in his own body on the tree, *he might destroy him that had the power of death that is, the devil*, by whose malice death first entered into the world, *and* who is the executioner of God's wrath upon sinners but his dominion is now broken, and his kingdom overthrown, by the death and resurrection of Jesus, who died and rose again, that he might *deliver them who through fear of death were all their life-time subject to bondage*, the sting of death, which is sin, being taken out of their consciences, and all their dismal apprehensions of the consequence of death being utterly removed *For verily he took not on him the nature of angels, but he took on him the seed of Abraham*, assuming the human nature, as a descendant from Abraham after the flesh *Wherefore*, we may infer from hence that, *in all things it behoved him to be made like unto his brethren*, sin only excepted, *that*, experiencing in his own person all the infirmities and miseries incident to the human nature, *he might be a merciful and faithful High-priest*, touched with tender sympathy towards them, and with all fidelity discharging his office, *in things pertaining to God, to make reconciliation for the sins of the people* by the fullest satisfaction paid to the divine justice, and appearing, as their great High priest, in the presence of God, with his own all-atoning blood *For in that he himself hath suffered, being tempted, he knows what sore temptation is to his people, can tenderly feel for them, and is able to succour them that are tempted* and make them with himself triumphant over all their enemies *Note*, (1) Christ is very man, as well as very God it was as necessary that he should suffer in our nature, as it was essential to the efficacy of those sufferings, that he should be God incarnate (2) Satan, sin, and death, are all vanquished since the Saviour bled, they have no more power to hurt his redeemed people, and we may now triumph over them, since life and immortality are before us, through our crucified Jesus (3) Christ hath made reconciliation between the offended God and the sinful soul since he hath offered the atonement, justice is satisfied, and grace enthroned (4) It is our comfort under all our present trials and sufferings, that we have one to go to, who hath felt all our sorrows, knows our infirmity, and hath now power great as his love to succour and save to the uttermost all that come unto God by him

CHAP III

In this chapter the apostle applies what he had said in the chapter foregoing concerning the priesthood of Christ 1 In a serious pathetic exhortation, that this great high priest that was discovered to them, might be seriously considered by them, ver 1—7 and then adds many weighty counsels and cautions from ver 7, to the end

1. WHerefore, holy brethren, partakers of [a] the
heavenly calling, consider [b] the apostle and
[c] high priest of our profession, Christ Jesus, 2 Who
was faithful to him that † appointed him, as also [d] Moses
was faithful in all his house 3 For this *man* was
counted worthy of more glory than Moses, in as much
as [e] he who hath builded the house hath more honour
than the house 4 For every house is builded by some
man, but [f] he that built all things *is* God 5 And
Moses verily *was* faithful in all his house as a servant, for
a testimony of those things which were to be spoken after,
6 But Christ as a Son over his own house [g] whose
house are we, [h] if we hold fast the confidence and the rejoicing of the hope firm unto the end

a Phil iii 14 b Rom xv 8 c Chap iv 14 & vi 20 & vii 1 & ix 11 † Gr made 1 Sam xii 6 d Num xii 7 e Zech vi 12 Mat xvi 18 f Eph ii 10 g 1 Cor iii 16, & vi 19 2 Cor vi 16 Eph ii 21, 1 Tim iii 15 1 Pet ii 5 h Mat xxiv 13 Ver 14 Chap vi 11

v 1—6 We have here the application of the foregoing considerations The excellency of our great High-priest should draw up our hearts in all holy affection and humble adoration to him

Wherefore, holy brethren, renewed in the spirit of your minds, *partakers of the heavenly calling*, admitted to all the blessings and privileges of the gospel, *consider the apostle and high priest of our profession, Christ Jesus*, sent of God, appointed to his office on purpose to make reconciliation, and whom we profess to believe in as the author of all blessedness, consider his transcendent dignity, and the characters he bears towards us.

1 With what fidelity he discharged his trust as a prophet *Who was faithful to him that appointed him*, revealing to us all his Father's will, *as also Moses*, who was his eminent type, *was faithful in all his house*, communicating to the church in the wilderness, among whom Christ in the divine Shechinah dwelt, as in his own house, all the statutes and ordinances delivered unto him

2 How far superior he is to Moses, as the builder of his own church *For this man* (*ουτος*), this incarnate Jesus, *was counted worthy of more glory than Moses, in as much as he who hath builded the house hath more honour than the house* The master, owner, and builder of the house must needs be far above any member of the family which inhabits it, and Moses, though so distinguished, was but one of the many faithful in the church, of which the Lord Jesus is the maker and builder, therefore must be far inferior to him *For every house is builded by some man, but he that built all things*, and regulated, furnished, and set in order every thing pertaining to his church, whether under the Jewish or evangelical dispensation, *is God*, even that Jesus who shares all the incommunicable attributes of deity, and is *very God*, as well as very man

3 Moses was but a servant, Christ is the Son over his own house *And Moses verily was faithful in all his house as a servant* merely, *for a testimony of those things which were to be spoken after*; to foretel and prefigure in the rites enjoined by him, according to divine command, the great things that under the gospel should be more fully and clearly revealed *But Christ* is infinitely his superior, *as a Son over his own house*, the church erected by him, and purchased with his blood, *whose house are we* that believe, the happy members of his family, *if we hold fast the confidence and the rejoicing of the hope*, which the gospel inspires, *unto the end*, which will prove the reality of our profession, and our assured interest in all the blessings of his holy family *Note*, (1) Christ is the glorious object, who should ever be in our eye the more we consider him, the more shall we honour, love, and serve him (2) Those who are brethren in Christ, and truly partakers of the heavenly calling, will prove it by the holiness of their walk and conversation (3) They who are living members of Christ never fail, but hold fast their confidence and rejoicing of hope stedfast unto the end

7 Wherefore as the holy Ghost saith, [i] To day if ye
will hear his voice, 8 Harden not your hearts, as in
the provocation, in [k] the day of temptation in the wil-
derness 9 When your fathers tempted me, proved
me, and saw my works forty years 10 Wherefore I
was grieved with that generation, and said, They do al-
way err in *their* heart, and they have not known my
ways 11 So I sware in my wrath, † [m] They shall not
enter into my rest 12 [n] Take heed, brethren, lest there
be in any of you an evil heart of unbelief, in departing
from the living God 13 [o] But exhort one another
daily while it is called, To-day, lest any of you be hard-
ened through the deceitfulness of sin 14 For we are
made partakers of Christ, [p] if we hold the beginning of
our confidence stedfast unto the end, 15 While it is
said, [q] To-day if ye will hear his voice, harden not your
hearts, as in the provocation 16 For [r] some, when
they had heard, did provoke [s] howbeit not all that
came out of Egypt by Moses 17 But with whom was
he grieved forty years? *was it* not with them that had
sinned, [t] whose carcases fell in the wilderness? 18
And [u] to whom sware he that they should not enter
into his rest, but to them that believed not? 19
So we see that [x] they could not enter in because of
unbelief

i Psal xcv 7 Ver 15 Chap iv 7 k Exod xvii 2 &c l Deut xxix 2 &c † Gr If they shall, &c m Num xiv 21 23 Deut i 35 n Chap iv 1 11 & xii 15 o Chap x 25 p Ver 6 q Ver 7 Chap iv 7 r Num xiv 4 s Deut i 36 t Num xiv 22, 29 &c & xxvi 65 Jude 5 u Num xiv 30 Deut i 34 x Num xx 12

v 7—19 As it is not nominal profession, but persevering fidelity, which can prove the truth of our relation to Jesus, the apostle proceeds to caution and warn them by former examples

Wherefore as the Holy Ghost saith, (Psal xcv 7) *To-day if ye will hear his voice*, without delay, or trifling with God's patience any longer, *harden not your hearts* against all the calls and warnings of God, *as your fathers did in the provocation, in the day of temptation in the wilderness, when*, by their murmurings, unbelief, and disobedience, *your fathers tempted me, proved me*, how mindful I am of my promise, and how long-suffering, *and saw my works forty years*, receiving the strongest evidences of my faithfulness, power, and grace *Wherefore*, wearied out with their perverseness, and incorrigible ingratitude and infidelity, *I was grieved with that generation, and said, They do alway err in their heart*, stubborn, and wilfully rebellious, *and they have not known my ways*, they delight not in them, and chuse their own delusions *So I sware in my wrath*, justly offended by their continued impenitence, *they shall not enter into my rest*, the land of promise, the type of that eternal rest which remaineth for the faithful above *Note*, (1) Whilst the day of life and hope is prolonged, we are called to seize and improve the precious moment on which eternity depends (2) Continued hardness of heart against the calls of grace, and the warnings of providence, must infallibly issue in everlasting ruin (3) God bears long, but he will not bear always He will swear in his wrath, that the incorrigible shall not enter into his rest

The example which he had quoted, the apostle applies,

1 For their caution *Take heed, brethren, lest there be in any of you*, as was in them, *an evil heart of unbelief, in departing from the living God* *Note*, (1) Unbelief is the damning sin (2) There may be much heart unbelief under the most specious profession of faith (3) Where unbelief prevails, departure from God our Saviour necessarily follow (4) It calls for all our watchfulness and prayer, that our souls do not suffer shipwreck on this fatal rock

2 He suggests the means of preventing the so much to be dreaded evil *But exhort* and encourage *one another daily, while it is called To-day*, improve every opportunity during the fleeting moment of life, to excite each other to watchfulness and holy diligence, *lest any of you*, who have made profession of the gospel, *be hardened through the deceitfulness of sin*, your conscience lulled asleep, and your souls perverted and seduced from the simplicity of the gospel *Note*, (1) Christian brethren should maintain a holy jealousy over each other (2) Since the time is so short, we need be earnest to redeem it for the best purposes (3) Sin comes with a most alluring aspect, and lurks often under the most specious appearances (4) Wherever sin gains possession of the heart, hardness and insensibility naturally follow, so that they who are in the most fatal danger, are the least apprized of it

3 He encourages them to end well as they had begun *For we are made partakers of Christ*, or, *we have been* admitted to all the blessings and privileges which spring from vital union with him; *if we hold the beginning of our confidence* (*υποστασεως*), or *substance* in him, *stedfast unto the end*, and perseveringly abide in this holy fellowship, without which our former profession would be proved hypocritical and insincere *Note*, (1) Every believer is a partaker of Christ, and all things are our's, as we are in his grace, merit, righteousness, and Spirit (2) To prove our

union

union with Christ real, we must continue faithfully attached to him, even unto the end

4 He returns to the subject he began with, to fortify them against apostasy Improve the present moment, *while it is said, To-day if ye will hear his voice, harden not your hearts, as in the provocation*, to-morrow you may be launched into eternity, and time be to you no more *For some, when they had heard*, notwithstanding every warning, *did provoke* God to abandon them *howbeit not all that came out of Egypt by Moses*, Caleb and Joshua, and those under twenty years of age, still survived *But with whom was he grieved forty years? was it not with them that had sinned*, who bore the righteous vengeance due to their iniquities, *and whose carcases fell in the wilderness? And to whom sware he that they should not enter into his rest*, nor possess the promised Canaan, *but to them that believed not*, and rejected their own mercies? *So we see that they could not enter in because of unbelief* *Note*, (1) Unbelief of God's promises is among the most common and highly provoking iniquities (2) They who wilfully reject the counsel of God against their own souls, have only themselves to blame for their ruin (3) Far the greater part of mankind, yea of professing Christians, live and die in their sins The remnant that is saved is very small, two only out of the miriads of Israel entred into the land of rest (4) Such fearful instances should awaken in us a holy jealousy to make our calling and election sure

CHAP IV

The apostle, 1 Inculcates on the Hebrews holy jealousy, ver 1, 2 2 He shews the excellence of the gospel rest above the earthly Canaan, ver 3—10 Then, 3 Concludes with proper and powerful arguments and motives to faith and obedience

a Chap xiii 15 1 [a] LET us therefore, fear lest a promise being left
us of entring into his rest, any of you should
seem to come short of it 2 For unto us was the gos-
pel preached, as well as unto them but the word preach-
b Chap. iii 12, 19 ed did not profit them, [b] not being mixed with faith in
them that heard *it* 3 For we which have believed do
c Ps xcv 11 Chap iii 11, 18 enter into rest, as he said, [c] As I have sworn in my wrath,
If they shall enter into my rest although the works
were finished from the foundation of the world 4 For
he spake in a certain place of the seventh *day* on this
d Gen ii 2 Ex xxxi 17 wise, [d] And God did rest the seventh day from all his
works 5 And in this *place* again, If they shall enter
into my rest 6 Seeing therefore it remaineth that some
must enter therein, and they to whom it was first preach-
e Chap iii 19 ed [e] entred not in because of unbelief 7 Again, he
limiteth a certain day, saying in David, To-day, after so
f Ps xcv 7 Chap iii 7 long a time, as it is said, [f] To day if ye will hear his
voice, harden not your hearts 8 For if † Jesus had
† i e Joshua So Acts vii 45 given them rest, then would he not afterward have spoken
g Rev xiv 13 of another day 9 [g] There remaineth therefore ‡ a rest
‡ Or a sabbatism to the people of God 10 For he that is entred into
his rest, he also hath ceased from his own works, as God
did from his

v 1—10 The apostle, in the view of the foregoing observations,

1 Exhorts them to holy jealousy *Let us fear therefore* for ourselves, *lest a promise being left us of entring into his rest*, into a state of happy peace with God here, and the eternal enjoyment of him hereafter, *any of you should seem to come short of it*, overcome by temptation, apostatizing from your professions, or faultering in your Christian course, so as, like Israel of old, to fail of the promised inheritance *For unto us was the gospel preached*, clearly and plainly, *as well as unto them*, more obscurely in types and figures *but the word preached did not profit them*, to any saving purpose, *not being mixed with faith in them that heard it*, and therefore never incorporated with their hearts, as the food, when digested, affords nourishment to the body Nor will the gospel profit us any more than it did them, unless it be received by faith into the soul *Note*, (1) The same gospel in substance was preached under the Old Testament as well as the New, and only by faith then, any more than at present, could any man be justified and saved (2) The word is preached to multitudes who never profit thereby, for unless the Lord gives the discerning ear, and enables us to mix it with faith in our hearts, we hear in vain (3) It is a dreadful thing to hear of gospel grace, and yet to come short of it, and perish in our sins (4) The way to ensure our entrance into the promised rest, is by constant watchfulness and holy caution They who do not fear, will fall

2 He shews the surpassing excellency of that spiritual rest, to which, under the gospel, believers are admitted *For we which have believed do enter into rest*, through Christ, having present peace with God by virtue of our union with our exalted Head, and are already sat down with him in heavenly places *As he said, As I have sworn in my wrath, If they shall enter into my rest*, which implied a promise, that true believers should enter into rest, *although the works were finished from the foundation of the world*, and a sabbatical rest enjoined in consequence thereof Yet the rest here spoken of is different from that, *for he spake in a certain place of the seventh day on this wise*, (Gen ii 2) *And God did rest the seventh day from all his works*, hallowing it for ever after as a day of holy rest, but this was not the rest concerning which God sware unto the Israelites *And in this place again, If they shall enter into my rest*, As I live, saith the Lord, they shall not, which being spoken by David to the people of his own days, could not refer to the land of Canaan, of which for some hundreds of years they had been in possession *Seeing therefore it remaineth, that some must enter therein*, as is implied in the very threatning, *and they to whom it was first preached*, the generality of them at least, *entred not in* to the typical rest of Canaan, *because of their unbelief* *Again he limiteth*, and fixes *a certain day* to come, *saying in David*, (Ps xcv 7, 8) *To-day, after so long a time* had elapsed from their settlement in Canaan, *as it is said, To-day if ye will hear his voice, harden not your hearts*, and ye shall enter into the promised rest Now this must be different from the possession of the land of Canaan, *For if Jesus*, Joshua, *had given them rest*, and none farther was to have been expected, *then would he not afterward have spoken of another day*, as he doth in that Psalm Since then neither the sabbath nor the land of Canaan are meant in this passage of scripture, *there remaineth therefore a rest to the people of God*, a rest into which the spiritual Joshua should bring his faithful followers, a present, a spiritual rest, through faith in Jesus Christ, far preferable to either of these, and this the earnest and foretaste of an eternal rest in glory everlasting *For he that is entred into his rest*, the Lord Jesus Christ, since his ascension into heaven, having finished the work of his people's salvation which he had undertaken, *he also hath ceased from his own works*, having nothing more to do or suffer as the meritorious cause of their acceptance with God, all being finished on the cross therefore he rests in glory, *as God did* rest *from his* works of creation and all who believe in Jesus rest with him in the present enjoyment of the divine favour, and in their title to eternal blessedness

11 Let us labour therefore to enter into that rest,
lest any man fall [h] after the same example of † unbelief
h Chap iii 19 † Or disobedience 12 For [i] the word of God *is* quick, and powerful, and
i Jer xxiii 29 2 Cor x 4, 5 [k] sharper than any two-edged sword, piercing even to
k Is xlix 2 Eph vi 17 Rev i 16 & ii 16 the dividing asunder of soul and spirit, and of the joints
l 1 Cor xiv 24 and marrow, [l] and *is* a discerner of the thoughts and in-
m Ps xxxiii 13, 14 & xc 8 & cxxxix 11, 12 tents of the heart 13 [m] Neither is there any creature
n Prov xv 11 that is not manifest in his sight [n] but all things *are*
naked and opened unto the eyes of him with whom we
o Chap iii 1 have to do 14 Seeing then that we have [o] a great
p Chap vii 26 & ix 12, 24 high priest, [p] that is passed into the heavens, Jesus the
q Chap x 23 Son of God, [q] let us hold fast *our* profession 15 For
r Chap ii 18 we have not an high priest [r] which cannot be touched
s Luke xxii 28 with the feeling of our infirmities, but [s] was in all
t 2 Cor v 21 Chap vii 26 1 Pet i 22 points tempted like as we are, [t] *yet* without sin 16
u Eph ii 18 & iii 12 Chap x 19, &c [u] Let us therefore come boldly unto the throne of grace,
that we may obtain mercy, and find grace to help in
time of need

v 11—16 Such a glorious rest being promised,

1 The apostle exhorts them to secure a part therein *Let us labour therefore to enter into that rest*, in opposition to every discouragement and difficulty from sin, Satan, and the world, which may be laid in our way, considering the awful examples above-mentioned, *lest any man fall after the same example of unbelief*, and perish in their sins *Note*, The way to heaven is strait, and the gate narrow we must *strive* if we would enter in, the slothful never went to glory

2 He enforces his exhortation by the strongest argument *For the word of God*, the uncreated word, the Son, our Lord, and shortly to be our Judge, *is quick*, having life in and of himself, *and* the author of it to all his creatures, *powerful* in agency, *and* omnipotent, *sharper than any two-edged sword*, in his gospel word brought home to the conscience by the operation of the Holy Ghost, *piercing even to the dividing asunder of soul and spirit, and of the joints and marrow*, entering into the inmost recesses of the heart, carrying the deepest conviction, and working effectually to bring the whole inner man into obedience to himself, *and is a discerner of the thoughts and intents of the heart*, intimately acquainted with every secret of the soul *Neither is there any creature*, in heaven or in earth, *that is not manifest in his sight*, nor can their inmost thoughts be hid from him, *but all things are naked and opened unto the eyes of him with whom we have to do*, (γυμνα και τετραχηλισμενα) As the sacrifices were flayed, laid open, and their entrails inspected with nicest care, so distinctly is every imagination of our hearts bare and exposed to him whose eyes are as a flame of fire, and at whose bar we must shortly give an account How awakening a consideration! and

4 what

what watchfulness and diligence should it excite in us, that we may be found of him in peace, and enter among his faithful ones into the promised rest.

Some by the word of God suppose the written word is meant, whose quickening, powerful, piercing, discerning efficacy is so great; and this, no doubt, is included, as being the instrument which the Lord makes use of; but I conceive the context and expressions shew that Christ personally is here described and spoken of.

3. He returns to the consideration of the priesthood of Christ, mentioned (*chap.* iii. 1.) as an encouraging motive to quicken their diligence, considering the power and grace which were engaged for their support. *Seeing then that we have a great high-priest*, whose excellence is so superlative; and that, having offered the all-atoning sacrifice, *is passed into the heavens*, into the holiest of all, to the immediate presence of God, even *Jesus the Son of God*, one in essence with the Father, and as Mediator exalted to the highest dignity and glory, able to succour and save his people to the uttermost: therefore *let us hold fast our profession*, unwavering; *for we have not an high-priest which cannot be touched with the feeling of our infirmities*, but one who tenderly sympathizes with every pang we feel in body or soul, and *was in all points tempted like as we are, only without sin*. His love and compassions therefore being great as his power, we may confidently expect salvation to the uttermost, and comfortably labour when we are assured it shall not be in vain in the Lord. *Note*, (1.) Christ is passed into the heavens, and for his people appears in the presence of God, to plead their cause, and ensure their salvation. (2.) It is an unspeakable comfort to us under every temptation, that Jesus hath endured it before us, knows our weakness, feels for our distress, and will proportion his grace to our necessities. (3.) This should embolden us under the severest conflicts to hold fast our profession, nor ever to be moved away from the hope of the gospel, seeing he is near that strengtheneth us.

4. The glorious high-priesthood of Jesus should encourage us to draw near to God in prayer. *Let us therefore*, having such an all-prevailing advocate, *come boldly to a throne of grace*, where our reconciled God in majesty and love unspeakable appears, inviting our applications, with humble reverence, and filial confidence; *that we may obtain mercy*, and pardons multiplied from day to day, *and grace to help in every time of need*, in time, manner, measure, vouchsafed according to our danger, trials, and distresses, till he shall land us safe on the shores of eternal rest. *Note*, (1.) They who know the inestimable privilege of having a throne of grace to go to, will not fail to be found there often upon their knees. (2.) There is nothing we can want, of which we are not assured of a supply, when by prayer and supplication with thanksgiving we make our requests known to a reconciled God. (3.) All our hopes of mercy or grace rise purely from the great High-priest, who lives to make intercession for us; for in him God is always well pleased, and with us for his sake. (4.) Humble boldness becomes a child of God when approaching that throne, where grace reigns through righteousness unto eternal life by Jesus Christ our Lord.

CHAP. V.

In this chapter the apostle continues his discourse upon the priesthood of Christ, a sweet subject, which he would not too soon dismiss. And here, 1. He explains the nature of the priestly office in general, ver. 1—3. 2. The proper and regular call thereto must be to this office, ver. 4—6. 3. The requisite qualifications for the work, ver. 7—9. 4. The peculiar order of the priesthood of Christ; it was not after the order of Aaron, but Melchisedec, ver. 6, 7, 10. 5. He reproves the Hebrews, that they had not made those improvements in knowledge as might have made them capable of looking into the more abstruse and mysterious parts of scripture, ver. 11—14.

1 FOR every high priest taken from among men,
^a is ordained for men ^b in things *pertaining* to
God, ^c that he may offer both gifts and sacrifices for
sins: 2 ^d Who can have compassion on the ignorant,
and on them that are out of the way; for that he him-
self also is compassed with infirmity. 3 And by reason
hereof he ought, as for the people, ^e so also for himself,
to offer for sins. 4 And ^f no man taketh this honour
unto himself, but he that is called of God, ^g as *was*
Aaron. 5 ^h So also Christ glorified not himself to be
made an high priest; but he that said unto him, ^i Thou
art my Son, to day have I begotten thee. 6 As he
saith also in another *place*, ^k Thou *art* a priest for ever
after the order of Melchisedec. 7 Who in the days of
his flesh, when he had ^l offered up prayers and suppli-
cations, ^m with strong crying and tears, unto him ^n that
was able to save him from death, ^o and was heard, ^p in
that he feared; 8 Though he were a Son, yet learned
he ^q obedience by the things which he suffered; 9
And ^r being made perfect, he became ^s the author of
eternal salvation unto all them that obey him; 10
Called of God an high priest ^t after the order of Mel-
chisedec.

v. 1—10. We have here,

1. An account of the sacerdotal office in general. *For every high priest taken from among men*, under the legal dispensation, *is* of the same nature with his brethren, and *ordained for men in things pertaining to God*, on their behalf to minister in holy things, *that he may offer both gifts and sacrifices for sins*, according to the law, as the type and figure of him, who in his own person, is both high priest and sacrifice, should, in the fulness of time, offer the true atonement, and make the perfect reconciliation for sin, causing the persons and prayers of his people to be accepted by the Father; *who can bear with, and have compassion on the ignorant*, sympathizing with them; *and having pity on them that are out of the way*, desirous to bring them back again to God, and peace of conscience: *for that he himself also is compassed with infirmity*, and liable to every affliction under which his brethren groan. *And by reason hereof*, since he himself is a poor infirm creature, and guilty sinner, as well as others, *he ought, as for the people, so for himself, to offer an* atoning sacrifice. But herein the surpassing glory of the great High-priest of our profession most eminently appears; for while, as partaker of the human nature, with infinitely greater compassion, he feels for the erring, and the ignorant, and stands to offer his all-prevailing sacrifice for them, he doth it purely on their account, not on his own, being himself without sin.

2. A divine appointment was necessary for the office of priesthood. *And no man taketh this honour unto himself, but he that is called of God, as was Aaron*, appointed thereto by the Lord's immediate order and authority. *So also Christ glorified not himself to be made an high priest*, assuming that honour in his human nature without a divine warrant; *but he* was solemnly called and qualified for this office by him, *that said unto him, Thou art my Son, to-day have I begotten thee*, intimating the dignity of his person who was to be invested with the pontifical office. *As he saith also in another place*, (Psal. cx. 4.) *Thou art a priest for ever after the order of Melchisedec*, an order prior and superior to that of Aaron, Christ having an eternal and unchangeable priesthood, ever living, and alone sufficient to manage all the concerns of his people. *Note*, (1.) Before we presume to minister in holy things, we must produce a divine call, lest intruding into an office for which we have no commission, we should expose ourselves to shame as intruders, instead of reaping honour by the service. (2.) The High-priest which God hath himself appointed, we may be assured he will accept, and all our oblations in his hands shall be received as sacrifices of a sweet smell.

3. We are told how he executed his office, and how effectual it was on the behalf of his people. *Who in the days of his flesh*, when here below, oppressed with manifold and severe afflictions, *he had offered up prayers and supplications, with strong crying and tears*, especially in his agonizing struggle in the garden, looking up *unto him that was able to save him from death*, and the terrors which distressed his innocent soul, *and was heard*, in the support ministred to him, and in his glorious resurrection from the dead, *because he feared*, and with holy reverence submitted to his Father's will. *Though he were a Son*, the eternal Son of the Father, and one with him in nature and perfections, yet, having condescended to take our nature upon him, *learned he obedience by the things which he suffered*, approving himself cheerfully submissive to his Father's will, and yielding himself up to death, even the death of the cross. *And being made perfect*, fully accomplishing by his obedience and sufferings the work which he had undertaken, and thereby being consecrated for the exercise of his priesthood in heaven, *he became the Author of eternal salvation*, purchasing it by his blood, securing it by his advocacy, and applying it by his Spirit to the souls of his people; a salvation not only from present guilt and corruption, but including all the blessings of glory everlasting, which he secured *unto all them that obey him*, and follow him as the Captain of their salvation; *called of God*, and fully qualified for his office, *an high priest after the order of Melchisedec*, ever living to make intercession for his people, and therefore a Saviour unto them to the uttermost. *Note*, (1.) God's adopted sons, like their great Head, are to expect sufferings, and under them to learn obedience and submission. (2.) None ever in the human nature endured any thing like what the Son of God hath suffered voluntarily for our sake: how dare we then murmur or complain? (3.) In his agony the Saviour prayed, to teach us whither we should look under all our difficulties; and if with faith and fervent, like him, we cry, we shall as assuredly be heard and delivered. (4.) The salvation which the Son of God hath obtained for us is complete and everlasting. He hath borne the penalty of sin, and fulfilled the righteousness of the law, that we might have all the benefit, and be entitled to the eternal reward of glory. (5.) All who hope to reign with him, must be ruled by him,

and, cheerfully yielding themselves to his holy will, take up their cross, and follow the captain of their salvation, and, unless we do this, our hope in him is but delusion

11 [u] Of whom we have many things to say, and hard
to be uttered, seeing ye are dull of hearing 12 For
when for the time ye ought to be teachers, ye have need
that one teach you again which *be* the first principles of
the oracles of God, and are become such as [x] have need
of milk, and not of strong meat 13 For every one
that useth milk, † *is* unskilful in the word of righteous-
ness for [y] he is a babe 14 But strong meat belong-
eth to them that are ‡ of full age, *even* those who by rea-
son of use have their senses exercised [z] to discern both
good and evil

v 11—14 The apostle pauses for a moment, and stays the further consideration of the subject which he was upon, to introduce a needful rebuke of their dulness and inattention to the great things of God's word Having mentioned the second time that remarkable personage Melchisedec, he observes, *Of whom we have many things to say, and hard to be uttered,* difficult to be understood in themselves, and the more so to you, *seeing ye are dull of hearing,* slothful and negligent to search into the sacred oracles, that you might become more deeply acquainted with their important contents *For when for the time ye ought to be teachers,* considering all the means and advantages which you have enjoyed, *ye have need,* so little progress have ye made in the school of Christ, *that one teach you again which be the first principles of the oracles of God,* as the child must learn his letters in order to spell and read, *and,* rather declining than advancing in knowledge, *are become such as have need of milk, and not of strong meat,* as babes at the breast, instead of that state of manhood to which you should, ere this, have arrived *For every one that useth milk,* and cannot relish or digest any thing beyond the first principles of the doctrine of Christ, *is unskilful,* and unexperienced *in the word of righteousness* in the gospel, where Christ's divine righteousness is revealed, and we are taught how to walk and please God, *for* such a one *is a babe* in understanding *But strong meat,* the sublimer doctrines of truth, *belong to them that are of full age,* and may, comparatively, be stiled perfect men (τελειοι) *even those, who by reason of use,* being experimentally acquainted with the blessed gospel, *have their senses exercised to discern both good and evil,* accurate to discover truth and detect error, and as eager to embrace and pursue the one, as to detest and avoid the other *Note,* (1) They who have long enjoyed the richest advantages, are expected to shew proportionable improvement in grace and knowledge (2) It is a great grief to ministers, and the sin and shame of their people, that, after years of labour, many of them have yet to learn the first principles of gospel truth (3) The Scripture is suited to every state, there is milk for babes, and strong meat for men, it is the wisdom of a minister to be able to divide to every man his portion in due season (4) The word of God contains mysteries, wherein the most deep read and experienced have much to learn, whilst the grand truths are plain and obvious, and such as the weakest capacities may comprehend

CHAP VI

In this chapter the apostle exhorts the Hebrews to make a better proficiency in religion than they had done, as the best way to prevent apostasy, the dreadful nature of which he sets forth, ver 1—9 and then expresses his good hopes concerning them, that they would persevere in faith and holiness, and sets before them the great encouragement they have from God, both with respect to their duty and happiness, from ver 9 to the end

1 THEREFORE, [a] leaving the principles of the
doctrine of Christ, let us go on unto ‖ perfec-
tion, not laying again the foundation of repentance [b] from
dead works, and of faith towards God 2 Of the
doctrine of baptisms, and [c] of laying on of hands, and of
resurrection of the dead, and of eternal judgment 3
And this will we do, [e] if God permit 4 [f] For *it is* im-
possible for those who were once [g] enlightened, and have
tasted of [h] the heavenly gift, and [i] were made partakers
of the holy Ghost, 5 And [k] have tasted the good word
of God, and the powers of [l] the world to come, 6 If
they shall fall away, to renew them again unto repent-
ance seeing [m] they crucify to themselves the Son of God
afresh, and put *him* to an open shame 7 For the earth
which drinketh in the rain that cometh oft upon it, and
bringeth forth herbs meet for them by whom it is dressed,
receiveth blessing from God 8 [n] But that which bear-
eth thorns and briers *is* rejected, and *is* nigh unto
cursing, whose end is to be burned

v 1—8 The apostle here,

1 Exhorts the Hebrews to advance in spiritual attainments *Therefore, leaving the principles of the doctrine of Christ, let us go on unto perfection,* to a more advanced state of grace and understanding, *not laying again the foundation,* and continuing still to insist on the first principles of the Christian doctrine, but proceeding to greater heighths in heavenly wisdom The principles I speak of are those, (1) *Of repentance from dead works,* implying a sense of the evil and danger of sin, the wages of which is death, an abhorrence of it, and real conversion of heart from the love and practice of all iniquity *And* (2) *Of faith towards God,* since all who come to him must believe his being, attributes, and perfections, and especially that he is our reconciled God in the Son of his love, Christ Jesus And these two principles *of* Christianity were typified under the Mosaical dispensation by *the doctrine of baptisms,* or diverse washings prescribed to the temple worshippers, which signified the purification of the conscience, through faith in the blood of Jesus, and by the power of his Spirit, *and of laying on of hands* upon the head of the sacrifice, with penitent confession of sin, in token of transferring their guilt to their substitute (3) *And of the resurrection of the dead,* which may be reckoned another first principle of Christianity *And* (4) *Of eternal judgment,* when every man must appear to give account at God's bar, and to receive his sentence to be happy or miserable for ever, in body and soul, according to his deeds These having been so often insisted upon, we design to leave them to your serious reflection, and pass on to sublimer things *And this will we do, if God permit* *Note,* (1) When the foundation of religion is laid, the superstructure must be raised in an increase of knowledge, grace, and holiness (2) All we purpose must be undertaken in dependance upon God's support, for without him we can do nothing aright

2 To quicken them to diligence, he sets before them the fearful case of apostates *For it is impossible for those who were once enlightned,* and so far received the knowledge of the truth as to make profession of it, *and have tasted of the heavenly gift,* in some superficial impressions made upon their conscience, though their heart hath remained unchanged, *and were made partakers of the Holy Ghost,* in some of his miraculous operations, *and have tasted of the good word of God,* receiving it, as the stony ground hearers, for a while with joy, *and of the powers of the world to come,* enabled to perform many wonderful works, *if,* after all this, *they shall fall away* from the gospel to judaism, or heathenism, the case is desperate, it is impossible *to renew them again unto repentance seeing they crucify to themselves the Son of God afresh,* approving the wickedness of those who nailed him to the tree as an impostor, *and put him to an open shame,* by assenting to the black calumnies of his murderers, turning from him as a deceiver, and renouncing his gospel as an untruth, for such apostacy, being a sin against the very remedy, cannot but be necessarily fatal *Note,* (1) Hypocrites may go far, and come short of heaven they may have many right notions in religion, make a fair profession, feel pangs of conviction, and transient flashes of joy under the ordinances, yea, they might have possessed even the power of miracles, and yet never have been partakers of the grace of God in truth (2) Satan will often seek to distress the souls of the sincere, when under darkness or temptation with these terrible declarations, let it therefore be remembered, that it is never impossible to renew those unto repentance, in whom the Lord still awakens a desire to repent and turn to him

3 The different states of the gracious soul and the apostate are here described *For the earth which drinketh in the rain that cometh oft upon it, and bringeth forth herbs meet for them by whom it is dressed, receiveth blessing from God,* so the faithful heart, watered with the dew of divine influences from the Lord, brings forth the fruits of righteousness, which by Jesus Christ are acceptable and well pleasing to God, who blesses his own work, and gives a more abundant increase of every holy and gracious disposition *But that ground which,* after all the culture bestowed upon it, still *beareth thorns and briers is rejected* by the owner as barren, *and is nigh unto cursing, whose end is to be burned* so where, amidst the means of grace, unbelief and hardness of heart remain, and after all their professions men turn aside to error in principle, and ungodliness in practice, such are in God's sight reprobate, his curse lieth upon them, which soon shall be fearfully executed, when, cast into the belly of hell, they shall lie down in everlasting burnings, and none can quench them

9 But, beloved, we are persuaded better things of
you, and things that accompany salvation, though we
thus speak 10 [o] For God *is* [p] not unrighteous, to for-
get [q] your work and labour of love which ye have shewed
toward his name, in that ye have ministred to the saints,
and do minister 11 And we desire, that [r] every one
of you do shew the same diligence, [s] to the full assurance
of hope unto the end 12 That ye be not slothful, but
followers

followers of them who through faith and patience inherit
the promises 13 For when God made promise to Abra-
r Gen xxii 16, 17 ham, because he could swear by no greater, he sware
by himself, 14 Saying, Surely, blessing, I will bless
thee, and multiplying, I will multiply thee 15 And
s Rom ii 7 so after he had patiently endured, he obtained the pro-
mise 16 For men verily swear by the greater and
t Ex xxii 11 an oath for confirmation is to them an end of all strife
17 Wherein God willing more abundantly to shew unto
the heirs of promise the immutability of his counsel,
† Gr mediated by an oath † confirmed it by an oath 18 That by two immuta-
ble things, in which it was impossible for God to lye, we
might have a strong consolation, who have fled for re-
fuge to lay hold upon the hope set before us 19 Which
hope we have as an anchor of the soul, both sure and
stedfast, and which entreth into that within the vail,
y Chap ix 24 20 y Whither the forerunner is for us entred, even Jesus,
z Chap iii 1 & v 6 & vii 17 z made an high priest for ever after the order of Melchi-
sedec

v 9—20 The apostle, from the most awful warnings, passes on to the most powerful encouragements to steadfastness and perseverance.

1 He professes his good opinion of them, in general at least *But, beloved, we are persuaded better things of you, and things that accompany salvation, though we thus speak*, that ye will never prove apostates, but are actually partakers of those blessings of justification, adoption, and grace, which cannot but issue in eternal glory

2 He suggests the reason on which his confidence was built *For God is not unrighteous* or unfaithful *to* his promises, and therefore will not *forget your work and labour of love*, the genuine principle of all holy obedience, and assured proof of your interest in all the blessings of the everlasting covenant, *which love ye have shewed toward his name, in that ye have ministred to the saints, and do continue to minister* unto them under all their afflictions *Note*, (1) Our love to God must appear in every work and labour of love for the good of his people (2) They who give genuine proofs of their faith unfeigned, by a conversation such as becometh godliness, will find God faithful to his promises, and their bounteous rewarder

3 He exhorts them to persevere *And we desire, that every one of you do shew the same diligence*, in every good word and work, your fruits of righteousness abiding and abounding, *to the full assurance of hope unto the end*, growing up to a more satisfied confidence of your interest in the eternal blessedness, and carried as a ship under full sails into the port of eternal rest See therefore *that ye be not slothful, but* diligent in every means of grace, and in the duties of your calling, as *followers of them who* have trod before this holy path, and, *through faith and patience* amidst every trial, persevering unto the end, are now gone to *inherit the promises* in glory everlasting *Note*, (1) If we have good hope through grace, we should seek to grow up to the full assurance of hope unto the end (2) Diligence in religion, as in every thing else, is the only way to thrive (3) The examples of those who are gone to glory before us should encourage and quicken us to follow them (4) Where faith and patience are implanted in the heart, there perseverance is the necessary fruit

4 The faithfulness of God to his promises should engage their fidelity to him *For when God made promise to Abraham*, (Gen xxii 16, 17) concerning the Messiah, his future seed, *because he could swear by no greater, he sware by himself*, to give him the strongest assurance of the fulfilment of the promise, *Saying, Surely*, as I live, my being and perfections are engaged to accomplish my word, *blessing, I will bless thee, and multiplying, I will multiply thee*, so that thou shalt be a father of many nations, and on thy spiritual seed shall thy blessing descend to the latest ages *And so after he had patiently endured*, through manifold afflictions, *he obtained the promise* of a son, the pledge of that Messiah who should descend from him, and at last departed himself in the faith, and entered the eternal world of glory *For men verily swear by the greater*, solemnly appealing to God as the witness of truth, and avenger of falshood, *and an oath for confirmation is to them an end of all strife*, this being judged the most solemn and decisive evidence, which can be given to silence doubt, and terminate dispute *Wherein God willing more abundantly to shew unto the heirs of promise the immutability of his counsel, confirmed it by an oath*, in condescension to our weakness, and to give us the utmost satisfaction with regard to the unchangeableness of his purposes of grace toward his people, and of the certainty of the accomplishment of every promise he had made, whatever difficulties might seem to prevent it *that by two immutable things*, the promise and oath of God, *in which it was impossible for God to lye, we might have a strong consolation*, filled with the sweetest delight, and supported under all our trials, *who have fled for refuge*, as the man-slayer to the appointed city, (Num xxxv 11, 12) with eagerness, under an awakened sense of our guilt and danger, *to lay hold upon the hope set before us*, even Christ, the rock of his people's confidence *which hope we have as an anchor of the soul, both sure and stedfast, and which entreth into that within the vail*, Christ, the object of our hope, being ascended into heaven, thither the grace of hope follows him, keeping the soul unmoved amidst all the storms of temptation *whither the forerunner*, our representative, *is for us entred, even Jesus*, the exalted Saviour, gone to prepare a place for us, *made an high priest for ever after the order of Melchisedec* *Note*, (1) In Christ there is a refuge provided for the chief of sinners, and all who flee to him shall not only be safe but happy (2) Since the promises are confirmed by two such immutable things as the counsel and oath of God, with what confidence ought we to trust upon them? (3) In this tempestuous world we should be hourly exposed to shipwreck, if hope did not enable us to ride out the storm, having cast anchor within the vail (4) Where our forerunner is entered for us, we must follow Is he in heaven? there shall we be shortly with him where he is, that we may behold and share his glory

CHAP VII

In this chapter, 1 We have a more particular account of Melchisedec, ver 1, 2, 3 2 The excellency of his priesthood above that of Aaron, ver 4—11 3 An accommodation of all to Christ, to shew the superior excellency of his person, office, and covenant, from ver 11 to the end

1. FOR this a Melchisedec, king of Salem, priest of a Gen xiv 18, &c
the most high God, who met Abraham return-
ing from the slaughter of the kings, and blessed him
2 To whom also Abraham gave a tenth part of all
first being by interpretation King of righteousness, and
after that also King of Salem, which is King of peace,
3 Without father, without mother, without † descent, † Gr genealogy or pedigree
having neither beginning of days, nor end of life, but
made like unto the Son of God, abideth a priest conti-
nually

v 1—3 Thrice had the apostle quoted the testimony borne to the Son of God out of the Psalms, as an high priest after the order of Melchisedec of this remarkable person he here gives an account, and we may therein trace the resemblance he bore to his great antitype

1 His name was Melchisedec, or king of righteousness, the figure of him on whose shoulders the universal government should rest, who, with the most distinguished rectitude, should administer the affairs of his kingdom, and is the author of everlasting righteousness to his people

2 He was *king of Salem*, that is, of *peace* So is Christ eminently the prince of peace, having procured it for us by his blood, applying it by his Spirit, and setting up his throne of peace within our hearts

3 He was said to be *a priest of the most high God* So was Jesus consecrated to this office by his Father, and through his sacrifice alone can we obtain reconciliation and acceptance with God

4 He blessed Abraham returning from the slaughter of the kings, is his superior And as Abraham gave him a tenth of all, he must needs be a priest of a higher rank and order than Levi or Aaron, who descended from this patriarch, and thus hath our incarnate Lord a priesthood infinitely excelling the Aaronical, and of far more extensive influence, ministring in behalf of Gentiles as well as Jews

5 Melchisedec' original is entirely concealed, no mention is made of his father or mother, of his birth or death, that he might more strikingly represent the Son of God, who abideth a priest continually, appointed to his office before the worlds were, and to the end of time continuing to exercise it on the behalf of his people, without predecessor, partner, or successor, alone appearing before the throne, and ever living to make intercession for us

4 Now consider how great this man *was*, b unto whom b Gen xiv 20
even the patriarch Abraham gave the tenth of the spoils
5. And verily c they that are of the sons of Levi, who c Num xviii 21, 26
receive the office of the priesthood, have a commandment
to take tithes of the people according to the law, that is,
of their brethren, though they come out of the loins of
Abraham 6 But he whose ‖ descent is not counted ‖ Or pedigree
from them, d received tithes of Abraham, and blessed d Gen xiv
him e that had the promises 7 And without all con-
tradiction, the less is blessed of the better 8 And here e Rom iv 13 Gal iii 16
men that die receive tithes but there he receiveth them,
of whom it is witnessed that he liveth 9 And, as I
may so say, Levi also who receiveth tithes, payed tithes
in Abraham 10 For he was yet in the loins of his
father when Melchisedec met him

v. 4—10 To guard the Hebrews from their attachment to the abolished priesthood of Levi, and lead them to the great High Priest of their profession, Christ Jesus, he shews his surpassing excellence above Aaron or his sons (1.) Because they, being in Abraham's loins, paid tythes to Melchisedec, and though commissioned afterwards to receive tythes of their brethren, yet virtually now, as included in their father, they paid tithes to this priest of God, acknowledged him as their superior, who was but the type of our Lord (2.) Because the less is blessed by the greater, and herein therefore Abraham himself, though favoured with such distinguished promises, was inferior to Melchisedec, and much more must his sons be who should descend from him, and how much more excellent still than they must he then be, of whom Melchisedec was only the representative? (3.) They were all dying men, and the succession and descent of the sons of Levi are well known, but Melchisedec's generation is concealed, we only hear of him that he liveth, as the figure of him who really hath an unchangeable priesthood, and actually lives for ever to intercede on the behalf of his people *Note*, If Abraham's paying tithes was reckoned the act of those who were then in his loins, and imputed to them as done by their covenant-head, we see how Adam's sin, and Christ's righteousness, are severally imputed to the natural descendants of the one, and the spiritual seed of the other

f Gal. ii. 21. ver. 19. Chap. viii. 7.
11 f If therefore perfection were by the Levitical
priesthood, (for under it the people received the law)
what further need *was there* that another priest should
rise after the order of Melchisedec, and not be called
after the order of Aaron? 12 For the priesthood being
changed, there is made of necessity a change also of the
law. 13 For he of whom these things are spoken per-
taineth to another tribe, of which no man gave attend-
g Mat. i. 3. Luke iii. 33.
ance at the altar. 14 For *it is* evident that g our Lord
sprang out of Juda; of which tribe Moses spake nothing
concerning priesthood. 15 And it is yet far more evi-
h Chap. v. 6. & vi. 20.
dent: for that h after the similitude of Melchisedec there
ariseth another priest, 16 Who is made, not after the
law of a carnal commandment, but after the power of
i Ps. cx. 4.
an endless life. 17 For he testifieth, i Thou *art* a
priest for ever after the order of Melchisedec. 18 For
there is verily a disannulling of the commandment going
k Rom. viii. 3. Gal. iv. 9.
before, for k the weakness and unprofitableness thereof.
l Acts xiii. 39. Rom. viii. 3. Gal. ii. 16. Chap. ix. 9.
19 For l the law made nothing perfect, but the bring-
m Eph. ii. 18. & iii. 12. Chap. iv. 16.
ing in of a better hope *did*; by the which m we draw
nigh unto God. 20 And inasmuch as not without an
oath *he was made priest*, 21 (For those priests were made
without an oath; but this with an oath, by him that
n Ps. cx. 4.
said unto him, n The Lord sware, and will not repent,
o Chap. viii. 6. & ix. 15. & xii. 24.
Thou *art* a priest for ever after the order of Melchisedec)
22 By so much o was Jesus made a surety of a better
testament. 23 And they truly were many priests, be-
cause they were not suffered to continue by reason of
death: 24 But this *man*, because he continueth ever, hath
an unchangeable priesthood. 25 Wherefore he is
Or, ever. p Rom. viii. 34.
able also to save them || to the uttermost, that come unto
God by him, seeing he ever liveth p to make intercession
q Chap. iv. 15.
for them. 26 For such an high priest became us, q *who*
is holy, harmless, undefiled, separate from sinners, and
r Eph. i. 20. Chap. viii. 1.
r made higher than the heavens; 27 Who needeth not
s Lev. ix. 7. & xvi. 6, 15. Chap. v. 3. & ix. 7.
daily, as those high priests, to offer up sacrifice, s first for
t Chap. ix. 12, 28. & x. 12.
his own sins, and then for the people's: for t this he did
once, when he offered up himself. 28 For the law
u Chap. v. 1, 2.
maketh u men high priests, which have infirmity; but
x Chap. ii. 10. & v. 9.
the word of the oath, which was since the law, *maketh* the
Son, x who is || consecrated for evermore.
|| Gr. perfected.

v. 11—28 Had perfection been by the Levitical priesthood, so that the consciences of the worshippers had thereby been fully purged from sin, and had the state of the church under the legal dispensation been complete, there could be no need that a new and higher order of priesthood should afterwards be instituted, after the order of Melchisedec and not after the order of Aaron, and such a change of the priesthood implied a change of the whole ceremonial law, which was inseparably interwoven therewith both law and priesthood therefore were to be abolished, in order to introduce another dispensation, more excellent and glorious than the former even that of the gospel. That such a change of the priesthood and law is made, is evident

1 Because our Lord, the priest who should rise after the order of Melchisedec, sprung from the tribe of Judah, not from Levi, and therefore, according to the law, was forbidden to offer at the altar

2 The priesthood of Christ was of an entirely different nature from that of the sons of Levi They *were made after the law of a carnal commandment*, which settled their succession, appointed the rites of their consecration, and those who filled the office were dying men, but Christ is made an high priest of a more excellent kind, *after the power of an endless life*, acting without either partner or successor, living to discharge his office in the behalf of his people for ever and ever

3 The efficacy of the gospel priesthood was far superior to that under the law, which was abrogated because of its weakness and unprofitableness, being insufficient to purge the conscience from guilt, or to secure unto the sinner justification to life, making nothing *perfect*, and was designed merely to lead us to Christ that we might be justified by faith But Christ hath brought in a *better hope*, his own sacrifice and abiding priesthood give boldness and access to God, and sure hope of favour and acceptance before him

4 The superior excellence of Christ's priesthood appears in the manner of his consecration The Levitical priests were made without an oath, but he, with an oath, to denote the immutability, efficacy, and eternity of his sacerdotal character *By so much was Jesus made a surety of a better testament*, or *covenant*, having undertaken completely to answer all the divine requirements on the behalf of his redeemed, that he might secure to them the accomplishment of all the promised blessings, a covenant far better than the Mosaical, both in the clearness of the light which accompanies its administration, and the extensiveness of its efficacy, as reaching to Gentiles as well as Jews

5 The Aaronical high priests, as mortal men, were many, succeeding each other, as death removed them from their office, but this glorious person, whom Melchisedec typified, hath an unchangeable priesthood that never passes from him, because he liveth for ever to discharge his sacerdotal functions *wherefore* we may assuredly conclude that Jesus *is able to save them to the uttermost, that come unto God by him, seeing he ever liveth to make intercession for them*, and therefore they can be in no circumstances of distress or danger from which he cannot deliver them, and his exaltation at the right hand of God is on purpose for their benefit, that he may so manage all their affairs as effectually to secure their final salvation, whilst coming to God by him they receive continual pardon, grace, and strength, to preserve them unto the end

6 Christ appears transcendently glorious above all other priests in his moral qualifications *For such an high priest became us*, and no other could have stood us in any stead, but one who is *holy, harmless, undefiled and separate from sinners*, both in nature and practice, *and made higher than the heavens*, in dignity above the angelic host, or rather, in purity of nature, excelling them. *Who needeth not daily, as those high priests* of the Levitical order, *to offer up sacrifice, first for their own sins, and then for the sins of the people*, on the great day of atonement, for Christ, having no sin of his own to expiate, needed no sacrifice, and as to his people's iniquities, his one sacrifice was available for ever *for this he did once, when he offered up himself* without spot to God, as their everlasting propitiation *For the law maketh men high priests, which have infirmity*, and, being sinners as well as others, must offer for themselves as well as the people, *but the word of the oath which was since the law, maketh the Son high priest, who is consecrated for evermore*, or *perfected*, who being in nature sinless and impeccable, never could need a sacrifice for himself, but having offered one of eternal efficacy on the behalf of his people, lives for ever to plead it in the presence of God, that they might reap the unutterably blessed fruits of it in their final and everlasting salvation

CHAP VIII

In this chapter the apostle pursues his former subject, the priesthood of Christ And, 1 He sums up what he had already said, ver 1 2 2 He sets before them the necessary parts of the priestly office, ver 3, 4, 5 And, 3 Largely illustrates the excellency of the priesthood of Christ, by considering the excellency of the new dispensation of the covenant of grace, of which Christ is the mediator, ver 6 to the end

1 NOW of the things which we have spoken, *this is*
the sum: We have such an high priest, a who
a Eph. i. 20. Chap. i. 3. & x. 12. & xii. 2.
is set on the right hand of the throne of the Majesty in
the heavens; 2 A minister || of the sanctuary, and of
|| Or, of holy things. b Chap. ix. 11.
b the true tabernacle, which the Lord pitched, and not man.

v. 1, 2 We have here a summary of the foregoing observations *Now of the things which we have spoken, this is the sum We have such an high priest*, so great and glorious, *who is set on the right hand of the throne of the Majesty in the heavens*, invested with all power and authority to secure all blessedness for his people in time and in eternity, *a minister of the sanctuary*, officiating as our high priest in heaven, which the Jewish sanctuary typified, *and of the true tabernacle* in his human nature, of which the

the earthly tabernacle was the figure, *which God pitched, and not man*, having prepared for him a body, wherein the fulness of the godhead should reside. And with what confidence should this inspire us, when we consider who now ministers for us before the throne of God!

3 For [c] every high priest is ordained to offer gifts
and sacrifices: wherefore [d] *it is* of necessity that this man
have somewhat also to offer. 4 For if he were on earth,
he should not be a priest, seeing that there are priests that
offer gifts according to the law: 5 Who serve unto the
example [e] and shadow of heavenly things, as Moses was
admonished of God, when he was about to make the ta-
bernacle: [f] For see (saith he) *that* thou make all things
according to the pattern shewed to thee in the mount.
6 But now [g] hath he obtained a more excellent ministry,
by how much also he is the mediator of a better † co-
venant, which was established upon better promises.
7 For if that first *covenant* had been faultless, then
should no place have been sought for the second. 8 For
finding fault with them, he saith, [h] Behold, the days
come, saith the Lord, when I will make a new covenant
with the house of Israel, and with the house of Judah:
9 Not according to the covenant that I made with their
fathers in the day when I took them by the hand to lead
them out of the land of Egypt; because they continued
not in my covenant, and I regarded them not, saith the
Lord. 10 For [i] this *is* the covenant that I will make
with the house of Israel after those days, saith the Lord;
I will ‡ put my laws into their mind, and write them in
their hearts: and [k] I will be to them a God, and they
shall be to me a people: 11 And [l] they shall not teach
every man his neighbour, and every man his brother,
saying, Know the Lord: for all shall know me, from
the least to the greatest. 12 For I will be merciful to
their unrighteousness, and [m] their sins and their iniquities
will I remember no more. 13 In that he saith, A new
covenant, he hath made the first old. Now that which
decayeth and waxeth old, *is* ready to vanish away.

c Chap. v. 1. d Eph. v. 2. Chap. ix. 14. e Col. ii. 17. Chap. x. 1. f Exod. xxv. 40. Acts vii. 44. g 2 Cor. iii. 6. Chap. vii. 22. † Or testament. h Jer. xxxi. 31—34. i Chap. x. 16. ‡ Gr. give. k Zech. viii. 8. l Isa. liv. 13. John vi. 45. 1 John ii. 27. m Chap. x. 17.

v. 3—13. The apostle proceeds,

1. To set forth the office of the high priest, and Christ's conformity thereto. *For every high priest is ordained to offer gifts and sacrifices*, the blood of which he afterwards carried into the holy place: *wherefore it is of necessity that this* glorious person *have somewhat also to offer*, a sacrifice suitable to his dignity, with the blood of which he might appear within the veil, before the throne of God in glory. *For if he were on earth*, and had continued here below, *he should not be a priest*, nor could have discharged the most peculiar part of his pontifical office, the appearing within the veil with the blood of the sacrifice, *seeing that there are priests that offer gifts according to the law*, and none of any other tribe but that of Levi could be admitted there: *who serve unto the example and shadow of heavenly things*, that priesthood and service being merely typical of Christ, *as Moses was admonished of God, when he was about to make the tabernacle: For see (saith he) that thou make all things according to the pattern shewed to thee in the mount.* Necessary therefore was it that Christ, having offered his own body a sacrifice on the cross, should, with the blood which he had shed, appear in the presence of God, and discharge that glorious high priesthood whereunto he had been appointed.

2. He shews the transcendent excellency of Christ's ministry above that of the sons of Aaron, as being *the mediator of a better covenant, established upon better promises.* The covenant of grace, as revealed in the gospel, far exceeding the Sinai covenant, whether considered as a *political covenant of peculiarity*, and ensuring to the people temporal blessings, merely as the fruit of an external obedience to the letter of the law; or if we admit its latitude to be more extensive, and that *it included spiritual and eternal blessings*, yet as that dispensation was clothed with darkness and terror, the gospel far exceeds it, as containing a more clear revelation of God's grace, extending its promises to Gentiles as well as Jews, being accompanied with a more abundant measure of the Spirit, and more particularly and fully leading the soul to seek and expect, not so much temporal, as spiritual and heavenly blessings. *For if that first covenant*, entered into with the Jews at Sinai, *had been faultless*, (for however well suited to answer the purposes of God at that time, yet it was deficient, and wanted much of that light and clearness, with which afterwards God intended to reveal his designs of grace) could that have been sufficient to accomplish the great end God had in view, *then should no place have been sought for the second*, as we find was the case. *For God finding fault with them*, and reproving the Jews by the prophet Jeremiah, *he saith, Behold, the days come, saith the Lord, when I will make* or finish *a new covenant with the house of Israel, and with the house of Judah*, a covenant of absolute promises, and sure to all the spiritual Israel, Gentiles as well as Jews: *not according to the covenant that I made with their fathers in the day when I took them by the hand to lead them out of the land of Egypt, because they continued not in my covenant*, but unfaithfully departed from it, *and I regarded them not, saith the Lord*, withdrew my favour from them, and no longer, as a husband, vouchsafed them my love and protection. *For this is the covenant that I will make with the house of Israel after those days, saith the Lord*, with the spiritual Israel of all nations, *I will put my laws into their mind, and write them in their hearts*, giving them the clearest views of my designs of grace, and engaging their souls to my love and service, by the powerful operations of my Spirit, making a deeper and more abiding impression upon their hearts, than the letters of law made on the tables of stone: *and I will be to them a God*, absolutely and everlastingly reconciled to them, and causing them to experience my continual protection and blessing, *and they shall be to me a people*, engaged to serve me by the most effectual ties of gratitude as well as duty, and secured in their allegiance by my effectual grace, so that they shall never depart from me. *And they shall not need to teach every man his neighbour, and every man his brother, saying, Know the Lord*, as under the former dispensation, where all the typical service required constant explication; but under the clearer dispensation of light and truth in the gospel this would be less necessary; not that the ministry of the word, or private instructions among Christians, should be set aside, but that in those days the knowledge of divine things should be more universally diffused, and all believers be under the more abundant teachings of the Spirit: *for all shall know me from the least unto the greatest*, as their reconciled God and Father in the great Redeemer, whatever difference there may be as to the degree of their attainments. *For I will be merciful to their unrighteousness*, through the propitiation of their great high priest, *and their sins and their iniquities will I remember no more*, pardoning them freely, fully, and for ever. Now *in that he saith, A new covenant, he hath made the first old*, abolishing the Mosaical dispensation, because of its weakness and unprofitableness. *Now that which decayeth and waxeth old*, as is the case with the Jewish œconomy at present, that, like a person dying with age, *is ready to vanish away*, the time being at hand, when, by the destruction of the temple, the whole service must cease, never to be resumed again. *Note*, (1.) Our fidelity to God in the covenant of grace depends upon his having engaged for our stability. (2.) God freely and for ever pardons the sins of his people; they shall sink as a stone in the abyss of water, and never rise up again. (3.) The dispensation of the covenant of grace, under which we live, should be matter of our unspeakable comfort and unceasing thankfulness, wherein all the riches of God's grace, without a veil, are laid open before his chosen people, and their eternal happiness infallibly secured.

CHAP. IX.

The apostle, in pursuance of his main design, proceeds to treat, 1. Of the tabernacle, the place of worship, ver. 1—6. 2. Of the worship and services performed in the tabernacle, ver. 6, 7. 3. Delivers the spiritual sense and the main design of all, ver. 8. to the end.

1 THEN verily the first *covenant* had also ‖ ordi-
nances of divine service, and a worldly sanctuary.
2 For there was a tabernacle made, [a] the first, [b] wherein
was the candlestick, and [c] the table, and the shew-
bread, which is called the sanctuary. 3 And [d] after the
second veil, the tabernacle which is called the holiest of
all: 4 Which had the golden censer, and [e] the ark of
the covenant overlaid round about with gold, wherein *was*
[f] the golden pot that had manna, and [g] Aaron's rod that
budded, and [h] the tables of the covenant; 5 And [i] over
it the cherubims of glory shadowing the mercy-seat: of
which we cannot now speak particularly.

‖ Or ceremonies. a Exod. xl. 4. b Exod. xxvi. 35. c Exod. xxv. 30. Lev. xxiv. 5, 8. d Exod. xxvi. 31. e Exod. xxv. 10, & xxvi. 33. f Exod. xvi. 33, 34. g Numb. xvii. 10. h Exod. xxv. 21. Deut. x. 2, 5. 1 Kings viii. 9. 2 Chron. v. 10. i Exod. xxv. 18, 22.

v. 1—5. The apostle begins with an account of the tabernacle, where the chief part of the service under the Mosaical dispensation, or first covenant, was performed. It consisted of two parts.

1. *The outward*, where stood the candlestick of beaten gold, and the table, with the shew-bread laid thereon; and this was called the sanctuary, where the daily service of God was performed. The whole building was figurative of Christ's body; the candlestick pointed him out as the true light who should come into the world, where, without him, spiritual darkness must have been for ever spread abroad; and the table of shew-bread pointed him out as the living bread that cometh down from heaven, and giveth life unto the world, upon whom his people, consecrated to be spiritual priests, feed, and maintain the most endeared communion thereby with each other.

2. *The inward*, which a second veil separated from the outer part of the tabernacle, and was called the holiest of all, the figure of heaven itself, into which none entered but the high priest alone once a year, on the great day of expiation, with *the golden censer* full of incense, which typified Christ entering then in heaven for his

his people, and there stood *the ark of the covenant overlaid round about with gold*, which signified him who was to be the end of the law for righteousness to every one that believeth, wherein were the tables of the law written with the finger of God, and, by the side of it, *the golden pot that had manna*, which was miraculously preserved from putrefaction, signifying the daily living bread with which Christ feeds his Israel in this howling wilderness, giving them meat to eat which the world knoweth not of. There also was *Aaron's rod that budded*, from a dry stick producing flowers and fruit, emblematical of him who rose as the rod out of the stem of Jesse, to be by divine appointement our high priest for ever. And over the ark were the cherubims of beaten gold, two winged figures, *that shadowed the mercy-seat*, over which the glorious shekinah dwelt, and on which the blood was sprinkled in the great day of atonement, intimating to us that Christ, as our propitiatory, interposes between the wrath of a holy God and the transgressors of his law, to save us from the eternal ruin which must otherwise necessarily ensue. But into the mystical meaning of these things the apostle waves to enter, *of which we cannot now speak particularly*. Let us not therefore too curiously pry into them, nor affect to be wise above that which is written.

6. Now when these things were thus ordain'd, [k] the
priests went always into the first tabernacle, accomplishing
the service *of God*. 7 But into the second *went* the high
priest alone once every year, not without blood, which
he offered for himself, and *for* the errors of the people.

[k] Num xxviii 3. [l] Ex xxx 10. Lev xvi 2, 15, 34. Ver 25.

v 6, 7. The tabernacle being prepared, we are told what service was performed in it.

1. In the outer part of the tabernacle the ordinary priests every day officiated, burning incense, trimming the lamps, and accomplishing all the service appointed them.

2. Into the *second* tabernacle, within the vail, went *the high priest alone once a year*, on one day only, and then *not without blood, which he offered* as an atonement *for himself and for the errors of the people*, intimating hereby that there was no access to God but through the blood of atonement, even the blood of him whom all the sacrifices represented, and whose intercession on the behalf of his people could only be available.

8 [m] The holy Ghost this signifying, [n] that the way in-
to the holiest of all was not yet made manifest, while as
the first tabernacle was yet standing. 9. Which *was* a
figure for the time then present, in which were offered
both gifts and sacrifices, [o] that could not make him that
did the service perfect, as pertaining to the conscience,
10 *Which stood* only in [p] meats, and drinks, and [q] divers
washings, and carnal † ordinances imposed *on them* until
the time of reformation. 11 But Christ being come an
high priest of good things to come, [s] by a greater and
more perfect tabernacle, not made with hands, that is to
say, not of this building, 12 Neither by the blood of
goats and calves, but [t] by his own blood he entred
in [u] once into the holy place, [x] having obtained eternal
redemption *for us*. 13 For if [y] the blood of bulls and
of goats, and [z] the ashes of an heifer sprinkling the un-
clean, sanctifieth to the purifying of the flesh, 14 How
much more [a] shall the blood of Christ, [b] who through the
eternal Spirit [c] offered himself without ‡ spot to God,
[d] purge your conscience from [e] dead works [f] to serve the
living God?

[m] Chap x 19, 20. [n] John xiv 6. [o] Chap vii 18. Gal iii 21. [p] Lev xi 2. [q] Num xix 7, &c. † Or rites or ceremonies. [r] Chap ii 17. [s] Chap viii 2. [t] Acts xx 28. Eph i 7. 1 Pet i 19. Rev i 5. [u] Ver 26, 28. [x] Dan ix 24. [y] Lev xvi 14, 16. [z] Num xix 2, 17, &c. [a] 1 Pet i 19. 1 John i 7. Rev i 5. [b] Rom i 4. [c] Eph v 2. ‡ Or fault. [d] Chap x 22. [e] Chap vi 1. [f] Luke i 74. 1 Pet iv 2.

v 8—14. The apostle here proceeds to declare the design of the Holy Ghost in these ritual services.

1. He signified hereby, *that the way into the holiest of all was not yet made manifest, while as the first tabernacle was yet standing*: in that dark dispensation, the way of access to a throne of grace, and of admission into heaven itself through the blood and righteousness of the Redeemer, was not so clearly and fully laid open, as it should afterwards be under the gospel.

2. The tabernacle was *a figure for the time then present*, suited to that more obscure dispensation, and the shadow of good things to come, till he who was the substance of them should appear, and then it would become useless.

3. The gifts and sacrifices there offered could not make the worshippers perfect, but though they were available to the purifying of the flesh, and exculpated them from suffering the temporal punishments, due to them as offenders against God considered as their political sovereign, they could not purge the conscience from moral evil, appease the fears of guilt, or secure from eternal punishment, any further than they led them to Christ, who was in these sacrifices prefigured, that so they might be justified by faith; for these sacrifices could little avail, standing *only in meats, and drinks, and divers washings, and carnal ordinances*, and rites which accompanied them, and may be considered as a burden *imposed on them until the time of reformation*, when Christ in his gospel should free his spiritual Israel from this heavy yoke.

4. Christ hath appeared and accomplished all that was here prefigured concerning him. *But Christ being come an high priest of good things to come*, on purpose to procure all spiritual and eternal blessings for his people, *by a greater and more perfect tabernacle*, even of his own body, wherein dwelt all the fulness of the godhead, *not made with hands, that is to say, not of this building*, but formed by the Holy Ghost from the substance of a virgin; *neither by the blood of goats and calves*, which was all the Levitical priests could offer, *but by* a sacrifice infinitely more excellent hath made the atonement, even by offering his own body on the tree, and with *his own blood*, of everlasting efficacy, *he entered in once into the holy place*, even into heaven itself, there for ever to abide, and plead the merit of that sacrifice which he had offered, *having obtained eternal redemption for us* by this one oblation. *For if the blood of bulls and of goats, and the ashes of an heifer sprinkling the unclean, sanctifieth to the purifying of the flesh*, and under the Mosaical œconomy readmitted those who were unclean, and excluded from the public worship, to the congregation of the faithful, *how much more shall the blood of Christ*, the efficacy of which is so infinitely greater, *who through the eternal Spirit*, which dwelt in his perfectly pure human nature, *offered himself without spot unto God*, a lamb meet to bleed on God's altar, how shall not this, I say, much more *purge your conscience from dead works*, from all your sins, however great and aggravated, the wages of which must have been eternal death, and restore you *to serve the living God*, in all holy and willing obedience, regarding him now as your reconciled God and Father, through the Son of his love Christ Jesus? *Note*, (1.) The redemption which the Saviour hath obtained for his people is *eternal*, not merely from present sin and guilt, but includes the purchase of everlasting glory for them. (2.) The oblation which he once offered effectually accomplished this, and left nothing for them to do, but freely to come and receive the unsearchable riches of his grace. (3.) The excellence and availableness of Christ's sacrifice arises from the dignity of his person; he who offered his human nature upon the cross was very God, and that gave infinite value to the blood which he shed. (4.) Sin must eternally have destroyed all the human race but for this one oblation; nothing else could purge the sinner's conscience, but this is all-sufficient to save to the uttermost, and cleanse us from *all* sin. (5.) All whose consciences are purged by the blood of sprinkling, experience also the power of changing grace upon their hearts, and are thenceforward both inclined and enabled in righteousness and true holiness to serve the living God.

15 And [g] for this cause he is the Mediator of the
new testament, [h] that by means of death, [i] for the re-
demption of the transgressions that were under the first
testament, they which are called might receive the pro-
mise of eternal inheritance. 16 For where a testament
is, there must also of necessity be the death of the testator.
17 For [k] a testament *is* of force after men are dead:
otherwise it is of no strength at all whilst the testator
liveth. 18 Whereupon, [l] neither the first *testament* was
‡ dedicated without blood. 19 For when Moses had
spoken every precept to all the people according to the
law, [m] he took the blood of calves and of goats, with
water, and scarlet wool, and hyssop, and sprinkled both
the book and all the people, 20 Saying, [n] This *is* the
blood of the testament which God hath enjoined unto
you. 21 Moreover, [o] he sprinkled likewise with blood
both the tabernacle, and all the vessels of the ministry.
22 And almost all things are by the law purged with
blood, and [p] without shedding of blood is no remis-
sion.

[g] 1 Tim ii 5. Chap vii 22. [h] Rom v 6. 1 Pet iii 18. [i] Rom iii 25. [k] Gal iii 15. [l] Ex xxiv 6, &c. ‡ Or purified. [m] Ex xxiv 5, 6. Lev xvi 14, 15. [n] Ex xxiv 8. Mat xxvi 28. [o] Ex xxix 12, 36. Lev viii 15, & xvi 14, 16. [p] Lev xvii 11.

v 15—22. The covenant of grace is here considered under the nature of a *testamentary disposition*, we receiving all spiritual blessings, as the legacies left by our dying Lord.

And for this cause he is the Mediator of the New Testament, securing for his people, and bequeathing to them every blessing, *that by means of death*, whereby the covenant was ratified, and the full atonement made, *for the redemption of the transgressions that were under the first testament*, the efficacy of his sacrifice reaching back to the beginning, as well as to the end of time, *they which are called* to faith in him, in whatever age they may have lived, *might receive the promise of eternal inheritance*, which is inseparably connected with faith in his atoning blood. *For*, as among men, *where a testament* or will *is* made, *there must also of necessity be the death of the testator*, before the legacies bequeathed can be claimed, or paid, so was it necessary that Christ should die; *for a testament is of force only after men are dead: otherwise it is of no strength at all while the testator liveth. Whereupon, neither the first testament was dedicated without blood* of slain beasts, which typified the death and blood shedding of the great Redeemer. *For when Moses had spoken every precept to all the people according to the law, he took the blood of calves and of goats*, which had been

sacrificed,

ſacrificed, *with water, and ſcarlet wool, and hyſſop, and ſprinkled both the book and all the people*, in token of the ratification of all that was contained in the ſacred volume, and of the application of the bleſſings and benefits contained in the teſtament to the ſouls of the faithful, and this was figurative of that blood and water which flowed from the wounded ſide of the Redeemer, which, in its virtue, effectually cleanſes the conſciences of thoſe who believe from all guilt and defilement And thus Moſes bid them particularly to obſerve, *Saying, This is the blood of the teſtament which God hath enjoined unto you*, whereby it is ratified, and his faithfulneſs engaged for the fulfilment of all the promiſes therein contained *Moreover, he ſprinkled likewiſe with blood both the tabernacle, and all the veſſels of the miniſtry*, when they were made *And almoſt all things are by the law purged with blood*, wherein the ſacrifice and death of Chriſt were conſtantly held forth to them as the alone meritorious cauſe of the ſinner's acceptance, *and* that *without* the *ſhedding of* his *blood* there *is no remiſſion* of ſins

23 *It was* therefore neceſſary that the patterns of
things in the heavens ſhould be purified with theſe,
but the heavenly things themſelves with better ſa-
crifices than theſe 24 For Chriſt is not entred into
the holy places made with hands, [q] *which are* the
figures of the true, [r] but into heaven itſelf, [s] now to
appear in the preſence of God for us 25 Nor
yet that he ſhould offer himſelf often, [t] as the high
prieſt entreth into the holy place, every year with
blood of others 26 (For then muſt he often have
ſuffered ſince the foundation of the world) but now
[u] once [x] in the end of the world, hath he appeared to
put away ſin by the ſacrifice of himſelf 27 And
as it is appointed unto men once to die, but after
this the judgment 28 So [y] Chriſt was once [z] offered
to bear the ſins [a] of many, and unto them that look
for him ſhall he appear the ſecond time, without ſin,
unto ſalvation

[q] Chap viii 5 [r] Chap vi 20. [s] Rom viii 34 Chap vii 25 1 John ii 1 [t] Ex xxx 10 Lev xvi 34. Ver 7 [u] Chap. vii 27 & x 10. 1 Pe. iii 18 [x] 1 Cor x. 11 Eph. i 10 [y] Rom vi 10 1 Pet iii. 18 [z] 1 Pet ii. 24 [a] Mat xxvi 28 Rom v 15 1 John iii 5.

v 23—28 From what he had advanced, the apoſtle argues,

That *it was therefore neceſſary*, by divine appointment, *that the pattern of things in the heavens*, the tabernacle and all the veſſels, *ſhould be purified with theſe* typical ſacrifices, and ſprinklings of blood, *but the heavenly things themſelves with better ſacrifices than theſe*, even the offering of Jeſus himſelf, who by his own blood ratified the covenant of grace, and being through his ſacrifice conſecrated to his office as the great high prieſt, entered into heaven, there to preſent his blood before the throne, and prepare manſions for the reception of his people *For Chriſt is not*, like the Jewiſh high prieſts, *entered into the holy places made with hands, which are the figures of the true, but into heaven itſelf, now to appear in the preſence of God for us*, and effectually to inſure to us all the bleſſings which, by his blood-ſhedding, he hath purchaſed *nor* was his ſacrifice incomplete, as *yet* again to require *that he ſhould offer himſelf often, as the high prieſt entreth into the holy place, every year with the blood of others*, of the animals which were ſacrificed *(for then muſt he often have ſuffered ſince the foundation of the world)* and the fall of man, *but now once in the end of the world*, at the cloſe of the Jewiſh œconomy, and at the beginning of the laſt and moſt excellent diſpenſation, under the goſpel, *hath he appeared to put away ſin by the ſacrifice of himſelf*, ſuffering in the human nature, and, by the divine glory of his perſon, offering ſuch a complete and all-ſufficing ſacrifice, as never needed a repetition, the efficacy thereof extending to every believer to the lateſt ages of time *And as it is appointed unto men once to die*, returning to the duſt from whence they came, and *but* once, for *after this* bodily death is *the* final *judgment*, when all muſt appear at God's bar, and ſtand or fall to eternity *ſo Chriſt was once offered* upon the croſs *to bear the ſins of many*, and made there a full atonement by his one oblation, *and unto them that look for him*, in faith and love, expecting his return, *ſhall he appear*, not as a ſuffering but a glorified Saviour, *without ſin*, having taken it all away, and being now manifeſted to bring his people *unto* that complete and perfect *ſalvation* in glory, which he hath obtained for them *Note*, (1) Die we muſt, ſuch is the divine decree, highly therefore doth it import us to prepare for this awful change (2) Judgment follows cloſe at the heels of death, and as the tree falleth, it muſt lie for ever (3) Chriſt hath borne *the ſins of many*, not of every individual of the human ſpecies, but of *the many* ſons whom he is appointed to bring unto glory (4) He that ſuffered upon a croſs ſhall ſhortly appear upon the throne, and a terrible judge will he be found to thoſe who have not embraced him as a Saviour (5) It is the character of his redeemed people that they *look* for the day of his appearing, earneſtly expecting his arrival, that they may obtain their perfect conſummation both in body and ſoul in his kingdom of everlaſting glory

CHAP X

To wean the Hebrews from the Levitical diſpenſation, he proceeds in this chapter, 1 *To lay low the whole of that prieſthood and ſervice*, ver 1—7 2 *He raiſes and exalts the prieſthood of Chriſt very high, that he might effectually recommend him and his goſpel to them*, ver 7—19 3 *He ſhews to believers the honours and dignities of their ſtate, and calls them to ſuitable duties*, ver 19, to the end

1 FOR the law having [a] a ſhadow of good things to
come, *and* not the very image of the things,
[b] can never with thoſe ſacrifices which they offered year
by year continually make the comers thereunto [c] perfect
2 For then, † would they not have ceaſed to be offered?
becauſe that the worſhippers once purged ſhould have
had no more conſcience of ſins 3 But in thoſe *ſacrifices*
[d] *there is* a remembrance again *made* of ſins every year
4 For [e] *it is* not poſſible that the blood of bulls and of
goats ſhould take away ſins 5 Wherefore when he
cometh into the world, he ſaith, [f] Sacrifice and offering
thou wouldſt not, but a body haſt thou prepared me
6 In burnt-offerings and *ſacrifices* for ſin thou haſt had
no pleaſure 7 Then, ſaid I, Lo, I come (*in the volume*
of the book it is written of me) to do thy will, O God
8 Above, when he ſaid, Sacrifice, and offering, and
burnt offerings, and *offering* for ſin thou wouldſt not,
neither hadſt pleaſure *therein*, (which are offered by the
law,) 9 Then ſaid he, Lo I come to do thy will, O
God He taketh away the firſt, that he may eſtabliſh
the ſecond 10 [g] By the which will we are ſanctified,
[h] through the offering of the body of Jeſus Chriſt once
for all 11 And every prieſt ſtandeth daily miniſtring
and offering oftentimes the ſame ſacrifices, [i] which can
never take away ſins 12 [k] But this man, after he had
offered one ſacrifice for ſins, for ever ſat down on the right
hand of God, 13 From henceforth expecting [l] till his
enemies be made his footſtool 14 For by one offering
he hath perfected [m] for ever them that are ſanctified
15 *Whereof* the holy Ghoſt alſo is a witneſs to us for
after that he had ſaid before, 16 [n] This *is* the cove-
nant that I will make with them after thoſe days, ſaith
the Lord, I will put my laws into their hearts, and in
their minds will I write them 17 ‡ And their ſins
and iniquities will I remember no more 18 Now
where remiſſion of theſe *is*, *there is* no more offering for
ſin

[a] Col ii 17 Chap viii 5 & ix 23 [b] Chap ix 9 [c] Ver 14 † Or, they would have ceaſed to be offered becauſe &c [d] Lev xvi 21 [e] Mic vi 7 Chap ix 13 [f] Pſ xl 6 &c Iſa i 11 Jer vi 20 Amos v 21 [g] John xvii 19 [h] Chap ix 12 & xiii 12 [i] Chap ix 9 [k] Chap i 3 [l] Pſ cx 1 1 Cor xv 25 Chap i 13 [m] Chap ix 12 [n] Jer xxxi 33 34 Chap viii 10 12 ‡ Some copies read, Then he ſaid, And their ſins &c.

v 1—18 The weakneſs and unprofitableneſs of the Levitical inſtitutions ſhould engage the Hebrews to receive, with greater cordiality, the bleſſed goſpel *For*,

1 *The law having a ſhadow of good things to come, and not the very image of the things*, all being figurative and typical of Chriſt, who ſhould, in the fulneſs of time, appear as the ſubſtance, *can never by theſe ſacrifices which they*, who were high prieſts, *offered from year to year continually make the comers thereunto perfect*, ſo as to ſatisfy God's juſtice, obtain reconciliation, and pacify the guilty conſcience *For then*, if this great end had been fully anſwered, *would they not have ceaſed to be offered?* What uſe would there have been for their repetition? *becauſe that the worſhippers once purged ſhould have had no more conſcience of ſins*, not have been under any further condemnation or diſtreſs of ſoul *But in thoſe ſacrifices there is a remembrance again made of ſins every year*, which ſhews that the former ſacrifices had not perfectly atoned for them Nor indeed could they, *for it is not poſſible that the blood of bulls and of goats ſhould take away ſins*, making an adequate compenſation to Divine Juſtice, or that the death of a beaſt ſhould be a proper and effectual atonement for the ſin of the ſoul A better ſacrifice than theſe was required, and all the uſe of theſe typical ones was to lead them to Chriſt, whoſe blood alone could ſatisfy for ſin *Wherefore*,

2 *When he cometh into the world he ſaith, Sacrifice and offering thou wouldſt not, but a body haſt thou prepared me*, in which to make that atonement for which the legal ſacrifices were ineffectual *In burnt-offerings and ſacrifices for ſin thou haſt had no pleaſure Then, ſaid I, Lo! I come* (as *in the volume of the book* of prophecy *it is written of me*) *to do thy will, O God*, well pleaſed and content to ſuffer all that Juſtice demands to make ſatisfaction for the ſins of my people *Above when he ſaid, Sacrifice, and offering, and burnt-offerings, and offering for ſin thou wouldſt not, neither hadſt pleaſure therein, (which are offered by the law,) then ſaid he, Lo, I come to do thy will, O God*, and to take away ſin by the ſacrifice of myſelf *He taketh away the firſt* covenant, with all the legal ſacrifices, becauſe of their inſufficiency, *that he may eſtabliſh the ſecond*, thro his own all atoning blood

3 In virtue of his oblation the moſt invaluable bleſſings are ſecured to us *By the which will* of God, as fulfilled in Chriſt, *we are ſanctified*, our ſins expiated, and our conſciences purged from their defilement, *through the offering of the body of Jeſus once for all*, wherein may be obſerved another ſingular excellence of our High-prieſt *and* his ſacrifice above all others, for *every prieſt* STANDETH, with awful diſtance, and continues DAILY *miniſtring, and offering* OFTENTIMES THE SAME SACRIFICES, all *which* things ſhewed the imperfection of that diſpenſation, and after all, theſe *can never take away ſin*, ſo as to ſatisfy God's juſtice, or relieve the guilty conſcience, *but this man*, the glorious Jeſus, *after he had offered* ONE *ſacrifice for ſins*, fully accompliſhed his work, and never needed to offer another, and *for ever* SAT DOWN, in a ſtate of endleſs reſt and moſt tranſcendent dignity, *on the right hand of God*, *from henceforth expecting till all his enemies be made his footſtool*, and Satan, ſin, the world, and death, ſhall at laſt be deſtroyed for ever *For by one offering he hath perfected for ever them that are ſanctified*, in his blood and righteouſneſs they ſtand complete before God, are regarded by him as without ſpot, and, through the powerful efficacy of divine faith, their hearts are renewed and dedicated to God *Whereof the Holy Ghoſt alſo is a witneſs to us for after that he had ſaid before, This is the covenant that I will make with them after thoſe days, ſaith the Lord, I will put my laws into their hearts, and in their minds will I write them, and their ſins and iniquities will I remember no more*, ſo that they ſhall be abſolutely, fully, and for ever done away *Now where remiſſion of theſe is*, in ſo complete a manner, *there is no more offering for ſin*, the one oblation of Chriſt's body on the croſs having ſatisfied to the uttermoſt *Note*, (1) All God's people are ſanctified, as well as juſtified, by the offering of the body of Jeſus once for all, thereby all grace, as well as pardon, was purchaſed for them (2) In Chriſt we are perfected for ever, and our title to glory was as complete when he died on the tree as when we ſhall appear before his throne (3) The abſolute and everlaſting pardon of ſin is one of the peculiar bleſſings of the covenant of grace (4) All the enemies of Chriſt and his people muſt ſooner or later become his footſtool he is ſat down on his throne, and ſhall reign till they are utterly deſtroyed

19 ° Having therefore, brethren, † boldneſs to enter
ᵖ into the holieſt by the blood of Jeſus, 20 ᑫ By a new
and living way which he hath ‡ conſecrated for us,
through the vail, that is to ſay, his fleſh, 21 And
having ʳ an high prieſt over the houſe of God 22 Let
us draw near with ˢ a true heart, ᵗ in full aſſurance of
faith, having our hearts ſprinkled ᵘ from an evil conſcience, and our bodies ˣ waſhed with pure water 23
ʸ Let us hold faſt the profeſſion of our faith without
wavering (for ᶻ he *is* faithful that promiſed) 24 And
let us conſider one another to provoke unto love, and to
good works 25 ᵃ Not forſaking the aſſembling of ourſelves together, as the manner of ſome *is*, but ᵇ exhorting *one another* and ſo much the more as ye ſee the day
approaching

° Rom v 2 Eph ii 18 & iii 12 † Or liberty ᵖ Chap ix 8 12 ᑫ John xiv 6 ‡ Or made new ʳ Chap iv 14 16 ˢ John iv 23 ᵗ Eph iii 12 Jam i 6 1 John iii 21 ᵘ Chap ix 14 ˣ Ezek xxxvi 25 ʸ Chap iv 14 ᶻ 1 Cor i 9 1 Theſ v 24 2 Theſ iii 3 ᵃ Acts ii 42 ᵇ Chap iii 13

v 19—25 The apoſtle, having concluded the doctrinal part of the epiſtle, proceeds to make a practical improvement of the whole

He reminds them of the ineſtimable privileges which through their great High-prieſt they enjoyed *Having therefore, brethren, boldneſs to enter into the holieſt*, and freedom and confidence in approaching a reconciled God, *by the blood of Jeſus*, ſprinkled with which we are aſſured of preſent and eternal acceptance before him, *by a new and living way which he hath conſecrated*, who is himſelf the way, the truth, and the life, and they who walk in him ſhall never die, and this *through the vail, that is to ſay, his fleſh*, for, when his body was broken on the tree, the vail of the temple was rent in twain from the top to the bottom, to ſhew, that every obſtruction in our way to a throne of grace and glory was now removed *and having an High-prieſt*, one ſo great and glorious, *over the houſe of God*, *let us*,

1 *Draw near* to God in every act of worſhip, and in the moſt endeared communion, *with a true heart*, in all ſimplicity and godly ſincerity, and *in full aſſurance of faith* in the all-ſufficiency of our Redeemer, and our reconciliation with God through him, *having our hearts ſprinkled from an evil conſcience*, with his atoning blood, which ſpeaks peace from all guilt and condemnation, *and our bodies waſhed with pure water*, cleanſed by the powerful operations of the Holy Ghoſt, which the Jewiſh waſhing prefigured

2 *Let us hold faſt the profeſſion of our faith without wavering* not ſeduced by temptation, diſmayed with oppoſition, or diſtruſting the grace engaged for our ſupport *for he is faithful that promiſed*, and we may ſafely repoſe on his word our everlaſting all

Yea, 3 *Let us conſider one another*, our reſpective trial, dangers, wants, and weakneſs, in order *to provoke each other unto love* toward Jeſus and the brethren, *and to good works*, ſuch as may adorn our high profeſſion

4 Let us be united in heart and worſhip, *not forſaking the aſſembling of ourſelves together, as the manner of ſome is*, who, on weak and frivolous pretences, abſent from the congregation of the faithful and the communion of the Lord, a ſad ſymptom of declenſion, and often the prelude to apoſtacy

5 Let us never be ſlack and remiſs in holy jealouſy over ourſelves and our brethren, *but be exhorting one another* to give all diligence to make our calling and election ſure, in the uſe of every appointed means of grace *and ſo much the more as ye ſee the day approaching*, when the whole Jewiſh polity and nation ſhall be deſtroyed, or when death muſt place you before the judgment-ſeat of Chriſt An awful conſideration! which, the more deeply it dwells upon our minds will excite our moſt awakened ſollicitude to be always ready for our great change

26 For ᶜ if we ſin wilfully ᵈ after that we have received the knowledge of the truth, there remaineth no
more ſacrifice for ſins, 27 But a certain fearful looking for of judgment, and ᵉ fiery indignation, which
ſhall devour the adverſaries 28 ᶠ He that deſpiſed
Moſes law died without mercy, ᵍ under two or three
witneſſes 29 ʰ Of how much ſorer puniſhment, ſuppoſe ye, ſhall he be thought worthy, who hath troden
under foot the Son of God, and hath counted ⁱ the blood
of the covenant wherewith he was ſanctified, an unholy
thing, and ᵏ hath done deſpite unto the Spirit of grace?
30 For we know him that hath ſaid, ˡ Vengeance *belongeth* unto me, I will recompenſe, ſaith the Lord
And again, ᵐ The Lord ſhall judge his people 31 ⁿ *It
is* a fearful thing to fall into the hands of the living
God

ᶜ Num xv 30 Chap vi 4, & 1 John v 16 ᵈ 2 Pet ii 20, 21 ᵉ Ezek xxxvi 5 Zeph i 18 & iii 8 2 Theſ i 8 ᶠ Ex xxxii 27 Lev xxiv 14 Num xv 35—36 ᵍ Deut xvii 6 & xix 15 ʰ Chap xii 25 ⁱ Chap xiii 20 ᵏ Acts v 3, 9 ˡ Deut xxxii 35 Rom xii 19 ᵐ Deut xxxii 36 Pſ l 4 ⁿ Luke xii 5 Chap xii 29

v 26—31 To awaken their more abundant concern, the apoſtle ſets before them the dreadful evil and danger of apoſtacy

For if we ſin wilfully, after that we have received the knowledge of the truth, which doth not mean every ſin that through infirmity or temptation we may be drawn into nor even deliberate or repeated acts of ſin, but ſuch a courſe of iniquity, embraced with full conſent of the mind, as leads to an utter rejection of the goſpel, and denial of Jeſus Chriſt in which caſe, the only remedy being rejected, *there remaineth no more ſacrifice for ſins*, nor any poſſibility of pardon, *but a certain fearful looking for of judgment, and fiery indignation, which ſhall devour the adverſaries*, ſuch as ſhortly muſt ſeize the infidel Jews, when they ſhall be buried in the ruins of their city, and awaits the finally impenitent in the great day of God's wrath, when the wicked ſhall be caſt into hell, where their worm dieth not, and the fire is not quenched Even *he that deſpiſed Moſes's law died without mercy, under two or three witneſſes*, and no ſacrifice was appointed for preſumptuous ſins *of how much ſorer puniſhment then, ſuppoſe ye, ſhall he be thought worthy*, whoſe offence is ſo infinitely more aggravated, *who hath troden under foot the Son of God*, treating him with the direſt inſolence and contempt as an impoſtor, denying his Deity, deſpiſing his atonement and righteouſneſs, and mocking at his grace, *and hath counted the blood of the covenant, wherewith he was ſanctified, an unholy thing*, of leſs efficacy than the blood of bulls and goats, yea, as the Jews intimated at his crucifixion, viler than that of the greateſt miſcreants, *and hath done deſpite unto the Spirit of grace*, imputing his miracles to diabolical power, and calling his operations upon the hearts of men deluſion and enthuſiaſm Such blaſphemy is unpardonable, and muſt bring down the heavieſt wrath of an offended God *For we know him that hath ſaid, Vengeance belongeth unto me, I will recompenſe, ſaith the Lord*, and puniſh incorrigible offenders according to their wickedneſs *And again, The Lord ſhall judge his people*, will detect the hypocrites, and as ſurely deſtroy the apoſtates as he will ſave the faithful *It is a fearful thing to fall into the hands of the living God*, whoſe wrath, if it be kindled, yea but a moment, who may abide it? Let us hear and tremble, and watch and pray, that we come not into this condemnation, and periſh with these deſpiſers

32 But ° call to remembrance the former days, in which
ᵖ after ye were illuminated, ye endured ᑫ a great fight of
afflictions 33 Partly whilſt ye were made ʳ a gazing-
ſtock, both by reproaches and afflictions, and partly
whilſt ˢ ye became companions of them that were ſo uſed
34 For ye had compaſſion of me in my bonds, and
ᵗ took joyfully the ſpoiling of your goods, knowing ‖ in
yourſelves that ᵘ ye have in heaven a better and an enduring ſubſtance 35 ˣ Caſt not away therefore your
confidence, ʸ which hath great recompenſe of reward
36 For ᶻ ye have need of patience, that after ye have
done the will of God, ye might receive the promiſe
37 For ᵃ yet a little while, and he that ſhall come will
come, and will not tarry 38 Now ᵇ the juſt ſhall live
by

° Gal iii 4 2 John 8 ᵖ Chap vi 4 ᑫ Phil i 29 Col ii 1 ʳ 1 Cor iv 9 ˢ Phil iv 14 1 Theſ ii 14 ᵗ Matt v 12 Acts v 41 Jam i 2 ‖ Or that ye have in or for your ſelves ᵘ Matt vi 20 & xix 21 Luke xii 33 ˣ Tim vi 19 ˣ Chap iv 14 ʸ Matt v 12 & x 32 ᶻ Luke xxi 19 ᵃ Heb vi Luke xviii 8 2 Pet iii 9 ᵇ Hab ii 4 Rom i 17 Gal iii 11

by faith . but if *any man* draw back, my soul shall have
c 1 Thes v 9 Chap vi 9 no pleasure in him 39 But [c] we are not of them who
d John iii 16 draw back unto perdition, but of them [d] that believe to
the saving of the soul

v 32—39 To excite the faithful steadily to persevere,

1 He reminds them of the past sufferings which they had so nobly undergone *But call to remembrance the former days, in which, after ye were illuminated*, and brought to the knowledge of the truth as it is in Jesus, *ye endured a great fight of afflictions*, and quitted yourselves manfully, as became those who were listed under the banner of the cross, *partly whilst ye were made a gazing-stock, both by reproaches and afflictions*, pointed at, treated as despicable and ridiculous, and as criminals exposed in the theatres to wild beasts, worried with the unrelenting malice and enmity of the wicked world, *and partly whilst ye became companions of them that were so used*, nobly owning them in their sufferings for righteousness sake, sympathizing with them, and affording them every assistance *For ye had compassion of me in my bonds*, tenderly affected for me, and supporting me to the utmost of your ability, *and took joyfully the spoiling of your goods*, content, yea glorying in your sufferings and losses, *knowing in yourselves*, from the fullest assurance of God's promises and the experience of his grace, *that ye have in heaven a better and an enduring substance*, which none can take from you, *Note*, (1) Every Christian must expect and welcome the cross (2) Though we may be skreened by Divine Providence and human laws from grosser violations of our property, the lash of slander, the bitterness of reproach, and the trial of cruel mockings, these we shall assuredly meet if we belong to Christ (3) God can make his people joyful under all their trials, and neither ashamed nor afraid to suffer for his sake (4) If we are of the body of Christ, none of his members suffer with whom we do not sympathize, and we shall own and honour them under their reproaches for his name's sake (5) If we gain heaven at last, we need be little concerned what we may lose by the way

2 He exhorts them to stand fast in the prospect of the glory which was before them *Cast not away therefore your confidence*, boldness and holy resolution, *which hath great recompence of reward*, and will secure for you a crown of glory which fadeth not away, and that will infinitely overbalance all your losses and sufferings *For ye have need of patience*, whilst the conflict continues, that ye may not be weary and faint in your mind, and *that after ye have done the will of God*, faithfully obedient to his word, and resigned to his providence, *ye might receive the promise* of the eternal inheritance *For yet a little while*, a very short moment, *and he that shall come will come, and will not tarry*, to execute vengeance upon his enemies, to vindicate the injuries of his people, and save them with his uttermost salvation *Note*, (1.) Faith and patience, held fast, secure our perseverance (2) Whatever trials oppress us, it is our comfort that the Judge standeth at the door, and that death shall quickly release us from every burden

3 He encourages and warns them alternately *Now the just shall live by faith*, or *the just by faith shall live*, in spite of every effort of sin, the world, and Satan, to destroy the life of God in their souls, yea, they shall live with him to eternity *but if any man draw back* from Christ and his gospel as apostates, *my soul*, saith God, *shall have no pleasure in him*, but, contrariwise, he will be the object of my abhorrence, and suffer all my furious indignation *But we are not of them who draw back unto perdition*, such confidence have I towards you, *but of them that* truly *believe to the saving of the soul*, faithful unto death, that we may receive the crown of life *Note*, (1) Many go far in profession, who after all prove apostates (2) They who have true faith will never draw back unto perdition (3) Past experience of God's keeping us should encourage our increasing confidence in his grace He will never leave nor forsake us, and then shall we never leave nor forsake him

CHAP XI

The apostle having, in the close of the foregoing chapter, recommended the grace of faith and a life of faith as the best preservative against apostasy, he now enlarges upon the nature and fruits of this excellent grace 1 The nature of it, and the honour it reflects upon all that live in the exercise of it, ver 1, 2, 3 2 The great examples we have in the Old Testament of those that lived by faith, and did and suffered extraordinary things by the strength of this grace, ver 4—39 And, 3 The advantages that we have in the gospel for the exercise of this grace above what they had that lived in the times of the Old Testament, ver 39, 40

† Or ground, or subsistence 1 NOW faith is the † substance of things hoped
a Rom viii 24 2 Cor iv 18 for, the evidence [a] of things not seen 2 For
b Ver 39 [b] by it the elders obtained a good report 3 Through
c Gen i 1 Ps xxxiii 6 faith we understand that [c] the worlds were framed by
John i 3 Chap i 2 the word of God, so that things which are seen were not
2 Pet iii 5 made of things which do appear.

v 1—3 We have here,

1 An account of the nature and effects of divine faith *Now faith is the substance of things hoped for*, giving such a realizing view of the promises, and such a subsistence of them to the mind, as if they were actually in our possession, *and the evidence of things not seen*, demonstrating as assuredly the certainty of the invisible things revealed in the divine word, as a mathematical proposition, when solved, carries the clearest conviction along with it

2 All the saints from the beginning have lived under its blessed influence *For by it the elders obtained a good report*, and were enabled so to walk as to obtain God's approbation of their conduct This from the first being the divine principle on which alone any work acceptable to God could ever be performed

3 One of the first articles of faith is this, *That the worlds were framed by the word of God*, who from nothing spake them into being, *so that the things which are seen*, even all the visible objects of creation, *were not made of things which do appear*, from any pre-existent matter, but from that chaotic mass, which was produced at the word of the Almighty.

4 By faith [d] Abel offered unto God a more excellent d Gen iv 4
sacrifice than Cain, by which he obtained witness that
he was righteous, God testifying of his gifts and by it
he being dead, [e] yet † speaketh 5 By faith [f] Enoch e Gen iv 10 Mat xxiii 35 Chap xii 24
was translated that he should not see death ; and was not † Or is spoken of
found, because God had translated him for before his f Gen v 24 Wisd iv 10 Ecclus xliv 16 & xlix 14
translation he had this testimony, that he pleased God.
6 But without faith *it is* impossible to please *him* for
[g] he that cometh to God, must believe that he is, and g Chap. x 22
that he is a rewarder of them that diligently seek him
7. By faith [h] Noah being warned of God of things not h Gen vi 13 Ecclus xliv 17
seen as yet, moved with fear, [i] prepared an ark to the i 1 Pet iii. 20
saving of his house, by the which he condemned the k Rom iii 22 & iv 13 Phil iii. 9
world, and became heir of [k] the righteousness which is
by faith

v 4—7 The apostle here begins to instance the power of divine faith in many of the eminent servants of God, and he begins with the antediluvian worthies

1 Abel *By Faith Abel offered unto God a more excellent sacrifice than Cain*, who only brought of the fruit of the ground, but offered no atoning sacrifice in acknowledgment of his sin, whilst Abel to his mincha or meat-offering added the blood of the firstlings of his flock, the type of the great atonement whereon his faith rested, *by which he obtained witness of God that he was righteous*, either by some visible token, as fire from heaven on his sacrifice, or by the witness of the Spirit in his heart, *God testifying of his works*, that they were accepted through the righteousness of faith, *and by it he, being dead, yet speaketh*, the record of it in the scripture instructs us, that, since the fall of man, the only way of access to God is through the atoning sacrifice of Jesus, and also that vengeance awaits the murderer and persecutor, against whom the blood of innocence and the cries of oppression cry for judgment *Note*, (1) The only access to God for sinners from the beginning was through the blood of Jesus (2) There is a great difference between those who worship God in formality, and faith It is not the act, but the way in which we present our prayers, which makes the acceptable offering (3) They who are righteous by faith, and have obtained witness from God, may expect the world's enmity The first most eminent saint recorded in scripture was a martyr for religion

2 Enoch *By faith Enoch was translated that he should not see death*, caught up to the paradise of God in body and soul, and instantly undergoing the change that fitted him for an eternal mansion in glory, *and was not found, because God had translated him for before his translation* to the realms of bliss, *he had this testimony, that he pleased God*, in a course of humble and holy walking, under the influence of divine faith in the expected seed of the woman; *see Jude 14, 15* *But without faith* in him *it is impossible to please* God *for he that cometh to God*, in any act of religious worship, *must believe that he is* such as he hath revealed himself to the sons of men, who never could have known either his being or attributes but by revelation, *and that he is a rewarder of them that diligently seek him*, in the use of all the ordinances which he hath appointed *Note*, (1) No service can please God, but what springs from faith as its origin (2.) God is the portion and exceeding great reward of all his people (3) There are appointed means, in which, God hath told us, they who wait upon him shall assuredly obtain his blessing, and in the use of them we cannot be too diligent

3 Noah *By faith Noah, being warned of God of things not seen as yet*, which reason could never have suggested, nor mortal know but by divine revelation, *moved with fear* and religious awe at the apprehension of the approaching judgments, *prepared an ark* according to God's direction, in defiance of the scoffs of the men of that generation, *to the saving of his house* from the approaching deluge, *by the which he condemned the world* his preaching and labours in building the ark witnessed against that

im-unbelieving world, who paid no regard to his works or word during the space of a hundred and twenty years, and thus left them without excuse, whilst he himself *became* hereby *heir of the righteousness which is by faith*, entitled to the complete salvation which the righteousness of that Redeemer in the fulness of time should purchase, whom the ark represented, and he by faith apprehended *Note*, (1) God sends his warnings before his judgments the latter come not till the former have been despised (2) Faith begets holy fear, silences all objections, and sets us to work for God in defiance of all opposition (3) They who will ever be saved from the deluge of wrath, must by faith take shelter in Christ their ark, for out of him there is no hope

8 By faith [l] Abraham, when he was called to go out
into a place which he should after receive for an inherit-
ance, obeyed, and he went out, not knowing whither
he went 9 By faith he sojourned in the land of pro-
mise, as *in* a strange country, dwelling in tabernacles
with Isaac and Jacob, the heirs with him of the same
promise 10 For he looked for [m] a city which hath
foundations [n] whose builder and maker *is* God 11
Through faith also [o] Sarah herself received strength to
conceive seed, and [p] was delivered of a child when she
was past age, because she judged [q] him faithful who had
promised 12 Therefore sprang there even of one,
and him as good as dead, [r] *so many* as the stars of the
sky in multitude, and as the sand which is by the sea-
shore innumerable 13 These all died in faith, not
having received the promises, but [s] having seen them
afar off, and were persuaded of *them*, and embraced *them*,
and [u] confessed that they were strangers and pilgrims on
the earth 14 For they that say such things declare
plainly that they seek a country 15 And truly, if they
had been mindful of that *country*, from whence they
came out, they might have had opportunity to have re-
turned 16 But now they desire a better *country*, that
is, an heavenly wherefore God is not ashamed [x] to be
called their God for [y] he hath prepared for them a city.
17 By faith [z] Abraham, when he was tried, offered up
Isaac and he that had received the promises, [a] offered up
his only begotten *son* 18 Of whom it was said, That
[b] in Isaac shall thy seed be called 19 Accounting that
[c] God was able to raise *him* up, even from the dead,
from whence also he received him in a figure

[l] Gen. xii 1 4 [m] Chap xi 22 & xiii 14 [n] Chap iii 4 Rev xxi 2 [o] Gen xvii 19 & xxi 2 [p] Luke i 36 [q] Rom. iv 21 Chap x 23 [r] Rom iv 19 [s] Gen xv 5 & xxii 17 & xxvi 4 Rom iv 18 [t] Ver 27 [u] Gen. xxiii 4 & xlvii 9 1 Chron xxix 15 Ps xxxix 12 & cxix 19 1 Pet i 17 & ii 11 [x] Ex iii 6 Mat xxii 32 Acts vii 32 [y] Phil iii 20 Chap. xiii 14 [z] Gen xxii 1 &c [a] Jam ii 21 [b] Gen xxi 12 Rom ix 7 [c] Rom iv 17, 19, 21

v 8—19 From the antediluvian patriarchs the apostle passes on to consider the case of the great father of the faithful, an example that should have peculiar weight with those who valued themselves on being his descendants

1 He mentions Abraham's call *By faith Abraham, when he was called to go out* from the land of his nativity *into a place which he should after receive for an inheritance, obeyed* without hesitation, fully persuaded of the truth, power, and grace of God to fulfil his promises *and he went out*, under divine guidance, and trusting on divine direction, *not knowing whither he went*, neither the country itself, nor the way which led to it *Note*, (1) Implicit faith is due to God's word, and though we know not how, yet we may be assured, however improbable it may appear to sense and reason, it shall be fulfilled in the appointed season (2) They who would go to the heavenly Canaan must, at God's call, come forth out of a world that lieth in wickedness (3) The inheritance of glory is secured to the faithful, and, whatever difficulties are in the way, they shall possess it at last

2 His sojourning in Canaan *By faith he sojourned in the land of promise, as in a strange country*, though proprietor of it by the divine grant, yet not holding the least part in possession, *dwelling in tabernacles*, without any settled abode, *with Isaac and Jacob the heirs with him of the same promise*, Jacob being fifteen years old at Abraham's death *For he looked for a city which hath foundations*, even the state of eternal glory above, which is represented as a city, (Rev xxii 14) *whose builder and maker is God*, he having prepared the heavenly mansions for his chosen *Note*, (1) The saints of God are here resident in tabernacles of clay, but mansions of glory await them in a better world (2) Faith, which realizes our hopes above, necessarily draws both our affections and desires after that blest world to which we go (3) All the trials of this mortal state will be regarded by us as light and transient, when we abidingly keep in view the far more exceeding and eternal weight of glory

3 The faith of Sarah is observed as closely connected with that of her husband Abraham *Through faith also Sarah herself*, though naturally barren, and now past the time of child-bearing, *received strength to conceive seed, and was delivered of a child when she was past age*, being ninety years old, *because*, notwithstanding she at first hesitated and laughed, as if the thing was impossible, yet her faith soon got the better of her unbelief; for *she judged him faithful who had promised*, and that he was able to perform what he had said *Therefore sprang there even of one, and him as good as dead* through old age, *so many as the stars of the sky in multitude, and as the sand which is by the sea-shore innumerable*. *Note*, Nothing is impossible with God when he promises, we may trust, and not be afraid

4 *These all*, Abraham, Sarah, Isaac, and Jacob, *died in faith, not having received the promises*, neither possessing the land of Canaan, nor having seen the Messiah incarnate, *but*, in the fullest assurance that what God had spoken was as good as done, and sure in the event, *having seen them afar off*, looking forward to the distant ages when the time of their accomplishment should arrive, *and were as fully persuaded of them* as if they had lived to see them fulfilled, *and embraced them* with confidence and holy joy, *and*, under the influence of them, *confessed that they were strangers and pilgrims on the earth*, regarding themselves as such, looking for their heavenly home, and living above the world on the glorious hopes which God through Christ had given unto them *For they that say such things*, and professedly and practically die unto the world, *declare plainly that they seek a country*, and look to a better world as their native land *And truly if they had been mindful of that country from whence they came out, they might have had opportunity to have returned* to Ur of the Chaldees again, *but now they desire a better country, that is, an heavenly*, even that inheritance incorruptible, undefiled, and that fadeth not away, which God in Christ, as their covenant God, had revealed unto them, and which they by faith embraced *Wherefore God is not ashamed to be called their God*, in a peculiar and most endeared relation: *for he hath prepared for them a city*, a glorious abode with himself, eternal in the heavens! *Note*, (1) In this world we live by faith, not by sight, and yet the certain approach of the promised inheritance can even here, as if possessed, fill us with joy and peace in believing (2) True faith hath ever this effect, to make us overcome the world, and live as strangers and pilgrims on the earth; we place not our affections upon it, but pass through it as a foreign land, with a holy indifference about its gains, honours, or interests, contentedly put up with any accommodations which we meet with, hasten on with diligence towards our native home, consort with our own countrymen who are travelling the same road, and speak the same language, and are happy the nearer we arrive to that land where our affections are placed, and whither our footsteps bend! (3) None that are truly converted to God from the kingdom of darkness and sin, ever think of returning thither again; but, whatever difficulties are in the way, or whatever temptations solicit, they stedfastly cleave to Christ as their portion, and follow him in the regeneration (4) The heavenly country may well be the object of the believer's desires, when every thing there is so infinitely preferable to what can ever be found in this miserable world (5) They who live in faith will die in faith, that which carries them victorious through the conflicts of life, will make them triumphant over the terrors of death (6) If God be our God, therein is comprehended all possible blessedness more heart cannot desire, nor imagination conceive

5 The apostle returns to mention another and the most eminent instance of Abraham's faith *By faith Abraham, when he was tried*, as never mortal was before, to prove the strength and truth of his faith and obedience, *offered up Isaac*, took every step which evidenced his intention fully to comply with the divine command (*see Gen* xxii) *and he that had received the promises offered up his only begotten son*, in whom alone these promises were to have been fulfilled, *of whom it was said, that in Isaac shall thy seed be called*, amidst innumerable objections, which sense, reason, nature, yea even religion, might seem to suggest, he staggered not, looking to the uplifted knife, we still shudder with horror and distress, and what must he then feel that stands ready to plunge it in that dear sacrifice, *thy son, thy only son, Isaac, whom thou lovest!* We start from the scene; but Abraham, herein more than human, dares obey, his faith triumphed over every suggestion, *accounting* (λογισάμενος) reasoning and concluding from the most substantial grounds of evidence, *that God*, by whose command he knew with the most infallible assurance that he now acted, *was able to raise him up even from the dead, from whence also he received him in a figure*, he knew that God could as easily reanimate Isaac on the altar as produce him from the bodies of his parents, that were, for the purposes of his generation, as good as dead, and that the divine promise should somehow receive its accomplishment, he rested in the fullest confidence *Note*, (1) God knows the purposes that are in the hearts of his people, and what they design in obedience to his will he regards as acts really performed (2) Where God commands, we must stop our ears to all the reasonings of unbelief, fear, and selfishness. Duty is ours, events are in his disposal (3) This was the figure and type of the death and resurrection of Christ (4) We marvel at Abraham's obedience to God's command, *though his son is spared*, with what astonishment and wonder then should we contemplate the love of God, *who spared not his own Son*, but even for us sinners gave him up to death, even the death of the cross!

20 By

20 By faith [d] Isaac blessed Jacob and Esau, concern-
ing things to come 21 By faith [e] Jacob, when he was
a dying, blessed both the sons of Joseph, and [f] worship-
ped, *leaning* upon the top of his staff 22 By faith
[g] Joseph, when he died, made mention of the departing
of the children of Israel, and gave commandment con-
cerning his bones. 23 By faith [h] Moses, when he was
born, was hid three months of his parents because they
saw *he was* a proper child, and they were not afraid of
[i] the king's commandment 24 By faith [k] Moses,
when he was come to years, refused to be called the son
of Pharaoh's daughter, 25 [l] Choosing rather to suffer
affliction with the people of God, than to enjoy the plea-
sures of sin for a season, 26 Esteeming [m] the reproach
of Christ greater riches than the treasures in Egypt
for he had respect unto [n] the recompence of the reward
27 By faith [o] he forsook Egypt, not fearing the wrath
of the king for he endured as [p] seeing him who is in-
visible. 28 Through faith [q] he kept the passover, and
the sprinkling of blood, lest he that destroyed the first-
born, should touch them 29 By faith [r] they passed
through the Red sea, as by dry *land* which the Egyp-
tians assaying to do, were drowned 30 By faith [s] the
walls of Jericho fell down, after they were compassed
about seven days 31 By faith [t] the harlot Rahab pe-
rished not with them that † believed not, when [u] she had
received the spies with peace.

d Gen. xxvii. 27, 39. e Gen. xlviii. 15, 20. f Gen. xlvii. 31. g Gen. l. 24, 25. Ex. xiii. 19. h Ex. ii. 2. Acts vii. 20. i Ex. i. 16, 22. k Ex. ii. 10, 11. l Ps. lxxxiv. 10. m Chap. xiii. 13. n Chap. x. 35. o Ex. x. 28, 29. & xiii. 17, 18. p Ver. 13. q Ex. xii. 21. r Ex. xiv. 22. s Josh. vi. 20. t Josh. ii. 23. Jam. ii. 25. † Or, were disobedient. u Josh. ii. 1.

v. 20—31. The apostle proceeds to other eminent instances of faith

1 *Isaac* He had been mentioned before, another instance of his faith is here given, when, in the confidence of the promise, he left his parting benediction with his children, and by divine determination, though undesignedly, being blind, conveyed the principal blessing to his younger son *By faith Isaac blessed Jacob, and Esau concerning things to come*, to Esau he gave the fatness of the earth, but to Jacob the mercies of a covenant God

2 Jacob *By faith* in the promises of God to Abraham, *Jacob, when he was a dying, blessed both the sons of Joseph*, by a prophetic spirit foretelling the superior greatness of Ephraim, and crossing his hands designedly, that his right hand might rest on the head of the youngest, *and worshipped God, leaning upon the top of his staff* *Note*, (1) The worship of God will be the believer's exercise to the last when old age and weakness will not permit him to bend his knees, he will still bow upon his bed, or lean upon his staff, and pour out his humble prayer (2) Parents cannot more properly finish their course than by leaving with their children, that surround their dying beds, the profession of their faith, and their final benediction

3 *Joseph* *By faith Joseph, when he died*, firmly persuaded of that inheritance in Canaan which was assigned to Abraham and his seed, *made mention of the departing of the children of Israel* out of Egypt, *and gave commandment concerning his bones*, solemnly charging them, under the sanction of an oath, that, when in the expected future day they departed to possess the promised land, his bones might be carried thither The dust of Canaan was more eligible in his eyes than the noblest sepulchres of Egypt *Note*, The testimony of dying saints to the truth of God's promises is a happy means to confirm the faith of their surviving brethren

4 The parents of Moses *By faith Moses, when he was born*, ordained to be the great lawgiver and deliverer of Israel, and a most eminent type of Jesus the spiritual Redeemer, *was hid three months of his parents, because they saw he was a proper child*, or *fair to God*, eminently beautiful, and probably some divine tokens appeared of his future greatness, *and they were not afraid of the king's commandment*, though, if discovered, their lives had paid for their disobedience to his bloody edict They were persuaded that, by a Hebrew, God would work their deliverance, and probably by some divine intimation perceived this child should be the person *Note*, (1) When Parents are eminent for their faith, there is a happy prospect that their children will rise up heirs of the same grace (2) In days of suffering we may lawfully use every prudent means for our preservation (3) An ingenuous countenance often bespeaks the ingenuous mind

5 Moses Much is spoken of him, for he is famous among the worthies, and hath his name in the first rank. Three eminent instances of his faith are here recorded

(1) *By faith* in the promises made to his ancestors, and of the blessings in a better world, *Moses, when he was come to years*, arrived at maturity, highly honoured, and eminent for wisdom and learning, *refused to be called the son of Pharaoh's daughter*, with all the dignities and advantages thence arising, perhaps even of succeeding to the throne of Egypt, *choosing rather to suffer affliction with the people of God*, as a despised Hebrew, *than to enjoy* all the glories of the highest human grandeur, *and the pleasures of sin*, however alluring, which are but *for a season*, and must in their issue plunge both body and soul into eternal misery *esteeming the reproach of Christ*, and all the contempt, scorn, and persecutions, which, for the sake of their fidelity to his worship, and faith in his promises, Israel endured, *greater riches than the treasures in Egypt*, and what in the issue would prove unspeakably his gain in the eternal world, *for he had respect unto the recompense of reward*, and looked off from the tempting objects of a flattering but deceitful world, to the substantial portion which he expected in the enjoyment of God for ever and ever *Note*, (1) Faith appears then most gloriously triumphant over the world, when, in the midst of greatness and grandeur, the soul can look down on these trifles, and be ready to part with all for the sake of Christ and his cause (2) The pleasures of sin, of the sweetest sins, are momentary, but the punishment of them is eternal They judge therefore as wisely as religiously who live in holy self-denial (3) All the greatest advantages cannot pay us for the least sin, so the greatest sufferings to be chosen rather than offend God, and we shall never see cause to regret what we forego or endure for our fidelity to him (4) The reproach of Christ is our truest honour far from being ashamed of it, we should glory therein as our greatest riches (5) There is a recompence of reward, the prospect of which should ever animate our souls, and teach us to count every thing beside dung and dross, so that we may but gain the glorious prize

2 *By faith he forsook Egypt*, carrying up with him the children of Israel, confident of the Lord's protection, and *not fearing the wrath of the enraged king*, nor the mighty hosts with which he pursued them in their way, *for he endured*, undismayed and unshaken, *as seeing him who is invisible*, higher than the kings of the earth, and able to save to the uttermost *Note*, (1) They who will be faithful to God must expect troubles, and be fearless of the wrath of man (2) A believing view of the invisible God will strengthen us, amidst all present difficulties, steadily to persevere

3 *Through faith* in God's deliverance of his people from Egypt, and of the greater redemption which should be obtained for Israel by the Lamb slain from the foundation of the world, *he kept the passover, and* observed the peculiar rite then enjoined of *the sprinkling of* the *blood* on the door-post of their houses, *lest he that destroyed the first-born* of the Egyptians *should touch them*, if the blood prevented not his entrance *Note*, (1) Christ is our passover (2) His blood upon our consciences is our only protection from the wrath of God (3) If we are spared, when others perish, we must acknowledge it to be an act of sovereign grace to us, and own ourselves entirely indebted for it to our adored Redeemer

(4) *By faith* in the power and promise of God, Moses stretched forth his rod, and the divided waters opened a passage for the discouraged hosts of Israel, and under his guidance, while he led the way, *they passed through the Red sea as by dry land which the Egyptians* daringly *assaying to do were drowned*, the waters closing upon them, and every man of that terrible host perished *Note*, They who persecute God's Israel, only rush upon their own ruin

6 *By Faith*, which Joshua, Caleb, and others exercised in God's power and veracity, *the walls of Jericho fell down* of their own accord, when they blew and shouted, *after they were compassed about seven days*, according to the divine command *Note*, (1) When God is for us, all opposition must fall before us (2) The weakest means in his hands are sufficient to bring about the greatest events

7 Rahab, a woman, a Canaanite, brings up the rear of faithful worthies *By faith* in the promise that God would assuredly give the land of Canaan to the Israelites, *the harlot Rahab*, who before had been a woman of infamous character, but now turned unto God, whose grace abounds toward the chief of sinners, *perished not with them that believed not*, of the Canaanites, but with her whole family was preserved, *when she had* given that real proof of her faith, in that she *received*, concealed, and dismissed *the spies* of Israel in peace *Note*, (1) The ruin of sinners is their unbelief (2) They who cleave to God's people, and faithfully determine to share their weal and woe, will never have reason to repent their choice

32 And what shall I more say? for the time would
fail me to tell of [x] Gideon, and *of* [y] Barak, and *of* [z] Sam-
son, and *of* [a] Jephthah, *of* [b] David also and [c] Samuel, and
of the prophets 33 Who through faith subdued king-
doms, wrought righteousness, obtained promises, [d] stop-
ped the mouths of lions, 34 [e] Quenched the violence
of fire, [f] escaped the edge of the sword, [g] out of weak-
ness were made strong, waxed valiant in fight, turned
to flight the armies of the aliens 35 [h] Women receiv-
ed their dead raised to life again and [i] others were tor-
tured, not accepting deliverance, [k] that they might ob-
tain a better resurrection 36 And [l] others had trial of
cruel mockings and scourgings, yea moreover, [m] of bonds
and imprisonment 37 They were stoned, they were

x Judg. vi. 11. y Judg. iv. 6. z Judg. xiii. 24. a Judg. xi. 1. & xii. 7. b 1 Sam. xvi. 1, 13. & xvii. 45. c 1 Sam. i. 20. & xii. 20. d Judg. xiv. 5, 6. 1 Sam. xvii. 34. Dan. vi. 22. e Dan. iii. 25. f 1 Sam. xx. 1. 1 Kings xix. 3. 2 Kings vi. 16. g 2 Kin. xx. 7. Job xlii. 10. h 1 Kin. xvii. 22. 2 Kin. iv. 35. i 2 Mac. vi. 19, 28. & vii. 7. k Ver. 26. l 2 Mac. vii. 7. m Gen. xxxix. 20. Judg. xvi. 21. Jer. xx. 2. n 1 Kin. xxii. 27. 2 Chron. xxiv. 21.

n 1 Sam xxii 18 1 Kings xix 10 Jer xxvi 23 p 2 Kings i 8 Mat iii 4 q 1 Sam xxvi 20 r 1 Kings xviii 4 & xviii 4 s Ver 2 t 1 Pet i 12 u Chap xi 22 & viii 6

sawn asunder, were tempted, [o] were slain with the sword
[p] they wandered about in sheep-skins, and goat-skins,
being destitute, afflicted, tormented 38 (Of whom
the world was not worthy) [q] they wandered in deserts,
and *in* mountains, and [r] *in* dens and caves of the earth
39 And these all [s] having obtained a good report through
faith, [t] received not the promise 40 [u] God having
provided [u] some better thing for us, that they without us
should not be made perfect

v 32—40 Unable to enter particularly into the case of every eminent believer recorded in the Old Testament, the apostle recites a cluster of distinguished names, and of the mighty effects which their faith produced

1 He recites some of their distinguished names *And what shall I more say?* when the field is so vast, *for the time would fail me*, if I enlarged on every individual, *to tell of Gideon* and his noble exploits recorded (*Judges* vi, vii, viii), *and of Barak*, who before him was alike eminent for his faith and victory, (*Judges* iv) *and of Sampson*, in life and death so signally remarkable, (*Judges* xiv 19 xvi 27—30) *and of Jephthah*, before whose faith the routed Ammonites fell, (*Judges* xi 23—33) *and of David also*, the man after God's own heart, so famous in sacred history for dependance on God, (2 *Sam* xxiii 1—5) *and Samuel and of the prophets*, who did and suffered so nobly in the cause of God and truth, under the mighty influence of divine faith

2 He mentions many of the glorious acts of faith, which these and other worthies like them shewed, and any one conversant in the book of God may apply them to several of the saints there recorded *Who* (1) *through faith subdued kingdoms*, as Joshua, David, &c (2) *Wrought righteousness* in their private and public capacities, governing with equity, and in their conversation were examples of every thing good and gracious, (3) *Obtained promises*, God remarkably appearing for them, as he had assured them he would in the hour of trial, (4) *Stopped the mouths of lions*, as David, Sampson, Daniel, and still the same faith will produce the same effects, in stopping the mouth of the old lion that he cannot devour, (5) *Quenched the violence of fire*, so as to remain unhurt in the midst of the flames, (*Dan* iii 13—27) (6) *Escaped the edge of the sword*, when in the most imminent danger of their lives, (7.) *Out of weakness were made strong*, their national affairs restored from the nearest prospect of ruin, their bodily health recovered, when their disease seemed desperate, (2 *Kings* xx 17) and though, in comparison with their foes, weak as infancy, yet, in divine strength, became more than conquerors, (8) *Waxed valiant in fight*, and trusting in the Lord, marvellously overcame in the day of battle, (9) *Turned to flight the armies of the aliens*, though more, and, to human view, incomparably mightier than they (10) *Women received their dead raised to life again*, as in the cases of the widow of Zarephath and the Shunamite *And*, with respect to the power of faith, is evident in the most acute sufferings, we read that, (11) *Others were tortured*, willingly submitting to the most dreadful torments, *not accepting deliverance*, when only to be obtained at the price of their conscience, and some base compliances, rather welcoming death itself than deny the faith, *that they might obtain a better resurrection*, the prospect of eternal glory raising them superior to all the pangs of nature, and all the terrors of death (12) *And others had trial of cruel mockings*, ridiculed, treated as despicable, and loaded with every opprobrious name, *and* with ... smarted under severe *scourgings, yea moreover*, endured the pain and shame *of bonds and imprisonment* Such hath been the saints' portion, more or less, in every age (13) They were murdered in a variety of ways *They were*, some of them *stoned, they were sawn asunder*, as the Jewish tradition affirms Isaiah was, at the command of the cruel Manasseh, they *were tempted* to deny their profession and save their lives, by complying with the commands of their persecutors, they *were slain with the sword* of tyrants and blood-thirsty men, and where some escaped the fury of their foes by flight, their life was imbittered and scarce preferable to death itself so, (14) *They wandered about in sheep-skins and goat skins*, having no better covering to protect them from the inclemency of the skies, *being destitute* of any abode, of cloath and necessary food, *afflicted* with various miseries, and *tormented* with endless insult and abuses, (*of whom indeed the world was not worthy*) nor deserved so great a blessing as their examples, prayers, and admonitions, and by the wicked they were treated as unfit for human society, and driven out from among men to dreary solitudes, *they wandered in deserts, and in mountains, and in dens and caves of the earth*, seeking refuge among wild beasts, more hospitable than their savage persecutors, and, in the midst of all their sufferings, faith enabled them to persevere, and brought them at last to their eternal rest For,

3 Their faith was at last crowned with the enjoyment of that Redeemer in whom they trusted *These all having obtained a good report through faith*, enrolled in the sacred records as names held up for imitation to the latest ages, *received not the promise*, saw not that Messiah incarnate in whom their faith centered *God having provided some better thing for us*, the manifestation of his Son in the flesh, to whom they had constantly respect, *that they without us should not be made perfect*, since not by any legal sacrifices, but by the offering of the body of Jesus, both their sins and ours were expiated, and that by the same grace revealed in him we might be saved even as they According therefore to the peculiar advantages which we enjoy under the gospel dispensation, a peculiar obligation is laid upon us, that our faith should be suitably operative, engaging us to all chearful obedience, and willing sufferers for our Redeemer's sake

CHAP XII

The apostle, in this chapter, applies what he has collected in the chapter foregoing, and makes use of it as a great motive to patience and perseverance in the Christian faith and state, pressing home the argument, 1 *From a greater example than he had yet mentioned, and that is Christ himself,* ver 1—3 2 *From the gentle and gracious nature of the afflictions they endured in their Christian course,* ver 4—18 3 *From the communion and conformity between the state of the gospel church on earth, and the triumphant church in heaven, from* ver 18 *to the end of the chapter.*

1 WHerefore, seeing we also are compassed about
with [a] so great a cloud of witnesses, [b] let us
lay aside every weight, and the sin which doth so easily
beset *us*, and [c] let us run [d] with patience the race that is
set before us. 2 Looking unto Jesus the author and
finisher of *our* faith, [e] who, for the joy that was set be-
fore him, endured the cross, despising the shame, and [f] is
set down at the right hand of the throne of God 3 For
consider him [g] that endured such contradiction of sinners
against himself, lest you be wearied and faint in your
minds.

a Chap. xi 1—40. b 1 Pet ii 1, 2 c 1 Cor ix 24 Phil. iii 13, 14 d Rom xii. 12 Chap. x 36 e Luke xxiv. 26 Phil. ii 8, &c 1 Pet i 11 f Ps cx. 1 Chap i 3, 13 & viii 1. g Mat xi 24. & xxvii 39, &c.

v. 1—3 Having proposed to them such bright examples, the apostle urges the Hebrews,

1 To imitate their faith, patience, and perseverance *Wherefore, seeing we also are compassed about with so great a cloud of witnesses*, who, having finished the glorious course themselves, are now looking on our conduct, *let us*, animated by their examples, and roused to imitation of their excellencies, *lay aside every weight* that would retard our speed, all inordinate attachment to earth and earthly things, *and the sin which doth so easily beset us*, that which from our circumstances, station in life, connections, and constitution, is ever sollicitıng our consent, and would ensnare our souls, particularly the great and capital sins of unbelief, pride, and lust, under whatever specious pretences they may appear. *and let us run with patience*, not discouraged at difficulties, nor fainting under temptation, but eager to finish *the race that is set before us*, and to win the glorious prize *Note*, (1) We have a race before us, the course is circumscribed by our mortal days, the word of God marks out our path; saints and angels are spectators, death is the goal, and glory the reward of fidelity What services then can we refuse? What sufferings shall dismay us? (2) Faith and patience are the mighty graces which can enable us to hold on, and to hold out, till we finish our course with joy

2 The only way that in faith and patience we can persevere is here described *Looking unto Jesus* (αφορωντες), turning away our eyes from sin, the world, and every ensnaring object which would seduce our affections, and keeping him singly in our view, who is *the author, and* alone can be *the finisher of our faith*, by grace and strength derived from him, enabling us to follow his perfect pattern, *who, for the joy that was set before him*, that God's perfections might be glorified, full satisfaction made to Divine Justice, his people's eternal redemption secured, and himself, as Mediator, be crowned with glory and honour, *endured the cross*, with all its horrors, exercising the most astonishing patience and unshaken fortitude, *despising the shame* of that ignominious tree, *and is* now, in consequence thereof, *sat down at the right hand of the throne of God*, exalted to the highest dignity and majesty in the heavens *For consider him that endured such contradiction of sinners against himself*, (αναλογισασθε) compare your sufferings with his, the infinite disproportion between your persons and him, the invincible patience and undisturbed composure with which he bore every insult and torment, reflect upon this often and deeply, *lest ye be weary and faint in your minds*, and let the eye of faith, fixed on him, draw out of his fulness the needful supplies of strength to follow his blessed footsteps. *Note*, (1) Faith is the gift of Jesus, and he who begins must finish the work with power in our hearts (2) When we consider what the Son of God for our sakes freely endured, we shall be ashamed to complain of the comparatively trivial cross which we sustain, and boldly set our faces as a flint against all sufferings and reproaches, which for his sake we may be called to bear (3) Great and long-continued trials are apt to weary out our feeble minds, so that we are ready to sink under them, but Jesus is before us, he saith, Look unto me, and that re-

viving sight uncloses the dying eye, reanimates the dejected spirit, rouses the fainting heart, and, inspired with renewed vigour, we run our heavenly race, made more than conquerors through his love.

4 [b] Ye have not yet resisted unto blood, striving against
sin. 5 And ye have forgotten the exhortation which
speaketh unto you as unto children, [i] My son, despise not
thou the chastening of the Lord, nor faint when thou art
rebuked of him: 6 For [k] whom the Lord loveth he
chasteneth, and scourgeth every son whom he receiveth.
7 If ye endure chastening, [l] God dealeth with you as
with sons; for what son is he whom the father chasteneth
not? 8 But if ye be without chastisement, [m] whereof all
are partakers, then are ye bastards and not sons. 9 Fur-
thermore, we have had fathers of our flesh, which corrected
us, and we gave *them* reverence: shall we not much rather
be in subjection unto [n] the Father of spirits, and live?
10 For they verily for a few days chastened *us* after their
own pleasure, but he for our profit, that we might be par-
takers of his holiness. 11 Now no chastening for the
present seemeth to be joyous, but grievous: nevertheless,
afterward it yieldeth [o] the peaceable fruit of righteousness,
unto them which are exercised thereby. 12 Wherefore
[p] lift up the hands which hang down, and the feeble knees;
13 And [q] make straight paths for your feet, lest that
which is lame be turned out of the way; [r] but let it rather
be healed. 14 [s] Follow peace with all *men*, [t] and holi-
ness, [u] without which no man shall see the Lord: 15
[x] Looking diligently, lest any man † fail of the grace of
God; [y] lest any root of bitterness springing up, trouble
you, and thereby many be defiled; 16 Lest there *be*
any fornicator, or profane person, as Esau, [a] who for one
morsel of meat sold his birthright. 17 For ye know how
that afterward [b] when he would have inherited the blessing,
he was rejected: for he [c] found no place of repentance,
though he sought it carefully with tears.

[h] Chap. x. 3-. [i] Job v. 17. Prov. iii. 11, 12. [k] Ps. xciv. 12. Jam. i. 12. Rev. iii. 19. [l] Deut. viii. 5. 2 Sam. vii. 14. [m] Ps. lxxiii. 15. 1 Pet. v. 9. [n] Num. xvi. 22. & xxvii. 16. Job xii. 10. Eccles. xii. 7. Isa. lvii. 16. Zech. xii. 1. [o] Jam. iii. 18. [p] Job iv. 3, 4. Isa. xxxv. 3. [q] Prov. iv. 26. [r] Gal. vi. 1. [s] Ps. xxxiv. 14. Rom. xii. 18. [t] 2 Cor. vii. 1. [u] Matt. v. 8. 2 Cor. vii. 1. Eph. v. 5. Rev. xxi. 27. [x] 2 Cor. vi. 1. [y] Chap. iv. 1. [†] Or fall from. Gal. v. 4. [z] Deut. xxix. 18. Chap. iii. 12. [a] Eph. v. 3. Col. iii. 5. 1 Thess. iv. 3. [a] Gen. xxv. 33. [b] Gen. xxvii. 36—38. [c] Chap. vi. 6.

v. 4—17. In support of what he had said before, the apostle,

1. Suggests the most engaging arguments to persevere.

(1.) God had hitherto preserved them in life. *Ye have not yet resisted unto blood, striving against sin*, and as he had not called them to the severest conflicts, it would be shameful indeed if they sunk under lesser trials. *Note*, (1.) Our warfare lies against sin, the deadly foe, who, if not vanquished, will destroy us body and soul for ever. We need be resolute, therefore, when our all is at stake. (2.) We are to acknowledge with thankfulness the kindness of our adored Lord, who proportions our trials to our strength.

(2.) The sufferings they had endured were the kind chastisements of a Father's rod, however evil the instruments might be who were the immediate authors of them. *And ye have forgotten*, or, *Have ye forgotten the exhortation which speaketh unto you as unto children? My son, despise not thou the chastening of the Lord*, on the one hand, neither slighting the affliction, unsuitably affected thereby, or stubborn under the rod; *nor*, on the other, *faint when thou art rebuked of him*, sinking under unbelief, impatient under the trial, or overwhelmed with despair. *For whom the Lord loveth he chasteneth* for their good, *and scourgeth every son whom he receiveth* into the bosom of his love. *If ye endure chastening*, far from counting it a token of wrath, *God herein dealeth with you as with sons*, with the kindest intention of your correction and amendment; *for what son is he whom the father chasteneth not?* There is no child of God but needs the gracious scourge, and our heavenly Father will not, like a foolishly-fond parent, spare the needful stroke. *But if ye be without chastisement, whereof all* the true members of his family *are partakers, then are ye bastards, and not sons*, to be neglected, and not counted worth correction, would prove you to be a spurious race, whom God abandons to their own ways. *Furthermore, we have had fathers of our flesh, which corrected us, and we gave them reverence*, were in duty bound to submit to their parental discipline, and to love them the more for their care in rebuking the evil they discovered in us: *shall we not much rather then be in subjection to the Father of Spirits*, from whose immediate hand our immortal souls are derived, meekly submitting to him, whose authority over us is so much greater, *and* thus, that we may *live* in a state of holy communion with him and subjection to him, till he shall have purged out all our evil, and prepared us for a place in his better house above. *For they verily for a few days chastened us after their own pleasure*, and much passion, self-will, and weakness mixed with their corrections; *but he*, who is infinitely wise as well as boundless in love, never scourges us *but for our profit, that*, in the blessed issue of the affliction which he is pleased to lay upon us, *we might be partakers of his holiness*, cleansed from the dross of corrupt affections, and renewed after his blessed image. *Now no chastening for the present seemeth to be joyous, but grievous*, and the flesh cannot but groan under the scourge; *nevertheless*, whilst faith supports us comfortably under the trial, we afterwards continually see cause to bless God for our suffering, since *afterward it yieldeth the peaceable fruit of righteousness, unto them which are exercised thereby*, and we can say, by happy experience, it is good for me that I have been afflicted. *Note*, (1.) God's corrections must not be made light of on the one hand, nor should we on the other despair on account of them; but, humbling our souls under the mighty hand of the Lord, should patiently wait, in confidence that he will lift us up. (2.) God's chastisements are all sent out of pure love to his children, and therefore with dutiful submission, and lowly resignation should be received. (3.) Though the Lord may leave others to themselves, yet he will not suffer his children to err without visiting their iniquities with a rod. It is a sad symptom of being an alien from his family, never to be visited with his corrections. (4.) If we are bound to reverence our earthly parents, and submit to their arbitrary and often self-willed corrections, how much more should the chastisements of our heavenly Father be embraced with thankfulness, to whom we owe so much higher reverence, who never afflicts without cause, and so wisely and graciously orders his afflictive dispensations in time, manner, measure, as shall be exactly suited to our wants, and effectually tend to our profiting. (5.) Far from judging of God's anger by the severity or length of our trials, we should from thence conclude his love is great towards us. He afflicts that he may purge us more thoroughly from our dross, and faith can make us rejoice even in these fires, under the confidence that peaceable fruits of righteousness shall be produced out of those trials, that to flesh and blood are most grievous.

2. He exhorts them not to faint or be disheartened, but to be vigorous in their Christian course. *Wherefore lift up the hands which hang down, and the feeble knees*, cast away every desponding fear, and press with earnestness to the goal, encouraging each other nobly to persevere in the face of every difficulty and danger, depending on Almighty Grace. *And make straight paths for your feet*, desiring to remove every obstacle at which yourselves or your brethren might stumble, *lest that which is lame be turned out of the way* of truth and righteousness, and the weak offended or perverted from the paths of godliness, *but let it rather be healed*, the feeble-minded supported, the disheartened encouraged, the weak confirmed, the fallen lifted up and restored again. *Note*, We should labour to be assisting to each other in our heavenly way, and attentive to the good of our brethren's souls, as to our own.

3. He particularly directs them what to pursue. *Follow peace with all men*, desiring earnestly to maintain it in every relation, and with all persons, as far as is consistent with a good conscience, *and holiness* in heart and life and all manner of conversation, *without which no man shall see the Lord*, or be admitted to the beatific vision in glory everlasting. *Note*, Peace and holiness are essential to our hopes as Christians; we deceive ourselves if we think we can ever be saved, whilst enslaved by passion and vile affections.

4. He gives them a solemn caution against apostacy, enforced by Esau's fearful example. *Looking diligently*, watching over each other with holy jealousy, *lest any man* who hath made profession of the gospel, *fail of the grace of God*, and apostatize from the faith, *lest any root of bitterness springing up trouble you, and thereby many be defiled*, seduced by their heresies, and perverted by their ill examples: *lest there be any fornicator, or profane person, as Esau, who for one morsel of meat sold his birthright*, despising the sacred as well as civil privileges which were annexed thereto; and his punishment was suited to his crime, *for ye know how that afterward, when he would have inherited the blessing*, and prevailed upon his father to retract what he had given to Jacob, *he was rejected* by him, *for he found no place for repentance*, nor would Isaac change his mind or reverse his word, *though he sought it diligently with tears*. *Note*, (1.) Apostates from the truth are the most dangerous enemies, and bitter opposers. (2.) Many, for the gratification of a bestial appetite, have, like Esau, renounced their sacred birthright, and too late they will rue their sin and folly.

18 For ye are not come unto [d] the mount that might
be touched, and that burned with fire, nor unto black-
ness, and darkness, and tempest, 19 And the sound of a
trumpet, and the voice of words, which *voice* they that
heard, [e] intreated that the word should not be spoken to
them any more: 20 (For they could not endure that
which was commanded, [f] And if so much as a beast
touch the mountain, it shall be stoned or thrust through
with a dart: 21 And so terrible was the sight, *that* Moses
said, I exceedingly fear and quake:) 22 But ye are
come unto [g] mount Sion, and unto [h] the city of the living
God, the heavenly Jerusalem, and [i] to an innumerable
company of angels, 23 To the general assembly and
church of [k] the first born [l] which are written in heaven,
and to God the judge of all, and to the spirits of just men
[m] made perfect, 24 And to Jesus [n] the mediator of the

[d] Ex. xix. 12, 18, 19. [e] Ex. xx. 19. Deut. v. 5, 25. & xviii. 16. [f] Ex. xix. 13. [g] Gal. iv. 26. Rev. iii. 12. & xxi. 2, 10. [h] Phil. iii. 20. [i] Jude xiv. [k] Ex. iv. 22. Jam. i. 18. [l] Luke x. 20. Phil. iv. 3. [m] Phil. iii. 12. [n] 1 Tim. ii. 5. Chap. viii. 6. & ix. 15.

new covenant, and to [o] the blood of ſprinkling, that
ſpeaketh better things [p] than *that of* Abel 25 See that
ye refuſe not him that ſpeaketh For [q] if they eſcaped
not who refuſed him, that ſpake on earth, much more
ſhall not we eſcape, if we turn away from him that *ſpeaketh*
from heaven 26 [r] Whoſe voice then ſhook the earth
but now he hath promiſed, ſaying, Yet once more I ſhake
not the earth only, but alſo heaven 27 And this *word*,
[s] Yet once more, ſignifieth [t] the removing of thoſe things
that are ſhaken, as of things that are made, that thoſe
things which cannot be ſhaken may remain 28 Where-
fore, we receiving [u] a kingdom which cannot be moved,
let us have grace, whereby we may ſerve God acceptably,
with reverence and godly fear 29 For [x] our God *is* a
conſuming fire

o Ex xxiv 8 Chap x 22 1 Pet i 2 p Gen iv 10 Chap xi 4 q Chap ii 2 & iii 17 & x 28 r Ex xix 18 s Hag ii 6 t Pſ cii 26 Mat xxiv 35 2 Pet iii 10 Rev xxi 1 u Iſa ix 7 Dan ii 44 & vii 14 Luke i 33 x Ex xxiv 17 Deut iv 24 & ix 3 Pſ l 3 2 Theſſ i 8

v 18—29 To guard the Hebrews particularly from revolting back to Judaiſm, he ſets before them the excellence of the goſpel church and worſhip above the judaical

1 He reminds them of that diſpenſation of terror and bondage from which they had been delivered *For ye are not come unto the mount that might be touched*, which was a palpable earthly ſubſtance, and not like the ſpiritual Zion, *and that burned with fire*, when God in terrible pomp deſcended thereon, *nor unto blackneſs and darkneſs*, which covered that typical diſpenſation, *and tempeſt*, emblematical of the ſtorms of wrath which hang over the head of the tranſgreſſors, *and the ſound of a trumpet*, which with louder and ſtill louder blaſts ſpread terrible diſmay throughout the hoſts of Iſrael, *and the voice of words*, in the moſt awful manner articulately pronouncing the ten commandments, *which voice they that heard, intreated that the word ſhould not be ſpoken to them any more*, ſo terrified were they at it, and begged that Moſes might be their mediator, and that through him they might receive the revelation of the Divine Will (*for they could not endure that which was commanded*, ſo unable were they to anſwer the demands of this perfect law, and dreaded its awful ſanction, particularly that fearful edict, *and if ſo much as a beaſt touch the mountain*, during the time that the Divine Preſence is there manifeſted, *he ſhall be ſtoned or thruſt through with a dart And ſo terrible was the ſight, that Moſes* himſelf *ſaid, I exceedingly fear and quake*), ſo dark and terrible was that diſpenſation under which they had been held, and this ſhould with hearty eagerneſs engage them to receive and hold faſt that milder, brighter, ſpiritual diſpenſation of goſpel grace, when God, without one terror ſpread around him, invited poor ſinners, through his dear Son, to approach his throne and live. This more glorious ſtate the apoſtle,

2 Deſcribes. *But ye are come unto mount Zion*, the ſpiritual goſpel church, where God, well pleaſed, takes up his bleſt abode, and accepts the worſhip and ſervice there performed, *and unto the city of the living God*, built on Chriſt the foundation, guarded by Almighty Power, and bleſt with the moſt tranſcendent privileges, *the heavenly Jeruſalem*, where all the inhabitants are ſpiritualized in temper and affections, and made meet for their eternal manſions in glory, and *to the innumerable company of angels*, your fellow ſervants, who miniſter unto them who ſhall be heirs of ſalvation, *to the general aſſembly and church of the firſt-born which are written in heaven*, in the Lamb's book of life, the noble army of ſaints, whether militant in earth or triumphant in heaven, *and to God the judge of all*, is reconciled now to you in the Son of his love, and having boldneſs to approach the throne in that great day, when he ſhall judge the world by him to whom all judgment is committed, *and to the ſpirits of juſt men made perfect*, now entered into their eternal reſt and perfected in holineſs, with whom you maintain communion, as influenced by the ſame ſpirit, juſtified by the ſame blood, members of the ſame body, purſuing the ſame end, and ready to join their ſervice in the immediate preſence of God and of the Lamb, *and to Jeſus the Mediator of the new covenant*, through whom all theſe invaluable privileges and bleſſings are derived down to us, *and to the blood of ſprinkling, that ſpeaketh better things than that of Abel* his blood cried for vengeance, but the blood which Jeſus ſhed, ſprinkled by faith upon our conſciences, ſpeaks peace, and comfort, and eternal bleſſedneſs as it infinitely exceeds in excellence that of Abel's ſacrifice, much more ſhall it obtain acceptance and favour with God for all thoſe, who, ſprinkled therewith, boldly appear in the preſence of the Moſt High and Moſt Holy

3 From theſe conſiderations he proceeds to exhort them to take heed to themſelves. *See that ye refuſe not him that ſpeaketh* in the goſpel *for if they eſcaped not who refuſed him that ſpake on earth*, even Moſes who delivered the ſacred oracles of the law to the people, *much more ſhall not we eſcape, if we turn away from him that ſpeaketh from heaven*, that Lord of life and glory who came down from heaven, and is returned thither again, and by the inſpiration of his Spirit, which, in ſuch an aſtoniſhing manner, he hath ſent from thence, ſpeaks now in his goſpel word *whoſe voice then ſhook the earth*, when Sinai trembled at his preſence *but now he hath promiſed, ſaying, Yet once more I ſhake not the earth only, but alſo heaven*, the Jewiſh church, with all their civil and eccleſiaſtical polity *And this word, Yet once more, ſignifieth the removing of thoſe things that are ſhaken, as of things that are made*, not for a perpetuity, but for a while only, as was the caſe of the Jewiſh tabernacle and œconomy, *that thoſe things which cannot be ſhaken may remain*, and that the goſpel church worſhip and privileges may endure unalterable unto the end of time *Wherefore, we receiving a kingdom which cannot be moved*, and by faith admitted to a participation of the privileges of that kingdom of goſpel grace, which will iſſue ſhortly in a kingdom of glory, *let us* remember, eſteem, and value our diſtinguiſhed mercies, *and have grace* to hold faſt the doctrine of truth, and beg a more abundant meaſure of the Spirit, *whereby we may ſerve God acceptably*, through Jeſus Chriſt, *with reverence and godly fear*, under a ſenſe of our own ſinfulneſs and unworthineſs *For our God is a conſuming fire*, and will execute fearful vengeance on every apoſtate from the faith and practice of the goſpel *Note*, (1) They who have received the grace of God in truth, have a kingdom that cannot be moved. (2) Conſtant worſhip and waiting upon God is the appointed way wherein he hath promiſed to beſtow on us the grace which can enable us to ſerve him acceptably (3) The fire of eternal vengeance will aſſuredly light down upon the apoſtate and impenitent ſoul

CHAP XIII

The apoſtle concludes with recommending ſeveral excellent duties to them, as the proper fruits of faith, ver 1—18 then beſpeaks their prayers for him, and offers up his prayers to God for them, gives them ſome hope of ſeeing himſelf and Timothy, and ends with the general ſalutation and benediction, ver 18 to the end

1 [a] LET brotherly love continue 2. [b] Be not for-
getful to entertain ſtrangers for thereby [c] ſome
have entertained angels unawares 3 [d] Remember them
that are in bonds, as bound with them, *and* them which
ſuffer adverſity, as being yourſelves alſo in the body 4
Marriage *is* honourable in all, and the bed undefiled but
[e] whoremongers and adulterers God will judge 5 *Let
your* converſation *be* without covetouſneſs, *and* [f] *be* content
with ſuch things as ye have for he hath ſaid, [g] I will
never leave thee, nor forſake thee 6 So that we may
boldly ſay, [h] The Lord *is* my helper, and I will not fear
what man ſhall do unto me 7 [i] Remember them which
have the rule over you, who have ſpoken unto you the
word of God whoſe faith follow, conſidering the end of
their converſation 8 Jeſus Chriſt the ſame yeſterday,
and to day, and for ever 9 [k] Be not carried about with
divers and ſtrange doctrines for *it is* a good thing that
the heart be eſtabliſhed with grace, [l] not with meats,
which have not profited them that have been occupied
therein 10 [m] We have an altar whereof they have no
right to eat which ſerve the tabernacle 11 For [n] the
bodies of thoſe beaſts, whoſe blood is brought into the
ſanctuary by the high prieſt for ſin, are burnt without the
camp 12 Wherefore Jeſus alſo, that he might ſanctify
the people with his own blood, ſuffered [o] without the
gate 13 Let us go forth therefore unto him without
the camp, [p] bearing his reproach 14 [q] For here we
have no continuing city, but we ſeek one to come 15
[r] By him therefore let us offer [s] the ſacrifice of praiſe to
God continually, that is, [t] the fruit of *our* lips, giving
thanks to his name 16 But to do good and to com-
municate forget not for [u] with ſuch ſacrifices God is well
pleaſed 17 [x] Obey them that have the rule over you,
and ſubmit yourſelves for [y] they watch for your ſouls,
as they that muſt give an account that they may do it
with joy, and not with grief for that *is* unprofitable for
you

a Rom xii 10. 1 Pet i 22 & ii 17 & v 8 (?) b Rom xii 13 1 Pet iv 9 c Gen xviii 2 & xix 1 d Mat xxv 36 Rom xii 15. 1 Co xii 26 Col iv 18 e 1 Co vi 9 Gal v 19, 21 Eph v 5 f Mat vi 25, 34 Phil iv 11 12 1 Tim vi 6, 8 g Deut xxxi 6 8 Joſh i 5 1 Chro. xxviii 20 h Pſ xxvii 1 [illegible]

v 1—17 Having warned them againſt apoſtacy, and ſet before them the excellency of the goſpel diſpenſation, he concludes with exhorting them to the practice of thoſe duties which muſt adorn their holy profeſſion

1 To mutual and fervent charity *Let brotherly love continue*, cultivate this bleſſed temper, and abide and abound in the exerciſe of it towards each other

2 To hoſpitality *Be not forgetful to entertain ſtrangers*, thoſe who travelled to preach the goſpel or by perſecution were driven from their native home, or whoſe diſtreſſed circumſtances pleaded for this kind relief, *for thereby ſome have entertained angels unawares*, as Abraham and Lot

3 To Chriſtian ſympathy with the afflicted *Remember them that are in bonds, as bound with them*, and tenderly feeling for their miſeries, *and them which ſuffer adverſity, as being yourſelves alſo in the body*, and liable to the ſame ſufferings, and fellow members in the ſame myſtical body of Chriſt

4. To chastity. *Marriage is honourable in all*, when entered into according to the divine prescription, *and the bed undefiled* by any forbidden and impure embraces: *but whoremongers and adulterers God will judge*, and execute upon them condign punishment, if they repent not of the evil of their ways.

5. To contentment. *Let your conversation be without covetousness*, free from the immoderate pursuit of worldly wealth, inordinate care about it, idolatrous delight in and reluctance to part with it, *and be content with such things as ye have*, satisfied in the portion which God's providence hath allotted you, and envying none their superior affluence: *for he*, who is able to supply all your wants, whilst in the way of duty and honest industry you depend upon him, *hath said, I will never leave thee, nor forsake thee*, for what was spoken particularly to Joshua shall be fulfilled to every faithful soul, respecting all their concerns, temporal and spiritual, who shall be under the Divine blessing, guidance, and protection. *So that we may boldly say*, with the psalmist, *The Lord is my helper, and I will not fear what man shall do unto me*; greater is he that is for us than all that are against us, and the devices of wicked men, or wicked devils, he can over-rule, and even make them work together for our good.

6. To imitate their dead pastors, and to obey their living guides.

(1.) To imitate the good examples of their departed spiritual teachers. *Remember them which have the rule over you, who have spoken unto you the word of God* in time past, and have now finished their testimony; *whose faith follow*, hold fast the doctrines which they preached, and copy after the holy lives they led, *considering the end of their conversation*, how singly they aimed at the glory of God in life, and what a happy exit they made at death; and well may we desire that our last end may be like theirs. And though the best of ministers are dying men, the great Shepherd and Bishop of Souls ever lives to feed his redeemed flock, *Jesus Christ*, the glorious object of our faith and hope, *the same*, unchangeable in nature, grace, and love towards his people, *yesterday*, in all past ages, *now*, *and for ever* the portion of his saints, as your faithful guides have taught you. *Be not* therefore *carried about with strange and divers doctrines*, different from that unadulterated gospel which they preached to you: *for it is a good thing that the heart be established with grace*, and fixed in its dependance on the sovereign grace of God in Jesus Christ, as the foundation of all hope, and peace, and holiness, in time and eternity; and *not* to be seduced by judaizing teachers *with* any pretences that the Mosaic ritual is still in force, and a difference of *meats* and drinks, and such like things necessary to be observed, in order to acceptance with God, all *which* are now abrogated, *and have not profited them that have been occupied therein*; even when they were in force, they were unable to purge the conscience, and make him who did the service perfect, and much less can they now profit, when they are abolished. *We* need none of the Levitical sacrifices to feast upon, we *have* one infinitely better, *an altar* and sacrifice, *whereof they have no right to eat which serve the tabernacle, for* no part of the sin offering under the law was to be eaten, but *the bodies of those beasts, whose blood is brought into the sanctuary*, on the great day of atonement, *by the high priest for the sin* of the people, *are burnt without the camp. Wherefore* they who remain subject to this law, can have no more right to feed upon the body and blood of Christ, which are received by the faithful in the Lord's Supper, than the Levitical priests had to feed upon the flesh of the atoning sacrifice; in exact correspondence with which *Jesus also, that he might sanctify the people*, his spiritual Israel, *with his own blood, suffered without the gate*, before he went up to heaven, the true sanctuary, there to plead the atonement which he had made. *Let us go forth therefore unto him without the camp, bearing his reproach*, turning our backs upon the temple and all its ritual service, founding no expectations upon them, but cleaving in faith and love to Christ alone, content to be treated with every insult, reproach, or cruelty for his sake, boldly carrying our cross to Calvary after him, and, if need be, ready to die for his sake. *For here we have no continuing city*; this polluted world is not our rest, nor do we desire to take up our rest here below, *but we seek one to come*, a city that hath abiding foundations, whose maker and builder is God, where saints, and angels, and Jesus himself dwelleth. *By him therefore let us offer the sacrifice of praise to God continually*, since all sacrifices of atonement are at an end, and praise and blessing for redeeming love, are the services now required at our hands, *that is, the fruit of our lips, giving thanks to his name*, an oblation well pleasing and acceptable to God through Jesus Christ. Not that we must rest merely in words, *but* our works also must testify our grateful acknowledgment of the divine mercy; therefore *to do good, and to communicate* of your substance to the needy, especially to those of the houshold of faith; and, according to your ability, *forget not: for with such sacrifices God is well pleased*, and for the Saviour's sake will bless the offerer.

(2.) They are enjoined, as to follow the examples of their departed pastors, so to obey their living guides. *Obey them that have the rule over you*, your spiritual teachers, who instruct you in the word of God, *and submit yourselves* meekly to their reproofs and admonitions: *for they watch for your souls*, to guard you from deceivers, to warn you from approaching danger, to feed you in the pastures of ordinances, and to help you on your heavenly way; and this they do with all holy jealousy, zeal, and diligence, knowing the solemn reckoning which they must one day make, *as they that must give account: that they may do it with joy, and not with grief: for that* would be not only grievous to them, but most *unprofitable for you*, whose condemnation would be highly aggravated by all their fruitless labours bestowed upon you. *Note*, (1.) Ministers can never too often or too deeply consider the awful account they must one day give before their eternal judge. (2.) When we have delivered our souls, then it becomes our people's care to see that their profiting appears; if they trifle with our message, their blood lies upon their own head.

18 ᵃ Pray for us: for we trust ᵇ we have a good con-
science, in all things willing to live honestly. 19 But I
beseech you ᶜ the rather to do this, that I may be restored
to you the sooner. 20 Now ᵈ the God of peace, ᵉ that
brought again from the dead our Lord Jesus, ᶠ that great
shepherd of the sheep, through ᵍ the blood of the ever-
lasting covenant, 21 ʰ Make you perfect in every good
work to do his will, working in you that which is well
pleasing in his sight, through Jesus Christ; ⁱ to whom *be*
glory for ever and ever. Amen. 22 And I beseech
you, brethren, suffer the word of exhortation: for ᵏ I
have written a letter unto you in few words. 23 Know
ye, that *our* brother Timothy is set at liberty; with whom,
if he come shortly, I will see you. 24 Salute all them
that have the rule over you, and all the saints. They of
Italy salute you. 25 Grace *be* with you all. Amen.

a Eph vi 19. Col iv 3. 2 Thess. iii 1. b Acts xxiii 1. & xxiv 16. 2 Cor i 12. c Philem 22. d Rom xv 33. e Acts ii 24. f Isa xl 11. Ezek xxxiv 23. John x 11. 1 Pet ii 25. & v 4. g Zech ix 11. Chap x 29. h Phil i 13. 1 Pet v 10. i Rev i 6. k 1 Pet v 12.

v. 18—25. The apostle here,

1. Recommends himself to their prayers. *Pray for us*, that we may be wise, vigilant, zealous, successful; and this will be your own benefit, for the more our people pray for us, the more profiting will they receive from us: *for we trust we have a good conscience, in all things willing to live honestly*, to discharge our awful trust with fidelity, and so to behave as to confute the calumnies of our enemies, approving ourselves to God, and enjoying the testimony of a good conscience. *But I beseech you the rather to do this, that I may be restored to you the sooner*, and that, being delivered from my present confinement, you may again reap the fruit of my labours among you. *Note*, (1.) Every faithful minister, however maligned by wicked men, hath the testimony of God and a good conscience; and that is his rejoicing. (2.) Mercies are doubly sweet which come in answer to prayer.

2. He in return offers up his own prayers on their behalf. *Now the God of peace*, our reconciled God, *that* hath spoken peace to our consciences, and hath *brought again from the dead our Lord Jesus, that great shepherd of the sheep*, in token of his perfect satisfaction in his undertaking, *through the blood of the everlasting covenant*, shed to procure our peace and pardon, and all the blessings of grace and glory for his redeemed, *make you perfect in every good work to do his will*, enabling you to go from strength to strength, till you arrive at the perfection of knowledge, holiness, and blessedness in glory everlasting, *working in you*, by his own almighty grace, *that which is pleasing in his sight through Jesus Christ*, by whom alone every spiritual gift descends upon us, *to whom be glory for ever and ever. Amen!* whose is the work, and to whom the praise is to be ascribed. *Note*, (1.) Our peace with God is bought with the blood of the everlasting covenant, and he is thereby become our God for ever and ever. (2.) Every thing pleasing in us to God, is his own work; left to ourselves, evil, and only evil continually, is the native produce of our fallen hearts. (3.) God must have all the glory of our salvation, from the beginning to the end; for we are nothing, and he is all in all.

3. He exhorts them very affectionately to attend to what he had said, and informs them of Timothy's release. *Now I beseech you, brethren*, dearly beloved, *suffer the word of exhortation*, take in good part what I have said, and receive the comfort it is intended to communicate to you, *for I have written a letter unto you in few words*, when the subject would have admitted of great enlargement. *Know ye, that our brother Timothy is set at liberty* from his bonds for Christ; *with whom, if he come* to me *shortly*, and it please the Lord that I regain my liberty, *I will see you*.

4. He concludes with his affectionate salutation. *Salute all them that have the rule over you*, your faithful ministers, *and all the saints* in Christ Jesus. *They of Italy salute you*, wishing you the best of blessings. *Grace be with you all. Amen!* May the sovereign and everlasting love of God in Christ, with all its transcendently-blessed effects, be with you in time, and continue to influence and guide you, till you arrive at his kingdom of glory in eternity!

THE

THE

EVANGELICAL EXPOSITOR;

OR, A

PRACTICAL COMMENT

UPON THE

GENERAL EPISTLE of JAMES.

THE writer of this epistle was James, the son of Alpheus, who was cousin-german to Christ, and one of the twelve apostles, Mat. x. 3 *He is called a pillar,* Gal ii 9. *And this epistle of his cannot be disputed, without loosening a foundation stone*

It is called a general epistle, because (as some think) not directed to any particular person or church, but such a one as we call a circular letter Others think it is called general or catholic, to distinguish it from the epistles of Ignatius, Barnabas, Polycarp, and others that were noted in the primitive times, but not generally received in the church, and on that account not canonical, as this is

The time when this epistle was written is uncertain, probably about the year 60 The design of it is, to reprove Christians for their great degeneracy, both in faith and manners, and to prevent the spreading of those libertine doctrines, which threatned the destruction of all practical godliness It was also a special intention of the author of this epistle, to awaken the Jewish nation to a sense of the greatness and nearness of those judgments which were coming upon them; and to support all true Christians in the way of their duty, under those calamities and persecutions they might meet with The truths laid down are very momentous and necessary to be maintained, and the rules for practice, as here stated, are such as ought to be observed in our times as well as in preceding ages

CHAP I

After the inscription and salutation, ver 1 *Christians are taught how to carry it when under the cross,* ver 2—12 *He warns them not to impute to God any temptations to sin, since he cannot be the author of sin, but is the author of all good,* ver 13—18 *All passion, and rash anger, and vile affections ought to be suppressed The word of God should be made our chief study And what we hear and know of it, we must take care to practise; otherwise our religion will prove but a vain thing To which is added, an account wherein pure religion consists,* ver 19—27

1. JAMES [a] a servant of God and of the Lord Jesus
Christ, to [b] the twelve tribes [c] which are scattered
abroad, greeting. 2 My brethren, [d] count it
all joy when ye fall into divers temptations
3 Knowing *this*, that [e] the trying of your faith worketh
patience 4 But let patience have *her* perfect work, that
ye may be perfect and entire, wanting nothing 5 If
any of you lack wisdom, [f] let him ask of God, that giveth
to all men liberally, and upbraideth not, [g] and it shall
be given him 6 [h] But let him ask in faith, nothing
wavering for he that wavereth is like a wave of the sea,
driven with the wind, and tossed 7 For let not that
man think that he shall receive any thing of the Lord
8 A double-minded man is unstable in all his ways 9
Let the brother of low degree rejoice in that he is exalted
10 But the rich, in that he is made low because [i] as
the flower of the grass he shall pass away 11 For the
sun is *no sooner* risen with a burning heat, *but* it withereth
the grass, and the flower thereof falleth, and the grace
of the fashion of it perisheth so also shall the rich man
fade away in his ways 12 Blessed *is* the man that endureth
temptation for when he is tried, he shall receive
[k] the crown of life, [l] which the Lord hath promised to
them that love him

a Tit i 1 b Acts xxvi. 7 c Deut xxxii 26 John vii 35 Acts viii 1 1 Pet i 1 d Mat v 12. Acts v 41 Rom v 3 Heb. x 34 1 Pet iv 13, 16 e Rom v 3 1 Pet i 7 f 1 Kings iii 9 Mat vii 7 & xxi 22 John xiv 13 & xv 7 & xvi 26 g Jer xxix 12 1 John v 14 h Mark xi 24 1 Tim ii 8

v 1—12 We have here,

1 The inscription of the epistle *James,* who counts it his highest honour to subscribe himself *a servant of God, and,* or even, *of the Lord Jesus Christ, to the twelve tribes which are scattered abroad* wherever dispersed throughout the world, sendeth *greeting,* wishing that all blessings may descend upon them, whether of this world or a better

2 He exhorts them, under the persecutions and troubles which for Christ's sake they endured, to rejoice *My brethren count it all joy when ye fall into divers temptations,* and by Divine Providence are permitted to be variously exercised by the malice of the wicked; esteem their reproaches your honour, and your losses your truest gain, *knowing this,* by divine testimony, and happy experience, *that the trying of your faith worketh patience.* Your faith is proved genuine by this blessed effect, and every exercise of it tends to confirm your heart in meek and humble resignation *But let patience have her perfect work,* be the trials never so many, never so grievous, never so long continued, bear up under

under them with a persevering stedfastness, *that ye may be perfect and entire, wanting nothing*, rising to the highest eminence of grace, and holding out till you reach the perfection of holiness in heaven. *Note*, (1.) Surrounded as we are with temptation, and beset with corruption, we have need of patience, that we faint not under our trials. (2.) Philosophy may enjoin submission, but Christianity only can teach us to rejoice under affliction. (3.) Faith is the root of all graces; as that is vigorous, they will be in exercise. (4.) The sharpest conflicts which we have to sustain, prove in their issue, when rightly improved, the greatest blessings to our souls.

3. If we would act aright under our trials, we must be upon our knees often, to beg divine direction. *If any of you lack wisdom*, and know not how to act in any emergence, *let him ask of God, that giveth to all men*, who apply according to his word, *liberally, and upbraideth not*, never weary in granting, nor ever reproaching his supplicants with their unworthiness, or the multitude of the favours which he bestows, *and it shall be given him*, all the counsel and assistance which such an one needs shall be bestowed in answer to his prayer. *But let him ask in faith, nothing wavering*, not distrusting the faithfulness, power, and grace of God in Christ, however difficult and embarrassed his circumstances may be: *for he that wavereth is like a wave of the sea, driven with the wind, and tossed*, the sport of every gust of temptation, restless, impatient, fluctuating, unsettled in principle and practice. *For let not that man think that he shall receive any thing of the Lord*, whilst he dishonours him by his unbelief and fickleness. Such *a double-minded man*, divided between hope and fear, Christ and the world, halting between both, and willing to reconcile the incompatible services of God and Mammon, *is unstable in all his ways*, and having no fixed end in view, can never prosper in his soul, nor expect an answer to his prayers. *Note*, (1.) We have every encouragement to approach a throne of grace, and every possible assurance of finding relief there. How perverse and foolish then must we be, if we make not use of this invaluable privilege! (2.) They who come to God with their requests, must honour him by their confidence in his power, truth, and love: unbelief shuts out the blessing. (3.) When the heart is unstable and wavering, prayer cannot ascend with acceptance before God.

4. *Let the brother of low degree rejoice in that he is exalted* to the infinite riches of grace, and the transcendent dignity of an heir of glory; *but the rich brother, in that he is made low*, taught, amidst all his affluence and grandeur, true poverty of spirit, and lowliness of mind, and ready ever to part with any thing he possesses for the sake of Christ, *because he* knows the fleeting and perishing nature of all worldly wealth, and that *as a flower of the grass he shall pass away*, and leave it all behind. *For the sun is no sooner risen with a burning heat, but it withereth the grass, and the flower thereof falleth, and the grace of the fashion of it perisheth: so also shall the rich man fade away in his ways*. Often in this world riches make themselves wings, and fly away as an eagle towards heaven, and death at furthest will prove their vanity.

5. A blessing is pronounced upon faithful perseverance. *Blessed is the man that endureth temptation*, far from proving our hurt, our trials in their issue tend to advance our truest felicity: *for when he is tried*, as gold in the furnace, and comes forth brighter from the fires, *he shall receive the crown of life* and glory, *which the Lord*, the righteous Judge, *hath promised*, and will at the great day of his appearing assuredly give *to them that love him*. *Note*, (1.) We must be tried before we can be crowned. (2.) Where the love of God is in the heart, many waters cannot quench it, neither can any of the floods of persecution or temptation drown it. (3.) The reward of fidelity is still the gift of God, who freely promises, by his grace supports, and of his mercy bestows, the crown of life.

13 Let no man say when he is tempted, I am tempt-
ed of God: for God cannot be tempted with evil, nei-
ther tempteth he any man: 14 But every man is
tempted, when he is drawn away of his own lust and
enticed. 15 Then when lust hath conceived, [a] it bring-
eth forth sin: and sin when it is finished, [b] bringeth forth
death. 16 Do not err, my beloved brethren. 17
[c] Every good gift, and every perfect gift is from above,
and cometh down from the Father of lights, [d] with whom
is no variableness, neither shadow of turning. 18 [e] Of
his own will begat he us with the word of truth, that we
should be a kind of first fruits of his creatures.

[a] Ps. vii. 14. [b] Rom. vi. 23 ... Rom. xi. ... Jer. ii. ... Rev. v. ...

v. 13—18. Concerning the cause of all the evil of sin which we fall into, when brought into temptation, we are taught,

1. That it is not to be imputed to God. *Let no man say when he is tempted* to commit sin, in order to excuse himself from suffering, *I am tempted of God*, for this is abominably impious, since God, who is in his nature perfectly holy, *cannot himself be tempted with evil, neither tempteth he any man* to iniquity, whatever providential afflictions he may lay upon them. *Note*, We are very apt to cast our sins at God's door, and to blame him for putting us in such temptations, whereas our trials are designed to exercise our graces, not to draw out our corruptions.

2. We have only ourselves to blame for all the evil which is in us. *But every man is tempted, when he is drawn away of his own lust, and enticed*, foolishly and perversely following the bait which Satan lays, beguiled by his enticements, and dragged by the cords of corrupt affections from the paths of truth and holiness. *Then when lust hath conceived*, in thought and desire, *it bringeth forth sin*, gaining the consent of the will to the perpetration of iniquity; *and sin when it is finished*, in the act, and impenitently persisted in, *bringeth forth death* of body and soul for ever. *Do not err, my beloved brethren*, by entertaining false and injurious conceptions of the blessed God in this matter. *Note*, (1.) The root of all evil is in our fallen hearts. (2.) Sin enslaves by flattery; it is the deceitfulness of unrighteousness which proves our ruin; and false hope supports vain confidence, till it appears that there is a lie in our right hand. (3.) If we do not destroy the power of sin, we may be assured it will finally destroy us.

3. All good which is in us proceeds wholly from God. *Every good gift, and every perfect gift*, every bounty of providence, and every spiritual endowment, which tends to the perfection of our nature in knowledge and holiness, *is from above, and cometh down from the Father of lights*, the Author of all light, natural, moral, spiritual, or eternal, *with whom is no variableness, neither shadow of turning*. The sun that gilds the firmament is obscured often by clouds, rises and sets, is eclipsed, and moves to and fro between the tropics, but God knows no change, nothing but good, without the shadow of evil, can proceed from him. *Of his own will begat he us with the word of truth*, not for any desert of ours, but of his sovereign pleasure, sending us his gospel, and making it effectual, through the power of the Spirit, to quicken our souls from the death of sin, and raise us to newness of life, *that*, as his adopted and regenerate sons, *we should be a kind of first-fruits of his creatures*, consecrated to him, and devoted to his immediate service. *Note*, (1.) All glorying must be excluded, if all good be of grace; for what then have we, which we have not received? (2.) Those who are born of God, owe it to his sovereign will and pleasure, not to any thing in themselves, they lying in the same corrupted mass of mankind as others, till separated by his grace. (3.) All who are begotten by the word of truth in the gospel, must from that moment consider themselves as consecrated to God's service, and bound to live to his glory.

19 Wherefore, my beloved brethren, let every man
be [t] swift to hear, [u] slow to speak, [x] slow to wrath. 20 [t] Eccles. v. 1.
For the wrath of man worketh not the righteousness of [u] Prov. x. 19. & xiii. 3.
God. 21 Wherefore [y] lay apart all filthiness, and su- & xvii. 27. Eccles. v. 2.
perfluity of naughtiness, and receive [z] with meekness the [x] Prov. xvi. 32. Eccles.
ingrafted word, [a] which is able to save your souls. 22 vii. 9. Col. iii. 8.
But [b] be ye doers of the word, and not hearers only, de- [y] Rom. xiii.
ceiving your own selves. 23 For [c] if any man be a 12. Col. iii.
hearer of the word, and not a doer, he is like unto a 8. 1 Pet. ii. 1.
man beholding his natural face in a glass: 24 For he [z] Ps. xxv. 9.
beholdeth himself, and goeth his way, and straightway [a] Rom. i.
forgetteth what manner of man he was. 25 But [d] whoso 16. 1 Cor. i.
looketh into the perfect [e] law of liberty, and continueth 21. & xv. 1.
therein, he being not a forgetful hearer, but a doer of the [b] Mat. vii.
work, [f] this man shall be blessed in his deed. 26 If 21. Rom. ii. 13.
any man among you seem to be religious, and bridleth [c] Luke vi. 47. &c.
not his tongue, but deceiveth his own heart, this man's Chap. ii. 14, &c.
religion is vain. 27 Pure religion and undefiled before [d] 2 Cor. iii. 18.
God and the Father, is this, [g] To visit the fatherless and [e] Chap. ii. 12.
widows in their affliction, *and* to keep himself unspotted [f] John xiii. 17.
from the world. [g] Ps. xxxiv. 13. & xxxix. 1. 1 Pet. iii. 10. [h] Mat. xxv. 36. [i] John xvii. 15. 1 John v. 18.

v. 19—27. The apostle here enjoins them,

1. To restrain their passions. *Wherefore, my beloved brethren, let every man be swift to hear* God's word, *slow to speak*, not daring to censure the ways of providence and grace, *slow to wrath*, not disputing or quarrelling with the truth of God, or treating those who differ in point of controversy with contempt or anger: *for the wrath of man worketh not the righteousness of God*, the cause of God cannot be served by our selfish passions, nor with such a spirit may we hope to speak aright, or to convince others. *Note*, (1.) We should not be obstinate in our own opinion, but be willing to hear the objections of others. (2.) God's cause is not to be served by noise and anger, but by meekness and the word of truth. Whoever is in the right, they that are angry are sure to be wrong.

2. To put away every other vile and corrupt affection. *Wherefore lay apart all filthiness, and superfluity of naughtiness*, every defiling lust, and malicious temper; *and receive with meekness the ingrafted word*, that it may take fast hold of your affections, and be incorporated with your hearts, bowing before it with all humility, and receiving it on God's authority with faith and love, *which is able to save your souls*, when thus accompanied by the power of the Spirit. *Note*, Corrupt affection unrestrained

tertained disincline and indispose the soul for receiving God's word, turn us away from hearing it, and prejudice us against the truth

3 We must be not only hearers of the truth, but practise it also, else it can profit us nothing *But be ye doers of the word, and not hearers only, deceiving your own selves*, by any fallacious conclusions to the ruin of your souls *For if any man be a hearer of the word* merely, resting upon that as of any avail; *and is not a doer* of what he hears, *he is like a man beholding his natural face in a glass*, *for he beholdeth himself, and* hastily passing by, *straightway forgetteth what manner of man he was* Such is the careless and cursory hearer of the word he may discover, whilst under the word, in a transient glance, something of the sinfulness and depravity of his nature, and his need of Christ; but it makes no deep or lasting impression no sooner is he gone forth into the world, than he forgets his convictions, and continues utterly unchanged in temper and conduct *But whoso looketh into the perfect law of liberty*, attentively viewing himself in the glass of the gospel, wherein we are called from the bondage of corruption into the glorious liberty of the sons of God, *and continueth therein*, careful to hold fast in principle, and to correspond in practice with the things therein revealed, *he being not a forgetful hearer, but a doer of the work*, diligent to obey what God commands, *this man shall be blessed in his deed*, made happy in God's present service, and his end be everlasting life *Note*, (1) True religion consists not in profession merely, but in practice, without which Christianity is but an empty name. (2) Many by hearing pick up some right notions in their heads, whose hearts are never savingly affected. (3) The word of God is as the faithful mirrour, that knows not to flatter if we attentively view ourselves in that glass, we shall see the horrid deformity of our fallen spirits, and the foul spots of native corruption, and learn to entertain the lowliest thoughts of our vile selves, and wretched services, when we see them all polluted with sin (4) They are only blessed, who, having discovered their real state, are seriously led to the fountain open for sin and for uncleanness, and in a Saviour's blood, and by the power of his grace, have their filthiness cleansed, and their nature renewed after his image, so as henceforth to walk and please God

4 He marks the difference between true and false religion *If any man among you seem to be religious*, making such a profession, *and yet bridleth not his tongue*, from railing, reproach, slander, profaneness, bitterness, or proud talkativeness to display his own talents, *this man's religion is vain* however plausible he may appear, his heart is rotten, and whilst he would build up his own excellence by detracting from others' worth, his hypocrisy is visible through the mask *Pure religion, and undefiled before God and the Father*, that religion which he approves, is dictated by his word, and aims at his glory, *is this, To visit the fatherless and widows in their affliction*, stretching out the kind hand of charity to relieve, sympathizing with them, and affording them every assistance which they need, and we can give, *and to keep himself unspotted from the world*, neither polluted by the lust of the flesh, the lust of the eye, or the pride of life, but preserved pure for God amidst the overflowings of ungodliness *Note*, (1) We have to do with a heart-searching God, who requireth truth in the inward parts (2) Where the soul is right with God, there purity and charity will be manifest in every word and work (3) This world is full of defilement, it will need much watchfulness to keep our garments unspotted

CHAP II

In this chapter the apostle condemns all partiality to the rich, and despising the poor, ver 1—7 He shews that the whole law is to be fulfilled, and that mercy should be followed, as well as justice, ver 8—13 He exposes the error and folly of those that boast of faith without works, telling us that this is but a dead faith and such a faith as devils have, not the faith of Abraham, or of Rahab, ver 14, to the end

1 MY brethren, have not the faith of our Lord
Jesus Christ, [a] *the Lord* of glory, [b] with respect
of persons 2 For if there come unto your † assembly
a man with a gold ring, in goodly apparel, and there
come in also a poor man in vile raiment; 3 And ye have
respect to him that weareth the gay clothing, and say
unto him, Sit thou here in a good place and say to the
poor, Stand thou there, or sit here under my footstool
4 Are ye not then partial in yourselves, and are become
judges of evil thoughts? 5 Hearken, my beloved
brethren, [c] Hath not God chosen the poor of this world,
rich in faith, and heirs of the kingdom, [d] which he
hath promised to them that love him? 6 But [e] ye
have despised the poor Do not rich men oppress you,
[f] and draw you before the judgment seats? 7 Do not
they blaspheme that worthy name by the which ye are
called

[a] 1 Cor ii 8 [b] Lev xix 15 Deut i 17 & xvi 19 Prov xxviii 21 Mat xxii 16 Ver 9 † Gr Synagogue [c] Luke vi 20 John vii 48 1 Cor i 28 [d] Luke xii 32 1 Tim vi 18, 19 Rev ii 9 [e] Ex xx 16 Prov xiv 17 Mat v 3 Chap i 12 [f] 1 Cor xi 2 [g] Chap v 6

v 1—7 The apostle here,

1 In general warns them against all undue respect of persons, because of their rank in life *My brethren, have not the faith of our Lord Jesus Christ*, which centres in him as the object, and is derived from him as the author and finisher of it, *the Lord of glory, with respect of persons*, acting with undue partiality, unbecoming the disciples of Jesus, who is himself exalted to the highest glory, and hath prepared eternal mansions for his people, without distinction of rich or poor, and therefore we should make none in the merits of any cause which comes before us *Note*, A sight of Christ, and the glory provided for his people, stamps vanity on all the puny differences which here subsist between men

2. He gives an instance of the great evil and injustice of all such partiality *For if there come into your assembly*, for religious worship, or rather into your court, where causes civil or ecclesiastical are determining, *a man with a gold ring, in goodly apparel, and there come in also a poor man*, who is a party in the cause to be tried, *in vile raiment*, making a wretched appearance, *and ye have respect to him that weareth the gay clothing, and*, with evident partiality on his side, *say unto him*, with great deference, *Sit thou here in a good place*, *and say to the poor*, with insolence and contempt, *Stand thou there*, at a distance, *or sit here under my footstool*, in any despicable place, *are ye not then partial in yourselves, and are become judges of evil thoughts?* disposed to favour the rich, and oppress the poor, and how criminal is such a behaviour? *Hearken, my beloved brethren, Hath not God chosen the poor of this world, rich in faith, and heirs of the kingdom, which he hath promised to them that love him?* Is not the gospel chiefly preached to them? and are they not for the most part called to the participation of all its glorious privileges of grace here and glory hereafter? and if God hath so highly honoured them, we surely ought not to treat them with disdain or partiality *But ye have despised the poor*, to your shame and guilt be it spoken *Do not rich men*, to whom you pay such undue deference, *oppress you, and draw you before judgment-seats*, with litigious suits, and exercise the most cruel tyranny over you? *Do not they*, who are high in the world, prove your bitterest persecutors, and *blaspheme that worthy name by the which ye are called?* and then surely you have no cause to caress them *Note*, (1) All partiality in judgment is in God's sight abominable (2) Among the poor, God's saints are chiefly to be found, and the riches of faith, and heirship of glory, are infinitely more valuable than the wealth of both the Indies, or the widest earthly domains (3) They who love God, however poor, can never be despicable, since they are possessed of the highest dignity, as heirs of God, and joint heirs with Christ

8 If ye fulfil the royal law, according to the scripture,
[h] Thou shalt love thy neighbour as thyself, ye do well
9 But [i] if ye have respect to persons, ye commit sin,
and are convinced of the law as transgressors, 10 For
whosoever shall keep the whole law, and yet offend in
one *point*, [k] he is guilty of all 11 For he that said,
[l] Do not commit adultery, said also, Do not kill Now
if thou commit no adultery, yet if thou kill, thou art be-
come a transgressor of the law 12 So speak ye, and
so do, as they that shall be judged by the [m] law of li-
berty 13 For [n] he shall have judgment without mer-
cy, that hath shewed no mercy, and [o] mercy rejoiceth
against judgment

[h] Lev xix 18 Mat xxii 39 Rom xiii 9 Gal v 14 [i] Lev [illegible] 15 Ver 1 [k] Deut xxvii 26 Mat v 19 Gal iii 10 [l] Ex xx 13, 14 Deut v 17 [m] Chap i 25 [n] Mat v [illegible] & xviii 35 & xxv 41 42 [o] 1 John [illegible]

v 8—13 The apostle,

1 Lays down the only proper rule of conduct *If ye fulfil the royal law*, enacted by the King of kings, *according to the scripture*, where he hath revealed his will to us, and among the most eminent precepts stands this, *Thou shalt love thy neighbour as thyself*, treating every man with that benevolence, kindness, and impartiality, which, if in their case, you would reasonably expect from them, *ye do well*, such a conduct is honourable, and becoming your profession *But if ye have respect to persons*, shewing more favour to the rich than to the poor, *ye commit sin, and are convinced of the law as transgressors*, (*Lev* xix 15) and one such wilful iniquity must issue in your eternal ruin *For whosoever shall keep the whole law*, admitting that it were possible, *and yet* should *offend in one point, he is guilty of all*, such an allowed transgression would be as evident a contempt of the authority of the lawgiver, as if he broke every precept, and, as the wages of every sin is death, must expose the soul to the wrath of God *For he that said, Do not commit adultery, said also, Do not kill Now if thou commit no adultery, yet if thou kill, thou art become a transgressor of the law*, and liable to suffer its awful penalty

2 He exhorts them to behave as becometh the gospel which they profess *So speak ye, and so do*, in every word and work seek to approve yourselves to God, *as they that shall be judged by the law of liberty*, and who being brought under the gospel dispensation of light and grace, have the strongest obligations to shew an impartial, genuine, universal, and chearful obedience to the Redeemer's commands

3 He ſupports his exhortation by a moſt awful conſideration *For he ſhall have judgment without mercy, that hath ſhewed no mercy*, but hath been partial to the rich, and oppreſſive to the poor; whilſt, on the other hand, where by divine grace the heart hath been influenced to exerciſe fervent charity, there *mercy rejoiceth againſt judgment*, ſuch a one ſhall not be afraid of appearing at God's bar, but through the great Redeemer ſhall have boldneſs, and find favour with God in that day *Note*, A ſolemn ſenſe upon our minds of an approaching judgment, will neceſſarily have the moſt powerful influence on our conduct

14 [p] What *doth it* profit, my brethren, though a man
ſay he hath faith, and have not works? can faith ſave
him? 15 If a brother or ſiſter be naked, and deſtitute
of daily food, 16 And one of you ſay unto them,
Depart in peace, be ye warmed and filled [q] notwith-
ſtanding ye give them not thoſe things which are needful
to the body, what *doth it* profit? 17 Even ſo faith,
if it hath not works, is dead, being alone 18 Yea, a
man may ſay, Thou haſt faith, and I have works ſhew
me thy faith † without thy works, and [r] I will ſhew
thee my faith by my works 19 Thou believeſt that
[s] there is one God, thou doſt well [t] the devils alſo be-
lieve and tremble 20 But wilt thou know, O vain
man, that faith without works is dead? 21 Was not
Abraham our father juſtified by works, [u] when he had
offered Iſaac his ſon upon the altar? 22 ‡ Seeſt thou
[x] how faith wrought with his works, and by works was
faith made perfect? 23 And the ſcripture was fulfilled,
which ſaid, [y] Abraham believed God, and it was imputed
unto him for righteouſneſs and he was called [z] the
friend of God 24 Ye ſee then how that by works a
man is juſtified, and not by faith only 25 Likewiſe
alſo was not Rahab the harlot juſtified by works, when
ſhe had received the meſſengers, and had ſent them out
another way? 26 For as the body without the § ſpirit
is dead, ſo faith without works is dead alſo

p Mat vii 26 Chap i 22
q Job xxxi 20. 1 John iii 17
† Some read, By thy works
r Chap ii 23
s Deut vi 4
t Mark i 24 & v 7
u Gen xxii 9 12
‡ Or, thou ſeeſt
x Heb xi 17
y Gen xv 6 Rom iv 3 Gal iii 6
z 2 Chron xx 7 Iſa xli 8
a Joſh ii 1 Heb xi 31
§ Or breath

v 14—26 The apoſtle having ſpoken of the royal law, proceeds to ſhew the influence of faith on all holy obedience, not, as many vainly ſuggeſt, in oppoſition to Paul, or to correct his doctrine, their word proceeded from that one Spirit, who is truth itſelf, and cannot contradict his own revelation Paul ſpeaks of faith as juſtifying the ſinner in the ſight of God, James ſpeaks of it as juſtifying us in the ſight of men, by the effects which it produces in juſtified perſons, for which Paul was equally an advocate *See Gal* v 6 1 *Theſ* i 3 *Tit* iii 8

1 True faith ever produces genuine fruit, and worketh by love, without which the profeſſion of faith is uſeleſs, *What doth it profit, my brethren, though a man ſay he hath faith, and have not works?* *Saying* and *having* are very different things What can a mere boaſted name ſignify? *Can faith*, ſuch a faith, *ſave him?* *If a brother or ſiſter be naked, and deſtitute of daily food*, and the neceſſaries of life, *and one of you*, pretending to charity, *ſay unto them, Depart in peace, be ye warmed and filled notwithſtanding ye give them not thoſe things which are needful to the body, what doth it profit?* ſuch empty words have nothing of godlike charity in them, and are mere ſounding braſs, and tinkling cymbal *Even ſo faith, if it hath not works, is dead, being alone*, an empty profeſſion, without real life and power *Yea, a man may ſay* to a vaunting hypocrite who pleads his faith, *Thou haſt faith*, in name, *and I have works, ſhew me thy faith*, to which thou makeſt ſuch vain pretenſions, *without thy works*, of which if thou art deſtitute, how wilt thou prove its genuineneſs and reality? *and I will ſhew thee my faith by my works*, which are the only indiſputable evidence before men of its truth *Thou mayeſt* perhaps ſay thou art no atheiſt, *thou believeſt that there is one God*, ſo far *thou doſt well* but what influence hath this faith upon thee? *the devils alſo believe and tremble*, and their faith is perhaps herein more operative than thine *But wilt thou know, O vain man, that faith without works is dead?* and wants every proof of its ſoundneſs and ſincerity *Note*, (1) To rehearſe the articles of our creed, if we have not the truth of faith in our heart, will not advance us above the devils (2) All pretences to faith are but deluſion, where men's works deny him in whom they profeſs to believe

2 He ſupports what he advances with ſcripture evidence

[1] In the caſe of Abraham *Was not Abraham our Father juſtified by works*, and proved to be a true believer, *when he had offered Iſaac his ſon upon the altar?* then his juſtification in the ſight of God, which he had many years before obtained, (*Rom* iv 10, 11) became evident, and the ſincerity of his faith apparent to all men *Seeſt thou how faith wrought with his works*, effectually engaging him to obey God's command, *and by works was faith made perfect*, manifeſted to be right in kind, and in the moſt vigorous exerciſe *And the ſcripture was fulfilled*, and ſeen to be true, *which ſaid*, many years before that event, (*See Gen* xv 6) *Abraham believed God, and it was imputed unto him for righteouſneſs and he was called the friend of God* *Ye ſee then*, by this inſtance, *how that by works a man is juſtified*, and the reality of his character as a believer diſcovered, *and not by faith only* which is ſuch only in name, without producing any genuine fruit that demonſtrates its living influence, or, though it be real, can only appear to men by the effects which it produces

[2] In the caſe of Rahab *Likewiſe alſo was not Rahab the harlot juſtified by works*, and did ſhe not give a ſolid proof of the faith ſhe poſſeſſed before the ſpies arrived at her houſe, that God would infallibly give the land of Canaan to Iſrael, *when*, in conſequence thereof, great as the danger was to which ſhe muſt expoſe herſelf, *ſhe had received the meſſengers*, who came to ſpy out the country, *and had ſent them out another way?*

From the whole therefore it appears evident, that nominal faith, or the mere profeſſion of it, without any living fruits of grace produced from it, is mere hypocriſy *For as the body without the ſpirit is dead, ſo faith without works is dead alſo* Where that vital principle is implanted, its powerful energy will be ſeen, and we may aſſuredly conclude, where no fruits of grace appear in the temper and converſation, that the ſoul is as really dead in ſin, as the body is dead when the ſpirit is departed, and nothing but the lifeleſs clay remains.

CHAP III

The apoſtle here reproves all arrogance of talk or behaviour 1 *Thoſe who profeſs religion, ought eſpecially to govern their tongues*, ver 1—12 2 *True wiſdom makes men meek, and avoiders of ſtrife and envy and hereby may eaſily be diſtinguiſhed from a wiſdom that is earthly, and hypocritical*, ver 13, *to the end*

1 MY brethren, [a] be not many maſters, knowing
that [b] we ſhall receive the greater condemna-
tion 2 For [c] in many things we offend all If any
man offend not in word, the ſame *is* a perfect man,
and able alſo to bridle the whole body 3 Behold, [d] we
put bits in the horſes mouths, that they may obey us,
and we turn about their whole body 4 Behold alſo
the ſhips, which though they be ſo great, and are driven
of fierce winds, yet are they turned about with a very
ſmall helm, whitherſoever the governor liſteth 5 Even
ſo the tongue is a little member, and [g] boaſteth great
things Behold how great † a matter a little fire kind-
leth! 6 And [h] the tongue *is* a fire, a world of iniqui-
ty ſo is the tongue amongſt our members, that [i] it de-
fileth the whole body, and ſetteth on fire the ‡ courſe of
nature, and it is ſet on fire of hell 7 For every kind of
beaſts, and of birds, and of ſerpents, and things in the
ſea, is tamed, and hath been tamed of § mankind 8
But the tongue can no man tame, *it is* an unruly evil,
[k] full of deadly poiſon 9 Therewith bleſs we God,
even the Father, and therewith curſe we men, [l] which
are made after the ſimilitude of God 10 Out of the
ſame mouth proceedeth bleſſing and curſing My bre-
thren, theſe things ought not ſo to be 11 Doth a
fountain ſend forth at the ſame ‖ place ſweet *water* and
bitter? 12 Can the fig tree, my brethren, bear olive
berries? either a vine, figs? ſo *can* no fountain both
yield ſalt water and freſh

a Mat xxiii 8 Rom ii 20 1 Pet v 3
b Luke vi 37
c 1 Kings viii 46 2 Chron vi 36 Prov xx 9 Eccleſ vii 20 1 John i 8
d Pſ xxxiv 13 Eccluſ xix 16 Chap i 26
g Mat xii 37
Pſ xxxii 9
Pſ xii 3, 4 & lxxiii 8, 9
† Or wood
h Prov xvi 27
i Mat xv 11 18, 19
‡ Or wheel
§ Or, the nature of man
k Pſ cxl 3 Rom iii 13
l Gen i 27, & ix 6
‖ Or hole

v 1—12 They who have the leaſt pretenſions to true godlineſs, are often the moſt talkative profeſſors of it to bridle the tongue is therefore among the proofs of living faith

1 He warns them againſt a magiſterial and cenſorious behaviour *My brethren, be not many maſters*, affect not to ſet up for teachers, (διδάσκαλοι), loving to hear yourſelves talk, and liberally dealing out reproof and cenſure, *knowing that we ſhall receive the greater condemnation*, by being thus forward to pronounce ſentence on others, when we do not truly firſt judge ourſelves *for* if we were duly ſenſible of our own faults, we ſhould be leſs rigid in our judgment of others, ſeeing *in many things we offend all*, and the more we know of our own hearts, the more ſhall we be obliged to own, that our cenſure can nowhere ſo juſtly light as upon ourſelves, for we muſt be conſcious to more evil within, than we can know of all the world beſide

2 He enjoins them to bridle their tongues *If any man offend not in word*, and hath ſuch a guard over himſelf as to utter nothing raſh, opprobrious, falſe, or ſinful, *the ſame is a perfect man*, a finiſhed Chriſtian, far advanced in the divine life, *and able alſo to bridle the whole body*, and reſtrain the irregular appetites and paſſions which war againſt the ſoul *Behold, we put bits in the horſes mouths, that they may obey us, and we turn about their whole body*, governing and directing thereby all their motions *Behold alſo the ſhips, which though they be ſo great, and are driven of fierce winds, yet are they turned about with a very ſmall helm, whitherſoever* the governor or pilot *liſteth* *Even ſo the tongue is a little member, and* boaſteth

boasteth great things, and, according as it is under government, or lawless, is capable of doing much good, or much evil

3 The evil of an unruly tongue is great *Behold how great a matter a little fire kindleth!* what a conflagration blazes from a single spark! *And the tongue*, when let loose, *is a fire, a world of iniquity*, pouring forth the abominations of the heart *so is the tongue amongst our members, that it defileth the whole body, and setteth on fire the course of nature*, in nations, churches, families, spreading sedition, treasons, heresies, blasphemies, divisions, enmity, in every age, in every station, its baleful influence appears *and it is set on fire of hell*, infected with the old serpent's venom, promoting the interests of Satan's kingdom by profaneness, rage, lying, lewdness, murder, and all the train of evils which flow from thence, the punishment of which will be, that in hell it shall be tormented in flames unquenchable *For every kind of beasts*, the most savage, *and of birds*, however untractable in their nature, yea, *and of serpents, and things in the sea, is tamed, and hath been tamed of mankind*, mastered by their power, and rendered gentle by human art *but the tongue can no man tame*, nothing short of almighty power and grace can restrain or cure its malignity *it is an unruly evil, full of deadly poison*, deadly to the owner, and mortal as far as its influence extends. *Therewith bless we God, even the Father*, in prayer and praise speaking good of his name, *and* this is indeed the proper use of our tongues, but alas, how horrid is that perversion of speech, when *therewith curse we men, which are made after the similitude of God* Yet such is the inconsistence of some professors of religion, that *out of the same mouth proceedeth blessing and cursing*, worship in one breath, and then reviling, slandering, and backbiting in the next *My brethren, these things ought not so to be*, such behaviour is utterly incongruous, and contradictory to the truth of the gospel *Doth a fountain send forth at the same place sweet water and bitter? Can the fig tree, my brethren, bear olive-berries? either a vine, figs? so can no fountain both yield salt water and fresh* and as impossible is it for a heart, in which true grace is implanted, to be guilty habitually of such gross inconsistencies

13 Who *is* a wise man and endued with knowledge
amongst you? [n] let him shew out of a good conversation
his works [o] with meekness of wisdom 14 But if ye
have [p] bitter envying and strife in your hearts, [q] glory
not, and lye not against the truth 15 This wisdom
descendeth not from above, but *is* earthly, [r] sensual, de-
vilish 16 For [s] where envying and strife *is*, there *is*
confusion, and every evil work 17 But the wisdom
[t] that is from above, is first [u] pure, then peaceable, gen-
tle, *and* easy to be intreated, full of mercy [x] and good
fruits, [y] without partiality, and [z] without hypocrisy 18
And [a] the fruit of righteousness is sown in peace of them
that make peace

n Mat v 16 Chap. ii 18
o Chap i 21 1 Pet iii 15
p Rom xiii 13
q Rom ii 17 23
r Jude 19
s 1 Cor iii 3 Gal v 20
t Chap i 17
u Mat v 8
x Luke vi 36
y Gal v 22
z Chap ii 1 &c
y Rom xii 9
a Prov xi 18 Hos x 12 Mat v 9 Ibid

2 13—18 Nothing is more desireable than true wisdom The apostle here teaches us,

1 In what way that will shew itself *Who is a wise man and endued with knowledge amongst you? let him shew out of a good conversation his works with meekness of wisdom*, and prove his pretensions, not by arrogant boasts, but by his humility, meekness, holy conversation, and every good word and work, which may prove him a partaker of the grace of God in truth, and of the wisdom which maketh wise unto salvation

2 A contrary conduct evidently demonstrates the folly and falshood of pretended sophists *But if ye have bitter envying and strife in your hearts*, live under the power of a contentious and disputing spirit, evident in the bitter words which proceed out of your mouths, *glory not* in any fancied attainments, or zeal for orthodoxy, *and lye not against the truth*, by pretending to contend for that, to which your temper proves you an utter stranger *This wisdom descendeth not from above*, and never had God for its author, *but is earthly*, in its principle and end, *sensual*, the offspring of the fallen nature, and *devilish*, the image of Satan, and cultivated by him to advance the interest of his kingdom *for where envying and strife is, there is confusion, and every evil work*, that tend to ruin both our own souls, and all that are around us

3 How different and lovely are the effects and influence of true wisdom! *But the wisdom that is from above*, coming down from the Father of lights, the gift of his grace to his peculiar people, *is first pure*, engaging us to all purity in doctrine, manners, temper, speech, and conduct, *then peaceable*, breathing nothing but love and quietness, averse to noisy broils and hot dispute, maintaining peace where it subsists, and seeking to heal every breach which division hath created It is *gentle*, affable, courteous, condescending, ready to recede from its own in matters of property to avoid litigation, and mild, where in sentiment any difference subsists, never urging its own opinion with violence, willing patiently to hear the judgment of others *easy to be intreated*, and ready to forgive every offence, not rigidly obstinate, but flexible to the advice of the wiser and more experienced *full of mercy and good fruits*, benevolent, generous, liberal, willing to the utmost to help and relieve the distresses of the afflicted *without partiality*, in judging or censuring others, *and without hypocrisy*, speaking and acting always with simplicity and godly sincerity, without disguise or design *And the fruit of righteousness*, even all the gracious produce above described, and eternal life hereafter, *is sown in peace of them that make peace*, they who are possessed of the peaceable wisdom above described, are the persons who go forth bearing the precious seed, and shall see in their own hearts, and under their ministry, the plenteous success of their labours both here and hereafter, *for the work of righteousness shall be peace, and the effect of righteousness quietness and assurance for ever*

CHAP. IV

In this chapter we are directed to consider, 1 Some causes of contention besides those mentioned in the foregoing chapter, and to watch against them, ver 1—5 2 We are taught to abandon the friendship of this world, so as to submit and subject ourselves entirely to God, ver 4—10 3 All detraction and rash judgment of others is to be carefully avoided, ver 11, 12 4 We must preserve a constant regard, and pay the utmost deference to the disposals of divine providence, ver 13, to the end

1 FROM whence *come* wars and fightings among
you? *come they* not hence, *even* of your lusts
[a] that war in your members? 2 Ye lust, and have not
[b] ye kill, and desire to have, and cannot obtain ye fight
and war, yet ye have not, because ye ask not 3 [c] Ye
ask, and receive not, [d] because ye ask amiss, that ye may
consume it upon your lusts 4 [e] Ye adulterers, and
adulteresses, know ye not that [f] the friendship of the
world is enmity with God? [g] whosoever therefore will be
a friend of the world, is the enemy of God 5 Do ye
think that the scripture saith in vain, [h] The spirit that
dwelleth in us lusteth to envy? 6. But he giveth more
grace wherefore he saith, [i] God resisteth the proud, but
giveth grace unto the humble 7 Submit yourselves
therefore to God, [k] resist the devil, and he will flee from
you 8 [l] Draw nigh to God, and he will draw nigh to
you [m] cleanse *your* hands, ye sinners, and purify *your*
hearts, ye double minded 9. [n] Be afflicted, and mourn,
[o] and weep let your laughter be turned to mourning,
and *your* joy to heaviness 10 [p] Humble yourselves in
the sight of the Lord, [q] and he shall lift you up

a Rom viii 23 Gal v 17 1 Pet ii 11
b Chap. v 6
c Job xxvii 9 Ps xviii 41 Prov i 28 Isa i 15. J xiv 12 Mic iii 4 Zech vii 13
d 1 John v 14
e Ps lxxiii 27
f 1 John ii 15
g John v 44 & xvii 14 Gal i 10
h Gen vi 5 & viii 21 Num xi 29 Prov xxi 10
i Isa cxxxviii 6 Prov iii 34 Mat xxiii 12 Luke xvi 14
1 Pet v 5
k Eph iv 27 1 Pet v 9
l 2 Chr xv 2
m Isa i 16
n Mat v 4
o Chap v 1
p Luke xiv 11 & xviii 14 1 Pet v 6
q Job xxii 29

2 1—10 Inordinate desire after earthly things is the usual ground of contention, against this therefore the apostle warns them

1 He ascribes to this the wars and contentions which then were notorious among them *From whence come wars and fightings among you?* which some suppose hath reference to the many seditions of the Jewish people against the Roman government, but rather refers to the contentions and law suits which were maintained by those who made profession of Christianity, and which were so unbecoming of the name they bore *come they not hence, even of your lusts that war in your members?* Yes to the pride and covetousness of your hearts do these owe their origin, and tend to the ruin of religion, and the peace of the church, provoking God to withdraw his spirit from you *Ye lust*, and long to gratify your criminal passions, *and have not* what you pursue after *ye kill*, impatient to inherit, and wishing those dead whom you expect to succeed, *and desire to have*, grasping covetously after abundance, *and cannot obtain*, disappointment blasts your pursuits *ye fight and war*, contending fiercely for superiority, wealth, and victory, *yet ye have not*, your schemes and designs are defeated, *because ye ask not*, neglecting to seek counsel of God in your enterprizes, and not desiring his direction and blessing And if *ye ask, ye receive not, because ye ask amiss*, neither praying for right things, nor with a right view, but eager after earthly gain, *that ye may consume it upon your lusts*, not to employ it for God's glory and the good of mankind *Note*, (1) Nothing is more contrary to the spirit of Christianity, than covetousness and fierce disputes (2) They who do not seek God's blessing, justly meet with disappointment in all their enterprizes (3) To ask amiss is as bad as not to ask at all, nor may we expect an answer to those prayers which worldly-mindedness and selfishness, not God's glory, dictates

2 He solemnly warns them against intimate connection with the world that lieth in wickedness *Ye adulterers and adulteresses*, whose affections are alienated from Christ, to whom ye were once in profession and baptism espoused, *know ye not that the friendship of the world is enmity with God* all undue attachment to the pleasures, interest, honours of the world, and delight in the company of the worldly-minded, is utterly inconsistent with fidelity to God, and real friendship with him, nay, are virtually a profession of enmity against him *Whosoever therefore*

therefore will be a friend of the world, and at all events is resolved to keep fair with the men of the world, and to advance his interests here below, he *is*, and must be, *the enemy of God*. *Do ye think that the scripture saith in vain*, in many passages describing the deadly corruption of the natural heart, *The spirit that dwelleth in us lusteth to envy?* and, till renewed by grace, is ever with an evil eye regarding the superior prosperity and affluence of others, and grasping after the like abundance: this spirit must therefore be mortified, or we must be condemned with the world.

3. He directs them how to overcome the world. *But he*, even God, *giveth more grace* than the world can spread snares, and hath infinitely greater riches to bestow, than this poor earth can proffer. *Wherefore he saith, God resisteth the proud*, who make flesh their arm, and place their happiness and confidence in worldly things, vain of their own wisdom, riches, or attainments; these he fights against, blasts their designs, and ruins their confidences: *but he giveth grace unto the humble*, who, sensible of their own wretchedness, wants, and weakness, bow down at his feet for relief. *Submit yourselves therefore to God*, to his guidance and government, obedient to his will and word, resigned to his providence, and content with the portion which he allots you, whatever it be. *Resist the devil, and he will flee from you*, as a vanquished foe, unable to contend with those who have put on the whole armour of God, and appear resolved to fight manfully under Christ's banner. *Draw nigh to God*, in fervent prayer for help, *and he will draw nigh to you*, with comfort, strength, and salvation in every time of need, and will make you more than conquerors.

4. He exhorts them to put away every evil thing, and with real penitence to return to God. *Cleanse your hands, ye sinners*, in the atoning blood of Jesus, that you may lift them up with acceptance before the throne of grace; *and purify your hearts, ye double-minded*, from pride, envy, covetousness, and hypocrisy; seeking that grace which can alone be effectual for this blessed purpose. *Be afflicted, and mourn, and weep* over the deep corruption and sinfulness of your hearts, and under a sense of your past grievous departures from God. *Let your laughter be turned to mourning, and your joy to heaviness*, ashamed and confounded at your past basenefs, ingratitude, and unfaithfulness to a dying Redeemer. *Humble yourselves in the sight of the Lord*, acknowledging your vileness, and imploring his pardoning grace and help; *and he shall lift you up* with the arms of his love, and recover you from your backsliding, restore you to his favour, and bring you at last to his presence and glory. *Note*, (1.) They who would find acceptance with God, must approach him as cleansed with atoning blood, and without hypocrisy desiring indeed to be received into the arms of his mercy. (2.) They who have unfaithfully departed from God, need with shame, remorse, and mourning, return to him, humbling their souls before him, that he may lift them up. (3.) None perish, who cast themselves at the footstool of divine mercy: it is God's delight to revive the spirit of the humble, and to heal the broken-hearted.

11 Speak not evil one of another, brethren. He that
speaketh evil of *his* brother, [r] and judgeth *his* brother,
speaketh evil of the law, and judgeth the law: but if
thou judge the law, thou art not a doer of the law, but
a judge. 12 There is one lawgiver, who is able to
save, [s] and to destroy: [t] who art thou that judgest another?
13 [u] Go to now, ye that say, To-day or to-morrow
we will go into such a city, and continue there
a year, and buy, and sell, and get gain: 14 Whereas
ye know not what *shall be* on the morrow. For what *is*
your life? [x] It is even a vapour that appeareth for a
little time, and then vanisheth away. 15 For that ye
ought to say, [y] If the Lord will, we shall live, and do
this, or that. 16 But now ye rejoice in your boastings:
[z] all such rejoicing is evil. 17 Therefore [a] to
him that knoweth to do good, and doeth it not, to him
it is sin.

r Matt. vii. 1. Rom. ii. 1. 1 Cor. iv. 5. — s Matt. x. 28. — t Rom. xiv. 4. — u Prov. xxvii. 1. Luke xii. 18. — x Job vii. 7. Psal. cii. 3. Chap. i. 10. 1 Pet. i. 24. — y Acts xviii. 21. 1 Cor. iv. 19. Heb. vi. 3. — z 1 Cor. v. 6. — a Luke xii. 47. John ix. 41. Rom. i. 20, 21, 32.

v. 11—17. The former subject is here resumed, concerning the right government of the tongue; and we are,

1. Warned against all reviling and rash censure. *Speak not evil one of another, brethren*, inventing falsehoods, exposing the infirmities, publishing the failings, divulging the secrets, aggravating the offences, or detracting from the excellencies one of another. *He that speaketh evil of his brother, and judgeth his brother*, in things which God hath left indifferent, *speaketh evil of the law, and judgeth the law*, arraigning the wisdom, equity, and goodness of the lawgiver, as if he permitted what he ought to condemn: *but if thou thus arrogantly judge the law*, and pretend to decide what is fit to be enjoined, and what not, *thou art not a doer of the law, but a judge*. *There is one lawgiver, who is able to save, and to destroy*, invested with supreme authority to enact laws, able to reward the faithful, and punish the disobedient. This is his prerogative; to invade it, is the highest insolence. *Who art thou*, a poor, despicable, perishing worm, *that judgest another*, and darest thus to usurp the throne of God? *Note*, (1.) Where we cannot in conscience speak well of a person, it is our duty at least to be silent. (2.) Since God hath reserved the power to himself to determine concerning men's everlasting state, and hath given us his law as our only rule of duty, it becomes us to make nothing sin, which he hath not declared to be evil; nor ought we to erect another court of judicature over our brethren, who make men's opinions, not the word of God, is to decide.

2. He inculcates constant dependance upon divine providence. *Go to now, ye* who forget your entire dependance upon God's disposal of you, and *that say*, with self-sufficiency and disregard of him, *To-day or to-morrow we will go into such a city, and continue there a year, and buy, and sell, and get gain*, as if your time, and the success of your enterprizes, were in your own hands, and owing to your own wisdom and diligence. *Whereas ye know not what shall be on the morrow*, or whether you shall ever live to the rising of another sun. *For what is your life? It is even a vapour that appeareth for a little time, and then vanisheth away*, so fleeting, so transitory, and every hour in jeopardy; the consideration of which should teach you to speak less confidently. *For that ye ought to say, If the Lord will, we shall live, and do this, or that*, adding this humble proviso, and owning your dependance for life, ability, or success in every enterprize, upon him, in whose hands our breath is, and whose are all your ways. (Dan. v. 23.) *But now ye rejoice in your boastings*, and talk as if you ceased to be creatures under the care and keeping of your great Creator. *All such rejoicing* in your own self-sufficiency *is evil*, most offensive to God, and bringing great guilt upon your souls. *Therefore to him that knoweth to do good, and doeth it not, to him it is sin*, highly aggravated, as he wilfully opposes the dictates of his own conscience, and treasures up thereby wrath against the day of wrath. *Note*, (1.) In all our ways we should consider God, and in every undertaking beg his blessing, and commit ourselves to his guidance. (2.) Our lives are fleeting things; we have not a moment we can call our own. It is folly to be planning schemes for years to come, when we know not what a day may bring forth. (3.) When we know better, and do worse, we are most inexcusable, and shall lie down under peculiar condemnation.

CHAP. V.

In this chapter the apostle denounces the judgments of God upon those rich men that oppress the poor, ver. 1—6. Hereupon all the faithful are exhorted to patience under their trials and sufferings, ver. 7—11. The sin of swearing is cautioned against, ver. 12. We are directed how to carry it, both under affliction, and in prosperity, ver. 13. Prayer for the sick, and anointing with oil, are prescribed, ver. 14, 15. Christians are directed to acknowledge their faults one to another, and to pray one for another, and the efficacy of prayer is proved, ver. 16—18. And lastly, it is recommended to us to do what we can for the reducing of them that stray from the ways of truth.

1 [a] GO to now, ye rich men, weep and howl for your
miseries that shall come upon *you*. 2 Your
riches are corrupted, and [b] your garments are moth-eaten.
3 Your gold and silver is cankered; and the rust of
them shall be a witness against you, and shall eat your
flesh as it were fire. [c] Ye have heaped treasure together
for the last days. 4 Behold, [d] the hire of the labourers
which have reaped down your fields, which is of you
kept back by fraud, crieth: and [e] the cries of them
which have reaped are entered into the ears of the Lord
of sabaoth. 5 [f] Ye have lived in pleasure on the earth,
and been wanton; ye have nourished your hearts, as in a
day of slaughter. 6 Ye have condemned *and* killed
the just; *and* he doth not resist you. 7 Be patient, therefore,
brethren, unto the coming of the Lord. Behold,
the husbandman waiteth for the precious fruit of the
earth, and hath long patience for it, until he receive [h] the
early and latter rain. 8 Be ye also patient; stablish
your hearts: for [i] the coming of the Lord draweth nigh.
9 [k] Grudge not one against another, brethren, lest ye
be condemned: behold, the judge standeth before the
door. 10 Take, my brethren, the prophets, who have
spoken in the name of the Lord, for an example of suffering
affliction, and of patience. 11 Behold, [n] we
count them happy which endure. Ye have heard of the
patience [o] of Job, and have seen [p] the end of the Lord;
that [q] the Lord is very pitiful, and of tender mercy.

a Prov. xi. 28. Luke vi. 24. 1 Tim. vi. 9. — b Matt. vi. 20. — c Rom. ii. 5. — d Lev. xix. 13. Jer. xxii. 13. Mal. iii. 5. Ecclus. xxxiv. 22. — e Deut. xxiv. 15. — f Job xxi. 13. Amos vi. 1. Luke xvi. 19, 25. — g Chap. iv. 2. — h Deut. xi. 14. Jer. v. 24. Joel ii. 23. — i Phil. iv. 5. Heb. x. 25, 37. — k Chap. iv. 11. — l Matt. xxiv. 33. 1 Cor. iv. 5. — m Matt. v. 12. — n Psal. xciv. 12. Matt. v. 10, 11. — o Job i. 21, 22. — p Job xlii. 10. — q Numb. xiv. 18. Psal. ciii. 8.

v. 1—11. The apostle addresseth himself,

1. To the rich oppressors. *Go to now, ye rich men*, whose portion is in this world only, *weep and howl for your miseries that shall come upon you*, both temporal and eternal. *Your riches are corrupted*, your hoarded store putrify, *and your garments are moth-eaten*,

eaten. Your gold and silver is cankered, laid by in useless bags, *and the rust of them* which by time they have contracted like iron, *shall be a witness against you*, to upbraid your covetousness and avarice, *and shall eat your flesh as it were fire*, bringing down divine vengeance upon your guilty heads. *Ye have heaped treasure together for the last days*, to provide for distant years to come, but which will be a prey to the destroyer of your city and nation, and serve only to be a treasure of wrath against the day of wrath. *Behold the hire of the labourers which have reaped down your fields, which is of you kept back by fraud, crieth* against you for judgment, *and the cries of them that reaped*, complaining of your injustice and oppression, *are entered into the ears of the Lord of sabaoth*, who will avenge their quarrel. *Ye have lived in pleasure on the earth, and been wanton*, indulging every brutish appetite, and making provision for the flesh to fulfil the lusts thereof: *ye have nourished your hearts, as in a day of slaughter*, faring sumptuously on the spoil of iniquity, fattening yourselves as beasts for the slaughter. *Ye have condemned and killed the just*, both the Lord himself, and many of his righteous servants, *and he doth not resist you*, meekly and patiently resigned to suffer. *Note*, (1.) Though wicked men prosper for a while, God keeps a strict account of all their ways, and will bring them shortly into judgment for these things. (2.) Riches are to be used, not to be hoarded in bags, or barns, or wardrobes; then they prove a blessing. Hoarded, they are only treasures of wrath. (3.) Though the poor may groan under the yoke of oppression without redress, there is one who hears their appeal, and will vindicate their cause. (4.) Pleasure, luxury, and indulgence may for a while lull the sinner's soul asleep, but he will soon be awakened from his golden dream, and startled with the fearful looking-for of judgment, when too late he will begin to weep and howl in vain.

2. He addresses himself to the persecuted poor saints. [1.] *Be patient therefore, brethren, unto the coming of the Lord*, who will come, and will not tarry, to espouse your cause, and release you from the power of your oppressors. *Behold, the husbandman waiteth for the precious fruit of the earth, and hath long patience for it, until he receive the early and latter rain*, expecting the desired harvest, when he hopes to reap the fruit of all his toils. *Be ye also patient, stablish your hearts: for the coming of the Lord draweth nigh*, when your redemption from every misery will be compleated for ever. [2.] *Grudge not one against another, brethren*, groan not under your sufferings through envy, fretfulness, or desire of revenge, *lest ye be condemned: behold, the judge standeth before the door*, and that consideration should powerfully plead with you to wait with patience, and refer yourselves entirely to his determination. [3.] *Take, my brethren, the prophets, who have spoken in the name of the Lord*, faithfully discharging their commission, *for an example of suffering affliction, and of patience*, whose noble behaviour bravely imitate under the like persecutions. *Behold, we count them happy which endure* with meekness and resignation to the will of God, because their end must be peace and blessedness eternal. *Ye have heard of the patience of Job*, how eminently exemplary; *and have seen the end of the Lord*, the happy issue which God put to his troubles; or that perfect pattern of submission to the will of God which Jesus himself shewed under all his sufferings: *that the Lord is very pitiful, and of tender mercy*, sympathizing with his suffering saints, and delivering them out of all their afflictions. We need not therefore be discouraged under any cross; the victory is secured, and the end of it shall be our eternal glory.

12 But above all things, my brethren, ᵗ swear not, ᵗ Ex. xx. 7. Mat. v. 34.
neither by heaven, neither by the earth, neither by any
other oath: but let your yea be yea, and your nay nay;
lest ye fall into condemnation. 13 ʳ Is any among you ʳ Mat. xxvi. 38. [illegible]
afflicted? let him pray. Is any merry? ˢ let him sing ˢ Eph. v. 19. Col. iii. 16.
psalms. 14 Is any sick among you? let him call for
the elders of the church; and let them pray over him,
ᵗ anointing him with oil in the name of the Lord. 15 ᵗ Mark vi. 13. & xvi. 18.
And the prayer of faith shall save the sick, and the Lord ᵘ Isa. xxxiii. 24. Mat. ix. 2.
shall raise him up; and ᵘ if he have committed sins,
they shall be forgiven him. 16 Confess your faults one
to another, and pray one for another, that ye may be
healed. ˣ the effectual fervent prayer of a righteous ˣ Gen. xx. 17. & xxxii. 28. Num. xi. 2. [illegible]
man availeth much. 17 Elias was a man ʸ subject to
like passions as we are, and ᶻ he prayed earnestly that it
might not rain: ᵃ and it rained not on the earth by the
space of three years and six months. 18 And ᵇ he
prayed again, and the heaven gave rain, and the earth
brought forth her fruit. 19 Brethren, ᶜ if any of you
do err from the truth, and one convert him; 20 Let
him know, that he which converteth a sinner from the
error of his way, ᵈ shall save a soul from death, and
ᵉ shall hide a multitude of sins.

v. 12—20. The apostle here,

1. Warns them against all profane swearing. *But above all things, my brethren, swear not, neither by heaven, neither by the earth, neither by any other oath: but let your yea be yea, and your nay nay*, except in solemn cases, where an appeal to God is lawful, never exceed a simple affirmation or denial in your conversation, *lest ye fall into condemnation*, and bring guilt upon your souls. *Note*, Swearing is of all sins most unprofitable, and while it offers the highest affront to God, affords not even momentary pleasure to the offender.

2. He teaches them how to behave in adversity and prosperity. *Is any among you afflicted? let him pray*, humbly spreading his case before the Lord, that he may obtain the needful relief. *Is any merry?* in prosperous circumstances, and happy in his soul, *let him sing psalms*, and praise the gracious giver of every good gift.

3. *Is any sick among you? let him call for the elders of the church, and let them pray over him, anointing him with oil in the name of the Lord*, as the symbol of the miraculous power with which the elders were invested, *and the prayer of faith shall save* and recover *the sick, and the Lord shall raise him up, and if he have committed sins*, which may have brought such a visitation upon him, *they shall be forgiven him*. *Note*, The removal of sickness is a great mercy, but the pardon of sin still far greater, for which we are especially called upon to offer up our prayers.

4. *Confess your faults one to another*, and take shame to yourselves where you have offended your brother. Or if any thing lies particularly upon your conscience, communicate it to some pious friend, or able minister of Christ, *and pray one for another* over the sins you confess and bewail, *that they may be healed*, their guilt pardoned, and their power subdued.

5. He shews the great efficacy of prayer. *The effectual fervent prayer of a righteous man availeth much*, a memorable example of which we have in the case of *Elias*, who *was a man subject to like passions as we are*, liable, as other poor corrupted creatures, to many sinful infirmities, *and he prayed earnestly that it might not rain*, as a punishment upon Ahab and rebellious Israel, and a means to convince them of the greatness of their sins, *and it rained not on the earth by the space of three years and six months*, so long the land of Israel was parched with drought, and a severe famine followed. *And he prayed again, and the heaven gave rain, and the earth brought forth her fruit*; and as the effect of Elijah's prayer was so wonderful, we may comfortably be assured, that when we like him pray with faith and fervency, our prayers too shall receive an answer of peace.

6. He concludes with warmly recommending a zeal for the conversion of men's souls. *Brethren, if any of you do err from the truth*, in principle or in practice, backsliding from Christ, *and one convert him*, recovering him back again to the great Shepherd's fold, *let him know, that he which converteth a sinner from the error of his ways, shall save a soul from death*, preventing that eternal ruin which must otherwise have ensued, *and shall hide a multitude of sins*, which, when the sinner is converted, shall be forgiven and blotted out, as well as be a means of preventing all the evil which must have ensued from his ill example and influence. *Note*, (1.) Nothing is so valuable an acquisition as an immortal soul: one such won to Christ is better than the riches of both the Indies. (2.) They who truly turn to God, will have a veil of eternal oblivion cast on their past offences: they shall be remembered no more. (3.) Death eternal, of body and soul, is the wages of sin, and unless we are saved from it now, we must be undone for ever.

THE

EVANGELICAL EXPOSITOR;

OR, A

PRACTICAL COMMENT

UPON THE

First EPISTLE GENERAL of PETER.

TWO epistles we have inrolled in the sacred canon of the scripture, written by Peter, an eminent apostle of Jesus Christ The design of this first epistle is, 1. To explain more fully the doctrines of Christianity to these newly converted Jews 2 To direct and persuade them to an holy conversation, in the faithful discharge of all personal and relative duties, whereby they would secure their own peace, and effectually confute the slanders and reproaches of their enemies. 3 To prepare them for sufferings This seems to be his principal intention; for he hath something to this purpose in every chapter, and doth, by a great variety of arguments, encourage them to patience and perseverance in the faith, lest the persecution and sad calamities that were coming upon them should prevail with them to apostatize from Christ and the gospel

CHAP I

In which the apostle describes the persons to whom he writes, and salutes them, ver 1, 2 Blesseth God for their regeneration to a lively hope of eternal salvation, ver 3—5 In the hopes of which salvation he shews they had great cause of rejoicing, though for a little while they were in heaviness and affliction for the trial of their faith, which would produce joy unspeakable and full of glory, ver 6—9 This is that salvation which the ancient prophets foretold, and the angels desire to look into, ver 10—12 He exhorteth them to sobriety and holiness, which he presseth from the consideration of the blood of Jesus, the invaluable price of man's redemption, ver 13—20 And to brotherly love, from the consideration of their regeneration, and the excellency of their spiritual state, ver 22—25.

1 PETER an apostle of Jesus Christ, to the
strangers [a] scattered throughout Pontus, Galatia, Cappadocia, Asia, and Bithynia, 2
[b] Elect [c] according to the foreknowledge of
God the Father, [d] through sanctification of the Spirit
unto obedience, and [e] sprinkling of the blood of Jesus
Christ [f] Grace unto you, and peace be multiplied.

[a] John vii 35 Jam i 1
[b] Rom xi 5 Eph i 4
[c] Rom viii 29
[d] 2 Thes ii 13
[e] Heb. xii. 24
[f] Rom i 7 1 Cor i 3 2 Pet i 2

v 1, 2 This epistle opens with,

1 The writer name and title *Peter, an apostle of Jesus Christ*, by his immediate appointment, and sent especially to the circumcision

2 The persons to whom it is addressed *To the strangers scattered throughout Pontus, Galatia, Cappadocia, Asia, and Bithynia*; dispersed by various providences through these provinces, and now called to the faith of Christ, *elect according to the foreknowledge of God the Father*, who from eternity designed you for salvation, as the objects whom his sovereign grace was pleased to chuse, *through sanctification of the Spirit unto obedience*, this blessed author of all grace effectually calling and converting your souls to the love and practice of true holiness, *and bringing you to the sprinkling of the blood of Jesus Christ*, for pardon and peace with God, which only by the sacrifice of the Redeemer could be obtained *Note*, (1) God hath an elect, whom before the worlds were, he determined to bring unto glory (2) These in the fulness of time are called to faith in a Redeemer, and, as miserable sinners, apply to the blood of sprinkling for the pardon of their iniquities (3) The Spirit of God sanctifies all those whom the Father chuses, and prepares them for the inheritance which is prepared for them

3 The salutation *Grace unto you, and peace be multiplied*; may the pardoning, healing, sanctifying, comforting, preserving grace of our God be with you, and peace, the blessed effect thereof, be diffused in the church, your families, and in your own souls *Note*, We need nothing more to make us happy, than grace and peace; and if we possess all the world beside, and lack these, we are poor and miserable

3 [g] Blessed *be* the God and Father of our Lord Jesus
Christ, which [h] according to his abundant mercy, [i] hath
begotten us again unto a lively hope, [k] by the resurrection of Jesus Christ from the dead, 4 To an inheritance
incorruptible and undefiled and [l] that fadeth not away,
[m] reserved in heaven for you, 5. [n] Who are kept by the
power of God through faith unto salvation ready to be
revealed in the last time. 6 [o] Wherein ye greatly re-
joice, though now [p] for a season (if need be) [q] ye are in
heaviness through manifold temptations 7 That [r] the
trial of your faith being much more precious than of
gold that perisheth, though [s] it be tried with fire, [t] might
be found unto praise and honour and glory at the ap-
pearing of Jesus Christ 8. [u] Whom having not seen,
ye love, [x] in whom though now ye see *him* not, yet
believing,

[g] 2 Cor i 3 Eph i 3
[h] Tit iii 5
[i] John iii 3, 5 Jam i 18
[k] 1 Cor xv 20
[l] Chap v 4
[m] Col i 5
[n] John x 28 & xvii 11, 15 Jude 1
[o] Mat v 12 Chap iv 13
[p] 2 Cor iv 17
[q] Jam i 2
[r] Jam i 3
[s] Job xxiii 10 Prov xvii 3 Isa xlviii 10 Zech xiii 9
[t] Rom ii 10 1 Cor iv 5
[u] 1 John iv 20
[x] John xx 29 2 Cor v 7 Heb xi. 1, 27.

believing, ye rejoice with joy unspeakable and full of
y Rom vi glory 9 Receiving y the end of your faith, *even* the
salvation of *your* souls

v 3—9 The apostle begins,

1 With thanksgiving for the inestimable blessings which through the gospel they enjoyed *Blessed be the God and Father of our Lord Jesus Christ, which, according to his abundant mercy,* without the least respect to our deserts, of his sovereign grace *hath begotten us again unto a lively hope,* when we had nothing in prospect before us but misery and despair, *by the resurrection of Jesus Christ from the dead,* who was delivered for our offences, and raised again for our justification, that we, beholding in him the justice of God satisfied, might be emboldened to approach a reconciled God, and not only by his grace be quickened to newness of life here, but be entitled also *to an inheritance incorruptible, undefiled, and that fadeth not away, reserved in heaven for you,* prepared by eternal love, and sure to every one of his redeemed, *who are kept,* not by your own strength or sufficiency, *but by the power of God,* engaged to protect you from all your enemies, and to preserve you, *through faith* of his operation in your hearts, *unto salvation* completed in glory, and which is *ready to be revealed in the last time,* when Jesus shall appear, and take his faithful followers to their eternal mansions of blessedness above *Note,* (1) We can never enough be thankful, when we remember the abundant mercy of our God and Father in Jesus Christ to our sinful souls (2) Every blessing flows from boundless and unmerited grace (3) The resurrection of Jesus from the dead is the grand foundation of our hope, and it is a lively hope, animating the soul to patience, purity, and perseverance, and never faileth till it is swallowed up in fruition (4) Heaven, with all its glories, is our *inheritance,* our title is secured, nay possession is taken by the Forerunner for us entered (5) Whatever enemies, snares, dangers, temptations, beset us in our way to heaven, we shall be more than conquerors, if God be our keeper, and if he implants true faith in our hearts, which never faileth (6) The time is short ere all the promises shall receive their accomplishment, and our salvation be perfected for ever

2 Having mentioned the salvation which was in prospect, he shews how that afforded comfort and support under all their trials *Wherein ye greatly rejoice,* looking forward and onward to your glorious hope, *though now for a season (if need be) ye are in heaviness through manifold temptations,* which though you cannot but feel as men, you can rejoice under them as Christians, and they are sent, *that the trial of your faith, being much more precious than of gold which perisheth, though it be tried in the fire, may be found unto praise and honour and glory, at the appearing of Jesus Christ,* when its purity, genuineness, and excellence, shall be acknowledged, brightened, and strengthened, by all the conflicts it hath sustained in the Saviour's service, *whom, having not seen, ye love* with fervent and supreme affection, faith realizing his amiableness to your souls, *in whom, though now ye see him not, yet believing, ye rejoice with joy unspeakable and full of glory,* the lively foretaste of the eternal bliss, *receiving the end of your faith, even the salvation of your souls,* begun already, and to be completed shortly in glory *Note,* (1) A Christian hath cause of rejoicing in God and the hope set before him at all times, and even in the midst of grief and trouble this consolation the world cannot take away (2) Though our lot as Christians in this world is manifold temptations, and our nature cannot but groan under the burden, yet we must remember there is a *need be* for every pang we feel, and that will reconcile us to them (3) The bitterest afflictions to flesh and blood are often the most profitable medicines to our souls, and when we come to glory we shall see, that these were indeed blessings in disguise (4) The trial of our faith tends to its confirmation and establishment, and like gold, when tortured in the furnace, we come forth from our troubles the brighter, and leave the dross of corruption behind (5) Fidelity will be crowned when Jesus shall appear, and all our trials then will end in immortal honour and eternal glory (6) Jesus is precious to the believing soul, and the realizing views of him, which faith presents, bring down the foretaste of heavenly blessedness

z Mat xiii 17 Luke x 24 a Gen xlix 10 Dan ii 44 Hag ii 7 Zech vi 12 b 2 Pet i 21 c Is xxii 6 & liii 3 &c Dan ix 26 Luke xxiv 26 Acts xxvi 22 d Dan ix 24 & xii 9 13 e Heb xi 13 39 f Acts ii 4 g Dan viii 13 & xii 5 6 Eph iii 10

10 z Of which salvation the prophets have enquired,
and searched diligently, a who prophesied of the grace
that should come unto you 11 Searching what or what
manner of time b the Spirit of Christ which was in them
did signify, when it testified beforehand c the sufferings
of Christ, and the glory that should follow 12 d Unto
whom it was revealed, e that not unto themselves, but
unto us they did minister the things which are now re-
ported unto you, by them that have preached the gospel
unto you, with f the holy Ghost sent down from heaven,
g which things the angels desire to look into

v 10—12 The salvation of the gospel, on which their faith fixed, was that which the blessed prophets had foretold, and after which they earnestly enquired *Of which salvation the prophets have enquired, and searched diligently* into the meaning of their own prophecies which by inspiration they delivered, digging deep into the golden mine, that themselves might share the treasure, *who prophesied of the grace that should come unto you* through the incarnate Saviour *Searching,* with eagerness, *what or what manner of time the Spirit of Christ, which was in them, did signify, when it testified beforehand the sufferings of Christ* for the sins of his people, *and the glory that should follow,* when, having offered his one atonement, he should ascend to the throne of Majesty on high They wished to know the exact time, and what would be the state of the world, when this great event should come to pass *Unto whom it was revealed, that not unto themselves, but unto us they did minister,* the events predicted were not to be fulfilled in their days, but ours, and they foretold *the things which are now reported unto you by them that have preached the gospel unto you, with the holy Ghost sent down from heaven,* who by his miraculous operations, and by the communication of his gifts and graces, bears his sacred testimony to the truth of our report *which things the angels desire to look into,* bending forward as the cherubims over the mercy-seat, with wonder and delight contemplating the glories of gospel-grace, admiring and adoring *Note,* (1) The mysteries of gospel-grace were not only the subject which engaged the holy prophets researches, but they afford matter for angelic contemplation, wonder, and praise (2) The word of God must be searched, and diligently examined there are treasures hid in it which will abundantly repay our pains (3) The Holy Ghost sent down from heaven still continues to make the gospel effectual to our salvation, and on his mighty operation all the success of our preaching depends

13 Wherefore h gird up the loins of your mind, i be h Lu xii 35 Eph vi 14
sober, and hope † to the end, for the grace that is to be i Luke xxi 34 Rom xiii 13
brought unto you at the revelation of Jesus Christ, 14 1 Thes v 6 † Gr perfectly
As obedient children, k not fashioning yourselves accord- k Rom xii 2 Chap iv 2
ing to the former lusts, l in your ignorance 15 But l Acts xvii 30
as he which hath called you is holy, so m be ye holy in m 2 Cor vii 1 Heb xii 14
all manner of conversation 16. Because it is written, n Lev xi 44 & xix 2 & xx 7
n Be ye holy, for I am holy 17 And if ye call on the o Deut x 17 Acts x 34 Rom ii 11
Father, o who without respect of persons judgeth accord- p Phil ii 12 Heb xii 28
ing to every man's work, p pass the time of your q sojourn- q 2 Cor v 6 Heb xi 13 Chap ii 11
ing here in fear 18 Forasmuch as ye know r that ye r 1 Cor vi 20 & vii 23
were not redeemed with corruptible things, *as* silver and s Ezek xx 18
gold, from your vain conversation s *received* by tradition t Acts xx 28 Eph i 7 Heb ix 12, 14 Rev v 9
from your fathers, 19 But t with the precious blood u Ex xii 5 Isa liii 7 John i 29, 36
of Christ, u as of a lamb x without blemish and without x Heb ix 14 & vii 26 Chap ii 22
spot 20 y Who verily was foreordained before the y Rom xvi 25 Eph iii 9 Col i 26 2 Tim i 9 10
foundation of the world, but was manifest in z these last z Gal iv 4 Eph i 10 Heb i 2
times for you, 21 a Who by him do believe in God a Rom iv 24
b that raised him up from the dead, and c gave him glory, b Acts ii 24 c Acts iii 13 Phil ii 9 Heb ii 9
that your faith and hope might be in God

v 13—21 From the foregoing considerations the apostle,

1 Enforces the practice of true godliness in sundry particulars *Wherefore,* (1) *Gird up the loins of your mind,* be disentangled from every thing in the world which would retard you in your heavenly course, and be strong in the Lord and the power of his might to fight the good fight of faith (2) *Be sober,* temperately using every creature-comfort, and with holy vigilance preparing for the Master's return *And,* (3) *Hope unto the end,* never dismayed nor discouraged by the temptations to which you may be exposed, but patiently persevering, and confidently waiting *for the grace that is to be brought unto you at the revelation of Jesus Christ,* when the work of grace shall be completed, and an eternity of glory succeed, the hope of which, as an anchor of the soul, will enable us to ride out every storm (4) Behave *as obedient children* to your heavenly Father, dutiful in observing his command, and submitting to his disposal and correction, *not fashioning yourselves according to the former lusts, in your ignorance,* not conformed to the corrupt manners, maxims, and pursuits of a world which lieth in wickedness, among whom we all had our conversation in time past, fulfilling the desires of the flesh and of the mind, and knowing not the dreadful ruin which hung over our heads To these ways let us never return, *but as he which hath called you is holy, so be ye holy in all manner of conversation,* proposing to yourselves nothing short of his complete and perfect image, and in every state, condition, and circumstance, desiring that your hearts, lips, and lives, may exactly correspond with his holy will *Because it is written* in that word which is our eternal rule of duty, *Be ye holy, for I am holy* (5) Maintain a holy jealousy over yourselves *And if,* as becometh your profession, *ye call* in ceaseless prayer *on the Father* for that grace which alone can enable you for all that he commands, *who, without respect of persons, judgeth according to every man's work,* and thereby proves whether they are obedient children or not, *pass the time of your sojourning here in fear,* in a filial fear of offending God, and holy jealousy over your own hearts, knowing that your present state is your pilgrimage, and that, if you are faithful, you shall shortly reach

the

the happy rest, where all your fears will end, and your felicity be completed for ever.

2. To encourage and engage them to the practice which he recommends, he suggests the most powerful motives. *Forasmuch as ye know that ye were not redeemed with corruptible things as silver and gold, from your vain conversation*, from the foolish traditions and corrupt manners and ways *received by tradition from your fathers*, to redeem you from which, all the perishing treasures of this world would be a price too despicable to be mentioned; *but* an infinitely greater hath been paid for you; ye are redeemed *with the precious blood of Christ, as of a lamb without blemish and without spot*, who offered himself as your ransom to God, pure from all defilement, a lamb fit to bleed on God's altar, and of such transcendent dignity in his person as to add infinite value to his sacrifice. *Who verily was fore-ordained before the foundation of the world*, by an eternal decree, to be the one great propitiation, *but was manifested in these last times for you*, becoming incarnate, and making the brightest displays of the glory of his grace, *who by him do believe in God* as your reconciled and covenant God, *that raised him from the dead* in testimony of his acceptance of the sacrifice which he had offered for our justification, *and gave him glory*, exalting him to the mediatorial throne, *that your faith and hope might be in God*, assured, through the divine Messiah, of present favour and acceptance with him, and expecting, according to his promise, all the blessings of grace here and of glory hereafter.

d Acts xv. 9.
e Rom. xii. 9, 10. 1 Thes. iv. 9. Heb. xiii. 1. Chap. iii. 8. 1 John iii. 18.
f John i. 13. & iii. 3.
g Jam. i. 18.
h Eccl. [illegible] Isa. xl. 6. Jam. i. 10.
i Isa. xl. 8. Luke xvi. 17.
Ver. 23.

22 Seeing ye have purified your souls in obeying the
truth through the Spirit, unto unfeigned [e] love of the
brethren, *see that* ye love one another with a pure heart
fervently: 23 [f] Being born again, not of corruptible
seed, but of incorruptible, [g] by the word of God, which
liveth and abideth for ever. 24 For [h] all flesh *is* as grass,
and all the glory of man as the flower of grass. The grass
withereth, and the flower thereof falleth away: 25 But
[i] the word of the Lord endureth for ever. And this is
the word which by the gospel is preached unto you.

v. 22—25. The apostle proceeds,

1. To inculcate the exercise of fervent charity. *Seeing ye have purified your souls in obeying the truth through the Spirit*, and have so graciously begun to advance in all holiness of heart and temper, being led by him especially *unto unfeigned love of the brethren*, *see* therefore *that*, under his blessed influences and according to the gospel word, *ye love one another with a pure heart fervently*, with still increasing and more enlarged affection: *being born again*, and made partakers of a divine nature, *not of corruptible seed, but of incorruptible, by the word of God which liveth and abideth for ever*, unchangeably the same, and communicating a dignity and honour to which the highest human pedigree cannot pretend. *Note*, (1.) The gospel truth, through the Spirit embraced and obeyed, is the effectual means of purifying the soul. (2.) Unfeigned love of the brethren is among the surest evidences of the Spirit's work upon the heart. (3.) They who have made the highest advancements in the divine life have need be exhorted to increase more and more. (4.) If we have received the engrafted word into our souls, we have a divine principle which shall live and abide for ever, till it is perfected in glory.

2. He sets forth the vanity of man. *All flesh is grass*, weak and perishing, *and all the glory of man*, his pomp, wealth, affluence, wisdom, and endowments of every kind, are *as the flower of grass*, that soon fades and decays. *The grass withereth, and the flower thereof falleth away*; one stroke of sickness, or accident, or the ravages of age, make all human greatness droop, and death consigns it to the grave: *but the word of the Lord endureth for ever*, and they who are begotten by it have in their hearts eternal life begun. *And this is the word which by the gospel is preached unto you*, whose effects are so everlastingly blessed. *Note*, A deep sense of the vanity of man, and of his present state of corruption, will serve greatly to draw off our minds from the trifles of time, to look to the abiding glories of eternity which in the gospel are revealed unto us.

CHAP. II.

The general exhortation to holiness is continued and enforced by several reasons taken from the foundation on which Christians are built, Jesus Christ, and from their spiritual blessings and privileges in him, ver. 1—12. Particular directions are given how subjects ought to obey the magistrates, and servants their masters, patiently suffering in well-doing, in imitation of Christ.

a Eph. iv. 22, 25, 31. Col. iii. 8. Heb. xii. 1. Jam. i. 21.
b Mat. xviii. 3.
c 1 Cor. iii. 2.
d Ps. xxxiv. 8. Heb. vi.

1 WHerefore [a] laying aside all malice, and all guile,
and hypocrisies, and envies, and all evil speak-
ings, 2 As [b] new-born babes desire [c] the sincere milk
of the word, that ye may grow thereby: 3 If so be ye
have [d] tasted that the Lord *is* gracious. 4 To whom

e Ps. cxviii. 22. Mat. xxi. 42. Acts iv. 11.
f Eph. ii. 21, 22.
g Heb. iii. 6.
h Isa. lxi. 6. & lxvi. 21. Ver. 9. Rev. i. 6.
i Hos. xiv. 2. Mal. i. 11. Rom. xii. 1. Heb. xiii. 15, 16.
k Phil. iv. 18.
l Isa. xxviii. 16. Rom. ix. 33.
† Or, An honour.
m Ps. cxviii. 22. Mat. xxi. 42. Acts iv. 11.
n Isa. viii. 14. Luke ii. 34. Rom. ix. 33.
o 1 Cor. i. 23.
p Exod. ix. 16. Rom. ix. 22. 1 Thes. v. 9. Jude 4.
q Deut. x. 15. Ver. 5.
r Exod. xix. 5, 6. Deut. vii. 6. & xiv. 2. & xxvi. 18.
s Tit. ii. 14.
t Isa. xliii. 21.
u Acts xxvi. 18. Col. i. 13.
x Hos. i. 10. & ii. 23. Rom. ix. 25.

coming, *as unto* a living stone, [e] disallowed indeed of
men, but chosen of God, *and* precious, 5 [f] Ye also as
lively stones, are built up [g] a spiritual house, [h] an holy
priesthood, to offer up [i] spiritual sacrifices, [k] acceptable
to God by Jesus Christ. 6 Wherefore also it is con-
tained in the scripture, [l] Behold, I lay in Sion a chief
corner stone, elect, precious: and he that believeth on
him, shall not be confounded. 7 Unto you therefore
which believe *he is* † precious: but unto them which be
disobedient, [m] the stone which the builders disallowed,
the same is made the head of the corner, 8 And [n] a
stone of stumbling, and a rock of offence, *even to them*
which stumble at the word, being disobedient: [p] where-
unto also they were appointed. 9 But ye *are* a chosen
generation, [q] a royal priesthood, an holy nation, [r] a pe-
culiar people; that ye should shew forth the praises of
him [u] who hath called you out of darkness into his mar-
vellous light: 10 [x] Which in time past *were* not a
people, but *are* now the people of God: which had not
obtained mercy, but now have obtained mercy.

v. 1—10. The apostle proceeds,

1. To exhort the Hebrews to shew a temper suitable to their profession. *Wherefore laying aside all malice*, every thing spiteful, envious, and revengeful, *and all guile*, every thing deceitful in word or behaviour, *and hypocrisies*, whether in the profession of religion towards God, or in pretences of respect and friendship towards men, *and envies*, repining at the prosperity of others, *and all evil speakings*, which proceed from these vile tempers in the heart; in opposition to all which, *as new-born babes desire the sincere milk of the word*, the pure unadulterated gospel, *that ye may grow thereby* in every divine and holy temper, unto the measure of the stature of the fulness of Christ: *if so be*, or *forasmuch as, ye have tasted that the Lord is gracious*, experimentally proving the riches of his mercy, and having begun to enjoy a sweet savour of that grace, which, though but a taste compared with what it shall be, is yet so precious and reviving. *Note*, (1.) All malice, guile, hypocrisy, and slander, are direct contradictions to the Christian character. (2.) By nature all evil cleaves to us closer than our garments; but it must be put off as filthy rags, if we mean with comfort to appear in the presence of God. (3.) The word of God supplies milk for babes, and strong meat for men; and they who feel an appetite for it verily shall be fed and nourished up in the words of sound doctrine. (4.) The grace which is in Jesus Christ is rich and free to the poorest and most miserable sinner; and to those who have tasted of it he will indeed be precious.

2. He described that blessed Jesus, the true foundation of the sinner's hope, of whose grace they had been made partakers. *To whom coming* by faith, *as unto a living stone*, even Christ, who is the only foundation, everlastingly durable, and never to be shaken, *a living stone*, the head of vital influence, and communicating to all his members life and stability; *disallowed indeed of men*, rejected and slighted by the Jewish rulers, and all unbelievers, who will not come to him that they may have life; *but chosen of God, and precious*, appointed by him from eternity to bear the massy structure of his church, as most excellent in himself, and most able to exalt the glory of God, and to secure the salvation of his redeemed. Coming therefore to him, *ye also, as lively stones*, animated by virtue of union with him, *are built up a spiritual house*, in which God the Spirit is pleased to take up his blest abode, *an holy priesthood*, consecrated to God's immediate service, and devoted to his glory, not *to offer up* the blood of beasts, but the better *spiritual sacrifices* of your bodies, souls, and spirits, in prayer and praise, which are *acceptable to God by Jesus Christ*. *Note*, (1.) Every child of God is the temple of the Deity, where his Spirit abidingly dwells. (2.) They who reject Christ as their foundation, must build on the sand, and be swept away by the deluge of wrath. (3.) All Christians are consecrated as priests to God, and must approve their peculiar relation to him by their unreserved devotedness to his service.

3. He supports what he had advanced by the testimony of Isaiah. *Wherefore also it is contained in the scripture, Behold*, with wonder, love, and praise, behold, *I lay in Sion*, in my holy mountain, *a chief corner-stone*, the great Messiah, on whom all his people's hopes are built, *elect*, and chosen for this blessed purpose, to unite Jews and Gentiles, and the whole body of the redeemed, in one glorious church, *precious* in my sight, and who should be above all things dear to those who are grounded on him as their foundation: *and he that believeth on him shall not be confounded*, neither here nor hereafter, having confidence, through a Redeemer's blood and righteousness, to approach a throne of grace, and boldness to appear before a throne of glory. *Unto you therefore which believe he is precious*, Jesus is inexpressibly amiable in your eyes, you count your relation to him the highest honour, and firmly trust your everlasting hopes upon him: *but unto them which be disobedient* and unbelieving, as in other scripture observes, *the stone which the builders*, the few the priests

priests and rulers, *disallowed* and rejected, *the same*, as was foretold, *is made the head of the corner*, exalted to the greatest honour, and setting up his gospel church in defiance of their enmity and opposition. *And*, as Isaiah in another place prophecies, he is become *a stone of stumbling and a rock of offence, even to them which stumble at the word*, and through pride and prejudice, unable to bear the humbling manner in which the Messiah appeared, and the doctrines which he taught, *being disobedient* and infidel, having rejected him as the promised hope of Israel, and split upon this rock, *whereunto also they were appointed*, according to God's sovereignty and righteous judgment. *Note*, (1) Faith in Jesus will prevent all shame, the hope founded upon him shall never fail us, either in time or in eternity. (2) Christ is indeed precious to the believer, so precious, that, compared with the excellency of the knowledge of him, he counts all things beside but dung and loss. (3) They who disbelieve the gospel, and disobey God's word, rush on their ruin, and must suffer shipwreck in eternity.

4 He reminds them of the rich and invaluable blessings and privileges which in the Redeemer they had obtained. *But ye are a chosen generation*, elect to infinitely greater privileges than those which the visible church of Israel enjoyed, *a royal priesthood*, having an unction from the Holy One, and made kings and priests unto God, *Rev.* i 6. victorious over your spiritual foes, separated for God, and to reign with him in glory for ever, *an holy nation*, consecrated to the Lord, and in spirit and temper conformed to his image, *a peculiar people*, in a nobler sense than ever Israel was of old, appointed to the highest dignity, and enriched with the most distinguishing blessings; *that ye should shew forth the praises of him who* by his grace *hath called you out of darkness into his marvellous light* of gospel truth, brought from the cloudy dispensation of legal institutions into that bright day, which the Sun of righteousness makes, arisen with healing in his wings. *Which in time past were not a people*, having been disowned and divorced of God, *Hos.* i 9, 10. ii 23. *but are now the people of God*, through Jesus admitted into the covenant of grace, and acknowledged as the Lord's; *which had not obtained mercy, but now have obtained mercy*, even pardon, grace, and all the blessings of eternal redemption.

11 Dearly beloved, I beseech *you* as strangers and
pilgrims, [t] abstain from fleshly lusts, [u] which war against
the soul, 12 [x] Having your conversation honest among
the Gentiles: that whereas they speak against you as evil-
doers, [y] they may by *your* good works, which they shall
behold, glorify God [z] in the day of visitation. 13
[a] Submit yourselves to every ordinance of man for the
Lord's sake: whether it be to the king, as supreme,
14 Or unto governors, as unto them that are sent by
him [b] for the punishment of evil doers, and [c] for the
praise of them that do well. 15 For so is the will of
God, that [d] with well-doing ye may put to silence the
ignorance of foolish men: 16 [e] As free, and [f] not
using *your* liberty for a cloke of maliciousness, but [g] as
the servants of God. 17 [h] Honour all men. [i] Love
the brotherhood. [k] Fear God. Honour the king.

[t] 1 Chron. xxix 15. Psal. xxxix 12. & cxix 19. Heb. xi 13. Chap. i 17. [u] Rom. xiii 14. Gal. v 16. [x] Jam. iv 1. [y] 2 Cor. viii 21. Phil. ii 15. Chap. iii 16. [y] Mat. v 16. [z] Luke xix 44. [a] Rom. xiii 1, 5. Tit. iii 1. [b] Rom. xiii 4. [c] Rom. xiii 3. [d] Tit. ii 8. [e] Gal. v 1, 13. [f] Jude 4. [g] 1 Cor. vii 22. [h] Rom. xii 10. Phil. ii 3. [i] Chap. i 22. & iii 8. [k] Prov. xxiv 21. Mat. xxii 21.

v. 11—17. Whilst they are in the flesh, the best of men have need be warned and exhorted to work out their own salvation with fear and trembling. The apostle therefore admonishes them,

1. To guard against all worldly and carnal affection. *Dearly beloved, I beseech you, as* becomes *strangers and pilgrims*, for such you profess yourselves to be upon the earth, *abstain from fleshly lusts*, subduing every inordinate appetite, and every covetous desire, *which war against the soul*, and threaten it defilement and destruction. *Having your conversation honest among the Gentiles*, adorning your profession by every thing commendable and excellent, *that whereas they speak against you as evil doers*, and misrepresent you as a wicked, refractory, and lawless people, *they may be convinced by your good works, which they shall behold*, and be ashamed of their unjust aspersion, compelled to *glorify God in the day of visitation*, either when in a day of judgment he shall punish them for their ill usage of you, or in mercy, when turning the hearts of the disobedient to the wisdom of the just, he shall lead them to approve and imitate your good conversation.

2. To be obedient to magistrates. *Submit yourselves to every ordinance of man for the Lord's sake*, under whatever form of government you live, or whoever they be whom the Divine Providence sets over you, *whether it be to the king, as supreme; or unto governors, as unto them that are sent by him*, and bear his commission, *for the punishment of evil doers, and for the praise of them that do well*, from whom faithful and obedient subjects have nothing to fear, have every thing to hope for. *For so is the will of God, that with well-doing ye may put to silence the ignorance of foolish men*, by your loyalty and cheerful submission to the civil government, confuting the calumnies of those who would brand you as seditious. *As free* indeed from the tyranny

of sin, Satan, and the curse of the law, *and not using your liberty for a cloke of maliciousness*, to cover any treasonable design, or other malignant evil, *but as the servants of God*, conscientiously observant of his holy will in all things, and obedient to magistrates not only for wrath but also for conscience sake.

3 He adds four short but important precepts. *Honour all men* according to their rank and station. *Love the brotherhood*, high or low, rich or poor, bear them an unfeigned regard as members of Christ, shew it in every act of kindness to their bodies or their souls. *Fear God* with all reverence, and filial awe of offending. *Honour the king*, as his representative upon earth, and governing by his authority.

18 [l] Servants, *be* subject to *your* masters, with all fear,
not only to the good and gentle, but also to the froward.
19 For [m] this *is* thank worthy, if a man for conscience
toward God endure grief, suffering wrongfully. 20 For
[n] what glory *is it*, if when ye be buffeted for your faults,
ye shall take it patiently? [o] but if, when ye do well, and
suffer *for it*, ye take it patiently, this *is* acceptable with
God. 21 For even [p] hereunto were ye called: because
[q] Christ also suffered for us, [r] leaving us an example,
that ye should follow his steps: 22 [s] Who did no sin,
neither was guile found in his mouth: 23 [t] Who
when he was reviled, reviled not again, when he suffered,
he threatned not, but committed † himself to him that
judgeth righteously: 24 [u] Who his own self bare our
sins in his own body on the tree, [x] that we being dead
to sin should live unto righteousness: [y] by whose stripes
ye were healed. 25 For [z] ye were as sheep going
astray, but are now returned unto [a] the Shepherd and
Bishop of your souls.

[l] Eph. vi 5. Col. iii 22. Tit. ii 9. [m] Mat. v 10. Chap. iii 14. [n] Chap. iv 15. [o] Chap. iii 14. & iv 14, 16. [p] Mat. xvi 24. Acts xiv 22. 1 Thes. iii 3. [q] Chap. iii 18. [r] John xiii 15. [s] Isa. liii 9. 2 Cor. v 21. [t] Chap. ii 20. [t] Mat. xxvii 39. † Or, his cause. [u] Isa. liii 4, &c. Mat. viii 17. Heb. ix 28. [x] Rom. vi 2, 11. & vii 6. [y] Isa. liii 5. [z] Isa. liii 6. [a] Ezek. xxxiv 23. & xxxvii 24. John x 11. Heb. xiii 20. Chap. v 4.

v. 18—25. As the Jews very hardly bore a foreign yoke, as unwilling were they to submit to any Gentile masters; and those of them who believed in Christ were by their judaizing teachers persuaded to think that they owed no obedience to unbelieving masters. To correct so dangerous an imagination, the apostle,

1. Inculcates the duty of *servants*. *Be subject to your masters, with all fear* and reverence, and be obedient to all their lawful commands; *not only to the good and gentle, but also to the froward*, if such is your lot to be placed under their power. *For this is thank-worthy*, a matter of real commendation, and a singular gift of God, *if a man for conscience toward God endure grief, suffering wrongfully*, and bearing patiently the ill usage of a cruel master, to whom he hath given no just cause of provocation. *For what glory is it, if when ye be buffeted for your faults, ye shall take it patiently?* this can bring no credit to your religion, you receive but the just reward of your deeds. *But if, when ye do well*, faithful to your trust, and true to your profession, *and suffer* for your conscientious regard to God and his service, *ye take it patiently*, with all meekness, and without murmuring, *this is acceptable to God*, and a sure proof of the truth of his grace in your hearts. *Note*, (1) The spirit of independence, which is in men, hardly brooks subjection, and correction still less. (2) Patient suffering for well doing is our distinguished honour. (3) Though the duty of servants is submission, yet their guilt is not the less who abuse their authority over them, and they will find a Master shortly, who will call them to account, with whom there is no respect of person.

2 He enforces what he had enjoined with the most powerful arguments. *For even hereunto were ye called*. The cross every Christian must be content to bear; and we should the more readily take it up, *because Christ also suffered for us* as our substitute, and to make atonement for us, or *for you*, as many copies read, for the meanest servant as well as for the highest of the sons of men, *leaving us an example* of patience and long-suffering under all the most cruel and unjust treatment which he met with, *that ye should follow his steps*, and be conformed to his blessed pattern: *who*, grievously as he suffered, yet *did no sin, neither was guile found in his mouth*, his bitterest enemies could not so much as fix upon him the shadow of a crime. *Who, when he was reviled, reviled not again*, but observed an admirable silence, as the sheep before her shearers is dumb. *When he suffered, he threatned not*, nor discovered the least anger at his tormentors, *but committed himself* and his cause *to him that judgeth righteously*, and to whom vengeance belongeth. *Who his own self bare our sins in his own body on the tree*, submitting, as our surety, with his own blood to pay the penalty due to our iniquities, *that we, being dead to sins*, as crucified with him, *should live unto righteousness*, quickened by his Spirit to newness of life. *By whose stripes ye were healed*, and the deadly wounds of your souls, far worse than those which the most cruel masters can make in your bodies, were cured by the sovereign balm of that blood which streamed from his scourging. *For ye were as sheep going astray*, foolish, disobedient, deceived, in time past, *but are now* by grace recovered, and *returned unto the Shepherd and Bishop of your souls*, the blessed and adored Jesus. *Note*, (1) Christ's example should

abun-

animate us with chearfulness to take up every cross which in his providence he is pleased to lay upon us (2) Our sufferings, however cruel or unjust, will never be an excuse for our impatience under them, or for any anger toward the instruments of them, however wicked or unreasonable (3) All the sins of the redeemed were laid upon the Saviour on the tree he bore them There never will one sin be pardoned, but those whose price were then paid there never will be one sin remembered any more against those whose surety he then appeared (4) The doctrine of imputation is inculcated in both testaments, nor can it be more strange that we should be justified by Christ's righteousness, than that we should be healed by his stripes (5) All whose sins he bore are raised from the death of sin unto the life of righteousness We are deceived, if we live in our iniquities and flatter ourselves with hope in Christ (6) By nature, by practice, we have all gone far astray Reader, art *thou* then returned by faith in the atoning blood to the great Shepherd of souls? art thou under his government, and dost thou tread in the footsteps of his flock?

CHAP III

Wherein the apostle describes the duties of husbands and wives, ver 1—7 He exhorts Christians to unity, love, compassion, peace, and patience under sufferings, to oppose the slanders of their enemies, not by returning evil for evil, or railing for railing, but by blessing, by a ready account of their faith and hope, and by keeping a good conscience, ver 8—17 To encourage them to this, he proposeth the example of Christ, who suffered, the just for the unjust, but yet punished the old world for their disobedience, and saved the few that were faithful in the days of Noah

1 LIKEWISE, ᵃ ye wives, *be* in subjection to your
own husbands, that if any obey not the word,
ᵇ they also may without the word be won by the con-
versation of the wives, 2 ᶜ While they behold your
chaste conversation *coupled* with fear 3 ᵈ Whose adorn-
ing, let it not be that outward *adorning* of plaiting the
hair, and of wearing of gold, or of putting on of appa-
rel 4 But *let it be* ᵉ the hidden man of the heart, in
that which is not corruptible, *even the ornament* of a meek
and quiet spirit, which is in the sight of God of great
price 5 For after this manner in the old time the holy
women also who trusted in God adorned themselves, be-
ing in subjection unto their own husbands, 6 Even
as Sara obeyed Abraham, ᶠ calling him lord whose
† daughters ye are as long as ye do well, and are not
afraid with any amazement 7 ᵍ Likewise, ye husbands,
dwell with them according to knowledge, giving honour
unto the wife as unto the weaker ʰ vessel, and as being
heirs together of the grace of life, ⁱ that your prayers
be not hindered

a 1 Cor xiv 34 Eph v 22 Col iii 18 Tit ii 5
b 1 Co vii 16
c Chap ii 12
d 1 Tim ii 9 Tit ii 3
e Ps xlv 13 Rom ii 29 & vii 22 2 Cor iv 16
f Gen xviii 12
† Gr Children
g Eph v 25 Col iii 19
h 1 Cor xii
i 1 Thes iv 4
i Mat v 23, 24

v 1—7 The apostle proceeds to the duty of husbands and wives

1 The duty of wives *Likewise ye wives, be in subjection to your own husbands*, whether Christian, Jewish, or heathen, regarding them as your superiors by creation and the ordinance of God, *that, if any obey not the word*, and are yet strangers to the faith of Christ, *they also may without the word*, though they should refuse to attend the preaching of the gospel, *be won by the conversation of the wives*, struck with your exemplary, engaging, and amiable conduct, *while they behold your chaste conversation*, circumspect in every word and action, and your chastity *coupled with fear*, shewing them that reverence, attention, desire to please, and fear to offend, which cannot but attract their notice and gain their high esteem *Whose adorning, let it not be that outward adorning of plaiting the hair, and of wearing of gold, or of putting on of apparel*, not making dress and finery your study, expensive, negligent of your family concerns, or desirous to attract others eyes besides your husband's, *but*, whilst careful of modest neatness of person, most careful of that which will render you above all other things amiable in their eyes, putting on *the hidden man of the heart*, the adornings of grace, truth, and holiness, *in that which is not corruptible*, and infinitely preferable to the poor and fading splendor of gay apparel, *even the ornament of a meek and quiet spirit*, gentle, mild, tractable, silencing every rising of anger, and the emotions of fretfulness, *which is* the great secret of happiness in a married state, and *in the sight of God of great price*, and highly approved by him *For after this manner in the old time the holy women also who trusted in God adorned themselves, being in subjection unto their own husbands*, delighting in their station, and never desiring to invert or change God's established order, *even as Sarah obeyed Abraham* with all dutiful subjection, *calling him lord*, and paying him due reverence and respect as her superior *whose daughters ye are*, in a spiritual sense, *as long as ye do well*, and copy her meek, dutiful, and humble example, *and are not afraid with any amazement*, not terrified from your duty by any menaces, not obedient through slavish fear of your husbands, but from the nobler principles of love and duty *Note*, Wives should seriously consider this word of God, and make conscience of observing it the advice is of infinite importance, not only to their comfort in this world, but is essential to all their hopes in a better

2 The duty of husbands *Likewise, ye husbands, dwell with them according to knowledge*, delighting in their company, their persons, their conversation, with purity and tender affection discharging every duty of the conjugal state; *giving honour unto the wife*, treating her with respect, making her your bosom friend, consulting her comfort and happiness, providing in the best manner for her which your circumstances will afford, bearing with and concealing her infirmities, considering her *as the weaker vessel*, to whom peculiar delicacy and tenderness is due, *and as* your equal in all Christian privileges, *being heirs together of the grace of life*, *that your prayers be not hindered*, or the effects of them defeated, as they must be by unchristian strifes, or austerity Let those who bear the honoured name of husband then remember the duties of their station Such a conduct will engage affection and submission, and supersede the exercise of authority

8 Finally, ᵏ *be ye* all of one mind, ˡ having compas-
sion one of another, ᵐ love as brethren, *be* pitiful, *be*
courteous 9 ⁿ Not rendering evil for evil, or railing
for railing, but contrariwise, blessing knowing that ye
are thereunto called ᵒ that ye should inherit a blessing
10 For ᵖ he that will love life, and see good days, ᵠ let
him refrain his tongue from evil, and his lips that they
speak no guile 11 ʳ Let him eschew evil, and do
good, ˢ let him seek peace, and ensue it 12 For the
eyes of the Lord *are* over the righteous, and his ears *are*
open ᵗ unto their prayers, but the face of the Lord *is*
† against them that do evil 13 And ᵘ who *is* he that
will harm you, if ye be followers of that which is good?
14 ˣ But and if ye suffer for righteousness sake, happy
are ye and ʸ be not afraid of their terror, neither be
troubled, 15 But sanctify the Lord God in your hearts
and ᶻ *be* ready to *give* an answer to every man that asketh
you a reason of the hope that is in you ᵃ with meekness
and fear 16 ᵇ Having a good conscience, that where-
as they speak evil of you as of evil-doers, they may be
ashamed that falsly accuse your good conversation in
Christ 17 For *it is* better, if the will of God be so,
that ye suffer for well-doing than for evil-doing

k Rom xii 16 & xv 5 1 Cor i 10 Phil ii 2 1 Eph iv 32
m 1 Thes iv 9 Chap i 22
n Prov xx 22 Mat v 39 Rom xii 17 1 Thes v 15
o Mat xxv 34
p Ps xxxiv 12, &c
q Jam i 26
r Ps xxxvii 27 Isa i 16 3 John 11
s Rom xii 18 Heb xii 14
t John ix 31 Jam v 16
† Gr Upon
u Prov xvi 7 Rob xii 7
x Mat v 10, &c Chap ii 19 & iv 14
y Isa viii 12, 13 Jer i 8
z Ps cxix 46 Acts iv 8 Col iv 6
a 2 Tim ii 25
b Chap ii 12

v 8—17 The apostle passes on to more general exhortations

1 He enjoins the exercise of Christian charity *Finally, be ye all of one mind*, united in the great points of Christian doctrine, and harmonizing in mutual affection, *having compassion one of another*, bearing with tender sympathy each others burdens, *love as brethren*, out of a pure heart, fervently, *be pitiful* of each other's wants, weakness, and infirmities, *be courteous*, obliging, friendly, condescending *not rendering evil for evil, or railing for railing*, however cruelly or unkindly treated by professed enemies or pretended friends, *but, contrariwise, blessing*, praying for those who most despitefully use you *knowing that ye are thereunto called, that ye should inherit a blessing*, both temporal, spiritual, and eternal, which promise God hath annexed to such a gracious conduct *Note*, To love those who are kind to us, is in some sort but natural, but to love our enemies, and return their bitterness with blessing, this is the work of supernatural grace

2 Having mentioned the blessing which they should inherit, who walked according to the rule laid down, he quotes a passage from the Book of Psalms, shewing the way to a truly happy life *For he that will love life, and see good days* of prosperity and comfort in this world, *let him refrain his tongue from evil, and his lips that they speak no guile*, sincere in all his conversation, without dissimulation, and cautious never to utter a rash, hasty, or passionate expression *let him eschew* and avoid *evil* of every kind, which misery, as its shadow, ever attends, *and do good* to all, according to his abilities and opportunities *let him seek peace*, as the richest acquisition, *and ensue it*, using every lawful means to preserve it inviolate in all his connections and relations, and to heal every breach which may be made *For the eyes of the Lord are over the righteous*, observing, approving, and directing them in all their holy conversation, *and his ears are open to their prayers*, regarding every request they make, and ready to fulfil all their petitions *but the face of the Lord is against them that do evil*, with frowns of righteous indignation he beholds their crooked ways, and winged vengeance cuts off the remembrance of them from the earth *See* Ps xxxiv 16 *Note*, (1) Godliness hath the promise of this life, as well as of that which is to come (2) What an encouragement have we to approach a throne of grace, when God assures us of his constant attention to our prayers?

prayers? (3) They who persist in their iniquities must perish without remedy.

3 He suggests the most encouraging motives for their patient suffering; *And who is he that will harm you, if ye be followers of that which is good?* What have you to fear from men or devils, if God is on your side? And will not such an inoffensive conduct disarm even your very enemies? *But and if ye suffer for righteousness sake*, and your religion exasperates your persecutors, *happy are ye* in this honourable cross, *and be not afraid of their terror, neither be troubled* at any of their menaces, frowns, or cruelty; *but sanctify the Lord God in your hearts*, set him before you, to it, filled with holy fear of offending him, relying on his power, faithfulness, wisdom, and mercy, you may defy all the impotent wrath of men, *and be ready always to give an answer*, and to make your defence and apology *to every man that asketh you a reason of the hope that is in you with meekness and fear*, with all dispassionate calmness and holy reverence of God, whose cause you plead; or this may refer to him that asketh the reason of their Christian hope, if he appears with meekness and fear, willing to hear your defence, then faithfully deliver your souls. *Having a good conscience* towards God and towards men, and acting so uprightly and irreproachably, *that whereas they speak evil of you as of evil doers, they may be ashamed that falsly accuse your good conversation in Christ*, and let your lives give the lye to their slanders, and turn them to their own confusion. *For it is better, if the will of God be so*, that ye are appointed to suffer, *that ye suffer for well-doing than for evil doing*, for it is bitter indeed when sin and suffering meet together, the burden is then grievously insupportable. *Note*, (1) To suffer for righteousness sake is our honour and happiness. (2) The more we live in the fear of God, the less shall we be influenced by the fear of men. (3) We never need be ashamed of our principles, but should readily and freely vindicate them, whenever we can gain an attentive hearing. (4) The purest innocence is not a defence from the aspersions of malice. (5) The surest way to confound the slanders of malevolence is *to live them down*.

18 For [c] Christ also hath once suffered for sins, the
just for the unjust, (that he might bring us to God) be-
ing put to death in the flesh, [d] but quickened by the
Spirit. 19 By which also he went and [e] preached unto
the spirits in prison, 20 Which sometime were dis-
obedient, [f] when once the long-suffering of God waited in
the days of Noah, while [g] the ark was a preparing, where-
in few, that is, eight souls, were saved by water. 21
[i] The like figure whereunto, *even* baptism, doth also now
save us, (not the putting away of [k] the filth of the flesh,
[l] but the answer of a good conscience towards God) by the
resurrection of Jesus Christ. 22 Who is gone into hea-
ven, and [m] is on the right hand of God; [n] angels and
authorities and powers being made subject unto him.

c Rom. v. 6. Heb. ix. 26, 28. Chap. ii. 21. d Rom. i. 4. 2 Cor. xiii. 4. e Chap. i. 12. & iv. 6. f Gen. vi. 3. g Heb. xi. 7. h Gen. vii. 7. ... 2 Pet. ii. ... i Eph. v. 26. k Tit. iii. 5. l Rom. x. 10. m Psal. cx. 1. Rom. viii. ... Eph. i. 20. n Eph. i. 21.

v. 18—22. We have here,

1. The example of Christ proposed as our encouragement to suffer patiently for him. *For Christ also hath once suffered for sins, the just for the unjust*, he who was perfectly pure and holy giving himself a sacrifice for us, to bear the sins of such polluted wretches as we are, *that*, having made a perfect and full satisfaction to Divine Justice, and obtained reconciliation through his own blood, he might *bring us to God* into a state of favour and acceptance with him, *being put to death in the flesh* and suffering in his human nature the penalty of sin, *but quickened by the Spirit*, by that eternal Spirit of the Son of God, which had taken the human nature into union with himself, or *by the Holy Ghost*, who is one in operation and agency with the Son. *Note* (1) The sufferings of Jesus were the real penalty due to our iniquities, and God laid them upon him in all their bitterness. (2) He was the *just* one; had he not been so, he could not have satisfied for the unjust. (3) By the sufferings of Jesus sinners have access to and acceptance with God. (4) If he voluntarily endured so much for us, shall we shrink from any cross which we may be called to bear for him?

2. He mentions what Christ did in the old world. *By which also he went and preached unto the spirits* which are now *in prison*, by his spirit enlightening Noah, and sending him forth as a preacher of righteousness to them, *which sometime were disobedient*, and would neither believe nor attend to the warnings which Christ sent them, *when once the long suffering of God waited*, during an hundred and twenty years, *in the days of Noah, while the ark was a preparing*, who continued preaching, and building that immense structure which was a living sermon to them, *wherein few, that is, eight souls were saved by water*, passing safely through the deluge which covered the earth, whilst the rest of the world perished in the waters, and went down into the prison of hell. *The like figure whereunto, even baptism, doth also now save us*, is the antitype of the ark, (*not* the mere external ordinance, the applying water to the body *for the putting away of the filth of the flesh*, which of itself could be of no avail, *but* is the outward and visible sign of an inward and spiritual grace, even *the answer of a good conscience towards God*, pledging our fidelity to him in return for the privileges to which we are admitted, *by the resurrection of Jesus Christ*, who is the author of our life and salvation, being raised for our justification, the head of vital influence to his people, and shall raise them up at the last day. *Note*, (1) God warns before he strikes. (2) Though he is long-suffering, he will not always bear with sinners. (3) They who reject the counsel of God against their own soul, have themselves only to blame for their destruction. (4) Few ever were or will be saved in any age. (5) Baptism saveth, not as a mere ceremony performed, but as a seal of that covenant which is established through a Redeemer, and a symbol of that grace, which out of his fulness we have received.

3. Christ is now exalted to the throne of majesty on high. *Who is gone into heaven, and is on the right hand of God, angels and authorities and powers being made subject unto him*; he is possessed of universal dominion, appointed to be head over all things to his church; and whatever any of his members may endure, he will support and bring them safely through; and, as surely as they suffer with him, they shall reign with him.

CHAP. IV.

The work of a Christian is twofold, doing the will of God, and suffering his pleasure. This chapter directs us in both. The duties we are here exhorted to employ ourselves in, are the mortification of sin, living to God, sobriety, prayer, charity, hospitality, and the best improvement of our talents, which the apostle presseth upon Christians from the consideration of the time they have lost in their sins, and the approaching end of all things, ver. 1—12. *The directions for sufferings are, that we should not be surprized at them, but rejoice in them, only taking care not to suffer as evil doers. He intimates, that their trials were near at hand, but their souls were in danger as well as their bodies, and the best way to preserve them was to commit them to God in well doing.*

1 FOrasmuch then [a] as Christ hath suffered for us in
the flesh, arm yourselves likewise with the same
mind: for [b] he that hath suffered in the flesh hath ceased
from sin; 2 [c] That he no longer [d] should live the rest
of his time in the flesh, to the lusts of men, [e] but to the
will of God. 3 For [f] the time past of our life may suf-
fice us to have wrought [g] the will of the Gentiles, when
we walked in lasciviousness, lusts, excess of wine, revel-
lings, banquetings, and abominable idolatries: 4 Where-
in they think it strange, that you run not with them to
the same excess of riot, [h] speaking evil of *you*: 5 Who
shall give account to him that is ready [i] to judge the quick
and the dead. 6 For, for this cause was [k] the gospel
preached also to them that are dead, that they might be
judged according to men in the flesh, but live according
to God in the Spirit.

a Chap. ii. 18. b Rom. vi. 7. c Rom. xiv. 7. Chap. ii. 1. d Gal. ii. 20. e 1 Thes. iv. 10. Heb. ix. 14. f Ezek. xliv. 6. & xlv. 9. Eph. iv. 17. g Rom. i. ... 1 Cor. xii. 2. h Acts xiii. 45. Chap. iii. 16. i Acts x. 42. & xvii. 31. 2 Tim. iv. 1. k Chap. iii. 19.

v. 1—6. The apostle here,

1. Draws an inference from what he had advanced. *Forasmuch then as Christ hath suffered for us in the flesh, arm yourselves likewise with the same mind*, with patience and holy resolution; *for he that hath suffered in the flesh*, crucifying the body of sin through union with a dying Saviour, and willingly taking up any cross which the Divine Providence may lay upon him, *hath ceased from sin*, from his former corrupt principles and practice, and is professionally by his baptism mortified to every corrupt affection, as a dead man ceases from the actions of life; *that he no longer should live the rest of his time in the flesh, to the will of men*, but the little space which yet remains he is earnest to redeem, and fain would spend it according *to the will of God*. *Note*, (1) Nothing so effectually mortifies sin as a believing view of the cross of Christ. (2) The will of God, not our vile affections, must be our guide. If we live after the flesh, we shall die eternally, whilst the paths of grace and holiness alone can lead us to immortal life and glory.

2. The apostle argues on the reasonableness of living unto God, from the consideration of the abuse they had made of the time that was past. *For the time past of our life may suffice us to have wrought the will of the Gentiles, when* (with shame and grief and anguish we remember it) *we walked in lasciviousness, lusts, excess of wine, revellings* and riot, *banquetings* and luxurious carousals, *and abominable idolatries*, joining with the Gentiles in these horrid deeds: *wherein they think it strange that you run not with them still to the same excess of riot* as before, *speaking evil of you* and your religion, as if it made you morose, unsociable, and poor despicable objects: *who shall give account to him that is ready to judge the quick and the dead*, at the great day of his appearing and glory. *Note*, (1) The remembrance of our former evil ways should often dwell upon our minds for our deep humiliation before God. (2) They who have tasted the bitterness of sin, can be tempted by no consideration to return to those destructive ways which they have forsaken. (3) The conduct of a Christian appears very strange to an ungodly world, and they

wonder what there is in religion which, for the sake of it, can induce men to forego all that they call enjoyment (4) They who speak evil of our good conversation in Christ, must shortly give a solemn account of their hard speeches before an awful tribunal

3 The former saints of God were thus censured of the world, and lived by grace *For this cause was the gospel preached also to them that are now dead* in Christ, and departed in his faith and fear, *that they might be judged according to men in the flesh*, and undergo reproach, persecution, and some of them even death itself for those tenets which the carnal world derides and abhors, *but* might, notwithstanding all their sufferings in the body, *live according to God in the Spirit*, under the mighty influence of his grace, in a holy conformity to his will, and expecting, through the power of the Holy Ghost, to be raised up at the last day to live with God eternally

7 But [l] the end of all things is at hand [m] be ye there-
fore sober, and [n] watch unto prayer 8 And [o] above all
things have fervent charity among yourselves for [p] cha-
rity shall cover the multitude of sins 9 [q] Use hospita-
lity one to another [r] without grudging 10 [s] As every
man hath received the gift, *even so* minister the same one
to another, [t] as good stewards of [u] the manifold grace of
God 11 [x] If any man speak, *let him speak* as the oracles
of God, if any man minister, *let him do it* as of the ability
which God giveth [y] that God in all things may be glo-
rified through Jesus Christ, [z] to whom be praise and
dominion for ever and ever. Amen

l Rom xiii 12 Phil iv 5 Jam v 8 m 1 Thes v 6 Chap v 8 n Luke xxi 36 Eph vi 18 Col iv 2 o Col iii 14 Chap i 22 p Prov x 12 Jam v 20 q Rom xii 13 Heb. xiii 2 r 2 Cor ix 7 s Rom. xii. 6 t Luk xii 42 1 Cor iv 1, 2 Tit i 7 u 1 Cor xii 4 Eph iv 11 x Rom xii 6 &c y Eph v 20 z 1 Tim vi 16 Chap v 11 Rev v 13

v 7—11 We have here an awful position *But the end of all things is at hand* The Jewish state was soon to be destroyed, where dwelt the most inveterate persecutors of the Christian name, and to every individual is this truth most applicable, to whom death and eternity are approaching, and judgment is at the door, from which awful considerations the apostle enforces the following exhortations

1 *Be ye therefore sober*, temperate in all things, not inordinately pursuing, nor immoderately using any thing in this world, knowing how short the time is *And*,

2 *Watch unto prayer*, be on your guard against the numberless temptations which beset you, and especially be looking up by ceaseless prayer for strength to resist and overcome them *Note*, Prayer is our great preservative, we shall never fail, whilst we continue waiting upon God

3 *And above all things have fervent charity among yourselves*, cordially and tenderly affected towards each other *for charity shall cover the multitude of sins*, engaging you kindly to overlook the offences of your brethren, to cast the veil of oblivion over their many infirmities, and to conceal them from the censorious world

4 *Use hospitality one towards another without grudging*, freely and chearfully receiving those who, for righteousness sake, are driven from place to place, or are travelling to spread the glad tidings of salvation, and trusting on the Divine Providence for their maintenance

5 *As every man hath received the gift*, whatever talents he is blessed with, whether of wealth, abilities, or grace, *even so minister the same one to another*, laying out yourselves for your mutual edification and comfort, *as good stewards of the manifold grace of God*, from whom you have received all that you possess, and to whom you are accountable for the due improvement of it *If any man speak*, therefore, as called to the office of a preacher, *let him speak as the oracles of God*, with strict adherence to the sacred doctrines therein revealed, presuming to add nothing thereunto, nor to diminish ought therefrom *If any man minister* in the office of a deacon, or out of his worldly substance to the necessitous, *let him do it as of the ability which God giveth*, with all fidelity, chearfulness and diligence, *that God in all things may be glorified through Jesus Christ*, and his name exalted in the advancement of his church and his kingdom in the world, *to whom be praise and dominion for ever and ever*, to the incarnate Saviour, and to the Father through him *Amen!* *Note*, (1) Whatever we possess, we are but stewards, and must give an account to the great Master for the talents committed to our trust (2) God's glory should be the great end of all our conversation, and in our lips and lives we should endeavour to shew forth his praise

12. Beloved, think it not strange concerning [a] the fiery
trial which is to try you, as though some strange thing
happened unto you 13 [b] But rejoice, in as much as
[c] ye are partakers of Christ's sufferings, [d] that when his
glory shall be revealed, ye may be glad also with exceed-
ing joy 14 [e] If ye be reproached for the name of Christ,
happy *are ye*, for the spirit of glory and of God [f] resteth
upon you on their part he is evil spoken of, but on
your part he is glorified 15 But [g] let none of you suf-
fer as a murderer, or *as* a thief, or *as* an evil doer, [h] or a
busy-body in other men's matters 16 Yet [i] if *any man*
suffer as a Christian, let him not be ashamed, but let him
glorify God on this behalf 17 For [k] the time *is come*
that judgment must begin at the house of God and [l] if
it first *begin* at us, [m] what shall the end *be* of them that
obey not the gospel of God? 18 [n] And if the righteous
scarcely be saved, where shall the ungodly and the sinner
appear? 19 Wherefore, let them that suffer according
to the will of God, [o] commit the keeping of their souls
to him in well-doing as unto a faithful Creator

a Isa xlviii 10 Zech. xiii 9 1 Cor iii 13 Chap i 7 b Mat v 12 Acts v 41 Jam i 2 c 2 Cor iv 10. Col i 24 2 Tim ii 10 Rev i 9 d Chap i 5, 6 e Mat v 11 Jam i 12 Chap ii 20 & iii 14 f 2 Cor xii 9. g Chap ii 20 h 1 Thes iv 11 i Chap iii 14. k Isa x 12 Jer xxv 29 & xlix 12 Ezek ix 6 Mal iii 5 l Luke xxiii 31 m Luke x 12 14 n Prov xi 31 Luke xxiii 31 o Ps xxxi 5 Luke xxiii 46 2 Tim i 12

v 12—19 The apostle here,

1 Encourages them to bear up boldly under their expected trials *Beloved, think it not strange concerning the fiery trial which is to try you* as gold in the furnace, *as if some strange thing happened unto you*, and your sufferings were uncommon, and such as God's children might not have expected *But*, however severe your trials may be, *rejoice in them*, *forasmuch as ye are partakers of Christ's sufferings*, and herein conformed to your glorious head, *that when his glory shall be revealed, ye may be glad also with exceeding joy*, and reign with him, as you have suffered for him And, in the lesser trials of reviling and slander, *if ye are reproached for the name of Christ*, branded with some opprobrious name, and made the objects of derision and contempt, *happy are ye*, let it be your delight to be thus vile, and gladly bear this honourable badge of infamy, *for the Spirit of glory and of God resteth upon you*, to comfort you under these reproaches, and to give you an earnest of that eternal glory to which these trials are the way *on their part he is evil spoken of*, and his blessed operations reviled and blasphemed, *but on your part he is glorified*, and his name exalted by your faith and patience, and by the praises given him for the supports and comforts which you experience from him *Note*, (1) We must count no affliction strange, however grievous for the time, it is only permitted to be, because God sees we have much dross, and need that furnace to purge us from it (2) Our sufferings for Christ are our real honour, and should be our highest joy (3) In a day of recompence we shall never regret what we have endured for Christ and his cause (4) We need not wonder at any reproaches cast on ourselves, when even the blessed Spirit of God himself sustains the like blasphemies, and his operations are branded as delusion and enthusiasm

2 He admonishes them to give their enemies no such handle against them as they desired to have *But let none of you suffer as a murderer, or as a thief, or as an evil-doer*, justly chargeable with any criminal conduct whatever, *or as a busy body in other men's matters*, prying into the concerns of his neighbours which do not belong to him, and neglecting his own *Yet if any man suffer as a Christian*, and if, however innocent, through enmity to him on account of his religion, any of these atrocious crimes are charged upon him, *let him not be ashamed* of such malignant abuse, *but let him glorify God on this behalf*, that he is counted worthy to suffer shame for the name of Christ, and enabled to despise these calumnies

3 He supports what he had advanced by the most weighty considerations *For the time is come that judgment must begin at the house of God*, not only in the destruction of the Jewish temple, but in very severe visitations upon his spiritual church and people, who need the correction of his rod *and if it first begin at us*, and we undergo the severe discipline of the cross, *what shall the end be of them that obey not the gospel of God?* How fearful will be the vengeance executed upon the finally-impenitent and unbelieving! *And if the righteous scarcely be saved*, plucked as brands from the burning, and hardly escaping, like Lot from the flames of Sodom, *where shall the ungodly and the sinner appear*, who wilfully and obstinately reject all the warnings of God's providence, and the word of his grace, determined to abide in their iniquities, whatever the consequence may be How terrible, sure, and inevitable must be their eternal perdition! *Wherefore, let them that suffer according to the will of God*, patiently and submissively, *commit the keeping of their souls to him in well doing as unto a faithful Creator*, content to refer themselves to him, resigned to his will, and ready to do or suffer according to his pleasure, satisfied in his faithfulness to all his promises, and sure to reap their fulfilment in a blessed eternity *Note*, (1) God corrects his own children that they might not be condemned with the world (2) If the Lord chastises his own people for the evil he sees in them, shall the rebellious sinner go unpunished? No, verily, there is vengeance hanging over his devoted head (3) The gate of heaven is strait, they who strive to enter, scarcely are able, how surely then must they be excluded, who never so much as set their faces heavenwards! (4) Come what will, we know that our sufferings are sent of God, and that his faithfulness, power, and love, are engaged to bring us safely through them, and this is sufficient to make us easy, yea, happy under them

CHAP V

In which the apostle gives particular directions first to the elders, how to behave themselves towards their flock, in the four first verses, them to the younger, to be obedient and humble, and to cast their care upon God, in the three next verses. From thence to the end he exhorts all to sobriety, watchfulness against temptations, and stedfastness in the faith, praying earnestly for them; and so concludes his epistle with a solemn doxology, mutual salutations, and his apostolical benediction.

1 THE elders which are among you I exhort, who am also an elder, and a witness of the sufferings of Christ, and also a partaker of the glory that
shall be revealed. 2 Feed the flock of God which is among you, taking the oversight *thereof*, not by constraint, but willingly; not for filthy lucre, but of a ready
mind; 3 Neither as being lords over *God's* heritage,
but being ensamples to the flock. 4 And when the
chief Shepherd shall appear, ye shall receive a crown of
glory that fadeth not away. 5 Likewise, ye younger,
submit yourselves unto the elder. Yea, all *of you* be subject one to another, and be clothed with humility: for God resisteth the proud, and giveth grace unto the
humble. 6 Humble yourselves therefore under the mighty hand of God, that he may exalt you in due time:
7 Casting all your care upon him; for he careth for you.

v 1—7. The apostle here,

1. Exhorts the presbyters to a diligent discharge of their sacred trust. *The elders which are among you I exhort, who am also an elder,* put in trust with the same gospel, *and a witness of the sufferings of Christ,* bearing testimony to what I have seen, and ready to suffer with him and for him, *and a partaker of the glory which shall be revealed,* when the great Shepherd and Bishop of souls shall appear to reward his faithful ministers. In the view and expectation of which, *feed the flock of God which is among you* with fidelity, diligence, and zeal, preaching the sound doctrine, and maintaining the wholsome discipline of the gospel, considering at what a price this ransomed flock was purchased; *taking the oversight thereof not by constraint, but willingly,* watching over them with wisdom, and holy solicitude to promote their spiritual and eternal good; *not by constraint,* as compelled to do it against your inclinations, *but willingly,* delighting in your blessed office and employment, *not for filthy lucre,* as the motive to undertake the charge, *but of a ready mind,* free from every mercenary view, and influenced purely by zeal for the Redeemer and love towards immortal souls; *neither as being lords over God's heritage,* and ruling with arrogance and haughtiness, as if you had dominion over men's consciences, *but being ensamples to the flock,* in all humility, meekness, and holy conversation. And then know, for your encouragement, that *when the chief Shepherd shall appear,* who hath appointed you to serve under him, *ye shall receive a crown of glory that fadeth not away,* the blessed reward of your fidelity. *Note,* (1.) The office of a presbyter is an high and honourable employment, and calls for suitable zeal and faithfulness to discharge it aright. (2.) None should ever enter the ministry by constraint, at the solicitation of friends, or moved to it for maintenance; but as prompted by a desire to glorify God, and to be instrumental in the salvation of lost souls. (3.) They who would profit others by their preaching, must second it by their examples, else how can we think that others will believe us, if it appears by our ill conduct that we do not believe ourselves? (4.) The reward of faithful ministers shall be eminently glorious, they shall shine as the stars in the firmament for ever and ever.

2. He addresses himself to the younger, and all private members of the church. *Likewise ye younger, submit yourselves unto the elder,* be guided by their advice, and attentive to their admonitions: *yea, all of you be subject one to another,* paying that deference and respect that is due to every one according to his station, age, rank, or office; *and be clothed with humility,* as a shining garb, which gives beauty to the whole conversation, and adds a lustre to every other grace: *for God resisteth the proud,* that is the character of all others which God abhors, *and he giveth grace to the humble,* who are peculiarly his delight, and enriched by him abundantly, and prepared for his presence in glory. *Humble yourselves therefore under the mighty hand of God,* enduring meekly whatever affliction he is pleased to send upon you, and submissive to those whom he hath set over you, *that he may exalt you in due time,* lifting you above all your tribulations, and bringing you to a throne at his right hand: *casting all your care upon him,* whatever difficulties and trials you may be involved in, *for he careth for you,* will preserve your bodies and souls, give you a happy issue out of all your afflictions, and cause them to work together for your eternal felicity. *Note,* (1.) It is the wisdom of young men to pay deference and obedience to the advice and admonition of their more aged and experienced friends. (2.) God is the enemy of the proud, is often in their chief; and in the unequal contest with Omnipotence, they must needs be undone. (3.) Humility is our greatest ornament, and in God's sight of great price, and those who possess it he delighteth to honour. (4.) God's time must be expected; he will send us relief in due season, if we faint not. (5.) None ever cast their care upon God, and were confounded.

8 Be sober, be vigilant; because your adversary
the devil, as a roaring lion, walketh about, seeking whom
he may devour: 9 Whom resist stedfast in the faith,
knowing that the same afflictions are accomplished in
your brethren that are in the world. 10 But the God
of all grace, who hath called us unto his eternal glory
by Christ Jesus, after that ye have suffered a while,
make you perfect, stablish, strengthen, settle *you*.
11 To him *be* glory and dominion for ever and ever.
Amen.

v 8—11. The apostle, in the view of the subtle enemy which they had to contend against,

1. Admonishes them to be on their guard. *Be sober, be vigilant;* weaned from all inordinate attachment to present things, and watchful in the use of every divine ordinance against the wiles of the great deceiver, *because your adversary the devil,* ever waiting for your halting, *as a roaring lion,* fierce and cruel, *walketh about, seeking whom he may devour,* restless and indefatigable in his attempts to murder immortal souls, and maliciously endeavouring to terrify those, whom he is not permitted to destroy. *Note,* We have a deadly foe to conflict with, powerful, wily, watchful, experienced in deceit; we need be ever on our guard against his snare.

2. The only way in which we can overcome is here set before us. *Whom resist stedfast in the faith,* lifting up this impenetrable shield against all the fiery darts of the wicked one, and encouraged by the examples and the victories of our suffering fellow Christians, *knowing that the same afflictions are accomplished in your brethren that are in the world,* they war against the same enemy, and are supported under all their trials, and through faith made more than conquerors. *Note,* (1.) The examples of others should be our encouragement. (2.) They who in faith resist the devil, will find the weakness of all his efforts, and that before this terrible shield he will be compelled to fly.

3. He offers up his fervent prayers on their behalf. *But the God of all grace,* the fountain and giver of it to all his people, never deserting them in any of their trials, *who hath called us unto his eternal glory by Jesus Christ,* to partake of unutterable blessedness in his presence for ever, through the redemption obtained by his dear Son, *after that ye have suffered a while* here below, *make you perfect* in holiness and happiness, and in your way to this state of complete felicity *stablish* you in the truth, *strengthen* your hearts with his grace, and *settle you* on that foundation from which you never can be moved. *To him be glory and dominion for ever and ever,* be his name adored for all his past mercies and protection, and may we be enabled still to trust upon his care and love. *Amen!*

12 By Silvanus, a faithful brother unto you (as I suppose), I have written briefly, exhorting, and testifying,
that this is the true grace of God wherein ye stand.
13 The *church that is* at Babylon, elected together with
you, saluteth you; and *so doth* Marcus my son. 14
Greet ye one another with a kiss of charity. Peace *be*
with you all that are in Christ Jesus. Amen.

v 12—14. He concludes,

1. With giving an account of his design in this epistle, and the person who was the bearer of it. *By Silvanus, a faithful brother unto you (as I suppose,* and conclude from the most substantial ground,) *I have written briefly* this short epistle, *exhorting, and testifying, that this is the true grace of God wherein ye stand,* in the doctrine and practice of which you have hitherto persevered, and I trust will continue even unto the end. *Note,* They who have begun well, must stand fast in the same grace which they have experienced.

2. He presents the salutations of the church at Babylon, from whence he seems to have written this epistle. *The church that is at Babylon, elected together with you,* through Jesus Christ unto life and glory, *saluteth you* in all Christian wishes of peace and prosperity: *and so doth Marcus my son,* who was either really such, or spiritually; some suppose he means the evangelist Mark, who was sister's son to Barnabas.

3. He exhorts them to fervent charity among themselves. *Greet ye one another with a kiss of charity,* in token of your mutual, unfeigned affection.

4. He pronounces his parting benediction upon them. *Peace be with you all that are in Christ Jesus,* and every blessing, spiritual, temporal, or eternal, which is the happy portion of those that are united to him their living head. May this portion, reader, be thine and mine. *Amen!*

Margin references: a Luke xxiv 48. Acts [illegible] b Rom viii 17, 18. Rev i 9. c John xxi 15. Acts xx 28. d 1 Cor ix 17. e 1 Tim iii 3, 8. Tit i 7. f Matt xx 25, 26. 2 Cor i 24. g Ps xxxiii 12. & lxxiv 2. h Phil iii 17. 2 Thes iii 9. 1 Tim iv 12. i Isa xl 11. Chap ii 25. k 1 Cor ix 25. Chap i 4. l Rom xii 10. Eph v 21. m Jam iv 6. n Prov xvi 5. Isa ii 11. & lvii 15. o Isa lvii 15. & lxvi 2. p Jam iv 10. q Ps xxxvii 5. & lv 22. Mat vi 25. Phil iv 6. r Luke xxi 36. 1 Thes v 6. Chap iv 7. s Job i 7. & ii 2. t Eph vi 11, 13. Jam iv 7. u 1 Thes iii 3. x 1 Cor i 9. y 2 Cor iv 17. Chap i 6. z Heb xiii 21. a Rom xvi 25. 2 Thes iii 3. b 1 Tim vi 16. Chap iv 11. Rev i 6. c 2 Cor i 19. d Heb xiii 22. e 1 Pet i 1. f Acts xii 12, 25. g Rom xvi 16. 1 Cor xvi 20. 2 Cor xiii 12. 1 Thes v 26.

THE

EVANGELICAL EXPOSITOR;

OR, A

PRACTICAL COMMENT

UPON THE

Second General Epiſtle of PETER.

THE penman of this epiſtle appears plainly to be the ſame who wrote the foregoing He was one of the three apoſtles that were preſent at Chriſt's transfiguration, ver 18 and ſays expreſsly, that he had written a former epiſtle to them, chap iii 1 *and the deſign of this ſecond epiſtle is the ſame with that of the former, as is evident from the firſt verſe of the third chapter, whence obſerve, that, in the things of God, we have need of* precept upon precept, and line upon line, *and all little enough to keep them in remembrance, and theſe are the things which ſhould be moſt faithfully recorded, and frequently remembred by us*

CHAP I

In this chapter we have, 1 An introduction, ver 1—4 2 An exhortation to advance and improve in all Chriſtian graces, ver 5, 6, 7 To enforce this exhortation, he adds, (1) A repreſentation of the very great advantage which will thereby accrue to them, ver 8—11 (2) A promiſe of the beſt aſſiſtance the apoſtle was able to give, to facilitate and forward this good work, ver 12—15 3 A declaration of the certain truth and divine original of the goſpel of Chriſt, in the grace whereof they were exhorted to increaſe and perſevere

a Rom i 12 2 Cor iv 13 Tit i 4
b Or of our God and Saviour Tit ii 13
b Rom i 7 1 Pet i 2 Jude 2
c John xvii 3
d 2 Cor vii 1
e 2 Cor iii 18 Eph iv 24 Heb xii 10 1 John iii 2
f Chap ii 18 20

1 SIMON Peter, a ſervant and an apoſtle of
Jeſus Chriſt, to them that have obtained [a]like
precious faith with us, through the righteouſ
neſs | of God, and our Saviour Jeſus Chriſt
2 [b]Grace and peace be multiplied unto you through
the knowledge of God, and of Jeſus our Lord, 3 Ac-
cording as his divine power hath given unto us all things
that *pertain* unto life and godlineſs, [c]through the know-
ledge of him that hath called us to glory and virtue
4 [d]Whereby are given unto us exceeding great and
precious promiſes, that by theſe you might [e]be par
takers of the divine nature, [f]having eſcaped the cor-
ruption that is in the world through luſt

ver 1—4 The apoſtle, being about to finiſh his glorious courſe, addreſſes his laſt epiſtle to his Hebrew brethren We have,

1 The writer *Simon Peter, a ſervant and an apoſtle of Jeſus Chriſt* In the dignity to which he was advanced he did not forget, that his office was not ſo much to rule as to ſerve the meaneſt member of the Redeemer's church

2 The perſons to whom the epiſtle is addreſſed *To them that have obtained like precious faith with us,* and are intereſted in the ſame glorious ſalvation, *through the righteouſneſs of God, or of our God and Saviour Jeſus Chriſt,* which is the meritorious cauſe by which we have obtained a ſure title to eternal bleſſedneſs *Note,* (1) Divine faith may well be called precious,

5

ſeeing the effects of it are ſo unſpeakably glorious (2) Whatever faith we poſſeſs, it is becauſe of our lot among the choſen, who are the objects of Chriſt's ſovereign love and undeſerved favour (3) In the divine righteouſneſs of God our Saviour we ſtand complete before God, and may by right claim all the bleſſings of perfect obedience

3 His apoſtolical benediction *Grace and peace,* with all the bleſſings of the everlaſting goſpel, *be multiplied unto you,* in more abundant manifeſtation and deeper inward experience of them, *through the knowledge of God,* as your covenant and reconciled God, *and of Jeſus our Lord,* in all the bleſſed offices and relations he bears towards us his redeemed people

4 The ground on which he built his confidence that his prayers for them ſhould be heard and anſwered *According as his divine power hath given unto us* freely *all things that pertain unto life and godlineſs,* beſtowing every bleſſing and mean of grace which can conduce to the furtherance of the divine life in our ſouls, till it is perfected above, *through the knowledge of him that hath called us to glory and virtue;* our acquaintance with Jeſus, and acknowledgment of him as the only Saviour of ſouls, being effectual to engage us in the purſuit of glory as our end, and with fortitude unſhaken to walk in all his holy ways *Whereby* (*ſi' ων*) or *by whom,* even through the grace of theſe divine Perſons, *are given unto us exceeding great and precious promiſes,* above all our conceptions, as well as beyond all our deſerts, *that by theſe you might be partakers of the divine nature,* or a divine nature, by the goſpel word, and the great and precious promiſes therein revealed, wherein beholding as in a glaſs the glory of God in the face of Jeſus Chriſt, you are transformed into the ſame image, not partaking of the divine eſſence, but formed anew after the divine likeneſs in righteouſneſs and true holineſs; *having eſcaped the corruption that is in the world through luſt,* flying from out of the world which lieth in wickedneſs, as from a city infected with the plague, and renouncing all the corrupt principles and practices that, through the natural concupiſcence which reigns in every fallen heart, in time paſt defiled your whole body, ſoul, and ſpirit *Note,* (1) All that is good in us comes alone from the divine power and grace (2) The goſpel calls us to glory and virtue, and at the ſame time communicates the effectual ability for the performance of all that it commands (3) The

know

knowledge of God, as he is revealed to us in the gospel of his dear Son, is the grand means of engaging our hearts towards him (4) Exceeding great indeed and precious are those promises, that reach to the deepest state of human guilt and misery, and extend to an eternity of glory in the highest (5) They who, by the transforming vision of God in the gospel, are truly made partakers of a divine nature, will shew it by their deadness to the world, and the subdual of every sensual appetite

g Chap. i. 3 — 5 And besides this, g giving all diligence, add to
your faith, virtue, and to virtue, knowledge, 6 And
to knowledge, temperance, and to temperance, patience,
h Gal. v. 10. 1 Thess. iii. 12. & v. 15 — and to patience, godliness, 7 And to godliness, h bro-
therly kindness, and to brotherly kindness, charity 8
For if these things be in you, and abound, they make
i Gr. Idle. John xv. 2. Tit. iii. 14 — *you that ye shall* neither *be* † barren, i nor unfruitful in
the knowledge of our Lord Jesus Christ 9 But he that
k Isa. lix. 10. 1 John ii. 9, 11 — lacketh these things, k is blind, and cannot see far off,
and hath forgotten that he was purged from his old sins
l 1 John iii. 19 — 10 Wherefore the rather, brethren, give diligence l to
make your calling and election sure, for if ye do these
m Rev. iii. 11 — things, m ye shall never fall 11 For so an entrance
shall be ministred unto you abundantly into the everlast-
ing kingdom of our Lord and Saviour Jesus Christ

v 5—11 Because they had already received so much from God, they were bound to make their profiting appear We have,

1 A golden chain of graces, which we are called to put on *And besides this,* or for this cause, seeing you are partakers of a divine nature, *giving all diligence* to increase with the increase of God, *add to your faith virtue,* courage and boldness in the profession of the gospel, *and to virtue knowledge,* prudently considering the company, place, and time, when our courage in vindicating the cause of Christ may be most successfully exerted, *and to knowledge temperance,* keeping our passions and appetites under strict government, and using all the creatures with a holy moderation, *and to temperance patience* under every provocation, bearing with the injuries, reproaches, and perverseness of others, and meekly submissive under every affliction, *and to patience godliness,* exercising yourselves in every act of devotion and means of grace, from a principle of love to God, and desire of nearer communion with him, *and to godliness brotherly kindness,* feeling the tenderest sympathy and compassion towards your fellow Christians, and ready to every good word and work that may be helpful to them, *and to brotherly kindness charity,* having your heart enlarged to all mankind, with universal benevolence towards every human creature, and a desire to promote their temporal, spiritual, and eternal welfare, not excluding even your greatest and most inveterate enemies

2 These graces will adorn our profession, as the want of them must necessarily prove us destitute of true Christianity *For if these things be in you, and abound,* in lively exercise, *they make you that ye shall neither be barren nor unfruitful in the knowledge of our Lord Jesus Christ, but* as trees of righteousness, the planting of the Lord, full of life, sap, and fruitfulness, which redounds to his glory Whilst *he that lacketh these things is blind,* whatever pretences to wisdom he may make, *and cannot see afar off,* at best hath but a glimmering, and notional apprehension of divine truth, being a stranger to that realizing faith which brings near the distant objects of an eternal world; *and hath forgotten that he was purged from his old sins,* unfaithful to the profession which he made at his baptism, and negligent in his application to that blood which alone can cleanse him from his iniquities

3 He exhorts all believers to diligence in their Christian course *Wherefore the rather, brethren,* considering how many have a name to live who are really dead in trespasses, *give diligence to make your calling and election sure,* in the lively use of every means of grace, which may bring the fullest assurance of it to our own souls, and in the practice of all holy conversation, which may demonstrate to others that we are indeed chosen vessels, and called unto glory, *for, if ye do these things,* and live in the exercise of the graces above mentioned, *ye shall never fall,* so as finally to apostatize from Christ, and perish with the world *For so an entrance shall be ministred unto you abundantly into the everlasting kingdom of our Lord and Saviour Jesus Christ,* when at the last, triumphant over death and the grave, you shall be admitted into all the glories of the eternal world, and so shall be for ever with the Lord *Note,* (1) Though our election be sure in God's purpose, and in the event to all his people, yet He, who hath connected the means with the end, requires our diligence and care to work out our own salvation with fear and trembling (2) They shall shortly enter an eternal world of glory, who now walk under the influences of a Saviour's grace

n Rom. xv. 14, 15. o 1 John ii. 21. — 12 Wherefore I will not be negligent n to put you
always in remembrance of these things, o though ye know
Chap. iii. 1 — them, and be established in the present truth 13 Yea,
I think it meet, p as long as I am in this tabernacle, q to — p 2 Cor. v. 1. q Chap. iii. 1
stir you up by putting you in remembrance 14 r Know- — r Deut. iv. 21, 22 & xxxi. 14
ing that shortly I must put off *this* my tabernacle, even — 2 Tim. iv. 6
as s our Lord Jesus Christ hath shewed me 15 More- — s John xxi. 18, 19.
over, I will endeavour that you may be able after my
decease to have these things always in remembrance

v 12—15 The apostle appears careful to discharge his own solemn trust towards them

Wherefore I will not be negligent to put you always in remembrance of these things, as matters of the last importance, *though ye know them* in a good measure, *and be established in the present truth,* fully satisfied in general of the necessity of holiness, in order to an entrance into the kingdom of heaven *Yea, I think it meet, as long as I am in this tabernacle* of clay, *to stir you up by putting you in remembrance,* that your hearts may be suitably affected, and your practice correspondent with your Christian principles And hereunto I give the greater diligence, *knowing that I must shortly put off this my tabernacle* of the body, and be soon silent in the dust, *even as our Lord Jesus Christ hath shewed me Moreover I will endeavour,* both by my labours among you and these epistles, which when I am dead will yet speak, *that ye may be able, after my decease, to have these things always in remembrance* *Note,* (1) Even the truths we know, we need be often reminded of, and urged to shew their influence on our conduct (2) A minister's work is never done till he closes his eyes his death-bed must be his farewel sermon (3) We live in houses of clay, whose foundation is in the dust, but, blessed be God, we need not regret the dissolution of this wretched tabernacle, when we are to exchange it for a mansion of glory

16 For we have not followed t cunningly devised fa- — t 1 Cor. i. 17 & ii. 1
bles when we made known unto you the power and
coming of our Lord Jesus Christ, but u were eye witnesses — u Matt. xvii. 1, 2. John i. 14. 1 John i. 1 & iv. 14
of his majesty 17 For he received from God the Fa-
ther honour and glory, when there came such a voice to
him from the excellent glory, x This is my beloved Son, — x Matt. iii. 17 & xvii. 5
in whom I am well pleased 18 And this voice which
came from heaven we heard, when we were with him in
y the holy mount 19 We have also a more sure word — y Exod. iii. 5. Josh. v. 15.
of prophecy, whereunto ye do well that ye take heed,
as unto z a light that shineth in a dark place, until the — z Ps. cxix. 105. John v. 35
day dawn, and a the day-star arise in your hearts 20 — a Rev. ii. 28 & xxii. 16
Knowing this first, that b no prophecy of the scripture — b Rom. xii. 6.
is of any private interpretation. 21 For c the prophecy — c 2 Tim. iii. 16. 1 Pet. i. 11
came not † in old time d by the will of man e but — † Or, at any time. d Num. xvi. 28
holy men of God spake *as they were* moved by the Holy — e Luke i. 70
Ghost

v 16—21 We have here a reason given for the importunity and seriousness with which he pressed the foregoing exhortations *For we have not followed cunningly devised fables,* like the Gentile legends or Jewish traditions, *when we made known unto you the power and coming of our Lord Jesus Christ,* at the last great day of his appearing and glory, to judge the assembled world of men and angels *But,*

1 We *were eye-witnesses of his majesty* on the mount of transfiguration, and attest that of which we had the fullest demonstration, not only seeing his glorified body shining in all the brightness of the meridian sun, but hearing the voice of God. *For he there received from God the Father honour and glory,* who bore the fullest testimony to the transcendent dignity of his divine character as his Son Messiah, *when there came such a voice to him from the excellent glory,* the bright cloud which overshadowed him, the symbol of the divine presence, saying, *This is my beloved Son, in whom I am well pleased,* in his person, offices, and all his undertakings *And this voice, which came from heaven, we heard* distinctly and clearly, *when we were with him on the holy mount* So that they could not be mistaken themselves in the things which they testified

2 *We have also a more sure word of prophecy,* wherein a more direct attestation is borne to the power and coming of Jesus to judgment than might be inferred from what we saw and heard. Or, *We have a most sure word of prophecy,* wherein this second appearing of the Lord to judgment is most expresly and repeatedly affirmed, *whereunto ye do well that ye take heed, as unto a light that shineth in a dark place* (and a dark world indeed would this be without the word of God), *until the day,* the great the expected day of our final redemption, *dawn, and the day-star arise in your hearts,* to shine henceforward with unclouded lustre on his chosen, when the Lord shall be our everlasting light, and our God our glory *Knowing this first, that,* till the day of Christ appears, we may surely depend upon his prophetic word as our guide, for *no prophecy of the scripture is of any private interpretation* (ἐπιλύσεως) is not of human invention or composition, but of celestial origin *for the prophecy came not in old time by the will of man; but holy men of God,* whom he had sanctified to be instruments in his hands to deliver his messages, *spake as they were moved by the Holy Ghost,* directing and dictating both

the

the matter and expression *Note*, (1) The scriptures alone are our guide to glory All our wisdom is ignorance, and our light darkness, without a divine revelation (2) The more diligently we take heed to the word of God, read, mark, learn, and inwardly digest it, the more surely shall we walk in holiness and happiness here, and be brought to the perfection of both in heaven hereafter (3) The scriptures carry their own divine authority along with them, and, through the energy of that Spirit who indited them, impress this full conviction on the conscience (4) Though the Bible was written by men, we must say, as of the tables which Moses hewed, that the writing was of God They were but organs and instruments, and did not themselves often comprehend the full meaning of what they delivered With what sacred reverence and awe then should we open that holy book, where God himself is heard still speaking!

CHAP II

The apostle here gives them fair warning of false teachers, by whom they might be in danger of being seduced To prevent this, 1 He describes these seducers as impious in themselves and very pernicious to others, ver 1, 2, 3 *2 He assures them of the punishment that shall be inflicted on them,* ver 3, 4, 5, 6 *3 He tells us how contrary the method is which God takes with those who fear him,* ver 7, 8, 9 *4 He fills up the rest of the chapter with a farther description of those seducers of whom he would have them beware*

1 BUT [a] there were false prophets also among the
people, even as [b] there shall be false teachers a-
mong you, [c] who privily shall bring in damnable heresies,
even denying the Lord [d] that bought them, [e] and bring
upon themselves swift destruction 2 And many shall
follow their † pernicious ways, by reason of whom the
way of truth shall be evil spoken of 3 And [f] through
covetousness shall they with feigned words [g] make mer-
chandise of you [h] whose judgment now of a long time
lingereth not, and their damnation slumbereth not 4
For if [i] God spared not the angels [k] that sinned, but [l] cast
them down to hell, and delivered *them* into chains of dark-
ness, to be reserved unto judgment, 5 And spared not
the old world, [m] but saved Noah the eighth *person*, [n] a
preacher of righteousness, bringing in the flood upon the
world of the ungodly, 6 And turning the cities of
Sodom and Gomorrah into ashes, condemned *them* with
an overthrow, [p] making *them* an ensample unto those that
after should live ungodly, 7 And [q] delivered just Lot,
vexed with the filthy conversation of the wicked 8
(For that righteous man dwelling among them, [r] in see-
ing and hearing, vexed his righteous soul from day to
day, with *their* unlawful deeds) 9 [s] The Lord know-
eth how to deliver the godly out of temptations, and to
reserve the unjust unto the day of judgment to be pu-
nished

v 1—9 False teachers in the church have ever been more dangerous and destructive than all the persecutions of the enemies without Against these the apostle here warns the people

1 He describes them *But there were false prophets also among the people* of Israel of old, *even as there shall be false teachers among you, who*, under pretences to divine inspiration, *privily shall bring in damnable heresies*, craftily perverting the word of God, and adulterating the doctrines of the gospel, *even denying the Lord that bought them*, redeemed them from Egypt with his mighty hand, and in a long succession of miracles repeatedly delivered them out of the hands of their enemies, *Deut* xxxii 6 yet they both doctrinally and practically renounced and disowned him, *and*, as the dreadful consequence of their disobedience, *bring upon themselves swift destruction*, which shall quickly come upon them to the uttermost *And many shall follow their pernicious ways*, seduced by their cunning and ill example, *by reason of whom the way of truth shall be evil spoken of*, and blasphemed by the enemies of the Christian name *and through covetousness shall they with feigned words make merchandise of you*, influenced merely by the detestable principle of avarice, and, amidst all their specious profession, making religion their trade, and designing wholly their secular advantage *Note*, (1) They who enter the ministry for gain must needs be deceivers, and perish in their wickedness (2) Deluding teachers are sure to find followers, error being much more acceptable to the fallen heart than holy truth

2 He foretells their destruction *Whose judgment, now of a long time suspended, yet lingereth not, and their damnation slumbereth not*, but soon shall it terribly overtake them in the midst of their security and sensuality *Note*, Vengeance against sinners is often slow, but always sure Three awful instances are here produced of God's judgment

(1) The fallen angels *For if God spared not the angels that sinned, but cast them down to hell*, though creatures of so much higher rank than men, *and*, on their first offence, *delivered them into chains of darkness, to be reserved unto judgment* in the great day, much less will he spare these obstinate offenders

(2) The antediluvian world *And God spared not the old world*, when abandoned to wickedness *but saved Noah, the eighth person*, with whom only seven more escaped in the ark, *a preacher of righteousness*, both of the righteousness of faith, and that moral righteousness to which he exhorted the men of his generation calling them to repent of their iniquities and, when they continued obstinate against his warnings God issued forth the dread decree, opening the windows of heaven, *bringing in the flood upon the world of the ungodly*, and swallowing them up in the mighty waters If therefore he executed such vengeance upon them, let not other incorrigible sinners think it possible to escape

(3) The destruction of Sodom *And turning the cities of Sodom and Gomorrah into ashes, he condemned them with an overthrow*, raining fire and brimstone upon them, *making them an ensample unto those that after should live ungodly*, that, taking warning by their fearful punishment, they might avoid or repent of their crimes before it be too late, otherwise the same wrath must fall seize upon the ungodly and the sinner

3 For the encouragement of the faithful, he mentions the wonderful escape of Lot from the flames When God destroyed the cities where he dwelt, he *delivered just Lot, vexed with the filthy conversation of the wicked*, grieved for the dishonour brought thereby upon God, and for the ruin which must infallibly descend upon their devoted heads *for that righteous man, dwelling among them, in seeing and hearing, vexed his righteous soul from day to day with their unlawful deeds*, enduring the most painful reflections in the view of their wickedness and the vengeance which hung over them *The Lord knoweth*, as is evident by this instance, *how to deliver the godly out of temptations*, and he will do it in his own good time, *and to reserve the unjust unto the day of judgment to be punished*, who, though they should escape any signal stroke of divine vengeance in this life, are reserved unto the last dreadful day, when their iniquities shall receive their just reward

10 But chiefly [t] them that walk after the flesh, in the
lust of uncleanness, and [u] despise government presump-
tuous *are they*, self willed, they are not afraid to speak
evil of dignities 11 Whereas [x] angels, which are
greater in power and might, bring not railing accusation
against them before the Lord 12 But these, [y] as na-
tural brute beasts, made to be taken and destroyed, speak
evil of the things that they understand not, and shall
utterly perish in their own corruption, 13 [z] And shall
receive the reward of unrighteousness, *as* they that count
it pleasure to riot in the day time [a] Spots *they are*, and
blemishes, sporting themselves with their own deceivings
while [b] they feast with you, 14 Having eyes full of
‖ adultery, and that cannot cease from sin, beguiling
unstable souls an heart they have exercised with covet-
ous practices cursed children 15 Which have for-
saken the right way, and are gone astray, following the
way of [c] Balaam *the son* of Bosor, who loved the wages
of unrighteousness, 16 But was rebuked for his ini-
quity the dumb ass, speaking with man's voice, forbad
the madness of the prophet 17 [d] These are wells with-
out water, clouds that are carried with a tempest, to
whom the mist of darkness is reserved for ever 18 For
when [e] they speak great swelling *words* of vanity, they
allure through the lusts of the flesh, through much wan-
tonness, those [f] that were ‖ clean escaped from them who
live in error 19 While they promise them [g] liberty,
they themselves are [h] the servants of corruption for of
whom a man is overcome, of the same is he brought in
bondage 20 For [i] if after they have [k] escaped the pol-
lutions of the world, [l] through the knowledge of the
Lord and Saviour Jesus Christ, they are again entangled
therein and overcome, the latter end is worse with them
than the beginning 21 For [m] it had been better for
them not to have known the way of righteousness, than
after they have known *it*, to turn from the holy com-
mandment delivered unto them 22 But it is happened
unto them according to the true proverb, [n] The dog *is*
turned to his own vomit again, and, The sow that was
washed, to her wallowing in the mire

v 10—22 The apostle here,

1 At large describes the seducing teachers, whose practices copied after the vilest of those ungodly workers whom he had mentioned, and who with them must perish *But chiefly them* will

Marginal references: [a] Deut xiii 1 [b] Mat xxiv 11 Acts xx 30 1 Tim iv 1 1 John iv 1 [c] Jude 4 [d] Acts xx 28 1 Cor vi 20 [e] Phil iii 19 † Or lascivious ways, as some read it [f] Rom xvi 18 [g] 1 Tim vi 5 Tit i 11 [h] 2 Cor ii 17 [h] Deut xxxii 35 Jude 4 [k] Jude 6 [l] John viii 44 1 John iii 8 [l] Luke viii 31 [m] Gen vii 23 1 Pet iii 20 [n] 1 Pet iii 19 [o] Gen xix 24 Jude 7 [p] Jude 7 Num xxvi 10 [q] Gen xix 16 [r] Psal cxix 158 Ezek ix 4 [s] 1 Cor x 13 [t] Jude 4 10 16 [u] Jude 8 [x] Jude 9 [y] Jer xii 3 Jude 10 [z] Phil iii 19 [a] Jude 12 [b] 1 Cor xi 20 21 ‖ Gr An adulteress [c] Num xxii 5 23 28 Jude 11 [d] Jude 12, 13 [e] Jude 16 [f] Acts ii 40 ‖ Some read, for a little, or in a little [g] Gal v 13 1 Pet ii 16 [h] John viii 34 Rom vi 16 [i] Mat xii 45 Heb vi 4 x 26 [k] Chap i 4 [l] Chap i 2 [m] Luke xii 47 48 [n] Prov xxvi 11

will God reserve unto judgment, *that walk after the flesh, in the lust of uncleanness*, like the men of Sodom, *and despise government*, seditious and refractory, unwilling to submit to any restraint. *Presumptuous are they*, and *self-willed*, *they are not afraid to speak evil of dignities*, reviling both the ministers and apostles of Christ, and the civil magistrates set over them for the restraint of evil-doers. *Whereas angels, which are greater in power and might* than every earthly potentate, yet *bring not a railing accusation against them before the Lord*, reviling their persons or government. *But these* despisers of God's ordinances, *as natural brute beasts, made to be taken and destroyed* by men, for whose use they were created, *speak evil of the things that they understand not*, reviling persons and things civil and religious, of whose excellence they have not the least knowledge, *and shall utterly perish in their own corruptions*, abandoned to their wicked hearts and left to their ruin. *And shall receive the reward of unrighteousness, as they that count it pleasure to riot in the day-time*, daring and impudent in sin, not even waiting for the night to cover their shame. *Spots they are, and blemishes*, a reproach to the name of Christian which they presume to bear, *sporting themselves with their own deceivings, whilst they feast with you*, and live in the indulgence of their sins, whilst they outwardly appear to maintain communion with you, *having eyes full of adultery*, whose wanton looks bespeak the impurity of their hearts, *and that cannot cease from sin*, enslaved by their sensual appetites, and inveterate in the indulgence of them, *beguiling unstable souls*, as Satan beguiled Eve through his subtilty, and tempting them to comply with their corrupt and lewd desires. *An heart they have exercised with covetous practices*, all their contrivances and pursuits being to amass wealth. *Cursed children*, under the wrath of a holy God, *which have forsaken the right way* of salvation by Jesus Christ *and are gone astray* from the paths of truth and holiness, *following the way of Balaam the son of Bosor, who loved the wages of unrighteousness*, and, notwithstanding his specious professions to Balak's messengers, really coveted the king of Moab's offers, *but was rebuked for his iniquity* in a very signal manner, *the dumb ass*, on which he rode, *speaking with man's voice*, by miraculous power, *forbad the madness of the prophet* in presuming to go, after the warnings to the contrary which he had received, or to attempt the cursing of that people whom the Lord had blessed. *These are wells without water*, pretending to piety, but disappointing those who, like the thirsty traveller, come to them for the water of life, *clouds that are carried with a tempest*, that promise rain, but prove noxious vapours, *to whom the mist of darkness is reserved for ever*, going from the darkness of sin and error to the horrible and eternal darkness of hell. *For when they speak great swelling words of vanity*, pretending to high flights of science, and boasting their vast attainments, *they allure through the lusts of the flesh, through much wantonness*, by temptations suited to the corrupt inclinations of their hearers, *those that were clean escaped from them who live in error*, and had made a creditable profession for a season, but now relapse into all their former abominations. *While they promise them liberty*, a carnal liberty to live as they list, without restraint, *they themselves are the servants of corruption*, the veriest slaves in nature to base and vile affections: *for of whom a man is overcome, of the same is he brought into bondage*, and no bondage so dreadful as that of sin and Satan. *Note*, (1.) The sins of lewdness are the dreadful rock on which unstable souls make shipwreck of the faith. (2.) They who have hearts set on their covetousness are hardly turned away from their vile pursuits, though conscience, like the faithful monitor of Balaam, often startle and rebukes them. (3.) None are so far escaped from the world, but they have need to watch and pray that they fall not into temptation. (4.) However speciously the snare may be laid, and whatever liberty we may promise ourselves in sin, to our cost we shall find the dire delusion, and prove how fearful is the bondage of corruption.

2. He warns them, by all the dreadful consequences of apostacy, to beware of these seducers. *For if after they have escaped the pollutions of the world, through the knowledge of the Lord and Saviour Jesus Christ*, and from the preaching of the gospel have been laid under such restraints as for a while to appear creditable in their profession, *they are again entangled therein and overcome*, so as to become thorough slaves to their lusts and appetites, *the latter end is worse with them than the beginning*, and their state more guilty than when they lay before in utter darkness, ignorance, and error. *For it had been better for them not to have known the way of righteousness*, or to have heard of Christ and his salvation, *than, after they have known it, to turn from the holy commandment delivered unto them*. *But it hath happened unto them according to the true proverb, The dog is turned to his own vomit again; and, The sow, that was washed, to her wallowing in the mire*. *Note*, (1.) Under convictions of sin, many for a while manifest their former lewdness, who soon return to their forsaken iniquities with greediness, when the impressions which have been made die away. (2.) Whatever outward reformation may be made, if the heart is not right with God, all is still wrong within, the swinish nature is not changed by the washing, and apostacy will inevitably be the issue. (3.) None perish with such aggravated guilt as those who have made the fairest profession, and seemed to begin well, but fail in their course, and relapse into iniquity. Woeful will be the end of apostates.

CHAP. III.

The apostle, drawing towards the conclusion of his second epistle, begins this last chapter of it with repeating the account of his design and scope in writing a second time to them, ver. 1, 2. 2. He proceeds to mention one thing that induced him to write this second epistle, namely, the coming of scoffers, whom he describes, ver. 3—7. 3. He instructs and establishes them in the coming of our Lord Jesus Christ to judgment, ver. 8, 9, 10. 4. He sets forth the use and improvement which Christians ought to make of Christ's second coming, and that dissolution and renovation of things, which will accompany that solemn coming of our Lord, ver. 11—18.

1 THIS second epistle, beloved, I now write unto
you; in both which [a] I stir up your pure minds [a] Chap. i. 13.
by way of remembrance: 2 That ye may be mindful
of the words which were spoken before by the holy pro-
phets, [b] and of the commandment of us the apostles of [b] Jude 17.
the Lord and Saviour: 3 [c] Knowing this first, that
there shall come in the last days scoffers, [d] walking after [c] 1 Tim. iv. 1. 2 Tim. iii. 1.
their own lusts, 4 And saying, [e] Where is the promise [d] Jude 18.
of his coming? for since the fathers fell asleep, [f] all [e] Chap. ii. 10.
things continue as *they were* from the beginning of the [e] Is. v. 19. Jer. xvii. 15. Ez. xii. 22.
creation. 5 For this they willingly are ignorant of,
that [g] by the word of God the heavens were of old, and [f] Eccles. i. 9.
[h] the earth standing out of the water, and in the water: [g] Gen. i. 6. Ps. xxxiii. 6. Heb. xi. 3.
6 [i] Whereby the world that then was, being overflowed
with water, perished: 7 But [k] the heavens and the [h] Ps. xxiv. 2. & cxxxvi. 6.
earth which are now, by the same word are kept in store, [i] Gen. vii. 11.
reserved unto fire against the day of judgment, [l] and per- [k] Chap. ii. 5. Ver. 10.
dition of ungodly men. [l] 2 Thess. i. 8.

v. 1—7. The apostle sets forth his design of writing both these epistles. *This second epistle, beloved, I now write unto you, in both which I stir up your pure minds by way of remembrance*, that you may be guarded against the arts of deceivers, and *that ye may be mindful of the words which were spoken before by the holy prophets, and of the commandments of us the apostles of the Lord and Saviour*, who, in perfect conformity with the inspired penmen of the old scriptures, as in other things, so particularly with regard to the coming of the Lord to judgment, have forewarned and admonished you. *Knowing this first, that there shall come in the last days scoffers* at revelation, and all its glorious and distinguishing doctrines, *walking after their own lusts*, given up to sensuality and brutish appetites, *and* with daring infidelity, and defiance of the divine declarations, *saying, Where is the promise of his coming*, so much talked of? when is this Jesus of Nazareth to come and take vengeance on his enemies, and to destroy the world? *for since the fathers fell asleep* (say they) during so many hundred years, *all things continue as they were from the beginning of the creation*. Thus they vainly argue, and, because judgment is not speedily executed upon the workers of iniquity, they would conclude that there is nothing to be feared. For, though the scripture assures them that God hath already eminently manifested his righteous wrath by the general destruction of an ungodly world, *this they willingly and wilfully are ignorant of, that the heavens were of old created* by the almighty word, *and the earth standing out of the water and in the water*, rising from the abyss of waters which covered it at the first, moistened still by this element and compacted together, and surrounded with waters above, and full of water in its bowels: *whereby the world that then was, being overflowed* at the general deluge, *perished*, and the scoffers of that day met their righteous doom. *But the heavens and the earth which are now, by the same almighty word are kept in store* as treasures, *reserved unto fire against the day of judgment, and perdition of ungodly men*. And however the scoffers of this day may despise God's warnings, yet the evident marks which still remain of what he hath done by the deluge, are speaking evidence of his power to fulfil a more terrible denunciation, when his fire shall descend, and a general conflagration ensue. A day, which will speak terror and dismay through an ungodly world, and too late convince those infidel mockers, that it is a fearful thing to fall into the hands of the living God.

8 But, beloved, be not ignorant of this one thing, that
one day *is* with the Lord as a thousand years, and [m] a thou- [m] Ps. xc. 4.
sand years as one day. 9 [n] The Lord is not slack con- [n] Hab. ii. 3.
cerning his promise, (as some men count slackness) [o] but Heb. x. 37.
is long-suffering to us-ward, [p] not willing that any should [o] Isa. xxx. 18. Ver. 15.
perish, [q] but that all should come to repentance. 10 But [p] Ez. xviii. 23, 32. & xxxiii. 11.
[r] the day of the Lord will come as a thief in the night, [q] 1 Tim. ii. 4.
in the which [s] the heavens shall pass away with a great [r] Mat. xxiv. 43. 1 Thess. v. 2. Rev. iii. 3. & xvi. 15.
noise, and the elements shall melt with fervent heat, the [s] Ps. cii. 26. Isa. li. 6. Mat. xxiv. 35. Rev. xx. 11. & xxi. 1.
earth also and the works that are therein shall be burnt
up.

up 11 Seeing then that all theſe things ſhall be diſ-
ſolved, what manner of perſons ought ye to be [t] in *all*
holy converſation and godlineſs, 12 Looking for, and
† haſtening unto [u] the coming of the day of God, where-
in [x] the heavens being on fire ſhall be diſſolved, and the
elements ſhall melt with fervent heat?

t 1 Pet i 15.
† Or haſting the coming
u Tit ii 13
x Iſa xxxiv 4

v 8—12 The apoſtle having warned them againſt the ſcoffers, encourages the ſaints of God to expect their Lord's ſecond coming

1 He will *ſurely* come *But, beloved, be not ignorant of this one thing, that one day is with the Lord as a thouſand years, and a thouſand years as one day* Though we meaſure time by ſucceſſion, to the eternal God the paſt, the preſent, and the future appear in one comprehenſive view, and is nothing compared with his eternity *The Lord is not ſlack concerning his promiſe (as ſome men count ſlackneſs)* too impatient for his appearing, *but is long-ſuffering to us ward, not willing that any* of his redeemed people ſhould periſh, *but that all ſhould come to repentance*, called in due time to the acknowledgment of the truth, and ſaved by grace, and when the number of his elect ſhall be accompliſhed, then he will haſten his kingdom, will come at the appointed period, and not tarry a moment longer *Note*, (1) The great deſign God hath in view is the ſalvation of his own people (2) The way in which any can meet the Lord with comfort is, by being converted and turned to him now by faith, the impenitent and unbelieving muſt aſſuredly periſh

2 He will come *ſuddenly* *But the day of the Lord will come as a thief in the night* with ſuch a terrible ſurprize to the ungodly world, *in the which the heavens ſhall paſs away with a great noiſe*, when nature in convulſions ſhall utter her expiring groans, *and the elements ſhall melt with fervent heat*, diſſolved amidſt the univerſal conflagration, *the earth alſo and the works that are therein ſhall be burnt up*, and not a wreck remain of all its glorious ſtructures

3 What influence ought ſuch an expectation to have upon us? *Seeing then that all theſe things ſhall be diſſolved, what manner of perſons ought ye to be in all holy converſation and godlineſs?* How dead to the world, how looſe to its enjoyment, how patient under the preſent momentary afflictions, how wholly engroſſed with one great concern, to ſecure a part in that eternal world whither we are going, *looking for, and haſtening unto the coming of the day of the Lord*, keeping it abidingly in view, and living in a conſtant preparation for that ſolemn hour, *when the heavens being on fire ſhall be diſſolved, and the elements ſhall melt with fervent heat?* *Note*, It is the character of a diſciple of Jeſus, that he is ever looking for his Lord's return as the glorious hope which animates him for every duty, and ſupports him under all his trials

y Iſa lxv 17 & lxvi 22. Rev xxi 1 27
z 1 Cor i 8 Eph v 27 Phil i 10 1 Theſ iii 13 & v 23
a Rom ii 4 1 Pet iii 20 Ver 9
b Rom viii 19 1 Cor xv 24 1 Theſ iv 15

13 Nevertheleſs we, according to his promiſe, look for
[y] new heavens and a new earth, wherein dwelleth righte-
ouſneſs 14 Wherefore, beloved, ſeeing that ye look
for ſuch things, be diligent that ye may be found of him
in peace, [z] without ſpot, and blameleſs 15 And ac-
count *that* [a] the long-ſuffering of our Lord *is* ſalvation,
even as our beloved brother Paul alſo, according to the
wiſdom given unto him, hath written unto you, 16 As
alſo in all *his* epiſtles, [b] ſpeaking in them of theſe things,
in which are ſome things hard to be underſtood, which
they that are unlearned and unſtable wreſt, as *they do* alſo
the other ſcriptures, unto their own deſtruction 17 Ye
therefore, beloved, [c] ſeeing ye know *theſe things* before,
[d] beware leſt ye alſo, being led away with the error of the
wicked, fall from your own ſtedfaſtneſs 18 But [e] grow
in grace, and *in* the knowledge of our Lord and Saviour
Jeſus Chriſt [f] To him *be* glory both now and for ever
Amen

c Mark xiii 23
d Eph iv 14 Chap i 10 & ii 18
e Eph iv 15. 1 Pet ii 2
f 2 Pet iv 11 Rev i 6 & v 13

v 13—18 We have here,

1 The Chriſtian's expectation when this heaven and earth ſhall be diſſolved *Nevertheleſs we, according to his promiſe, look for a new heaven and a new earth, wherein dwelleth righteouſneſs*, even that bleſſed abode which Everlaſting Love hath prepared for the redeemed from the earth, where nothing ſhall ever enter which defileth, and where our bliſs and glory will be eternal

2 He exhorts them, in the proſpect of ſuch an inheritance,

(1) To be faithful in their holy profeſſion *Wherefore, beloved, ſeeing that ye look for ſuch things, be diligent* in the uſe of every appointed means of grace, and in all holy watchfulneſs, *that ye may be found of him in peace*, poſſeſſing a ſure intereſt in his love, *without ſpot* of ſin, *and blameleſs* in his preſence at that great day *Note*, They are truly ſafe and happy for ever, whoſe conſciences are now purged through the Saviour's blood, and by the power of his grace

(2) Patiently to perſevere, though the time ſhould yet be diſtant *And account that the long-ſuffering of our Lord is ſalvation*, and that the reaſon of his delay is for the benefit of his people's ſouls, that his elect may all be finally gathered in, *even as our beloved brother Paul alſo, according to the wiſdom given unto him, hath written unto you, as alſo in all his epiſtles, ſpeaking in them of theſe things*, of God's long-ſuffering, and the coming of the Lord to judgment, *in which* doctrines *are ſome things hard to be underſtood*, being of a ſublime and ſpiritual nature, *which they that are unlearned and unſtable*, who are not divinely taught of God, and whoſe principles are fluctuating and unſettled, *wreſt* and diſtort from their true meaning, *as they do alſo the other Scriptures, unto their own deſtruction* *Note*, The more dangerous it is to be ignorant in the Scriptures, the more diligently ſhould we ſearch them, and pray God to enlighten our minds that we may be made wiſe unto ſalvation

(3) To beware of all deceivers *Ye therefore, beloved, ſeeing ye know theſe things before*, that Chriſt will ſurely come and take vengeance of the ungodly, *beware leſt ye alſo, being led away with the error of the wicked*, by their flatteries and ſeductions, *fall from your own ſtedfaſtneſs*, and depart from the purity of that goſpel, which you have hitherto ſo nobly maintained *Note*, (1) When deluding teachers are at work, we need be deeply on our guard (2) They who fall into erroneous principles, grow ſoon unſettled in their practice, and ſhew the baleful influence of this poiſon

(4) To advance in the divine life *But grow in grace, and in the knowledge of our Lord and Saviour Jeſus Chriſt*, gaining a deeper and more experimental acquaintance with his love, a more unſhaken dependance upon him, and an increaſe of every divine and ſpiritual diſpoſition in conſequence thereof

3 He concludes with an aſcription of praiſe to the Divine Redeemer *To him be glory both now and for ever* May every creature in heaven and earth unite in ceaſeleſs worſhip, praiſe, and adoration to the great Immanuel! *Amen!*

THE EVANGELICAL EXPOSITOR; OR, A PRACTICAL COMMENT UPON THE First General Epistle of JOHN.

THIS epistle is universally ascribed to the apostle John, and it indeed contains in itself the fullest evidence, that it flowed from the same pen which wrote the Gospel and Revelations. Though the precise time when he wrote is not certain, it seems, from chap ii 18 *& iv 1 to have been a little before the destruction of Jerusalem. The epistle is stiled General, as not being addressed to any particular church, but to the body of Christian believers throughout the world, in order to confirm their faith in the glory and divinity of the Lord Jesus, to maintain the sacred doctrines of his person and offices against heretical seducers, to quicken them to the practice of righteousness and true holiness, and to engage them to the exercise of fervent charity towards each, that, thus united, they might be preserved from the world which lieth in wickedness, and come to the eternal enjoyment of their ever blessed God and Saviour.*

CHAP I.

Evidence given concerning Christ's person and excellency, ver 1, 2. *The knowledge thereof gives us communion with God and Christ,* ver 3. *And joy,* ver 4. *A description of God,* ver. 5. *How we are thereupon to walk,* ver 6. *The benefit of all such walking,* ver 7. *The way to forgiveness,* ver 9. *The evil of denying our sin,* ver 8, 9, 10.

1 THAT [a] which was from the beginning, which we have heard, which we have seen with our eyes, [b] which we have looked upon, and [c] our hands have handled of the
word of life; 2 (For the life [d] was manifested, and we
have seen *it*, and [e] bear witness, and shew unto you [f] that
eternal life, [g] which was with the Father, and was manifested unto us) 3 That which we have seen and heard
declare we unto you, that ye also may have fellowship
with us: and truly [h] our fellowship *is* with the Father,
and with his Son Jesus Christ. 4 And these things write
we unto you, [i] that your joy may be full.

V. 1—4. The blessed penman of this epistle immediately enters into his subject. Full of Christ, he breaks forth,

That which was from the beginning, that glorious and divine person, who from eternity is the Son, subsisted with the Father in the same undivided essence, *which*, in the fulness of time, became incarnate, *we have heard* preaching his everlasting gospel, *which we have seen with our eyes*, living and dying, *which we have looked upon*, attentively regarding him both before and after his resurrection from the dead, *and our hands have handled*, so that we have the strongest and most indubitable evidence of his true humanity, and of the reality of his resurrection in the same body, which before his death he had assumed into personal union with himself, who emphatically bears the name *of the word of life*, being the fountain of natural life to every creature, and the giver of spiritual and eternal life to his redeemed people, (*for the life*, the Lord of life and glory, *was manifested* in the flesh, *and we have seen it, and bear witness, and shew unto you that eternal life*, who from everlasting existed in the unity of the Godhead, *which was with the Father*, one with him in co-essential glory, *and was*, in the fulness of time, according to the prophetic word, *manifested to us* in the human nature) *that adored personage, which we have seen and heard*, and concerning whom we are most incontestibly assured that our record is true, *HIM we declare unto you*, as God and Man in one Christ, as the only and all-sufficient Saviour, through whom all blessings in time and eternity are obtained for his people, and we publish his offices, glory and gospel, *that ye also may have fellowship with us* in all the inestimable privileges which he bestows on his chosen, on us and all who believe on his name: *and truly* this communion is of the most transcendently-glorious nature, for *our fellowship is with the Father* himself, *and with his Son Jesus Christ*, in and through whom we are admitted into the nearest, most honourable and eternal union and friendship with the God of glory. *And these things write we unto you, that your joy may be full*, abounding with consolation in the experience of the present invaluable privileges of pardon, adoption, and grace, and advancing to the perfection of joy in heaven, and to the pleasure which are at God's right hand for evermore.

Note, (1.) It is the dignity of every faithful soul that he is admitted into communion with God, and is one with Jesus, as a member of his body mystical. (2.) They who know the Saviour experimentally, as united to him in faith and love, have within them a fund of never-ending consolation, a well of living water springing up into everlasting life.

5 [k] This then is the message which we have heard of him, and declare unto you, that [l] God is light, and in
him is no darkness at all. 6 [m] If we say that we have
fellowship with him, and walk in darkness, we lie, and
do

a John i. 1. b John i. 14. 2 Pet. i. 16. c Chap. iv. 14. Luke xxiv. 39. John xx. 27. d 1 Tim. iii. 16. e Chap. v. 11. f Chap. v. 20. g John i. 1, 2. h John xvii. 21. 1 Cor. i. 9. Chap. ii. 24. i John xv. 11. & xvi. 24. 2 John 12.

k Chap. iii. 11. l John i. 9. & viii. 12. & ix. 5. & xii. 35, 36. m 2 Cor. vi. 14. Chap. ii. 4.

do not the truth 7 But if we walk in the light, as
he is in the light, we have fellowship one with another,
and [n] the blood of Jesus Christ his Son cleanseth us from
all sin

n 1 Cor vi 11 Heb ix 14 1 Pet i 19 Rev i

v 5—7 Having mentioned the Author of the everlasting gospel, the apostle passes on to the message which they had received from him to deliver unto men

1 Concerning God *This then is the message which we have heard of him, and declare unto you, that God is light*, a Spirit absolutely pure, infinite in all perfections, without the least shadow or possibility of imperfection, *and in him is no darkness at all* *Note*, Our poor and finite ideas are unable adequately to comprehend the divine excellencies, nay, angels before him vail their faces, for he dwelleth in that light which no creature can approach unto, so as fully to discern his glory What we know of him is rather by removing every defect from him, and saying what he is not, rather than what he is

2 Concerning those who professed to believe in him [1] *If we say that we have fellowship with him*, through the gospel of his dear Son, *and* yet notwithstanding *walk in darkness*, the allowed servants of sin, which is so opposite to his essential purity, *we lye, and do not the truth*, our falshood is evident to his all-searching eye, and our practice contradicts our professions, and proves our hypocrisy *But*, [2] *if we walk in the light* of truth and holiness, under the guidance of his Spirit, and according to our Christian profession, *as he is in the light*, resembling him in his communicable perfections, then *we have fellowship one with another*, we dwell in God, and God in us, enjoying the most distinguishing communion with him in spirit, *and the blood of Jesus Christ his Son cleanseth us from all sin*, compleatly justified in God's sight, free from all condemnation, and assured also that the being of sin in us shall be shortly for ever rooted out Blessed and happy are they whom this blood cleanses, and who are admitted into this holy fellowship!

8 [o] If we say that we have no sin, we deceive our-
selves, and the truth is not in us 9 [p] If we confess
our sins, he is faithful and just to forgive us our sins,
and to cleanse us from all unrighteousness 10 If we
say that we have not sinned, we make him a lyar, and
his word is not in us

o 1 Kings viii 46 2 Chron vi 36 Job xv 14 Prov xx 9 Eccles vii 20 Jam iii 2
p Ps xxxii 5 Prov xxviii 13

v 8—10 The apostle, to prevent all misconception, as if perfection were to be attained here below, plainly declares, that sin still cleaves to those who are nearest and dearest to God For,

1 *If we say that we have no sin*, not that we never had, but that we have it not now, if we, even the highest apostles, dare make such an arrogant boast, *we deceive ourselves, and the truth is not in us*, we are under a most dangerous error and delusion And he repeats the admonition, v 10 to guard more strongly against all the pride of pretended perfectionists *If we say that we have not sinned, we make him a lyar*, by directly contradicting his truth, because being by nature corrupted creatures, we remain, and must remain whilst in the body, imperfect, *and*, if we deny it, *his word is not in us*, which every where supposes and declares us to be such, for if we were not, the exercise of faith in the atoning blood, and of daily repentance, would be at an end.

2 *If we confess our sins*, and humbly, through faith in Jesus Christ, apply for the promised mercy of God, *he is faithful and just to forgive us our sins* faithful to the covenant of grace, and to his promise made therein to the Redeemer on the behalf of his people *just*, because having received the ransom of atoning blood, it is become an act of justice to pardon those who plead it, *and to cleanse them from all unrighteousness* *Note*, Our acceptance with God stands not on the footing of mercy only, but is secured to us by that very perfection of holiness which seemed most strongly to militate against the sinner's hope

CHAP II

Here the apostle encourages against sins of infirmity, ver 1, 2 *Shews the true knowledge and love of God*, ver 3—6 *Renews the precept of fraternal love*, ver 7—11 *Addresses Christians of several ages*, ver 12—14 *Warns against worldly love*, ver 15—17 *Against seducers*, ver 18, 19 *Shews the security of true Christians*, ver 20—27, *And advises to abide in Christ*, ver 28, 29

1 MY little children, these things I write unto you,
that ye sin not And if any man sin, [a] we
have an advocate with the Father, Jesus Christ the right-
eous 2 And [b] he is the propitiation for our sins and
not for ours only, but [c] also for *the sins of* the whole
world 3 And hereby we do know that we know him,
if we keep his commandments 4 [d] He that saith, I
know him, and keepeth not his commandments, is a
lyar, and the truth is not in him 5 But [e] whoso keep-
eth his word, [f] in him verily is the love of God perfect-
ed [g] hereby know we that we are in him 6 [h] He that
saith he abideth in him, [i] ought himself also so to walk,
even as he walked.

a Rom viii 34 1 Tim ii 5 Heb vii 25 & ix 24
b Rom iii 25 Chap i 7
c John i 29 Chap iv 14
d Chap i 6 & iv 20
e John xiv 21 23
f Chap iv 12
g Chap iv 13
h John xv 4
i Matt xi 29 John xiii 15 1 Pet ii 21

v 1—6 We have here,

1 The design which the apostle chiefly aimed at in what he had written *My little children*, whom I regard with the tenderest sensations of paternal love, *these things write I unto you, that ye sin not*, watchful against every surprize and temptation, and never allowing yourselves in the practice of it *And if any man*, through the infirmity of his nature, be drawn aside from the way of God's commandments, *we have an advocate with the Father, Jesus Christ the righteous*, who shall still plead our cause, when we with shame and sorrow return to him, whose everlasting righteousness shall stand us in stead before the throne of God *And he is the abiding propitiation for our sins*, having made the full atonement, and obtained eternal redemption for us, paying that ransom which is available not only for all past, but for all future transgressions to our lives end *and not for our sins only*, who were once, as Jews, his peculiar and covenant people, *but for the sins of the whole world*, of Gentile believers also, who are admitted to the participation of the same privilege, and become the children of God through faith in Jesus Christ *Note*, (1) The advocacy of Jesus is founded upon his everlasting righteousness, and perfect atonement, and therefore is ever available no cause put into his hand can miscarry (2) Whilst with holy jealousy we watch against sin, we must not, if at any time cast down, sink into despair we have one before the throne, who ever liveth to make intercession for us, and God for his sake will abundantly pardon (3) Christ's salvation is universal to sinners of all ranks and nations, who come to God by him none shall be in any wise cast out

2 The rule of judgment concerning our real knowledge of Christ *And hereby we do know that we know him*, and have the fullest demonstration of our real acquaintance with him, and of our genuine faith and love, *if we keep his commandments*, and unreservedly yield up ourselves to be guided by his holy word and will *He that saith, I know him, and keepeth not his commandments*, living in the allowed and habitual practice of iniquity, *is a lyar, and the truth is not in him*, however confident his boasts may be, and however high his pretensions *But whoso keepeth his word*, in doctrine and practice, faithfully desiring to correspond therewith in all things, *in him verily is the love of God perfected*, its prevailing influence, and unfeigned sincerity is *hereby* manifested, and by this *know we that we are in him*, vitally united to the living head, eternally interested in all the privileges of his gospel, in which the hypocrite hath neither part nor lot *He that saith he abideth in him, ought himself also so to walk, even as he walked*, copying the divine pattern, and, though at an humble distance, following the footsteps of the holy Jesus *Note*, The profession of Christianity, without the practice of true godliness, is but an empty name They who are truly Christ's, will prove it not only in their lips, but by their lives

7 Brethren, [k] I write no new commandment unto
you, but an old commandment [l] which ye had from the
beginning the old commandment is the word which ye
have heard from the beginning 8 Again, [m] a new
commandment I write unto you, which thing is true in
him and in you because [n] the darkness is past, and [o] the
true light now shineth 9 [p] He that saith he is in the
light, and hateth his brother, is in darkness even until
now. 10 [q] He that loveth his brother abideth in the
light, and [r] there is none occasion of [||] stumbling in him
11 But he that hateth his brother is in darkness, and
[s] walketh in darkness, and knoweth not whither he go-
eth, because that darkness hath blinded his eyes

k 2 John 5
l Chap iii 11 2 John 5
m John xiii 34
n Rom xiii 12 1 Thes v 5, 8
o John i 9 & viii 12
p 1 Cor xiii 2 2 Pet i 9 Chap iii 14 15
q Chap iii 14
r 2 Pet i 10
|| Or scandal
s John xii 35

v 7—11 The apostle, as the most distinguishing character of true discipleship, and the great command of the divine Master, earnestly inculcates the great duty of brotherly love

Brethren, I write no new commandment unto you, but remind you of *an old commandment which ye had from the beginning*, written upon the heart of man in innocence, and enforced in that revelation which God from the first made unto men *The old commandment is the word which ye have heard from the beginning*, wherein love is enjoined as the fulfilling of the law *Again a new commandment I write unto you*, the same indeed in substance, but enforced by new motives, encouragements, assistances, and examples, *which thing is true in him and in you*, manifested most strikingly in that divine pattern of love which he set before you, and which you have in a gracious measure humbly imitated *because the darkness* of the former dispensation *is past, and the true light now shineth*, the Sun of righteousness is arisen, and the shadows are fled, the glorious gospel bringing us forth out of darkness into the meridian light of truth, and demanding from us a conversation suitable to the peculiar advantages which we enjoy

He

9 L

He that ſaith he is in the light, and profeſſes faith in Jeſus, the light of the world, *and hateth his brother*, *is in darkneſs even until now*, a ſtranger to the godlike ſpirit of charity which the goſpel breathes, and covered with the black night of ſin and error *He that loveth his brother*, as a fellow-member of Chriſt's myſtical body, and becauſe he is the child of the ſame heavenly Father, *abideth in the light* of truth, *and there is no occaſion of ſtumbling in him*, he will carefully avoid whatever would offend or weaken his brother's ſoul *But he that hateth his brother*, and harbours an uncharitable, envious, proud, and revengeful diſpoſition, *is in darkneſs*, under the evident dominion of Satan and ſin, *and walketh in darkneſs*, all his ways being perverſe before God, *and knoweth not whither he goeth*, nor is aware of the dreadful iſſue of his ways, *becauſe that the darkneſs* of his fallen heart *hath blinded his eyes* to all the dire conſequences of ſin *Note*, (1) Charity is the diſtinguiſhing characteriſtic of the Chriſtian (2) If there be a creature living, againſt whom we harbour allowed envy, malice, or revenge, in whoſe miſery we ſhould delight, or whoſe good we deſire not to promote, we brand ourſelves the children of darkneſs

e 1 Jn xxiv f Acts ii 3 & x 43 & xiii 38 — 12 I write to you, little children, becauſe [e] your ſins
are forgiven you for his name's ſake 13 I write unto
you, fathers, becauſe ye have known him that is from
the beginning I write unto you, young men, becauſe
ye have overcome the wicked one I write unto you,
little children, becauſe ye have known the Father 14
I have written unto you, fathers, becauſe ye have known
him that is from the beginning I have written unto
u Eph vi 10. x Ver 13 Chap iv 4 — you, young men, becauſe [u] ye are ſtrong, and the word
of God abideth in you, and [x] ye have overcome the
wicked one 15 Love not the world, neither the things
y Mat vi 24 Jam iv 4 — that are in the world [y] If any man love the world, the
love of the Father is not in him. 16 For all that is in
z Rom xiii 14 — the world, [z] the luſt of the fleſh, and [a] the luſt of the
a Eccleſ v 11 — eyes, and the pride of life, is not of the Father, but is
b 1 Cor vii 31 Jam i 10 1 Pet i 24 — of the world 17 And [b] the world paſſeth away, and
the luſt thereof but he that doth the will of God
abideth for ever.

v 12—17 The great duty of love is equally the concern of all ranks and degrees of Chriſtians, whatever their ſeveral attainments may be in the divine life

1 He addreſſes himſelf to Chriſtians in every ſtage of their profeſſion

I write unto you, little children, and as a powerful incentive to the exerciſe of charity, urge this duty upon you, *becauſe your ſins are forgiven you for his name's ſake*, and having much forgiven, you ſhould love much *Note*, The loweſt in the Chriſtian life hath received the free and full pardon of all their ſins, this being the firſt great privilege of the goſpel, of which every babe in Chriſt is immediately a partaker

I write unto you, fathers, becauſe ye have known him that is from the beginning, and by long acquaintance with his grace and love, are peculiarly called and engaged to ſhew the ſame divine charity to others, and none are ſo far advanced, as leſs to need the word of exhortation

I write unto you, young men, becauſe ye have overcome the wicked one, and have been made more than conqueror over ſin, and Satan, and the world, through him that loved you And to impreſs more deeply my exhortation, I repeat my words,

I write unto you, little children, becauſe ye have known the Father, and, young as you are in the Chriſtian life, have taſted of the goodneſs and love of your heavenly Father *I have written unto you, fathers*, grown old in the happy experience of the good ways of Chriſt, *becauſe ye have known him that is from the beginning*, and entered deep into the myſteries of his everlaſting grace, and his tranſcendent excellencies *I have written unto you, young men, becauſe ye are ſtrong* in faith and knowledge, and the exerciſe of every heavenly temper *and the word of God abideth in you*, Chriſt being formed in your hearts, and his goſpel dwelling in you richly, and influencing all your converſation, *and ye have overcome the wicked one*, and hitherto effectually defeated all his efforts againſt your ſouls, and will, I truſt, go on ſtill conquering, and to conquer, and bleſſed are they who are thus ſtrong in the Lord, and in the power of his might

He ſolemnly warns them all, whatever their ſeveral attainments may be, to beware of this preſent evil world *Love not the world*, ſet not your affections thereon, neither inordinately ſeek, nor be immoderately delighted with, *the things that are in the world* *If any man* ſupremely *love the world*, and ſet his heart upon it, as his home and his happineſs, *the love of the Father is not in him*, it is evident that ſuch an one is not the object of his choice and regard, hath never experienced a ſenſe of his love, nor felt any real heart attachment to God in Chriſt, as his portion and exceeding great joy *For all that is in the world*, to engage and ſeduce the heart from God, *the luſt of the fleſh*, whatever miniſters to the lawleſs gratification of appetite, and leads to exceſs, ſloth, intemperance, luxury, drunkenneſs, revellings, and every kind of impurity, *and the luſt of the eyes*, the gain, poſſeſſions, wealth, and glittering riches which the covetous eye gazes upon with ſuch rapture, and eager deſire after them, *and the pride of life*, the pomp and ſplendor of titles, ſhew, equipage, honours, magnificence, which gratify the vanity, and inflame the ambition of the fallen mind, of all and either of theſe we muſt ſay, that it *is not of the Father*, worldly things were not given to be thus abuſed, nor are theſe the objects on which God's children place their affections, *but* we know, that each of theſe things *is of the world*, they are the flattering baits which the god of this world, the devil, ſpreads to enſnare the ſenſual and earthly hearts of fallen men, and to ſeduce them from their true Lord and Maſter *And the world paſſeth away, and the luſt thereof*, great and deſireable as the things of it appear in the eye of ſenſe, they are poor, periſhing, unſatisfactory in the enjoyment, and tranſitory, often in time flying our graſp, and certainly at death muſt fail us *but he that doth the will of God abideth for ever*, hath a more enduring ſubſtance, his fidelity to death ſhall be crowned with immortal life and glory, his pleaſures in eternity ſhall be infinitely ſuperior to all the delights of ſenſe, and his inheritance above incorruptible, undefiled, and which fadeth not away Oh! that thou mayeſt be wiſe, reader, and learn to weigh time and eternity, this world and the next, in the balances of the ſanctuary!

18 Little children, [c] it is the laſt time and as ye — c Heb i 2
have heard that [d] antichriſt ſhall come, [e] even now are — d 2 Theſ ii 3, &c Chap iv 3 2 John 7
there many antichriſts, [f] whereby we know that it is
the laſt time 19 [g] They went out from us, but they — e Mat xxiv 5, 24
were not of us for [h] if they had been of us, they would — f 1 Tim iv 1 2 Tim iii 1
no doubt have continued with us but *they went out*,
that they might [i] be made manifeſt that they were not all — g Deut xiii 13 Acts xx 30
of us 20 But [k] ye have an unction from the Holy — h Mat xxiv 24 John vi 37 & x 28, 29 2 Tim ii 19.
One, and [l] ye know all things 21 I have not written — i 1 Cor xi 19
unto you, becauſe ye know not the truth but becauſe — k 2 Cor i 21 Heb i 9 Ver 27
ye know it, and that no lye is of the truth 22 [m] Who — l John xiv 26 & xvi 13 Ver 27
is a lyar but he that denieth that Jeſus is the Chriſt? he — m Chap iv 3 2 John 7
is antichriſt that denieth the Father and the Son 23 — n John xv 23 2 John 9
[n] Whoſoever denieth the Son, the ſame hath not the Fa- — o John vii 10 & xiv 9 Chap iv 15
ther (*but*) [o] *he that acknowledgeth the Son, hath the Fa-* — p 2 John 6
ther alſo. 24 Let that therefore abide in you [p] which — q John xiv 23 Chap i 3
ye have heard from the beginning If that which ye — r John xvii 3 Chap i 2 & v 11
have heard from the beginning ſhall remain in you, [q] ye — s Chap iii 7 2 John 7
alſo ſhall continue in the Son and in the Father 25 — t Jer xxxi 33 34 Heb viii 10 11
[r] And this is the promiſe that he hath promiſed us, *even* — u John xiv 26 & xvi 13 Ver 20
eternal life 26 Theſe things have I written unto you — † Or, it
[s] concerning them that ſeduce you 27 But the anoint-
ing which ye have received of him abideth in you, and
[t] ye need not that any man teach you but, as the ſame
anointing [u] teacheth you of all things, and is truth, and
is no lye and even as it hath taught you, ye ſhall abide
in † him

v 18—27 As the myſtery of iniquity had begun already to work, the apoſtle,

1 Reminds them, that the Jewiſh diſpenſation was now ready to expire utterly with the deſtruction of their temple, city, and nation *Little children, it is the laſt time and as ye have heard that Antichriſt ſhall come, even now are there many Antichriſts*, either thoſe who among the Jewiſh people ſet up themſelves for the Meſſiah, or rather, who under the Chriſtian profeſſion oppoſed and denied the perſon, offices, and goſpel of Chriſt, broaching their heretical tenets, and perverting many from the truth *They went out from us*, from our communion and ſociety, *but they were not of us*, nor had ever truly been renewed by grace *for if they had been of us*, and partakers of the like precious faith with us, *they would no doubt have continued with us*, and perſevered in the principles and practice of the goſpel *but they went out, that they might be made manifeſt that they were not all of us*, but from the beginning were falſe-hearted profeſſors, who never taſted of the grace of God in truth *Note*, They who fall away finally, we may aſſuredly conclude, never were truly converted, whatever ſpecious profeſſions they might have made

2 He encourages them to truſt, and not be afraid, ſince no ſeducers ſhould ever be able to move them from their ſtedfaſtneſs *But ye have an unction from the Holy One*, from the Spirit of grace and truth, which through the exalted Saviour hath been beſtowed upon you, *and ye know all things* neceſſary to preſerve you from the wiles of deceivers, and to bring you to everlaſting ſalvation *I have not written unto you, becauſe ye know not the truth, but becauſe ye know it*, and are eſtabliſhed in the principles of the goſpel, and the fundamental doctrines of Chriſt, *and know that no lye is of the truth*, but the very reverſe, and prove the hypocriſy and apoſtacy of thoſe who by fraud and error would ſupport their heretical doctrines *Note*, They who are truly taught of God ſhall be preſerved from every fatal deluſion

3 He particularly points out these seducers, by their tenets *Who is a liar*, and to be deemed an impostor, *but he that denieth that Jesus is the Christ*, rejecting him as the true Messiah? *He is antichrist*, and bears the brand of this hateful name, *that denieth the Father and the Son*, either confounding the persons in the Godhead, or dividing the substance, or denying that flood of evidence, wherewith God the Father hath borne witness to the mission and incarnation of his dear Son *Whosoever denieth the Son*, his personality and essential Deity, or the office he bears as Mediator, *the same hath not the Father*, holds not the true doctrine of the persons in the undivided Godhead, and of the relation which God the Father bears to God the Son, and therein denies all that revelation which he hath made of pardon and reconciliation, through the substitution of the incarnate Redeemer *but he that acknowledges the Son, hath the Father also*, he that receives the Lord Jesus by faith as the only Saviour, and confesses him to be the eternal Son of God, he hath the true knowledge of God the Father, and an interest in his favour and love

[The last clause of this text is wanting in many editions, but appears in others, of great authority, and is admitted into our version, though marked with Italics, as a supplement which elucidates the foregoing part of the verse]

4 He exhorts them to cleave to the old truth, for novelty of doctrine is the sure proof of error *Let that therefore abide in you which ye have heard from the beginning*, when the gospel was first preached unto you *If that which ye have heard from the beginning shall remain in you, ye also shall continue in the Son and in the Father*, and holding the profession of your faith unwavering, shall enjoy the most happy communion with the Father through the Son, until you come to his kingdom in glory *And this is the promise that he hath promised us, even eternal life*, which he will infallibly fulfil to those who abide in him, and will bring them to the beatific vision and enjoyment of his blessed self for ever and ever

5 He mentions one great purpose of this epistle *These things have I written unto you concerning them that* labour to *seduce* and pervert *you* from the simplicity which is in Christ *But the anointing which ye have received of him abideth in you*, the Spirit which he hath given you shall continue to teach, direct, and lead you aright, *and ye need not that any man teach you*, cannot want the help of these pretended wise men to instruct you above what is written *but, as the same anointing teacheth you of all things*, and hath opened your eyes to see in the revealed word all things that pertain unto life and godliness, *and is truth, and is no lye*, but directly contrary to the spirit of error which actuates these seducers *and even as it hath taught you, ye shall abide in him*, your living head, and continue under the blessed influence and guidance of his truth and grace unto the end.

x Chap iii 2
y Chap iv 17
z Acts xxii 14
a Chap ii 7 10

28 And now, little children, abide in him, that [x] when
he shall appear we may have confidence, [y] and not be
ashamed before him at his coming 29 [z] If ye know
that he is righteous, ye know that [a] every one that doth
righteousness is born of him.

v 28, 29 From what he had said, the apostle closes with this affectionate exhortation to them

And now, little children, abide in him, maintaining the closest communion with Jesus, and walking in the lively exercise of faith and hope, and love towards him, unmoved from the doctrines of his gospel by the wiles of deceivers, *that when he shall appear* on the throne of judgment at the last day, *we may have confidence* and boldness to appear in his presence, *and not be ashamed before him at his coming*, when we your ministers shall not be disappointed of our hopes, but meet you as our joy and crown, and, together with you, stand forth without fault, and blameless, acknowledged by him as his people, and admitted into the joy of our Lord *If*, or *since*, *ye know that he is righteous*, perfectly righteous himself, the lover and author of all righteousness in his redeemed, *ye know that every one that doth righteousness is born of him*, and thereby gives a demonstration that he is a partaker of a divine nature, and hath the possession of spiritual life, which is the pledge of that which will be eternal *Note*, (1) They only will have boldness in a day of judgment who are found in Christ, and perseveringly cleave to him (2) Everlasting shame and contempt will cover those, who ungratefully, unfaithfully, and perversely have departed from the truth, and shall be disowned of Jesus in the day of his appearing and glory (3) The evidence of a divine nature must be manifested in a good conversation, for whatever conceits men may entertain of themselves, it is by their fruits they must be known

CHAP III

The apostle here magnifies the love of God in our adoption, ver 1, 2 *He thereupon argues for holiness*, ver. 3 *and against sin*, ver 4—10 *He presseth brotherly love*, ver 11—18 *How to assure our hearts before God*, ver 19—22 *The precept of faith*, ver 23 *And the good of obedience*, ver 24.

a John i 12
b John xv 18 & xvi 3 & xvii 25
c Isa lvi 5 Rom viii 15 Gal iii 26 & iv 6
d Rom viii 18 2 Cor iv 17
e 1 Cor xv 49 Phil iii 21 Col iii 4
f John xix 3 1 Cor xiii 12
g 2 Pet i 4

1 BEhold what manner of love the Father hath be-
stowed upon us, that [a] we should be called the
sons of God therefore the world knoweth us not, [b] be-
cause it knew him not 2 Beloved, [c] now are we the
sons of God, and [d] it doth not yet appear what we shall
be but we know that, when he shall appear, [e] we shall
be like him, for [f] we shall see him as he is 3 And
[g] every man that hath this hope in him purifieth himself,
even as he is pure

v 1—3 The apostle here,

1 Breaks forth with admiration in the view of the love of God towards his people *Behold*, with wonder and amaze, *what manner of love the Father hath bestowed upon us* in Jesus Christ, *that we*, by nature and practice so vile, corrupt, and sinful, *should*, notwithstanding, be adopted into his family, and *be called the sons of God*, advanced to that transcendent dignity and honour *therefore the world*, who have their minds wholly engrossed with sensible objects, and have no discernment of spiritual things, *knoweth us not*, far from esteeming and valuing us, they deride and persecute us for that image which we bear, *because it knew him not*, they are ignorant of God, and when this Son appeared incarnate, they nailed him to a tree *Note*, (1) The meanest child of God hath a dignity infinitely greater than the first-born of princes (2) It will be matter of everlasting wonder and praise to the redeemed, that ever God should set his love upon them (3) If we are treated with derision and contempt by this wicked world we should remember the cross which Jesus bore, and be ashamed to murmur

2 He declares the high expectations of God's children *Beloved, now are we the sons of God*, this is our present honour, *and it doth not yet appear what we shall be*, greater blessedness is in store for us than eye hath seen, or ear heard, or it hath entered into the heart of man to conceive *but we know that when he shall appear*, who is our head, even Christ, *we shall be with him*, admitted to his presence, and partakers of all his glory, *for we shall see him as he is*, and our bodies as well as souls shall be fashioned after his bright image *Note*, The day of judgment will be a day of triumph to every redeemed soul; then at last they shall be perfected in holiness and happiness for ever

3 Such a hope cannot but have the most powerful influence upon our conduct *And every man that hath this hope in him purifieth himself, even as he is pure*, setting Christ's glorious pattern before him, and earnestly desirous to obtain a holy conformity to him in all things *Note*, The hope that doth not lead us to holiness, is but the hope of the hypocrite, which perisheth

h Rom iv 15 Chap v 17
i Chap i 2
k Isa liii 6, &c 1 Tim i 15 Heb ix 26
l 2 Cor v 21 Heb iv 15 1 Pet ii 22
m Chap ii 4 & iv 8
n 2 John 7 Chap ii 26
o Rom ii 13 Chap ii 29
p Matt xiii 38 John viii 44
q Ver 5
r Chap v 18
s 1 Pet i 23
t Chap iv 8

4 Whosoever committeth sin, transgresseth also the
law for [h] sin is the transgression of the law 5 And ye
know that [i] he was manifested [k] to take away our sins,
and [l] in him is no sin 6 Whosoever abideth in him
sinneth not [m] whosoever sinneth hath not seen him,
neither known him 7 Little children, [n] let no man
deceive you [o] He that doth righteousness is righteous,
even as he is righteous 8 [p] He that committeth sin is
of the devil, for the devil sinneth from the beginning
For this purpose [q] the Son of God was manifested, that
he might destroy the works of the devil 9 [r] Whoso-
ever is born of God, doth not commit sin, for [s] his seed
remaineth in him and he cannot sin, because he is born
of God 10 In this the children of God are manifest,
and the children of the devil Whosoever doth not
righteousness is not of God, [t] neither he that loveth not
his brother

v 4—10 Nothing can more strongly urge the believer to strive against sin, than the arguments which the apostle here urges upon him

1 Sin is the breach of God's holy law *Whosoever committeth sin, transgresseth also the law for sin is the transgression of the law* Every deviation from that perfect rule brings guilt upon the conscience, and so far clouds our hope, and where sin is the allowed practice, there all hope toward God must be delusion

2 The very end of Christ's redemption was to cleanse us from all iniquity *And ye know that he was manifested* in the flesh on purpose *to take away our sins*, both the guilt of them from the conscience, and to break the power of them in our hearts, *and in him is no sin* All therefore, who belong to him, must shew that the design of his incarnation is answered respecting them in their deliverance from the bondage of corruption, and in their growing conformity to his blessed image

3 An allowed and habitual course of sin is utterly contradictory to real union with Christ *Whosoever abideth in him*, as the branch in the vine, deriving constant supplies of grace out of his fulness, *sinneth not* with freedom, choice, delight, and perseverance, but hates sin as the greatest evil, and desires to keep at the [illegible] distance from it *whosoever sinneth*, determinedly, with [illegible], and full purpose to abide in the practice of it, *hath*

not seen him, neither known him, but is an utter stranger to Christ, and his great salvation

4 It is the most fatal deceit to imagine, that without the practice of righteousness we can be ever like him or with him *Little children, let no man deceive you* with any vain suggestions *he that doth righteousness,* in the constant and habitual course of his temper and conduct, and conscientiously towards God and man desires to be found without offence, *he is righteous, even as he is righteous,* and thus resembles in a measure the Holy One of God

5 The allowed and avowed practice of sin is a virtual compact with the devil, and renunciation of Jesus Christ *He that committeth sin,* as his trade, delight, and choice, *is of the devil,* bears his image, and is under his influence, *for the devil sinneth from the beginning,* was the author of evil, and continues to spread the dreadful poison, having tempted angels from their allegiance, and seduced man in paradise, with unrelenting malice he persists in labouring for men's eternal ruin *For this purpose the Son of God was manifested that he might destroy the works of the devil,* and rescue his people from Satan's hateful power, breaking his yoke from off their neck now, and by and by destroying the very being of sin in them, all who are his chosen, therefore, experience his power, and are delivered from the bonds of the wicked one

6 Every regenerate soul cannot but renounce his connection with iniquity *Whosoever is born of God, doth not commit sin,* 'tis contrary to that divine nature which he hath received, and he can never sin in the same manner that he did before, *for his seed remaineth in him,* he has that principle of grace implanted in his heart, that makes sin odious and hateful to him *and he cannot sin,* not that he is literally impeccable, but that the new nature he hath received is utterly averse to it, opposes the carnal mind, and never suffers him to rest under the power of evil, *because he is born of God*

7 *In this the children of God are manifest, and the children of the devil,* their works always evidence what spirit is in them *whosoever doth not righteousness is not of God,* hath no part nor lot in his kingdom, *neither he that loveth not his brother,* these two things, neglect of godliness, and an uncharitable spirit, are the sure brands of Satan's slaves

11 For this is the message that ye heard from the
beginning, that we should love one another 12 Not
as Cain, *who* was of that wicked one, and slew his bro-
ther And wherefore slew he him? Because his own
works were evil, and his brother's righteous 13 Mar-
vel not, my brethren, if the world hate you 14 We
know that we have passed from death unto life, because
we love the brethren He that loveth not *his* brother
abideth in death 15 Whosoever hateth his brother
is a murderer and ye know that no murderer hath
eternal life abiding in him 16 Hereby perceive we the
love of God, because he laid down his life for us and
we ought to lay down our lives for the brethren 17
But whoso hath this world's good, and seeth his
brother have need, and shutteth up his bowels *of compassion*
from him, how dwelleth the love of God in him? 18
My little children, let us not love in word, neither in
tongue, but in deed and in truth 19 And hereby we
know that we are of the truth, and shall assure our
hearts before him 20 For if our heart condemn us,
God is greater than our heart, and knoweth all things
21 Beloved, if our heart condemn us not, *then* have we
confidence towards God 22 And whatsoever we ask,
we receive of him, because we keep his commandments,
and do those things that are pleasing in his sight

v 11—22 The apostle having mentioned the want of brotherly love as the sure evidence of exclusion from God's favour, enforces the practice of that most excellent of graces, charity *For,*

1 *This is the message that ye heard from the beginning,* and one of the chief precepts of the Redeemer, *that we should love one another*

2 He mentions the dire example of the wicked Cain, to shew the hatefulness of such a spirit as he possessed *Not as Cain, who was of that wicked one,* a child of the devil, *and slew his brother And wherefore slew he him? Because his own works were evil, and his brother's righteous,* and he could not bear the rebukes of his pious example, and the approbation which God testified of Abel's sacrifice, when his own was rejected And if this w[illegible] the cause to Cain, and the enmity between the seed of the woman and the seed of the serpent appeared then so malignant, *marvel not, my brethren, that the world hate you;* the same diabolical nature will produce exactly similar effects *Note,* (1) Anger, envy, and hatred in the heart, is murder begun (2) We need not wonder at the world's enmity; such is the lot of all the saint

3 Brotherly love is the sure proof of our spiritual life *We know that we have passed from death unto life, because we love the brethren,* to love them as children of God, and for the sake of him whose image they bear, evidences the life of God in our own souls

4 The contrary is as sure a sign of the remaining power of spiritual death over the soul *He that loveth not his brother abideth in death,* in a state of nature, and of wrath under the curse of the law For *whosoever hateth his brother, is,* in the eye of the law, *a murderer and ye know that no murderer,* who continues under the power of his malignant spirit, *hath eternal life abiding in him,* nor the least prospect of attaining it, eternal death is the wages of his sin

5 The love of Jesus to us should engage our love to our brethren *Hereby perceive we the love of God* the Son towards us, *because he laid down his life for us* on the accursed tree, an instance of love so stupendous, as passes all understanding *and we,* animated by such an example, *ought,* if duty so requires, *to lay down our lives for the brethren,* and if our lives must be thus offered for their service, how much more our substance, when their necessities call for our relief? *But whoso hath this world's good, and seeth his brother have need, and shutteth up his bowels of compassion from him, how dwelleth the love of God in him?* Such a conduct must necessarily shew the absence of that divine principle, and prove the hypocrisy of every pretension to the high relation of children of God *My little children, let us not love in word, nor in tongue,* merely, but give the more substantial evidences of our charity *in deed and in truth,* acting according to our professions, with an open hand and open heart towards every Christian brother, for his sake whose love we in common share

6 *And hereby we know that we are of the truth,* such a conversation demonstrates the reality of our interest in the redemption which is in Jesus Christ, *and shall assure our hearts before him,* bearing witness to our simplicity and godly sincerity, and giving us rejoicing in the testimony of our conscience *For if our heart condemn us* of allowed hypocrisy, and we cannot stand before our own tribunal within, *God is greater than our heart, and knoweth all things,* and must therefore much more condemn us, as his piercing eyes can discover hidden iniquities which we pass by unregarded *Beloved, if our hearts condemn us not,* not the stupified hearts, and seared consciences of the unregenerate, but the enlightened minds of the faithful, where, tho' many infirmities may be seen and lamented, allowed guile is not harboured, this consciousness of our simplicity gives an humble boldness to the soul, and *then have we confidence towards God,* a holy freedom and liberty of soul in our approaches to a throne of grace *And whatsoever we ask, we receive of him, because we keep his commandments, and do those things that are pleasing in his sight,* asking always according to his will, and aiming at his glory in all our conversation

23 And this is his commandment, that we should
believe on the name of his Son Jesus Christ, and love
one another, as he gave us commandment 24 And
he that keepeth his commandments dwelleth in him,
and he in him and hereby we know that he abideth in
us, by the Spirit which he hath given us.

v 23, 24 We have here,

1 The great commandments of the gospel *And this is his commandment,* (1) *That we should believe on the name of his Son Jesus Christ,* as the only and all-sufficient Saviour of lost sinners, renouncing every other hope and dependence, and with satisfaction resting our souls on him for pardon and acceptance with God, *and,* (2) That we should, in consequence of faith in him, *love one another, as he gave us commandment,* exercising the most enlarged, unfeigned, and cordial affection towards all the members of his body mystical in particular, and shewing a general benevolence to mankind

2 Great will be the blessedness resulting from hence *And he that keepeth his commandments,* from this principle of faith which worketh by love, *dwelleth in him, and he in him,* abiding in a state of vital union with the exalted Jesus *and hereby we know that he abideth in us, by the Spirit which he hath given us,* whose mighty energy effectually influences our hearts and conduct, and who bears witness to his own work to our increasing comfort and joy

CHAP IV

In this chapter the apostle exhorts to try spirits, ver 1 Gives a rule to try by, ver 2, 3 Shews who are of the world, and who of God, ver 4—6 Urges Christian love by divers considerations, ver 7—16 Describes our love to God, and the effect of it, ver 17—21

1 BEloved, believe not every spirit, but try the
spirits whether they are of God because many
false prophets are gone out into the world 2 Hereby
know ye the Spirit of God every spirit that confesseth
that Jesus Christ is come in the flesh, is of God 3 And
every spirit that confesseth not that Jesus Christ is come

in

in the flesh, is not of God and this is that *spirit* of anti-
f 2 Thes ii — christ [f] whereof you have heard that it should come, and
g Chap ii 18 — [g] even now already is it in the world

v 1—3 The apostle,

1 Warns them against seducing teachers *Beloved, believe not every spirit*, nor credit rashly each pretender to inspiration, *but try the spirits*, by the infallible oracles of truth, *whether they are of God*, and speak agreeable to his revealed will *because many false prophets are gone out into the world*, and we need be on our guard, proving all things, and holding fast that which is good

2 He gives them a certain rule to direct their judgment in this matter *Hereby know ye the Spirit of God*, and those who are influenced by it *every Spirit that confesseth that Jesus Christ is come in the flesh*, or that *confesseth Jesus Christ who is come in the flesh*, receiving him in his divine person and mediatorial character and offices, as the true Messiah, from whom alone life and salvation are to be expected, he *is of God*, and speaks according to his mind and will *And every spirit that confesseth not that Jesus Christ is come in the flesh*, but denies his divine glory, his real incarnation, and mediatorial undertaking, *is not of God*, but is under the spirit of satan and delusion *and this is that spirit of antichrist*, that is enmity against Christ and his gospel, *whereof you have heard that it should come, and even now already is it in the world*, the mystery of iniquity having already begun to work, and woe to those over whom it prevails!

4 Ye are of God, little children, and have overcome
r John xii 31 1 Cor ii 12 Eph ii 2 & vi 12 — them because greater is he that is in you than [r] he that is
in the world. 5 [h] They are of the world · therefore speak
h John iii 31 — they of the world, and [i] the world heareth them 6 We
i John xv 19 & xvii 14 — are of God [k] he that knoweth God, heareth us, he that
k John viii 47 x 27 1 Cor iv 37 2 Cor x 7 1 Is. viii 20 John xiv 17 — is not of God, heareth not us. Hereby know we [l] the Spi-
rit of truth, and the spirit of error

v 4—6 To encourage them against the fears of being drawn aside by seducers, the apostle,

1 Assures them, that as they belonged to God, they were safe *Ye are of God, little children, and have overcome them* hitherto, and shall be still superior to all their arts *because greater is he that is in you than he that is in the world*, and he will preserve you from the power of evil

2 He describes those seducers *They are of the world* whatever pretences they make, they are wholly engrossed and influenced by the riches, honours, and pleasures of this life *therefore speak they of the world*, expect a temporal Messiah, and seek a worldly kingdom, *and the world heareth them*, greedily drinking in a doctrine so suited to their carnal hearts

3 He shews the different character of God's true ministers and people *We are of God*, appointed by him, and owned of him, having his glory singly in view, and walking under the guidance and influence of his word and Spirit *he that knoweth God, heareth us*, and receives our testimony as divine, *he that is not of God*, not enlightened by him, nor born of him, *heareth not us*, disregarding the doctrine, and counting it foolishness *Hereby know we the Spirit of truth and the spirit of error* *Note*, They who reject the warnings of God's ministers, speaking according to his holy word, evidently shew themselves to be under the Spirit of error

m Chap. iii 11 — 7 [m] Beloved, let us love one another for love is of
n Chap iii 11 Ver 16 — God, and [n] every one that loveth, is born of God, and
knoweth God 8 He that loveth not, knoweth not
God for [o] God is love 9 [p] In this was manifested
p John iii 16 Rom v 8 Chap iii 16 — the love of God towards us, because that God sent his
q Chap v 11 — only begotten Son into the world, [q] that we might live
r John xv 16 Rom v 8, 10 — through him 10 Herein is love, [r] not that we loved
God, but that he loved us, and sent his Son [s] *to be* the
s Rom iii 25 Chap ii 2 — propitiation for our sins 11 Beloved, [t] if God so loved
t Mat xviii 33 John xv 12, 13 Chap iii 16 — us, we ought also to love one another 12 [u] No man
u Ex xxxiii 20 John i 18 1 Tim vi 16 — hath seen God at any time If we love one another, God
x Chap ii 5 Ver 18 — dwelleth in us, and [x] his love is perfected in us. 13
y Chap iii 24 — [y] Hereby know we that [z] we dwell in him, and he in us,
z John xiv 20 & xvii 21 — because he hath given us of his Spirit

v 7—13 The apostle returns to recommend the exercise of fervent charity, as the genuine evidence of a right spirit *Beloved, let us love one another for love is of God*, his genuine offspring, and his brightest image, *and every one that loveth, is born of God, and knoweth God*, he evidences hereby his experimental acquaintance with God, and shews himself a child of his family of love *He that loveth not, knoweth not God*, whatever he may pretend, *for God is love*, and the true knowledge of him hath ever a transforming efficacy, to change us into his blessed image *In this was manifested the love of God towards us*, and shone forth with the most distinguished lustre, *because that God sent his only begotten Son into the world*, to become incarnate, to live and die for us, *that we might live through him*, redeemed from the sentence of death, quickened to newness of life, and through his divine righteousness intitled to immortal bliss and glory *Herein is love*, surpassing strange! *not that we loved God!* no, just the reverse, we were sinners, ungodly, enemies, *but* even when we had every thing which could render us the objects of his loathing, even then, *that* he might magnify the wonders of his grace, *he loved us, and* gave the most astonishing demonstration of it, when he *sent his Son to be the propitiation for our sins*, with his own blood making atonement for us, and purging us from our iniquities by this amazing sacrifice *Beloved, if God so loved us, we ought also to love one another*, who can possibly offend us so highly as we have offended God? yet he forgives and pardons abundantly, yea, he spared not his own Son, but freely gave him up for us all what then can we with-hold from our brethren, when we have such an example before us? Surely, if we belong to him, we shall be like him, and prove it by this Spirit of love *No man indeed hath seen God at any time*, for he is a Spirit invisible and incorporeal But *if we love one another, God dwelleth in us*, by his Spirit manifesting his presence in our hearts, *and his love is perfected in us*, our love to him is proved to be sincere and genuine, and will grow up unto absolute perfection in glory *Hereby know we that we dwell in him, and he in us, because he hath given us of his Spirit*, whereby we become one with him, united to him in faith and love, and experiencing the most gracious manifestations of his presence with our soul Thou God of life and love, give me more abundantly of this blessed Spirit!

14 And [a] we have seen and do testify, that the Father
a Chap i 2 — sent the Son [b] *to be* the Saviour of the world 15 [c] Who-
b Mat i 21 c Chap v 1 — soever shall confess that Jesus is the Son of God, [d] God
d Chap iii 24 Ver 13 — dwelleth in him, and he in God 16 And we have
e Ver 8 — known and believed the love that God hath to us [e] God
is love, and he that dwelleth in love, dwelleth in God,
and God in him

v 14—16 We have here,

1 The apostolick testimony *And we have seen and do testify, that the Father sent the Son*, in his infinite grace and love, *to be the Saviour of the world*, of both Jews and Gentiles, even of all that believe in him, without exception

2 The true evangelical confession *Whosoever shall confess that Jesus is the Son of God*, owning him as the divine and true Messiah, and making open profession of his faith, in the face of every danger, *God dwelleth in him, and he in God*, being happily joined to him in one Spirit for eternity

3 The experience of all true Christians *And we have known and believed the love that God hath to us*, the astonishing manifestation of which, in sending his Son, leaves us no room to doubt of his transcendent and distinguishing grace towards us *God is love*, pure, perfect love, *and he that dwelleth in love, dwelleth in God, and God in him*, there subsists a holy union between them, and it will be everlasting

f Gr love is made perfect with us — 17 Herein [f] is our love made perfect, [f] that we may
f Chap ii 28 — have boldness in the day of judgment because [g] as he is,
g 2 Tim ii 12 or 1 Pet. i 15 — so are we in this world 18 There is no fear in love;
h Ver 7 — but perfect love casteth out fear because fear hath tor-
ment he that feareth [h] is not made perfect in love 19
i Chap ii 3. & iii 17 — We love him, because he first loved us 20 [i] If a man
say, I love God, and hateth his brother, he is a liar for
he that loveth not his brother whom he hath seen, how
can he love God whom he hath not seen? 21 And this
k Lev xix 18 Mat xxii 39 John xiii 34. & xv 12 Chap iii 34 — commandment have we from him, that he who loveth
God [k] love his brother also

v 17—21 The apostle proceeds to set forth the blessed effects of Christian love *Herein is our love made perfect*, proved to be genuine and sincere, by our union of heart to God, and charity to the brethren, and where this is the case, then, it being evident *that* we are born of God,

1 *We may have boldness in the day of judgment*, and confidently appear before the throne of Jesus, assured of acceptance in that great day *because, as he is, so are we in this world*, and he cannot but receive into the bosom of his love those who bear his own bright image

2 We are delivered from all slavish fear *There is no fear in love*, nothing distressing, terrifying, and servile, *but perfect love casteth out fear*, a real consciousness of love to God, and of an interest in his favour, silences all fearful apprehensions of death or judgment *because fear hath torment*, and where it prevails, must make the soul miserable and unhappy *he that feareth*, and trembles before God as his enemy, *is not made perfect in love*, nor hath yet seen him in the delightful character of a reconciled God and Father *We love him, because he first loved us*, his love, shed abroad in the heart, must kindle ours, and the view of those amazing manifestations of it which he hath made, should every day add fuel to the sacred fire, and raise the flame of holy affections still higher and higher, till at last we are wholly assimilated to his image, and made absolutely perfect in love

3 Love to God necessarily includes love to the brethren *If a man say, I love God, and hateth his brother, he is a lyar;* his uncharitableness proves the hypocrisy of his pretensions *for he that loveth not his brother whom he hath seen,* with his bodily eyes, and beheld his distresses, which should excite compassion, or the divine image in him, which should engage his regards, *how can he love God, whom he hath not seen?* how absurd is the supposition! *And this commandment have we from him, that he who loveth God, love his brother also,* and prove thereby the unfeigned sincerity of his professions

CHAP V

In this chapter the apostle asserts, 1 The dignity of believers, ver 1 Then, 2 Their obligations to love, and the trial of it, ver 1—3 Then 3 Their victory, ver 4, 5 Then, 4 The credibility and confirmation of their faith, ver 6—10 Then, 5 The advantage of their faith in eternal life, ver 11—13 Then, 6 The audience of their prayers, unless for those that have sinned unto death, ver 14—17 Then 7 Their preservation from sin and Satan, ver 18 Then, 8 Their happy distinction from the world, ver 19 Then, 9 Their true knowledge of God, ver 20 Lastly, from which they must depart from idols, ver 21

a John i 12 Chap ii 23 & iv 2 15 1 a Whosoever believeth that Jesus is the Christ,
is born of God and every one that loveth
him that begat, loveth him also that is begotten of him
2 By this we know that we love the children of God,
when we love God and keep his commandments 3
b John xiv 15, 21 23, & xv 10 2 John 6 For b this is the love of God, that we keep his com-
c Mat xi 30 mandments, and his commandments are not grievous,
d Chap iv 4 For d whatsoever is born of God overcometh the
e 1 Cor xv 57 Chap iv 15 world and this is the victory that overcometh the
world, *even* our faith 5 Who is he that overcometh
the world, but e he that believeth that Jesus is the Son
of God?

v 1—5 The apostle shews,

1 The genuine marks of a child of God *Whosoever believeth that Jesus is the Christ,* the true Messiah, placing his whole dependance for pardon, life, and salvation upon him, *is born of God,* adopted into his blessed family, and dignified with all the honours of a son and heir of the Almighty *and every one that loveth him that begat,* the blessed God, the Author of all grace to his people, *loveth him also that is begotten of him,* and delights in his image wherever it appears

2 *By this we know that we love the children of God,* as his children, and purely for his sake, *when we love God* unfeignedly, *and keep his commandments,* from a principle of faith which worketh by love *For this is the love of God,* the most undoubted evidence of it, *that we keep his commandments,* counting them all holy, just, and good, and having respect unto them without partiality or hypocrisy, *and his commandments are not grievous,* love makes the labour light, and the obedience cheerful and willing

3 This is what will gain the conquest over an ensnaring world *For whatsoever is born of God,* and partakes of a new and a divine nature, *overcometh the world,* and triumphs over both its terrors and allurements *and this is the victory that overcometh the world, even our faith,* which realizing unseen and eternal things, [illegible] upon all present objects, and deriving strength from the Redeemer's fulness, enables us to be more than conquerors over all our trials *Who is he that overcometh the world?* none ever did or can *but he that believeth that Jesus is the Son of God* and depending upon him for life and salvation, [illegible] Lord, give and increase this victorious faith!

6 This is he that came by water and blood, *even*
Jesus Christ, not by water only, but by water and
f John xix 34 blood and f it is the Spirit that beareth witness, be-
g John xvi 13 cause g the Spirit is truth 7 For there are three that
h Mat iii 16 17 & xvii 5 bear record in heaven, h the Father, the Word, and the
i John x 30 Holy Ghost, and i these three are one 8 And there
are three that bear witness in earth, the Spirit, and the
water, and the blood and these three agree in one 9
k John viii 17, 18 If we receive k the witness of men, the witness of God is
greater for this is the witness of God, which he hath
testified of his Son

v 6—9 [illegible] Messiah being [illegible] consequence [illegible] which [illegible] the [illegible]

[illegible] at his baptism [illegible] upon the cross [illegible] moment, and the blood and water which flowed from his wounded side declared the purposes of his coming, both to pay a ransom for our sins, and to cleanse us from the defilement of them, by the renewal of our nature through the mighty energy of his Spirit, for which glorious purposes faith looks to Jesus Christ, as appointed of the Father to his mediatorial office, and able and willing in both these respects to perfect the salvation of his people

2 Christ hath the strongest attestation born to his divine person and character *It is the Spirit that beareth witness,* in the miraculous powers bestowed upon the ministers of the gospel, and to the consciences of believers, *because the Spirit is truth* itself, and his testimony cannot deceive *For there are three that bear record in heaven, the Father, the Word, and the Holy Ghost, the Father,* at his baptism and transfiguration, bore witness to him, *the Son* repeatedly asserted his own divine glory and office, and appealed to the miracles he wrought, for a proof of the truth of what he advanced *the Holy Ghost,* by his descent on Jesus at his baptism, and the miraculous powers with which he invested the apostles and others, added his full attestation to the great Redeemer *and these three,* though personally distinct, *are,* in essence, *one* *And there are three that bear witness in earth, the Spirit,* in his gifts and graces, *the water,* wherewith every believer is baptized in the name of the Son of God, as a divine person, *and the blood,* which Jesus shed upon the cross, and instituted in his last supper a constant memorial of it to be observed in his church, *and these three agree in one,* and bear testimony to the divine character and complete redemption of our adored Immanuel *If we receive the witness of men,* attesting any fact, and every court of human judicature admits their oath and evidence as satisfactory, *the witness of God is greater,* which both Father, Son, and Spirit, severally bears to the dignity and glory of the Lord Jesus, and with whom the appointed witnesses on earth agree *for this is the witness of God, which he hath testified of his Son,* as the true and divine Messiah, whom we by faith and love must embrace, and in whom alone salvation can be attained

10 He that believeth on the Son of God l hath the l Rom viii 16 Gal iv 6
witness in himself: he that believeth not God, m hath
made him a lyar, because he believed not the record that m John iii 33 & v 38
God gave of his Son 11 And this is the record, that
God hath given to us eternal life, and n this life is in n John i 4 Chap iv 9
his Son 12 o He that hath the Son hath life *and* o John iii 36 & v 24
he that hath not the Son of God hath not life 13
p These things have I written unto you, that believe p John xx 31
on the name of the Son of God, that ye may know
that ye have eternal life, and that ye may believe on
the name of the Son of God

v 10—13 We have here,

1 The happy state of the true believer *He that believeth on the Son of God hath the witness in himself,* he feels the suitableness of the Saviour to his state of guilt and misery, and knows by happy experience his excellence, fulness, and all sufficiency *He that believeth not God,* and receiveth not his testimony concerning his only-begotten Son, *hath made him a lyar,* and denied his truth, *because he believeth not the record that God gave of his Son,* and submits not to the witness which he hath born to the character of Jesus as the true Messiah

2 The perpetuity of his felicity *And this is the record, that God hath given to us eternal life,* the earnest, foretaste, and beginning of it, and the sure title to it through the Redeemer's righteousness, *and this life is in his Son,* secured by him, treasured up in him, and communicated from him to his people *He that hath the Son,* is by faith united to him, and interested in his redemption, *hath life,* hath spiritual life here, and possesses the title to eternal life hereafter, *and he that hath not the Son of God,* who hath not by faith embraced him, and departs from him, *hath not life,* [illegible] and the wrath of God abideth on him

3 The knowledge he hath of his invaluable privileges *These things have I written unto you that believe on the name of the Son of God, that ye may know that ye have eternal life,* and rejoice in this distinguished gift of God, *and that ye may believe on the name of the Son of God,* engaged more steadfastly to cleave to him, and with unshaken perseverance maintain your holy profession *Note,* (1) [illegible] life [illegible] in Christ Jesus, is to be known, the Lord [illegible] knowledge [illegible] [illegible] who have [illegible] well [illegible] be encouraged to persevere, assured that their labour shall not be in vain [illegible]

14 And this is the confidence that we have in him, q John xiv 13 & xv 7
that if we ask any thing according to his will, he heareth Chap iii 22
us 15 And if we know that he heareth us, whatso- r 1 Ki xiii 6 Jam v 14 15
ever we ask, we know that we have the petitions that s Mat xii 31 32
we desired of him 16 If any man see his brother sin a Heb vi 4 & x 26
sin *which is* not unto death, he shall ask, and he shall t Jer vii 16
give him life for them that sin not unto death There
is a sin unto death t I do not say that he shall pray John xvii 9
for

for it 17 [u] All unrighteousness is sin and there is a
sin not unto death

v. 14—17 The apostle adds, to all the other blessings flowing from faith in Christ,

1 Access to God in prayer, and the sure answer to all our petitions *And this is the confidence that we have in him*, and boldness to approach a throne of grace, *that if we ask any thing according to his will, he heareth us*, accepts our prayers, and will grant our requests *And if we know that he heareth us, whatsoever we ask, we know that we have the petitions that we desired of him*, in manner, time, and measure bestowed, as he sees most for his own glory and our good *Note*, (1) If we would obtain an answer to our prayers, God's revealed will must be the rule of them (2) When we pray in faith, we may confidently rest ourselves upon God's promise he will hear and help us

2 Our prayers for others, as well as for ourselves, shall meet with kind acceptance *If any man see his brother sin a sin which is not unto death*, though it deserves death as its wages, yet is not in its nature unpardonable, *he shall ask* God to pardon his offending brother, *and he will*, in answer to his prayer, *give him life for them that sin not unto death*, and renew them again unto repentance *There is a sin unto death*, which never can be forgiven, either in this life, or in that which is to come, *I do not say, that he shall pray for it* blasphemy against the Holy Ghost, and wilful apostacy, seem to be beyond the reach of prayer *All unrighteousness indeed is sin*, and if God were to execute his righteous law on the offender, he must perish But every sin is not unpardonable *there is a sin not unto death*, for which prayer can be available, and pardon and restoration may be obtained What an encouragement is this to fervent and continual intercession on the behalf of others!

18 We know that [x] whosoever is born of God sinneth
not, but he that is begotten of God [y] keepeth himself,
and that wicked one toucheth him not 19 *And* we
know that we are of God, and [z] the whole world lieth
in [†] wickedness 20 And we know that the Son of
God is come, and [b] hath given us an understanding
[c] that we may know him that is true and we are in
him [e] that is true, *even* in his Son Jesus Christ [d] This is
the true God, [e] and eternal life 21 Little children,
[f] keep yourselves from idols Amen.

[u] Chap. iii. 4
[x] Chap. iii. 9
[y] Jam. i. 27
[z] Eph. ii. 2
† Or, the wicked one
[a] Luke xxiv. 45
[b] John xvii. 3
[c] Rev. iii. 14
[d] Isa. ix. 6 & xliv. 6
John xx. 28
Rom. ix. 5
1 Tim. iii. 16 Tit. ii. 13
[e] Ver. 11, 12
[f] 1 Cor. x. 7, 14

v. 18—21 The apostle concludes,

1 With a recapitulation of the believer's privileges and practice *We know that whosoever is born of God sinneth not*, that unpardonable sin, nor continues allowedly in any course of iniquity, *but he that is begotten of God*, and thus partaker of a new and divine nature, *keepeth himself, and that wicked one toucheth him not*, the power of Satan is broken, and he never can again bring the redeemed soul into the like connection with himself, that it should perish by apostacy *Note*, A truly regenerate soul can never die eternally

2 He mentions their happy separation from the world *And we know that we are of God*, his children, renewed in the spirit of our minds, and separated for him to be a peculiar people from the corrupted mass of mankind *and the whole world*, beside those who are born of God, *lieth in wickedness*, (ἐν τῷ πονηρῷ) in the wicked one, under his power, influence, and dominion, and must be condemned together with him *Note*, It is most indubitably certain, that the far greater part of the world, even the Christian world, lieth in wickedness, and is certain, that they will perish everlastingly It becomes us therefore seriously to enquire, whether we are of the world, for then must we be condemned with the world When but few shall be saved, it should awaken our solicitude to be of that few

3 They knew the Son of God, and enjoyed a blessed union with him *And we know that the Son of God is come*, in the human nature, to take away our sins by the sacrifice of himself *and hath given us an understanding, that we may know him that is true*, by his Spirit opening the eyes of our mind, and shining into our hearts, to give us the light of the knowledge of his glory *and we are in him that is true*, vitally united to him who is the truth itself, *even in his Son Jesus Christ*, as living members of his mystical body And *this* Jesus *is the true God*, the self-existent Jehovah, *and eternal life*, the purchaser, fountain, and bestower of it on all his people, and they who know him now by faith, will live eternally with him in glory *Note*, (1) Either Jesus Christ is the true God, or the scriptures are a fiction (2) They who know him as their Saviour, by real union of heart with him, can never perish, but shall have everlasting life

4 He closes with a solemn admonition *Little children*, dear to me as the offspring of eternal love, *keep yourselves from idols* abhorring and avoiding the hated idolatry of paganism, and the use of images as mediums of worship, and let the triune God be the only object of your adoration *Amen!*

THE

EVANGELICAL EXPOSITOR;

OR, A

PRACTICAL COMMENT

UPON THE

SECOND EPISTLE of JOHN.

SINCE in Christ Jesus there is neither male nor female, but all, without distinction of sex, are admitted to the privileges of the gospel, we need not wonder to have an inspired epistle directed to an honourable matron and her children The stile marks the penman, and the similitude of expression shews him to be the same who wrote the foregoing Epistle, and probably about the same time, accordingly it hath been generally received in the church as canonical

The apostle here salutes an honourable matron and her children, ver 1—3 *Recommends to them faith and love,* ver 5, 6 *Warns them of deceivers,* ver 7 *and to take heed to themselves,* ver 8 *Teaches how to treat those that bring not the doctrine of Christ,* ver 10, 11 *And referring other things to personal discourse, concludes the epistle,* ver 12, 13

1 THE elder unto the elect lady, and her
children, [a] whom I love [b] in the truth
and not I only, but also all they that have
known the truth 2 For the truth's
sake [c] which dwelleth in us, and shall be with us for
ever 3 [d] Grace be with you, mercy *and* peace from
God the Father, and from the Lord Jesus Christ, the
Son of the Father, in truth and love 4 [e] I rejoiced
greatly, that I found of thy children walking in truth,
as we have received a commandment from the Father
5 And now I beseech thee, lady, [f] not as though I
wrote a new commandment unto thee, but that which
we had from the beginning, [f] that we love one another.
6 And [g] this is love, that we walk after his commandments
This is the commandment, that [h] as ye have
heard from the beginning, ye should walk in it

a 1 John iii 18 3 John 1
b Or truly
c 1 John ii 24
d 1 Tim i 2 2 Tim i 2
e 3 John 3
e 1 John ii 7 & iii 11
f John xiii 34 & xv 12 Eph v 2 1 Pet iv 8 1 John iii 23 & iv 21
g John xiv 15 21 & xv 10 1 John ii 5 & v 3
h 1 John ii 24

v 1—6 The epistle opens,

1 With the inscription *The elder*, John, now far advanced in age, and by office an elder, as well as an apostle, *unto the elect lady*, chosen, among the not many noble, to be a partaker of the gospel salvation, *and to her children*, heirs with her of the same promises, *whom I love in the truth*, unfeignedly, and for the sake of him whose image they bear *and not I only, but also all they that have known the truth*, who cannot but respect and delight in those who adorn so eminently the doctrine of God our Saviour in all things, *for the truth's sake which dwelleth in us*, which renders the possessor more respectable than all riches, birth, or titles, *and shall be with us for ever*, for this truth is an incorruptible seed, and, when planted in the heart, springs up unto eternal life

2 We have the apostolic benediction *Grace be with you*, in all its happy fruits and effects, of pardon, strength, and consolation, with *mercy and peace*, and every blessing that we can ask, or the Lord hath promised to give, *from God the Father, and from the Lord Jesus Christ*, to whom we are indebted for all, and who is *the Son of the Father, in truth and love*, one with him in essence and glory, the divine Son of the divine Father, and the object of his eternal love

3 His congratulation *I rejoiced greatly, that I found of thy children walking in truth*, as it is in Jesus, and in their spirit and conduct a credit to the holy profession which they make, guided by the oracles of God, *as we have received a commandment from the Father* *Note*, (1) It is a singular joy to ministers, to behold the rising generation ornaments to religion (2) We then walk in the truth, when we make God's word our constant rule of conduct

4 His request and exhortation *And now I beseech thee, lady*, as the chief design of my epistle, *not as though I wrote a new commandment unto thee, but that which we had from the beginning, that we love one another*, out of a pure heart fervently, from the divine principle of faith which worketh by love *And this is love*, the infallible test of true love to God and man, *that we walk after his commandments*, with an universal and conscientious respect to all his holy will *This is the commandment, that, as ye have heard from the beginning, ye should walk in it*, under the influence of this great law of love *Note*, Kind exhortations are preferable to authoritative commands, and usually much more available

7 For [i] many deceivers are entred into the world,
[k] who confess not that Jesus Christ is come in the flesh
[l] This is a deceiver and an antichrist 8 [m] Look to
yourselves, [n] that we lose not those things which we have
wrought, [o] but that we receive a full reward. 9 [p] Who-
soever transgresseth, and abideth not in the doctrine of
Christ, hath not God he that abideth in the doctrine of
Christ, he hath both the Father and the Son 10 If
there come any unto you, and bring not this doctrine,
receive

i Mat xxiv 24 1 John iv 1
k 1 John iv 2, 3
l 1 John ii 22 & iv 3
m Mark xiii 9
n Gal iii 4
o Heb x 35
p 1 John ii 23

receive him not into your houſe, [q] neither bid him God
ſpeed 11 For he that biddeth him God ſpeed, is par-
taker of his evil deeds 12 [r] Having many things to
write unto you, I would not *write* with paper and ink,
but I truſt to come unto you, and ſpeak face to face,
[s] that our joy may be full 13 The children of thy
elect ſiſter greet thee Amen

[q] Rom xvi 17 Gal i 8, 9 Tit iii 10
[r] 3 John 13
[s] Rom i 12 2 Tim i 4

v 7—13 The apoſtle proceeds,

1 To warn and guard this honoured family againſt the wiles of ſeducers *For many deceivers are entered into the world, who confeſs not that Jeſus Chriſt is come in the fleſh*, broaching the moſt fatal and heretical doctrines, as that Jeſus Chriſt aſſumed not a real human nature, but lived and died in appearance only, or that he who was born at Nazareth was not the true expected Meſſiah *This is a deceiver and an antichriſt*, an avowed enemy to the Redeemer's glory and goſpel, and a deſtroyer of the ſouls of men Therefore *look to yourſelves* with holy jealouſy and watchfulneſs, *that we loſe not thoſe things which we have wrought*, and be at laſt diſappointed of our hopes of you, whilſt you come finally ſhort of the grace of God, and, after all the moſt promiſing appearances, be ſeduced by the error of the wicked, *but* hold faſt the truth, and, whereunto ye have already attained, walk by the ſame rule, mind the ſame things, *that we receive a full reward*, when you ſhall appear our joy and crown in the great day, and we with you ſhall obtain the glorious recompenſe promiſed to thoſe who are faithful unto death *Whoſoever tranſgreſſeth, and abideth not in the doctrine of Chriſt, hath not God*, is not influenced by his Spirit, and hath no part in his ſalvation *he that abideth in the doctrine of Chriſt*, with regard to his divine Perſon, real incarnation, mediatorial offices, and complete redemption, profeſſing boldly his faith in defiance of all oppoſition, *he hath both the Father and the Son*, is admitted into a holy and happy communion with them, and hath the moſt aſſured intereſt in their love and favour

2 They are enjoined not to give the leaſt countenance to theſe ſeducers *If there come any unto you, and bring not this doctrine, receive him not into your houſe*, nor afford him ought of that hoſpitable entertainment which you kindly give to the faithful miniſters of Chriſt, *neither bid him God ſpeed*, nor wiſh the leaſt ſucceſs to ſuch ungodly attempts as the propagation of theſe poiſonous errors *for he that biddeth him God ſpeed, is partaker of his evil deeds*, and an abettor of his wickedneſs Note, We need be very cautious not only to keep from evil ourſelves, but to avoid being partakers of other men's ſins

3 He concludes with informing the lady, that he hoped ſhortly to have a more full perſonal conference with her on this ſubject *Having many things to write unto you, I would not write with paper and ink, but I truſt to come unto you, and ſpeak face to face*, more at large, *that our joy may be full*, and we may be happy together in the experience of the true grace of God, and be preſerved from all deluders *The children of thy elect ſiſter greet thee!* How happy is it where grace thus diffuſes itſelf through a whole family, and thoſe who are united by the ties of blood are thus more nearly united in the bonds of God's everlaſting love! *Amen!* Would God that this were the caſe in every family!

THE

EVANGELICAL EXPOSITOR;

OR, A

PRACTICAL COMMENT

UPON THE

THIRD EPISTLE of JOHN.

THE epistle to Gaius, like the former, is written to an individual, but of general use to the church, and universally admitted as canonical. Whether this Gaius is the same whom the apostle Paul calls his host, Rom xvi 23 *is uncertain*

In this epistle the apostle congratulates Gaius upon the prosperity of his soul, ver 1, 2 *Upon the fame he had among good Christians,* ver 3, 4 *Upon his charity and hospitality to the servants of Christ,* ver 5, 6 *He complains of contemptuous treatment by an ambitious Diotrephes,* ver 9, 10 *Recommends Demetrius,* ver 12 *And hopes to visit Gaius shortly,* ver 13, 14

1 THE elder unto the well beloved Gaius,
[a] whom I love in the truth 2 Beloved,
I wish above all things, that thou mayest
prosper and be in health, even as thy soul
prospereth 3 For I rejoiced greatly when the brethren
came and testified of the truth that is in thee, even [b] as
thou walkest in the truth 4 I have no greater joy
than to hear [c] that my children walk in truth 5 Be-
loved, thou dost faithfully whatsoever thou dost to the
brethren, and to strangers, 6 Which have born wit-
ness of thy charity before the church whom if thou
bring forward on their journey [†] after a godly sort, thou
shalt do well 7 Because that for his name's sake they
went forth, [d] taking nothing of the Gentiles 8 We
therefore ought to receive such, that we might be fellow-
helpers to the truth

a 2 John 1
b 2 John 4
c 1 Cor iv 15 Philem 10
† Gr Worthy of God
d 1 Cor ix 12

Ver 1—8 We have here,

1 The inscription and salutation *The elder,* John *unto the well beloved Gaius, whom I love in the truth,* as a faithful member of Jesus Christ *Beloved, I wish above all things, that thou mayest prosper, and be in health, even as thy soul prospereth,* and may your success in all temporal things and your bodily health, bear pace with your spiritual prosperity *Note,* (1) The true prosperity, and that which is most desirable, is the health of the soul (2) Bodily health is a singular mercy, especially as it enables us more eminently to improve our spiritual gifts and graces for the good of mankind

2 He testifies the satisfaction he felt in the report which he had heard *For I rejoiced greatly when the brethren came and testified of the truth that is in thee,* of thy faith, and love unfeigned, *even as thou walkest in the truth* adorning, with all manner of holy conversation thy Christian profession *I have no greater joy than to hear that my children walk in truth* *Note,* It is a most sincere and heartfelt delight to every faithful minister of Christ to behold the children, whom they have begotten in the gospel, walk worthy of their vocation

3 He commends his kind and charitable conduct *Beloved, thou dost faithfully whatsoever thou dost to the brethren, and to strangers,* such hospitality and generosity are the genuine characteristics of thy faithful heart, and have been justly praised by those *which have born witness of thy charity before the church,* and gratefully acknowledged the kindnesses which they received *whom if thou bring forward on their journey after a godly sort,* and assist those itinerant preachers of the gospel who devote their time and labour to this blessed work of spreading the glad tidings through the earth, *thou shalt do well,* and act a noble part in thus advancing the blessed cause of our divine Redeemer, *because that for his name's sake they went forth,* giving up all the world, that they might addict themselves wholly to the ministry, and with a spirit uninfluenced by any mercenary views, *taking nothing of the Gentiles,* but preaching the gospel of God freely *We therefore,* who wish well to that service, and whom God hath blessed with ability, *ought to receive such,* and afford them a comfortable maintenance, *that we might be fellow-helpers to the truth,* and, though not ordained to be preachers, may hereby receive a preacher's reward *Note,* They who devote themselves to the ministry, foregoing all worldly pursuits for the love of Christ and of immortal souls, deserve every kindness at our hands that we can shew them

9 I wrote unto the church but Diotrephes, who
loveth to have the preeminence among them, receiveth
us not 10 Wherefore if I come, I will remember his
deeds which he doth, prating against us with malicious
words and not content therewith, neither doth he him-
self receive the brethren, and forbiddeth them that would,
and casteth *them* out of the church 11 Beloved, [e] fol-
low not that which is evil, but that which is good
[f] He that doth good, is of God but he that doth evil
hath not seen God 12 Demetrius [g] hath good report
of all men, and of the truth itself yea, and we *also* bear
record, [h] and ye know that our record is true 13 [i] I
had many things to write, but I will not with ink and
pen write unto thee 14 But I trust I shall shortly see
thee, and we shall speak [‡] face to face Peace *be* to thee
Our friends salute thee Greet the friends by name

e Ps xxxvii 27 Isa i 16 17
f 1 John iii 6
g 1 Tim iii 7
h John xxi 24
i 2 John 12
‡ Gr Mouth to mouth

Ver 9—14

v 9—14 The apostle here,

1 Points out a man of a very different character *I wrote unto the church*, or, as some render the words, *I would have wrote unto the church but Diotrephes, who loveth to have the preeminence among them*, and proudly lords it over them, *receiveth us not*, and pays no regard to our apostolic injunctions *Wherefore if*, or *when, I come, I will remember his deeds which he doeth*, and severely animadvert upon his imperious and uncharitable conduct, *prating against us with malicious words*, assuming the most insolent airs, and daring even to cast reproach on the divinely-constituted apostles of the Son of God *and not content therewith, neither doth he himself receive the brethren* to any hospitable entertainment in his house, *and forbiddeth them that would, and*, when any notwithstanding disobey his mandates, and receive, assist, and further in their way those faithful ministers of Christ, who travel, preaching his gospel, he *casteth them out of the church*, merely for presuming to disobey his wicked commands, and usurped authority *Note*, (1) Nothing is more contrary to the spirit of a Christian minister than over-bearing arrogance and pride (2) They are doubly wicked, who neither will do good themselves, and those who are willing to do it, they hinder

2 He dissuades Gaius from copying so bad an example *Beloved, follow not that which is evil, but that which is good*, let no height of station or office lead you to copy a bad man; but ever imitate the excellent and the generous *He that doth good, is of God*, proves that he is born of him, and partakes of his Spirit *but he that doth evil, hath not seen God*, whatever pretensions to religion he may make, he is a stranger to all experimental knowledge of divine things

3 He mentions Demetrius as an excellent man, and worthy of imitation *Demetrius hath good report of all men*, all who know him bear testimony to his amiable and pious conversation, *and of the truth itself*, every one, who would speak the truth, must acknowledge his excellence, and we, who are ministers of truth, declare our full approbation of him *and ye know that our record is true*, and may be assuredly depended upon *Note*, It is a noble character indeed so to behave as to be entitled to universal applause, and to be approved of God and all men of truth and integrity

4 He concludes his epistle with the hopes of a personal interview shortly *I had many things to write, but I will not with ink and pen write unto thee but I trust I shall shortly see thee, and we shall speak face to face*, when I can more fully communicate all my mind *Peace be to thee*, prosperity of every kind attend thee in body and soul *Our friends salute thee*, joining in all Christian wishes *Greet the friends* with thee *by name*, presenting to each my most affectionate remembrances.

THE EVANGELICAL EXPOSITOR; OR, A PRACTICAL COMMENT UPON THE GENERAL EPISTLE of JUDE.

THIS epistle, written shortly before the destruction of Jerusalem, is stiled general or catholic, for that it is not immediately directed to any particular person, family or church, but to the whole society of Christians of that time, lately converted to the faith of Christ, whether from Judaism or Paganism. And it is and will be of standing, lasting, and special use in and to the church as long as Christianity, that is, as time shall last.

Some of the chief things contained in it summarily are, 1. *An account of the penman of it, a character of the church, the blessings and privileges of that happy society,* ver. 1, 2. 2. *The occasion of writing this epistle,* ver. 3. 3. *A character of evil and perverse men, who were already sprung up in that infant state of the church, and would be succeeded by others of the like evil spirit and temper in after-times,* ver. 4. 4. *A caution against hearkening to and following after such, from the severity of God towards the unbelieving, murmuring Israelites, at their coming out of Egypt, the angels that fell, the instance of Sodom and Gomorrah, their sin and punishment,* ver. 5, 6, 7. 5. *To these the apostle likens the seducers, against whom he was warning them, and describes them at large, from* ver. 8—13 *inclusive.* 6. *Then (as specially suitable to his argument) he cites an ancient prophesy of Enoch, foretelling and describing the future judgment,* ver. 14, 15. 7. *Enlargeth on the seducer's character, and guards against the offence which honest minds might be apt to take at the so early permission of such things, by shewing that it was foretold long before that so it must be,* ver. 16, 17, 18, 19. 8. *Exhorts them to* perseverance in the faith, fervency in prayer, watchfulness against falling from the love of God, and a lively hope of eternal life, *ver.* 20, 21. 9. *Directs them how to carry themselves towards the erroneous and scandalous,* ver. 22, 23. *And,* 10. *Closes with an admirable doxology in the two last verses.*

We have here, I. *The preface or introduction to the epistle,* ver. 1, 2.

1 JUDE the servant of Jesus Christ, and [a] brother
of James, to them that are sanctified by God
the Father, and [b] preserved in Jesus Christ, *and*
called.
2 Mercy unto you and peace and love
be multiplied.
3 Beloved, when I gave all diligence to
write unto you of [c] the common salvation, it was need-
ful for me to write unto you, and exhort you, that [d] ye
should earnestly contend for the faith which was once de-
livered unto the saints.
4 For [e] there are certain men
crept in unawares, [f] who were before of old ordained to
this condemnation, ungodly men, [g] turning the grace
of our God into lasciviousness, and [h] denying the only
Lord God, and our Lord Jesus Christ.

a Luke vi. 16. Acts i. 13. b John xvii. 11. 1 Pet. i. 5. c [illegible] Phil. i. [illegible] 1 Tim. i. [illegible] & vi. 12. [illegible] Tim. i. 13. e 2 Pet. ii. 1. f Rom. ix. 21, 22. 1 Pet. ii. 8. g 2 Pet. ii. 19. h [illegible] Pet. i. 16. [illegible] Pet. ii. 1.

v. 1—4. The epistle opens,

1. With an account of the sacred penman, *Jude the servant of Jesus Christ*, whose highest honour it is to minister in the [illegible], *and brother of James*, the son of Alpheus.

2. The persons to whom it is addressed. *To them that are sanctified by God the Father*, set apart for himself in the purpose of his eternal love, *and preserved in Jesus Christ*, as the glorious covenant-head of his people, who loses none of those whom the Father hath given him, *and called*, in the fulness of time, to an actual participation of those gospel privileges which Jesus hath purchased, and God the Father promised to bestow on the redeemed, of pardon, grace, holiness and comfort here, and of everlasting blessedness hereafter. *Note*, (1.) All those who are called to partake of the grace of the gospel, are sanctified. Hope toward God, without holiness, is but delusion. (2.) Christ's people are preserved by him, and none can ever pluck them out of his hands.

3. The apostolical benediction. *Mercy unto you* from a pardoning God, *and peace*, flowing from a sense of his reconciliation, *and love*, both to him and toward each other, *be multiplied*.

3. He exhorts them to hold fast the truth which they had received both [illegible] and [illegible]. *Beloved, when I gave all [illegible] of the common salvation,* which [illegible]

lievers enjoy through our adored Redeemer and Saviour, *it was become needful for me to write unto you*, because of the multitude of deceivers, *and exhort you, that ye should earnestly contend for the faith which was once delivered unto the saints*, firmly holding fast the unadulterated doctrines of truth, and zealously maintaining them against all heretical opposers. *Note*, (1.) The salvation of the gospel is a common salvation for Jews and Gentiles, and sinners of every kind, without exception. (2.) They who have received the truth, in the light and love of it, need be exhorted still to stand fast against all the wiles of deceivers. (3.) That faith which God, by his inspired servants, once delivered to his saints, for the use of his church to the latest ages, we must contend for, not with anger, or carnal weapons, but with holy zeal, tempered with meekness, and arguments drawn from the sacred treasury of the Scriptures.

5. He describes the false teachers against whom they need be on their guard. *For there are certain men crept in unawares*, by craft and subtilty into the church and the ministry, *who were before of old ordained to this condemnation*, in God's wise and righteous counsels, *ungodly men*, whose spirit, temper, and conduct, are directly opposite to the divine will and word, *turning the grace of our God into lasciviousness*, perverting the richest doctrines of grace to the vilest purposes of impurity, and abusing them to encourage men in all immorality with the hopes of impunity, *denying the only Lord God*, in works, if not in words, practical, if not speculative atheists, *and rejecting also the gospel testimony concerning the person, character, and offices of our Lord Jesus Christ*. *Note*, (1.) Deceivers were rife in every age, we need not wonder therefore if such ungodly men are found in our own, perverting the glorious grace of the gospel. (2.) They who are vile upon principle, and plead God's word to countenance their impurities, are of all men most desperately wicked. (3.) When ungodly men meet their appointed condemnation, they receive but the just reward of their deeds.

5 ⁱ I will therefore put you in remembrance, though
ye once knew this, ᵏ how that the Lord having saved the
people out of the land of Egypt, afterward ˡ destroyed
them that believed not. 6 And ᵐ the angels which
kept not their first estate, but left their own habitation,
ⁿ he hath reserved in everlasting chains under darkness,
unto the judgment of the great day. 7 Even as ᵒ Sodom
and Gomorrah, and the cities about them in like
manner giving themselves over to fornication, and going
after † strange flesh, are set forth for an example, suffering
the vengeance of eternal fire.

i 2 Pet. iii. 1. k 1 Cor. x. 9. l Num. xiv. 29, 37. & xxvi. 64. Heb. iii. 17, 19. m John viii. 44. n 2 Pet. ii. 4. o Gen. xix. 24. Deut. xxix. 23. 2 Pet. ii. 6. † Gr. Other.

v. 5—7. The apostle, to inforce his warnings, reminds them of the judgment which God formerly executed on such ungodly men. *I will therefore put you in remembrance, though ye once knew this*, the perpetual memory of which needs to be preserved, and it is good to be often reminded of these things, that they may be present before our minds, and the impression of them more deep and lively.

Three awful instances of divine vengeance here stand forth to warn and deter others from the like crimes. Remember,

1. *How that the Lord having saved the people out of the land of Egypt, afterward destroyed them that believed not*, though he had done so great things for them; and if he spared not these, let not the perverters of the gospel, whose crime is so much more aggravated, expect a less fearful doom. *And* remember also,

2. That *the angels*, those creatures of such superior excellence and dignity, *which kept not their first estate*, were not content with the station allotted them, *but left their own habitation*, affecting to be as the Most High, and were therefore hurled from those bright regions which were before their blest abode, *he hath reserved in everlasting chains under darkness*, like criminals fast bound in prison, and kept in custody under his eternal and unchangeable decree, in spiritual darkness, misery, and black despair, *unto the judgment of the great day*, when sentence will finally be executed upon them, and their torment be complete as eternal. And if God thus punished rebel angels, what severity shall not they meet with, who fight against the word of his truth, and the honour of his Son! Apostates in heaven or earth must perish together.

3. Another instance of God's wrath is produced. *Even as Sodom and Gomorrah, and the cities about them*, Admah and Zeboim, *in like manner* abandoned to impurity, *giving themselves over to fornication, and going after strange flesh*, guilty of the most shocking acts of uncleanness, and the most unnatural crimes, *are set forth for an example* of God's tremendous wrath, *suffering the vengeance of eternal fire*, the liveliest image of what the damned must endure in the lake which burneth with fire and brimstone for ever and ever. Wo to those who are partakers of their sins! the same fearful vengeance awaits them.

8 ᵖ Likewise also these filthy dreamers defile the flesh,
despise dominion, and ᵠ speak evil of dignities. 9 Yet
ʳ Michael the archangel, when contending with the devil
he disputed about the body of Moses, ˢ durst not bring
against him a railing accusation, but said, ᵗ The Lord
rebuke thee. 10 But ᵘ these speak evil of those things
which they know not: but what they know naturally as
brute beasts, in those things they corrupt themselves.
11 Wo unto them, for they have gone in the way of
ˣ Cain, and ʸ ran greedily after the error of Balaam for
reward, and perished in ᶻ the gainsaying of Core. 12
ᵃ These are spots in your ᵇ feasts of charity, when they
feast with you, feeding themselves without fear: ᶜ clouds
they are without water, carried about of winds; trees
whose fruit withereth, without fruit, twice dead, ᵈ plucked
up by the roots; 13 ᵉ Raging waves of the sea, ᶠ foaming
out their own shame; wandering stars, ᵍ to whom is
reserved the blackness of darkness for ever.

p 2 Pet. ii. 10, 11. q Ex. xxii. 28. r Dan. x. 13. & xii. 1. Rev. xii. 7. s 2 Pet. ii. 11. t Zech. iii. 2. u 2 Pet. ii. 12. x Gen. iv. 5. y Num. xxii. 21. 2 Pet. ii. 15. Rev. ii. 14. z Num. xvi. 1. a 2 Pet. ii. 13. b 1 Cor. xi. 21. c Prov. xxv. 14. 2 Pet. ii. 17. d Mat. xv. 13. e Isa. lvii. 20. f Phil. iii. 19. g 2 Pet. ii. 17.

v. 8—13. The apostle describes these seducing teachers as guilty of the same crimes, which had before brought down wrath both on sinning angels and ungodly men.

1. Their impurities were great. *Likewise also these filthy dreamers defile the flesh*, sleeping and waking their minds are ever running after impure objects, dishonouring their own bodies by their lewd practices, and drawing in others to gratify their lawless appetites.

2. They cast off all respect for lawful authority. They *despise dominion*, treating the civil government with insolence and contempt, *and speak evil of dignities*, reviling the persons of magistrates, and those who are high in office, whether in church or state. *Yet even Michael the archangel*, eminent as his rank and station is, *when contending with the devil about the body of Moses, durst not bring a railing accusation against him*, wicked as he was, *but said, The Lord rebuke thee*.

Some refer this to a contention which they suppose really passed on the mountain where Moses died, whose dead body, they conceive the devil desired to possess, in order to lead Israel to idolatry, though nothing is mentioned of this in the Scriptures.

Others by Michael suppose, that Christ, the great angel of the covenant, is meant, and by the body of Moses, understand the Mosaical œconomy, and refer to *Zech.* iii. 1, 2. but though the former sense hath its difficulties, the latter seems unnatural and strained. However, the argument is plain, that if the devil himself, wicked as he is, was not rebuked with railing, much less ought any magistrates or rulers, which God hath ordained, in church or state, to be treated with insolence and malignity. *But these seducers speak evil of those things which they know not*, ignorant of the excellence and importance of religion and of the Scriptures, and of the usefulness of that ministry and magistracy against which they rail: *but what they know naturally, as brute beasts*, governed merely by their sensitive appetites, *in those things they corrupt themselves*, giving a loose to all their brutish passions, without fear or shame, till they bring upon themselves swift destruction. *Note*, When men live like beasts they may expect to perish like devils.

3. They copied the vilest examples. *Wo unto them!* the most fearful vengeance hangs over them, *for they have gone in the way of Cain*, filled with his malignant spirit of envy, hatred, and murder towards the righteous, *and ran greedily after the error of Balaam for reward*, ambitious, proud, covetous, and, like that wicked prophet, infatuate after gain, *and they have perished in the gainsaying of Core*, like those rebels who rose up against Moses and Aaron, and ready with them to be swallowed up in the yawning pit of hell. *Note*, Companions with sinners must expect to share their plagues.

4. He describes these deluders under a variety of images. *These are spots in your feasts of charity, when they feast with you, feeding themselves without fear*, whether in a way of civil intercourse, or religious communion, they let loose their luxurious appetites, without any fear of that judgment which awaits them: *clouds they are without water*, that seem to promise rain, but prove like noxious meteors, or noisome fog, *carried about with winds*, variable, and tossed to and fro by every blast of error; *trees whose fruit withereth*, deceiving our expectation, and bring nothing to maturity, *without fruit*, their specious appearances, like blasted fruit, drop off, and the hypocrite and apostate is detected, *twice dead*, by nature and by a revolt from their profession, *plucked up by the roots*, and thus irrecoverably ruined, all hope respecting them is become desperate, and they are now only fit fuel for the flames: *raging waves of the sea*, turbulent, ungovernable, *foaming out their own shame*, belching forth their blasphemies against Christ and reproaches against his cause and people; *wandering stars*, resembling fiery meteors that kindle in the atmosphere, and, after a momentary blaze, are extinguished, or, like the comets, wandering wide from the system of truth and holiness; *to whom is reserved the blackness of darkness for ever*, in that place where total despair completes the misery of the damned, whose worm dieth not, and their fire is not quenched.

14 And Enoch also, ʰ the seventh from Adam,
prophesied of these, saying, Behold, ⁱ the Lord cometh
with

h Gen. v. 18. i Dan. vii. 10. Zech. xiv. 5. Mat. xxv. 31. 2 Thes. i. 7.

with ten thouſand of his ſaints, 15 To execute judg-
ment upon all, and to convince all that are ungodly
among them, of all their ungodly deeds which they have
ungodly committed, and of all their [k] hard *ſpeeches*, which
ungodly ſinners have ſpoken againſt him 16 Theſe
are murmurers, complainers, [l] walking after their own
luſts, and [m] their mouth ſpeaketh great ſwelling *words*,
having men's perſons in admiration becauſe of advantage

k 1 Sam ii 3 Iſ xxxi 18 & xxiv 4 Mal iii 13
l 2 Pet ii 10
m 2 Pet ii 18

v 14—16 We have here,

1 A prophecy of Enoch's recorded concerning theſe men *And Enoch alſo, the ſeventh from Adam*, in the line of deſcent, *propheſied of theſe, ſaying, Behold, the Lord cometh with ten thouſand of his ſaints*, in glorious majeſty, ſwift to avenge the wrongs of his people, and the blaſphemies againſt himſelf, *to execute judgment upon all*, who muſt ſtand at his bar, and receive from his lips their deciſive ſentence, *and to convince all that are ungodly among them*, by the vengeance he will inflict, *of all their ungodly deeds which they have ungodly committed*, in defiance of his authority, *and of all their hard ſpeeches, which ungodly ſinners have ſpoken againſt him* Note, (1) There is a dreadful day of judgment at hand, when vengeance ſhall overtake the ungodly (2) However impious and ſtout-hearted ſinners may now be, every impenitent heart in that day will tremble, and every hardened face gather blackneſs (3) Though mockers now make light of ridiculing the word, the ways, and the people of God, they will find a fearful reckoning for their hard ſpeeches in the day of recompenſe

2 A further deſcription of theſe wicked men *Theſe are murmurers*, againſt God and his providences, *complainers*, diſcontented with their condition in life, finding fault with the doctrines and diſpenſations of the Lord, *walking after their own luſts*, gratifying every vile and ſenſual appetite without reſtraint *and their mouth ſpeaketh great ſwelling words*, making a pretended oſtentation of their knowledge and piety, when in the very depth of error, and in the gall of bitterneſs, *having men's perſons in admiration becauſe of advantage*, careſſing and flattering thoſe, however vile, who are rich, in order to make gain of them Note, (1) Diſcontent with our lot is, in God's ſight, rebellion againſt his providence (2) Men-pleaſers, and ſmooth-tongued flatterers of the great, have the ſure brand upon them of miniſters of Satan

17 [n] But, beloved, remember ye the words which
were ſpoken before of the apoſtles of our Lord Jeſus
Chriſt 18 *How* that they told you [o] there ſhould be
mockers in the laſt time, [p] who ſhould walk after their
own ungodly luſts 19 Theſe be they [q] who ſeparate
themſelves, [r] ſenſual, having not the Spirit 20 But
ye, beloved, building up yourſelves [s] on your moſt holy
faith, [t] praying in the holy Ghoſt, 21 Keep yourſelves
in the love of God, looking for the mercy of our Lord
Jeſus Chriſt unto eternal life 22 And of ſome have
compaſſion, making a difference 23 And others [u] ſave
with fear, pulling *them* out of the fire, hating [x] even
[y] the garment ſpotted by the fleſh 24 [z] Now unto
him that is able to keep you from falling, and to pre-
ſent *you* [a] faultleſs before the preſence of his glory with
exceeding joy, 25 [b] To the only wiſe [c] God our Sa-
viour, *be* glory and majeſty, dominion and power, both
now and ever Amen

n 2 Pet iii 2
o 1 Tim iv 1 2 Tim iii 1 2 Pet iii 3
p Ver 16
q Prov xviii 1 Ezek xiv 7 Hoſ iv 14 & ix 10
r 1 Cor ii 14 Jam iii 15
s Col i 23 & ii 7
t Rom viii 26 Eph vi 18
u Rom xi 14 1 Tim iv 16
x 1 Theſ v 22
y Zech iii 4 Rev iii 4
z Rom xvi 25 Eph iii 20 1 Tim i 17
a Eph i 4 Col i 22
b Rom xvi 27
c 1 Tim i 17 & ii 3 Tit iii 4

v 17—25 The apoſtle concludes,

1 With his kind admonitions *But, beloved*, be deaf to the arts of theſe ſeducers, and *remember ye the words which were ſpoken before of the apoſtles of our Lord Jeſus Chriſt*, which now have received their fulfilment, and ſhould confirm the doctrine which they taught *how that they told you there ſhould be mockers in the laſt time, who ſhould walk after their own ungodly luſts*, ſcoffing at the religion of Jeſus, that without reſtraint they might give a looſe to every lawleſs paſſion And *theſe be they*, of whom the apoſtles ſpake, *who ſeparate themſelves*, fomenting factions, and, under pretences of purer worſhip, forming new ſects and parties, withdrawing from the communion of the apoſtolic church, who, notwithſtanding all their profeſſions of piety, they are utterly *ſenſual*, the ſlaves of worldly-mindedneſs and fleſhly luſts, *having not the Spirit*, and ſtrangers to his gracious influence Note, (1) The only way to be preſerved from the wiles of deceivers is to cleave to our bibles (2) We need not think it ſtrange that ſo many diviſions rend the church, and ſo many factious ſpirits endeavour to draw away diſciples after them, how elſe ſhould the ſcripture be fulfilled? (3) We muſt not be aſhamed of mocking, remember who will mock laſt See Prov i 26

2 With warm exhortations *But ye, beloved, building up yourſelves on your moſt holy faith*, on the glorious foundation of it, Jeſus Chriſt, continuing ſtedfaſt in your holy profeſſion, and ſeeking to eſtabliſh each other in the truth, *praying in the Holy Ghoſt*, under his gracious teaching and influences, who helpeth our infirmities, *keep yourſelves in the love of God*, uſe all appointed means to preſerve and increaſe the heavenly life, and to approve yourſelves in all holy obedience and humble religion, *looking for the mercy of our Lord Jeſus unto eternal life*, and that compleat felicity, both in body and ſoul, for which you muſt own yourſelves wholly indebted to the riches of his ſovereign grace *And of ſome have compaſſion, making a difference* between thoſe who err wilfully, and thoſe who are miſled thro' weakneſs and the wiles of deceivers, whom with all kindneſs and tenderneſs labour to recover from the ſnare *and others ſave with fear*, uſing that ſharpneſs, ſeverity, and terror with them, which their more dangerous caſe requires, *pulling them*, if poſſible, *out of the fire*, which is ready to conſume them, *hating even the garment ſpotted by the fleſh*, deteſting all impure converſation, and teſtifying an unremitting diſpleaſure againſt ſin, and whatever would lead thereto, as the Jews were under the law obliged to ſhun every touch that communicated defilement, and the garment that had the ſpot of leproſy muſt be burned Note, (1) Faith in lively exerciſe is the great preſervative from all deluſion (2) Prayer muſt be our daily employment, *ſpiritual* prayer, not the taſk of the lip and the knee, but the warm effuſions of the heart, where the Holy Ghoſt abides (3) They who would keep themſelves in the love of God, muſt carefully ſhun whatever they know muſt offend him (4) Mercy, not merit, muſt be our hope, even in a judgment-day, and eternal life be expected merely as the ſovereign gift of God in Jeſus Chriſt (5) We ſhould ſhow a holy jealouſy over our brethren, tenderly deſirous to ſnatch them from the dangers to which they are expoſed, kindly warning them, and, where ſharpneſs is needful, faithfully declaring thoſe terrors of the Lord, which may rouſe the lethargic conſcience

3 He cloſes with a ſolemn doxology *Now unto him that is able to keep you from falling*, that bleſſed Jeſus, in and by whom alone you can be preſerved (*See* ver 1) from all evil or apoſtacy, *and to preſent you faultleſs*, in his own divine righteouſneſs, *before the preſence of his glory*, in the great day of his appearing, *with exceeding joy*, when every tear ſhall be wiped from your eyes, and eternal triumphs fill your happy ſouls, *to the only wiſe God our Saviour*, in whom dwell all the treaſures of wiſdom and knowledge, *be glory and majeſty, dominion and power, both now and ever Amen* Note, (1) We are in his hands who is not only able, but hath engaged to keep us from falling, therefore we may truſt, and not be afraid (2) Whatever infirmities ſtill cleave to us, we ſhall be preſented faultleſs before the throne, for if we are Chriſt's, we are complete in him (3) The ſervice of eternity will begin even here below, and every redeemed ſoul will delight to proclaim the Saviour's praiſe.

THE

EVANGELICAL EXPOSITOR;

OR, A

PRACTICAL COMMENT

UPON THE

Revelation of St. JOHN the Divine.

WE are now entering upon the last volume in the canon of the scriptures, and the most difficult of the whole to be understood; as must needs be the case with prophecies which wait for the key of time to open them.

It is generally admitted, that this book contains an account of the state of the church to the end of time, then at least we shall fully understand its contents. Mean time, whilst we are humbly searching what and what manner of time the Spirit speaking in it doth signify, we shall find much profitable matter for our souls health, and though we may mistake in the application of some of the prophecies, yet shall we obtain the blessing promised to those who read and hear the things written in this book, ver. 3.

I concur with those who suppose, that the events from Chap. iv. *to the end follow in a regular series, and am content to select from the labours of the most wise and judicious interpreters, the sense which appears most probable, though withal acknowledging, that in many places the prophecies are covered with deep obscurity, and the wisest conjectures dubious. We must be content for a while to wait the explication of them.* The vision is for an appointed time, and in the end it shall speak.

CHAP. I.

This chapter is a general preface to the whole book, and contains, 1. *An inscription, declaring the original and the design of it,* ver. 1, 2. 2. *The apostolical benediction pronounced on all those that shall pay a due regard to the contents of this book,* ver. 3—8. 3. *A glorious vision or appearance of the Lord Jesus Christ to the apostle John, when he delivered to him this revelation, from* ver. 9, *to the end of the chapter.*

1 THE revelation of Jesus Christ, which God
gave unto him, to shew unto his servants
things [a] which must shortly come to pass;
and [b] he sent and signified *it* by his angel
unto his servant John: 2 Who bare record of the
Word of God, and of [c] the testimony of Jesus Christ,
and of all things [d] that he saw. 3 [e] Blessed *is* he that
readeth, and they that hear the words of this prophecy,
and keep those things which are written therein: for
[f] the time is at hand.

[a] Chap. iv. 1. [b] Chap. xxii. 16. [c] 1 Cor. i. 6. Ver. 9. Chap. vi. 9. & xii. 17. 1 John v. 11. [d] Luke xi. 28. Chap. xxii. 7. [f] Rom. xiii. 11. Jam. v. 8. 1 Pet. iv. 7. Chap. xxii. 10.

v. 1—3. The book opens,

1. With a preface, declaring its sacred contents. *The revelation of Jesus Christ,* which comes from him, as the great prophet of his church, and which *God gave unto him, to shew unto his servants things which must shortly come to pass,* some of them to be quickly accomplished, and the rest in order till the end of time: *and he sent and signified it by his angel,* whom he employed on this errand, *unto his servant John, who bare record of the word of God,* and had before, in his gospel and epistles, spoken of the glory and offices of the incarnate word, *and* was one of the faithful witnesses *of the testimony of Jesus Christ,* of his gospel, *and of all things that he saw,* the miracles, life, death, and resurrection of the great Redeemer, and those amazing visions which are here recorded.

2. A blessing is pronounced on the hearers, readers, and observers of this book. *Blessed is he that readeth, and they that hear the words of this prophecy,* attentively remarking the prophecies here revealed, and enquiring into the mind of the Spirit, *and keep those things which are written therein,* retaining them in their memory, and directed by them in their practice: *for the time is at hand,* when their fulfilment will begin. *Note,* (1.) They who diligently study the scriptures, will find the happy fruit of their labours. (2.) The shorter the period of time allotted to us is, the greater diligence should we give to improve it.

4 JOHN to the seven churches which are in Asia:
Grace *be* unto you, and peace, from him [g] which
is, and [h] which was, and which is to come; and [i] from
the seven spirits which are before his throne; 5 And
from Jesus Christ, *who is* [k] the faithful witness, *and*
[l] the first begotten of the dead, and [m] the prince of the
kings of the earth. Unto him [n] that loved us, and
[o] washed us from our sins in his own blood, 6 And
hath

[g] Ex. iii. 14. Ver. 8. [h] John i. 1. [i] Zech. iii. 9. & iv. 10. Chap. iii. 1. & iv. 5. & v. 6. [k] John viii. 14. Chap. iii. 14. [l] 1 Cor. xv. 20. Col. i. 18. [m] Chap. xvii. 14. & xix. 16. [n] Gal. ii. 20. [o] Heb. ix. 14. 1 John i. 7.

ᵖ hath made us kings and prieſts, unto God and his
Father, ᵠ to him *be* glory and dominion for ever and
ever Amen 7. ʳ Behold, he cometh with clouds,
and every eye ſhall ſee him, and ˢ they *alſo* which pierced
him and all kindreds of the earth ſhall wail becauſe of
him even ſo, Amen 8 ᵗ I am Alpha and Omega,
the beginning and the ending, ſaith the Lord, ᵘ which is,
and which was, and which is to come, the Almighty

p Ex xix 6 1 Pet ii 5, 9 Chap v 10 & xx 6 q 1 Tim vi 16 Heb xiii 21 1 Pet iv 11 & v 11 r Dan vii 13 Mat xxiv 30 & xxvi 64 Acts i 11 Jude 14 s Zech xii 10, John xix 37 t Iſa xli 4 & xliv 6 & xlviii 12 Ver 11 Chap xxi 6 & xxii 13 u Ver 4 Chap iv 8 & xi 17 & xvi 5

v 4—8 The apoſtle,

1 Addreſſes *the ſeven churches which are in Aſia* and adds his benediction, *Grace be unto you* in all its fulneſs of bleſſings, *and peace* in your conſciences from a ſenſe of redeeming love, flowing *from him which is, and which was, and which is to come*, from the eternal Father, in his nature and perfections unchangeably the ſame for ever and ever *and from the ſeven ſpirits which are before his throne*, even that Holy Ghoſt whoſe gifts and graces are various and perfect, having all fulneſs to communicate to theſe ſeven churches, and to all the members of them *and from Jeſus Chriſt*, through whom as Mediator all the bleſſings of the triune God deſcend upon his people, *who is the faithful witneſs*, the anointed prophet to declare the Father's will, *and the firſt-begotten of the dead*, who roſe as our glorious high-prieſt, with his own blood to appear in the preſence of God for us, *and the prince of the kings of the earth*, exalted to the mediatorial throne, and become the Head of all principalities and powers, as the univerſal *King* to protect his people and ſubdue their enemies

2 He aſcribes glory to the incarnate Jeſus *Unto him that loved us* with an everlaſting love, *and waſhed us from our ſins in his own blood*, which he ſhed to redeem us from all iniquity, *and hath made us kings and prieſts unto God and his Father*, inveſting us with dominion over all the power of evil, and conſecrating us for his bleſſed ſervice, to offer thoſe ſpiritual ſacrifices which are acceptable to God by Jeſus Chriſt, *to him*, even to this amiable and adorable Jeſus, *be glory and dominion for ever and ever Amen!* *Note*, (1) Jeſus by his blood hath purged our ſins, and nothing but this could ever have cleanſed our guilty ſouls (2) Every child of God is now conſecrated to the higheſt office and dignity, is heir to a throne of glory, and hath acceſs with boldneſs into the holieſt of all through atoning blood (3) They who know the divine Redeemer, and are intereſted in his love, will be ceaſeleſs in their adorations of him

3 With rapture the apoſtle looks forward to the glorious coming of Jeſus as the eternal judge, and as preſent for the comfort and joy of his people, cries out, *Behold*, with wonder and delight, *he cometh with clouds* in awful majeſty, ſurrounded with angels and archangels, ten thouſand times ten thouſand, and thouſands of thouſands, *and every eye ſhall ſee him*, ſeated on the throne of judgment, *and they alſo which pierced him*, with impious and bloody cruelty nailed him to the tree, *and all kindreds of the earth ſhall wail becauſe of him*, whoſe guilt unpardoned now ſhall ſtare them in the face, and horrors unutterable ſeize upon their conſciences, whilſt with tranſport the faithful ſhall welcome his arrival, approving and applauding all his righteous deciſions, and are now waiting for the day of his appearing, *even ſo, Amen!* come quickly *Note*, (1) A day of judgment will ſpread terror through a wicked world Wo then to thoſe who have pierced the Redeemer, whether in his own perſon, or in the inſults ſhewn to his people they ſhall receive a fearful recompence (2) Bleſſed and happy are they who, in the proſpect of that day, can comfortably ſay, *Even ſo, Amen!*

4 The great Judge deſcribes his own tranſcendent honour *I am Alpha and Omega, the beginning and the ending, ſaith the Lord*, the ſum and ſubſtance of the ſcriptures, poſſeſſing all perfection, and accompliſhing all my pleaſure, *which is, and which was, and which is to come, the Almighty*, the ſelf-exiſtent and incomprehenſible Jehovah, able to ſave or deſtroy to the uttermoſt

9 I John, who alſo am your brother, and ˣ compa
nion in tribulation, and ʸ in the kingdom and patience
of Jeſus Chriſt, was in the iſle that is called Patmos,
ᶻ for the word of God, and for the teſtimony of Jeſus
Chriſt 10 ᵃ I was in the Spirit on ᵇ the Lord's day,
and heard behind me a great voice, ᶜ as of a trumpet,
11 Saying, ᵈ I am Alpha and Omega, ᵉ the firſt and
the laſt and, What thou ſeeſt, write in a book, and
ſend *it* unto the ſeven churches which are in Aſia, unto
Epheſus, and unto Smyrna, and unto Pergamos, and
unto Thyatira, and unto Sardis, and unto Philadelphia,
and unto Laodicea. 12 And I turned to ſee the voice
that ſpake with me And being turned, ᶠ I ſaw ſeven
golden candleſticks; 13 And ᵍ in the midſt of the ſe-
ven candleſticks, ʰ *one* like unto the Son of man, ⁱ cloth-
ed with a garment down to the foot, and ᵏ girt about the
paps with a golden girdle 14 His head and ˡ *his* hairs
were white like wool, as white as ſnow; and ᵐ his eyes
were as a flame of fire, 15 And ⁿ his feet like unto
fine braſs, as if they burned in a furnace, and ᵒ his voice
as the ſound of many waters 16 And ᵖ he had in his
right hand ſeven ſtars and ᵠ out of his mouth went a
ſharp two-edged ſword and ʳ his countenance *was* as the
ſun ſhineth in his ſtrength 17 And ˢ when I ſaw him,
I fell at his feet as dead ᵗ and ᵘ he laid his right hand
upon me, ſaying unto me, Fear not, ᵘ I am the firſt
and the laſt 18 ˣ *I am* he that liveth, and was dead,
and behold, ʸ I am alive for evermore, Amen, and ᶻ have
the keys of hell and of death 19 Write ᵃ the things
which thou haſt ſeen, ᵇ and the things which are, ᶜ and
the things which ſhall be hereafter 20 The myſtery
of the ᵈ ſeven ſtars which thou ſaweſt in my right hand,
ᵉ and the ſeven golden candleſticks The ſeven ſtars
ᶠ are the angels of the ſeven churches and ᵍ the ſeven
candleſticks which thou ſaweſt, are the ſeven churches

s 1 Theſſ ii 7 t Chap iv 11 x 1 Tim i 8 y Rom viii 17 2 Tim ii 12 z Ver 2 Chap vi 9 a Chap iv 2 & xvii 3 & xxi 10 b John xx 26 Acts xx 7 1 Cor xvi 2 c Chap iv 1 d Ver 8 e Ver 17 f Ver 20 g Chap ii 1 h Ezek i 26 Dan vii 13 & x 16 Chap xiv 14 i Lev xvi 4, 32 Dan x 5 k Ex xxix 5 l Dan vii 9 m Dan x 6 Chap ii 18 & xix 12

n Ezek i 7 Dan x 6 Chap ii 18 o Dan x 6 Chap xiv 2 p Ver 20 Chap ii 1 & iii 1 q Iſa xlix 2 Eph vi 17 Heb iv 12 Chap ii 12, 16 & xix 15, 21 r Acts xxvi 13 Chap x 1 s Ezek i 28 t Dan viii 18 & x 10. u Ver 11 Chap ii 8 & xxii 13 x Rom vi 9 y Chap iv 9 z Pſ lxviii 20 Chap xx 1 a Ver 12 b Chap ii, 1 &c c Chap iv 1 &c d Ver 16 e Ver 12, 13 f Mal ii 7 g Zech iv 2 Mat v 15 Phil ii 15

v 9—20 We have here the glorious viſion which appeared to the divine penman of this book

1 He calls himſelf *John, your brother and companion in tribulation, and in the kingdom and patience of Jeſus Chriſt*, for all his ſervants follow him with their croſs to glory and muſt expect and be content patiently to ſuffer for his great name's ſake He was now in baniſhment in the iſle of Patmos, for his fidelity to his bleſſed Maſter, and, though removed far from earthly comforters, ſtill he found that preſence of God which made his lonely abode a paradiſe of delights He was *in the Spirit on the Lord's day*, whilſt on that holy day, obſerved by the Chriſtian church in memory of the Saviour's reſurrection, he was employed in ſacred meditation and prayer, he felt the deſcending power of the Holy One, and was filled with prophetic inſpiration *Note*, They who on the Lord's day employ in ſpiritual exerciſes their time and thoughts, retiring from the world and all its cares and avocations, will find a bleſſed intercourſe with heaven, and experience that communion with God which is a foretaſte of eternal bleſſedneſs

2 He declares what he heard and ſaw A great voice, as of a trumpet behind him, awakened his attention, and he heard diſtinctly the voice of Jeſus, ſaying, *I am Alpha and Omega, the firſt and the laſt*, and commanding him to write what in viſion he was now about to ſee and hear, and ſend it to the ſeven churches of Aſia, whoſe names are ſpecified Turning to ſee from whence the voice proceeded, a glorious perſonage meets his aſtoniſhed ſight, whoſe majeſty he deſcribes *I ſaw ſeven golden candleſticks*, ſeven branches ſpringing from the ſame ſtem, like that which ſtood in the tabernacle of old, the emblems of that light of truth and fire of love which Jeſus ſends into the midſt of his church and people, and which they in their converſation hold forth to the world *And in the midſt of the ſeven golden candleſticks one* ſtood, as the prieſt when he came to trim the lamps, *like unto the Son of man, clothed with a garment down to the foot*, the figure of his complete and ſpotleſs righteouſneſs, *and girt about the paps with a golden girdle*, far ſurpaſſing the coſtly girdle of the ephod, and intimating how ready and able he is to diſcharge his ſacerdotal office on their behalf *his head and his hairs were white like wool*, as the Ancient of days, *as white as ſnow*, *and his eyes were as a flame of fire*, piercing and penetrating into the inmoſt ſecrets of men's ſouls, and darting lightning againſt his foes, *and his feet like unto fine braſs, as if they burned in a furnace*, mighty to ſupport the concerns of his church and people, and to tread down their enemies, *and his voice as the ſound of many waters*, ſpreading to the diſtant corners of the earth his bleſſed goſpel word, and terrible in his providences and judgments as the roaring waves *And he had in his right hand ſeven ſtars*, the faithful biſhops of his church, whom he upholds and preſerves, and who ſhine bright in the luſtre of his grace; *and out of his mouth went a ſharp two-edged ſword*, even the ſword of his law and goſpel, pricking man to the heart, and hewing down all oppoſition, *and his countenance was as the ſun ſhineth in his ſtrength*, reviving as the light and warmth of his invigorating beams *And when I ſaw him, I fell at his feet as dead*, overcome with the brightneſs of his glory *And he laid his right hand upon me*, to revive my intimidated mind by his mighty grace, ſaying unto me, *Fear not, I am the firſt and the laſt*, in kindneſs and love unchangeable *I am he that liveth*, eſſentially poſſeſſed of life in and of myſelf, *and was dead*, in that human nature which I aſſumed, *and behold I am alive for evermore, Amen!* ſo it is, infallibly certain and true, *and I have the keys of hell and of death*, to ſave or to deſtroy according to my ſovereign pleaſure, to unlock the gates of the grave to my people, and ſhut up in the priſon of eternal darkneſs the wicked *Write the things which thou haſt ſeen, and the things which are, and the things which ſhall be hereafter* until the end of time *The myſtery of the ſeven ſtars which thou ſaweſt in my right hand, and the ſeven golden candleſticks The ſeven ſtars are the angels*, or meſſengers, *of the ſeven churches and the ſeven candleſticks, which thou ſaweſt, are the ſeven churches* May we by faith behold the ſame Jeſus, and feel the enlivening influence of his preſence with our ſouls!

CHAP II

The apostle John, according to the command which he received, proceeds to write the epistles to the angels or ministers of the seven churches of Ephesus, from ver 1—8 Of Smyrna, from ver 8—12 3 Of Pergamos, from ver 12—18 4 Of Thyatira, from ver 18 to the end

1 UNTO the angel of the church of Ephesus,
write, These things saith [a] he that holdeth the
seven stars in his right hand, [b] who walketh in the midst
of the seven golden candlesticks; 2 [c] I know thy works,
and thy labour, and thy patience, and how thou canst
not bear them which are evil and [d] thou hast tried them
[e] which say they are apostles, and are not, and hast found
them liars 3 And hast born, and hast patience, and
for my name's sake [f] hast laboured, and hast not fainted
4 Nevertheless, I have *somewhat* against thee, because
thou hast left thy first love 5 Remember therefore
from whence thou art fallen, [g] and repent, and do the
first works, [i] or else I will come unto thee quickly, and
will remove thy candlestick out of his place, except thou
repent 6 But this thou hast, that thou hatest the deeds
of [i] the Nicolaitans, which I also hate 7 [k] He that
hath an ear, let him hear what the Spirit saith unto the
churches, To him that overcometh will I give [l] to eat
of [m] the tree of life, which is in the midst of the paradise
of God

[a] Chap i 16 20 [b] Chap i 13 [c] Ver 9 13 19. Chap iii 1 8, 15 [d] 1 John iv 1 [e] 2 Cor xi 13 [f] Gal vi 9 [g] Chap iii 19 [h] Mat xxi 41 43 Chap iii 3 [i] Ver 15 [k] Mat xi 15 & xiii 9 43 Ver xi 17 29 Chap iii 6, 13 22 [l] Chap xxii 2 14 [m] Gen ii 9

v 1—7 The first epistle is directed to the angel of the church of Ephesus We have,

1 The preface, informing us who dictated what the apostle wrote, even that glorious Personage *that holdeth the seven stars in his right hand, and who walketh in the midst of the seven golden candlesticks* Note, The Lord Jesus is he who makes his ministers bright stars he gives them purity of doctrine and holiness of life, and enables them to shine to his own glory May we each be upheld in his almighty arms, and be fed with oil from the living Source, shining brighter and stronger till we come to the eternal temple above!

2 The contents

(1) The epistle contains matter of great commendation *I know* and approve *thy works* as a minister of zeal, and the works of the church in general as exemplary, *and thy patience* under persecutions, *and how thou canst not bear them which are evil*, abhorring their principles and practices, and removing them from communion with you *and thou hast tried them which say they are apostles, and are not, and hast found them liars*, detecting their impostures, and demonstrating the falsehood of their pretended commission from Christ *and hast born* many conflicts, *and hast patience, and for my name's sake hast laboured* with fidelity, *and hast not fainted* Note, They who are put in trust with the ministry may expect many trials They have need of peculiar faith and patience, that they may persevere in their labours, and faint not

(2) Here is a needful rebuke and admonition *Nevertheless, I have somewhat against thee, because thou hast left thy first love*, and grown colder of late in affection to me and my ways And such a backsliding in heart the Lord Jesus observes, and cannot but be highly displeased with *Remember therefore from whence thou art fallen, and repent, and do the first works, or else I will come unto thee quickly, and will remove thy candlestick out of his place, except thou repent* Note, (1) They who are fallen should remember how much they have lost, and with grief and shame consider their ways (2) They who truly repent will return to their first works, and then they will return again to a sense of the divine grace and love (3) The churches that neglect Christ's admonition may expect to be visited with his judgments

(3) A word of encouragement is added *But this thou hast, that thou hatest the deeds of the Nicolaitans, which I also hate*, their idolatrous, vicious, and impure principles and practices *Note*, True Christians will maintain a holy hatred to all the ways of sin

3 The conclusion Where we have, (1) A solemn call to attention *He that hath an ear, let him hear what the Spirit saith unto the churches* Note, The scriptures are of general use for all ages, and what was written of old was written for our instruction, as much as for those to whom it was more immediately addressed (2) A gracious promise *To him that overcometh*, and perseveres unto the end, manfully fighting under my banners against sin, Satan, and the world, *will I give to eat of the tree of life, which is in the midst of the paradise of God*, admitting him to all the blessings and happiness of the celestial paradise, infinitely surpassing that from which Adam for his transgression was ejected Note, In Christ Jesus, and by his grace, we shall be advanced to higher glories than even man in innocence enjoyed

8 And unto the angel of the church in Smyrna, write,
These things saith [n] the first and the last, which was dead,
and is alive 9 [o] I know thy works, and tribulation,
and poverty, (but [p] thou art rich) and *I know* the blas-
phemy of [q] them which say they are Jews, and are not,
[q] but are the synagogue of Satan 10 Fear none of those
things which thou shalt suffer behold, the devil shall
cast some of you into prison, that ye may be tried, and
ye shall have tribulation ten days [r] be thou faithful unto
death, and I will give thee [s] a crown of life 11 [t] He
that hath an ear, let him hear what the Spirit saith unto
the churches, He that overcometh, shall not be hurt of
[u] the second death

[n] Chap i 8, 17 18 [o] Ver 2 [p] Luke xii 21 1 Tim vi 18 Jam ii 5 [q] Rom ii 28 29 & ix 6 [q] Chap iii 9 [r] Mat x 22 & xxiv 13 [s] 2 Tim iv 8 Jam i 12 Chap iii 11 [t] Ver 7 Chap xiii 9 [u] Chap xx 14 & xxi 8

v 8—11 The form of the epistles is similar We have,

1 The preface to the church of Smyrna *These things saith the first and the last* the Creator and Judge of all, the Author and Finisher of his people's salvation, *who was dead, and is alive*, delivered for our offences, to make the one great atonement is raised again for our justification, and lives for ever to secure our eternal blessedness

2 The contents (1) Their commendation *I know thy works, and tribulation*, how zealously thou hast laboured, and how much thou hast suffered, *and thy poverty, (but thou art rich)* for whatever we lose for Christ, and the gospel's sake, it shall procure us much more substantial treasures in a better world *And I know the blasphemy of them which say they are Jews, and are not, but are the synagogue of Satan*, who, whilst they pretended a peculiar covenant-title to God's favour, and zealously urged the mosaic ritual as essential to salvation, were in fact Satan's emissaries and the bitter enemies of the spiritual Israel (2) Warning is given them of approaching trials *Fear none of those things which thou shalt suffer*, so as to be terrified from the path of duty *behold, the devil*, by cruel persecutors his instruments, *shall cast some of you into prison, that ye may be tried*, and your faith and constancy proved in the furnace of affliction, *and ye shall have tribulation ten days*, either so many years, or for a considerable though indefinite space of time Note, God's people need not fear the malice of their most invenomed persecutors If he be for them, no matter who may be against them (3) An encouraging promise is added *Be thou faithful unto death, and I will give thee a crown of life*, and then, though it be won by martyrdom, our gain will be unspeakably great

3 The conclusion *He that hath an ear, let him hear what the Spirit saith unto the churches*, what encouragements there are to fidelity, and how watchful God is over his chosen *He that overcometh* in the holy warfare, and is finally victorious over his spiritual foes, *shall not be hurt of the second death*, hath nothing to fear, hath every thing to hope for in eternity

12 And to the angel of the church in Pergamos,
write, These things saith [x] he, which hath the sharp sword
with two edges, 13 [y] I know thy works, and where
thou dwellest, [z] *even* where Satan's seat *is* and thou
holdest fast my name, and hast not denied my faith, even
in those days wherein Antipas *was* my faithful martyr,
who was slain among you, where Satan dwelleth 14
But I have a few things against thee, because thou hast
there them that hold the doctrine of [a] Balaam, who
taught Balac to cast a stumbling-block before the child-
ren of Israel, [b] to eat things sacrificed unto idols, and to
commit fornication 15 So hast thou also them that
hold the doctrine of [c] the Nicolaitans, which thing I
hate 16 Repent, or else I will come unto thee quick-
ly, and [d] will fight against them with the sword of my
mouth. 17 [e] He that hath an ear, let him hear what
the Spirit saith unto the churches, To him that over-
cometh will I give to eat of [f] the hidden [g] manna, and
will give him a white stone, and in the stone [h] a new
name written, which no man knoweth, saving he that
receiveth *it*

[x] Chap i 16 [y] Ver 2 [z] Ver 9 [a] Num xxv 1 & xxxi 16 [b] Acts xv 29 Ver 20 [c] Ver 6 [d] Isa xi 4 2 Thes ii 8 Chap i 16, & xix 15, 21 [e] Ver 7 [f] John iv 32 [g] John vi 58 [h] Chap. iii 12 & xix. 12

v 12—17 Here is, as before,

1 The preface, to the angel of the church of Pergamos *These things saith he, which hath the sharp sword with two edges*, the sword of his word and his providence, to defend the faithful, and to cut off all enemies and apostates

2 The contents (1) Notice is taken of their perilous situation *I know thy works*, and behold with satisfaction whatever is excellent among you, *and where thou dwellest, even where Satan's seat is*, environed with enemies *and thou holdest fast my name, and hast not denied my faith*, amidst the fire of hottest persecution, *even in those days wherein Antipas was my faithful martyr, who was slain among you, where Satan dwelleth*, and manifests his bloody

bloody rage against my loyal subjects. *Note,* Steady fidelity in perilous days is doubly commendable. (2.) A reproof is given them for what was amiss. *But I have a few things against thee, because thou hast there them that hold the doctrine of Balaam, who taught Balac to cast a stumbling-block before the children of Israel, to eat things sacrificed unto idols, and to commit fornication.* Some such seducing teachers were among them, who inculcated the lawfulness of eating idol-sacrifices, and of fornication. *So hast thou also them that hold the doctrine of the Nicolaitans, which thing I hate,* and countenance their impure and abominable practices. *Note,* God hates all impurity, and they who make light of fornication will feel the heavy wrath of an offended God, which it provokes. (3.) They are warned instantly to repent. *Repent, or else I will come unto thee quickly* in judgment, *and will fight against thee with the sword of my mouth;* and no sword is so fatal to the body as the denunciations of his wrath are to the guilty soul. *Note,* By speedy repentance alone we can prevent the threatened judgments. And not only must we cleanse our hearts from the love of sin, but separate ourselves from all communion with scandalous offenders, lest we become by connivance partakers of their guilt and ruin.

3. The conclusion. *He that hath an ear, let him hear what the Spirit saith unto the churches. To him that overcometh,* faithful in the arduous conflict, *will I give to eat of the hidden manna,* feeding him with the abundant grace and consolations of my Spirit and my gospel, *and will give him a white stone,* absolving him from all his iniquities, *and in the stone a new name written,* the name of a child of God and heir of glory, securing to him an eternity of inconceivable blessedness, *which no man knoweth saving he that receiveth it.*

18 And unto the angel of the church in Thyatira,
write, These things saith the Son of God, [i] who hath
his eyes like unto a flame of fire, and his feet *are* like fine
brass; 19 [k] I know thy works, and charity, and ser-
vice, and faith, and thy patience, and thy works, and
the last *to be* more than the first. 20 Notwithstanding,
I have a few things against thee, because thou sufferest
that woman [l] Jezebel, which calleth herself a prophetess,
to teach and seduce my servants [m] to commit fornication,
and to eat things sacrificed unto idols. 21 And I gave her
space [n] to repent of her fornication, and she repented not.
22 Behold, I will cast her into a bed, and them that
commit adultery with her into great tribulation, except
they repent of their deeds. 23 And I will kill her
children with death; and all the churches shall know
that [o] I am he that searcheth the reins and hearts: and
I [p] will give unto every one of you according to your
works. 24 But unto you I say, and unto the rest in
Thyatira, As many as have not this doctrine, and which
have not known the depths of Satan, as they speak,
[q] I will put upon you none other burden. 25 But that
which ye have *already,* hold fast till I come. 26 And
he that overcometh, and keepeth [r] my works unto the
end, [s] to him will I give power over the nations: 27
(And [t] he shall rule them with a rod of iron; as the
vessels of a potter shall they be broken to shivers:) even
as I received of my Father. 28 And I will give him
[x] the morning star. 29 [y] He that hath an ear, let him
hear what the Spirit saith unto the churches.

v. 18—29. The fourth epistle is directed to the angel of the church of Thyatira.

1. The picture describes the Son of God, who directs to the sacred penman. *These things saith the Son of God, who hath his eyes like unto a flame of fire,* infinite in wisdom and knowledge, discerning the secrets of all hearts; *and his feet are like fine brass,* almighty to support his people amidst every danger, and to tread his enemies and theirs into the dust.

2. The contents. (1.) They are highly commended. *I know thy works,* and am pleased with them, *and thy charity, and service, and faith, and thy patience, and thy works; and the last to be more than the first,* that in all divine graces and good conversation thou art increasing with the increase of God, growing more exemplary and eminent. *Note,* It is well for us when he who knoweth our hearts bears witness that our last works are more than the first. (2.) They are reproved for what was blameable among them. *Notwithstanding, I have a few things against thee, because thou sufferest that woman Jezebel, which calleth herself a prophetess,* (probably some woman of eminence among them who pretended to inspiration, and had her abettors and followers) *to teach, and to seduce my servants to commit fornication, and to eat things sacrificed unto idols,* perverting their souls, and leading them to corporal and spiritual idolatries and impurities. *And I gave her space to repent of her fornication, and she repented not;* therefore behold swift vengeance shall overtake her and her adherents. *Behold, I will cast her into a bed* of languishing and misery, *and them that commit adultery with her into great tribulation,* the partakers of her sins shall partake of her plagues, *except they repent of their deeds,* and prevent the threatened judgments: *and I will kill her children with death,* as surely as the sons of Ahab perished by the sword of Jehu: *and all the churches shall know that I am he that searcheth the reins and hearts,* and can discover every hidden principle and secret of the soul, distinguishing the hypocrite from the faithful, *and I will give unto every one of you according to your works.* *Note,* (1.) They who abuse the patience of God, and harden themselves in sin, instead of repenting of their iniquities, will bring aggravated guilt and ruin upon their souls. (2.) God's omniscience cannot be deceived, nor his justice eluded; the faithless professor will be detected and sentenced at his impartial tribunal. 3. He encourages the faithful among them. *But unto you I say, and unto the rest in Thyatira, As many as have not this doctrine, and which have not known the depths of Satan,* abhorring all such impure principles and practices, which impostors, influenced by deep Satanical subtlety, seek to inculcate, *I will put upon you none other burden,* nor add any farther injunctions or restraints than those revealed in my word. *But that which ye have already,* the doctrines and precepts of the gospel which you have embraced, *hold fast till I come* to take you to my eternal rest, and deliver you from all your temptations for ever. *Note,* (1.) The Lord knows how to separate between the precious and the vile, and will secure his own people amidst all the arts of deceivers. (2.) They who would meet Christ with comfort at his coming, must hold fast his truth in principle and practice, and never be moved away from the hope of the gospel.

3. The conclusion. *And he that overcometh, and keepeth my works unto the end,* patiently and faithfully persevering in the profession and practice of the gospel, *to him will I give power over the nations,* when he shall sit with me on my throne at the great day, *(and he shall rule them with a rod of iron,* breaking in pieces all the wicked of the earth, *as the vessels of a potter shall they be broken to shivers) even as I received,* in my office-capacity, a kingdom *of my Father:* he shall share my glory, and reign with me for ever, *and I will give him the morning-star,* so that he shall shine bright in eternal glory as the stars for ever and ever. *He that hath an ear, let him hear what the Spirit saith unto the churches.* Lord, open thou mine ears, and make me earnestly take heed to the things that are spoken!

CHAP. III.

Here we have three more of the epistles of Christ to the churches. 1. To Sardis, ver. 1—7. *2. To Philadelphia, ver.* 7—14. *3. To Laodicea, ver.* 14—22.

1 AND unto the angel of the church in Sardis, write,
These things saith [a] he that hath the seven Spi-
rits of God, and the seven stars; [b] I know thy works,
that thou hast a name that thou livest, and art dead.
2 Be watchful, and strengthen the things which remain,
that are ready to die: for I have not found thy works
perfect before God. 3 [c] Remember therefore how thou
hast received and heard, and hold fast, [d] and repent.
If therefore thou shalt not watch, I will come on thee
as a thief, and thou shalt not know what hour I will come
upon thee. 4 Thou hast [f] a few names even in Sardis,
which have not [g] defiled their garments; and they shall
walk with me [h] in white: for they are worthy. 5 He
that overcometh, the same shall be clothed in white rai-
ment; and I will not [i] blot out his name out of [k] the
book of life, but [l] I will confess his name before my
Father, and before his angels. 6 [m] He that hath an
ear, let him hear what the Spirit saith unto the church-
es.

v. 1—6. To the angel of the church of Sardis is this epistle directed.

1. It comes from him *that hath the seven Spirits of God,* who is the divine Mediator, hath all variety and fulness of the gifts and grace of the Spirit to bestow, *and the seven stars,* guiding and directing his ministering servants, and giving them all their light and influence.

2. The contents are melancholy. 1. *I know thy works, that thou hast a name that thou livest, and art dead,* amidst all thy specious appearances of religion, I know that thy professions in general are hypocritical, and many who have a name among the members of the church are really dead in trespasses and sins, and others too cold and lukewarm. *Be watchful, and strengthen the things which remain, that are ready to die,* before all vital godliness be utterly destroyed: *for I have not found thy works perfect before God;* they are but as the carcass, when the spirit is fled, thy duties lifeless, thy services insincere. *Remember therefore how thou hast received and heard, and hold fast, and repent.* *Note,* (1.) A form of godliness will avail nothing, if the power of it be

be lost. (2.) They, who feel their souls under decays, need jealously watch, and cry to God for quickening influences to revive his work in their hearts. (3.) The way to recover from our backslidings is to consider how we departed, what God's word hath said of the sin and danger of such a conduct, to repent of our unfaithfulness, and still to cleave to those promises that preserve the soul from despair, and encourage us to return to God. [2.] He sharply threatens them. *If therefore thou shalt not watch*, but goest on careless and secure, *I will come on thee as a thief, and thou shalt not know what hour I will come upon thee*. *Note*, Christ's appearing at death or judgment will be very terrible and surprising to the backslider in heart, when too late he will be startled from the slumbers of security. [3.] He encourages the few faithful among them. *Thou hast a few names even in Sardis*, cold and careless as the generality of professors are, *which have not defiled their garments*, who have kept themselves unspotted from the world, and maintained becoming purity of doctrine and holiness amidst abounding ungodliness, *and they shall walk with me in white*, as sacred priests, and triumphant conquerors, decked with glory, honour, and immortality, *for they are worthy*, and meet for the inheritance among the saints in light.

3. The conclusion. *He that overcometh, the same shall be clothed in white raiment*, shining in splendid robes of righteousness and victory, *and I will not blot out his name out of the book of life, but I will confess his name before my Father, and before his angels*, in the great day of my appearing to judge the world. *He that hath an ear, let him hear what the Spirit saith unto the churches*. *Note*, They who fight manfully under Christ's banner, will be acknowledged by him with the most distinguished favour and honour, when he shall come to reward their fidelity.

7 And to the angel of the church in Philadelphia,
write, These things saith [n] he that is holy, [o] he that is
true, he that hath [p] the key of David, [q] he that openeth,
and no man shutteth; and [r] shutteth, and no man open-
eth; 8 [s] I know thy works: behold, I have set before
thee [t] an open door, and no man can shut it: for thou
hast a little strength, and hast kept my word, and hast
not denied my name. 9 Behold, I will make [u] them of
the synagogue of Satan (which say they are Jews, and
are not, but do lie) behold, [x] I will make them to come
and worship before thy feet, and to know that I have
loved thee. 10 Because thou hast kept the word of my
patience, [y] I also will keep thee from the hour of temp-
tation, which shall come upon all the world, to try them
that dwell upon the earth. 11 Behold, [z] I come quick-
ly: [a] hold that fast which thou hast, that no man take
[b] thy crown. 12 Him that overcometh, will I make
[c] a pillar in the temple of my God, and he shall go no
more out: and [d] I will write upon him the name of my
God, and the name of the city of my God, *which is*
new Jerusalem, which cometh down out of heaven
from my God: and [e] I *will write upon him* my new name.
13 [f] He that hath an ear, let him hear what the Spirit
saith unto the churches.

n Acts iii. 14. o Chap. i. 5. Ver. 14. p Isa. xxii. 22. Luke i. 32. Chap. i. 18. q Mat. xvi. 19. r Job xii. 14. s Chap. ii. 2. t 1 Cor. xvi. 9. 2 Cor. ii. 12. u Chap. ii. 9. x Isa. xlix. 23. & lx. 14. y 1 Cor. x. 13. 2 Pet. ii. 9. z Phil. iv. 5. Chap. i. 3. & xxii. 7, 12. a Chap. ii. 25. Ver. 3. b Chap. ii. 10. c 1 Kings vii. 21. d Chap. ii. 17. & xiv. 1. & xxii. 4. e Gal. iv. 26. Heb. xii. 22. Chap. xxi. 2, 10. f Chap. xxii. 4. g Chap. ii. 7.

v. 7—13. The sixth epistle is directed to the angel of the church of Philadelphia. We have,

1. The preface. *These things saith he that is holy, he that is true*, who by nature is essential truth and holiness, the substance of all the prophecies and promises, the true Messiah, *he that hath the key of David*, on whose shoulder is the government laid, *he that openeth* the gates of the grave and the kingdom of heaven to his people, *and no man shutteth*, no creature can exclude those from his eternal glory whom he hath chosen for himself, *and shutteth* up the wicked in the dreadful prison of eternal torment, *and no man openeth*, or can open the gates of the impassible gulph, to rescue the damned from thence.

2. The contents. [1.] *I know thy works*, and regard them with delight and approbation. *Behold, I have set before thee an open door*, that my word should run, and have free access, and be glorified, *and no man can shut it*, or obstruct the progress of the gospel: *for thou hast a little strength*, and some measure, though it be small, of true grace and spiritual attainments, *and hast kept my word* with fidelity and stedfastness, *and hast not denied my name*, nor revolted from the profession of the faith amidst the wiles of deceivers, and the persecutions of avowed enemies. *Behold, I will make them of the synagogue of Satan (which say they are Jews and are not, but do lie) behold*, with thankfulness and delight, *I will make them*, who, under pretence of zeal for Judaism, corrupt the doctrine of Christianity, and whose practice is vicious as their principles are erroneous, *to come and worship before thy feet*, humbled into the dust, and brought with humble confession of their faults to take shame to themselves, *and to know that I have loved thee*, with distinguishing favour and regard. *Note*, Sooner or later the bitterest persecutors of God's people shall be made to [illegible] how dear they are to him; and

be covered with everlasting confusion in the view of their malice against them. [2.] A gracious promise is given to the faithful. *Because thou hast kept the word of my patience*, and maintained the profession of the unadulterated gospel, amidst the malignant opposition of envenomed foes, *I also will keep thee from the hour of temptation*, that thou shalt not apostatize from the truth under those fiery persecutions, *which shall*, under the bloody heathen emperors of Rome, *come upon all the world, to try them that dwell upon the earth*, and shew who are true and false professors. *Note*, (1.) They who steadily cleave to Christ, shall be kept in the most dangerous days. (2.) We must prepare for temptation; it will come; and if we are unprepared, we shall be in imminent danger. [3.] He adds a glorious encouragement. *Behold, I come quickly*; the time therefore of suffering cannot but be momentary: *hold that fast which thou hast*, with holy resolution cleaving to the word of truth, *that no man take thy crown*, nor by fraud or violence seduce or intimidate thee from the truth of the gospel, and rob thee of the reward of fidelity. *Note*, A sense of the speedy coming of Jesus for our help, is the greatest support under every affliction.

3. The conclusion. *Him that overcometh, will I make a pillar in the temple of my God, and he shall go no more out*, admitted into the eternal presence of God in glory, and there shall be ever with the Lord, enjoying that beatific vision. *And I will write upon him the name of my God*, as one of the redeemed from the earth, *and the name of the city of my God, which is the new Jerusalem, which cometh down out of heaven from my God*, as a citizen, intitled to all the blessings and privileges of that celestial city: *and I will write upon him my new name*, acknowledging him for a Christian indeed, and bringing him to share in all the glories of my kingdom. *He that hath an ear, let him hear what the Spirit saith unto the churches*, and well worthy is it of our deepest and most serious attention.

14 And unto the angel of the church of the Laodi-
ceans, write, These things saith [h] the Amen, [i] the faith-
ful and true witness, [k] the beginning of the creation of
God; 15 [l] I know thy works, that thou art neither
cold nor hot: I would thou wert cold or hot. 16. So
then because thou art lukewarm, and neither cold nor
hot, I will spue thee out of my mouth. 17 Because
thou sayst, [m] I am rich, and increased with goods, and
have need of nothing; and knowest not that thou art
wretched, and miserable, and poor, and blind, and na-
ked: 18 I counsel thee [n] to buy of me gold tried in the
fire, that thou mayst be rich; and [o] white raiment, that
thou mayst be clothed, and *that* the shame of thy na-
kedness do not appear; and anoint thine eyes with eye-
salve, that thou mayst see. 19 [p] As many as I love, I
rebuke and chasten: be zealous therefore, and repent.
20 Behold, I stand at the door and knock: If any man
hear my voice, and open the door, [q] I will come in to
him, and will sup with him, and he with me. 21 To
him that overcometh [r] will I grant to sit with me in my
throne, even as I also overcame, and am set down with
my Father in his throne. 22 [s] He that hath an ear, let
him hear what the Spirit saith unto the churches.

h Isa. lxv. 16. i Chap. i. 5. & xix. 11. & xxii. 6. k Col. i. 15. l Chap. ii. 2. m Hos. xii. 8. 1 Cor. iv. 8. n Isa. lv. 1. Mat. xiii. 44. & xxv. 9. o 2 Cor. v. 3. Chap. vii. 13. & xvi. 15. & xix. 8. p Job v. 17. Prov. iii. 12. Heb. xii. 5, 6. Jam. i. 12. q Cant. v. 2. John xiv. 23. r Mat. xix. 28. Luke xxii. 30. 1 Cor. vi. 2. 2 Tim. ii. 12. Chap. ii. 26, 27. s Chap. ii. 7.

v. 14—22. The last epistle is directed to the angel of the church of Laodicea. We have,

1. The preface. *These things saith the Amen, the faithful and true witness*, whose testimony is infallible, and neither can nor will deceive his people, or fail of the accomplishment of his promises; *the beginning of the creation of God*, the author of life and being to every creature, the head of vital influence to his people, having in all things the pre-eminence, and possessing universal dominion in heaven and earth.

2. The contents. [1.] A melancholy account is given of their state. *I know thy works, that thou art neither cold nor hot*, but listless and lukewarm: *I would thou wert cold or hot*, either be sincerely zealous, or make no profession, rather than disgrace it by an unsuitable conduct. [2.] A threatening is added. *So then because thou art lukewarm, and neither cold nor hot, I will spue thee out of my mouth*, as loathsome and nauseous. [3.] The cause of their declension is remarked. *Because thou sayst, I am rich, and increased with goods, and have need of nothing*, filled with spiritual gifts, abounding in worldly wealth; and thus they flattered themselves with high imaginations of their own excellence, *and knowest not that thou art wretched, and miserable, and poor, and blind, and naked*, insensible to thy spiritual wants and poverty, ignorant of all true wisdom, destitute of real grace and righteousness, and exposed to the storm of divine wrath. *Note*, (1.) Nothing is more fatal to the soul, than a vain conceit of our own excellencies. (2.) Many flatter themselves confident of heaven, whose ways lead down to death and hell. [4.] He gives them the kindest advice. *I counsel thee to buy of me*, that is, to come to me out of my fulness to receive freely the supply of every want, *gold tried in the fire, that thou mayst be rich*, the gold

of my Spirit, wisdom, and grace, and all the spiritual treasures which I bestow on my redeemed, *and white raiment, that thou mayest be cloath d*, even that spotless and everlasting righteousness which I have wrought out, *and* will put upon thee, *that the shame of thy nakedness do not appear*, but that all thy guilt and deformity may be for ever hid from the eyes of divine purity and justice *and anoint thine eyes with eye-salve, that thou mayest see* the things that make for thy everlasting peace, and all the mysteries of gospel-grace, no longer blinded by ignorance, prejudice, and worldly lusts *Note*, They who would be spiritually rich, and cloathed, and wise unto salvation, must come to Christ out of his fulness to buy, and, blessed be his name, the purchase is to be made without money and without price, for he freely gives to the miserable and the destitute [5] A gracious encouragement is yet given them to repent *As many as I love, I rebuke and chasten*, the reproofs of my word, and the corrections of my providence, are the rod of love *be zealous, therefore*, cast off this lukewarm spirit, let the fire of zeal and love kindle in your hearts, *and repent* of past unfaithfulness *Behold*, such is my patience and condescensions, *I yet stand*, waiting to be gracious, *at the door* of your hearts *if any man hear my voice*, attends to my calls and warnings, *and open the door*, in faith and penitence to receive me with eager welcome into his soul, *I will come in to him, and will sup with him, and he with me*, honouring him with my presence, and love, and blessed communion *Note* (1) The Lord's chastisements are signs, not of his wrath, but of his love (2) Christ, by his providences, word, and spirit, knocks at the door of our hearts, and they who welcome him in, shall find him not only as a guest that tarrieth for a night, but whose communion shall make us blessed for eternity

3 The conclusion *To him that overcometh* the corruptions of his nature, and the temptations of the world, *will I grant to sit with me in my throne, even as I also overcame, and am set down with my Father in his throne*, to such infinite and transcendent glory and dignity shall he be exalted in the great day of my appearing, and come to reign with me triumphant over every foe for ever and ever *He that hath an ear, let him hear what the Spirit saith unto the churches*, for these things are written for our learning to the latest ages, and blessed are they who attend to the warnings, reproofs, exhortations, encouragements, and instructions here revealed, and feel their mighty influence

CHAP IV.

In this chapter the prophetical scene begins, and as the epistolary part opened with a vision of Christ, chap 1 so this part is introduced with a glorious appearance of the great God, whose throne is in heaven, compassed about with the heavenly host John, 1 Records the heavenly sight he saw, from ver 1—8 And then, 2 The heavenly songs he heard, from ver 8, to the end

1. AFter this I looked, and behold, a door *was* open-
ed in heaven and the first voice which I heard,
was as it were of a trumpet talking with me, which said,
Come up hither, and I will shew thee things which
a Chap i 10 must be hereafter 2 And immediately [a] I was in the
b Isa vi 1 spirit and behold, [b] a throne was set in heaven, and
Jer xvii 12 *one* sat on the throne 3 And [c] he that sat, was to look
c Chap xxi 11—19 upon like a jasper, and a sardine stone and *there was*
d Gen ix [d] a rainbow round about the throne, in sight like unto
13—16 Isa liv 9, 10 an emerald. 4 And round about the throne *were* four
and twenty seats and upon the seats I saw four and
twenty elders sitting, clothed in white raiment, and
e Chap v 10 they had [e] on their heads crowns of gold 5 And out
f Exod xix 16, Ex xviii of the throne proceeded [f] lightnings and thundrings, and
13, 14 voices And *there were* [g] seven lamps of fire burning be-
g Chap iii 1 fore the throne, which are the seven Spirits of God 6
h 1 Kings vii 23 [h] And before the throne *there was* a sea of glass like unto
crystal And in the midst of the throne, and round
i Ezek i 5—10 about the throne *were* [i] four beasts full of eyes before
and behind. 7 And the first beast *was* like a lion, and
the second beast like a calf, and the third beast had a
face as a man, and the fourth beast was like a flying
eagle.

v 1—7 Prepared by what he had seen for further discoveries, a door is opened to him in heaven, and the voice of Jesus, which he had heard before, loud and solemn as the trumpet which was heard of old from Sinai's top, calls him to come up thither, that he might be informed of the great events of providence relative to the church. Instantly a sacred rapture seized his spirit, and a glorious vision presents itself to his view

1 He saw a throne of majesty and judgment, compassed with a rainbow beautiful as the emerald, the emblem of that everlasting covenant which God hath established with his people, on whom no deluge of wrath shall ever descend. (*See Gen* ix 13, &c)

2 Upon the throne sat the eternal Jehovah, the antient of days, the Creator, Governor, and Judge of all, shining like the jasper and sardine stone, with brightness infinitely surpassing those precious stones which glittered in the high priest's breast-plate, inexpressibly glorious in holiness, and every divine perfection

3 Around the throne were four and twenty elders seated cloathed with white raiment, and on their heads they had crowns of gold, the representatives of the whole body of the faithful now perfected in holiness, admitted to their eternal rest, brought into God's immediate presence, enjoying that beatific vision, and crowned with glory, honour, and immortality

4 Out of the throne proceeded lightnings, and thundrings and voices, signifying the mighty and powerful energy of the gospel word, which spread like lightning through the world, or those tremendous judgments which he executes on the earth

5 There were seven lamps burning before the throne, which are the seven spirits of God, the emblem of the variety and perfection of the gifts and graces which the Holy Ghost bestows

6 Before the throne was a sea of glass, like unto chrystal, in allusion, as is supposed, to the molten sea, where the priests washed, (*Exod* xxx 18, 19) the figure of Christ's blood, which cleanseth from all sin

7 In the midst of the throne, and round about it, were four living creatures, full of eyes before and behind, the first like a lion, the second like an ox, the third with the face of a man, and the fourth like a flying eagle, the same as *Ezek* i 5 and seem to represent the ministers of grace, who are themselves alive to God by his Spirit, the happy instruments of quickening others, standing between God and the people, to speak in his name, full of light and spiritual understanding, bold in the cause of truth as lions, indefatigable in labour as the ox, possessed of all prudence and compassion as men, soaring high as the eagle in the knowledge of divine mysteries, and winging their flight heavenward, with unremitting zeal and ardor.

8 And the four beasts had each [a] of them six wings a Isa vi 2,
about him, and *they were* full of eyes within, and they 3
rest not day and night, saying, Holy, holy, holy, Lord
God almighty, which was, and is, and is to come 9
And when those beasts give glory, and honour, and
thanks to him that sat on the throne, who liveth for
ever and ever, 10 The four and twenty elders fall
down before him that sat on the throne, and worship
him that liveth for ever and ever, and cast their crowns
before the throne, saying, 11 [b] Thou art worthy, O b Rom xi
Lord, to receive glory, and honour, and power for 36 Prov
thou hast created all things, and for thy pleasure they xvi 4
are, and were created.

v 8—11 The four living creatures, like the seraphim, (*Isa* vi 2) had six wings, and they were full of eyes within, deep-read in the knowledge of their own hearts, and attending to the notices of God's Spirit in their souls, and with ceaseless adorations they worship the eternal, unchangeable, holy, and triune Jehovah

When these representatives of the gospel ministers thus led the song of heaven, the elders, who represented the church of the redeemed, joined in their adorations, casting their crowns before the throne, and, humbly prostrate, ascribed eternal glory, honour, and power to the ever-living Jehovah, the Creator and Ruler of all, by whose sovereign pleasure every creature exists, and is designed to shew forth his praise *Note*, (1) All things are of God, and for God his own glory is the end of all his works, and should be the design of ours (2) God's saints on earth are called upon to join the services of heaven, and to unite in the same sacred ascriptions of praise to him that liveth for ever and ever (3) The highest are the humblest beings they who approach nearest to the throne, are most deeply sensible, that to sovereign grace alone they owe their unutterable bliss, and therefore cast down their golden crowns before their Lord, and say, Thou, and thou alone, art worthy to receive the glory

CHAP V

In the foregoing chapter the prophetical scene was opened in the sight and hearing of the apostle He saw God on the throne of glory and government, surrounded with his holy ones, and receiving their adorations Now the counsels and decrees of God are set before the apostle, as in a book, which God held in his right hand, and this book is represented, 1 As sealed in the hand of God, from ver 1—6 2 As taken into the hand of Christ the Redeemer, to be unsealed and opened, from ver. 6, to the end

1 AND I saw in the right hand of him that sat on
the throne, a book written within and on the
backside, [a] sealed with seven seals 2 And I saw a a Isa xxix 11
strong

ſtrong angel proclaiming with a loud voice, Who is
worthy to open the book, and to looſe the ſeals thereof?
3 And no man in heaven, nor in earth, neither under
the earth, was able to open the book, neither to look
thereon 4 And I wept much becauſe no man was
found worthy to open, and to read the book, neither to
look thereon 5 And one of the elders ſaith unto me,
Weep not behold, the [b] Lion of the tribe of Juda,
[c] the root of David, hath prevailed to open the book,
and to looſe the ſeals thereof

b Gen xlix 9
c Iſa xi 1, 10.

v 1—5 We have here,

1 The prophetic volume, which was in the hand of him that ſat on the throne, containing the events which in ſucceeding ages ſhould befal his church It *was written within and on the backſide*, like Ezekiel's roll Or, *on the backſide* may be joined with the following clauſe, as ſealed there with ſeven ſeals, not probably all on the outſide, but as there were ſeven parchment rolls, one under the other, when the firſt ſeal was opened, and the volume unrolled, then the ſecond ſeal and volume appeared Known to God from the beginning are all his works, but they are inſcrutable by us, till in his word he is pleaſed to reveal his deſigns, or by his providence to accompliſh his eternal purpoſes

2 The proclamation iſſued forth by a ſtrong angel *Who is worthy to open the book, and to looſe the ſeals thereof?* but no creature was found in heaven, earth, or hell, capable of penetrating into the divine decrees, or of foretelling the events of futurity This is God's prerogative alone

3 The grief of the apoſtle at finding no creature who dared eſſay the arduous taſk He wept bitterly, that he could not gain a knowledge of the things contained in the book, apprehending them to be of ſignal importance

4 One of the elders kindly obſerved his tears, and cheared his afflicted heart, ſaying, *Weep not behold, the Lion of the tribe of Judah*, the mighty Lord and Saviour, *the root of David*, not only after the fleſh his offspring, but, as God, the ſource of all honour and bleſſedneſs to his people, *hath prevailed to open the book, and to looſe the ſeven ſeals thereof* Note, God's people are often needleſly afflicting themſelves with fears were their eyes more ſteadily fixed upon their great Redeemer, their tears never need to flow

6 And I beheld, and lo, in the midſt of the throne,
and of the four beaſts, and in the midſt of the elders
ſtood a Lamb as it had been [d] ſlain, having [e] ſeven
horns, and [f] ſeven eyes, which are the ſeven [g] Spirits of
God ſent forth into all the earth 7 And he came and
took the book out of the right hand of him that ſat up-
on the throne 8 And when he had taken the book,
the four beaſts, and four *and* twenty elders fell down be-
fore the Lamb, having every one of them harps and
golden vials full of odours [h] which are the prayers of
ſaints. 9. And they ſung a new ſong, ſaying, Thou
art worthy to take the book, and to open the ſeals
thereof for thou waſt ſlain, [i] and haſt [k] redeemed us to
God by thy blood, out of every kindred, and tongue,
and people, and nation, 10 And haſt made us unto
our God [l] kings and prieſts and we ſhall reign on the
earth 11 And I beheld, and I heard the voice of ma-
ny angels round about the throne, and the beaſts, and
elders [m] and the number of them was ten thouſand
times ten thouſand, and thouſands of thouſands, [n] 12
Saying with a loud voice, Worthy is the Lamb that was
ſlain, to receive power, and riches, and wiſdom, and
ſtrength, and honour, and glory, and bleſſing 13 And
every creature which is in heaven, and on the earth, and
under the earth, and ſuch as are in the ſea, and all that
are in them, heard I, ſaying, Bleſſing, and honour, and
glory, and power, *be* unto him that ſitteth upon the
throne, and unto the Lamb for ever and ever [o] 14
And the four beaſts ſaid, Amen And the four and
twenty elders fell down and worſhipped him that liveth
for ever and ever [p]

d John i 29 Heb ix 14.
e Dan viii —4 Pſal cxxxii 17
f Col ii 3
g Zech iii 9 iv 10
h Pſ cxli 2 Chap viii 3 4
i Iſa liii 7—10
k Luke i 71 75
l Chap i 6
m Gen xxxii 8 1 John v 7 1 Pet ii 13
n 5 Rom viii 37
n Pſ xxxiv 7 2 Kings vi 16 17
n Dan vii 10 Pſal lxviii 17
o Acts xx
p Heb xii

v 6—14 Behold, the wonderful perſonage appears, alone found worthy to unlooſe the ſeals, and unfold this ſacred volume

1 He is deſcribed, *as a Lamb* that *had been ſlain*, and by his own blood having taken away the ſins of the world, ſtood as our great *High prieſt*, juſt before the throne, within the circle of the elders and the living creatures, as the advocate of his redeemed, and ever pleading the oblation he once offered in his own body on the tree He had *ſeven horns*, denoting the perfection of his power and dominion as the univerſal *King* over his church, to protect his people, and puſh his enemies till he hath conſumed them and his *ſeven eyes, which are the ſeven Spirits of God ſent forth into all the earth*, repreſent the treaſures of wiſdom, grace, and knowledge, which as the great *prophet* he poſſeſſes, and diſpenſes to all his miniſters and members, according to their various wants *He came*, as fully qualified in the virtue of his all-ſufficient merit, *and took the book out of the right hand of him that ſat upon the throne*, who readily gave it to him, acknowledging thereby, that he was worthy to unlooſe the ſeals, and reveal the myſterious contents

2 Inſtantly all heaven reſounds with praiſe, the church triumphant in heaven begin the ſong, angels repeat the ſound, and every creature joins the ſacred choir, and echoes loud allelujahs

[1] The four beaſts and four and twenty elders fall down before the Lamb with humble adoration, their hearts, like their golden lyres, tuned to their Redeemer's praiſe, and vials full of the moſt grateful incenſe, even the prayers of the ſaints, breathed before him their ſweet perfume United in ſacred chorus, high they raiſed their voices, and uttered this moſt glorious ſong, ſaying, *Thou art worthy to take the book, and to open the ſeals thereof*, qualified fully for the diſcharge of thy mediatorial office, *for thou waſt ſlain*, for our tranſgreſſions, *and haſt redeemed us to God by thy blood, out of every kindred, and tongue, and people, and nation*, that we thy choſen might be delivered from the bondage of ſin, Satan, and death, and reſtored to favour and communion with the Moſt High, *and haſt made us unto our God*, now reconciled in a covenant of everlaſting love, *kings and prieſts and we ſhall reign on the earth*, exalted to the higheſt dignity and honour, and ruled ſuperior to all our ſpiritual enemies Who can without ſome glow of the ſame ſacred rapture read their ſong, or not long to join with them before the throne?

[2] The angels, who, without the living creatures and the elders, in ſhining ranks innumerable compaſſed the throne, joined their adorations, and cried, *Worthy is the Lamb that was ſlain, to receive power, and riches, and wiſdom, and ſtrength, and honour, and glory, and bleſſing*

[3] The whole creation echoes back the ſound All in heaven, earth, or ſea, whether angels, the ſpirits of the juſt departed, the living here below, creatures animate or inanimate, all, all utter forth their united praiſes, *ſaying, Bleſſing, and honour, and glory, and power, be unto him that ſitteth upon the throne, and unto the Lamb for ever and ever!* The ſame divine glory is aſcribed to each of the ſacred Perſons, as being one in eſſence, and alike the objects of every creature's worſhip and adoration

[4] The four living creatures cloſe with their ſolemn *Amen*, and the four and twenty elders, the repreſentatives of the church, with humble proſtration fell down and worſhipped him that liveth for ever and ever Oh when ſhall I join this heavenly choir, and with them in heart and lip unite in theſe eternal praiſes of God and of the Lamb!

CHAP VI

Hitherto the waters of the ſanctuary have been as thoſe in Ezekiel's viſion, only to the ankles, or to the knees, or to the loins at leaſt, but here they begin to be a river that cannot be paſſed over The viſions which John ſaw, the epiſtles to the churches, the ſongs of praiſe, in the two foregoing chapters, had ſome things dark and hard to be underſtood, and yet they were rather milk for babes, than meat for ſtrong men, but now we are to launch into the deep, and our buſineſs is not ſo much to fathom it, as to let down our net to take a draught

In this chapter ſix of the ſeven ſeals are opened, and the viſions attending them are related, the firſt ſeal in ver 1 2. the ſecond ſeal in ver 3, 4 the third ſeal in ver 5, 6 the fourth ſeal in ver 7, 8 the fifth ſeal in ver 9—11 the ſixth ſeal in ver 12, 13, &c

1 AND I ſaw when the Lamb opened one [a] of the
ſeals, and I heard, as it were the noiſe of thun-
der, one of the four beaſts, ſaying, Come, and ſee 2
And I ſaw, and behold, a white horſe, and he that ſat
on him had a bow, and a crown was given unto him,
and he went forth conquering and to conquer [b].

a Mat. xxviii 18.
b Iſ xlv 5 Ez cx 3 1 Cor xv 25

v 1, 2 The ſix firſt ſeals are ſuppoſed to contain the events relative to the church under the heathen emperors, till in the reign of Conſtantine paganiſm was utterly ſubverted, about the year 323

On the Lamb's opening the firſt ſeal, one of the living creatures, with a voice loud as the thunder, ſummoned the apoſtle's attention, and bid him come and ſee the viſion When lo! *a white horſe* appeared, and one ſat thereon, carrying a bow, and a crown on his head, and he went forth conquering and to conquer This repreſents the miniſtration of the goſpel, which brings joy, and peace, and triumph to the ſoul, of which the white horſe is the emblem The bow of Jeſus, like that of Jonathan, returns not empty the arrows of his goſpel, through the power of the Spirit, become effectual to ſubdue the ſinners ſouls his crown denotes his victories and dignity He muſt prevail, and, in ſpite of all oppoſition, his goſpel ſhall go on conquering and to conquer, till in the hearts of his redeemed every corruption is ſubdued, till throughout the world his truth is diffuſed, and to the lateſt ages he will continue his conqueſts, till the kingdoms of the earth ſhall become the kingdoms of the Lord and of his Chriſt Haſten, O Lord, that happy day

3 And when he had opened the ſecond ſeal, I heard
the ſecond beaſt ſay, Come, and ſee. 4. And there went
c Zech iii 6 out another horſe *that was* red c and *power* was given to
him that ſat thereon, to take peace from the earth, and
that they ſhould kill one another and there was given
unto him a great ſword

v 3, 4 The ſecond ſeal being opened, he hath a ſummons repeated from the ſecond beaſt to come and ſee And behold, another red horſe, and one armed with a ſword ſat thereon, to whom power was given to take peace from the earth And this ſeems to prefigure the bloody wars, which, during the reigns of Trajan and Adrian, conſumed innumerable multitudes of Jews and Romans, the common perſecutors of Chriſtianity, till about the year 138 *Note*, (1) Perſecutors of God's people ſhall have blood given them to drink (2) The Lord can ſet his enemies at variance among themſelves, and makes often one wicked nation to be the ſcourge of his vengeance upon another

5 And when he had opened the third ſeal, I heard
the third beaſt ſay, Come, and ſee. And I beheld, and
lo, a black horſe, and he that ſat on him had a pair of
balances in his hand 6 And I heard a voice in the
midſt of the four beaſts ſay, A meaſure of wheat for a
d Lev xxvi 26 Lam v 10 Ezek iv 16 penny, and three meaſures of barley for a penny d, and
ſee thou hurt not the oil and the wine

v 5, 6 The third ſeal opens, and another ſummons bids him come and ſee, when lo, a black horſe, the emblem of famine, appeared, and one with a pair of balances ſat on him; when one of the beaſts cried, A meaſure of wheat for a penny, and three meaſures of barley for a penny, and ſee thou hurt not the oil and the wine The famine would fall chiefly on the poor, who for the price of a whole day's labour, could but juſt procure bread for their ſubſiſtence, which happened under the reigns of the two Antonines, between the years 138 and 179 *Note*, When one judgment is not effectual to lead ſinners to repentance, a ſecond follows at its heels.

7 And when he had opened the fourth ſeal, I heard
the voice of the fourth beaſt ſay, Come and ſee 8
And I looked, and behold, a pale horſe, and his name
e Chap xx 6, 14 that ſat on him was Death, and hell e followed with
him and power was given unto them over the fourth
part of the earth, to kill with ſword, and with hunger,
f Ezek v 17 xiv 21 xxxiii 27 and with death, and with the beaſts of the earth f

v 7, 8 The fourth ſeal being opened, the fourth beaſt bids him come and ſee when behold, a pale horſe, Death ſat thereon, and the grave attended him, to devour the corpſes of the fallen, or hell, to receive their ſouls By war, by famine, by peſtilence, and the beaſts of the earth, permiſſion is given them to ſlay even a fourth part of the earth and hiſtory informs us of the dreadful deſolations which waſted the Roman empire, from the reign of Maximinus to Dioclehan, in righteous vengeance for their bloody perſecutions of Chriſtianity *Note*, (1) Death marches as a conqueror through the earth, and, when attended with hell at his feet, is indeed a king of terrors (2) God's quiver is never exhauſted, and when he contends, he muſt prevail

9 And when he had opened the fifth ſeal, I ſaw un-
g Lev iv 7. der the altar g the ſouls of them that were ſlain for the
word of God, and for the teſtimony which they held
10 And they cried with a loud voice, ſaying, How
long, O Lord, holy and true, doſt thou not judge and
h Job xxiv 12 avenge our blood on them that dwell on the earth h?
11 And white robes were given unto every one of
them, and it was ſaid unto them, that they ſhould reſt
yet for a little ſeaſon, until their fellow-ſervants alſo, and
their brethren, that ſhould be killed as they *were*, ſhould
be fulfilled

v 9—11 On opening the fifth ſeal a new ſcene is diſcloſed The ſouls of the martyrs appear at the foot of the altar of incenſe, who had been ſlain for the word of God, and for the teſtimony which they held; and they united in their fervent ſupplication, *ſaying, How long, O Lord, holy and true, doſt thou not* diſplay thy perfections, and *judge and avenge our blood on them that dwell on the earth?* In anſwer to their prayer, and in token of their acceptance, *white robes*, the emblems of righteouſneſs and honour, *were given unto every one of them*, *and it was ſaid unto them, that they ſhould reſt yet for a little ſeaſon*, patiently expecting their final triumphs over all their foes, *until their fellow ſervants alſo, and their brethren, that ſhould be killed as they were, ſhould be fulfilled*, and then a period ſhould be put to the bloody perſecutions of the pagan emperors, by the acceſſion of Conſtantine, about the year 323. *Note*, (1) The blood of martyrs, and the ſufferings of the perſecuted, cry for vengeance to a holy God, and it will ſurely come upon the heads of their enemies (2) The time for the exerciſe of faith and patience is *a little ſeaſon*, but the glory which ſhall follow will be eternal

12 And I beheld when he had opened the ſixth ſeal,
and lo, there was a great earthquake, and the ſun be-
came black as ſackcloth of hair, and the moon became
as blood, 13 And the ſtars of heaven fell unto the
earth, even as a fig-tree caſteth her untimely figs when
ſhe is ſhaken of a mighty wind: 14 And the heaven
departed as a ſcroll when it is rolled together, and every
mountain and iſland were removed out of their places i. i Iſa xiii 9—19 xxiv 23 xxxiv 4. Ezek xxxii 7 8 Hag ii 21, 22 Mat xxiv 29
15 And the kings of the earth, and the great men, and
the rich men, the chief captains, and the mighty men,
and every bondman, and every freeman hid k themſelves
in the dens, and in the rocks of the mountains, 16 k Iſa ii 17—21
And ſaid to the mountains and rocks, Fall on us, l and l Hoſ x. 8
hide us from the face of him that ſitteth on the throne,
and from the wrath of the Lamb 17 For the great
day of his wrath is come, and who ſhall be able to
ſtand m? m Pſ ii 12

v 12—17 On opening the ſixth ſeal, a dreadful earthquake ſeemed to threaten univerſal deſtruction The luminaries of heaven grew dark as ſackcloth, the ſtars dropped, extinguiſhed from their ſpheres, as when the ſtorm ſhakes down the untimely figs, the heaven itſelf departed as a ſcroll, every iſland and mountain fled affrighted, and univerſal conſternation ſeized all ranks and degrees, from the king upon the throne, to the meaneſt ſlave, who ſought for ſhelter in dens and caves, and in their horror wiſhed to be for ever covered under the rocks and mountains, from the face of him who ſat upon the throne, and from the wrath of the Lamb, for now by woful experience they felt his terrible vengeance, which they could neither flee from nor reſiſt

This viſion ſeems to repreſent the utter and irrecoverable overthrow of heatheniſm, when that wonderful revolution was brought about in the empire, and under Conſtantine idolatry was aboliſhed, the idols of paganiſm deſtroyed, and all thoſe who had before been the inveterate enemies of the Chriſtian name, covered with confuſion

And what is here preſented in viſion, will be moſt emphatically verified in the great day of the perdition of ungodly men When trembling before the intolerable wrath of the offended Judge, in vain the mountains and rocks will be invoked to fall on the ſinner's guilty head naked and defenceleſs he muſt be expoſed to all the furious blaſts of vengeance, and ſink down into everlaſting burnings, under black unfathomable deſpair! Lord, gather not my ſoul with ſinners!

CHAP VII

After the opening of the ſix ſeals, which foretold great calamities in the world, and before the ſound of the ſeven trumpets, which gave notice of great corruptions ariſing in the church, a ſhort reſpite is given to the church, from the years 323 to 337 We have, 1 An account of the reſtraint laid upon the winds, ver 1—3 2 The ſealing of the ſervants of God, ver 4—9 3 The ſongs of angels and ſaints on this occaſion, ver 9—13 4 A deſcription of the honour and happineſs of thoſe that had faithfully ſerved Chriſt, and ſuffered for him, ver 13, &c

1. AND after theſe things, I ſaw four angels ſtand-
ing on the four corners of the earth, holding
the four winds a of the earth, that the wind ſhould not a Jer xlix 36 Dan vii 2
blow on the earth, nor on the ſea, nor on any tree 2
And I ſaw another angel aſcending from the eaſt, having
the ſeal of the living God and he cried with a loud
voice to the four angels, to whom it was given to hurt
the earth and the ſea, 3 Saying, Hurt not the earth,
neither the ſea, nor the trees, till we have ſealed b the ſer- b Ezek ix 4, 6 &c xi 22, 23
vants of our God in their foreheads

v 1—3 The winds and ſtorms of perſecution are now for a while huſhed in peace, and the church enjoys undiſturbed tranquillity, whilſt miniſtring angels, at the command of the great and uncreated angel of the covenant, who bore the impreſs of the living God, and beſtows his Spirit upon his people, whereby they are ſealed unto the day of redemption, reſtrain for a while the deſolating judgments which had before deſtroyed the earth

4 And I heard the number of them which were sealed
and there were sealed an hundred *and* forty *and* four thou-
c Gen xxxii 28 & xvii ...9 sand, of all the tribes of the children of Israel c 5 Of
the tribe of Juda *were* sealed twelve thousand Of the
tribe of Reuben *were* sealed twelve thousand Of the
tribe of Gad *were* sealed twelve thousand 6 Of the
tribe of Aser *were* sealed twelve thousand Of the tribe
of Nephthalim *were* sealed twelve thousand. Of the
tribe of Manasses *were* sealed twelve thousand 7 Of
the tribe of Simeon *were* sealed twelve thousand Of the
tribe of Levi *were* sealed twelve thousand Of the tribe
of Issachar *were* sealed twelve thousand 8. Of the tribe
of Zabulon *were* sealed twelve thousand Of the tribe
of Joseph *were* sealed twelve thousand Of the tribe of
Benjamin *were* sealed twelve thousand.

v 4—8 The saints, who are here sealed out of the twelve tribes, are the emblems of the elect of God out of all nations in all ages The tribes of Dan and Ephraim, as ringleaders in idolatry, are omitted, a brand of just reproach being set upon them for such apostacy from God *Note*, God's people are sealed ones, he knoweth those that are his.

9 After this I beheld, and lo, a great multitude, which
no man could number, of all nations, and kindreds, and
people, and tongues, stood before the throne, and before
the Lamb, clothed with white robes, and palms in their
d John xii 13 hands, d 10 And cried with a loud voice, saying, Sal-
vation to our God which sitteth upon the throne, and
unto the Lamb. 11 And all the angels stood round
about the throne, and *about* the elders, and the four beasts,
and fell before the throne on their faces, and worshipped
e Heb xii 2. God, e 12 Saying, Amen Blessing, and glory, and
wisdom, and thanksgiving, and honour, and power, and
f Chap v 11—13 might *be* unto our God for ever and ever f Amen

v 9—12 We have here a glorious scene of the happy state of the church, either during the Millenium, as some suppose, or when the redeemed shall be finally entered into their eternal rest

1 They are a great multitude which no man could number, though few comparatively in any one age or nation, yet, when collected in the great congregation, they will be innumerable

2 They stand before the throne and before the Lamb, with holy boldness and sure acceptance, *clothed with white robes*, the emblems of honour, joy, and purity, *and palms in their hands*, in token of their glorious victories obtained over all their foes, for all God's saints shall assuredly be finally triumphant over their foes

3 They lifted up their voices in loud hallelujahs, crying, *Salvation to our God which sitteth upon the throne, and unto the Lamb*, all glory, praise, and adoration be ascribed to him, for that complete salvation which he hath wrought out for us, and freely bestowed upon us

4 The angelic host, with the elders and living creatures which stood before the throne, immediately joined in their adorations, and falling *on their faces, worshipped God, saying, Amen! Blessing, and glory, and wisdom, and thanksgiving, and honour, and power, and might be unto our God for ever and ever Amen!* The inhabitants of heaven have all one mind and employment, ceaseless in the praises of their common Lord May we now delight to join their song, and prepare hereby for the happy service of eternity!

13 And one of the elders answered, saying unto me,
What are these which are arrayed in white robes? and
whence came they? 14 And I said unto him, Sir, thou
knowest And he said to me, These are they which came
g Chap vi 9—11 out of great tribulation, g and have washed their robes,
h Acts xiv 22 and made them white in the blood of the Lamb h 15
i Heb ix 14 Eph v 25. Therefore are they before the throne of God, and serve
him day and night in his temple i and he that sitteth on
j Ps cxxxiv the throne shall dwell among them 16 They shall
k Isa xlix 10 hunger no more, k neither thirst any more, neither shall
the sun light on them, nor any heat. 17 For the Lamb
which is in the midst of the throne, shall feed them, and
l Ps xxiii 2 shall lead them unto living fountains of waters l and
m Isa xxv 8 Chap xxi 4 God shall wipe away all tears from their eyes m

v 13—17 Whilst John, with holy rapture, beheld the heavenly vision, one of the elders questioned him, whether he understood what he saw, and knew who these were and whence they came? With humble acknowledgment of his ignorance, and desire of information, he replied, Sir, thou knowest The elder thereupon kindly undertook to inform him

1 *These*, saith he, *are they who came out of great tribulation*, through various affliction and the fire of persecution, *and have washed their robes, and made them white in the blood of the Lamb Therefore are they before the throne of God*, not on account of their own deserts or sufferings, but as having overcome through the blood of Jesus, applied to their hearts by faith for their complete justification before God *Note*, Our title to eternal blessedness depends not upon what we do or suffer for Christ, but upon what he hath done and suffered for us, when he perfected his people by one oblation once offered

2 He informs him of the distinguished dignity and glory to which these once-suffering saints were admitted They *are before the throne of God*, admitted to the immediate presence of the Eternal Majesty, *and serve him day and night in his celestial temple*, without ceasing *and he that sitteth on the throne shall dwell among them* for ever, as the author and source of their eternal felicity *They shall hunger no more, neither thirst any more*, knowing no more these painful cravings, *neither shall the sun light on them, nor any heat*, no fire of persecution, nor furnace of affliction or temptation shall there be ever apprehended *For the Lamb which is in the midst of the throne*, possessed of all dominion and power, *shall feed them* with his rich provision, *and shall lead them unto fountains of living waters*, to refresh and comfort their souls, which from his presence shall drink in pleasures as out of a river *and God shall wipe away all tears from their eyes*, no sin, no sorrow shall be there, nor one salt tear ever again trickle down their faces, but unutterable and uninterrupted consolations shall be their eternal happy portion Bring me, dear Lord, to share this blessedness among thy saints in light

CHAP VIII

We have already seen what occurred upon opening six of the seals, we come now to the opening of the seventh, which introduced the sounding of the seven trumpets, and a direful scene now opens most expositors agree, the seven seals represent the intervals between the apostles time and the reign of Constantine, but the seven trumpets are designed to represent the rise of antichrist, some time after the empire became Christian In this chapter we have the preface, or prelude, to the sounding of the trumpets, ver 1—7 2 The sounding of four of the trumpets, ver 7, &c

1 AND when he had opened the seventh seal, there
was silence in heaven about the space of half an
hour 2 And I saw the seven a angels which stood be- a 2 Kings xix 35
fore God, and to them were given seven trumpets b b Jer iv 10 Hos v 8
3 And another angel came and stood at the altar, having c Lev xvi 12
a golden c censer, and there was given unto him much d Ex xxx 7, 38
d incense, that he should offer *it* with the prayers of all
saints upon the golden altar which was before the throne e e Psal cxl 2
4 And the smoke of the incense *which came* with the
prayers f of the saints, ascended up before God out of the f Luke i 10
angel's hand 5 And the angel took the censer, and
filled it with fire of the altar, and cast *it* into the earth, g g Ezek x 2
and there were voices, and thunderings, and lightnings,
and an earthquake h 6 And the seven angels which h Chap xi 15 & xvi 17, 18
had the seven trumpets, prepared themselves to sound

v 1—6 The former seals related to the events which should happen to the Roman empire whilst pagan, the last seal includes the dreadful judgments of God upon the degenerate Christian empire, after the short state of prosperity enjoyed under Constantine, represented here by the silence observed in heaven for *half an hour*, when a new scene opens to view

1 Seven angels present themselves before God, the instruments of his providence, and seven trumpets are given them to proclaim the judgments in so many successive periods about to be executed on the earth

2 Another angel, the Lord of the angelic host, and the uncreated angel of the covenant appears, and as the great high-priest of his people, offers upon the golden altar much incense, making the prayers of his saints acceptable before the throne of God, through his own sacrifice and intercession *Note*, (1) God's saints are known by their continual life of prayer, they who never pray have no part or lot in Christ's salvation (2) Not for their own sakes do our prayers come up with acceptance before the throne, but for his, who ever liveth to make intercession for us

3 Having secured a gracious answer to his people's prayers, this great angel gives the signal for his judgments to break forth upon his enemies; filling his censer with fire from the altar, he cast it into the earth, the Roman empire, and terrible thunderings, lightenings, and voices followed, and a great earthquake, emblems of the dreadful vengeance ready to be executed, and immediately the angels prepared to sound their trumpets.

7 The first angel sounded, and there followed hail i Ex ix 24, 25 Ps xi 6 & xviii 13 Isa xxviii 2 & xxix 6 & xxx 30
i and fire mingled with blood, and they were cast upon Ezek xxxviii 22
the earth and the third part of the trees was burnt up, k k Isa ii 13 Zech xi 2
and all green grass was burnt up. 8 And the second
angel

angel founded, and as it were a great mountain burning
with fire was caſt into the ſea, and the third part of the
l Ex vii 17, 18 ſea became blood l 9 And the third part of the crea-
tures which were in the ſea, and had life, died, and the
the third part of the ſhips were deſtroyed 10 And the
m Iſa xiv 12—15 Dan viii 10 third angel ſounded, and there fell a great ſtar m from
heaven, burning as it were a lamp, and it fell upon the
third part of the rivers, and upon the fountains of wa-
n Iſa xxx 4, 8 Hoſ xiii 15, 16 Ex vii 20, 21 ters n 11 And the name of the ſtar is called Worm-
wood and the third part of the waters became worm-
wood, and many men died of the waters, becauſe
o Ex xv 23 they were made bitter o 12 And the fourth angel
ſounded, and the third part of the ſun was ſmitten, and
the third part of the moon, and the third part of the
p Ezek xxxii 7, 8 Iſa xviii 9, 11 ſtars, p ſo as the third part of them was darkned and
the day ſhone not for a third part of it, and the night
likewiſe 13 And I beheld, and heard an angel flying
through the midſt of heaven, ſaying with a loud voice,
Wo, wo, wo to the inhabitants of the earth, by reaſon
of the other voices of the trumpets of the three angels
which are yet to ſound.

v 7—13

1 The firſt trumpet ſounds, and hail, fire, and blood mingled therewith, like one of the plagues of Egypt, followed, by which a third part of the trees, and every green thing was conſumed, denoting the civil wars between the ſons of Conſtantine, which ended, after prodigious ſlaughter, with the deſtruction of his family, between the years 337—379, and the Goths alſo then began to break in and ravage the empire

2 The ſecond trumpet ſounds the alarm, and a burning mountain, hurled into the ſea, converts the third part of it into blood, and ſlays the third part of all the creatures that lived therein, or failed upon it And this is ſuppoſed to refer to the irruptions of the Goths and Vandals into the empire, when under Alaric they penetrated into Italy, and ſacked Rome itſelf, between the years 379 and 412

3 The third trumpet is blown, and a falling ſtar, called Wormwood, embittered the third part of the waters, and a great mortality enſued, and this denotes the fearful deſolations wrought by the Goths and Vandals between the years 412 and 493, under Genſeric, they ravaged Italy, plundered Rome about the year 455, and afterwards, under Odoacer, they took Rome, dethroned Auguſtulus, and their general aſſumed the title of king

4 The fourth trumpet ſounds, and a total eclipſe of all the luminaries of heaven over the third part of the earth followed, ſignifying the dreadful darkneſs and ignorance that, under the barbarous nations, which ravaged the empire, generally prevailed The ſeat of empire was alſo under Odoacer tranſlated from Rome to Ravenna, and though no alteration was then made in the government, yet when Juſtinian afterwards recovered Italy from the Goths, and erected the exarchate of Ravenna, Rome was only a petty dukedom, her ſenate and councils were aboliſhed, and it became ſubject to the exarch of Ravenna Whilſt, with attentive expectation, John waited for the ſounding of the other trumpets, a mighty angel, flying through the midſt of heaven, cried aloud, *Wo, wo, wo to the inhabitants of the earth, by reaſon of the other voices of the trumpets of the three angels which are yet to ſound* *Note*, (1) God warns before he ſtrikes (2) Leſſer judgments, when ſlighted, will aſſuredly be followed with others more tremendous

CHAP IX

In this chapter we have an account of the ſounding of the fifth and ſixth trumpets, the appearances that attended them, and the events that were to follow the fifth trumpet, ver 1—13 the ſixth, ver 13, &c.

1 AND the fifth angel ſounded, and I ſaw a ſtar fall
from heaven unto the earth and to him was
a Chap xx 1—3 given the key of the bottomleſs pit a 2 And he opened
the bottomleſs pit, and there aroſe a ſmoke out of the pit,
as the ſmoke of a great furnace, and the ſun and the air
b Gen xix 28 were darkned, by reaſon of the ſmoke of the pit b 3
c Iſa xiv 31 Gen xv 17 Ex x 4, 15 Jud vi 5 Jer xxxiii 4 And there came out of the ſmoke locuſts upon the earth, c
and unto them was given power, as the ſcorpions of the
earth have power 4 And it was commanded them
that they ſhould not hurt the graſs of the earth, neither
d Joel ii 9 Pſ 3 & 9 Jer xvii 7 any green thing, neither any tree, d but only thoſe men
which have not the ſeal of God in their foreheads. 5
And to them it was given that they ſhould not kill them,
but that they ſhould be tormented five months and their
torment *was* as the torment of a ſcorpion when he ſtriketh
a man 6 And in thoſe days ſhall men ſeek death, and
ſhall not find it, and ſhall deſire to die, and death ſhall

2

flee from them e 7 And the ſhapes of the locuſts *were* e Jer viii 3
like unto horſes prepared unto battle, f and on their heads f Joel ii 4
were as it were crowns like gold, g and their faces *were* as g Nah iii 17
the faces of men 8 And they had hair as the hair of
women, and their teeth were as *the teeth* of lions h 9 h Joel i 6 & ii 5
And they had breaſtplates, as it were breaſtplates of iron,
and the ſound of their wings *was* as the ſound of chariots
of many horſes running to battle. i 10 And they had tails
like unto ſcorpions, and there were ſtings in their tails
and their power *was* to hurt men five months 11 And i Iſa ix 15
they had a king over them, *which is* the angel of the
bottomleſs pit, whoſe name in the Hebrew tongue *is*
Abaddon, but in the Greek tongue hath *his* name Apol-
lyon k 12 One wo is paſt, *and* behold there come two k 2 Theſ ii 3
woes more hereafter

v 1—12 The fifth trumpet is ſuppoſed to refer to the riſe of the impoſtor Mahomet, who is the ſtar here ſpoken of, infecting the earth like a peſtilential meteor with his abominable falſehoods, permiſſion being given him to open the bottomleſs pit, and a cloud of errors, black as the darkneſs of hell itſelf, immediately burſt out, and covered the Eaſt, innumerable multitudes of Saracens, thick as locuſts, under his banners, ruſhed forth they chiefly conſiſted of cavalry, made dreadful incurſions into the empire, with turbans like crowns on their heads, wore long hair like women, ſtrong as lions, defended with armour, weapon proof, and ruſhed with irreſiſtible fury on their foes. Satan, the angel of the bottomleſs pit, the great deſtroyer of men, was at their head and ſuch was the miſery which they every where ſpread through the apoſtate church, that death appeared preferable to life, but to the elect of God, the ſealed in the earth, the power of theſe deſtroyers reached not, they were not to be deceived by the wiles of impoſture, nor terrified from their profeſſion by any danger or threatnings The ſpace contained within this ſeal extends from 568 to 675 *Note*, (1) The heavieſt judgments upon the world are thoſe, when God lets looſe the great deceiver, and becauſe men turn away from the truth, he gives them up to ſtrong deluſions, to believe a lye (2) Hereſy and error, like the ſcorpion's ſting, infuſe baleful poiſon into the ſoul (3) Satan, and all his emiſſaries, are under a divine reſtraint, God ſaith unto them, Hitherto ſhall ye come, and no further (4.) Whatever prevalence of deluſion there may be, God's people ſhall every one of them be preſerved in the moſt trying times

One wo is now paſt, two more are yet to come

13 And the ſixth angel ſounded, and I heard a voice
from the four horns of the golden altar, l which is before l Ex xxx 6
God, 14 Saying to the ſixth angel which had the trum-
pet, Looſe the four angels which are bound in the great
river Euphrates 15 And the four angels were looſed,
which were prepared for an hour, and a day, and a month,
and a year, for to ſlay the third part of men 16 And
the number of the army of the horſemen *were* two hundred
thouſand thouſand and I heard the number of them
17. And thus I ſaw the horſes in the viſion, and them
that ſat on them, having breaſt-plates of fire, and of ja-
cinct, and brimſtone and the heads of the horſes *were* as
the heads of lions, and out of their mouths iſſued fire, and
ſmoke, and brimſtone 18 By theſe three was the third
part of men killed, by the fire and by the ſmoke, and by
the brimſtone which iſſued out of their mouths 19 For
their power is in their mouths, and in their tails m for m Iſa ix 15
their tails *were* like unto ſerpents, and had heads, and
with them they do hurt 20 And the reſt of the men
which were not killed by theſe plagues, yet repented not
of the works of their hands, that they ſhould not worſhip
devils, and idols of gold and ſilver, and braſs, and ſtone,
and of wood which neither can ſee, nor hear, nor walk n n Pſ cxv 4
21. Neither repented they of their murders, nor of their
ſorceries, nor of their fornication, nor of their thefts

v 13—21 On the ſounding of the ſixth angel, the voice of Chriſt is heard from the four horns of the golden altar, which is before God, the emblem of the prevalence of his interceſſion for all his people in the four parts of the earth his command to the ſixth angel is, that he ſhould looſe the four angels that were bound in the great river Euphrates, and let them have power for an hour, and a day, and a month, and a year, to ſlay the third part of men This may be referred to the inteſtine quarrels among the ſucceſſors of Mahomet, which for about fifty years prevented them from ſpreading their conqueſts in the empire, but afterwards, from 675 to 750, they carried their arms far and wide through Egypt, Africa, and Spain their forces were innumerable and invincible, chiefly conſiſting of cavalry, and breathing forth threatning and ſlaughter through the earth, and, like ſcorpions, they infuſed their poiſonous tenets wherever their

aim

arms prevailed Yet all theſe heavy judgments reclaimed not thoſe who bore the Chriſtian name, but diſhonoured it by the vileſt abominations, nor did they repent of their idolatries, the worſhip of dæmons and images, unable to hear or anſwer their more ſtupid votaries, but continued in the practice of murder, ſorcery, fornication, and theft, and all thoſe miſcalled pious frauds which prieſtcraft invented to beguile the ſuperſtitious therefore more deadly woes are yet in ſtore for them *Note*, (1) God ſends his judgments that ſinners may turn from the evil of their ways (2) They who under God's viſitations harden their hearts, muſt inevitably periſh at the laſt

CHAP. X

This chapter is an introduction to the latter part of the propheces of this book Here we have, 1 A remarkable deſcription of a very glorious angel with an open book in his hand, ver 1—3 2 *An account of ſeven thunders which the apoſtle heard, as echoing to this voice of the angel, and communicated ſome diſcoveries, which the apoſtle was not yet allowed to write* 3 *The ſolemn oath taken by him who had the book in his hand, ver* 5—7 4 *The charge given to the apoſtle, and obſerved by him, ver* 8—11.

1 AND I ſaw another mighty angel [a] come down
from heaven, clothed with a cloud, [b] and a
rainbow *was* upon his head, [c] and his face *was* as it were
the ſun, and his feet as pillars of fire 2 And he had
in his hand a little book open and he ſet his right foot
upon the ſea, and *his* left *foot* on the earth, [d] 3 And cried
with a loud voice, as *when* a lion roareth and when he
had cried, ſeven thunders uttered their voices 4 And
when the ſeven thunders had uttered their voices, I was
about to write and I heard a voice from heaven, ſaying
unto me, Seal up thoſe things which the ſeven thunders
uttered, and write them not 5 And the angel which I
ſaw ſtand upon the ſea, and upon the earth, lifted up his
hand to heaven, [e] 6 And ſware by him that liveth for
ever and ever, who created heaven, and the things that
therein are, and the earth, and the things that therein
are, and the ſea and the things which are therein, that
there ſhould be time no longer. 7. But in the days of
the voice of the ſeventh angel, when he ſhall begin to
ſound, the myſtery of God ſhould be finiſhed, [f] as he
hath declared to his ſervants the prophets. [g]

a Dan x 5, 6 & xii 7 b Pſ civ 3 Ez xxxv 5 c Gen ix 13, 17 Ez k i 28 Chap i 15 d Pſ ii 8 e Gen xiv 22 Dan xii 7 f Rom x. 25 26 Eph iii 4, 6. g Iſa ix 5, 5 Dan ii 44 & vii. 25 & xii 6, 7 Zech xiv 9.

v 1—7 Another viſion intervenes between the ſixth and ſeventh trumpet, as before between the ſixth and ſeventh ſeal

1 A glorious angel, even the ſame divine perſonage whoſe voice was heard before, giving the angels their commiſſion, (chap vii 2) comes down from heaven clothed with a cloud, and around his head the rainbow glowed the token of his mindfulneſs of his everlaſting covenant, his countenance like the ſun, chearing the hearts of his people, and his feet as pillars of fire, firm to ſupport the intereſts of his church, and terrible to tread down her enemies In his hand he held a little book, the laſt volume of the roll which he had opened, and was about to reveal the contents of it, and, ſetting one foot on the earth, the other on the ſea, *to intimate his univerſal dominion*, loud as the lion roars he uttered his voice, and inſtant ſeven mighty thunderings, the emblems of the judgments about to follow, echoed back the ſound Being about to minute down the articulate denunciations uttered by theſe thunders, *John is reſtrained by a* voice from heaven, ſaying, *Seal up theſe things, and write them not*

2 The angel that ſtood on the earth and ſea then lifted up his hand to heaven, and, with a ſolemn oath, ſware by the great Creator of all things, *that there ſhould be time no longer*, but that when the time, and times and half a time (*Dan* xii 7) are expired, the 1260 years of the reign of Antichriſt, then an end ſhould be put to the Antichriſtian tyranny for ever, and that, within the period of the ſeventh trumpet, the myſtery of God ſhould be finiſhed, his deſigns of grace accompliſhed, and his great ſalvation ſpread from pole to pole As of old had been ſhewn to his prophets, (*Dan* vii 25—28 xii 6, 7 *Zech* xiv. 9)

8 And the voice which I heard from heaven ſpake
unto me again, and ſaid, Go, *and* take the little book
which is open in the hand of the angel which ſtandeth
upon the ſea, and upon the earth 9. And I went unto the
angel, and ſaid unto him, Give me the little book
And he ſaid unto me, Take *it*, and eat it up [h], and it
ſhall make thy belly bitter, but it ſhall be in thy mouth
ſweet as honey 10 And I took the little book out of
the angel's hand, and ate it up [i]; and it was in my mouth
ſweet as honey and as ſoon as I had eaten it, my belly
was bitter 11 And he ſaid unto me, Thou muſt pro-
pheſy again before many peoples, and nations, and
tongues, and kings

h Ezek ii 8, 3 i Jer xv 16

v 8—11 The ſame voice which he had heard from heaven,

1. Commands him to go and take the volume out of the angel's hand who ſtood on the earth and ſea, who gave it to him and bid him eat it up, digeſting the awful contents therein revealed, telling him, that though ſweet in his mouth, it would make his belly bitter; deſireable as it was to know the events of futurity, the awful deſolations about to come upon the earth, and the ſufferings of the church, could not but inwardly grieve and afflict him

2 The apoſtle obeyed, and found the word true which had been ſpoken, ſweet as the book was in his mouth, as honey, his belly was made bitter as gall, and the burdens he foreſaw deeply affected him; but he muſt not conceal the ſecrets communicated to him; he is commanded to propheſy concerning the events which muſt ſucceſſively come to paſs before many people and nations, and tongues and kings *Note*, Preachers muſt firſt themſelves digeſt and be deeply affected with the truths which they deliver to others

CHAP XI

In this chapter we have an account, 1 *Of the meaſuring reed given to the apoſtle to take the dimenſions of the temple,* ver 1, 2 2 *Of the two witneſſes of God,* ver 3—14 3 *Of the ſounding of the ſeventh trumpet, and what followed upon it,* ver 14, &c

1. AND there was given me a reed [a] like unto a rod
and the angel ſtood, ſaying, Riſe, and meaſure
[b] the temple of God, [c] and the altar, and them that
worſhip therein [d] 2 But the court which is without the
temple leave out, and meaſure it not, for it is given unto
the Gentiles [e] and the holy city ſhall they tread under
foot [f] forty *and* two months [g] 3 And I will give *power*
unto my two witneſſes, [h] and they ſhall propheſy a thou-
ſand two hundred *and* threeſcore days clothed in ſack-
cloth. 4 Theſe are the two olive-trees, [i] and the two
candleſticks [k] ſtanding before the God of the earth 5
And if any man will hurt them, fire proceedeth out of
their mouth, [l] and devoureth their enemies and if any
man will hurt them, he muſt in this manner be killed 6
Theſe have power to ſhut heaven, that it rain not in the
days of their propheſy [m] and have power over waters to
turn them to blood [n], and to ſmite the earth with all
plagues as often as they will 7 And when they ſhall
have finiſhed their teſtimony, the beaſt [o] that aſcendeth
out of the bottomleſs pit, ſhall make war againſt them,
and ſhall overcome them, and kill them 8 And their
dead bodies *ſhall lie* in the ſtreets of the great city, which
ſpiritually is called Sodom and Egypt, [p] where alſo our
Lord was crucified 9 And they of the people, and
kindreds, and tongues, and nations, ſhall ſee their dead
bodies three days and a half, and ſhall not ſuffer their
dead bodies to be put in graves 10 And they that
dwell upon the earth ſhall rejoice over them, and make
merry, and ſhall ſend gifts [q] one to another, becauſe theſe
two prophets tormented them that dwelt on the earth
11 And after three days and a half, the Spirit of life
from God entred into them [r] and they ſtood upon their
feet [s], and great fear fell upon them which ſaw them
12 And they heard a great voice from heaven, ſaying
unto them, Come up hither And they aſcended up to
[t] heaven in a cloud, and their enemies beheld them 13
And the ſame hour was there a great earthquake, and
the tenth part of the city fell, and in the earthquake
were ſlain of men ſeven thouſand, and the remnant were
affrighted, and gave glory to the God of heaven

a Ezek xl 3 Zech ii 1 b Iſ viii 20 Cal vi 16 c 1 Co iii 16 17 2 Cor vi 16 Eph ii 21 22 1 Pet ii 5 e Luke xxi 24 Luke xx 4 f Chap xiii 5 h Deut xvii 6 & xix 15 Mat xviii 16 2 Cor xiii 1 i Zech iv 3, 11 k Mal v 14, 16 l 2 Kings i 10, 12 Jer v 14 & xxiii 29 m 1 Kings xvii 1 Jam v 17 n Ex vii 17 o Dan vii 21 2 Theſſ ii 9 p Chap xvi 19 & xvii 18 & xviii 10, 21 q Eſth ix 22 r Luke i 19 Mat xi 14 & xvii 11, 12 t Iſa xxxvii 1, 10 Mat xi 23

v 1—13 A general deſcription is here given of the ſtate both of the true and the antichriſtian church, during 1260 years, from the time that the temporal power of the pope roſe about 750

1 John is commanded to meaſure the temple of God, and the altar, and the worſhippers, for in the worſt of times, and the darkeſt days, God would ſtill maintain his church, and ſome ſhould be preſerved from the general apoſtacy, a remnant according to the election of grace The outer court he was not meaſure, that is left to the Gentiles; thoſe indeed who profeſs to bear the Chriſtian name, but by the idolatry, ſuperſtitions, and frauds which they encourage and maintain, are returned in reality to the worſhip of Paganiſm, Popery being heatheniſm revived and during forty-two months, or 1260 years, theſe Gentile Papiſts ſhall tread the holy city under foot, and exerciſe their tyrannical government over the profeſſors of the Chriſtian name

During

2 During the prevalence of the antichristian tyranny, God will not leave the world without warning, nor the corruptors of his worship without witness, a succession of faithful ministers shall arise, a few indeed, here spoken of but as two, and clothed in sackcloth, deeply affected with the miseries of the church, and the persecutors of the faithful remnant. *These are the two olive-trees*, &c like Zerubbabel and Joshua (Zech iv 6—14) whom God will supply with the continual influences of his grace, and endue them with light and zeal to remonstrate against the corruptions of the antichristian church. And if any attempt to hurt them, the word of the Lord, which proceedeth out of their mouths as fire, denounces spiritual and eternal death upon them. These have power, like Elijah, to shut up heaven, and to bring the heaviest plagues, like those of Egypt, on their enemies, even the spiritual plagues of a famine of the word, obduracy of heart, and all the dreadful judgments that, in answer to their prayers, God will inflict on their persecutors, and which they denounce upon them, not from a spirit of revenge, but for the vindication of God's injured honour.

3 The witnesses shall be slain, *while they are performing their testimony*, though God will always raise up others, and avenge their blood on their persecutors, and their dead bodies shall be forbid burial, and be insulted in the streets of that great city, spiritually called Sodom and Egypt, where also our Lord was crucified, Rome papal being notorious for filthiness as Sodom, like Egypt, the cruel oppressor of God's people, and red with the blood of the martyrs of Jesus, which is, as it were, afresh to crucify him.

Some suppose that this slaying the witnesses by the antichristian beast, and his adherents, is yet to come, and that the *three days and half*, v 9 refer not to the time and times and half time, or 1260 years, the whole period of popery, but to some more dreadful persecution, and general prevalence of the power of antichrist, which towards the close of this period will be permitted, and for a short space the inhabitants of the papal countries will congratulate each other, as if they had now finally triumphed over those who troubled their consciences with remonstrances against their impieties, idolatries, and all their abominations.

4 *After three days and half*, at the close of the period of 1260 years, the witnesses are miraculously raised to life, to the terror of their enemies, not the same persons, but others, endued with their spirit, boldness, and zeal, and God, in testimony of his approbation, caught them up to heaven in the sight of their enemies, not literally, but figuratively, he exalted them to a state of eminent dignity and safety, above all the malice of their foes and thereupon a great earthquake shook down great part of the city of the beast, and seven thousand men were slain, a vast number of his dependents and abettors, men of note and influence fell, and his jurisdiction was in part demolished, whilst the remnant, affrighted by these prodigies, renounced their idolatries and superstitions, and, converted to the faith of Jesus, glorified God. *Note*, (1) The enemies of God's witnessing servants shall one day, with confusion, behold their exaltation, and know that God hath sent them. (2) When God's judgments are in the earth, the inhabitants thereof should learn righteousness, and they who fly to God for refuge, and give him glory, shall be saved from fear of evil.

14 The second wo is past, *and* behold, the third wo
cometh quickly. 15 And the seventh angel sounded,
and there were great voices in heaven, saying, The king-
doms of this world are become *the kingdoms* of our Lord,
and of his Christ, [u] and he shall reign for ever and ever.
16 And the four and twenty elders which sit before God
[w] on their seats, fell upon their faces, and worshipped God,
17 Saying, We give thee thanks, O Lord God almighty,
which art, and wast, and art to come; because thou hast
taken to thee thy great power, and hast reigned. 18 And
the nations were angry, [x] and thy wrath is come, and the
time of the dead that they should be judged, and that thou
shouldst give reward unto thy servants the prophets, and
to the saints, and them that fear thy name, small and great,
and shouldst destroy them which destroy the earth. 19
And the temple of God was opened in heaven, and there
was seen in his temple the ark of his testament [y]: and
there were lightnings, and voices, and thunderings, and an
earthquake, and great hail [z].

u [illegible]
w Ch. iv 4
x Ps. xcix 1
y [illegible]
z [illegible]

v. 14—19 The seventh trumpet sounds, and lo, the third and last woe is denounced, when the Mahometan and Papal power, the eastern and western antichrists are to be utterly destroyed. On which,

1 Loud acclamations of joy fill all the courts of heaven, the wished-for time is come when Jesus shall erect his throne, and all nations shall bow before the sceptre of his grace, and become a willing people in the day of his power, owning him as their rightful king, who shall reign over his redeemed for ever and ever. And for this the four and twenty elders pour forth their thanks to the Lord, and in humble adoration prostrate themselves before his throne, ascribing praise to the eternal and almighty Jesus, that he hath now signally made bare his arm, avenging the deaths of his martyred servants, and in return for the indignation shewn by the antichristian persecutors, pouring forth his vials of wrath upon them, whilst his faithful ministers and people now receive their glorious reward, they see their foes become their footstool, and enjoy peace, comfort, mutual communion, and the free liberty of all gospel ordinances in their highest purity. And every gracious soul, looking forward to this happy season, cannot but pray that God would hasten it in his good time.

2 *The temple of God was opened in heaven*, the exercise of the true evangelical worship was now restored, *and there was seen in his temple the ark of his testament*, intimating the peculiar manifestations of God's presence to all his people, the boldness that they will have to approach the holiest of all, and the sweet communion which they shall enjoy with their Lord, seeing him, as it were, face to face.

3 *And there were lightnings, and voices, and thunderings, and an earthquake, and great hail*, as if the dissolution of all things was at hand, intimating the entire demolition of all the church's enemies. *Note*, Though the struggle be long and sharp, the gospel shall be finally triumphant, and the truth at last prevail over all opposition.

CHAP XII

In this chapter we have, 1 *An account of the contest between the church and antichrist, the seed of the woman, and the seed of the serpent*, ver 1—6 2 *War in heaven*, ver 7—14 3 *As it was carried on in the wilderness*, ver 14, &c.

1 AND there appeared a great wonder in heaven, a
woman clothed with the sun, [a] and the moon
under her feet, and upon her head a crown of twelve stars.
2 And she being with child, cried, travailing in birth,
[b] and pained to be delivered. 3 And there appeared
another wonder in heaven; and behold, a great red dra-
gon, having seven heads and ten horns, and seven crowns
upon his head. 4 And his tail drew the third part of
the stars of heaven, and did cast them to the earth: and
the dragon stood before the woman which was ready to be
delivered, for to devour [c] her child as soon as it was born.
5 And she brought forth a man child [d] which was to
rule all nations with a rod of iron: and her child was
caught up unto God, and to his throne [e]. 6 And the
woman fled into the wilderness, [f] where she hath a place
prepared of God, that they should feed her [g] there a
thousand two hundred *and* threescore days.

a Mal. iv 2
b Isa. liv 1 & lxvi 7, 9 Gal. iv 19 1 John v 1, 4
c 1 Pet. v 8
d Isa. vi 7, 8 Ps. ii 9
e 2 Chron. xxii 11 & xxiii 11
f Ps. lxxxvii 5, 6 Mat. xvi 18
g Jer. iii 15

v 1—6 The same period as before is here described of 1260 years, during which,

1 A great wonder appears in heaven, the church of Christ, represented under the figure of a woman clothed with the sun, with Christ and his righteousness, having the moon under her feet, regarding all sublunary things with holy contempt, upon her head was a crown of twelve stars, the doctrines of the gospel dispensed by the apostles, and being with child, she cried out, travailing and ready to be delivered.

2 A great red dragon appears, representing satan, as acting by his wicked emissaries of Rome papal, with seven heads, ten horns, and seven crowns upon his head, signifying the dignity and supremacy, in spirituals and temporals, which the bishop of Rome usurped, and his tyrannical dominion over the bodies and souls of men, drawing into superstition and idolatry multitudes both ministers and people, who seemed before as stars in the heavens, and bringing them down to the earthly and sensual religion of the church of Rome, and with unwearied opposition and implacable enmity striving to destroy every faithful Christian, and to suppress the progress of the true religion of Jesus in the earth, ready to devour the child, for which the woman travailed, as soon as it was born.

3 God disappointed the malice of the dragon, a man-child was born, the emblem of all the spiritual seed of the woman, who in succession should arise, and, in defiance of the malice of the antichristian foe, be preserved, and finally prevail over all their enemies, taken under God's immediate protection, and secured as if caught up to the throne of God whilst the mother, the church, though in obscurity during this dark period of 1260 years, hath a place provided for her, as in the valleys of Piedmont, and other retreats, where the true religion of Jesus was preserved amidst the abounding corruption of the church of Rome, till the reformation took place. *Note*, God will ever have a church in the darkest day, and will in the desert feed his people, as he did Israel of old with living manna.

7 And there was war in heaven, Michael [h] and his
angels fought against the dragon, and the dragon fought

and

and his angels 8 And prevailed not, neither was their
place found any more in heaven 9 And the great
dragon was cast out, that old serpent, i called the devil
and Satan, which deceiveth the whole world, he was cast
out into the earth, and his angels were cast out with him
10 And I heard a loud voice saying in heaven, Now is
come salvation, and strength, and the kingdom of our
God, and the power of his Christ for the accuser of
our brethren k is cast down, which accused them before
our God day and night 11 And they overcame him
by the blood of the Lamb, and by the word of their
testimony, l and they loved not their lives m unto the
death 12 Therefore rejoice, n ye heavens, and ye that
dwell in them Wo to the inhabiters of the earth, and
of the sea for the devil is come down unto you, having
great wrath, because he knoweth that he hath but a short
time

i Gen. iii. 4. 2 Cor. xi. 3. k Job i. 8. ii. 2. Zech. iii. 1. l Eph. vi. 17. m Acts xx. 24. n Isa. xlix. 13. Ps. xcvi. 10, 11.

v. 7—12 Another representation of this period is here made 1 *There was war in heaven*, in the church, *Michael and his angels*, the Lord Jesus and his ministers, with the sword of the Spirit, which is the word of God, *fought against the dragon and his angels*, his popish emissaries, and all the legions of ecclesiastics in that idolatrous church The issue of the combat was, that in spite of all the dragon's efforts he could not prevail to extinguish the truth, he was foiled in the glorious reformation, when many states threw off the antichristian yoke, and, like a falling star, from their towering height of power and dominion, Satan, that old serpent, and his instruments of the church of Rome, were cast down, and at the end of this period the conquest will be completed

2 Hereupon a triumphant song is sung by the church of the redeemed, who glorify God for this exertion of his power and strength in the salvation of his people from the accuser of the brethren, who by means of the antichristian persecutors, with pretended crimes, sought occasion to harrass and oppress them, night and day and night accused them before God But they *overcame by the blood of the Lamb*, which removed all condemnation, *and by the word of their testimony*, the sword of the spirit which confounded their enemies, and so faithfully adhered they to Christ and his pure gospel, that for his sake they readily laid down their lives, and submitted to death armed with its greatest terrors *Note*, (1) All our victories are gained through the blood of the Lamb (2) They who know in whom they have believed, will rather part with their lives than deny the faith

3 The saints and angels of God are called upon to rejoice in this victory, *v.* 12 whilst a woe is denounced on the inhabiters of the earth and sea, on the earthly-minded, and carnal professors of Christianity, for though the kingdom of the beast be on the decline, and hath but a short time to endure, yet therein Satan will exert his utmost efforts to deceive and destroy the souls of men, and many of them will fall a prey unto his teeth

13 And when the dragon saw that he was cast unto
the earth, he persecuted the woman which brought forth
the man *child* 14 And to the woman were given two
wings of a great eagle, o that she might fly into the wil-
derness, into her place where she is nourished for a
time, and times, and half a time, p from the face of the
serpent 15 And the serpent cast out of his mouth wa-
ter as a flood, q after the woman, that he might cause
her to be carried away of the flood 16 And the earth
helped the woman, and the earth opened her mouth, and
swallowed up the flood which the dragon cast out of his
mouth 17 And the dragon was wroth with the wo-
man, and went to make war with the remnant of her
seed, which keep the commandments of God, and have
the testimony of Jesus Christ

o Exod. xix. 4. p Dan. vii. 25. xii. 7. q Isa. lix. 19. Jer. xlvi. 7, 8. Isa. xxvii. 1.

v. 13—17 By the reformation the power of Satan and the church of Rome being greatly broken, like one cast down from heaven to earth, he muttered up all his wiles and fury, and in the Jesuits raised up a new set of instruments to persecute, with unheard-of cruelty, the mother of the man-child, the true church, reformed from the errors of popery But God supplied her with eagles' wings, and bore her safe to a resting-place during her wilderness state, *v.* 14 until the period of the reign of antichrist, and the 1260 years come to an end In vain the serpent cast out a flood of errors, heresies, and persecutions, and endeavoured by fraud and force to stop the progress of the reformation, and swallow up the church, *the earth* helped her, the secular powers, many princes and states, who were themselves under the influence of temporal motives, opposed the antichristian tyranny, and persecution and the dragon, enraged to be thus foiled, retired to rally all his forces, and renewed with all his fury his attacks upon the woman and the remnant of her seed, which survived his former persecutions, whose distinguishing character is given, *they keep the commandments of God, and have the testimony of Jesus Christ*, maintaining his pure and undulterated gospel, in opposition to all the human impositions, and traditions of the papal church *Note*, Whilst we hold the testimony of Jesus, and keep his commandments, we must be finally more than conquerors

CHAP XIII

We have in this chapter a farther discovery and description of the church's enemies, not other enemies than are mentioned before, but described after another manner, that the methods of their enmity may more fully appear, they are represented as two beasts, the first you have an account of, ver 1—10 the second, ver 11

1 AND I stood upon the sand of the sea, and saw a
beast rise up out of the sea, a having seven heads b
and ten horns, and upon his horns ten crowns, and upon
his heads the name of blasphemy c 2 d And the beast
which I saw was like unto a leopard, and his feet *were as*
the feet of a bear, and his mouth as the mouth of a lion
and the dragon gave him his power, d and his seat, and
great authority 3 And I saw one of his heads, as it
were wounded to death; and his deadly wound was
healed and all the world e wondered after the beast 4
And they worshipped the dragon f which gave power
unto the beast and they worshipped the beast, saying,
Who *is* like unto the beast? who is able to make war
with him? 5 And there was given unto him a mouth,
speaking great things, and blasphemies g, and power was
given unto him to continue forty *and* two months 6
And he opened his mouth in blasphemy against God, to
blaspheme his name, and his tabernacle, and them that
dwell in heaven 7 And it was given unto him to make
war with the saints, and to overcome them and power
was given him over all kindreds, and tongues, and na-
tions 8 And all that dwell upon the earth shall worship
him, whose names are not written in the book of life of
the Lamb h slain from the foundation of the world 9
If any man have an ear, let him hear 10 He that
leadeth into captivity, shall go into captivity i He that
killeth with the sword, must be killed with the sword
Here is the patience and the faith of the saints.

a Dan. vii. 8. b Chap. xvii. c Isa. lxv. 7. Ezek. xx. 27. d Dan. vii. 4. 3. e Luke ii. 1. f Cor. x. 20. g Dan. xi. 36. h 1 Pet. i. 19. i Mat. vii. 2.

v. 1—10 Another vision relative to the same events as the foregoing here appears

1 A beast rises out of the sea, with seven heads, ten horns, and crowns upon his horns, and names of blasphemy thereon, like a leopard, with the feet of a bear and the mouth of a lion, denoting the fierceness, cruelty, and strength of the antichristian, idolatrous, and blasphemous state which should arise out of the commotions which had shaken the empire To this beast, that is, to the pope and his adherents, the devil would delegate his power and authority, enabling the man of sin to work his lying miracles, and establish his seat and capital at Rome, where, during the reign of paganism, Satan especially dwelt

2 A deadly wound was given to the beast; which some refer to the sacking of the city of Rome by the Goths, and the removal of the supreme authority from thence during the exarchate of Ravenna, and others, to the blow the church of Rome received at the reformation, and this wound was healed, either Rome itself, under the papal government, rose to unexpected greatness, and was held in veneration by the wondering world, or this may refer to the recovery of the papal interest since the reformation, and which it is supposed will flourish more than ever before the final downfall of popery

3 The people, who wondered after the beast, worshipped the dragon, the idolatrous worship of the church of Rome being, in fact, the adoration of Satan himself, and they worshipped the beast, his delegate, ascribing divine honours and titles to the pope, exalting him above all princes and potentates, and ascribing to him a kind of omnipotence upon earth would he, by horrid blasphemies, assuming the very prerogatives of the most high God, pretended, by the plenitude of his power, to sin, nay, to alter God's revealed will, to have dominion over men's consciences, and to enact canons equally, or more obligatory than the laws of God himself, blaspheming his name, and his tabernacle the church, and them that dwell in heaven, the citizens of the New Jerusalem, the faithful whom he anathematizes, or the saints and angels whose names he uses in his idolatrous worship During the period of 1260 years his dominion will endure, and by Divine Providence he will be permitted to make war with the saints who refuse to submit to his tyrannical yoke, and to overcome them, obliging all, whose names are not written in the book of life, to worship him and submit to his idolatrous decrees *Note*, Amidst the most fatal delusions and prevalence of iniquity, God's chosen ones shall be secured

4 For the comfort of God's people, a ſolemn note of attention is added, and they are called to hear This antichriſtian power, that enſlaves and deſtroys others, ſhall as ſurely be ſubdued and deſtroyed in its turn, and God's ſaints, now with patience enduring their perſecutions, muſt with faith confidently expect that this will be the iſſue *Note*, It requires much faith and patience, in ſuffering times, to hold faſt the promiſes of God and wait their fulfilment

11 And I beheld another beaſt coming up out of the
earth, and he had two horns like a lamb, and he ſpake as
a dragon [k] 12 And he exerciſeth all the power of the k Chap xi 7
firſt beaſt before him, and cauſeth the earth, and them
which dwell therein, to worſhip the firſt beaſt, whoſe
deadly wound was healed 13 And he doth great won-
ders, ſo that he maketh fire come down from heaven on
the earth, in the ſight of men [l] 14. And deceiveth them l 1 Kings xviii 37 2 Kings i 10, 12
that dwell on the earth, by *the means of* thoſe miracles
which he had power to do in the ſight of the beaſt, ſaying
to them that dwell on the earth, that they ſhould make
an image to the beaſt which had the wound by a ſword,
and did live 15 And he had power to give life unto
the image of the beaſt, that the image of the beaſt ſhould
both ſpeak, and cauſe that as many as would not worſhip
the image of the beaſt, ſhould be killed 16 And he
cauſeth all, both ſmall and great, rich and poor, free and
bond, to receive a mark in their right hand, or in their
foreheads 17 And that no man might buy or ſell, ſave
he that had the mark, or the name of the beaſt, or the
number of his name 18 Here is wiſdom Let him
that hath underſtanding count the number of the beaſt
for it is the number of a man; and his number is ſix
hundred threeſcore *and* ſix

v 11—18 Another beaſt, or the ſame power under another form, appears like a lamb with two horns, the ſymbol of his dominion temporal and ſpiritual, who with all pretended meekneſs and humility, hath all the pride and rage of the old dragon, exerciſing all the power of the firſt beaſt, and cauſing all the earth to worſhip him, and own his univerſal, temporal as well as ſpiritual juriſdiction, with lying miracles ſupporting his idolatrous worſhip, deceiving the inhabitants of the earth, and leading them to erect the image of the firſt beaſt whoſe deadly wound was healed, and pay their adoration to the idol, blindly and implicitly ſubmitting to the authority of the pope, and the conſtitutions of paganiſm revived in the church of Rome, giving life to the image of the beaſt, enforcing all the canons and laws of his idolatrous worſhip, by excommunications, fire, and ſword, making it death to refuſe obedience to the papal power, ſetting a mark upon all the votaries of the beaſt, and excluding thoſe who would not ſubmit to make profeſſion of this ſyſtem of error and blaſphemy, from all intercourſe with the worſhippers of the beaſt, as unworthy of every bleſſing of ſociety *Here is wiſdom Let him that hath underſtanding count the number of the beaſt for it is the number of a man, and his number is ſix hundred three ſcore and ſix*, concerning which number there have been many learned conjectures I incline to concur with thoſe who refer it to the time when popery ſhould riſe to her ſtrength about the year 756, which, if we add 666 to the time in which John wrote, will bring it nearly to that very period from whence the 1260 years of the antichriſtian tyranny are to be reckoned But however dark and myſterious theſe prophetic hints may be, one thing we are ſure of, that is plain and obvious, that God will always maintain his own church in the world, in defiance of oppoſition, and that all her foes ſhall finally become her footſtool

CHAP XIV

After an account of the great trials and ſufferings which the ſervants of God had endured, we have a more pleaſant ſcene opening, the day begins now to dawn, and here we have repreſented, 1 *The Lord Jeſus at the head of his faithful followers*, ver 1—6 2 *Three angels ſent ſucceſſively to proclaim the fall of Babylon, and the things antecedent and conſequent to ſo great an event*, ver. 6—14 3 *The viſion of the harveſt*, ver 14, &c.

1 AND I looked, and lo, a Lamb ſtood on the mount
Sion, [a] and with him an hundred forty *and* four a Heb xii 22 24
thouſand, having his Father's name written in their fore-
heads [b] 2 And I heard a voice from heaven, as the voice b Chap xvii 1, 15
of many waters, [b] and as the voice of a great thunder. and
I heard the voice of harpers [c] harping with their harps c 1 Chron xxv 1 7 Pſ lxviii 25
3 And they ſung as it were a new ſong [d] before the d Chap v 9
throne, and before the four beaſts, and the elders and
no man could learn that ſong, but the hundred *and* forty
and four thouſand, which were redeemed from the earth
4 Theſe are they which were not defiled with women [e] e Chap xvii 5 Ezek 6
for they are virgins theſe are they which follow the
Lamb whitherſoever he goeth: theſe were redeemed from 2 Cor xi 2
among men, *being* the firſt-fruits [f] unto God, and to the f Rom xvi 5 1 Cor xv 20
Lamb 5 And in their mouth was found no guile
for they are without fault [g] before the throne of God g Jude 24 Col i 22 Eph i 4

v 1—5 Dark and gloomy as the former ſcene appeared, the ſun now ariſes to diſpel the night of idolatry, ignorance, and error

1 The Lamb of God is ſeen on mount Zion with all his redeemed, ſealed in their foreheads, in oppoſition to thoſe who had the mark of the beaſt, over whom they are made triumphant, innumerable multitudes, as the drops of the ocean, with voices united, raiſing a chorus loud as thunder, yet melodious as the trembling harps which mingled with their concert, ſung that ſong of praiſe which none but the redeemed from the earth can learn

2 The character of thoſe happy ſouls is given They are virgins, not defiled with the idolatries of the great whore, they follow the Lamb wherefoever he goeth, faithful to his goſpel doctrines, and obſervant of his ordinances, they are a peculiar people, even the firſt fruits to God and to the Lamb, ſpecially appropriated to his ſervice, and without guile before the throne of God, as waſhed in the blood and clothed in the righteouſneſs of their Redeemer, uncorrupt by error of doctrine and immorality of conduct, and at laſt perfected in holineſs Bleſſed and happy are they who ſhall be found to anſwer theſe characters of the redeemed from the earth!

6 And I ſaw another angel fly in the midſt of heaven,
having the everlaſting goſpel [h] to preach unto them that h Iſ lxi 6, 3 Gen iii 15
dwell on the earth, and to every nation, and kindred,
and tongue, and people, 7 Saying with a loud voice,
Fear God, and give glory to him, for the hour of his
judgment is come and worſhip him that made heaven
and earth, and the ſea, and the fountains of waters 8
And there followed another angel, ſaying, Babylon [i] is
fallen, is fallen, that great city, becauſe ſhe made all i Iſa xx 9 Chap xvi 19 & xvii 18
nations drink of the wine of the wrath of her fornica
tion 9 And the third angel followed them, ſaying
with a loud voice, If any man worſhip the beaſt and his
image, and receive *his* mark in his forehead, or in his
hand, 10. The ſame ſhall drink of the wine [k] of the k Jer xxv 15 Iſa li 17 22 Pſ lxxv 8
wrath of God, which is poured out without mixture,
into the cup of his indignation, and he ſhall be tor-
mented with fire and brimſtone [l], in the preſence of the l Mat xiii 49, 50
holy angels, and in the preſence of the Lamb 11
And the ſmoke of their torment aſcendeth up for ever
and ever [m] and they have no reſt day nor night, who m Mark ix 43 44
worſhip the beaſt and his image, and whoſoever re-
ceiveth the mark of his name 12 Here is the patience
of the ſaints [n] here *are* they that keep the command- n Chap xiii 10
ments of God, and the faith of Jeſus

v 6—12 Three angels, or meſſengers, are ſent from heaven to proclaim the fall of Babylon

1 One bearing the everlaſting goſpel through the midſt of heaven, cries aloud to all people, nations, and languages, to fear, worſhip, and glorify God, the great Creator, in oppoſition to all idols, his judgments upon his enemies ſpeedily approaching And this may refer either to the preaching of Luther, Calvin, and the other reformers, or to the future period, when, before the final overthrow of popery, a noble army of preachers of the pure goſpel, animated with holy zeal, ſhall be raiſed up to plead the cauſe of God and truth

2 Another angel followed, crying, *Babylon is fallen, is fallen* and the cauſe of her doom is aſſigned, becauſe ſhe intoxicated the nations with her fornications and idolatries, which provoke the fearful wrath of God againſt her. And this ſeems to be the language of triumph of the faithful, who ſhall live in that day when Rome, with all her abominations, ſhall be utterly deſtroyed

3 A third angel followed, denouncing the moſt terrible woes on the antichriſtian party, who ſhall henceforth perſiſt in this idolatrous religion, even the eternal torments of hell, intolerable as endleſs, muſt be their portion, in the preſence of the holy angels, who will applaud the righteous judgment of God and of the Lamb, who inflicts it upon them, *and the ſmoke of their torment aſcendeth up for ever and ever, and they have no reſt, day nor night* How fearful the ſcene! how loudly doth it preach to us, *Flee from idolatry!*

4 *Here is the patience of the ſaints*; the bleſſed iſſue and effect of it *here* in glory *are they who keep the commandments of God, and the faith of Jeſus*, in oppoſition to all the corruptions of deceivers and perſecutors, great and eternal will be their reward

4 13 And

13 And I heard a voice from heaven [o], saying unto me, Write, Blessed are the dead which die in the Lord [p], from henceforth yea, saith the Spirit, that they may rest from their labours, and their works do follow them 14 And I looked, and behold, a white cloud, and upon the cloud *one* sat, like unto the Son of man [q], having on his head a golden crown [r], and in his hand a sharp sickle. 15 And another angel came out of the temple, crying with a loud voice to him that sat on the cloud, Thrust in thy sickle, and reap for the time is come for thee to reap, for the harvest of the earth is ripe [s] 16 And he that sat on the cloud, thrust in his sickle on the earth, and the earth was reaped 17 And another angel came out of the temple which is in heaven, he having also a sharp sickle 18 And another angel came out from the altar, which had power over fire, and cried with a loud cry to him that had the sharp sickle, saying, Thrust in thy sharp sickle, and gather the clusters of the vine of the earth [t], for her grapes are fully ripe 19 And the angel thrust in his sickle into the earth, and gathered the vine of the earth, and cast *it* into the great wine-press of the wrath of God [u] 20 And the wine press was trodden without the city, and blood [x] came out of the wine press, even unto the horse-bridles, by the space of a thousand *and* six hundred furlongs.

v 13—20 For the further encouragement of the church we have here,

1 A voice from heaven, declaring the blessedness of all who die in the faith and favour of Jesus, whether martyrs or others, their sufferings are all ended, they enter upon the beginnings of their eternal rest, and their works shall follow them, to bear witness to their fidelity Lord Jesus, may this blessedness be mine!

2 A new vision succeeds under the figure of the harvest and vintage The Lord Jesus appears seated on a cloud, with a golden crown, and sharp sickle in his hands, and an angel, the representative of the ministers of Jesus, cried to him in prayer out of the temple, that he would put in his sickle, and execute vengeance on the wicked, whose provocations made them ripe for judgment in answer to their cry, the sickle is thrust into the earth A second angel with another sharp sickle appears, and a third from out of the temple cries to him to put in his sickle, and gather the grapes of the earth into the wine-press of the wrath of God, and the blood came out of the wine-press up to the horses bridles, for the space of one thousand and six hundred furlongs These judgments, if considered as the same, may refer either to the great destruction which shall be made of the enemies of Christ's church, in the day when the papal tyranny shall be destroyed, and the most dreadful slaughter be made of all the adherents of the beast or it may refer to the final day of judgment, as others suppose, and perdition of ungodly men But if the events alluded to are supposed to be different, then the first may be applied to the destruction of the kingdom of the beast and his subjects, and the last to the general judgment Whichever it be, it is the comfort of the faithful, that however many or inveterate their enemies may be, they shall inevitably be rooted out at the last, and perish for ever

CHAP. XV

This chapter contains an useful introduction or preparation for the pouring out of the vials, in which we have, 1 A sight of those angels in heaven that were to have the execution of this great work, and with what acclamations of joy the heavenly host applauded the great design, ver 1—5 2 A sight of those angels coming out of heaven to receive those vials which they were to pour out, and the great commotions that this caused in the world, ver 5, &c

1. AND I saw another sign in heaven, great and marvellous, seven angels, having the seven last plagues, for in them is filled up the wrath of God 2 And I saw as it were a sea of glass [a], mingled with fire; and them that had gotten the victory over the beast, and over his image, and over his mark, *and* over the number of his name, stand on the sea of glass, having the harps of God 3 And they sing the song of Moses [b] the servant of God, and the song of the Lamb, saying, Great and marvellous are thy works, Lord God almighty; just and true are thy ways, thou King of saints 4 Who shall not fear thee, [c] O Lord, and glorify thy name? for *thou* only *art* holy for all nations shall come and worship before thee [d]; for thy judgments are made manifest

v 1—4 The former chapters gave a general view of the judgments which were ready to fall on the antichristian foe, and we have here preparation made for the execution of them

1 Seven angels, the ministers of wrath, appear with the seven last plagues, ready to execute them on the enemies of the church

2 The church triumphant in heaven is seen standing on a sea of glass mingled with fire, the emblem of their multitude, spotless purity, and tried integrity, and in the view of their deliverance from all their persecuting foes, and the judgments God was about to inflict upon them, they sung aloud his praises, as Israel of old, when having passed through the Red Sea, they beheld the carcases of the Egyptians on the shore They ascribe glory to God for his providential works, acknowledge the truth and justice of all his ways, and that he is most worthy to be feared and adored, who in his judgments manifests his love to his people, and his wrath against their enemies

5 And after that, I looked, and behold, the temple of the tabernacle of the testimony [e] in heaven was opened 6 And the seven angels came out of the temple, having the seven plagues, clothed in pure and white linnen, and having their breasts girded with golden girdles [f], 7 And one of the four beasts gave unto the seven angels seven golden vials [g] full of the wrath of God, who liveth for ever and ever 8 And the temple was filled with smoke [h] from the glory of God, and from his power, and no man was able to enter into the temple [i], till the seven plagues of the seven angels were fulfilled

v 5—8 A further vision presents itself to the enraptured apostle

1 *The temple of the tabernacle of the testimony in heaven was opened*, the holiest place of all, alluding to the temple on mount Zion, was laid open, and from thence came forth the seven angels with the seven last plagues, cloathed in fine linnen, and girded with golden girdles, bringing the answer of the prayers which God's suffering saints had put up before the mercy-seat

2 One of the beasts puts into their hands seven vials full of the wrath of the ever-living God, which they are sent forth to pour on the earth And hereupon the temple was filled with smoak, the emblem of these judgments, from the glory of God, *so that no man was able to enter into the temple, till the seven plagues of the seven angels were fulfilled*, nor were they by any means to be averted

CHAP XVI

In this chapter we have an account of the pouring forth of these vials that were filled with the wrath of God, and they were poured out upon the whole antichristian empire, and on every thing appertaining to it 1 Upon the earth, ver 2 the sea, 3 Upon the sea, ver 3 Upon the rivers and fountains of waters, ver 4 Upon which there the heavenly hosts proclaim and applaud the righteousness of the judgments of God 4 The fourth vial was poured out on the sun, ver 8 the fifth on the seat of the beast, the sixth on the river Euphrates, the seventh in the air, upon which the cities of the nations fell, and great Babylon came in remembrance before God

1. AND I heard a great voice out of the temple, saying to the seven angels, Go your ways, and pour out the vials of the wrath of God upon the earth 2 And the first went and poured out his vial upon the earth, and there fell a noisome and grievous sore [a] upon the men which had the mark of the beast, and *upon* them which worshipped his image [b]. 3 And the second angel poured out his vial upon the sea, and it became as the blood [c] of a dead man and every living soul died in the sea 4 And the third angel poured out his vial upon the rivers and fountains of waters, and they became blood [d] 5 And I heard the angel of the waters say, Thou art righteous, O Lord, which art, and wast, and shalt be, because thou hast judged thus 6 For they have shed the blood of saints and prophets, and thou hast given them blood to drink [e], for they are worthy 7 And I heard another out of the altar say, Even so, Lord God almighty, true and righteous [f] *are* thy judgments.

v 1—7. Whether theſe vials have already begun to be poured forth, or whether all of them are to be referred to ſome future day of vengeance on the antichriſtian beaſt, is matter of diſpute I am moſt inclined to the latter opinion, and that the events can only ſhow the meaning of the judgments but I ſhall give the ſentiments of thoſe who ſuppoſe them already begun

1 The firſt vial, which brings a noiſome and grievous ſore upon the men who worſhipped the beaſt, is ſuppoſed to refer to the great corruptions of worſhip and manners, and the wars which aroſe among the popiſh princes, after the death of Lewis, ſurnamed the pious, between the years 830 and 988

2 The ſecond vial was poured upon the ſea, and it became congealed as the blood of a dead man, and every living creature died alluding, as is ſuggeſted, to the wars which were ſet on foot for the recovery of the holy land from the Saracens, wherein ſuch innumerable multitudes of papiſts loſt their lives, between 1040 and 1190

3 The third vial is poured on the rivers, and turns them into blood, and is referred to the civil wars of Italy between the Guelphs and Gibelines, the popes and the emperors, carried on with vaſt effuſion of blood, from the year 1200 to about 1370

For theſe judgments, the angel who laſt poured out his vial upon the waters, aſcribes glory to God, acknowledging the righteouſneſs of his puniſhments, in giving thoſe in return blood to drink, who had ſhed ſo profuſely the blood of ſaints to which another angel, from under the altar ſaid, *Amen*, concurring in the ſolemn aſcription of praiſe to God for theſe his righteous judgments *Note*, God will make every creature ſubſervient to his glory even the damnation of the wicked ſhall redound to the praiſe of his juſtice and holineſs, and ſaints and angels ſhall adore him for his awful judgments, as well as for his mercies

8. And the fourth angel poured out his vial upon the
ſun [g], and power was given unto him to ſcorch men
with fire [h] 9 And men were ſcorched with a great
heat, and blaſphemed the name of God [i], which hath
power over theſe plagues and they repented not, to give
him glory [k] 10. And the fifth angel poured out his
vial upon the ſeat of the beaſt [l], and his kingdom was
full of darkneſs, and they gnawed [m] their tongues for
pain, 11 And blaſphemed the God of heaven, becauſe
of their pains and their ſores, and repented not of their
deeds 12 And the ſixth angel poured out his vial
upon the great river Euphrates, and the water thereof
was dried up [n], that the way of the kings of the eaſt
might be prepared 13 And I ſaw three unclean ſpirits
like frogs [o], *come* out of the mouth of the dragon [p], and
out of the mouth of the beaſt, and out of the mouth of
the falſe prophet 14 For they are the ſpirits of devils,
working miracles [q], which go forth unto the kings of
the earth, and of the whole world, to gather them to the
battle of that great day of God almighty 15 Behold,
I come as a thief [r] Bleſſed *is* he that watcheth, and
keepeth his garments [s], leſt he walk naked, and they
ſee his ſhame 16. And he gathered them together into
a place, called in the Hebrew tongue, Armageddon [t].

g Ch xxxvii 9, 10 h I ſ cxxi 6 i I a viii 21 k Joſh vii 19 l 1 Sam iii 10 2 Kings 37 47 m Ex x 21, 23 Iſa v 30 ix 1 n Iſa xliv 27, 28 Jer l 38 Iſa li 36 37 o Ex viii 2 1 Kings xxii 22 p Chap xii 13 q 2 Theſ ii 9, 10 r Chap xxii 7 1 Theſ v 2 2 Pet iii 10 s Mat xxii 11 12 t Judg iv 15 v 19 2 Kings xxiii 29, 30 Zech xii 11, 12

v 8—16 We have here,

1 The fourth vial poured out upon the ſun, and this may refer to the terrible calamities which happened between 1378 and 1530, through the contentions about the papal chair, ſeveral popes at a time claiming it, and excommunicating each other, and through their intrigues and ambition horrid ravages and furious wars raged Yet, far from being affected with theſe providences, the adherents to popery repented not, but blaſphemed God the more, and ſet themſelves more fiercely to perſecute thoſe whom he raiſed up, burning thoſe faithful witneſſes Jerome and Huſs, who teſtified againſt their abominations

2 The fifth vial was poured on the ſeat of the beaſt, and darkneſs followed in his kingdom, and his ſubjects gnawed their tongues for pain, where, as in the foregoing vials, there is a manifeſt alluſion to the plagues of Egypt And this is interpreted of the ſtroke given to the pope's dominion by the reformation, between 1530 and 1650, which excited the blaſphemies of the antichriſtian power, and, far from bringing them to repentance, though it cut them to the heart with vexation, excited their bitter imprecations upon the reformed, as heretics and apoſtates, on whom they denounced the heavieſt vengeance

3 The ſixth vial is poured upon the river Euphrates, and ſuppoſed to imply the deſtruction of the Ottoman empire, in order to open a way for the converſion of the eaſtern nations to Chriſtianity, the river being dried up, to prepare a paſſage for the kings of the eaſt to come into the church

Hereupon the devil, perceiving his kingdom every where ſhaken, rallies all his forces, and by his emiſſaries, the eccleſiaſtics of Rome, repreſented by unclean ſpirits like frogs, ſends forth to gather the kings of the antichriſtian party to his banners, and by lying wonders and falſe miracles engages them, in ſupport of the papal cauſe, to aſſemble for war againſt the ſaints in a place called Armageddon, which ſhould be as fatal to the enemies of the church as Megiddo, where the army of Siſera fell before the ſword of Barak

A warning is added, *v* 15 addreſſed to the faithful in the view of this day *Behold, I come as a thief*, ſuddenly and unexpectedly, when theſe enemies apprehend themſelves moſt ſecure *Bleſſed is he that watcheth, and keepeth his garments, leſt he walk naked, and they ſee his ſhame* *Note*, The uncertainty of the coming of our Lord ſhould engage us to maintain conſtant watchfulneſs, that we may not be ſurprized, but ready with joy to welcome his arrival

17 And the ſeventh angel poured out his vial into
the air [u], and there came a great voice out of the tem- u Eph ii 2 & vi 12
ple of heaven, from the throne, ſaying, It is done [x] 18 x John xix 30.
And there were voices, and thunders, and lightnings,
and there was a great earthquake, ſuch as was not ſince
men were upon the earth, ſo mighty an earthquake [y], y Joel iii 16
and ſo great 19 And the great city was divided into Chap xi 13
three parts [z], and the cities of the nations fell, and great z Ezek v 12
Babylon came in remembrance before God, to give unto
her the cup of the wine of the fierceneſs of his wrath [a] a Pſ lxxv 8. Jer xxv 15
20 And every iſland fled away, and the mountains were
not found [b] 21 And there fell upon men a great hail b Iſa ii
out of heaven, *every ſtone* about the weight of a talent [c] c Joſh x 11
and men blaſphemed God becauſe of the plague of the Ex ix —
hail, for the plague thereof was exceeding great 6 Iſa xx 6 3, Ezek xxxviii 2

v 17—21 The ſeventh and laſt vial is poured into the air, the place where Satan's illuſions are practiſed And now a voice from heaven exulting cries, *It is done*, the ruin of Antichriſt is compleated Tremendous voices, thunders, and lightning followed, and ſuch an earthquake as had never been before, denoting the entire diſſolution of this perſecuting ſtate Rome itſelf, the ſeat of the papal empire, is ſhattered in pieces, and all the other cities of the antichriſtian empire ſunk into ruins The time is now come for myſtical Babylon's overthrow, and God's fearful vengeance is poured out upon her The whole body of her adherents, whether dwelling in iſlands or mountains, ſhall utterly be deſtroyed, as if ſwallowed up by an earthquake And, as one means of compleating their ruin, they who attempt to flee for their lives, ſhall, like the Amorites, (*Joſh* x 11) be conſumed with hail-ſtones, each vaſt as a talent, and die impenitent under all their judgments, ſtill blaſpheming the hand that lies ſo heavy upon them *Note*, The ſoreſt judgment is an hard and impenitent heart where that abides, there all God's viſitations tend but to exaſperate and provoke deeper blaſphemies

CHAP XVII

This chapter is another repreſentative of thoſe things that had been revealed before, concerning the wickedneſs and ruin of antichriſt. This antichriſt had been before repreſented as a beaſt, and is now deſcribed as a great whore And here, 1 The apoſtle is invited to ſee this vile woman, ver 1, 2 2 He tells us what an appearance ſhe made, ver 3—6 3 The myſtery of it is explained to him, ver 7—12 And, 4 Her ruin foretold, ver 13, &c

1 AND there came one of the ſeven angels which had
the ſeven vials, and talked with me, [a] ſaying un- a Zech i 5
to me, Come hither, I will ſhew unto thee the judgment
of the great whore, that ſitteth upon many waters [b] 2 b Chap xviii 7 Jer li 1
With whom the kings of the earth have committed for-
nication, and the inhabiters of the earth have been made
drunk with the wine of her fornication 3 So he carried
me away in the ſpirit [c] into the wilderneſs [d] and I ſaw a c Ezek viii 3
woman ſit upon a ſcarlet-coloured beaſt, full of names of d Chap xii 6.
blaſphemy, having ſeven heads and ten horns [e] 4 And e Chap xiii 1
the woman was arrayed in purple, and ſcarlet colour, and
decked with gold, and precious ſtone and pearls, having
a golden cup in her hand, [f] full of abominations and f Jer li 7
filthineſs of her fornication 5 And upon her forehead
was a name written, MYSTERY, [g] BABYLON THE GREAT, g 2 Theſ ii 7
THE MOTHER OF HARLOTS AND ABOMINATIONS OF THE
EARTH 6 And I ſaw the woman drunken with the h Jer xlvi 10
blood of the ſaints, and with the blood of the martyrs of
Jeſus and when I ſaw her, I wondered with great ad-
miration 7 And the angel ſaid unto me, Wherefore
didſt thou marvel? I will tell thee the myſtery of
the woman, and of the beaſt that carrieth her, which
hath

4

hath the ſeven heads and ten horns. 8 The beaſt that
thou ſaweſt was, and is not; and ſhall aſcend out of the
i Chap xix 20. bottomleſs pit, and go into perdition [i] and they that
dwell on the earth ſhall wonder (whoſe names were not
written in the book of life from the foundation of the
k Eph i 4. world) [k] when they behold the beaſt that was, and is not,
and yet *is*. 9. And here is the mind which hath wiſ-
dom The ſeven heads are ſeven mountains, on which
the woman ſitteth 10 And there are ſeven kings five
are fallen, and one is, *and* the other is not yet come,
and when he cometh, he muſt continue a ſhort ſpace
11 And the beaſt that was and is not, even he is the
eighth, and is of the ſeven, and goeth into perdition 12
l Dan ii 42 & vii 7 24 And the ten horns [l] which thou ſaweſt, are ten kings,
which have received no kingdom as yet, but receive
power as kings one hour with the beaſt 13 Theſe
have one mind, and ſhall give their power and ſtrength
unto the beaſt

v 1—13 An angel farther explains to the apoſtle what was meant by the viſion before him, who this great whore was on whom God's judgments were to be executed, whilſt proudly ſeated upon the waters, the emblem of her vaſt juriſdiction, and having made the kings and inhabitants of the earth drunk with her idolatries and ſorceries, ſhe flattered herſelf ſhe ſhould ſit as a queen, and ſee no ſorrow

Inſtant in viſion John was carried into the wilderneſs, and there he beheld the antichriſtian whore ſeated upon a ſcarlet-coloured beaſt, the papacy, ſcarlet being the colour in which the pope and cardinals are dreſſed, or to denote the ſanguinary edicts executed by her This beaſt was full of names of blaſphemy, the blaſphemous titles and prerogatives of infallibility, ſupremacy, &c being challenged by the popes of Rome, which is ſeated on ſeven hills, ſignified by the ſeven heads, and uſurped authority over many potent kingdoms This woman appeared in all the attire of an harlot, intimating the vaſt pomp and profuſion of rich cloaths and ornaments uſed by the Romiſh church, to deck their Prieſts, idols, and images In her hand was a cup of philters, to intoxicate her paramours, and lead them to all her abominable wickedneſſes in doctrine, worſhip, and manners, and upon her forehead her name was written, *Myſtery*, (2 *Theſ* ii 7) with deep deſign and craft carrying on her iniquitous deſigns, *Babylon the great*, like Babylon of old, for oppreſſion, pride, and idolatry, *the mother of harlots, and abominations of the earth*, the parent and patroneſs of every wickedneſs, and ſhe was drunk with the blood of martyrs A character ſo horrid, infamous, and hideous, greatly excited John's aſtoniſhment

Obſerving his amazement, the angel explains the viſion This beaſt *was* of old, when Rome was the ſeat of pagan idolatry and perſecution, *and is not*, Rome pagan having been deſtroyed, *and yet is*, the ſame under the papal government in tyranny and idolatry as formerly it is the offspring of hell, and is doomed to return thither The men of the Roman empire in general, God's elect excepted, ſhall wonder after this beaſt with ſuperſtitious veneration *And here is the mind which hath wiſdom*, let ſuch one who is intelligent mark theſe characters, and they will be led to what is prefigured by them (1) *The ſeven heads are ſeven mountains, on which the woman ſitteth*, Rome, the capital of her empire, being built on ſeven hills (2) *There are ſeven kings*, or ſucceſſive forms of government, *five are fallen*, the kings, conſuls, dictators, decemvirs, and military tribunes, no longer ſubſiſt *One is*, the pagan emperors that then reigned when the viſion was given *and one is not yet come*, the Chriſtian emperors, which are to endure but a ſhort ſpace *The beaſt is the eighth*, in order, or if the empire, as under the pagan and Chriſtian emperors, be conſidered as one form of government, the papacy *is one of the ſeven kings*, and will be as ſurely deſtroyed as the former (3) Another mark of this beaſt is the ten horns, which are ſo many kings, which had not yet received their kingdoms, but were to ariſe about the ſame time when the papal power ſhould grow to its height, even when the empire was divided into about that number of kingdoms, and all theſe princes ſubmitted to the papal yoke, and conſented to uphold the authority of the Roman pontiſs

14 Theſe ſhall make war with the Lamb, and the
Lamb ſhall overcome them for he is Lord of lords,
m Chap vi 15—17 & xix 16 and King of kings, [m] and they that are with him, *are*
n Luke xiv 24 called, [n] and choſen, and faithful 15 And he ſaid unto
o Jam ii 5 me, The waters which thou ſaweſt, where the whore
p 2 Pet i 10 ſitteth, are peoples, and multitudes, and nations, and
q Dan ii 44 tongues 16 And the ten horns which thou ſaweſt
upon the beaſt, theſe ſhall hate the whore, and ſhall make
r Dan vii 11 Lev xxi 9 her deſolate and naked, and ſhall eat her fleſh, and burn
her with fire [r] 17 For God hath put in their hearts to
s Prov xxi 1 fulfil his will, [s] and to agree, and give their kingdom unto
the beaſt, until the words of God ſhall be fulfilled 18.
And the woman which thou ſaweſt, is that great city, [t] t Chap xv 19
which reigneth over the kings of the earth

v 14—18 The riſe of the papal power had been ſhown, here we have its downfal

1 Theſe kings will make war with the Lamb, endeavouring by fire and ſword to compel his people to ſubmit with implicit obedience to the papal ſee, but he ſhall ſtrengthen them with conſtancy to reſiſt, and even in martyrdom to conquer, *for he is Lord of lords, and King of kings*, mighty to ſupport his ſuffering ſaints, who being choſen by his grace, and called by his word, are enabled to approve themſelves faithful in defiance of all oppoſition

2 The ſame kingdoms that have exerted their power to ſupport the throne of the beaſt, ſhall, through God's over-ruling providence, be made the means of his deſtruction Though God for a while ſuffers them to give their kingdoms to the beaſt, yet, when the time appointed is accompliſhed, their ſucceſſors in theſe kingdoms ſhall be as much turned to hate and deſtroy the whore, whoſe dominion for a while ſhould extend over the nations and kings of the earth, as their predeceſſors were zealous to maintain the papal uſurpations, they ſhall treat her with every indignity, and deſtroy her by the moſt tormenting death Whence we may obſerve, (1) That there never will be another univerſal monarchy erected by any of the ſtates of Chriſtendom (2) That the very powers that have been the pillars of popery, ſhall be the chief inſtruments in pulling down the papal throne

CHAP XVIII

We have here, 1 *An angel proclaiming the fall of Babylon*, ver 1, 2 2 *Aſſigning the reaſons of her fall*, ver 3 3 *Giving warning to all that belonged to God, to come out of her*, ver 4, 5 *and to aſſiſt in her deſtruction*, ver 6—8 4 *The great lamentation made for her by thoſe that had been large ſharers in her ſinful pleaſures and profits*, ver 9—20 5 *The great joy that there would be among others at the ſight of her irrecoverable ruin*, ver 20, &c

1. AND after theſe things I ſaw another angel come
down from heaven, having great power, and
the earth was lightned with his glory [a] 2 And he a Ezek xliii 2—5
cried mightily with a ſtrong voice, ſaying, Babylon the
great is fallen, is fallen, and is become the habitation of
devils, and the hold of every foul ſpirit, and a cage of
every unclean and hateful bird [b] 3 For all nations b Iſa xiii 19—22 & xiv 23
have drunk of the wine of the wrath of her fornication, Jer l 39 & li 37, 62
[c] and the kings of the earth have committed fornication c Chap xvii 17
with her, and the merchants of the earth are waxed rich,
through the abundance of her delicacies.

v 1—3 Deſcending from heaven with brightneſs like the ſun, an angel, inveſted with great power, cries, *Babylon the great is fallen, is fallen*, her long-expected doom is come, and as ſhe hath been filled with abominations, her deſerted palaces and ruined habitations *ſhall become the den of dragons, the hold of every foul ſpirit, and the cage of every unclean and hateful bird* and the cauſe of her ruin is aſcribed to her idolatries, adulteries, and the merchandize of ſouls, which enabled her and her eccleſiaſtics to riot in wealth and luxury

4 And I heard another voice from heaven, ſaying,
Come out of her, my people, [d] that ye be not partakers d Iſa xlviii 20 & lii 11
of her ſins, and that ye receive not of her plagues 5 Jer l 8 & li 45
For her ſins have reached unto heaven, [e] and God hath
remembred her iniquities. 6 Reward her even as ſhe e Gen xix 13
rewarded you, and double unto her double, [f] according f Ex xxi 23, 24 &c
to her works in the cup which ſhe hath filled, fill to Zech. 4—9
her double 7 How much ſhe hath glorified herſelf, Jer xvi 18
and lived deliciouſly, ſo much torment and ſorrow give
her for ſhe ſaith in her heart, I ſit a queen, [g] and am g Iſa xlvii 5—8
no widow, and ſhall ſee no ſorrow 8 Therefore ſhall
her plagues come in one day, death, and mourning, and
famine, [h] and ſhe ſhall be utterly burnt with fire, for h Iſa xlvii 9—11
ſtrong *is* the Lord God who judgeth her 9 And the
kings of the earth, who have committed fornication, and
lived deliciouſly with her, ſhall bewail her, and lament
for her, [i] when they ſhall ſee the ſmoke of her burning, i Ezek xxvii
10 Standing afar off for the fear of her torment, ſaying, 1—37
Alas, alas, that great city Babylon, that mighty city!
for in one hour is thy judgment come 11 And the
merchants of the earth ſhall weep and mourn over her,
for no man buyeth her merchandize any more

The merchandize of gold and ſilver, and precious ſtones,
and of pearls, and fine linnen, and purple and ſilk, and
ſcarlet, and all thyine wood, and all manner of veſſels of
ivory, and all manner of veſſels of moſt precious wood,
and of braſs, and iron, and marble, 13 And cinnamon,
and odours, and ointments, and frankincenſe, and wine,
and oil, and fine flour, and wheat, and beaſts, and ſheep,
k 2 Pet ii 3 and horſes, and chariots, and ſlaves, and ſouls of men k
14 And the fruits that thy ſoul luſted after, are depart-
ed from thee, and all things which were dainty and
goodly, are departed from thee, and thou ſhalt find
them no more at all 15 The merchants of theſe
things which were made rich by her, ſhall ſtand afar off,
for fear of her torment, weeping and wailing, 16 And
ſaying, Alas, alas, that great city that was cloathed in
fine linnen, and purple, and ſcarlet, and decked with
gold, and precious ſtones, and pearls 17 For in one
hour ſo great riches is come to nought And every ſhip-
maſter, and all the company in ſhips, and ſailors, and as
many as trade by ſea, ſtood afar off, 18 And cried,
when they ſaw the ſmoke of her burning, ſaying, What
city is like unto this great city ? 19 And they caſt duſt
l Ezek xxvii 30 Job ii 12 on their heads, l and cried, weeping and wailing, ſaying,
Alas, alas, that great city, wherein were made rich all
that had ſhips in the ſea, by reaſon of her coſtlineſs for
in one hour is ſhe made deſolate 20 Rejoice over her,
m Eph … thou heaven, and ye holy apoſtles, and prophets, m for
God hath avenged you on her 21 And a mighty an-
gel took up a ſtone like a great mill ſtone, and caſt it
into the ſea, ſaying, Thus with violence ſhall that great
city Babylon be thrown down, and ſhall be found no
n Jer li 63 … more at all n 22 And the voice of harpers and muſi-
o Neh ix … cians, and of pipers, and of trumpeters, ſhall be heard
no more at all in thee, o and no craftſman, of whatſo-
o Ezek xxiv 8 … ever craft *he be*, ſhall be found any more in thee, and
the ſound of a mill ſtone ſhall be heard no more at all in
p Jer xxv 10 thee p 23 And the light of a candle ſhall ſhine no
more at all in thee, and the voice of the bridegroom
q Jer vii 34 & xxv 11 and of the bride ſhall be heard no more at all in thee q
for thy merchants were the great men of the earth, for
by thy ſorceries were all nations deceived 24 And in
her was found the blood of prophets, and of ſaints, and
r Mat xxiii 34—35 of all that were ſlain upon the earth r

v 4—24 We have here,

1 Warning given to the people of God to ſeparate themſelves from Babylon myſtical, and, becauſe of her enormous provocations againſt God, to retaliate upon her righteous vengeance She proudly vaunted her imperial ſtate, and boaſted of her ſecurity, but ſudden deſtruction ſhall overtake her, and, hurled from the ſummit of grandeur, death, mourning, and famine ſhall ſeize her, and by the judgment of the Almighty Lord ſhe ſhall be utterly burnt with fire *Note*, (1) They who would be ſaved from the ruin of the wicked, muſt ſeparate themſelves from their ſociety (2) God will give righteous judgment to the ſinner and repay him according to the multitude of his ungodlineſs

2 A doleful lamentation is taken up for her fall by the kings and merchants of the earth, and ſailors, the cardinals, prieſts, monks, jeſuits, and other eccleſiaſtics, who trafficked in diſpenſations, indulgencies, &c making merchandize of the ſouls of men Standing afar off, and beholding the ſmoke of her burning, they will bewail her ſudden and irrecoverable ruin, and therewith the loſs of all that grandeur, wealth, and luxury, in which they had long indulged themſelves a ſorrow of the world which worketh death, and but aggravates the miſeries complained of

3 The ſaints of God, with the apoſtles and prophets, are called to triumph over her, and to rejoice in her fall for when the wicked fall there is ſhouting, not from a ſpirit of private revenge, but from a delight to behold God glorified in his righteous judgments

4 To give a ſign of Babylon's irrecoverable ruin, a mighty angel hurls a mill-ſtone into the ſea, intimating, that all joy ſhould for ever ceaſe, every kind of traffick be at an end, the neceſſaries of life fail, no light appear, no bridal ſong any more be heard, but ſolitude and ſilence reign in her deſolate palaces; becauſe by her ſorceries and idolatries ſhe had bewitched the earth, and at her hands was required the blood of all the martyrs which had been ſlain on the earth by her cruel edicts and perſecutions *Note*, The ſinner who ſinks down into the abyſs of hell under the wrath of God, is loſt for ever, and ſhall never riſe up again

CHAP XIX

In this chapter we have, 1 A farther account of the triumphant ſong of angels and ſaints for the fall of Babylon, ver 1—4. 2 *The marriage between Chriſt and the church proclaimed and perfected,* ver 5—10 3 *Another warlike expedition of the glorious head and huſband of the church, with the ſucceſs of it,* ver 10, &c

1 AND after theſe things I heard a great voice of
much people in heaven, ſaying, Alleluia, Sal-
vation, and glory, and honour, and power unto the
Lord our God : 2 For true and righteous *are* his
judgments, a for he hath judged the great whore, which a Chap …
did corrupt the earth with her fornication, and hath
avenged the blood of his ſervants at her hand b 3 And b Chap xvi 6 …
again they ſaid, Alleluia c And her ſmoke roſe up for c … 18
ever and ever 4 And the four and twenty elders, and
the four beaſts d fell down and worſhipped God that ſat d Chap iv 4—6
on the throne, ſaying, Amen, Alleluia

v 1—4 A command being given in *v* 20 of the former chapter, to the ſaints of God, to rejoice over Babylon fallen, we have here their ſong of praiſe on that occaſion. They cried, *Alleluia*, aſcribing ſalvation, and glory, and honour, and power, to the Lord their God, acknowledging his righteous judgments in the vengeance executed on the great whore, for her lewdneſs, idolatry, and cruelty, and they repeated loud Alleluias, whilſt the *ſmoke of her torment aroſe up for ever and ever* The four living creatures, and the elders, the repreſentatives of the miniſters and the church of the redeemed, hereupon joined in their adorations before the throne, and joyfully cried, Amen! Alleluia! *Note*, Even the torment of the damned will afford matter of praiſe to God's ſaints, and glory to himſelf

5 And a voice came out of the throne, ſaying, Praiſe
our God, all ye his ſervants, and ye that fear him, both
ſmall and great e 6 And I heard as it were the voice e Pſ cxxxiv 1 …
of a great multitude, and as the voice of many waters,
and as the voice of mighty thundrings, ſaying, Alleluia
for the Lord God omnipotent reigneth, f 7 Let us be f Pſ … 1
glad and rejoice, and give honour to him for the mar-
riage of the Lamb is come, and his wife hath made her-
ſelf ready g 8 And to her was granted, that ſhe ſhould g 2 Cor xi 2 …
be arrayed in fine linnen, clean and white for the fine
linnen is the righteouſneſs of ſaints h 9 And he ſaith h … Mat xxii
unto me, Write, Bleſſed are they which *are* called unto
the marriage-ſupper of the Lamb i And he ſaith unto i Luke xiv … 6
me, Theſe are the true ſayings of God k 10 And I fell k Chap xxi 5
at his feet to worſhip him And he ſaid unto me, See
thou do it not l I am thy fellow ſervant, and of thy bre- l Acts … 10
thren that have the teſtimony of Jeſus worſhip God
for the teſtimony of Jeſus is the ſpirit of propheсy

v 5—10 The ſong of triumph over Babylon being ended, a voice from the throne enjoins the hoſt of the redeemed to unite in the praiſes of their common Lord, and inſtantly innumerable voices, loud as cataracts of water, or mighty thunders, poured forth their Hallelujahs *For the Lord God omnipotent reigneth*, ſince the antichriſtian powers are broken, his kingdom of grace is extended through the earth, and his dominion univerſal over a willing people *The marriage of the Lamb is come, and his wife hath made herſelf ready*, therefore *let us be glad, and rejoice, and give honour to him* And this many refer to the converſion of the Jews, who will now be brought into the church, and be publicly in profeſſion joined to the Lord as his people

1 The dreſs of the Lamb's wife is deſcribed She is arrayed in fine linnen, clean and white, and that is interpreted to ſignify the *righteouſneſs of ſaints*, both imputed and implanted, whereby the church becomes meet for the boſom of her Lord, beautiful in the comelineſs he put upon her

2 They are declared bleſſed, who are invited, and come to the marriage-ſupper of the Lamb, partaking of all the privileges and ordinances of the goſpel, thereby admitted to the higheſt communion with Jeſus, and joined to the Lord in one Spirit

3 The angel cloſes with a ſolemn aſſurance of the truth of this revelation, which ſhould not fail of its accompliſhment and, overcome with the brightneſs of his glory, John fell at his feet, and was ready to pay him divine honour, not conſidering what he did but the angel rebuked him for his inconſiderate deſign He owns himſelf unworthy of that honour, which was due to God alone, and, glorious as he appeared, was but the apoſtle's fellow-ſervant, bearing teſtimony to the ſame Jeſus, and now revealing what the Saviour directed to him, who inſpired the prophets, and ſent him to deliver this meſſage

4

to John for the church's use and comfort *Note*, The highest created being hath no more title to our worship than the lowest, it is the same idolatry to worship an angel as a worm

11 And I saw heaven opened, and behold, a white horse, and he that sat upon him *was* called faithful and true, and in righteousness he doth judge and make war. 12 His eyes *were* as a flame of fire, and on his head were many crowns, and he had a name written that no man knew but he himself 13 And he *was* clothed with a vesture dipt in blood and his name is called, The Word of God 14 And the armies which were in heaven followed him upon white horses, clothed in fine linen, white and clean 15 And out of his mouth goeth a sharp sword, that with it he should smite the nations and he shall rule them with a rod of iron; and he treadeth the wine-press of the fierceness and wrath of almighty God 16 And he hath on his vesture and on his thigh a name written, KING OF KINGS, AND LORD OF LORDS 17 And I saw an angel standing in the sun, and he cried with a loud voice, saying to all the fowls that fly in the midst of heaven, Come and gather your selves together unto the supper of the great God, 18 That ye may eat the flesh of kings, and the flesh of captains, and the flesh of mighty men, and the flesh of horses, and of them that sit on them, and the flesh of all men, both free and bond, both small and great 19 And I saw the beast, and the kings of the earth, and their armies gathered together, to make war against him that sat on the horse, and against his army. 20 And the beast was taken, and with him the false prophet that wrought miracles before him, with which he deceived them that had received the mark of the beast, and them that worshipped his image These both were cast alive into a lake of fire burning with brimstone 21 And the remnant were slain with the sword of him that sat upon the horse, which *sword* proceeded out of his mouth: and all the fowls were filled with their flesh.

v 11—21. The Lord Jesus here appears in Majesty to execute vengeance on the beast and his adherents, now assembled to make their last efforts

1 A most magnificent description is given of the Captain of our salvation. He is seated on a white horse, the emblem of victory, he is called *faithful and true*, performing all his promises to his people, and in righteousness executing vengeance on his enemies His eyes, bright as the flame, pierce into the secrets of the soul, and his many crowns of gold denote his universal dominion, his name and nature, as Jehovah, none can comprehend, his bloody vesture bespeaks his conquest over his slaughtered foes, and one of the names, whereby he hath revealed himself, is, *The Word of God* Close behind him followed his faithful warriors, his saints arrayed in robes of righteousness and garments of salvation, from his mouth proceeds the sharp sword of his denunciations of vengeance, before which his foes must fall as a potter's vessel before an iron rod, so shall they be broken to pieces, and as grapes laid in the wine-press, so shall he trample them in his fury, and on his vesture, where it hung down over his thigh, was this illustrious motto wrought, KING OF KINGS, AND LORD OF LORDS

2 A call is given to all the fowls of the air, to assemble on this dread occasion, and feast on the corpses of all the antichristian host, both great and small, who are now about to perish together

3 The army of the ungodly, Papist, Pagan, and Mahometan, assembles under the conduct of the beast, the battle is joined, the victory decisive, the beast and false prophet, which wrought the lying wonders, are taken, and the ringleaders in the antichristian apostacy are cast together, body and soul, into the burning lake, and all their adherents fall by the sword of him that sat on the white horse, and the fowls are gorged with their carcases And now, all foes being subdued, the glorious millennium commences, when the kingdoms of the world become the kingdoms of the Lord and of his Christ

CHAP XX

This chapter is thought, by some, to be the darkest part of all this prophecy, it is very probable the things contained in it are not yet accomplished, and therefore it is the wiser way to content ourselves with general observations, than to be positive and particular in our explications of it Here we have an account, 1 Of the binding of Satan for a thousand years, ver 1—3 2 The reign of the saints with Christ for the same time, ver 4—6 3 Of the loosing of Satan, and the conflict of the church with Gog and Magog, ver 7—10 4 Of the day of judgment, ver 11, &c.

1 AND I saw an angel come down from heaven, having the key of the bottomless pit, and a great chain in his hand 2 And he laid hold on the dragon that old serpent, which is the devil and Satan, and bound him a thousand years 3 And cast him into the bottomless pit, and shut him up, and set a seal upon him, that he should deceive the nations no more, till the thousand years should be fulfilled and after that he must be loosed for a little season 4 And I saw thrones, and they sat upon them, and judgment was given unto them and *I saw* the souls of them that were beheaded for the witness of Jesus, and for the word of God, and which had not worshipped the beast, neither his image, neither had received his mark upon their foreheads, or in their hands, and they lived and reigned with Christ a thousand years 5 But the rest of the dead lived not again until the thousand years were finished This *is* the first resurrection 6 Blessed and holy *is* he that hath part in the first resurrection on such the second death hath no power, but they shall be priests of God, and of Christ, and shall reign with him a thousand years

v 1—6 The *fourth period* now commences

1 Satan, the great deceiver, is bound by the angel of the everlasting covenant, and cast into the bottomless pit, restrained from all exercise of his power, and permitted no more, during a thousand years, to trouble the peaceful and happy state of the church, when they are expired, for a little season he will again be loosed

2 The reign of the saints with Christ begins, which some interpret literally of the resurrection of saints and martyrs, with whom Christ will personally dwell upon earth, during a thousand years before the general resurrection, but I rather concur with those who interpret this of the glorious state of the church during this period, when the faithful, who are one in spirit with all the former martyrs and confessors, who had faithfully opposed the antichristian tyranny, and now behold judgment executed upon their foes, these and their successors shall reign in a state of great dignity, peace, prosperity, and joy, Satan being no longer able to interrupt their repose, whilst all their former enemies are so entirely subdued, as figuratively to be called dead, and during this period none will be found to interrupt or disturb the felicity of the saints This happy state may metaphorically be well stiled *the first resurrection*, and is a figure of that which shall follow at the end of time

3 The happiness of these souls is great *Blessed and holy is he that hath part in the first resurrection on such the second death hath no power, but they shall be priests of God, and of Christ, and shall reign with him a thousand years*, in body, soul, and spirit devoted to him, and experiencing the felicity of his service here as the pledge of that eternal glory and blessedness which they expect hereafter

7 And when the thousand years are expired, Satan shall be loosed out of his prison, 8 And shall go out to deceive the nations which are in the four quarters of the earth, Gog and Magog, to gather them together to battle the number of whom *is* as the sand of the sea 9 And they went up on the breadth of the earth, and compassed the camp of the saints about, and the beloved city, and fire came down from God out of heaven, and devoured them 10 And the devil that deceived them was cast into the lake of fire and brimstone, where the beast and the false prophet *are*, and shall be tormented day and night for ever and ever

v 7—10 *The fifth period* begins with the loosing of Satan, the thousand years being expired His going forth once more to deceive, his prevalence over the nations, whom once more he will assemble, even Gog and Magog, the figure of those enemies of the church so named of old, and they shall surround the camp of the saints and the beloved city, but fire from heaven shall consume them, and the devil that deceived them will now be finally shut up in the eternal prison of hell, with the beast and the false prophet, to be tormented for ever and ever To what event this refers, who are the nations meant by Gog and Magog, or what time this period occupies, is utterly mysterious, and where we must be content to be ignorant The events themselves alone can unfold the prophecy

11 And I saw a great white throne, and him that sat on it, from whose face the earth and the heaven fled away, and there was found no place for them 12 And I saw the dead, both small and great, stand before God, and the books were opened and another book was

opened, which is *the book* of life and the dead were judged
out of those things which were written in the books, ac-
z Mat xxv 31, 46 & xvi 27 2 Cor v 10 1 Cor xi 31 32 1 Thes iv 15, 17 — cording to their works [z] 13 And the sea gave up the
dead which were in it, and death and hell delivered up
the dead which were in them and they were judged
every man according to their works 14 And death
and hell were cast into the lake of fire This is the se-
cond death 15 And whosoever was not found written
t Mat iii 12 Mark ix 13, 48 — in the book of life, was cast into the lake of fire [t]

v 11—15 *The sixth period* seems evidently to refer to the final judgment, which is here awfully described

1 The Judge appears on his magnificent throne, and before him the elementary heavens vanish, and the earth flies away

2 All, both small and great, appear at his tremendous bar, the sea and the grave give up their dead, the books are opened of God's omniscience, where every work and secret thought of men are recorded, and they are judged accordingly, whilst in the book of life of the Lamb their names are found written who shall never enter into condemnation *Note*, Before this awful day arrives, we should judge ourselves that we may not then be judged of the Lord, and so continually live under the apprehension and influence of it, that we may then have nothing to fear

3 The issue of the great assize is, that *death and hell*, the grave, for ever were abolished, and the wicked who existed in their separate state, now raised to life, even all who are not found written in the book of life, are cast into the lake of fire *this is the second death*, inexpressibly more dreadful than the first, for here immortality itself will be a curse, and the torment be intolerable and eternal Lord, gather not my soul with sinners in that day !

CHAP XXI

Hitherto the prophecy of this book has presented to us a very remarkable mixture of light and shade, prosperity and adversity, mercy and judgment, in the conduct of Divine Providence towards the church in the world, now, at the close of all, the day breaks, and the shadows flee away, a new world now appears, the former being passed away. Some are willing to understand all that is said in these two last chapters, of the state of the church even here on earth, in the glory of the latter days, but others, more probably, take it as a representation of the perfect and triumphant state of the church in heaven Let but the faithful saints and servants of God wait a while, and they shall not only see, but enjoy the perfect holiness and happiness of that world. In this chapter you have, 1 An introduction to the vision of the new Jerusalem, ver 1—9 2 The vision itself, ver. 10, &c

a Isa lxv 17 & lxvi 22 — 1 AND I saw a new heaven, and a new earth [a] for
the first heaven and the first earth were passed
b Isa lvii 20 — away, and there was no more sea [b] 2 And I John
c Heb xi 10 — saw the holy city, [c] new Jerusalem, coming down from
God out of heaven, prepared as a bride adorned for her
d Jude 24 — husband [d] 3 And I heard a great voice out of heaven,
saying, Behold, the tabernacle of God *is* with men, and
e Ex xxxvii 27 — he will dwell with them, [e] and they shall be his people,
f Ps cxliv 15 — and God himself shall be with them, *and be* their God [f]
4 And God shall wipe away all tears from their eyes, [g]
g Isa li 11 — and there shall be no more death, neither sorrow, nor
crying, neither shall there be any more pain for the
former things are passed away 5 And he that sat upon
h Isa xliii 19 — the throne said, Behold, I make all things new [h] And
he said unto me, Write for these words are true and
i Ps xxxiii — faithful 6 And he said unto me, It is done [i] I am
k Chap i 8 — Alpha and Omega, the beginning and the end [k] I will
give unto him that is athirst, of the fountain of the water
l John vii 37, 38 — of life freely [l] 7 He that overcometh shall inherit all
m Heb viii 13 — things, and I will be his God, and he shall be my son [m]
8 But the fearful, and unbelieving, and the abominable,
and murderers, and whoremongers, and sorcerers, and
idolaters, and all liars, shall have their part in the lake
n 2 Cor vi 9, 1 Gal v 19, 21 — which burneth with fire and brimstone [n] which is the
second death

v 1—8 *The last glorious period* now commences of the heavenly felicity of God's saints, if that may be so called, which, though it hath a beginning, never will have an end

The blessedness of the heavenly state is here described under the most august representations

1 A new heaven and earth rise, where there is no sea, all storms, calamities, and trouble being at an end, and an eternal rest remaining for the people of God

2 A glorious city appears in view, such as earth never beheld, the new Jerusalem whose maker and builder is God, beautiful as a bride adorned to meet the bridegroom, the emblem of the church of the redeemed, who will then be perfected in holiness and happiness for ever

3 The unutterable felicity of God's saints is described by a voice from heaven, declaring (1) The residence of God in the midst of his people, admitting them into the nearest relation with his blessed self, taking them for his own, and offering himself as their eternal portion (2) He will for ever banish sin, sorrow, and death from the celestial mansions, the former imperfect state is passed away, and that of perfect happiness is come

4 The certainty of this bliss and blessedness is confirmed by the word of him that sitteth on the throne, *Behold, I make all things new* And again he said, *Write, for these words are true and faithful* And he added, *It is done*, the work of redemption is completely finished *I am Alpha and Omega, the beginning and the end*, who will assuredly accomplish what I have begun. *I will give unto him that is athirst* for spiritual blessings in heavenly things, to drink *of the fountain of the water of life freely*, admitting him, of my sovereign grace and favour, to all the unutterable delights of never-ending consolations in my immediate presence and glory *He that overcometh shall inherit all things, and I will be his God, and he shall be my son*, entitled to all the dignity and honour of that transcendently glorious relation

5 The dreadful ruin of the wicked shall be as sure as the happiness of the saints, they are described as *fearful*, ashamed of the cross of Christ, and dreading the sufferings of his service; *unbelieving*, distrustful of his promises, and rejecting his word, *abominable*, the slaves of corrupt affections, *murderers, whoremongers, sorcerers, idolaters, and all liars*, these are doomed to suffer endless torment *in the lake which burneth with fire and brimstone which is the second death* Wo to those on whom these sins are found, they are assuredly brands for the burning

9 And there came unto me one of the seven angels, [o] — o Chap xv 1
which had the seven vials full of the seven last plagues,
and talked with me, saying, Come hither, I will shew
thee the bride, the Lamb's wife [p] 10 And he carried — p Mat xxii
me away in the spirit to a great and high mountain, and
shewed me that great city, the holy [q] Jerusalem, descend-
ing out of heaven from God, 11 Having the glory of — q Mat iv 5
God [r] and her light *was* like unto a stone most precious, — r Ex xl 35
even like a jasper-stone, [s] clear as crystal, 12 And had — 1 Kings viii 11
a wall great and high, [t] and had twelve gates, and at the — s Isa xl 19, 20
gates twelve angels, *and* names written thereon, which — t Isa xxvi 1
are *the names* of the twelve tribes of the children of Israel — & lx 18
13 On the east, three gates, on the north, three gates,
on the south, three gates, and on the west, three gates [u] — u Ezek xlviii 31, 34
14 And the wall of the city had twelve foundations, [w] — w Eph ii 20
and in them the names of the twelve apostles of the — Heb xi 10
Lamb 15 And he that talked with me had a golden — Isa xxviii 16
reed to measure the city, [x] and the gates thereof, and the — x Zech ii 1, 2
wall thereof 16 And the city lieth four-square, and
the length is as large as the breadth and he measured the
city with the reed, twelve thousand furlongs [y] the length, — y Ezek xlviii 3
and the breadth, and the height of it are equal 17
And he measured the wall thereof, an hundred *and* forty
and four cubits, according to the measure of a man, that
is, of the angel 18 And the building of the wall of it
was of jasper, and the city was pure gold, like unto clear
glass 19 And the foundations of the wall of the city
were garnished with all manner of precious stones [z] The — z Isa liv 11, 12
first foundation *was* jasper, the second, sapphire, the
third, a chalcedony, the fourth, an emerald, 20 The
fifth, sardonyx, the sixth, sardius, the seventh, chryso-
lite, the eighth, beryl, the ninth, a topaz, the tenth, a
chrysoprasus; the eleventh, a jacinth, the twelfth, an
amethyst [a] 21 And the twelve gates were twelve pearls; — a Ex xxviii 17, 21
every several gate was of one pearl, and the street of the
city was pure gold, as it were transparent glass

v 9—21 One of those ministring spirits who had lately been employed in pouring out the vials of wrath, leads the enraptured John to take a nearer view from a neighbouring mountain of the glorious city, the emblem of the church, the Lamb's wife, which he saw descending from heaven

The glory of God, the divine Shechinah, was visible in the midst of her, affording her the brightest light, Jesus the sun of righteousness shining upon her; a vast high wall, and angels the guard waiting at her gates, inscribed with the names of the twelve tribes, through which the seed of the Lord entered into the city, denoted her invincible defence and security The gates stood three on each side, looking to the four quarters of the heaven, open for the faithful who should come from all lands, the twelve foundations of the wall bore the names of the apostles on whom the church is built, Jesus Christ himself being the chief corner stone, the city, on being measured, appeared four square, to signify the perfection, stability, and uni-

formity

formity of the church above, it was fifteen hundred miles on each side, intimating its vast extent, and the heighth of the walls proportionable to its length and breadth, even one hundred and forty-four cubits, the building was of jasper, and the city of pure gold like chrystal, denoting its magnificence, durability, and glory, and the foundations garnished with every precious stone, brighter than those which glittered in the high priest's breast-plate, (*Exod* xxviii 15—21) and the gates were each of one massy pearl, and the street of the city was of burnished gold, polished like chrystal Every thing excellent and dazzling in the sight of mortals, is here heaped together with amazing profusion, and yet how faintly can all these images convey the delights, blessedness, and perfection of the heavenly state, where such good things are prepared as pass man's understanding!

22 And I saw no temple therein for the Lord God
Almighty, and the Lamb, are the temple of it 23
And the city had no need of the sun, neither of the moon
b 1 Cor xv 28 to shine in it b for the glory of God did lighten it, c and
c 1 Kings viii 10 11 Isa lx 19, 20 the Lamb is the light thereof 24 And the nations of
them which are saved, d shall walk in the light of it. e
and the kings of the earth do bring their glory and ho-
d Isa xlix 20 & lxvi 19 nour into it 25 And the gates of it shall not be shut at
all by day f for there shall be no night there 26 And
e Isa lx 1, 3 they shall bring the glory and honour of the nations into
f Jer xlix 31 it 27 And there shall in no wise enter into it any thing
g Isa lii 1 that defileth, g neither *whatsoever* worketh abomination, or
h 2 Tim iv 7 2 Thes ii 11, 12 Hab i 13 Jer xliv 4 *maketh* a lye h but they which are written in the Lamb's
book of life

v 22—27

1 No temple was found in this celestial city, immediate communion with the eternal God being there enjoyed, which renders all the present ordinances of approach to God needless

2 No sun nor moon were wanted, where the uncreated Light himself abode, the glory of God and the Lamb, one in essential union with the Father and Spirit, is the light thereof

3 There all the nations, saved through the atoning blood of Jesus, walk in the light of the Lord, and the potentates, who through grace partake of his salvation, bring thither their glory and honour, counting that they reign indeed when made kings and priests unto God in this eternal state of blessedness

4 The gates stand open continually by day, and there is no night there, nor fear of invading foes, all that hath ever appeared valuable and glorious among the nations here, with infinitely surpassing excellencies found there, and every thing defiling is forbidden admission, no liar, no idolater especially can enter there, but only those whose names are written in the book of life of the Lamb *Note*, Into the present churches upon earth hypocrites will insinuate themselves, but into heaven nothing unholy or impure can be admitted, all there are perfected in holiness

CHAP XXII

In this chapter we have, 1 A further description of the heavenly state of the church, ver 1—6 2 A confirmation of this and all the other visions of this book, ver 6—20 3 The conclusion, ver 20, 21

1 AND he shewed me a pure river of water of life,
a Gen ii 10 clear as crystal, a proceeding out of the throne
b Ezek xlvii 1 [illegible] of God and of the Lamb b 2 In the midst of the street
of it, and of either side the river, *was there* the tree of life c
c Gen ii 9 which bare twelve *manner* of fruits, and yielded her fruit
every month and the leaves of the tree *were* for the
healing of the nations 3 And there shall be no more
d Gen iii 16, 17 curse d but the throne of God and of the Lamb shall be
in it, and his servants shall serve him 4 And they
e Mat v 8 [illegible] shall see his face, and his name *shall be* in their fore-
heads f 5 And there shall be no night there, and they
need no candle, neither light of the sun, for the Lord
God giveth them light, g and they shall reign for ever
h 2 Cor iv 17 and ever h

v 1—5 The angelic guide here further leads the apostle to view some other emblematical glories of this celestial city

1 *A river of water of life, clear as crystal*, flowing from *the throne of God, and of the Lamb*, the figure of those eternal consolations, and that vital influence immediately derived from communion with the fountain of eternal bliss.

2 *The tree of life*, the emblem of Jesus the Lord of life and glory, here spread its branches on both sides the river, or several in a row were planted on the river's bank, yielding perpetual fruit, new every month, and the very leaves are for the healing of the nations, intimating the rich provision of unceasing delights that is here made for the faithful, and their perfect preservation in soul and body from all decay or infirmity

3 No curse can there enter, the eternal felicity and impeccability of the saints are secured, and before the throne of God and of the Lamb they shall pay their unceasing adorations, enjoy the beatific vision of the God of glory, and bear his bright image on them visible as if his name was engraven on their foreheads

4 No night is there, nor need they the sun or a candle, where the Lord God is their everlasting light, and they reign with him for ever and ever O blessed abode! my soul, aspire after it, and eager press for an entrance into this everlasting kingdom of thy God and Saviour

6 And he said unto me, These things *are* faithful and
true And the Lord God of the holy prophets sent his
angel to shew unto his servants the things which must
shortly be done 7 Behold, I come quickly i blessed i Heb x 37.
is he that keepeth the sayings of the prophecy of this
book 8 And I John saw these things, and heard *them*.
And when I had heard and seen, I fell down to worship
before the feet of the angel, which shewed me these things.
9 Then saith he unto me, See *thou do it* not for I am
thy fellow-servant, and of thy brethren the prophets, and
of them which keep the sayings of this book worship
God. k 10 And he saith unto me, Seal not the sayings k Mat iv 10
of the prophecy of this book for the time is at hand l l Chap i 3
11 He that is unjust, let him be unjust still and he
that is filthy, let him be filthy still and he that is righte-
ous, let him be righteous still and he that is holy, let
him be holy still m 12 And behold, I come quickly, m Eph v 27
and my reward *is* with me, n to give every man accord- n Isa xl 10 & lxii 11
ing as his work shall be o 13 I am Alpha and Omega, o 2 Cor v 10
the beginning and the end, p the first and the last 14 p Chap i 8 11
Blessed are they that do his commandments, q that they
may have right to the tree of life, and may enter in q Chap xii 17 & xiv 12
through the gates into the city 15 For without *are* dogs,
r and sorcerers, and whoremongers, and murderers, and ido- r Mat vii 6. Phil iii 2
laters, and whosoever loveth and maketh a lye 16 I Jesus Mat xxii 13 Chap xxi 8
have sent mine angel to testify unto you these things in
the churches I am the root and the offspring of David, s s Mat xxii 42 45
and the bright and morning star t 17 And the Spirit t Num.xxiv. 17 Mal iv 2
and the bride say, Come And let him that heareth say,
Come And let him that is athirst, come And whoso-
ever will, let him take the water of life freely u 18 For u Isa lv 1.
I testify unto every man that heareth the words of the
prophecy of this book, If any man shall add unto these
things, God shall add unto him the plagues that are
written in this book 19 And if any man shall take
away from the words of the book of this prophecy, God
shall take away his part out of the book of life, and out
of the holy city, and *from* the things which are written in
this book w Deut iv. 2 & xii 32 Mal iv 4

v 6—19 We have here,

1 A solemn ratification given by the angel of the certainty of these events *These sayings are faithful and true*, and he was sent expressly from the Lord Jesus to reveal to John the things that would begin shortly to be accomplished, and continue fulfilling until the end of time

2 The Lord Jesus himself speaks *Behold, I come quickly*, prepare to meet me, the whole period of time is comparatively short and momentary *blessed is he that keepeth the sayings of the prophecy of this book*, faithfully adhere to the gospel word, and confidently expect the fulfilment of the promises

3 Overcome with what he heard and saw, and scarce himself through rapture, he fell before the angel, and is ready to adore him, but again is reproved and prevented; God is the only worthy object of adoration, angels are but our fellow-servants

4 The Lord again addresses him, and bids him not seal up the prophecies of this book, but deliver them to the churches, the time for their fulfilment now approaching, and when they are accomplished, men's everlasting state will be fixed unchangeably He that in the great day is found filthy and unjust, must remain so for ever under the wrath of God, and he that is found righteous in the Lord, and made holy by his Spirit, shall be eternally blessed

5 He repeats his assurance for the comfort of his people *Behold, I come quickly, and my reward is with me to give to every man according as his works shall be*, whether good or bad *I am Alpha and Omega, the beginning and the end, the first and the last*, unchangeable in love to my people, eternally the same in faithfulness, grace, and power, to protect and preserve them for ever And it will shortly appear how *blessed are they that do his commandments*, and approve their fidelity to God, *that they may have right*, through the promise, *to the tree of life, and may enter in through the gates into the city*, partaking of all the inconceivable blessedness prepared for the faithful whilst those who shall be

found

found disobedient, unholy, and profane, shall be eternally excluded from these bright mansions *For without are dogs, and sorcerers, and whoremongers, and murderers, and idolaters, and whosoever loveth or maketh a lye*, whoever lives and dies under the guilt of any of these things perishes irrecoverably

6 The Lord Jesus confirms to him what the angel had told him *I Jesus*, your Lord and Master, *have sent mine angel to testify unto you these things in*, or *concerning*, *the churches*, and their future state and condition *I am the root and offspring of David*, as God, his root, as man, his offspring, *and the bright and morning star*, leading my people in paths of everlasting peace

7 *The spirit and the bride say, Come*, welcoming the Saviour, and waiting the fulfilment of his promise *And let him that heareth*, even every faithful soul take up the word and *say, Come And let him that is athirst* for spiritual blessings, *come and whosoever will, let him take of the water of life freely*, and out of these wells of salvation the Scriptures draw the living streams of grace and consolation *For I testify unto every man that heareth the words of the prophecy of this book, if any man shall add unto these things*, now the canon of revelation is complete, by new pretended visions, or wilful perversion of their meaning, *God shall add unto him the plagues that are written in this book and if any man shall take away from the words of the book of this prophecy, God shall take away his part out of the book of life, and out of the holy city, and from the things which are written in this book* An awful sanction, which guards the sacred records, and binds the heaviest vengeance upon those who dare, by base adulterations, to add thereto, or to diminish therefrom

20 He which testifieth these things saith, Surely I
come quickly Amen Even so, come, Lord Jesus [x] x Chap. i. 7
21 The grace of our Lord Jesus Christ *be* with you all [y] y 2 Thes. iii. 17, 18
Amen.

v 20, 21. The Lord Jesus closes his Revelation,

1 With a solemn confirmation of the whole *He which testifieth these things saith, Surely I come quickly*, certainly and speedily, for the comfort and salvation of my people

2 The apostle, in the name of all the faithful, professes his confidence in the promise, *Amen!* Lord, I believe, fulfil it in due season *Even so* be it, *come, Lord Jesus*, and bring our complete and final salvation!

3 He concludes with his benediction *The grace of our Lord Jesus Christ be with you all!* May you experience the riches of his sovereign favour and love, be strengthened by his Spirit mightily in the inner man, faithfully to stand in every evil day, comfortably and confidently persevering in the truth, may you, when all your conflicts end, enter into that eternal state of rest and blessedness which is here revealed *Amen!* Such are my prayers for thee, reader, may we now, without ceasing, be found uniting our supplications before a throne of grace, and together may we meet around a throne of glory, and spend a happy eternity in the praises of our adored Jesus! *Amen!*

F I N I S.

CPSIA information can be obtained
at www.ICGtesting.com
Printed in the USA
BVOW10s1413231017
498409BV00021B/1019/P